# SKY SPORTS

# FOOTBALL YEARBOOK 2004-2005

EDITORS: GLENDA ROLLIN AND JACK ROLLIN



headl

First published in 2004
by HEADLINE BOOK PUBLISHING

10 9 8 7 6 5 4 3 2 1



**Front cover photographs:** (left) John Terry (Chelsea) – *Empics/Nigel French*; (centre and background) Thierry Henry (Arsenal) – *Actionimages/Roy Beardsworth*; (right) Maurice Ross (Rangers) and Roy Keane (Manchester United) – *Colorsport/Andrew Cowie.*

**Spine photograph:** Wayne Rooney (England) and Dario Simic (Croatia) – *Getty Images/Ross Kinnaird.*

**Back cover photographs:** (top) Jay-Jay Okocha (Bolton Wanderers) – *Actionimages/Darren Walsh*; (bottom) Chris Sutton (Celtic) – *Getty Images/Matthew Stockman.*

Cataloguing in Publication Data is available from the British Library

ISBN 0 7553 1310 0 (hardback)
ISBN 0 7553 1311 9 (trade paperback)

Typeset by Wearset Ltd, Boldon, Tyne and Wear

Printed and bound in Great Britain by
Mackays of Chatham PLC,
Chatham, Kent

Headline's policy is to use papers that are natural, renewable and recyclable products and made from wood grown in sustainable forests. The logging and manufacturing processes are expected to conform to the environmental regulations of the country of origin.

HEADLINE BOOK PUBLISHING
A division of Hodder Headline
338 Euston Road
London NW1 3BH

www.headline.co.uk
www.hodderheadline.com

# CONTENTS

# FOREWORD

The Yearbook has been a constant companion throughout my 30-year career in sports broadcasting, from my time as a cub reporter on the *Hartlepool Mail* to my current role of fronting 'Gillette Soccer Saturday'. I have dog-eared copies around the house dating back to the first edition in 1970 when I was earning a living for the first time in my life.

We live and die on our translation of football facts on the show and, trust me, you don't want to 'die' on live TV! I know that any errors will be leapt upon with relish by Rodney Marsh (not to mention the viewers at home). So you can be sure that every desk in the building is complete with a copy of the ever-expanding tome that is now sponsored by us here at Sky Sports.

It's the bible as far as we're concerned and the 'Soccer Saturday' stats man Dave Todd has a pile of recent copies next to him all season long in the production gallery. He'll prompt us with valuable nuggets of information and significant milestones and occasionally set us straight after a quick flick through the old blue faithful. It's a constant, reliable reference source and I'm delighted that Sky Sports is now so intrinsically linked with it. And of course, if modern technology can occasionally let you down, the Yearbook never will!

Like the Yearbook, 'Soccer Saturday' has – we hope – built itself a reputation as a definitive source of information. This is our ninth season in a purely football format and if we can carry on with a blend of information and entertainment half as long as the Yearbook, we'll be doing something right.

**Jeff Stelling, Presenter, Sky Sports**

Jeff Stelling and the team on 'Gillette Soccer Saturday'

# INTRODUCTION

The 35th edition of the Yearbook, our second with new sponsors Sky Sports, has been expanded to a record 1,056 pages. Among the innovations are an A to Z index of names with a cross reference to the Players Directory, enabling readers to check on the whereabouts of any specific player during the 2003–04 season. The who's who style directory again provides a season-by-season account of individual player's appearances and goals. With the increase in interest in non-League football, all Conference clubs have been given the same style of recognition as the FA Premier League and Football League teams.

As far as the club pages are concerned, a more uniform approach has been made to individual entries, without losing any of the essential information, including records over the previous ten seasons, latest sequences and runs of scoring and non-scoring.

For the first time, every match played in the Champions League, including the qualifying competition, has full teams and line-ups and Euro 2004 takes into account both qualifying and final tournaments.

The usual detailed and varied coverage involves Scottish, Welsh and Irish football, amateur, schools, university, reserve team, extensive non-League information, awards, records and an international directory. Football and the law, women's football, referees and the work of chaplains are also featured.

The Editors would like to express their appreciation of the response from FA Premier League and Football League clubs when requesting information. Thanks are also due to Alan Elliott for the Scottish section, Tony Brown for sequences and instances of match results in the records section and Ian Nannestad for the obituaries and additional information on foreign players. Thanks are also due to John English, who provided invaluable and conscientious reading of the proofs.

# ACKNOWLEDGEMENTS

The Editors would like to express appreciation of the following individuals and organisations for their co-operation: David Barber, Dawn Keleher and Gary Simmonds (Football Association), David C. Thomson (Scottish League), Heather Elliott, Dr Malcolm Brodie, Wally Goss (AFA), Rev. Nigel Sands, Edward Grayson, Ken Goldman, Grahame Lloyd, Marshall Gillespie, Valery Karpoushkin, Andrew Howe, Mike Kelleher, Ester Kristiansson and Wendy McCance (Headline Book Publishing). The highest praise is due to the ubiquitous Lorraine Jerram, Headline's Managing Editor and finally sincere thanks to John Anderson, Simon Dunnington, Geoff Turner, Brian Tait and the staff at Wearset for their efforts in the production of this book, which was much appreciated throughout the year.

**ROBERT WINGFIELD HENNESSY**

7 August 1941 – 24 December 2003

A promising Irish schoolboy footballer in his native Dublin, he came to England hopefully to start a professional career with Southend United in the late 1950s. This did not materialise, but instead he furthered his journalistic ambitions initially with the Press Association and then as a freelance, contributing to various national newspapers on both sides of the water, including *Sunday Independent*, *Evening Herald*, *Daily Star* and *News of the World*. He also took on the responsibility of keeping track of Irish lads coming into football in England and had a comprehensive network of contacts in this field. His other interest originally as a chorister in Dublin, continued as a member of the Reading Male Voice Choir. A keen supporter of Aldershot Football Club past and present, he always signed off with the cry 'Up the Shots!' In recent years, he became the diarist for *Rothmans Football Yearbook* and then *Sky Sports Football Yearbook*, bringing his own individual style to the season's milestones. As a friend, he is sorely missed; he always had time to help others. He is survived by wife Lynda, son James and daughter Carly, brother David and sister Ruth.

# EDITORIAL

Was it déjà vu? No, we had seen it all before. Even Sven's worst nightmare was causing a language problem, though it is reported he does not dream. Anyway Michael Owen opened the scoring after a park pitch defensive error; the Portuguese speaking opposition equalised. Felipe Scolari was again in charge. It all had a familiar ring to it. The story unravelled a little but the tail end was the same, out of the competition when the all too familiar much promise had been shown.

Euro 2004 was not exactly similar to World Cup 2002 in other respects. There was what seemed to be a good excuse for complaint. The object of this was the unsuspecting Swiss referee Herr Meier. By disallowing what many thought to be a legitimate goal by Sol Campbell because John Terry was impeding the goalkeeper, some critics felt this was the neatest steal since Robin Hood played copse (sic) and robbers in Sherwood Forest.

Poor Urs. He had the press laying into him and much of the enraged populace would have been happy to drag him through the streets without the aid of four plumed horses. We were truly in the mire as the tabloids would say. The far too serious side of this event was the death threats he apparently received; alas the ugly side of the beautiful game is never far away.

Well, if we are content with this explanation of what went wrong, fine. Surely it is not as simple as that because we have to discuss the next horror, the penalty shoot-out, not England at its best is this particular art. Rather we have perfected the way out. It started with Beckham converting the ball instead of hitting the target. But he should not have taken the first shot. It was said the earth moved . . . possibly not for the first time.

Having missed against France, his second failure in a row after slipping up in Turkey, Owen should have been the first up. Nit picking? No, using the old loaf. And who knows what might have happened against Portugal if this had gone in. Unfortunately, too, David James did not stop any of the Portuguese shots, so there is room for improvement at both ends. Shameful, too, Portugal are our oldest allies!

But we are getting ahead of ourselves. Before the Portugal match a kind of heady euphoria had taken over, not entirely unjustified given the none-too-clever look of the so-called fancied teams in the tournament. Wayne Rooney was scaring defences, scoring goals and even in some sections of the English press being compared with Pele – the white Pele of course, a term last used on Zico, more of a Brazilian. One hopes that in 40 years time, Rooney will not be producing his 100 best players of all time.

After the collapse at the end of the French affair, both the Swiss and Croats had been banished with goals piling up in the process. This was a competition we could win. There was even talk of Sven popping the question to Nancy, though perhaps someone had his or her wires crossed with all this discussion of diamonds; a confusion of formation and clusters.

Alas, the fantasy of Euro gold was about to fade with our traditional exit from the penalty spot. Inevitably the cross of St George became a flag of inconvenience; the mark of sorrow. But as long as we have to persist with this lottery, what do you expect? The game deserves better than suffering this farce to settle a cup-tie. At the start of our domestic season any goalkeeper having the audacity to stop any kind of a penalty was likely to be marched off to the Tower. At its end the goalkeeper could get away with rushing almost closer to the ball than the kicker with the freedom of any city available as a prize for cheating.

When was the last penalty shoot-out kick ordered to be re-taken?

Players could put an end to the lottery whenever they wanted. Wonder what would happen if the penalty taker missed every time on purpose? In simple times undecided matches were solved by the team winning the most corners. If away goals can count double, why not away corners. At least attacking intent would be rewarded.

Shoot-outs – this apparently essential method of deciding matches of varying importance is dismissed as a footnote in records, the exact kicking order often not given and the game itself treated as a draw! There will be no more sudden death (golden) or slow death (silver) goals. The same shoot-out mentality for the spectacular had the Christians losing heavily to the lions – and with no overtime. If animals were involved in penalty shoot-outs the RSPCA would rightly go to court and close the circus down.

Still back to basics and trying to fathom out problems affecting performance at international level. Our next target is the World Cup in 2006 in Germany, 40 years after we had that dramatic victory over them at Wembley, which remains our only trophy of note at top level. Misty eyes recall the event, mostly by those who were not around when it happened.

Fundamentally our game needs overhauling. There must be enough wiseacres at top level who can come up with answers and provide the right direction for the future. We await the event with interest. If the League of Positive Thinking was unable to agree its fixture list, you might write them off, but it could be their members were debating the matter. So one hopes the same process is ticking over in the brains of those in charge of our destiny.

But where are we going wrong? Certainly the opening of borders across the continent would seem to be having a poor effect on the standard of international teams. Without decrying the exceptional performance of Latvia in reaching the finals in Portugal at all, they are not one of the leading football nations of the world. Yet they might easily have beaten Germany.

The Germans with Italy, France and Spain led the parade of the fallen from grace, others merely slipped on Greece, whose Otto Rehhagel tactics proved correct. Ironically the Greek team included three players who could claim past and present time in English football! With England the first four named countries above, are those with the strongest potential at both club and international level, but the former is outperforming the latter. UEFA are said to be attempting to curb the number of foreign players per club – yet this seems to be running in the face of EU regulations on freedom of movement of labour.

Football has always considered itself to be beyond the law of the land, preferring everyone in the game to adhere to its own brand. Slowly but surely they have found the courts ruling against them, though it has been a long process.

Even so club football has continued to make strides with the influx of foreign players especially in the FA Premier League. At this point praise is due to Arsene Wenger and the Arsenal players for their awesome achievement in remaining unbeaten throughout the League season in what is arguably the most competitive domestic environment in the world.

The growth in interest in the Champions League and re-vamping of the UEFA Cup for the new season has tended to overshadow events at national level. And it appears to be at the expense of developing talent for the home grown variety.

Tactically, too, we seem outflanked at times. One criticism levelled at Eriksson is that he is not too clever when it comes to substitutions. He prefers quantity at the expense of quality at crucial stages of games – and he only has three in competitive matches. He must have inherited the Alf Ramsey gene for not really understanding the subleties of replacements. Often the game plan goes out of the window when something unexpected occurs and a retreat into the defensive shell follows.

Talking of days or yore, at least with Euro 2004 fading from memory and two years before World Cup 2006, we will be spared the TV panelists on a daily basis when an older generation yearned for a return of the cardboard cut-out Alf Ramsey in the famous Monty Python skit.

There is enough money being pumped into football in this country. But it is clearly not used for the overall benefit of the areas in need, too much at the top not enough at the bottom. And the national team manager is allegedly being the highest paid in Europe is no guarantee of success.

However it was a welcome relief to see that at intermediate levels, the England set up was cutting back on fixtures – well under half of those of the previous season. Again it is the quantity factor which has often impeded progress. Clubs will always feel they have the right to more say since it is they who pay the players on a regular basis. But there are enough clubs in financial difficulties, so there has to be something drastically wrong with the economics as they stand at present.

Let us be honest, the real curse of football is losing. It is Hell, or certainly L. None of us like it. Winning is uncomplicated, can be savoured and recalled throughout time, losing leads to irrational thoughts and unacceptable behaviour, scratching around for excuses and fretting until the next game

Wayne Rooney scores the opening goal past Switzerland's goalkeeper Jorg Stiel in England's 3-0 Group B win in Coimbra during the UEFA European Championship in Portugal. (Empics)

France goalkeeper Fabien Barthez dives to his right to save David Beckham's penalty during his country's 2-1 win in the opening Group B game of the European Championships in Lisbon, Portugal. (Actionimages)

which might or might not wipe away the misery. We used to be good at losing. We still lose, but are rubbish at it now.

Managers and teams will analyse defeats, but often gloss over victory without realising the fine line which can exist between the W and L columns, not to mention the D in the middle. Going to the dogs and riding to hounds sounds the same, but they have completely different connotations. Unlike Shrove Tuesday and Mardi Gras which appear to be world's apart but have exactly the same meaning. Pure match results are not always what they seem to be.

Naturally managers remain the scapegoat for all ills. The attitude to them differs widely from those attributed to players. While the core cell of the football brain is knowing exactly what you are going to do with the ball before you receive it, the manager must not look ahead of his immediate job. He knows he will get the sack one day, but woe betide him for trying to line up his next berth – unlike players who can frequently sort out their next club move without overmuch criticism.

There needs to be vast improvement in the discipline of players, more consistency for the poor officials who have to control them. We have to address the other problem of matches taking more than 90 minutes, when the fourth official could easily take the responsibility for timing, stopping the watch at crucial moments and ending the ludicrous situation of the last minute recorded as many as six or seven minutes over.

Offside is difficult enough to flag, we now have to contend with subtle diversions and interpretations of what is or what is not interferring with play. Assistant referees need wide perpherical vision and spectators in the stand often have a better view of what constitutes on or offside. The eyes have yet to be produced which can cover the length of the pitch.

Goalkeepers are still given far too much leniency when challenged by attackers even forgetting the Meier incident in Euro 2004. Allowing them to take goal kicks on either side of the goal is a built-in safeguard for time-wasting. Nobody wants to see goalkeepers whacked into the back of the net, but if they have not managed to get their hands on the ball and have not been impeded in doing so, play must be allowed to continue.

Bounce-ups after play is stopped for injury in the middle of the park must return at the expense of this other nonsense of inviting players to kick the ball in a certain direction. Where in the laws does this instruct referees to order players to do this particular action?

Club v country will always be a battle for supremacy, but the calendar must reflect fairness to players, clubs, national interests and equally the followers of the game, without whom none of it would exist. Moreover it must not be put down as other business and forgotten about.

Meanwhile the football marquee is packed, the caravan and its entourage moves on around the globe as the game never ends. Euro 2004 is dead, long live World Cup 2006, when one hopes the fun will be just as intense.

# SKY SPORTS FOOTBALL YEARBOOK HONOURS

Even though Arsenal carried all before them in the FA Premier League, there was strong challenge in most areas of the team of the season from other clubs for Sky Sports Football Yearbook. In fact, no fewer than 45 different players received votes spread throughout the League.

However, five Arsenal players made the final selection, namely Ashley Cole, Sol Campbell, Patrick Vieira, Thierry Henry and Robert Pires. Runners-up Chelsea contributed central defender John Terry and midfield player Frank Lampard but third-placed Manchester United were solely represented by right-back Gary Neville, who had lost his place in the previous year and had to be content then with a place on the substitutes bench.

Liverpool, who finished fourth, had Steven Gerrard in midfield while Alan Shearer, who enjoyed an Indian summer of his long career, ousted Ruud Van Nistelrooy as one of the two strikers.

Again the members favoured a 4-4-2 formation for this 2003–04 Team of the Season and their deliberations were concluded with the goalkeeping role going to Southampton's Finn Antti Niemi who was one of eight different players for this position among those receiving votes.

Among those just missing a place in the final line-up, Lauren, the Arsenal right-back was so well represented that he earned a place as substitute and the Portuguese international discovery Cristiano Ronaldo also found a place for himself on the bench with the versatile Arsenal defender Kolo Toure completing the squad.

Manager of the Year was not surprisingly Arsène Wenger of Arsenal in view of the excellent consistency shown by his players during the season and overall comparing this team with the 2002–03 version only Cole, Campbell, Vieira and Henry retained their places, all Arsenal players, in fact. Interestingly enough, because the voting took place before Euro 2004, there was not one vote for Everton's Wayne Rooney, who was one of the substitutes last time – such are the changing fortunes in the game.

Henry achieved both the Football Writers' Association accolade as Player of the Year and was similarly honoured as Professional Footballers' Association Footballer of the Year.

### Sky Sports Football Yearbook Team of the Season 2003–04

Antti Niemi
*(Southampton)*

| | | | |
|---|---|---|---|
| Gary Neville *(Manchester U)* | John Terry *(Chelsea)* | Sol Campbell *(Arsenal)* | Ashley Cole *(Arsenal)* |
| Steven Gerrard *(Liverpool)* | Frank Lampard *(Chelsea)* | Patrick Vieira *(Arsenal)* | Robert Pires *(Arsenal)* |
| | Alan Shearer *(Newcastle U)* | Thierry Henry *(Arsenal)* | |

**Manager**
Arsène Wenger *(Arsenal)*

*Substitutes:*
Lauren (Arsenal)
Kolo Toure (Arsenal)
Cristiano Ronaldo (Manchester U)

# THE FOOTBALL RECORDS

## LANDMARKS

Arsenal became the third team to avoid defeat in one season and only the second to achieve it at the top level. They won 26 and drew 12 of their 38 FA Premier League games. Preston NE in 1888–89 had won 18 and drawn 4 of their 22 Football League matches, while in 1893–94 Liverpool had won 22 and drawn 6 of 28 of their Second Division games.

During 2003–04, Arsenal also overtook Liverpool's record of 13 unbeaten games from the start of the season, set a club record when they reached their 24th unbeaten match and later established the top flight record of 30 unbeaten games from the start of the season.

Wayne Rooney, at 17 years 317 days became England's youngest goalscorer. Michael Owen, at 18 years 164 days had been the previous holder of this title. Rooney scored his important goal against Macedonia, while Owen had opened his account against Morocco in 1998.

There were more personal milestones for Alan Shearer at Newcastle United. He scored his 250th career League goal, his 100th under Sir Bobby Robson, his 100th at home and topped 300 in his career. He was also joint leading goalscorer in the UEFA Cup with six goals.

Henrik Larsson, in his last season with Celtic, overtook the European scoring records of both Ian Rush (Liverpool) and Peter Lorimer (Leeds U) with his 31st goal in Europe. He also became Celtic's leading post-war goalscorer when he scored his 169th League goal in 232 matches. Michael Owen subsequently overhauled Rush's record at Liverpool.

Celtic created a record with 25 consecutive wins in the Scottish Premier League, beating the previous Scottish League record held by Morton.

Ruud Van Nistelrooy of Manchester United set a new FA Premier League record by scoring in 10 consecutive matches for a total of 15 goals.

Northern Ireland ended their goal famine, but only after 1298 minutes of international football.

There were two Champions League records in goalscoring, the highest aggregate number of goals was achieved when Monaco beat Deportivo La Coruna 8-3 and the highest margin of victory was reached when Juventus beat Olympiakos 7-0.

In Euro 2004, Rooney became European Championship Finals youngest marksman at the age of 18 years 236 days. This honour lasted four days until Johan Vonlanthen set a new record for Switzerland at 18 years 141 days.

Mikael Antoine-Curier was with seven different Football League clubs in 2003–04: Burnley, Oldham Athletic, Kidderminster Harriers, Rochdale, Sheffield Wednesday, Notts County and Grimsby Town, made League appearances for the last six named and was not on loan to any of them.

In 2003–04 Neil Redfearn completed League appearances for 13 different Football League clubs in his career: Bolton Wanderers, Lincoln City, Doncaster Rovers, Crystal Palace, Watford, Oldham Athletic, Barnsley, Charlton Athletic, Bradford City, Wigan Athletic, Halifax Town, Boston United and Rochdale.

## THE EXPORT GAME

From the end of the 2002–03 season and into 2003–04, the movement of players has not only been incoming, but also outgoing. The following is a list of players who have moved abroad, either permanently, returning from loan periods or going on temporary transfers:

Acimovic, Tottenham H to Lille (loan).
Acuna, Newcastle U to Rosario Central.
Alpay, Aston Villa to Incheon U.
Andre, returned from loan to Nantes from Bolton.
Baggio, Blackburn R to Ancona.
Balaban, Aston Villa to Empoli, FC Brugge.
Baldacchino, Carlisle U to Gretna.
Bardsley, Manchester U to Antwerp (loan).
Barrett, Portsmouth to Dundee (loan).
Barthez, Manchester U to Marseille (loan).
Beckham, Manchester U to Real Madrid.
Belmadi, returned from loan to Marseille from Manchester C.
Benarbia, Manchester C to Al Rayan.
Bennett, Rochdale to Albion R.
Berg, Blackburn R to Rangers.
Blondel, Tottenham H to FC Brugge.
Buchan, Stockport Co to Peterhead.
Bulent, Bolton W to Genclerbirligi.
Caldwell, G. Newcastle U to Hibernian.
Cansdell-Sheriff, Leeds U to Aarhus.
Cas, Grimsby T to RBC.
Chapuis, Leeds U to Strasbourg.
Dacourt, Leeds U to Roma.
Delgado, Southampton to Aucas (loan).
De Lucas, returned from loan to Alaves from Chelsea.
Diarra, Liverpool to Bastia (loan).
Di Cesare, Chelsea to Avellino (loan).
Diomede, Liverpool to Ajaccio.
Djordjic, Manchester U to Red Star Belgrade (loan).
Doyle, Leicester C to Ayr U.
Fangzho, Manchester U to Antwerp (loan).
Festa, Portsmouth to Cagliari.
Figueroa, Birmingham C to Cruz Azul.
Forschelet, Bolton W to Chateauraux (loan).
George, Ipswich T to Mallorca.
Grabbi, Blackburn R to Ancona.
Gudjonsson, returned from loan to Betis from Aston Villa.
Hadji, Aston Villa to Espanyol.
Hakan Sukur, Blackburn R to Galatasaray.
Heath, Manchester U to Antwerp (loan).
Herrera, Fulham to Estudiantes (loan).
Jardel, Bolton W to Ancona (loan).
Jensen, Manchester C to Borussia Dortmund.
Johnson, Manchester U to Antwerp (loan).
Jones, Wolverhampton W to St Patrick's Ath.
Jordao, WBA to Amadora.
Juan, Arsenal to Fluminense.
Karelse, Newcastle U to AGOW.
Kawaguchi, Portsmouth to Nordsjaelland.
Keenan, Chelsea to Westerlo (loan).
Kelly, Wycombe W to Cowdenbeath.
Kendrick, Newcastle U to 1860 Munich.
Kerr, Newcastle U to Livingston (loan).
Kirovski, Birmingham C to La Galazy.
Knissel, Chelsea to Dundee (loan).
Lucic, returned from loan to AIK Stockholm from Leeds U.
Marlet, Fulham to Marseille (loan).
Marsden, Southampton to Busan Icons.
McKinlay, Leicester C to Ross Co (loan).
Mendy, returned from loan to Paris St Germain from Bolton W.
Milosevic, Leeds U to Celtic.
Molloy, Derby to Drogheda.
O'Donnell, Sheffield W to Motherwell.
Ouaddou, Fulham to Rennes (loan).
Peeters, Sunderland to Mechelen.
Pelzer, Manchester C to Eintracht Trier.
Raul Bravo, returned from loan to Real Madrid from Leeds U.
Ricardo, Manchester U to Santander (loan).

## THE EXPORT GAME – *continued*

Rodrigo, returned from loan to Botafogo from Everton.
Roque Junior, returned from loan to AC Milan from Leeds U.
Roussel, Wolverhampton W to Genk.
Salva, returned from loan to Valencia from Bolton W.
Sjolund, Liverpool to Djurgaarden.
Skora, Preston NE to Kilmarnock (loan).
Slaven, Carlisle U to Cowdenbeath (loan).
Sofiane, West Ham U to Lille.
Sommeil, Manchester C to Marseille (loan).
Stepanovs, Arsenal to Beveren (loan).
Strupar, Derby Co to Dynamo Zagreb.
Svard, Arsenal to FC Copenhagen (loan).
Swierczewski, returned from loan to Marseille from Birmingham C.
Ten Heuvel, Sheffield U to De Graafschap.
Toda, returned from loan to Shimizu S-Pulse from Tottenham H.
Townsley, Oxford U to Gretna.
Valakari, Derby Co to Dallas Burn.
Van Bronckhorst, Arsenal to Barcelona (loan).
Van der Gouw, West Ham U to RKC.
Vignal, Liverpool to Espanyol, Rennes (loan).
Vuoso, Manchester C to Sant Laguna (loan).
Wake, Carlisle U to Gretna.
Warmuz, Arsenal to Borussia Dortmund.
Wome, Fulham to Bologna (loan).
Xavier, Liverpool to Hanover (loan).
Zivkovic, Portsmouth to Stuttgart.
Zola, Chelsea to Cagliari.
Zvagno, Derby Co to Ancona.

## THE YOUNG ONES

In addition to the full internationals who appear in the Players Directory, there are many other foreign imports with intermediate honours, those with Under-21 appearances not included in this section are as follows:

**DENMARK**
Bischoff; Svard.

**FRANCE**
Aliadiere; Bellion; Chapuis; Cisse, E; Clichy; Dalmat; Domi; Kanoute; Legwinski; Le Tallec; Malbranque; Sakho; Sinama-Pongolle; Tebily.

**GERMANY**
Hitzlsperger; Huth.

**ITALY**
Cudicini.

**POLAND**
Abbott; Olszar.

**PORTUGAL**
Costa.

**SWEDEN**
Tidman.

**FRANCE B INTERNATIONALS**
Bonnissel; Sommeil.

**YOUTH INTERNATIONALS**
**CZECH REPUBLIC**
Papadopoulos.

**DENMARK**
Ellegaard.

**FRANCE**
Folly; Sibierski; Sofiane.

**GERMANY**
Volz.

**HOLLAND**
Owusu-Abeyie.

**PORTUGAL**
Oliviera; Vaz Te.

**SPAIN**
Fabregas.

# CHAMPIONS LEAGUE AND EUROPEAN CUP RECORDS

## ALL-TIME EUROPEAN CUP AND CHAMPIONS LEAGUE TOP SCORERS

| | | |
|---|---|---|
| 1955–56 | Milos Milutinovic (Partizan Belgrade) | 8 |
| 1956–57 | Dennis Viollet (Manchester United) | 9 |
| 1957–58 | Alfredo Di Stefano (Real Madrid) | 10 |
| 1958–59 | Just Fontaine (Reims) | 10 |
| 1959–60 | Ferenc Puskas (Real Madrid) | 12 |
| 1960–61 | Jose Aguas (Benfica) | 11 |
| 1961–62 | Alfredo Di Stefano (Real Madrid) | |
| | Ferenc Puskas (Real Madrid) | |
| | Justo Tejada (Real Madrid) | 7 |
| 1962–63 | Jose Altafini (AC Milan) | 14 |
| 1963–64 | Vladimir Kovacevic (Partizan Belgrade) | |
| | Ferenc Puskas (Real Madrid) | |
| | Alessandro Mazzola (Internazionale) | 7 |
| 1964–65 | Jose Torres (Benfica) | 9 |
| 1965–66 | Eusebio (Benfica) | |
| | Florian Albert (Ferencvaros) | 7 |
| 1966–67 | Paul Van Himst (Anderlecht) | |
| | Jurgen Piepenberg (Vorwaerts) | 6 |
| 1967–68 | Eusebio (Benfica) | 6 |
| 1968–69 | Denis Law (Manchester United) | 9 |
| 1969–70 | Mick Jones (Leeds United) | 8 |
| 1970–71 | Antonis Antoniadis (Panathinaikos) | 10 |
| 1971–72 | Sylvester Takac (Standard Liege) | |
| | Johan Cruyff (Ajax) | |
| | Lou Macari (Celtic) | 5 |
| 1972–73 | Gerd Muller (Bayern Munich) | 11 |
| 1973–74 | Gerd Muller (Bayern Munich) | 9 |
| 1974–75 | Gerd Muller (Bayern Munich) | 6 |
| 1975–76 | Josef Heynckes (Moenchengladbach) | |
| | Carlos Santillana (Real Madrid) | 6 |
| 1976–77 | Gerd Muller (Bayern Munich) | |
| | Franco Cucinotta (Zurich) | 5 |
| 1977–78 | Allan Simonsen (Moenchengladbach) | 5 |
| 1978–79 | Claudio Sulser (Grasshoppers) | 11 |
| 1979–80 | Soren Lerby (Ajax) | 10 |
| 1980–81 | Karl-Heinz Rummenigge (Bayern Munich) | |
| | Terry McDermott (Liverpool) | |
| | Graeme Souness (Liverpool) | 6 |
| 1981–82 | Dieter Hoeness (Bayern Munich) | 7 |
| 1982–83 | Paolo Rossi (Juventus) | 6 |
| 1983–84 | Viktor Sokol (Dynamo Minsk) | 6 |
| 1984–85 | Michel Platini (Juventus) | |
| | Torbjorn Nilsson (IFK Gothenburg) | 7 |
| 1985–86 | Torbjorn Nilsson (IFK Gothenburg) | 7 |
| 1986–87 | Borislav Cvetkovic (Red Star Belgrade) | 7 |
| 1987–88 | Rabah Madjer (Porto) | |
| | Jean-Marc Ferreri (Bordeaux) | |
| | Michel (Real Madrid) | |
| | Rui Aguas (Benfica) | |
| | Ally McCoist (Rangers) | |
| | Gheorghe Hagi (Steaua) | 4 |
| 1988–89 | Marco Van Basten (AC Milan) | 10 |
| 1989–90 | Romario (PSV Eindhoven) | |
| | Jean-Pierre Papin (Marseille) | 6 |
| 1990–91 | Peter Pacult (Tirol) | |
| | Jean-Pierre Papin (Marseille) | 6 |
| 1991–92 | Jean-Pierre Papin (Marseille) | 7 |
| 1992–93 | Romario (PSV Eindhoven) | 7 |
| 1993–94 | Ronald Koeman (Barcelona) | |
| | Wynton Rufer (Werder Bremen) | 8 |
| 1994–95 | George Weah (Paris St Germain) | 7 |
| 1995–96 | Jari Litmanen (Ajax) | 9 |
| 1996–97 | Ally McCoist (Rangers) | 6 |
| 1997–98 | Alessandro Del Piero (Juventus) | 10 |
| 1998–99 | Andrei Shevchenko (Dynamo Kiev) | 10 |
| 1999–2000 | Mario Jardel (Porto) | |
| | Rivaldo (Barcelona) | |
| | Raul (Real Madrid) | 10 |
| 2000–01 | Andrei Shevchenko (AC Milan) | |
| | Mario Jardel (Galatasaray) | 9 |
| 2001–02 | Ruud Van Nistelrooy (Manchester United) | 10 |
| 2002–03 | Ruud Van Nistelrooy (Manchester United) | 14 |
| 2203–04 | Fernando Morientes (Monaco) | 9 |

## EUROPEAN CUP AND CHAMPIONS LEAGUE RECORDS

### CHAMPIONS LEAGUE ATTENDANCES AND GOALS FROM GROUP STAGES ONWARDS

| *Season* | *Attendances* | *Average* | *Goals* | *Games* |
|---|---|---|---|---|
| 1992–93 | 873,251 | 34,930 | 56 | 25 |
| 1993–94 | 1,202,289 | 44,529 | 71 | 27 |
| 1994–95 | 2,328,515 | 38,172 | 140 | 61 |
| 1995–96 | 1,874,316 | 30,726 | 159 | 61 |
| 1996–97 | 2,093,228 | 34,315 | 161 | 61 |
| 1997–98 | 2,868,271 | 33,744 | 239 | 85 |
| 1998–99 | 3,608,331 | 42,451 | 238 | 85 |
| 1999–2000 | 5,490,709 | 34,973 | 442 | 157 |
| 2000–01 | 5,773,486 | 36,774 | 449 | 157 |
| 2001–02 | 5,417,716 | 34,508 | 393 | 157 |
| 2002–03 | 6,461,112 | 41,154 | 431 | 157 |
| 2003–04 | 4,611,214 | 36,890 | 309 | 125 |

### HIGHEST AVERAGE ATTENDANCE IN ONE EUROPEAN CUP SEASON
1959–60 50,545 from a total attendance of 2,780,000.

### HIGHEST SCORE IN A EUROPEAN CUP MATCH
Feyenoord (Holland)12, KR Reykjavik (Iceland) 0
*(First Round First Leg 1969–70)*

### HIGHEST AGGREGATE
Benfica (Portugal) 18, Dudelange (Luxembourg) 0
*(Preliminary Round 1965–66)*

### MOST GOALS OVERALL
49 Alfredo Di Stefano (Real Madrid) *(1955–64)*
46 Eusebio (Benfica) *(1959–74)*
43 Raul (Real Madrid) *(1995–2003)*
36 Gerd Muller (Bayern Munich) *(1969–77)*

### CHAMPIONS LEAGUE BIGGEST WINS
Juventus 7, Olympiakos 0 10.12.2003
Marseille 6, CKSA Moscow 0 17.3.93
Leeds U 6, Besiktas 0 26.9.2000
Real Madrid 6, Genk 0 25.9.2002

### FIRST TEAM TO SCORE SEVEN GOALS
Paris St Germain 7, Rosenborg 2 24.10.2000

### HIGHEST AGGREGATE OF GOALS
Monaco 8, La Coruna 3 05.11.2003

### HIGHEST SCORING DRAW
Hamburg 4, Juventus 4 13.9.2000

### GREATEST COMEBACKS
Werder Bremen beat Anderlecht 5-3 after being three goals down in 33 minutes on 8.12.1993. They scored five goals in 23 second-half minutes.
La Coruna beat Paris St Germain 4-3 after being three goals down in 55 minutes on 7.3.2001. They scored four goals in 27 second-half minutes.

### MOST GOALS IN CHAMPIONS LEAGUE MATCH
4, Marco Van Basten AC Milan v IFK Gothenburg (33, 53 (pen), 61, 62 mins) 4-0 25.11.1992.
4, Simone Inzaghi Lazio v Marseille (17, 37, 38, 71 mins) 5-1 14.3.2000.

### WINS WITH TWO DIFFERENT CLUBS
Miodrag Belodedici (Steaua) 1986; (Red Star Belgrade) 1991.
Ronald Koeman (PSV Eindhoven) 1988; (Barcelona) 1992.
Dejan Savicevic (Red Star Belgrade) 1991; (AC Milan) 1994.
Marcel Desailly (Marseille) 1993; (AC Milan) 1994.
Frank Rijkaard (AC Milan) 1989, 1990; (Ajax) 1995.
Vladimir Jugovic (Red Star Belgrade) 1991; (Juventus) 1996.
Didier Deschamps (Marseille) 1993; (Juventus) 1996.
Paulo Sousa (Juventus) 1996; (Borussia Dortmund) 1997.
Christian Panucci (AC Milan) 1994; (Real Madrid) 1998.
Jimmy Rimmer (Mancheser U) 1968, (Aston Villa) 1982 but as a non-playing substitute.

### MOST WINS WITH DIFFERENT CLUBS
Clarence Seedorf (Ajax) 1995; (Real Madrid) 1998; (AC Milan) 2003.

### MOST WINNERS MEDALS
6 Francisco Gento (Real Madrid) 1956, 1957, 1958, 1959, 1960, 1966.
5 Alfredo Di Stefano (Real Madrid) 1956, 1957, 1958, 1959, 1960.
5 Jose Maria Zarraga (Real Madrid) 1956, 1957, 1958, 1959, 1960.
4 Jose-Hector Rial (Real Madrid) 1956, 1957, 1958, 1959.
4 Marquitos (Real Madrid) 1956, 1957, 1959, 1960.
4 Phil Neal (Liverpool) 1977, 1978, 1981, 1984.

### MOST GOALS SCORED IN FINALS
7 Alfredo Di Stefano (Real Madrid), 1956 (1), 1957 (1 pen), 1958 (1), 1959 (1), 1960 (3).
7 Ferenc Puskas (Real Madrid), 1960 (4), 1962 (3).

### MOST FINAL APPEARANCES PER COUNTRY
Italy 23 (10 wins, 13 defeats).
Spain 19 (10 wins, 9 defeats).
Germany 13 (6 wins, 7 defeats).
England 11 (9 wins, 2 defeats).

### MOST CLUB FINAL WINNERS

| | | |
|---|---|---|
| Real Madrid (Spain) | 9 | 1956, 1957, 1958, 1959, 1960, 1966, 1998, 2000, 2002. |
| AC Milan (Italy) | 6 | 1963, 1969, 1989, 1990, 1994, 2003. |

### MOST APPEARANCES IN FINAL
Real Madrid 12; AC Milan 9.

### MOST EUROPEAN CUP APPEARANCES
Paolo Maldini (AC Milan)

| *Season* | *European Cup* | *Cup* | *UEFA Cup* | *Super* | *WCC* |
|---|---|---|---|---|---|
| 1985-86 | 0 | 6 | 0 | 0 | |
| 1987-88 | 0 | 2 | 0 | 0 | |
| 1988-89 | 7 | 0 | 0 | 0 | |
| 1989-90 | 8 | 0 | 2 | 1 | |
| 1990-91 | 4 | 0 | 2 | 0 | |
| 1992-93 | 10 | 0 | 0 | 0 | |
| 1993-94 | 10 | 0 | 2 | 1 | |
| 1994-95 | 11 | 0 | 2 | 0 | |
| 1995-96 | 0 | 8 | 0 | 0 | |
| 1996-97 | 6 | 0 | 0 | 0 | |
| 1999-2000 | | 6 | 0 | 0 | 0 |
| 2000-01 | 14 | 0 | 0 | 0 | |
| 2001-02 | 0 | 4 | 0 | 0 | |
| 2002-03 | 19 | 0 | 0 | 0 | |
| 2003-04 | 9 | 0 | 0 | 1 | |
| *Total* | 104 | 20 | 8 | 3 | |

### MOST SUCCESSFUL MANAGER
Bob Paisley (Liverpool) 1977, 1978, 1981.

### FASTEST GOALS SCORED IN CHAMPIONS LEAGUE
20.07 sec Gilberto Silva for Arsenal at PSV Eindhoven 25 September 2002.
20.12 sec Alessandro Del Piero for Juventus at Manchester United 1 October 1997.

### MOST SUCCESSIVE CHAMPIONS LEAGUE APPEARANCES
Rosenborg (Norway) 9 1995–96 – 2003–04.

### MOST SUCCESSIVE WINS IN THE CHAMPIONS LEAGUE
Barcelona (Spain) 11 2002–03.

# OTHER BRITISH FOOTBALL RECORDS

## ALL-TIME PREMIER LEAGUE CHAMPIONSHIP SEASONS ON POINTS AVERAGE

| | Team | Season | P | W | D | L | F | A | Pts | Pts Av |
|---|---|---|---|---|---|---|---|---|---|---|
| 1 | Manchester U | 1999–2000 | 38 | 28 | 7 | 3 | 97 | 45 | 91 | 2.39 |
| 2 | Arsenal | 2003–04 | 38 | 26 | 12 | 0 | 73 | 26 | 90 | 2.36 |
| 3 | Arsenal | 2001–02 | 38 | 26 | 9 | 3 | 79 | 36 | 87 | 2.28 |
| 4 | Manchester U | 1993–94 | 42 | 27 | 11 | 4 | 80 | 38 | 92 | 2.19 |
| 5 | Manchester U | 2002–03 | 38 | 25 | 8 | 5 | 74 | 34 | 83 | 2.18 |
| 6 | Manchester U | 1995–96 | 38 | 25 | 7 | 6 | 73 | 35 | 82 | 2.15 |
| 7 | Blackburn R | 1994–95 | 42 | 27 | 8 | 7 | 80 | 39 | 89 | 2.11 |
| 8 | Manchester U | 2000–01 | 38 | 24 | 8 | 6 | 79 | 31 | 80 | 2.10 |
| 9 | Manchester U | 1998–99 | 38 | 22 | 13 | 3 | 80 | 37 | 79 | 2.07 |
| 10 | Arsenal | 1997–98 | 38 | 23 | 9 | 6 | 68 | 33 | 78 | 2.05 |
| 11 | Manchester U | 1992–93 | 42 | 24 | 12 | 6 | 67 | 31 | 84 | 2.00 |
| 12 | Manchester U | 1996–97 | 38 | 21 | 12 | 5 | 76 | 44 | 75 | 1.97 |

## TOP TEN WORLD TRANSFERS

| | Player | Clubs | Fee (£m) | Year |
|---|---|---|---|---|
| 1 | Zinedine Zidane | Juventus to Real Madrid | 46.5 | 2001 |
| 2 | Luis Figo | Barcelona to Real Madrid | 37.4 | 2000 |
| 3 | Hernan Crespo | Parma to Lazio | 35.7 | 2000 |
| 4 | Gianluigi Buffon | Parma to Juventus | 34 | 2001 |
| 5 | Christian Vieri | Lazio to Internationale | 31 | 1999 |
| 6 | Rio Ferdinand | Leeds U to Manchester U | 30 | 2002 |
| 7 | Giazka Mendieta | Valencia to Lazio | 29 | 2001 |
| 8 | Ronaldo | Internazionale to Real Madrid | 28.9 | 2002 |
| 9 | Juan Sebastian Veron | Lazio to Manchester United | 28.1 | 2001 |
| 10 | Rui Costa | Fiorentina to AC Milan | 28 | 2001 |

*Source: National Press.*

## TOP TEN BRITISH TRANSFERS (incoming only)

| | Player | Clubs | Fee (£m) | Year |
|---|---|---|---|---|
| 1 | Rio Ferdinand | Leeds U to Manchester U | 30 | 2002 |
| 2 | Juan Sebastian Veron | Lazio to Manchester U | 28.1 | 2001 |
| 3 | Ruud Van Nistelrooy | PSV Eindhoven to Manchester U | 19 | 2001 |
| 4 | Rio Ferdinand | West Ham U to Leeds U | 18 | 2000 |
| 5 | José Antonio Reyes | Sevill to Arsenal | 17.6 | 2004 |
| 6 | Damien Duff | Blackburn R to Chelsea | 17 | 2003 |
| 7 | Hernan Crespo | Inernazionale to Chelsea | 16.8 | 2003 |
| 8 | Adrian Mutu | Parma to Chelsea | 15.8 | 2003 |
| 9 | Alan Shearer | Blackburn R to Newcastle U | 15 | 1996 |
| | Jimmy Floyd Hasselbaink | Atletico Madrid to Chelsea | 15 | 2000 |

*Source: National Press.*

## REAL MADRID

Real Madrid's origins include teams called Madrid FC and Foot-Ball-Sky! In 1904 they became the only club side to be admitted to FIFA. Two years later their membership was cancelled as only national associations were deemed to be eligible.

## CHARLIE DAVIS

Centre-half Charlie Davis has the unique record of playing for three different Football League clubs in their first season in the competition: Torquay United 1927–28, York City 1929–30 and Mansfield Town 1931–32.

## TOP TEN PREMIER LEAGUE AVERAGE ATTENDANCES 2003–04

| | | |
|---|---|---|
| 1 | Manchester U | 67,641 |
| 2 | Newcastle U | 51,966 |
| 3 | Manchester C | 46,830 |
| 4 | Liverpool | 42,677 |
| 5 | Chelsea | 41,272 |
| 6 | Everton | 38,837 |
| 7 | Arsenal | 38,079 |
| 8 | Leeds U | 36,666 |
| 9 | Aston Villa | 36,622 |
| 10 | Tottenham H | 34,872 |

## TOP TEN GOALSCORERS IN WORLD CUP FINAL TOURNAMENTS

| | | | |
|---|---|---|---|
| 1 | Gerd Muller (West Germany) | 1970, 74 | 14 |
| 2 | Just Fontaine (France) | 1958 | 13 |
| 3 | Pele (Brazil) | 1958, 70 | 12 |
| 4 | Ronaldo (Brazil) | 1998, 2002 | 12 |
| 5 | Sandor Kocsis (Hungary) | 1954 | 11 |
| 6 | Jurgen Klinsmann (Germany) | 1990, 98 | 11 |
| 7 | Helmut Rahn (West Germany) | 1954, 58 | 10 |
| | Teofilo Cubillas (Peru) | 1970, 78 | 10 |
| | Grzegorz Lato (Poland) | 1974, 82 | 10 |
| | Gary Lineker (England) | 1986, 90 | 10 |
| | Gabriel Batistuta (Argentina) | 1994, 2002 | 10 |

## TOP TEN FOOTBALL LEAGUE AVERAGE ATTENDANCES 2002–03

| | | |
|---|---|---|
| 1 | West Ham U | 31,167 |
| 2 | Sunderland | 27,119 |
| 3 | WBA | 24,765 |
| 4 | Nottingham F | 24,759 |
| 5 | Ipswich T | 24,520 |
| 6 | Sheffield W | 22,336 |
| 7 | Derby Co | 22,200 |
| 8 | Sheffield U | 21,646 |
| 9 | Norwich C | 19,074 |
| 10 | Crystal Palace | 17,344 |

## TOP TEN ALL-TIME ENGLAND GOALSCORERS

| | | |
|---|---|---|
| 1 | Bobby Charlton | 49 |
| 2 | Gary Lineker | 48 |
| 3 | Jimmy Greaves | 44 |
| 4 | Tom Finney | 30 |
| 5 | Nat Lofthouse | 30 |
| 6 | Alan Shearer | 30 |
| 7 | Vivian Woodward | 29 |
| 8 | Steve Bloomer | 28 |
| 9 | David Platt | 27 |
| 10 | Bryan Robson & Michael Owen | 26 |

## TOP TEN AVERAGE ATTENDANCES

| | | | |
|---|---|---|---|
| 1 | Manchester United | 2003–04 | 67,641 |
| 2 | Manchester United | 2002–03 | 67,630 |
| 3 | Manchester United | 2001–02 | 67,586 |
| 4 | Manchester United | 2000–01 | 67,544 |
| 5 | Manchester United | 1999–2000 | 58,017 |
| 6 | Manchester United | 1967–68 | 57,552 |
| 7 | Newcastle United | 1947–48 | 56,283 |
| 8 | Tottenham Hotspur | 1950–51 | 55,509 |
| 9 | Manchester United | 1998–99 | 55,188 |
| 10 | Manchester United | 1997–98 | 55,168 |

## TOP TEN AVERAGE WORLD CUP FINAL CROWDS

| | | | |
|---|---|---|---|
| 1 | In USA | 1994 | 68,604 |
| 2 | In Brazil | 1950 | 60,772 |
| 3 | In Mexico | 1970 | 52,311 |
| 4 | In England | 1966 | 50,458 |
| 5 | In Italy | 1990 | 48,368 |
| 6 | In Mexico | 1986 | 46,956 |
| 7 | In West Germany | 1974 | 46,684 |
| 8 | In France | 1998 | 43,366 |
| 9 | In Argentina | 1978 | 42,374 |
| 10 | In South Korea/Japan | 2002 | 42,274 |

## TOP TEN ALL-TIME ENGLAND CAPS

| | | |
|---|---|---|
| 1 | Peter Shilton | 125 |
| 2 | Bobby Moore | 108 |
| 3 | Bobby Charlton | 106 |
| 4 | Billy Wright | 105 |
| 5 | Bryan Robson | 90 |
| 6 | Kenny Sansom | 86 |
| 7 | Ray Wilkins | 84 |
| 8 | Gary Lineker | 80 |
| 9 | John Barnes | 79 |
| 10 | Stuart Pearce | 78 |

## TOP TEN PREMIERSHIP APPEARANCES

| | | |
|---|---|---|
| 1 | Gary Speed | 414 |
| 2 | Alan Shearer | 381 |
| 3 | Teddy Sheringham | 375 |
| 4 | Ryan Giggs | 375 |
| 5 | Gareth Southgate | 339 |
| 6 | David James | 345 |
| 7 | Sol Campbell | 354 |
| 8 | Nigel Winterburn | 352 |
| 9 | David Seaman | 344 |
| 10 | Tim Sherwood | 341 |

## MOST GOALS FOR IN A SEASON

| | | Goals | Games |
|---|---|---|---|
| **FA PREMIER LEAGUE** | | | |
| 1999–2000 | Manchester U | 97 | 38 |
| **FOOTBALL LEAGUE** | | | |
| **Division 1** | | | |
| 1930–31 | Aston V | 128 | 42 |
| **Division 2** | | | |
| 1926–27 | Middlesbrough | 122 | 42 |
| **Division 3(S)** | | | |
| 1927–28 | Millwall | 127 | 42 |
| **Division 3(N)** | | | |
| 1928–29 | Bradford C | 128 | 42 |
| **Division 3** | | | |
| 1961–62 | QPR | 111 | 46 |
| **Division 4** | | | |
| 1960–61 | Peterborough U | 134 | 46 |
| **SCOTTISH PREMIER LEAGUE** | | | |
| 2001–02 | Celtic | 94 | 38 |
| **SCOTTISH LEAGUE** | | | |
| **Premier Division** | | | |
| 2003–04 | Celtic | 105 | 38 |
| 1991–92 | Rangers | 101 | 44 |
| 1982–83 | Dundee U | 90 | 36 |
| 1982–83 | Celtic | 90 | 36 |
| 1986–87 | Celtic | 90 | 44 |
| **Division 1** | | | |
| 1957–58 | Hearts | 132 | 34 |
| **Division 2** | | | |
| 1937–38 | Raith R | 142 | 34 |
| **New Division 1** | | | |
| 1993–94 | Dunfermline Ath | 93 | 44 |
| 1981–82 | Motherwell | 92 | 39 |
| **New Division 2** | | | |
| 1987–88 | Ayr U | 95 | 39 |
| **New Division 3** | | | |
| 2003–04 | Stranraer | 87 | 36 |

## FEWEST GOALS AGAINST IN A SEASON

| | | Goals | Games |
|---|---|---|---|
| **FA PREMIER LEAGUE** | | | |
| 1998–99 | Arsenal | 17 | 38 |
| **FOOTBALL LEAGUE** (minimum 42 games) | | | |
| **Division 1** | | | |
| 1978–79 | Liverpool | 16 | 42 |
| **Division 2** | | | |
| 1924–25 | Manchester U | 23 | 42 |
| 2002–03 | Wigan Ath | 25 | 46 |
| **Division 3(S)** | | | |
| 1921–22 | Southampton | 21 | 42 |
| **Division 3(N)** | | | |
| 1953–54 | Port Vale | 21 | 46 |
| **Division 3** | | | |
| 1995–96 | Gillingham | 20 | 46 |
| **Division 4** | | | |
| 1980–81 | Lincoln C | 25 | 46 |
| **SCOTTISH PREMIER LEAGUE** | | | |
| 2001–02 | Celtic | 18 | 38 |
| **SCOTTISH LEAGUE** (minimum 30 games) | | | |
| **Premier Division** | | | |
| 1989–90 | Rangers | 19 | 36 |
| 1986–87 | Rangers | 23 | 44 |
| 1987–88 | Celtic | 23 | 44 |
| **Division 1** | | | |
| 1913–14 | Celtic | 14 | 38 |
| **Division 3** | | | |
| 1966–67 | Morton | 20 | 38 |
| **New Division 1** | | | |
| 1996–97 | St Johnstone | 23 | 36 |
| 1980–81 | Hibernian | 24 | 39 |
| 1993–94 | Falkirk | 32 | 44 |
| **New Division 2** | | | |
| 1987–88 | St Johnstone | 24 | 39 |
| 1990–91 | Stirling Alb | 24 | 39 |
| **New Division 3** | | | |
| 1995–96 | Brechin C | 21 | 36 |

## FEWEST GOALS FOR IN A SEASON

| | | Goals | Games |
|---|---|---|---|
| **FA PREMIER LEAGUE** | | | |
| 2002–03 | Sunderland | 21 | 38 |
| **FOOTBALL LEAGUE** (minimum 42 games) | | | |
| **Division 1** | | | |
| 1984–85 | Stoke C | 24 | 42 |
| **Division 2** | | | |
| 1971–72 | Watford | 24 | 42 |
| 1994–95 | Leyton Orient | 30 | 46 |
| **Division 3(S)** | | | |
| 1950–51 | Crystal Palace | 33 | 46 |
| **Division 3(N)** | | | |
| 1923–24 | Crewe Alex | 32 | 42 |
| **Division 3** | | | |
| 1969–70 | Stockport Co | 27 | 46 |
| **Division 4** | | | |
| 1981–82 | Crewe Alex | 29 | 46 |
| **SCOTTISH PREMIER LEAGUE** | | | |
| 2001–02 | St Johnstone | 24 | 38 |
| **SCOTTISH LEAGUE** (minimum 30 games) | | | |
| **Premier Division** | | | |
| 1988–89 | Hamilton A | 19 | 36 |
| 1991–92 | Dunfermline Ath | 22 | 44 |
| **Division 1** | | | |
| 1993–94 | Brechin C | 30 | 44 |
| 1966–67 | Ayr U | 20 | 34 |
| **Division 2** | | | |
| 1923–24 | Lochgelly U | 20 | 38 |
| **New Division 1** | | | |
| 1980–81 | Stirling Alb | 18 | 39 |
| 1995–96 | Dumbarton | 23 | 36 |
| **New Division 2** | | | |
| 1994–95 | Brechin C | 22 | 36 |
| **New Division 3** | | | |
| 1995–96 | Alloa | 26 | 36 |

## MOST GOALS AGAINST IN A SEASON

| | | Goals | Games |
|---|---|---|---|
| **FA PREMIER LEAGUE** | | | |
| 1993–94 | Swindon T | 100 | 42 |
| **FOOTBALL LEAGUE** | | | |
| **Division 1** | | | |
| 1930–31 | Blackpool | 125 | 42 |
| **Division 2** | | | |
| 1898–99 | Darwen | 141 | 34 |
| **Division 3(S)** | | | |
| 1929–30 | Merthyr T | 135 | 42 |
| **Division 3(N)** | | | |
| 1927–28 | Nelson | 136 | 42 |
| **Division 3** | | | |
| 1959–60 | Accrington S | 123 | 46 |
| **Division 4** | | | |
| 1959–60 | Hartlepools U | 109 | 46 |
| **SCOTTISH PREMIER LEAGUE** | | | |
| 1999–2000 | Aberdeen | 83 | 36 |
| **SCOTTISH LEAGUE** | | | |
| **Premier Division** | | | |
| 1984–85 | Morton | 100 | 36 |
| 1987–88 | Morton | 100 | 44 |
| **Division 1** | | | |
| 1931–32 | Leith Ath | 137 | 38 |
| **Division 2** | | | |
| 1931–32 | Edinburgh C | 146 | 38 |
| **New Division 1** | | | |
| 1988–89 | Queen of the S | 99 | 39 |
| 1992–93 | Cowdenbeath | 109 | 44 |
| **New Division 2** | | | |
| 1977–78 | Meadowbank T | 89 | 39 |
| **New Division 3** | | | |
| 2003–04 | East Stirling | 118 | 36 |

## GOALS PER GAME (from 1992–93)

| Goals per game | Premier | | Division 1 | | Division 2 | | Division 3 | |
|---|---|---|---|---|---|---|---|---|
| | Games | Goals | Games | Goals | Games | Goals | Games | Goals |
| 0 | 428 | 0 | 563 | 0 | 550 | 0 | 534 | 0 |
| 1 | 892 | 892 | 1231 | 1231 | 1236 | 1236 | 1223 | 1223 |
| 2 | 1184 | 2368 | 1651 | 3302 | 1713 | 3426 | 1607 | 3214 |
| 3 | 981 | 2943 | 1389 | 4167 | 1430 | 4290 | 1389 | 4167 |
| 4 | 669 | 2676 | 932 | 3728 | 901 | 3604 | 844 | 3376 |
| 5 | 347 | 1735 | 507 | 2535 | 474 | 2370 | 429 | 2145 |
| 6 | 184 | 1104 | 233 | 1398 | 189 | 1134 | 202 | 1212 |
| 7 | 80 | 560 | 80 | 560 | 94 | 658 | 86 | 602 |
| 8 | 34 | 272 | 28 | 224 | 24 | 192 | 29 | 232 |
| 9 | 7 | 63 | 5 | 45 | 11 | 99 | 8 | 72 |
| 10 | 0 | 0 | 3 | 30 | 2 | 20 | 2 | 20 |
| 11 | 0 | 0 | 2 | 22 | 0 | 0 | 1 | 11 |
| | **4806** | **12613** | **6624** | **17242** | **6624** | **17029** | **6354** | **16274** |

## GOALS PER GAME (Football League to 1991–92))

| Goals per game | Division 1 | | Division 2 | | Division 3 | | Division 4 | | Division 3(S) | | Division 3(N) | |
|---|---|---|---|---|---|---|---|---|---|---|---|---|
| | Games | Goals | Games | Goals | Games | Goals | Games | Goals | Games | Goals | Games | Goals |
| 0 | 2465 | 0 | 2665 | 0 | 1446 | 0 | 1438 | 0 | 997 | 0 | 803 | 0 |
| 1 | 5606 | 5606 | 5836 | 5836 | 3225 | 3225 | 3106 | 3106 | 2073 | 2073 | 1914 | 1914 |
| 2 | 8275 | 16550 | 8609 | 17218 | 4569 | 9138 | 4441 | 8882 | 3314 | 6628 | 2939 | 5878 |
| 3 | 7731 | 23193 | 7842 | 23526 | 3784 | 11352 | 4041 | 12123 | 2996 | 8988 | 2922 | 8766 |
| 4 | 6230 | 24920 | 5897 | 23588 | 2837 | 11348 | 2784 | 11136 | 2445 | 9780 | 2410 | 9640 |
| 5 | 3751 | 18755 | 3634 | 18170 | 1566 | 7830 | 1506 | 7530 | 1554 | 7770 | 1599 | 7995 |
| 6 | 2137 | 12822 | 2007 | 12042 | 769 | 4614 | 786 | 4716 | 870 | 5220 | 930 | 5580 |
| 7 | 1092 | 7644 | 1001 | 7007 | 357 | 2499 | 336 | 2352 | 451 | 3157 | 461 | 3227 |
| 8 | 542 | 4336 | 376 | 3008 | 135 | 1080 | 143 | 1144 | 209 | 1672 | 221 | 1768 |
| 9 | 197 | 1773 | 164 | 1476 | 64 | 576 | 35 | 315 | 76 | 684 | 102 | 918 |
| 10 | 83 | 830 | 68 | 680 | 13 | 130 | 8 | 80 | 33 | 330 | 45 | 450 |
| 11 | 37 | 407 | 19 | 209 | 2 | 22 | 7 | 77 | 15 | 165 | 15 | 165 |
| 12 | 12 | 144 | 17 | 204 | 1 | 12 | 0 | 0 | 7 | 84 | 8 | 96 |
| 13 | 4 | 52 | 4 | 52 | 0 | 0 | 0 | 0 | 2 | 26 | 4 | 52 |
| 14 | 2 | 28 | 1 | 14 | 0 | 0 | 0 | 0 | 0 | 0 | 0 | 0 |
| 17 | 0 | 0 | 0 | 0 | 0 | 0 | 0 | 0 | 0 | 0 | 1 | 17 |
| | **38164** | **117060** | **38140** | **113030** | **18768** | **51826** | **18631** | **51461** | **15042** | **46577** | **14374** | **46466** |

| New Overall Totals (since 1992) | | Totals (up to1991–92) | | Complete Overall Totals (since 1888–89) | |
|---|---|---|---|---|---|
| Games | 24408 | Games | 143119 | Games | 167527 |
| Goals | 63158 | Goals | 426420 | Goals | 489578 |

## TOP TEN PREMIERSHIP GOALSCORERS

| | | | | | |
|---|---|---|---|---|---|
| **1** | Alan Shearer | 243 | **6** | Dwight Yorke | 120 |
| **2** | Andy Cole | 163 | **7** | Michael Owen | 118 |
| **3** | Les Ferdinand | 148 | **8** | Ian Wright | 113 |
| **4** | Robbie Fowler | 143 | **9** | Thierry Henry | 112 |
| **5** | Teddy Sheringham | 138 | **10** | Dion Dublin | 111 |

## MOST CUP GOALS IN A CAREER

**FA CUP (Pre-Second World war)**
Henry Cursham 48 (Notts Co)

**FA CUP (post-war)**
Ian Rush 43 (Chester, Liverpool)

**LEAGUE CUP**
Geoff Hurst 49 (West Ham U, Stoke C)
Ian Rush 49 (Chester, Liverpool, Newcastle U)

## SCORED IN EVERY PREMIERSHIP GAME

Arsenal 2001–02 38 matches

## MOST FA CUP FINAL GOALS

Ian Rush (Liverpool) 5: 1986(2), 1989(2), 1992(1)

## MOST LEAGUE GOALS IN A SEASON

| | | Goals | Games |
|---|---|---|---|
| **FA PREMIER LEAGUE** | | | |
| 1993–94 | Andy Cole (Newcastle U) | 34 | 40 |
| 1994–95 | Alan Shearer (Blackburn R) | 34 | 42 |
| **FOOTBALL LEAGUE** | | | |
| **Division 1** | | | |
| 1927–28 | Dixie Dean (Everton) | 60 | 39 |
| **Division 2** | | | |
| 1926–27 | George Camsell (Middlesbrough) | 59 | 37 |
| **Division 3(S)** | | | |
| 1936–37 | Joe Payne (Luton T) | 55 | 39 |
| **Division 3(N)** | | | |
| 1936–37 | Ted Harston (Mansfield T) | 55 | 41 |
| **Division 3** | | | |
| 1959–60 | Derek Reeves (Southampton) | 39 | 46 |
| **Division 4** | | | |
| 1960–61 | Terry Bly (Peterborough U) | 52 | 46 |
| **FA CUP** | | | |
| 1887–88 | Jimmy Ross (Preston NE) | 20 | 8 |
| **LEAGUE CUP** | | | |
| 1986–87 | Clive Allen (Tottenham H) | 12 | 9 |
| **SCOTTISH PREMIER LEAGUE** | | | |
| 2000–01 | Henrik Larsson (Celtic) | 35 | 37 |
| **SCOTTISH LEAGUE** | | | |
| **Division 1** | | | |
| 1931–32 | William McFadyen (Motherwell) | 52 | 34 |
| **Division 2** | | | |
| 1927–28 | Jim Smith (Ayr U) | 66 | 38 |

## MOST LEAGUE GOALS IN A CAREER

**FOOTBALL LEAGUE**

| **Arthur Rowley** | Goals | Games | Season |
|---|---|---|---|
| WBA | 4 | 24 | 1946–48 |
| Fulham | 27 | 56 | 1948–50 |
| Leicester C | 251 | 303 | 1950–58 |
| Shrewsbury T | 152 | 236 | 1958–65 |
| | 434 | 619 | |

**SCOTTISH LEAGUE**

| **Jimmy McGrory** | Goals | Games | Season |
|---|---|---|---|
| Celtic | 1 | 3 | 1922–23 |
| Clydebank | 13 | 30 | 1923–24 |
| Celtic | 396 | 375 | 1924–38 |
| | 410 | 408 | |

## HAT-TRICKS

**Career**
34 Dixie Dean (Tranmere R, Everton, Notts Co, England)

**Division 1 (one season post-war)**
6 Jimmy Greaves (Chelsea), 1960–61

**Three for one team one match**
West, Spouncer, Hooper, Nottingham F v Leicester Fosse, Division 1, 21 April 1909
Barnes, Ambler, Davies, Wrexham v Hartlepools U, Division 4, 3 March 1962
Adcock, Stewart, White, Manchester C v Huddersfield T, Division 2, 7 Nov 1987
Loasby, Smith, Wells, Northampton T v Walsall, Division 3S, 5 Nov 1927
Bowater, Hoyland, Readman, Mansfield T v Rotherham U, Division 3N, 27 Dec 1932

## MOST GOALS IN A GAME

| | |
|---|---|
| **FA PREMIER LEAGUE** | |
| 19 Sept 1999 | Alan Shearer (Newcastle U) 5 goals v Sheffield W |
| 4 Mar 1995 | Andy Cole (Manchester U) 5 goals v Ipswich T |
| **FOOTBALL LEAGUE** | |
| **Division 1** | |
| 14 Dec 1935 | Ted Drake (Arsenal) 7 goals v Aston V |
| **Division 2** | |
| 5 Feb 1955 | Tommy Briggs (Blackburn R) 7 goals v Bristol R |
| 23 Feb 1957 | Neville Coleman (Stoke C) 7 goals v Lincoln C |
| **Division 3(S)** | |
| 13 April 1936 | Joe Payne (Luton T) 10 goals v Bristol R |
| **Division 3(N)** | |
| 26 Dec 1935 | Bunny Bell (Tranmere R) 9 goals v Oldham Ath |
| **Division 3** | |
| 16 Sept 1969 | Steve Earle (Fulham) 5 goals v Halifax T |
| 24 April 1965 | Barrie Thomas (Scunthorpe U) 5 goals v Luton T |
| 20 Nov 1965 | Keith East (Swindon T) 5 goals v Mansfield T |
| 2 Oct 1971 | Alf Wood (Shrewsbury T) 5 goals v Blackburn R |
| 10 Sept 1983 | Tony Caldwell (Bolton W) 5 goals v Walsall |
| 4 May 1987 | Andy Jones (Port Vale) 5 goals v Newport Co |
| 3 April 1990 | Steve Wilkinson (Mansfield T) 5 goals v Birmingham C |
| 5 Sept 1998 | Giuliano Grazioli (Peterborough U) 5 goals v Barnet |
| 6 April 2002 | Lee Jones (Wrexham) 5 goals v Cambridge U |
| **Division 4** | |
| 26 Dec 1962 | Bert Lister (Oldham Ath) 6 goals v Southport |
| **FA CUP** | |
| 20 Nov 1971 | Ted MacDougall (Bournemouth) 9 goals v Margate (*1st Round*) |
| **LEAGUE CUP** | |
| 25 Oct 1989 | Frankie Bunn (Oldham Ath) 6 goals v Scarborough |
| **SCOTTISH LEAGUE** | |
| **Premier Division** | |
| 17 Nov 1984 | Paul Sturrock (Dundee U) 5 goals v Morton |
| **Premier League** | |
| 23 Aug 1996 | Marco Negri (Rangers) 5 goals v Dundee U |
| **Division 1** | |
| 14 Sept 1928 | Jimmy McGrory (Celtic) 8 goals v Dunfermline Ath |
| **Division 2** | |
| 1 Oct 1927 | Owen McNally (Arthurlie) 8 goals v Armadale |
| 2 Jan 1930 | Jim Dyet (King's Park) 8 goals v Forfar Ath |
| 18 April 1936 | John Calder (Morton) 8 goals v Raith R |
| 20 Aug 1937 | Norman Hayward (Raith R) 8 goals v Brechin C |
| **SCOTTISH CUP** | |
| 12 Sept 1885 | John Petrie (Arbroath) 13 goals v Bon Accord (*1st Round*) |

## HIGHEST WINS

**Highest win in a First-Class Match**
*(Scottish Cup 1st Round)*

| | | | | |
|---|---|---|---|---|
| Arbroath | 36 | Bon Accord | 0 | 12 Sept 1885 |

**Highest win in an International Match**

| | | | | |
|---|---|---|---|---|
| England | 13 | Ireland | 0 | 18 Feb 1882 |

**Highest win in a FA Cup Match**

| | | | | |
|---|---|---|---|---|
| Preston NE *(1st Round)* | 26 | Hyde U | 0 | 15 Oct 1887 |

**Highest win in a League Cup Match**

| | | | | |
|---|---|---|---|---|
| West Ham U *(2nd Round, 2nd Leg)* | 10 | Bury | 0 | 25 Oct 1983 |
| Liverpool *(2nd Round, 1st Leg)* | 10 | Fulham | 0 | 23 Sept 1986 |

**Highest win in an FA Premier League Match**

| | | | | |
|---|---|---|---|---|
| Manchester U | 9 | Ipswich T | 0 | 4 March 1995 |
| Nottingham F | 1 | Manchester U | 8 | 6 Feb 1999 |

**Highest win in a Football League Match**

**Division 1 – highest home win**

| | | | | |
|---|---|---|---|---|
| WBA | 12 | Darwen | 0 | 4 April 1892 |
| Nottingham F | 12 | Leicester Fosse | 0 | 21 April 1909 |

**Division 1 – highest away win**

| | | | | |
|---|---|---|---|---|
| Newcastle U | 1 | Sunderland | 9 | 5 Dec 1908 |
| Cardiff C | 1 | Wolverhampton W | 9 | 3 Sept 1955 |

**Division 2 – highest home win**

| | | | | |
|---|---|---|---|---|
| Newcastle U | 13 | Newport Co | 0 | 5 Oct 1946 |

**Division 2 – highest away win**

| | | | | |
|---|---|---|---|---|
| Burslem PV | 0 | Sheffield U | 10 | 10 Dec 1892 |

**Division 3 – highest home win**

| | | | | |
|---|---|---|---|---|
| Gillingham | 10 | Chesterfield | 0 | 5 Sept 1987 |

**Division 3 – highest away win**

| | | | | |
|---|---|---|---|---|
| Barnet | 1 | Peterborough U | 9 | 5 Sept 1998 |

**Division 3(S) – highest home win**

| | | | | |
|---|---|---|---|---|
| Luton T | 12 | Bristol R | 0 | 13 April 1936 |

**Division 3(S – highest away win**

| | | | | |
|---|---|---|---|---|
| Northampton T | 0 | Walsall | 8 | 2 Feb 1947 |

**Division 3(N – highest home win**

| | | | | |
|---|---|---|---|---|
| Stockport Co | 13 | Halifax T | 0 | 6 Jan 1934 |

**Division 3(N) – highest away win**

| | | | | |
|---|---|---|---|---|
| Accrington S | 0 | Barnsley | 9 | 3 Feb 1934 |

**Division 4 – highest home win**

| | | | | |
|---|---|---|---|---|
| Oldham Ath | 11 | Southport | 0 | 26 Dec 1962 |

**Division 4 – highest away win**

| | | | | |
|---|---|---|---|---|
| Crewe Alex | 1 | Rotherham U | 8 | 8 Sept 1973 |

**Highest wins in a Scottish League Match**

**Scottish Premier Division – highest home win**

| | | | | |
|---|---|---|---|---|
| Aberdeen | 8 | Motherwell | 0 | 26 March 1979 |

**Scottish Premier Division – highest away win**

| | | | | |
|---|---|---|---|---|
| Hamilton A | 0 | Celtic | 8 | 5 Nov 1988 |

**Scottish Division 1 – highest home win**

| | | | | |
|---|---|---|---|---|
| Celtic | 11 | Dundee | 0 | 26 Oct 1895 |

**Scottish Division 1 – highest away win**

| | | | | |
|---|---|---|---|---|
| Airdrieonians | 1 | Hibernian | 11 | 24 Oct 1950 |

**Scottish Division 2 – highest home win**

| | | | | |
|---|---|---|---|---|
| Airdrieonians | 15 | Dundee Wanderers | 1 | 1 Dec 1894 |

**Scottish Division 2 – highest away win**

| | | | | |
|---|---|---|---|---|
| Alloa Ath | 0 | Dundee | 10 | 8 March 1947 |

## MOST HOME WINS IN A SEASON

Brentford won all 21 games in Division 3(S), 1929–30

## RECORD AWAY WINS IN A SEASON

Doncaster R won 18 of 21 games in Division 3(N), 1946–47

## CONSECUTIVE AWAY WINS

**FA PREMIER LEAGUE**
Arsenal 8 games 2001–02

## FEWEST WINS IN A SEASON

| | | *Wins* | *Games* |
|---|---|---|---|
| **FA PREMIER LEAGUE** | | | |
| 1993–94 | Swindon T | 5 | 42 |
| 2002–03 | Sunderland | 4 | 38 |
| **FOOTBALL LEAGUE** | | | |
| **Division 1** | | | |
| 1889–90 | Stoke C | 3 | 22 |
| 1912–13 | Woolwich Arsenal | 3 | 38 |
| 1984–85 | Stoke C | 3 | 42 |
| **Division 2** | | | |
| 1899–1900 | Loughborough T | 1 | 34 |
| 1983–84 | Cambridge U | 4 | 42 |
| **Division 3(S)** | | | |
| 1929–30 | Merthyr T | 6 | 42 |
| 1925–26 | QPR | 6 | 42 |
| **Division 3(N)** | | | |
| 1931–32 | Rochdale | 4 | 40 |
| **Division 3** | | | |
| 1973–74 | Rochdale | 2 | 46 |
| **Division 4** | | | |
| 1976–77 | Southport | 3 | 46 |
| **SCOTTISH PREMIER LEAGUE** | | | |
| 1998–99 | Dunfermline Ath | 4 | 36 |
| **SCOTTISH LEAGUE** | | | |
| **Premier Division** | | | |
| 1975–76 | St Johnstone | 3 | 36 |
| 1982–83 | Kilmarnock | 3 | 36 |
| 1987–88 | Morton | 3 | 44 |
| **Division 1** | | | |
| 1891–92 | Vale of Leven | 0 | 22 |
| **Division 2** | | | |
| 1905–06 | East Stirlingshire | 1 | 22 |
| 1974–75 | Forfar Ath | 1 | 38 |
| **New Division 1** | | | |
| 1988–89 | Queen of the S | 2 | 39 |
| 1992–93 | Cowdenbeath | 3 | 44 |
| **New Division 2** | | | |
| 1975–76 | Forfar Ath | 4 | 26 |
| 1987–88 | Stranraer | 4 | 39 |
| **New Division 3** | | | |
| 2002–03 | East Stirling | 2 | 36 |
| 2003–04 | East Stirling | 2 | 36 |

## UNDEFEATED AT HOME OVERALL

Liverpool 85 games (63 League, 9 League Cup, 7 European, 6 FA Cup), Jan 1978–Jan 1981

## UNDEFEATED IN A SEASON

**FA PREMIER LEAGUE**

| | | |
|---|---|---|
| 2003–04 | Arsenal | 38 games |

**FOOTBALL LEAGUE**

| | | |
|---|---|---|
| 1889–90 | Preston NE | 22 games |

**Division 2**

| | | |
|---|---|---|
| 1893–94 | Liverpool | 22 games |

## UNDEFEATED AWAY

Arsenal 19 games FA Premier League 2001–02 and 2003–04 (only Preston NE with 11 in 1888–89 had previously remained unbeaten away) in the top flight

## HIGHEST AGGREGATE SCORES

**Highest Aggregate Score England**
**Division 3(N)**

| | | | | |
|---|---|---|---|---|
| Tranmere R | 13 | Oldham Ath | 4 | 26 Dec 1935 |

**Highest Aggregate Score Scotland**
**Division 2**

| | | | | |
|---|---|---|---|---|
| Airdrieonians | 15 | Dundee Wanderers | 1 | 1 Dec 1894 |

## MOST WINS IN A SEASON

| | | Wins | Games |
|---|---|---|---|
| **FA PREMIER LEAGUE** | | | |
| 1999–2000 | Manchester U | 28 | 38 |
| **FOOTBALL LEAGUE** | | | |
| **Division 1** | | | |
| 1960–61 | Tottenham H | 31 | 42 |
| 2001–02 | Manchester C | 31 | 46 |
| **Division 2** | | | |
| 1919–20 | Tottenham H | 32 | 42 |
| **Division 3(S)** | | | |
| 1927–28 | Millwall | 30 | 42 |
| 1929–30 | Plymouth Arg | 30 | 42 |
| 1946–47 | Cardiff C | 30 | 42 |
| 1950–51 | Nottingham F | 30 | 46 |
| 1954–55 | Bristol C | 30 | 46 |
| **Division 3(N)** | | | |
| 1946–47 | Doncaster R | 33 | 42 |
| **Division 3** | | | |
| 1971–72 | Aston V | 32 | 46 |
| **Division 4** | | | |
| 1975–76 | Lincoln C | 32 | 46 |
| 1985–86 | Swindon T | 32 | 46 |
| **SCOTTISH PREMIER LEAGUE** | | | |
| 2000–01 | Celtic | 31 | 38 |
| 2002–03 | Rangers | 31 | 38 |
| | Celtic | 31 | 38 |
| 2003–04 | Celtic | 31 | 38 |
| **SCOTTISH LEAGUE** | | | |
| **Premier Division** | | | |
| 1995–96 | Rangers | 27 | 36 |
| 1984–85 | Aberdeen | 27 | 36 |
| 1991–92 | Rangers | 33 | 44 |
| 1992–93 | Rangers | 33 | 44 |
| **Division 1** | | | |
| 1920–21 | Rangers | 35 | 42 |
| **Division 2** | | | |
| 1966–67 | Morton | 33 | 38 |
| **New Division 1** | | | |
| 1998–99 | Hibernian | 28 | 36 |
| **New Division 2** | | | |
| 1983–84 | Forfar Ath | 27 | 39 |
| 1987–88 | Ayr U | 27 | 39 |
| **New Division 3** | | | |
| 1994–95 | Forfar Ath | 25 | 36 |

## MOST POINTS IN A SEASON

*(three points for a win)*

| | | Points | Games |
|---|---|---|---|
| **FA PREMIER LEAGUE** | | | |
| 1993–94 | Manchester U | 92 | 42 |
| **FOOTBALL LEAGUE** | | | |
| **Division 1** | | | |
| 1998–99 | Sunderland | 105 | 46 |
| 1984–85 | Everton | 90 | 42 |
| 1987–88 | Liverpool | 90 | 40 |
| **Division 2** | | | |
| 1998–99 | Fulham | 101 | 46 |
| **Division 3** | | | |
| 2001–02 | Plymouth Arg | 102 | 46 |
| **Division 4** | | | |
| 1985–86 | Swindon T | 102 | 46 |
| **SCOTTISH PREMIER LEAGUE** | | | |
| 2001–02 | Celtic | 103 | 38 |
| **SCOTTISH LEAGUE** | | | |
| **Premier League** | | | |
| 1995–96 | Rangers | 87 | 36 |
| **New Division 1** | | | |
| 1998–99 | Hibernian | 89 | 36 |
| **New Division 2** | | | |
| 1995–96 | Stirling Alb | 81 | 36 |
| **New Division 3** | | | |
| 1994–95 | Forfar Ath | 80 | 36 |

## MOST POINTS IN A SEASON

*(under old system of two points for a win)*

| | | Points | Games |
|---|---|---|---|
| **FOOTBALL LEAGUE** | | | |
| **Division 1** | | | |
| 1978–79 | Liverpool | 68 | 42 |
| **Division 2** | | | |
| 1919–20 | Tottenham H | 70 | 42 |
| **Division 3** | | | |
| 1971–72 | Aston V | 70 | 46 |
| **Division 3(S)** | | | |
| 1950–51 | Nottingham F | 70 | 46 |
| 1954–55 | Bristol C | 70 | 46 |
| **Division 3(N)** | | | |
| 1946–47 | Doncaster R | 72 | 42 |
| **Division 4** | | | |
| 1975–76 | Lincoln C | 74 | 46 |
| **SCOTTISH LEAGUE** | | | |
| **Premier Division** | | | |
| 1984–85 | Aberdeen | 59 | 36 |
| 1992–93 | Rangers | 73 | 44 |
| **Division 1** | | | |
| 1920–21 | Rangers | 76 | 42 |
| **Division 2** | | | |
| 1966–67 | Morton | 69 | 38 |
| **New Division 1** | | | |
| 1976–77 | St Mirren | 62 | 39 |
| 1993–94 | Falkirk | 66 | 44 |
| **New Division 2** | | | |
| 1983–84 | Forfar Ath | 63 | 39 |

## FEWEST POINTS IN A SEASON

| | | Points | Games |
|---|---|---|---|
| **FA PREMIER LEAGUE** | | | |
| 2002–03 | Sunderland | 19 | 38 |
| **FOOTBALL LEAGUE** (minimum 34 games) | | | |
| **Division 1** | | | |
| 1984–85 | Stoke C | 17 | 42 |
| **Division 2** | | | |
| 1904–05 | Doncaster R | 8 | 34 |
| 1899–1900 | Loughborough T | 8 | 34 |
| **Division 3** | | | |
| 1997–98 | Doncaster R | 20 | 46 |
| **Division 3(S)** | | | |
| 1924–25 & 1929–30 | Merthyr T | 21 | 42 |
| 1925–26 | QPR | 21 | 42 |
| **Division 3(N)** | | | |
| 1931–32 | Rochdale | 11 | 40 |
| **Division 4** | | | |
| 1976–77 | Workington | 19 | 46 |
| **SCOTTISH PREMIER LEAGUE** | | | |
| 2001–02 | St Johnstone | 21 | 38 |
| **SCOTTISH LEAGUE** (minimum 30 games) | | | |
| **Premier Division** | | | |
| 1975–76 | St Johnstone | 11 | 36 |
| 1987–88 | Morton | 16 | 44 |
| **Division 1** | | | |
| 1954–55 | Stirling Alb | 6 | 30 |
| **Division 2** | | | |
| 1936–37 | Edinburgh C | 7 | 34 |
| **New Division 1** | | | |
| 1988–89 | Queen of the S | 10 | 39 |
| 1992–93 | Cowdenbeath | 13 | 44 |
| **New Division 2** | | | |
| 1987–88 | Berwick R | 16 | 39 |
| 1987–88 | Stranraer | 16 | 39 |
| **New Division 3** | | | |
| 2003–04 | East Stirling | 8 | 36 |

## FEWEST DEFEATS IN A SEASON

*(Minimum 20 games)*

| FA PREMIER LEAGUE | | Defeats | Games |
|---|---|---|---|
| 1998–99 | Manchester U | 3 | 38 |
| 1998–99 | Chelsea | 3 | 38 |
| 1999–2000 | Manchester U | 3 | 38 |
| 2001–02 | Arsenal | 3 | 38 |
| **FOOTBALL LEAGUE** | | | |
| **Division 1** | | | |
| 1888–89 | Preston NE | 0 | 22 |
| 1990–91 | Arsenal | 1 | 38 |
| 1987–88 | Liverpool | 2 | 40 |
| 1968–69 | Leeds U | 2 | 42 |
| **Division 2** | | | |
| 1893–94 | Liverpool | 0 | 28 |
| 1897–98 | Burnley | 2 | 30 |
| 1905–06 | Bristol C | 2 | 38 |
| 1963–64 | Leeds U | 3 | 42 |
| 2002–03 | Wigan Ath | 4 | 46 |
| **Division 3** | | | |
| 1966–67 | QPR | 5 | 46 |
| 1989–90 | Bristol R | 5 | 46 |
| 1997–98 | Notts Co | 5 | 46 |
| **Division 3(S)** | | | |
| 1921–22 | Southampton | 4 | 42 |
| 1929–30 | Plymouth Arg | 4 | 42 |
| **Division 3(N)** | | | |
| 1953–54 | Port Vale | 3 | 46 |
| 1946–47 | Doncaster R | 3 | 42 |
| 1923–24 | Wolverhampton W | 3 | 42 |
| **Division 4** | | | |
| 1975–76 | Lincoln C | 4 | 46 |
| 1981–82 | Sheffield U | 4 | 46 |
| 1981–82 | Bournemouth | 4 | 46 |
| **SCOTTISH PREMIER LEAGUE** | | | |
| 2001–02 | Celtic | 1 | 38 |
| **SCOTTISH LEAGUE** | | | |
| **Premier Division** | | | |
| 1995–96 | Rangers | 3 | 36 |
| 1987–88 | Celtic | 3 | 44 |
| **Division 1** | | | |
| 1898–99 | Rangers | 0 | 18 |
| 1920–21 | Rangers | 1 | 42 |
| **Division 2** | | | |
| 1956–57 | Clyde | 1 | 36 |
| 1962–63 | Morton | 1 | 36 |
| 1967–68 | St Mirren | 1 | 36 |
| **New Division 1** | | | |
| 1975–76 | Partick T | 2 | 26 |
| 1976–77 | St Mirren | 2 | 39 |
| 1992–93 | Raith R | 4 | 44 |
| 1993–94 | Falkirk | 4 | 44 |
| **New Division 2** | | | |
| 1975–76 | Raith R | 1 | 26 |
| 1975–76 | Clydebank | 3 | 26 |
| 1983–84 | Forfar Ath | 3 | 39 |
| 1986–87 | Raith R | 3 | 39 |
| 1998–99 | Livingston | 3 | 36 |
| **New Division 3** | | | |
| 2000–01 | Hamilton A | 4 | 36 |

## MOST LEAGUE MEDALS

Phil Neal (Liverpool) 8: 1976, 1977, 1979, 1980, 1982, 1983, 1984, 1986
Alan Hansen (Liverpool) 8: 1979, 1980, 1982, 1983, 1984, 1986, 1988, 1990
Ryan Giggs (Manchester U) 8: 1993, 1994, 1996, 1997, 1999, 2000, 2001, 2003

## LEAGUE CHAMPIONSHIP HAT-TRICKS

| | |
|---|---|
| **Huddersfield T** | 1923–24 to 1925–26 |
| **Arsenal** | 1932–33 to 1934–35 |
| **Liverpool** | 1981–82 to 1983–84 |
| **Manchester U** | 1998–99 to 2000–01 |

## MOST DEFEATS IN A SEASON

| FA PREMIER LEAGUE | | Defeats | Games |
|---|---|---|---|
| 1994–95 | Ipswich T | 29 | 42 |
| **FOOTBALL LEAGUE** | | | |
| **Division 1** | | | |
| 1984–85 | Stoke C | 31 | 42 |
| 2003–04 | Wimbledon | 33 | 46 |
| **Division 2** | | | |
| 1938–39 | Tranmere R | 31 | 42 |
| 1992–93 | Chester C | 33 | 46 |
| 2000–01 | Oxford U | 33 | 46 |
| **Division 3** | | | |
| 1997–98 | Doncaster R | 34 | 46 |
| **Division 3(S)** | | | |
| 1924–25 | Merthyr T | 29 | 42 |
| 1952–53 | Walsall | 29 | 46 |
| 1953–54 | Walsall | 29 | 46 |
| **Division 3(N)** | | | |
| 1931–32 | Rochdale | 33 | 40 |
| **Division 4** | | | |
| 1987–88 | Newport Co | 33 | 46 |
| **SCOTTISH PREMIER LEAGUE** | | | |
| 2001–02 | St Johnstone | 27 | 38 |
| **SCOTTISH LEAGUE** | | | |
| **Premier Division** | | | |
| 1984–85 | Morton | 29 | 36 |
| **Division 1** | | | |
| 1920–21 | St Mirren | 31 | 42 |
| **Division 2** | | | |
| 1962–63 | Brechin C | 30 | 36 |
| 1923–24 | Lochgelly | 30 | 38 |
| **New Division 1** | | | |
| 1988–89 | Queen of the S | 29 | 39 |
| 1995–96 | Dumbarton | 31 | 36 |
| 1992–93 | Cowdenbeath | 34 | 44 |
| **New Division 2** | | | |
| 1987–88 | Berwick R | 29 | 39 |
| **New Division 3** | | | |
| 2003–04 | East Stirling | 32 | 36 |

## MOST DRAWN GAMES IN A SEASON

| FA PREMIER LEAGUE | | Draws | Games |
|---|---|---|---|
| 1993–94 | Manchester C | 18 | 42 |
| 1993–94 | Sheffield U | 18 | 42 |
| 1994–95 | Southampton | 18 | 42 |
| **FOOTBALL LEAGUE** | | | |
| **Division 1** | | | |
| 1978–79 | Norwich C | 23 | 42 |
| **Division 3** | | | |
| 1997–98 | Cardiff C | 23 | 46 |
| 1997–98 | Hartlepool U | 23 | 46 |
| **Division 4** | | | |
| 1986–87 | Exeter C | 23 | 46 |
| **SCOTTISH LEAGUE** | | | |
| **Premier Division** | | | |
| 1993–94 | Aberdeen | 21 | 44 |
| **New Division 1** | | | |
| 1986–87 | East Fife | 21 | 44 |

## LONGEST WINNING SEQUENCE

| FA PREMIER LEAGUE | Team | Games |
|---|---|---|
| 2001–02 and 2002–03 | Arsenal | 14 |
| **FOOTBALL LEAGUE** | | |
| **Division 1** | | |
| 1959–60 (2) and 1960–61 (11) | Tottenham H | 13 |
| 1891–92 | Preston NE | 13 |
| 1891–92 | Sunderland | 13 |
| **Division 2** | | |
| 1904–05 | Manchester U | 14 |
| 1905–06 | Bristol C | 14 |
| 1950–51 | Preston NE | 14 |
| **Division 3** | | |
| 1985–86 | Reading | 13 |
| **FROM SEASON'S START** | | |
| **Division 1** | | |
| 1960–61 | Tottenham H | 11 |
| 1992–93 | Newcastle U | 11 |
| 2000–01 | Fulham | 11 |
| **Division 3** | | |
| 1985–86 | Reading | 13 |
| **SCOTTISH LEAGUE** | | |
| **Premier League** | | |
| 2003–04 | Celtic | 25 |

## LONGEST SEQUENCE OF CONSECUTIVE SCORING (Individual)

**FA PREMIER LEAGUE**
Ruud Van Nistelroy
(Manchester U) 15 in 10 games 2003–04

**FOOTBALL LEAGUE RECORD**
Tom Phillipson
(Wolverhampton W) 23 in 13 games 1926–27

## LONGEST UNBEATEN SEQUENCE

| FA PREMIER LEAGUE | Team | Games |
|---|---|---|
| May 2003–May 2004 | Arsenal | 40 |
| **FOOTBALL LEAGUE** | | |
| **Division 1** | | |
| Nov 1977–Dec 1978 | Nottingham F | 42 |

## LONGEST UNBEATEN CUP SEQUENCE

Liverpool 25 rounds League/Milk Cup 1980–84

## LONGEST UNBEATEN SEQUENCE IN A SEASON

| FA PREMIER LEAGUE | Team | Games |
|---|---|---|
| 2003–04 | Arsenal | 38 |
| **FOOTBALL LEAGUE** | | |
| **Division 1** | | |
| 1920–21 | Burnley | 30 |

## LONGEST UNBEATEN START TO A SEASON

| FA PREMIER LEAGUE | Team | Games |
|---|---|---|
| 2003–04 | Arsenal | 38 |
| **FOOTBALL LEAGUE** | *Team* | *Games* |
| **Division 1** | | |
| 1973–74 | Leeds U | 29 |
| 1987–88 | Liverpool | 29 |

## LONGEST SEQUENCE WITHOUT A WIN IN A SEASON

| FOOTBALL LEAGUE | Team | Games |
|---|---|---|
| **Division 2** | | |
| 1983–84 | Cambridge U | 31 |

## NO DEFEATS IN A SEASON

**FA PREMIER LEAGUE**
2003–04 Arsenal won 26, drew 12

**FOOTBALL LEAGUE**
**Division 1**
1888–89 Preston NE won 18, drew 4

**Division 2**
1893–94 Liverpool won 22, drew 6

## LONGEST SEQUENCE WITHOUT A WIN FROM SEASON'S START

| FOOTBALL LEAGUE | Team | Games |
|---|---|---|
| **Division 1** | | |
| 1990–91 | Sheffield U | 16 |

## LONGEST SEQUENCE OF CONSECUTIVE DEFEATS

| FOOTBALL LEAGUE | Team | Games |
|---|---|---|
| **Division 2** | | |
| 1898–99 | Darwen | 18 |

## A CENTURY OF LEAGUE AND CUP GOALS IN CONSECUTIVE SEASONS

| George Camsell | League | Cup | Season |
|---|---|---|---|
| Middlesbrough | 59 | 5 | 1926–27 |
| (101 goals) | 33 | 4 | 1927–28 |

(*Camsell's cup goals were all scored in the FA Cup.*)

| Steve Bull | | | |
|---|---|---|---|
| Wolverhampton W | 34 | 18 | 1987–88 |
| (102 goals) | 37 | 13 | 1988–89 |

(*Bull had 12 in the Sherpa Van Trophy, 3 Littlewoods Cup, 3 FA Cup in 1987–88; 11 Sherpa Van Trophy, 2 Littlewoods Cup in 1988–89.*)

## PENALTIES

**Most in a Season (individual)**

| Division 1 | Goals | Season |
|---|---|---|
| Francis Lee (Manchester C) | 13 | 1971–72 |

**Most awarded in one game**
Five Crystal Palace (4 – 1 scored, 3 missed) v Brighton & HA (1 scored), Div 2 1988–89

**Most saved in a Season**
**Division 1**
Paul Cooper (Ipswich T) 8 (of 10) 1979–80

## GOALKEEPING RECORDS

*(without conceding a goal)*

**BRITISH RECORD (all competitive games)**
Chris Woods, Rangers, in 1196 minutes from 26 November 1986 to 31 January 1987.

**FOOTBALL LEAGUE**
Steve Death, Reading, 1103 minutes from 24 March to 18 August 1979.

## MOST SUCCESSFUL MANAGERS

**Sir Alex Ferguson CBE**
**Manchester U**
16 major trophies in 14 seasons:
8 Premier League, 5 FA Cup, 1 European Cup, 1 Cup-Winners' Cup, 1 League Cup.

**Aberdeen**
1976–86 – 9 trophies:
3 League, 4 Scottish Cup, 1 League Cup, 1 Cup-Winners' Cup.

**Bob Paisley**
**Liverpool**
1974–83 – 13 trophies:
6 League, 3 European Cup, 3 League Cup, 1 UEFA Cup.

## MOST LEAGUE APPEARANCES (750+ matches)

1005 Peter Shilton (286 Leicester City, 110 Stoke City, 202 Nottingham Forest, 188 Southampton, 175 Derby County, 34 Plymouth Argyle, 1 Bolton Wanderers, 9 Leyton Orient) 1966–97

931 Tony Ford (355 Grimsby T, 9 Sunderland (loan), 112 Stoke C, 114 WBA, 68 Grimsby T, 5 Bradford C (loan), 76 Scunthorpe U, 103 Mansfield T, 89 Rochdale) 1975–2002

909 Graeme Armstrong (204 Stirling A, 83 Berwick R, 353 Meadowbank T, 268 Stenhousemuir, 1 Alloa) 1975–2001

863 Tommy Hutchison (165 Blackpool, 314 Coventry City, 46 Manchester City, 92 Burnley, 178 Swansea City, 68 Alloa) 1965–91

824 Terry Paine (713 Southampton, 111 Hereford United) 1957–77

790 Neil Redfearn (35 Bolton W, 10 Lincoln C (loan), 90 Lincoln C, 46 Doncaster R, 57 Crystal Palace, 24 Watford, 62 Oldham Ath, 292 Barnsley, 30 Charlton Ath, 17 Bradford C, 22 Wigan Ath, 42 Halifax T, 54 Boston U, 9 Rochdale) 1982–2004

782 Robbie James (484 Swansea C, 48 Stoke C, 87 QPR, 23 Leicester C, 89 Bradford C, 51 Cardiff C) 1973–94

777 Alan Oakes (565 Manchester C, 211 Chester C, 1 Port Vale) 1959–84

771 John Burridge (27 Workington, 134 Blackpool, 65 Aston Villa, 6 Southend U (loan), 88 Crystal Palace, 39 QPR, 74 Wolverhampton W, 6 Derby Co (loan), 109 Sheffield U, 62 Southampton, 67 Newcastle U, 65 Hibernian, 3 Scarborough, 4 Lincoln C, 3 Aberdeen, 3 Dumbarton, 3 Falkirk, 4 Manchester C, 3 Darlington, 6 Queen of the South) 1968–96

770 John Trollope (all for Swindon Town) 1960–80†

764 Jimmy Dickinson (all for Portsmouth) 1946–65

761 Roy Sproson (all for Port Vale) 1950–72

760 Mick Tait (64 Oxford U, 106 Carlisle U, 33 Hull C, 240 Portsmouth, 99 Reading, 79 Darlington, 139 Hartlepool U) 1975–97

758 Ray Clemence (48 Scunthorpe United, 470 Liverpool, 240 Tottenham Hotspur) 1966–87

758 Billy Bonds (95 Charlton Ath, 663 West Ham U) 1964–88

757 Pat Jennings (48 Watford, 472 Tottenham Hotspur, 237 Arsenal) 1963–86

757 Frank Worthington (171 Huddersfield T, 210 Leicester C, 84 Bolton W, 75 Birmingham C, 32 Leeds U, 19 Sunderland, 34 Southampton, 31 Brighton & HA, 59 Tranmere R, 23 Preston NE, 19 Stockport Co) 1966–88

† record for one club

**CONSECUTIVE**

401 Harold Bell (401 Tranmere R; 459 in all games) 1946–55

**FA CUP**

88 Ian Callaghan (79 Liverpool, 7 Swansea C, 2 Crewe Alex)

**MOST SENIOR MATCHES**

1390 Peter Shilton (1005 League, 86 FA Cup, 102 League Cup, 125 Internationals, 13 Under-23, 4 Football League XI, 20 European Cup, 7 Texaco Cup, 5 Simod Cup, 4 European Super Cup, 4 UEFA Cup, 3 Screen Sport Super Cup, 3 Zenith Data Systems Cup, 2 Autoglass Trophy, 2 Charity Shield, 2 Full Members Cup, 1 Anglo-Italian Cup, 1 Football League play-offs, 1 World Club Championship)

## YOUNGEST PLAYERS

**FA Premier League appearance**
Aaron Lennon, 16 years 129 days, Leeds U v Tottenham H, 23.8.2003.

**FA Premier League scorer**
James Milner, 16 years 357 days, Leeds U v Sunderland 26.12.2002

**Football League appearance**
Albert Geldard, 15 years 158 days, Bradford Park Avenue v Millwall, Division 2, 16.9.29; and Ken Roberts, 15 years 158 days, Wrexham v Bradford Park Avenue, Division 3N, 1.9.51
*If leap years are included, Ken Roberts was 157 days*

**Football League scorer**
Ronnie Dix, 15 years 180 days, Bristol Rovers v Norwich City, Division 3S, 3.3.28.

**Division 1 appearance**
Derek Forster, 15 years 185 days, Sunderland v Leicester City, 22.8.64.

**Division 1 scorer**
Jason Dozzell, 16 years 57 days as substitute Ipswich Town v Coventry City, 4.2.84

**Division 1 hat-tricks**
Alan Shearer, 17 years 240 days, Southampton v Arsenal, 9.4.88
Jimmy Greaves, 17 years 10 months, Chelsea v Portsmouth, 25.12.57

**FA Cup appearance (any round)**
Andy Awford, 15 years 88 days as substitute Worcester City v Boreham Wood, 3rd Qual. rd, 10.10.87

**FA Cup proper appearance**
Lee Holmes, 15 years 277 days, Derby Co v Brentford 4.1.2003

**FA Cup Final appearance**
Curtis Weston, 17 years 119 days, Milwall v Manchester U, 2004

**FA Cup Final scorer**
Norman Whiteside, 18 years 18 days, Manchester United v Brighton & Hove Albion, 1983

**FA Cup Final captain**
David Nish, 21 years 212 days, Leicester City v Manchester City, 1969

**League Cup Final scorer**
Norman Whiteside, 17 years 324 days, Manchester United v Liverpool, 1983

**League Cup Final captain**
Barry Venison, 20 years 7 months 8 days, Sunderland v Norwich City, 1985

## OLDEST PLAYERS

**FA Premier League appearance**
John Burridge 43 years 5 months, Manchester C v QPR 14.5.1995

**Football League appearance**
Neil McBain, 52 years 4 months, New Brighton v Hartlepools United, Div 3N, 15.3.47 (McBain was New Brighton's manager and had to play in an emergency)

**Division 1 appearance**
Stanley Matthews, 50 years 5 days, Stoke City v Fulham, 6.2.65

## RECORD ATTENDANCES

**FA PREMIER LEAGUE**
67,758 Manchester U v Southampton, Old Trafford 31.1.2004

**FOOTBALL LEAGUE**
83,260 Manchester U v Arsenal, Maine Road 17.1.1948

**SCOTTISH LEAGUE**
118,567 Rangers v Celtic, Ibrox Stadium 2.1.1939

**FA CUP FINAL**
126,047* Bolton W v West Ham U, Wembley 28.4.1923

**EUROPEAN CUP**
135,826 Celtic v Leeds U, semi-final at Hampden Park 15.4.1970

**SCOTTISH CUP**
146,433 Celtic v Aberdeen, Hampden Park 24.4.37

**WORLD CUP**
199,854† Brazil v Uruguay, Maracana, Rio 16.7.50

* It has been estimated that as many as 70,000 more broke in without paying.
† 173,830 paid.

## SENDINGS-OFF

**SEASON**
451 (League alone) 2003–04
*(Before rescinded cards taken into account)*

**DAY**
19 (League) 13 Dec 2003

**FA CUP FINAL**
Kevin Moran, Manchester U v Everton 1985

**QUICKEST**
Walter Boyd, Swansea C v Darlington Div 3 as substitute in zero seconds 23 Nov 1999

**MOST IN ONE GAME**
Five: Chesterfield (2) v Plymouth Arg (3) 22 Feb 1997
Five: Wigan Ath (1) v Bristol R (4) 2 Dec 1997
Five: Exeter C (3) v Cambridge U (2) 23 Nov 2002

**MOST IN ONE TEAM**
Wigan Ath (1) v Bristol R (4) 2 Dec 1997
Hereford U (4) v Northampton T (0) 11 Nov 1992

## RED CARDS RESCINDED 2003–04

The following players had their sendings-off rescinded by the referee after the game during the season:

**LEAGUE**
Parker (Charlton Ath) 23 August
Coles (Bristol C) 21 October
Munroe (Macclesfield T) 21 October
Rae (Wolverhampton W) 1 November
Santos (Ipswich T) 13 December
Diouf (Liverpool) 7 January
Bull (Brentford) 17 January
Jones (Rochdale) 14 February

**FA CUP**
Mayers, Smith, (Stalybridge C) 18 November
Gwilliam (Bishop's Stortford) 8 November
McKeevor (Weston-Super-Mare) 6 December

**CARLING CUP**
Furlong (QPR) 12 August

## MONTH BY MONTH RED CARDS IN PREMIERSHIP AND FOOTBALL LEAGUE 2003–04

| | Games | Reds | Average |
|---|---|---|---|
| Aug | 216 | 57 | 0.26 |
| Sep | 230 | 73 | 0.32 |
| Oct | 219 | 55 | 0.25 |
| Nov | 199 | 42 | 0.21 |
| Dec | 209 | 51 | 0.24 |
| Jan | 180 | 31 | 0.17 |
| Feb | 189 | 35 | 0.19 |
| Mar | 247 | 45 | 0.18 |
| Apr | 242 | 43 | 0.18 |
| May | 105 | 19 | 0.18 |
| Total | **2036** | **451** | **0.22** |

## PREMIER LEAGUE EVER-PRESENT CLUBS

| | *P* | *W* | *D* | *L* | *F* | *A* | *Pts* |
|---|---|---|---|---|---|---|---|
| Manchester U | 468 | 292 | 107 | 69 | 927 | 429 | 983 |
| Arsenal | 468 | 244 | 131 | 93 | 756 | 415 | 863 |
| Liverpool | 468 | 223 | 122 | 123 | 759 | 486 | 791 |
| Chelsea | 468 | 203 | 135 | 130 | 704 | 519 | 744 |
| Leeds U | 468 | 189 | 125 | 154 | 641 | 579 | 692 |
| Aston Villa | 468 | 181 | 135 | 152 | 581 | 525 | 678 |
| Tottenham H | 468 | 163 | 122 | 183 | 616 | 653 | 611 |
| Everton | 468 | 145 | 131 | 192 | 572 | 644 | 566 |
| Southampton | 468 | 144 | 123 | 201 | 553 | 672 | 555 |

## LESLIE ROBERTS

From 1920 to 1937 Leslie Roberts, an inside-forward, played for 16 teams: Aston Villa, Bristol Rovers, Chesterfield, Sheffield Wednesday, Merthyr, Bournemouth, Bolton Wanderers, Swindon Town, Brentford, Manchester City, Exeter City, Crystal Palace, Chester, Rotherham United, Scunthorpe & Lindsey United and New Brighton. He made League appearances for all except Villa, Rovers, Wednesday and Scunthorpe who were then outside the League. He made 300 League appearances and scored 92 goals.

# INTERNATIONAL RECORDS

## MOST GOALS IN AN INTERNATIONAL

| | | |
|---|---|---|
| **Record/World Cup** | Archie Thompson (Australia) 13 goals v American Samoa | 11.4.2001 |
| **England** | Malcolm Macdonald (Newcastle U) 5 goals v Cyprus, at Wembley | 16.4.1975 |
| | Willie Hall (Tottenham H) 5 goals v Ireland, at Old Trafford | 16.11.1938 |
| | Steve Bloomer (Derby Co) 5 goals v Wales, at Cardiff | 16.3.1896 |
| | Howard Vaughton (Aston Villa) 5 goals v Ireland, at Belfast | 18.2.1882 |
| **Northern Ireland** | Joe Bambrick (Linfield) 6 goals v Wales, at Belfast | 1.2.1930 |
| **Wales** | John Price (Wrexham) 4 goals v Ireland, at Wrexham | 25.2.1882 |
| | Mel Charles (Cardiff C) 4 goals v Ireland, at Cardiff | 11.4.1962 |
| | Ian Edwards (Chester) 4 goals v Malta, at Wrexham | 25.10.1978 |

## MOST GOALS IN AN INTERNATIONAL CAREER

| | | *Goals* | *Games* |
|---|---|---|---|
| **England** | Bobby Charlton (Manchester U) | 49 | 106 |
| **Scotland** | Denis Law (Huddersfield T, Manchester C, Torino, Manchester U) | 30 | 55 |
| | Kenny Dalglish (Celtic, Liverpool) | 30 | 102 |
| **Northern Ireland** | David Healy (Manchester U, Preston NE) | 14 | 35 |
| **Wales** | Ian Rush (Liverpool, Juventus) | 28 | 73 |
| **Republic of Ireland** | Niall Quinn (Arsenal, Manchester C, Sunderland) | 21 | 91 |

## HIGHEST SCORES

| | | | | | |
|---|---|---|---|---|---|
| **Record/World Cup Match** | Australia | 31 | American Samoa | 0 | 2001 |
| **European Championship** | Spain | 12 | Malta | 1 | 1983 |
| **Olympic Games** | Denmark | 17 | France | 1 | 1908 |
| | Germany | 16 | USSR | 0 | 1912 |
| **Other International Match** | Libya | 21 | Oman | 0 | 1966 |
| **European Cup** | Feyenoord | 12 | K R Reykjavik | 2 | 1969 |
| **European Cup-Winners' Cup** | Sporting Lisbon | 16 | Apoel Nicosia | 1 | 1963 |
| **Fairs & UEFA Cups** | Ajax | 14 | Red Boys | 0 | 1984 |

## GOALSCORING RECORDS

| | | |
|---|---|---|
| **World Cup Final** | Geoff Hurst (England) 3 goals v West Germany | 1966 |
| **World Cup Final tournament** | Just Fontaine (France) 13 goals | 1958 |
| **Career** | Artur Friedenreich (Brazil) 1329 goals | 1910–30 |
| | Pele (Brazil) 1281 goals | *1956–78 |
| | Franz 'Bimbo' Binder (Austria, Germany) 1006 goals | 1930–50 |
| **World Cup Finals fastest** | Hakan Sukur (Turkey) 10.8 secs v South Korea | 2002 |

**Pele subsequently scored two goals in Testimonial matches making his total 1283.*

## MOST CAPPED INTERNATIONALS IN THE BRITISH ISLES

| | | | |
|---|---|---|---|
| **England** | Peter Shilton | 125 appearances | 1970–90 |
| **Northern Ireland** | Pat Jennings | 119 appearances | 1964–86 |
| **Scotland** | Kenny Dalglish | 102 appearances | 1971–86 |
| **Wales** | Neville Southall | 92 appearances | 1982–97 |
| **Republic of Ireland** | Steve Staunton | 102 appearances | 1988–2002 |

## LONDON INTERNATIONAL VENUES

Eleven different venues in the London area have staged full England international games: Kennington Oval, Richmond Athletic Ground, Queen's Club, Crystal Palace, Craven Cottage, The Den, Stamford Bridge, Highbury, Wembley, Selhurst Park and White Hart Lane.

# FOOTBALL AND THE LAW

Trade Mark registration, ticket touting, racist chanting, drugs and personal injury insurance, all were tips of a never ending iceberg, spanning oceans of legal territories.

Tottenham Hotspur followed Arsenal under Trade Mark law to resist a street trader's claim of 30 years' sales near to but not outside the White Hart Lane ground that the merchandise brand 'Tottenham' is not the sole property of the club, because it denotes an area of London as well as the football club.

The club succeeded in claiming 'Tottenham' as a Trade Mark in respect of a variety of goods and services it wished to commercialise as part of a club merchandising programme because the club's football fame superseded any geographical association to justify registration under section 3 (1) (b) and (c) of the Trade Marks Act 1994.

Linked to that trade element, a ticket tout who offered a ticket to a plain clothes officer for £100 with evidence of access to other tickets was subject to a banning order under section 14A of the Football Spectators Act after the offer for sale contrary to section 166 of the Criminal Justice and Public Order Act 1994. This section followed Lord Justice Taylor's Hillsborough Report targeting such activities as a focus for public disorder.

Rio Ferdinand's well publicised suspension for failing to take a drug test was part of a wider sporting scenario. It was reflected at international level when the Welsh FA claimed that Russia should have been ejected from Euro 2004 finals because UEFA failed to punish Russia's Egor Titov who failed a drug test after he appeared in the first leg play-off. UEFA ruled that Wales failed to prove Titov was under the influence of a performance enhancing drug in the second leg, and teams are not liable when one member commits an offence.

The different approach when an offending athlete can cause a track and field team's disqualification demonstrates the variations and variances in this area of punishment.

Nearer to reality on the playing field, Southampton's David Howells' injury in the Premiership prevented a return to that level, but nevertheless he played in eight reserve team matches before he retired finally.

His compensation claim under an insurance policy failed because it required proof of total inability to carry on his occupation as a professional player for 12 months and would never be able to participate again. The purpose of the policy was to provide cover in the event of permanent total disablement from employment as a professional footballer.

Coincidentally it has echoes of a similar case 50 years ago when a West Ham United player lost an eye in the then Football League competition but transferred to non-League Cambridge United and continued playing there. The underwriters recovered a £750 payment under a policy because he had undertaken never to play professional football again. Times change, problems remain the same.

Finally, in the context of developing multi-racialism in sport and society generally, a Port Vale supporter was found guilty of racist chanting against a visiting group of Oldham Athletic supporters, '*You're just a town full of Pakis*', contrary to the Football (Offences) Act 1991.

A local Stoke-on-Trent District Judge found the phrase was 'mere doggerel' and that it amounted to no more than claiming *'Our town is better than your town*'.

Moreover, he held that the word 'Paki' was held to have been no more insulting or racist than use of the words 'Pom', 'Brit' or 'Yank'.

The Crown Prosecution Service appealed and the High Court held that the use of the word had to be examined in the context of each case, but there was no doubt that the accused defendant had used it in a racially derogatory and insulting sense, contrary to the Act of Parliament.

EDWARD GRAYSON
Founder President, British Association for Sport and the Law.

# DAILY ROUND-UP 2003–04

**JULY 2003**

**Chelsea's Roman roubles ... Eriksson linked with the Bridge ... Ronaldinho snubs Man Utd ... FA to crack down on verbal abuse ... EU threat to TV deals ... Larsson equals a Euro record.**

1 £150 million coup gives Russian billionaire Roman Abramovich the keys to Chelsea. Beckham passes medical to sign for Real Madrid and swaps No. 7 for 23. Mark Palios one-time Tranmere now FA supremo vows to put the game first.
2 Dunn leaves Blackburn in a £5.5 million transfer to Birmingham.
3 Nyarko back with Everton after two-year absence. Van Nistelrooy admits he will miss Becks influence on the pitch.
4 Liverpool declare interest in Leeds' Kewell. Zola turns down chance to stay at Chelsea.
5 Row between Sheff Utd and Tranmere over Neil Warnock trying to obtain David Kelly as his assistant.
6 Vieira ends speculation by agreeing new contract with Arsenal.
7 Millwall raise £2.5 million from a share issue.
8 Eriksson caught on camera visiting Abramovich. UEFA likely to introduce a group stage for the 2004-05 UEFA Cup after the first round, but with eight groups of five teams.
9 Kewell move from Leeds to Liverpool alleged to pan out at £4 million for him (equal amounts from both clubs) and only £3 million for United, on day when Gerard Houllier collects his honorary OBE. Rumours persist about Eriksson being tapped for the Chelsea job.
10 Chelsea line up West Ham's Johnson at £6 million and chase Inter's Vieri. Dacourt to leave Leeds for Roma. Ronaldinho making positive noises Man Utd way. BBC back in focus to show England live.
11 England fans obtaining black market tickets for the Istanbul fixture will be banned from entering stadium. Villa hope to sign Sunderland pair McCann and Sorensen for £5 million. Les Ferdinand becomes Leicester's seventh summer signing. Man Utd raise bid for Ronaldinho to £19 million. Chelsea add Geremi from Real Madrid for £6.9 million.
12 FL decide to withhold sponsorship and TV money from Luton for the present.
13 Tim Howard, Man Utd's American goalkeeper who cost £2.3 million from New York/New Jersey MetroStars gets work permit through his Hungarian wife. Abramovich said to have been trying to buy United before Chelsea. Sunderland, £30 million in the red, appeal to the PFA for help.
14 Man Utd take an interest in Kleberson, Brazilian cap of Atletico Paranaense. Luton in receivership. Sunderland hoping to avoid administration.
15 Veron likely to be signed by Chelsea if they improve bid. Zamora heading for Tottenham at £1.5 million.
16 Man Utd's hopes of landing Ronaldinho from PSG stalling on size of offer as they prepare for USA trip.
17 FA to tighten up rules about people buying into clubs.
18 PL referees told to toughen up on players and managers who use verbal abuse to officials. Southampton reluctantly prepare for Bridge's departure to the Stamford variety at £7 million. AFC Wimbledon raise £1 million needed for controlling interest in Kingstonian ground which they share.
19 Spurs chairman Daniel Levy denies takeover talks.
20 Ronaldinho dumps United for Barcelona.
21 Duff costs Chelsea £17 million in biggest summer buy to date, taking their spending to £36.9 million. West Ham cop £2.5 million for Sinclair, off to Man City. Venezuelan billionaire interested in buying Villa. Spurs Thatcher becomes Leicester's ninth close season capture.
22 With Ronaldinho off to Spain, Sir Alex turns his attention to Newcastle's Dyer.
23 Man Utd beat Celtic 4-0 in front of 66,722 in Seattle. Birmingham agree £2.5 million deal for Luciano Figueroa (Rosario Central). Barry Town out of Ch Lge despite 2-1 win over Vardar (2-4) on aggregate.
24 EU threat on UK TV rights. Perugia president Luciano Gaucci having signed Colonel Gaddafi's son Saadi, wants to include a female player in his team.
25 Arsenal snap up German goalkeeper Jens Lehmann from Borussia Dortmund for £1.25 million. Chelsea double your money bid for Real's Raul rejected.
26 Rooney stretchered off as Everton beat Rangers 3-2 in friendly at Ibrox.
27 Rooney likely to miss season's start because of ankle ligament damage.
28 Veron resigned to joining Chelsea. Beckham likely to start Real career on right side of midfield, not in a central role.
29 Threat of more qualifying matches for European teams in WC, also next Club World Championship to be held in Mexico in 2005. Referee Alan Kaye charged by FA for failing to send off Viduka in a friendly. Nantes midfield player Eric Djemba-Djemba signs for Man Utd at £3.5 million.
30 Ch Lge: Celtic 4-0 winners in Kaunas; Larsson equals British record with 30 goals for one club, previously Rush (Liverpool) and Lorimer (Leeds) had reached this total. Sir Alex denies Veron sale.
31 New PL assessors will include Keith Burkinshaw, Peter Shreeves, Graham Mackrell, Joe Jordan and Kenny Hibbitt, representing former managers, secretary and players. Macedonia sack coach Nikola Ilievski citing poor results. John Aston ex-Man Utd full-back dies at 81.

**AUGUST 2003**

**MOTD returns to BBC ... First trophy for Man Utd ... Larsson breaks record ... Beckham shines after staccato start ... Sir Alex sees red ... First managerial casualty.**

1 Fashanu quits as Barry chairman after eight months. Iversen joins Wolves. OFT fine FA £158,000 for replica shirt price-fixing.

2 Bell's Cup kicks off Scottish season with most convincing win Inverness 5-0 at Gretna. Beckham debut for rich boys Real in Workers Stadium, Beijing; a 4-0 stroll against Dragon XI. Arsenal attract 44,396 to Celtic in 1-1 draw. Chelsea parade some newcomers in 2-1 win at Palace.

3 Geoff Thomas ex-England midfield player urgently needs life-saving bone marrow donor.

4 Didier Domi ex-Newcastle joins Leeds on loan from PSG. Soton expect to sign McCann, Rangers winger. Opposition on both sides of the border for Rangers – Celtic joining PL. With Stevenage, Telford and Woking going full-time, just half the Conf remain part-timers.

5 West Ham's Cole lined up for Chelsea in £6.6 million move and owner Abramovich even muses about Beckham. Sunderland's Phillips linked with Soton.

6 Celtic end the Kaunas affair with a mercy killing own goal. No Norwegian rhapsody for Bohemians. Watchmakers Tissot to clock all 92 managers in new award.

7 Barcelona are £115 million in debt. Chelsea finally sign Veron in deal for £12.5 million.

8 MOTD to return to BBC. Argentina may have new Maradona in Carlos Alberto Tevez, 19, Boca Juniors striker.

9 FL opens in sadness: Ray Harford dies and Watford's Jimmy Davis on loan striker from Man Utd killed in car crash. Their match is postponed. 20,000 plus crowds at Derby, Ipswich, Forest and Sheff Utd, but only 1145 for Wimbledon. Palace have two dismissed but Freedman hat-trick gives them 3-2 win. West Ham goalscoring debutant sub David Connolly lashes boss Roeder for not starting him. In Div 2 Hartlepool trailing 3-1 at Peterborough win 4-3. First League goals for winger Brad Maylett in six seasons – a hat-trick for Swansea in Div 3. New boys Doncaster and Yeovil win 3-1 away. SPL starts: Celtic drop two points, Rangers have two point lead. Chelsea's latest capture: Adrian Mutu from Parma, a snip at £15.8 million.

10 Man Utd win Com Shd on penalties against Arsenal. Conf ex-League teams live on Sky: Aldershot 2 Accrington 1.

11 EU to question television deals. Di Canio signs for Charlton on free transfer. Ambitious Ryman Hornchurch ask manager Mick Marsden to resign, ex-Aldershot boss George Borg expected to replace him.

12 Winger Cristiano Ronaldo, 18, will cost Man Utd £12.24 million from Sporting Lisbon. UEFA Cup start, Intertoto at final first leg stage. Debut for C Cup: Highest win and only five figure gate sees WBA beat Brentford 4-0 before 10,440; lowest crowd 1986 for Wycombe's 2-0 win over Wimbledon!

13 Ch Lge: Chelsea open with 2-0 success in Zilina; Newcastle 1-0 winners over Partizan; Celtic take four off MTK and Larsson strikes a record 31st in Europe, but Rangers held by FC Copenhagen. Bolton sign hot-shot Jardel from Sporting Lisbon.

14 UEFA Cup: UEFA's first female referee Nicole Pegitnat, 36, a Swiss, controls AIK v Fylkir first leg. Man City have too much firepower for TNS.

15 FA take belated action over midland derby brawl in March between Villa and Birmingham, fining each £5,000 and issuing warnings. Cardiff spend over £1 million on Lee (Rotherham) and Langley (QPR). Arsenal turn down bid by Everton for ex-player Jeffers.

16 PL starts with Blackburn taking five goals off Wolves, Man Utd four from Bolton. Arsenal with Campbell red-carded for professional foul and scorer Henry taunting crowd, beat Everton 2-1 as do newcomers Portsmouth against Aston Villa. Spurs' Hoddle blames ref Styles for penalty decision at Birmingham. Palace's Hughes sent off in first senior game for 16 months. Sunderland suffer 17th defeat. In Div 2 Kuqi scores twice for Sheff Wed and is then sent off in draw with Oldham. Second-half hat-trickster Lee Trundle rescues Swansea, 2-0 down at Cheltenham.

17 Chelsea start where they left off last season beating Liverpool, this time 2-1 at Anfield. Man City win 3-0 at Charlton. Two more goals for the Shearer collection as Newcastle draw 2-2 at Leeds. Becks jeered but Real beat Valencia 6-5 on penalties to win some silverware. Man Utd said to be interested in Brazilian wonderboy Freddie Adu just 14.

18 Southgate's absence from England squad appears to spell end after 55 caps.

19 The Republic beat Australia 2-1 in full international while their Under-21s win 5-1 in Poland. Others at this level see Croatia beat England 3-0 with Pennant sent off at Upton Park and Scotland lose 3-1 in Norway. Middlesbrough interested in loan of Gaizka Mendieta (Lazio).

20 Euro 2004: Wales concede second half goal in Serbia. Friendlies: England beat Croatia 3-1, Scotland goalless in Norway, thanks to goalkeeper Douglas. Chelsea closing in on Inter's Hernan Crespo at £16.8 million, Bordeaux midfield man Alexei Smertin for £3.8 million and loan Carlton Cole to Charlton.

21 Hoddle facing misconduct charge over remarks about referee Styles. Italian Serie B clubs threaten boycott because of FA wanting four more clubs in it.

22 Blackburn eyeing prospects of securing Ferguson the Scottish international from Rangers. Sunderland preparing to let Flo go.

23 Sir Alex red carded at Newcastle after remarks to officials; Man Utd win 2-1 and record-breaker Van Nistelrooy makes it 15 goals in ten consecutive games. With thousands of English holidaymakers present, Beckham flops as Real lose Spanish Super Cup first leg 2-1 to Mallorca.

24 Arsenal hit Middlesbrough 4-0 at the Riverside.

25 Crystal Palace top Div 1 without playing. Barnsley's 2-0 win at Blackpool keeps them goal difference ahead of Wrexham in Div 2 and Oxford 3-0 against Swansea are a point ahead in Div 3. Conf top two result: Hereford 4 Aldershot 3, crowd 4985.

26 Ch Lge: Chelsea ease 3-0 against Zilina. Intertoto winners Schalke, Villarreal and Perugia will enter UEFA Cup. Portsmouth rampage on 4-0 over Bolton.

27 Ch Lge: Newcastle stunned by Partizan 1-0 winners on the night and 4-3 on penalties. Late show for Rangers 2-1 victors over FC Copenhagen while Celtic 1-0 against MTK. In PL, Wolves restrict Man Utd to one goal, Arsenal beat Aston Villa 2-0. Now hero Beckham, dubbed 'Lord of the Earrings' scores on home debut for Real in 3-0 return win over Mallorca.

28 UEFA Cup: mass exit for Coleraine, Cwmbran, Derry, Portadown and Shelbourne, plus TNS taken out by Man City, but Dundee go through after 4-0 over Vllaznia.
29 AC Milan win the Super Cup beating Porto 1-0 in Monaco. Carlisle sack manager Roddy Collins after poorest start for 46 years. McManaman joins Man City after four year exile with Real Madrid, Chelsea bargain basement capture of Spurs goalkeeper Sullivan for £500,000. UEFA expects to generate £393 million this season, a drop of 15 percent.
30 Under-fire Houllier becomes first Liverpool manager to win four times at Everton in 3-0 shock. Spurs crash 3-0 at home to Fulham. First point for Wolves goalless with Pompey, whose boss Harry Redknapp is sent off. Twenty-second Cole goal helps Blackburn draw 2-2 at Chelsea. Port Vale edge ahead in Div 2 after 1-0 win over Brentford. Becks scores in two minutes for Real.
31 Manchester gloom: Utd go down to late Beattie goal at Southampton, defence dodgy City lose 2-1 at home to Arsenal.

**SEPTEMBER 2003**

**Chelsea spending tops £100 million ... Rooney England's youngest marksman ... England fans warned over Turkey trot ... Arsenal hit 52 reds ... Big spat at Old Trafford ... Man Utd profits up.**

1 Chelsea's spending spree reaches £106.8 million with capture of Makelele for £13.9 million as transfer window shuts. PFA warn against long-term loan deals. Manager Jones gets three year contract at struggling Wolves.
2 Beckham yellow card in Real's 1-1 draw at Villarreal. Bottom six in Div 1 were all relegated from PL in last three years.
3 Man Utd decide to take £11.1 million from Beckham deal now rather than wait for Real to pay £12 over four years. Bosnich appeal against nine-month ban for improper conduct and breach of doping regulations turned down. Leeds boy wonder Milner loaned to Swindon. Row between Wales and Newcastle over Bellamy's fitness boils over. Campbell to dispute misconduct charge as will Portsmouth manager Redknapp. Fulham look to a Cottage return.
4 Millwall's Richard Sadlier forced to retire with injury at 24. Yankey goal beats the Aussies as England ladies score first goal in six matches.
5 U-21s: Kirkland gifts Macedonia an equalizer as England are held 1-1, Wales sink 8-1 in Italy, the Republic beat Russia 2-0 and Northern Ireland lose 1-0 to Ukraine.
6 Rooney at 17 years 317 days, becomes youngest goalscorer for England in 2-1 win in hostile Macedonia; Beckham is booked, gets a death threat but hits the winning penalty. Wales are harpooned by an 11 minute second half hat-trick from Filippo Inzaghi as Italy cruise it 4-0. Scotland beat Faroes 3-1 in a game of goalkeeping errors, the Republic lose the plot in the 1-1 draw with Russia and Northern Ireland go over 1000 minutes without a goal but make a point in the Ukraine. Chelsea's Veron is booed off as Argentina are held 2-2 by Chile.
7 Eriksson predicts dire consequences for any England supporter foolish enough to travel to Istanbul. Man Utd's Forlan starts the 5 -0 Uruguay goal rush against Bolivia and Angel scores for Colombia in the 2-1 defeat with Brazil all in WC.
8 Latest Chelsea signing: Peter Kenyon, chief executive of Mancheser United, the architect of much of the Old Trafford club's global development over three years.
9 U-21s: Tottenham's Helder Postiga scuppers England hopes, blatantly handling the ball for Portugal's second goal in the 2-1 win; Wales scrape a 0-0 draw with Finland, the Scots win 1-0 in Germany and Northern Ireland record first win in three years beating Armenia 3-1. The Republic draw 2-2 in a full international with Turkey. Cardiff get green light for new stadium complex and crisis-club Oldham are on amber until mid-October.
10 Goals from Owen and Rooney see off mighty Liechtenstein, Wales get a play-off point against the Finns despite Koumas red card, still no goals for Northern Ireland and Scotland lose 2-1 in Germany plus Ross with a red card. Definite Euro 2004 qualifiers: France, Czech Republic, Sweden and Bulgaria. Alan Pardew thought to be interesting West Ham, quits as Reading manager.
11 England ladies lose 4-0 to Germany in Darmstadt.
12 Hartlepool's 8-1 win over Grimsby is two goals short of their best League win, one adrift of the Mariners worst defeat.
13 Liverpool win 3-1 at Blackburn but lose Carragher (broken leg) after a red-card Neill challenge and Baros (broken ankle). Forest's David Johnson also breaks his leg. Referee Styles hands out two red cards, ten yellow and three penalties in Everton's 2-2 draw with Newcastle. Pires in diving accusation as Arsenal held 1-1 by Portsmouth. Trevor Birch quits as Chelsea chief executive. It's a W formation in Div 1: Wigan, West Brom and West Ham top the table.
14 Anelka treble helps Man City to third place after 4-1 win over Villa.
15 Leeds crash 4-0 at Leicster.
16 Ch Lge: Greek tragedy for Panathinaikos 5-0 losers at Man Utd; Rangers recover to beat Stuttgart 2-1 and Chelsea win 1-0 against Sparta Prague. Becks' Real give Marseille goal start and win 4-2.
17 Ch Lge: Inter do a mini-Italian job on Arsenal 3-0 at Highbury and Henry fluffs a penalty; Celtic beaten 2-1 by Bayern Munich. All four Italian teams confirm success in two days. Eriksson seeks peace talks with Turkey. Hoddle charged with misconduct after opening day remarks about referee Styles.
18 Reading chairman Madejeski drops legal action against Pardew who will become Hammers boss on 18 October. With 210 yellow and 16 red cards in 48 Premiership games, an unwanted record looms. Women's pro game in USA folds on eve of WC finals.
19 Carlton Palmer dismissed as Stockport manager. Hitherto unbeaten Hereford go for a 4-1 Burton in Conf. Green light for Wimbledon's Milton Keynes move.
20 Much-changed Chelsea top after 5-0 cruise at Wolves. Spurs flounder to 3-1 home defeat by Soton. First reverse for Portsmouth 2-1 to Blackburn at Fratton. Ex-Derby goalkeeper Poom heads equaliser for

Sunderland against old club. Dunfermline parade on their new artificial surface but it's grassless and goalless with Hibs.

21 Vieira becomes Arsenal's 52nd dismissal in seven years after alleged over-reaction by Van Nistelrooy who also hits the bar with an injury-time penalty, followed by a bust-up in the tunnel after the 0-0 draw at Man Utd. Hoddle and Gorman axed by Spurs. Middlesbrough's first win 1-0 v Everton.

22 FA to investigate Old Trafford fracas. Raddy Antic ex-Real Madrid, Barcelona coach and Luton player under Pleat tops list of Spurs vacancy fillers.

23 Groundshare talks held between Everton and Liverpool. Hoddle linked with Reading. C Cup action: Unbeaten Birmingham slip up 1-0 at Blackpool and Clemence misses a penalty; Fulham also lose by the minimum at Wigan; shoot-out saves Charlton against Luton and a penalty each in hat-tricks for Defoe (West Ham) at Cardiff plus Angel (Villa) at Wycombe. CIS Cup scalp for Brechin against Premier Killie, but Dobbie gets three as Hibs slaughter Montrose 9-0.

24 Six Arsenal players: Lauren, Lehmann, Vieira, Parlour, Cole and Keown plus two from Man Utd: Giggs and Ronaldo charged with varying offences. Arsenal accused of failing to control their players. UEFA Cup: Newcastle take five off Breda; Owen breaks Rush's Euro record in Liverpool's 1-1 against Olimpija; Soton held by Steaua and Blackburn slump 3-1 to Genclerbirligi in Ankara, but late Anelka penalty spares Man City blushes against Lokeren. Hearts beat Zeljeznicar 2-0 but Dundee lose 2-1 at Dens to Perugia. C Cup: Leeds need penalties to beat Swindon after goalkeeper Robinson does an injury-time Poom and Middlesbrough require extra time against Brighton.

25 English and Turkish FA officials meet in Switzerland to decide how to keep England fans away from Euro 2004 group decider. Preston and Bradford charged with misconduct after incidents on 13 September. FL to introduce ten-point deduction for clubs in administration from next season. Paul Simpson confirmed as Carlisle manager with John Ward No. 2. Sir Jack Hayward prepared to write off £40 million owed to him by Wolves and seek new owner.

26 Quiet Highbury: Arsenal 3 Newcastle (one booking) 2.

27 Van Nistelrooy hat-trick in Man Utd's 4-1 win at Leicester. Southampton lose unbeaten record 1-0 to Middlesbrough, but Birmingham roll on with fifth clean sheet in 2-0 win over Portsmouth. Lunchtime 2-1 win at Bradford puts Sheff Utd top of Div One. Crowd of 5639 at Milton Keynes see Wimbledon come back to draw 2-2 with Burnley. Leyton Orient sack manager Paul Brush after losing 3-0 at Huddersfield. Beckham injures foot in Real's 2-0 defeat in Valencia.

28 Lisbie treble as Charlton edge Liverpool 3-2. Everton take four off sorry Leeds as Watson is treble-shooter. Caretaker Pleat collects a point for Spurs at Man City. Tranmere dismiss manager Ray Mathias and assistant Kelham O'Hanlon.

29 PFA and Managers agree in condemnation of players' conduct but another managerial casualty: Martin Wilkinson at Northampton.

30 Ch Lge: Arsenal goalless draw with Lokomotiv Moscow and Celtic wear down Lyon to win 2-0. Man Utd announce 22 percent increase in pre-tax profits to £39.3 million thanks to Beckham sale. Chesterfield draw 1-1 with Bournemouth but are alone among the 92 without a win. Fourth manager to be sacked in five days as Lawrie Sanchez leaves Wycombe, but Sir Alex to stay with Utd until 2007.

## OCTOBER 2003

**More Shearer records ... Rio Ferdinand misses drug test ... Mutiny threat by England players – but qualify for Euro 2004 ... Scots and Welsh for play-offs ... heavy financial loss for Leeds ... Fine day for Arsenal.**

1 Ch Lge: Shocks for Chelsea beaten by two goals in four minutes by ten-man Besiktas and Man Utd 2-1 (two in two minutes) losers in Stuttgart, but Rangers draw against Panathinaikos. Gascoigne trials with Al Jazira in UAE.

2 Under-fire Peter Reid gets Leeds backing. Coppell linked with Reading. Women's WC hosts USA take semi-final place 1-0 v Norway and Sweden edge Brazil 2-1.

3 New £57 million three year deal from next season with Barclays Premiership replacing Barclaycard. Beckham pronouncd fit for Turkey tie. Women's WC quarter-finals: Germany slam Russia 7-1 and Canada surprisingly beat China 1-0.

4 Shearer's 250th career League goal sinks old mates Soton for first Newcastle win. Goalkeeper Taylor's dismissal leads to Birmingham losing 3-0 to Man Utd. Spurs revival continues 3-0 over Everton but Rooney gets his fifth yellow of the season. Pires memorable 25 yard swerver as Arsenal win 2-1 at Liverpool, but Owen injury worries Eriksson. Under-fire Reid sees Leeds beat Blackburn 3-1. Improving Sunderland topple Div 1 leaders Sheff Utd 1-0 at Bramall Lane, Brighton 3-0 winners over Blackpool now top of Div 2 and free-scoring Hull's 5-1 win at Northampton opens four point gap in Div 3. SPL: Celtic top after 1-0 win at Ibrox. Liverpool's Otsemobor injured in bar shooting. Rumours continue over some PL players alleged involvement in rape story.

5 Crespo late strike earns edgy Chelsea a 2-1 win at Middlesbrough.

6 Rio Ferdinand said to have refused routine drug test two weeks ago. Women's WC semi-final surprise: USA lose 3-0 to Germany, Canada 2-1 to Sweden.

7 Ferdinand protests innocence but FA make him unavailable for Turkey. Man Utd fury, England squad threatens mutiny. Two Leeds players questioned by police over alleged assault on a woman. Bellamy fined £750 for threatening behaviour in incident six months earlier. Irish investors buy stake in Man Utd.

8 Unhappy England players call off boycott after protest statement. Improper conduct findings: Campbell fined £20,000 from Com Shd match; Harry Redknapp £3,000 and two match ban from Wolves game; Brevett £1,000 and costs resulting from Bolton match in April. Scotland likely to be without six regulars against Lithuania. Bryan Robson to become Nigeria coach.

9 Leeds suspend Morris. Wales without five players due to injuries and suspensions. Managerial appointments: Steve Coppell (Reading), Colin Calderwood (Northampton) and Paul Simpson (Carlisle).

10 Eriksson's agent denies Chelsea connection. U-21s: England lose 1-0 in Turkey and Chelsea's Johnson sent off; Scotland edge Lithuania 3-2; Northern Ireland win again 1-0 in Greece; the Republic 2-0 in Switzerland, but Wales are beaten 1-0 by Serbia.

11 Euro 2004: Beckham fluffs a penalty, is confronted by Alpay but a goalless end is enough in intimidating Istanbul; Scotland 1-0 v Lithuania, thanks to sub Fletcher; Wales also in play-offs despite losing 3-2 to Serbia, but the Republic miss out after 2-0 defeat by the Swiss. Northern Ireland suffer a Greek penalty after McCartney red-carded taking goal draught to 1242 minutes over 13 games. Denmark, Germany, Greece, England, Italy and Switzerland join the qualifiers; Slovenia, Norway, Holland, Latvia (the surprise), Scotland, Spain, Turkey, Croatia, Wales and Russia for the play-offs. USA take third place in Womens WC beating Canada 3-1.

12 Womens WC Final: Germany beat Sweden 2-1 in sudden death. Brian Little appointed Tranmere manager. Tommy Taylor resigns at Farnborough, coach Ian McDonald sacked.

13 Scotland paired with Holland, Wales against Russia in Euro 2004 play-offs. Other ties: Croatia v Slovenia, Spain v Norway and Latvia v Turkey, whose Alpay involved with Beckham in half-time altercation is part of a UEFA investigation. ITV's delayed coverage of Turkey game was a record for them averaging 4.5 million viewers. LDV starts.

14 Chelsea make a Brummie point for the top as do Sheff Utd 2-0 at WBA in Div 1. Ipswich hit Burnley for six. FA ask Ferdinand for phone data over drug test. Arsenal revealed as top of PL Fair Play table! LDV hat-tricks for Murphy (Blackpool), Lee Jones (Wrexham).

15 Arsenal – surprisingly to some – admit misconduct charges, Man Utd request personal hearings. Mark McGhee and assistant Archie Knox axed by Millwall; Wise is caretaker player-manager. Sammy McIlroy quits as Northern Ireland boss to take over at Stockport. UEFA Cup: mixed fortunes: Liverpool coast it, Man City and Newcastle cruise in and Hearts slide through but out go Blackburn, Southampton and Dundee all counting missed chances. Trouble involving variety of fans in Breda.

16 Man Utd ready for Ferdinand court battle. England may be second seeds in Portugal. Gascoigne prances with Wolves.

17 FIFA supremo Blatter blasts England players over boycott threat. Coventry green light for new stadium complex. Glentoran fined £5000, deducted five points and axed from CIS Cup Final for registration irregularity.

18 Cudicini clanger costs Chelsea first defeat 2-1 at Arsenal, after Crespo over the goal-line – comes back on to score. Berger is Pompey goal king in downing old Liverpool mates. Man City six goal slickers but Wright-Phillips red card tackle. Caretaker Wise one of two sent off as Millwall knock Sheff Utd off Div 1 top 2-0. Dons slump six degrees under to Forest. Div 2: Plymouth 5-1 at slipping Port Vale. Chesterfield win at the 14th attempt. Div 3: Bobby Gould resigns at Cheltenham after 1-0 defeat by Rochdale, Ian Britton sacked at Kidderminster and Mark Patterson quits at Leigh RMI.

19 FIFA to force English FA to ban players immediately after red card offences from next season. Jan Molby returns to Kidderminster as director of football. Rangers held at Motherwell drop three points behind Celtic. Barry Town with £1 million debts may fold. Inter axe coach Hector Cuper after 28 months.

England captain David Beckham is confronted by Turkey players after missing a penalty. The match in Istanbul in October saw England progress into the European Championship finals after a 0-0 draw. (Actionimages)

20 Sir Alex gets two-match touchline ban and £10,000 fine for Newcastle red card. Derby County sold to business consortium. Charlton's 1-0 win at Blackburn their third in a row, Rovers fourth consecutive home defeat.

21 Ch Lge: English leaders Arsenal suffer 2-1 electric shock against Dynamo, Scottish counterparts Celtic wastefully go down to ten-man Anderlecht 1-0. Lokomotiv shunt Inter 3-0 in Moscow. PL Newcastle give Fulham two goals start and win 3-2. Div 1 cellar-dwelling Dons shock WBA at Hawthorns. Div 2 leaders Brighton crash 4-0 at Brentford, but Div 3 pacemakers ten-man Hull hold on at Bury. Scotland lose a B international 1-0 to Germany.

22 Ch Lge: Chelsea's second half revival hits Lazio 2-1 and Man Utd win 1-0 at Ibrox against Rangers with rare Phil Neville strike. Becks injures hamstring in Real's latest win. In Div 2 Plymouth top after 3-1 win at Sheff Wed. Kallon, Inter striker, tested positive for a drug on 27 Sept, second such in Serie A after Blasi (Parma).

23 Villa pay up Alpay's contract.

24 UK Sport announce two players tested positive for cocaine and ecstasy. Morris gets ten days leave of absence from Leeds. PL referee supremo Phillip Don axed.

25 Man Utd rest three and lose 3-1 at home to Fulham. Game of two halves: Leicester three up at Wolves concede four. Fourth win in a row for Newcastle 3-0 v Portsmouth, fourth such defeat for Blackburn to a brace of Beattie goals for Saints. Another clean sheet for Birmingham. Norwich only 100 percent team at home in England. Macclesfield chop manager David Moss after defeat by Southend. Carlisle already ten points adrift at foot of Div 3. FA Cup: Conf casualty Dagenham lose Essex derby at Thurrock, formed as Purfleet only in 1985. Albany NL Shildon whack Stocksbridge 6-0 to enter first round for first time in 42 years. Rangers in goalless draw at Livingston trail Celtic by five points.

26 Arsenal held 1-1 at Charlton, but sneak point ahead of Chelsea again. Bell's Cup final: Inverness 2 Airdrie 0.

27 No tunnel vision for UEFA over Istanbul. Spurs announce loss of £7.1 million before tax. Abramovich seems likely to escape Russian tycoon tax investigation. John Askey is Macclesfield boss.

28 Record pre-tax loss of £49.5 million hits Leeds, now £78 million in debt. On the pitch Man Utd beat them 3-1 in the C Cup; Smith in bottle incident. In another tie reserve-looking Arsenal scrape through on penalties against Rotherham. Brighton appoint Mark McGhee manager. FA Cup replay: full-time Ryman Grays knock-out part-time Conf Margate on penalties. CIS Cup: Dunfermline edge out St Johnstone 3-2.

29 C Cup: extra time out for Newcastle against WBA; Liverpool in odd goal in seven win at Blackburn who have Neill sent off again. Chelsea recover from Notts scare; CIS Cup produces a hat-trick for Ravanelli (Dundee). Wales have four injury worries. Gazza having turned down Darlington plays for Wolves stiffs.

30 Have a fine day: Arsenal £175,000 and conduct warning; Lauren four matches, £40,000; Keown three, £20,000; Vieira one, £20,000; Parlour one, £10,000; Cole £10,000; England £4,400 for Turkey tunnel tandrums. FIFA hold up Barthez loan to Marseille until next window. David Hodgson to be appointed Darlington manager with Mick Tait staying as youth team coach.

31 Sir Alex unhappy about the leniency shown to Arsenal by FA. Becks appoints Terry Bryne, Watford director of football, as his personal manager.

## NOVEMBER 2003

**Reid axed at Leeds ... Millwall get Wise to themselves ... French on a roll ... Dutch batter Scots and Wales also crash out Euro 2004 ... Arsenal's season start record.**

1 Shock! horror! all three top Premier teams kick-off at 3 pm – and win; Arsenal 4-1 at falling Leeds, Chelsea ruining Rooney's 18th celebrations 1-0 and Man Utd 3-0 over Portsmouth. Sorensen saves a Shearer penalty as ten-man Villa draw 1-1 at Newcastle. Okocha hits the bar three times as Bolton win 1-0 at Spurs. In Div 1 top team Wigan crack five past Palace, Liddell breaks club aggregate scoring record. Late night Dons win but Milton Keynes crowd is only 3334. In Scotland, Forfar edge Hamilton 4-3 as both sides finish with nine players.

2 Fifth straight defeat for Blackburn as Leicester Foxes bound to 18th, leaving Rovers and Leeds as underdogs. Last minute Murphy penalty lifts Liverpool at Fulham.

3 Holland brace breaks down Brummie dyke for Charlton. Palace chairman Simon Jordan removes Steve Kember as boss with Kit Symons as caretaker. Steve Wignall becomes 17th managerial casualty of season axed by Southend and Dave Webb comes back as caretaker, his fourth time at Roots Hall. Morris returns to train at Leeds, but Viduka faces fine for reporting late last week. Gazza plays it again at Wolves.

4 Ch Lge: When in Rome, Chelsea hit Lazio for four clear goals in ten-a-side ending, unpleasant Mihajlovic dismissed plus another Johnson red card; Man Utd take three off Rangers; Real Madrid drop first point in Belgrade; ten-man AC Milan win in Brugge. Forest chopped down 4-1 by Walsall in Div 1. LDV: Rock bottom Carlisle beat Huddersfield 2-0 in second round. National Game U-23 team first to be captained by a black player Roscoe D'Sane (Aldershot), draw 2-2 with Belgium U-21, Shrewsbury's Rodgers scoring both home goals.

5 Ch Lge: Late Cole delivery fuels Arsenal hopes; Celtic sparked by first half fireworks; Monaco's 8-3 win over La Coruna is the highest goals aggregate in the competition's history and eight the most by one team. LDV: Stockport edge Wrexham 5-4 in slow death (silver goal) win. Tony Adams appointed Wycombe manager and caretaker Gorman stays as assistant. FIFA to monitor FA's actions over recent misconduct in domestic football. Saadi al Gaddafi has tested positive for a performance-enhancing drug at Perugia.

6 UEFA Cup: Liverpool splash to a 1-1 draw in soggy Bucharest; Swiss roll over for Newcastle in Basle; Holding role for Groclin Poles at Man City; Hearts take Bordeaux direct. UEFA raise prize money for Euro 2004 by 66 percent. PFA's Gordon Taylor blasts back at FIFA's Blatter. Bryan Robson shown Nigerian door as they cannot afford his six-month £180,000 wages.

7 Sinisa Mihajlovic gets Ch Lge record eight-match ban following his two yellow cards and the spitting episode against Chelsea's Mutu. Viduka in row with Reid at Leeds. England beach ball international Bowes earns plucky Thurrock a replay against Luton.

8 Ljungberg deflected goal edges Arsenal 2-1 against plucky Spurs in 133rd derby. Charlton celebrate boss Alan Curbishley's 46th birthday by climbing to fourth after 3-1 win over Fulham. Pompey six chimes toll ominously for Leeds. In Div 1 West Ham discard three goal lead to lose 4-3 to new leaders WBA. Eleven no-win Bantams Nicky Law bombed out of Bradford job on website message. FA Cup: Burton at Torquay and Scarborough home to Doncaster start giant-killing. Ford fiesta in merited draw at Port Vale. Harrold hat-trick in his first such tie for Brentford. Cheltenham and Wycombe impress new managers. Weston super nightmare for Farnborough. A third of managers are said to be suffering cardiac problems. Nearly three times as many PL goals have been scored this season by a right rather than a left foot.

9 Status quo in PL charts as Chelsea whack ten-man Newcastle 5-0 and Man Utd win 2-1 at Liverpool. Leicester stun Man City 3-0. FA Cup: more mini-giants tumble as Ryman Hornchurch beat Darlington 2-0, Accrington defeat Huddersfield 1-0 and Ryman Canvey hold Southend in bucket and spade tie, but Shildon ship seven at Notts after being only 3-2 adrift. Proudlock treble for Sheff Wed downs Salisbury.

10 New Leeds chief executive Trevor Birch informs Peter Reid that his rolling contract has stopped; Eddie Gray becomes caretaker with Paul Hart and George Graham names in the frame. Dennis Wise expected to be confirmed as player-manager at Millwall. Blackburn end poor run at Everton's expense. Foreign Legion Chelsea have five players in England squad – more than any other club. UEFA to use silver goal (slow death) in Euro 2004 play-offs.

11 Spurs Gardner in England squad replacing reprieved Southgate forced to cry off with injury. Cameron only Scottish doubt. Wales likely to be without Davies, Pembridge, Savage and long-term injury Bellamy. FA row with Sir Alex still simmering. Gerrard pledges loyalty to Liverpool with long contract agreement after Kirkland and Carragher do too, but Owen hints at looking to other shores. Gray makes peace with Viduka. QPR beat Brentford in Div 2 west London derby and go second on goal difference to Plymouth. West Ham £44 million in debt.

12 Savage boost for Wales. Flu-boy Rooney recovering for England. Vassell scores four for Villa in 5-2 friendly win in Dubai, but is injured; Smith in as replacement. Man Utd hunt Chinese striker Dong Fangzhuo, 18, of Dalian Shide. Keith Alexander, Lincoln manager, in hospital after collapsing. Merson in domestic strife. Paul McGrath former Republic international now of no fixed abode.

13 Returned empty bottle from 28 October lands Leeds' Smith in bother with police; FA axe him from England squad! Ferdinand pleads not guilty. O'Leary dismisses Leeds link. England ladies pan Scotland 5-0 at Preston.

14 FA chief Palios under fire and players unhappy again. UEFA to step up drug testing. Summit planned to tackle domestic discipline.

15 Euro 2004: Hero McFadden as brave Scots clog Dutch; Wales dig deep for draw against rough Russia; little Latvia shake Turks; Slovenia hold Croatia and Spain's own goal late show edges Norway. Norwich lose 100 percent home record in Div 1. QPR impressively beat Plymouth 3-0 and replace them top of Div 2. Hull lead in Div 3 shrinks to a point after losing to Huddersfield. Euro U-21s: Croatia take two goal lead over Scots. Friendly in Gelsenkirchen against Germany gives France a record 14th consecutive win (2-0) beating the 1984 Platini era. Conf coincidence: Stevenage 2-1 half and full-time against Accrington watched by 2121.

16 Rooney and Joe Cole sizzle but sliced-open defence fails to save home bacon against the Danes. Gorman leaves Wycombe. Crespo scores in Argentina's 3-0 WC win over Bolivia.

17 Wales sweat on Russian plea to UEFA for Giggs ban after retaliation in Moscow. Dutch camp in turmoil. UEFA to investigate another Turkey tunnel affair. FL to raise inferior comparison with PL to Parliament. G-14 clubs want more money for their players on international duty.

18 Giggs charged with misconduct for Moscow elbow and is doubtful with injury. Robbie Keane scores twice for Republic in 3-0 v Canada. Morris charged with rape. Sir Alex sues over share of Rock of Gibraltar. FA Cup: Grazioli double for Barnet in three red card game ends Stalybridge (two reds) interest as does Forbes treble for Luton as Thurrock lose at Luton. Owen pledges future with Liverpool. Euro U-21s: O'Connor goal not enough for Scots.

19 Euro 2004: Six-shooting Dutch (Van Nistelrooy three) make it Scotland the grave; Russia shake wailing Wales; No chickening-out for Latvia against the Turks; Croatia and Spain both recover their poise. WC: Ronaldo saves Brazil blushes at 3-3 after Forlan brace and Silva own goal for Uruguay. FA Cup: own goal leaves Ford in reverse; Southend win on the late tide. Mark Ansell, Villa deputy chief executive to quit. West Ham to bow to shareholders verdict. Colombia part company with coach Francisco Maturana. Police let Smith off hook.

20 Euro 2004: England take B pot luck in final draw with Spain, Italy and Germany in other pots, but UEFA again worn over hooligan issue. Chelsea game in Turkey in doubt. Doug Ellis stands down as Villa chief executive but remains chairman.

21 Sheikh Abdul bin Mubarak al-Khalifa may rescue Leeds. Hungary dispense with coach Imre Gellei.

22 Arsenal eclipse Liverpool's unbeaten PL record from season's start, their 13th such win and Wenger's 230th in a 3-0 victory at Birmingham, despite six out with suspension and injury. Man Utd hoist PL gate record at 67,748 for 2-1 edge over Blackburn. Chelsea 1-0 winners at Southampton where Strachan rumoured for Leeds. Two more Shearer goals for reviving Newcastle, his 100th under Sir Bobby. Di Canio diving storm as Charlton draw at Leicester. Draws enough respectively for WBA and QPR to head Div 1 and 2, but Oxford lead Div 3 from slipping Hull. Conf: Shrewsbury 4 Hereford 1 crowd: 6585. AFC Wimbledon attract 2307 for a Vase game.

23 Spurs give Villa a late goal start and beat them 2-1.

24 Saha brace lifts Fulham to fifth against Pompey. Bradford appoint Bryan Robson as manager. WBA leave out Hughes after his arrest following a serious motoring incident. Dundee £20 million in debt go into administration and two players Novo and Sancho charged with alleged assault. West Ham splash out £500,000 on Forest's Harewood, while the midlanders buy a King from Gillingham for £950,000.

25 Ch Lge: Henry inspired Arsenal goal-blitz Inter 5-1. Celtic draw with Bayern to top tight Group A. Chelsea will play Besiktas on neutral ground. FA refuse to bottle out over Smith throw and will shortly announce date for Ferdinand. Dundee axe 15 players including Ravanelli and Burley plus other staff. Lee Hughes charged with causing death by dangerous driving. In the Conf Hereford give Halifax a goal start and beat them 7-1. Man Utd youth team attracts 5214 to Rushden.

26 Ch Lge: Man Utd single strike in Greece and Chelsea with a Czech point qualify for knock-out stage, but Rangers lose out in Stuttgart. AC Milan and Real Madrid – with Becks scoring and making one – confirm places with away wins. Turkey unhappy about UEFA neutralising their fixtures. FIFA World Player of the Year short list: Henry, Zidane and Ronaldo. Administration looms for Leeds. Death announced of Ted Bates, 85, Mr Southampton.

27 Palios revolution at FA: Trevor Brooking new director of football development, communications man Paul Barber leaves and Eriksson hand forced with contract extension ploy. UEFA Cup: Pole dancing delight over draw with Man City; Bordeaux break Hearts; minimum winning efforts see Liverpool and Newcastle through. Becks collects his OBE.

28 Strachan pledges Saintlyhood. Gazza agrees his Premiership ambitions are doomed. Eriksson will not respond quickly to FA advances.

29 More shock, horror – Leeds win at Charlton as Sheikh promises the readies. Subbed Rooney fury as Bolton defeat Everton. Blackburn win but Souness sent off for calling ref Poll a Spurs fan. Female Wolves fan injured by firework in pre-match display. UEFA worn England over two friendlies – trouble and no Euro 2004. In Div 1 WBA with identical home and away form after 3-0 at Forest. Robson turns Bradford fortunes to win after 2-0 down to Millwall. QPR storm on in Div 2 with 3-0 against Sheff Wed. Oxford still rowing in front of Div 3. Japan beat England 1-0 in WYC. Blatter blasts Man Utd for Ferdinand stance.

30 West London celebrates: Lampard penalty against Man Utd lifts Chelsea top as Fulham and Van der Sar hold Arsenal goalless. Own goal hits Man City against Middlesbrough. Euro 2004 draw: England face France, Switzerland and Croatia in Group B. Group A: Portugal, Greece, Spain, Russia; Group C: Sweden, Bulgaria, Denmark, Italy; Group D: Czech Republic, Latvia, Germany, Holland. Partick sack Gerry Collins.

**DECEMBER 2003**

**Arsenal's youngest goalscorer ... Sir Alex heart scare ... Van Nistelrooy equals Law total ... Celtic's record run ... EU force new TV deal ... Eight month ban for Ferdinand.**

1 Ferdinand hearing for 18 December; Giggs fined £7,500, Ronaldo £4,000 over Arsenal fracas. Man Utd secure £36,000 four year deal with Vodafone. Further administration fears for Leeds.

2 C Cup: Beattie strikes for Saints win south coast battle with Pompey; All-change Gunners savage Wolves as Fabregas becomes their youngest goalscorer at 16 years 212 days, beating Cliff Bastin's 1930 record. Joe Cole fined £15,000 and banned for two games for seven month old misconduct case. Ch Lge: Galatasaray give themselves a lifeline on neutral ground against Juventus. Blatter still wants 16 team top leagues. Leeds keep hoping for Sheikh sheckels. Middle East crisis: Egypt 1 England Youth 0. Peter Hetherston accused of criticising female assistant referee last month and a male one on Saturday, quits as Albion Rovers manager.

3 C Cup: WBA too good for understrength Man Utd; Bolton stun Liverpool at Anfield; Spurs ease past Man City, Villa stroll it against Palace, Middlesbrough need penalties to oust Everton and Chelsea as usual 1-0 against Reading. WC 2006 Euro Zone draw puts four home countries and the Republic in separate pots. Notts County haul themselves out of financial morass.

4 Sir Alex treated for Blair type irregular heart beat. Man Utd revive interest in young Chinese cracker. Blatter hits out at FA over Ferdinand delay. Leeds in creditors deal, but more queries over Dundee survival.

5 WC 2006: England, Wales and Northern Ireland in Group 6; Republic in Group 4 and Scotland Group 5. Overall draw gives countries with potential travelling support for Germany every chance! Sir Alex gets away with apology over his Arsenal favouritism remark to FA. Giggs two-match ban for Russian elbow. Bye bye to consistent England Youth failing to score again 0-0 v Colombia.

6 Chelsea and Arsenal still one and two in order despite respectively drawing 1-1 at Leeds and Leicester, where Cole was red-carded. Man Utd doubles for Van Nistelrooy and Forlan against Villa. Keane treble snares Wolves in 5-2 Spurs romp. Rovers return 4-0 from wilting Birmingham, who had Dugarry sent off. Two in a minute men Fulham hold fourth place. FA Cup: Telford's Moore three stings on bumbling Brentford; Accrington hold Bournemouth; Taylor hat-trick hero for Blackpool; Two penalty stops Wilson saves ten-man Macclesfield from defeat. Managerless Partick achieve first League win. Becks helps Real to their first in Barcelona for 20 years.

7 Saints alive – they score three to clip Parker's two fine strikes for Charlton. Rooney first half only in goalless Everton and Man City. FA Cup: Scarborough claim Vale scalp.

8 Sunderland's Healy fractures leg after tackle by Safri to mar McAllister's 200th Coventry appearance in 1-1 draw. Hammers chairman Terence Brown claims Defoe 'not right in the head'. Souness in hot water over Poll stancing. Gazza offered opening by Sheff Wed.

9 Ch Lge: Van Nistelrooy scores his 28th goal in 30 European matches to equal Denis Law's club record and Man Utd march on; Chelsea ignore the Turkish terrace menace in Gelsenkirchen for victory but Rangers in retreat from Europe. Out of favour Balaban leaves Villa for Empoli. Conf local derby no goals Shrewsbury and Telford but 6738 there.

10 Ch Lge: Arsenal full steam ahead after Lokomotiv shunt, but Celtic suffer costly late derailment to Lyon in debatable handling offence. Juventus 7-0 win over Olympiakos is a competition record winning margin. Last 16 comprise Spain (4), England (3), France, Germany and Italy (2 each), Czech Republic, Portugal and Russia (one each). Scotland B draw 1-1 with Turkey at Tannadice. Boa Morte fined £4,000 and suspended one game for a first class stamp. Alvin McDonald sacked after two months at Northwich.

11 FL rebel against transfer window pain and threat to shut door on players agreement with PFA. Pleat-Hughton Spurs dynamic duo to stay for season. Stockport bigger in China than Man Utd!

12 Barnsley out of administration. Northwich appoint Shaun Teale as manager.

13 Man Utd climb top after derby day win as Chelsea fall to Bolton, starting line-up just £3.2 million. Rooney: good, bad and lucky; scores and stays on after getting pushy at Pompey. Liverpool second best to Saints. Two off plus boss Adams as Leicester lose to Birmingham. Shearer hits 100 and 101 home goals for Newcastle in Spurs defeat. Riverside draught: no goals in 397 mins, Boro seven clean sheets in a row. In Div 1 'Head man' Defoe nails Sunderland for Hammers win after Black Cats led 2-0. QPR sweep on in Div 2. Eight-man Southend win at Swansea in Div 3. SPL record 15th consecutive win for Celtic as Larsson hits his 200th goal for them.

14 Bergkamp strike enough for Arsenal top up. Leeds win again. Rangers lose 2-0 at Dunfermline, now eight points adrift of Celtic. Eriksson alleged to be backing Ferdinand in drug affair. WCC: Boca beat AC Milan 3-1 on penalties after 1-1 draw in Yokohama. Spanish record six off (three apiece) in Barcelona 3 Espaynol 1 local derby,

15 FA Cup: Accrington beat Bournemouth on penalties. Prof McKenzie to step down at Leeds. FL want British Cup.

16 EU force Sky to fall with eight PL games going to terrestrial TV from next season. C Cup: Arsenal 2-0 at WBA, Bolton 1-0 in extra time against Saints. FA Cup: Lawrence hat-trick including two penalties downs Wycombe; Macclesfield shoot-out success at Cambridge; Barnsley edge out Bristol City all in replays. LDV: Conf survivors Halifax surprise Lincoln. Fulham to return to the Cottage. Andy Preece loses Bury job, Graham Barrow is caretaker. Chinese millionaire said to be planning Leeds takeaway. Gazza wage demands too much for Wednesday.

17 C Cup: Angel delights Villa against Chelsea, who plan more signings during the New Year transfer window; Middlesbrough need penalties to knock out Spurs. FA Cup: shoot-out gives Scunthorpe nod over Sheff Wed. Blatter's latest salvo aimed at foreign mercenaries in English game. Frank Yallop new Canada coach.

18 Scottish sensation: Celtic lose CIS Cup game 2-1 to the Hibees of Edinburgh. Barcelona claim record membership of 108,929, their best since 1986. Becks scores but Real need extra time to beat lowly Leganes 4-3 in Copa del Rey.

19 Ferdinand hammered with eight-month ban, £50,000 fine and hearing costs; Man Utd to appeal. FIFA satisfied with punishment but Blatter warns against court action. Sir Jack hands over to son Rick Hayward as Wolves chairman. Carlisle chairman John Courtenay given 150 hours community service for involvement in brawl with Lincoln last season. Iain Dowie resigns as Oldham boss and will join Palace. New Div 3 leaders, new boys Doncaster. Brazil (of course) beat Spain 1-0 for Youth title.

20 Arsenal held 1-1 at Bolton, Chelsea beat Fulham 1-0 leaving both teams top-tied with same points, goals and difference. Rooney revives Everton on 124th anniversary of club's first game. Flying Angel in Villa's first away win since January. Di Canio wobbly after substitution. Weather hits seven PL, Fl matches one Conf and seven Scottish. Defoe controversial red card in Div 1 where WBA stay top despite losing 1-0 at Coventry. Late goals down QPR at Oldham giving Plymouth two-point Div 2 lead.

21 Rio (and Man Utd) reclaim leading role in PL with 2-1 win at Spurs. Soton up to fourth after another south coast success over Pompey.

22 Another point for Leeds. Campbell offered life at Highbury. Dowie appointed Palace manager, Martin Ling sheds caretaker role for full job at Orient. Pavel Nedved is European Footballer of the Year, leaving Henry II part two after the Arsenal striker was runner-up to Zinedine Zidane for the FIFA World Player a week earlier. Other players of the year: Petrov (Celtic) for Bulgaria, Mutu for Romania.

23 FA deny wanting two-year ban for Ferdinand. Darlington in administration. Davie Hay given Livingston nod after caretaker role following Marcio Maximo axing in October. Gerry Britton and Derek Whyte appointed joint player-managers of Partick quickly make their point. Optimistic noises at Leeds, share issue at Spurs. Chris Coleman against delivering Saha to Man Utd. Birmingham say bye bye to summer buy Figueroa.

24 Spurs to shop for Sheff Utd's Brown in January sales. John Mortimore named as new Soton President.

25 Shock, horror, probe – Government to make club finances more accountable in New Year.

26 A 3-2 ding-dong with Everton keeps Man Utd merrily on high; Henry the second – and the third goals as Arsenal devour Wolves, Henry racks up his 42nd goal in 68 matches of all sorts in 2003. A 42 second opener and 4-2 finale as Charlton pull a cracker against Chelsea. Festive fare sees Fulham snatch fourth from Soton. Trotters roasted in Liverpool revenge. Double Berger for Pompey against Spurs. Ten games without a win for Man City. Norwich topping Div 1 is Delia's recipe as WBA draw again. Ipswich indulge themselves despite Defoe goal for West Ham. Dowie bow has Palace hitting the woodwrk three times, missing a penalty as food-poison victims Millwall win 1-0. Plymouth lead Div 2 and pass 5000th League goal in process. Div 3 has Doncaster still ahead. Crowd control: 737,317 with PL 337,878; Div 1 228,231; Div 2 95,239; Div 3 75,969. Conf Shrewsbury 5059, while Dorset derby 3734 for Claridge's Weymouth 8-0 grilling of Dorchester; a non-league gate bettered only by two in Conf.

27 Abramovich reported to be seeking Steve McClaren as coach and Eriksson as Chelsea manager by August. One more year for Sir Bobby at Newcastle. Saha still a Man Utd target. SPL: Celtic sting the Hibees to a six rout revenge. S Cup: Spartans put Alloa to sword in extra time replay. Unbeaten AFC Wimbledon's 20-20 vision and 7-0 over Raynes Park watched by nearly 4000.

28 Mills boob bombs out to Man Utd – Riverside goal draught ends after 411 minutes as does Boro's 11 undefeated run and games without conceding. Wolves beat Leeds 3-1 but need to overcome relegation tradition of cellar dwellers at half-way mark. Charlton latest to occupy fourth place after downing sad Spurs. Chelsea treble shooters. Vassell ends his 362 scoreless days at Villa Park with brace against Fulham. Supersub Rooney sticks it for Toffees. Norwich celebrate on top of Div 1 with four goals at Derby, but Ipswich upset by Palace. Plymouth sixth win on trot confirms top billing in Div 2, Tony Adams Wycombe adrift at the bottom. Ex-Southender Rawle skittles old mates for Oxford head boys of Div 3 after 15th unbeaten game while Doncaster pay treble Price at Hull where 23,006 turn up. Free-fall Dundee bow to Rangers who are eight points behind Celtic.

29 Pires destroys Saints again for Arsenal. Big bucks Bolton fan Eddie Davies boost for club with share increase. Colin Addison leaves Forst Green in mutual move.

30 Martin O'Neill gets the OBE. WBA a draw at the Dons. Alan Buckley leaves Rochdale in mutual accord. Port Vale saved from administration for the time being. Ottmar Hitzfeld Bayern Munich boss dismisses link with England job. Freddy Shepherd, Newcastle chairman bemoans season so far. Defoe five match suspension. Henry the first in France at least as P of Y 2003. Len Forge, 81, long-serving local Southend soccer admin man awarded MBE.

31 Steve Parkin back as Rochdale manager. Darlington facing administration may go back to Feethams. Rangers nab Gordon Rae from Dundee. Sir Bobby hits back at Toon critics.

## JANUARY

**Sir Alex under Irish whip . . . Offside law confusion . . . Leeds may sell ground . . . Giant-killing for Telford . . . Eriksson wants winter break . . . Saha, Reyes, Parker in big money moves.**

1 First light window move sees Dabizas loan to Leicester from Newcastle. Conf rules OK? Chester three in last five minutes win 6-2 at Leigh completing holiday double as do Aldershot and Gravesend. Boss man Claridge sent off as Weymouth held 2-2 in Dr Martens derby at Dorchester watched by 4116, better than all Conf except Aldershot and Exeter, where City goalie Bittner sent off for second time v Hereford! Roberto Mancini mentioned as possible Spurs No. 1. Gary Neville to lead England players delegation in clear-the-air talks with FA over Ferdinand issue.

2 Delay likely in Ferdinand appeal. Spurs in dispute with Kanoute wanting to play for Mali. Arsenal's Tavlaridis loaned to Lille.

3 FA Cup: Gills upset Charlton, no change for Crewe as Telford's 13th League victims, Tranmere hold Bolton stiffs and Chelsea bogged down level at plucky Watford who are lucky with first goal but denied penalty. Last gasps: winner for Pompey, equaliser for Wolves. Kanoute treble but Palace's Butterfield wrongly dismissed by referee D'Urso. Birmingham turn League reverse to victory over Blackburn. Penalty miss costs Luton's Forbes another hat-trick. Draws for Accrington, Scarborough. Toons of glory for Sir Bobby's men at Soton. Div 2 leaders Plymouth 7-0 v Chesterfield had six in first half. SPL: Celtic club record 18th consecutive win as Auld Firm clash leaves Rangers 11 points behind.

4 FA Cup: Lehmann gift but Arsenal make their presence felt at Leeds. Cheltenham fall to Fulham in last minute. Scholes double for Man Utd at Villa. Yeovil hold out for 70 minutes against Liverpool.

5 PSV winger Robben bobs up on Reds list and gets Sir Alex an accusation. FA did not believe Ferdinand version. Houllier criticised by fans. Loan deal has Javi Moreno at Bolton from Atletico Madrid. Steve Bull may make a comeback with Pelsall Villa. Clubless Rivaldo aims for Brazil champs Cruzeiro. Tommy (TG) Jones, Everton and Wales centre-half, dies at 86.

6 No bottling out for the FA – Smith gets two-match ban. Now Sir Alex upsets Fulham over Saha and will pay Ferdinand during the ban. Pompey edged out at Villa 2-1. UEFA to start referee swapping.

7 Man Utd steal three point lead after 2-1 win at Bolton while Arsenal are held at Everton and faltering Chelsea lose at home to Liverpool. Shearer proves Leeds downfall again with 12th against them in Newcastle's 2000th home League game. Spurs revival continues at Brummie expense. Saha unhappy with Fulham. Billy Dearden quits as Notts Co manager. Gazza fails to agree with Oldham. John Charles, 72, suffers heart attack in Italy.

8 Carlton Cole and Titus Bramble not to be charged with rape. Under-fire Ranieri may face Roman's Russian roulette. Berkovic moves to Pompey. Kanoute and 16 other PL players heading for ACN finals. Trapattoni linked with Spurs.

9 Summertime news: Strachan will leave Saints, Man Utd to sign Liam Miller (Celtic). Lehmann and Phillips to be charged with improper conduct after the alleged stamping incident in December. WBA move two points closer to Norwich after 2-0 v Walsall. Gary Mills appointed Notts Co manager.

10 Another alphabetical topping – Arsenal and Man Utd, same points, difference, goals following the Gunners 4-1 destruction of Boro. Charlton occupy fourth place, Bolton odd goal in seven win at Blackburn. Man City 14 without a win lose at Portsmouth. Saha so good for Fulham. Robbie Keane causes more grief for Leeds. Div 1: Bradford latest to find hole in Norwich home record. Div 2: QPR close gap on Plymouth to two points. Div 3: Hull back at top after 1-0 at Darlington while Oxford held goalless by Lincoln. Graham Barrow confirmed as Bury boss, Kelham O'Hanlon is No. 2. SC: Spartans carry the non-league flag after 4-1 win at Arbroath. AFC Wimbledon held at Sandhurst end 38 consecutive win streak. Manchester smile: Utd head Fair Play, City second, but bung deal accusation against Reds. City board escape plane crash drama.

11 Man Utd edge ahead after goalless with Newcastle, but ace whistler Durkin in bother after denying Silvestre goal and Shearer penalty. Ruel Fox (Norwich) was the last visitor to score a spot kick at Old Trafford in 1993. Chelsea find four goals again. Veron and family menaced by machete burglar.

12 LMA question Brooking credentials. Clear the air talks betweeen players and FA. Wigan prepare to pay club record £2 million for Jason Roberts (WBA). Durkin admits error over penalty. Maradona the Musical getting rave reviews in Buenos Aires. Gary McAllister resigns as Coventry manager due to wife's ill-health.

13 FA Cup: Tranmere show Bolton to have little in reserve; off day for Accrington; Dons graduate at Stoke; Cobblers earn Utd tie. Seaman retires after Saturday's injured shoulder, City replace him with Hammers James. Brooking to end media work. Concern over lack of a Leeds buyer. George Reynolds resigns as Darlington chairman. Roy Hodgson sacked as UAE coach.

14 FA Cup: Scarborough Seadogs snaffle Southend Shrimpers to set up dream tie with four-play Chelsea; Man City end winless streak at Leicester. Saha interesting Chelsea. Man Utd may ditch Ferdinand appeal, but youth player Phil Marsh injured in car crash. Ravanelli off to Perugia. Frome Town enlist white witch to end ground curse.

15 Cash-strapped Leeds may have to sell Smith and Viduka – quickly. Eric Black appointed manager of Coventry from caretaker role. Trapattoni again linked with Spurs. Steve McMahon resigns at Blackpool then changes mind. Charlton to leave out Parker, unsettled by transfer interest from Chelsea. AFC Wimbledon announce profit of £164,750 to June. Homeless Margate in turmoil as local council refuse ground redevelopment. Leigh chucked out of the Trophy for fielding an ineligible player.

16 Ferdinand will start ban but will appeal. Women players give Blatter bum's rush over shorter kit. Leeds may have another week's grace before administration.

17 Shocks and goals day: Miller grinds Wolves a goal to ko Man Utd. Leeds bottom after losing to Saints and may have to sell Elland Road. Charlton win at Everton. Leicester concede two in last minute to draw 3-3 with Boro. Liverpool rage over ref Rennie ignoring penalty claims allegedly for Doherty handball in losing at Spurs. Div 1 goal deluge 54 in all. Ipswich beat Crewe 6-4, Rotherham and leaders Norwich share eight, West Ham and Sheff Utd six between themselves after the Hammers led 3-1, Coventry win 6-1 at Walsall, Palace 5-1 at Watford, Wigan 4-2 at Preston. Plymouth and QPR carry on winning as do Bristol City and Port Vale in the Div 2 pecking order. Hull score three in eight second-half minutes in top of the Div 3 table clash with Oxford to win 4-2. Dons tail: Milton Keynes version 3623, AFC 3215 – but united in 1-0 defeats.

18 With a disputed free-kick and challenged penalty a Henry double puts Arsenal top at Villa. Chelsea held by Brummies. Saha heading for Old Trafford at £12 million.

19 Saha-less Fulham beaten 3-1 at Newcastle. PL refereeing body tell whistler Halsey he was correct with quick free-kick at Villa. Ferdinand sends 125 page appeal to FA. Chelsea's summer post-dated Petr Cech deal for Rennes goalkeeper at £8.5 million. Irish racing tycoon John Magnier increases stake in Man Utd to over 25%. Eriksson wants 16 day winter break from 2005. Leeds players asked to defer wages. Gabbiadini retires through injury on eve of 36th birthday. Bristol Rovers and Ray Graydon to part company, Phil Bater caretaker. Toshack is Murcia coach choice.

20 C Cup: Juninho goal leaves Arsenal semi-detached. LDV: Blackpool beach Halifax, Sheff Wed four spree over Scunny, silver lining for Colchester's McGleish at Northampton and four star Southend stall QPR. Birmingham announce profit of £3.3 million. Barnet out of Trophy – ineligible player syndrome. Coaches instructions may not fall on deaf earpieces. Cameroon to experiment with all-in-one strip.

21 C Cup: Angel brace not enough for Bolton high five. Miller rescues point for Wolves. S Cup: Dons dump Dundee. Lawrie Sanchez is new Northern Ireland boss. Becks sent off for Real gets standing ovation. Accrington to go full-time after summer.

22 Dundee will start next season ten points worse off unless they come out of administration by 31 May. Wimbledon hopeful of takeover.

23 Man Utd: the anatomy of a transfer – Saha signs in £12.85 million deal (£11.5 million to Fulham, £575,000 PL levy, £750,000 agents fee). Wales want Euro 2004 place because Russia's Titov tested positive for drug in play-off. Lincoln overturn Doncaster at Belle Vue. Kanchelskis, 35, joins Moscow Dynamo.

24 FA Cup: Ref Knight denies Seadogs penalty in McCain Theatre of Chips as Chelsea spoil Scarborough fare; Colchester earn replay against Coventry; Swansea's goal-a-tie Trundle puts Preston to flight; Cheyrou double edges it for Liverpool against Newcastle; Arsenal sans holidaying Henry beat Boro 4-1 with two from Ljungberg; winning braces for Blake (Burnley), Taylor (Portsmouth). Another clean sheet in Div 2 for ten in a row unbeaten Plymouth as QPR stumble at Bournemouth. Hull four points clear in Div 3 after 2-0 at Cheltenham. No change in top SPL ratings. Brazil's 1938 WC star Leonidas, 90, dies.

25 FA Cup: Hammers riveting display at Wolves; Everton leave it late to birthday boy Jeffers for Fulham replay; Forlan penalty miss for Man Utd but Cobblers keeper Harper keeps score down to three; threesome, too, for Sheff Utd at Forest; Spurs and Man City to play again.

26 Man Utd to review their transfer procedures. Leeds get more time to find salvation. FA Cup draw pairs Arsenal with Chelsea and possibly the two Mancunians together, but only three PL teams guaranteed – five maximum – to go through. Kanoute double for Mali. Miklos Feher, 24, Benfica and Hungary forward, dies after collapsing Sunday in League game. Rinse too far: Seadogs goalie Walker finds mum has washed Chelsea autographs out of shirt. Everton seek return of 50 balls kicked into crowd by Rooney in pre-match warm-ups.

27 Arsenal snap surprise signing of Jose Antonio Reyes, 20, from Sevilla – a snip at £17.6 million. C Cup: ten-man Villa win 2-0 but lose 5-4 on aggregate to Bolton. Man Utd challenged by Irish shareholders Magnier and McManus. Leeds still ducking and diving to stay afloat. Long-term injury Bellamy on comeback trail. Republic to get Landsdowne Road expansion. Keith Alexander to return to Lincoln post after medical clearance.

28 Sir Alex gets £4 million one year rolling contract to keep M and M sweet? C Cup semi-final off – Boro pitch ok, ground and around icy. But Derby beat the freeze and leapfrog Forest in Div 1. Lua Lua sent off for Congo. Winter break for PL next season. FIFA to accept drug code. Antic gets a job coaching Celta Vigo.

29 No curbs for Parker, off to Chelsea for £10 million. Leeds players agree to wage deferral. Magnier wants probe into Man Utd transfer deals as Dong Fangzhou, 18, finally arrives there. PL to adopt points deduction for clubs in administration from next season. A week after Newcastle sold Cort to Wolves, they claim another £2 million with Solano joining Villa. Fulham woo a McBride as Saha replacement. FIFA

keeping eye on Ferdinand appeal. Cureton comeback in England from Busan Icons (South Korea). Gazza escapes car crash. Best arrested for drunk driving.

30 Sir Alex accuses critics of horseying around his family. England line up games with Japan and Iceland. Boa Morte in racial abuse claim. Hasselbaink charged with misconduct over FA Cup tie. Man City home in on Belgian cap Daniel Van Buyten (Marseille). Nigeria expel Babayaro and Yakubu for breaches of discipline.

31 Offside law tweaking helps Man Utd winner over spirited Saints; record PL gate too. Five goals in 18 minutes as Villa whack Leicester whose goalie Walker has to wrestle pitch invader. Bless the McBride as Fulham down Spurs. Best-ever goalless Merseyside draw thanks to keepers. Charlton suffer minus Parker. Leeds make it six defeats in a row as Boro score three. In Div 1 crucial win for Norwich over Sheff Utd. Plymouth and QPR both beaten in Div 2. Waterlogging causes 11 Nationwide postponements plus 12 in Scotland.

**FEBRUARY**

**Goal rushes ... John Charles dies ... Coca Cola to sponsor Football League ... Chelsea-Arsenal in Euro pairing ... Celtic milestones ... Hayter quickest treble.**

1 Arsenal back on top after Man City own goal misery, Anelka dismissal and rocket from Henry. Lampard at the double for Chelsea. Becks red card for Real. Geoff Thomas has bone marrow transplant op, thanks to donor sister Kay. Deaths of former managers Ally MacLeod, 72, Scotland and Bob Stokoe 73, Sunderland.

2 Window shopping closes with minimal sales in the PL but deals lower down still in evidence, though Defoe goes to Spurs for £7 million with Zamora moving to West Ham in the transaction. Liverpool-Newcastle reserve game sees comebacks from injury for Baros, Sinama-Pongolle, Bellamy and Bowyer. Coach Wadsworth axed from Congo job. John Hollins heading for China and Stockport Tiger Stars.

3 Boro make the C Cup final as Keown embrace leads to his 13th and Arsenal's 54th red under Wenger but wonder boy Reyes scores – at the wrong end. FA Cup: Coventry whither on the Vine hat-trick for productive Colchester. UEFA reject Wales Euro appeal. FIFA centenary match France v Brazil two days before FA Cup final would threaten Arsenal. Oldham out of administration as three USA based Englishmen finance takeover. CIS Cup: Dundee in administration suffer last minute defeat to cash-strapped Livingston.

4 FA Cup: Man City's ten men turn 3-0 half-time deficit into 4-3 win at Spurs; Fulham home in extra time despite another Jeffers last gasp equaliser for Everton. Kenyon finally takes up his role at Chelsea. Nigeria want to recall expelled players. Livingston players may play for free in cup final.

5 Istanbul awarded 2005 Ch Lge final, with Lisbon getting the UEFA version. Brighton's plans for new ground hit. Coventry give free tickets to fans who travelled to Colchester. Hibs pull off Auld Firm double beating Rangers on penalties having disposed of Celtic earlier in the CIS Cup. Alpay to join Incheon United (South Korea). Danny Wallace ex-Saints and MS sufferer to have benefit at St Mary's. Emlyn Hughes suffering from brain cancer.

6 Some 30 Man Utd supporters delay 4.20 pm race at Hereford in protest over M and M interference at Old Trafford. Derby debt said to have risen to £35.2 million. Kenyon makes it plain: Chelsea must win something. More time for Leeds.

7 PL 29-goal rush and see-saw sevens see Spurs 4-3 winners over Pompey and Man Utd shaken by gallant Everton rally at three down to draw level before ton-up Van Nistelrooy's 101st seals it 89 minutes. Club record 24th unbeaten PL game for Arsenal at Wolves. Speed in 400th PL game, Shearer 300th as Newcastle hit fourth place in similar 3-1 victory over Leicester. Leeds teetering after reverse at Villa. Van der Sar holds Saints at bay for Fulham. Debutant ex-Huddersfield Stead does it for Blackburn. In Div 1 Norwich win 1-0 at nine-man Wimbledon. Powering Palace fifth success in six matches stun Sheff Utd 3-0. Forest end boss Paul Hart's reign. Div 2: Moss gathers sub Wotton penalty as Pilgrims progress halted v Bournemouth. QPR cut deficit to three points. Div 3: Hull gain three point lead after 2-1 over York. Another 4-3 in Conf as Tamworth beat nine-man Leigh. S Cup game at Clyde abandoned in snow. Seven in one place as Stranraer swamp struggling East Stirling in Div 3. Senegal lose in ANC.

8 Chelsea 1-0 again, but goalless tale of two City's. Celebrating Oldham let in fans for free all 13,007 of them and then beat Grimsby by six. The defeat costs Paul Groves his Mariners job, Graham Rodger becomes caretaker. Nigeria put Cameroon out. John Charles recovering from having part of right foot amputated.

9 Hearts Murrayfield move next season. Blatter wants to restrict subs to five per team in international friendlies. Merson to seek treatment for personal problems. Batty axed at Leeds. Wembley's £757 million cost causes consternation.

10 Leeds revive 4-1 leapfrogging over victims Wolves. Henry hits 100th and 101st Premiership goals against Saints. Walker fumble as Leicester concede draw to Bolton. LDV: Blackpool and Southend first leg wins line-up possible all seasiders final. Joe Kinnear takes root at Forest. Hoddle's possible second coming at Southampton, attracting little local fan mail. Six Livingston players axed, another six asked to take wage cut. Dundee, Livingston and Motherwell in administration, Dunfermline heading towards it and Scottish FA threaten all with relegation.

11 Goals aplenty again 24 in seven and Man Utd ship another three as Job's worthy effort sneaks it for Boro. Chelsea move a point behind second place. Four more for Spurs at Charlton. Man City 14 League without a win as Owen back on goal standard for Liverpool. Brummies threesome against Everton. Scots also hit 23 in five games, Motherwell and Partick get five apiece. M and M increase Man Utd stake. FA Cup: Telford's reign ends with Millwall defeat. Tunisia beat Nigeria on penalties, Morocco easily defeat Mali.

12 American sports tycoon Malcolm Glazer with 16.31% share in Man Utd may launch takeover bid. Brian Horton and Port Vale part company. Sheff Wed announce debt of £29.6 million. UEFA warn clubs in debt may face European competition exclusion.

13 Strachan takes early leave from Soton, Youth supremo Steve Wigley becomes caretaker. Martin Foyle appointed at Port Vale. New Boston owner John Sutnick sacks boss Neil Thompson and chief executive Dave Pickett. Jim Rodwell becomes caretaker. Liverpool to drop Diouf and Diao after late return from Senegal duty. Confusion reigns over new offside change. Nigeria pip Mali for African third place.

14 FA Cup: No iffs, just a butt from Gary Neville as ten man Utd beat City 4-2 in Mancunian affair. Fulham held by Hammers, Sunderland by Brummies. Dichio seals it for Millwall and Hume goal sparks Tranmere victory. Div 1: Palace rock Stoke 6-3 as Johnson hat-trick keeps momentum going. Norwich stay five points clear after 2-0 at Coventry. Div 2: Inactive Plymouth, but QPR's 1-1 draw at Brentford allows Bristol City to close in on points. Div 3: Hull only draw at Carlisle and Doncaster's 1-0 win over Huddersfield edges them within a point. SPL: Rangers snatch draw at Aberdeen, Celtic score twice in last nine minutes to beat Dundee Utd 2-1 and extend lead to gaping 13 points. Trophy kit note: Tamworth pack wrong shirts, decline Aldershot offer and buy set of England locally – still draw 1-1. Tunisia beat Morocco for their first African Nations Cup trophy.

15 FA Cup: Two-goal Reyes lifts Arsenal after Mutu lead, fourth successive season Chelsea have lost to the Gunners in it; Liverpool denied by Pompey fight back; battling Colchester concede just one at Sheff Utd.

16 Becks speaks out for Sven. Lehmann fined £10,000 for misconduct over Saints game. Bolton want more tickets for C Cup final.

17 England double-Dutch victories: U-21 3-2, U-19 2-0. Injury toll mounts for home countries ahead of full internationals. England venue in Portugal houses two impoverished third division clubs. Terry Gibson quits Wycombe No. 2 post to join Sanchez at Northern Ireland, facing 30 goalless minutes to equal world record 1272. Wales and Scots minus key men. Div 2: Plymouth woe at Tranmere, leaves ten-on-a-spin Bristol City top after 2-1 at Grimsby. LDV: Southend reach their first ever final. Dunfermline players agree pay cut, so do the Livingston six and Forest Green.

18 King on the rebound for England draw. Earnshaw treble slays Scots. Northern Ireland score only after new famine 1298 minutes as Norway win 4-1. Republic hold Brazil scoreless. Subs are us: England 9, Wales 6, Scots 4, N. Ireland 3, Republic 1. Scots U-21 pipped late by Hungary. Elsewhere PL scorers include Solano (Peru), Mutu (Romania), Pahars (Latvia) and debutant Saha (France). Howard Wilkinson turns down a Chinese offer, but Steve Cotterill his ex-No. 2 becomes Leicester coach. FA force Pompey to stage women's international despite pitch concerns. Goa Div 3 title race: one team wins 55-1, the other 61-1. All four now suspended. Tommy Eglington, Everton and dual Irish cap, dies at 81.

19 FIFA ban Viduka from Leeds match over tug-of-war with Aussies. Leeds threaten legal action. Roy Keane signalling possible Republic comeback. Zidane extends contract with Real to 2007. England ladies beat Danes 2-0 at Fratton.

20 Scholes charged with misconduct over Doriva clash on 11th. French coach Jacques Santini may not call on Arsenal men for centenary game. Russia not to appeal Titov one-year ban. Div 1: QPR held by Peterborough.

21 Despite 27 second joy, Chelsea left with title mountain to climb after Arsenal's six-day repeat 2-1, now 17 games since they lost to the Blues. Uphill task, too, for Man Utd failing to beat gutsy Leeds. Wolves bottom-out to 18th as ref Harold Webb signals his first ever PL goal in 560 minutes play! Rovers goalie Friedel equalises late against Charlton but is beaten shortly after. Saints recover to share six goals with two-goal Rooney tuning in the Everton hit parade. Man City end 14 League game winless streak at Bolton. Div 1: As Norwich draw with West Ham, WBA close gap winning at slipping Sheff Utd. Only four points separate 4th and 12th. Div 2: Bristol City slickers 11 on the spin lead from Argyle 2-1 to the good over Port Vale. Heffernan four for Notts. Div 3: Doncaster's 2-1 success at Mansfield overtakes Hull, 1-0 losers at home to Torquay. John Charles, 72, gentle giant, dies.

22 More four play: another Spurs quartet – but also visiting Leicester, while Aston Villa and Birmingham share theirs in another midland scrap. FA Cup: misery for Houllier and Liverpool, downed late in Pompey replay. SPL; Celtic break Morton's 1963-64 (Div 2) Scottish record with 24th straight victory, though the Greenock club had had 25 dating back the previous season. Roque Maspoli, Uruguay's WC winning goalie in 1950, dies at 86.

23 Highbury Reds green light for £357 million Ashburton Grove 60,000 all-seater stadium, but might still turn amber over opposition. Micky Adams £500 fine for December confrontation with ref Riley. Silvestre out with injury for a month. Van Nistelrooy re-runs his 'missing Becks' speech. Bradford heading for administration.

24 Ch Lge: Edu twice nicely for Arsenal in 3-2 at Celta Vigo; Kahn boob costs Bayern a Real draw; holders Milan held at Sparta; Two months in cold storage, Lokomotiv chip it 2-1 over Monaco. FA Cup: Hammer horror as Fulham take three. Div 1: ten man Sheff Utd rediscover winning formula at Crewe, Millwall move into play-off zone. Div 2: 84th minute sub Hayter sets FL fast scoring hat-trick in 2 mins 20 secs as Bournemouth hit Wrexham for six, but parents already left for home! S Cup: Dunfermline win postponed tie at Clyde. Boss Steve Evans will bounce back at Boston next week.

25 Keane stamping off for 11th red leaves ten-man Man Utd 2-1 down to Porto on Sir Alex's 100th Ch Lge game; Lyon inflict Sociedad's first home European defeat in 26; La Coruna edge Juventus 1-0 and own goal gives Chelsea win in Stuttgart. FA Cup: Black Cats bad luck for Birmingham with Smith extra time brace for Sunderland. Div 1: Forest make a point but now 17 games without a win. LDV: Peerless Blackpool ensure Tangerine and Shrimpers final beach party. Glazer increases Man Utd stake to 16.69%. Thatcher, ex-England U-21 skipper given FIFA permission to play for Wales. Jacques Georges, ex-UEFA President, dies at 87.

26 UEFA Cup: Wins for Celtic, Liverpool while Newcastle draw at Valerenga. Four Italians – two defeats with Turkish delight, two draws. Leeds consortium withdraws.

27 Coca-Cola to sponsor FL in £15 million three year deal from 2004-05. Sir Alex begs fans not to demonstrate at Cheltenham races. Fourteen goal Friday: No kidding for Doncaster high five against Harriers, while Daggers wrecked by Shipp's red card as Hereford equal Conf record with 9-0 win there. Chris Coleman selects Fulham team from hospital bed after recovering from virus. Bradford back in administration. Conf regional second division to go ahead.

28 Sir Alex fumes at ref Wiley over no-penalty for Van der Sar clash with Saha as Man Utd draw at Fulham, leaving Arsenal – 300 unbeaten League days – 2-1 winners against Charlton nine points ahead. Chelsea snatch lucky 1-0 at Man City to go second. First win in ten for Everton, Wolves goalless at Leicester move to 17th on a day all six PL games kick off at 3 pm! Div 1: WBA upset by Rotherham, Palace scrape 1-0 win as Gillingham's Southall has one penalty try saved, the replay hitting the bar. Forest end 17 match no-win run. Div 2: Bristol City lose in injury-time at Sheff Wed, Plymouth top again. Jevons hits post with Grimsby penalty, but then scores four goals in 6-1 v Barnsley. Div 3: Hull lose, Oxford draw, Torquay make ground to fourth. Frozen pitches cause six FL postponements, two more for snow reason, one Conf and only three SL survive. Gaddafi ducking and diving for a PL club? No more sudden or slow deaths as FIFA junket to terminate golden and silver goals, allow only six friendly subs, authorise artificial pitches, new offside interpretation but veto 20 min h-t, one piece kits.

29 C Cup Final: Trotters let in two in seven mins including debatable penalty as Boro lift first trophy since Amateur Cup in 1898 and ref Riley ignores claim for Ehiogu hands. PL: Crucial point each for Leeds against Liverpool and Pompey for whom loan raider Lua Lua scores against his own Toon. SPL: Half of Auld Firm looking infirm as Rangers lose at Dundee Utd leaving Celtic 16 pts ahead; Hearts only 13 behind second place! Blatter still bleating about size of PL. Becks said to have earned £4 million from football in 2003, £6.7 million from sponsorships.

**MARCH**

**Man Utd big profit ... Leicester three in strife ... Winter break OK? ... Ferdinand ban stands ... Leeds takeover ... Eriksson signs new FA contract.**

1 Home Office announce 19% rise in football related arrests last year. Chelsea to snatch Arjen Robben for £13.5 million, to Man Utd rage. Bradford players agree pay cut. Sir Bobby wrings hands over failure to prevent Lua Lua playing against Newcastle. Wilkinson goes Chinese after all – with Shanghai Shenua.

2 Man Utd top of income league for seventh successive year, the 2002-03 figure was £167.4 million ahead of Juventus, AC Milan, Real Madrid, Bayern Munich and Internazionale with Arsenal 7th on £99.51, Chelsea only 10th. Bates bows out at the Bridge. Div 1: Norwich and WBA grapple goalless at the top; Forest win again; Sheff Utd beat Millwall in return to play-off frame; Hammers draw at Burnley. Clarke dismissed in third minute for a tackle after 25 secs, but Coventry win 1-0 at Cardiff. Div 2: QPR injury-time winner, Bristol City held at home by lowly Wycombe. Houllier had death threat.

3 UEFA Cup: Liverpool stride forward as do tentative Newcastle; Celtic lose a leg but march on, too. PL: Boro cut down at Birmingham. Walter Smith gets No. 2 slot at Man Utd. Paul Sturrock in Saints frame as Hoddle drops out of picture. On the cards for Hearts to play SPL game with Celtic down under.

4 Nine Leicester players arrested in Spain for alleged attacks on women; one released, six detained overnight. Meet the managers: Sturrock in at Soton; Paul Hart at Barnsley after Thordarson sacking; Nicky Law with Rodger No. 2 at Grimsby. Owen had death threats, too. UEFA Cup draw: Celtic v Barcelona; Newcastle v Mallorca; Liverpool v Marseille. Pele's 100 living legends includes one dead (Foe) and two American women. Bradford put up for sale, Wimbledon may go into liquidation. Arsenal's half-year debt rises to £61.7 million.

5 The Leicester three: Dickov, Gillespie and Sinclair charged with sexual aggression and put in prison, others released. Sir Alex may settle for around £2.5 million from the dispute over Rock of Gibraltar, but Magnier to press ahead with transfer inquisition. Man Utd hope to add 7500 seats at Old Trafford. Keane gets one-match ban in Europe, Scholes asks for personal hearing over clash with Doriva. Doncaster held at Swansea. Morris axed by Leeds.

6 FA Cup: After Keane-Brown error leading to first successful domestic penalty by opposition at Man Utd since December 1993, Van Nistelrooy double ends Fulham resistance. Arsenal high five but Pompey fans chime in happily – only singing when they're losing and have Sheringham late consolation. PL: Birmingham's win over Bolton completes double over C Cup finalists in three days. Div l: WBA catch Norwich after 3-0 v Coventry; Ashton treble for Crewe hits Wigan; Stoke rack up 28 from possible 30 points. Div 2: McCormick penalty save from Notts Heffernan earns Plymouth point, Bristol City lose, QPR only draw. Fifth successive win for Swindon. Div 3: Hull lose to Benin's D'Jaffo debut goal for Mansfield, Oxford lose 18 match home record to Huddersfield. S Cup: giant-killers Inverness topple Motherwell. Dr Martens: Crawley have record 4522 crowd for 2-1 v Weymouth, better than all Conf, eight Div 3, two Div 2. Abramovich, 37, richest man in Britain £7.2 bn from oil, aluminium, pharmaceuticals and bacon.

7 FA Cup: Millwall unwisely allow Muscat to take penalty – Achterberg saves to earn Tranmere replay. Smith goal puts Sunderland into semi-finals against Sheff Utd, repaying debt for knocking Black Cats out for Watford last season. Div 1: clear on top for Norwich after E Anglian derby win over Ipswich. S Cup: Celtic beat Rangers, yet again.

8 Micky Adams stands by his Leicester players on day Walkers Stadium hosts independent schools Boodle & Dunthorne Cup final. FA Cup draw ensures one FL team in final. Brian Talbot leaves Rushden, may go to Oldham.

9 Ch Lge: Porto's Costinha draws Man Utd to account for late expensive exit after Reds denied a Scholes goal; blank check but Chelsea in credit; La Coruna bullish in Juventus upset and Lyon again increase stock 1-0. Div l: Etherington treble as Hammers do Dons down 5-0 to go third. Bates unwanted by Sheff Wed, sues Chelsea for £2 million.

10 Ch Lge: Arsenal ease after early Henry double; AC Milan coast to 4-1 over Sparta; Lokomotiv run on empty with ten men at Monaco who scrape home on back of away goal; Zidane enough for Real. Div 1: Sunderland lose a man and two points to Preston. Div 2: Tranmere ship three at Brighton. Talbot confirmed at Oldham, Barry Hunter acting player-manager for Diamonds. Besiktas fined £34,000 for crowd trouble v Chelsea in Dortmund! Wolves Butler fined £3000 for improper conduct at Middlesbrough. Coleman back at Fulham.

11 UEFA Cup: Celtic (one goal, one red card) beat Barcelona (no goals, two reds); Magpies four late goal swoop crushes Mallorca, but Marseille catch Liverpool similarly for a draw. Cudicini breaks hand in training. Steve Tilson gets Southend job, Paul Brush as assistant.

12 Leicester three bailed and on way home. Sir Alex reveals he had pacemaker fitted. Ch Lge draw sees Arsenal v Chelsea! FA Cup committee against winter break. Div 2: Bristol City 1-0 v Rushden secures second spot for now.

13 PL: All the threes including points: first three away wins, next three home; no goals for losers; two enough for Londoners Arsenal – though Rovers Souness unhappy with whistler Wiley – Chelsea and Fulham; one apiece for Charlton (who go fourth), Everton and embattled Leicester at Birmingham. Div 1: Norwich slip up at Cardiff but have game in hand of WBA 2-1 winners at Crewe. Div 2; Argyle edge ten man Swindon, QPR win 4-1 at Hartlepool. Peterborough hit six against Wrexham. Div 3: Doncaster snatch draw, Hull win and Huddersfield move to third. Bottom battlers Carlisle beat failing Oxford 2-0. SPL: Rangers drop another two points. Oxford beat Cambridge 2-0 to level Varsity series 46 all in 120th meeting.

14 PL: Manchester derby and Utd not at the races in City's 4-1 win. Own goal misery for Newcastle at Spurs. Sturrock Saints are winners and Niemi nabs Owen penalty – 10th miss in 23 – and Ganea spot kick saved by Sorensen as Villa cruise 4-0 at Wolves. CIS Cup final: skint Livingston beat Hibs 2-0 for first trophy. Celtic held by Motherwell after 25 straight wins. Leeds still hopeful of salvation. Brentford axe Wally Downes.

15 Eriksson pressing for his winter break. Thai consortium may wrap up Liverpool interest. Garry Thompson caretaker at Brentford.

16 FA Cup: Tranmere run ends as Millwall reach first semi-final since 1937. Div 1: Victorious but late Norwich and last minute WBA extend gap to third place by 11 points. Bent treble for Ipswich. Div 2: Two goal wins enough for both Plymouth and QPR. Div 3: Doncaster 1-0 at Yeovil, Hull 2-0 at home to Orient, Huddersfield held by Rochdale. G-14 clubs thumbs down to Blatter's CWC. Leicester three survive night on the boos in reserve game at Soton. FA to overhaul banning system. Falkirk interested in groundshare with Dunfermline.

17 PL: Owen twice on the goal standard as Liverpool down Pompey 3-0. Div 1: Hammers cruise to third place after 4-2 v Alex. Div 3: Oxford return to winning ways. SPL: Celtic 2-1 at Dundee have 19 point lead with game played more than Rangers. Becks scores but Real lose Spanish Cup Final to Zaragoza.

18 FA uphold Ferdinand ban, but forget to invite witness for Hasselbaink misconduct hearing. Managerial moves: Martin Allen bounds from Barnet to Brentford; John Taylor sacked at Cambridge; Brian Flynn mutual parting at Swansea. Wimbledon hopeful of a buyer. Cole and Yorke unhappy at Blackburn. Charlton's Peter Varney against a winter break. S Cup: Livingston win again in Dons replay.

19 Leeds takeover by Yorkshire based consortium in £22 million deal; Gerald Krasner chairman, Peter Lorimer on the board. Wales fail in second Euro 2004 appeal. Darlington hopeful of salvation. Bristol Rovers may sign Ian Atkins (Oxford manager) – in the summer!

20 High winds, safety worries cause a few postponements, two abandoned games; tragedy outside Walkers Stadium as visiting supporter killed by flying debris. PL: Late goal salvaging yields Leicester a point against ten-man Everton; Liverpool three points (for fourth place) over Wolves; Man Utd two in a 3-0 win v Spurs and Middlesbrough one to satisfy a 5-3 feast against Birmingham. Rovers in good Stead for Souness, Arsenal and Chelsea 2-1 each. Div 1: Palace halt Norwich progress, Boy Bowditch hat-trick for Ipswich. Div 2: Plymouth, QPR draw, Bristol City lose. Div 3: Doncaster snatch late equaliser, Torquay go third. Oxford suspend boss Atkins. Winchester and Sudbury reach Vase final. Waterlogged pitches prevent seven SL games.

21 Div 1: Millwall miss two penalties but nail ten-man Hammers 4-1; massive police presence – one Bobby for every 13 fans. LDV final: bracing Blackpool tower over Southend. SPL: Celtic's Larsson cracks club post-war scoring record with 169th League goal and 232nd overall. Rome derby abandoned on erroneous rumour of child fatality outside ground causing disturbances.

22 Leeds off the bottom with a 2-1 win over Man City. Honeymoon period over for Becks at Real? Divorce pending for Ranieri at Chelsea? Oxford in a fix appoint Graham Rix in temporary charge, while Bristol Rovers give joint custody to Russell Osman and Kevan Broadhurst. Gheorghe Hagi is new Galatasaray coach.

23 Ch Lge: AC Milan celebrate Maldini's 130th European game with 4-1 comeback against La Coruna; Porto lead Lyon 2-0. Div 1: Sunderland climb into the frame after 2-1 win over Gillingham. Conf: Exeter – not to lose points – break into top five after 3-2 at Scarborough. Barnet threaten High Court action over Allen. Bellamy in coach bust-up. Cambridge confusion over new appointee Claude Le Roy.

24 Ch Lge: Drawing Chelsea lose lead, dogged by Arsenal again; Real second half recovery against Monaco for 4-2 win, but Becks booked to miss return. Div 1: Millwall in the frame as Dons lose again. Div 2: Bristol City defeated at Tranmere. Trevor Birch heading for Villa this summer. Stuart Baxter, Engand U-19 coach, is South Arica's No. 1. Bobby Moore's 1970 shirt v Brazil fetches nearly £60,000. Duncan Ferguson charged with misconduct relating to Leicester game. Managers in the toils: Joe Kinnear, Dennis Wise and Stan Ternent charged with various misdemeanours. Spurs make a £3.2 million operating profit.

25 UEFA Cup: Spanish eyes of ref Ibanez an area of Liverpool woe as Biscan red-carded and penalty leads to Marseille win; Spanish saunter for Newcastle; Celtic draw inspiration. Transfer deadline activity for

FL, plenty of moves, little money spent. Brian Laws leaves Scunthorpe post. Darlington facing liquidation, Telford in administration.

26 Bolton manager Sam Allardyce facing two charges relating to remarks over ref Riley. Eriksson reported visiting home of Chelsea supremo Kenyon. Darlington owe money to Manager David Hodgson.

27 Super sub birthday boy Hasselbaink's late 13 minute treble for 102 goals in his 200th PL game savages plucky Wolves at 5-2 as Sven shadow hovers over Ranieri. Viduka hit and miss before Birmingham strike Leeds 4-1. Delap bicycle kicks Saints to win over Spurs, while Pompey pedal their first away win at Blackburn. Div 1: Top four Norwich, WBA, Sunderland and West Ham all win, Millwall draw, Sheff Utd lose 2-1 at Cardiff. Div 2: Only 6th place Bournemouth manage victory, leaders Plymouth and QPR draw. Chesterfield 4 Grimsby 4 crowd 4444! Wycombe first away success. Div 3: Doncaster held at Oxford, Hull beat Rushden 1-0. Richards all four for Northampton at Macclesfield. Conf: Hereford have 5850 for Shrewsbury and go top. Trophy: Hednesford wreck Aldershot 2-0; Canvey draw at Telford. Eriksson squad includes Defoe, Wright-Phillips, Thompson (Celtic), Green (Norwich) and Samuel (Villa),

28 Surprise surprise – £4 million man Eriksson signs two-year extension to England contract! Sunday Specials: Saha late goal earns draw for Man Utd at Arsenal; point for Liverpool at Leicester keeps fourth place as Newcastle lose 1-0 at Bolton. SPL: Celtic win at Rangers to go 19 points ahead. Women's PL cup final: Charlton 1 Fulham 0. Rooney's girl birthday bash ends in family brawl.

29 Becks among host of injured non-starters for home countries friendlies. Antic resigns at Celta Vigo.

30 Gerrard to skipper England. whose U-21's draw 2-2 in Sweden, but Romania beat the Scots 2-0 at the same level. U-19 England draw 1-1 in Germany. Div 2: Swindon share six goals at Port Vale after 3-0 down. Leeds to get £15 million kit deal with Diadora. Iraq national team to visit England. Australia beat South Africa 1-0 at QPR. Fabio Capello latest Chelsea rumour. Man Utd half year profit £26.8 million, making them richest sports club worldwide. SPL: more groundshare likely: Dundee Utd and Dundee at Tannadice, Clyde at Kilmarnock if promoted.

31 Friendlies galore: turn-up for England losing 1-0 in Gothenburg – last win over Swedes 1968; Scots downed, too, 2-1 by Romania; Northern Ireland's shock success in 16 against Estonia; Earnshaw ensures Wales victory in Hungary and Republic's Robbie Keane injury time goal checks Czechs after their 20 game unbeaten run also at 2-1; Crespo winner for Argentina in WC; France held in Holland after 14 straight wins; Greece unbeaten in 15. Germans deny 1954 WC doping. John Askey reverts to assistant at Macclesfield. Leeds fans aiming to buy Elland Road.

## APRIL

**Wise men reach final . . . Milan crash . . . ton down for East Stirling . . . More Henry milestones . . . Germany routed . . . Arsenal triumph**

1 UEFA may investigate post-match confrontation between Savage (Wales) and Hungarian coach Lothar Matthaus. Brian Horton in at Macclesfield. Hasselbaink escapes Scarborough punishment. Wage cut agreed by Telford players.

2 G-14 clubs to take on FIFA over compensation for World Cup players. Ranieri named Manager of the Month! Kenny Jackett in frame as next Swansea manager.

3 FA Cup: Scholes shoots Man Utd to victory after early Gunners misfiring and despite late sub entry by Henry. PL: Chelsea (unbeaten in 28 League games over 14 years v Spurs) win 1-0. Newcastle go fourth 4-2 over Everton. Another four conceded by Wolves at home to Saints whose Lundekvam scores first goal in 250 PL attempts. Brummie goalie Taylor holds old Fulham mates. FL: Bottom dogs day: Wimbledon win at Wigan, Wycombe at home to Port Vale and Carlisle at Swansea. Div 1 leaders Norwich 5-3 romp at Burnley. Both Plymouth and QPR (crucially at Bristol City) lose in Div 2. Doncaster edge three points ahead but Hull have game in hand. Trophy: Canvey get their penalties right, Hednesford (one off) hold Aldershot (two off) 1-1 to reach final, too. SPL: Celtic (76 home without defeat) need injury time equaliser against Hearts. SL: Div 2 and 3 leaders Airdrie and Stranraer hit six each. Conf: Garry Hill resigns at Dagenham.

4 FA Cup: Lions Den leads his Wise men to promised final after Oster bar strike and late McAteer dismissal costs Sunderland. PL: Liverpool's turn for 4th after 4-0 over Blackburn, another brace for Owen. Freddy Adu, 14 years 10 months, sub debut for DC United v San Jose, highest paid pro in MLS. Dundee unlikely to share.

5 Leeds late strike ends Leicester fight back, but Viduka red carded. Jackett wraps up Swansea post.

6 Ch Lge: Ranieri revenge and a Bridge too far for Arsenal at Highbury as Chelsea reach semis with Monaco giving Real a royal going over in the Principality. Div 1: Sunderland win demotes Dons at MK. FIFA make a profit of £60 million. Exeter having escaped points deduction for administration, cleared over player registration. Everton not to appeal four match ban on Ferguson.

7 Ch Lge: La Coruna stunner and awesome foursome destroys Milan; more Iberian delight as Porto draw at ten man Lyon to progress. Div 1: Millwall down to earth held by Cardiff and goal hero Cahill sent off. Clyde reprieved from closure for a year.

8 UEFA Cup: Newcastle and Celtic in 1-1 draws – Sir Bobby's bitter return to PSV not aided by all-round criticism of ref Veissiere, while Larsson rescues Celts against Villarreal; ten-man Bordeaux overtaken by Valencia, but Marseille edge Inter 1-0. PL to issue code of conduct. Man Utd to field second reserve team in Pontin's. Wales cause splash in Bath: beat England 2-1 in University Games Final.

9 PL: Hooray Henry hat-trick turns tables on Liverpool in Gunners 4-2 comeback. Everton ease to 3-1 over Spurs who have scorer Carr red carded. Div 1: Norwich 2-0 against Wigan while Sunderland win second game after cup defeat, beating Sheff Utd by three clear goals. Derby disallowed goal gives West Ham a point. Sir Alex tells Wes Brown not to go to Euro 2004 because of Ferdinand ban. Injured Millwall skipper Muscat to miss cup final. Bates nearer Sheff Wed takeover. Canvey reach Conf with seven games to go!

10 PL: Wolves squander 2-0 lead, fluff penalty and concede late equaliser at Man City. Leicester critically lose to Fulham as do Blackburn to Leeds in 10th home defeat, but Portsmouth draw at Charlton. Chelsea concede title hope after draw with Boro and Man Utd recover to beat Birmingham 2-1. Baptismal brace for Fulham's John. Div 1: Millwall mauled four times at Coventry, WBA leave it late against Gillingham. Div 2: Plymouth, QPR win, Bristol City held at Swindon. Wycombe relegated after 2-1 defeat by Tranmere. Div 3: Akinfenwa in (winner) off (red card) in Doncaster 2-1 at Bristol Rovers. but Hull beaten 3-2 by Northampton. Huddersfield keep third after 1-0 v Southend. S Cup: Caley and Dunfermline to replay. SL: Hamilton chasing Morton for second in Div 2 beat them 6-1. East Stirling concede 100th goal.

11 PL: Arsenal point nearer, Henry hits foot of post at Newcastle. S Cup: Larsson's 35th goal as Celtic beat Livingston 3-1 to reach final. Becks and Real slump 3-0 at home to Osasuna, AC Milan need late penalty to beat Empoli.

12 PL: Chelsea score two but lose at Villa. Another brace for John but Fulham edged 4-3 by Rovers return. Charlton's first win at Liverpool for half a century. Birmingham goalie Taylor sent off and they crash 3-1 at Pompey. Dave Jones rants at ref Rennie for two missed penalty awards as Bolton beat Wolves 2-1. Div 1: Norwich 1-0 at Reading extend lead as WBA two reds one late in each half draw at Millwall. Sunderland pay the penalty at Ipswich. Sheff Utd recover to beat the Dons 2-1. Hammers suffer red card and 1-0 reverse at Palace. Derby 3-2 over fellow strugglers Bradford. Div 2: QPR snatch last minute share of six goals at Barnsley. Swindon take three at Luton. Div 3: Doncaster promoted after 2-0 success over Cambridge. Hull win odd goal in five at Swansea. Huddersfield lose to ten-man Harriers. Crawley reach Conf.

13 PL: Martyn holds up old mates as Everton draw at Leeds. Gary Neville achieves three points for Man Utd at Leicester expense. Div 1: Decisive win for Wigan over Cardiff. Div 2: Bristol City edge Plymouth 1-0. Conf: Shrewsbury move third after goalless with Chester watched by 5827. Roy Keane back in international favour.

14 UEFA Cup: The SS men (Shearer, Speed) storm Newcastle into the semi-finals 2-1 over PSV, but Celtic finds its a Villarreal nightmare. SPL: Rangers drop two points to Livingston. Chelsea hierarchy no closer to deciding Tinkerman Ranieri's future. Brian Laws back at Scunthorpe helm after club coup. Bryan Robson may leave Bradford at end of season. Halifax may go part-time.

15 Middlesbrough take 2-0 lead in first leg of Youth Cup final at Villa. Henry favourite to retain PFA player crown.

16 PL: Foursome Henry strikes his 150th for Arsenal as Leeds are swamped 5-0. Walsall sack manager Colin Lee after Plymouth show interest in him. Barry Town fail in attempt to stop Airbus UK taking their Welsh place despite ground share with Conwy.

17 PL: Pompey win over Man Utd set in Stone, but Man City crumble 3-1 to Soton. Wolves even have penalty saved but still beat Boro 2-0. Tinker tailor Ranieri not suiting Chelsea masters seeking other material after goalless with Everton. Van der Sar saves Gerrard spot kick in another blank at Anfield. Norwich hit managerless Walsall for five. Dichio cup final place in jeopardy after dismissal in Millwall draw at Forest. Div 2: Plymouth crash 4-1 in ten-a-side at Oldham; QPR held by Stockport. Tranmere take five off Bournemouth. Div 3: ten man Doncaster lose 1-0 at Torquay, Hull draw at Macclesfield while ten-man Huddersfield rally to beat Scunthorpe 3-2. Bottom pair Carlisle and free-falling York both beaten 2-0. Conf: Chester back in FL after four years, Hereford and Shrewsbury in play-offs, jitters for beaten Exeter, Aldershot and drawing Barnet. John Still Dagenham boss.

18 O'Brien gets a red in Newcastle 0-0 at Villa. SPL: Celtic take title after 1-0 at Killie. Div 1: crucial win for WBA at Sunderland gives them massive 12 point advantage. Conf: Morecambe still chasing a play-off berth despite 1-1 with Margate. Adu, 14, becomes youngest MLS goalscorer.

19 Maradona seriously ill after drug overdose. George Hardwick, Middlesbrough and England captain, dies at 84. Boro clinch Youth Cup with 1-0 second leg win over Villa. Tim Harris confirmed as Forest Green boss.

20 Ch Lge: ten-man Monaco in pole position as Chelsea hit the skids 3-1, aided by Ranieri's sub standard half-time tweaking. PL: Man Utd close point behind the Blues after 2-0 v Charlton. Div 1: Millwall lose again, six without a win now. Div 3: Huddersfield successful at Northampton, Hull held at Southend. S Cup: Dunfermline win Caley replay 3-2. Keane back in Irish squad. Motherwell out of administration. Bobby Williamson appointed Plymouth manager. Ronnie Simpson, Celtic and Scottish international goalkeeper dies at 73.

21 Ch Lge: Iberian blank as La Coruna (one late red) hold Porto. Div 1: Palace promote Norwich to PL after beating ten man Sunderland 3-0, shooting themselves goal difference off the play-offs. SPL; Celtic's run ends in injury time to Aberdeen. Wimbledon facing tax man problem. Rix confirmed as Oxford manager. Israel can stage home games in Tel Aviv. Ron Atkinson resigns as ITV pundit after his 'off-air' racist comment on Desailly had been heard in many countries.

22 UEFA Cup: blankety-blank ties – Newcastle with Marseille, similarly Spanish affair, Villarreal and Valencia. Leeds turn down second takeover bid. Bristol Rovers to appoint Ian Atkins next week. Stockport and Brighton fined after incident between players. Rivaldo interesting Bolton. Boro dispense with their Brazilian Ricardinho who did not play in their seniors. Rushden appoint Ernie Tippett as boss. Managers to leave: Shaun Teale (Northwich) and Darron Gee (Tamworth).

23 Desailly three match ban for Monaco nudge. Porto coach Jose Mourinho denies Chelsea connection.

24 PL; square up then all square after Leicester's ex-Man City Dickov has penalty saved by James. But Murphy spot kick gives Liverpool win at Man Utd, his third successful strike at Old Trafford in four years. Davies does in old Saints mates for Bolton, Stead again on Rovers target. Solano off but Villa win at Boro. Div 1: Sunderland draw at Wigan promotes WBA before they beat Bradford. Palace with Johnson treble close in seventh place. Div 2: Debut delight for Plymouth boss Williamson title-clinching win over QPR. Port Vale relegate Notts. Div 3: Huddersfield draw and attract 23,495 record gate at Hull.

Carlisle win at Mansfield as Glennon saves Lawrence penalty, but York almost down. Conf: bumber crowds total 35,034; Exeter get 8256 but still miss out as Barnet win and Aldershot draw to take remaining play-off berths. SL: Inverness only two points off Clyde. Albion win 8-1 at hapless East Stirling. Monaco miss chance of going top after losing 1-0 at home to Nantes.

25 PL: Arsenal's title triumph at Tottenham, as Spurs salvage honour with a draw. Leeds slump to Pompey, Wolves held at Birmingham, Chelsea edged out by Shearer special, Barca beat Real 2-1 at the Bernabeu. Henry keeps his PFA player title, Young Player: Chelsea's Parker; merit award Dario Gradi. Eddie Hopkinson, Bolton and England goalkeeper dies at 69.

26 Glazer increases stake in Man Utd to 18.25%. FA await tape of two Citys brawl. Millwall unhappy about final ticket share. Inverness interested in groundshare with Aberdeen if promoted. St Johnstone sack manager Billy Stark.

27 Blatter's latest: get rid of your draws. Woodgate injury worries Newcastle and Eriksson. Keane may be unfit for Irish return. Roberto Baggio, 37, awaiting last Italian hurrah. U-21: Scots and Republic both draw 2-2 at Denmark and Poland respectively; Northern Ireland U-23 lose 1-0 to Serbia.

28 Scots lose 1-0 in Denmark, the Republic draw goalless in Poland and Northern Ireland hold Serbia 1-1. Arsenal pay £3 million for the removal of Robin Van Persie from Feyenoord in the summer. Dave Jones, Wolves boss, charged over remarks re-ref Rennie. U-19: England beaten 2-1 by Slovenia.

29 Conf play-offs: Goalie Bull prevents Bulls stampede before Aldershot earn draw with Hereford; Clist clincher leaves Barnet fair in taming of the Shrews. Duff dislocates shoulder for second time this season. Becks linked with Chelsea. Wales Euro appeal goes to arbitration on 12 May. UEFA to issue video over offside law! Marcello Lippi to quit Juventus at end of term. Man Utd say Van Nistelrooy not moving anywhere.

30 Div 1: Ipswich draw at Sheff Utd. Bad day for Fulham's Knight – three match ban, but Desailly has one knocked off. Simply the Wurst: Germany's Bild labels team as sausages after 5-1 Romanian rout. Telford sack boss Mick Jones. Ex-Daggers Garry Hill moves down the District Line to Hornchurch. Southend get OK for new ground. Larsson comeback for Sweden Euro 2004. St Johnstone appoint John Connolly (QoS) as manager.

**MAY**

**Leeds lose PL place ... Chelsea and Newcastle blow Europe ... Arsenal stay unbeaten ... Houllier axed ... Cup Final babe ... Porto's Euro Cup**

1 PL: Leicester down despite draw, even Wolves win unlikely to save them; Rovers Stead does for Man Utd, but Man City hit Newcastle; Chelsea late four play cracks Saints; Arsenal held to draw by Brummies; Fulham pinch point at Pompey. Div 1: Hammers sting Watford Hornets as Sunderland draw, Wigan lose. Palace Johnson follows up his saved penalty to endanger Walsall along with ten man Gillingham beaten 5-2 by Coventry. Millwall slip out of frame, but only three points separate seven challenging clubs. Div 2: QPR early strike beats Swindon. Div 3: Hull promoted after 2-1 at Yeovil, but Carlisle's gallant fight ends in relegation and York confirmed to accompany them after 19th game without a win. Becks unhappy being subbed in Real defeat.

2 PL: Leeds demoted after 4-1 reverse at Bolton as Viduka gets second red in five games. Liverpool fourth a point ahead of Villa after both win. SPL: Celtic beaten by Dunfermline.

3 Conf shoot-outs: Tretton red rag but Bull saves two after D'Sane miss as Shots stop the Hereford Bulls, while Clist becomes villain of the Barnet story, Howie saving his spot kick after Rodgers had levelled tie for Shrews in normal time. Coventry axe manager Black.

4 Ch Lge: Porto gamble with long-term injury Derlei pays off with penalty as La Coruna lose Naybet (red) and the tie. PL: Arsenal draw at Pompey. Div 1: Norwich and WBA both lose but City get the title. Stan Ternent to leave Burnley post at season's end. UEFA U-17: England 2 Ukraine 0. FIFA drug code may enrage Olympics version.

5 Ch Lge: Chelsea lose two goal lead, draw and mourn Monaco reaching final watched by Jose Mourinho eyeing final opponents and next job? Newcastle have Woodgate, Jenas, Bellamy and Dyer injured, Lua-Lua refusing to return from Pompey. Leicester and Man City charged with misconduct over fracas last month. The Jags achieve first away win of season: Hibs 1 Partick 2.

6 UEFA Cup: Marseille goodbye to the Magpies with Drogba brace; all-Spanish affair sees Mista spot on for Valencia against Villarreal. Peter Reid gets Coventry job, Steve McMahon leaves Blackpool. Player possibilies: Trezeguet, Juventus to Barcelona £6.7 million, Stam, Lazio to AC Milan. UEFA U-17 England 3 Portugal 1. Bunch of potential Euro 2004 hooligans jailed include a schoolmaster.

7 Celtic interested in Rivaldo. Dundee hoping to come out of administration.

8 PL: Cudicini saves Van Nistelrooy penalty then gifts him an equaliser in Chelsea's 1-1 draw at Man Utd. Fourth place Liverpool convince in 3-0 at Birmingham. Puzzling penalty award by ref Webb for Villa in draw at Soton. Rare Spurs win. Leeds share six with Charlton. Div 2: QPR clinch promotion 3-1 at Sheff Wed. Hartlepool play-off berth after 1-1 at Swindon on goal difference over Port Vale, whose 2-0 victory relegates opponents Rushden along with Grimsby beaten at ten-man Tranmere after leading. Div 3: Automatic lift for Torquay on goal difference after 2-1 at Southend at expense of Huddersfield held at ten-man Cheltenham. Similar agony for Yeovil 3-2 winners who lose out to their victims Lincoln! Northampton take the other place in 2-1 success at Mansfield. SPL: Celtic make it six in a row wins over Rangers. SL: Div 1 top clash sees Inverness leapfrog Clyde but if they stay there groundshare must be agreed with Aberdeen. Div 2: Free-fall Morton overtaken by Hamilton. Div 3: promoted teams Stirling and Stranraer 2-2.

9 PL: Van der Sar gift to Reyes and Arsenal record on track. Newcastle held by finally relegated Wolves, but Shearer penalty saved by Jones. FL: Drama at Wigan 49 seconds from end as Deane equalises for West Ham and destroys Latics play-off hopes to reprieve Palace beaten at Coventry. Ipswich draw suffi-

cient but Sheff Utd lose out after six shared at Preston. Banks save keeps Gillingham from relegation but Walsall win not enough for them.

10 Arsenal's Henry gets back-to-back FWA recognition. FL claim crowds best for 40 years, glossing over fact they had four divisions then! Non-league restructure complete with Conf N & S, Northern Premier, Southern Premier, Northern First, Southern E & W plus Isthmian First. Thai Premier aims for Liverpool cash tie-up. Eddie Gray axed but has year consultancy at Leeds. Gordon Strachan and Iain Dowie in frame. Pompey hierachy in rift with management.

11 Now a Mr Jersey mega-bucks vies with Thai PM for Anfield bid. Paul Merson appointed player-manager of Walsall, Brian Horton confirmed at Macclesfield. Bradford players told to find new teams and the club might move to Odsal stadium. Wimbledon High Court relief. Dennis Wilshaw, Wolves and England, scorer of four v Scots 1955, dies at 78.

12 Magpies miss out on fourth pecking order virtually handing it to Liverpool after pulsating three-all draw at Soton. UEFA U-17: England lose semi-final in overtime to Spain 2-1. Iraq reach Olympic finals after 3-1 win over Saudi. FL to change designations next season: Coca-Cola League Championship, League Championship One and Two!

13 Wales finally turned down by Sport Arbitration Court over Euro 2004. Liverpool reject offer by Jersey-based Steve Morgan. FL need Bradford assurance for next term. FL to have father Clive Oliver, 41, and son Michael, 18, as referee and assistant. Graeme Souness fined £10,000 for his Poll outburst.

14 David Platt axed as U-21 manager. Div 1 play-off: Johnson edges it 3-2 for Palace over Sunderland, but crowd trouble spoils. Peace breaks out at Pompey. Death of Jesus Gil, long-time Atletico Madrid owner, 71.

15 PL: Arsenal, the new Invincibles, make it unbeaten in the competition and 40 in a sequence after Leicester take lead. Newcastle draw at Liverpool gives them UEFA Cup place as Villa lose 2-0 to Man Utd who finish with nine men! Amazing 5-1 wins for Man City and Pompey over Everton and Boro respectively. Ranieri feted by Chelsea fans following 1-0 over Leeds. Play-offs: Div 1: Narrow lead for Ipswich against Hammers; Div 2: Bristol City draw at Hartlepool; Div 3: Huddersfield 2-1 at Lincoln. SL Hamilton finally overhaul Morton for promotion spot. East Stirling achieve second win – again at Elgin's expense.

16 Play-offs: Div 2: Brighton edge it 1-0 at Swindon; Div 3: Mansfield take 2-0 lead at Northampton. Conf: Shrews keeper Howie shoot-out hat-trick heroics end their on-loan spell in Conf against part-time Aldershot after 1-1 draw. Hampshire consolation in Vase victory for Winchester 2-0 against Sudbury. Becks sent off again for Real. France – naturally – win the UEFA U-17 final 2-1 v Spain; England, of course, lose third place on penalties to Portugal.

17 Eriksson selects his 23 for Euro 2004, including Robinson Spurs recent goalie capture from Leeds. Div 1 play-off: Another shoot-out sees Palace beat Sunderland after see-saw and despite Gray dismissal. FIFA defy doping code. Becks banned by Real from playing in Keown benefit, still manages four kicks. Gravesend give boss Andy Ford full-time job.

18 Div 1 play-off: Hammers through after 2-0 over Ipswich. Heskey moves to Birmingham for £6.25 million and Liverpool try for Smith after Leeds turn down Man Utd bid. Spurs appoint Frank Arnesen from PSV as technical director. National Game XI lose 3-2 to Republic; Scotland and Wales 0-0. Livingston saved and Bradford players agree differed payments.

19 UEFA Cup final: early Barthez departure at half-time, red carded for clattering Mista and Valencia go on to beat Marseille 2-0 with Carboni, 39, the oldest winner and finalist. Play-offs: Div 2: Bristol City late, late showing downs Hartlepool 2-1. Div 3: Huddersfield recover two-goal deficit to level with Lincoln. Leeds' Smith interesting Liverpool. Forest's Walker, 38, retires.

20 Play-offs: Div 2: Sickener for Swindon as Brighton force penalty shoot-out in last minute and win it; Div 3: Stags at bay do for Cobblers on penalties, too, after going 3-1 down on the day. Gerard Houllier expected to be relieved at Liverpool shortly. Everton bid £7 million for Smith. Marseille to report ref Collina over Barthez red. National Game XI lose 2-0 to Wales; Scotland 2 Republic 0. FIFA Centenary match attracts 79,344 France and Brazil goalless, first half wearing old style kit. Becks and Posh to settle in Madrid. Leicester three are cleared of charges.

21 Martin Laursen heading to Villa from AC Milan for £3 million. Cameroon WC points penalty for kit violation removed. Margate decide to go into Conf Div 2 South over ground problems, giving Leigh reprieve.

22 FA Cup final: Ronaldo flies, Van Nistelrooy bags a brace in Man Utd 3-0 romp over Millwall whose young Lion Curtis Weston at 17 years 119 days becomes youngest in final history. S Cup final: Celtic 3-1 winners over Dunfermline with Larsson's duo taking him to 242 goals in 316 games in swansong outing.

23 Trophy final: pint-pulling Pitman Brindley own goal agony turns to winning ecstasy as Hednesford shock Canvey 3-2. Suspended Becks watches as Real lose fifth in a row and slump to finishing fourth in Spain!

24 Exit Houllier. Real sack ex-Man Utd coach Queirox and appoint Jose Camacho. Tony Mowbray becomes Hibs boss, Aberdeen sack Steve Paterson. Charlton sign Stephan Andersen goalkeeper from AB Copenhagen, Frandsen from Bolton to Wigan.

25 Man Utd to stop transfer dealings with Sir Alex agent son Jason and Walter Smith leaves assistant job. Leeds latest takeover collapses. Darlingon future assured, Bradford uncertainty. U-21: Republic 3 Scots 1. Aldershot to go full-time. Grimsby to relieve Nicky Law of managerial role. It's the Rhyl thing: fourth trophy of season 6-0 v Halkyn U.

26 Ch Lge final: Mourinho masterminds mauling of Monaco 3-0 prior to Porto parting. Smith from Leeds to Man Utd £7.05 million as Elland Road confirm Kevin Blackwell as manager. Rafael Benitez, Valencia boss, tempting Liverpool as Thais move closer to Anfield. Dundee hopeful of salvation.

27 Keane return as Republic edge Romania 1-0, merited draw for makeshift Wales who spoil Berg's 100th and Scotland again look to McFadden for win in Estonia; England U-21 Quashie becomes only second

New Chelsea manager Jose Mourinho reflects on his European Champions League final success with Porto against Monaco in Gelsenkirchen, Germany. (Colorsport)

black player for Scotland. Telford go into liquidation and reprieve Northwich from Conf relegation. Growth of women's game: now 101,173 official players.

28 Jimmy Calderwood gets Aberdeen post, Russell Slade moves from Scarborough to Grimsby managerial slot. Fabio Capello, Roma to Juventus hot-seat.

29 Div 1 play-off: Hammer blow as Shipperley bursts bubble with megabucks shot spiralling Palace into Premiership. Lost in Africa? – no, The Valley: Nigeria 3 Republic 0.

30 Div 2 play-off: Knight penalty and a grey day for Bristol City as Brighton crusade rocks on. Scots win again 4-1 v T & T, so do Wales 1-0 over Canada, while ten-man Japan beat Iceland 3-2 in Manchester! Brazil's Masters XI beat Exeter 1-0 at St James' Park in re-run of 1914 game in Rio.

31 Ranieri finally runs into the Roman road block. Div 3 play-off: Penalties are us: Huddersfield promoted at the expense of Mansfield. Healy scores, misses a penalty, Williams is dismissed but the Sanchez Irish wagon rolls on in a Barbados draw. Nigeria 2 Jamaica 0 – at The Valley of course. FA want Peter Taylor back as U-21 boss. SPL clubs veto Caley promotion, Partick reprieved.

**JUNE**

**Santini gets the Spurs job . . . now it's Sir Trevor . . . good EURO start for England . . . then usual penalty exit . . . favourites falter all round**

1 O-Day: England – Japan one-to-one, Owen – Ono and Sven uses only nine subs. Becks gets ankle injury. Annual Waltz of the Entrenadors – dance cards to be marked: Mourinho to Chelsea, Queiroz back to Man Utd, Steve Cotterill to Burnley and Rafael Benitez sobs on quitting Valencia leaving gap for Ranieri if he fancies one of his ex-clubs. Trevor Birch sets in as chief executive at Everton, Bill Kenwright becomes chairman and Sir Philip Carter life president. WC: Forlan scores for Uruguay but they lose at home again.

2 Diamond geezer Sven picks his Euro gems. Republic beat Jamaica 1-0 at The Valley. Taylor unlikely to run U-21s.

3 Jacques Santini, French national coach, takes over Spurs! Real Madrid blocking Chelsea attempt to join G-14 pack. WBA pay club record £2.7 million for FC Copenhagen's Martin Albrechtsen. Charlton's Rufus forced to retire with injury. Mourinho sends Veron on loan to Inter. Healy again on mark as Northern Ireland beat St Kitts & company 2-0. Sam Ellis is new Leeds assistant manager.

4 Terry has a hamstring problem. Alan Murray becomes assistant manager at Blackburn, Tony Parkes reverting to the stiffs. Mourinho's successor at Porto is ex-Chievo boss Luigi Del Neri. Danny Wilson leaves Bristol City post.

5 England boost for 11 subs Sven as six-pack of goals upsets Iceland trolley. Robbie Keane on target for tasty Irish treat against flakey Dutch. Brian Tinnion gets Bristol City player-manager role.

6 Healy double for Northern Ireland against T & T makes him their leading scorer. Germany destroyed in 50th WC anniversary clash with Hungary – thanks to Magyars boss 150-capped German Lothar

Matthaus. Baros double for Czechs, one for Larsson in Sweden come-back. Valencia agree terms with Ranieri.

7 Icelandic players had been told to go easy against England! FA fuious with UEFA over fans warning. Colin Hendry named as Blackpool manager. Conf to restart League Cup next season adding North and South sections too. WC: another crash for Uruguay 5-0 in Colombia. Brazil and Argentina both held.

8 UEFA Cup farce as Charlton lose out Fair Play place on ballot. Keith Millen appointed assistant at Bristol City. Soton sign Jelle van Damme from Ajax for £2.5 million. Euro U-21 final: Italy 3 Serbia & M 0. The Italians and third place winners Portugal qualify for Olympics.

9 Euro 2004 refs include Riley and Collina. Plymouth boss Sturrock gives No. 2 job to old Argyle assistant Kevin Summerfield.

10 Martin Jol is No. 2 at Spurs. Entente Cordiale boils over ahead of England – France.

11 It's Sir Trevor Brooking and Mark Hughes OBE. Man Utd sign Gabriel Heinze in £6.9 million deal from PSG. Second tier FL clubs attempt to reduce demotion to three clubs rejected.

12 Euro shock start: Greek tragedy – for Portugal; Spanish sub sinks ten Russians.

13 Ice-cool Zidane dead-ball double at the death freeze-frames England after Lampard lead and Barthez denying Becks penalty; UK based hoolies riot. Swiss (one red) and Croats stay goalless.

14 Larsson brace laces Swedish nap hand over Bulgaria; Italy – as usual – start slowly with a Danish draw. Bradford deadline for survival: 8 July. Steve Burr new Northwich boss ex-Hucknall. TV audience for French match said to be record 30 million at home, pubs and clubs. Portugal based England hoolies riot.

15 Heinz late goal variety keeps Czechs ahead of Latvia; Ruud awakening saves Dutch point against Germany. One riot at a ground and England are out say UEFA who are relaxing goalie cards. AFC Telford United appoint Brendan McNally manager.

16 Exit ten man Russia shown door by Portugal; Spain slip up on Greece to set up mother and mother of all life and death games with hosts. Liverpool appoint Rafael Benitez, Bryan Robson resigns at Bradford, Scarborough give job to Nick Henry, Dunfermline to announce Davie Hayas boss.

17 Rooney tunes of glory for England over ten-man Swiss as the Everton babe at 18 years 236 days becomes Euro finals youngest marksman; Croatia merit draw with France. UEFA spit spot gets Totti three match ban. Colin Todd appointed at Bradford.

18 Swede dreams as Italians only draw; Bulgaria see red as Danes put them out. Exit Phil Thompson as Liverpool No. 2 and Thais no longer interested.

19 Czechs cash in winning streak as Dutch in the red finish overdrawn in five star entertainer; Latvia claim Riley penalty turn down robbed them of German victory. Chelsea said to be interested in Gerrard and Rooney. Intertoto under way.

20 Here we Figo as Nuno Gomes edges Portugal into last eight against traditional under achievers Spain; mousey Greeks lose to Russia but stil squeak through.

21 Rooney rules as careering England rein in Croatia 4-2; France head group after stirring themselves against the Swiss for whom Johan Vonlanthen at 18 years 141 days eclipses the Roon as youngest Euro marksman.

22 Italians stitched up by Denmark-Sweden draw despite beating Bulgaria. Rooney hailed as latterday Pele. Inverness given thumbs up by SPL and Partick demoted.

23 'Wurst yet' as German sausage men skinned out of it by Czechs; Dutch treated to comfortable Latvian romp.

24 Traditional England exit via penalty spot, Rooney off injured, controversy over referee Meier disallowing Campbell goal at 1-1. Some rioting in UK. Rudi Voller resigns German post, Inaki Saez (Spain) and Giovanni Trapattoni (Italy) likely to follow.

25 Now Fragile French slip up as Greeks say 'I'm all right Jacques' allowing Santini to leave early for Spurs.

26 Another shoot-out and Holland edge Sweden who hit bar and post in goalless draw. Becks says he was not fit in Euro 2004.

27 Another brace from Anfield bit player Baros in starring role as Czechs beat Danes 3-0. UEFA praise behaviour of England fans in Portugal.

28 Meier receives the backing of FIFA. Merk will referee the final.

29 Newcastle move in for Milner at £5 million. Bates to sue Sheff Wed chairman. Valencia the same to Benitez.

30 Figo fires flair-flecked Portugal who hold nerve against flakey Dutch. Greeks threaten strike over money. Meier admits he received death threats.

**JULY**

**Greece are the surprise EURO 2004 winners**

1 Greeks steal the silver on the corner to bounce out the Czechs. Dennis Rommedahl moves from PSV to Charlton for £2 million. Milton Keynes Dons aka Wimbledon come out of administration.

2 Chelsea home in on PSV's Mateja Kezman. Viduka moving to Middlesbrough.

3 Wenger says Rooney is going to Man Utd. England fans given thumbs up for conduct in Portugal. It's King Otto Rehhagel v Felipe Scolari on the eve of the final.

4 Euro 2004: Greeks corner the Euro market again; the myth becomes legend as Portugal's stock slumps.

# ENGLISH LEAGUE TABLES 2003–04

## FA BARCLAYCARD PREMIERSHIP

| | | | *Home* | | | | | *Away* | | | | | *Total* | | | | | | |
|---|---|---|---|---|---|---|---|---|---|---|---|---|---|---|---|---|---|---|---|
| | | *P* | *W* | *D* | *L* | *F* | *A* | *W* | *D* | *L* | *F* | *A* | *W* | *D* | *L* | *F* | *A* | *GD* | *Pts* |
| 1 | Arsenal | 38 | 15 | 4 | 0 | 40 | 14 | 11 | 8 | 0 | 33 | 12 | 26 | 12 | 0 | 73 | 26 | 47 | 90 |
| 2 | Chelsea | 38 | 12 | 4 | 3 | 34 | 13 | 12 | 3 | 4 | 33 | 17 | 24 | 7 | 7 | 67 | 30 | 37 | 79 |
| 3 | Manchester U | 38 | 12 | 4 | 3 | 37 | 15 | 11 | 2 | 6 | 27 | 20 | 23 | 6 | 9 | 64 | 35 | 29 | 75 |
| 4 | Liverpool | 38 | 10 | 4 | 5 | 29 | 15 | 6 | 8 | 5 | 26 | 22 | 16 | 12 | 10 | 55 | 37 | 18 | 60 |
| 5 | Newcastle U | 38 | 11 | 5 | 3 | 33 | 14 | 2 | 12 | 5 | 19 | 26 | 13 | 17 | 8 | 52 | 40 | 12 | 56 |
| 6 | Aston Villa | 38 | 9 | 6 | 4 | 24 | 19 | 6 | 5 | 8 | 24 | 25 | 15 | 11 | 12 | 48 | 44 | 4 | 56 |
| 7 | Charlton Ath | 38 | 7 | 6 | 6 | 29 | 29 | 7 | 5 | 7 | 22 | 22 | 14 | 11 | 13 | 51 | 51 | 0 | 53 |
| 8 | Bolton W | 38 | 6 | 8 | 5 | 24 | 21 | 8 | 3 | 8 | 24 | 35 | 14 | 11 | 13 | 48 | 56 | –8 | 53 |
| 9 | Fulham | 38 | 9 | 4 | 6 | 29 | 21 | 5 | 6 | 8 | 23 | 25 | 14 | 10 | 14 | 52 | 46 | 6 | 52 |
| 10 | Birmingham C | 38 | 8 | 5 | 6 | 26 | 24 | 4 | 9 | 6 | 17 | 24 | 12 | 14 | 12 | 43 | 48 | –5 | 50 |
| 11 | Middlesbrough | 38 | 8 | 4 | 7 | 25 | 23 | 5 | 5 | 9 | 19 | 29 | 13 | 9 | 16 | 44 | 52 | –8 | 48 |
| 12 | Southampton | 38 | 8 | 6 | 5 | 24 | 17 | 4 | 5 | 10 | 20 | 28 | 12 | 11 | 15 | 44 | 45 | –1 | 47 |
| 13 | Portsmouth | 38 | 10 | 4 | 5 | 35 | 19 | 2 | 5 | 12 | 12 | 35 | 12 | 9 | 17 | 47 | 54 | –7 | 45 |
| 14 | Tottenham H | 38 | 9 | 4 | 6 | 33 | 27 | 4 | 2 | 13 | 14 | 30 | 13 | 6 | 19 | 47 | 57 | –10 | 45 |
| 15 | Blackburn R | 38 | 5 | 4 | 10 | 25 | 31 | 7 | 4 | 8 | 26 | 28 | 12 | 8 | 18 | 51 | 59 | –8 | 44 |
| 16 | Manchester C | 38 | 5 | 9 | 5 | 31 | 24 | 4 | 5 | 10 | 24 | 30 | 9 | 14 | 15 | 55 | 54 | 1 | 41 |
| 17 | Everton | 38 | 8 | 5 | 6 | 27 | 20 | 1 | 7 | 11 | 18 | 37 | 9 | 12 | 17 | 45 | 57 | –12 | 39 |
| 18 | Leicester C | 38 | 3 | 10 | 6 | 19 | 28 | 3 | 5 | 11 | 29 | 37 | 6 | 15 | 17 | 48 | 65 | –17 | 33 |
| 19 | Leeds U | 38 | 5 | 7 | 7 | 25 | 31 | 3 | 2 | 14 | 15 | 48 | 8 | 9 | 21 | 40 | 79 | –39 | 33 |
| 20 | Wolverhampton W | 38 | 7 | 5 | 7 | 23 | 35 | 0 | 7 | 12 | 15 | 42 | 7 | 12 | 19 | 38 | 77 | –39 | 33 |

## NATIONWIDE FOOTBALL LEAGUE DIVISION 1

| | | | *Home* | | | | | *Away* | | | | | *Total* | | | | | | |
|---|---|---|---|---|---|---|---|---|---|---|---|---|---|---|---|---|---|---|---|
| | | *P* | *W* | *D* | *L* | *F* | *A* | *W* | *D* | *L* | *F* | *A* | *W* | *D* | *L* | *F* | *A* | *GD* | *Pts* |
| 1 | Norwich C | 46 | 18 | 3 | 2 | 44 | 15 | 10 | 7 | 6 | 35 | 24 | 28 | 10 | 8 | 79 | 39 | 40 | 94 |
| 2 | WBA | 46 | 14 | 5 | 4 | 34 | 16 | 11 | 6 | 6 | 30 | 26 | 25 | 11 | 10 | 64 | 42 | 22 | 86 |
| 3 | Sunderland | 46 | 13 | 8 | 2 | 33 | 15 | 9 | 5 | 9 | 29 | 30 | 22 | 13 | 11 | 62 | 45 | 17 | 79 |
| 4 | West Ham U | 46 | 12 | 7 | 4 | 42 | 20 | 7 | 10 | 6 | 25 | 25 | 19 | 17 | 10 | 67 | 45 | 22 | 74 |
| 5 | Ipswich T | 46 | 12 | 3 | 8 | 49 | 36 | 9 | 7 | 7 | 35 | 36 | 21 | 10 | 15 | 84 | 72 | 12 | 73 |
| 6 | Crystal Palace | 46 | 10 | 8 | 5 | 34 | 25 | 11 | 2 | 10 | 38 | 36 | 21 | 10 | 15 | 72 | 61 | 11 | 73 |
| 7 | Wigan Ath | 46 | 11 | 8 | 4 | 29 | 16 | 7 | 9 | 7 | 31 | 29 | 18 | 17 | 11 | 60 | 45 | 15 | 71 |
| 8 | Sheffield U | 46 | 11 | 6 | 6 | 37 | 25 | 9 | 5 | 9 | 28 | 31 | 20 | 11 | 15 | 65 | 56 | 9 | 71 |
| 9 | Reading | 46 | 11 | 6 | 6 | 29 | 25 | 9 | 4 | 10 | 26 | 32 | 20 | 10 | 16 | 55 | 57 | –2 | 70 |
| 10 | Millwall | 46 | 11 | 8 | 4 | 28 | 15 | 7 | 7 | 9 | 27 | 33 | 18 | 15 | 13 | 55 | 48 | 7 | 69 |
| 11 | Stoke C | 46 | 11 | 7 | 5 | 35 | 24 | 7 | 5 | 11 | 23 | 31 | 18 | 12 | 16 | 58 | 55 | 3 | 66 |
| 12 | Coventry C | 46 | 9 | 9 | 5 | 34 | 22 | 8 | 5 | 10 | 33 | 32 | 17 | 14 | 15 | 67 | 54 | 13 | 65 |
| 13 | Cardiff C | 46 | 10 | 6 | 7 | 40 | 25 | 7 | 8 | 8 | 28 | 33 | 17 | 14 | 15 | 68 | 58 | 10 | 65 |
| 14 | Nottingham F | 46 | 8 | 9 | 6 | 33 | 25 | 7 | 6 | 10 | 28 | 33 | 15 | 15 | 16 | 61 | 58 | 3 | 60 |
| 15 | Preston NE | 46 | 11 | 7 | 5 | 43 | 29 | 4 | 7 | 12 | 26 | 42 | 15 | 14 | 17 | 69 | 71 | –2 | 59 |
| 16 | Watford | 46 | 9 | 8 | 6 | 31 | 28 | 6 | 4 | 13 | 23 | 40 | 15 | 12 | 19 | 54 | 68 | –14 | 57 |
| 17 | Rotherham U | 46 | 8 | 8 | 7 | 31 | 27 | 5 | 7 | 11 | 22 | 34 | 13 | 15 | 18 | 53 | 61 | –8 | 54 |
| 18 | Crewe Alex | 46 | 11 | 3 | 9 | 33 | 26 | 3 | 8 | 12 | 24 | 40 | 14 | 11 | 21 | 57 | 66 | –9 | 53 |
| 19 | Burnley | 46 | 9 | 6 | 8 | 37 | 32 | 4 | 8 | 11 | 23 | 45 | 13 | 14 | 19 | 60 | 77 | –17 | 53 |
| 20 | Derby Co | 46 | 11 | 5 | 7 | 39 | 33 | 2 | 8 | 13 | 14 | 34 | 13 | 13 | 20 | 53 | 67 | –14 | 52 |
| 21 | Gillingham | 46 | 10 | 1 | 12 | 28 | 34 | 4 | 8 | 11 | 20 | 33 | 14 | 9 | 23 | 48 | 67 | –19 | 51 |
| 22 | Walsall | 46 | 8 | 7 | 8 | 29 | 31 | 5 | 5 | 13 | 16 | 34 | 13 | 12 | 21 | 45 | 65 | –20 | 51 |
| 23 | Bradford C | 46 | 6 | 3 | 14 | 23 | 35 | 4 | 3 | 16 | 15 | 34 | 10 | 6 | 30 | 38 | 69 | –31 | 36 |
| 24 | Wimbledon | 46 | 3 | 4 | 16 | 21 | 40 | 5 | 1 | 17 | 20 | 49 | 8 | 5 | 33 | 41 | 89 | –48 | 29 |

## NATIONWIDE FOOTBALL LEAGUE DIVISION 2

| | | | *Home* | | | | | *Away* | | | | | *Total* | | | | | | |
|---|---|---|---|---|---|---|---|---|---|---|---|---|---|---|---|---|---|---|---|
| | | *P* | *W* | *D* | *L* | *F* | *A* | *W* | *D* | *L* | *F* | *A* | *W* | *D* | *L* | *F* | *A* | *GD* | *Pts* |
| 1 | Plymouth Arg | 46 | 17 | 5 | 1 | 52 | 13 | 9 | 7 | 7 | 33 | 28 | 26 | 12 | 8 | 85 | 41 | 44 | 90 |
| 2 | QPR | 46 | 16 | 7 | 0 | 47 | 12 | 6 | 10 | 7 | 33 | 33 | 22 | 17 | 7 | 80 | 45 | 35 | 83 |
| 3 | Bristol C | 46 | 15 | 6 | 2 | 34 | 12 | 8 | 7 | 8 | 24 | 25 | 23 | 13 | 10 | 58 | 37 | 21 | 82 |
| 4 | Brighton & HA | 46 | 17 | 4 | 2 | 39 | 11 | 5 | 7 | 11 | 25 | 32 | 22 | 11 | 13 | 64 | 43 | 21 | 77 |
| 5 | Swindon T | 46 | 12 | 7 | 4 | 41 | 23 | 8 | 6 | 9 | 35 | 35 | 20 | 13 | 13 | 76 | 58 | 18 | 73 |
| 6 | Hartlepool U | 46 | 10 | 8 | 5 | 39 | 24 | 10 | 5 | 8 | 37 | 37 | 20 | 13 | 13 | 76 | 61 | 15 | 73 |
| 7 | Port Vale | 46 | 15 | 6 | 2 | 45 | 28 | 6 | 4 | 13 | 28 | 35 | 21 | 10 | 15 | 73 | 63 | 10 | 73 |
| 8 | Tranmere R | 46 | 13 | 7 | 3 | 36 | 18 | 4 | 9 | 10 | 23 | 38 | 17 | 16 | 13 | 59 | 56 | 3 | 67 |
| 9 | Bournemouth | 46 | 11 | 8 | 4 | 35 | 25 | 6 | 7 | 10 | 21 | 26 | 17 | 15 | 14 | 56 | 51 | 5 | 66 |
| 10 | Luton T | 46 | 14 | 6 | 3 | 44 | 27 | 3 | 9 | 11 | 25 | 39 | 17 | 15 | 14 | 69 | 66 | 3 | 66 |
| 11 | Colchester U | 46 | 11 | 8 | 4 | 33 | 23 | 6 | 5 | 12 | 19 | 33 | 17 | 13 | 16 | 52 | 56 | –4 | 64 |
| 12 | Barnsley | 46 | 7 | 12 | 4 | 25 | 19 | 8 | 5 | 10 | 29 | 39 | 15 | 17 | 14 | 54 | 58 | –4 | 62 |
| 13 | Wrexham | 46 | 9 | 6 | 8 | 27 | 21 | 8 | 3 | 12 | 23 | 39 | 17 | 9 | 20 | 50 | 60 | –10 | 60 |
| 14 | Blackpool | 46 | 9 | 5 | 9 | 31 | 28 | 7 | 6 | 10 | 27 | 37 | 16 | 11 | 19 | 58 | 65 | –7 | 59 |
| 15 | Oldham Ath | 46 | 9 | 8 | 6 | 37 | 25 | 3 | 13 | 7 | 29 | 35 | 12 | 21 | 13 | 66 | 60 | 6 | 57 |
| 16 | Sheffield W | 46 | 7 | 9 | 7 | 25 | 26 | 6 | 5 | 12 | 23 | 38 | 13 | 14 | 19 | 48 | 64 | –16 | 53 |
| 17 | Brentford | 46 | 9 | 5 | 9 | 34 | 38 | 5 | 6 | 12 | 18 | 31 | 14 | 11 | 21 | 52 | 69 | –17 | 53 |
| 18 | Peterborough U | 46 | 5 | 8 | 10 | 36 | 33 | 7 | 8 | 8 | 22 | 25 | 12 | 16 | 18 | 58 | 58 | 0 | 52 |
| 19 | Stockport Co | 46 | 6 | 8 | 9 | 31 | 36 | 5 | 11 | 7 | 31 | 34 | 11 | 19 | 16 | 62 | 70 | –8 | 52 |
| 20 | Chesterfield | 46 | 9 | 7 | 7 | 34 | 31 | 3 | 8 | 12 | 15 | 40 | 12 | 15 | 19 | 49 | 71 | –22 | 51 |
| 21 | Grimsby T | 46 | 10 | 5 | 8 | 36 | 26 | 3 | 6 | 14 | 19 | 55 | 13 | 11 | 22 | 55 | 81 | –26 | 50 |
| 22 | Rushden & D | 46 | 9 | 5 | 9 | 37 | 34 | 4 | 4 | 15 | 23 | 40 | 13 | 9 | 24 | 60 | 74 | –14 | 48 |
| 23 | Notts Co | 46 | 6 | 9 | 8 | 32 | 27 | 4 | 3 | 16 | 18 | 51 | 10 | 12 | 24 | 50 | 78 | –28 | 42 |
| 24 | Wycombe W | 46 | 5 | 7 | 11 | 31 | 39 | 1 | 12 | 10 | 19 | 36 | 6 | 19 | 21 | 50 | 75 | –25 | 37 |

## NATIONWIDE FOOTBALL LEAGUE DIVISION 3

| | | | *Home* | | | | | *Away* | | | | | *Total* | | | | | | |
|---|---|---|---|---|---|---|---|---|---|---|---|---|---|---|---|---|---|---|---|
| | | *P* | *W* | *D* | *L* | *F* | *A* | *W* | *D* | *L* | *F* | *A* | *W* | *D* | *L* | *F* | *A* | *GD* | *Pts* |
| 1 | Doncaster R | 46 | 17 | 4 | 2 | 47 | 13 | 10 | 7 | 6 | 32 | 24 | 27 | 11 | 8 | 79 | 37 | 42 | 92 |
| 2 | Hull C | 46 | 16 | 4 | 3 | 50 | 21 | 9 | 9 | 5 | 32 | 23 | 25 | 13 | 8 | 82 | 44 | 38 | 88 |
| 3 | Torquay U | 46 | 15 | 6 | 2 | 44 | 18 | 8 | 6 | 9 | 24 | 26 | 23 | 12 | 11 | 68 | 44 | 24 | 81 |
| 4 | Huddersfield T | 46 | 16 | 4 | 3 | 42 | 18 | 7 | 8 | 8 | 26 | 34 | 23 | 12 | 11 | 68 | 52 | 16 | 81 |
| 5 | Mansfield T | 46 | 13 | 5 | 5 | 44 | 25 | 9 | 4 | 10 | 32 | 37 | 22 | 9 | 15 | 76 | 62 | 14 | 75 |
| 6 | Northampton T | 46 | 13 | 4 | 6 | 30 | 23 | 9 | 5 | 9 | 28 | 28 | 22 | 9 | 15 | 58 | 51 | 7 | 75 |
| 7 | Lincoln C | 46 | 9 | 11 | 3 | 36 | 23 | 10 | 6 | 7 | 32 | 24 | 19 | 17 | 10 | 68 | 47 | 21 | 74 |
| 8 | Yeovil T | 46 | 14 | 3 | 6 | 40 | 19 | 9 | 2 | 12 | 30 | 38 | 23 | 5 | 18 | 70 | 57 | 13 | 74 |
| 9 | Oxford U | 46 | 14 | 8 | 1 | 34 | 13 | 4 | 9 | 10 | 21 | 31 | 18 | 17 | 11 | 55 | 44 | 11 | 71 |
| 10 | Swansea C | 46 | 9 | 8 | 6 | 36 | 26 | 6 | 6 | 11 | 22 | 35 | 15 | 14 | 17 | 58 | 61 | –3 | 59 |
| 11 | Boston U | 46 | 11 | 7 | 5 | 35 | 21 | 5 | 4 | 14 | 15 | 33 | 16 | 11 | 19 | 50 | 54 | –4 | 59 |
| 12 | Bury | 46 | 10 | 7 | 6 | 29 | 26 | 5 | 4 | 14 | 25 | 38 | 15 | 11 | 20 | 54 | 64 | –10 | 56 |
| 13 | Cambridge U | 46 | 6 | 7 | 10 | 26 | 32 | 8 | 7 | 8 | 29 | 35 | 14 | 14 | 18 | 55 | 67 | –12 | 56 |
| 14 | Cheltenham T | 46 | 11 | 4 | 8 | 37 | 38 | 3 | 10 | 10 | 20 | 33 | 14 | 14 | 18 | 57 | 71 | –14 | 56 |
| 15 | Bristol R | 46 | 9 | 7 | 7 | 29 | 26 | 5 | 6 | 12 | 21 | 35 | 14 | 13 | 19 | 50 | 61 | –11 | 55 |
| 16 | Kidderminster H | 46 | 9 | 5 | 9 | 28 | 29 | 5 | 8 | 10 | 17 | 30 | 14 | 13 | 19 | 45 | 59 | –14 | 55 |
| 17 | Southend U | 46 | 8 | 4 | 11 | 27 | 29 | 6 | 8 | 9 | 24 | 34 | 14 | 12 | 20 | 51 | 63 | –12 | 54 |
| 18 | Darlington | 46 | 10 | 4 | 9 | 30 | 28 | 4 | 7 | 12 | 23 | 33 | 14 | 11 | 21 | 53 | 61 | –8 | 53 |
| 19 | Leyton Orient | 46 | 8 | 9 | 6 | 28 | 27 | 5 | 5 | 13 | 20 | 38 | 13 | 14 | 19 | 48 | 65 | –17 | 53 |
| 20 | Macclesfield T | 46 | 8 | 9 | 6 | 28 | 25 | 5 | 4 | 14 | 26 | 44 | 13 | 13 | 20 | 54 | 69 | –15 | 52 |
| 21 | Rochdale | 46 | 7 | 8 | 8 | 28 | 26 | 5 | 6 | 12 | 21 | 32 | 12 | 14 | 20 | 49 | 58 | –9 | 50 |
| 22 | Scunthorpe U | 46 | 7 | 10 | 6 | 36 | 27 | 4 | 6 | 13 | 33 | 45 | 11 | 16 | 19 | 69 | 72 | –3 | 49 |
| 23 | Carlisle U | 46 | 8 | 5 | 10 | 23 | 27 | 4 | 4 | 15 | 23 | 42 | 12 | 9 | 25 | 46 | 69 | –23 | 45 |
| 24 | York C | 46 | 7 | 6 | 10 | 22 | 29 | 3 | 8 | 12 | 13 | 37 | 10 | 14 | 22 | 35 | 66 | –31 | 44 |

# FOOTBALL LEAGUE PLAY-OFFS 2003–04

▪ *Denotes player sent off.*

## DIV 1 SEMI-FINALS FIRST LEG

Friday, 14 May 2004

**Crystal Palace (0) 3** *(Shipperley 52, Butterfield 64, Johnson 87)*

**Sunderland (0) 2** *(Stewart 51 (pen), Kyle 85)* 25,287

*Crystal Palace:* Vaesen; Butterfield, Granville, Leigertwood, Popovic, Riihilahti, Routledge, Gray, Johnson, Shipperley (Powell), Hughes (Derry).
*Sunderland:* Poom; Williams (Bjorklund), McCartney, Robinson, Breen, Babb, McAteer (Thornton), Whitley, Kyle, Stewart (Smith), Oster.

Saturday, 15 May 2004

**Ipswich T (0) 1** *(Bent D 57)*

**West Ham U (0) 0** 28,435

*Ipswich T:* Davis; Wilnis, Richards, Miller, McGreal (Kuqi), Elliott, Magilton (Bart-Williams), Wright, Naylor, Bent D (Bowditch), Westlake.
*West Ham U:* Bywater; Repka, Lomas, Mullins, Melville, Dailly, Carrick, Connolly, Harewood (Deane), Zamora (McAnuff), Etherington (Reo-Coker).

## DIV 2 SEMI-FINALS FIRST LEG

Saturday, 15 May 2004

**Hartlepool U (0) 1** *(Porter 74)*

**Bristol C (1) 1** *(Rougier 5)* 7211

*Hartlepool U:* Provett; Barron, Robertson, Nelson (Clarke), Westwood, Tinkler, Sweeney (Danns), Boyd, Williams E, Porter (Robinson P), Humphreys.
*Bristol C:* Phillips; Carey, Hill, Doherty (Burnell), Butler, Coles, Rougier (Murray), Tinnion, Peacock, Roberts (Wilkshire), Woodman.

Sunday, 16 May 2004

**Swindon T (0) 0**

**Brighton & HA (0) 1** *(Carpenter 72)* 14,034

*Swindon T:* Evans; O'Hanlon, Duke (Smith), Gurney, Nicholas (Fallon), Heywood, Howard, Igoe, Mooney, Parkin, Hewlett.
*Brighton & HA:* Roberts; Virgo, Harding, Cullip, Butters, Carpenter, Reid (Hart), Oatway, Knight, Iwelumo, Jones N.

## DIV 3 SEMI-FINALS FIRST LEG

Saturday, 15 May 2004

**Lincoln C (0) 1** *(Fletcher 51)*

**Huddersfield T (1) 2** *(Onuora 5, Mirfin 72)* 9202

*Lincoln C:* Marriott; Bailey, Gain (Liburd), Weaver (McCombe), Bloomer, Futcher, Butcher, Richardson (Green), Fletcher, Yeo, Ellison.
*Huddersfield T:* Rachubka; Sodje, Lloyd, Holdsworth, Yates (Scott), Mirfin, Worthington, Schofield, Booth, Onuora (Abbott), Edwards.

Sunday, 16 May 2004

**Northampton T (0) 0**

**Mansfield T (1) 2** *(Day 40, Mendes 67)* 6960

*Northampton T:* Harper; Low, Ullathorne, Sampson (Taylor), Willmott, Westwood▪, Trollope, Richards (Youngs), Asamoah, Smith (Reid), Hargreaves.
*Mansfield T:* Pilkington; Hassell, Baptiste (MacKenzie), Curtis, Day, Eaton, Lawrence, Williamson, Mendes (D'Jaffo), Disley (Larkin), Corden.

## DIV 1 SEMI-FINALS SECOND LEG

Monday, 17 May 2004

**Sunderland (2) 2** *(Kyle 42, Stewart 45)*

**Crystal Palace (0) 1** *(Powell 90)* 34,536

*Sunderland:* Poom; McCartney, Bjorklund (Williams), McAteer, Breen, Babb, Oster, Whitley, Kyle, Stewart (Smith), Thornton (Robinson).
*Crystal Palace:* Vaesen; Butterfield (Freedman), Granville (Powell), Leigertwood, Popovic, Riihilahti (Derry), Routledge, Gray▪, Johnson, Shipperley, Hughes.
*aet; Crystal Palace won 5-4 on penalties: Oster (missed), Johnson (scored), Smith (scored), Freedman (scored), Babb (scored), Shipperley (scored), Robinson (scored), Popovic (scored), Breen (scored), Derry (saved), McAteer (saved), Routledge (saved), Whitley (saved), Hughes (scored).*

Tuesday, 18 May 2004

**West Ham U (0) 2** *(Etherington 50, Dailly 71)*

**Ipswich T (0) 0** 34,002

*West Ham U:* Bywater; Repka, Lomas, Mullins, Melville, Dailly, Carrick, Connolly (Reo-Coker), Harewood, Zamora (Deane), Etherington.
*Ipswich T:* Davis; Wilnis, Richards, Miller, Naylor, Elliott, Magilton (Reuser), Wright, Bent, Kuqi (Armstrong), Westlake.

Brighton & Hove Albion's Leon Knight scores the winning goal from the penalty spot in the Division 2 play-off final at the Millennium Stadium, Cardiff. (Empics)

Liam Lawrence of Mansfield and Andy Holdsworth of Huddersfield (stripes) in battle during the Division 3 play-off final at the Millennium Stadium, Cardiff. (Actionimages)

**DIV 2 SEMI-FINALS SECOND LEG**

Wednesday, 19 May 2004

**Bristol C (0) 2** *(Goodfellow 88, Roberts 90)*

**Hartlepool U (0) 1** *(Sweeney 63)* 18,434

*Bristol C:* Phillips; Carey, Hill, Doherty, Butler (Lita), Coles, Rougier, Tinnion, Peacock (Murray), Roberts, Woodman (Goodfellow).
*Hartlepool U:* Provett; Barron (Clarke), Robertson, Nelson, Westwood (Danns), Tinkler, Sweeney, Boyd, Williams E, Porter (Robinson P), Humphreys.

Thursday, 20 May 2004

**Brighton & HA (0) 1** *(Virgo 120)*

**Swindon T (0) 2** *(Parkin 81, Fallon 97)* 6876

*Brighton & HA:* Roberts; Virgo, Harding, Cullip, Butters, Carpenter, Reid (Hart), Oatway, Knight (Hinshelwood), Iwelumo, Jones N (Piercy).
*Swindon T:* Evans; O'Hanlon, Smith (Nicholas), Gurney, Howard (Fallon), Heywood, Miglioranzi, Igoe (Reeves), Mooney, Parkin, Hewlett.
*aet; Brighton & HA won 4-3 on penalties: Parkin (scored), Carpenter (scored), Heywood (scored), Iwelumo (scored), Mooney (saved), Piercy (scored), Fallon (scored), Virgo (scored), Gurney (missed).*

**DIV 3 SEMI-FINALS SECOND LEG**

Wednesday, 19 May 2004

**Huddersfield T (0) 2** *(Schofield 60 (pen), Edwards 83)*

**Lincoln C (2) 2** *(Butcher 38, Bailey 39)* 19,467

*Huddersfield T:* Rachubka; Sodje, Lloyd, Holdsworth, Yates, Mirfin, Worthington, Schofield, Booth, Onuora (McAliskey), Edwards.
*Lincoln C:* Marriott; Bailey, Gain, McCombe, Bloomer (Green), Futcher, Butcher, Richardson (Wilford), Fletcher, Yeo, Ellison.

Thursday, 20 May 2004

**Mansfield T (0) 1** *(Curtis 68)*

**Northampton T (2) 3** *(Richards 36, Hargreaves 42, Smith 46)* 9243

*Mansfield T:* Pilkington; Hassell, Baptiste, Curtis, Day, Eaton, Lawrence, Williamson (MacKenzie), Mendes (D'Jaffo), Disley (Larkin), Corden.
*Northampton T:* Harper; Low (Taylor), Ullathorne, Sampson, Willmott, Reid, Trollope, Richards (Asamoah) (Reeves), Sabin, Smith, Hargreaves.
*aet; Mansfield T won 5-4 on penalties: Reeves (scored), Corden (scored), Smith (scored), Lawrence (scored), Reid (scored), MacKenzie (scored), Sabin (saved), D'Jaffo (scored), Willmott (scored), Larkin (scored).*

**DIV 1 FINAL**

Saturday, 29 May 2004

(at Millennium Stadium, Cardiff)

**Crystal Palace (0) 1** *(Shipperley 62)*

**West Ham U (0) 0** 72,523

*Crystal Palace:* Vaesen; Butterfield (Powell), Granville, Leigertwood, Popovic, Riihilahti, Routledge, Derry, Johnson, Shipperley, Hughes.
*West Ham U:* Bywater; Repka, Lomas, Mullins, Melville, Dailly, Carrick, Connolly (Hutchison), Harewood (Reo-Coker), Zamora (Deane), Etherington.
*Referee:* G. Poll (Hertfordshire).

**DIV 2 FINAL**

Sunday, 30 May 2004

(at Millennium Stadium, Cardiff)

**Brighton & HA (0) 1** *(Knight 84 (pen))*

**Bristol C (0) 0** 65,167

*Brighton & HA:* Roberts; Virgo, Harding, Cullip, Butters, Carpenter (Reid), Hart, Oatway, Knight, Iwelumo, Jones N (Piercy).
*Bristol C:* Phillips; Carey, Hill, Doherty, Butler (Goodfellow), Coles, Rougier, Tinnion (Wilkshire), Miller (Murray), Roberts, Woodman.
*Referee:* R. Beeby (Northamptonshire).

**DIV 3 FINAL**

Monday, 31 May 2004

(at Millennium Stadium, Cardiff)

**Huddersfield T (0) 0**

**Mansfield T (0) 0** 37,298

*Huddersfield T:* Rachubka; Sodje, Lloyd (Edwards), Holdsworth, Yates, Mirfin, Worthington (Fowler), Schofield, Booth, Abbott (McAliskey), Carss.
*Mansfield T:* Pilkington; Hassell, Baptiste, Curtis, Day, Eaton, Lawrence, Williamson (MacKenzie), Mendes (D'Jaffo), Disley (Larkin), Corden.
*aet; Huddersfield T won 4-1 on penalties: Edwards (scored), Corden (saved), Schofield (scored), Lawrence (missed), Carss (scored), MacKenzie (scored), Fowler (scored).*
*Referee:* M. Clattenburg (Co. Durham).

# LEADING GOALSCORERS 2003–04

| | League | Carling Cup | FA Cup | Other | Total |
|---|---|---|---|---|---|
| **FA BARCLAYCARD PREMIERSHIP** | | | | | |
| Thierry Henry *(Arsenal)* | 30 | 0 | 3 | 6 | 39 |
| Alan Shearer *(Newcastle U)* | 22 | 0 | 0 | 6 | 28 |
| Ruud Van Nistelrooy *(Manchester U)* | 20 | 0 | 6 | 4 | 30 |
| Louis Saha *(Manchester U)* | 20 | 0 | 2 | 0 | 22 |
| *(including 19 League goals and 2 FA Cup goals for Fulham)* | | | | | |
| Mikael Forssell *(Birmingham C)* | 17 | 0 | 2 | 0 | 19 |
| Nicolas Anelka *(Manchester C)* | 16 | 0 | 4 | 4 | 24 |
| Juan Pablo Angel *(Aston Villa)* | 16 | 7 | 0 | 0 | 23 |
| Michael Owen *(Liverpool)* | 16 | 0 | 1 | 2 | 19 |
| Ayegbeni Yakubu *(Portsmouth)* | 16 | 2 | 1 | 0 | 19 |
| Robert Pires *(Arsenal)* | 14 | 0 | 1 | 4 | 19 |
| James Beattie *(Southampton)* | 14 | 3 | 0 | 0 | 17 |
| Robbie Keane *(Tottenham H)* | 14 | 1 | 1 | 0 | 16 |
| Jimmy Floyd Hasselbaink *(Chelsea)* | 12 | 2 | 1 | 2 | 17 |
| Les Ferdinand *(Leicester C)* | 12 | 0 | 1 | 0 | 13 |
| Kevin Phillips *(Southampton)* | 12 | 0 | 0 | 1 | 13 |
| Mark Viduka *(Leeds U)* | 11 | 0 | 1 | 0 | 12 |
| Andy Cole *(Blackburn R)* | 11 | 0 | 0 | 0 | 11 |
| **NATIONWIDE DIVISION 1** | | | | | |
| Andy Johnson *(Crystal Palace)* | 27 | 4 | 0 | 1 | 32 |
| Marlon Harewood *(West Ham U)* | 25 | 0 | 1 | 0 | 26 |
| *(including 12 League goals for Nottingham F)* | | | | | |
| Robert Earnshaw *(Cardiff C)* | 21 | 5 | 0 | 0 | 26 |
| Robbie Blake *(Burnley)* | 19 | 1 | 2 | 0 | 22 |
| Dean Ashton *(Crewe Alex)* | 19 | 1 | 0 | 0 | 20 |
| Nathan Ellington *(Wigan Ath)* | 18 | 1 | 0 | 0 | 19 |
| Ricardo Fuller *(Preston NE)* | 17 | 0 | 2 | 0 | 19 |
| Darren Bent *(Ipswich T)* | 16 | 0 | 0 | 1 | 17 |
| Steve Jones *(Crewe Alex)* | 15 | 1 | 0 | 0 | 16 |
| Martin Butler *(Rotherham U)* | 15 | 0 | 0 | 0 | 15 |
| David Healy *(Preston NE)* | 15 | 0 | 0 | 0 | 15 |
| Marcus Stewart *(Sunderland)* | 14 | 0 | 0 | 2 | 16 |
| Darren Huckerby *(Norwich C)* | 14 | 0 | 0 | 0 | 14 |
| Dougie Freedman *(Crystal Palace)* | 13 | 2 | 0 | 0 | 15 |
| Patrick Agyemang *(Gillingham)* | 13 | 0 | 0 | 0 | 13 |
| *(including 7 League goals for Wimbledon)* | | | | | |
| Andy Reid *(Nottingham F)* | 13 | 0 | 0 | 0 | 13 |
| Peter Thorne *(Cardiff C)* | 13 | 0 | 0 | 0 | 13 |
| **DIVISION 2** | | | | | |
| Leon Knight *(Brighton & HA)* | 25 | 0 | 0 | 2 | 27 |
| Stephen McPhee *(Port Vale)* | 25 | 0 | 1 | 1 | 27 |
| Paul Heffernan *(Notts Co)* | 20 | 0 | 1 | 0 | 21 |
| Sam Parkin *(Swindon T)* | 19 | 3 | 0 | 1 | 23 |
| Tommy Mooney *(Swindon T)* | 19 | 1 | 0 | 0 | 20 |
| Kevin Gallen *(QPR)* | 17 | 0 | 0 | 0 | 17 |
| Scott Taylor *(Blackpool)* | 16 | 3 | 6 | 2 | 27 |
| Eugene Dadi *(Tranmere R)* | 16 | 1 | 2 | 0 | 19 |
| Paul Furlong *(QPR)* | 16 | 0 | 0 | 0 | 16 |
| Onandi Lowe *(Rushden & D)* | 15 | 1 | 0 | 0 | 16 |
| Lee Peacock *(Bristol C)* | 14 | 2 | 0 | 0 | 16 |
| David Friio *(Plymouth Arg)* | 14 | 0 | 1 | 0 | 15 |
| Steve Howard *(Luton T)* | 14 | 1 | 0 | 0 | 15 |
| James Hayter *(Bournemouth)* | 14 | 0 | 0 | 0 | 14 |
| Billy Paynter *(Port Vale)* | 13 | 0 | 1 | 0 | 14 |
| Eifion Williams *(Hartlepool U)* | 13 | 0 | 0 | 1 | 14 |
| Glynn Hurst *(Chesterfield)* | 13 | 0 | 0 | 0 | 13 |
| **DIVISION 3** | | | | | |
| Steve MacLean *(Scunthorpe U)* | 23 | 1 | 0 | 1 | 25 |
| David Graham *(Torquay U)* | 22 | 1 | 0 | 0 | 23 |
| Leon Constantine *(Southend U)* | 21 | 0 | 0 | 4 | 25 |
| Liam Lawrence *(Mansfield T)* | 18 | 0 | 3 | 0 | 21 |
| Greg Blundell *(Doncaster R)* | 18 | 2 | 0 | 0 | 20 |
| Ben Burgess *(Hull C)* | 18 | 0 | 0 | 0 | 18 |
| Lee Trundle *(Swansea C)* | 16 | 0 | 5 | 0 | 21 |
| Matt Tipton *(Macclesfield T)* | 16 | 0 | 3 | 0 | 19 |
| Gary Fletcher *(Lincoln C)* | 16 | 0 | 0 | 3 | 19 |
| Jon Stead *(Huddersfield T)* | 16 | 2 | 0 | 0 | 18 |
| Gary Alexander *(Leyton Orient)* | 15 | 0 | 1 | 0 | 16 |
| Danny Allsopp *(Hull C)* | 15 | 0 | 0 | 0 | 15 |
| Steve Basham *(Oxford U)* | 14 | 1 | 0 | 0 | 15 |
| Barry Conlon *(Darlington)* | 14 | 0 | 0 | 0 | 14 |
| Stuart Elliott *(Hull C)* | 14 | 0 | 0 | 0 | 14 |
| Andy Booth *(Huddersfield T)* | 13 | 1 | 0 | 0 | 14 |
| Paul Tait *(Bristol R)* | 12 | 0 | 0 | 0 | 12 |

*Other matches consist of European games, LDV Vans Trophy, Community Shield and Football League play-offs. Only goals scored in the respective divisions count in the table. Players listed in order of League goals total.*

# REVIEW OF THE SEASON

Arsenal's remarkable achievement in completing the 2003–04 season without losing a match understandably dominated the domestic scene. Taking all matches into an overall context of performance the disappointments came in varying degrees in cup competitions.

As far as the Champions League was concerned elimination looked a distinct possibility only for the Gunners to turn it around in spectacular fashion against Internazionale before losing it crucially against Chelsea in the quarter-finals. Manchester United accounted for them in the FA Cup, Middlesbrough in the Carling Cup; both reverses at the semi-final stage.

But these irritations should not have detracted from the quality of the football they showed during the campaign. At times they appeared to be unplayable. If the opposition could withstand the onslaught it was a mere short-lived respite.

When squad systems tend to provide more players with opportunities of first team action, it was surprising that Arsenal used only 22 players. Two of these made a single appearance, one from the start, another as substitute.

Ironically in view of their generally poor Euro 2004 to come, the French contingent had a glorious time in the League. Thierry Henry, honoured as both Football Writers' Association Player of the Year and similarly recognised by the Professional Footballers' Association, was in sparkling form and top scorer with 30 League goals. Robert Pires weighed in with a valuable 14 himself. In midfield, too, Patrick Vieira despite missing a chunk of the season with injury was a formidable forager.

Left-back Ashley Cole further enhanced his reputation and Sol Campbell was solid in the middle of the back four. During the season he was partnered by Kolo Toure who was arguably the most improved player in the squad, while right-back Lauren was consistently reliable.

Midfield also provided other options with the Brazilians Gilberto Silva and Edu – the latter a useful replacement at strategic times – plus Freddie Ljungberg the Swede. At the half-way stage of the season manager Arsène Wenger made the shrewd capture of the Spaniard Jose Antonio Reyes from Sevilla to add a further dimension to attacking potential.

With two matches unbeaten at the start of the previous season Arsenal's sequence extended to 40 games. Their next target was the overall record at the beginning of 2004–05. Analysing this outstanding achievement records were broken at regular intervals throughout.

First it was not unlucky 13 because this match set a new Premiership record. Next came 31 unbeaten which embraced the previous season's two. Eight days later and it was 30 for the season itself. Two weeks on from that and it was 31 unbeaten for a single season. Obviously since there were no defeats it was also a Premier record along those lines.

Of those 22 players called upon, only goalkeeper Jens Lehmann was ever present. Henry and Toure missed one each, though the latter's total included one as a substitute. Pires was absent on two occasions, three of his outings being from the substitutes bench. Campbell missed three games. As they became known, the New Invincibles had made their mark.

Runners-up were Chelsea bolstered by the millions provided by owner Roman Abramovich. Their frustration, too, came chiefly in the Champions League where having achieved the apparently more difficult task of

Arsenal's Ashley Cole, Dennis Bergkamp, Thierry Henry, Edu and Patrick Vieira celebrate winning the FA Barclaycard Premiership at White Hart Lane after the 2-2 draw with Tottenham Hotspur. (Empics)

Liverpool's Anthony Le Tallec finds himself surrounded by Everton's Gary Naysmith, Alessandro Pistone, Tony Hibbert and Alan Stubbs. This Merseyside derby at the end of January ended 0-0. (Empics)

disposing of Arsenal, failed in the semi-finals when manager Claudio Ranieri made a hash of his half-time tinkering against Monaco and signalled the probability of losing his job at the same time.

With a clutch of new foreign signings it was difficult to find a suitable combination but runners-up spot might have suited a club with less ambition. Still Chelsea finished higher than their previous best of winning the Football League Championship in 1955.

In February, Chelsea overtook Manchester United who had to settle for the consolation prize of the FA Cup. It was during United's worst spell of taking just two points from a possible 12. United were knocked out of the Champions League by the eventual winners Porto. Because of the gap which developed pretty rapidly, the top three of the Premier League did not appear in much threat from elsewhere. So fourth place and its guarantee of a place in the Champions League provided almost as much excitement as Arsenal carrying on their unbeaten run.

Ultimately it was Liverpool who snatched it after a succession of clubs strove for the coveted position. Such is the pressure on Premier League clubs, it was not enough to save manager Gerard Houllier, who eventually walked out alone from Anfield. To emphasise the situation, Liverpool were 15 points adrift of Manchester United and a massive 30 behind Arsenal.

The mini-leagues within the Premier are well known; the top three followed by the half dozen vying for places in Europe, those who are unlikely to be relegated and then the half dozen who have to worry about their futures in the top flight.

Newcastle United had to settle for fifth place after looking at one time capable of fourth. The other downside to their season was in losing on penalties to Partizan Belgrade in the Champions League and to Marseille in the semi-final of the UEFA Cup. But they were at least making a mark in Europe in the latter competition.

Aston Villa were edged out of this spot on goal difference after a second half of the season revival and Charlton Athletic, too, had strong claims for fourth place themselves until mid-January when results became erratic.

Bolton Wanderers reached the final of the Carling Cup and a top half of the table finish was satisfactory. Fulham were as high as fourth on Boxing Day but fared less well subsequently. Birmingham City were another in the same category but suffered, too, in failing to consolidate when they did so.

For Middlesbrough the Carling Cup provided them with some silverware at last following too long a period without such success. A mixture of games with few goals, others free-scoring was not conducive to consistency in the League.

Southampton were fourth in mid-December and might have done better as overall they failed to score in 16 matches. A surprise start on the south coast for Portsmouth was spoilt and only herculean efforts at the end shot them to safety.

Tottenham Hotspur bade farewell to manager Glenn Hoddle and soldiered on without a replacement but for the most part were treading water in the lower reaches as were Blackburn Rovers, another team worried by the drop. Similarly Manchester City drifted down after looking promising in the opening weeks.

Everton like Blackburn had done well in the previous season, but found the going tough especially away where they won only one game. However, the unlucky trio were Leicester City, Leeds United and Wolverhampton Wanderers. Leicester and Wolves, two of the promoted teams along with Pompey, were unable to sustain small flurries of optimism and for Leeds came their first demotion from the Premier League after a season dominated by enormous financial problems.

In the Football League, Norwich City were never headed after December and a win at local rivals Ipswich Town. They were joined in promotion by West Bromwich Albion who had a run of nine undefeated games towards the end, though finishing with a hat-trick of defeats when others could not take advantage.

The final play-off quartet were Sunderland, West Ham United, Ipswich and Crystal Palace who needed penalties to oust Sunderland, but West Ham had an easier time with Ipswich. In the final Palace, who had been as low as 21st in December, edged the Hammers in the all-London finale for third spot towards the Premiership.

Before this stage of course mid-April had proved to be a dreadful one for Sunderland after a fine run. The Hammers, too, had faltered earlier in the same month, but pulled their game together, while Ipswich faltered a little at a crucial time.

There were few points separating these teams and those missing out including Wigan Athletic, Sheffield United, Reading and Milwall. Indeed in the final table there were only five points from fourth to tenth place. Wigan were still third in March, United shortly afterwards. However, Reading seemed unable to move from just outside the play-off area in the last half of the season.

For Millwall whose outstanding achievement was to reach the FA Cup final for the first time, this drastically affected their chances of a place in the play-offs and they won only the last of their remaining nine games.

Third from bottom in early December, Stoke City had a better second half to edge into the top half but a mid-table look was evident from an early point at Coventry City. On the other hand Cardiff City managed only one run of three consecutive wins and a club record seven non-scoring games plunged Nottingham Forest into trouble until a change at the top and survival.

Two wins in the last 17 was not good enough for Preston North End and one win in the first nine outings for Watford was a burden. There was only one goal in the first seven matches for Rotherham United and Crewe Alexandra had to be content with the odd win here and there to keep them safe.

Seven games without a win at the turn of the year led to later concerns for Burnley and Derby County were firmly entrenched in the bottom four until the last couple of matches. Gillingham, too, lived dangerously and only goal difference saved them at the death.

The relegated trio were Walsall, Bradford City and Wimbledon. Walsall lost five in a row out of the last six and Bradford were never out of 23rd place from the end of October. For Wimbledon a move to Milton Keynes improved attendances but 12 games with one goal a point was a recipe for disaster.

Save for a small blip in February, Plymouth Argyle were consistent over the second half of the season and had a seven point lead over their promotion rivals Queens Park Rangers to take the Second Division championship.

Rangers for their part held off a challenge from Bristol City, who had 11 consecutive wins, but probably at the wrong time. City then joined Brighton & Hove Albion, Swindon Town and Hartlepool United in the play-offs. United had only secured a berth on goal difference from Port Vale.

City drew at United and won at home, but Brighton having won at Swindon lost at home and needed penalties to see them through to the final which oddly enough Brighton won against City with another penalty.

Brighton had quietly chipped away on the points scale to reach their goal, Swindon's own unbeaten 11 run had probably also been timed too early and Hartlepool blossomed from five wins in a row in April.

Port Vale had ended with three straight wins – still not enough and Tranmere Rovers with only one win in the first nine had too much ground to make up. Bournemouth won just one of their last eight, while Luton Town slipped from fifth at the end of February.

James Beattie scores Southampton's first goal in the 3-3 draw with Newcastle United at St Mary's Stadium in May. An injury-time equaliser from Darren Ambrose briefly kept alive Newcastle's Champions League hopes. (Actionimages)

Colchester United, fourth in mid-November, started a decline and 11 matches without a win from January from the same position hit Barnsley severely. One win in the last nine ruled Wrexham out of a play-off chance and consolation prize for Blackpool was the LDV Vans Trophy for the second time in their history.

Oldham Athletic managed to stay away from serious problems and fourth place in mid-October flattered Sheffield Wednesday. Brentford needed a late revival after 19 games with just one win. Peterborough United, 13 without a win earlier in the season, hauled themselves away from relegation towards the close as did Stockport County after just one victory in 15.

Chesterfield appeared entrenched in the relegation zone at the turn of the year, but scraped enough points to push themselves clear. In fact, only three points separated Brentford from Grimsby Town, the first of the demoted quartet. They were erratic throughout and went down with Rushden & Diamonds, Notts County and Wycombe Wanderers. Rushden scored only seven goals in their last 13 and one win in the last dozen was not sufficient for Notts' continuing in the division. Wycombe, bottom from Boxing Day, were never able to extricate themselves.

Doncaster Rovers' accomplishment in winning the Third Division title having just regained Football League status was an exceptional achievement after an understandably tentative opening. One win in seven from the middle of October was Hull City's poorest spell in an otherwise fine season. The third automatically promoted team was Torquay United who lost only two of their last 16 to judge the run-in and edge out Huddersfield Town on goal difference.

Huddersfield had seemed assured of third place at least but merely drew two of their last three. So it was the play-offs for them, Mansfield Town, Northampton Town and Lincoln City. Mansfield won at Northampton, Huddersfield at Lincoln who only drew in the second leg. However, Northampton turned the tables at Mansfield only to lose on penalties.

Mansfield had not had such a good second half of the season as the first, but Northampton were as low as 19th at the end of October. Lincoln, with no goals in their first three matches, improved until almost falling out of the top zone near the close.

In the play-off final, penalties were again required to see Huddersfield through at Mansfield's expense. Once again this season a team lost out on goal difference. It was Yeovil Town who had accompanied Doncaster from the Conference. They had needed to win their last five, not just four of them.

Oxford United tumbled crazily winning just two of their last 16 having led the table in late December. Swansea City, too, had too many stretches without victory after a good first half of the campaign.

Boston United removed to safety after six wins in the last 11 but seven defeats in a row mid-season kept Bury away from a challenge. Cambridge United had to pick up the pace from March when they were slipping and Cheltenham Town were still hovering above the relegation zone around the New Year. Bristol Rovers went 10 games without a win when better results might have made a significant difference.

A marked improvement for a time from February finally saved Kidderminster Harriers and Southend United's eight without defeat banished their worries. One win in 18 and only 11 goals could have proved dire for Darlington and it was as well Leyton Orient had points in hand when only one win came in the last 15.

Four wins in the last seven gave Macclesfield Town the necessary life-line and two wins in the last four were enough for Rochdale. Scunthorpe United with one win in the last dozen had also had sufficient points at the time. Not so, Carlisle United and York City the relegation pair.

Carlisle's had been a magnificent effort since they had had just one win in the first 21 and on 13 December were 15 points below the next club. But for York goalscoring was always a problem and they failed to win any of their last 20. Their places are taken by Chester City and Shrewsbury Town, both of whom are former Football League clubs.

Neil Shipperley celebrates his winning goal for Crystal Palace in the First Division play-off final against West Ham United at the Millennium Stadium, Cardiff. (Actionimages)

# INTRODUCTION TO THE CLUB SECTION

The *Sky Sports Football Yearbook* features a who's who style players directory which incorporates the total appearances and goals for each player as in earlier editions of *Rothmans Football Yearbook*, but additionally, includes more personal information and a season-by-season account of the individual player's record. It is again presented in an A to Z form for easy reference (see pages 430 to 564). There is also each club's full record in the last ten seasons and the latest sequences recorded for wins, draws and defeats, etc. In addition, the individual club's record scoring and non-scoring runs are also included.

For the first time, an additional A to Z of players has been included to enable readers to locate any player who appeared with a club during the 2003–04 season. Every club is given a number to facilitate easy reference.

Once again the club section comprises four pages, the first two featuring new entries in the *Sky Sports Fact File* and *Did you know?* series. Record transfer fees are usually left to the discretion of the club concerned. The third and fourth pages of this section present a complete record of the League season, including date, venue, opponents, results, half-time score, League position, goalscorers, attendances and complete line-ups including substitutes where used. This comprises every League game in the 2003–04 season. Again, goal times have been added; though not official they give an indication of when goals were scored. These appear as superior figures $^{10, 20, 30}$.

Players shown red cards are indicated thus ■.

Squad numbers have not been included; those used are the familiar ones, 1–11, substitutes are recognised as follows: the first substitute number 12, the second number 13 and the third number 14. However, if there is a subsitute goalkeeper he is represented by number 15, *but only* if he replaces the first choice goalkeeper or another outfield player. Otherwise, he adopts one of the other three substitute numbers, as there have been several instances where a goalkeeper has been used as an outfield player because of injuries during the game. Players replaced are respectively noted with superior figures $^{1, 2, 3}$ and $^{g}$ for goalkeeper. These third and fourth pages also include consolidated lists of goalscorers for the club in League, Carling Cup, FA Cup, LDV Vans Trophy and European matches, plus a summary of results in all these major competitions.

The continual increase in the number of matches played on Sundays has resulted in the League positions after the weekend's results. Full holiday programmes are also recorded, but the position after mid-week fixtures will not normally have been updated. Attendance figures quoted for the Nationwide Football League are those that appeared in the Press at the time. But those in the FA Barclaycard Premiership are official. The attendance statistics published on pages 598–599 are those officially issued by the FA Premier League but not those concerning the Football League at the end of the season. In the totals at the top of each column on page 4 of the club section, substitute appearances are listed separately by the '+', but have been amalgamated in the totals which feature in the players historical section in the directory mentioned above. Thus, these appearances include those as substitute. In fact, the directory features those names appearing on the FA Premier League and Football League's retained lists, which are published at the end of May. Each player's height and weight where known, plus birth date and place plus source, together with total League goals and appearances for each club represented, can be found as in previous editions. The player's details remain under the club which retain him at the end of the season. An '*' by a player's name indicates that he was given a free transfer at the end of the 2003–04 season, a dagger '†' against a name means that he is a non-contract player, a double dagger '‡' indicates that the player's registration was cancelled during the season and a section mark '§' shows the player to be a trainee, scholar or associated schoolboy who has made either League or senior appearances. The symbol '#' indicates players 24 and over who are out of contract, but who were offered re-engagement by their clubs. Appearances by players in the play-offs are not included in their career totals. International appearances of foreign players reflect latest information available.

# ARSENAL FA Premiership

## FOUNDATION

Formed by workers at the Royal Arsenal, Woolwich in 1886, they began as Dial Square (name of one of the workshops), and included two former Nottingham Forest players, Fred Beardsley and Morris Bates. Beardsley wrote to his old club seeking help and they provided the new club with a full set of red jerseys and a ball. The club became known as the 'Woolwich Reds' although their official title soon after formation was Woolwich Arsenal.

***Arsenal Stadium, Highbury, London N5 1BU.***

***Telephone:*** (020) 7704 4000.

***Fax:*** (020) 7704 4001.

***Ticket Office:*** (020) 7704 4242.

***Website:*** www.arsenal.com

***Email:*** info@arsenal.com

***Ground Capacity:*** 38,500.

***Record Attendance:*** 73,295 v Sunderland, Div 1, 9 March 1935.

***At Wembley:*** 73,707 v RC Lens, UEFA Champions League, 25 November 1998.

***Pitch Measurements:*** 110yd × 73yd.

***Chairman:*** Peter Hill-Wood.

***Vice-chairman:*** David Dein.

***Managing Director:*** K. Edelman.

***Secretary:*** David Miles.

***Manager:*** Arsène Wenger.

***Assistant Manager:*** Pat Rice.

***Physio:*** Gary Lewin.

***Colours:*** Red shirts with white sleeves, white shorts, red stockings with yellow trim.

***Change Colours:*** Blue shirts with red trim, blue shorts, blue stockings with red and yellow trim.

***Year Formed:*** 1886.

***Turned Professional:*** 1891.

***Ltd Co:*** 1893.

***Previous Names:*** 1886, Dial Square; 1886, Royal Arsenal; 1891, Woolwich Arsenal; 1914 Arsenal.

***Club Nickname:*** 'Gunners'.

***Previous Grounds:*** 1886, Plumstead Common; 1887, Sportsman Ground; 1888, Manor Ground; 1890, Invicta Ground; 1893, Manor Ground; 1913, Highbury.

## HONOURS

*FA Premier League:* Champions 1997–98, 2001–02, 2003–04. Runners-up 1998–99, 1999–2000, 2000–01, 2002–03.

*Football League:* Division 1 – Champions 1930–31, 1932–33, 1933–34, 1934–35, 1937–38, 1947–48, 1952–53, 1970–71, 1988–89, 1990–91; Runners-up 1925–26, 1931–32, 1972–73; Division 2 – Runners-up 1903–04.

*FA Cup:* Winners 1930, 1936, 1950, 1971, 1979, 1993, 1998, 2002, 2003; Runners-up 1927, 1932, 1952, 1972, 1978, 1980, 2001.

*Double performed:* 1970–71, 1997–98, 2001–02.

*Football League Cup:* Winners 1987, 1993; Runners-up 1968, 1969, 1988.

***European Competitions:*** *Fairs Cup:* 1963–64, 1969–70 (winners), 1970–71. *European Cup:* 1971–72, 1991–92. *UEFA Champions League:* 1998–99, 1999–2000, 2000–01, 2001–02, 2002–03, 2003–04. *UEFA Cup:* 1978–79, 1981–82, 1982–83, 1996–97, 1997–98, 1999–2000 (runners-up). *European Cup-Winners' Cup:* 1979–80 (runners-up), 1993–94 (winners), 1994–95 (runners-up).

## SKY SPORTS FACT FILE

During his lengthy association with Arsenal, skipper Tony Adams lifted more trophies than any other captain of the club. The nine such honours consisted of four Championships, three FA Cups, one each for the League Cup and Cup-Winners' Cup.

***First Football League Game:*** 2 September 1893, Division 2, v Newcastle U (h) D 2–2 – Williams; Powell, Jeffrey; Devine, Buist, Howat; Gemmell, Henderson, Shaw (1), Elliott (1), Booth.

***Record League Victory:*** 12–0 v Loughborough T, Division 2, 12 March 1900 – Orr; McNichol, Jackson; Moir, Dick (2), Anderson (1); Hunt, Cottrell (2), Main (2), Gaudie (3), Tennant (2).

***Record Cup Victory:*** 11–1 v Darwen, FA Cup 3rd rd, 9 January 1932 – Moss; Parker, Hapgood; Jones, Roberts, John; Hulme (2), Jack (3), Lambert (2), James, Bastin (4).

***Record Defeat:*** 0–8 v Loughborough T, Division 2, 12 December 1896.

***Most League Points (2 for a win):*** 66, Division 1, 1930–31.

***Most League Points (3 for a win):*** 90, Premier League 2003–04.

***Most League Goals:*** 127, Division 1, 1930–31.

***Highest League Scorer in Season:*** Ted Drake, 42, 1934–35.

***Most League Goals in Total Aggregate:*** Cliff Bastin, 150, 1930–47.

***Most League Goals in One Match:*** 7, Ted Drake v Aston Villa, Division 1, 14 December 1935.

***Most Capped Player:*** Kenny Sansom, 77 (86), England, 1981–88.

***Most League Appearances:*** David O'Leary, 558, 1975–93.

***Youngest League Player:*** Gerry Ward, 16 years 321 days v Huddersfield T, 22 August 1953 (Jermaine Pennant, 16 years 319 days v Middlesbrough, League Cup, 30 November 1999).

***Record Transfer Fee Received:*** A reported £22,900,000 from Real Madrid for Nicolas Anelka, August 1999.

***Record Transfer Fee Paid:*** A reported £11,000,000 to Bordeaux for Sylvain Wiltord, August 2000.

***Football League Record:*** 1893 Elected to Division 2; 1904–13 Division 1; 1913–19 Division 2; 1919–92 Division 1; 1992– FA Premier League.

## MANAGERS

Sam Hollis 1894–97
Tom Mitchell 1897–98
George Elcoat 1898–99
Harry Bradshaw 1899–1904
Phil Kelso 1904–08
George Morrell 1908–15
Leslie Knighton 1919–25
Herbert Chapman 1925–34
George Allison 1934–47
Tom Whittaker 1947–56
Jack Crayston 1956–58
George Swindin 1958–62
Billy Wright 1962–66
Bertie Mee 1966–76
Terry Neill 1976–83
Don Howe 1984–86
George Graham 1986–95
Bruce Rioch 1995–96
Arsène Wenger September 1996–

## LATEST SEQUENCES

***Longest Sequence of League Wins:*** 14, 10.2.2002 – 18.8.2002.

***Longest Sequence of League Defeats:*** 7, 12.2.1977 – 12.3.1977.

***Longest Sequence of League Draws:*** 6, 4.3.1961 – 1.4.1961.

***Longest Sequence of Unbeaten League Matches:*** 40, 7.5.2003 – 15.5.2004.

***Longest Sequence Without a League Win:*** 23, 28.9.1912 – 1.3.1913.

***Successive Scoring Runs:*** 55 from 19.5.2001.

***Successive Non-scoring Runs:*** 6 from 25.2.1987.

## TEN YEAR LEAGUE RECORD

| | | P | W | D | L | F | A | Pts | Pos |
|---|---|---|---|---|---|---|---|---|---|
| 1994-95 | PR Lge | 42 | 13 | 12 | 17 | 52 | 49 | 51 | 12 |
| 1995-96 | PR Lge | 38 | 17 | 12 | 9 | 49 | 32 | 63 | 5 |
| 1996-97 | PR Lge | 38 | 19 | 11 | 8 | 62 | 32 | 68 | 3 |
| 1997-98 | PR Lge | 38 | 23 | 9 | 6 | 68 | 33 | 78 | 1 |
| 1998-99 | PR Lge | 38 | 22 | 12 | 4 | 59 | 17 | 78 | 2 |
| 1999-2000 | PR Lge | 38 | 22 | 7 | 9 | 73 | 43 | 73 | 2 |
| 2000-01 | PR Lge | 38 | 20 | 10 | 8 | 63 | 38 | 70 | 2 |
| 2001-02 | PR Lge | 38 | 26 | 9 | 3 | 79 | 36 | 87 | 1 |
| 2002-03 | PR Lge | 38 | 23 | 9 | 6 | 85 | 42 | 78 | 2 |
| 2003-04 | PR Lge | 38 | 26 | 12 | 0 | 73 | 26 | 90 | 1 |

## DID YOU KNOW ?

Arsenal players Kanu and Lauren each achieved Olympic gold medal honours for their country. Kanu captained Nigeria to their 1996 triumph in Atlanta, while Lauren helped Cameroon to the title at the Sydney Olympics in 2000.

## ARSENAL 2003–04 LEAGUE RECORD

| *Match No.* | *Date* | *Venue* | *Opponents* | *Result* | *H/T Score* | *Lg. Pos.* | *Goalscorers* | *Attendance* |
|---|---|---|---|---|---|---|---|---|
| 1 | Aug 16 | H | Everton | W 2-1 | 1-0 | — | Henry (pen) [35], Pires [58] | 38,014 |
| 2 | 24 | A | Middlesbrough | W 4-0 | 3-0 | 1 | Henry [5], Silva [13], Wiltord 2 [22, 60] | 29,450 |
| 3 | 27 | H | Aston Villa | W 2-0 | 0-0 | — | Campbell [57], Henry [90] | 38,010 |
| 4 | 31 | A | Manchester C | W 2-1 | 0-1 | 1 | Wiltord [48], Ljungberg [72] | 46,436 |
| 5 | Sept 13 | H | Portsmouth | D 1-1 | 1-1 | 1 | Henry (pen) [40] | 38,052 |
| 6 | 21 | A | Manchester U | D 0-0 | 0-0 | 1 | | 67,639 |
| 7 | 26 | H | Newcastle U | W 3-2 | 1-1 | — | Henry 2 (1 pen) [18, 80 (p)], Silva [67] | 38,112 |
| 8 | Oct 4 | A | Liverpool | W 2-1 | 1-1 | 1 | Hyypia (og) [31], Pires [68] | 44,374 |
| 9 | 18 | H | Chelsea | W 2-1 | 1-1 | 1 | Edu [5], Henry [75] | 38,172 |
| 10 | 26 | A | Charlton Ath | D 1-1 | 1-1 | 1 | Henry [39] | 26,639 |
| 11 | Nov 1 | A | Leeds U | W 4-1 | 3-0 | 1 | Henry 2 [8, 33], Pires [17], Silva [50] | 36,491 |
| 12 | 8 | H | Tottenham H | W 2-1 | 0-1 | 1 | Pires [69], Ljungberg [79] | 38,101 |
| 13 | 22 | A | Birmingham C | W 3-0 | 1-0 | 1 | Ljungberg [4], Bergkamp [80], Pires [88] | 29,588 |
| 14 | 30 | H | Fulham | D 0-0 | 0-0 | 2 | | 38,063 |
| 15 | Dec 6 | A | Leicester C | D 1-1 | 0-0 | 2 | Silva [60] | 32,108 |
| 16 | 14 | H | Blackburn R | W 1-0 | 1-0 | 1 | Bergkamp [11] | 37,677 |
| 17 | 20 | A | Bolton W | D 1-1 | 0-0 | 2 | Pires [57] | 27,492 |
| 18 | 26 | H | Wolverhampton W | W 3-0 | 2-0 | 2 | Craddock (og) [13], Henry 2 [20, 89] | 38,003 |
| 19 | 29 | A | Southampton | W 1-0 | 1-0 | — | Pires [35] | 32,151 |
| 20 | Jan 7 | A | Everton | D 1-1 | 1-0 | — | Kanu [29] | 38,726 |
| 21 | 10 | H | Middlesbrough | W 4-1 | 2-0 | 2 | Henry (pen) [38], Queudrue (og) [45], Pires [57], Ljungberg [68] | 38,117 |
| 22 | 18 | A | Aston Villa | W 2-0 | 1-0 | 1 | Henry 2 (1 pen) [29, 53 (p)] | 39,380 |
| 23 | Feb 1 | H | Manchester C | W 2-1 | 1-0 | 1 | Tarnat (og) [39], Henry [83] | 38,103 |
| 24 | 7 | A | Wolverhampton W | W 3-1 | 1-1 | 1 | Bergkamp [9], Henry [58], Toure [63] | 29,392 |
| 25 | 10 | H | Southampton | W 2-0 | 1-0 | — | Henry 2 [31, 90] | 38,007 |
| 26 | 21 | A | Chelsea | W 2-1 | 2-1 | 1 | Vieira [15], Edu [21] | 41,926 |
| 27 | 28 | H | Charlton Ath | W 2-1 | 2-0 | 1 | Pires [2], Henry [4] | 38,137 |
| 28 | Mar 13 | A | Blackburn R | W 2-0 | 0-0 | 1 | Henry [57], Pires [87] | 28,627 |
| 29 | 20 | H | Bolton W | W 2-1 | 2-1 | 1 | Pires [16], Bergkamp [24] | 38,053 |
| 30 | 28 | H | Manchester U | D 1-1 | 0-0 | 1 | Henry [50] | 38,184 |
| 31 | Apr 9 | H | Liverpool | W 4-2 | 1-2 | — | Henry 3 [31, 50, 78], Pires [49] | 38,119 |
| 32 | 11 | A | Newcastle U | D 0-0 | 0-0 | 1 | | 52,141 |
| 33 | 16 | H | Leeds U | W 5-0 | 3-0 | — | Pires [6], Henry 4 (1 pen) [27, 33 (p), 50, 67] | 38,094 |
| 34 | 25 | A | Tottenham H | D 2-2 | 2-0 | 1 | Vieira [3], Pires [35] | 36,097 |
| 35 | May 1 | H | Birmingham C | D 0-0 | 0-0 | 1 | | 38,061 |
| 36 | 4 | A | Portsmouth | D 1-1 | 0-1 | — | Reyes [50] | 20,140 |
| 37 | 9 | A | Fulham | W 1-0 | 1-0 | 1 | Reyes [9] | 18,102 |
| 38 | 15 | H | Leicester C | W 2-1 | 0-1 | 1 | Henry (pen) [47], Vieira [66] | 38,419 |

**Final League Position: 1**

### GOALSCORERS

*League (73):* Henry 30 (7 pens), Pires 14, Bergkamp 4, Ljungberg 4, Silva 4, Vieira 3, Wiltord 3, Edu 2, Reyes 2, Campbell 1, Kanu 1, Toure 1, own goals 4.
*Carling Cup (9):* Aladiere 4, Kanu 2, Edu 1, Fabregas Soler 1, Wiltord 1.
*FA Cup (15):* Ljungberg 4, Henry 3, Reyes 2, Toure 2, Bentley 1, Bergkamp 1, Edu 1, Pires 1.
*Community Shield (1):* Henry 1.
*Champions League (16):* Henry 5, Pires 4, Edu 3, Ljungberg 2, Cole 1, Reyes 1.

| Lehmann J 38 | Lauren E 30 + 2 | Cole A 32 | Vieira P 29 | Campbell S 35 | Toure K 36 + 1 | Ljungberg F 27 + 3 | Silva G 29 + 3 | Wiltord S 8 + 4 | Henry T 37 | Pires R 33 + 3 | Keown M 3 + 7 | Parlour R 16 + 9 | Edu13 + 17 | Bergkamp D 21 + 7 | Cygan P 10 + 8 | Aliadiere J 3 + 7 | Kanu N 3 + 7 | Clichy G 7 + 5 | Hoyte J — + 1 | Reyes J 7 + 6 | Bentley D 1 | Match No. |
|---|---|---|---|---|---|---|---|---|---|---|---|---|---|---|---|---|---|---|---|---|---|---|
| 1 | 2 | 3 | 4 | 5■ | 6 | 7 | 8 | $9^{1}$ | 10 | $11^{2}$ | 12 | 13 | | | | | | | | | | 1 |
| 1 | 2 | 3 | 4 | 5 | 6 | $7^{1}$ | 8 | $9^{2}$ | 10 | $11^{3}$ | | 12 | 14 | 13 | | | | | | | | 2 |
| 1 | 2 | 3 | 4 | 5 | 6 | $7^{1}$ | 8 | $9^{2}$ | 10 | 11 | | 12 | | 13 | | | | | | | | 3 |
| 1 | 2 | 3 | 4 | | 6 | $7^{1}$ | 8 | $9^{2}$ | 10 | $11^{3}$ | 5 | 12 | 14 | 13 | | | | | | | | 4 |
| 1 | 2 | 3 | 4 | 5 | 6 | 12 | | 13 | 9 | 11 | | 7 | $8^{1}$ | $10^{2}$ | | | | | | | | 5 |
| 1 | 2 | 3 | 4■ | | 6 | 11 | 8 | | 9 | | 5 | 7 | 12 | $10^{1}$ | | | | | | | | 6 |
| 1 | 2 | $3^{3}$ | $4^{1}$ | | 6 | 11 | 8 | 9 | 10 | 13 | 5 | $7^{2}$ | 12 | | 14 | | | | | | | 7 |
| 1 | 2 | 3 | | 5 | 6 | | 4 | 12 | 10 | 11 | | 7 | 8 | | | $9^{1}$ | | | | | | 8 |
| 1 | 2 | 3 | | 5 | 6 | | 4 | $9^{3}$ | 10 | $11^{2}$ | | $7^{1}$ | 8 | 12 | 13 | | 14 | | | | | 9 |
| 1 | 2 | 3 | | 5 | 6 | $7^{2}$ | 4 | 12 | 9 | 11 | | 8 | | $10^{1}$ | | | 13 | | | | | 10 |
| 1 | 2 | 3 | | 5 | 6 | $7^{1}$ | 4 | | 9 | $11^{2}$ | | 8 | 12 | 10 | | 13 | | | | | | 11 |
| 1 | $2^{3}$ | 3 | | 5 | 6 | 7 | $4^{1}$ | | 10 | 11 | | 8 | 13 | 12 | 14 | | $9^{2}$ | | | | | 12 |
| 1 | | 3 | | 5 | 2 | 7 | | | $9^{2}$ | $11^{3}$ | | | 4 | 10 | 6 | 13 | 12 | $8^{1}$ | 14 | | | 13 |
| 1 | | 3 | | 5 | 2 | $7^{2}$ | $4^{1}$ | | 9 | 11 | | | 8 | 10 | 6 | 13 | 12 | | | | | 14 |
| 1 | | 3■ | | 5 | 2 | $7^{1}$ | 4 | 13 | | 11 | 12 | | 8 | $10^{3}$ | 6 | $9^{2}$ | | 14 | | | | 15 |
| 1 | | 3 | 4 | 5 | 2 | $7^{2}$ | 8 | | 9 | 11 | | 12 | 13 | $10^{1}$ | 6 | | | | | | | 16 |
| 1 | | | 4 | 5 | 2 | 7 | 8 | | 9 | 11 | | 12 | | $10^{1}$ | 6 | | | 3 | | | | 17 |
| 1 | | | 4 | 5 | 2 | $7^{2}$ | | | 9 | $11^{1}$ | | 8 | 12 | 10 | 6 | 13 | | 3 | | | | 18 |
| 1 | 12 | | 4 | 5 | 2 | $7^{2}$ | | | 9 | $11^{1}$ | | 8 | 13 | $10^{3}$ | 6 | | 14 | 3 | | | | 19 |
| 1 | 12 | 3 | 4 | 5 | $2^{1}$ | $7^{2}$ | 13 | | 10 | 11 | | 8 | 14 | | 6 | | $9^{3}$ | | | | | 20 |
| 1 | 2 | 3 | 4 | 5 | | $7^{1}$ | 8 | | 10 | $11^{3}$ | | 12 | 14 | | 6 | $9^{2}$ | 13 | | | | | 21 |
| 1 | 2 | 3 | 4 | 5 | 14 | $7^{1}$ | 8 | | 10 | $11^{2}$ | | 12 | 13 | | 6 | | $9^{3}$ | | | | | 22 |
| 1 | 2 | 3 | | 5 | 6 | $7^{1}$ | 4 | | 9 | $11^{2}$ | | 8 | 12 | $10^{3}$ | 13 | | | | | 14 | | 23 |
| 1 | 2 | 3 | 4 | 5 | 6 | | 7 | | 9 | 11 | | | 8 | $10^{1}$ | | | | | | 12 | | 24 |
| 1 | 2 | 3 | 4 | 5 | 6 | | 8 | | 10 | 11 | | 7 | | | | | | 12 | | $9^{1}$ | | 25 |
| 1 | 2 | | 4 | 5 | 6 | 12 | 7 | | 9 | 11 | | | 8 | $10^{1}$ | | | | 3 | | | | 26 |
| 1 | 2 | 3 | 4 | 5 | 6 | $7^{1}$ | 12 | | 9 | $11^{2}$ | | | 8 | $10^{3}$ | 13 | | | | | 14 | | 27 |
| 1 | 2 | 3 | 4 | 5 | 6 | | 7 | | 10 | $11^{1}$ | | | 8 | | 12 | | | 13 | | $9^{2}$ | | 28 |
| 1 | 2 | 3 | 4 | 5 | 6 | 12 | $7^{1}$ | | 9 | $11^{2}$ | | | 8 | 10 | 13 | | | | | | | 29 |
| 1 | 2 | | 4 | 5 | 6 | $7^{3}$ | 12 | | 10 | $11^{2}$ | | | 8 | 13 | 14 | | | 3 | | $9^{1}$ | | 30 |
| 1 | 2 | 3 | 4 | 5 | 6 | $7^{2}$ | 8 | | 9 | $11^{1}$ | 13 | | 12 | 10 | | | | | | | | 31 |
| 1 | 2 | $3^{3}$ | 4 | 5 | 6 | | 7 | $11^{1}$ | 10 | 12 | | | 8 | 13 | | | | 14 | | $9^{2}$ | | 32 |
| 1 | 2 | | 4 | 5 | 6 | | $8^{1}$ | 7 | 9 | $11^{2}$ | | 13 | 12 | $10^{3}$ | | | | 3 | | 14 | | 33 |
| 1 | 2 | 3 | 4 | 5 | 6 | | 8 | | 9 | 11 | | $7^{1}$ | 12 | $10^{2}$ | | | | | | 13 | | 34 |
| 1 | 2 | 3 | 4 | 5 | 6 | $11^{1}$ | 8 | | 10 | 12 | 13 | | | $7^{2}$ | | 14 | | | | $9^{3}$ | | 35 |
| 1 | 2 | 3 | 4 | 5 | 6 | $7^{3}$ | | | 10 | | 13 | 8 | | | | 14 | 12 | | | $9^{2}$ | $11^{1}$ | 36 |
| 1 | 2 | 3 | 4 | 5 | 6 | $7^{1}$ | | | 10 | $11^{2}$ | 12 | 8 | | | | 14 | | 13 | | $9^{3}$ | | 37 |
| 1 | 2 | 3 | 4 | 5 | 6 | $7^{2}$ | 8 | | 9 | $11^{1}$ | 13 | | 12 | $10^{3}$ | | | | | | 14 | | 38 |

**Carling Cup**

| | | | |
|---|---|---|---|
| Third Round | Rotherham U | (h) | 1-1 |
| Fourth Round | Wolverhampton W | (h) | 5-1 |
| Fifth Round | WBA | (a) | 2-0 |
| Semi-Final | Middlesbrough | (h) | 0-1 |
| | | (a) | 1-2 |

**FA Cup**

| | | | |
|---|---|---|---|
| Third Round | Leeds U | (a) | 4-1 |
| Fourth Round | Middlesbrough | (h) | 4-1 |
| Fifth Round | Chelsea | (h) | 2-1 |
| Sixth Round | Portsmouth | (a) | 5-1 |
| Semi-Final (at Villa Park) | Manchester U | | 0-1 |

**Champions League**

| | | | |
|---|---|---|---|
| Group B | Internazionale | (h) | 0-3 |
| | Lokomotiv Moscow | (a) | 0-0 |
| | Dynamo Kiev | (a) | 1-2 |
| | | (h) | 1-0 |
| | Internazionale | (a) | 5-1 |
| | Lokomotiv Moscow | (h) | 2-0 |
| First KO Round | Celta Vigo | (a) | 3-2 |
| | | (h) | 2-0 |
| Quarter-Finals | Chelsea | (a) | 1-1 |
| | | (h) | 1-2 |

# ASTON VILLA FA Premiership

## FOUNDATION

Cricketing enthusiasts of Villa Cross Wesleyan Chapel, Aston, Birmingham decided to form a football club during the winter of 1874–75. Football clubs were few and far between in the Birmingham area and in their first game against Aston Brook St Mary's Rugby team they played one half rugby and the other soccer. In 1876 they were joined by a Scottish soccer enthusiast George Ramsay who was immediately appointed captain and went on to lead Aston Villa from obscurity to one of the country's top clubs in a period of less than 10 years.

***Villa Park, Birmingham B6 6HE.***

***Telephone:*** (0121) 327 2299.

***Fax:*** (0121) 322 2107.

***Ticket Office:*** (0121) 327 5353.

***Website:*** avfc.co.uk

***Email:*** postmaster@astonvilla-fc.co.uk

***Ground Capacity:*** 42,573.

***Record Attendance:*** 76,588 v Derby Co, FA Cup 6th rd, 2 March 1946.

***Pitch Measurements:*** 115yd × 72yd.

***Chairman:*** H. D. Ellis.

***Chief Executive:*** B. Langham.

***Club Secretary/Operations Director:*** S. M. Stride.

***Manager:*** David O'Leary.

***Assistant Manager:*** Roy Aitken.

***Physio:*** Alan Smith.

***Colours:*** Claret and blue shirts, white shorts, sky blue stockings.

***Change Colours:*** White shirts, sky blue shorts, white stockings.

***Year Formed:*** 1874.

***Turned Professional:*** 1885.

***Ltd Co.:*** 1896.

***Public Ltd Company:*** 1969.

***Club Nickname:*** 'The Villans'.

***Previous Grounds:*** 1874 Wilson Road and Aston Park (also used Aston Lower Grounds for some matches); 1876 Wellington Road, Perry Barr; 1897 Villa Park.

## HONOURS

*FA Premier League:* Runners-up 1992–93.

*Football League:* Division 1 – Champions 1893–94, 1895–96, 1896–97, 1898–99, 1899–1900, 1909–10, 1980–81; Runners-up 1888–89, 1902–03, 1907–08, 1910–11, 1912–13, 1913–14, 1930–31, 1932–33, 1989–90; Division 2 – Champions 1937–38, 1959–60; Runners-up 1974–75, 1987–88; Division 3 – Champions 1971–72.

*FA Cup:* Winners 1887, 1895, 1897, 1905, 1913, 1920, 1957; Runners-up 1892, 1924, 2000.

*Double Performed:* 1896–97.

*Football League Cup:* Winners 1961, 1975, 1977, 1994, 1996; Runners-up 1963, 1971.

***European Competitions:*** *European Cup:* 1981–82 (winners), 1982–83. *UEFA Cup:* 1975–76, 1977–78, 1983–84, 1990–91, 1993–94, 1994–95, 1996–97, 1997–98, 1998–99, 2001–02. *World Club Championship:* 1982. *European Super Cup:* 1982–83 (winners). *Intertoto Cup:* 2000, 2001 (winners), 2002.

## SKY SPORTS FACT FILE

Aston Villa's record run of League wins from 1910 included seven victories by the odd goal. In the first six of the overall sequence inside-right Joey Walters scored in each match out of his total of 13 for the season.

***First Football League Game:*** 8 September 1888, Football League, v Wolverhampton W (a) D 1–1 – Warner; Cox, Coulton; Yates, H. Devey, Dawson; A. Brown, Green (1), Allen, Garvey, Hodgetts.

***Record League Victory:*** 12–2 v Accrington S, Division 1, 12 March 1892 – Warner; Evans, Cox; Harry Devey, Jimmy Cowan, Baird; Athersmith (1), Dickson (2), John Devey (4), L. Campbell (4), Hodgetts (1).

***Record Cup Victory:*** 13–0 v Wednesbury Old Ath, FA Cup 1st rd, 30 October 1886 – Warner; Coulton, Simmonds; Yates, Robertson, Burton (2); R. Davis (1), A. Brown (3), Hunter (3), Loach (2), Hodgetts (2).

***Record Defeat:*** 1–8 v Blackburn R, FA Cup 3rd rd, 16 February 1889.

***Most League Points (2 for a win):*** 70, Division 3, 1971–72.

***Most League Points (3 for a win):*** 78, Division 2, 1987–88.

***Most League Goals:*** 128, Division 1, 1930–31.

***Highest League Scorer in Season:*** 'Pongo' Waring, 49, Division 1, 1930–31.

***Most League Goals in Total Aggregate:*** Harry Hampton, 215, 1904–15.

***Most League Goals in One Match:*** 5, Harry Hampton v Sheffield W, Division 1, 5 October 1912; 5, Harold Halse v Derby Co, Division 1, 19 October 1912; 5, Len Capewell v Burnley, Division 1, 29 August 1925; 5, George Brown v Leicester C, Division 1, 2 January 1932; 5, Gerry Hitchens v Charlton Ath, Division 2, 18 November 1959.

***Most Capped Player:*** Steve Staunton 64 (102), Republic of Ireland.

***Most League Appearances:*** Charlie Aitken, 561, 1961–76.

***Youngest League Player:*** Jimmy Brown, 15 years 349 days v Bolton W, 17 September 1969.

***Record Transfer Fee Received:*** £12,600,000 from Manchester U for Dwight Yorke, August 1998.

***Record Transfer Fee Paid:*** £9,500,000 to River Plate for Juan Pablo Angel, January 2001.

***Football League Record:*** 1888 Founder Member of the League; 1936–38 Division 2; 1938–59 Division 1; 1959–60 Division 2; 1960–67 Division 1; 1967–70 Division 2; 1970–72 Division 3; 1972–75 Division 2; 1975–87 Division 1; 1987–88 Division 2; 1988–92 Division 1; 1992– FA Premier League.

## MANAGERS

George Ramsay 1884–1926
*(Secretary-Manager)*
W. J. Smith 1926–34
*(Secretary-Manager)*
Jimmy McMullan 1934–35
Jimmy Hogan 1936–44
Alex Massie 1945–50
George Martin 1950–53
Eric Houghton 1953–58
Joe Mercer 1958–64
Dick Taylor 1964–67
Tommy Cummings 1967–68
Tommy Docherty 1968–70
Vic Crowe 1970–74
Ron Saunders 1974–82
Tony Barton 1982–84
Graham Turner 1984–86
Billy McNeill 1986–87
Graham Taylor 1987–90
Dr Jozef Venglos 1990–91
Ron Atkinson 1991–94
Brian Little 1994–98
John Gregory 1998–2002
Graham Taylor OBE 2002–03
David O'Leary May 2003–

## LATEST SEQUENCES

***Longest Sequence of League Wins:*** 9, 15.10.1910 – 10.12.1910.

***Longest Sequence of League Defeats:*** 11, 23.3.1963 – 4.5.1963.

***Longest Sequence of League Draws:*** 6, 12.9.1981 – 10.10.1981.

***Longest Sequence of Unbeaten League Matches:*** 15, 12.3.1949 – 27.8.1949.

***Longest Sequence Without a League Win:*** 12, 27.12.1986 – 25.3.1987.

***Successive Scoring Runs:*** 35 from 10.11.1895.

***Successive Non-scoring Runs:*** 5 from 29.2.1992.

## TEN YEAR LEAGUE RECORD

| | | P | W | D | L | F | A | Pts | Pos |
|---|---|---|---|---|---|---|---|---|---|
| 1994-95 | PR Lge | 42 | 11 | 15 | 16 | 51 | 56 | 48 | 18 |
| 1995-96 | PR Lge | 38 | 18 | 9 | 11 | 52 | 35 | 63 | 4 |
| 1996-97 | PR Lge | 38 | 17 | 10 | 11 | 47 | 34 | 61 | 5 |
| 1997-98 | PR Lge | 38 | 17 | 6 | 15 | 49 | 48 | 57 | 7 |
| 1998-99 | PR Lge | 38 | 15 | 10 | 13 | 51 | 46 | 55 | 6 |
| 1999-2000 | PR Lge | 38 | 15 | 13 | 10 | 46 | 35 | 58 | 6 |
| 2000-01 | PR Lge | 38 | 13 | 15 | 10 | 46 | 43 | 54 | 8 |
| 2001-02 | PR Lge | 38 | 12 | 14 | 12 | 46 | 47 | 50 | 8 |
| 2002-03 | PR Lge | 38 | 12 | 9 | 17 | 42 | 47 | 45 | 16 |
| 2003-04 | PR Lge | 38 | 15 | 11 | 12 | 48 | 44 | 56 | 6 |

## DID YOU KNOW ?

The immediate post-war boom in attendances began for many clubs in the 1945–46 transitional season. Aston Villa, second in the League North, averaged crowds of 32,822 in the competition and had a season high of 76,588 for an FA Cup tie with Derby County.

## ASTON VILLA 2003–04 LEAGUE RECORD

| *Match No.* | *Date* | *Venue* | *Opponents* | *Result* | *H/T Score* | *Lg. Pos.* | *Goalscorers* | *Attendance* |
|---|---|---|---|---|---|---|---|---|
| 1 | Aug 16 | A | Portsmouth | L 1-2 | 0-1 | — | Barry (pen) [84] | 20,101 |
| 2 | 24 | H | Liverpool | D 0-0 | 0-0 | 16 | | 42,573 |
| 3 | 27 | A | Arsenal | L 0-2 | 0-0 | — | | 38,010 |
| 4 | 30 | H | Leicester C | W 3-1 | 3-0 | 13 | Thatcher (og) [8], Angel 2 [10, 16] | 32,274 |
| 5 | Sept 14 | A | Manchester C | L 1-4 | 1-0 | 15 | Angel [31] | 46,687 |
| 6 | 20 | H | Charlton Ath | W 2-1 | 1-0 | 11 | Alpay [37], Samuel [55] | 31,410 |
| 7 | 27 | A | Chelsea | L 0-1 | 0-1 | 13 | | 41,182 |
| 8 | Oct 5 | H | Bolton W | D 1-1 | 0-0 | 15 | Angel [58] | 30,229 |
| 9 | 19 | A | Birmingham C | D 0-0 | 0-0 | 14 | | 29,546 |
| 10 | 25 | H | Everton | D 0-0 | 0-0 | 14 | | 36,146 |
| 11 | Nov 1 | A | Newcastle U | D 1-1 | 1-1 | 13 | Dublin [11] | 51,975 |
| 12 | 8 | H | Middlesbrough | L 0-2 | 0-1 | 16 | | 29,898 |
| 13 | 23 | A | Tottenham H | L 1-2 | 0-0 | 18 | Allback [66] | 33,140 |
| 14 | 29 | H | Southampton | W 1-0 | 1-0 | 17 | Dublin [45] | 31,285 |
| 15 | Dec 6 | A | Manchester U | L 0-4 | 0-2 | 18 | | 67,621 |
| 16 | 14 | H | Wolverhampton W | W 3-2 | 2-1 | 16 | Angel 2 [21, 23], Barry [48] | 36,964 |
| 17 | 20 | A | Blackburn R | W 2-0 | 0-0 | 13 | Moore S [62], Angel [75] | 20,722 |
| 18 | 26 | A | Leeds U | D 0-0 | 0-0 | 12 | | 38,513 |
| 19 | 28 | H | Fulham | W 3-0 | 1-0 | 10 | Angel [33], Vassell 2 [69, 82] | 35,617 |
| 20 | Jan 6 | H | Portsmouth | W 2-1 | 1-0 | — | Angel [22], Vassell [85] | 28,625 |
| 21 | 10 | A | Liverpool | L 0-1 | 0-1 | 10 | | 43,771 |
| 22 | 18 | H | Arsenal | L 0-2 | 0-1 | 12 | | 39,380 |
| 23 | 31 | A | Leicester C | W 5-0 | 0-0 | 11 | Vassell 2 [50, 60], Crouch 2 [57, 68], Dublin [64] | 31,056 |
| 24 | Feb 7 | H | Leeds U | W 2-0 | 1-0 | 8 | Angel (pen) [45], Johnsen [59] | 39,171 |
| 25 | 11 | A | Fulham | W 2-1 | 2-1 | — | Angel [13], Vassell [32] | 16,153 |
| 26 | 22 | H | Birmingham C | D 2-2 | 1-0 | 7 | Vassell [21], Hitzlsperger [47] | 40,061 |
| 27 | 28 | A | Everton | L 0-2 | 0-0 | 7 | | 39,353 |
| 28 | Mar 14 | A | Wolverhampton W | W 4-0 | 3-0 | 7 | Hitzlsperger [7], Mellberg [18], Angel 2 [24, 59] | 29,386 |
| 29 | 20 | H | Blackburn R | L 0-2 | 0-2 | 8 | | 37,532 |
| 30 | 27 | A | Charlton Ath | W 2-1 | 1-1 | 7 | Vassell [24], Samuel [54] | 26,238 |
| 31 | Apr 4 | H | Manchester C | D 1-1 | 1-0 | 7 | Angel [26] | 37,602 |
| 32 | 10 | A | Bolton W | D 2-2 | 1-0 | 7 | Crouch [18], Hendrie [53] | 26,374 |
| 33 | 12 | H | Chelsea | W 3-2 | 1-1 | 6 | Vassell (pen) [39], Hitzlsperger [49], Hendrie [52] | 41,112 |
| 34 | 18 | H | Newcastle U | D 0-0 | 0-0 | 6 | | 40,786 |
| 35 | 24 | A | Middlesbrough | W 2-1 | 1-1 | 6 | Barry [45], Crouch [89] | 31,243 |
| 36 | May 2 | H | Tottenham H | W 1-0 | 1-0 | 5 | Angel [5] | 42,573 |
| 37 | 8 | A | Southampton | D 1-1 | 1-1 | 5 | Angel (pen) [39] | 32,054 |
| 38 | 15 | H | Manchester U | L 0-2 | 0-2 | 6 | | 42,573 |

**Final League Position: 6**

### GOALSCORERS

*League (48):* Angel 16 (2 pens), Vassell 9 (1 pen), Crouch 4, Barry 3 (1 pen), Dublin 3, Hitzlsperger 3, Hendrie 2, Samuel 2, Allback 1, Alpay 1, Johnsen 1, Mellberg 1, Moore S 1, own goal 1.
*Carling Cup (15):* Angel 7 (1 pen), Hitzlsperger 2, McCann 2, Samuel 1, Vassell 1 (pen), Whittingham 1, own goal 1.
*FA Cup (1):* Barry 1.

| Sorensen T 38 | Delaney M 23 + 2 | Samuel J 38 | McCann G 28 | Johnsen R 21 + 2 | Alpay O 4 + 2 | Hendrie L 32 | Barry G 36 | Angel J 33 | Allback M 7 + 8 | Whittingham P 20 + 12 | Crouch P 6 + 10 | Hitzlsperger T 22 + 10 | Mellberg O 33 | Vassell D 26 + 6 | De la Cruz U 20 + 8 | Dublin D 12 + 11 | Kinsella M 2 | Hadji M — + 1 | Postma S — + 2 | Moore S 2 + 6 | Ridgewell L 5 + 6 | Solano N 10 | Moore L — + 7 | Match No. |
|---|---|---|---|---|---|---|---|---|---|---|---|---|---|---|---|---|---|---|---|---|---|---|---|---|
| 1 | 2 | 3 | 4 | 5 | 6 | 7 | 8■ | $9^{1}$ | 10 | $11^{2}$ | 12 | 13 | | | | | | | | | | | | 1 |
| 1 | 2 | 3 | 4 | 5 | | $7^{1}$ | 8 | $9^{2}$ | | 11 | | | 6 | 10 | 12 | 13 | | | | | | | | 2 |
| 1 | 2 | 3 | | 5 | | 8 | 6 | 9 | | 11 | | | 4 | 12 | 7 | | $10^{1}$ | | | | | | | 3 |
| 1 | 2 | 3 | 4 | $5^{1}$ | 12 | $7^{2}$ | | 9 | | 11 | | 8 | 6 | $10^{3}$ | 13 | 14 | | | | | | | | 4 |
| 1 | 2 | 3 | 4 | $5^{2}$ | 12 | 7 | | $9^{3}$ | 10 | 11 | | 8 | $6^{1}$ | | | 14 | | 13 | | | | | | 5 |
| 1 | 5 | 3 | 4 | | 6 | 7 | 8 | 9 | $10^{1}$ | 11 | | | | 12 | 2 | | | | | | | | | 6 |
| 1 | 2 | 3 | 4 | | 6 | 10 | 8 | 9 | | $11^{1}$ | | | | 12 | 7 | 5 | | | | | | | | 7 |
| $1^{G}$ | 2 | 3 | 4 | | 6 | 7 | 8 | 9 | 12 | $11^{1}$ | | | 5 | 10 | | | | | 15 | | | | | 8 |
| 1 | 2 | 3 | 4 | 5 | | $11^{1}$ | 8 | 9 | | 12 | | | 6 | 10 | 7 | | | | | | | | | 9 |
| 1 | 2 | 3 | 4 | | | | $8^{2}$ | 9 | | 11 | | 12 | 6 | 10 | 13 | 5 | $7^{1}$ | | | | | | | 10 |
| 1 | 2 | 3 | 4■ | 5 | | | 8 | $9^{1}$ | 12 | 11 | | 10 | | | $7^{2}$ | 6 | | | | 13 | | | | 11 |
| 1 | 2 | 3 | 4 | 5 | | $7^{1}$ | $8^{2}$ | 9 | $10^{3}$ | 11 | | 13 | 6 | 12 | | 14 | | | | | | | | 12 |
| 1 | $2^{1}$ | 3 | | 5 | | $7^{2}$ | 6 | | 9 | 11 | | 8 | 4 | 10 | | 12 | | | | 13 | | | | 13 |
| 1 | | 3 | 4 | | | $7^{3}$ | 8 | $9^{1}$ | 12 | $11^{2}$ | | 13 | 6 | 10 | 2 | 5 | | | | 14 | | | | 14 |
| 1 | 2 | 3 | 4 | | | 7 | 8 | $9^{1}$ | 12 | $11^{2}$ | | 13 | 6 | 10 | | 5 | | | | | | | | 15 |
| $1^{G}$ | 2 | 3 | 4 | | | | 8 | 9 | $11^{1}$ | | | 7 | 6 | 10 | 12 | 5 | | | 15 | | | | | 16 |
| 1 | 2 | 3 | 4 | | | $7^{1}$ | $8^{2}$ | 9 | | 11 | | 13 | 6 | 14 | 12 | 5 | | | | $10^{3}$ | | | | 17 |
| 1 | 2 | 3 | 4 | | | $7^{2}$ | 8 | 9 | | 11 | | 13 | 6 | 12 | | 5 | | | | $10^{1}$ | | | | 18 |
| 1 | $2^{3}$ | 3 | 4 | 5 | | $7^{1}$ | 8 | $9^{2}$ | | 11 | | 12 | 6 | 10 | | | | | | 13 | 14 | | | 19 |
| 1 | 2 | 3 | 4 | | | 7 | 8 | $9^{3}$ | | $11^{1}$ | 14 | 12 | 6 | $10^{2}$ | | 5 | | | | 13 | | | | 20 |
| 1 | 2 | 3 | $4^{1}$ | 13 | | $7^{2}$ | 8 | 9 | | 11 | | 12 | 6 | $10^{3}$ | | 5 | | | | 14 | | | | 21 |
| 1 | 2 | 3 | | 5 | | $7^{1}$ | $8^{3}$ | 9 | $10^{2}$ | 11 | 13 | 4 | 6 | | 12 | | | | | | 14 | | | 22 |
| 1 | $2^{3}$ | 3 | 4 | | | | 11 | | 13 | 12 | 9 | $8^{2}$ | 6 | $10^{1}$ | 14 | 5 | | | | | | 7 | | 23 |
| 1 | | 3 | | 12 | | $7^{3}$ | 11 | 9 | | | 13 | 8 | 6 | $10^{2}$ | 2 | $5^{1}$ | | | | | 14 | 4 | | 24 |
| 1 | $2^{1}$ | 3 | | 5 | | $7^{3}$ | $11^{2}$ | 9 | | 13 | | 8 | 6 | 10 | 12 | | | | | | 14 | 4 | | 25 |
| 1 | | 3 | | $5^{1}$ | | $7^{3}$ | $11^{2}$ | 9 | | 13 | | 8 | 6 | 10 | 2 | 12 | | | | | | 4 | 14 | 26 |
| 1 | | 3 | | 5 | | 7 | 11 | 9 | | | 12 | 8 | 6 | $10^{1}$ | 2 | | | | | | | 4 | | 27 |
| 1 | | 3 | | 5 | | $7^{1}$ | 11 | $9^{2}$ | | 12 | 13 | 8 | 6 | $10^{3}$ | 2 | | | | | | | 4 | 14 | 28 |
| 1 | | 3 | | | | 7 | $11^{1}$ | 9 | | 12 | 13 | 8 | 6 | $10^{2}$ | 2 | | | | | | 5 | $4^{3}$ | 14 | 29 |
| 1 | | 3 | 4 | 5 | | 7 | $11^{2}$ | 9 | | | | 8 | 6 | $10^{1}$ | 2 | | | | | | 13 | | 12 | 30 |
| 1 | | 3 | 4 | 5 | | 7 | 11 | $9^{1}$ | | | 12 | 8 | 6 | $10^{2}$ | 2 | | | | | | | | 13 | 31 |
| 1 | | 3 | 4 | | | $7^{1}$ | 11 | | | 12 | $9^{2}$ | 8 | 6 | $10^{3}$ | 2 | 13 | | | | | 5 | | 14 | 32 |
| 1 | | 3 | 4 | 5 | | $7^{1}$ | 11 | | | 12 | $9^{3}$ | 8 | 6 | $10^{2}$ | 2 | 13 | | | | | | | 14 | 33 |
| 1 | | 3 | | $5^{3}$ | | 7 | 11 | | 13 | 12 | $9^{2}$ | 8 | 6 | 10 | 2 | | | | | | 14 | $4^{1}$ | | 34 |
| 1 | 14 | 3 | 4 | 5 | | | $11^{1}$ | $9^{2}$ | | 12 | 13 | 8 | 6 | $10^{3}$ | 2 | | | | | | | 7■ | | 35 |
| 1 | 12 | 3 | 4 | | | | 11 | $9^{2}$ | 13 | | $10^{3}$ | 8 | 6 | | 2 | 14 | | | | | 5 | $7^{1}$ | | 36 |
| 1 | | 3 | 4 | 6 | | $7^{1}$ | 11 | $9^{2}$ | | 12 | 14 | 8 | | $10^{3}$ | 2 | 13 | | | | | 5 | | | 37 |
| 1 | | 3 | 4 | | | $7^{1}$ | $11^{3}$ | 9 | 13 | 12 | $10^{2}$ | 8 | 6 | | 2 | 14 | | | | | 5 | | | 38 |

**Carling Cup**

| | | | |
|---|---|---|---|
| Second Round | Wycombe W | (a) | 5-0 |
| Third Round | Leicester C | (h) | 1-0 |
| Fourth Round | Crystal Palace | (h) | 3-0 |
| Fifth Round | Chelsea | (h) | 2-1 |
| Semi-Final | Bolton W | (a) | 2-5 |
| | | (h) | 2-0 |

**FA Cup**

| | | | |
|---|---|---|---|
| Third Round | Manchester U | (h) | 1-2 |

# BARNSLEY — FL Championship 1

### FOUNDATION

Many clubs owe their inception to the church and Barnsley are among them, for they were formed in 1887 by the Rev. T. T. Preedy, curate of Barnsley St Peter's and went under that name until it was dropped in 1897 a year before being admitted to the Second Division of the Football League.

***Oakwell Stadium, Barnsley S71 1ET.***

***Telephone:*** (01226) 211 211.

***Fax:*** (01226) 211 444.

***Ticket Office:*** (01226) 211 211

***Website:*** www.barnsleyfc.co.uk

***Email:*** thereds@barnsleyfc.co.uk

***Ground Capacity:*** 23,009.

***Record Attendance:*** 40,255 v Stoke C, FA Cup 5th rd, 15 February 1936.

***Pitch Measurements:*** 110yd × 75yd.

***Chairman:*** Peter Ridsdale.

***Manager:*** Paul Hart.

***First Team Coach:*** Colin Walker.

***Physio:*** Robert Magnusson.

***Secretary:*** Chris Patzelt.

***Sales and Marketing Manager:*** Graham Barlow.

***Colours:*** Red shirts, white shorts, red stockings.

***Change Colours:*** All black.

***Year Formed:*** 1887.

***Turned Professional:*** 1888.

***Ltd Co.:*** 1899.

***Previous Name:*** 1887, Barnsley St Peter's; 1897, Barnsley.

***Club Nickname:*** 'The Tykes', 'Reds' or 'Colliers'.

***First Football League Game:*** 1 September 1898, Division 2, v Lincoln C (a) L 0–1 – Fawcett; McArtney, Nixon; King, Burleigh, Porteous; Davis, Lees, Murray, McCullough, McGee.

***Record League Victory:*** 9–0 v Loughborough T, Division 2, 28 January 1899 – Greaves; McArtney, Nixon; Porteous, Burleigh, Howard; Davis (4), Hepworth (1), Lees (1), McCullough (1), Jones (2). 9–0 v Accrington S, Division 3 (N), 3 February 1934 – Ellis; Cookson, Shotton; Harper, Henderson, Whitworth; Spence (2), Smith (1), Blight (4), Andrews (1), Ashton (1).

***Record Cup Victory:*** 6–0 v Blackpool, FA Cup 1st rd replay, 20 January 1910 – Mearns; Downs, Ness; Glendinning, Boyle (1), Utley; Bartrop, Gadsby (1), Lillycrop (2), Tufnell (2), Forman. 6–0 v Peterborough U, League Cup 1st rd 2nd leg, 15 September 1981 – Horn; Joyce, Chambers, Glavin (2), Banks, McCarthy, Evans, Parker (2), Aylott (1), McHale, Barrowclough (1).

### HONOURS

*Football League:* Division 1 – Runners-up 1996–97; Division 3 (N) – Champions 1933–34, 1938–39, 1954–55; Runners-up 1953–54; Division 3 – Runners-up 1980–81; Division 4 – Runners-up 1967–68; Promoted 1978–79.

*FA Cup:* Winners 1912; Runners-up 1910.

*Football League Cup:* best season: 5th rd, 1982.

### SKY SPORTS FACT FILE

Despite finishing only 11th in Division Two in 1926–27, Barnsley scored in all but three of their 42 League games. That season Frank Eaton became their first player to score as many as five goals in one League match.

***Record Defeat:*** 0–9 v Notts Co, Division 2, 19 November 1927.

***Most League Points (2 for a win):*** 67, Division 3 (N), 1938–39.

***Most League Points (3 for a win):*** 82, Division 1, 1999–2000.

***Most League Goals:*** 118, Division 3 (N), 1933–34.

***Highest League Scorer in Season:*** Cecil McCormack, 33, Division 2, 1950–51.

***Most League Goals in Total Aggregate:*** Ernest Hine, 123, 1921–26 and 1934–38.

***Most League Goals in One Match:*** 5, Frank Eaton v South Shields, Division 3N, 9 April 1927; 5, Peter Cunningham v Darlington, Division 3N, 4 February 1933; 5, Beau Asquith v Darlington, Division 3N, 12 November 1938; 5, Cecil McCormack v Luton T, Division 2, 9 September 1950.

***Most Capped Player:*** Gerry Taggart, 35 (50), Northern Ireland.

***Most League Appearances:*** Barry Murphy, 514, 1962–78.

***Youngest League Player:*** Alan Ogley, 16 years 226 days v Bristol R, 18 September 1962.

***Record Transfer Fee Received:*** £4,250,000 from Blackburn R for Ashley Ward, December 1998.

***Record Transfer Fee Paid:*** £1,500,000 to Partizan Belgrade for Georgi Hristov, July 1997.

***Football League Record:*** 1898 Elected to Division 2; 1932–34 Division 3 (N); 1934–38 Division 2; 1938–39 Division 3 (N); 1946–53 Division 2; 1953–55 Division 3 (N); 1955–59 Division 2; 1959–65 Division 3; 1965–68 Division 4; 1968–72 Division 3; 1972–79 Division 4; 1979–81 Division 3; 1981–92 Division 2; 1992–97 Division 1; 1997–98 FA Premier League; 1998–2002 Division 1; 2002–04 Division 2; 2004– FL1.

## MANAGERS

Arthur Fairclough 1898–1901 *(Secretary-Manager)*
John McCartney 1901–04 *(Secretary-Manager)*
Arthur Fairclough 1904–12
John Hastie 1912–14
Percy Lewis 1914–19
Peter Sant 1919–26
John Commins 1926–29
Arthur Fairclough 1929–30
Brough Fletcher 1930–37
Angus Seed 1937–53
Tim Ward 1953–60
Johnny Steele 1960–71 *(continued as General Manager)*
John McSeveney 1971–72
Johnny Steele *(General Manager)* 1972–73
Jim Iley 1973–78
Allan Clarke 1978–80
Norman Hunter 1980–84
Bobby Collins 1984–85
Allan Clarke 1985–89
Mel Machin 1989–93
Viv Anderson 1993–94
Danny Wilson 1994–98
John Hendrie 1998–99
Dave Bassett 1999–2000
Nigel Spackman 2001
Steve Parkin 2001–02
Glyn Hodges 2002–03
Gudjon Thordarson 2003–04
Paul Hart March 2004–

## LATEST SEQUENCES

***Longest Sequence of League Wins:*** 10, 5.3.1955 – 23.4.1955.

***Longest Sequence of League Defeats:*** 9, 14.3.1953 – 25.4.1953.

***Longest Sequence of League Draws:*** 7, 28.3.1911 – 22.4.1911.

***Longest Sequence of Unbeaten League Matches:*** 21, 1.1.1934 – 5.5.1934.

***Longest Sequence Without a League Win:*** 26, 13.12.1952 – 26.8.1953.

***Successive Scoring Runs:*** 44 from 2.10.1926.

***Successive Non-scoring Runs:*** 6 from 7.10.1899.

## TEN YEAR LEAGUE RECORD

| | | *P* | *W* | *D* | *L* | *F* | *A* | *Pts* | *Pos* |
|---|---|---|---|---|---|---|---|---|---|
| 1994-95 | Div 1 | 46 | 20 | 12 | 14 | 63 | 52 | 72 | 6 |
| 1995-96 | Div 1 | 46 | 14 | 18 | 14 | 60 | 66 | 60 | 10 |
| 1996-97 | Div 1 | 46 | 22 | 14 | 10 | 76 | 55 | 80 | 2 |
| 1997-98 | PR Lge | 38 | 10 | 5 | 23 | 37 | 82 | 35 | 19 |
| 1998-99 | Div 1 | 46 | 14 | 17 | 15 | 59 | 56 | 59 | 13 |
| 1999-2000 | Div 1 | 46 | 24 | 10 | 12 | 88 | 67 | 82 | 4 |
| 2000-01 | Div 1 | 46 | 15 | 9 | 22 | 49 | 62 | 54 | 16 |
| 2001-02 | Div 1 | 46 | 11 | 15 | 20 | 59 | 86 | 48 | 23 |
| 2002-03 | Div 2 | 46 | 13 | 13 | 20 | 51 | 64 | 52 | 19 |
| 2003-04 | Div 2 | 46 | 15 | 17 | 14 | 54 | 58 | 62 | 12 |

## DID YOU KNOW ?

Goalkeeper Norman Rimmington celebrated his 80th birthday on 29 November 2003. Barnsley debut 1946 after wartime appearances. Later youth team coach, groundsman and even physio at the club after five years with the then Hartlepools United.

## BARNSLEY 2003–04 LEAGUE RECORD

| Match No. | Date | Venue | Opponents | Result | | H/T Score | Lg. Pos. | Goalscorers | Attendance |
|---|---|---|---|---|---|---|---|---|---|
| 1 | Aug 9 | H | Colchester U | W | 1-0 | 0-0 | — | Gorre (pen) [47] | 8450 |
| 2 | 16 | A | Bournemouth | D | 2-2 | 1-2 | 7 | Ireland [38], Gorre [57] | 5960 |
| 3 | 23 | H | Brighton & HA | W | 1-0 | 0-0 | 3 | Betsy [68] | 7918 |
| 4 | 25 | A | Blackpool | W | 2-0 | 1-0 | 1 | Fallon [29], Lumsdon [51] | 6039 |
| 5 | 30 | H | Notts Co | D | 1-1 | 0-0 | 2 | Gorre [47] | 9087 |
| 6 | Sept 6 | A | Chesterfield | W | 2-0 | 1-0 | 1 | Kay [10], Ireland [67] | 5605 |
| 7 | 13 | A | Port Vale | L | 1-3 | 1-1 | 3 | Fallon [8] | 7809 |
| 8 | 16 | H | Oldham Ath | D | 1-1 | 0-0 | — | Lumsdon [61] | 10,102 |
| 9 | 20 | H | Swindon T | D | 1-1 | 0-1 | 5 | Fallon [77] | 9006 |
| 10 | 27 | A | Plymouth Arg | L | 0-2 | 0-1 | 8 | | 8695 |
| 11 | 30 | A | QPR | L | 0-4 | 0-0 | — | | 11,854 |
| 12 | Oct 4 | H | Rushden & D | W | 2-0 | 1-0 | 8 | Betsy [32], Gorre [57] | 8461 |
| 13 | 18 | A | Wycombe W | W | 2-1 | 2-0 | 8 | Rankin 2 [28, 33] | 4446 |
| 14 | 21 | A | Peterborough U | W | 3-2 | 1-2 | — | Betsy [35], Rankin [47], Carson [63] | 3909 |
| 15 | 25 | H | Grimsby T | D | 0-0 | 0-0 | 5 | | 10,092 |
| 16 | 28 | H | Wrexham | W | 2-1 | 1-0 | — | Gorre [24], Rankin [64] | 8916 |
| 17 | Nov 1 | A | Brentford | L | 1-2 | 0-0 | 2 | Fallon [90] | 4789 |
| 18 | 15 | H | Tranmere R | W | 2-0 | 1-0 | 2 | Rankin [23], Gorre (pen) [64] | 9663 |
| 19 | 22 | A | Bristol C | L | 1-2 | 0-1 | 3 | Burns [51] | 10,031 |
| 20 | 29 | H | Stockport Co | D | 3-3 | 1-2 | 4 | Betsy 2 [5, 76], Gorre [68] | 9047 |
| 21 | Dec 13 | H | Sheffield W | D | 1-1 | 1-1 | 4 | Kay [26] | 20,438 |
| 22 | 20 | A | Luton T | W | 1-0 | 0-0 | 3 | Kay [90] | 6162 |
| 23 | 26 | A | Hartlepool U | W | 2-1 | 1-1 | 3 | Betsy 2 [45, 69] | 6520 |
| 24 | 28 | H | Chesterfield | L | 0-1 | 0-0 | 4 | | 11,664 |
| 25 | Jan 10 | A | Colchester U | D | 1-1 | 0-1 | 4 | Betsy [79] | 3507 |
| 26 | 17 | H | Bournemouth | D | 1-1 | 0-1 | 5 | Lumsdon [80] | 7934 |
| 27 | 24 | A | Brighton & HA | L | 0-1 | 0-1 | 8 | | 6033 |
| 28 | 27 | H | Blackpool | W | 3-0 | 1-0 | — | Nardiello 2 [11, 61], Stallard [54] | 7918 |
| 29 | 31 | A | Notts Co | D | 1-1 | 0-1 | 4 | Betsy (pen) [87] | 7355 |
| 30 | Feb 7 | H | Hartlepool U | D | 2-2 | 0-1 | 5 | Nardiello [56], Hayward [80] | 9220 |
| 31 | 14 | A | Wrexham | L | 0-1 | 0-1 | 7 | | 4086 |
| 32 | 21 | H | Wycombe W | D | 0-0 | 0-0 | 8 | | 8507 |
| 33 | 28 | A | Grimsby T | L | 1-6 | 0-4 | 9 | Nardiello [47] | 5603 |
| 34 | Mar 2 | H | Peterborough U | L | 0-1 | 0-0 | — | | 7547 |
| 35 | 6 | H | Luton T | D | 0-0 | 0-0 | 11 | | 8656 |
| 36 | 13 | A | Sheffield W | L | 1-2 | 0-1 | 11 | Williams (pen) [74] | 25,664 |
| 37 | 16 | A | Oldham Ath | D | 1-1 | 1-0 | — | Nardiello [34] | 5837 |
| 38 | 20 | H | Port Vale | D | 0-0 | 0-0 | 11 | | 8267 |
| 39 | 27 | A | Swindon T | D | 1-1 | 1-1 | 11 | Nardiello (pen) [34] | 7305 |
| 40 | Apr 3 | H | Plymouth Arg | W | 1-0 | 0-0 | 10 | Birch [81] | 9266 |
| 41 | 10 | A | Rushden & D | W | 3-2 | 3-1 | 10 | Murphy [10], Betsy [41], Neil [45] | 4063 |
| 42 | 12 | H | QPR | D | 3-3 | 1-1 | 10 | Ireland [22], Nardiello [85], Murphy [89] | 10,402 |
| 43 | 17 | H | Brentford | L | 0-2 | 0-1 | 12 | | 9824 |
| 44 | 24 | A | Tranmere R | L | 0-2 | 0-0 | 13 | | 7612 |
| 45 | May 2 | H | Bristol C | L | 0-1 | 0-1 | 13 | | 10,865 |
| 46 | 8 | A | Stockport Co | W | 3-2 | 2-0 | 12 | Wroe [10], Birch [16], Neil [72] | 6581 |

**Final League Position: 12**

### GOALSCORERS

*League (54):* Betsy 10 (1 pen), Gorre 7 (2 pens), Nardiello 7 (1 pen), Rankin 5, Fallon 4, Ireland 3, Kay 3, Lumsdon 3, Birch 2, Murphy 2, Neil 2, Burns 1, Carson 1, Hayward 1, Stallard 1, Williams 1 (pen), Wroe 1.
*Carling Cup (1):* Gorre 1 (pen).
*FA Cup (4):* Betsy 1, Kay 1, Monk 1, Rankin 1.
*LDV Vans Trophy (0).*

| Ilic S 25 / Ward G 1 | O'Callaghan B 25 + 4 | Gallimore T 20 / Baker T — + 1 | Kay A 39 + 4 | Handyside P 28 | Ireland C 43 | Betsy K 42 + 3 | Hayward S 24 + 8 | Fallon R 12 + 4 | Gorre D 16 + 3 | Mulligan D 2 + 2 | Rankin I 9 + 11 | Lumsdon C 17 + 11 | Gibbs P — + 3 | Austin N 32 + 5 | Neil A 17 + 14 | Crooks L 20 + 3 | Carson S 9 + 2 | Burns J 16 + 6 | Walters J 7 + 1 | Monk G 14 + 3 | Warhurst P 3 + 1 | Caig T 3 | Stallard M 10 | Nardiello D 14 + 2 | Beresford M 14 | Boulding M 5 + 1 | Rocastle C 4 + 1 | Davies A 1 + 3 | Williams R 3 + 1 | Atkinson R — + 1 | Murphy D 10 | Shuker C 9 | Birch G 8 | Alcock D — + 1 | Turnbull R 3 | Tonge D — + 1 | Wroe N 1 + 1 | *Match No.* |
|---|---|---|---|---|---|---|---|---|---|---|---|---|---|---|---|---|---|---|---|---|---|---|---|---|---|---|---|---|---|---|---|---|---|---|---|---|---|---|
| 1 | 2 | 3 | 4 | 5 | 6 | 7 | 8 | $9^{1}$ | $10^{2}$ | $11^{3}$ | 12 | 13 | 14 | | | | | | | | | | | | | | | | | | | | | | | | | 1 |
| 1 | 11 | 3 | 4 | 5 | 6 | 7 | | $9^{1}$ | $10^{2}$ | 14 | 12 | 8 | | $2^{3}$ | 13 | | | | | | | | | | | | | | | | | | | | | | | 2 |
| 1 | 2 | 3 | 4 | 5 | 6 | 7 | 12 | $9^{2}$ | $10^{3}$ | 13 | | 8▮ | 14 | $11^{1}$ | | | | | | | | | | | | | | | | | | | | | | | | 3 |
| 1 | 7 | 3 | 4 | 5 | 6 | 11 | | $9^{1}$ | 10 | | 12 | 8 | | | | 2 | | | | | | | | | | | | | | | | | | | | | | 4 |
| 1 | 2 | 3 | 4 | 5 | 6 | 7 | | 9 | 10 | | | $8^{1}$ | 12 | | | 11 | | | | | | | | | | | | | | | | | | | | | | 5 |
| 1 | 2 | 3 | 4▮ | 5 | 6 | 7 | 12 | $9^{2}$ | $10^{3}$ | | 13 | | | 14 | $8^{1}$ | 11 | | | | | | | | | | | | | | | | | | | | | | 6 |
| 1 | $4^{3}$ | 3 | 8 | 5 | 6 | 10 | 12 | $9^{1}$ | 13 | | 14 | 7 | | 2 | | $11^{2}$ | | | | | | | | | | | | | | | | | | | | | | 7 |
| 1 | | 3 | 4 | 5 | 6 | 7 | 8 | 9 | 10 | | | 11 | | | | 2 | | | | | | | | | | | | | | | | | | | | | | 8 |
| 1 | 4 | 3 | | 5 | 6 | 7 | $8^{1}$ | 9 | 10 | | | 11 | | 12 | | 2 | | | | | | | | | | | | | | | | | | | | | | 9 |
| 1 | $4^{1}$ | 3 | 12 | $5^{2}$ | 6 | 7 | | 9 | 10 | | | 11 | | 8 | | 2 | 13 | | | | | | | | | | | | | | | | | | | | | 10 |
| 1 | 12 | 3 | 4 | 5 | 6 | 13 | | 9 | 14 | $11^{2}$ | | 7 | | $8^{1}$ | $10^{3}$ | 2 | | | | | | | | | | | | | | | | | | | | | | 11 |
| 1 | 4 | 3 | 12 | 5 | 6 | 7 | $8^{1}$ | $9^{2}$ | $10^{3}$ | | | 11 | | 14 | 13 | 2 | | | | | | | | | | | | | | | | | | | | | | 12 |
| 1 | 10 | 3 | 8 | | 5 | 7 | | 12 | | | $9^{1}$ | $11^{3}$ | | 2 | 13 | 6 | $4^{2}$ | 14 | | | | | | | | | | | | | | | | | | | | 13 |
| 1 | 2 | 3 | $4^{3}$ | $5^{1}$ | 6 | 7 | | | | | 9 | 11 | | 13 | 12 | 8 | $10^{2}$ | 14 | | | | | | | | | | | | | | | | | | | | 14 |
| 1 | 2 | 3 | $4^{2}$ | 5 | 6 | 7 | 12 | 13 | | | 9 | | | | | 11 | $10^{1}$ | 8 | | | | | | | | | | | | | | | | | | | | 15 |
| 1 | 2 | 3 | | 5 | 6 | 7 | $8^{3}$ | 12 | $10^{1}$ | | $9^{2}$ | | | 14 | 13 | 4 | 11 | | | | | | | | | | | | | | | | | | | | | 16 |
| 1 | 2 | $3^{2}$ | 12 | 5 | 6 | 10 | 8 | 13 | | | 9 | | | 7 | | $4^{1}$ | 11 | | | | | | | | | | | | | | | | | | | | | 17 |
| 1 | 2 | 3 | | | 6 | 7 | 8 | | $11^{1}$ | | $9^{2}$ | 12 | | 5 | 13 | | | 4 | 10 | | | | | | | | | | | | | | | | | | | 18 |
| 1 | 5 | 3 | 12 | | 6 | 7 | 8 | | $11^{2}$ | | 9 | | | 2 | | | | 4 | $10^{1}$ | 13 | | | | | | | | | | | | | | | | | | 19 |
| 1 | 2 | | 4 | | 6 | 9 | 8 | | 11 | | 12 | | | $3^{1}$ | | | | 7 | 10 | 5 | | | | | | | | | | | | | | | | | | 20 |
| 1 | 2 | $3^{1}$ | 7 | | 6 | 9 | 12 | | | | $11^{3}$ | 13 | | | | | 14 | $4^{2}$ | 10 | 5 | 8▮ | | | | | | | | | | | | | | | | | 21 |
| 1 | $2^{2}$ | | 7 | | 6 | 9 | 8 | | | | 14 | | | 3 | 12 | | $11^{1}$ | 4 | $10^{3}$ | 5 | 13 | | | | | | | | | | | | | | | | | 22 |
| 1 | | | 7 | | 6 | 9 | $8^{1}$ | | | | | 12 | | 3 | 13 | | 11 | 4 | $10^{2}$ | 5 | 2 | | | | | | | | | | | | | | | | | 23 |
| 1 | $2^{1}$ | | $7^{2}$ | | 6 | 9 | $8^{3}$ | | | | 12 | 14 | | 3 | 13 | | 11 | 4 | 10 | 5 | | | | | | | | | | | | | | | | | | 24 |
| 1 | $2^{3}$ | | 7 | | 6 | 9 | | | | | $10^{2}$ | | | 3 | 12 | 13 | $11^{1}$ | 8 | 14 | 5 | 4 | | | | | | | | | | | | | | | | | 25 |
| | 12 | | 10 | $4^{2}$ | 6 | 9 | | | | | 13 | 8 | | $2^{1}$ | 3 | 11 | | 7 | | 5 | | 1 | | | | | | | | | | | | | | | | 26 |
| | 12 | | 8 | 4 | $6^{1}$ | 9 | | | | | | $11^{2}$ | | 3 | 13 | 7 | | 2 | | 5 | | 1 | 10 | | | | | | | | | | | | | | | 27 |
| | 12 | | 3 | 4 | 6 | 9 | | | $11^{2}$ | | | 13 | | 2 | | $7^{1}$ | | 14 | | 5 | | 1 | 10 | $8^{3}$ | | | | | | | | | | | | | | 28 |
| | | | $3^{3}$ | 4 | 6 | 9 | | | | | 13 | 11 | | 2 | 12 | $7^{2}$ | | 14 | | $5^{1}$ | | | 10 | 8 | 1 | | | | | | | | | | | | | 29 |
| | 6 | | 2 | | | 9 | 13 | | | | 12 | 11▮ | | $3^{1}$ | 7 | $4^{2}$ | | | | 5 | | | 10 | 8 | 1 | | | | | | | | | | | | | 30 |
| | $2^{1}$ | | $3^{2}$ | 4 | 6 | | 12 | | | | | | | | 7 | | | | | 5 | | | 10 | 8 | 1 | 9 | 11 | 13 | | | | | | | | | | 31 |
| | | | $2^{3}$ | 4 | 6 | 7 | 12 | | 13 | | | | | | $3^{1}$ | | | | | 5 | | | 10 | 8 | 1 | $9^{2}$ | 11 | 14 | | | | | | | | | | 32 |
| | | | 2 | 4 | 6▮ | 9 | | | | | | | | 3 | 12 | | | | | $5^{1}$ | | | 10 | 8 | 1 | 13 | $11^{2}$ | 7 | | | | | | | | | | 33 |
| | | | 3 | 5 | 6 | 7 | $4^{1}$ | | | | | | | 2 | 13 | | | | | | | | 10 | 8 | 1 | 9 | $11^{2}$ | | 12 | | | | | | | | | 34 |
| | | | 6 | 5 | | 7 | 4 | | | | | | | 2 | $11^{1}$ | | | | | | | | 10 | 8 | 1 | 9 | | 12 | $3^{2}$ | 13 | | | | | | | | 35 |
| | | | $11^{1}$ | 5 | | 7 | 4 | | | | | 12 | | 2 | 10 | | | 13 | | | | | | $8^{2}$ | 1 | 9 | 14 | | $3^{3}$ | | 6 | | | | | | | 36 |
| | | | 7 | 5 | 6 | 10 | $4^{1}$ | | | | | 12 | | 2 | 11 | | | 13 | | | | | $9^{2}$ | 8 | 1 | | | | | | 3 | | | | | | | 37 |
| | | | 5 | | 6 | 9 | 4 | | | | | | | 2 | 11 | | | 7 | | | | | | 8 | 1 | | | | | | 3 | 10 | | | | | | 38 |
| | | | 3 | | 5 | 12 | 4 | | | | | 13 | | 2 | $11^{2}$ | | | 7 | | | | | | 8 | 1 | | | | | | 6 | $9^{1}$ | 10 | | | | | 39 |
| | | | 6 | | 5 | 9 | 4 | | | | | 15 | | 2 | 8 | | | $7^{1}$ | | | | | | 12 | $1^{G}$ | | | | | | 3 | 11 | 10 | | | | | 40 |
| | | | 6 | | 5 | 9 | 4 | | | | | | | 2 | 8 | | | 7 | | | | | | | 1 | | | | | | 3 | 11 | 10 | | | | | 41 |
| | | | 6 | | 5 | 9 | 4 | | | | | | | 2 | $8^{1}$ | | | 7 | | | | | | 12 | $1^{G}$ | | | | | | 3 | 11 | 10 | 15 | | | | 42 |
| | | | 2 | $5^{3}$ | 6 | $9^{1}$ | 4 | | | | | $7^{2}$ | | 3 | | 12 | | | | | | | | 8 | | | | | | | | 11 | 10 | | 1 | 14 | 13 | 43 |
| | | | 6 | | $5^{2}$ | 9 | $4^{1}$ | | | | | 14 | | 2 | 7 | 12 | | | | 13 | | | | 8 | | | | | | | 3 | 11 | $10^{3}$ | | 1 | | | 44 |
| 1 | 2 | 13 | 6▮ | | 5 | 9 | 4 | | $8^{2}$ | | | | | | 7 | | | | | 12 | | | | | | | | | | | 3 | $11^{1}$ | 10 | | | | | 45 |
| | | | 6 | | 5 | 12 | | | | | | | | 2 | 7 | 4 | | | | | | | | | | | | | 9 | | $3^{1}$ | 11 | 10 | | 1 | | 8 | 46 |

**Carling Cup**

| | | | |
|---|---|---|---|
| First Round | Blackpool | (h) | 1-2 |

**LDV Vans Trophy**

| | | | |
|---|---|---|---|
| First Round | Notts Co | (a) | 0-0 |
| Second Round | Sheffield W | (a) | 0-1 |

**FA Cup**

| | | | |
|---|---|---|---|
| First Round | York C | (a) | 2-1 |
| Second Round | Bristol C | (a) | 0-0 |
| | | (h) | 2-1 |
| Third Round | Scunthorpe U | (h) | 0-0 |
| | | (a) | 0-2 |

# BIRMINGHAM CITY

## FA Premiership

### FOUNDATION

In 1875, cricketing enthusiasts who were largely members of Trinity Church, Bordesley, determined to continue their sporting relationships throughout the year by forming a football club which they called Small Heath Alliance. For their earliest games played on waste land in Arthur Street, the team included three Edden brothers and two James brothers.

***St Andrews Stadium, Birmingham B9 4NH.***
***Telephone:*** (0121) 772 0101.
***Fax:*** (0121) 766 7866.
***Ticket Office:*** (0121) 202 5333.
***Website:*** www.bcfc.com
***Email:*** reception@bcfc.com
***Ground Capacity:*** 29,949.
***Record Attendance:*** 66,844 v Everton, FA Cup 5th rd, 11 February 1939.
***Pitch Measurements:*** 110yd × 74yd.
***Chairman:*** David Gold.
***Vice-chairman:*** Jack Wiseman.
***Managing Director:*** Karren Brady.
***Secretary:*** Julia Shelton.
***Manager:*** Steve Bruce.
***Assistant Manager:*** Eric Black.
***Physio:*** Steve Brannigan.
***Colours:*** Blue shirts, white shorts, blue stockings.
***Change Colours:*** All red.
***Year Formed:*** 1875.
***Turned Professional:*** 1885.
***Ltd Co.:*** 1888.
***Previous Names:*** 1875, Small Heath Alliance; 1888, dropped 'Alliance'; 1905, Birmingham; 1945, Birmingham City.
***Club Nickname:*** 'Blues'.
***Previous Grounds:*** 1875, waste ground near Arthur St; 1877, Muntz St, Small Heath; 1906, St Andrews.
***First Football League game:*** 3 September 1892, Division 2, v Burslem Port Vale (h) W 5–1 – Charsley; Bayley, Speller; Ollis, Jenkyns, Devey; Hallam (1), Edwards (1), Short (1), Wheldon (2), Hands.
***Record League Victory:*** 12–0 v Walsall T Swifts, Division 2, 17 December 1892 – Charsley; Bayley, Jones; Ollis, Jenkyns, Devey; Hallam (2), Walton (3), Mobley (3), Wheldon (2), Hands (2). 12–0 v Doncaster R, Division 2, 11 April 1903 – Dorrington; Goldie, Wassell; Beer, Dougherty (1), Howard; Athersmith (1), Leonard (3), McRoberts (1), Wilcox (4), Field (1). Aston, (1 og).

### HONOURS

*Football League:* Promoted from Division 1 (play offs) 2001–02; Division 2 – Champions 1892–93, 1920–21, 1947–48, 1954–55, 1994–95; Runners-up 1893–94, 1900–01, 1902–03, 1971–72, 1984–85; Division 3 Runners-up 1991–92.
*FA Cup:* Runners-up 1931, 1956.
*Football League Cup:* Winners 1963; Runners-up 2001.
*Leyland Daf Cup:* Winners 1991.
*Auto Windscreens Shield:* Winners 1995.
***European Competitions:*** *European Fairs Cup:* 1955–58, 1958–60 (runners-up), 1960–61 (runners-up), 1961–62.

### SKY SPORTS FACT FILE

Trevor Francis scored 16 times in only 22 League appearances during his first season with Birmingham City in 1970–71 including a spell of 13 in eight games, one of which gave him four goals against Bolton Wanderers when still only aged 16.

***Record Cup Victory:*** 9–2 v Burton W, FA Cup 1st rd, 31 October 1885 – Hedges; Jones, Evetts (1); F. James, Felton, A. James (1); Davenport (2), Stanley (4), Simms, Figures, Morris (1).

***Record Defeat:*** 1–9 v Sheffield W, Division 1, 13 December 1930. 1–9 v Blackburn R, Division 1, 5 January 1895.

***Most League Points (2 for a win):*** 59, Division 2, 1947–48.

***Most League Points (3 for a win):*** 89, Division 2, 1994–95.

***Most League Goals:*** 103, Division 2, 1893–94 (only 28 games).

***Highest League Scorer in Season:*** Joe Bradford, 29, Division 1, 1927–28.

***Most League Goals in Total Aggregate:*** Joe Bradford, 249, 1920–35.

***Most League Goals in One Match:*** 5, Walter Abbott v Darwen, Division 2, 26 November, 1898; 5, John McMillan v Blackpool, Division 2, 2 March 1901; 5, James Windridge v Glossop, Division 2, 23 January 1915.

***Most Capped Player:*** Malcolm Page, 28, Wales.

***Most League Appearances:*** Frank Womack, 491, 1908–28.

***Youngest League Player:*** Trevor Francis, 16 years 7 months v Cardiff C, 5 September 1970.

***Record Transfer Fee Received:*** £3,500,000 from Leicester C for Gary Rowett, July 2000.

***Record Transfer Fee Paid:*** £4,375,000 to Blackburn R for David Dunn, July 2003.

***Football League Record:*** 1892 elected to Division 2; 1894–96 Division 1; 1896–1901 Division 2; 1901–02 Division 1; 1902–03 Division 2; 1903–08 Division 1; 1908–21 Division 2; 1921–39 Division 1; 1946–48 Division 2; 1948–50 Division 1; 1950–55 Division 2; 1955–65 Division 1; 1965–72 Division 2; 1972–79 Division 1; 1979–80 Division 2; 1980–84 Division 1; 1984–85 Division 2; 1985–86 Division 1; 1986–89 Division 2; 1989–92 Division 3; 1992–94 Division 1; 1994–95 Division 2; 1995–2002 Division 1; 2002– FA Premier League.

## MANAGERS

Alfred Jones 1892–1908
*(Secretary-Manager)*
Alec Watson 1908–10
Bob McRoberts 1910–15
Frank Richards 1915–23
Billy Beer 1923–27
Leslie Knighton 1928–33
George Liddell 1933–39
Harry Storer 1945–48
Bob Brocklebank 1949–54
Arthur Turner 1954–58
Pat Beasley 1959–60
Gil Merrick 1960–64
Joe Mallett 1965
Stan Cullis 1965–70
Fred Goodwin 1970–75
Willie Bell 1975–77
Jim Smith 1978–82
Ron Saunders 1982–86
John Bond 1986–87
Garry Pendrey 1987–89
Dave Mackay 1989–91
Lou Macari 1991
Terry Cooper 1991–93
Barry Fry 1993–96
Trevor Francis 1996–2001
Steve Bruce December 2001–

## LATEST SEQUENCES

***Longest Sequence of League Wins:*** 13, 17.12.1892 – 16.9.1893.

***Longest Sequence of League Defeats:*** 8, 28.9.1985 – 23.11.1985.

***Longest Sequence of League Draws:*** 8, 18.9.1990 – 23.10.1990.

***Longest Sequence of Unbeaten League Matches:*** 20, 3.9.1994 – 2.1.1995.

***Longest Sequence Without a League Win:*** 17, 28.9.1985 – 18.1.1986.

***Successive Scoring Runs:*** 24 from 24.9.1892.

***Successive Non-scoring Runs:*** 6 from 1.10.1949.

## TEN YEAR LEAGUE RECORD

| | | P | W | D | L | F | A | Pts | Pos |
|---|---|---|---|---|---|---|---|---|---|
| 1994-95 | Div 2 | 46 | 25 | 14 | 7 | 84 | 37 | 89 | 1 |
| 1995-96 | Div 1 | 46 | 15 | 13 | 18 | 61 | 64 | 58 | 15 |
| 1996-97 | Div 1 | 46 | 17 | 15 | 14 | 52 | 48 | 66 | 10 |
| 1997-98 | Div 1 | 46 | 19 | 17 | 10 | 60 | 35 | 74 | 7 |
| 1998-99 | Div 1 | 46 | 23 | 12 | 11 | 66 | 37 | 81 | 4 |
| 1999-2000 | Div 1 | 46 | 22 | 11 | 13 | 65 | 44 | 77 | 5 |
| 2000-01 | Div 1 | 46 | 23 | 9 | 14 | 59 | 48 | 78 | 5 |
| 2001-02 | Div 1 | 46 | 21 | 13 | 12 | 70 | 49 | 76 | 5 |
| 2002-03 | PR Lge | 38 | 13 | 9 | 16 | 41 | 49 | 48 | 13 |
| 2003-04 | PR Lge | 38 | 12 | 14 | 12 | 43 | 48 | 50 | 10 |

## DID YOU KNOW ?

Birmingham became the first Football League club to pay a wartime benefit to a professional player with goalkeeper Harry Hibbs's testimonial against Aston Villa on 13 April 1940. Birmingham won 2-1. Hibbs had made 388 League and Cup appearances.

## BIRMINGHAM CITY 2003–04 LEAGUE RECORD

| *Match No.* | *Date* | *Venue* | *Opponents* | *Result* | *H/T Score* | *Lg. Pos.* | *Goalscorers* | *Attendance* |
|---|---|---|---|---|---|---|---|---|
| 1 | Aug 16 | H | Tottenham H | W 1-0 | 1-0 | — | Dunn (pen) [36] | 29,358 |
| 2 | 23 | A | Southampton | D 0-0 | 0-0 | 7 | | 31,656 |
| 3 | 30 | A | Newcastle U | W 1-0 | 0-0 | 6 | Dunn [61] | 52,006 |
| 4 | Sept 14 | H | Fulham | D 2-2 | 1-1 | 8 | Forssell 2 [45, 82] | 27,250 |
| 5 | 20 | A | Leeds U | W 2-0 | 0-0 | 7 | Savage (pen) [79], Forssell [84] | 34,305 |
| 6 | 27 | H | Portsmouth | W 2-0 | 1-0 | 4 | Clemence [21], Lazaridis [60] | 29,057 |
| 7 | Oct 4 | A | Manchester U | L 0-3 | 0-1 | 5 | | 67,633 |
| 8 | 14 | H | Chelsea | D 0-0 | 0-0 | — | | 29,460 |
| 9 | 19 | H | Aston Villa | D 0-0 | 0-0 | 4 | | 29,546 |
| 10 | 25 | A | Bolton W | W 1-0 | 1-0 | 4 | Forssell [31] | 25,023 |
| 11 | Nov 3 | H | Charlton Ath | L 1-2 | 0-1 | — | Dugarry [64] | 27,225 |
| 12 | 8 | A | Wolverhampton W | D 1-1 | 0-0 | 5 | Forssell [49] | 28,831 |
| 13 | 22 | H | Arsenal | L 0-3 | 0-1 | 5 | | 29,588 |
| 14 | 30 | A | Liverpool | L 1-3 | 1-1 | 8 | Forssell [33] | 42,683 |
| 15 | Dec 6 | H | Blackburn R | L 0-4 | 0-0 | 9 | | 29,359 |
| 16 | 13 | A | Leicester C | W 2-0 | 1-0 | 8 | Morrison [42], Forssell [66] | 30,639 |
| 17 | 26 | H | Manchester C | W 2-1 | 0-1 | 8 | Kenna [81], Forssell [87] | 29,520 |
| 18 | 28 | A | Everton | L 0-1 | 0-0 | 9 | | 39,631 |
| 19 | Jan 7 | A | Tottenham H | L 1-4 | 0-3 | — | Savage (pen) [68] | 30,025 |
| 20 | 10 | H | Southampton | W 2-1 | 1-1 | 8 | Clemence [16], Kenna [67] | 29,071 |
| 21 | 18 | A | Chelsea | D 0-0 | 0-0 | 9 | | 41,073 |
| 22 | 31 | H | Newcastle U | D 1-1 | 0-1 | 9 | John [90] | 29,513 |
| 23 | Feb 8 | A | Manchester C | D 0-0 | 0-0 | 10 | | 46,967 |
| 24 | 11 | H | Everton | W 3-0 | 2-0 | — | Johnson D [8], Lazaridis [39], Forssell [49] | 29,004 |
| 25 | 22 | A | Aston Villa | D 2-2 | 0-1 | 8 | Forssell [60], John [90] | 40,061 |
| 26 | Mar 3 | H | Middlesbrough | W 3-1 | 1-0 | — | Taylor Martin [23], Savage [57], Forssell [79] | 29,369 |
| 27 | 6 | H | Bolton W | W 2-0 | 1-0 | 5 | Forssell [24], Hughes [69] | 28,003 |
| 28 | 13 | H | Leicester C | L 0-1 | 0-0 | 6 | | 29,491 |
| 29 | 20 | A | Middlesbrough | L 3-5 | 2-4 | 7 | Forssell 2 [23, 59], Morrison [44] | 30,231 |
| 30 | 27 | H | Leeds U | W 4-1 | 1-1 | 6 | Hughes 2 [12, 67], Forssell 2 (1 pen) [69, 82 (p)] | 29,069 |
| 31 | Apr 3 | A | Fulham | D 0-0 | 0-0 | 6 | | 14,667 |
| 32 | 10 | H | Manchester U | L 1-2 | 1-0 | 6 | Grainger [39] | 29,548 |
| 33 | 12 | A | Portsmouth | L 1-3 | 0-1 | 8 | John [67] | 20,079 |
| 34 | 17 | A | Charlton Ath | D 1-1 | 0-0 | 8 | Morrison [84] | 25,184 |
| 35 | 25 | H | Wolverhampton W | D 2-2 | 2-1 | 9 | Forssell [34], Morrison [41] | 29,494 |
| 36 | May 1 | A | Arsenal | D 0-0 | 0-0 | 10 | | 38,061 |
| 37 | 8 | H | Liverpool | L 0-3 | 0-1 | 10 | | 29,553 |
| 38 | 15 | A | Blackburn R | D 1-1 | 0-1 | 10 | John [83] | 26,070 |

**Final League Position: 10**

### GOALSCORERS

*League (43):* Forssell 17 (1 pen), John 4, Morrison 4, Hughes 3, Savage 3 (2 pens), Clemence 2, Dunn 2 (1 pen), Kenna 2, Lazaridis 2, Dugarry 1, Grainger 1, Johnson D 1, Taylor Martin 1.
*Carling Cup (0).*
*FA Cup (6):* Forssell 2, Hughes 2, Clemence 1, Morrison 1.

| Taylor Maik 34 | Kenna J 14 + 3 | Clapham J 22 + 3 | Cunningham K 36 | Purse D 9 | Clemence S 32 + 3 | Johnson D 35 | Savage R 31 | Horsfield G 2 + 1 | Dugarry C 12 + 2 | Dunn D 20 + 1 | Tebily O 17 + 10 | John S 7 + 22 | Devlin P — + 2 | Upson M 30 | Lazaridis S 25 + 5 | Morrison C 19 + 13 | Cisse A 5 + 10 | Forssell M 32 | Figueroa L — + 1 | Carter D 1 + 4 | Bennett I 4 + 2 | Hughes B 17 + 9 | Kirovski J — + 6 | Taylor Martin 11 + 1 | Barrowman A — + 1 | Grainger M 3 + 1 | *Match No.* |
|---|---|---|---|---|---|---|---|---|---|---|---|---|---|---|---|---|---|---|---|---|---|---|---|---|---|---|---|
| 1 | 2 | 3 | 4 | 5 | 6 | 7 | $8^{1}$ | $9^{2}$ | $10^{3}$ | 11 | 12 | 13 | 14 | | | | | | | | | | | | | | 1 |
| 1 | 2 | 3 | 4 | | 6 | $7^{1}$ | 8 | $9^{2}$ | | 11 | | $10^{3}$ | 12 | 5 | 13 | 14 | | | | | | | | | | | 2 |
| 1 | 2 | 3 | 4 | | 6 | 7 | 8 | 12 | | $10^{2}$ | 13 | $9^{1}$ | | 5 | $11^{3}$ | | 14 | | | | | | | | | | 3 |
| 1 | $2^{2}$ | 3 | | 5■ | $6^{1}$ | 7 | 8 | | | 11 | 13 | $10^{3}$ | | 4 | 12 | 14 | | 9 | | | | | | | | | 4 |
| 1 | | 3 | 4 | | 6 | 2 | 8 | | $10^{3}$ | $7^{2}$ | 12 | | | 5 | 11 | 13 | 14 | $9^{1}$ | | | | | | | | | 5 |
| 1 | | 3 | 4 | | 6 | 2 | 8 | | $10^{2}$ | 7 | 12 | | | 5 | $11^{1}$ | | 13 | $9^{3}$ | 14 | | | | | | | | 6 |
| 1■ | | 3 | 4 | | $6^{1}$ | 2 | | | $10^{2}$ | 7 | 12 | | | 5 | $11^{6}$ | | 8 | 9 | | 13 | 15 | | | | | | 7 |
| 1 | | 3 | 4 | | $6^{2}$ | 7 | | | $10^{1}$ | 9 | 2 | 12 | | 5 | 11 | | 8 | | | | | 13 | | | | | 8 |
| | | 3 | 4 | | 6 | $2^{1}$ | 8 | | $10^{2}$ | 7 | 12 | | | 5 | $11^{3}$ | 13 | 14 | 9 | | | 1 | | | | | | 9 |
| 1 | 12 | 3 | 4 | | 6 | | | | $10^{2}$ | 7 | $2^{1}$ | | | 5 | $11^{3}$ | 13 | 8 | 9 | | | | 14 | | | | | 10 |
| 1 | | 3 | 4 | | 6 | | | | 10 | 7 | $2^{1}$ | 14 | | 5 | $11^{3}$ | 12 | $8^{2}$ | 9 | | | | 13 | | | | | 11 |
| 1 | | 3 | 4 | | 6 | 2 | 8 | | $10^{1}$ | 7 | | 13 | | 5 | 12 | | | 9 | | | | $11^{2}$ | | | | | 12 |
| 1 | | 3 | 4 | | 6 | 2 | 7 | | | 10 | | 12 | | 5 | $11^{3}$ | 13 | $8^{1}$ | $9^{2}$ | | | | 14 | | | | | 13 |
| | | 3 | 4 | | $6^{2}$ | 2 | 8 | | $10^{3}$ | 7 | 12 | | | $5^{1}$ | 11 | 13 | | 9 | | | 1 | | 14 | | | | 14 |
| 1 | $2^{2}$ | 3 | 4 | | 12 | 7 | $6^{1}$ | | 10■ | 8 | 5 | | | | $11^{3}$ | 14 | 13 | 9 | | | | | | | | | 15 |
| 1 | 2 | 3 | 4 | | $6^{1}$ | 7 | $8^{3}$ | | | 11 | | 13 | | 5 | 12 | 10 | 14 | $9^{2}$ | | | | | | | | | 16 |
| 1 | 2 | | 4 | | $6^{2}$ | 7 | 8 | | | $11^{1}$ | | 12 | | 5 | 3 | $10^{3}$ | 13 | 9 | | | | | 14 | | | | 17 |
| 1 | $2^{3}$ | | 4 | | 6 | 7 | 8 | | | | | $10^{1}$ | | 5 | 3 | 12 | 13 | 9 | | | | $11^{2}$ | 14 | | | | 18 |
| 1 | 2 | | 4 | 5 | $6^{2}$ | 7 | 8 | | | 11 | 12 | | | | | 10 | | $9^{3}$ | | $3^{1}$ | | 13 | 14 | | | | 19 |
| 1 | 2 | | 4 | 5 | 6 | 7 | | | | $11^{1}$ | 3 | | | | | $10^{2}$ | | 9 | | 12 | | 8 | 13 | | | | 20 |
| 1 | 3 | | 4 | 5 | 6 | 7 | 8 | | | | 2 | $10^{2}$ | | | 12 | $9^{1}$ | | | | 13 | | $11^{3}$ | 14 | | | | 21 |
| 1 | 3 | | 4 | 5 | | $7^{1}$ | 8 | | | | 2 | 12 | | | 11 | 10 | | 9 | | | | 6 | | | | | 22 |
| 1 | $3^{1}$ | 12 | 4 | 5 | | 7 | 8 | | 14 | | 2 | $10^{3}$ | | | 11 | 13 | | $9^{2}$ | | | | 6 | | | | | 23 |
| 1 | | | 4 | 5 | | 7 | $8^{2}$ | | 13 | | 2 | 12 | | 3 | $11^{1}$ | 10 | | $9^{3}$ | | | | 6 | | 14 | | | 24 |
| 1 | $3^{2}$ | | 4 | 5 | $6^{1}$ | 7 | 8 | | $10^{3}$ | 12 | 2 | 13 | | | | 14 | | 9 | | | | 11 | | | | | 25 |
| 1 | 12 | | 4 | | 6 | 7 | $8^{1}$ | | | | 2 | 13 | | 3 | | $10^{3}$ | | $9^{2}$ | | 14 | | 11 | | 5 | | | 26 |
| 1 | 12 | | 4 | | $6^{3}$ | $7^{1}$ | 8 | | | | 2 | 13 | | 3 | | 10 | 14 | $9^{2}$ | | | | 11 | | 5 | | | 27 |
| 1 | | | $4^{2}$ | | $6^{1}$ | | 8 | | | | 2 | 12 | | 3 | 11 | 10 | | 9 | | | | 7 | | 5 | 13 | | 28 |
| 1 | | | 4 | | 6 | $7^{1}$ | | | | | | 12 | | 5 | 11 | 10 | | 9 | | | | 8 | | 2 | | 3 | 29 |
| 1 | | | 4 | | 6 | 7 | | | | | 13 | 12 | | 5 | 11 | $10^{2}$ | | $9^{1}$ | | | | 8 | | 2 | | 3 | 30 |
| 1 | | 13 | 4 | | 12 | 7 | 8 | | | | | 14 | | 5 | 11 | $10^{3}$ | | 9 | | | | $6^{2}$ | | 2 | | $3^{1}$ | 31 |
| 1 | | 14 | 4 | | $6^{1}$ | 7 | 8 | | | | | 12 | | 5 | $3^{2}$ | 10 | | 9 | | | | 11 | | 2 | | $13^{3}$ | 32 |
| 1■ | | 3 | 4 | | 12 | 7 | $8^{1}$ | | | | $2^{6}$ | 10 | | 5 | | 13 | | $9^{2}$ | | | 15 | 11 | | 6 | | | 33 |
| 1 | | 3 | 4 | | 6 | 7 | 8 | | | | | 12 | | 5 | | 10 | | $9^{1}$ | | | | 11 | | 2 | | | 34 |
| 1 | | 3 | 4 | | 6 | 7 | 8 | | | | | 12 | | 5 | $11^{2}$ | 10 | | 9 | | | | 13 | | $2^{1}$ | | | 35 |
| | | 3 | 4 | | 6 | 7 | 8 | | | $10^{2}$ | 2 | 12 | | 5 | 11 | $9^{1}$ | | | | | 1 | 13 | | | | | 36 |
| | | $3^{3}$ | 4■ | | $6^{1}$ | 7 | $8^{2}$ | | | | 2 | 12 | | 5 | 11 | 10 | 14 | 9 | | | 1 | 13 | | | | | 37 |
| 1 | | 3 | | | $6^{2}$ | 7 | 8 | | | | $2^{1}$ | 12 | | 5 | 11 | 10 | | 9 | | | | 13 | | 4 | | | 38 |

**Carling Cup**
Second Round Blackpool (a) 0-1

**FA Cup**

| | | | |
|---|---|---|---|
| Third Round | Blackburn R | (h) | 4-0 |
| Fourth Round | Wimbledon | (h) | 1-0 |
| Fifth Round | Sunderland | (a) | 1-1 |
| | | (h) | 0-2 |

# BLACKBURN ROVERS FA Premiership

## FOUNDATION

It was in 1875 that some Public School old boys called a meeting at which the Blackburn Rovers club was formed and the colours blue and white adopted. The leading light was John Lewis, later to become a founder of the Lancashire FA, a famous referee who was in charge of two FA Cup Finals, and a vice-president of both the FA and the Football League.

***Ewood Park, Blackburn BB2 4JF.***

***Telephone:*** 08701 113 232.

***Fax:*** (01254) 671 042.

***Website:*** www.rovers.co.uk

***Email:*** enquiries@rovers.co.uk

***Ground Capacity:*** 31,367.

***Record Attendance:*** 62,522 v Bolton W, FA Cup 6th rd, 2 March 1929.

***Pitch Measurements:*** 115yd × 72yd.

***Chairman:*** R. D. Coar BSC.

***Vice-chairman:*** R. L. Matthewman.

***Manager:*** Graeme Souness.

***Physio:*** Dave Fevre.

***Assistant Manager:*** Alan Murray.

***Secretary:*** Tom Finn.

***Colours:*** Blue and white halved shirts, white shorts with navy blue strip, white stockings with navy blue trim.

***Change Colours:*** TBC.

***Year Formed:*** 1875.

***Turned Professional:*** 1880.

***Ltd Co.:*** 1897.

***Club Nickname:*** Rovers.

***Previous Grounds:*** 1875, all matches played away; 1876, Oozehead Ground; 1877, Pleasington Cricket Ground; 1878, Alexandra Meadows; 1881, Leamington Road; 1890, Ewood Park.

***First Football League Game:*** 15 September 1888, Football League, v Accrington (h) D 5–5 – Arthur; Beverley, James Southworth; Douglas, Almond, Forrest; Beresford (1), Walton, John Southworth (1), Fecitt (1), Townley (2).

***Record League Victory:*** 9–0 v Middlesbrough, Division 2, 6 November 1954 – Elvy; Suart, Eckersley; Clayton, Kelly, Bell; Mooney (3), Crossan (2), Briggs, Quigley (3), Langton (1).

## HONOURS

*FA Premier League:* Champions 1994–95; Runners-up 1993–94.

*Football League:* Division 1 – Champions 1911–12, 1913–14; 1991–92 (play-offs); Runners-up 2000–01; Division 2 – Champions 1938–39; Runners-up 1957–58; Division 3 – Champions 1974–75; Runners-up 1979–80.

*FA Cup:* Winners 1884, 1885, 1886, 1890, 1891, 1928; Runners-up 1882, 1960.

*Football League Cup:* Winners 2002.

*Full Members' Cup:* Winners 1987.

***European Competitions:*** *European Cup:* 1995–96. *UEFA Cup:* 1994–95, 1998–99, 2002–03, 2003–04.

## SKY SPORTS FACT FILE

When Johnny McIntyre scored his four goals in five second-half minutes for Blackburn Rovers against Everton on 16 September 1922, the teams had been level 1-1 at half-time, Rovers having equalised just before the break during the 5-1 win.

***Record Cup Victory:*** 11–0 v Rossendale, FA Cup 1st rd, 13 October 1884 – Arthur; Hopwood, McIntyre; Forrest, Blenkhorn, Lofthouse; Sowerbutts (2), J. Brown (1), Fecitt (4), Barton (3), Birtwistle (1).

***Record Defeat:*** 0–8 v Arsenal, Division 1, 25 February 1933.

***Most League Points (2 for a win):*** 60, Division 3, 1974–75.

***Most League Points (3 for a win):*** 91, Division 1, 2000–01.

***Most League Goals:*** 114, Division 2, 1954–55.

***Highest League Scorer in Season:*** Ted Harper, 43, Division 1, 1925–26.

***Most League Goals in Total Aggregate:*** Simon Garner, 168, 1978–92.

***Most League Goals in One Match:*** 7, Tommy Briggs v Bristol R, Division 2, 5 February 1953.

***Most Capped Player:*** Henning Berg, 58 (100), Norway.

***Most League Appearances:*** Derek Fazackerley, 596, 1970–86.

***Youngest League Player:*** Harry Dennison, 16 years 155 days v Bristol C, 8 April 1911.

***Record Transfer Fee Received:*** £15,000,000 from Newcastle U for Alan Shearer, July 1996.

***Record Transfer Fee Paid:*** £7,500,000 to Manchester U for Andy Cole, December 2001.

***Football League Record:*** 1888 Founder Member of the League; 1936–39 Division 2; 1946–48 Division 1; 1948–58 Division 2; 1958–66 Division 1; 1966–71 Division 2; 1971–75 Division 3; 1975–79 Division 2; 1979–80 Division 3; 1980–92 Division 2; 1992–99 FA Premier League; 1999–2001 Division 1; 2001– FA Premier League.

## MANAGERS

Thomas Mitchell 1884–96
*(Secretary-Manager)*
J. Walmsley 1896–1903
*(Secretary-Manager)*
R. B. Middleton 1903–25
Jack Carr 1922–26
*(Team Manager under Middleton to 1925)*
Bob Crompton 1926–30
*(Hon. Team Manager)*
Arthur Barritt 1931–36
*(had been Secretary from 1927)*
Reg Taylor 1936–38
Bob Crompton 1938–41
Eddie Hapgood 1944–47
Will Scott 1947
Jack Bruton 1947–49
Jackie Bestall 1949–53
Johnny Carey 1953–58
Dally Duncan 1958–60
Jack Marshall 1960–67
Eddie Quigley 1967–70
Johnny Carey 1970–71
Ken Furphy 1971–73
Gordon Lee 1974–75
Jim Smith 1975–78
Jim Iley 1978
John Pickering 1978–79
Howard Kendall 1979–81
Bobby Saxton 1981–86
Don Mackay 1987–91
Kenny Dalglish 1991–95
Ray Harford 1995–97
Roy Hodgson 1997–98
Brian Kidd 1998–99
Tony Parkes 1999–2000
Graeme Souness March 2000–

## LATEST SEQUENCES

***Longest Sequence of League Wins:*** 8, 1.3.1980 – 7.4.1980.

***Longest Sequence of League Defeats:*** 7, 12.3.1966 – 16.4.1966.

***Longest Sequence of League Draws:*** 5, 11.10.1975 – 1.11.1975.

***Longest Sequence of Unbeaten League Matches:*** 23, 30.9.1987 – 27.3.1988.

***Longest Sequence Without a League Win:*** 16, 11.11.1978 – 24.3.1979.

***Successive Scoring Runs:*** 32 from 24.4.1954.

***Successive Non-scoring Runs:*** 4 from 12.12.1908.

## TEN YEAR LEAGUE RECORD

| | | P | W | D | L | F | A | Pts | Pos |
|---|---|---|---|---|---|---|---|---|---|
| 1994-95 | PR Lge | 42 | 27 | 8 | 7 | 80 | 39 | 89 | 1 |
| 1995-96 | PR Lge | 38 | 18 | 7 | 13 | 61 | 47 | 61 | 7 |
| 1996-97 | PR Lge | 38 | 9 | 15 | 14 | 42 | 43 | 42 | 13 |
| 1997-98 | PR Lge | 38 | 16 | 10 | 12 | 57 | 52 | 58 | 6 |
| 1998-99 | PR Lge | 38 | 7 | 14 | 17 | 38 | 52 | 35 | 19 |
| 1999-2000 | Div 1 | 46 | 15 | 17 | 14 | 55 | 51 | 62 | 11 |
| 2000-01 | Div 1 | 46 | 26 | 13 | 7 | 76 | 39 | 91 | 2 |
| 2001-02 | PR Lge | 38 | 12 | 10 | 16 | 55 | 51 | 46 | 10 |
| 2002-03 | PR Lge | 38 | 16 | 12 | 10 | 52 | 43 | 60 | 6 |
| 2003-04 | PR Lge | 38 | 12 | 8 | 18 | 51 | 59 | 44 | 15 |

## DID YOU KNOW ?

In Blackburn Rovers' Second Division championship winning season of 1938–39 the five forwards accounted for all but nine of the team's 94 goals: Albert Clarke 21, Billy Rogers 18, Len Butt and Jack Weddle 16 each plus Bobby Langton 14.

## BLACKBURN ROVERS 2003–04 LEAGUE RECORD

| *Match No.* | *Date* | *Venue* | *Opponents* | *Result* | | *H/T Score* | *Lg. Pos.* | *Goalscorers* | *Attendance* |
|---|---|---|---|---|---|---|---|---|---|
| 1 | Aug 16 | H | Wolverhampton W | W | 5-1 | 2-0 | — | Amoruso [17], Thompson [29], Emerton [53], Cole 2 [79, 87] | 26,270 |
| 2 | 23 | A | Bolton W | D | 2-2 | 0-2 | 4 | Jansen [50], Yorke [90] | 27,423 |
| 3 | 25 | H | Manchester C | L | 2-3 | 1-1 | — | Sinclair (og) [44], Amoruso [61] | 23,353 |
| 4 | 30 | A | Chelsea | D | 2-2 | 1-1 | 9 | Cole 2 [1, 58] | 41,066 |
| 5 | Sept 13 | H | Liverpool | L | 1-3 | 1-1 | 10 | Jansen [8] | 30,074 |
| 6 | 20 | A | Portsmouth | W | 2-1 | 2-0 | 9 | Neill [35], Cole [43] | 20,029 |
| 7 | 28 | H | Fulham | L | 0-2 | 0-1 | 11 | | 21,985 |
| 8 | Oct 4 | A | Leeds U | L | 1-2 | 0-2 | 11 | Baggio [86] | 35,039 |
| 9 | 20 | H | Charlton Ath | L | 0-1 | 0-1 | — | | 19,939 |
| 10 | 25 | A | Southampton | L | 0-2 | 0-0 | 16 | | 31,620 |
| 11 | Nov 2 | A | Leicester C | L | 0-2 | 0-0 | 19 | | 30,975 |
| 12 | 10 | H | Everton | W | 2-1 | 2-0 | — | Babbel [6], Yorke [13] | 22,179 |
| 13 | 22 | A | Manchester U | L | 1-2 | 0-2 | 17 | Emerton [62] | 67,748 |
| 14 | 29 | H | Tottenham H | W | 1-0 | 0-0 | 16 | Carr (og) [78] | 22,802 |
| 15 | Dec 6 | A | Birmingham C | W | 4-0 | 0-0 | 14 | Ferguson [66], Neill [68], Tugay [82], Gallagher [88] | 29,359 |
| 16 | 14 | A | Arsenal | L | 0-1 | 0-1 | 14 | | 37,677 |
| 17 | 20 | H | Aston Villa | L | 0-2 | 0-0 | 16 | | 20,722 |
| 18 | 26 | H | Middlesbrough | D | 2-2 | 1-1 | 16 | Babbel 2 [3, 90] | 25,452 |
| 19 | 28 | A | Newcastle U | W | 1-0 | 0-0 | 14 | Gallagher [71] | 51,648 |
| 20 | Jan 7 | A | Wolverhampton W | D | 2-2 | 1-0 | — | Cole [14], Yorke [78] | 27,393 |
| 21 | 10 | H | Bolton W | L | 3-4 | 3-2 | 16 | Gresko [3], Yorke [24], Cole [34] | 23,538 |
| 22 | 17 | A | Manchester C | D | 1-1 | 0-0 | 16 | Flitcroft [55] | 47,090 |
| 23 | Feb 1 | H | Chelsea | L | 2-3 | 1-2 | 16 | Flitcroft [3], Gallagher [87] | 24,867 |
| 24 | 7 | A | Middlesbrough | W | 1-0 | 1-0 | 14 | Stead [39] | 28,307 |
| 25 | 11 | H | Newcastle U | D | 1-1 | 0-0 | — | Stead [85] | 23,459 |
| 26 | 21 | A | Charlton Ath | L | 2-3 | 0-2 | 15 | Cole [74], Friedel [89] | 26,322 |
| 27 | 28 | H | Southampton | D | 1-1 | 0-1 | 15 | Cole [52] | 21,970 |
| 28 | Mar 13 | H | Arsenal | L | 0-2 | 0-0 | 16 | | 28,627 |
| 29 | 20 | A | Aston Villa | W | 2-0 | 2-0 | 15 | Flitcroft [26], Stead [36] | 37,532 |
| 30 | 27 | H | Portsmouth | L | 1-2 | 1-1 | 16 | Taylor, Martin (og) [37] | 22,855 |
| 31 | Apr 4 | A | Liverpool | L | 0-4 | 0-3 | 16 | | 41,559 |
| 32 | 10 | H | Leeds U | L | 1-2 | 0-1 | 16 | Short [90] | 26,611 |
| 33 | 12 | A | Fulham | W | 4-3 | 1-2 | 16 | Cole [23], Douglas [49], Amoruso [51], Stead [75] | 13,981 |
| 34 | 17 | H | Leicester C | W | 1-0 | 1-0 | 15 | Dabizas (og) [42] | 22,749 |
| 35 | 24 | A | Everton | W | 1-0 | 0-0 | 13 | Stead [81] | 38,884 |
| 36 | May 1 | H | Manchester U | W | 1-0 | 0-0 | 13 | Stead [84] | 29,616 |
| 37 | 8 | A | Tottenham H | L | 0-1 | 0-1 | 13 | | 35,687 |
| 38 | 15 | H | Birmingham C | D | 1-1 | 1-0 | 15 | Cole [24] | 26,070 |

**Final League Position: 15**

### GOALSCORERS

*League (51):* Cole 11, Stead 6, Yorke 4, Amoruso 3, Babbel 3, Flitcroft 3, Gallagher 3, Emerton 2, Jansen 2, Neill 2, Baggio 1, Douglas 1, Ferguson 1, Friedel 1, Gresko 1, Short 1, Thompson 1, Tugay 1, own goals 4.
*Carling Cup (3):* Yorke 2, Ferguson 1.
*FA Cup (0).*
*UEFA Cup (2):* Emerton 1, Jansen 1.

| Friedel B 36 | Neill L 30 + 2 | Gresko V 22 + 2 | Amoruso L 11 + 1 | Taylor Martin 10 + 1 | Tugay K 30 + 6 | Thompson D 10 + 1 | Flitcroft G 29 + 2 | Jansen M 9 + 10 | Yorke D 15 + 8 | Emerton B 31 + 6 | Grabbi C — + 5 | Cole A 27 + 7 | Reid S 9 + 7 | Babbel M 23 + 2 | Gallagher P 12 + 14 | Johansson N 7 + 7 | Ferguson B 14 + 1 | Baggio D — + 9 | Todd A 19 | Short C 19 | Mahon A 1 + 2 | Douglas J 14 | Danns N — + 1 | Gray M 14 | Stead J 13 | Andresen M 11 | Enckelman P 2 | *Match No.* |
|---|---|---|---|---|---|---|---|---|---|---|---|---|---|---|---|---|---|---|---|---|---|---|---|---|---|---|---|---|
| 1 | 2 | 3 | 4 | 5 | 6 | 7$^{1}$ | 8 | 9$^{2}$ | 10 | 11 | 12 | 13 | | | | | | | | | | | | | | | | 1 |
| 1 | 2 | 3$^{1}$ | 4 | 5 | 6 | 7 | 8$^{3}$ | 9$^{2}$ | 10 | 11 | 12 | 13 | 14■ | | | | | | | | | | | | | | | 2 |
| 1 | 2 | 3 | 4 | 5 | 6 | 12 | 8$^{3}$ | 13 | 10$^{2}$ | 7 | 14 | 9 | 11$^{1}$ | | | | | | | | | | | | | | | 3 |
| 1 | 2 | 3 | 4 | 12 | 6$^{1}$ | 7 | 8 | 10$^{2}$ | | | | 9 | 11$^{3}$ | 5 | 13 | 14 | | | | | | | | | | | | 4 |
| 1 | 2■ | 3 | 4 | | 12 | 11$^{3}$ | 8$^{1}$ | 10$^{2}$ | 13 | 7 | | 9 | | 5 | | | 6 | 14 | | | | | | | | | | 5 |
| 1 | 2$^{1}$ | 3 | 4 | | 6$^{3}$ | 11 | | 10$^{2}$ | 13 | 7 | | 9 | | 5 | | 12 | 8 | 14 | | | | | | | | | | 6 |
| 1 | | 3$^{3}$ | 4 | 5 | 12 | 11 | 8 | 10 | | 7 | 14 | 9 | | 2$^{2}$ | | 13 | 6$^{1}$ | | | | | | | | | | | 7 |
| 1 | | 3 | | 5 | 6$^{1}$ | 11 | 8$^{3}$ | | 10 | 7 | 12 | 9 | 2$^{2}$ | | | 4 | 14 | 13 | | | | | | | | | | 8 |
| 1 | | 3$^{3}$ | | 5 | 6 | 11 | 8$^{1}$ | 12 | | 7$^{2}$ | | 9 | 2 | | 13 | | 10 | 14 | 4 | | | | | | | | | 9 |
| 1 | 12 | 3$^{3}$ | | 5 | 6 | 11$^{1}$ | 8 | 13 | | 7$^{2}$ | | 9■ | 2 | | 14 | | 10 | | 4 | | | | | | | | | 10 |
| 1 | 2 | 3$^{1}$ | | | 13 | 11 | 8$^{2}$ | | 10 | 7 | | 9 | 12 | 5 | | | 4 | | 6 | | | | | | | | | 11 |
| 1 | 2 | 3 | | | | | 8 | 9$^{1}$ | 10$^{2}$ | 11 | | | 7 | 5 | 13 | | 4 | 12 | 6 | | | | | | | | | 12 |
| 1 | | 3 | | | | | 8$^{3}$ | 9$^{2}$ | 10 | 11 | | | 7$^{1}$ | 2 | 13 | 12 | 4 | 14 | 6 | 5 | | | | | | | | 13 |
| 1 | | 3 | | | 6 | | | 12 | 10 | 7 | | | 13 | 2 | 9$^{1}$ | 11$^{2}$ | 8 | | 4 | 5 | | | | | | | | 14 |
| 1 | 11 | 3 | | | 6 | | | | 10$^{1}$ | 7 | | 12 | | 2 | 9 | | 8 | | 4 | 5 | | | | | | | | 15 |
| 1 | 11 | 3$^{2}$ | | | 6 | | | | 10 | 7 | | 12 | 13 | 2$^{3}$ | 9$^{1}$ | | 8 | 14 | 4 | 5 | | | | | | | | 16 |
| 1 | 3$^{2}$ | 12 | | | 6$^{3}$ | | 14 | 13 | 10 | 7 | | 9 | | 2 | 11$^{1}$ | | 8 | | 4 | 5 | | | | | | | | 17 |
| 1 | 3 | | | 5 | 12 | | 7$^{1}$ | | 10$^{3}$ | 11 | | 13 | | 2 | 9 | 6$^{2}$ | 8 | | 4 | | 14 | | | | | | | 18 |
| 1 | 2 | 3 | | | 6 | | 14 | 12 | 13 | 7 | | 9$^{2}$ | | 5 | 10$^{1}$ | | 8$^{3}$ | | 4 | | 11 | | | | | | | 19 |
| 1 | 3 | 11$^{3}$ | | 5 | 6 | | 8 | | 12 | 7 | | 9 | | 2 | 10$^{1}$ | 13 | | 14 | | 4$^{2}$ | | | | | | | | 20 |
| 1 | 2$^{1}$ | 3 | | 5 | 6 | | | 12 | 8 | 7 | | 9 | | 4 | 10$^{2}$ | | | 13 | | | | 11$^{3}$ | 14 | | | | | 21 |
| 1 | 2 | 3 | | | 6 | | 8 | | 10 | 7 | | 9 | | 5 | | 4 | | | | | | 11 | | | | | | 22 |
| 1 | 2 | | | | 6 | | 8 | | 10$^{2}$ | 7 | | 9 | | 5 | 13 | | | | 4 | | 12 | 11$^{1}$ | | 3 | | | | 23 |
| 1 | 2 | | | | 13 | | 8 | 12 | | 7 | | | | 5 | 9$^{1}$ | | | | 6 | 4 | | 11 | | 3 | 10$^{2}$ | | | 24 |
| 1 | 2 | | | | 6 | | 8 | | | 7 | | 9$^{1}$ | | 5 | 13 | 12 | | | 4 | | | 11$^{2}$ | | 3 | 10 | | | 25 |
| 1 | 2 | | | | 14 | | 8$^{3}$ | | 13 | 7 | | 12 | | 5 | 9 | | | | 6$^{2}$ | 4 | | 11 | | 3 | 10$^{1}$ | | | 26 |
| 1 | 2 | | | | 6 | | | 13 | 12 | 7 | | 9 | | 5 | 10$^{1}$ | | | | | 4 | | 11$^{2}$ | | 3 | | 8 | | 27 |
| 1 | 2 | 13 | | | 6 | | | 10$^{1}$ | 12 | 7 | | 9 | | 14 | | | | | 5$^{3}$ | 4 | | 11$^{2}$ | | 3 | | 8 | | 28 |
| 1 | 2$^{2}$ | | 12 | | 6 | | 8 | | | 7 | | 9 | | 13 | | | | | 5 | 4 | | | | 3 | 10$^{1}$ | 11 | | 29 |
| 1 | 2 | | | | 6 | | 8 | | 12 | 7 | | 9 | 13 | | 14 | | | | 5 | 4 | | | | 3$^{3}$ | 10$^{2}$ | 11$^{1}$ | | 30 |
| 1 | | | | | 6 | | 8$^{3}$ | | | 7 | | 12 | 14 | 2 | 9$^{1}$ | 13 | | | 5 | 4$^{2}$ | | | | 3 | 10 | 11 | | 31 |
| 1 | 2 | | 5 | | 6 | | 8 | 12 | | 7 | | 9 | 11$^{2}$ | | 13 | | | | | 4 | | | | 3 | 10$^{1}$ | | | 32 |
| 1 | 2 | 3 | 5 | | 6 | | 8 | | | 12 | | 9$^{1}$ | | | 13 | | | | | 4 | | 11 | | | 10$^{2}$ | 7 | | 33 |
| 1 | 2 | 3 | 5 | | 6 | | 8 | | | 12 | | 9 | | | | | | | | 4 | | 11 | | | 10 | 7$^{1}$ | | 34 |
| 1 | 2 | | 5 | | 6 | | 8 | | | 12 | | 9$^{2}$ | | | 13 | | | | | 4 | | 11 | | 3 | 10 | 7$^{1}$ | | 35 |
| 1 | 2 | | | | 6$^{1}$ | | 8 | | | 12 | | 9$^{2}$ | | 5 | 13 | 4 | | | | | | 11 | | 3 | 10 | 7 | | 36 |
| | 2$^{2}$ | | | | 6 | | 8$^{3}$ | | | 12 | | 9 | 13 | | 14 | 5 | | | | 4 | | 11 | | 3 | 10 | 7$^{1}$ | 1 | 37 |
| | 14 | | | | 6 | | 8 | | | 12 | | 9 | 2$^{1}$ | | 13 | 5 | | | | 4 | | 11 | | 3$^{2}$ | 10 | 7$^{3}$ | 1 | 38 |

**Carling Cup**
Third Round Liverpool (h) 3-4

**FA Cup**
Third Round Birmingham C (a) 0-4

**UEFA Cup**
First Round Genclerbirligi (a) 1-3
(h) 1-1

# BLACKPOOL FL Championship 1

## FOUNDATION

Old boys of St John's School who had formed themselves into a football club decided to establish a club bearing the name of their town and Blackpool FC came into being at a meeting at the Stanley Arms Hotel in the summer of 1887. In their first season playing at Raikes Hall Gardens, the club won both the Lancashire Junior Cup and the Fylde Cup.

***Bloomfield Road Ground, Seasiders Way, Blackpool FY1 6JJ.***

***Telephone:*** 0870 443 1953.

***Fax:*** (01253) 405 011.

***Ticket Office:*** 0870 443 1953

***Website:*** www.blackpoolfc.co.uk

***Email:*** info@blackpoolfc.co.uk, secretary@blackpoolfc.co.uk

***Ground Capacity:*** 9,500.

***Record Attendance:*** 38,098 v Wolverhampton W, Division 1, 17 September 1955.

***Pitch Measurements:*** 112yd × 74yd.

***Chairman:*** Karl Oyston.

***Secretary:*** Peter Collins.

***Manager:*** Colin Hendry.

***Assistant Manager:*** Mark Seagraves.

***Physio:*** Phil Horner.

***Colours:*** Tangerine shirts, white shorts, tangerine stockings.

***Change Colours:*** All black.

***Year Formed:*** 1887.

***Turned Professional:*** 1887.

***Ltd Co.:*** 1896.

***Previous Name:*** 'South Shore' combined with Blackpool in 1899, twelve years after the latter had been formed on the breaking up of the old 'Blackpool St John's' club.

***Club Nickname:*** 'The Seasiders'.

***Previous Grounds:*** 1887, Raikes Hall Gardens; 1897, Athletic Grounds; 1899, Raikes Hall Gardens; 1899, Bloomfield Road.

***First Football League game:*** 5 September 1896, Division 2, v Lincoln C (a) L 1–3 – Douglas; Parr, Bowman; Stuart, Stirzaker, Norris; Clarkin, Donnelly, R. Parkinson, Mount (1), J. Parkinson.

***Record League Victory:*** 7–0 v Reading, Division 2, 10 November 1928 – Mercer; Gibson, Hamilton, Watson, Wilson, Grant, Ritchie, Oxberry (2), Hampson (5), Tufnell, Neal. 7–0 v Preston NE (away), Division 1, 1 May 1948 – Robinson; Shimwell, Crosland; Buchan, Hayward, Kelly; Hobson, Munro (1), McIntosh (5), McCall, Rickett (1). 7–0 v Sunderland, Division 1, 5 October 1957 – Farm;

## HONOURS

*Football League:* Division 1 – Runners-up 1955–56; Division 2 – Champions 1929–30; Runners-up 1936–37, 1969–70; Promoted from Division 3 – 2000–01 (play-offs); Division 4 – Runners-up 1984–85.

*FA Cup:* Winners 1953; Runners-up 1948, 1951.

*Football League Cup:* Semi-final 1962.

*Anglo-Italian Cup:* Winners 1971; Runners-up 1972.

*LDV Vans Trophy:* Winners 2002, 2004.

## SKY SPORTS FACT FILE

When Philip Doughty made his debut for Blackpool on 7 December 2002 as substitute in an FA Cup tie against Torquay United, he was still a member of the club's Centre of Excellence. At 16 years 92 days he became their youngest debutant.

Armfield, Garrett, Kelly (J), Gratrix, Kelly (H), Matthews, Taylor (2), Charnley (2), Durie (2), Perry (1).

***Record Cup Victory:*** 7–1 v Charlton Ath, League Cup 2nd rd, 25 September 1963 – Harvey; Armfield, Martin; Crawford, Gratrix, Cranston; Lea, Ball (1), Charnley (4), Durie (1), Oates (1).

***Record Defeat:*** 1–10 v Small Heath, Division 2, 2 March 1901 and v Huddersfield T, Division 1, 13 December 1930.

***Most League Points (2 for a win):*** 58, Division 2, 1929–30 and Division 2, 1967–68.

***Most League Points (3 for a win):*** 86, Division 4, 1984–85.

***Most League Goals:*** 98, Division 2, 1929–30.

***Highest League Scorer in Season:*** Jimmy Hampson, 45, Division 2, 1929–30.

***Most League Goals in Total Aggregate:*** Jimmy Hampson, 246, 1927–38.

***Most League Goals in One Match:*** 5, Jimmy Hampson v Reading, Division 2, 10 November 1928; 5, Jimmy McIntosh v Preston NE, Division 1, 1 May 1948.

***Most Capped Player:*** Jimmy Armfield, 43, England.

***Most League Appearances:*** Jimmy Armfield, 568, 1952–71.

***Youngest League Player:*** Trevor Sinclair, 16 years 170 days v Wigan Ath, 19 August 1989.

***Record Transfer Fee Received:*** £1,500,000 from Southampton for Brett Ormerod, December 2001.

***Record Transfer Fee Paid:*** £275,000 to Millwall for Chris Malkin, October 1996.

***Football League Record:*** 1896 Elected to Division 2; 1899 Failed re-election; 1900 Re-elected; 1900–30 Division 2; 1930–33 Division 1; 1933–37 Division 2; 1937–67 Division 1; 1967–70 Division 2; 1970–71 Division 1; 1971–78 Division 2; 1978–81 Division 3; 1981–85 Division 4; 1985–90 Division 3; 1990–92 Division 4; 1992–2000 Division 2; 2000–01 Division 3; 2001–04 Division 2; 2004– FL1.

## MANAGERS

Tom Barcroft 1903–33
*(Secretary-Manager)*
John Cox 1909–11
Bill Norman 1919–23
Maj. Frank Buckley 1923–27
Sid Beaumont 1927–28
Harry Evans 1928–33
*(Hon. Team Manager)*
Alex 'Sandy' Macfarlane 1933–35
Joe Smith 1935–58
Ronnie Suart 1958–67
Stan Mortensen 1967–69
Les Shannon 1969–70
Bob Stokoe 1970–72
Harry Potts 1972–76
Allan Brown 1976–78
Bob Stokoe 1978–79
Stan Ternent 1979–80
Alan Ball 1980–81
Allan Brown 1981–82
Sam Ellis 1982–89
Jimmy Mullen 1989–90
Graham Carr 1990
Bill Ayre 1990–94
Sam Allardyce 1994–96
Gary Megson 1996–97
Nigel Worthington 1997–99
Steve McMahon 2000–04
Collin Hendry June 2004–

## LATEST SEQUENCES

***Longest Sequence of League Wins:*** 9, 21.11.1936 – 1.1.1937.

***Longest Sequence of League Defeats:*** 8, 26.11.1898 – 7.1.1899.

***Longest Sequence of League Draws:*** 5, 4.12.1976 – 1.1.1977.

***Longest Sequence of Unbeaten League Matches:*** 17, 6.4.1968 – 21.9.1968.

***Longest Sequence Without a League Win:*** 19, 19.12.1970 – 24.4.1971.

***Successive Scoring Runs:*** 33 from 23.2.1929.

***Successive Non-scoring Runs:*** 5 from 12.4.1975.

## TEN YEAR LEAGUE RECORD

| | | P | W | D | L | F | A | Pts | Pos |
|---|---|---|---|---|---|---|---|---|---|
| 1994-95 | Div 2 | 46 | 18 | 10 | 18 | 64 | 70 | 64 | 12 |
| 1995-96 | Div 2 | 46 | 23 | 13 | 10 | 67 | 40 | 82 | 3 |
| 1996-97 | Div 2 | 46 | 18 | 15 | 13 | 60 | 47 | 69 | 7 |
| 1997-98 | Div 2 | 46 | 17 | 11 | 18 | 59 | 67 | 62 | 12 |
| 1998-99 | Div 2 | 46 | 14 | 14 | 18 | 44 | 54 | 56 | 14 |
| 1999-2000 | Div 2 | 46 | 8 | 17 | 21 | 49 | 77 | 41 | 22 |
| 2000-01 | Div 2 | 46 | 22 | 6 | 18 | 74 | 58 | 72 | 7 |
| 2001-02 | Div 2 | 46 | 14 | 14 | 18 | 66 | 69 | 56 | 16 |
| 2002-03 | Div 2 | 46 | 15 | 13 | 18 | 56 | 64 | 58 | 13 |
| 2003-04 | Div 2 | 46 | 16 | 11 | 19 | 58 | 65 | 59 | 14 |

## DID YOU KNOW ?

During his record breaking season of 1929–30, Jimmy Hampson scored his 100th goal for the club in only his 97th match on 4 January. His second goal in a hat-trick of a 5-1 Blackpool win against Southampon hoisted the century.

## BLACKPOOL 2003–04 LEAGUE RECORD

| *Match No.* | *Date* | *Venue* | *Opponents* | *Result* | | *H/T Score* | *Lg. Pos.* | *Goalscorers* | *Attendance* |
|---|---|---|---|---|---|---|---|---|---|
| 1 | Aug 9 | A | QPR | L | 0-5 | 0-2 | — | | 14,581 |
| 2 | 16 | H | Wycombe W | W | 3-2 | 2-2 | 15 | Taylor 2 [44, 45], Hilton [61] | 5960 |
| 3 | 23 | A | Oldham Ath | W | 3-2 | 0-1 | 10 | Danns [56], Douglas [69], Taylor [81] | 6745 |
| 4 | 25 | H | Barnsley | L | 0-2 | 0-1 | 13 | | 6039 |
| 5 | 30 | A | Swindon T | D | 2-2 | 2-2 | 13 | Douglas [10], Taylor [27] | 6219 |
| 6 | Sept 13 | H | Bournemouth | L | 1-2 | 1-0 | 18 | Wellens [37] | 5607 |
| 7 | 16 | A | Brentford | D | 0-0 | 0-0 | — | | 3818 |
| 8 | 20 | A | Stockport Co | W | 3-1 | 0-1 | 16 | Grayson [56], Clarke C [61], Murphy [68] | 5420 |
| 9 | 27 | H | Notts Co | W | 2-1 | 2-1 | 15 | Southern [11], Danns [43] | 6206 |
| 10 | 30 | H | Grimsby T | L | 0-1 | 0-0 | — | | 5491 |
| 11 | Oct 4 | A | Brighton & HA | L | 0-3 | 0-2 | 17 | | 6483 |
| 12 | 11 | A | Colchester U | D | 1-1 | 0-1 | 17 | Taylor [52] | 3265 |
| 13 | 18 | H | Hartlepool U | W | 4-0 | 3-0 | 16 | Douglas [4], Taylor 3 (1 pen) [20, 40, 72 (p)] | 6871 |
| 14 | 21 | H | Rushden & D | L | 2-3 | 1-1 | — | Murphy 2 [4, 62] | 5234 |
| 15 | 25 | A | Plymouth Arg | L | 0-1 | 0-1 | 18 | | 12,372 |
| 16 | Nov 1 | A | Sheffield W | W | 1-0 | 0-0 | 18 | Taylor [79] | 21,450 |
| 17 | 11 | H | Wrexham | L | 0-1 | 0-0 | — | | 4864 |
| 18 | 15 | H | Chesterfield | W | 1-0 | 1-0 | 16 | Taylor [41] | 5252 |
| 19 | 22 | A | Peterborough U | W | 1-0 | 0-0 | 14 | Taylor [48] | 4411 |
| 20 | 29 | H | Bristol C | W | 1-0 | 0-0 | 11 | Taylor [58] | 5989 |
| 21 | Dec 13 | H | Luton T | L | 0-1 | 0-1 | 12 | | 5739 |
| 22 | 26 | H | Tranmere R | W | 2-1 | 1-0 | 10 | Murphy [9], Johnson [79] | 8340 |
| 23 | 28 | A | Wrexham | L | 2-4 | 2-4 | 13 | Taylor [23], Flynn [45] | 6171 |
| 24 | Jan 10 | H | QPR | L | 0-1 | 0-1 | 14 | | 7329 |
| 25 | 14 | A | Port Vale | L | 1-2 | 0-2 | — | Sheron [73] | 4523 |
| 26 | 17 | A | Wycombe W | W | 3-0 | 2-0 | 14 | Coid [12], Taylor [27], Davis [67] | 4834 |
| 27 | 24 | H | Oldham Ath | D | 1-1 | 1-0 | 12 | Coid [25] | 7508 |
| 28 | 27 | A | Barnsley | L | 0-3 | 0-1 | — | | 7918 |
| 29 | 31 | H | Swindon T | D | 2-2 | 1-0 | 13 | Taylor [14], Dinning [64] | 6463 |
| 30 | Feb 7 | A | Tranmere R | D | 1-1 | 1-0 | 13 | Taylor [36] | 7919 |
| 31 | 20 | A | Hartlepool U | D | 1-1 | 0-0 | — | Sheron [74] | 5497 |
| 32 | 28 | H | Plymouth Arg | L | 0-1 | 0-0 | 16 | | 7253 |
| 33 | Mar 2 | A | Rushden & D | D | 0-0 | 0-0 | — | | 3764 |
| 34 | 6 | H | Port Vale | W | 2-1 | 0-1 | 14 | Dinning (pen) [54], Wellens [60] | 6878 |
| 35 | 13 | A | Luton T | L | 2-3 | 0-1 | 15 | Dinning (pen) [69], Blinkhorn [79] | 6343 |
| 36 | 16 | H | Brentford | D | 1-1 | 0-1 | — | Wellens [53] | 4617 |
| 37 | 24 | A | Bournemouth | W | 2-1 | 1-0 | — | Sheron [45], Murphy [86] | 6436 |
| 38 | 27 | H | Stockport Co | D | 1-1 | 0-0 | 14 | Sheron [62] | 7604 |
| 39 | 30 | H | Colchester U | D | 0-0 | 0-0 | — | | 5473 |
| 40 | Apr 3 | A | Notts Co | L | 1-4 | 0-3 | 15 | Sheron [47] | 5100 |
| 41 | 10 | H | Brighton & HA | W | 3-1 | 1-0 | 14 | Sheron [24], Matias [58], Murphy [79] | 6194 |
| 42 | 12 | A | Grimsby T | W | 2-0 | 1-0 | 12 | Murphy [23], Coid [53] | 4775 |
| 43 | 17 | H | Sheffield W | W | 4-1 | 2-1 | 11 | Murphy 2 [10, 86], Sheron 2 [26, 79] | 7388 |
| 44 | 24 | A | Chesterfield | L | 0-1 | 0-1 | 12 | | 4117 |
| 45 | May 1 | H | Peterborough U | L | 1-4 | 1-2 | 14 | Bullock [28] | 7200 |
| 46 | 8 | A | Bristol C | L | 1-2 | 0-2 | 14 | Southern (pen) [78] | 19,101 |

**Final League Position: 14**

### GOALSCORERS

*League (58):* Taylor 16 (1 pen), Murphy 9, Sheron 8, Coid 3, Dinning 3 (2 pens), Douglas 3, Wellens 3, Danns 2, Southern 2 (1 pen), Blinkhorn 1, Bullock 1, Clarke C 1, Davis 1, Flynn 1, Grayson 1, Hilton 1, Johnson 1, Matias 1.
*Carling Cup (4):* Taylor 3, Southern 1.
*FA Cup (10):* Taylor 6, Burns 1, Coid 1, Richardson 1, Southern 1.
*LDV Vans Trophy (13):* Murphy 4, Sheron 3, Coid 2, Taylor 2, Blinkhorn 1, Southern 1.

| Barnes P 19 | Grayson S 28 + 5 | Hilton K 12 + 2 | Flynn M 29 + 1 | Davis S 22 + 7 | Danns N 12 | Wellens R 40 + 1 | Bullock M 33 + 11 | Sheron M 28 + 10 | Taylor S 30 + 1 | Coid D 30 + 5 | Richardson L 24 + 4 | Clarke C 11 + 7 | Douglas J 15 + 1 | Jones L 21 | Walker R 3 + 6 | Evans G 21 + 2 | Southern K 15 + 13 | Murphy J 27 + 3 | Doherty S — + 1 | Jaszczun T 5 + 2 | Elliott S 28 | Jones B 5 | Burns J 3 + 8 | McMahon S 7 + 5 | Johnson S 3 + 1 | Wiles S — + 4 | Dinning T 10 | Hessey S 4 + 2 | Blinkhorn M 4 + 8 | Matias P 7 | Donnelly C 8 + 1 | Clancy S 1 + 1 | Mangan A — + 2 | Edge L 1 | Match No. |
|---|---|---|---|---|---|---|---|---|---|---|---|---|---|---|---|---|---|---|---|---|---|---|---|---|---|---|---|---|---|---|---|---|---|---|---|
| 1 | 2[1] | 3 | 4[2] | 5 | 6 | 7■ | 8 | 9 | 10 | 11[3] | 12 | 13 | 14 |  |  |  |  |  |  |  |  |  |  |  |  |  |  |  |  |  |  |  |  |  | 1 |
|  |  | 3 | 4 | 5 | 6■ | 7[2] | 8[1] | 9[3] | 10 | 13 | 2 | 12 | 11 | 1 | 14 |  |  |  |  |  |  |  |  |  |  |  |  |  |  |  |  |  |  |  | 2 |
|  | 12 | 3 | 4[2] | 5 | 6 |  | 8 | 9 | 10[3] | 11[1] | 2 | 13 | 7 | 1 | 14 |  |  |  |  |  |  |  |  |  |  |  |  |  |  |  |  |  |  |  | 3 |
|  | 12 | 3 | 4[2] | 5 | 6 | 7 |  | 9 | 10 | 11[3] | 2[1] | 13 | 8 | 1 | 14 |  |  |  |  |  |  |  |  |  |  |  |  |  |  |  |  |  |  |  | 4 |
|  | 2 | 3[1] | 4 | 5 |  | 8 | 13 | 9[2] | 10 | 11 | 6 | 12 | 7 | 1 |  |  |  |  |  |  |  |  |  |  |  |  |  |  |  |  |  |  |  |  | 5 |
|  |  |  |  | 5 | 6 | 7 | 8 | 9[1] | 10 |  | 2 | 4 | 11[2] | 1 | 12 | 3 | 13 |  |  |  |  |  |  |  |  |  |  |  |  |  |  |  |  |  | 6 |
|  | 4 |  |  | 5 | 8 | 7[2] | 12 | 9 | 10 |  | 2[1] | 6 | 11 | 1 |  | 3 | 13 |  |  |  |  |  |  |  |  |  |  |  |  |  |  |  |  |  | 7 |
|  | 4 |  |  | 5 | 8■ | 7 | 12 | 9[3] | 10[1] |  | 2[2] | 6 | 11 | 1 |  | 3 | 13 | 14 |  |  |  |  |  |  |  |  |  |  |  |  |  |  |  |  | 8 |
|  | 2 |  |  | 5 | 8[1] | 7 | 12 | 9 | 10[3] | 13 |  | 6 | 11 | 1 |  | 3[2] | 4 | 14 |  |  |  |  |  |  |  |  |  |  |  |  |  |  |  |  | 9 |
|  | 2 |  |  | 5 | 8 | 7 | 12 | 9[1] | 10 | 3[3] |  | 6[2] | 11 | 1 |  |  | 4 | 13 | 14 |  |  |  |  |  |  |  |  |  |  |  |  |  |  |  | 10 |
|  | 4 | 3 |  | 5 |  | 7 | 12 | 13 | 10 | 2[1] |  | 6 | 11 | 1 |  |  | 8[2] | 9 |  |  |  |  |  |  |  |  |  |  |  |  |  |  |  |  | 11 |
|  | 6 | 3 |  | 5 |  | 7[2] | 8 |  | 10 | 2 | 13 | 12 | 11 | 1 |  |  | 4[1] | 9 |  |  |  |  |  |  |  |  |  |  |  |  |  |  |  |  | 12 |
| 1 | 2 | 3 |  | 5 | 6 | 7 | 8[2] | 12 | 10 | 13 |  | 4 | 11[1] |  |  | 14 |  | 9[3] |  |  |  |  |  |  |  |  |  |  |  |  |  |  |  |  | 13 |
| 1 | 2[2] | 3 |  | 5 | 6 | 7 | 8[1] | 12 | 10 | 13 |  | 4 | 11 |  |  |  |  | 9 |  |  |  |  |  |  |  |  |  |  |  |  |  |  |  |  | 14 |
| 1 | 2 |  |  | 5 | 6 | 7 | 12 |  | 13 | 3[1] |  | 4 | 11■ |  |  | 8 | 10[2] | 9 |  |  |  |  |  |  |  |  |  |  |  |  |  |  |  |  | 15 |
| 1 | 2 |  | 12 | 5 |  | 7[3] | 8 | 13 | 10[1] |  |  | 6 | 11 |  |  | 3 | 4 | 9[2] |  | 14 |  |  |  |  |  |  |  |  |  |  |  |  |  |  | 16 |
|  | 2[1] | 13 | 5 |  |  | 14 | 7 | 8[3] | 10 | 11 | 12 | 6 |  |  |  |  | 4 | 9 |  | 3[2] |  | 1 |  |  |  |  |  |  |  |  |  |  |  |  | 17 |
|  |  |  | 5 |  |  | 7 | 8 |  | 10 | 11 | 2 |  |  |  |  |  | 4 | 9 |  | 3 | 6 | 1 |  |  |  |  |  |  |  |  |  |  |  |  | 18 |
|  |  |  | 5 | 12 |  | 7 | 8[1] |  | 10 | 11 | 2 |  |  |  |  | 13 | 4 | 9 |  | 3[2] | 6 | 1 |  |  |  |  |  |  |  |  |  |  |  |  | 19 |
|  | 12 |  | 5 | 13 |  | 7[1] | 8[2] |  | 10 | 11 | 2 |  |  |  |  | 3 | 4 | 9 |  |  | 6 | 1 |  |  |  |  |  |  |  |  |  |  |  |  | 20 |
|  | 2[2] |  | 5 | 12 |  | 8 | 4[3] | 9[1] | 10 | 7 |  |  |  |  |  | 3 |  |  |  |  | 6 | 1 | 13 | 14 | 11 |  |  |  |  |  |  |  |  |  | 21 |
|  | 12 |  | 5 | 6 |  | 7[1] | 8 |  | 10 | 11 | 2 |  |  | 1 |  | 3 |  | 9 |  |  |  |  | 13 |  | 4[2] |  |  |  |  |  |  |  |  |  | 22 |
|  | 2[1] | 13 | 5 |  |  |  | 7 |  | 10 | 11 |  | 12 |  | 1 |  | 3[2] |  | 9 |  |  | 6 |  | 14 | 4 | 8[3] |  |  |  |  |  |  |  |  |  | 23 |
|  | 2 | 4[1] |  | 5 |  | 7 | 8[2] | 12 | 10 | 11 |  |  |  | 1 |  | 3 |  | 9 |  |  | 6 |  |  |  | 13 |  |  |  |  |  |  |  |  |  | 24 |
|  | 2[2] | 4 |  | 5 |  | 7 | 8 | 12 | 10 | 11 |  |  |  | 1 |  | 3[1] |  | 9 |  |  | 6 |  |  | 13 |  |  |  |  |  |  |  |  |  |  | 25 |
|  | 2 | 3 |  | 5 |  | 7[1] | 8[3] | 13 | 10[2] | 11 |  |  |  | 1 |  |  |  | 9 |  |  | 6 |  | 12 | 4 |  | 14 |  |  |  |  |  |  |  |  | 26 |
| 1 | 2[1] |  | 5 |  |  |  | 8[3] | 9[2] | 10 | 11 | 12 |  |  |  | 13 | 3 |  |  |  |  | 6 |  |  | 7 |  | 14 | 4 |  |  |  |  |  |  |  | 27 |
| 1 |  |  | 5 |  |  |  | 8[2] | 9 | 10 | 11 | 2 |  |  |  |  | 3 |  |  |  |  | 6 |  | 12 | 7[1] |  | 13 | 4 |  |  |  |  |  |  |  | 28 |
| 1 | 12 |  | 5 |  |  | 7■ | 8 | 9[2] | 10 | 11 | 2[1] |  |  |  |  | 3 | 13 |  |  |  | 6 |  |  |  |  |  | 4 |  |  |  |  |  |  |  | 29 |
|  | 2 |  | 5 |  |  | 7 | 14 | 13 | 10[3] | 11 | 4 |  |  | 1 | 9[2] | 3 | 12 |  |  |  | 6 |  |  | 8[1] |  |  |  |  |  |  |  |  |  |  | 30 |
|  | 5 |  |  |  |  |  | 8 | 13 | 10[3] | 11 | 2 |  |  | 1 | 9[2] | 3 | 12 |  |  |  | 6 |  |  | 7[1] |  |  | 4 | 14 |  |  |  |  |  |  | 31 |
| 1 | 2 |  | 5 |  |  | 7 | 8[1] | 10 |  | 11 |  |  |  |  |  | 3 | 4 | 9 |  |  | 6 |  |  |  |  |  |  |  | 12 |  |  |  |  |  | 32 |
| 1 | 2 |  | 5 |  |  | 7 | 12 | 9[1] |  |  | 3 |  |  |  | 13 | 11 | 8 |  |  |  | 6 |  |  |  |  |  | 4 |  | 10[2] |  |  |  |  |  | 33 |
| 1 | 2 |  | 5 | 12 |  | 7 | 11 | 9 |  |  |  |  |  |  |  | 3 | 8 |  |  |  | 6 |  |  |  |  |  | 4 |  | 10[1] |  |  |  |  |  | 34 |
| 1 | 2 |  |  | 5 |  | 7 | 12 | 9[3] |  |  |  |  |  |  | 10 | 3[2] |  |  |  | 13 | 6 |  |  | 11[1] |  |  | 8 | 4 | 14 |  |  |  |  |  | 35 |
|  |  |  | 5 | 14 |  | 7 | 8 | 13 |  |  | 2 |  |  | 1 |  |  | 12 | 9 |  | 3 | 6 |  |  |  |  |  | 11[3] | 4[1] | 10[2] |  |  |  |  |  | 36 |
|  |  |  | 5 | 13 |  | 7 | 8[2] | 10[3] |  | 11 | 2 |  |  | 1 |  |  | 12 | 9 |  |  | 6 |  |  |  |  |  | 4 | 3[1] | 14 |  |  |  |  |  | 37 |
|  |  |  | 5 |  |  | 7 | 8 | 10 |  | 12 | 2 |  |  | 1 |  |  |  | 9 |  | 3[1] | 6 |  |  |  |  |  | 4[2] |  |  | 11 | 13 |  |  |  | 38 |
| 1 | 2 |  | 5 |  |  | 7[1] | 8 | 10[2] |  | 3■ |  |  |  |  |  |  | 12 | 9 |  |  | 6 |  |  |  |  |  |  | 14 | 13 | 11[3] | 4 |  |  |  | 39 |
| 1 | 2 |  |  | 5 |  | 7 | 8 | 10[2] |  | 3 |  |  |  |  |  |  | 12 | 9 |  |  | 6 |  | 14 |  |  |  |  |  | 13 | 11[3] | 4[1] |  |  |  | 40 |
| 1 |  |  | 5 | 13 |  | 7 | 8[2] | 10[3] |  | 3 | 2 |  |  |  |  |  | 12 | 9 |  |  | 6 |  |  |  |  |  |  |  | 14 | 11[1] | 4 |  |  |  | 41 |
| 1 |  |  | 5 |  |  | 8 |  | 10 |  | 11[3] | 2 |  |  |  |  |  | 14 | 9[2] |  |  | 6 |  | 12 |  |  |  |  | 3[1] | 13 | 7 | 4 |  |  |  | 42 |
| 1 |  |  | 5 |  |  | 7[2] | 8[1] | 10 |  |  | 2 |  |  |  |  |  | 12 | 9 |  |  | 6 |  | 3[3] | 13 |  |  |  |  |  | 11 | 4 | 14 |  |  | 43 |
| 1■ | 2 |  | 5 |  |  | 7 | 12 |  |  |  |  |  |  |  |  |  | 8[6] | 9 |  |  | 6 |  | 3 | 13 |  |  |  |  | 10[2] | 11[1] | 4 |  | 15 |  | 44 |
| 1 |  |  | 5 |  |  | 7 | 8 | 10[3] |  |  | 2 |  |  |  |  |  |  | 9 |  |  | 6 |  | 11 | 13 |  | 14 |  |  | 12 |  | 4[2] | 3[1] |  |  | 45 |
|  |  |  | 5 |  |  | 7 | 8 | 10 |  | 3[1] | 2 |  |  |  |  |  | 11 | 9 |  |  | 6 |  | 12 |  |  |  |  |  |  |  | 4[2] |  | 13 | 1 | 46 |

**Carling Cup**

| | | | |
|---|---|---|---|
| First Round | Barnsley | (a) | 2-1 |
| Second Round | Birmingham C | (h) | 1-0 |
| Third Round | Crystal Palace | (h) | 1-3 |

**FA Cup**

| | | | |
|---|---|---|---|
| First Round | Boreham Wood | (h) | 4-0 |
| Second Round | Oldham Ath | (a) | 5-2 |
| Third Round | Portsmouth | (a) | 1-2 |

**LDV Vans Trophy**

| | | | |
|---|---|---|---|
| First Round | Tranmere R | (h) | 3-2 |
| Second Round | Doncaster R | (h) | 1-0 |
| Quarter-Final | Stockport Co | (a) | 1-0 |
| Semi-Final | Halifax T | (h) | 3-2 |
| Northern Final | Sheffield W | (h) | 1-0 |
| | | (a) | 2-0 |
| Final | Southend U | | 2-0 |

*(at Millennium Stadium)*

# BOLTON WANDERERS FA Premiership

## FOUNDATION

In 1874 boys of Christ Church Sunday School, Blackburn Street, led by their master Thomas Ogden, established a football club which went under the name of the school and whose president was Vicar of Christ Church. Membership was 6d (two and a half pence). When their president began to lay down too many rules about the use of church premises, the club broke away and formed Bolton Wanderers in 1877, holding their earliest meetings at the Gladstone Hotel.

***Reebok Stadium, Burnden Way, Lostock, Bolton BL6 6JW.***

***Telephone:*** (01204) 673 673.

***Fax:*** (01204) 673 773.

***Ticket Office:*** 0871 871 2932.

***Website:*** www.bwfc.co.uk

***Email:*** reception@bwfc.co.uk

***Ground Capacity:*** 27,879.

***Record Attendance:*** 69,912 v Manchester C, FA Cup 5th rd, 18 February 1933.

***Pitch Measurements:*** 114yd × 74yd.

***Chairman:*** P. A. Gartside.

***Vice-chairman:*** W. B. Warburton.

***Secretary:*** Simon Marland.

***Manager:*** Sam Allardyce.

***Assistant Manager:*** P. Brown.

***Physio:*** Mark Taylor.

***Colours:*** All white.

***Change Colours:*** All sky blue.

***Year Formed:*** 1874.

***Turned Professional:*** 1880.

***Ltd Co.:*** 1895.

***Previous Name:*** 1874, Christ Church FC; 1877, Bolton Wanderers.

***Club Nickname:*** 'The Trotters'.

***Previous Grounds:*** Park Recreation Ground and Cockle's Field before moving to Pike's Lane ground 1881; 1895, Burnden Park; 1997, Reebok Stadium.

***First Football League Game:*** 8 September 1888, Football League, v Derby Co (h) L 3–6 – Harrison; Robinson, Mitchell; Roberts, Weir, Bullough, Davenport (2), Milne, Coupar, Barbour, Brogan (1).

***Record League Victory:*** 8–0 v Barnsley, Division 2, 6 October 1934 – Jones; Smith, Finney; Goslin, Atkinson, George Taylor; George T. Taylor (2), Eastham, Milsom (1), Westwood (4), Cook, (1 og).

## HONOURS

*Football League:* Division 1 – Champions 1996–97; Promoted from Division 1 (play-offs) 2000–01. Division 2 – Champions 1908–09, 1977–78; Runners-up 1899–1900, 1904–05, 1910–11, 1934–35, 1992–93; Division 3 – Champions 1972–73.

*FA Cup:* Winners 1923, 1926, 1929, 1958; Runners-up 1894, 1904, 1953.

*Football League Cup:* Runners-up 1995, 2004.

*Freight Rover Trophy:* Runners-up 1986.

*Sherpa Van Trophy:* Winners 1989.

## SKY SPORTS FACT FILE

Jimmy Seddon, centre-half of Bolton Wanderers in their three 1920s FA Cup-winning teams, joined the club in 1913 and despite contracting trench-foot during the First World War made 337 peacetime League appearances and played for England.

***Record Cup Victory:*** 13–0 v Sheffield U, FA Cup 2nd rd, 1 February 1890 – Parkinson; Robinson (1), Jones; Bullough, Davenport, Roberts; Rushton, Brogan (3), Cassidy (5), McNee, Weir (4).

***Record Defeat:*** 1–9 v Preston NE, FA Cup 2nd rd, 10 December 1887.

***Most League Points (2 for a win):*** 61, Division 3, 1972–73.

***Most League Points (3 for a win):*** 98, Division 1, 1996–97.

***Most League Goals:*** 100, Division 1, 1996–97.

***Highest League Scorer in Season:*** Joe Smith, 38, Division 1, 1920–21.

***Most League Goals in Total Aggregate:*** Nat Lofthouse, 255, 1946–61.

***Most League Goals in One Match:*** 5, Tony Caldwell v Walsall, Division 3, 10 September 1983.

***Most Capped Player:*** Mark Fish, 34 (62), South Africa.

***Most League Appearances:*** Eddie Hopkinson, 519, 1956–70.

***Youngest League Player:*** Ray Parry, 15 years 267 days v Wolverhampton W, 13 October 1951.

***Record Transfer Fee Received:*** £4,500,000 from Liverpool for Jason McAteer, September 1995.

***Record Transfer Fee Paid:*** £3,500,000 for Dean Holdsworth from Wimbledon, October 1997.

***Football League Record:*** 1888 Founder Member of the League; 1899–1900 Division 2; 1900–03 Division 1; 1903–05 Division 2; 1905–08 Division 1; 1908–09 Division 2; 1909–10 Division 1; 1910–11 Division 2; 1911–33 Division 1; 1933–35 Division 2; 1935–64 Division 1; 1964–71 Division 2; 1971–73 Division 3; 1973–78 Division 2; 1978–80 Division 1; 1980–83 Division 2; 1983–87 Division 3; 1987–88 Division 4; 1988–92 Division 3; 1992–93 Division 2; 1993–95 Division 1; 1995–96 FA Premier League; 1996–97 Division 1; 1997–98 FA Premier League; 1998–2001 Division 1; 2001– FA Premier League.

## MANAGERS

Tom Rawthorne 1874–85 *(Secretary)*
J. J. Bentley 1885–86 *(Secretary)*
W. G. Struthers 1886–87 *(Secretary)*
Fitzroy Norris 1887 *(Secretary)*
J. J. Bentley 1887–95 *(Secretary)*
Harry Downs 1895–96 *(Secretary)*
Frank Brettell 1896–98 *(Secretary)*
John Somerville 1898–1910
Will Settle 1910–15
Tom Mather 1915–19
Charles Foweraker 1919–44
Walter Rowley 1944–50
Bill Ridding 1951–68
Nat Lofthouse 1968–70
Jimmy McIlroy 1970
Jimmy Meadows 1971
Nat Lofthouse 1971 *(then Admin. Manager to 1972)*
Jimmy Armfield 1971–74
Ian Greaves 1974–80
Stan Anderson 1980–81
George Mulhall 1981–82
John McGovern 1982–85
Charlie Wright 1985
Phil Neal 1985–92
Bruce Rioch 1992–95
Roy McFarland 1995–96
Colin Todd 1996–99
Sam Allardyce October 1999–

## LATEST SEQUENCES

***Longest Sequence of League Wins:*** 11, 5.11.1904 – 2.1.1905.

***Longest Sequence of League Defeats:*** 11, 7.4.1902 – 18.10.1902.

***Longest Sequence of League Draws:*** 6, 25.1.1913 – 8.3.1913.

***Longest Sequence of Unbeaten League Matches:*** 23, 13.10.1990 – 9.3.1991.

***Longest Sequence Without a League Win:*** 26, 7.4.1902 – 10.1.1903.

***Successive Scoring Runs:*** 24 from 22.11.1996.

***Successive Non-scoring Runs:*** 5 from 3.1.1898.

## TEN YEAR LEAGUE RECORD

| | | *P* | *W* | *D* | *L* | *F* | *A* | *Pts* | *Pos* |
|---|---|---|---|---|---|---|---|---|---|
| 1994-95 | Div 1 | 46 | 21 | 14 | 11 | 67 | 45 | 77 | 3 |
| 1995-96 | PR Lge | 38 | 8 | 5 | 25 | 39 | 71 | 29 | 20 |
| 1996-97 | Div 1 | 46 | 28 | 14 | 4 | 100 | 53 | 98 | 1 |
| 1997-98 | PR Lge | 38 | 9 | 13 | 16 | 41 | 61 | 40 | 18 |
| 1998-99 | Div 1 | 46 | 20 | 16 | 10 | 78 | 59 | 76 | 6 |
| 1999-2000 | Div 1 | 46 | 21 | 13 | 12 | 69 | 50 | 76 | 6 |
| 2000-01 | Div 1 | 46 | 24 | 15 | 7 | 76 | 45 | 87 | 3 |
| 2001-02 | PR Lge | 38 | 9 | 13 | 16 | 44 | 62 | 40 | 16 |
| 2002-03 | PR Lge | 38 | 10 | 14 | 14 | 41 | 51 | 44 | 17 |
| 2003-04 | PR Lge | 38 | 14 | 11 | 13 | 48 | 56 | 53 | 8 |

## DID YOU KNOW?

Bolton Wanderers' record run of scoring in 24 consecutive matches in 1996–97 equalled their original feat in 1888–89 when they registered in all 22 games and the first two in 1889–90. Their goals total then was 70; in 1996–97 it was 60.

## BOLTON WANDERERS 2003–04 LEAGUE RECORD

| Match No. | Date | Venue | Opponents | Result | | H/T Score | Lg. Pos. | Goalscorers | Attendance |
|---|---|---|---|---|---|---|---|---|---|
| 1 | Aug 16 | A | Manchester U | L | 0-4 | 0-1 | — | | 67,647 |
| 2 | 23 | H | Blackburn R | D | 2-2 | 2-0 | 18 | Djorkaeff (pen) [3], Davies [25] | 27,423 |
| 3 | 26 | A | Portsmouth | L | 0-4 | 0-0 | — | | 20,118 |
| 4 | 30 | H | Charlton Ath | D | 0-0 | 0-0 | 17 | | 23,098 |
| 5 | Sept 13 | H | Middlesbrough | W | 2-0 | 1-0 | 14 | Davies [23], N'Gotty [81] | 26,419 |
| 6 | 20 | A | Newcastle U | D | 0-0 | 0-0 | 12 | | 52,014 |
| 7 | 27 | H | Wolverhampton W | D | 1-1 | 0-1 | 15 | Davies [85] | 27,043 |
| 8 | Oct 5 | A | Aston Villa | D | 1-1 | 0-0 | 14 | Nolan [46] | 30,229 |
| 9 | 18 | A | Manchester C | L | 2-6 | 1-1 | 16 | Nolan [25], Campo [60] | 47,101 |
| 10 | 25 | H | Birmingham C | L | 0-1 | 0-1 | 18 | | 25,023 |
| 11 | Nov 1 | A | Tottenham H | W | 1-0 | 0-0 | 15 | Nolan [73] | 35,191 |
| 12 | 8 | H | Southampton | D | 0-0 | 0-0 | 14 | | 25,619 |
| 13 | 22 | A | Leeds U | W | 2-0 | 2-0 | 14 | Davies [16], Giannakopoulos [17] | 36,558 |
| 14 | 29 | H | Everton | W | 2-0 | 1-0 | 11 | Frandsen [26], Djorkaeff [46] | 27,350 |
| 15 | Dec 6 | A | Fulham | L | 1-2 | 0-0 | 13 | Davies [53] | 14,393 |
| 16 | 13 | A | Chelsea | W | 2-1 | 1-1 | 10 | N'Gotty [39], Terry (og) [90] | 40,491 |
| 17 | 20 | H | Arsenal | D | 1-1 | 0-0 | 10 | Pedersen [83] | 27,492 |
| 18 | 26 | A | Liverpool | L | 1-3 | 0-1 | 10 | Pedersen [85] | 42,987 |
| 19 | 28 | H | Leicester C | D | 2-2 | 1-1 | 12 | Thatcher (og) [35], Campo [55] | 27,407 |
| 20 | Jan 7 | H | Manchester U | L | 1-2 | 0-2 | — | Neville G (og) [89] | 27,668 |
| 21 | 10 | A | Blackburn R | W | 4-3 | 2-3 | 11 | Nolan 2 [1, 78], Djorkaeff [43], Giannakopoulos [73] | 23,538 |
| 22 | 17 | H | Portsmouth | W | 1-0 | 0-0 | 10 | Davies [53] | 26,558 |
| 23 | 31 | A | Charlton Ath | W | 2-1 | 1-1 | 8 | Pedersen [1], Nolan [78] | 26,220 |
| 24 | Feb 7 | H | Liverpool | D | 2-2 | 1-0 | 9 | Hunt [11], Djorkaeff [58] | 27,552 |
| 25 | 10 | A | Leicester C | D | 1-1 | 1-1 | — | Walker (og) [33] | 26,674 |
| 26 | 21 | H | Manchester C | L | 1-3 | 1-2 | 11 | Nolan [22] | 27,301 |
| 27 | Mar 6 | A | Birmingham C | L | 0-2 | 0-1 | 11 | | 28,003 |
| 28 | 13 | H | Chelsea | L | 0-2 | 0-0 | 13 | | 26,717 |
| 29 | 20 | A | Arsenal | L | 1-2 | 1-2 | 13 | Campo [41] | 38,053 |
| 30 | 28 | H | Newcastle U | W | 1-0 | 1-0 | 13 | Pedersen [4] | 27,360 |
| 31 | Apr 3 | A | Middlesbrough | L | 0-2 | 0-1 | 13 | | 30,104 |
| 32 | 10 | H | Aston Villa | D | 2-2 | 0-1 | 12 | Pedersen [48], Davies [86] | 26,374 |
| 33 | 12 | A | Wolverhampton W | W | 2-1 | 1-1 | 12 | Pedersen [43], Davies [90] | 28,695 |
| 34 | 17 | H | Tottenham H | W | 2-0 | 1-0 | 12 | Campo [7], Pedersen [65] | 26,440 |
| 35 | 24 | A | Southampton | W | 2-1 | 0-1 | 10 | Nolan [77], Davies [78] | 31,712 |
| 36 | May 2 | H | Leeds U | W | 4-1 | 0-1 | 7 | Djorkaeff 2 [47, 53], Harte (og) [55], Nolan [78] | 27,420 |
| 37 | 8 | A | Everton | W | 2-1 | 1-0 | 7 | Djorkaeff 2 [14, 87] | 40,190 |
| 38 | 15 | H | Fulham | L | 0-2 | 0-1 | 8 | | 27,383 |

**Final League Position: 8**

### GOALSCORERS

*League (48):* Davies 9, Nolan 9, Djorkaeff 8 (1 pen), Pedersen 7, Campo 4, Giannakopoulos 2, N'Gotty 2, Frandsen 1, Hunt 1, own goals 5.
*Carling Cup (15):* Jardel 3, Okocha 3, Giannakopoulos 2, Nolan 2, Pedersen 2, Davies 1, Djorkjaeff 1 (pen), N'Gotty 1.
*FA Cup (2):* Nolan 1, Shakes 1.

| Jaaskelainen J 38 | Hunt N 28 + 3 | Gardner R 20 + 2 | Campo I 37 + 1 | N'Gotty B 32 + 1 | Laville F 5 | Giannakopoulos S 17 + 14 | Nolan K 37 | Pedersen H 19 + 14 | Davies K 38 | Okocha J 33 + 2 | Facey D — + 1 | Frandsen P 22 + 11 | Djorkaeff Y 24 + 3 | Barness A 11 + 4 | Charlton S 28 + 3 | Jardel M — + 7 | Emerson25 + 1 | Little G — + 4 | Ba I — + 9 | Javi Moreno1 + 7 | Otsemobor J 1 | Howey S 2 + 1 | Vaz Te R — + 1 | *Match No.* |
|---|---|---|---|---|---|---|---|---|---|---|---|---|---|---|---|---|---|---|---|---|---|---|---|---|
| 1 | 2 | 3 | 4 | 5 | 6 | $7^1$ | $8^2$ | $9^3$ | 10 | 11 | 12 | 13 | 14 | | | | | | | | | | | 1 |
| 1 | 2 | 3 | 4 | 5 | 6 | 12 | $7^2$ | $9^3$ | 10 | $11^1$ | | 13 | 8 | 14 | | | | | | | | | | 2 |
| 1 | | 3 | 4 | 5 | 6 | 12 | | 9 | $10^3$ | 11 | | $8^1$ | 7 | $2^2$ | 13 | 14 | | | | | | | | 3 |
| 1 | 2 | 3 | 4 | | 6 | 12 | 8 | $9^1$ | 10 | 11 | | | 7 | | | | 5 | | | | | | | 4 |
| 1 | $2^3$ | 3 | 4 | 12 | $6^1$ | 7 | 8 | 13 | 9 | 11 | | 14 | $10^2$ | | | | 5 | | | | | | | 5 |
| 1 | | 3 | 4 | 2 | | $7^1$ | 8 | 12 | 9 | 11 | | 13 | $10^2$ | | 6 | | 5 | | | | | | | 6 |
| 1 | | 3 | $4^1$ | $2^3$ | | | 7 | $9^2$ | 10 | 11 | | 12 | 8 | | 6 | 13 | 5 | 14 | | | | | | 7 |
| 1 | | 3 | 4 | 2 | | $11^2$ | $7^1$ | | 9 | 10 | | 8 | | | 6 | 12 | 5 | 13 | | | | | | 8 |
| 1 | | 3 | 4 | 2 | | 11 | 7 | | 9 | 10 | | $8^1$ | | | 6 | 12 | $5^2$ | 13 | | | | | | 9 |
| 1 | | 3 | $4^2$ | 2 | | $7^1$ | $11^3$ | 12 | 9 | 10 | | 8 | | | 6 | 13 | 5 | 14 | | | | | | 10 |
| 1 | 2 | 3 | 4 | 5 | | $7^1$ | 11 | 12 | 9 | 10 | | 8 | | | 6 | | | | | | | | | 11 |
| 1 | 2 | 3 | 4 | 5 | | $11^1$ | 7 | 12 | $9^2$ | 10 | | 8 | | | 6 | 13 | | | | | | | | 12 |
| 1 | 2 | 3 | 4 | 5 | | 11 | $7^1$ | 12 | 9 | 10 | | 8 | | | 6 | | | | | | | | | 13 |
| 1 | 2 | 3 | 4 | 5 | | $7^1$ | 11 | | 9 | 10 | | 8 | 12 | | 6 | | | | | | | | | 14 |
| 1 | 2 | 3 | $4^3$ | 5 | | 12 | $7^2$ | | 9 | 11 | | $8^1$ | 10 | | 6 | 13 | | | 14 | | | | | 15 |
| 1 | 2 | 3 | 4 | 5 | | 12 | $7^1$ | 13 | 9 | 11 | | 8 | $10^2$ | | 6 | | | | | | | | | 16 |
| 1 | 2 | 3 | $4^2$ | | | | $7^1$ | 12 | 9 | 11 | | 8 | 10 | | 6 | | 5 | | 13 | | | | | 17 |
| 1 | 2 | 3 | $4^3$ | | | 13 | 7 | 12 | 9 | $11^2$ | | 8 | $10^1$ | | 6 | | 5 | | 14 | | | | | 18 |
| 1 | 2 | 3 | 4 | 5 | | $7^1$ | 8 | 12 | 9 | 11 | | | 10 | | 6 | | | | | | | | | 19 |
| 1 | 2 | $3^1$ | $4^2$ | 5 | | | $7^3$ | | 9 | 11 | | 8 | 10 | | 6 | | 12 | | 13 | 14 | | | | 20 |
| 1 | 2 | | 4 | 5 | | 13 | 7 | 12 | $9^1$ | 11 | | $8^2$ | 10 | | $3^3$ | | 6 | | | 14 | | | | 21 |
| 1 | 2 | | 4 | 5 | | 13 | 7 | 12 | 9 | $11^2$ | | | $10^1$ | 3 | | | 6 | | 14 | $8^3$ | | | | 22 |
| 1 | 2 | | 4 | 5 | | $7^2$ | 11 | $9^1$ | $10^3$ | | | 8 | | 3 | 12 | | 6 | | 13 | 14 | | | | 23 |
| 1 | 2 | | 4 | 5 | | | 7 | 9 | 10 | | | $8^1$ | 11 | 3 | 13 | | 6 | | $12^2$ | | | | | 24 |
| 1 | | | 4 | 5 | | | 7 | 9 | 10 | | | 8 | $11^1$ | 2 | 3 | | 6 | | | 12 | | | | 25 |
| 1 | 12 | | 4 | | | | 7 | 9 | 10 | 14 | | $8^2$ | $11^3$ | 3 | 6 | | | | | 13 | $2^1$ | 5 | | 26 |
| 1 | 2 | | 4 | 5 | | 13 | 7 | 12 | 9 | $11^3$ | | $8^2$ | $10^1$ | 3 | 6 | | | | 14 | | | | | 27 |
| 1 | 2 | | 4 | 5 | | $7^1$ | 8 | 10 | 9 | 11 | | | | | 3 | | 6 | | 12 | | | | | 28 |
| 1 | 2 | | 4 | 5 | | 7 | $8^1$ | 9 | 10 | 11 | | 12 | | | 3 | | 6 | | | | | | | 29 |
| 1 | $2^2$ | | 4 | $5^1$ | | 7 | 8 | 9 | 10 | 11 | | 13 | | | 3 | | 6 | | | | | 12 | | 30 |
| 1 | 2 | | $4^3$ | | | 7 | $8^1$ | 9 | $10^2$ | 11 | | 12 | | 3 | | | 6 | | | 13 | | 5 | 14 | 31 |
| 1 | 14 | | 13 | 5 | | 12 | $4^2$ | 9 | 10 | 11 | | 8 | $7^1$ | 2 | $3^3$ | | $6^1$ | | | | | | | 32 |
| 1 | 2 | | 4 | 5 | | $7^2$ | 11 | 9 | 10 | 12 | | $8^1$ | 13 | 3 | | | 6 | | | | | | | 33 |
| 1 | $2^3$ | | 4 | 5 | | 13 | 7 | 9 | 10 | $11^1$ | | 12 | $8^2$ | 14 | 3 | | 6 | | | | | | | 34 |
| 1 | 12 | | 4 | 5 | | 14 | 7 | $9^2$ | 10 | 11 | | 13 | $8^3$ | $2^1$ | 3 | | 6 | | | | | | | 35 |
| 1 | 2 | | 4 | 5 | | 14 | 7 | $9^2$ | $10^3$ | 11 | | | 8 | 12 | 3 | | $6^1$ | | | 13 | | | | 36 |
| 1 | $2^1$ | 13 | 4 | 5 | | | $7^2$ | $9^3$ | 10 | 11 | | 14 | 8 | 12 | 3 | | 6 | | | | | | | 37 |
| 1 | 2 | 12 | 4 | 5 | | 13 | 7 | 14 | 9 | 11 | | $8^2$ | $10^3$ | | $3^1$ | | 6 | | | | | | | 38 |

**Carling Cup**

| | | | |
|---|---|---|---|
| Second Round | Walsall | (h) | 3-1 |
| Third Round | Gillingham | (h) | 2-0 |
| Fourth Round | Liverpool | (a) | 3-2 |
| Fifth Round | Southampton | (h) | 1-0 |
| Semi-Final | Aston Villa | (h) | 5-2 |
| | | (a) | 0-2 |
| Final | Middlesbrough | | 1-2 |
| (at Millennium Stadium) | | | |

**FA Cup**

| | | | |
|---|---|---|---|
| Third Round | Tranmere R | (a) | 1-1 |
| | | (h) | 1-2 |

# BOSTON UNITED FL Championship 2

## FOUNDATION

Although it was 1934 before the name Boston United first appeared, football had been played in the town since the late 1800s and indeed, always on the same site as the present York Street stadium. In fact Boston Football Club was established in March 1870 playing their first match against Louth the following month. Before the First World War, there were two clubs, Boston Town, whose headquarters were The Coach and Horses, and Boston Swifts, who used The Indian Queen. In fact, as both public houses were situated on Main Ridge and the pitch was virtually just opposite, it was not surprising that for the first forty years or so, that was what the ground was called. Swifts never reappeared after the First World War and it was left to the club called simply Boston to achieve the first giant-killing in the FA Cup by beating Bradford Park Avenue 1-0 on 12 December 1925. The club was now competing in the Midland League and subsequently reformed under the new title of Boston United.

***York Street Ground, York Street, Boston, Lincolnshire.***

***Telephone:*** (01205) 364 406.

***Fax:*** (01205) 354 063.

***Ticket Office:*** (01205) 364 406, (01205) 365 525.

***Website:*** www.bostonunited.co.uk

***Email:*** jan.mclucas1@playing4success.org.uk

***Ground Capacity:*** 6,639.

***Record Attendance:*** 10,086 v Corby Town, Friendly, 1955.

***Chairman:*** Jon Sotnick.

***Vice-chairman:*** Nigel Clempson.

***Director of Football:*** James Rodwell.

***Secretary:*** John Blackwell.

***Manager:*** Steve Evans.

***Coach:*** Paul Raynor.

## HONOURS

*FA Cup:* best season: 3rd rd, 1926, 1956, 1972, 1974.
*Football League Cup:* never past 1st rd.
*Conference:* Champions 2001–02.
*Dr. Martens:* Champions 1999–2000. Runners-up: 1998–99.
*Unibond League:* Runners-up 1995–96, 1997–98.
*Unibond Challenge Cup:* Runners-up 1996–97.
*FA Trophy:* Runners-up 1984–85.
*Northern Premier League:* Champions 1972–73, 1973–74, 1976–77, 1977–78.
*Northern Premier League Cup:* Winners 1974, 1976.
*Northern Premier League Challenge Shield:* Winners 1974, 1975, 1977, 1978.
*Lincolnshire Senior Cup:* Winners 1935, 1937, 1938, 1946, 1950, 1955, 1956, 1960, 1977, 1979, 1986, 1988, 1989.
*Non-League Champions of Champions Cup:* Winners 1973, 1977.
*East Anglian Cup:* Winners 1961.
*Central Alliance League:* Champions 1961–62.
*United Counties League:* Champions 1965–66.
*West Midlands League:* Champions 1966–67, 1967–68.
*Eastern Professional Floodlit Cup:* Winners 1972.

## SKY SPORTS FACT FILE

In successive seasons 1970–71 and 1971–72, Boston United put out two Fourth Division teams in the FA Cup, respectively beating Southport 2-0 and Hartlepool United 2-1 while members of the Northern Premier League.

***Physio:*** Jim Woods.

***Colours:*** Amber and black.

***Change Colours:*** White with blue edgings.

***Year formed:*** 1934.

***Club Nickname:*** 'The Pilgrims'.

***First Football League Game:*** 10 August 2002, Division 3, v Bournemouth (h), D 2–2 – Bastock; Hocking, Chapman, Morley (Rodwell), Warburton, Ellender, Gould (1), Bennett, Clare, Elding (Cook), Weatherstone S. (1 og).

### MANAGERS

George Kerr/Dave Cusack
Dave Cusack
Peter Morris
Mel Sterland
Greg Fee
Steve Evans 1998–2002
Neil Thompson 2002–04
Steve Evans March 2004–

***Record League Victory:*** 6–0 v Shrewsbury T, Division 3, 21 December 2002 – Bastock; Costello, Chapman, Redfearn (1), Balmer, Hocking (McCarthy), Weatherstone S, Higgins, Douglas (1), Logan (2) (Thompson L), Angel (Gould (1)). (1 og).

***Record Transfer Fee Received:*** £50,000 from Bolton W for David Norris, February 2000.

***Record Transfer Fee Paid:*** £30,000 to Scarborough for Paul Ellender, August 2001.

***Football League Record:*** 2002 Promoted to Division 3; 2004– FL2.

## LATEST SEQUENCES

***Longest Sequence of League Wins:*** 4, 19.4.2003 – 3.5.2003.

***Longest Sequence of League Defeats:*** 6, 29.10.2002 – 14.12.2002.

***Longest Sequence of League Draws:*** 3, 29.3.2003 – 2.4.2003.

***Longest Sequence of Unbeaten League Matches:*** 6, 19.4.2002 – 16.8.2003.

***Longest Sequence Without a League Win:*** 6, 28.12.2002 – 1.2.2003.

***Successive Scoring Runs:*** 7 from 4.10.2003.

***Successive Non-scoring Runs:*** 5 from 29.10.2002.

### TEN YEAR LEAGUE RECORD

| | | P | W | D | L | F | A | Pts | Pos |
|---|---|---|---|---|---|---|---|---|---|
| 1994-95 | NP pr | 42 | 20 | 11 | 11 | 80 | 43 | 71 | 5 |
| 1995-96 | NP pr | 42 | 23 | 6 | 13 | 86 | 59 | 75 | 2 |
| 1996-97 | NP pr | 44 | 22 | 13 | 9 | 74 | 47 | 79 | 6 |
| 1997-98 | NP pr | 42 | 22 | 12 | 8 | 55 | 40 | 78 | 2 |
| 1998-99 | SL pr | 42 | 17 | 16 | 9 | 69 | 51 | 67 | 2 |
| 1999-2000 | SL pr | 42 | 27 | 11 | 4 | 102 | 39 | 92 | 1 |
| 2000-01 | Conf. | 42 | 13 | 17 | 12 | 74 | 63 | 56 | 12 |
| 2001-02 | Conf. | 42 | 25 | 9 | 8 | 84 | 42 | 84 | 1 |
| 2002-03 | Div 3 | 46 | 15 | 13 | 18 | 55 | 56 | 54* | 15 |
| 2003-04 | Div 3 | 46 | 16 | 11 | 19 | 50 | 54 | 59 | 11 |

**4 pts deducted at start of season.*

### DID YOU KNOW ?

Jim Smith who has had successful careers as player and manager, with most recently his No.2 spot at Portsmouth, spent three years as a wing-half with Boston United after leaving Lincoln City and returning to the League with Colchester United.

## BOSTON UNITED 2003–04 LEAGUE RECORD

| Match No. | Date | Venue | Opponents | Result | | H/T Score | Lg. Pos. | Goalscorers | Atten-dance |
|---|---|---|---|---|---|---|---|---|---|
| 1 | Aug 9 | A | Macclesfield T | D | 0-0 | 0-0 | — | | 2222 |
| 2 | 16 | H | Huddersfield T | D | 2-2 | 1-0 | 14 | Redfearn [22], Ellender [67] | 3452 |
| 3 | 22 | A | Swansea C | L | 0-3 | 0-0 | — | | 9041 |
| 4 | 25 | H | Carlisle U | W | 1-0 | 1-0 | 14 | Redfearn [30] | 2527 |
| 5 | 30 | A | Hull C | L | 1-2 | 0-1 | 20 | Ellender [55] | 13,091 |
| 6 | Sept 6 | H | Scunthorpe U | D | 1-1 | 1-1 | 19 | Beevers [23] | 3154 |
| 7 | 13 | A | Bristol R | L | 0-2 | 0-0 | 21 | | 6845 |
| 8 | 17 | H | Cambridge U | L | 1-2 | 0-1 | — | Weatherstone [59] | 2452 |
| 9 | 20 | H | Bury | W | 1-0 | 0-0 | 19 | Duffield [57] | 2260 |
| 10 | 27 | A | Darlington | L | 0-3 | 0-0 | 20 | | 4519 |
| 11 | 30 | A | Yeovil T | L | 0-2 | 0-2 | — | | 5093 |
| 12 | Oct 4 | H | Oxford U | D | 1-1 | 1-0 | 22 | Jones [35] | 2664 |
| 13 | 11 | H | Cheltenham T | W | 3-1 | 2-1 | 20 | Bennett [28], Balmer [33], Angel [57] | 2283 |
| 14 | 18 | A | York C | D | 1-1 | 0-1 | 21 | Weatherstone [58] | 3190 |
| 15 | 21 | A | Southend U | W | 2-0 | 0-0 | — | Thompson L [59], Weatherstone [76] | 2463 |
| 16 | 25 | H | Torquay U | W | 4-0 | 1-0 | 15 | Redfearn [4], Thompson L [61], Duffield 2 [81, 90] | 2431 |
| 17 | Nov 1 | A | Mansfield T | L | 1-2 | 1-1 | 17 | Weatherstone [27] | 5161 |
| 18 | 15 | H | Leyton Orient | W | 3-0 | 1-0 | 14 | Jones [24], Redfearn 2 [82, 86] | 2619 |
| 19 | 22 | A | Doncaster R | L | 0-3 | 0-1 | 15 | | 5211 |
| 20 | 29 | H | Kidderminster H | D | 2-2 | 0-1 | 15 | Boyd 2 [62, 69] | 2147 |
| 21 | Dec 13 | H | Northampton T | D | 1-1 | 1-1 | 15 | Thompson L [38] | 2756 |
| 22 | 20 | A | Rochdale | L | 0-1 | 0-1 | 18 | | 2049 |
| 23 | 26 | H | Lincoln C | L | 0-1 | 0-0 | 21 | | 5708 |
| 24 | 28 | A | Scunthorpe U | W | 1-0 | 1-0 | 18 | Duffield [12] | 4346 |
| 25 | Jan 3 | A | Carlisle U | L | 1-2 | 1-1 | 19 | Jones [10] | 5296 |
| 26 | 10 | H | Macclesfield T | W | 3-1 | 2-0 | 15 | Jones [14], Boyd [39], Douglas [77] | 2300 |
| 27 | 17 | A | Huddersfield T | L | 0-2 | 0-0 | 17 | | 9603 |
| 28 | Feb 7 | A | Lincoln C | D | 1-1 | 1-1 | 19 | Redfearn [6] | 7114 |
| 29 | 14 | A | Cheltenham T | L | 0-1 | 0-0 | 19 | | 3434 |
| 30 | 18 | H | Swansea C | D | 1-1 | 0-1 | — | Boyd [87] | 2573 |
| 31 | 21 | H | York C | W | 2-0 | 0-0 | 18 | Duffield [55], Jones [81] | 2490 |
| 32 | 28 | A | Torquay U | L | 0-2 | 0-1 | 18 | | 3000 |
| 33 | Mar 3 | H | Southend U | L | 0-2 | 0-1 | — | | 2780 |
| 34 | 6 | H | Rochdale | W | 2-0 | 1-0 | 19 | Ellender [20], Jones [76] | 2466 |
| 35 | 13 | A | Northampton T | L | 0-2 | 0-0 | 21 | | 6243 |
| 36 | 16 | A | Cambridge U | W | 1-0 | 1-0 | — | Balmer [6] | 3294 |
| 37 | 20 | H | Bristol R | W | 1-0 | 1-0 | 14 | Thomas [38] | 2450 |
| 38 | 27 | A | Bury | W | 3-1 | 2-1 | 11 | Cropper [8], Thomas 2 [25, 88] | 2693 |
| 39 | 31 | H | Hull C | L | 1-2 | 0-1 | — | Ellender [66] | 4741 |
| 40 | Apr 3 | H | Darlington | W | 1-0 | 1-0 | 11 | Melton [45] | 2573 |
| 41 | 9 | A | Oxford U | D | 0-0 | 0-0 | — | | 6050 |
| 42 | 12 | H | Yeovil T | W | 3-2 | 2-1 | 11 | Hurst [14], Noble [45], Thompson L [90] | 2848 |
| 43 | 17 | H | Mansfield T | L | 1-2 | 0-0 | 11 | Balmer [69] | 3826 |
| 44 | 24 | A | Leyton Orient | W | 3-1 | 0-0 | 10 | Beevers [57], Noble [89], Thompson L [90] | 3580 |
| 45 | May 1 | H | Doncaster R | D | 0-0 | 0-0 | 10 | | 4671 |
| 46 | 8 | A | Kidderminster H | L | 0-2 | 0-1 | 11 | | 3047 |

**Final League Position: 11**

### GOALSCORERS

*League (50):* Jones 6, Redfearn 6, Duffield 5, Thompson L 5, Boyd 4, Ellender 4, Weatherstone 4, Balmer 3, Thomas 3, Beevers 2, Noble 2, Angel 1, Bennett 1, Cropper 1, Douglas 1, Hurst 1, Melton 1.
*Carling Cup (1):* Redfearn 1 (pen).
*FA Cup (0).*
*LDV Vans Trophy (3):* Akinfenwa 1, Beevers 1, Duffield 1.

| Bastock P 46 | Sutch D 6 | Chapman B 33 + 4 | Hocking M 16 + 6 | Greaves M 34 + 3 | Ellender P 42 | Potter G 11 + 1 | Bennett T 35 | Douglas S 14 + 15 | Duffield P 12 + 17 | Rusk S 16 + 3 | Redfearn N 19 + 4 | Logan R 4 + 4 | Jones G 31 + 2 | Balmer S 25 + 1 | Beevers L 40 | Angel M 12 + 11 | Thompson L 20 + 15 | Weatherstone S 14 + 3 | White A 3 + 3 | Clarke R 1 + 3 | Hogg C 10 | Akinfenwa A 2 + 1 | Boyd A 14 | Morrow S — + 2 | Noble D 14 | Brown J 3 + 2 | Sabin E 2 | Melton S 9 | Thomas D 8 | Cropper D 4 + 1 | Holland C 3 + 2 | Hurst K 3 + 4 | Match No. |
|---|---|---|---|---|---|---|---|---|---|---|---|---|---|---|---|---|---|---|---|---|---|---|---|---|---|---|---|---|---|---|---|---|---|
| 1 | 2 | 3¹ | 4 | 5 | 6 | 7 | 8 | 9² | 10³ | 11 | 12 | 13 | 14 | | | | | | | | | | | | | | | | | | | | 1 |
| 1 | 2 | 3 | 4 | 5 | 6 | | 8 | 9 | | | 11 | 7 | 10 | | | | | | | | | | | | | | | | | | | | 2 |
| 1 | 2³ | 3² | 4 | | 6 | 7 | 8 | 9¹ | 12 | | 13 | 10 | | 5 | 11 | 14 | | | | | | | | | | | | | | | | | 3 |
| 1 | 2 | 3 | | | 6 | 7 | 8 | 12 | 10 | | 4 | 9¹ | | | 5 | 11² | 13 | | | | | | | | | | | | | | | | 4 |
| 1 | 2 | 3 | 4▮ | 12 | 6 | | 8 | 9² | 10¹ | 14 | 7 | 13 | | | 5 | 11³ | | | | | | | | | | | | | | | | | 5 |
| 1 | | 3 | | 5 | 6 | | 8 | 12 | | 7 | 10 | 9² | | 4 | 2 | 11¹ | | 13 | | | | | | | | | | | | | | | 6 |
| 1 | | 3³ | | 5 | 8 | 2² | | 9¹ | 12 | 11 | 13 | | | 4 | 6 | | 14 | 7 | 10 | | | | | | | | | | | | | | 7 |
| 1 | | 3 | 4 | | 6 | 7 | | 9¹ | 12 | 2 | 8 | 13 | | | 5² | | | 11 | 10 | | | | | | | | | | | | | | 8 |
| 1 | | 3 | 4 | 14 | 6 | 7 | 5 | 12 | 9 | 2 | 8² | 13³ | | | | | | 11 | 10¹ | | | | | | | | | | | | | | 9 |
| 1 | | 3³ | 4 | 5² | 6 | 7 | 8 | 9¹ | 10 | 2 | | | | | | | 12 | 11 | 13 | 14 | | | | | | | | | | | | | 10 |
| 1 | | 12 | 4 | 5 | | 7 | 8 | | 9² | 2 | | | 10³ | 6 | | | 13 | 11 | 14 | 3¹ | | | | | | | | | | | | | 11 |
| 1 | | 3 | 4 | 6³ | | | 8 | 12² | 13 | | | | 10¹ | 5 | 2 | 11 | 7 | 9 | | 14 | | | | | | | | | | | | | 12 |
| 1 | | | 4 | | 6 | | 8▮ | | | | | | 10¹ | 5 | 3 | 11 | 7 | 9 | 12 | | 2 | | | | | | | | | | | | 13 |
| 1 | | | 4¹ | 12 | 6 | | 8 | | 13 | | | | 10 | 5 | 3 | 11³ | 7 | 14 | | | 2 | 9² | | | | | | | | | | | 14 |
| 1 | | | | 4 | 6 | | 8 | 9² | 12 | | | | 10¹ | 5 | 3 | | 7 | 11 | | | 2 | 13 | | | | | | | | | | | 15 |
| 1 | | | | 4 | 6 | | | 12 | 13 | | 8 | | 10² | 5 | 3 | | 7 | 11 | | | 2 | 9¹ | | | | | | | | | | | 16 |
| 1 | | 12 | | 4 | 6¹ | | | 13 | 9 | 11 | | | 10² | 5 | 3 | | 7 | 8 | | | 2 | | | | | | | | | | | | 17 |
| 1 | | 3 | | 4 | 6 | | 8 | | 12 | | 11 | | 10¹ | 5 | 2 | | 7 | | | | | | 9 | | | | | | | | | | 18 |
| 1 | | 3 | | 4 | 6 | | 8³ | | 12 | 14 | 11 | | 10 | 5 | 2 | 13 | 7² | | | | | | 9¹ | | | | | | | | | | 19 |
| 1 | 2 | | | 4 | 6 | | | | | | 8 | | 10 | 5 | 3 | 11 | 7 | | | | | | 9 | | | | | | | | | | 20 |
| 1 | | | 4 | 5 | | | | | 12 | 13 | 6 | | 10³ | | 3 | 11² | 7¹ | 8 | | | 2 | | 9 | 14 | | | | | | | | | 21 |
| 1 | | 3³ | 4 | | | | | | 12 | 11 | 6 | | 10¹ | | 5▮ | 13 | 7² | 8 | | | 2 | | 9 | 14 | | | | | | | | | 22 |
| 1 | | 3▮ | | 4 | 6 | | | | 10 | 11 | 8¹ | | 13 | | 5 | 12 | | 7² | | | 2 | | 9 | | | | | | | | | | 23 |
| 1 | | 3 | 4 | 5 | 6 | | 8 | | 9 | 7 | | | 10 | | 2 | | | | | | | | 11 | | | | | | | | | | 24 |
| 1 | | 3³ | 4 | 5 | 6 | 14 | 8 | 13 | 9² | | 12 | | 10 | | | | | 7 | | | 2 | | 11¹ | | | | | | | | | | 25 |
| 1 | | | | 4 | 6 | 3 | 8 | 12 | 13 | 7 | 11² | | 10¹ | 5 | 2 | | | | | | | | 9 | | | | | | | | | | 26 |
| 1 | | | 4 | 5 | 6 | 3³ | 8 | 10 | 13 | 7¹ | 11 | | | | 2 | | 14 | 12 | | | | | 9² | | | | | | | | | | 27 |
| 1 | | 3 | | 4 | 6 | 11 | 8 | | | | 7 | | 10 | | 5 | | 12 | | | | 2¹ | | 9 | | | | | | | | | | 28 |
| 1 | | 12 | | 2 | 6 | | 8³ | 14 | 13 | | 4 | | 10 | 5 | 3 | 11¹ | 7 | | | | | | 9² | | | | | | | | | | 29 |
| 1 | | 12 | | 2 | 6 | | 8 | 14 | 13 | | 4² | | 10 | 5 | 3¹ | 11³ | 7 | | | | | | 9 | | | | | | | | | | 30 |
| 1 | | 3 | | 4 | 6 | | 8 | 12 | 11 | | | | 10¹ | 5 | 2 | | 7 | | | | | | 9 | | | | | | | | | | 31 |
| 1 | | 3 | | | 6¹ | | 4 | 13 | 9 | | | | 10² | 5 | 2 | 12 | 11 | | | | | | | | 7 | 8 | | | | | | | 32 |
| 1 | | 3 | | 4 | 6 | | 8¹ | 12 | 13 | | 11³ | | | 5▮ | 2 | | 14 | | | | | | | | 7 | 10² | 9 | | | | | | 33 |
| 1 | | 3 | | | 6 | | 4 | 12 | 13 | | | | 10² | 5 | 2 | 11¹ | 7 | | | | | | | | 8³ | 14 | 9 | | | | | | 34 |
| 1 | | 3 | | 4 | 6 | | 8 | 13 | | | | | 10 | 5 | 2 | 12 | 11 | | | | | | | | 7¹ | 9² | | | | | | | 35 |
| 1 | | 3 | 12 | 4 | 6 | | 8 | 9³ | | | | | 10 | 5¹ | 2 | 11² | 7 | | | 13 | | | | | | 14 | | | | | | | 36 |
| 1 | | 3 | | 5 | 6 | | 4 | 9 | | | | | 10¹ | | 2 | | 12 | | | | | | | | 8 | | | 7 | 11 | | | | 37 |
| 1 | | 3 | | 5 | 6 | | 4 | 9² | | | | | | | 2 | | 12 | | | | | | | | 8³ | | | 7 | 11 | 10¹ | 14 | 13 | 38 |
| 1 | | 3¹ | 12 | 5 | 6 | | 8 | 9³ | | | | | | | 2 | | 13 | | | | | | | | 7 | | | | 11 | 10 | 4² | 14 | 39 |
| 1 | | 3 | 12 | 5¹ | 6 | | 4 | 9³ | | | | | | | 2 | | 13 | | | | | | | | 8 | | | 7 | 11² | 10 | 14 | | 40 |
| 1 | | 3 | 12 | | 6 | | 4 | | | | | | 10² | 5¹ | 2 | 13 | 14 | | | | | | | | 8 | | | 7 | | 9³ | 11 | | 41 |
| 1 | | 3¹ | 12 | | 6 | | 4 | | | | | | 10 | 5 | 2 | 14 | 13 | | | | | | | | 8 | | | 7 | | | 11³ | 9² | 42 |
| 1 | | | | 2 | 6 | | 4 | | | | | | 10³ | 5¹ | 3 | 12 | 13 | | | | | | | | 8 | | | 7 | 11 | 14 | | 9² | 43 |
| 1 | | 3 | 12 | 5 | 6 | | | | | 11² | | | 10 | | 2 | 13 | 14 | | | | | | | | 4 | | | 7 | 8¹ | | | 9³ | 44 |
| 1 | | 3 | | 5 | 6 | | | | | 11¹ | | | 10 | | 2 | 12 | 9² | | | | | | | | 4 | | | 7 | 8 | | | 13 | 45 |
| 1 | | 3¹ | | 5 | 6 | | | | | 11 | | | 10 | 12 | 2² | | 9 | | | | | | | | 4 | | | 7 | 8 | | | 13 | 46 |

**Carling Cup**
First Round Reading (h) 1-3

**LDV Vans Trophy**
First Round Swindon T (h) 2-1
Second Round Brighton & HA (a) 1-3

**FA Cup**
First Round Macclesfield T (a) 0-3

# AFC BOURNEMOUTH FL Championship 1

## FOUNDATION

There was a Bournemouth FC as early as 1875, but the present club arose out of the remnants of the Boscombe St John's club (formed 1890). The meeting at which Boscombe FC came into being was held at a house in Gladstone Road in 1899. They began by playing in the Boscombe and District Junior League.

***The Fitness First Stadium at Dean Court, Bournemouth, Dorset BH7 7AF.***

***Telephone:*** (01202) 726 300.

***Fax:*** (01202) 726 301.

***Ticket Office:*** (01202) 726 303.

***Website:*** www.afcb.co.uk

***Email:*** admin@afcb.co.uk

***Ground Capacity:*** 9,600 seats, rising to 12,000 all-seater.

***Record Attendance:*** 28,799 v Manchester U, FA Cup 6th rd, 2 March 1957.

***Pitch Measurements:*** 105m × 78m.

***Chairman:*** P. I. Phillips.

***Vice-chairman:*** A. H. Kaye.

***Secretary:*** K. R. J. MacAlister.

***Manager:*** Sean O'Driscoll.

***Acting Assistant Manager:*** Joe Roach.

***Physio:*** Jim Marshall.

***Colours:*** Red shirts with black centre panel, black shorts, black stockings.

***Change Colours:*** Sky blue and navy shirts, sky blue shorts, sky blue stockings.

***Year Formed:*** 1899.

***Turned Professional:*** 1912.

***Ltd Co.:*** 1914.

***Previous Names:*** 1890, Boscombe St Johns; 1899, Boscombe FC; 1923, Bournemouth & Boscombe Ath FC; 1971, AFC Bournemouth.

***Club Nickname:*** 'Cherries'.

***Previous Grounds:*** 1899, Castlemain Road, Pokesdown; 1910, Dean Court.

***First Football League Game:*** 25 August 1923, Division 3 (S), v Swindon T (a) L 1–3 – Heron; Wingham, Lamb; Butt, C. Smith, Voisey; Miller, Lister (1), Davey, Simpson, Robinson.

***Record League Victory:*** 7–0 v Swindon T, Division 3 (S), 22 September 1956 – Godwin; Cunningham, Keetley; Clayton, Crosland, Rushworth; Siddall (1), Norris (2), Arnott (1), Newsham (2), Cutler (1). 10–0 win v Northampton T at start of 1939–40 expunged from the records on outbreak of war.

***Record Cup Victory:*** 11–0 v Margate, FA Cup 1st rd, 20 November 1971 – Davies; Machin (1), Kitchener, Benson, Jones, Powell, Cave (1), Boyer, MacDougall (9 incl. 1p), Miller, Scott (De Garis).

## HONOURS

*Football League:* Division 3 – Champions 1986–87; Promoted from Division 3, 2002–03 (play-offs); Division 3 (S) – Runners-up 1947–48; Division 4 – Runners-up 1970–71; Promotion from Division 4 1981–82 (4th).

*FA Cup:* best season: 6th rd, 1957.

*Football League Cup:* best season: 4th rd, 1962, 1964.

*Associate Members' Cup:* Winners 1984.

*Auto Windscreens Shield:* Runners-up 1998.

## SKY SPORTS FACT FILE

In 1926–27 Bournemouth reached the fourth round of the FA Cup and held Bolton Wanderers to a 2-2 draw at Dean Court and even led 2-0 in the replay before losing 6-2. Bolton said they would invite them to the final if they reached Wembley and kept both promises.

***Record Defeat:*** 0–9 v Lincoln C, Division 3, 18 December 1982.

***Most League Points (2 for a win):*** 62, Division 3, 1971–72.

***Most League Points (3 for a win):*** 97, Division 3, 1986–87.

***Most League Goals:*** 88, Division 3 (S), 1956–57.

***Highest League Scorer in Season:*** Ted MacDougall, 42, 1970–71.

***Most League Goals in Total Aggregate:*** Ron Eyre, 202, 1924–33.

***Most League Goals in One Match:*** 4, Jack Russell v Clapton Orient, Division 3S, 7 January 1933; 4, Jack Russell v Bristol C, Division 3S, 28 January 1933; 4, Harry Mardon v Southend U, Division 3S, 1 January 1938; 4, Jack McDonald v Torquay U, Division 3S, 8 November 1947; 4, Ted MacDougall v Colchester U, 18 September 1970; 4, Brian Clark v Rotherham U, 10 October 1972, 4, Luther Blissett v Hull C, 29 November 1988; 4, James Hayter v Bury, Division 2, 21 October 2000.

***Most Capped Player:*** Gerry Peyton, 7 (33), Republic of Ireland.

***Most League Appearances:*** Sean O'Driscoll, 423, 1984–95.

***Youngest League Player:*** Jimmy White, 15 years 321 days v Brentford, 30 April 1958.

***Record Transfer Fee Received:*** £800,000 from Everton for Joe Parkinson, March 1994.

***Record Transfer Fee Paid:*** £210,000 to Gillingham for Gavin Peacock, August 1989.

***Football League Record:*** 1923 Elected to Division 3 (S) and remained a Third Division club for record number of years until 1970; 1970–71 Division 4; 1971–75 Division 3; 1975–82 Division 4; 1982–87 Division 3; 1987–90 Division 2; 1990–92 Division 3; 1992–2002 Division 2; 2002–03 Division 3; 2003–04 Division 2; 2004– FL1.

### MANAGERS

Vincent Kitcher 1914–23
*(Secretary-Manager)*
Harry Kinghorn 1923–25
Leslie Knighton 1925–28
Frank Richards 1928–30
Billy Birrell 1930–35
Bob Crompton 1935–36
Charlie Bell 1936–39
Harry Kinghorn 1939–47
Harry Lowe 1947–50
Jack Bruton 1950–56
Fred Cox 1956–58
Don Welsh 1958–61
Bill McGarry 1961–63
Reg Flewin 1963–65
Fred Cox 1965–70
John Bond 1970–73
Trevor Hartley 1974–75
John Benson 1975–78
Alec Stock 1979–80
David Webb 1980–82
Don Megson 1983
Harry Redknapp 1983–92
Tony Pulis 1992–94
Mel Machin 1994–2000
Sean O'Driscoll August 2000–

## LATEST SEQUENCES

***Longest Sequence of League Wins:*** 7, 22.8.1970 – 23.9.1970.

***Longest Sequence of League Defeats:*** 7, 13.8.1994 – 13.9.1994.

***Longest Sequence of League Draws:*** 5, 25.4.2000 – 12.8.2000.

***Longest Sequence of Unbeaten League Matches:*** 18, 6.3.1982 – 28.8.1982.

***Longest Sequence Without a League Win:*** 14, 6.3.1974 – 27.4.1974.

***Successive Scoring Runs:*** 31 from 28.10.2000.

***Successive Non-scoring Runs:*** 6 from 1.2.1975.

### TEN YEAR LEAGUE RECORD

| | | P | W | D | L | F | A | Pts | Pos |
|---|---|---|---|---|---|---|---|---|---|
| 1994-95 | Div 2 | 46 | 13 | 11 | 22 | 49 | 69 | 50 | 19 |
| 1995-96 | Div 2 | 46 | 16 | 10 | 20 | 51 | 70 | 58 | 14 |
| 1996-97 | Div 2 | 46 | 15 | 15 | 16 | 43 | 45 | 60 | 16 |
| 1997-98 | Div 2 | 46 | 18 | 12 | 16 | 57 | 52 | 66 | 9 |
| 1998-99 | Div 2 | 46 | 21 | 13 | 12 | 63 | 41 | 76 | 7 |
| 1999-2000 | Div 2 | 46 | 16 | 9 | 21 | 59 | 62 | 57 | 16 |
| 2000-01 | Div 2 | 46 | 20 | 13 | 13 | 79 | 55 | 73 | 7 |
| 2001-02 | Div 2 | 46 | 10 | 14 | 22 | 56 | 71 | 44 | 21 |
| 2002-03 | Div 3 | 46 | 20 | 14 | 12 | 60 | 48 | 74 | 4 |
| 2003-04 | Div 2 | 46 | 17 | 15 | 14 | 56 | 51 | 66 | 9 |

### DID YOU KNOW?

After a 1-1 draw with Queens Park Rangers in the Division Three (South) Cup semi-final in 1945–46, the replay at Loftus Road after three periods of extra time was decided on sudden death after 136 minutes with a Jack Kirkham goal for Bournemouth!

## AFC BOURNEMOUTH 2003–04 LEAGUE RECORD

| Match No. | Date | Venue | Opponents | Result | | H/T Score | Lg. Pos. | Goalscorers | Attendance |
|---|---|---|---|---|---|---|---|---|---|
| 1 | Aug 9 | A | Port Vale | L | 1-2 | 0-0 | — | Hayter [73] | 6465 |
| 2 | 16 | H | Barnsley | D | 2-2 | 2-1 | 17 | Fletcher S 2 [27, 39] | 5960 |
| 3 | 23 | A | QPR | L | 0-1 | 0-0 | 19 | | 13,065 |
| 4 | 25 | H | Swindon T | D | 2-2 | 1-2 | 20 | Maher [21], Hayter [61] | 6606 |
| 5 | 30 | A | Wrexham | W | 1-0 | 1-0 | 17 | Purches S [8] | 4929 |
| 6 | Sept 6 | H | Bristol C | D | 0-0 | 0-0 | 17 | | 6756 |
| 7 | 13 | A | Blackpool | W | 2-1 | 0-1 | 13 | Purches S [49], Broadhurst [51] | 5607 |
| 8 | 16 | H | Sheffield W | W | 1-0 | 0-0 | — | Elliott [90] | 8219 |
| 9 | 20 | H | Rushden & D | W | 2-1 | 0-1 | 7 | Feeney 2 [69, 71] | 6464 |
| 10 | 27 | A | Colchester U | L | 0-1 | 0-0 | 10 | | 3602 |
| 11 | 30 | A | Chesterfield | D | 1-1 | 0-1 | — | Fletcher S [80] | 3131 |
| 12 | Oct 4 | H | Hartlepool U | D | 2-2 | 0-1 | 12 | Holmes [79], Feeney [81] | 6342 |
| 13 | 11 | A | Notts Co | W | 1-0 | 0-0 | 11 | Fletcher S [54] | 4419 |
| 14 | 18 | H | Brighton & HA | W | 1-0 | 1-0 | 5 | Feeney [15] | 7908 |
| 15 | 21 | H | Luton T | W | 6-3 | 4-2 | — | Fletcher S 2 [7, 45], Stock 2 [34, 62], O'Connor [42], Elliott [67] | 6388 |
| 16 | 25 | A | Oldham Ath | D | 1-1 | 1-1 | 3 | Feeney [45] | 5850 |
| 17 | Nov 1 | A | Tranmere R | D | 1-1 | 0-1 | 5 | Feeney [72] | 7123 |
| 18 | 15 | H | Peterborough U | L | 1-2 | 0-2 | 8 | Feeney [73] | 6963 |
| 19 | 22 | A | Stockport Co | L | 2-3 | 0-2 | 10 | Hayter [67], Feeney [76] | 4622 |
| 20 | 29 | H | Brentford | W | 1-0 | 0-0 | 6 | Elliott [64] | 6674 |
| 21 | Dec 13 | H | Grimsby T | D | 0-0 | 0-0 | 7 | | 5837 |
| 22 | 20 | A | Wycombe W | L | 0-2 | 0-1 | 9 | | 5205 |
| 23 | 26 | H | Plymouth Arg | L | 0-2 | 0-2 | 13 | | 8901 |
| 24 | 28 | A | Bristol C | L | 0-2 | 0-1 | 14 | | 13,807 |
| 25 | Jan 3 | A | Swindon T | L | 1-2 | 1-1 | 14 | Hayter [5] | 7158 |
| 26 | 10 | H | Port Vale | W | 2-1 | 0-1 | 13 | O'Connor (pen) [50], Fletcher S [55] | 5926 |
| 27 | 17 | A | Barnsley | D | 1-1 | 1-0 | 13 | Hayter [31] | 7934 |
| 28 | 24 | H | QPR | W | 1-0 | 0-0 | 11 | Feeney [58] | 8909 |
| 29 | Feb 7 | A | Plymouth Arg | D | 0-0 | 0-0 | 11 | | 13,371 |
| 30 | 14 | H | Notts Co | W | 1-0 | 0-0 | 11 | Hayter [83] | 6332 |
| 31 | 21 | A | Brighton & HA | L | 0-3 | 0-3 | 11 | | 6441 |
| 32 | 24 | H | Wrexham | W | 6-0 | 2-0 | — | Purches S [3], Cummings [45], Feeney [59], Hayter 3 [86, 87, 88] | 5899 |
| 33 | 28 | H | Oldham Ath | W | 1-0 | 0-0 | 8 | Hayter [61] | 6594 |
| 34 | Mar 6 | H | Wycombe W | W | 1-0 | 1-0 | 8 | Cummings [20] | 7311 |
| 35 | 13 | A | Grimsby T | D | 1-1 | 0-1 | 8 | Warhurst (og) [73] | 5015 |
| 36 | 17 | A | Sheffield W | W | 2-0 | 2-0 | — | Fletcher C [11], Fletcher S [21] | 18,799 |
| 37 | 24 | H | Blackpool | L | 1-2 | 0-1 | — | Fletcher S [51] | 6436 |
| 38 | 27 | A | Rushden & D | W | 3-0 | 1-0 | 6 | Stock [37], Hayter [48], Feeney [62] | 4500 |
| 39 | Apr 3 | H | Colchester U | D | 1-1 | 0-1 | 6 | Hayter [86] | 6896 |
| 40 | 10 | A | Hartlepool U | L | 1-2 | 1-1 | 8 | Hayter [31] | 5544 |
| 41 | 12 | H | Chesterfield | D | 2-2 | 0-2 | 8 | Hayter [77], Holmes [80] | 7081 |
| 42 | 17 | H | Tranmere R | L | 1-5 | 0-1 | 9 | Allen (og) [71] | 7063 |
| 43 | 20 | A | Luton T | D | 1-1 | 0-1 | — | Feeney [75] | 6485 |
| 44 | 24 | A | Peterborough U | W | 1-0 | 0-0 | 8 | Fletcher C [81] | 4831 |
| 45 | May 1 | H | Stockport Co | D | 0-0 | 0-0 | 8 | | 7541 |
| 46 | 8 | A | Brentford | L | 0-1 | 0-0 | 9 | | 9485 |

**Final League Position: 9**

### GOALSCORERS

*League (56):* Hayter 14, Feeney 12, Fletcher S 9, Elliott 3, Purches S 3, Stock 3, Cummings 2, Fletcher C 2, Holmes 2, O'Connor 2 (1 pen), Broadhurst 1, Maher 1, own goals 2.
*Carling Cup (0).*
*FA Cup (2):* Browning 1, Elliott 1.
*LDV Vans Trophy (0).*

| Moss N 46 | Purches S 42 | Cummings W 42 | Broadhurst K 36 + 3 | Fletcher C 40 | Browning M 41 + 1 | Elliott W 23 + 16 | O'Connor G 28 + 9 | Hayter J 37 + 7 | Fletcher S 40 + 1 | Thomas D 2 + 8 | Holmes D 10 + 16 | Feeney W 34 + 6 | Stock B 11 + 8 | Tindall J 2 + 17 | Connell A 1 + 6 | Maher S 23 + 6 | Young N 5 + 5 | Buxton L 24 + 2 | Cooke S 3 | Jorgensen C 16 + 1 | Williams G — + 1 | *Match No.* |
|---|---|---|---|---|---|---|---|---|---|---|---|---|---|---|---|---|---|---|---|---|---|---|
| 1 | 2 | 3 | 4 | 5 | 6 | 7 | 8 | $9^1$ | $10^2$ | $11^3$ | 12 | 13 | 14 | | | | | | | | | 1 |
| 1 | 2 | $3^2$ | 4 | 5 | 6 | 7 | 8 | 9 | 10 | $11^1$ | | 12 | | 13 | | | | | | | | 2 |
| 1 | 2 | $3^1$ | 4 | 5 | 6 | 12 | $8^2$ | 7 | 10 | | $9^3$ | 13 | | 11 | 14 | | | | | | | 3 |
| 1 | 2 | | 3 | 5 | 6 | 7 | 8 | 9 | 10 | | | $11^1$ | | | 12 | 4 | | | | | | 4 |
| 1 | 2 | 3 | 4 | 5 | 8 | | 7 | 9 | 10 | | 12 | $11^1$ | | | | $6^2$ | 13 | | | | | 5 |
| 1 | 4 | $3^1$ | 6 | 5 | 8 | 7 | 11 | 9 | 10 | 12 | | | | | | | 2 | | | | | 6 |
| 1 | 4 | 3 | 6 | 5 | 8 | $7^2$ | 11 | 9 | 10 | | | 12 | | | | 13 | $2^1$ | | | | | 7 |
| 1 | 2 | 3 | 4 | 5 | 11 | 7 | $8^2$ | $9^1$ | 10 | | | 12 | | 13 | | 6 | | | | | | 8 |
| 1 | 2 | 3 | 4 | 5 | 8 | $7^3$ | $11^1$ | $9^2$ | 10 | | 13 | 12 | | 14 | | 6 | | | | | | 9 |
| 1 | 8 | 3■ | 2 | 5 | $4^2$ | 7 | $11^1$ | 12 | 10 | | 14 | 9 | 13 | | | $6^3$ | | | | | | 10 |
| 1 | 8 | 3 | 2 | 5 | | $7^3$ | 11 | 13 | 10 | $12^2$ | 14 | 9 | | 4 | | $6^1$ | | | | | | 11 |
| 1 | 2 | 3 | 4 | 5 | | 7 | 11 | $8^1$ | 10 | | 12 | $9^2$ | | 13 | | $6^3$ | 14 | | | | | 12 |
| 1 | 2 | | 3 | 5 | 4 | $7^1$ | 11 | 8 | 10 | 12 | $9^2$ | | | 13 | | $6^3$ | 14 | | | | | 13 |
| 1 | 3 | | 4 | 5 | 6 | 7 | $11^1$ | 8 | 10 | | | $9^2$ | 12 | 14 | $13^3$ | | 2 | | | | | 14 |
| 1 | 2 | 3 | 4 | 5 | $6^2$ | $7^1$ | $11^3$ | 8 | 10 | 12 | | 9 | 13 | 14 | | | | | | | | 15 |
| 1 | 2 | 3 | 4 | 5 | 6 | $7^2$ | $11^1$ | 8 | 10 | | | 9 | | 12 | | 13 | | | | | | 16 |
| 1 | 2 | $3^2$ | 4 | 5 | | 12 | $11^1$ | 8 | 10 | | | 9 | $7^3$ | 14 | | 13 | | 6 | | | | 17 |
| 1 | 7 | 2 | $4^1$ | 5 | 6 | $11^3$ | $8^2$ | 12 | 10 | | | 9 | 13 | 14 | | | | 3 | | | | 18 |
| 1 | $7^3$ | 3 | 4 | 5 | 6 | 12 | 13 | 8 | 10 | | | 9 | $11^2$ | 14 | | | | $2^1$ | | | | 19 |
| 1 | 2 | 3 | $4^3$ | 5 | 6 | $7^2$ | 11 | | 10 | | | 9 | $8^1$ | 12 | | 14 | | 13 | | | | 20 |
| 1 | 2 | 3 | 4 | | 6 | 7 | $8^1$ | 12 | 10 | | | 9 | 11■ | | | 5 | | | | | | 21 |
| 1 | 2 | 3 | 4 | 5 | 6 | $7^3$ | 11 | 12 | 10 | 13 | | $9^1$ | $8^2$ | | 14 | | | | | | | 22 |
| 1 | 2 | 3 | 4 | $5^1$ | 7 | 12 | | 11 | 10 | | | 9 | | | | 8 | | 6 | | | | 23 |
| 1 | 2 | 3 | 4 | | 8 | $7^1$ | | 11 | $10^2$ | 13 | | 9 | | | 12 | 6 | | 5 | | | | 24 |
| 1 | $2^1$ | 3 | | | 6 | 12 | 8 | 11 | 10 | 13 | | 7 | | | $9^2$ | 5 | | 4 | | | | 25 |
| 1 | | 3 | 4 | 5 | 6 | 12 | 8 | 11 | 10 | | 13 | $9^2$ | | | | | | 2 | $7^1$ | | | 26 |
| 1 | | | | 5 | 4 | 12 | 11 | 2 | 10 | 13 | $7^3$ | 9 | $6^2$ | | 14 | | | 8 | $3^1$ | | | 27 |
| 1 | | 3 | 4 | 5 | 6 | 12 | $11^1$ | 8 | 10 | | 13 | $9^2$ | | | | | | 2 | $7^3$ | 14 | | 28 |
| 1 | 2 | 3 | 4 | 5 | 6 | 13 | 12 | 11 | $10^3$ | | | $9^2$ | | | | 14 | | 8 | | $7^1$ | | 29 |
| 1 | 8 | 3 | $4^2$ | 5 | 6 | $11^3$ | | 12 | 10 | | 14 | $9^1$ | | | | 13 | | 2 | | 7 | | 30 |
| 1 | 2 | 3 | | 5 | 8 | 11 | | | $10^2$ | | 12 | 9 | | | | 6 | | $4^1$ | | 7 | 13 | 31 |
| 1 | $4^3$ | 3 | | 5 | 8 | 11 | 12 | 13 | $10^2$ | | | 9 | 14 | | | 6 | | 2 | | $7^1$ | | 32 |
| 1 | 4 | 3 | | 5 | 8 | 12 | | 9 | 10 | | | $11^1$ | | 13 | | 6 | | 2 | | $7^2$ | | 33 |
| 1 | 4 | 3 | 12 | 5 | 8 | | | $11^2$ | 10 | | 13 | $9^1$ | | | | 6 | | 2 | | 7 | | 34 |
| 1 | 4 | 3 | | 5 | 8 | 12 | 13 | 11 | 10 | | 14 | $9^2$ | | | | $6^3$ | | 2 | | $7^1$ | | 35 |
| 1 | $4^2$ | 3 | 12 | 5 | 8 | | | $11^3$ | $10^1$ | | 14 | 9 | 13 | | | 6 | | 2 | | 7 | | 36 |
| 1 | 4 | 3 | 5 | | $8^2$ | 12 | | $11^1$ | 10 | | 14 | 9 | 13 | | | 6 | | $2^3$ | | 7 | | 37 |
| 1 | 4 | 3 | $5^2$ | | | | 12 | 11 | 10 | | 14 | $9^3$ | 8 | 13 | | 6 | | 2 | | $7^1$ | | 38 |
| 1 | 4 | 3 | | 5 | 13 | | 12 | 11 | 10 | | 14 | $9^2$ | $8^3$ | | | $6^1$ | | 2 | | 7 | | 39 |
| 1 | 2 | 3 | 14 | 5 | 4 | 12 | $11^3$ | 9 | 13 | | 10 | | $8^2$ | | | $6^1$ | | | | 7 | | 40 |
| 1 | $4^2$ | 3 | 5 | | 8 | 12 | 13 | 11 | $10^3$ | | 9 | | | 14 | | 6 | | $2^1$ | | 7 | | 41 |
| 1 | 4 | 3 | 6 | 5 | 8 | 12 | 13 | $11^1$ | | | 10 | 9 | | | | | 14 | $2^3$ | | $7^2$ | | 42 |
| 1 | $4^1$ | 3 | 6 | 5 | 8 | | | 11 | | | 10 | 9 | | 12 | | | | 2 | | 7 | | 43 |
| 1 | 4 | 3 | 6 | 5 | 8 | | 12 | 11 | | | $10^3$ | $9^2$ | | 13 | | | 14 | 2 | | $7^1$ | | 44 |
| 1 | | 3 | 6 | 5 | 4 | 11 | 7 | 9 | | | 10 | | 8 | | | | 2 | | | | | 45 |
| 1 | 4 | 3 | 6 | 5 | 7 | 13 | 11 | 9 | | | 10 | | $8^2$ | | | | $2^1$ | 12 | | | | 46 |

**Carling Cup**

| | | | |
|---|---|---|---|
| First Round | Watford | (a) | 0-1 |

**LDV Vans Trophy**

| | | | |
|---|---|---|---|
| First Round | Yeovil T | (a) | 0-2 |

**FA Cup**

| | | | |
|---|---|---|---|
| First Round | Bristol R | (h) | 1-0 |
| Second Round | Accrington S | (h) | 1-1 |
| | | (a) | 0-0 |

# BRADFORD CITY — FL Championship 1

## FOUNDATION

Bradford was a rugby stronghold around the turn of the century but after Manningham RFC held an archery contest to help them out of financial difficulties in 1903, they were persuaded to give up the handling code and turn to soccer. So they formed Bradford City and continued at Valley Parade. Recognising this as an opportunity of spreading the dribbling code in this part of Yorkshire, the Football League immediately accepted the new club's first application for membership of the Second Division.

***Bradford & Bingley Stadium, Valley Parade, Bradford, West Yorkshire BD8 7DY.***

***Telephone:*** (01274) 773 355.

***Fax:*** (01274) 773 356.

***Ticket Office:*** (01274) 770 022.

***Website:*** www.bradfordcityfc.co.uk

***Email:*** bradfordcityfc@compuserve.com

***Ground Capacity:*** 25,136.

***Record Attendance:*** 39,146 v Burnley, FA Cup 4th rd, 11 March 1911.

***Pitch Measurements:*** 110yd × 73yd.

***Managing Director:*** Shaun Harvey.

***Chief Executive:*** Julian Rhodes.

***Secretary:*** Jon Pollard.

***Manager:*** Colin Todd.

***Assistant Manager:*** Bobby Davison.

***Physio:*** Steve Redmond.

***Colours:*** Claret and amber shirts, white shorts with claret and amber trim, claret stockings with amber and black trim.

***Change Colours:*** All black.

***Year Formed:*** 1903.

***Turned Professional:*** 1903.

***Ltd Co.:*** 1908.

***Club Nickname:*** 'The Bantams'.

***First Football League Game:*** 1 September 1903, Division 2, v Grimsby T (a) L 0–2 – Seymour; Wilson, Halliday; Robinson, Millar, Farnall; Guy, Beckram, Forrest, McMillan, Graham.

***Record League Victory:*** 11–1 v Rotherham U, Division 3 (N), 25 August 1928 – Sherlaw; Russell, Watson; Burkinshaw (1), Summers, Bauld; Harvey (2), Edmunds (3), White (3), Cairns, Scriven (2).

***Record Cup Victory:*** 11–3 v Walker Celtic, FA Cup 1st rd (replay), 1 December 1937 – Parker; Rookes, McDermott; Murphy, Mackie, Moore; Bagley (1), Whittingham (1), Deakin (4 incl. 1p), Cooke (1), Bartholomew (4).

## HONOURS

*Football League:* Division 1 – Runners-up 1998–99; Division 2 – Champions 1907–08; Promoted from Division 2 1995–96 (play-offs); Division 3 – Champions 1984–85; Division 3 (N) – Champions 1928–29; Division 4 – Runners-up 1981–82.

*FA Cup:* Winners 1911.

*Football League Cup:* best season: 5th rd, 1965, 1989.

***European Competitions:*** *Intertoto Cup:* 2000.

## SKY SPORTS FACT FILE

Identical twins David and Peter Jackson (1954–61) were regulars for Bradford City. Two other similar pairs of City brothers were Alan and Christopher Rhodes (1963–64) and Alan and Alec Smith (1967–68).

***Record Defeat:*** 1–9 v Colchester U, Division 4, 30 December 1961.

***Most League Points (2 for a win):*** 63, Division 3 (N), 1928–29.

***Most League Points (3 for a win):*** 94, Division 3, 1984–85.

***Most League Goals:*** 128, Division 3 (N), 1928–29.

***Highest League Scorer in Season:*** David Layne, 34, Division 4, 1961–62.

***Most League Goals in Total Aggregate:*** Bobby Campbell, 121, 1981–84, 1984–86.

***Most League Goals in One Match:*** 7, Albert Whitehurst v Tranmere R, Division 3N, 6 March 1929.

***Most Capped Player:*** Jamie Lawrence, Jamaica.

***Most League Appearances:*** Cec Podd, 502, 1970–84.

***Youngest League Player:*** Robert Cullingford, 16 years 141 days v Mansfield T, 22 April 1970.

***Record Transfer Fee Received:*** £2,000,000 from Newcastle U for Des Hamilton, July 1997 and £2,000,000 from Newcastle U for Andrew O'Brien, March 2001.

***Record Transfer Fee Paid:*** £2,500,000 to Leeds U for David Hopkin, July 2000.

***Football League Record:*** 1903 Elected to Division 2; 1908–22 Division 1; 1922–27 Division 2; 1927–29 Division 3 (N); 1929–37 Division 2; 1937–61 Division 3; 1961–69 Division 4; 1969–72 Division 3; 1972–77 Division 4; 1977–78 Division 3; 1978–82 Division 4; 1982–85 Division 3; 1985–90 Division 2; 1990–92 Division 3; 1992–96 Division 2; 1996–99 Division 1; 1999–2001 FA Premier League; 2001–04 Division 1; 2004– FL1.

## MANAGERS

Robert Campbell 1903–05
Peter O'Rourke 1905–21
David Menzies 1921–26
Colin Veitch 1926–28
Peter O'Rourke 1928–30
Jack Peart 1930–35
Dick Ray 1935–37
Fred Westgarth 1938–43
Bob Sharp 1943–46
Jack Barker 1946–47
John Milburn 1947–48
David Steele 1948–52
Albert Harris 1952
Ivor Powell 1952–55
Peter Jackson 1955–61
Bob Brocklebank 1961–64
Bill Harris 1965–66
Willie Watson 1966–69
Grenville Hair 1967–68
Jimmy Wheeler 1968–71
Bryan Edwards 1971–75
Bobby Kennedy 1975–78
John Napier 1978
George Mulhall 1978–81
Roy McFarland 1981–82
Trevor Cherry 1982–87
Terry Dolan 1987–89
Terry Yorath 1989–90
John Docherty 1990–91
Frank Stapleton 1991–94
Lennie Lawrence 1994–95
Chris Kamara 1995–98
Paul Jewell 1998–2000
Chris Hutchings 2000
Jim Jefferies 2000–01
Nicky Law 2002–03
Bryan Robson 2003–04
Colin Todd June 2004–

## LATEST SEQUENCES

***Longest Sequence of League Wins:*** 10, 26.11.1983 – 3.2.1984.

***Longest Sequence of League Defeats:*** 8, 21.1.1933 – 11.3.1933.

***Longest Sequence of League Draws:*** 6, 30.1.1976 – 13.3.1976.

***Longest Sequence of Unbeaten League Matches:*** 21, 11.1.1969 – 2.5.1969.

***Longest Sequence Without a League Win:*** 16, 28.8.1948 – 20.11.1948.

***Successive Scoring Runs:*** 30 from 26.12.1961.

***Successive Non-scoring Runs:*** 7 from 18.4.1925.

## TEN YEAR LEAGUE RECORD

| | | P | W | D | L | F | A | Pts | Pos |
|---|---|---|---|---|---|---|---|---|---|
| 1994-95 | Div 2 | 46 | 16 | 12 | 18 | 57 | 64 | 60 | 14 |
| 1995-96 | Div 2 | 46 | 22 | 7 | 17 | 71 | 69 | 73 | 6 |
| 1996-97 | Div 1 | 46 | 12 | 12 | 22 | 47 | 72 | 48 | 21 |
| 1997-98 | Div 1 | 46 | 14 | 15 | 17 | 46 | 59 | 57 | 13 |
| 1998-99 | Div 1 | 46 | 26 | 9 | 11 | 82 | 47 | 87 | 2 |
| 1999-2000 | PR Lge | 38 | 9 | 9 | 20 | 38 | 68 | 36 | 17 |
| 2000-01 | PR Lge | 38 | 5 | 11 | 22 | 30 | 70 | 26 | 20 |
| 2001-02 | Div 1 | 46 | 15 | 10 | 21 | 69 | 76 | 55 | 15 |
| 2002-03 | Div 1 | 46 | 14 | 10 | 22 | 51 | 73 | 52 | 19 |
| 2003-04 | Div 1 | 46 | 10 | 6 | 30 | 38 | 69 | 36 | 23 |

## DID YOU KNOW?

Revenge of the stiffs: two days after Worksop Town had beaten Bradford City in an FA Cup second reound replay on 15 December 1955 after a 2-2 draw at Valley Parade, City's reserves beat Worksop 2-1 on the same ground.

## BRADFORD CITY 2003–04 LEAGUE RECORD

| *Match No.* | *Date* | *Venue* | *Opponents* | *Result* | *H/T Score* | *Lg. Pos.* | *Goalscorers* | *Attendance* |
|---|---|---|---|---|---|---|---|---|
| 1 | Aug 9 | H | Norwich C | D 2-2 | 0-1 | — | Muirhead [84], Branch [90] | 13,159 |
| 2 | 16 | A | Cardiff C | W 2-0 | 1-0 | 7 | Gray [6], Emanuel [69] | 16,421 |
| 3 | 23 | H | Gillingham | L 0-1 | 0-0 | 10 | | 10,317 |
| 4 | 26 | A | West Ham U | L 0-1 | 0-1 | — | | 30,370 |
| 5 | 30 | H | Sunderland | L 0-4 | 0-3 | 19 | | 14,116 |
| 6 | Sept 13 | H | Preston NE | W 2-1 | 0-1 | 16 | Branch [59], Summerbee [71] | 11,243 |
| 7 | 16 | A | Crystal Palace | W 1-0 | 1-0 | — | Branch [42] | 13,514 |
| 8 | 20 | A | Burnley | L 0-4 | 0-1 | 17 | | 12,719 |
| 9 | 27 | H | Sheffield U | L 1-2 | 1-1 | 18 | Windass [28] | 11,067 |
| 10 | 30 | H | Derby Co | L 1-2 | 0-1 | — | Gray [59] | 10,143 |
| 11 | Oct 4 | A | Reading | D 2-2 | 1-1 | 21 | Evans [44], Gray [55] | 12,594 |
| 12 | 11 | H | Ipswich T | L 0-1 | 0-1 | 21 | | 10,229 |
| 13 | 14 | A | Crewe Alex | D 2-2 | 0-0 | — | Evans [55], Muirhead [87] | 5867 |
| 14 | 18 | A | Watford | L 0-1 | 0-0 | 22 | | 10,381 |
| 15 | 25 | H | Nottingham F | L 1-2 | 1-0 | 23 | Branch [5] | 11,654 |
| 16 | Nov 1 | A | Wimbledon | L 1-2 | 1-0 | 23 | Gray [34] | 3334 |
| 17 | 5 | A | Coventry C | D 0-0 | 0-0 | — | | 11,862 |
| 18 | 8 | H | Walsall | D 1-1 | 1-1 | 23 | Branch [5] | 9629 |
| 19 | 22 | A | Stoke C | L 0-1 | 0-1 | 23 | | 11,661 |
| 20 | 29 | H | Millwall | W 3-2 | 0-2 | 23 | Cadamarteri [52], Gray [69], Branch [90] | 10,107 |
| 21 | Dec 6 | A | Walsall | L 0-1 | 0-0 | 23 | | 6876 |
| 22 | 9 | H | WBA | L 0-1 | 0-0 | — | | 11,198 |
| 23 | 13 | A | Wigan Ath | L 0-1 | 0-0 | 23 | | 7256 |
| 24 | 20 | H | Rotherham U | L 0-2 | 0-1 | 23 | | 10,923 |
| 25 | 26 | A | Sunderland | L 0-3 | 0-1 | 23 | | 29,639 |
| 26 | 28 | H | Coventry C | W 1-0 | 1-0 | 23 | Windass [34] | 11,432 |
| 27 | Jan 10 | A | Norwich C | W 1-0 | 1-0 | 23 | Armstrong [45] | 16,360 |
| 28 | 17 | H | Cardiff C | L 0-1 | 0-0 | 23 | | 11,132 |
| 29 | 24 | H | Crystal Palace | L 1-2 | 1-2 | 23 | Wallwork [27] | 10,310 |
| 30 | 31 | A | Gillingham | L 0-1 | 0-1 | 23 | | 7836 |
| 31 | Feb 7 | H | West Ham U | L 1-2 | 1-0 | 23 | Atherton [35] | 13,078 |
| 32 | 14 | A | Ipswich T | L 1-3 | 1-2 | 23 | Windass [44] | 21,478 |
| 33 | 21 | H | Crewe Alex | W 2-1 | 0-0 | 23 | Windass [51], Wallwork [79] | 9935 |
| 34 | 28 | A | Nottingham F | L 1-2 | 1-1 | 23 | Windass [19] | 26,021 |
| 35 | Mar 6 | A | Rotherham U | W 2-1 | 2-0 | 23 | Wallwork 2 [40, 45] | 6796 |
| 36 | 9 | H | Watford | W 2-0 | 2-0 | — | Evans [9], Windass [22] | 17,143 |
| 37 | 13 | H | Wigan Ath | D 0-0 | 0-0 | 23 | | 11,744 |
| 38 | 20 | A | Sheffield U | L 0-2 | 0-0 | 23 | | 20,052 |
| 39 | 27 | H | Burnley | L 1-2 | 1-1 | 23 | Cadamarteri [18] | 13,677 |
| 40 | Apr 3 | A | Preston NE | L 0-1 | 0-0 | 23 | | 12,367 |
| 41 | 10 | H | Reading | W 2-1 | 1-1 | 23 | Wetherall [12], Emanuel [53] | 10,287 |
| 42 | 12 | A | Derby Co | L 2-3 | 0-1 | 23 | Atherton [67], Wolleaston [79] | 21,593 |
| 43 | 17 | H | Wimbledon | L 2-3 | 0-2 | 23 | Sanasy [72], Cadamarteri [75] | 9011 |
| 44 | 24 | A | WBA | L 0-2 | 0-0 | 23 | | 26,143 |
| 45 | May 1 | H | Stoke C | L 0-2 | 0-1 | 23 | | 10,147 |
| 46 | 9 | A | Millwall | L 0-1 | 0-0 | 23 | | 9635 |

**Final League Position: 23**

### GOALSCORERS

*League (38):* Branch 6, Windass 6, Gray 5, Wallwork 4, Cadamarteri 3, Evans 3, Atherton 2, Emanuel 2, Muirhead 2, Armstrong 1, Sanasy 1, Summerbee 1, Wetherall 1, Wolleaston 1.
*Carling Cup (0).*
*FA Cup (1):* Gray 1 (pen).

| Paston M 13 | Edds G 19 + 4 | Jacobs W 11 + 2 | Evans P 20 + 3 | Wetherall D 34 | Francis S 25 + 5 | Gray A 33 | Kearney T 13 + 4 | Windass D 34 + 2 | Branch M 29 + 4 | Heckingbottom P 43 | Emanuel L 18 + 10 | Muirhead B 12 + 16 | Gavin J 37 + 1 | Wolleaston R 6 + 8 | Standing M 2 + 4 | Combe A 21 | Summerbee N 33 + 2 | Beresford M 5 | Sanasy K 2 + 3 | Cornwall L 2 + 1 | Forrest D 2 + 11 | Bower M 11 + 3 | McHugh F 3 | Cadamarteri D 14 + 4 | Atherton P 27 | Farrelly G 14 | Armstrong A 6 | Wallwork R 7 | Davies C 1 + 1 | Vaesen N 6 | Penford T 3 + 1 | *Match No.* |
|---|---|---|---|---|---|---|---|---|---|---|---|---|---|---|---|---|---|---|---|---|---|---|---|---|---|---|---|---|---|---|---|---|
| 1 | 2 | $3^1$ | 4 | 5 | 6 | 7 | $8^2$ | 9 | 10 | 11 | 12 | 13 | | | | | | | | | | | | | | | | | | | | 1 |
| 1 | 2 | 3 | 4 | 5 | 8 | 7 | | 9 | 10 | 6 | 12 | $11^1$ | | | | | | | | | | | | | | | | | | | | 2 |
| 1 | 2 | 3 | 4 | 5 | 6 | 10 | | $9^3$ | 7 | $8^2$ | $11^1$ | 12 | 13 | 14 | | | | | | | | | | | | | | | | | | 3 |
| 1 | 2 | 3 | 4 | 5 | 7 | 10 | | $8^2$ | $9^1$ | 11 | | | 6 | 12 | 13 | | | | | | | | | | | | | | | | | 4 |
| 1 | 2 | 3 | | 5 | 6 | 10 | | $8^1$ | 9 | 7 | 13 | | 4 | 12 | $11^2$ | | | | | | | | | | | | | | | | | 5 |
| | $2^1$ | 3 | | 5 | 12 | 8 | | 9 | 10 | 6 | 13 | 11 | 4 | | | 1 | $7^2$ | | | | | | | | | | | | | | | 6 |
| | | | 4 | 5 | 8 | 11 | | $9^1$ | 10 | 3 | 2 | | 6 | | | | 7 | 1 | 12 | | | | | | | | | | | | | 7 |
| | 12 | | $4^3$ | 5 | 2 | 8 | | 9 | 10 | 3 | 11 | 13 | $6^1$ | | | | $7^2$ | 1 | | 14 | | | | | | | | | | | | 8 |
| | 2 | | 4 | 5 | 12 | 10 | | 9■ | $8^2$ | 6 | $3^1$ | 14 | 11 | 13 | | | $7^3$ | 1 | | | | | | | | | | | | | | 9 |
| 1 | 2 | | 4 | 5 | | 10 | | 8 | 9 | 3 | | $11^1$ | 6 | 12 | | | 7 | | | | | | | | | | | | | | | 10 |
| 1 | 2 | | 4 | 5 | 12 | 10 | | 8 | | 3 | 13 | 11 | 6 | | | | $7^1$ | | | $9^2$ | | | | | | | | | | | | 11 |
| | 2 | 12 | 4 | 5 | 13 | 10 | 8 | | | $3^1$ | | 11 | $6^3$ | | | | 7 | 1 | | $9^2$ | 14 | | | | | | | | | | | 12 |
| | 2 | 3 | 4 | 5 | 12 | 10 | $8^1$ | | | | | 11 | 6 | | | | 7 | 1 | | | 9 | | | | | | | | | | | 13 |
| 1 | 2 | 3 | 4 | $5^1$ | 8 | 10 | 12 | | | | | 11 | 6 | 13 | 14 | | $7^3$ | | | | $9^2$ | | | | | | | | | | | 14 |
| | 2 | | 4 | | | 10 | | 8 | $9^1$ | 5 | 3 | 11 | 6 | | | 1 | 7 | | | | 12 | | | | | | | | | | | 15 |
| | $2^2$ | | 4 | | 7 | 10 | | 8 | 9 | 11 | $3^1$ | 12 | 6 | | | 1 | | | | | 13 | $5^1$ | | | | | | | | | | 16 |
| | 12 | | | | | 10 | 11 | 8 | 9 | 3 | 2 | | 6 | | | 1 | $7^1$ | | | | | 5 | 4 | | | | | | | | | 17 |
| | | | | | | 10 | $11^1$ | 8 | 9 | 4 | | 3 | 6 | | | 1 | 2 | | | | | 5 | 7 | 12 | | | | | | | | 18 |
| | 11 | | | | 2 | 10 | 13 | | 9 | 3 | | 12 | 6 | | | 1 | 7 | | | | | 5 | $8^2$ | | $4^1$ | | | | | | | 19 |
| | | | | | 2 | 10 | 4 | 9 | 13 | 3 | | $11^1$ | 6 | | | 1 | 7 | | | | | | | $12^2$ | 5 | 8 | | | | | | 20 |
| | | | | | 2 | 10 | 4 | 9 | 12 | 3 | $11^1$ | | 6 | | | 1 | 7 | | | | | | | | 5 | 8 | | | | | | 21 |
| | | | | | 2 | 10 | 4 | 8 | 9 | 3 | | | 6 | | | 1 | 7 | | | | | | | | 5 | 11 | | | | | | 22 |
| 1 | | | | | 2 | 10 | 4 | $8^1$ | $9^2$ | 3 | | | 6■ | | 12 | | 7 | | | | | 13 | | | 5 | 11 | | | | | | 23 |
| 1 | | | 13 | | 2 | 10 | 4 | | 9 | 3 | | $12^2$ | 6 | | $8^3$ | | $7^1$ | | | | 14 | | | | 5 | 11 | | | | | | 24 |
| 1 | | 12 | | | $2^1$ | 10 | 4 | $8^3$ | 9 | 3 | | $7^2$ | 6 | | 13 | | | | | | 14 | | | | 5 | 11 | | | | | | 25 |
| | | | 4 | 5 | | 10 | $7^1$ | 8 | | 3 | | 12 | | | | 1 | | | | | | 6 | | | 2 | 11 | 9 | | | | | 26 |
| | | | 13 | 5 | 2 | 10 | | | | 3 | | 12 | 6 | | | 1 | $7^1$ | | | | | | | 8 | 4 | $11^2$ | 9 | | | | | 27 |
| | | | | 5 | $2^1$ | 11 | | | $10^2$ | 3 | 12 | 13 | 6 | | | 1 | 7 | | | | | | | 8 | 4 | | 9 | | | | | 28 |
| | | | | 5 | | 10 | | | | 3 | 13 | 12 | 6 | | | 1 | $7^1$ | | | | | | | $8^2$ | 2 | 11 | 9 | 4 | | | | 29 |
| | | | 12 | 5 | $2^1$ | 10 | | | | 3 | | $7^6$ | 6 | | | 1■ | | | | | 13 | | | | 4 | $11^2$ | 9 | 8 | 15 | | | 30 |
| | | | | 5 | 2 | 10 | | 12 | 13 | 3 | | | 6 | | | 1 | $7^1$ | | | | | | | | 4 | 11 | $9^2$ | 8 | | | | 31 |
| | | | $8^2$ | 5 | | $10^1$ | | 9 | 12 | 3 | 13 | | | | | | $7^3$ | | | | | 6 | | 14 | 2 | 11 | | 4 | | 1 | | 32 |
| | | | | 5 | 2 | $10^1$ | | 9 | | 3 | | 12 | 6 | | | | 13 | | | | | | | 8 | 4 | $11^2$ | | 7 | | 1 | | 33 |
| | | | | 5 | 2 | | | 9 | | 3 | 8 | | 6■ | | | | 12 | | | | | | | 10 | 4 | $11^1$ | | 7 | | 1 | | 34 |
| | | | 8 | 5 | 2 | | | 9 | | 3 | $11^1$ | 12 | 6 | | | | | | | | | | | 10 | 4 | | | 7 | | 1 | | 35 |
| | | | 8 | 5 | 2 | | | 9 | | 3 | $11^2$ | 12 | 6 | | | | 7 | | | | 13 | | | $10^1$ | 4 | | | | | 1 | | 36 |
| | | | 8 | 5 | 2 | | | 9 | $10^1$ | 3 | 11 | 12 | | | | | 7 | | | | | 6 | | | 4 | | | | | 1 | | 37 |
| | | 2 | 8 | | | | 6 | 9 | $10^1$ | 3 | 11 | | | 12 | | | 7 | | | | | 5 | | | 4 | | | | 1 | | | 38 |
| | 12 | $2^1$ | | 5 | | | | 9 | 8 | 3 | 11 | | | | | 1 | 7 | | | | | 6 | | 10 | 4 | | | | | | | 39 |
| | 2 | | | 5 | | | | 8 | 9 | 3 | $11^1$ | | | 12 | | 1 | 7 | | | | | 6 | | 10 | 4 | | | | | | | 40 |
| | 2 | | | 5 | | | | $8^2$ | 9■ | 3 | 12 | | 6 | 11 | | 1 | 7 | | | | 13 | | | $10^1$ | 4 | | | | | | | 41 |
| | $2^1$ | | | 5 | | | | 9 | 10 | 3 | $11^2$ | 12 | $6^3$ | 8 | | 1 | 7 | | | | | 14 | | 13 | 4 | | | | | | | 42 |
| 1 | 2 | | | 5 | | | | $9^2$ | $10^3$ | 3 | | | 6 | 8 | | | 7 | | 13 | | 12 | | | 11 | $4^1$ | | | | | | 14 | 43 |
| 1 | | | | 5 | | | 12 | $9^3$ | | 3 | 11 | | 6 | 8 | | | 7 | | 14 | | | 13 | | 10 | $4^2$ | | | | | | $2^1$ | 44 |
| | | | | 5 | | | 13 | 12 | $9^3$ | | 3 | | 6 | $8^1$ | | 1 | 7 | | 11 | | 14 | | | 10 | $2^2$ | | | | | | 4 | 45 |
| | 13 | $2^1$ | | $5^2$ | | | | | 9 | 3 | 12 | | 6 | 8 | | 1 | | | 11 | | 14 | 4 | | $10^3$ | | | | | | | 7 | 46 |

**Carling Cup**
First Round Darlington (h) 0-0

**FA Cup**
Third Round Luton T (h) 1-2

# BRENTFORD FL Championship 1

## FOUNDATION

Formed as a small amateur concern in 1889 they were very successful in local circles. They won the championship of the West London Alliance in 1893 and a year later the West Middlesex Junior Cup before carrying off the Senior Cup in 1895. After winning both the London Senior Amateur Cup and the Middlesex Senior Cup in 1898 they were admitted to the Second Division of the Southern League.

***Griffin Park, Braemar Road, Brentford, TW8 0NT.***

***Telephone:*** 0870 9009229.

***Fax:*** (0208) 380 9937.

***Ground Capacity:*** 12,416.

***Record Attendance:*** 38,678 v Leicester C, FA Cup 6th rd, 26 February 1949.

***Pitch Measurements:*** 111yd × 74yd.

***Chairman:*** Eddie Rogers.

***Executive Director:*** John McGlashon.

***Secretary:*** Lisa Hall.

***Manager:*** Martin Allen.

***First Team Coach:*** Adrian Whitbread.

***Physio:*** Matt Hirons.

***Colours:*** Red and white stripes.

***Change Colours:*** Blue and yellow stripes.

***Year Formed:*** 1889.

***Turned Professional:*** 1899.

***Ltd Co.:*** 1901.

***Club Nickname:*** 'The Bees'.

***Previous Grounds:*** 1889, Clifden Road; 1891, Benns Fields, Little Ealing; 1895, Shotters Field; 1898, Cross Road, S. Ealing; 1900, Boston Park; 1904, Griffin Park.

***First Football League Game:*** 28 August 1920, Division 3, v Exeter C (a) L 0–3 – Young; Hodson, Rosier, Elliott J, Levitt, Amos, Smith, Thompson, Spreadbury, Morley, Henery.

***Record League Victory:*** 9–0 v Wrexham, Division 3, 15 October 1963 – Cakebread; Coote, Jones; Slater, Scott, Higginson; Summers (1), Brooks (2), McAdams (2), Ward (2), Hales (1), (1 og).

***Record Cup Victory:*** 7–0 v Windsor & Eton (away), FA Cup 1st rd, 20 November 1982 – Roche; Rowe, Harris (Booker), McNichol (1), Whitehead, Hurlock (2), Kamara, Joseph (1), Mahoney (3), Bowles, Roberts.
*N.B.* 8–0 v Uxbridge, FA Cup, 3rd Qual rd, 31 October 1903.

## HONOURS

*Football League:* Division 1 best season: 5th, 1935–36; Division 2 – Champions 1934–35; Division 3 – Champions 1991–92, 1998–99; Division 3 (S) – Champions 1932–33, Runners-up 1929–30, 1957–58; Division 4 – Champions 1962–63.

*FA Cup:* best season: 6th rd, 1938, 1946, 1949, 1989.

*Football League Cup:* best season: 4th rd, 1983.

*Freight Rover Trophy:* Runners-up 1985.

*LDV Vans Trophy:* Runners-up 2001.

## SKY SPORTS FACT FILE

In 1937–38 Brentford were invited to play in the Scottish Exhibition Cup with Chelsea, Everton, Sunderland, Celtic, Rangers, Hearts and Aberdeen. Brentford did well to reach the final and were only beaten 1-0 by Hearts at Ibrox.

***Record Defeat:*** 0–7 v Swansea T, Division 3 (S), 8 November 1924 and v Walsall, Division 3 (S), 19 January 1957.

***Most League Points (2 for a win):*** 62, Division 3 (S), 1932–33 and Division 4, 1962–63.

***Most League Points (3 for a win):*** 85, Division 2, 1994–95 and Division 3, 1998–99.

***Most League Goals:*** 98, Division 4, 1962–63.

***Highest League Scorer in Season:*** Jack Holliday, 38, Division 3 (S), 1932–33.

***Most League Goals in Total Aggregate:*** Jim Towers, 153, 1954–61.

***Most League Goals in One Match:*** 5, Jack Holliday v Luton T, Division 3S, 28 January 1933; Billy Scott v Barnsley, Division 2, 15 December 1934; Peter McKennan v Bury, Division 2, 18 February 1949.

***Most Capped Player:*** John Buttigieg, 22 (98), Malta.

***Most League Appearances:*** Ken Coote, 514, 1949–64.

***Youngest League Player:*** Danis Salman, 15 years 243 days v Watford, 15 November 1975.

***Record Transfer Fee Received:*** £2,500,000 from Wimbledon for Hermann Hreidarsson, October 1999.

***Record Transfer Fee Paid:*** £750,000 to Crystal Palace for Hermann Hreidarsson, September 1998.

***Football League Record:*** 1920 Original Member of Division 3; 1921–33 Division 3 (S); 1933–35 Division 2; 1935–47 Division 1; 1947–54 Division 2; 1954–62 Division 3 (S); 1962–63 Division 4; 1963–66 Division 3; 1966–72 Division 4; 1972–73 Division 3; 1973–78 Division 4; 1978–92 Division 3; 1992–93 Division 1; 1993–98 Division 2; 1998–99 Division 3; 1999–04 Division 2; 2004– FL1.

## MANAGERS

Will Lewis 1900–03 *(Secretary-Manager)*
Dick Molyneux 1902–06
W. G. Brown 1906–08
Fred Halliday 1908–12, 1915–21, 1924–26 *(only Secretary to 1922)*
Ephraim Rhodes 1912–15
Archie Mitchell 1921–24
Harry Curtis 1926–49
Jackie Gibbons 1949–52
Jimmy Blain 1952–53
Tommy Lawton 1953
Bill Dodgin Snr 1953–57
Malcolm Macdonald 1957–65
Tommy Cavanagh 1965–66
Billy Gray 1966–67
Jimmy Sirrel 1967–69
Frank Blunstone 1969–73
Mike Everitt 1973–75
John Docherty 1975–76
Bill Dodgin Jnr 1976–80
Fred Callaghan 1980–84
Frank McLintock 1984–87
Steve Perryman 1987–90
Phil Holder 1990–93
David Webb 1993–97
Eddie May 1997
Micky Adams 1997–98
Ron Noades 1998–2000
Ray Lewington 2001
Steve Coppell 2001–02
Wally Downes 2002–04
Martin Allen March 2004–

## LATEST SEQUENCES

***Longest Sequence of League Wins:*** 9, 30.4.1932 – 24.9.1932.

***Longest Sequence of League Defeats:*** 9, 20.10.1928 – 25.12.1928.

***Longest Sequence of League Draws:*** 5, 16.3.1957 – 6.4.1957.

***Longest Sequence of Unbeaten League Matches:*** 26, 20.2.1999 – 16.10.1999.

***Longest Sequence Without a League Win:*** 16, 19.2.1994 – 7.5.1994.

***Successive Scoring Runs:*** 26 from 4.3.1963.

***Successive Non-scoring Runs:*** 7 from 7.3.2000.

## TEN YEAR LEAGUE RECORD

| | | *P* | *W* | *D* | *L* | *F* | *A* | *Pts* | *Pos* |
|---|---|---|---|---|---|---|---|---|---|
| 1994-95 | Div 2 | 46 | 25 | 10 | 11 | 81 | 39 | 85 | 2 |
| 1995-96 | Div 2 | 46 | 15 | 13 | 18 | 43 | 49 | 58 | 15 |
| 1996-97 | Div 2 | 46 | 20 | 14 | 12 | 56 | 43 | 74 | 4 |
| 1997-98 | Div 2 | 46 | 11 | 17 | 18 | 50 | 71 | 50 | 21 |
| 1998-99 | Div 3 | 46 | 26 | 7 | 13 | 79 | 56 | 85 | 1 |
| 1999-2000 | Div 2 | 46 | 13 | 13 | 20 | 47 | 61 | 52 | 17 |
| 2000-01 | Div 2 | 46 | 14 | 17 | 15 | 56 | 70 | 59 | 14 |
| 2001-02 | Div 2 | 46 | 24 | 11 | 11 | 77 | 43 | 83 | 3 |
| 2002-03 | Div 2 | 46 | 14 | 12 | 20 | 47 | 56 | 54 | 16 |
| 2003-04 | Div 2 | 46 | 14 | 11 | 21 | 52 | 69 | 53 | 17 |

## DID YOU KNOW ?

Ken Coote, the Brentford player with the most League games to his credit, made a total of 559 senior appearances during his time at Griffin Park. Never once booked by a referee he was also honoured by playing for London in the 1958 Fairs Cup Final.

## BRENTFORD 2003–04 LEAGUE RECORD

| Match No. | Date | Venue | Opponents | Result | | H/T Score | Lg. Pos. | Goalscorers | Attendance |
|---|---|---|---|---|---|---|---|---|---|
| 1 | Aug 9 | A | Tranmere R | L | 1-4 | 0-2 | — | Hunt (pen) [64] | 7307 |
| 2 | 16 | H | Peterborough U | L | 0-3 | 0-1 | 23 | | 4463 |
| 3 | 23 | A | Wrexham | L | 0-1 | 0-1 | 23 | | 4048 |
| 4 | 25 | H | Oldham Ath | W | 2-1 | 1-1 | 19 | Hutchinson [42], Rougier [58] | 4073 |
| 5 | 30 | A | Port Vale | L | 0-1 | 0-0 | 23 | | 5257 |
| 6 | Sept 6 | H | Plymouth Arg | L | 1-3 | 1-1 | 23 | May [27] | 5688 |
| 7 | 13 | A | Rushden & D | W | 1-0 | 1-0 | 21 | Hunt [19] | 4396 |
| 8 | 16 | H | Blackpool | D | 0-0 | 0-0 | — | | 3818 |
| 9 | 20 | H | Hartlepool U | W | 2-1 | 1-1 | 18 | Sonko [13], Wright [48] | 4501 |
| 10 | 27 | A | Chesterfield | W | 2-1 | 0-0 | 17 | Hunt [63], Wright [82] | 3257 |
| 11 | 30 | A | Colchester U | D | 1-1 | 1-0 | — | Rougier [36] | 3343 |
| 12 | Oct 4 | H | Sheffield W | L | 0-3 | 0-2 | 18 | | 8631 |
| 13 | 18 | H | Luton T | W | 4-2 | 1-0 | 18 | Hunt [12], Tabb 2 [58, 65], May [87] | 5579 |
| 14 | 21 | H | Brighton & HA | W | 4-0 | 2-0 | — | Hunt 2 (2 pens) [8, 87], Tabb [36], May [78] | 6532 |
| 15 | 25 | A | Notts Co | L | 0-2 | 0-1 | 17 | | 4145 |
| 16 | Nov 1 | H | Barnsley | W | 2-1 | 0-0 | 15 | Hutchinson [47], Rougier [58] | 4789 |
| 17 | 11 | A | QPR | L | 0-1 | 0-1 | — | | 15,865 |
| 18 | 15 | A | Wycombe W | W | 2-1 | 1-0 | 13 | Hutchinson [29], Tabb [90] | 6445 |
| 19 | 22 | H | Grimsby T | L | 1-3 | 1-1 | 16 | Hunt (pen) [10] | 4685 |
| 20 | 29 | A | Bournemouth | L | 0-1 | 0-0 | 16 | | 6674 |
| 21 | Dec 13 | A | Stockport Co | D | 1-1 | 0-0 | 16 | Jackman (og) [66] | 4081 |
| 22 | 20 | H | Swindon T | L | 0-2 | 0-0 | 18 | | 5077 |
| 23 | 26 | H | Bristol C | L | 1-2 | 0-0 | 19 | May [63] | 5912 |
| 24 | 28 | A | Plymouth Arg | L | 0-2 | 0-0 | 19 | | 17,882 |
| 25 | Jan 3 | A | Oldham Ath | D | 1-1 | 1-0 | 19 | May [13] | 4990 |
| 26 | 10 | H | Tranmere R | D | 2-2 | 1-1 | 19 | Hunt [18], May [62] | 4105 |
| 27 | 17 | A | Peterborough U | D | 0-0 | 0-0 | 19 | | 4658 |
| 28 | 24 | H | Wrexham | L | 0-1 | 0-0 | 19 | | 4567 |
| 29 | 31 | H | Port Vale | W | 3-2 | 1-1 | 18 | Tabb [2], Hunt [48], Rougier [56] | 4306 |
| 30 | Feb 7 | A | Bristol C | L | 1-3 | 0-1 | 18 | Hutchinson [77] | 13,029 |
| 31 | 14 | H | QPR | D | 1-1 | 0-1 | 18 | O'Connor [51] | 8418 |
| 32 | 21 | A | Luton T | L | 1-4 | 0-1 | 18 | Wright [63] | 6273 |
| 33 | 28 | H | Notts Co | L | 2-3 | 2-1 | 20 | Evans [16], Hutchinson [40] | 4478 |
| 34 | Mar 2 | A | Brighton & HA | L | 0-1 | 0-0 | — | | 6007 |
| 35 | 6 | A | Swindon T | L | 1-2 | 1-1 | 22 | May [30] | 7649 |
| 36 | 13 | H | Stockport Co | L | 0-2 | 0-0 | 23 | | 6615 |
| 37 | 16 | A | Blackpool | D | 1-1 | 1-0 | — | Hunt (pen) [17] | 4617 |
| 38 | 20 | H | Rushden & D | W | 3-2 | 3-0 | 22 | Tabb [26], Hunt [27], Talbot [36] | 4616 |
| 39 | 27 | A | Hartlepool U | W | 2-1 | 2-1 | 20 | Tabb [2], Dobson [33] | 5206 |
| 40 | Apr 3 | H | Chesterfield | D | 1-1 | 0-0 | 22 | Evans [89] | 4962 |
| 41 | 10 | A | Sheffield W | D | 1-1 | 0-0 | 21 | Sonko [69] | 20,004 |
| 42 | 12 | H | Colchester U | W | 3-2 | 1-0 | 20 | Tabb [45], Sonko [58], Harrold [78] | 5017 |
| 43 | 17 | A | Barnsley | W | 2-0 | 1-0 | 17 | Talbot [2], Tabb [61] | 9824 |
| 44 | 24 | H | Wycombe W | D | 1-1 | 0-0 | 18 | Harrold [72] | 7145 |
| 45 | May 1 | A | Grimsby T | L | 0-1 | 0-0 | 19 | | 6856 |
| 46 | 8 | H | Bournemouth | W | 1-0 | 0-0 | 17 | Rhodes [83] | 9485 |

**Final League Position: 17**

## GOALSCORERS

*League (52):* Hunt 11 (5 pens), Tabb 9, May 7, Hutchinson 5, Rougier 4, Sonko 3, Wright 3, Evans 2, Harrold 2, Talbot 2, Dobson 1, O'Connor 1, Rhodes 1, own goal 1.
*Carling Cup (0).*
*FA Cup (7):* Harrold 3, Frampton 1, O'Connor 1, Rougier 1, own goal 1.
*LDV Vans Trophy (5):* Hunt 2 (2 pens), Tabb 2, Dobson 1.

| Smith P 24 | Dobson M 42 | Sonner M 30 + 9 | Sonko I 42 + 1 | Roget L 15 | Frampton A 10 + 6 | Smith J 12 + 5 | Hutchinson E 36 | Beadle P 1 | O'Connor K 36 + 7 | Hunt S 38 + 2 | Fieldwick L 4 + 1 | Tabb J 22 + 14 | Peters M 2 + 7 | Rougier T 29 + 2 | Evans S 14 + 11 | Blackman L — + 3 | Hughes S 1 + 8 | May B 38 + 3 | Julian A 13 | Wright T 18 + 7 | Kitamirike J 21 + 1 | Harrold M 5 + 8 | Wells D — + 1 | Olugbodi J — + 2 | Rhodes A — + 3 | Bull R 20 | Talbot S 15 | Nelson S 9 | Fitzgerald S 9 | *Match No.* |
|---|---|---|---|---|---|---|---|---|---|---|---|---|---|---|---|---|---|---|---|---|---|---|---|---|---|---|---|---|---|---|
| 1 | 2 | 3 | 4 | $5^{1}$ | $6^{2}$ | 7 | $8^{3}$ | 9■ | 10 | 11 | 12 | 13 | 14 | | | | | | | | | | | | | | | | | 1 |
| 1 | 2 | 3 | 4 | 5 | | $7^{1}$ | 6 | | 11 | | | 8 | $10^{2}$ | 9 | 12 | 13 | | | | | | | | | | | | | | 2 |
| 1 | 2 | $3^{2}$ | 4 | 5 | | $7^{1}$ | 6 | | 11 | | | | 12 | 9 | 8 | 13 | 10 | | | | | | | | | | | | | 3 |
| 1 | 2 | 3 | 4 | | | 7 | 6 | | 11 | 12 | 5 | | | $9^{1}$ | 8 | | | 10 | | | | | | | | | | | | 4 |
| | 2 | $3^{1}$ | 4 | 5 | | $7^{2}$ | 6 | | 11 | 12 | | 13 | | 9 | 8 | | | 10 | 1 | | | | | | | | | | | 5 |
| | 2 | | 4 | 5■ | | $7^{1}$ | 6 | | | 11 | 3 | 13 | $9^{2}$ | 8 | 12 | | | 10 | 1 | | | | | | | | | | | 6 |
| | | 2 | 4 | 5 | | 7 | 6 | | $8^{1}$ | 11 | 3 | | | 9 | | | 12 | $10^{2}$ | 1 | 13 | | | | | | | | | | 7 |
| 1 | 2 | 12 | 4 | 5 | | $7^{2}$ | 6 | | 8 | 11 | $3^{1}$ | 13 | | $9^{3}$ | | | | 10 | | 14 | | | | | | | | | | 8 |
| 1 | 2 | 3 | 4 | | | | 6 | | 7 | 11 | | 12 | | $9^{1}$ | 13 | | | $10^{2}$ | | 8 | 5 | | | | | | | | | 9 |
| 1 | 2 | 3 | 4 | | | 12 | 6 | | 8 | 11 | | | | $7^{1}$ | | | | 9 | | 10■ | 5 | | | | | | | | | 10 |
| 1 | 2 | 3 | 4 | | | 12 | 6 | | 8 | 11 | | | | $7^{1}$ | | | | $9^{2}$ | | 10 | 5 | 13 | | | | | | | | 11 |
| 1 | 2 | $3^{1}$ | | $4^{2}$ | | | $6^{3}$ | | 8 | 11 | | 12 | | 7 | | | | 9 | | 10 | 5 | | 13 | 14 | | | | | | 12 |
| 1 | 2 | 3 | 12 | $4^{1}$ | | 13 | | | 8 | 11 | | 14 | | 7 | $6^{2}$ | | | 9 | | $10^{3}$ | 5 | | | | | | | | | 13 |
| 1 | $2^{1}$ | 3 | 4 | | 12 | | 6 | | 8 | 11 | | $10^{2}$ | 13 | 7 | | | | 9 | | | 5 | | | | | | | | | 14 |
| 1 | 2 | 3 | | | 4 | | $6^{2}$ | | 8 | 11 | | 10 | | $7^{1}$ | 12 | | | 9 | | | 5 | | | 13 | | | | | | 15 |
| 1 | 2 | 3 | 4 | | | | 6 | | 8 | 11 | | $9^{2}$ | 13 | 7 | | | 12 | | | | 5 | $10^{1}$ | | | | | | | | 16 |
| 1 | 2 | 3 | 4 | | | | 6 | | $8^{1}$ | 11 | | $10^{2}$ | | 7 | 12 | | | $9^{3}$ | | 13 | 5 | 14 | | | | | | | | 17 |
| 1 | $2^{1}$ | 3 | 4 | | 12 | | 6 | | 8 | 11 | | 14 | | $7^{2}$ | | | 13 | 9 | | $10^{3}$ | 5 | | | | | | | | | 18 |
| 1 | 2 | 3 | 4 | | | 12 | $6^{1}$ | | 8 | $11^{3}$ | | 10 | | $7^{2}$ | | | 13 | 9 | | | 5 | 14 | | | | | | | | 19 |
| 1 | 2 | $3^{1}$ | 4 | | | 6 | | | 8 | 11 | | 10 | 14 | $7^{2}$ | 12 | | 13 | $9^{3}$ | | | 5 | | | | | | | | | 20 |
| 1 | 2 | 3 | 4 | 6 | | | | | 10 | 11 | | 8 | | | 7 | | | 12 | | $9^{1}$ | 5 | | | | | | | | | 21 |
| 1 | 2 | 3 | | 4 | | $7^{1}$ | | | 8 | 11 | | 10 | | 12 | 6 | | | 13 | | $9^{2}$ | 5 | | | | | | | | | 22 |
| 1 | 2 | 3 | 4 | 6 | | | | | 8 | 11 | | | | | 7 | | | $9^{1}$ | | 10 | 5 | | | | 12 | | | | | 23 |
| 1 | 2 | 3 | 4 | 6■ | | | | | 8 | 11 | | | | | $7^{1}$ | | 12 | 9 | | 10 | 5 | | | | | | | | | 24 |
| 1 | 2 | 3 | 4 | 6 | 13 | 12 | | | 8 | 11 | | | | | 7 | | | $9^{1}$ | | $10^{2}$ | 5■ | | | | | | | | | 25 |
| 1 | 2 | | 4 | 5 | 6 | | | | 12 | 11 | | | | $7^{2}$ | 8■ | | 13 | 9 | | $10^{1}$ | | | | | | 3 | | | | 26 |
| 1 | | 2 | 4 | | 5 | 8 | | | 12 | 11 | | 13 | | $7^{1}$ | 6 | | | 9 | | $10^{2}$ | | | | | | 3■ | | | | 27 |
| | | 2 | 4 | | 5 | $6^{1}$ | | | $8^{2}$ | 11 | | 10 | | 7 | | | 12 | 9 | 1 | 13 | | | | | | 3 | | | | 28 |
| | 2 | | 4 | | | | $6^{2}$ | | 8 | 11 | | 10 | 12 | $7^{1}$ | | 13 | | 9 | 1 | | 5 | | | | | 3 | | | | 29 |
| | 2 | | 4 | | | | 6 | | 8 | 11 | | 10 | 12 | 7 | | | | | 1 | $9^{1}$ | 5 | | | | | 3 | | | | 30 |
| | 2 | 3 | 4 | | | | 6 | | 8 | 11 | | 10 | | 7 | | | | 9 | 1 | | 5 | | | | | | | | | 31 |
| | 2 | 12 | 4 | | | | 6 | | 8 | | | 14 | | $7^{3}$ | 13 | | | $9^{2}$ | 1 | 10 | 5 | | | | | $3^{1}$ | 11 | | | 32 |
| | 2 | | 4 | | 5 | | 6 | | | | | 12 | | 7 | 8 | | | $9^{1}$ | 1 | 10 | | | | | | 3 | 11 | | | 33 |
| | 2 | 3 | 4 | | $5^{1}$ | | 8 | | 13 | | | 14 | | | $11^{3}$ | | | 9 | | $10^{2}$ | 12 | | | | | 6 | 7 | 1■ | | 34 |
| | 2 | 5 | 4 | | | | $6^{2}$ | | 7 | | | 10 | | 12 | 8 | | | 9 | | 13 | | | | | | 3 | $11^{1}$ | 1 | | 35 |
| | 2 | 5 | 4 | | | | $6^{2}$ | | 10 | 11 | | 13 | | $7^{1}$ | | | | 9 | | 12 | | | | | | 3 | 8 | 1 | | 36 |
| | 2 | 5 | 4 | | | | $8^{2}$ | | 12 | 11 | | | | $7^{1}$ | 13 | | | $9^{3}$ | 1 | | | 14 | | | | 3 | 10 | | 6 | 37 |
| | 2 | | 4 | | 13 | | 6 | | 12 | $11^{3}$ | | $7^{2}$ | | | 14 | | | 9 | 1 | | | $10^{1}$ | | | | 3 | 8 | | 5 | 38 |
| | 2 | 13 | 4 | | 12 | | 6 | | $10^{2}$ | $11^{3}$ | | $7^{1}$ | | | | | | 9 | 1 | | | 14 | | | | 3 | 8 | | 5 | 39 |
| | 2 | 12 | 4 | | | | 6 | | $7^{3}$ | 11 | | $10^{2}$ | | | 13 | | | 9 | 1 | | | 14 | | | | 3 | $8^{1}$ | | 5 | 40 |
| | 2 | 12 | 4 | | $11^{1}$ | | 6 | | $10^{3}$ | $7^{2}$ | | 14 | | | | | | 9 | | 13 | | | | | | 3 | 8 | 1 | 5 | 41 |
| | 2 | 12 | 4 | | $5^{1}$ | | 6 | | 13 | 11 | | $7^{2}$ | | | | | | 14 | | $10^{3}$ | | 9 | | | | 3 | 8 | 1 | | 42 |
| | 2 | 12 | 4 | | | | 6 | | 7 | $11^{3}$ | | 10 | | | 13 | | | $9^{2}$ | | | | 14 | | | | 3 | $8^{1}$ | 1 | 5 | 43 |
| | $2^{2}$ | 12 | 4 | | | | $6^{1}$ | | 8 | 11 | | 10 | | | | | | 9 | | | | 13 | | | | 3 | 7 | 1 | 5 | 44 |
| | | 12 | 4 | | 2 | | 6 | | 13 | $11^{2}$ | | 7 | | | | | | 9 | | | | 10 | | | 14 | $3^{3}$ | $8^{1}$ | 1 | 5 | 45 |
| | 2 | | 4 | | 12 | | 6 | | | 11 | | 7 | | | | | | 9 | | | | $10^{2}$ | | | 13 | 3 | $8^{1}$ | 1 | 5 | 46 |

**Carling Cup**
First Round WBA (a) 0-4

**LDV Vans Trophy**
First Round Barnet (a) 3-3
Second Round Peterborough U (a) 2-3

**FA Cup**
First Round Gainsborough T (h) 7-1
Second Round Telford U (a) 0-3

# BRIGHTON & HOVE ALBION FL Championship

## FOUNDATION

A professional club Brighton United was formed in November 1897 at the Imperial Hotel, Queen's Road, but folded in March 1900 after less than two seasons in the Southern League at the County Ground. An amateur team, Brighton & Hove Rangers was then formed by some prominent United supporters and after one season at Withdean, decided to turn semi-professional and play at the County Ground. Rangers were accepted into the Southern League but then also folded June 1901. John Jackson the former United manager organised a meeting at the Seven Stars public house, Ship Street on 24 June 1901 at which a new third club Brighton & Hove United was formed. They took over Rangers' place in the Southern League and pitch at County Ground. The name was changed to Brighton & Hove Albion before a match was played because of objections by Hove FC.

***Withdean Stadium, Tongdean Lane, Brighton, East Sussex BN1 5JD.***

***Telephone:*** (01273) 695 400.

***Fax:*** (01273) 648 179.

***Ticket Office:*** (01273) 776 992.

***Website:*** www.seagulls.co.uk

***Email:*** seagulls@bhafc.co.uk

***Ground Capacity:*** 6,973.

***Record Attendance:*** 36,747 v Fulham, Division 2, 27 December 1958.

***Pitch Measurements:*** 110yd × 70yd.

***Chairman:*** Dick Knight.

***Chief Executive:*** Martin Perry.

***Secretary:*** Derek J. Allan.

***Manager:*** Mark McGhee.

***Assistant Manager:*** Bob Booker.

***Physio:*** Malcolm Stuart.

***Colours:*** Blue and white striped shirts, white shorts, white stockings.

***Change Colours:*** All yellow.

***Year Formed:*** 1901.

***Turned Professional:*** 1901.

***Ltd Co.:*** 1904.

***Previous Grounds:*** 1901, County Ground; 1902, Goldstone Ground.

***Club Nickname:*** 'The Seagulls'.

***First Football League Game:*** 28 August 1920, Division 3, v Southend U (a) L 0–2 – Hayes; Woodhouse, Little; Hall, Comber, Bentley; Longstaff, Ritchie, Doran, Rodgerson, March.

## HONOURS

*Football League:* Division 1 best season: 13th, 1981–82; Division 2 – Champions 2001–02; Runners-up 1978–79; Promoted from Division 2 2003–04 (play-offs); Division 3 (S) – Champions 1957–58; Runners-up 1953–54, 1955–56; Division 3 – Champions 2000–01; Runners-up 1971–72, 1976–77, 1987–88; Division 4 – Champions 1964–65.

*FA Cup:* Runners-up 1983.

*Football League Cup:* best season: 5th rd, 1979.

## SKY SPORTS FACT FILE

Centre-forward Billy 'Bullet' Jones signed by Brighton & Hove Albion from Birmingham, scored 22 goals in the 1909–10 Southern League title campaign. Top scorer the next season he switched back to his former club, before returning in 1914–15.

***Record League Victory:*** 9–1 v Newport Co, Division 3 (S), 18 April 1951 – Ball; Tennant (1p), Mansell (1p); Willard, McCoy, Wilson; Reed, McNichol (4), Garbutt, Bennett (2), Keene (1). 9–1 v Southend U, Division 3, 27 November 1965 – Powney; Magill, Baxter; Leck, Gall, Turner; Gould (1), Collins (1), Livesey (2), Smith (3), Goodchild (2).

***Record Cup Victory:*** 10–1 v Wisbech, FA Cup 1st rd, 13 November 1965 – Powney; Magill, Baxter; Collins (1), Gall, Turner; Gould, Smith (2), Livesey (3), Cassidy (2), Goodchild (1), (1 og).

***Record Defeat:*** 0–9 v Middlesbrough, Division 2, 23 August 1958.

***Most League Points (2 for a win):*** 65, Division 3 (S), 1955–56 and Division 3, 1971–72.

***Most League Points (3 for a win):*** 92, Division 3, 2000–01.

***Most League Goals:*** 112, Division 3 (S), 1955–56.

***Highest League Scorer in Season:*** Peter Ward, 32, Division 3, 1976–77.

***Most League Goals in Total Aggregate:*** Tommy Cook, 114, 1922–29.

***Most League Goals in One Match:*** 5, Jack Doran v Northampton T, Division 3S, 5 November 1921; 5, Adrian Thorne v Watford, Division 3S, 30 April 1958.

***Most Capped Player:*** Steve Penney, 17, Northern Ireland.

***Most League Appearances:*** 'Tug' Wilson, 509, 1922–36.

***Youngest League Player:*** Ian Chapman, 16 years 259 days v Birmingham C, 14 February 1987.

***Record Transfer Fee Received:*** £1,500,000 from Tottenham H for Bobby Zamora, July 2003.

***Record Transfer Fee Paid:*** £500,000 to Manchester U for Andy Ritchie, October 1980.

***Football League Record:*** 1920 Original Member of Division 3; 1921–58 Division 3 (S); 1958–62 Division 2; 1962–63 Division 3; 1963–65 Division 4; 1965–72 Division 3; 1972–73 Division 2; 1973–77 Division 3; 1977–79 Division 2; 1979–83 Division 1; 1983–87 Division 2; 1987–88 Division 3; 1988–96 Division 2; 1996–2001 Division 3; 2001–02 Division 2; 2002–03 Division 1; 2003–04 Division 2; 2004– FLC.

### MANAGERS

John Jackson 1901–05
Frank Scott-Walford 1905–08
John Robson 1908–14
Charles Webb 1919–47
Tommy Cook 1947
Don Welsh 1947–51
Billy Lane 1951–61
George Curtis 1961–63
Archie Macaulay 1963–68
Fred Goodwin 1968–70
Pat Saward 1970–73
Brian Clough 1973–74
Peter Taylor 1974–76
Alan Mullery 1976–81
Mike Bailey 1981–82
Jimmy Melia 1982–83
Chris Cattlin 1983–86
Alan Mullery 1986–87
Barry Lloyd 1987–93
Liam Brady 1993–95
Jimmy Case 1995–96
Steve Gritt 1996–98
Brian Horton 1998–99
Jeff Wood 1999
Micky Adams 1999–2001
Peter Taylor 2001–02
Martin Hinshelwood 2002
Steve Coppell 2002–03
Mark McGhee October 2003–

### LATEST SEQUENCES

***Longest Sequence of League Wins:*** 9, 2.10.1926 – 20.11.1926.

***Longest Sequence of League Defeats:*** 12, 17.8.2002 – 26.10.2002.

***Longest Sequence of League Draws:*** 6, 16.2.1980 – 15.3.1980.

***Longest Sequence of Unbeaten League Matches:*** 16, 8.10.1930 – 28.1.1931.

***Longest Sequence Without a League Win:*** 15, 21.10.1972 – 27.1.1973

***Successive Scoring Runs:*** 31 from 4.2.1956.

***Successive Non-scoring Runs:*** 6 from 8.11.1924.

### TEN YEAR LEAGUE RECORD

| | | *P* | *W* | *D* | *L* | *F* | *A* | *Pts* | *Pos* |
|---|---|---|---|---|---|---|---|---|---|
| 1994-95 | Div 2 | 46 | 14 | 17 | 15 | 54 | 53 | 59 | 16 |
| 1995-96 | Div 2 | 46 | 10 | 10 | 26 | 46 | 69 | 40 | 23 |
| 1996-97 | Div 3 | 46 | 13 | 10 | 23 | 53 | 70 | 47 | 23 |
| 1997-98 | Div 3 | 46 | 6 | 17 | 23 | 38 | 66 | 35 | 23 |
| 1998-99 | Div 3 | 46 | 16 | 7 | 23 | 49 | 66 | 55 | 17 |
| 1999-2000 | Div 3 | 46 | 17 | 16 | 13 | 64 | 46 | 67 | 11 |
| 2000-01 | Div 3 | 46 | 28 | 8 | 10 | 73 | 35 | 92 | 1 |
| 2001-02 | Div 2 | 46 | 25 | 15 | 6 | 66 | 42 | 90 | 1 |
| 2002-03 | Div 1 | 46 | 11 | 12 | 23 | 49 | 67 | 45 | 23 |
| 2003-04 | Div 2 | 46 | 22 | 11 | 13 | 64 | 43 | 77 | 4 |

### DID YOU KNOW ?

In 1922–23 Brighton & Hove Albion had a lengthy first round tussle with crack amateurs Corinthians, making their bow in the FA Cup. The teams drew 1-1 at Hove, similarly at Crystal Palace, before the tie was decided at Stamford Bridge, 1-0 to Brighton.

## BRIGHTON & HOVE ALBION 2003–04 LEAGUE RECORD

| *Match No.* | *Date* | *Venue* | *Opponents* | *Result* | | *H/T Score* | *Lg. Pos.* | *Goalscorers* | *Atten-dance* |
|---|---|---|---|---|---|---|---|---|---|
| 1 | Aug 9 | A | Oldham Ath | W | 3-1 | 2-0 | — | Henderson (pen) [23], Knight 2 [44, 62] | 6522 |
| 2 | 18 | H | QPR | W | 2-1 | 1-1 | — | Knight 2 [12, 68] | 6536 |
| 3 | 23 | A | Barnsley | L | 0-1 | 0-0 | 8 | | 7918 |
| 4 | 25 | H | Luton T | W | 2-0 | 1-0 | 3 | Coyne (og) [16], Oatway [85] | 6604 |
| 5 | 30 | A | Plymouth Arg | D | 3-3 | 2-1 | 4 | Connolly (og) [14], Butters [36], Knight [73] | 9289 |
| 6 | Sept 6 | H | Swindon T | D | 2-2 | 1-1 | 5 | Hart [15], Henderson (pen) [75] | 6534 |
| 7 | 13 | A | Colchester U | L | 0-1 | 0-0 | 8 | | 4169 |
| 8 | 16 | H | Chesterfield | W | 1-0 | 1-0 | — | Knight [33] | 6054 |
| 9 | 20 | H | Sheffield W | W | 2-0 | 1-0 | 2 | Knight [8], McPhee [83] | 6602 |
| 10 | 27 | A | Hartlepool U | D | 0-0 | 0-0 | 3 | | 5443 |
| 11 | 30 | A | Rushden & D | W | 3-1 | 1-0 | — | Butters [42], Knight [53], Rehman [77] | 4634 |
| 12 | Oct 4 | H | Blackpool | W | 3-0 | 2-0 | 1 | Coid (og) [2], McPhee 2 [38, 73] | 6483 |
| 13 | 11 | H | Grimsby T | W | 3-0 | 0-0 | 1 | Rehman [53], Knight 2 (1 pen) [55, 90 (p)] | 6286 |
| 14 | 18 | A | Bournemouth | L | 0-1 | 0-1 | 1 | | 7908 |
| 15 | 21 | A | Brentford | L | 0-4 | 0-2 | — | | 6532 |
| 16 | 25 | H | Stockport Co | L | 0-1 | 0-0 | 2 | | 6171 |
| 17 | Nov 1 | A | Peterborough U | D | 2-2 | 1-2 | 4 | Knight 2 [26, 68] | 5929 |
| 18 | 15 | H | Bristol C | L | 1-4 | 1-3 | 7 | Knight (pen) [45] | 6305 |
| 19 | 22 | A | Notts Co | W | 2-1 | 2-1 | 4 | Knight 2 [19, 37] | 5051 |
| 20 | 29 | H | Wrexham | W | 2-0 | 1-0 | 3 | Piercy [11], Carpenter [65] | 5642 |
| 21 | Dec 12 | H | Port Vale | D | 1-1 | 1-0 | — | Knight (pen) [16] | 5811 |
| 22 | 20 | A | Tranmere R | L | 0-1 | 0-0 | 4 | | 7616 |
| 23 | 26 | H | Wycombe W | W | 4-0 | 2-0 | 4 | Carpenter [31], Piercy 2 [42, 63], McPhee [49] | 6141 |
| 24 | 28 | A | Swindon T | L | 1-2 | 0-1 | 5 | Knight [55] | 9269 |
| 25 | Jan 10 | H | Oldham Ath | D | 0-0 | 0-0 | 5 | | 6036 |
| 26 | 17 | A | QPR | L | 1-2 | 1-2 | 7 | Cullip [45] | 17,839 |
| 27 | 24 | H | Barnsley | W | 1-0 | 1-0 | 6 | Knight (pen) [32] | 6033 |
| 28 | 31 | H | Plymouth Arg | W | 2-1 | 2-0 | 5 | Benjamin [12], Knight [34] | 6379 |
| 29 | Feb 7 | A | Wycombe W | D | 1-1 | 1-1 | 6 | Benjamin [34] | 6567 |
| 30 | 10 | A | Luton T | L | 0-2 | 0-1 | — | | 6846 |
| 31 | 14 | A | Grimsby T | L | 1-2 | 1-1 | 8 | Benjamin [18] | 3673 |
| 32 | 21 | H | Bournemouth | W | 3-0 | 3-0 | 5 | Hart [6], Benjamin [13], Knight (pen) [24] | 6441 |
| 33 | 28 | A | Stockport Co | D | 1-1 | 0-1 | 7 | Virgo [52] | 5038 |
| 34 | Mar 2 | H | Brentford | W | 1-0 | 0-0 | — | Carpenter [58] | 6007 |
| 35 | 10 | H | Tranmere R | W | 3-0 | 3-0 | — | Hart [7], Benjamin [18], Knight [31] | 5994 |
| 36 | 13 | A | Port Vale | D | 1-1 | 1-1 | 5 | Knight (pen) [11] | 5646 |
| 37 | 16 | A | Chesterfield | W | 2-0 | 0-0 | — | Butters [49], Iwelumo [83] | 4478 |
| 38 | 20 | H | Colchester U | W | 2-1 | 1-0 | 4 | Iwelumo [30], Knight [87] | 6156 |
| 39 | 27 | A | Sheffield W | L | 1-2 | 1-1 | 5 | Carpenter [14] | 19,707 |
| 40 | Apr 3 | H | Hartlepool U | W | 2-0 | 0-0 | 4 | Knight [68], Iwelumo [90] | 6257 |
| 41 | 10 | A | Blackpool | L | 1-3 | 0-1 | 4 | Piercy [83] | 6194 |
| 42 | 12 | H | Rushden & D | D | 0-0 | 0-0 | 5 | | 6320 |
| 43 | 17 | H | Peterborough U | W | 1-0 | 1-0 | 5 | Knight (pen) [11] | 6285 |
| 44 | 24 | A | Bristol C | D | 0-0 | 0-0 | 6 | | 17,088 |
| 45 | May 1 | H | Notts Co | W | 1-0 | 0-0 | 4 | Wilson (og) [74] | 6618 |
| 46 | 8 | A | Wrexham | W | 2-0 | 1-0 | 4 | Iwelumo [8], Lawrence (og) [50] | 4542 |

**Final League Position: 4**

## GOALSCORERS

*League (64):* Knight 25 (7 pens), Benjamin 5, Carpenter 4, Iwelumo 4, McPhee 4, Piercy 4, Butters 3, Hart 3, Henderson 2 (2 pens), Rehman 2, Cullip 1, Oatway 1, Virgo 1, own goals 5.
*Carling Cup (1):* McPhee 1.
*FA Cup (1):* McPhee 1.
*LDV Vans Trophy (6):* McPhee 3 (1 pen), Carpenter 1, Knight 1, Robinson 1.
*Play-Offs (3):* Carpenter 1, Knight 1 (pen), Virgo 1.

| Roberts B 32 | Watson P 14 + 1 | Jones N 34 + 2 | Hinshelwood A 16 + 1 | Cullip D 40 | Mayo K 31 + 2 | Rodger S 7 | Oatway C 29 + 2 | Knight L 43 + 1 | Henderson D 10 | Carpenter R 40 + 2 | Pethick R 6 + 8 | McPhee C 17 + 12 | Hart G 35 + 7 | Harding D 17 + 6 | Butters G 43 | Piercy J 8 + 16 | Flitney R 3 | Kuipers M 9 + 1 | Rehman Z 9 + 2 | Marney D — + 3 | Robinson J 1 + 8 | Beck D — + 1 | Wilkinson S — + 2 | Yeates M 9 | El-Abd A 6 + 5 | Lee D 1 + 3 | Virgo A 20 + 2 | Benjamin T 10 | Jones S 2 + 1 | Iwelumo C 10 | Reid P 4 + 1 | *Match No.* |
|---|---|---|---|---|---|---|---|---|---|---|---|---|---|---|---|---|---|---|---|---|---|---|---|---|---|---|---|---|---|---|---|---|
| 1 | 2 | 11 | 4 | 5 | 3 | 7[1] | 8 | 9[2] | 10[3] | 6 | 12 | 13 | 14 | | | | | | | | | | | | | | | | | | | 1 |
| 1 | 2 | 11 | 4 | 5 | 3 | 8[1] | 12 | 9 | 10 | 6 | | | 7 | | | | | | | | | | | | | | | | | | | 2 |
| 1 | 2[2] | 11 | 4 | 5[1] | 3 | 7 | | 9 | 10 | 6 | 12 | | 8 | 13 | | | | | | | | | | | | | | | | | | 3 |
| 1 | | 11 | 4 | | 3 | | 8 | 9[2] | 10[1] | 6 | 2 | 12 | 7 | | 5 | 13 | | | | | | | | | | | | | | | | 4 |
| 1 | | | 2 | 4 | 3 | | 8 | 9 | 10 | 6 | | | 7 | 11 | 5 | | | | | | | | | | | | | | | | | 5 |
| 1 | | | 2 | 4 | 3 | 11 | 8 | 9 | 10 | 6[2] | | | 7[1] | 13 | 5 | 12 | | | | | | | | | | | | | | | | 6 |
| 1 | | | 2 | 4 | 3 | 11[1] | 8[2] | 9 | 10 | 12 | 13 | | 7 | 6[3] | 5 | 14 | | | | | | | | | | | | | | | | 7 |
| | | 11 | 2 | 4 | 3 | 8 | 6 | 9 | 10[2] | | 12 | 13 | 7[1] | | 5 | | 1 | | | | | | | | | | | | | | | 8 |
| | | 11 | 2 | 4 | 3 | 8 | 6[1] | 9[2] | 10 | 12 | | 13 | 7 | | 5 | | | 1 | | | | | | | | | | | | | | 9 |
| | | 11 | 2 | 4[1] | 3 | | | 9 | 10 | 6 | 8 | | 7 | 12 | 5 | | | 1 | | | | | | | | | | | | | | 10 |
| | | 11 | 2 | | 3 | | | 9 | | 6 | 4 | 10 | 7[1] | | 5 | 12 | | 1 | 8 | | | | | | | | | | | | | 11 |
| | | 11 | 2 | | 3 | | | 9 | | 6 | 4 | 10 | | | 5 | 7[1] | | 1 | 8 | 12 | | | | | | | | | | | | 12 |
| | | 11 | 2 | 4 | 3 | | | 9 | | 6 | | 10 | 7 | | 5 | | | 1 | 8 | | | | | | | | | | | | | 13 |
| | 12 | 11[1] | 2 | 4 | 3 | | | 9[2] | | 6 | 13 | 10[3] | 7 | | 5 | | | 1 | 8 | | 14 | | | | | | | | | | | 14 |
| | | 11[1] | 2 | 4 | 3 | | | 9 | | 6 | | 10[2] | 7 | | 5 | 12 | | 1 | 8 | | | 13 | | | | | | | | | | 15 |
| | 2 | 11[1] | | 4 | 3 | | | 9[2] | | 6 | | 10 | 7 | | 5 | 12 | | 1 | 8 | | | | 13 | | | | | | | | | 16 |
| | 2 | 11[1] | | 4 | 3 | | | 9 | | 6 | 8 | 10 | 7 | | 5 | | | 1 | | | | | 12 | | | | | | | | | 17 |
| 1 | | | 2 | 4 | 3 | | | 9 | | 6 | 12 | 10[3] | 7[1] | | 5 | 13 | | | 8[2] | | 14 | | | 11 | | | | | | | | 18 |
| 1 | | 11 | | 4 | 3 | | | 9 | | 6 | 12 | 10[2] | | 13 | 5 | 7[■] | | | | | | | | 8[1] | 2 | | | | | | | 19 |
| 1 | | 11 | | 4 | 3 | | | 9[2] | | 6 | 13 | 10[3] | 12 | 14 | 5 | 7[1] | | | | | | | | 8 | 2 | | | | | | | 20 |
| 1 | | 11[2] | | | 3 | | | 9 | | | 6 | 10 | 7[1] | | 5 | 12 | | | 4 | | | | | 8 | 2 | 13 | | | | | | 21 |
| 1 | 2 | 11 | | 4 | 3 | | | 9 | | 6 | | 10[1] | 7 | | 5 | 12 | | | | | | | | 8 | | | | | | | | 22 |
| | 2 | 11 | | 4 | 3 | | 12 | | | 6[1] | | 10 | 7[3] | | 5 | 9 | 1 | | 13 | 14 | | | | 8[2] | | | | | | | | 23 |
| | 2 | 11[■] | | 4 | 3 | | | 12 | | 6 | | 10[1] | 7 | | 5 | 9[2] | 1 | | 13 | | | | | 8 | | | | | | | | 24 |
| 1 | 2 | | | 4 | 3 | | 8 | 9 | | | | 10[2] | 7 | 12 | 5 | | | | 6[1] | 13 | | | | 11[3] | | | 14 | | | | | 25 |
| 1 | 2 | | | 4 | 3[3] | | 8 | 9 | | 6 | | 12 | 7[2] | | 5 | | | | | | 13 | | | 11[1] | | | 14 | 10 | | | | 26 |
| 1[6] | 7 | | | 4 | 3 | | 8 | 9[2] | | 6 | | 11[1] | 12 | | 5 | | | 15 | | | | | | | 13 | | 2 | 10 | | | | 27 |
| 1 | 7 | | | 4 | 3 | | 8 | 9[2] | | 6 | | 13 | 12 | | 5 | 11[1] | | | | | | | | | | | 2 | 10 | | | | 28 |
| 1[6] | 7 | | | 4 | 3 | | 8 | 9 | | 6 | | 12 | 11[2] | | 5 | | | | | | 13 | | | | | | 2 | 10[1] | 15 | | | 29 |
| | 7[1] | 12[2] | | 4 | 3 | | 8 | 9[■] | | 6 | | 13 | 11[3] | | 5 | | | | | | 14 | | | | | | 2 | 10 | 1 | | | 30 |
| | | | | 4 | 3 | | 8 | 9 | | 6 | | 12 | | | 5 | | | | | | 11[1] | | | | 2 | | 7 | 10 | 1 | | | 31 |
| 1 | | 11 | | 4 | | | 8[1] | 9 | | 6 | | | 7 | 3 | 5 | | | | | | | | | | | 12 | 2 | 10 | | | | 32 |
| 1 | | 11 | | 4 | | | 8 | | | 6 | | 9[2] | 7 | 3 | 5 | | | | | | 12 | | | | | 13 | 2 | 10[1] | | | | 33 |
| 1 | | 11[1] | | 4 | 12 | | 8 | 9[2] | | 6 | | | 7 | 3 | 5 | | | | | | 13 | | | | | | 2 | 10 | | | | 34 |
| 1 | | 11 | | 4 | | | 8 | 9 | | 6 | | | 7[1] | 3 | 5 | 12 | | | | | | | | | 13 | | 2[2] | 10 | | | | 35 |
| 1 | | 11[1] | | 4 | 12 | | 8 | 9 | | 6 | | | 7 | 3 | 5 | 10[2] | | | | | 13 | | | | | | 2 | | | | | 36 |
| 1 | | 11 | | 4 | | | 8 | 9 | | 6 | | | 7 | 3 | 5 | | | | | | | | | | | | 2 | | | 10 | | 37 |
| 1 | | 11[1] | | 4[2] | | | 8 | 9 | | 6 | | | 7 | 3 | 5 | 12 | | | | | | | | | 13 | | 2 | | | 10 | | 38 |
| 1 | | 11 | | 4[1] | | | 8 | 9 | | 6 | | | | 3 | 5 | | | | | | | | | | 12 | 7 | 2 | | | 10 | | 39 |
| 1 | | 11 | | | | | 8 | 9 | | 6 | | | 7 | 3 | 5 | | | | | | | | | | 4 | | 2 | | | 10 | | 40 |
| 1 | | 11[3] | 12 | | | | 8 | 9 | | 6 | | 14 | 7[2] | 3 | 5 | 13 | | | | | | | | | 2 | | 4 | | | 10[1] | | 41 |
| 1 | | 11 | | 4 | | | 8[2] | 9[3] | | 6 | | 13 | 7[1] | 3 | 5 | 12 | | | | | | | | | | | 2 | | | 10 | 14 | 42 |
| 1 | | 13 | | 4 | | | 8 | 9 | | 6 | | | 12 | 3 | 5 | 7[2] | | | | | | | | | | | 2 | | | 10 | 11[1] | 43 |
| 1 | | 11[2] | | 4 | | | 8 | 9 | | 6 | | | 12 | 3 | 5 | 13 | | | | | | | | | | | 2 | | | 10[1] | 7 | 44 |
| 1 | | 11 | | 4 | | | 8[1] | 9 | | 6 | | | 12 | 3 | 5 | 13 | | | | | | | | | | | 2 | | | 10[2] | 7 | 45 |
| 1 | | 11[1] | | 4 | | | 8 | 9 | | | | 13 | 7[2] | 3 | 5 | 12 | | | | | | | | | 14 | | 2 | | | 10[3] | 6 | 46 |

**Carling Cup**

| | | | |
|---|---|---|---|
| First Round | Bristol R | (a) | 1-0 |
| Second Round | Middlesbrough | (a) | 0-1 |

**LDV Vans Trophy**

| | | | |
|---|---|---|---|
| First Round | Forest Green R | (h) | 2-0 |
| Second Round | Boston U | (h) | 3-1 |
| Quarter-Final | QPR | (a) | 1-2 |

**FA Cup**

| | | | |
|---|---|---|---|
| First Round | Lincoln C | (a) | 1-3 |

**Play-Offs**

| | | | |
|---|---|---|---|
| Semi-Final | Swindon T | (a) | 1-0 |
| | | (h) | 1-2 |
| Final | Bristol C | | 1-0 |

*(at Millennium Stadium)*

# BRISTOL CITY FL Championship 1

## FOUNDATION

The name Bristol City came into being in 1897 when the Bristol South End club, formed three years earlier, decided to adopt professionalism and apply for admission to the Southern League after competing in the Western League. The historic meeting was held at The Albert Hall, Bedminster. Bristol City employed Sam Hollis from Woolwich Arsenal as manager and gave him £40 to buy players. In 1900 they merged with Bedminster, another leading Bristol club.

***Ashton Gate, Bristol BS3 2EJ.***

***Telephone:*** (0117) 9630 630.

***Fax:*** (0117) 9630 700.

***Ticket Office:*** 0870 112 1897.

***Website:*** www.bcfc.co.uk

***Ground Capacity:*** 21,497.

***Record Attendance:*** 43,335 v Preston NE, FA Cup 5th rd, 16 February 1935.

***Pitch Measurements:*** 115yd × 75yd.

***Chairman:*** Stephen Lansdown.

***Chief Executive:*** Colin Sexstone.

***Secretary:*** Michelle McDonald.

***Player Manager:*** Brian Tinnion.

***Assistant Manager:*** Frank Barlow.

***Physio:*** Gill Holt.

***Colours:*** All red.

***Change Colours:*** Yellow shirts, green shorts, yellow stockings.

***Year Formed:*** 1894.

***Turned Professional:*** 1897.

***Ltd Co.:*** 1897. Bristol City Football Club Ltd.

***Previous Name:*** 1894, Bristol South End; 1897, Bristol City.

***Club Nickname:*** 'Robins'.

***Previous Grounds:*** 1894, St John's Lane; 1904, Ashton Gate.

***First Football League Game:*** 7 September 1901, Division 2, v Blackpool (a) W 2–0 – Moles; Tuft, Davies; Jones, McLean, Chambers; Bradbury, Connor, Boucher, O'Brien (2), Flynn.

***Record League Victory:*** 9–0 v Aldershot, Division 3 (S), 28 December 1946 – Eddols; Morgan, Fox; Peacock, Roberts, Jones (1); Chilcott, Thomas, Clark (4 incl. 1p), Cyril Williams (1), Hargreaves (3).

## HONOURS

*Football League:* Division 1 – Runners-up 1906–07; Division 2 – Champions 1905–06; Runners-up 1975–76, 1997–98; Division 3 (S) – Champions 1922–23, 1926–27, 1954–55; Runners-up 1937–38; Division 3 – Runners-up 1964–65, 1989–90.

*FA Cup:* Runners-up 1909.

*Football League Cup:* Semi-final 1971, 1989.

*Welsh Cup:* Winners 1934.

*Anglo-Scottish Cup:* Winners 1978.

*Freight Rover Trophy:* Winners 1986; Runners-up 1987.

*Auto Windscreens Shield:* Runners-up 2000.

*LDV Vans Trophy:* Winners 2003.

## SKY SPORTS FACT FILE

In the first two post-Second World War seasons, Bristol City provided the leading goalscorers in the Third Division (South). Don Clark hit 36 in 1946–47, while Len Townsend registered 31 in the following campaign, when Clark contributed 22.

***Record Cup Victory:*** 11–0 v Chichester C, FA Cup 1st rd, 5 November 1960 – Cook; Collinson, Thresher; Connor, Alan Williams, Etheridge; Tait (1), Bobby Williams (1), Atyeo (5), Adrian Williams (3), Derrick, (1 og).

***Record Defeat:*** 0–9 v Coventry C, Division 3 (S), 28 April 1934.

***Most League Points (2 for a win):*** 70, Division 3 (S), 1954–55.

***Most League Points (3 for a win):*** 91, Division 3, 1989–90.

***Most League Goals:*** 104, Division 3 (S), 1926–27.

***Highest League Scorer in Season:*** Don Clark, 36, Division 3 (S), 1946–47.

***Most League Goals in Total Aggregate:*** John Atyeo, 314, 1951–66.

***Most League Goals in One Match:*** 6, Tommy 'Tot' Walsh v Gillingham, Division 3S, 15 January 1927.

***Most Capped Player:*** Billy Wedlock, 26, England.

***Most League Appearances:*** John Atyeo, 597, 1951–66.

***Youngest League Player:*** Nyrere Kelly, 16 years 213 days v Hartlepool U, 16 October 1982.

***Record Transfer Fee Received:*** £3,500,000 from Wolverhampton W for Ade Akinbiyi, September 1999.

***Record Transfer Fee Paid:*** £1,200,000 to Gillingham for Ade Akinbiyi, May 1998.

***Football League Record:*** 1901 Elected to Division 2; 1906–11 Division 1; 1911–22 Division 2; 1922–23 Division 3 (S); 1923–24 Division 2; 1924–27 Division 3 (S); 1927–32 Division 2; 1932–55 Division 3 (S); 1955–60 Division 2; 1960–65 Division 3; 1965–76 Division 2; 1976–80 Division 1; 1980–81 Division 2; 1981–82 Division 3; 1982–84 Division 4; 1984–90 Division 3; 1990–92 Division 2; 1992–95 Division 1; 1995–98 Division 2; 1998–99 Division 1; 1999–04 Division 2; 2004– FL1.

### MANAGERS

Sam Hollis 1897–99
Bob Campbell 1899–1901
Sam Hollis 1901–05
Harry Thickett 1905–10
Sam Hollis 1911–13
George Hedley 1913–17
Jack Hamilton 1917–19
Joe Palmer 1919–21
Alex Raisbeck 1921–29
Joe Bradshaw 1929–32
Bob Hewison 1932–49
*(under suspension 1938–39)*
Bob Wright 1949–50
Pat Beasley 1950–58
Peter Doherty 1958–60
Fred Ford 1960–67
Alan Dicks 1967–80
Bobby Houghton 1980–82
Roy Hodgson 1982
Terry Cooper 1982–88
*(Director from 1983)*
Joe Jordan 1988–90
Jimmy Lumsden 1990–92
Denis Smith 1992–93
Russell Osman 1993–94
Joe Jordan 1994–97
John Ward 1997–98
Benny Lennartsson 1998–99
Tony Pulis 1999
Tony Fawthrop 2000
Danny Wilson 2000–04
Brian Tinnion June 2004–

### LATEST SEQUENCES

***Longest Sequence of League Wins:*** 14, 9.9.1905 – 2.12.1905.

***Longest Sequence of League Defeats:*** 7, 3.10.1970 – 7.11.1970.

***Longest Sequence of League Draws:*** 4, 6.11.1999 – 27.11.1999.

***Longest Sequence of Unbeaten League Matches:*** 24, 9.9.1905 – 10.2.1906.

***Longest Sequence Without a League Win:*** 15, 29.4.1933 – 4.11.1933.

***Successive Scoring Runs:*** 25 from 26.12.1905.

***Successive Non-scoring Runs:*** 6 from 10.9.1910.

### TEN YEAR LEAGUE RECORD

| | | P | W | D | L | F | A | Pts | Pos |
|---|---|---|---|---|---|---|---|---|---|
| 1994-95 | Div 1 | 46 | 11 | 12 | 23 | 42 | 63 | 45 | 23 |
| 1995-96 | Div 2 | 46 | 15 | 15 | 16 | 55 | 60 | 60 | 13 |
| 1996-97 | Div 2 | 46 | 21 | 10 | 15 | 69 | 51 | 73 | 5 |
| 1997-98 | Div 2 | 46 | 25 | 10 | 11 | 69 | 39 | 85 | 2 |
| 1998-99 | Div 1 | 46 | 9 | 15 | 22 | 57 | 80 | 42 | 24 |
| 1999-2000 | Div 2 | 46 | 15 | 19 | 12 | 59 | 57 | 64 | 9 |
| 2000-01 | Div 2 | 46 | 18 | 14 | 14 | 70 | 56 | 68 | 9 |
| 2001-02 | Div 2 | 46 | 21 | 10 | 15 | 68 | 53 | 73 | 7 |
| 2002-03 | Div 2 | 46 | 24 | 11 | 11 | 79 | 48 | 83 | 3 |
| 2003-04 | Div 2 | 46 | 23 | 13 | 10 | 58 | 37 | 82 | 3 |

### DID YOU KNOW?

On 30 January 1935 Bristol City met a Portsmouth boasting all but one of their FA Cup winning team in a fourth round replay. Before 42,885 spectators, City won this Wednesday afternoon affair 2-0 with goals from Ted Harston and Jack Hodge.

## BRISTOL CITY 2003–04 LEAGUE RECORD

| Match No. | Date | Venue | Opponents | Result | | H/T Score | Lg. Pos. | Goalscorers | Attendance |
|---|---|---|---|---|---|---|---|---|---|
| 1 | Aug 9 | H | Notts Co | W | 5-0 | 2-0 | — | Peacock 2 [12, 37], Miller [50], Matthews 2 [71, 88] | 12,050 |
| 2 | 16 | A | Chesterfield | D | 1-1 | 1-1 | 3 | Coles [10] | 4302 |
| 3 | 23 | H | Hartlepool U | D | 1-1 | 0-0 | 11 | Peacock [56] | 10,730 |
| 4 | 26 | A | Colchester U | L | 1-2 | 0-0 | — | Peacock [66] | 3079 |
| 5 | 30 | H | Grimsby T | W | 1-0 | 0-0 | 7 | Roberts [90] | 10,033 |
| 6 | Sept 6 | A | Bournemouth | D | 0-0 | 0-0 | 9 | | 6756 |
| 7 | 13 | A | Oldham Ath | D | 1-1 | 1-0 | 9 | Butler [35] | 5921 |
| 8 | 16 | H | Tranmere R | W | 2-0 | 0-0 | — | Brown A [23], Peacock [76] | 9365 |
| 9 | 20 | H | Port Vale | L | 0-1 | 0-0 | 12 | | 11,369 |
| 10 | 27 | A | QPR | D | 1-1 | 0-0 | 11 | Miller [76] | 14,913 |
| 11 | 30 | A | Plymouth Arg | W | 1-0 | 1-0 | — | Peacock [27] | 13,923 |
| 12 | Oct 4 | H | Swindon T | W | 2-1 | 0-1 | 6 | Peacock [52], Brown A [74] | 14,294 |
| 13 | 10 | H | Peterborough U | D | 1-1 | 1-0 | — | Tinnion [24] | 11,053 |
| 14 | 18 | A | Wrexham | D | 0-0 | 0-0 | 7 | | 4405 |
| 15 | 21 | A | Wycombe W | L | 0-3 | 0-1 | — | | 4613 |
| 16 | 25 | H | Sheffield W | D | 1-1 | 0-1 | 11 | Peacock [70] | 13,668 |
| 17 | Nov 1 | H | Luton T | D | 1-1 | 1-1 | 9 | Burnell [2] | 9735 |
| 18 | 15 | A | Brighton & HA | W | 4-1 | 3-1 | 9 | Wilkshire [26], Miller [31], Brown A [45], Hill [85] | 6305 |
| 19 | 22 | H | Barnsley | W | 2-1 | 1-0 | 6 | Miller 2 [38, 90] | 10,031 |
| 20 | 29 | A | Blackpool | L | 0-1 | 0-0 | 9 | | 5989 |
| 21 | Dec 13 | A | Rushden & D | D | 1-1 | 0-1 | 9 | Miller [71] | 4340 |
| 22 | 20 | H | Stockport Co | W | 1-0 | 0-0 | 6 | Peacock [69] | 10,478 |
| 23 | 26 | A | Brentford | W | 2-1 | 0-0 | 5 | Lita 2 [77, 82] | 5912 |
| 24 | 28 | H | Bournemouth | W | 2-0 | 1-0 | 3 | Peacock [40], Brown A [56] | 13,807 |
| 25 | Jan 10 | A | Notts Co | W | 2-1 | 1-1 | 3 | Peacock [11], Goodfellow [90] | 6403 |
| 26 | 17 | H | Chesterfield | W | 4-0 | 1-0 | 3 | Doherty [44], Lita [84], Carey [86], Goodfellow [89] | 11,807 |
| 27 | 24 | A | Hartlepool U | W | 2-1 | 0-0 | 3 | Peacock [54], Tinnion [76] | 5375 |
| 28 | 27 | H | Colchester U | W | 1-0 | 1-0 | — | Goodfellow [45] | 10,733 |
| 29 | Feb 7 | H | Brentford | W | 3-1 | 1-0 | 3 | Miller [4], Hill [88], Lita [90] | 13,029 |
| 30 | 14 | A | Peterborough U | W | 1-0 | 0-0 | 3 | Doherty [75] | 4449 |
| 31 | 17 | A | Grimsby T | W | 2-1 | 1-1 | — | Miller [10], Brown A [88] | 5272 |
| 32 | 21 | H | Wrexham | W | 1-0 | 1-0 | 1 | Wilkshire [3] | 13,871 |
| 33 | 28 | A | Sheffield W | L | 0-1 | 0-0 | 2 | | 24,154 |
| 34 | Mar 2 | H | Wycombe W | D | 1-1 | 0-0 | — | Goodfellow [59] | 12,291 |
| 35 | 6 | A | Stockport Co | L | 0-2 | 0-1 | 2 | | 5050 |
| 36 | 12 | H | Rushden & D | W | 1-0 | 1-0 | — | Lita [29] | 12,559 |
| 37 | 20 | H | Oldham Ath | L | 0-2 | 0-2 | 3 | | 11,037 |
| 38 | 24 | A | Tranmere R | L | 0-1 | 0-0 | — | | 6712 |
| 39 | 27 | A | Port Vale | L | 1-2 | 0-0 | 3 | Peacock [90] | 6724 |
| 40 | Apr 3 | H | QPR | W | 1-0 | 1-0 | 3 | Roberts [40] | 19,041 |
| 41 | 10 | A | Swindon T | D | 1-1 | 1-0 | 3 | Roberts [45] | 14,540 |
| 42 | 13 | H | Plymouth Arg | W | 1-0 | 0-0 | — | Peacock [85] | 19,045 |
| 43 | 17 | A | Luton T | L | 2-3 | 0-1 | 3 | Roberts [59], Coles [89] | 6944 |
| 44 | 24 | H | Brighton & HA | D | 0-0 | 0-0 | 3 | | 17,088 |
| 45 | May 2 | A | Barnsley | W | 1-0 | 1-0 | 3 | Rougier [21] | 10,865 |
| 46 | 8 | H | Blackpool | W | 2-1 | 2-0 | 3 | Roberts 2 [19, 21] | 19,101 |

**Final League Position: 3**

### GOALSCORERS

*League (58):* Peacock 14, Miller 8, Roberts 6, Brown A 5, Lita 5, Goodfellow 4, Coles 2, Doherty 2, Hill 2, Matthews 2, Tinnion 2, Wilkshire 2, Burnell 1, Butler 1, Carey 1, Rougier 1.
*Carling Cup (5):* Peacock 2, Bell 1 (pen), Coles 1, Miller 1.
*FA Cup (6):* Amankwaah 2, Matthews 1, Roberts 1, Wilkshire 1, own goal 1.
*LDV Vans Trophy (0).*
*Play-Offs (3):* Goodfellow 1, Roberts 1, Rougier 1.

| Phillips S 46 | Carey L 41 | Hill M 40 + 2 | Burnell J 14 + 3 | Butler T 37 + 1 | Coles D 45 | Wilkshire L 35 + 2 | Doherty T 28 + 5 | Peacock L 39 + 2 | Miller L 32 + 10 | Bell M 20 + 7 | Roberts C 24 + 14 | Tinnion B 36 + 9 | Matthews L 1 + 7 | Brown A 29 + 1 | Lita L 2 + 24 | Fortune C 1 + 5 | Woodman C 14 + 7 | Amankwaah K 4 + 1 | Clist S 1 | Brown M 1 + 1 | Goodfellow M 7 + 8 | Murray S 4 + 2 | Rougier T 5 + 1 | *Match No.* |
|---|---|---|---|---|---|---|---|---|---|---|---|---|---|---|---|---|---|---|---|---|---|---|---|---|
| 1 | 2 | 3 | $4^1$ | 5 | 6 | 7 | $8^2$ | 9 | $10^3$ | 11 | 12 | 13 | 14 | | | | | | | | | | | 1 |
| 1 | 2 | 3 | 4 | 5 | 6 | $7^1$ | 8 | 9 | $10^2$ | $11^3$ | 12 | 14 | 13 | | | | | | | | | | | 2 |
| 1 | 2 | 3 | $4^1$ | 5 | 6 | 7 | $8^3$ | 9 | $10^2$ | 11 | 12 | 14 | 13 | | | | | | | | | | | 3 |
| 1 | 2 | 3 | 4 | 5 | 6 | $7^1$ | 8 | 9 | $10^2$ | $11^3$ | 12 | 14 | 13 | | | | | | | | | | | 4 |
| 1 | 2 | $3^3$ | $4^2$ | 5 | 6 | $7^1$ | 8 | 9 | 12 | 11 | 10 | 13 | | 14 | | | | | | | | | | 5 |
| 1 | 2 | 3 | 4 | 5 | 6 | 7 | | 9 | 12 | 13 | $10^1$ | 8 | | $11^2$ | | | | | | | | | | 6 |
| 1 | 2 | $3^1$ | 4 | 5 | 6 | $7^3$ | | | $9^2$ | 12 | 10 | 8 | 13 | 11 | 14 | | | | | | | | | 7 |
| 1 | 2 | 3 | 4 | 5 | 6■ | | 12 | 9 | $10^3$ | | $7^2$ | $8^1$ | 13 | 11 | | 14 | | | | | | | | 8 |
| 1 | 2 | 3 | $4^1$ | 5 | 6 | 13 | 12 | | 10 | | $7^2$ | 8 | $9^3$ | 11 | 14 | | | | | | | | | 9 |
| 1 | | | | 5 | 6 | 7 | 4 | | 9■ | 3 | $10^1$ | 8 | | 11 | 12 | | 2 | | | | | | | 10 |
| 1 | | 6 | 4 | 5 | | 7 | | $9^1$ | 10 | $3^2$ | | 8 | | 11 | 12 | 13 | 2 | | | | | | | 11 |
| 1 | | 12 | $4^2$ | 5 | 6 | 7 | | 9 | $10^3$ | $3^1$ | 13 | 8 | | 11 | 14 | | 2 | | | | | | | 12 |
| 1 | | 13 | 4 | 5 | 6 | $7^1$ | | 9 | $10^3$ | 3 | 12 | 8 | | $11^2$ | 14 | | 2 | | | | | | | 13 |
| 1 | 2 | | | 5 | 6 | 7 | 4 | 9 | $10^1$ | 3 | 12 | 8 | | $11^2$ | | | 13 | | | | | | | 14 |
| 1 | 2 | | 12 | 5 | 6■ | 7 | 4■ | 9 | $10^2$ | $3^3$ | 13 | 8 | | $11^1$ | | | 14 | | | | | | | 15 |
| 1 | $2^2$ | 3 | | 5 | 6 | 7 | 4 | 9 | | | $10^1$ | 8 | | | 12 | | 11 | 13 | | | | | | 16 |
| 1 | | 6 | 8 | 5 | 4 | 7 | | 9 | 13 | | 10 | 11 | | | $12^2$ | | 3 | $2^1$ | | | | | | 17 |
| 1 | 4 | 6 | 13 | 12 | 5 | 7 | | | $10^3$ | | 9 | $8^2$ | 14 | 11 | | | $3^1$ | 2 | | | | | | 18 |
| 1 | 2 | 6 | | | 5 | 7 | | 13 | 9 | | $10^2$ | 8 | | 11 | 12 | | $3^1$ | 4 | | | | | | 19 |
| 1 | 2 | 3 | | | 6 | 7 | | 12 | 9 | 13 | 10 | 8 | | $4^2$ | | | 11 | $5^1$ | | | | | | 20 |
| 1 | 2 | 6 | | | 5 | 7 | | 9 | $10^2$ | | 12 | 8 | | 11 | 13 | | 3 | | $4^1$ | | | | | 21 |
| 1 | 2 | 6 | | | 5 | 7 | 12 | 9 | $10^2$ | | 8 | $4^1$ | | 11 | 13 | | 3 | | | | | | | 22 |
| 1 | 2 | 3 | | 6 | 5 | 7 | 12 | 9 | $10^2$ | | $8^3$ | $4^1$ | | 11 | 13 | | 14 | | | | | | | 23 |
| 1 | 2 | 3 | | 6 | 5 | 7 | 4 | $9^1$ | 10 | | 8 | | | 11 | 12 | | | | | | | | | 24 |
| 1 | 2 | 3 | | 6 | $5^1$ | | 4 | 9 | $10^2$ | 12 | | 8 | | 7 | 13 | | | | | $11^3$ | 14 | | | 25 |
| 1 | 2 | 3 | | $6^3$ | 5 | | 4 | 9 | $10^2$ | 12 | | 8 | | $11^1$ | 13 | | 14 | | | | 7 | | | 26 |
| 1 | 2 | 6 | | | 5 | | 4 | 9 | 10 | | | 8 | | 11 | | | 3 | | | | 7 | | | 27 |
| 1 | 2 | 6 | | | 5 | | $4^1$ | 9 | $10^3$ | 12 | 13 | 8 | | 11 | 14 | | 3 | | | | $7^2$ | | | 28 |
| 1 | 2 | 6 | | | 5 | 7 | | 9 | $10^2$ | | 12 | $4^3$ | | 11 | 13 | 14 | 3 | | | | $8^1$ | | | 29 |
| 1 | 2 | 3 | | 6 | 5 | $7^1$ | 12 | 9 | $10^2$ | | | 4 | | 11 | 13 | | | | | 14 | $8^3$ | | | 30 |
| 1 | 2 | 3 | | $6^2$ | 5 | $7^3$ | 4 | 9 | $10^1$ | | | 8 | | 11 | 12 | | 13 | | | | 14 | | | 31 |
| 1 | 2 | 3 | 12 | 6 | 5 | 7 | $4^1$ | 9 | $10^2$ | | | $8^3$ | | 11 | 13 | | | | | | 14 | | | 32 |
| 1 | 2 | $3^2$ | | 6 | 5 | $7^1$ | 4 | 9 | 10 | | 12 | 8 | | 11 | | | 13 | | | | | | | 33 |
| 1 | 2 | $6^3$ | | | 5 | $7^1$ | 4 | 9 | $10^2$ | 3 | | 12 | | 11 | 13 | 14 | | | | | 8 | | | 34 |
| 1 | 2 | | | 6 | 5 | $7^1$ | 4 | 9 | $10^2$ | 3 | 12 | 8 | | $11^3$ | 13 | | | | | | 14 | | | 35 |
| 1 | 2 | 3 | | 6 | 5 | | $4^2$ | 9 | 12 | | 7 | 8 | | $11^3$ | $10^1$ | 13 | | | | | 14 | | | 36 |
| 1 | 2 | $3^3$ | 4 | 6 | 5 | $7^1$ | | $9^2$ | 13 | 12 | 8 | 11 | | | 10 | | | | | | 14 | | | 37 |
| 1 | 2 | 3 | | 6 | 5 | 7 | | | 9 | | 10 | 11 | | | 12 | 4 | | | | | $8^1$ | | | 38 |
| 1 | 2 | 3 | | 6 | 5 | $7^2$ | 4 | 9 | | | 12 | 8 | | | | | 13 | | | | | 11 | $10^1$ | 39 |
| 1 | 2 | 3 | | 6 | 5 | 12 | 4 | 9 | 13 | 11 | $10^2$ | $8^1$ | | | | | | | | | | 7 | | 40 |
| 1 | 2 | 3 | | 6 | 5 | | 4 | 9 | 12 | 11 | $10^1$ | 8 | | | | | | | | | | 7 | | 41 |
| 1 | 2 | 3 | | 6 | 5 | $8^1$ | 4 | 9 | 13 | 11 | $10^2$ | 12 | | | | | | | | | | $7^3$ | 14 | 42 |
| 1 | 2 | 3 | | 5 | 6 | $7^1$ | 4 | 9 | 13 | $11^2$ | $10^3$ | 12 | | | | | | | | | 14 | | 8 | 43 |
| 1 | 2 | 3 | | $6^2$ | 5 | $7^1$ | 4 | 9 | | 11 | 10 | 12 | | | | | | | | | 13 | 14 | $8^3$ | 44 |
| 1 | 2 | 3 | | 6 | 5 | | 4 | 9 | | 11 | $10^1$ | 8 | | | 12 | | | | | | | | 7 | 45 |
| 1 | 2 | 3 | | 6 | 5 | | 4 | 9 | 12 | $11^2$ | $10^1$ | 8 | | | | | | | | | | 13 | 7 | 46 |

**Carling Cup**

| | | | |
|---|---|---|---|
| First Round | Swansea C | (h) | 4-1 |
| Second Round | Watford | (h) | 1-0 |
| Third Round | Southampton | (h) | 0-3 |

**FA Cup**

| | | | |
|---|---|---|---|
| First Round | Bradford PA | (a) | 5-2 |
| Second Round | Barnsley | (h) | 0-0 |
| | | (a) | 1-2 |

**LDV Vans Trophy**

| | | | |
|---|---|---|---|
| First Round | Plymouth Arg | (a) | 0-4 |

**Play-Offs**

| | | | |
|---|---|---|---|
| Semi-Final | Hartlepool U | (a) | 1-1 |
| | | (h) | 2-1 |
| Final | Brighton & HA | | 0-1 |
| *(at Millennium Stadium)* | | | |

# BRISTOL ROVERS FL Championship 2

## FOUNDATION

Bristol Rovers were formed at a meeting in Stapleton Road, Eastville, in 1883. However, they first went under the name of the Black Arabs (wearing black shirts). Changing their name to Eastville Rovers in their second season, they won the Gloucestershire Senior Cup in 1888–89. Original members of the Bristol & District League in 1892, this eventually became the Western League and Eastville Rovers adopted professionalism in 1897.

***The Memorial Stadium, Filton Avenue, Horfield, Bristol BS7 0BF.***

***Telephone:*** (0117) 909 6648.

***Fax:*** (0117) 908 5530.

***Ticket Office:*** (0117) 909 8848 (matchdays only).

***Website:*** www.bristolrovers.co.uk

***Email:*** admin@bristolrovers.co.uk

***Ground Capacity:*** 11,679.

***Record Attendance:*** 11,433 v Sunderland, Worthington Cup 3rd rd, 31 October 2000 (Memorial Stadium). 9464 v Liverpool, FA Cup 4th rd, 8 February 1992 (Twerton Park). 38,472 v Preston NE, FA Cup 4th rd, 30 January 1960 (Eastville).

## HONOURS

*Football League:* Division 2 best season: 4th, 1994–95; Division 3 (S) – Champions 1952–53; Division 3 – Champions 1989–90; Runners-up 1973–74.

*FA Cup:* best season: 6th rd, 1951, 1958.

*Football League Cup:* best season: 5th rd, 1971, 1972.

***Pitch Measurements:*** 101m × 68m.

***Chairman:*** Geoff Dunford.

***Vice-chairman:*** Ron Craig.

***Company Secretary:*** Toni Watola. ***Director of Administration:*** Rod Wesson.

***Manager:*** Ian Atkins.

***Assistant Manager:*** Kevan Broadhurst.

***Physio:*** Phil Kite.

***Colours:*** Blue and white quartered shirts, white shorts, blue stockings.

***Change Colours:*** Sky blue shirts with navy sash, navy shorts, sky blue stockings.

***Year Formed:*** 1883. ***Turned Professional:*** 1897. ***Ltd Co.:*** 1896.

***Previous Names:*** 1883, Black Arabs; 1884, Eastville Rovers; 1897, Bristol Eastville Rovers; 1898, Bristol Rovers. ***Club Nickname:*** 'Pirates'.

***Previous Grounds:*** 1883, Purdown; Three Acres, Ashley Hill; Rudgeway, Fishponds; 1897, Eastville; 1986, Twerton Park; 1996, The Memorial Stadium.

***First Football League Game:*** 28 August 1920, Division 3, v Millwall (a) L 0–2 – Stansfield; Bethune, Panes; Boxley, Kenny, Steele; Chance, Bird, Sims, Bell, Palmer.

***Record League Victory:*** 7–0 v Brighton & HA, Division 3 (S), 29 November 1952 – Hoyle; Bamford, Fox; Pitt, Warren, Sampson; McIlvenny, Roost (2), Lambden (1), Bradford (1), Petherbridge (2), (1 og). 7–0 v Swansea T, Division 2, 2 October 1954 – Radford; Bamford, Watkins; Pitt, Muir, Anderson; Petherbridge, Bradford (2), Meyer, Roost (1), Hooper (2), (2 og). 7–0 v Shrewsbury T, Division 3, 21 March 1964 – Hall; Hillard, Gwyn Jones; Oldfield, Stone (1), Mabbutt; Jarman (2), Brown (1), Biggs (1p), Hamilton, Bobby Jones (2).

## SKY SPORTS FACT FILE

Shortest first team career of any Bristol Rovers player was that experienced by David Smith aged 17. Signed as an apprentice he made his debut as a substitute against Walsall on 24 April 1982, coming on in the last ten minutes of the 2-1 win.

***Record Cup Victory:*** 6–0 v Merthyr Tydfil, FA Cup 1st rd, 14 November 1987 – Martyn; Alexander (Dryden), Tanner, Hibbitt, Twentyman, Jones, Holloway, Meacham (1), White (2), Penrice (3) (Reece), Purnell.

***Most League Points (2 for a win):*** 64, Division 3 (S), 1952–53.

***Most League Points (3 for a win):*** 93, Division 3, 1989–90.

***Most League Goals:*** 92, Division 3 (S), 1952–53.

***Highest League Scorer in Season:*** Geoff Bradford, 33, Division 3 (S), 1952–53.

***Most League Goals in Total Aggregate:*** Geoff Bradford, 242, 1949–64.

***Most League Goals in One Match:*** 4, Sidney Leigh v Exeter C, Division 3S, 2 May 1921; 4, Jonah Wilcox v Bournemouth, Division 3S, 12 December 1925; 4, Bill Culley v QPR, Division 3S, 5 March 1927; Frank Curran v Swindon T, Division 3S, 25 March 1939; Vic Lambden v Aldershot, Division 3S, 29 March 1947; George Petherbridge v Torquay U, Division 3S, 1 December 1951; Vic Lambden v Colchester U, Division 3S, 14 May 1952; Geoff Bradford v Rotherham U, Division 2, 14 March 1959; Robin Stubbs v Gillingham, Division 2, 10 October 1970; Alan Warboys v Brighton & HA, Division 3, 1 December 1973; Jamie Cureton v Reading, Division 2, 16 January 1999.

***Most Capped Player:*** Vitalijs Astafjevs, 31 (105), Latvia.

***Most League Appearances:*** Stuart Taylor, 546, 1966–80.

***Youngest League Player:*** Ronnie Dix, 15 years 180 days v Norwich C, 3 March 1928.

***Record Transfer Fee Received:*** £2,000,000 from Fulham for Barry Hayles, November 1998 and £2,000,000 from WBA for Jason Roberts, July 2000.

***Record Transfer Fee Paid:*** £370,000 to QPR for Andy Tillson, November 1992.

***Football League Record:*** 1920 Original Member of Division 3; 1921–53 Division 3 (S); 1953–62 Division 2; 1962–74 Division 3; 1974–81 Division 2; 1981–90 Division 3; 1990–92 Division 2. 1992–93 Division 1; 1993–2001 Division 2; 2001–04 Division 3; 2004– FL2.

## MANAGERS

Alfred Homer 1899–1920 *(continued as Secretary to 1928)*
Ben Hall 1920–21
Andy Wilson 1921–26
Joe Palmer 1926–29
Dave McLean 1929–30
Albert Prince-Cox 1930–36
Percy Smith 1936–37
Brough Fletcher 1938–49
Bert Tann 1950–68 *(continued as General Manager to 1972)*
Fred Ford 1968–69
Bill Dodgin Snr 1969–72
Don Megson 1972–77
Bobby Campbell 1978–79
Harold Jarman 1979–80
Terry Cooper 1980–81
Bobby Gould 1981–83
David Williams 1983–85
Bobby Gould 1985–87
Gerry Francis 1987–91
Martin Dobson 1991
Dennis Rofe 1992
Malcolm Allison 1992–93
John Ward 1993–96
Ian Holloway 1996–2001
Garry Thompson 2001
Gerry Francis 2001
Garry Thompson 2001–02
Ray Graydon 2002–04
Ian Atkins April 2004–

## LATEST SEQUENCES

***Longest Sequence of League Wins:*** 12, 18.10.1952 – 17.1.1953.

***Longest Sequence of League Defeats:*** 8, 26.10.2002 – 21.12.2002.

***Longest Sequence of League Draws:*** 5, 1.11.1975 – 22.11.1975.

***Longest Sequence of Unbeaten League Matches:*** 32, 7.4.1973 – 27.1.1974.

***Longest Sequence Without a League Win:*** 20, 5.4.1980 – 1.11.1980.

***Successive Scoring Runs:*** 26 from 26.3.1927.

***Successive Non-scoring Runs:*** 6 from 14.10.1922.

## TEN YEAR LEAGUE RECORD

| | | P | W | D | L | F | A | Pts | Pos |
|---|---|---|---|---|---|---|---|---|---|
| 1994-95 | Div 2 | 46 | 22 | 16 | 8 | 70 | 40 | 82 | 4 |
| 1995-96 | Div 2 | 46 | 20 | 10 | 16 | 57 | 60 | 70 | 10 |
| 1996-97 | Div 2 | 46 | 15 | 11 | 20 | 47 | 50 | 56 | 17 |
| 1997-98 | Div 2 | 46 | 20 | 10 | 16 | 70 | 64 | 70 | 5 |
| 1998-99 | Div 2 | 46 | 13 | 17 | 16 | 65 | 56 | 56 | 13 |
| 1999-2000 | Div 2 | 46 | 23 | 11 | 12 | 69 | 45 | 80 | 7 |
| 2000-01 | Div 2 | 46 | 12 | 15 | 19 | 53 | 57 | 51 | 21 |
| 2001-02 | Div 3 | 46 | 11 | 12 | 23 | 40 | 60 | 45 | 23 |
| 2002-03 | Div 3 | 46 | 12 | 15 | 19 | 50 | 57 | 51 | 20 |
| 2003-04 | Div 3 | 46 | 14 | 13 | 19 | 50 | 61 | 55 | 15 |

## DID YOU KNOW ?

Goalscoring was the department for John Lewis before the turn of the 19th century. During Bristol Rovers' first season in the Southern League he scored a hat-trick in a 5-0 FA Cup third qualifying round win over Eastleigh on 28 October 1899.

## BRISTOL ROVERS 2003–04 LEAGUE RECORD

| Match No. | Date | Venue | Opponents | Result | H/T Score | Lg. Pos. | Goalscorers | Attendance |
|---|---|---|---|---|---|---|---|---|
| 1 | Aug 9 | A | Scunthorpe U | W 2-1 | 1-0 | — | Barrett [13], Hodges [85] | 4186 |
| 2 | 16 | H | Rochdale | D 0-0 | 0-0 | 9 | | 7575 |
| 3 | 23 | A | Carlisle U | W 2-0 | 2-0 | 4 | Carlisle 2 [38, 43] | 4764 |
| 4 | 25 | H | Macclesfield T | D 2-2 | 2-2 | 5 | Tait [30], Quinn [33] | 7064 |
| 5 | 30 | A | Huddersfield T | L 1-2 | 0-1 | 8 | Tait [90] | 8486 |
| 6 | Sept 6 | H | Kidderminster H | W 1-0 | 0-0 | 5 | Hodges [70] | 6791 |
| 7 | 13 | H | Boston U | W 2-0 | 0-0 | 3 | Tait 2 [67, 80] | 6845 |
| 8 | 16 | A | Torquay U | L 1-2 | 0-2 | — | Street [63] | 3691 |
| 9 | 20 | A | York C | L 1-2 | 1-2 | 9 | Agogo [21] | 3968 |
| 10 | 27 | H | Cheltenham T | W 2-0 | 1-0 | 7 | Tait [43], Carlisle (pen) [88] | 8013 |
| 11 | 30 | H | Mansfield T | L 1-3 | 0-3 | — | Tait (pen) [90] | 8451 |
| 12 | Oct 4 | A | Doncaster R | L 1-5 | 0-3 | 11 | Haldane [61] | 5439 |
| 13 | 11 | A | Darlington | W 4-0 | 1-0 | 9 | Haldane [38], Savage [64], Rammell 2 [77, 90] | 4268 |
| 14 | 18 | H | Cambridge U | L 0-2 | 0-0 | 12 | | 6440 |
| 15 | 21 | H | Leyton Orient | D 1-1 | 1-0 | — | Tait [34] | 5333 |
| 16 | 25 | A | Oxford U | D 0-0 | 0-0 | 11 | | 6644 |
| 17 | Nov 1 | A | Swansea C | D 0-0 | 0-0 | 12 | | 7536 |
| 18 | 15 | H | Bury | L 1-2 | 0-0 | 15 | Haldane [51] | 7019 |
| 19 | 22 | A | Lincoln C | L 1-3 | 1-1 | 13 | Carlisle [18] | 3882 |
| 20 | 29 | H | Hull C | W 2-1 | 1-1 | 13 | Williams R [33], Agogo [87] | 6331 |
| 21 | Dec 13 | H | Yeovil T | L 0-1 | 0-1 | 13 | | 9812 |
| 22 | 20 | A | Southend U | W 1-0 | 1-0 | 12 | Savage [16] | 3771 |
| 23 | 26 | H | Northampton T | L 1-2 | 0-0 | 12 | Carlisle (pen) [47] | 7695 |
| 24 | 28 | A | Kidderminster H | L 0-1 | 0-0 | 14 | | 3411 |
| 25 | Jan 10 | H | Scunthorpe U | W 1-0 | 1-0 | 11 | Carlisle (pen) [45] | 5789 |
| 26 | 13 | A | Macclesfield T | L 1-2 | 0-1 | — | Haldane [62] | 1542 |
| 27 | 17 | A | Rochdale | D 2-2 | 0-2 | 12 | Doughty (og) [74], Agogo [83] | 2497 |
| 28 | 24 | H | Carlisle U | W 1-0 | 0-0 | 12 | Carlisle (pen) [52] | 8485 |
| 29 | Feb 7 | A | Northampton T | L 0-2 | 0-1 | 13 | | 5068 |
| 30 | 14 | H | Darlington | L 0-3 | 0-0 | 15 | | 6011 |
| 31 | 17 | H | Huddersfield T | D 1-1 | 0-0 | — | Hyde [69] | 6262 |
| 32 | 21 | A | Cambridge U | L 1-3 | 1-2 | 17 | Barrett [31] | 3256 |
| 33 | 28 | H | Oxford U | D 1-1 | 0-1 | 16 | Haldane [82] | 6556 |
| 34 | Mar 2 | A | Leyton Orient | D 1-1 | 1-0 | — | Tait [44] | 3575 |
| 35 | 6 | H | Southend U | D 1-1 | 1-0 | 17 | Tait [15] | 5625 |
| 36 | 13 | A | Yeovil T | L 0-4 | 0-2 | 20 | | 8726 |
| 37 | 16 | H | Torquay U | D 2-2 | 1-2 | — | Tait [28], Parker [52] | 6461 |
| 38 | 20 | A | Boston U | L 0-1 | 0-1 | 21 | | 2450 |
| 39 | 27 | H | York C | W 3-0 | 2-0 | 18 | Williams D [18], Barrett [20], Gibb [46] | 6723 |
| 40 | Apr 3 | A | Cheltenham T | W 2-1 | 2-1 | 15 | Barrett [34], Agogo [43] | 5088 |
| 41 | 10 | H | Doncaster R | L 1-2 | 0-0 | 17 | Agogo [59] | 8571 |
| 42 | 12 | A | Mansfield T | D 0-0 | 0-0 | 17 | | 4735 |
| 43 | 17 | H | Swansea C | W 2-1 | 1-1 | 15 | Hyde [31], Agogo [82] | 7843 |
| 44 | 24 | A | Bury | D 0-0 | 0-0 | 15 | | 2683 |
| 45 | May 1 | H | Lincoln C | W 3-1 | 1-1 | 12 | Tait 2 [7, 64], Thorpe [80] | 8562 |
| 46 | 8 | A | Hull C | L 0-3 | 0-0 | 15 | | 22,562 |

**Final League Position: 15**

### GOALSCORERS

*League (50):* Tait 12 (1 pen), Carlisle 7 (4 pens), Agogo 6, Haldane 5, Barrett 4, Hodges 2, Hyde 2, Rammell 2, Savage 2, Gibb 1, Parker 1, Quinn 1, Street 1, Thorpe 1, Williams D 1, Williams R 1, own goal 1.
*Carling Cup (0).*
*FA Cup (0).*
*LDV Vans Trophy (1):* Haldane 1.

| Miller K 44 | Boxall D 23 + 1 | Anderson I 37 + 2 | Edwards C 40 + 2 | Barrett A 45 | Quinn R 23 + 12 | Carlisle W 22 + 3 | Savage D 37 + 1 | Tait P 28 + 5 | Agogo M 28 + 10 | Street K 8 + 5 | Willock C — + 5 | Hodges L 5 + 8 | Hyde G 33 + 4 | Austin K 21 + 2 | Bryant S 7 + 5 | Haldane L 16 + 11 | Parker S 13 + 2 | Rammell A 1 + 4 | Hobbs S — + 2 | Williams R 15 + 4 | U'ddin A 1 | Gilroy D 1 + 3 | Arndale N 1 + 2 | Matthews L 9 | Clarke R 2 | Thorpe L 8 + 2 | Twigg G 7 + 1 | Anderson J 8 | Williams D 6 | Gibb A 8 | Lescott A 8 | Henriksen B 1 + 3 | Match No. |
|---|---|---|---|---|---|---|---|---|---|---|---|---|---|---|---|---|---|---|---|---|---|---|---|---|---|---|---|---|---|---|---|---|---|
| 1 | 2 | 3 | 4 | 5 | 6 | 7 | 8 | 9 | 10[1] | 11[2] | 12 | 13 | | | | | | | | | | | | | | | | | | | | | 1 |
| 1 | 2 | 3 | 4 | 5■ | 6 | 7[2] | 8 | 9 | 10[3] | 11[1] | | 12 | 13 | 14 | | | | | | | | | | | | | | | | | | | 2 |
| 1 | 2 | 3 | 4 | 5 | 6 | 7[1] | 8 | 9 | 10[2] | 11 | 13 | | 12 | | | | | | | | | | | | | | | | | | | | 3 |
| 1 | 2 | 3 | 4 | 5 | 6[3] | 7[2] | 8 | 9 | 10 | 11[1] | 12 | | 13 | | 14 | | | | | | | | | | | | | | | | | | 4 |
| 1 | 2 | 3 | 4 | | 6[1] | 12 | 8 | 9 | 10[2] | 11[3] | 13 | 14 | 7 | 5 | | | | | | | | | | | | | | | | | | | 5 |
| 1 | 2 | 3 | 4 | 5 | 6 | | 8 | 9 | 10[1] | 11[2] | 12 | 13 | 7 | | | | | | | | | | | | | | | | | | | | 6 |
| 1 | 2 | 3 | 4 | 5 | 6[1] | 12 | 8 | 9 | 10 | 13 | | 11[2] | 7 | | | | | | | | | | | | | | | | | | | | 7 |
| 1 | 2 | 3 | 4 | 5 | 6 | 7 | | 9[1] | 10 | 12 | | 11 | 8 | | | | | | | | | | | | | | | | | | | | 8 |
| 1 | 2 | 3 | 4 | 5 | 6[1] | 7 | 12 | 9 | 10 | 11[2] | | 13 | 8[3] | | 14■ | | | | | | | | | | | | | | | | | | 9 |
| 1 | 2 | 3 | 4 | 5 | 12 | 7 | 8 | 9 | 10[3] | 13 | | 11[2] | 6[1] | | | 14 | | | | | | | | | | | | | | | | | 10 |
| 1 | 2 | 3 | 4 | 5 | | | 8 | 9 | 10[2] | 7[1] | | 11 | 6 | | 12 | 13 | | | | | | | | | | | | | | | | | 11 |
| 1 | 2 | 3 | 4[3] | 5 | 6 | | 7 | 9 | 10[2] | 12 | | 11[1] | 8■ | | | 13 | 14 | | | | | | | | | | | | | | | | 12 |
| 1 | 2 | 3 | 4 | 5 | 6 | 7 | 8 | 9[3] | | 12 | | | 11[2] | 13 | | 10[1] | | 14 | | | | | | | | | | | | | | | 13 |
| 1 | 2 | 3 | 4 | 5 | 6 | 7[1] | 11 | 9 | | | | | | | 8 | 10[2] | | 13 | 12 | | | | | | | | | | | | | | 14 |
| 1 | 12 | 3■ | 4 | 5 | 6 | 13 | 7[3] | 9 | | | | | 8 | 11 | 14 | 10[2] | 2[1] | | | | | | | | | | | | | | | | 15 |
| 1 | | 3 | 4 | 5 | 6 | | 7 | 9 | | | | | 8 | 11 | | 10[1] | 2 | 12 | | | | | | | | | | | | | | | 16 |
| 1 | | 3 | 4 | 5 | 6 | | 7 | | | | | | 8 | | | 10 | 2 | 9 | | 11 | | | | | | | | | | | | | 17 |
| 1 | | 3 | 4 | 5 | | 7 | 8 | 9 | | | | | 6 | | | 10 | 2 | | | 11 | | | | | | | | | | | | | 18 |
| 1 | | | 4 | 5 | | 7 | 8 | 9 | | | | | 6 | | | 10[1] | 2 | | | 11 | 3 | 12 | | | | | | | | | | | 19 |
| 1 | | 3 | 4 | 5 | 12 | 7 | 8 | | 9 | | | | 6 | | | 10[1] | 2 | | | 11 | | | | | | | | | | | | | 20 |
| 1 | | 3 | 4 | 5 | | 7 | 8 | | 9 | | | | 6 | | | 10[1] | 2 | 12 | | 11 | | | | | | | | | | | | | 21 |
| 1 | 2 | 3 | 4■ | 5 | 12 | 7 | 8 | | 9 | | | | 6 | | | 10[1] | | | | 11[2] | | 13 | | | | | | | | | | | 22 |
| 1 | | 3 | 4 | 5 | | 7 | 8 | | 9[1] | | | | 6 | | | 10 | 2 | | | 11 | | 12 | | | | | | | | | | | 23 |
| 1 | | 3 | 4 | 5 | 6 | 7 | 8 | | 9[1] | | | | | | | | 2 | | 12 | 11 | | 10 | | | | | | | | | | | 24 |
| 1 | | 3 | | 5 | 12 | 7 | 8 | | 9[1] | | | | 6 | 4 | | 10[2] | 2 | | | 11 | | | 13 | | | | | | | | | | 25 |
| 1 | | 3 | | 5 | | 7 | 8[1] | | 9[2] | | | | 6 | 4 | 12 | 13 | 2 | | | 11 | | | | 10 | | | | | | | | | 26 |
| 1 | | 3[2] | 4 | 5 | 13 | 7 | 8 | 14 | 12 | | | | 6 | 2[1] | | 9[3] | | | | 11 | | | | 10 | | | | | | | | | 27 |
| 1 | 2 | | 4 | 5 | 12 | 7 | 8 | 13 | 14 | | | | 6 | 3 | | 9[1] | | | | 11[3] | | | | 10[2] | | | | | | | | | 28 |
| 1 | 2 | | 4 | 5 | | 7 | 8 | 9 | 12 | | | | 6 | 3 | | 13 | | | | 11[2] | | | | 10[1] | | | | | | | | | 29 |
| 1 | 2 | 3 | 4 | 5 | | 7 | 8 | 9[2] | 10 | | | 12 | 6 | | | 13 | | | | 11[1] | | | | | | | | | | | | | 30 |
| | 2 | 11 | 4 | 5 | | | 8 | | 9 | | | | 6 | 3 | 7 | 10 | | | | | | | | | 1 | | | | | | | | 31 |
| 1 | 2 | 3 | 4 | 5 | | | 8 | | 9 | | | 12 | | 6 | 7 | 10[1] | | | | 11 | | | | | | | | | | | | | 32 |
| 1 | 2 | 3 | | 5 | 6 | | 8 | 12 | 9[1] | | | | 11[2] | 4 | 7 | 13 | | | | | | | | 10 | | | | | | | | | 33 |
| 1 | 2 | 3■ | | 5 | 6 | | 11 | 9[1] | 12 | | | | 8 | 4 | 7 | | | | | 13 | | | | 10[2] | | | | | | | | | 34 |
| 1 | 2[1] | 3 | 12 | 5 | 6 | | 11 | 9 | 13 | | | | 8 | 4 | 7[3] | 14 | | | | | | | | 10[2] | | | | | | | | | 35 |
| 1 | | 3 | 12 | 5 | 6 | | 11 | 9[3] | | | | | 8■ | 4 | 7[1] | | | | | 13 | | | 2 | 10[2] | | 14 | | | | | | | 36 |
| 1 | | | 4 | 5 | 6 | | 11 | 9 | 13 | | | | 8[2] | 3 | | | 2[1] | | | 14 | | | 12 | 10 | | | 7[3] | | | | | | 37 |
| 1 | | | 4 | 5 | 6[3] | | 11 | 9 | 13 | | | 12 | 8 | 3 | | | 2[1] | | | 14 | | | | | | 10[2] | 7 | | | | | | 38 |
| 1 | | | 4 | 5 | 12 | | | 14 | 9[2] | | | | | 3 | | | | | | | | | | | | 10[3] | 7[1] | 6 | 11 | 2 | 8 | 13 | 39 |
| 1 | | 12 | 4 | 5 | 13 | | | | 9[2] | | | | | 3 | | 14 | | | | | | | | | | 10[3] | 7[1] | 6 | 11 | 2 | 8 | | 40 |
| 1 | | 12 | 4[1] | 5 | | | | | 9 | | | | | 3■ | | 13 | | | | | | | | | | 10[2] | 7[3] | 6 | 11 | 2 | 8 | 14 | 41 |
| 1 | | 3[3] | 4 | 5 | 12 | | | | 9[2] | | | | 8[1] | 11 | | 13 | | | | | | | | | | 10 | 14 | 6 | | 2 | 7 | | 42 |
| 1 | | 3 | 4 | 5 | 12 | | | 13 | 14 | | | | 8[1] | 11 | | | | | | | | | | | | 10[2] | | 6 | | 2 | 7 | 9[3] | 43 |
| | | 3[1] | 4 | 5 | 12 | | | 9 | 10 | | | | 13[3] | | | | | | | | | | | | 1 | 14 | 7[2] | 6 | 11 | 2 | 8 | | 44 |
| 1 | | | 4 | 5 | 11 | | | 9 | 12 | | | | | | | | 13 | | | | | | | | | 10[2] | 3[1] | 6 | 7 | 2 | 8 | | 45 |
| 1 | | 3[1] | 4 | 5 | 12 | | 8 | 9[3] | 13 | | | | | | | | | | | | | | | | | 10[2] | | 6 | 11 | 2 | 7 | 14 | 46 |

**Carling Cup**
First Round Brighton & HA (h) 0-1

**LDV Vans Trophy**
First Round Southend U (a) 1-2

**FA Cup**
First Round Bournemouth (a) 0-1

# BURNLEY — FL Championship

## FOUNDATION

The majority of those responsible for the formation of the Burnley club in 1881 were from the defunct rugby club Burnley Rovers. Indeed, they continued to play rugby for a year before changing to soccer and dropping 'Rovers' from their name. The changes were decided at a meeting held in May 1882 at the Bull Hotel.

***Turf Moor, Harry Potts Way, Burnley, Lancashire BB10 4BX.***

***Telephone:*** 0870 443 1882.

***Fax:*** (01282) 700 014.

***Ticket Office:*** 0870 443 1914.

***Website:*** www.burnleyfootballclub.com

***Email:*** info@burnleyfootballclub.net

***Ground Capacity:*** 22,500.

***Record Attendance:*** 54,775 v Huddersfield T, FA Cup 3rd rd, 23 February 1924.

***Pitch Measurements:*** 112yd × 70yd.

***Chairman:*** Barry Kilby.

***Vice-chairman:*** Ray Ingleby.

***Chief Executive:*** Dave Edmundson.

***Secretary:*** Cathy Pickup.

***Manager:*** Steve Cotterill.

***Physio:*** Ian Liversedge.

***Colours:*** Claret and blue.

***Change Colours:*** White with blue trim.

***Year Formed:*** 1882.

***Turned Professional:*** 1883.

***Ltd Co.:*** 1897.

***Previous Name:*** 1881, Burnley Rovers; 1882, Burnley.

***Club Nickname:*** 'The Clarets'.

***Previous Grounds:*** 1881, Calder Vale; 1882, Turf Moor.

***First Football League Game:*** 8 September 1888, Football League, v Preston NE (a) L 2–5 – Smith; Lang, Bury, Abrams, Friel, Keenan, Brady, Tait, Poland (1), Gallocher (1), Yates.

***Record League Victory:*** 9–0 v Darwen, Division 1, 9 January 1892 – Hillman; Walker, McFettridge, Lang, Matthews, Keenan, Nicol (3), Bowes, Espie (1), McLardie (3), Hill (2).

***Record Cup Victory:*** 9–0 v Crystal Palace, FA Cup 2nd rd (replay), 10 February 1909 – Dawson; Barron, McLean; Cretney (2), Leake, Moffat; Morley, Ogden, Smith (3), Abbott (2), Smethams (1). 9–0 v New Brighton, FA Cup 4th rd, 26 January 1957 – Blacklaw; Angus, Winton; Seith, Adamson, Miller; Newlands (1), McIlroy (3), Lawson (3), Cheesebrough (1), Pilkington (1). 9–0 v Penrith, FA Cup 1st rd, 17 November 1984 – Hansbury; Miller, Hampton, Phelan, Overson (Kennedy), Hird (3 incl. 1p), Grewcock (1), Powell (2), Taylor (3), Biggins, Hutchison.

## HONOURS

*Football League:* Division 1 – Champions 1920–21, 1959–60; Runners-up 1919–20, 1961–62; Division 2 – Champions 1897–98, 1972–73; Runners-up 1912–13, 1946–47, 1999–2000; Promoted from Division 2, 1993–94 (play-offs); Division 3 – Champions 1981–82; Division 4 – Champions 1991–92. Record 30 consecutive Division 1 games without defeat 1920–21.

*FA Cup:* Winners 1914; Runners-up 1947, 1962.

*Football League Cup:* Semi-final 1961, 1969, 1983.

*Anglo-Scottish Cup:* Winners 1979.

*Sherpa Van Trophy:* Runners-up 1988.

***European Competitions:*** *European Cup:* 1960–61. *European Fairs Cup:* 1966–67.

## SKY SPORTS FACT FILE

On 9 January 1954 Burnley defeated Manchester United 5-3 at Turf Moor in a third round FA Cup tie. Burnley took a 2-0 lead only for United to level with just over five minutes played. Burnley led again, but United's equaliser was their last goal.

***Record Defeat:*** 0–10 v Aston Villa, Division 1, 29 August 1925 and v Sheffield U, Division 1, 19 January 1929.

***Most League Points (2 for a win):*** 62, Division 2, 1972–73.

***Most League Points (3 for a win):*** 88, Division 2, 1999–2000.

***Most League Goals:*** 102, Division 1, 1960–61.

***Highest League Scorer in Season:*** George Beel, 35, Division 1, 1927–28.

***Most League Goals in Total Aggregate:*** George Beel, 178, 1923–32.

***Most League Goals in One Match:*** 6, Louis Page v Birmingham C, Division 1, 10 April 1926.

***Most Capped Player:*** Jimmy McIlroy, 51 (55), Northern Ireland.

***Most League Appearances:*** Jerry Dawson, 522, 1907–28.

***Youngest League Player:*** Tommy Lawton, 16 years 174 days v Doncaster R, 28 March 1936.

***Record Transfer Fee Received:*** £750,000 from Luton T for Steve Davis, June 1995.

***Record Transfer Fee Paid:*** £1,000,000 to Stockport C for Ian Moore, November 2000. £1,000,000 to Bradford C for Robbie Blake, January 2002.

***Football League Record:*** 1888 Original Member of the Football League; 1897–98 Division 2; 1898–1900 Division 1; 1900–13 Division 2; 1913–30 Division 1; 1930–47 Division 2; 1947–71 Division 1; 1971–73 Division 2; 1973–76 Division 1; 1976–80 Division 2; 1980–82 Division 3; 1982–83 Division 2; 1983–85 Division 3; 1985–92 Division 4; 1992–94 Division 2; 1994–95 Division 1; 1995–2000 Division 2; 2000–04 Division 1; 2004– FLC.

## MANAGERS

Arthur F. Sutcliffe 1893–96
*(Secretary-Manager)*
Harry Bradshaw 1896–99
*(Secretary-Manager)*
Ernest Magnall 1899–1903
*(Secretary-Manager)*
Spen Whittaker 1903–10
R. H. Wadge 1910–11
*(Secretary-Manager)*
John Haworth 1911–25
Albert Pickles 1925–32
Tom Bromilow 1932–35
Alf Boland 1935–39
*(Secretary-Manager)*
Cliff Britton 1945–48
Frank Hill 1948–54
Alan Brown 1954–57
Billy Dougall 1957–58
Harry Potts 1958–70
*(General Manager to 1972)*
Jimmy Adamson 1970–76
Joe Brown 1976–77
Harry Potts 1977–79
Brian Miller 1979–83
John Bond 1983–84
John Benson 1984–85
Martin Buchan 1985
Tommy Cavanagh 1985–86
Brian Miller 1986–89
Frank Casper 1989–91
Jimmy Mullen 1991–96
Adrian Heath 1996–97
Chris Waddle 1997–98
Stan Ternent 1998–2004
Steve Cotterill June 2004–

## LATEST SEQUENCES

***Longest Sequence of League Wins:*** 10, 16.11.1912 – 18.1.1913.

***Longest Sequence of League Defeats:*** 8, 2.1.1995 – 25.2.1995.

***Longest Sequence of League Draws:*** 6, 21.2.1931 – 28.3.1931.

***Longest Sequence of Unbeaten League Matches:*** 30, 6.9.1920 – 25.3.1921.

***Longest Sequence Without a League Win:*** 24, 16.4.1979 – 17.11.1979.

***Successive Scoring Runs:*** 27 from 13.2.1926.

***Successive Non-scoring Runs:*** 6 from 9.8.1997.

## TEN YEAR LEAGUE RECORD

| | | P | W | D | L | F | A | Pts | Pos |
|---|---|---|---|---|---|---|---|---|---|
| 1994-95 | Div 1 | 46 | 11 | 13 | 22 | 49 | 74 | 46 | 22 |
| 1995-96 | Div 2 | 46 | 14 | 13 | 19 | 56 | 68 | 55 | 17 |
| 1996-97 | Div 2 | 46 | 19 | 11 | 16 | 71 | 55 | 68 | 9 |
| 1997-98 | Div 2 | 46 | 13 | 13 | 20 | 55 | 65 | 52 | 20 |
| 1998-99 | Div 2 | 46 | 13 | 16 | 17 | 54 | 73 | 55 | 15 |
| 1999-2000 | Div 2 | 46 | 25 | 13 | 8 | 69 | 47 | 88 | 2 |
| 2000-01 | Div 2 | 46 | 21 | 9 | 16 | 50 | 54 | 72 | 7 |
| 2001-02 | Div 1 | 46 | 21 | 12 | 13 | 70 | 62 | 75 | 7 |
| 2002-03 | Div 1 | 46 | 15 | 10 | 21 | 65 | 89 | 55 | 16 |
| 2003-04 | Div 1 | 46 | 13 | 14 | 19 | 60 | 77 | 53 | 19 |

## DID YOU KNOW ?

Burnley failed to score in only three League games during 1965–66 when they finished third in the First Division. Interestingly enough it was not a high scoring season for them as they managed just 47 goals and even conceded 55.

## BURNLEY 2003–04 LEAGUE RECORD

| Match No. | Date | Venue | Opponents | Result | | H/T Score | Lg. Pos. | Goalscorers | Attendance |
|---|---|---|---|---|---|---|---|---|---|
| 1 | Aug 9 | H | Crystal Palace | L | 2-3 | 2-2 | — | Blake [11], Roche [19] | 12,976 |
| 2 | 16 | A | WBA | L | 1-4 | 1-1 | 24 | Blake [28] | 22,489 |
| 3 | 23 | H | Wigan Ath | L | 0-2 | 0-1 | 24 | | 13,231 |
| 4 | 25 | A | Gillingham | W | 3-0 | 2-0 | 19 | Moore I [27], West [30], Blake [77] | 7645 |
| 5 | 30 | H | Crewe Alex | W | 1-0 | 0-0 | 15 | Chaplow [52] | 11,495 |
| 6 | Sept 6 | A | Stoke C | W | 2-1 | 2-0 | 10 | May [18], Chadwick [27] | 14,867 |
| 7 | 13 | A | Norwich C | L | 0-2 | 0-0 | 13 | | 16,407 |
| 8 | 16 | H | Nottingham F | L | 0-3 | 0-1 | — | | 12,530 |
| 9 | 20 | H | Bradford C | W | 4-0 | 1-0 | 12 | Moore I [43], Chadwick 2 [54, 60], Blake [68] | 12,719 |
| 10 | 27 | A | Wimbledon | D | 2-2 | 2-0 | 11 | Blake 2 [21, 37] | 5639 |
| 11 | 30 | A | Watford | D | 1-1 | 0-1 | — | Chadwick [54] | 11,573 |
| 12 | Oct 4 | H | Walsall | W | 3-1 | 1-1 | 8 | Facey 3 [4, 82, 87] | 10,532 |
| 13 | 14 | A | Ipswich T | L | 1-6 | 0-5 | — | Facey [49] | 22,048 |
| 14 | 18 | A | West Ham U | D | 2-2 | 1-1 | 13 | Facey [38], Moore I [82] | 31,474 |
| 15 | 25 | H | Millwall | D | 1-1 | 0-0 | 16 | Moore I [60] | 10,435 |
| 16 | Nov 1 | H | Cardiff C | D | 1-1 | 0-0 | 15 | Chaplow [52] | 10,886 |
| 17 | 8 | A | Sheffield U | L | 0-1 | 0-1 | 18 | | 20,967 |
| 18 | 15 | A | Derby Co | L | 0-2 | 0-1 | 18 | | 21,960 |
| 19 | 22 | H | Rotherham U | D | 1-1 | 1-0 | 18 | Blake [35] | 12,928 |
| 20 | 25 | H | Reading | W | 3-0 | 1-0 | — | Blake [5], Chaplow [47], Chadwick [54] | 9473 |
| 21 | 29 | A | Sunderland | D | 1-1 | 0-1 | 16 | Moore I [72] | 29,852 |
| 22 | Dec 6 | H | Sheffield U | W | 3-2 | 3-2 | 14 | Blake 2 (1 pen) [17, 45 (p)], Moore I [34] | 11,452 |
| 23 | 13 | H | Coventry C | L | 1-2 | 0-2 | 16 | Blake [53] | 10,358 |
| 24 | 20 | A | Preston NE | L | 3-5 | 1-1 | 18 | Moore I [24], Gnohere [64], Blake (pen) [78] | 18,802 |
| 25 | 26 | A | Crewe Alex | L | 1-3 | 0-1 | 19 | Blake (pen) [89] | 9512 |
| 26 | 28 | H | Stoke C | L | 0-1 | 0-0 | 21 | | 12,812 |
| 27 | Jan 10 | A | Crystal Palace | D | 0-0 | 0-0 | 20 | | 15,276 |
| 28 | 17 | H | WBA | D | 1-1 | 0-0 | 19 | Blake [68] | 13,106 |
| 29 | 31 | A | Wigan Ath | D | 0-0 | 0-0 | 19 | | 11,147 |
| 30 | Feb 7 | H | Gillingham | W | 1-0 | 0-0 | 19 | Little [83] | 10,400 |
| 31 | 21 | H | Ipswich T | W | 4-2 | 2-0 | 17 | Little [26], May [28], Chaplow [61], Blake [90] | 12,418 |
| 32 | 24 | A | Reading | D | 2-2 | 1-1 | — | Moore I [23], May [67] | 10,543 |
| 33 | 28 | A | Millwall | L | 0-2 | 0-1 | 18 | | 10,148 |
| 34 | Mar 2 | H | West Ham U | D | 1-1 | 1-1 | — | Branch [31] | 12,440 |
| 35 | 6 | H | Preston NE | D | 1-1 | 1-0 | 18 | Blake [19] | 15,837 |
| 36 | 13 | A | Coventry C | L | 0-4 | 0-3 | 21 | | 12,953 |
| 37 | 17 | A | Nottingham F | D | 1-1 | 1-0 | — | Chaplow [15] | 26,885 |
| 38 | 27 | A | Bradford C | W | 2-1 | 1-1 | 19 | Blake [8], Moore I [90] | 13,677 |
| 39 | Apr 3 | H | Norwich C | L | 3-5 | 3-2 | 20 | Wood [7], May [30], Blake [38] | 12,417 |
| 40 | 10 | A | Walsall | W | 1-0 | 0-0 | 19 | Blake (pen) [56] | 7769 |
| 41 | 12 | H | Watford | L | 2-3 | 1-1 | 20 | McGregor [30], Adebola [86] | 11,413 |
| 42 | 17 | A | Cardiff C | L | 0-2 | 0-0 | 21 | | 13,525 |
| 43 | 20 | H | Wimbledon | W | 2-0 | 2-0 | — | Branch [26], Ntimban-Zeh (og) [45] | 13,555 |
| 44 | 24 | H | Derby Co | W | 1-0 | 1-0 | 17 | Branch [42] | 16,189 |
| 45 | May 1 | A | Rotherham U | L | 0-3 | 0-2 | 19 | | 9157 |
| 46 | 9 | H | Sunderland | L | 1-2 | 1-1 | 19 | Little [11] | 18,852 |

**Final League Position: 19**

### GOALSCORERS

*League (60):* Blake 19 (4 pens), Moore I 9, Chadwick 5, Chaplow 5, Facey 5, May 4, Branch 3, Little 3, Adebola 1, Gnohere 1, McGregor 1, Roche 1, West 1, Wood 1, own goal 1.
*Carling Cup (3):* Blake 1, Chadwick 1, Moore I 1.
*FA Cup (5):* Moore I 3, Blake 2.

| Jensen B 46 | Camara M 45 | Roche L 21 + 4 | Chaplow R 30 + 9 | Branch G 30 + 8 | Gnohere A 12 + 2 | Little G 33 + 1 | Weller P 25 + 8 | Moore A 5 + 8 | Blake R 44 + 1 | Chadwick L 23 + 13 | West D 25 + 7 | Grant T 34 + 3 | O'Neill M — + 4 | May D 34 + 1 | Moore I 38 + 2 | Todd A 7 | Farrelly G 9 + 3 | Facey D 12 + 2 | McGregor M 20 + 3 | McEveley J — + 4 | Orr B 1 + 3 | Wood N 8 + 2 | Townsend R — + 1 | Scott P — + 2 | Adebola D — + 3 | Johnrose L 4 + 3 | Pilkington J — + 1 | *Match No.* |
|---|---|---|---|---|---|---|---|---|---|---|---|---|---|---|---|---|---|---|---|---|---|---|---|---|---|---|---|---|
| 1 | 2 | 3 | $4^{1}$ | 5 | 6 | 7 | $8^{2}$ | $9^{3}$ | 10 | 11 | 12 | 13 | 14 | | | | | | | | | | | | | | | 1 |
| 1 | 2 | $3^{2}$ | 12 | 6 | | 7 | 8 | $9^{1}$ | 10 | 11 | 13 | 4 | | 5 | | | | | | | | | | | | | | 2 |
| 1 | 3 | | 12 | 5 | 13 | 7 | 8 | 14 | $10^{2}$ | $11^{3}$ | 2 | $4^{1}$ | | 6 | 9 | | | | | | | | | | | | | 3 |
| 1 | 3 | | 12 | 5 | | 7 | 8 | 13 | 10 | $11^{1}$ | 2 | 4 | | 6 | $9^{2}$ | | | | | | | | | | | | | 4 |
| 1 | 3 | | $4^{1}$ | 5 | 12 | 7 | | 13 | 10 | 11 | 2 | 8 | | 6 | $9^{2}$ | | | | | | | | | | | | | 5 |
| 1 | 3 | | | 10 | | | 12 | | 8 | 11 | 2 | 4 | | 5 | 13 | 6 | $7^{1}$ | $9^{2}$ | | | | | | | | | | 6 |
| 1 | 3 | 12 | | $10^{2}$ | | | | | 8 | 11 | $2^{1}$ | 4 | | 6 | 13 | 5 | 7 | 9 | | | | | | | | | | 7 |
| 1 | 2 | $3^{1}$ | 13 | 14 | | | 12 | | $8^{3}$ | 7 | | 4 | | 6 | 9 | 5 | $11^{2}$ | 10 | | | | | | | | | | 8 |
| 1 | 3 | | 12 | 13 | | | 14 | | 8 | 11 | 2 | $4^{3}$ | | $6^{2}$ | 9 | 5 | $7^{1}$ | 10 | | | | | | | | | | 9 |
| 1 | 3 | | 12 | 13 | | | 4 | | $8^{2}$ | $7^{1}$ | 2 | | | 6■ | 9 | 5 | 11 | 10 | | | | | | | | | | 10 |
| 1 | 3 | | 13 | 12 | | | 4 | | 8 | 7 | 2 | | | $6^{1}$ | 9 | 5 | $11^{2}$ | 10 | | | | | | | | | | 11 |
| 1 | 3 | | 4 | 6 | | | 7 | | 8 | 11 | 2 | | | | 9 | 5 | | 10 | | | | | | | | | | 12 |
| 1 | 6 | 3 | 4 | 5 | | | 7 | | 8 | | 2 | | | | 9 | | 11 | 10 | | | | | | | | | | 13 |
| 1 | 3 | | 4 | 5 | 6 | | $7^{1}$ | | $8^{2}$ | 11 | 2 | 12 | | | 9 | | 13 | 10 | | | | | | | | | | 14 |
| 1 | 3 | | 4 | 5 | 6 | | $7^{1}$ | | 8 | $11^{2}$ | 2 | 12 | | | 9 | | 13 | 10 | | | | | | | | | | 15 |
| 1 | 3 | | 4 | 5 | 6 | $7^{1}$ | | | $8^{2}$ | 13 | 2 | 11 | | | 9 | | 12 | 10 | | | | | | | | | | 16 |
| 1 | 3 | 13 | 4 | $5^{3}$ | 6 | | | | 12 | $7^{1}$ | 2 | 8 | | | 9 | | 11 | $10^{2}$ | 14 | | | | | | | | | 17 |
| 1 | 3 | 12 | 4 | 13 | 6■ | 7 | | | 10 | | $2^{1}$ | 8 | | 5 | 9 | | $11^{2}$ | | | | | | | | | | | 18 |
| 1 | 3 | | 4 | 11 | 6 | 7 | | | 10 | | 2 | 8 | | 5 | $9^{1}$ | | | 12 | | | | | | | | | | 19 |
| 1 | 3 | | $4^{1}$ | $11^{2}$ | 6 | 7 | 12 | | 10 | $13^{3}$ | 2 | 8 | | 5 | 9 | | | 14 | | | | | | | | | | 20 |
| 1 | 3 | 12 | 4 | | | 7 | 13 | | 10 | $11^{2}$ | $2^{1}$ | 8 | | 5 | 9 | | | | 6 | | | | | | | | | 21 |
| 1 | 3 | 2 | 4 | | 6 | 7 | $12^{2}$ | | 10 | $11^{1}$ | 13 | 8 | | | 9 | | | | 5 | | | | | | | | | 22 |
| 1 | 3 | $2^{1}$ | | | 6■ | 7 | 8 | | 10 | $11^{3}$ | 12 | 4 | | 13 | 9 | | | | $5^{2}$ | 14 | | | | | | | | 23 |
| 1 | $3^{1}$ | | 4 | 12 | 6 | 7 | $11^{2}$ | | 10 | 13 | $2^{3}$ | 8 | | 5 | 9 | | | | | 14 | | | | | | | | 24 |
| 1 | 3 | | $4^{3}$ | 5 | 6 | $7^{1}$ | 11 | | 10 | 12 | $2^{2}$ | 8 | | | 9 | | | | 13 | 14 | | | | | | | | 25 |
| 1 | $3^{1}$ | | 4 | 5 | | | 11 | | 10 | $7^{2}$ | 2 | 8 | 12 | 6 | 9 | | | | | 13 | | | | | | | | 26 |
| 1 | 3 | 2 | $4^{1}$ | 12 | | 13 | 11 | | 10 | $7^{2}$ | | 8 | | 5 | 9 | | | | 6 | | | | | | | | | 27 |
| 1 | 3 | 2 | | $10^{2}$ | | 11 | | 13 | 8 | $7^{1}$ | 12 | 4 | | 5 | 9 | | | | 6 | | | | | | | | | 28 |
| 1 | 3 | 2 | 4 | | | $7^{1}$ | | | 10 | | | 8 | | 5 | 9 | | | | 6 | | 12 | 11 | | | | | | 29 |
| 1 | 3 | 2 | 4 | | | 7 | | $11^{1}$ | | 12 | | 8 | | 5 | 9 | | | | 6 | | | 10 | | | | | | 30 |
| 1 | 3 | 2 | 4 | | | 7 | $11^{1}$ | | 10 | | | 8 | | 5 | 9 | | | | 6 | | 12 | | | | | | | 31 |
| 1 | 3 | 2 | $4^{1}$ | | | 7 | 11 | | 10 | | | 8 | | 5 | 9 | | | | 6 | | 12 | | | | | | | 32 |
| 1 | 3 | $2^{1}$ | | 13 | | $7^{3}$ | | $11^{2}$ | 10 | 14 | 12 | | | 5 | 9 | | | | 6 | | 8 | 4 | | | | | | 33 |
| 1 | 3 | $2^{1}$ | | 10 | | 7 | | 13 | 8 | $11^{2}$ | 12 | 4 | | 5 | 9 | | | | 6 | | | | | | | | | 34 |
| 1 | 3 | | 4 | $10^{1}$ | | 7 | | 12 | 8 | | 2 | 11 | | 5 | 9 | | | | 6 | | | | | | | | | 35 |
| 1 | | | 4 | | | 7 | 3 | $11^{3}$ | 10 | | $2^{2}$ | 8 | | $5^{1}$ | 9 | | | | 6 | | | 12 | 13 | 14 | | | | 36 |
| 1 | 3 | | 4 | 6 | | 7 | 12 | | 10 | | 2 | $8^{2}$ | | 5 | 9 | | | | 13 | | | $11^{1}$ | | | | | | 37 |
| 1 | 3 | | $4^{1}$ | 6 | | 7 | 13 | | $10^{2}$ | | 2 | 8 | | 5 | 9 | | | | | | | 11 | | | 12 | | | 38 |
| 1 | 3 | 2 | 12 | 6 | | 7 | $8^{3}$ | 13 | 10 | 14 | | $4^{2}$ | | 5 | 9 | | | | | | | $11^{1}$ | | | | | | 39 |
| 1 | 3 | 2 | $12^{2}$ | 6 | | 11 | $8^{1}$ | | 10 | 14 | | 4 | | | $9^{3}$ | | | | 5 | | | 7 | | | | 13 | | 40 |
| 1 | 3 | 2 | | 6 | | 7 | $11^{3}$ | | 10 | $12^{2}$ | | 4 | | | 9 | | | | 5 | | | $8^{1}$ | | | 13 | 14 | | 41 |
| 1 | 3 | 2 | 4 | 10 | | 7 | | | 9 | 11 | | $8^{1}$ | | 5 | | | | | 6 | | | | | | | 12 | | 42 |
| 1 | 3 | 2 | $4^{3}$ | 10 | | 7 | $11^{2}$ | 13 | $9^{1}$ | 12 | | | | 5 | | | | | 6 | | | | | | | 8 | 14 | 43 |
| 1 | 3 | 2 | 4 | 10 | | $7^{1}$ | 11 | | $9^{2}$ | 13 | | | | 5 | | | | | 6 | | | 12 | | | | 8 | | 44 |
| 1 | $3^{1}$ | $2^{3}$ | $4^{2}$ | 10 | | 7 | 11 | | 9 | 12 | | | 13 | 5 | | | | | 6 | | | | | | 14 | 8 | | 45 |
| 1 | $2^{3}$ | | $4^{2}$ | 3 | | 7 | $11^{1}$ | | 10 | 12 | | | 13 | 5 | 9 | | | | 6 | | | | | 14 | | 8 | | 46 |

**Carling Cup**

| | | | |
|---|---|---|---|
| First Round | Chesterfield | (a) | 0-0 |
| Second Round | Scunthorpe U | (a) | 3-2 |
| Third Round | Wolverhampton W | (a) | 0-2 |

**FA Cup**

| | | | |
|---|---|---|---|
| Third Round | Mansfield T | (a) | 2-0 |
| Fourth Round | Gillingham | (h) | 3-1 |
| Fifth Round | Millwall | (a) | 0-1 |

# BURY FL Championship 2

## FOUNDATION

A meeting at the Waggon & Horses Hotel, attended largely by members of Bury Wesleyans and Bury Unitarians football clubs, decided to form a new Bury club. This was officially formed at a subsequent gathering at the Old White Horse Hotel, Fleet Street, Bury on 24 April 1885.

***Gigg Lane, Bury BL9 9HR.***

***Telephone:*** (0161) 764 4881.

***Fax:*** (0161) 764 5521.

***Website:*** www.buryfc.co.uk

***Email:*** admin@buryfc.co.uk

***Ground Capacity:*** 11,669.

***Record Attendance:*** 35,000 v Bolton W, FA Cup 3rd rd, 9 January 1960.

***Pitch Measurements:*** 112yd × 70yd.

***Secretary:*** Jill Neville.

***Manager:*** Graham Barrow.

***Assistant Manager:*** Kelham O'Hanlon.

***Physio:*** Lee Nobes.

***Colours:*** White shirts, royal blue shorts, white stockings.

***Change Colours:*** All navy blue.

***Year Formed:*** 1885.

***Turned Professional:*** 1885.

***Ltd Co.:*** 1897.

***Club Nickname:*** 'Shakers'.

***First Football League Game:*** 1 September 1894, Division 2, v Manchester C (h) W 4–2 – Lowe; Gillespie, Davies; White, Clegg, Ross; Wylie, Barbour (2), Millar (1), Ostler (1), Plant.

***Record League Victory:*** 8–0 v Tranmere R, Division 3, 10 January 1970 – Forrest; Tinney, Saile; Anderson, Turner, McDermott; Hince (1), Arrowsmith (1), Jones (4), Kerr (1), Grundy, (1 og).

***Record Cup Victory:*** 12–1 v Stockton, FA Cup 1st rd (replay), 2 February 1897 – Montgomery; Darroch, Barbour; Hendry (1), Clegg, Ross (1); Wylie (3), Pangbourn, Millar (4), Henderson (2), Plant, (1 og).

***Record Defeat:*** 0–10 v Blackburn R, FA Cup pr rd, 1 October 1887. 0–10 v West Ham U, Milk Cup 2nd rd 2nd leg, 25 October 1983.

***Most League Points (2 for a win):*** 68, Division 3, 1960–61.

## HONOURS

*Football League:* Division 1 best season: 4th, 1925–26; Division 2 – Champions 1894–95, 1996–97; Runners-up 1923–24; Division 3 – Champions 1960–61; Runners-up 1967–68; Promoted from Division 3 (3rd) 1995–96.

*FA Cup:* Winners 1900, 1903.

*Football League Cup:* Semi-final 1963.

## SKY SPORTS FACT FILE

Billy Hibbert was leading scorer for Bury in four consecutive seasons from 1907–08 and was capped by England against Scotland in 1910. Later with Newcastle United, Bradford City and Oldham Athletic he also coached in the USA and Spain.

***Most League Points (3 for a win):*** 84, Division 4, 1984–85 and Division 2, 1996–97.

***Most League Goals:*** 108, Division 3, 1960–61.

***Highest League Scorer in Season:*** Craig Madden, 35, Division 4, 1981–82.

***Most League Goals in Total Aggregate:*** Craig Madden, 129, 1978–86.

***Most League Goals in One Match:*** 5, Eddie Quigley v Millwall, Division 2, 15 February 1947; 5, Ray Pointer v Rotherham U, Division 2, 2 October 1965.

***Most Capped Player:*** Bill Gorman, 11 (13), Republic of Ireland and (4), Northern Ireland.

***Most League Appearances:*** Norman Bullock, 506, 1920–35.

***Youngest League Player:*** Brian Williams, 16 years 133 days v Stockport Co, 18 March 1972.

***Record Transfer Fee Received:*** £1,100,000 from Ipswich T for David Johnson, November 1997.

***Record Transfer Fee Paid:*** £200,000 to Ipswich T for Chris Swailes, November 1997 and to Swindon T for Darren Bullock, February 1999.

***Football League Record:*** 1894 Elected to Division 2; 1895–1912 Division 1; 1912–24 Division 2; 1924–29 Division 1; 1929–57 Division 2; 1957–61 Division 3; 1961–67 Division 2; 1967–68 Division 3; 1968–69 Division 2; 1969–71 Division 3; 1971–74 Division 4; 1974–80 Division 3; 1980–85 Division 4; 1985–96 Division 3; 1996–97 Division 2; 1997–99 Division 1; 1999–2002 Division 2; 2002–04 Division 3; 2004– FL2.

## MANAGERS

T. Hargreaves 1887
*(Secretary-Manager)*
H. S. Hamer 1887–1907
*(Secretary-Manager)*
Archie Montgomery 1907–15
William Cameron 1919–23
James Hunter Thompson 1923–27
Percy Smith 1927–30
Arthur Paine 1930–34
Norman Bullock 1934–38
Jim Porter 1944–45
Norman Bullock 1945–49
John McNeil 1950–53
Dave Russell 1953–61
Bob Stokoe 1961–65
Bert Head 1965–66
Les Shannon 1966–69
Jack Marshall 1969
Les Hart 1970
Tommy McAnearney 1970–72
Alan Brown 1972–73
Bobby Smith 1973–77
Bob Stokoe 1977–78
David Hatton 1978–79
Dave Connor 1979–80
Jim Iley 1980–84
Martin Dobson 1984–89
Sam Ellis 1989–90
Mike Walsh 1990–95
Stan Ternent 1995–98
Neil Warnock 1998–99
Andy Preece 2000–04
Graham Barrow January 2004–

## LATEST SEQUENCES

***Longest Sequence of League Wins:*** 9, 26.9.1960 – 19.11.1960.

***Longest Sequence of League Defeats:*** 8, 18.8.2001 – 25.9.2001.

***Longest Sequence of League Draws:*** 6, 6.3.1999 – 3.4.1999.

***Longest Sequence of Unbeaten League Matches:*** 18, 4.2.1961 – 29.4.1961.

***Longest Sequence Without a League Win:*** 19, 1.4.1911 – 2.12.1911.

***Successive Scoring Runs:*** 24 from 1.9.1894.

***Successive Non-scoring Runs:*** 6 from 11.1.1969.

## TEN YEAR LEAGUE RECORD

| | | P | W | D | L | F | A | Pts | Pos |
|---|---|---|---|---|---|---|---|---|---|
| 1994-95 | Div 3 | 42 | 23 | 11 | 8 | 73 | 36 | 80 | 4 |
| 1995-96 | Div 3 | 46 | 22 | 13 | 11 | 66 | 48 | 79 | 3 |
| 1996-97 | Div 2 | 46 | 24 | 12 | 10 | 62 | 38 | 84 | 1 |
| 1997-98 | Div 1 | 46 | 11 | 19 | 16 | 42 | 58 | 52 | 17 |
| 1998-99 | Div 1 | 46 | 10 | 17 | 19 | 35 | 60 | 47 | 22 |
| 1999-2000 | Div 2 | 46 | 13 | 18 | 15 | 61 | 64 | 57 | 15 |
| 2000-01 | Div 2 | 46 | 16 | 10 | 20 | 45 | 59 | 58 | 16 |
| 2001-02 | Div 2 | 46 | 11 | 11 | 24 | 43 | 75 | 44 | 22 |
| 2002-03 | Div 3 | 46 | 18 | 16 | 12 | 57 | 56 | 70 | 7 |
| 2003-04 | Div 3 | 46 | 15 | 11 | 20 | 54 | 64 | 56 | 12 |

## DID YOU KNOW ?

In June 1947 Bury went on tour to Denmark and recorded victories over Esbjerg 2-0, Aarhus 3-0 and Aalborg 5-2 before losing to a strong Danish representative XI 5-4. Ten years earlier they had won all three matches in the same country.

## BURY 2003–04 LEAGUE RECORD

| *Match No.* | *Date* | *Venue* | *Opponents* | *Result* | | *H/T Score* | *Lg. Pos.* | *Goalscorers* | *Attendance* |
|---|---|---|---|---|---|---|---|---|---|
| 1 | Aug 9 | A | Swansea C | L | 2-4 | 1-1 | — | Preece [20], Connell [85] | 8826 |
| 2 | 16 | H | Scunthorpe U | L | 2-3 | 1-1 | 21 | Porter [45], Preece [76] | 2761 |
| 3 | 23 | A | Kidderminster H | W | 2-0 | 1-0 | 14 | Porter [28], Seddon [88] | 2548 |
| 4 | 25 | H | Lincoln C | W | 2-1 | 0-1 | 10 | Unsworth [81], Preece (pen) [90] | 2576 |
| 5 | 30 | A | Southend U | L | 0-1 | 0-0 | 17 | | 3172 |
| 6 | Sept 6 | H | Huddersfield T | W | 2-1 | 1-0 | 11 | Swailes [24], Connell [83] | 4591 |
| 7 | 13 | H | Cheltenham T | D | 1-1 | 1-0 | 11 | Preece (pen) [35] | 2753 |
| 8 | 16 | A | Mansfield T | L | 3-5 | 1-3 | — | Connell 2 [21, 78], Seddon [58] | 4145 |
| 9 | 20 | A | Boston U | L | 0-1 | 0-0 | 18 | | 2260 |
| 10 | 27 | H | Doncaster R | L | 1-3 | 1-2 | 18 | Preece (pen) [28] | 3606 |
| 11 | 30 | H | York C | W | 2-0 | 1-0 | — | Porter [37], O'Neill [71] | 2282 |
| 12 | Oct 4 | A | Torquay U | L | 1-3 | 1-1 | 18 | Porter [38] | 2732 |
| 13 | 11 | A | Cambridge U | W | 2-1 | 2-0 | 14 | Connell [32], Porter [39] | 5106 |
| 14 | 18 | H | Oxford U | L | 0-4 | 0-1 | 17 | | 2930 |
| 15 | 21 | H | Hull C | D | 0-0 | 0-0 | — | | 3896 |
| 16 | 25 | A | Darlington | W | 3-1 | 1-1 | 16 | Seddon [35], Connell [56], Singh [82] | 3516 |
| 17 | Nov 1 | H | Yeovil T | W | 2-1 | 1-1 | 13 | O'Shaughnessy [35], Unsworth [88] | 3086 |
| 18 | 15 | A | Bristol R | W | 2-1 | 0-0 | 12 | Barrett (og) [70], O'Neill [90] | 7019 |
| 19 | 22 | H | Northampton T | W | 1-0 | 0-0 | 11 | O'Neill [72] | 2683 |
| 20 | 29 | A | Macclesfield T | L | 0-1 | 0-1 | 12 | | 2312 |
| 21 | Dec 6 | A | Hull C | L | 0-2 | 0-1 | 12 | | 11,308 |
| 22 | 13 | H | Rochdale | L | 1-2 | 0-1 | 12 | Dunfield [49] | 3646 |
| 23 | 20 | A | Leyton Orient | L | 0-2 | 0-0 | 14 | | 3475 |
| 24 | 26 | H | Carlisle U | L | 1-3 | 1-1 | 14 | Porter (pen) [30] | 3345 |
| 25 | 28 | A | Huddersfield T | L | 0-1 | 0-1 | 17 | | 10,217 |
| 26 | Jan 3 | A | Lincoln C | L | 1-2 | 0-2 | 18 | Porter [90] | 3870 |
| 27 | 10 | H | Swansea C | W | 2-0 | 0-0 | 13 | Swailes [62], Daly [86] | 2799 |
| 28 | 17 | A | Scunthorpe U | D | 0-0 | 0-0 | 15 | | 3869 |
| 29 | 24 | H | Kidderminster H | D | 0-0 | 0-0 | 14 | | 2526 |
| 30 | Feb 7 | A | Carlisle U | L | 1-2 | 1-1 | 18 | Seddon [25] | 4954 |
| 31 | 14 | H | Cambridge U | W | 1-0 | 1-0 | 14 | Seddon [2] | 2322 |
| 32 | 21 | A | Oxford U | D | 1-1 | 0-0 | 16 | Dunfield [47] | 6473 |
| 33 | 24 | H | Southend U | D | 1-1 | 0-1 | — | Seddon [90] | 1670 |
| 34 | 28 | H | Darlington | D | 1-1 | 0-1 | 13 | Barrass [57] | 2766 |
| 35 | Mar 6 | H | Leyton Orient | D | 1-1 | 0-0 | 14 | Seddon [63] | 2355 |
| 36 | 13 | A | Rochdale | D | 0-0 | 0-0 | 14 | | 4225 |
| 37 | 16 | H | Mansfield T | W | 3-0 | 2-0 | — | Seddon 2 [26, 60], Swailes (pen) [43] | 2199 |
| 38 | 20 | A | Cheltenham T | W | 2-1 | 0-1 | 11 | Swailes [74], Porter [82] | 3435 |
| 39 | 27 | H | Boston U | L | 1-3 | 1-2 | 12 | Swailes (pen) [13] | 2693 |
| 40 | Apr 3 | A | Doncaster R | L | 1-3 | 0-0 | 14 | Singh [88] | 6221 |
| 41 | 9 | H | Torquay U | W | 2-1 | 1-1 | — | Seddon [35], Nugent [67] | 2770 |
| 42 | 13 | A | York C | D | 1-1 | 1-1 | — | Seddon [16] | 3111 |
| 43 | 17 | A | Yeovil T | L | 1-2 | 1-0 | 14 | Nugent [35] | 5172 |
| 44 | 24 | H | Bristol R | D | 0-0 | 0-0 | 13 | | 2683 |
| 45 | May 1 | A | Northampton T | L | 2-3 | 2-1 | 15 | Cartledge [10], Nugent [45] | 6179 |
| 46 | 8 | H | Macclesfield T | W | 2-0 | 0-0 | 12 | Porter [85], Whaley [90] | 3569 |

**Final League Position: 12**

### GOALSCORERS

*League (54):* Seddon 11, Porter 9 (1 pen), Connell 6, Preece 5 (3 pens), Swailes 5 (2 pens), Nugent 3, O'Neill 3, Dunfield 2, Singh 2, Unsworth 2, Barrass 1, Cartledge 1, Daly 1, O'Shaughnessy 1, Whaley 1, own goal 1.
*Carling Cup (0).*
*FA Cup (1):* Porter 1.
*LDV Vans Trophy (2):* Preece 1, Thompson 1.

| Garner G 46 | Unsworth L 27 | Woodthorpe C 39 | Clegg G 4 + 2 | Swailes D 42 | Strong G 10 | Duxbury L 36 + 1 | Nugent D 20 + 6 | Porter C 19 + 18 | Preece A 10 + 4 | Singh H 20 + 8 | Barrass M 19 + 3 | Connell L 23 + 5 | Seddon G 28 + 12 | Charnock P 3 | O'Shaughnessy P 21 + 6 | Gunby S 1 + 4 | Thornley B 5 | O'Neill J 10 + 13 | Whaley S 3 + 7 | Kennedy T 22 + 5 | Whelan G 13 | Dunfield T 28 + 2 | Gulliver P 10 | Thompson J 1 | Daly J 7 | Challinor D 15 | Cartledge J 7 + 4 | Flitcroft D 17 | Match No. |
|---|---|---|---|---|---|---|---|---|---|---|---|---|---|---|---|---|---|---|---|---|---|---|---|---|---|---|---|---|---|
| 1 | $2^{1}$ | 3 | $4^{2}$ | 5 | 6 | 7 | 8 | 9 | $10^{3}$ | 11 | 12 | 13 | 14 | | | | | | | | | | | | | | | | 1 |
| 1 | 2 | 3 | $4^{1}$ | 5 | 6 | 7 | 12 | $9^{2}$ | 10 | 11 | | 8 | 13 | | | | | | | | | | | | | | | | 2 |
| 1 | 2 | 3 | | 5 | 6 | $8^{3}$ | | $9^{2}$ | 10 | 11 | 12 | | 13 | $4^{1}$ | 7 | 14 | | | | | | | | | | | | | 3 |
| 1 | 2 | 3 | | 5 | 6 | 8 | 9 | | 10 | 11 | | | 12 | $4^{1}$ | 7 | | | | | | | | | | | | | | 4 |
| 1 | 2 | 3 | | 5 | 6 | 8 | 9 | | 10 | 11 | | | 12 | $4^{1}$ | 7 | | | | | | | | | | | | | | 5 |
| 1 | 2 | 3 | | 5 | 6 | 8 | $9^{3}$ | | 10 | $7^{2}$ | | 12 | | | $4^{1}$ | | 11 | 14 | 13 | | | | | | | | | | 6 |
| 1 | 2 | 3 | | 5 | 6 | 8 | $9^{2}$ | 12 | 10 | $11^{3}$ | | 14 | 13 | | $4^{1}$ | | 7 | | | | | | | | | | | | 7 |
| 1 | 2 | $3^{3}$ | | 5 | 6 | $8^{2}$ | | 12 | $9^{1}$ | 11 | | 10 | 13 | | 4 | | 7 | | | 14 | | | | | | | | | 8 |
| 1 | 2 | 3 | | 5 | 6 | $8^{3}$ | | 12 | | 13 | | 10 | 7 | | $4^{1}$ | 14 | 11 | $9^{2}$ | | | | | | | | | | | 9 |
| 1 | 2 | 3 | | 5 | $6^{1}$ | 12 | | 13 | 9 | $11^{2}$ | | 8 | $10^{3}$ | | 4 | | 7 | 14 | | | | | | | | | | | 10 |
| 1 | | 3 | | 5 | | 2 | | 9 | | 11 | | 7 | $10^{2}$ | | 4 | | | 13 | 12 | | 6 | $8^{1}$ | | | | | | | 11 |
| 1 | 2▪ | 5 | | | | 4 | | 9 | | 11 | | 7 | $10^{1}$ | | | 3 | | 13 | 12 | | 6 | $8^{2}$ | | | | | | | 12 |
| 1 | 3 | 6 | | 5 | | 8 | | $9^{2}$ | 12 | $11^{3}$ | | 7 | 13 | | 4 | 14 | | $10^{1}$ | | | | | 2 | | | | | | 13 |
| 1 | | | | 5 | | $7^{1}$ | | | 12 | 3 | | 2 | 10 | | 11 | | | 9 | | | 6 | 8 | 4 | | | | | | 14 |
| 1 | 3 | | | 5 | | 6 | 9 | | | 11 | | 2 | 10 | | 8 | | | | | | 7 | | 4 | | | | | | 15 |
| 1 | 2 | | | 5 | | 6 | 9 | | | 11 | | 7 | $10^{1}$ | | 8 | | | 12 | | | 3 | | 4 | | | | | | 16 |
| 1 | 3 | | | 5 | | 4 | $9^{1}$ | | | 11 | | 2 | 10 | | 7 | | | 12 | | | 8 | | 6 | | | | | | 17 |
| 1 | 2 | 3 | | 5 | | 6 | | $9^{1}$ | 10 | | | 7 | | | | | | 11 | 12 | | 8 | | 4 | | | | | | 18 |
| 1 | 2 | 3 | | 5 | | 6 | | 9 | 12 | | | 7 | $10^{1}$ | | | | | 11 | | | | 8 | 4 | | | | | | 19 |
| 1 | 2 | 3 | | 5 | | $6^{2}$ | | $9^{1}$ | 12 | | | 7 | 10 | | | | | 11 | | 13 | | 8 | 4 | | | | | | 20 |
| 1 | 2 | 3 | | 5 | | $6^{2}$ | | 12 | | | | 7 | $10^{1}$ | | 11 | | | 9 | | 13 | | 8 | 4 | | | | | | 21 |
| 1 | $2^{1}$ | | $3^{3}$ | 5 | | | | 12 | | | 6 | 11 | 10 | | $7^{2}$ | 13 | | 9 | | 14 | | 8 | 4 | | | | | | 22 |
| 1 | | 6 | | 5 | | $4^{3}$ | 12 | $9^{2}$ | | | 2 | 3 | 13 | | 7 | | | 10 | | 14 | | 8 | | $11^{1}$ | | | | | 23 |
| 1 | 4 | 3 | 12 | 5 | | | | 9 | | | $2^{1}$ | 13 | 14 | | 7 | | | $10^{3}$ | | 11 | 6 | $8^{2}$ | | | | | | | 24 |
| 1 | | 6 | | 5 | | 7 | 12 | $9^{1}$ | | | 2 | 3 | 10 | | | | | | | 11 | 4 | 8 | | | | | | | 25 |
| 1 | 6 | 3 | $11^{1}$ | 5 | | 4 | | 12 | | | 2 | | 10 | | | | | | | | 7 | 8 | | | 9 | | | | 26 |
| 1 | | 3 | | 5 | | 6 | | $9^{3}$ | | | | 2 | 12 | | 13 | | | 14 | | 11 | 7 | $8^{2}$ | | | $10^{1}$ | 4 | | | 27 |
| 1 | | 3 | | 5 | | 6 | | $9^{1}$ | | | | 2 | | | | | | 12 | | 11 | 7 | 8 | | | 10 | 4 | | | 28 |
| 1 | | 3 | | 5 | | 6 | | $9^{1}$ | | | $2^{2}$ | 7 | 12 | | | | | 13 | | 11 | 8 | | | | 10 | 4 | | | 29 |
| 1 | | | | 5 | | 6 | | 12 | | 13 | | $2^{1}$ | 10 | | | | | | | 11 | | $8^{2}$ | | | 9 | 4 | 3 | 7 | 30 |
| 1 | | | | 5 | | 6 | | | | | | $2^{3}$ | 10 | | 12 | | | 13 | 14 | 11 | | $8^{2}$ | | | 9 | 4 | 3 | $7^{1}$ | 31 |
| 1 | 2 | 3 | | 5 | | 6 | 12 | | | | | 13 | $10^{1}$ | | | | | | | 11 | | $8^{2}$ | | | 9▪ | 4 | | 7 | 32 |
| 1 | $2^{1}$ | 3 | | 5 | | 6 | 13 | 9 | | | 12 | | 10 | | | | | | | 11 | | 8 | | | | 4 | | $7^{2}$ | 33 |
| 1 | | 3 | 13 | 5 | | | 12 | 9 | | | 2 | | $10^{2}$ | | 6 | | | | | 11 | | 8 | | | | 4 | | $7^{1}$ | 34 |
| 1 | | 3 | | 5 | | 6 | 9 | 13 | | 12 | 2 | | $10^{2}$ | | | | | | | 11 | | $8^{1}$ | | | | 4 | | 7 | 35 |
| 1 | | 3 | | 5 | | 6 | 9 | 12 | | | 2 | | $10^{1}$ | | | | | | | 11 | | 8 | | | | 4 | | 7 | 36 |
| 1 | | 3 | | 5 | | 6 | $9^{2}$ | 12 | | 13 | 2 | | $10^{1}$ | | | | | | | $11^{3}$ | | 8 | | | | 4 | 14 | 7 | 37 |
| 1 | | 3 | | 5 | | 6 | $9^{3}$ | 12 | | 13 | 2 | | $10^{1}$ | | | | | | | 11 | | $8^{2}$ | | | | 4 | 14 | 7 | 38 |
| 1 | | $3^{3}$ | | 5 | | $6^{1}$ | 9 | 13 | | 12 | 2 | | $10^{2}$ | | | | | | | 11 | | 8 | | | | 4 | 14 | 7 | 39 |
| 1 | | 3 | | 5 | | $6^{2}$ | 9 | 12 | | 10 | 2 | | | | 13 | | | | | $11^{3}$ | | $8^{1}$ | | | | 4 | 14 | 7 | 40 |
| 1 | | 3 | | 5 | | | $9^{1}$ | 12 | | 8 | 2 | | $10^{2}$ | | 13 | | | | | 11 | | 6 | | | | 4 | | 7 | 41 |
| 1 | | 3 | | 5 | | | 9 | 12 | | $7^{3}$ | 2 | | $10^{1}$ | | 14 | | | | 13 | 11 | | 8 | | | | | $4^{2}$ | 6 | 42 |
| 1 | | 6 | | $5^{3}$ | | | 9 | 12 | | 7 | 2 | | $10^{1}$ | | 13 | | | | 14 | 11 | | $8^{2}$ | | | | | 3 | 4 | 43 |
| 1 | 5 | 6 | | | | | 10 | $9^{2}$ | | | 2 | | | | $7^{1}$ | | | 13 | 4 | 11 | | 12 | | | | | 3 | 8 | 44 |
| 1 | 5 | 6 | | | | | 10 | $9^{3}$ | | 13 | 2 | | | | $7^{1}$ | | | 14 | 4 | 11 | | 12 | | | | | 3 | $8^{2}$ | 45 |
| 1 | 5 | 6 | | | | | $9^{3}$ | 12 | | 13 | 2 | | $10^{1}$ | | | | | 14 | 4 | 11 | | $8^{2}$ | | | | | 3 | 7 | 46 |

**Carling Cup**
First Round — Tranmere R — (a) — 0-1

**LDV Vans Trophy**
Second Round — Oldham Ath — (h) — 2-1
Quarter-Final — Scunthorpe U — (h) — 0-1

**FA Cup**
First Round — Rochdale — (h) — 1-2

# CAMBRIDGE UNITED FL Championship 2

## FOUNDATION

The football revival in Cambridge began soon after World War II when the Abbey United club (formed 1912) decided to turn professional in 1949. In 1951 they changed their name to Cambridge United. They were competing in the United Counties League before graduating to the Eastern Counties League in 1951 and the Southern League in 1958.

***Abbey Stadium, Newmarket Road, Cambridge CB5 8LN.***

***Telephone:*** (01223) 566 500.

***Fax:*** (01223) 566 502.

***Website:*** www.cambridge-united.co.uk

***Email:*** web@cambridge-united.co.uk

***Ground Capacity:*** 9,217.

***Record Attendance:*** 14,000 v Chelsea, Friendly, 1 May 1970.

***Pitch Measurements:*** 110yd × 74yd.

***Chairman:*** G. Harwood.

***Vice-chairman:*** R. Hunt.

***Secretary:*** A. Pincher.

***Manager:*** Herve Renard.

***Assistant Manager:*** Dale Brooks.

***Physio:*** Anthony Cooke.

***Colours:*** Amber shirts, black shorts, amber stockings.

***Change Colours:*** All white with mid-blue trim.

***Year Formed:*** 1912.

***Turned Professional:*** 1949.

***Ltd Co.:*** 1948.

***Previous Name:*** 1919, Abbey United; 1951, Cambridge United.

***Club Nickname:*** The 'U's'.

***First Football League Game:*** 15 August 1970, Division 4, v Lincoln C (h) D 1–1 – Roberts; Thompson, Meldrum (1), Slack, Eades, Hardy, Leggett, Cassidy, Lindsey, McKinven, Harris.

***Record League Victory:*** 6–0 v Darlington, Division 4, 18 September 1971 – Roberts; Thompson, Akers, Guild, Eades, Foote, Collins (1p), Horrey, Hollett, Greenhalgh (4), Phillips, (1 og). 6–0 v Hartlepool U, Division 4, 11 February 1989 – Vaughan; Beck, Kimble, Turner, Chapple (1), Daish, Clayton, Holmes, Taylor (3 incl. 1p), Bull (1), Leadbitter (1).

## HONOURS

*Football League:* Division 2 best season: 5th, 1991–92; Division 3 – Champions 1990–91; Runners-up 1977–78, 1998–99; Division 4 – Champions 1976–77; Promoted from Division 4 1989–90 (play-offs).

*FA Cup:* best season: 6th rd, 1990 (shared record for Fourth Division club), 1991.

*Football League Cup:* best season: 5th rd, 1993.

*LDV Vans Trophy:* Runners-up 2002.

## SKY SPORTS FACT FILE

In 1927–28 when still known as Abbey United, the club hit their highest score in defeating Godmanchester 14-1 in the Chatteris Engineering Works Cup. The score was all the more amazing as they played for 75 minutes with ten men through injury.

***Record Cup Victory:*** 5–1 v Bristol C, FA Cup 5th rd second replay, 27 February 1990 – Vaughan; Fensome, Kimble, Bailie (O'Shea), Chapple, Daish, Cheetham (Robinson), Leadbitter (1), Dublin (2), Taylor (1), Philpott (1).

***Record Defeat:*** 0–7 v Sunderland, League Cup 2nd rd, 1 October 2002.

***Most League Points (2 for a win):*** 65, Division 4, 1976–77.

***Most League Points (3 for a win):*** 86, Division 3, 1990–91.

***Most League Goals:*** 87, Division 4, 1976–77.

***Highest League Scorer in Season:*** David Crown, 24, Division 4, 1985–86.

***Most League Goals in Total Aggregate:*** John Taylor, 86, 1988–92; 1996–2001.

***Most League Goals in One Match:*** 5, Steve Butler v Exeter C, Division 2, 4 April 1994.

***Most Capped Player:*** Tom Finney, 7 (15), Northern Ireland.

***Most League Appearances:*** Steve Spriggs, 416, 1975–87.

***Youngest League Player:*** Andy Sinton, 16 years 228 days v Wolverhampton W, 2 November 1982.

***Record Transfer Fee Received:*** £1,000,000 from Manchester U for Dion Dublin, August 1992 and £1,000,000 from Leicester C for Trevor Benjamin, July 2000.

***Record Transfer Fee Paid:*** £192,000 to Luton T for Steve Claridge, November 1992.

***Football League Record:*** 1970 Elected to Division 4; 1973–74 Division 3; 1974–77 Division 4; 1977–78 Division 3; 1978–84 Division 2; 1984–85 Division 3; 1985–90 Division 4; 1990–91 Division 3; 1991–92 Division 2; 1992–93 Division 1; 1993–95 Division 2; 1995–99 Division 3; 1999– 2002 Division 2; 2002–04 Division 3; 2004– FL2.

## MANAGERS

Bill Whittaker 1949–55
Gerald Williams 1955
Bert Johnson 1955–59
Bill Craig 1959–60
Alan Moore 1960–63
Roy Kirk 1964–66
Bill Leivers 1967–74
Ron Atkinson 1974–78
John Docherty 1978–83
John Ryan 1984–85
Ken Shellito 1985
Chris Turner 1985–90
John Beck 1990–92
Ian Atkins 1992–93
Gary Johnson 1993–95
Tommy Taylor 1995–96
Roy McFarland 1996–2001
John Beck 2001
John Taylor 2002–04
Claude Le Roy 2004
Herve Renard March 2004–

## LATEST SEQUENCES

***Longest Sequence of League Wins:*** 7, 19.2.1977 – 1.4.1977.

***Longest Sequence of League Defeats:*** 7, 8.4.1985 – 30.4.1985.

***Longest Sequence of League Draws:*** 6, 6.9.1986 – 30.9.1986.

***Longest Sequence of Unbeaten League Matches:*** 14, 9.9.1972 – 10.11.1972.

***Longest Sequence Without a League Win:*** 31, 8.10.1983 – 23.4.1984.

***Successive Scoring Runs:*** 26 from 9.4.2002.

***Successive Non-scoring Runs:*** 5 from 29.9.1973.

## TEN YEAR LEAGUE RECORD

| | | P | W | D | L | F | A | Pts | Pos |
|---|---|---|---|---|---|---|---|---|---|
| 1994-95 | Div 2 | 46 | 11 | 15 | 20 | 52 | 69 | 48 | 20 |
| 1995-96 | Div 3 | 46 | 14 | 12 | 20 | 61 | 71 | 54 | 16 |
| 1996-97 | Div 3 | 46 | 18 | 11 | 17 | 53 | 59 | 65 | 10 |
| 1997-98 | Div 3 | 46 | 14 | 18 | 14 | 63 | 57 | 60 | 16 |
| 1998-99 | Div 3 | 46 | 23 | 12 | 11 | 78 | 48 | 81 | 2 |
| 1999-2000 | Div 2 | 46 | 12 | 12 | 22 | 64 | 65 | 48 | 19 |
| 2000-01 | Div 2 | 46 | 14 | 11 | 21 | 61 | 77 | 53 | 19 |
| 2001-02 | Div 2 | 46 | 7 | 13 | 26 | 47 | 93 | 34 | 24 |
| 2002-03 | Div 3 | 46 | 16 | 13 | 17 | 67 | 70 | 61 | 12 |
| 2003-04 | Div 3 | 46 | 14 | 14 | 18 | 55 | 67 | 56 | 13 |

## DID YOU KNOW ?

When Cambridge United beat Derby County 3-0 on the opening day of the 1980–81 season, it was their best starting result since entering the League. In addition the crowd of 9,558 was better than any home game of the previous season.

## CAMBRIDGE UNITED 2003–04 LEAGUE RECORD

| *Match No.* | *Date* | *Venue* | *Opponents* | *Result* | | *H/T Score* | *Lg. Pos.* | *Goalscorers* | *Attendance* |
|---|---|---|---|---|---|---|---|---|---|
| 1 | Aug 9 | A | Huddersfield T | D | 2-2 | 1-1 | — | Chillingworth [18], Kitson [89] | 10,319 |
| 2 | 16 | H | Macclesfield T | W | 3-1 | 1-0 | 8 | Chillingworth 2 [10, 63], Revell [89] | 3089 |
| 3 | 23 | A | Rochdale | D | 2-2 | 2-0 | 9 | Revell [32], Kitson [38] | 2204 |
| 4 | 25 | H | Hull C | L | 0-2 | 0-2 | 12 | | 4571 |
| 5 | 30 | A | Carlisle U | D | 0-0 | 0-0 | 15 | | 4571 |
| 6 | Sept 3 | H | Lincoln C | D | 0-0 | 0-0 | — | | 4458 |
| 7 | 13 | H | Torquay U | D | 1-1 | 1-1 | 17 | Guttridge [9] | 3723 |
| 8 | 17 | A | Boston U | W | 2-1 | 1-0 | — | Guttridge [41], Angus [88] | 2452 |
| 9 | 20 | A | Cheltenham T | W | 3-0 | 1-0 | 8 | Kitson 2 [30, 60], Opara [87] | 3728 |
| 10 | 27 | H | Mansfield T | L | 1-2 | 0-1 | 10 | Fleming [81] | 4068 |
| 11 | 30 | H | Doncaster R | D | 3-3 | 2-0 | — | Tudor [9], Kitson 2 [36, 55] | 3492 |
| 12 | Oct 4 | A | York C | L | 0-2 | 0-1 | 14 | | 3481 |
| 13 | 11 | H | Bury | L | 1-2 | 0-2 | 15 | Duncan [80] | 5106 |
| 14 | 18 | A | Bristol R | W | 2-0 | 0-0 | 13 | Turner [68], Walker [77] | 6440 |
| 15 | 21 | A | Swansea C | W | 2-0 | 1-0 | — | Kitson 2 [1, 59] | 6211 |
| 16 | 25 | H | Yeovil T | L | 1-4 | 1-1 | 13 | Kitson [44] | 4072 |
| 17 | Nov 1 | A | Kidderminster H | D | 2-2 | 0-1 | 14 | Kitson [59], Williams [63] | 2401 |
| 18 | 15 | H | Oxford U | D | 1-1 | 1-0 | 14 | Duncan [21] | 4430 |
| 19 | 22 | A | Scunthorpe U | L | 0-4 | 0-2 | 14 | | 3397 |
| 20 | 29 | H | Leyton Orient | L | 1-4 | 0-3 | 16 | Turner [83] | 3910 |
| 21 | Dec 13 | H | Darlington | W | 1-0 | 1-0 | 14 | Guttridge (pen) [45] | 2822 |
| 22 | 19 | A | Northampton T | W | 2-1 | 1-0 | — | Guttridge (pen) [28], Tann [88] | 4910 |
| 23 | 26 | H | Southend U | L | 0-1 | 0-1 | 13 | | 5368 |
| 24 | 28 | A | Lincoln C | D | 2-2 | 1-2 | 12 | Guttridge [14], Webb [88] | 5074 |
| 25 | Jan 3 | A | Hull C | L | 0-2 | 0-1 | 13 | | 14,271 |
| 26 | 10 | H | Huddersfield T | L | 1-2 | 0-1 | 16 | Tann [90] | 3667 |
| 27 | 17 | A | Macclesfield T | W | 1-0 | 0-0 | 13 | Guttridge [49] | 2151 |
| 28 | 24 | H | Rochdale | D | 0-0 | 0-0 | 13 | | 3221 |
| 29 | Feb 7 | A | Southend U | L | 0-1 | 0-1 | 17 | | 4289 |
| 30 | 14 | A | Bury | L | 0-1 | 0-1 | 18 | | 2322 |
| 31 | 17 | H | Carlisle U | D | 2-2 | 0-1 | — | Bridges [53], Guttridge [56] | 3280 |
| 32 | 21 | H | Bristol R | W | 3-1 | 2-1 | 15 | Revell [13], Guttridge [25], Bridges [51] | 3256 |
| 33 | 28 | A | Yeovil T | L | 1-4 | 1-3 | 17 | Webb [45] | 5694 |
| 34 | Mar 2 | H | Swansea C | L | 0-1 | 0-1 | — | | 2713 |
| 35 | 6 | H | Northampton T | L | 0-1 | 0-0 | 21 | | 4298 |
| 36 | 13 | A | Darlington | W | 4-3 | 2-1 | 18 | Easter 2 [30, 65], Webb [41], Guttridge [81] | 5056 |
| 37 | 16 | H | Boston U | L | 0-1 | 0-1 | — | | 3294 |
| 38 | 20 | A | Torquay U | L | 0-3 | 0-2 | 22 | | 2975 |
| 39 | 27 | H | Cheltenham T | W | 2-1 | 2-0 | 19 | Turner [5], Tudor (pen) [10] | 3909 |
| 40 | Apr 3 | A | Mansfield T | D | 1-1 | 0-0 | 19 | Tudor [90] | 4342 |
| 41 | 9 | H | York C | W | 2-0 | 1-0 | — | Guttridge [24], Dunning (og) [86] | 5120 |
| 42 | 12 | A | Doncaster R | L | 0-2 | 0-0 | 19 | | 9644 |
| 43 | 17 | H | Kidderminster H | D | 0-0 | 0-0 | 20 | | 3765 |
| 44 | 24 | A | Oxford U | D | 2-2 | 0-0 | 18 | Chillingworth 2 [72, 87] | 5830 |
| 45 | May 1 | H | Scunthorpe U | W | 3-2 | 2-0 | 16 | Nicholls [37], Chillingworth 2 [39, 77] | 4498 |
| 46 | 8 | A | Leyton Orient | W | 1-0 | 1-0 | 13 | Guttridge [8] | 5482 |

**Final League Position: 13**

## GOALSCORERS

*League (55):* Guttridge 11 (2 pens), Kitson 10, Chillingworth 7, Revell 3, Tudor 3 (1 pen), Turner 3, Webb 3, Bridges 2, Duncan 2, Easter 2, Tann 2, Angus 1, Fleming 1, Nicholls 1, Opara 1, Walker 1, Williams 1, own goal 1.
*Carling Cup (1):* Walker 1.
*FA Cup (5):* Turner 2, Guttridge 1, Kitson 1, Tann 1.
*LDV Vans Trophy (0).*

| Marshall S 45 | Murray F 34 + 4 | Bimson S 21 + 3 | Tann A 31 + 3 | Angus S 39 + 1 | Venus M 21 | Tudor S 30 + 6 | Guttridge L 46 | Kitson D 17 | Chillingworth D 10 + 3 | Walker J 23 | Revell A 10 + 10 | Nacca F 2 + 7 | Turner J 17 + 19 | Fleming T 17 + 1 | Opara L 1 + 7 | Duncan A 37 | Goodhind W 25 + 1 | Taylor J 6 + 3 | Bridges D 11 + 10 | Williams G 4 | Gleeson D 3 + 4 | Dutton B — + 3 | Webb D 19 + 2 | Peat N 3 + 3 | McCafferty N 5 + 1 | Lockett R 1 + 1 | Easter J 10 + 5 | Nicholls A 15 + 1 | Robinson M 1 + 2 | Clarke C — + 1 | Fuller A — + 1 | Smith S 1 + 1 | Daniels D — + 1 | Ruddy J 1 | Quinton D — + 1 | *Match No.* |
|---|---|---|---|---|---|---|---|---|---|---|---|---|---|---|---|---|---|---|---|---|---|---|---|---|---|---|---|---|---|---|---|---|---|---|---|---|
|1|2|3|4|5|6|$7^1$|8|$9^2$|$10^3$|11|12|13|14| | | | | | | | | | | | | | | | | | | | | | |1|
|1|$2^2$|3|4|5|6|$7^1$|8|9|$10^3$|11|12|13|14| | | | | | | | | | | | | | | | | | | | | | |2|
|1|3| |4|5|6|$7^1$|8|9| |$11^2$|$10^3$|12|14|2|13| | | | | | | | | | | | | | | | | | | | |3|
|1|$2^1$|3|4|5|6|12|8|9| |11|$10^2$| |13|7| | | | | | | | | | | | | | | | | | | | | |4|
|1| |3| |5|6|12|8|9|$10^1$|11|$7^2$| |13|2| |4| | | | | | | | | | | | | | | | | | | |5|
|1| |3| |5|6|12|8|9|$10^1$|11|$7^2$| |13|2| |4| | | | | | | | | | | | | | | | | | | |6|
|1|13|3| |5■|6|$12^2$|8|9|$10^1$|11|$7^3$| |14|2| |4| | | | | | | | | | | | | | | | | | | |7|
|1|2|3| |5|6| |8|9|$10^2$|$11^1$| |12|13|7| |4| | | | | | | | | | | | | | | | | | | |8|
|1|$2^2$|3| |5|6| |8|$9^3$| |11| |12|$10^1$|7|13|4|14| | | | | | | | | | | | | | | | | | |9|
|1|$7^1$|$3^2$| | |6|12|8|9■| |11| | |10|4|13|5|2| | | | | | | | | | | | | | | | | | |10|
|1|12|$3^1$|13|2|$6^2$|7|8|9| |$11^3$| | |10|4|14|5| | | | | | | | | | | | | | | | | | | |11|
|1| |$3^2$| |2|6|7|8|9| |11| | |$10^1$|4|12|5| |13| | | | | | | | | | | | | | | | | |12|
|1| |3| |$2^2$|6|7|8| |$10^1$|11| | |12|4|9|5| |13| | | | | | | | | | | | | | | | | |13|
|1|12|3| |5|6|$7^1$|8| | |11| | |$10^2$|2|13|4| |9| | | | | | | | | | | | | | | | | |14|
|1|12|3| |5|6|$7^3$|$8^1$|9| |11| | | |2|13|4| |$10^2$|14| | | | | | | | | | | | | | | | |15|
|1| |3|12|$5^1$|6|7|$8^3$|9| |11| | |13|2| |4| |$10^2$|14| | | | | | | | | | | | | | | | |16|
|1| |3|12|5| | |$8^1$|9| |11| | |13|7| |4|2■| |$6^2$|$10^3$|14| | | | | | | | | | | | | | |17|
|1|$11^1$|3|2|5| |$7^3$|8|9| | | |12|13|6| |4| | |14|$10^2$| | | | | | | | | | | | | | | |18|
|1|$11^3$|3|5|2| |7|8|$9^2$| | | |12| |6| |4| |14|13|$10^1$| | | | | | | | | | | | | | | |19|
|1|11|$3^1$|6|5| |7|8| | | | | |10|12| |4|2| | |$9^2$| |13| | | | | | | | | | | | | |20|
|1|3| |6|5| |11|$8^1$| | | | |7|$10^2$| | |4|2|9|12| | |13| | | | | | | | | | | | | |21|
|1|$11^1$| |3|5|6| |8| | | | |$7^2$|10| | |4|2| |12| |13| |9| | | | | | | | | | | | |22|
|1| | |6|5|3| |8| | | | | |10| | |4|2| |$7^2$| | |12|9|13|$11^1$| | | | | | | | | | |23|
|1|3| |6| |5| |8| | | | | |10| | |4|2|$11^2$|12| | | |9|13|$7^1$| | | | | | | | | | |24|
|1|10| |6|5|3| |8| | | | | | | | |4|2|$9^1$|7| | | | | |11|12| | | | | | | | | |25|
|1|$3^2$| |6| |5|11|8| | | |12| |$10^1$| | |4|2| | | | | |9|13|7| | | | | | | | | | |26|
|1|3| |6|5| |$7^2$|8| | | |12| |$10^1$| | |4|2| | | | | |9|11|13| | | | | | | | | | |27|
|1|3| |6|5| |7|8| | | |12| |$10^1$| | |4|2| | | | | |9|11| | | | | | | | | | | |28|
|1|3| | |5| |7|8| | | |12| |13| | |$4^1$|2| | | | | |9|11|6| |$10^2$| | | | | | | | |29|
|1|3| |6|$5^1$| | |8| | | |10| |12| | |4|2| |$7^2$| | | |9| | | |13|11| | | | | | | |30|
|1|3| |6|5| | |8| | | |$10^1$| |12| | |4|2| |7| | | |9| | | | |11| | | | | | | |31|
|1|3| |6|5| | |8| | | |$10^1$| | | | |4|2| |7| | | |9| | | |12|11| | | | | | | |32|
|1|3| |6|5| |14|8| | | |$10^1$| |12| | |4|2| |$7^2$| | | |9| | | |$13^3$|11| | | | | | | |33|
|1|3| |6|$5^3$| |$7^1$|8| | | |$10^2$| |12| | |4| | |2| |14| |9| | | |13|11| | | | | | | |34|
|1|3| |6| | |7|8| | | | | | | | |4| | |2| |5| |9| | | |10|11| | | | | | | |35|
|1|$3^1$| |6|12| |$11^3$|8| | | | | |13| | |4|2| |7| |5| |9| | | |$10^2$| |14| | | | | | |36|
|1|3| |6| | |$7^2$|8| | | |13| |12| | |4|2| | | |$5^1$| |9| | | |10|11| | | | | | | |37|
|1|3|12|6|5| |$4^1$|$8^3$| | | |13| |10| | | |2| |14| | | |9| | | |$7^2$|11| | | | | | | |38|
|1|3| |$5^1$| | |$7^3$|$8^2$| | |6|12| |10| | |4|2| |13| | | | | | | |9|11| |14| | | | | |39|
|1|7|3| |$5^2$| |11|8| | |6|12| | | | |4|2| | | | | | | | | | |9|13|$10^1$| | | | | | |40|
|1|3| |4|5| |7|8| |12| | | | | | | |2| |6| | | | | | |$10^1$|$9^2$|11| | |13| | | | |41|
|1|3| |$4^1$|5| |7|8| |12| | | |10| | | |2| |13| | | |14| | | |9|$11^2$| | | |$6^3$| | | |42|
|1|3| |4|5| |7|8| |12|6| | |$10^2$| | | |2| | | | | |13| | | |$9^1$|$11^3$|14| | | | | | |43|
|1|$3^1$|12|4|5| |7|8| |$10^2$|6| | | | | | |2| | | | | |9| | | | |11| | | |13| | | |44|
|1| |3|4|2| |$7^2$|8| |10|6| | | | | |$5^1$| | | | |12| |9| | | | |11| | | | |13| | |45|
| |3|12|4|2| |$7^1$|$8^3$| |$10^2$|6| | | | | |5| | | | | | |9| | | |13|11| | | | | |1|14|46|

**Carling Cup**
First Round | Gillingham | (h) | 1-2

**LDV Vans Trophy**
First Round | Wycombe W | (a) | 0-1

**FA Cup**
First Round | Lancaster C | (a) | 2-1
Second Round | Macclesfield T | (a) | 1-1
| | (h) | 2-2

# CARDIFF CITY FL Championship

## FOUNDATION

Credit for the establishment of a first class professional football club in such a rugby stronghold as Cardiff, is due to members of the Riverside club formed in 1899 out of a cricket club of that name. Cardiff became a city in 1905 and in 1908 the South Wales and Monmouthshire FA granted Riverside permission to call themselves Cardiff City. The club turned professional under that name in 1910.

***Ninian Park, Cardiff CF11 8SX.***

***Telephone:*** (029) 2022 1011.

***Fax:*** (029) 2034 1148.

***Ticket Office:*** 0845 345 1400.

***Website:*** www.cardiffcityfc.co.uk

***Email:*** info@cardiffcityfc.co.uk

***Ground Capacity:*** 21,508.

***Record Attendance:*** 62,634, Wales v England, 17 October 1959.

***Club Record Attendance:*** 57,893 v Arsenal, Division 1, 22 April 1953.

***Pitch Measurements:*** 110yd × 75yd.

***Owner:*** Sam Hammam.

***Vice-chairman:*** Steve Borley.

***Chief Executive:*** David Temme.

***Club Secretary:*** Jason Turner.

***Manager:*** Lennie Lawrence.

***Assistant Manager:*** Ian Butterworth.

***Physio:*** Clive Goodyear.

***Colours:*** All blue.

***Change Colours:*** All red.

***Year Formed:*** 1899.

***Turned Professional:*** 1910.

***Ltd Co.:*** 1910.

## HONOURS

*Football League:* Division 1 – Runners-up 1923–24; Division 2 – Runners-up 1920–21, 1951–52, 1959–60; Division 2 – 2002–03 (play-offs); Division 3 (S) – Champions 1946–47; Division 3 – Champions 1992–93. Runners-up 1975–76, 1982–83, 2000–01; Division 4 – Runners-up 1987–88.

*FA Cup:* Winners 1927 (only occasion the Cup has been won by a club outside England); Runners-up 1925.

*Football League Cup:* Semi-final 1966.

*Welsh Cup:* Winners 22 times (joint record).

*Charity Shield:* Winners 1927.

***European Competitions:*** *European Cup-Winners' Cup:* 1964–65, 1965–66, 1967–68 (semi-finalists), 1968–69, 1969–70, 1970–71, 1971–72, 1973–74, 1974–75, 1976–77, 1977–78, 1988–89, 1992–93, 1993–94.

***Previous Names:*** 1899, Riverside; 1902, Riverside Albion; 1908, Cardiff City.

***Club Nickname:*** 'Bluebirds'.

***Previous Grounds:*** Riverside, Sophia Gardens, Old Park and Fir Gardens. Moved to Ninian Park, 1910.

***First Football League Game:*** 28 August 1920, Division 2, v Stockport Co (a) W 5–2 – Kneeshaw; Brittan, Leyton; Keenor (1), Smith, Hardy; Grimshaw (1), Gill (2), Cashmore, West, Evans (1).

***Record League Victory:*** 9–2 v Thames, Division 3 (S), 6 February 1932 – Farquharson; E. L. Morris, Roberts; Galbraith, Harris, Ronan; Emmerson (1), Keating (1), Jones (1), McCambridge (1), Robbins (5).

## SKY SPORTS FACT FILE

In Cardiff City's first Cup-Winners' Cup venture in 1964–65, victory over Esbjerg was followed by a clash with Sporting Lisbon. In Portugal, City won 2-1 with goals by Greg Farrell and Derek Tapscott, sealing the tie with a goalless draw.

***Record Cup Victory:*** 8–0 v Enfield, FA Cup 1st rd, 28 November 1931 – Farquharson; Smith, Roberts; Harris (1), Galbraith, Ronan; Emmerson (2), Keating (3); O'Neill (2), Robbins, McCambridge.

***Record Defeat:*** 2–11 v Sheffield U, Division 1, 1 January 1926.

***Most League Points (2 for a win):*** 66, Division 3 (S), 1946–47.

***Most League Points (3 for a win):*** 86, Division 3, 1982–83.

***Most League Goals:*** 95, Division 3, 2000–01.

***Highest League Scorer in Season:*** Robert Earnshaw, 31, Division 2, 2002–03.

***Most League Goals in Total Aggregate:*** Len Davies, 128, 1920–31.

***Most League Goals in One Match:*** 5, Hugh Ferguson v Burnley, Division 1, 1 September 1928; 5, Walter Robbins v Thames, Division 3S, 6 February 1932; 5, William Henderson v Northampton T, Division 3S, 22 April 1933.

***Most Capped Player:*** Alf Sherwood, 39 (41), Wales.

***Most League Appearances:*** Phil Dwyer, 471, 1972–85.

***Youngest League Player:*** John Toshack, 16 years 236 days v Leyton Orient, 13 November 1965.

***Record Transfer Fee Received:*** £500,000 from Coventry C for Simon Haworth, June 1997.

***Record Transfer Fee Paid:*** £1,700,000 to Stoke C for Peter Thorne, September 2001.

***Football League Record:*** 1920 Elected to Division 2; 1921–29 Division 1; 1929–31 Division 2; 1931–47 Division 3 (S); 1947–52 Division 2; 1952–57 Division 1; 1957–60 Division 2; 1960–62 Division 1; 1962–75 Division 2; 1975–76 Division 3; 1976–82 Division 2; 1982–83 Division 3; 1983–85 Division 2; 1985–86 Division 3; 1986–88 Division 4; 1988–90 Division 3; 1990–92 Division 4; 1992–93 Division 3; 1993–95 Division 2; 1995–99 Division 3; 1999–2000 Division 2; 2000–01 Division 3; 2001–03 Division 2; 2003–04 Division 1; 2004– FLC.

## MANAGERS

Davy McDougall 1910–11
Fred Stewart 1911–33
Bartley Wilson 1933–34
B. Watts-Jones 1934–37
Bill Jennings 1937–39
Cyril Spiers 1939–46
Billy McCandless 1946–48
Cyril Spiers 1948–54
Trevor Morris 1954–58
Bill Jones 1958–62
George Swindin 1962–64
Jimmy Scoular 1964–73
Frank O'Farrell 1973–74
Jimmy Andrews 1974–78
Richie Morgan 1978–82
Len Ashurst 1982–84
Jimmy Goodfellow 1984
Alan Durban 1984–86
Frank Burrows 1986–89
Len Ashurst 1989–91
Eddie May 1991–94
Terry Yorath 1994–95
Eddie May 1995
Kenny Hibbitt *(Chief Coach)* 1995
Phil Neal 1996
Russell Osman 1996–97
Kenny Hibbitt 1996–98
Frank Burrows 1998–99
Billy Ayre 1999–2000
Bobby Gould 2000
Alan Cork 2000–02
Lennie Lawrence February 2002–

## LATEST SEQUENCES

***Longest Sequence of League Wins:*** 9, 26.10.1946 – 28.12.1946.

***Longest Sequence of League Defeats:*** 7, 4.11.1933 – 25.12.1933.

***Longest Sequence of League Draws:*** 6, 29.11.1980 – 17.1.1981.

***Longest Sequence of Unbeaten League Matches:*** 21, 21.9.1946 – 1.3.1947.

***Longest Sequence Without a League Win:*** 15, 21.11.1936 – 6.3.1937.

***Successive Scoring Runs:*** 23 from 24.10.1992.

***Successive Non-scoring Runs:*** 8 from 20.12.1952.

## TEN YEAR LEAGUE RECORD

| | | *P* | *W* | *D* | *L* | *F* | *A* | *Pts* | *Pos* |
|---|---|---|---|---|---|---|---|---|---|
| 1994-95 | Div 2 | 46 | 9 | 11 | 26 | 46 | 74 | 38 | 22 |
| 1995-96 | Div 3 | 46 | 11 | 12 | 23 | 41 | 64 | 45 | 22 |
| 1996-97 | Div 3 | 46 | 20 | 9 | 17 | 56 | 54 | 69 | 7 |
| 1997-98 | Div 3 | 46 | 9 | 23 | 14 | 48 | 52 | 50 | 21 |
| 1998-99 | Div 3 | 46 | 22 | 14 | 10 | 60 | 39 | 80 | 3 |
| 1999-2000 | Div 2 | 46 | 9 | 17 | 20 | 45 | 67 | 44 | 21 |
| 2000-01 | Div 3 | 46 | 23 | 13 | 10 | 95 | 58 | 82 | 2 |
| 2001-02 | Div 2 | 46 | 23 | 14 | 9 | 75 | 50 | 83 | 4 |
| 2002-03 | Div 2 | 46 | 23 | 12 | 11 | 68 | 43 | 81 | 6 |
| 2003-04 | Div 1 | 46 | 17 | 14 | 15 | 68 | 58 | 65 | 13 |

## DID YOU KNOW ?

Despite an indifferent start to 1975–76 producing only two wins and two draws in the first eight games, Cardiff City won promotion in second place. They also had eight clean sheets from their last nine games with only one goal conceded.

## CARDIFF CITY 2003–04 LEAGUE RECORD

| Match No. | Date | Venue | Opponents | Result | | H/T Score | Lg. Pos. | Goalscorers | Attendance |
|---|---|---|---|---|---|---|---|---|---|
| 1 | Aug 9 | A | Rotherham U | D | 0-0 | 0-0 | — | | 8176 |
| 2 | 16 | H | Bradford C | L | 0-2 | 0-1 | 19 | | 16,421 |
| 3 | 23 | A | Nottingham F | W | 2-1 | 2-0 | 14 | Earnshaw [2], Kavanagh [7] | 23,407 |
| 4 | 25 | H | Derby Co | W | 4-1 | 2-0 | 16 | Lee [30], Kavanagh (pen) [40], Earnshaw [55], Collins [70] | 15,091 |
| 5 | 30 | A | Walsall | D | 1-1 | 0-0 | 11 | Whalley [90] | 8974 |
| 6 | Sept 13 | H | Gillingham | W | 5-0 | 4-0 | 6 | Thorne [18], Earnshaw 4 (1 pen) [21, 35, 45 (p), 74] | 15,057 |
| 7 | 16 | A | Reading | L | 1-2 | 1-0 | — | Thorne [12] | 15,810 |
| 8 | 20 | A | Sheffield U | L | 3-5 | 0-0 | 14 | Earnshaw 2 [46, 64], Langley [69] | 21,323 |
| 9 | 27 | H | Crewe Alex | W | 3-0 | 1-0 | 9 | Thorne 2 [44, 85], Earnshaw [52] | 14,385 |
| 10 | 30 | H | Wigan Ath | D | 0-0 | 0-0 | — | | 15,143 |
| 11 | Oct 4 | A | Crystal Palace | L | 1-2 | 0-1 | 11 | Kavanagh [60] | 16,160 |
| 12 | 14 | A | Sunderland | D | 0-0 | 0-0 | — | | 26,835 |
| 13 | 18 | A | Coventry C | W | 3-1 | 3-1 | 11 | Whalley [28], Gordon [32], Earnshaw (pen) [40] | 11,767 |
| 14 | 25 | H | West Ham U | D | 0-0 | 0-0 | 12 | | 19,202 |
| 15 | 28 | H | Watford | W | 3-0 | 1-0 | — | Earnshaw [32], Vidmar [77], Kavanagh [87] | 14,011 |
| 16 | Nov 1 | A | Burnley | D | 1-1 | 0-0 | 9 | Earnshaw [75] | 10,886 |
| 17 | 8 | H | Stoke C | W | 3-1 | 1-0 | 8 | Earnshaw 2 [24, 71], Gabbidon [81] | 15,227 |
| 18 | 22 | A | Wimbledon | W | 1-0 | 1-0 | 8 | Croft [15] | 5056 |
| 19 | 25 | H | WBA | D | 1-1 | 0-0 | — | Earnshaw (pen) [65] | 17,678 |
| 20 | 29 | H | Ipswich T | L | 2-3 | 0-2 | 9 | Earnshaw (pen) [58], Thorne [86] | 17,833 |
| 21 | Dec 6 | A | Stoke C | W | 3-2 | 2-1 | 7 | Thorne 3 [34, 40, 72] | 12,208 |
| 22 | 9 | H | Preston NE | D | 2-2 | 0-0 | — | Langley [63], Thorne [90] | 13,703 |
| 23 | 13 | A | Norwich C | L | 1-4 | 0-1 | 8 | Thorne [59] | 18,428 |
| 24 | 20 | H | Millwall | L | 1-3 | 1-1 | 10 | Thorne [30] | 14,610 |
| 25 | 26 | H | Walsall | L | 0-1 | 0-0 | 11 | | 17,531 |
| 26 | 28 | A | Watford | L | 1-2 | 0-0 | 12 | Thorne [53] | 15,512 |
| 27 | Jan 10 | H | Rotherham U | W | 3-2 | 3-2 | 11 | Thorne [24], Kavanagh [38], Earnshaw [45] | 13,021 |
| 28 | 17 | A | Bradford C | W | 1-0 | 0-0 | 10 | Langley [72] | 11,132 |
| 29 | 31 | H | Nottingham F | D | 0-0 | 0-0 | 11 | | 17,913 |
| 30 | Feb 7 | A | Derby Co | D | 2-2 | 0-0 | 12 | Earnshaw [60], Kavanagh [62] | 20,958 |
| 31 | 14 | A | WBA | L | 1-2 | 0-0 | 12 | Lee [80] | 25,196 |
| 32 | 21 | H | Sunderland | W | 4-0 | 2-0 | 11 | Kavanagh [18], Langley [27], Gabbidon [48], Lee [80] | 17,337 |
| 33 | 28 | A | West Ham U | L | 0-1 | 0-0 | 11 | | 31,858 |
| 34 | Mar 2 | H | Coventry C | L | 0-1 | 0-0 | — | | 14,376 |
| 35 | 13 | H | Norwich C | W | 2-1 | 2-0 | 14 | Parry [17], Earnshaw [20] | 16,317 |
| 36 | 16 | H | Reading | L | 2-3 | 1-2 | — | Earnshaw [42], Bullock [72] | 14,051 |
| 37 | 20 | A | Crewe Alex | W | 1-0 | 0-0 | 12 | Williams (og) [70] | 6650 |
| 38 | 27 | H | Sheffield U | W | 2-1 | 1-1 | 10 | Langley [45], Robinson [63] | 13,666 |
| 39 | Apr 3 | A | Gillingham | W | 2-1 | 1-0 | 10 | Earnshaw [36], Bullock [86] | 7852 |
| 40 | 7 | A | Millwall | D | 0-0 | 0-0 | — | | 9584 |
| 41 | 10 | H | Crystal Palace | L | 0-2 | 0-0 | 11 | | 16,656 |
| 42 | 13 | A | Wigan Ath | L | 0-3 | 0-1 | — | | 8052 |
| 43 | 17 | H | Burnley | W | 2-0 | 0-0 | 11 | Langley (pen) [78], Campbell [80] | 13,525 |
| 44 | 24 | A | Preston NE | D | 2-2 | 0-1 | 11 | Campbell [51], Gabbidon [56] | 11,972 |
| 45 | May 1 | H | Wimbledon | D | 1-1 | 0-0 | 11 | Robinson [82] | 15,337 |
| 46 | 9 | A | Ipswich T | D | 1-1 | 1-1 | 13 | Bullock [41] | 28,703 |

**Final League Position: 13**

### GOALSCORERS

*League (68):* Earnshaw 21 (4 pens), Thorne 13, Kavanagh 7 (1 pen), Langley 6 (1 pen), Bullock 3, Gabbidon 3, Lee 3, Campbell 2, Robinson 2, Whalley 2, Collins 1, Croft 1, Gordon 1, Parry 1, Vidmar 1, own goal 1.
*Carling Cup (6):* Earnshaw 5, Campbell 1.
*FA Cup (0).*

| Alexander N 24 + 1 | Weston R 23 + 1 | Barker C 33 + 6 | Boland W 33 + 4 | Gabbidon D 41 | Vidmar T 45 | Bonner M 14 + 6 | Kavanagh G 27 | Earnshaw R 44 + 2 | Campbell A 6 + 19 | Robinson J 31 + 3 | Collins J 15 + 5 | Bowen J — + 2 | Maxwell L — + 1 | Whalley G 16 + 6 | Lee A 17 + 6 | Langley R 39 + 5 | Thorne P 19 + 4 | Gordon G 7 + 8 | Croft G 23 + 4 | Gray J 5 + 4 | Fleetwood S — + 2 | Prior S 4 + 3 | Margetson M 22 | Parry P 14 + 3 | Bullock L 4 + 7 | *Match No.* |
|---|---|---|---|---|---|---|---|---|---|---|---|---|---|---|---|---|---|---|---|---|---|---|---|---|---|---|
| 1 | $2^1$ | 3 | 4 | 5 | 6 | 7 | 8 | $9^2$ | 10 | $11^3$ | 12 | 13 | 14 | | | | | | | | | | | | | 1 |
| 1 | 2 | 3 | 7 | 5 | 4 | 12 | $8^1$ | $9^2$ | 13 | 11 | | | | $6^3$ | 10 | 14 | | | | | | | | | | 2 |
| 1 | 2 | 3 | 4 | 5 | 6 | 12 | 8 | $9^2$ | | $11^1$ | | | | | 10 | 7 | 13 | | | | | | | | | 3 |
| 1 | 2 | 3 | 4 | | 6 | | 8 | 9 | | $11^1$ | 5 | | | 12 | $10^2$ | 7 | 13 | | | | | | | | | 4 |
| 1 | 2 | 3 | $4^1$ | | 6 | | 8 | 9 | | $11^2$ | 5 | | | 13 | $10^■$ | 7 | 12 | | | | | | | | | 5 |
| 1 | 2 | 3 | 4 | | 6 | | 8 | 9 | | 11 | 5 | | | | | 7 | $10^1$ | 12 | | | | | | | | 6 |
| 1 | 2 | 3 | 4 | | 6 | | 8 | 9 | | $11^1$ | 5 | 12 | | | | 7 | 10 | | | | | | | | | 7 |
| 1 | 2 | 3 | 4 | | 6 | $11^1$ | 8 | 9 | | | 5 | | | | | 7 | 10 | 12 | | | | | | | | 8 |
| 1 | 2 | 3 | $4^3$ | 5 | 6 | 11 | 8 | $9^1$ | 12 | | 13 | | | | | 7 | $10^2$ | | 14 | | | | | | | 9 |
| 1 | 2 | 3 | 4 | 5 | 6 | 11 | 8 | 9 | | | | | | | | 7 | 10 | | | | | | | | | 10 |
| 1 | $2^2$ | 3 | $4^■$ | 5 | 6 | $11^1$ | 8 | 9 | $12^■$ | | | | | | | 7 | 10 | | 13 | | | | | | | 11 |
| 1 | $2^2$ | 3 | 4 | 5 | 6 | 12 | 8 | 9 | $10^3$ | $11^1$ | | | | | | 7 | | | 13 | 14 | | | | | | 12 |
| 1 | | 3 | | 5 | 6 | 8 | | 9 | | 11 | | | | $4^1$ | | 7 | | 10 | 2 | 12 | | | | | | 13 |
| 1 | | 3 | | 5 | 6 | 4 | 8 | 9 | | 11 | 12 | | | | | 7 | | $10^1$ | 2 | | | | | | | 14 |
| 1 | | 3 | | 5 | 6 | 4 | 8 | $9^3$ | | 11 | 12 | | | | | $7^2$ | | $10^1$ | 2 | 13 | 14 | | | | | 15 |
| 1 | | 3 | $4^2$ | 5 | 6 | 7 | 8 | 9 | | 11 | 12 | | | | | | | 10 | | 13 | | $2^1$ | | | | 16 |
| 1 | | 3 | 12 | 5 | 6 | $4^1$ | 8 | 9 | | 11 | | | | | | 13 | | 10 | 2 | $7^2$ | | | | | | 17 |
| 1 | | 3 | 12 | 5 | 6 | 4 | | 9 | | $11^1$ | | | | | | 7 | | 10 | 2 | 8 | | | | | | 18 |
| 1 | | 3 | 12 | 5 | 6 | 4 | | 9 | | $11^1$ | | | | | | 7 | 13 | $10^2$ | 2 | 8 | | | | | | 19 |
| 1 | | 3 | 12 | 5 | 6 | $4^1$ | | 9 | | 11 | | | | | | $7^2$ | 10 | 13 | 2 | 8 | | | | | | 20 |
| 1 | | 3 | 4 | 5 | 6 | 14 | | $9^2$ | 13 | $11^3$ | | | | | | 7 | 10 | | 2 | $8^1$ | | 12 | | | | 21 |
| 1 | | 3 | 8 | 5 | 6 | $4^2$ | | 9 | 13 | $11^1$ | | | | 12 | | 7 | 10 | | 2 | | | | | | | 22 |
| 1 | 12 | 3 | 4 | 5 | 6 | | | 9 | $11^2$ | | | | | 8 | 13 | 7 | 10 | | $2^1$ | | | | | | | 23 |
| 1 | 2 | 3 | $4^1$ | 5 | 6 | 12 | 8 | 9 | 13 | | | | | $11^2$ | | 7 | 10 | | | | | | | | | 24 |
| | 2 | | $11^1$ | 5 | 6 | | 8 | 9 | 12 | | | | | 4 | | 7 | 10 | | | | | 3 | 1 | | | 25 |
| | 2 | 12 | 11 | $5^1$ | 6 | 13 | 8 | 14 | $9^3$ | | | | | $4^2$ | | 7 | 10 | | | | | 3 | 1 | | | 26 |
| | 2 | | 4 | 5 | 6 | | 8 | 9 | | | | | | 13 | | 7 | 10 | | 12 | | | $3^1$ | 1 | $11^2$ | | 27 |
| | $2^2$ | 12 | 4 | 5 | 6 | | 8 | $9^3$ | | | | | | 13 | 14 | 7 | 10 | | $3^■$ | | | | 1 | $11^1$ | | 28 |
| | 2 | 3 | 4 | 5 | 6 | | 8 | $9^1$ | 12 | | | | | 13 | 14 | 7 | $10^3$ | | | | | | 1 | $11^2$ | | 29 |
| | 2 | 3 | 4 | 5 | 6 | | 8 | $9^1$ | 12 | | | | | | 13 | 7 | $10^2$ | | | | | | 1 | 11 | | 30 |
| | 2 | 3 | $4^1$ | 5 | 6 | | 8 | 9 | 14 | 12 | | | | | 13 | $7^2$ | $10^3$ | | | | | | 1 | 11 | | 31 |
| | 2 | 3 | 4 | 5 | 6 | | $8^3$ | $9^1$ | 12 | 13 | | | | | 14 | 7 | 10 | | | | | | 1 | $11^2$ | | 32 |
| | $2^1$ | 3 | 4 | 5 | 6 | | 8 | 9 | 14 | 13 | | | | | 10 | $7^2$ | | | | | | 12 | 1 | $11^3$ | | 33 |
| 15 | | 3 | | 5 | 6 | | $8^G$ | 9 | 13 | $11^2$ | | | | 4 | 10 | 12 | | | $2^1$ | | | | $1^■$ | 7 | | 34 |
| | | 3 | 4 | 5 | 6 | | | 9 | | 7 | | | | 8 | $10^3$ | 12 | | 14 | $2^2$ | | | 13 | 1 | $11^1$ | | 35 |
| | | 3 | $4^1$ | 5 | 6 | | | 9 | | 11 | | | | 8 | 10 | 7 | | | 2 | | | | 1 | | 12 | 36 |
| | | 12 | | 5 | 6 | | | 9 | | 11 | 3 | | | 4 | $10^2$ | 7 | | 13 | 2 | | | | 1 | | $8^1$ | 37 |
| | | 12 | $4^3$ | 5 | 6 | | | $9^2$ | 13 | $11^1$ | 3 | | | 8 | 10 | 7 | | | 2 | | | | 1 | | 14 | 38 |
| | | 12 | | $5^1$ | 6 | | | 9 | 13 | $11^3$ | 2 | | | 4 | 10 | 7 | | | 3 | | | | 1 | $8^2$ | 14 | 39 |
| | | | | 5 | 6 | | | 9 | 12 | $11^3$ | 2 | | | 4 | $10^2$ | 7 | | 13 | 3 | | | | 1 | $8^1$ | 14 | 40 |
| | | | | 5 | $6^■$ | | | 9 | 12 | $11^3$ | 2 | | | 4 | $10^2$ | 7 | | 13 | 3 | | | | 1 | $8^1$ | 14 | 41 |
| | | | | 5 | 6 | | | 9 | 12 | 11 | 2 | | | 4 | 10 | $7^2$ | | | 3 | | | | 1 | $8^1$ | 13 | 42 |
| | | | 8 | 5 | 6 | | | $9^1$ | 12 | $11^3$ | 2 | | | $4^2$ | 10 | 7 | | | 3 | | | | 1 | 13 | 14 | 43 |
| | 2 | 3 | 4 | 5 | | | | 12 | 9 | $11^1$ | 6 | | | | 10 | $7^2$ | | | | | | | 1 | 13 | 8 | 44 |
| | | | 4 | 5 | 6 | | | $9^2$ | $10^3$ | 11 | 2 | | | | | 12 | | 14 | 3 | | 13 | | 1 | $8^1$ | 7 | 45 |
| | | 12 | 4 | $5^1$ | 6 | | | 9 | | $11^2$ | 2 | | | | 10 | 7 | | | 3 | | | | 1 | 13 | 8 | 46 |

**Carling Cup**

| | | | |
|---|---|---|---|
| First Round | Leyton Orient | (h) | 4-1 |
| Second Round | West Ham U | (h) | 2-3 |

**FA Cup**

| | | | |
|---|---|---|---|
| Third Round | Sheffield U | (h) | 0-1 |

# CARLISLE UNITED Conference National

## FOUNDATION

Carlisle United came into being in 1903 through the amalgamation of Shaddongate United and Carlisle Red Rose. The new club was admitted to the Second Division of the Lancashire Combination in 1905–06, winning promotion the following season. Devonshire Park was officially opened on 2 September 1905, when St Helens Town were the visitors. Despite defeat in a disappointing 3-2 start, a respectable mid-table position was achieved.

***Brunton Park, Carlisle CA1 1LL.***

***Telephone:*** (01228) 526 237.

***Fax:*** (01228) 530 138.

***Website:*** www.carlisleunited.co.uk

***Email:*** enquiries@carlisleunited.co.uk

***Ground Capacity:*** 14,496.

***Record Attendance:*** 27,500 v Birmingham C, FA Cup 3rd rd, 5 January 1957 and v Middlesbrough, FA Cup 5th rd, 7 February 1970.

***Pitch Measurements:*** 117yd × 72yd.

***Chairman:*** John Courtenay.

***Vice-chairman:*** Andrew Jenkins.

***Secretary:*** Sarah McKnight.

***Manager:*** Paul Simpson.

***Assistant Manager:*** Dennis Booth.

***Physio:*** Neil Dalton.

***Colours:*** Blue shirts, white shorts, blue stockings.

***Change Colours:*** White shirts, blue shorts, white stockings.

***Year Formed:*** 1903.

***Ltd Co.:*** 1921.

***Previous Name:*** 1903, Shaddongate United; 1904, Carlisle United.

***Club Nicknames:*** 'Cumbrians' or 'The Blues'.

***Previous Grounds:*** 1903, Milholme Bank; 1905, Devonshire Park; 1909, Brunton Park.

***First Football League Game:*** 25 August 1928, Division 3 (N), v Accrington S (a) W 3–2 – Prout; Coulthard, Cook; Harrison, Ross, Pigg; Agar (1), Hutchison, McConnell (1), Ward (1), Watson.

***Record League Victory:*** 8–0 v Hartlepool U, Division 3 (N), 1 September 1928 – Prout; Smiles, Cook; Robinson (1) Ross, Pigg; Agar (1), Hutchison (1), McConnell (4), Ward (1), Watson. 8–0 v Scunthorpe U, Division 3 (N), 25 December 1952 – MacLaren; Hill, Scott; Stokoe, Twentyman, Waters; Harrison (1), Whitehouse (5), Ashman (2), Duffett, Bond.

***Record Cup Victory:*** 6–0 v Shepshed Dynamo, FA Cup 1st rd, 16 November 1996 – Caig; Hopper, Archdeacon (pen), Walling, Robinson, Pounewatchy, Peacock (1), Conway (1) (Jansen), Smart (McAlindon (1)), Hayward, Aspinall (Thorpe), (2 og).

## HONOURS

*Football League:* Division 1 best season: 22nd, 1974–75; Promoted from Division 2 (3rd) 1973–74; Division 3 – Champions 1964–65, 1994–95; Runners-up 1981–82; Promoted from Division 3 1996–97; Division 4 – Runners-up 1963–64.

*FA Cup:* best season: 6th rd 1975.

*Football League Cup:* Semi-final 1970.

*Auto Windscreens Shield:* Winners 1997; Runners-up 1995.

*LDV Vans Trophy:* Runners-up 2003.

## SKY SPORTS FACT FILE

In 1978–79 Carlisle United drew a club record 22 League matches in finishing sixth in Division Three. It was one short of a Football League record set the same season. Clean sheets were plentiful, 19 in all and only 42 goals were conceded.

***Record Defeat:*** 1–11 v Hull C, Division 3 (N), 14 January 1939.

***Most League Points (2 for a win):*** 62, Division 3 (N), 1950–51.

***Most League Points (3 for a win):*** 91, Division 3, 1994–95.

***Most League Goals:*** 113, Division 4, 1963–64.

***Highest League Scorer in Season:*** Jimmy McConnell, 42, Division 3 (N), 1928–29.

***Most League Goals in Total Aggregate:*** Jimmy McConnell, 126, 1928–32.

***Most League Goals in One Match:*** 5, Hugh Mills v Halifax T, Division 3N, 11 September 1937; 5, Jim Whitehouse v Scunthorpe U, Division 3N, 25 December 1952.

***Most Capped Player:*** Eric Welsh, 4, Northern Ireland.

***Most League Appearances:*** Allan Ross, 466, 1963–79.

***Youngest League Player:*** John Slaven, 16 years 162 days v Scunthorpe U, 16 March 2002.

***Record Transfer Fee Received:*** £1,500,000 from Crystal Palace for Matt Jansen, February 1998.

***Record Transfer Fee Paid:*** £121,000 to Notts Co for David Reeves, December 1993.

***Football League Record:*** 1928 Elected to Division 3 (N); 1958–62 Division 4; 1962–63 Division 3; 1963–64 Division 4; 1964–65 Division 3; 1965–74 Division 2; 1974–75 Division 1; 1975–77 Division 2; 1977–82 Division 3; 1982–86 Division 2; 1986–87 Division 3; 1987–92 Division 4; 1992–95 Division 3; 1995–96 Division 2; 1996–97 Division 3; 1997–98 Division 2; 1998–04 Division 3; 2004– Conference.

## LATEST SEQUENCES

***Longest Sequence of League Wins:*** 6, 27.8.1994 – 17.9.1994.

***Longest Sequence of League Defeats:*** 12, 27.9.2003 – 13.12.2003.

***Longest Sequence of League Draws:*** 6, 11.2.1978 – 11.3.1978.

***Longest Sequence of Unbeaten League Matches:*** 19, 1.10.1994 – 11.2.1995.

***Longest Sequence Without a League Win:*** 14, 19.1.1935 – 19.4.1935.

***Successive Scoring Runs:*** 26 from 23.8.1947.

***Successive Non-scoring Runs:*** 5 from 24.8.1968.

## MANAGERS

Harry Kirkbride 1904–05 *(Secretary-Manager)*
McCumiskey 1905–06 *(Secretary-Manager)*
Jack Houston 1906–08 *(Secretary-Manager)*
Bert Stansfield 1908–10
Jack Houston 1910–12
Davie Graham 1912–13
George Bristow 1913–30
Billy Hampson 1930–33
Bill Clarke 1933–35
Robert Kelly 1935–36
Fred Westgarth 1936–38
David Taylor 1938–40
Howard Harkness 1940–45
Bill Clark 1945–46 *(Secretary-Manager)*
Ivor Broadis 1946–49
Bill Shankly 1949–51
Fred Emery 1951–58
Andy Beattie 1958–60
Ivor Powell 1960–63
Alan Ashman 1963–67
Tim Ward 1967–68
Bob Stokoe 1968–70
Ian MacFarlane 1970–72
Alan Ashman 1972–75
Dick Young 1975–76
Bobby Moncur 1976–80
Martin Harvey 1980
Bob Stokoe 1980–85
Bryan 'Pop' Robson 1985
Bob Stokoe 1985–86
Harry Gregg 1986–87
Cliff Middlemass 1987–91
Aidan McCaffery 1991–92
David McCreery 1992–93
Mick Wadsworth *(Director of Coaching)* 1993–96
Mervyn Day 1996–97
David Wilkes and John Halpin (*Directors of Coaching*), and Michael Knighton 1997–99
Martin Wilkinson 1999–2000
Ian Atkins 2000–01
Roddy Collins 2001–02; 2002–03
Paul Simpson October 2003–

## TEN YEAR LEAGUE RECORD

| | | P | W | D | L | F | A | Pts | Pos |
|---|---|---|---|---|---|---|---|---|---|
| 1994-95 | Div 3 | 42 | 27 | 10 | 5 | 67 | 31 | 91 | 1 |
| 1995-96 | Div 2 | 46 | 12 | 13 | 21 | 57 | 72 | 49 | 21 |
| 1996-97 | Div 3 | 46 | 24 | 12 | 10 | 67 | 44 | 84 | 3 |
| 1997-98 | Div 2 | 46 | 12 | 8 | 26 | 57 | 73 | 44 | 23 |
| 1998-99 | Div 3 | 46 | 11 | 16 | 19 | 43 | 53 | 49 | 23 |
| 1999-2000 | Div 3 | 46 | 9 | 12 | 25 | 42 | 75 | 39 | 23 |
| 2000-01 | Div 3 | 46 | 11 | 15 | 20 | 42 | 65 | 48 | 22 |
| 2001-02 | Div 3 | 46 | 12 | 16 | 18 | 49 | 56 | 52 | 17 |
| 2002-03 | Div 3 | 46 | 13 | 10 | 23 | 52 | 78 | 49 | 22 |
| 2003-04 | Div 3 | 46 | 12 | 9 | 25 | 46 | 69 | 45 | 23 |

## DID YOU KNOW?

A few days after leaving his position as player-manager of Bury, Andy Preece made his debut for Carlisle United and opened the scoring against Torquay United on 20 December 2003, to end a run of 12 consecutive defeats.

## CARLISLE UNITED 2003–04 LEAGUE RECORD

| Match No. | Date | Venue | Opponents | Result | | H/T Score | Lg. Pos. | Goalscorers | Attendance |
|---|---|---|---|---|---|---|---|---|---|
| 1 | Aug 9 | H | York C | L | 1-2 | 1-2 | — | Raven [4] | 7261 |
| 2 | 16 | A | Yeovil T | L | 0-3 | 0-2 | 23 | | 6347 |
| 3 | 23 | H | Bristol R | L | 0-2 | 0-2 | 23 | | 4764 |
| 4 | 25 | A | Boston U | L | 0-1 | 0-1 | 24 | | 2527 |
| 5 | 30 | H | Cambridge U | D | 0-0 | 0-0 | 24 | | 4571 |
| 6 | Sept 6 | A | Darlington | L | 0-2 | 0-2 | 24 | | 5889 |
| 7 | 13 | H | Rochdale | W | 3-2 | 3-0 | 24 | Simpson [10], Foran [17], McGill [22] | 4532 |
| 8 | 16 | A | Northampton T | L | 0-2 | 0-0 | — | | 4156 |
| 9 | 20 | A | Southend U | D | 2-2 | 0-2 | 24 | Henderson [47], Foran [79] | 4620 |
| 10 | 27 | H | Swansea C | L | 1-2 | 1-0 | 24 | Foran (pen) [42] | 4854 |
| 11 | 30 | H | Leyton Orient | L | 0-1 | 0-0 | — | | 4650 |
| 12 | Oct 4 | A | Kidderminster H | L | 1-2 | 0-0 | 24 | Murphy [63] | 2488 |
| 13 | 12 | A | Hull C | L | 1-2 | 0-1 | 24 | McDonagh [59] | 19,050 |
| 14 | 18 | H | Macclesfield T | L | 0-1 | 0-0 | 24 | | 4366 |
| 15 | 21 | H | Scunthorpe U | L | 1-4 | 0-1 | — | Farrell [87] | 3437 |
| 16 | 25 | A | Huddersfield T | L | 1-2 | 0-2 | 24 | Kelly [74] | 9050 |
| 17 | Nov 1 | A | Lincoln C | L | 0-2 | 0-1 | 24 | | 4044 |
| 18 | 15 | H | Mansfield T | L | 0-2 | 0-0 | 24 | | 4154 |
| 19 | 22 | A | Cheltenham T | L | 1-2 | 1-1 | 24 | Simpson [19] | 3414 |
| 20 | 29 | H | Doncaster R | L | 0-1 | 0-0 | 24 | | 4344 |
| 21 | Dec 13 | A | Oxford U | L | 1-2 | 0-2 | 24 | Foran (pen) [78] | 6111 |
| 22 | 20 | H | Torquay U | W | 2-0 | 1-0 | 24 | Preece [16], Arnison [53] | 3600 |
| 23 | 26 | A | Bury | W | 3-1 | 1-1 | 24 | Gray [41], McGill [57], Henderson [69] | 3345 |
| 24 | 28 | H | Darlington | D | 1-1 | 1-1 | 24 | McGill [10] | 8369 |
| 25 | Jan 3 | H | Boston U | W | 2-1 | 1-1 | 24 | Chapman (og) [15], Fryatt [61] | 5296 |
| 26 | 10 | A | York C | L | 0-2 | 0-1 | 24 | | 4804 |
| 27 | 17 | H | Yeovil T | W | 2-0 | 1-0 | 24 | Simpson [21], Farrell [75] | 5455 |
| 28 | 24 | A | Bristol R | L | 0-1 | 0-0 | 24 | | 8485 |
| 29 | Feb 7 | H | Bury | W | 2-1 | 1-1 | 24 | Simpson [31], Gray [53] | 4954 |
| 30 | 14 | H | Hull C | D | 1-1 | 0-0 | 24 | Preece [56] | 7176 |
| 31 | 17 | A | Cambridge U | D | 2-2 | 1-0 | — | Simpson 2 [7, 83] | 3280 |
| 32 | 21 | A | Macclesfield T | D | 1-1 | 1-1 | 24 | McGill [24] | 3256 |
| 33 | Mar 6 | A | Torquay U | L | 1-4 | 0-2 | 24 | McGill [73] | 3366 |
| 34 | 9 | H | Huddersfield T | W | 1-0 | 0-0 | — | Duffield [72] | 4782 |
| 35 | 13 | H | Oxford U | W | 2-0 | 0-0 | 24 | Cowan [52], Farrell [76] | 5492 |
| 36 | 16 | H | Northampton T | D | 1-1 | 0-0 | — | Farrell [82] | 6269 |
| 37 | 20 | A | Rochdale | L | 0-2 | 0-1 | 24 | | 4755 |
| 38 | 23 | A | Scunthorpe U | W | 3-2 | 1-1 | — | Duffield [15], Boyd [55], Billy [77] | 2326 |
| 39 | 27 | H | Southend U | L | 1-2 | 0-0 | 24 | Farrell [87] | 6173 |
| 40 | Apr 3 | A | Swansea C | W | 2-1 | 1-1 | 24 | Farrell (pen) [26], Duffield [60] | 5238 |
| 41 | 10 | H | Kidderminster H | W | 1-0 | 0-0 | 24 | Farrell [79] | 7296 |
| 42 | 12 | A | Leyton Orient | D | 1-1 | 0-0 | 24 | McGill [81] | 4182 |
| 43 | 17 | H | Lincoln C | L | 0-2 | 0-0 | 24 | | 7875 |
| 44 | 24 | A | Mansfield T | W | 3-2 | 2-2 | 23 | Gray [12], Preece [21], Langmead [66] | 5361 |
| 45 | May 1 | H | Cheltenham T | D | 1-1 | 1-0 | 23 | McGill [9] | 9524 |
| 46 | 8 | A | Doncaster R | L | 0-1 | 0-0 | 23 | | 9720 |

**Final League Position: 23**

### GOALSCORERS

*League (46):* Farrell 7 (1 pen), McGill 7, Simpson 6, Foran 4 (2 pens), Duffield 3, Gray 3, Preece 3, Henderson 2, Arnison 1, Billy 1, Boyd 1, Cowan 1, Fryatt 1, Kelly 1, Langmead 1, McDonagh 1, Murphy 1, Raven 1, own goal 1.
*Carling Cup (1):* Russell 1.
*FA Cup (0).*
*LDV Vans Trophy (4):* Wake 2, Rundle 1, Schumacher 1.

| Glennon M 44 | Birch M 2 | Murphy P 33 + 2 | McGill B 42 + 2 | Kelly D 9 + 1 | Raven P 13 | Foran R 20 + 3 | Simpson P 25 | Livingstone S 6 | Farrell C 21 + 9 | Billy C 39 | Rundle A 6 + 17 | Wake B 2 + 13 | Baldacchino R — + 1 | Maddison L 2 | Russell C 3 + 3 | Summerbell M 4 + 2 | Shelley B 28 + 3 | Andrews L 33 + 4 | McDonagh W 23 + 4 | Byrne D 9 + 2 | Henderson K 10 + 9 | Molloy D 3 + 4 | Keen P 2 + 1 | Smith S 4 | Jack M — + 3 | Arnison P 20 + 6 | Schumacher S 4 | Cowan T 20 | Gray K 25 | Fryatt M 9 + 1 | Preece A 23 + 2 | Warhurst P — + 1 | Langmead K 3 + 8 | Duffield P 10 | Boyd M 9 | *Match No.* |
|---|---|---|---|---|---|---|---|---|---|---|---|---|---|---|---|---|---|---|---|---|---|---|---|---|---|---|---|---|---|---|---|---|---|---|---|---|
| 1 | $2^{1}$ | 3 | 4 | 5 | 6 | $7^{2}$ | $8^{3}$ | 9■ | 10 | 11 | 12 | 13 | 14 | | | | | | | | | | | | | | | | | | | | | | | 1 |
| 1 | $2^{1}$ | | 4 | 5 | 6 | 10 | 11 | 9 | | 7 | 12 | | | 3 | $8^{2}$ | 13 | | | | | | | | | | | | | | | | | | | | 2 |
| 1 | | 3 | 4 | $5^{3}$ | 6 | 9 | 11 | | $10^{2}$ | 7 | 12 | 13 | | | | 8 | $2^{1}$ | 14 | | | | | | | | | | | | | | | | | | 3 |
| 1 | | | $4^{2}$ | | 6 | 9 | $11^{3}$ | | 10 | 7 | 12 | 13 | | 3■ | | 8 | $2^{1}$ | 5 | 14 | | | | | | | | | | | | | | | | | 4 |
| 1 | | 3 | 12 | 5 | | 9 | | | $10^{2}$ | 7 | $11^{1}$ | 13 | | | | 8 | 2 | 6 | $4^{3}$ | 14 | | | | | | | | | | | | | | | | 5 |
| 1 | | 6 | 12 | 5 | | 9 | | | $10^{2}$ | $7^{1}$ | 11 | 14 | | | 13 | 8 | 2 | 4 | $3^{3}$ | | | | | | | | | | | | | | | | | 6 |
| 1 | | 3 | 4 | | 6 | 9 | $8^{3}$ | | 12 | 7 | $11^{2}$ | | | | 13 | | 2 | 5 | | 14 | $10^{1}$ | | | | | | | | | | | | | | | 7 |
| 1 | | 3 | 4 | | 6 | 9 | $8^{3}$ | | | $7^{2}$ | | 14 | | | | 12 | 2 | 5 | 13 | 11 | $10^{1}$ | | | | | | | | | | | | | | | 8 |
| 1 | | $3^{2}$ | 8 | | 6 | 9 | | | | 7 | | 12 | | | | | 2 | 5 | 4 | 11 | $10^{1}$ | 13 | | | | | | | | | | | | | | 9 |
| 1 | | 3 | 8 | | $6^{2}$ | 9 | | | | 7 | | 12 | | | | | 2 | 5 | 4 | 11 | $10^{1}$ | 13 | | | | | | | | | | | | | | 10 |
| 1 | | 3 | $8^{1}$ | 12 | | 9 | | | 13 | 7 | 14 | $10^{2}$ | | | | | 2 | 5 | 4 | 6 | | $11^{3}$ | | | | | | | | | | | | | | 11 |
| 1 | | 11 | 8 | 5 | | 9 | | | | 7 | 12 | 13 | | | | | 2 | 4 | 6 | $3^{2}$ | | $10^{1}$ | | | | | | | | | | | | | | 12 |
| 1 | | 6 | 8 | 5 | | $9^{2}$ | | | | 7 | 12 | | | | | | 2 | 4■ | 11 | 3 | 13 | $10^{1}$ | | | | | | | | | | | | | | 13 |
| 1 | | | $4^{2}$ | | | 9 | | 5 | 12 | 7 | 11 | 13 | | | | | 2 | 6 | 8 | 3 | $10^{1}$ | | | | | | | | | | | | | | | 14 |
| | | | 8 | | | 9 | | 5 | 12 | $7^{3}$ | $11^{2}$ | 13 | | | | | 2 | 6 | 4 | $10^{1}$ | | | 1 | 3 | 14 | | | | | | | | | | | 15 |
| 1 | | | $8^{2}$ | $6^{1}$ | | 9■ | | 5 | 10 | 7 | | 12 | | | | | 2 | 4 | 11 | | | | | 3 | 13 | | | | | | | | | | | 16 |
| 1 | | | 8 | 5 | $6^{2}$ | | | 9■ | $11^{1}$ | 7 | 12 | $10^{3}$ | | | | | 13 | | | 3 | 14 | | | | | 2 | 4 | | | | | | | | | 17 |
| 1 | | | $8^{2}$ | | | | | | $10^{3}$ | 7 | 13 | 14 | | | 11 | | 12 | 4 | 5 | | 9 | | | $3^{1}$ | | 2 | 6 | | | | | | | | | 18 |
| 1 | | | | | | | 11 | | | 7 | | | | | 9 | | 5 | 4 | 6 | | 10 | 12 | | 3 | | 2 | $8^{1}$ | | | | | | | | | 19 |
| 1 | | | | | | $9^{1}$ | 8 | | | 11 | | | | | 12 | | 2 | 5 | | | 10 | 13 | | | | $7^{2}$ | 4 | 3 | 6 | | | | | | | 20 |
| 1 | | | 10 | | 6 | 9 | $11^{1}$ | | | 7 | 12 | | | | | | | $4^{2}$ | 8 | | 13 | | | | | 2 | | 3 | 5 | | | | | | | 21 |
| 1 | | | 8 | | 6 | | $11^{2}$ | | | 7 | | | | | | | | 13 | 4 | | 12 | | | | | 2 | | 3 | 5 | $9^{1}$ | 10 | | | | | 22 |
| 1 | | 12 | 8 | | 6 | | $11^{1}$ | | 13 | 7 | | | | | | | | | 4 | | 14 | | | | | 2 | | 3 | 5 | $9^{3}$ | $10^{2}$ | | | | | 23 |
| 1 | | 12 | 8 | | $6^{1}$ | | $11^{2}$ | | | 7 | | | | | | | | | 4 | | 13 | | | | | 2 | | 3 | 5 | 9 | 10 | | | | | 24 |
| 1 | | $6^{1}$ | 8 | | | | 11 | | | 7 | | | | | | | | | 4 | | 12 | | | | | 2 | | 3 | 5 | 9 | 10 | | | | | 25 |
| 1 | | 6 | 8 | | | | 11 | | 12 | 7 | | | | | | | | | 4 | | 13 | | | | | 2 | | 3 | $5^{2}$ | $9^{1}$ | 10 | | | | | 26 |
| 1 | | 3 | 8 | | | | 11 | | 12 | 7 | | | | | | | | 6 | 4 | | $9^{1}$ | | | | | 2 | | | 5 | | 10 | | | | | 27 |
| 1 | | 6 | 8 | | | | $11^{1}$ | | | 7 | 12 | | | | | | | 4 | | | $9^{2}$ | | | | | 2 | | 3 | 5 | 13 | 10 | | | | | 28 |
| 1 | | 6 | 8 | | | | 11 | | 12 | 7 | | | | | | | | 4 | | | | | | | | 2 | | 3 | 5 | $9^{1}$ | 10 | | | | | 29 |
| 1 | | 6 | 8 | | | 12 | $11^{1}$ | | | 7 | | | | | | | | 4 | | | | | | | | 2 | | 3 | 5 | 9 | 10 | | | | | 30 |
| 1 | | $6^{2}$ | 8 | | | | 11 | | 12 | 7 | | | | | | | | 4 | 13 | | | | | | | 2 | | 3 | 5 | $9^{1}$ | 10 | | | | | 31 |
| 1 | | 6 | 8 | | | | 11 | | | 7 | | | | | | | | 4 | | | | | | | | $2^{1}$ | | 3 | 5 | 9 | 10 | 12 | | | | 32 |
| 1 | | 6 | 8 | | | | 11 | | 9 | $7^{2}$ | 12 | | | | | | 2 | 4 | | | | | | | | | | 3 | 5 | | $10^{1}$ | | 13 | | | 33 |
| 1 | | 6 | 8 | | | | | | 9 | 7 | | | | | | | | | 4 | | | | | | | 2 | | 3 | 5 | | 10 | | | 11 | | 34 |
| 1 | | 6 | $8^{1}$ | | | | | | 9 | 7 | 13 | | | | | | 12 | 14 | 4 | | | | | | | 2 | | $3^{3}$ | 5 | | 10 | | | $11^{2}$ | | 35 |
| 1 | | 6 | 8 | | | | | | 9 | 7 | | | | | | | 3 | 12 | $4^{1}$ | | | | | | | 2 | | | 5 | | 10 | | 13 | $11^{2}$ | | 36 |
| 1■ | | 6 | 4 | | | | | | 9 | 7 | 12 | | | | | | 3 | | | | | | 15 | | | $2^{1}$ | | | 5 | | $10^{2}$ | | 13 | $11^{6}$ | 8 | 37 |
| 1 | | 6 | 4 | | | | | | 9 | 7 | 12 | | | | | | 3 | 2 | | | | | | | | | | | 5 | | 13 | | $10^{2}$ | $11^{1}$ | 8 | 38 |
| 1 | | 6 | 4 | | | | | | 9 | $7^{1}$ | 13 | | | | | | 3 | 2 | | | | | | | | 12 | | | 5 | | 14 | | $10^{2}$ | $11^{3}$ | 8 | 39 |
| | | 3 | 4 | | | | 8 | | $9^{1}$ | | | | | | | | 2 | 6 | | | | | 1 | | | 12 | | | 5 | | $10^{2}$ | | 13 | 11 | 7 | 40 |
| 1 | | 3 | 4 | | | | 8 | | 9 | | | | | | | | 2 | 6 | | | | | | | | 12 | | | $5^{1}$ | | $10^{2}$ | | 13 | 11 | 7 | 41 |
| 1 | | 6 | 8 | | | 12 | | | 9 | | | | | | | | 2 | 4 | | | | | | | | | | 3 | 5■ | | 10 | | | $11^{1}$ | 7 | 42 |
| 1 | | 6 | 8 | | | 12 | | | 9 | | 13 | | | | | | 2 | 4 | | | | | | | | | | $3^{2}$ | 5 | | 10 | | 14 | $11^{3}$ | $7^{1}$ | 43 |
| 1 | | 6 | $8^{1}$ | | | 11 | | | $9^{2}$ | | | | | | | | 2 | 4 | | | | | | | | 12 | | 3 | 5 | | 10 | | 13 | | 7 | 44 |
| 1 | | 6 | 4 | | | $11^{2}$ | 8 | | $9^{3}$ | | | | | | | | 2 | 5 | 12 | | | | | | | 13 | | 3 | | | 10 | | 14 | | $7^{1}$ | 45 |
| 1 | | 6 | $7^{1}$ | | | | $8^{3}$ | | | | $11^{2}$ | | | | | | 2 | 5 | 4 | | 13 | | | | 14 | 12 | | 3 | | | 10 | | 9 | | | 46 |

**Carling Cup**
First Round Walsall (a) 1-2

**LDV Vans Trophy**
First Round Rochdale (h) 2-0
Second Round Huddersfield T (h) 2-0
Quarter-Final Sheffield W (h) 0-3

**FA Cup**
First Round Oldham Ath (a) 0-3

# CHARLTON ATHLETIC FA Premiership

## FOUNDATION

The club was formed on 9 June 1905, by a group of 14- and 15-year-old youths living in streets by the Thames in the area which now borders the Thames Barrier. The club's progress through local leagues was so rapid that after the First World War they joined the Kent League where they spent a season before turning professional and joining the Southern League in 1920. A year later they were elected to the Football League's Division 3 (South).

***The Valley, Floyd Road, Charlton, London SE7 8BL.***

***Telephone:*** (020) 8333 4000.

***Fax:*** (020) 8333 4001.

***Website:*** www.cafc.co.uk

***Email:*** info@cafc.co.uk

***Ground Capacity:*** 26,875.

***Record Attendance:*** 75,031 v Aston Villa, FA Cup 5th rd, 12 February 1938 (at The Valley).

***Pitch Measurements:*** 111yd × 73yd.

***Chairman:*** M. A. Simons.

***Vice Chairman:*** R. A. Murray.

***Chief Executive:*** P. D. Varney.

***Secretary:*** Chris Parkes.

***Manager:*** Alan Curbishley.

***Assistant Manager:*** Keith Peacock.

***Physio:*** George Cooper.

***Colours:*** Red shirts, white shorts, red stockings.

***Change Colours:*** All yellow.

***Year Formed:*** 1905.

***Turned Professional:*** 1920.

***Ltd Co.:*** 1919.

***Club Nickname:*** 'Addicks'.

***Previous Grounds:*** 1906, Siemen's Meadow; 1907, Woolwich Common; 1909, Pound Park; 1913, Horn Lane; 1920, The Valley; 1923, Catford (The Mount); 1924, The Valley; 1985, Selhurst Park; 1991, Upton Park; 1992, The Valley.

***First Football League Game:*** 27 August 1921, Division 3 (S), v Exeter C (h) W 1–0 – Hughes; Mitchell, Goodman; Dowling (1), Hampson, Dunn; Castle, Bailey, Halse, Green, Wilson.

***Record League Victory:*** 8–1 v Middlesbrough, Division 1, 12 September 1953 – Bartram; Campbell, Ellis; Fenton, Ufton, Hammond; Hurst (2), O'Linn (2), Leary (1), Firmani (3), Kiernan.

## HONOURS

*Football League:* Division 1 – Champions 1999–2000; Runners-up 1936–37; Promoted from Division 1, 1997–98 (play-offs); Division 2 – Runners-up 1935–36, 1985–86; Division 3 (S) – Champions 1928–29, 1934–35; Promoted from Division 3 (3rd) 1974–75, 1980–81.

*FA Cup:* Winners 1947; Runners-up 1946.

*Football League Cup:* best season: 4th rd, 1963, 1966, 1979.

*Full Members' Cup:* Runners-up 1987.

## SKY SPORTS FACT FILE

Swedish international centre-forward Hans Jeppson, recommended to Charlton Athletic by ex-player Dai Astley, the coach of Djurgaarden, was tremendously popular at The Valley. In 11 League games as an amateur in 1950–51 he scored nine goals en route to Italy.

***Record Cup Victory:*** 7–0 v Burton A, FA Cup 3rd rd, 7 January 1956 – Bartram; Campbell, Townsend; Hewie, Ufton, Hammond; Hurst (1), Gauld (1), Leary (3), White, Kiernan (2).

***Record Defeat:*** 1–11 v Aston Villa, Division 2, 14 November 1959.

***Most League Points (2 for a win):*** 61, Division 3 (S), 1934–35.

***Most League Points (3 for a win):*** 91, Division 1, 1999–2000.

***Most League Goals:*** 107, Division 2, 1957–58.

***Highest League Scorer in Season:*** Ralph Allen, 32, Division 3 (S), 1934–35.

***Most League Goals in Total Aggregate:*** Stuart Leary, 153, 1953–62.

***Most League Goals in One Match:*** 5, Wilson Lennox v Exeter C, Division 3S, 2 February 1929; 5, Eddie Firmani v Aston Villa, Division 1, 5 February 1955; 5, John Summers v Huddersfield T, Division 2, 21 December 1957; 5, John Summers v Portsmouth, Division 2, 1 October 1960.

## MANAGERS

Bill Rayner 1920–25
Alex McFarlane 1925–27
Albert Lindon 1928
Alex McFarlane 1928–32
Jimmy Seed 1933–56
Jimmy Trotter 1956–61
Frank Hill 1961–65
Bob Stokoe 1965–67
Eddie Firmani 1967–70
Theo Foley 1970–74
Andy Nelson 1974–79
Mike Bailey 1979–81
Alan Mullery 1981–82
Ken Craggs 1982
Lennie Lawrence 1982–91
Steve Gritt/Alan Curbishley 1991–95
Alan Curbishley June 1995–

***Most Capped Player:*** Mark Kinsella, 33 (48), Republic of Ireland.

***Most League Appearances:*** Sam Bartram, 583, 1934–56.

***Youngest League Player:*** Paul Konchesky, 16 years 93 days v Oxford U, 16 August 1997.

***Record Transfer Fee Received:*** £10,000,000 from Chelsea for Scott Parker, January 2004.

***Record Transfer Fee Paid:*** £4,750,000 to Wimbledon for Jason Euell, July 2001.

***Football League Record:*** 1921 Elected to Division 3 (S); 1929–33 Division 2; 1933–35 Division 3 (S); 1935–36 Division 2; 1936–57 Division 1; 1957–72 Division 2; 1972–75 Division 3; 1975–80 Division 2; 1980–81 Division 3; 1981–86 Division 2; 1986–90 Division 1; 1990–92 Division 2; 1992–98 Division 1; 1998–99 FA Premier League; 1999–2000 Division 1; 2000– FA Premier League.

## LATEST SEQUENCES

***Longest Sequence of League Wins:*** 12, 26.12.1999 – 7.3.2000.

***Longest Sequence of League Defeats:*** 10, 11.4.1990 – 15.9.1990.

***Longest Sequence of League Draws:*** 6, 13.12.1992 – 16.1.1993.

***Longest Sequence of Unbeaten League Matches:*** 15, 4.10.1980 – 20.12.1980.

***Longest Sequence Without a League Win:*** 16, 26.2.1955 – 22.8.1955.

***Successive Scoring Runs:*** 25 from 26.12.1935.

***Successive Non-scoring Runs:*** 5 from 6.9.1922.

## TEN YEAR LEAGUE RECORD

| | | P | W | D | L | F | A | Pts | Pos |
|---|---|---|---|---|---|---|---|---|---|
| 1994-95 | Div 1 | 46 | 16 | 11 | 19 | 58 | 66 | 59 | 15 |
| 1995-96 | Div 1 | 46 | 17 | 20 | 9 | 57 | 45 | 71 | 6 |
| 1996-97 | Div 1 | 46 | 16 | 11 | 19 | 52 | 66 | 59 | 15 |
| 1997-98 | Div 1 | 46 | 26 | 10 | 10 | 80 | 49 | 88 | 4 |
| 1998-99 | PR Lge | 38 | 8 | 12 | 18 | 41 | 56 | 36 | 18 |
| 1999-2000 | Div 1 | 46 | 27 | 10 | 9 | 79 | 45 | 91 | 1 |
| 2000-01 | PR Lge | 38 | 14 | 10 | 14 | 50 | 57 | 52 | 9 |
| 2001-02 | PR Lge | 38 | 10 | 14 | 14 | 38 | 49 | 44 | 14 |
| 2002-03 | PR Lge | 38 | 14 | 7 | 17 | 45 | 56 | 49 | 12 |
| 2003-04 | PR Lge | 38 | 14 | 11 | 13 | 51 | 51 | 53 | 7 |

## DID YOU KNOW?

Charlton Athletic began their longest unbeaten run in inauspicious circumstances during the 1980–81 season in a goalless draw at Barnsley. Derek Hales hit the crossbar with a 27th minute penalty kick.

## CHARLTON ATHLETIC 2003–04 LEAGUE RECORD

| *Match No.* | *Date* | *Venue* | *Opponents* | *Result* | *H/T Score* | *Lg. Pos.* | *Goalscorers* | *Atten-dance* |
|---|---|---|---|---|---|---|---|---|
| 1 | Aug 17 | H | Manchester C | L 0-3 | 0-2 | — | | 25,846 |
| 2 | 23 | A | Wolverhampton W | W 4-0 | 4-0 | 8 | Euell [5], Jensen [15], Bartlett 2 [25, 33] | 27,327 |
| 3 | 26 | H | Everton | D 2-2 | 1-1 | — | Euell 2 (2 pens) [25, 49] | 26,314 |
| 4 | 30 | A | Bolton W | D 0-0 | 0-0 | 11 | | 23,098 |
| 5 | Sept 13 | H | Manchester U | L 0-2 | 0-1 | 12 | | 26,046 |
| 6 | 20 | A | Aston Villa | L 1-2 | 0-1 | 14 | Lisbie [86] | 31,410 |
| 7 | 28 | H | Liverpool | W 3-2 | 2-1 | 12 | Lisbie 3 [31, 43, 83] | 26,530 |
| 8 | Oct 4 | A | Portsmouth | W 2-1 | 0-1 | 9 | Fortune [77], Bartlett [90] | 20,122 |
| 9 | 20 | A | Blackburn R | W 1-0 | 1-0 | — | Hreidarsson [33] | 19,939 |
| 10 | 26 | H | Arsenal | D 1-1 | 1-1 | 9 | Di Canio (pen) [28] | 26,639 |
| 11 | Nov 3 | A | Birmingham C | W 2-1 | 1-0 | — | Holland 2 [11, 59] | 27,225 |
| 12 | 8 | H | Fulham | W 3-1 | 1-0 | 4 | Stuart [10], Johansson 2 [69, 76] | 26,285 |
| 13 | 22 | A | Leicester C | D 1-1 | 0-1 | 4 | Di Canio (pen) [84] | 30,242 |
| 14 | 29 | H | Leeds U | L 0-1 | 0-1 | 5 | | 26,425 |
| 15 | Dec 7 | A | Southampton | L 2-3 | 0-2 | 6 | Parker 2 [46, 65] | 30,513 |
| 16 | 13 | A | Middlesbrough | D 0-0 | 0-0 | 7 | | 26,721 |
| 17 | 20 | H | Newcastle U | D 0-0 | 0-0 | 7 | | 26,469 |
| 18 | 26 | H | Chelsea | W 4-2 | 2-1 | 5 | Hreidarsson [1], Holland [35], Johansson [48], Euell [53] | 26,752 |
| 19 | 28 | A | Tottenham H | W 1-0 | 0-0 | 4 | Cole [68] | 34,534 |
| 20 | Jan 7 | A | Manchester C | D 1-1 | 0-1 | — | Di Canio [84] | 44,307 |
| 21 | 10 | H | Wolverhampton W | W 2-0 | 1-0 | 4 | Euell 2 [38, 79] | 26,123 |
| 22 | 17 | A | Everton | W 1-0 | 1-0 | 4 | Stuart [41] | 36,322 |
| 23 | 31 | H | Bolton W | L 1-2 | 1-1 | 4 | Johansson [12] | 26,220 |
| 24 | Feb 8 | A | Chelsea | L 0-1 | 0-1 | 5 | | 41,255 |
| 25 | 11 | H | Tottenham H | L 2-4 | 0-2 | — | Stuart [51], Perry [81] | 26,645 |
| 26 | 21 | H | Blackburn R | W 3-2 | 2-0 | 5 | Cole [10], Euell [36], Jensen [90] | 26,322 |
| 27 | 28 | A | Arsenal | L 1-2 | 0-2 | 5 | Jensen [59] | 38,137 |
| 28 | Mar 13 | H | Middlesbrough | W 1-0 | 1-0 | 4 | Holland [25] | 26,229 |
| 29 | 20 | A | Newcastle U | L 1-3 | 0-2 | 6 | Jensen [54] | 51,847 |
| 30 | 27 | H | Aston Villa | L 1-2 | 1-1 | 8 | Cole [8] | 26,238 |
| 31 | Apr 10 | H | Portsmouth | D 1-1 | 1-0 | 9 | Bartlett [8] | 26,369 |
| 32 | 12 | A | Liverpool | W 1-0 | 0-0 | 7 | Bartlett [63] | 40,003 |
| 33 | 17 | H | Birmingham C | D 1-1 | 0-0 | 7 | Holland [86] | 25,184 |
| 34 | 20 | A | Manchester U | L 0-2 | 0-1 | — | | 67,477 |
| 35 | 24 | A | Fulham | L 0-2 | 0-1 | 8 | | 16,585 |
| 36 | May 1 | H | Leicester C | D 2-2 | 0-1 | 9 | Fortune [53], Di Canio (pen) [76] | 26,043 |
| 37 | 8 | A | Leeds U | D 3-3 | 1-2 | 8 | Holland [11], Euell 2 (1 pen) [76 (p), 79] | 38,986 |
| 38 | 15 | H | Southampton | W 2-1 | 1-0 | 7 | Euell [36], Cole [53] | 26,598 |

**Final League Position: 7**

### GOALSCORERS

*League (51):* Euell 10 (3 pens), Holland 6, Bartlett 5, Cole 4, Di Canio 4 (3 pens), Jensen 4, Johansson 4, Lisbie 4, Stuart 3, Fortune 2, Hreidarsson 2, Parker 2, Perry 1.
*Carling Cup (4):* Di Canio 1, Jensen 1, Lisbie 1, Parker 1.
*FA Cup (2):* Cole 1, own goal 1.

| Royce S 1 | Kishishev R 30 + 3 | Konchesky P 17 + 4 | Rowett G 1 | Hreidarsson H 33 | Fish M 23 | Holland M 38 | Euell J 24 + 7 | Bartlett S 13 + 6 | Lisbie K 5 + 4 | Parker S 20 | Young L 21 + 3 | Jensen C 27 + 4 | Johansson J 16 + 10 | Kiely D 37 | Fortune J 21 + 7 | Stuart G 23 + 5 | Cole C 8 + 13 | Di Canio P 23 + 8 | Powell C 11 + 5 | Perry C 25 + 4 | Campbell-Ryce J — + 2 | Svensson M 1 + 2 | Thomas J — + 1 | *Match No.* |
|---|---|---|---|---|---|---|---|---|---|---|---|---|---|---|---|---|---|---|---|---|---|---|---|---|
| 1 | $2^{1}$ | 3 | 4 | 5 | 6■ | 7 | 8 | $9^{2}$ | $10^{3}$ | 11 | 12 | 13 | 14 | | | | | | | | | | | 1 |
| | $7^{1}$ | | | 3 | 6 | 4 | 8 | $9^{2}$ | | 11■ | 2 | $10^{3}$ | | 1 | 5 | 12 | 13 | 14 | | | | | | 2 |
| | $7^{2}$ | | | 3 | 6 | 4 | 8 | $9^{1}$ | | 11 | 2 | 10 | | 1 | 5 | 13 | 12 | | | | | | | 3 |
| | 7 | | | 3 | 6 | 4 | 8 | $9^{2}$ | 12 | 11 | 2 | $10^{1}$ | 13 | 1 | 5 | | | | | | | | | 4 |
| | 2 | | | | | $4^{1}$ | 9■ | 12 | 13 | $11^{2}$ | | 8 | 14 | 1 | 5 | 7 | | $10^{3}$ | 3 | 6 | | | | 5 |
| | $7^{2}$ | | | | 6 | 4 | | 9 | 12 | 11 | 2 | 8 | | 1 | 5 | 13 | | $10^{1}$ | 3 | | | | | 6 |
| | 12 | | | | $6^{3}$ | 4 | | 9 | $10^{2}$ | 11 | 2 | 8 | 13 | 1 | 14 | $7^{1}$ | | | 3 | 5 | | | | 7 |
| | | | | | $6^{2}$ | 4 | | 9 | 10 | 11 | 2 | $8^{1}$ | | 1 | 13 | 7 | | 12 | 3 | 5 | | | | 8 |
| | 12 | | | 3 | 6 | 4 | 13 | | | 11 | $2^{1}$ | 8 | $9^{2}$ | 1 | 14 | 7 | | $10^{3}$ | | 5 | | | | 9 |
| | 2 | | | 3 | 6 | 4 | 12 | | | 11 | | 8 | $9^{2}$ | 1 | | 7 | | $10^{1}$ | | 5 | 13 | | | 10 |
| | 2 | | | 3 | 6 | 4 | $10^{1}$ | | 12 | $11^{2}$ | | 8 | $9^{3}$ | 1 | 13 | 7 | | | | 5 | | 14 | | 11 |
| | 2 | | | 3 | 6 | 4 | 12 | | $9^{2}$ | $11^{3}$ | | $8^{1}$ | 10 | 1 | | 7 | | 13 | 14 | 5 | | | | 12 |
| | 2 | | | 3 | $11^{2}$ | 4 | 8 | | $9^{1}$ | | | | | 1 | 6 | 7 | 12 | $10^{3}$ | 14 | 5 | | 13 | | 13 |
| | $2^{1}$ | | | 3 | 6 | 4 | 9 | | | 11 | | $8^{3}$ | | 1 | 12 | 7 | 13 | | | 5 | 14 | $10^{2}$ | | 14 |
| | 2 | | | 3 | | 4 | 9 | | | 11 | | 8 | | 1 | 6 | 7 | 12 | $10^{1}$ | | 5 | | | | 15 |
| | 2 | | | 3 | | 4 | 9 | | | 11 | | 8 | | 1 | 6 | 7 | | 10 | | 5 | | | | 16 |
| | 2 | | | 3 | | 4 | 9 | | | 11 | | 8 | | 1 | 6 | 7 | 12 | $10^{1}$ | | 5 | | | | 17 |
| | 2 | 13 | | 3 | | 4 | 9 | | | 11 | | | 8 | 1 | 6 | $7^{2}$ | | $10^{1}$ | 12 | 5 | | | | 18 |
| | 2 | 11 | | 3 | 6 | 4 | 9 | | | 7 | | | $8^{1}$ | 1 | | | 12 | 10 | | 5 | | | | 19 |
| | 2 | $11^{2}$ | | 3 | 6 | 4 | $8^{1}$ | | | 7 | | 14 | $9^{3}$ | 1 | | 12 | 13 | 10 | | 5 | | | | 20 |
| | 2 | 13 | | 3 | 6 | 4 | 8 | | | 11 | | | 9 | 1 | | $7^{2}$ | 12 | $10^{1}$ | | 5 | | | | 21 |
| | 2 | 11 | | 3 | 6 | 4 | 8 | | | | 14 | | 12 | 1 | 13 | $7^{3}$ | $9^{1}$ | $10^{2}$ | | 5 | | | | 22 |
| | 2 | 13 | | 3 | 6 | 4 | $8^{1}$ | | | | | $11^{2}$ | 9 | 1 | | 7 | 12 | 10 | | 5 | | | | 23 |
| | 2 | $11^{2}$ | | 3 | 6 | 4 | | 13 | | | 12 | 8 | 9 | 1 | | $7^{1}$ | | 10 | | 5 | | | | 24 |
| | $7^{1}$ | 11 | | 3 | 6 | 4 | 13 | $10^{3}$ | | | 2 | 8 | | 1 | | 12 | $9^{2}$ | 14 | | 5 | | | | 25 |
| | 7 | 14 | | 3 | $6^{1}$ | 4 | 8 | | | | 2 | 13 | | 1 | 12 | 11 | $9^{2}$ | $10^{3}$ | | 5 | | | | 26 |
| | $7^{1}$ | | | 3 | 6 | 4 | | | | | 2 | 8 | 12 | 1 | 5 | 11 | 9 | 10 | | | | | | 27 |
| | 7 | 11 | | 3 | 6 | 4 | | 13 | | | 2 | 8 | 12 | 1 | | | $9^{2}$ | $10^{1}$ | | 5 | | | | 28 |
| | $7^{1}$ | 11 | | $3^{3}$ | | 4 | | 13 | | | 2 | 8 | 12 | 1 | 6 | | $9^{2}$ | 10 | 14 | 5 | | | | 29 |
| | $7^{1}$ | 3 | | | | 4 | $8^{2}$ | 14 | | | 2 | 11 | 12 | 1 | 6 | | 9 | $10^{3}$ | 13 | 5 | | | | 30 |
| | | 11 | | 6 | | 4 | 8 | $9^{1}$ | | | 2 | 7 | $10^{2}$ | 1 | 5 | | 12 | 13 | 3 | | | | | 31 |
| | 2 | 11 | | 6 | | 7 | 12 | 9 | | | 5 | 8 | $10^{1}$ | 1 | 4 | | | | 3 | | | | | 32 |
| | $7^{1}$ | 11 | | 6 | | 4 | 13 | $9^{3}$ | | | 2 | 8 | $10^{2}$ | 1 | 5 | | 12 | 14 | 3 | | | | | 33 |
| | | 11 | | 6 | | 4 | 14 | 9 | | | 2 | 8 | $10^{3}$ | 1 | 5 | $7^{2}$ | | 13 | $3^{1}$ | 12 | | | | 34 |
| | | 11 | | 6 | | 4 | 8 | | | | 2 | 10 | 14 | 1 | 5 | $7^{3}$ | $9^{1}$ | 13 | $3^{2}$ | 12 | | | | 35 |
| | | $11^{2}$ | | 6 | | 4 | 8 | | | | 2 | | 9 | 1 | 5 | 7 | | $10^{1}$ | 3 | 12 | | | 13 | 36 |
| | 14 | 11 | | 6 | | 4 | 8 | 12 | | | 2 | | 9 | 1 | 5 | $7^{3}$ | | $10^{2}$ | $3^{1}$ | 13 | | | | 37 |
| | 7 | 11 | | 3 | | 4 | 8 | 9 | | | 2 | 13 | | 1 | 5 | | $12^{2}$ | $10^{1}$ | | 6 | | | | 38 |

**Carling Cup**

| | | | |
|---|---|---|---|
| Second Round | Luton T | (h) | 4-4 |
| Third Round | Everton | (a) | 0-1 |

**FA Cup**

| | | | |
|---|---|---|---|
| Third Round | Gillingham | (a) | 2-3 |

# CHELSEA FA Premiership

## FOUNDATION

Chelsea may never have existed but for the fact that Fulham rejected an offer to rent the Stamford Bridge ground from Mr H. A. Mears who had owned it since 1904. Fortunately he was determined to develop it as a football stadium rather than sell it to the Great Western Railway and got together with Frederick Parker, who persuaded Mears of the financial advantages of developing a major sporting venue. Chelsea FC was formed in 1905, and when admission to the Southern League was denied, they immediately gained admission to the Second Division of the Football League.

***Stamford Bridge, London SW6 1HS.***

***Telephone:*** 0870 300 1212.

***Fax:*** (020) 7381 4831.

***Ticket Office:*** (020) 7915 2951.

***Website:*** www.chelseafc.com

***Ground Capacity:*** 42,449.

***Record Attendance:*** 82,905 v Arsenal, Division 1, 12 October 1935.

***Pitch Measurements:*** 113yd × 74yd.

***Chief Executive:*** Peter Kenyon.

***Secretary:*** David Barnard.

***Head Coach:*** Jose Mourinho.

***Assistant Manager:*** Gwyn Williams.

***Physio:*** Mike Banks.

***Colours:*** Royal blue shirts and shorts, white stockings.

***Change Colours:*** Black shirts, silver shorts, black stockings.

***Year Formed:*** 1905.

***Turned Professional:*** 1905.

***Ltd Co.:*** 1905.

***Club Nickname:*** 'The Blues'.

***First Football League Game:*** 2 September 1905, Division 2, v Stockport Co (a) L 0–1 – Foulke; Mackie, McEwan; Key, Harris, Miller; Moran, J. T. Robertson, Copeland, Windridge, Kirwan.

***Record League Victory:*** 9–2 v Glossop N E, Division 2, 1 September 1906 – Byrne; Walton, Miller; Key (1), McRoberts, Henderson; Moran, McDermott (1), Hilsdon (5), Copeland (1), Kirwan (1).

## HONOURS

*FA Premier League:* Runners-up 2003–04.

*Football League:* Division 1 – Champions 1954–55; Division 2 – Champions 1983–84, 1988–89; Runners-up 1906–07, 1911–12, 1929–30, 1962–63, 1976–77.

*FA Cup:* Winners 1970, 1997, 2000; Runners-up 1915, 1967, 1994, 2002.

*Football League Cup:* Winners 1965, 1998; Runners-up 1972.

*Full Members' Cup:* Winners 1986.

*Zenith Data Systems Cup:* Winners 1990.

***European Competitions:*** *Champions League:* 1999–2000, 2003–04 (semi-finals). *European Fairs Cup:* 1958–60, 1965–66, 1968–69. *European Cup-Winners' Cup:* 1970–71 (winners), 1971–72, 1994–95, 1997–98 (winners), 1998–99 (semi-finals). *UEFA Cup:* 2000–01, 2001–02, 2002–03. *Super Cup:* 1998–99 (winners).

## SKY SPORTS FACT FILE

Alan Birchenall was the first £100,000 transfer for Chelsea when joining Crystal Palace in June 1970, having been the second signing at the same figure when the striker was recruited from Sheffield United in November 1967.

***Record Cup Victory:*** 13–0 v Jeunesse Hautcharage, ECWC, 1st rd 2nd leg, 29 September 1971 – Bonetti; Boyle, Harris (1), Hollins (1p), Webb (1), Hinton, Cooke, Baldwin (3), Osgood (5), Hudson (1), Houseman (1).

***Record Defeat:*** 1–8 v Wolverhampton W, Division 1, 26 September 1953.

***Most League Points (2 for a win):*** 57, Division 2, 1906–07.

***Most League Points (3 for a win):*** 99, Division 2, 1988–89.

***Most League Goals:*** 98, Division 1, 1960–61.

***Highest League Scorer in Season:*** Jimmy Greaves, 41, 1960–61.

***Most League Goals in Total Aggregate:*** Bobby Tambling, 164, 1958–70.

***Most League Goals in One Match:*** 5, George Hilsdon v Glossop, Division 2, 1 September 1906; 5, Jimmy Greaves v Wolverhampton W, Division 1, 30 August 1958; 5, Jimmy Greaves v Preston NE, Division 1, 19 December 1959; 5, Jimmy Greaves v WBA, Division 1, 3 December 1960; 5, Bobby Tambling v Aston Villa, Division 1, 17 September 1966; 5, Gordon Durie v Walsall, Division 2, 4 February 1989.

***Most Capped Player:*** Marcel Desailly, 67 (116), France.

***Most League Appearances:*** Ron Harris, 655, 1962–80.

***Youngest League Player:*** Ian Hamilton, 16 years 138 days v Tottenham H, 18 March 1967.

***Record Transfer Fee Received:*** £12,000,000 from Rangers for Tore Andre Flo, November 2000.

***Record Transfer Fee Paid:*** £17,000,000 to Blackburn R for Damien Duff, July 2003.

***Football League Record:*** 1905 Elected to Division 2; 1907–10 Division 1; 1910–12 Division 2; 1912–24 Division 1; 1924–30 Division 2; 1930–62 Division 1; 1962–63 Division 2; 1963–75 Division 1; 1975–77 Division 2; 1977–79 Division 1; 1979–84 Division 2; 1984–88 Division 1; 1988–89 Division 2; 1989–92 Division 1; 1992– FA Premier League.

### MANAGERS

John Tait Robertson 1905–07
David Calderhead 1907–33
Leslie Knighton 1933–39
Billy Birrell 1939–52
Ted Drake 1952–61
Tommy Docherty 1962–67
Dave Sexton 1967–74
Ron Suart 1974–75
Eddie McCreadie 1975–77
Ken Shellito 1977–78
Danny Blanchflower 1978–79
Geoff Hurst 1979–81
John Neal 1981–85 *(Director to 1986)*
John Hollins 1985–88
Bobby Campbell 1988–91
Ian Porterfield 1991–93
David Webb 1993
Glenn Hoddle 1993–96
Ruud Gullit 1996–98
Gianluca Vialli 1998–2000
Claudio Ranieri 2000–04
Jose Mourinho June 2004–

## LATEST SEQUENCES

***Longest Sequence of League Wins:*** 8, 15.3.1989 – 8.4.1989.

***Longest Sequence of League Defeats:*** 7, 1.11.1952 – 20.12.1952.

***Longest Sequence of League Draws:*** 6, 20.8.1969 – 13.9.1969.

***Longest Sequence of Unbeaten League Matches:*** 27, 29.10.1988 – 8.4.1989.

***Longest Sequence Without a League Win:*** 21, 3.11.1987 – 2.4.1988.

***Successive Scoring Runs:*** 27 from 29.10.1988.

***Successive Non-scoring Runs:*** 9 from 14.3.1981.

### TEN YEAR LEAGUE RECORD

| | | P | W | D | L | F | A | Pts | Pos |
|---|---|---|---|---|---|---|---|---|---|
| 1994-95 | PR Lge | 42 | 13 | 15 | 14 | 50 | 55 | 54 | 11 |
| 1995-96 | PR Lge | 38 | 12 | 14 | 12 | 46 | 44 | 50 | 11 |
| 1996-97 | PR Lge | 38 | 16 | 11 | 11 | 58 | 55 | 59 | 6 |
| 1997-98 | PR Lge | 38 | 20 | 3 | 15 | 71 | 43 | 63 | 4 |
| 1998-99 | PR Lge | 38 | 20 | 15 | 3 | 57 | 30 | 75 | 3 |
| 1999-2000 | PR Lge | 38 | 18 | 11 | 9 | 53 | 34 | 65 | 5 |
| 2000-01 | PR Lge | 38 | 17 | 10 | 11 | 68 | 45 | 61 | 6 |
| 2001-02 | PR Lge | 38 | 17 | 13 | 8 | 66 | 38 | 64 | 6 |
| 2002-03 | PR Lge | 38 | 19 | 10 | 9 | 68 | 38 | 67 | 4 |
| 2003-04 | PR Lge | 38 | 24 | 7 | 7 | 67 | 30 | 79 | 2 |

### DID YOU KNOW?

When Chelsea won the FA Youth Cup in 1959–60 they had a mixture of opponents: West Thurrock, Colchester United, Ford United, Portsmouth, Aston Villa, Bristol City and Preston North End. They retained their title the following season.

## CHELSEA 2003–04 LEAGUE RECORD

| Match No. | Date | Venue | Opponents | Result | | H/T Score | Lg. Pos. | Goalscorers | Attendance |
|---|---|---|---|---|---|---|---|---|---|
| 1 | Aug 17 | A | Liverpool | W | 2-1 | 1-0 | — | Veron [25], Hasselbaink [87] | 44,080 |
| 2 | 23 | H | Leicester C | W | 2-1 | 2-1 | 3 | Nalis (og) [3], Mutu [45] | 41,074 |
| 3 | 30 | H | Blackburn R | D | 2-2 | 1-1 | 5 | Mutu [45], Hasselbaink (pen) [63] | 41,066 |
| 4 | Sept 13 | H | Tottenham H | W | 4-2 | 2-1 | 4 | Lampard [35], Mutu 2 [37, 75], Hasselbaink [90] | 41,165 |
| 5 | 20 | A | Wolverhampton W | W | 5-0 | 2-0 | 2 | Lampard [17], Hasselbaink [36], Duff [52], Crespo 2 [67, 90] | 29,208 |
| 6 | 27 | H | Aston Villa | W | 1-0 | 1-0 | 2 | Hasselbaink [43] | 41,182 |
| 7 | Oct 5 | A | Middlesbrough | W | 2-1 | 1-0 | 3 | Gudjohnsen [17], Crespo [88] | 29,170 |
| 8 | 14 | A | Birmingham C | D | 0-0 | 0-0 | — | | 29,460 |
| 9 | 18 | A | Arsenal | L | 1-2 | 1-1 | 3 | Crespo [8] | 38,172 |
| 10 | 25 | H | Manchester C | W | 1-0 | 1-0 | 2 | Hasselbaink [34] | 41,143 |
| 11 | Nov 1 | A | Everton | W | 1-0 | 0-0 | 2 | Mutu [49] | 40,189 |
| 12 | 9 | H | Newcastle U | W | 5-0 | 3-0 | 2 | Johnson [25], Crespo [40], Lampard (pen) [42], Duff [78], Gudjohnsen [84] | 41,322 |
| 13 | 22 | A | Southampton | W | 1-0 | 0-0 | 2 | Melchiot [47] | 32,149 |
| 14 | 30 | H | Manchester U | W | 1-0 | 1-0 | 1 | Lampard (pen) [30] | 41,932 |
| 15 | Dec 6 | A | Leeds U | D | 1-1 | 0-1 | 1 | Duff [70] | 36,305 |
| 16 | 13 | H | Bolton W | L | 1-2 | 1-1 | 3 | Crespo [22] | 40,491 |
| 17 | 20 | A | Fulham | W | 1-0 | 0-0 | 3 | Crespo [62] | 18,431 |
| 18 | 26 | A | Charlton Ath | L | 2-4 | 1-2 | 3 | Terry [10], Gudjohnsen [73] | 26,752 |
| 19 | 28 | H | Portsmouth | W | 3-0 | 0-0 | 3 | Bridge [65], Lampard [73], Geremi [82] | 41,552 |
| 20 | Jan 7 | H | Liverpool | L | 0-1 | 0-1 | — | | 41,533 |
| 21 | 11 | A | Leicester C | W | 4-0 | 2-0 | 3 | Hasselbaink [12], Dabizas (og) [44], Mutu [88], Babayaro [90] | 31,547 |
| 22 | 18 | H | Birmingham C | D | 0-0 | 0-0 | 3 | | 41,073 |
| 23 | Feb 1 | A | Blackburn R | W | 3-2 | 2-1 | 3 | Lampard 2 [25, 35], Johnson [88] | 24,867 |
| 24 | 8 | H | Charlton Ath | W | 1-0 | 1-0 | 3 | Hasselbaink (pen) [28] | 41,255 |
| 25 | 11 | A | Portsmouth | W | 2-0 | 1-0 | — | Parker [17], Crespo [79] | 20,110 |
| 26 | 21 | H | Arsenal | L | 1-2 | 1-2 | 3 | Gudjohnsen [1] | 41,926 |
| 27 | 28 | A | Manchester C | W | 1-0 | 0-0 | 2 | Gudjohnsen [82] | 47,304 |
| 28 | Mar 13 | A | Bolton W | W | 2-0 | 0-0 | 2 | Terry [71], Duff [74] | 26,717 |
| 29 | 20 | H | Fulham | W | 2-1 | 2-1 | 2 | Gudjohnsen [7], Duff [30] | 41,459 |
| 30 | 27 | H | Wolverhampton W | W | 5-2 | 1-1 | 2 | Melchiot [4], Lampard [70], Hasselbaink 3 [77, 87, 90] | 41,215 |
| 31 | Apr 3 | A | Tottenham H | W | 1-0 | 1-0 | 2 | Hasselbaink [38] | 36,101 |
| 32 | 10 | H | Middlesbrough | D | 0-0 | 0-0 | 2 | | 41,011 |
| 33 | 12 | A | Aston Villa | L | 2-3 | 1-1 | 2 | Crespo 2 [11, 90] | 41,112 |
| 34 | 17 | H | Everton | D | 0-0 | 0-0 | 2 | | 41,169 |
| 35 | 25 | A | Newcastle U | L | 1-2 | 1-1 | 2 | Cole J [5] | 52,016 |
| 36 | May 1 | H | Southampton | W | 4-0 | 0-0 | 2 | Cranie (og) [59], Lampard 2 [75, 83], Johnson [85] | 41,321 |
| 37 | 8 | A | Manchester U | D | 1-1 | 1-0 | 2 | Gronkjaer [19] | 67,609 |
| 38 | 15 | H | Leeds U | W | 1-0 | 1-0 | 2 | Gronkjaer [20] | 41,281 |

**Final League Position: 2**

### GOALSCORERS

*League (67):* Hasselbaink 12 (2 pens), Crespo 10, Lampard 10 (2 pens), Gudjohnsen 6, Mutu 6, Duff 5, Johnson 3, Gronkjaer 2, Melchiot 2, Terry 2, Babayaro 1, Bridge 1, Cole J 1, Geremi 1, Parker 1, Veron 1, own goals 3.
*Carling Cup (6):* Cole J 2, Gudjohnsen 2 (1 pen), Hasselbaink 2.
*FA Cup (8):* Mutu 3, Gudjohnsen 2 (1 pen), Hasselbaink 1, Lampard 1, Terry 1.
*Champions League (21):* Lampard 4, Gudjohnsen 3, Bridge 2, Crespo 2, Hasselbaink 2, Duff 1, Gallas 1, Gronkjaer 1, Huth 1, Johnson 1, Mutu 1, own goals 2.

| Cudicini C 26 | Johnson G 17 + 2 | Bridge W 33 | Lampard F 38 | Terry J 33 | Desailly M 15 | Gronkjaer J 19 + 12 | Geremi19 + 6 | Gudjohnsen E 17 + 9 | Duff D 17 + 6 | Veron J 5 + 2 | Gallas W 23 + 6 | Hasselbaink J 22 + 8 | Cole J 18 + 17 | Melchiot M 20 + 3 | Mutu A 21 + 4 | Crespo H 13 + 6 | Petit E 3 + 1 | Babayaro C 5 + 1 | Makelele C 26 + 4 | Huth R 8 + 8 | Stanic M — + 2 | Sullivan N 4 | Parker S 7 + 4 | Nicolas A 1 + 1 | Ambrosio M 8 | Oliveira F — + 1 | *Match No.* |
|---|---|---|---|---|---|---|---|---|---|---|---|---|---|---|---|---|---|---|---|---|---|---|---|---|---|---|---|
| 1 | $2^1$ | 3 | 4 | 5 | 6 | 7 | 8 | $9^2$ | $10^3$ | 11 | 12 | 13 | 14 | | | | | | | | | | | | | | 1 |
| 1 | | 3 | 4 | 5 | 6 | 12 | 8■ | 13 | $7^3$ | 11 | | $9^2$ | 14 | 2 | $10^1$ | | | | | | | | | | | | 2 |
| 1 | 2 | $3^1$ | 4 | 5 | 6 | | 8 | | $11^2$ | 7 | | 9 | 12 | | $10^3$ | 14 | 13 | | | | | | | | | | 3 |
| 1 | | | 8 | 5 | 6 | $7^2$ | | | $11^1$ | | 13 | 9 | 12 | 2 | 10 | | $4^3$ | 3 | 14 | | | | | | | | 4 |
| 1 | $2^3$ | | 8 | 5 | | $7^1$ | | 10 | 11 | | 6 | $9^2$ | 12 | | | 13 | | 3 | 4 | 14 | | | | | | | 5 |
| 1 | 2 | 3 | 8 | | 6 | 12 | | | 11 | $7^2$ | 5 | 9 | 13 | | $10^1$ | | $4^3$ | | 14 | | | | | | | | 6 |
| 1 | 2 | 3 | 8 | 5 | | $7^1$ | | $10^2$ | 11 | | | $9^3$ | 12 | | 13 | 14 | | | 4 | 6 | | | | | | | 7 |
| 1 | 2 | 3 | 8 | 5 | | | 7 | 12 | 13 | | | $9^1$ | $11^2$ | | | 10 | | | 4 | 6 | | | | | | | 8 |
| 1 | 2 | 3 | 8 | | | 12 | $7^2$ | | $11^3$ | | | 13 | 14 | 5 | $10^1$ | 9 | | | 4 | 6 | | | | | | | 9 |
| 1 | | 3 | 8 | 5 | | $11^2$ | 13 | | 12 | | 6 | $9^3$ | $7^1$ | 2 | 10 | | | | 4 | 14 | | | | | | | 10 |
| 1 | | 3 | 8 | 5 | | | 7 | 12 | 13 | | 6 | 9 | $11^1$ | 2 | $10^2$ | | | | 4 | | | | | | | | 11 |
| 1 | $2^3$ | 3 | 7 | 5 | | | | 12 | 11 | 8 | 6 | | 13 | | $10^2$ | $9^1$ | | | 4 | 14 | | | | | | | 12 |
| 1 | | 3 | 7 | 5 | | 12 | | 10 | $11^3$ | | 6 | $9^2$ | $8^1$ | 2 | 13 | | | | 4 | | 14 | | | | | | 13 |
| 1 | | 3 | 8 | 5 | | 12 | 7 | | 14 | | 6 | 13 | $11^3$ | 2 | $10^2$ | $9^1$ | | | 4 | | | | | | | | 14 |
| 1 | | 3 | 8 | 5 | | 12 | | | 11 | | 6 | $9^1$ | $7^2$ | 2 | 10 | 13 | | | 4 | | | | | | | | 15 |
| 1 | 2 | 3 | $8^3$ | 5 | 6 | $7^1$ | 14 | | 11 | | | 12 | 13 | | 10 | $9^2$ | | | 4 | | | | | | | | 16 |
| 1 | 2 | 3 | 8 | 5 | 6 | 7 | 13 | | $11^1$ | | 14 | | $12^2$ | | 10 | $9^3$ | | | 4 | | | | | | | | 17 |
| 1 | 2 | 3 | $8^2$ | 5 | 6 | $7^1$ | 13 | 12 | | | 14 | 9 | $11^3$ | | 10 | | | | 4 | | | | | | | | 18 |
| | | 3 | 8 | 5 | | 7 | 11 | 9 | | | 6 | | | 2 | 10 | | | | 4 | | | 1 | | | | | 19 |
| 1 | 2 | 3 | 8 | 5 | | 13 | 7 | 12 | | | 6 | | $11^2$ | | 10 | $9^1$ | | | 4 | | | | | | | | 20 |
| 1 | | | 8 | 5 | 6 | $7^2$ | 13 | $10^3$ | | | 12 | 9 | $11^1$ | 2 | 14 | | | 3 | 4 | | | | | | | | 21 |
| 1 | $2^1$ | 3 | 8 | | 6 | $11^2$ | | 10 | 13 | | 5 | 9 | $7^3$ | 12 | 14 | | | | 4 | | | | | | | | 22 |
| 1 | 2 | 3 | 8 | 5 | | 12 | | 14 | | | 6 | 9 | | 13 | $10^3$ | | $11^2$ | | 4 | | | | $7^1$ | | | | 23 |
| | 7 | 3 | 8 | | | 11 | | 12 | | | 6 | $9^1$ | | 2 | 10 | | | | | 5 | | 1 | | 4 | | | 24 |
| | | 3 | 8 | 5 | | 11 | | $9^1$ | | | 6 | 12 | 14 | 2 | $10^2$ | 13 | | | 4 | | | 1 | $7^3$ | | | | 25 |
| | | 3 | 8 | 5 | | 12 | $11^3$ | 9■ | | | 6 | 13 | 14 | 2 | $10^2$ | | | | 4 | | | 1 | $7^1$ | | | | 26 |
| 1 | 2 | 3 | 4 | 5 | | | $7^3$ | 13 | | | 6 | $9^2$ | $8^1$ | | | 10 | | | 12 | 14 | | | 11 | | | | 27 |
| | | 3 | 4 | 5 | 6 | $7^1$ | 8 | | $11^3$ | | 2 | 9 | 13 | | | $10^2$ | | | | 12 | | | 14 | | 1 | | 28 |
| | | 3 | 4 | 5 | 6 | $7^2$ | 8 | 9 | $11^1$ | | 2 | | 12 | | | 10 | | | | | | | 13 | | 1 | | 29 |
| | | | 8 | 5 | | | $7^1$ | $9^2$ | 13 | | 6 | 12 | $11^3$ | 2 | | 10 | | 3 | 4 | | | | 14 | | 1 | | 30 |
| | | 3 | 8 | 5 | | 14 | | $10^3$ | 11 | | 6 | $9^1$ | 13 | 2 | | 12 | | | 4 | | | | $7^2$ | | 1 | | 31 |
| | | | 8 | 5 | 6 | $7^1$ | 12 | 10 | | 14 | 2 | 9 | 11 | | | | | $3^2$ | $4^3$ | 13 | | | | | 1 | | 32 |
| | | 3 | 4 | 5 | | 13 | 8 | | $11^2$ | | 12 | | 14 | $2^1$ | $10^3$ | 9 | | | | 6 | | | 7 | | 1 | | 33 |
| | | 3 | 4 | | 6 | 13 | 8 | | | | $2^1$ | 9 | $11^3$ | 12 | 10 | | | | | 5 | | | $7^2$ | | 1 | 14 | 34 |
| | | 3 | 8 | 5 | $6^2$ | | 7 | 10 | | | | 12 | 11 | 2 | | $9^1$ | | | 4 | 13 | | | | | 1 | | 35 |
| 1 | 13 | 3 | $4^1$ | 5 | | $7^2$ | 8 | 10 | | 14 | | 9 | $11^3$ | 2 | | | | | 12 | 6 | | | | | | | 36 |
| 1 | 12 | 3 | 8 | 5 | | $7^3$ | 11 | 9 | | | | | $10^2$ | $2^1$ | | | | 14 | 4 | 6■ | | | 13 | | | | 37 |
| 1 | $7^3$ | 3 | $8^2$ | $5^1$ | | 11 | | 9 | | | 6 | | 10 | 2 | | | | | 4 | 12 | 14 | | | 13 | | | 38 |

**Carling Cup**

| | | | |
|---|---|---|---|
| Third Round | Notts Co | (h) | 4-2 |
| Fourth Round | Reading | (a) | 1-0 |
| Fifth Round | Aston Villa | (a) | 1-2 |

**FA Cup**

| | | | |
|---|---|---|---|
| Third Round | Watford | (a) | 2-2 |
| | | (h) | 4-0 |
| Fourth Round | Scarborough | (a) | 1-0 |
| Fifth Round | Arsenal | (a) | 1-2 |

**Champions League**

| | | | |
|---|---|---|---|
| Third Qualifying Round | Zilina | (a) | 2-0 |
| | | (h) | 3-0 |
| Group G | Sparta Prague | (a) | 1-0 |
| | Besiktas | (h) | 0-2 |
| | Lazio | (h) | 2-1 |
| | | (a) | 4-0 |
| | Sparta Prague | (h) | 0-0 |
| | Besiktas | (n) | 2-0 |
| First KO Round | Stuttgart | (a) | 1-0 |
| | | (h) | 0-0 |
| Quarter-Finals | Arsenal | (h) | 1-1 |
| | | (a) | 2-1 |
| Semi-Final | Monaco | (a) | 1-3 |
| | | (h) | 2-2 |

# CHELTENHAM TOWN FL Championship 2

## FOUNDATION

Although a scratch team representing Cheltenham played a match against Gloucester in 1884, the earliest recorded match for Cheltenham Town FC was a friendly against Dean Close School on 12 March 1892. The School won 4–3 and the match was played at Prestbury (half a mile from Whaddon Road). Cheltenham Town played Wednesday afternoon friendlies at a local cricket ground until entering the Mid Gloucester League. In those days the club played in deep red coloured shirts and were nicknamed 'the Rubies'. The club moved to Whaddon Lane for season 1901–02 and changed to red and white colours two years later.

***Whaddon Road, Cheltenham, Gloucester GL52 5NA.***

***Telephone:*** (01242) 573 558.

***Fax:*** (01242) 224 675.

***Website:*** www.ctfc.com

***Email:*** info@cheltenhamtownfc.com

***Ground Capacity:*** 7,289.

***Record Attendance:*** at Whaddon Road: 8,326 v Reading, FA Cup 1st rd, 17 November 1956; at Cheltenham Athletic Ground: 10,389 v Blackpool, FA Cup 3rd rd, 13 January 1934.

***Pitch Measurements:*** 111yd × 72yd.

***Chairman:*** Paul Godfrey.

***Vice-chairman:*** Colin Farmer.

***Secretary:*** Paul Godfrey.

***Manager:*** John Ward.

***Assistant Manager:*** Keith Downing.

***Physio:*** Ian Weston.

***Colours:*** Red and white striped shirts, black shorts, black stockings.

***Change Colours:*** Blue and black striped shirts, black shorts, blue stockings.

***Year Formed:*** 1892.

***Turned Professional:*** 1932.

***Ltd Co.:*** 1937.

***Club Nickname:*** 'The Robins'.

***Previous Grounds:*** Grafton Cricket Ground, Whaddon Lane, Carter's Field (pre 1932).

## HONOURS

*Football League:* Promoted from Division 3 (play-offs) 2001–02.

*FA Cup:* best season: 5th rd 2002.

*Football League Cup:* never past 2nd rd.

*Football Conference:* Champions 1998–99, runners-up 1997–98.

*Trophy:* Winners 1997–98.

*Southern League:* Champions 1984–85; *Southern League Cup:* Winners 1957–58, runners-up 1968–69, 1984–85; *Southern League Merit Cup:* Winners 1984–85; *Southern League Championship Shield:* Winners 1985.

*Gloucestershire Senior Cup:* Winners 1998–99; *Gloucestershire Northern Senior Professional Cup:* Winners 30 times; *Midland Floodlit Cup:* Winners 1985–86, 1986–87, 1987–88; *Mid Gloucester League:* Champions 1896–97; *Gloucester and District League:* Champions 1902–03, 1905–06; *Cheltenham League:* Champions 1910–11, 1913–14; *North Gloucestershire League:* Champions 1913–14; *Gloucestershire Northern Senior League:* Champions 1928–29, 1932–33; *Gloucestershire Northern Senior Amateur Cup:* Winners 1929–30, 1930–31, 1932–33, 1933–34, 1934–35; *Leamington Hospital Cup:* Winners 1934–35.

## SKY SPORTS FACT FILE

For their first season in the Southern League in 1935–36, Cheltenham Town secured two experienced Football League players in inside-forwards Alex Findlay (Bristol Rovers, Wrexham) and Jim Black (Charlton Athletic, Aldershot).

***Record League Victory:*** 11–0 v Bourneville Ath, Birmingham Combination, 29 April 1933 – Davis; Jones, Williams; Lang (1), Blackburn, Draper; Evans, Hazard (4), Haycox (4), Goodger (1), Hill (1).

***Record Cup Victory:*** 12–0 v Chippenham R, FA Cup 3rd qual. rd, 2 November 1935 – Bowles; Whitehouse, Williams; Lang, Devonport (1), Partridge (2); Perkins, Hackett, Jones (4), Black (4), Griffiths (1).

***Record Defeat:*** 0–7 v Crystal Palace, League Cup 2nd rd, 2 October 2002.
*N.B.* 1–10 v Merthyr T, Southern League, 8 March 1952.

***Most League Points (2 for a win):*** 60, Southern League Division 1, 1963–64.

***Most League Points (3 for a win):*** 86, Southern League Premier Division, 1994–95.

***Most League Goals:*** 115, Southern League, 1957–58.

***Highest League Scorer in Season:*** Dave Lewis, 33 (53 in all competitions), Southern League Division 1, 1974–75.

***Most League Goals in Total Aggregate:*** Dave Lewis, 205 (290 in all competitions), 1970–83.

***Most Capped Player:*** Grant McCann, 4 (9), Northern Ireland.

***Most League Appearances:*** Roger Thorndale, 523 (702 in all competitions), 1958–76.

***Record Transfer Fee Received:*** £60,000 from Southampton for Christer Warren, 1995.

***Record Transfer Fee Paid:*** £57,000 to West Ham U for Grant McCann, January 2003.

***Football League Record:*** 1999 Promoted to Division 3; 2002 Division 2; 2003–04 Division 3; 2004– FL2.

## MANAGERS

George Blackburn 1932–34
George Carr 1934–37
Jimmy Brain 1937–48
Cyril Dean 1948–50
George Summerbee 1950–52
William Raeside 1952–53
Arch Anderson 1953–58
Ron Lewin 1958–60
Peter Donnelly 1960–61
Tommy Cavanagh 1961
Arch Anderson 1961–65
Harold Fletcher 1965–66
Bob Etheridge 1966–73
Willie Penman 1973–74
Dennis Allen 1974–79
Terry Paine 1979
Alan Grundy 1979–82
Alan Wood 1982–83
John Murphy 1983–88
Jim Barron 1988–90
John Murphy 1990
Dave Lewis 1990–91
Ally Robertson 1991–92
Lindsay Parsons 1992–95
Chris Robinson 1995–97
Steve Cotterill 1997–2002
Graham Allner 2002–03
Bobby Gould 2003
John Ward November 2003–

## LATEST SEQUENCES

***Longest Sequence of League Wins:*** not more than 3.

***Longest Sequence of League Defeats:*** 5, 13.1.2001 – 13.2.2001.

***Longest Sequence of League Draws:*** 5, 5.4.2003 – 21.4.2003.

***Longest Sequence of Unbeaten League Matches:*** 16, 1.12.2001 – 12.3.2002.

***Longest Sequence Without a League Win:*** 10, 16.4.2002 – 14.9.2002.

***Successive Scoring Runs:*** 15 from 15.2.2003.

***Successive Non-scoring Runs:*** 4 from 12.9.1999.

## TEN YEAR LEAGUE RECORD

| | | *P* | *W* | *D* | *L* | *F* | *A* | *Pts* | *Pos* |
|---|---|---|---|---|---|---|---|---|---|
| 1994–95 | Sth L | 42 | 25 | 11 | 6 | 87 | 39 | 86 | 2 |
| 1995–96 | Sth L | 42 | 21 | 11 | 10 | 76 | 57 | 74 | 3 |
| 1996–97 | Sth L | 42 | 21 | 11 | 10 | 76 | 44 | 74 | 2 |
| 1997–98 | Conf. | 42 | 23 | 9 | 10 | 63 | 43 | 78 | 2 |
| 1998-99 | Conf. | 42 | 22 | 14 | 6 | 71 | 36 | 80 | 1 |
| 1999-2000 | Div 3 | 46 | 20 | 10 | 16 | 50 | 42 | 70 | 8 |
| 2000-01 | Div 3 | 46 | 18 | 14 | 14 | 59 | 52 | 68 | 9 |
| 2001-02 | Div 3 | 46 | 21 | 15 | 10 | 66 | 49 | 78 | 4 |
| 2002-03 | Div 2 | 46 | 10 | 18 | 18 | 53 | 68 | 48 | 21 |
| 2003-04 | Div 3 | 46 | 14 | 14 | 18 | 57 | 71 | 56 | 14 |

## DID YOU KNOW ?

Cheltenham Town clinched the Southern League title in 1984–85 in dramatic fashion on the last day of the season. A penalty by Brian Hughes lifted them to a 2-1 win over Alvechurch in what proved to be their last game in the competition.

## CHELTENHAM TOWN 2003–04 LEAGUE RECORD

| *Match No.* | *Date* | *Venue* | *Opponents* | *Result* | *H/T Score* | *Lg. Pos.* | *Goalscorers* | *Attendance* |
|---|---|---|---|---|---|---|---|---|
| 1 | Aug 9 | A | Southend U | L 0-2 | 0-1 | — | | 4403 |
| 2 | 16 | H | Swansea C | L 3-4 | 2-1 | 22 | Cozic [17], McCann 2 (1 pen) [30, 60 (p)] | 4660 |
| 3 | 23 | A | Hull C | D 3-3 | 3-2 | 22 | Spencer 3 [31, 39, 40] | 12,522 |
| 4 | 25 | H | Kidderminster H | W 2-1 | 0-0 | 18 | Victory [79], McCann [81] | 4179 |
| 5 | 30 | A | Leyton Orient | W 4-1 | 4-1 | 10 | Odejayi [23], Jones D [32], Taylor 2 [34, 41] | 3785 |
| 6 | Sept 5 | H | Northampton T | W 4-3 | 0-2 | — | Taylor [56], Forsyth 2 (2 pens) [76, 89], Devaney [90] | 5002 |
| 7 | 13 | A | Bury | D 1-1 | 0-1 | 8 | Odejayi [71] | 2753 |
| 8 | 16 | H | Oxford U | D 0-0 | 0-0 | — | | 5319 |
| 9 | 20 | H | Cambridge U | L 0-3 | 0-1 | 15 | | 3728 |
| 10 | 27 | A | Bristol R | L 0-2 | 0-1 | 17 | | 8013 |
| 11 | 30 | A | Scunthorpe U | L 2-5 | 1-2 | — | Taylor [44], McCann (pen) [88] | 2857 |
| 12 | Oct 4 | H | Yeovil T | W 3-1 | 2-1 | 16 | Devaney [4], Yates [15], Brayson [46] | 4960 |
| 13 | 11 | A | Boston U | L 1-3 | 1-2 | 16 | McCann [22] | 2283 |
| 14 | 18 | H | Rochdale | L 0-2 | 0-1 | 19 | | 3105 |
| 15 | 21 | H | Darlington | W 2-1 | 1-1 | — | Victory [31], Devaney [90] | 2745 |
| 16 | 25 | A | Mansfield T | L 0-4 | 0-2 | 18 | | 4095 |
| 17 | Nov 1 | H | York C | D 1-1 | 0-0 | 19 | Spencer [85] | 3431 |
| 18 | 15 | A | Torquay U | L 1-3 | 0-0 | 20 | Spencer [56] | 2653 |
| 19 | 22 | H | Carlisle U | W 2-1 | 1-1 | 18 | Taylor 2 [33, 50] | 3414 |
| 20 | 29 | A | Huddersfield T | D 0-0 | 0-0 | 18 | | 8442 |
| 21 | Dec 13 | H | Doncaster R | L 1-3 | 1-2 | 21 | Yates [19] | 3884 |
| 22 | 26 | H | Macclesfield T | W 3-2 | 1-0 | 20 | Spencer [30], Taylor [57], Devaney [72] | 4237 |
| 23 | 28 | A | Northampton T | L 0-1 | 0-1 | 21 | | 5118 |
| 24 | Jan 9 | H | Southend U | D 1-1 | 0-0 | — | Cort (og) [87] | 4451 |
| 25 | 13 | A | Lincoln C | D 0-0 | 0-0 | — | | 3464 |
| 26 | 17 | A | Swansea C | D 0-0 | 0-0 | 21 | | 6474 |
| 27 | 24 | H | Hull C | L 0-2 | 0-0 | 21 | | 4536 |
| 28 | 31 | H | Leyton Orient | W 1-0 | 1-0 | 17 | Brayson [45] | 3336 |
| 29 | Feb 7 | A | Macclesfield T | W 2-1 | 2-1 | 14 | Whitaker (og) [26], McCann [27] | 2061 |
| 30 | 10 | A | Kidderminster H | D 0-0 | 0-0 | — | | 3803 |
| 31 | 14 | H | Boston U | W 1-0 | 0-0 | 13 | Brough [62] | 3434 |
| 32 | 21 | A | Rochdale | D 0-0 | 0-0 | 12 | | 2449 |
| 33 | 28 | H | Mansfield T | W 4-2 | 1-0 | 12 | Henry [42], Spencer [61], Brayson [70], Odejayi [90] | 3818 |
| 34 | Mar 6 | H | Lincoln C | W 3-2 | 1-2 | 12 | McCann [32], Finnigan [87], Odejayi [90] | 3783 |
| 35 | 9 | A | Darlington | L 1-2 | 1-2 | — | McCann [45] | 3921 |
| 36 | 13 | A | Doncaster R | D 1-1 | 0-0 | 12 | Devaney [50] | 7510 |
| 37 | 17 | A | Oxford U | L 0-1 | 0-1 | — | | 5916 |
| 38 | 20 | H | Bury | L 1-2 | 1-0 | 13 | Brayson [28] | 3435 |
| 39 | 27 | A | Cambridge U | L 1-2 | 0-2 | 14 | Brayson [71] | 3909 |
| 40 | Apr 3 | H | Bristol R | L 1-2 | 1-2 | 16 | Brough [30] | 5088 |
| 41 | 10 | A | Yeovil T | D 0-0 | 0-0 | 16 | | 6613 |
| 42 | 12 | H | Scunthorpe U | W 2-1 | 1-1 | 14 | Brayson [45], Spencer [49] | 3409 |
| 43 | 17 | A | York C | W 2-0 | 0-0 | 12 | Nogan (og) [59], Brayson (pen) [90] | 3221 |
| 44 | 24 | H | Torquay U | L 1-3 | 0-1 | 12 | Spencer [81] | 4900 |
| 45 | May 1 | A | Carlisle U | D 1-1 | 0-1 | 13 | Odejayi [85] | 9524 |
| 46 | 8 | H | Huddersfield T | D 1-1 | 0-1 | 14 | Duff S [75] | 5814 |

**Final League Position: 14**

### GOALSCORERS

*League (57):* Spencer 9, McCann 8 (2 pens), Brayson 7 (1 pen), Taylor 7, Devaney 5, Odejayi 5, Brough 2, Forsyth 2 (2 pens), Victory 2, Yates 2, Cozic 1, Duff S 1, Finnigan 1, Henry 1, Jones D 1, own goals 3.
*Carling Cup (1):* McCann 1.
*FA Cup (7):* McCann 3 (1 pen), Brayson 1, Spencer 1, Taylor 1, Yates 1.
*LDV Vans Trophy (1):* Devaney 1.

| Book S 4 + 1 | Griffin A 10 + 5 | Victory J 44 | Finnigan J 32 + 1 | Duff S 13 + 2 | Duff M 42 | Devaney M 32 + 8 | Yates M 20 + 1 | Brayson P 20 + 11 | Odejayi K 14 + 16 | McCann G 43 | Brough J 23 + 3 | Cleverley B 2 + 6 | Spencer D 29 + 7 | Cozic B 7 | Fyfe G 15 + 5 | Amankwaah K 11 + 1 | Taylor B 19 + 9 | Forsyth R 16 + 11 | Higgs S 42 | Jones D 14 | Howells L 7 + 2 | Bird D 18 + 6 | Dobson C — + 2 | Corbett L — + 1 | Wilson B 14 | Henry K 8 + 1 | Hynes P 2 + 2 | Gill J 5 + 2 | *Match No.* |
|---|---|---|---|---|---|---|---|---|---|---|---|---|---|---|---|---|---|---|---|---|---|---|---|---|---|---|---|---|---|
| 1 | 2 | 3 | 4 | $5^{1}$ | 6 | $7^{2}$ | 8 | 9 | 10 | $11^{3}$ | 12 | 13 | 14 | | | | | | | | | | | | | | | | 1 |
| 1 | $2^{3}$ | 3 | | | 6 | 12 | 8 | | 10 | 11 | $5^{1}$ | 13 | 9 | $4^{2}$ | 7 | 14 | | | | | | | | | | | | | 2 |
| 1 | | 3 | | | 6 | 12 | 8 | | 10 | 11 | $5^{3}$ | | $9^{1}$ | $7^{2}$ | 4 | 2 | 14 | 13 | | | | | | | | | | | 3 |
| | | 3 | | | 6 | 12 | 8 | | $10^{3}$ | 11 | | | $9^{2}$ | 7 | $4^{1}$ | 2 | 14 | 13 | 1 | 5 | | | | | | | | | 4 |
| | 12 | 3 | | | $6^{1}$ | 13 | 8 | | 10 | 11 | | | | $7^{2}$ | 4 | 2 | $9^{3}$ | 14 | 1 | 5 | | | | | | | | | 5 |
| | $2^{3}$ | 3 | | | 6 | 7 | 8 | 12 | $10^{1}$ | | | | | $11^{2}$ | 4 | | 9 | 13 | 1 | 5 | 14 | | | | | | | | 6 |
| | | 3 | | | 6 | $12^{2}$ | 8 | 13 | 10 | 11 | | | | $7^{1}$ | $4^{3}$ | 2 | 9 | 14 | 1 | 5 | | | | | | | | | 7 |
| | | 3 | | | 6■ | | 8 | | 10 | 11 | | | | | | 2 | 9 | 4 | 1 | 5 | 7 | | | | | | | | 8 |
| | | 3 | | 12 | $6^{1}$ | 13 | $8^{2}$ | 14 | 10 | 11 | | | | | | $2^{3}$ | 9 | 4 | 1 | 5 | 7 | | | | | | | | 9 |
| | | 3 | | 6 | | | 8 | | $10^{1}$ | | | | 9 | $7^{2}$ | $4^{3}$ | 2 | 12 | | 1 | 5 | 11 | 14 | 13 | | | | | | 10 |
| | | 3 | | $6^{1}$ | | 7 | 8 | | 12 | 11 | | | 10 | | $4^{2}$ | $2^{3}$ | 9 | 13 | 1 | 5 | | 14 | | | | | | | 11 |
| | | 3 | | | | 7 | 8 | 12 | | $11^{1}$ | | | | | $10^{2}$ | 2 | 9 | 4 | 1 | 5 | 13 | 6 | | | | | | | 12 |
| 1■ | | 3 | 12 | | | 7 | 8 | $10^{1}$ | | 11 | | 14 | 13 | | $6^{3}$ | 2 | 9 | | | 5 | | $4^{2}$ | | | | | | | 13 |
| | | 3 | 4 | | 6 | 10 | 8 | | | 11 | | 12 | $9^{1}$ | | $7^{2}$ | 2 | 13 | | 1 | $5^{3}$ | | | 14 | | | | | | 14 |
| | | 3 | | | 6 | 7 | 8 | 9 | | 11 | | | 12 | | | | $10^{1}$ | | 1 | 5 | 4 | 2 | | | | | | | 15 |
| | | 3 | 8 | | 6 | 7 | | 9 | | $11^{1}$ | | 12 | 13 | | | | $10^{2}$ | | 1 | 5 | 4 | 2 | | | | | | | 16 |
| | | 3 | 4 | | 6 | 7 | 8 | 9 | | | $5^{2}$ | | 12 | | | | $10^{1}$ | | 1 | 2 | 11 | | | 13 | | | | | 17 |
| | | | $4^{2}$ | | 6 | 12 | 8 | 9 | | 3 | 5 | $11^{3}$ | 10 | | | | 13 | 14 | 1 | | $7^{1}$ | 2 | | | | | | | 18 |
| | 13 | | 11 | | 6 | 7 | 8 | | | 3 | 5 | | 10 | | 12 | | $9^{2}$ | $4^{1}$ | 1 | | | 2 | | | | | | | 19 |
| | | 3 | 4 | | 6 | 7 | 8 | | | 11 | 5 | | 10 | | | | 9 | | 1 | | | 2 | | | | | | | 20 |
| | | 3 | 4 | | 6 | 8 | $7^{3}$ | 12 | 13 | $11^{1}$ | 5 | | 10 | | | | $9^{2}$ | | 1 | | | 14 | | | 2 | | | | 21 |
| | | 3 | 8 | | 6 | 7 | 12 | 13 | 14 | 11 | 5 | | $10^{2}$ | | | | $9^{3}$ | $4^{1}$ | 1 | | | | | | 2 | | | | 22 |
| 15 | | 3 | 8 | | 6 | 7 | | 12 | | $11^{2}$ | 5 | | 10 | | | | $9^{1}$ | 4 | $1^{G}$ | | | 13 | | | 2 | | | | 23 |
| | | 3 | 8 | 13 | 6 | 7 | | 12 | | $11^{3}$ | $5^{2}$ | | 10 | | | | $9^{1}$ | 4 | 1 | | | 14 | | | 2 | | | | 24 |
| | | 3 | 8 | 5 | 6 | 12 | | | | 11 | | | 10 | | | | $9^{1}$ | $4^{2}$ | 1 | | | 7 | | | 2 | 13 | | | 25 |
| | | 3 | 8 | 5 | 6 | 7 | | | | 11 | | | 10 | | | | | | 1 | | | 4 | | | 2 | 9 | | | 26 |
| | | 3 | 10 | 5 | 6 | $7^{3}$ | | | | 11 | 14 | | 9■ | | | | $12^{2}$ | | 1 | | | $4^{1}$ | | | 2 | 8 | 13 | | 27 |
| | | 3 | 8 | 5 | 6 | 7 | | 9 | 12 | $11^{1}$ | | | | | | | | | 1 | | | 2 | | | | 4 | 10 | | 28 |
| | 14 | 3 | 8 | $5^{2}$ | 6 | 7 | | 9 | $10^{1}$ | 11 | 13 | | | | | | | 12 | 1 | | | $2^{3}$ | | | | 4 | | | 29 |
| | 2 | 3 | 8 | | 6 | 7 | | $9^{2}$ | $10^{3}$ | 11 | 5 | | | | | | | 12 | 1 | | | 13 | | | | $4^{1}$ | 14 | | 30 |
| | 2 | 3 | 8 | | 6 | 7 | | 9 | 12 | 11 | 5 | | | | | | | | 1 | | | | | | | 4 | $10^{1}$ | | 31 |
| | 2 | 3 | 8 | | 6 | 7 | | 9 | | 11 | 5 | | 10 | | | | | | 1 | | | | | | | 4 | | | 32 |
| | 2 | 3 | 8 | | 6 | 7 | | $9^{1}$ | 12 | 11 | 5 | | 10 | | | | | | 1 | | | | | | | 4 | | | 33 |
| | $2^{3}$ | 3 | 8 | | 6 | 7 | | $9^{1}$ | 12 | 11 | 5 | 13 | 10 | | | | | $4^{2}$ | 1 | | | | | | | | | 14 | 34 |
| | 2 | 3 | 8 | | 6 | 7 | | $9^{1}$ | 12 | 11 | 5 | | 10 | | | | | 4 | 1 | | | | | | | | | | 35 |
| | 14 | 3 | 8 | | 6 | 7 | | | 12 | $11^{3}$ | 5 | 9 | $10^{1}$ | | | | 13 | $4^{2}$ | 1 | | | | | | | | | 2 | 36 |
| | | 3 | 8 | 4 | 6 | 10 | | 12 | 13 | 11 | 5 | | $9^{2}$ | | | | 14 | $7^{1}$ | 1 | | | | | | | | | $2^{3}$ | 37 |
| | | 3 | 8 | | 6 | 7 | | 9 | 13 | 11 | 5 | | 12 | | | | $10^{2}$ | $4^{1}$ | 1 | | | | | | | | | 2 | 38 |
| | | 3 | 8 | | 6 | 7 | | 9 | 13 | 11 | 5 | | $10^{2}$ | | 12 | | | $4^{1}$ | 1 | | | | | | | | | 2 | 39 |
| | | 3 | 8 | | 6 | 7 | | 9 | $10^{2}$ | 11 | 5 | | 12 | | 13 | | | $4^{1}$ | 1 | | | | | | 2 | | | | 40 |
| | | 3 | 8 | | 6 | 7 | | | 12 | 11 | 5 | | $9^{1}$ | | 10 | | | | 1 | | | 4 | | | 2 | | | | 41 |
| | | 3 | 8 | | 6 | $7^{2}$ | | 12 | | 11 | $5^{3}$ | | 9 | | $10^{1}$ | | | 13 | 1 | | | 4 | | | 2 | | | 14 | 42 |
| | 13 | 3 | 8 | 5 | 6 | | | 9 | 12 | $11^{3}$ | | | $10^{1}$ | | 14 | | | | 1 | | | 4 | | | 2 | | | $7^{2}$ | 43 |
| | $7^{1}$ | 3 | $8^{2}$ | 5 | 6 | | | 9 | 12 | 11 | | | 10 | | 13 | | | | 1 | | | 4 | | | 2 | | | | 44 |
| | | 3 | 8 | 5 | 6 | | | $9^{2}$ | 13 | 11 | | | 10 | | $7^{1}$ | | | 12 | 1 | | | 4 | | | 2 | | | | 45 |
| | | 3 | | 5 | 6 | | | 12 | $9^{1}$ | 11 | | | 10■ | | $7^{2}$ | | 13 | 4 | 1 | | | 8 | | | 2 | | | | 46 |

**Carling Cup**
First Round — QPR (h) 1-2

**LDV Vans Trophy**
First Round — Colchester U (h) 1-3

**FA Cup**
First Round — Hull C (h) 3-1
Second Round — Leyton Orient (h) 3-1
Third Round — Fulham (a) 1-2

# CHESTER CITY FL Championship 2

## FOUNDATION

All students of soccer history have read about the medieval games of football in Chester, but the present club was not formed until 1884 through the amalgamation of King's School Old Boys with Chester Rovers. For many years Chester were overshadowed in Cheshire by Northwich Victoria and Crewe Alexandra who had both won the Senior Cup several times before Chester's first success in 1894–95. The final against Macclesfield saw Chester face the team that had not only beaten them in the previous year's final, but also knocked them out of the FA Cup two seasons in succession. The final was held at the Drill Field, Northwich and Chester had the support of more than 1000 fans. Chester won 2-1.

***The Deva Stadium, Bumpers Lane, Chester CH1 4LT.***

***Telephone:*** (01244) 371 376.

***Fax:*** (01244) 390 265.

***Website:*** www.chestercityfc.net

***Email:*** info@chestercityfc.net

***Ground Capacity:*** 6,000.

***Record Attendance:*** 20,500 v Chelsea, FA Cup 3rd rd (replay), 16 January 1952 (at Sealand Road).

***Pitch Measurements:*** 115yd × 75yd.

***Chairman:*** Stephen Vaughan.

***Vice-chairman:*** Darren Liversage.

***Chief Executive:*** David Burford.

***Secretary:*** Tony Allan.

***Manager:*** Mark Wright.

***Assistant Manager:*** David Moss.

***Physio:*** Joe Hinnigan.

***Colours:*** Blue and white striped shirts, blue shorts, blue stockings.

***Change Colours:*** Yellow shirts, navy blue shorts, yellow stockings.

***Year Formed:*** 1885.

***Turned Professional:*** 1902.

***Ltd Co.:*** 1909.

***Previous Name:*** Chester until 1983.

***Club Nickname:*** 'Blues' and 'City'.

***Previous Grounds:*** 1885, Faulkner Street; 1898, The Old Showground; 1901, Whipcord Lane; 1906, Sealand Road; 1990, Moss Rose Ground, Macclesfield; 1992, Deva Stadium, Bumpers Lane.

***First Football League Game:*** 2 September 1931, Division 3 (N), v Wrexham (a) D 1–1 – Johnson; Herod, Jones; Keeley, Skitt, Reilly; Thompson, Ranson, Jennings (1), Cresswell, Hedley.

## HONOURS

*Football League:* Division 3 – Runners-up 1993–94; Division 3 (N) – Runners-up 1935–36; Division 4 – Runners-up 1985–86.

*Conference:* Champions 2003–04.

*FA Cup:* best season: 5th rd, 1977, 1980.

*Football League Cup:* Semi-final 1975.

*Welsh Cup:* Winners 1908, 1933, 1947.

*Debenhams Cup:* Winners 1977.

## SKY SPORTS FACT FILE

In the 1978–79 season Chester had their then best run in the FA Youth Cup reaching the last 32, thanks in no small measure to the goalscoring exploits of a 15-year-old Flintshire schoolboy by the name of Ian Rush.

***Record League Victory:*** 12–0 v York C, Division 3 (N), 1 February 1936 – Middleton; Common, Hall; Wharton, Wilson, Howarth; Horsman (2), Hughes, Wrightson (4), Cresswell (2), Sargeant (4).

***Record Cup Victory:*** 6–1 v Darlington, FA Cup 1st rd, 25 November 1933 – Burke; Bennett, Little; Pitcairn, Skitt, Duckworth; Armes (3), Whittam, Mantle (2), Cresswell (1), McLachlan.

***Record Defeat:*** 2–11 v Oldham Ath, Division 3 (N), 19 January 1952.

***Most League Points (2 for a win):*** 56, Division 3 (N), 1946–47 and Division 4, 1964–65.

***Most League Points (3 for a win):*** 84, Division 4, 1985–86.

***Most League Goals:*** 119, Division 4, 1964–65.

***Highest League Scorer in Season:*** Dick Yates, 36, Division 3 (N), 1946–47.

***Most League Goals in Total Aggregate:*** Stuart Rimmer, 135, 1985–88, 1991–98.

***Most League Goals in One Match:*** 5, Tom Jennings v Walsall, Division 3N, 30 January 1932; 5, Barry Jepson v York C, Division 4, 8 February 1958.

***Most Capped Player:*** Bill Lewis, 13 (27), Wales.

***Most League Appearances:*** Ray Gill, 406, 1951–62.

***Youngest League Player:*** Aidan Newhouse, 15 years 350 days v Bury, 7 May 1988.

***Record Transfer Fee Received:*** £300,000 from Liverpool for Ian Rush, May 1980.

***Record Transfer Fee Paid:*** £95,000 to Boston U for Daryl Clare, November 2002.

***Football League Record:*** 1931 Elected Division 3 (N); 1958–75 Division 4; 1975–82 Division 3; 1982–86 Division 4; 1986–92 Division 3; 1992–93 Division 2; 1993–94 Division 3; 1994–95 Division 2; 1995–2000 Division 3; 2000–04 Conference; 2004– FL2.

## MANAGERS

Charlie Hewitt 1930–36
Alex Raisbeck 1936–38
Frank Brown 1938–53
Louis Page 1953–56
John Harris 1956–59
Stan Pearson 1959–61
Bill Lambton 1962–63
Peter Hauser 1963–68
Ken Roberts 1968–76
Alan Oakes 1976–82
Cliff Sear 1982
John Sainty 1982–83
John McGrath 1984
Harry McNally 1985–92
Graham Barrow 1992–94
Mike Pejic 1994–95
Derek Mann 1995
Kevin Ratcliffe 1995–99
Terry Smith 1999
Ian Atkins 2000
Graham Barrow 2000–01
Gordon Hill 2001
Steve Mungall 2001
Andy Porter/Dean Spink 2001–02
Mark Wright September 2002–

## LATEST SEQUENCES

***Longest Sequence of League Wins:*** 8, 12.4.78 – 26.8.78.

***Longest Sequence of League Defeats:*** 9, 30.4.94 – 13.9.94.

***Longest Sequence of League Draws:*** 6, 11.10.86 – 1.11.86.

***Longest Sequence of Unbeaten League Matches:*** 18, 27.10.34 – 16.2.35.

***Longest Sequence Without a League Win:*** 25, 19.9.61 – 3.3.62.

## TEN YEAR LEAGUE RECORD

| | | P | W | D | L | F | A | Pts | Pos |
|---|---|---|---|---|---|---|---|---|---|
| 1994-95 | Div 2 | 46 | 6 | 11 | 29 | 37 | 84 | 29 | 23 |
| 1995-96 | Div 3 | 46 | 18 | 16 | 12 | 72 | 53 | 70 | 8 |
| 1996-97 | Div 3 | 46 | 18 | 16 | 12 | 55 | 43 | 70 | 6 |
| 1997-98 | Div 3 | 46 | 17 | 10 | 19 | 60 | 61 | 61 | 14 |
| 1998-99 | Div 3 | 46 | 13 | 18 | 15 | 57 | 66 | 57 | 14 |
| 1999-2000 | Div 3 | 46 | 10 | 9 | 27 | 44 | 79 | 39 | 24 |
| 2000-01 | Conf. | 42 | 16 | 14 | 12 | 49 | 43 | 62 | 8 |
| 2001-02 | Conf. | 42 | 15 | 9 | 18 | 54 | 51 | 54 | 14 |
| 2002-03 | Conf. | 42 | 21 | 12 | 9 | 59 | 31 | 75 | 4 |
| 2003-04 | Conf. | 42 | 27 | 11 | 4 | 85 | 34 | 92 | 1 |

## DID YOU KNOW ?

Chester's election to the Football League in 1931 was a close-run affair. On the first ballot they finished equal on 27 with Nelson. But on the second vote it was Chester 28 Nelson 20 and they went on to finish third in the table.

# CHESTERFIELD — FL Championship 1

## FOUNDATION

Chesterfield are fourth only to Stoke, Notts County and Nottingham Forest in age for they can trace their existence as far back as 1866, although it is fair to say that they were somewhat casual in the first few years of their history playing only a few friendlies a year. However, their rules of 1871 are still in existence showing an annual membership of 2s (10p), but it was not until 1891 that they won a trophy (the Barnes Cup) and followed this a year later by winning the Sheffield Cup, Barnes Cup and the Derbyshire Junior Cup.

***Recreation Ground, St Margarets Drive, Saltergate, Chesterfield, Derbyshire S40 4SX.***

***Telephone:*** (01246) 209 765.

***Fax:*** (01246) 556 799.

***Ticket Office:*** (01246) 209 765.

***Email:*** reception@chesterfield-fc.co.uk.

***Ground Capacity:*** 8,509.

***Record Attendance:*** 30,968 v Newcastle U, Division 2, 7 April 1939.

***Pitch Measurements:*** 113yd × 71yd.

***Chairman:*** Barrie Hubbard.

***Vice-chairman:*** Jason Elliott.

***Chief Executive:*** Mike Warner.

***Manager:*** Roy McFarland.

***Assistant Manager:*** Lee Richardson.

***Physio:*** Jamie Hewitt.

***Secretary:*** Alan Walters.

***Colours:*** Blue shirts, blue shorts, white stockings.

***Change Colours:*** All black.

***Year Formed:*** 1866.

***Turned Professional:*** 1891.

***Ltd Co:*** 1871.

***Previous Name:*** Chesterfield Town.

***Club Nicknames:*** 'Blues' or 'Spireites'.

***First Football League Game:*** 2 September 1899, Division 2, v Sheffield W (a) L 1–5 – Hancock; Pilgrim, Fletcher; Ballantyne, Bell, Downie; Morley, Thacker, Gooing, Munday (1), Geary.

***Record League Victory:*** 10–0 v Glossop NE, Division 2, 17 January 1903 – Clutterbuck; Thorpe, Lerper; Haig, Banner, Thacker; Tomlinson (2), Newton (1), Milward (3), Munday (2), Steel (2).

***Record Cup Victory:*** 5–0 v Wath Ath (a), FA Cup 1st rd, 28 November 1925 – Birch; Saxby, Dennis; Wass, Abbott, Thompson; Fisher (1), Roseboom (1), Cookson (2), Whitfield (1), Hopkinson.

## HONOURS

*Football League:* Division 2 best season: 4th, 1946–47; Division 3 (N) – Champions 1930–31, 1935–36; Runners-up 1933–34; Promoted to Division 2 (3rd) – 2000–01; Division 4 – Champions 1969–70, 1984–85.

*FA Cup:* Semi-final 1997.

*Football League Cup:* best season: 4th rd, 1965.

*Anglo-Scottish Cup:* Winners 1981.

## SKY SPORTS FACT FILE

Although they lost their opening three League games in 1994–95 scoring just one goal, Chesterfield went on to gain promotion through the play-offs in a season during which they completed 58 League and Cup matches in five different competitions.

***Record Defeat:*** 0–10 v Gillingham, Division 3, 5 September 1987.

***Most League Points (2 for a win):*** 64, Division 4, 1969–70.

***Most League Points (3 for a win):*** 91, Division 4, 1984–85.

***Most League Goals:*** 102, Division 3 (N), 1930–31.

***Highest League Scorer in Season:*** Jimmy Cookson, 44, Division 3 (N), 1925–26.

***Most League Goals in Total Aggregate:*** Ernie Moss, 161, 1969–76, 1979–81 and 1984–86.

***Most League Goals in One Match:*** 4, Jimmy Cookson v Accrington S, Division 3N, 16 January 1926; 4, Jimmy Cookson v Ashington, Division 3N, 1 May 1926; 4, Jimmy Cookson v Wigan Borough, Division 3N, 4 September 1926; 4, Tommy Lyon v Southampton, Division 2, 3 December 1938.

***Most Capped Player:*** Walter McMillen, 4 (7), Northern Ireland; Mark Williams, 4 (30), Northern Ireland.

***Most League Appearances:*** Dave Blakey, 613, 1948–67.

***Youngest League Player:*** Dennis Thompson, 16 years 160 days v Notts Co, 26 December 1950.

***Record Transfer Fee Received:*** £750,000 from Southampton for Kevin Davies, May 1997.

***Record Transfer Fee Paid:*** £250,000 to Watford for Jason Lee, August 1998.

***Football League Record:*** 1899 Elected to Division 2; 1909 failed re-election; 1921–31 Division 3 (N); 1931–33 Division 2; 1933–36 Division 3 (N); 1936–51 Division 2; 1951–58 Division 3 (N); 1958–61 Division 3; 1961–70 Division 4; 1970–83 Division 3; 1983–85 Division 4; 1985–89 Division 3; 1989–92 Division 4; 1992–95 Division 3; 1995–2000 Division 2; 2000–01 Division 3; 2001–04 Division 2; 2004– FL1.

## MANAGERS

E. Russell Timmeus 1891–95
*(Secretary-Manager)*
Gilbert Gillies 1895–1901
E. F. Hind 1901–02
Jack Hoskin 1902–06
W. Furness 1906–07
George Swift 1907–10
G. H. Jones 1911–13
R. L. Weston 1913–17
T. Callaghan 1919
J. J. Caffrey 1920–22
Harry Hadley 1922
Harry Parkes 1922–27
Alec Campbell 1927
Ted Davison 1927–32
Bill Harvey 1932–38
Norman Bullock 1938–45
Bob Brocklebank 1945–48
Bobby Marshall 1948–52
Ted Davison 1952–58
Duggie Livingstone 1958–62
Tony McShane 1962–67
Jimmy McGuigan 1967–73
Joe Shaw 1973–76
Arthur Cox 1976–80
Frank Barlow 1980–83
John Duncan 1983–87
Kevin Randall 1987–88
Paul Hart 1988–91
Chris McMenemy 1991–93
John Duncan 1993–2000
Nicky Law 2000–02
Dave Rushbury 2002–03
Roy McFarland May 2003–

## LATEST SEQUENCES

***Longest Sequence of League Wins:*** 10, 6.9.1933 – 4.11.1933.

***Longest Sequence of League Defeats:*** 9, 22.10.1960 – 27.12.1960.

***Longest Sequence of League Draws:*** 5, 19.9.1990 – 6.10.1990.

***Longest Sequence of Unbeaten League Matches:*** 21, 26.12.1994 – 29.4.1995.

***Longest Sequence Without a League Win:*** 18, 11.9.1999 – 3.1.2000.

***Successive Scoring Runs:*** 46 from 25.12.1929.

***Successive Non-scoring Runs:*** 7 from 23.9.1977.

## TEN YEAR LEAGUE RECORD

| | | *P* | *W* | *D* | *L* | *F* | *A* | *Pts* | *Pos* |
|---|---|---|---|---|---|---|---|---|---|
| 1994-95 | Div 3 | 42 | 23 | 12 | 7 | 62 | 37 | 81 | 3 |
| 1995-96 | Div 2 | 46 | 20 | 12 | 14 | 56 | 51 | 72 | 7 |
| 1996-97 | Div 2 | 46 | 18 | 14 | 14 | 42 | 39 | 68 | 10 |
| 1997-98 | Div 2 | 46 | 16 | 17 | 13 | 46 | 44 | 65 | 10 |
| 1998-99 | Div 2 | 46 | 17 | 13 | 16 | 46 | 44 | 64 | 9 |
| 1999-2000 | Div 2 | 46 | 7 | 15 | 24 | 34 | 63 | 36 | 24 |
| 2000-01 | Div 3 | 46 | 25 | 14 | 7 | 79 | 42 | 80* | 3 |
| 2001-02 | Div 2 | 46 | 13 | 13 | 20 | 53 | 65 | 52 | 18 |
| 2002-03 | Div 2 | 46 | 14 | 8 | 24 | 43 | 73 | 50 | 20 |
| 2003-04 | Div 2 | 46 | 12 | 15 | 19 | 49 | 71 | 51 | 20 |

**9 pts deducted.*

## DID YOU KNOW ?

Champions of Division Four in 1984–85, Chesterfield owed much to their defence as they failed to score in 14 games, while in another 15 they managed just one goal. Defensively they recorded 21 clean sheets in the League.

## CHESTERFIELD 2003–04 LEAGUE RECORD

| Match No. | Date | Venue | Opponents | Result | | H/T Score | Lg. Pos. | Goalscorers | Attendance |
|---|---|---|---|---|---|---|---|---|---|
| 1 | Aug 9 | A | Wrexham | D | 0-0 | 0-0 | — | | 5688 |
| 2 | 16 | H | Bristol C | D | 1-1 | 1-1 | 16 | O'Hare[31] | 4302 |
| 3 | 23 | A | Wycombe W | D | 3-3 | 2-2 | 18 | Brandon[16], Hudson[45], Rushbury[90] | 4529 |
| 4 | 25 | H | Plymouth Arg | D | 1-1 | 0-0 | 17 | Brandon[50] | 4089 |
| 5 | 30 | A | QPR | L | 0-3 | 0-1 | 21 | | 12,986 |
| 6 | Sept 6 | H | Barnsley | L | 0-2 | 0-1 | 22 | | 5605 |
| 7 | 13 | H | Notts Co | L | 0-1 | 0-0 | 24 | | 4367 |
| 8 | 16 | A | Brighton & HA | L | 0-1 | 0-1 | — | | 6054 |
| 9 | 20 | A | Grimsby T | L | 0-4 | 0-1 | 24 | | 4141 |
| 10 | 27 | H | Brentford | L | 1-2 | 0-0 | 24 | Payne (pen)[77] | 3257 |
| 11 | 30 | H | Bournemouth | D | 1-1 | 1-0 | — | Robinson[33] | 3131 |
| 12 | Oct 4 | A | Stockport Co | D | 0-0 | 0-0 | 24 | | 4764 |
| 13 | 11 | A | Rushden & D | L | 1-2 | 1-2 | 24 | Robinson[14] | 3817 |
| 14 | 18 | H | Swindon T | W | 3-0 | 2-0 | 23 | Robinson 2[11, 19], Cade[71] | 3506 |
| 15 | 21 | H | Hartlepool U | L | 1-2 | 0-1 | — | Cade[53] | 3411 |
| 16 | 25 | A | Colchester U | L | 0-1 | 0-1 | 24 | | 3115 |
| 17 | Nov 1 | H | Port Vale | W | 1-0 | 0-0 | 23 | Robinson[60] | 4088 |
| 18 | 15 | A | Blackpool | L | 0-1 | 0-1 | 23 | | 5252 |
| 19 | 22 | H | Oldham Ath | D | 1-1 | 1-0 | 23 | Blatherwick[30] | 3565 |
| 20 | 29 | A | Luton T | L | 0-1 | 0-1 | 23 | | 5453 |
| 21 | Dec 13 | H | Tranmere R | D | 2-2 | 2-1 | 23 | Hurst[2], Allott[45] | 3123 |
| 22 | 20 | A | Sheffield W | D | 0-0 | 0-0 | 24 | | 25,296 |
| 23 | 26 | H | Peterborough U | W | 2-1 | 0-1 | 23 | Robinson[48], Hurst[75] | 4376 |
| 24 | 28 | A | Barnsley | W | 1-0 | 0-0 | 22 | Hurst[80] | 11,664 |
| 25 | Jan 3 | A | Plymouth Arg | L | 0-7 | 0-6 | 23 | | 13,109 |
| 26 | 10 | H | Wrexham | W | 2-1 | 0-0 | 22 | Blatherwick[70], Evatt[86] | 3585 |
| 27 | 17 | A | Bristol C | L | 0-4 | 0-1 | 23 | | 11,807 |
| 28 | 24 | H | Wycombe W | D | 2-2 | 0-1 | 22 | Brandon[75], Evatt[82] | 3576 |
| 29 | 31 | H | QPR | W | 4-2 | 1-1 | 21 | McMaster[31], Evatt[50], Hurst[65], Hudson[79] | 4567 |
| 30 | Feb 7 | A | Peterborough U | W | 2-0 | 0-0 | 19 | Hurst[47], McMaster[77] | 5446 |
| 31 | 14 | H | Rushden & D | W | 2-0 | 1-0 | 19 | Hurst[2], Reeves (pen)[59] | 4361 |
| 32 | 21 | A | Swindon T | L | 0-2 | 0-1 | 19 | | 6814 |
| 33 | Mar 2 | A | Hartlepool U | L | 0-2 | 0-0 | — | | 4736 |
| 34 | 7 | H | Sheffield W | W | 3-1 | 1-0 | 19 | Hurst 2[45, 59], Brandon[75] | 7695 |
| 35 | 13 | A | Tranmere R | W | 3-2 | 1-0 | 17 | Hurst 2[21, 86], Jones (og)[83] | 7370 |
| 36 | 16 | H | Brighton & HA | L | 0-2 | 0-0 | — | | 4478 |
| 37 | 20 | A | Notts Co | D | 1-1 | 0-0 | 18 | Richardson (og)[77] | 7808 |
| 38 | 23 | H | Colchester U | L | 1-2 | 0-1 | — | Hurst[50] | 3787 |
| 39 | 27 | H | Grimsby T | D | 4-4 | 1-2 | 18 | Hurst[19], Reeves 3 (2 pens)[66, 73 (p), 90 (p)] | 4444 |
| 40 | Apr 3 | A | Brentford | D | 1-1 | 0-0 | 21 | Evatt[90] | 4962 |
| 41 | 10 | H | Stockport Co | L | 0-3 | 0-2 | 22 | | 5901 |
| 42 | 12 | A | Bournemouth | D | 2-2 | 2-0 | 21 | Allott[21], De Bolla[27] | 7081 |
| 43 | 17 | A | Port Vale | D | 1-1 | 1-0 | 22 | Evatt[34] | 5582 |
| 44 | 24 | H | Blackpool | W | 1-0 | 1-0 | 21 | Niven[20] | 4117 |
| 45 | May 1 | A | Oldham Ath | L | 0-2 | 0-0 | 22 | | 8177 |
| 46 | 8 | H | Luton T | W | 1-0 | 0-0 | 20 | Hurst[88] | 6285 |

**Final League Position: 20**

### GOALSCORERS

*League (49):* Hurst 13, Robinson 6, Evatt 5, Brandon 4, Reeves 4 (3 pens), Allott 2, Blatherwick 2, Cade 2, Hudson 2, McMaster 2, De Bolla 1, Niven 1, O'Hare 1, Payne 1 (pen), Rushbury 1, own goals 2.
*Carling Cup (0).*
*FA Cup (2):* Davies 1, Evatt 1.
*LDV Vans Trophy (5):* Brandon 2, Cade 1, Robinson 1, Warhurst 1.

| Muggleton C 46 | Uhlenbeek G 36 + 1 | O'Hare A 40 | Dawson K 22 + 2 | Blatherwick S 36 | Payne S 20 | Brandon C 39 + 4 | Hudson M 32 + 3 | Allott M 35 + 5 | Hurst G 28 + 1 | Evatt I 43 | Reeves D 18 + 13 | Searle D 4 + 1 | Davies G 18 + 10 | Burt J — + 1 | Rushbury A — + 5 | Folan C 4 + 3 | Innes M 17 + 5 | De Bolla M 3 + 5 | Smith A — + 3 | Howson S 6 + 3 | Robinson M 17 + 15 | Cade J 9 + 1 | Warhurst P 3 + 1 | O'Halloran M 1 + 2 | Niven D 22 | McMaster J 4 + 2 | N'Toya T 3 + 3 | Fullarton J — + 1 | *Match No.* |
|---|---|---|---|---|---|---|---|---|---|---|---|---|---|---|---|---|---|---|---|---|---|---|---|---|---|---|---|---|---|
| 1 | 2 | 3 | 4 | 5 | 6 | 7 | 8 | $9^{1}$ | 10 | 11 | 12 | | | | | | | | | | | | | | | | | | 1 |
| 1 | 2 | 3 | 4 | | 6 | $7^{1}$ | 8 | 9 | $10^{2}$ | 5 | | 11 | 12 | 13 | | | | | | | | | | | | | | | 2 |
| 1 | 2 | 3 | 4 | | 6 | 7 | 8 | 9 | $10^{1}$ | 5 | 12 | $11^{2}$ | | | 13 | | | | | | | | | | | | | | 3 |
| 1 | 2 | 3 | 4 | | 6 | 7 | 8 | $9^{2}$ | $10^{1}$ | 5 | 12 | 11 | | | | 13 | | | | | | | | | | | | | 4 |
| 1 | 2 | 3 | 4 | | $6^{2}$ | $7^{3}$ | 8 | 9 | $10^{1}$ | 5 | 12 | 11 | | | 14 | 13 | | | | | | | | | | | | | 5 |
| 1 | 2 | $3^{2}$ | 4 | | 6 | 7 | 8 | 11 | | 5 | $9^{1}$ | | 12 | | | 10 | 13 | | | | | | | | | | | | 6 |
| 1 | 2 | $3^{2}$ | $4^{1}$ | 5 | 6 | 7 | 8 | 12 | | 11 | | 13 | | | | 10 | | $9^{3}$ | 14 | | | | | | | | | | 7 |
| 1 | 2 | 3 | $4^{1}$ | 5 | 6 | 7 | 8 | 9 | | 11 | | | 12 | | | $10^{2}$ | | | 13 | | | | | | | | | | 8 |
| 1 | 2▮ | | 12 | 5 | 6 | 7 | 8 | 9 | | 11 | | | $4^{2}$ | | 13 | $10^{3}$ | | | | $3^{1}$ | 14 | | | | | | | | 9 |
| 1 | 2 | | 4 | 5 | 6 | 7 | 8 | $9^{2}$ | | 3 | | | 12 | | | | | | 13 | | 10 | $11^{1}$ | | | | | | | 10 |
| 1 | 2 | 3 | $4^{1}$ | 5 | 6 | 12 | 8 | 13 | | 11 | | | 7 | | | | | | | | $9^{2}$ | 10 | | | | | | | 11 |
| 1 | | 3 | | 5▮ | 6 | 7 | 8 | 12 | | 11 | | | 2 | | | | | | | 4 | $9^{1}$ | 10 | | | | | | | 12 |
| 1 | | 3 | | 5 | 6 | 7 | 8 | 12 | | 11 | | | 2 | | | | | 13 | | $4^{2}$ | 9 | $10^{1}$ | | | | | | | 13 |
| 1 | 2 | 3 | | | 6 | 12 | 13 | 7 | | 5 | | | 4 | | | | $8^{2}$ | $11^{1}$ | | | 9 | $10^{3}$ | 14 | | | | | | 14 |
| 1 | 2 | 3 | | | 6 | 12 | 8 | 7 | | 5 | | | $11^{1}$ | | | | | | | | 9 | 10 | 4 | | | | | | 15 |
| 1 | 2▮ | 3 | | | 6 | 7 | 8 | 11 | 12 | 5 | | | $4^{1}$ | | | | | | | | 9 | 10 | | | | | | | 16 |
| 1 | 2 | 3 | 12 | 5 | 6 | 7 | | 11 | | | $9^{2}$ | | | | | | | | | $4^{1}$ | 13 | 10 | 8 | | | | | | 17 |
| 1 | | 3 | | 5 | 6 | 7 | | 8 | | 11 | 12 | | $2^{2}$ | | 13 | | | | | | $9^{1}$ | 10 | 4 | | | | | | 18 |
| 1 | 2 | 3 | 4 | 5 | 6 | $7^{3}$ | 12 | 10 | | 11 | $9^{2}$ | | | | | | $8^{1}$ | | | | 13 | 14 | | | | | | | 19 |
| 1 | 2 | 3 | 4 | 5 | | 7 | | 8 | | 11 | $9^{2}$ | | | | 12 | | $10^{1}$ | | | 6 | 13 | | | | | | | | 20 |
| 1 | 2 | $3^{3}$ | $4^{2}$ | 5 | | | 8 | $7^{1}$ | 10 | 6 | 12 | | 13 | | | | 11 | | | | | | | 14 | 9 | | | | 21 |
| 1 | 2 | | | 5 | | 7 | 8 | 11 | 10 | 6 | 12 | | | | | | 3 | | | | $9^{1}$ | | | | 4 | | | | 22 |
| 1 | 2 | | | 5 | | 7 | 8 | 9 | 11 | 6 | 12 | | | | | | 3 | | | | $10^{1}$ | | | | 4 | | | | 23 |
| 1 | 2 | | 5 | | | 12 | 8 | 7 | 10 | 11 | 13 | | | | | | 3 | | | 6 | $9^{2}$ | | | | $4^{1}$ | | | | 24 |
| 1 | 2 | 3 | | 5 | | 7 | 8 | 9 | 10 | 6 | | | 12 | | | | $11^{2}$ | | | | 13 | | | | $4^{1}$ | | | | 25 |
| 1 | 2 | 3 | | 5 | | 7 | | 11 | $10^{2}$ | 6 | | | | | | | $8^{1}$ | | | 12 | 9 | | | | 4 | 13 | | | 26 |
| 1 | 2 | 3 | | 5 | | 7 | 12 | 11 | 10 | $6^{2}$ | | | | | | | $8^{1}$ | | | 13 | 14 | | | | 4 | $9^{3}$ | | | 27 |
| 1 | 2 | 3 | | $5^{2}$ | | 7 | 8 | 11 | 10 | 6 | 12 | | | | | | 13 | | | | $9^{1}$ | | | | $4^{3}$ | 14 | | | 28 |
| 1 | 2 | 3 | | 5 | | 7 | 8 | | 10 | 6 | 9 | | | | | | | | | | | | | | 4 | 11 | | | 29 |
| 1 | | 3 | 2 | 5 | | 7 | 8 | | 10 | 6 | 9 | | 12 | | | | | | | | | | | | 4 | $11^{1}$ | | | 30 |
| 1 | 2 | 3 | | 5 | | 7 | $4^{1}$ | 8 | 10 | 6 | $9^{2}$ | | 11 | | | | 12 | | | | 13 | | | | | | | | 31 |
| 1 | 2 | 3 | | 5 | | $7^{1}$ | 8 | 12 | 10 | 6 | 9 | | $4^{2}$ | | | | | | | 13 | 14 | | | | | $11^{3}$ | | | 32 |
| 1 | 2 | 3 | | 5 | 4 | $7^{1}$ | 8 | | 10 | 6 | $9^{2}$ | | 12 | | | | 11 | | | | 13 | | | | | | | | 33 |
| 1 | 2 | 3 | | 5 | | 7 | 8 | 11 | 10 | 6 | $9^{1}$ | | 4 | | | | | | | | 12 | | | | | | | | 34 |
| 1 | 2 | 3 | | 5 | | 7 | 8 | 11 | 10 | 6 | | | | | | | | | | | 9 | | | | 4 | | | | 35 |
| 1 | 2 | $3^{1}$ | | 5 | | 7 | $8^{2}$ | 11 | 10 | 6 | $9^{3}$ | | 12 | | | | 13 | | | | 14 | | | | 4 | | | | 36 |
| 1 | 2 | 3 | | 5 | | 7 | | 8 | 10▮ | 11 | 12 | | 6 | | | | | | | | $9^{1}$ | | | | 4 | | | | 37 |
| 1 | 2 | 3 | | 5 | | 7 | | 11 | 10 | 6 | 13 | | $8^{1}$ | | | | 12 | | | | $9^{2}$ | | | | 4 | | | | 38 |
| 1 | 12 | $3^{1}$ | 2 | 5 | | 7 | | 11 | 10 | 6 | 9 | | | | | | 8▮ | | | | | | | | 4 | | | | 39 |
| 1 | 2 | | 6 | 5 | | 7 | | 8 | | 11 | 9 | | | | | | 3 | 12 | | | | | | | 4 | | $10^{1}$ | | 40 |
| 1 | $2^{3}$ | 3 | 4 | $5^{2}$ | | | | 11 | | 6 | 9 | | 7 | | | | | 13 | | | 12 | | | | 8 | | $10^{1}$ | 14 | 41 |
| 1 | | 3 | 5 | | | | | $11^{2}$ | | 6 | 12 | | 7 | | | 13 | 8 | $9^{3}$ | | | $10^{1}$ | | | 2 | 4 | | 14 | | 42 |
| 1 | | 3 | | 5 | | $7^{1}$ | | | 10 | 6 | 9 | | 2 | | | | 8 | 13 | | | | | | 12 | 4 | | $11^{2}$ | | 43 |
| 1 | | 3 | 6 | 5 | | $7^{2}$ | 8 | | 10 | | $9^{1}$ | | 2 | | | | 11 | | | | 12 | | | | 4 | | 13 | | 44 |
| 1 | | 3 | 6 | 5 | | 7 | 8 | | 10 | | $9^{1}$ | | 2 | | | | $11^{2}$ | | | | 12 | | | | 4 | | 13 | | 45 |
| 1 | | 3 | $2^{1}$ | 5 | | 7 | 8 | $11^{3}$ | 10 | 6 | $9^{2}$ | | 12 | | | | | 14 | | | 13 | | | | 4 | | | | 46 |

**Carling Cup**

| | | | |
|---|---|---|---|
| First Round | Burnley | (h) | 0-0 |

**LDV Vans Trophy**

| | | | |
|---|---|---|---|
| First Round | Macclesfield T | (h) | 2-1 |
| Second Round | Lincoln C | (a) | 3-4 |

**FA Cup**

| | | | |
|---|---|---|---|
| First Round | Tranmere R | (a) | 2-3 |

# COLCHESTER UNITED FL Championship 1

## FOUNDATION

Colchester United was formed in 1937 when a number of enthusiasts of the much older Colchester Town club decided to establish a professional concern as a limited liability company. The new club continued at Layer Road which had been the amateur club's home since 1909.

***Layer Road Ground, Colchester, Essex CO2 7JJ.***

***Telephone:*** 0845 330 2975.

***Fax:*** (01206) 715 303.

***Ticket Office:*** 0845 330 2975.

***Website:*** www.cu-fc.com

***Email:*** editor@colchesterunited.net

***Ground Capacity:*** 6,180.

***Record Attendance:*** 19,072 v Reading, FA Cup 1st rd, 27 November 1948.

***Pitch Measurements:*** 110yd × 71yd.

***Chairman:*** Peter Heard.

***Chief Executive:*** Marie Partner.

***Secretary:*** Andy Gardner.

***Manager:*** Phil Parkinson.

***Assistant Manager:*** Geraint Williams.

***Physio:*** Stuart Ayles.

***Colours:*** Blue and white stripes.

***Change Colours:*** All red.

***Year Formed:*** 1937.

***Turned Professional:*** 1937.

***Ltd Co.:*** 1937.

***Club Nickname:*** 'The U's'.

***First Football League Game:*** 19 August 1950, Division 3 (S), v Gillingham (a) D 0–0 – Wright; Kettle, Allen; Bearryman, Stewart, Elder; Jones, Curry, Turner, McKim, Church.

***Record League Victory:*** 9–1 v Bradford C, Division 4, 30 December 1961 – Ames; Millar, Fowler; Harris, Abrey, Ron Hunt; Foster, Bobby Hunt (4), King (4), Hill (1), Wright.

***Record Cup Victory:*** 7–1 v Yeovil T (away), FA Cup 2nd rd (replay), 11 December 1958 – Ames; Fisher, Fowler; Parker, Milligan, Hammond; Williams (1), McLeod (2), Langman (4), Evans, Wright. 7–1 v Yeading, FA Cup 1st rd (replay), 22 November 1994 – Cheesewright; Betts, English, Cawley, Caesar, Locke (Dennis), Fry, Brown (2), Whitton (2) (Thompson), Kinsella (1), Abrahams (2).

## HONOURS

*Football League:* Promoted from Division 3 – 1997–98 (play-offs); Division 4 – Runners-up 1961–62.

*FA Cup:* best season: 6th rd, 1971.

*Football League Cup:* best season: 5th rd, 1975.

*Auto Windscreens Shield:* Runners-up 1997.

*GM Vauxhall Conference:* Winners 1991–92.

*FA Trophy:* Winners 1992.

## SKY SPORTS FACT FILE

Dubbed the wing-half with the Betty Grable legs, Jimmy Elder joined Colchester United from Portsmouth in 1950 and made 212 League and Cup appearances. His other more significant claim to fame was that he never missed a penalty.

***Record Defeat:*** 0–8 v Leyton Orient, Division 4, 15 October 1989.

***Most League Points (2 for a win):*** 60, Division 4, 1973–74.

***Most League Points (3 for a win):*** 81, Division 4, 1982–83.

***Most League Goals:*** 104, Division 4, 1961–62.

***Highest League Scorer in Season:*** Bobby Hunt, 38, Division 4, 1961–62.

***Most League Goals in Total Aggregate:*** Martyn King, 130, 1956–64.

***Most League Goals in One Match:*** 4, Bobby Hunt v Bradford C, Division 4, 30 December 1961; 4, Martyn King v Bradford C, Division 4, 30 December 1961; 4, Bobby Hunt v Doncaster R, Division 4, 30 April 1962.

***Most Capped Player:*** None.

***Most League Appearances:*** Micky Cook, 613, 1969–84.

***Youngest League Player:*** Lindsay Smith, 16 years 218 days v Grimsby T, 24 April 1971.

***Record Transfer Fee Received:*** £2,250,000 from Newcastle U for Lomano Lua-Lua, September 2000.

***Record Transfer Fee Paid:*** £50,000 to Peterborough U for Neil Gregory, March 1998 and £50,000 to Norwich C for Adrian Coote, December 2001.

***Football League Record:*** 1950 Elected to Division 3 (S); 1958–61 Division 3; 1961–62 Division 4; 1962–65 Division 3; 1965–66 Division 4; 1966–68 Division 3; 1968–74 Division 4; 1974–76 Division 3, 1976–77 Division 4; 1977–81 Division 3; 1981–90 Division 4; 1990–92 GM Vauxhall Conference; 1992–98 Division 3; 1998–04 Division 2; 2004– FL1.

## MANAGERS

Ted Fenton 1946–48
Jimmy Allen 1948–53
Jack Butler 1953–55
Benny Fenton 1955–63
Neil Franklin 1963–68
Dick Graham 1968–72
Jim Smith 1972–75
Bobby Roberts 1975–82
Allan Hunter 1982–83
Cyril Lea 1983–86
Mike Walker 1986–87
Roger Brown 1987–88
Jock Wallace 1989
Mick Mills 1990
Ian Atkins 1990–91
Roy McDonough 1991–94
George Burley 1994
Steve Wignall 1995–99
Mick Wadsworth 1999
Steve Whitton 1999–2003
Phil Parkinson February 2003–

## LATEST SEQUENCES

***Longest Sequence of League Wins:*** 7, 29.11.1968 – 1.2.1969.

***Longest Sequence of League Defeats:*** 8, 9.10.1954 – 4.12.1954.

***Longest Sequence of League Draws:*** 6, 21.3.1977 – 11.4.1977.

***Longest Sequence of Unbeaten League Matches:*** 20, 22.12.1956 – 19.4.1957.

***Longest Sequence Without a League Win:*** 20, 2.3.1968 – 31.8.1968.

***Successive Scoring Runs:*** 24 from 15.9.1962.

***Successive Non-scoring Runs:*** 5 from 7.4.1981.

## TEN YEAR LEAGUE RECORD

| | | P | W | D | L | F | A | Pts | Pos |
|---|---|---|---|---|---|---|---|---|---|
| 1994-95 | Div 3 | 42 | 16 | 10 | 16 | 56 | 64 | 58 | 10 |
| 1995-96 | Div 3 | 46 | 18 | 18 | 10 | 61 | 51 | 72 | 7 |
| 1996-97 | Div 3 | 46 | 17 | 17 | 12 | 62 | 51 | 68 | 8 |
| 1997-98 | Div 3 | 46 | 21 | 11 | 14 | 72 | 60 | 74 | 4 |
| 1998-99 | Div 2 | 46 | 12 | 16 | 18 | 52 | 70 | 52 | 18 |
| 1999-2000 | Div 2 | 46 | 14 | 10 | 22 | 59 | 82 | 52 | 18 |
| 2000-01 | Div 2 | 46 | 15 | 12 | 19 | 55 | 59 | 57 | 17 |
| 2001-02 | Div 2 | 46 | 15 | 12 | 19 | 65 | 76 | 57 | 15 |
| 2002-03 | Div 2 | 46 | 14 | 16 | 16 | 52 | 56 | 58 | 12 |
| 2003-04 | Div 2 | 46 | 17 | 13 | 16 | 52 | 56 | 64 | 11 |

## DID YOU KNOW ?

On 2 February 1956 Colchester United visited Reading in what was the Elm Park club's first Football League match under floodlights as well as the initial such illuminated fixture in the Third Division (South). Colchester won 3-1.

## COLCHESTER UNITED 2003–04 LEAGUE RECORD

| *Match No.* | *Date* | *Venue* | *Opponents* | *Result* | | *H/T Score* | *Lg. Pos.* | *Goalscorers* | *Attendance* |
|---|---|---|---|---|---|---|---|---|---|
| 1 | Aug 9 | A | Barnsley | L | 0-1 | 0-0 | — | | 8450 |
| 2 | 15 | H | Swindon T | L | 0-1 | 0-0 | — | | 3339 |
| 3 | 23 | A | Port Vale | L | 3-4 | 2-1 | 21 | McGleish 2 [26, 38], Andrews [88] | 5133 |
| 4 | 26 | H | Bristol C | W | 2-1 | 0-0 | — | McGleish 2 [47, 55] | 3079 |
| 5 | 30 | A | Tranmere R | D | 1-1 | 1-1 | 19 | Andrews [30] | 6745 |
| 6 | Sept 6 | H | QPR | D | 2-2 | 1-0 | 18 | Vine [10], McGleish (pen) [75] | 3835 |
| 7 | 13 | H | Brighton & HA | W | 1-0 | 0-0 | 15 | Andrews [67] | 4169 |
| 8 | 16 | A | Wycombe W | W | 2-1 | 2-0 | — | Andrews [25], Vine [27] | 4401 |
| 9 | 20 | A | Peterborough U | W | 2-1 | 1-0 | 11 | Fagan [36], Keith [90] | 4690 |
| 10 | 27 | H | Bournemouth | W | 1-0 | 0-0 | 6 | Duguid [75] | 3602 |
| 11 | 30 | H | Brentford | D | 1-1 | 0-1 | — | Vine [76] | 3343 |
| 12 | Oct 4 | A | Notts Co | L | 0-3 | 0-1 | 10 | | 4187 |
| 13 | 11 | H | Blackpool | D | 1-1 | 1-0 | 13 | Andrews [2] | 3265 |
| 14 | 18 | A | Grimsby T | L | 0-2 | 0-1 | 13 | | 5021 |
| 15 | 21 | A | Stockport Co | W | 3-1 | 2-0 | — | Fagan [26], Andrews [34], Vine [47] | 3683 |
| 16 | 25 | H | Chesterfield | W | 1-0 | 1-0 | 8 | Andrews [10] | 3115 |
| 17 | 31 | A | Wrexham | W | 1-0 | 1-0 | — | Andrews [35] | 4269 |
| 18 | Nov 15 | H | Sheffield W | W | 3-1 | 1-0 | 4 | McGleish [27], Andrews [81], Fagan [90] | 5018 |
| 19 | 22 | A | Rushden & D | L | 0-4 | 0-2 | 5 | | 4149 |
| 20 | 29 | H | Plymouth Arg | L | 0-2 | 0-2 | 8 | | 4332 |
| 21 | Dec 13 | H | Oldham Ath | W | 2-1 | 0-0 | 5 | Duguid [48], Vine [72] | 2897 |
| 22 | 20 | A | Hartlepool U | D | 0-0 | 0-0 | 5 | | 4135 |
| 23 | 26 | H | Luton T | D | 1-1 | 1-1 | 6 | McGleish [12] | 5083 |
| 24 | 28 | A | QPR | L | 0-2 | 0-1 | 9 | | 15,720 |
| 25 | Jan 10 | H | Barnsley | D | 1-1 | 1-0 | 10 | Andrews [25] | 3507 |
| 26 | 17 | A | Swindon T | L | 0-2 | 0-1 | 11 | | 6014 |
| 27 | 27 | A | Bristol C | L | 0-1 | 0-1 | — | | 10,733 |
| 28 | 31 | H | Tranmere R | D | 1-1 | 0-1 | 14 | Izzet [89] | 3099 |
| 29 | Feb 7 | A | Luton T | L | 0-1 | 0-0 | 14 | | 5662 |
| 30 | 21 | H | Grimsby T | W | 2-0 | 0-0 | 14 | Fagan [65], Izzet [90] | 2922 |
| 31 | 24 | H | Port Vale | L | 1-4 | 1-3 | — | McGleish (pen) [10] | 2539 |
| 32 | Mar 2 | H | Stockport Co | W | 2-1 | 0-0 | — | Vine [50], Andrews [60] | 2513 |
| 33 | 6 | H | Hartlepool U | L | 1-2 | 1-1 | 15 | Halford [35] | 3348 |
| 34 | 13 | A | Oldham Ath | D | 0-0 | 0-0 | 13 | | 5937 |
| 35 | 16 | H | Wycombe W | D | 1-1 | 1-1 | — | Fagan (pen) [8] | 3092 |
| 36 | 20 | A | Brighton & HA | L | 1-2 | 0-1 | 14 | Izzet [69] | 6156 |
| 37 | 23 | A | Chesterfield | W | 2-1 | 1-0 | — | Halford [31], Andrews [82] | 3787 |
| 38 | 27 | H | Peterborough U | D | 0-0 | 0-0 | 13 | | 3754 |
| 39 | 30 | A | Blackpool | D | 0-0 | 0-0 | — | | 5473 |
| 40 | Apr 3 | A | Bournemouth | D | 1-1 | 1-0 | 12 | Halford [35] | 6896 |
| 41 | 10 | H | Notts Co | W | 4-1 | 2-0 | 12 | Fagan 3 [9, 17, 53], Williams [78] | 3782 |
| 42 | 12 | A | Brentford | L | 2-3 | 0-1 | 13 | White [53], Fagan [80] | 5017 |
| 43 | 17 | H | Wrexham | W | 3-1 | 2-1 | 13 | Williams [16], Halford [45], McGleish [82] | 3077 |
| 44 | 24 | A | Sheffield W | W | 1-0 | 0-0 | 11 | Keith [48] | 20,464 |
| 45 | May 1 | H | Rushden & D | W | 2-0 | 0-0 | 11 | McGleish (pen) [81], Johnson [90] | 4618 |
| 46 | 8 | A | Plymouth Arg | L | 0-2 | 0-1 | 11 | | 19,868 |

**Final League Position: 11**

## GOALSCORERS

*League (52):* Andrews 12, McGleish 10 (3 pens), Fagan 9 (1 pen), Vine 6, Halford 4, Izzet 3, Duguid 2, Keith 2, Williams 2, Johnson 1, White 1.
*Carling Cup (2):* Fagan 1, Pinault 1.
*FA Cup (8):* Vine 4, Keith 2, McGleish 1, own goal 1.
*LDV Vans Trophy (14):* McGleish 6, Andrews 2, Vine 2, Brown J 1, Izzet 1, Keith 1, Pinault 1.

| Brown S 40 | Stockley S 44 | Myers A 21 | Pinault T 31 + 9 | Fitzgerald S 22 + 1 | White A 30 + 3 | Duguid K 30 | Izzet K 43 + 1 | Fagan C 30 + 7 | McGleish S 25 + 9 | Keith J 16 + 12 | Bowry B 18 + 6 | Vine R 30 + 5 | Hadland P — + 1 | Baldwin P 1 + 3 | Andrews W 32 + 9 | Chilvers L 29 + 3 | Halford G 15 + 3 | Johnson G 14 + 4 | Cade J 6 + 9 | McKinney R 5 | Tierney P 2 | Brown W 16 | Williams G 5 + 2 | Gerken D 1 | *Match No.* |
|---|---|---|---|---|---|---|---|---|---|---|---|---|---|---|---|---|---|---|---|---|---|---|---|---|---|
| 1 | 2 | 3 | 4[1] | 5 | 6 | 7 | 8 | 9[2] | 10 | 11 | 12 | 13 | | | | | | | | | | | | | 1 |
| 1 | 2 | 3 | 4 | 5 | 6 | 7 | 8 | 9 | 12 | 11[2] | | 10[1] | 13 | | | | | | | | | | | | 2 |
| 1 | 2 | 3 | 4[1] | 5 | 6[2] | 7 | 8 | 9[3] | 10 | 11 | 12 | | | 13 | 14 | | | | | | | | | | 3 |
| 1 | 2 | 3 | 4 | 5 | | 7 | 8 | 12 | 10 | | | 9 | | 6 | 11[1] | | | | | | | | | | 4 |
| 1 | 2 | 3[1] | 4 | 5 | | 7 | 8 | | 10 | | | 9 | | 12 | 11 | 6 | | | | | | | | | 5 |
| 1 | 2 | 3 | 4 | 5 | | 7 | 8 | | 10 | | | 9 | | | 11 | 6 | | | | | | | | | 6 |
| 1 | 2 | 3[2] | 4[1] | 5 | | 7 | 8 | 14 | 10 | | 12 | 9 | | 13 | 11[3] | 6 | | | | | | | | | 7 |
| 1 | 2 | 3■ | 4[1] | 5 | | 7 | 8 | 13 | 10 | | 12 | 9 | | | 11[2] | 6 | | | | | | | | | 8 |
| 1 | 2 | 3[1] | 4 | 5 | | 7 | 8 | 10 | | 12 | | 9 | | | 11 | 6 | | | | | | | | | 9 |
| 1 | 2 | 3[2] | 4 | 5 | | 7 | 8 | 13 | 10 | 12 | | 11 | | | 9[1] | 6 | | | | | | | | | 10 |
| 1 | 2 | | 4 | 5 | | 3 | 8 | 7 | 10 | | | 11 | | | 9 | 6 | | | | | | | | | 11 |
| 1 | 2 | | 4 | 5 | | 7 | 8 | 3 | 10[1] | 12 | | 9 | | | 11 | 6 | | | | | | | | | 12 |
| 1 | 2[1] | 3 | 4 | 5 | 6 | 7 | 8[2] | 10 | 12 | | 13 | 9 | | | 11 | | | | | | | | | | 13 |
| 1 | 2[2] | 3 | 4 | 5 | | 7 | 8 | | 10 | 12 | | 11 | | | 9[1] | 6 | 13 | | | | | | | | 14 |
| 1 | 2 | 3 | 4 | 5 | | 7 | 8 | 10 | 12 | 13 | | 11[2] | | | 9[1] | 6 | | | | | | | | | 15 |
| 1 | 2 | 3 | 4 | 5 | 12 | 7 | 8 | 10 | 13 | 14 | | 11[3] | | | 9[2] | 6[1] | | | | | | | | | 16 |
| 1 | 2 | 3 | 4 | 5 | 6 | 7 | 8 | 10 | 12 | 13 | | 11[2] | | | 9[1] | | | | | | | | | | 17 |
| 1 | 2 | 3[1] | 4 | 5 | 12 | 7 | | 9 | 10[2] | | 8 | 11 | | | 13 | 6 | | | | | | | | | 18 |
| 1 | 2 | 3 | 4[1] | 5 | | 7 | 12 | 10■ | 13 | | 8 | 11 | | | 9[2] | 6 | | | | | | | | | 19 |
| 1 | 2 | 3 | 4 | 5[1] | | 7 | 8 | 10 | | 12 | | 11 | | | 9 | 6 | | | | | | | | | 20 |
| 1 | 2 | | 4 | | 5 | 7 | 8 | | 10 | | | 11 | | | 9[1] | 6 | | 3 | 12 | | | | | | 21 |
| 1 | 2 | 3 | 4 | 12 | 5■ | 7 | 8 | 13 | 10[2] | | | 11[3] | | | 9[1] | 6 | | 14 | | | | | | | 22 |
| 1 | 2 | 3 | 4 | | 5 | | 8 | 7 | 10[1] | | | 11 | | | 9 | 6 | | | 12 | | | | | | 23 |
| 1 | 2 | 3 | | | 5[2] | 7■ | 8 | 9 | 10[1] | | | 11 | | | 12 | 6 | | 4 | 13 | | | | | | 24 |
| 1 | 2 | | | 5 | 12 | 3■ | 8 | 7 | 10 | 11 | 4[3] | 13 | | | 9[2] | 6[1] | 14 | | | | | | | | 25 |
| 1 | 2 | | 4 | 5 | 6[1] | | | 7 | 10 | 11 | | | | | 9 | 8 | 3 | | 12 | | | | | | 26 |
| | 2 | | 4 | | 5 | 3 | 8[1] | 7■ | 10 | 11 | | | | | 9[2] | 6 | 12 | | 13 | 1 | | | | | 27 |
| | 2 | | 4 | | 5 | 7 | 8 | 13 | 10 | 11 | | 12 | | | 9[2] | 6 | | | | 1 | 3[1] | | | | 28 |
| 1 | 2[1] | | 4[2] | | 5 | 7 | 8[3] | 9 | 12 | 11 | | 10 | | | 13 | 6 | | | 14 | | 3 | | | | 29 |
| 1 | 2 | | | | 5 | 3 | 8 | 9 | 13 | 12 | 4 | 11[2] | | | 10 | | | | 7[1] | | | 6 | | | 30 |
| 1 | 2[1] | | 13 | | 5 | 3 | 8 | 7 | 10 | 11 | 4[2] | 12 | | | 9 | | | | | | | 6 | | | 31 |
| | | | 4 | | 5 | 2[1] | 7 | | 10[2] | | 12 | 11 | | | 9 | 8 | 3 | 13 | | 1 | | 6 | | | 32 |
| | | | 12 | | 5 | | 7 | | | 13 | 8[1] | 11 | | | 9 | 3 | 2 | 4[2] | 10 | 1 | | 6 | | | 33 |
| | 2 | | | | 5 | | 8 | 12 | | | 11 | 10 | | | 9[1] | 4 | 3[2] | 7 | 13 | 1 | | 6 | | | 34 |
| 1 | 2 | | 12 | | 5 | | 11 | 9 | | 14 | 8[1] | 10 | | | 13 | 4 | | 3[2] | 7[3] | | | 6 | | | 35 |
| 1 | 2 | | 4 | | 5 | | 11 | 9 | | 13 | 8[1] | 10[3] | | | 12 | | 3 | 14 | 7[2] | | | 6■ | | | 36 |
| 1 | 2 | | 4[1] | | 5 | | 11 | 9 | | | 8 | 10[2] | | | 12 | | 3 | 13 | 7 | | | 6 | | | 37 |
| 1 | 2 | | 4 | | 5[1] | | 8 | 10 | | | | | | | 9■ | 12 | 3 | 11 | 7[2] | | | 6 | 13 | | 38 |
| 1 | 2 | | | | 5 | | 7 | 10 | | 11 | 8[1] | | | | 9 | 12 | 3 | 4 | | | | 6 | | | 39 |
| 1 | 2 | | 12 | | 5 | | 7 | 10 | | 11 | 8 | | | | 9[1] | 4 | 3 | 6 | | | | | | | 40 |
| 1 | 2 | | 12 | | 5 | | 7 | 10 | | 11[3] | 8[1] | | | | | 13 | 3[2] | 4 | 14 | | | 6 | 9 | | 41 |
| | 2 | | 12 | | 5 | | 7 | 10 | | | 8[1] | 13 | | | | 4[3] | 3 | 11 | 14 | | | 6 | 9[2] | 1 | 42 |
| 1 | 2 | | 12 | | 5 | | 7 | 10 | 13 | 11 | 8 | | | | | | 3 | 4[1] | | | | 6 | 9[2] | | 43 |
| 1 | 2 | | 12 | | 5 | | 7 | | 10 | 11 | 8 | | | | 13 | | 3 | 4[1] | | | | 6 | 9[2] | | 44 |
| 1 | 2 | | | | 5 | | 7 | | 10 | 11 | 8 | | | | 12 | | 3 | 4 | | | | 6 | 9[1] | | 45 |
| 1 | 2 | | 12 | | 5 | | 7 | | 10 | 11 | 8[1] | | | | 9 | | 3 | 4[2] | | | | 6 | 13 | | 46 |

**Carling Cup**

| | | | |
|---|---|---|---|
| First Round | Plymouth Arg | (h) | 2-1 |
| Second Round | Rotherham U | (a) | 0-1 |

**LDV Vans Trophy**

| | | | |
|---|---|---|---|
| First Round | Cheltenham T | (a) | 3-1 |
| Second Round | Yeovil T | (a) | 2-2 |
| Quarter-Final | Wycombe W | (a) | 3-2 |
| Semi-Final | Northampton T | (a) | 3-2 |
| Southern Final | Southend U | (h) | 2-3 |
| | | (a) | 1-1 |

**FA Cup**

| | | | |
|---|---|---|---|
| First Round | Oxford U | (h) | 1-0 |
| Second Round | Aldershot T | (h) | 1-0 |
| Third Round | Accrington S | (a) | 0-0 |
| | | (h) | 2-1 |
| Fourth Round | Coventry C | (a) | 1-1 |
| | | (h) | 3-1 |
| Fifth Round | Sheffield U | (a) | 0-1 |

# COVENTRY CITY FL Championship

## FOUNDATION

Workers at Singers' cycle factory formed a club in 1883. The first success of Singers' FC was to win the Birmingham Junior Cup in 1891 and this led in 1894 to their election to the Birmingham and District League. Four years later they changed their name to Coventry City and joined the Southern League in 1908 at which time they were playing in blue and white quarters.

***Highfield Road Stadium, King Richard Street, Coventry CV2 4FW.***

***Telephone:*** 0870 421 1987.

***Fax:*** 0870 421 1988.

***Ticket Office:*** 0870 421 1987.

***Website:*** www.ccfc.co.uk

***Email:*** info@ccfc.co.uk

***Ground Capacity:*** 23,633.

***Record Attendance:*** 51,455 v Wolverhampton W, Division 2, 29 April 1967.

***Pitch Measurements:*** 110yd × 75yd.

***Chairman:*** Mike McGinnity.

***Chief Executive:*** Graham Hover.

***Manager:*** Peter Reid.

***Assistant Manager:*** Adrian Heath.

***Physio:*** Michael McBride.

***Colours:*** Sky blue shirts with white and navy side panel, sky blue shorts with white and navy side panel, sky blue stockings with white and navy turnover and centre white stripe.

***Change Colours:*** White shirts with red front panel, red shorts, white stockings.

***Year Formed:*** 1883.

***Turned Professional:*** 1893.

***Ltd Co.:*** 1907.

***Previous Names:*** 1883, Singers FC; 1898, Coventry City FC.

***Club Nickname:*** 'Sky Blues'.

***Previous Grounds:*** 1883, Binley Road; 1887, Stoke Road; 1899, Highfield Road.

***First Football League Game:*** 30 August 1919, Division 2, v Tottenham H (h) L 0–5 – Lindon; Roberts, Chaplin, Allan, Hawley, Clarke, Sheldon, Mercer, Sambrooke, Lowes, Gibson.

***Record League Victory:*** 9–0 v Bristol C, Division 3 (S), 28 April 1934 – Pearson; Brown, Bisby; Perry, Davidson, Frith; White (2), Lauderdale, Bourton (5), Jones (2), Lake.

***Record Cup Victory:*** 8–0 v Rushden & D, League Cup 2nd rd, 2 October 2002 – Debec; Caldwell, Quinn, Betts (1p), Konjic (Shaw), Davenport, Pipe, Safri (Stanford), Mills (2) (Bothroyd (2)), McSheffery (3), Partridge.

## HONOURS

*Football League:* Division 1 best season: 6th, 1969–70; Division 2 – Champions 1966–67; Division 3 – Champions 1963–64; Division 3 (S) – Champions 1935–36; Runners-up 1933–34; Division 4 – Runners-up 1958–59.

*FA Cup:* Winners 1987.

*Football League Cup:* Semi-final 1981, 1990.

***European Competitions:*** *European Fairs Cup:* 1970–71.

## SKY SPORTS FACT FILE

Though Clarrie Bourton hogged the scoring headlines for Coventry City between the wars, much credit for his haul of goals went to the skilful creativity of Jock Lauderdale who also contributed 60 goals in five seasons.

***Record Defeat:*** 2–10 v Norwich C, Division 3 (S), 15 March 1930.

***Most League Points (2 for a win):*** 60, Division 4, 1958–59 and Division 3, 1963–64.

***Most League Points (3 for a win):*** 66, Division 1, 2001–02.

***Most League Goals:*** 108, Division 3 (S), 1931–32.

***Highest League Scorer in Season:*** Clarrie Bourton, 49, Division 3 (S), 1931–32.

***Most League Goals in Total Aggregate:*** Clarrie Bourton, 171, 1931–37.

***Most League Goals in One Match:*** 5, Clarrie Bourton v Bournemouth, Division 3S, 17 October 1931; 5, Arthur Bacon v Gillingham, Division 3S, 30 December 1933.

***Most Capped Player:*** Magnus Hedman 44 (56), Sweden.

***Most League Appearances:*** Steve Ogrizovic, 507, 1984–2000.

***Youngest League Player:*** Ben Mackey, 16 years 167 days v Ipswich T, 12 April 2003.

***Record Transfer Fee Received:*** £12,500,000 from Internazionale for Robbie Keane, July 2000.

***Record Transfer Fee Paid:*** £6,000,000 to Wolverhampton W for Robbie Keane, August 1999.

***Football League Record:*** 1919 Elected to Division 2; 1925–26 Division 3 (N); 1926–36 Division 3 (S); 1936–52 Division 2; 1952–58 Division 3 (S); 1958–59 Division 4; 1959–64 Division 3; 1964–67 Division 2; 1967–92 Division 1; 1992–2001 FA Premier League; 2001–04 Division 1; 2004– FLC.

## LATEST SEQUENCES

***Longest Sequence of League Wins:*** 6, 25.4.1964 – 5.9.1964.

***Longest Sequence of League Defeats:*** 9, 30.8.1919 – 11.10.1919.

***Longest Sequence of League Draws:*** 6, 1.11.2003 – 29.11.2003.

***Longest Sequence of Unbeaten League Matches:*** 25, 26.11.1966 – 13.5.1967.

***Longest Sequence Without a League Win:*** 19, 30.8.1919 – 20.12.1919.

***Successive Scoring Runs:*** 25 from 10.9.1966.

***Successive Non-scoring Runs:*** 11 from 11.10.1919.

## MANAGERS

H. R. Buckle 1909–10
Robert Wallace 1910–13
*(Secretary-Manager)*
Frank Scott-Walford 1913–15
William Clayton 1917–19
H. Pollitt 1919–20
Albert Evans 1920–24
Jimmy Kerr 1924–28
James McIntyre 1928–31
Harry Storer 1931–45
Dick Bayliss 1945–47
Billy Frith 1947–48
Harry Storer 1948–53
Jack Fairbrother 1953–54
Charlie Elliott 1954–55
Jesse Carver 1955–56
Harry Warren 1956–57
Billy Frith 1957–61
Jimmy Hill 1961–67
Noel Cantwell 1967–72
Bob Dennison 1972
Joe Mercer 1972–75
Gordon Milne 1972–81
Dave Sexton 1981–83
Bobby Gould 1983–84
Don Mackay 1985–86
George Curtis 1986–87
*(became Managing Director)*
John Sillett 1987–90
Terry Butcher 1990–92
Don Howe 1992
Bobby Gould 1992–93
Phil Neal 1993–95
Ron Atkinson 1995–96
*(became Director of Football)*
Gordon Strachan 1996–2001
Roland Nilsson 2001–02
Gary McAllister 2002–04
Eric Black 2004
Peter Reid May 2004–

## TEN YEAR LEAGUE RECORD

| | | P | W | D | L | F | A | Pts | Pos |
|---|---|---|---|---|---|---|---|---|---|
| 1994-95 | PR Lge | 42 | 12 | 14 | 16 | 44 | 62 | 50 | 16 |
| 1995-96 | PR Lge | 38 | 8 | 14 | 16 | 42 | 60 | 38 | 16 |
| 1996-97 | PR Lge | 38 | 9 | 14 | 15 | 38 | 54 | 41 | 17 |
| 1997-98 | PR Lge | 38 | 12 | 16 | 10 | 46 | 44 | 52 | 11 |
| 1998-99 | PR Lge | 38 | 11 | 9 | 18 | 39 | 51 | 42 | 15 |
| 1999-2000 | PR Lge | 38 | 12 | 8 | 18 | 47 | 54 | 44 | 14 |
| 2000-01 | PR Lge | 38 | 8 | 10 | 20 | 36 | 63 | 34 | 19 |
| 2001-02 | Div 1 | 46 | 20 | 6 | 20 | 59 | 53 | 66 | 11 |
| 2002-03 | Div 1 | 46 | 12 | 14 | 20 | 46 | 62 | 50 | 20 |
| 2003-04 | Div 1 | 46 | 17 | 14 | 15 | 67 | 54 | 65 | 12 |

## DID YOU KNOW?

The first player to be officially loaned out to another in the Football League in the modern era was John Docker from Coventry City to Torquay United on a month's temporary transfer in July 1967, making five appearances, his sole League experience.

## COVENTRY CITY 2003–04 LEAGUE RECORD

| Match No. | Date | Venue | Opponents | Result | | H/T Score | Lg. Pos. | Goalscorers | Attendance |
|---|---|---|---|---|---|---|---|---|---|
| 1 | Aug 16 | H | Walsall | D | 0-0 | 0-0 | 15 | | 15,377 |
| 2 | 23 | A | Ipswich T | D | 1-1 | 1-1 | 19 | Doyle [31] | 22,419 |
| 3 | 27 | H | Nottingham F | L | 1-3 | 0-1 | — | Whing [46] | 17,586 |
| 4 | 30 | A | Sheffield U | L | 1-2 | 0-1 | 23 | Suffo [67] | 20,102 |
| 5 | Sept 13 | H | Stoke C | W | 4-2 | 2-1 | 18 | Suffo [5], Barrett [10], Adebola [58], Morrell [75] | 13,982 |
| 6 | 16 | A | Preston NE | L | 2-4 | 1-2 | — | Staunton (pen) [42], Morrell [77] | 11,886 |
| 7 | 20 | A | Reading | W | 2-1 | 1-1 | 18 | Adebola [35], Morrell [76] | 15,371 |
| 8 | 27 | H | Wigan Ath | D | 1-1 | 0-0 | 20 | Morrell [89] | 14,862 |
| 9 | Oct 1 | H | Crewe Alex | W | 2-0 | 0-0 | — | McAllister [49], Morrell [73] | 11,557 |
| 10 | 4 | A | Millwall | L | 1-2 | 0-0 | 18 | Staunton (pen) [72] | 9849 |
| 11 | 15 | H | Wimbledon | W | 1-0 | 0-0 | — | Pead [63] | 10,872 |
| 12 | 18 | H | Cardiff C | L | 1-3 | 1-3 | 16 | Doyle [11] | 11,767 |
| 13 | 21 | A | Watford | D | 1-1 | 0-0 | — | Staunton [90] | 13,487 |
| 14 | 25 | A | Derby Co | W | 3-1 | 2-0 | 15 | Warnock [11], Suffo 2 [38, 80] | 21,641 |
| 15 | Nov 1 | H | West Ham U | D | 1-1 | 1-1 | 14 | Barrett [38] | 19,126 |
| 16 | 5 | H | Bradford C | D | 0-0 | 0-0 | — | | 11,862 |
| 17 | 8 | A | Sunderland | D | 0-0 | 0-0 | 15 | | 27,247 |
| 18 | 22 | H | Gillingham | D | 2-2 | 0-0 | 16 | Joachim 2 [55, 90] | 13,432 |
| 19 | 25 | A | Norwich C | D | 1-1 | 0-1 | — | McAllister (pen) [49] | 16,414 |
| 20 | 29 | A | Crystal Palace | D | 1-1 | 0-1 | 15 | Jackson [90] | 14,622 |
| 21 | Dec 2 | A | Rotherham U | L | 0-2 | 0-2 | — | | 5524 |
| 22 | 8 | H | Sunderland | D | 1-1 | 1-1 | — | McAllister (pen) [22] | 12,913 |
| 23 | 13 | A | Burnley | W | 2-1 | 2-0 | 14 | Suffo [8], Weller (og) [40] | 10,358 |
| 24 | 20 | H | WBA | W | 1-0 | 0-0 | 12 | Jackson [89] | 17,616 |
| 25 | 26 | H | Sheffield U | L | 0-1 | 0-0 | 15 | | 21,132 |
| 26 | 28 | A | Bradford C | L | 0-1 | 0-1 | 17 | | 11,432 |
| 27 | Jan 10 | H | Watford | D | 0-0 | 0-0 | 15 | | 12,226 |
| 28 | 17 | A | Walsall | W | 6-1 | 1-1 | 14 | Morrell 2 [6, 57], McSheffrey 2 [48, 82], Joachim [70], Roper (og) [76] | 8264 |
| 29 | 31 | H | Ipswich T | D | 1-1 | 1-0 | 15 | Warnock [45] | 14,441 |
| 30 | Feb 7 | A | Nottingham F | W | 1-0 | 1-0 | 14 | Suffo [4] | 23,075 |
| 31 | 14 | H | Norwich C | L | 0-2 | 0-1 | 14 | | 15,757 |
| 32 | 21 | A | Wimbledon | W | 3-0 | 2-0 | 14 | Joachim [9], Suffo [40], Gudjonsson [63] | 5905 |
| 33 | 28 | H | Derby Co | W | 2-0 | 2-0 | 12 | McSheffrey [20], Joachim [33] | 16,042 |
| 34 | Mar 2 | A | Cardiff C | W | 1-0 | 0-0 | — | McSheffrey (pen) [71] | 14,376 |
| 35 | 6 | A | WBA | L | 0-3 | 0-1 | 13 | | 25,414 |
| 36 | 13 | H | Burnley | W | 4-0 | 3-0 | 10 | Joachim [10], McSheffrey 2 (1 pen) [33, 39 (p)], Konjic [78] | 12,953 |
| 37 | 17 | H | Preston NE | W | 4-1 | 4-0 | — | Gudjonsson 2 [2, 27], Doyle [8], McSheffrey [11] | 13,142 |
| 38 | 20 | A | Wigan Ath | L | 1-2 | 0-2 | 10 | Warnock [72] | 8784 |
| 39 | 27 | H | Reading | L | 1-2 | 0-1 | 11 | McSheffrey [67] | 15,811 |
| 40 | Apr 3 | A | Stoke C | L | 0-1 | 0-1 | 11 | | 12,855 |
| 41 | 10 | H | Millwall | W | 4-0 | 2-0 | 12 | Joachim 2 [6, 58], Deloumeaux [12], McSheffrey (pen) [87] | 12,546 |
| 42 | 12 | A | Crewe Alex | L | 1-3 | 0-0 | 12 | Lowe [83] | 7475 |
| 43 | 17 | A | West Ham U | L | 0-2 | 0-1 | 13 | | 27,890 |
| 44 | 24 | H | Rotherham U | D | 1-1 | 0-0 | 12 | Morrell [56] | 13,572 |
| 45 | May 1 | A | Gillingham | W | 5-2 | 3-0 | 12 | Doyle [8], Morrell [24], McSheffrey 2 [31, 85], Shaw [90] | 10,388 |
| 46 | 9 | H | Crystal Palace | W | 2-1 | 2-0 | 12 | Konjic [4], Doyle [27] | 22,195 |

**Final League Position: 12**

### GOALSCORERS

*League (67):* McSheffrey 11 (3 pens), Morrell 9, Joachim 8, Suffo 7, Doyle 5, Gudjonsson 3, McAllister 3 (2 pens), Staunton 3 (2 pens), Warnock 3, Adebola 2, Barrett 2, Jackson 2, Konjic 2, Deloumeaux 1, Lowe 1, Pead 1, Shaw 1, Whing 1, own goals 2.
*Carling Cup (2):* Adebola 1, Barrett 1.
*FA Cup (4):* Joachim 3, McSheffrey 1.

| Shearer S 29 + 1 | Whing A 26 + 2 | Warnock S 42 + 2 | McAllister G 14 | Konjic M 36 + 6 | Staunton S 34 + 1 | Barrett G 20 + 11 | Safri Y 31 | Adebola D 15 + 13 | Suffo P 20 + 7 | Doyle M 38 + 2 | Morrell A 19 + 11 | Mansouri Y 9 + 5 | Davenport C 31 + 2 | O'Neill K — + 1 | Jorgensen C 4 + 4 | Shaw R 11 + 8 | Joachim J 27 + 2 | Pead C 6 + 11 | Arphexad P 5 | Ward G 12 | Gordon D 3 + 2 | Jackson J 2 + 3 | Pitt C 1 | McSheffrey G 16 + 3 | Deloumeaux E 19 | Gudjonsson B 17 + 1 | Grainger M 7 | Clarke P 5 | Kerr B 5 + 4 | Olszar S 1 + 4 | Lowe O 1 + 1 | Giddings S — + 1 | *Match No.* |
|---|---|---|---|---|---|---|---|---|---|---|---|---|---|---|---|---|---|---|---|---|---|---|---|---|---|---|---|---|---|---|---|---|---|
| 1 | 2 | 3 | 4 | 5 | 6 | 7 | 8■ | $9^{1}$ | 10 | 11 | 12 | | | | | | | | | | | | | | | | | | | | | | 1 |
| 1 | 2 | 3 | $4^{2}$ | 5 | $6^{3}$ | 7 | 8 | $9^{1}$ | 10 | 11 | 12 | 13 | 14 | | | | | | | | | | | | | | | | | | | | 2 |
| 1 | 2 | 3 | | 5 | | 7 | $8^{1}$ | 9 | 4 | $11^{2}$ | 10 | 12 | 6 | $13^{3}$ | 14 | | | | | | | | | | | | | | | | | | 3 |
| 1 | 2 | 3 | 4 | 5 | | $7^{1}$ | | 9 | 10 | 11 | 12 | 8 | 6 | | | | | | | | | | | | | | | | | | | | 4 |
| 1 | 2 | $3^{3}$ | $4^{1}$ | 5 | 6 | 7 | 8 | 9 | $10^{2}$ | 11 | 12 | 13 | | | | 14 | | | | | | | | | | | | | | | | | 5 |
| 1 | $2^{3}$ | $3^{2}$ | 4 | 5 | 6 | $7^{1}$ | 8 | 9 | 10■ | 11■ | 12 | | | | 13 | 14 | | | | | | | | | | | | | | | | | 6 |
| 1 | | 3 | | 5 | 6 | 12 | 8 | 9 | $10^{1}$ | 11 | 7 | 4 | | | | 2 | | | | | | | | | | | | | | | | | 7 |
| 1 | 2 | | 4 | 5 | 6 | $7^{1}$ | 8 | 9 | 12 | | 10 | $11^{2}$ | | | 13 | 3 | | | | | | | | | | | | | | | | | 8 |
| 1 | 2 | 12 | 4 | 5 | 3 | 7 | $8^{1}$ | $9^{3}$ | | | 10 | 13 | | | $11^{2}$ | 6 | 14 | | | | | | | | | | | | | | | | 9 |
| 1 | 2 | 12 | 4 | $5^{2}$ | 3 | $7^{3}$ | 8 | $9^{1}$ | | | 10 | | 13 | | 11 | 6 | 14 | | | | | | | | | | | | | | | | 10 |
| 1 | 2 | 3 | | 12 | $6^{1}$ | 7 | 8 | 9 | | | 10 | $4^{2}$ | | | 11 | 5 | | 13 | | | | | | | | | | | | | | | 11 |
| 1 | $2^{2}$ | $3^{1}$ | | 12 | 6 | 13 | 8 | 9 | 4 | 11 | 10 | | | | $7^{3}$ | 5 | | 14 | | | | | | | | | | | | | | | 12 |
| | 2 | 3 | | 5 | 6 | $7^{1}$ | 8 | 12 | 9 | 11 | 10 | | | | | 4 | | | 1 | | | | | | | | | | | | | | 13 |
| | 2 | 3 | | 5 | $6^{2}$ | 7 | $8^{3}$ | 12 | 9 | 11 | $10^{1}$ | 13 | | | | 4 | | 14 | 1 | | | | | | | | | | | | | | 14 |
| | 2 | 3 | 4 | 5 | | $7^{1}$ | 8 | | 9 | 11 | 10 | | | | | 6 | | 12 | 1 | | | | | | | | | | | | | | 15 |
| | 2 | 3 | 4 | 5 | | $7^{1}$ | 8 | 12 | 9 | 11 | 10 | | | | | 6 | | | 1 | | | | | | | | | | | | | | 16 |
| 15 | $2^{2}$ | 3 | 4 | 5 | 11 | | 8 | | $9^{1}$ | 7 | 12 | | 6 | | | | 10 | 13 | $1^{G}$ | | | | | | | | | | | | | | 17 |
| | | 3 | | 5 | 4 | $7^{2}$ | 8 | 12 | $9^{1}$ | 11 | 13 | | 6 | | | | 10 | 2 | | 1 | | | | | | | | | | | | | 18 |
| | | 3 | 4 | 5 | | | 8 | 9 | 12 | 11 | $7^{1}$ | | $6^{2}$ | | | | 10 | 2 | | 1 | 13 | | | | | | | | | | | | 19 |
| | | 3 | $4^{2}$ | 5 | 14 | | 8 | $9^{1}$ | 12 | 11 | $7^{3}$ | | 6 | | | | 10 | 2 | | 1 | | 13 | | | | | | | | | | | 20 |
| | 12 | 3 | | 5 | 4 | 11 | $8^{3}$ | | 13 | 14 | | $7^{2}$ | 6 | | | | 9 | $2^{1}$ | | 1 | | 10 | | | | | | | | | | | 21 |
| | | $11^{3}$ | $4^{1}$ | 5 | 3 | 12 | 8 | | 9 | 7 | 13 | | 6 | | | | $10^{2}$ | 2 | | 1 | | 14 | | | | | | | | | | | 22 |
| | 2 | 11 | | $5^{1}$ | 3 | | | 14 | $9^{2}$ | 7 | $10^{3}$ | 4 | 6 | | | 12 | | 13 | | 1 | | 8 | | | | | | | | | | | 23 |
| | $2^{1}$ | 11 | | 5 | 3 | | 8 | | 13 | $7^{3}$ | $10^{2}$ | 4 | 6 | | | 12 | 9 | | | 1 | | 14 | | | | | | | | | | | 24 |
| | 2 | $11^{1}$ | | 5 | 3 | | 8 | 12 | $9^{2}$ | 7 | 13 | 4 | 6 | | | | 10 | | | 1 | | | | | | | | | | | | | 25 |
| | 2 | 11 | | 5 | 3 | | 8 | 13 | 12 | | 9 | $4^{1}$ | 6 | | | | 10 | | | 1 | | | $7^{2}$ | | | | | | | | | | 26 |
| | 2 | $11^{2}$ | | 5 | | | 4 | $9^{1}$ | 12 | 7 | | | 6 | | | | 10 | 13 | | 1 | 3 | | | 8 | | | | | | | | | 27 |
| | $2^{2}$ | $11^{1}$ | | 5 | | | | 12 | | 7 | 9 | | 6 | | | 13 | 10 | 14 | | 1 | 3 | | | 8 | $4^{3}$ | | | | | | | | 28 |
| | | $11^{2}$ | | 5 | 3 | 12 | | | | 7 | | | 6 | | | 2 | 10 | | | 1 | 13 | | | $9^{1}$ | 4 | 8 | | | | | | | 29 |
| 1 | 2 | 11 | | | 5 | | | | 9 | 7 | | | 6 | | | | 10 | 12 | | | $3^{1}$ | | | | 4 | 8 | | | | | | | 30 |
| 1 | 2 | | | 12 | $5^{1}$ | 13 | | | 9 | 7 | | | 6 | | | | 10 | $11^{3}$ | | | | | | 14 | 4 | $8^{2}$ | 3 | | | | | | 31 |
| 1 | | $11^{3}$ | | 5 | | 12 | $8^{2}$ | | 9 | 7 | | | | | | 13 | 10 | | | | | | | 14 | 2 | $4^{1}$ | 3 | 6 | | | | | 32 |
| 1 | | $11^{1}$ | | 12 | | | 8 | 13 | | 7 | | | 5 | | | | 10 | | | | | | | 9 | 2 | $4^{2}$ | 3 | 6 | | | | | 33 |
| 1 | | 11 | | | 5 | | | 13 | | 7 | | | 6 | | | | $10^{2}$ | 12 | | | | | | 9 | 2 | $8^{1}$ | 3 | 4■ | | | | | 34 |
| 1 | | $11^{2}$ | | | 5 | | | 12 | | 7 | | | 6 | | | | 10 | 13 | | | | | | 9 | 2 | $8^{1}$ | 3 | 4 | | | | | 35 |
| 1 | | 11 | | 12 | $5^{1}$ | 13 | | 14 | | 7 | | | 6 | | | | $10^{3}$ | | | | | | | 9 | $4^{2}$ | 8 | 3 | 2 | | | | | 36 |
| 1 | | 11 | | 12 | 5 | | | | | 7 | | | 6 | | | | $10^{2}$ | | | | | | | 9 | 2 | 8 | 3 | | $4^{1}$ | 13 | | | 37 |
| 1 | | 11 | | 5 | 3 | | | 12 | | $7^{1}$ | | | 6 | | | | 10 | | | | | | | $9^{2}$ | 2 | 8 | | | 4 | 13 | | | 38 |
| 1 | | $11^{1}$ | | 5 | 3 | 12 | | | | $7^{2}$ | | | 6 | | | | 10 | | | | | | | 9 | 2 | 8 | | | 4 | 13 | | | 39 |
| 1 | 12 | 11 | | 5 | 3 | 13 | | | | $7^{1}$ | | | 6 | | | | 10 | | | | | | | 9 | 2 | $8^{2}$ | | | $4^{3}$ | 14 | | | 40 |
| 1 | 2 | 11 | | 5 | $3^{2}$ | $7^{1}$ | | | | | | | 6 | | | | 10 | | | | | | | 12 | 4 | $8^{3}$ | | | 13 | 9 | 14 | | 41 |
| 1 | $2^{1}$ | 3 | | | 5 | 12 | | | | 7 | | | 6 | | | | 10 | | | | | | | 9 | 4 | 13 | | | $11^{2}$ | | 8 | | 42 |
| 1 | | 11 | | 5 | 3 | 12 | $8^{3}$ | | | 7 | 13 | | 6 | | | | $10^{2}$ | | | | | | | 9 | 2 | $4^{1}$ | | | 14 | | | | 43 |
| 1 | | 11 | | 5 | 3 | $7^{3}$ | 8 | | | 13 | 12 | | $6^{2}$ | | | | $10^{1}$ | | | | | | | 9 | 2 | 4 | | | 14 | | | | 44 |
| 1 | | 3 | | 5 | | $7^{1}$ | 8 | | | 11 | 10 | | 6 | | | 12 | | | | | | | | 9 | 2 | $4^{2}$ | | | 13 | | | | 45 |
| 1 | | $3^{3}$ | | 5 | | $11^{2}$ | 8 | | | 7 | $10^{1}$ | | 6 | | 13 | 12 | | | | | | | | 9 | 2 | 4 | | | | | | 14 | 46 |

**Carling Cup**

| | | | |
|---|---|---|---|
| First Round | Peterborough U | (h) | 2-0 |
| Second Round | Tottenham H | (h) | 0-3 |

**FA Cup**

| | | | |
|---|---|---|---|
| Third Round | Peterborough U | (h) | 2-1 |
| Fourth Round | Colchester U | (h) | 1-1 |
| | | (a) | 1-3 |

# CREWE ALEXANDRA FL Championship

## FOUNDATION

The first match played at Crewe was on 1 December 1877 against Basford, the leading North Staffordshire team of that time. During the club's history they have also played in a number of other leagues including the Football Alliance, Football Combination, Lancashire League, Manchester League, Central League and Lancashire Combination. Two former players, Aaron Scragg in 1899 and Jackie Pearson in 1911, had the distinction of refereeing FA Cup finals. Pearson was also capped for England against Ireland in 1892.

***The Alexandra Stadium, Gresty Road, Crewe, Cheshire CW2 6EB.***

***Telephone:*** (01270) 213 014.

***Fax:*** (01270) 216 320.

***Ticket Office:*** (01270) 252 610.

***Website:*** www.crewealex.net

***Email:*** info@crewealex.net

***Ground Capacity:*** 10,107.

***Record Attendance:*** 20,000 v Tottenham H, FA Cup 4th rd, 30 January 1960.

***Pitch Measurements:*** 112yd × 74yd.

***Chairman:*** John Bowler.

***Vice-chairman:*** Norman Hassall.

***Business Operations Manager:*** Alison Bowler.

***Finance Operations Manager:*** Andrew Blakemore.

***Manager:*** Dario Gradi MBE.

***Assistant Manager:*** Neil Baker.

***Physio:*** Matt Radcliffe.

***Colours:*** Red shirts, white shorts, red stockings.

***Change Colours:*** Silver shirts, navy shorts, silver stockings.

***Year Formed:*** 1877.

***Turned Professional:*** 1893.

***Ltd Co.:*** 1892.

***Club Nickname:*** 'Railwaymen'.

***First Football League Game:*** 3 September 1892, Division 2, v Burton Swifts (a) L 1–7 – Hickton; Moore, Cope; Linnell, Johnson, Osborne; Bennett, Pearson (1), Bailey, Barnett, Roberts.

***Record League Victory:*** 8–0 v Rotherham U, Division 3 (N), 1 October 1932 – Foster; Pringle, Dawson; Ward, Keenor (1), Turner (1); Gillespie, Swindells (1), McConnell (2), Deacon (2), Weale (1).

## HONOURS

*Football League:* Divison 2 – Runners-up 2002–03; Promoted from Division 2 1996–97 (play-offs).

*FA Cup:* Semi-final 1888.

*Football League Cup:* best season: 3rd rd, 1975, 1976, 1979, 1993, 1999, 2000, 2002.

*Welsh Cup:* Winners 1936, 1937.

## SKY SPORTS FACT FILE

Len Hales, an amateur inside-left, joined his local club Crewe Alexandra in 1889 at 17. Loaned briefly to Stoke City, he returned to play for England v Germany in the unofficial international in 1900, before transferring to Stoke again.

***Record Cup Victory:*** 8–0 v Hartlepool U, Auto Windscreens Shield 1st rd, 17 October 1995 – Gayle; Collins (1), Booty, Westwood (Unsworth), Macauley (1), Whalley (1), Garvey (1), Murphy (1), Savage (1) (Rivers (1p)), Lennon, Edwards, (1 og). 8–0 v Doncaster R, LDV Vans Trophy 3rd rd, 10 November 2002 – Bankole; Wright, Walker, Foster, Tierney; Lunt (1), Brammer, Sorvel, Vaughan (1) (Bell); Ashton (3) (Miles), Jack (2) (Jones (1)).

***Record Defeat:*** 2–13 v Tottenham H, FA Cup 4th rd replay, 3 February 1960.

***Most League Points (2 for a win):*** 59, Division 4, 1962–63.

***Most League Points (3 for a win):*** 86, Division 2, 2002–03.

***Most League Goals:*** 95, Division 3 (N), 1931–32.

***Highest League Scorer in Season:*** Terry Harkin, 35, Division 4, 1964–65.

***Most League Goals in Total Aggregate:*** Bert Swindells, 126, 1928–37.

***Most League Goals in One Match:*** 5, Tony Naylor v Colchester U, Division 3, 24 April 1993.

***Most Capped Player:*** Clayton Ince, 34, Trinidad & Tobago.

***Most League Appearances:*** Tommy Lowry, 436, 1966–78.

***Youngest League Player:*** Steve Walters, 16 years 119 days v Peterborough U, 6 May 1988.

***Record Transfer Fee Received:*** £3,000,000 from Derby Co for Seth Johnson, May 1999.

***Record Transfer Fee Paid:*** £650,000 to Torquay U for Rodney Jack, June 1998.

***Football League Record:*** 1892 Original Member of Division 2; 1896 Failed re-election; 1921 Re-entered Division 3 (N); 1958–63 Division 4; 1963–64 Division 3; 1964–68 Division 4; 1968–69 Division 3; 1969–89 Division 4; 1989–91 Division 3; 1991–92 Division 4; 1992–94 Division 3; 1994–97 Division 2; 1997–2002 Division 1; 2002–03 Division 2; 2003–04 Division 1; 2004– FLC.

## MANAGERS

W. C. McNeill 1892–94 *(Secretary-Manager)*
J. G. Hall 1895–96 *(Secretary-Manager)*
R. Roberts *(1st team Secretary-Manager)* 1897
J. B. Blomerley 1898–1911 *(Secretary-Manager, continued as Hon. Secretary to 1925)*
Tom Bailey *(Secretary only)* 1925–38
George Lillycrop *(Trainer)* 1938–44
Frank Hill 1944–48
Arthur Turner 1948–51
Harry Catterick 1951–53
Ralph Ward 1953–55
Maurice Lindley 1956–57
Willie Cook 1957–58
Harry Ware 1958–60
Jimmy McGuigan 1960–64
Ernie Tagg 1964–71 *(continued as Secretary to 1972)*
Dennis Viollet 1971
Jimmy Melia 1972–74
Ernie Tagg 1974
Harry Gregg 1975–78
Warwick Rimmer 1978–79
Tony Waddington 1979–81
Arfon Griffiths 1981–82
Peter Morris 1982–83
Dario Gradi June 1983–

## LATEST SEQUENCES

***Longest Sequence of League Wins:*** 7, 30.4.1994 – 3.9.1994.

***Longest Sequence of League Defeats:*** 10, 16.4.1979 – 22.8.1979.

***Longest Sequence of League Draws:*** 5, 31.8.1987 – 18.9.1987.

***Longest Sequence of Unbeaten League Matches:*** 17, 25.3.1995 – 16.9.1995.

***Longest Sequence Without a League Win:*** 30, 22.9.1956 – 6.4.1957.

***Successive Scoring Runs:*** 26 from 7.4.1934.

***Successive Non-scoring Runs:*** 9 from 6.11.1974.

## TEN YEAR LEAGUE RECORD

| | | P | W | D | L | F | A | Pts | Pos |
|---|---|---|---|---|---|---|---|---|---|
| 1994-95 | Div 2 | 46 | 25 | 8 | 13 | 80 | 68 | 83 | 3 |
| 1995-96 | Div 2 | 46 | 22 | 7 | 17 | 77 | 60 | 73 | 5 |
| 1996-97 | Div 2 | 46 | 22 | 7 | 17 | 56 | 47 | 73 | 6 |
| 1997-98 | Div 1 | 46 | 18 | 5 | 23 | 58 | 65 | 59 | 11 |
| 1998-99 | Div 1 | 46 | 12 | 12 | 22 | 54 | 78 | 48 | 18 |
| 1999-2000 | Div 1 | 46 | 14 | 9 | 23 | 46 | 67 | 51 | 19 |
| 2000-01 | Div 1 | 46 | 15 | 10 | 21 | 47 | 62 | 55 | 14 |
| 2001-02 | Div 1 | 46 | 12 | 13 | 21 | 47 | 76 | 49 | 22 |
| 2002-03 | Div 2 | 46 | 25 | 11 | 10 | 76 | 40 | 86 | 2 |
| 2003-04 | Div 1 | 46 | 14 | 11 | 21 | 57 | 66 | 53 | 18 |

## DID YOU KNOW ?

The season before Crewe Alexandra recorded their record League victory, they achieved wins of 8-1 on two occasions, beating Lincoln City on 5 December and York City on 20 February 1932, when the club finished sixth in Division Three (North).

## CREWE ALEXANDRA 2003–04 LEAGUE RECORD

| Match No. | Date | Venue | Opponents | Result | | H/T Score | Lg. Pos. | Goalscorers | Attendance |
|---|---|---|---|---|---|---|---|---|---|
| 1 | Aug 9 | A | Wimbledon | L | 1-3 | 1-1 | — | Brammer [8] | 1145 |
| 2 | 16 | H | Ipswich T | W | 1-0 | 0-0 | 11 | Lunt [69] | 6982 |
| 3 | 23 | A | Millwall | D | 1-1 | 0-0 | 13 | Ashton [58] | 9504 |
| 4 | 25 | H | Walsall | W | 1-0 | 0-0 | 6 | Jones S [66] | 7026 |
| 5 | 30 | A | Burnley | L | 0-1 | 0-0 | 13 | | 11,495 |
| 6 | Sept 13 | A | Rotherham U | W | 2-0 | 1-0 | 11 | Ashton (pen) [45], Walker [57] | 5495 |
| 7 | 16 | H | West Ham U | L | 0-3 | 0-0 | — | | 9575 |
| 8 | 20 | H | Nottingham F | W | 3-1 | 0-0 | 10 | Lunt [64], Ashton [74], Jones S [88] | 8685 |
| 9 | 27 | A | Cardiff C | L | 0-3 | 0-1 | 12 | | 14,385 |
| 10 | Oct 1 | A | Coventry C | L | 0-2 | 0-0 | — | | 11,557 |
| 11 | 4 | H | Watford | L | 0-1 | 0-0 | 16 | | 7055 |
| 12 | 14 | H | Bradford C | D | 2-2 | 0-0 | — | Jones S [45], Ashton [49] | 5867 |
| 13 | 18 | H | Derby Co | W | 3-0 | 2-0 | 14 | Barrowman [10], Ashton [24], Rix [78] | 8656 |
| 14 | 21 | H | Preston NE | W | 2-1 | 2-0 | — | Lunt [10], Foster [28] | 7012 |
| 15 | 25 | A | Stoke C | D | 1-1 | 0-0 | 11 | Jones S [53] | 17,569 |
| 16 | Nov 1 | H | Reading | W | 1-0 | 1-0 | 12 | Jones S [15] | 7091 |
| 17 | 4 | A | Sheffield U | L | 0-2 | 0-1 | — | | 17,396 |
| 18 | 8 | A | Gillingham | L | 0-2 | 0-0 | 13 | | 6923 |
| 19 | 22 | H | Sunderland | W | 3-0 | 0-0 | 12 | Ashton [53], Jones S 2 [55, 63] | 9807 |
| 20 | 29 | A | Norwich C | L | 0-1 | 0-1 | 12 | | 16,367 |
| 21 | Dec 6 | H | Gillingham | D | 1-1 | 1-0 | 13 | Jones S [11] | 6271 |
| 22 | 9 | A | Crystal Palace | W | 3-1 | 2-0 | — | Ashton 2 [8, 86], Varney [16] | 12,259 |
| 23 | 13 | A | WBA | D | 2-2 | 2-1 | 11 | Jones S [18], Wright [45] | 22,825 |
| 24 | 20 | H | Wigan Ath | L | 2-3 | 2-2 | 13 | Jones B [10], Jones S [17] | 7873 |
| 25 | 26 | H | Burnley | W | 3-1 | 1-0 | 12 | Ashton [37], Jones S 2 [55, 90] | 9512 |
| 26 | 28 | A | Preston NE | D | 0-0 | 0-0 | 11 | | 15,830 |
| 27 | Jan 10 | H | Wimbledon | W | 1-0 | 0-0 | 9 | Jones S [62] | 6234 |
| 28 | 17 | A | Ipswich T | L | 4-6 | 1-2 | 13 | Ashton [35], McGreal (og) [48], Richards (og) [66], Robinson [82] | 22,071 |
| 29 | 31 | H | Millwall | L | 1-2 | 0-1 | 14 | Roberts (og) [65] | 6685 |
| 30 | Feb 7 | A | Walsall | D | 1-1 | 0-1 | 15 | Foster [85] | 6871 |
| 31 | 21 | A | Bradford C | L | 1-2 | 0-0 | 15 | Rix [66] | 9935 |
| 32 | 24 | H | Sheffield U | L | 0-1 | 0-0 | — | | 6525 |
| 33 | Mar 3 | A | Derby Co | D | 0-0 | 0-0 | — | | 19,861 |
| 34 | 6 | A | Wigan Ath | W | 3-2 | 2-2 | 15 | Ashton 3 (2 pens) [20 (p), 26 (p), 90] | 8367 |
| 35 | 13 | H | WBA | L | 1-2 | 0-0 | 15 | Ashton [63] | 8335 |
| 36 | 17 | A | West Ham U | L | 2-4 | 0-4 | — | Jones S 2 [61, 72] | 31,158 |
| 37 | 20 | H | Cardiff C | L | 0-1 | 0-0 | 15 | | 6650 |
| 38 | 23 | H | Stoke C | W | 2-0 | 1-0 | — | Lunt 2 [25, 61] | 10,014 |
| 39 | 27 | A | Nottingham F | L | 0-2 | 0-2 | 15 | | 24,347 |
| 40 | Apr 3 | H | Rotherham U | D | 0-0 | 0-0 | 16 | | 6749 |
| 41 | 10 | A | Watford | L | 1-2 | 0-1 | 16 | Ashton (pen) [61] | 18,041 |
| 42 | 12 | H | Coventry C | W | 3-1 | 0-0 | 15 | Higdon [46], Symes [64], Ashton (pen) [90] | 7475 |
| 43 | 17 | A | Reading | D | 1-1 | 1-1 | 15 | Lunt [39] | 14,729 |
| 44 | 24 | H | Crystal Palace | L | 2-3 | 0-2 | 18 | Ashton [47], Lunt [73] | 8136 |
| 45 | May 1 | A | Sunderland | D | 1-1 | 0-1 | 18 | Ashton [76] | 25,311 |
| 46 | 9 | H | Norwich C | L | 1-3 | 0-2 | 18 | Ashton [82] | 9833 |

**Final League Position: 18**

### GOALSCORERS

*League (57):* Ashton 19 (5 pens), Jones S 15, Lunt 7, Foster 2, Rix 2, Barrowman 1, Brammer 1, Higdon 1, Jones B 1, Robinson 1, Symes 1, Varney 1, Walker 1, Wright 1, own goals 3.
*Carling Cup (2):* Ashton 1 (pen), Jones S 1.
*FA Cup (0).*

| Ince C 36 | Wright D 40 | Vaughan D 29+2 | Brammer D 16 | Foster S 45 | Moses A 15+6 | Lunt K 43+2 | Cochrane J 37+2 | Robinson J 1+8 | Jones S 43+2 | Rix B 18+8 | McCready C 15+7 | Bell L —+3 | Varney L 5+3 | Ashton D 43+1 | Smart A —+6 | Sorvel N 26+5 | Walker R 17+3 | Edwards P 2+8 | Tonkin A 20+6 | Barrowman A 3+1 | Jones B 23+4 | Higdon M 7+3 | Roberts M —+2 | Hignett C 11+4 | Tomlinson S —+1 | Williams B 10 | Symes M 1+3 | *Match No.* |
|---|---|---|---|---|---|---|---|---|---|---|---|---|---|---|---|---|---|---|---|---|---|---|---|---|---|---|---|---|
| 1 | 2 | 3 | 4 | 5 | $6^{1}$ | 7 | $8^{2}$ | $9^{3}$ | 10 | 11 | 12 | 13 | 14 | | | | | | | | | | | | | | | 1 |
| 1 | 2 | | 4 | 5 | 6 | 7 | 8 | | 10 | $11^{1}$ | 3 | 12 | | 9 | | | | | | | | | | | | | | 2 |
| 1 | $2^{1}$ | 3 | 4 | 5 | 6 | 7 | 8 | | 10 | 11 | 12 | | | $9^{2}$ | 13 | | | | | | | | | | | | | 3 |
| 1 | | 3 | 4 | 5 | 6 | 7 | 8 | | 10 | 11 | 2 | | | 9 | | | | | | | | | | | | | | 4 |
| 1 | 2 | 3 | 4 | 5 | $6^{1}$ | 7 | $8^{3}$ | | 10 | $11^{2}$ | 12 | | | 9 | 13 | 14 | | | | | | | | | | | | 5 |
| 1 | 2 | $3^{1}$ | 4 | 5 | | 7 | 8 | | $10^{2}$ | $11^{3}$ | | | | 9 | | 12 | 6 | 13 | 14 | | | | | | | | | 6 |
| 1 | 2 | | 4 | 5 | | 7 | $8^{1}$ | | $10^{2}$ | 11 | | | | 9 | | 12 | 6 | 13 | 3 | | | | | | | | | 7 |
| 1 | 2 | 3 | 4 | 5 | | 7 | 8 | | 10 | 11 | | | | 9 | | | 6 | | | | | | | | | | | 8 |
| 1 | $2^{1}$ | 3 | 4 | 5 | | 7 | 8 | | | | 12 | | 13 | 9 | | | 6 | $10^{2}$ | 11 | | | | | | | | | 9 |
| 1 | 2 | 3 | | 5 | | $4^{2}$ | 8 | | 10 | $7^{1}$ | | 12 | | 9 | | 11 | 6 | 13 | | | | | | | | | | 10 |
| 1 | 2 | 3 | | 5 | | 7 | $8^{1}$ | | 10 | 12 | $4^{2}$ | | | 9 | | 11 | 6 | 13 | | | | | | | | | | 11 |
| 1 | 2 | 3 | | 5 | | 4 | 8 | | 10 | $7^{1}$ | | | | 9 | | 11 | 6 | | | 12 | | | | | | | | 12 |
| 1 | 2 | 3 | $4^{1}$ | 5 | | 7 | $8^{3}$ | | 10 | 13 | | | | 9 | | 12 | 6 | | | $11^{2}$ | 14 | | | | | | | 13 |
| 1 | 2 | 3 | | 5 | | 4 | 8 | | 10 | 12 | | | | $9^{2}$ | 13 | 11 | 6 | | | $7^{1}$ | | | | | | | | 14 |
| 1 | 2 | 3 | | 5 | | 4 | 8 | | $10^{1}$ | | | | | 9 | | 11 | 6 | | 12 | 7 | | | | | | | | 15 |
| 1 | 2 | 11 | | 5 | | 4 | 8 | | 10 | | | | | 9 | | 7 | 6 | | 3 | | | | | | | | | 16 |
| 1 | 2 | $11^{1}$ | | 5 | | $4^{2}$ | 8 | | 10 | 12 | | | | 9 | 13 | 7 | $6^{3}$ | | 3 | | 14 | | | | | | | 17 |
| 1 | 2 | 11 | | 5 | | $4^{1}$ | $8^{2}$ | 14 | $10^{3}$ | 12 | 6 | | | 9 | 13 | $7^{1}$ | | | 3 | | | | | | | | | 18 |
| 1 | 2 | 11 | | 5 | | | 8 | | 10 | 7 | 6 | | | 9 | | | | | 3 | | 4 | | | | | | | 19 |
| 1 | 2 | $11^{1}$ | | 5 | | 12 | 8 | | 10 | 7 | 6 | | 13 | 9 | | | | | 3 | | $4^{2}$ | | | | | | | 20 |
| 1 | 2 | | | 5 | 13 | 7 | 8 | | 10 | $11^{1}$ | 6 | | | 9 | | | $12^{2}$ | | 3 | | 4 | | | | | | | 21 |
| 1 | 2 | | | 5 | 12 | 7 | 8 | | 10 | | $6^{1}$ | | $11^{2}$ | $9^{3}$ | 13 | | | | 3 | | 4 | 14 | | | | | | 22 |
| 1 | 2 | | | 5 | 12 | 7 | 8 | | 10 | | 6 | | 11 | 9 | | | | | 3 | | $4^{1}$ | | | | | | | 23 |
| 1 | 2 | | | 5 | | 7 | 8 | 12 | 10 | | | | $11^{1}$ | 9 | | | | | 3 | | 4 | 6 | | | | | | 24 |
| 1 | 2 | | | 5 | | 7 | $8^{1}$ | 12 | 10 | | | | $11^{2}$ | 9 | | | | | 3 | | 4 | 6 | 13 | | | | | 25 |
| 1 | 2 | | | 5 | | 7 | $8^{1}$ | | 10 | 12 | | | 11 | 9 | | | | | 3 | | 4 | 6 | | | | | | 26 |
| 1 | 2 | | | 5 | | 7 | $8^{1}$ | 13 | 10 | $11^{2}$ | | | | 9 | | 12 | | | 3 | | 4 | $6^{3}$ | 14 | | | | | 27 |
| 1 | 2 | | | 5 | | 7 | | 13 | 10 | $11^{3}$ | | | | $9^{2}$ | | 8 | 12 | 14 | 3 | | $4^{1}$ | 6 | | | | | | 28 |
| 1 | 2 | | | 5 | | 8 | | 12 | 10 | $7^{1}$ | | | | | | 11 | | 9 | 3 | | 4 | 6 | | | | | | 29 |
| 1 | 2 | | | 5 | 6 | 8 | | | 10 | $7^{2}$ | | | | 9 | | $11^{1}$ | | 12 | 3 | | 4 | 13 | | | | | | 30 |
| 1 | 2 | 12 | | 5 | 6 | 4 | $8^{2}$ | | 10 | 13 | | | | $9^{3}$ | | 11 | | 14 | $3^{1}$ | | | | | 7 | | | | 31 |
| 1 | 2 | 6 | | 5 | $4^{3}$ | 12 | $8^{2}$ | | 10 | 13 | | | | 9 | | $11^{1}$ | | | 3 | | 14 | | | 7 | | | | 32 |
| 1 | 2 | | | 5 | | 4 | 12 | 13 | 10 | $7^{1}$ | | | | 9 | | 11 | 6 | | | | 3 | | | $8^{2}$ | | | | 33 |
| 1 | $2^{1}$ | | | 5 | | 4 | 8 | | 10 | | | | | 9 | | 11 | 6 | | 12 | | 3 | | | 7 | | | | 34 |
| 1 | | 3 | | 5 | | 4 | $8^{2}$ | 13 | 10 | | | | | 9 | | 11 | 6 | | 12 | | 2 | | | $7^{1}$ | | | | 35 |
| $1^{G}$ | | 3 | | 5 | | 4 | 8 | | 10 | | 13 | | | 9 | | 11 | 6 | | 12 | | $2^{2}$ | | | $7^{1}$ | 15 | | | 36 |
| | | 7 | | 5 | 12 | 4 | $8^{3}$ | | 10 | | $6^{1}$ | | | 9 | | 11 | | 13 | $3^{2}$ | | 2 | | | 14 | | 1 | | 37 |
| | | 3 | | 5 | 12 | 4 | 8 | | 10 | | 6 | | | 9 | | 11 | | | | | 2 | | | $7^{1}$ | | 1 | | 38 |
| | | 3 | | 5 | 12 | 4 | $8^{2}$ | | 10 | | $6^{1}$ | | | 9 | | 11 | | | | | 2 | | | 7 | | 1 | 13 | 39 |
| | 2 | 7 | | 5 | 6 | 4 | 8 | | 12 | | | | | 9 | | 11 | | | | | 3 | | | $10^{1}$ | | 1 | | 40 |
| | 2 | $7^{2}$ | $4^{1}$ | 5 | 6 | 8 | 12 | | 13 | | | | | 9 | | 11 | | | | | 3 | | | $10^{3}$ | | 1 | 14 | 41 |
| | 2 | | 4 | 5 | 6 | 7 | 8 | | 10 | | 13 | | | 12 | | | | | | | $3^{2}$ | 11 | | | | 1 | $9^{1}$ | 42 |
| | 2 | 3 | $8^{2}$ | 5 | 6 | 7 | | | 10 | | $4^{1}$ | | | $9^{3}$ | | 11 | 12 | | | | | | | 13 | | 1 | 14 | 43 |
| | 2 | $7^{2}$ | 4 | 5 | 6 | 8 | | | $10^{3}$ | | $3^{1}$ | | | 9 | | 11 | | | | | 12 | 13 | | 14 | | 1 | | 44 |
| | 2 | 13 | 4 | | 6 | 7 | | | 10 | | 12 | | | 9 | | 11 | $5^{1}$ | | | | 3 | | | $8^{2}$ | | 1 | | 45 |
| | 2 | 3 | 8 | 5 | 6 | 7 | | | 10 | | $4^{1}$ | | | 9 | | $11^{2}$ | | | 12 | | | | | 13 | | 1 | | 46 |

**Carling Cup**

| | | | |
|---|---|---|---|
| First Round | Wrexham | (h) | 2-0 |
| Second Round | Leicester C | (a) | 0-1 |

**FA Cup**

| | | | |
|---|---|---|---|
| Third Round | Telford U | (h) | 0-1 |

# CRYSTAL PALACE FA Premiership

## FOUNDATION

There was a Crystal Palace club as early as 1861 but the present organisation was born in 1905 after the formation of a club by the company that controlled the Crystal Palace (building), had been rejected by the FA who did not like the idea of the Cup Final hosts running their own club. A separate company had to be formed and they had their home on the old Cup Final ground until 1915.

***Selhurst Park, London SE25 6PU.***

***Telephone:*** (020) 8768 6000.

***Fax:*** (020) 8653 1750.

***Ticket Office:*** 0871 200 0071

***Website:*** www.cpfc.co.uk

***Email:*** info@cpfc.co.uk

***Ground Capacity:*** 26,500.

***Record Attendance:*** 51,482 v Burnley, Division 2, 11 May 1979.

***Pitch Measurements:*** 110yd × 74yd.

***Chairman:*** Simon Jordan.

***Vice-chairman:*** Dominic Jordan.

***Chief Executive:*** Phil Alexander.

***Manager:*** Iain Dowie.

***Assistant Manager:*** Kit Symons.

***Physio:*** Steve Allen.

***Colours:*** Red and blue vertical striped shirts, red shorts, red stockings.

## HONOURS

*Football League:* Division 1 – Champions 1993–94; Promoted from Division 1, 1996–97 (play-offs), 2003–04 (play-offs); Division 2 – Champions 1978–79; Runners-up 1968–69; Division 3 – Runners-up 1963–64; Division 3 (S) – Champions 1920–21; Runners-up 1928–29, 1930–31, 1938–39; Division 4 – Runners-up 1960–61.

*FA Cup:* Runners-up 1990.

*Football League Cup:* Semi-final 1993, 1995, 2001.

*Zenith Data Systems Cup:* Winners 1991.

***European Competition:*** *Intertoto Cup:* 1998.

***Change Colours:*** White shirts with blue trim, blue shorts, white stockings.

***Year Formed:*** 1905.

***Turned Professional:*** 1905.

***Ltd Co.:*** 1905.

***Club Nickname:*** 'The Eagles'.

***Previous Grounds:*** 1905, Crystal Palace; 1915, Herne Hill; 1918, The Nest; 1924, Selhurst Park.

***First Football League Game:*** 28 August 1920, Division 3, v Merthyr T (a) L 1–2 – Alderson; Little, Rhodes; McCracken, Jones, Feebury; Bateman, Conner, Smith, Milligan (1), Whibley.

***Record League Victory:*** 9–0 v Barrow, Division 4, 10 October 1959 – Rouse; Long, Noakes; Truett, Evans, McNichol; Gavin (1), Summersby (4 incl. 1p), Sexton, Byrne (2), Colfar (2).

***Record Cup Victory:*** 8–0 v Southend U, Rumbelows League Cup 2nd rd (1st leg), 25 September 1989 – Martyn; Humphrey (Thompson (1)), Shaw, Pardew, Young, Thorn, McGoldrick, Thomas, Bright (3), Wright (3), Barber (Hodges (1)).

## SKY SPORTS FACT FILE

Crystal Palace had two players selected for the London representative team which took part in the Inter-Cities Fairs Cup in 1957. On 16 September against Lausanne they provided Peter Berry (right-wing) and Geoff Truett (wing-half).

***Record Defeat:*** 0–9 v Burnley, FA Cup 2nd rd replay, 10 February 1909. 0–9 v Liverpool, Division 1, 12 September 1990.

***Most League Points (2 for a win):*** 64, Division 4, 1960–61.

***Most League Points (3 for a win):*** 90, Division 1, 1993–94.

***Most League Goals:*** 110, Division 4, 1960–61.

***Highest League Scorer in Season:*** Peter Simpson, 46, Division 3 (S), 1930–31.

***Most League Goals in Total Aggregate:*** Peter Simpson, 153, 1930–36.

***Most League Goals in One Match:*** 6, Peter Simpson v Exeter C, Division 3S, 4 October 1930.

***Most Capped Player:*** Aleksandrs Kolinko 23 (51), Latvia.

***Most League Appearances:*** Jim Cannon, 571, 1973–88.

***Youngest League Player:*** Phil Hoadley, 16 years 112 days v Bolton W, 27 April 1968.

***Record Transfer Fee Received:*** £4,500,000 from Tottenham H for Chris Armstrong, June 1995.

***Record Transfer Fee Paid:*** £2,750,000 to RC Strasbourg for Valerien Ismael, January 1998.

***Football League Record:*** 1920 Original Members of Division 3; 1921–25 Division 2; 1925–58 Division 3 (S); 1958–61 Division 4; 1961–64 Division 3; 1964–69 Division 2; 1969–73 Division 1; 1973–74 Division 2; 1974–77 Division 3; 1977–79 Division 2; 1979–81 Division 1; 1981–89 Division 2; 1989–92 Division 1; 1992–93 FA Premier League; 1993–94 Division 1; 1994–95 FA Premier League; 1995–97 Division 1; 1997–98 FA Premier League; 1998–2004 Division 1; 2004– FA Premier League.

## LATEST SEQUENCES

***Longest Sequence of League Wins:*** 8, 9.2.1921 – 26.3.1921.

***Longest Sequence of League Defeats:*** 8, 10.1.1998 – 14.3.1998.

***Longest Sequence of League Draws:*** 5, 21.9.2002 – 19.10.2002.

***Longest Sequence of Unbeaten League Matches:*** 18, 22.2.1969 – 13.8.1969.

***Longest Sequence Without a League Win:*** 20, 3.3.1962 – 8.9.1962.

***Successive Scoring Runs:*** 24 from 27.4.1929.

***Successive Non-scoring Runs:*** 9 from 19.11.1994.

## MANAGERS

John T. Robson 1905–07
Edmund Goodman 1907–25 *(had been Secretary since 1905 and afterwards continued in this position to 1933)*
Alec Maley 1925–27
Fred Mavin 1927–30
Jack Tresadern 1930–35
Tom Bromilow 1935–36
R. S. Moyes 1936
Tom Bromilow 1936–39
George Irwin 1939–47
Jack Butler 1947–49
Ronnie Rooke 1949–50
Charlie Slade and Fred Dawes *(Joint Managers)* 1950–51
Laurie Scott 1951–54
Cyril Spiers 1954–58
George Smith 1958–60
Arthur Rowe 1960–62
Dick Graham 1962–66
Bert Head 1966–72 *(continued as General Manager to 1973)*
Malcolm Allison 1973–76
Terry Venables 1976–80
Ernie Walley 1980
Malcolm Allison 1980–81
Dario Gradi 1981
Steve Kember 1981–82
Alan Mullery 1982–84
Steve Coppell 1984–93
Alan Smith 1993–95
Steve Coppell *(Technical Director)* 1995–96
Dave Bassett 1996–97
Steve Coppell 1997–98
Attilio Lombardo 1998
Terry Venables *(Head Coach)* 1998–99
Steve Coppell 1999–2000
Alan Smith 2000–01
Steve Bruce 2001
Trevor Francis 2001–03
Steve Kember 2003
Iain Dowie December 2003–

## TEN YEAR LEAGUE RECORD

| | | *P* | *W* | *D* | *L* | *F* | *A* | *Pts* | *Pos* |
|---|---|---|---|---|---|---|---|---|---|
| 1994-95 | PR Lge | 42 | 11 | 12 | 19 | 34 | 49 | 45 | 19 |
| 1995-96 | Div 1 | 46 | 20 | 15 | 11 | 67 | 48 | 75 | 3 |
| 1996-97 | Div 1 | 46 | 19 | 14 | 13 | 78 | 48 | 71 | 6 |
| 1997-98 | PR Lge | 38 | 8 | 9 | 21 | 37 | 71 | 33 | 20 |
| 1998-99 | Div 1 | 46 | 14 | 16 | 16 | 58 | 71 | 58 | 14 |
| 1999-2000 | Div 1 | 46 | 13 | 15 | 18 | 57 | 67 | 54 | 15 |
| 2000-01 | Div 1 | 46 | 12 | 13 | 21 | 57 | 70 | 49 | 21 |
| 2001-02 | Div 1 | 46 | 20 | 6 | 20 | 70 | 62 | 66 | 10 |
| 2002-03 | Div 1 | 46 | 14 | 17 | 15 | 59 | 52 | 59 | 14 |
| 2003-04 | Div 1 | 46 | 21 | 10 | 15 | 72 | 61 | 73 | 6 |

## DID YOU KNOW ?

In 1905–06 Crystal Palace went from first qualifying round of the FA Cup to the first round proper. On the way, they had trounced first season Chelsea 7-0, highest score by a non-league club against a League team in the competition.

## CRYSTAL PALACE 2003–04 LEAGUE RECORD

| *Match No.* | *Date* | *Venue* | *Opponents* | *Result* | | *H/T Score* | *Lg. Pos.* | *Goalscorers* | *Attendance* |
|---|---|---|---|---|---|---|---|---|---|
| 1 | Aug 9 | A | Burnley | W | 3-2 | 2-2 | — | Freedman 3 (1 pen) [6 (p), 32, 67] | 12,976 |
| 2 | 16 | H | Watford | W | 1-0 | 1-0 | 3 | Shipperley [14] | 15,333 |
| 3 | 23 | A | Wimbledon | W | 3-1 | 0-1 | 1 | Butterfield [59], Freedman (pen) [65], Hughes [89] | 6113 |
| 4 | 26 | H | Sheffield U | L | 1-2 | 0-2 | — | Johnson (pen) [76] | 15,466 |
| 5 | 30 | A | Millwall | D | 1-1 | 0-0 | 5 | Watson [67] | 14,425 |
| 6 | Sept 13 | A | Sunderland | L | 1-2 | 0-0 | 9 | Johnson [89] | 27,324 |
| 7 | 16 | H | Bradford C | L | 0-1 | 0-1 | — | | 13,514 |
| 8 | 20 | H | WBA | D | 2-2 | 0-0 | 15 | Freedman [59], Johnson [90] | 17,477 |
| 9 | 27 | A | Norwich C | L | 1-2 | 1-1 | 15 | Derry [2] | 16,425 |
| 10 | Oct 1 | A | West Ham U | L | 0-3 | 0-2 | — | | 31,861 |
| 11 | 4 | H | Cardiff C | W | 2-1 | 1-0 | 15 | Routledge [45], Shipperley [47] | 16,160 |
| 12 | 14 | H | Derby Co | D | 1-1 | 1-0 | — | Butterfield [45] | 14,344 |
| 13 | 18 | H | Rotherham U | D | 1-1 | 0-1 | 15 | Freedman [57] | 18,715 |
| 14 | 21 | H | Ipswich T | L | 3-4 | 2-2 | — | Johnson [5], Freedman 2 (1 pen) [18, 86 (p)] | 15,483 |
| 15 | 25 | A | Gillingham | L | 0-1 | 0-0 | 19 | | 8889 |
| 16 | Nov 1 | A | Wigan Ath | L | 0-5 | 0-2 | 20 | | 6796 |
| 17 | 8 | H | Preston NE | D | 1-1 | 0-0 | 20 | Johnson [84] | 14,608 |
| 18 | 22 | A | Walsall | D | 0-0 | 0-0 | 21 | | 6910 |
| 19 | 25 | A | Stoke C | W | 1-0 | 1-0 | — | Johnson [27] | 10,277 |
| 20 | 29 | H | Coventry C | D | 1-1 | 1-0 | 19 | Edwards [9] | 14,622 |
| 21 | Dec 6 | A | Preston NE | L | 1-4 | 0-0 | 20 | Derry [71] | 12,836 |
| 22 | 9 | H | Crewe Alex | L | 1-3 | 0-2 | — | Butterfield [78] | 12,259 |
| 23 | 13 | H | Nottingham F | W | 1-0 | 1-0 | 21 | Johnson [12] | 16,935 |
| 24 | 20 | A | Reading | W | 3-0 | 2-0 | 19 | Johnson 2 [40, 90], Routledge [43] | 12,743 |
| 25 | 26 | H | Millwall | L | 0-1 | 0-1 | 20 | | 19,737 |
| 26 | 28 | A | Ipswich T | W | 3-1 | 0-1 | 18 | Johnson 2 [61, 86], Gray [65] | 27,629 |
| 27 | Jan 10 | H | Burnley | D | 0-0 | 0-0 | 18 | | 15,276 |
| 28 | 17 | A | Watford | W | 5-1 | 3-0 | 15 | Johnson 2 (1 pen) [9, 45 (p)], Routledge [39], Gray [73], Freedman [90] | 15,017 |
| 29 | 24 | A | Bradford C | W | 2-1 | 2-1 | 14 | Johnson [13], Shipperley [15] | 10,310 |
| 30 | 31 | H | Wimbledon | W | 3-1 | 1-0 | 13 | Johnson 2 [32, 89], Granville [59] | 20,552 |
| 31 | Feb 7 | A | Sheffield U | W | 3-0 | 1-0 | 11 | Johnson [42], Popovic [57], Shipperley [87] | 23,816 |
| 32 | 14 | H | Stoke C | W | 6-3 | 4-2 | 8 | Johnson 3 (2 pens) [5, 9 (p), 33 (p)], Hughes [45], Shipperley [55], Routledge [90] | 16,715 |
| 33 | 21 | A | Derby Co | L | 1-2 | 1-0 | 10 | Hughes [16] | 21,856 |
| 34 | 28 | H | Gillingham | W | 1-0 | 0-0 | 9 | Butterfield [53] | 17,485 |
| 35 | Mar 6 | H | Reading | D | 2-2 | 2-1 | 10 | Freedman [33], Johnson [44] | 17,853 |
| 36 | 13 | A | Nottingham F | L | 2-3 | 0-2 | 12 | Shipperley [58], Granville [76] | 28,306 |
| 37 | 20 | H | Norwich C | W | 1-0 | 1-0 | 11 | Routledge [41] | 23,798 |
| 38 | 27 | A | WBA | L | 0-2 | 0-0 | 12 | | 24,990 |
| 39 | Apr 6 | A | Rotherham U | W | 2-1 | 2-0 | — | Shipperley 2 [11, 27] | 6001 |
| 40 | 10 | A | Cardiff C | W | 2-0 | 0-0 | 10 | Johnson [55], Routledge [87] | 16,656 |
| 41 | 12 | H | West Ham U | W | 1-0 | 0-0 | 9 | Freedman [66] | 23,977 |
| 42 | 17 | H | Wigan Ath | D | 1-1 | 0-1 | 9 | Granville [79] | 18,799 |
| 43 | 21 | H | Sunderland | W | 3-0 | 1-0 | — | Johnson (pen) [24], Shipperley [63], Freedman [80] | 18,291 |
| 44 | 24 | A | Crewe Alex | W | 3-2 | 2-0 | 7 | Johnson 3 (1 pen) [30, 36, 56 (p)] | 8136 |
| 45 | May 1 | H | Walsall | W | 1-0 | 0-0 | 5 | Johnson [88] | 21,518 |
| 46 | 9 | A | Coventry C | L | 1-2 | 0-2 | 6 | Freedman [64] | 22,195 |

**Final League Position: 6**

### GOALSCORERS

*League (72):* Johnson 27 (6 pens), Freedman 13 (3 pens), Shipperley 9, Routledge 6, Butterfield 4, Granville 3, Hughes 3, Derry 2, Gray 2, Edwards 1, Popovic 1, Watson 1.
*Carling Cup (6):* Johnson 4 (2 pens), Freedman 2 (1 pen).
*FA Cup (0).*
*Play-Offs (5):* Shipperley 2, Johnson 1, Powell 1, own goal 1.

| Clarke M 4 | Butterfield D 45 | Routledge W 32 + 12 | Symons K 12 + 3 | Popovic T 34 | Powell D 10 | Derry S 25 + 12 | Johnson A 40 + 2 | Freedman D 20 + 15 | Shipperley N 40 | Watson B 8 + 8 | Borrowdale G 14 + 9 | Smith J 13 + 2 | Riihilahti A 24 + 7 | Hughes M 34 | Mullins H 10 | Black T 12 + 13 | Berthelin C 17 | Fleming C 15 + 2 | Myhre T 15 | Granville D 21 | Heeroo G — + 1 | Edwards R 6 + 1 | Gray J 24 | Hudson M 14 | Leigertwood M 7 + 5 | Soares T — + 3 | Vaesen N 10 | *Match No.* |
|---|---|---|---|---|---|---|---|---|---|---|---|---|---|---|---|---|---|---|---|---|---|---|---|---|---|---|---|---|
| 1 | 2 | 11■ | 4¹ | 5 | 6 | 7■ | 8 | 9 | 10 | 3³ | 12² | 13 | 14 | | | | | | | | | | | | | | | 1 |
| 1 | 2 | 12 | | 5 | 6 | 7² | 8¹ | 9 | 10 | 3 | | 4 | 13 | 11■ | | | | | | | | | | | | | | 2 |
| 1 | 2 | | 4 | | 6¹ | | 13 | 9² | 10 | 7 | 12 | 3 | 14 | 11 | 5³ | 8 | | | | | | | | | | | | 3 |
| 1 | 2 | 12 | 4 | | | 7³ | 13 | 9² | 10 | 14 | 3¹ | 6 | | 11 | 5 | 8 | | | | | | | | | | | | 4 |
| | 2 | 7 | | | 6 | 4 | 10 | | | 8 | | 3 | 11 | | 5 | 9■ | 1 | | | | | | | | | | | 5 |
| | 7 | 3³ | 4² | | | 8 | 9 | | 10 | 13 | 12 | 2¹ | 14 | 11 | 5 | | 1 | 6 | | | | | | | | | | 6 |
| | 3 | 12 | | 5 | | 7² | 9 | | 10 | 13 | 14 | 6³ | | 11 | 4 | 8 | 1 | 2¹ | | | | | | | | | | 7 |
| | 2 | 13 | 12 | 5¹ | | 7 | 8 | 9² | 10 | | 3 | 6³ | | 11 | 4 | | 1 | 14 | | | | | | | | | | 8 |
| | 2 | | | | 6 | 7 | 8 | 9 | 10 | | 3¹ | | 12 | 11 | 4 | | 1 | 5 | | | | | | | | | | 9 |
| | 2 | 12 | | | 5³ | 7 | 8 | 9 | 10¹ | | 13 | 3² | 6 | 11 | 4 | | 1 | 14 | | | | | | | | | | 10 |
| | 2 | 7 | | | 5 | 6 | | 9 | 10 | | 12 | | | 11 | 4 | 8¹ | 1 | 3 | | | | | | | | | | 11 |
| | 2 | 7 | 4 | | 5■ | 6 | | 9 | 10 | 12 | | | | 11¹ | | 8 | 1 | 3 | | | | | | | | | | 12 |
| | 2 | 7 | | | 5 | 6¹ | 8 | 9 | 10 | | | | 12 | | 4 | 11 | 1 | 3 | | | | | | | | | | 13 |
| | 2 | 7 | | 5 | 6¹ | 4 | 8 | 9 | 10 | | | 13 | 12 | | | 11² | 1 | 3 | | | | | | | | | | 14 |
| | | 12 | 4 | 5 | | 7 | 8 | 9 | 10 | | 13 | 3 | 6 | | | 11¹ | | 2² | 1 | | | | | | | | | 15 |
| | 7 | 12 | | 5 | | 8 | 11 | 9 | 10 | 13 | 14 | 2 | 6² | | | | | 4¹ | 1 | 3³ | | | | | | | | 16 |
| | 7¹ | 12 | 4 | 5 | | 6 | 11 | 9 | 10 | 8³ | | 2 | | | | 13 | | 3² | 1 | | 14 | | | | | | | 17 |
| | 7 | 12 | 4³ | 5 | | | 8 | 9¹ | 10 | 6² | 2 | | | 11 | | 13 | | 3 | 1 | | | 14 | | | | | | 18 |
| | 7 | 12 | 13 | 5 | | 4 | 10³ | 9² | | 14 | 2 | | | 11 | | 8¹ | | 6 | 1 | | | 3 | | | | | | 19 |
| | 7 | 12 | | 5 | | 4 | 10¹ | 9 | | 13 | 2 | | | 11² | | 8 | | 3 | 1 | | | 6 | | | | | | 20 |
| | 2 | 12 | 4■ | 5 | | 8 | | | 10 | | 3 | | 11 | 7 | | 9¹ | | | 1 | | | 6 | | | | | | 21 |
| | 2 | 7 | 4 | | | 8 | | 9 | 10 | | 3 | | 11 | | | 12 | | 6¹ | 1 | | | 5 | | | | | | 22 |
| | 7 | 9 | 12 | 5 | | | 10² | 13 | | | 3 | 2¹ | 6 | 11 | | | | | 1 | | | 4 | 8 | | | | | 23 |
| | 2 | 7 | | 5 | | 12 | 9 | | 10 | | 3 | | 6 | 11¹ | | | | | 1 | | | 4 | 8 | | | | | 24 |
| | 2 | 7 | 4 | 5 | | | 9 | 12 | 10 | | 3¹ | | 6² | 11 | | 13 | | | 1 | | | | 8 | | | | | 25 |
| | 2 | 7 | 4 | 5 | | 12 | 9 | | 10 | | 3 | | 6 | 11¹ | | | | | 1 | | | | 8 | | | | | 26 |
| | 11 | 7 | | 5¹ | | | 9 | 13 | 10² | 4 | 14 | 6 | | | | 12 | | 2³ | 1 | 3 | | | 8 | | | | | 27 |
| | 2 | 7³ | | | | 12 | 9² | 13 | 10 | 8¹ | 5 | | 6 | | | 14 | | | 1 | 3 | | | 11 | 4 | | | | 28 |
| | 2 | 7³ | | | | 12 | 9² | 13 | 10 | | 5 | | 6 | 11¹ | | 14 | | | 1 | 3 | | | 8 | 4 | | | | 29 |
| | 2 | 7 | | 5 | | | 9 | | 10 | | | | 6 | 11 | | | 1 | | | 3 | | | 8 | 4 | | | | 30 |
| | 2 | 7 | | 5 | | 12 | 9 | | 10 | | | | 6 | 11¹ | | | 1 | | | 3 | | | 8 | 4 | | | | 31 |
| | 2 | 7 | | 5 | | 13 | 9¹ | 12 | 10 | | | | 6³ | 11² | | | 1 | | | 3 | | | 8 | 4 | 14 | | | 32 |
| | 2 | 7³ | | 5 | | 12 | 9² | 13 | 10 | | | | 6¹ | 11 | | 14 | 1 | | | 3 | | | 8 | 4 | | | | 33 |
| | 2 | 7¹ | | 5 | | 6 | 9² | | 10 | | | | | 11 | | | 1 | | | 3 | | | 8 | 4■ | 12 | 13 | | 34 |
| | 2 | 7 | | 5 | | 6¹ | 9 | 10 | | | | | | 11 | | | 1 | | | 3 | | | 8 | 4 | | 12 | | 35 |
| | 2 | 7 | | 5 | | 4¹ | 9 | 12 | 10 | | | | | 11 | | | 1 | | | 3 | | | 8 | | 6 | | | 36 |
| | 2 | 7 | | 5 | | | 9 | 12 | 10¹ | | | | | 11 | | | | | | 3 | | | 8 | 4 | 6 | | 1 | 37 |
| | 2 | 7 | | 5 | | | 9 | | 10 | | | | | 11 | | 12 | | | | 3 | | | 8 | 4 | 6¹ | | 1 | 38 |
| | 2 | 7 | | 5 | | | 9 | | 10 | | | | 6¹ | 11 | | | | | | 3 | | | 8 | 4 | 12 | | 1 | 39 |
| | 2 | 7 | | 5 | | 13 | 9 | 12 | 10¹ | | | | 6³ | 11² | | | | | | 3 | | | 8 | 4 | 14 | | 1 | 40 |
| | 2 | 7 | | 5 | | 12 | 9² | 10³ | | | | | 6¹ | 11 | | | | | | 3 | | | 8 | 4 | 14 | 13 | 1 | 41 |
| | 2² | 7 | | 5 | | 12 | 9 | 13 | 10 | | | | 6¹ | 11 | | | | | | 3 | | | 8 | 4 | | | 1 | 42 |
| | 2 | 7³ | | 5 | | 12 | 9 | 13 | 10² | | | | 6¹ | 11 | | 14 | | | | 3 | | | 8 | | 4 | | 1 | 43 |
| | 2 | 7 | | 5 | | 8 | 9 | 12 | 10¹ | | | | 6 | | | 13 | | | | 3 | | | 11² | | 4 | | 1 | 44 |
| | 2² | 7 | | 5 | | 8¹ | 9 | 12 | 10 | 14 | | | 6³ | | | 13 | | | | 3 | | | 11 | | 4 | | 1 | 45 |
| | 2 | 7 | | 5 | | 12 | 9 | 13 | 10³ | | | | 6² | 11 | | 14 | | | | 3 | | | 8 | | 4¹ | | 1 | 46 |

**Carling Cup**

| | | | |
|---|---|---|---|
| First Round | Torquay U | (a) | 1-1 |
| Second Round | Doncaster R | (h) | 2-1 |
| Third Round | Blackpool | (a) | 3-1 |
| Fourth Round | Aston Villa | (a) | 0-3 |

**FA Cup**

| | | | |
|---|---|---|---|
| Third Round | Tottenham H | (a) | 0-3 |

**Play-Offs**

| | | | |
|---|---|---|---|
| Semi-Final | Sunderland | (h) | 3-2 |
| | | (a) | 1-2 |
| Final | West Ham U | | 1-0 |
| *(at Millennium Stadium)* | | | |

# DARLINGTON FL Championship 2

## FOUNDATION

A football club was formed in Darlington as early as 1861 but the present club began in 1883 and reached the final of the Durham Senior Cup in their first season, losing to Sunderland in a replay after complaining that they had suffered from intimidation in the first. On 5 April 1884, Sunderland had defeated Darlington 4-3. Darlington's objection was upheld by the referee and the replay took place on 3 May. The new referee for the match was Major Marindin, appointed by the Football Association to ensure fair play. Sunderland won 2-0. The following season Darlington won this trophy and for many years were one of the leading amateur clubs in their area.

***New Stadium, Neasham Road, Darlington DL2 1GR.***

***Telephone:*** (01325) 387 000.

***Fax:*** (01325) 387 050.

***Ticket Office:*** (01325) 387 030.

***Website:*** darlington-fc.net

***Email:*** carol@newstadium.fsnet.co.uk

***Ground Capacity:*** 25,000.

***Record Attendance:*** 21,023 v Bolton W, League Cup 3rd rd, 14 November 1960.

***Pitch Measurements:*** 105m × 68m.

***Chief Executive:*** Andy Battison.

***Secretary:*** Lisa Charlton.

***Manager:*** David Hodgson.

***Physio:*** Paul Gough.

***Colours:*** Black and white shirts, black shorts, black stockings.

***Change Colours:*** All black.

***Year Formed:*** 1883.

***Turned Professional:*** 1908.

***Ltd Co.:*** 1891.

***Previous Grounds:*** Feethams Ground; 2003, Reynolds Arena, Hurworth Moor.

***Club Nickname:*** 'The Quakers'.

***First Football League Game:*** 27 August 1921, Division 3 (N), v Halifax T (h) W 2–0 – Ward; Greaves, Barbour; Dickson (1), Sutcliffe, Malcolm; Dolphin, Hooper (1), Edmunds, Wolstenholme, Winship.

***Record League Victory:*** 9–2 v Lincoln C, Division 3 (N), 7 January 1928 – Archibald; Brooks, Mellen; Kelly, Waugh, McKinnell; Cochrane (1), Gregg (1), Ruddy (3), Lees (3), McGiffen (1).

***Record Cup Victory:*** 7–2 v Evenwood T, FA Cup 1st rd, 17 November 1956 – Ward; Devlin, Henderson; Bell (1p), Greener, Furphy; Forster (1), Morton (3), Tulip (2), Davis, Moran.

## HONOURS

*Football League:* Division 2 best season: 15th, 1925–26; Division 3 (N) – Champions 1924–25; Runners-up 1921–22; Division 4 – Champions 1990–91; Runners-up 1965–66.

*FA Cup:* best season: 5th rd, 1958.

*Football League Cup:* best season: 5th rd, 1968.

*GM Vauxhall Conference:* Champions 1989–90.

## SKY SPORTS FACT FILE

Though Mark Hooper made his name as a diminutive right-winger with Darlington, he actually began as a schoolboy goalkeeper. Later with a local steelworks, Willington and Cockfield. Debut 1924 then to Sheffield Wednesday in 1927.

***Record Defeat:*** 0–10 v Doncaster R, Division 4, 25 January 1964.

***Most League Points (2 for a win):*** 59, Division 4, 1965–66.

***Most League Points (3 for a win):*** 85, Division 4, 1984–85.

***Most League Goals:*** 108, Division 3 (N), 1929–30.

***Highest League Scorer in Season:*** David Brown, 39, Division 3 (N), 1924–25.

***Most League Goals in Total Aggregate:*** Alan Walsh, 90, 1978–84.

***Most League Goals in One Match:*** 5, Tom Ruddy v South Shields, Division 2, 23 April 1927; 5, Maurice Wellock v Rotherham U, Division 3N, 15 February 1930.

***Most Capped Player:*** Jason Devos, 3 (46), Canada.

***Most League Appearances:*** Ron Greener, 442, 1955–68.

***Youngest League Player:*** Dale Anderson, 16 years 254 days v Chesterfield, 4 May 1987.

***Record Transfer Fee Received:*** £400,000 from Dundee U for Jason Devos, October 1998.

***Record Transfer Fee Paid:*** £95,000 to Motherwell for Nick Cusack, January 1992.

***Football League Record:*** 1921 Original Member Division 3 (N); 1925–27 Division 2; 1927–58 Division 3 (N); 1958–66 Division 4; 1966–67 Division 3; 1967–85 Division 4; 1985–87 Division 3; 1987–89 Division 4; 1989–90 GM Vauxhall Conference; 1990–91 Division 4; 1991–2004 Division 3; 2004– FL2.

## LATEST SEQUENCES

***Longest Sequence of League Wins:*** 6, 6.2.2000 – 7.3.2000.

***Longest Sequence of League Defeats:*** 8, 31.8.1985 – 19.10.1985.

***Longest Sequence of League Draws:*** 5, 31.12.1988 – 28.1.1989.

***Longest Sequence of Unbeaten League Matches:*** 17, 27.4.1968 – 19.10.1968.

***Longest Sequence Without a League Win:*** 19, 27.4.1988 – 8.11.1988.

***Successive Scoring Runs:*** 22 from 3.12.1932.

***Successive Non-scoring Runs:*** 7 from 5.9.1975.

## MANAGERS

Tom McIntosh 1902–11
W. L. Lane 1911–12
*(Secretary-Manager)*
Dick Jackson 1912–19
Jack English 1919–28
Jack Fairless 1928–33
George Collins 1933–36
George Brown 1936–38
Jackie Carr 1938–42
Jack Surtees 1942
Jack English 1945–46
Bill Forrest 1946–50
George Irwin 1950–52
Bob Gurney 1952–57
Dick Duckworth 1957–60
Eddie Carr 1960–64
Lol Morgan 1964–66
Jimmy Greenhalgh 1966–68
Ray Yeoman 1968–70
Len Richley 1970–71
Frank Brennan 1971
Ken Hale 1971–72
Allan Jones 1972
Ralph Brand 1972–73
Dick Conner 1973–74
Billy Horner 1974–76
Peter Madden 1976–78
Len Walker 1978–79
Billy Elliott 1979–83
Cyril Knowles 1983–87
Dave Booth 1987–89
Brian Little 1989–91
Frank Gray 1991–92
Ray Hankin 1992
Billy McEwan 1992–93
Alan Murray 1993–95
Paul Futcher 1995
David Hodgson/Jim Platt
*(Director of Coaching)* 1995
Jim Platt 1995–96
David Hodgson 1996–2000
Gary Bennett 2000–01
Tommy Taylor 2001–02
Mick Tait 2003
David Hodgson November 2003–

## TEN YEAR LEAGUE RECORD

| | | *P* | *W* | *D* | *L* | *F* | *A* | *Pts* | *Pos* |
|---|---|---|---|---|---|---|---|---|---|
| 1994-95 | Div 3 | 42 | 11 | 8 | 23 | 43 | 57 | 41 | 20 |
| 1995-96 | Div 3 | 46 | 20 | 18 | 8 | 60 | 42 | 78 | 5 |
| 1996-97 | Div 3 | 46 | 14 | 10 | 22 | 64 | 78 | 52 | 18 |
| 1997-98 | Div 3 | 46 | 14 | 12 | 20 | 56 | 72 | 54 | 19 |
| 1998-99 | Div 3 | 46 | 18 | 11 | 17 | 69 | 58 | 65 | 11 |
| 1999-2000 | Div 3 | 46 | 21 | 16 | 9 | 66 | 36 | 79 | 4 |
| 2000-01 | Div 3 | 46 | 12 | 13 | 21 | 44 | 56 | 49 | 20 |
| 2001-02 | Div 3 | 46 | 15 | 11 | 20 | 60 | 71 | 56 | 15 |
| 2002-03 | Div 3 | 46 | 12 | 18 | 16 | 58 | 59 | 54 | 14 |
| 2003-04 | Div 3 | 46 | 14 | 11 | 21 | 53 | 61 | 53 | 18 |

## DID YOU KNOW ?

Of the unchanged eleven who played for Darlington in the abortive three games in 1939–40 prior to wartime regional matches, only two players had previously appeared in peacetime games for them: Hugh Foulkes and Joe Hodgson and none subsequently.

## DARLINGTON 2003–04 LEAGUE RECORD

| Match No. | Date | Venue | Opponents | Result | | H/T Score | Lg. Pos. | Goalscorers | Attendance |
|---|---|---|---|---|---|---|---|---|---|
| 1 | Aug 9 | A | Hull C | L | 1-4 | 1-1 | — | Conlon [41] | 14,675 |
| 2 | 16 | H | Kidderminster H | L | 0-2 | 0-0 | 24 | | 11,600 |
| 3 | 22 | A | Northampton T | L | 0-1 | 0-1 | — | | 5020 |
| 4 | 25 | H | Leyton Orient | W | 2-1 | 0-0 | 22 | Clarke M [79], Hughes [90] | 4660 |
| 5 | 30 | A | Rochdale | L | 2-4 | 2-2 | 23 | McGurk [30], Pearson [43] | 2518 |
| 6 | Sept 6 | H | Carlisle U | W | 2-0 | 2-0 | 20 | Conlon 2 [6, 13] | 5889 |
| 7 | 13 | H | Doncaster R | W | 2-1 | 0-0 | 16 | Wainwright 2 [59, 67] | 5518 |
| 8 | 16 | A | York C | D | 1-1 | 1-1 | — | Conlon [45] | 3867 |
| 9 | 20 | A | Torquay U | D | 2-2 | 1-2 | 16 | Liddle [13], Clark [73] | 2420 |
| 10 | 27 | H | Boston U | W | 3-0 | 0-0 | 11 | Liddle [65], Clarke M [72], Clark [78] | 4519 |
| 11 | 30 | H | Southend U | D | 0-0 | 0-0 | — | | 4369 |
| 12 | Oct 4 | A | Mansfield T | L | 1-3 | 1-1 | 15 | Clark [45] | 4621 |
| 13 | 11 | H | Bristol R | L | 0-4 | 0-1 | 17 | | 4268 |
| 14 | 18 | A | Yeovil T | L | 0-1 | 0-1 | 20 | | 4892 |
| 15 | 21 | A | Cheltenham T | L | 1-2 | 1-1 | — | Morgan [42] | 2745 |
| 16 | 25 | H | Bury | L | 1-3 | 1-1 | 21 | Liddle [4] | 3516 |
| 17 | Nov 1 | A | Oxford U | L | 1-3 | 1-0 | 23 | McGurk [23] | 4962 |
| 18 | 15 | H | Lincoln C | D | 0-0 | 0-0 | 22 | | 4601 |
| 19 | 22 | A | Swansea C | L | 0-1 | 0-1 | 23 | | 5651 |
| 20 | 29 | H | Scunthorpe U | D | 2-2 | 1-0 | 23 | Conlon [39], Wainwright [59] | 3606 |
| 21 | Dec 6 | H | York C | W | 3-0 | 2-0 | 21 | Conlon [11], Wainwright [35], James [78] | 4115 |
| 22 | 13 | A | Cambridge U | L | 0-1 | 0-1 | 23 | | 2822 |
| 23 | 20 | H | Macclesfield T | L | 0-1 | 0-0 | 23 | | 2920 |
| 24 | 26 | H | Huddersfield T | L | 0-1 | 0-1 | 23 | | 6205 |
| 25 | 28 | A | Carlisle U | D | 1-1 | 1-1 | 23 | Matthews [40] | 8369 |
| 26 | Jan 3 | A | Leyton Orient | L | 0-1 | 0-1 | 23 | | 3737 |
| 27 | 10 | H | Hull C | L | 0-1 | 0-1 | 23 | | 6847 |
| 28 | 17 | A | Kidderminster H | D | 1-1 | 0-1 | 23 | McGurk [90] | 2550 |
| 29 | 31 | H | Rochdale | W | 1-0 | 0-0 | 23 | Hughes [80] | 5689 |
| 30 | Feb 7 | A | Huddersfield T | W | 2-0 | 1-0 | 23 | Clark (pen) [22], Maddison [54] | 11,014 |
| 31 | 14 | A | Bristol R | W | 3-0 | 0-0 | 22 | Liddle [74], Conlon 2 [80, 90] | 6011 |
| 32 | 17 | H | Northampton T | L | 1-2 | 0-0 | — | Willmott (og) [47] | 4764 |
| 33 | 21 | H | Yeovil T | W | 3-2 | 2-1 | 21 | Conlon [20], Wainwright 2 [33, 80] | 4500 |
| 34 | 28 | A | Bury | D | 1-1 | 1-0 | 21 | Conlon [19] | 2766 |
| 35 | Mar 6 | A | Macclesfield T | W | 1-0 | 0-0 | 20 | Russell [53] | 2293 |
| 36 | 9 | H | Cheltenham T | W | 2-1 | 2-1 | — | McGurk [14], Conlon [39] | 3921 |
| 37 | 13 | H | Cambridge U | L | 3-4 | 1-2 | 17 | Convery [26], Keltie [85], Clarke M [86] | 5056 |
| 38 | 20 | A | Doncaster R | D | 1-1 | 0-0 | 17 | Convery [59] | 7178 |
| 39 | 27 | H | Torquay U | D | 1-1 | 1-0 | 20 | Conlon [2] | 4317 |
| 40 | Apr 3 | A | Boston U | L | 0-1 | 0-1 | 20 | | 2573 |
| 41 | 10 | H | Mansfield T | W | 1-0 | 0-0 | 20 | Clarke M [48] | 4946 |
| 42 | 12 | A | Southend U | L | 2-3 | 2-0 | 21 | Graham [6], Valentine (pen) [33] | 5132 |
| 43 | 17 | H | Oxford U | W | 2-0 | 1-0 | 18 | Valentine [26], Conlon [71] | 4212 |
| 44 | 24 | A | Lincoln C | D | 1-1 | 1-0 | 17 | Wainwright [37] | 6187 |
| 45 | May 1 | H | Swansea C | L | 1-2 | 0-0 | 21 | Graham [65] | 5487 |
| 46 | 8 | A | Scunthorpe U | W | 1-0 | 1-0 | 18 | Conlon [5] | 4801 |

**Final League Position: 18**

### GOALSCORERS

*League (53):* Conlon 14, Wainwright 7, Clark 4 (1 pen), Clarke M 4, Liddle 4, McGurk 4, Convery 2, Graham 2, Hughes 2, Valentine 2 (1 pen), James 1, Keltie 1, Maddison 1, Matthews 1, Morgan 1, Pearson 1, Russell 1, own goal 1.
*Carling Cup (0).*
*FA Cup (0).*
*LDV Vans Trophy (1):* Sheeran 1.

| Collett A 9 | McGurk D 22 + 5 | Valentine R 33 + 7 | Liddle C 43 | Clarke M 44 + 1 | Hutchinson J 38 + 1 | Keltie C 23 + 8 | Nicholls A 25 + 1 | Conlon B 38 + 1 | Mellanby D 5 + 2 | Maddison N 30 + 2 | Hughes C 24 + 6 | Robson G 3 + 3 | Bossy F 4 + 2 | Clark I 20 + 14 | Wainwright N 30 + 5 | Sheeran M — + 6 | Pearson G 11 + 7 | Price M 36 | Coghlan M — + 3 | Morgan A 4 + 1 | Convery M 17 + 8 | Turnbull R 1 | James C 10 | Alexander J — + 3 | Matthews L 6 | Russell C 6 + 6 | Teggart N 9 + 6 | Close B 8 + 4 | Graham D 7 + 2 | Mason C — + 1 | *Match No.* |
|---|---|---|---|---|---|---|---|---|---|---|---|---|---|---|---|---|---|---|---|---|---|---|---|---|---|---|---|---|---|---|---|
| 1 | 2 | 3 | 4 | 5 | $6^{1}$ | 7 | 8 | 9 | $10^{2}$ | 11 | 12 | 13 | | | | | | | | | | | | | | | | | | | 1 |
| 1 | 2 | 3 | 4 | | | 7 | $8^{2}$ | 9 | | $11^{1}$ | 12 | $10^{3}$ | 6 | 5 | 13 | 14 | | | | | | | | | | | | | | | 2 |
| 1 | 2 | $3^{2}$ | 4 | 10 | | 7 | $8^{3}$ | 9 | | $11^{1}$ | 12 | 13 | 6 | 14 | | | 5 | | | | | | | | | | | | | | 3 |
| 1 | 2 | 3 | 4 | 5 | 12 | $7^{1}$ | | 9 | 13 | 14 | 8 | $10^{2}$ | $6^{3}$ | | | | 11 | | | | | | | | | | | | | | 4 |
| 1 | 2 | 3 | 4 | 10 | 6 | 7 | | 9 | | | 8 | $11^{2}$ | 12 | 13 | | | $5^{1}$ | | | | | | | | | | | | | | 5 |
| 1 | 2 | 3 | 4 | 10 | 6 | 7 | 8 | 9 | | | 11 | | | | | | 5■ | | | | | | | | | | | | | | 6 |
| 1 | 2 | 3 | 4 | 10 | 6 | 7 | 8 | 9 | | | $11^{2}$ | | | 12 | 13 | | $5^{1}$ | | | | | | | | | | | | | | 7 |
| 1 | 2 | 3 | 4 | 10 | 6 | 7 | 8 | 9 | | | | | | | 11 | | 5■ | | | | | | | | | | | | | | 8 |
| 1 | 2 | $3^{2}$ | 4 | 10 | 5 | 7 | 8 | 9 | 14■ | | 13 | | $6^{3}$ | 12 | $11^{1}$ | | | | | | | | | | | | | | | | 9 |
| | 2 | 3 | 4 | 10 | 5 | 7 | 8 | 9 | | | 6 | | | 11 | | | | 1 | | | | | | | | | | | | | 10 |
| | 2 | 3 | 4 | 10 | 5 | 7 | 8 | 9 | | | 6 | | | 11 | | | | 1 | | | | | | | | | | | | | 11 |
| | 2■ | 3 | 4 | 10 | 5 | 7 | 8 | 9 | | | 6 | | | 11 | | | | 1 | | | | | | | | | | | | | 12 |
| | 2 | 3 | 4 | 10 | 5 | $7^{1}$ | 8 | $9^{2}$ | | | $6^{3}$ | | | 11 | | 12 | | 1 | 14 | 13 | | | | | | | | | | | 13 |
| | | 3 | 4 | 10 | $2^{1}$ | | 8 | | 9 | $11^{2}$ | | | | 12 | $7^{3}$ | 13 | 5 | 1 | | 6 | 14 | | | | | | | | | | 14 |
| | 2 | 3 | 4 | 12 | 6 | 7 | | | $9^{1}$ | | | | | 10 | $11^{2}$ | | 5 | 1 | | 8 | 13 | | | | | | | | | | 15 |
| | 2 | $3^{1}$ | 4 | 10 | 6 | 7 | 13 | | $9^{2}$ | | | | | 12 | $11^{3}$ | | 5 | 1 | | 8 | 14 | | | | | | | | | | 16 |
| | 2■ | | 4 | 10 | 6 | 7 | $8^{1}$ | | 9■ | 12 | $3^{2}$ | 13 | 14 | | | | $5^{3}$ | 1 | | 11 | | | | | | | | | | | 17 |
| | | 3 | 4 | 5 | 6 | 7 | 8 | 9 | | 10 | | | | | 11 | | | | | | | 1 | 2 | | | | | | | | 18 |
| | | $3^{2}$ | 4 | 5 | 6 | $7^{3}$ | $8^{1}$ | 9 | | 10 | | | | 12 | 11 | | 13 | 1 | | | 14 | | 2 | | | | | | | | 19 |
| | | 3■ | 4 | 5 | 6 | $7^{2}$ | 8 | 9■ | | 10 | | | | 12 | $11^{1}$ | | 13 | 1 | | | | | 2 | | | | | | | | 20 |
| | | 3 | 4 | 5 | 6 | | $8^{1}$ | 9 | | $10^{2}$ | | | | 11 | $7^{3}$ | | | 1 | 13 | | 12 | | 2 | 14 | | | | | | | 21 |
| | 12 | | 4 | 5 | 6 | | 8 | | | $7^{3}$ | | | | 11 | 9 | | $2^{1}$ | 1 | 14 | | | | 3 | 13 | $10^{2}$ | | | | | | 22 |
| | | | 4 | 5 | 6 | | $8^{1}$ | | | 7 | 3 | | | 11 | 9 | | | 1 | | | 12 | | 2 | | 10 | | | | | | 23 |
| | | | 4 | 5 | 6 | 12 | 7 | | | $8^{3}$ | 3 | | | $11^{2}$ | 9 | | | 1 | | | 13 | | 2 | 14 | $10^{1}$ | | | | | | 24 |
| | | 13 | 4 | 5 | 6 | 12 | 7 | 9 | | $8^{1}$ | $3^{2}$ | | | | 11 | | | 1 | | | | | 2 | | 10 | | | | | | 25 |
| | | 12 | 4 | 5 | 6 | | 11 | 9 | | 8 | 3 | | | | $7^{1}$ | | | 1 | | | | | 2 | | 10 | | | | | | 26 |
| | 13 | 3 | 4 | 5 | $6^{2}$ | | 7 | 9 | | $8^{3}$ | 14 | | | | 11 | 12 | | 1 | | | | | $2^{1}$ | | 10 | | | | | | 27 |
| | 2 | $3^{1}$ | 4 | 5 | | | 6 | 9 | | 8 | | | | $11^{2}$ | 10 | 12 | | 1 | | | 7 | | | | | 13 | | | | | 28 |
| | 12 | | 4 | 5 | 6 | | $3^{2}$ | $9^{1}$ | | 8 | 2 | | | 11 | $10^{3}$ | 13 | | 1 | | | 7 | | | | | 14 | | | | | 29 |
| | | 12 | 4 | 5 | 6 | | | 9 | | 8 | 2 | | | 3 | 11 | | | 1 | | | $7^{1}$ | | | | | 13 | $10^{2}$ | | | | 30 |
| | | 12 | 4 | 5 | 6 | | | 9 | | $8^{1}$ | $2^{2}$ | | | 3 | 11 | | 13 | 1 | | | $7^{3}$ | | | | | 14 | 10 | | | | 31 |
| | | 12 | 4 | 5 | 6 | | | 9 | | $8^{2}$ | $2^{1}$ | | | 3■ | 11 | | 13 | 1 | | | $7^{3}$ | | | | | 14 | 10 | | | | 32 |
| | 13 | 12 | 4 | 5 | 6 | | | $9^{2}$ | | $8^{3}$ | 2 | | | $3^{1}$ | 11 | | 14 | 1 | | | 7 | | | | | | 10■ | | | | 33 |
| | | 12 | 4 | 5 | 6 | | | 9 | | 8 | 2 | | | 3 | $11^{2}$ | | | 1 | | | 7 | | | | | 13 | $10^{1}$ | | | | 34 |
| | 2 | 3 | 4 | 5 | | 12 | | 9 | | $8^{1}$ | 6 | | | | 11 | | | 1 | | | $7^{2}$ | | | | | 10 | | 13 | | | 35 |
| | 2 | 3 | 4 | 5 | | 13 | | 9 | | | 6 | | | 12 | $11^{2}$ | | | 1 | | | $7^{1}$ | | | | | $10^{3}$ | 14 | 8 | | | 36 |
| | 2 | 3 | 4 | 5 | | 13 | | 9 | | $8^{3}$ | 6 | | | 12 | $11^{2}$ | | | 1 | | | $7^{1}$ | | | | | 10 | | 14 | | | 37 |
| | | 3 | 4 | $5^{2}$ | 6 | 12 | | 9 | | 8 | 2 | | | | | | | 1 | | | $7^{1}$ | | | | | 11 | $10^{3}$ | 13 | 14 | | 38 |
| | | 3 | 4 | 5 | 6 | | | 9 | | 8 | $2^{1}$ | | | | 12 | | | 1 | | | $7^{3}$ | | | | | $11^{2}$ | 10 | 13 | 14 | | 39 |
| | | | 4 | 5 | 6 | 13 | | 9 | | $8^{2}$ | | | | 12 | 2 | | | 1 | | | 14 | | | | | $3^{1}$ | $10^{3}$ | 7 | 11 | | 40 |
| | 12 | 3 | | 5 | 6 | 2 | | 9 | | $8^{1}$ | | | | 13 | 11 | | | 1 | | | $7^{2}$ | | | | | | 14 | 4 | $10^{3}$ | | 41 |
| | 2 | 3 | | 5 | 6■ | 13 | | 9 | | $8^{2}$ | | | | 12 | 11 | | | 1 | | | $7^{1}$ | | | | | | 14 | 4 | $10^{3}$ | | 42 |
| | | 3 | 4 | 5 | 6 | 8 | | $9^{3}$ | | | | | | 12 | 11 | | 13 | 1 | | | $7^{1}$ | | | | | | 14 | $2^{2}$ | 10 | | 43 |
| | | 3 | 4 | 5 | 6 | 7 | | $9^{2}$ | | | | | | 8 | 11 | | 12 | 1 | | | | | | | | | 13 | $2^{1}$ | 10 | | 44 |
| | | 3 | 4 | 5 | | $6^{3}$ | | 12 | | 8 | 14 | | | $11^{2}$ | 13 | | | 1 | | | 7 | | | | | | $10^{1}$ | 2 | 9 | | 45 |
| | 2 | 3 | | 5 | 6 | | | $9^{2}$ | | 8 | | | | $11^{3}$ | 12 | | | 1 | | | $7^{1}$ | | | | | | 13 | 4 | 10 | 14 | 46 |

**Carling Cup**

| | | | |
|---|---|---|---|
| First Round | Bradford C | (a) | 0-0 |
| Second Round | Wolverhampton W | (a) | 0-2 |

**LDV Vans Trophy**

| | | | |
|---|---|---|---|
| First Round | Hull C | (h) | 1-3 |

**FA Cup**

| | | | |
|---|---|---|---|
| First Round | Hornchurch | (a) | 0-2 |

# DERBY COUNTY FL Championship

## FOUNDATION

Derby County was formed by members of the Derbyshire County Cricket Club in 1884, when football was booming in the area and the cricketers thought that a football club would help boost finances for the summer game. To begin with, they sported the cricket club's colours of amber, chocolate and pale blue, and went into the game at the top immediately entering the FA Cup.

***Pride Park Stadium, Derby DE24 8XL.***

***Telephone:*** (01332) 202 202.

***Fax:*** (01332) 667 519.

***Ticket Office:*** (01332) 209 209.

***Website:*** www.dcfc.co.uk

***Email:*** derby.county@dcfc.co.uk

***Ground Capacity:*** 33,597.

***Record Attendance:*** 41,826 v Tottenham H, Division 1, 20 September 1969.

***Pitch Measurements:*** 110yd × 72yd.

***Chairman:*** John Sleightholme.

***Chief Executive:*** Jeremy Keith.

***Secretary:*** Keith Pearson ACIS.

***Manager:*** George Burley.

***Physio:*** Peter Melville.

***Colours:*** White shirts with black piping, black shorts, white stockings.

## HONOURS

*Football League:* Division 1 – Champions 1971–72, 1974–75; Runners-up 1895–96, 1929–30, 1935–36, 1995–96; Division 2 – Champions 1911–12, 1914–15, 1968–69, 1986–87; Runners-up 1925–26; Division 3 (N) Champions 1956–57; Runners-up 1955–56.

*FA Cup:* Winners 1946; Runners-up 1898, 1899, 1903.

*Football League Cup:* Semi-final 1968.

*Texaco Cup:* Winners 1972.

***European Competitions:*** *European Cup:* 1972–73, 1975–76. *UEFA Cup:* 1974–75, 1976–77. *Anglo-Italian Cup:* Runners-up 1993.

***Change Colours:*** Royal blue shirts, white and royal blue shorts, royal blue stockings.

***Year Formed:*** 1884.

***Turned Professional:*** 1884.

***Ltd Co.:*** 1896.

***Club Nickname:*** 'The Rams'.

***Previous Grounds:*** 1884, Racecourse Ground; 1895, Baseball Ground; 1997, Pride Park.

***First Football League Game:*** 8 September 1888, Football League, v Bolton W (a) W 6–3 – Marshall; Latham, Ferguson, Williamson; Monks, W. Roulstone; Bakewell (2), Cooper (2), Higgins, H. Plackett, L. Plackett (2).

***Record League Victory:*** 9–0 v Wolverhampton W, Division 1, 10 January 1891 – Bunyan; Archie Goodall, Roberts; Walker, Chalmers, Roulstone (1); Bakewell, McLachlan, Johnny Goodall (1), Holmes (2), McMillan (5). 9–0 v Sheffield W, Division 1, 21 January 1899 – Fryer; Methven, Staley; Cox, Archie Goodall, May; Oakden (1), Bloomer (6), Boag, McDonald (1), Allen, (1 og).

### SKY SPORTS FACT FILE

When Derby County won the FA Cup in 1946 the total aggregate of attendances for the 11 matches which included the two-legged rounds operating that season was in excess of 500,000. The highest Baseball Ground crowd was 32,000 on three occasions.

***Record Cup Victory:*** 12–0 v Finn Harps, UEFA Cup 1st rd 1st leg, 15 September 1976 – Moseley; Thomas, Nish, Rioch (1), McFarland, Todd (King), Macken, Gemmill, Hector (5), George (3), James (3).

***Record Defeat:*** 2–11 v Everton, FA Cup 1st rd, 1889–90.

***Most League Points (2 for a win):*** 63, Division 2, 1968–69 and Division 3 (N), 1955–56 and 1956–57.

***Most League Points (3 for a win):*** 84, Division 3, 1985–86 and Division 3, 1986–87.

***Most League Goals:*** 111, Division 3 (N), 1956–57.

***Highest League Scorer in Season:*** Jack Bowers, 37, Division 1, 1930–31; Ray Straw, 37 Division 3 (N), 1956–57.

***Most League Goals in Total Aggregate:*** Steve Bloomer, 292, 1892–1906 and 1910–14.

***Most League Goals in One Match:*** 6, Steve Bloomer v Sheffield W, Division 1, 2 January 1899.

***Most Capped Players:*** Deon Burton, 41 (98), Jamaica and Mart Poom, 41 (48), Estonia`.

***Most League Appearances:*** Kevin Hector, 486, 1966–78 and 1980–82.

***Youngest League Player:*** Lee Holmes, 15 years 268 days v Grimsby T, 26 December 2002.

***Record Transfer Fee Received:*** £7,000,000 rising to £9,000,000 for Seth Johnson from Leeds U, October 2001.

***Record Transfer Fee Paid:*** £3,000,000 rising to £4,000,000 for Lee Morris from Sheffield U, October 1999.

***Football League Record:*** 1888 Founder Member of the Football League; 1907–12 Division 2; 1912–14 Division 1; 1914–15 Division 2; 1915–21 Division 1; 1921–26 Division 2; 1926–53 Division 1; 1953–55 Division 2; 1955–57 Division 3 (N); 1957–69 Division 2; 1969–80 Division 1; 1980–84 Division 2; 1984–86 Division 3; 1986–87 Division 2; 1987–91 Division 1; 1991–92 Division 2; 1992–96 Division 1; 1996–2002 FA Premier League; 2002–04 Division 1; 2004– FLC.

## MANAGERS

W. D. Clark 1896–1900
Harry Newbould 1900–06
Jimmy Methven 1906–22
Cecil Potter 1922–25
George Jobey 1925–41
Ted Magner 1944–46
Stuart McMillan 1946–53
Jack Barker 1953–55
Harry Storer 1955–62
Tim Ward 1962–67
Brian Clough 1967–73
Dave Mackay 1973–76
Colin Murphy 1977
Tommy Docherty 1977–79
Colin Addison 1979–82
Johnny Newman 1982
Peter Taylor 1982–84
Roy McFarland 1984
Arthur Cox 1984–93
Roy McFarland 1993–95
Jim Smith 1995–2001
Colin Todd 2001–02
John Gregory 2002–03
George Burley June 2003–

## LATEST SEQUENCES

***Longest Sequence of League Wins:*** 9, 15.3.1969 – 19.4.1969.

***Longest Sequence of League Defeats:*** 8, 12.12.1987 – 10.2.1988.

***Longest Sequence of League Draws:*** 6, 26.3.1927 – 18.4.1927.

***Longest Sequence of Unbeaten League Matches:*** 22, 8.3.1969 – 20.9.1969.

***Longest Sequence Without a League Win:*** 20, 15.12.1990 – 23.4.1991.

***Successive Scoring Runs:*** 29 from 3.12.1960.

***Successive Non-scoring Runs:*** 8 from 30.10.1920.

## TEN YEAR LEAGUE RECORD

| | | P | W | D | L | F | A | Pts | Pos |
|---|---|---|---|---|---|---|---|---|---|
| 1994-95 | Div 1 | 46 | 18 | 12 | 16 | 66 | 51 | 66 | 9 |
| 1995-96 | Div 1 | 46 | 21 | 16 | 9 | 71 | 51 | 79 | 2 |
| 1996-97 | PR Lge | 38 | 11 | 13 | 14 | 45 | 58 | 46 | 12 |
| 1997-98 | PR Lge | 38 | 16 | 7 | 15 | 52 | 49 | 55 | 9 |
| 1998-99 | PR Lge | 38 | 13 | 13 | 12 | 40 | 45 | 52 | 8 |
| 1999-2000 | PR Lge | 38 | 9 | 11 | 18 | 44 | 57 | 38 | 16 |
| 2000-01 | PR Lge | 38 | 10 | 12 | 16 | 37 | 59 | 42 | 17 |
| 2001-02 | PR Lge | 38 | 8 | 6 | 24 | 33 | 63 | 30 | 19 |
| 2002-03 | Div 1 | 46 | 15 | 7 | 24 | 55 | 74 | 52 | 18 |
| 2003-04 | Div 1 | 46 | 13 | 13 | 20 | 53 | 67 | 52 | 20 |

## DID YOU KNOW ?

On 7 February 1973 Derby County were trailing Tottenham Hotspur 3-1 at White Hart Lane in a fourth round FA Cup replay with 12 minutes remaining. Before the end of full-time Derby had levelled the scores and won 5-3 in the extra period.

## DERBY COUNTY 2003–04 LEAGUE RECORD

| Match No. | Date | Venue | Opponents | Result | H/T Score | Lg. Pos. | Goalscorers | Attendance |
|---|---|---|---|---|---|---|---|---|
| 1 | Aug 9 | H | Stoke C | L 0-3 | 0-2 | — | | 21,517 |
| 2 | 16 | A | Gillingham | D 0-0 | 0-0 | 21 | | 7850 |
| 3 | 23 | H | Reading | L 2-3 | 1-3 | 22 | Taylor (pen) [7], Svensson [81] | 18,970 |
| 4 | 25 | A | Cardiff C | L 1-4 | 0-2 | 22 | Svensson [48] | 15,091 |
| 5 | 30 | H | WBA | L 0-1 | 0-0 | 24 | | 21,499 |
| 6 | Sept 13 | A | Walsall | W 1-0 | 0-0 | 22 | Junior [80] | 8726 |
| 7 | 17 | H | Watford | W 3-2 | 1-1 | — | Taylor [18], Svensson [73], Junior [88] | 18,459 |
| 8 | 20 | H | Sunderland | D 1-1 | 0-0 | 20 | Taylor [89] | 22,535 |
| 9 | 27 | A | Nottingham F | D 1-1 | 1-1 | 21 | Junior [25] | 29,059 |
| 10 | 30 | A | Bradford C | W 2-1 | 1-0 | — | Morris 2 [45, 79] | 10,143 |
| 11 | Oct 4 | H | West Ham U | L 0-1 | 0-0 | 20 | | 22,810 |
| 12 | 11 | H | Wigan Ath | D 2-2 | 1-2 | 16 | Taylor (pen) [40], Morris [62] | 19,151 |
| 13 | 14 | A | Crystal Palace | D 1-1 | 0-1 | — | Zavagno [74] | 14,344 |
| 14 | 18 | A | Crewe Alex | L 0-3 | 0-2 | 18 | | 8656 |
| 15 | 21 | A | Norwich C | L 1-2 | 0-0 | — | Taylor (pen) [61] | 16,346 |
| 16 | 25 | H | Coventry C | L 1-3 | 0-2 | 21 | Holmes [52] | 21,641 |
| 17 | Nov 1 | A | Preston NE | L 0-3 | 0-1 | 21 | | 12,839 |
| 18 | 8 | H | Ipswich T | D 2-2 | 2-0 | 22 | Kennedy [44], Dichio [45] | 19,976 |
| 19 | 15 | H | Burnley | W 2-0 | 1-0 | 19 | Morris [20], Taylor (pen) [90] | 21,960 |
| 20 | 22 | A | Millwall | D 0-0 | 0-0 | 20 | | 10,308 |
| 21 | 29 | H | Wimbledon | W 3-1 | 1-1 | 20 | Herzig (og) [13], Tudgay [52], Holmes [53] | 22,025 |
| 22 | Dec 6 | A | Ipswich T | L 1-2 | 0-1 | 21 | Tudgay [73] | 25,018 |
| 23 | 13 | A | Rotherham U | D 0-0 | 0-0 | 22 | | 7320 |
| 24 | 26 | A | WBA | D 1-1 | 0-0 | 22 | Costa [86] | 26,412 |
| 25 | 28 | H | Norwich C | L 0-4 | 0-0 | 22 | | 23,783 |
| 26 | Jan 10 | A | Stoke C | L 1-2 | 1-1 | 22 | Morris [1] | 16,402 |
| 27 | 17 | H | Gillingham | W 2-1 | 1-0 | 22 | Vincent [14], Edwards [61] | 20,473 |
| 28 | 28 | H | Sheffield U | W 2-0 | 0-0 | — | Tudgay [70], McLeod [90] | 23,603 |
| 29 | 31 | A | Reading | L 1-3 | 0-2 | 21 | Johnson [59] | 14,382 |
| 30 | Feb 7 | H | Cardiff C | D 2-2 | 0-0 | 21 | Taylor [49], Osman [90] | 20,958 |
| 31 | 14 | A | Wigan Ath | L 0-2 | 0-1 | 21 | | 9146 |
| 32 | 21 | H | Crystal Palace | W 2-1 | 0-1 | 21 | Manel [70], Osman [76] | 21,856 |
| 33 | 28 | A | Coventry C | L 0-2 | 0-2 | 22 | | 16,042 |
| 34 | Mar 3 | H | Crewe Alex | D 0-0 | 0-0 | — | | 19,861 |
| 35 | 13 | H | Rotherham U | W 1-0 | 0-0 | 22 | Peschisolido [61] | 21,741 |
| 36 | 16 | A | Watford | L 1-2 | 1-1 | — | Peschisolido [10] | 13,931 |
| 37 | 20 | H | Nottingham F | W 4-2 | 3-1 | 22 | Taylor [4], Peschisolido 2 [28, 31], Tudgay [82] | 32,390 |
| 38 | 23 | A | Sheffield U | D 1-1 | 1-1 | — | Taylor (pen) [25] | 21,351 |
| 39 | 27 | A | Sunderland | L 1-2 | 0-1 | 22 | Taylor (pen) [64] | 30,838 |
| 40 | Apr 3 | H | Walsall | L 0-1 | 0-0 | 22 | | 23,574 |
| 41 | 10 | A | West Ham U | D 0-0 | 0-0 | 22 | | 28,207 |
| 42 | 12 | H | Bradford C | W 3-2 | 1-0 | 22 | Osman [36], Taylor [64], Combe (og) [84] | 21,593 |
| 43 | 17 | H | Preston NE | W 5-1 | 4-0 | 19 | Manel 2 [2, 37], Tudgay 2 [27, 32], Junior (pen) [76] | 24,162 |
| 44 | 24 | A | Burnley | L 0-1 | 0-1 | 21 | | 16,189 |
| 45 | May 1 | H | Millwall | W 2-0 | 1-0 | 20 | Bolder [40], Reich [72] | 26,056 |
| 46 | 9 | A | Wimbledon | L 0-1 | 0-1 | 20 | | 6509 |

**Final League Position: 20**

### GOALSCORERS

*League (53):* Taylor 11 (6 pens), Tudgay 6, Morris 5, Junior 4 (1 pen), Peschisolido 4, Manel 3, Osman 3, Svensson 3, Holmes 2, Bolder 1, Costa 1, Dichio 1, Edwards 1, Johnson 1, Kennedy 1, McLeod 1, Reich 1, Vincent 1, Zavagno 1, own goals 2.
*Carling Cup (1):* Taylor 1.
*FA Cup (0).*

| Oakes A 10 | Hunt L 1 | Jackson R 34 + 2 | Caldwell G 6 + 3 | Mills P 13 + 6 | Elliott S 2 + 2 | Costa C 23 + 11 | Taylor I 42 | Morris L 21 + 2 | McLeod I 4 + 6 | Huddlestone T 42 + 1 | Labarthe G — + 3 | Bolder A 11 + 13 | Boertien P 10 + 8 | Grant L 36 | Zavagno L 16 + 1 | Johnson M 39 | Bradbury L 7 | Svensson M 9 + 1 | Valakari S 14 + 6 | Junior6 + 6 | Holmes L 17 + 6 | Tudgay M 20 + 9 | Dichio D 6 | Walton D 3 + 2 | Kennedy P 5 | Mawene Y 30 | Doyle N 1 + 1 | Edwards R 10 + 1 | Manel12 + 4 | Vincent J 7 | Reich M 9 + 4 | Osman L 17 | Whelan N 3 + 5 | Kenna J 9 | Peschisolido P 11 | *Match No.* |
|---|---|---|---|---|---|---|---|---|---|---|---|---|---|---|---|---|---|---|---|---|---|---|---|---|---|---|---|---|---|---|---|---|---|---|---|---|
| 1 | $2^{1}$ | 3 | 4 | 5 | 6 | 7 | 8 | $9^{2}$ | $10^{3}$ | 11 | 12 | 13 | 14 | | | | | | | | | | | | | | | | | | | | | | | 1 |
| | | 2 | 5 | | | 7 | 8 | 12 | $10^{1}$ | 4 | | 13 | 11 | 1 | 3 | 6 | $9^{2}$ | | | | | | | | | | | | | | | | | | | 2 |
| | | 2 | $5^{1}$ | 12 | | 7 | 8 | 9 | | 4 | | | 3 | 1 | | 6 | | 10 | $11^{2}$ | 13 | | | | | | | | | | | | | | | | 3 |
| | | 2 | | 5 | | 7■ | 8 | $9^{1}$ | | 4 | | 13 | 3 | 1 | | 6 | | 10 | 12 | $11^{2}$ | | | | | | | | | | | | | | | | 4 |
| 1 | | 2 | | 5 | | 7 | 8 | 9 | | 4 | | | 3 | | | $6^{1}$ | | 10 | 11 | 12 | | | | | | | | | | | | | | | | 5 |
| 1 | | 2 | 12 | 5 | | | 8 | 11 | | 4 | | | 13 | | $3^{2}$ | 6 | | 10 | 7 | $9^{1}$ | | | | | | | | | | | | | | | | 6 |
| 1 | | 2 | 12 | 5 | | | 8 | 11 | | 4 | | | 13 | | $3^{2}$ | $6^{1}$ | | 10 | $7^{3}$ | 9 | 14 | | | | | | | | | | | | | | | 7 |
| 1 | | 2 | 6 | 5 | | | 8 | $7^{1}$ | | 4 | | | 3 | | | | | 10 | 12 | 9 | 11 | | | | | | | | | | | | | | | 8 |
| 1 | | 2 | 12 | 5 | | 13 | 8 | 14 | | 4 | | | | | 3 | 6 | | 10 | $7^{1}$ | $9^{3}$ | $11^{2}$ | | | | | | | | | | | | | | | 9 |
| 1 | | 2 | 5 | | | $7^{1}$ | 8 | 9 | | 4 | | | | | 3 | 6 | | 10 | 12 | | 11 | | | | | | | | | | | | | | | 10 |
| 1 | | | 2 | 5 | | 7 | 8 | $9^{2}$ | | 4 | | | | | 3 | 6 | | $10^{1}$ | 12 | | 11 | 13 | | | | | | | | | | | | | | 11 |
| 1 | | 2 | | 5 | | | 8 | 9 | | 4 | | | | | 3 | 6 | | | 7 | | 11 | 10 | | | | | | | | | | | | | | 12 |
| 1 | | 2 | | 5 | 12 | 11 | 8 | $9^{2}$ | | 4 | | | | | 3 | $6^{1}$ | | | 7 | | 10 | 13 | | | | | | | | | | | | | | 13 |
| | | 2 | | 5 | 12 | 13 | 8■ | $9^{2}$ | | 4 | | | | 1 | $3^{1}$ | 6 | | | $7^{3}$ | | 11 | 14 | 10 | | | | | | | | | | | | | 14 |
| | | 2 | | | | 12 | 8 | $9^{1}$ | | 4 | | | | 1 | 3 | 6 | | | $7^{2}$ | | 11 | 13 | 10 | 5 | | | | | | | | | | | | 15 |
| | | 2 | | 12 | | $11^{1}$ | | 9 | | 4 | | 13 | | 1 | 3 | 6 | | 14 | $7^{3}$ | | 8 | | 10 | $5^{2}$ | | | | | | | | | | | | 16 |
| | | | | 2 | 6 | 13 | | $9^{3}$ | | | | 4 | 12 | 1 | | | | | 7 | | $11^{2}$ | 14 | 10 | | $3^{1}$ | 5 | 8 | | | | | | | | | 17 |
| | | | | 2 | | 12 | 8 | 9 | | 4 | | | | 1 | | 6 | | | $7^{1}$ | | 11 | | 10 | | 3 | 5 | | | | | | | | | | 18 |
| | | 2 | | 12 | | $7^{2}$ | 8 | 9 | | 4 | | | 14 | 1 | | 6 | | | 13 | | $11^{3}$ | | 10 | | 3 | $5^{1}$ | | | | | | | | | | 19 |
| | | 2 | | | | | 8 | 9 | | 4 | | 13 | 12 | 1 | | 6 | $10^{3}$ | | $7^{2}$ | | $11^{1}$ | 14 | | | 3 | 5 | | | | | | | | | | 20 |
| | | 2 | | 12 | | 7 | 8 | | | $4^{3}$ | | 14 | | 1 | 13 | $6^{1}$ | 9 | | | | $11^{2}$ | 10 | | | 3 | 5 | | | | | | | | | | 21 |
| | | 2 | | 12 | | 7 | 8 | | 13 | | | 4 | | 1 | 3 | $6^{1}$ | 9 | | $11^{3}$ | | 14 | $10^{2}$ | | | | 5 | | | | | | | | | | 22 |
| | | 2 | | | | 7 | $8^{1}$ | | | | | 4 | | 1 | 3 | | 9 | | 12 | | 11 | 10 | | 6 | | 5 | | | | | | | | | | 23 |
| | | 2 | | | | 12 | 8 | 11 | | 4 | | 7 | | 1 | 3 | 6 | 9 | | | | | $10^{1}$ | | | | 5 | | | | | | | | | | 24 |
| | | 2 | | | | 12 | 8 | 9 | 13 | $4^{1}$ | | 7 | | 1 | 3 | 6 | | | | | $11^{2}$ | 10 | | | | 5 | | | | | | | | | | 25 |
| | | | | | | 12 | 8 | 11 | | 4 | | $7^{2}$ | | 1 | 2 | 6 | $9^{1}$ | | | | | 13 | | | | 5 | | 3 | 10 | | | | | | | 26 |
| | | | | | | $7^{2}$ | 8 | | | 4 | 12 | 13 | | 1 | | 6 | | | | | | 9 | | | | 5 | | 2 | $10^{1}$ | 3 | 11 | | | | | 27 |
| | | | | | | 7 | | | 12 | 4 | | 13 | | 1 | | 6 | | | | | | 9 | | | | 5 | | 2 | $10^{2}$ | 3 | $11^{1}$ | 8 | | | | 28 |
| | | 12 | | | | 7 | | | | 4 | | | | 1 | | $6^{1}$ | | | | | | 9 | | | | 5 | | 2 | $10^{2}$ | 3 | 11 | 8 | 13 | | | 29 |
| | | 12 | | | | $7^{2}$ | 8 | | 13 | 4 | | | | 1 | | 6 | | | | | | 14 | | | | 5 | | $2^{1}$ | | 3 | 11 | 10 | $9^{3}$ | | | 30 |
| | | 2 | | | | | 8 | | 10 | 7 | | | | 1 | | 6 | | | | | | | | | | 5 | | 4 | 12 | $3^{1}$ | 13 | 11 | $9^{2}$ | | | 31 |
| | | 3 | | | | $7^{2}$ | 8 | | $9^{3}$ | $4^{1}$ | | 12 | | 1 | | 6 | | | | | | | | | | 5 | | 2 | 14 | | 11 | 10 | 13 | | | 32 |
| | | 3 | | | | | 8 | | 13 | 12 | | 4 | | 1 | | 6 | | | | | | 14 | | | | 5 | | $2^{1}$ | 10■ | | $11^{3}$ | 7 | $9^{2}$ | | | 33 |
| | | 2 | | | | 12 | 8 | | 13 | 4 | | | 3 | 1 | | 6 | | | | | | $9^{2}$ | | | | 5 | | | $10^{3}$ | | $11^{1}$ | 7 | 14 | | | 34 |
| | | 3 | | | | $7^{1}$ | 8 | | | 4 | | | 13 | 1 | | $6^{2}$ | | | | | 12 | 9 | | | | 5 | | | | | | 11 | 14 | 2 | $10^{3}$ | 35 |
| | | $6^{1}$ | | | | $7^{2}$ | 8 | | | 4 | 14 | | 3 | 1 | | | | | | | 12 | $9^{3}$ | | 13 | | 5 | | | | | | 11 | | 2 | 10 | 36 |
| | | $2^{1}$ | | | | $7^{2}$ | 8 | | | 4 | | | 12 | 1 | | 6 | | | | | 13 | 9 | | | | 5 | | | | | | 11 | | 3 | 10 | 37 |
| | | | | | | 12 | 8 | | | 4 | | 7 | 3 | 1 | | $6^{3}$ | | | | | | $9^{2}$ | | 14 | | 5 | | 2 | $10^{1}$ | | | 11 | 13 | | | 38 |
| | | | | | | | 8 | | | 4 | | 12 | 11 | 1 | | 6 | | | | | | | | | | 5 | | $2^{1}$ | 9 | | | 7 | | 3 | 10 | 39 |
| | | | | | | $7^{3}$ | 8 | | | 4 | | | $3^{2}$ | 1 | | 6■ | | | | 12 | | | | | | 5 | | 13 | 9 | | 14 | 11 | | 2 | $10^{1}$ | 40 |
| | | 2 | | | | | 8 | | | 4 | | 12 | | 1 | | | | | | | $11^{1}$ | 9 | | | | 5 | | | 13 | 3 | | 7 | | 6 | $10^{2}$ | 41 |
| | | 2 | | 12 | | $7^{2}$ | 8 | | | 4 | | 13 | | 1 | | | | | | | | 9 | | | | 5 | | | 14 | $3^{1}$ | | 11 | | $6^{3}$ | 10 | 42 |
| | | 3 | | | | | $8^{1}$ | | | 4 | | 2 | | 1 | | 6 | | | | 12 | | $9^{2}$ | | | | 5 | 13 | | $11^{3}$ | | 14 | 7 | | | 10 | 43 |
| | | 3 | | | | | 8 | | | 4 | | $2^{2}$ | | 1 | | 6 | | | | 12 | | 9 | | | | 5 | | | 11 | | 13 | 7 | | | $10^{1}$ | 44 |
| | | 3 | | | | | 8 | | | 4 | | 14 | | 1 | | $6^{3}$ | | | | 13 | 12 | 9 | | | | 5 | | | $11^{2}$ | | $7^{1}$ | | | 2 | 10 | 45 |
| | | | | | | 12 | 8 | | | 4 | | 3 | | 1 | | 6 | | | | $11^{1}$ | | 9 | | | | 5 | | | | | 7 | | | 2 | 10 | 46 |

**Carling Cup**
First Round Huddersfield T (a) 1-2

**FA Cup**
Third Round Ipswich T (a) 0-3

# DONCASTER ROVERS FL Championship 1

## FOUNDATION

In 1879, Mr Albert Jenkins assembled a team to play a match against the Yorkshire Institution for the Deaf. The players remained together as Doncaster Rovers, joining the Midland Alliance in 1889 and the Midland Counties League in 1891.

***The Earth Stadium, Belle Vue, Doncaster DN4 5HT.***

***Telephone:*** (01302) 539 441.

***Fax:*** (01302) 539 679.

***Ticket Office:*** (01302) 379 328.

***Website:*** www.doncasterroversfc.co.uk

***Email:*** info@doncasterroversfc.co.uk

***Ground Capacity:*** 9,975.

***Record Attendance:*** 3,7149 v Hull C, Division 3 (N), 2 October 1948.

***Pitch Measurements:*** 110yd × 76yd.

***Chairman:*** John Ryan.

***Vice-chairman:*** Stuart Highfield JP.

***Secretary:*** Joan Oldale.

***Manager:*** Dave Penney.

***Assistant Manager:*** Micky Walker.

***Physio***: Barry Windle.

***Colours:*** Red and white broad hooped shirts, red shorts, red stockings.

***Change Colours:*** All blue.

***Year Formed:*** 1879.

***Turned Professional:*** 1885.

***Ltd Co.:*** 1905 & 1920.

***Club Nickname:*** 'Rovers'.

***Previous Grounds:*** Intake Ground 1880–1916; Benetthorpe Ground 1920–1922; Low Pasture, Belle Vue 1922.

***Record League Victory:*** 10–0 v Darlington, Division 4, 25 January 1964: Potter; Raine, Meadows, Windross (1), White, Ripley (2), Robinson, Book (2), Hale (4), Jeffrey, Broadbent (1).

***Record Cup Victory:*** 7–0 v Blyth Spartans, FA Cup 1st rd, 27 November 1937: Imrie; Shaw, Rodgers, McFarlane, Bycroft, Cyril Smith, Burton (1), Killourhy (4), Morgan (2), Malam, Dutton.

## HONOURS

*Football League:* Division 2 best season: 7th, 1901–02; Division 3 Champions 2003–04; Division 3 (N) Champions – 1934–35, 1946–47, 1949–50; Runners-up: 1937–38, 1938–39; Division 4 Champions 1965–66, 1968–69; Runners-up: 1983–84. Promoted 1980–81 (3rd).

*FA Cup:* best season 5th rd, 1952, 1954, 1955, 1956.

*Football League Cup:* best season: 5th rd, 1976.

*Sheffield County Cup:* Winners 1891, 1912, 1936, 1938, 1956, 1968, 1976, 1986.

*Midland Counties League:* Champions 1897, 1899.

*Conference Trophy:* Winners 1999, 2000.

*Sheffield & Hallamshire Senior Cup:* Winners 2001, 2002.

## SKY SPORTS FACT FILE

In 1928–29 Tom Keetley scored over half of the Doncaster Rovers total of 76 League goals in Division Three (North). His tally of 40 was six more than achieved by Colin Booth for the club in 1962–63 when Rovers scored 64 in Division Four.

***Record Defeat:*** 0–12 v Small Heath, Division 2, 11 April 1903.

***Most League Points (2 for a win):*** 72, Division 3 (N), 1946–47.

***Most League Points (3 for a win):*** 92, Division 3, 2003–04.

***Most League Goals:*** 123, Division 3 (N), 1946–47.

***Highest League Scorer in Season:*** Clarrie Jordan, 42, Division 3 (N), 1946–47.

***Most League Goals in Total Aggregate:*** Tom Keetley, 180, 1923–29.

***Most Capped Player:*** Len Graham, 14, Northern Ireland.

***Most League Appearances:*** Fred Emery, 417, 1925–36.

***Record Transfer Fee Received:*** £275,000 from QPR for Rufus Brevett, February 1991.

***Record Transfer Fee Paid:*** £120,000 to Rushden & D for Justin Jackson, September 2001.

***Football League Record:*** 1901 Elected to Division 2; 1903 Failed re-election; 1904 Re-elected; 1905 Failed re-election; 1923 Re-elected to Divison 3 (N); 1935–37 Division 2; 1937–47 Division 3 (N); 1947–48 Division 2; 1948–50 Division 3 (N); 1950–58 Division 2; 1958–59 Division 3; 1959–66 Division 4; 1966–67 Division 3; 1967–69 Division 4; 1969–71 Division 3; 1971–81 Division 4; 1981–83 Division 3; 1983–84 Division 4; 1984–88 Division 3; 1988–92 Division 4; 1992–98 Division 3; 1998–2003 Conference; 2003–04 Division 3; 2004– FL1.

## LATEST SEQUENCES

***Longest Sequence of League Wins:*** 10, 22.1.1947 – 4.4.1947.

***Longest Sequence of League Defeats:*** 9, 14.1.1905 – 1.4.1905.

***Longest Sequence of League Draws:*** 4, 29.10.1932 – 19.11.1932.

***Longest Sequence of Unbeaten League Matches:*** 20, 26.12.1968 – 12.4.1969.

***Longest Sequence Without a League Win:*** 20, 9.8.1997 – 29.11.1997.

***Successive Scoring Runs:*** 27 from 10.11.1934.

***Successive Non-scoring Runs:*** 7 from 27.9.1947.

## MANAGERS

Arthur Porter 1920–21
Harry Tufnell 1921–22
Arthur Porter 1922–23
Dick Ray 1923–27
David Menzies 1928–36
Fred Emery 1936–40
Bill Marsden 1944–46
Jackie Bestall 1946–49
Peter Doherty 1949–58
Jack Hodgson & Sid Bycroft (*Joint Managers*) 1958
Jack Crayston 1958–59 (*continued as Secretary-Manager to 1961*)
Jackie Bestall (TM) 1959–60
Norman Curtis 1960–61
Danny Malloy 1961–62
Oscar Hold 1962–64
Bill Leivers 1964–66
Keith Kettleborough 1966–67
George Raynor 1967–68
Lawrie McMenemy 1968–71
Morris Setters 1971–74
Stan Anderson 1975–78
Billy Bremner 1978–85
Dave Cusack 1985–87
Dave Mackay 1987–89
Billy Bremner 1989–91
Steve Beaglehole 1991–93
Ian Atkins 1994
Sammy Chung 1994–96
Kerry Dixon (*Player–Manager*) 1996–97
Dave Cowling 1997
Mark Weaver 1997–98
Ian Snodin 1998–99
Steve Wignall 1999–2001
Dave Penney March 2002–

## TEN YEAR LEAGUE RECORD

| | | *P* | *W* | *D* | *L* | *F* | *A* | *Pts* | *Pos* |
|---|---|---|---|---|---|---|---|---|---|
| 1994-95 | Div 3 | 42 | 17 | 10 | 15 | 58 | 43 | 61 | 9 |
| 1995-96 | Div 3 | 46 | 16 | 11 | 19 | 49 | 60 | 59 | 13 |
| 1996-97 | Div 3 | 46 | 14 | 10 | 22 | 52 | 65 | 52 | 19 |
| 1997-98 | Div 3 | 46 | 4 | 8 | 34 | 30 | 113 | 20 | 24 |
| 1998-99 | Conf. | 42 | 12 | 12 | 18 | 51 | 55 | 48 | 16 |
| 1999-2000 | Conf. | 42 | 15 | 9 | 18 | 46 | 48 | 54 | 12 |
| 2000-01 | Conf. | 42 | 15 | 13 | 14 | 47 | 43 | 58 | 9 |
| 2001-02 | Conf. | 42 | 18 | 13 | 11 | 68 | 46 | 67 | 4 |
| 2002-03 | Conf. | 42 | 22 | 12 | 8 | 73 | 47 | 78 | 3 |
| 2003-04 | Div 3 | 46 | 27 | 11 | 8 | 79 | 37 | 92 | 1 |

## DID YOU KNOW?

Doncaster Rovers were the only Football League club in the 1946–47 season to score eight or more goals on two occasions. They defeated Carlisle United 9-2 on 25 January and Barrow 8-0 on 13 March in gaining promotion.

## DONCASTER ROVERS 2003–04 LEAGUE RECORD

| Match No. | Date | Venue | Opponents | Result | | H/T Score | Lg. Pos. | Goalscorers | Attendance |
|---|---|---|---|---|---|---|---|---|---|
| 1 | Aug 9 | A | Leyton Orient | W | 3-1 | 1-0 | — | Blundell [45], Fortune-West 2 [51, 66] | 5194 |
| 2 | 16 | H | Southend U | W | 2-0 | 1-0 | 2 | Foster [12], Green [55] | 5592 |
| 3 | 23 | A | Lincoln C | D | 0-0 | 0-0 | 3 | | 5051 |
| 4 | 25 | H | Huddersfield T | D | 1-1 | 0-1 | 4 | Fortune-West [47] | 7367 |
| 5 | 30 | A | Northampton T | L | 0-1 | 0-0 | 6 | | 4933 |
| 6 | Sept 8 | H | Hull C | D | 0-0 | 0-0 | — | | 7132 |
| 7 | 13 | A | Darlington | L | 1-2 | 0-0 | 13 | Paterson (pen) [53] | 5518 |
| 8 | 16 | H | Yeovil T | L | 0-1 | 0-1 | — | | 4716 |
| 9 | 20 | H | Oxford U | W | 2-0 | 1-0 | 12 | Ryan [39], Green [83] | 5040 |
| 10 | 27 | A | Bury | W | 3-1 | 2-1 | 9 | Fortune-West [11], Blundell [36], McIndoe [53] | 3606 |
| 11 | 30 | A | Cambridge U | D | 3-3 | 0-2 | — | Tierney [57], Albrighton [64], Ryan [75] | 3492 |
| 12 | Oct 4 | H | Bristol R | W | 5-1 | 3-0 | 8 | Tierney [12], Brown [41], McIndoe 3 (1 pen) [45, 57, 82 (p)] | 5439 |
| 13 | 11 | A | Macclesfield T | W | 3-1 | 1-1 | 5 | Blundell [45], Green [49], McIndoe (pen) [53] | 2831 |
| 14 | 18 | H | Mansfield T | W | 4-2 | 1-1 | 5 | Blundell [38], Green [53], McIndoe (pen) [70], Brown [77] | 8500 |
| 15 | 21 | H | Rochdale | W | 2-1 | 1-1 | — | Tierney [2], Brown [75] | 5890 |
| 16 | 25 | A | Kidderminster H | W | 2-0 | 1-0 | 2 | Blundell [16], Brown [60] | 3393 |
| 17 | Nov 1 | H | Torquay U | W | 1-0 | 1-0 | 2 | Green [21] | 6863 |
| 18 | 15 | A | York C | L | 0-1 | 0-0 | 4 | | 5942 |
| 19 | 22 | H | Boston U | W | 3-0 | 1-0 | 3 | Brown 2 [31, 54], Melligan [53] | 5211 |
| 20 | 29 | A | Carlisle U | W | 1-0 | 0-0 | 2 | Fortune-West [68] | 4344 |
| 21 | Dec 13 | A | Cheltenham T | W | 3-1 | 2-1 | 2 | McIndoe (pen) [12], Morley [24], Melligan [51] | 3884 |
| 22 | 19 | H | Swansea C | W | 3-1 | 2-0 | — | McIndoe (pen) [11], Green [20], Blundell [90] | 6566 |
| 23 | 26 | H | Scunthorpe U | W | 1-0 | 0-0 | 1 | Blundell [67] | 8961 |
| 24 | 28 | A | Hull C | L | 1-3 | 1-1 | 2 | Fortune-West [39] | 23,006 |
| 25 | Jan 3 | A | Huddersfield T | L | 1-3 | 0-1 | 3 | Blundell [72] | 13,044 |
| 26 | 10 | H | Leyton Orient | W | 5-0 | 3-0 | 3 | Fortune-West 3 [6, 14, 18], Blundell [56], Hynes [80] | 6293 |
| 27 | 17 | A | Southend U | W | 2-0 | 2-0 | 2 | Fortune-West [4], McIndoe [7] | 4308 |
| 28 | 23 | H | Lincoln C | L | 0-2 | 0-1 | — | | 8774 |
| 29 | 30 | H | Northampton T | W | 1-0 | 1-0 | — | Green [8] | 6017 |
| 30 | Feb 7 | A | Scunthorpe U | D | 2-2 | 0-1 | 2 | McIndoe (pen) [83], Fortune-West [90] | 5681 |
| 31 | 14 | H | Macclesfield T | W | 1-0 | 1-0 | 2 | Blundell [45] | 5525 |
| 32 | 21 | A | Mansfield T | W | 2-1 | 0-1 | 1 | Blundell 2 [60, 67] | 7724 |
| 33 | 27 | H | Kidderminster H | W | 5-0 | 2-0 | — | Albrighton [5], Blundell 2 [45, 78], Ravenhill [56], Mulligan [90] | 7594 |
| 34 | Mar 5 | A | Swansea C | D | 1-1 | 0-1 | — | Brown [56] | 8045 |
| 35 | 13 | H | Cheltenham T | D | 1-1 | 0-0 | 1 | Brown [90] | 7510 |
| 36 | 16 | A | Yeovil T | W | 1-0 | 0-0 | — | Ravenhill [72] | 7587 |
| 37 | 20 | H | Darlington | D | 1-1 | 0-0 | 1 | Akinfenwa [86] | 7178 |
| 38 | 27 | A | Oxford U | D | 0-0 | 0-0 | 1 | | 8483 |
| 39 | 30 | A | Rochdale | D | 1-1 | 0-0 | — | Albrighton [90] | 4601 |
| 40 | Apr 3 | H | Bury | W | 3-1 | 0-0 | 1 | Blundell 2 [47, 68], Akinfenwa [73] | 6221 |
| 41 | 10 | A | Bristol R | W | 2-1 | 0-0 | 1 | Ravenhill [51], Akinfenwa [61] | 8571 |
| 42 | 12 | H | Cambridge U | W | 2-0 | 0-0 | 1 | Akinfenwa [60], Green [65] | 9644 |
| 43 | 17 | A | Torquay U | L | 0-1 | 0-1 | 1 | | 5808 |
| 44 | 24 | H | York C | W | 3-1 | 2-0 | 1 | Blundell [5], Brown 2 [8, 57] | 7843 |
| 45 | May 1 | A | Boston U | D | 0-0 | 0-0 | 1 | | 4671 |
| 46 | 8 | H | Carlisle U | W | 1-0 | 0-0 | 1 | Blundell [69] | 9720 |

**Final League Position: 1**

### GOALSCORERS

*League (79):* Blundell 18, Fortune-West 11, Brown 10, McIndoe 10 (6 pens), Green 8, Akinfenwa 4, Albrighton 3, Ravenhill 3, Tierney 3, Melligan 2, Ryan 2, Foster 1, Hynes 1, Morley 1, Mulligan 1, Paterson 1 (pen).
*Carling Cup (4):* Blundell 2, Barnes 1 (pen), Fortune-West 1.
*FA Cup (0).*
*LDV Vans Trophy (1):* Tierney 1.

| Warrington A 46 | Marples S 16 | Beech C 11 | Foster S 44 | Ryan T 41 + 1 | Green P 38 + 5 | Paterson J 7 + 1 | Doolan J 36 + 3 | Blundell G 41 + 3 | Fortune-West L 28 + 11 | McIndoe M 45 | Ravenhill R 14 + 22 | Tierney F 10 + 3 | Morley D 15 + 6 | Barnes P 2 + 5 | Price J 17 + 2 | McGrath J 4 + 7 | Albrighton M 27 + 1 | Burton S 1 + 5 | Brown C 17 + 5 | Gill R — + 1 | O'Brien R 1 | Melligan J 21 | Rigoglioso A 5 + 12 | Hynes P — + 5 | Mulligan D 14 | Akinfenwa A 4 + 5 | Black C 1 | Maloney J — + 1 | Match No. |
|---|---|---|---|---|---|---|---|---|---|---|---|---|---|---|---|---|---|---|---|---|---|---|---|---|---|---|---|---|---|
| 1 | 2 | 3 | 4 | 5 | 6[1] | 7[2] | 8[3] | 9 | 10 | 11 | 12 | 13 | 14 | | | | | | | | | | | | | | | | 1 |
| 1 | 2 | 3 | 4 | 5 | 6 | 7[2] | 8[1] | 9 | 10[3] | 11 | 12 | 13 | | 14 | | | | | | | | | | | | | | | 2 |
| 1 | 2 | 3 | 4 | 5 | 6 | 7 | 8 | 9 | 10 | 11 | | | | | | | | | | | | | | | | | | | 3 |
| 1 | 2 | 3 | 4 | 5 | 6 | 7 | 8 | 9 | 10 | 11 | | | | | | | | | | | | | | | | | | | 4 |
| 1 | 2 | 3[1] | 4 | 5 | 6 | 7 | 8 | 9 | 10 | 11 | | | | 12 | | | | | | | | | | | | | | | 5 |
| 1 | 2 | 3 | 4 | 5 | 6[1] | 7 | 8 | 9 | 10[2] | 11 | 12 | | | 13 | | | | | | | | | | | | | | | 6 |
| 1 | | 3[1] | 4 | 5 | 6 | 7[2] | 8 | 9 | 12 | 11 | | 13 | 2 | 10 | | | | | | | | | | | | | | | 7 |
| 1 | | 3[2] | 4 | 5 | 6 | 12 | 8 | 9[3] | 10■ | 11 | | 7[1] | 13 | 14 | 2 | | | | | | | | | | | | | | 8 |
| 1 | | | 4 | 5 | 6 | | 8 | 9[1] | 10 | 11 | | 7[2] | 3 | 12 | 2 | 13 | | | | | | | | | | | | | 9 |
| 1 | | | 4 | 5 | 6 | | 8 | 9 | 10 | 11 | | 7 | 3 | | 2 | | | | | | | | | | | | | | 10 |
| 1 | | | 4 | 5 | 6 | | 8 | 9[3] | | 11 | 12 | 7 | 3[2] | 10[1] | 2 | | 13 | 14 | | | | | | | | | | | 11 |
| 1 | | | 4 | 5 | 6[1] | | 8 | | | 11 | 12 | 7 | | | 2 | 13 | 3 | 9[3] | 10[2] | 14 | | | | | | | | | 12 |
| 1 | | | 4 | 5 | 6 | | 8 | 9[3] | | 11 | 12 | 7[1] | 13 | | 2 | | 3 | 14 | 10[2] | | | | | | | | | | 13 |
| 1 | | | 4 | 5 | 6[1] | | 8 | 9 | | 11 | 12 | 7 | | | 2 | | 3 | | 10 | | | | | | | | | | 14 |
| 1 | | | 4 | 5 | 6 | | 8 | 9 | 12 | 11 | | 7[1] | | | 2 | | 3 | | 10 | | | | | | | | | | 15 |
| 1 | | 3 | 4 | | 6[2] | | 8 | 9 | 12 | 11 | 13 | | | | 2 | 14 | 5 | | 10[3] | | 7[1] | | | | | | | | 16 |
| 1 | | | 4 | 5 | 6[1] | | 8[2] | 9 | 12 | 11 | 14 | | 13 | | 2 | 7 | 3 | | 10[3] | | | | | | | | | | 17 |
| 1 | 2 | | 4 | 5 | 8 | | | 9 | 12 | 11 | 6 | | | | | 7[2] | 3 | 13 | 10[1] | | | | | | | | | | 18 |
| 1 | 2 | | 4 | 5 | 6 | | 8[2] | 9[3] | 12 | 11 | 13 | | | | | | 3 | 14 | 10[1] | | | 7 | | | | | | | 19 |
| 1 | 2 | | 4 | 5 | 6[1] | | 8 | 9 | 10 | 11 | 12 | | 3 | | | | | | | | | 7 | | | | | | | 20 |
| 1 | 2 | | 4 | 5 | 6[2] | | | 9[1] | 10 | 11 | 8 | | 3 | | | | | | | | | 7 | 13 | 12 | | | | | 21 |
| 1 | 2 | | 4 | 5 | 6[1] | | 8 | 9 | 10[3] | 11 | 12 | | 3 | | | | | | | | | 7[2] | 13 | 14 | | | | | 22 |
| 1 | 2 | | 4 | 5 | 6[3] | | 8 | 9 | 10[2] | 11 | 12 | 7[1] | 3 | | | | | | | | | | 14 | 13 | | | | | 23 |
| 1 | 2 | | 4 | 5 | | | | 9 | 10 | 11 | 6 | | 3 | | | | | | | | | 7 | 8 | | | | | | 24 |
| 1 | 2 | | 4 | 5 | 6[1] | | 12 | 9 | 10 | 11 | | | 3 | | | | | | | | | 7[2] | 8 | 13 | | | | | 25 |
| 1 | | | 4 | 5 | 6[1] | | 8 | 9 | 10[3] | 11 | 12 | | | | 2 | | 3 | | | | | 7[2] | 13 | 14 | | | | | 26 |
| 1 | | | 4 | 5 | 6 | | 8[1] | 9 | 10[2] | 11 | 12 | | | | 2 | | 3 | | 13 | | | 7[3] | 14 | | | | | | 27 |
| 1 | | | 4 | 5 | 6 | | 8[1] | 9[2] | 10 | 11 | 12 | | | | 2 | | 3 | 13 | | | | 7[3] | 14 | | | | | | 28 |
| 1 | | 5[2] | 4 | | 6 | | 8[1] | 9 | 10 | 11 | 12 | | 13 | | 2 | | 3 | | | | | | 7 | | | | | | 29 |
| 1 | | 5[1] | 4 | 12 | 6 | | 8[3] | 9 | 10 | 11 | | | | | 2■ | 14 | 3 | | 13 | | | | 7[2] | | | | | | 30 |
| 1 | | | 4 | 5 | 8[1] | | | 7[2] | 10 | 11 | 6 | | | | 2 | 12 | 3 | | 9 | | | | 13 | | | | | | 31 |
| 1 | | | 4 | 5 | 8 | | | 9[1] | 10 | 11 | 6 | | | | | | 3 | | 12 | | | 7 | | | 2 | | | | 32 |
| 1 | | | 4 | 5 | 8 | | | 9 | 10[1] | 11 | 6[2] | | | | | 13 | 3 | | 12 | | | 7[3] | 14 | | 2 | | | | 33 |
| 1 | | | 4 | 5 | 8[1] | | 12 | | 10[3] | 11 | 6 | | | | | | 3 | | 9[2] | | | 7 | 13 | | 2 | 14 | | | 34 |
| 1 | | | 4 | 5 | 8 | | 12 | 9[2] | 13 | 11 | 6[1] | | | | | | 3 | | 10 | | | 7 | | | 2[3] | 14 | | | 35 |
| 1 | | | 4 | 5 | | | 8 | 12 | 10 | 11 | 6 | | | | | | 3 | | 9[1] | | | 7 | | | 2 | | | | 36 |
| 1 | | | 4 | 5 | 12 | | 8 | 13 | 10[3] | 11 | 6[1] | | | | | | 3 | | 9 | | | 7[2] | | | 2 | 14 | | | 37 |
| 1 | | | 4 | 5 | 6 | | 8 | 13 | 10[3] | 11 | 12 | | | | | | 3 | | 9[2] | | | | | | 2 | 14 | 7[1] | | 38 |
| 1 | | | | 5 | 12 | | 8[1] | 9 | 10[3] | 11 | 6 | | 3 | | | | 4 | | | | | 7[2] | 13 | | 2 | 14 | | | 39 |
| 1 | | | | 5 | 6[1] | | 8 | 9 | 13 | 11 | 12 | | 3 | | | | 4 | | | | | 7[3] | 14 | | 2 | 10[2] | | | 40 |
| 1 | | | 5 | | | | 8 | 9 | | 11 | 6 | | 3 | | 12 | | 4 | | | | | 7[1] | | | 2 | 10■ | | | 41 |
| 1 | | | 4 | | 12 | | 8[3] | 9 | | 11[1] | 6 | | 3 | | 5 | | | | 13 | | | 7 | 14 | | 2 | 10[2] | | | 42 |
| 1 | | | 4 | 5 | 13 | | 8[1] | 9 | 12 | | 6 | | 3 | | 14 | 11 | | | | | | 7[3] | | | 2■ | 10[2] | | | 43 |
| 1 | 3 | | 5 | 6 | 7[2] | | 8[1] | 9 | 13 | 11 | 12 | | 14 | | | | 4 | | 10[3] | | | | | | 2 | | | | 44 |
| 1 | 2 | | 4 | 5 | 6 | | 8[2] | 9 | 12 | 11 | 13 | | | | | 14 | 3 | | 10[1] | | | 7[3] | | | | | | | 45 |
| 1 | | | 4 | 5 | 13 | | | 9 | | 11[2] | 12 | 7[1] | | | | 6[3] | 3 | | 10 | | | | 8 | | 2 | | | 14 | 46 |

**Carling Cup**
First Round Grimsby T (h) 3-2
Second Round Crystal Palace (a) 1-2

**LDV Vans Trophy**
First Round Chester C (a) 1-0
Second Round Blackpool (a) 0-1

**FA Cup**
First Round Scarborough (a) 0-1

# EVERTON

## FA Premiership

### FOUNDATION

St Domingo Church Sunday School formed a football club in 1878 which played at Stanley Park. Enthusiasm was so great that in November 1879 they decided to expand membership and changed the name to Everton playing in black shirts with a scarlet sash and nicknamed the 'Black Watch'. After wearing several other colours, royal blue was adopted in 1901.

***Goodison Park, Liverpool L4 4EL.***

***Telephone:*** (0151) 330 2200.

***Fax:*** (0151) 286 9112.

***Ticket Office:*** 0870 442 1878.

***Website:*** www.evertonfc.com

***Email:*** everton@evertonfc.com

***Ground Capacity:*** 40,565.

***Record Attendance:*** 78,299 v Liverpool, Division 1, 18 September 1948.

***Pitch Measurements:*** 110yd × 70yd.

***Chairman:*** Bill Kenwright CBE.

***Chief Executive:*** Trevor Birch.

***Secretary:*** David Harrison.

***Manager:*** David Moyes.

***Assistant Manager:*** Alan Irvine.

***Physio:*** Mick Rathbone.

***Head of Physiotherapy:*** Mick Rathbone, Bsc (Hons), MCSP.

***Colours:*** Blue shirts, white shorts, white stockings.

***Change Colours:*** White shirts, blue shorts, blue stockings.

***Year Formed:*** 1878.

***Turned Professional:*** 1885.

***Ltd Co.:*** 1892.

***Previous Name:*** 1878, St Domingo FC; 1879, Everton.

***Club Nickname:*** 'The Toffees'.

***Previous Grounds:*** 1878, Stanley Park; 1882, Priory Road; 1884, Anfield Road; 1892, Goodison Park.

***First Football League Game:*** 8 September 1888, Football League, v Accrington (h) W 2–1 – Smalley; Dick, Ross; Holt, Jones, Dobson; Fleming (2), Waugh, Lewis, E. Chadwick, Farmer.

### HONOURS

*Football League:* Division 1 – Champions 1890–91, 1914–15, 1927–28, 1931–32, 1938–39, 1962–63, 1969–70, 1984–85, 1986–87; Runners-up 1889–90, 1894–95, 1901–02, 1904–05, 1908–09, 1911–12, 1985–86; Division 2 – Champions 1930–31; Runners-up 1953–54.

*FA Cup:* Winners 1906, 1933, 1966, 1984, 1995; Runners-up 1893, 1897, 1907, 1968, 1985, 1986, 1989.

*Football League Cup:* Runners-up 1977, 1984.

*League Super Cup:* Runners-up 1986.

*Simod Cup:* Runners-up 1989.

*Zenith Data Systems Cup:* Runners-up 1991.

***European Competitions:*** *European Cup:* 1963–64, 1970–71. *European Cup-Winners' Cup:* 1966–67, 1984–85 (winners), 1995–96. *European Fairs Cup:* 1962–63, 1964–65, 1965–66. *UEFA Cup:* 1975–76, 1978–79, 1979–80.

### SKY SPORTS FACT FILE

In 1962–63 Everton judged their championship race to perfection. Goodison Park was an undefeated fortress and, never out of the top three all season, they remained unbeaten in the last 12 matches when only four points were dropped in drawn affairs.

***Record League Victory:*** 9–1 v Manchester C, Division 1, 3 September 1906 – Scott; Balmer, Crelley; Booth, Taylor (1), Abbott (1); Sharp, Bolton (1), Young (4), Settle (2), George Wilson. 9–1 v Plymouth Arg, Division 2, 27 December 1930 – Coggins; Williams, Cresswell; McPherson, Griffiths, Thomson; Critchley, Dunn, Dean (4), Johnson (1), Stein (4).

***Record Cup Victory:*** 11–2 v Derby Co, FA Cup 1st rd, 18 January 1890 – Smalley; Hannah, Doyle (1); Kirkwood, Holt (1), Parry; Latta, Brady (3), Geary (3), Chadwick, Millward (3).

***Record Defeat:*** 4–10 v Tottenham H, Division 1, 11 October 1958.

***Most League Points (2 for a win):*** 66, Division 1, 1969–70.

***Most League Points (3 for a win):*** 90, Division 1, 1984–85.

***Most League Goals:*** 121, Division 2, 1930–31.

***Highest League Scorer in Season:*** William Ralph 'Dixie' Dean, 60, Division 1, 1927–28 (All-time League record).

***Most League Goals in Total Aggregate:*** William Ralph 'Dixie' Dean, 349, 1925–37.

***Most League Goals in One Match:*** 6, Jack Southworth v WBA, Division 1, 30 December 1893.

***Most Capped Player:*** Neville Southall, 92, Wales.

***Most League Appearances:*** Neville Southall, 578, 1981–98.

***Youngest League Player:*** Joe Royle, 16 years 282 days v Blackpool, 15 January 1966.

***Record Transfer Fee Received:*** £10,000,000 from Arsenal for Francis Jeffers, June 2001.

***Record Transfer Fee Paid:*** £5,750,000 to Middlesbrough for Nick Barmby, October 1996.

***Football League Record:*** 1888 Founder Member of the Football League; 1930–31 Division 2; 1931–51 Division 1; 1951–54 Division 2; 1954–92 Division 1; 1992– FA Premier League.

### MANAGERS

W. E. Barclay 1888–89
*(Secretary-Manager)*
Dick Molyneux 1889–1901
*(Secretary-Manager)*
William C. Cuff 1901–18
*(Secretary-Manager)*
W. J. Sawyer 1918–19
*(Secretary-Manager)*
Thomas H. McIntosh 1919–35
*(Secretary-Manager)*
Theo Kelly 1936–48
Cliff Britton 1948–56
Ian Buchan 1956–58
Johnny Carey 1958–61
Harry Catterick 1961–73
Billy Bingham 1973–77
Gordon Lee 1977–81
Howard Kendall 1981–87
Colin Harvey 1987–90
Howard Kendall 1990–93
Mike Walker 1994
Joe Royle 1994–97
Howard Kendall 1997–98
Walter Smith 1998–2002
David Moyes March 2002–

### LATEST SEQUENCES

***Longest Sequence of League Wins:*** 12, 24.3.1894 – 13.10.1894.

***Longest Sequence of League Defeats:*** 6, 26.12.1996 – 29.1.1997.

***Longest Sequence of League Draws:*** 5, 4.5.1977 – 16.5.1977.

***Longest Sequence of Unbeaten League Matches:*** 20, 29.4.1978 – 16.12.1978.

***Longest Sequence Without a League Win:*** 14, 6.3.1937 – 4.9.1937.

***Successive Scoring Runs:*** 40 from 15.3.1930.

***Successive Non-scoring Runs:*** 6 from 3.3.1951.

### TEN YEAR LEAGUE RECORD

| | | *P* | *W* | *D* | *L* | *F* | *A* | *Pts* | *Pos* |
|---|---|---|---|---|---|---|---|---|---|
| 1994-95 | PR Lge | 42 | 11 | 17 | 14 | 44 | 51 | 50 | 15 |
| 1995-96 | PR Lge | 38 | 17 | 10 | 11 | 64 | 44 | 61 | 6 |
| 1996-97 | PR Lge | 38 | 10 | 12 | 16 | 44 | 57 | 42 | 15 |
| 1997-98 | PR Lge | 38 | 9 | 13 | 16 | 41 | 56 | 40 | 17 |
| 1998-99 | PR Lge | 38 | 11 | 10 | 17 | 42 | 47 | 43 | 14 |
| 1999-2000 | PR Lge | 38 | 12 | 14 | 12 | 59 | 49 | 50 | 13 |
| 2000-01 | PR Lge | 38 | 11 | 9 | 18 | 45 | 59 | 42 | 16 |
| 2001-02 | PR Lge | 38 | 11 | 10 | 17 | 45 | 57 | 43 | 15 |
| 2002-03 | PR Lge | 38 | 17 | 8 | 13 | 48 | 49 | 59 | 7 |
| 2003-04 | PR Lge | 38 | 9 | 12 | 17 | 45 | 57 | 39 | 17 |

### DID YOU KNOW ?

Versatile Jack Taylor is the only Everton player to have made 100 consecutive appearances from his debut. From 5 September 1896 to 24 March 1899 he completed a total of 122 from a career at the club totalling 400 alone in the League.

## EVERTON 2003–04 LEAGUE RECORD

| Match No. | Date | Venue | Opponents | Result | H/T Score | Lg. Pos. | Goalscorers | Attendance |
|---|---|---|---|---|---|---|---|---|
| 1 | Aug 16 | A | Arsenal | L 1-2 | 0-1 | — | Radzinski 84 | 38,014 |
| 2 | 23 | H | Fulham | W 3-1 | 3-0 | 9 | Naysmith 7, Unsworth 20, Watson 35 | 37,604 |
| 3 | 26 | A | Charlton Ath | D 2-2 | 1-1 | — | Watson 26, Rooney 72 | 26,314 |
| 4 | 30 | H | Liverpool | L 0-3 | 0-1 | 14 | | 40,200 |
| 5 | Sept 13 | H | Newcastle U | D 2-2 | 0-0 | 13 | Radzinski 67, Ferguson (pen) 88 | 40,228 |
| 6 | 21 | A | Middlesbrough | L 0-1 | 0-1 | 15 | | 28,113 |
| 7 | 28 | H | Leeds U | W 4-0 | 3-0 | 10 | Watson 3 27, 37, 52, Ferguson 39 | 39,151 |
| 8 | Oct 4 | A | Tottenham H | L 0-3 | 0-1 | 12 | | 36,103 |
| 9 | 19 | H | Southampton | D 0-0 | 0-0 | 13 | | 35,775 |
| 10 | 25 | A | Aston Villa | D 0-0 | 0-0 | 13 | | 36,146 |
| 11 | Nov 1 | H | Chelsea | L 0-1 | 0-0 | 16 | | 40,189 |
| 12 | 10 | A | Blackburn R | L 1-2 | 0-2 | — | Radzinski 49 | 22,179 |
| 13 | 22 | H | Wolverhampton W | W 2-0 | 2-0 | 15 | Radzinski 16, Kilbane 19 | 40,190 |
| 14 | 29 | A | Bolton W | L 0-2 | 0-1 | 18 | | 27,350 |
| 15 | Dec 7 | H | Manchester C | D 0-0 | 0-0 | 17 | | 37,871 |
| 16 | 13 | A | Portsmouth | W 2-1 | 2-1 | 15 | Carsley 27, Rooney 42 | 20,099 |
| 17 | 20 | H | Leicester C | W 3-2 | 1-1 | 11 | Carsley 33, Rooney 71, Radzinski 79 | 37,007 |
| 18 | 26 | A | Manchester U | L 2-3 | 1-2 | 14 | Neville G (og) 13, Ferguson 90 | 67,642 |
| 19 | 28 | H | Birmingham C | W 1-0 | 0-0 | 11 | Rooney 69 | 39,631 |
| 20 | Jan 7 | H | Arsenal | D 1-1 | 0-1 | — | Radzinski 75 | 38,726 |
| 21 | 10 | A | Fulham | L 1-2 | 0-1 | 12 | Kilbane 81 | 17,308 |
| 22 | 17 | H | Charlton Ath | L 0-1 | 0-1 | 14 | | 36,322 |
| 23 | 31 | A | Liverpool | D 0-0 | 0-0 | 14 | | 44,056 |
| 24 | Feb 7 | H | Manchester U | L 3-4 | 0-3 | 15 | Unsworth 49, O'Shea (og) 65, Kilbane 75 | 40,190 |
| 25 | 11 | A | Birmingham C | L 0-3 | 0-2 | — | | 29,004 |
| 26 | 21 | A | Southampton | D 3-3 | 2-0 | 16 | Rooney 2 7, 78, Ferguson 32 | 31,875 |
| 27 | 28 | H | Aston Villa | W 2-0 | 0-0 | 14 | Radzinski 78, Gravesen 83 | 39,353 |
| 28 | Mar 13 | H | Portsmouth | W 1-0 | 0-0 | 14 | Rooney 78 | 40,105 |
| 29 | 20 | A | Leicester C | D 1-1 | 0-0 | 14 | Rooney 75 | 31,650 |
| 30 | 27 | H | Middlesbrough | D 1-1 | 0-0 | 14 | Radzinski 78 | 38,210 |
| 31 | Apr 3 | A | Newcastle U | L 2-4 | 1-2 | 14 | Gravesen 12, Yobo 81 | 52,155 |
| 32 | 9 | H | Tottenham H | W 3-1 | 3-0 | — | Unsworth 17, Naysmith 24, Yobo 40 | 38,086 |
| 33 | 13 | A | Leeds U | D 1-1 | 1-0 | — | Rooney 13 | 39,835 |
| 34 | 17 | A | Chelsea | D 0-0 | 0-0 | 13 | | 41,169 |
| 35 | 24 | H | Blackburn R | L 0-1 | 0-0 | 15 | | 38,884 |
| 36 | May 1 | A | Wolverhampton W | L 1-2 | 1-0 | 15 | Osman 3 | 29,395 |
| 37 | 8 | H | Bolton W | L 1-2 | 0-1 | 16 | Ferguson 68 | 40,190 |
| 38 | 15 | A | Manchester C | L 1-5 | 0-3 | 17 | Campbell 60 | 47,152 |

**Final League Position: 17**

### GOALSCORERS

*League (45):* Rooney 9, Radzinski 8, Ferguson 5 (1 pen), Watson 5, Kilbane 3, Unsworth 3, Carsley 2, Gravesen 2, Naysmith 2, Yobo 2, Campbell 1, Osman 1, own goals 2.
*Carling Cup (4):* Ferguson 2 (1 pen), Chadwick 1, Linderoth 1.
*FA Cup (5):* Ferguson 2 (2 pens), Jeffers 2, Kilbane 1.

| Wright R 4 | Pistone A 20 + 1 | Unsworth D 22 + 4 | Stubbs A 25 + 2 | Yobo J 27 + 1 | Linderoth T 23 + 4 | Watson S 22 + 2 | Gravesen T 29 + 1 | Chadwick N 1 + 2 | Radzinski T 28 + 6 | Pembridge M 4 | Li Tie4 + 1 | Rooney W 26 + 8 | Naysmith G 27 + 2 | Simonsen S 1 | Ferguson D 13 + 7 | Hibbert T 24 + 1 | Kilbane K 26 + 4 | Martyn N 33 + 1 | Jeffers F 5 + 13 | Carsley L 15 + 6 | McFadden J 11 + 12 | Weir D 9 + 1 | Campbell K 8 + 9 | Nyarko A 7 + 4 | Clarke P 1 | Osman L 3 + 1 | *Match No.* |
|---|---|---|---|---|---|---|---|---|---|---|---|---|---|---|---|---|---|---|---|---|---|---|---|---|---|---|---|
| 1 | 2 | $3^{1}$ | 4 | 5 | $6^{2}$ | 7 | 8 | 9 | 10 | $11^{3}$ | 12■ | 13 | 14 | | | | | | | | | | | | | | 1 |
| 1 | 2 | 3 | 4 | 5 | 6 | 7 | | 12 | 10 | 8 | | $9^{1}$ | 11 | | | | | | | | | | | | | | 2 |
| 1 | 2 | 3 | 4 | 5 | 6 | 7 | | | 10 | 8 | | 9 | 11 | | | | | | | | | | | | | | 3 |
| | 2 | $3^{1}$ | 4 | 5 | $6^{2}$ | 7 | 12 | | 10 | 8 | | 9 | 11 | 1 | 13 | | | | | | | | | | | | 4 |
| $1^{6}$ | | | 4 | 5 | 6 | $7^{1}$ | 8 | | 10 | | | $9^{2}$ | 3■ | | 12 | 2 | 11 | 15 | 13 | | | | | | | | 5 |
| | | | 4 | 5 | $6^{1}$ | $7^{2}$ | 8 | | 10 | | | 9 | 3 | | 12 | 2 | $11^{3}$ | 1 | | 13 | 14 | | | | | | 6 |
| | | 3 | 4 | 5 | 12 | $7^{3}$ | 8 | | $10^{2}$ | | | 13 | | | 9 | 2 | 14 | 1 | | 6 | $11^{1}$ | | | | | | 7 |
| | | 3 | $4^{3}$ | 5 | | 7 | 8 | | $10^{2}$ | | | 12 | | | 9 | 2 | 13 | 1 | | 6 | $11^{1}$ | 14 | | | | | 8 |
| | | | | 4 | 12 | 7 | 8 | | | | | | 3 | | | 2 | 13 | 1 | 10 | $6^{1}$ | $11^{2}$ | 5 | 9 | | | | 9 |
| | | | 12 | 4 | 7 | | 8 | | | | $6^{1}$ | 10 | 3 | | 13 | 2 | 11 | 1 | | | | 5 | $9^{2}$ | | | | 10 |
| | | | 12 | 4 | $6^{3}$ | | 8 | | $10^{2}$ | | | 9 | 3 | | | 2 | 11 | 1 | 13 | | 14 | $5^{1}$ | | 7 | | | 11 |
| | | 12 | | 5 | 4 | | 8 | | 10 | | | | $3^{2}$ | | | 2 | $11^{3}$ | 1 | 13 | | 14 | | 9 | $7^{1}$ | 6 | | 12 |
| | | 3 | 4 | 5 | 6 | | 8 | | 10 | | | $9^{1}$ | | | | 2 | 11 | 1 | 12 | | $7^{2}$ | | | | | 13 | 13 |
| | | 3 | 4 | 5 | $6^{1}$ | | $8^{2}$ | | 10 | | | $9^{3}$ | | | | 2 | 11 | 1 | 14 | 7 | 12 | | | 13 | | | 14 |
| | | 5 | 4 | | | | 8 | | 10 | | 6 | $9^{3}$ | 3 | | | $2^{1}$ | 12 | 1 | $11^{2}$ | 7 | 14 | | 13 | | | | 15 |
| | 2 | 5 | 4 | | | $7^{1}$ | 8 | | $10^{2}$ | | | 12 | 3 | | | | 11 | 1 | | 6 | 13 | | 9 | | | | 16 |
| | $2^{2}$ | 5 | 4 | | | | 8 | | 10 | | | 12 | 3 | | 14 | 13 | 11 | 1 | | 6 | $7^{1}$ | | $9^{3}$ | | | | 17 |
| | | 5 | 4 | | $7^{1}$ | | 8 | | | | 6 | $10^{3}$ | 3 | | 13 | 2 | 11 | 1 | 12 | | 14 | | $9^{2}$ | | | | 18 |
| | | 5 | 4 | 13 | | | 6 | | $10^{3}$ | | | 12 | 3 | | 9 | 2 | 11 | 1 | 14 | $7^{1}$ | | | | $8^{2}$ | | | 19 |
| | | 5 | 4 | | 12 | | | | $10^{2}$ | | $6^{1}$ | 8 | 3 | | 9 | 2 | $11^{3}$ | 1 | 14 | 7 | | | 13 | | | | 20 |
| | | 5 | | | 6 | | | | $10^{3}$ | | | 12 | 3 | | 13 | 2 | 11 | 1 | 8 | $7^{1}$ | 14 | 4 | $9^{2}$ | | | | 21 |
| | 2 | 5 | 4 | | | | 6 | | 12 | | | 8 | 3 | | 9 | | 11 | 1 | $10^{1}$ | $7^{2}$ | | | 13 | | | | 22 |
| | 5 | | 4 | | | 12 | 6 | | $10^{3}$ | | | $8^{1}$ | 3 | | 9 | 2 | 11 | 1 | 14 | 13 | | | | $7^{2}$ | | | 23 |
| | $3^{1}$ | 5 | 4 | | | $7^{2}$ | 8 | | 14 | | | 13 | 12 | | 9 | 2 | 11 | 1 | $10^{3}$ | 6 | | | | | | | 24 |
| | 12 | $5^{1}$ | 4 | | | | 8 | | $7^{3}$ | | | 10 | 3 | | $9^{2}$ | 2 | 11 | 1 | | 6 | 14 | | 13 | | | | 25 |
| | 3 | 5 | | 4 | 6 | 7 | 8 | | | | | 10 | | | 9 | 2 | 11 | 1 | | | | | | | | | 26 |
| | $3^{1}$ | 12 | 4 | 5 | 6 | $7^{2}$ | 8 | | 13 | | | 10 | | | $9^{3}$ | 2 | 11 | 1 | | | | | 14 | | | | 27 |
| | | | 4 | 5 | 6 | 7 | | | 12 | | | 10 | 3 | | $9^{1}$ | 2 | 11 | 1 | | | | | | 8 | | | 28 |
| | 2 | | 4 | 5 | 6 | 7 | 8 | | 12 | | | $10^{2}$ | 3 | | 9■ | | | 1 | | | $11^{1}$ | | 13 | | | | 29 |
| | 2 | 12 | $4^{1}$ | 5 | 6 | $7^{2}$ | 8 | | 10 | | | 9 | 3 | | | | 11 | 1 | 13 | | | | | | | | 30 |
| | 2 | 4 | | 5 | $6^{1}$ | 7 | 8 | | 10 | | | | 3 | | | | $11^{2}$ | 1 | | | 13 | | 9 | 12 | | | 31 |
| | 2 | 4 | | 5 | 6 | 7 | $8^{1}$ | | 10 | | | | 3 | | | | 11 | 1 | 13 | 12 | $9^{2}$ | | | | | | 32 |
| | 2 | 4 | | 5 | $6^{2}$ | $7^{3}$ | $8^{1}$ | | 10 | | | 9 | 3 | | | | 11 | 1 | | 12 | 14 | | | 13 | | | 33 |
| | 2 | | | 4 | 6 | 12 | $8^{1}$ | | $10^{3}$ | | | 9 | 3 | | | | 11 | 1 | 14 | 13 | $7^{2}$ | 5 | | | | | 34 |
| | 2 | 12 | | 4 | 6 | 7 | $8^{2}$ | | $10^{3}$ | | | 9 | $3^{1}$ | | | | 11 | 1 | | | 14 | 5 | | 13 | | | 35 |
| | 3 | | | 4 | | | | | 10 | | | 9 | | | | 2 | | 1 | 12 | 6 | $7^{1}$ | 5 | 13 | $8^{2}$ | | 11 | 36 |
| | $3^{2}$ | | | 6 | | 4 | | | 12 | | | 9 | | | 10 | 2 | | 1 | | 13 | 11 | $5^{3}$ | 14 | $8^{1}$ | | 7 | 37 |
| | | | 4 | 6 | 12 | $2^{3}$ | | 14 | $10^{1}$ | | | 9 | | | | 3 | | 1 | | 8 | $7^{2}$ | 5 | 13 | | | 11 | 38 |

**Carling Cup**

| | | | |
|---|---|---|---|
| Second Round | Stockport Co | (h) | 3-0 |
| Third Round | Charlton Ath | (h) | 1-0 |
| Fourth Round | Middlesbrough | (a) | 0-0 |

**FA Cup**

| | | | |
|---|---|---|---|
| Third Round | Norwich C | (h) | 3-1 |
| Fourth Round | Fulham | (h) | 1-1 |
| | | (a) | 1-2 |

# FULHAM

## FA Premiership

### FOUNDATION

Churchgoers were responsible for the foundation of Fulham, which first saw the light of day as Fulham St Andrew's Church Sunday School FC in 1879. They won the West London Amateur Cup in 1887 and the championship of the West London League in its initial season of 1892–93. The name Fulham had been adopted in 1888.

***Craven Cottage, Stevenage Road, London SW6 6HH***
***Telephone:*** 0870 442 1222.
***Fax:*** (020) 8336 0514.
***Ticket Office:*** 0870 442 1234
***Website:*** www.fulhamfc.co.uk
***Email:*** enquiries@fulhamfc.com
***Ground Capacity:*** 22,400.
***Record Attendance:*** 49,335 v Millwall, Division 2, 8 October 1938.
***Pitch Measurements:*** 110yd × 75yd.
***Chairman:*** Mohammed Al Fayed.
***Chief Executive:*** Jim Hone.
***Secretary:*** Lee Hoos.
***Manager:*** Chris Coleman.
***Assistant Manager:*** Steve Kean.
***Physio:*** Jason Palmer
***Colours:*** White shirts, black shorts, white stockings.
***Change Colours:*** Blue shirts, white shorts, blue stockings.
***Year Formed:*** 1879.
***Turned Professional:*** 1898.
***Ltd Co.:*** 1903.
***Reformed:*** 1987.
***Previous Name:*** 1879, Fulham St Andrew's; 1888, Fulham.
***Club Nickname:*** 'Cottagers'.
***Previous Grounds:*** 1879, Star Road, Fulham; c.1883, Eel Brook Common, 1884, Lillie Road; 1885, Putney Lower Common; 1886, Ranelagh House, Fulham; 1888, Barn Elms, Castelnau; 1889, Purser's Cross (Roskell's Field), Parsons Green Lane; 1891, Eel Brook Common; 1891, Half Moon, Putney; 1895, Captain James Field, West Brompton; 1896, Craven Cottage.
***First Football League Game:*** 3 September 1907, Division 2, v Hull C (h) L 0–1 – Skene; Ross, Lindsay; Collins, Morrison, Goldie; Dalrymple, Freeman, Bevan, Hubbard, Threlfall.
***Record League Victory:*** 10–1 v Ipswich T, Division 1, 26 December 1963 – Macedo; Cohen, Langley; Mullery (1), Keetch, Robson (1); Key, Cook (1), Leggat (4), Haynes, Howfield (3).
***Record Cup Victory:*** 7–0 v Swansea C, FA Cup 1st rd, 11 November 1995 – Lange; Jupp (1), Herrera, Barkus (Brooker (1)), Moore, Angus, Thomas (1), Morgan, Brazil (Hamill), Conroy (3) (Bolt), Cusack (1).

### HONOURS

*Football League:* Division 1 – Champions 2000–01; Division 2 – Champions 1948–49, 1998–99; Runners-up 1958–59; Division 3 (S) – Champions 1931–32; Division 3 – Runners-up 1970–71, 1996–97.

*FA Cup:* Runners-up 1975.

*Football League Cup:* best season: 5th rd, 1968, 1971, 2000.

***European Competitions:*** *UEFA Cup:* 2002–03. *Intertoto Cup:* 2002 (winners)

### SKY SPORTS FACT FILE

In 1921–22 Fulham were particularly miserly at conceding home goals. In their 21 games they let in only eight, while in the following season their defence was especially sound away from home when they lost only 20 goals.

***Record Defeat:*** 0–10 v Liverpool, League Cup 2nd rd 1st leg, 23 September 1986.

***Most League Points (2 for a win):*** 60, Division 2, 1958–59 and Division 3, 1970–71.

***Most League Points (3 for a win):*** 101, Division 2, 1998–99.

***Most League Goals:*** 111, Division 3 (S), 1931–32.

***Highest League Scorer in Season:*** Frank Newton, 43, Division 3 (S), 1931–32.

***Most League Goals in Total Aggregate:*** Gordon Davies, 159, 1978–84, 1986–91.

***Most League Goals in One Match:*** 5, Fred Harrison v Stockport Co, Division 2, 5 September 1908; 5, Bedford Jezzard v Hull C, Division 2, 8 October 1955; 5, Jimmy Hill v Doncaster R, Division 2, 15 March 1958; 5, Steve Earle v Halifax T, Division 3, 16 September 1969.

***Most Capped Player:*** Johnny Haynes, 56, England.

***Most League Appearances:*** Johnny Haynes, 594, 1952–70.

***Youngest League Player:*** Tony Mahoney, 17 years 38 days v Cardiff C, 6 November 1976.

***Record Transfer Fee Received:*** £11,500,000 from Manchester U for Louis Saha, January 2004.

***Record Transfer Fee Paid:*** £11,500,000 to Lyon for Steve Marlet, August 2001.

***Football League Record:*** 1907 Elected to Division 2; 1928–32 Division 3 (S); 1932–49 Division 2; 1949–52 Division 1; 1952–59 Division 2; 1959–68 Division 1; 1968–69 Division 2; 1969–71 Division 3; 1971–80 Division 2; 1980–82 Division 3; 1982–86 Division 2; 1986–92 Division 3; 1992–94 Division 2; 1994–97 Division 3; 1997–99 Division 2; 1999–2001 Division 1; 2001– FA Premier League.

## MANAGERS

Harry Bradshaw 1904–09
Phil Kelso 1909–24
Andy Ducat 1924–26
Joe Bradshaw 1926–29
Ned Liddell 1929–31
Jim MacIntyre 1931–34
Jimmy Hogan 1934–35
Jack Peart 1935–48
Frank Osborne 1948–64
*(was Secretary-Manager or General Manager for most of this period)*
Bill Dodgin Snr 1949–53
Duggie Livingstone 1956–58
Bedford Jezzard 1958–64
*(General Manager for last two months)*
Vic Buckingham 1965–68
Bobby Robson 1968
Bill Dodgin Jnr 1969–72
Alec Stock 1972–76
Bobby Campbell 1976–80
Malcolm Macdonald 1980–84
Ray Harford 1984–96
Ray Lewington 1986–90
Alan Dicks 1990–91
Don Mackay 1991–94
Ian Branfoot 1994–96
*(continued as General Manager)*
Micky Adams 1996–97
Ray Wilkins 1997–98
Kevin Keegan 1998–99
*(Chief Operating Officer)*
Paul Bracewell 1999–2000
Jean Tigana 2000–03
Chris Coleman April 2003–

## LATEST SEQUENCES

***Longest Sequence of League Wins:*** 12, 7.5.2000 – 18.10.2000.

***Longest Sequence of League Defeats:*** 11, 2.12.1961 – 24.2.1962.

***Longest Sequence of League Draws:*** 6, 14.10.1995 – 18.11.1995.

***Longest Sequence of Unbeaten League Matches:*** 15, 26.1.1999 – 13.4.1999.

***Longest Sequence Without a League Win:*** 15, 25.2.1950 – 23.8.1950.

***Successive Scoring Runs:*** 26 from 28.3.1931.

***Successive Non-scoring Runs:*** 6 from 21.8.1971.

## TEN YEAR LEAGUE RECORD

| | | *P* | *W* | *D* | *L* | *F* | *A* | *Pts* | *Pos* |
|---|---|---|---|---|---|---|---|---|---|
| 1994-95 | Div 3 | 42 | 16 | 14 | 12 | 60 | 54 | 62 | 8 |
| 1995-96 | Div 3 | 46 | 12 | 17 | 17 | 57 | 63 | 53 | 17 |
| 1996-97 | Div 3 | 46 | 25 | 12 | 9 | 72 | 38 | 87 | 2 |
| 1997-98 | Div 2 | 46 | 20 | 10 | 16 | 60 | 43 | 70 | 6 |
| 1998-99 | Div 2 | 46 | 31 | 8 | 7 | 79 | 32 | 101 | 1 |
| 1999-2000 | Div 1 | 46 | 17 | 16 | 13 | 49 | 41 | 67 | 9 |
| 2000-01 | Div 1 | 46 | 30 | 11 | 5 | 90 | 32 | 101 | 1 |
| 2001-02 | PR Lge | 38 | 10 | 14 | 14 | 36 | 44 | 44 | 13 |
| 2002-03 | PR Lge | 38 | 13 | 9 | 16 | 41 | 50 | 48 | 14 |
| 2003-04 | PR Lge | 38 | 14 | 10 | 14 | 52 | 46 | 52 | 9 |

## DID YOU KNOW ?

Jim Hammond was popularly known by Fulham fans as the 'Galloping Hairpin'. From 1929 to 1938 he was a consistent scorer with exactly 150 League and Cup goals. He was England's 12th man against Australia in 1932 and a Sussex cricketer.

## FULHAM 2003–04 LEAGUE RECORD

| *Match No.* | *Date* | *Venue* | *Opponents* | *Result* | *H/T Score* | *Lg. Pos.* | *Goalscorers* | *Attendance* |
|---|---|---|---|---|---|---|---|---|
| 1 | Aug 16 | H | Middlesbrough | W 3-2 | 1-1 | — | Marlet [18], Inamoto [56], Saha [70] | 14,546 |
| 2 | 23 | A | Everton | L 1-3 | 0-3 | 11 | Hayles [69] | 37,604 |
| 3 | 30 | A | Tottenham H | W 3-0 | 1-0 | 7 | Hayles 2 [23, 67], Boa Morte [71] | 33,421 |
| 4 | Sept 14 | A | Birmingham C | D 2-2 | 1-1 | 9 | Saha [1], Boa Morte [78] | 27,250 |
| 5 | 20 | H | Manchester C | D 2-2 | 0-0 | 10 | Malbranque [73], Saha [79] | 16,124 |
| 6 | 28 | A | Blackburn R | W 2-0 | 1-0 | 7 | Boa Morte [5], Saha [65] | 21,985 |
| 7 | Oct 4 | H | Leicester C | W 2-0 | 1-0 | 4 | Boa Morte 2 [36, 73] | 14,612 |
| 8 | 18 | H | Wolverhampton W | D 0-0 | 0-0 | 6 | | 17,031 |
| 9 | 21 | H | Newcastle U | L 2-3 | 2-1 | — | Clark [6], Saha [8] | 15,241 |
| 10 | 25 | A | Manchester U | W 3-1 | 1-1 | 5 | Clark [3], Malbranque [66], Inamoto [79] | 67,727 |
| 11 | Nov 2 | H | Liverpool | L 1-2 | 1-1 | 6 | Saha [40] | 17,682 |
| 12 | 8 | A | Charlton Ath | L 1-3 | 0-1 | 7 | Davis [89] | 26,285 |
| 13 | 24 | H | Portsmouth | W 2-0 | 2-0 | — | Saha 2 [30, 33] | 15,624 |
| 14 | 30 | A | Arsenal | D 0-0 | 0-0 | 4 | | 38,063 |
| 15 | Dec 6 | H | Bolton W | W 2-1 | 0-0 | 4 | Davis [75], Sava [76] | 14,393 |
| 16 | 14 | A | Leeds U | L 2-3 | 0-1 | 4 | Saha 2 [47, 86] | 30,544 |
| 17 | 20 | H | Chelsea | L 0-1 | 0-0 | 5 | | 18,431 |
| 18 | 26 | H | Southampton | W 2-0 | 1-0 | 4 | Saha 2 (1 pen) [19, 63 (p)] | 15,640 |
| 19 | 28 | A | Aston Villa | L 0-3 | 0-1 | 5 | | 35,617 |
| 20 | Jan 7 | A | Middlesbrough | L 1-2 | 0-1 | — | Hayles [90] | 27,869 |
| 21 | 10 | H | Everton | W 2-1 | 1-0 | 6 | Saha (pen) [45], Malbranque [46] | 17,308 |
| 22 | 19 | A | Newcastle U | L 1-3 | 0-2 | — | Davis [74] | 50,104 |
| 23 | 31 | H | Tottenham H | W 2-1 | 1-1 | 7 | Malbranque (pen) [45], McBride [67] | 17,024 |
| 24 | Feb 7 | A | Southampton | D 0-0 | 0-0 | 7 | | 31,820 |
| 25 | 11 | H | Aston Villa | L 1-2 | 1-2 | — | Boa Morte [1] | 16,153 |
| 26 | 21 | A | Wolverhampton W | L 1-2 | 0-1 | 9 | Malbranque [84] | 28,424 |
| 27 | 28 | H | Manchester U | D 1-1 | 0-1 | 8 | Boa Morte [64] | 18,306 |
| 28 | Mar 13 | H | Leeds U | W 2-0 | 0-0 | 9 | Davis [71], Boa Morte [83] | 17,104 |
| 29 | 20 | A | Chelsea | L 1-2 | 1-2 | 9 | Pembridge [19] | 41,459 |
| 30 | 27 | A | Manchester C | D 0-0 | 0-0 | 9 | | 46,522 |
| 31 | Apr 3 | H | Birmingham C | D 0-0 | 0-0 | 10 | | 14,667 |
| 32 | 10 | A | Leicester C | W 2-0 | 0-0 | 8 | John 2 [66, 89] | 28,392 |
| 33 | 12 | H | Blackburn R | L 3-4 | 2-1 | 10 | John 2 [26, 45], Boa Morte [60] | 13,981 |
| 34 | 17 | A | Liverpool | D 0-0 | 0-0 | 10 | | 42,042 |
| 35 | 24 | H | Charlton Ath | W 2-0 | 1-0 | 7 | Malbranque (pen) [18], Davis [64] | 16,585 |
| 36 | May 1 | A | Portsmouth | D 1-1 | 0-0 | 8 | McBride [85] | 20,056 |
| 37 | 9 | H | Arsenal | L 0-1 | 0-1 | 9 | | 18,102 |
| 38 | 15 | A | Bolton W | W 2-0 | 1-0 | 9 | McBride 2 [45, 78] | 27,383 |

**Final League Position: 9**

### GOALSCORERS

*League (52):* Saha 13 (2 pens), Boa Morte 9, Malbranque 6 (2 pens), Davis 5, Hayles 4, John 4, McBride 4, Clark 2, Inamoto 2, Marlet 1, Pembridge 1, Sava 1.
*Carling Cup (0).*
*FA Cup (9):* Malbranque 2 (1 pen), Saha 2, Boa Morte 1, Davis 1, Hayles 1, Inamoto 1, McBride 1.

| Van der Sar E 37 | Volz M 32 + 1 | Bonnissel J 16 | Djetou M 19 + 7 | Goma A 23 | Clark L 25 | Legwinski S 30 + 2 | Inamoto J 15 + 7 | Saha L 20 + 1 | Marlet S 1 | Malbranque S 38 | Hayles B 10 + 16 | Boa Morte L 32 + 1 | Knight Z 30 + 1 | Buari M 1 + 2 | Sava F — + 6 | Pembridge M 9 + 3 | Leacock D 3 + 1 | Crossley M 1 | Melville A 9 | Davis S 22 + 2 | Pratley D — + 1 | Harley J 3 + 1 | Green A 4 | Petta B 3 + 6 | Bocanegra C 15 | Pearce I 12 + 1 | McBride B 5 + 11 | John C 3 + 5 | Rehman Z — + 1 | Match No. |
|---|---|---|---|---|---|---|---|---|---|---|---|---|---|---|---|---|---|---|---|---|---|---|---|---|---|---|---|---|---|---|
| 1 | 2 | 3 | 4 | 5 | 6 | 7 | 8 | 9[1] | 10[2] | 11 | 12 | 13 | | | | | | | | | | | | | | | | | | 1 |
| 1 | 2 | 3 | 4[2] | 5 | 6 | 7[1] | 8[3] | 9 | | 11 | 12 | 10 | 13 | 14 | | | | | | | | | | | | | | | | 2 |
| 1 | 2 | 3 | | 5 | 6 | 7 | 8 | 12 | | 11 | 9[1] | 10 | 4 | | | | | | | | | | | | | | | | | 3 |
| 1 | 2 | 3 | 12 | 5 | 6 | 7■ | 8[1] | 9[2] | | 11[3] | | 10 | 4 | | 13 | 14 | | | | | | | | | | | | | | 4 |
| 1 | 2 | 3 | | 5 | 6 | 7 | 8 | 9 | | 11 | | 10[1] | 4 | | | 12 | | | | | | | | | | | | | | 5 |
| 1 | 2[2] | 3 | | 5 | 6 | | 8 | 9 | | 7 | | 10[1] | 4 | 12 | | 11 | 13 | | | | | | | | | | | | | 6 |
| 1 | | 3 | 12 | 5 | 6 | 13 | 8[2] | 9[3] | | 7 | 14 | 10 | 4 | | | 11 | 2[1] | | | | | | | | | | | | | 7 |
| 1 | | 3 | | 5 | 6 | 7 | 8[1] | 9 | | 10 | 12 | | 4 | | | 11 | 2 | | | | | | | | | | | | | 8 |
| 1 | | 3 | | 5 | 6 | 7 | 12 | 9 | | 8 | 13 | | 4 | 10[2] | | 11[1] | 2 | | | | | | | | | | | | | 9 |
| 1 | 2 | 3[3] | 14 | 5 | 6 | 7 | 12 | 9 | | 8 | 13 | 10[2] | 4 | | | 11[1] | | | | | | | | | | | | | | 10 |
| | 2 | 3 | 13 | | 6 | 7 | | 9[1] | | 8 | 12 | 10■ | 4 | | | 11[2] | | 1 | 5 | | | | | | | | | | | 11 |
| 1 | 2 | 3 | | | 6 | 7 | 8[3] | 9 | | 11 | 12[2] | 10[1] | 4 | | | | | | 5 | 14 | 13 | | | | | | | | | 12 |
| 1 | 2 | 3 | | | 6 | 7 | 12 | 9[2] | | 11 | 10[1] | | 4 | | 13 | | | | 5 | 8 | | | | | | | | | | 13 |
| 1 | 2 | 3 | | | 10 | 7 | 8 | 9[1] | | 11 | 12 | | 4 | | | | | | 5 | 6 | | | | | | | | | | 14 |
| 1 | 2 | 3 | 14 | | 10 | 7 | 8[2] | 9[1] | | 11 | 12 | | 4 | | 13 | | | | 5 | 6[3] | | | | | | | | | | 15 |
| 1 | 2[1] | | | | 8 | 7 | | 9 | | 11 | 12 | 10[2] | 4 | | 13 | | | | 5 | 6 | | 3 | | | | | | | | 16 |
| 1 | 2 | | 13 | | 8 | 7 | | 9 | | 11 | 12 | 10 | 4 | | | | | | 5 | 6[2] | | 3[1] | | | | | | | | 17 |
| 1 | 2 | 3[1] | 6 | 5 | 10 | | 8 | 9 | | 7 | | 11 | 4 | | | | | | | | | 12 | | | | | | | | 18 |
| 1 | 2 | | 6 | 5 | 10 | | 8[1] | 9 | | 7[2] | 12 | 11 | 4 | | 13 | | | | | | | 3 | | | | | | | | 19 |
| 1 | | | 2 | | 8 | 7[1] | | 9 | | 11 | 12 | 10 | 4 | | | | | | 5 | 6 | | | 3 | | | | | | | 20 |
| 1 | | | 2 | | 8 | 7 | | 9 | | 11 | | 10[1] | 4 | | | | | | 5 | 6 | | | 3 | 12 | | | | | | 21 |
| 1 | 12 | | 2 | 5 | 8 | 7[1] | | | | 11 | 9[2] | 10 | 4 | | 13 | | | | | 6 | | | | | 3 | | | | | 22 |
| 1 | 2 | | 7 | | 8 | | | | | 11 | 9[2] | 10[1] | 4 | | | | | | | 6 | | | | 12 | 3 | 5 | 13 | | | 23 |
| 1 | 2 | | 6 | | 10[3] | 14 | 13 | | | 7[1] | | 11 | 4 | | | | | | | 8[2] | | | | 12 | 3 | 5 | 9 | | | 24 |
| 1 | 2 | | 7[1] | | 10[2] | | | | | 8 | 12 | 11 | 4 | | | | | | | 6 | | | | 13 | 3■ | 5 | 9 | | | 25 |
| 1 | 2 | | 12 | | | 7 | | | | 8 | 10[2] | 11 | 4[1] | | | | | | | 6 | | | | 13 | 3 | 5 | 9 | | | 26 |
| 1 | 2 | | | 4 | | 7 | 12 | | | 8[1] | | 10 | | | | 13 | | | | 6 | | | 3 | 11[2] | | 5 | 9 | | | 27 |
| 1 | 2 | | | | | 7 | | | | 8 | 9[1] | 10 | 4 | | | 11 | | | | 6 | | | 3 | | | 5 | 12 | | | 28 |
| 1 | 2 | | | | | 7 | | | | 8 | 9[1] | 10 | 4 | | | 11[2] | | | | 6 | | | | | 3 | 5 | 12 | 13 | | 29 |
| 1 | 2 | | 8 | 5 | | | | | | 7 | 9[1] | 10 | 4 | | | 11 | | | | 6 | | | | | 3 | | 12 | | | 30 |
| 1 | 2 | | 8[2] | 5 | | 7 | | | | 11 | 9[1] | 10 | 4 | | | | | | | 6 | | | | | 3 | 12 | 13 | | | 31 |
| 1 | 2 | | 8 | 5 | | 7 | | | | 11[1] | 9[2] | 10 | 4 | | | | | | | 6 | | | | | 3 | | 12 | 13 | | 32 |
| 1 | 2 | | 8 | 5 | | 7 | | | | 11[3] | 12 | 10 | 4 | | | | | | | 6[2] | | | | 13 | 3 | | 14 | 9[1] | | 33 |
| 1 | 2 | | 4 | 5 | | 7 | 12 | | | 11 | | 10 | | | | | | | | | | | | 8[3] | 3[1] | 6 | 13 | 9[2] | 14 | 34 |
| 1 | 2 | | 4 | 5 | | 7 | 13 | | | 11 | | 10[2] | | | | | | | | 12 | | | | 8[1] | 3 | 6 | 14 | 9[3] | | 35 |
| 1 | 2 | | 8[1] | 5 | | 7 | 10 | | | 11 | | 9[2] | | | | | | | | 6 | | | | | 3 | 4 | 12 | 13 | | 36 |
| 1 | 2 | | 8[2] | 5 | | 7 | 10[1] | | | 11 | | 9 | | | | | | | | 6 | | | | | 3 | 4 | 12 | 13 | | 37 |
| 1 | 2 | | 8 | 5 | | 7 | | | | 11 | | 10 | | | | | | | | 6 | | | | | 3 | 4 | 9[1] | 12 | | 38 |

**Carling Cup**

| | | | |
|---|---|---|---|
| Second Round | Wigan Ath | (a) | 0-1 |

**FA Cup**

| | | | |
|---|---|---|---|
| Third Round | Cheltenham T | (h) | 2-1 |
| Fourth Round | Everton | (a) | 1-1 |
| | | (h) | 2-1 |
| Fifth Round | West Ham U | (h) | 0-0 |
| | | (a) | 3-0 |
| Sixth Round | Manchester U | (a) | 1-2 |

# GILLINGHAM FL Championship

## FOUNDATION

The success of the pioneering Royal Engineers of Chatham excited the interest of the residents of the Medway Towns and led to the formation of many clubs including Excelsior. After winning the Kent Junior Cup and the Chatham District League in 1893, Excelsior decided to go for bigger things and it was at a meeting in the Napier Arms, Brompton, in 1893 that New Brompton FC came into being, buying and developing the ground which is now Priestfield Stadium. Changed name to Gillingham in 1913, when they also changed their strip from black and white stripes to predominantly blue.

***Priestfield Stadium, Redfern Avenue, Gillingham, Kent ME7 4DD.***

***Telephone:*** (01634) 300 000.

***Fax:*** (01634) 850 986.

***Ticket Office:*** (01634) 300 000.

***Website:*** www.gillinghamfootballclub.com

***Email:*** info@gillinghamfootballclub.com

***Ground Capacity:*** 11,400.

***Record Attendance:*** 23,002 v QPR, FA Cup 3rd rd, 10 January 1948.

***Pitch Measurements:*** 114yd × 75yd.

***Chairman:*** P. D. P. Scally.

***Vice-chairman:*** P. A. Spokes.

***Chief Executive:*** P. D. P. Scally.

***Secretary:*** Mrs G. E. Poynter.

***Manager:*** Andy Hessenthaler.

***First Team Coach:*** P. W. Jones.

***Physio:*** S. Webster.

***Colours:*** All blue.

***Change Colours:*** All yellow.

***Year Formed:*** 1893.

***Turned Professional:*** 1894.

***Ltd Co.:*** 1893.

***Previous Name:*** 1893, New Brompton; 1913, Gillingham.

***Club Nickname:*** 'The Gills'.

***First Football League Game:*** 28 August 1920, Division 3, v Southampton (h) D 1–1 – Branfield; Robertson, Sissons; Battiste, Baxter, Wigmore; Holt, Hall, Gilbey (1), Roe, Gore.

***Record League Victory:*** 10–0 v Chesterfield, Division 3, 5 September 1987 – Kite; Haylock, Pearce, Shipley (2) (Lillis), West, Greenall (1), Pritchard (2), Shearer (2), Lovell, Elsey (2), David Smith (1).

## HONOURS

*Football League:* Promoted from Division 2 1999–2000 (play-offs); Division 3 – Runners-up 1995-96; Division 4 – Champions 1963–64; Runners-up 1973–74.

*FA Cup:* best season: 6th rd, 2000.

*Football League Cup:* best season: 4th rd, 1964, 1997.

## SKY SPORTS FACT FILE

In 1931–32 Gillingham pulled off the remarkable feat of being the only club to achieve the double over champions Fulham in Division Three (South). They also became the sole side to prevent the Cottagers from scoring at home.

***Record Cup Victory:*** 10–1 v Gorleston, FA Cup 1st rd, 16 November 1957 – Brodie; Parry, Hannaway; Riggs, Boswell, Laing; Payne, Fletcher (2), Saunders (5), Morgan (1), Clark (2).

***Record Defeat:*** 2–9 v Nottingham F, Division 3 (S), 18 November 1950.

***Most League Points (2 for a win):*** 62, Division 4, 1973–74.

***Most League Points (3 for a win):*** 85, Division 2, 1999–2000.

***Most League Goals:*** 90, Division 4, 1973–74.

***Highest League Scorer in Season:*** Ernie Morgan, 31, Division 3 (S), 1954–55; Brian Yeo, 31, Division 4, 1973–74.

***Most League Goals in Total Aggregate:*** Brian Yeo, 135, 1963–75.

***Most League Goals in One Match:*** 6, Fred Cheesmur v Merthyr T, Division 3S, 26 April 1930.

***Most Capped Player:*** Mamady Sidibe, 7, Mali.

***Most League Appearances:*** John Simpson, 571, 1957–72.

***Youngest League Player:*** Billy Hughes, 15 years 275 days v Southend U, 13 April 1976.

***Record Transfer Fee Received:*** £1,500,000 from Manchester C for Robert Taylor, November 1999.

***Record Transfer Fee Paid:*** £600,000 to Reading for Carl Asaba, August 1998.

***Football League Record:*** 1920 Original Member of Division 3; 1921 Division 3 (S); 1938 Failed re-election; Southern League 1938–44; Kent League 1944–46; Southern League 1946–50; 1950 Re-elected to Division 3 (S); 1958–64 Division 4; 1964–71 Division 3; 1971–74 Division 4; 1974–89 Division 3; 1989–92 Division 4; 1992–96; Division 3; 1996–2000 Division 2; 2000–04 Division 1; 2004– FLC.

## MANAGERS

W. Ironside Groombridge 1896–1906 *(Secretary-Manager) (previously Financial Secretary)*
Steve Smith 1906–08
W. I. Groombridge 1908–19 *(Secretary-Manager)*
George Collins 1919–20
John McMillan 1920–23
Harry Curtis 1923–26
Albert Hoskins 1926–29
Dick Hendrie 1929–31
Fred Mavin 1932–37
Alan Ure 1937–38
Bill Harvey 1938–39
Archie Clark 1939–58
Harry Barratt 1958–62
Freddie Cox 1962–65
Basil Hayward 1966–71
Andy Nelson 1971–74
Len Ashurst 1974–75
Gerry Summers 1975–81
Keith Peacock 1981–87
Paul Taylor 1988
Keith Burkinshaw 1988–89
Damien Richardson 1989–93
Mike Flanagan 1993–95
Neil Smillie 1995
Tony Pulis 1995–99
Peter Taylor 1999–2000
Andy Hessenthaler June 2000–

## LATEST SEQUENCES

***Longest Sequence of League Wins:*** 7, 18.12.1954 – 29.1.1955.

***Longest Sequence of League Defeats:*** 10, 20.9.1988 – 5.11.1988.

***Longest Sequence of League Draws:*** 5, 28.8.1993 – 18.9.1993.

***Longest Sequence of Unbeaten League Matches:*** 20, 13.10.1973 – 10.2.1974.

***Longest Sequence Without a League Win:*** 15, 1.4.1972 – 2.9.1972.

***Successive Scoring Runs:*** 20 from 31.10.1959.

***Successive Non-scoring Runs:*** 6 from 11.2.1961.

## TEN YEAR LEAGUE RECORD

| | | P | W | D | L | F | A | Pts | Pos |
|---|---|---|---|---|---|---|---|---|---|
| 1994-95 | Div 3 | 42 | 10 | 11 | 21 | 46 | 64 | 41 | 19 |
| 1995-96 | Div 3 | 46 | 22 | 17 | 7 | 49 | 20 | 83 | 2 |
| 1996-97 | Div 2 | 46 | 19 | 10 | 17 | 60 | 59 | 67 | 11 |
| 1997-98 | Div 2 | 46 | 19 | 13 | 14 | 52 | 47 | 70 | 8 |
| 1998-99 | Div 2 | 46 | 22 | 14 | 10 | 75 | 44 | 80 | 4 |
| 1999-2000 | Div 2 | 46 | 25 | 10 | 11 | 79 | 48 | 85 | 3 |
| 2000-01 | Div 1 | 46 | 13 | 16 | 17 | 61 | 66 | 55 | 13 |
| 2001-02 | Div 1 | 46 | 18 | 10 | 18 | 64 | 67 | 64 | 12 |
| 2002-03 | Div 1 | 46 | 16 | 14 | 16 | 56 | 65 | 62 | 11 |
| 2003-04 | Div 1 | 46 | 14 | 9 | 23 | 48 | 67 | 51 | 21 |

## DID YOU KNOW ?

Winning the championship of the Fourth Division in 1963–64 was largely due to the Gillingham defence which conceded only 30 goals and included 24 clean sheets. They were unbeaten at home and totalled 60 points, a then club record.

## GILLINGHAM 2003–04 LEAGUE RECORD

| Match No. | Date | Venue | Opponents | Result | | H/T Score | Lg. Pos. | Goalscorers | Attendance |
|---|---|---|---|---|---|---|---|---|---|
| 1 | Aug 9 | A | Sheffield U | D | 0-0 | 0-0 | — | | 21,569 |
| 2 | 16 | H | Derby Co | D | 0-0 | 0-0 | 13 | | 7850 |
| 3 | 23 | A | Bradford C | W | 1-0 | 0-0 | 8 | Hope [77] | 10,317 |
| 4 | 25 | H | Burnley | L | 0-3 | 0-2 | 11 | | 7645 |
| 5 | 30 | A | Watford | D | 2-2 | 0-1 | 16 | Shaw [52], Spiller [63] | 12,793 |
| 6 | Sept 6 | H | Millwall | W | 4-3 | 2-1 | 11 | Sidibe [28], Shaw [43], King [81], Nosworthy [87] | 8237 |
| 7 | 13 | A | Cardiff C | L | 0-5 | 0-4 | 14 | | 15,057 |
| 8 | 16 | H | Norwich C | L | 1-2 | 1-0 | — | King [40] | 8022 |
| 9 | 20 | H | West Ham U | W | 2-0 | 0-0 | 13 | King [57], Benjamin [82] | 11,418 |
| 10 | 27 | A | Rotherham U | D | 1-1 | 1-0 | 13 | Spiller [36] | 5501 |
| 11 | 29 | A | Walsall | L | 1-2 | 0-1 | — | Brown (pen) [48] | 6395 |
| 12 | Oct 4 | H | WBA | L | 0-2 | 0-2 | 17 | | 8883 |
| 13 | 14 | A | Reading | L | 1-2 | 0-0 | — | King [73] | 13,011 |
| 14 | 18 | A | Wigan Ath | L | 0-1 | 0-0 | 20 | | 6696 |
| 15 | 25 | H | Crystal Palace | W | 1-0 | 0-0 | 20 | Perpetuini [83] | 8889 |
| 16 | Nov 1 | A | Ipswich T | W | 4-3 | 2-1 | 18 | Wallace [14], Sidibe [45], Shaw [53], Saunders [90] | 24,788 |
| 17 | 4 | H | Sunderland | L | 1-3 | 1-1 | — | Shaw [37] | 9066 |
| 18 | 8 | H | Crewe Alex | W | 2-0 | 0-0 | 16 | Shaw [64], Spiller [70] | 6923 |
| 19 | 15 | H | Wimbledon | L | 1-2 | 1-1 | 17 | Nosworthy [41] | 9041 |
| 20 | 22 | A | Coventry C | D | 2-2 | 0-0 | 17 | Johnson T 2 [66, 85] | 13,432 |
| 21 | 29 | H | Stoke C | W | 3-1 | 2-0 | 14 | Shaw [26], Hope [45], Sidibe [83] | 7888 |
| 22 | Dec 6 | A | Crewe Alex | D | 1-1 | 0-1 | 16 | Perpetuini [49] | 6271 |
| 23 | 13 | H | Preston NE | L | 0-1 | 0-1 | 17 | | 7602 |
| 24 | 26 | H | Watford | W | 1-0 | 0-0 | 17 | Hills (pen) [56] | 8971 |
| 25 | 28 | A | Millwall | W | 2-1 | 1-0 | 15 | Hessenthaler [21], James [90] | 12,084 |
| 26 | Jan 10 | H | Sheffield U | L | 0-3 | 0-1 | 16 | | 8353 |
| 27 | 17 | A | Derby Co | L | 1-2 | 0-1 | 18 | Johnson T [69] | 20,473 |
| 28 | 31 | H | Bradford C | W | 1-0 | 1-0 | 16 | Agyemang [16] | 7836 |
| 29 | Feb 7 | A | Burnley | L | 0-1 | 0-0 | 18 | | 10,400 |
| 30 | 21 | H | Reading | L | 0-1 | 0-1 | 20 | | 8600 |
| 31 | 25 | A | Nottingham F | D | 0-0 | 0-0 | — | | 26,473 |
| 32 | 28 | A | Crystal Palace | L | 0-1 | 0-0 | 20 | | 17,485 |
| 33 | Mar 6 | H | Nottingham F | W | 2-1 | 1-1 | 19 | Agyemang [34], Spiller [82] | 9096 |
| 34 | 13 | A | Preston NE | D | 0-0 | 0-0 | 19 | | 13,111 |
| 35 | 16 | A | Norwich C | L | 0-3 | 0-0 | — | | 23,198 |
| 36 | 20 | H | Rotherham U | W | 2-0 | 2-0 | 17 | Ashby [15], Sidibe [19] | 8047 |
| 37 | 23 | A | Sunderland | L | 1-2 | 1-1 | — | Agyemang [28] | 23,262 |
| 38 | 27 | A | West Ham U | L | 1-2 | 1-1 | 21 | Spiller [32] | 34,551 |
| 39 | Apr 3 | H | Cardiff C | L | 1-2 | 0-1 | 21 | Hope [59] | 7852 |
| 40 | 6 | H | Wigan Ath | L | 0-3 | 0-2 | — | | 7410 |
| 41 | 10 | A | WBA | L | 0-1 | 0-1 | 21 | | 24,524 |
| 42 | 12 | H | Walsall | W | 3-0 | 1-0 | 21 | Agyemang 2 [45, 67], Spiller [90] | 8244 |
| 43 | 17 | H | Ipswich T | L | 1-2 | 1-0 | 22 | Hills (pen) [8] | 9641 |
| 44 | 24 | A | Wimbledon | W | 2-1 | 0-0 | 20 | Hessenthaler [62], Agyemang [79] | 5049 |
| 45 | May 1 | H | Coventry C | L | 2-5 | 0-3 | 21 | Wales [64], Sidibe [72] | 10,388 |
| 46 | 9 | A | Stoke C | D | 0-0 | 0-0 | 21 | | 19,240 |

**Final League Position: 21**

### GOALSCORERS

*League (48):* Agyemang 6, Shaw 6, Spiller 6, Sidibe 5, King 4, Hope 3, Johnson T 3, Hessenthaler 2, Hills 2 (2 pens), Nosworthy 2, Perpetuini 2, Ashby 1, Benjamin 1, Brown 1 (pen), James 1, Saunders 1, Wales 1, Wallace 1.
*Carling Cup (4):* Hills 1, King 1, Nosworthy 1, Saunders 1.
*FA Cup (4):* Henderson 1, Johnson T 1, Sidibie 1, Smith 1.

| Brown J 22 | Southall N 34 + 1 | Hills J 27 + 2 | Hope C 37 | Ashby B 22 + 1 | Cox I 32 + 1 | Spiller D 32 + 7 | Saunders M 8 + 13 | Sidibe M 34 + 7 | Nosworthy N 26 + 1 | Shaw P 20 + 1 | Johnson T 6 + 9 | Perpetuini D 14 + 6 | Rose R 12 + 5 | King M 9 + 2 | Bartram V 1 | Wallace R 10 + 4 | Hessenthaler A 27 + 9 | Smith P 31 + 2 | Brown W 4 | Benjamin T 1 + 3 | Bossu B 3 + 1 | Jarvis M 2 + 8 | James K 12 + 5 | Vaesen N 5 | Henderson D 4 | Johnson L 18 + 2 | Agyemang P 20 | Crofts A 1 + 7 | Pouton A 14 + 5 | Hirschfeld L 2 | Banks S 13 | Wales G 3 + 3 | Match No. |
|---|---|---|---|---|---|---|---|---|---|---|---|---|---|---|---|---|---|---|---|---|---|---|---|---|---|---|---|---|---|---|---|---|---|
| 1 | 2 | 3 | 4 | 5 | 6 | 7 | 8 | $9^1$ | 10 | 11 | 12 | | | | | | | | | | | | | | | | | | | | | | 1 |
| 1 | 2 | 3 | 4 | | 6 | 7 | | 9 | 5 | $11^1$ | 10 | 8 | 12 | | | | | | | | | | | | | | | | | | | | 2 |
| 1 | 2 | 3 | 4 | 5 | 6 | $7^1$ | 12 | 13 | 9 | $8^2$ | $10^3$ | 11 | | 14 | | | | | | | | | | | | | | | | | | | 3 |
| 1 | 2 | 3 | 4 | 5 | 6 | 7 | | 12 | $9^2$ | 11 | $10^1$ | 8 | | 13 | | | | | | | | | | | | | | | | | | | 4 |
| 1 | 2 | 3 | 4 | 5 | 6 | 7 | | 9 | | 8 | | 11 | | 10 | | | | | | | | | | | | | | | | | | | 5 |
| | 2 | 3 | 4 | $5^1$ | 6 | 7 | | $9^2$ | 12 | 8 | | $11^3$ | | 10 | 1 | 13 | 14 | | | | | | | | | | | | | | | | 6 |
| 1 | 2 | 3 | 4 | $5^1$ | 6 | $7^3$ | 12 | $9^2$ | 11 | 8 | | | | 10 | | 13 | 14 | | | | | | | | | | | | | | | | 7 |
| 1 | | 3 | 4 | 12 | 6 | 7 | 5 | | 2 | $11^1$ | 13 | | | 10 | | $9^2$ | $8^3$ | 14 | | | | | | | | | | | | | | | 8 |
| 1 | | | 4 | | 6 | 7 | 5 | $9^3$ | 2 | $11^2$ | | 12 | | 10 | | | $8^1$ | 13 | 3 | 14 | | | | | | | | | | | | | 9 |
| 1 | | | 4 | | 5 | 7 | 6 | 9 | 2 | | | 11 | | $10^1$ | | | | 8 | 3 | 12 | | | | | | | | | | | | | 10 |
| | | | 4 | | 5 | $7^2$ | 6 | 9 | 2 | | 12 | 11 | | | | | 13 | 8 | 3 | $10^1$ | 1 | | | | | | | | | | | | 11 |
| 1 | | 12 | 4 | | 5 | 7 | | $9^3$ | 2 | | 13 | $11^2$ | | 10 | | | 8 | 6 | $3^1$ | 14 | | | | | | | | | | | | | 12 |
| 1 | | $3^2$ | 4 | 5 | 6 | 14 | $7^3$ | 12 | 2 | | | 13 | | 10 | | $9^1$ | 8 | 11 | | | | | | | | | | | | | | | 13 |
| 1 | 7 | 3 | 4 | $5^1$ | 6 | | | 12 | 2 | 13 | | | | $10^2$ | | 9 | 8 | 11 | | | | | | | | | | | | | | | 14 |
| 1 | 7 | 3 | 4■ | 5 | 6 | | 12 | 13 | 2 | $10^1$ | | 14 | | | | $9^2$ | $8^3$ | 11 | | | | | | | | | | | | | | | 15 |
| 1 | 7 | | 4 | | 5 | | 14 | 10 | 2 | $11^3$ | $12^2$ | 13 | 3 | | | $9^1$ | 8 | 6 | | | | | | | | | | | | | | | 16 |
| 1 | 7 | | 4 | | 5 | 12 | | 9 | 2 | 10 | | 11 | $3^2$ | | | | $8^1$ | 6 | | | | 13 | | | | | | | | | | | 17 |
| 1 | 2 | 3 | | 5 | | 7 | | 9 | 4 | 10 | | 11 | | | | | $8^1$ | 6 | | | | | 12 | | | | | | | | | | 18 |
| 1 | 11 | 3 | 4 | 5 | $2^1$ | $7^2$ | | | 8 | 10 | | | | | | 9 | 12 | 6 | | | | | 13 | | | | | | | | | | 19 |
| 1 | 11 | 3 | 4 | | 5 | | 14 | 9 | 2 | $10^3$ | 12 | 13 | | | | $8^1$ | $7^2$ | 6 | | | | | | | | | | | | | | | 20 |
| 1 | 11 | 3 | 4 | | 5 | | 12 | 9 | 2 | $8^1$ | $10^3$ | 13 | | | | | $7^2$ | 6 | | | | | 14 | | | | | | | | | | 21 |
| 1 | 7 | 3 | 4 | | 5 | | | 9 | 2 | 10 | | 11 | | | | | | 8 | | | | | 6 | | | | | | | | | | 22 |
| $1^G$ | $7^1$ | 3 | 4 | | 5 | | 13 | 9 | 2 | 10 | | $11^2$ | | | | | 12 | 8 | | | 15 | | 6 | | | | | | | | | | 23 |
| | | 3 | 4 | | 5 | 14 | 13 | 9 | 2 | $10^1$ | 12 | $11^2$ | | | | | 8 | 6 | | | | | $7^3$ | 1 | | | | | | | | | 24 |
| | | 3 | 4 | | 5 | 14 | 13 | $9^1$ | 2 | 10 | 12 | $11^2$ | | | | | $8^3$ | 6 | | | | | 7 | 1 | | | | | | | | | 25 |
| | $11^1$ | 3 | 4 | | 5 | $7^3$ | 12 | 9 | 2 | | $8^2$ | | | | | | | 6 | | | | | 13 | 1 | 10 | 14 | | | | | | | 26 |
| | | 3■ | 4 | | 5■ | $7^1$ | 8 | | 2 | | $11^3$ | | | | | | 12 | 6 | | | | | | 1 | $10^2$ | 13 | 9 | 14 | | | | | 27 |
| | | | 4 | 5 | | 11 | | | 2 | | | | 12 | | | | $7^2$ | 6 | | | | | 13 | 1 | $10^3$ | $3^1$ | 9 | 14 | 8 | | | | 28 |
| 1 | | | 4 | 5 | | $11^2$ | 12 | | | | | | 13 | | | 14 | 7 | 6 | | | | | 2 | | $10^3$ | 3 | 9 | | $8^1$ | | | | 29 |
| | 14 | 3 | | 5 | | 11 | | 12 | | | $13^3$ | | | | | $10^2$ | 7 | 6 | | | 1 | | 2 | | | 4 | 9 | | $8^1$ | | | | 30 |
| | 2 | $3^2$ | | 5 | | 12 | | 9 | | | | | 13 | | | $10^3$ | 7 | 11 | | | 1 | | 4 | | | 6 | $8^1$ | | 14 | | | | 31 |
| | $11^1$ | | | 5 | | 12 | | 9 | | | | | 3 | | | $10^2$ | 7 | 6 | | | | | 2 | | | 4 | 8 | | 13 | 1 | | | 32 |
| | 2 | | | 5 | | $11^2$ | | 9 | | | | | 3 | | | | 8 | 7 | | | | | 6 | | | 4 | $10^1$ | 13 | 12 | 1 | | | 33 |
| | 2 | | | 5 | | 7 | | 9 | | | | | 3 | | | | | 6 | | | | 11 | | | | 4 | 10 | | 8 | | 1 | | 34 |
| | 2 | | | 5■ | | 11 | | 9 | | | | | 3 | | | | | 7 | | | | | 6 | | | 4 | $10^1$ | 12 | 8 | | 1 | | 35 |
| | 2 | | | 5 | | 11 | | 9 | | | | | 3 | | | 13 | 12 | 7 | | | | | $6^1$ | | | 4 | $10^2$ | 14 | $8^3$ | | 1 | | 36 |
| | 2 | | | 5 | | $11^1$ | | 9 | | | | | 3 | | | | 12 | 7 | | | | 13 | $6^2$ | | | 4 | 10 | | 8 | | 1 | | 37 |
| | 2 | | 5 | | | $11^1$ | | $9^3$ | | | | | 3 | | | | 7 | $6^2$ | | | | 12 | | | | 4 | 10 | 13 | 8 | | 1 | 14 | 38 |
| | 2 | | 5 | | | 11 | | 9 | | | | | 3 | | | | 7 | | | | | | | | | 4 | 10 | | 6 | | 1 | 8 | 39 |
| | 2 | | 5 | | 12 | $11^3$ | | 9 | | | | | $3^1$ | | | | 7 | | | | | 13 | | | | 4 | $10^2$ | 14 | 6 | | 1 | 8 | 40 |
| | 2 | 12 | 6 | | 5 | $7^2$ | | 9 | | | | | $3^1$ | | | | 13 | | | | | 14 | | | | 4 | $10^3$ | 11 | 8 | | 1 | | 41 |
| | 2 | $3^1$ | 6 | | 5 | 11 | | 9 | | | | | 12 | | | | $7^2$ | 8 | | | | 14 | | | | 4 | $10^3$ | | 13 | | 1 | | 42 |
| | 2 | $3^1$ | 6 | | 5 | 11 | | 9 | | | | | | | | | 7 | 8 | | | | 13 | | | | 4 | $10^2$ | | 12 | | 1 | | 43 |
| | 2 | | 6 | | 5 | 11 | 12 | 9 | | | | | | | | | $7^1$ | | | | | $3^2$ | | | | 4 | 10 | | 8 | | 1 | 13 | 44 |
| | 2 | $3^2$ | 6 | | 5 | 11 | 12 | 9 | | | | | | | | | 7■ | | | | | | | | | 4 | 10 | | $8^1$ | | 1 | 13 | 45 |
| | 2 | 3 | 6 | 5 | 4 | 13 | 11 | 12 | | | | | | | | | 7 | | | | | 14 | | | | | $9^3$ | | $8^2$ | | 1 | $10^1$ | 46 |

**Carling Cup**

| | | | |
|---|---|---|---|
| First Round | Cambridge U | (a) | 2-1 |
| Second Round | Stoke C | (a) | 2-0 |
| Third Round | Bolton W | (a) | 0-2 |

**FA Cup**

| | | | |
|---|---|---|---|
| Third Round | Charlton Ath | (h) | 3-2 |
| Fourth Round | Burnley | (a) | 1-3 |

# GRIMSBY TOWN FL Championship 2

## FOUNDATION

Grimsby Pelham FC, as they were first known, came into being at a meeting held at the Wellington Arms in September 1878. Pelham is the family name of big landowners in the area, the Earls of Yarborough. The receipts for their first game amounted to 6s. 9d. (approx. 39p). After a year, the club name was changed to Grimsby Town.

***Blundell Park, Cleethorpes, North East Lincolnshire DN35 7PY.***

***Telephone:*** (01472) 605 050.

***Fax:*** (01472) 693 665.

***Ticket Office:*** (01472) 605 050.

***Website:*** www.gtfc.co.uk.

***Email:*** mariners@gtfc.co.uk

***Ground Capacity:*** 10,033.

***Record Attendance:*** 31,657 v Wolverhampton W, FA Cup 5th rd, 20 February 1937.

***Pitch Measurements:*** 111yd × 75yd.

***Chairman:*** P. W. Furneaux.

***Chief Executive:*** Ian Fleming.

***Manager:*** Russell Slade.

***Assistant Manager:*** Graham Rodger.

***Physio:*** Paul Mitchell.

***Colours:*** Black and white striped shirts, black shorts, black stockings.

***Change Colours:*** Sky blue shirts with navy trim, sky blue shorts with navy trim, sky blue stockings with navy trim.

***Year Formed.*** 1878.

***Turned Professional:*** 1890. ***Ltd Co.:*** 1890.

***Previous Name:*** 1878, Grimsby Pelham; 1879, Grimsby Town.

***Club Nickname:*** 'The Mariners'.

***Previous Grounds:*** 1880, Clee Park; 1889, Abbey Park; 1899, Blundell Park.

***First Football League Game:*** 3 September 1892, Division 2, v Northwich Victoria (h) W 2–1 – Whitehouse; Lundie, T. Frith; C. Frith, Walker, Murrell; Higgins, Henderson, Brayshaw, Riddoch (2), Ackroyd.

***Record League Victory:*** 9–2 v Darwen, Division 2, 15 April 1899 – Bagshaw; Lockie, Nidd; Griffiths, Bell (1), Nelmes; Jenkinson (3), Richards (1), Cockshutt (3), Robinson, Chadburn (1).

***Record Cup Victory:*** 8–0 v Darlington, FA Cup 2nd rd, 21 November 1885 – G. Atkinson; J. H. Taylor, H. Taylor; Hall, Kimpson, Hopewell; H. Atkinson (1), Garnham, Seal (3), Sharman, Monument (4).

## HONOURS

*Football League:* Division 1 best season: 5th, 1934–35; Division 2 – Champions 1900–01, 1933–34; Runners-up 1928–29; Promoted from Division 2 1997–98 (play-offs); Division 3 (N) – Champions 1925–26, 1955–56; Runners-up 1951–52; Division 3 – Champions 1979–80; Runners-up 1961–62; Division 4 – Champions 1971–72; Runners-up 1978–79; 1989–90.

*FA Cup:* Semi-finals, 1936, 1939.

*Football League Cup:* best season: 5th rd, 1980, 1985.

*League Group Cup:* Winners 1982.

*Auto Windscreen Shield:* Winners 1998.

## SKY SPORTS FACT FILE

Though his 20-year career with Grimsby Town spanned the war years, goalkeeper George Tweedy still made 350 League appearances and was capped for England against Hungary in 1936. His service included a brief return after retirement.

***Record Defeat:*** 1–9 v Arsenal, Division 1, 28 January 1931.

***Most League Points (2 for a win):*** 68, Division 3 (N), 1955–56.

***Most League Points (3 for a win):*** 83, Division 3, 1990–91.

***Most League Goals:*** 103, Division 2, 1933–34.

***Highest League Scorer in Season:*** Pat Glover, 42, Division 2, 1933–34.

***Most League Goals in Total Aggregate:*** Pat Glover, 180, 1930–39.

***Most League Goals in One Match:*** 6, Tommy McCairns v Leicester Fosse, Division 2, 11 April 1896.

***Most Capped Player:*** Pat Glover, 7, Wales.

***Most League Appearances:*** John McDermott, 553, 1987– .

***Youngest League Player:*** Tony Ford, 16 years 143 days v Walsall, 4 October 1975.

***Record Transfer Fee Received:*** £1,500,000 from Everton for John Oster, July 1997.

***Record Transfer Fee Paid:*** £500,000 to Preston NE for Lee Ashcroft, August 1998.

***Football League Record:*** 1892 Original Member Division 2; 1901–03 Division 1; 1903 Division 2; 1910 Failed re-election; 1911 re-elected Division 2; 1920–21 Division 3; 1921–26 Division 3 (N); 1926–29 Division 2; 1929–32 Division 1; 1932–34 Division 2; 1934–48 Division 1; 1948–51 Division 2; 1951–56 Division 3 (N); 1956–59 Division 2; 1959–62 Division 3; 1962–64 Division 2; 1964–68 Division 3; 1968–72 Division 4; 1972–77 Division 3; 1977–79 Division 4; 1979–80 Division 3; 1980–87 Division 2; 1987–88 Division 3; 1988–90 Division 4; 1990–91 Division 3; 1991–92 Division 2; 1992–97 Division 1; 1997–98 Division 2; 1998–2003 Division 1; 2003–04 Division 2; 2004– FL2.

## MANAGERS

H. N. Hickson 1902–20
*(Secretary-Manager)*
Haydn Price 1920
George Fraser 1921–24
Wilf Gillow 1924–32
Frank Womack 1932–36
Charles Spencer 1937–51
Bill Shankly 1951–53
Billy Walsh 1954–55
Allenby Chilton 1955–59
Tim Ward 1960–62
Tom Johnston 1962–64
Jimmy McGuigan 1964–67
Don McEvoy 1967–68
Bill Harvey 1968–69
Bobby Kennedy 1969–71
Lawrie McMenemy 1971–73
Ron Ashman 1973–75
Tom Casey 1975–76
Johnny Newman 1976–79
George Kerr 1979–82
David Booth 1982–85
Mike Lyons 1985–87
Bobby Roberts 1987–88
Alan Buckley 1988–94
Brian Laws 1994–96
Kenny Swain 1997
Alan Buckley 1997–2000
Lennie Lawrence 2000–01
Paul Groves 2001–04
Nicky Law 2004
Russell Slade May 2004

## LATEST SEQUENCES

***Longest Sequence of League Wins:*** 11, 19.1.1952 – 29.3.1952.

***Longest Sequence of League Defeats:*** 9, 30.11.1907 – 18.1.1908.

***Longest Sequence of League Draws:*** 5, 6.2.1965 – 6.3.1965.

***Longest Sequence of Unbeaten League Matches:*** 19, 16.2.1980 – 30.8.1980.

***Longest Sequence Without a League Win:*** 18, 10.10.1981 – 16.3.1982.

***Successive Scoring Runs:*** 33 from 6.10.1928.

***Successive Non-scoring Runs:*** 6 from 11.3.2000.

## TEN YEAR LEAGUE RECORD

| | | P | W | D | L | F | A | Pts | Pos |
|---|---|---|---|---|---|---|---|---|---|
| 1994-95 | Div 1 | 46 | 17 | 14 | 15 | 62 | 56 | 65 | 10 |
| 1995-96 | Div 1 | 46 | 14 | 14 | 18 | 55 | 69 | 56 | 17 |
| 1996-97 | Div 1 | 46 | 11 | 13 | 22 | 60 | 81 | 46 | 22 |
| 1997-98 | Div 2 | 46 | 19 | 15 | 12 | 55 | 37 | 72 | 3 |
| 1998-99 | Div 1 | 46 | 17 | 10 | 19 | 40 | 52 | 61 | 11 |
| 1999-2000 | Div 1 | 46 | 13 | 12 | 21 | 41 | 67 | 51 | 20 |
| 2000-01 | Div 1 | 46 | 14 | 10 | 22 | 43 | 62 | 52 | 18 |
| 2001-02 | Div 1 | 46 | 12 | 14 | 20 | 50 | 72 | 50 | 19 |
| 2002-03 | Div 1 | 46 | 9 | 12 | 25 | 48 | 85 | 39 | 24 |
| 2003-04 | Div 2 | 46 | 13 | 11 | 22 | 55 | 81 | 50 | 21 |

## DID YOU KNOW?

Already assured of promotion in 1901, Grimsby Town visited Middlesbrough on the last day. The title was up for grabs with Small Heath, who had a better goal average. Grimsby drew goalless but with their rivals losing, achieved it by a point.

## GRIMSBY TOWN 2003–04 LEAGUE RECORD

| Match No. | Date | Venue | Opponents | Result | | H/T Score | Lg. Pos. | Goalscorers | Attendance |
|---|---|---|---|---|---|---|---|---|---|
| 1 | Aug 9 | A | Plymouth Arg | D | 2-2 | 1-1 | — | Boulding [28], Anderson [64] | 9590 |
| 2 | 16 | H | Port Vale | L | 1-2 | 1-0 | 18 | Boulding [39] | 4816 |
| 3 | 23 | A | Luton T | W | 2-1 | 1-0 | 16 | Anderson [34], Boulding [77] | 5827 |
| 4 | 25 | H | Wycombe W | W | 3-1 | 1-0 | 8 | Barnard [27], Boulding [52], Cas [79] | 4512 |
| 5 | 30 | A | Bristol C | L | 0-1 | 0-0 | 10 | | 10,033 |
| 6 | Sept 6 | H | Peterborough U | D | 1-1 | 0-1 | 13 | Boulding [80] | 4710 |
| 7 | 12 | A | Hartlepool U | L | 1-8 | 0-4 | — | Rowan [48] | 5528 |
| 8 | 16 | H | Swindon T | L | 1-2 | 1-0 | — | Boulding [23] | 3535 |
| 9 | 20 | H | Chesterfield | W | 4-0 | 1-0 | 15 | Campbell [23], Hockless [56], Cas [73], Edwards [80] | 4141 |
| 10 | 27 | A | Sheffield W | D | 0-0 | 0-0 | 18 | | 21,918 |
| 11 | 30 | A | Blackpool | W | 1-0 | 0-0 | — | Crane [72] | 5491 |
| 12 | Oct 4 | H | QPR | L | 0-1 | 0-0 | 15 | | 5447 |
| 13 | 11 | A | Brighton & HA | L | 0-3 | 0-0 | 16 | | 6286 |
| 14 | 18 | H | Colchester U | W | 2-0 | 1-0 | 17 | Onuora [41], Boulding [84] | 5021 |
| 15 | 21 | H | Notts Co | W | 2-0 | 1-0 | — | Boulding 2 [23, 63] | 4274 |
| 16 | 25 | A | Barnsley | D | 0-0 | 0-0 | 13 | | 10,092 |
| 17 | Nov 1 | A | Rushden & D | L | 1-3 | 1-0 | 17 | Anderson [40] | 4185 |
| 18 | 15 | H | Stockport Co | D | 1-1 | 0-0 | 17 | Mansaram [72] | 4014 |
| 19 | 22 | A | Brentford | W | 3-1 | 1-1 | 15 | Onuora [45], Boulding 2 [84, 88] | 4685 |
| 20 | 29 | H | Tranmere R | L | 0-1 | 0-0 | 15 | | 4406 |
| 21 | Dec 13 | A | Bournemouth | D | 0-0 | 0-0 | 15 | | 5837 |
| 22 | 26 | H | Oldham Ath | D | 3-3 | 1-2 | 16 | Jevons 2 [9, 76], Boulding [57] | 6172 |
| 23 | 28 | A | Peterborough U | D | 0-0 | 0-0 | 16 | | 5245 |
| 24 | Jan 3 | A | Wycombe W | L | 1-4 | 1-2 | 17 | Onuora [8] | 4519 |
| 25 | 10 | H | Plymouth Arg | D | 0-0 | 0-0 | 17 | | 5007 |
| 26 | 17 | A | Port Vale | L | 1-5 | 1-4 | 18 | Jevons [34] | 5133 |
| 27 | 20 | H | Wrexham | L | 1-3 | 0-2 | — | Jevons [73] | 3572 |
| 28 | Feb 8 | A | Oldham Ath | L | 0-6 | 0-5 | 20 | | 13,007 |
| 29 | 14 | H | Brighton & HA | W | 2-1 | 1-1 | 20 | Rankin [5], Jevons [75] | 3673 |
| 30 | 17 | H | Bristol C | L | 1-2 | 1-1 | — | Anderson (pen) [31] | 5272 |
| 31 | 21 | A | Colchester U | L | 0-2 | 0-0 | 20 | | 2922 |
| 32 | 24 | H | Luton T | W | 3-2 | 0-1 | — | Jevons 2 (1 pen) [55, 69 (p)], Ford [90] | 3143 |
| 33 | 28 | H | Barnsley | W | 6-1 | 4-0 | 17 | Jevons 4 (1 pen) [23, 31, 55 (p), 75], Armstrong [27], Rankin [41] | 5603 |
| 34 | Mar 2 | A | Notts Co | L | 1-3 | 1-2 | — | Crane [11] | 6011 |
| 35 | 6 | A | Wrexham | L | 0-3 | 0-3 | 17 | | 3127 |
| 36 | 13 | H | Bournemouth | D | 1-1 | 1-0 | 18 | Rowan [11] | 5015 |
| 37 | 17 | A | Swindon T | L | 0-2 | 0-2 | — | | 6954 |
| 38 | 20 | H | Hartlepool U | L | 0-2 | 0-1 | 20 | | 4303 |
| 39 | 27 | A | Chesterfield | D | 4-4 | 2-1 | 21 | Anderson [35], Lawrence [42], Barnard [86], Rankin [87] | 4444 |
| 40 | Apr 3 | H | Sheffield W | W | 2-0 | 2-0 | 19 | Mansaram [6], Crane [33] | 6641 |
| 41 | 10 | A | QPR | L | 0-3 | 0-1 | 20 | | 14,488 |
| 42 | 12 | H | Blackpool | L | 0-2 | 0-1 | 22 | | 4775 |
| 43 | 17 | H | Rushden & D | W | 1-0 | 0-0 | 21 | Jevons (pen) [80] | 3890 |
| 44 | 24 | A | Stockport Co | L | 1-2 | 0-2 | 22 | Hockless [70] | 5924 |
| 45 | May 1 | H | Brentford | W | 1-0 | 0-0 | 20 | Rankin [70] | 6856 |
| 46 | 8 | A | Tranmere R | L | 1-2 | 1-0 | 21 | Mansaram [24] | 10,301 |

**Final League Position: 21**

## GOALSCORERS

*League (55):* Boulding 12, Jevons 12 (3 pens), Anderson 5 (1 pen), Rankin 4, Crane 3, Mansaram 3, Onuora 3, Barnard 2, Cas 2, Hockless 2, Rowan 2, Armstrong 1, Campbell 1, Edwards 1, Ford 1, Lawrence 1.
*Carling Cup (2):* Anderson 1 (pen), Campbell 1.
*FA Cup (3):* Boulding 1, Cas 1, Jevons 1.
*LDV Vans Trophy (1):* Mansaram 1.

| Davison A 32 | Crowe J 27 + 5 | Barnard D 34 | Hamilton D 20 + 7 | Ford S 21 + 5 | Crane T 37 | Cas M 13 + 7 | Campbell S 39 | Boulding M 27 | Ten Heuvel L 3 + 1 | Anderson I 24 + 5 | Groves P 7 + 4 | Rowan J 9 + 5 | Mansaram D 11 + 20 | Parker W — + 4 | Bolder C 6 + 1 | McDermott J 21 | Edwards M 32 + 1 | Hockless G 4 + 9 | Soames D — + 10 | Nimmo L — + 2 | Daws N 17 | Onuora I 18 + 1 | Young G 10 + 7 | Jevons P 21 + 8 | Pouton A 5 | Thorpe L 5 + 1 | Coldicott S 13 + 1 | Rankin I 12 | Pettinger A 3 | Armstrong C 9 | Fettis A 11 | Warhurst P 5 + 2 | Thorrington J 2 + 1 | Antoine-Curier M 3 + 2 | Lawrence J 5 | Match No. |
|---|---|---|---|---|---|---|---|---|---|---|---|---|---|---|---|---|---|---|---|---|---|---|---|---|---|---|---|---|---|---|---|---|---|---|---|---|
| 1 | 2 | 3 | $4^1$ | 5 | 6 | 7 | 8 | $9^2$ | $10^3$ | 11 | 12 | 13 | 14 | | | | | | | | | | | | | | | | | | | | | | | 1 |
| 1 | $2^2$ | 3 | 4 | 5 | 6 | 7 | 8 | $9^3$ | $10^1$ | 11■ | 12 | 13 | 14 | | | | | | | | | | | | | | | | | | | | | | | 2 |
| 1 | 2 | 3 | 4 | 5 | 6 | $7^1$ | 8 | 9 | $10^2$ | $11^3$ | 12 | 13 | 14 | | | | | | | | | | | | | | | | | | | | | | | 3 |
| 1 | 2 | $3^2$ | 4 | 5 | 6 | $7^1$ | 11 | 9 | | | $8^3$ | 10 | 12 | 13 | 14 | | | | | | | | | | | | | | | | | | | | | 4 |
| 1 | 7 | 3 | | 5 | 6 | | 11 | 9 | 12 | | 4 | 10 | | 13 | $8^1$ | $2^2$ | | | | | | | | | | | | | | | | | | | | 5 |
| 1 | | | | 5 | 6 | 7 | 11 | 9 | | | 4 | $10^2$ | | | $8^1$ | 2 | 3 | 12 | 13 | | | | | | | | | | | | | | | | | 6 |
| 1 | 2 | 3 | | 5 | 6 | 7 | 11 | $9^1$ | | | 4 | $10^2$ | | | | | | 8 | 12 | 13 | | | | | | | | | | | | | | | | 7 |
| 1 | 12 | 3 | | 5 | 6 | 7 | 11 | 9 | | | | $10^3$ | | | $4^1$ | 2 | | $8^2$ | 13 | 14 | | | | | | | | | | | | | | | | 8 |
| 1 | 12 | 3 | | $5^3$ | 6 | 7 | 11 | $9^2$ | | | | | 13 | | | 2 | 14 | $8^1$ | | | 4 | 10 | | | | | | | | | | | | | | 9 |
| 1 | | 3 | 4 | | 6 | $7^1$ | 11 | 9 | | | | | | | | 2 | 5 | 12 | | | 8 | 10 | | | | | | | | | | | | | | 10 |
| 1 | 7 | 3 | 4 | | 6 | | 11 | $9^1$ | | | | | 12 | | | 2 | $5^2$ | | | | 8 | 10 | 13 | | | | | | | | | | | | | 11 |
| 1 | $7^1$ | 3 | 4 | | 6 | | 11 | 9 | | 12 | | | | | | 2 | 5 | | | | 8 | 10 | | | | | | | | | | | | | | 12 |
| 1 | 3 | | 4 | | $6^3$ | | 7 | $9^2$ | | $11^1$ | | | | | | 2 | 5 | 13 | 12 | | 8 | 10 | 14 | | | | | | | | | | | | | 13 |
| 1 | 13 | 3 | 4 | $12^2$ | 6 | 14 | 7 | 9 | | $11^3$ | | | | | | 2 | $5^1$ | | | | 8 | 10 | | | | | | | | | | | | | | 14 |
| 1 | | 3 | 4 | | 6 | 12 | 7 | 9 | | $11^1$ | | | 13 | | | 2 | 5 | | | | 8 | $10^2$ | | | | | | | | | | | | | | 15 |
| 1 | 12 | 3 | 4 | | 6 | $8^1$ | 7 | 9 | | 11 | | | | | | 2 | 5 | | | | | 10 | | | | | | | | | | | | | | 16 |
| 1 | 3 | | 4 | | | 8 | 7 | 9 | | $11^1$ | | | | | | 2 | 5 | | | | | 10 | 6 | 12 | | | | | | | | | | | | 17 |
| 1 | 4 | | 8 | | 6 | 12 | $7^1$ | 9 | | $11^3$ | | | 13 | | | 2 | 5 | | | | | $10^2$ | 3 | 14 | | | | | | | | | | | | 18 |
| 1 | 4 | 3 | 8 | | 6 | 13 | 7 | 9 | | $11^2$ | 12 | | | | | $2^1$ | 5 | | | | | 10 | | | | | | | | | | | | | | 19 |
| 1 | 4 | 3 | $8^1$ | | 6 | 12 | 7 | 9 | | $11^3$ | | | 13 | | | 2 | 5 | | | | | $10^2$ | | 14 | | | | | | | | | | | | 20 |
| 1 | 4■ | 3 | 12 | | 6 | | $11^3$ | 9 | | 13 | | | 14 | | | 2 | 5 | | | | | 10 | | $8^2$ | $7^1$ | | | | | | | | | | | 21 |
| 1 | | 3 | $4^1$ | 14 | 6■ | 12 | 7 | $9^2$ | | | | | 13 | | | 2 | 5 | | | | | $10^3$ | | 11 | 8 | | | | | | | | | | | 22 |
| 1 | | | 4 | 13 | 6 | 2 | 7 | 9 | | | | | 12 | | | | 5 | | | | | $10^1$ | $3^2$ | 11 | 8 | | | | | | | | | | | 23 |
| 1 | | | 4 | | 6 | 2 | $7^2$ | 9 | | | | | 12 | | | 3 | 5 | | | | | $10^1$ | 13 | 11 | 8 | | | | | | | | | | | 24 |
| 1 | | $3^3$ | | 6 | | 12 | | 9 | | $7^1$ | 4 | | $10^2$ | | | 2 | 5 | | | | | 13 | 14 | 11 | 8 | | | | | | | | | | | 25 |
| 1 | 3 | | 12 | 6 | | | | | | 7 | $4^1$ | 13 | 9 | | | 2 | 5 | | | | $8^3$ | $10^2$ | 14 | 11 | | | | | | | | | | | | 26 |
| 1 | 4 | | 12 | 6 | | | | 9 | | $7^1$ | | | 13 | | | 2 | 5 | | | | 8 | $10^2$ | 3 | 11 | | | | | | | | | | | | 27 |
| 1 | 2 | 3 | | 12 | 6 | | 7 | 9 | | 13 | $4^1$ | | | | | | 5■ | | | | 8 | | | $11^2$ | | 10 | | | | | | | | | | 28 |
| 1■ | 2 | 3 | 12 | 5 | 6 | | 7 | | | 11 | | | $9^3$ | | | | | | 13 | | 4 | | | 14 | | | $8^1$ | $10^2$ | | | | | | | | 29 |
| 1 | 2 | | 12 | 5 | 6 | | 7 | | | $11^3$ | | | $9^2$ | | | | | | 13 | | 4 | | 3 | 14 | | | $8^1$ | 10 | | | | | | | | 30 |
| 1 | | 3 | 4 | 5 | 6 | | $7^2$ | | | 11 | | | 12 | | | | 2 | | | | 8 | | | 13 | | $9^1$ | | 10 | | | | | | | | 31 |
| 1 | | 3 | | 2 | 6 | | 7 | | | $11^1$ | | | $9^2$ | | | | | | 14 | | 4 | | | 12 | | 13 | $8^3$ | 10 | | 5 | | | | | | 32 |
| | | 3 | 12 | $2^3$ | 6■ | | 7 | | | | | | | 14 | | | | | | | 4 | | 13 | 11 | | 9 | $8^1$ | $10^2$ | 1 | 5 | | | | | | 33 |
| | | 3 | | $2^2$ | 6 | | 7 | | | | | | 12 | 13 | | | | 8 | | | 4 | | | 11 | | 10 | | $9^1$ | 1 | 5 | | | | | | 34 |
| | | 3 | 8 | | 6 | | 7 | | | | | | $9^1$ | | | | 2 | 14 | 12 | | 4 | | 13 | 11 | | $10^3$ | | | 1 | $5^2$ | | | | | | 35 |
| | | 3 | 12 | | | | 11 | | | | | $9^2$ | 13 | | | | 6 | 14 | | | | | 2 | 10 | | | $8^1$ | | | 5 | 1 | 4 | $7^3$ | | | 36 |
| | | 3 | | | | | 11 | | | 12 | | $9^2$ | 13 | | 8 | | 6 | | | | | | 2 | 10 | | | | | | 5 | 1 | 4 | $7^1$ | | | 37 |
| | 12 | 3 | | | | | 11 | | | | | $9^3$ | 13 | | 7 | | $6^1$ | | | | | | 2 | 10 | | | $8^2$ | | | 5 | 1 | 4 | | 14 | | 38 |
| | 2 | 3 | | | | | | | | 11 | | | 13■ | | | | | | | | | | $5^1$ | 12 | | | 8 | 10 | | 4 | 1 | 6 | | $9^2$ | 7 | 39 |
| | 2 | | | 5 | 6 | | | | | 7 | | 13 | $9^1$ | | | | 3 | | | | | | | 11 | | | 8 | 10 | | | 1 | | | $12^2$ | 4 | 40 |
| | 2 | | | 5 | 6 | | | | | 7 | | 10 | | | | | 3 | | | | | | | 11 | | | 12 | | | $4^2$ | 1 | 13 | 14 | $9^3$ | $8^1$ | 41 |
| | 2 | | | 5 | 6 | | | | | $7^2$ | | | | | 4 | | 3 | 13 | 12 | | | | | 11 | | | 8 | | | | 1 | 10 | | $9^1$ | | 42 |
| | 2 | $3^1$ | | 12 | 6 | | 8 | | | 7 | | | $9^2$ | | | | 5 | | 13 | | | | | 11 | | | 4 | 10 | | | 1 | | | | | 43 |
| | $2^2$ | 3 | | | 6 | | 8 | | | 7 | | | $9^1$ | | | | 5 | 12 | | | | | | 11 | | | 4 | 10 | | | 1 | 13 | | | | 44 |
| | 2 | 3 | | | 6 | | 8 | | | | | | $9^1$ | | | | 5 | 12 | | | | | | 11 | | | 4 | 10 | | | 1 | | | | 7 | 45 |
| | 2 | 3 | | | | | $8^1$ | | | 12 | | | $9^2$ | | | | 6 | 13 | | | | | 5 | 11 | | | 4 | 10 | | | 1 | | | | 7 | 46 |

**Carling Cup**
First Round Doncaster R (a) 2-3

**LDV Vans Trophy**
First Round Sheffield W (a) 1-1

**FA Cup**
First Round QPR (h) 1-0
Second Round Peterborough U (a) 2-3

# HARTLEPOOL UNITED FL Championship 1

## FOUNDATION

The inspiration for the launching of Hartlepool United was the West Hartlepool club which won the FA Amateur Cup in 1904–05. They had been in existence since 1881 and their Cup success led in 1908 to the formation of the new professional concern which first joined the North-Eastern League. In those days they were Hartlepools United and won the Durham Senior Cup in their first two seasons.

***Victoria Park, Clarence Road, Hartlepool TS24 8BZ.***

***Telephone:*** (01429) 272 584.

***Fax:*** (01429) 863 007.

***Ticket Office:*** (01429) 272 584.

***Website:*** www.hartlepoolunited.co.uk

***Email:*** hufc@btconnect.com

***Ground Capacity:*** 7,629.

***Record Attendance:*** 17,426 v Manchester U, FA Cup 3rd rd, 5 January 1957.

***Pitch Measurements:*** 100 × 66 metres.

***Chairman:*** Ken Hodcroft.

***Secretary:*** Maureen Smith.

***Manager:*** Neale Cooper.

***Assistant Manager:*** Martin Scott.

***Physio:*** John Murray.

***Colours:*** White with royal blue pinstripe shirts, blue shorts, white stockings.

***Change Colours:*** All red.

***Year Formed:*** 1908.

***Turned Professional:*** 1908.

***Ltd Co.:*** 1908.

***Previous Names:*** 1908, Hartlepools United; 1968, Hartlepool; 1977, Hartlepool United.

***Club Nickname:*** 'The Pool'.

***First Football League Game:*** 27 August 1921, Division 3 (N), v Wrexham (a) W 2–0 – Gill; Thomas, Crilly; Dougherty, Hopkins, Short; Kessler, Mulholland (1), Lister (1), Robertson, Donald.

***Record League Victory:*** 10–1 v Barrow, Division 4, 4 April 1959 – Oakley; Cameron, Waugh; Johnson, Moore, Anderson; Scott (1), Langland (1), Smith (3), Clark (2), Luke (2), (1 og).

***Record Cup Victory:*** 6–0 v North Shields, FA Cup 1st rd, 30 November 1946 – Heywood; Brown, Gregory; Spelman, Lambert, Jones; Price, Scott (2), Sloan (4), Moses, McMahon.

## HONOURS

*Football League:* Division 3 – Runners-up 2002–03; Division 3 (N) – Runners-up 1956–57.

*FA Cup:* best season: 4th rd, 1955, 1978, 1989, 1993.

*Football League Cup,* best season: 4th rd, 1975.

## SKY SPORTS FACT FILE

In successive seasons 1955–56 and 1956–57 Hartlepool United won 18 home League games. The former season saw them finish fourth with 57 points, the latter with two more points as runners-up in the Third Division (North).

***Record Defeat:*** 1–10 v Wrexham, Division 4, 3 March 1962.

***Most League Points (2 for a win):*** 60, Division 4, 1967–68.

***Most League Points (3 for a win):*** 85, Division 3, 2002–03.

***Most League Goals:*** 90, Division 3 (N), 1956–57.

***Highest League Scorer in Season:*** William Robinson, 28, Division 3 (N), 1927–28; Joe Allon, 28, Division 4, 1990–91.

***Most League Goals in Total Aggregate:*** Ken Johnson, 98, 1949–64.

***Most League Goals in One Match:*** 5, Harry Simmons v Wigan Borough, Division 3N, 1 January 1931; 5, Bobby Folland v Oldham Ath, Division 3N, 15 April 1961.

***Most Capped Player:*** Ambrose Fogarty, 1 (11), Republic of Ireland.

***Most League Appearances:*** Wattie Moore, 447, 1948–64.

***Youngest League Player:*** David Foley, 16 years 105 days v Port Vale, 25 August 2003.

***Record Transfer Fee Received:*** £750,000 from Ipswich T for Tommy Miller, July 2001.

***Record Transfer Fee Paid:*** £75,000 to Notts Co for Gary Jones, March 1999; £75,000 to Mansfield T for Darrell Clarke, July 2001.

***Football League Record:*** 1921 Original Member of Division 3 (N); 1958–68 Division 4; 1968–69 Division 3; 1969–91 Division 4; 1991–92 Division 3; 1992–94 Division 2; 1994–2003 Division 3; 2003–04 Division 2; 2004– FL1.

## LATEST SEQUENCES

***Longest Sequence of League Wins:*** 7, 30.3.2002 – 13.8.2002.

***Longest Sequence of League Defeats:*** 8, 27.1.1993 – 27.2.1993.

***Longest Sequence of League Draws:*** 5, 24.2.2001 – 17.3.2001.

***Longest Sequence of Unbeaten League Matches:*** 21, 2.12.2000 – 31.3.2001.

***Longest Sequence Without a League Win:*** 18, 9.1.1993 – 3.4.1993.

***Successive Scoring Runs:*** 17 from 28.2.1964.

***Successive Non-scoring Runs:*** 11 from 9.1.1993.

## MANAGERS

Alfred Priest 1908–12
Percy Humphreys 1912–13
Jack Manners 1913–20
Cecil Potter 1920–22
David Gordon 1922–24
Jack Manners 1924–27
Bill Norman 1927–31
Jack Carr 1932–35
*(had been Player-Coach since 1931)*
Jimmy Hamilton 1935–43
Fred Westgarth 1943–57
Ray Middleton 1957–59
Bill Robinson 1959–62
Allenby Chilton 1962–63
Bob Gurney 1963–64
Alvan Williams 1964–65
Geoff Twentyman 1965
Brian Clough 1965–67
Angus McLean 1967–70
John Simpson 1970–71
Len Ashurst 1971–74
Ken Hale 1974–76
Billy Horner 1976–83
Johnny Duncan 1983
Mike Docherty 1983
Billy Horner 1984–86
John Bird 1986–88
Bobby Moncur 1988–89
Cyril Knowles 1989–91
Alan Murray 1991–93
Viv Busby 1993
John MacPhail 1993–94
David McCreery 1994–95
Keith Houchen 1995–96
Mick Tait 1996–99
Chris Turner 1999–2002
Mike Newell 2002–03
Neale Cooper June 2003–

## TEN YEAR LEAGUE RECORD

| | | P | W | D | L | F | A | Pts | Pos |
|---|---|---|---|---|---|---|---|---|---|
| 1994-95 | Div 3 | 42 | 11 | 10 | 21 | 43 | 69 | 43 | 18 |
| 1995-96 | Div 3 | 46 | 12 | 13 | 21 | 47 | 67 | 49 | 20 |
| 1996-97 | Div 3 | 46 | 14 | 9 | 23 | 53 | 66 | 51 | 20 |
| 1997-98 | Div 3 | 46 | 12 | 23 | 11 | 61 | 53 | 59 | 17 |
| 1998-99 | Div 3 | 46 | 13 | 12 | 21 | 52 | 65 | 51 | 22 |
| 1999-2000 | Div 3 | 46 | 21 | 9 | 16 | 60 | 49 | 72 | 7 |
| 2000-01 | Div 3 | 46 | 21 | 14 | 11 | 71 | 54 | 77 | 4 |
| 2001-02 | Div 3 | 46 | 20 | 11 | 15 | 74 | 48 | 71 | 7 |
| 2002-03 | Div 3 | 46 | 24 | 13 | 9 | 71 | 51 | 85 | 2 |
| 2003-04 | Div 2 | 46 | 20 | 13 | 13 | 76 | 61 | 73 | 6 |

## DID YOU KNOW?

David Lindsay, a prolific scoring centre-forward, hit 21 goals in only 37 League games for Hartlepools United in 1934–35. Previously with East Fife, Cowdenbeath, Newcastle, Bury, Ashton National and Northampton, he later turned out for Barrow and York.

## HARTLEPOOL UNITED 2003–04 LEAGUE RECORD

| *Match No.* | *Date* | *Venue* | *Opponents* | *Result* | *H/T Score* | *Lg. Pos.* | *Goalscorers* | *Attendance* |
|---|---|---|---|---|---|---|---|---|
| 1 | Aug 9 | A | Peterborough U | W 4-3 | 1-2 | — | Strachan [38], Robinson P [55], Robson [70], Nelson [85] | 5965 |
| 2 | 16 | H | Tranmere R | D 0-0 | 0-0 | 6 | | 5357 |
| 3 | 23 | A | Bristol C | D 1-1 | 0-0 | 12 | Gabbiadini [73] | 10,730 |
| 4 | 25 | H | Port Vale | W 2-0 | 1-0 | 5 | Robinson P [2], Gabbiadini (pen) [88] | 5314 |
| 5 | 30 | A | Luton T | L 2-3 | 1-3 | 9 | Clarke [40], Robinson P (pen) [71] | 5515 |
| 6 | Sept 6 | H | Oldham Ath | D 0-0 | 0-0 | 12 | | 5728 |
| 7 | 12 | H | Grimsby T | W 8-1 | 4-0 | — | Groves (og) [19], Robinson P 3 (1 pen) [20 (p), 56, 80], Strachan [28], Humphreys [31], Gabbiadini [60], Williams E [66] | 5528 |
| 8 | 16 | A | Stockport Co | W 2-1 | 1-1 | — | Williams E [8], Gabbiadini [54] | 4021 |
| 9 | 20 | A | Brentford | L 1-2 | 1-1 | 6 | Tinkler [42] | 4501 |
| 10 | 27 | H | Brighton & HA | D 0-0 | 0-0 | 7 | | 5443 |
| 11 | 30 | H | Wrexham | W 2-0 | 2-0 | — | Clarke 2 [23, 37] | 4677 |
| 12 | Oct 4 | A | Bournemouth | D 2-2 | 1-0 | 5 | Tinkler [10], Strachan [90] | 6342 |
| 13 | 10 | H | Sheffield W | D 1-1 | 0-0 | — | Gabbiadini [84] | 7448 |
| 14 | 18 | A | Blackpool | L 0-4 | 0-3 | 9 | | 6871 |
| 15 | 21 | A | Chesterfield | W 2-1 | 1-0 | — | Evatt (og) [26], Robinson P [78] | 3411 |
| 16 | 25 | H | Wycombe W | D 1-1 | 1-1 | 7 | Barron [40] | 5153 |
| 17 | Nov 1 | A | Notts Co | L 0-1 | 0-0 | 8 | | 5011 |
| 18 | .15 | H | Rushden & D | W 2-1 | 1-0 | 6 | Strachan (pen) [41], Wilkinson [75] | 4944 |
| 19 | 22 | A | Plymouth Arg | L 0-2 | 0-1 | 8 | | 9000 |
| 20 | 29 | H | Swindon T | W 2-0 | 1-0 | 5 | Strachan (pen) [18], Wilkinson [86] | 4493 |
| 21 | Dec 13 | A | QPR | L 1-4 | 0-3 | 10 | Williams E [71] | 15,003 |
| 22 | 20 | H | Colchester U | D 0-0 | 0-0 | 8 | | 4135 |
| 23 | 26 | H | Barnsley | L 1-2 | 1-1 | 11 | Williams E [22] | 6520 |
| 24 | 28 | A | Oldham Ath | W 2-0 | 1-0 | 10 | Williams E [45], Porter [79] | 6243 |
| 25 | Jan 10 | H | Peterborough U | W 1-0 | 1-0 | 6 | Williams E [37] | 4855 |
| 26 | 17 | A | Tranmere R | D 0-0 | 0-0 | 8 | | 7418 |
| 27 | 24 | H | Bristol C | L 1-2 | 0-0 | 9 | Tinkler [70] | 5375 |
| 28 | 27 | A | Port Vale | W 5-2 | 2-1 | — | Shuker [6], Humphreys [31], Nelson [69], Williams E [74], Clarke [83] | 4845 |
| 29 | Feb 7 | A | Barnsley | D 2-2 | 1-0 | 9 | Williams E [27], Tinkler [67] | 9220 |
| 30 | 14 | A | Sheffield W | L 0-1 | 0-0 | 10 | | 20,732 |
| 31 | 20 | H | Blackpool | D 1-1 | 0-0 | — | Robertson [51] | 5497 |
| 32 | 28 | A | Wycombe W | W 4-3 | 3-2 | 11 | Williams E 2 [4, 46], Robertson [10], Tinkler (pen) [39] | 4731 |
| 33 | Mar 2 | H | Chesterfield | W 2-0 | 0-0 | — | Williams E [52], Tinkler [71] | 4736 |
| 34 | 6 | A | Colchester U | W 2-1 | 1-1 | 5 | Nelson [17], Istead [78] | 3348 |
| 35 | 13 | H | QPR | L 1-4 | 0-0 | 7 | Porter [88] | 6519 |
| 36 | 16 | H | Stockport Co | D 2-2 | 1-2 | — | Williams E [10], Porter [58] | 4674 |
| 37 | 20 | A | Grimsby T | W 2-0 | 1-0 | 6 | Boyd 2 [29, 87] | 4303 |
| 38 | 27 | H | Brentford | L 1-2 | 1-2 | 9 | Boyd [38] | 5206 |
| 39 | Apr 3 | A | Brighton & HA | L 0-2 | 0-0 | 9 | | 6257 |
| 40 | 6 | H | Luton T | W 4-3 | 1-2 | — | Sweeney [14], Boyd 2 (1 pen) [53, 90 (p)], Robertson [55] | 4434 |
| 41 | 10 | H | Bournemouth | W 2-1 | 1-1 | 6 | Boyd 2 [38, 69] | 5544 |
| 42 | 12 | A | Wrexham | W 2-1 | 1-0 | 6 | Clarke [41], Danns [63] | 3786 |
| 43 | 17 | H | Notts Co | W 4-0 | 1-0 | 6 | Humphreys [42], Boyd 2 [55, 56], Robertson [69] | 5629 |
| 44 | 24 | A | Rushden & D | W 2-0 | 0-0 | 5 | Williams E [56], Boyd [79] | 4568 |
| 45 | May 1 | H | Plymouth Arg | L 1-3 | 1-2 | 6 | Boyd [11] | 7437 |
| 46 | 8 | A | Swindon T | D 1-1 | 0-1 | 6 | Boyd [71] | 11,627 |

**Final League Position: 6**

### GOALSCORERS

*League (76):* Williams E 13, Boyd 12 (1 pen), Robinson P 7 (2 pens), Tinkler 6 (1 pen), Clarke 5, Gabbiadini 5 (1 pen), Strachan 5 (2 pens), Robertson 4, Humphreys 3, Nelson 3, Porter 3, Wilkinson 2, Barron 1, Danns 1, Istead 1, Robson 1, Shuker 1, Sweeney 1, own goals 2.
*Carling Cup (3):* Robinson P 2 (2 pens), Istead 1.
*FA Cup (5):* Gabbiadini 2, Brackstone 1, Humphreys 1, Porter 1.
*LDV Vans Trophy (3):* Clarke 2, Williams E 1.
*Play-Offs (2):* Porter 1, Sweeney 1.

| Williams A 1 | Arnison P 2 + 2 | Robson M 17 + 6 | Nelson M 38 + 2 | Westwood C 45 | Jordan A 4 + 1 | Clarke D 23 + 10 | Humphreys R 46 | Williams E 39 + 2 | Robinson P 19 + 12 | Strachan G 34 + 2 | Istead S 1 + 30 | Henderson K 1 + 2 | Provett J 45 | Barron M 32 | Tinkler M 43 + 1 | Gabbiadini M 9 + 6 | Foley D — + 1 | Boyd A 10 + 8 | Easter J — + 3 | McCann R — + 4 | Robinson M 4 | Brackstone J 5 + 1 | Richardson M 3 | Sweeney A 8 + 3 | Craddock D 9 + 1 | Wilkinson J 2 + 2 | Byrne D 2 | Porter J 18 + 9 | Shuker C 14 | Robertson H 18 | Walker S 5 + 1 | Carson S 1 + 2 | Danns N 8 + 1 | *Match No.* |
|---|---|---|---|---|---|---|---|---|---|---|---|---|---|---|---|---|---|---|---|---|---|---|---|---|---|---|---|---|---|---|---|---|---|---|
| 1 | 2 | 3 | 4 | 5 | 6 | 7 | 8 | $9^{1}$ | $10^{2}$ | 11 | 12 | 13 | | | | | | | | | | | | | | | | | | | | | | 1 |
| | | $3^{2}$ | 4 | 5 | 6 | $7^{1}$ | 8 | $9^{3}$ | 10 | 11 | 12 | | 1 | 2 | 13 | 14 | | | | | | | | | | | | | | | | | | 2 |
| | | 12 | 4 | 5 | 6 | $7^{3}$ | 3 | | 10 | 11 | 14 | $9^{2}$ | 1 | 2 | $8^{1}$ | 13 | | | | | | | | | | | | | | | | | | 3 |
| | | 3 | 4 | 5 | 12 | 7 | 8 | | $9^{3}$ | 11 | 13 | | 1 | $2^{1}$ | $6^{2}$ | 10 | 14 | | | | | | | | | | | | | | | | | 4 |
| | | 3 | 4 | 5 | | 7 | 8 | | $9^{3}$ | 11 | 12 | 13 | 1 | 2 | $6^{1}$ | $10^{2}$ | | 14 | | | | | | | | | | | | | | | | 5 |
| | $2^{2}$ | 3 | 4 | 5 | | | 8 | 12 | $9^{3}$ | 11 | 13 | | 1 | 6 | 7 | $10^{1}$ | | 14 | | | | | | | | | | | | | | | | 6 |
| | | 3 | 4 | 5 | | 12 | 7 | 9 | $8^{2}$ | $11^{1}$ | | | 1 | 2 | 6 | $10^{3}$ | | | 13 | 14 | | | | | | | | | | | | | | 7 |
| | | 12 | 4 | 5 | $3^{2}$ | | 7 | 9 | $8^{1}$ | 11 | 14 | | 1 | 2 | 6 | $10^{3}$ | | | | 13 | | | | | | | | | | | | | | 8 |
| | | 3 | 4 | 5 | | | 7 | 9 | $8^{1}$ | 11 | 12 | | 1 | $2^{2}$ | 6 | 10 | | | | 13 | | | | | | | | | | | | | | 9 |
| | | | 4 | 5 | | $7^{1}$ | 6 | 9 | $8^{2}$ | 11 | 12 | | 1 | 2 | 3 | 10 | | | 13 | | | | | | | | | | | | | | | 10 |
| | | | 4 | 5 | | 7 | 8 | 9 | $10^{2}$ | $11^{3}$ | 12 | | 1 | 2 | $6^{1}$ | | | 13 | | 14 | 3 | | | | | | | | | | | | | 11 |
| | | | 4 | 5 | | 7 | 8 | 9 | $10^{1}$ | 11 | | | 1 | 2 | 6 | 12 | | 13 | | | $3^{2}$ | | | | | | | | | | | | | 12 |
| | 12 | | 4 | | | 7 | 8 | 9 | $2^{2}$ | 11 | | | 1 | 5 | 6 | 10 | | 13 | | | $3^{1}$ | | | | | | | | | | | | | 13 |
| | | | 4 | 5 | | $7^{2}$ | 8 | | $9^{1}$ | 11 | | | 1 | 2 | 6 | 10 | | 12 | 13 | | $3^{3}$ | 14 | | | | | | | | | | | | 14 |
| | 12 | | 4 | 5 | | $7^{1}$ | 8 | $9^{2}$ | 13 | 11 | | | 1 | 2 | 6 | | | 14 | | | | 3 | $10^{3}$ | | | | | | | | | | | 15 |
| | | | 4 | 5 | | $7^{1}$ | 8 | 9 | 12 | 11 | | | 1 | 2 | $6^{2}$ | 13 | | | | | | 3 | $10^{3}$ | 14 | | | | | | | | | | 16 |
| | | | 4 | 5 | | 7 | 8 | 9 | 12 | 11 | | | 1 | 2 | 6 | 13 | | | | | | $3^{1}$ | $10^{2}$ | | | | | | | | | | | 17 |
| | | 3 | 4 | 2 | | 7 | 8 | 9 | | 11 | | | 1 | | $6^{1}$ | | | | | | | | | 12 | 5 | 10 | | | | | | | | 18 |
| | | 3 | 4 | 2 | | $7^{3}$ | 8 | 9 | 12 | $11^{1}$ | | | 1 | | 6 | 13 | | | | | | | | 14 | 5 | $10^{2}$ | | | | | | | | 19 |
| | | 3 | 4 | 5 | | | 8 | 9 | | 11 | | | 1 | 2 | 6 | | | | | | | | | | | 12 | $7^{1}$ | 10 | | | | | | 20 |
| | | 3 | 4 | 5 | | | 8 | 9 | 12 | 11 | | | 1 | 2 | | | | | | | | | | | | | $6^{1}$ | 10 | 7 | | | | | 21 |
| | | $3^{1}$ | 4 | 5 | | | 8 | 9 | 12 | 11 | | | 1 | 2 | 6 | | | | | | | | | | | 13 | | $10^{2}$ | 7 | | | | | 22 |
| | | | 4 | 5 | | 12 | 8 | 9 | 13 | 11 | 14 | | 1 | 2 | $6^{1}$ | | | | | | | $3^{3}$ | | | | | | $10^{2}$ | 7 | | | | | 23 |
| | | 3 | 4 | 5 | | | 8 | 9 | $10^{1}$ | 11 | 13 | | 1 | 2 | 6 | | | | | | | | | | | | | 12 | $7^{2}$ | | | | | 24 |
| | | 12 | 4 | 5 | | | 8 | $9^{2}$ | $13^{3}$ | 11 | 14 | | 1 | 2 | 6 | | | | | | | $3^{1}$ | | | | | | 10 | 7 | | | | | 25 |
| | | 3 | 4 | 5 | | 13 | 8 | 9 | | $11^{2}$ | 12 | | 1 | 2 | 6 | | | | | | | | | | | | | $10^{1}$ | 7 | | | | | 26 |
| | | $3^{2}$ | 4 | 5 | | 12 | 8 | 9 | 13 | 11 | 14 | | 1 | 2 | $6^{1}$ | | | | | | | | | | | | | $10^{3}$ | 7 | | | | | 27 |
| | | 3 | 4 | 5 | | 12 | 8 | $9^{3}$ | $10^{2}$ | 11 | 14 | | 1 | 2 | 6 | | | | | | | | | | | | | 13 | $7^{1}$ | | | | | 28 |
| | | 12 | 4 | 2 | | | 8 | 9 | $10^{3}$ | 11 | 13 | | 1 | | 6 | | | | | | | | | | | | | 14 | $7^{2}$ | $3^{1}$ | 5 | | | 29 |
| | | | 4 | 5 | | 12 | 8 | 9 | $10^{2}$ | $11^{1}$ | | | 1 | $2^{3}$ | 6 | | | | | | | | | | | | | 13 | 7 | 3 | 14 | | | 30 |
| | | | 4 | 5 | | 11 | 8 | $9^{2}$ | $10^{1}$ | | | | 1 | 2 | 6 | | | | | | | | | | | | | 12 | 7 | 3 | | 13 | | 31 |
| | | 13 | | 5 | | $11^{2}$ | 8 | 9 | | | 12 | | 1 | 2 | 6 | | | | | | | | | | 14 | | | $10^{3}$ | $7^{1}$ | 3 | 4 | | | 32 |
| | | 12 | 4 | 5 | | | 8 | $9^{2}$ | | $11^{1}$ | 13 | | 1 | 2 | 6 | | | | | | | | | | | | | 10 | 7 | 3 | | | | 33 |
| | | $11^{3}$ | 4 | 5 | | 12 | 8 | $9^{1}$ | | | 13 | | 1 | 2 | 6 | | | | | | | | | | | | | 10 | $7^{2}$ | 3 | | 14 | | 34 |
| | | | 4 | 5 | | | 11 | 9 | 12 | | 13 | | 1 | $2^{1}$ | 8 | | | | | | | | | | | | | 10 | | 3 | | $7^{2}$ | 6 | 35 |
| | | | 2 | 5 | | 13 | $11^{2}$ | 9 | | | 8 | | 1 | | $6^{1}$ | | | 12 | | | | | | | | | | 10 | | 3 | 4 | | 7 | 36 |
| | | | 2 | 5 | | | 11 | 9 | | | 12 | | 1 | | 6 | | | 7 | | | | | | | | | | $10^{1}$ | | 3 | 8 | | 4 | 37 |
| | | | $4^{1}$ | 2 | | 13 | 11 | 9 | | 12 | 14 | | 1 | | 6 | | | 8 | | | | | | | | | | 10 | | 3 | $5^{2}$ | | $7^{3}$ | 38 |
| | | | | 5 | | $7^{1}$ | 8 | $9^{2}$ | | 11 | 12 | | 1 | | 2 | | | 6 | | | | | | 10 | 4 | | | 13 | | 3 | | | | 39 |
| | | | | 5 | | $7^{2}$ | 8 | 12 | | 11 | 13 | | 1 | | 6 | | | 10 | | | | | | 4 | 2 | | | $9^{1}$ | | 3 | | | | 40 |
| | | | | 5 | | $7^{1}$ | 8 | | 13 | $11^{3}$ | 12 | | 1 | | 6 | | | 10 | | | | | | 4 | 2 | | | $9^{2}$ | | 3 | | | 14 | 41 |
| | | | | 5 | | 7 | 11 | $9^{2}$ | | | 12 | | 1 | | 6 | | | $10^{1}$ | | | | | | 4 | 2 | | | 13 | | 3 | | | 8 | 42 |
| | | | | 5 | | $7^{1}$ | 11 | 9 | | 13 | 12 | | 1 | | 6 | | | $10^{3}$ | | | | | | 4 | 2 | | | 14 | | 3 | | | $8^{2}$ | 43 |
| | | | 12 | 5 | | $7^{3}$ | $11^{2}$ | 9 | | | 13 | | 1 | | 6 | | | 10 | | | | | | 4 | $2^{1}$ | | | 14 | | 3 | | | 8 | 44 |
| | | | 12 | $5^{1}$ | | 13 | 11 | $9^{3}$ | | | 14 | | 1 | | 6 | | | 8 | | | | | | $4^{2}$ | 2 | | | 10 | | 3 | | | 7 | 45 |
| | | | 4 | 5 | | | 11 | 9 | 12 | | | | 1 | 2 | 6 | | | 8 | | | | | | 7 | | | | $10^{1}$ | | 3 | | | | 46 |

**Carling Cup**

| | | | |
|---|---|---|---|
| First Round | Sheffield W | (a) | 2-2 |
| Second Round | WBA | (h) | 1-2 |

**LDV Vans Trophy**

| | | | |
|---|---|---|---|
| First Round | Oldham Ath | (a) | 3-3 |

**FA Cup**

| | | | |
|---|---|---|---|
| First Round | Whitby T | (h) | 4-0 |
| Second Round | Burton A | (a) | 1-0 |
| Third Round | Sunderland | (a) | 0-1 |

**Play-Offs**

| | | | |
|---|---|---|---|
| Semi-Final | Bristol C | (h) | 1-1 |
| | | (a) | 1-2 |

# HUDDERSFIELD TOWN FL Championship 1

## FOUNDATION

A meeting, attended largely by members of the Huddersfield & District FA, was held at the Imperial Hotel in 1906 to discuss the feasibility of establishing a football club in this rugby stronghold. However, it was not until a man with both the enthusiasm and the money to back the scheme came on the scene, that real progress was made. This benefactor was Mr Hilton Crowther and it was at a meeting at the Albert Hotel in 1908, that the club formally came into existence with a capital of £2,000 and joined the North-Eastern League.

***The Alfred McAlpine Stadium, Stadium Way, Huddersfield HD1 6PX.***

***Telephone:*** (01484) 484 100.

***Fax:*** (01484) 484 101.

***Ticket Office:*** (01484) 484 123.

***Website:*** www.htafc.com

***Email:*** info@htafc.com

***Ground Capacity:*** 25,000.

***Record Attendance:*** 67,037 v Arsenal, FA Cup 6th rd, 27 February 1932 (at Leeds Road); 23,678 v Liverpool, FA Cup 3rd rd, 12 December 1999 (at Alfred McAlpine Stadium).

***Pitch Measurements:*** 115yd × 76yd.

***Chairman:*** Ken Davy.

***Chief Executive:*** Andrew Watson.

***Secretary:*** Ann Hough.

***Manager:*** Peter Jackson.

***Assistant Manager:*** Terry Yorath.

***Physio:*** Lee Martin.

***Colours:*** Blue and white stripes. ***Change Colours:*** Red and black stripes.

***Year Formed:*** 1908.

***Turned Professional:*** 1908. ***Ltd Co.:*** 1908.

***Club Nickname:*** 'The Terriers'.

***Previous Ground:*** 1908, Leeds Road; 1994, The Alfred McAlpine Stadium.

***First Football League Game:*** 3 September 1910, Division 2, v Bradford PA (a) W 1–0 – Mutch; Taylor, Morris; Beaton, Hall, Bartlett; Blackburn, Wood, Hamilton (1), McCubbin, Jee.

***Record League Victory:*** 10–1 v Blackpool, Division 1, 13 December 1930 – Turner; Goodall, Spencer; Redfern, Wilson, Campbell; Bob Kelly (1), McLean (4), Robson (3), Davies (1), Smailes (1).

***Record Cup Victory:*** 7–0 v Lincoln U, FA Cup 1st rd, 16 November 1991 – Clarke; Trevitt, Charlton, Donovan (2), Mitchell, Doherty, O'Regan (1), Stapleton (1) (Wright), Roberts (2), Onuora (1), Barnett (Ireland).

## HONOURS

*Football League:* Division 1 – Champions 1923–24, 1924–25, 1925–26; Runners-up 1926–27, 1927–28, 1933–34; Division 2 – Champions 1969–70; Runners-up 1919–20, 1952–53; Promoted from Division 2 1994–95 (play-offs); Promoted from Division 3 2003–04 (play-offs); Division 4 – Champions 1979–80.

*FA Cup:* Winners 1922; Runners-up 1920, 1928, 1930, 1938.

*Football League Cup:* Semi-final 1968.

*Autoglass Trophy:* Runners-up 1994.

## SKY SPORTS FACT FILE

In 1924–25, the middle season of the trio of Huddersfield Town First Division championships, the team conceded only 28 goals in what was the season before the offside law was changed. No opponent scored more than two goals against them.

*N.B.* 11-0 v Heckmondwike (a), FA Cup pr rd, 18 September 1909 – Doggart; Roberts, Ewing; Hooton, Stevenson, Randall; Kenworthy (2), McCreadie (1), Foster (4), Stacey (4), Jee.

***Record Defeat:*** 1–10 v Manchester C, Division 2, 7 November 1987.

***Most League Points (2 for a win):*** 66, Division 4, 1979–80.

***Most League Points (3 for a win):*** 82, Division 3, 1982–83.

***Most League Goals:*** 101, Division 4, 1979–80.

***Highest League Scorer in Season:*** Sam Taylor, 35, Division 2, 1919–20; George Brown, 35, Division 1, 1925–26.

***Most League Goals in Total Aggregate:*** George Brown, 142, 1921–29; Jimmy Glazzard, 142, 1946–56.

***Most League Goals in One Match:*** 5, Dave Mangnall v Derby Co, Division 1, 21 November 1931; 5, Alf Lythgoe v Blackburn R, Division 1, 13 April 1935.

***Most Capped Player:*** Jimmy Nicholson, 31 (41), Northern Ireland.

***Most League Appearances:*** Billy Smith, 520, 1914–34.

***Youngest League Player:*** Denis Law, 16 years 303 days v Notts Co, 24 December 1956.

***Record Transfer Fee Received:*** £2,700,000 from Sheffield W for Andy Booth, July 1996.

***Record Transfer Fee Paid:*** £1,200,000 to Bristol R for Marcus Stewart, July 1996.

***Football League Record:*** 1910 Elected to Division 2; 1920–52 Division 1; 1952–53 Division 2; 1953–56 Division 1; 1956–70 Division 2; 1970–72 Division 1; 1972–73 Division 2; 1973–75 Division 3; 1975–80 Division 4; 1980–83 Division 3; 1983–88 Division 2; 1988–92 Division 3; 1992–95 Division 2; 1995–2001 Division 1; 2001–03 Division 2; 2003–04 Division 3; 2004– FL1.

## MANAGERS

Fred Walker 1908–10
Richard Pudan 1910–12
Arthur Fairclough 1912–19
Ambrose Langley 1919–21
Herbert Chapman 1921–25
Cecil Potter 1925–26
Jack Chaplin 1926–29
Clem Stephenson 1929–42
David Steele 1943–47
George Stephenson 1947–52
Andy Beattie 1952–56
Bill Shankly 1956–59
Eddie Boot 1960–64
Tom Johnston 1964–68
Ian Greaves 1968–74
Bobby Collins 1974
Tom Johnston 1975–78
*(had been General Manager since 1975)*
Mike Buxton 1978–86
Steve Smith 1986–87
Malcolm Macdonald 1987–88
Eoin Hand 1988–92
Ian Ross 1992–93
Neil Warnock 1993–95
Brian Horton 1995–97
Peter Jackson 1997–99
Steve Bruce 1999–2000
Lou Macari 2000–02
Mick Wadsworth 2002–03
Peter Jackson June 2003–

## LATEST SEQUENCES

***Longest Sequence of League Wins:*** 11, 5.4.1920 – 4.9.1920.

***Longest Sequence of League Defeats:*** 7, 8.10.1955 – 19.11.1955.

***Longest Sequence of League Draws:*** 6, 3.3.1987 – 3.4.1987.

***Longest Sequence of Unbeaten League Matches:*** 27, 24.1.1925 – 17.10.1925.

***Longest Sequence Without a League Win:*** 22, 4.12.1971 – 29.4.1972.

***Successive Scoring Runs:*** 21 from 5.12.1931.

***Successive Non-scoring Runs:*** 7 from 22.1.1972.

## TEN YEAR LEAGUE RECORD

| | | P | W | D | L | F | A | Pts | Pos |
|---|---|---|---|---|---|---|---|---|---|
| 1994-95 | Div 2 | 46 | 22 | 15 | 9 | 79 | 49 | 81 | 5 |
| 1995-96 | Div 1 | 46 | 17 | 12 | 17 | 61 | 58 | 63 | 8 |
| 1996-97 | Div 1 | 46 | 13 | 15 | 18 | 48 | 61 | 54 | 20 |
| 1997-98 | Div 1 | 46 | 14 | 11 | 21 | 50 | 72 | 53 | 16 |
| 1998-99 | Div 1 | 46 | 15 | 16 | 15 | 62 | 71 | 61 | 10 |
| 1999-2000 | Div 1 | 46 | 21 | 11 | 14 | 62 | 49 | 74 | 8 |
| 2000-01 | Div 1 | 46 | 11 | 15 | 20 | 48 | 57 | 48 | 22 |
| 2001-02 | Div 2 | 46 | 21 | 15 | 10 | 65 | 47 | 78 | 6 |
| 2002-03 | Div 2 | 46 | 11 | 12 | 23 | 39 | 61 | 45 | 22 |
| 2003-04 | Div 3 | 46 | 23 | 12 | 11 | 68 | 52 | 81 | 4 |

## DID YOU KNOW ?

Having been rejected as a teenager by Huddersfield Town, Dave Mangnall returned to the club ten years later and despite limited senior chances scored 61 goals in only 79 League games, including his best season 1931–32 with 33 in 34 matches.

## HUDDERSFIELD TOWN 2003–04 LEAGUE RECORD

| Match No. | Date | Venue | Opponents | Result | | H/T Score | Lg. Pos. | Goalscorers | Attendance |
|---|---|---|---|---|---|---|---|---|---|
| 1 | Aug 9 | H | Cambridge U | D | 2-2 | 1-1 | — | Stead 2 [30, 59] | 10,319 |
| 2 | 16 | A | Boston U | D | 2-2 | 0-1 | 13 | Stead [55], Hughes [60] | 3452 |
| 3 | 23 | H | York C | L | 0-1 | 0-1 | 17 | | 9850 |
| 4 | 25 | A | Doncaster R | D | 1-1 | 1-0 | 19 | Booth [7] | 7367 |
| 5 | 30 | H | Bristol R | W | 2-1 | 1-0 | 16 | Edwards [32], Stead [78] | 8486 |
| 6 | Sept 6 | A | Bury | L | 1-2 | 0-1 | 18 | Scott [72] | 4591 |
| 7 | 13 | H | Northampton T | W | 3-0 | 3-0 | 12 | Stead 2 [17, 35], Carss (pen) [33] | 8285 |
| 8 | 16 | A | Rochdale | D | 1-1 | 1-1 | — | Worthington [23] | 4626 |
| 9 | 20 | A | Swansea C | L | 0-2 | 0-1 | 17 | | 8048 |
| 10 | 27 | H | Leyton Orient | W | 3-0 | 1-0 | 13 | Yates [31], Scott [62], Booth [83] | 8942 |
| 11 | 30 | H | Kidderminster H | W | 1-0 | 1-0 | — | Stead [12] | 8275 |
| 12 | Oct 4 | A | Southend U | W | 2-1 | 1-1 | 9 | Booth [45], Schofield [89] | 4205 |
| 13 | 11 | H | Torquay U | W | 1-0 | 0-0 | 6 | Carss [80] | 9117 |
| 14 | 18 | A | Lincoln C | L | 1-3 | 1-0 | 7 | Booth [5] | 5718 |
| 15 | 21 | A | Yeovil T | L | 1-2 | 1-1 | — | Stead [42] | 5274 |
| 16 | 25 | H | Carlisle U | W | 2-1 | 2-0 | 7 | Booth [38], Stead [45] | 9050 |
| 17 | Nov 1 | A | Scunthorpe U | L | 2-6 | 0-2 | 9 | Booth 2 [46, 72] | 4715 |
| 18 | 15 | H | Hull C | W | 3-1 | 2-1 | 8 | Stead [32], Booth [41], Schofield [80] | 13,893 |
| 19 | 22 | A | Mansfield T | D | 3-3 | 2-1 | 10 | Schofield [15], Stead 2 [31, 64] | 5828 |
| 20 | 29 | H | Cheltenham T | D | 0-0 | 0-0 | 10 | | 8442 |
| 21 | Dec 13 | A | Macclesfield T | L | 0-4 | 0-1 | 10 | | 3059 |
| 22 | 20 | H | Oxford U | D | 1-1 | 1-0 | 11 | Stead [38] | 9368 |
| 23 | 26 | A | Darlington | W | 1-0 | 1-0 | 11 | Booth [28] | 6205 |
| 24 | 28 | H | Bury | W | 1-0 | 1-0 | 9 | Swailes (og) [31] | 10,217 |
| 25 | Jan 3 | H | Doncaster R | W | 3-1 | 1-0 | 7 | Stead 2 [42, 69], Worthington [82] | 13,044 |
| 26 | 10 | A | Cambridge U | W | 2-1 | 1-0 | 6 | Stead (pen) [44], Worthington [85] | 3667 |
| 27 | 17 | H | Boston U | W | 2-0 | 0-0 | 6 | Sodje [71], Lloyd [86] | 9603 |
| 28 | 25 | A | York C | W | 2-0 | 0-0 | 5 | Schofield [88], Mirfin [89] | 6969 |
| 29 | Feb 7 | H | Darlington | L | 0-2 | 0-1 | 7 | | 11,014 |
| 30 | 14 | A | Torquay U | W | 1-0 | 0-0 | 6 | Clarke N [71] | 3821 |
| 31 | 17 | A | Bristol R | D | 1-1 | 0-0 | — | Abbott [86] | 6262 |
| 32 | 21 | H | Lincoln C | W | 2-1 | 0-1 | 5 | Sodje [48], Abbott [67] | 11,553 |
| 33 | Mar 2 | H | Yeovil T | W | 3-1 | 1-0 | — | Abbott [40], Schofield 2 [46, 60] | 9395 |
| 34 | 6 | A | Oxford U | W | 1-0 | 1-0 | 4 | Sodje [41] | 7278 |
| 35 | 9 | A | Carlisle U | L | 0-1 | 0-0 | — | | 4782 |
| 36 | 13 | H | Macclesfield T | W | 4-0 | 1-0 | 3 | Booth [21], Abbott [47], Sodje [69], McAliskey [90] | 9729 |
| 37 | 16 | H | Rochdale | D | 1-1 | 0-1 | — | Lloyd [49] | 10,884 |
| 38 | 27 | H | Swansea C | W | 3-0 | 0-0 | 3 | Schofield 2 [51, 85], Lloyd [89] | 11,250 |
| 39 | Apr 3 | A | Leyton Orient | D | 1-1 | 1-1 | 3 | Booth [9] | 4137 |
| 40 | 10 | H | Southend U | W | 1-0 | 1-0 | 3 | Abbott [30] | 10,680 |
| 41 | 12 | A | Kidderminster H | L | 1-2 | 0-1 | 3 | Sall (og) [84] | 4051 |
| 42 | 17 | H | Scunthorpe U | W | 3-2 | 1-2 | 3 | Mirfin [5], McAliskey 2 [87, 90] | 12,108 |
| 43 | 20 | A | Northampton T | W | 1-0 | 0-0 | — | Booth [53] | 6873 |
| 44 | 24 | A | Hull C | D | 0-0 | 0-0 | 3 | | 23,495 |
| 45 | May 1 | H | Mansfield T | L | 1-3 | 1-2 | 3 | McAliskey [14] | 18,633 |
| 46 | 8 | A | Cheltenham T | D | 1-1 | 1-0 | 4 | Booth [16] | 5814 |

**Final League Position: 4**

## GOALSCORERS

*League (68):* Stead 16 (1 pen), Booth 13, Schofield 8, Abbott 5, McAliskey 4, Sodje 4, Lloyd 3, Worthington 3, Carss 2 (1 pen), Mirfin 2, Scott 2, Clarke N 1, Edwards 1, Hughes 1, Yates 1, own goals 2.
*Carling Cup (6):* Stead 2, Booth 1, Carss 1, Holdsworth 1, Thorrington 1.
*FA Cup (0).*
*LDV Vans Trophy (0).*
*Play-Offs (4):* Edwards 1, Mirfin 1, Onuora 1, Schofield 1 (pen).

| Gray I 17 | Booty M 3 + 1 | Edwards R 11 + 6 | Yates S 35 | Hughes I 12 + 1 | Fowler L 27 + 2 | Schofield D 38 + 2 | Thompson T 1 + 1 | Newby J 10 + 4 | Stead J 26 | Carss T 35 + 1 | Worthington J 36 + 3 | Thorrington J 3 + 2 | Sodje E 37 + 2 | Booth A 36 + 1 | Scott P 16 + 3 | Holdsworth A 31 + 5 | Brown N 13 + 8 | Mirfin D 15 + 6 | Ahmed A — + 1 | Lloyd A 30 + 1 | Mattis D 2 + 3 | Clarke N 25 + 1 | Holland C — + 3 | Senior P 16 | Onibuje F — + 2 | Abbott P 12 + 1 | Rachubka P 13 | McAliskey J 5 + 3 | Onuora I — + 3 | Harkins G 1 + 2 | Match No. |
|---|---|---|---|---|---|---|---|---|---|---|---|---|---|---|---|---|---|---|---|---|---|---|---|---|---|---|---|---|---|---|---|
| 1 | 2 | 3 | 4 | 5 | $6^{1}$ | 7 | $8^{2}$ | 9 | 10 | 11 | 12 | 13 | | | | | | | | | | | | | | | | | | | 1 |
| 1 | 12 | $3^{1}$ | 4 | 5 | 6 | $7^{2}$ | | 9 | 10 | 11 | | 8 | 2 | 13 | | | | | | | | | | | | | | | | | 2 |
| 1 | 2 | | 4 | 5 | 6 | 12 | | 8 | 10 | $11^{2}$ | 13 | $7^{1}$ | 3 | 9 | | | | | | | | | | | | | | | | | 3 |
| 1 | 2 | | $4^{2}$ | 5 | 6 | 12■ | | $8^{1}$ | 10 | 11 | | 7 | 3 | 9 | 13 | | | | | | | | | | | | | | | | 4 |
| 1 | | 3 | | 5 | 6 | 7 | | $8^{2}$ | 10 | 11 | | | 2 | $9^{1}$ | 4 | 13 | 12 | | | | | | | | | | | | | | 5 |
| 1 | | 3 | | 5 | | 8 | | 9 | 10 | 11 | 7 | | 2■ | | 6 | $4^{1}$ | | 12 | | | | | | | | | | | | | 6 |
| 1 | | 3 | | 5 | 6 | | 12 | | 10 | 11 | 7 | | 2 | $9^{2}$ | 4 | $8^{1}$ | 13 | | | | | | | | | | | | | | 7 |
| 1 | | 3 | | 5 | 6 | | | $8^{1}$ | 10 | 11 | 7 | | 2 | 9 | 4 | | | | 12 | | | | | | | | | | | | 8 |
| 1 | | $3^{2}$ | | 5■ | 2 | | | $10^{1}$ | 8 | 11 | 7 | | | 9 | 4■ | 13 | 12 | 6 | | | | | | | | | | | | | 9 |
| 1 | | | $5^{1}$ | | 8 | 11 | | 12 | 10 | | 7 | | | $9^{3}$ | 4 | $3^{2}$ | | 6 | | 2 | 13 | 14 | | | | | | | | | 10 |
| 1 | | | 5 | | 8 | 3 | | | 10 | 11 | 7 | | 12 | 9 | 2 | $4^{1}$ | | 6 | | | | | | | | | | | | | 11 |
| 1 | | | 5 | | $4^{1}$ | 2 | | | 10 | $11^{2}$ | 8 | | 3 | 9 | | | | 6 | | 13 | 12 | 7 | | | | | | | | | 12 |
| 1 | | | 5 | | 8 | 2 | | | 10 | 11 | 7 | | 3 | 9 | | 4 | | | | | | 6 | | | | | | | | | 13 |
| 1 | | | 5 | | 8 | 3 | | | | 11 | 7 | | 2 | 9 | 10 | $4^{1}$ | 12 | | | | | 6 | | | | | | | | | 14 |
| 1 | | | $5^{1}$ | | $8^{2}$ | 3 | | | 10 | 11 | 7 | | 2 | 9 | | 4 | 12 | | | | | 6 | 13 | | | | | | | | 15 |
| 1 | | | 5■ | | 8 | 3 | | | 10 | 11 | 7 | | 2 | 9 | | 4 | | | | | | 6 | | | | | | | | | 16 |
| 1 | | | $5^{1}$ | | 8■ | 3 | | | $10^{2}$ | 11 | | | 2 | 9 | | 4 | 13 | | | | 7 | 6 | 12 | | | | | | | | 17 |
| | | | | 5 | | 8 | | | 10 | 11 | 7 | 12 | | $9^{1}$ | 2 | | 4 | | | 3 | | 6 | | 1 | | | | | | | 18 |
| | | | | 5 | 8 | 9 | | | 10 | 11 | 7 | | | | 2 | | 4 | | | 3 | | 6 | | 1 | | | | | | | 19 |
| | | 13 | | $5^{1}$ | 8 | 7 | | | 10 | $11^{2}$ | | | 12 | 9 | $2^{3}$ | | 4 | | | 3 | | 6 | | 1 | 14 | | | | | | 20 |
| | | 11 | | | $8^{1}$ | 7 | | | 10 | | | | 2 | 9 | 4 | 12 | 6 | | | 3 | | 5■ | | 1 | | | | | | | 21 |
| | | | 5 | | 8■ | $7^{1}$ | | | 10 | | | | 6 | $9^{2}$ | 11 | | 2 | | | 3 | 12 | 4 | | 1 | 13 | | | | | | 22 |
| | | 14 | 5 | | $8^{2}$ | $7^{1}$ | | | 10 | | 12 | | 2 | 9 | $11^{3}$ | 13 | 4 | | | 3 | | 6 | | 1 | | | | | | | 23 |
| | | 11 | 5 | | 8 | | | | 10 | | 7 | | 2 | 9 | | 4 | 6 | | | 3 | | | | 1 | | | | | | | 24 |
| | | 11 | 5 | 12 | | 8 | | | 10 | | 7 | | 2 | | | 4 | 9 | | | $3^{1}$ | | 6 | | 1 | | | | | | | 25 |
| | | $11^{1}$ | 5 | | | 8 | | | 10 | | 7 | | 2 | | | 4 | 9 | | | 3 | | 6 | 12 | 1 | | | | | | | 26 |
| | | | 5 | | 8 | 11 | | 12 | $10^{1}$ | | 7 | | 2 | | | 4 | 9 | | | 3 | | 6 | | 1 | | | | | | | 27 |
| | | | 5 | | 8 | 11 | | $10^{1}$ | | | 7 | | 2 | | | 4 | 9 | 12 | | 3 | | 6 | | 1 | | | | | | | 28 |
| | | | 5 | | $8^{1}$ | 11 | | $10^{2}$ | | 12 | 7 | | 2 | | | 4 | 9 | 13 | | 3 | | 6 | | 1 | | | | | | | 29 |
| | | | 5 | | $8^{2}$ | 10 | | | | 11■ | 7 | | 2 | $9^{1}$ | | 4 | 12 | 13 | | 3 | | 6 | | 1 | | | | | | | 30 |
| | | | 5 | | $8^{2}$ | 10 | | 12 | | 11 | 7 | | $2^{1}$ | 9 | | 4 | | | | 3 | | 6 | | 1 | | 13 | | | | | 31 |
| | | | 5 | | | 8 | | | | 11 | 7 | | 2 | 9 | | 12 | $4^{1}$ | 13 | | $3^{2}$ | | 6 | | 1 | | 10 | | | | | 32 |
| | | 13 | 5 | | 12 | 11 | | | | | $7^{1}$ | | 2 | 9 | | 4 | | | | 3 | $8^{2}$ | 6 | | 1 | | 10 | | | | | 33 |
| | | 12 | 5 | | | 8 | | | | 11 | 7 | | 2 | 9 | | 4 | | | | 3 | | 6 | | | | $10^{1}$ | 1 | | | | 34 |
| | | | $5^{2}$ | | | $8^{1}$ | | 12 | | 11 | 7 | | 2 | 9 | | 4 | | 13 | | 3 | | 6 | | | | 10 | 1 | | | | 35 |
| | | 12 | | | | 8 | | | | 11 | $7^{1}$ | | 2 | $9^{2}$ | | 4 | | 5 | | 3 | | 6 | | | | 10 | 1 | 13 | | | 36 |
| | | | | | | $8^{2}$ | | | | 11 | 7 | | 2 | 9 | 12 | 4 | | 5 | | 3 | | $6^{1}$ | | | | 10 | 1 | 13 | | | 37 |
| | | | 5 | | | 8 | | | | 11 | 7 | | 2 | 9 | | 4 | | 6 | | 3 | | | | | | $10^{1}$ | 1 | | 12 | | 38 |
| | | | 5 | | | $8^{1}$ | | | | 11 | 7 | | 2 | 9■ | | 4 | | 6 | | 3 | | | | | | 10■ | 1 | | | 12 | 39 |
| | | | 5 | | | 8 | | | | 11 | 7 | | 2 | 9 | | 4 | | 6 | | 3 | | | | | | 10 | 1 | | | | 40 |
| | | | $5^{2}$ | | | 8 | | | | $11^{1}$ | 7 | | 2 | 9 | | 4 | | 6 | | 3 | | | | | | 10 | 1 | 12 | | 13 | 41 |
| | | 12 | 5 | | | 10■ | | | | 11 | $7^{2}$ | | 2■ | | 13 | 4 | | 6 | | 3 | | | | | | | 1 | 9 | | $8^{1}$ | 42 |
| | | | 5 | | | 8 | | | | 11 | 7 | | 2 | 9 | | 4 | | 6 | | 3 | | | | | | | 1 | 10 | | | 43 |
| | | | 5 | | | 8 | | | | 11 | 7 | | 2 | 9 | | 4 | | 6 | | 3 | | | | | | | 1 | 10 | | | 44 |
| | | | 5 | | 12 | | | | | 11 | 7 | | | 9 | $2^{1}$ | 4 | | 6 | | $3^{2}$ | | | | | | 8 | 1 | 10 | 13 | | 45 |
| | | | 5 | | | | | | | 11 | 7 | | | 9 | $2^{1}$ | 4 | 12 | 6 | | 3 | | | | | | $8^{2}$ | 1 | 10 | 13 | | 46 |

**Carling Cup**

| | | | |
|---|---|---|---|
| First Round | Derby Co | (h) | 2-1 |
| Second Round | Sunderland | (a) | 4-2 |
| Third Round | Reading | (a) | 0-1 |

**LDV Vans Trophy**

| | | | |
|---|---|---|---|
| Second Round | Carlisle U | (a) | 0-2 |

**FA Cup**

| | | | |
|---|---|---|---|
| First Round | Accrington S | (a) | 0-1 |

**Play-Offs**

| | | | |
|---|---|---|---|
| Semi-Final | Lincoln C | (a) | 2-1 |
| | | (h) | 2-2 |
| Final *(at Millennium Stadium)* | Mansfield T | | 0-0 |

# HULL CITY — FL Championship 1

## FOUNDATION

The enthusiasts who formed Hull City in 1904 were brave men indeed. More than that they were audacious for they immediately put the club on the map in this Rugby League fortress by obtaining a three-year agreement with the Hull Rugby League club to rent their ground! They had obtained quite a number of conversions to the dribbling code, before the Rugby League forbade the use of any of their club grounds by Association Football clubs. By that time, Hull City were well away having entered the FA Cup in their initial season and the Football League, Second Division after only a year.

***KC Stadium, The Circle, Walton Street, Anlaby Road, Hull HU3 6HU.***

***Telephone:*** 0870 837 0003.

***Fax:*** (01482) 304 882.

***Ticket Office:*** 0870 837 0004.

***Website:*** www.hullcityafc.net

***Email:*** info@hulltigers.com

***Ground Capacity:*** 25,400.

***Record Attendance:*** KC Stadium: 23,495 v Huddersfield T, Division 3, 24 April 2004. Boothferry Park: 55,019 v Manchester U, FA Cup 6th rd, 26 February 1949.

***Pitch Measurements:*** 105m × 68m.

***Chairman & Chief Executive:*** Adam Pearson.

***Secretary:*** Phil Hough.

***Manager:*** Peter Taylor.

***Assistant Manager:*** Colin Murphy.

***Physio:*** Simon Maltby.

***Colours:*** Amber and black.

***Change Colours:*** All white.

***Year Formed:*** 1904. ***Turned Professional:*** 1905.

***Ltd Co.:*** 1905.

***Club Nickname:*** 'The Tigers'.

***Previous Grounds:*** 1904, Boulevard Ground (Hull RFC); 1905, Anlaby Road (Hull CC); 1944, Boulevard Ground; 1946, Boothferry Park; 2002, Kingston Communications Stadium.

***First Football League Game:*** 2 September 1905, Division 2, v Barnsley (h) W 4–1 – Spendiff; Langley, Jones; Martin, Robinson, Gordon (2); Rushton, Spence (1), Wilson (1), Howe, Raisbeck.

***Record League Victory:*** 11–1 v Carlisle U, Division 3 (N), 14 January 1939 – Ellis; Woodhead, Dowen; Robinson (1), Blyth, Hardy; Hubbard (2), Richardson (2), Dickinson (2), Davies (2), Cunliffe (2).

## HONOURS

*Football League:* Division 2 best season: 3rd, 1909–10; Division 3 (N) – Champions 1932–33, 1948–49; Division 3 – Champions 1965–66; Runners-up 1958–59, 2003–04; Division 4 – Runners-up 1982–83.

*FA Cup:* Semi-final 1930.

*Football League Cup:* best season: 4th, 1974, 1976, 1978.

*Associate Members' Cup:* Runners-up 1984.

## SKY SPORTS FACT FILE

Hull City suffered when unable to play in the 1945–46 season due to ground problems. But despite having to use 43 different players the following term, they finished midway in the Third Division (North) with gates averaging 19,673.

***Record Cup Victory:*** 8–2 v Stalybridge Celtic (a), FA Cup 1st rd, 26 November 1932 – Maddison; Goldsmith, Woodhead; Gardner, Hill (1), Denby; Forward (1), Duncan, McNaughton (1), Wainscoat (4), Sargeant (1).

***Record Defeat:*** 0–8 v Wolverhampton W, Division 2, 4 November 1911.

***Most League Points (2 for a win):*** 69, Division 3, 1965–66.

***Most League Points (3 for a win):*** 90, Division 4, 1982–83.

***Most League Goals:*** 109, Division 3, 1965–66.

***Highest League Scorer in Season:*** Bill McNaughton, 39, Division 3 (N), 1932–33.

***Most League Goals in Total Aggregate:*** Chris Chilton, 195, 1960–71.

***Most League Goals in One Match:*** 5, Ken McDonald v Bristol C, Division 2, 17 November 1928; 5, Simon 'Slim' Raleigh v Halifax T, Division 3N, 26 December 1930.

***Most Capped Player:*** Theo Whitmore, Jamaica.

***Most League Appearances:*** Andy Davidson, 520, 1952–67.

***Youngest League Player:*** Matthew Edeson, 16 years 63 days v Fulham, 10 October 1992.

***Record Transfer Fee Received:*** £750,000 from Middlesbrough for Andy Payton, November 1991.

***Record Transfer Fee Paid:*** £210,000 to Leicester C for Lawrie Dudfield, July 2001.

***Football League Record:*** 1905 Elected to Division 2; 1930–33 Division 3 (N); 1933–36 Division 2; 1936–49 Division 3 (N); 1949–56 Division 2; 1956–58 Division 3 (N); 1958–59 Division 3; 1959–60 Division 2; 1960–66 Division 3; 1966–78 Division 2; 1978–81 Division 3; 1981–83 Division 4; 1983–85 Division 3; 1985–91 Division 2; 1991–92 Division 3; 1992–96 Division 2; 1996–2004 Division 3; 2004– FL1.

## MANAGERS

James Ramster 1904–05
*(Secretary-Manager)*
Ambrose Langley 1905–13
Harry Chapman 1913–14
Fred Stringer 1914–16
David Menzies 1916–21
Percy Lewis 1921–23
Bill McCracken 1923–31
Haydn Green 1931–34
John Hill 1934–36
David Menzies 1936
Ernest Blackburn 1936–46
Major Frank Buckley 1946–48
Raich Carter 1948–51
Bob Jackson 1952–55
Bob Brocklebank 1955–61
Cliff Britton 1961–70
*(continued as General Manager to 1971)*
Terry Neill 1970–74
John Kaye 1974–77
Bobby Collins 1977–78
Ken Houghton 1978–79
Mike Smith 1979–82
Bobby Brown 1982
Colin Appleton 1982–84
Brian Horton 1984–88
Eddie Gray 1988–89
Colin Appleton 1989
Stan Ternent 1989–91
Terry Dolan 1991–97
Mark Hateley 1997–98
Warren Joyce 1998–2000
Brian Little 2000–02
Jan Molby 2002
Peter Taylor October 2002–

## LATEST SEQUENCES

***Longest Sequence of League Wins:*** 10, 23.2.1966 – 20.4.1966.

***Longest Sequence of League Defeats:*** 8, 7.4.1934 – 8.9.1934.

***Longest Sequence of League Draws:*** 5, 30.3.1929 – 15.4.1929.

***Longest Sequence of Unbeaten League Matches:*** 19, 13.3.2001 – 22.9.2001.

***Longest Sequence Without a League Win:*** 27, 27.3.1989 – 4.11.1989.

***Successive Scoring Runs:*** 26 from 10.4.1990.

***Successive Non-scoring Runs:*** 6 from 13.11.1920.

## TEN YEAR LEAGUE RECORD

| | | *P* | *W* | *D* | *L* | *F* | *A* | *Pts* | *Pos* |
|---|---|---|---|---|---|---|---|---|---|
| 1994-95 | Div 2 | 46 | 21 | 11 | 14 | 70 | 57 | 74 | 8 |
| 1995-96 | Div 2 | 46 | 5 | 16 | 25 | 36 | 78 | 31 | 24 |
| 1996-97 | Div 3 | 46 | 13 | 18 | 15 | 44 | 50 | 57 | 17 |
| 1997-98 | Div 3 | 46 | 11 | 8 | 27 | 56 | 83 | 41 | 22 |
| 1998-99 | Div 3 | 46 | 14 | 11 | 21 | 44 | 62 | 53 | 21 |
| 1999-2000 | Div 3 | 46 | 15 | 14 | 17 | 43 | 43 | 59 | 14 |
| 2000-01 | Div 3 | 46 | 19 | 17 | 10 | 47 | 39 | 74 | 6 |
| 2001-02 | Div 3 | 46 | 16 | 13 | 17 | 57 | 51 | 61 | 11 |
| 2002-03 | Div 3 | 46 | 14 | 17 | 15 | 58 | 53 | 59 | 13 |
| 2003-04 | Div 3 | 46 | 25 | 13 | 8 | 82 | 44 | 88 | 2 |

## DID YOU KNOW ?

In 1932–33 Hull City owed much to their fine home record in winning the Third Division (North) title. They were unbeaten and dropped only three points. Walsall were the only team to prevent Hull from scoring at home.

## HULL CITY 2003–04 LEAGUE RECORD

| Match No. | Date | Venue | Opponents | Result | | H/T Score | Lg. Pos. | Goalscorers | Attendance |
|---|---|---|---|---|---|---|---|---|---|
| 1 | Aug 9 | H | Darlington | W | 4-1 | 1-1 | — | Burgess [26], Price J [49], Thelwell [50], Allsopp [82] | 14,675 |
| 2 | 16 | A | Oxford U | L | 1-2 | 0-2 | 10 | Allsopp [77] | 6618 |
| 3 | 23 | H | Cheltenham T | D | 3-3 | 2-3 | 10 | Elliott [7], Price J [42], Allsopp [51] | 12,522 |
| 4 | 25 | A | Cambridge U | W | 2-0 | 2-0 | 6 | Price J [5], Allsopp [21] | 4571 |
| 5 | 30 | H | Boston U | W | 2-1 | 1-0 | 4 | Elliott [34], Green [90] | 13,091 |
| 6 | Sept 8 | A | Doncaster R | D | 0-0 | 0-0 | — | | 7132 |
| 7 | 13 | H | Southend U | W | 3-2 | 1-1 | 2 | Allsopp [43], Dawson [59], Elliott [74] | 12,545 |
| 8 | 16 | A | Leyton Orient | D | 1-1 | 1-1 | — | Burgess [33] | 3728 |
| 9 | 20 | A | Rochdale | W | 2-0 | 0-0 | 2 | Green [63], Burgess [67] | 4215 |
| 10 | 27 | H | Kidderminster H | W | 6-1 | 2-1 | 2 | Burgess 2 [5, 81], Allsopp [44], Dawson [57], France [84], Green [90] | 13,683 |
| 11 | 30 | H | Swansea C | W | 1-0 | 1-0 | — | Elliott [27] | 20,903 |
| 12 | Oct 4 | A | Northampton T | W | 5-1 | 2-0 | 1 | Elliott [20], Allsopp [42], Price J [67], Burgess [82], Forrester [90] | 6011 |
| 13 | 12 | H | Carlisle U | W | 2-1 | 1-0 | 1 | Burgess [13], Forrester [75] | 19,050 |
| 14 | 18 | A | Torquay U | D | 1-1 | 0-1 | 1 | Elliott [78] | 3720 |
| 15 | 21 | A | Bury | D | 0-0 | 0-0 | — | | 3896 |
| 16 | 25 | H | Lincoln C | W | 3-0 | 1-0 | 1 | Holt [45], Allsopp [52], Green [80] | 17,453 |
| 17 | Nov 1 | H | Macclesfield T | D | 2-2 | 1-1 | 1 | Hinds [8], Allsopp [57] | 15,053 |
| 18 | 15 | A | Huddersfield T | L | 1-3 | 1-2 | 1 | Forrester [90] | 13,893 |
| 19 | 22 | H | Yeovil T | D | 0-0 | 0-0 | 2 | | 14,367 |
| 20 | 29 | A | Bristol R | L | 1-2 | 1-1 | 4 | Burgess [5] | 6331 |
| 21 | Dec 6 | H | Bury | W | 2-0 | 1-0 | 2 | Price J [17], Burgess [47] | 11,308 |
| 22 | 13 | A | Scunthorpe U | D | 1-1 | 0-0 | 3 | Elliott [70] | 6426 |
| 23 | 20 | H | Mansfield T | L | 0-1 | 0-0 | 5 | | 15,005 |
| 24 | 26 | A | York C | W | 2-0 | 0-0 | 4 | Burgess [56], Forrester (pen) [69] | 7923 |
| 25 | 28 | H | Doncaster R | W | 3-1 | 1-1 | 3 | Price J 3 [3, 66, 77] | 23,006 |
| 26 | Jan 3 | H | Cambridge U | W | 2-0 | 1-0 | 2 | Elliott 2 [42, 59] | 14,271 |
| 27 | 10 | A | Darlington | W | 1-0 | 1-0 | 1 | Elliott [30] | 6847 |
| 28 | 17 | H | Oxford U | W | 4-2 | 0-0 | 1 | Burgess [58], Allsopp 2 [63, 66], Crosby (og) [80] | 21,491 |
| 29 | 24 | A | Cheltenham T | W | 2-0 | 0-0 | 1 | Allsopp [58], Burgess [60] | 4536 |
| 30 | Feb 7 | H | York C | W | 2-1 | 0-0 | 1 | Allsopp [56], Walters [74] | 19,099 |
| 31 | 14 | A | Carlisle U | D | 1-1 | 0-0 | 1 | Green [81] | 7176 |
| 32 | 21 | H | Torquay U | L | 0-1 | 0-1 | 2 | | 15,222 |
| 33 | 28 | A | Lincoln C | L | 0-2 | 0-0 | 2 | | 7069 |
| 34 | Mar 6 | A | Mansfield T | L | 0-1 | 0-0 | 2 | | 6859 |
| 35 | 13 | H | Scunthorpe U | W | 2-1 | 2-0 | 2 | Burgess 2 [12, 30] | 19,076 |
| 36 | 16 | H | Leyton Orient | W | 3-0 | 1-0 | — | Elliott [20], Burgess [78], France [90] | 15,531 |
| 37 | 27 | H | Rochdale | W | 1-0 | 0-0 | 2 | Delaney [79] | 16,050 |
| 38 | 31 | A | Boston U | W | 2-1 | 1-0 | — | Elliott [19], Allsopp [61] | 4741 |
| 39 | Apr 3 | A | Kidderminster H | D | 1-1 | 0-1 | 2 | Burgess [68] | 3853 |
| 40 | 10 | H | Northampton T | L | 2-3 | 1-3 | 2 | Elliott [7], Dawson [69] | 18,017 |
| 41 | 12 | A | Swansea C | W | 3-2 | 1-1 | 2 | Allsopp [10], Burgess 2 [60, 87] | 5993 |
| 42 | 17 | A | Macclesfield T | D | 1-1 | 1-0 | 2 | Joseph [6] | 3801 |
| 43 | 20 | A | Southend U | D | 2-2 | 1-2 | — | Lewis [42], Ashbee [67] | 5389 |
| 44 | 24 | H | Huddersfield T | D | 0-0 | 0-0 | 2 | | 23,495 |
| 45 | May 1 | A | Yeovil T | W | 2-1 | 1-0 | 2 | Green (pen) [11], Ashbee [76] | 8760 |
| 46 | 8 | H | Bristol R | W | 3-0 | 0-0 | 2 | Price J [58], Delaney [60], Elliott [73] | 22,562 |

**Final League Position: 2**

### GOALSCORERS

*League (82):* Burgess 18, Allsopp 15, Elliott 14, Price J 9, Green 6 (1 pen), Forrester 4 (1 pen), Dawson 3, Ashbee 2, Delaney 2, France 2, Hinds 1, Holt 1, Joseph 1, Lewis 1, Thelwell 1, Walters 1, own goal 1.
*Carling Cup (0).*
*FA Cup (1):* Price 1.
*LDV Vans Trophy (4):* Forrester 1, France 1, Webb 1, Williams 1.

| Fettis A 3 | Thelwell A 22 + 4 | Delaney D 46 | Ashbee I 39 | Joseph M 32 | Hinds R 34 + 5 | Price J 29 + 4 | Green S 38 + 4 | Allsopp D 31 + 5 | Burgess B 44 | Elliott S 42 | Whittle J 15 + 3 | Forrester J 6 + 15 | Keates D 9 + 5 | Musselwhite P 17 + 1 | Melton S — + 5 | Holt A 6 + 19 | Kuipers M 3 | Dawson A 32 + 1 | Webb D — + 4 | France R 7 + 21 | Myhill B 23 | Marshall L 10 + 1 | Walters J 5 + 11 | Peat N — + 1 | Lewis J 13 | Wiseman S — + 2 | *Match No.* |
|---|---|---|---|---|---|---|---|---|---|---|---|---|---|---|---|---|---|---|---|---|---|---|---|---|---|---|---|
| 1 | 2 | 3 | 4 | 5 | $6^{1}$ | 7 | 8 | $9^{2}$ | 10 | $11^{3}$ | 12 | 13 | 14 | | | | | | | | | | | | | | 1 |
| $1^{6}$ | 2 | 3 | 4 | 5 | 6 | 7 | 8 | 9 | 10 | $11^{1}$ | | 12 | | 15 | | | | | | | | | | | | | 2 |
| | 2 | 3 | 4 | 5 | $6^{3}$ | 7 | $8^{2}$ | 9 | 10 | $11^{1}$ | 14 | 12 | 13 | 1 | | | | | | | | | | | | | 3 |
| | 2 | 3 | 4 | | 6 | 7 | | 9 | 10 | $11^{2}$ | 5 | | $8^{1}$ | 1 | 12 | 13 | | | | | | | | | | | 4 |
| | $2^{2}$ | 3 | 4 | | 6 | 7 | 8 | 9 | $10^{3}$ | $11^{1}$ | 5 | 13 | 12 | 1 | 14 | | | | | | | | | | | | 5 |
| | | 3 | 4 | | 6 | 12 | 8 | 9 | $10^{2}$ | $11^{1}$ | 5 | | 7 | | | | 1 | 2 | 13 | | | | | | | | 6 |
| | | 3 | 4 | | $6^{1}$ | 7 | 8 | 9 | 10 | $11^{2}$ | 5 | | | | 12 | 13 | 1 | 2 | | | | | | | | | 7 |
| | | 3 | 4 | | 6 | | 8 | | 10 | 11 | 5 | $9^{1}$ | $7^{2}$ | | 12 | | 1 | 2 | 13 | | | | | | | | 8 |
| | | 6 | 4 | | 2 | | 8 | 9 | 10 | $11^{1}$ | 5 | | 7 | 1 | | 12 | | 3 | | | | | | | | | 9 |
| | | 6 | | | 2 | $7^{3}$ | 8 | $9^{1}$ | 10 | $11^{2}$ | 5 | 12 | 4 | 1 | | 13 | | 3 | | 14 | | | | | | | 10 |
| | | 6 | 4 | | 2 | 7 | 8 | 9 | 10 | $11^{1}$ | 5 | | | 1 | | 12 | | 3 | | | | | | | | | 11 |
| | | 6 | 4 | | 2 | $7^{1}$ | 8 | $9^{2}$ | 10 | $11^{3}$ | 5 | 13 | 12 | 1 | | 14 | | 3 | | | | | | | | | 12 |
| | 12 | 6 | 4 | | $2^{1}$ | $7^{3}$ | 8 | 9 | 10 | | 5 | 13 | | 1 | | $11^{2}$ | | 3 | | 14 | | | | | | | 13 |
| | 2 | 6 | 4 | | | $7^{3}$ | $8^{1}$ | $9^{2}$ | 10 | 11 | 5 | 12 | | 1 | | 13 | | 3 | | 14 | | | | | | | 14 |
| | 2 | 6 | 4■ | | | $7^{3}$ | 12 | $9^{2}$ | 10 | | 5 | 13 | $8^{1}$ | 1 | | 11 | | 3 | | 14 | | | | | | | 15 |
| | 2 | 6 | 4 | | 12 | $7^{3}$ | 8 | $9^{2}$ | $10^{1}$ | | 5 | | | 1 | | 11 | | 3 | 13 | 14 | | | | | | | 16 |
| | | 6 | | 2 | 4 | $7^{2}$ | 8 | 9 | $10^{1}$ | 11 | 5 | | | 1 | | 12 | | 3 | | 13 | | | | | | | 17 |
| 1 | | 6 | 4 | 5 | 3 | 7 | 8 | $9^{1}$ | 10 | $11^{2}$ | | 12 | | | | | | 2 | | 13 | | | | | | | 18 |
| | | 6 | 4 | 5 | 2 | 7 | 8 | | $10^{1}$ | 11 | | $9^{2}$ | | 1 | | | | 3 | 13 | 12 | | | | | | | 19 |
| | | 6 | 4 | 5 | 2 | 9 | $8^{1}$ | | 10 | $11^{2}$ | | | 12 | 1 | | 13 | | 3 | | 7 | | | | | | | 20 |
| | | 6 | 4 | 5 | 2 | 9 | $7^{1}$ | | 10 | 11 | | | 8 | 1 | | 12 | | 3 | | | | | | | | | 21 |
| | | 6 | 4 | 5 | 2 | 7 | 12 | | 10 | 9 | | | $8^{1}$ | 1 | | $11^{2}$ | | 3 | | 13 | | | | | | | 22 |
| | | 6 | 4 | 5 | 2 | $9^{3}$ | 7 | 12 | $10^{2}$ | 11 | | | $8^{1}$ | | | 13 | | 3 | | 14 | 1 | | | | | | 23 |
| | | 6 | 4 | 5 | 2 | 7 | 8 | | 10 | 11 | | $9^{1}$ | | 1 | | 12 | | 3 | | | | | | | | | 24 |
| | 12 | 6 | 4 | 5 | 2 | $7^{3}$ | $8^{1}$ | 13 | 10 | 11 | | $9^{2}$ | | | | | | 3 | | 14 | 1 | | | | | | 25 |
| | 12 | 6 | 4 | 5 | 2 | $7^{2}$ | $8^{1}$ | | 10 | 11 | | $9^{3}$ | | | | 14 | | 3 | | 13 | 1 | | | | | | 26 |
| | 7 | 6 | 4 | 5 | 2 | 8 | | 12 | 10 | $11^{2}$ | | $9^{1}$ | | | | 13 | | 3 | | | 1 | | | | | | 27 |
| | | 6 | 4 | 5 | 2 | 7 | $8^{3}$ | $9^{2}$ | 10 | $11^{1}$ | 14 | 12 | | | | 13 | | 3 | | | 1 | | | | | | 28 |
| | | 6 | 4 | 5 | 2 | | 8 | $9^{2}$ | 10 | 11 | | | | | | 12 | | $3^{1}$ | | 7 | 1 | 13 | | | | | 29 |
| | | 6 | 4 | 5 | 13 | | 8 | $9^{2}$ | 10 | $11^{3}$ | | | | | | 14 | | 3 | | $7^{1}$ | 1 | 2 | 12 | | | | 30 |
| | | 6 | | 5 | 7 | | 8 | $9^{3}$ | 10 | $11^{2}$ | $4^{1}$ | | | | 12 | 13 | | 3 | | | 1 | 2 | 14 | | | | 31 |
| | 4 | 6 | | 5 | $7^{2}$ | | 8 | | $10^{1}$ | 11 | | 12 | | | | $3^{3}$ | | | | 13 | 1 | 2 | 9 | 14 | | | 32 |
| | 4 | 6 | | 5 | $3^{3}$ | 13 | $7^{2}$ | | 10 | 11 | | 12 | | | | 14 | | | | | 1 | 2 | $9^{1}$ | | 8 | | 33 |
| | 3 | $6^{2}$ | 4 | 5 | 13 | $7^{1}$ | | | 10 | | | 12 | | | | 11 | | | | 14 | 1 | 2 | $9^{3}$ | | 8 | | 34 |
| | 3 | 6 | 4 | 5 | | 7 | | 12 | 10 | 11 | | | | | | | | | | | 1 | 2 | $9^{1}$ | | 8 | | 35 |
| | 3 | 6 | 4 | 5 | | $7^{3}$ | 12 | 13 | 10 | $11^{1}$ | | | | | | | | | | 14 | 1 | 2 | $9^{2}$ | | 8 | | 36 |
| | $3^{1}$ | 6 | 4 | 5 | | 7 | 12 | $9^{3}$ | 10 | $11^{2}$ | | | | | | | | | | 13 | 1 | 2 | 14 | | 8 | | 37 |
| | 3 | 6 | | 5 | 7 | | 4 | $9^{2}$ | 10 | 11 | | | | | | | | | | 12 | 1 | $2^{1}$ | 13 | | 8 | | 38 |
| | 3 | 6 | | | 5 | | 4 | $9^{1}$ | 10 | 11 | | | | | | | | | | 7 | 1 | $2^{2}$ | 12 | | 8 | 13 | 39 |
| | $3^{1}$ | 6 | 4 | 5 | $2^{3}$ | | 8 | 9 | 10 | 11 | | | | | | | | 12 | | $7^{2}$ | 1 | | 13 | | | 14 | 40 |
| | 5 | 6 | 4 | 2 | 12 | | $7^{2}$ | $9^{3}$ | 10 | $11^{1}$ | | | | | | | | 3 | | 13 | 1 | | 14 | | 8 | | 41 |
| | 2 | 6 | 4 | 5 | | | 7 | $9^{2}$ | 10 | $11^{1}$ | | | | | | | | 3 | | 12 | 1 | | 13 | | 8 | | 42 |
| | $2^{1}$ | 6 | 4 | 5 | 12 | | $7^{2}$ | $9^{3}$ | 10 | 11 | | | | | | | | 3 | | 13 | 1 | | 14 | | 8 | | 43 |
| | 2 | 6 | 4 | 5 | | | 7 | $9^{2}$ | $10^{1}$ | 11 | | | | | | | | 3 | | 12 | 1 | | 13 | | 8 | | 44 |
| | | 6 | 4 | 5 | 2 | 12 | $10^{1}$ | 9 | | $11^{2}$ | | | | | | | | 3 | | 7 | 1 | | 13 | | 8 | | 45 |
| | 14 | 6 | 4 | 5 | $2^{1}$ | $13^{3}$ | 11 | 9 | | 10 | | 12 | | | | | | 3 | | 7 | 1 | | | | $8^{2}$ | | 46 |

**Carling Cup**
First Round Wigan Ath (a) 0-2

**LDV Vans Trophy**
First Round Darlington (a) 3-1
Second Round Scunthorpe U (h) 1-3

**FA Cup**
First Round Cheltenham T (a) 1-3

# IPSWICH TOWN — FL Championship

## FOUNDATION

Considering that Ipswich Town only reached the Football League in 1938, many people outside of East Anglia may be surprised to learn that this club was formed at a meeting held in the Town Hall as far back as 1878 when Mr T. C. Cobbold, MP, was voted president. Originally it was the Ipswich Association FC to distinguish it from the older Ipswich Football Club which played rugby. These two amalgamated in 1888 and the handling game was dropped in 1893.

***Portman Road, Ipswich, Suffolk IP1 2DA.***

***Telephone:*** (01473) 400 500.

***Fax:*** (01473) 400 040.

***Ticket Office:*** (01473) 400 555.

***Website:*** www.itfc.co.uk

***Email:*** enquiries@itfc.co.uk

***Ground Capacity:*** 30,311.

***Record Attendance:*** 38,010 v Leeds U, FA Cup 6th rd, 8 March 1975.

***Pitch Measurements:*** 101m × 65m.

***Chairman:*** David Sheepshanks.

***Chief Executive:*** Derek Bowden.

***Secretary:*** David Rose.

***Assistant Club Secretary:*** Sally Webb.

***Manager:*** Joe Royle.

***Assistant Manager:*** Willie Donachie.

***Physio:*** David Williams.

***Colours:*** Blue and white.

***Change Colours:*** Orange and black.

***Year Formed:*** 1878.

***Turned Professional:*** 1936.

***Ltd Co.:*** 1936.

***Club Nicknames:*** 'Blues' or 'Town' or 'Tractor Boys'.

***First Football League Game:*** 27 August 1938, Division 3 (S), v Southend U (h) W 4–2 – Burns; Dale, Parry; Perrett, Fillingham, McLuckie; Williams, Davies (1), Jones (2), Alsop (1), Little.

## HONOURS

*Football League:* Division 1 – Champions 1961–62; Runners-up 1980–81, 1981–82; Promoted from Division 1 1999–2000 (play-offs); Division 2 – Champions 1960–61, 1967–68, 1991–92; Division 3 (S) – Champions 1953–54, 1956–57.

*FA Cup:* Winners 1978.

*Football League Cup:* Semi-final 1982, 1985.

*Texaco Cup:* Winners 1973.

***European Competitions:*** *European Cup:* 1962–63. *European Cup-Winners' Cup:* 1978–79. *UEFA Cup:* 1973–74, 1974–75, 1975–76, 1977–78, 1979–80, 1980–81 (winners), 1981–82, 1982–83, 2001–02, 2002–03.

## SKY SPORTS FACT FILE

On Good Friday 20 April 1962 Ipswich Town had a then record crowd of 30,649 for the visit of Arsenal. The match ended in a 2-2 draw. The following day Ipswich drew similarly at Chelsea and on Easter Monday won 3-0 at Highbury.

**Record League Victory:** 7–0 v Portsmouth, Division 2, 7 November 1964 – Thorburn; Smith, McNeil; Baxter, Bolton, Thompson; Broadfoot (1), Hegan (2), Baker (1), Leadbetter, Brogan (3). 7–0 v Southampton, Division 1, 2 February 1974 – Sivell; Burley, Mills (1), Morris, Hunter, Beattie (1), Hamilton (2), Viljoen, Johnson, Whymark (2), Lambert (1) (Woods). 7–0 v WBA, Division 1, 6 November 1976 – Sivell; Burley, Mills, Talbot, Hunter, Beattie (1), Osborne, Wark (1), Mariner (1) (Bertschin), Whymark (4), Woods.

**Record Cup Victory:** 10–0 v Floriana, European Cup prel. rd, 25 September 1962 – Bailey; Malcolm, Compton; Baxter, Laurel, Elsworthy (1); Stephenson, Moran (2), Crawford (5), Phillips (2), Blackwood.

**Record Defeat:** 1–10 v Fulham, Division 1, 26 December 1963.

### MANAGERS

Mick O'Brien 1936–37
Scott Duncan 1937–55
*(continued as Secretary)*
Alf Ramsey 1955–63
Jackie Milburn 1963–64
Bill McGarry 1964–68
Bobby Robson 1969–82
Bobby Ferguson 1982–87
Johnny Duncan 1987–90
John Lyall 1990–94
George Burley 1994–2002
Joe Royle October 2002–

**Most League Points (2 for a win):** 64, Division 3 (S), 1953–54 and 1955–56.

**Most League Points (3 for a win):** 87, Division 1, 1999–2000.

**Most League Goals:** 106, Division 3 (S), 1955–56.

**Highest League Scorer in Season:** Ted Phillips, 41, Division 3 (S), 1956–57.

**Most League Goals in Total Aggregate:** Ray Crawford, 203, 1958–63 and 1966–69.

**Most League Goals in One Match:** 5, Alan Brazil v Southampton, Division 1, 16 February 1981.

**Most Capped Player:** Allan Hunter, 47 (53), Northern Ireland.

**Most League Appearances:** Mick Mills, 591, 1966–82.

**Youngest League Player:** Jason Dozzell, 16 years 56 days v Coventry C, 4 February 1984.

**Record Transfer Fee Received:** £6,000,000 from Newcastle U for Kieron Dyer, July 1999; £6,000,000 from Arsenal for Richard Wright, July 2001.

**Record Transfer Fee Paid:** £4,750,000 to Sampdoria for Matteo Sereni, July 2001.

**Football League Record:** 1938 Elected to Division 3 (S); 1954–55 Division 2; 1955–57 Division 3 (S); 1957–61 Division 2; 1961–64 Division 1; 1964–68 Division 2; 1968–86 Division 1; 1986–92 Division 2; 1992–95 FA Premier League; 1995–2000 Division 1; 2000–02 FA Premier League; 2002–04 Division 1; 2004– FLC.

### LATEST SEQUENCES

**Longest Sequence of League Wins:** 8, 23.9.1953 – 31.10.1953.

**Longest Sequence of League Defeats:** 10, 4.9.1954 – 16.10.1954.

**Longest Sequence of League Draws:** 7, 10.11.1990 – 21.12.1990.

**Longest Sequence of Unbeaten League Matches:** 23, 8.12.1979 – 26.4.1980.

**Longest Sequence Without a League Win:** 21, 28.8.1963 – 14.12.1963.

**Successive Scoring Runs:** 28 from 1.5.1953.

**Successive Non-scoring Runs:** 7 from 28.2.1995.

### TEN YEAR LEAGUE RECORD

| | | P | W | D | L | F | A | Pts | Pos |
|---|---|---|---|---|---|---|---|---|---|
| 1994-95 | PR Lge | 42 | 7 | 6 | 29 | 36 | 93 | 27 | 22 |
| 1995-96 | Div 1 | 46 | 19 | 12 | 15 | 79 | 69 | 69 | 7 |
| 1996-97 | Div 1 | 46 | 20 | 14 | 12 | 68 | 50 | 74 | 4 |
| 1997-98 | Div 1 | 46 | 23 | 14 | 9 | 77 | 43 | 83 | 5 |
| 1998-99 | Div 1 | 46 | 26 | 8 | 12 | 69 | 32 | 86 | 3 |
| 1999-2000 | Div 1 | 46 | 25 | 12 | 9 | 71 | 42 | 87 | 3 |
| 2000-01 | PR Lge | 38 | 20 | 6 | 12 | 57 | 42 | 66 | 5 |
| 2001-02 | PR Lge | 38 | 9 | 9 | 20 | 41 | 64 | 36 | 18 |
| 2002-03 | Div 1 | 46 | 19 | 13 | 14 | 80 | 64 | 70 | 7 |
| 2003-04 | Div 1 | 46 | 21 | 10 | 15 | 84 | 72 | 73 | 5 |

### DID YOU KNOW ?

The first Ipswich Town player to score a hat-trick once the club turned professional was Jack Blackwell in a preliminary round FA Cup tie against Eastern Counties United on 19 September 1936. Ipswich won 7-0.

## IPSWICH TOWN 2003–04 LEAGUE RECORD

| *Match No.* | *Date* | *Venue* | *Opponents* | *Result* | | *H/T Score* | *Lg. Pos.* | *Goalscorers* | *Attendance* |
|---|---|---|---|---|---|---|---|---|---|
| 1 | Aug 9 | H | Reading | D | 1-1 | 0-0 | — | Miller T (pen) [90] | 24,830 |
| 2 | 16 | A | Crewe Alex | L | 0-1 | 0-0 | 17 | | 6982 |
| 3 | 23 | H | Coventry C | D | 1-1 | 1-1 | 20 | Bent M [17] | 22,419 |
| 4 | 26 | A | Wigan Ath | L | 0-1 | 0-0 | — | | 8292 |
| 5 | 30 | H | West Ham U | L | 1-2 | 0-1 | 22 | Wright [65] | 29,679 |
| 6 | Sept 13 | A | WBA | L | 1-4 | 0-1 | 24 | Naylor [63] | 24,954 |
| 7 | 16 | H | Walsall | W | 2-1 | 1-1 | — | Armstrong (pen) [13], Bent D [67] | 20,912 |
| 8 | 20 | H | Wimbledon | W | 4-1 | 2-1 | 19 | Armstrong [24], Naylor [26], Bent D [68], Counago (pen) [81] | 23,428 |
| 9 | 27 | A | Watford | W | 2-1 | 0-0 | 16 | Kuqi [52], Magilton [82] | 15,350 |
| 10 | 30 | A | Sunderland | L | 2-3 | 1-1 | — | Bent D [36], Naylor [51] | 24,840 |
| 11 | Oct 4 | H | Rotherham U | W | 2-1 | 0-0 | 14 | Counago 2 (1 pen) [53, 70 (p)] | 21,859 |
| 12 | 11 | A | Bradford C | W | 1-0 | 1-0 | 9 | Mahon [42] | 10,229 |
| 13 | 14 | H | Burnley | W | 6-1 | 5-0 | — | Counago 2 [20, 22], Wright [28], Bart-Williams [30], Chaplow (og) [40], Kuqi [90] | 22,048 |
| 14 | 18 | H | Stoke C | W | 1-0 | 1-0 | 6 | Richards [43] | 22,122 |
| 15 | 21 | A | Crystal Palace | W | 4-3 | 2-2 | — | Naylor 2 [26, 45], Counago [78], Kuqi [89] | 15,483 |
| 16 | 25 | A | Preston NE | D | 1-1 | 0-1 | 7 | Counago (pen) [65] | 14,863 |
| 17 | Nov 1 | H | Gillingham | L | 3-4 | 1-2 | 7 | Westlake [18], Counago [60], Miller T [74] | 24,788 |
| 18 | 8 | A | Derby Co | D | 2-2 | 0-2 | 7 | Miller T (pen) [56], Bent D [65] | 19,976 |
| 19 | 22 | H | Sheffield U | W | 3-0 | 1-0 | 6 | Kuqi (pen) [43], Westlake [67], Bent D [90] | 25,004 |
| 20 | 29 | A | Cardiff C | W | 3-2 | 2-0 | 4 | Miller T (pen) [29], Santos [33], Bart-Williams [82] | 17,833 |
| 21 | Dec 3 | A | Nottingham F | D | 1-1 | 0-0 | — | Bent D [62] | 21,558 |
| 22 | 6 | H | Derby Co | W | 2-1 | 1-0 | 3 | Bent D [1], Mawene (og) [69] | 25,018 |
| 23 | 13 | A | Millwall | D | 0-0 | 0-0 | 4 | | 9829 |
| 24 | 21 | H | Norwich C | L | 0-2 | 0-1 | 5 | | 30,152 |
| 25 | 26 | A | West Ham U | W | 2-1 | 0-0 | 4 | Counago 2 (1 pen) [70 (p), 79] | 35,021 |
| 26 | 28 | H | Crystal Palace | L | 1-3 | 1-0 | 5 | Wright [11] | 27,629 |
| 27 | Jan 10 | A | Reading | D | 1-1 | 0-0 | 6 | McGreal [72] | 17,362 |
| 28 | 17 | H | Crewe Alex | W | 6-4 | 2-1 | 5 | Miller T 2 [3, 9], Kuqi 2 [55, 88], Reuser [72], Counago [74] | 22,071 |
| 29 | 31 | A | Coventry C | D | 1-1 | 0-1 | 5 | Westlake [58] | 14,441 |
| 30 | Feb 7 | H | Wigan Ath | L | 1-3 | 0-2 | 7 | Kuqi [60] | 22,093 |
| 31 | 14 | H | Bradford C | W | 3-1 | 2-1 | 4 | Kuqi [28], Westlake [45], Bent D [52] | 21,478 |
| 32 | 21 | A | Burnley | L | 2-4 | 0-2 | 4 | Miller T [65], Reuser [88] | 12,418 |
| 33 | 28 | H | Preston NE | W | 2-0 | 0-0 | 4 | Miller T [72], Westlake [90] | 23,359 |
| 34 | Mar 2 | A | Stoke C | L | 0-2 | 0-1 | — | | 11,435 |
| 35 | 7 | A | Norwich C | L | 1-3 | 0-0 | 7 | Miller T (pen) [87] | 23,942 |
| 36 | 13 | H | Millwall | L | 1-3 | 0-2 | 9 | Bent D [52] | 23,582 |
| 37 | 16 | A | Walsall | W | 3-1 | 0-0 | — | Bent D 3 [48, 59, 90] | 6562 |
| 38 | 20 | H | Watford | W | 4-1 | 2-1 | 8 | Bowditch 3 [5, 24, 61], Wright [90] | 23,524 |
| 39 | 27 | A | Wimbledon | W | 2-1 | 0-0 | 8 | Bent D [72], Kuqi [73] | 6389 |
| 40 | Apr 4 | H | WBA | L | 2-3 | 1-0 | 9 | Miller T [43], Bent D [78] | 24,608 |
| 41 | 10 | A | Rotherham U | W | 3-1 | 0-1 | 5 | Wright [67], Bent D [88], Kuqi [90] | 6561 |
| 42 | 12 | H | Sunderland | W | 1-0 | 1-0 | 4 | Miller T (pen) [45] | 26,801 |
| 43 | 17 | A | Gillingham | W | 2-1 | 0-1 | 4 | Reuser [62], Bent D [67] | 9641 |
| 44 | 24 | H | Nottingham F | L | 1-2 | 1-1 | 4 | Bowditch [34] | 27,848 |
| 45 | 30 | A | Sheffield U | D | 1-1 | 0-0 | — | Westlake [71] | 24,184 |
| 46 | May 9 | H | Cardiff C | D | 1-1 | 1-1 | 5 | Kuqi [26] | 28,703 |

**Final League Position: 5**

### GOALSCORERS

*League (84):* Bent D 16, Counago 11 (4 pens), Kuqi 11 (1 pen), Miller T 11 (5 pens), Westlake 6, Naylor 5, Wright 5, Bowditch 4, Reuser 3, Armstrong 2 (1 pen), Bart-Williams 2, Bent M 1, Magilton 1, Mahon 1, McGreal 1, Richards 1, Santos 1, own goals 2.
*Carling Cup (2):* Bowditch 1, Counago 1 (pen).
*FA Cup (4):* Kuqi 1, Miller 1, Naylor 1, Reuser 1.
*Play-Offs (1):* Bent D 1.

| Davis K 45 | Wilnis F 41 | Makin C 5 | Naylor R 28 + 11 | Diallo D 16 + 3 | Santos G 28 + 6 | Magilton J 46 | Bent M 4 | Counago P 18 + 11 | Bent D 32 + 5 | Miller T 27 + 7 | Richards M 41 + 3 | Bowditch D 7 + 9 | Reuser M 3 + 14 | Wright J 42 + 3 | Westlake I 30 + 9 | Armstrong A 5 + 2 | Bart-Williams C 23 + 3 | Mahon A 7 + 4 | Kuqi S 29 + 7 | Nash G — + 1 | Mitchell S — + 2 | McGreal J 18 | Elliott M 10 | Price L 1 | *Match No.* |
|---|---|---|---|---|---|---|---|---|---|---|---|---|---|---|---|---|---|---|---|---|---|---|---|---|---|
| 1 | $2^1$ | 3 | 4 | 5 | $6^2$ | 7 | 8 | 9 | $10^3$ | 11 | 12 | 13 | 14 | | | | | | | | | | | | 1 |
| 1 | 2 | 3 | 4 | 5 | $6^2$ | 7 | 9 | 12 | 10 | 8 | | | $11^1$ | 13 | | | | | | | | | | | 2 |
| 1 | 2 | 3 | 4 | 5 | $6^2$ | 7 | 8 | $9^3$ | $10^1$ | 11 | | 12 | | 13 | 14 | | | | | | | | | | 3 |
| 1 | 2 | 6 | 4 | 5 | | 7 | 9 | 12 | $10^1$ | $8^2$ | $3^3$ | 14 | | 11 | 13 | | | | | | | | | | 4 |
| 1 | 2 | $3^2$ | 4 | 5 | $6^3$ | 7 | | 9 | 12 | 8 | 13 | | | 14 | $11^1$ | 10 | | | | | | | | | 5 |
| 1 | 2 | | 4 | 5 | 12 | 7 | | $9^2$ | 13 | | 3 | 14 | | 8 | | $10^1$ | 6 | $11^3$ | | | | | | | 6 |
| 1 | 2 | | 12 | 5 | 6 | $7^1$ | | 13 | 10 | | 3 | | | 8 | 14 | $9^2$ | 4 | $11^3$ | | | | | | | 7 |
| 1 | 2 | | 12 | $5^1$ | 6 | 7 | | 13 | $10^3$ | | 3 | 14 | | 8 | | $9^2$ | 4 | 11 | | | | | | | 8 |
| 1 | 2 | | 5 | | 6 | 7 | | 12 | 10 | | 3 | | | 8 | $11^2$ | $9^1$ | 4 | | 13 | | | | | | 9 |
| 1 | 2 | | 5 | | 6 | 7 | | $9^2$ | 10 | | 3 | | | 8 | | 12 | 4 | 13 | $11^1$ | | | | | | 10 |
| 1 | 2 | | 5 | | 6 | 7 | | 9 | | | 3 | | | 8 | 12 | | 4 | $11^1$ | 10 | | | | | | 11 |
| 1 | 2 | | 5 | | 6 | 7 | | $9^1$ | | | 3 | | | 8 | 12 | | 4 | 11 | 10 | | | | | | 12 |
| 1 | 2 | | 5 | | $6^2$ | $7^1$ | | 9 | | | 3 | | | 8 | 12 | | 4 | 11 | 10 | 13 | | | | | 13 |
| 1 | 2 | | 5 | | 6 | $7^2$ | | 9 | | 13 | 3 | | | 8 | 12 | | 4 | $11^1$ | 10 | | | | | | 14 |
| 1 | 2 | | 5 | | 6 | 7 | | $9^1$ | | 12 | 3 | | | 8 | 11 | | 4 | | 10 | | | | | | 15 |
| 1 | 2 | | 5 | | 6 | 7 | | 9 | | 12 | 3 | | | 8 | 11 | | $4^1$ | | 10 | | | | | | 16 |
| 1 | 2 | | 5 | | 6 | 7 | | 9 | | 12 | 3 | | | 8 | 11 | | $4^1$ | | 10 | | | | | | 17 |
| 1 | 5 | | | | 6 | 7 | | $9^1$ | 8 | 4 | 3 | $12^2$ | | 2 | 11 | 13 | | | $10^3$ | | 14 | | | | 18 |
| 1 | 2 | | 5 | | 6 | $7^1$ | | | 9 | 12 | 3 | | | 8 | 11 | | 4 | | 10 | | | | | | 19 |
| 1 | 2 | | 5 | | 6 | $7^1$ | | | 9 | 12 | 3 | | | 8 | 11 | | 4 | | 10 | | | | | | 20 |
| 1 | $2^1$ | | 5 | | 6 | 7 | | | 9 | 12 | 3 | | | 8 | 11 | | 4 | | 10 | | | | | | 21 |
| 1 | | | $5^1$ | | | 7 | | | 9 | 8 | 3 | | | 2 | 11 | | 4 | 12 | 10 | | | 6 | | | 22 |
| 1 | 2 | | | | 6■ | 7 | | 12 | 9 | | 3 | | 14 | 8 | $11^2$ | | 4 | $13^3$ | $10^1$ | | | 5 | | | 23 |
| 1 | 2 | | 12 | | $6^1$ | 7 | | 13 | 9 | | 3 | | | 8 | $11^2$ | | 4 | 14 | $10^3$ | | | 5 | | | 24 |
| 1 | 2 | | 6 | | 12 | 7 | | 13 | $9^3$ | $8^2$ | 3 | | 14 | 11 | | | 4 | | 10 | | | $5^1$ | | | 25 |
| 1 | 2 | | 5 | | 6 | 7 | | 9 | 12 | | 3 | 14 | 13 | $8^3$ | 11 | | $4^2$ | | $10^1$ | | | | | | 26 |
| 1 | 2 | | 5 | | | 7 | | $9^1$ | | $8^2$ | 3 | 12 | 13 | 11 | | | 4 | | 10 | | | 6 | | | 27 |
| 1 | | | 5 | 12 | 13 | $7^2$ | | 9 | | 8 | 3 | | 14 | 2 | $11^3$ | | $4^1$ | | 10 | | | 6 | | | 28 |
| 1 | $2^1$ | | 9 | 5 | $6^2$ | 7 | | | 13 | $4^3$ | 3 | | 11 | 8 | 14 | | 12 | | 10 | | | | | | 29 |
| 1 | | | 6 | 5 | 14 | 7 | | $9^2$ | 13 | 8 | 3 | | $11^3$ | 2 | 12 | | $4^1$ | | 10 | | | | | | 30 |
| 1 | | | 5 | 2 | | 7 | | | 9 | 4 | 3 | | | 8 | 11 | | | | 10 | | | 6 | | | 31 |
| 1 | $2^1$ | | 4 | $5^2$ | | 7 | | 13 | 9 | 3 | 12 | | 14 | 8 | 11 | | | | $10^3$ | | | 6 | | | 32 |
| 1 | 2 | | 13 | | 6 | $7^1$ | | $9^2$ | 10 | 4 | 3 | | | 8 | 11 | | 12 | | | | | 5 | | | 33 |
| 1 | 2 | | 14 | 12 | 6 | $7^2$ | | 13 | 9 | 4 | 3 | | | 8 | 11 | | | | $10^3$ | | | $5^1$ | | | 34 |
| 1 | $2^1$ | | 13 | 5■ | 6 | 7 | | 12 | 9 | 4 | 3 | | | 8 | 11 | | | | $10^2$ | | | | | | 35 |
| 1 | 2 | | 12 | $5^1$ | $6^2$ | 7 | | | 9 | 4 | 3 | 14 | 13 | 8 | 11 | | | | $10^3$ | | | | | | 36 |
| 1 | 2 | | 5 | | | 7 | | | 10 | 4 | 3 | $9^1$ | | 8 | 11 | | | | 12 | | | | 6 | | 37 |
| 1 | 2 | | | | | $7^2$ | | | $10^1$ | 4 | 3 | 9 | | 8 | 11 | | | | 12 | | 13 | 5 | 6 | | 38 |
| 1 | 2 | | | | | 7 | | | 10 | 4 | 3 | $9^1$ | | 8 | $11^2$ | | 12 | | 13 | | | 5 | 6 | | 39 |
| 1 | 2 | | | | 6 | 7 | | | 10 | 4 | 3 | $9^1$ | 13 | 8 | $11^2$ | | | | 12 | | | | 5 | | 40 |
| 1 | | | | $5^1$ | 13 | $7^2$ | | | 10 | 8 | 3 | $9^3$ | 14 | 2 | 11 | | | | 12 | | | 4 | 6 | | 41 |
| 1 | 2 | | | | 12 | 7 | | | 9 | 4 | 3 | | | 8 | 11 | | | | $10^1$ | | | 5 | 6 | | 42 |
| | $2^1$ | | 13 | 12 | | 7 | | | 9 | $4^3$ | 3 | | 14 | 8 | 11 | | | | $10^2$ | | | 5 | 6 | 1 | 43 |
| 1 | 2 | | 12 | $5^3$ | | $7^2$ | | | 10 | | 3 | $9^1$ | 14 | 8 | 11 | | | | 13 | | | 4 | 6 | | 44 |
| 1 | 2 | | 12 | | | 7 | | | 10 | $4^2$ | 3 | $9^1$ | 13 | 8 | 11 | | | | | | | 5 | 6 | | 45 |
| 1 | 2 | | 12 | | | $7^1$ | | | 9 | 4 | 3 | | 13 | 8 | 11 | | | | $10^2$ | | | 5 | 6 | | 46 |

**Carling Cup**

| | | | |
|---|---|---|---|
| First Round | Kidderminster H | (h) | 1-0 |
| Second Round | Notts Co | (a) | 1-2 |

**FA Cup**

| | | | |
|---|---|---|---|
| Third Round | Derby Co | (h) | 3-0 |
| Fourth Round | Sunderland | (h) | 1-2 |

**Play-Offs**

| | | | |
|---|---|---|---|
| Semi-Final | West Ham U | (h) | 1-0 |
| | | (a) | 0-2 |

# KIDDERMINSTER HARRIERS FL Championship 2

### FOUNDATION

Kidderminster Harriers were originally formed as a rugby team and played their first game as a soccer club on 18 September 1886 away to Wilden. Harriers won 2-1 with goals from Arthur Millward and William Colsey. Millward was vice-captain and later Kidderminster's first representative on the executive of the Birmingham County FA in 1897. Colsey was to die in tragic circumstances following an accidental injury sustained in a match only two months later.

***Aggborough Stadium, Hoo Road, Kidderminster DY10 1NB.***

***Telephone:*** (01562) 823 931.

***Fax:*** (01562) 827 329.

***Ticket Office:*** (01562) 823 931.

***Website:*** www.harriers.co.uk

***Email:*** info@harriers.co.uk

***Ground Capacity:*** 6,419.

***Record Attendance:*** 9,155 v Hereford U, 27 November 1948.

***Chairman:*** Colin Youngjohns.

***Vice-chairman:*** Barry Norgrove.

***Secretary:*** Roger Barlow.

***Manager:*** Jan Molby.

***Assistant Manager:*** Garry Barnett.

***Physio:*** Jim Conway.

***Colours:*** Red shirts, white shorts, red stockings.

***Change Colours:*** Navy shirts, white shorts, navy stockings.

***Year Formed:*** 1886.

### HONOURS

*FA Cup:* best season: 5th rd 1994

*Football League Cup:* never past 2nd rd.

*Conference:* Champions 1993–94, 1999–2000; Runners-up 1996–97.

*FA Trophy:* 1986–87 (winners); 1990–91, 1994–95 (runners-up).

*Spalding Challenge Cup:* Winners 1996–97.

*Welsh FA Cup:* Runners-up 1985–86, 1988–89.

*Southern League Cup:* Winners 1979–80.

*Worcester Senior Cup:* (22)

*Birmingham Senior Cup:* (7)

*Staffordshire Senior Cup:* (4)

*West Midland League:* Champions (6); Runners-up (3)

*Southern Premier:* Runners-up (1)

*West Midland League Cup:* Winners (7)

*Keys Cup:* Winners (7)

*Border Counties Floodlit League:* Champions: (3)

*Camkin Floodlit Cup:* Winners (3)

*Bass County Vase:* Winners (1)

*Conference Fair Play Trophy:* (5)

### SKY SPORTS FACT FILE

Centre-forward Johnny Dent joined Kidderminster Harriers in 1937–38. They won the Birmingham League championship twice and he scored 93 goals. He had previous League experience with Durham City, Huddersfield Town and Nottingham Forest.

***Club Nickname:*** 'Harriers'.

***First Football League Game:*** 12 August 2000, Division 3, v Torquay U (h) W 2–0 – Clarke; Clarkson, Stamps, Webb, Hinton, Smith, Bennett, Horne (1), Foster, Hadley (1), Ducros (Bird).

***Record League Victory:*** 4–0 v Swansea C (a), Division 3, 29 October 2002 – Brock; Coleman, Shilton (1), Stamps, Hinton (Bennett), Ayres, Melligan (1), Flynn, Broughton (1) (Foster), Henriksen (1), Williams (Parrish).

***Record Cup Victory:*** 4–0 v Halesowen T, FA Cup 1st rd replay, 16 November 1987.
*N.B.* 25–0 v Hereford, Birmingham Senior Cup, 1889–90.

***Record Defeat:*** 0–13 v Darwen, FA Cup 1st rd replay, 24 January 1891.

### MANAGERS

Leslie Smith
Amos Moss
John Spilsbury
Dudley Kernick
Archie Styles
Stan Lloyd
Harold Cox
Stan Jones
Ron Whitehouse
Alan Grundy
John Chambers
Graham Allner 1983–99
Jan Molby 1999–2002
Ian Britton 2002–03
Jan Molby October 2003–

***Most League Points (3 for a win):*** 66, Division 3, 2001–02.

***Most League Goals:*** 62, Division 3, 2002–03.

***Record Transfer Fee Received:*** £380,000 from WBA for Lee Hughes, July 1997.

***Record Transfer Fee Paid:*** £80,000 to Nuneaton Borough for Andy Ducros, July 2000.

***Football League Record:*** 2000 Promoted to Division 3; 2004– FL2.

## LATEST SEQUENCES

***Longest Sequence of League Wins:*** 4, 3.11.2001 – 24.11.2001.

***Longest Sequence of League Defeats:*** 4, 16.9.2003 – 30.9.2003.

***Longest Sequence Without a League Win:*** 9, 23.8.2003 – 30.9.2003.

***Longest Sequence of League Draws:*** 4, 26.8.2002 – 14.9.2002.

***Longest Sequence of Unbeaten League Matches:*** 9, 24.8.2002 – 5.10.2002.

***Successive Scoring Runs:*** 10 from 3.11.2001.

***Successive Non-scoring Runs:*** 4 from 10.3.2001.

### TEN YEAR LEAGUE RECORD

| | | *P* | *W* | *D* | *L* | *F* | *A* | *Pts* | *Pos* |
|---|---|---|---|---|---|---|---|---|---|
| 1994-95 | Conf. | 42 | 16 | 9 | 17 | 63 | 61 | 57 | 11 |
| 1995-96 | Conf. | 42 | 18 | 10 | 14 | 78 | 66 | 64 | 7 |
| 1996-97 | Conf. | 42 | 26 | 7 | 9 | 84 | 42 | 85 | 2 |
| 1997-98 | Conf. | 42 | 11 | 14 | 17 | 56 | 63 | 47 | 17 |
| 1998-99 | Conf. | 42 | 14 | 9 | 19 | 56 | 52 | 51 | 15 |
| 1999-2000 | Conf. | 42 | 26 | 7 | 9 | 75 | 40 | 85 | 1 |
| 2000-01 | Div 3 | 46 | 13 | 14 | 19 | 47 | 61 | 53 | 16 |
| 2001-02 | Div 3 | 46 | 19 | 9 | 18 | 56 | 47 | 66 | 10 |
| 2002-03 | Div 3 | 46 | 16 | 15 | 15 | 62 | 63 | 63 | 11 |
| 2003-04 | Div 3 | 46 | 14 | 13 | 19 | 45 | 59 | 55 | 16 |

### DID YOU KNOW?

In the 1985–86 season Kidderminster Harriers defeated a Football League club for the first time – but it was Shrewsbury Town in the Welsh Cup. Goals by Kim Casey, John Horne and Paul Davies ensured a 3-1 victory.

## KIDDERMINSTER HARRIERS 2003–04 LEAGUE RECORD

| Match No. | Date | Venue | Opponents | Result | H/T Score | Lg. Pos. | Goalscorers | Attendance |
|---|---|---|---|---|---|---|---|---|
| 1 | Aug 9 | H | Mansfield T | W 2-1 | 1-0 | — | Henriksen 2 (1 pen) 15, 74 (p) | 3180 |
| 2 | 16 | A | Darlington | W 2-0 | 0-0 | 4 | Williams D 50, Bishop 57 | 11,600 |
| 3 | 23 | H | Bury | L 0-2 | 0-1 | 8 | | 2548 |
| 4 | 25 | A | Cheltenham T | L 1-2 | 0-0 | 11 | Williams D 50 | 4179 |
| 5 | 30 | H | Oxford U | D 1-1 | 0-0 | 11 | Willis 82 | 3262 |
| 6 | Sept 6 | A | Bristol R | L 0-1 | 0-0 | 16 | | 6791 |
| 7 | 13 | A | Macclesfield T | D 1-1 | 1-0 | 18 | Williams D 40 | 1988 |
| 8 | 16 | H | Scunthorpe U | L 0-2 | 0-0 | — | | 2162 |
| 9 | 20 | H | Lincoln C | L 1-2 | 1-2 | 21 | Dyer 11 | 2462 |
| 10 | 27 | A | Hull C | L 1-6 | 1-2 | 21 | Williams J 21 | 13,683 |
| 11 | 30 | A | Huddersfield T | L 0-1 | 0-1 | — | | 8275 |
| 12 | Oct 4 | H | Carlisle U | W 2-1 | 0-0 | 21 | Bishop 56, Williams D 83 | 2488 |
| 13 | 11 | H | Southend U | L 1-2 | 1-1 | 23 | Melligan 84 | 2429 |
| 14 | 18 | A | Swansea C | D 0-0 | 0-0 | 22 | | 6825 |
| 15 | 21 | A | Northampton T | W 1-0 | 1-0 | — | Parrish 22 | 4089 |
| 16 | 25 | H | Doncaster R | L 0-2 | 0-1 | 23 | | 3393 |
| 17 | Nov 1 | H | Cambridge U | D 2-2 | 1-0 | 21 | Parrish 41, Williams J 80 | 2401 |
| 18 | 15 | A | Rochdale | W 1-0 | 1-0 | 19 | Gadsby 35 | 2498 |
| 19 | 22 | H | Torquay U | L 1-2 | 1-1 | 20 | Williams D 12 | 2725 |
| 20 | 29 | A | Boston U | D 2-2 | 1-0 | 21 | Hinton (pen) 35, White 54 | 2147 |
| 21 | Dec 13 | H | Leyton Orient | W 2-1 | 1-1 | 20 | Peters (og) 31, Gadsby 66 | 2605 |
| 22 | 21 | A | York C | L 0-1 | 0-0 | 20 | | 2973 |
| 23 | 26 | A | Yeovil T | W 2-1 | 1-0 | 19 | Williams J 45, Parrish 73 | 5640 |
| 24 | 28 | H | Bristol R | W 1-0 | 0-0 | 16 | Bennett 47 | 3411 |
| 25 | Jan 10 | A | Mansfield T | L 0-1 | 0-1 | 19 | | 4574 |
| 26 | 17 | H | Darlington | D 1-1 | 1-0 | 20 | Murray 7 | 2550 |
| 27 | 24 | A | Bury | D 0-0 | 0-0 | 19 | | 2526 |
| 28 | 31 | A | Oxford U | L 1-2 | 1-1 | 21 | Murray 45 | 6057 |
| 29 | Feb 7 | H | Yeovil T | L 0-1 | 0-0 | 21 | | 3255 |
| 30 | 10 | H | Cheltenham T | D 0-0 | 0-0 | — | | 3803 |
| 31 | 14 | A | Southend U | L 0-3 | 0-1 | 21 | | 3716 |
| 32 | 21 | H | Swansea C | W 2-0 | 0-0 | 20 | Foster 59, Christiansen 66 | 3407 |
| 33 | 27 | A | Doncaster R | L 0-5 | 0-2 | — | | 7594 |
| 34 | Mar 2 | H | Northampton T | W 2-1 | 1-0 | — | Keates 29, Bennett 47 | 2699 |
| 35 | 6 | H | York C | W 4-1 | 3-1 | 15 | Foster (pen) 10, Bennett 35, Yates 45, Murray 67 | 2569 |
| 36 | 13 | A | Leyton Orient | D 1-1 | 0-1 | 15 | Yates (pen) 81 | 3764 |
| 37 | 16 | A | Scunthorpe U | W 2-0 | 1-0 | — | Foster 18, Keates 54 | 2512 |
| 38 | 20 | H | Macclesfield T | L 1-4 | 0-3 | 15 | Rickards 84 | 2666 |
| 39 | 27 | A | Lincoln C | D 1-1 | 0-0 | 15 | Brown 46 | 4797 |
| 40 | Apr 3 | H | Hull C | D 1-1 | 1-0 | 17 | Brown 22 | 3853 |
| 41 | 10 | A | Carlisle U | L 0-1 | 0-0 | 18 | | 7296 |
| 42 | 12 | H | Huddersfield T | W 2-1 | 1-0 | 16 | Hatswell 30, Lloyd (og) 54 | 4051 |
| 43 | 17 | A | Cambridge U | D 0-0 | 0-0 | 16 | | 3765 |
| 44 | 24 | H | Rochdale | L 0-1 | 0-1 | 16 | | 3580 |
| 45 | May 1 | A | Torquay U | D 1-1 | 0-1 | 19 | Hatswell 73 | 5515 |
| 46 | 8 | H | Boston U | W 2-0 | 1-0 | 16 | Bastock (og) 22, Williams J 73 | 3047 |

**Final League Position: 16**

## GOALSCORERS

*League (45):* Williams D 5, Williams J 4, Bennett 3, Foster 3 (1 pen), Murray 3, Parrish 3, Bishop 2, Brown 2, Gadsby 2, Hatswell 2, Henriksen 2 (1 pen), Keates 2, Yates 2 (1 pen), Christiansen 1, Dyer 1, Hinton 1 (pen), Melligan 1, Rickards 1, White 1, Willis 1, own goals 3.
*Carling Cup (0).*
*FA Cup (6):* Bennett 4, Burton 1, Williams J 1.
*LDV Vans Trophy (0).*

| Brock S 37 | Coleman K 10 | Shilton S 9 + 5 | Stamps S 34 + 1 | Hinton C 41 + 1 | Willis A 12 | Bennett D 34 + 4 | Flynn S 4 + 2 | Henriksen B 14 + 8 | Bishop A 8 + 3 | Williams D 28 | Ward G 17 + 4 | Williams J 28 + 16 | Smith A 19 + 3 | Parrish S 16 + 11 | Murray A 19 + 3 | Gadsby M 23 + 9 | Dyer L 5 + 2 | Betts R 8 + 1 | Antoine-Curier M — + 1 | Melligan J 5 | Lewis M 1 + 3 | Hatswell W 32 | Burton S 10 + 2 | White A 6 + 1 | Rickards S 5 + 8 | Jenkins L 5 + 2 | Christiansen J 11 + 10 | Foster I 10 + 1 | Keates D 8 | Sall A 6 + 1 | Yates M 14 | Viveash A 7 | Danby J 9 | Brown S 8 | Clarke L 3 + 1 | McHale C — + 1 | *Match No.* |
|---|---|---|---|---|---|---|---|---|---|---|---|---|---|---|---|---|---|---|---|---|---|---|---|---|---|---|---|---|---|---|---|---|---|---|---|---|---|
| 1 | 2 | 3 | 4 | 5 | 6 | 7 | 8 | $9^{1}$ | $10^{2}$ | 11 | 12 | 13 | | | | | | | | | | | | | | | | | | | | | | | | | 1 |
| 1 | 2 | 3 | 4 | 5 | 6 | $7^{2}$ | 8 | $9^{3}$ | 12 | 11 | 13 | $10^{1}$ | 14 | | | | | | | | | | | | | | | | | | | | | | | | 2 |
| 1 | $2^{1}$ | 3 | 4 | 5 | 6 | 7 | 8 | 9 | $10^{2}$ | 11 | | 13 | 12 | | | | | | | | | | | | | | | | | | | | | | | | 3 |
| 1 | 2 | 3 | $4^{1}$ | 5 | 6■ | 7 | 8 | 9 | 10 | 11 | | | 12 | | | | | | | | | | | | | | | | | | | | | | | | 4 |
| 1 | 2 | 12 | 4 | 5 | 6 | | | 9 | $10^{2}$ | 11 | $7^{3}$ | 13 | | $3^{1}$ | 8 | 14 | | | | | | | | | | | | | | | | | | | | | 5 |
| 1 | $2^{2}$ | | 4 | 5 | 6 | 10 | 12 | 9 | 13 | 11 | $7^{3}$ | 14 | | | | $8^{1}$ | 3 | | | | | | | | | | | | | | | | | | | | 6 |
| 1 | 2 | 12 | 4 | 5 | | | 13 | $9^{3}$ | 10 | 11 | | 14 | 6 | | $7^{2}$ | | $3^{1}$ | 8 | | | | | | | | | | | | | | | | | | | 7 |
| 1 | | | 2 | $5^{1}$ | 6 | 12 | | 9 | 10 | 11 | | 13 | $4^{3}$ | | $8^{2}$ | 14 | 3 | 7 | | | | | | | | | | | | | | | | | | | 8 |
| 1 | | | 2 | $5^{3}$ | 6 | 12 | | 9 | $10^{2}$ | 11 | | 13 | 4 | | | $8^{1}$ | 3 | 7 | 14 | | | | | | | | | | | | | | | | | | 9 |
| 1 | | | 2 | 5 | 6 | 7 | | 12 | | 11 | 8 | 9 | 4 | | | | 3 | $10^{1}$ | | | | | | | | | | | | | | | | | | | 10 |
| 1 | | 3 | 2 | | 6 | $7^{2}$ | | 9 | 12 | $11^{3}$ | 8 | $10^{1}$ | 5 | 14 | | | 13 | 4 | | | | | | | | | | | | | | | | | | | 11 |
| 1 | | $3^{3}$ | 4 | | 6 | 12 | | 9 | $10^{2}$ | 11 | $8^{1}$ | | 5 | | | 13 | 14 | 2 | | 7 | | | | | | | | | | | | | | | | | 12 |
| 1 | | 3 | 2 | | 6 | 12 | | $9^{1}$ | | 11 | 8 | 13 | 5 | | | 14 | | $4^{3}$ | | 7 | $10^{2}$ | | | | | | | | | | | | | | | | 13 |
| 1 | 3 | | $5^{1}$ | 12 | | 4 | | | | 11 | 8 | 9 | 2 | 10 | | | | | | 7 | | 6 | | | | | | | | | | | | | | | 14 |
| 1 | 4 | 12 | | 5 | | 8 | | | | 11 | 10 | 9 | 2 | $3^{1}$ | | | | | | 7 | | 6 | | | | | | | | | | | | | | | 15 |
| 1 | $2^{3}$ | 3 | | 5 | | 10 | | | | 11 | $8^{1}$ | $9^{2}$ | 4 | 12 | | | | | | 7 | 13 | 6 | 14 | | | | | | | | | | | | | | 16 |
| 1 | | 12 | | 5 | | 8 | | | | 7 | | $9^{2}$ | 4 | 11 | | 2 | | | | | 13 | 6 | 3 | $10^{1}$ | | | | | | | | | | | | | 17 |
| 1 | | | | 5 | | 8 | | 12 | | 11 | | 10 | 2 | 3 | | 7 | | | | | | 6 | 4 | $9^{1}$ | | | | | | | | | | | | | 18 |
| 1 | | | | 5 | | 4 | | 9 | | 7 | | $10^{1}$ | $2^{2}$ | 11 | | 13 | | 12 | | | 14 | 6 | 3 | $8^{3}$ | | | | | | | | | | | | | 19 |
| 1 | | 12 | 13 | 5 | | 8 | | | | 7 | | $9^{1}$ | 4 | $11^{2}$ | | 2 | | | | | | 6 | 3 | 10 | | | | | | | | | | | | | 20 |
| 1 | | | 3 | 5 | | 8 | | 12 | | 11 | | $10^{1}$ | 2 | | | 7 | | | | | | 6 | $4^{2}$ | 9 | 13 | | | | | | | | | | | | 21 |
| 1 | | $3^{2}$ | 2 | 5 | | 8 | | 12 | | 11 | | 13 | 4 | | | 7 | | | | | | 6 | $10^{3}$ | $9^{1}$ | 14 | | | | | | | | | | | | 22 |
| 1 | | | 2 | 5 | | 8 | | | | 11 | 10 | $9^{2}$ | $4^{1}$ | 3 | | 12 | | | | | | 6 | | 13 | | 7 | | | | | | | | | | | 23 |
| 1 | | | 2 | 5 | | 8 | | 12 | | 11 | 4 | 9 | | 7 | | 13 | | | | | | 6 | | | $10^{1}$ | $3^{2}$ | | | | | | | | | | | 24 |
| 1 | | | 3 | 5 | | 8 | | 13 | | | 11 | 12 | 2 | $7^{1}$ | 10 | 4 | | | | | | 6 | | | | | $9^{2}$ | | | | | | | | | | 25 |
| 1 | | | | 5 | | 8 | | 12 | | 11 | 7 | $9^{1}$ | 2 | | 4 | 3 | | | | | | 6 | | | | | 10 | | | | | | | | | | 26 |
| 1 | | | 3 | 5 | | 8 | | 12 | | 11 | $7^{3}$ | $9^{1}$ | | 13 | $4^{2}$ | 2 | | | | | | 6 | | | 14 | | 10 | | | | | | | | | | 27 |
| 1 | | | 3 | 5 | | 8 | | $9^{1}$ | | 11 | $7^{2}$ | 12 | | 13 | 4 | 2 | | | | | | 6 | | | | | 10 | | | | | | | | | | 28 |
| 1 | | | 3 | 5 | | 8 | | | | 11 | 13 | 12 | | | 4 | 2 | | $7^{2}$ | | | | 6 | | | $9^{1}$ | | 10 | | | | | | | | | | 29 |
| 1 | | | 3 | 5 | | 8 | | | | | | 9 | | | 4 | 2 | | | | | | 6 | | | 7 | | 12 | $10^{1}$ | 11 | | | | | | | | 30 |
| 1 | | | 3 | 5 | | 8 | | | | | 7 | 12 | | | 4 | 2 | | | | | | | | | | | 9 | $10^{1}$ | 11 | 6 | | | | | | | 31 |
| 1 | | | 3 | 5 | | 8 | | | | | | 12 | | 13 | 4 | 2 | | | | | | 6 | | | 7 | | $10^{1}$ | $9^{2}$ | 11 | | | | | | | | 32 |
| 1 | | | 3■ | | | 8 | | | | | 12 | 9 | | 13 | 4 | $2^{1}$ | | | | | | $6^{2}$ | | | 14 | | $10^{3}$ | | 11 | 5 | 7 | | | | | | 33 |
| 1 | | | 3 | 2 | | 8 | | | | | | 9 | | 12 | 4 | | | | | | | 6 | | | | | | $10^{1}$ | 11 | | 7 | 5 | | | | | 34 |
| 1 | | | 3 | 2 | | 8 | | | | | | $9^{3}$ | | 12 | 4 | | | | | | | $6^{2}$ | | | | | 14 | $10^{1}$ | 11 | 13 | 7 | 5 | | | | | 35 |
| 1 | | | | 2 | | 8 | | | | | | $9^{2}$ | | 12 | 4 | $3^{1}$ | | | | | | 6 | | | 13 | | 14 | $10^{3}$ | 11■ | | 7 | 5 | | | | | 36 |
| | | | 3 | 2 | | 4 | | | | | | 9 | | 11 | | | | | | | | 6 | | | 12 | | 13 | $10^{1}$ | $8^{2}$ | | 7 | 5 | 1 | | | | 37 |
| | | | 3 | 2 | | 8 | | | | | | 9 | | $11^{2}$ | 4 | | | | | | | 6 | | | 12 | | 13 | $10^{1}$ | | | 7 | 5 | 1 | | | | 38 |
| | | | 3 | 2 | | 4 | | | | | | $9^{2}$ | | | | 8 | | | | | | 6 | | | | | 12 | $10^{1}$ | | | 7 | 5 | 1 | 11 | 13 | | 39 |
| | | | 3 | 2 | | $8^{1}$ | | | | | | 9 | | | 4 | 12 | | | | | | 6 | | | | | 14 | 13 | | | 7 | 5 | 1 | $11^{3}$ | $10^{2}$ | | 40 |
| | | | $3^{2}$ | 2 | | | | | | | | 9 | | 12 | 4 | 5 | | | | | | 6 | 13 | | | $11^{1}$ | 14 | | | | 7 | | 1 | 8 | $10^{3}$ | | 41 |
| | | | | 2 | | | | | | | | 12 | | 11 | | 3 | | | | | | 6 | 4 | | | 13 | $9^{1}$ | 10■ | | 5 | 7 | | 1 | $8^{2}$ | | | 42 |
| | | | | 2 | | | | | | | | 12 | | $11^{2}$ | 13 | $8^{1}$ | | | | | | 6 | 4 | | | 3 | 9 | | | 5■ | 7 | | 1 | 10 | | | 43 |
| | | | | 2 | | | | | | | | 9 | | 12 | $8^{3}$ | 3 | | | | | | 6 | 4 | | | 13 | 14 | | | 5 | $7^{2}$ | | 1 | 11 | $10^{1}$ | | 44 |
| | | | | 2 | | | | | | | $4^{1}$ | $9^{3}$ | | 11 | 12 | 13 | | | | | | 6 | 3 | | 14 | 5 | 10 | | | | 7 | | 1 | $8^{2}$ | | | 45 |
| 1 | | | 2 | 5 | | | | | | | | 9 | | 11 | 12 | 3 | | | | | | 6 | | | $8^{2}$ | | 13 | | | 4 | $7^{3}$ | | | $10^{1}$ | | 14 | 46 |

**Carling Cup**

| | | | |
|---|---|---|---|
| First Round | Ipswich T | (a) | 0-1 |

**LDV Vans Trophy**

| | | | |
|---|---|---|---|
| First Round | QPR | (a) | 0-2 |

**FA Cup**

| | | | |
|---|---|---|---|
| First Round | Northwich Vic | (h) | 2-1 |
| Second Round | Woking | (a) | 3-0 |
| Third Round | Wolverhampton W | (h) | 1-1 |
| | | (a) | 0-2 |

# LEEDS UNITED FL Championship

## FOUNDATION

Immediately the Leeds City club (founded in 1904) was wound up by the FA in October 1919, following allegations of illegal payments to players, a meeting was called by a Leeds solicitor, Mr Alf Masser, at which Leeds United was formed. They joined the Midland League playing their first game in that competition in November 1919. It was in this same month that the new club had discussions with the directors of a virtually bankrupt Huddersfield Town who wanted to move to Leeds in an amalgamation. But Huddersfield survived even that crisis.

***Elland Road, Leeds, West Yorkshire LS11 0ES.***

***Telephone:*** (0113) 367 6000.

***Fax:*** (0113) 367 6050.

***Ticket Office:*** 0845 121 1992.

***Website:*** www.leedsunited.com

***Email:*** football@leedsunited.com

***Ground Capacity:*** 40,232.

***Record Attendance:*** 57,892 v Sunderland, FA Cup 5th rd (replay), 15 March 1967.

***Pitch Measurements:*** 105m × 68m.

***Chairman:*** Gerald Krasner.

***Managing Director:*** David Richmond.

***Secretary:*** Ian Silvester.

***Manager:*** Kevin Blackwell.

***Head Coach:*** Sam Ellis.

***Physio:*** Dave Hancock.

***Colours:*** All white.

***Change Colours:*** Sky blue shirts, navy blue shorts, sky blue stockings.

***Year Formed:*** 1919, as Leeds United after disbandment (by FA order) of Leeds City (formed in 1904).

***Turned Professional:*** 1920.

***Ltd Co.:*** 1920.

***Club Nickname:*** 'The Whites'.

## HONOURS

*Football League:* Division 1 – Champions 1968–69, 1973–74, 1991–92; Runners-up 1964–65, 1965–66, 1969–70, 1970–71, 1971–72; Division 2 – Champions 1923–24, 1963–64, 1989–90; Runners-up 1927–28, 1931–32, 1955–56.

*FA Cup:* Winners 1972; Runners-up 1965, 1970, 1973.

*Football League Cup:* Winners 1968; Runners-up 1996.

***European Competitions:*** *European Cup:* 1969–70, 1974–75 (runners-up). *Champions League:* 1992–93, 2000–01 (semi-finalists). *European Cup-Winners' Cup:* 1972–73 (runners-up). *European Fairs Cup:* 1965–66, 1966–67 (runners-up), 1967–68 (winners), 1968–69, 1970–71 (winners). *UEFA Cup:* 1971–72, 1973–74, 1979–80, 1995–96, 1998–99, 1999–2000 (semi-finalists), 2001–02, 2002–03.

***First Football League Game:*** 28 August 1920, Division 2, v Port Vale (a) L 0–2 – Down; Duffield, Tillotson; Musgrove, Baker, Walton; Mason, Goldthorpe, Thompson, Lyon, Best.

***Record League Victory:*** 8–0 v Leicester C, Division 1, 7 April 1934 – Moore; George Milburn, Jack Milburn; Edwards, Hart, Copping; Mahon (2), Firth (2), Duggan (2), Furness (2), Cochrane.

## SKY SPORTS FACT FILE

Leeds United have had two players who scored more than half of their team's League goals in a season. Tom Jennings did so in 1926–27 with 35 of 69 and 30 years later John Charles equalled the achievement with 38 of 72.

***Record Cup Victory:*** 10–0 v Lyn (Oslo), European Cup 1st rd 1st leg, 17 September 1969 – Sprake; Reaney, Cooper, Bremner (2), Charlton, Hunter, Madeley, Clarke (2), Jones (3), Giles (2) (Bates), O'Grady (1).

***Record Defeat:*** 1–8 v Stoke C, Division 1, 27 August 1934.

***Most League Points (2 for a win):*** 67, Division 1, 1968–69.

***Most League Points (3 for a win):*** 85, Division 2, 1989–90.

***Most League Goals:*** 98, Division 2, 1927–28.

***Highest League Scorer in Season:*** John Charles, 42, Division 2, 1953–54.

***Most League Goals in Total Aggregate:*** Peter Lorimer, 168, 1965–79 and 1983–86.

***Most League Goals in One Match:*** 5, Gordon Hodgson v Leicester C, Division 1, 1 October 1938.

***Most Capped Player:*** Lucas Radebe, 58 (70), South Africa.

***Most League Appearances:*** Jack Charlton, 629, 1953–73.

***Youngest League Player:*** Peter Lorimer, 15 years 289 days v Southampton, 29 September 1962.

***Record Transfer Fee Received:*** £28,250,000 from Manchester U for Rio Ferdinand, July 2002 (see Manchester United page 249).

***Record Transfer Fee Paid:*** £18,000,000 to West Ham United for Rio Ferdinand, November 2000.

***Football League Record:*** 1920 Elected to Division 2; 1924–27 Division 1; 1927–28 Division 2; 1928–31 Division 1; 1931–32 Division 2; 1932–47 Division 1; 1947–56 Division 2; 1956–60 Division 1; 1960–64 Division 2; 1964–82 Division 1; 1982–90 Division 2; 1990–92 Division 1; 1992–2004 FA Premier League; 2004– FLC.

## MANAGERS

Dick Ray 1919–20
Arthur Fairclough 1920–27
Dick Ray 1927–35
Bill Hampson 1935–47
Willis Edwards 1947–48
Major Frank Buckley 1948–53
Raich Carter 1953–58
Bill Lambton 1958–59
Jack Taylor 1959–61
Don Revie OBE 1961–74
Brian Clough 1974
Jimmy Armfield 1974–78
Jock Stein CBE 1978
Jimmy Adamson 1978–80
Allan Clarke 1980–82
Eddie Gray MBE 1982–85
Billy Bremner 1985–88
Howard Wilkinson 1988–96
George Graham 1996–98
David O'Leary 1998–2002
Terry Venables 2002–03
Peter Reid 2003
Eddie Gray *(Caretaker)* 2003–04
Kevin Blackwell May 2004–

## LATEST SEQUENCES

***Longest Sequence of League Wins:*** 9, 26.9.1931 – 21.11.1931.

***Longest Sequence of League Defeats:*** 6, 28.12.2003 – 7.2.2004.

***Longest Sequence of League Draws:*** 5, 19.4.1997 – 9.8.1997.

***Longest Sequence of Unbeaten League Matches:*** 34, 26.10.1968 – 26.8.1969.

***Longest Sequence Without a League Win:*** 17, 1.2.1947 – 26.5.1947.

***Successive Scoring Runs:*** 30 from 27.8.1927.

***Successive Non-scoring Runs:*** 6 from 30.1.1982.

## TEN YEAR LEAGUE RECORD

| | | *P* | *W* | *D* | *L* | *F* | *A* | *Pts* | *Pos* |
|---|---|---|---|---|---|---|---|---|---|
| 1994-95 | PR Lge | 42 | 20 | 13 | 9 | 59 | 38 | 73 | 5 |
| 1995-96 | PR Lge | 38 | 12 | 7 | 19 | 40 | 57 | 43 | 13 |
| 1996-97 | PR Lge | 38 | 11 | 13 | 14 | 28 | 38 | 46 | 11 |
| 1997-98 | PR Lge | 38 | 17 | 8 | 13 | 57 | 46 | 59 | 5 |
| 1998-99 | PR Lge | 38 | 18 | 13 | 7 | 62 | 34 | 67 | 4 |
| 1999-2000 | PR Lge | 38 | 21 | 6 | 11 | 58 | 43 | 69 | 3 |
| 2000-01 | PR Lge | 38 | 20 | 8 | 10 | 64 | 43 | 68 | 4 |
| 2001-02 | PR Lge | 38 | 18 | 12 | 8 | 53 | 37 | 66 | 5 |
| 2002-03 | PR Lge | 38 | 14 | 5 | 19 | 58 | 57 | 47 | 15 |
| 2003-04 | PR Lge | 38 | 8 | 9 | 21 | 40 | 79 | 33 | 19 |

## DID YOU KNOW ?

The first Leeds United player to score a hat-trick in an FA Cup tie was Walter Butler in a 7-0 win over Leeds Steelworks on 25 September 1920. He had been signed from – Leeds Steelworks. Later with Doncaster Rovers and Darlington.

## LEEDS UNITED 2003–04 LEAGUE RECORD

| *Match No.* | *Date* | *Venue* | *Opponents* | *Result* | | *H/T Score* | *Lg. Pos.* | *Goalscorers* | *Attendance* |
|---|---|---|---|---|---|---|---|---|---|
| 1 | Aug 17 | H | Newcastle U | D | 2-2 | 1-1 | — | Viduka $^{24}$, Smith $^{57}$ | 36,766 |
| 2 | 23 | A | Tottenham H | L | 1-2 | 1-1 | 13 | Smith $^{5}$ | 34,350 |
| 3 | 26 | H | Southampton | D | 0-0 | 0-0 | — | | 34,721 |
| 4 | 30 | A | Middlesbrough | W | 3-2 | 1-0 | 12 | Sakho $^{16}$, Camara $^{77}$, Viduka $^{90}$ | 30,414 |
| 5 | Sept 15 | A | Leicester C | L | 0-4 | 0-2 | — | | 30,460 |
| 6 | 20 | H | Birmingham C | L | 0-2 | 0-0 | 16 | | 34,305 |
| 7 | 28 | A | Everton | L | 0-4 | 0-3 | 18 | | 39,151 |
| 8 | Oct 4 | H | Blackburn R | W | 2-1 | 2-0 | 16 | Johnson 2 $^{11, 27}$ | 35,039 |
| 9 | 18 | H | Manchester U | L | 0-1 | 0-0 | 17 | | 40,153 |
| 10 | 25 | A | Liverpool | L | 1-3 | 1-1 | 19 | Smith $^{42}$ | 43,599 |
| 11 | Nov 1 | H | Arsenal | L | 1-4 | 0-3 | 20 | Smith $^{64}$ | 36,491 |
| 12 | 8 | A | Portsmouth | L | 1-6 | 1-2 | 20 | Smith $^{19}$ | 20,122 |
| 13 | 22 | H | Bolton W | L | 0-2 | 0-2 | 20 | | 36,558 |
| 14 | 29 | A | Charlton Ath | W | 1-0 | 1-0 | 20 | Milner $^{9}$ | 26,425 |
| 15 | Dec 6 | H | Chelsea | D | 1-1 | 1-0 | 19 | Pennant $^{18}$ | 36,305 |
| 16 | 14 | H | Fulham | W | 3-2 | 1-0 | 19 | Duberry $^{41}$, Viduka $^{46}$, Matteo $^{88}$ | 30,544 |
| 17 | 22 | A | Manchester C | D | 1-1 | 1-0 | — | Viduka $^{24}$ | 47,126 |
| 18 | 26 | H | Aston Villa | D | 0-0 | 0-0 | 19 | | 38,513 |
| 19 | 28 | A | Wolverhampton W | L | 1-3 | 1-1 | 19 | Duberry $^{3}$ | 29,139 |
| 20 | Jan 7 | A | Newcastle U | L | 0-1 | 0-1 | — | | 52,130 |
| 21 | 10 | H | Tottenham H | L | 0-1 | 0-0 | 19 | | 35,365 |
| 22 | 17 | A | Southampton | L | 1-2 | 0-2 | 20 | Kilgallon $^{75}$ | 31,976 |
| 23 | 31 | H | Middlesbrough | L | 0-3 | 0-0 | 20 | | 35,970 |
| 24 | Feb 7 | A | Aston Villa | L | 0-2 | 0-1 | 20 | | 39,171 |
| 25 | 10 | H | Wolverhampton W | W | 4-1 | 2-1 | — | Smith $^{14}$, Matteo $^{41}$, Milner $^{62}$, Viduka $^{90}$ | 36,867 |
| 26 | 21 | A | Manchester U | D | 1-1 | 0-0 | 20 | Smith $^{67}$ | 67,744 |
| 27 | 29 | H | Liverpool | D | 2-2 | 2-2 | 20 | Bakke $^{29}$, Viduka $^{34}$ | 39,932 |
| 28 | Mar 13 | A | Fulham | L | 0-2 | 0-0 | 20 | | 17,104 |
| 29 | 22 | H | Manchester C | W | 2-1 | 1-1 | — | McPhail $^{23}$, Viduka (pen) $^{76}$ | 36,998 |
| 30 | 27 | A | Birmingham C | L | 1-4 | 1-1 | 19 | Viduka $^{3}$ | 29,069 |
| 31 | Apr 5 | H | Leicester C | W | 3-2 | 2-0 | — | Duberry $^{11}$, Viduka $^{13}$, Smith $^{86}$ | 34,036 |
| 32 | 10 | A | Blackburn R | W | 2-1 | 1-0 | 18 | Caldwell $^{2}$, Viduka $^{89}$ | 26,611 |
| 33 | 13 | H | Everton | D | 1-1 | 0-1 | — | Milner $^{50}$ | 39,835 |
| 34 | 16 | A | Arsenal | L | 0-5 | 0-3 | — | | 38,094 |
| 35 | 25 | H | Portsmouth | L | 1-2 | 0-1 | 18 | Harte (pen) $^{83}$ | 39,273 |
| 36 | May 2 | A | Bolton W | L | 1-4 | 1-0 | 19 | Viduka (pen) $^{27}$ | 27,420 |
| 37 | 8 | H | Charlton Ath | D | 3-3 | 2-1 | 20 | Kilgallon $^{29}$, Pennant $^{41}$, Smith (pen) $^{69}$ | 38,986 |
| 38 | 15 | A | Chelsea | L | 0-1 | 0-1 | 19 | | 41,281 |

**Final League Position: 19**

### GOALSCORERS

*League (40):* Viduka 11 (2 pens), Smith 9 (1 pen), Duberry 3, Milner 3, Johnson Seth 2, Kilgallon 2, Matteo 2, Pennant 2, Bakke 1, Caldwell 1, Camara 1, Harte 1 (pen), McPhail 1, Sakho 1.
*Carling Cup (4):* Roque Junior 2, Harte 1, Robinson 1.
*FA Cup (1):* Viduka 1.

| Robinson P 36 | Kelly G 37 | Matteo D 33 | Morris J 11 + 1 | Radebe L 11 + 3 | Camara Z 13 | Sakho L 9 + 8 | Johnson Seth 24 + 1 | Viduka M 30 | Smith A 35 | Wilcox J 3 + 3 | Domi D 9 + 3 | Batty D 10 + 2 | Lennon A — + 11 | Pennant J 34 + 2 | Harte I 21 + 2 | Richardson F 2 + 2 | Roque Junior J 5 | Olembe S 8 + 4 | Bridges M 1 + 9 | Milner J 27 + 3 | Barmby N 1 + 5 | Duberry M 19 | Chapuis C — + 1 | McPhail S 8 + 4 | Kilgallon M 7 + 1 | Bakke E 8 + 2 | Carson S 2 + 1 | Caldwell S 13 | Johnson Simon 1 + 4 | *Match No.* |
|---|---|---|---|---|---|---|---|---|---|---|---|---|---|---|---|---|---|---|---|---|---|---|---|---|---|---|---|---|---|---|
| 1 | 2 | 3 | 4 | 5 | 6 | $7^1$ | 8 | 9 | 10 | $11^2$ | 12 | 13 | | | | | | | | | | | | | | | | | | 1 |
| 1 | 2 | 3 | 4 | 5 | 6 | $7^1$ | 8 | $9^2$ | 10 | $11^3$ | 12 | | 13 | 14 | | | | | | | | | | | | | | | | 2 |
| 1 | 2 | 5 | $4^2$ | | 6 | 11 | 8 | 9 | 10 | 12 | | 13 | | $7^1$ | $3^3$ | 14 | | | | | | | | | | | | | | 3 |
| 1 | 2 | 6 | 4 | 12 | 5 | $11^1$ | 8 | 9 | 10 | | | | 13 | 7 | $3^2$ | | | | | | | | | | | | | | | 4 |
| 1 | 2 | | 4 | 12 | 6 | $11^2$ | 8 | 9 | 10 | | $5^3$ | | 13 | 7 | | | $3^1$ | 14 | | | | | | | | | | | | 5 |
| 1 | 2 | | 4 | | 6 | $11^1$ | | 9 | 10 | | | | 12 | 7 | 3 | | 5■ | 8 | | | | | | | | | | | | 6 |
| 1 | 2 | 3 | 4 | | 6 | $11^3$ | $8^2$ | 9 | 10 | | | | 12 | $7^1$ | | | 5 | 13 | 14 | | | | | | | | | | | 7 |
| 1 | 2 | 5 | 4 | | 6 | 12 | 11 | $9^2$ | 10 | | | 8 | | $7^1$ | | | | 3 | 13 | | | | | | | | | | | 8 |
| 1 | 2 | 5 | | | 6 | 12 | 8 | $9^3$ | 10 | | | 4 | 13 | $7^2$ | | | | 3 | 14 | $11^1$ | | | | | | | | | | 9 |
| 1 | 2 | 5 | | | 6 | 12 | $8^3$ | 9 | 10 | | | 4 | 13 | $7^2$ | | | | 3 | | $11^1$ | 14 | | | | | | | | | 10 |
| 1 | 2 | | | | 6 | $11^1$ | 8 | | 10 | | | 4 | 12 | 7 | | | 5 | 3 | $9^2$ | 13 | | | | | | | | | | 11 |
| 1 | 2 | 5 | 8 | | | 12 | 10 | | 9 | | | | | $7^1$ | | | $6^2$ | 3 | 13 | 11 | | 4 | | | | | | | | 12 |
| 1 | | | $8^2$ | 5 | 2 | 11 | $10^1$ | 9 | | | | $4^3$ | | | 3 | | | 13 | | 7 | 12 | 6 | 14 | | | | | | | 13 |
| 1 | 2 | 4 | | 5 | | | | 9 | 10 | | | 8 | | 7 | 3 | | | | | 11 | | 6 | | | | | | | | 14 |
| 1 | 2 | 4 | | 5 | | | 13 | 9 | 10 | | 12 | | | 7 | 3 | | | | | $11^2$ | | 6 | | $8^1$ | | | | | | 15 |
| 1 | 2 | 4 | | 5 | | | | 9 | 10 | | | 8 | | 7 | 3 | | | | | 11 | | 6 | | | | | | | | 16 |
| 1 | 2 | 4 | | $5^1$ | | | | 9 | 8 | | | $10^3$ | | $7^2$ | 3 | | | | 13 | 11 | | 6 | | 12 | 14 | | | | | 17 |
| 1 | 2 | $4^2$ | | | | | | 9 | 8 | | | 10 | 12 | $7^1$ | 3 | | | | | 11 | | 6 | | | 5 | 13 | | | | 18 |
| 1 | 2 | 4■ | | | | 12 | | 9 | 10 | | | | | $7^1$ | 3 | | | | | 13 | | 6 | | $11^2$ | 5 | 8 | | | | 19 |
| 1 | 2 | 4 | | | | 12 | $8^2$ | 9 | | | | $11^3$ | | 7 | 3 | | | 14 | 13 | $10^1$ | | 6 | | | 5 | | | | | 20 |
| 1 | 2 | 4 | | | | 12 | | $9^2$ | | | | | | 7 | 3 | | | $8^1$ | 13 | 14 | $10^3$ | 6 | | | 5 | 11 | | | | 21 |
| 1 | 2 | | $10^1$ | | 6 | | 8 | | 9 | | | | | 7 | 3 | | | | 12 | 11 | | | | | 5 | 4 | | | | 22 |
| 1■ | 2 | 4 | 12 | | | | $8^2$ | | 9 | | | | | 7 | 3 | | | | 13 | $10^6$ | | 6 | | | 5 | $11^1$ | 15 | | | 23 |
| 1 | 2 | 4 | | | | | 8 | 9 | 10 | | 3 | | 12 | $7^1$ | | 13 | | | | 11 | | | | | | $6^2$ | | 5 | | 24 |
| 1 | 2 | 4 | | | | | 8 | 9 | 10 | | $3^1$ | | | 7 | 12 | | | | | 11 | | | | | | 6 | | 5 | | 25 |
| | 2 | 4 | | | | 12 | 8 | | 9 | | 3 | | | 7 | | | | | | $10^1$ | | | | 11 | | 6 | 1 | 5 | | 26 |
| 1 | 2 | 4 | | | | | 8 | 9 | $10^2$ | | 3 | | | 7 | | | | | | 11 | | | | 12 | | $6^1$ | | 5 | 13 | 27 |
| 1 | 2 | 4 | | | | | 8 | 9 | 10 | | 3 | | | 7 | | | | | | $11^1$ | | | | 6 | | | | 5 | 12 | 28 |
| 1 | 2 | 4 | | | | | 8 | 9 | 10 | | 3 | | | 7 | | | | | | 11 | | | | 6 | | | | 5 | | 29 |
| 1 | 2 | 4 | | | | | 8 | 9 | 10 | | 3 | | | 7 | | | | | | $11^1$ | | | | 6 | | | | 5 | 12 | 30 |
| 1 | 2 | 4 | | | | | 8 | 9■ | 10 | | 3 | | | 7 | 12 | | | | | $11^1$ | | 6 | | | | | | 5 | | 31 |
| 1 | 2 | 4 | | | | | $8^2$ | 9 | $10^1$ | | | | | 7 | 3 | | | | | 11 | | 6 | | 12 | | 13 | | 5 | | 32 |
| 1 | 2 | 4 | | 8 | | | | 9 | 10 | | | | | 7 | 3 | | | | | 11 | | 6 | | | | | | 5 | | 33 |
| 1 | 2 | 4 | | $8^2$ | | | | $9^1$ | 10 | | | | | 7 | 3 | | | | | 11 | 13 | 6 | | | | | | 5 | 12 | 34 |
| 1 | 2 | $4^2$ | | $8^3$ | | | | | 9 | | | | 14 | 7 | 3 | | | | | 11 | 12 | 6 | | 13 | | | | 5 | $10^1$ | 35 |
| 1 | 2 | 4 | | | | | | 9■ | 10 | 12 | | | | 7 | 3 | | | | | $11^1$ | | 6 | | 8 | | | | 5 | | 36 |
| 1 | $2^2$ | 4 | | 12 | | | | | 9 | 13 | | | | 7 | 3 | $11^1$ | | | | 10 | | 6 | | 8 | 5 | | | | | 37 |
| | 2 | 4 | | 5 | | | | | 9 | $11^1$ | | | | 12 | 3 | 7 | | $8^2$ | | 10 | 13 | 6 | | | | | 1 | | | 38 |

**Carling Cup**

| | | | |
|---|---|---|---|
| Second Round | Swindon T | (h) | 2-2 |
| Third Round | Manchester U | (h) | 2-3 |

**FA Cup**

| | | | |
|---|---|---|---|
| Third Round | Arsenal | (h) | 1-4 |

# LEICESTER CITY FL Championship

## FOUNDATION

In 1884 a number of young footballers who were mostly old boys of Wyggeston School, held a meeting at a house on the Roman Fosse Way and formed Leicester Fosse FC. They collected 9d (less than 4p) towards the cost of a ball, plus the same amount for membership. Their first professional, Harry Webb from Stafford Rangers, was signed in 1888 for 2s 6d (12p) per week, plus travelling expenses.

***The Walkers Stadium, Filbert Way, Leicester LE2 7FL.***

***Telephone:*** 0870 040 6000.

***Ticket Office:*** 0870 040 6000.

***Website:*** www.lcfc.co.uk

***Ground Capacity:*** 32,500.

***Record Attendance:*** 47,298 v Tottenham H, FA Cup 5th rd, 18 February 1928.

***Pitch Measurements:*** 110yd × 76yd.

***Chairman:*** Jim McCahill.

***Chief Executive:*** Tim Davies.

***Secretary:*** Andrew Neville.

***Manager:*** Micky Adams.

***Assistant Manager:*** Alan Cork.

***Physio:*** David Rennie.

***Colours:*** Blue shirts, white shorts, blue stockings.

***Change Colours:*** All black.

***Year Formed:*** 1884.

***Turned Professional:*** 1888.

***Ltd Co:*** 1897.

***Previous Name:*** 1884, Leicester Fosse; 1919, Leicester City.

***Club Nickname:*** 'Foxes'.

***Previous Grounds:*** 1884, Victoria Park; 1887, Belgrave Road; 1888, Victoria Park; 1891, Filbert Street.

***First Football League Game:*** 1 September 1894, Division 2, v Grimsby T (a) L 3–4 – Thraves; Smith, Bailey; Seymour, Brown, Henrys; Hill, Hughes, McArthur (1), Skea (2), Priestman.

***Record League Victory:*** 10–0 v Portsmouth, Division 1, 20 October 1928 – McLaren; Black, Brown; Findlay, Carr, Watson; Adcock, Hine (3), Chandler (6), Lochhead, Barry (1).

***Record Cup Victory:*** 8–1 v Coventry C (a), League Cup 5th rd, 1 December 1964 – Banks; Sjoberg, Norman (2); Roberts, King, McDerment; Hodgson (2), Cross, Goodfellow, Gibson (1), Stringfellow (2), (1 og).

## HONOURS

*Football League:* Division 1 – Runners-up 1928–29; Promoted from Division 1 1993–94 (play-offs) and 1995–96 (play-offs); Division 2 – Champions 1924–25, 1936–37, 1953–54, 1956–57, 1970–71, 1979–80; Runners-up 1907–08.

*FA Cup:* Runners-up 1949, 1961, 1963, 1969.

*Football League Cup:* Winners 1964, 1997, 2000; Runners-up 1965, 1999.

***European Competitions:*** *European Cup-Winners' Cup:* 1961–62. *UEFA Cup:* 1997–98, 2000–01.

## SKY SPORTS FACT FILE

The first four figure transfer fee paid by Leicester City for a player was £3,000 in June 1923 when they secured Arthur Chandler from Queens Park Rangers. By September 1986 and the capture of Steve Moran from Southampton their highest was £300,000.

***Record Defeat:*** 0–12 (as Leicester Fosse) v Nottingham F, Division 1, 21 April 1909.

***Most League Points (2 for a win):*** 61, Division 2, 1956–57.

***Most League Points (3 for a win):*** 77, Division 2, 1991–92.

***Most League Goals:*** 109, Division 2, 1956–57.

***Highest League Scorer in Season:*** Arthur Rowley, 44, Division 2, 1956–57.

***Most League Goals in Total Aggregate:*** Arthur Chandler, 259, 1923–35.

***Most League Goals in One Match:*** 6, John Duncan v Port Vale, Division 2, 25 December 1924; 6, Arthur Chandler v Portsmouth, Division 1, 20 October 1928.

***Most Capped Player:*** John O'Neill, 39, Northern Ireland.

***Most League Appearances:*** Adam Black, 528, 1920–35.

***Youngest League Player:*** Dave Buchanan, 16 years 192 days v Oldham Ath, 1 January 1979.

***Record Transfer Fee Received:*** £11,000,000 from Liverpool for Emile Heskey, March 2000.

***Record Transfer Fee Paid:*** £5,500,000 to Wolverhampton W for Ade Akinbiyi, July 2001.

***Football League Record:*** 1894 Elected to Division 2; 1908–09 Division 1; 1909–25 Division 2; 1925–35 Division 1; 1935–37 Division 2; 1937–39 Division 1; 1946–54 Division 2; 1954–55 Division 1; 1955–57 Division 2; 1957–69 Division 1; 1969–71 Division 2; 1971–78 Division 1; 1978–80 Division 2; 1980–81 Division 1; 1981–83 Division 2; 1983–87 Division 1; 1987–92 Division 2; 1992–94 Division 1; 1994–95 FA Premier League; 1995–96 Division 1; 1996–2002 FA Premier League; 2002–03 Division 1; 2003–04 FA Premier League; 2004– FLC.

## MANAGERS

Frank Gardner 1884–92
Ernest Marson 1892–94
J. Lee 1894–95
Henry Jackson 1895–97
William Clark 1897–98
George Johnson 1898–1912
Jack Bartlett 1912–14
Louis Ford 1914–15
Harry Linney 1915–19
Peter Hodge 1919–26
Willie Orr 1926–32
Peter Hodge 1932–34
Arthur Lochhead 1934–36
Frank Womack 1936–39
Tom Bromilow 1939–45
Tom Mather 1945–46
John Duncan 1946–49
Norman Bullock 1949–55
David Halliday 1955–58
Matt Gillies 1958–68
Frank O'Farrell 1968–71
Jimmy Bloomfield 1971–77
Frank McLintock 1977–78
Jock Wallace 1978–82
Gordon Milne 1982–86
Bryan Hamilton 1986–87
David Pleat 1987–91
Gordon Lee 1991
Brian Little 1991–94
Mark McGhee 1994–95
Martin O'Neill 1995–2000
Peter Taylor 2000–01
Dave Bassett 2001–02
Micky Adams April 2002–

## LATEST SEQUENCES

***Longest Sequence of League Wins:*** 7, 28.2.1993 – 27.3.1993.

***Longest Sequence of League Defeats:*** 8, 17.3.2001 – 28.4.2001.

***Longest Sequence of League Draws:*** 6, 21.8.1976 – 18.9.1976.

***Longest Sequence of Unbeaten League Matches:*** 19, 6.2.1971 – 18.8.1971.

***Longest Sequence Without a League Win:*** 18, 12.4.1975 – 1.11.1975.

***Successive Scoring Runs:*** 31 from 12.11.1932.

***Successive Non-scoring Runs:*** 7 from 21.11.1987.

## TEN YEAR LEAGUE RECORD

| | | *P* | *W* | *D* | *L* | *F* | *A* | *Pts* | *Pos* |
|---|---|---|---|---|---|---|---|---|---|
| 1994-95 | PR Lge | 42 | 6 | 11 | 25 | 45 | 80 | 29 | 21 |
| 1995-96 | Div 1 | 46 | 19 | 14 | 13 | 66 | 60 | 71 | 5 |
| 1996-97 | PR Lge | 38 | 12 | 11 | 15 | 46 | 54 | 47 | 9 |
| 1997-98 | PR Lge | 38 | 13 | 14 | 11 | 51 | 41 | 53 | 10 |
| 1998-99 | PR Lge | 38 | 12 | 13 | 13 | 40 | 46 | 49 | 10 |
| 1999-2000 | PR Lge | 38 | 16 | 7 | 15 | 55 | 55 | 55 | 8 |
| 2000-01 | PR Lge | 38 | 14 | 6 | 18 | 39 | 51 | 48 | 13 |
| 2001-02 | PR Lge | 38 | 5 | 13 | 20 | 30 | 64 | 28 | 20 |
| 2002-03 | Div 1 | 46 | 26 | 14 | 6 | 73 | 40 | 92 | 2 |
| 2003-04 | PR Lge | 38 | 6 | 15 | 17 | 48 | 65 | 33 | 18 |

## DID YOU KNOW ?

In 2003–04 Les Ferdinand became the oldest debutant for Leicester City at 36 years 251 days on 16 August. That honour had previously been held by Ben Davies who first appeared at 35 years 182 days on 8 December 1923.

## LEICESTER CITY 2003–04 LEAGUE RECORD

| Match No. | Date | Venue | Opponents | Result | | H/T Score | Lg. Pos. | Goalscorers | Attendance |
|---|---|---|---|---|---|---|---|---|---|
| 1 | Aug 16 | H | Southampton | D | 2-2 | 2-0 | 0 | Dickov (pen) 5, Ferdinand 10 | 31,621 |
| 2 | 23 | A | Chelsea | L | 1-2 | 1-2 | 14 | Scowcroft 40 | 41,074 |
| 3 | 26 | H | Middlesbrough | D | 0-0 | 0-0 | — | | 30,823 |
| 4 | 30 | A | Aston Villa | L | 1-3 | 0-3 | 16 | Izzet 53 | 32,274 |
| 5 | Sept 15 | H | Leeds U | W | 4-0 | 2-0 | — | Nalis 20, Dickov 2 23, 80, Scowcroft 90 | 30,460 |
| 6 | 20 | A | Liverpool | L | 1-2 | 0-1 | 13 | Bent 90 | 44,094 |
| 7 | 27 | H | Manchester U | L | 1-4 | 0-3 | 16 | Sinclair 73 | 32,044 |
| 8 | Oct 4 | A | Fulham | L | 0-2 | 0-1 | 19 | | 14,612 |
| 9 | 19 | H | Tottenham H | L | 1-2 | 1-0 | 20 | Dickov 38 | 31,521 |
| 10 | 25 | A | Wolverhampton W | L | 3-4 | 3-0 | 20 | Ferdinand 2 12, 15, Scimeca 35 | 28,578 |
| 11 | Nov 2 | H | Blackburn R | W | 2-0 | 0-0 | 18 | Bent 75, Howey 82 | 30,975 |
| 12 | 9 | A | Manchester C | W | 3-0 | 1-0 | 15 | Stewart 12, Dickov (pen) 53, Bent 58 | 46,966 |
| 13 | 22 | H | Charlton Ath | D | 1-1 | 1-0 | 16 | Ferdinand 39 | 30,242 |
| 14 | 29 | A | Portsmouth | W | 2-0 | 1-0 | 13 | Ferdinand 31, Bent 59 | 20,140 |
| 15 | Dec 6 | H | Arsenal | D | 1-1 | 0-0 | 15 | Hignett 90 | 32,108 |
| 16 | 13 | H | Birmingham C | L | 0-2 | 0-1 | 17 | | 30,639 |
| 17 | 20 | A | Everton | L | 2-3 | 1-1 | 17 | Ferdinand 45, Scowcroft 58 | 37,007 |
| 18 | 26 | H | Newcastle U | D | 1-1 | 0-0 | 18 | Dickov 67 | 32,148 |
| 19 | 28 | A | Bolton W | D | 2-2 | 1-1 | 17 | Bent 18, Ferdinand 90 | 27,407 |
| 20 | Jan 7 | A | Southampton | D | 0-0 | 0-0 | — | | 31,053 |
| 21 | 11 | H | Chelsea | L | 0-4 | 0-2 | 18 | | 31,547 |
| 22 | 17 | A | Middlesbrough | D | 3-3 | 0-1 | 18 | Dickov 2 49, 65, Bent 76 | 27,124 |
| 23 | 31 | H | Aston Villa | L | 0-5 | 0-0 | 18 | | 31,056 |
| 24 | Feb 7 | A | Newcastle U | L | 1-3 | 0-2 | 18 | Ferdinand 80 | 52,125 |
| 25 | 10 | H | Bolton W | D | 1-1 | 1-1 | — | Ferdinand 16 | 26,674 |
| 26 | 22 | A | Tottenham H | D | 4-4 | 1-3 | 19 | Doherty (og) 9, Ferdinand 51, Thatcher 74, Bent 79 | 35,218 |
| 27 | 28 | H | Wolverhampton W | D | 0-0 | 0-0 | 19 | | 31,768 |
| 28 | Mar 13 | A | Birmingham C | W | 1-0 | 0-0 | 17 | Ferdinand 53 | 29,491 |
| 29 | 20 | H | Everton | D | 1-1 | 0-0 | 17 | Bent 90 | 31,650 |
| 30 | 28 | H | Liverpool | D | 0-0 | 0-0 | 18 | | 32,013 |
| 31 | Apr 5 | A | Leeds U | L | 2-3 | 0-2 | — | Dickov 77, Izzet 79 | 34,036 |
| 32 | 10 | H | Fulham | L | 0-2 | 0-0 | 19 | | 28,392 |
| 33 | 13 | A | Manchester U | L | 0-1 | 0-0 | — | | 67,749 |
| 34 | 17 | A | Blackburn R | L | 0-1 | 0-1 | 19 | | 22,749 |
| 35 | 24 | H | Manchester C | D | 1-1 | 0-1 | 19 | Scowcroft 66 | 31,457 |
| 36 | May 1 | A | Charlton Ath | D | 2-2 | 1-0 | 20 | Bent 5, Ferdinand 88 | 26,043 |
| 37 | 8 | H | Portsmouth | W | 3-1 | 2-0 | 18 | Taylor (og) 6, Dickov 27, Scowcroft 71 | 31,536 |
| 38 | 15 | A | Arsenal | L | 1-2 | 1-0 | 18 | Dickov 26 | 38,419 |

**Final League Position: 18**

### GOALSCORERS

*League (48):* Ferdinand 12, Dickov 11 (2 pens), Bent 9, Scowcroft 5, Izzet 2, Hignett 1, Howey 1, Nalis 1, Scimeca 1, Sinclair 1, Stewart 1, Thatcher 1, own goals 2.
*Carling Cup (1):* Dickov 1 (pen).
*FA Cup (3):* Bent 1, Dickov 1, Ferdinand 1.

| Walker I 37 | Curtis J 14 + 1 | Rogers A 7 + 1 | Elliott M 3 + 4 | Thatcher B 28 + 1 | Scimeca R 28 + 1 | Gillespie K 7 + 5 | Izzet M 30 | Dickov P 28 + 7 | Ferdinand L 20 + 9 | Scowcroft J 33 + 2 | Stewart J 16 + 9 | Nalis L 11 + 9 | Deane B — + 5 | Howey S 13 | Impey A 11 + 2 | Hignett C 3 + 10 | Sinclair F 11 + 3 | Taggart G 9 | Bent M 28 + 5 | Coyne D 1 + 3 | McKinlay B 15 + 1 | Davidson C 8 + 5 | Heath M 13 | Brooker P — + 3 | Dabizas N 18 | Guppy S 9 + 6 | Freund S 13 + 1 | Benjamin T 2 + 2 | Canero P 2 + 5 | *Match No.* |
|---|---|---|---|---|---|---|---|---|---|---|---|---|---|---|---|---|---|---|---|---|---|---|---|---|---|---|---|---|---|---|
| 1 | 2 | 3 | 4 | 5 | 6 | $7^1$ | 8 | $9^2$ | $10^3$ | 11 | 12 | 13 | 14 | | | | | | | | | | | | | | | | | 1 |
| 1 | 2 | 3■ | | 5 | 6■ | 12 | 8 | $9^2$ | | 10 | | $11^3$ | 13 | 4 | $7^1$ | 14 | | | | | | | | | | | | | | 2 |
| 1 | 2 | 3 | | 5 | 6 | 7 | 8 | $9^2$ | | 10 | | $11^1$ | 12 | 4 | | 13 | | | | | | | | | | | | | | 3 |
| 1 | $2^3$ | 3 | | 5 | 6 | 7 | 8 | $9^2$ | 10■ | 11 | 13 | 12 | | $4^1$ | 14 | | | | | | | | | | | | | | | 4 |
| 1 | 2 | | | 5 | | | 8 | $9^3$ | | 7 | 12 | 11 | 13 | | 14 | $4^1$ | 3 | 6 | $10^2$ | | | | | | | | | | | 5 |
| 1 | 2 | | | 3 | 12 | | 4 | 9 | | 11 | $13^3$ | $8^1$ | 14 | | | $7^2$ | 6 | 5 | 10 | | | | | | | | | | | 6 |
| $1^G$ | 2 | 12 | | $3^1$ | 4 | | 8 | 9 | | 7 | 13 | 11 | | | | | 6 | $5^2$ | 10 | 15 | | | | | | | | | | 7 |
| 1 | | 3 | | | 7 | 14 | 8 | 12 | 13 | 10 | | $11^2$ | | $4^1$ | 2 | | 6 | 5 | $9^3$ | | | | | | | | | | | 8 |
| 1 | 2 | 3 | | | 4 | $7^1$ | 8 | $9^2$ | $10^3$ | 11 | 12 | | | | | 13 | 6 | 5 | 14 | | | | | | | | | | | 9 |
| 1 | 2 | 3 | 4 | | 6 | $7^1$ | 8 | $9^3$ | $10^2$ | 11 | | 12 | | | | 13 | | 5 | 14 | | | | | | | | | | | 10 |
| 1 | | | 12 | 13 | | $7^2$ | 6 | 14 | $9^3$ | 8 | 11 | | | 5 | 2 | | $3^1$ | | 10 | | 4 | | | | | | | | | 11 |
| 1 | | | | 3 | 6 | | 8 | $9^2$ | 12 | 7 | 11 | | | 5 | 2 | 13 | | | $10^1$ | | 4 | | | | | | | | | 12 |
| 1 | | | | 3 | 6 | | 8 | 12 | $9^1$ | 7 | 11 | | | 5 | 2 | | | | 10 | | 4 | | | | | | | | | 13 |
| 1 | 2 | | | 3 | 6 | | 8 | | $9^2$ | 7 | 11 | | | 5 | | 12 | | | $10^1$ | | 4 | 13 | | | | | | | | 14 |
| 1 | | | | 3 | 6 | 13 | | 12 | $9^2$ | 7 | 11 | | | 5 | 2 | 14 | | | $10^1$ | | $4^3$ | 8 | | | | | | | | 15 |
| 1■ | 13 | | 5■ | $3^1$ | 6 | | 8 | $10^G$ | $9^2$ | 7 | 11 | | | | 2 | | | | 12 | 15 | | 4 | | | | | | | | 16 |
| 1 | | | 12 | 3 | 6 | | 8 | 13 | 9 | 7 | $11^3$ | | | $5^1$ | 2 | | | | 10 | | $4^2$ | 14 | | | | | | | | 17 |
| 1 | 2 | | 12 | 3 | 6 | | 8 | 9 | 10 | 7 | $11^2$ | | | $5^1$ | | | | | | | 4 | 13 | | | | | | | | 18 |
| | 2 | | | 3 | 6 | | 8 | $9^1$ | 12 | 7 | 13 | | | | | $11^3$ | | | $10^2$ | 1 | | 4 | 5 | 14 | | | | | | 19 |
| 1 | | | | 3 | | | 8 | 12 | $10^1$ | 7 | 11 | | | 5 | 2 | | | | 9 | | | 6 | | | 4 | | | | | 20 |
| 1 | | | | | | | | 9 | 12 | 7 | 11 | $8^3$ | | 5 | 2 | 13 | | | $10^1$ | | $4^2$ | 3 | | 14 | 6 | | | | | 21 |
| 1 | 2 | | | | 5 | 14 | | $9^2$ | 12 | 7 | 8 | | | | | 13 | | | $10^1$ | | $4^3$ | 3 | | | 6 | 11 | | | | 22 |
| 1 | $2^1$ | | 13 | 3 | 5 | $7^2$ | | | | 9 | | | | | | 14 | 12 | | 10 | | $4^3$ | 6 | | | 8 | 11 | | | | 23 |
| 1 | | | | 3 | 6 | | | 9 | 13 | $7^2$ | 14 | | | | $2^1$ | | 12 | 5 | 10 | | | 4 | | | | $11^3$ | 8 | | | 24 |
| 1 | | | | 3 | 2 | | | 9 | 10 | 12 | 13 | $8^3$ | | | | | | 5 | $7^1$ | | | 14 | | | 6 | $11^2$ | 4 | | | 25 |
| 1 | | | | 3 | 2 | | | $9^3$ | $10^1$ | 7■ | | 8 | | | | | 14 | $5^2$ | 12 | | | 13 | | | 6 | 11 | 4 | | | 26 |
| 1 | | | | | 2 | | 8 | 9 | 12 | $7^1$ | 3 | | | | | | | | 10 | | | | 5 | | 6 | 11 | 4 | | | 27 |
| 1 | | | | 3 | 2 | | 8 | | 10 | | | 12 | | | | | | | 9 | | 4 | | 5 | | 6 | | $7^1$ | $11^2$ | 13 | 28 |
| 1 | | | | 3 | 2 | | 8 | 9 | $10^3$ | | | 12 | | | | | | | 7 | | | | 5 | | 6 | 13 | $4^1$ | $11^2$ | 14 | 29 |
| 1 | | | | 3 | 2 | | 7 | 9 | 10 | | | $11^1$ | | | | | | | 8 | | | | 5 | | 6 | 12 | 4 | | | 30 |
| 1 | | | | 3 | 2 | | 8 | 13 | $10^3$ | 7 | | 12 | | | | | | | 9 | | | | 5 | | 6 | $11^2$ | $4^1$ | | 14 | 31 |
| 1 | | | | 3 | 2 | | 8 | 9 | | 7 | | 12 | | | | | | | 10 | | | | 5 | | $6^2$ | 11 | $4^1$ | | 13 | 32 |
| 1 | | | | 3 | 2 | 13 | 8 | $9^3$ | | 12 | $11^1$ | | | | | | | | 10 | | 4 | | 5 | | 6 | 14 | $7^2$ | | | 33 |
| 1 | | | | 3 | | | 8 | 9 | $10^2$ | 7 | | | | | | | 2 | | 11 | | $4^1$ | | $5^3$ | | 6 | 13 | 12 | | 14 | 34 |
| 1 | | | | 3 | | | 8 | 9 | $10^2$ | 7 | | 12 | | | | | $2^3$ | | 13 | | | | 5 | | 6 | 14 | $4^1$ | | 11 | 35 |
| 1 | | | | | | | 8 | $9^3$ | 13 | 11 | 3 | | | | | | 2 | | 10 | | 12 | | 5 | | 6■ | 14 | $4^1$ | | $7^2$ | 36 |
| 1 | | | | | | | $8^1$ | 9 | 13 | 7 | 3 | 12 | | | | | 2 | | $10^3$ | | 4 | | 5 | | 6 | $11^2$ | | 14 | | 37 |
| $1^G$ | | | | | | | | $9^2$ | | 7 | 3 | 11 | | | | | 2 | | 10 | 15 | 4 | | 5 | 12 | 6 | | $8^1$ | 13 | | 38 |

**Carling Cup**

| | | | | | | | |
|---|---|---|---|---|---|---|---|
| Second Round | Crewe Alex | (h) | 1-0 | | | | |
| Third Round | Aston Villa | (a) | 0-1 | | | | |

**FA Cup**

| | | | |
|---|---|---|---|
| Third Round | Manchester C | (a) | 2-2 |
| | | (h) | 1-3 |

# LEYTON ORIENT FL Championship 2

## FOUNDATION

There is some doubt about the foundation of Leyton Orient, and, indeed, some confusion with clubs like Leyton and Clapton over their early history. As regards the foundation, the most favoured version is that Leyton Orient was formed originally by members of Homerton Theological College who established Glyn Cricket Club in 1881 and then carried on through the following winter playing football. Eventually many employees of the Orient Shipping Line became involved and so the name Orient was chosen in 1888.

***Matchroom Stadium, Brisbane Road, Leyton, London E10 5NE.***

***Telephone:*** (020) 8926 1111.

***Fax:*** (020) 8926 1110.

***Website:*** leytonorient.com

***Email:*** info@leytonorient.net

***Ground Capacity:*** 11,127.

***Record Attendance:*** 34,345 v West Ham U, FA Cup 4th rd, 25 January 1964.

***Pitch Measurements:*** 110yd × 80yd.

***Chairman:*** Barry Hearn.

***Chief Executive:*** Steve Dawson.

***Manager:*** Martin Ling.

***Physio:*** Tony Flynn.

***Secretary:*** Lindsey Freeman.

***Colours:*** Red shirts with black panels under arm, red shorts with black panels down sides, red stockings with black trim.

***Change Colours:*** All black with red trim.

***Year Formed:*** 1881.

***Turned Professional:*** 1903.

***Ltd Co.:*** 1906.

***Previous Names:*** 1881, Glyn Cricket and Football Club; 1886, Eagle Football Club; 1888, Orient Football Club; 1898, Clapton Orient; 1946, Leyton Orient; 1966, Orient; 1987, Leyton Orient.

***Club Nickname:*** 'The O's'.

***Previous Grounds:*** 1884, Glyn Road; 1896, Whittles Athletic Ground; 1900, Millfields Road; 1930, Lea Bridge Road; 1937, Brisbane Road.

***First Football League Game:*** 2 September 1905, Division 2, v Leicester Fosse (a) L 1–2 – Butler; Holmes, Codling; Lamberton, Boden, Boyle; Kingaby (1), Wootten, Leigh, Evenson, Bourne.

***Record League Victory:*** 8–0 v Crystal Palace, Division 3 (S), 12 November 1955 – Welton; Lee, Earl; Blizzard, Aldous, McKnight; White (1), Facey (3), Burgess (2), Heckman, Hartburn (2). 8–0 v Rochdale, Division 4, 20 October 1987 – Wells; Howard, Dickenson (1), Smalley (1), Day, Hull, Hales (2), Castle (Sussex), Shinners (2), Godfrey (Harvey), Comfort (2). 8–0 v Colchester U,

## HONOURS

*Football League:* Division 1 best season: 22nd, 1962–63; Division 2 – Runners-up 1961–62; Division 3 – Champions 1969–70; Division 3 (S) – Champions 1955–56; Runners-up 1954–55; Promoted from Division 4 1988–89 (play-offs).

*FA Cup:* Semi-final 1978.

*Football League Cup:* best season: 5th rd, 1963.

## SKY SPORTS FACT FILE

A full house Good Friday crowd of 32,821 at White Hart Lane saw Tottenham Hotspur entertain the then Clapton Orient for the first time on 9 April 1909. Though Spurs were destined for promotion, a 76th minute goal by George Scott won it for Orient.

Division 4, 15 October 1988 – Wells; Howard, Dickenson, Hales (1p), Day (1), Sitton (1), Baker (1), Ward, Hull (3), Juryeff, Comfort (1). 8–0 v Doncaster R, Division 3, 28 December 1997 – Hyde; Channing, Naylor, Smith (1p), Hicks, Clark, Ling, Joseph R, Griffiths (3) (Harris), Richards (2) (Baker (1)), Inglethorpe (1) (Simpson).

***Record Cup Victory:*** 9–2 v Chester, League Cup 3rd rd, 15 October 1962 – Robertson; Charlton, Taylor; Gibbs, Bishop, Lea; Deeley (1), Waites (3), Dunmore (2), Graham (3), Wedge.

***Record Defeat:*** 0–8 v Aston Villa, FA Cup 4th rd, 30 January 1929.

***Most League Points (2 for a win):*** 66, Division 3 (S), 1955–56.

***Most League Points (3 for a win):*** 75, Division 4, 1988–89.

***Most League Goals:*** 106, Division 3 (S), 1955–56.

***Highest League Scorer in Season:*** Tom Johnston, 35, Division 2, 1957–58.

***Most League Goals in Total Aggregate:*** Tom Johnston, 121, 1956–58, 1959–61.

***Most League Goals in One Match:*** 4, Wally Leigh v Bradford C, Division 2, 13 April 1906; 4, Albert Pape v Oldham Ath, Division 2, 1 September 1924; 4, Peter Kitchen v Millwall, Division 3, 21 April 1984.

***Most Capped Players:*** Tunji Banjo, 7 (7), Nigeria; John Chiedozie, 7 (9), Nigeria; Tony Grealish, 7 (45), Eire.

***Most League Appearances:*** Peter Allen, 432, 1965–78.

***Youngest League Player:*** Paul Went, 15 years 327 days v Preston NE, 4 September 1965.

***Record Transfer Fee Received:*** £600,000 from Notts Co, for John Chiedozie, August 1981.

***Record Transfer Fee Paid:*** £175,000 to Wigan Ath for Paul Beesley, October 1989.

***Football League Record:*** 1905 Elected to Division 2; 1929–56 Division 3 (S); 1956–62 Division 2; 1962–63 Division 1; 1963–66 Division 2; 1966–70 Division 3; 1970–82 Division 2; 1982–85 Division 3; 1985–89 Division 4; 1989–92 Division 3; 1992–95 Division 2; 1995–2004 Division 3; 2004– FL2.

## MANAGERS

Sam Omerod 1905–06
Ike Ivenson 1906
Billy Holmes 1907–22
Peter Proudfoot 1922–29
Arthur Grimsdell 1929–30
Peter Proudfoot 1930–31
Jimmy Seed 1931–33
David Pratt 1933–34
Peter Proudfoot 1935–39
Tom Halsey 1939
Bill Wright 1939–45
Willie Hall 1945
Bill Wright 1945–46
Charlie Hewitt 1946–48
Neil McBain 1948–49
Alec Stock 1949–59
Les Gore 1959–61
Johnny Carey 1961–63
Benny Fenton 1963–64
Dave Sexton 1965
Dick Graham 1966–68
Jimmy Bloomfield 1968–71
George Petchey 1971–77
Jimmy Bloomfield 1977–81
Paul Went 1981
Ken Knighton 1981
Frank Clark 1982–91 *(Managing Director)*
Peter Eustace 1991–94
Chris Turner/John Sitton 1994–95
Pat Holland 1995–96
Tommy Taylor 1996–2001
Paul Brush 2001–03
Martin Ling January 2004–

## LATEST SEQUENCES

***Longest Sequence of League Wins:*** 10, 21.1.1956 – 30.3.1956.

***Longest Sequence of League Defeats:*** 9, 1.4.1995 – 6.5.1995.

***Longest Sequence of League Draws:*** 6, 30.11.1974 – 28.12.1974.

***Longest Sequence of Unbeaten League Matches:*** 13, 30.10.1954 – 19.2.1955.

***Longest Sequence Without a League Win:*** 23, 6.10.1962 – 13.4.1963.

***Successive Scoring Runs:*** 24 from 3.5.2003.

***Successive Non-scoring Runs:*** 8 from 19.11.1994.

## TEN YEAR LEAGUE RECORD

| | | P | W | D | L | F | A | Pts | Pos |
|---|---|---|---|---|---|---|---|---|---|
| 1994-95 | Div 2 | 46 | 6 | 8 | 32 | 30 | 75 | 26 | 24 |
| 1995-96 | Div 3 | 46 | 12 | 11 | 23 | 44 | 63 | 47 | 21 |
| 1996-97 | Div 3 | 46 | 15 | 12 | 19 | 50 | 58 | 57 | 16 |
| 1997-98 | Div 3 | 46 | 19 | 12 | 15 | 62 | 47 | 66 | 11 |
| 1998-99 | Div 3 | 46 | 19 | 15 | 12 | 68 | 59 | 72 | 6 |
| 1999-2000 | Div 3 | 46 | 13 | 13 | 20 | 47 | 52 | 52 | 19 |
| 2000-01 | Div 3 | 46 | 20 | 15 | 11 | 59 | 51 | 75 | 5 |
| 2001-02 | Div 3 | 46 | 13 | 13 | 20 | 55 | 71 | 52 | 18 |
| 2002-03 | Div 3 | 46 | 14 | 11 | 21 | 51 | 61 | 53 | 18 |
| 2003-04 | Div 3 | 46 | 13 | 14 | 19 | 48 | 65 | 53 | 19 |

## DID YOU KNOW ?

Though Leyton Orient were but briefly in the First Division in 1962–63, they did have other successes reaching the fifth round in both FA Cup and League Cup, notably accounting for Newcastle United in the former, Derby County in the latter.

## LEYTON ORIENT 2003–04 LEAGUE RECORD

| Match No. | Date | Venue | Opponents | Result | | H/T Score | Lg. Pos. | Goalscorers | Attendance |
|---|---|---|---|---|---|---|---|---|---|
| 1 | Aug 9 | H | Doncaster R | L | 1-3 | 0-1 | — | Lockwood (pen) [77] | 5194 |
| 2 | 16 | A | Mansfield T | D | 1-1 | 0-1 | 16 | Alexander [90] | 3920 |
| 3 | 23 | H | Yeovil T | W | 2-0 | 1-0 | 13 | Thorpe [4], Brazier [78] | 4431 |
| 4 | 25 | A | Darlington | L | 1-2 | 0-0 | 17 | Thorpe [59] | 4660 |
| 5 | 30 | H | Cheltenham T | L | 1-4 | 1-4 | 22 | Purser [29] | 3785 |
| 6 | Sept 6 | A | Torquay U | L | 1-2 | 0-0 | 23 | Newey [86] | 2362 |
| 7 | 13 | A | Lincoln C | D | 0-0 | 0-0 | 23 | | 3940 |
| 8 | 16 | H | Hull C | D | 1-1 | 1-1 | — | Hunt D [45] | 3728 |
| 9 | 20 | H | Scunthorpe U | D | 1-1 | 0-1 | 22 | Ibehre [90] | 3663 |
| 10 | 27 | A | Huddersfield T | L | 0-3 | 0-1 | 23 | | 8942 |
| 11 | 30 | A | Carlisle U | W | 1-0 | 0-0 | — | Ibehre [66] | 4650 |
| 12 | Oct 4 | H | Macclesfield T | W | 2-0 | 2-0 | 19 | McGhee [14], Alexander [25] | 3585 |
| 13 | 11 | H | Swansea C | L | 1-2 | 0-2 | 19 | Tate [88] | 4393 |
| 14 | 18 | A | Southend U | W | 2-1 | 1-0 | 15 | Alexander [27], McSweeney (og) [89] | 6077 |
| 15 | 21 | A | Bristol R | D | 1-1 | 0-1 | — | Ibehre [80] | 5333 |
| 16 | 25 | H | Northampton T | D | 1-1 | 0-0 | 17 | Alexander [89] | 4130 |
| 17 | Nov 1 | H | Rochdale | W | 2-1 | 1-0 | 15 | Lockwood (pen) [23], Alexander [88] | 3623 |
| 18 | 15 | A | Boston U | L | 0-3 | 0-1 | 16 | | 2619 |
| 19 | 22 | H | York C | D | 2-2 | 2-0 | 17 | Miller [3], Thorpe [35] | 3593 |
| 20 | 29 | A | Cambridge U | W | 4-1 | 3-0 | 14 | Purser 2 [17, 45], Thorpe [34], Miller [54] | 3910 |
| 21 | Dec 13 | A | Kidderminster H | L | 1-2 | 1-1 | 16 | Zakuani [7] | 2605 |
| 22 | 20 | H | Bury | W | 2-0 | 0-0 | 15 | Zakuani [60], Alexander [61] | 3475 |
| 23 | 26 | A | Oxford U | L | 1-2 | 1-1 | 15 | Alexander [26] | 9477 |
| 24 | 28 | H | Torquay U | D | 0-0 | 0-0 | 15 | | 4288 |
| 25 | Jan 3 | H | Darlington | W | 1-0 | 1-0 | 11 | Toner [9] | 3737 |
| 26 | 10 | A | Doncaster R | L | 0-5 | 0-3 | 12 | | 6293 |
| 27 | 17 | H | Mansfield T | W | 3-1 | 1-1 | 11 | Alexander 2 [6, 82], Newey [70] | 4072 |
| 28 | 24 | A | Yeovil T | W | 2-1 | 2-0 | 11 | Peters [25], Alexander [28] | 6299 |
| 29 | 31 | A | Cheltenham T | L | 0-1 | 0-1 | 11 | | 3336 |
| 30 | Feb 7 | H | Oxford U | W | 1-0 | 0-0 | 10 | Alexander [64] | 5433 |
| 31 | 21 | H | Southend U | W | 2-1 | 0-1 | 10 | Broughton (og) [67], Bramble (og) [81] | 6119 |
| 32 | 24 | A | Swansea C | L | 1-2 | 1-1 | — | Purser [31] | 4727 |
| 33 | 28 | A | Northampton T | L | 0-1 | 0-0 | 11 | | 5784 |
| 34 | Mar 2 | H | Bristol R | D | 1-1 | 0-1 | — | Ibehre [47] | 3575 |
| 35 | 6 | A | Bury | D | 1-1 | 0-0 | 11 | Mackie [73] | 2355 |
| 36 | 13 | H | Kidderminster H | D | 1-1 | 1-0 | 11 | Alexander [24] | 3764 |
| 37 | 16 | A | Hull C | L | 0-3 | 0-1 | — | | 15,531 |
| 38 | 20 | H | Lincoln C | L | 0-2 | 0-1 | 12 | | 3637 |
| 39 | 27 | A | Scunthorpe U | D | 1-1 | 0-1 | 13 | Purser [80] | 2822 |
| 40 | Apr 3 | H | Huddersfield T | D | 1-1 | 1-1 | 12 | Alexander [5] | 4137 |
| 41 | 10 | A | Macclesfield T | L | 0-1 | 0-0 | 13 | | 2156 |
| 42 | 12 | H | Carlisle U | D | 1-1 | 0-0 | 15 | Alexander [69] | 4182 |
| 43 | 17 | A | Rochdale | L | 0-3 | 0-1 | 17 | | 2417 |
| 44 | 24 | H | Boston U | L | 1-3 | 0-0 | 19 | Scott [87] | 3580 |
| 45 | May 1 | A | York C | W | 2-1 | 2-1 | 17 | Peters [28], Alexander [45] | 3462 |
| 46 | 8 | H | Cambridge U | L | 0-1 | 0-1 | 19 | | 5482 |

**Final League Position: 19**

### GOALSCORERS

*League (48):* Alexander 15, Purser 5, Ibehre 4, Thorpe 4, Lockwood 2 (2 pens), Miller 2, Newey 2, Peters 2, Zakuani 2, Brazier 1, Hunt D 1, Mackie 1, McGhee 1, Scott 1, Tate 1, Toner 1, own goals 3.
*Carling Cup (1):* Ibehre 1.
*FA Cup (3):* Alexander 1, Lockwood 1, Purser 1.
*LDV Vans Trophy (1):* Lockwood 1 (pen).

| Harrison L 19 + 1 | Miller J 27 + 7 | Hunt D 35 + 3 | Ebdon M 10 + 4 | Lockwood M 24 + 1 | Jones B 29 + 2 | Purser W 29 + 12 | Newey T 31 + 3 | Alexander G 44 | Tate C 5 + 18 | Brazier M 5 | Harnwell J 1 + 2 | Ibehre J 17 + 18 | Toner C 19 + 8 | Morris G 27 | Joseph M 23 + 1 | Stephens K — + 1 | Thorpe L 15 + 2 | Heald G 4 | McCormack A 8 + 2 | Peters M 39 | Downer S 1 + 2 | Forbes B — + 10 | McGhee D 10 | Saah B 4 + 2 | Zakuani G 9 + 1 | Cooper S 9 | Hammond D 6 + 2 | Akinfenwa A — + 1 | Barnard D 17 + 6 | Mackie J 20 | Sam L 5 + 5 | Hunt W 6 | Scott A 8 | Duncan D — + 1 | *Match No.* |
|---|---|---|---|---|---|---|---|---|---|---|---|---|---|---|---|---|---|---|---|---|---|---|---|---|---|---|---|---|---|---|---|---|---|---|---|
| 1 | 5 | $2^1$ | $4^2$ | 3 | 6 | 7 | $8^3$ | 9 | 10 | 11 | 12 | 13 | 14 | | | | | | | | | | | | | | | | | | | | | | 1 |
| | 5 | 10 | $4^1$ | 3 | 6 | 7 | $8^3$ | 9 | 12 | 11 | | | | 1 | $2^2$ | 13 | 14 | | | | | | | | | | | | | | | | | | 2 |
| | 4 | 12 | 13 | 3 | 6 | $7^2$ | $8^3$ | 9 | | 11 | 14 | | | 1 | $2^1$ | | 10 | 5 | | | | | | | | | | | | | | | | | 3 |
| | 4 | 13 | 12 | 3 | 6 | $7^3$ | $8^1$ | 9 | 14 | 11 | | | | 1 | 2 | | $10^2$ | 5 | | | | | | | | | | | | | | | | | 4 |
| 15 | $4^G$ | 12 | | 3 | $6^2$ | 7 | | 9 | | 11 | 8 | | | 1■ | 2 | | $10^1$ | 5 | 13 | | | | | | | | | | | | | | | | 5 |
| 1 | $6^1$ | 2 | 7 | 3■ | | 13 | 8 | 9■ | | | | 12 | | | 4 | | 10 | 5 | $11^2$ | | | | | | | | | | | | | | | | 6 |
| 1 | | $7^2$ | 4 | 3 | 6 | 12 | $8^1$ | 9 | | | | | | | 2 | | 10 | | 11■ | 5 | 13 | | | | | | | | | | | | | | 7 |
| 1 | 12 | 7 | 4 | 3 | 6 | | 8 | $9^2$ | 13 | | | | | | 2 | | 10 | | $11^1$ | 5 | | | | | | | | | | | | | | | 8 |
| 1 | 6 | 7 | $4^3$ | | 3 | | 8 | $9^1$ | 10 | | | 12 | | | 2 | | | | 11 | $5^2$ | 13 | 14 | | | | | | | | | | | | | 9 |
| 1 | 4 | 2 | 8 | | $3^3$ | 12 | $11^2$ | 9 | 13 | | | 10 | | | | | | | | 5 | | 14 | 6 | $7^1$ | | | | | | | | | | | 10 |
| 1 | | 2 | 8 | | $3^3$ | $7^2$ | $11^1$ | 9 | | | | 10 | | | | | | | | 5 | 4 | 12 | 6 | 13 | 14 | | | | | | | | | | 11 |
| 1 | | 2 | 8 | 3 | 6 | 7 | $11^3$ | $9^2$ | 12 | | | $10^1$ | | | | | | | | 5 | | 13 | 4 | 14 | | | | | | | | | | | 12 |
| 1 | | 2 | 8 | 3 | $6^3$ | $7^1$ | | $9^2$ | 12 | | | 10 | | | | | 13 | | 11 | 5 | | 14 | 4 | | | | | | | | | | | | 13 |
| 1 | | 8 | | $3^1$ | 12 | 7 | | 9 | | | | | | | | | 10■ | | 11 | 5 | | | 4 | | | 2 | 6 | | | | | | | | 14 |
| 1 | | 8 | 12 | | $3^1$ | $7^2$ | 13 | 9 | | | | 14 | | | | | $10^3$ | | 11 | 5 | | | 4 | | | 2 | 6 | | | | | | | | 15 |
| 1 | | 7 | 12 | | $3^3$ | 13 | $8^2$ | 9 | | | | 10 | | | | | | | 11■ | 5 | | 14 | 4 | | | $2^1$ | 6 | | | | | | | | 16 |
| 1 | 12 | $8^1$ | | 3 | | $7^2$ | 11 | 9 | | | | 10 | | | 2 | | | | 14 | 5 | | 13 | 4 | | | | $6^3$ | | | | | | | | 17 |
| 1 | 8 | | | $3^2$ | | 7 | 11 | 9 | | | | 10 | 12 | | 2 | | | | | 5 | | 13 | 4 | | | | $6^1$ | | | | | | | | 18 |
| 1 | 8 | | | 3 | | $7^1$ | $4^3$ | 9 | | | | | 12 | | 2 | | 10 | | | 5 | | 13 | | | 11 | | $6^2$ | 14 | | | | | | | 19 |
| | 4 | 8 | | 3 | | $7^2$ | 11 | 9 | | | | 12 | | 1 | $2^3$ | | $10^1$ | | | 5 | | | | | 6 | | 13 | | 14 | | | | | | 20 |
| | 4 | 8 | | 3 | | $7^2$ | 11 | 9 | | | | 12 | 13 | 1 | 2 | | $10^1$ | | | 5 | | | | | $6^3$ | | 14 | | | | | | | | 21 |
| 1 | 4 | 7 | | 3 | | | 11 | 9 | | | | | 8 | | 2 | | 10 | | | 5 | | | | | 6 | | | | | | | | | | 22 |
| 1 | 4 | 8 | | 3 | | 12 | 11■ | $9^1$ | | | | 13 | 7 | | 2 | | $10^2$ | | | 5 | | | | | $6^3$ | | | | 14 | | | | | | 23 |
| | 4 | 6 | | 3 | | 7 | $11^2$ | 9 | 12 | | | $10^1$ | $8^3$ | 1 | 2 | | | | | 5 | | 13 | | | | | | | 14 | | | | | | 24 |
| | 4 | 8 | | 3 | | | 11 | | 12 | | | 9 | $7^2$ | 1 | 2 | | $10^1$ | | | 5 | | | | | 6 | | | | 13 | | | | | | 25 |
| | 4 | 8 | | $3^1$ | 12 | 7 | | 9 | | | | 13 | 11 | 1 | $2^3$ | | $10^2$ | | | 5 | | | | | 6 | | | | 14 | | | | | | 26 |
| | 4 | 8 | | | 3 | 12 | $11^2$ | 9 | | | | $10^1$ | 7 | 1 | 2 | | | | | 5 | | | | | | | | | | 6 | 13 | | | | 27 |
| | 4 | 8 | | | 3 | 12 | 11 | 9 | | | | $10^1$ | 7 | 1 | $2^2$ | | | | | 5 | | | | | | | | | 13 | 6 | | | | | 28 |
| | 4 | 8 | | | 3 | $10^1$ | $11^2$ | 9 | 12 | | | | 7 | 1 | | | | | | 5 | | | | | | | | | 2 | 6 | 13 | | | | 29 |
| | $4^1$ | 8 | | | 2 | 10 | 12 | 9 | 13 | | | | 7 | 1 | | | | | | 5 | | | | | | | | | 3 | 6 | $11^2$ | | | | 30 |
| | 4 | 8 | | | 3 | 7 | 11 | 9 | | | | 12 | | 1 | | | | | | 5 | | | | | | | | | 2 | 6 | $10^1$ | | | | 31 |
| | $4^3$ | 8 | | | 3 | 11 | 12 | 9 | 13 | | | $10^2$ | $7^1$ | 1 | | | | | | 5 | | | | | | | | | 2 | 6 | 14 | | | | 32 |
| | | 4 | | | $3^2$ | 10 | 8 | 9 | 13 | | | 12 | 7 | 1 | | | | | | 5 | | | | | | | | | 2 | 6 | $11^1$ | | | | 33 |
| | 12 | 4 | | | $3^2$ | 10 | $11^3$ | 9 | 14 | | | 13 | 8 | 1 | | | | | | 5 | | | | | | | | | $2^1$ | 6 | 7 | | | | 34 |
| | 12 | 4 | | | | $7^1$ | $11^2$ | 9 | | | | 10 | 8 | 1 | 2 | | | | | 5 | | | | | | | | | 3 | 6 | 13 | | | | 35 |
| | 13 | 4■ | | | | $7^1$ | $11^2$ | 9 | | | | 10 | 8 | 1 | 2 | | | | | 5 | | | | | | | | | 3 | 6 | 12 | | | | 36 |
| | 12 | 8 | | | | 13 | 11 | 9 | 14 | | | $10^3$ | 7 | 1 | 3 | | | | | 5 | | | $4^1$ | | | | | | $2^2$ | 6 | | | | | 37 |
| | 4 | | | | 3 | 7 | $11^3$ | 9 | 13 | | | 14 | $8^2$ | 1 | 12 | | | | | 5 | | | | 10 | | | | | $2^1$ | 6 | | | | | 38 |
| | 4 | | | | 3 | 12 | | | 9 | | | 13 | $8^2$ | 1 | | | | | | 5 | | | | | | 2 | | | | 6 | $7^1$ | 10 | 11 | | 39 |
| | 4 | | | | 3 | 12 | | 9 | $10^3$ | | | 14 | 13 | 1 | | | | | | 5 | | | | | | 2 | | | $8^2$ | 6 | | 7 | $11^1$ | | 40 |
| | $4^2$ | | | | 3 | 12 | | 9 | $10^3$ | | | 14 | 13 | 1 | | | | | | 5 | | | | | | 2 | | | 8 | 6 | | $7^1$ | 11 | | 41 |
| 1 | | | | | 3 | 7 | | 9 | 12 | | | $10^1$ | 13 | | | | | | | 5 | | | | | | 4 | | | 2 | 6 | | 8■ | $11^2$ | | 42 |
| 1 | | | | 12 | $3^1$ | 7 | | 9 | 13 | | | $10^3$ | 14 | | | | | | | 5 | | | | | | 2 | | | 4 | 6 | | $8^2$ | 11 | | 43 |
| | 12 | 10 | | 3 | | $7^2$ | | 9 | 13 | | | 14 | | 1 | | | | | | 5 | | | | | | $2^1$ | | | 4 | 6 | | $8^3$ | 11 | | 44 |
| | | 7 | | 3 | | | | 9 | | | | 12 | 8 | 1 | | | | | | 5 | | | | 11 | 4 | | | | 2 | 6 | | | $10^1$ | | 45 |
| | | 7 | | 3 | $5^1$ | 12 | | 9 | | | | 13 | 8■ | 1 | | | | | | | | | | $10^2$ | 4 | | | | 2 | 6 | | | $11^3$ | 14 | 46 |

**Carling Cup**
First Round Cardiff C (a) 1-4

**LDV Vans Trophy**
First Round Dagenham & R (a) 1-4

**FA Cup**
First Round Grantham T (a) 2-1
Second Round Cheltenham T (a) 1-3

# LINCOLN CITY — FL Championship 2

## FOUNDATION

The original Lincoln Football Club was established in the early 1860's and was one of the first provisional clubs to affiliate to the Football Association. In their early years, they regularly played matches against the famous Sheffield Club and later became known as Lincoln Lindum. The present organisation was formed at a public meeting held in the Monson Arms Hotel in June 1884 and won the Lincolnshire Cup in only their third season. They were founder members of the Midland League in 1889 and that competition's first champions.

***Sincil Bank Stadium, Lincoln LN5 8LD.***

***Telephone:*** (01522) 880 011.

***Fax:*** (01522) 880 020.

***Ticket Office:*** (01522) 880 011.

***Website:*** www.redimps.com

***Ground Capacity:*** 9,800.

***Record Attendance:*** 23,196 v Derby Co, League Cup 4th rd, 15 November 1967.

***Pitch Measurements:*** 110yd × 71yd.

***Chairman:*** Rob Bradley.

***Vice-chairman:*** Kevin Cooke.

***General Manager:*** Dave Roberts.

***Secretary:*** Fran Martin.

***Manager:*** Keith Alexander.

***Assistant Manager:*** Gary Simpson.

***Physio:*** Keith Oakes.

***Colours:*** Red and white.

***Change Colours:*** Navy blue.

***Year Formed:*** 1884.

***Turned Professional:*** 1892.

***Ltd Co.:*** 1895.

***Club Nickname:*** 'The Red Imps'.

***Previous Grounds:*** 1883, John O'Gaunt's; 1894, Sincil Bank.

***First Football League Game:*** 3 September 1892, Division 2, v Sheffield U (a) L 2–4 – W. Gresham; Coulton, Neill; Shaw, Mettam, Moore; Smallman, Irving (1), Cameron (1), Kelly, J. Gresham.

***Record League Victory:*** 11–1 v Crewe Alex, Division 3 (N), 29 September 1951 – Jones; Green (1p), Varney; Wright, Emery, Grummett (1); Troops (1), Garvey, Graver (6), Whittle (1), Johnson (1).

***Record Cup Victory:*** 8–1 v Bromley, FA Cup 2nd rd, 10 December 1938 – McPhail; Hartshorne, Corbett; Bean, Leach, Whyte (1); Hancock, Wilson (1), Ponting (3), Deacon (1), Clare (2).

## HONOURS

*Football League:* Division 2 best season: 5th, 1901–02; Promotion from Division 3, 1997–98; Division 3 (N) – Champions 1931–32, 1947–48, 1951–52; Runners-up 1927–28, 1930–31, 1936–37; Division 4 – Champions 1975–76; Runners-up 1980–81.

*FA Cup:* best season: 1st rd of Second Series (5th rd equivalent), 1887, 2nd rd (5th rd equivalent), 1890, 1902.

*Football League Cup:* best season: 4th rd, 1968.

*GM Vauxhall Conference:* Champions 1987–88.

## SKY SPORTS FACT FILE

Lincoln City owed much to Allan Hall whose goals had helped considerably in the 1931–32 promotion season. They were in his debt the following term when despite missing a third of the games he scored 23 valuable goals to keep them up.

***Record Defeat:*** 3–11 v Manchester C, Division 2, 23 March 1895.

***Most League Points (2 for a win):*** 74, Division 4, 1975–76.

***Most League Points (3 for a win):*** 77, Division 3, 1981–82.

***Most League Goals:*** 121, Division 3 (N), 1951–52.

***Highest League Scorer in Season:*** Allan Hall, 41, Division 3 (N), 1931–32.

***Most League Goals in Total Aggregate:*** Andy Graver, 143, 1950–55 and 1958–61.

***Most League Goals in One Match:*** 6, Frank Keetley v Halifax T, Division 3N, 16 January 1932; 6, Andy Graver v Crewe Alex, Division 3N, 29 September 1951.

***Most Capped Player:*** David Pugh, 3 (7), Wales; George Moulson, 3, Republic of Ireland.

***Most League Appearances:*** Grant Brown, 407, 1989–2002.

***Youngest League Player:*** Shane Nicholson, 16 years 172 days v Burnley, 22 November 1986.

***Record Transfer Fee Received:*** £500,000 from Port Vale for Gareth Ainsworth, September 1997.

***Record Transfer Fee Paid:*** £75,000 to Carlisle U for Dean Walling, September 1997; £75,000 to Bury for Tony Battersby, August 1998.

***Football League Record:*** 1892 Founder member of Division 2. Remained in Division 2 until 1920 when they failed re-election but also missed seasons 1908–09 and 1911–12 when not re-elected. 1921–32 Division 3 (N); 1932–34 Division 2; 1934–48 Division 3 (N); 1948–49 Division 2; 1949–52 Division 3 (N); 1952–61 Division 2; 1961–62 Division 3; 1962–76 Division 4; 1976–79 Division 3; 1979–81 Division 4; 1981–86 Division 3; 1986–87 Division 4; 1987–88 GM Vauxhall Conference; 1988–92 Division 4; 1992–98 Division 3; 1998–99 Division 2; 1999–2004 Division 3; 2004– FL2.

## MANAGERS

David Calderhead 1900–07
John Henry Strawson 1907–14
*(had been Secretary)*
George Fraser 1919–21
David Calderhead Jnr. 1921–24
Horace Henshall 1924–27
Harry Parkes 1927–36
Joe McClelland 1936–46
Bill Anderson 1946–65
*(General Manager to 1966)*
Roy Chapman 1965–66
Ron Gray 1966–70
Bert Loxley 1970–71
David Herd 1971–72
Graham Taylor 1972–77
George Kerr 1977–78
Willie Bell 1977–78
Colin Murphy 1978–85
John Pickering 1985
George Kerr 1985–87
Peter Daniel 1987
Colin Murphy 1987–90
Allan Clarke 1990
Steve Thompson 1990–93
Keith Alexander 1993–94
Sam Ellis 1994–95
Steve Wicks *(Head Coach)* 1995
John Beck 1995–98
Shane Westley 1998
John Reames 1998–99
Phil Stant 2000–01
Alan Buckley 2001–02
Keith Alexander May 2002–

## LATEST SEQUENCES

***Longest Sequence of League Wins:*** 10, 1.9.1930 – 18.10.1930.

***Longest Sequence of League Defeats:*** 12, 21.9.1896 – 9.1.1897.

***Longest Sequence of League Draws:*** 5, 21.2.1981 – 7.3.1981.

***Longest Sequence of Unbeaten League Matches:*** 18, 11.3.1980 – 13.9.1980.

***Longest Sequence Without a League Win:*** 19, 22.8.1978 – 23.12.1978.

***Successive Scoring Runs:*** 37 from 1.3.1930.

***Successive Non-scoring Runs:*** 5 from 15.11.1913.

## TEN YEAR LEAGUE RECORD

| | | P | W | D | L | F | A | Pts | Pos |
|---|---|---|---|---|---|---|---|---|---|
| 1994-95 | Div 3 | 42 | 15 | 11 | 16 | 54 | 55 | 56 | 12 |
| 1995-96 | Div 3 | 46 | 13 | 14 | 19 | 57 | 73 | 53 | 18 |
| 1996-97 | Div 3 | 46 | 18 | 12 | 16 | 70 | 69 | 66 | 9 |
| 1997-98 | Div 3 | 46 | 20 | 15 | 11 | 60 | 51 | 72 | 3 |
| 1998-99 | Div 2 | 46 | 13 | 7 | 26 | 42 | 74 | 46 | 23 |
| 1999-2000 | Div 3 | 46 | 15 | 14 | 17 | 67 | 69 | 59 | 15 |
| 2000-01 | Div 3 | 46 | 12 | 15 | 19 | 58 | 66 | 51 | 18 |
| 2001-02 | Div 3 | 46 | 10 | 16 | 20 | 44 | 62 | 46 | 22 |
| 2002-03 | Div 3 | 46 | 18 | 16 | 12 | 46 | 37 | 70 | 6 |
| 2003-04 | Div 3 | 46 | 19 | 17 | 10 | 68 | 47 | 74 | 7 |

## DID YOU KNOW ?

In 1983 Lincoln City players were persuaded to make a stab at the Hit Parade and recorded a 45 rpm disc with proceeds destined for the Red Imps Association. On one side was 'You'll Never Walk Alone', backed by 'The Lincolnshire Poacher'.

## LINCOLN CITY 2003–04 LEAGUE RECORD

| *Match No.* | *Date* | *Venue* | *Opponents* | *Result* | | *H/T Score* | *Lg. Pos.* | *Goalscorers* | *Attendance* |
|---|---|---|---|---|---|---|---|---|---|
| 1 | Aug 9 | H | Oxford U | L | 0-1 | 0-1 | — | | 4543 |
| 2 | 16 | A | Torquay U | L | 0-1 | 0-0 | 19 | | 2920 |
| 3 | 23 | H | Doncaster R | D | 0-0 | 0-0 | 21 | | 5051 |
| 4 | 25 | A | Bury | L | 1-2 | 1-0 | 23 | Fletcher [25] | 2576 |
| 5 | 30 | H | York C | W | 3-0 | 1-0 | 21 | Fletcher [21], Butcher [72], Mayo (pen) [88] | 3892 |
| 6 | Sept 3 | A | Cambridge U | D | 0-0 | 0-0 | — | | 4458 |
| 7 | 13 | H | Leyton Orient | D | 0-0 | 0-0 | 20 | | 3940 |
| 8 | 16 | A | Southend U | W | 2-0 | 1-0 | — | Richardson [10], Butcher [78] | 2874 |
| 9 | 20 | A | Kidderminster H | W | 2-1 | 2-1 | 13 | Richardson [32], Butcher [43] | 2462 |
| 10 | 27 | H | Rochdale | D | 1-1 | 1-1 | 14 | Richardson [44] | 4141 |
| 11 | 30 | H | Northampton T | D | 0-0 | 0-0 | — | | 3928 |
| 12 | Oct 4 | A | Swansea C | D | 2-2 | 2-1 | 13 | Butcher [11], Mayo (pen) [15] | 7914 |
| 13 | 11 | A | Scunthorpe U | W | 3-1 | 2-0 | 11 | Futcher [5], Fletcher [30], Green [57] | 5045 |
| 14 | 18 | H | Huddersfield T | W | 3-1 | 0-1 | 9 | Fletcher [61], Richardson [65], Yeo [90] | 5718 |
| 15 | 21 | H | Macclesfield T | W | 3-2 | 1-0 | — | Gain [24], Butcher [56], Green [90] | 3441 |
| 16 | 25 | A | Hull C | L | 0-3 | 0-1 | 9 | | 17,453 |
| 17 | Nov 1 | H | Carlisle U | W | 2-0 | 1-0 | 7 | Yeo [45], Fletcher [50] | 4044 |
| 18 | 15 | A | Darlington | D | 0-0 | 0-0 | 7 | | 4601 |
| 19 | 22 | H | Bristol R | W | 3-1 | 1-1 | 7 | Yeo [11], Futcher [56], Fletcher [87] | 3882 |
| 20 | 29 | A | Yeovil T | L | 1-3 | 0-0 | 8 | Yeo [50] | 4867 |
| 21 | Dec 13 | A | Mansfield T | W | 2-1 | 1-1 | 8 | Butcher [3], Gain [50] | 5797 |
| 22 | 26 | A | Boston U | W | 1-0 | 0-0 | 6 | Mayo (pen) [61] | 5708 |
| 23 | 28 | H | Cambridge U | D | 2-2 | 2-1 | 7 | Fletcher 2 [9, 41] | 5074 |
| 24 | Jan 3 | H | Bury | W | 2-1 | 2-0 | 6 | Fletcher [4], Green [28] | 3870 |
| 25 | 10 | A | Oxford U | D | 0-0 | 0-0 | 7 | | 6679 |
| 26 | 13 | H | Cheltenham T | D | 0-0 | 0-0 | — | | 3464 |
| 27 | 17 | H | Torquay U | L | 1-3 | 1-1 | 7 | Mayo [39] | 3873 |
| 28 | 23 | A | Doncaster R | W | 2-0 | 1-0 | — | Ryan (og) [12], Fletcher [58] | 8774 |
| 29 | Feb 7 | H | Boston U | D | 1-1 | 1-1 | 8 | Richardson [40] | 7114 |
| 30 | 14 | H | Scunthorpe U | D | 1-1 | 1-0 | 8 | Gain [35] | 5324 |
| 31 | 17 | A | York C | W | 4-1 | 1-0 | — | Mayo (pen) [44], Green [58], Gain [61], Yeo [76] | 3396 |
| 32 | 21 | A | Huddersfield T | L | 1-2 | 1-0 | 8 | Richardson [19] | 11,553 |
| 33 | 28 | H | Hull C | W | 2-0 | 0-0 | 8 | Gain [78], Mayo [85] | 7069 |
| 34 | Mar 6 | A | Cheltenham T | L | 2-3 | 2-1 | 8 | Richardson 2 (1 pen) [3, 45 (p)] | 3783 |
| 35 | 13 | H | Mansfield T | W | 4-1 | 0-1 | 8 | Fletcher 2 [55, 69], Green [71], Yeo [89] | 6034 |
| 36 | 16 | H | Southend U | D | 2-2 | 0-2 | — | Green [51], Yeo [90] | 3943 |
| 37 | 20 | A | Leyton Orient | W | 2-0 | 1-0 | 6 | Fletcher 2 [3, 49] | 3637 |
| 38 | 27 | H | Kidderminster H | D | 1-1 | 0-0 | 6 | Richardson [89] | 4797 |
| 39 | 30 | A | Macclesfield T | D | 0-0 | 0-0 | — | | 2016 |
| 40 | Apr 3 | A | Rochdale | W | 3-0 | 0-0 | 5 | Fletcher 2 [58, 67], Yeo [66] | 4224 |
| 41 | 10 | H | Swansea C | W | 2-1 | 0-1 | 4 | Gain [57], Yeo [82] | 5455 |
| 42 | 12 | A | Northampton T | D | 1-1 | 0-1 | 5 | Yeo [84] | 7160 |
| 43 | 17 | A | Carlisle U | W | 2-0 | 0-0 | 5 | Gain [48], Bailey [90] | 7875 |
| 44 | 24 | H | Darlington | D | 1-1 | 0-1 | 5 | Green [54] | 6187 |
| 45 | May 1 | A | Bristol R | L | 1-3 | 1-1 | 6 | Richardson [24] | 8562 |
| 46 | 8 | H | Yeovil T | L | 2-3 | 0-0 | 7 | Wilford [82], Yeo [87] | 8154 |

**Final League Position: 7**

### GOALSCORERS

*League (68):* Fletcher 16, Yeo 11, Richardson 10 (1 pen), Gain 7, Green 7, Butcher 6, Mayo 6 (4 pens), Futcher 2, Bailey 1, Wilford 1, own goal 1.
*Carling Cup (0).*
*FA Cup (3):* Bloomer 1, Mayo 1 (pen), Yeo 1.
*LDV Vans Trophy (7):* Fletcher 2, Bailey 1, Green 1, Mayo 1 (pen), Richardson 1, Yeo 1.
*Play-Offs (3):* Bailey 1, Butcher 1, Fletcher 1.

| Marriott A 46 | Mayo P 31 | Bloomer M 14 + 13 | Weaver S 39 | Morgan P 41 | Futcher B 43 | Liburd R 19 + 5 | Butcher R 26 + 6 | May R 1 + 4 | Yeo S 13 + 28 | Gain P 42 | Remy E — + 1 | Pearce A — + 3 | Fletcher G 42 | Sedgemore B 24 + 3 | McNamara N 2 + 8 | Bailey M 34 + 1 | Cropper D 5 + 16 | Willis S — + 3 | Richardson M 34 + 4 | Green F 28 + 7 | Wattley D 1 + 2 | Carbon M 1 | McCombe J 8 | Ellison K 11 | Sandwith K 1 + 2 | Rocastle C — + 2 | Wilford A — + 5 | *Match No.* |
|---|---|---|---|---|---|---|---|---|---|---|---|---|---|---|---|---|---|---|---|---|---|---|---|---|---|---|---|---|
| 1 | 3 | 2 | $4^1$ | 5 | 6 | 7 | 8 | $9^2$ | 10▪ | 11 | 12 | 13 | | | | | | | | | | | | | | | | 1 |
| 1 | 3 | 2 | 4 | 5 | 6 | $7^1$ | 8 | 12 | 10 | | | | 9 | $11^2$ | 13 | | | | | | | | | | | | | 2 |
| 1 | 3 | 12 | 4 | 5 | 6 | $7^2$ | 8 | | | $11^3$ | | | 9 | | | $2^1$ | 10 | 13 | 14 | | | | | | | | | 3 |
| 1 | 3 | 12 | 4 | 5 | 6 | $7^2$ | 8 | | 13 | 11 | | | $9^1$ | | | 2 | $10^3$ | | 14 | | | | | | | | | 4 |
| 1 | 3 | | 4 | 5 | 6 | $7^1$ | 8 | | 12 | 11 | | | $9^3$ | | 14 | 2 | $10^2$ | | 13 | | | | | | | | | 5 |
| 1 | 3 | | 4 | 5 | 6 | $7^1$ | 8 | | 12 | 11 | | | 9 | | | 2 | 13 | | $10^2$ | | | | | | | | | 6 |
| 1 | 3 | | 4 | 5 | 6 | $7^1$ | $8^2$ | | 12 | 11 | | | 9 | | | 2 | | 13 | 10 | | | | | | | | | 7 |
| 1 | 3 | | 4 | 5 | 6 | $7^1$ | 8 | | 12 | 11 | | | $9^3$ | | | 2 | 13 | | $10^2$ | 14 | | | | | | | | 8 |
| 1 | 3 | | 4 | 5 | 6 | $7^3$ | 8 | | | 11 | | | $9^2$ | | | 2 | 12 | | $10^1$ | 13 | 14 | | | | | | | 9 |
| 1 | 3 | | $4^2$ | 5 | 6 | 7 | 8 | | 12 | 11 | | | $9^1$ | | | 2 | | | 10 | 13 | | | | | | | | 10 |
| 1 | 3 | 12 | 4 | $5^1$ | 6 | $7^3$ | 8 | | 13 | 11 | | | $9^2$ | | | 2 | | | 10 | 14 | | | | | | | | 11 |
| 1 | 3▪ | 12 | 4 | 5 | 6 | 7 | 8 | | | 11 | | | $9^1$ | | | 2 | | | 10 | | | | | | | | | 12 |
| 1 | 3 | 12 | 4 | 5 | 6 | 7 | 8 | | | | | | $9^1$ | | | 2▪ | 13 | | $10^3$ | $11^2$ | 14 | | | | | | | 13 |
| 1 | | 12 | 4 | 5 | 6 | $7^3$ | 8 | | 13 | 3 | | | 9 | 14 | | $2^2$ | | | $10^1$ | 11 | | | | | | | | 14 |
| 1 | 3 | | 4 | 5 | 6 | 2 | 8 | | 10 | 11 | | | 9 | | | | | | | 7 | | | | | | | | 15 |
| 1 | 3 | 12 | 4 | 5 | | $2^2$ | 8 | 13 | 10 | $11^3$ | | | 9 | | | | | 14 | | 7 | | $6^1$ | | | | | | 16 |
| 1 | $3^2$ | 12 | 4 | 5 | 6 | 2 | 8 | | $10^1$ | 11 | | | 9 | 13 | 14 | | | | | $7^3$ | | | | | | | | 17 |
| 1 | 3 | 2 | 4 | 5 | 6 | $7^1$ | 8 | | 10 | | | 12 | 9 | | 13 | | | | | $11^2$ | | | | | | | | 18 |
| 1 | 3 | 2 | 4 | 5 | 6 | | 7 | 12 | 8 | 11 | | | $9^1$ | | 10 | | | | | | | | | | | | | 19 |
| 1 | 3 | 2 | $4^1$ | 5 | 6 | | 8 | 12 | 10 | 11 | | | 9 | | 7 | | | | | | | | | | | | | 20 |
| 1 | 3 | 12 | 4 | 5 | 6 | | 7 | | 10 | 11 | | | | | 13 | 2 | $8^2$ | | $9^1$ | | | | | | | | | 21 |
| 1 | 3 | | 4 | 5 | 6 | | $7^2$ | | $10^1$ | 11 | | | 9 | | 13 | 2 | $8^3$ | | 14 | 12 | | | | | | | | 22 |
| 1 | 3 | 14 | 4 | 5 | 6 | | $7^2$ | | 12 | 11 | | | 9 | 13 | | 2 | | | $10^3$ | $8^1$ | | | | | | | | 23 |
| 1 | 3 | | 4 | 5 | 6 | | | | 12 | 11 | | | $9^1$ | 7 | 14 | 2 | 13 | | $10^2$ | $8^3$ | | | | | | | | 24 |
| 1 | 3 | | 4 | 5 | 6 | | 12 | | 13 | 11 | | | $9^2$ | 7 | | 2 | 14 | | $10^3$ | $8^1$ | | | | | | | | 25 |
| 1 | 3 | | 4 | 5 | 6 | | | | $10^2$ | 11 | | | 9 | 7 | | 2 | 12 | | $8^1$ | 13 | | | | | | | | 26 |
| 1 | 3 | | $4^1$ | 5 | 6 | | | | 12 | $11^3$ | | | 9 | 7 | 14 | 2 | 13 | | $10^2$ | 8 | | | | | | | | 27 |
| 1 | 3 | | 4 | 5 | 6 | | 11 | | 12 | | | | 9 | 7 | | 2 | 13 | | $10^2$ | $8^1$ | | | | | | | | 28 |
| 1 | | 3 | 4 | 5 | 6 | | | | 12 | 11 | | | 9 | 7 | | 2 | | | 10 | $8^1$ | | | | | | | | 29 |
| 1 | 3 | | 4 | 5 | 6 | | | | 12 | 11 | | | $9^1$ | 7 | | 2 | 13 | | $10^2$ | 8 | | | | | | | | 30 |
| 1 | 3 | | 4 | 5 | 6 | 14 | | | 12 | 11 | | | $9^1$ | 7 | | $2^3$ | 13 | | $10^2$ | 8 | | | | | | | | 31 |
| 1 | 3 | | $4^1$ | 5 | 6 | 14 | | | 12 | 11 | | | 9 | $7^3$ | | 2 | 13 | | $10^2$ | 8 | | | | | | | | 32 |
| 1 | 3 | 13 | 4 | 5 | 6 | 14 | | | | 11 | | | 9 | $7^3$ | | $2^2$ | 12 | | $10^1$ | 8 | | | | | | | | 33 |
| 1 | | 6 | 4 | 5 | | 3▪ | | | 9 | 11 | | 12 | | 7 | | | 13 | | $10^2$ | $8^1$ | 2 | | | | | | | 34 |
| 1 | | 12 | 4 | 5 | | 13 | | | 14 | $3^2$ | | | 9 | 7 | | $2^1$ | | | 10 | $8^3$ | | | 6 | 11 | | | | 35 |
| 1 | | 2 | | 5 | 6 | | | | 12 | 3 | | | 9 | $7^1$ | | | 13 | | $10^2$ | 8 | | | 4 | $11^3$ | 14 | | | 36 |
| 1 | | 2 | | 5 | 6 | | | | 12 | 3 | | | $9^1$ | 7 | | | 13 | | $10^2$ | $8^3$ | | | 4 | 11 | 14 | | | 37 |
| 1 | | 2 | $4^3$ | $5^1$ | 6 | | | | 13 | 3 | | | 9 | $7^2$ | | 12 | | | 10 | 8 | | | | 11 | | 14 | | 38 |
| 1 | | 5 | | | 6 | 12 | | | 8 | $3^1$ | | | 9 | 7 | | 2 | | | $10^2$ | 13 | | | 4 | 11 | | | | 39 |
| 1 | | 5 | | | 6 | | 12 | | 13 | 3 | | | $9^1$ | 7 | | 2 | | | 10 | $8^2$ | | | 4 | $11^3$ | | 14 | | 40 |
| 1 | | | | 5 | 6 | | 12 | | 13 | 3 | | | 9 | 7 | | 2 | | | $10^3$ | $8^1$ | | | 4 | $11^2$ | | | 14 | 41 |
| 1 | | | | 5 | 6 | | 12 | | 13 | 3 | | | 9 | 7 | | 2 | | | $10^1$ | $8^2$ | | | $4^3$ | 11 | | | 14 | 42 |
| 1 | | 14 | | $5^3$ | 6 | | 12 | | 13 | 3 | | | 9 | 7 | | 2 | | | 10 | $8^1$ | | | 4 | $11^2$ | | | | 43 |
| 1 | | | 4 | | 6 | | 7 | | 12 | 3 | | | 9 | $5^1$ | | 2 | | | $10^2$ | 8 | | | | | 11 | | 13 | 44 |
| 1 | | 5 | 4 | | 6 | | 7 | | 12 | 3 | | | | $8^1$ | | 2 | | | $9^2$ | 10 | | | | 11 | | | 13 | 45 |
| 1 | | 5 | 4 | | 6 | | 12 | | 13 | 3 | | | 9 | $7^1$ | | 2 | | | $10^3$ | $8^2$ | | | | 11 | | | 14 | 46 |

**Carling Cup**
First Round Stockport Co (h) 0-1

**LDV Vans Trophy**
First Round Telford U (h) 3-1
Second Round Chesterfield (h) 4-3
Quarter-Final Halifax T (a) 0-1

**FA Cup**
First Round Brighton & HA (h) 3-1
Second Round Southend U (a) 0-3

**Play-Offs**
Semi-Final Huddersfield T (h) 1-2
(a) 2-2

# LIVERPOOL

## FA Premiership

### FOUNDATION

But for a dispute between Everton FC and their landlord at Anfield in 1892, there may never have been a Liverpool club. This dispute persuaded the majority of Evertonians to quit Anfield for Goodison Park, leaving the landlord, Mr John Houlding, to form a new club. He originally tried to retain the name 'Everton' but when this failed, he founded Liverpool Association FC on 15 March 1892.

***Anfield Stadium, Liverpool L4 0TH.***

***Telephone:*** (0151) 263 2361.

***Fax:*** (0151) 260 8813.

***Ticket Office:*** 0870 220 2345.

***Website:*** www.liverpoolfc.tv

***Email:*** customercontact@liverpoolfc.tv

***Ground Capacity:*** 45,362.

***Record Attendance:*** 61,905 v Wolverhampton W, FA Cup 4th rd, 2 February 1952.

***Pitch Measurements:*** 111yd × 74yd.

***Chairman:*** David Moores.

***Chief Executive:*** Rick Parry BSC, FCA.

***Secretary:*** Bryce Morrison.

***Manager:*** Rafael Benitez.

***Physio:*** Dave Galley.

***Colours:*** All red.

***Change Colours:*** Yellow shirts, black shorts, yellow stockings.

***Year Formed:*** 1892.

***Turned Professional:*** 1892.

***Ltd Co.:*** 1892.

***Club Nicknames:*** 'Reds' or 'Pool'.

***First Football League Game:*** 2 September 1893, Division 2, v Middlesbrough Ironopolis (a) W 2–0 – McOwen; Hannah, McLean; Henderson, McQue (1), McBride; Gordon, McVean (1), M. McQueen, Stott, H. McQueen.

***Record League Victory:*** 10–1 v Rotherham T, Division 2, 18 February 1896 – Storer; Goldie, Wilkie; McCartney, McQue, Holmes; McVean (3), Ross (2), Allan (4), Becton (1), Bradshaw.

### HONOURS

*Football League:* Division 1 – Champions 1900–01, 1905–06, 1921–22, 1922–23, 1946–47, 1963–64, 1965–66, 1972–73, 1975–76, 1976–77, 1978–79, 1979–80, 1981–82, 1982–83, 1983–84, 1985–86, 1987–88, 1989–90 (Liverpool have a record number of 18 League Championship wins); Runners-up 1898–99, 1909–10, 1968–69, 1973–74, 1974–75, 1977–78, 1984–85, 1986–87, 1988–89, 1990–91, 2001–02; Division 2 – Champions 1893–94, 1895–96, 1904–05, 1961–62.

*FA Cup:* Winners 1965, 1974, 1986, 1989, 1992, 2001; Runners-up 1914, 1950, 1971, 1977, 1988, 1996;

*Football League Cup:* Winners 1981, 1982, 1983, 1984, 1995, 2001, 2003; Runners-up 1978, 1987.

*League Super Cup:* Winners 1986.

***European Competitions:*** *European Cup:* 1964–65, 1966–67, 1973–74, 1976–77 (winners), 1977–78 (winners), 1978–79, 1979–80, 1980–81 (winners), 1981–82, 1982–83, 1983–84 (winners), 1984–85 (runners-up). *Champions League:* 2001–02, 2002–03. *European Cup-Winners' Cup:* 1965–66 (runners-up), 1971–72, 1974–75, 1992–93, 1996–97 (s-f.). *European Fairs Cup:* 1967–68, 1968–69, 1969–70, 1970–71. *UEFA Cup:* 1972–73 (winners), 1975–76 (winners), 1991–92, 1995–96, 1997–98, 1998–99, 2000–01 (winners), 2002–03, 2003–04. *Super Cup:* 1977 (winners), 1978, 1984, 2001 (winners). *World Club Championship:* 1981 (runners-up), 1984 (runners-up).

### SKY SPORTS FACT FILE

On 3 May 1980 Avi Cohen scored the second Liverpool goal after 50 minutes against Aston Villa. They went on to win 4-1 and clinch the championship. It was his only goal for the club and earlier in the game Cohen had put through his own goal.

***Record Cup Victory:*** 11–0 v Stromsgodset Drammen, ECWC 1st rd 1st leg, 17 September 1974 – Clemence; Smith (1), Lindsay (1p), Thompson (2), Cormack (1), Hughes (1), Boersma (2), Hall, Heighway (1), Kennedy (1), Callaghan (1).

***Record Defeat:*** 1–9 v Birmingham C, Division 2, 11 December 1954.

***Most League Points (2 for a win):*** 68, Division 1, 1978–79.

***Most League Points (3 for a win):*** 90, Division 1, 1987–88.

***Most League Goals:*** 106, Division 2, 1895–96.

***Highest League Scorer in Season:*** Roger Hunt, 41, Division 2, 1961–62.

***Most League Goals in Total Aggregate:*** Roger Hunt, 245, 1959–69.

***Most League Goals in One Match:*** 5, Andy McGuigan v Stoke C, Division 1, 4 January 1902; 5, John Evans v Bristol R, Division 2, 15 September 1954; 5, Ian Rush v Luton T, Division 1, 29 October 1983.

***Most Capped Player:*** Ian Rush, 67 (73), Wales.

***Most League Appearances:*** Ian Callaghan, 640, 1960–78.

***Youngest League Player:*** Max Thompson, 17 years 128 days v Tottenham H, 8 May 1974.

***Record Transfer Fee Received:*** £12,500,000 from Leeds U for Robbie Fowler, November 2001.

***Record Transfer Fee Paid:*** £11,000,000 to Leicester C for Emile Heskey, March 2000.

***Football League Record:*** 1893 Elected to Division 2; 1894–95 Division 1; 1895–96 Division 2; 1896–1904 Division 1; 1904–05 Division 2; 1905–54 Division 1; 1954–62 Division 2; 1962–92 Division 1; 1992– FA Premier League.

## MANAGERS

W. E. Barclay 1892–96
Tom Watson 1896–1915
David Ashworth 1920–23
Matt McQueen 1923–28
George Patterson 1928–36
*(continued as Secretary)*
George Kay 1936–51
Don Welsh 1951–56
Phil Taylor 1956–59
Bill Shankly 1959–74
Bob Paisley 1974–83
Joe Fagan 1983–85
Kenny Dalglish 1985–91
Graeme Souness 1991–94
Roy Evans 1994–98
*(then Joint Manager)*
Gerard Houllier 1998–2004
Rafael Benitez June 2004–

## LATEST SEQUENCES

***Longest Sequence of League Wins:*** 12, 21.4.1990 – 6.10.1990.

***Longest Sequence of League Defeats:*** 9, 29.4.1899 – 14.10.1899.

***Longest Sequence of League Draws:*** 6, 19.2.1975 – 19.3.1975.

***Longest Sequence of Unbeaten League Matches:*** 31, 4.5.1987 – 16.3.1988.

***Longest Sequence Without a League Win:*** 14, 12.12.1953 – 20.3.1954.

***Successive Scoring Runs:*** 29 from 27.4.1957.

***Successive Non-scoring Runs:*** 5 from 22.12.1906.

## TEN YEAR LEAGUE RECORD

| | | P | W | D | L | F | A | Pts | Pos |
|---|---|---|---|---|---|---|---|---|---|
| 1994-95 | PR Lge | 42 | 21 | 11 | 10 | 65 | 37 | 74 | 4 |
| 1995-96 | PR Lge | 38 | 20 | 11 | 7 | 70 | 34 | 71 | 3 |
| 1996-97 | PR Lge | 38 | 19 | 11 | 8 | 62 | 37 | 68 | 4 |
| 1997-98 | PR Lge | 38 | 18 | 11 | 9 | 68 | 42 | 65 | 3 |
| 1998-99 | PR Lge | 38 | 15 | 9 | 14 | 68 | 49 | 54 | 7 |
| 1999-2000 | PR Lge | 38 | 19 | 10 | 9 | 51 | 30 | 67 | 4 |
| 2000-01 | PR Lge | 38 | 20 | 9 | 9 | 71 | 39 | 69 | 3 |
| 2001-02 | PR Lge | 38 | 24 | 8 | 6 | 67 | 30 | 80 | 2 |
| 2002-03 | PR Lge | 38 | 18 | 10 | 10 | 61 | 41 | 64 | 5 |
| 2003-04 | PR Lge | 38 | 16 | 12 | 10 | 55 | 37 | 60 | 4 |

## DID YOU KNOW?

In successive seasons 1980–81 and 1981–82, Liverpool were initially paired with Oulu in the European Cup. After a 1-1 draw in Finland, Liverpool won the return 10-1 and the following term had 1-0 and 7-0 victories against them.

## LIVERPOOL 2003–04 LEAGUE RECORD

| *Match No.* | *Date* | | *Venue* | *Opponents* | *Result* | | *H/T Score* | *Lg. Pos.* | *Goalscorers* | *Attendance* |
|---|---|---|---|---|---|---|---|---|---|---|
| 1 | Aug | 17 | H | Chelsea | L | 1-2 | 0-1 | — | Owen (pen) $^{79}$ | 44,080 |
| 2 | | 24 | A | Aston Villa | D | 0-0 | 0-0 | 17 | | 42,573 |
| 3 | | 27 | H | Tottenham H | D | 0-0 | 0-0 | — | | 43,778 |
| 4 | | 30 | A | Everton | W | 3-0 | 1-0 | 10 | Owen 2 $^{39, 52}$, Kewell $^{80}$ | 40,200 |
| 5 | Sept | 13 | A | Blackburn R | W | 3-1 | 1-1 | 7 | Owen 2 (1 pen) $^{12 (p), 68}$, Kewell $^{90}$ | 30,074 |
| 6 | | 20 | H | Leicester C | W | 2-1 | 1-0 | 6 | Owen (pen) $^{20}$, Heskey $^{75}$ | 44,094 |
| 7 | | 28 | A | Charlton Ath | L | 2-3 | 1-2 | 8 | Smicer $^{15}$, Owen (pen) $^{52}$ | 26,530 |
| 8 | Oct | 4 | H | Arsenal | L | 1-2 | 1-1 | 8 | Kewell $^{14}$ | 44,374 |
| 9 | | 18 | A | Portsmouth | L | 0-1 | 0-1 | 9 | | 19,126 |
| 10 | | 25 | H | Leeds U | W | 3-1 | 1-1 | 10 | Owen $^{35}$, Murphy $^{57}$, Sinama-Pongolle $^{84}$ | 43,599 |
| 11 | Nov | 2 | A | Fulham | W | 2-1 | 1-1 | 7 | Heskey $^{17}$, Murphy (pen) $^{89}$ | 17,682 |
| 12 | | 9 | H | Manchester U | L | 1-2 | 0-0 | 8 | Kewell $^{76}$ | 44,159 |
| 13 | | 22 | A | Middlesbrough | D | 0-0 | 0-0 | 9 | | 34,268 |
| 14 | | 30 | H | Birmingham C | W | 3-1 | 1-1 | 6 | Gerrard (pen) $^{34}$, Kewell $^{69}$, Heskey $^{78}$ | 42,683 |
| 15 | Dec | 6 | A | Newcastle U | D | 1-1 | 1-0 | 5 | Murphy $^{6}$ | 52,151 |
| 16 | | 13 | H | Southampton | L | 1-2 | 0-1 | 9 | Heskey $^{75}$ | 41,762 |
| 17 | | 26 | H | Bolton W | W | 3-1 | 1-0 | 9 | Hyypia $^{30}$, Sinama-Pongolle $^{47}$, Smicer $^{54}$ | 42,987 |
| 18 | | 28 | A | Manchester C | D | 2-2 | 0-1 | 6 | Smicer $^{66}$, Hamann $^{80}$. | 47,201 |
| 19 | Jan | 7 | A | Chelsea | W | 1-0 | 1-0 | — | Cheyrou $^{33}$ | 41,533 |
| 20 | | 10 | H | Aston Villa | W | 1-0 | 1-0 | 5 | Delaney (og) $^{36}$ | 43,771 |
| 21 | | 17 | A | Tottenham H | L | 1-2 | 0-1 | 5 | Kewell $^{75}$ | 36,104 |
| 22 | | 21 | A | Wolverhampton W | D | 1-1 | 1-0 | — | Cheyrou $^{42}$ | 29,380 |
| 23 | | 31 | H | Everton | D | 0-0 | 0-0 | 5 | | 44,056 |
| 24 | Feb | 7 | A | Bolton W | D | 2-2 | 0-1 | 6 | Hyypia $^{51}$, Gerrard $^{69}$ | 27,552 |
| 25 | | 11 | H | Manchester C | W | 2-1 | 1-0 | — | Owen $^{3}$, Gerrard $^{51}$ | 43,257 |
| 26 | | 29 | A | Leeds U | D | 2-2 | 2-2 | 6 | Kewell $^{21}$, Baros $^{42}$ | 39,932 |
| 27 | Mar | 14 | A | Southampton | L | 0-2 | 0-0 | 8 | | 32,056 |
| 28 | | 17 | H | Portsmouth | W | 3-0 | 2-0 | — | Hamann $^{6}$, Owen 2 $^{28, 58}$ | 34,663 |
| 29 | | 20 | H | Wolverhampton W | W | 1-0 | 0-0 | 4 | Hyypia $^{90}$ | 43,795 |
| 30 | | 28 | A | Leicester C | D | 0-0 | 0-0 | 4 | | 32,013 |
| 31 | Apr | 4 | H | Blackburn R | W | 4-0 | 3-0 | 4 | Owen 2 $^{7, 24}$, Todd (og) $^{22}$, Heskey $^{79}$ | 41,559 |
| 32 | | 9 | A | Arsenal | L | 2-4 | 2-1 | — | Hyypia $^{5}$, Owen $^{42}$ | 38,119 |
| 33 | | 12 | H | Charlton Ath | L | 0-1 | 0-0 | 4 | | 40,003 |
| 34 | | 17 | H | Fulham | D | 0-0 | 0-0 | 4 | | 42,042 |
| 35 | | 24 | A | Manchester U | W | 1-0 | 0-0 | 4 | Murphy (pen) $^{63}$ | 67,647 |
| 36 | May | 2 | H | Middlesbrough | W | 2-0 | 0-0 | 4 | Murphy (pen) $^{50}$, Heskey $^{53}$ | 42,031 |
| 37 | | 8 | A | Birmingham C | W | 3-0 | 1-0 | 4 | Owen $^{29}$, Heskey $^{51}$, Gerrard $^{86}$ | 29,553 |
| 38 | | 15 | H | Newcastle U | D | 1-1 | 0-1 | 4 | Owen $^{67}$ | 44,172 |

**Final League Position: 4**

### GOALSCORERS

*League (55):* Owen 16 (4 pens), Heskey 7, Kewell 7, Murphy 5 (3 pens), Gerrard 4 (1 pen), Hyypia 4, Smicer 3, Cheyrou 2, Hamann 2, Sinama-Pongolle 2, Baros 1, own goals 2.
*Carling Cup (6):* Heskey 2, Murphy 2 (1 pen), Kewell 1, Smicer 1.
*FA Cup (5):* Cheyrou 2, Heskey 1, Murphy 1 (pen), Owen 1.
*UEFA Cup (14):* Kewell 3, Gerrard 2, Heskey 2, Owen 2, Baros 1, Hamann 1, Hyypia 1, Le Tallec 1, Traore 1.

| Dudek J 30 | Carragher J 22 | Riise J 22 + 6 | Biscan I 27 + 2 | Henchoz S 15 + 3 | Hyypia S 38 | Kewell H 36 | Murphy D 19 + 12 | Heskey E 25 + 10 | Owen M 29 | Cheyrou B 9 + 3 | Finnan S 19 + 3 | Baros M 6 + 7 | Diouf E 20 + 6 | Gerrard S 34 | Smicer V 15 + 5 | Le Tallec A 3 + 10 | Diao S 2 + 1 | Welsh J — + 1 | Sinama-Pongolle F 3 + 12 | Traore D 7 | Kirkland C 6 | Hamann D 25 | Otsemobor J 4 | Luzi-Bernardi P — + 1 | Jones P 2 | *Match No.* |
|---|---|---|---|---|---|---|---|---|---|---|---|---|---|---|---|---|---|---|---|---|---|---|---|---|---|---|
| 1 | 2 | 3 | $4^{1}$ | $5^{2}$ | 6 | 7 | 8 | 9 | 10 | $11^{3}$ | 12 | 13 | 14 | | | | | | | | | | | | | 1 |
| 1 | 2 | 3 | 12 | 5 | 6 | 7 | $8^{1}$ | $9^{2}$ | 10 | | | 13 | 11 | 4 | | | | | | | | | | | | 2 |
| 1 | 3 | | 5 | | 6 | 7 | 12 | | 10 | | 2 | 9 | 11 | 4 | $8^{1}$ | | | | | | | | | | | 3 |
| 1 | 3 | 12 | 5 | | 6 | 7 | 13 | 14 | 10 | | 2 | $9^{3}$ | $11^{1}$ | 4 | $8^{2}$ | | | | | | | | | | | 4 |
| 1 | $3^{2}$ | 13 | 5 | | 6 | 11 | | 12 | 10 | | 2 | $9^{1}$ | 7 | $4^{3}$ | 8 | 14 | | | | | | | | | | 5 |
| 1 | | 3 | 5 | | 6 | 11 | 12 | 9 | 10 | | 2 | | $7^{2}$ | 4 | $8^{1}$ | 13 | | | | | | | | | | 6 |
| 1 | | 3 | 5 | | 6 | 11 | 12 | 9 | 10 | | 2 | | $7^{2}$ | 4 | $8^{1}$ | 13 | | | | | | | | | | 7 |
| 1 | | 3 | 5 | | 6 | 9 | | 12 | $10^{1}$ | | 2 | | 7 | 4 | $11^{2}$ | 13 | $8^{3}$ | 14 | | | | | | | | 8 |
| 1 | | 3 | 4 | 5 | 6 | 10 | | 9 | | | 2 | | $7^{2}$ | 8 | $11^{1}$ | 12 | | | 13 | | | | | | | 9 |
| 1 | | 3 | 5 | | 6 | $11^{2}$ | 12 | 9 | $10^{3}$ | | 2 | | 7 | 4 | $8^{1}$ | 13 | | | 14 | | | | | | | 10 |
| 1 | | | $5^{1}$ | 12 | 6 | 11 | 7 | $9^{2}$ | $10^{3}$ | | 2 | | | 4 | 8 | 13 | | | 14 | 3 | | | | | | 11 |
| 1 | | | 5 | | 6 | 11 | 8 | 9 | | | 2 | | $7^{1}$ | 4 | $10^{2}$ | 12 | | | 13 | 3 | | | | | | 12 |
| | | | 5 | | 6 | 11 | 8 | 9 | $10^{3}$ | | $2^{2}$ | | $7^{1}$ | 4 | 12 | | 13 | | 14 | 3 | 1 | | | | | 13 |
| | | 12 | 5 | | 6 | 11 | 14 | 9 | | | | | $7^{2}$ | 8 | 13 | | 2 | | $10^{3}$ | $3^{1}$ | 1 | 4 | | | | 14 |
| | | 3 | 5 | | 6 | | 8 | 9 | | | | | 11 | 7 | 12 | | | | $10^{1}$ | | 1 | 4 | 2 | | | 15 |
| | | 3 | 5 | | 6 | | 7 | 9 | | | | | $11^{2}$ | 8 | 10 | 13 | | | 12 | | 1 | $4^{1}$ | 2 | | | 16 |
| | | 3 | 5 | | 6 | $11^{2}$ | 7 | 12 | | | | | 13 | 8 | $10^{3}$ | 14 | | | $9^{1}$ | | 1 | 4 | 2 | | | 17 |
| 1 | | 3 | 5 | 12 | 6 | 11 | 7 | 9 | | | | | 13 | $8^{2}$ | $10^{3}$ | | | | 14 | | | 4 | $2^{1}$ | | | 18 |
| $1^{6}$ | | 12 | 5 | 2 | 6 | 10 | 8 | 9 | | $11^{1}$ | | | 7■ | | | | | | | 3 | | 4 | | 15 | | 19 |
| | | 3 | 5 | 2 | 6 | 11 | 8 | 9 | $10^{1}$ | 13 | | | $7^{2}$ | | | | | | 12 | | | 4 | | | 1 | 20 |
| | | 12 | $5^{2}$ | 2 | 6 | 11 | 8 | 9 | 10 | 7 | 13 | | | | | | | | | $3^{1}$ | | 4 | | | 1 | 21 |
| 1 | 3 | | $5^{1}$ | 12 | 6 | 11 | 13 | 9 | 10 | $7^{2}$ | 2 | | | 8 | | | | | | | | 4 | | | | 22 |
| 1 | 3 | | | 5 | 6 | 11 | | | 10 | 9 | 2 | | | 7 | | 8 | | | | | | 4 | | | | 23 |
| 1 | 3 | | | 5 | 6 | 11 | 12 | | 10 | $9^{2}$ | 2 | | | 7 | | $8^{1}$ | | | 13 | | | 4 | | | | 24 |
| 1 | 3 | | 14 | 5 | 6 | $11^{2}$ | 12 | 13 | 10 | $9^{3}$ | 2 | | | 7 | | $8^{1}$ | | | | | | 4 | | | | 25 |
| | 3 | | | 5 | 6 | 11 | 7 | 12 | 10 | | 2 | $9^{1}$ | | 8 | | | | | | | 1 | 4 | | | | 26 |
| 1 | 3 | 12 | 2 | $5^{1}$ | 6 | 11 | | 13 | 10 | | | 9 | $7^{2}$ | 8 | | | | | | | | 4 | | | | 27 |
| 1 | 2 | 3 | 5 | | 6 | $11^{1}$ | 7 | 9 | 10 | 13 | | | 12 | $8^{2}$ | | | | | | | | 4 | | | | 28 |
| 1 | 2 | 3 | 5 | | 6 | $11^{2}$ | $7^{1}$ | $9^{3}$ | 10 | | | 14 | 13 | 8 | | | | | 12 | | | 4 | | | | 29 |
| 1 | 2 | | 5 | | 6 | 11 | 12 | 9 | | $7^{1}$ | | $10^{2}$ | | 8 | | | | | 13 | 3 | | 4 | | | | 30 |
| 1 | 2 | 3 | 5 | | 6 | 11 | 12 | $9^{2}$ | $10^{3}$ | | | 14 | $7^{1}$ | 8 | | | | | 13 | | | 4 | | | | 31 |
| 1 | 2 | 3 | 5 | | 6 | 11 | 12 | $9^{2}$ | 10 | | | 13 | $7^{1}$ | 8 | | | | | | | | 4 | | | | 32 |
| 1 | 2 | 3 | | 5 | 6 | 11 | | $9^{2}$ | 10 | | | 12 | $7^{1}$ | 8 | 13 | | | | | | | 4 | | | | 33 |
| 1 | 2 | 3 | | 5 | 6 | $11^{2}$ | | 13 | 10 | $9^{3}$ | | 14 | 12 | 8 | $7^{1}$ | | | | | | | 4 | | | | 34 |
| 1 | 3 | 11 | | 5 | 6 | $9^{3}$ | 7 | 12 | $10^{1}$ | 14 | $2^{2}$ | | | 8 | 13 | | | | | | | 4 | | | | 35 |
| 1 | 2 | 3 | | $5^{1}$ | 6 | 9 | 7 | 12 | 10 | | 13 | | | 8 | $11^{2}$ | | | | | | | 4 | | | | 36 |
| 1 | 5 | 3 | | | 6 | 11 | 7 | 9 | 10 | | 2 | | | 8 | | | | | | | | 4 | | | | 37 |
| 1 | 5 | 3 | | | 6 | 11 | 7 | 9 | 10 | | 2 | | | 8 | | | | | | | | 4 | | | | 38 |

**Carling Cup**

| | | | |
|---|---|---|---|
| Third Round | Blackburn R | (a) | 4-3 |
| Fourth Round | Bolton W | (h) | 2-3 |

**FA Cup**

| | | | |
|---|---|---|---|
| Third Round | Yeovil T | (a) | 2-0 |
| Fourth Round | Newcastle U | (h) | 2-1 |
| Fifth Round | Portsmouth | (h) | 1-1 |
| | | (a) | 0-1 |

**UEFA Cup**

| | | | |
|---|---|---|---|
| First Round | Olimpija | (a) | 1-1 |
| | | (h) | 3-0 |
| Second Round | Steaua | (a) | 1-1 |
| | | (h) | 1-0 |
| Third Round | Levski | (h) | 2-0 |
| | | (a) | 4-2 |
| Fourth Round | Marseille | (h) | 1-1 |
| | | (a) | 1-2 |

# LUTON TOWN FL Championship 1

## FOUNDATION

Formed by an amalgamation of two leading local clubs, Wanderers and Excelsior a works team, at a meeting in Luton Town Hall in April 1885. The Wanderers had three months earlier changed their name to Luton Town Wanderers and did not take too kindly to the formation of another Town club but were talked around at this meeting. Wanderers had already appeared in the FA Cup and the new club entered in its inaugural season.

***Kenilworth Road Stadium, 1 Maple Road, Luton, Beds LU4 8AW.***

***Telephone:*** (01582) 411 622.

***Fax:*** (01582) 405 070.

***Ticket Office:*** (01582) 416 976.

***Website:*** www.lutontown.co.uk

***Email:*** commercial@lutontown.co.uk

***Ground Capacity:*** 9,975.

***Record Attendance:*** 30,069 v Blackpool, FA Cup 6th rd replay, 4 March 1959.

***Pitch Measurements:*** 110yd × 72yd.

***Chairman:*** Bill Tomlins.

***Secretary:*** Cherry Newbery.

***Manager:*** Mike Newell.

***Director of Football:*** Mick Harford.

***Physio:*** Paul Coleman.

***Colours:*** White shirts with orange and black trim, black shorts with orange and white trim, black stockings with two white hoops.

***Change Colours:*** Orange shirts with white and royal trim, royal shorts with orange and white trim, royal stockings with two white hoops.

***Year Formed:*** 1885.

***Turned Professional:*** 1890.

***Ltd Co.:*** 1897.

***Club Nickname:*** 'The Hatters'.

***Previous Grounds:*** 1885, Excelsior, Dallow Lane; 1897, Dunstable Road; 1905, Kenilworth Road.

***First Football League Game:*** 4 September 1897, Division 2, v Leicester Fosse (a) D 1–1 – Williams; McCartney, McEwen; Davies, Stewart, Docherty; Gallacher, Coupar, Birch, McInnes, Ekins (1).

***Record League Victory:*** 12–0 v Bristol R, Division 3 (S), 13 April 1936 – Dolman; Mackey, Smith; Finlayson, Nelson, Godfrey; Rich, Martin (1), Payne (10), Roberts (1), Stephenson.

## HONOURS

*Football League:* Division 1 best season: 7th, 1986–87; Division 2 – Champions 1981–82; Runners-up 1954–55, 1973–74; Division 3 – Runners-up 1969–70, 2001–02; Division 4 – Champions 1967–68; Division 3 (S) – Champions 1936–37; Runners-up 1935–36.

*FA Cup:* Runners-up 1959.

*Football League Cup:* Winners 1988; Runners-up 1989.

*Simod Cup:* Runners-up 1988.

## SKY SPORTS FACT FILE

Despite a modest season in Division Three (South) in 1932–-33, Luton Town enjoyed a useful FA Cup run to the sixth round, accounting for Kingstonian, Stockport County, Barnsley, Tottenham Hotspur and Halifax Town en route.

***Record Cup Victory:*** 9–0 v Clapton, FA Cup 1st rd (replay after abandoned game), 30 November 1927 – Abbott; Kingham, Graham; Black, Rennie, Fraser; Pointon, Yardley (4), Reid (2), Woods (1), Dennis (2).

***Record Defeat:*** 0–9 v Small Heath, Division 2, 12 November 1898.

***Most League Points (2 for a win):*** 66, Division 4, 1967–68.

***Most League Points (3 for a win):*** 97, Division 3, 2001–02.

***Most League Goals:*** 103, Division 3 (S), 1936–37.

***Highest League Scorer in Season:*** Joe Payne, 55, Division 3 (S), 1936–37.

***Most League Goals in Total Aggregate:*** Gordon Turner, 243, 1949–64.

***Most League Goals in One Match:*** 10, Joe Payne v Bristol R, Division 3S, 13 April 1936.

***Most Capped Player:*** Mal Donaghy, 58 (91), Northern Ireland.

***Most League Appearances:*** Bob Morton, 495, 1948–64.

***Youngest League Player:*** Mike O'Hara, 16 years 32 days v Stoke C, 1 October 1960.

***Record Transfer Fee Received:*** £2,500,000 from Arsenal for John Hartson, January 1995.

***Record Transfer Fee Paid:*** £850,000 to Odense for Lars Elstrup, August 1989.

***Football League Record:*** 1897 Elected to Division 2; 1900 Failed re-election; 1920 Division 3; 1921–37 Division 3 (S); 1937–55 Division 2; 1955–60 Division 1; 1960–63 Division 2; 1963–65 Division 3; 1965–68 Division 4; 1968–70 Division 3; 1970–74 Division 2; 1974–75 Division 1; 1975–82 Division 2; 1982–96 Division 1; 1996–2001 Division 2; 2001–02 Division 3; 2002–04 Division 2; 2004– FL1.

## MANAGERS

Charlie Green 1901–28
*(Secretary-Manager)*
George Thomson 1925
John McCartney 1927–29
George Kay 1929–31
Harold Wightman 1931–35
Ted Liddell 1936–38
Neil McBain 1938–39
George Martin 1939–47
Dally Duncan 1947–58
Syd Owen 1959–60
Sam Bartram 1960–62
Bill Harvey 1962–64
George Martin 1965–66
Allan Brown 1966–68
Alec Stock 1968–72
Harry Haslam 1972–78
David Pleat 1978–86
John Moore 1986–87
Ray Harford 1987–89
Jim Ryan 1900–91
David Pleat 1991–95
Terry Westley 1995
Lennie Lawrence 1995–2000
Ricky Hill 2000
Lil Fuccillo 2000
Joe Kinnear 2001–03
Mike Newell June 2003–

## LATEST SEQUENCES

***Longest Sequence of League Wins:*** 12, 19.2.2002 – 6.4.2002.

***Longest Sequence of League Defeats:*** 8, 11.11.1899 – 6.1.1900.

***Longest Sequence of League Draws:*** 5, 28.8.1971 – 18.9.1971.

***Longest Sequence of Unbeaten League Matches:*** 19, 8.4.1969 – 7.10.1969.

***Longest Sequence Without a League Win:*** 16, 9.9.1964 – 6.11.1964.

***Successive Scoring Runs:*** 25 from 24.10.1931.

***Successive Non-scoring Runs:*** 5 from 10.4.1973.

## TEN YEAR LEAGUE RECORD

| | | *P* | *W* | *D* | *L* | *F* | *A* | *Pts* | *Pos* |
|---|---|---|---|---|---|---|---|---|---|
| 1994-95 | Div 1 | 46 | 15 | 13 | 18 | 61 | 64 | 58 | 16 |
| 1995-96 | Div 1 | 46 | 11 | 12 | 23 | 40 | 64 | 45 | 24 |
| 1996-97 | Div 2 | 46 | 21 | 15 | 10 | 71 | 45 | 78 | 3 |
| 1997-98 | Div 2 | 46 | 14 | 15 | 17 | 60 | 64 | 57 | 17 |
| 1998-99 | Div 2 | 46 | 16 | 10 | 20 | 51 | 60 | 58 | 12 |
| 1999-2000 | Div 2 | 46 | 17 | 10 | 19 | 61 | 65 | 61 | 13 |
| 2000-01 | Div 2 | 46 | 9 | 13 | 24 | 52 | 80 | 40 | 22 |
| 2001-02 | Div 3 | 46 | 30 | 7 | 9 | 96 | 48 | 97 | 2 |
| 2002-03 | Div 2 | 46 | 17 | 14 | 15 | 67 | 62 | 65 | 9 |
| 2003-04 | Div 2 | 46 | 17 | 15 | 14 | 69 | 66 | 66 | 10 |

## DID YOU KNOW?

John O'Rourke arriving at Luton Town midway through the 1963–64 season produced a remarkable goals return for the number of League games played. Signed from Chelsea he registered 64 goals in 84 matches before moving on to Middlesbrough.

## LUTON TOWN 2003–04 LEAGUE RECORD

| *Match No.* | *Date* | *Venue* | *Opponents* | *Result* | *H/T Score* | *Lg. Pos.* | *Goalscorers* | *Attendance* |
|---|---|---|---|---|---|---|---|---|
| 1 | Aug 9 | H | Rushden & D | W 3-1 | 0-1 | — | Thorpe 2 [50, 59], Spring [90] | 6878 |
| 2 | 16 | A | Stockport Co | W 2-1 | 1-0 | 1 | Neilson [32], Howard [56] | 4566 |
| 3 | 23 | H | Grimsby T | L 1-2 | 0-1 | 7 | Nicholls (pen) [85] | 5827 |
| 4 | 25 | A | Brighton & HA | L 0-2 | 0-1 | 12 | | 6604 |
| 5 | 30 | H | Hartlepool U | W 3-2 | 3-1 | 6 | Howard 2 [6, 23], McSheffrey [14] | 5515 |
| 6 | Sept 6 | A | Notts Co | D 1-1 | 1-0 | 8 | Coyne [43] | 7505 |
| 7 | 13 | A | Plymouth Arg | L 1-2 | 0-0 | 12 | McSheffrey [58] | 9894 |
| 8 | 16 | H | Port Vale | W 2-0 | 1-0 | — | McSheffrey [31], Foley [71] | 5079 |
| 9 | 20 | H | QPR | D 1-1 | 0-0 | 9 | McSheffrey [60] | 8339 |
| 10 | 27 | A | Oldham Ath | L 0-3 | 0-2 | 14 | | 6077 |
| 11 | Oct 1 | A | Swindon T | D 2-2 | 0-1 | — | McSheffrey (pen) [65], Forbes [67] | 7573 |
| 12 | 6 | H | Tranmere R | W 3-1 | 1-0 | — | Perrett [45], McSheffrey [64], Forbes [72] | 5002 |
| 13 | 11 | H | Wycombe W | W 3-1 | 0-0 | 8 | McSheffrey 2 [76, 89], Perrett [85] | 5695 |
| 14 | 18 | A | Brentford | L 2-4 | 0-1 | 10 | Forbes 2 [48, 88] | 5579 |
| 15 | 21 | A | Bournemouth | L 3-6 | 2-4 | — | Purches (og) [10], Hughes [25], Forbes [60] | 6388 |
| 16 | 25 | H | Peterborough U | D 1-1 | 1-0 | 12 | Forbes [29] | 6067 |
| 17 | Nov 1 | A | Bristol C | D 1-1 | 1-1 | 14 | McSheffrey [18] | 9735 |
| 18 | 15 | H | Wrexham | W 3-2 | 1-2 | 12 | Forbes [45], Robinson [52], Mansell [58] | 5505 |
| 19 | 22 | A | Sheffield W | D 0-0 | 0-0 | 13 | | 21,027 |
| 20 | 29 | H | Chesterfield | W 1-0 | 1-0 | 10 | Howard [3] | 5453 |
| 21 | Dec 13 | A | Blackpool | W 1-0 | 1-0 | 6 | Robinson [35] | 5739 |
| 22 | 20 | H | Barnsley | L 0-1 | 0-0 | 7 | | 6162 |
| 23 | 26 | A | Colchester U | D 1-1 | 1-1 | 9 | Mansell [28] | 5083 |
| 24 | 28 | H | Notts Co | W 2-0 | 1-0 | 7 | Forbes [4], Boyce [79] | 7181 |
| 25 | Jan 10 | A | Rushden & D | D 2-2 | 2-1 | 8 | Forbes [6], Holmes [39] | 5823 |
| 26 | 17 | H | Stockport Co | D 2-2 | 1-1 | 9 | Griffin (og) [32], Howard [85] | 5920 |
| 27 | Feb 7 | H | Colchester U | W 1-0 | 0-0 | 10 | Showunmi [52] | 5662 |
| 28 | 10 | H | Brighton & HA | W 2-0 | 1-0 | — | Holmes [27], Nicholls (pen) [77] | 6846 |
| 29 | 14 | A | Wycombe W | D 0-0 | 0-0 | 9 | | 6407 |
| 30 | 21 | H | Brentford | W 4-1 | 1-0 | 6 | Boyce [10], Showunmi 3 [49, 66, 80] | 6273 |
| 31 | 24 | A | Grimsby T | L 2-3 | 1-0 | — | Howard 2 [19, 80] | 3143 |
| 32 | 28 | A | Peterborough U | W 2-1 | 1-0 | 5 | Howard [26], Brkovic [77] | 6628 |
| 33 | Mar 6 | A | Barnsley | D 0-0 | 0-0 | 7 | | 8656 |
| 34 | 13 | H | Blackpool | W 3-2 | 1-0 | 6 | Boyce [25], Holmes [66], Showunmi [74] | 6343 |
| 35 | 16 | A | Port Vale | L 0-1 | 0-0 | — | | 5048 |
| 36 | 20 | H | Plymouth Arg | D 1-1 | 1-0 | 7 | Coyne [42] | 8499 |
| 37 | 27 | A | QPR | D 1-1 | 0-1 | 8 | Showunmi [76] | 17,695 |
| 38 | Apr 3 | H | Oldham Ath | D 1-1 | 1-1 | 8 | Showunmi [34] | 5966 |
| 39 | 6 | A | Hartlepool U | L 3-4 | 2-1 | — | Howard [3], Leary 2 [31, 59] | 4434 |
| 40 | 10 | A | Tranmere R | L 0-1 | 0-1 | 9 | | 7937 |
| 41 | 12 | H | Swindon T | L 0-3 | 0-3 | 9 | | 7008 |
| 42 | 17 | H | Bristol C | W 3-2 | 1-0 | 8 | Howard [26], Boyce [56], Keane [90] | 6944 |
| 43 | 20 | H | Bournemouth | D 1-1 | 1-0 | — | Howard [15] | 6485 |
| 44 | 24 | A | Wrexham | L 1-2 | 0-1 | 10 | Howard [63] | 3239 |
| 45 | May 1 | H | Sheffield W | W 3-2 | 0-2 | 9 | Howard 2 [54, 90], O'Leary [78] | 7157 |
| 46 | 8 | A | Chesterfield | L 0-1 | 0-0 | 10 | | 6285 |

**Final League Position: 10**

### GOALSCORERS

*League (69):* Howard 14, Forbes 9, McSheffrey 9 (1 pen), Showunmi 7, Boyce 4, Holmes 3, Coyne 2, Leary 2, Mansell 2, Nicholls 2 (2 pens), Perrett 2, Robinson 2, Thorpe 2, Brkovic 1, Foley 1, Hughes 1, Keane 1, Neilson 1, O'Leary 1, Spring 1, own goals 2.
*Carling Cup (8):* Foley 2, Bayliss 1, Coyne 1, Howard 1, McSheffrey 1, Pitt 1, Thorpe 1.
*FA Cup (8):* Forbes 5 (1 pen), Boyce 1, Mansell 1, Robinson 1 (pen).
*LDV Vans Trophy (3):* Judge 1, Leary 1 (pen), Showunmi 1.

| Beckwith R 13 | Spring M 24 | Pitt C 11 + 1 | Neilson A 11 + 3 | Boyce E 42 | Coyne C 44 | Nicholls K 21 | Hughes P 20 + 2 | Howard S 34 | Thorpe T 2 | Foley K 32 + 1 | Brkovic A 24 + 8 | Hillier I 8 + 3 | McSheffrey G 18 | Crowe D — + 8 | Davis S 34 + 2 | Bayliss D 6 | Showunmi E 18 + 8 | Forbes A 21 + 6 | Leary M 8 + 6 | Perrett R 5 + 1 | Mansell L 12 + 4 | Brill D 4 + 1 | Robinson S 32 + 2 | Judge M — + 1 | Beresford M 11 | Holmes P 11 + 5 | Davies C 4 + 2 | Hyldgaard M 18 | Keane K 14 + 1 | O'Leary S 3 + 2 | Underwood P 1 | *Match No.* |
|---|---|---|---|---|---|---|---|---|---|---|---|---|---|---|---|---|---|---|---|---|---|---|---|---|---|---|---|---|---|---|---|---|
| 1 | 2 | $3^1$ | 4 | 5 | 6 | 7 | 8 | 9 | 10 | 11 | 12 | | | | | | | | | | | | | | | | | | | | | 1 |
| 1 | | 11 | 4 | 5 | 6 | 7 | 8 | 9 | 10 | 2 | 12 | $3^1$ | | | | | | | | | | | | | | | | | | | | 2 |
| 1 | $2^1$ | 3 | 4 | 5 | 6 | 7 | 8 | 9 | | 11 | 12 | | $10^2$ | 13 | | | | | | | | | | | | | | | | | | 3 |
| 1 | 4 | 11 | | | 6 | 7 | 8 | 9■ | | 2 | | | $10^1$ | 12 | 3 | 5 | | | | | | | | | | | | | | | | 4 |
| 1 | 4 | $11^2$ | $3^3$ | 5 | 6 | | 8 | 9 | | 2 | 13 | | $10^1$ | 12 | 14 | 7 | | | | | | | | | | | | | | | | 5 |
| 1 | 4 | | $3^2$ | 2 | 6 | | 8■ | 9 | | 7 | $11^1$ | | 10 | 12 | 13 | 5 | | | | | | | | | | | | | | | | 6 |
| 1 | 4 | | | 2 | 6 | | 8 | | | 7 | 11 | 12 | 10 | 13 | 3 | $5^1$ | $9^2$ | | | | | | | | | | | | | | | 7 |
| 1 | 4 | | | 2 | 6 | | 8 | | | 7 | 11 | | 10 | | 3 | 5 | 12 | $9^1$ | | | | | | | | | | | | | | 8 |
| 1 | 4 | 12 | | 2 | 6 | | | 9 | | 11 | 8 | | $10^1$ | | 3 | 5 | | | 7 | | | | | | | | | | | | | 9 |
| 1■ | | $11^6$ | | 5 | 6 | | 4 | 9 | | | $7^2$ | $2^1$ | 10 | | 3 | | | | 8 | 12 | 13 | 15 | | | | | | | | | | 10 |
| 1 | | 11 | | 2 | 6 | | 8 | | | 7 | | | 10 | | 3■ | | | $9^1$ | 12 | 5 | | | 4 | | | | | | | | | 11 |
| 1 | 4 | 11 | | 2 | 6 | | 8 | | | $7^1$ | | | 10 | | 3 | | | 9 | | 5 | | | 12 | | | | | | | | | 12 |
| | 4 | 11 | | 2 | 6 | | 8 | | | | | | 10 | | 3 | | 12 | $9^1$ | | 5 | 13 | 1 | $7^2$ | | | | | | | | | 13 |
| | 4 | $11^1$ | | 2 | 6 | | 8 | | | 7 | | 3 | 10 | | | | | 9 | | 5 | | 1 | | 12 | | | | | | | | 14 |
| 1 | 4 | 11 | | 2 | 6 | | $8^2$ | | | $7^1$ | | 3 | 10 | | | | | 9 | | 5 | 12 | | 13 | | | | | | | | | 15 |
| | 4 | | 12 | 5 | 6 | | | | | 2 | 11 | 3■ | 10 | | | | | 9 | | | $8^1$ | | 7 | | 1 | | | | | | | 16 |
| | 4 | | $2^1$ | 5 | 6 | | | | | | 11 | 12 | 10 | | 3 | | 13 | $9^2$ | | | 7 | | 8 | | 1 | | | | | | | 17 |
| | 4 | | | 5 | 6 | | | | | 2 | 11 | | 10 | | 3 | | | 9 | | | 7 | | 8 | | 1 | | | | | | | 18 |
| | 4 | | | 2 | | | | 10 | | | 6 | 3 | 8 | | | | | 9 | 12 | | 5 | | 7 | | 1 | $11^1$ | | | | | | 19 |
| | 4 | | | 5 | 6 | | | 10 | | | $11^1$ | 2 | 7 | | 3 | | | 9 | | | | | 8 | | 1 | 12 | | | | | | 20 |
| | 4 | | | 5 | 6 | | | 10 | | 2 | $11^1$ | | | | 3 | | | 9 | 12 | | 7 | | 8 | | 1 | | | | | | | 21 |
| | 4 | | | 5 | 6 | | | 10 | | 2 | 11 | | | | 3 | | | 9 | | | 7 | | 8 | | 1 | | | | | | | 22 |
| | 4 | | | 5 | 6 | | | 10 | | 2 | 11 | | | | 3 | | | 9 | | | $7^1$ | | 8 | | 1 | 12 | | | | | | 23 |
| | $4^3$ | | | 5 | 6 | | | 10 | | 2 | $11^2$ | 14 | | | 3 | | 12 | $9^1$ | | | 7 | | 8 | | 1 | 13 | | | | | | 24 |
| | | | | 5 | 6 | | | 10 | | 2 | 11 | $3^1$ | | | | | | 9 | 12 | | 7 | | 8 | | 1 | 4 | | | | | | 25 |
| | | | | | 6 | | | 10 | | 2 | 11 | | | | 3 | | 12 | 9■ | | | $7^1$ | | 8 | | 1 | 4 | 5 | | | | | 26 |
| | 4 | | | 5 | 6 | 8 | | 10 | | 2 | | | | 12 | 3 | | $9^1$ | | | | | | 7 | | | 11 | | 1 | | | | 27 |
| | 4 | | | 5 | 6 | $7^3$ | | 10 | | 2 | 12 | | | 13 | 3 | | $9^2$ | | 14 | | | | 8 | | | $11^1$ | | 1 | | | | 28 |
| | 4 | | | 5 | 6 | 7 | | 10 | | | 12 | | | | 3 | | 9 | | | | | | 8 | | | $11^1$ | | 1 | 2 | | | 29 |
| | | | 12 | 5 | 6 | 7 | 13 | 10 | | | | | | | 3 | | 9 | | $4^3$ | | | | $8^2$ | | | 11 | | 1 | $2^1$ | 14 | | 30 |
| | | | | 5 | 6 | $7^2$ | 13 | 10 | | | 12 | | | | 3 | | 9 | | 4 | | | | 8 | | | $11^1$ | | 1 | 2 | | | 31 |
| | | | 12 | 5 | 6 | 7 | 8 | 10 | | | 11 | | | | 3 | | 9 | | | | | | 4 | | | | | 1 | $2^1$ | | | 32 |
| | | | | 5 | 6 | 7 | 8 | 10 | | | $11^1$ | | | | 3 | | 9 | | | | | | 4 | | | 12 | | 1 | 2 | | | 33 |
| | | | | 5 | 6 | 7 | 8 | 10 | | | | | | | 3 | | 9 | | | | | | 4 | | | 11 | | 1 | 2 | | | 34 |
| | | | | 5 | 6 | 7 | $8^1$ | 10 | | | 12 | | | | 3 | | 9 | | | | | | 4 | | | 11 | | 1 | 2 | | | 35 |
| | | | 2 | 5 | $6^2$ | 7■ | 8 | 10 | | | | | | 12 | | | $9^1$ | | | | | | 4 | | | 11 | 13 | 1 | 3 | | | 36 |
| | | | 3 | 5 | | 7 | $8^3$ | | | 13 | 10 | | | | | | 9 | 14 | | | | | 4 | | | $12^2$ | 6 | 1 | 2 | | $11^1$ | 37 |
| | | | $4^2$ | 5 | 6 | | | 10 | | $11^1$ | 8 | | | | 3 | | 9 | 12 | | | | | 7 | | | | | 1 | 2 | 13 | | 38 |
| | | | | | 6 | | | 10 | | 7 | 11 | | | | 3 | | 9 | 12 | 4 | | | | 8 | | | | 5 | 1 | $2^1$ | | | 39 |
| | | | | 5 | 6 | | | 10 | | 2 | $11^1$ | | | | 3 | | 9 | 12 | 4 | | 7 | | 8 | | | | | 1 | | | | 40 |
| | | | | 5 | 6 | 7 | | 10 | | 2 | | | | | 3 | | 9 | 12 | $4^1$ | | $11^2$ | | 8 | | | | | 1 | 13 | | | 41 |
| | | | | 5 | 6 | 7 | | 10 | | 11 | 8 | | | | 3 | | 12 | $9^1$ | | | | | 4 | | | | | 1 | 2 | | | 42 |
| | | | | $5^3$ | 6 | 7 | | 10 | | 2 | $11^2$ | | | | 3 | | 12 | $9^1$ | 13 | | | | 8 | | | | 14 | 1 | 4 | | | 43 |
| | | | | | 6 | $7^2$ | | 10 | | 2 | | | | | 3 | | 9 | 12 | 8 | | 13 | | | | | | 5 | 1 | $4^1$ | 11 | | 44 |
| | | | 4 | 5 | 6 | 7 | | 10 | | 2 | | | | | 3 | | 12 | $9^1$ | | | | 1 | 8 | | | | | | | 11 | | 45 |
| | | | 4 | 5 | 6 | 7 | | | | 2 | | | | | 3 | | 9 | 10 | | | | 1 | 8 | | | | | | | 11 | | 46 |

**Carling Cup**

| | | | |
|---|---|---|---|
| First Round | Yeovil T | (h) | 4-1 |
| Second Round | Charlton Ath | (a) | 4-4 |

**LDV Vans Trophy**

| | | | |
|---|---|---|---|
| First Round | Stevenage B | (a) | 1-0 |
| Second Round | Rushden & D | (a) | 2-1 |
| Quarter-Final | Southend U | (a) | 0-3 |

**FA Cup**

| | | | |
|---|---|---|---|
| First Round | Thurrock | (a) | 1-1 |
| | | (h) | 3-1 |
| Second Round | Rochdale | (a) | 2-0 |
| Third Round | Bradford C | (a) | 2-1 |
| Fourth Round | Tranmere R | (h) | 0-1 |

# MACCLESFIELD TOWN FL Championship 2

## FOUNDATION

From the mid-19th Century until 1874, Macclesfield Town FC played under rugby rules. In 1891 they moved to the Moss Rose and finished champions of the Manchester & District League in 1906 and 1908. By 1911, they had carried off the Cheshire Senior Cup five times. Macclesfield were founder members of the Cheshire County League in 1919.

***Moss Rose Ground, London Road, Macclesfield, Cheshire SK11 7SP.***

***Telephone:*** (01625) 264 686.

***Fax:*** (01625) 264 692.

***Ticket Office:*** (01625) 264 686.

***Website:*** www.mtfc.co.uk

***Email:*** admin@mtfc.co.uk

***Ground Capacity:*** 6,208.

***Pitch Measurements:*** 100m × 66m.

***Chairman:*** Robert Bickerton.

***Deputy Chairman:*** Alan Cash.

***Secretary:*** Colin Garlick.

***Manager:*** Brian Horton.

***Assistant Manager:*** John Askey.

***Physio:*** Paul Lake.

***Colours:*** Blue shirts, white shorts, blue stockings.

***Change Colours:*** White shirts, blue shorts, white stockings.

***Year formed:*** 1874.

***Club Nickname:*** 'The Silkmen'.

***Previous Ground:*** 1874, Rostron Field; 1891, Moss Rose.

***First Football League Game:*** 9 August 1997, Division 3, v Torquay U (h) W 2–1 – Price; Tinson, Rose, Payne (Edey), Howarth, Sodje (1), Askey, Wood, Landon (1) (Power), Mason, Sorvel.

***Record League Victory:*** 5–2 v Mansfield T, Division 3, 2 November 1999 – Martin; Ingram, Rioch, Collins, Tinson, Sedgemore (1), Askey (1), Priest (1), Barker (2), Davies (Wood), Durkan.

## HONOURS

*Football League:* Division 3 – Runners-up 1997–98.

*FA Cup:* best season: 3rd rd, 1968, 1988, 2002, 2003, 2004.

*Football League Cup:* never past 2nd rd.

*Vauxhall Conference:* Champions 1994–95, 1996–97.

*FA Trophy:* Winners 1969–70, 1995–96; Runners-up 1988–89.

*Bob Lord Trophy:* Winners 1993–94; Runners-up 1995–96, 1996–97.

*Vauxhall Conference Championship Shield:* Winners 1996, 1997, 1998.

*Northern Premier League:* Winners 1968–69, 1969–70, 1986–87; Runners-up 1984–85.

*Northern Premier League Challenge Cup:* Winners 1986–87; Runners-up 1969–70, 1970–71, 1982–83.

*Northern Premier League Presidents Cup:* Winners 1986–87; Runners-up 1984–85.

*Cheshire Senior Cup:* Winners 20 times; Runners-up 11.

## SKY SPORTS FACT FILE

The first goal scored by a Macclesfield Town player in the Conference was by Steve Burr against Maidstone United on 22 August 1987 in front of a crowd of 850. He went on to register 65 League goals in four seasons.

***Record Win:*** 15–0 v Chester St Marys, Cheshire Senior Cup, 2nd rd, 16 February 1886.

***Record Defeat:*** 1–13 v Tranmere R reserves, 3 May 1929.

***Most League Points (3 for a win):*** 82, Division 3, 1997–98.

***Most League Goals:*** 66, Division 3, 1999–2000.

***Highest League Scorer in Season:*** Richard Barker, 16, Division 3, 1999–2000.

***Most League Goals in Total Aggregate:*** John Askey, 31, 1997–2003.

***Most Capped Player:*** George Abbey, 10, Nigeria.

***Most League Appearances:*** Darren Tinson, 263, 1997–2003.

***Youngest League Player:*** Peter Griffiths, 18 years 44 days v Reading, 26 September 1998.

***Record Transfer Fee Received:*** £300,000 from Stockport Co for Rickie Lambert, June 2002.

***Record Transfer Fee Paid:*** £35,000 to Vauxhall Motors for Matt Haddrell, March 2003.

***Football League Record:*** 1997 Promoted to Division 3; 1998–99 Division 2; 1999–2004 Division 3; 2004– FL2.

## MANAGERS

**Since 1967**
Keith Goalen 1967–68
Frank Beaumont 1968–72
Billy Haydock 1972–74
Eddie Brown 1974
John Collins 1974
Willie Stevenson 1974
John Collins 1975–76
Tony Coleman 1976
John Barnes 1976
Brian Taylor 1976
Dave Connor 1976–78
Derek Partridge 1978
Phil Staley 1978–80
Jimmy Williams 1980–81
Brian Booth 1981–85
Neil Griffiths 1985–86
Roy Campbell 1986
Peter Wragg 1986–93
Sammy McIlroy 1993–2000
Peter Davenport 2000
Gil Prescott 2001
David Moss 2001–03
John Askey 2003–04
Brian Horton April 2004–

## LATEST SEQUENCES

***Longest Sequence of League Wins:*** 5, 16.10.1999 – 6.11.1999.

***Longest Sequence of League Defeats:*** 6, 26.12.1998 –6.2.1999.

***Longest Sequence of League Draws:*** 3, 27.9.1997 – 11.10.1997.

***Longest Sequence of Unbeaten League Matches:*** 8, 16.10.1999 – 27.11.1999.

***Longest Sequence Without a League Win:*** 10, 21.11.1998 – 6.2.1999.

***Successive Scoring Runs:*** 14 from 11.10.2003.

***Successive Non-scoring Runs:*** 5 from 18.12.1998.

## TEN YEAR LEAGUE RECORD

| | | P | W | D | L | F | A | Pts | Pos |
|---|---|---|---|---|---|---|---|---|---|
| 1994-95 | Conf. | 42 | 24 | 8 | 10 | 70 | 40 | 80 | 1 |
| 1995-96 | Conf. | 42 | 22 | 9 | 11 | 66 | 49 | 75 | 4 |
| 1996-97 | Conf. | 42 | 27 | 9 | 6 | 80 | 30 | 90 | 1 |
| 1997-98 | Div 3 | 46 | 23 | 13 | 10 | 63 | 44 | 82 | 2 |
| 1998-99 | Div 2 | 46 | 11 | 10 | 25 | 43 | 63 | 43 | 24 |
| 1999-2000 | Div 3 | 46 | 18 | 11 | 17 | 66 | 61 | 65 | 13 |
| 2000-01 | Div 3 | 46 | 14 | 14 | 18 | 51 | 62 | 56 | 14 |
| 2001-02 | Div 3 | 46 | 15 | 13 | 18 | 41 | 52 | 58 | 13 |
| 2002-03 | Div 3 | 46 | 14 | 12 | 20 | 57 | 63 | 54 | 16 |
| 2003-04 | Div 3 | 46 | 13 | 13 | 20 | 54 | 69 | 52 | 20 |

## DID YOU KNOW ?

Billy Johnston, who captained Macclesfield Town to their 1930 Cheshire Cup victory, had been a regular member of Manchester United's FA Cup team in 1927–28. After two seasons with the Silkmen, he returned to Old Trafford.

## MACCLESFIELD TOWN 2003–04 LEAGUE RECORD

| *Match No.* | *Date* | *Venue* | *Opponents* | *Result* | | *H/T Score* | *Lg. Pos.* | *Goalscorers* | *Attendance* |
|---|---|---|---|---|---|---|---|---|---|
| 1 | Aug 9 | H | Boston U | D | 0-0 | 0-0 | — | | 2222 |
| 2 | 16 | A | Cambridge U | L | 1-3 | 0-1 | 17 | Carruthers [61] | 3089 |
| 3 | 23 | H | Torquay U | D | 1-1 | 1-0 | 19 | Miles [8] | 1970 |
| 4 | 25 | A | Bristol R | D | 2-2 | 2-2 | 20 | Miles [2], Anderson (og) [16] | 7064 |
| 5 | 30 | H | Yeovil T | W | 4-1 | 2-0 | 14 | Carruthers 2 [8, 78], Whitaker 2 [21, 90] | 2221 |
| 6 | Sept 6 | A | Mansfield T | L | 2-3 | 2-1 | 17 | Tipton [14], Miles [38] | 4209 |
| 7 | 13 | H | Kidderminster H | D | 1-1 | 0-1 | 19 | Little [90] | 1988 |
| 8 | 16 | A | Swansea C | L | 0-3 | 0-2 | — | | 6641 |
| 9 | 20 | A | Northampton T | D | 0-0 | 0-0 | 20 | | 4332 |
| 10 | 27 | H | York C | D | 0-0 | 0-0 | 19 | | 2311 |
| 11 | 30 | H | Rochdale | W | 2-1 | 0-0 | — | Burgess (og) [67], Whitaker [74] | 2152 |
| 12 | Oct 4 | A | Leyton Orient | L | 0-2 | 0-2 | 20 | | 3585 |
| 13 | 11 | H | Doncaster R | L | 1-3 | 1-1 | 21 | Carruthers [17] | 2831 |
| 14 | 18 | A | Carlisle U | W | 1-0 | 0-0 | 18 | Tipton [68] | 4366 |
| 15 | 21 | A | Lincoln C | L | 2-3 | 0-1 | — | Tipton 2 [55, 79] | 3441 |
| 16 | 25 | H | Southend U | L | 1-2 | 0-0 | 20 | Little [90] | 1821 |
| 17 | Nov 1 | A | Hull C | D | 2-2 | 1-1 | 20 | Carruthers [6], Whitaker [90] | 15,053 |
| 18 | 15 | H | Scunthorpe U | D | 2-2 | 1-1 | 21 | Whitaker [38], Tipton [86] | 2205 |
| 19 | 22 | A | Oxford U | L | 1-3 | 1-2 | 22 | Priest [4] | 6676 |
| 20 | 29 | H | Bury | W | 1-0 | 1-0 | 20 | Tipton [25] | 2312 |
| 21 | Dec 13 | H | Huddersfield T | W | 4-0 | 1-0 | 18 | Tipton 2 (1 pen) [13, 76 (p)], Miles [64], Priest [88] | 3059 |
| 22 | 20 | A | Darlington | W | 1-0 | 0-0 | 16 | Brackenridge [62] | 2920 |
| 23 | 26 | A | Cheltenham T | L | 2-3 | 0-1 | 17 | Brackenridge [83], Haddrell [86] | 4237 |
| 24 | 28 | H | Mansfield T | D | 1-1 | 0-0 | 19 | Tipton [90] | 3578 |
| 25 | Jan 10 | A | Boston U | L | 1-3 | 0-2 | 20 | Little [61] | 2300 |
| 26 | 13 | H | Bristol R | W | 2-1 | 1-0 | — | Little [42], Miles [73] | 1542 |
| 27 | 17 | H | Cambridge U | L | 0-1 | 0-0 | 18 | | 2151 |
| 28 | 24 | A | Torquay U | L | 1-4 | 1-3 | 20 | Little [45] | 2770 |
| 29 | 31 | A | Yeovil T | D | 2-2 | 2-1 | 20 | Tipton (pen) [20], Carruthers [39] | 5257 |
| 30 | Feb 7 | H | Cheltenham T | L | 1-2 | 1-2 | 20 | Miles [10] | 2061 |
| 31 | 14 | A | Doncaster R | L | 0-1 | 0-1 | 23 | | 5525 |
| 32 | 21 | H | Carlisle U | D | 1-1 | 1-1 | 22 | Potter [29] | 3256 |
| 33 | 28 | A | Southend U | L | 0-1 | 0-0 | 23 | | 4107 |
| 34 | Mar 6 | H | Darlington | L | 0-1 | 0-0 | 23 | | 2293 |
| 35 | 13 | A | Huddersfield T | L | 0-4 | 0-1 | 23 | | 9729 |
| 36 | 16 | H | Swansea C | W | 2-1 | 1-0 | — | Tipton [8], Harsley [68] | 1513 |
| 37 | 20 | A | Kidderminster H | W | 4-1 | 3-0 | 23 | Tipton 2 (1 pen) [5 (p), 78], Carruthers [29], Harsley [37] | 2666 |
| 38 | 27 | H | Northampton T | L | 0-4 | 0-4 | 23 | | 2634 |
| 39 | 30 | H | Lincoln C | D | 0-0 | 0-0 | — | | 2016 |
| 40 | Apr 4 | A | York C | W | 2-0 | 2-0 | 22 | Parkin [19], Potter [27] | 3855 |
| 41 | 10 | H | Leyton Orient | W | 1-0 | 0-0 | 21 | Carruthers [60] | 2156 |
| 42 | 12 | A | Rochdale | W | 2-1 | 0-1 | 18 | Tipton 2 (1 pen) [62, 82 (p)] | 4942 |
| 43 | 17 | H | Hull C | D | 1-1 | 0-1 | 19 | Tipton [64] | 3801 |
| 44 | 24 | A | Scunthorpe U | L | 0-1 | 0-0 | 22 | | 4334 |
| 45 | May 1 | H | Oxford U | W | 2-1 | 2-1 | 18 | Ashton (og) [17], Louis (og) [44] | 2763 |
| 46 | 8 | A | Bury | L | 0-2 | 0-0 | 20 | | 3569 |

**Final League Position: 20**

### GOALSCORERS

*League (54):* Tipton 16 (4 pens), Carruthers 8, Miles 6, Little 5, Whitaker 5, Brackenridge 2, Harsley 2, Potter 2, Priest 2, Haddrell 1, Parkin 1, own goals 4.
*Carling Cup (1):* Whitaker 1.
*FA Cup (7):* Tipton 3 (1 pen), Carruthers 2, Little 1, Miles 1.
*LDV Vans Trophy (1):* Adams 1.

|Myhill B 15|Abbey G 23 + 2|Adams D 27|Welch M 33 + 5|Haddrell M 4 + 6|Munroe K 35 + 1|Little C 18 + 6|Smith D 7 + 3|Miles J 23 + 6|Carruthers M 30 + 9|Whitaker D 33 + 3|Tipton M 34 + 4|Hitchen S 8 + 1|Macauley S 16|Flitcroft D 14 + 1|Widdrington T 34 + 1|Priest C 26 + 3|Ross N 1 + 5|Clark S 1 + 3|Beresford D 5|Wilson S 31 + 1|Jones R 1|Brackenridge S 2 + 5|Carragher M 18|Carr M 7|Beswetherick J 3 + 1|Robinson N — + 1|Harsley P 16|Potter G 16|Parkin J 12|Payne S 13|Olsen J — + 2|*Match No.*|
|---|---|---|---|---|---|---|---|---|---|---|---|---|---|---|---|---|---|---|---|---|---|---|---|---|---|---|---|---|---|---|---|---|
|1|2|3|4|$5^{1}$|6|7|8|9|10|11|12|||||||||||||||||||||1|
|1|4|3||12|6|$7^{2}$|11|9|10||13|$2^{1}$|5|8||||||||||||||||||2|
|1|2|3|||6|$7^{1}$|8|9|10|11|12||5|4||||||||||||||||||3|
|1|2|3|14||6||12|9|10|11|13||5|$4^{1}$|$7^{2}$|$8^{3}$||||||||||||||||4|
|1|2|3|12||6||8|9|10|11|7||$5^{1}$|4||||||||||||||||||5|
|1|2|3|4||6||8|9|10|11|$7^{1}$|||5|||12|||||||||||||||6|
|1|2|3|||6|12|8|9|10|11|||5|4|||$7^{1}$|||||||||||||||7|
|1|$3^{1}$|2|4||6|13|$8^{2}$|9|10|11||12|5|$7^{3}$|14|||||||||||||||||8|
|1|12|3|4||6|$7^{1}$||9|10|11||2|5||8|||||||||||||||||9|
|1||3|$4^{1}$||6|$7^{2}$||9|10|11||2|5|12|8|||13||||||||||||||10|
|1||3|4|12|6|13||$9^{1}$|10|11||2||8|7|||$5^{2}$||||||||||||||11|
|1||3|5||6|||$9^{1}$|10|11||2||8|4|||12|7|||||||||||||12|
|1||3|||6|||$9^{2}$|10|11||2|5■|$8^{1}$|4|12||13|7|||||||||||||13|
|1|3||5||6|12|||10|11|$9^{1}$|2||8|4|13|||$7^{2}$|||||||||||||14|
|$1^{G}$|2|3|5|12|6■|13|||$10^{1}$|11|9|||8|4||||$7^{2}$|15||||||||||||15|
||2|3|5■|12|6|13|||10|11|$9^{3}$|||$8^{2}$|4|14|||$7^{1}$|1||||||||||||16|
||2|3|||6|7■|||10|11|9||||4|8||||1|5|||||||||||17|
||2|3||5|6|||9|10|11|7||||4|8||||1||||||||||||18|
|||3|6|5||||9||11|$10^{1}$|2||$7^{2}$|4|8|12|||1||13||||||||||19|
||2|3|4||6||||10|11|9||||7|8||||1|||5|||||||||20|
||2|3|5||6|7||9||11|10||||4|8||||1||||||||||||21|
|||2|5||6|$7^{2}$||9|12|11|$10^{1}$||||4|8||||1||13|3|||||||||22|
|||3|5|12|6|$7^{3}$||$9^{2}$|13|11|10||||$4^{1}$|8||||1||14|2|||||||||23|
|||3|5||6|7||12|10|11|9|||||4||||1||$8^{1}$|2|||||||||24|
|||3■|4|$5^{1}$||7||12|10|11|9||6|||8||||1|||2|||||||||25|
|||3|5||6|7||9||11|10|||||8||||1||12|$2^{1}$|4||||||||26|
|||3|$5^{1}$|12|6|7||9|13|11|$10^{2}$|||||8||||1||$4^{3}$||2|14|||||||27|
||||5||6|7|$12^{2}$|9||11|10■|||||8||||1||13|4|$2^{1}$|3|||||||28|
||||||6|7|||10|11|9||5||4|8||||1|||2||3|||||||29|
||||||6|7||9|10|11|||5||4|$8^{1}$||||1|||2||3|12||||||30|
|||$3^{2}$|12||6|||13|9|7|10||$5^{1}$||4|||||1|||2||||8|11||||31|
||2||12||6|||13||7|$9^{2}$||5||4|||||1|||$3^{1}$||||8|11|10|||32|
||2||4||6|||12|13|11|9||5||8|||||1|||||||$7^{1}$|3|$10^{2}$|||33|
||$2^{1}$||12|||7|14|13||11|9||$5^{3}$||4|||||1|||||||8|3|$10^{2}$|6||34|
||||5|||$7^{1}$||$9^{2}$|13|12|10||||4|8■||||1||||2|||11|3||6||35|
||||5||||||10|12|9||||4|8||||1||||2|||7|3|$11^{1}$|6||36|
||||5||||||10||9||||4|8||||1||||2|||7|3|11|6||37|
||12||5||6||||$10^{2}$||9||||11|||||1||||$2^{1}$|||7|3|8|4|13|38|
||2||5||12||||10||9||||4|8||||1|||||||$7^{1}$|3|$11^{2}$|6|13|39|
||3||5||||||12||9||||4|8||||1|||2||||7|11|$10^{1}$|6||40|
||2||5||||||12||9||||4|8||||1|||7||||$11^{1}$|3|10|6||41|
||3||5||||||||9||||4|8||||1|||2||||7|11|10|6||42|
||3||5||||||10||9||||4|8||||1|||2||||7|11||6||43|
||||5||6||||10||9||||11|8|12|||1|||2||||$7^{1}$|3||4||44|
||||5||6||||12||$9^{2}$||||11|8|13|||1|||2||||7|3|$10^{1}$|4||45|
||||5||6||||13|12|9||||11|$8^{3}$|14|||1|||2■||||7|3|$10^{2}$|$4^{1}$||46|

**Carling Cup**

| | | | |
|---|---|---|---|
| First Round | Sheffield U | (h) | 1-2 |

**LDV Vans Trophy**

| | | | |
|---|---|---|---|
| First Round | Chesterfield | (a) | 1-2 |

**FA Cup**

| | | | |
|---|---|---|---|
| First Round | Boston U | (h) | 3-0 |
| Second Round | Cambridge U | (h) | 1-1 |
| | | (a) | 2-2 |
| Third Round | Swansea C | (a) | 1-2 |

# MANCHESTER CITY FA Premiership

## FOUNDATION

Manchester City was formed as a Limited Company in 1894 after their predecessors Ardwick had been forced into bankruptcy. However, many historians like to trace the club's lineage as far back as 1880 when St Mark's Church, West Gorton added a football section to their cricket club. They amalgamated with Gorton Athletic in 1884 as Gorton FC. Because of a change of ground they became Ardwick in 1887.

***City of Manchester Stadium, SportCity, Manchester M11 3FF.***

***Telephone:*** 0870 062 1894.

***Fax:*** (0161) 438 7999.

***Ticket Office:*** 0870 062 1894.

***Website:*** www.mcfc.co.uk

***Email:*** mcfc@mcfc.co.uk

***Ground Capacity:*** 48,000.

***Record Attendance:*** 84,569 v Stoke C, FA Cup 6th rd, 3 March 1934 (British record for any game outside London or Glasgow).

***Chairman:*** John Wardle.

***Vice-chairman:*** Bryan Bodek.

***Secretary:*** J. B. Halford.

***Manager:*** Kevin Keegan.

***Assistant Manager:*** TBA.

***Physio:*** Rob Harris.

***Colours:*** Sky blue shirts, white shorts, sky blue stockings.

***Change Colours:*** White shirts with purple flash, navy blue shorts, white stockings.

***Year Formed:*** 1887 as Ardwick FC; 1894 as Manchester City.

***Turned Professional:*** 1887 as Ardwick FC.

***Ltd Co.:*** 1894.

## HONOURS

*Football League:* Division 1 – Champions 1936–37, 1967–68, 2001–02; Runners-up 1903–04, 1920–21, 1976–77, 1999–2000; Division 2 – Champions 1898–99, 1902–03, 1909–10, 1927–28, 1946–47, 1965–66; Runners-up 1895–96, 1950–51, 1987–88; Promoted from Division 2 (play-offs) 1998–99.

*FA Cup:* Winners 1904, 1934, 1956, 1969; Runners-up 1926, 1933, 1955, 1981.

*Football League Cup:* Winners 1970, 1976; Runners-up 1974.

***European Competitions:*** *European Cup:* 1968–69. *European Cup-Winners' Cup:* 1969–70 (winners), 1970–71. *UEFA Cup:* 1972–73, 1976–77, 1977–78, 1978–79, 2003–04.

***Previous Names:*** 1887, Ardwick FC (formed through the amalgamation of West Gorton and Gorton Athletic, the latter having been formed in 1880); 1894, Manchester City.

***Club Nicknames:*** 'Blues' or 'The Citizens'.

***Previous Grounds:*** 1880, Clowes Street; 1881, Kirkmanshulme Cricket Ground; 1882, Queens Road; 1884, Pink Bank Lane; 1887, Hyde Road (1894–1923 as City); 1923, Maine Road; 2003, City of Manchester Stadium.

***First Football League Game:*** 3 September 1892, Division 2, v Bootle (h) W 7–0 – Douglas; McVickers, Robson; Middleton, Russell, Hopkins; Davies (3), Morris (2), Angus (1), Weir (1), Milarvie.

***Record League Victory:*** 10–1 v Huddersfield T, Division 2, 7 November 1987 – Nixon; Gidman, Hinchcliffe, Clements, Lake, Redmond, White (3), Stewart (3), Adcock (3), McNab (1), Simpson.

## SKY SPORTS FACT FILE

The first League game played at Maine Road was on 25 August 1923 against Sheffield United. A crowd of 58,159 saw Manchester City win 2-1 with goals from Horace Barnes after 68 minutes and Tom Johnson three minutes later.

***Record Cup Victory:*** 10–1 v Swindon T, FA Cup 4th rd, 29 January 1930 – Barber; Felton, McCloy; Barrass, Cowan, Heinemann; Toseland, Marshall (5), Tait (3), Johnson (1), Brook (1).

***Record Defeat:*** 1–9 v Everton, Division 1, 3 September 1906.

***Most League Points (2 for a win):*** 62, Division 2, 1946–47.

***Most League Points (3 for a win):*** 99, Division 1, 2001–02.

***Most League Goals:*** 108, Division 2, 1926–27, 108, Division 1, 2001–02.

***Highest League Scorer in Season:*** Tommy Johnson, 38, Division 1, 1928–29.

***Most League Goals in Total Aggregate:*** Tommy Johnson, 158, 1919–30.

***Most League Goals in One Match:*** 5, Fred Williams v Darwen, Division 2, 18 February 1899; 5, Tom Browell v Burnley, Division 2, 24 October 1925; 5, Tom Johnson v Everton, Division 1, 15 September 1928; 5, George Smith v Newport Co, Division 2, 14 June 1947.

***Most Capped Player:*** Colin Bell, 48, England.

***Most League Appearances:*** Alan Oakes, 565, 1959–76.

***Youngest League Player:*** Glyn Pardoe, 15 years 314 days v Birmingham C, 11 April 1961.

***Record Transfer Fee Received:*** £4,925,000 from Ajax for Georgi Kinkladze, May 1998.

***Record Transfer Fee Paid:*** £10,000,000 to Paris St Germain for Nicolas Anelka, June 2002.

***Football League Record:*** 1892 Ardwick elected founder member of Division 2; 1894 Newly-formed Manchester C elected to Division 2; Division 1 1899–1902, 1903–09, 1910–26, 1928–38, 1947–50, 1951–63, 1966–83, 1985–87, 1989–92; Division 2 1902–03, 1909–10, 1926–28, 1938–47, 1950–51, 1963–66, 1983–85, 1987–89; 1992–96 FA Premier League; 1996–98 Division 1; 1998–99 Division 2; 1999–2000 Division 1; 2000–01 FA Premier League; 2001–02 Division 1; 2002– FA Premier League.

## MANAGERS

Joshua Parlby 1893–95
*(Secretary-Manager)*
Sam Omerod 1895–1902
Tom Maley 1902–06
Harry Newbould 1906–12
Ernest Magnall 1912–24
David Ashworth 1924–25
Peter Hodge 1926–32
Wilf Wild 1932–46
*(continued as Secretary to 1950)*
Sam Cowan 1946–47
John 'Jock' Thomson 1947–50
Leslie McDowall 1950–63
George Poyser 1963–65
Joe Mercer 1965–71
*(continued as General Manager to 1972)*
Malcolm Allison 1972–73
Johnny Hart 1973
Ron Saunders 1973–74
Tony Book 1974–79
Malcolm Allison 1979–80
John Bond 1980–83
John Benson 1983
Billy McNeill 1983–86
Jimmy Frizzell 1986–87
*(continued as General Manager)*
Mel Machin 1987–89
Howard Kendall 1990
Peter Reid 1990–93
Brian Horton 1993–95
Alan Ball 1995–96
Steve Coppell 1996
Frank Clark 1996–98
Joe Royle 1998–2001
Kevin Keegan May 2001–

## LATEST SEQUENCES

***Longest Sequence of League Wins:*** 9, 8.4.1912 – 28.9.1912.

***Longest Sequence of League Defeats:*** 8, 23.8.1995 – 14.10.1995.

***Longest Sequence of League Draws:*** 6, 5.4.1913 – 6.9.1913.

***Longest Sequence of Unbeaten League Matches:*** 22, 16.11.1946 – 19.4.1947.

***Longest Sequence Without a League Win:*** 17, 26.12.1979 – 7.4.1980.

***Successive Scoring Runs:*** 44 from 3.10.1936.

***Successive Non-scoring Runs:*** 6 from 30.1.1971.

## TEN YEAR LEAGUE RECORD

| | | *P* | *W* | *D* | *L* | *F* | *A* | *Pts* | *Pos* |
|---|---|---|---|---|---|---|---|---|---|
| 1994-95 | PR Lge | 42 | 12 | 13 | 17 | 53 | 64 | 49 | 17 |
| 1995-96 | PR Lge | 38 | 9 | 11 | 18 | 33 | 58 | 38 | 18 |
| 1996-97 | Div 1 | 46 | 17 | 10 | 19 | 59 | 60 | 61 | 14 |
| 1997-98 | Div 1 | 46 | 12 | 12 | 22 | 56 | 57 | 48 | 22 |
| 1998-99 | Div 2 | 46 | 22 | 16 | 8 | 69 | 33 | 82 | 3 |
| 1999-2000 | Div 1 | 46 | 26 | 11 | 9 | 78 | 40 | 89 | 2 |
| 2000-01 | PR Lge | 38 | 8 | 10 | 20 | 41 | 65 | 34 | 18 |
| 2001-02 | Div 1 | 46 | 31 | 6 | 9 | 108 | 52 | 99 | 1 |
| 2002-03 | PR Lge | 38 | 15 | 6 | 17 | 47 | 54 | 51 | 9 |
| 2003-04 | PR Lge | 38 | 9 | 14 | 15 | 55 | 54 | 41 | 16 |

## DID YOU KNOW ?

When Manchester City won the Second Division championship in 1965–66, they were unbeaten at home. Of the 21 different players called upon during the campaign only Mike Summerbee was ever present on League duty.

## MANCHESTER CITY 2003–04 LEAGUE RECORD

| Match No. | Date | Venue | Opponents | Result | | H/T Score | Lg. Pos. | Goalscorers | Attendance |
|---|---|---|---|---|---|---|---|---|---|
| 1 | Aug 17 | A | Charlton Ath | W | 3-0 | 2-0 | — | Anelka (pen) [13], Sibierski [23], Jihai [83] | 25,846 |
| 2 | 23 | H | Portsmouth | D | 1-1 | 0-1 | 5 | Sommeil [90] | 46,287 |
| 3 | 25 | A | Blackburn R | W | 3-2 | 1-1 | — | Tarnat [4], Barton [59], Anelka [87] | 23,353 |
| 4 | 31 | H | Arsenal | L | 1-2 | 1-0 | 4 | Lauren (og) [10] | 46,436 |
| 5 | Sept 14 | H | Aston Villa | W | 4-1 | 0-1 | 3 | Anelka 3 (2 pens) [48 (p), 68 (p), 83], Tarnat [90] | 46,687 |
| 6 | 20 | A | Fulham | D | 2-2 | 0-0 | 5 | Knight (og) [46], Wanchope [90] | 16,124 |
| 7 | 28 | H | Tottenham H | D | 0-0 | 0-0 | 5 | | 46,842 |
| 8 | Oct 4 | A | Wolverhampton W | L | 0-1 | 0-0 | 6 | | 29,386 |
| 9 | 18 | H | Bolton W | W | 6-2 | 1-1 | 5 | Wright-Phillips 2 [27, 56], Distin [48], Anelka 2 [58, 72], Reyna [84] | 47,101 |
| 10 | 25 | A | Chelsea | L | 0-1 | 0-1 | 7 | | 41,143 |
| 11 | Nov 1 | A | Southampton | W | 2-0 | 1-0 | 5 | Fowler [4], Wanchope [85] | 31,952 |
| 12 | 9 | H | Leicester C | L | 0-3 | 0-1 | 6 | | 46,966 |
| 13 | 22 | A | Newcastle U | L | 0-3 | 0-0 | 8 | | 52,159 |
| 14 | 30 | H | Middlesbrough | L | 0-1 | 0-1 | 9 | | 46,824 |
| 15 | Dec 7 | A | Everton | D | 0-0 | 0-0 | 10 | | 37,871 |
| 16 | 13 | A | Manchester U | L | 1-3 | 0-2 | 12 | Wright-Phillips [52] | 67,643 |
| 17 | 22 | H | Leeds U | D | 1-1 | 0-1 | — | Sibierski [82] | 47,126 |
| 18 | 26 | A | Birmingham C | L | 1-2 | 1-0 | 13 | Fowler [14] | 29,520 |
| 19 | 28 | H | Liverpool | D | 2-2 | 1-0 | 13 | Anelka (pen) [30], Fowler [90] | 47,201 |
| 20 | Jan 7 | H | Charlton Ath | D | 1-1 | 1-0 | — | Fowler [39] | 44,307 |
| 21 | 10 | A | Portsmouth | L | 2-4 | 2-1 | 15 | Anelka [21], Sibierski [45] | 20,120 |
| 22 | 17 | H | Blackburn R | D | 1-1 | 0-0 | 15 | Anelka [50] | 47,090 |
| 23 | Feb 1 | A | Arsenal | L | 1-2 | 0-1 | 15 | Anelka [89] | 38,103 |
| 24 | 8 | H | Birmingham C | D | 0-0 | 0-0 | 16 | | 46,967 |
| 25 | 11 | A | Liverpool | L | 1-2 | 0-1 | — | Wright-Phillips [50] | 43,257 |
| 26 | 21 | A | Bolton W | W | 3-1 | 2-1 | 14 | Fowler 2 [27, 31], Charlton (og) [50] | 27,301 |
| 27 | 28 | H | Chelsea | L | 0-1 | 0-0 | 16 | | 47,304 |
| 28 | Mar 14 | H | Manchester U | W | 4-1 | 2-1 | 15 | Fowler [3], Macken [32], Sinclair [73], Wright-Phillips [90] | 47,284 |
| 29 | 22 | A | Leeds U | L | 1-2 | 1-1 | — | Anelka [44] | 36,998 |
| 30 | 27 | H | Fulham | D | 0-0 | 0-0 | 15 | | 46,522 |
| 31 | Apr 4 | A | Aston Villa | D | 1-1 | 0-1 | 15 | Distin [82] | 37,602 |
| 32 | 10 | H | Wolverhampton W | D | 3-3 | 2-2 | 15 | Anelka [25], Sibierski [39], Wright-Phillips [90] | 47,248 |
| 33 | 12 | A | Tottenham H | D | 1-1 | 1-0 | 15 | Anelka [25] | 35,282 |
| 34 | 17 | H | Southampton | L | 1-3 | 0-1 | 17 | Anelka [78] | 47,152 |
| 35 | 24 | A | Leicester C | D | 1-1 | 1-0 | 17 | Tarnat [45] | 31,457 |
| 36 | May 1 | H | Newcastle U | W | 1-0 | 0-0 | 17 | Wanchope [59] | 47,266 |
| 37 | 8 | A | Middlesbrough | L | 1-2 | 1-2 | 17 | Wanchope [35] | 34,734 |
| 38 | 15 | H | Everton | W | 5-1 | 3-0 | 16 | Wanchope 2 [16, 30], Anelka [41], Sibierski [89], Wright-Phillips [90] | 47,152 |

**Final League Position: 16**

### GOALSCORERS

*League (55):* Anelka 16 (4 pens), Fowler 7, Wright-Phillips 7, Wanchope 6, Sibierski 5, Tarnat 3, Distin 2, Barton 1, Jihai 1, Macken 1, Reyna 1, Sinclair 1, Sommeil 1, own goals 3.
*Carling Cup (4):* Wright-Phillips 2, Fowler 1, Macken 1.
*FA Cup (12):* Anelka 4 (1 pen), Macken 2, Bosvelt 1, Distin 1, Fowler 1, Siberski 1, Tarnat 1, Wright-Phillips 1.
*UEFA Cup (12):* Anelka 4 (2 pens), Fowler 1, Huckerby 1, Jihai 1, Negouai 1, Siberski 1, Sinclair 1, Sommeil 1, Wright-Phillips 1.

| Seaman D 19 | Jihai S 29 + 4 | Tarnat M 32 | Sommeil D 18 | Distin S 38 | Barton J 24 + 4 | Wright-Phillips S 32 + 2 | Sibierski A 18 + 15 | Anelka N 31 + 1 | Fowler R 23 + 8 | Sinclair T 20 + 9 | Wanchope P 12 + 10 | Tiatto D 1 + 4 | Berkovic E 1 + 3 | Bosvelt P 22 + 3 | McManaman S 20 + 2 | Reyna C 19 + 4 | Dunne R 28 + 1 | Ellegaard K 2 + 2 | Macken J 7 + 8 | James D 17 | Van Buyten D 5 | Jordan S — + 2 | Elliott S — + 2 | *Match No.* |
|---|---|---|---|---|---|---|---|---|---|---|---|---|---|---|---|---|---|---|---|---|---|---|---|---|
| 1 | 2 | 3 | 4 | 5 | 6 | 7 | 8 | 9 | $10^1$ | $11^2$ | 12 | 13 | | | | | | | | | | | | 1 |
| 1 | 2 | 3 | 4 | 5 | 6 | 7 | $8^2$ | 9 | $10^1$ | 11 | 12 | | 13 | | | | | | | | | | | 2 |
| 1 | 2 | 3 | 4 | 5 | 6 | 7 | 8 | 9 | | 11 | | | | 10 | | | | | | | | | | 3 |
| 1 | 2 | 3 | 4 | 5 | 6 | $7^3$ | $8^2$ | 9 | 12 | 11 | | 13 | 14 | $10^1$ | | | | | | | | | | 4 |
| 1 | 2 | 3 | 4 | 5 | $6^1$ | 7 | 12 | 9 | | 11 | $10^2$ | | | | 8 | 13 | | | | | | | | 5 |
| 1 | 2 | | 4 | 5 | 6 | $7^3$ | 12 | $9^1$ | 13 | 11 | 10 | 3 | | 14 | $8^2$ | | | | | | | | | 6 |
| 1 | 2 | 3 | 4 | 5 | | 7 | 12 | 9 | 13 | $11^1$ | $10^2$ | | | 6 | $8^3$ | 14 | | | | | | | | 7 |
| 1 | 2 | 3 | 4 | 5 | | 7 | $11^1$ | $9^2$ | 13 | 12 | 10 | | | 8 | | 6 | | | | | | | | 8 |
| 1 | 2 | 3 | 4 | 5 | $6^3$ | 7■ | 12 | 9 | $10^2$ | | | 13 | | | $11^1$ | 8 | 14 | | | | | | | 9 |
| 1 | 2 | 3 | 4 | 5 | 6 | 7 | 12 | 9 | $10^2$ | 11 | 13 | | | | | $8^1$ | | | | | | | | 10 |
| 1 | 2 | 3 | | 5 | 6 | | 12 | | $10^1$ | 7 | 9 | | | | 11 | 8 | 4 | | | | | | | 11 |
| | 2 | 3 | | 5 | $6^2$ | | 8 | 9 | 12 | | $10^1$ | | 11 | 13 | 7 | | 4 | 1 | | | | | | 12 |
| 1 | 2 | 3 | | 5 | 6 | | 14 | 9 | $10^1$ | 11 | | | $13^3$ | $8^2$ | 7 | | 4 | | 12 | | | | | 13 |
| | $2^1$ | | 4 | 5 | $6^2$ | 7 | 13 | 9 | 12 | 11 | 10 | | | | | 8 | 3 | 1 | | | | | | 14 |
| $1^G$ | 2 | | 4 | 5 | 6 | $7^1$ | | 9 | 10 | 11 | 12 | | | | 8 | | 3 | 15 | | | | | | 15 |
| 1 | 2 | | 4 | 5 | 6 | 7 | | 9 | 10 | $11^1$ | 12 | | | | 8 | | 3 | | | | | | | 16 |
| 1 | 2 | | 4 | 5 | $6^1$ | 7 | 12 | 9 | $10^2$ | | 13 | | | | $11^3$ | 8 | 3 | | 14 | | | | | 17 |
| 1 | 2 | | 4 | 5 | 6 | 7 | 12 | 9 | $10^2$ | 13 | | | | | $11^1$ | 8 | 3 | | | | | | | 18 |
| 1 | | $3^2$ | 2 | 5 | | 7 | 12 | 9 | 10 | 13 | | | | $6^3$ | $11^1$ | 8 | 4 | | 14 | | | | | 19 |
| 1 | | 3 | 4 | 5 | 13 | 12 | $7^1$ | 9 | $10^3$ | 11 | | | | 6 | | $8^2$ | 2 | | 14 | | | | | 20 |
| $1^G$ | | 3 | 4 | 5 | 6 | | 8 | 9 | 10 | 7 | | | | 11 | | | 2 | 15 | | | | | | 21 |
| | 2 | 3 | | 5 | 6 | 12 | 7 | 9 | | $11^2$ | | 13 | | 8 | | | 4 | | $10^1$ | 1 | | | | 22 |
| | 2 | 3 | | 5 | 6 | 10 | | 9■ | 12 | 11 | | | | $7^1$ | 13 | $8^2$ | 4 | | | 1 | | | | 23 |
| | 12 | 3 | | 5 | 13 | 2 | 7 | | 10 | | | | | $8^2$ | 14 | $11^3$ | $4^1$ | | 9 | 1 | 6 | | | 24 |
| | | 3 | | 5 | 12 | 2 | 13 | | 10 | | | | | 7 | 11 | $8^1$ | 4 | | $9^2$ | 1 | 6 | | | 25 |
| | 12 | 3 | | 5 | | 2 | 8 | | $10^3$ | 7 | | | | | $11^2$ | 6 | 4 | | $9^1$ | 1 | | 13 | 14 | 26 |
| | | 3 | | 5 | | 2 | 7 | | 10 | 12 | | | | | 11 | 8 | 4 | | $9^1$ | 1 | 6 | | | 27 |
| | 13 | 3 | | 5 | | 2 | $8^2$ | | 10 | 14 | | | | 12 | $11^3$ | $7^1$ | 4 | | 9 | 1 | 6 | | | 28 |
| | 12 | 3 | | 5 | 8 | 2 | 11 | 9 | 10 | | | | | $7^1$ | | | 4 | | | 1 | 6■ | | | 29 |
| | 2 | 3 | | 5 | | 7 | $11^3$ | $9^1$ | $10^2$ | 14 | 12 | | | 4 | | 8 | 6 | | 13 | 1 | | | | 30 |
| | 2 | 3 | | 5 | | 7 | | 12 | 13 | 14 | $10^1$ | | | 6 | 11 | $8^3$ | 4 | | $9^2$ | 1 | | | | 31 |
| | 2 | 3 | | 5 | 12 | 7 | 8 | 9 | $10^2$ | | 13 | | | $6^1$ | 11 | | 4 | | | 1 | | | | 32 |
| | $2^1$ | 3 | | 5 | | 7 | 8 | 9 | $10^2$ | 12 | 13 | | | 6 | 11 | | 4 | | | 1 | | | | 33 |
| | 2 | 3 | | 5 | | 7 | 8 | 9 | $10^3$ | 13 | 14 | | | $6^1$ | $11^2$ | 12 | 4 | | | 1 | | | | 34 |
| | 2 | 3 | | 5 | 6 | 7 | 12 | $9^1$ | | 11 | 10 | | | 8 | | | 4 | | | 1 | | | | 35 |
| | 2 | 3 | | 5 | 6 | 7 | | 9 | | $11^1$ | $10^2$ | | | 8 | | 12 | 4 | | 13 | 1 | | | | 36 |
| | 2 | 3 | | 5 | 6 | 7 | 12 | $9^3$ | | | $10^2$ | | | $8^1$ | | 11 | 4 | | 13 | 1 | | | 14 | 37 |
| | 2 | 3 | | 5 | $6^1$ | 7 | 12 | 9 | | | $10^2$ | | | 8 | | $11^3$ | 4 | | 13 | 1 | | 14 | | 38 |

**Carling Cup**

| | | | |
|---|---|---|---|
| Third Round | QPR | (a) | 3-0 |
| Fourth Round | Tottenham H | (a) | 1-3 |

**FA Cup**

| | | | |
|---|---|---|---|
| Third Round | Leicester C | (h) | 2-2 |
| | | (a) | 3-1 |
| Fourth Round | Tottenham H | (h) | 1-1 |
| | | (a) | 4-3 |
| Fifth Round | Manchester U | (a) | 2-4 |

**UEFA Cup**

| | | | |
|---|---|---|---|
| Qualifying Round | TNS | (h) | 5-0 |
| | | (a) | 2-0 |
| First Round | Lokeren | (h) | 3-2 |
| | | (a) | 1-0 |
| Second Round | Groclin | (h) | 1-1 |
| | | (a) | 0-0 |

# MANCHESTER UNITED FA Premiership

## FOUNDATION

Manchester United was formed as comparatively recently as 1902 after their predecessors, Newton Heath, went bankrupt. However, it is usual to give the date of the club's foundation as 1878 when the dining room committee of the carriage and waggon works of the Lancashire and Yorkshire Railway Company formed Newton Heath L and YR Cricket and Football Club. They won the Manchester Cup in 1886 and as Newton Heath FC were admitted to the Second Division in 1892.

***Sir Matt Busby Way, Old Trafford, Manchester M16 0RA.***
***Telephone:*** (0161) 868 8000.
***Fax:*** (0161) 868 8804.
***Ticket Office:*** 0870 442 1968.
***Website:*** www.manutd.com
***Email:*** enquiries@manutd.co.uk
***Ground Capacity:*** 68,190.
***Record Attendance:*** 76,962 Wolverhampton W v Grimsby T, FA Cup semi-final, 25 March 1939.
***Club Record Attendance:*** 70,504 v Aston Villa, Division 1, 27 December 1920.
***Pitch Measurements:*** 116yd × 76yd.
***Chief Executive:*** David Gill.
***Secretary:*** Kenneth R. Merrett.
***Manager:*** Sir Alex Ferguson CBE.
***Assistant Manager:*** Carlos Queiroz. ***Physio:*** Robert Swire.
***Colours:*** Red shirts, white or black shorts, black or white stockings.
***Change Colours:*** All black.
***Year Formed:*** 1878 as Newton Heath LYR; 1902, Manchester United.
***Turned Professional:*** 1885. ***Ltd Co.:*** 1907.
***Previous Name:*** 1880, Newton Heath; 1902, Manchester United.
***Club Nickname:*** 'Red Devils'.
***Previous Grounds:*** 1880, North Road, Monsall Road; 1893, Bank Street; 1910, Old Trafford (played at Maine Road 1941–49).
***First Football League Game:*** 3 September 1892, Division 1, v Blackburn R (a) L 3–4 – Warner; Clements, Brown; Perrins, Stewart, Erentz; Farman (1), Coupar (1), Donaldson (1), Carson, Mathieson.

## HONOURS

*FA Premier League* – Champions 1992–93, 1993–94, 1995–96, 1996–97, 1998–99, 1999–2000, 2000–01, 2002–03; Runners-up 1994–95, 1997–98.

*Football League:* Division 1 – Champions 1907–08, 1910–11, 1951–52, 1955–56, 1956–57, 1964–65, 1966–67; Runners-up 1946–47, 1947–48, 1948–49, 1950–51, 1958–59, 1963–64, 1967–68, 1979–80, 1987–88, 1991–92. Division 2 – Champions 1935–36, 1974–75; Runners-up 1896–97, 1905–06, 1924–25, 1937–38.

*FA Cup:* Winners 1909, 1948, 1963, 1977, 1983, 1985, 1990, 1994, 1996, 1999, 2004; Runners-up 1957, 1958, 1976, 1979, 1995.

*Football League Cup:* Winners 1992; Runners-up 1983, 1991, 1994, 2003.

***European Competitions:*** *European Cup:* 1956–57 (s-f), 1957–58 (s-f), 1965–66 (s-f), 1967–68 (winners), 1968–69 (s-f). *Champions League:* 1993–94, 1994–95, 1996–97 (s-f), 1997–98, 1998–99 (winners), 1999–2000, 2000–01, 2001–02 (s-f), 2002–03, 2003–04. *European Cup-Winners' Cup:* 1963–64, 1977–78, 1983–84, 1990–91 (winners). 1991–92. *Inter Cities Fairs Cup:* 1964–65. *UEFA Cup:* 1976–77, 1980–81, 1982–83, 1984–85, 1992–93, 1995–96. *Super Cup:* 1991 (winners), 1999 (runners-up). *Inter-Continental Cup:* 1999 (winners), 1968 (runners-up).

## SKY SPORTS FACT FILE

In the 1955–56 season Manchester United completed a highly successful championship win with a 1-0 victory over Portsmouth on 21 April. A Dennis Viollet goal gave the Old Trafford club an eleven-point margin over runners-up Blackpool.

**Record League Victory (as Newton Heath):** 10–1 v Wolverhampton W, Division 1, 15 October 1892 – Warner; Mitchell, Clements; Perrins, Stewart (3), Erentz; Farman (1), Hood (1), Donaldson (3), Carson (1), Hendry (1).

**Record League Victory (as Manchester U):** 9–0 v Ipswich T, FA Premier League, 4 March 1995 – Schmeichel; Keane (1) (Sharpe), Irwin, Bruce (Butt), Kanchelskis, Pallister, Cole (5), Ince (1), McClair, Hughes (2), Giggs.

**Record Cup Victory:** 10–0 v RSC Anderlecht, European Cup prel. rd 2nd leg, 26 September 1956 – Wood; Foulkes, Byrne; Colman, Jones, Edwards; Berry (1), Whelan (2), Taylor (3), Viollet (4), Pegg.

**Record Defeat:** 0–7 v Blackburn R, Division 1, 10 April 1926. 0–7 v Aston Villa, Division 1, 27 December 1930. 0–7 v Wolverhampton W, Division 2, 26 December 1931.

**Most League Points (2 for a win):** 64, Division 1, 1956–57.

**Most League Points (3 for a win):** 92, FA Premier League, 1993–94.

**Most League Goals:** 103, Division 1, 1956–57 and 1958–59.

**Highest League Scorer in Season:** Dennis Viollet, 32, 1959–60.

**Most League Goals in Total Aggregate:** Bobby Charlton, 199, 1956–73.

**Most Capped Player:** Bobby Charlton, 106, England.

**Most League Appearances:** Bobby Charlton, 606, 1956–73.

**Youngest League Player:** Jeff Whitefoot, 16 years 105 days v Portsmouth, 15 April 1950.

**Record Transfer Fee Received:** £25,000,000 from Real Madrid for David Beckham, July 2003.

**Record Transfer Fee Paid:** £30,000,000 to Leeds U for Rio Ferdinand, July 2002 (see also Leeds United page 217).

**Football League Record:** 1892 Newton Heath elected to Division 1; 1894–1906 Division 2; 1906–22 Division 1; 1922–25 Division 2; 1925–31 Division 1; 1931–36 Division 2; 1936–37 Division 1; 1937–38 Division 2; 1938–74 Division 1; 1974–75 Division 2; 1975–92 Division 1; 1992– FA Premier League.

### MANAGERS

J. Ernest Mangnall 1903–12
John Bentley 1912–14
John Robson 1914–21
*(Secretary-Manager from 1916)*
John Chapman 1921–26
Clarence Hilditch 1926–27
Herbert Bamlett 1927–31
Walter Crickmer 1931–32
Scott Duncan 1932–37
Walter Crickmer 1937–45
*(Secretary-Manager)*
Matt Busby 1945–69
*(continued as General Manager then Director)*
Wilf McGuinness 1969–70
Sir Matt Busby 1970–71
Frank O'Farrell 1971–72
Tommy Docherty 1972–77
Dave Sexton 1977–81
Ron Atkinson 1981–86
Sir Alex Ferguson November 1986–

### LATEST SEQUENCES

**Longest Sequence of League Wins:** 14, 15.10.1904 – 3.1.1905.

**Longest Sequence of League Defeats:** 14, 26.4.1930 – 25.10.1930.

**Longest Sequence of League Draws:** 6, 30.10.1988 – 27.11.1988.

**Longest Sequence of Unbeaten League Matches:** 29, 26.12.1998 – 25.9.1999.

**Longest Sequence Without a League Win:** 16, 19.4.1930 – 25.10.1930.

**Successive Scoring Runs:** 27 from 11.10.1958.

**Successive Non-scoring Runs:** 5 from 22.2.1902.

### TEN YEAR LEAGUE RECORD

| | | P | W | D | L | F | A | Pts | Pos |
|---|---|---|---|---|---|---|---|---|---|
| 1994-95 | PR Lge | 42 | 26 | 10 | 6 | 77 | 28 | 88 | 2 |
| 1995-96 | PR Lge | 38 | 25 | 7 | 6 | 73 | 35 | 82 | 1 |
| 1996-97 | PR Lge | 38 | 21 | 12 | 5 | 76 | 44 | 75 | 1 |
| 1997-98 | PR Lge | 38 | 23 | 8 | 7 | 73 | 26 | 77 | 2 |
| 1998-99 | PR Lge | 38 | 22 | 13 | 3 | 80 | 37 | 79 | 1 |
| 1999-2000 | PR Lge | 38 | 28 | 7 | 3 | 97 | 45 | 91 | 1 |
| 2000-01 | PR Lge | 38 | 24 | 8 | 6 | 79 | 31 | 80 | 1 |
| 2001-02 | PR Lge | 38 | 24 | 5 | 9 | 87 | 45 | 77 | 3 |
| 2002-03 | PR Lge | 38 | 25 | 8 | 5 | 74 | 34 | 83 | 1 |
| 2003-04 | PR Lge | 38 | 23 | 6 | 9 | 64 | 35 | 75 | 3 |

### DID YOU KNOW ?

By coincidence on 21 April 1993, a 2-0 win against Crystal Palace virtually assured Manchester United of the first Premier League title. That day Mark Hughes achieved his 100th League goal for the club.

## MANCHESTER UNITED 2003–04 LEAGUE RECORD

| Match No. | Date | Venue | Opponents | Result | | H/T Score | Lg. Pos. | Goalscorers | Attendance |
|---|---|---|---|---|---|---|---|---|---|
| 1 | Aug 16 | H | Bolton W | W | 4-0 | 1-0 | — | Giggs 2 [35, 74], Scholes [77], Van Nistelrooy [87] | 67,647 |
| 2 | 23 | A | Newcastle U | W | 2-1 | 0-1 | 2 | Van Nistelrooy [51], Scholes [59] | 52,165 |
| 3 | 27 | H | Wolverhampton W | W | 1-0 | 1-0 | — | O'Shea [10] | 67,648 |
| 4 | 31 | A | Southampton | L | 0-1 | 0-0 | 2 | | 32,066 |
| 5 | Sept 13 | A | Charlton Ath | W | 2-0 | 1-0 | 2 | Van Nistelrooy 2 [62, 81] | 26,046 |
| 6 | 21 | H | Arsenal | D | 0-0 | 0-0 | 3 | | 67,639 |
| 7 | 27 | A | Leicester C | W | 4-1 | 3-0 | 3 | Keane [15], Van Nistelrooy 3 [16, 45, 52] | 32,044 |
| 8 | Oct 4 | H | Birmingham C | W | 3-0 | 1-0 | 2 | Van Nistelrooy (pen) [36], Scholes [57], Giggs [82] | 67,633 |
| 9 | 18 | A | Leeds U | W | 1-0 | 0-0 | 2 | Keane [81] | 40,153 |
| 10 | 25 | H | Fulham | L | 1-3 | 1-1 | 3 | Forlan [45] | 67,727 |
| 11 | Nov 1 | H | Portsmouth | W | 3-0 | 1-0 | 3 | Forlan [37], Ronaldo [80], Keane [82] | 67,639 |
| 12 | 9 | A | Liverpool | W | 2-1 | 0-0 | 3 | Giggs 2 [59, 70] | 44,159 |
| 13 | 22 | H | Blackburn R | W | 2-1 | 2-0 | 3 | Van Nistelrooy [24], Kleberson [38] | 67,748 |
| 14 | 30 | A | Chelsea | L | 0-1 | 0-1 | 3 | | 41,932 |
| 15 | Dec 6 | H | Aston Villa | W | 4-0 | 2-0 | 3 | Van Nistelrooy 2 [16, 45], Forlan 2 [89, 90] | 67,621 |
| 16 | 13 | H | Manchester C | W | 3-1 | 2-0 | 2 | Scholes 2 [7, 73], Van Nistelrooy [34] | 67,643 |
| 17 | 21 | A | Tottenham H | W | 2-1 | 2-0 | 1 | O'Shea [15], Van Nistelrooy [25] | 35,910 |
| 18 | 26 | H | Everton | W | 3-2 | 2-1 | 1 | Butt [9], Kleberson [44], Bellion [68] | 67,642 |
| 19 | 28 | A | Middlesbrough | W | 1-0 | 1-0 | 1 | Mills (og) [14] | 34,738 |
| 20 | Jan 7 | A | Bolton W | W | 2-1 | 2-0 | — | Scholes [24], Van Nistelrooy [39] | 27,668 |
| 21 | 11 | H | Newcastle U | D | 0-0 | 0-0 | 1 | | 67,622 |
| 22 | 17 | A | Wolverhampton W | L | 0-1 | 0-0 | 2 | | 29,396 |
| 23 | 31 | H | Southampton | W | 3-2 | 2-1 | 2 | Saha [18], Scholes [37], Van Nistelrooy [61] | 67,758 |
| 24 | Feb 7 | A | Everton | W | 4-3 | 3-0 | 2 | Saha 2 [9, 29], Van Nistelrooy 2 [24, 89] | 40,190 |
| 25 | 11 | H | Middlesbrough | L | 2-3 | 1-2 | — | Van Nistelrooy [45], Giggs [63] | 67,346 |
| 26 | 21 | H | Leeds U | D | 1-1 | 0-0 | 2 | Scholes [64] | 67,744 |
| 27 | 28 | A | Fulham | D | 1-1 | 1-0 | 3 | Saha [14] | 18,306 |
| 28 | Mar 14 | A | Manchester C | L | 1-4 | 1-2 | 3 | Scholes [35] | 47,284 |
| 29 | 20 | H | Tottenham H | W | 3-0 | 1-0 | 3 | Giggs [30], Ronaldo [89], Bellion [90] | 67,644 |
| 30 | 28 | A | Arsenal | D | 1-1 | 0-0 | 3 | Saha [86] | 38,184 |
| 31 | Apr 10 | A | Birmingham C | W | 2-1 | 0-1 | 3 | Ronaldo [60], Saha [78] | 29,548 |
| 32 | 13 | H | Leicester C | W | 1-0 | 0-0 | — | Neville G [56] | 67,749 |
| 33 | 17 | A | Portsmouth | L | 0-1 | 0-1 | 3 | | 20,125 |
| 34 | 20 | H | Charlton Ath | W | 2-0 | 1-0 | — | Saha [28], Neville G [65] | 67,477 |
| 35 | 24 | H | Liverpool | L | 0-1 | 0-0 | 3 | | 67,647 |
| 36 | May 1 | A | Blackburn R | L | 0-1 | 0-0 | 3 | | 29,616 |
| 37 | 8 | H | Chelsea | D | 1-1 | 0-1 | 3 | Van Nistelrooy [77] | 67,609 |
| 38 | 15 | A | Aston Villa | W | 2-0 | 2-0 | 3 | Ronaldo [4], Van Nistelrooy [10] | 42,573 |

**Final League Position: 3**

### GOALSCORERS

*League (64):* Van Nistelrooy 20 (1 pen), Scholes 9, Giggs 7, Saha 7, Forlan 4, Ronaldo 4, Keane 3, Bellion 2, Kleberson 2, Neville G 2, O'Shea 2, Butt 1, own goal 1.
*Carling Cup (3):* Bellion 1, Djemba-Djemba 1, Fowler 1.
*FA Cup (15):* Van Nistelrooy 6 (1 pen), Scholes 4, Ronaldo 2, Forlan 1, Silvestre 1, own goal 1.
*Champions League (15):* Van Nistelrooy 4 (1 pen), Forlan 2, Fortune 2, Butt 1, Djemba-Djemba 1, Giggs 1, Neville P 1, Scholes 1, Silvestre 1, Solskjaer 1.

| Howard T 32 | Neville P 29 + 2 | Fortune Q 18 + 5 | Ferdinand R 20 | Keane R 25 + 3 | Silvestre M 33 + 1 | Solskjaer O 7 + 6 | Butt N 12 + 9 | Van Nistelrooy R 31 + 1 | Scholes P 24 + 4 | Giggs R 29 + 4 | Djemba-Djemba E 10 + 5 | Ronaldo C 15 + 14 | Forlan D 10 + 14 | O'Shea J 32 + 1 | Neville G 30 | Kleberson J 10 + 2 | Bellion D 4 + 10 | Fletcher D 17 + 5 | Brown W 15 + 2 | Saha L 9 + 3 | Carroll R 6 | *Match No.* |
|---|---|---|---|---|---|---|---|---|---|---|---|---|---|---|---|---|---|---|---|---|---|---|
| 1 | 2 | 3 | 4 | 5 | 6 | $7^1$ | $8^2$ | 9 | 10 | $11^3$ | 12 | 13 | 14 | | | | | | | | | 1 |
| 1 | 2 | | 4 | 5 | 6 | $7^1$ | | 9 | 10 | $11^2$ | 8 | 12 | 13 | 3 | | | | | | | | 2 |
| 1 | 3 | | | 5 | | $7^3$ | | 9 | 12 | 13 | 8 | $11^2$ | 10 | 6 | 2 | $4^1$ | 14 | | | | | 3 |
| 1 | $3^2$ | 13 | | 5 | 6 | | 14 | 9 | | 11 | $8^3$ | 12 | 10 | 4 | 2 | $7^1$ | | | | | | 4 |
| 1 | 10 | $3^1$ | 4 | $5^2$ | 12 | 13 | 8 | 9 | | 11 | | 7 | | 6 | 2 | | | | | | | 5 |
| 1 | 8 | 11 | 4 | 5 | 6 | | | 9 | | 10 | | 7 | 12 | $3^1$ | 2 | | | | | | | 6 |
| 1 | 8 | 3 | 4 | $5^1$ | | | 13 | 9 | $10^3$ | $11^2$ | 12 | | 14 | 6 | 2 | | | 7 | | | | 7 |
| 1 | $8^2$ | 3 | 4 | $5^1$ | 6 | | 13 | 9 | 10 | 11 | | | 12 | | 2 | | | 7 | | | | 8 |
| 1 | 8 | $3^1$ | 4 | 5 | 6 | | 13 | 9 | 10 | | | $11^2$ | 14 | 12 | 2 | | | $7^3$ | | | | 9 |
| 1 | | 12 | 4 | | $6^1$ | | 5 | 9 | 13 | 11 | $8^3$ | $7^2$ | 10 | 3 | 2 | | 14 | | | | | 10 |
| 1 | | 3 | 4 | 12 | | | 5 | 9 | | $11^3$ | $8^1$ | 13 | $10^2$ | 6 | 2 | | 14 | 7 | | | | 11 |
| 1 | 8 | $11^1$ | 4 | 5 | 6 | | | 9 | | 7 | | | 10 | 3 | 2 | | | 12 | | | | 12 |
| 1 | 10 | $11^1$ | 4 | 5 | 6 | | | $9^3$ | | 12 | | 13 | 14 | 3 | 2 | 8 | $7^2$ | | | | | 13 |
| 1 | $8^2$ | $11^1$ | 4 | 5 | 6 | | | 9 | | 7 | | 12 | 10 | 3 | 2 | 13 | | | | | | 14 |
| 1 | $8^1$ | 3 | 4 | 5 | 6 | | | $9^2$ | 12 | $11^3$ | | 7 | 13 | | 2 | 10 | 14 | | | | | 15 |
| 1 | 8 | | 4 | 5 | 6 | | | 9 | 10 | 11 | | 12 | | 3 | 2 | $7^1$ | | | | | | 16 |
| 1 | 8 | | 4 | $5^1$ | 6 | | 12 | 9 | 10 | 11 | | 13 | | 3 | 2 | | | $7^2$ | | | | 17 |
| 1 | | 11 | 4 | | $6^2$ | | 5 | | 12 | | 13 | 7 | 10 | $3^1$ | 2 | 8 | 9 | | | | | 18 |
| 1 | 8 | 3 | 4 | 5 | 6 | | 12 | $9^1$ | 10 | 11 | | | | | 2 | | | 7■ | | | | 19 |
| 1 | 8 | 13 | 4 | $5^1$ | 6 | | 12 | 9 | 10 | $11^2$ | | | | 3 | 2 | | | 7 | | | | 20 |
| 1 | $8^2$ | 13 | 4 | 5 | 6 | | | 9 | 10 | $11^1$ | | | 12 | 3 | $2^3$ | 7 | 14 | | | | | 21 |
| 1 | $8^1$ | 3 | $4^3$ | 5 | 6 | | | 9 | 10 | | | 11 | 12 | 2 | | | 13 | $7^2$ | 14 | | | 22 |
| 1 | 8 | 3 | | 5 | 6 | | 12 | 9 | 11 | | | $7^1$ | | 2 | | | | 13 | 4 | $10^2$ | | 23 |
| 1 | | 13 | | 5 | 6 | | | 9 | 8 | 11 | | 12 | | 3 | 2 | | | $7^1$ | 4 | $10^2$ | | 24 |
| 1 | 12 | 3 | | | 6 | | $5^2$ | 9 | 8 | 11 | | 14 | 13 | 2 | | $7^3$ | | | $4^1$ | 10 | | 25 |
| 1 | $5^3$ | 3 | | 12 | $6^2$ | 14 | 8 | 9 | 10 | 11 | | | | 4 | 2 | $7^1$ | | | 13 | | | 26 |
| | 5 | 3 | | 4 | | | | 12 | 8 | 13 | | 11 | $9^1$ | 2 | | | | $7^2$ | 6 | 10 | 1 | 27 |
| 1 | 2 | | | | 6 | 13 | 5 | 9 | 10 | $11^1$ | | $7^2$ | 12 | 3 | | | | 8 | 4 | | | 28 |
| | 2 | | | 5 | 6 | $7^1$ | 13 | 9 | $8^3$ | 11 | | 12 | $10^2$ | 3 | | | 14 | | 4 | | 1 | 29 |
| | | | | 5 | 6 | 12 | | 9 | 10 | 11 | $8^2$ | | | 3 | 2 | | | $7^1$ | 4 | 13 | 1 | 30 |
| | 14 | | | | 6 | $11^2$ | | | 8 | $9^3$ | $5^1$ | 13 | 12 | 3 | 2 | | | 7 | 4 | 10 | 1 | 31 |
| | | | | | 6 | | 5 | | 8 | | 12 | 11 | $9^2$ | 3 | 2 | | $7^1$ | 13 | 4 | 10 | 1 | 32 |
| | | | | | 6 | 7 | $5^3$ | | 11 | 9 | $8^1$ | 12 | | $3^2$ | 2 | | 14 | 13 | 4 | 10 | 1 | 33 |
| 1 | 3 | | | 12 | 6 | | $5^1$ | 9 | | 13 | 8 | 14 | | | 2 | | 11 | $7^3$ | 4 | $10^2$ | | 34 |
| 1 | $8^2$ | | | 5 | 6 | 12 | | | | 9 | | 11 | | $3^1$ | 2 | | 13 | 7 | 4 | 10 | | 35 |
| 1 | 5 | | | | 6 | 10 | $7^3$ | | | 9 | $8^2$ | | 12 | 3 | 2 | $11^1$ | 14 | 13 | 4 | | | 36 |
| 1 | $5^2$ | | | | 6 | 12 | | 9 | $8^3$ | 10 | | $11^1$ | | 3 | 2 | 13 | | 7 | 4 | 14 | | 37 |
| 1 | 5 | | | | 6 | | | $9^2$ | 10 | 11 | 12 | 7■ | | $3^1$ | 2 | | | 8■ | 4 | 13 | | 38 |

**Carling Cup**

| | | | |
|---|---|---|---|
| Third Round | Leeds U | (a) | 3-2 |
| Fourth Round | WBA | (a) | 0-2 |

**FA Cup**

| | | | |
|---|---|---|---|
| Third Round | Aston Villa | (a) | 2-1 |
| Fourth Round | Northampton T | (a) | 3-0 |
| Fifth Round | Manchester C | (h) | 4-2 |
| Sixth Round | Fulham | (h) | 2-1 |
| Semi-Final (at Villa Park) | Arsenal | | 1-0 |
| Final *(at Millennium Stadium)* | Millwall | | 3-0 |

**Champions League**

| | | | |
|---|---|---|---|
| Group E | Panathinaikos | (h) | 5-0 |
| | Stuttgart | (a) | 1-2 |
| | Rangers | (a) | 1-0 |
| | | (h) | 3-0 |
| | Panathinaikos | (a) | 1-0 |
| | Stuttgart | (h) | 2-0 |
| First KO Round | Porto | (a) | 1-2 |
| | | (h) | 1-1 |

# MANSFIELD TOWN — FL Championship 2

## FOUNDATION

The club was formed as Mansfield Wesleyans in 1897, and changed their name to Mansfield Wesley in 1906 and Mansfield Town in 1910. This was after the Mansfield Wesleyan Chapel trustees had requested that the club change its name as 'it has no longer had any connection with either the chapel or school'. The new club participated in the Notts and Derby District League, but in the following season 1911–12 joined the Central Alliance.

***Field Mill Ground, Quarry Lane, Mansfield, Notts NG18 5DA.***

***Telephone:*** 0870 756 3160.

***Fax:*** (01623) 482 495.

***Ticket Office:*** (0870) 756 3160.

***Website:*** www.mansfieldtown.net

***Email:*** mtfc@stags.plus.com

***Ground Capacity:*** 9,899.

***Record Attendance:*** 24,467 v Nottingham F, FA Cup 3rd rd, 10 January 1953.

***Pitch Measurements:*** 114yd × 70yd.

***Chairman:*** Keith Haslam.

***Secretary:*** Christine Reynolds.

***Manager:*** Keith Curle.

***Assistant Manager:*** John Gannon.

***Physio:*** Derek French.

***Colours:*** Amber shirts, blue shorts, blue stockings.

***Change Colours:*** White shirts with orange and blue flash, orange shorts, orange stockings.

***Year Formed:*** 1897.

***Turned Professional:*** 1906.

***Ltd Co.:*** 1922.

***Previous Name:*** 1897, Mansfield Wesleyans; 1906, Mansfield Wesley; 1910, Mansfield Town.

***Previous Grounds:*** 1897–99, Westfield Lane; 1899–1901, Ratcliffe Gate; 1901–12, Newgate Lane; 1912–16, Ratcliffe Gate.

***Club Nickname:*** 'The Stags'.

***First Football League Game:*** 29 August 1931, Division 3 (S), v Swindon T (h) W 3–2 – Wilson; Clifford, England; Wake, Davis, Blackburn; Gilhespy, Readman (1), Johnson, Broom (2), Baxter.

***Record League Victory:*** 9–2 v Rotherham U, Division 3 (N), 27 December 1932 – Wilson; Anthony, England; Davies, S. Robinson, Slack; Prior, Broom, Readman (3), Hoyland (3), Bowater (3).

***Record Cup Victory:*** 8–0 v Scarborough (a), FA Cup 1st rd, 22 November 1952 – Bramley; Chessell, Bradley; Field, Plummer, Lewis; Scott, Fox (3), Marron (2), Sid Watson (1), Adam (2).

## HONOURS

*Football League:* Division 2 best season: 21st, 1977–78; Division 3 – Champions 1976–77; Promoted to Division 2 (3rd) 2001–02; Division 4 – Champions 1974–75; Division 3 (N) – Runners-up 1950–51.

*FA Cup:* best season: 6th rd, 1969.

*Football League Cup:* best season: 5th rd, 1976.

*Freight Rover Trophy:* Winners 1987.

## SKY SPORTS FACT FILE

On 28 August 1937 Harold Crawshaw scored a hat-trick on his debut for Mansfield Town against Northampton Town in a 4-1 win. He went on to score 25 League goals in total and missed just one match. Previously with Portsmouth, he later joined Nottingham Forest.

***Record Defeat:*** 1–8 v Walsall, Division 3 (N), 19 January 1933.

***Most League Points (2 for a win):*** 68, Division 4, 1974–75.

***Most League Points (3 for a win):*** 81, Division 4, 1985–86.

***Most League Goals:*** 108, Division 4, 1962–63.

***Highest League Scorer in Season:*** Ted Harston, 55, Division 3 (N), 1936–37.

***Most League Goals in Total Aggregate:*** Harry Johnson, 104, 1931–36.

***Most League Goals in One Match:*** 7, Ted Harston v Hartlepools U, Division 3N, 23 January 1937.

***Most Capped Player:*** John McClelland, 6 (53), Northern Ireland.

***Most League Appearances:*** Rod Arnold, 440, 1970–83.

***Youngest League Player:*** Cyril Poole, 15 years 351 days v New Brighton, 27 February 1937.

***Record Transfer Fee Received:*** £655,000 from Tottenham H for Colin Calderwood, July 1993.

***Record Transfer Fee Paid:*** £150,000 to Carlisle U for Lee Peacock, October 1997.

***Football League Record:*** 1931 Elected to Division 3 (S); 1932–37 Division 3 (N); 1937–47 Division 3 (S); 1947–58 Division 3 (N); 1958–60 Division 3; 1960–63 Division 4; 1963–72 Division 3; 1972–75 Division 4; 1975–77 Division 3; 1977–78 Division 2; 1978–80 Division 3; 1980–86 Division 4; 1986–91 Division 3; 1991–92 Division 4; 1992–93 Division 2; 1993–2002 Division 3; 2002–03 Division 2; 2003–04 Division 3; 2004– FL2.

## MANAGERS

John Baynes 1922–25
Ted Davison 1926–28
Jack Hickling 1928–33
Henry Martin 1933–35
Charlie Bell 1935
Harold Wightman 1936
Harold Parkes 1936–38
Jack Poole 1938–44
Lloyd Barke 1944–45
Roy Goodall 1945–49
Freddie Steele 1949–51
George Jobey 1952–53
Stan Mercer 1953–55
Charlie Mitten 1956–58
Sam Weaver 1958–60
Raich Carter 1960–63
Tommy Cummings 1963–67
Tommy Eggleston 1967–70
Jock Basford 1970–71
Danny Williams 1971–74
Dave Smith 1974–76
Peter Morris 1976–78
Billy Bingham 1978–79
Mick Jones 1979–81
Stuart Boam 1981–83
Ian Greaves 1983–89
George Foster 1989–93
Andy King 1993–96
Steve Parkin 1996–99
Bill Dearden 1999–2002
Stuart Watkiss 2002
Keith Curle December 2002–

## LATEST SEQUENCES

***Longest Sequence of League Wins:*** 7, 13.9.1991 – 26.10.1991.

***Longest Sequence of League Defeats:*** 7, 18.1.1947 – 15.3.1947.

***Longest Sequence of League Draws:*** 5, 18.10.1986 – 22.11.1986.

***Longest Sequence of Unbeaten League Matches:*** 20, 14.2.1976 – 21.8.1976.

***Longest Sequence Without a League Win:*** 14, 25.3.2000 – 2.9.2000.

***Successive Scoring Runs:*** 27 from 1.10.1962.

***Successive Non-scoring Runs:*** 8 from 25.3.2000.

## TEN YEAR LEAGUE RECORD

| | | P | W | D | L | F | A | Pts | Pos |
|---|---|---|---|---|---|---|---|---|---|
| 1994-95 | Div 3 | 42 | 18 | 11 | 13 | 84 | 59 | 65 | 6 |
| 1995-96 | Div 3 | 46 | 11 | 20 | 15 | 54 | 64 | 53 | 19 |
| 1996-97 | Div 3 | 46 | 16 | 16 | 14 | 47 | 45 | 64 | 11 |
| 1997-98 | Div 3 | 46 | 16 | 17 | 13 | 64 | 55 | 65 | 12 |
| 1998-99 | Div 3 | 46 | 19 | 10 | 17 | 60 | 58 | 67 | 8 |
| 1999-2000 | Div 3 | 46 | 16 | 8 | 22 | 50 | 65 | 56 | 17 |
| 2000-01 | Div 3 | 46 | 15 | 13 | 18 | 64 | 72 | 68 | 13 |
| 2001-02 | Div 3 | 46 | 24 | 7 | 15 | 72 | 60 | 79 | 3 |
| 2002-03 | Div 2 | 46 | 12 | 8 | 26 | 66 | 97 | 44 | 23 |
| 2003-04 | Div 3 | 46 | 22 | 9 | 15 | 76 | 62 | 75 | 5 |

## DID YOU KNOW?

Absenteeism was rife in the area when Mansfield Town met Sheffield United in an FA Cup replay at Field Mill on a Wednesday afternoon 31 January 1931. Locals were not disappointed as the Stags won through 2-1 after extra time.

## MANSFIELD TOWN 2003–04 LEAGUE RECORD

| Match No. | Date | Venue | Opponents | Result | | H/T Score | Lg. Pos. | Goalscorers | Atten-dance |
|---|---|---|---|---|---|---|---|---|---|
| 1 | Aug 9 | A | Kidderminster H | L | 1-2 | 0-1 | — | Corden [65] | 3180 |
| 2 | 16 | H | Leyton Orient | D | 1-1 | 1-0 | 15 | Dimech [13] | 3920 |
| 3 | 23 | A | Southend U | W | 3-0 | 1-0 | 11 | Christie 3 [42, 51, 90] | 3837 |
| 4 | 26 | H | Scunthorpe U | W | 5-0 | 2-0 | — | Day [9], Mendes [18], Lawrence 2 [65, 90], Christie [72] | 5142 |
| 5 | 30 | A | Swansea C | L | 1-4 | 1-1 | 9 | Vaughan [44] | 6991 |
| 6 | Sept 6 | H | Macclesfield T | W | 3-2 | 1-2 | 6 | Artell [7], Mendes [52], Lawrence (pen) [69] | 4209 |
| 7 | 13 | A | Oxford U | D | 1-1 | 0-0 | 7 | MacKenzie [79] | 5625 |
| 8 | 16 | H | Bury | W | 5-3 | 3-1 | — | Mendes [30], Corden 2 [36, 44], Lawrence 2 [63, 88] | 4145 |
| 9 | 20 | H | Yeovil T | L | 0-1 | 0-1 | 7 | | 5270 |
| 10 | 27 | A | Cambridge U | W | 2-1 | 1-0 | 6 | Disley [34], Lawrence (pen) [74] | 4068 |
| 11 | 30 | A | Bristol R | W | 3-1 | 3-0 | — | Mendes [10], Disley 2 [13, 41] | 8451 |
| 12 | Oct 4 | H | Darlington | W | 3-1 | 1-1 | 2 | Vaughan [13], Christie [59], Corden [65] | 4621 |
| 13 | 11 | H | York C | W | 2-0 | 1-0 | 2 | Artell [31], Beardsley [76] | 4914 |
| 14 | 18 | A | Doncaster R | L | 2-4 | 1-1 | 4 | Lawrence [21], Corden [81] | 8500 |
| 15 | 21 | A | Torquay U | L | 0-1 | 0-1 | — | | 2773 |
| 16 | 25 | H | Cheltenham T | W | 4-0 | 2-0 | 6 | Lawrence 2 (2 pens) [8, 86], Larkin 2 [45, 53] | 4095 |
| 17 | Nov 1 | H | Boston U | W | 2-1 | 1-1 | 4 | Mendes 2 [33, 51] | 5161 |
| 18 | 15 | A | Carlisle U | W | 2-0 | 0-0 | 2 | Corden [54], Mendes [63] | 4154 |
| 19 | 22 | H | Huddersfield T | D | 3-3 | 1-2 | 4 | Day [45], Artell [62], Disley [90] | 5828 |
| 20 | 29 | A | Northampton T | W | 3-0 | 1-0 | 3 | Christie [5], Lawrence (pen) [66], Disley [80] | 5019 |
| 21 | Dec 13 | H | Lincoln C | L | 1-2 | 1-1 | 5 | Lawrence (pen) [34] | 5797 |
| 22 | 20 | A | Hull C | W | 1-0 | 0-0 | 4 | MacKenzie [84] | 15,005 |
| 23 | 26 | H | Rochdale | W | 1-0 | 0-0 | 3 | Larkin [56] | 6963 |
| 24 | 28 | A | Macclesfield T | D | 1-1 | 0-0 | 4 | Christie [71] | 3578 |
| 25 | Jan 10 | H | Kidderminster H | W | 1-0 | 1-0 | 4 | Day [26] | 4574 |
| 26 | 17 | A | Leyton Orient | L | 1-3 | 1-1 | 7 | Buxton [33] | 4072 |
| 27 | 24 | H | Southend U | W | 1-0 | 1-0 | 4 | Corden (pen) [15] | 4292 |
| 28 | 27 | A | Scunthorpe U | D | 0-0 | 0-0 | — | | 3113 |
| 29 | Feb 7 | A | Rochdale | L | 0-3 | 0-2 | 4 | | 3157 |
| 30 | 14 | A | York C | W | 2-1 | 1-0 | 4 | Lawrence [29], Pacquette [53] | 4068 |
| 31 | 21 | H | Doncaster R | L | 1-2 | 1-0 | 4 | Lawrence (pen) [15] | 7724 |
| 32 | 28 | A | Cheltenham T | L | 2-4 | 0-1 | 5 | Christie [64], Corden [83] | 3818 |
| 33 | Mar 6 | H | Hull C | W | 1-0 | 0-0 | 6 | D'Jaffo [69] | 6859 |
| 34 | 13 | A | Lincoln C | L | 1-4 | 1-0 | 6 | Lawrence (pen) [37] | 6034 |
| 35 | 16 | A | Bury | L | 0-3 | 0-2 | — | | 2199 |
| 36 | 23 | H | Swansea C | D | 1-1 | 0-1 | — | Lawrence (pen) [51] | 4058 |
| 37 | 27 | A | Yeovil T | D | 1-1 | 0-0 | 7 | Day [79] | 6002 |
| 38 | 30 | H | Torquay U | W | 2-1 | 2-1 | — | Larkin [5], Mendes [10] | 4552 |
| 39 | Apr 3 | H | Cambridge U | D | 1-1 | 0-0 | 7 | Mendes [61] | 4342 |
| 40 | 6 | H | Oxford U | W | 3-1 | 3-1 | — | Mendes [16], Larkin [19], Day [37] | 5132 |
| 41 | 10 | A | Darlington | L | 0-1 | 0-0 | 6 | | 4946 |
| 42 | 12 | H | Bristol R | D | 0-0 | 0-0 | 6 | | 4735 |
| 43 | 17 | A | Boston U | W | 2-1 | 0-0 | 6 | Larkin [15], Ellender (og) [59] | 3826 |
| 44 | 24 | H | Carlisle U | L | 2-3 | 2-2 | 6 | Lawrence 2 (1 pen) [29 (p), 45] | 5361 |
| 45 | May 1 | A | Huddersfield T | W | 3-1 | 2-1 | 5 | Day [20], Mendes [38], Lawrence [76] | 18,633 |
| 46 | 8 | H | Northampton T | L | 1-2 | 0-1 | 5 | Larkin [54] | 8065 |

**Final League Position: 5**

## GOALSCORERS

*League (76):* Lawrence 18 (10 pens), Mendes 11, Christie 8, Corden 8 (1 pen), Larkin 7, Day 6, Disley 5, Artell 3, MacKenzie 2, Vaughan 2, Beardsley 1, Buxton 1, D'Jaffo 1, Dimech 1, Pacquette 1, own goal 1.
*Carling Cup (1):* own goal 1.
*FA Cup (10):* Lawrence 3 (2 pens), MacKenzie 3, Christie 1, Curtis 1, Larkin 1, Mendes 1.
*LDV Vans Trophy (1):* Day 1.
*Play-Offs (3):* Curtis 1, Day 1, Mendes 1.

| Pilkington K 46 | Hassell B 33 + 1 | Clarke J 11 + 1 | Curtis T 34 + 4 | Artell D 24 + 2 | Dimech L 17 + 3 | Lawrence L 41 | Williamson L 29 + 6 | Christie I 24 + 3 | Larkin C 19 + 18 | Corden W 40 + 4 | Disley C 18 + 16 | White A 2 + 12 | Mendes J 36 + 3 | MacKenzie N 25 + 7 | Beardsley C 2 + 13 | Vaughan T 32 | Day R 40 + 1 | John-Baptiste A 14 + 3 | Mulligan L — + 1 | Mitchell C — + 1 | Curle T — + 1 | Eaton A 3 | Buxton J 9 | Pacquette R 3 + 2 | D'Jaffo L 4 + 4 | *Match No.* |
|---|---|---|---|---|---|---|---|---|---|---|---|---|---|---|---|---|---|---|---|---|---|---|---|---|---|---|
| 1 | 2 | 3 | 4 | 5 | 6 | $7^{1}$ | 8 | $9^{2}$ | $10^{3}$ | 11 | 12 | 13 | 14 | | | | | | | | | | | | | 1 |
| 1 | 2 | 3 | 4 | 5 | 6 | | 8 | 9 | | $11^{1}$ | 13 | $10^{2}$ | $7^{3}$ | 12 | 14 | | | | | | | | | | | 2 |
| 1 | 2 | | | 5 | | 7 | 4 | 9 | $10^{1}$ | 11 | | | 12 | $8^{2}$ | | 3 | 6 | 13 | | | | | | | | 3 |
| 1 | 2 | | | 5 | | 7 | 4 | 9 | | 11 | | | 10 | 8 | | 3 | 6 | | | | | | | | | 4 |
| 1 | $2^{2}$ | | | 5 | | 7 | 4■ | 9■ | 12 | $11^{1}$ | 14 | 13 | 10 | $8^{3}$ | | 3 | 6 | | | | | | | | | 5 |
| 1 | 2 | | 12 | 5 | | 7 | 4 | 9 | | $11^{2}$ | 13 | | 10 | $8^{1}$ | | 3 | 6 | | | | | | | | | 6 |
| 1 | 2 | | 4 | 5 | | 7 | | | | $11^{2}$ | $10^{1}$ | | 9 | 8 | 12 | 3 | 6 | | 13 | | | | | | | 7 |
| 1 | 2 | | 4 | $5^{2}$ | | 7 | | | | 11 | $10^{1}$ | | 9 | 8 | 12 | 3 | 6 | 13 | | | | | | | | 8 |
| 1 | | $2^{2}$ | 4 | | | 7 | | | | 11 | $10^{1}$ | | 9 | 8 | 12 | $5^{3}$ | 6 | 3 | | 13 | 14 | | | | | 9 |
| 1 | 2 | | 4 | 12 | 13 | 7 | | 9■ | $10^{3}$ | | 11 | | | $8^{1}$ | 14 | $3^{2}$ | 6■ | 5 | | | | | | | | 10 |
| 1 | | 2 | $4^{2}$ | | 6 | 7 | | $9^{3}$ | 12 | 13 | $11^{1}$ | | 10 | 8 | 14 | 3 | 5 | | | | | | | | | 11 |
| 1 | | 3 | 4 | | 2 | 7 | | $9^{1}$ | 12 | 13 | $11^{2}$ | | $10^{3}$ | 8 | 14 | 6 | 5 | | | | | | | | | 12 |
| 1 | | 2 | 4 | 5 | 3 | 7 | 12 | | $10^{2}$ | $11^{1}$ | 13 | | | 8 | 9 | 6 | | | | | | | | | | 13 |
| 1 | | $2^{2}$ | 4 | 5 | 6 | 7 | 8 | 9 | 12 | 14 | | | | $11^{3}$ | $10^{1}$ | 3 | 13 | | | | | | | | | 14 |
| 1 | | 2 | $4^{2}$ | 5 | 6 | 7 | 8 | $9^{3}$ | 12 | $11^{1}$ | 13 | 14 | 10 | | | 3 | | | | | | | | | | 15 |
| 1 | | | 12 | 5 | 2 | 7 | $6^{1}$ | | 10 | 11 | 13 | | 9 | $8^{2}$ | | 3 | 4 | | | | | | | | | 16 |
| 1 | 2 | | 12 | 5 | | 7 | 4 | | $10^{2}$ | 11 | | | 9 | $8^{1}$ | 13 | 3 | 6 | | | | | | | | | 17 |
| 1 | 2 | | 4 | 5 | | 7 | 8 | | $10^{2}$ | $11^{1}$ | 12 | | 9 | | 13 | 3 | 6 | | | | | | | | | 18 |
| 1 | 2 | | 4 | 5 | | 7 | $8^{1}$ | 13 | 10 | $11^{2}$ | 12 | | $9^{3}$ | 14 | | 3 | 6 | | | | | | | | | 19 |
| 1 | 2 | | 4 | 5 | | 7 | 8 | $9^{1}$ | 13 | | 11 | | $10^{2}$ | 12 | | 3 | 6 | | | | | | | | | 20 |
| 1 | 2 | | 4 | 5 | | 7 | 8 | 9 | 13 | $11^{2}$ | | | 10 | 12 | | | 6 | | | | | $3^{1}$ | | | | 21 |
| 1 | 2 | | 4 | 5 | | 7 | 8 | $9^{1}$ | | 13 | $11^{2}$ | | 10 | 12 | | 3 | 6 | | | | | | | | | 22 |
| 1 | 2 | 12 | 4 | | 6 | | 7 | | 10 | 11 | 8 | | 9 | | | $3^{1}$ | 5 | | | | | | | | | 23 |
| 1 | 2 | 3 | 4 | | 6 | 7 | 8 | 9 | | 11 | | | 10 | | | | 5 | | | | | | | | | 24 |
| 1 | 2 | 3 | 4 | | 6 | $7^{1}$ | 8 | 9 | 12 | 11 | | | 10 | | | | 5 | | | | | | | | | 25 |
| 1 | 2 | | 4 | 5 | | | 8 | 12 | $10^{1}$ | $11^{2}$ | | 13 | 9 | 7 | | | 6 | | | | | | 3 | | | 26 |
| 1 | | | | 12 | 6 | | | 9 | 13 | 11 | $7^{2}$ | | 10 | 8 | | $3^{1}$ | 5 | 4 | | | | | 2 | | | 27 |
| 1 | 2 | | 4 | | 6 | 7 | | 9 | 12 | $11^{2}$ | | 13 | $10^{1}$ | 8 | | | 5 | | | | | | 3 | | | 28 |
| 1 | 2 | | | | 6 | 7 | 4 | 13 | $8^{1}$ | $11^{2}$ | 14 | | $9^{3}$ | 12 | | | 5 | | | | | | 3 | 10 | | 29 |
| 1 | | | | 5 | 12 | 7 | 4 | 9 | 13 | 11 | $8^{1}$ | | | | | 3 | 6 | | | | | | 2 | $10^{2}$ | | 30 |
| 1 | | | | 5 | | 7 | 4 | 9 | 13 | $11^{1}$ | 8 | | 12 | | | 3 | 6 | | | | | | 2 | $10^{2}$ | | 31 |
| 1 | 12 | | | 5 | 4 | 7 | | $9^{3}$ | 13 | 11 | 8 | | $10^{2}$ | | | 3 | 6 | | | | | | $2^{1}$ | 14 | | 32 |
| 1 | 2 | | 12 | | 6 | 7 | 4 | 9 | | 11 | $8^{1}$ | | | | | 3 | 5 | | | | | | | 13 | $10^{2}$ | 33 |
| 1 | 2 | | 4 | 5 | | 7 | | 9 | 12 | $11^{1}$ | 8 | 13 | | | | 3 | 6 | | | | | | | | $10^{2}$ | 34 |
| 1 | 2 | | 4 | 5 | 6 | | 7 | $9^{1}$ | 12 | $11^{3}$ | | 13 | 8 | | | | | 14 | | | | | $3^{2}$ | | 10 | 35 |
| 1 | 2 | | $4^{1}$ | | | 7 | 14 | | 13 | $11^{2}$ | 12 | | 9 | 8 | | 3■ | 5 | 6 | | | | | | | $10^{3}$ | 36 |
| 1 | 2 | | 4 | | | 7 | 12 | | 14 | 11 | $10^{3}$ | | $9^{2}$ | 8 | 13 | 3 | 5 | $6^{1}$ | | | | | | | | 37 |
| 1 | 2 | | 4 | | | 7 | 13 | | $10^{3}$ | $11^{2}$ | 12 | 14 | 9 | $8^{1}$ | | 3 | 5 | 6 | | | | | | | | 38 |
| 1 | 2 | | 4 | | | 7 | 12 | | $10^{2}$ | 11 | | 13 | $9^{3}$ | $8^{1}$ | 14 | 3 | 5 | 6 | | | | | | | | 39 |
| 1 | 2 | | 4 | | | 7 | 6 | | $10^{2}$ | 11 | | 12 | $9^{1}$ | 8 | 13 | | 5 | 3 | | | | | | | | 40 |
| 1 | 2 | | 4 | | | 7 | 6 | | $10^{2}$ | $11^{1}$ | 12 | 13 | 9 | $8^{3}$ | 14 | | 5 | 3 | | | | | | | | 41 |
| 1 | | | 4 | | | 7 | 6 | | 10 | 11 | $8^{2}$ | 12 | $9^{1}$ | 13 | | | 5 | 3 | | | | | 2 | | | 42 |
| 1 | 2 | | 4 | | | 7 | 12 | | $10^{2}$ | 11 | 13 | $9^{3}$ | | $8^{1}$ | | 3 | 5 | 6 | | | | | | | 14 | 43 |
| 1 | 2 | | 4 | | | 7 | | | 10 | 11 | 12 | | $9^{2}$ | 8 | | $3^{1}$ | 5 | 6 | | | | | | | 13 | 44 |
| 1 | 2 | | 4 | | 12 | 7 | $8^{1}$ | | 13 | 11 | $10^{2}$ | | $9^{3}$ | | | | 5 | 6 | | | | 3 | | | 14 | 45 |
| 1 | | 2 | $4^{2}$ | | | 7 | 8 | | 10 | $11^{1}$ | 12 | | 9 | | | | 5 | 6 | | | | 3 | | | 13 | 46 |

**Carling Cup**

| | | | |
|---|---|---|---|
| First Round | Sunderland | (h) | 1-2 |

**FA Cup**

| | | | |
|---|---|---|---|
| First Round | Bishop's Stortford | (h) | 6-0 |
| Second Round | Wycombe W | (a) | 1-1 |
| | | (h) | 3-2 |
| Third Round | Burnley | (h) | 0-2 |

**LDV Vans Trophy**

| | | | |
|---|---|---|---|
| First Round | Stockport Co | (h) | 1-2 |

**Play-Offs**

| | | | |
|---|---|---|---|
| Semi-Final | Northampton T | (a) | 2-0 |
| | | (h) | 1-3 |
| Final | Huddersfield T | | 0-0 |
| *(at Millennium Stadium)* | | | |

# MIDDLESBROUGH FA Premiership

## FOUNDATION

A previous belief that Middlesbrough Football Club was founded at a tripe supper at the Corporation Hotel has proved to be erroneous. In fact, members of Middlesbrough Cricket Club were responsible for forming it at a meeting in the gymnasium of the Albert Park Hotel in 1875.

***Riverside Stadium, Middlesbrough TS3 6RS.***

***Telephone:*** (01642) 877 700.

***Fax:*** (01642) 877 840.

***Ticket Office:*** (01642) 877 745.

***Website:*** www.mfc.co.uk

***Email:*** enquiries@mfc.co.uk

***Ground Capacity:*** 35,120.

***Record Attendance:*** Ayresome Park: 53,536 v Newcastle U, Division 1, 27 December 1949. Riverside Stadium: 34,814 v Newcastle U, FA Premier League, 5 March 2003.

***Pitch Measurements:*** 105m × 68m.

***Chairman:*** Steve Gibson.

***Chief Executive:*** Keith Lamb.

***Secretary:*** Karen Nelson.

***Manager:*** Steve McClaren.

***Physio:*** Grant Downie.

## HONOURS

*Football League:* Division 1 – Champions 1994–95; Runners-up 1997–98; Division 2 – Champions 1926–27, 1928–29, 1973–74; Runners-up 1901–02, 1991–92; Division 3 – Runners-up 1966–67, 1986–87.

*FA Cup:* Runners-up 1997.

*Football League Cup:* Winners 2004; Runners-up 1997, 1998.

*Amateur Cup:* Winners 1895, 1898.

*Anglo-Scottish Cup:* Winners 1976.

*Zenith Data Systems Cup:* Runners-up 1990.

***Colours:*** Red shirts with white chest band, red shorts, red stockings.

***Change Colours:*** Navy blue shirts with maroon trim, navy blue shorts, navy blue stockings.

***Year Formed:*** 1876; re-formed 1986.

***Turned Professional:*** 1889; became amateur 1892, and professional again, 1899.

***Ltd Co:*** 1892.

***Club Nickname:*** 'Boro'.

***Previous Grounds:*** 1877, Old Archery Ground, Albert Park; 1879, Breckon Hill; 1882, Linthorpe Road Ground; 1903, Ayresome Park; 1995, Cellnet Riverside Stadium.

***First Football League Game:*** 2 September 1899, Division 2, v Lincoln C (a) L 0–3 – Smith; Shaw, Ramsey; Allport, McNally, McCracken; Wanless, Longstaffe, Gettins, Page, Pugh.

***Record League Victory:*** 9–0 v Brighton & HA, Division 2, 23 August 1958 – Taylor; Bilcliff, Robinson; Harris (2p), Phillips, Walley; Day, McLean, Clough (5), Peacock (2), Holliday.

***Record Cup Victory:*** 7–0 v Hereford U, Coca-Cola Cup 2nd rd, 1st leg, 18 September 1996 – Miller; Fleming (1), Branco (1), Whyte, Vickers, Whelan, Emerson (1), Mustoe, Stamp, Juninho, Ravanelli (4).

## SKY SPORTS FACT FILE

George Camsell had a sixth sense as a marksman and 20-20 vision when playing for Durham City – his games and goals ratio in fact. Transferred to Middlesbrough for only £600 in October 1925 he took just eight years to top his 250th career League goal.

***Record Defeat:*** 0–9 v Blackburn R, Division 2, 6 November 1954.

***Most League Points (2 for a win):*** 65, Division 2, 1973–74.

***Most League Points (3 for a win):*** 94, Division 3, 1986–87.

***Most League Goals:*** 122, Division 2, 1926–27.

***Highest League Scorer in Season:*** George Camsell, 59, Division 2, 1926–27 (Second Division record).

***Most League Goals in Total Aggregate:*** George Camsell, 325, 1925–39.

***Most League Goals in One Match:*** 5, Andy Wilson v Nottingham F, Division 1, 6 October 1923; 5, George Camsell v Manchester C, Division 2, 25 December 1926; 5, George Camsell v Aston Villa, Division 1, 9 September 1935; 5, Brian Clough v Brighton & HA, Division 2, 22 August 1958.

***Most Capped Player:*** Wilf Mannion, 26, England.

***Most League Appearances:*** Tim Williamson, 563, 1902–23.

***Youngest League Player:*** Stephen Bell, 16 years 323 days v Southampton, 30 January 1982; Sam Lawrie, 16 years 323 days v Arsenal, 3 November 1951.

***Record Transfer Fee Received:*** £12,000,000 from Atletico Madrid for Juninho, July 1997.

***Record Transfer Fee Paid:*** £8,100,500 to Empoli for Massimo Maccarone, July 2002.

***Football League Record:*** 1899 Elected to Division 2; 1902–24 Division 1; 1924–27 Division 2; 1927–28 Division 1; 1928–29 Division 2; 1929–54 Division 1; 1954–66 Division 2; 1966–67 Division 3; 1967–74 Division 2; 1974–82 Division 1; 1982–86 Division 2; 1986–87 Division 3; 1987–88 Division 2; 1988–89 Division 1; 1989–92 Division 2; 1992–93 FA Premier League; 1993–95 Division 1; 1995–97 FA Premier League; 1997–98 Division 1; 1998– FA Premier League.

## MANAGERS

John Robson 1899–1905
Alex Mackie 1905–06
Andy Aitken 1906–09
J. Gunter 1908–10
*(Secretary-Manager)*
Andy Walker 1910–11
Tom McIntosh 1911–19
Jimmy Howie 1920–23
Herbert Bamlett 1923–26
Peter McWilliam 1927–34
Wilf Gillow 1934–44
David Jack 1944–52
Walter Rowley 1952–54
Bob Dennison 1954–63
Raich Carter 1963–66
Stan Anderson 1966–73
Jack Charlton 1973–77
John Neal 1977–81
Bobby Murdoch 1981–82
Malcolm Allison 1982–84
Willie Maddren 1984–86
Bruce Rioch 1986–90
Colin Todd 1990–91
Lennie Lawrence 1991–94
Bryan Robson 1994–2001
Steve McClaren July 2001–

## LATEST SEQUENCES

***Longest Sequence of League Wins:*** 9, 16.2.1974 – 6.4.1974.

***Longest Sequence of League Defeats:*** 8, 26.12.1995 – 17.2.1996.

***Longest Sequence of League Draws:*** 8, 3.4.1971 – 1.5.1971.

***Longest Sequence of Unbeaten League Matches:*** 24, 8.9.1973 – 19.1.1974.

***Longest Sequence Without a League Win:*** 19, 3.10.1981 – 6.3.1982.

***Successive Scoring Runs:*** 26 from 21.9.1946.

***Successive Non-scoring Runs:*** 4 from 24.11.1923.

## TEN YEAR LEAGUE RECORD

| | | P | W | D | L | F | A | Pts | Pos |
|---|---|---|---|---|---|---|---|---|---|
| 1994-95 | Div 1 | 46 | 23 | 13 | 10 | 67 | 40 | 82 | 1 |
| 1995-96 | PR Lge | 38 | 11 | 10 | 17 | 35 | 50 | 43 | 12 |
| 1996-97 | PR Lge | 38 | 10 | 12 | 16 | 51 | 60 | 39 | 19 |
| 1997-98 | Div 1 | 46 | 27 | 10 | 9 | 77 | 41 | 91 | 2 |
| 1998-99 | PR Lge | 38 | 12 | 15 | 11 | 48 | 54 | 51 | 9 |
| 1999-2000 | PR Lge | 38 | 14 | 10 | 14 | 46 | 52 | 52 | 12 |
| 2000-01 | PR Lge | 38 | 9 | 15 | 14 | 44 | 44 | 42 | 14 |
| 2001-02 | PR Lge | 38 | 12 | 9 | 17 | 35 | 47 | 45 | 12 |
| 2002-03 | PR Lge | 38 | 13 | 10 | 15 | 48 | 44 | 49 | 11 |
| 2003-04 | PR Lge | 38 | 13 | 9 | 16 | 44 | 52 | 48 | 11 |

## DID YOU KNOW ?

In 1914–15 Middlesbrough had a remarkable sequence of scoring just one goal in 13 of 15 consecutive League games. Thirteen was an important number that season, for on 13 February they defeated Tottenham Hotspur 7-5!

## MIDDLESBROUGH 2003–04 LEAGUE RECORD

| Match No. | Date | Venue | Opponents | Result | | H/T Score | Lg. Pos. | Goalscorers | Attendance |
|---|---|---|---|---|---|---|---|---|---|
| 1 | Aug 16 | A | Fulham | L | 2-3 | 1-1 | — | Marinelli[10], Nemeth[81] | 14,546 |
| 2 | 24 | H | Arsenal | L | 0-4 | 0-3 | 19 | | 29,450 |
| 3 | 26 | A | Leicester C | D | 0-0 | 0-0 | — | | 30,823 |
| 4 | 30 | H | Leeds U | L | 2-3 | 0-1 | 19 | Nemeth[60], Juninho[62] | 30,414 |
| 5 | Sept 13 | A | Bolton W | L | 0-2 | 0-1 | 19 | | 26,419 |
| 6 | 21 | H | Everton | W | 1-0 | 1-0 | 17 | Job[6] | 28,113 |
| 7 | 27 | A | Southampton | W | 1-0 | 1-0 | 14 | Christie[13] | 30,772 |
| 8 | Oct 5 | H | Chelsea | L | 1-2 | 0-1 | 17 | Nemeth[46] | 29,170 |
| 9 | 18 | H | Newcastle U | L | 0-1 | 0-1 | 18 | | 34,081 |
| 10 | 26 | A | Tottenham H | D | 0-0 | 0-0 | 17 | | 32,641 |
| 11 | Nov 1 | H | Wolverhampton W | W | 2-0 | 0-0 | 14 | Mendieta[73], Juninho[83] | 30,303 |
| 12 | 8 | A | Aston Villa | W | 2-0 | 1-0 | 12 | Zenden[30], Ricketts (pen)[49] | 29,898 |
| 13 | 22 | H | Liverpool | D | 0-0 | 0-0 | 13 | | 34,268 |
| 14 | 30 | A | Manchester C | W | 1-0 | 1-0 | 10 | Jihai (og)[30] | 46,824 |
| 15 | Dec 6 | H | Portsmouth | D | 0-0 | 0-0 | 11 | | 28,083 |
| 16 | 13 | H | Charlton Ath | D | 0-0 | 0-0 | 11 | | 26,721 |
| 17 | 26 | A | Blackburn R | D | 2-2 | 1-1 | 11 | Juninho 2[31, 51] | 25,452 |
| 18 | 28 | H | Manchester U | L | 0-1 | 0-1 | 15 | | 34,738 |
| 19 | Jan 7 | H | Fulham | W | 2-1 | 1-0 | — | Job[15], Nemeth[67] | 27,869 |
| 20 | 10 | A | Arsenal | L | 1-4 | 0-2 | 14 | Maccarone (pen)[86] | 38,117 |
| 21 | 17 | H | Leicester C | D | 3-3 | 1-0 | 13 | Juninho[8], Maccarone[89], Curtis (og)[90] | 27,124 |
| 22 | 31 | A | Leeds U | W | 3-0 | 0-0 | 12 | Zenden[53], Job[77], Ricketts (pen)[89] | 35,970 |
| 23 | Feb 7 | H | Blackburn R | L | 0-1 | 0-1 | 13 | | 28,307 |
| 24 | 11 | A | Manchester U | W | 3-2 | 2-1 | — | Juninho 2[34, 38], Job[80] | 67,346 |
| 25 | 21 | A | Newcastle U | L | 1-2 | 1-0 | 13 | Zenden[33] | 52,156 |
| 26 | Mar 3 | A | Birmingham C | L | 1-3 | 0-1 | — | Nemeth[75] | 29,369 |
| 27 | 9 | H | Tottenham H | W | 1-0 | 0-0 | — | Nemeth[73] | 31,789 |
| 28 | 13 | A | Charlton Ath | L | 0-1 | 0-1 | 12 | | 26,229 |
| 29 | 20 | H | Birmingham C | W | 5-3 | 4-2 | 10 | Mendieta[5], Maccarone 2[21, 45], Southgate[30], Nemeth[90] | 30,231 |
| 30 | 27 | A | Everton | D | 1-1 | 0-0 | 11 | Yobo (og)[83] | 38,210 |
| 31 | Apr 3 | H | Bolton W | W | 2-0 | 1-0 | 11 | Nolan (og)[8], Greening[51] | 30,104 |
| 32 | 10 | A | Chelsea | D | 0-0 | 0-0 | 11 | | 41,011 |
| 33 | 12 | H | Southampton | W | 3-1 | 2-0 | 9 | Juninho[23], Nemeth[32], Maccarone[49] | 30,768 |
| 34 | 17 | A | Wolverhampton W | L | 0-2 | 0-1 | 11 | | 27,975 |
| 35 | 24 | H | Aston Villa | L | 1-2 | 1-1 | 12 | Job[41] | 31,243 |
| 36 | May 2 | A | Liverpool | L | 0-2 | 0-0 | 12 | | 42,031 |
| 37 | 8 | H | Manchester C | W | 2-1 | 2-1 | 11 | Maccarone[8], Nemeth[32] | 34,734 |
| 38 | 15 | A | Portsmouth | L | 1-5 | 1-3 | 11 | Zenden[27] | 20,134 |

**Final League Position: 11**

## GOALSCORERS

*League (44):* Nemeth 9, Juninho 8, Maccarone 6 (1 pen), Job 5, Zenden 4, Mendieta 2, Ricketts 2 (2 pens), Christie 1, Greening 1, Marinelli 1, Southgate 1, own goals 4.
*Carling Cup (9):* Zenden 2 (1 pen), Christie 1, Job 1, Juninho 1, Maccarone 1, Mendieta 1, Ricketts 1, own goal 1.
*FA Cup (3):* Job 1, Zenden 1, own goal 1.

| Schwarzer M 36 | Parnaby S 8 + 5 | Wright A 2 | Southgate G 27 | Riggott C 14 + 3 | Doriva 19 + 2 | Boateng G 35 | Marinelli C 1 | Christie M 7 + 3 | Juninho 26 + 5 | Greening J 17 + 8 | Cooper C 17 + 2 | Job J 19 + 5 | Nemeth S 17 + 15 | Davies A 8 + 2 | Downing S 7 + 13 | Mendieta G 30 + 1 | Stockdale R — + 2 | Ricketts M 7 + 16 | Mills D 28 | Zenden B 31 | Queudrue F 31 | Maccarone M 13 + 10 | Nash C 1 | Ehiogu U 16 | Jones B 1 | Morrison J — + 1 | *Match No.* |
|---|---|---|---|---|---|---|---|---|---|---|---|---|---|---|---|---|---|---|---|---|---|---|---|---|---|---|---|
| 1 | 2 | 3 | 4 | 5 | 6 | $7^{1}$ | $8^{2}$ | 9 | $10^{3}$ | 11 | 12 | 13 | 14 | | | | | | | | | | | | | | 1 |
| 1 | 2 | 3 | 4 | $5^{1}$ | 8 | 7 | | 9 | 11 | | 6 | | $10^{2}$ | 12 | 13 | | | | | | | | | | | | 2 |
| 1 | 2 | | 4 | | | 6 | | 12 | 10 | 11 | $3^{2}$ | $8^{3}$ | $9^{1}$ | 5 | | 7 | 13 | 14 | | | | | | | | | 3 |
| 1 | $3^{2}$ | | 4 | | | 6 | | 12 | 10 | 11 | | $8^{1}$ | $9^{3}$ | 5 | | 7 | 13 | 14 | 2 | | | | | | | | 4 |
| 1 | | | 4 | | | 6 | | | $10^{1}$ | 7 | 3 | 12 | $9^{2}$ | 5 | | 8 | | 13 | 2 | 11 | | | | | | | 5 |
| 1 | | | 4 | 12 | 6 | 8 | | $9^{2}$ | | $7^{3}$ | 5 | $10^{1}$ | 13 | | | | | 14 | 2 | 11 | 3 | | | | | | 6 |
| 1 | | | | 4 | 6 | 8 | | $9^{2}$ | | 7 | 5 | $10^{1}$ | 12 | | | | | 13 | 2 | 11 | 3 | | | | | | 7 |
| 1 | | | | 5 | $6^{1}$ | 8 | | $9^{3}$ | 12 | 11 | 4 | | $10^{2}$ | | 13 | 7 | | 14 | 2 | | 3 | | | | | | 8 |
| 1 | | | 4 | | $6^{1}$ | 8 | | 9 | 12 | 13 | 5 | | $10^{3}$ | | | 7 | | | 2 | $11^{2}$ | 3 | 14 | | | | | 9 |
| 1 | | | 4 | | 6 | 8 | | $9^{3}$ | 12 | 13 | 5 | | $10^{1}$ | 2 | | 7 | | | | $11^{2}$ | 3 | 14 | | | | | 10 |
| 1 | | | 4 | | $6^{1}$ | 8 | | 13 | 12 | 14 | 5 | | $9^{2}$ | | | 7 | | | 2 | 11 | 3 | $10^{3}$ | | | | | 11 |
| | | | 4 | | 6 | 8 | | | $10^{1}$ | 12 | 5 | | | | | 7 | | $9^{2}$ | 2 | 11 | 3 | 13 | 1 | | | | 12 |
| 1 | | | 4 | | 6 | 8 | | | 10 | | 5 | | 12 | 2 | | 7 | | $9^{1}$ | | 11 | 3 | | | | | | 13 |
| 1 | | | 4 | 14 | $6^{1}$ | $8^{2}$ | | | 10 | 12 | 5 | | 13 | | | 7 | | $9^{3}$ | 2 | 11 | 3 | | | | | | 14 |
| 1 | | | 4 | | | 6 | | | $10^{2}$ | 7 | 5 | | 13 | | | 8 | | $9^{1}$ | 2 | 11 | 3 | 12 | | | | | 15 |
| 1 | | | 4 | 5 | | 6 | | | | $7^{1}$ | | | 9 | | 12 | 8 | | 13 | 2 | 11 | 3 | $10^{2}$ | | | | | 16 |
| 1 | | | 4 | | | 6 | | | $10^{1}$ | 12 | 5 | | | 2 | 7 | 8 | | 9 | | 11 | 3 | | | | | | 17 |
| 1 | $12^{2}$ | | 4 | | | 6 | | | 10 | $7^{3}$ | | | | | 13 | 8 | | 9 | 2 | 11 | $3^{1}$ | 14 | | 5 | | | 18 |
| | | | 4 | | | 6 | | | 10 | | | 8 | 9 | | 7 | | | | 2 | 11 | 3 | | | 5 | 1 | | 19 |
| 1 | | | 4 | 13 | $6^{1}$ | 8 | | | 12 | | | $10^{3}$ | 9 | | 7 | | | | 2 | 11 | 3 | 14 | | $5^{2}$ | | | 20 |
| 1 | | | | 5 | | 6 | | | 10 | | $4^{3}$ | $8^{1}$ | 9 | 14 | 7 | 13 | | | 2 | $11^{2}$ | 3 | 12 | | | | | 21 |
| 1 | 14 | | 4 | 5 | 6 | 8 | | | $10^{2}$ | | | 12 | | $2^{3}$ | | 7 | | 13 | | 11 | 3 | $9^{1}$ | | | | | 22 |
| 1 | $8^{2}$ | | 4 | 5 | 6 | | | | 10 | | | 14 | 12 | | 13 | $7^{1}$ | | | 2 | 11 | 3 | $9^{3}$ | | | | | 23 |
| 1 | 13 | | 4 | 5 | 6 | | | | $10^{1}$ | | 12 | 9 | | | 7 | $8^{2}$ | | | 2 | 11 | 3 | | | | | | 24 |
| 1 | $3^{1}$ | | 4 | | $6^{2}$ | 8 | | | 10 | | | 9 | | | 12 | 7 | | 13 | 2 | 11 | | | | 5 | | | 25 |
| 1 | | | 4 | | 12 | 6 | | | | $8^{2}$ | | $9^{3}$ | 13 | | $7^{1}$ | | | 10 | 2 | 11■ | 3 | 14 | | 5 | | | 26 |
| 1 | 14 | | 4 | | $6^{1}$ | 8 | | | 10 | | | $9^{2}$ | 13 | $2^{3}$ | | 7 | | | | 11 | 3 | 12 | | 5 | | | 27 |
| 1 | 2 | | 4 | | $6^{2}$ | 8 | | | 10 | 14 | | $9^{1}$ | 13 | | | $7^{3}$ | | | | 11 | 3 | 12 | | 5 | | | 28 |
| 1 | | | 4 | | 6 | | | | $8^{1}$ | 11 | | $9^{2}$ | 12 | | 13 | 7 | | 14 | 2 | | 3 | $10^{3}$ | | 5 | | | 29 |
| 1 | 14 | | 4 | 5 | $13^{3}$ | 6 | | | 8 | | | 9 | 12 | | | 7 | | | $2^{1}$ | 11 | 3 | $10^{2}$ | | | | | 30 |
| 1 | | | | 4 | | 6 | | | $8^{3}$ | 11 | | $9^{1}$ | 12 | | 13 | 7 | | 14 | 2 | 3 | | $10^{2}$ | | 5 | | | 31 |
| 1 | 2 | | | | | 6 | | | 8 | 11 | 4 | | $9^{2}$ | | 12 | 7 | | 13 | | | 3 | $10^{1}$ | | 5 | | | 32 |
| 1 | | | | | | 6 | | | $8^{3}$ | 12 | 4 | | $9^{2}$ | | 13 | $7^{1}$ | | 14 | 2 | 11 | 3 | 10 | | 5 | | | 33 |
| 1 | | | | 4 | | 6 | | | 8 | | | 12 | $9^{1}$ | | | 7 | | 13 | 2 | 11 | $3^{2}$ | 10 | | 5 | | | 34 |
| 1 | | | | 4 | | 6 | | | 8 | | | 9 | 12 | | 13 | 7 | | | $2^{1}$ | 11 | $3^{2}$ | 10 | | 5 | | | 35 |
| 1 | | | | $4^{1}$ | | 6 | | | | 7 | | $9^{3}$ | 13 | | 12 | 8 | | 14 | 2 | 11 | 3 | $10^{2}$ | | 5 | | | 36 |
| 1 | | | | | | 6 | | | | 7 | | 9 | 8 | | 12 | 4 | | | 2 | 11 | 3 | $10^{1}$ | | 5 | | | 37 |
| 1 | | | | | | 6 | | | | 7 | | 9 | $10^{1}$ | | $11^{2}$ | 8 | | 12 | 2 | 3 | 4 | | | 5 | | 13 | 38 |

**Carling Cup**

| | | | |
|---|---|---|---|
| Second Round | Brighton & HA | (h) | 1-0 |
| Third Round | Wigan Ath | (a) | 2-1 |
| Fourth Round | Everton | (h) | 0-0 |
| Fifth Round | Tottenham H | (a) | 1-1 |
| Semi-Final | Arsenal | (a) | 1-0 |
| | | (h) | 2-1 |
| Final | Bolton W | | 2-1 |

*(at Millennium Stadium)*

**FA Cup**

| | | | |
|---|---|---|---|
| Third Round | Notts Co | (h) | 2-0 |
| Fourth Round | Arsenal | (a) | 1-4 |

# MILLWALL FL Championship

## FOUNDATION

Formed in 1885 as Millwall Rovers by employees of Morton & Co, a jam and marmalade factory in West Ferry Road. The founders were predominantly Scotsmen. Their first headquarters was The Islanders pub in Tooke Street, Millwall. Their first trophy was the East End Cup in 1887.

***The Den, Zampa Road, London SE16 3LN.***

***Telephone:*** (020) 7232 1222.

***Fax:*** (020) 7231 3663.

***Ticket Office:*** (020) 7231 9999.

***Website:*** www.millwallfc.co.uk

***Email:*** questions@millwallplc.com

***Ground Capacity:*** 20,146.

***Record Attendance:*** 20,093 v Arsenal, FA Cup 3rd rd, 10 January 1994.

***Pitch Measurements:*** 100m × 68m.

***Chairman:*** Theo Paphitis.

***Chief Executive:*** Ken Brown

***Secretary:*** Yvonne Haines.

***Manager:*** Dennis Wise.

***Assistant Manager:*** Ray Wilkins.

***Physio:*** Gerry Docherty.

***Colours:*** Blue and white shirts, blue shorts, blue stockings.

***Change Colours:*** Green and white shirts, green shorts, green stockings.

***Year Formed:*** 1885.

***Turned Professional:*** 1893.

***Ltd Co.:*** 1894.

***Previous Names:*** 1885, Millwall Rovers; 1889, Millwall Athletic; 1985, Millwall Football & Athletic Company.

***Club Nickname:*** 'The Lions'.

***Previous Grounds:*** 1885, Glengall Road, Millwall; 1886, Back of 'Lord Nelson'; 1890, East Ferry Road; 1901, North Greenwich; 1910, The Den, Cold Blow Lane; 1993, The Den, Bermondsey.

***First Football League Game:*** 28 August 1920, Division 3, v Bristol R (h) W 2–0 – Lansdale; Fort, Hodge; Voisey (1), Riddell, McAlpine; Waterall, Travers, Broad (1), Sutherland, Dempsey.

***Record League Victory:*** 9–1 v Torquay U, Division 3 (S), 29 August 1927 – Lansdale, Tilling, Hill, Amos, Bryant (3), Graham, Chance, Hawkins (3), Landells (1), Phillips (2), Black. 9–1 v Coventry C, Division 3 (S), 19 November 1927 – Lansdale, Fort, Hill, Amos, Collins (1), Graham, Chance, Landells (4), Cock (2), Phillips (2), Black.

## HONOURS

*Football League:* Division 1 best season: 3rd, 1993–94; Division 2 – Champions 1987–88, 2000–01; Division 3 (S) – Champions 1927–28, 1937–38; Runners-up 1952–53; Division 3 – Runners-up 1965–66, 1984–85; Division 4 – Champions 1961–62; Runners-up 1964–65.

*FA Cup:* Runners-up 2004; Semi-final 1900, 1903, 1937 (first Division 3 side to reach semi-final).

*Football League Cup:* best season: 5th rd, 1974, 1977, 1995.

*Football League Trophy:* Winners 1983.

*Auto Windscreens Shield:* Runners-up 1999.

## SKY SPORTS FACT FILE

Wally Davis was the scourge of Southern League defences playing for Millwall in the years leading up to the First World War. He registered 67 in 114 League games, including scoring on his League debut on 4 November 1911 v West Ham United.

***Record Cup Victory:*** 7–0 v Gateshead, FA Cup 2nd rd, 12 December 1936 – Yuill; Ted Smith, Inns; Brolly, Hancock, Forsyth; Thomas (1), Mangnall (1), Ken Burditt (2), McCartney (2), Thorogood (1).

***Record Defeat:*** 1–9 v Aston Villa, FA Cup 4th rd, 28 January 1946.

***Most League Points (2 for a win):*** 65, Division 3 (S), 1927–28 and Division 3, 1965–66.

***Most League Points (3 for a win):*** 93, Division 2, 2000–01.

***Most League Goals:*** 127, Division 3 (S), 1927–28.

***Highest League Scorer in Season:*** Richard Parker, 37, Division 3 (S), 1926–27.

***Most League Goals in Total Aggregate:*** Teddy Sheringham, 93, 1984–91.

***Most League Goals in One Match:*** 5, Richard Parker v Norwich C, Division 3S, 28 August 1926.

***Most Capped Player:*** Eamonn Dunphy, 22 (23), Republic of Ireland.

***Most League Appearances:*** Barry Kitchener, 523, 1967–82.

***Youngest League Player:*** Moses Ashikodi, 15 years 240 days v Brighton & HA, 22 February 2003.

***Record Transfer Fee Received:*** £2,300,000 from Liverpool for Mark Kennedy, March 1995.

***Record Transfer Fee Paid:*** £800,000 to Derby Co for Paul Goddard, December 1989.

***Football League Record:*** 1920 Original Members of Division 3; 1921 Division 3 (S); 1928–34 Division 2; 1934–38 Division 3 (S); 1938–48 Division 2; 1948–58 Division 3 (S); 1958–62 Division 4; 1962–64 Division 3; 1964–65 Division 4; 1965–66 Division 3; 1966–75 Division 2; 1975–76 Division 3; 1976–79 Division 2; 1979–85 Division 3; 1985–88 Division 2; 1988–90 Division 1; 1990–92 Division 2; 1992–96 Division 1; 1996–2001 Division 2; 2001–04 Division 1; 2004– FLC.

## MANAGERS

F. B. Kidd 1894–99
*(Hon. Treasurer/Manager)*
E. R. Stopher 1899–1900
*(Hon. Treasurer/Manager)*
George Saunders 1900–11
*(Hon. Treasurer/Manager)*
Herbert Lipsham 1911–19
Robert Hunter 1919–33
Bill McCracken 1933–36
Charlie Hewitt 1936–40
Bill Voisey 1940–44
Jack Cock 1944–48
Charlie Hewitt 1948–56
Ron Gray 1956–57
Jimmy Seed 1958–59
Reg Smith 1959–61
Ron Gray 1961–63
Billy Gray 1963–66
Benny Fenton 1966–74
Gordon Jago 1974–77
George Petchey 1978–80
Peter Anderson 1980–82
George Graham 1982–86
John Docherty 1986–90
Bob Pearson 1990
Bruce Rioch 1990–92
Mick McCarthy 1992–96
Jimmy Nicholl 1996–97
John Docherty 1997
Billy Bonds 1997–98
Keith Stevens May 1998–2000
*(then Joint Manager)*
(*plus* Alan McLeary 1999–2000)
Mark McGhee 2000–03
Dennis Wise December 2003–

## LATEST SEQUENCES

***Longest Sequence of League Wins:*** 10, 10.3.1928 – 25.4.1928.

***Longest Sequence of League Defeats:*** 11, 10.4.1929 – 16.9.1929.

***Longest Sequence of League Draws:*** 5, 22.12.1973 – 12.1.1974.

***Longest Sequence of Unbeaten League Matches:*** 19, 22.8.1959 – 31.10.1959.

***Longest Sequence Without a League Win:*** 20, 26.12.1989 – 5.5.1990.

***Successive Scoring Runs:*** 22 from 8.12.1923.

***Successive Non-scoring Runs:*** 6 from 20.12.1947.

## TEN YEAR LEAGUE RECORD

| | | P | W | D | L | F | A | Pts | Pos |
|---|---|---|---|---|---|---|---|---|---|
| 1994-95 | Div 1 | 46 | 16 | 14 | 16 | 60 | 60 | 62 | 12 |
| 1995-96 | Div 1 | 46 | 13 | 13 | 20 | 43 | 63 | 52 | 22 |
| 1996-97 | Div 2 | 46 | 16 | 13 | 17 | 50 | 55 | 61 | 14 |
| 1997-98 | Div 2 | 46 | 14 | 13 | 19 | 43 | 54 | 55 | 18 |
| 1998-99 | Div 2 | 46 | 17 | 11 | 18 | 52 | 59 | 62 | 10 |
| 1999-2000 | Div 2 | 46 | 23 | 13 | 10 | 76 | 50 | 82 | 5 |
| 2000-01 | Div 2 | 46 | 28 | 9 | 9 | 89 | 38 | 93 | 1 |
| 2001-02 | Div 1 | 46 | 22 | 11 | 13 | 69 | 48 | 77 | 4 |
| 2002-03 | Div 1 | 46 | 19 | 9 | 18 | 59 | 69 | 66 | 9 |
| 2003-04 | Div 1 | 46 | 18 | 15 | 13 | 55 | 48 | 69 | 10 |

## DID YOU KNOW ?

In the 1927–28 Third Division (South) championship season, Millwall were unbeaten at home, only Swindon Town and Crystal Palace escaping with a draw. Yet Swindon led the Lions 3-1 at half-time before a second-half revival.

## MILLWALL 2003–04 LEAGUE RECORD

| Match No. | Date | Venue | Opponents | Result | | H/T Score | Lg. Pos. | Goalscorers | Attendance |
|---|---|---|---|---|---|---|---|---|---|
| 1 | Aug 9 | H | Wigan Ath | W | 2-0 | 0-0 | — | Wise 53, Cahill 74 | 10,898 |
| 2 | 16 | A | Sunderland | W | 1-0 | 1-0 | 2 | Whelan 7 | 24,877 |
| 3 | 23 | H | Crewe Alex | D | 1-1 | 0-0 | 4 | Whelan 90 | 9504 |
| 4 | 26 | A | Stoke C | D | 0-0 | 0-0 | — | | 13,087 |
| 5 | 30 | H | Crystal Palace | D | 1-1 | 0-0 | 8 | Peeters 90 | 14,425 |
| 6 | Sept 6 | A | Gillingham | L | 3-4 | 1-2 | 9 | Ifill 11, Peeters 2 61, 69 | 8237 |
| 7 | 13 | A | Watford | L | 1-3 | 1-2 | 12 | Ifill 34 | 11,305 |
| 8 | 16 | H | Wimbledon | W | 2-0 | 1-0 | — | Harris (pen) 44, Whelan 90 | 7855 |
| 9 | 20 | H | Walsall | W | 2-1 | 1-1 | 6 | Ward 16, Harris (pen) 80 | 9262 |
| 10 | 28 | A | West Ham U | D | 1-1 | 0-1 | 8 | Cahill 74 | 31,626 |
| 11 | 30 | A | WBA | L | 1-2 | 1-2 | — | Nethercott 45 | 22,909 |
| 12 | Oct 4 | H | Coventry C | W | 2-1 | 0-0 | 7 | Ifill 63, Harris 85 | 9849 |
| 13 | 11 | A | Rotherham U | D | 0-0 | 0-0 | 7 | | 5461 |
| 14 | 14 | H | Preston NE | L | 0-1 | 0-0 | — | | 8015 |
| 15 | 18 | H | Sheffield U | W | 2-0 | 0-0 | 7 | Harris (pen) 53, Ifill 66 | 10,046 |
| 16 | 25 | A | Burnley | D | 1-1 | 0-0 | 10 | Whelan 53 | 10,435 |
| 17 | Nov 1 | H | Nottingham F | W | 1-0 | 1-0 | 8 | Braniff 45 | 9635 |
| 18 | 8 | A | Norwich C | L | 1-3 | 0-3 | 11 | Ward 90 | 16,423 |
| 19 | 15 | A | Reading | L | 0-1 | 0-1 | 11 | | 14,090 |
| 20 | 22 | H | Derby Co | D | 0-0 | 0-0 | 11 | | 10,308 |
| 21 | 29 | A | Bradford C | L | 2-3 | 2-0 | 11 | Cahill 19, Chadwick 24 | 10,107 |
| 22 | Dec 6 | H | Norwich C | D | 0-0 | 0-0 | 11 | | 9850 |
| 23 | 13 | H | Ipswich T | D | 0-0 | 0-0 | 12 | | 9829 |
| 24 | 20 | A | Cardiff C | W | 3-1 | 1-1 | 11 | Roberts 5, Cahill 65, Sweeney 84 | 14,610 |
| 25 | 26 | A | Crystal Palace | W | 1-0 | 1-0 | 10 | Harris 18 | 19,737 |
| 26 | 28 | H | Gillingham | L | 1-2 | 0-1 | 10 | Chadwick 56 | 12,084 |
| 27 | Jan 10 | A | Wigan Ath | D | 0-0 | 0-0 | 12 | | 7047 |
| 28 | 17 | H | Sunderland | W | 2-1 | 1-1 | 11 | Dichio 2 39, 62 | 13,048 |
| 29 | 31 | A | Crewe Alex | W | 2-1 | 1-0 | 10 | Dichio 2 44, 90 | 6685 |
| 30 | Feb 7 | H | Stoke C | D | 1-1 | 1-1 | 10 | Dichio 23 | 9034 |
| 31 | 21 | A | Preston NE | W | 2-1 | 1-0 | 9 | Ifill 45, Cahill 77 | 12,903 |
| 32 | 24 | H | Rotherham U | W | 2-1 | 1-0 | — | Harris 38, Cahill 90 | 8254 |
| 33 | 28 | H | Burnley | W | 2-0 | 1-0 | 5 | Ifill 12, Sweeney 52 | 10,148 |
| 34 | Mar 2 | A | Sheffield U | L | 1-2 | 0-0 | — | Ifill 69 | 19,579 |
| 35 | 13 | A | Ipswich T | W | 3-1 | 2-0 | 6 | Harris 2 30, 48, Ward 37 | 23,582 |
| 36 | 21 | H | West Ham U | W | 4-1 | 1-0 | 7 | Dailly (og) 34, Cahill 2 46, 56, Chadwick 80 | 14,055 |
| 37 | 24 | A | Wimbledon | W | 1-0 | 1-0 | — | Cahill 43 | 3037 |
| 38 | 27 | A | Walsall | D | 1-1 | 0-0 | 5 | Ifill 88 | 6486 |
| 39 | Apr 7 | H | Cardiff C | D | 0-0 | 0-0 | — | | 9584 |
| 40 | 10 | A | Coventry C | L | 0-4 | 0-2 | 7 | | 12,546 |
| 41 | 12 | H | WBA | D | 1-1 | 1-0 | 7 | Dichio 19 | 13,304 |
| 42 | 17 | A | Nottingham F | D | 2-2 | 0-0 | 7 | Livermore 46, Chadwick 84 | 22,263 |
| 43 | 20 | H | Watford | L | 1-2 | 1-0 | — | Dichio 16 | 10,263 |
| 44 | 24 | H | Reading | L | 0-1 | 0-1 | 10 | | 12,535 |
| 45 | May 1 | A | Derby Co | L | 0-2 | 0-1 | 10 | | 26,056 |
| 46 | 9 | H | Bradford C | W | 1-0 | 0-0 | 10 | Harris (pen) 58 | 9635 |

**Final League Position: 10**

### GOALSCORERS

*League (55):* Cahill 9, Harris 9 (4 pens), Ifill 8, Dichio 7, Chadwick 4, Whelan 4, Peeters 3, Ward 3, Sweeney 2, Braniff 1, Livermore 1, Nethercott 1, Roberts 1, Wise 1, own goal 1.
*Carling Cup (0).*
*FA Cup (8):* Cahill 3, Braniff 1, Dichio 1, Harris 1, Ifill 1, Wise 1.

| Warner T 28 | Lawrence M 34 + 2 | Ryan R 28 + 2 | Cahill T 40 | Nethercott S 11 + 3 | Ward D 46 | Wise D 26 + 5 | Juan2 + 1 | Harris N 26 + 12 | Ifill P 29 + 4 | Roberts A 29 + 4 | Whelan N 8 + 7 | Hearn C 3 + 4 | Craig T 8 + 1 | Peeters B 16 + 4 | Sadlier R — + 2 | Dunne A 4 + 4 | Muscat K 27 | Fofana A 9 + 7 | Livermore D 35 + 1 | Robinson P 7 + 2 | Sweeney P 21 + 8 | Braniff K 6 + 10 | Elliott M 14 + 7 | Chadwick N 11 + 4 | Quigley M — + 1 | Dichio D 15 | Robinson T — + 1 | Marshall A 16 | Sutton J 2 + 2 | Gueret W 2 | McCammon M 3 + 4 | Cogan B — + 3 | Dolan J — + 1 | Weston C — + 1 | Match No. |
|---|---|---|---|---|---|---|---|---|---|---|---|---|---|---|---|---|---|---|---|---|---|---|---|---|---|---|---|---|---|---|---|---|---|---|---|
| 1 | 2 | 3 | 4 | 5 | 6 | 7 | $8^{1}$ | 9 | $10^{2}$ | 11 | 12 | 13 | | | | | | | | | | | | | | | | | | | | | | | 1 |
| 1 | 2 | 3 | 4 | 5 | 6 | 7 | | 9 | | 11 | 10 | $8^{1}$ | 12 | | | | | | | | | | | | | | | | | | | | | | 2 |
| 1 | $2^{3}$ | $3^{2}$ | 4 | 5 | 6 | 7 | 12 | 9 | | 11 | 8 | 13 | | $10^{1}$ | 14 | | | | | | | | | | | | | | | | | | | | 3 |
| 1 | | | 4 | 5 | 6 | 7 | $2^{3}$ | 12 | | 11 | 10 | $8^{2}$ | 3 | $9^{1}$ | 13 | 14 | | | | | | | | | | | | | | | | | | | 4 |
| 1 | | | 4 | 5 | 6 | 8 | | 9 | 7 | 11 | $10^{1}$ | 12 | $3^{2}$ | 13 | | | 2 | | | | | | | | | | | | | | | | | | 5 |
| 1 | $2^{1}$ | | 4 | 5 | 6 | 8 | | 12 | 7 | 11 | $10^{2}$ | | 3 | 9 | | | | 13 | | | | | | | | | | | | | | | | | 6 |
| 1 | | | 4 | 5 | 6 | 7 | | 12 | 10 | $8^{3}$ | | | $3^{2}$ | 9 | | | 2■ | $11^{1}$ | 13 | 14 | | | | | | | | | | | | | | | 7 |
| 1 | | 3 | 4 | 5 | 6 | 8 | | 9 | 7 | | 12 | | | 10 | | | 2 | $11^{1}$ | | | | | | | | | | | | | | | | | 8 |
| 1 | | $3^{2}$ | 4 | 5 | 6 | 8 | | 9 | 7 | | 12 | | | $10^{1}$ | | 13 | 2 | | 11 | | | | | | | | | | | | | | | | 9 |
| 1 | 13 | | 4 | 5 | 6 | 7 | | 12 | 10 | $11^{1}$ | | | 3 | 9 | | $2^{2}$ | | | 8 | | | | | | | | | | | | | | | | 10 |
| 1 | 2 | | 4 | 5 | 6 | 7 | | $9^{2}$ | 11 | | 12 | | $3^{1}$ | 10 | | | | | 8 | 13 | | | | | | | | | | | | | | | 11 |
| 1 | 2 | | 4■ | | 6 | 8 | | 12 | $7^{2}$ | 13 | 10 | | 3 | $9^{1}$ | | | | 14 | $11^{3}$ | 5 | | | | | | | | | | | | | | | 12 |
| 1 | | | 4 | | 6 | 8 | | 12 | 7 | | 10 | | 3 | $9^{1}$ | | | 2 | 13 | $11^{2}$ | 5 | | | | | | | | | | | | | | | 13 |
| 1 | | | 4 | 12 | 6 | 8 | | 9 | $7^{3}$ | 10 | 13 | | | 14 | | $2^{2}$ | 3 | | $11^{1}$ | 5 | | | | | | | | | | | | | | | 14 |
| 1 | | 3 | | | 6 | 12■ | | 9 | 7 | 4 | 13 | | | $10^{2}$ | | | 2 | $11^{1}$ | 8■ | 5 | | | | | | | | | | | | | | | 15 |
| 1 | | 3 | | | 6 | | | $9^{1}$ | 7 | 4 | 12 | | | $10^{2}$ | | | 2 | | 8 | 5 | 11 | 13 | | | | | | | | | | | | | 16 |
| 1 | | 3 | 4 | | 6 | | | | | 8 | $10^{2}$ | 12 | | 9 | | | 2 | $11^{1}$ | | 5 | 7 | 13 | | | | | | | | | | | | | 17 |
| 1 | 12 | 3 | 4 | | 6 | | | | 10 | 8 | | | | $9^{2}$ | | | 2 | 14 | $11^{3}$ | $5^{1}$ | 7 | 13 | | | | | | | | | | | | | 18 |
| 1 | 5 | 3 | 4 | | 6 | | | | 10 | 12 | | | | | | | 2 | $11^{2}$ | 8 | | 7 | $9^{1}$ | 13 | | | | | | | | | | | | 19 |
| 1 | 5 | 3 | $4^{1}$ | | 6 | | | | 7 | 8 | | | | $9^{2}$ | | | 2 | 13 | 11 | | 10 | 12 | | | | | | | | | | | | | 20 |
| 1 | 5 | $3^{1}$ | $10^{3}$ | 12 | 6 | 14 | | | | $4^{2}$ | | | | | | | 2 | 11 | 8 | | 7 | 13 | | 9 | | | | | | | | | | | 21 |
| 1 | 5 | | 4 | 13 | 6 | | | | | 8 | | | | $10^{1}$ | | | 2■ | $11^{2}$ | 3 | | 7 | 12 | | 9 | | | | | | | | | | | 22 |
| 1 | 5 | | 4 | | 6 | 12 | | | | 8 | | | | | | | 2 | $11^{1}$ | 3 | | 7 | $10^{2}$ | | 9 | 13 | | | | | | | | | | 23 |
| 1 | 5 | | 4 | | 6 | 8 | | $9^{1}$ | | 11 | | | | | | 14 | | | $3^{3}$ | | $7^{2}$ | 12 | 2 | 10 | | | 13 | | | | | | | | 24 |
| 1 | 5 | | 4 | | 6 | 8 | | $9^{1}$ | | 2 | | | | 13 | | | | 14 | 3 | | $7^{3}$ | 12 | 11 | $10^{2}$ | | | | | | | | | | | 25 |
| 1 | 5 | | 4 | | 6 | 12 | | 9 | | 8 | | | | 13 | | | 2 | $11^{1}$ | 3 | | 7 | | | $10^{2}$ | | | | | | | | | | | 26 |
| 1 | 5 | 12 | 4 | | 6 | 8 | | $9^{3}$ | 13 | $11^{2}$ | | | | | | | 2 | | 3 | | $7^{1}$ | 10 | 14 | | | | | | | | | | | | 27 |
| 1 | 5 | | | | 6 | 8 | | 4 | 12 | $11^{2}$ | | | | | | | 2 | | 3 | | 7 | $9^{1}$ | 13 | | | 10 | | | | | | | | | 28 |
| | 5 | | | | 6 | | | | 11 | 8 | | | | | | | 2 | 12 | 3 | | $7^{1}$ | $9^{2}$ | 4 | | | 10 | | 1 | 13 | | | | | | 29 |
| | 5 | 12 | 4 | | 6 | 8 | | 9 | 14 | $11^{3}$ | | | | | | | 2 | | $3^{1}$ | | $7^{2}$ | | 13 | | | 10 | | 1 | | | | | | | 30 |
| | 5 | 3 | 4 | | 6 | | | 12 | $9^{2}$ | 11 | | | | | | | | | 2 | | $7^{1}$ | 13 | 8 | | | 10 | | | | 1 | | | | | 31 |
| | 5 | $3^{2}$ | 4 | | 6 | 8 | | 9 | $7^{1}$ | | | | | | | | 2 | | 11 | | 12 | | 13 | | | 10 | | | | 1 | | | | | 32 |
| | 5 | 3 | 4 | | 6 | 8 | | 9 | $10^{1}$ | | | | | | | | 2 | | | | 7 | | 11 | | | | | 1 | | | 12 | | | | 33 |
| | 5 | 3 | 4 | | 6 | | | 12 | 9 | | | | | | | | 2 | | 11 | | $7^{1}$ | | $8^{2}$ | | | 10 | | 1 | | | 13 | | | | 34 |
| | 5 | 3 | 4 | | 6 | | | 12 | $8^{2}$ | | | | | | | 13 | 2 | | 7 | | | | 11 | | | 10 | | 1 | | | $9^{1}$ | | | | 35 |
| | 5 | 3 | 4 | | 6 | | | 9 | 7 | 11 | | | | | | | 2 | | 8 | | | | | 12 | | $10^{1}$ | | 1 | | | | | | | 36 |
| | 5 | 3 | 4 | | 6 | 13 | | $9^{3}$ | $7^{1}$ | 11 | | | | | | | 2 | | $8^{2}$ | | 14 | | | 12 | | 10 | | 1 | | | | | | | 37 |
| | 5 | 3 | 4 | | 6 | 8 | | $9^{1}$ | 12 | 13 | | | | | | | 2 | | | | 14 | | $11^{2}$ | $7^{3}$ | | 10 | | 1 | | | | | | | 38 |
| | 2 | 3 | 4■ | | 6 | | | $9^{1}$ | | $11^{3}$ | | | | | | 5 | | | 8 | | 13 | 12 | 14 | $7^{2}$ | | 10 | | 1 | | | | | | | 39 |
| | 5 | $3^{1}$ | $4^{3}$ | | 6 | | | $9^{2}$ | | 12 | | | | | | 2 | | | 11 | | 7 | | 8 | 10 | | | | 1 | 13 | | 14 | | | | 40 |
| | 5 | $3^{2}$ | 4 | | 6 | 8 | | 12 | | 11 | | | | | | | | | 7 | | 13 | | 2 | | | 10 | | 1 | | | $9^{1}$ | | | | 41 |
| | 5 | 3 | 4 | | 6 | 8 | | $9^{1}$ | $7^{2}$ | | | | | | | | | | 11 | | 12 | | $2^{G}$ | 13 | | 10■ | | 1 | | | 15 | | | | 42 |
| | 5 | 3 | $4^{1}$ | | 6 | 8 | | 12 | $11^{2}$ | | | | | | | | | | 2 | | $7^{3}$ | | 13 | 9 | | 10 | | 1 | | | | 14 | | | 43 |
| | 5 | 3 | | | 6 | 8 | | 12 | 7 | | | | | | | | | | 2 | | 13 | | 4 | 9 | | $10^{1}$ | | 1 | | | $11^{2}$ | | | | 44 |
| | 5 | 3 | | | 6 | | | $9^{1}$ | 7 | | | $4^{3}$ | | | | | | | 11 | | 13 | $8^{2}$ | 2 | 12 | | | | 1 | 10 | | | 14 | | | 45 |
| | $5^{2}$ | 3 | 4 | | 6 | | | 9 | 11 | | | | | | | | | | 8 | | $7^{3}$ | | 2 | | | | | 1 | $10^{1}$ | | | 12 | 13 | 14 | 46 |

**Carling Cup**

| | | | |
|---|---|---|---|
| First Round | Oxford U | (h) | 0-1 |

**FA Cup**

| | | | |
|---|---|---|---|
| Third Round | Walsall | (h) | 2-1 |
| Fourth Round | Telford U | (a) | 2-0 |
| Fifth Round | Burnley | (h) | 1-0 |
| Sixth Round | Tranmere R | (h) | 0-0 |
| | | (a) | 2-1 |
| Semi-Final *(at Old Trafford)* | Sunderland | | 1-0 |
| Final *(at Millennium Stadium)* | Manchester U | | 0-3 |

# NEWCASTLE UNITED FA Premiership

## FOUNDATION

It stemmed from a newly formed club called Stanley in 1881. In October 1882 they changed their name to Newcastle East End to avoid confusion with two other local clubs, Stanley Nops and Stanley Albion. Shortly afterwards another club Rosewood merged with them. Newcastle West End had been formed in August 1882 and they played on a pitch which was part of the Town Moor. Moved to Brandling Park 1885 and St James' Park 1886 (home of Newcastle Rangers). West End went out of existence after a bad run and the remaining committee men invited East End to move to St James' Park. They accepted and, at a meeting in Bath Lane Hall in 1892, changed their name to Newcastle United.

***St James' Park, Newcastle-upon-Tyne NE1 4ST.***
***Telephone:*** (0191) 201 8400.
***Fax:*** (0191) 201 8600.
***Ticket Office:*** (0191) 261 1571.
***Website:*** www.nufc.co.uk
***Email:*** admin@nufc.co.uk
***Ground Capacity:*** 52,193.
***Record Attendance:*** 68,386 v Chelsea, Division 1, 3 September 1930.
***Pitch Measurements:*** 105m × 68m.
***Chairman:*** W. F. Shepherd.
***Deputy Chairman:*** D. S. Hall.
***Secretary:*** R. Cushing.
***Manager:*** Sir Bobby Robson CBE.
***Coaches:*** John Carver, David Geddis, Tommy Craig, Simon Smith.
***Physios:*** Derek Wright, Paul Ferris.
***Colours:*** Black and white striped shirts, black shorts, black stockings.
***Change Colours:*** Marine/atlantic blue shirts, white shorts and stockings with marine blue piping.
***Year Formed:*** 1881.
***Turned Professional:*** 1889.
***Ltd Co.:*** 1890.
***Previous Names:*** 1881, Stanley; 1882, Newcastle East End; 1892, Newcastle United.
***Club Nickname:*** 'The Magpies'.
***Previous Grounds:*** 1881, South Byker; 1886, Chillingham Road, Heaton, 1892, St James' Park.

## HONOURS

*FA Premier League:* Runners-up 1995–96, 1996–97; *Football League:* Division 1 – Champions 1904–05, 1906–07, 1908–09, 1926–27, 1992–93; Division 2 – Champions 1964–65; Runners-up 1897–98, 1947–48.

*FA Cup:* Winners 1910, 1924, 1932, 1951, 1952, 1955; Runners-up 1905, 1906, 1908, 1911, 1974, 1998, 1999.

*Football League Cup:* Runners-up 1976.

*Texaco Cup:* Winners 1974, 1975.

***European Competitions:*** *Champions League:* 1997–98, 2002–03, 2003–04. *European Fairs Cup:* 1968–69 (winners), 1969–70, 1970–71. *UEFA Cup:* 1977–78, 1994–95, 1996–97, 1999–2000, 2003–04 (semi-final). *European Cup Winners' Cup:* 1998–99. *Anglo-Italian Cup:* Winners 1972–73. *Intertoto Cup:* 2001 (runners-up).

## SKY SPORTS FACT FILE

Newcastle United have had five players who scored on their first full international appearances: Jackie Milburn (England 1948), Ronald Orr (1902), Willie Cowan (1924) and Bobby Mitchell (1951) all Scotland plus Billy Foulkes (Wales 1951). Cowan's later given as og!

***First Football League Game:*** 2 September 1893, Division 2, v Royal Arsenal (a) D 2–2 – Ramsay; Jeffery, Miller; Crielly, Graham, McKane; Bowman, Crate (1), Thompson, Sorley (1), Wallace. Graham and not Crate scored according to some reports.

***Record League Victory:*** 13–0 v Newport Co, Division 2, 5 October 1946 – Garbutt; Cowell, Graham; Harvey, Brennan, Wright; Milburn (2), Bentley (1), Wayman (4), Shackleton (6), Pearson.

***Record Cup Victory:*** 9–0 v Southport (at Hillsborough), FA Cup 4th rd, 1 February 1932 – McInroy; Nelson, Fairhurst; McKenzie, Davidson, Weaver (1); Boyd (1), Jimmy Richardson (3), Cape (2), McMenemy (1), Lang (1).

***Record Defeat:*** 0–9 v Burton Wanderers, Division 2, 15 April 1895.

***Most League Points (2 for a win):*** 57, Division 2, 1964–65.

***Most League Points (3 for a win):*** 96, Division 1, 1992–93.

***Most League Goals:*** 98, Division 1, 1951–52.

***Highest League Scorer in Season:*** Hughie Gallacher, 36, Division 1, 1926–27.

***Most League Goals in Total Aggregate:*** Jackie Milburn, 177, 1946–57.

***Most League Goals in One Match:*** 6, Len Shackleton v Newport Co, Division 2, 5 October 1946.

***Most Capped Player:*** Shay Given, 51 (60), Republic of Ireland.

***Most League Appearances:*** Jim Lawrence, 432, 1904–22.

***Youngest League Player:*** Steve Watson, 16 years 223 days v Wolverhampton W, 10 November 1990.

***Record Transfer Fee Received:*** £8,000,000 from Liverpool for Dieter Hamann, July 1999.

***Record Transfer Fee Paid:*** £15,000,000 to Blackburn R for Alan Shearer, July 1996.

***Football League Record:*** 1893 Elected to Division 2; 1898–1934 Division 1; 1934–48 Division 2; 1948–61 Division 1; 1961–65 Division 2; 1965–78 Division 1; 1978–84 Division 2; 1984–89 Division 1; 1989–92 Division 2; 1992–93 Division 1; 1993– FA Premier League.

## MANAGERS

Frank Watt 1895–32
*(Secretary-Manager)*
Andy Cunningham 1930–35
Tom Mather 1935–39
Stan Seymour 1939–47
*(Hon. Manager)*
George Martin 1947–50
Stan Seymour 1950–54
*(Hon. Manager)*
Duggie Livingstone 1954–56
Stan Seymour 1956–58
*(Hon. Manager)*
Charlie Mitten 1958–61
Norman Smith 1961–62
Joe Harvey 1962–75
Gordon Lee 1975–77
Richard Dinnis 1977
Bill McGarry 1977–80
Arthur Cox 1980–84
Jack Charlton 1984
Willie McFaul 1985–88
Jim Smith 1988–91
Ossie Ardiles 1991–92
Kevin Keegan 1992–97
Kenny Dalglish 1997–98
Ruud Gullit 1998–99
Sir Bobby Robson
September 1999–

## LATEST SEQUENCES

***Longest Sequence of League Wins:*** 13, 25.4.1992 – 18.10.1992.

***Longest Sequence of League Defeats:*** 10, 23.8.1977 – 15.10.1977.

***Longest Sequence of League Draws:*** 4, 20.1.1990 – 24.2.1990.

***Longest Sequence of Unbeaten League Matches:*** 14, 22.4.1950 – 30.9.1950.

***Longest Sequence Without a League Win:*** 21, 14.1.1978 – 23.8.1978.

***Successive Scoring Runs:*** 25 from 15.4.1939.

***Successive Non-scoring Runs:*** 6 from 31.12.1938.

## TEN YEAR LEAGUE RECORD

| | | P | W | D | L | F | A | Pts | Pos |
|---|---|---|---|---|---|---|---|---|---|
| 1994-95 | PR Lge | 42 | 20 | 12 | 10 | 67 | 47 | 72 | 6 |
| 1995-96 | PR Lge | 38 | 24 | 6 | 8 | 66 | 37 | 78 | 2 |
| 1996-97 | PR Lge | 38 | 19 | 11 | 8 | 73 | 40 | 68 | 2 |
| 1997-98 | PR Lge | 38 | 11 | 11 | 16 | 35 | 44 | 44 | 13 |
| 1998-99 | PR Lge | 38 | 11 | 13 | 14 | 48 | 54 | 46 | 13 |
| 1999-2000 | PR Lge | 38 | 14 | 10 | 14 | 63 | 54 | 52 | 11 |
| 2000-01 | PR Lge | 38 | 14 | 9 | 15 | 44 | 50 | 51 | 11 |
| 2001-02 | PR Lge | 38 | 21 | 8 | 9 | 74 | 52 | 71 | 4 |
| 2002-03 | PR Lge | 38 | 21 | 6 | 11 | 63 | 48 | 69 | 3 |
| 2003-04 | PR Lge | 38 | 13 | 17 | 8 | 52 | 40 | 56 | 5 |

## DID YOU KNOW ?

On 10 March 1928 Newcastle United were engaged in an enthralling 7-5 win against Aston Villa played in snow, sunshine and showers, with the scores fluctuating 4-0, 4-1, 4-2, 7-2, before Villa came back with three in eight minutes.

## NEWCASTLE UNITED 2003–04 LEAGUE RECORD

| *Match No.* | *Date* | *Venue* | *Opponents* | *Result* | | *H/T Score* | *Lg. Pos.* | *Goalscorers* | *Atten-dance* |
|---|---|---|---|---|---|---|---|---|---|
| 1 | Aug 17 | A | Leeds U | D | 2-2 | 1-1 | — | Shearer 2 (1 pen) [20 (p), 88] | 36,766 |
| 2 | 23 | H | Manchester U | L | 1-2 | 1-0 | 15 | Shearer [26] | 52,165 |
| 3 | 30 | H | Birmingham C | L | 0-1 | 0-0 | 18 | | 52,006 |
| 4 | Sept 13 | A | Everton | D | 2-2 | 0-0 | 17 | Shearer 2 (2 pens) [59, 82] | 40,228 |
| 5 | 20 | H | Bolton W | D | 0-0 | 0-0 | 19 | | 52,014 |
| 6 | 26 | A | Arsenal | L | 2-3 | 1-1 | — | Robert [28], Bernard [71] | 38,112 |
| 7 | Oct 4 | H | Southampton | W | 1-0 | 1-0 | 16 | Shearer [44] | 52,127 |
| 8 | 18 | A | Middlesbrough | W | 1-0 | 1-0 | 12 | Ameobi [21] | 34,081 |
| 9 | 21 | A | Fulham | W | 3-2 | 1-2 | — | Robert [18], Shearer 2 (1 pen) [51 (p), 58] | 15,241 |
| 10 | 25 | H | Portsmouth | W | 3-0 | 2-0 | 8 | Speed [17], Shearer (pen) [28], Ameobi [61] | 52,161 |
| 11 | Nov 1 | H | Aston Villa | D | 1-1 | 1-1 | 8 | Robert [45] | 51,975 |
| 12 | 9 | A | Chelsea | L | 0-5 | 0-3 | 10 | | 41,322 |
| 13 | 22 | H | Manchester C | W | 3-0 | 0-0 | 6 | Ameobi [57], Shearer 2 [77, 85] | 52,159 |
| 14 | 29 | A | Wolverhampton W | D | 1-1 | 1-1 | 7 | Shearer [31] | 29,344 |
| 15 | Dec 6 | H | Liverpool | D | 1-1 | 0-1 | 7 | Shearer (pen) [63] | 52,151 |
| 16 | 13 | H | Tottenham H | W | 4-0 | 1-0 | 5 | Robert 2 [35, 55], Shearer 2 [59, 66] | 52,138 |
| 17 | 20 | A | Charlton Ath | D | 0-0 | 0-0 | 6 | | 26,469 |
| 18 | 26 | A | Leicester C | D | 1-1 | 0-0 | 6 | Ambrose [90] | 32,148 |
| 19 | 28 | H | Blackburn R | L | 0-1 | 0-0 | 7 | | 51,648 |
| 20 | Jan 7 | H | Leeds U | W | 1-0 | 1-0 | — | Shearer [4] | 52,130 |
| 21 | 11 | A | Manchester U | D | 0-0 | 0-0 | 7 | | 67,622 |
| 22 | 19 | H | Fulham | W | 3-1 | 2-0 | — | O'Brien [4], Speed [41], Robert [54] | 50,104 |
| 23 | 31 | A | Birmingham C | D | 1-1 | 1-0 | 6 | Speed [37] | 29,513 |
| 24 | Feb 7 | H | Leicester C | W | 3-1 | 2-0 | 4 | Ameobi [30], Taggart (og) [37], Jenas [59] | 52,125 |
| 25 | 11 | A | Blackburn R | D | 1-1 | 0-0 | — | Bellamy [52] | 23,459 |
| 26 | 21 | H | Middlesbrough | W | 2-1 | 0-1 | 4 | Bellamy [63], Shearer (pen) [83] | 52,156 |
| 27 | 29 | A | Portsmouth | D | 1-1 | 1-0 | 4 | Bellamy [34] | 20,134 |
| 28 | Mar 14 | A | Tottenham H | L | 0-1 | 0-0 | 5 | | 36,088 |
| 29 | 20 | H | Charlton Ath | W | 3-1 | 2-0 | 5 | Shearer 2 [2, 77], Jenas [35] | 51,847 |
| 30 | 28 | A | Bolton W | L | 0-1 | 0-1 | 5 | | 27,360 |
| 31 | Apr 3 | H | Everton | W | 4-2 | 2-1 | 5 | Bellamy [5], Dyer [21], Shearer 2 [52, 90] | 52,155 |
| 32 | 11 | H | Arsenal | D | 0-0 | 0-0 | 5 | | 52,141 |
| 33 | 18 | A | Aston Villa | D | 0-0 | 0-0 | 5 | | 40,786 |
| 34 | 25 | H | Chelsea | W | 2-1 | 1-1 | 5 | Ameobi [44], Shearer [48] | 52,016 |
| 35 | May 1 | A | Manchester C | L | 0-1 | 0-0 | 6 | | 47,266 |
| 36 | 9 | H | Wolverhampton W | D | 1-1 | 1-0 | 6 | Bowyer [38] | 52,139 |
| 37 | 12 | A | Southampton | D | 3-3 | 2-2 | — | Ameobi [7], Bowyer [35], Ambrose [90] | 31,815 |
| 38 | 15 | A | Liverpool | D | 1-1 | 1-0 | 5 | Ameobi [25] | 44,172 |

**Final League Position: 5**

### GOALSCORERS

*League (52):* Shearer 22 (7 pens), Ameobi 7, Robert 6, Bellamy 4, Speed 3, Ambrose 2, Bowyer 2, Jenas 2, Bernard 1, Dyer 1, O'Brien 1, own goal 1.
*Carling Cup (1):* Robert 1.
*FA Cup (4):* Dyer 2, Robert 2.
*Champions League (1):* Solano 1.
*UEFA Cup (24):* Shearer 6, Bellamy 5, Ameobi 3, Bramble 3, Robert 3, Ambrose 1, Jenas 1, Speed 1, own goal 1.

| Given S 38 | Hughes A 34 | Bernard O 35 | Speed G 37 + 1 | O'Brien A 27 + 1 | Woodgate J 18 | Bowyer L 17 + 7 | Dyer K 25 | Shearer A 37 | Bellamy C 13 + 3 | Robert L 31 + 4 | Jenas J 26 + 5 | Ameobi F 18 + 8 | Solano N 8 + 4 | Griffin A 5 | Bramble T 27 + 2 | Chopra M 1 + 5 | Viana H 5 + 11 | Ambrose D 10 + 14 | Lua-Lua L 2 + 5 | Caldwell S 3 + 2 | Bridges M — + 6 | Taylor S 1 | Brittain M — + 1 | *Match No.* |
|---|---|---|---|---|---|---|---|---|---|---|---|---|---|---|---|---|---|---|---|---|---|---|---|---|
| 1 | 2 | $3^1$ | 4 | 5 | 6 | $7^2$ | 8 | 9 | 10 | $11^3$ | 12 | 13 | 14 | | | | | | | | | | | 1 |
| 1 | 3 | | 4 | 5 | | $7^1$ | 8 | 9 | | $11^3$ | 12 | $10^2$ | | 2 | 6 | 13 | 14 | | | | | | | 2 |
| 1 | | | 3 | 5 | | 12 | 8 | 9 | | 13 | 7 | $10^3$ | $6^1$ | 2 | 4 | 14 | $11^2$ | | | | | | | 3 |
| 1 | | 3 | $4^1$ | 5 | | 7 | 8 | 9 | 10 | 11■ | 12 | | | 2 | 6 | | | | | | | | | 4 |
| 1 | | 3 | $8^1$ | | 5 | | 7 | 9 | 10 | 11 | 12 | 13 | $6^2$ | 2 | 4 | | | | | | | | | 5 |
| 1 | 2 | 3 | 12 | 5 | | $8^1$ | 7 | 9 | 10 | $11^3$ | $4^2$ | 13 | | | 6 | | | 14 | | | | | | 6 |
| 1 | 2 | 3 | 4 | 5 | | 11 | 7 | 9 | 10 | | 8 | | | | 6 | | | | | | | | | 7 |
| 1 | 2 | 3 | 4 | 5 | | $11^1$ | 7 | 9 | | 12 | 8 | 10 | | | 6 | | | | | | | | | 8 |
| 1 | 2 | 3 | 4 | 5 | | 7 | | 9 | | $11^1$ | 8 | 10 | | | 6 | | | 12 | | | | | | 9 |
| 1 | 2 | 3 | 4 | 5 | | $7^2$ | | 9 | | $11^3$ | 8 | $10^1$ | | | 6 | | 12 | 13 | 14 | | | | | 10 |
| 1 | 2 | 3 | 4 | | | 7 | | 9 | | 11 | 8 | 10 | | | 6 | | | | | 5 | | | | 11 |
| 1 | 2 | 3 | 4 | 5■ | | 7 | | | | $11^1$ | 8 | 9 | | | 6 | | $10^2$ | | 12 | 13 | | | | 12 |
| 1 | 2 | 3 | 4 | | 5 | 12 | $7^1$ | 9 | | $11^3$ | 8 | $10^2$ | | | 6 | | | 14 | 13 | | | | | 13 |
| 1 | 2 | 3 | 4 | | 5 | $11^2$ | 7 | 9 | | | 8 | 12 | 13 | | 6 | | | | $10^1$ | | | | | 14 |
| 1 | $2^1$ | 3 | 4 | | 5 | | 7 | 9 | | 11 | 8 | 10 | 12 | | 6 | | | | | | | | | 15 |
| 1 | 2 | 3 | $4^3$ | 12 | $5^1$ | | 7 | 9 | | $11^2$ | 8 | 10 | 14 | | 6 | | | 13 | | | | | | 16 |
| 1 | 5 | 3 | 4 | 6 | | | 7 | 9 | | $11^2$ | 8 | $10^1$ | 2 | | | | | 13 | 12 | | | | | 17 |
| 1 | $2^1$ | 3 | 4 | 5 | | | | 9 | | 11 | 8 | | 7 | | 6 | 13 | | 12 | $10^2$ | | | | | 18 |
| 1 | 2 | 3 | $4^1$ | 5 | | | | 9 | | 11 | 8 | | $7^3$ | | 6 | $10^2$ | 12 | 14 | 13 | | | | | 19 |
| 1 | 2 | 3 | 4 | | 5 | | 10 | 9 | | $11^1$ | 8 | | $7^2$ | | 6 | | 12 | 13 | | | | | | 20 |
| 1 | 2 | 3 | 4 | 6 | 5 | | 10 | 9 | | 11 | 8 | | $7^1$ | | | | | 12 | | | | | | 21 |
| 1 | 2 | 3 | 4 | 6 | 5 | | 10 | $9^1$ | | $11^2$ | 8 | 12 | $7^3$ | | | | 13 | 14 | | | | | | 22 |
| 1 | 2 | 3 | 4 | 6 | 5 | | 10 | 9 | 12 | $11^2$ | 8 | | | | | | 13 | $7^1$ | | | | | | 23 |
| 1 | 2 | 3 | 4 | 6 | 5 | | $7^1$ | $9^3$ | 13 | | 8 | $10^2$ | | | | | 11 | 12 | | | 14 | | | 24 |
| 1 | 2 | 3 | 4 | 5 | | | 7 | 9 | 10 | 11 | 8 | | | | 6 | | | | | | | | | 25 |
| 1 | 2 | 3 | 4 | 5 | | 12 | 8 | 9 | 10 | 11 | | | | | 6 | | | $7^1$ | | | | | | 26 |
| 1 | 2 | 3 | 4 | 5 | | $7^3$ | $8^1$ | 9 | 10 | $11^2$ | 12 | | | | 6 | | 13 | | | | 14 | | | 27 |
| 1 | $2^1$ | 3 | 4 | 6 | 5 | $7^2$ | | 9 | 10 | 11 | 8 | 12 | | | | | | 13 | | | | | | 28 |
| 1 | $2^1$ | 3 | 4 | 6 | 5 | 13 | | 9 | | 11 | 8 | 10 | | | 12 | | | $7^2$ | | | | | | 29 |
| 1 | | 3 | 4 | | 5 | $7^3$ | | 9 | 10 | $11^2$ | $8^1$ | 12 | | | 6 | | 13 | 14 | | | | 2 | | 30 |
| 1 | 2 | 3 | 4 | | 5 | 13 | 8 | 9 | 10 | $11^1$ | | 12 | | | 6 | | | $7^2$ | | | | | | 31 |
| 1 | 2 | 3 | 4 | 6 | 5 | 12 | | 9 | 10 | $11^2$ | 8 | | | | | | 13 | $7^1$ | | | | | | 32 |
| 1 | 2 | 3 | 4 | 6■ | 5 | 13 | 7 | 9 | $10^3$ | $11^2$ | $8^1$ | | | | | | 12 | | | | 14 | | | 33 |
| 1 | 2 | 3 | 4 | 6 | $5^1$ | | | 9 | | 11 | | $10^2$ | | | 12 | | 8 | 7 | | | 13 | | | 34 |
| 1 | 2 | 3 | 4 | 6 | | | | 9 | | $11^3$ | | $10^2$ | | | 5 | 12 | 8 | $7^1$ | | | 13 | | 14 | 35 |
| 1 | 2 | 3 | 4 | | | 8 | | 9 | | $11^1$ | | 10 | | | 6 | 13 | 12 | $7^2$ | | 5 | | | | 36 |
| 1 | 2 | 3 | 4 | | | 8 | $11^1$ | 9 | | 12 | | 10 | | | $6^2$ | | | 7 | | 5 | 13 | | | 37 |
| 1 | 3 | | 4 | 5 | | 8 | 11 | 9 | 13 | 12 | | $10^2$ | | $2^3$ | 6 | | | $7^1$ | | 14 | | | | 38 |

**Carling Cup**

| | | | |
|---|---|---|---|
| Third Round | WBA | (h) | 1-2 |

**FA Cup**

| | | | |
|---|---|---|---|
| Third Round | Southampton | (a) | 3-0 |
| Fourth Round | Liverpool | (a) | 1-2 |

**Champions League**

| | | | |
|---|---|---|---|
| Third Qualifying Round | Partizan Belgrade | (a) | 1-0 |
| | | (h) | 0-1 |

**UEFA Cup**

| | | | |
|---|---|---|---|
| First Round | NAC Breda | (h) | 5-0 |
| | | (a) | 1-0 |
| Second Round | Basle | (a) | 3-2 |
| | | (h) | 1-0 |
| Third Round | Valerenga | (a) | 1-1 |
| | | (h) | 3-1 |
| Fourth Round | Mallorca | (h) | 4-1 |
| | | (a) | 3-0 |
| Quarter-Finals | PSV Eindhoven | (a) | 1-1 |
| | | (h) | 2-1 |
| Semi-Final | Marseille | (h) | 0-0 |
| | | (a) | 0-2 |

# NORTHAMPTON TOWN FL Championship 2

## FOUNDATION

Formed in 1897 by school teachers connected with the Northampton and District Elementary Schools' Association, they survived a financial crisis at the end of their first year when they were £675 in the red and became members of the Midland League – a fast move indeed for a new club. They achieved Southern League membership in 1901.

***Sixfields Stadium, Upton Way, Northampton NN5 5QA.***

***Telephone:*** (01604) 757 773.

***Fax:*** (01604) 751 613.

***Ticket Office:*** (01604) 588 338.

***Website:*** www.ntfc.co.uk

***Email:*** secretary@ntfc.co.uk

***Ground Capacity:*** 7,653.

***Record Attendance:*** (at County Ground): 24,523 v Fulham, Division 1, 23 April 1966; (at Sixfields Stadium): 7,557 v Manchester C, Division 2, 26 September 1998.

***Pitch Measurements:*** 116yd × 72yd.

***Chairman:*** David Cardoza.

***Chief Executive:*** Peter Miller.

***Secretary:*** Norman Howells.

***Manager:*** Colin Calderwood.

***Director of Football:*** John Deehan.

***Physio:*** Denis Casey.

***Colours:*** Claret shirts, white shorts, claret stockings.

***Change Colours:*** White shirt, claret shorts, white stockings.

***Year Formed:*** 1897.

***Turned Professional:*** 1901.

***Ltd Co.:*** 1901.

***Previous Ground:*** 1897, County Ground; 1994, Sixfields Stadium.

***Club Nickname:*** 'The Cobblers'.

***First Football League Game:*** 28 August 1920, Division 3, v Grimsby T (a) L 0–2 – Thorpe; Sproston, Hewison; Jobey, Tomkins, Pease; Whitworth, Lockett, Thomas, Freeman, MacKechnie.

***Record League Victory:*** 10–0 v Walsall, Division 3 (S), 5 November 1927 – Hammond; Watson, Jeffs; Allen, Brett, Odell; Daley, Smith (3), Loasby (3), Hoten (1), Wells (3).

***Record Cup Victory:*** 10–0 v Sutton T, FA Cup prel rd, 7 December 1907 – Cooch; Drennan, Lloyd Davies, Tirrell (1), McCartney, Hickleton, Badenock (3), Platt (3), Lowe (1), Chapman (2), McDiarmid.

## HONOURS

*Football League:* Division 1 best season: 21st, 1965–66; Division 2 – Runners-up 1964–65; Division 3 – Champions 1962–63; Promoted from Division 3 1996–97 (play-offs); Division 3 (S) – Runners-up 1927–28, 1949–50; Division 4 – Champions 1986–87; Runners-up 1975–76.

*FA Cup:* best season: 5th rd, 1934, 1950, 1970.

*Football League Cup:* best season: 5th rd, 1965, 1967.

## SKY SPORTS FACT FILE

Lloyds, a paper factory team from Sittingbourne, reached the first round of the FA Cup and on 26 November 1932 were beaten 8-1 by Northampton Town for whom Albert Dawes scored five goals to equal his club's individual scoring feat.

***Record Defeat:*** 0–11 v Southampton, Southern League, 28 December 1901.

***Most League Points (2 for a win):*** 68, Division 4, 1975–76.

***Most League Points (3 for a win):*** 99, Division 4, 1986–87.

***Most League Goals:*** 109, Division 3, 1962–63 and Division 3 (S), 1952–53.

***Highest League Scorer in Season:*** Cliff Holton, 36, Division 3, 1961–62.

***Most League Goals in Total Aggregate:*** Jack English, 135, 1947–60.

***Most League Goals in One Match:*** 5, Ralph Hoten v Crystal Palace, Division 3S, 27 October 1928.

***Most Capped Player:*** E. Lloyd Davies, 12 (16), Wales.

***Most League Appearances:*** Tommy Fowler, 521, 1946–61.

***Youngest League Player:*** Adrian Mann, 16 years 297 days v Bury, 5 May 1984.

***Record Transfer Fee Received:*** £265,000 from Watford for Richard Hill, July 1987.

***Record Transfer Fee Paid:*** £165,000 to Oldham Ath for Josh Low, July 2003.

***Football League Record:*** 1920 Original Member of Division 3; 1921 Division 3 (S); 1958–61 Division 4; 1961–63 Division 3; 1963–65 Division 2; 1965–66 Division 1; 1966–67 Division 2; 1967–69 Division 3; 1969–76 Division 4; 1976–77 Division 3; 1977–87 Division 4; 1987–90 Division 3; 1990–92 Division 4; 1992–97 Division 3; 1997–99 Division 2; 1999–2000 Division 3; 2000–03 Division 2; 2003–04 Division 3; 2004– FL2.

## LATEST SEQUENCES

***Longest Sequence of League Wins:*** 8, 27.8.1960 – 19.9.1960.

***Longest Sequence of League Defeats:*** 8, 26.10.1935 – 21.12.1935.

***Longest Sequence of League Draws:*** 6, 18.9.1983 – 15.10.1983.

***Longest Sequence of Unbeaten League Matches:*** 21, 27.9.1986 – 6.2.1987.

***Longest Sequence Without a League Win:*** 18, 26.3.1969 – 20.9.1969.

***Successive Scoring Runs:*** 27 from 23.8.1986.

***Successive Non-scoring Runs:*** 7 from 7.4.1939.

## MANAGERS

Arthur Jones 1897–1907
*(Secretary-Manager)*
Herbert Chapman 1907–12
Walter Bull 1912–13
Fred Lessons 1913–19
Bob Hewison 1920–25
Jack Tresadern 1925–30
Jack English 1931–35
Syd Puddefoot 1935–37
Warney Cresswell 1937–39
Tom Smith 1939–49
Bob Dennison 1949–54
Dave Smith 1954–59
David Bowen 1959–67
Tony Marchi 1967–68
Ron Flowers 1968–69
Dave Bowen 1969–72
*(continued as General Manager and Secretary to 1985 when joined the board)*
Billy Baxter 1972–73
Bill Dodgin Jnr 1973–76
Pat Crerand 1976–77
Bill Dodgin Jnr 1977
John Petts 1977–78
Mike Keen 1978–79
Clive Walker 1979–80
Bill Dodgin Jnr 1980–82
Clive Walker 1982–84
Tony Barton 1984–85
Graham Carr 1985–90
Theo Foley 1990–92
Phil Chard 1992–93
John Barnwell 1993–95
Ian Atkins 1995–99
Kevin Wilson 1999–2001
Kevan Broadhurst 2001–03
Terry Fenwick 2003
Martin Wilkinson 2003
Colin Calderwood October 2003–

## TEN YEAR LEAGUE RECORD

| | | *P* | *W* | *D* | *L* | *F* | *A* | *Pts* | *Pos* |
|---|---|---|---|---|---|---|---|---|---|
| 1994-95 | Div 3 | 42 | 10 | 14 | 18 | 45 | 67 | 44 | 17 |
| 1995-96 | Div 3 | 46 | 18 | 13 | 15 | 51 | 44 | 67 | 11 |
| 1996-97 | Div 3 | 46 | 20 | 12 | 14 | 67 | 44 | 72 | 4 |
| 1997-98 | Div 2 | 46 | 18 | 17 | 11 | 52 | 37 | 71 | 4 |
| 1998-99 | Div 2 | 46 | 10 | 18 | 18 | 43 | 57 | 48 | 22 |
| 1999-2000 | Div 3 | 46 | 25 | 7 | 14 | 63 | 45 | 82 | 3 |
| 2000-01 | Div 2 | 46 | 15 | 12 | 19 | 46 | 59 | 57 | 18 |
| 2001-02 | Div 2 | 46 | 14 | 7 | 25 | 54 | 79 | 49 | 20 |
| 2002-03 | Div 2 | 46 | 10 | 9 | 27 | 40 | 79 | 39 | 24 |
| 2003-04 | Div 3 | 46 | 22 | 9 | 15 | 58 | 51 | 75 | 6 |

## DID YOU KNOW ?

In 1949–50 Northampton Town were runners-up to Notts County in Division Three (South) and also reached the fifth round of the FA Cup beating Walthamstow Avenue, Torquay United, plus both Southampton and Bournemouth in replays on the way.

## NORTHAMPTON TOWN 2003–04 LEAGUE RECORD

| Match No. | Date | Venue | Opponents | Result | H/T Score | Lg. Pos. | Goalscorers | Attendance |
|---|---|---|---|---|---|---|---|---|
| 1 | Aug 9 | H | Torquay U | L 0-1 | 0-0 | — | | 5675 |
| 2 | 16 | A | York C | L 0-1 | 0-1 | 20 | | 3870 |
| 3 | 22 | H | Darlington | W 1-0 | 1-0 | — | Smith M [43] | 5020 |
| 4 | 25 | A | Yeovil T | W 2-0 | 2-0 | 9 | Reid [5], Low [41] | 6105 |
| 5 | 30 | H | Doncaster R | W 1-0 | 0-0 | 5 | Dudfield [76] | 4933 |
| 6 | Sept 5 | A | Cheltenham T | L 3-4 | 2-0 | — | Dudfield 2 [24, 32], Smith M (pen) [73] | 5002 |
| 7 | 13 | A | Huddersfield T | L 0-3 | 0-3 | 14 | | 8285 |
| 8 | 16 | H | Carlisle U | W 2-0 | 0-0 | — | Smith M (pen) [58], Trollope [77] | 4156 |
| 9 | 20 | H | Macclesfield T | D 0-0 | 0-0 | 10 | | 4332 |
| 10 | 27 | A | Oxford U | L 0-3 | 0-3 | 16 | | 6518 |
| 11 | 30 | A | Lincoln C | D 0-0 | 0-0 | — | | 3928 |
| 12 | Oct 4 | H | Hull C | L 1-5 | 0-2 | 17 | Trollope [78] | 6011 |
| 13 | 11 | A | Rochdale | D 1-1 | 0-0 | 18 | Smith M [51] | 2710 |
| 14 | 17 | H | Scunthorpe U | D 1-1 | 1-0 | — | Smith M [9] | 4827 |
| 15 | 21 | H | Kidderminster H | L 0-1 | 0-1 | — | | 4089 |
| 16 | 25 | A | Leyton Orient | D 1-1 | 0-0 | 19 | Low [59] | 4130 |
| 17 | Nov 1 | A | Southend U | W 1-0 | 0-0 | 18 | Trollope [60] | 5085 |
| 18 | 17 | H | Swansea C | W 2-1 | 1-0 | — | Walker [44], Smith M [58] | 4010 |
| 19 | 22 | A | Bury | L 0-1 | 0-0 | 16 | | 2683 |
| 20 | 29 | H | Mansfield T | L 0-3 | 0-1 | 17 | | 5019 |
| 21 | Dec 13 | A | Boston U | D 1-1 | 1-1 | 17 | Lincoln [33] | 2756 |
| 22 | 19 | H | Cambridge U | L 1-2 | 0-1 | — | Asamoah [72] | 4910 |
| 23 | 26 | A | Bristol R | W 2-1 | 0-0 | 16 | Asamoah [75], Walker [86] | 7695 |
| 24 | 28 | H | Cheltenham T | W 1-0 | 1-0 | 13 | Walker [10] | 5118 |
| 25 | Jan 10 | A | Torquay U | L 1-3 | 0-2 | 17 | Sampson [55] | 2585 |
| 26 | 17 | H | York C | W 2-1 | 2-0 | 14 | Walker [20], Parkin (og) [45] | 5003 |
| 27 | 30 | A | Doncaster R | L 0-1 | 0-1 | — | | 6017 |
| 28 | Feb 3 | H | Yeovil T | W 2-0 | 0-0 | — | Hargreaves [58], Smith M [70] | 4363 |
| 29 | 7 | H | Bristol R | W 2-0 | 1-0 | 12 | Vieira [31], Smith M [77] | 5068 |
| 30 | 14 | H | Rochdale | W 3-1 | 0-1 | 9 | Hargreaves [69], Reid [80], Vieira [86] | 4540 |
| 31 | 17 | A | Darlington | W 2-1 | 0-0 | — | Smith M (pen) [75], Richards [76] | 4764 |
| 32 | 21 | A | Scunthorpe U | L 0-1 | 0-0 | 9 | | 3566 |
| 33 | 28 | H | Leyton Orient | W 1-0 | 0-0 | 9 | Low [73] | 5784 |
| 34 | Mar 2 | A | Kidderminster H | L 1-2 | 0-1 | — | Hargreaves [56] | 2699 |
| 35 | 6 | A | Cambridge U | W 1-0 | 0-0 | 9 | Willmott [90] | 4298 |
| 36 | 13 | H | Boston U | W 2-0 | 0-0 | 9 | Morison [72], Sampson [86] | 6243 |
| 37 | 16 | A | Carlisle U | D 1-1 | 0-0 | — | Trollope [83] | 6269 |
| 38 | 27 | A | Macclesfield T | W 4-0 | 4-0 | 9 | Richards 4 [18, 23, 26, 39] | 2634 |
| 39 | Apr 3 | H | Oxford U | W 2-1 | 0-1 | 9 | Richards [63], Trollope [73] | 6799 |
| 40 | 10 | A | Hull C | W 3-2 | 3-1 | 8 | Richards [2], Sabin 2 [20, 31] | 18,017 |
| 41 | 12 | H | Lincoln C | D 1-1 | 1-0 | 8 | Trollope [44] | 7160 |
| 42 | 17 | H | Southend U | D 2-2 | 1-2 | 8 | Smith M (pen) [24], Taylor [83] | 5919 |
| 43 | 20 | H | Huddersfield T | L 0-1 | 0-0 | — | | 6873 |
| 44 | 24 | A | Swansea C | W 2-0 | 2-0 | 8 | Sabin 2 [34, 43] | 4985 |
| 45 | May 1 | H | Bury | W 3-2 | 1-2 | 7 | Smith M [41], Richards [60], Asamoah [74] | 6179 |
| 46 | 8 | A | Mansfield T | W 2-1 | 1-0 | 6 | Sabin [19], Ullathorne [70] | 8065 |

**Final League Position: 6**

### GOALSCORERS

*League (58):* Smith M 11 (4 pens), Richards 8, Trollope 6, Sabin 5, Walker 4, Asamoah 3, Dudfield 3, Hargreaves 3, Low 3, Reid 2, Sampson 2, Vieira 2, Lincoln 1, Morison 1, Taylor 1, Ullathorne 1, Willmott 1, own goal 1.
*Carling Cup (3):* Dudfield 1, Hargreaves 1 (pen), Low 1.
*FA Cup (10):* Smith 3 (1 pen), Richards 2, Walker 2, Asamoah 1, Hargreaves 1, Low 1.
*LDV Vans Trophy (5):* Dudfield 2, Walker 2, Low 1.
*Play-Offs (3):* Hargreaves 1, Richards 1, Smith 1.

| Thompson G 7 + 1 | Chambers L 19 + 5 | Clark P 6 | Trollope P 43 | Willmott C 35 + 1 | Reid P 33 | Low J 28 + 5 | Richards M 27 + 14 | Dudfield L 12 + 7 | Smith M 43 + 1 | Reeves M 9 + 5 | Asamoah D 4 + 27 | Burgess O 3 + 6 | Hargreaves C 41 + 1 | Harsley P 5 + 9 | Sampson I 35 + 2 | Youngs T 2 + 10 | Carruthers C 19 + 5 | Westwood A 8 + 1 | Harper L 39 | Doig C 9 | Morison S 2 + 3 | Walker R 11 + 1 | Lyttle D 23 + 4 | Lincoln G 4 + 3 | Sadler M 7 | Vieira M 7 + 3 | Abidallah N — + 1 | Ullathorne R 13 | Sabin E 9 + 2 | Taylor J 3 + 5 | Amoo R — + 1 | Match No. |
|---|---|---|---|---|---|---|---|---|---|---|---|---|---|---|---|---|---|---|---|---|---|---|---|---|---|---|---|---|---|---|---|---|
| 1 | 2¹ | 3 | 4 | 5 | 6 | 7 | 8 | 9² | 10 | 11 | 12 | 13 | | | | | | | | | | | | | | | | | | | | 1 |
| 1 | 2 | 3 | 4 | 5 | 6 | 7¹ | 8² | 13 | 10 | | 12 | 9³ | 11 | 14 | | | | | | | | | | | | | | | | | | 2 |
| 1 | 2 | 3 | 4 | 5² | 6 | 7 | | 9 | 10 | 8¹ | | 12 | 11 | | 13 | | | | | | | | | | | | | | | | | 3 |
| 1 | 2 | 3 | 4 | | 6 | 7 | 12 | 9² | 10¹ | | | 8 | 11 | 13 | 5 | | | | | | | | | | | | | | | | | 4 |
| 1 | 2 | 3 | 4 | | 6 | 7 | 12 | 9² | 10¹ | | | | 11 | 8 | 5 | 13 | | | | | | | | | | | | | | | | 5 |
| 1 | 2 | 3³ | | | 6 | 7 | 12 | 9 | 10¹ | | | 13 | 11 | 8 | 5 | | 14 | 4² | | | | | | | | | | | | | | 6 |
| | 3 | | 4 | | 6 | 7 | 12 | 9¹ | 10 | 8² | | 13 | 11 | | 5 | | 2 | | 1 | | | | | | | | | | | | | 7 |
| | 2 | | 4 | | 6 | 7¹ | 8 | 9² | 10 | | | 12 | 11 | | | 13 | 3 | | 1 | 5 | | | | | | | | | | | | 8 |
| | 2 | | 4 | | 6 | 7 | | 9 | 10² | | 12 | 8¹ | 11 | | | 13 | 3 | | 1 | 5 | | | | | | | | | | | | 9 |
| | 2 | | 8 | 5¹ | 6 | 7 | 10 | 9 | | | | | 11 | | | 12 | 3 | | 1 | 4 | | | | | | | | | | | | 10 |
| | 2 | | 8 | 5 | 6 | 7 | 12 | 9² | | | | | 11 | | 13 | | 3 | | 1 | 4 | 10¹ | | | | | | | | | | | 11 |
| 15 | 2 | | 4 | 5 | 8 | 7 | 12 | 10² | 13 | | | | 11 | | | | 3 | | 1■ | 6⁶ | 9¹ | | | | | | | | | | | 12 |
| | 2 | | 4 | 5 | | 7 | 12 | 9¹ | 10 | | | 13 | 11³ | 8² | 3 | | | | 1 | 6 | 14 | | | | | | | | | | | 13 |
| | 2 | | 8 | 5 | | 7² | 9¹ | | 10 | 12 | 13 | | 14 | 11 | 4 | | 3³ | | 1 | 6 | | | | | | | | | | | | 14 |
| 1 | | | 8 | 5 | | 2 | 9³ | 12 | 10 | | 13 | | 11¹ | 7 | 4² | | 3 | | | 6 | | 14 | | | | | | | | | | 15 |
| | 12 | | 8 | 5 | | 2 | 13 | 14 | 10³ | 7¹ | | | 11 | | 4 | | 3 | | 1 | 6 | | 9² | | | | | | | | | | 16 |
| | 2 | | 4 | 5 | | 7 | 12 | | 10 | 8 | | | 11 | | 6 | | 3 | | 1 | | | 9¹ | | | | | | | | | | 17 |
| | | | | 5 | | 7 | | 12 | 10 | 8² | 14 | | 11 | 13 | 4 | | 3 | | 1 | | | 9³ | 2 | 6¹ | | | | | | | | 18 |
| | 4 | | 6³ | 5 | | 7¹ | 12 | 13 | 10 | 8² | | | 11 | | | | | | 1 | | | 9 | 2 | 14 | 3 | | | | | | | 19 |
| | 14 | | 6¹ | 5 | | 7 | 12 | | 10 | | 13 | | 11 | | 4 | | | | 1 | | | 9 | 2³ | 8² | 3 | | | | | | | 20 |
| | | | 4¹ | 5 | 6 | | 8 | 14 | 10 | | 13 | | 11 | 12 | | | | | 1 | | | 9³ | 2 | 7² | 3 | | | | | | | 21 |
| | | | | 5■ | 6 | | 8 | | 10 | | 13 | | 11 | 12 | 4 | | 14 | | 1 | | | 9³ | 2 | 7² | 3¹ | | | | | | | 22 |
| | | | 7 | 5 | 6 | | 8² | | 10 | | 13 | | 11 | 12 | 4 | | 14 | | 1 | | | 9¹ | 2 | | 3³ | | | | | | | 23 |
| | | | 7 | 5 | 6 | | 12 | | 10² | | 8 | | 11 | 13 | 4 | | 14 | | 1 | | | 9¹ | 2 | | 3³ | | | | | | | 24 |
| | | | 7 | | 6 | | 13 | | 10 | | 8 | | 11 | 12 | 4 | | | 5 | 1 | | | 9² | 2¹ | 14 | 3³ | | | | | | | 25 |
| | | | 7 | 5 | 6 | | | | 10³ | | 8² | | 11 | 12 | 4 | | 3 | | 1 | | | 9 | 2¹ | | | 13 | 14 | | | | | 26 |
| | | | 7² | 5 | 6 | | 8³ | 12 | 10 | | 9¹ | | 11 | | 4 | | 3 | | 1 | | | | 2 | 13 | | 14 | | | | | | 27 |
| | 14 | | 7 | 5 | 6 | | 8 | | 10² | 13 | 12 | | 11 | | | | 3 | 4³ | 1 | | | | 2 | | | 9¹ | | | | | | 28 |
| | | | 7 | 5 | 6 | | 8¹ | | 10 | 12 | 13 | | 11 | | 4 | | 3 | | 1 | | | | 2 | | | 9² | | | | | | 29 |
| | | | 7 | 5 | 6 | | 8³ | | 10 | 12 | 13 | | 11 | | 4 | 14 | 3² | | 1 | | | | 2 | | | 9¹ | | | | | | 30 |
| | | | 7 | 5 | 6 | | 8¹ | | 10 | 14 | 13 | | 11 | | 4 | 12 | 3² | | 1 | | | | 2 | | | 9³ | | | | | | 31 |
| | | | 7 | 5 | 6 | | 8 | | 10 | | 13 | | 11 | | 4¹ | 12 | | | 1 | | | | 2 | | | 9² | | 3 | | | | 32 |
| | | | 7 | 5 | 6■ | 12 | 8² | | 11 | | 13 | | | | 4 | 10¹ | 14 | | 1 | | | | 2 | | | 9³ | | 3 | | | | 33 |
| | | | 8² | 5 | 6 | 7 | 9³ | | 10 | | 12 | | 11 | | 4¹ | 13 | | | 1 | | | | 2 | | | 14 | | 3 | | | | 34 |
| | 14 | | 8 | 5 | 6 | 12 | 9 | | 10 | | 13 | | 11 | | 4³ | 7² | | | 1 | | | | 2¹ | | | | | 3 | | | | 35 |
| | 6 | | 7 | 5 | | 13 | | | 10 | 11² | 12 | | | | 4 | | | | 1 | | 14 | | 2¹ | | | 9³ | | 3 | 8 | | | 36 |
| | 6 | | 7 | 5 | | 13 | 8¹ | | 10 | 11² | 12 | | | | 4 | | | | 1 | | 14 | | 2 | | | | | 3 | 9³ | | | 37 |
| | 5 | | 7¹ | | 6 | 12 | 8 | | 10² | | | | 11 | | 4 | 13 | | | 1 | | | | 2 | | | | | 3 | 9³ | 14 | | 38 |
| | | | 6 | 12 | 5 | 7¹ | 8² | | 10³ | | | | 11 | | 4 | | | | 1 | | | | 2 | | | | | 3 | 13 | 9 | 14 | 39 |
| | | | 7 | 5² | 6 | | 8³ | | 10 | | 12 | | 11 | | 4 | | | 13 | 1 | | | | 2 | | | | | 3 | 9¹ | 14 | | 40 |
| | | | 7 | | 6 | 2² | 8¹ | | 10³ | | 12 | | 11 | | 4 | | | 5 | 1 | | | | 13 | | | | | 3 | 14 | 9 | | 41 |
| | | | 7 | | 6 | 2 | 8³ | | 10 | | 13 | | 11 | | 4 | | | 5² | 1 | | | | 12 | | | | | 3 | 9¹ | 14 | | 42 |
| | | | 7 | 5 | 6 | 2 | 14 | | 10 | | 12 | | 11 | | 4 | | | | 1 | | | | 13 | | | | | 3² | 9¹ | 8³ | | 43 |
| | | | 7 | 5 | | 2 | 8² | | 10¹ | | 13 | | 11 | | 4 | 12 | 3 | 6 | 1 | | | | | | | | | | 9 | | | 44 |
| | 13 | | 7 | 5 | | 2² | 8³ | | 10 | | 12 | | 11 | | 4 | | 3¹ | 6 | 1 | | | | | | | | | | 9■ | 14 | | 45 |
| | | | 7 | 5 | | 2¹ | 8² | | 10³ | | 13 | | 11 | | 4 | | | 6 | 1 | | | | 12 | | | | | 3 | 9 | 14 | | 46 |

**Carling Cup**

| | | | |
|---|---|---|---|
| First Round | Norwich C | (h) | 1-0 |
| Second Round | Portsmouth | (a) | 2-5 |

**LDV Vans Trophy**

| | | | |
|---|---|---|---|
| Second Round | Hereford U | (a) | 1-1 |
| Quarter-Final | Peterborough U | (h) | 2-1 |
| Semi-Final | Colchester U | (h) | 2-3 |

**FA Cup**

| | | | |
|---|---|---|---|
| First Round | Plymouth Arg | (h) | 3-2 |
| Second Round | Weston-Super-Mare | (h) | 4-1 |
| Third Round | Rotherham U | (h) | 1-1 |
| | | (a) | 2-1 |
| Fourth Round | Manchester U | (h) | 0-3 |

**Play-Offs**

| | | | |
|---|---|---|---|
| Semi-Final | Mansfield T | (h) | 0-2 |
| | | (a) | 3-1 |

# NORWICH CITY

# FA Premiership

## FOUNDATION

Formed in 1902, largely through the initiative of two local schoolmasters who called a meeting at the Criterion Cafe, they were shocked by an FA Commission which in 1904 declared the club professional and ejected them from the FA Amateur Cup. However, this only served to strengthen their determination. New officials were appointed and a professional club established at a meeting in the Agricultural Hall in March 1905.

***Carrow Road, Norwich NR1 1JE.***
***Telephone:*** (01603) 760 760.
***Fax:*** (01603) 613 886.
***Ticket Office:*** 0870 444 1902.
***Website:*** www.canaries.co.uk
***Email:*** reception@ncfc-canaries.co.uk
***Ground Capacity:*** 24,349.
***Record Attendance:*** 43,984 v Leicester C, FA Cup 6th rd, 30 March 1963.
***Pitch Measurements:*** 114yd × 74yd.
***Chairman:*** Roger Munby.
***Vice-chairman:*** Barry Skipper.
***Chief Executive:*** Neil Doncaster.
***Secretary:*** Kevan Platt.
***Manager:*** Nigel Worthington.
***Assistant Manager:*** Doug Livermore.
***Physio:*** Neil Reynolds, MCSP, SRP.
***Colours:*** Yellow shirts, green shorts, yellow stockings.
***Change Colours:*** Green and black shirts, green shorts, green stockings.
***Year Formed:*** 1902.
***Turned Professional:*** 1905.
***Ltd Co.:*** 1905.
***Club Nickname:*** 'The Canaries'.
***Previous Grounds:*** 1902, Newmarket Road; 1908, The Nest, Rosary Road; 1935, Carrow Road.
***First Football League Game:*** 28 August 1920, Division 3, v Plymouth Arg (a) D 1–1 – Skermer; Gray, Gadsden; Wilkinson, Addy, Martin; Laxton, Kidger, Parker, Whitham (1), Dobson.
***Record League Victory:*** 10–2 v Coventry C, Division 3 (S), 15 March 1930 – Jarvie; Hannah, Graham; Brown, O'Brien, Lochhead (1); Porter (1), Anderson, Hunt (5), Scott (2), Slicer (1).

## HONOURS

*FA Premier League:* best season: 3rd 1992–93.

*Football League:* Division 1 – Champions 2003–04; Division 2 – Champions 1971–72, 1985–86; Division 3 (S) – Champions 1933–34; Division 3 – Runners-up 1959–60.

*FA Cup:* Semi-finals 1959, 1989, 1992.

*Football League Cup:* Winners 1962, 1985; Runners-up 1973, 1975.

***European Competitions:*** *UEFA Cup:* 1993–94.

## SKY SPORTS FACT FILE

Having lost both legs of their 1945–46 FA Cup tie with Brighton & Hove Albion, Norwich City exacted revenge on their opponents when drawn together the following season. On 30 November 1946 the Canaries won 7-2, Les Eyre scoring five.

***Record Cup Victory:*** 8–0 v Sutton U, FA Cup 4th rd, 28 January 1989 – Gunn; Culverhouse, Bowen, Butterworth, Linighan, Townsend (Crook), Gordon, Fleck (3), Allen (4), Phelan, Putney (1).

***Record Defeat:*** 2–10 v Swindon T, Southern League, 5 September 1908.

***Most League Points (2 for a win):*** 64, Division 3 (S), 1950–51.

***Most League Points (3 for a win):*** 94, Division 1, 2003–04.

***Most League Goals:*** 99, Division 3 (S), 1952–53.

***Highest League Scorer in Season:*** Ralph Hunt, 31, Division 3 (S), 1955–56.

***Most League Goals in Total Aggregate:*** Johnny Gavin, 122, 1945–54, 1955–58.

***Most League Goals in One Match:*** 5, Tommy Hunt v Coventry C, Division 3S, 15 March 1930; 5, Roy Hollis v Walsall, Division 3S, 29 December 1951.

***Most Capped Player:*** Mark Bowen, 35 (41), Wales.

***Most League Appearances:*** Ron Ashman, 592, 1947–64.

***Youngest League Player:*** Ryan Jarvis, 16 years 282 days v Walsall, 19 April 2003.

***Record Transfer Fee Received:*** £5,000,000 from Blackburn R for Chris Sutton, July 1994. £5,000,000 from Coventry C for Craig Bellamy, August 2000.

***Record Transfer Fee Paid:*** £1,000,000 to Leeds U for Jon Newsome, June 1994.

***Football League Record:*** 1920 Original Member of Division 3; 1921 Division 3 (S): 1934–39 Division 2; 1946–58 Division 3 (S); 1958–60 Division 3; 1960–72 Division 2; 1972–74 Division 1; 1974–75 Division 2; 1975–81 Division 1; 1981–82 Division 2; 1982–85 Division 1; 1985–86 Division 2; 1986–92 Division 1; 1992–95 FA Premier League; 1995–2004 Division 1; 2004– FA Premier League.

## MANAGERS

John Bowman 1905–07
James McEwen 1907–08
Arthur Turner 1909–10
Bert Stansfield 1910–15
Major Frank Buckley 1919–20
Charles O'Hagan 1920–21
Albert Gosnell 1921–26
Bert Stansfield 1926
Cecil Potter 1926–29
James Kerr 1929–33
Tom Parker 1933–37
Bob Young 1937–39
Jimmy Jewell 1939
Bob Young 1939–45
Cyril Spiers 1946–47
Duggie Lochhead 1947–50
Norman Low 1950–55
Tom Parker 1955–57
Archie Macaulay 1957–61
Willie Reid 1961–62
George Swindin 1962
Ron Ashman 1962–66
Lol Morgan 1966–69
Ron Saunders 1969–73
John Bond 1973–80
Ken Brown 1980–87
Dave Stringer 1987–92
Mike Walker 1992–94
John Deehan 1994–95
Martin O'Neill 1995
Gary Megson 1995–96
Mike Walker 1996–98
Bruce Rioch 1998–2000
Bryan Hamilton 2000
Nigel Worthington January 2001–

## LATEST SEQUENCES

***Longest Sequence of League Wins:*** 10, 23.11.1985 – 25.1.1986.

***Longest Sequence of League Defeats:*** 7, 1.4.1995 – 6.5.1995.

***Longest Sequence of League Draws:*** 7, 15.1.1994 – 26.2.1994.

***Longest Sequence of Unbeaten League Matches:*** 20, 31.8.1950 – 30.12.1950.

***Longest Sequence Without a League Win:*** 25, 22.9.1956 – 23.2.1957.

***Successive Scoring Runs:*** 25 from 31.8.1963.

***Successive Non-scoring Runs:*** 5 from 21.2.1925.

## TEN YEAR LEAGUE RECORD

| | | P | W | D | L | F | A | Pts | Pos |
|---|---|---|---|---|---|---|---|---|---|
| 1994-95 | PR Lge | 42 | 10 | 13 | 19 | 37 | 54 | 43 | 20 |
| 1995-96 | Div 1 | 46 | 14 | 15 | 17 | 59 | 55 | 57 | 16 |
| 1996-97 | Div 1 | 46 | 17 | 12 | 17 | 63 | 68 | 63 | 13 |
| 1997-98 | Div 1 | 46 | 14 | 13 | 19 | 52 | 69 | 55 | 15 |
| 1998-99 | Div 1 | 46 | 15 | 17 | 14 | 62 | 61 | 62 | 9 |
| 1999-2000 | Div 1 | 46 | 14 | 15 | 17 | 45 | 50 | 57 | 12 |
| 2000-01 | Div 1 | 46 | 14 | 12 | 20 | 46 | 58 | 54 | 15 |
| 2001-02 | Div 1 | 46 | 22 | 9 | 15 | 60 | 51 | 75 | 6 |
| 2002-03 | Div 1 | 46 | 19 | 12 | 15 | 60 | 49 | 69 | 8 |
| 2003-04 | Div 1 | 46 | 28 | 10 | 8 | 79 | 39 | 94 | 1 |

## DID YOU KNOW ?

Despite finishing 14th in the First Division in 1982–83, Norwich City had the distinction of being the first club to take six points off champions elect Liverpool, the system having just been changed. City won 1-0 at home, 2-0 at Anfield.

## NORWICH CITY 2003–04 LEAGUE RECORD

| Match No. | Date | Venue | Opponents | Result | | H/T Score | Lg. Pos. | Goalscorers | Attendance |
|---|---|---|---|---|---|---|---|---|---|
| 1 | Aug 9 | A | Bradford C | D | 2-2 | 1-0 | — | Rivers (pen) [44], Easton [47] | 13,159 |
| 2 | 16 | H | Rotherham U | W | 2-0 | 2-0 | 6 | Easton [9], Rivers [30] | 16,263 |
| 3 | 23 | A | Sheffield U | L | 0-1 | 0-1 | 9 | | 24,285 |
| 4 | 26 | H | Wimbledon | W | 3-2 | 2-0 | — | Francis [10], Rivers 2 (1 pen) [27 (p), 56] | 16,082 |
| 5 | 30 | A | Nottingham F | L | 0-2 | 0-1 | 12 | | 21,058 |
| 6 | Sept 13 | H | Burnley | W | 2-0 | 0-0 | 10 | Crouch [58], Roberts [90] | 16,407 |
| 7 | 16 | A | Gillingham | W | 2-1 | 0-1 | — | Francis [28], Crouch [67] | 8022 |
| 8 | 20 | A | Stoke C | D | 1-1 | 0-1 | 8 | Huckerby [67] | 10,672 |
| 9 | 27 | H | Crystal Palace | W | 2-1 | 1-1 | 4 | Huckerby (pen) [38], MacKay [89] | 16,425 |
| 10 | 30 | H | Reading | W | 2-1 | 1-1 | — | Huckerby [17], McVeigh [87] | 16,387 |
| 11 | Oct 4 | A | Wigan Ath | D | 1-1 | 0-1 | 6 | Roberts [63] | 9346 |
| 12 | 15 | A | West Ham U | D | 1-1 | 0-1 | — | Crouch [63] | 31,308 |
| 13 | 18 | A | WBA | L | 0-1 | 0-1 | 8 | | 24,966 |
| 14 | 21 | H | Derby Co | W | 2-1 | 0-0 | — | Roberts (pen) [81], Mulryne [90] | 16,346 |
| 15 | 25 | H | Sunderland | W | 1-0 | 1-0 | 3 | Francis [33] | 16,427 |
| 16 | Nov 1 | A | Walsall | W | 3-1 | 0-1 | 3 | Henderson [52], McVeigh [60], Crouch [64] | 8331 |
| 17 | 8 | H | Millwall | W | 3-1 | 3-0 | 3 | Henderson 2 [15, 30], McVeigh [22] | 16,423 |
| 18 | 15 | H | Watford | L | 1-2 | 0-1 | 3 | Jarvis [88] | 16,420 |
| 19 | 22 | A | Preston NE | D | 0-0 | 0-0 | 2 | | 14,775 |
| 20 | 25 | H | Coventry C | D | 1-1 | 1-0 | — | Henderson [35] | 16,414 |
| 21 | 29 | H | Crewe Alex | W | 1-0 | 1-0 | 2 | Huckerby [39] | 16,367 |
| 22 | Dec 6 | A | Millwall | D | 0-0 | 0-0 | 2 | | 9850 |
| 23 | 13 | H | Cardiff C | W | 4-1 | 1-0 | 2 | Huckerby [34], Roberts [54], Fleming [71], Vidmar (og) [79] | 18,428 |
| 24 | 21 | A | Ipswich T | W | 2-0 | 1-0 | 1 | McKenzie 2 [37, 76] | 30,152 |
| 25 | 26 | H | Nottingham F | W | 1-0 | 1-0 | 1 | Svensson [14] | 16,429 |
| 26 | 28 | A | Derby Co | W | 4-0 | 0-0 | 1 | Fleming [51], MacKay [78], McVeigh [81], McKenzie (pen) [88] | 23,783 |
| 27 | Jan 10 | H | Bradford C | L | 0-1 | 0-1 | 1 | | 16,360 |
| 28 | 17 | A | Rotherham U | D | 4-4 | 3-2 | 1 | Roberts [29], McKenzie [33], Huckerby (pen) [45], Francis [90] | 7448 |
| 29 | 31 | H | Sheffield U | W | 1-0 | 0-0 | 1 | Roberts [59] | 18,977 |
| 30 | Feb 7 | A | Wimbledon | W | 1-0 | 1-0 | 1 | Huckerby [16] | 7368 |
| 31 | 14 | A | Coventry C | W | 2-0 | 1-0 | 1 | Holt [38], Brennan [85] | 15,757 |
| 32 | 21 | H | West Ham U | D | 1-1 | 0-0 | 1 | Huckerby [76] | 23,940 |
| 33 | Mar 2 | H | WBA | D | 0-0 | 0-0 | — | | 23,223 |
| 34 | 7 | H | Ipswich T | W | 3-1 | 0-0 | 1 | MacKay 2 [50, 59], Huckerby [88] | 23,942 |
| 35 | 13 | A | Cardiff C | L | 1-2 | 0-2 | 1 | McKenzie [55] | 16,317 |
| 36 | 16 | H | Gillingham | W | 3-0 | 0-0 | — | Pouton (og) [63], Mulryne [65], McVeigh [67] | 23,198 |
| 37 | 20 | A | Crystal Palace | L | 0-1 | 0-1 | 1 | | 23,798 |
| 38 | 27 | H | Stoke C | W | 1-0 | 1-0 | 1 | Svensson [45] | 23,565 |
| 39 | Apr 3 | A | Burnley | W | 5-3 | 2-3 | 1 | Svensson 2 [14, 62], Huckerby 2 [32, 89], McKenzie [51] | 12,417 |
| 40 | 9 | H | Wigan Ath | W | 2-0 | 0-0 | — | Svensson [55], Huckerby [72] | 23,446 |
| 41 | 12 | A | Reading | W | 1-0 | 0-0 | 1 | Mulryne [86] | 18,460 |
| 42 | 17 | H | Walsall | W | 5-0 | 2-0 | 1 | Francis [2], McKenzie [45], Svensson 2 [51, 86], Huckerby [73] | 23,558 |
| 43 | 24 | A | Watford | W | 2-1 | 1-0 | 1 | Francis [29], McKenzie [48] | 19,290 |
| 44 | May 1 | H | Preston NE | W | 3-2 | 2-1 | 1 | McKenzie [2], Francis [28], Huckerby [84] | 23,673 |
| 45 | 4 | A | Sunderland | L | 0-1 | 0-1 | — | | 35,174 |
| 46 | 9 | A | Crewe Alex | W | 3-1 | 2-0 | 1 | Fleming [28], Roberts 2 (1 pen) [31, 88 (p)] | 9833 |

**Final League Position: 1**

### GOALSCORERS

*League (79):* Huckerby 14 (2 pens), McKenzie 9 (1 pen), Roberts 8 (2 pens), Francis 7, Svensson 7, McVeigh 5, Crouch 4, Henderson 4, MacKay 4, Rivers 4 (2 pens), Fleming 3, Mulryne 3, Easton 2, Brennan 1, Holt 1, Jarvis 1, own goals 2.
*Carling Cup (0).*
*FA Cup (1):* Brennan 1.

| Green R 46 | Briggs K 1 + 2 | Drury A 42 | Fleming C 46 | MacKay M 45 | Holt G 46 | Rivers M 7 + 5 | Francis D 39 + 2 | Nielsen D 2 | McVeigh P 36 + 8 | Easton C 8 + 2 | Edworthy M 42 + 1 | Mulryne P 14 + 20 | Abbey Z 1 + 2 | Hammond E — + 4 | Roberts I 13 + 28 | Jarvis R — + 12 | Henderson I 14 + 5 | Harper K 9 | Huckerby D 36 | Crouch P 14 + 1 | Notman A — + 1 | Shackell J 4 + 2 | Brennan J 7 + 8 | McKenzie L 12 + 6 | Svensson M 16 + 4 | Cooper K 6 + 4 | *Match No.* |
|---|---|---|---|---|---|---|---|---|---|---|---|---|---|---|---|---|---|---|---|---|---|---|---|---|---|---|---|
| 1 | 2¹ | 3 | 4 | 5 | 6 | 7² | 8 | 9 | 10³ | 11 | 12 | 13 | 14 | | | | | | | | | | | | | | 1 |
| 1 | | 3 | 4 | 5 | 6 | 7 | 8 | 9¹ | 10² | 11 | 2 | | 12 | 13 | | | | | | | | | | | | | 2 |
| 1 | | 3 | 4 | 5 | 6 | 10¹ | 7 | | 8 | 11³ | 2 | | 9² | 12 | 13 | 14 | | | | | | | | | | | 3 |
| 1 | | 3 | 4 | 5 | 6 | 7¹ | 8 | | 10² | 11 | 2 | | | 13 | 9 | | 12 | | | | | | | | | | 4 |
| 1 | | 3 | 4 | 5 | 6 | 7² | 8 | | 10 | 12 | 2 | 11¹ | | 13 | 9³ | 14 | | | | | | | | | | | 5 |
| 1 | | 3 | 4 | 5 | 6 | | 8 | | 12 | 11¹ | 2 | | | | 13 | | | 7³ | 9 | 10² | 14 | | | | | | 6 |
| 1 | | 3 | 4 | 5 | 6 | | 8 | | 12 | 11¹ | 2 | 13 | | | 14 | | | 7² | 9 | 10³ | | | | | | | 7 |
| 1 | | 3 | 4 | 5 | 6 | | 8² | | 12 | 11¹ | 2 | 13 | | | 14 | | | 7³ | 9 | 10 | | | | | | | 8 |
| 1 | | 3 | 4 | 5 | 6 | | 8 | | 11 | | 2 | 12 | | | 13 | | | 7¹ | 9 | 10² | | | | | | | 9 |
| 1 | | | 4 | 5 | 6 | | 8 | | 11 | | 2 | 7 | | | 12 | | | | 9 | 10¹ | | 3 | | | | | 10 |
| 1 | | 3 | 4 | 5 | 6 | | 8¹ | | 11 | 12² | 2 | 7 | | | 10 | | 13 | | 9 | | | | | | | | 11 |
| 1 | | 3 | 4 | 5 | 6 | 12 | 8 | | 11 | | 2 | 13 | | | 14 | | | 7² | 9¹ | 10³ | | | | | | | 12 |
| 1 | | 3 | 4 | 5 | 6³ | 11¹ | 8 | | 12 | | 2 | 10 | | | 9² | | | 7 | | 13 | | 14 | | | | | 13 |
| 1 | | 3 | 4 | 5 | 6 | 10³ | 8 | | 11¹ | | 2 | 12 | | | 13 | 14 | | 7■ | | 9² | | | | | | | 14 |
| 1 | | 3 | 4 | 5 | 6 | 12 | 8 | | 11 | | 2² | 13 | | | 14 | | | 7¹ | 9 | 10³ | | | | | | | 15 |
| 1 | | 3 | 4 | 5 | 6 | | 8 | | 11 | | | 7 | | | 12 | | 13 | 2² | 9¹ | 10■ | | | | | | | 16 |
| 1 | 12 | 3 | 4 | 5 | 6 | | 8 | | 11 | | | 2¹ | | | 13 | 14 | 7 | | 9³ | 10² | | | | | | | 17 |
| 1 | 12 | 3 | 4 | 5 | 6 | 13 | 8 | | 11³ | 2¹ | | | | | 10 | 14 | 7² | | 9 | | | | | | | | 18 |
| 1 | | 3 | 4 | 5 | 6 | | 8 | | 11 | | 2 | | | | 12 | | 7 | | 9 | 10¹ | | | | | | | 19 |
| 1 | | 3 | 4 | 5■ | 6 | | 8¹ | | 11 | | 2 | 12 | | | 13 | 14 | 7 | | 9³ | 10² | | | | | | | 20 |
| 1 | | 3 | 4 | 5 | 6 | | | | 11² | | 2 | 8 | | | | 12 | 7¹ | | 9 | 10 | | | 13 | | | | 21 |
| 1 | | 3² | 4 | 5 | 6 | | | | 11 | | 2 | 8 | | | | 12 | 7 | | 9¹ | 10 | | | 13 | | | | 22 |
| 1 | | 3 | 4 | | 6 | | | | 11² | | 2 | 8 | | | 10¹ | 13 | 7 | | 9 | | | 5 | 12 | | | | 23 |
| 1 | | 3 | 4 | 5 | 6 | | | | 11 | | 2 | 8 | | | 12 | 13 | 7³ | | | | | | 14 | 9² | 10¹ | | 24 |
| 1 | | 3 | 4 | 5 | 6 | | 13 | | 11³ | | 2 | 8² | | | 12 | | 7 | | | | | | 14 | 9 | 10¹ | | 25 |
| 1 | | 3 | 4 | 5 | 6 | | 8 | | 11 | | 2 | | | | 12 | 13 | 7³ | | | | | | 14 | 9² | 10¹ | | 26 |
| 1 | | 3 | 4 | 5 | 6 | 12 | 14 | | 11² | | 2 | 8³ | | | 13 | | 7¹ | | 10 | | | | | 9 | | | 27 |
| 1 | | 3 | 4 | 5 | 6 | 12 | 7 | | 11² | | 2¹ | | | | 8 | | 13 | | 10 | | | | | 9 | | | 28 |
| 1 | | 3 | 4 | 5 | 6 | | 7¹ | | 11 | | 2 | 12 | | | 10 | | | | 9 | | | | 8 | | | | 29 |
| 1 | | 3 | 4 | 5 | 6 | | 7 | | 11 | | 2 | | | | 9¹ | | | | 10² | | | | 8 | 13 | 12 | | 30 |
| 1 | | 3 | 4 | 5 | 6 | | 7 | | 11 | | 2 | | | | 9¹ | | | | 10² | | | | 8 | 13 | 12 | | 31 |
| 1 | | 3 | 4 | 5 | 6 | | 7 | | 11 | | 2 | | | | 9¹ | | | | 10 | | | | 8 | | 12 | | 32 |
| 1 | | 3¹ | 4 | 5 | 6 | | 7 | | 11³ | | 2 | 12 | | | 9² | | | | 10 | | | | 8 | 14 | 13 | | 33 |
| 1 | | | 4 | 5 | 6 | | 8 | | 11 | | 2 | 12 | | | 13 | | 7¹ | | 9 | | | 14 | 3³ | | 10² | | 34 |
| 1 | | 3 | 4 | 5 | 6 | | 8 | | 11³ | | 2 | 12 | | | 13 | | | | 9 | | | | 7¹ | 14 | 10² | | 35 |
| 1 | | | 4 | 5 | 6 | | 8¹ | | 11 | | 2 | 12 | | | 13 | 14 | 7³ | | 9² | | | 3 | | | 10 | | 36 |
| 1 | | | 4 | 5 | 6 | | | | 11² | | 2 | 8 | | | 12 | | 7³ | | 9 | | | 3¹ | | 13 | 10 | 14 | 37 |
| 1 | | 3 | 4 | 5 | 6 | | 8 | | 11 | | 2 | | | | 12 | | | | 7 | | | | | 9² | 10¹ | 13 | 38 |
| 1 | | 3 | 4 | 5 | 6 | | 7 | | 11³ | | 2 | 12 | | | 13 | | | | 9 | | | | | 8¹ | 10² | 14 | 39 |
| 1 | | 3 | 4 | 5 | 6 | | 7 | | | | 2 | 12 | | | | | | | 9 | | | | 13 | 8² | 10 | 11¹ | 40 |
| 1 | | 3 | 4 | 5 | 6 | | 8 | | 11¹ | | 2 | 12 | | | 13 | | | | 9 | | | | 14 | | 10² | 7³ | 41 |
| 1 | | 3 | 4 | 5 | 6 | | 7 | | 12 | | 2 | 13 | | | 14 | | | | 9 | | | | | 8¹ | 10³ | 11² | 42 |
| 1 | | 3 | 4 | 5 | 6 | | 7 | | 14 | | 2 | 12 | | | 13 | | | | 9 | | | | | 8¹ | 10² | 11³ | 43 |
| 1 | | 3 | 4 | 5 | 6 | | 7 | | 13 | | 2 | 12 | | | 14 | | | | 9 | | | | | 8² | 10³ | 11¹ | 44 |
| 1 | | 3 | 4 | 5 | 6 | | 7 | | 13 | | 2 | 12 | | | 14 | | | | 9 | | | | | 8² | 10³ | 11¹ | 45 |
| 1 | | 3 | 4 | 5 | 6 | | 7¹ | | | | 2 | 8 | | | 11 | | 12 | | 9³ | | | | | 13 | 10² | 14 | 46 |

**Carling Cup**
First Round Northampton T (a) 0-1

**FA Cup**
Third Round Everton (a) 1-3

# NOTTINGHAM FOREST FL Championship

## FOUNDATION

One of the oldest football clubs in the world, Nottingham Forest was formed at a meeting in the Clinton Arms in 1865. Known originally as the Forest Football Club, the game which first drew the founders together was 'shinney', a form of hockey. When they determined to change to football in 1865, one of their first moves was to buy a set of red caps to wear on the field.

***The City Ground, Nottingham NG2 5FJ.***

***Telephone:*** (0115) 982 4444.

***Fax:*** (0115) 982 4455.

***Ticket Office:*** (0115) 982 4445.

***Website:*** www.nottinghamforest.co.uk

***Email:*** info@nottinghamforest.co.uk

***Ground Capacity:*** 30,602.

***Record Attendance:*** 49,946 v Manchester U, Division 1, 28 October 1967.

***Pitch Measurements:*** 112yd × 74yd.

***Chairman:*** Nigel Doughty.

***Chief Executive:*** Mark Arthur.

***Secretary:*** Paul White.

***Manager:*** Joe Kinnear.

***Physios:*** Gary Fleming and Steve Devine.

***Colours:*** Red shirts, white shorts, red stockings.

***Change Colours:*** All white.

***Year Formed:*** 1865.

***Turned Professional:*** 1889.

***Ltd Co.:*** 1982.

***Club Nickname:*** 'Reds'.

***Previous Grounds:*** 1865, Forest Racecourse; 1879, The Meadows; 1880, Trent Bridge Cricket Ground; 1882, Parkside, Lenton; 1885, Gregory, Lenton; 1890, Town Ground; 1898, City Ground.

***First Football League Game:*** 3 September 1892, Division 1, v Everton (a) D 2–2 – Brown; Earp, Scott; Hamilton, A. Smith, McCracken; McCallum, W. Smith, Higgins (2), Pike, McInnes.

***Record League Victory:*** 12–0 v Leicester Fosse, Division 1, 12 April 1909 – Iremonger; Dudley, Maltby; Hughes (1), Needham, Armstrong; Hooper (3), Marrison, West (3), Morris (2), Spouncer (3 incl. 1p).

***Record Cup Victory:*** 14–0 v Clapton (away), FA Cup 1st rd, 17 January 1891 – Brown; Earp, Scott; A. Smith, Russell, Jeacock; McCallum (2), 'Tich' Smith (1), Higgins (5), Lindley (4), Shaw (2).

***Record Defeat:*** 1–9 v Blackburn R, Division 2, 10 April 1937.

## HONOURS

*Football League:* Division 1 – Champions 1977–78, 1997–98; Runners-up 1966–67, 1978–79; Division 2 – Champions 1906–07, 1921–22; Runners-up 1956–57; Division 3 (S) – Champions 1950–51.

*FA Cup:* Winners 1898, 1959; Runners-up 1991.

*Football League Cup:* Winners 1978, 1979, 1989, 1990; Runners-up 1980, 1992.

*Anglo-Scottish Cup:* Winners 1977;

*Simod Cup:* Winners 1989.

*Zenith Data Systems Cup:* Winners: 1992.

***European Competitions:*** *European Fairs Cup:* 1961–62, 1967–68. *European Cup:* 1978–79 (winners), 1979–80 (winners), 1980–81. *Super Cup:* 1979–80 (winners), 1980–81 (runners-up). *World Club Championship:* 1980. *UEFA Cup:* 1983–84, 1984–85, 1995–96.

## SKY SPORTS FACT FILE

Nottingham Forest met three different Nottingham teams in the first round of the FA Cup on three separate occasions in the early years: 1878 Notts FC (later County) 3-1; 1886 Notts Olympic 3-0 and 1887 Notts Swifts 2-1.

***Most League Points (2 for a win):*** 70, Division 3 (S), 1950–51.

***Most League Points (3 for a win):*** 94, Division 1, 1997–98.

***Most League Goals:*** 110, Division 3 (S), 1950–51.

***Highest League Scorer in Season:*** Wally Ardron, 36, Division 3 (S), 1950–51.

***Most League Goals in Total Aggregate:*** Grenville Morris, 199, 1898–1913.

***Most League Goals in One Match:*** 4, Enoch West v Sunderland, Division 1, 9 November 1907; 4, Tommy Gibson v Burnley, Division 2, 25 January 1913; 4, Tom Peacock v Port Vale, Division 2, 23 December 1933; 4, Tom Peacock v Barnsley, Division 2, 9 November 1935; 4, Tom Peacock v Port Vale, Division 2, 23 November 1935; 4, Tom Peacock v Doncaster R, Division 2, 26 December 1935; 4, Tommy Capel v Gillingham, Division 3S, 18 November 1950; 4, Wally Ardron v Hull C, Division 2, 26 December 1952; 4, Tommy Wilson v Barnsley, Division 2, 9 February 1957; 4, Peter Withe v Ipswich T, Division 1, 4 October 1977.

***Most Capped Player:*** Stuart Pearce, 76 (78), England.

***Most League Appearances:*** Bob McKinlay, 614, 1951–70.

***Youngest League Player:*** Craig Westcarr, 16 years 257 days v Burnley, 13 October 2001.

***Record Transfer Fee Received:*** £8,500,000 from Liverpool for Stan Collymore, June 1995.

***Record Transfer Fee Paid:*** £3,500,000 to Celtic for Pierre van Hooijdonk, March 1997.

***Football League Record:*** 1892 Elected to Division 1; 1906–07 Division 2; 1907–11 Division 1; 1911–22 Division 2; 1922–25 Division 1; 1925–49 Division 2; 1949–51 Division 3 (S); 1951–57 Division 2; 1957–72 Division 1; 1972–77 Division 2; 1977–92 Division 1; 1992–93 FA Premier League; 1993–94 Division 1; 1994–97 FA Premier League; 1997–98 Division 1; 1998–99 FA Premier League; 1999–2004 Division 1; 2004– FLC.

## MANAGERS

Harry Radford 1889–97 *(Secretary-Manager)*
Harry Haslam 1897–1909 *(Secretary-Manager)*
Fred Earp 1909–12
Bob Masters 1912–25
John Baynes 1925–29
Stan Hardy 1930–31
Noel Watson 1931–36
Harold Wightman 1936–39
Billy Walker 1939–60
Andy Beattie 1960–63
Johnny Carey 1963–68
Matt Gillies 1969–72
Dave Mackay 1972
Allan Brown 1973–75
Brian Clough 1975–93
Frank Clark 1993–96
Stuart Pearce 1996–97
Dave Bassett 1997–98 *(previously General Manager from February)*
Ron Atkinson 1998–99
David Platt 1999–2001
Paul Hart 2001–04
Joe Kinnear February 2004–

## LATEST SEQUENCES

***Longest Sequence of League Wins:*** 7, 9.5.1979 – 1.9.1979.

***Longest Sequence of League Defeats:*** 14, 21.3.1913 – 27.9.1913.

***Longest Sequence of League Draws:*** 7, 29.4.1978 – 2.9.1978.

***Longest Sequence of Unbeaten League Matches:*** 42, 26.11.1977 – 25.11.1978.

***Longest Sequence Without a League Win:*** 19, 8.9.1998 – 16.1.1999.

***Successive Scoring Runs:*** 22 from 28.3.1931.

***Successive Non-scoring Runs:*** 7 from 13.12.2003.

## TEN YEAR LEAGUE RECORD

| | | P | W | D | L | F | A | Pts | Pos |
|---|---|---|---|---|---|---|---|---|---|
| 1994-95 | PR Lge | 42 | 22 | 11 | 9 | 72 | 43 | 77 | 3 |
| 1995-96 | PR Lge | 38 | 15 | 13 | 10 | 50 | 54 | 58 | 9 |
| 1996-97 | PR Lge | 38 | 6 | 16 | 16 | 31 | 59 | 34 | 20 |
| 1997-98 | Div 1 | 46 | 28 | 10 | 8 | 82 | 42 | 94 | 1 |
| 1998-99 | PR Lge | 38 | 7 | 9 | 22 | 35 | 69 | 30 | 20 |
| 1999-2000 | Div 1 | 46 | 14 | 14 | 18 | 53 | 55 | 56 | 14 |
| 2000-01 | Div 1 | 46 | 20 | 8 | 18 | 55 | 53 | 68 | 11 |
| 2001-02 | Div 1 | 46 | 12 | 18 | 16 | 50 | 51 | 54 | 16 |
| 2002-03 | Div 1 | 46 | 20 | 14 | 12 | 82 | 50 | 74 | 6 |
| 2003-04 | Div 1 | 46 | 15 | 15 | 16 | 61 | 58 | 60 | 14 |

## DID YOU KNOW ?

Tom McInnes was the first Nottingham Forest player to be an ever present in the League team in 1892–93 with 30 appearances. A left-winger he repeated the achievement in 1895–96 and played in a total of 185 League and Cup games scoring 55 goals.

## NOTTINGHAM FOREST 2003–04 LEAGUE RECORD

| *Match No.* | *Date* | *Venue* | *Opponents* | *Result* | *H/T Score* | *Lg. Pos.* | *Goalscorers* | *Attendance* |
|---|---|---|---|---|---|---|---|---|
| 1 | Aug 9 | H | Sunderland | W 2-0 | 2-0 | — | Harewood [19], Louis-Jean [41] | 23,729 |
| 2 | 16 | A | Reading | L 0-3 | 0-0 | 12 | | 16,833 |
| 3 | 23 | H | Cardiff C | L 1-2 | 0-2 | 18 | Harewood [70] | 23,407 |
| 4 | 27 | A | Coventry C | W 3-1 | 1-0 | — | Reid 2 [19, 61], Johnson [65] | 17,586 |
| 5 | 30 | H | Norwich C | W 2-0 | 1-0 | 9 | Johnson [30], Harewood (pen) [51] | 21,058 |
| 6 | Sept 13 | H | Sheffield U | W 3-1 | 1-0 | 5 | Harewood 2 (1 pen) [3 (p), 55], Reid [71] | 25,209 |
| 7 | 16 | A | Burnley | W 3-0 | 1-0 | — | Harewood [7], Reid [76], Taylor [82] | 12,530 |
| 8 | 20 | A | Crewe Alex | L 1-3 | 0-0 | 5 | Harewood [54] | 8685 |
| 9 | 27 | H | Derby Co | D 1-1 | 1-1 | 6 | Reid [27] | 29,059 |
| 10 | Oct 1 | H | Preston NE | L 0-1 | 0-1 | — | | 22,278 |
| 11 | 4 | A | Stoke C | L 1-2 | 0-2 | 9 | Williams [90] | 13,755 |
| 12 | 14 | H | Rotherham U | D 2-2 | 2-0 | — | Harewood 2 [31, 37] | 20,168 |
| 13 | 18 | H | Wimbledon | W 6-0 | 3-0 | 10 | Harewood 2 (1 pen) [24 (p), 37], Reid [45], Taylor [63], Dawson [65], Morgan [81] | 23,520 |
| 14 | 22 | A | West Ham U | D 1-1 | 1-0 | — | Reid [5] | 29,544 |
| 15 | 25 | A | Bradford C | W 2-1 | 0-1 | 8 | Jess [78], Reid [90] | 11,654 |
| 16 | Nov 1 | A | Millwall | L 0-1 | 0-1 | 10 | | 9635 |
| 17 | 4 | A | Walsall | L 1-4 | 1-2 | — | Reid [42] | 7321 |
| 18 | 8 | H | Watford | D 1-1 | 0-0 | 12 | Bopp [54] | 21,229 |
| 19 | 22 | A | Wigan Ath | D 2-2 | 0-1 | 13 | Thompson [51], Harewood [67] | 10,403 |
| 20 | 29 | H | WBA | L 0-3 | 0-2 | 13 | | 27,331 |
| 21 | Dec 3 | H | Ipswich T | D 1-1 | 0-0 | — | Morgan [68] | 21,558 |
| 22 | 6 | A | Watford | D 1-1 | 0-0 | 12 | Reid [89] | 14,988 |
| 23 | 13 | A | Crystal Palace | L 0-1 | 0-1 | 15 | | 16,935 |
| 24 | 26 | A | Norwich C | L 0-1 | 0-1 | 18 | | 16,429 |
| 25 | 28 | H | West Ham U | L 0-2 | 0-1 | 20 | | 27,491 |
| 26 | Jan 10 | A | Sunderland | L 0-1 | 0-1 | 21 | | 26,340 |
| 27 | 17 | H | Reading | L 0-1 | 0-1 | 21 | | 23,116 |
| 28 | 31 | A | Cardiff C | D 0-0 | 0-0 | 22 | | 17,913 |
| 29 | Feb 7 | H | Coventry C | L 0-1 | 0-1 | 22 | | 23,075 |
| 30 | 14 | H | Walsall | D 3-3 | 1-3 | 22 | Impey [3], King [56], Taylor [90] | 25,012 |
| 31 | 21 | A | Rotherham U | D 1-1 | 0-0 | 22 | Jess [90] | 9046 |
| 32 | 25 | H | Gillingham | D 0-0 | 0-0 | — | | 26,473 |
| 33 | 28 | H | Bradford C | W 2-1 | 1-1 | 21 | Reid [9], Taylor [90] | 26,021 |
| 34 | Mar 2 | A | Wimbledon | W 1-0 | 1-0 | — | Taylor [4] | 6317 |
| 35 | 6 | A | Gillingham | L 1-2 | 1-1 | 20 | Barmby [27] | 9096 |
| 36 | 13 | H | Crystal Palace | W 3-2 | 2-0 | 16 | Williams 2 [4, 74], Reid [13] | 28,306 |
| 37 | 17 | H | Burnley | D 1-1 | 0-1 | — | Taylor [80] | 26,885 |
| 38 | 20 | A | Derby Co | L 2-4 | 1-3 | 19 | Taylor [45], Williams [67] | 32,390 |
| 39 | 27 | H | Crewe Alex | W 2-0 | 2-0 | 16 | King 2 [8, 20] | 24,347 |
| 40 | Apr 3 | A | Sheffield U | W 2-1 | 1-0 | 15 | King [24], Taylor [74] | 22,339 |
| 41 | 10 | H | Stoke C | D 0-0 | 0-0 | 15 | | 28,758 |
| 42 | 12 | A | Preston NE | D 2-2 | 2-1 | 16 | King [4], Williams [45] | 15,117 |
| 43 | 17 | H | Millwall | D 2-2 | 0-0 | 16 | Reid [55], Johnson [70] | 22,263 |
| 44 | 24 | A | Ipswich T | W 2-1 | 1-1 | 15 | Johnson 2 [12, 55] | 27,848 |
| 45 | May 1 | H | Wigan Ath | W 1-0 | 0-0 | 15 | Johnson [57] | 29,172 |
| 46 | 9 | A | WBA | W 2-0 | 1-0 | 14 | Williams [4], Johnson [90] | 26,821 |

**Final League Position: 14**

### GOALSCORERS

*League (61):* Reid 13, Harewood 12 (3 pens), Taylor 8, Johnson 7, Williams 6, King 5, Jess 2, Morgan 2, Barmby 1, Bopp 1, Dawson 1, Impey 1, Louis-Jean 1, Thompson 1.
*Carling Cup (2):* Bopp 2.
*FA Cup (1):* King 1 (pen).

| Ward D 32 | Louis-Jean M 37 + 1 | Oyen D 4 | Gunnarsson B 9 + 4 | Thompson J 26 + 6 | Walker D 23 + 2 | Jess E 21 + 13 | Stewart M 11 + 2 | Johnson D 10 + 7 | Harewood M 19 | Reid A 46 | Sonner D 19 + 9 | Morgan W 30 + 2 | Williams G 38 + 1 | Dawson M 30 | Westcarr C — + 3 | Bopp E 9 + 6 | McPhail S 13 + 1 | Taylor G 28 + 6 | Robertson G 12 + 4 | Gardner R 1 + 1 | King M 23 + 1 | Doig C 7 + 3 | Chopra M 3 + 2 | Cash B — + 1 | Rogers A 12 | Impey A 15 + 1 | Roche B 6 + 2 | Barmby N 6 | Evans P 8 | Gerrard P 8 | *Match No.* |
|---|---|---|---|---|---|---|---|---|---|---|---|---|---|---|---|---|---|---|---|---|---|---|---|---|---|---|---|---|---|---|---|
| 1 | 2 | 3 | $4^1$ | 5 | 6 | 7 | 8 | 9 | 10 | 11 | 12 | | | | | | | | | | | | | | | | | | | | 1 |
| 1 | 2 | | $4^1$ | 5 | 6 | 7 | 8 | 9 | 10 | 11 | | 3 | 12 | | | | | | | | | | | | | | | | | | 2 |
| 1 | 2 | 3 | | 5 | | $8^1$ | 7 | $9^2$ | 10 | $11^3$ | | 12 | 4 | 6 | 13 | 14 | | | | | | | | | | | | | | | 3 |
| 1 | 2 | 3 | | 5 | | | | 9 | 10 | 11 | 4 | | 7 | 6 | | | 8 | | | | | | | | | | | | | | 4 |
| 1 | 2 | | | 5 | | | | 9 | 10 | 11 | 4 | 3 | 7 | 6 | | | 8 | | | | | | | | | | | | | | 5 |
| 1 | 2 | | | 5 | | | 12 | $9^2$ | 10 | 11 | 4 | 3 | $7^1$ | 6 | | | 8 | 13 | | | | | | | | | | | | | 6 |
| 1 | 2 | | | 5 | | | | | 10 | 11 | 4 | 3 | 7 | 6 | | | 8 | 9 | | | | | | | | | | | | | 7 |
| 1 | 2 | | | 5 | | | | | 10 | 11 | 4 | 3 | 7 | 6 | | | 8 | 9 | | | | | | | | | | | | | 8 |
| 1 | 2 | | | 5■ | | $12^2$ | | | 10 | 11 | 4 | 3 | 7 | 6 | | | 8 | $9^1$ | 13 | | | | | | | | | | | | 9 |
| 1 | 2 | | | 5 | | 12 | | | 10 | 11 | 4 | 3 | 7 | | | | 8 | $9^1$ | 6 | | | | | | | | | | | | 10 |
| 1 | 2 | | | 5 | | 9 | 7 | | 10 | 11 | | $3^2$ | 4 | 6 | | | $8^1$ | 12 | 13 | | | | | | | | | | | | 11 |
| 1 | 2 | | | | | 7 | 8 | | 10 | 11 | | 3 | | 5 | | | 4 | 9 | 6 | | | | | | | | | | | | 12 |
| 1 | 2 | | | | 6 | 4 | 7 | | $10^2$ | $11^3$ | 12 | 3 | $8^1$ | 5 | | 13 | | 9 | | 14 | | | | | | | | | | | 13 |
| 1 | 2 | | 12 | | 6 | $7^2$ | $8^1$ | | 10 | 11 | 13 | 3 | 4 | 5 | | | | 9 | | | | | | | | | | | | | 14 |
| 1 | 2 | | 12 | 5 | | 7 | $8^1$ | | 10 | 11 | 13 | 3 | 4 | $6^3$ | | | $9^2$ | | 14 | | | | | | | | | | | | 15 |
| 1 | $2^3$ | | | 5 | 6 | $8^2$ | 7 | | 10 | 11 | | 3 | $4^1$ | | | 13 | 12 | 9 | 14 | | | | | | | | | | | | 16 |
| 1 | | | | 5 | 6 | 9 | $7^1$ | | 10 | 11 | | 3 | 4 | | | 12 | 8 | | 2 | | | | | | | | | | | | 17 |
| 1 | 2 | | 4 | 5 | | | | | 10 | 11 | | | | 6 | | 7 | 8 | 9 | 3 | | | | | | | | | | | | 18 |
| 1 | 2 | | 4 | 5 | 12 | | | | 10 | 11 | | | | $6^1$ | | 7 | 8 | 9 | 3 | | | | | | | | | | | | 19 |
| 1 | 2 | | $4^2$ | $5^1$ | 6 | 8 | | | | 10 | | 12 | 11 | | | 7 | | 9 | 3 | | 13 | | | | | | | | | | 20 |
| 1 | 2 | | | | 6 | $8^1$ | | | | 11 | 12 | 5 | 4 | | | 7 | | 9 | 3 | | 10 | | | | | | | | | | 21 |
| 1 | $2^1$ | | 12 | 5 | | 13 | | | | 11 | 4 | 6 | 8 | | | 7 | | $9^2$ | 3 | | 10 | | | | | | | | | | 22 |
| 1 | | | 12 | 2 | 6 | $9^1$ | | | | 11 | $8^3$ | 5■ | 4 | | 14 | 7 | | | $3^2$ | | 10 | 13 | | | | | | | | | 23 |
| 1 | | | | 2 | 6 | $8^1$ | 12 | | | 11 | | 3 | 4 | | | 7 | | 9 | | | 10 | 5 | | | | | | | | | 24 |
| 1 | 2 | | | 3 | | 12 | $7^1$ | | | 11 | | | 4 | 5 | | | | 9 | | 8 | 10 | 6 | | | | | | | | | 25 |
| 1 | 2 | | $4^1$ | 7 | 6 | 12 | | | | 11 | | 5 | 8 | | | 13 | | $9^2$ | 3 | | 10 | | | | | | | | | | 26 |
| 1 | 2 | | $4^1$ | | 6 | | | | | 11 | 8 | 5 | 7 | | | 12 | | 9 | 3 | | 10 | | | | | | | | | | 27 |
| 1 | 2 | 3 | | | 6 | | | | | 11 | 4 | | 7 | | | 8 | | 9 | | | 10 | 5 | | | | | | | | | 28 |
| 1 | 2 | | | | 6 | | | | | 11 | $4^1$ | | 7 | | | 8 | | 12 | 3 | | $10^2$ | 5 | 9 | 13 | | | | | | | 29 |
| 1 | 2 | | | 5 | 6 | 12 | | | | 11 | 4 | | $8^1$ | | | | | 13 | | | 10 | | $9^2$ | | 3 | 7 | | | | | 30 |
| 1 | | | 4 | 2 | $6^3$ | 12 | | | | 11 | 8 | | | 5 | | | | 13 | | | 10 | 14 | $9^2$ | | 3 | $7^1$ | | | | | 31 |
| $1^6$ | | | $4^1$ | 2 | 6 | 12 | | | | 11 | 8 | | | 5 | | | | $9^2$ | | | 10 | | 13 | | 3 | 7 | 15 | | | | 32 |
| | 2 | | | 12 | 6 | 13 | | | | 11 | $8^2$ | | 4 | 5 | | | | 14 | | | 10■ | | | | 3 | $7^1$ | 1 | $9^3$ | | | 33 |
| | 2 | | | 13 | 6 | 12 | | | | 11 | | | 4 | 5 | | | | $9^2$ | | | 10 | | | | 3 | 7 | 1 | $8^1$ | | | 34 |
| | 2 | | | $4^3$ | 6 | 12 | | | | 11 | 13 | 5 | | | | | | $9^1$ | | | 10 | | 14 | | 3■ | 7 | 1 | $8^2$ | | | 35 |
| | 2 | | | 13 | 12 | 8 | | 14 | | 11 | 4 | 6 | $7^2$ | 5 | | | | 9 | | | | | | | $3^1$ | | 1 | $10^3$ | | | 36 |
| | $2^3$ | | | 12 | $6^1$ | 8 | | 13 | | 11 | 4 | 3 | 7 | 5 | | | | 9 | | | | | | | | 14 | 1 | $10^2$ | | | 37 |
| | 2 | | | | | 8 | | 12 | | 11 | 4 | 6 | 7 | 5 | | | | 9 | | | | | | | | 3 | 1 | $10^1$ | | | 38 |
| | 2 | | | 12 | | | | 13 | | 11 | | 6 | $8^1$ | 5 | | | | 9 | | | $10^2$ | 3 | | | | 7 | | | 4 | 1 | 39 |
| | 2 | | | | | | | 12 | | 11 | | 6 | 8 | 5 | | | | 9 | | | $10^1$ | 3 | | | | 7 | | | 4 | 1 | 40 |
| | 2 | | | | | 12 | | 13 | | 11 | | 6 | $8^1$ | 5 | | | | 9 | | | $10^2$ | 3 | | | | 7 | | | 4 | 1 | 41 |
| | 2 | | | | | 13 | | 12 | | $11^2$ | | 6 | 8 | 5 | | | | 9 | | | $10^1$ | | | | 3 | 7 | | | 4 | 1 | 42 |
| | | | | | | 7 | | $9^1$ | | 11 | 12 | 6■ | $8^2$ | 5 | | | | | | | 10 | 13 | | | 3 | 2 | | | 4 | 1 | 43 |
| | | | | 13 | | $7^1$ | | 9 | | 11 | 12 | 6 | $8^2$ | 5 | | | | | | | 10 | | | | 3 | 2 | | | 4 | 1 | 44 |
| | | | | | 6 | $7^1$ | | $9^2$ | | 11 | 12 | | 8 | 5 | 13 | | | | | | 10 | | | | 3 | 2 | 15 | | 4 | $1^6$ | 45 |
| | 12 | | | | 6 | 7 | | 9 | | 11 | | | 8 | 5 | | | | | | | 10 | | | | 3 | $2^1$ | | | 4 | 1 | 46 |

**Carling Cup**

| | | | |
|---|---|---|---|
| First Round | Port Vale | (a) | 0-0 |
| Second Round | Tranmere R | (a) | 0-0 |
| Third Round | Portsmouth | (h) | 2-4 |

**FA Cup**

| | | | |
|---|---|---|---|
| Third Round | WBA | (h) | 1-0 |
| Fourth Round | Sheffield U | (h) | 0-3 |

# NOTTS COUNTY FL Championship 2

## FOUNDATION

According to the official history of Notts County 'the true date of Notts' foundation has to be the meeting at the George Hotel on 7 December 1864'. However, in the same opening chapter is the following: *The Nottingham Guardian* on 28 November 1862 carried the following report: 'The opening of the Nottingham Football Club commenced on Tuesday last at Cremorne Gardens. A side was chosen by W. Arkwright and Chas Deakin. A very spirited game resulted in the latter scoring two goals and two rouges against one and one.'

***The Meadow Lane Stadium, Meadow Lane, Nottingham NG2 3HJ.***

***Telephone:*** (0115) 952 9000.

***Fax:*** (0115) 955 3994.

***Ticket Office:*** (0115) 955 7210.

***Website:*** www.nottscountyfc.co.uk

***Email:*** info@nottscountyfc.co.uk

***Ground Capacity:*** 20,300.

***Record Attendance:*** 47,310 v York C, FA Cup 6th rd, 12 March 1955.

***Pitch Measurements:*** 113yd × 72yd.

***Operations Manager:*** Mark Durkin.

***Secretary:*** Tony Cuthbert.

***Manager:*** Gary Mills.

***Assistant Manager:*** John Gaunt.

***Physio:*** John Haselden.

***Colours:*** Black with white striped shirts, black shorts, white stockings.

***Change Colours:*** Pale blue.

***Year Formed:*** 1862* *(see Foundation).*

***Turned Professional:*** 1885.

***Ltd Co.:*** 1888.

***Club Nickname:*** 'Magpies'.

***Previous Grounds:*** 1862, The Park; 1864, The Meadows; 1877, Beeston Cricket Ground; 1880, Castle Ground; 1883, Trent Bridge; 1910, Meadow Lane.

***First Football League Game:*** 15 September 1888, Football League, v Everton (a) L 1–2 – Holland; Guttridge, McLean; Brown, Warburton, Shelton; Hodder, Harker, Jardine, Moore (1), Wardle.

***Record League Victory:*** 11–1 v Newport Co, Division 3 (S), 15 January 1949 – Smith; Southwell, Purvis; Gannon, Baxter, Adamson; Houghton (1), Sewell (4), Lawton (4), Pimbley, Johnston (2).

***Record Cup Victory:*** 15–0 v Rotherham T (at Trent Bridge), FA Cup 1st rd, 24 October 1885 – Sherwin; Snook, H. T. Moore; Dobson (1), Emmett (1), Chapman; Gunn (1), Albert Moore (2), Jackson (3), Daft (2), Cursham (4), (1 og).

## HONOURS

*Football League:* Division 1 best season: 3rd, 1890–91, 1900–01; Division 2 – Champions 1896–97, 1913–14, 1922–23; Runners-up 1894–95, 1980–81; Promoted from Division 2 1990–91 (play-offs); Division 3 (S) – Champions 1930–31, 1949–50; Runners-up 1936–37; Division 3 – Champions 1997–98; Runners-up 1972–73; Promoted from Division 3 1989–90 (play-offs); Division 4 – Champions 1970–71; Runners-up 1959–60.

*FA Cup:* Winners 1894; Runners-up 1891.

*Football League Cup:* best season: 5th rd, 1964, 1973, 1976.

*Anglo-Italian Cup:* Winners 1995; Runners-up 1994.

## SKY SPORTS FACT FILE

Notts County first toured abroad in 1910 when they visited Denmark. They played three matches against Danish representative teams drawing the first 2-2 and winning the following two games 4-2 and 2-1 in early June.

***Record Defeat:*** 1–9 v Blackburn R, Division 1, 16 November 1889. 1–9 v Aston Villa, Division 1, 29 September 1888. 1–9 v Portsmouth, Division 2, 9 April 1927.

***Most League Points (2 for a win):*** 69, Division 4, 1970–71.

***Most League Points (3 for a win):*** 99, Division 3, 1997–98.

***Most League Goals:*** 107, Division 4, 1959–60.

***Highest League Scorer in Season:*** Tom Keetley, 39, Division 3 (S), 1930–31.

***Most League Goals in Total Aggregate:*** Les Bradd, 124, 1967–78.

***Most League Goals in One Match:*** 5, Robert Jardine v Burnley, Division 1, 27 October 1888; 5, Daniel Bruce v Port Vale, Division 2, 26 February 1895; 5, Bertie Mills v Barnsley, Division 2, 19 November 1927.

***Most Capped Player:*** Kevin Wilson, 15 (42), Northern Ireland.

***Most League Appearances:*** Albert Iremonger, 564, 1904–26.

***Youngest League Player:*** Tony Bircumshaw, 16 years 54 days v Brentford, 3 April 1961.

***Record Transfer Fee Received:*** £2,500,000 from Derby Co for Craig Short, September 1992.

***Record Transfer Fee Paid:*** £685,000 to Sheffield U for Tony Agana, November 1991.

***Football League Record:*** 1888 Founder Member of the Football League; 1893–97 Division 2; 1897–1913 Division 1; 1913–14 Division 2; 1914–20 Division 1; 1920–23 Division 2; 1923–26 Division 1; 1926–30 Division 2; 1930–31 Division 3 (S); 1931–35 Division 2; 1935–50 Division 3 (S); 1950–58 Division 2; 1958–59 Division 3; 1959–60 Division 4; 1960–64 Division 3; 1964–71 Division 4; 1971–73 Division 3; 1973–81 Division 2; 1981–84 Division 1; 1984–85 Division 2; 1985–90 Division 3; 1990–91 Division 2; 1991–95 Division 1; 1995–97 Division 2; 1997–98 Division 3; 1998–2004 Division 2; 2004– FL2.

## LATEST SEQUENCES

***Longest Sequence of League Wins:*** 10, 3.12.1997 – 31.1.1998.

***Longest Sequence of League Defeats:*** 7, 3.9.1983 – 16.10.1983.

***Longest Sequence of League Draws:*** 5, 2.12.1978 – 26.12.1978.

***Longest Sequence of Unbeaten League Matches:*** 19, 26.4.1930 – 6.12.1930.

***Longest Sequence Without a League Win:*** 20, 3.12.1996 – 31.3.1997.

***Successive Scoring Runs:*** 35 from 26.4.1930.

***Successive Non-scoring Runs:*** 5 from 30.11.1912.

## MANAGERS

Edwin Browne 1883–93 *(Secretary-Manager)*
Tom Featherstone 1893 *(Secretary-Manager)*
Tom Harris 1893–1913 *(Secretary-Manager)*
Albert Fisher 1913–27
Horace Henshall 1927–34
Charlie Jones 1934–35
David Pratt 1935
Percy Smith 1935–36
Jimmy McMullan 1936–37
Harry Parkes 1938–39
Tony Towers 1939–42
Frank Womack 1942–43
Major Frank Buckley 1944–46
Arthur Stollery 1946–49
Eric Houghton 1949–53
George Poyser 1953–57
Tommy Lawton 1957–58
Frank Hill 1958–61
Tim Coleman 1961–63
Eddie Lowe 1963–65
Tim Coleman 1965–66
Jack Burkitt 1966–67
Andy Beattie *(General Manager)* 1967
Billy Gray 1967–68
Jimmy Sirrel 1969–75
Ron Fenton 1975–77
Jimmy Sirrel 1978–82 *(continued as General Manager to 1984)*
Howard Wilkinson 1982–83
Larry Lloyd 1983–84
Richie Barker 1984–85
Jimmy Sirrel 1985–87
John Barnwell 1987–88
Neil Warnock 1989–93
Mick Walker 1993–94
Russell Slade 1994–95
Howard Kendall 1995
Colin Murphy 1995 *(continued as General Manager to 1996)*
Steve Thompson 1996
Sam Allardyce 1997–99
Gary Brazil 1999–2000
Jocky Scott 2000–01
Gary Brazil 2001
Billy Dearden 2002–04
Gary Mills January 2004–

## TEN YEAR LEAGUE RECORD

| | | P | W | D | L | F | A | Pts | Pos |
|---|---|---|---|---|---|---|---|---|---|
| 1994-95 | Div 1 | 46 | 9 | 13 | 24 | 45 | 66 | 40 | 24 |
| 1995-96 | Div 2 | 46 | 21 | 15 | 10 | 63 | 39 | 78 | 4 |
| 1996-97 | Div 2 | 46 | 7 | 14 | 25 | 33 | 59 | 35 | 24 |
| 1997-98 | Div 3 | 46 | 29 | 12 | 5 | 82 | 43 | 99 | 1 |
| 1998-99 | Div 2 | 46 | 14 | 12 | 20 | 52 | 61 | 54 | 16 |
| 1999-2000 | Div 2 | 46 | 18 | 11 | 17 | 61 | 55 | 65 | 8 |
| 2000-01 | Div 2 | 46 | 19 | 12 | 15 | 62 | 66 | 69 | 8 |
| 2001-02 | Div 2 | 46 | 13 | 11 | 22 | 59 | 71 | 50 | 19 |
| 2002-03 | Div 2 | 46 | 13 | 16 | 17 | 62 | 70 | 55 | 15 |
| 2003-04 | Div 2 | 46 | 10 | 12 | 24 | 50 | 78 | 42 | 23 |

## DID YOU KNOW ?

Defeats in the last two League games cost Notts County promotion in the 1936–37 season. Spurred by the capture of Hughie Gallacher from Derby County in late September after an indifferent start to the campaign, the Scot hit 25 goals in 32 League games.

## NOTTS COUNTY 2003–04 LEAGUE RECORD

| Match No. | Date | Venue | Opponents | Result | | H/T Score | Lg. Pos. | Goalscorers | Attendance |
|---|---|---|---|---|---|---|---|---|---|
| 1 | Aug 9 | A | Bristol C | L | 0-5 | 0-2 | — | | 12,050 |
| 2 | 16 | H | Wrexham | L | 0-1 | 0-0 | 24 | | 4768 |
| 3 | 23 | A | Swindon T | L | 0-4 | 0-2 | 24 | | 5758 |
| 4 | 25 | H | Peterborough U | L | 0-1 | 0-1 | 24 | | 5177 |
| 5 | 30 | A | Barnsley | D | 1-1 | 0-0 | 24 | Heffernan [90] | 9087 |
| 6 | Sept 6 | H | Luton T | D | 1-1 | 0-1 | 24 | Barras [61] | 7505 |
| 7 | 13 | A | Chesterfield | W | 1-0 | 0-0 | 23 | Bolland [48] | 4367 |
| 8 | 16 | H | Rushden & D | L | 1-3 | 1-1 | — | Stallard [27] | 4250 |
| 9 | 20 | H | Tranmere R | D | 2-2 | 1-1 | 22 | Stallard [4], Platt [71] | 4215 |
| 10 | 27 | A | Blackpool | L | 1-2 | 1-2 | 23 | Stallard (pen) [21] | 6206 |
| 11 | Oct 1 | A | Sheffield W | L | 1-2 | 0-1 | — | Stallard [62] | 20,354 |
| 12 | 4 | H | Colchester U | W | 3-0 | 1-0 | 21 | Heffernan 2 [23, 86], Riley [76] | 4187 |
| 13 | 11 | H | Bournemouth | L | 0-1 | 0-0 | 22 | | 4419 |
| 14 | 18 | A | Stockport Co | D | 2-2 | 0-0 | 22 | Caskey [59], Platt [85] | 4727 |
| 15 | 21 | A | Grimsby T | L | 0-2 | 0-1 | — | | 4274 |
| 16 | 25 | H | Brentford | W | 2-0 | 1-0 | 22 | Platt [26], Caskey [90] | 4145 |
| 17 | Nov 1 | H | Hartlepool U | W | 1-0 | 0-0 | 20 | Baldry [63] | 5011 |
| 18 | 15 | A | Port Vale | L | 0-1 | 0-0 | 22 | | 4900 |
| 19 | 22 | H | Brighton & HA | L | 1-2 | 1-2 | 22 | Heffernan (pen) [35] | 5051 |
| 20 | 29 | A | Oldham Ath | W | 1-0 | 1-0 | 22 | Heffernan [4] | 5190 |
| 21 | Dec 13 | H | Wycombe W | D | 1-1 | 0-1 | 22 | Heffernan [74] | 5014 |
| 22 | 20 | A | Plymouth Arg | L | 0-3 | 0-1 | 22 | | 9923 |
| 23 | 26 | H | QPR | D | 3-3 | 2-2 | 22 | Heffernan 3 (1 pen) [6, 28, 72 (p)] | 7702 |
| 24 | 28 | A | Luton T | L | 0-2 | 0-1 | 23 | | 7181 |
| 25 | Jan 6 | A | Peterborough U | L | 2-5 | 1-2 | — | Riley 2 [44, 47] | 3855 |
| 26 | 10 | H | Bristol C | L | 1-2 | 1-1 | 23 | Butler (og) [42] | 6403 |
| 27 | 17 | A | Wrexham | W | 1-0 | 1-0 | 22 | Parkinson [31] | 4212 |
| 28 | 24 | H | Swindon T | L | 1-2 | 0-1 | 23 | Heffernan (pen) [66] | 6663 |
| 29 | 31 | H | Barnsley | D | 1-1 | 1-0 | 23 | Parkinson [26] | 7355 |
| 30 | Feb 7 | A | QPR | L | 2-3 | 0-0 | 23 | Parkinson [66], Richardson [90] | 14,412 |
| 31 | 14 | A | Bournemouth | L | 0-1 | 0-0 | 23 | | 6332 |
| 32 | 21 | H | Stockport Co | W | 4-1 | 2-0 | 23 | Heffernan 4 (1 pen) [2, 27, 73 (p), 85] | 5618 |
| 33 | 28 | A | Brentford | W | 3-2 | 1-2 | 21 | Richardson [12], Heffernan [72], Scully [82] | 4478 |
| 34 | Mar 2 | H | Grimsby T | W | 3-1 | 2-1 | — | Antoine-Curier [17], Heffernan [28], Scoffham [83] | 6011 |
| 35 | 6 | H | Plymouth Arg | D | 0-0 | 0-0 | 21 | | 8057 |
| 36 | 13 | A | Wycombe W | D | 1-1 | 1-0 | 21 | Heffernan [17] | 5125 |
| 37 | 16 | A | Rushden & D | L | 1-2 | 0-2 | — | Scully [62] | 4030 |
| 38 | 20 | H | Chesterfield | D | 1-1 | 0-0 | 23 | Fenton [51] | 7808 |
| 39 | 27 | A | Tranmere R | L | 0-4 | 0-2 | 23 | | 7308 |
| 40 | Apr 3 | H | Blackpool | W | 4-1 | 3-0 | 23 | Scully [23], Heffernan 2 [29, 78], Scoffham [33] | 5100 |
| 41 | 10 | A | Colchester U | L | 1-4 | 0-2 | 23 | Richardson [88] | 3782 |
| 42 | 12 | H | Sheffield W | D | 0-0 | 0-0 | 23 | | 9601 |
| 43 | 17 | A | Hartlepool U | L | 0-4 | 0-1 | 23 | | 5629 |
| 44 | 24 | H | Port Vale | L | 1-2 | 0-2 | 23 | Heffernan [90] | 5834 |
| 45 | May 1 | A | Brighton & HA | L | 0-1 | 0-0 | 23 | | 6618 |
| 46 | 8 | H | Oldham Ath | D | 1-1 | 0-0 | 23 | Barras [90] | 6715 |

**Final League Position: 23**

### GOALSCORERS

*League (50):* Heffernan 20 (4 pens), Stallard 4 (1 pen), Parkinson 3, Platt 3, Richardson 3, Riley 3, Scully 3, Barras 2, Caskey 2, Scoffham 2, Antoine-Curier 1, Baldry 1, Bolland 1, Fenton 1, own goal 1.
*Carling Cup (4):* Stallard 2 (1 pen), Baldry 1, Barras 1.
*FA Cup (9):* Platt 3, Fenton 2, Barras 1, Heffernan 1, Nicholson 1, Richardson 1.
*LDV Vans Trophy (0).*

| Garden S 12+1 | Jenkins S 17 | Nicholson K 16+7 | Richardson I 40 | Fenton N 42+1 | Barras T 38+2 | Bolland P 35+4 | Brough M 5+5 | Platt C 19 | Stallard M 18+4 | Baraclough I 30+4 | Francis W —+3 | Hackworth T 4+8 | Heffernan P 31+7 | Mildenhall S 28 | Baldry S 32+3 | Caskey D 29+4 | Riley P 13+6 | McFaul S 2+4 | Livesey D 9+2 | Murray A 1+2 | Rhodes C —+1 | Harrad S —+8 | Pipe D 18 | Parkinson A 10+4 | Boertien P 5 | McHugh F 9+4 | McGoldrick D 2+2 | Scully T 6+4 | Oakes S 14 | Antoine-Curier M 4 | Scoffham S 4+11 | Arphexad P 3 | Williams M 5+2 | Bewers J —+3 | Wilson K 2+1 | Deeney S 3 | *Match No.* |
|---|---|---|---|---|---|---|---|---|---|---|---|---|---|---|---|---|---|---|---|---|---|---|---|---|---|---|---|---|---|---|---|---|---|---|---|---|---|
| 1 | 2 | 3 | 4 | 5 | 6 | $7^1$ | 8 | $9^2$ | $10^3$ | 11 | 12 | 13 | 14 | | | | | | | | | | | | | | | | | | | | | | | | 1 |
| | 2 | $3^1$ | $4^2$ | 5 | 6 | 8 | | | 9 | 11 | | 12 | 10 | 1 | 7 | 13 | | | | | | | | | | | | | | | | | | | | | 2 |
| | | $3^2$ | 4 | $5^3$ | 6 | 2 | | 9 | 10 | 11 | | | 12 | 1 | 7 | $8^1$ | 13 | 14 | | | | | | | | | | | | | | | | | | | 3 |
| | | 12 | 4 | 5 | 6 | | | 9 | $10^2$ | 11 | | 14 | 8■ | 1 | 7 | 13 | $3^1$ | $2^3$ | | | | | | | | | | | | | | | | | | | 4 |
| | 2 | 12 | $4^1$ | 5 | 6 | 7 | 13 | 9 | | $11^2$ | | | 14 | 1 | 10 | 8 | $3^3$ | | | | | | | | | | | | | | | | | | | | 5 |
| | | | 4 | | 6 | 2 | | 9 | 12 | 11 | | | 10 | 1 | 7 | 8 | | $3^1$ | 5 | | | | | | | | | | | | | | | | | | 6 |
| | 2 | | 3 | | 6 | $8^1$ | 12 | 9 | 10 | 11 | | | | 1 | 7 | 4 | | | 5 | | | | | | | | | | | | | | | | | | 7 |
| | | $3^3$ | | 5 | 6 | 2 | 12 | $9^2$ | 10 | 11 | | 13 | | 1 | 7 | $8^1$ | 14 | | 4 | | | | | | | | | | | | | | | | | | 8 |
| | | 12 | $3^1$ | 5 | 6 | $2^2$ | 8 | 9 | 10 | 11 | | | | 1 | 7 | 13 | | | 4 | | | | | | | | | | | | | | | | | | 9 |
| | 2 | 3 | 4 | 5 | $6^2$ | | | $9^1$ | 10 | 11 | | | 12 | 1 | 7 | 8 | | | 13 | | | | | | | | | | | | | | | | | | 10 |
| | | $3^2$ | | 5 | 6 | $2^3$ | | 9 | 10 | 11 | | | 12 | 1 | 7 | $8^1$ | 13 | 14 | 4 | | | | | | | | | | | | | | | | | | 11 |
| | $2^1$ | 12 | 3 | 5 | 6 | | 13 | | 9 | 11 | | | 10 | 1 | $7^2$ | 8 | $4^3$ | 14 | | | | | | | | | | | | | | | | | | | 12 |
| | 2 | | $3^2$ | 5 | 6 | 12 | | | 9 | 11 | | 13 | 10 | 1 | 7 | 8 | $4^1$ | | | | | | | | | | | | | | | | | | | | 13 |
| | 2 | | | 5 | 6 | 7 | 8 | 9 | | 11 | | 12 | $10^1$ | 1 | | 3 | | | 4 | | | | | | | | | | | | | | | | | | 14 |
| | 2 | | | 5 | 6 | 3 | $7^2$ | 9 | | 11 | | | 10 | 1 | 12 | 8 | 13 | | $4^1$ | | | | | | | | | | | | | | | | | | 15 |
| | 2 | 12 | $3^1$ | 5 | 6 | | | 9 | | 11 | | | 10 | 1 | 7 | 8 | 4 | | | | | | | | | | | | | | | | | | | | 16 |
| | 2 | 12 | 3 | 5 | 6 | | | 9 | $10^2$ | 11 | | | 13 | 1 | 7 | 8 | $4^1$ | | | | | | | | | | | | | | | | | | | | 17 |
| | 2 | 7 | 3 | 5 | $6^2$ | $4^3$ | | 9 | 10 | $11^1$ | 14 | | 12 | 1 | | 8 | | | 13 | | | | | | | | | | | | | | | | | | 18 |
| | $2^1$ | 13 | $3^2$ | 5 | | | | 9 | 12 | 11 | | | 10 | 1 | 7 | 8 | 6 | | 4 | | | | | | | | | | | | | | | | | | 19 |
| | | 3 | 2 | 5 | | 8 | | 9■ | 12 | | | | $10^1$ | 1 | 7 | | 4 | 13 | $6^2$ | 11 | | | | | | | | | | | | | | | | | 20 |
| | 2 | 3 | 6 | 5 | | $4^2$ | | | $9^1$ | 11 | | 12 | 10 | 1 | 7 | 8 | | | | 13 | | | | | | | | | | | | | | | | | 21 |
| | 2 | 3 | 6 | $5^1$ | 12 | 4 | | | 9 | 11 | | | 10 | 1 | 7 | $8^2$ | | | | 13 | | | | | | | | | | | | | | | | | 22 |
| | $2^1$ | 3 | 6 | 12 | 5 | 4 | | 9 | | 11 | | | 10 | 1 | 7 | | 8 | | | | | | | | | | | | | | | | | | | | 23 |
| | 2 | 3 | 6 | | 5 | $8^2$ | | 9 | 14 | 11 | | 13 | $10^3$ | 1 | 7 | 12 | $4^1$ | | | | | | | | | | | | | | | | | | | | 24 |
| | | 3 | 6 | 2 | 5 | $8^1$ | 12 | | 9 | | | $10^2$ | | 1 | $7^3$ | 4 | 11 | | | | 14 | 13 | | | | | | | | | | | | | | | 25 |
| | | 3 | 6 | 2 | 5 | $8^2$ | 7 | | 9 | | 13 | $10^1$ | | 1 | | 4 | 11 | | | | | 12 | | | | | | | | | | | | | | | 26 |
| | | 3 | 6 | 5 | | 7 | | | 9 | $11^2$ | | 10 | | 1 | | 4 | 12 | | | | | 13 | $2^1$ | 8 | | | | | | | | | | | | | 27 |
| | | | | 5 | | 7 | | | | 11 | | $9^1$ | 10 | 1 | | 4 | | | | | | 12 | 2 | 8 | 3 | $6^2$ | 13 | | | | | | | | | | 28 |
| 15 | | | 6■ | 5 | 13 | $7^1$ | | | | 11 | | | 10 | $1^G$ | | 4 | | | | | | $12^2$ | 2 | 9 | 3 | 8 | | | | | | | | | | | 29 |
| 1 | | $3^1$ | 6 | 5 | | 12 | | | | 7 | | | 10 | | | $4^2$ | | | | | | 13 | 2 | 9 | 11 | 8 | | | | | | | | | | | 30 |
| 1 | | | | 6 | 5 | 7 | | | | 12 | | | 10 | | | | | | | | | 13 | 2 | 9 | 3 | 4 | $11^2$ | $8^1$ | | | | | | | | | 31 |
| 1 | | | 6 | 2 | 5 | $8^1$ | | | | | | | $10^3$ | | | $4^2$ | | | | | | | 7 | | 3 | 12 | | 13 | 11 | 9 | 14 | | | | | | 32 |
| 1 | | | 3 | 6 | 5 | 8 | | | | | | | 10 | | 7 | 4 | | | | | | | 2 | | | $11^1$ | | 12 | | $9^2$ | 13 | | | | | | 33 |
| 1 | | | 3 | 6 | 5 | 8 | | | | | | | 10 | | 7 | $4^2$ | | | | | | | 2 | | | 12 | | | 11 | $9^1$ | 13 | | | | | | 34 |
| 1 | | | 3 | $6^1$ | 5 | 8 | | | | 12 | | | 10 | | $7^3$ | 4 | | | | | | | 2 | | | | | 14 | 11 | $9^2$ | 13 | | | | | | 35 |
| | | | 3 | 6 | 5 | 8 | | | | | | | $10^2$ | | 7 | $4^1$ | | | | | | | 2 | | | 12 | | 9 | 11 | | 13 | 1 | | | | | 36 |
| | | | 3 | 6 | 5 | 8 | | | | 12 | | | 10 | | $7^2$ | $4^1$ | | | | | | | 2 | | | | | 13 | 11 | | 9 | 1 | | | | | 37 |
| | | | 3 | 6 | 5 | 4 | | | | | | | 10 | | | | | | | | | | $2^1$ | 8 | | 12 | | 7 | 11 | | 13 | 1 | $9^2$ | | | | 38 |
| 1 | | | 2 | 6 | 5 | 4 | | | | $3^1$ | | | $10^3$ | | 12 | | | | | | | | | $9^2$ | | 7 | | 8 | 11 | | 13 | | 14 | | | | 39 |
| 1 | | | 3 | 6 | 5 | | | | | | | | 10 | | 7 | | 12 | | | | | | 2 | 13 | | 4 | | $8^1$ | $11^3$ | | $9^2$ | | | 14 | | | 40 |
| 1 | | | 3 | 6 | 5 | 12 | | | | | | | 10 | | 7 | | | | | | | | 2 | 13 | | $4^1$ | 14 | $8^3$ | 11 | | $9^2$ | | | | | | 41 |
| 1 | | | 3 | 6 | 5 | 8 | | | | | | | 10 | | 7 | | | | | | | | 2 | $9^2$ | | | $4^1$ | | 11 | | 12 | | 13 | | | | 42 |
| 1 | | | 3 | 6 | 5 | 8 | | | | | | | 10 | | 7 | | $4^1$ | | | | | | $2^3$ | 12 | | | | | 11 | | 13 | | $9^2$ | | 14 | | 43 |
| | | | 3 | 6 | 5 | 12 | | | | 13 | | | 10 | | $7^2$ | | | | | | | | 2 | 14 | | $4^1$ | | | 11 | | 9 | | $8^3$ | | | 1 | 44 |
| | | | $4^2$ | 6 | 5 | 8 | | | | 11 | | | | | 12 | | | | | | | | $2^1$ | 9 | | | | | $7^3$ | | 13 | | 10 | 14 | 3 | 1 | 45 |
| | | | 2 | 6 | 5 | 4 | | | | 11 | | | | | 7 | | | | | | | 13 | | $9^1$ | | | | | $8^3$ | | 12 | | $10^2$ | 14 | 3 | 1 | 46 |

**Carling Cup**

| | | | |
|---|---|---|---|
| First Round | Preston NE | (a) | 0-0 |
| Second Round | Ipswich T | (h) | 2-1 |
| Third Round | Chelsea | (a) | 2-4 |

**FA Cup**

| | | | |
|---|---|---|---|
| First Round | Shildon | (h) | 7-2 |
| Second Round | Gravesend | (a) | 2-1 |
| Third Round | Middlesbrough | (a) | 0-2 |

**LDV Vans Trophy**

| | | | |
|---|---|---|---|
| First Round | Barnsley | (h) | 0-0 |

# OLDHAM ATHLETIC FL Championship 1

## FOUNDATION

It was in 1895 that John Garland, the landlord of the Featherstall and Junction Hotel, decided to form a football club. As Pine Villa they played in the Oldham Junior League. In 1899 the local professional club, Oldham County, went out of existence and one of the liquidators persuaded Pine Villa to take over their ground at Sheepfoot Lane and change their name to Oldham Athletic.

***Boundary Park, Oldham OL1 2PA.***

***Telephone:*** 0870 753 2000.

***Fax:*** (0161) 652 6501.

***Ticket Office:*** 0870 753 2000.

***Website:*** www.oldhamathletic.co.uk

***Email:*** info@oldhamathletic.co.uk

***Ground Capacity:*** 13,595.

***Record Attendance:*** 46,471 v Sheffield W, FA Cup 4th rd, 25 January 1930.

***Pitch Measurements:*** 110yd × 74yd.

***Chairman:*** Barry Chatow.

***Managing Director:*** Simon Corney.

***Chief Executive/Secretary:*** Alan Hardy.

***Manager:*** Brian Talbot.

***Assistant Manager:*** John Sheridan.

***Physio:*** Lee Nobes.

***Colours:*** Royal blue shirts with white piping, royal blue shorts, white stockings.

***Change Colours:*** Black shirts with silver piping, black shorts, black stockings.

***Year Formed:*** 1895.

***Turned Professional:*** 1899.

***Ltd Co.:*** 1906.

***Previous Name:*** 1895, Pine Villa; 1899, Oldham Athletic.

***Club Nickname:*** 'The Latics'.

***Previous Grounds:*** 1895, Sheepfoot Lane; 1900, Hudson Field; 1906, Sheepfoot Lane; 1907, Boundary Park.

***First Football League Game:*** 9 September 1907, Division 2, v Stoke (a) W 3–1 – Hewitson; Hodson, Hamilton; Fay, Walders, Wilson; Ward, W. Dodds (1), Newton (1), Hancock, Swarbrick (1).

***Record League Victory:*** 11–0 v Southport, Division 4, 26 December 1962 – Bollands; Branagan, Marshall; McCall, Williams, Scott; Ledger (1), Johnstone, Lister (6), Colquhoun (1), Whitaker (3).

## HONOURS

*Football League:* Division 1 – Runners-up 1914–15; Division 2 – Champions 1990–91; Runners-up 1909–10; Division 3 (N) – Champions 1952–53; Division 3 – Champions 1973–74; Division 4 – Runners-up 1962–63.

*FA Cup:* Semi-final 1913, 1990, 1994.

*Football League Cup:* Runners-up 1990.

## SKY SPORTS FACT FILE

During the 1929–30 season, Oldham Athletic established an attendance record for the club in League games. On 21 April the visit of Blackpool attracted a crowd of 45,120 with receipts of £2,458 for this Second Division encounter.

***Record Cup Victory:*** 10–1 v Lytham, FA Cup 1st rd, 28 November 1925 – Gray; Wynne, Grundy; Adlam, Heaton, Naylor (1), Douglas, Pynegar (2), Ormston (2), Barnes (3), Watson (2).

***Record Defeat:*** 4–13 v Tranmere R, Division 3 (N), 26 December 1935.

***Most League Points (2 for a win):*** 62, Division 3, 1973–74.

***Most League Points (3 for a win):*** 88, Division 2, 1990–91.

***Most League Goals:*** 95, Division 4, 1962–63.

***Highest League Scorer in Season:*** Tom Davis, 33, Division 3 (N), 1936–37.

***Most League Goals in Total Aggregate:*** Roger Palmer, 141, 1980–94.

***Most League Goals in One Match:*** 7, Eric Gemmell v Chester, Division 3N, 19 January 1952.

***Most Capped Player:*** Gunnar Halle, 24 (64), Norway.

***Most League Appearances:*** Ian Wood, 525, 1966–80.

***Youngest League Player:*** Wayne Harrison, 15 years 11 months v Notts Co, 27 October 1984.

***Record Transfer Fee Received:*** £1,700,000 from Aston Villa for Earl Barrett, February 1992.

***Record Transfer Fee Paid:*** £750,000 to Aston Villa for Ian Olney, June 1992.

***Football League Record:*** 1907 Elected to Division 2; 1910–23 Division 1; 1923–35 Division 2; 1935–53 Division 3 (N); 1953–54 Division 2; 1954–58 Division 3 (N); 1958–63 Division 4; 1963–69 Division 3; 1969–71 Division 4; 1971–74 Division 3; 1974–91 Division 2; 1991–92 Division 1; 1992–94 FA Premier League; 1994–97 Division 1; 1997–2004 Division 2; 2004– FL1.

## MANAGERS

David Ashworth 1906–14
Herbert Bamlett 1914–21
Charlie Roberts 1921–22
David Ashworth 1923–24
Bob Mellor 1924–27
Andy Wilson 1927–32
Jimmy McMullan 1933–34
Bob Mellor 1934–45
*(continued as Secretary to 1953)*
Frank Womack 1945–47
Billy Wootton 1947–50
George Hardwick 1950–56
Ted Goodier 1956–58
Norman Dodgin 1958–60
Jack Rowley 1960–63
Les McDowall 1963–65
Gordon Hurst 1965–66
Jimmy McIlroy 1966–68
Jack Rowley 1968–69
Jimmy Frizzell 1970–82
Joe Royle 1982–94
Graeme Sharp 1994–97
Neil Warnock 1997–98
Andy Ritchie 1998–2001
Mick Wadsworth 2001–02
Iain Dowie 2002–03
Brian Talbot March 2004–

## LATEST SEQUENCES

***Longest Sequence of League Wins:*** 10, 12.1.1974 – 12.3.1974.

***Longest Sequence of League Defeats:*** 8, 15.12.1934 – 2.2.1935.

***Longest Sequence of League Draws:*** 5, 26.12.1982 – 15.1.1983.

***Longest Sequence of Unbeaten League Matches:*** 20, 1.5.1990 – 10.11.1990.

***Longest Sequence Without a League Win:*** 17, 4.9.1920 – 18.12.1920.

***Successive Scoring Runs:*** 25 from 15.1.1927.

***Successive Non-scoring Runs:*** 6 from 4.2.1922.

## TEN YEAR LEAGUE RECORD

| | | *P* | *W* | *D* | *L* | *F* | *A* | *Pts* | *Pos* |
|---|---|---|---|---|---|---|---|---|---|
| 1994-95 | Div 1 | 46 | 16 | 13 | 17 | 60 | 60 | 61 | 14 |
| 1995-96 | Div 1 | 46 | 14 | 14 | 18 | 54 | 50 | 56 | 18 |
| 1996-97 | Div 1 | 46 | 10 | 13 | 23 | 51 | 66 | 43 | 23 |
| 1997-98 | Div 2 | 46 | 15 | 16 | 15 | 62 | 54 | 61 | 13 |
| 1998-99 | Div 2 | 46 | 14 | 9 | 23 | 48 | 66 | 51 | 20 |
| 1999-2000 | Div 2 | 46 | 16 | 12 | 18 | 50 | 55 | 60 | 14 |
| 2000-01 | Div 2 | 46 | 15 | 13 | 18 | 53 | 65 | 58 | 15 |
| 2001-02 | Div 2 | 46 | 18 | 16 | 12 | 77 | 65 | 70 | 9 |
| 2002-03 | Div 2 | 46 | 22 | 16 | 8 | 68 | 38 | 82 | 5 |
| 2003-04 | Div 2 | 46 | 12 | 21 | 13 | 66 | 60 | 57 | 15 |

## DID YOU KNOW ?

With 110 League goals for Oldham Athletic in six years from 1947 despite his best years lost in the war, Eric Gemmell was only part-time, working as a salesman. In summer he was a cricket professional in the Levenshulme League.

## OLDHAM ATHLETIC 2003–04 LEAGUE RECORD

| *Match No.* | *Date* | *Venue* | *Opponents* | *Result* | | *H/T Score* | *Lg. Pos.* | *Goalscorers* | *Attendance* |
|---|---|---|---|---|---|---|---|---|---|
| 1 | Aug 9 | H | Brighton & HA | L | 1-3 | 0-2 | — | Murray [82] | 6522 |
| 2 | 16 | A | Sheffield W | D | 2-2 | 1-1 | 20 | Sheridan J (pen) [5], Antoine-Curier [55] | 24,630 |
| 3 | 23 | H | Blackpool | L | 2-3 | 1-0 | 20 | Eyre [1], Antoine-Curier [90] | 6745 |
| 4 | 25 | A | Brentford | L | 1-2 | 1-1 | 21 | Holden [17] | 4073 |
| 5 | 30 | H | Rushden & D | W | 3-2 | 1-1 | 20 | Sheridan J (pen) [11], Haining [75], O'Halloran [90] | 5469 |
| 6 | Sept 6 | A | Hartlepool U | D | 0-0 | 0-0 | 19 | | 5728 |
| 7 | 13 | H | Bristol C | D | 1-1 | 0-1 | 19 | Zola Makongo [54] | 5921 |
| 8 | 16 | A | Barnsley | D | 1-1 | 0-0 | — | Vernon [65] | 10,102 |
| 9 | 20 | A | Wycombe W | W | 5-2 | 3-0 | 17 | Murray 2 [1, 85], Hall D [16], Zola Makongo [21], Killen (pen) [75] | 4725 |
| 10 | 27 | H | Luton T | W | 3-0 | 2-0 | 16 | Sheridan J (pen) [30], Zola Makongo [45], Holden [47] | 6077 |
| 11 | 30 | H | Stockport Co | W | 2-0 | 1-0 | — | Sheridan J (pen) [11], Vernon [46] | 7015 |
| 12 | Oct 4 | A | Peterborough U | D | 2-2 | 1-1 | 11 | Cooksey [8], Sheridan J (pen) [57] | 4465 |
| 13 | 11 | H | Port Vale | W | 2-1 | 0-0 | 9 | Killen [71], Eyres [87] | 6913 |
| 14 | 18 | A | Tranmere R | L | 1-2 | 1-0 | 11 | Eyre [30] | 8202 |
| 15 | 21 | A | Wrexham | L | 0-4 | 0-2 | — | | 3963 |
| 16 | 25 | H | Bournemouth | D | 1-1 | 1-1 | 15 | Vernon [30] | 5850 |
| 17 | Nov 1 | A | Plymouth Arg | D | 2-2 | 1-1 | 16 | Beharall 2 [10, 63] | 11,205 |
| 18 | 15 | H | Swindon T | L | 0-1 | 0-0 | 18 | | 5282 |
| 19 | 22 | A | Chesterfield | D | 1-1 | 0-1 | 18 | Zola Makongo [55] | 3565 |
| 20 | 29 | H | Notts Co | L | 0-1 | 0-1 | 19 | | 5190 |
| 21 | Dec 13 | A | Colchester U | L | 1-2 | 0-0 | 19 | Eyres [66] | 2897 |
| 22 | 20 | H | QPR | W | 2-1 | 0-1 | 19 | Cooksey [67], Eyre [86] | 5603 |
| 23 | 26 | A | Grimsby T | D | 3-3 | 2-1 | 17 | Johnson [19], Cooksey [32], Vernon [73] | 6172 |
| 24 | 28 | H | Hartlepool U | L | 0-2 | 0-1 | 18 | | 6243 |
| 25 | Jan 3 | H | Brentford | D | 1-1 | 0-1 | 18 | Vernon [54] | 4990 |
| 26 | 10 | A | Brighton & HA | D | 0-0 | 0-0 | 18 | | 6036 |
| 27 | 17 | H | Sheffield W | W | 1-0 | 1-0 | 15 | Vernon [17] | 9316 |
| 28 | 24 | A | Blackpool | D | 1-1 | 0-1 | 16 | Vernon [68] | 7508 |
| 29 | 31 | A | Rushden & D | L | 1-4 | 0-2 | 17 | Johnson [55] | 4591 |
| 30 | Feb 8 | H | Grimsby T | W | 6-0 | 5-0 | 16 | Vernon 3 [9, 16, 45], Griffin [27], Johnson [34], Zola Makongo [88] | 13,007 |
| 31 | 14 | A | Port Vale | L | 0-1 | 0-0 | 17 | | 6035 |
| 32 | 21 | H | Tranmere R | D | 1-1 | 0-0 | 17 | Vernon [60] | 6916 |
| 33 | 28 | A | Bournemouth | L | 0-1 | 0-0 | 18 | | 6594 |
| 34 | Mar 6 | A | QPR | D | 1-1 | 1-0 | 18 | Murray [45] | 13,696 |
| 35 | 13 | H | Colchester U | D | 0-0 | 0-0 | 19 | | 5937 |
| 36 | 16 | H | Barnsley | D | 1-1 | 0-1 | — | Murray [53] | 5837 |
| 37 | 20 | A | Bristol C | W | 2-0 | 2-0 | 16 | Cooksey [26], Murray [36] | 11,037 |
| 38 | 27 | H | Wycombe W | L | 2-3 | 2-2 | 17 | Murray [18], Eyre [44] | 5758 |
| 39 | Apr 3 | A | Luton T | D | 1-1 | 1-1 | 17 | Crowe [33] | 5966 |
| 40 | 10 | H | Peterborough U | D | 1-1 | 0-1 | 18 | Vernon [90] | 5688 |
| 41 | 12 | A | Stockport Co | D | 1-1 | 1-1 | 19 | Haining [1] | 8617 |
| 42 | 17 | H | Plymouth Arg | W | 4-1 | 3-0 | 16 | Johnson [34], Owen [42], Eyres [45], Murray [67] | 6924 |
| 43 | 20 | H | Wrexham | D | 1-1 | 1-1 | — | Holden [45] | 5646 |
| 44 | 24 | A | Swindon T | W | 2-1 | 1-0 | 15 | Murray [8], Johnson [74] | 8506 |
| 45 | May 1 | H | Chesterfield | W | 2-0 | 0-0 | 15 | Eyre 2 [50, 81] | 8177 |
| 46 | 8 | A | Notts Co | D | 1-1 | 0-0 | 15 | Holden [61] | 6715 |

**Final League Position: 15**

### GOALSCORERS

*League (66):* Vernon 12, Murray 9, Eyre 6, Johnson 5, Sheridan J 5 (5 pens), Zola Makongo 5, Cooksey 4, Holden 4, Eyres 3, Antoine-Curier 2, Beharall 2, Haining 2, Killen 2 (1 pen), Crowe 1, Griffin 1, Hall D 1, O'Halloran 1, Owen 1.
*Carling Cup (1):* Antoine-Curier 1.
*FA Cup (5):* Cooksey 2, Eyre 1, Johnson 1, Zola Makongo 1.
*LDV Vans Trophy (4):* Vernon 2, Boshell 1, Zola Makongo 1.

| Pogliacomi L 46 | Murray P 41 | Boshell D 16 + 6 | Hall D 28 + 3 | Ndiwa L 3 + 1 | Haining W 30 + 1 | Eyre J 42 + 1 | Sheridan D 18 + 9 | Killen C 7 + 6 | Vernon S 28 + 17 | Walker R 1 | O'Halloran M 2 + 11 | Roca C — + 7 | Antoine-Curier M 5 + 3 | Clegg M 28 + 4 | Sheridan J 19 + 3 | Holden D 37 + 2 | Eyres D 22 + 7 | Hudson M 15 | Cooksey E 22 + 14 | Zola Makongo C 21 + 4 | Beharall D 7 | Hall C — + 1 | Wolfenden M — + 1 | Tierney M — + 2 | Johnson J 18 + 2 | Griffin A 25 + 1 | Owen G 15 | Fleming C — + 1 | Wilkinson W 2 + 3 | Bonner M 6 + 1 | Crowe D 2 + 3 | Lomax K — + 1 | Barlow M — + 1 | *Match No.* |
|---|---|---|---|---|---|---|---|---|---|---|---|---|---|---|---|---|---|---|---|---|---|---|---|---|---|---|---|---|---|---|---|---|---|---|
| 1 | 2 | $3^1$ | 4 | 5 | $6^2$ | 7 | 8 | $9^3$ | 10 | 11 | 12 | 13 | 14 | | | | | | | | | | | | | | | | | | | | | 1 |
| 1 | 2 | | 4■ | 5 | 6 | 10 | 11 | | 12 | | $7^2$ | | $9^1$ | 3 | 8 | 13 | | | | | | | | | | | | | | | | | | 2 |
| 1 | 7 | 12 | 4 | 5 | | $10^3$ | 11 | | 14 | | | 13 | 9 | $2^2$ | $8^1$ | 6 | 3 | | | | | | | | | | | | | | | | | 3 |
| 1 | 2 | | $4^1$ | 13 | 6 | 9 | 11 | | 14 | | | | $10^2$ | | 12 | 5 | 3 | 7 | $8^3$ | | | | | | | | | | | | | | | 4 |
| 1 | 2 | | | | 6 | 10 | | | 12 | | 13 | 14 | $9^1$ | $7^2$ | $8^3$ | 5 | 3 | 4 | 11 | | | | | | | | | | | | | | | 5 |
| 1 | 2 | | 4 | | $6^2$ | 7 | | | 12 | | 14 | | $9^1$ | 13 | 8 | 11 | 3 | 5 | | $10^3$ | | | | | | | | | | | | | | 6 |
| 1 | 7 | | 4 | | | 11 | | | $9^1$ | | 13 | | 12 | 6 | $8^3$ | 2 | 3 | 5 | 14 | $10^2$ | | | | | | | | | | | | | | 7 |
| 1 | 7 | | 4 | | | 11 | 12 | 13 | $9^2$ | | | | 14 | 2 | $8^1$ | 6 | 3 | 5 | | $10^3$ | | | | | | | | | | | | | | 8 |
| 1 | 7 | | 4 | | | 11 | 12 | 13 | $9^3$ | | 14 | | | 2 | $8^1$ | 6 | 3 | 5 | | $10^2$ | | | | | | | | | | | | | | 9 |
| 1 | 7 | | 5 | | | $11^3$ | 12 | 13 | $9^2$ | | | | | 2 | $8^1$ | 4 | 3 | 6 | 14 | 10 | | | | | | | | | | | | | | 10 |
| 1 | 7 | | 4 | | | 11 | 12 | 13 | $9^3$ | | 14 | | | 2 | $8^1$ | 6 | 3 | 5 | | $10^2$ | | | | | | | | | | | | | | 11 |
| 1 | | 12 | 4 | | | $7^1$ | 6 | 10■ | $9^3$ | | 13 | | | 2 | 8 | | | 5 | 11 | | $3^2$ | 14 | | | | | | | | | | | | 12 |
| 1 | 7 | | 4 | | | 11 | 12 | $9^2$ | 13 | | | | | 2 | $8^1$ | 6 | $3^3$ | 5 | 14 | 10 | | | | | | | | | | | | | | 13 |
| 1 | 7 | | 4 | | | 11 | 12 | | $9^2$ | | 13 | | | 2 | $8^3$ | 6 | $3^1$ | 5 | 14 | 10 | | | | | | | | | | | | | | 14 |
| 1 | 7 | | $4^1$ | | | 11 | 3 | $9^3$ | 12 | | 13 | | | 2 | $8^2$ | 6 | | | 14 | 10 | 5 | | | | | | | | | | | | | 15 |
| 1 | 7 | | 4 | | | 11 | 12 | | 9 | | | | | 2 | $8^1$ | 6 | | | 3 | 10 | 5 | | | | | | | | | | | | | 16 |
| 1 | 7■ | | 12 | | $4^1$ | 11 | 13 | | $9^2$ | | 14 | | | $2^3$ | 8■ | 6 | | | 3 | 10 | 5 | | | | | | | | | | | | | 17 |
| 1 | | $8^3$ | $4^2$ | | 7 | 11 | | | 9 | | 13 | 12 | | $2^1$ | | 6 | | | 3 | 10 | 5 | | 14 | | | | | | | | | | | 18 |
| 1 | | $8^1$ | 4 | | 11 | | | | 9 | | 7 | | | 2 | | 6 | | | 3 | 10 | 5 | | | 12 | | | | | | | | | | 19 |
| 1 | | | $4^3$ | | 2 | 11 | | | $9^2$ | | | 13 | | 12 | | 7 | | 6 | 3 | 10 | $5^1$ | | | | 8 | 14 | | | | | | | | 20 |
| 1 | 7 | $6^1$ | 4 | | 5 | $9^2$ | | | 13 | | | | | 2 | | | 12 | | 11 | 10 | | | | | 8 | 3 | | | | | | | | 21 |
| 1 | 4 | 12 | | | 5 | 9 | | | 13 | | | | | 2 | | | $11^1$ | 6 | 7 | $10^2$ | | | | | 8 | 3 | | | | | | | | 22 |
| 1 | 7 | $4^1$ | | | 5 | 9 | | | 13 | | | 14 | | 2 | | | 12 | 6 | $11^3$ | $10^2$ | | | | | 8 | 3 | | | | | | | | 23 |
| 1 | | $4^3$ | | | 5 | 9 | | | 13 | | | 14 | | 2 | | 12 | 11 | 6 | 7 | $10^2$ | | | | | 8 | $3^1$ | | | | | | | | 24 |
| 1 | 2 | 12 | 4 | | 5 | 11 | $7^1$ | | 9 | | | | | | 8 | 6 | | | 13 | | | | | | 10 | $3^2$ | | | | | | | | 25 |
| 1 | 2 | 8 | 4 | | 5 | 7 | | | $9^1$ | | | | | | 12 | 6 | | | 11 | | | | | 13 | 10 | $3^2$ | | | | | | | | 26 |
| 1 | 2 | 7 | 4 | | | | | | $9^1$ | | | | | 12 | $8^2$ | 5 | 13 | | 11 | | | | | | 10 | 3 | 6 | | | | | | | 27 |
| 1 | 2 | 8 | 4 | | 5 | | | | $9^1$ | | | | | | | 7 | | | 11 | | | | | | 10 | 3 | 6 | 12 | | | | | | 28 |
| 1 | 7 | 8 | $4^1$ | | 5 | $12^2$ | | | $9^3$ | | | | | 13 | | 2 | | | 11 | 14 | | | | | 10 | 3 | 6 | | | | | | | 29 |
| 1 | 7 | 4 | 12 | | $5^1$ | 11 | | | $9^3$ | | | | | | $8^2$ | 2 | 13 | | | 14 | | | | | 10 | 3 | 6 | | | | | | | 30 |
| 1 | 7 | $4^2$ | | | 5 | 8 | | | $9^3$ | | | | | 2 | 12 | | 13 | | $11^1$ | 14 | | | | | 10 | 3 | 6 | | | | | | | 31 |
| 1 | $7^3$ | $4^1$ | | | 5 | 11 | | 13 | 9 | | | | | 2 | 8 | | 12 | | 14 | $10^2$ | | | | | | 3 | 6 | | | | | | | 32 |
| 1 | 7 | 4 | | | 5 | 8 | | 12 | $9^2$ | | | | | $2^1$ | | 3 | 11 | | 14 | 13 | | | | | 10 | | $6^3$ | | | | | | | 33 |
| 1 | 7 | $4^2$ | | | | 8 | | 9■ | 12 | | | | | 2 | | 5 | 11 | | 13 | $10^1$ | | | | | | 3 | 6 | | | | | | | 34 |
| 1 | 7 | 12 | | | | 8 | $4^1$ | 9 | 13 | | | | | 2 | | 5 | 11 | | | $10^2$ | | | | | | 3 | 6 | | | | | | | 35 |
| 1 | 7 | 12 | | | | $8^1$ | 4 | $9^2$ | 10 | | | | | 2 | | 5 | | | 11 | | | | | | | 3 | 6 | | 13 | | | | | 36 |
| 1 | 7 | $4^2$ | | | 12 | 9 | 8 | | 10 | | | | | 2 | | 5 | | | 11 | | | | | | | 3 | $6^1$ | | 13 | | | | | 37 |
| 1 | 7 | | | | 5 | 8 | $4^1$ | | $9^2$ | | | | | 2 | | 6 | | | 11 | | | | | | 13 | 3 | | | $10^3$ | 12 | 14 | | | 38 |
| 1 | 7 | | | | 5 | 8 | 4 | | | | | | | | | 2 | | | 11 | | | | | | 12 | 3 | 6 | | $9^1$ | | 10 | | | 39 |
| 1 | 7 | | 12 | | $5^1$ | 9 | 4 | | 14 | | | | | | | 2 | 13 | | $11^2$ | | | | | | 8 | 3 | 6 | | | | $10^3$ | | | 40 |
| 1 | 7 | | | | 5 | 9 | 12 | | $10^1$ | | | | | | | 2 | $11^2$ | | 13 | | | | | | $8^3$ | 3 | 6 | | 14 | 4 | | | | 41 |
| 1 | 7 | | | | 5 | $9^1$ | 8 | | 12 | | | | | | | 2 | $11^2$ | | 13 | | | | | | 10■ | 3 | 6 | | | 4 | | | | 42 |
| 1 | 7 | | 6 | | 5 | $9^1$ | $8^2$ | | 12 | | | | | | | 2 | 11 | | 13 | | | | | | $10^3$ | 3 | | | | 4 | 14 | | | 43 |
| 1 | 7 | | 6 | | 5 | $9^1$ | 8 | | 12 | | | | | | | 2 | $11^2$ | | 13 | | | | | | 10 | 3 | | | | 4 | | | | 44 |
| 1 | 7 | | 6 | | 5 | 9 | 8 | | $10^1$ | | | | | | | 2 | 11 | | | | | | | | | 3 | | | | 4 | 12 | | | 45 |
| 1 | 7 | | 6 | | 5 | 9 | $8^2$ | | $10^3$ | | | | | | | 2 | $11^1$ | | 12 | | | | | | | 3 | | | | 4 | | 13 | 14 | 46 |

**Carling Cup**
First Round Scunthorpe U (a) 1-2

**LDV Vans Trophy**
First Round Hartlepool U (h) 3-3
Second Round Bury (a) 1-2

**FA Cup**
First Round Carlisle U (h) 3-0
Second Round Blackpool (h) 2-5

# OXFORD UNITED FL Championship 2

## FOUNDATION

There had been an Oxford United club around the time of World War I but only in the Oxfordshire Thursday League and there is no connection with the modern club which began as Headington in 1893, adding 'United' a year later. Playing first on Quarry Fields and subsequently Wootten's Fields, they owe much to a Dr Hitchings for their early development.

***The Kassam Stadium, Grenoble Road, Oxford OX4 4XP.***

***Telephone:*** (01865) 337 500.

***Fax:*** (01865) 337 555.

***Ticket Office:*** (01865) 337 533.

***Website:*** www.oufc.co.uk

***Email:*** admin@oufc.co.uk

***Ground Capacity:*** 12,973.

***Record Attendance:*** 22,730 v Preston NE, FA Cup 6th rd, 29 February 1964.

***Pitch Measurements:*** 115yd × 74yd.

***Chairman:*** Firoz Kassam.

***Manager:*** Graham Rix.

***Physio:*** Neil Sullivan.

***Secretary:*** Mick Brown.

***Colours:*** Yellow shirts, navy shorts, navy stockings.

***Change Colours:*** All black.

***Year Formed:*** 1893.

***Turned Professional:*** 1949.

***Ltd Co.:*** 1949.

***Club Nickname:*** 'The U's'.

***Previous Names:*** 1893, Headington; 1894, Headington United; 1960, Oxford United.

***Previous Grounds:*** 1893, Headington Quarry; 1894, Wootten's Field; 1898, Sandy Lane Ground; 1902, Britannia Field; 1909, Sandy Lane; 1910, Quarry Recreation Ground; 1914, Sandy Lane; 1922, The Paddock Manor Road; 1925, Manor Ground; 2001, The Kassam Stadium.

***First Football League Game:*** 18 August 1962, Division 4, v Barrow (a) L 2–3 – Medlock; Beavon, Quartermain; R. Atkinson, Kyle, Jones; Knight, G. Atkinson (1), Houghton (1), Cornwell, Colfar.

***Record League Victory:*** 7–0 v Barrow, Division 4, 19 December 1964 – Fearnley; Beavon, Quartermain; R. Atkinson (1), Kyle, Jones; Morris, Booth (3), Willey (1), G. Atkinson (1), Harrington (1).

## HONOURS

*Football League:* Division 1 best season: 12th, 1997–98; Division 2 – Champions 1984–85; Runners-up 1995–96; Division 3 – Champions 1967–68, 1983–84; Division 4 – Promoted 1964–65 (4th).

*FA Cup:* best season: 6th rd, 1964 (shared record for 4th Division club).

*Football League Cup:* Winners 1986.

## SKY SPORTS FACT FILE

On 24 November 1984 Oxford United scored their 50th League and Cup goal of the season in beating Leeds United 5-2. It was their tenth successive home win. But it required a determined comeback because Leeds had led 2-0 after 22 minutes.

***Record Cup Victory:*** 9–1 v Dorchester T, FA Cup 1st rd, 11 November 1995 – Whitehead; Wood (2), Ford M (1), Smith, Elliott, Gilchrist, Rush (1), Massey (Murphy), Moody (3), Ford R (1), Angel (Beauchamp (1)).

***Record Defeat:*** 0–7 v Sunderland, Division 1, 19 September 1998.

***Most League Points (2 for a win):*** 61, Division 4, 1964–65.

***Most League Points (3 for a win):*** 95, Division 3, 1983–84.

***Most League Goals:*** 91, Division 3, 1983–84.

***Highest League Scorer in Season:*** John Aldridge, 30, Division 2, 1984–85.

***Most League Goals in Total Aggregate:*** Graham Atkinson, 77, 1962–73.

***Most League Goals in One Match:*** 4, Tony Jones v Newport Co, Division 4, 22 September 1962; 4, Arthur Longbottom v Darlington, Division 4, 26 October 1963; 4, Richard Hill v Walsall, Division 2, 26 December 1988; 4, John Durnin v Luton T, 14 November 1992.

***Most Capped Player:*** Jim Magilton, 18 (52\), Northern Ireland.

***Most League Appearances:*** John Shuker, 478, 1962–77.

***Youngest League Player:*** Jason Seacole, 16 years 149 days v Mansfield T, 7 September 1976.

***Record Transfer Fee Received:*** £1,600,000 from Leicester C for Matt Elliott, January 1997.

***Record Transfer Fee Paid:*** £475,000 to Aberdeen for Dean Windass, August 1998.

***Football League Record:*** 1962 Elected to Division 4; 1965–68 Division 3; 1968–76 Division 2; 1976–84 Division 3; 1984–85 Division 2; 1985–88 Division 1; 1988–92 Division 2; 1992–94 Division 1; 1994–96 Division 2; 1996–99 Division 1; 1999–2001 Division 2; 2001–04 Division 3; 2004– FL2.

### MANAGERS

Harry Thompson 1949–58
*(Player-Manager)* 1949-51
Arthur Turner 1959–69
*(continued as General Manager to 1972)*
Ron Saunders 1969
Gerry Summers 1969–75
Mick Brown 1975–79
Bill Asprey 1979–80
Ian Greaves 1980–82
Jim Smith 1982–85
Maurice Evans 1985–88
Mark Lawrenson 1988
Brian Horton 1988–93
Denis Smith 1993–97
Malcolm Crosby 1997
Malcolm Shotton 1998–99
Denis Smith 2000
David Kemp 2000–01
Mark Wright 2001
Ian Atkins 2001–04
Graham Rix March 2004–

### LATEST SEQUENCES

***Longest Sequence of League Wins:*** 6, 6.4.1985 – 24.4.1985.

***Longest Sequence of League Defeats:*** 7, 4.5.1991 – 7.9.1991.

***Longest Sequence of League Draws:*** 5, 7.10.1978 – 28.10.1978.

***Longest Sequence of Unbeaten League Matches:*** 20, 17.3.1984 – 29.9.1984.

***Longest Sequence Without a League Win:*** 27, 14.11.1987 – 27.8.1988.

***Successive Scoring Runs:*** 17 from 10.9.1983.

***Successive Non-scoring Runs:*** 6 from 26.3.1988.

### TEN YEAR LEAGUE RECORD

| | | *P* | *W* | *D* | *L* | *F* | *A* | *Pts* | *Pos* |
|---|---|---|---|---|---|---|---|---|---|
| 1994-95 | Div 2 | 46 | 21 | 12 | 13 | 66 | 52 | 75 | 7 |
| 1995-96 | Div 2 | 46 | 24 | 11 | 11 | 76 | 39 | 83 | 2 |
| 1996-97 | Div 1 | 46 | 16 | 9 | 21 | 64 | 68 | 57 | 17 |
| 1997-98 | Div 1 | 46 | 16 | 10 | 20 | 60 | 64 | 58 | 12 |
| 1998-99 | Div 1 | 46 | 10 | 14 | 22 | 48 | 71 | 44 | 23 |
| 1999-2000 | Div 2 | 46 | 12 | 9 | 25 | 43 | 73 | 45 | 20 |
| 2000-01 | Div 2 | 46 | 7 | 6 | 33 | 53 | 100 | 27 | 24 |
| 2001-02 | Div 3 | 46 | 11 | 14 | 21 | 53 | 62 | 47 | 21 |
| 2002-03 | Div 3 | 46 | 19 | 12 | 15 | 57 | 47 | 69 | 8 |
| 2003-04 | Div 3 | 46 | 18 | 17 | 11 | 55 | 44 | 71 | 9 |

### DID YOU KNOW ?

At the start of their last season under their previous name, Oxford United had an excellent start to the campaign remaining unbeaten in their first 13 League games, dropping just four points. They finished runners-up in the Southern League.

## OXFORD UNITED 2003–04 LEAGUE RECORD

| Match No. | Date | Venue | Opponents | Result | | H/T Score | Lg. Pos. | Goalscorers | Attendance |
|---|---|---|---|---|---|---|---|---|---|
| 1 | Aug 9 | A | Lincoln C | W | 1-0 | 1-0 | — | Basham [6] | 4543 |
| 2 | 16 | H | Hull C | W | 2-1 | 2-0 | 5 | Basham 2 [23, 28] | 6618 |
| 3 | 23 | A | Scunthorpe U | D | 1-1 | 1-0 | 5 | Crosby (pen) [43] | 3617 |
| 4 | 25 | H | Swansea C | W | 3-0 | 0-0 | 1 | Crosby (pen) [85], Alsop [87], Rawle [89] | 6725 |
| 5 | 30 | A | Kidderminster H | D | 1-1 | 0-0 | 3 | Rawle [80] | 3262 |
| 6 | Sept 6 | H | Southend U | W | 2-0 | 1-0 | 1 | Basham [26], Wanless [47] | 5567 |
| 7 | 13 | H | Mansfield T | D | 1-1 | 0-0 | 1 | Wanless [64] | 5625 |
| 8 | 16 | A | Cheltenham T | D | 0-0 | 0-0 | — | | 5319 |
| 9 | 20 | A | Doncaster R | L | 0-2 | 0-1 | 4 | | 5040 |
| 10 | 27 | H | Northampton T | W | 3-0 | 3-0 | 3 | Basham 2 [1, 41], Whitehead [32] | 6518 |
| 11 | Oct 1 | H | Torquay U | W | 1-0 | 0-0 | — | Alsop [70] | 5479 |
| 12 | 4 | A | Boston U | D | 1-1 | 0-1 | 4 | Louis [88] | 2664 |
| 13 | 11 | H | Yeovil T | W | 1-0 | 1-0 | 4 | Basham [13] | 6301 |
| 14 | 18 | A | Bury | W | 4-0 | 1-0 | 2 | Whitehead 2 [29, 79], Basham 2 [83, 84] | 2930 |
| 15 | 21 | A | York C | D | 2-2 | 1-1 | — | Brass (og) [5], Hackett [85] | 3022 |
| 16 | 25 | H | Bristol R | D | 0-0 | 0-0 | 3 | | 6644 |
| 17 | Nov 1 | H | Darlington | W | 3-1 | 0-1 | 3 | Rawle [52], Whitehead [74], Wanless [89] | 4962 |
| 18 | 15 | A | Cambridge U | D | 1-1 | 0-1 | 3 | Rawle [90] | 4430 |
| 19 | 22 | H | Macclesfield T | W | 3-1 | 2-1 | 1 | Alsop [29], Hunt [45], Wanless [70] | 6676 |
| 20 | 29 | A | Rochdale | W | 2-1 | 1-0 | 1 | Basham [30], Alsop [51] | 2282 |
| 21 | Dec 13 | H | Carlisle U | W | 2-1 | 2-0 | 1 | Robinson [3], Crosby (pen) [31] | 6111 |
| 22 | 20 | A | Huddersfield T | D | 1-1 | 0-1 | 2 | Rawle [72] | 9368 |
| 23 | 26 | H | Leyton Orient | W | 2-1 | 1-1 | 2 | Crosby (pen) [33], Alsop [90] | 9477 |
| 24 | 28 | A | Southend U | W | 1-0 | 0-0 | 1 | Rawle [68] | 6449 |
| 25 | Jan 6 | A | Swansea C | D | 0-0 | 0-0 | — | | 8896 |
| 26 | 10 | H | Lincoln C | D | 0-0 | 0-0 | 2 | | 6679 |
| 27 | 17 | A | Hull C | L | 2-4 | 0-0 | 3 | Basham [77], Bound [90] | 21,491 |
| 28 | 31 | H | Kidderminster H | W | 2-1 | 1-1 | 3 | Basham [7], McCarthy [77] | 6057 |
| 29 | Feb 7 | A | Leyton Orient | L | 0-1 | 0-0 | 3 | | 5433 |
| 30 | 11 | H | Scunthorpe U | W | 3-2 | 2-2 | — | Wanless [30], Rawle [34], Steele [88] | 5118 |
| 31 | 14 | A | Yeovil T | L | 0-1 | 0-1 | 3 | | 7404 |
| 32 | 21 | H | Bury | D | 1-1 | 0-0 | 3 | Whitehead [49] | 6473 |
| 33 | 28 | A | Bristol R | D | 1-1 | 1-0 | 3 | Rawle [13] | 6556 |
| 34 | Mar 3 | H | York C | D | 0-0 | 0-0 | — | | 5091 |
| 35 | 6 | H | Huddersfield T | L | 0-1 | 0-1 | 3 | | 7278 |
| 36 | 13 | A | Carlisle U | L | 0-2 | 0-0 | 4 | | 5492 |
| 37 | 17 | H | Cheltenham T | W | 1-0 | 1-0 | — | Crosby (pen) [25] | 5916 |
| 38 | 27 | H | Doncaster R | D | 0-0 | 0-0 | 5 | | 8483 |
| 39 | Apr 3 | A | Northampton T | L | 1-2 | 1-0 | 6 | Basham [22] | 6799 |
| 40 | 6 | A | Mansfield T | L | 1-3 | 1-3 | — | Whitehead [34] | 5132 |
| 41 | 9 | H | Boston U | D | 0-0 | 0-0 | — | | 6050 |
| 42 | 12 | A | Torquay U | L | 0-3 | 0-1 | 7 | | 5114 |
| 43 | 17 | A | Darlington | L | 0-2 | 0-1 | 7 | | 4212 |
| 44 | 24 | H | Cambridge U | D | 2-2 | 0-0 | 9 | McCarthy [75], Louis [86] | 5830 |
| 45 | May 1 | A | Macclesfield T | L | 1-2 | 1-2 | 9 | Hunt [36] | 2763 |
| 46 | 8 | H | Rochdale | W | 2-0 | 2-0 | 9 | Basham [33], Whitehead [39] | 5134 |

**Final League Position: 9**

### GOALSCORERS

*League (55):* Basham 14, Rawle 8, Whitehead 7, Alsop 5, Crosby 5 (5 pens), Wanless 5, Hunt 2, Louis 2, McCarthy 2, Bound 1, Hackett 1, Robinson 1, Steele 1, own goal 1.
*Carling Cup (2):* Basham 1, Louis 1.
*FA Cup (0).*
*LDV Vans Trophy (0).*

| Woodman A 41 | McNiven S 41 | Robinson M 40 | Bound M 33 + 4 | Crosby A 41 + 1 | Townsley D 9 + 2 | Brown D 12 | Wanless P 38 | Basham S 38 | Alsop J 26 + 3 | Ashton J 30 + 4 | Whitehead D 37 + 7 | Hackett C 6 + 16 | Oldfield D 1 + 2 | Hunt J 36 + 5 | Scott A 2 + 4 | Rawle M 10 + 21 | Waterman D 6 + 7 | McCarthy P 28 + 1 | Louis J 6 + 14 | Steele L 3 + 13 | Foran R 3 + 1 | Omoyinmi M 1 + 2 | Quinn B 5 + 1 | Walker R 3 + 1 | Cox S 5 | Pitt C 5 + 3 | Winters T — + 1 | Match No. |
|---|---|---|---|---|---|---|---|---|---|---|---|---|---|---|---|---|---|---|---|---|---|---|---|---|---|---|---|---|
| 1 | 2 | 3 | 4 | 5 | 6[1] | 7 | 8 | 9[2] | 10 | 11 | 12 | 13 | | | | | | | | | | | | | | | | 1 |
| 1 | 2 | 3 | 4 | 5 | 7 | 11[1] | 8 | 9[2] | 10■ | 6 | 12 | | 13 | | | | | | | | | | | | | | | 2 |
| 1 | 2 | 3 | 4 | 5 | 7[2] | | 8 | 9[3] | 10[1] | 6 | 13 | | 12 | 11 | 14 | | | | | | | | | | | | | 3 |
| 1 | 2 | 3 | 4 | 5 | 11[1] | 7[2] | 8 | 9[3] | 10 | 6 | 12 | | | 13 | | 14 | | | | | | | | | | | | 4 |
| 1 | 2 | 3 | 4 | 5 | 7 | 8[1] | 11 | 9 | | 6 | | | 10[2] | 12 | | 13 | | | | | | | | | | | | 5 |
| 1 | 2 | 3 | 4 | 5 | 7 | 11[1] | 8 | 9[2] | 10 | 6[3] | | | | 12 | | 13 | 14 | | | | | | | | | | | 6 |
| 1 | 2 | 3 | 4 | 5[3] | 7[1] | 11 | 8 | 9 | | 6 | 12 | | | | 13 | 10[2] | 14 | | | | | | | | | | | 7 |
| 1 | 2 | 3 | 4 | 5 | 7[1] | | 8 | 9[2] | | 6 | 11 | 13 | | 12 | 14 | 10[3] | | | | | | | | | | | | 8 |
| 1 | 2 | 3[1] | 4 | 5 | 7[3] | | 8 | | 9■ | 6 | 11[2] | 12 | | 14 | 10 | 13 | | | | | | | | | | | | 9 |
| 1 | 2 | 3 | 4 | | 12 | | 8 | 9[2] | 10[3] | 6 | 7 | | | 11[1] | 13 | | | 5 | 14 | | | | | | | | | 10 |
| 1 | 2 | 3 | 4 | | | | 8 | 9 | 10[1] | 6 | 7 | | | 11 | | | | 5 | 12 | | | | | | | | | 11 |
| 1 | 2[3] | 3 | 4 | | | | 8[1] | 9 | | 6 | 7 | 12 | | 11 | 10[2] | 13 | | 5 | 14 | | | | | | | | | 12 |
| 1 | 2 | 3 | 4 | 12 | 13 | | 8 | 9[2] | | 6 | 7 | | | 11 | | 14 | | 5[1] | 10[3] | | | | | | | | | 13 |
| 1 | 2 | 3 | 4 | 5 | | | 8 | 9[1] | | 6 | 7[2] | 12 | | 11[3] | | | 14 | 13 | 10 | | | | | | | | | 14 |
| 1 | 2 | 3 | 4 | 5 | | | 8[1] | 9[3] | 10[2] | 6 | 7 | 12 | | 11 | | | 13 | | 14 | | | | | | | | | 15 |
| 1 | 2[1] | 3 | 4 | 5 | | | 8 | 9 | 10 | 6 | 7 | 12 | | 11 | | | | | | | | | | | | | | 16 |
| 1 | 2 | 3 | 4 | 5 | | | 8 | 9[2] | 10 | 6[1] | 7 | 12 | | 11 | | 13 | | | | | | | | | | | | 17 |
| 1 | 2[3] | 3 | 4 | 5 | | | 8 | 9 | 12 | 6 | 7 | 13 | | 11[2] | | 14 | | | 10[1] | | | | | | | | | 18 |
| 1 | 2[1] | 3 | 4 | 5 | | | 8[2] | 9 | 10[3] | 6 | 7 | 12 | | 11 | | | 13 | | 14 | | | | | | | | | 19 |
| 1 | | 3 | | 5 | | 11 | 8 | 9 | 10 | 6 | 7 | | | | | | 4 | 2 | | | | | | | | | | 20 |
| 1 | 2 | 3 | 12 | 5 | | | 8 | 9[2] | 10 | 6[1] | 7 | | | 11 | | | | 4 | 13 | | | | | | | | | 21 |
| 1 | 2[2] | 3 | 5 | 4 | | | 8 | 9[1] | 10■ | 12 | 7 | | | 11 | | 13 | | 6 | | | | | | | | | | 22 |
| 1 | 2[1] | 3 | 5 | 4 | | | 8 | 9[2] | 10 | | 7 | | | 11 | | 12 | | 6 | | 13 | | | | | | | | 23 |
| 1 | 2 | 3 | 5 | 4 | | | 8 | 9[2] | 10 | 12 | 7 | | | 11 | | 13 | | 6[1] | | | | | | | | | | 24 |
| 1 | 2 | 3 | 5 | 4 | | | 8[1] | 9 | | 12 | 7 | | | 11 | | 13 | | 6 | 10[2] | | | | | | | | | 25 |
| 1 | 2 | 3 | 5 | 4 | | | 8 | 9[2] | | | 7 | | | 11 | | 12 | | 6 | 10[1] | | 13 | | | | | | | 26 |
| 1 | 2 | 3 | 5 | 4 | | | 8 | 9 | | | 7[2] | | | 11 | | 13 | | 6 | 12 | | 10[1] | | | | | | | 27 |
| 1 | 2[3] | 3 | 12 | 4 | | | 8 | 9[1] | | 6 | 7 | | | 11 | | 13 | | 5 | | 14 | 10[2] | | | | | | | 28 |
| 1 | 2 | 3 | | 4 | | | 8[2] | 9[3] | | 6 | 7 | | | 11 | | 13 | | 5 | 12 | 14 | 10[1] | | | | | | | 29 |
| 1 | 2[2] | 3 | 12 | 4 | | | 7 | 9[3] | 10 | 6 | 13 | | | 11 | | 8[1] | | 5 | | 14 | | | | | | | | 30 |
| 1 | 2[2] | 3 | | 4 | | | 7[1] | 9[3] | 10 | 6 | 12 | 13 | | 11 | | 8 | | 5 | | 14 | | | | | | | | 31 |
| 1 | 2[1] | 3 | | 4 | | | 8 | | 10 | 6[2] | 7 | | | 11 | | 12 | | 5 | 13 | 9[3] | | 14 | | | | | | 32 |
| 1 | 2 | 3 | 5 | 4 | | | 8 | | 9 | | 7 | | | 11 | | 10[1] | | 6 | 12[2] | 13 | | | | | | | | 33 |
| 1 | 2[1] | 3 | 5 | 4 | | | | | 9 | | 7 | 12 | | 11 | | 14 | 13 | 6 | | 10[3] | | | 8[2] | | | | | 34 |
| 1 | 2[1] | 3 | 5 | 4 | | | | | 9 | | 7 | 12 | | 11 | | 10[3] | | 6 | 13 | 14 | | | 8[2] | | | | | 35 |
| 1 | 2[3] | 3 | 5 | 4 | | | | | 9[2] | | 7 | 12 | | 11[1] | | 10 | | 6 | 13 | 14 | | | 8 | | | | | 36 |
| 1 | 2 | 3 | 5 | 4 | | | | 9[2] | 10 | | 7 | | | 11 | | | 12 | 6 | | | | | 8[1] | 13 | | | | 37 |
| | | 3 | | 4 | | | 8 | 9 | 12 | | 6 | 10 | | 11[1] | | 13 | 2 | 5 | | | | | | | 1 | 7[2] | | 38 |
| | | 3 | | 4 | | | 8 | 9 | 13 | 12 | 6 | 7[3] | | | | | 2 | 5 | | 14 | | | | 10[1] | 1 | 11[2] | | 39 |
| | | 3 | | 5 | | | 8[1] | 9 | | 6 | 4 | 7 | | 11 | | 10 | 2 | | | | | | | | 1 | 12 | | 40 |
| 1 | 2 | | 12 | 5 | | 3 | | 9 | | 6 | 4 | 7[1] | | 8 | | 13 | | | | 14 | | | | 10[3] | | 11[2] | | 41 |
| 1 | | | 4 | 5■ | | 3 | 8[1] | 9[2] | | 6 | 7 | 12 | | 11 | | 10 | 2 | | | | | | | | | 13 | | 42 |
| 1 | 2[1] | | 4 | 5 | | 3 | 8[3] | 9[2] | | | 7 | 12 | | 11 | | | | 6 | | 13 | | | | 10 | | 14 | | 43 |
| 1 | 2 | | | 5 | | | | | | | 4 | 7 | | 8 | | 10[2] | 3 | 6 | 12 | 13 | | 9 | | | | 11[1] | | 44 |
| | 2 | | | | | 3 | | | | 6 | 4 | 7[2] | | 8 | | 12 | | 5 | 10 | 9[3] | | 14 | 13 | | 1 | 11[1] | | 45 |
| | 2 | | 5[2] | 4 | | 11 | | 9[3] | 10[1] | | 3 | | | 8 | | | | 6 | 12 | 13 | | | 7 | | 1 | | 14 | 46 |

**Carling Cup**

| | | | |
|---|---|---|---|
| First Round | Millwall | (a) | 1-0 |
| Second Round | Reading | (h) | 1-3 |

**LDV Vans Trophy**

| | | | |
|---|---|---|---|
| First Round | Rushden & D | (h) | 0-1 |

**FA Cup**

| | | | |
|---|---|---|---|
| First Round | Colchester U | (a) | 0-1 |

# PETERBOROUGH UNITED FL Championship 1

## FOUNDATION

The old Peterborough & Fletton club, founded in 1923, was suspended by the FA during season 1932–33 and disbanded. Local enthusiasts determined to carry on and in 1934 a new professional club, Peterborough United, was formed and entered the Midland League the following year. Peterborough's first success came in 1939–40, but from 1955–56 to 1959–60 they won five successive titles. During the 1958–59 season they were undefeated in the Midland League. They reached the third round of the FA Cup, won the Northamptonshire Senior Cup, the Maunsell Cup and were runners-up in the East Anglian Cup.

***London Road Stadium, Peterborough PE2 8AL.***

***Telephone:*** (01733) 563 947.

***Fax:*** (01733) 344 140.

***Website:*** www.theposh.com

***Email:*** info@pufc-theposh.com

***Ground Capacity:*** 15,314.

***Record Attendance:*** 30,096 v Swansea T, FA Cup 5th rd, 20 February 1965.

***Pitch Measurements:*** 112yd × 71yd.

***Chairman:*** Alfred Hand.

***Vice-chairman:*** Steve Holt.

***Executive Director:*** Bob Symns.

***Secretary:*** Julie Etherington.

***Manager:*** Barry Fry.

***Physio:*** Paul Showler.

***Colours:*** All blue.

***Change Colours:*** All white.

***Year Formed:*** 1934.

***Turned Professional:*** 1934.

***Ltd Co.:*** 1934.

***Club Nickname:*** 'The Posh'.

***First Football League Game:*** 20 August 1960, Division 4, v Wrexham (h) W 3–0 – Walls; Stafford, Walker; Rayner, Rigby, Norris; Hails, Emery (1), Bly (1), Smith, McNamee (1).

***Record League Victory:*** 9–1 v Barnet (a) Division 3, 5 September 1998 – Griemink; Hooper (1), Drury (Farell), Gill, Bodley, Edwards, Davies, Payne, Grazioli (5), Quinn (2) (Rowe), Houghton (Etherington) (1).

## HONOURS

*Football League:* Division 1 best season: 10th, 1992–93; Division 2 1991–92 (play-offs). Promoted from Division 3 1999–2000 (play-offs); Division 4 – Champions 1960–61, 1973–74.

*FA Cup:* best season: 6th rd, 1965.

*Football League Cup:* Semi-final 1966.

## SKY SPORTS FACT FILE

Some 3,000 Peterborough United supporters went to Newcastle United for the FA Cup third round tie on 6 January 1962. Posh survived the shock of a disallowed Newcastle goal after five minutes before Terry Bly hit a 74th minute winner.

***Record Cup Victory:*** 7–0 v Harlow T, FA Cup 1st rd, 16 November 1991 – Barber; Luke, Johnson, Halsall (1), Robinson D, Welsh, Sterling (1) (Butterworth), Cooper G (2 incl. 1p), Riley (1) (Culpin (1)), Charlery (1), Kimble.

***Record Defeat:*** 1–8 v Northampton T, FA Cup 2nd rd (2nd replay), 18 December 1946.

***Most League Points (2 for a win):*** 66, Division 4, 1960–61.

***Most League Points (3 for a win):*** 82, Division 4, 1981–82.

***Most League Goals:*** 134, Division 4, 1960–61.

***Highest League Scorer in Season:*** Terry Bly, 52, Division 4, 1960–61.

***Most League Goals in Total Aggregate:*** Jim Hall, 122, 1967–75.

***Most League Goals in One Match:*** 5, Guiliano Grazioli v Barnet, Division 3, 5 September 1998.

***Most Capped Player:*** Tony Millington, 8 (21), Wales.

***Most League Appearances:*** Tommy Robson, 482, 1968–81.

***Youngest League Player:*** Matthew Etherington, 15 years 262 days v Brentford, 3 May 1997.

***Record Transfer Fee Received:*** £700,000 from Tottenham H for Simon Davies, December 1999.

***Record Transfer Fee Paid:*** £350,000 to Walsall for Martin O'Connor, July 1996.

***Football League Record:*** 1960 Elected to Division 4; 1961–68 Division 3, when they were demoted for financial irregularities; 1968–74 Division 4; 1974–79 Division 3; 1979–91 Division 4; 1991–92 Division 3; 1992–94 Division 1; 1994–97 Division 2; 1997–2000 Division 3; 2000–04 Division 2; 2004– FL1.

## MANAGERS

Jock Porter 1934–36
Fred Taylor 1936–37
Vic Poulter 1937–38
Sam Madden 1938–48
Jack Blood 1948–50
Bob Gurney 1950–52
Jack Fairbrother 1952–54
George Swindin 1954–58
Jimmy Hagan 1958–62
Jack Fairbrother 1962–64
Gordon Clark 1964–67
Norman Rigby 1967–69
Jim Iley 1969–72
Noel Cantwell 1972–77
John Barnwell 1977–78
Billy Hails 1978–79
Peter Morris 1979–82
Martin Wilkinson 1982–83
John Wile 1983–86
Noel Cantwell 1986–88 *(continued as General Manager)*
Mick Jones 1988–89
Mark Lawrenson 1989–90
Chris Turner 1991–92
Lil Fuccillo 1992–93
John Still 1994–95
Mick Halsall 1995–96
Barry Fry May 1996–

## LATEST SEQUENCES

***Longest Sequence of League Wins:*** 9, 1.2.1992 – 14.3.1992.

***Longest Sequence of League Defeats:*** 5, 8.10.1996 – 26.10.1996.

***Longest Sequence of League Draws:*** 8, 18.12.1971 – 12.2.1972.

***Longest Sequence of Unbeaten League Matches:*** 17, 17.12.1960 – 8.4.1961.

***Longest Sequence Without a League Win:*** 17, 23.9.1978 – 30.12.1978.

***Successive Scoring Runs:*** 33 from 20.9.1960.

***Successive Non-scoring Runs:*** 6 from 13.8.2002.

## TEN YEAR LEAGUE RECORD

| | | P | W | D | L | F | A | Pts | Pos |
|---|---|---|---|---|---|---|---|---|---|
| 1994-95 | Div 2 | 46 | 14 | 18 | 14 | 54 | 69 | 60 | 15 |
| 1995-96 | Div 2 | 46 | 13 | 13 | 20 | 59 | 66 | 52 | 19 |
| 1996-97 | Div 2 | 46 | 11 | 14 | 21 | 55 | 73 | 47 | 21 |
| 1997-98 | Div 3 | 46 | 18 | 13 | 15 | 63 | 51 | 67 | 10 |
| 1998-99 | Div 3 | 46 | 18 | 12 | 16 | 72 | 56 | 66 | 9 |
| 1999-2000 | Div 3 | 46 | 22 | 12 | 12 | 63 | 54 | 78 | 5 |
| 2000-01 | Div 2 | 46 | 15 | 14 | 17 | 61 | 66 | 59 | 12 |
| 2001-02 | Div 2 | 46 | 15 | 10 | 21 | 64 | 59 | 55 | 17 |
| 2002-03 | Div 2 | 46 | 14 | 16 | 16 | 51 | 54 | 58 | 11 |
| 2003-04 | Div 2 | 46 | 12 | 16 | 18 | 58 | 58 | 52 | 18 |

## DID YOU KNOW?

In 1952–53 Peterborough United made three important signings: full-back Al Woollard from Northampton Town – later sold to Newcastle – plus half-backs Johnny Anderson (ex-Forest and Manchester United) and Republic of Ireland international Paddy Sloan.

## PETERBOROUGH UNITED 2003–04 LEAGUE RECORD

| Match No. | Date | Venue | Opponents | Result | | H/T Score | Lg. Pos. | Goalscorers | Attendance |
|---|---|---|---|---|---|---|---|---|---|
| 1 | Aug 9 | H | Hartlepool U | L | 3-4 | 2-1 | — | Arber (pen) [18], Clarke A 2 [23, 51] | 5965 |
| 2 | 16 | A | Brentford | W | 3-0 | 1-0 | 10 | Clarke A [3], Arber [48], Boucaud [90] | 4463 |
| 3 | 23 | H | Sheffield W | L | 0-1 | 0-1 | 17 | | 10,194 |
| 4 | 25 | A | Notts Co | W | 1-0 | 1-0 | 11 | Clarke A [39] | 5177 |
| 5 | 30 | H | Stockport Co | L | 1-2 | 0-1 | 16 | McKenzie [90] | 4395 |
| 6 | Sept 6 | A | Grimsby T | D | 1-1 | 1-0 | 14 | Newton [18] | 4710 |
| 7 | 13 | A | Tranmere R | D | 0-0 | 0-0 | 14 | | 6726 |
| 8 | 16 | H | Plymouth Arg | D | 2-2 | 1-1 | — | Arber (pen) [34], Clarke A [81] | 4183 |
| 9 | 20 | H | Colchester U | L | 1-2 | 0-1 | 19 | Wood [57] | 4690 |
| 10 | 27 | A | Swindon T | L | 0-2 | 0-0 | 19 | | 6767 |
| 11 | 30 | A | Port Vale | L | 0-3 | 0-1 | — | | 5495 |
| 12 | Oct 4 | H | Oldham Ath | D | 2-2 | 1-1 | 20 | McKenzie 2 [21, 50] | 4465 |
| 13 | 10 | A | Bristol C | D | 1-1 | 0-1 | — | Logan [90] | 11,053 |
| 14 | 18 | H | QPR | D | 0-0 | 0-0 | 20 | | 7247 |
| 15 | 21 | H | Barnsley | L | 2-3 | 2-1 | — | McKenzie 2 [27, 41] | 3909 |
| 16 | 25 | A | Luton T | D | 1-1 | 0-1 | 21 | McKenzie [64] | 6067 |
| 17 | Nov 1 | H | Brighton & HA | D | 2-2 | 2-1 | 22 | McKenzie [15], Willock [29] | 5929 |
| 18 | 15 | A | Bournemouth | W | 2-1 | 2-0 | 20 | McKenzie [7], Woodhouse [21] | 6963 |
| 19 | 22 | H | Blackpool | L | 0-1 | 0-0 | 21 | | 4411 |
| 20 | 29 | A | Wycombe W | W | 2-1 | 1-0 | 20 | McKenzie [34], Logan [90] | 4669 |
| 21 | Dec 13 | A | Wrexham | L | 0-2 | 0-0 | 21 | | 3035 |
| 22 | 20 | H | Rushden & D | W | 3-1 | 0-0 | 20 | Willock [77], Woodhouse (pen) [84], Farrell [86] | 6167 |
| 23 | 26 | A | Chesterfield | L | 1-2 | 1-0 | 20 | Logan [13] | 4376 |
| 24 | 28 | H | Grimsby T | D | 0-0 | 0-0 | 20 | | 5245 |
| 25 | Jan 6 | H | Notts Co | W | 5-2 | 2-1 | — | Woodhouse [10], Logan 2 [28, 80], Farrell [56], Clarke A [83] | 3855 |
| 26 | 10 | A | Hartlepool U | L | 0-1 | 0-1 | 20 | | 4855 |
| 27 | 17 | H | Brentford | D | 0-0 | 0-0 | 20 | | 4658 |
| 28 | 24 | A | Sheffield W | L | 0-2 | 0-0 | 20 | | 21,474 |
| 29 | 31 | A | Stockport Co | D | 2-2 | 2-2 | 20 | Woodhouse [5], Clarke A [30] | 4653 |
| 30 | Feb 7 | H | Chesterfield | L | 0-2 | 0-0 | 21 | | 5446 |
| 31 | 14 | H | Bristol C | L | 0-1 | 0-0 | 21 | | 4449 |
| 32 | 20 | A | QPR | D | 1-1 | 1-0 | — | Platt [44] | 13,276 |
| 33 | 28 | H | Luton T | L | 1-2 | 0-1 | 22 | Willock [79] | 6628 |
| 34 | Mar 2 | A | Barnsley | W | 1-0 | 0-0 | — | Willock [46] | 7547 |
| 35 | 6 | A | Rushden & D | W | 1-0 | 1-0 | 20 | Willock [23] | 4855 |
| 36 | 13 | H | Wrexham | W | 6-1 | 2-1 | 20 | Willock 2 [24, 54], Platt [32], Burton [60], Clarke A [69], Farrell [76] | 4323 |
| 37 | 16 | A | Plymouth Arg | L | 0-2 | 0-0 | — | | 13,110 |
| 38 | 20 | H | Tranmere R | D | 0-0 | 0-0 | 19 | | 4185 |
| 39 | 27 | A | Colchester U | D | 0-0 | 0-0 | 19 | | 3754 |
| 40 | Apr 3 | H | Swindon T | W | 4-2 | 2-1 | 18 | Newton [3], Farrell [20], Logan [74], Thomson [89] | 4745 |
| 41 | 10 | A | Oldham Ath | D | 1-1 | 1-0 | 19 | Rea [37] | 5688 |
| 42 | 12 | H | Port Vale | W | 3-1 | 1-0 | 16 | Logan [45], Williams [55], Clarke A [67] | 4988 |
| 43 | 17 | A | Brighton & HA | L | 0-1 | 0-1 | 18 | | 6285 |
| 44 | 24 | H | Bournemouth | L | 0-1 | 0-0 | 19 | | 4831 |
| 45 | May 1 | A | Blackpool | W | 4-1 | 2-1 | 18 | Woodhouse 2 (1 pen) [19 (p), 26], Willock [53], Farrell [58] | 7200 |
| 46 | 8 | H | Wycombe W | D | 1-1 | 0-0 | 18 | Woodhouse [64] | 6398 |

**Final League Position: 18**

### GOALSCORERS

*League (58):* Clarke A 9, McKenzie 9, Willock 8, Logan 7, Woodhouse 7 (2 pens), Farrell 5, Arber 3 (2 pens), Newton 2, Platt 2, Boucaud 1, Burton 1, Rea 1, Thomson 1, Williams 1, Wood 1.
*Carling Cup (0).*
*FA Cup (6):* Clarke A 2, Logan 1, Newton 1, Thomson 1, Willock 1.
*LDV Vans Trophy (7):* McKenzie 3, Burton 1 (pen), Clarke A 1, Farrell 1, Logan 1.

| Tyler M 43 | Newton A 28 + 9 | Legg A 38 + 4 | Arber M 43 + 1 | Rea S 25 + 3 | Burton S 27 + 3 | Gill M 27 + 6 | Shields T 9 | Clarke A 28 + 17 | McKenzie L 19 | Boucaud A 7 + 1 | Farrell D 30 + 14 | Kanu C 16 + 5 | Jelleyman G 13 + 4 | Green F — + 3 | Pearce D 1 + 2 | Thomson S 28 + 7 | Wood N 2 + 1 | Logan R 12 + 17 | Nolan M — + 1 | Woodhouse C 26 + 1 | Willock C 22 + 7 | St Ledger-Hall S 1 + 1 | Fotiadis A — + 8 | Pullen J 3 | Williams T 20 + 1 | Platt C 17 + 1 | Jenkins S 6 + 2 | Semple R 1 + 1 | Branston G 14 | Match No. |
|---|---|---|---|---|---|---|---|---|---|---|---|---|---|---|---|---|---|---|---|---|---|---|---|---|---|---|---|---|---|---|
| 1 | 2 | 3 | 4 | 5 | 6 | 7 | 8 | 9 | 10 | $11^1$ | 12 | | | | | | | | | | | | | | | | | | | 1 |
| 1 | | $3^2$ | 4 | 5 | 6 | 7 | 8 | $9^1$ | $10^3$ | 11 | 12 | 2 | 13 | 14 | | | | | | | | | | | | | | | | 2 |
| 1 | 12 | 3 | 4 | 5 | $6^3$ | $7^1$ | 8 | 9 | 10 | $11^2$ | 13 | 2■ | | | 14 | | | | | | | | | | | | | | | 3 |
| 1 | 12 | 3 | 4 | 5 | $6^2$ | 7 | $8^3$ | 9 | 10 | $11^1$ | 14 | 2 | 13 | | | | | | | | | | | | | | | | | 4 |
| 1 | $11^1$ | 3 | 4 | 5 | | 8 | $6^2$ | 9 | 10 | 13 | 7 | 2 | | 12 | | | | | | | | | | | | | | | | 5 |
| 1 | 7 | 6 | | 5 | | 2 | 4 | 9 | 10 | $11^1$ | 8 | | 3 | | | 12 | | | | | | | | | | | | | | 6 |
| 1 | $11^2$ | $3^3$ | 4 | 5 | | 2 | 6 | 12 | 9 | | 7 | | 14 | 13 | | 8 | $10^1$ | | | | | | | | | | | | | 7 |
| 1 | 7 | 3 | 4 | 5 | | 2 | 6 | 9 | 10 | | 11 | | | | | 8 | | | | | | | | | | | | | | 8 |
| 1 | $7^1$ | 3 | 4 | 5■ | 12 | $8^2$ | $6^3$ | 9 | 10 | | 11 | 2 | | | | 13 | 14 | | | | | | | | | | | | | 9 |
| 1 | 12 | 3 | 4 | 5 | 6 | 7 | | $9^3$ | 10 | | 13 | $2^1$ | | | | 11 | $8^2$ | 14 | | | | | | | | | | | | 10 |
| 1 | $7^3$ | $3^1$ | 4 | | 6 | 5 | | 9 | | 8 | $11^2$ | 2 | | | 12 | 10 | | 13 | 14 | | | | | | | | | | | 11 |
| 1 | 7 | 12 | 4 | | 5 | 6 | | $9^3$ | 10 | 8 | $11^1$ | $2^2$ | | | 3 | 13 | | 14 | | | | | | | | | | | | 12 |
| 1 | $7^2$ | 3 | 4 | $5^3$ | 6 | 2 | | $9^1$ | 10 | | 12 | 13 | 11 | | | 8 | | 14 | | | | | | | | | | | | 13 |
| 1 | $7^3$ | 3 | 4 | | 6■ | 2 | | $9^2$ | 10 | | 11 | 13 | 12 | | | 8 | | | | $5^1$ | 14 | | | | | | | | | 14 |
| 1 | 12 | $3^3$ | 4 | | | 2 | | $9^2$ | 10 | | 11 | 5 | | | | 7 | | 13 | | 6 | $8^1$ | 14 | | | | | | | | 15 |
| 1 | 12 | | 4 | | 5 | $2^2$ | | $7^1$ | 10 | | 13 | | 3 | | | 11 | | $9^3$ | | 6 | 8 | | 14 | | | | | | | 16 |
| 1 | 12 | | 4 | 5 | | $2^2$ | | $9^3$ | 10 | | 11 | 13 | 3 | | | 8 | | 14 | | 6 | $7^1$ | | | | | | | | | 17 |
| 1 | | $3^1$ | 4 | 5 | 13 | 2 | | 12 | 10 | | | | 11 | | | 8 | | $9^2$ | | 6 | 7 | | | | | | | | | 18 |
| 1 | 12 | $3^3$ | 4 | 5 | | 2 | | 13 | 10 | | 14 | | 11 | | | 8 | | $9^2$ | | 6 | $7^1$ | | | | | | | | | 19 |
| | 12 | 13 | 4 | 5 | | | | $9^3$ | 10 | | $11^1$ | 2 | 3 | | | 8 | | 14 | | 6 | $7^2$ | | | 1 | | | | | | 20 |
| 1 | 7 | 12 | 4 | 14 | 5 | 2 | | $9^2$ | | | $11^3$ | | 3 | | | 8 | | $10^1$ | | 6 | | | 13 | | | | | | | 21 |
| | | 5 | 4 | | $6^1$ | 12 | | $9^2$ | | | 13 | 2 | 3 | | | 8 | | 10 | | 11 | $7^3$ | | 14 | 1 | | | | | | 22 |
| | 12 | 5 | 4 | | 6 | | | $9^1$ | | | 13 | 2 | 3 | | | $8^2$ | | 10 | | 11 | $7^3$ | | 14 | 1 | | | | | | 23 |
| 1 | | 11 | 4 | | 5 | | | 12 | | | 10 | 2 | 3 | | | 8 | | $9^2$ | | 6 | $7^1$ | | 13 | | | | | | | 24 |
| 1 | | 11 | 4 | $5^2$ | 13 | 2 | | 12 | | | 7 | | | | | 8 | | $9^3$ | | 6 | $10^1$ | | 14 | | 3 | | | | | 25 |
| 1 | | 11 | 4 | | 5 | 2■ | | 12 | | | $7^1$ | | | | | 8 | | $9^2$ | | 6 | 13 | | | | $3^3$ | 10 | 14 | | | 26 |
| 1 | | 11 | 4 | 5 | | 12 | | $9^2$ | | | $7^3$ | | | | | 8 | | 13 | | 6 | 14 | | | | 3 | 10 | $2^1$ | | | 27 |
| 1 | $7^3$ | 11 | 4 | $5^2$ | | | | 12 | | | 13 | 8 | | | | | | $9^1$ | | 6 | 14 | | | | 3 | 10 | 2■ | | | 28 |
| 1 | | 11 | 4 | | 5 | | | $9^2$ | | | | 6 | | | | 8 | | 12 | | 7 | | | 13 | | 3 | $10^1$ | 2 | | | 29 |
| 1 | | $3^1$ | 4 | $5^3$ | 6 | 7 | | 9 | | | 12 | $2^2$ | | | | 8 | | | | | | | 13 | | 11 | 10 | | 14 | | 30 |
| 1 | 2 | 6 | 4 | 5 | | | | $9^2$ | | | 11 | | 3 | | | 8 | | 12 | | 7 | 13 | | | | | $10^1$ | | | | 31 |
| 1 | 2 | 5 | 4 | | 6 | | | $9^1$ | | | 12 | | $3^2$ | | | 8 | | | | 7 | | | | | 13 | 10 | 11 | | | 32 |
| 1 | 7 | 3 | 4 | | 6 | | | $9^3$ | | | 12 | 13 | | | | $8^2$ | | 14 | | 11 | 10 | | | | $2^1$ | | | | 5 | 33 |
| 1 | 2 | 8 | 4 | 12 | $6^1$ | 14 | | 13 | | | 7 | | | | | | | | | | $10^2$ | | | | 3 | 9 | $11^3$ | | 5 | 34 |
| 1 | 2 | 8 | 4 | | 6 | | | 12 | | | 11 | | | | | | | 13 | | 7 | $10^1$ | | | | 3 | $9^2$ | | | 5 | 35 |
| 1 | 2 | $8^3$ | 4 | | 6 | 14 | | 12 | | | 11 | | | | | | | 13 | | 7 | $10^1$ | | | | 3 | $9^2$ | | | 5 | 36 |
| 1 | 2 | 8 | 4 | | 6 | 13 | | 12 | | | $7^1$ | | | | | | | 14 | | | 10 | | | | 3 | $9^3$ | $11^2$ | | 5 | 37 |
| 1 | 2 | 8 | 4 | 6 | | | | 12 | | | $11^1$ | | | | | | | | | 7 | 10 | | | | 3 | 9 | | | 5 | 38 |
| 1 | 2 | 8 | 4 | 5 | | | | | | | 11 | | | | | 12 | | | | 7 | 10 | | | | $3^1$ | 9 | | | 6 | 39 |
| 1 | 2 | 8 | | 5 | 4 | | | 14 | | | 11 | | | | | 12 | | 13 | | $7^1$ | $10^3$ | | | | 3 | $9^2$ | | | 6 | 40 |
| 1 | 7 | | 4 | 12 | $6^1$ | 2 | | 14 | | | $11^3$ | | | | | 8 | | 13 | | | $10^2$ | | | | 3 | 9 | | | 5 | 41 |
| 1 | $7^2$ | | 4 | 5 | | 2 | | $9^3$ | | | 11 | 13 | | | | 8 | | $10^1$ | | | 12 | | | | 3 | | 14 | | 6 | 42 |
| 1 | $7^1$ | 12 | 4 | 6 | | 2 | | 9 | | | $11^2$ | | | | | 8 | | $10^3$ | | | 14 | | | | 3 | 13 | | | 5 | 43 |
| 1 | 7 | 6 | 4 | | | 2 | | 12 | | | $11^2$ | | | | | 8 | | 14 | | 13 | $10^1$ | | | | 3 | $9^3$ | | | 5 | 44 |
| 1 | 2 | 8 | 4 | | $6^1$ | 14 | | 13 | | | 11 | | | | | 12 | | | | $7^3$ | 10 | | | | 3 | $9^2$ | | | 5 | 45 |
| 1 | 7 | 8 | 12 | | 6 | | | 13 | | | $9^2$ | | | | | 14 | | | | $11^3$ | 10 | 2 | | | 3 | | | 4 | $5^1$ | 46 |

**Carling Cup**

| | | | |
|---|---|---|---|
| First Round | Coventry C | (a) | 0-2 |

**LDV Vans Trophy**

| | | | |
|---|---|---|---|
| First Round | Torquay U | (h) | 3-2 |
| Second Round | Brentford | (h) | 3-2 |
| Quarter-Final | Northampton T | (a) | 1-2 |

**FA Cup**

| | | | |
|---|---|---|---|
| First Round | Hereford U | (h) | 2-0 |
| Second Round | Grimsby T | (h) | 3-2 |
| Third Round | Coventry C | (a) | 1-2 |

# PLYMOUTH ARGYLE FL Championship

## FOUNDATION

The club was formed in September 1886 as the Argyle Football Club by former public and private school pupils who wanted to continue playing the game. The meeting was held in a room above the Borough Arms (a Coffee House), Bedford Street, Plymouth. It was common then to choose a local street/terrace as a club name and Argyle or Argyll was a fashionable name throughout the land due to Queen Victoria's great interest in Scotland.

***Home Park, Plymouth, Devon PL2 3DQ.***

***Telephone:*** (01752) 562 561.

***Fax:*** (01752) 606 167.

***Ticket Office:*** (01752) 562 562.

***Email:*** argyle@pafc.co.uk

***Ground Capacity:*** 20,134.

***Record Attendance:*** 43,596 v Aston Villa, Division 2, 10 October 1936.

***Pitch Measurements:*** 110yd × 72yd.

***Chairman:*** Paul Stapleton.

***Vice-chairman:*** Peter Jones.

***Secretary:*** Carole Rowntree.

***Manager:*** Bobby Williamson.

***Physio:*** Paul Maxwell.

***Colours:*** Green shirts, white shorts, green stockings.

***Change Colours:*** White shirts, green shorts, white stockings.

***Year Formed:*** 1886.

***Turned Professional:*** 1903.

***Ltd Co.:*** 1903.

***Previous Name:*** 1886, Argyle Athletic Club; 1903, Plymouth Argyle.

***Club Nickname:*** 'The Pilgrims'.

***First Football League game:*** 28 August 1920, Division 3, v Norwich C (h) D 1–1 – Craig; Russell, Atterbury; Logan, Dickinson, Forbes; Kirkpatrick, Jack, Bowler, Heeps (1), Dixon.

***Record League Victory:*** 8–1 v Millwall, Division 2, 16 January 1932 – Harper; Roberts, Titmuss; Mackay, Pullan, Reed; Grozier, Bowden (2), Vidler (3), Leslie (1), Black (1), (1 og). 8–1 v Hartlepool U (a), Division 2, 7 May 1994 – Nicholls; Patterson (Naylor), Hill, Burrows, Comyn, McCall (1), Barlow, Castle (1), Landon (3), Marshall (1), Dalton (2).

***Record Cup Victory:*** 6–0 v Corby T, FA Cup 3rd rd, 22 January 1966 – Leiper; Book, Baird; Williams,

## HONOURS

*Football League:* Division 2 – Champions 2003–04; Division 3 (S) – Champions 1929–30, 1951–52; Runners-up 1921–22, 1922–23, 1923–24, 1924–25, 1925–26, 1926–27 (record of six consecutive years); Division 3 – Champions 1958–59, 2001–02; Runners-up 1974–75, 1985–86, Promoted 1995–96 (play-offs).

*FA Cup:* Semi-final 1984.

*Football League Cup:* Semi-final 1965, 1974.

## SKY SPORTS FACT FILE

On 7 March 1959 Plymouth Argyle entertained Mansfield Town. Taking a 3-0 lead in 20 minutes they were pulled back to 3-2 at the break. Mansfield equalised but in the last 20 minutes Argyle ran in five goals for an amazing 8-3 victory.

Nelson, Newman; Jones (1), Jackson (1), Bickle (3), Piper (1), Jennings.

***Record Defeat:*** 0–9 v Stoke C, Division 2, 17 December 1960.

***Most League Points (2 for a win):*** 68, Division 3 (S), 1929–30.

***Most League Points (3 for a win):*** 102, Division 3, 2001–02.

***Most League Goals:*** 107, Division 3 (S), 1925–26 and 1951–52.

***Highest League Scorer in Season:*** Jack Cock, 32, Division 3 (S), 1926–27.

***Most League Goals in Total Aggregate:*** Sammy Black, 180, 1924–38.

***Most League Goals in One Match:*** 5, Wilf Carter v Charlton Ath, Division 2, 27 December 1960.

***Most Capped Player:*** Moses Russell, 20 (23), Wales.

***Most League Appearances:*** Kevin Hodges, 530, 1978–92.

***Youngest League Player:*** Lee Phillips, 16 years 43 days v Gillingham, 29 October 1996.

***Record Transfer Fee Received:*** £750,000 from Southampton for Mickey Evans, March 1997.

***Record Transfer Fee Paid:*** £250,000 to Hartlepool U for Paul Dalton, June 1992.

***Football League Record:*** 1920 Original Member of Division 3; 1921–30 Division 3 (S); 1930–50 Division 2; 1950–52 Division 3 (S); 1952–56 Division 2; 1956–58 Division 3 (S); 1958–59 Division 3; 1959–68 Division 2; 1968–75 Division 3; 1975–77 Division 2; 1977–86 Division 3; 1986–95 Division 2; 1995–96 Division 3; 1996–98 Division 2; 1998–2002 Division 3; 2002–04 Division 2; 2004– FLC.

## MANAGERS

Frank Brettell 1903–05
Bob Jack 1905–06
Bill Fullerton 1906–07
Bob Jack 1910–38
Jack Tresadern 1938–47
Jimmy Rae 1948–55
Jack Rowley 1955–60
Neil Dougall 1961
Ellis Stuttard 1961–63
Andy Beattie 1963–64
Malcolm Allison 1964–65
Derek Ufton 1965–68
Billy Bingham 1968–70
Ellis Stuttard 1970–72
Tony Waiters 1972–77
Mike Kelly 1977–78
Malcolm Allison 1978–79
Bobby Saxton 1979–81
Bobby Moncur 1981–83
Johnny Hore 1983–84
Dave Smith 1984–88
Ken Brown 1988–90
David Kemp 1990–92
Peter Shilton 1992–95
Steve McCall 1995
Neil Warnock 1995–97
Mick Jones 1997–98
Kevin Hodges 1998–2000
Paul Sturrock 2000–04
Bobby Williamson April 2004–

## LATEST SEQUENCES

***Longest Sequence of League Wins:*** 9, 8.3.1986 – 12.4.1986.

***Longest Sequence of League Defeats:*** 9, 12.10.1963 – 7.12.1963.

***Longest Sequence of League Draws:*** 5, 26.2.2000 – 14.3.2000.

***Longest Sequence of Unbeaten League Matches:*** 22, 20.4.1929 – 21.12.1929.

***Longest Sequence Without a League Win:*** 13, 27.4.1963 – 2.10.1963.

***Successive Scoring Runs:*** 39 from 15.4.1939.

***Successive Non-scoring Runs:*** 5 from 20.9.1947.

## TEN YEAR LEAGUE RECORD

| | | *P* | *W* | *D* | *L* | *F* | *A* | *Pts* | *Pos* |
|---|---|---|---|---|---|---|---|---|---|
| 1994-95 | Div 2 | 46 | 12 | 10 | 24 | 45 | 83 | 46 | 21 |
| 1995-96 | Div 3 | 46 | 22 | 12 | 12 | 68 | 49 | 79 | 4 |
| 1996-97 | Div 2 | 46 | 12 | 18 | 16 | 47 | 58 | 54 | 19 |
| 1997-98 | Div 2 | 46 | 12 | 13 | 21 | 55 | 70 | 49 | 22 |
| 1998-99 | Div 3 | 46 | 17 | 10 | 19 | 58 | 54 | 61 | 13 |
| 1999-2000 | Div 3 | 46 | 16 | 18 | 12 | 55 | 51 | 66 | 12 |
| 2000-01 | Div 3 | 46 | 15 | 13 | 18 | 54 | 61 | 58 | 12 |
| 2001-02 | Div 3 | 46 | 31 | 9 | 6 | 71 | 28 | 102 | 1 |
| 2002-03 | Div 2 | 46 | 17 | 14 | 15 | 63 | 52 | 65 | 8 |
| 2003-04 | Div 2 | 46 | 26 | 12 | 8 | 85 | 41 | 90 | 1 |

## DID YOU KNOW ?

While the valiant near misses towards promotion by Plymouth Argyle in the 1920s have been well chronicled, the reserves in the Southern League from 1921 to 1939 recorded four first places, four runners-up and were never once lower than fifth.

## PLYMOUTH ARGYLE 2003–04 LEAGUE RECORD

| Match No. | Date | Venue | Opponents | Result | | H/T Score | Lg. Pos. | Goalscorers | Attendance |
|---|---|---|---|---|---|---|---|---|---|
| 1 | Aug 9 | H | Grimsby T | D | 2-2 | 1-1 | — | Keith [32], Coughlan [51] | 9590 |
| 2 | 16 | A | Rushden & D | L | 1-2 | 0-0 | 19 | Capaldi [77] | 4045 |
| 3 | 23 | H | Stockport Co | W | 3-1 | 3-1 | 14 | Keith [21], Hodges [23], Bent [28] | 7594 |
| 4 | 25 | A | Chesterfield | D | 1-1 | 0-0 | 16 | Friio [66] | 4089 |
| 5 | 30 | H | Brighton & HA | D | 3-3 | 1-2 | 15 | Coughlan [19], Stonebridge [81], Friio [89] | 9289 |
| 6 | Sept 6 | A | Brentford | W | 3-1 | 1-1 | 11 | Stonebridge [9], Evans 2 [58, 84] | 5688 |
| 7 | 13 | H | Luton T | W | 2-1 | 0-0 | 7 | Evans [82], Friio [90] | 9894 |
| 8 | 16 | A | Peterborough U | D | 2-2 | 1-1 | — | Wotton (pen) [10], Capaldi [84] | 4183 |
| 9 | 20 | A | Wrexham | D | 2-2 | 1-2 | 8 | Norris [31], Capaldi [49] | 3945 |
| 10 | 27 | H | Barnsley | W | 2-0 | 1-0 | 5 | Coughlan [38], Evans [75] | 8695 |
| 11 | 30 | H | Bristol C | L | 0-1 | 0-1 | — | | 13,923 |
| 12 | Oct 4 | A | Wycombe W | D | 0-0 | 0-0 | 9 | | 5708 |
| 13 | 11 | H | Tranmere R | W | 6-0 | 3-0 | 6 | Friio [7], Wotton [38], Gilbert [45], Keith [49], Evans [56], Norris [79] | 7610 |
| 14 | 18 | A | Port Vale | W | 5-1 | 3-0 | 2 | Keith [35], Friio 2 [38, 73], Adams [44], Wotton [47] | 5786 |
| 15 | 22 | A | Sheffield W | W | 3-1 | 1-0 | — | Friio 2 [22, 64], Wotton (pen) [62] | 20,090 |
| 16 | 25 | H | Blackpool | W | 1-0 | 1-0 | 1 | Keith [42] | 12,372 |
| 17 | Nov 1 | H | Oldham Ath | D | 2-2 | 1-1 | 1 | Wotton [17], Evans [50] | 11,205 |
| 18 | 15 | A | QPR | L | 0-3 | 0-1 | 3 | | 17,049 |
| 19 | 22 | H | Hartlepool U | W | 2-0 | 1-0 | 2 | Keith [45], Lowndes [48] | 9000 |
| 20 | 29 | A | Colchester U | W | 2-0 | 2-0 | 2 | Capaldi [4], Keith [11] | 4332 |
| 21 | Dec 13 | A | Swindon T | W | 3-2 | 1-0 | 2 | Capaldi [13], Norris [76], Keith [90] | 9374 |
| 22 | 20 | H | Notts Co | W | 3-0 | 1-0 | 1 | Lowndes [28], Evans 2 [79, 82] | 9923 |
| 23 | 26 | A | Bournemouth | W | 2-0 | 2-0 | 1 | Wotton [22], Norris [40] | 8901 |
| 24 | 28 | H | Brentford | W | 2-0 | 0-0 | 1 | Capaldi [48], Lowndes [63] | 17,882 |
| 25 | Jan 3 | H | Chesterfield | W | 7-0 | 6-0 | 1 | Hodges [4], Capaldi [11], Lowndes 2 [12, 18], Friio 3 [15, 36, 88] | 13,109 |
| 26 | 10 | A | Grimsby T | D | 0-0 | 0-0 | 1 | | 5007 |
| 27 | 17 | H | Rushden & D | W | 3-0 | 0-0 | 1 | Coughlan [47], Stonebridge [58], Wotton [90] | 13,021 |
| 28 | 24 | A | Stockport Co | W | 2-0 | 1-0 | 1 | Friio [29], Coughlan [62] | 6608 |
| 29 | 31 | A | Brighton & HA | L | 1-2 | 0-2 | 1 | Lowndes [88] | 6379 |
| 30 | Feb 7 | H | Bournemouth | D | 0-0 | 0-0 | 1 | | 13,371 |
| 31 | 17 | A | Tranmere R | L | 0-3 | 0-2 | — | | 7948 |
| 32 | 21 | H | Port Vale | W | 2-1 | 0-0 | 2 | Phillips [80], Stonebridge [90] | 11,330 |
| 33 | 28 | A | Blackpool | W | 1-0 | 0-0 | 1 | Stonebridge [54] | 7253 |
| 34 | Mar 2 | H | Sheffield W | W | 2-0 | 1-0 | — | Evans [7], Coughlan [77] | 17,218 |
| 35 | 6 | A | Notts Co | D | 0-0 | 0-0 | 1 | | 8057 |
| 36 | 13 | H | Swindon T | W | 2-1 | 1-0 | 1 | Keith [11], Evans (og) [84] | 16,080 |
| 37 | 16 | H | Peterborough U | W | 2-0 | 0-0 | — | Lowndes [55], Wotton (pen) [79] | 13,110 |
| 38 | 20 | A | Luton T | D | 1-1 | 0-1 | 1 | Adams [90] | 8499 |
| 39 | 27 | H | Wrexham | D | 0-0 | 0-0 | 1 | | 12,275 |
| 40 | Apr 3 | A | Barnsley | L | 0-1 | 0-0 | 1 | | 9266 |
| 41 | 10 | H | Wycombe W | W | 2-1 | 1-1 | 1 | Coughlan [39], Evans [80] | 14,806 |
| 42 | 13 | A | Bristol C | L | 0-1 | 0-0 | — | | 19,045 |
| 43 | 17 | A | Oldham Ath | L | 1-4 | 0-3 | 1 | Wotton [51] | 6924 |
| 44 | 24 | H | QPR | W | 2-0 | 0-0 | 1 | Evans [81], Friio [86] | 19,888 |
| 45 | May 1 | A | Hartlepool U | W | 3-1 | 2-1 | 1 | Hodges [12], Lowndes [42], Tinkler (og) [48] | 7437 |
| 46 | 8 | H | Colchester U | W | 2-0 | 1-0 | 1 | Friio [17], Norris [47] | 19,868 |

**Final League Position: 1**

### GOALSCORERS

*League (85):* Friio 14, Evans 11, Keith 9, Wotton 9 (3 pens), Lowndes 8, Capaldi 7, Coughlan 7, Norris 5, Stonebridge 5, Hodges 3, Adams 2, Bent 1, Gilbert 1, Phillips 1, own goals 2.
*Carling Cup (1):* Evans 1.
*FA Cup (2):* Friio 1, Stonebridge 1.
*LDV Vans Trophy (6):* Lowndes 2, Coughlan 1, Evans 1, Gilbert 1, Keith 1.

| Larrieu R 6 | Worrell D 18 | Hodges L 28 + 9 | Friio D 35 + 1 | Wotton P 31 + 7 | Coughlan G 46 | Norris D 42 + 3 | Bent J 13 + 5 | Stonebridge I 21 + 9 | Keith M 28 + 12 | Capaldi T 29 + 4 | Adams S 25 + 11 | Evans M 35 + 9 | Lowndes N 18 + 15 | Connolly P 28 + 1 | Beresford D — + 1 | Sturrock B — + 24 | Gilbert P 40 | Aljofree H 20 + 4 | McCormick L 40 | Phillips M 3 + 6 | Yetton S — + 1 | *Match No.* |
|---|---|---|---|---|---|---|---|---|---|---|---|---|---|---|---|---|---|---|---|---|---|---|
| 1 | 2 | 3 | 4 | 5 | 6 | $7^{1}$ | 8 | $9^{2}$ | $10^{3}$ | 11 | 12 | 13 | 14 | | | | | | | | | 1 |
| 1 | $2^{2}$ | $3^{1}$ | 4 | 5 | 6 | 7 | 8 | 12 | $10^{3}$ | 11 | 13 | 9 | 14 | | | | | | | | | 2 |
| 1 | 2 | 3 | 4 | 5 | 6 | $7^{2}$ | 8 | $9^{1}$ | $10^{3}$ | 11 | 13 | 12 | 14 | | | | | | | | | 3 |
| 1 | 2 | 3 | 4 | 5 | 6 | 12 | 8 | $9^{1}$ | $10^{3}$ | $11^{2}$ | 7 | 13 | 14 | | | | | | | | | 4 |
| 1 | | 3 | 4 | 5 | 6 | $7^{2}$ | 8 | 9 | | $11^{3}$ | 12 | 10 | | $2^{1}$ | 13 | 14 | | | | | | 5 |
| 1 | $2^{1}$ | $11^{3}$ | 4 | 5 | 6 | 7 | | $9^{2}$ | | | 8 | 10 | | 12 | | 13 | 3 | 14 | | | | 6 |
| | 2 | 11 | 4 | 5 | 6 | 7 | 12 | $9^{2}$ | 13 | | $8^{1}$ | 10 | | | | 14 | $3^{3}$ | | 1 | | | 7 |
| | 2 | | $4^{2}$ | 5 | 6 | 7 | 8 | $9^{1}$ | 12 | 11 | 13 | $10^{3}$ | | | | 14 | 3 | | 1 | | | 8 |
| | 2 | 3 | | 5 | 6 | 7 | 8 | $9^{1}$ | $10^{2}$ | 11 | 4 | 12 | | | | 13 | | | 1 | | | 9 |
| | 2 | 12 | | 5 | 6 | 7 | 8 | | $10^{2}$ | $11^{1}$ | 4 | 9 | | | | 13 | 3 | | 1 | | | 10 |
| | 2 | 13 | | 5 | 6 | 7 | 8 | 12 | $10^{1}$ | $11^{3}$ | 4 | 9 | | | | 14 | $3^{2}$ | | 1 | | | 11 |
| | 2 | 12 | | 5 | 6 | 7 | 8 | 13 | $10^{2}$ | 11 | $4^{1}$ | 9 | | | | | 3 | | 1 | | | 12 |
| | 2 | 12 | $4^{1}$ | 5 | 6 | 7 | | 9 | $10^{3}$ | | 8 | $11^{2}$ | 13 | | | 14 | 3 | | 1 | | | 13 |
| | 2 | | $4^{1}$ | 5 | 6 | 7 | 12 | 9 | $11^{2}$ | 13 | $8^{3}$ | 10 | | | | | 3 | 14 | 1 | | | 14 |
| | 2 | | $4^{1}$ | 5 | 6 | 7 | 12 | $9^{2}$ | 11 | 13 | 8 | 10 | | | | | 3 | | 1 | | | 15 |
| | 2 | | 4 | 5 | 6 | $7^{1}$ | 12 | $9^{2}$ | $11^{3}$ | 13 | 8 | 10 | 14 | | | | 3 | | 1 | | | 16 |
| | 2 | | 4■ | 5 | 6 | $7^{3}$ | 8 | $9^{2}$ | $11^{1}$ | 12 | | 10 | 13 | | | 14 | 3 | | 1 | | | 17 |
| | 2 | 11 | | 5 | 6 | 7 | $8^{1}$ | 9 | 12 | | 4 | $10^{2}$ | 13 | | | | 3 | | 1 | | | 18 |
| | | 8 | | 12 | 6 | 7 | | 13 | $10^{3}$ | 11 | $4^{1}$ | | $9^{2}$ | 2 | | 14 | 3 | 5 | 1 | | | 19 |
| | | 8 | | 4 | 6 | 7 | | | 10 | 11 | | 12 | $9^{1}$ | 2 | | | 3 | 5 | 1 | | | 20 |
| | | 8 | | 4 | 6 | 7 | | | 10 | 11 | | 12 | $9^{1}$ | 2 | | | 3 | 5 | 1 | | | 21 |
| | | 8 | 13 | 4 | 6 | 7 | | | $10^{2}$ | $11^{3}$ | | 12 | $9^{1}$ | 2 | | 14 | 3 | 5 | 1 | | | 22 |
| | | $11^{2}$ | 8 | 4 | 6 | 7 | | | $10^{1}$ | | 13 | 12 | $9^{3}$ | 2 | | 14 | 3 | 5 | 1 | | | 23 |
| | | 8 | 4 | | 6 | | | 12 | | 11 | | 10 | $9^{2}$ | 2 | | 13 | 3 | 5 | 1 | $7^{1}$ | | 24 |
| | | 8 | 4 | | 6 | 12 | | 13 | 14 | $11^{2}$ | | $10^{3}$ | 9 | 2 | | | 3 | 5 | 1 | $7^{1}$ | | 25 |
| | | 8 | 4 | 12 | 6 | 14 | | | 13 | $11^{1}$ | | $10^{2}$ | 9 | 2 | | | 3 | 5 | 1 | $7^{3}$ | | 26 |
| | | $11^{1}$ | 4 | 12 | 6 | 7 | | 8 | 13 | | | 10 | $9^{2}$ | 2 | | | 3 | 5 | 1 | | | 27 |
| | | 8 | $4^{3}$ | 12 | 6 | 7 | | $11^{1}$ | 13 | | 14 | $10^{2}$ | 9 | 2 | | | 3 | 5 | 1 | | | 28 |
| | | $11^{1}$ | 4 | 8 | 6 | $7^{2}$ | | | 12 | | 13 | 10 | 9 | 2 | | 14 | 3 | $5^{3}$ | 1 | | | 29 |
| | | $8^{1}$ | 4 | 12 | 6 | 7 | | | 13 | $11^{3}$ | | 10 | $9^{2}$ | 2 | | | 3 | 5 | 1 | 14 | | 30 |
| | | | $4^{1}$ | 12 | 6 | $7^{2}$ | | $11^{3}$ | | | 8 | 10 | 9 | 2 | | 13 | 3 | 5 | 1 | 14 | | 31 |
| | | | 4 | | 6 | $7^{1}$ | | 12 | | $11^{3}$ | 8 | 10 | $9^{2}$ | 2 | | 13 | 3 | 5 | 1 | 14 | | 32 |
| | | 13 | 4 | | 6 | 7 | | 12 | | $11^{2}$ | 8 | $10^{3}$ | $9^{1}$ | 2 | | 14 | 3 | 5 | 1 | | | 33 |
| | | 12 | 4 | | 6 | 7 | | $11^{1}$ | 10 | | 8 | $9^{2}$ | | 2 | | 13 | 3 | 5 | 1 | | | 34 |
| | | 12 | 4 | | 6 | 7 | | $11^{1}$ | $10^{3}$ | | 8 | $9^{2}$ | 14 | 2 | | 13 | 3 | 5 | 1 | | | 35 |
| | | | 4 | 5 | 6 | $7^{1}$ | 12 | | $10^{2}$ | 11 | 8 | $9^{3}$ | 13 | 2 | | 14 | 3 | | 1 | | | 36 |
| | | 12 | 4 | 5 | 6 | 7 | | | $10^{2}$ | 11 | 8 | $9^{1}$ | 13 | 2 | | | 3 | | 1 | | | 37 |
| | | | 4 | 5 | 6 | 7 | | | 12 | $11^{3}$ | 8 | $10^{2}$ | $9^{1}$ | 2 | | 13 | 3 | | 1 | 14 | | 38 |
| | | 12 | 4 | 5 | 6 | 7 | | $11^{2}$ | 13 | | $8^{1}$ | 10 | $9^{3}$ | 2 | | | 3 | | 1 | 14 | | 39 |
| | | 11 | $4^{1}$ | 5 | 6 | 7 | | 9 | $10^{2}$ | | 8 | 12 | | 2 | | 13 | 3 | | 1 | | | 40 |
| | | 8 | $4^{1}$ | 5 | 6 | 7 | | | $10^{3}$ | $11^{2}$ | 12 | 9 | 13 | 2 | | 14 | 3 | | 1 | | | 41 |
| | | 10 | | 5 | 6 | 7 | $8^{3}$ | | 12 | $11^{2}$ | $4^{1}$ | 9 | 13 | 2 | | | 3 | 14 | 1 | | | 42 |
| | | $8^{2}$ | 4 | 5■ | 6 | 7 | | | 10 | $11^{3}$ | 12 | 9 | | 2 | | | $3^{1}$ | 13 | 1 | 14 | | 43 |
| | | 8 | 4 | | 6 | 7 | | | $10^{1}$ | 11 | | 9 | 12 | 2 | | | 3 | 5 | 1 | | | 44 |
| | 2 | 8 | | | 6 | 7 | | 12 | $10^{3}$ | $11^{1}$ | 4 | | $9^{2}$ | | | 13 | 3 | 5 | 1 | | 14 | 45 |
| | | 8 | 4■ | 12 | 6 | 7 | | | $10^{3}$ | $11^{2}$ | 13 | $9^{1}$ | 14 | 2 | | | 3 | 5 | 1 | | | 46 |

**Carling Cup**
First Round — Colchester U — (a) — 1-2

**LDV Vans Trophy**
First Round — Bristol C — (h) — 4-0
Second Round — Wycombe W — (h) — 2-2

**FA Cup**
First Round — Northampton T — (a) — 2-3

# PORTSMOUTH — FA Premiership

### FOUNDATION

At a meeting held in his High Street, Portsmouth offices in 1898, solicitor Alderman J. E. Pink and five other business and professional men agreed to buy some ground close to Goldsmith Avenue for £4,950 which they developed into Fratton Park in record breaking time. A team of professionals was signed up by manager Frank Brettell and entry to the Southern League obtained for the new club's September 1899 kick-off.

***Fratton Park, Frogmore Road, Portsmouth PO4 8RA.***

***Telephone:*** (02392) 731 204.

***Fax:*** (02392) 734 129.

***Ticket Office:*** (02392) 618 777.

***Website:*** www.pompeyfc.co.uk

***Email:*** info@pompeyfc.co.uk

***Ground Capacity:*** 20,228.

***Record Attendance:*** 51,385 v Derby Co, FA Cup 6th rd, 26 February 1949.

***Pitch Measurements:*** 110yd × 72yd.

***Chairman:*** Milan Mandaric.

***Chief Executive:*** Peter Storrie.

***Secretary:*** Paul Weld.

***Manager:*** Harry Redknapp.

***Assistant Manager:*** Jim Smith.

***Physio:*** Gary Sadler.

***Colours:*** Blue shirts, white shorts, red stockings.

***Change Colours:*** All navy.

***Year Formed:*** 1898.

***Turned Professional:*** 1898.

***Ltd Co.:*** 1898.

***Club Nickname:*** 'Pompey'.

***First Football League Game:*** 28 August 1920, Division 3, v Swansea T (h) W 3–0 – Robson; Probert, Potts; Abbott, Harwood, Turner; Thompson, Stringfellow (1), Reid (1), James (1), Beedie.

***Record League Victory:*** 9–1 v Notts Co, Division 2, 9 April 1927 – McPhail; Clifford, Ted Smith; Reg Davies (1), Foxall, Moffat; Forward (1), Mackie (2), Haines (3), Watson, Cook (2).

### HONOURS

*Football League:* Division 1 – Champions 1948–49, 1949–50, 2002–03; Division 2 – Runners-up 1926–27, 1986–87; Division 3 (S) – Champions 1923–24; Division 3 – Champions 1961–62, 1982–83.

*FA Cup:* Winners 1939; Runners-up 1929, 1934.

*Football League Cup:* best season: 5th rd, 1961, 1986.

### SKY SPORTS FACT FILE

Though centre-half Reg Flewin had played twice for England in wartime internationals, Jimmy Dickinson was the first to be fully capped for his country from the players who appeared in Portsmouth's championship-winning team of 1948–49.

***Record Cup Victory:*** 7–0 v Stockport Co, FA Cup 3rd rd, 8 January 1949 – Butler; Rookes, Ferrier; Scoular, Flewin, Dickinson; Harris (3), Barlow, Clarke (2), Phillips (2), Froggatt.

***Record Defeat:*** 0–10 v Leicester C, Division 1, 20 October 1928.

***Most League Points (2 for a win):*** 65, Division 3, 1961–62.

***Most League Points (3 for a win):*** 98, Division 1, 2002–03.

***Most League Goals:*** 97, Division 1, 2002–03.

***Highest League Scorer in Season:*** Guy Whittingham, 42, Division 1, 1992–93.

***Most League Goals in Total Aggregate:*** Peter Harris, 194, 1946–60.

***Most League Goals in One Match:*** 5, Alf Strange v Gillingham, Division 3, 27 January 1923; 5, Peter Harris v Aston Villa, Division 1, 3 September 1958.

***Most Capped Player:*** Jimmy Dickinson, 48, England.

***Most League Appearances:*** Jimmy Dickinson, 764, 1946–65.

***Youngest League Player:*** Clive Green, 16 years 259 days v Wrexham, 21 August 1976.

***Record Transfer Fee Received:*** £4,500,000 from Aston Villa for Peter Crouch, March 2002.

***Record Transfer Fee Paid:*** £1,800,000 to Vitesse Arnhem for Dejan Stefanovic, July 2003.

***Football League Record:*** 1920 Original Member of Division 3; 1921 Division 3 (S); 1924–27 Division 2; 1927–59 Division 1; 1959–61 Division 2; 1961–62 Division 3; 1962–76 Division 2; 1976–78 Division 3; 1978–80 Division 4; 1980–83 Division 3; 1983–87 Division 2; 1987–88 Division 1; 1988–92 Division 2; 1992–2003 Division 1; 2003– FA Premier League.

## MANAGERS

Frank Brettell 1898–1901
Bob Blyth 1901–04
Richard Bonney 1905–08
Bob Brown 1911–20
John McCartney 1920–27
Jack Tinn 1927–47
Bob Jackson 1947–52
Eddie Lever 1952–58
Freddie Cox 1958–61
George Smith 1961–70
Ron Tindall 1970–73
*(General Manager to 1974)*
John Mortimore 1973–74
Ian St John 1974–77
Jimmy Dickinson 1977–79
Frank Burrows 1979–82
Bobby Campbell 1982–84
Alan Ball 1984–89
John Gregory 1989–90
Frank Burrows 1990–91
Jim Smith 1991–95
Terry Fenwick 1995–98
Alan Ball 1998–99
Tony Pulis 2000
Steve Claridge 2000–01
Graham Rix 2001–02
Harry Redknapp March 2002–

## LATEST SEQUENCES

***Longest Sequence of League Wins:*** 7, 17.8.2002 – 17.9.2002.

***Longest Sequence of League Defeats:*** 9, 21.10.1975 – 6.12.1975.

***Longest Sequence of League Draws:*** 5, 16.12.2000 – 13.1.2001.

***Longest Sequence of Unbeaten League Matches:*** 15, 18.4.1924 – 18.10.1924.

***Longest Sequence Without a League Win:*** 25, 29.11.1958 – 22.8.1959.

***Successive Scoring Runs:*** 23 from 30.8.1930.

***Successive Non-scoring Runs:*** 6 from 14.1.1939.

## TEN YEAR LEAGUE RECORD

| | | P | W | D | L | F | A | Pts | Pos |
|---|---|---|---|---|---|---|---|---|---|
| 1994-95 | Div 1 | 46 | 15 | 13 | 18 | 53 | 63 | 58 | 18 |
| 1995-96 | Div 1 | 46 | 13 | 13 | 20 | 61 | 69 | 52 | 21 |
| 1996-97 | Div 1 | 46 | 20 | 8 | 18 | 59 | 53 | 68 | 7 |
| 1997-98 | Div 1 | 46 | 13 | 10 | 23 | 51 | 63 | 49 | 20 |
| 1998-99 | Div 1 | 46 | 11 | 14 | 21 | 57 | 73 | 47 | 19 |
| 1999-2000 | Div 1 | 46 | 13 | 12 | 21 | 55 | 66 | 51 | 18 |
| 2000-01 | Div 1 | 46 | 10 | 19 | 17 | 47 | 59 | 49 | 20 |
| 2001-02 | Div 1 | 46 | 13 | 14 | 19 | 60 | 72 | 53 | 17 |
| 2002-03 | Div 1 | 46 | 29 | 11 | 6 | 97 | 45 | 98 | 1 |
| 2003-04 | PR Lge | 38 | 12 | 9 | 17 | 47 | 54 | 45 | 13 |

## DID YOU KNOW?

Much of the 1937–38 season was difficult for Portsmouth. The first win came on 20 November 4-0 over Derby County. But determined efforts and a last match four clear goals victory over Leeds United meant relegation escape by two points.

## PORTSMOUTH 2003–04 LEAGUE RECORD

| Match No. | Date | Venue | Opponents | Result | | H/T Score | Lg. Pos. | Goalscorers | Attendance |
|---|---|---|---|---|---|---|---|---|---|
| 1 | Aug 16 | H | Aston Villa | W | 2-1 | 1-0 | — | Sheringham [42], Berger [63] | 20,101 |
| 2 | 23 | A | Manchester C | D | 1-1 | 1-0 | 6 | Yakubu [24] | 46,287 |
| 3 | Aug 26 | H | Bolton W | W | 4-0 | 0-0 | — | Stone [48], Sheringham 3 (1 pen) [57, 88, 90 (p)] | 20,118 |
| 4 | 30 | A | Wolverhampton W | D | 0-0 | 0-0 | 3 | | 28,680 |
| 5 | Sept 13 | A | Arsenal | D | 1-1 | 1-1 | 5 | Sheringham [26] | 38,052 |
| 6 | 20 | H | Blackburn R | L | 1-2 | 0-2 | 8 | De Zeeuw [57] | 20,029 |
| 7 | 27 | A | Birmingham C | L | 0-2 | 0-1 | 9 | | 29,057 |
| 8 | Oct 4 | H | Charlton Ath | L | 1-2 | 1-0 | 10 | Sheringham [34] | 20,122 |
| 9 | 18 | H | Liverpool | W | 1-0 | 1-0 | 8 | Berger [4] | 19,126 |
| 10 | 25 | A | Newcastle U | L | 0-3 | 0-2 | 11 | | 52,161 |
| 11 | Nov 1 | A | Manchester U | L | 0-3 | 0-1 | 11 | | 67,639 |
| 12 | 8 | H | Leeds U | W | 6-1 | 2-1 | 11 | Stefanovic [17], O'Neil 2 [45, 71], Foxe [63], Berger [75], Yakubu [86] | 20,122 |
| 13 | 24 | A | Fulham | L | 0-2 | 0-2 | — | | 15,624 |
| 14 | 29 | H | Leicester C | L | 0-2 | 0-1 | 15 | | 20,140 |
| 15 | Dec 6 | A | Middlesbrough | D | 0-0 | 0-0 | 16 | | 28,083 |
| 16 | 13 | H | Everton | L | 1-2 | 1-2 | 18 | Roberts [15] | 20,099 |
| 17 | 21 | A | Southampton | L | 0-3 | 0-1 | 18 | | 31,697 |
| 18 | 26 | H | Tottenham H | W | 2-0 | 0-0 | 15 | Berger 2 [52, 68] | 20,010 |
| 19 | 28 | A | Chelsea | L | 0-3 | 0-0 | 16 | | 41,552 |
| 20 | Jan 6 | A | Aston Villa | L | 1-2 | 0-1 | — | Yakubu [49] | 28,625 |
| 21 | 10 | H | Manchester C | W | 4-2 | 1-2 | 17 | Stefanovic [19], Yakubu 2 [52, 77], Sheringham [58] | 20,120 |
| 22 | 17 | A | Bolton W | L | 0-1 | 0-0 | 17 | | 26,558 |
| 23 | 31 | H | Wolverhampton W | D | 0-0 | 0-0 | 17 | | 20,116 |
| 24 | Feb 7 | A | Tottenham H | L | 3-4 | 1-2 | 17 | Berkovic [39], Lua-Lua [73], Mornar [84] | 36,107 |
| 25 | 11 | H | Chelsea | L | 0-2 | 0-1 | — | | 20,110 |
| 26 | 29 | H | Newcastle U | D | 1-1 | 0-1 | 17 | Lua-Lua [89] | 20,134 |
| 27 | Mar 13 | A | Everton | L | 0-1 | 0-0 | 18 | | 40,105 |
| 28 | 17 | A | Liverpool | L | 0-3 | 0-2 | — | | 34,663 |
| 29 | 21 | H | Southampton | W | 1-0 | 0-0 | 19 | Yakubu [68] | 20,140 |
| 30 | 27 | A | Blackburn R | W | 2-1 | 1-1 | 17 | Sheringham [17], Yakubu [82] | 22,855 |
| 31 | Apr 10 | A | Charlton Ath | D | 1-1 | 0-1 | 17 | Yakubu [65] | 26,369 |
| 32 | 12 | H | Birmingham C | W | 3-1 | 1-0 | 17 | Stefanovic [45], Lua-Lua [62], Yakubu (pen) [73] | 20,079 |
| 33 | 17 | H | Manchester U | W | 1-0 | 1-0 | 16 | Stone [36] | 20,125 |
| 34 | 25 | A | Leeds U | W | 2-1 | 1-0 | 14 | Yakubu [9], Lua-Lua [51] | 39,273 |
| 35 | May 1 | H | Fulham | D | 1-1 | 0-0 | 14 | Yakubu [80] | 20,056 |
| 36 | 4 | H | Arsenal | D | 1-1 | 1-0 | — | Yakubu [30] | 20,140 |
| 37 | 8 | A | Leicester C | L | 1-3 | 0-2 | 14 | Quashie [66] | 31,536 |
| 38 | 15 | H | Middlesbrough | W | 5-1 | 3-1 | 13 | Yakubu 4 (1 pen) [4, 14 (p), 31, 83], Sheringham [80] | 20,134 |

**Final League Position: 13**

### GOALSCORERS

*League (47):* Yakubu 16 (2 pens), Sheringham 9 (1 pen), Berger 5, Lua-Lua 4, Stefanovic 3, O'Neil 2, Stone 2, Berkovic 1, De Zeeuw 1, Foxe 1, Mornar 1, Quashie 1, Roberts 1.
*Carling Cup (9):* Roberts 3, Sherwood 2, Yakubu 2, Taylor 1, own goal 1.
*FA Cup (7):* Taylor 3, Hughes 1, Schemmel 1, Sheringham 1, Yakubu 1.

| Hislop S 30 | Zivkovic B 17 + 1 | De Zeeuw A 36 | Faye A 27 | Foxe H 8 + 2 | Stefanovic D 32 | Stone S 29 + 3 | Quashie N 17 + 4 | Yakubu A 35 + 2 | Sheringham T 25 + 7 | Berger P 20 | Schemmel S 12 + 2 | Pericard V — + 6 | Harper K — + 7 | Primus L 19 + 2 | Smertin A 23 + 3 | Roberts J 4 + 6 | Sherwood T 7 + 6 | Taylor M 18 + 12 | O'Neil G 3 | Wapenaar H 5 | Burton D — + 1 | Srnicek P 3 | Hughes R 8 + 3 | Robinson C — + 1 | Pasanen P 11 + 1 | Berkovic E 10 + 1 | Mornar I 3 + 5 | Curtis J 5 + 1 | Lua-Lua L 10 + 5 | Todorov S 1 | Duffy R — + 1 | *Match No.* |
|---|---|---|---|---|---|---|---|---|---|---|---|---|---|---|---|---|---|---|---|---|---|---|---|---|---|---|---|---|---|---|---|---|
| 1 | 2 | 3 | $4^1$ | 5 | 6 | 7 | 8 | $9^2$ | 10 | 11 | 12 | 13 | | | | | | | | | | | | | | | | | | | | 1 |
| 1 | 3 | 5 | 4 | | 6 | 7 | 8 | $9^1$ | 10 | $11^2$ | 2 | 12 | 13 | | | | | | | | | | | | | | | | | | | 2 |
| 1 | 3 | 5 | 4 | | 6 | 7 | 8 | $9^1$ | 10 | 11 | $2^2$ | 12 | | 13 | | | | | | | | | | | | | | | | | | 3 |
| 1 | 3 | 5 | 4 | | 6 | $7^2$ | 8 | $9^1$ | 10 | 11 | 2 | 12 | | | 13 | | | | | | | | | | | | | | | | | 4 |
| 1 | 3 | 5 | 4 | | 6 | 7 | 8 | $9^2$ | $10^3$ | $11^1$ | 2 | | | | 12 | 13 | 14 | | | | | | | | | | | | | | | 5 |
| 1 | 3 | 5 | 4 | | 6 | 7 | $11^1$ | 9 | 10 | | 2 | 12 | | | | 13 | $8^2$ | | | | | | | | | | | | | | | 6 |
| 1 | 3 | 5 | $4^1$ | | 6 | 7 | | 9 | 10 | | 2 | | | | 8 | 13 | 12 | $11^2$ | | | | | | | | | | | | | | 7 |
| 1 | 3 | 5 | 4 | | 6 | 7 | | $9^1$ | 10 | $11^2$ | 2 | | | | $8^3$ | 12 | 14 | 13 | | | | | | | | | | | | | | 8 |
| 1 | 3 | 5 | 4 | 12 | $6^1$ | 7 | $8^2$ | 9 | 10 | 11 | 2 | | | | | | 13 | | | | | | | | | | | | | | | 9 |
| 1 | $3^1$ | 5 | $4^3$ | 12 | 6 | 7 | 8 | 9 | 10 | 11 | $2^2$ | | | | | | 14 | 13 | | | | | | | | | | | | | | 10 |
| 1 | $2^1$ | 3 | | 5 | 6 | 7 | 8 | 9 | 10 | 11 | | | | | | 12 | $4^2$ | 13 | | | | | | | | | | | | | | 11 |
| 1 | | 3 | | 5 | 6 | $7^1$ | | 9 | 10 | 11 | 2 | | | | | | 8 | 12 | 4 | | | | | | | | | | | | | 12 |
| | | 3 | | $5^2$ | 6 | $7^3$ | | 9 | 10 | 11■ | 2 | | | | 12 | | 8 | 13 | $4^1$ | 1 | 14 | | | | | | | | | | | 13 |
| | 2 | 3 | | $5^1$ | 6 | 7 | | 9 | 10 | 11 | | | | | 8 | | 4 | 12 | | 1 | | | | | | | | | | | | 14 |
| | 2 | 6 | $4^1$ | 5 | | 7■ | 12 | 9 | $10^2$ | $11^3$ | | | | 13 | 8 | | 14 | 3 | | | | 1 | | | | | | | | | | 15 |
| | 2 | | 4 | 5 | 6 | 7 | | 9 | $11^1$ | | | 12 | | | 8 | 10 | | 3 | | | | 1 | | | | | | | | | | 16 |
| | 12 | | | 5 | 6 | | | 13 | 10 | | $4^1$ | | | 2 | 8 | 9 | 7 | 3 | | 1 | | | $11^2$ | | | | | | | | | 17 |
| | 2 | 3 | | | 6 | 7 | | $9^2$ | 10 | 11 | | | | 5 | $8^1$ | 13 | $4^3$ | 12 | | 1 | | | 14 | | | | | | | | | 18 |
| | 3 | 5 | | | 6 | $7^1$ | | $9^3$ | | 11 | 12 | | | 2 | | 10 | | 13 | $4^2$ | 1 | | | 8 | 14 | | | | | | | | 19 |
| | $3^2$ | 6 | | | | | | 9 | 12 | 7 | | | 13 | 2 | $8^1$ | 10 | | 11 | | | | 1 | 4 | | 5 | | | | | | | 20 |
| 1 | | 6 | | | 3 | | | 9 | 10 | 7 | | | 12 | 2 | 8 | | | | | | | | 4 | | 5 | $11^1$ | | | | | | 21 |
| 1 | | 6 | | | 3■ | | | 9 | 10 | 7 | | | 13 | $2^2$ | 8 | | | 12 | | | | | $4^1$ | | 5 | 11 | | | | | | 22 |
| 1 | | 6 | 4 | | | 12 | 13 | 14 | 10 | 11 | | | | 2 | $8^2$ | | | 3 | | | | | | | 5 | $7^1$ | $9^3$ | | | | | 23 |
| 1 | | 6 | $4^3$ | | | 12 | 11 | 9 | $10^2$ | | | | | 5 | 8 | | | 3 | | | | | | | | $7^1$ | 13 | 2 | 14 | | | 24 |
| 1 | | 6 | 4 | | 3 | | 7 | 9 | | $11^2$ | | | | 2 | | | | 12 | | | | | | | 5 | $8^1$ | 10 | | 13 | | | 25 |
| 1 | | 6 | $4^2$ | | | | 11 | 9 | | | | | 12 | 2 | 7 | | | 3 | | | | | | | 5 | $8^1$ | 13 | | 10 | | | 26 |
| 1 | | 6 | 4 | | | $7^1$ | | 9 | 12 | | | | | 2 | | | | 13 | | | | | 8 | | 5 | $11^3$ | 14 | 3 | $10^2$ | | | 27 |
| 1 | | 6 | 4 | | 3 | 12 | | | | | | | | 5 | $7^1$ | | | 13 | | | | | 8 | | | | 11 | 2 | 10 | $9^2$ | | 28 |
| 1 | | 6 | 4 | | 3 | 7 | | $9^1$ | 10 | | | | | 2 | 8 | | | 11 | | | | | | | 5 | | | | 12 | | | 29 |
| 1 | | 6 | 4 | | 3 | 7 | | 9 | $10^2$ | | | | | 2 | 8 | | | $11^1$ | | | | | 12 | | 5 | | | | 13 | | | 30 |
| 1 | | 6 | 4 | | 3 | 7 | | 9 | $10^2$ | | | | | 2 | 8 | | | 11 | | | | | | | $5^1$ | 12 | | | 13 | | | 31 |
| 1 | | 6 | $4^2$ | | 5 | 7 | 14 | 9 | | | | | 13 | $2^1$ | 8 | | | 3 | | | | | | | 12 | $11^3$ | | | 10 | | | 32 |
| 1 | | 6 | 4 | | 5 | 7 | 13 | 9 | 12 | | | | | 2 | 8 | | | 3 | | | | | | | | $11^2$ | | | $10^1$ | | | 33 |
| 1 | | 6 | 4 | | 5 | $7^2$ | 11 | 9 | 12 | | | | 13 | 2 | 8 | | | 3 | | | | | | | | | | | $10^1$ | | | 34 |
| 1 | | 6 | 4 | | 5 | 7 | 11 | $9^1$ | 12 | | | | | $2^2$ | 8 | | | 3 | | | | | | | | | | | 10 | | 13 | 35 |
| 1 | | 6 | 4 | | 5 | 7 | 11 | $9^1$ | | | | | | | | | | 3 | | | | | 8 | | | | 12 | 2 | 10 | | | 36 |
| 1 | | 6 | $4^2$ | | 5 | $7^1$ | 11 | 9 | 12 | | | | | | 8 | | | 3 | | | | | | | | | 13 | 2 | 10 | | | 37 |
| 1 | | 6 | | | 5 | 7 | $11^3$ | 9 | 13 | | | | | | 4 | | | 3 | | | | | 14 | | $2^1$ | 8 | | 12 | $10^2$ | | | 38 |

**Carling Cup**

| | | | |
|---|---|---|---|
| Second Round | Northampton T | (h) | 5-2 |
| Third Round | Nottingham F | (a) | 4-2 |
| Fourth Round | Southampton | (a) | 0-2 |

**FA Cup**

| | | | |
|---|---|---|---|
| Third Round | Blackpool | (h) | 2-1 |
| Fourth Round | Scunthorpe U | (h) | 2-1 |
| Fifth Round | Liverpool | (a) | 1-1 |
| | | (h) | 1-0 |
| Sixth Round | Arsenal | (h) | 1-5 |

# PORT VALE — FL Championship 1

## FOUNDATION

Formed in 1876 as Port Vale, adopting the prefix 'Burslem' in 1884 upon moving to that part of the city. It was dropped in 1909.

***Vale Park, Burslem, Stoke-on-Trent ST6 1AW.***

***Telephone:*** (01782) 655 800.

***Fax:*** (01782) 834 981.

***Ticket Office:*** (01782) 811 707.

***Website:*** www.port-vale.co.uk

***Email:*** pvfc@port-vale.co.uk

***Ground Capacity:*** 18,982.

***Record Attendance:*** 49,768 v Aston Villa, FA Cup 5th rd, 20 February 1960.

***Pitch Measurements:*** 114yd × 75yd.

***Chairman:*** William A. Bratt.

***Secretary:*** Frederick W. Lodey.

***Manager:*** Martin Foyle.

***Assistant Manager:*** Dean Glover.

***Physio:*** Andrew Jackson.

***Colours:*** White shirts with black trim, black shorts, black stockings.

***Change Colours:*** All yellow.

***Year Formed:*** 1876.

***Turned Professional:*** 1885.

***Ltd Co.:*** 1911.

***Previous Name:*** 1876, Port Vale; 1884, Burslem Port Vale; 1909, Port Vale.

***Club Nickname:*** 'Valiants'.

***Previous Grounds:*** 1876, Limekin Lane, Longport; 1881, Westport; 1884, Moorland Road, Burslem; 1886, Athletic Ground, Cobridge; 1913, Recreation Ground, Hanley; 1950, Vale Park.

***First Football League Game:*** 3 September 1892, Division 2, v Small Heath (a) L 1–5 – Frail; Clutton, Elson; Farrington, McCrindle, Delves; Walker, Scarratt, Bliss (1), Jones. (Only 10 men).

***Record League Victory:*** 9–1 v Chesterfield, Division 2, 24 September 1932 – Leckie; Shenton, Poyser; Sherlock, Round, Jones; McGrath, Mills, Littlewood (6), Kirkham (2), Morton (1).

***Record Cup Victory:*** 7–1 v Irthlingborough, FA Cup 1st rd, 12 January 1907 – Matthews; Dunn, Hamilton; Eardley, Baddeley, Holyhead; Carter, Dodds (2), Beats, Mountford (2), Coxon (3).

***Record Defeat:*** 0–10 v Sheffield U, Division 2, 10 December 1892. 0–10 v Notts Co, Division 2, 26 February 1895.

## HONOURS

*Football League:* Division 2 – Runners-up 1993–94; Division 3 (N) – Champions 1929–30, 1953–54; Runners-up 1952–53; Division 4 – Champions 1958–59; Promoted 1969–70 (4th).

*FA Cup:* Semi-final 1954, when in Division 3.

*Football League Cup:* best season: 3rd rd 1992, 1997.

*Autoglass Trophy:* Winners 1993.

*Anglo-Italian Cup:* Runners-up 1996.

*LDV Vans Trophy:* Winners 2001.

## SKY SPORTS FACT FILE

During their 1929–30 Third Division (North) championship winning season, Port Vale relied heavily on three marksmen: Sam Jennings 24 goals, Albert Pynegar 21 and Philip Griffiths 14. Amazingly this trio miss a total of 38 games between them!

***Most League Points (2 for a win):*** 69, Division 3 (N), 1953–54.

***Most League Points (3 for a win):*** 89, Division 2, 1992–93.

***Most League Goals:*** 110, Division 4, 1958–59.

***Highest League Scorer in Season:*** Wilf Kirkham 38, Division 2, 1926–27.

***Most League Goals in Total Aggregate:*** Wilf Kirkham, 154, 1923–29, 1931–33.

***Most League Goals in One Match:*** 6, Stewart Littlewood v Chesterfield, Division 2, 24 September 1922.

***Most Capped Player:*** Tony Rougier, Trinidad & Tobago.

***Most League Appearances:*** Roy Sproson, 761, 1950–72.

***Youngest League Player:*** Malcolm McKenzie, 15 years 347 days v Newport Co, 12 April 1966.

***Record Transfer Fee Received:*** £2,000,000 from Wimbledon for Gareth Ainsworth, October 1998.

***Record Transfer Fee Paid:*** £500,000 to York C for Jon McCarthy, August 1995; £500,000 to Lincoln C for Gareth Ainsworth, September 1997.

***Football League Record:*** 1892 Original Member of Division 2. Failed re-election in 1896; Re-elected 1898; Resigned 1907; Returned in Oct, 1919, when they took over the fixtures of Leeds City; 1929–30 Division 3 (N); 1930–36 Division 2; 1936–38 Division 3 (N); 1938–52 Division 3 (S); 1952–54 Division 3 (N); 1954–57 Division 2; 1957–58 Division 3 (S); 1958–59 Division 4; 1959–65 Division 3; 1965–70 Division 4; 1970–78 Division 3; 1978–83 Division 4; 1983–84 Division 3; 1984–86 Division 4; 1986–89 Division 3; 1989–94 Division 2; 1994–2000 Division 1; 2000–04 Division 2; 2004– FL1.

## MANAGERS

Sam Gleaves 1896–1905
*(Secretary-Manager)*
Tom Clare 1905–11
A. S. Walker 1911–12
H. Myatt 1912–14
Tom Holford 1919–24
*(continued as Trainer)*
Joe Schofield 1924–30
Tom Morgan 1930–32
Tom Holford 1932–35
Warney Cresswell 1936–37
Tom Morgan 1937–38
Billy Frith 1945–46
Gordon Hodgson 1946–51
Ivor Powell 1951
Freddie Steele 1951–57
Norman Low 1957–62
Freddie Steele 1962–65
Jackie Mudie 1965–67
Sir Stanley Matthews
*(General Manager)* 1965–68
Gordon Lee 1968–74
Roy Sproson 1974–77
Colin Harper 1977
Bobby Smith 1977–78
Dennis Butler 1978–79
Alan Bloor 1979
John McGrath 1980–83
John Rudge 1984–99
Brian Horton 1999–2004
Martin Foyle February 2004–

## LATEST SEQUENCES

***Longest Sequence of League Wins:*** 8, 8.4.1893 – 30.9.1893.

***Longest Sequence of League Defeats:*** 9, 9.3.1957 – 20.4.1957.

***Longest Sequence of League Draws:*** 6, 26.4.1981 – 12.9.1981.

***Longest Sequence of Unbeaten League Matches:*** 19, 5.5.1969 – 8.11.1969.

***Longest Sequence Without a League Win:*** 17, 7.12.1991 – 21.3.1992.

***Successive Scoring Runs:*** 22 from 12.9.1992.

***Successive Non-scoring Runs:*** 4 from 10.2.1896.

## TEN YEAR LEAGUE RECORD

| | | P | W | D | L | F | A | Pts | Pos |
|---|---|---|---|---|---|---|---|---|---|
| 1994-95 | Div 1 | 46 | 15 | 13 | 18 | 58 | 64 | 58 | 17 |
| 1995-96 | Div 1 | 46 | 15 | 15 | 16 | 59 | 66 | 60 | 12 |
| 1996-97 | Div 1 | 46 | 17 | 16 | 13 | 58 | 55 | 67 | 8 |
| 1997-98 | Div 1 | 46 | 13 | 10 | 23 | 56 | 66 | 49 | 19 |
| 1998-99 | Div 1 | 46 | 13 | 8 | 25 | 45 | 75 | 47 | 21 |
| 1999-2000 | Div 1 | 46 | 7 | 15 | 24 | 48 | 69 | 36 | 23 |
| 2000-01 | Div 2 | 46 | 16 | 14 | 16 | 55 | 49 | 62 | 11 |
| 2001-02 | Div 2 | 46 | 16 | 10 | 20 | 51 | 62 | 58 | 14 |
| 2002-03 | Div 2 | 46 | 14 | 11 | 21 | 54 | 70 | 53 | 17 |
| 2003-04 | Div 2 | 46 | 21 | 10 | 15 | 73 | 63 | 73 | 7 |

## DID YOU KNOW ?

In 1969–70 Port Vale remained the longest unbeaten team in the Football League from the start of the season, stretching 18 matches. The run contained eight draws, five of which were goalless. But it helped towards fourth place and promotion.

## PORT VALE 2003–04 LEAGUE RECORD

| Match No. | Date | Venue | Opponents | Result | H/T Score | Lg. Pos. | Goalscorers | Attendance |
|---|---|---|---|---|---|---|---|---|
| 1 | Aug 9 | H | Bournemouth | W 2-1 | 0-0 | — | McPhee [67], Littlejohn [87] | 6465 |
| 2 | 16 | A | Grimsby T | W 2-1 | 0-1 | 2 | McPhee [65], Paynter [68] | 4816 |
| 3 | 23 | H | Colchester U | W 4-3 | 1-2 | 1 | Collins [34], Paynter [58], Armstrong [71], McPhee [73] | 5133 |
| 4 | 25 | A | Hartlepool U | L 0-2 | 0-1 | 4 | | 5314 |
| 5 | 30 | H | Brentford | W 1-0 | 0-0 | 1 | Paynter [63] | 5257 |
| 6 | Sept 6 | A | Stockport Co | D 2-2 | 0-2 | 3 | Paynter [82], Collins [90] | 5316 |
| 7 | 13 | H | Barnsley | W 3-1 | 1-1 | 1 | Lipa [23], Pilkington [55], Littlejohn [73] | 7809 |
| 8 | 16 | A | Luton T | L 0-2 | 0-1 | — | | 5079 |
| 9 | 20 | A | Bristol C | W 1-0 | 0-0 | 1 | Paynter [71] | 11,369 |
| 10 | 27 | H | Wycombe W | D 1-1 | 1-0 | 1 | McPhee [44] | 6822 |
| 11 | 30 | H | Peterborough U | W 3-0 | 1-0 | — | McPhee 2 [12, 67], Collins [86] | 5495 |
| 12 | Oct 4 | A | Wrexham | L 1-2 | 1-1 | 3 | Paynter [20] | 5822 |
| 13 | 11 | A | Oldham Ath | L 1-2 | 0-0 | 3 | Bridge-Wilkinson (pen) [76] | 6913 |
| 14 | 18 | H | Plymouth Arg | L 1-5 | 0-3 | 6 | McPhee [51] | 5786 |
| 15 | 21 | H | QPR | W 2-0 | 2-0 | — | Paynter [5], McPhee [9] | 5243 |
| 16 | 25 | A | Swindon T | D 0-0 | 0-0 | 4 | | 5313 |
| 17 | Nov 1 | A | Chesterfield | L 0-1 | 0-0 | 7 | | 4088 |
| 18 | 15 | H | Notts Co | W 1-0 | 0-0 | 5 | McPhee [56] | 4900 |
| 19 | 22 | A | Tranmere R | L 0-1 | 0-0 | 7 | | 7081 |
| 20 | 29 | H | Rushden & D | D 1-1 | 1-1 | 7 | Littlejohn [10] | 4586 |
| 21 | Dec 12 | A | Brighton & HA | D 1-1 | 0-1 | — | Littlejohn [50] | 5811 |
| 22 | 26 | A | Sheffield W | W 3-2 | 1-2 | 7 | Littlejohn [25], Paynter [54], Brooker [89] | 24,991 |
| 23 | 28 | H | Stockport Co | D 2-2 | 2-2 | 8 | McPhee 2 [4, 28] | 6237 |
| 24 | Jan 10 | A | Bournemouth | L 1-2 | 1-0 | 12 | McPhee [23] | 5926 |
| 25 | 14 | H | Blackpool | W 2-1 | 2-0 | — | Brooker [8], Bridge-Wilkinson [29] | 4523 |
| 26 | 17 | H | Grimsby T | W 5-1 | 4-1 | 4 | Lipa [18], Collins [20], Bridge-Wilkinson 2 [33, 74], Paynter [45] | 5133 |
| 27 | 27 | H | Hartlepool U | L 2-5 | 1-2 | — | Brooker [8], Cummins [87] | 4845 |
| 28 | 31 | A | Brentford | L 2-3 | 1-1 | 9 | McPhee 2 [30, 90] | 4306 |
| 29 | Feb 7 | H | Sheffield W | W 3-0 | 1-0 | 7 | Littlejohn [42], McPhee [72], Brooker [90] | 7958 |
| 30 | 14 | H | Oldham Ath | W 1-0 | 0-0 | 5 | McPhee [46] | 6035 |
| 31 | 21 | A | Plymouth Arg | L 1-2 | 0-0 | 7 | McPhee [53] | 11,330 |
| 32 | 24 | A | Colchester U | W 4-1 | 3-1 | — | Brooker [13], Brown W (og) [24], Cummins [27], Bridge-Wilkinson [73] | 2539 |
| 33 | Mar 2 | A | QPR | L 2-3 | 1-0 | — | Brooker [2], Littlejohn [89] | 12,593 |
| 34 | 6 | A | Blackpool | L 1-2 | 1-0 | 9 | Paynter [4] | 6878 |
| 35 | 13 | H | Brighton & HA | D 1-1 | 1-1 | 9 | Paynter [26] | 5646 |
| 36 | 16 | H | Luton T | W 1-0 | 0-0 | — | Cummins [84] | 5048 |
| 37 | 20 | A | Barnsley | D 0-0 | 0-0 | 9 | | 8267 |
| 38 | 27 | H | Bristol C | W 2-1 | 0-0 | 7 | Brooker [66], Bridge-Wilkinson [77] | 6724 |
| 39 | 30 | H | Swindon T | D 3-3 | 2-0 | — | Paynter [14], McPhee 2 [41, 58] | 5702 |
| 40 | Apr 3 | A | Wycombe W | L 1-2 | 1-1 | 7 | McPhee [7] | 4738 |
| 41 | 10 | H | Wrexham | W 1-0 | 0-0 | 7 | Cummins [52] | 5892 |
| 42 | 12 | A | Peterborough U | L 1-3 | 0-1 | 7 | Bridge-Wilkinson [90] | 4988 |
| 43 | 17 | H | Chesterfield | D 1-1 | 0-1 | 7 | Paynter [74] | 5582 |
| 44 | 24 | A | Notts Co | W 2-1 | 2-0 | 7 | McPhee [4], Brooker [34] | 5834 |
| 45 | May 1 | H | Tranmere R | W 2-1 | 1-1 | 7 | McPhee 2 [10, 90] | 6806 |
| 46 | 8 | A | Rushden & D | W 2-0 | 1-0 | 7 | McPhee 2 [14, 90] | 5240 |

**Final League Position: 7**

## GOALSCORERS

*League (73):* McPhee 25, Paynter 13, Brooker 8, Bridge-Wilkinson 7 (1 pen), Littlejohn 7, Collins 4, Cummins 4, Lipa 2, Armstrong 1, Pilkington 1, own goal 1.
*Carling Cup (0).*
*FA Cup (4):* Burns 1, McPhee 1, Paynter 1, own goal 1.
*LDV Vans Trophy (1):* McPhee 1.

| Delany D 14 | Cummins M 42 | Boyd M 20 + 2 | Collins S 43 | Burns L 19 + 8 | Pilkington G 44 | Brown R 17 | Armstrong I 4 + 16 | McPhee S 46 | Brooker S 29 + 3 | Bridge-Wilkinson M 27 + 5 | Lipa A 27 + 3 | Walsh M 12 + 1 | Littlejohn A 24 + 12 | Rowland S 26 + 3 | Paynter B 42 + 2 | Brisco N 20 + 7 | Birchall C 1 + 9 | Brightwell I 2 | Brain J 32 | Reid L 7 + 4 | James C 8 | *Match No.* |
|---|---|---|---|---|---|---|---|---|---|---|---|---|---|---|---|---|---|---|---|---|---|---|
| 1 | 2 | $3^{1}$ | 4 | $5^{2}$ | 6 | 7 | $8^{3}$ | 9 | 10 | 11 | 12 | 13 | 14 | | | | | | | | | 1 |
| 1 | $2^{1}$ | | 4 | | $6^{2}$ | 7 | | 9 | 10 | 11 | 3 | 5 | 8 | 12 | 13 | | | | | | | 2 |
| 1 | 2 | | 4 | | 6 | 7 | 12 | 9 | $10^{1}$ | $11^{2}$ | 3 | 5 | 8 | | 13 | | | | | | | 3 |
| 1 | 2 | | 4 | | 6 | 7 | 12 | 9 | | $11^{1}$ | 3 | 5 | 8 | | 10 | | | | | | | 4 |
| 1 | $2^{1}$ | | 4 | | 6 | 7 | | 9 | 10 | | 3 | 5 | 11 | | 8 | 12 | | | | | | 5 |
| 1 | | 2 | 4 | 5 | 6 | 7 | 12 | $9^{1}$ | 10 | | 3 | | 11 | | 8 | | | | | | | 6 |
| 1 | | 3 | 4 | 5 | 6 | 7 | | 9 | 10 | | 2 | | 11 | | 8 | | | | | | | 7 |
| 1 | | 3 | 4 | $5^{2}$ | 6 | $7^{3}$ | 12 | 9 | 10 | | 2 | | $11^{1}$ | 14 | 8 | 13 | | | | | | 8 |
| 1 | 2 | 11 | 4 | | 6 | 7 | | 9 | 10 | | 3 | 5 | | | 8 | | | | | | | 9 |
| 1 | | $2^{2}$ | 4 | 5 | 6 | 7 | 12 | 9 | 10 | | 3 | | $11^{1}$ | | 8 | | 13 | | | | | 10 |
| 1 | 2 | 8 | 4 | 5 | 6 | 7 | $11^{1}$ | 9 | | | 3 | | 12 | | 10 | | | | | | | 11 |
| 1 | 2 | $8^{2}$ | 4 | 5 | 6 | $7^{3}$ | $11^{1}$ | 9 | 12 | | 3 | | 13 | | 10 | 14 | | | | | | 12 |
| 1 | 2 | | 4 | 5 | 6 | | $8^{1}$ | 9 | | 11 | 3 | | 12 | | 10 | 7 | | | | | | 13 |
| 1 | 2 | | 4 | 13 | 6 | $7^{2}$ | 14 | 9 | | 12 | 3 | | 8 | | 10 | | $11^{3}$ | $5^{1}$ | | | | 14 |
| | 2 | | 4 | 5 | 6 | | | 9 | | | 3 | 7 | 8 | 11■ | 10 | | | | 1 | | | 15 |
| | 2 | 12 | 4 | 8 | 6 | | | 9 | | | 3 | 5 | $11^{1}$ | 7 | 10 | | | | 1 | | | 16 |
| | $2^{2}$ | 12 | 4 | $8^{1}$ | 6 | | | 9 | | | 3 | 5 | 11 | 7 | 10 | | | | 1 | 13 | | 17 |
| | 2 | 7 | 4 | 5 | 6 | | | 9 | | | | | 11 | | 10 | 8 | | | 1 | 3 | | 18 |
| | 2 | $7^{2}$ | 4 | 5 | 6 | | | 9 | | | 3 | | 12 | | 10 | 8 | 13 | | 1 | $11^{1}$ | | 19 |
| | 2 | 7 | 4 | 5 | 6 | | 12 | 9 | | | 3 | | 10 | | | $8^{1}$ | | | 1 | 11 | | 20 |
| | 2 | 7 | 4 | | 6 | | | 9 | $10^{2}$ | 13 | $3^{1}$ | | 12 | 5 | 11 | 8 | | | 1 | | | 21 |
| | 2 | $7^{2}$ | $4^{1}$ | | 6 | | | 9 | 12 | 13 | 3 | | 11 | 5 | 10 | 8 | | | 1 | | | 22 |
| | 2 | 7 | 4 | | $6^{1}$ | | | 9 | 13 | 12 | $3^{2}$ | | 11 | 5 | 10 | 8 | | | 1 | | | 23 |
| | 2 | 7 | 4 | | | | 13 | 9 | 10 | 12 | $3^{1}$ | | $11^{2}$ | 5 | 8 | 6 | | | 1 | | | 24 |
| | 2 | 7 | 4 | 12 | 6 | | | 9 | $10^{1}$ | 11 | 3 | | | | 8 | 5 | | | 1 | | | 25 |
| | 2 | 7 | 4 | | 6 | | 13 | 9 | $10^{2}$ | 11 | $3^{1}$ | | 12 | | 8 | 5 | | | 1 | | | 26 |
| | 2 | 7 | 4■ | | 6 | | | 9 | 10 | 11 | $3^{1}$ | | | 12 | 8 | 5 | | | 1 | | | 27 |
| | 2 | 5 | 4 | 14 | $6^{3}$ | | 12 | 9 | 10 | 11 | | | $7^{1}$ | $3^{2}$ | 8 | | | | 1 | 13 | | 28 |
| | 2 | | 4 | 5 | | | | 9 | 10 | 11 | | | 7 | 3 | 8 | 6 | | | 1 | | | 29 |
| | 2 | | | 5 | 6 | 4 | | 9 | $10^{1}$ | 11 | | | 7 | 3 | 8 | 12 | | | 1 | | | 30 |
| | $2^{1}$ | | | 5 | 6 | 4 | | 9 | 10 | 11 | | | 7 | 3 | 8 | 12 | | | 1 | | | 31 |
| | 2 | $7^{1}$ | 4 | | 6 | 3 | | 9 | $10^{2}$ | 11 | | | 13 | 5 | 8 | 12 | | | 1 | | | 32 |
| | 2 | | 4 | 12 | 6 | $3^{1}$ | | 9 | 10 | 11 | | | 13 | 5 | $8^{2}$ | 7 | | | 1 | | | 33 |
| | 2 | | 4 | 12 | 6 | | | 9 | | 11 | | $5^{1}$ | $7^{2}$ | 3 | 10 | $8^{3}$ | 14 | | 1 | 13 | | 34 |
| | 2 | | 4 | | 6 | | 12 | 9 | 10 | 11 | | 5 | $7^{1}$ | 3 | $8^{2}$ | | 13 | | 1 | | | 35 |
| | 2 | | 4 | | 6 | | 12 | 9 | 10 | 11 | | 5 | | 3 | 8 | $7^{1}$ | | | 1 | | | 36 |
| | 2 | | 4 | 12 | 6 | | | 9 | 10 | 11 | | $5^{1}$ | | 3 | 8 | 7 | | | 1 | | | 37 |
| | 2 | | 4 | | 6 | | | 9 | $10^{1}$ | 11 | | | | 5 | 8 | 7 | 12 | | 1 | | 3 | 38 |
| | 2 | | 4 | | 6 | | | 9 | $10^{1}$ | 11 | | | | 5 | 8 | 7 | 12 | | 1 | | 3 | 39 |
| | 2 | | | 4 | 6 | | 12 | 9 | | 11 | $7^{2}$ | | | $5^{3}$ | 10 | $8^{1}$ | 13 | | 1 | 14 | 3 | 40 |
| | $2^{2}$ | | 4 | 13 | 6 | | | 9 | $10^{3}$ | 11 | 12 | | 14 | 5 | 8 | $7^{1}$ | | | 1 | | 3 | 41 |
| | 2 | | 4 | 5 | 6 | | 12 | 9 | | 11 | $7^{2}$ | | 13 | 3 | $10^{1}$ | | | | 1 | | 8 | 42 |
| | 2 | | 4 | | 6 | | 12 | 9 | | 11 | | | 8 | 3 | 10 | | 13 | $5^{1}$ | 1 | $7^{2}$ | | 43 |
| | 2 | | 4 | 13 | 6 | | | $9^{3}$ | $10^{2}$ | $11^{1}$ | 12 | | | 5 | 8 | | 14 | | 1 | 7 | 3 | 44 |
| | 2 | | 4 | | 6 | | 12 | 9 | 10 | 11 | | | 13 | 5 | $8^{2}$ | | | | 1 | $7^{1}$ | 3 | 45 |
| | 2 | | 4 | | 6 | | | 9 | $10^{1}$ | 11 | | | | 5 | 8 | 12 | | | 1 | 7 | 3 | 46 |

**Carling Cup**
First Round Nottingham F (h) 0-0

**LDV Vans Trophy**
First Round Scarborough (a) 1-2

**FA Cup**
First Round Ford U (h) 2-2
(a) 2-1
Second Round Scarborough (h) 0-1

# PRESTON NORTH END FL Championship

## FOUNDATION

North End Cricket and Rugby Club which was formed in 1863, indulged in most sports before taking up soccer in about 1879. In 1881 they decided to stick to football to the exclusion of other sports and even a 16–0 drubbing by Blackburn Rovers in an invitation game at Deepdale, a few weeks after taking this decision, did not deter them for they immediately became affiliated to the Lancashire FA.

***Deepdale, Preston PR1 6RU.***
***Telephone:*** 0870 442 1964.
***Fax:*** (01772) 693 366.
***Website:*** www.pne.com
***Email:*** enquiries@pne.com
***Ticket Enquiries:*** 0870 442 1966.
***Ground Capacity:*** 20,600.
***Record Attendance:*** 42,684 v Arsenal, Division 1, 23 April 1938.
***Pitch Measurements:*** 110yd × 77yd.
***Chairman:*** Derek Shaw.
***Vice-chairman:*** David Taylor.
***Secretary:*** Janet Parr.
***Manager:*** Craig Brown.
***Physio:*** Andrew Balderston.
***Colours:*** White shirts, navy shorts, white stockings.
***Change Colours:*** Blue shirts, white shorts, blue stockings.
***Year Formed:*** 1881.
***Turned Professional:*** 1885.
***Ltd Co.:*** 1893.
***Club Nicknames:*** 'The Lilywhites' or 'North End'.
***First Football League Game:*** 8 September 1888, Football League, v Burnley (h) W 5–2 – Trainer; Howarth, Holmes; Robertson, W. Graham, J. Graham; Gordon (1), Ross (2), Goodall, Dewhurst (2), Drummond.
***Record League Victory:*** 10–0 v Stoke, Division 1, 14 September 1889 – Trainer; Howarth, Holmes; Kelso, Russell (1), Graham; Gordon, Jimmy Ross (2), Nick Ross (3), Thomson (2), Drummond (2).
***Record Cup Victory:*** 26–0 v Hyde, FA Cup 1st rd, 15 October 1887 – Addision; Howarth, Nick Ross; Russell (1), Thomson (5), Graham (1); Gordon (5), Jimmy Ross (8), John Goodall (1), Dewhurst (3), Drummond (2).
***Record Defeat:*** 0–7 v Blackpool, Division 1, 1 May 1948.
***Most League Points (2 for a win):*** 61, Division 3, 1970–71.
***Most League Points (3 for a win):*** 95, Division 2, 1999–2000.

## HONOURS

*Football League:* Division 1 – Champions 1888–89 (first champions) 1889–90; Runners-up 1890–91, 1891–92, 1892–93, 1905–06, 1952–53, 1957–58; Division 2 – Champions 1903–04, 1912–13, 1950–51, 1999–2000; Runners-up 1914–15, 1933–34; Division 3 – Champions 1970–71, 1995–96; Division 4 – Runners-up 1986–87.

*FA Cup:* Winners 1889, 1938; Runners-up 1888, 1922, 1937, 1954, 1964.

*Football League Cup:* best season: 4th rd, 2003.

*Double Performed:* 1888–89.

*Football League Cup:* best season: 4th rd, 1963, 1966, 1972, 1981.

## SKY SPORTS FACT FILE

On 28 December 1935 Preston North End defeated Huddersfield Town 4-0. The fourth goal was the 2,500th League goal scored by the club. On 13 April 1936 Preston completed their 1,600th League fixture with a 1-0 victory over Bolton Wanderers.

***Most League Goals:*** 100, Division 2, 1927–28 and Division 1, 1957–58.

***Highest League Scorer in Season:*** Ted Harper, 37, Division 2, 1932–33.

***Most League Goals in Total Aggregate:*** Tom Finney, 187, 1946–60.

***Most League Goals in One Match:*** 4, Jimmy Ross v Stoke, Division 1, 6 October 1888; 4, Nick Ross v Derby Co, Division 1, 11 January 1890; 4, George Drummond v Notts Co, Division 1, 12 December 1891; 4, Frank Becton v Notts Co, Division 1, 31 March 1893; 4, George Harrison v Grimsby T, Division 2, 3 November 1928; 4, Alex Reid v Port Vale, Division 2, 23 February 1929; 4, James McClelland v Reading, Division 2, 6 September 1930; 4, Dick Rowley v Notts Co, Division 2, 16 April 1932; 4, Ted Harper v Burnley, Division 2, 29 August 1932; 4, Ted Harper v Lincoln C, Division 2, 11 March 1933; 4, Charlie Wayman v QPR, Division 2, 25 December 1950; 4, Alex Bruce v Colchester U, Division 3, 28 February 1978.

***Most Capped Player:*** Tom Finney, 76, England.

***Most League Appearances:*** Alan Kelly, 447, 1961–75.

***Youngest League Player:*** Steve Doyle, 16 years 166 days v Tranmere R, 15 November 1974.

***Record Transfer Fee Received:*** £5,000,000 from Manchester C for Jon Macken March 2002.

***Record Transfer Fee Paid:*** £1,500,000 to Manchester U for David Healy, December 2000.

***Football League Record:*** 1888 Founder Member of League; 1901–04 Division 2; 1904–12 Division 1; 1912–13 Division 2; 1913–14 Division 1; 1914–15 Division 2; 1919–25 Division 1; 1925–34 Division 2; 1934–49 Division 1; 1949–51 Division 2; 1951–61 Division 1; 1961–70 Division 2; 1970–71 Division 3; 1971–74 Division 2; 1974–78 Division 3; 1978–81 Division 2; 1981–85 Division 3; 1985–87 Division 4; 1987–92 Division 3; 1992–93 Division 2; 1993–96 Division 3; 1996–2000 Division 2; 2000–04 Division 1; 2004– FLC.

## MANAGERS

Charlie Parker 1906–15
Vincent Hayes 1919–23
Jim Lawrence 1923–25
Frank Richards 1925–27
Alex Gibson 1927–31
Lincoln Hayes 1931–32
*Run by committee* 1932–36
Tommy Muirhead 1936–37
*Run by committee* 1937–49
Will Scott 1949–53
Scot Symon 1953–54
Frank Hill 1954–56
Cliff Britton 1956–61
Jimmy Milne 1961–68
Bobby Seith 1968–70
Alan Ball Sr 1970–73
Bobby Charlton 1973–75
Harry Catterick 1975–77
Nobby Stiles 1977–81
Tommy Docherty 1981
Gordon Lee 1981–83
Alan Kelly 1983–85
Tommy Booth 1985–86
Brian Kidd 1986
John McGrath 1986–90
Les Chapman 1990–92
Sam Allardyce 1992 (*Caretaker*)
John Beck 1992–94
Gary Peters 1994–98
David Moyes 1998–2002
Kelham O'Hanlon 2002 (*Caretaker*)
Craig Brown April 2002–

## LATEST SEQUENCES

***Longest Sequence of League Wins:*** 14, 25.12.1950 – 27.3.1951.

***Longest Sequence of League Defeats:*** 8, 22.9.1984 – 27.10.1984.

***Longest Sequence of League Draws:*** 6, 24.2.1979 – 20.3.1979.

***Longest Sequence of Unbeaten League Matches:*** 23, 8.9.1888 – 14.9.1889.

***Longest Sequence Without a League Win:*** 15, 14.4.1923 – 20.10.1923.

***Successive Scoring Runs:*** 30 from 15.11.1952.

***Successive Non-scoring Runs:*** 6 from 8.4.1897.

## TEN YEAR LEAGUE RECORD

| | | *P* | *W* | *D* | *L* | *F* | *A* | *Pts* | *Pos* |
|---|---|---|---|---|---|---|---|---|---|
| 1994-95 | Div 3 | 42 | 19 | 10 | 13 | 58 | 41 | 67 | 5 |
| 1995-96 | Div 3 | 46 | 23 | 17 | 6 | 78 | 38 | 86 | 1 |
| 1996-97 | Div 2 | 46 | 18 | 7 | 21 | 49 | 55 | 61 | 15 |
| 1997-98 | Div 2 | 46 | 15 | 14 | 17 | 56 | 56 | 59 | 15 |
| 1998-99 | Div 2 | 46 | 22 | 13 | 11 | 78 | 50 | 79 | 5 |
| 1999-2000 | Div 2 | 46 | 28 | 11 | 7 | 74 | 37 | 95 | 1 |
| 2000-01 | Div 1 | 46 | 23 | 9 | 14 | 64 | 52 | 78 | 4 |
| 2001-02 | Div 1 | 46 | 20 | 12 | 14 | 71 | 59 | 72 | 8 |
| 2002-03 | Div 1 | 46 | 16 | 13 | 17 | 68 | 70 | 61 | 12 |
| 2003-04 | Div 1 | 46 | 15 | 14 | 17 | 69 | 71 | 59 | 15 |

## DID YOU KNOW ?

In 1903–04 Preston North End opened what was to be a Second Division championship-winning season by beating Stockport County 5-1. They remained unbeaten in the first 13 League games, the longest sequence that term in the competition.

## PRESTON NORTH END 2003–04 LEAGUE RECORD

| *Match No.* | *Date* | *Venue* | *Opponents* | *Result* | *H/T Score* | *Lg. Pos.* | *Goalscorers* | *Attendance* |
|---|---|---|---|---|---|---|---|---|
| 1 | Aug 9 | H | West Ham U | L 1-2 | 1-1 | — | Lewis [2] | 18,246 |
| 2 | 16 | A | Wigan Ath | D 1-1 | 0-0 | 16 | Fuller [87] | 12,073 |
| 3 | 23 | H | Sunderland | L 0-2 | 0-2 | 21 | | 14,018 |
| 4 | 25 | A | WBA | L 0-1 | 0-1 | 23 | | 24,402 |
| 5 | 30 | H | Stoke C | W 1-0 | 1-0 | 18 | McKenna [19] | 12,965 |
| 6 | Sept 13 | A | Bradford C | L 1-2 | 1-0 | 21 | Fuller [10] | 11,243 |
| 7 | 16 | H | Coventry C | W 4-2 | 2-1 | — | Fuller 2 [35, 45], Cresswell [66], Keane [88] | 11,886 |
| 8 | 20 | H | Rotherham U | W 4-1 | 1-1 | 16 | Cresswell [11], Fuller [55], Alexander (pen) [65], O'Neil [73] | 12,340 |
| 9 | 27 | A | Walsall | L 1-2 | 0-0 | 17 | Fuller [62] | 6981 |
| 10 | Oct 1 | A | Nottingham F | W 1-0 | 1-0 | — | Abbott [36] | 22,278 |
| 11 | 4 | H | Wimbledon | W 1-0 | 1-0 | 10 | Fuller [29] | 13,801 |
| 12 | 14 | A | Millwall | W 1-0 | 0-0 | — | McKenna [51] | 8015 |
| 13 | 18 | A | Reading | L 2-3 | 1-1 | 12 | Fuller [20], Alexander (pen) [53] | 13,130 |
| 14 | 21 | A | Crewe Alex | L 1-2 | 0-2 | — | Etuhu [90] | 7012 |
| 15 | 25 | H | Ipswich T | D 1-1 | 1-0 | 13 | Healy [21] | 14,863 |
| 16 | Nov 1 | H | Derby Co | W 3-0 | 1-0 | 13 | Alexander (pen) [22], Healy [68], Fuller [72] | 12,839 |
| 17 | 4 | H | Watford | W 2-1 | 0-0 | — | Abbott [51], Healy [90] | 11,152 |
| 18 | 8 | A | Crystal Palace | D 1-1 | 0-0 | 9 | Healy [51] | 14,608 |
| 19 | 22 | H | Norwich C | D 0-0 | 0-0 | 10 | | 14,775 |
| 20 | 29 | A | Sheffield U | L 0-2 | 0-1 | 10 | | 21,003 |
| 21 | Dec 6 | H | Crystal Palace | W 4-1 | 0-0 | 10 | Etuhu [48], Alexander (pen) [50], Lewis [79], Healy [90] | 12,836 |
| 22 | 9 | A | Cardiff C | D 2-2 | 0-0 | — | Fuller [52], Healy [84] | 13,703 |
| 23 | 13 | A | Gillingham | W 1-0 | 1-0 | 9 | Fuller [3] | 7602 |
| 24 | 20 | H | Burnley | W 5-3 | 1-1 | 7 | Fuller 3 [18, 71, 82], Lewis [60], Healy [88] | 18,802 |
| 25 | 26 | A | Stoke C | D 1-1 | 0-0 | 7 | Healy [66] | 20,126 |
| 26 | 28 | H | Crewe Alex | D 0-0 | 0-0 | 8 | | 15,830 |
| 27 | Jan 10 | A | West Ham U | W 2-1 | 0-1 | 5 | Fuller [64], Healy [67] | 28,777 |
| 28 | 17 | H | Wigan Ath | L 2-4 | 1-2 | 7 | Etuhu [30], Alexander (pen) [86] | 19,161 |
| 29 | Feb 7 | H | WBA | W 3-0 | 1-0 | 8 | Lewis [33], Healy [75], Alexander (pen) [87] | 16,569 |
| 30 | 14 | A | Watford | L 0-2 | 0-1 | 9 | | 12,675 |
| 31 | 21 | H | Millwall | L 1-2 | 0-1 | 12 | Davis [70] | 12,903 |
| 32 | 28 | A | Ipswich T | L 0-2 | 0-0 | 13 | | 23,359 |
| 33 | Mar 2 | H | Reading | W 2-1 | 1-0 | — | Healy 2 [35, 89] | 11,745 |
| 34 | 6 | A | Burnley | D 1-1 | 0-1 | 11 | Alexander (pen) [58] | 15,837 |
| 35 | 10 | A | Sunderland | D 3-3 | 1-1 | — | Healy [43], Mears [79], Lewis [90] | 27,181 |
| 36 | 13 | H | Gillingham | D 0-0 | 0-0 | 11 | | 13,111 |
| 37 | 17 | A | Coventry C | L 1-4 | 0-4 | — | Fuller [48] | 13,142 |
| 38 | 20 | H | Walsall | L 1-2 | 0-1 | 13 | Alexander (pen) [53] | 11,551 |
| 39 | 27 | A | Rotherham U | L 0-1 | 0-1 | 13 | | 6268 |
| 40 | Apr 3 | H | Bradford C | W 1-0 | 0-0 | 12 | Gemmill [50] | 12,367 |
| 41 | 10 | A | Wimbledon | D 3-3 | 2-1 | 13 | McKenna [25], Lynch [43], Koumantarakis [84] | 2866 |
| 42 | 12 | H | Nottingham F | D 2-2 | 1-2 | 13 | Lucketti [34], McKenna [77] | 15,117 |
| 43 | 17 | A | Derby Co | L 1-5 | 0-4 | 14 | Mawene (og) [55] | 24,162 |
| 44 | 24 | H | Cardiff C | D 2-2 | 1-0 | 14 | Lewis [15], McKenna [46] | 11,972 |
| 45 | May 1 | A | Norwich C | L 2-3 | 1-2 | 14 | McKenna [5], Healy [48] | 23,673 |
| 46 | 9 | H | Sheffield U | D 3-3 | 1-2 | 15 | Alexander [24], Healy [54], Fuller [79] | 16,612 |

**Final League Position: 15**

## GOALSCORERS

*League (69):* Fuller 17, Healy 15, Alexander 9 (8 pens), Lewis 6, McKenna 6, Etuhu 3, Abbott 2, Cresswell 2, Davis 1, Gemmill 1, Keane 1, Koumantarakis 1, Lucketti 1, Lynch 1, Mears 1, O'Neil 1, own goal 1.
*Carling Cup (0).*
*FA Cup (6):* Fuller 2, Cresswell 1, Etuhu 1, Koumantarakis 1, O'Neil 1.

| Gould J 37 | Alexander G 45 | Edwards R 16 + 8 | O'Neil B 27 + 2 | Luckett C 37 | Jackson Michael 41 + 2 | Etuhu D 23 + 8 | Healy D 27 + 11 | Cresswell R 41 + 4 | Fuller R 37 + 1 | Lewis E 26 + 7 | Skora E — + 2 | Keane M 21 + 9 | Cartwright L 2 + 10 | McKenna P 39 | Lynch S 6 + 13 | Broomes M 30 | Davis C 16 + 6 | Lucas D 1 + 1 | Mears T 11 + 1 | Abbott P 2 + 7 | Koumantarakis G 1 + 6 | Lonergan A 8 | Burley C 1 + 3 | McCormack A 2 + 3 | Smith J — + 5 | Gemmill S 7 | Briscoe L 2 | Jackson Mark — + 1 | *Match No.* |
|---|---|---|---|---|---|---|---|---|---|---|---|---|---|---|---|---|---|---|---|---|---|---|---|---|---|---|---|---|---|
| 1 | 2 | 3 | 4 | 5 | 6 | $7^{1}$ | 8 | 9 | 10 | 11 | 12 | | | | | | | | | | | | | | | | | | 1 |
| 1 | 2 | 3 | 4 | 5 | 6 | $7^{2}$ | 12 | 9 | 10 | $11^{1}$ | | 8 | 13 | | | | | | | | | | | | | | | | 2 |
| 1 | 2 | $3^{3}$ | 13 | 5 | 6 | 4 | 12 | 9 | 10 | 11 | | $8^{2}$ | | $7^{1}$ | 14 | | | | | | | | | | | | | | 3 |
| 1■ | $2^{G}$ | | $4^{2}$ | 5 | 12 | | 13 | 9 | 10 | 11 | | 7 | | 8 | | 3 | $6^{1}$ | 15 | | | | | | | | | | | 4 |
| 1 | 2 | | 4 | 5 | 12 | 13 | 14 | $9^{3}$ | 10 | 11 | | $7^{2}$ | | 8 | | 3 | $6^{1}$ | | | | | | | | | | | | 5 |
| | 2■ | | $4^{2}$ | 5 | 6 | 12 | 13 | 9 | 10 | 11 | | 7 | | $8^{1}$ | | 3 | | 1 | | | | | | | | | | | 6 |
| 1 | 2 | | 4 | 5 | 6 | $7^{1}$ | | $9^{3}$ | 10 | $11^{2}$ | | 13 | 12 | 8 | 14 | 3 | | | | | | | | | | | | | 7 |
| 1 | $2^{2}$ | 3 | $8^{3}$ | 5 | 6 | | 12 | 9 | 10 | | | $11^{1}$ | 13 | 7 | 14 | 4 | | | | | | | | | | | | | 8 |
| 1 | | $3^{1}$ | 4 | 5 | 6 | | 12 | 9 | 10 | | | 11 | 13 | 8 | | $2^{2}$ | | | 7 | | | | | | | | | | 9 |
| 1 | 2 | 12 | 4 | 5 | 6 | 13 | $10^{1}$ | | | | | $11^{2}$ | 7 | 8 | 14 | 3 | | | | $9^{3}$ | | | | | | | | | 10 |
| 1 | 2 | | $4^{2}$ | 5 | 6 | 12 | $9^{3}$ | 13 | 10 | 11 | | 7 | | $8^{1}$ | | 3 | | | | 14 | | | | | | | | | 11 |
| 1 | 2 | 12 | 4 | 5 | 6 | | | $9^{3}$ | 10 | $11^{1}$ | | $7^{2}$ | 13 | 8 | | 3 | 14 | | | | | | | | | | | | 12 |
| 1 | 2 | 12 | 4 | 5 | 6 | | | $9^{1}$ | 10 | $11^{2}$ | | 7 | | 8 | | 3■ | 13 | | | | | | | | | | | | 13 |
| 1 | 2 | | $4^{2}$ | 5 | 6 | 12 | | 9 | 10■ | $11^{1}$ | | 7 | 13 | 8 | | 3 | | | | | | | | | | | | | 14 |
| 1 | 2 | 12 | $4^{1}$ | 5 | 6 | | $11^{3}$ | 9 | 10 | 13 | | | $7^{2}$ | 8 | | 3 | | | | 14 | | | | | | | | | 15 |
| 1 | 2 | | $4^{1}$ | 5 | 6 | | $11^{2}$ | $9^{3}$ | 10 | 12 | | 7 | 13 | 8 | 14 | | 3 | | | | | | | | | | | | 16 |
| 1 | 2 | | | 5 | 6 | 4 | $10^{1}$ | 9 | | 11 | | 7 | | 8 | | $3^{2}$ | 12 | | | 13 | | | | | | | | | 17 |
| 1 | 2 | 3 | $4^{2}$ | 5 | 6 | 12 | 10 | 9 | | $11^{3}$ | | $7^{1}$ | 14 | 8 | 13 | | | | | | | | | | | | | | 18 |
| 1 | 2 | $3^{1}$ | 11 | 5 | 6 | 7 | 10 | $9^{2}$ | | 12 | | | | 8 | | 4 | | | | 13 | | | | | | | | | 19 |
| 1 | 2 | $3^{1}$ | $4^{3}$ | | 6 | $8^{2}$ | 13 | 9 | 10 | 12 | | | | 11 | | 5 | 7 | | | 14 | | | | | | | | | 20 |
| 1 | $2^{2}$ | | $4^{1}$ | $5^{3}$ | 6 | 7 | 9 | 12 | 10 | 11 | | | 13 | 8 | | 3 | 14 | | | | | | | | | | | | 21 |
| 1 | 2 | | 4 | 5 | 6 | 7 | 12 | $9^{1}$ | $10^{2}$ | $11^{3}$ | | | | 8 | 13 | 3 | 14 | | | | | | | | | | | | 22 |
| 1 | 2 | | 4 | 5 | 6 | 7 | $11^{3}$ | $9^{1}$ | 10 | 12 | | 13 | 14 | $8^{2}$ | | 3 | | | | | | | | | | | | | 23 |
| 1 | 2 | | 4 | 5 | 6 | $7^{1}$ | 12 | $9^{2}$ | $10^{3}$ | 11 | | | | 8 | | 3 | 14 | | | 13 | | | | | | | | | 24 |
| 1 | 2 | | 4 | 5 | 6■ | 12 | 7 | $9^{2}$ | $10^{1}$ | 11 | | | | 8 | | | 3 | | | 13 | | | | | | | | | 25 |
| 1 | 2 | | 4 | 5 | 6 | $7^{2}$ | 8 | 12 | 10 | 11 | 13 | | | | | | 3 | | | $9^{1}$ | | | | | | | | | 26 |
| 1 | 2 | | 7 | 5 | | 12 | 11 | 9 | 10 | | | $3^{2}$ | | 8 | | | $4^{1}$ | | 6 | | 13 | | | | | | | | 27 |
| 1 | 2 | | $8^{2}$ | 5 | | 7 | | 9 | 10 | | | 12 | | 11 | | 6 | 4 | | $3^{1}$ | | 13 | | | | | | | | 28 |
| | 2 | 13 | | | 5 | $7^{1}$ | 8 | 9 | 10 | $11^{2}$ | | 12 | | $4^{3}$ | | 6 | | | 3 | | | 1 | 14 | | | | | | 29 |
| | 2 | 12 | 13 | | 5 | | 8 | 9 | 10 | 11 | | $4^{3}$ | | $7^{2}$ | | $6^{1}$ | | | 3 | | | 1 | 14 | | | | | | 30 |
| 1 | 2 | | $7^{1}$ | | 5 | | $8^{2}$ | 9 | 10 | 11 | | 3 | | | 13 | | 4 | | 6 | | | | 12 | | | | | | 31 |
| 1 | 2 | | | 5 | 6 | | 12 | 9 | 10 | $11^{1}$ | | 14 | | $7^{3}$ | 13 | | 4 | | $3^{2}$ | | | | 8 | | | | | | 32 |
| | 2 | 3 | | 5 | $6^{2}$ | | 8 | 9 | 10 | 12 | | 11 | | 7 | | | $4^{1}$ | | 13 | | | 1 | | | | | | | 33 |
| | 2 | 3 | | $5^{1}$ | 6 | $7^{2}$ | 8 | 9 | 10■ | 12 | | $11^{3}$ | | | 14 | | | | 4 | | | 1 | | 13 | | | | | 34 |
| | 2 | 5 | | | 6 | | 8 | 9 | 10 | 11 | | | | | 7 | | | | 3 | | | 1 | | $4^{1}$ | 12 | | | | 35 |
| | 2 | 5 | | | 6 | | 8 | $9^{1}$ | 10 | | | 12 | | | 7 | | 4 | | 3 | | | 1 | | | | 11 | | | 36 |
| | 2 | 5 | | | 6 | | 11 | 9■ | 10 | | | 12 | | $7^{2}$ | 13 | | 4 | | $3^{1}$ | | | 1 | | | | 8 | | | 37 |
| | 2 | $5^{1}$ | | | 6 | | 10 | 9 | | | | 3 | | 7 | 11 | | 4 | | | | 13 | 1 | | | $12^{2}$ | 8 | | | 38 |
| 1 | 2 | 3 | | | 6 | 8 | 10 | 9 | | | | 12 | | $7^{2}$ | | 5 | | | | | 13 | | | | 14 | $11^{3}$ | $4^{1}$ | | 39 |
| 1 | 2 | 12 | | 5 | 6 | 8 | | 9 | | | | | | 7 | 10 | 3 | $4^{1}$ | | | | | | | | | 11 | | | 40 |
| 1 | 2 | 12 | | 5 | 6 | $8^{3}$ | | 9 | | | | 14 | | 7 | 10 | $4^{2}$ | | | | | 13 | | | | | 11 | $3^{1}$ | | 41 |
| 1 | 2 | $3^{3}$ | | 5 | 6 | 8 | | 12 | 10 | | | | | 7 | 13 | 4 | | | | | $9^{2}$ | | | | 14 | $11^{1}$ | | | 42 |
| 1 | 2 | | | 5 | 6 | $8^{1}$ | 11 | 9 | 10 | | | | | 7 | 12 | 3 | | | | | | | | $4^{2}$ | | | | 13 | 43 |
| 1 | 2 | | | 5 | 6 | $4^{1}$ | 8 | 9 | 10 | 11 | | | | 7 | | 3 | | | | | | | | 12 | | | | | 44 |
| 1 | 2 | | | 5 | 6 | 4 | 10 | $9^{1}$ | 12 | 11 | | | | 7 | $8^{2}$ | 3■ | | | | | | | | | 13 | | | | 45 |
| 1 | 2 | | | 5 | | $6^{2}$ | 8 | 9 | 10 | 11 | | | | $7^{1}$ | | 3 | 4 | | | | 12 | | | 13 | | | | | 46 |

**Carling Cup**

| | | | |
|---|---|---|---|
| First Round | Notts Co | (h) | 0-0 |

**FA Cup**

| | | | |
|---|---|---|---|
| Third Round | Reading | (h) | 3-3 |
| | | (a) | 2-1 |
| Fourth Round | Swansea C | (a) | 1-2 |

# QUEENS PARK RANGERS FL Championship

## FOUNDATION

There is an element of doubt about the date of the foundation of this club, but it is believed that in either 1885 or 1886 it was formed through the amalgamation of Christchurch Rangers and St Jude's Institute FC. The leading light was George Wodehouse, whose family maintained a connection with the club until comparatively recent times. Most of the players came from the Queen's Park district so this name was adopted after a year as St Jude's Institute.

***Loftus Road Stadium, South Africa Road, Shepherds Bush, London W12 7PA.***

***Telephone:*** (020) 8743 0262.

***Fax:*** (020) 8749 0994.

***Ticket Office:*** 0870 112 1967.

***Website:*** www.qpr.premiumtv.co.uk

***Email:*** qpr.co.uk

***Ground Capacity:*** 19,091.

***Record Attendance:*** 35,353 v Leeds U, Division 1, 27 April 1974.

***Pitch Measurements:*** 112yd × 72yd.

***Chairman:*** Nick Blackburn.

***Chief Executive:*** David Davies.

***Secretary:*** Sheila Marson.

***Manager:*** Ian Holloway.

***Physio:*** Prav Mathema.

***Colours:*** Blue and white hooped shirts, white shorts, white stockings.

***Change Colours:*** Sky blue with navy trim shirts, sky blue shorts, sky blue stockings.

***Year Formed:*** 1885* (*see Foundation*).

***Turned Professional:*** 1898. ***Ltd Co.:*** 1899.

***Previous Name:*** 1885, St Jude's; 1887, Queens Park Rangers.

***Club Nicknames:*** 'Rangers' or 'Rs'.

***Previous Grounds:*** 1885* (*see Foundation*), Welford's Fields; 1888–99; London Scottish Ground, Brondesbury, Home Farm, Kensal Rise Green, Gun Club Wormwood Scrubs, Kilburn Cricket Ground; 1899, Kensal Rise Athletic Ground; 1901, Latimer Road, Notting Hill; 1904, Agricultural Society, Park Royal; 1907, Park Royal Ground; 1917, Loftus Road; 1931, White City; 1933, Loftus Road; 1962, White City; 1963, Loftus Road.

***First Football League Game:*** 28 August 1920, Division 3, v Watford (h) L 1–2 – Price; Blackman, Wingrove; McGovern, Grant, O'Brien; Faulkner, Birch (1), Smith, Gregory, Middlemiss.

***Record League Victory:*** 9–2 v Tranmere R, Division 3, 3 December 1960 – Drinkwater; Woods, Ingham; Keen, Rutter, Angell; Lazarus (2), Bedford (2), Evans (2), Andrews (1), Clark (2).

***Record Cup Victory:*** 8–1 v Bristol R (away), FA Cup 1st rd, 27 November 1937 – Gilfillan; Smith, Jefferson; Lowe, James, March; Cape, Mallett, Cheetham (3), Fitzgerald (3) Bott (2). 8–1 v Crewe Alex, Milk Cup 1st rd, 3 October 1983 – Hucker; Neill, Dawes, Waddock (1), McDonald (1), Fenwick, Micklewhite (1), Stewart (1), Allen (1), Stainrod (3), Gregory.

## HONOURS

*Football League:* Division 1 – Runners-up 1975–76; Division 2 – Champions 1982–83; Runners-up 1967–68, 1972–73, 2003–04; Division 3 (S) – Champions 1947–48; Runners-up 1946–47; Division 3 – Champions 1966–67.

*FA Cup:* Runners-up 1982.

*Football League Cup:* Winners 1967; Runners-up 1986. (In 1966–67 won Division 3 and Football League Cup).

***European Competitions:*** *UEFA Cup:* 1976–77, 1984–85.

## SKY SPORTS FACT FILE

In 1911–12 Queens Park Rangers were forced to play two home matches over Easter at White City because a coal strike prevented them using Park Royal. On Good Friday Rangers drew 1-1 with Southampton, and the following day defeated Stoke City 1-0.

***Record Defeat:*** 1–8 v Mansfield T, Division 3, 15 March 1965. 1–8 v Manchester U, Division 1, 19 March 1969.

***Most League Points (2 for a win):*** 67, Division 3, 1966–67.

***Most League Points (3 for a win):*** 85, Division 2, 1982–83.

***Most League Goals:*** 111, Division 3, 1961–62.

***Highest League Scorer in Season:*** George Goddard, 37, Division 3 (S), 1929–30.

***Most League Goals in Total Aggregate:*** George Goddard, 172, 1926–34.

***Most League Goals in One Match:*** 4, George Goddard v Merthyr T, Division 3S, 9 March 1929; 4, George Goddard v Swindon T, Division 3S, 12 April 1930; 4, George Goddard v Exeter C, Division 3S, 20 December 1930; 4, George Goddard v Watford, Division 3S, 19 September 1931; 4, Tom Cheetham v Aldershot, Division 3S, 14 September 1935; 4, Tom Cheetham v Aldershot, Division 3S, 12 November 1938.

***Most Capped Player:*** Alan McDonald, 52, Northern Ireland.

***Most League Appearances:*** Tony Ingham, 519, 1950–63.

***Youngest League Player:*** Frank Sibley, 16 years 97 days v Bristol C, 10 March 1964.

***Record Transfer Fee Received:*** £6,000,000 from Newcastle U for Les Ferdinand, June 1995.

***Record Transfer Fee Paid:*** £2,750,000 to Stoke C for Mike Sheron, July 1997.

***Football League Record:*** 1920 Original Members of Division 3; 1921–48 Division 3 (S); 1948–52 Division 2; 1952–58 Division 3 (S); 1958–67 Division 3; 1967–68 Division 2; 1968–69 Division 1; 1969–73 Division 2; 1973–79 Division 1; 1979–83 Division 2; 1983–92 Division 1; 1992–96 FA Premier League; 1996–2001 Division 1; 2001–04 Division 2; 2004– FLC.

## LATEST SEQUENCES

***Longest Sequence of League Wins:*** 8, 7.11.1931 – 28.12.1931.

***Longest Sequence of League Defeats:*** 9, 25.2.1969 – 5.4.1969.

***Longest Sequence of League Draws:*** 6, 29.1.2000 – 5.3.2000.

***Longest Sequence of Unbeaten League Matches:*** 20, 11.3.1972 – 23.9.1972.

***Longest Sequence Without a League Win:*** 20, 7.12.1968 – 7.4.1969.

***Successive Scoring Runs:*** 33 from 9.12.1961.

***Successive Non-scoring Runs:*** 6 from 18.3.1939.

## MANAGERS

James Cowan 1906–13
Jimmy Howie 1913–20
Ted Liddell 1920–24
Will Wood 1924–25
*(had been Secretary since 1903)*
Bob Hewison 1925–30
John Bowman 1930–31
Archie Mitchell 1931–33
Mick O'Brien 1933–35
Billy Birrell 1935–39
Ted Vizard 1939–44
Dave Mangnall 1944–52
Jack Taylor 1952–59
Alec Stock 1959–65
*(General Manager to 1968)*
Bill Dodgin Jnr 1968
Tommy Docherty 1968
Les Allen 1968–71
Gordon Jago 1971–74
Dave Sexton 1974–77
Frank Sibley 1977–78
Steve Burtenshaw 1978–79
Tommy Docherty 1979–80
Terry Venables 1980–84
Gordon Jago 1984
Alan Mullery 1984
Frank Sibley 1984–85
Jim Smith 1985–88
Trevor Francis 1988–90
Don Howe 1990–91
Gerry Francis 1991–94
Ray Wilkins 1994–96
Stewart Houston 1996–97
Ray Harford 1997–98
Gerry Francis 1998–2001
Ian Holloway February 2001–

## TEN YEAR LEAGUE RECORD

| | | *P* | *W* | *D* | *L* | *F* | *A* | *Pts* | *Pos* |
|---|---|---|---|---|---|---|---|---|---|
| 1994-95 | PR Lge | 42 | 17 | 9 | 16 | 61 | 59 | 60 | 8 |
| 1995-96 | PR Lge | 38 | 9 | 6 | 23 | 38 | 57 | 33 | 19 |
| 1996-97 | Div 1 | 46 | 18 | 12 | 16 | 64 | 60 | 66 | 9 |
| 1997-98 | Div 1 | 46 | 10 | 19 | 17 | 51 | 63 | 49 | 21 |
| 1998-99 | Div 1 | 46 | 12 | 11 | 23 | 52 | 61 | 47 | 20 |
| 1999-2000 | Div 1 | 46 | 16 | 18 | 12 | 62 | 53 | 66 | 10 |
| 2000-01 | Div 1 | 46 | 7 | 19 | 20 | 45 | 75 | 40 | 23 |
| 2001-02 | Div 2 | 46 | 19 | 14 | 13 | 60 | 49 | 71 | 8 |
| 2002-03 | Div 2 | 46 | 24 | 11 | 11 | 69 | 45 | 83 | 4 |
| 2003-04 | Div 2 | 46 | 22 | 17 | 7 | 80 | 45 | 83 | 2 |

## DID YOU KNOW ?

Despite a hiccup around the turn of the year in the 1982–3 season when two successive games ended in defeat including 4-0 at Wolverhampton Wanderers, Queens Park Rangers finished as Second Division champions ten points ahead of Wolves.

## QUEENS PARK RANGERS 2003–04 LEAGUE RECORD

| Match No. | Date | Venue | Opponents | Result | | H/T Score | Lg. Pos. | Goalscorers | Attendance |
|---|---|---|---|---|---|---|---|---|---|
| 1 | Aug 9 | H | Blackpool | W | 5-0 | 2-0 | — | Ainsworth 2 4, 69, Langley 43, Gallen 56, Palmer 90 | 14,581 |
| 2 | 18 | A | Brighton & HA | L | 1-2 | 1-1 | — | Padula 9 | 6536 |
| 3 | 23 | H | Bournemouth | W | 1-0 | 0-0 | 5 | Furlong 63 | 13,065 |
| 4 | 25 | A | Rushden & D | D | 3-3 | 2-1 | 6 | Ainsworth 2 37, 45, Furlong 53 | 5544 |
| 5 | 30 | H | Chesterfield | W | 3-0 | 1-0 | 3 | Thorpe 2 29, 67, Furlong 87 | 12,986 |
| 6 | Sept 6 | A | Colchester U | D | 2-2 | 0-1 | 4 | Furlong 2 49, 66 | 3835 |
| 7 | 13 | H | Wycombe W | D | 0-0 | 0-0 | 5 | | 13,618 |
| 8 | 16 | A | Wrexham | W | 2-0 | 1-0 | — | Bean 7, Rowlands 90 | 4539 |
| 9 | 20 | A | Luton T | D | 1-1 | 0-0 | 3 | Furlong 90 | 8339 |
| 10 | 27 | H | Bristol C | D | 1-1 | 0-0 | 4 | Padula 73 | 14,913 |
| 11 | 30 | H | Barnsley | W | 4-0 | 0-0 | — | Gallen 60, Rowlands 61, Ainsworth 63, Thorpe 77 | 11,854 |
| 12 | Oct 4 | A | Grimsby T | W | 1-0 | 0-0 | 2 | Sabin 90 | 5447 |
| 13 | 18 | A | Peterborough U | D | 0-0 | 0-0 | 3 | | 7247 |
| 14 | 21 | A | Port Vale | L | 0-2 | 0-2 | — | | 5243 |
| 15 | 25 | H | Tranmere R | D | 1-1 | 0-1 | 6 | Gallen 47 | 12,937 |
| 16 | Nov 1 | A | Stockport Co | W | 2-1 | 2-0 | 3 | Gallen 19, Rowlands 43 | 5461 |
| 17 | 11 | H | Brentford | W | 1-0 | 1-0 | — | Thorpe 42 | 15,865 |
| 18 | 15 | H | Plymouth Arg | W | 3-0 | 1-0 | 1 | Gallen 2 33, 75, Thorpe 72 | 17,049 |
| 19 | 22 | A | Swindon T | D | 1-1 | 0-1 | 1 | Rowlands 79 | 10,021 |
| 20 | 29 | H | Sheffield W | W | 3-0 | 1-0 | 1 | Palmer 13, Thorpe 85, McLeod 90 | 17,393 |
| 21 | Dec 13 | H | Hartlepool U | W | 4-1 | 3-0 | 1 | Gallen 2 27, 38, Padula 34, Ainsworth 50 | 15,003 |
| 22 | 20 | A | Oldham Ath | L | 1-2 | 1-0 | 2 | Thorpe 31 | 5603 |
| 23 | 26 | A | Notts Co | D | 3-3 | 2-2 | 2 | Palmer 3, Richardson (og) 10, Gallen 90 | 7702 |
| 24 | 28 | H | Colchester U | W | 2-0 | 1-0 | 2 | Gallen 12, Thorpe 57 | 15,720 |
| 25 | Jan 3 | H | Rushden & D | W | 1-0 | 1-0 | 2 | Gallen 24 | 14,141 |
| 26 | 10 | A | Blackpool | W | 1-0 | 1-0 | 2 | Rowlands 38 | 7329 |
| 27 | 17 | H | Brighton & HA | W | 2-1 | 2-1 | 2 | Rowlands 20, Gallen 43 | 17,839 |
| 28 | 24 | A | Bournemouth | L | 0-1 | 0-0 | 2 | | 8909 |
| 29 | 31 | A | Chesterfield | L | 2-4 | 1-1 | 2 | Thorpe 11, Palmer 63 | 4567 |
| 30 | Feb 7 | H | Notts Co | W | 3-2 | 0-0 | 2 | McLeod 54, Thorpe 69, Furlong 83 | 14,412 |
| 31 | 14 | A | Brentford | D | 1-1 | 1-0 | 2 | Furlong 20 | 8418 |
| 32 | 20 | H | Peterborough U | D | 1-1 | 0-1 | — | Gallen 90 | 13,276 |
| 33 | Mar 2 | H | Port Vale | W | 3-2 | 0-1 | — | Bircham 64, Cureton 2 77, 90 | 12,593 |
| 34 | 6 | H | Oldham Ath | D | 1-1 | 0-1 | 3 | Gallen (pen) 54 | 13,696 |
| 35 | 13 | A | Hartlepool U | W | 4-1 | 0-0 | 3 | Furlong 2 48, 74, Gallen 52, Rowlands 76 | 6519 |
| 36 | 16 | H | Wrexham | W | 2-0 | 0-0 | — | Carlisle 67, McLeod 88 | 13,363 |
| 37 | 20 | A | Wycombe W | D | 2-2 | 0-2 | 2 | Gallen 46, Rowlands 68 | 7634 |
| 38 | 27 | H | Luton T | D | 1-1 | 1-0 | 2 | Furlong 45 | 17,695 |
| 39 | Apr 3 | A | Bristol C | L | 0-1 | 0-1 | 2 | | 19,041 |
| 40 | 6 | A | Tranmere R | D | 0-0 | 0-0 | — | | 7699 |
| 41 | 10 | H | Grimsby T | W | 3-0 | 1-0 | 2 | Furlong 2 42, 86, Bircham 84 | 14,488 |
| 42 | 12 | A | Barnsley | D | 3-3 | 1-1 | 2 | Kay (og) 32, Furlong 2 74, 90 | 10,402 |
| 43 | 17 | H | Stockport Co | D | 1-1 | 1-0 | 2 | Rowlands 3 | 15,162 |
| 44 | 24 | A | Plymouth Arg | L | 0-2 | 0-0 | 2 | | 19,888 |
| 45 | May 1 | H | Swindon T | W | 1-0 | 1-0 | 2 | Rowlands 2 | 18,396 |
| 46 | 8 | A | Sheffield W | W | 3-1 | 1-0 | 2 | Gallen 35, Furlong 48, Carr (og) 69 | 29,313 |

**Final League Position: 2**

### GOALSCORERS

*League (80):* Gallen 17 (1 pen), Furlong 16, Rowlands 10, Thorpe 10, Ainsworth 6, Palmer 4, McLeod 3, Padula 3, Bircham 2, Cureton 2, Bean 1, Carlisle 1, Langley 1, Sabin 1, own goals 3.
*Carling Cup (4):* Rowlands 2, Ainsworth 1, Langley 1.
*FA Cup (0).*
*LDV Vans Trophy (6):* Gnohere 1, Pacquette 1, Padula 1, Palmer 1, McLeod 1, Thorpe 1.

| Day C 29 | Forbes T 30 | Padula G 36 | Palmer S 24 + 11 | Shittu D 18 + 2 | Carlisle C 32 + 1 | Langley R 1 | Ainsworth G 21 + 8 | Furlong P 31 + 5 | Gallen K 44 + 1 | Bircham M 36 + 2 | Rowlands M 41 + 1 | Sabin E 3 + 7 | Williams T 4 + 1 | Bean M 23 + 8 | McLeod K 26 + 9 | Oli D — + 3 | Thorpe T 22 + 9 | Edghill R 15 + 5 | Gnohere A 17 + 1 | Daly W — + 2 | Barton W 2 + 1 | Pacquette R — + 2 | Culkin N 5 | Rose M 15 + 5 | Marney D 1 + 1 | Cureton J 2 + 11 | Johnson R 10 + 1 | Camp L 12 | Bignot M 6 | *Match No.* |
|---|---|---|---|---|---|---|---|---|---|---|---|---|---|---|---|---|---|---|---|---|---|---|---|---|---|---|---|---|---|---|
| 1 | 2 | 3 | 4 | 5 | 6 | 7 | $8^1$ | $9^2$ | $10^3$ | 11 | 12 | 13 | 14 | | | | | | | | | | | | | | | | | 1 |
| 1 | 2▪ | 3 | 4 | 5 | 6 | | | 9 | | 8 | $7^1$ | $10^2$ | $11^3$ | 12 | 13 | 14 | | | | | | | | | | | | | | 2 |
| 1 | | 3 | 2 | 5 | 6 | | 7 | 9 | 12 | $8^2$ | 4 | | | 13 | 11 | | $10^1$ | | | | | | | | | | | | | 3 |
| 1 | | 3 | 4 | 5 | 6 | | 7 | $9^2$ | 10 | $8^1$ | 2 | | 11 | 12 | | | 13 | | | | | | | | | | | | | 4 |
| 1 | | 3 | 4 | 5 | | | $7^1$ | 9 | 10 | | 2 | | $6^2$ | 12 | 11 | | 8 | 13 | | | | | | | | | | | | 5 |
| 1 | | | 4 | 5 | | | $7^2$ | 9 | 8 | | 2 | | $6^3$ | 12 | 11 | 14 | $10^1$ | 13 | 3 | | | | | | | | | | | 6 |
| 1 | | 3 | 4 | 5 | | | 7 | 9 | 10 | | 2 | | | 8 | 11 | | | | 6 | | | | | | | | | | | 7 |
| 1 | | 3 | 4 | 5 | | | $7^1$ | $9^2$ | 10 | | 2 | 12 | | 8 | 11▪ | | | 13 | 6 | | | | | | | | | | | 8 |
| 1 | | 3 | $4^1$ | 5 | | | 13 | 9 | 10 | 12 | $7^3$ | | | 8 | $11^2$ | | 14 | 2 | 6 | | | | | | | | | | | 9 |
| 1 | 5 | 3 | 12 | | | | 13 | 9 | 10 | 7 | 4 | | | $8^3$ | $11^1$ | 14 | | $2^2$ | 6 | | | | | | | | | | | 10 |
| 1 | 5 | 3 | 4 | | | | 7 | | 9 | $11^1$ | 2 | | | 8 | | | 10 | | 6 | 12 | | | | | | | | | | 11 |
| 1 | 5 | 3 | 4 | | | | $7^1$ | 9 | 11 | 8 | 2 | 12 | | 6 | | | $10^2$ | | | | 13 | | | | | | | | | 12 |
| 1 | 5 | 3 | 4 | | | | 12 | $9^3$ | 10 | 8 | $7^1$ | 13 | | 6 | $11^2$ | | 14 | | | | 2 | | | | | | | | | 13 |
| 1 | 2 | 3 | 4 | | 12 | | 13 | | 9 | 6 | 7 | | | $8^3$ | 11 | | $10^2$ | | | | $5^1$ | 14 | | | | | | | | 14 |
| 1 | 5 | 3 | | | 6 | | $7^2$ | | 9 | 4 | 8 | 12 | | | 11 | | $10^1$ | 2 | | | | 13 | | | | | | | | 15 |
| 1 | 5 | 3 | 12 | | 4 | | 7 | | 9 | $6^1$ | 8 | | | | 11 | | 10 | 2 | | | | | | | | | | | | 16 |
| 1 | 5 | 3 | 12 | | 4 | | 13 | | 9 | 6 | $7^2$ | | | 8 | 11 | | 10 | $2^1$ | | | | | | | | | | | | 17 |
| 1 | 5 | 3 | | 12 | 4 | | | | 9 | 6 | 7 | | | 8 | 11 | | 10 | $2^1$ | | | | | | | | | | | | 18 |
| 1 | 5 | 3 | 13 | 12 | 4 | | 14 | | 9 | 6 | 7 | $11^3$ | | $8^2$ | | | 10 | $2^1$ | | | | | | | | | | | | 19 |
| 1 | 2 | $3^3$ | 4 | 5 | 6 | | $7^1$ | 12 | 9 | | 11 | | | $8^2$ | 13 | | 10 | 14 | | | | | | | | | | | | 20 |
| | 2 | $3^3$ | 4 | 5 | 6 | | 7 | 12 | $9^1$ | | 11 | | | 8 | 13 | | $10^2$ | | | | | | 1 | 14 | | | | | | 21 |
| 1 | 2 | 3 | $4^1$ | 5 | | | 7 | | 9 | 12 | | | | 8 | 11 | | 10 | | | | | | | 6 | | | | | | 22 |
| 1 | 2 | 3 | $4^1$ | 5 | 6 | | 13 | | 9 | 7 | 8 | 12 | | | $11^2$ | | 10 | | | | | | | | | | | | | 23 |
| 1 | 2 | 3 | 12 | $5^1$ | 6 | | | | 9 | $4^2$ | 7 | | | 8 | 11 | | 10 | | | | | | | 13 | | | | | | 24 |
| 1 | 2 | 3 | | 5 | 6 | | 12 | 9 | 10 | 4 | 7 | | | 8 | $11^1$ | | | | | | | | | | | | | | | 25 |
| 1 | 2 | 3 | | 5 | 6 | | | 9 | 10 | 4 | 7 | | | 8 | $11^1$ | | | | | | | | | 12 | | | | | | 26 |
| 1 | 2 | 3 | 12 | 5 | 6 | | | 9 | 10 | 4 | 11 | | | $8^1$ | | | | | | | | | | $7^2$ | 13 | | | | | 27 |
| 1 | 2 | 3 | 4 | 5 | | | | 9 | 10 | 6 | 8 | | | | | | 12 | | | | | | | 7 | $11^1$ | | | | | 28 |
| 1 | 2 | 3 | 4 | | 6 | | | $9^2$ | 10 | 7 | $11^3$ | 12 | | | 13 | | 8 | | | 14 | | | | $5^1$ | | | | | | 29 |
| | 5 | 3 | 4 | | 6 | | | 12 | 9 | 8 | 7 | | | | $11^2$ | | $10^1$ | | | | | | 1 | 2 | | 13 | | | | 30 |
| 1 | 2 | 3 | 4 | | 6 | | | 9 | 10 | 8 | 7 | $11^1$ | | | | | | | | | | | | 5 | | 12 | | | | 31 |
| | 2 | 3 | $4^3$ | | 6 | | | $9^1$ | 10 | 8 | | | | | 11 | | 12 | | 5 | | | | 1 | $7^2$ | | 13 | 14 | | | 32 |
| | 2 | 3 | | | 6 | | | 12 | 9 | 8 | 7 | | | | $11^2$ | | $10^1$ | | 5 | | | | 1 | | | 13 | 4 | | | 33 |
| | 2 | 3 | | | 6 | | | 12 | 9 | 8 | 7 | | | | $11^1$ | | $10^2$ | | 5 | | | | 1 | | | 13 | 4 | | | 34 |
| | 2 | | 12 | | 6 | | | 9 | 10 | $8^1$ | 7 | | | 13 | 11 | | | | 5 | | | | | 3 | | | $4^2$ | 1 | | 35 |
| | 2 | | | | 6 | | | 9 | 10 | 8 | 7 | | | | 11 | | 12 | | 5 | | | | | $3^1$ | | | 4 | 1 | | 36 |
| | $2^2$ | | | | 6 | | | 9 | 10 | $7^1$ | 3 | | | 12 | $11^3$ | | 8 | 13 | 5 | | | | | | | 14 | 4 | 1 | | 37 |
| | | | | | 6 | | | 9 | 11 | | 7 | | | $8^2$ | 12 | | $10^1$ | 2 | 5 | | | | | | | 13 | 4 | 1 | 3 | 38 |
| | | | 12 | | 6 | | | 9 | 10 | | 7 | | | $8^3$ | $11^2$ | | 13 | | 5 | | | | | 3 | | 14 | $4^1$ | 1 | 2 | 39 |
| | | | 12 | | 6 | | 11 | 9 | 10 | $4^1$ | $7^2$ | | | 8 | | | | 3 | 5 | | | | | 13 | | | | 1 | 2▪ | 40 |
| | | | 12 | | $6^2$ | | $11^3$ | 9 | 7 | 4 | | | | $8^1$ | 14 | | | 3 | 5 | | | | | 13 | | 10 | | 1 | 2 | 41 |
| | | | 4 | | | | $7^1$ | 9 | 11 | 8 | | | | $13^3$ | 12 | | 14 | 2 | 5 | | | | | 6 | | $10^2$ | | 1 | 3 | 42 |
| | | | 4 | | | | $11^3$ | 9 | 10 | 6 | $7^1$ | | | 8 | $12^2$ | | 13 | 2 | | | | | | 5 | | 14 | | 1 | 3 | 43 |
| | | $3^3$ | 12 | | 6 | | $11^2$ | 9 | 10 | $8^1$ | 7 | | | | 13 | | | 2 | | | | | | 5 | | 14 | 4 | 1 | | 44 |
| | | 3 | | | 6 | | 11 | 9 | 10 | 8 | 7 | | | | | | | 2 | | | | | | 5 | | | 4 | 1 | | 45 |
| | | 3 | | | $6^1$ | | 11 | 9 | 10 | 8 | $7^2$ | | | | | | | 2 | 12 | | | | | 5 | | 13 | 4 | 1 | | 46 |

**Carling Cup**

| | | | |
|---|---|---|---|
| First Round | Cheltenham T | (a) | 2-1 |
| Second Round | Sheffield U | (a) | 2-0 |
| Third Round | Manchester C | (h) | 0-3 |

**FA Cup**

| | | | |
|---|---|---|---|
| First Round | Grimsby T | (a) | 0-1 |

**LDV Vans Trophy**

| | | | |
|---|---|---|---|
| First Round | Kidderminster H | (h) | 2-0 |
| Second Round | Dagenham & R | (h) | 2-1 |
| Quarter-Final | Brighton & HA | (h) | 2-1 |
| Semi-Final | Southend U | (a) | 0-4 |

# READING FL Championship

## FOUNDATION

Reading was formed as far back as 1871 at a public meeting held at the Bridge Street Rooms. They first entered the FA Cup as early as 1877 when they amalgamated with the Reading Hornets. The club was further strengthened in 1889 when Earley FC joined them. They were the first winners of the Berks and Bucks Cup in 1878–79.

***Madejski Stadium, Junction 11, M4, Reading, Berks RG2 0FL.***

***Telephone:*** (0118) 968 1100.

***Fax:*** (0118) 968 1101.

***Ticket Office:*** (0118) 968 1000.

***Website:*** www.readingfc.co.uk

***Email:*** comments@readingfc.co.uk

***Ticket Office:*** (0118) 968 1000.

***Ground Capacity:*** 24,185.

***Record Attendance:*** 33,042 v Brentford, FA Cup 5th rd, 19 February 1927.

***Pitch Measurements:*** 102m × 68m.

***Chairman:*** John Madejski OBE, DL.

***Chief Executive:*** Nigel Howe.

***Secretary:*** Sue Hewett.

***Manager:*** Steve Coppell.

***Physio:*** Jon Fearn MSC, MMACP, MCSP.

## HONOURS

*Football League:* Division 1 – Runners-up 1994–95; Division 2 – Champions 1993–94; Runners-up 2001–02; Division 3 – Champions 1985–86; Division 3 (S) – Champions 1925–26; Runners-up 1931–32, 1934–35, 1948–49, 1951–52; Division 4 – Champions 1978–79.

*FA Cup:* Semi-final 1927.

*Football League Cup:* best season: 5th rd, 1996.

*Simod Cup:* Winners 1988.

***Colours:*** Blue and white hooped shirts, blue or white shorts, white stockings with blue bands.

***Change Colours:*** All white.

***Year Formed:*** 1871.

***Turned Professional:*** 1895.

***Ltd Co.:*** 1895.

***Club Nickname:*** 'The Royals'.

***Previous Grounds:*** 1871, Reading Recreation; Reading Cricket Ground; 1882, Coley Park; 1889, Caversham Cricket Ground; 1896, Elm Park; 1998, Madejski Stadium.

***First Football League Game:*** 28 August 1920, Division 3, v Newport Co (a) W 1–0 – Crawford; Smith, Horler; Christie, Mavin, Getgood; Spence, Weston, Yarnell, Bailey (1), Andrews.

***Record League Victory:*** 10–2 v Crystal Palace, Division 3 (S), 4 September 1946 – Groves; Glidden, Gulliver; McKenna, Ratcliffe, Young; Chitty, Maurice Edelston (3), McPhee (4), Barney (1), Deverell (2).

## SKY SPORTS FACT FILE

In 1927–28 Reading played Manchester United three times in a third round FA Cup tie. At home, despite one player carried off and another dismissed, Reading drew 1-1. The replay finished 2-2. At Villa Park Reading won 2-1 with a Bill Johnstone goal.

***Record Cup Victory:*** 6–0 v Leyton, FA Cup 2nd rd, 12 December 1925 – Duckworth; Eggo, McConnell; Wilson, Messer, Evans; Smith (2), Braithwaite (1), Davey (1), Tinsley, Robson (2).

***Record Defeat:*** 0–18 v Preston NE, FA Cup 1st rd, 1893–94.

***Most League Points (2 for a win):*** 65, Division 4, 1978–79.

***Most League Points (3 for a win):*** 94, Division 3, 1985–86.

***Most League Goals:*** 112, Division 3 (S), 1951–52.

***Highest League Scorer in Season:*** Ronnie Blackman, 39, Division 3 (S), 1951–52.

***Most League Goals in Total Aggregate:*** Ronnie Blackman, 158, 1947–54.

***Most League Goals in One Match:*** 6, Arthur Bacon v Stoke C, Division 2, 3 April 1931.

***Most Capped Player:*** Jimmy Quinn, 17 (46), Northern Ireland.

***Most League Appearances:*** Martin Hicks, 500, 1978–91.

***Youngest League Player:*** Peter Castle, 16 years 49 days v Watford, 30 April 2003.

***Record Transfer Fee Received:*** £1,750,000 from Newcastle U for Shaka Hislop, August 1995.

***Record Transfer Fee Paid:*** £800,000 to Brentford for Carl Asaba, August 1997.

***Football League Record:*** 1920 Original Member of Division 3; 1921–26 Division 3 (S); 1926–31 Division 2; 1931–58 Division 3 (S); 1958–71 Division 3; 1971–76 Division 4; 1976–77 Division 3; 1977–79 Division 4; 1979–83 Division 3; 1983–84 Division 4; 1984–86 Division 3; 1986–88 Division 2; 1988–92 Division 3; 1992–94 Division 2; 1994–98 Division 1; 1998–2002 Division 2; 2002–04 Division 1; 2004– FLC.

## MANAGERS

Thomas Sefton 1897–1901
*(Secretary-Manager)*
James Sharp 1901–02
Harry Matthews 1902–20
Harry Marshall 1920–22
Arthur Chadwick 1923–25
H. S. Bray 1925–26
*(Secretary only since 1922 and 1926–35)*
Andrew Wylie 1926–31
Joe Smith 1931–35
Billy Butler 1935–39
John Cochrane 1939
Joe Edelston 1939–47
Ted Drake 1947–52
Jack Smith 1952–55
Harry Johnston 1955–63
Roy Bentley 1963–69
Jack Mansell 1969–71
Charlie Hurley 1972–77
Maurice Evans 1977–84
Ian Branfoot 1984–89
Ian Porterfield 1989–91
Mark McGhee 1991–94
Jimmy Quinn/Mick Gooding 1994–97
Terry Bullivant 1997–98
Tommy Burns 1998–99
Alan Pardew 1999–2003
Steve Coppell October 2003–

## LATEST SEQUENCES

***Longest Sequence of League Wins:*** 13, 17.8.1985 – 19.10.1985.

***Longest Sequence of League Defeats:*** 7, 10.4.1998 – 15.8.1998.

***Longest Sequence of League Draws:*** 6, 23.3.2002 – 20.4.02.

***Longest Sequence of Unbeaten League Matches:*** 19, 21.4.1973 – 27.10.1973.

***Longest Sequence Without a League Win:*** 14, 30.4.1927 – 29.10.1927.

***Successive Scoring Runs:*** 32 from 1.10.1932.

***Successive Non-scoring Runs:*** 6 from 13.4.1925.

## TEN YEAR LEAGUE RECORD

| | | *P* | *W* | *D* | *L* | *F* | *A* | *Pts* | *Pos* |
|---|---|---|---|---|---|---|---|---|---|
| 1994-95 | Div 1 | 46 | 23 | 10 | 13 | 58 | 44 | 79 | 2 |
| 1995-96 | Div 1 | 46 | 13 | 17 | 16 | 54 | 63 | 56 | 19 |
| 1996-97 | Div 1 | 46 | 15 | 12 | 19 | 58 | 67 | 57 | 18 |
| 1997-98 | Div 1 | 46 | 11 | 9 | 26 | 39 | 78 | 42 | 24 |
| 1998-99 | Div 2 | 46 | 16 | 13 | 17 | 54 | 63 | 61 | 11 |
| 1999-2000 | Div 2 | 46 | 16 | 14 | 16 | 57 | 63 | 62 | 10 |
| 2000-01 | Div 2 | 46 | 25 | 11 | 10 | 86 | 52 | 86 | 3 |
| 2001-02 | Div 2 | 46 | 23 | 15 | 8 | 70 | 43 | 84 | 2 |
| 2002-03 | Div 1 | 46 | 25 | 4 | 17 | 61 | 46 | 79 | 4 |
| 2003-04 | Div 1 | 46 | 20 | 10 | 16 | 55 | 57 | 70 | 9 |

## DID YOU KNOW ?

During 1910–11 Reading had a highly impressive home record in the Southern League Second Division. They conceded just one goal in their 11 games and scored 31 on the way to winnning the title, but only on goal average and a point above third place.

## READING 2003–04 LEAGUE RECORD

| *Match No.* | *Date* | *Venue* | *Opponents* | *Result* | | *H/T Score* | *Lg. Pos.* | *Goalscorers* | *Attendance* |
|---|---|---|---|---|---|---|---|---|---|
| 1 | Aug 9 | A | Ipswich T | D | 1-1 | 0-0 | — | Sidwell $^{59}$ | 24,830 |
| 2 | 16 | H | Nottingham F | W | 3-0 | 0-0 | 4 | Sidwell $^{49}$, Murray $^{59}$, Goater $^{79}$ | 16,833 |
| 3 | 23 | A | Derby Co | W | 3-2 | 3-1 | 2 | Goater $^{3}$, Murray 2 $^{30, 36}$ | 18,970 |
| 4 | 25 | H | Rotherham U | D | 0-0 | 0-0 | 3 | | 14,047 |
| 5 | 30 | A | Wimbledon | W | 3-0 | 1-0 | 2 | Goater 2 $^{12, 59}$, Hughes $^{53}$ | 2066 |
| 6 | Sept 13 | A | West Ham U | L | 0-1 | 0-1 | 7 | | 32,634 |
| 7 | 16 | H | Cardiff C | W | 2-1 | 0-1 | — | Forster $^{62}$, Sidwell $^{79}$ | 15,810 |
| 8 | 20 | H | Coventry C | L | 1-2 | 1-1 | 7 | Forster $^{21}$ | 15,371 |
| 9 | 27 | A | Sunderland | L | 0-2 | 0-2 | 10 | | 22,420 |
| 10 | 30 | A | Norwich C | L | 1-2 | 1-1 | — | Forster $^{25}$ | 16,387 |
| 11 | Oct 4 | H | Bradford C | D | 2-2 | 1-1 | 12 | Sidwell $^{5}$, Hughes $^{78}$ | 12,594 |
| 12 | 14 | H | Gillingham | W | 2-1 | 0-0 | — | Murray $^{54}$, Sidwell $^{85}$ | 13,011 |
| 13 | 18 | H | Preston NE | W | 3-2 | 1-1 | 9 | Goater (pen) $^{39}$, Mackie $^{82}$, Forster $^{90}$ | 13,130 |
| 14 | 21 | H | Walsall | L | 0-1 | 0-1 | — | | 11,225 |
| 15 | 24 | A | Sheffield U | W | 2-1 | 2-1 | — | Williams $^{7}$, Forster $^{43}$ | 20,651 |
| 16 | Nov 1 | A | Crewe Alex | L | 0-1 | 0-1 | 11 | | 7091 |
| 17 | 8 | H | Wigan Ath | W | 1-0 | 0-0 | 10 | Hughes $^{69}$ | 13,819 |
| 18 | 15 | H | Millwall | W | 1-0 | 1-0 | 6 | Salako $^{23}$ | 14,090 |
| 19 | 22 | A | WBA | D | 0-0 | 0-0 | 7 | | 22,839 |
| 20 | 25 | A | Burnley | L | 0-3 | 0-1 | — | | 9473 |
| 21 | 29 | H | Watford | W | 2-1 | 0-0 | 6 | Cox (og) $^{59}$, Sidwell $^{88}$ | 14,521 |
| 22 | Dec 6 | A | Wigan Ath | W | 2-0 | 0-0 | 5 | Forster 2 $^{55, 89}$ | 7512 |
| 23 | 13 | A | Stoke C | L | 0-3 | 0-2 | 7 | | 11,212 |
| 24 | 20 | H | Crystal Palace | L | 0-3 | 0-2 | 9 | | 12,743 |
| 25 | 26 | H | Wimbledon | L | 0-3 | 0-2 | 9 | | 14,486 |
| 26 | 28 | A | Walsall | D | 1-1 | 0-1 | 9 | Shorey $^{72}$ | 8089 |
| 27 | Jan 10 | H | Ipswich T | D | 1-1 | 0-0 | 10 | Owusu $^{62}$ | 17,362 |
| 28 | 17 | A | Nottingham F | W | 1-0 | 1-0 | 9 | Murray $^{41}$ | 23,116 |
| 29 | 31 | H | Derby Co | W | 3-1 | 2-0 | 8 | Goater 2 $^{2, 51}$, Sidwell $^{41}$ | 14,382 |
| 30 | Feb 7 | A | Rotherham U | L | 1-5 | 1-2 | 9 | Goater (pen) $^{20}$ | 6405 |
| 31 | 21 | A | Gillingham | W | 1-0 | 1-0 | 8 | Goater $^{8}$ | 8600 |
| 32 | 24 | H | Burnley | D | 2-2 | 1-1 | — | Owusu $^{19}$, Harper $^{90}$ | 10,543 |
| 33 | 28 | H | Sheffield U | W | 2-1 | 2-1 | 8 | Shorey $^{25}$, Goater (pen) $^{33}$ | 15,545 |
| 34 | Mar 2 | A | Preston NE | L | 1-2 | 0-1 | — | Salako $^{82}$ | 11,745 |
| 35 | 6 | A | Crystal Palace | D | 2-2 | 1-2 | 8 | Owusu 2 $^{14, 56}$ | 17,853 |
| 36 | 13 | H | Stoke C | D | 0-0 | 0-0 | 8 | | 14,132 |
| 37 | 16 | A | Cardiff C | W | 3-2 | 2-1 | — | Ingimarsson $^{39}$, Kitson $^{45}$, Morgan $^{90}$ | 14,051 |
| 38 | 20 | H | Sunderland | L | 0-2 | 0-0 | 9 | | 18,019 |
| 39 | 27 | A | Coventry C | W | 2-1 | 1-0 | 9 | Salako $^{10}$, Goater $^{54}$ | 15,811 |
| 40 | Apr 3 | H | West Ham U | W | 2-0 | 1-0 | 7 | Kitson 2 $^{35, 52}$ | 21,718 |
| 41 | 10 | A | Bradford C | L | 1-2 | 1-1 | 9 | Kitson $^{25}$ | 10,287 |
| 42 | 12 | H | Norwich C | L | 0-1 | 0-0 | 10 | | 18,460 |
| 43 | 17 | H | Crewe Alex | D | 1-1 | 1-1 | 10 | Kitson $^{10}$ | 14,729 |
| 44 | 24 | A | Millwall | W | 1-0 | 1-0 | 9 | Goater $^{16}$ | 12,535 |
| 45 | May 1 | H | WBA | W | 1-0 | 0-0 | 9 | Sidwell $^{88}$ | 20,619 |
| 46 | 9 | A | Watford | L | 0-1 | 0-1 | 9 | | 17,979 |

**Final League Position: 9**

### GOALSCORERS

*League (55):* Goater 12 (3 pens), Sidwell 8, Forster 7, Kitson 5, Murray 5, Owusu 4, Hughes 3, Salako 3, Shorey 2, Harper 1, Ingimarsson 1, Mackie 1, Morgan 1, Williams 1, own goal 1.
*Carling Cup (7):* Forster 4, Harper 1, Salako 1, Sidwell 1.
*FA Cup (4):* Goater 2, own goals 2.

| Hahnemann M 36 | Murty G 37 + 1 | Shorey N 35 | Brown S 19 | Williams A 33 | Harper J 35 + 4 | Murray S 25 + 9 | Sidwell S 43 | Goater S 30 + 4 | Forster N 28 + 2 | Hughes A 42 + 1 | Mackie J 7 + 2 | Salako J 32 + 5 | Butler M — + 3 | Watson K 10 + 12 | Newman R 25 + 5 | Daley O — + 6 | Tyson N — + 8 | Savage B 6 + 9 | Ingimarsson I 24 + 1 | Henderson D — + 1 | Morgan D 3 + 10 | Owusu L 11 + 5 | Kitson D 10 + 7 | Brooker P 5 + 6 | Young J — + 1 | Ashdown J 10 | Gordon D — + 3 | *Match No.* |
|---|---|---|---|---|---|---|---|---|---|---|---|---|---|---|---|---|---|---|---|---|---|---|---|---|---|---|---|---|
| 1 | 2 | 3■ | 4 | $5^{1}$ | 6 | 7 | $8^{2}$ | $9^{3}$ | 10 | 11 | 12 | 13 | 14 | | | | | | | | | | | | | | | 1 |
| 1 | 2 | 3 | 4 | 5 | | 7 | 8 | 9 | 10 | 6 | | $11^{1}$ | | 12 | | | | | | | | | | | | | | 2 |
| 1 | 2 | | $4^{2}$ | 5 | 12 | 7 | 8 | $9^{3}$ | 10 | 11 | 13 | | 14 | $6^{1}$ | 3 | | | | | | | | | | | | | 3 |
| 1 | 2 | 3 | 4 | 5 | 6 | $7^{2}$ | 8 | $9^{3}$ | 10 | $11^{1}$ | | | 12 | | | 13 | 14 | | | | | | | | | | | 4 |
| 1 | 2 | 3 | 4 | 5 | $6^{1}$ | $7^{3}$ | 8 | 9 | 10 | $11^{2}$ | | 13 | | | 12 | 14 | | | | | | | | | | | | 5 |
| 1 | 2 | 3 | 4 | 5 | $6^{1}$ | $7^{2}$ | 8 | 9 | 10 | 11 | | | | 12 | | | 13 | | | | | | | | | | | 6 |
| 1 | 2 | 3 | 4 | 5 | 6 | 7 | $8^{1}$ | $9^{2}$ | 10 | 11 | | | | 12 | | | 13 | | | | | | | | | | | 7 |
| 1 | 2 | 3 | 4 | 5 | $6^{1}$ | $7^{2}$ | 8 | 9 | 10 | $11^{3}$ | | | | 12 | | 14 | 13 | | | | | | | | | | | 8 |
| 1 | 2 | 3 | 4 | 5 | $6^{2}$ | $7^{3}$ | 8 | 12 | 9 | 10 | | $11^{1}$ | | | 13 | 14 | | | | | | | | | | | | 9 |
| 1 | 2 | 3 | | 5 | | 7 | $8^{1}$ | 9 | 10 | 11 | 4 | | | 12 | $6^{2}$ | 13 | | | | | | | | | | | | 10 |
| 1 | | 3 | | 5 | | 7 | 8 | 9 | 10 | 11 | 4 | | | $6^{1}$ | 2 | 12 | | | | | | | | | | | | 11 |
| 1 | | 3 | 4 | 5 | $6^{2}$ | 7 | 8 | $9^{1}$ | 10 | 11 | | 13 | | 12 | 2 | | | | | | | | | | | | | 12 |
| 1 | | 3 | | 5 | 6 | 7 | 8 | 9 | 10 | $11^{1}$ | 4 | 12 | | | $2^{2}$ | | | 13 | | | | | | | | | | 13 |
| 1 | | 3 | $4^{2}$ | 5 | 6 | 7 | 8 | 9 | 10 | | | 11 | | | $2^{1}$ | | 12 | 13 | | | | | | | | | | 14 |
| 1 | | 3 | | 5 | 6 | 7 | 8 | | 10 | $9^{1}$ | | 11 | | 12 | 2 | | | | 4 | | | | | | | | | 15 |
| 1 | 12 | 3 | | 5 | 6 | $7^{3}$ | 8 | 13 | 9 | 10 | | $11^{2}$ | | | $2^{1}$ | | | 14 | 4 | | | | | | | | | 16 |
| 1 | 2 | 3 | | $5^{2}$ | 6 | $7^{3}$ | | $9^{1}$ | 10 | 8 | | 11 | | 12 | 13 | | | 14 | 4 | | | | | | | | | 17 |
| 1 | 2 | 3 | | | $6^{1}$ | | 8 | $9^{2}$ | 10 | 7 | | $11^{3}$ | | 12 | 5 | | | 13 | 4 | 14 | | | | | | | | 18 |
| 1 | 2 | 3 | | | 6 | $7^{1}$ | 8 | | 9 | 10 | | 11 | | | 5 | | | 12 | 4 | | | | | | | | | 19 |
| 1 | 2 | 3 | | | $6^{1}$ | $7^{3}$ | 8 | | 9 | 10 | | $11^{2}$ | | 12 | 5 | | 13 | 14 | 4 | | | | | | | | | 20 |
| 1 | 2 | 3 | | | | 12 | 8 | | 9 | $10^{1}$ | 5 | $11^{2}$ | | 6 | | | 13 | 7 | 4 | | | | | | | | | 21 |
| 1 | 2 | 3 | | | 13 | 12 | 8 | | 9 | $10^{2}$ | 5 | 11 | | 6 | | | | $7^{1}$ | 4 | | | | | | | | | 22 |
| 1 | 2 | 3 | | | $10^{2}$ | $7^{1}$ | 8 | | 9 | | 5 | 11 | | 6 | | | 12 | 13 | 4 | | | | | | | | | 23 |
| 1 | | 3 | 2 | | | 12 | 8 | | 9 | 10 | $5^{1}$ | $11^{2}$ | | 6 | | | | 7 | 4 | | 13 | | | | | | | 24 |
| 1 | 2 | 3 | | 5 | 12 | $7^{2}$ | 8 | | 9 | 10 | | 11 | | $6^{1}$ | | | | | 4 | | | 13 | | | | | | 25 |
| 1 | 2 | 3 | 4 | 5 | 11 | 12 | 8 | | 9 | $7^{1}$ | | | | | $6^{2}$ | | | | 13 | | | 10 | | | | | | 26 |
| 1 | 2 | 3 | 4 | 5 | 11 | 7 | | $9^{2}$ | | 8 | | | | | 6 | | | | | | 12 | $10^{1}$ | 13 | | | | | 27 |
| 1 | 2 | 3 | 4 | 5 | | $7^{1}$ | 8 | $9^{2}$ | 10 | 12 | | 11 | | 6 | | | | | | | | 13 | | | | | | 28 |
| 1 | 2 | 3 | 4 | 5 | 12 | | 8 | 9 | | 7 | | 11 | | $6^{1}$ | | | | | | | | 10 | | | | | | 29 |
| 1 | 2 | 3 | $4^{1}$ | 5 | | 13 | 8 | 9 | | $7^{2}$ | | 11 | | 6 | 12 | | | | | | | 10 | | | | | | 30 |
| 1 | 2 | 3 | | | 6 | 12 | 8 | $9^{2}$ | | 7 | | $11^{1}$ | | | 5 | | | | 4 | | | 10 | 13 | | | | | 31 |
| 1 | 2 | 3 | | | 6 | 12 | 8 | $9^{3}$ | | $7^{1}$ | | $11^{2}$ | | | 5 | | | | 4 | | 13 | 10 | 14 | | | | | 32 |
| 1 | $2^{2}$ | 3 | | 5 | 6 | 12 | 8 | $9^{3}$ | | $7^{1}$ | | 11 | | | 13 | | | | 4 | | | 10 | 14 | | | | | 33 |
| 1 | | 3 | | 5 | 6 | $7^{1}$ | 8 | | | 11 | | 13 | | | 2 | | | | 4 | | | 10■ | 12 | $9^{2}$ | | | | 34 |
| 1 | | 3 | | 5 | 6 | 7 | 8 | $9^{1}$ | | 2 | | 11 | | | | | | | 4 | | 13 | $10^{2}$ | 12 | | | | | 35 |
| $1^{6}$ | 2 | 3 | | 5 | 6 | | 8 | 9 | | 7 | | $11^{2}$ | | | | | | | 4 | | | $10^{1}$ | 12 | 13 | 15 | | | 36 |
| | 2 | | 5 | | 6 | | 8 | $9^{1}$ | | 7 | | $11^{2}$ | | | 3 | | | | 4 | | 12 | | 10 | 13 | | 1 | | 37 |
| | 2 | | 5 | | 6 | 12 | 8 | $9^{2}$ | | $7^{1}$ | | $11^{3}$ | | | 3 | | | | 4 | | 13 | | 10 | 14 | | 1 | | 38 |
| | 2 | | | | 6 | | 8■ | $9^{1}$ | | 7 | | 11 | | 12 | 3 | | | 13 | 4 | | $5^{3}$ | | $10^{2}$ | 14 | | 1 | | 39 |
| | 2 | | | | 6 | | $8^{1}$ | | | 3 | | 11 | | 12 | 5 | | | | 4 | | $10^{2}$ | 13 | 9 | 7 | | 1 | | 40 |
| | 2 | | | 5 | 8 | | | 12 | 13 | 3 | | $11^{2}$ | | | $6^{3}$ | | | | 4■ | | 10 | | 9 | $7^{1}$ | | 1 | 14 | 41 |
| | 2 | | | 5 | 6 | | 8 | 12 | 10 | $3^{2}$ | | 11 | | | | | | | 4 | | | | 9 | $7^{1}$ | | 1 | 13 | 42 |
| | 2 | | | 5 | 6 | | 8 | | 12 | | | 11 | | | 3 | | | | 4 | | 13 | $10^{2}$ | 9 | $7^{1}$ | | 1 | | 43 |
| | 2 | | | 5 | 4 | | 8 | $10^{2}$ | | 3 | | 11 | | | 6 | | | $7^{1}$ | | | 12 | 13 | 9 | | | 1 | | 44 |
| | 2 | | | 5 | 4 | | 8 | $10^{3}$ | | 3 | | $11^{2}$ | | | 6 | | | $7^{1}$ | | | 12 | | 9 | 14 | | 1 | 13 | 45 |
| | 2 | | | 5 | 4 | | 8 | $10^{2}$ | | 3 | | $11^{3}$ | | | 6 | | | $7^{1}$ | | | 12 | 13 | 9 | 14 | | 1 | | 46 |

**Carling Cup**

| | | | |
|---|---|---|---|
| First Round | Boston U | (a) | 3-1 |
| Second Round | Oxford U | (a) | 3-1 |
| Third Round | Huddersfield T | (h) | 1-0 |
| Fourth Round | Chelsea | (h) | 0-1 |

**FA Cup**

| | | | |
|---|---|---|---|
| Third Round | Preston NE | (a) | 3-3 |
| | | (h) | 1-2 |

# ROCHDALE

## FL Championship 2

### FOUNDATION

Considering the love of rugby in their area, it is not surprising that Rochdale had difficulty in establishing an Association Football club. The earlier Rochdale Town club formed in 1900 went out of existence in 1907 when the present club was immediately established and joined the Manchester League, before graduating to the Lancashire Combination in 1908.

***Spotland Stadium, Sandy Lane, Rochdale OL11 5DS.***

***Telephone:*** (01706) 644 648.

***Fax:*** (01706) 648 466.

***Website:*** www.rochdaleafc.co.uk

***Email:*** office@rochdaleafc.co.uk

***Ground Capacity:*** 10,208.

***Record Attendance:*** 24,231 v Notts Co, FA Cup 2nd rd, 10 December 1949.

***Pitch Measurements:*** 114yd × 76yd.

***Chairman:*** D. F. Kilpatrick.

***Secretary:*** Hilary Molyneux Dearden.

***Manager:*** Steve Parkin.

***Assistant Manager:*** Tony Ford

***Physio:*** Andy Thorpe.

***Colours:*** Blue shirts with white trim, blue shorts, blue stockings with white hoop on turnover.

***Change Colours:*** All black with fluorescent trim.

***Year Formed:*** 1907.

***Turned Professional:*** 1907.

***Ltd Co.:*** 1910.

***Club Nickname:*** 'The Dale'.

***First Football League Game:*** 27 August 1921, Division 3 (N), v Accrington Stanley (h) W 6–3 – Crabtree; Nuttall, Sheehan; Hill, Farrer, Yarwood; Hoad, Sandiford, Dennison (2), Owens (3), Carney (1).

***Record League Victory:*** 8–1 v Chesterfield, Division 3 (N), 18 December 1926 – Hill; Brown, Ward; Hillhouse, Parkes, Braidwood; Hughes, Bertram, Whitehurst (5), Schofield (2), Martin (1).

***Record Cup Victory:*** 8–2 v Crook T, FA Cup 1st rd, 26 November 1927 – Moody; Hopkins, Ward; Braidwood, Parkes, Barker; Tompkinson, Clennell (3) Whitehurst (4), Hall, Martin (1).

### HONOURS

*Football League:* Division 3 best season: 9th, 1969–70; Division 3 (N) – Runners-up 1923–24, 1926–27.

*FA Cup:* best season: 5th rd, 1990, 2003.

*Football League Cup:* Runners-up 1962 (record for 4th Division club).

### SKY SPORTS FACT FILE

Former Bristol City centre-half Jim Pearce's career with Rochdale spanned the Second World War years, yet he made no official League appearances for them. He played in the three abortive 1939–40 fixtures, in wartime and four FA Cup ties 1945–46.

***Record Defeat:*** 1–9 v Tranmere R, Division 3 (N), 25 December 1931.

***Most League Points (2 for a win):*** 62, Division 3 (N), 1923–24.

***Most League Points (3 for a win):*** 78, Division 3, 2001–02.

***Most League Goals:*** 105, Division 3 (N), 1926–27.

***Highest League Scorer in Season:*** Albert Whitehurst, 44, Division 3 (N), 1926–27.

***Most League Goals in Total Aggregate:*** Reg Jenkins, 119, 1964–73.

***Most League Goals in One Match:*** 6, Tommy Tippett v Hartlepools U, Division 3N, 21 April 1930.

***Most Capped Players:*** Patrick McCourt, 1, Northern Ireland and Lee McEvilly, 1, Northern Ireland.

***Most League Appearances:*** Graham Smith, 317, 1966–74.

***Youngest League Player:*** Zac Hughes, 16 years 105 days v Exeter C, 19 September 1987.

***Record Transfer Fee Received:*** £400,000 from West Ham U for Stephen Bywater, August 1998.

***Record Transfer Fee Paid:*** £150,000 to Stoke C for Paul Connor, March 2001.

***Football League Record:*** 1921 Elected to Division 3 (N); 1958–59 Division 3; 1959–69 Division 4; 1969–74 Division 3; 1974–92 Division 4; 1992–2004 Division 3; 2004– FL2.

## MANAGERS

Billy Bradshaw 1920
*Run by committee* 1920–22
Tom Wilson 1922–23
Jack Peart 1923–30
Will Cameron 1930–31
Herbert Hopkinson 1932–34
Billy Smith 1934–35
Ernest Nixon 1935–37
Sam Jennings 1937–38
Ted Goodier 1938–52
Jack Warner 1952–53
Harry Catterick 1953–58
Jack Marshall 1958–60
Tony Collins 1960–68
Bob Stokoe 1967–68
Len Richley 1968–70
Dick Conner 1970–73
Walter Joyce 1973–76
Brian Green 1976–77
Mike Ferguson 1977–78
Doug Collins 1979
Bob Stokoe 1979–80
Peter Madden 1980–83
Jimmy Greenhoff 1983–84
Vic Halom 1984–86
Eddie Gray 1986–88
Danny Bergara 1988–89
Terry Dolan 1989–91
Dave Sutton 1991–94
Mick Docherty 1995–96
Graham Barrow 1996–99
Steve Parkin 1999–2001
John Hollins 2001–02
Paul Simpson 2002–03
Alan Buckley 2003–04
Steve Parkin January 2004–

## LATEST SEQUENCES

***Longest Sequence of League Wins:*** 8, 29.9.1969 – 3.11.1969.

***Longest Sequence of League Defeats:*** 17, 14.11.1931 – 12.3.1932.

***Longest Sequence of League Draws:*** 6, 17.8.1968 – 14.9.1968.

***Longest Sequence of Unbeaten League Matches:*** 20, 15.9.1923 – 19.1.1924.

***Longest Sequence Without a League Win:*** 28, 14.11.1931 – 29.8.1932.

***Successive Scoring Runs:*** 29 from 8.1.1927.

***Successive Non-scoring Runs:*** 9 from 14.3.1980.

## TEN YEAR LEAGUE RECORD

| | | *P* | *W* | *D* | *L* | *F* | *A* | *Pts* | *Pos* |
|---|---|---|---|---|---|---|---|---|---|
| 1994-95 | Div 3 | 42 | 12 | 14 | 16 | 44 | 67 | 50 | 15 |
| 1995-96 | Div 3 | 46 | 14 | 13 | 19 | 57 | 61 | 55 | 15 |
| 1996-97 | Div 3 | 46 | 14 | 16 | 16 | 58 | 58 | 58 | 14 |
| 1997-98 | Div 3 | 46 | 17 | 7 | 22 | 56 | 55 | 58 | 18 |
| 1998-99 | Div 3 | 46 | 13 | 15 | 18 | 42 | 55 | 54 | 19 |
| 1999-2000 | Div 3 | 46 | 18 | 14 | 14 | 57 | 54 | 68 | 10 |
| 2000-01 | Div 3 | 46 | 18 | 17 | 11 | 59 | 48 | 71 | 8 |
| 2001-02 | Div 3 | 46 | 21 | 15 | 10 | 65 | 52 | 78 | 5 |
| 2002-03 | Div 3 | 46 | 12 | 16 | 18 | 63 | 70 | 52 | 19 |
| 2003-04 | Div 3 | 46 | 12 | 14 | 20 | 49 | 58 | 50 | 21 |

## DID YOU KNOW ?

On 14 January 1939 Rochdale achieved their highest away win in the League beating York City 7-0, courtesy of a hat-trick from Peter Vause, two goals from Joe Firth, a Jimmy Wynn penalty and another strike from Joe Duff.

## ROCHDALE 2003–04 LEAGUE RECORD

| Match No. | Date | Venue | Opponents | Result | | H/T Score | Lg. Pos. | Goalscorers | Atten-dance |
|---|---|---|---|---|---|---|---|---|---|
| 1 | Aug 9 | H | Yeovil T | L | 1-3 | 1-1 | — | Connor [45] | 4611 |
| 2 | 16 | A | Bristol R | D | 0-0 | 0-0 | 18 | | 7575 |
| 3 | 23 | H | Cambridge U | D | 2-2 | 0-2 | 18 | McEvilly (pen) [67], Connor [79] | 2204 |
| 4 | 25 | A | Torquay U | W | 3-1 | 0-0 | 13 | McEvilly (pen) [59], Betts 2 [63, 78] | 3003 |
| 5 | 30 | H | Darlington | W | 4-2 | 2-2 | 7 | McEvilly 2 (1 pen) [37 (p), 41], Connor [59], Bertos [65] | 2518 |
| 6 | Sept 6 | A | York C | W | 2-1 | 2-0 | 4 | Townson [15], Bertos [19] | 3982 |
| 7 | 13 | A | Carlisle U | L | 2-3 | 0-3 | 9 | Connor [76], Townson [79] | 4532 |
| 8 | 16 | H | Huddersfield T | D | 1-1 | 1-1 | — | Connor [1] | 4626 |
| 9 | 20 | H | Hull C | L | 0-2 | 0-0 | 14 | | 4215 |
| 10 | 27 | A | Lincoln C | D | 1-1 | 1-1 | 15 | Antoine-Curier [40] | 4141 |
| 11 | 30 | A | Macclesfield T | L | 1-2 | 0-0 | — | Shuker [51] | 2152 |
| 12 | Oct 4 | H | Scunthorpe U | W | 2-0 | 0-0 | 12 | Bertos [82], Brannan (pen) [89] | 2838 |
| 13 | 11 | H | Northampton T | D | 1-1 | 0-0 | 12 | Townson [72] | 2710 |
| 14 | 18 | A | Cheltenham T | W | 2-0 | 1-0 | 11 | Townson [31], Bertos [88] | 3105 |
| 15 | 21 | A | Doncaster R | L | 1-2 | 1-1 | — | Townson [4] | 5890 |
| 16 | 25 | H | Swansea C | L | 0-1 | 0-1 | 14 | | 2646 |
| 17 | Nov 1 | A | Leyton Orient | L | 1-2 | 0-1 | 16 | McEvilly (pen) [59] | 3623 |
| 18 | 15 | H | Kidderminster H | L | 0-1 | 0-1 | 17 | | 2498 |
| 19 | 22 | A | Southend U | L | 0-4 | 0-2 | 19 | | 3169 |
| 20 | 29 | H | Oxford U | L | 1-2 | 0-1 | 19 | Jones [54] | 2282 |
| 21 | Dec 13 | A | Bury | W | 2-1 | 1-0 | 19 | Bishop [18], Townson [83] | 3646 |
| 22 | 20 | H | Boston U | W | 1-0 | 1-0 | 17 | Griffiths [42] | 2049 |
| 23 | 26 | A | Mansfield T | L | 0-1 | 0-0 | 18 | | 6963 |
| 24 | 28 | H | York C | L | 1-2 | 0-1 | 20 | Townson (pen) [49] | 2764 |
| 25 | Jan 3 | H | Torquay U | W | 1-0 | 1-0 | 16 | Townson (pen) [36] | 2559 |
| 26 | 10 | A | Yeovil T | L | 0-1 | 0-1 | 18 | | 5806 |
| 27 | 17 | H | Bristol R | D | 2-2 | 2-0 | 19 | McCourt [20], Townson [37] | 2497 |
| 28 | 24 | A | Cambridge U | D | 0-0 | 0-0 | 18 | | 3221 |
| 29 | 31 | A | Darlington | L | 0-1 | 0-0 | 19 | | 5689 |
| 30 | Feb 7 | H | Mansfield T | W | 3-0 | 2-0 | 16 | Jones (pen) [12], Holt [27], Bertos [54] | 3157 |
| 31 | 14 | A | Northampton T | L | 1-3 | 1-0 | 17 | Townson [32] | 4540 |
| 32 | 21 | H | Cheltenham T | D | 0-0 | 0-0 | 19 | | 2449 |
| 33 | Mar 6 | A | Boston U | L | 0-2 | 0-1 | 22 | | 2466 |
| 34 | 9 | A | Swansea C | D | 1-1 | 1-0 | — | Bertos [26] | 5819 |
| 35 | 13 | H | Bury | D | 0-0 | 0-0 | 22 | | 4225 |
| 36 | 16 | A | Huddersfield T | D | 1-1 | 1-0 | — | Bertos [39] | 10,884 |
| 37 | 20 | H | Carlisle U | W | 2-0 | 1-0 | 20 | Jones (pen) [34], Holt [64] | 4755 |
| 38 | 27 | A | Hull C | L | 0-1 | 0-0 | 22 | | 16,050 |
| 39 | 30 | H | Doncaster R | D | 1-1 | 0-0 | — | McEvilly [73] | 4601 |
| 40 | Apr 3 | H | Lincoln C | L | 0-3 | 0-0 | 21 | | 4224 |
| 41 | 10 | A | Scunthorpe U | D | 2-2 | 2-2 | 22 | Bertos [3], Warner [24] | 3564 |
| 42 | 12 | H | Macclesfield T | L | 1-2 | 1-0 | 22 | Heald [32] | 4942 |
| 43 | 17 | H | Leyton Orient | W | 3-0 | 1-0 | 22 | Holt 2 [23, 58], McCourt [90] | 2417 |
| 44 | 24 | A | Kidderminster H | W | 1-0 | 1-0 | 21 | Bertos [38] | 3580 |
| 45 | May 1 | H | Southend U | D | 1-1 | 0-0 | 20 | Jones [58] | 3591 |
| 46 | 8 | A | Oxford U | L | 0-2 | 0-2 | 21 | | 5134 |

**Final League Position: 21**

### GOALSCORERS

*League (49):* Townson 10 (2 pens), Bertos 9, McEvilly 6 (4 pens), Connor 5, Holt 4, Jones 4 (2 pens), Betts 2, McCourt 2, Antoine-Curier 1, Bishop 1, Brannan 1 (pen), Griffiths 1, Heald 1, Shuker 1, Warner 1.
*Carling Cup (1):* Townson 1.
*FA Cup (2):* Bertos 1, Townson 1.
*LDV Vans Trophy (0).*

| Gilks M 12 | Evans W 45 | Simpkins M 25 + 2 | Beech C 9 + 5 | Burgess D 33 + 2 | Grand S 11 + 6 | Bertos L 40 | McClare S 33 + 5 | Shuker C 14 | Connor P 21 + 3 | McCourt P 6 + 18 | McEvilly L 15 + 15 | Betts R 4 + 1 | Doughty M 25 + 6 | Townson K 17 + 16 | Griffiths G 29 + 4 | Hill S 1 | Brannan G 11 | Antoine-Curier M 5 + 3 | Strachan C — + 1 | Edwards N 34 | Patterson R 3 + 4 | Jones G 26 | Warner S 10 + 4 | Bishop A 8 + 2 | Donovan K 4 + 3 | Pemberton M 1 | Holt G 14 | Livesey D 11 + 2 | Ndiwa L — + 1 | Smith J 1 | Smith S 13 | Heald G 10 | Flood W 6 | Redfearn N 9 | *Match No.* |
|---|---|---|---|---|---|---|---|---|---|---|---|---|---|---|---|---|---|---|---|---|---|---|---|---|---|---|---|---|---|---|---|---|---|---|---|
| 1 | 2 | 3 | $4^{1}$ | 5 | 6 | $7^{2}$ | 8 | 9 | 10 | $11^{3}$ | 12 | 13 | 14 | | | | | | | | | | | | | | | | | | | | | | 1 |
| 1 | 2 | 3 | 4 | 5 | 6 | $7^{2}$ | 8 | 9 | 10 | 12 | | | $11^{1}$ | 13 | | | | | | | | | | | | | | | | | | | | | 2 |
| 1 | 2 | 3 | 12 | 5 | 6 | | $8^{1}$ | 9■ | 10 | $11^{2}$ | 14 | 7 | 13 | $4^{3}$ | | | | | | | | | | | | | | | | | | | | | 3 |
| 1 | 2 | 6■ | | 5 | 12 | 7 | 8 | $9^{1}$ | 10 | | 11 | 4 | 3 | | | | | | | | | | | | | | | | | | | | | | 4 |
| 1 | 2 | 3 | 12 | 5 | 6 | 7 | $8^{1}$ | 9 | 10 | | 11 | 4 | | | | | | | | | | | | | | | | | | | | | | | 5 |
| 1 | 2 | 3 | | 5 | 6 | 7 | 8 | | 10■ | 12 | | 4 | $11^{2}$ | $9^{1}$ | 13 | | | | | | | | | | | | | | | | | | | | 6 |
| 1 | 2 | | | $5^{3}$ | 6 | 7 | 8 | | 9 | 12 | $10^{1}$ | | $11^{2}$ | 13 | 14 | 3 | 4 | | | | | | | | | | | | | | | | | | 7 |
| 1 | 2 | 3 | | 5 | | 7 | 8 | | 10 | | 12 | | 11 | $9^{1}$ | 6 | | 4 | | | | | | | | | | | | | | | | | | 8 |
| 1 | 2 | 3 | | 5 | | 7 | 8 | 9 | | 12 | 11 | | 13 | $10^{2}$ | 6 | | $4^{1}$ | | | | | | | | | | | | | | | | | | 9 |
| 1 | 2 | 3 | | 5 | 12 | 7 | 8 | $11^{2}$ | | | 10■ | | | 13 | 6 | | $4^{1}$ | 9 | | | | | | | | | | | | | | | | | 10 |
| 1 | 2 | 3 | | 5 | | 7 | $8^{2}$ | 11 | | | $10^{1}$ | | | 12 | 6 | | 4 | 9 | 13 | | | | | | | | | | | | | | | | 11 |
| | 2 | 3 | | 5 | | 7 | 8 | 11 | 10 | | | | | | 6 | | 4 | 9 | | 1 | | | | | | | | | | | | | | | 12 |
| | 2 | 3 | | | 6 | | 8 | $11^{1}$ | $10^{2}$ | 12 | | | 7 | 13 | 5 | | 4 | $9^{3}$ | | 1 | 14 | | | | | | | | | | | | | | 13 |
| | 2 | 3 | 12 | | 6 | 7 | $8^{1}$ | $11^{2}$ | | | | | 13 | $10^{3}$ | 5 | | 4 | 14 | | 1 | 9 | | | | | | | | | | | | | | 14 |
| | 2 | 3 | $4^{1}$ | $6^{3}$ | 12 | 7 | | 9 | | | 11 | | | $10^{2}$ | 5 | | 8 | 14 | | 1 | 13 | | | | | | | | | | | | | | 15 |
| | 2 | 3 | | 5 | | 7 | 8 | 11 | $10^{2}$ | 12 | 13 | | | | 6 | | 4 | $9^{1}$ | | 1 | | | | | | | | | | | | | | | 16 |
| | $2^{1}$ | 3 | | 5 | | 7 | 8 | 9 | | 13 | 11 | | $10^{2}$ | 12 | 6 | | 4 | | | 1 | | | | | | | | | | | | | | | 17 |
| | 2 | 13 | 12 | $5^{2}$ | 3 | 7 | 8 | | | 11 | $9^{3}$ | | | 10 | 6 | | | 14 | | 1 | | $4^{1}$ | | | | | | | | | | | | | 18 |
| | 2 | | | 5 | 3 | 7 | 8■ | | | 13 | $9^{1}$ | | $11^{2}$ | 12 | 6 | | | | | 1 | | $4^{3}$ | 14 | 10 | | | | | | | | | | | 19 |
| | 2 | 3 | 12 | 5 | | 7 | 8 | | | | 13 | | $11^{1}$ | 14 | 6 | | | | | 1 | $9^{2}$ | 4 | | $10^{3}$ | | | | | | | | | | | 20 |
| | 2 | 3 | 4 | 5 | | 7 | | | 9 | 13 | | | $11^{2}$ | 12 | 6 | | | | | 1 | | 8 | | $10^{1}$ | | | | | | | | | | | 21 |
| | 2 | $3^{3}$ | 4 | 5 | 14 | 7 | | | 9 | 13 | | | $11^{2}$ | 12 | 6 | | | | | 1 | | 8 | | $10^{1}$ | | | | | | | | | | | 22 |
| | 2 | 3 | 4 | $5^{2}$ | 13 | 7 | | | 9 | | | | $11^{3}$ | 12 | 6 | | | | | 1 | | 8 | | $10^{1}$ | 14 | | | | | | | | | | 23 |
| | 2 | 3 | 4 | | $6^{3}$ | 7 | 8 | | 9 | 13 | | | $11^{2}$ | 12 | 5 | | | | | 1 | | | | $10^{1}$ | 14 | | | | | | | | | | 24 |
| | 2 | 3 | 4 | 5 | | 7 | 8 | | $9^{1}$ | | | | $11^{2}$ | 10 | 6 | | | | | 1 | | | | 12 | 13 | | | | | | | | | | 25 |
| | 2 | | $4^{1}$ | 5 | | | 8 | | $9^{3}$ | 13 | | | 11 | 12 | 6 | | | | | 1 | | | 10 | 14 | 7 | $3^{2}$ | | | | | | | | | 26 |
| | 2 | | | 5 | | | 8 | | 12 | 11 | 13 | | 3 | $9^{2}$ | 6 | | | | | 1 | | 4 | | $10^{1}$ | 7 | | | | | | | | | | 27 |
| | 2 | 3 | | 5 | | | 8 | | 13 | 14 | | | $11^{3}$ | $9^{2}$ | 6 | | | | | 1 | | $4^{1}$ | 12 | 10 | 7 | | | | | | | | | | 28 |
| | 2 | 3 | | $5^{1}$ | 13 | | 8 | | 9 | 14 | | | $11^{3}$ | | $6^{2}$ | | | | | 1 | | 4 | 12 | | 7 | | 10 | | | | | | | | 29 |
| | 2 | 12 | | 5 | | 7 | 8 | | 9 | $11^{1}$ | | | 3 | | | | | | | 1 | | 4 | | | | | $10^{2}$ | 6 | 13 | | | | | | 30 |
| | 2 | 3 | | 5 | | 7 | 8 | | 9 | 12 | | | $11^{1}$ | 10 | | | | | | 1 | | 6■ | | | | | | 4 | | | | | | | 31 |
| | 2 | | | | | 7 | | | 12 | | | | 3 | $9^{1}$ | 6 | | | | | 1 | | 8 | 4 | | | | 10 | 5 | | 11 | | | | | 32 |
| | 2 | | | | | 7 | 8 | | $9^{2}$ | | 13 | | $11^{1}$ | 12 | 6 | | | | | 1 | | 4 | | | | | 10 | 5■ | | | 3 | | | | 33 |
| | 2 | | | 5 | | 7 | 8 | | | | 12 | | 3 | $9^{1}$ | | | | | | 1 | | 6 | | | | | 10 | 4 | | | 11 | | | | 34 |
| | 2 | | | $5^{1}$ | | 7 | 8 | | | 13 | 14 | | $11^{2}$ | $9^{3}$ | 12 | | | | | 1 | | 6 | | | | | 10 | 4 | | | 3 | | | | 35 |
| | 2 | | | | | 7 | 13 | | | | 9 | | | | 12 | | | | | 1 | | 6 | 11 | | | | 10 | $4^{1}$ | | | 3 | 5 | $8^{2}$ | | 36 |
| | 2 | | | | | 7 | | | | | $9^{2}$ | | | 13 | 6 | | | | | 1 | | 11 | 12 | | | | 10 | | | | 3 | 5 | 8 | $4^{1}$ | 37 |
| | 2 | | | | | 7 | 12 | | | | 13 | | 3 | | 6 | | | | | 1 | | 11 | $8^{2}$ | | | | 10 | | | | | 5 | 9 | $4^{1}$ | 38 |
| | 2 | | | | | 7 | | | | | 12 | | | $9^{1}$ | | | | | | 1 | | 8 | | | | | 10 | 6 | | | 3 | 5 | 11 | 4 | 39 |
| | 2 | | | | | 7 | | | | | 9 | | 13 | 12 | | | | | | 1 | | 8 | | | | | $10^{1}$ | 6 | | | 3 | 5 | $11^{2}$ | 4 | 40 |
| | 2 | | | 12 | | 7 | 13 | | | | 14 | | | | | | | | | 1 | | 10 | 4 | | | | $9^{3}$ | $6^{1}$ | | | 3 | 5 | $11^{2}$ | 8 | 41 |
| | | | | 6 | | $7^{1}$ | 12 | | | | 13 | | | 9 | $2^{3}$ | | | | | 1 | | 11 | 8 | | | | $10^{2}$ | 14 | | | 3 | 5 | | 4 | 42 |
| | 2 | | | 6 | | 7 | $8^{2}$ | | | 13 | 12 | | | | | | | | | 1 | | 9 | 11 | | | | $10^{1}$ | | | | 3 | 5 | | 4 | 43 |
| | 2 | | | | | 7 | 8 | | | | $9^{1}$ | | | | 6 | | | | | 1 | 12 | 10 | 11 | | | | | 13 | | | 3 | $5^{2}$ | | 4 | 44 |
| | 2 | | | 12 | | 7 | 8 | | | 13 | $9^{3}$ | | | | 6 | | | | | 1 | 14 | 10 | 11 | | | | | | | | 3 | $5^{1}$ | | $4^{2}$ | 45 |
| 1 | 2 | | | 5 | | 7 | 12 | | | $8^{1}$ | 13 | | 14 | $9^{2}$ | | | | | | | 10 | 6 | $11^{3}$ | | | | | 4 | | | 3 | | | | 46 |

**Carling Cup**
First Round | Stoke C | (a) | 1-2

**LDV Vans Trophy**
First Round | Carlisle U | (a) | 0-2

**FA Cup**
First Round | Bury | (a) | 2-1
Second Round | Luton T | (h) | 0-2

# ROTHERHAM UNITED FL Championship

## FOUNDATION

Rotherham were formed in 1870 before becoming Town in the late 1880s. Thornhill United were founded in 1877 and changed their name to Rotherham County in 1905. The Town amalgamated with Rotherham County to form Rotherham United in 1925.

***Millmoor Ground, Rotherham S60 1HR.***

***Telephone:*** (01709) 512 434.

***Fax:*** (01709) 512 762.

***Ticket Office:*** 0870 443 1884.

***Ground Capacity:*** 11,499.

***Record Attendance:*** 25,170 v Sheffield U, Division 2, 13 December 1952.

***Pitch Measurements.*** 115yd × 70yd.

***Chairman:*** Ken Booth.

***Chief Executive:*** Phil Henson.

***Manager:*** Ronnie Moore.

***Assistant Manager:*** John Breckin.

***Physio:*** Dennis Circuit.

***Colours:*** Red shirts with white trim, white shorts, red stockings.

***Change Colours:*** Black shirts with red trim, black shorts, black stockings.

***Year Formed:*** 1870.

***Turned Professional:*** 1905.

***Ltd Co.:*** 1920.

***Club Nickname:*** 'The Merry Millers'.

***Previous Names:*** 1877, Thornhill United; 1905, Rotherham County; 1925, amalgamated with Rotherham Town under Rotherham United.

***Previous Ground:*** 1870, Red House Ground; 1907, Millmoor.

***First Football League Game:*** 2 September 1893, Division 2, Rotherham T v Lincoln C (a) D 1–1 – McKay; Thickett, Watson; Barr, Brown, Broadhead; Longden, Cutts, Leatherbarrow, McCormick, Pickering, (1 og). 30 August 1919, Division 2, Rotherham Co v Nottingham F (h) W 2–0 – Branston; Alton, Baines; Bailey, Coe, Stanton; Lee (1), Cawley (1), Glennon, Lees, Lamb.

***Record League Victory:*** 8–0 v Oldham Ath, Division 3 (N), 26 May 1947 – Warnes; Selkirk, Ibbotson; Edwards, Horace Williams, Danny Williams; Wilson (2), Shaw (1), Ardron (3), Guest (1), Hainsworth (1).

***Record Cup Victory:*** 6–0 v Spennymoor U, FA Cup 2nd rd, 17 December 1977 – McAlister; Forrest, Breckin, Womble, Stancliffe, Green, Finney, Phillips (3), Gwyther (2) (Smith), Goodfellow, Crawford (1). 6–0 v Wolverhampton W, FA Cup 1st rd, 16 November 1985 – O'Hanlon; Forrest, Dungworth, Gooding (1), Smith (1), Pickering, Birch (2), Emerson, Tynan (1), Simmons (1), Pugh. 6–0 v Kings Lynn, FA Cup 2nd rd, 6 December 1997 – Mimms; Clark, Hurst (Goodwin), Garner (1) (Hudson) (1), Warner (Bass), Richardson (1), Berry (1), Thompson, Druce (1), Glover (1), Roscoe.

## HONOURS

*Football League:* Division 2 – runners-up 2000–01; Division 3 – Champions 1980–81; Runners-up 1999–2000; Division 3 (N) – Champions 1950–51; Runners-up 1946–47, 1947–48, 1948–49; Division 4 – Champions 1988–89; Runners-up 1991–92.

*FA Cup:* best season: 5th rd, 1953, 1968.

*Football League Cup:* Runners-up 1961.

*Auto Windscreens Shield:* Winners 1996.

## SKY SPORTS FACT FILE

On Boxing Day 2003 Will Hoskins, 17, with just thirty minutes of first team football for Rotherham United, was introduced as a substitute against Wigan Athletic in the 61st minute. His two goals in three minutes resulted in a 2-1 win.

***Record Defeat:*** 1–11 v Bradford C, Division 3 (N), 25 August 1928.

***Most League Points (2 for a win):*** 71, Division 3 (N), 1950–51.

***Most League Points (3 for a win):*** 91, Division 2, 2000–01.

***Most League Goals:*** 114, Division 3 (N), 1946–47.

***Highest League Scorer in Season:*** Wally Ardron, 38, Division 3 (N), 1946–47.

***Most League Goals in Total Aggregate:*** Gladstone Guest, 130, 1946–56.

***Most League Goals in One Match:*** 4, Roland Bastow v York C, Division 3N, 9 November 1935; 4, Roland Bastow v Rochdale, Division 3N, 7 March 1936; 4, Wally Ardron v Crewe Alex, Division 3N, 5 October 1946; 4, Wally Ardron v Carlisle U, Division 3N, 13 September 1947; 4, Wally Ardron v Hartlepools U, Division 3N, 13 October 1948; 4, Ian Wilson v Liverpool, Division 2, 2 May 1955; 4, Carl Gilbert v Swansea C, Division 3, 28 September 1971; 4, Carl Airey v Chester, Division 3, 31 August 1987; 4, Shaun Goater v Hartlepool U, Division 3, 9 April 1994; 4, Lee Glover v Hull C, Division 3, 28 December 1997; 4, Darren Byfield v Millwall, Division 1, 10 August 2002.

***Most Capped Player:*** Shaun Goater 14 (19), Bermuda.

***Most League Appearances:*** Danny Williams, 459, 1946–62.

***Youngest League Player:*** Kevin Eley, 16 years 72 days v Scunthorpe U, 15 May 1984.

***Record Transfer Fee Received:*** £850,000 from Cardiff C for Alan Lee, August 2003.

***Record Transfer Fee Paid:*** £150,000 to Millwall for Tony Towner, August 1980; £150,000 to Port Vale for Lee Glover, August 1996; £150,000 to Burnley for Alan Lee, September 2000; £150,000 to Reading for Martin Butler, September 2003.

***Football League Record:*** 1893 Rotherham Town elected to Division 2; 1896 Failed re-election; 1919 Rotherham County elected to Division 2; 1923–51 Division 3 (N); 1951–68 Division 2; 1968–73 Division 3; 1973–75 Division 4; 1975–81 Division 3; 1981–83 Division 2; 1983–88 Division 3; 1988–89 Division 4; 1989–91 Division 3; 1991–92 Division 4; 1992–97 Division 2; 1997–2000 Division 3; 2000–01 Division 2; 2001–04 Division 1; 2004– FLC.

## MANAGERS

Billy Heald 1925–29 *(Secretary only for long spell)*
Stanley Davies 1929–30
Billy Heald 1930–33
Reg Freeman 1934–52
Andy Smailes 1952–58
Tom Johnston 1958–62
Danny Williams 1962–65
Jack Mansell 1965–67
Tommy Docherty 1967–68
Jimmy McAnearney 1968–73
Jimmy McGuigan 1973–79
Ian Porterfield 1979–81
Emlyn Hughes 1981–83
George Kerr 1983–85
Norman Hunter 1985–87
Dave Cusack 1987–88
Billy McEwan 1988–91
Phil Henson 1991–94
Archie Gemmill/John McGovern 1994–96
Danny Bergara 1996–97
Ronnie Moore May 1997–

## LATEST SEQUENCES

***Longest Sequence of League Wins:*** 9, 2.2.1982 – 6.3.1982.

***Longest Sequence of League Defeats:*** 8, 7.4.1956 – 18.8.1956.

***Longest Sequence of League Draws:*** 6, 13.10.1969 – 22.11.1969.

***Longest Sequence of Unbeaten League Matches:*** 18, 13.10.1969 – 7.2.1970.

***Longest Sequence Without a League Win:*** 14, 8.10.1977 – 2.1.1978.

***Successive Scoring Runs:*** 30 from 3.4.1954.

***Successive Non-scoring Runs:*** 5 from 4.4.1986.

## TEN YEAR LEAGUE RECORD

| | | P | W | D | L | F | A | Pts | Pos |
|---|---|---|---|---|---|---|---|---|---|
| 1994-95 | Div 2 | 46 | 14 | 14 | 18 | 57 | 61 | 56 | 17 |
| 1995-96 | Div 2 | 46 | 14 | 14 | 18 | 54 | 62 | 56 | 16 |
| 1996-97 | Div 2 | 46 | 7 | 14 | 25 | 39 | 70 | 35 | 23 |
| 1997-98 | Div 3 | 46 | 16 | 19 | 11 | 67 | 61 | 67 | 9 |
| 1998-99 | Div 3 | 46 | 20 | 13 | 13 | 79 | 61 | 73 | 5 |
| 1999-2000 | Div 3 | 46 | 24 | 12 | 10 | 72 | 36 | 84 | 2 |
| 2000-01 | Div 2 | 46 | 27 | 10 | 9 | 79 | 55 | 91 | 2 |
| 2001-02 | Div 1 | 46 | 10 | 19 | 17 | 52 | 66 | 49 | 21 |
| 2002-03 | Div 1 | 46 | 15 | 14 | 17 | 62 | 62 | 59 | 15 |
| 2003-04 | Div 1 | 46 | 13 | 15 | 18 | 53 | 61 | 54 | 17 |

## DID YOU KNOW?

On 6 March 1937 and unusually at the time, left-back Albert Rhodes made a scoring debut for Rotherham United against Hartlepools United. Contemporary sources wrongly credited him with the other goal scored by Ernie Smith.

## ROTHERHAM UNITED 2003–04 LEAGUE RECORD

| Match No. | Date | Venue | Opponents | Result | | H/T Score | Lg. Pos. | Goalscorers | Attendance |
|---|---|---|---|---|---|---|---|---|---|
| 1 | Aug 9 | H | Cardiff C | D | 0-0 | 0-0 | — | | 8176 |
| 2 | 16 | A | Norwich C | L | 0-2 | 0-2 | 20 | | 16,263 |
| 3 | 23 | H | West Ham U | W | 1-0 | 1-0 | 15 | Byfield [14] | 8739 |
| 4 | 25 | A | Reading | D | 0-0 | 0-0 | 10 | | 14,047 |
| 5 | 30 | H | Wigan Ath | L | 0-3 | 0-0 | 17 | | 6660 |
| 6 | Sept 13 | H | Crewe Alex | L | 0-2 | 0-1 | 19 | | 5495 |
| 7 | 16 | A | Sheffield U | L | 0-5 | 0-2 | — | | 22,572 |
| 8 | 20 | A | Preston NE | L | 1-4 | 1-1 | 22 | Byfield [45] | 12,340 |
| 9 | 27 | H | Gillingham | D | 1-1 | 0-1 | 22 | Byfield (pen) [80] | 5501 |
| 10 | 30 | H | Stoke C | W | 3-0 | 1-0 | — | Byfield (pen) [45], Butler 2 [51, 90] | 5450 |
| 11 | Oct 4 | A | Ipswich T | L | 1-2 | 0-0 | 22 | Butler [59] | 21,859 |
| 12 | 11 | H | Millwall | D | 0-0 | 0-0 | 22 | | 5461 |
| 13 | 14 | A | Nottingham F | D | 2-2 | 0-2 | — | Byfield [51], Butler [56] | 20,168 |
| 14 | 18 | A | Crystal Palace | D | 1-1 | 1-0 | 23 | Swailes [32] | 18,715 |
| 15 | 21 | A | Sunderland | D | 0-0 | 0-0 | — | | 24,506 |
| 16 | 25 | H | WBA | L | 0-3 | 0-1 | 22 | | 7815 |
| 17 | Nov 1 | A | Watford | L | 0-1 | 0-0 | 22 | | 18,067 |
| 18 | 8 | H | Wimbledon | W | 3-1 | 2-0 | 21 | Butler [34], Swailes [38], McIntosh [54] | 5777 |
| 19 | 22 | A | Burnley | D | 1-1 | 0-1 | 22 | Mullin [51] | 12,928 |
| 20 | 29 | H | Walsall | W | 2-0 | 0-0 | 22 | Swailes [67], Butler [80] | 6101 |
| 21 | Dec 2 | H | Coventry C | W | 2-0 | 2-0 | — | Byfield [14], Barker S [39] | 5524 |
| 22 | 6 | A | Wimbledon | W | 2-1 | 1-0 | 17 | Barker S [45], McIntosh [67] | 3061 |
| 23 | 13 | H | Derby Co | D | 0-0 | 0-0 | 18 | | 7320 |
| 24 | 20 | A | Bradford C | W | 2-0 | 1-0 | 15 | Byfield (pen) [16], Mullin [90] | 10,923 |
| 25 | 26 | A | Wigan Ath | W | 2-1 | 0-0 | 14 | Hoskins 2 [81, 83] | 9235 |
| 26 | 28 | H | Sunderland | L | 0-2 | 0-2 | 16 | | 11,455 |
| 27 | Jan 10 | A | Cardiff C | L | 2-3 | 2-3 | 17 | Talbot [3], Mullin [9] | 13,021 |
| 28 | 17 | H | Norwich C | D | 4-4 | 2-3 | 17 | Butler 3 [28, 42, 65], Mullin [75] | 7448 |
| 29 | 31 | A | West Ham U | L | 1-2 | 1-1 | 18 | Repka (og) [23] | 34,483 |
| 30 | Feb 7 | H | Reading | W | 5-1 | 2-1 | 16 | Proctor 2 (1 pen) [24 (p), 79], Monkhouse [36], Butler [47], Barker R [90] | 6405 |
| 31 | 21 | H | Nottingham F | D | 1-1 | 0-0 | 16 | Monkhouse [65] | 9046 |
| 32 | 24 | A | Millwall | L | 1-2 | 0-1 | — | Proctor (pen) [89] | 8254 |
| 33 | 28 | A | WBA | W | 1-0 | 0-0 | 15 | Sedgwick [73] | 24,104 |
| 34 | Mar 6 | H | Bradford C | L | 1-2 | 0-2 | 16 | Hurst [74] | 6796 |
| 35 | 13 | A | Derby Co | L | 0-1 | 0-0 | 17 | | 21,741 |
| 36 | 16 | H | Sheffield U | D | 1-1 | 0-0 | — | Monkhouse [52] | 9793 |
| 37 | 20 | A | Gillingham | L | 0-2 | 0-2 | 20 | | 8047 |
| 38 | 27 | H | Preston NE | W | 1-0 | 1-0 | 17 | Butler [30] | 6268 |
| 39 | Apr 3 | A | Crewe Alex | D | 0-0 | 0-0 | 18 | | 6749 |
| 40 | 6 | H | Crystal Palace | L | 1-2 | 0-2 | — | Proctor [85] | 6001 |
| 41 | 10 | H | Ipswich T | L | 1-3 | 1-0 | 20 | Sedgwick [24] | 6561 |
| 42 | 12 | A | Stoke C | W | 2-0 | 1-0 | 18 | Morris [22], Butler [68] | 11,978 |
| 43 | 17 | H | Watford | D | 1-1 | 1-1 | 18 | Butler [4] | 7221 |
| 44 | 24 | A | Coventry C | D | 1-1 | 0-0 | 19 | Butler [75] | 13,572 |
| 45 | May 1 | H | Burnley | W | 3-0 | 2-0 | 16 | Butler [15], Stockdale [39], Proctor (pen) [85] | 9157 |
| 46 | 9 | A | Walsall | L | 2-3 | 0-0 | 17 | Proctor (pen) [55], Warne (pen) [89] | 11,049 |

**Final League Position: 17**

### GOALSCORERS

*League (53):* Butler 15, Byfield 7 (3 pens), Proctor 6 (4 pens), Mullin 4, Monkhouse 3, Swailes 3, Barker S 2, Hoskins 2, McIntosh 2, Sedgwick 2, Barker R 1, Hurst 1, Morris 1, Stockdale 1, Talbot 1, Warne 1 (pen), own goal 1.
*Carling Cup (4):* Sedgwick 2, Byfield 1, Swailes 1.
*FA Cup (2):* Barker R 1, Hurst 1.

| Pollitt M 43 | Barker S 36 | Minto S 28 + 4 | Daws N 3 + 1 | Swailes C 43 | McIntosh M 18 | Sedgwick C 40 | Talbot S 19 + 4 | Lee A 1 | Robins M 2 + 7 | Garner D 10 + 3 | Monkhouse A 17 + 10 | Byfield D 26 + 2 | Barker R 12 + 20 | Branston G 7 + 1 | Mullin J 35 + 3 | Scott R 8 + 2 | Hurst P 23 + 5 | Warne P 23 + 12 | Butler M 36 + 1 | Baudet J 8 + 3 | Robinson C 14 | Montgomery G 3 + 1 | Hoskins W — + 4 | Proctor M 16 + 1 | Stockdale R 16 | Gilchrist P 10 | Morris J 9 + 1 | *Match No.* |
|---|---|---|---|---|---|---|---|---|---|---|---|---|---|---|---|---|---|---|---|---|---|---|---|---|---|---|---|---|
| 1 | 2 | 3 | 4 | 5 | 6 | $7^{1}$ | 8 | 9 | $10^{2}$ | 11 | 12 | 13 | | | | | | | | | | | | | | | | 1 |
| 1 | 2 | 3 | 4 | 5 | 6■ | 7 | 8 | | $10^{1}$ | $11^{2}$ | 13 | 12 | $9^{3}$ | 14 | | | | | | | | | | | | | | 2 |
| 1 | 2 | 3 | | 5 | 6 | 4 | 8 | | | | 7 | 10 | 9 | | 11 | | | | | | | | | | | | | 3 |
| 1 | | 3 | | 5 | 6 | 7 | 8 | | | | $4^{1}$ | 10 | 9 | | 11 | 2 | 12 | | | | | | | | | | | 4 |
| 1 | 2 | 3 | | 5 | | $7^{2}$ | 8 | | 12 | | $4^{1}$ | 10 | 9 | 6 | 11 | | | 13 | | | | | | | | | | 5 |
| 1 | 2 | 3 | | 5 | | 7 | $8^{2}$ | | 12 | | $4^{1}$ | 10 | | 6 | 11 | | | | 9 | 13 | | | | | | | | 6 |
| 1 | 2 | 3 | 4 | 5 | | $7^{2}$ | $8^{1}$ | | | | | 10 | | | 11 | 13 | | 12 | 9 | 6 | | | | | | | | 7 |
| 1 | 2■ | 3 | | 5 | 6 | $7^{1}$ | 8 | | | | | 10 | | | 11 | 12 | | | 9 | | 4 | | | | | | | 8 |
| 1 | | 3 | | 5 | 6 | 7 | 8 | | | | $11^{1}$ | 10 | | | | 2 | | 12 | 9 | | 4 | | | | | | | 9 |
| 1 | | | | 5 | 6 | $7^{2}$ | | | 12 | | 13 | $10^{3}$ | 14 | | | 2 | 3 | 11 | $9^{1}$ | 4 | 8 | | | | | | | 10 |
| 1 | | | | 5 | 6■ | $7^{1}$ | 12 | | | | | $10^{2}$ | 13 | | | 2 | 3 | 11 | 9 | 8■ | 4 | | | | | | | 11 |
| 1 | | 3 | | 5 | 6 | 7 | 8 | | | | 12 | 10 | | | | 2 | 13 | $11^{1}$ | 9 | $4^{2}$ | | | | | | | | 12 |
| 1 | | 3 | | 5 | 6 | 7 | 12 | | | | | 10 | | | | 2 | | 11 | 9 | $4^{1}$ | 8 | | | | | | | 13 |
| 1■ | $6^{2}$ | 3 | | 5 | | 7 | 8 | | | | | $10^{1}$ | 12 | | | 2 | 13 | 11 | $9^{G}$ | | 4 | 15 | | | | | | 14 |
| 1 | 6 | 3 | | 5 | | 7 | $8^{1}$ | | | | | $10^{3}$ | 14 | | 12 | $2^{2}$ | 13 | 11 | 9 | | 4 | | | | | | | 15 |
| 1 | 2 | $3^{3}$ | | 5 | 6 | $7^{1}$ | 4 | | 12 | | 13 | $10^{2}$ | 9 | | 8 | | 14 | 11 | | | | | | | | | | 16 |
| | 2 | | | | 6 | $7^{2}$ | $8^{1}$ | | | | | 10 | 9 | | 12 | | 3 | 11 | 13 | 5 | 4 | 1 | | | | | | 17 |
| 1 | 2 | | | 5 | 6 | | 8■ | | 12 | | | | $10^{1}$ | | 7 | | 3 | 11 | $9^{2}$ | | 4 | | 13 | | | | | 18 |
| | 2 | | | 5 | 6 | 7 | | | | | | 10 | 9 | | 8 | | 3 | 11 | | | 4 | 1 | | | | | | 19 |
| | 2 | | | 5 | 6 | 7 | | | 13 | | | $10^{1}$ | 12 | | 8 | | 3 | 11 | $9^{2}$ | | 4 | 1 | | | | | | 20 |
| 1 | 2 | | | 5 | 6 | $7^{1}$ | 12 | | 14 | | | $10^{2}$ | 13 | | 8 | | 3 | 11 | $9^{3}$ | | 4 | | | | | | | 21 |
| 1 | 2 | | | 5 | 6 | 7 | | | | | | $10^{1}$ | 12 | | 8 | | 3 | 11 | 9 | | 4 | | | | | | | 22 |
| 1 | 2 | 12 | | 5 | $6^{1}$ | 7 | | | | | | 10 | | | 8 | | 3 | 11 | 9 | | 4 | | | | | | | 23 |
| 1 | 2 | | 12 | 5 | | 7 | $4^{1}$ | | | | | 10 | | 6 | 8 | | 3 | 11 | 9 | | | | | | | | | 24 |
| 1 | 2 | | | 5 | | 7 | 4 | | | | | $10^{1}$ | 12 | 6 | 8 | | 3 | 11 | $9^{2}$ | | | | 13 | | | | | 25 |
| 1 | $2^{1}$ | 12 | | 5 | | 7 | 4 | | | | | $10^{3}$ | 13 | 6 | 8 | | 3 | 11 | $9^{2}$ | | | | 14 | | | | | 26 |
| 1 | 2 | | | 5 | | 7 | $4^{2}$ | | | 13 | 12 | 10 | 9 | 6 | 8 | | 3 | $11^{1}$ | | | | | | | | | | 27 |
| 1 | 2 | 12 | | 5 | | 7 | | | | 4 | $11^{1}$ | 10 | | 6■ | 8 | | 3 | | 9 | | | | | | | | | 28 |
| 1 | 2 | 3 | | 5 | | 7 | | | | 4 | 13 | $10^{1}$ | 9 | | 8 | | $11^{2}$ | 12 | | 6 | | | | | | | | 29 |
| 1 | 2 | 6 | | 5 | | 7 | 12 | | | 4 | $11^{3}$ | | 13 | | $8^{1}$ | | 3 | 14 | $9^{2}$ | | | | | 10 | | | | 30 |
| 1 | 6 | 12 | | 5 | | 7 | | | | 4 | $11^{1}$ | | | | 8 | | 3 | | 9 | | | | | 10 | 2 | | | 31 |
| 1 | 6 | | | 5 | | $7^{2}$ | | | | $4^{1}$ | $11^{3}$ | | 13 | | 8 | | 3 | 12 | 9 | 14 | | | | 10 | 2 | | | 32 |
| 1 | 6 | | | 5 | | 7 | | | | 4 | 11 | | 12 | | 8 | | 3 | 13 | $9^{1}$ | | | | | $10^{2}$ | 2 | | | 33 |
| 1 | 6 | | | 5 | | $7^{2}$ | | | | $4^{3}$ | 11 | | 12 | | 8 | | 3 | 13 | 9 | 14 | | | | $10^{1}$ | 2 | | | 34 |
| 1 | | 11 | | 5 | | | | | | $7^{2}$ | | | $10^{3}$ | | 12 | | 3 | 8 | 9 | $6^{1}$ | | | 13 | 14 | 2 | 4 | | 35 |
| 1 | | 6 | | 5 | | | | | | | 11 | | | | 8 | | 3 | 7 | 9 | | | | | 10 | 2 | 4 | | 36 |
| 1 | | 6 | | 5 | | | | | | 13 | 11 | | 12 | | $8^{2}$ | | $3^{3}$ | $7^{1}$ | 9 | | | | | 10 | 2 | 4 | 14 | 37 |
| 1 | | 3 | | 5 | | $7^{1}$ | | | | 12 | 11 | | | | 8 | | | | 9 | | | | | 10 | 2 | 6 | 4 | 38 |
| 1 | 5 | 3 | | | | | | | | | 7 | | 12 | | 8 | | | 11 | 9 | | | | | $10^{1}$ | 2 | 6 | 4 | 39 |
| 1 | 5 | 3 | | | | | | | | | 7 | | 12 | | 8 | | | $11^{1}$ | 9 | | | | | 10 | 2 | 6 | 4 | 40 |
| 1 | 6 | 3 | | 5 | | $7^{1}$ | | | | | 11 | | 12 | | 8 | | | | 9 | | | | | 10 | 2 | | 4 | 41 |
| 1 | 6 | 3 | | 5 | | $7^{1}$ | | | | | | | | | 8 | | | 12 | 9 | | | | | 10 | 2 | 4 | 11 | 42 |
| 1 | 6 | 3 | | 5 | | 7 | | | | | 12 | | 13 | | 8 | | | | 9 | | | | | $10^{2}$ | 2 | $4^{1}$ | 11 | 43 |
| 1 | 6 | 3 | | 5 | | $7^{1}$ | | | | | 12 | | $10^{2}$ | | 8 | | | 13 | 9 | | | | | 11 | 2 | | 4 | 44 |
| 1 | 6 | 3 | | 5 | | $7^{2}$ | | | | | | | 12 | | 8 | | | 13 | $9^{1}$ | | | | | 10 | 2 | 4 | 11 | 45 |
| 1 | $6^{2}$ | 3 | | 5 | | 7 | | | | | 13 | | 12 | | 8 | | | 14 | $9^{1}$ | | | | | $10^{3}$ | 2 | 4 | 11 | 46 |

**Carling Cup**

| | | | |
|---|---|---|---|
| First Round | York C | (h) | 2-1 |
| Second Round | Colchester U | (h) | 1-0 |
| Third Round | Arsenal | (a) | 1-1 |

**FA Cup**

| | | | |
|---|---|---|---|
| Third Round | Northampton T | (a) | 1-1 |
| | | (h) | 1-2 |

# RUSHDEN & DIAMONDS FL Championship 2

## FOUNDATION

Rushden & Diamonds were formed in 1992 from an amalgamation of Rushden Town and Irthlingborough Diamonds. At the end of 1990–91, Rushden Town had been relegated to the Southern League Midland Division as their ground was unfit for Premier Division football. Irthlingborough Diamonds were competing in the United Counties League at the time. The idea for this merger came from Max Griggs (owner of Dr Martens), a local multi-millionaire businessman. He invested several million pounds and they were able to achieve Football League status in nine years.

***Nene Park, Diamond Way, Irthlingborough, Northants NN9 5QF.***

***Telephone:*** (01933) 652 000.

***Fax:*** (01933) 650 418.

***Ticket Office:*** (01933) 625 936.

***Website:*** www.thediamondsfc.com

***Email:*** dave.joyce@airwair.co.uk

***Ground Capacity:*** 6,441.

***Record Attendance:*** 6,431 v Leeds U, FA Cup 3rd rd, 2 January 1999.

***Pitch Measurements:*** 111yd × 75yd.

***Secretary:*** David Joyce.

***Manager:*** Ernie Tippett.

***Assistant Manager:*** Stewart Robson.

***Physio:*** Simon Parsell.

***Colours:*** White and blue.

***Change Colours:*** Yellow and black.

***Year formed:*** 1992.

***Turned Professional:*** 1992.

***Ltd Co.:*** 1992.

***Club Nickname:*** 'The Diamonds'.

## HONOURS

*Football League:* Division 3 – Champions 2002–03

*FA Cup:* best season 3rd rd 1999.

*Football League Cup:* never past 2nd rd.

*Conference:* Champions 2000–01.

*Conference Championship Shield:* Winners 2001.

*Southern League Midland Division:* Champions 1993–94.

*Premier Division:* Champions 1995–96.

*FA Trophy:* Semi-finalists 1994.

*Northants FA Hillier Senior Cup:* Winners 1993–94, 1998–99.

*Maunsell Premier Cup:* Winners 1994–95, 1998–99; Finalists 2001–02.

## SKY SPORTS FACT FILE

The Rushden Town portion of the club's history found itself drawn against neighbours Kettering Town in preliminary stages of the FA Cup in six of eight seasons from 1946–47 apart from the 1949–50 and 1951–52 seasons.

***First Football League Match:*** 11 August 2001, Division 3, v York C (a) W 1–0 – Turley; Mustafa, Underwood, Talbot (Setchell), Peters, Rodwell, Butterworth, Brady, Patmore (1) (Darby), Jackson, Mills (Carey).

***Record League Victory:*** 7–0 v Redditch U, Southern League, Midland Division, 7 May 1994 – Fox; Wooding (1), Johnson, Flower (1), Beech, Page, Coe, Mann (2), Nuttell (1), Watkins (1), Keast (1).

## MANAGERS

Roger Ashby 1992–97
Brian Talbot 1997–2004
Ernie Tippett April 2004–

***Record Cup Victory:*** 8–0 v Desborough T, Northants FA Hillier Senior Cup, 1st rd, 27 September 1994 – Fox; Wooding, Johnson, Flower, Keast, Page, Collins, Butterworth, Nuttell (2), Watkins (2), Mann (2). Subs:– Capone (2), Mason.

***Record Defeat:*** 0–8 v Coventry C, League Cup 2nd rd, 2 October 2002.

***Most League Points (3 for a win):*** 98, Southern League Midland Division, 1993–94.

***Most League Goals:*** 109, Southern League Midland Division, 1993–94.

***Highest League Scorer in Season:*** Darren Collins, 30 (40 in all competitions), Southern League Premier Division, 1995–96.

***Most League Goals in Total Aggregate:*** Darren Collins, 112 (153 in all competitions), 1994–2000.

***Most Capped Player:*** Onandi Lowe, 9, Jamaica.

***Most League Appearances:*** Garry Butterworth, 286 (371 in all competitions), 1994–2002.

***Record Transfer Fee Received:*** £25,000 from Kettering T for Darren Collins, November 2000.

***Record Transfer Fee Paid:*** Undisclosed to Kansas City Wizards for Onandi Lowe, February 2002.

***Football League Record:*** 2001 Promoted to Division 3; 2003–04 Division 2; 2004– FL2.

## LATEST SEQUENCES

***Longest Sequence of League Wins:*** 6, 29.10.2002 – 14.12.2002.

***Longest Sequence of League Defeats:*** 4, 27.8.2001 – 15.9.2001.

***Longest Sequence of League Draws:*** not more than 2.

***Longest Sequence of Unbeaten League Matches:*** 12, 18.9.2001 – 20.11.2001.

***Longest Sequence Without a League Win:*** 9, 20.3.2004 continuing

***Successive Scoring Runs:*** 16 from 26.1.2002.

***Successive Non-scoring Runs:*** 5 from 12.4.2004 continuing.

## TEN YEAR LEAGUE RECORD

| | | P | W | D | L | F | A | Pts | Pos |
|---|---|---|---|---|---|---|---|---|---|
| 1994-95 | SL pr | 42 | 19 | 11 | 12 | 99 | 65 | 68 | 5 |
| 1995-96 | SL pr | 42 | 29 | 7 | 6 | 99 | 41 | 94 | 1 |
| 1996-97 | Conf. | 42 | 14 | 11 | 17 | 61 | 63 | 53 | 12 |
| 1997-98 | Conf. | 42 | 23 | 5 | 14 | 79 | 57 | 74 | 4 |
| 1998-99 | Conf. | 42 | 20 | 12 | 10 | 71 | 42 | 72 | 4 |
| 1999-2000 | Conf. | 42 | 21 | 13 | 8 | 71 | 42 | 76 | 2 |
| 2000-01 | Conf. | 42 | 25 | 11 | 6 | 78 | 36 | 86 | 1 |
| 2001-02 | Div 3 | 46 | 20 | 13 | 13 | 69 | 53 | 73 | 6 |
| 2002-03 | Div 3 | 46 | 24 | 15 | 7 | 73 | 47 | 87 | 1 |
| 2003-04 | Div 2 | 46 | 13 | 9 | 24 | 60 | 74 | 48 | 22 |

## DID YOU KNOW ?

Former Rushden & Diamonds manager Brian Talbot's first connection with the club was when he was a guest player on the official opening of Irthlingborough Diamonds' floodlights at Nene Park. He made further appearances at the ground in later years.

## RUSHDEN & DIAMONDS 2003–04 LEAGUE RECORD

| *Match No.* | *Date* | *Venue* | *Opponents* | *Result* | | *H/T Score* | *Lg. Pos.* | *Goalscorers* | *Atten-dance* |
|---|---|---|---|---|---|---|---|---|---|
| 1 | Aug 9 | A | Luton T | L | 1-3 | 1-0 | — | Lowe [37] | 6878 |
| 2 | 16 | H | Plymouth Arg | W | 2-1 | 0-0 | 14 | Lowe [54], Jack [56] | 4045 |
| 3 | 23 | A | Tranmere R | W | 2-1 | 2-0 | 9 | Jack [6], Bell [33] | 7374 |
| 4 | 25 | H | QPR | D | 3-3 | 1-2 | 10 | Darby [16], Hall [82], Lowe [90] | 5544 |
| 5 | 30 | A | Oldham Ath | L | 2-3 | 1-1 | 12 | Lowe [38], Bignot [83] | 5469 |
| 6 | Sept 6 | H | Wycombe W | W | 2-0 | 1-0 | 7 | Jack [35], Lowe [85] | 4192 |
| 7 | 13 | H | Brentford | L | 0-1 | 0-1 | 11 | | 4396 |
| 8 | 16 | A | Notts Co | W | 3-1 | 1-1 | — | Lowe [29], Gray (pen) [49], Darby [81] | 4250 |
| 9 | 20 | A | Bournemouth | L | 1-2 | 1-0 | 13 | Lowe [2] | 6464 |
| 10 | 27 | H | Stockport Co | D | 2-2 | 1-1 | 12 | Gray [12], Edwards [86] | 4048 |
| 11 | 30 | H | Brighton & HA | L | 1-3 | 0-1 | — | Gray (pen) [50] | 4634 |
| 12 | Oct 4 | A | Barnsley | L | 0-2 | 0-1 | 16 | | 8461 |
| 13 | 11 | H | Chesterfield | W | 2-1 | 2-1 | 15 | Hunter [12], Jack [15] | 3817 |
| 14 | 18 | A | Sheffield W | D | 0-0 | 0-0 | 15 | | 22,599 |
| 15 | 21 | A | Blackpool | W | 3-2 | 1-1 | — | Burgess [45], Jack [46], Kitson [55] | 5234 |
| 16 | 25 | H | Wrexham | L | 2-3 | 0-2 | 16 | Kitson 2 [53, 66] | 4117 |
| 17 | Nov 1 | H | Grimsby T | W | 3-1 | 0-1 | 13 | Lowe 2 [68, 74], Hanlon [90] | 4185 |
| 18 | 15 | A | Hartlepool U | L | 1-2 | 0-1 | 15 | Jack [57] | 4944 |
| 19 | 22 | H | Colchester U | W | 4-0 | 2-0 | 12 | Lowe [4], Gray [39], Burgess [58], Bignot [81] | 4149 |
| 20 | 29 | A | Port Vale | D | 1-1 | 1-1 | 12 | Benjamin [31] | 4586 |
| 21 | Dec 13 | H | Bristol C | D | 1-1 | 1-0 | 13 | Talbot [4] | 4340 |
| 22 | 20 | A | Peterborough U | L | 1-3 | 0-0 | 14 | Kitson [49] | 6167 |
| 23 | 26 | H | Swindon T | W | 2-0 | 1-0 | 12 | Lowe 2 [23, 63] | 4845 |
| 24 | 28 | A | Wycombe W | W | 2-0 | 2-0 | 11 | Jack 2 [4, 35] | 5421 |
| 25 | Jan 3 | A | QPR | L | 0-1 | 0-1 | 12 | | 14,141 |
| 26 | 10 | H | Luton T | D | 2-2 | 1-2 | 11 | Kitson [17], Hunter [65] | 5823 |
| 27 | 17 | A | Plymouth Arg | L | 0-3 | 0-0 | 12 | | 13,021 |
| 28 | 31 | H | Oldham Ath | W | 4-1 | 2-0 | 10 | Jack [26], Lowe [36], Burgess [71], Hall [88] | 4591 |
| 29 | Feb 7 | A | Swindon T | L | 2-4 | 0-2 | 12 | Reeves (og) [53], Jack [77] | 7023 |
| 30 | 14 | A | Chesterfield | L | 0-2 | 0-1 | 12 | | 4361 |
| 31 | 21 | H | Sheffield W | L | 1-2 | 0-1 | 16 | Jack [88] | 5685 |
| 32 | 24 | H | Tranmere R | W | 2-1 | 0-0 | — | Lowe [50], Mills [71] | 3074 |
| 33 | 28 | A | Wrexham | D | 1-1 | 1-1 | 13 | Jack [30] | 3680 |
| 34 | Mar 2 | H | Blackpool | D | 0-0 | 0-0 | — | | 3764 |
| 35 | 6 | H | Peterborough U | L | 0-1 | 0-1 | 13 | | 4855 |
| 36 | 12 | A | Bristol C | L | 0-1 | 0-1 | — | | 12,559 |
| 37 | 16 | H | Notts Co | W | 2-1 | 2-0 | — | Edwards 2 [12, 36] | 4030 |
| 38 | 20 | A | Brentford | L | 2-3 | 0-3 | 13 | Burgess [76], Lowe [88] | 4616 |
| 39 | 27 | H | Bournemouth | L | 0-3 | 0-1 | 16 | | 4500 |
| 40 | Apr 3 | A | Stockport Co | L | 1-2 | 0-0 | 16 | Hunter [70] | 4717 |
| 41 | 10 | H | Barnsley | L | 2-3 | 1-3 | 16 | Gray [27], Hunter [82] | 4063 |
| 42 | 12 | A | Brighton & HA | D | 0-0 | 0-0 | 17 | | 6320 |
| 43 | 17 | A | Grimsby T | L | 0-1 | 0-0 | 19 | | 3890 |
| 44 | 24 | H | Hartlepool U | L | 0-2 | 0-0 | 20 | | 4568 |
| 45 | May 1 | A | Colchester U | L | 0-2 | 0-0 | 21 | | 4618 |
| 46 | 8 | H | Port Vale | L | 0-2 | 0-1 | 22 | | 5240 |

**Final League Position: 22**

### GOALSCORERS

*League (60):* Lowe 15, Jack 12, Gray 5 (2 pens), Kitson 5, Burgess 4, Hunter 4, Edwards 3, Bignot 2, Darby 2, Hall 2, Bell 1, Benjamin 1, Hanlon 1, Mills 1, Talbot 1, own goal 1.
*Carling Cup (1):* Lowe 1.
*FA Cup (0).*
*LDV Vans Trophy (2):* Gray 1 (pen), Jack 1.

| Turley B 25 | Bignot M 35 | Underwood P 30 | Bell D 31 + 6 | Hunter B 43 | Edwards A 29 | Hall P 28 + 5 | Gray S 33 + 2 | Darby D 9 + 3 | Lowe O 24 + 2 | Burgess A 32 + 5 | Jack R 44 + 1 | Mills G 25 + 5 | Sambrook A 14 + 6 | Dempster J 11 + 8 | Story O — + 5 | Talbot D 3 + 4 | Kitson P 18 + 10 | Hanlon R 18 + 9 | Evans P 2 | Ashdown J 19 | Benjamin T 5 + 1 | Okuonghae M — + 1 | Manangu E — + 1 | Quinn B 4 | Roget L 16 + 1 | Duffy R 4 + 4 | Kelly M 4 + 4 | *Match No.* |
|---|---|---|---|---|---|---|---|---|---|---|---|---|---|---|---|---|---|---|---|---|---|---|---|---|---|---|---|---|
| 1 | 2 | 3 | 4 | 5 | 6 | 7 | $8^{1}$ | $9^{2}$ | 10 | 11 | 12 | 13 | | | | | | | | | | | | | | | | 1 |
| 1 | 2 | 3 | 4 | 5 | 6 | 7 | | 12 | 10 | 11 | $9^{1}$ | 8 | | | | | | | | | | | | | | | | 2 |
| 1 | 2 | 3 | 4 | 5 | 6 | 7 | | 9 | | 11 | 10 | 8 | | | | | | | | | | | | | | | | 3 |
| 1 | 2 | 3 | 4 | 5 | 6 | 7 | 12 | $9^{2}$ | 13 | 11 | 10 | $8^{1}$ | | | | | | | | | | | | | | | | 4 |
| 1 | 2 | 3 | 4 | 5 | 6■ | $7^{3}$ | 12 | | 10 | $11^{1}$ | 9 | $8^{2}$ | 14 | 13 | | | | | | | | | | | | | | 5 |
| 1 | $2^{3}$ | 3 | $4^{1}$ | 5 | 6 | 7 | 8 | 13 | 10 | 11 | $9^{2}$ | 12 | 14 | | | | | | | | | | | | | | | 6 |
| 1 | 2 | 3 | 4 | 5 | | 7 | 8 | 12 | 10 | $11^{1}$ | 9 | | | 6 | | | | | | | | | | | | | | 7 |
| 1 | 2 | 3 | 4 | 5 | 6 | 7 | 11 | 9 | 10 | | 8 | | | | | | | | | | | | | | | | | 8 |
| 1 | 2 | 3 | 4 | 5 | 6 | 7 | 11 | $8^{2}$ | $10^{1}$ | | 9 | 12 | | | 13 | | | | | | | | | | | | | 9 |
| 1 | 2 | 3 | 4 | $5^{1}$ | 6 | 7 | 11 | $9^{3}$ | | | 10 | $8^{2}$ | | 12 | | 13 | 14 | | | | | | | | | | | 10 |
| 1 | 2 | 3 | $4^{3}$ | 5 | 6 | 7 | 11 | 9 | | | $10^{2}$ | $8^{1}$ | 12 | | | 13 | 14 | | | | | | | | | | | 11 |
| 1 | 2 | 3 | 12 | 5 | 6 | 7 | 11 | 9 | | | | $8^{3}$ | | | 13 | $4^{1}$ | $10^{2}$ | 14 | | | | | | | | | | 12 |
| 1 | 2 | 3 | 4 | 5 | 6 | $7^{1}$ | 8 | 9 | | 11 | 10 | 12 | | | | | | | | | | | | | | | | 13 |
| 1 | 2 | 3 | 4 | 5 | 6 | | 7 | | | 11 | 10 | 8 | | | | | 9 | | | | | | | | | | | 14 |
| 1 | 2 | 3 | 4 | 5 | 6 | 12 | 7 | | | 11 | 10 | $8^{1}$ | 13 | | | | $9^{2}$ | | | | | | | | | | | 15 |
| | 2 | 3 | 4 | 5 | 6 | 12 | $7^{1}$ | | | 11 | 10 | $8^{2}$ | | 13 | | | 9 | | 1 | | | | | | | | | 16 |
| | 2 | 3 | | 5 | 6 | 7 | $8^{1}$ | | $10^{2}$ | 11 | 9 | 4 | | | | | 12 | 13 | 1 | | | | | | | | | 17 |
| | 2 | 3 | | 5 | | 7■ | 11 | | | 12 | 9 | 4 | | 6 | | | | $8^{1}$ | | 1 | 10 | | | | | | | 18 |
| | 2 | 3 | | | $6^{1}$ | | 8 | | $9^{2}$ | 11 | 7 | | | 5 | | | | 4 | | 1 | 10 | 12 | 13 | | | | | 19 |
| | 2 | 3 | | 5 | | | 8 | | 9 | 11 | 7 | 12 | | 6 | | | 13 | $4^{1}$ | | 1 | $10^{2}$ | | | | | | | 20 |
| | 2 | 3 | 12 | 5 | | | | | 9 | 11 | 7 | 4■ | | 6 | | $8^{1}$ | 13 | | | 1 | $10^{2}$ | | | | | | | 21 |
| | 2 | $3^{3}$ | 13 | 5 | | 12 | | | 10 | 11 | 8 | 4 | 14 | 6 | | $7^{2}$ | $9^{1}$ | | | 1 | | | | | | | | 22 |
| | 2 | | 4 | 5 | | 7 | | | $10^{1}$ | 11 | 8 | | 3 | 6 | | | 9 | 12 | | 1 | | | | | | | | 23 |
| | 2 | | 13 | 5 | | $7^{1}$ | | | | $11^{2}$ | 8 | | 3 | 6 | | 12 | 9 | 4 | | 1 | 10 | | | | | | | 24 |
| | 2 | | 12 | 5 | | $7^{1}$ | | | 10 | 11 | 8 | | 3 | 6 | | | $9^{2}$ | 4 | | 1 | 13 | | | | | | | 25 |
| | 2 | | | 5 | | 7 | | | 10 | 11 | 8 | | 3 | | | | 9 | 4 | | 1 | | | | 6 | | | | 26 |
| | 2■ | | | $5^{2}$ | | 7 | | | 10 | 11 | 8 | | 3 | 13 | | 12 | 9 | $4^{1}$ | | 1 | | | | 6 | | | | 27 |
| | | | 12 | $5^{2}$ | | 7 | | | 10 | 11 | 9 | 8 | 2 | 13 | | | | $4^{1}$ | | 1 | | | | 3 | 6 | | | 28 |
| | | | $4^{1}$ | 5 | | 7 | | | 10 | 11 | 9 | 8 | 2 | | | | 12 | | | 1 | | | | 3 | 6 | | | 29 |
| | | | $4^{3}$ | 5 | | 7 | $3^{2}$ | | 10 | 11 | 9 | 8 | $2^{1}$ | 12 | | | 14 | 13 | | 1 | | | | | 6 | | | 30 |
| | 2 | 3 | $4^{1}$ | 5 | | 7 | 11 | | 10 | | 9 | 8 | | | | | | 12 | | 1 | | | | | 6 | | | 31 |
| | 2 | 3 | $4^{1}$ | 5 | 6 | 7 | 11 | | 10 | | 9 | $8^{2}$ | 12 | | | | | 13 | | 1 | | | | | | | | 32 |
| | 2 | 3 | | 5 | 6 | 12 | 11 | | | | 9 | 8 | | | | | $10^{2}$ | $7^{1}$ | | 1 | | | | | 4 | 13 | | 33 |
| | 2 | 3 | 4 | 5 | | $7^{1}$ | $11^{2}$ | | 10 | 13 | 9 | 8 | | | | | 12 | | | 1 | | | | | 6 | | | 34 |
| | 2 | 3 | $4^{3}$ | 5 | | $7^{2}$ | $11^{1}$ | | 10 | 12 | 9 | 8 | | | | | 13 | 14 | | 1 | | | | | 6 | | | 35 |
| | 2 | 3 | 11 | 5 | 6 | | $7^{1}$ | | | 12 | 10 | $8^{3}$ | | | | | $9^{2}$ | 14 | | 1 | | | | | 4 | 13 | | 36 |
| 1 | 2 | 3 | 4 | | 6 | $7^{1}$ | 11 | | 10 | | 9 | 8 | | | | | | 12 | | | | | | | 5 | | | 37 |
| 1 | 2 | 3 | $7^{3}$ | | 6 | 12 | 11 | | 13 | 14 | 9 | $8^{1}$ | | | | | 10 | $4^{2}$ | | | | | | | 5 | | | 38 |
| 1 | | | $11^{2}$ | 5 | 6 | | 7 | | | 3 | 10 | | 2 | | | | $9^{1}$ | 8 | | | | | | | 4 | 12 | 13 | 39 |
| 1 | | | $4^{2}$ | 5 | 6 | | 11 | | | 7 | 10 | | 3 | 2■ | | | $9^{1}$ | 8 | | | | | | | | 12 | 13 | 40 |
| 1 | | | 4 | 5 | 6 | | 3 | | | 11 | 7 | | $2^{1}$ | 12 | | | $9^{3}$ | 8 | | | | | | | 13 | $10^{2}$ | 14 | 41 |
| 1 | | | | 5 | | | 7 | | | 11 | 10 | | 2 | 3 | 12 | | | 8 | | | | | | | 6 | $9^{1}$ | 4 | 42 |
| 1 | | | $4^{1}$ | 5 | 6 | | 7 | | | 11 | 10 | | 3 | | | | | 8 | | | | | | | 2 | 9■ | 12 | 43 |
| 1 | | | | 5 | 6 | | 7 | | | 11 | 10 | | 3 | | 13 | | 12 | $8^{1}$ | | | | | | | 2 | $9^{2}$ | 4 | 44 |
| 1 | | | $4^{1}$ | 5■ | 6 | | 7 | | | 3 | 10 | | | 12 | | | 9 | 8 | | | | | | | 2 | | 11 | 45 |
| 1 | | | 4 | 5 | $6^{1}$ | | 7 | | | 3 | 10 | | | | 12 | | 9 | 8 | | | | | | | 2 | | 11 | 46 |

**Carling Cup**
First Round — West Ham U — (a) — 1-3

**LDV Vans Trophy**
First Round — Oxford U — (a) — 1-0
Second Round — Luton T — (h) — 1-2

**FA Cup**
First Round — Swansea C — (a) — 0-3

# SCUNTHORPE UNITED FL Championship 2

## FOUNDATION

The year of foundation for Scunthorpe United has often been quoted as 1910, but the club can trace its history back to 1899 when Brumby Hall FC, who played on the Old Showground, consolidated their position by amalgamating with some other clubs and changing their name to Scunthorpe United. The year 1910 was when that club amalgamated with North Lindsey United as Scunthorpe and Lindsey United. The link is Mr W. T. Lockwood whose chairmanship covers both years.

***Glanford Park, Doncaster Road, Scunthorpe DN15 8TD.***

***Telephone:*** (01724) 747 670.

***Fax:*** (01724) 857 986.

***Website:*** www.scunthorpe-united.co.uk

***Email:*** admin@scunthorpe-united.co.uk

***Ground Capacity:*** 9,182.

***Record Attendance:*** Old Showground: 23,935 v Portsmouth, FA Cup 4th rd, 30 January 1954. Glanford Park: 8,775 v Rotherham U, Division 4, 1 May 1989.

***Pitch Measurements:*** 110yd × 71yd.

***Chairman:*** J. S. Wharton.

***Vice-chairman:*** R. Garton.

***Manager:*** Brian Laws.

***Assistant Manager:*** R. Wilcox.

***Physio:*** N. Adkins.

***Colours:*** Claret shirts, blue shorts, white stockings.

***Change Colours:*** Red shirts, blue shorts, blue stockings.

***Year Formed:*** 1899.

***Turned Professional:*** 1912.

***Ltd Co.:*** 1912.

***Club Nickname:*** 'The Iron'.

***Previous Names:*** Amalgamated first with Brumby Hall then North Lindsey United to become Scunthorpe & Lindsey United, 1910; dropped '& Lindsey' in 1958.

***Previous Ground:*** 1899, Old Showground; 1988, Glanford Park.

***First Football League Game:*** 19 August 1950, Division 3 (N), v Shrewsbury T (h) D 0–0 – Thompson; Barker, Brownsword; Allen, Taylor, McCormick; Mosby, Payne, Gorin, Rees, Boyes.

***Record League Victory:*** 8–1 v Luton T, Division 3, 24 April 1965 – Sidebottom; Horstead, Hemstead; Smith, Neale, Lindsey; Bramley (1), Scott, Thomas (5), Mahy (1), Wilson (1). 8–1 v Torquay U (a), Division 3, 28 October 1995 – Samways; Housham, Wilson, Ford (1), Knill (1), Hope (Nicholson), Thornber, Bullimore (Walsh), McFarlane (4) (Young), Eyre (2), Paterson.

## HONOURS

*Football League:* Division 2 best season: 4th, 1961–62; Division 3 (N) – Champions 1957–58. Promoted from Division 3 1998–99 (play-offs).

*FA Cup:* best season: 5th rd, 1958, 1970.

*Football League Cup:* never past 3rd rd.

## SKY SPORTS FACT FILE

Scunthorpe United achieved promotion from fourth place in 1971–72, but it was a close run affair. Only eight goals were scored in the last 13 matches during which a mere ten points were gathered. One point separated them from unlucky Lincoln City.

***Record Cup Victory:*** 9–0 v Boston U, FA Cup 1st rd, 21 November 1953 – Malan; Hubbard, Brownsword; Sharpe, White, Bushby; Mosby (1), Haigh (3), Whitfield (2), Gregory (1), Mervyn Jones (2).

***Record Defeat:*** 0–8 v Carlisle U, Division 3 (N), 25 December 1952.

***Most League Points (2 for a win):*** 66, Division 3 (N), 1956–57, 1957–58.

***Most League Points (3 for a win):*** 83, Division 4, 1982–83.

***Most League Goals:*** 88, Division 3 (N), 1957–58.

***Highest League Scorer in Season:*** Barrie Thomas, 31, Division 2, 1961–62.

***Most League Goals in Total Aggregate:*** Steve Cammack, 110, 1979–81, 1981–86.

***Most League Goals in One Match:*** 5, Barrie Thomas v Luton T, Division 3, 24 April 1965.

***Most Capped Player:*** None.

***Most League Appearances:*** Jack Brownsword, 595, 1950–65.

***Youngest League Player:*** Mike Farrell, 16 years 240 days v Workington, 8 November 1975.

***Record Transfer Fee Received:*** £350,000 from Aston Villa for Neil Cox, February 1991.

***Record Transfer Fee Paid:*** £175,000 to Bristol C for Steve Torpey, February 2000.

***Football League Record:*** 1950 Elected to Division 3 (N); 1958–64 Division 2; 1964–68 Division 3; 1968–72 Division 4; 1972–73 Division 3; 1973–83 Division 4; 1983–84 Division 3; 1984–92 Division 4; 1992–99 Division 3; 1999–2000 Division 2; 2000–04 Division 3; 2004– FL2.

## MANAGERS

Harry Allcock 1915–53
*(Secretary-Manager)*
Tom Crilly 1936–37
Bernard Harper 1946–48
Leslie Jones 1950–51
Bill Corkhill 1952–56
Ron Suart 1956–58
Tony McShane 1959
Bill Lambton 1959
Frank Soo 1959–60
Dick Duckworth 1960–64
Fred Goodwin 1964–66
Ron Ashman 1967–73
Ron Bradley 1973–74
Dick Rooks 1974–76
Ron Ashman 1976–81
John Duncan 1981–83
Allan Clarke 1983–84
Frank Barlow 1984–87
Mick Buxton 1987–91
Bill Green 1991–93
Richard Money 1993–94
David Moore 1994–96
Mick Buxton 1996–97
Brian Laws February 1997–

## LATEST SEQUENCES

***Longest Sequence of League Wins:*** 6, 18.10.1969 – 25.11.1969.

***Longest Sequence of League Defeats:*** 8, 29.11.1997 – 20.1.1998.

***Longest Sequence of League Draws:*** 6, 2.1.1984 – 25.2.1984.

***Longest Sequence of Unbeaten League Matches:*** 15, 13.11.1971 – 26.2.1972.

***Longest Sequence Without a League Win:*** 14, 22.3.1975 – 6.9.1975.

***Successive Scoring Runs:*** 23 from 18.8.1951.

***Successive Non-scoring Runs:*** 7 from 19.4.1975.

## TEN YEAR LEAGUE RECORD

| | | *P* | *W* | *D* | *L* | *F* | *A* | *Pts* | *Pos* |
|---|---|---|---|---|---|---|---|---|---|
| 1994-95 | Div 3 | 42 | 18 | 8 | 16 | 68 | 63 | 62 | 7 |
| 1995-96 | Div 3 | 46 | 15 | 15 | 16 | 67 | 61 | 60 | 12 |
| 1996-97 | Div 3 | 46 | 18 | 9 | 19 | 59 | 62 | 63 | 13 |
| 1997-98 | Div 3 | 46 | 19 | 12 | 15 | 56 | 52 | 69 | 8 |
| 1998-99 | Div 3 | 46 | 22 | 8 | 16 | 69 | 58 | 74 | 4 |
| 1999-2000 | Div 2 | 46 | 9 | 12 | 25 | 40 | 74 | 39 | 23 |
| 2000-01 | Div 3 | 46 | 18 | 11 | 17 | 62 | 52 | 65 | 10 |
| 2001-02 | Div 3 | 46 | 19 | 14 | 13 | 74 | 56 | 71 | 8 |
| 2002-03 | Div 3 | 46 | 19 | 15 | 12 | 68 | 49 | 72 | 5 |
| 2003-04 | Div 3 | 46 | 11 | 16 | 19 | 69 | 72 | 49 | 22 |

## DID YOU KNOW ?

There were similarities in the Midland League championship winning seasons for Scunthorpe United in 1926–27 and 1938–39 though four more games were played in the latter season, when the extra quartet gave United four more points in draws.

## SCUNTHORPE UNITED 2003–04 LEAGUE RECORD

| *Match No.* | *Date* | *Venue* | *Opponents* | *Result* | | *H/T Score* | *Lg. Pos.* | *Goalscorers* | *Attendance* |
|---|---|---|---|---|---|---|---|---|---|
| 1 | Aug 9 | H | Bristol R | L | 1-2 | 0-1 | — | Beagrie (pen) [63] | 4186 |
| 2 | 16 | A | Bury | W | 3-2 | 1-1 | 11 | Torpey 2 [39, 50], Beagrie [63] | 2761 |
| 3 | 23 | H | Oxford U | D | 1-1 | 0-1 | 12 | Beagrie [63] | 3617 |
| 4 | 26 | A | Mansfield T | L | 0-5 | 0-2 | — | | 5142 |
| 5 | 30 | H | Torquay U | W | 2-1 | 0-1 | 13 | McLean [86], Calvo-Garcia [90] | 3080 |
| 6 | Sept 6 | A | Boston U | D | 1-1 | 1-1 | 14 | Sharp (pen) [45] | 3154 |
| 7 | 13 | H | Swansea C | D | 2-2 | 1-1 | 15 | Calvo-Garcia [9], McLean (pen) [60] | 3510 |
| 8 | 16 | A | Kidderminster H | W | 2-0 | 0-0 | — | Byrne [56], McLean [77] | 2162 |
| 9 | 20 | A | Leyton Orient | D | 1-1 | 1-0 | 11 | Kell [44] | 3663 |
| 10 | 27 | H | Southend U | D | 1-1 | 1-0 | 12 | McLean [6] | 3390 |
| 11 | 30 | H | Cheltenham T | W | 5-2 | 2-1 | — | McLean 3 (1 pen) [11, 51, 78 (p)], Beagrie [28], Torpey [80] | 2857 |
| 12 | Oct 4 | A | Rochdale | L | 0-2 | 0-0 | 10 | | 2838 |
| 13 | 11 | H | Lincoln C | L | 1-3 | 0-2 | 13 | Hayes [71] | 5045 |
| 14 | 17 | A | Northampton T | D | 1-1 | 0-1 | — | Kell [52] | 4827 |
| 15 | 21 | A | Carlisle U | W | 4-1 | 1-0 | — | Torpey [23], McLean [51], Sharp [64], Beagrie (pen) [83] | 3437 |
| 16 | 25 | H | York C | D | 0-0 | 0-0 | 12 | | 3807 |
| 17 | Nov 1 | H | Huddersfield T | W | 6-2 | 2-0 | 8 | Beagrie [17], Sparrow [24], Barwick [55], McLean 3 [59, 68, 87] | 4715 |
| 18 | 15 | A | Macclesfield T | D | 2-2 | 1-1 | 11 | Beagrie [15], McLean [54] | 2205 |
| 19 | 22 | H | Cambridge U | W | 4-0 | 2-0 | 9 | Hayes [13], McLean 3 [17, 72, 90] | 3397 |
| 20 | 29 | A | Darlington | D | 2-2 | 0-1 | 9 | Torpey [70], Beagrie (pen) [82] | 3606 |
| 21 | Dec 13 | H | Hull C | D | 1-1 | 0-0 | 9 | Beagrie (pen) [65] | 6426 |
| 22 | 20 | A | Yeovil T | L | 1-2 | 1-0 | 10 | Beagrie (pen) [39] | 5714 |
| 23 | 26 | A | Doncaster R | L | 0-1 | 0-0 | 10 | | 8961 |
| 24 | 28 | H | Boston U | L | 0-1 | 0-1 | 11 | | 4346 |
| 25 | Jan 10 | A | Bristol R | L | 0-1 | 0-1 | 14 | | 5789 |
| 26 | 17 | H | Bury | D | 0-0 | 0-0 | 16 | | 3869 |
| 27 | 27 | H | Mansfield T | D | 0-0 | 0-0 | — | | 3113 |
| 28 | Feb 7 | H | Doncaster R | D | 2-2 | 1-0 | 15 | Torpey [10], Butler [62] | 5681 |
| 29 | 11 | A | Oxford U | L | 2-3 | 2-2 | — | Torpey 2 [37, 44] | 5118 |
| 30 | 14 | A | Lincoln C | D | 1-1 | 0-1 | 16 | Taylor C [82] | 5324 |
| 31 | 21 | H | Northampton T | W | 1-0 | 0-0 | 14 | Ridley [72] | 3566 |
| 32 | 24 | A | Torquay U | L | 0-1 | 0-1 | — | | 2561 |
| 33 | Mar 6 | H | Yeovil T | W | 3-0 | 2-0 | 13 | McLean 2 [26, 60], Holloway [45] | 3355 |
| 34 | 9 | A | York C | W | 3-1 | 2-0 | — | Groves 2 [17, 56], McLean (pen) [33] | 2676 |
| 35 | 13 | A | Hull C | L | 1-2 | 0-2 | 13 | McLean [73] | 19,076 |
| 36 | 16 | H | Kidderminster H | L | 0-2 | 0-1 | — | | 2512 |
| 37 | 20 | A | Swansea C | L | 2-4 | 1-1 | 16 | Taylor C 2 [25, 83] | 4400 |
| 38 | 23 | H | Carlisle U | L | 2-3 | 1-1 | — | McLean 2 (1 pen) [28, 73 (p)] | 2326 |
| 39 | 27 | H | Leyton Orient | D | 1-1 | 1-0 | 16 | Sparrow [7] | 2822 |
| 40 | Apr 2 | A | Southend U | L | 2-4 | 1-3 | — | Sparrow [30], Torpey [49] | 4976 |
| 41 | 10 | H | Rochdale | D | 2-2 | 2-2 | 19 | McLean [5], Butler [22] | 3564 |
| 42 | 12 | A | Cheltenham T | L | 1-2 | 1-1 | 20 | Groves [29] | 3409 |
| 43 | 17 | A | Huddersfield T | L | 2-3 | 2-1 | 21 | Sodje (og) [8], McLean [42] | 12,108 |
| 44 | 24 | H | Macclesfield T | W | 1-0 | 0-0 | 20 | Torpey [55] | 4334 |
| 45 | May 1 | A | Cambridge U | L | 2-3 | 0-2 | 22 | Beagrie [65], Torpey [90] | 4498 |
| 46 | 8 | H | Darlington | L | 0-1 | 0-1 | 22 | | 4801 |

**Final League Position: 22**

### GOALSCORERS

*League (69):* MacLean 23 (4 pens), Beagrie 11 (5 pens), Torpey 11, Groves 3, Sparrow 3, Taylor C 3, Butler 2, Calvo-Garcia 2, Hayes 2, Kell 2, Sharp 2 (1 pen), Barwick 1, Byrne 1, Holloway 1, Ridley 1, own goal 1.
*Carling Cup (4):* Hayes 2, Beagrie 1, MacLean 1.
*FA Cup (7):* Torpey 3, Hayes 2, McCombe 1, Parton 1.
*LDV Vans Trophy (6):* Hayes 1, Jackson 1, Kell 1, MacLean 1, Sparrow 1, Torpey 1.

| Evans T 36 | Stanton N 31 + 2 | Sharp K 37 + 3 | Kell R 21 + 3 | Jackson M 15 + 2 | Byrne C 39 | Sparrow M 37 + 1 | Kilford I 11 + 7 | Hayes P 12 + 23 | Torpey S 42 + 1 | Beagrie P 28 + 4 | MacLean S 37 + 5 | McCombe J 8 + 7 | Calvo-Garcia A 8 + 4 | Graves W 12 + 9 | Ridley L 15 + 3 | Featherstone L 7 + 4 | Russell S 10 | Butler A 34 + 1 | Barwick T 27 + 3 | Keegan P — + 2 | Hunt J — + 1 | Gulliver P 2 | Smith J 1 | Taylor C 18 + 2 | Parton A — + 3 | Groves P 13 | Holloway D 5 | Williams M — + 1 | Match No. |
|---|---|---|---|---|---|---|---|---|---|---|---|---|---|---|---|---|---|---|---|---|---|---|---|---|---|---|---|---|---|
| 1 | 2 | 3 | 4 | 5 | 6 | 7 | 8 | 9¹ | 10 | 11 | 12 | | | | | | | | | | | | | | | | | | 1 |
| 1 | 2 | 3 | 4 | 5 | 6 | 7 | 8 | 9¹ | 10 | 11 | 12 | | | | | | | | | | | | | | | | | | 2 |
| 1 | 2 | 3 | 8 | 5 | 6 | 7 | | 9¹ | 10 | 11 | 12 | 4 | | | | | | | | | | | | | | | | | 3 |
| 1 | | 3 | 4 | 5 | 2 | | 8¹ | 9² | 10 | 11 | 7 | 6 | 12 | 13 | | | | | | | | | | | | | | | 4 |
| 1 | | 3 | 4 | 5 | 2 | | 8² | 9¹ | 10 | 11 | 12 | 6 | 13 | 7■ | | | | | | | | | | | | | | | 5 |
| 1 | | 2 | 4 | 5 | 6 | | | | 10 | | 9 | | 8 | 11 | 3 | 7 | | | | | | | | | | | | | 6 |
| 1 | 2 | 11² | 4¹ | 5 | 6 | 7 | 12 | 13 | 10 | | 9 | | 8 | | 3 | | | | | | | | | | | | | | 7 |
| | | 11 | 4³ | 12 | 2 | 7 | 8² | | 10 | | 9 | 5 | 6 | | 3¹ | 14 | 1 | | 13 | | | | | | | | | | 8 |
| | 2 | 3² | 8 | 5³ | 6 | 7 | | 12 | 10 | | 9¹ | 4 | 11 | | | 13 | 1 | 14 | | | | | | | | | | | 9 |
| | 2 | 3 | 4 | | 6 | 7 | | | 10 | 11 | 9 | 5 | | | | | 1 | 8 | | | | | | | | | | | 10 |
| | 2 | 3 | 4 | | 6 | 7 | | 12 | 10¹ | 11 | 9 | | 8² | | | | 1 | 5 | 13 | | | | | | | | | | 11 |
| | 2 | 3 | 4■ | | 6 | 7 | | 12 | 10 | 11² | 9¹ | | 8 | | | 13 | 1 | 5 | | | | | | | | | | | 12 |
| | 2 | 3¹ | 4 | | 6 | 7 | | 12 | 10 | 11 | 9 | | 8 | | | | 1 | 5 | | | | | | | | | | | 13 |
| | | 12 | 4 | 5 | 6 | 7³ | | 13 | 10 | 11 | 9² | | | 14 | | 3¹ | 1 | 2 | 8 | | | | | | | | | | 14 |
| | | 3² | | 2 | 6 | | 8³ | 12 | 10¹ | 11 | 9 | | | 4 | 13 | | 1 | 5 | 7 | 14 | | | | | | | | | 15 |
| | 12 | 3 | | 2¹ | 6 | | 8 | 13 | 10■ | 11 | 9 | | | 4² | | | 1 | 5 | 7 | | | | | | | | | | 16 |
| | | 3 | | 5 | 6 | 7 | 8² | | 10 | 11 | 9 | | | 14 | 12 | | 1 | 4¹ | 2³ | 13 | | | | | | | | | 17 |
| 1 | | | 8 | 4 | 6 | 7 | | 10 | | 11 | 9 | | | | 3 | | | 5 | 2 | | | | | | | | | | 18 |
| 1 | | 3 | 8¹ | 4 | 6 | 7 | 12 | 10 | | 11 | 9 | | | | | | | 5 | 2 | | | | | | | | | | 19 |
| 1 | | 3 | | 5 | 6 | 7 | 8² | 10¹ | 12 | 11 | 9 | | | 13 | | | | 4 | 2 | | | | | | | | | | 20 |
| 1 | | 3 | 8 | | | 7 | | 12 | 10 | 11 | 9¹ | 6 | | 2 | | | | 5 | 4 | | | | | | | | | | 21 |
| 1 | 2 | 3 | 8 | 12 | 6¹ | 7 | | 10³ | | 11² | 9 | | | | | 13 | | 5 | 4 | | 14 | | | | | | | | 22 |
| 1 | 2 | 3 | 8 | | 6 | 7 | | 12 | 10 | | 9 | | | 13 | | 11¹ | | 5 | 4² | | | | | | | | | | 23 |
| 1 | 2³ | 3 | 8 | | 6 | 7 | 12 | 13 | 10 | | 9 | | | 14 | | 11² | | 5 | 4¹ | | | | | | | | | | 24 |
| 1 | | | 8¹ | | 6 | 7 | 12 | 13 | 10 | | 9 | 14 | | 2 | 3 | 11² | | 5³ | 4 | | | | | | | | | | 25 |
| 1 | 2 | 3 | 13 | | 6 | 7² | 8 | 12 | 10 | | | 14 | | | | | | | 4¹ | | | 5 | 11³ | 9 | | | | | 26 |
| 1 | 5 | 3 | | | 6 | 7 | | 8¹ | 10 | 11 | | | | 2 | | | | | 4 | | | | | 9 | 12 | | | | 27 |
| 1 | 2 | 3 | 12 | | 6 | 7 | | 9² | 10 | 11 | | | | | | | | 5 | 4¹ | | | | | 8 | 13 | | | | 28 |
| 1 | 2 | 3 | | | 6 | 7 | | 12² | 10 | 11 | | 13 | | | | | | 5 | 8 | | | 4¹ | | 9 | | | | | 29 |
| 1 | 2 | 3 | | | 6 | 7 | | 9¹ | 10 | 11 | 12 | 13 | | | | | | 5 | 4² | | | | | 8 | | | | | 30 |
| 1 | 2¹ | 3 | | | 6 | 4 | 8² | | 10 | 11³ | 9 | 13 | | 12 | 14 | | | 5 | | | | | | 7 | | | | | 31 |
| 1 | 12 | 11³ | | | 6 | 7 | | | 10 | | 9 | 13 | | 2¹ | 3 | | | 5 | 4² | | | | | 8 | 14 | | | | 32 |
| 1 | 5 | 3¹ | | | | | | | 10 | | 9 | 6 | | 2 | 11 | | | | | | | | | 7 | | 4 | 8 | 12 | 33 |
| 1 | 6 | 11 | | | | | | | 10 | | 9 | 12■ | | 2¹ | 3 | | | 5 | 13 | | | | | 7 | | 4 | 8² | | 34 |
| 1 | 2 | 11¹ | | | 6 | | | | 10 | 12 | 9 | | | | 3 | | | 5 | | | | | | 7 | | 4 | 8 | | 35 |
| 1 | 2 | 3■ | | | 6 | 12 | | 13 | 10 | 11 | 9² | | | | | | | 5 | | | | | | 7 | | 4 | 8¹ | | 36 |
| 1 | 2 | | | | | 11 | | 13 | 10 | 12 | 9² | | | | 3 | | | 5 | 6¹ | | | | | 7 | | 4 | 8 | | 37 |
| 1 | 2 | 12 | | | | 7 | | 13 | 10 | | 9 | | | 8² | 3¹ | | | 5 | 6 | | | | | 11 | | 4 | | | 38 |
| 1 | 2 | 12 | | | | 7 | 13 | 14 | 10 | | 9³ | | | 8¹ | 3 | | | 5 | 6² | | | | | 11 | | 4 | | | 39 |
| 1 | | | | | 2 | 7 | | 12 | 10 | | 9 | | | | 3 | 8¹ | | 5 | 6 | | | | | 11 | | 4 | | | 40 |
| 1 | 2 | | | | | 7 | | 13 | 10 | 12 | 9 | | | | 3 | 8¹ | | 5 | 6 | | | | | 11² | | 4 | | | 41 |
| 1 | 2 | | | | 6³ | 7 | 13 | 14 | 10 | 12 | 9 | | | | 3 | | | 5 | 8² | | | | | 11¹ | | 4 | | | 42 |
| 1 | 2 | 3 | | | 6 | 7 | 12 | | 10 | 11 | 9 | | | | | | | 5 | 8¹ | | | | | | | 4 | | | 43 |
| 1 | 2 | 3 | | | 6 | 7 | | 13 | 10 | 11² | 9³ | | 12 | | | | | 5 | 8¹ | | | | | 14 | | 4 | | | 44 |
| 1 | 2¹ | 3 | | | 6 | 7 | | | 10 | 11 | 9 | | 13 | 12 | | | | 5 | 8³ | | | | | 14 | | 4² | | | 45 |
| 1 | 2 | 3 | 13 | | 6 | 4¹ | | 14 | 10 | 11³ | 9 | | 8² | 12 | | | | 5 | | | | | | 7 | | | | | 46 |

**Carling Cup**

| | | | |
|---|---|---|---|
| First Round | Oldham Ath | (h) | 2-1 |
| Second Round | Burnley | (h) | 2-3 |

**LDV Vans Trophy**

| | | | |
|---|---|---|---|
| First Round | Shrewsbury T | (h) | 2-1 |
| Second Round | Hull C | (a) | 3-1 |
| Quarter-Final | Bury | (a) | 1-0 |
| Semi-Final | Sheffield W | (a) | 0-4 |

**FA Cup**

| | | | |
|---|---|---|---|
| First Round | Shrewsbury T | (h) | 2-1 |
| Second Round | Sheffield W | (h) | 2-2 |
| | | (a) | 0-0 |
| Third Round | Barnsley | (a) | 0-0 |
| | | (h) | 2-0 |
| Fourth Round | Portsmouth | (a) | 1-2 |

# SHEFFIELD UNITED FL Championship

## FOUNDATION

In March 1889, Yorkshire County Cricket Club formed Sheffield United six days after an FA Cup semi-final between Preston North End and West Bromwich Albion had finally convinced Charles Stokes, a member of the cricket club, that the formation of a professional football club would prove successful at Bramall Lane. The United's first secretary, Mr J. B. Wostinholm was also secretary of the cricket club.

***Bramall Lane Ground, Cherry Street, Bramall Lane, Sheffield S2 4SU.***

***Telephone:*** 0870 787 1960.

***Fax:*** 0870 787 3345.

***Ticket Office:*** 0870 787 1799.

***Website:*** www.sufc.co.uk

***Email:*** info@sufc.co.uk

***Ground Capacity:*** 28,000.

***Record Attendance:*** 68,287 v Leeds U, FA Cup 5th rd, 15 February 1936.

***Pitch Measurements:*** 112yd × 72yd.

***Chairman:*** Derek Dooley.

***Vice-chairman:*** Terry Robinson.

***Secretary:*** Donna Fletcher.

***Manager:*** Neil Warnock.

***Assistant Manager:*** David Kelly.

***Physio:*** Dennis Pettitt.

***Colours:*** Red and white striped shirts, red shorts, red stockings.

***Change Colours:*** Orange and black shirts, black shorts, black stockings.

***Year Formed:*** 1889.

***Turned Professional:*** 1889.

***Ltd Co.:*** 1899.

***Club Nickname:*** 'The Blades'.

***First Football League Game:*** 3 September 1892, Division 2, v Lincoln C (h) W 4–2 – Lilley; Witham, Cain; Howell, Hendry, Needham (1); Wallace, Dobson, Hammond (3), Davies, Drummond.

***Record League Victory:*** 10–0 v Burslem Port Vale (a), Division 2, 10 December 1892 – Howlett; Witham, Lilley; Howell, Hendry, Needham; Drummond (1), Wallace (1), Hammond (4), Davies (2), Watson (2).

## HONOURS

*Football League:* Division 1 – Champions 1897–98; Runners-up 1896–97, 1899–1900; Division 2 – Champions 1952–53; Runners-up 1892–93, 1938–39, 1960–61, 1970–71, 1989–90; Division 4 – Champions 1981–82.

*FA Cup:* Winners 1899, 1902, 1915, 1925; Runners-up 1901, 1936.

*Football League Cup:* semi-final 2003.

## SKY SPORTS FACT FILE

On 5 October 1889 Sheffield United were involved in their first FA Cup tie, a first qualifying round game at Scarborough. Leading 2-1 at the interval, United won 6-1, contemporary reports variously reporting the crowd as 'large' and 'very good'.

***Record Cup Victory:*** 6–1 v Lincoln C, League Cup, 22 August 2000 – Tracey; Uhlenbeek, Weber, Woodhouse (Ford), Murphy, Sandford, Devlin (pen), Ribeiro (Santos), Bent (3), Kelly (1) (Thompson), Jagielka, og (1). 6–1 v Loughborough, FA Cup 4th qualifying rd, 6 December 1890; 6–1 v Scarborough (a), FA Cup 1st qualifying rd, 5 October 1889.

***Record Defeat:*** 0–13 v Bolton W, FA Cup 2nd rd, 1 February 1890.

***Most League Points (2 for a win):*** 60, Division 2, 1952–53.

***Most League Points (3 for a win):*** 96, Division 4, 1981–82.

***Most League Goals:*** 102, Division 1, 1925–26.

***Highest League Scorer in Season:*** Jimmy Dunne, 41, Division 1, 1930–31.

***Most League Goals in Total Aggregate:*** Harry Johnson, 205, 1919–30.

***Most League Goals in One Match:*** 5, Harry Hammond v Bootle, Division 2, 26 November 1892; 5, Harry Johnson v West Ham U, Division 1, 26 December 1927.

***Most Capped Player:*** Billy Gillespie, 25, Northern Ireland.

***Most League Appearances:*** Joe Shaw, 629, 1948–66.

***Youngest League Player:*** Steve Hawes, 17 years 47 days v WBA, 2 September 1995.

***Record Transfer Fee Received:*** £3,000,000 from Derby Co for Lee Morris, October 1999.

***Record Transfer Fee Paid:*** £1,200,000 to West Ham U for Don Hutchison, January 1996.

***Football League Record:*** 1892 Elected to Division 2; 1893–1934 Division 1; 1934–39 Division 2; 1946–49 Division 1; 1949–53 Division 2; 1953–56 Division 1; 1956–61 Division 2; 1961–68 Division 1; 1968–71 Division 2; 1971–76 Division 1; 1976–79 Division 2; 1979–81 Division 3; 1981–82 Division 4; 1982–84 Division 3; 1984–88 Division 2; 1988–89 Division 3; 1989–90 Division 2; 1990–92 Division 1; 1992–94 FA Premier League; 1994–2004 Division 1; 2004– FLC.

## MANAGERS

J. B. Wostinholm 1889–99
*(Secretary-Manager)*
John Nicholson 1899–1932
Ted Davison 1932–52
Reg Freeman 1952–55
Joe Mercer 1955–58
Johnny Harris 1959–68
*(continued as General Manager to 1970)*
Arthur Rowley 1968–69
Johnny Harris *(General Manager resumed Team Manager duties)* 1969–73
Ken Furphy 1973–75
Jimmy Sirrel 1975–77
Harry Haslam 1978–81
Martin Peters 1981
Ian Porterfield 1981–86
Billy McEwan 1986–88
Dave Bassett 1988–95
Howard Kendall 1995–97
Nigel Spackman 1997–98
Steve Bruce 1998–99
Adrian Heath 1999
Neil Warnock December 1999–

## LATEST SEQUENCES

***Longest Sequence of League Wins:*** 8, 14.9.1960 – 22.10.1960.

***Longest Sequence of League Defeats:*** 7, 19.8.1975 – 20.9.1975.

***Longest Sequence of League Draws:*** 6, 6.5.2001 – 8.9.2001.

***Longest Sequence of Unbeaten League Matches:*** 22, 2.9.1899 – 13.1.1900.

***Longest Sequence Without a League Win:*** 19, 27.9.1975 – 7.2.1976.

***Successive Scoring Runs:*** 34 from 30.3.1956.

***Successive Non-scoring Runs:*** 6 from 4.12.1993.

## TEN YEAR LEAGUE RECORD

| | | P | W | D | L | F | A | Pts | Pos |
|---|---|---|---|---|---|---|---|---|---|
| 1994-95 | Div 1 | 46 | 17 | 17 | 12 | 74 | 55 | 68 | 8 |
| 1995-96 | Div 1 | 46 | 16 | 14 | 16 | 57 | 54 | 62 | 9 |
| 1996-97 | Div 1 | 46 | 20 | 13 | 13 | 75 | 52 | 73 | 5 |
| 1997-98 | Div 1 | 46 | 19 | 17 | 10 | 69 | 54 | 74 | 6 |
| 1998-99 | Div 1 | 46 | 18 | 13 | 15 | 71 | 66 | 67 | 8 |
| 1999-2000 | Div 1 | 46 | 13 | 15 | 18 | 59 | 71 | 54 | 16 |
| 2000-01 | Div 1 | 46 | 19 | 11 | 16 | 52 | 49 | 68 | 10 |
| 2001-02 | Div 1 | 46 | 15 | 15 | 16 | 53 | 54 | 60 | 13 |
| 2002-03 | Div 1 | 46 | 23 | 11 | 12 | 72 | 52 | 80 | 3 |
| 2003-04 | Div 1 | 46 | 20 | 11 | 15 | 65 | 56 | 71 | 8 |

## DID YOU KNOW?

During their 1938–39 promotion season, Sheffield United recruited among others, Harold Hampson from Southport for £2,250. Elevation secured with two matches left, Hampson then celebrated against Tottenham Hotspur with a goal in ten seconds.

## SHEFFIELD UNITED 2003–04 LEAGUE RECORD

| *Match No.* | *Date* | *Venue* | *Opponents* | *Result* | | *H/T Score* | *Lg. Pos.* | *Goalscorers* | *Attendance* |
|---|---|---|---|---|---|---|---|---|---|
| 1 | Aug 9 | H | Gillingham | D | 0-0 | 0-0 | — | | 21,569 |
| 2 | 16 | A | West Ham U | D | 0-0 | 0-0 | 14 | | 28,972 |
| 3 | 23 | H | Norwich C | W | 1-0 | 1-0 | 7 | Page [23] | 24,285 |
| 4 | 26 | A | Crystal Palace | W | 2-1 | 2-0 | — | Ndlovu [18], Allison [45] | 15,466 |
| 5 | 30 | H | Coventry C | W | 2-1 | 1-0 | 3 | Brown (pen) [42], Lester [87] | 20,102 |
| 6 | Sept 13 | A | Nottingham F | L | 1-3 | 0-1 | 8 | Ndlovu (pen) [54] | 25,209 |
| 7 | 16 | H | Rotherham U | W | 5-0 | 2-0 | — | Tonge [12], Peschisolido 2 [22, 57], Ndlovu 2 [61, 83] | 22,572 |
| 8 | 20 | H | Cardiff C | W | 5-3 | 0-0 | 2 | Tonge [53], Ndlovu 3 (2 pens) [62, 78 (p), 89 (p)], Lester [85] | 21,323 |
| 9 | 27 | A | Bradford C | W | 2-1 | 1-1 | 1 | Ndlovu [29], McCall [54] | 11,067 |
| 10 | 30 | A | Wimbledon | W | 2-1 | 0-0 | — | Ward [62], Peschisolido [68] | 6016 |
| 11 | Oct 4 | H | Sunderland | L | 0-1 | 0-0 | 2 | | 27,008 |
| 12 | 14 | A | WBA | W | 2-0 | 2-0 | — | Tonge [9], Ward [37] | 27,195 |
| 13 | 18 | A | Millwall | L | 0-2 | 0-0 | 3 | | 10,046 |
| 14 | 21 | A | Wigan Ath | D | 1-1 | 0-1 | — | Lester [86] | 12,032 |
| 15 | 24 | H | Reading | L | 1-2 | 1-2 | — | Ward [10] | 20,651 |
| 16 | Nov 1 | A | Stoke C | D | 2-2 | 0-2 | 4 | Kozluk [53], Lester (pen) [90] | 14,217 |
| 17 | 4 | H | Crewe Alex | W | 2-0 | 1-0 | — | Armstrong [21], Lester (pen) [74] | 17,396 |
| 18 | 8 | H | Burnley | W | 1-0 | 1-0 | 2 | Tonge [45] | 20,967 |
| 19 | 22 | A | Ipswich T | L | 0-3 | 0-1 | 4 | | 25,004 |
| 20 | 29 | H | Preston NE | W | 2-0 | 1-0 | 3 | Brown (pen) [31], McCall [75] | 21,003 |
| 21 | Dec 6 | A | Burnley | L | 2-3 | 2-3 | 4 | Montgomery [24], Whitlow [31] | 11,452 |
| 22 | 9 | H | Walsall | W | 2-0 | 1-0 | — | Peschisolido [41], Montgomery [52] | 18,602 |
| 23 | 13 | H | Watford | D | 2-2 | 0-0 | 3 | Jagielka P [52], Lester (pen) [86] | 18,637 |
| 24 | 26 | A | Coventry C | W | 1-0 | 0-0 | 3 | Lester (pen) [56] | 21,132 |
| 25 | 28 | H | Wigan Ath | D | 1-1 | 1-1 | 3 | Lester [23] | 26,056 |
| 26 | Jan 10 | A | Gillingham | W | 3-0 | 1-0 | 3 | Peschisolido 3 [38, 58, 66] | 8353 |
| 27 | 17 | H | West Ham U | D | 3-3 | 1-3 | 3 | Peschisolido [5], Shaw [72], Jagielka P [90] | 22,787 |
| 28 | 28 | A | Derby Co | L | 0-2 | 0-0 | — | | 23,603 |
| 29 | 31 | A | Norwich C | L | 0-1 | 0-0 | 3 | | 18,977 |
| 30 | Feb 7 | H | Crystal Palace | L | 0-3 | 0-1 | 4 | | 23,816 |
| 31 | 21 | H | WBA | L | 1-2 | 0-0 | 6 | Moore (og) [57] | 24,805 |
| 32 | 24 | A | Crewe Alex | W | 1-0 | 0-0 | — | Montgomery [85] | 6525 |
| 33 | 28 | A | Reading | L | 1-2 | 1-2 | 7 | Gray [10] | 15,545 |
| 34 | Mar 2 | H | Millwall | W | 2-1 | 0-0 | — | Ward [58], Gray [62] | 19,579 |
| 35 | 13 | A | Watford | W | 2-0 | 1-0 | 4 | Lester [42], Gray [90] | 13,861 |
| 36 | 16 | A | Rotherham U | D | 1-1 | 0-0 | — | Lester (pen) [48] | 9793 |
| 37 | 20 | H | Bradford C | W | 2-0 | 0-0 | 3 | Morgan [60], Lester [62] | 20,052 |
| 38 | 23 | H | Derby Co | D | 1-1 | 1-1 | — | Gray [21] | 21,351 |
| 39 | 27 | A | Cardiff C | L | 1-2 | 1-1 | 6 | Ndlovu [25] | 13,666 |
| 40 | Apr 3 | H | Nottingham F | L | 1-2 | 0-1 | 6 | Wright [59] | 22,339 |
| 41 | 9 | A | Sunderland | L | 0-3 | 0-1 | — | | 27,472 |
| 42 | 12 | H | Wimbledon | W | 2-1 | 0-1 | 5 | Gray 2 [50, 67] | 19,391 |
| 43 | 17 | H | Stoke C | L | 0-1 | 0-1 | 8 | | 19,372 |
| 44 | 24 | A | Walsall | W | 1-0 | 0-0 | 8 | Lester (pen) [49] | 7873 |
| 45 | 30 | H | Ipswich T | D | 1-1 | 0-0 | — | Gray (pen) [64] | 24,184 |
| 46 | May 9 | A | Preston NE | D | 3-3 | 2-1 | 8 | Jagielka P [21], Gray 2 [38, 77] | 16,612 |

**Final League Position: 8**

### GOALSCORERS

*League (65):* Lester 12 (6 pens), Gray 9 (1 pen), Ndlovu 9 (3 pens), Peschisolido 8, Tonge 4, Ward 4, Jagielka P 3, Montgomery 3, Brown 2 (2 pens), McCall 2, Allison 1, Armstrong 1, Kozluk 1, Morgan 1, Page 1, Shaw 1, Whitlow 1, Wright 1, own goal 1.
*Carling Cup (2):* Lester 2 (1 pen).
*FA Cup (5):* Allison 2, Lester 1 (pen), Morgan 1, Peschisolido 1.

| Kenny P 27 | Jagielka P 43 | Armstrong C 4+8 | Morgan C 32 | Page R 30 | Rankine M 6+7 | Ndlovu P 28+8 | Brown M 14+1 | Lester J 25+7 | Allison W 14+25 | Tonge M 46 | Parkinson A 3+4 | Peschisolido P 12+15 | Ward A 20+3 | Kozluk R 42 | McCall S 37 | Montgomery N 32+4 | Whitlow M 13+4 | Gerrard P 16 | Cryan C —+1 | Harley J 5 | Wright A 21 | Baxter L 1 | Fettis A 2+1 | Boussatta D 3+3 | Kabba S —+1 | Sturridge D 2+2 | Shaw P 4+9 | Forte J 1+6 | Robinson C 4+1 | Gray A 14 | McLeod I 1+6 | Francis S 4+1 | Sestanovich A —+2 | Match No. |
|---|---|---|---|---|---|---|---|---|---|---|---|---|---|---|---|---|---|---|---|---|---|---|---|---|---|---|---|---|---|---|---|---|---|---|
| 1 | 2 | $3^{1}$ | 4 | 5 | 6 | 7 | 8 | $9^{2}$ | $10^{3}$ | 11 | 12 | 13 | 14 | | | | | | | | | | | | | | | | | | | | | 1 |
| 1 | 3 | | 6 | 5 | | 7 | | 9 | | 11 | | | 10 | 2 | 4 | 8 | | | | | | | | | | | | | | | | | | 2 |
| 1 | 2 | 12 | 6 | 5 | | $7^{1}$ | $8^{3}$ | $9^{2}$ | 10 | 11 | | 13 | | 3 | 4 | 14 | | | | | | | | | | | | | | | | | | 3 |
| $1^{G}$ | 2 | | 6 | 5 | 12 | 9 | 8■ | | 10 | 11 | | | | 3 | $4^{1}$ | 7 | 15 | | | | | | | | | | | | | | | | | 4 |
| | 2 | | 6 | 5 | 12 | $9^{3}$ | 8 | 13 | 10 | 11 | | 14 | | 3 | $4^{1}$ | $7^{2}$ | | 1 | | | | | | | | | | | | | | | | 5 |
| | 2 | 12 | 4■ | $5^{3}$ | 6 | 7 | | | $9^{2}$ | 11 | | 10 | 13 | $3^{1}$ | | 8 | | 1 | 14 | | | | | | | | | | | | | | | 6 |
| | 5 | 12 | $6^{3}$ | | | 7 | | | 13 | 11 | | 10 | $9^{2}$ | 2 | 4 | $8^{1}$ | 14 | 1 | | 3 | | | | | | | | | | | | | | 7 |
| | 5 | | | | 12 | 7 | | 13 | 14 | 11 | | $10^{3}$ | $9^{2}$ | 2 | $4^{1}$ | 8 | 6 | 1 | | 3 | | | | | | | | | | | | | | 8 |
| | 5 | | | | | 7 | 8 | | 12 | 11 | | 13 | $9^{1}$ | 2 | 4 | $10^{2}$ | 6 | 1 | | 3 | | | | | | | | | | | | | | 9 |
| | 5 | | | | | 7 | 8 | 12 | | 11 | | $10^{1}$ | 9 | | 4 | 2 | 6 | 1 | | 3 | | | | | | | | | | | | | | 10 |
| | 5 | 12 | | | | 7 | | 13 | 14 | 11 | | 10 | $9^{3}$ | 2 | 4 | $8^{2}$ | 6 | 1 | | $3^{1}$ | | | | | | | | | | | | | | 11 |
| | 5 | | 6 | | | 7 | 8 | | 12 | $11^{2}$ | | 13 | $9^{1}$ | 2 | 4 | 10 | 3 | 1 | | | | | | | | | | | | | | | | 12 |
| | 5 | 12 | 6 | | | 7 | 8 | | 13 | 11 | | 14 | $9^{2}$ | 2 | $4^{3}$ | $10^{1}$ | 3 | 1 | | | | | | | | | | | | | | | | 13 |
| | 5 | 12 | 6 | | | 7 | 8 | 13 | 14 | 11 | | $10^{1}$ | $9^{3}$ | 2 | $4^{2}$ | | 3 | 1 | | | | | | | | | | | | | | | | 14 |
| | 5 | 12 | 6 | | | 7 | 8 | $10^{2}$ | 14 | 11 | | 13 | 9 | 2 | $4^{3}$ | | $3^{1}$ | 1 | | | | | | | | | | | | | | | | 15 |
| | 5 | 12 | 6 | | | $7^{3}$ | | 10 | 13 | 11 | 14 | | 9 | 2 | 4 | $8^{1}$ | | 1 | | | $3^{2}$ | | | | | | | | | | | | | 16 |
| | 5 | 8 | 6 | | | $7^{3}$ | | $10^{1}$ | | 11 | 14 | 12 | 9 | 2 | $4^{2}$ | 13 | | 1 | | | 3 | | | | | | | | | | | | | 17 |
| | 5 | 8 | 6 | | | $7^{3}$ | | $10^{1}$ | 13 | 11 | 14 | 12 | $9^{2}$ | 2 | 4 | | | 1 | | | 3 | | | | | | | | | | | | | 18 |
| | 5 | 3 | 6 | | | 7 | 8 | $10^{1}$ | 14 | 11 | | 12 | $9^{3}$ | 2 | $4^{2}$ | 13 | | 1 | | | | | | | | | | | | | | | | 19 |
| | 5 | | 6 | | $7^{1}$ | 12 | 8 | $9^{2}$ | 10 | 11 | | | | 2 | $4^{3}$ | 13 | 14 | 1 | | | 3 | | | | | | | | | | | | | 20 |
| | 5 | | $6^{1}$ | | 12 | 7 | 10■ | | $9^{2}$ | 11 | | 13 | | | 4 | 8 | 2 | | | | 3 | $1^{G}$ | 15 | | | | | | | | | | | 21 |
| | 5 | | | 6 | | $7^{3}$ | 12 | 9 | 13 | 11 | | $10^{2}$ | | 2 | $4^{1}$ | 8 | | | | | 3 | | 1 | 14 | | | | | | | | | | 22 |
| | 5 | | | 6 | | 12 | 7 | 9 | | 11 | | $10^{2}$ | 13 | $2^{3}$ | 4 | $8^{1}$ | | | | | 3 | | 1 | 14 | | | | | | | | | | 23 |
| 1 | 5 | | | 6 | 12 | 7 | | $9^{3}$ | 13 | 11 | | | $10^{2}$ | 2 | $4^{1}$ | 8 | 14 | | | | 3 | | | | | | | | | | | | | 24 |
| 1 | 5 | | | 6 | | $7^{3}$ | | $9^{1}$ | 13 | 11 | | 12 | $10^{2}$ | 2 | 4 | 8 | | | | | 3 | | | | 14 | | | | | | | | | 25 |
| 1 | 5 | | 3 | 6 | | | | 9 | 8 | 11 | | 10 | | 2 | 4 | 7 | | | | | | | | | | | | | | | | | | 26 |
| 1 | 5 | | 3 | $6^{1}$ | | | | $9^{2}$ | 8 | 11 | | 10 | | 2 | 4 | 7 | | | | | | | | | | 12 | 13 | | | | | | | 27 |
| 1 | | | 5 | 6 | $4^{2}$ | | | | 8 | 11 | | 12 | | 2 | | 7 | | | | | 3 | | | | | $9^{1}$ | 10 | 13 | | | | | | 28 |
| 1 | 5 | | | 6 | | | | | 9 | 11 | | 12 | | 2 | $4^{1}$ | $7^{3}$ | | | | | 3 | | | | | 13 | $10^{2}$ | 14 | 8 | | | | | 29 |
| 1 | 5 | | | 6 | | 13 | | 12 | 14 | 11 | | 10 | | 2 | $4^{1}$ | 7 | | | | | 3 | | | | | $9^{3}$ | $8^{2}$ | | | | | | | 30 |
| 1 | 2 | | | 6 | | $7^{3}$ | | | 12 | 11 | | 10 | 9 | $3^{1}$ | $4^{2}$ | 8 | 5 | | | | | | | | | | 13 | | 14 | | | | | 31 |
| 1 | 2 | | | 6 | | 12 | | | | 11 | $7^{1}$ | | 9 | 3 | | 8 | 5■ | | | | | | | | | | 13 | $10^{2}$ | 4 | | | | | 32 |
| 1 | 2 | | | 6 | | 14 | | | 13 | 11 | $7^{3}$ | 12 | 9 | 3 | | 8 | $5^{2}$ | | | | | | | | | | | | $4^{1}$ | 10 | | | | 33 |
| 1 | 2 | | | 6 | 12 | | | | | 11 | $7^{2}$ | | 9 | 3 | | 8 | 5 | | | | | | | | | | 13 | | $4^{1}$ | 10 | | | | 34 |
| 1 | 2 | | 5 | 6 | 4 | | | $9^{3}$ | 13 | 11 | | | | 3 | | | | | | | 8 | | | $7^{1}$ | | | 12 | | | $10^{2}$ | 14 | | | 35 |
| 1 | 2 | | 5 | 6 | | 12 | | $9^{3}$ | 13 | 11 | | | | 3 | | 8 | | | | | 4 | | | $7^{1}$ | | | | | | $10^{2}$ | 14 | | | 36 |
| 1 | 2 | | 5 | 6 | | | | 9 | 12 | 11 | | | | 3 | $4^{1}$ | $8^{2}$ | | | | | | | | $7^{3}$ | | | | 13 | | 10 | 14 | | | 37 |
| 1 | 2 | | 5 | 6 | | $7^{1}$ | | 9 | 13 | 11 | | | | 3 | $4^{3}$ | 8 | | | | | | | | $12^{2}$ | | | | 14 | | 10 | | | | 38 |
| 1 | 2 | | 5 | 6 | | $7^{1}$ | | $9^{3}$ | 12 | 11 | | | | 3 | $4^{2}$ | | | | | | | | | | | | 13 | | | 10 | 14 | 8 | | 39 |
| 1 | 5 | | 6 | | | $7^{3}$ | | 9 | 12 | 11 | | | | | $4^{1}$ | $8^{2}$ | | | | | 3 | | | | | | 13 | | | 10 | | 2 | 14 | 40 |
| 1 | 5 | | 4 | $6^{3}$ | 8 | | | 12 | 13 | 11 | | | | 3 | | | | | | | $2^{1}$ | | | | | | 9 | | | $10^{2}$ | | 7 | 14 | 41 |
| 1 | | | 5 | 6 | | 12 | | 9 | | 11 | | | | 2 | 4 | 8 | | | | | 3 | | | | | | | | | 10 | | $7^{1}$ | | 42 |
| 1 | | | 5 | 6 | | $7^{3}$ | | 9 | 12 | 11 | | | | 2 | $4^{2}$ | $8^{1}$ | | | | | 3 | | | | | | 13 | 14 | | 10 | | | | 43 |
| 1 | 7 | | 5 | 6 | 12 | | | $9^{1}$ | 8 | $11^{2}$ | | | | 2 | 4 | | | | | | 3 | | | | | | 13 | | | $10^{3}$ | 14 | | | 44 |
| 1 | 7 | | 5 | 6 | | 12 | | $9^{3}$ | 8 | 11 | | | | $2^{2}$ | $4^{1}$ | | | | | | 3 | | | | | | | | | 10 | 14 | 13 | | 45 |
| 1 | 7 | | 5 | 6 | | | | | 8 | 11 | | | | 2 | $4^{1}$ | | | | | | 3 | | | | | | | 12 | | 10 | 9 | | | 46 |

**Carling Cup**

| | | | |
|---|---|---|---|
| First Round | Macclesfield T | (a) | 2-1 |
| Second Round | QPR | (h) | 0-2 |

**FA Cup**

| | | | |
|---|---|---|---|
| Third Round | Cardiff C | (a) | 1-0 |
| Fourth Round | Nottingham F | (a) | 3-0 |
| Fifth Round | Colchester U | (h) | 1-0 |
| Sixth Round | Sunderland | (a) | 0-1 |

# SHEFFIELD WEDNESDAY FL Championship 1

## FOUNDATION

Sheffield being one of the principal centres of early Association Football, this club was formed as long ago as 1867 by the Sheffield Wednesday Cricket Club (formed 1825) and their colours from the start were blue and white. The inaugural meeting was held at the Adelphi Hotel and the original committee included Charles Stokes who was subsequently a founder member of Sheffield United.

***Hillsborough, Sheffield S6 1SW.***

***Telephone:*** (0114) 221 2121.

***Fax:*** (0114) 221 2122.

***Ticket Office:*** (0114) 221 2400.

***Website:*** www.swfc.co.uk

***Email:*** enquiries@swfc.co.uk

***Ground Capacity:*** 39,814.

***Record Attendance:*** 72,841 v Manchester C, FA Cup 5th rd, 17 February 1934.

***Pitch Measurements:*** 115yd × 74yd.

***Chairman:*** Dave E. D. Allen.

***Vice-chairman:*** Mick G. Wright.

***Secretary:*** Kaven Walker.

***Manager:*** Chris Turner.

***Assistant Manager:*** Colin West.

***Physio:*** John Dickens.

***Colours:*** Blue and white striped shirts, black shorts, blue stockings.

***Change Colours:*** All silver.

***Year Formed:*** 1867 (fifth oldest League club).

***Turned Professional:*** 1887.

***Ltd Co.:*** 1899.

***Former Names:*** The Wednesday until 1929.

***Club Nickname:*** 'The Owls'.

***Previous Grounds:*** 1867, Highfield; 1869, Myrtle Road; 1877, Sheaf House; 1887, Olive Grove; 1899, Owlerton (since 1912 known as Hillsborough). Some games were played at Endcliffe in the 1880s. Until 1895 Bramall Lane was used for some games.

***First Football League Game:*** 3 September 1892, Division 1, v Notts Co (a) W 1–0 – Allan; Tom Brandon (1), Mumford; Hall, Betts, Harry Brandon; Spiksley, Brady, Davis, R. N. Brown, Dunlop.

***Record League Victory:*** 9–1 v Birmingham, Division 1, 13 December 1930 – Brown; Walker, Blenkinsop; Strange, Leach, Wilson; Hooper (3), Seed (2), Ball (2), Burgess (1), Rimmer (1).

## HONOURS

*Football League:* Division 1 – Champions 1902–03, 1903–04, 1928–29, 1929–30; Runners-up 1960–61; Division 2 – Champions 1899–1900, 1925–26, 1951–52, 1955–56, 1958–59; Runners-up 1949–50, 1983–84.

*FA Cup:* Winners 1896, 1907, 1935; Runners-up 1890, 1966, 1993.

*Football League Cup:* Winners 1991; Runners-up 1993.

***European Competitions:*** *European Fairs Cup:* 1961–62, 1963–64. *UEFA Cup:* 1992–93. *Intertoto Cup:* 1995.

## SKY SPORTS FACT FILE

On 31 August 1968 Sheffield Wednesday were at home to Manchester United, the reigning European Cup holders in a First Division match. This see-saw of a goal packed thriller went 1-0, 1-1, 1-2, 2-2, 2-3, 2-4, 3-4 at half time, 4-4, then 5-4 to the Owls.

***Record Cup Victory:*** 12–0 v Halliwell, FA Cup 1st rd, 17 January 1891 – Smith; Thompson, Brayshaw; Harry Brandon (1), Betts, Cawley (2); Winterbottom, Mumford (2), Bob Brandon (1), Woolhouse (5), Ingram (1).

***Record Defeat:*** 0–10 v Aston Villa, Division 1, 5 October 1912.

***Most League Points (2 for a win):*** 62, Division 2, 1958–59.

***Most League Points (3 for a win):*** 88, Division 2, 1983–84.

***Most League Goals:*** 106, Division 2, 1958–59.

***Highest League Scorer in Season:*** Derek Dooley, 46, Division 2, 1951–52.

***Most League Goals in Total Aggregate:*** Andy Wilson, 199, 1900–20.

***Most League Goals in One Match:*** 6, Doug Hunt v Norwich C, Division 2, 19 November 1938.

***Most Capped Player:*** Nigel Worthington, 50 (66), Northern Ireland.

***Most League Appearances:*** Andrew Wilson, 501, 1900–20.

***Youngest League Player:*** Peter Fox, 15 years 269 days v Orient, 31 March 1973.

***Record Transfer Fee Received:*** £2,750,000 from Blackburn R for Paul Warhurst, September 1993.

***Record Transfer Fee Paid:*** £4,500,000 to Celtic for Paolo Di Canio, August 1997.

***Football League Record:*** 1892 Elected to Division 1; 1899–1900 Division 2; 1900–20 Division 1; 1920–26 Division 2; 1926–37 Division 1; 1937–50 Division 2; 1950–51 Division 1; 1951–52 Division 2; 1952–55 Division 1; 1955–56 Division 2; 1956–58 Division 1; 1958–59 Division 2; 1959–70 Division 1; 1970–75 Division 2; 1975–80 Division 3; 1980–84 Division 2; 1984–90 Division 1; 1990–91 Division 2; 1991–92 Division 1; 1992–2000 FA Premier League; 2000–03 Division 1; 2003–04 Division 2; 2004– FL1.

### MANAGERS

Arthur Dickinson 1891–1920
*(Secretary-Manager)*
Robert Brown 1920–33
Billy Walker 1933–37
Jimmy McMullan 1937–42
Eric Taylor 1942–58
*(continued as General Manager to 1974)*
Harry Catterick 1958–61
Vic Buckingham 1961–64
Alan Brown 1964–68
Jack Marshall 1968–69
Danny Williams 1969–71
Derek Dooley 1971–73
Steve Burtenshaw 1974–75
Len Ashurst 1975–77
Jackie Charlton 1977–83
Howard Wilkinson 1983–88
Peter Eustace 1988–89
Ron Atkinson 1989–91
Trevor Francis 1991–95
David Pleat 1995–97
Ron Atkinson 1997–98
Danny Wilson 1998–2000
Peter Shreeves (Acting) 2000
Paul Jewell 2000–01
Peter Shreeves 2001
Terry Yorath 2001–02
Chris Turner November 2002–

### LATEST SEQUENCES

***Longest Sequence of League Wins:*** 9, 23.4.1904 – 15.10.1904.

***Longest Sequence of League Defeats:*** 8, 9.9.2000 – 17.10.2000.

***Longest Sequence of League Draws:*** 5, 24.10.1992 – 28.11.1992.

***Longest Sequence of Unbeaten League Matches:*** 19, 10.12.1960 – 8.4.1961.

***Longest Sequence Without a League Win:*** 20, 11.1.1975 – 30.8.1975.

***Successive Scoring Runs:*** 40 from 14.11.1959.

***Successive Non-scoring Runs:*** 8 from 8.3.1975.

### TEN YEAR LEAGUE RECORD

| | | P | W | D | L | F | A | Pts | Pos |
|---|---|---|---|---|---|---|---|---|---|
| 1994-95 | PR Lge | 42 | 13 | 12 | 17 | 49 | 57 | 51 | 13 |
| 1995-96 | PR Lge | 38 | 10 | 10 | 18 | 48 | 61 | 40 | 15 |
| 1996-97 | PR Lge | 38 | 14 | 15 | 9 | 50 | 51 | 57 | 7 |
| 1997-98 | PR Lge | 38 | 12 | 8 | 18 | 52 | 67 | 44 | 16 |
| 1998-99 | PR Lge | 38 | 13 | 7 | 18 | 41 | 42 | 46 | 12 |
| 1999-2000 | PR Lge | 38 | 8 | 7 | 23 | 38 | 70 | 31 | 19 |
| 2000-01 | Div 1 | 46 | 15 | 8 | 23 | 52 | 71 | 53 | 17 |
| 2001-02 | Div 1 | 46 | 12 | 14 | 20 | 49 | 71 | 50 | 20 |
| 2002-03 | Div 1 | 46 | 10 | 16 | 20 | 56 | 73 | 46 | 22 |
| 2003-04 | Div 2 | 46 | 13 | 14 | 19 | 48 | 64 | 53 | 16 |

### DID YOU KNOW ?

In 1902–03 Sheffield Wednesday bagged a hatful of trophies, chiefly winning the First Division championship, but also the Plymouth Bowl, while the reserves took the Midland League title, Sheffield Challenge Cup and Wharncliffe Charity Cup.

## SHEFFIELD WEDNESDAY 2003–04 LEAGUE RECORD

| Match No. | Date | Venue | Opponents | Result | H/T Score | Lg. Pos. | Goalscorers | Atten-dance |
|---|---|---|---|---|---|---|---|---|
| 1 | Aug 9 | A | Swindon T | W 3-2 | 3-1 | — | Owusu 2 [5, 20], Kuqi [25] | 10,573 |
| 2 | 16 | H | Oldham Ath | D 2-2 | 1-1 | 5 | Kuqi 2 [24, 52] | 24,630 |
| 3 | 23 | A | Peterborough U | W 1-0 | 1-0 | 2 | Kuqi [44] | 10,194 |
| 4 | 25 | H | Wrexham | L 2-3 | 1-1 | 9 | Quinn [2], Smith P [79] | 24,478 |
| 5 | Sept 1 | A | Wycombe W | W 2-1 | 2-1 | — | Owusu [5], Quinn [8] | 6444 |
| 6 | 6 | H | Tranmere R | W 2-0 | 0-0 | 2 | Smith P [57], Cooke [61] | 21,705 |
| 7 | 13 | H | Stockport Co | D 2-2 | 2-0 | 2 | Kuqi [17], Quinn [31] | 22,535 |
| 8 | 16 | A | Bournemouth | L 0-1 | 0-0 | — | | 8219 |
| 9 | 20 | A | Brighton & HA | L 0-2 | 0-1 | 10 | | 6602 |
| 10 | 27 | H | Grimsby T | D 0-0 | 0-0 | 9 | | 21,918 |
| 11 | Oct 1 | H | Notts Co | W 2-1 | 1-0 | — | McLaren 2 [23, 53] | 20,354 |
| 12 | 4 | A | Brentford | W 3-0 | 2-0 | 4 | Holt 2 [39, 45], Owusu [75] | 8631 |
| 13 | 10 | A | Hartlepool U | D 1-1 | 0-0 | — | Owusu [47] | 7448 |
| 14 | 18 | H | Rushden & D | D 0-0 | 0-0 | 4 | | 22,599 |
| 15 | 22 | H | Plymouth Arg | L 1-3 | 0-1 | — | Reddy [84] | 20,090 |
| 16 | 25 | A | Bristol C | D 1-1 | 1-0 | 10 | Proudlock [25] | 13,668 |
| 17 | Nov 1 | H | Blackpool | L 0-1 | 0-0 | 11 | | 21,450 |
| 18 | 15 | A | Colchester U | L 1-3 | 0-1 | 14 | Bromby [58] | 5018 |
| 19 | 22 | H | Luton T | D 0-0 | 0-0 | 17 | | 21,027 |
| 20 | 29 | A | QPR | L 0-3 | 0-1 | 17 | | 17,393 |
| 21 | Dec 13 | A | Barnsley | D 1-1 | 1-1 | 17 | N'Dumbu Nsungu [30] | 20,438 |
| 22 | 20 | H | Chesterfield | D 0-0 | 0-0 | 17 | | 25,296 |
| 23 | 26 | H | Port Vale | L 2-3 | 2-1 | 18 | Robins [21], Lee [30] | 24,991 |
| 24 | 28 | A | Tranmere R | D 2-2 | 2-0 | 17 | Lee [4], N'Dumbu Nsungu [21] | 9645 |
| 25 | Jan 3 | A | Wrexham | W 2-1 | 1-0 | 15 | N'Dumbu Nsungu [39], Quinn [65] | 8497 |
| 26 | 10 | H | Swindon T | D 1-1 | 0-0 | 15 | Robins [72] | 22,751 |
| 27 | 17 | A | Oldham Ath | L 0-1 | 0-1 | 16 | | 9316 |
| 28 | 24 | H | Peterborough U | W 2-0 | 0-0 | 16 | Robins [55], Proudlock [90] | 21,474 |
| 29 | 30 | H | Wycombe W | D 1-1 | 0-1 | — | Proudlock [62] | 19,596 |
| 30 | Feb 7 | A | Port Vale | L 0-3 | 0-1 | 17 | | 7958 |
| 31 | 14 | H | Hartlepool U | W 1-0 | 0-0 | 13 | N'Dumbu Nsungu (pen) [80] | 20,732 |
| 32 | 21 | A | Rushden & D | W 2-1 | 1-0 | 12 | N'Dumbu Nsungu 2 (2 pens) [13, 55] | 5685 |
| 33 | 28 | H | Bristol C | W 1-0 | 0-0 | 12 | Lee [90] | 24,154 |
| 34 | Mar 2 | A | Plymouth Arg | L 0-2 | 0-1 | — | | 17,218 |
| 35 | 7 | A | Chesterfield | L 1-3 | 0-1 | 12 | N'Dumbu Nsungu [66] | 7695 |
| 36 | 13 | H | Barnsley | W 2-1 | 1-0 | 12 | N'Dumbu Nsungu 2 [36, 56] | 25,664 |
| 37 | 17 | H | Bournemouth | L 0-2 | 0-2 | — | | 18,799 |
| 38 | 20 | A | Stockport Co | L 0-1 | 0-1 | 12 | | 8011 |
| 39 | 27 | H | Brighton & HA | W 2-1 | 1-1 | 12 | Brunt [8], Mustoe [90] | 19,707 |
| 40 | Apr 3 | A | Grimsby T | L 0-2 | 0-2 | 14 | | 6641 |
| 41 | 10 | H | Brentford | D 1-1 | 0-0 | 15 | Smith D [90] | 20,004 |
| 42 | 12 | A | Notts Co | D 0-0 | 0-0 | 15 | | 9601 |
| 43 | 17 | A | Blackpool | L 1-4 | 1-2 | 15 | Brunt [37] | 7388 |
| 44 | 24 | H | Colchester U | L 0-1 | 0-0 | 16 | | 20,464 |
| 45 | May 1 | A | Luton T | L 2-3 | 2-0 | 16 | Shaw J [23], Cooke [33] | 7157 |
| 46 | 8 | H | QPR | L 1-3 | 0-1 | 16 | Shaw J [59] | 29,313 |

**Final League Position: 16**

### GOALSCORERS

*League (48):* N'Dumbu Nsungu 9 (3 pens), Kuqi 5, Owusu 5, Quinn 4, Lee 3, Proudlock 3, Robins 3, Brunt 2, Cooke 2, Holt 2, McLaren 2, Shaw J 2, Smith P 2, Bromby 1, Mustoe 1, Reddy 1, Smith D 1.
*Carling Cup (2):* Lee 1, Wood 1.
*FA Cup (6):* Proudlock 3 (1 pen), Holt 1, N'Dumbu-Nsungu 1, Owusu 1.
*LDV Vans Trophy (9):* Robins 4, Proudlock 3, Lee 1, Reddy 1.

| Tidman O 9 | Geary D 41 | Barry-Murphy B 38 + 3 | Armstrong C 5 + 5 | Smith D 41 | Lee G 30 | Evans R 5 + 1 | Quinn A 23 + 1 | Owusu L 12 + 8 | Kuqi S 7 | Cooke T 19 + 4 | Wood R 10 + 2 | Haslam S 16 + 9 | Holt G 9 + 8 | McLaren P 23 + 2 | Smith P 12 + 7 | Mustoe R 22 + 3 | Pressman K 20 + 1 | Proudlock A 26 + 4 | N'Dumbu Nsungu G 20 + 4 | Beswetherick J 4 + 1 | Bromby L 29 | Nixon E — + 1 | Lucas D 17 | Reddy M 9 + 3 | Antoine-Curier M — + 1 | Robins M 14 + 1 | Burchill M 4 + 1 | Wilson M 3 | Olsen K 6 + 4 | Chambers A 8 + 3 | Shaw J 7 + 7 | McMahon L 9 + 1 | Brunt C 8 + 1 | Carr C — + 2 | *Match No.* |
|---|---|---|---|---|---|---|---|---|---|---|---|---|---|---|---|---|---|---|---|---|---|---|---|---|---|---|---|---|---|---|---|---|---|---|---|
| 1 | 2 | 3 | 4 | 5 | 6 | $7^1$ | $8^2$ | $9^3$ | 10 | 11 | 12 | 13 | 14 | | | | | | | | | | | | | | | | | | | | | | 1 |
| 1 | 2 | 3 | | 5 | 6 | $7^1$ | 8 | $9^2$ | 10■ | 11 | 4 | 12 | 13 | | | | | | | | | | | | | | | | | | | | | | 2 |
| 1 | 2 | 3 | | 5 | 6 | $11^3$ | 4 | $9^1$ | $10^2$ | 7 | | 13 | 12 | 8 | 14 | | | | | | | | | | | | | | | | | | | | 3 |
| 1 | $2^1$ | 3 | | 5 | 6 | $7^2$ | 8 | 12 | 10 | 11 | | | 9 | 4 | 13 | | | | | | | | | | | | | | | | | | | | 4 |
| 1 | 2■ | 3 | | 5 | 6 | $7^3$ | 8 | $9^1$ | | 11 | | 12 | $10^2$ | 4 | 13 | 14 | | | | | | | | | | | | | | | | | | | 5 |
| | 2 | 3 | 12 | 5 | 6 | 13 | | $9^3$ | | $11^2$ | | | 14 | 4 | 8 | $7^1$ | 1 | 10 | | | | | | | | | | | | | | | | | 6 |
| | 2 | $3^3$ | 12 | 5 | 6 | | $7^1$ | 13 | 10 | 11 | | | | 4 | 8 | | 1 | $9^2$ | 14 | | | | | | | | | | | | | | | | 7 |
| | | | | 5 | 6 | | 8 | 12 | 10 | $11^1$ | | 2 | | 4 | 7 | | 1 | 9 | | 3 | | | | | | | | | | | | | | | 8 |
| | | 12 | | 5 | | | 8 | 13 | $10^2$ | 11 | | 2 | | 4 | $7^3$ | | 1 | 9 | 14 | $3^1$ | 6 | | | | | | | | | | | | | | 9 |
| | | | | 5 | 6 | | 11 | 12 | | 7 | | 13 | | $4^1$ | | 8 | $1^G$ | 9 | 10 | $3^2$ | 2 | 15 | | | | | | | | | | | | | 10 |
| | 2 | $3^2$ | | 5 | 6 | | | 12 | | 11 | 13 | | 10 | 8 | | 7 | | $9^1$ | | | 4 | | 1 | | | | | | | | | | | | 11 |
| | 2 | 3 | | 5 | 6 | | | $9^1$ | | 11 | | 7 | $10^2$ | 8 | | | | | 12 | | 4 | | 1 | 13 | | | | | | | | | | | 12 |
| | 2 | 3 | | 5 | 6 | | | $9^3$ | | 11 | | 12 | $10^2$ | 8 | | $7^1$ | | 13 | | | 4 | | 1 | 14 | | | | | | | | | | | 13 |
| | 2 | 3 | | 5 | 6 | | | | | $11^1$ | | 12 | $10^2$ | 8 | | 7 | | 9 | | | 4 | | 1 | 13 | | | | | | | | | | | 14 |
| | 2 | $3^2$ | | 5 | 6 | | | 12 | | | | | 10 | 8 | 13 | 7 | | $9^1$ | | | 4 | | 1 | 11 | | | | | | | | | | | 15 |
| | 2 | | | 5 | 6 | | | 10 | | | 3 | | | 8 | | 7 | | 9 | | | 4 | | 1 | 11 | | | | | | | | | | | 16 |
| | 3 | | | 5 | 6 | | | 9 | | | $4^1$ | | | 8 | 12 | 7 | | 10 | | | 2 | | 1 | 11 | | | | | | | | | | | 17 |
| | 2 | $3^1$ | | 6 | 5 | | | 9 | | | | 12 | 13 | 8 | | 7 | 1 | $10^2$ | | | 4 | | | 11 | | | | | | | | | | | 18 |
| | 2 | $3^1$ | | 6 | 5 | | | 9 | | | | 7 | | | | 8 | 1 | 10 | | | 4 | | | 11 | 12 | | | | | | | | | | 19 |
| | | 3 | | 6 | 5 | | | 9 | | | 4 | 7 | 12 | | | 8 | 1 | $10^1$ | | | 2 | | | 11 | | | | | | | | | | | 20 |
| | 2 | 3 | | | 5 | | | | | | | 7 | 10■ | | | 4 | | 12 | 8 | | 6 | | 1 | $11^1$ | | 9 | | | | | | | | | 21 |
| | 2 | 3 | $4^1$ | | 5 | | | 13 | | | | 7 | $10^3$ | 12 | 14 | | | | 8 | | 6 | | 1 | $11^2$ | | 9 | | | | | | | | | 22 |
| | 2 | 3 | | | 5 | | | | | | | | | 8 | 7 | 4 | | | 10 | | 6 | | 1 | $11^1$ | | 9 | 12 | | | | | | | | 23 |
| | 2 | 12 | 14 | $3^1$ | 5 | | | | | | | 13 | | $8^2$ | 7 | 4 | | | 11 | | 6 | | 1 | | | 9 | $10^3$ | | | | | | | | 24 |
| | 2 | 12 | 14 | 6 | 5 | | 3 | | | | | 7 | 13 | | $8^1$ | 4 | | | 11 | | | | 1 | | | $9^2$ | $10^3$ | | | | | | | | 25 |
| | 2 | 3 | | 5 | | | 11 | | | | | 6 | | | 8 | 4 | | 12 | 7 | | | | 1 | | | 9 | $10^1$ | | | | | | | | 26 |
| | 2 | 3 | 12 | 5 | | | 11 | | | | | 6 | | | 8 | $4^1$ | | 13 | 7 | | | | 1 | | | 9 | $10^2$ | | | | | | | | 27 |
| | 2 | 3 | $4^1$ | 5 | | | 11 | | | 12 | | 6 | 13 | | 8 | | | 10 | | | | | 1 | | | $9^2$ | | 7 | | | | | | | 28 |
| | 2 | 3 | | 5 | | | 11 | | | 12 | | 6 | | | 4 | | | 10 | $7^1$ | | | | 1 | | | 9 | | 8 | | | | | | | 29 |
| | 2 | 3 | $4^2$ | 5 | | | 11 | | | | | 6 | | | 8 | | 15 | 10■ | 12 | | | | $1^G$ | | | 9 | | $7^1$ | 13 | | | | | | 30 |
| 1 | 2 | 3 | $11^2$ | 5 | | | 13 | | | | | 6 | | | 12 | | | 10 | 7 | | 4 | | | | | $9^1$ | | | 8 | | | | | | 31 |
| 1 | 2 | 3 | | 5 | | | 11 | | | | | 6 | | | | | | | 7 | | 4 | | | | | | | | 10 | 8 | 9 | | | | 32 |
| | | 3 | | 5 | 6 | | 11 | | | | 4 | 7 | | | | | 1 | | 10 | | 2 | | | | | | | | | 8 | 9 | | | | 33 |
| 1 | 2 | 3 | | 6 | $5^1$ | | 11 | | | | 8 | | | | | | | | 10 | 12 | 4 | | | | | | | | | 7 | 9 | | | | 34 |
| 1 | 2 | 11 | | 6 | 5 | | 8■ | | | | | | | | | | | | 10 | 3 | 4 | | | | | | | | | 7 | 9 | | | | 35 |
| | 2 | 3 | | | 5 | | 11 | | | | | | | | | 13 | 1 | $8^1$ | 10 | | 4 | | | | | | | | $9^2$ | 7 | 12 | 6 | | | 36 |
| | 2 | 3 | | | 5 | | | | | | | | | | | $7^1$ | 1 | $8^2$ | 10 | | 4 | | | | | | | | 9 | 11 | 12 | 6 | 13 | | 37 |
| | 2 | 3 | | $6^2$ | 5 | | | | | 12 | | | | | | $7^1$ | 1 | 9 | 10 | | 4 | | | | | | | | 13 | 11 | | 8 | | | 38 |
| | 2 | 3 | | 5 | | | | | | $7^1$ | | | | | | 8 | 1 | 9 | $10^2$ | | 4 | | | | | | | | | 12 | 13 | 11 | 6 | | 39 |
| | 2 | 3 | | 5 | | | | | | $7^2$ | | | | | | $8^1$ | 1 | 9 | 10■ | | 4 | | | | | | | | | 13 | 12 | 6 | 11 | | 40 |
| | 2 | 3 | | 5 | | | | | | $7^1$ | | | | 13 | | $8^2$ | 1 | 9 | $10^3$ | | 4 | | | | | | | | 14 | | 12 | 6 | 11 | | 41 |
| | 2 | | | 5 | | | 6■ | | | | 3 | | | $8^1$ | | | 1 | 10 | | | 4 | | | | | | | | 9 | 7 | 12 | | 11 | | 42 |
| | 2 | 3 | | 5 | | | 6 | | | | | | | 7 | | | 1 | $10^2$ | | | 4 | | | | | 12 | | | $9^1$ | | 8 | 13 | 11 | | 43 |
| | 2 | 3 | | 5 | | | 8 | | | 12 | 6 | | | $7^1$ | | 13 | 1 | $10^3$ | | | | | | | | $9^2$ | | | | | 14 | 4 | 11 | | 44 |
| | $2^3$ | 3 | | 5 | | | | | | $7^1$ | 6 | | | 8 | | | 1 | | | | | | | | | $9^2$ | | | 13 | 12 | 10 | 4 | 11 | 14 | 45 |
| | 2 | 3 | | $5^1$ | | | | | | 7 | 6 | | | 8 | | | 1 | | | | | | | | | 9 | | | | | 10 | 4 | 11 | 12 | 46 |

**Carling Cup**

| | | | |
|---|---|---|---|
| First Round | Hartlepool U | (h) | 2-2 |

**FA Cup**

| | | | |
|---|---|---|---|
| First Round | Salisbury C | (h) | 4-0 |
| Second Round | Scunthorpe U | (a) | 2-2 |
| | | (h) | 0-0 |

**LDV Vans Trophy**

| | | | |
|---|---|---|---|
| First Round | Grimsby T | (h) | 1-1 |
| Second Round | Barnsley | (h) | 1-0 |
| Quarter-Final | Carlisle U | (a) | 3-0 |
| Semi-Final | Scunthorpe U | (h) | 4-0 |
| Northern Final | Blackpool | (a) | 0-1 |
| | | (h) | 0-2 |

# SHREWSBURY TOWN FL Championship 2

## FOUNDATION

Shrewsbury School having provided a number of the early England and Wales international players it is not surprising that there was a Town club as early as 1876 which won the Birmingham Senior Cup in 1879. However, the present Shrewsbury Town club was formed in 1886 and won the Welsh FA Cup as early as 1891.

***Gay Meadow, Abbey Foregate, Shrewsbury SY2 6AB.***

***Telephone:*** (01743) 360 111.

***Fax:*** (01743) 236 384.

***Ticket Office:*** (01743) 360 111.

***Website:*** www.shrewsburytown.com

***Email:*** office@shrewsburytown.co.uk

***Ground Capacity:*** 8,000.

***Record Attendance:*** 18,917 v Walsall, Division 3, 26 April 1961.

***Pitch Measurements:*** 114yd × 74yd.

***Chairman:*** Roland Wycherley.

***Secretary:*** Judy Shone.

***Manager:*** Jimmy Quinn.

***Assistant Manager:*** Dave Cooke.

***Colours:*** Blue and amber.

***Change Colours:*** White and blue.

***Year Formed:*** 1886.

***Turned Professional:*** 1896.

***Ltd Co.:*** 1936.

***Club Nickname:*** 'Town', 'Blues' or 'Salop'. The name 'Salop' is a colloquialism for the county of Shropshire. Since Shrewsbury is the only club in Shropshire, cries of 'Come on Salop' are frequently used!

***Previous Ground:*** Old Shrewsbury Racecourse.

***First Football League Game:*** 19 August 1950, Division 3 (N), v Scunthorpe U (a) D 0–0 – Egglestone; Fisher, Lewis; Wheatley, Depear, Robinson; Griffin, Hope, Jackson, Brown, Barker.

***Record League Victory:*** 7–0 v Swindon T, Division 3 (S), 6 May 1955 – McBride; Bannister, Skeech; Wallace, Maloney, Candlin; Price, O'Donnell (1), Weigh (4), Russell, McCue (2).

***Record Cup Victory:*** 11–2 v Marine, FA Cup 1st rd, 11 November 1995 – Edwards, Seabury (Dempsey (1)), Withe (1), Evans (1), Whiston (2), Scott (1), Woods, Stevens (1), Spink (3) (Anthrobus), Walton, Berkley, (1 og).

## HONOURS

*Football League:* Division 2 best season: 8th, 1983–84, 1984–85; Division 3 – Champions 1978–79, 1993–94; Division 4 – Runners-up 1974–75.

*Conference:* Promotion 2003–04 (play-offs)

*FA Cup:* best season: 6th rd, 1979, 1982.

*Football League Cup:* Semi-final 1961.

*Welsh Cup:* Winners 1891, 1938, 1977, 1979, 1984, 1985; Runners-up 1931, 1948, 1980.

*Auto Windscreens Shield:* Runners-up 1996

## SKY SPORTS FACT FILE

Though goalscoring was a problem for newly elected Football League team Shrewsbury Town in 1950–51 – 43 in 46 matches – they succeeded in securing sufficient points to finish 20th. There was also a highly encouraging average crowd of 9,096.

***Record Defeat:*** 1–8 v Norwich C, Division 3 (S), 13 September 1952. 1–8 v Coventry C, Division 3, 22 October 1963.

***Most League Points (2 for a win):*** 62, Division 4, 1974–75.

***Most League Points (3 for a win):*** 79, Division 3, 1993–94.

***Most League Goals:*** 101, Division 4, 1958–59.

***Highest League Scorer in Season:*** Arthur Rowley, 38, Division 4, 1958–59.

***Most League Goals in Total Aggregate:*** Arthur Rowley, 152, 1958–65 (thus completing his League record of 434 goals).

***Most League Goals in One Match:*** 5, Alf Wood v Blackburn R, Division 3, 2 October 1971.

***Most Capped Player:*** Jimmy McLaughlin, 5 (12), Northern Ireland; Bernard McNally, 5, Northern Ireland.

***Most League Appearances:*** Mickey Brown, 418, 1986–91; 1992–94; 1996–2001.

***Youngest League Player:*** Graham French, 16 years 177 days v Reading, 30 September 1961.

***Record Transfer Fee Received:*** £500,000 from Crewe Alex for Dave Walton, October 1997.

***Record Transfer Fee Paid:*** £100,000 to Aldershot for John Dungworth, November 1979 and £100,000 to Southampton for Mark Blake, August 1990.

***Football League Record:*** 1950 Elected to Division 3 (N); 1951–58 Division 3 (S); 1958–59 Division 4; 1959–74 Division 3; 1974–75 Division 4; 1975–79 Division 3; 1979–89 Division 2; 1989–94 Division 3; 1994–97 Division 2; 1997–2003 Division 3; 2003–04 Conference; 2004– FL2.

## MANAGERS

W. Adams 1905–12
*(Secretary-Manager)*
A. Weston 1912–34
*(Secretary-Manager)*
Jack Roscamp 1934–35
Sam Ramsey 1935–36
Ted Bousted 1936–40
Leslie Knighton 1945–49
Harry Chapman 1949–50
Sammy Crooks 1950–54
Walter Rowley 1955–57
Harry Potts 1957–58
Johnny Spuhler 1958
Arthur Rowley 1958–68
Harry Gregg 1968–72
Maurice Evans 1972–73
Alan Durban 1974–78
Richie Barker 1978
Graham Turner 1978–84
Chic Bates 1984–87
Ian McNeill 1987–90
Asa Hartford 1990–91
John Bond 1991–93
Fred Davies 1994–97
*(previously Caretaker-Manager 1993–94)*
Jake King 1997–99
Kevin Ratcliffe 1999–2003
Jimmy Quinn May 2003–

## LATEST SEQUENCES

***Longest Sequence of League Wins:*** 7, 28.10.1995 – 16.12.1995.

***Longest Sequence of League Defeats:*** 8, 9.4.2003 – 3.5.2003.

***Longest Sequence of League Draws:*** 6, 30.10.1963 – 14.12.1963.

***Longest Sequence of Unbeaten League Matches:*** 16, 30.10.1993 – 26.2.1994.

***Longest Sequence Without a League Win:*** 17, 25.1.1992 – 11.4.1992.

***Successive Scoring Runs:*** 28 from 7.9.1960.

***Successive Non-scoring Runs:*** 6 from 1.1.1991.

## TEN YEAR LEAGUE RECORD

| | | *P* | *W* | *D* | *L* | *F* | *A* | *Pts* | *Pos* |
|---|---|---|---|---|---|---|---|---|---|
| 1994-95 | Div 2 | 46 | 13 | 14 | 19 | 54 | 62 | 53 | 18 |
| 1995-96 | Div 2 | 46 | 13 | 14 | 19 | 58 | 70 | 53 | 18 |
| 1996-97 | Div 2 | 46 | 11 | 13 | 22 | 49 | 74 | 46 | 22 |
| 1997-98 | Div 3 | 46 | 16 | 13 | 17 | 61 | 62 | 61 | 13 |
| 1998-99 | Div 3 | 46 | 14 | 14 | 18 | 52 | 63 | 56 | 15 |
| 1999-2000 | Div 3 | 46 | 9 | 13 | 24 | 40 | 67 | 40 | 22 |
| 2000-01 | Div 3 | 46 | 15 | 10 | 21 | 49 | 65 | 55 | 15 |
| 2001-02 | Div 3 | 46 | 20 | 10 | 16 | 64 | 53 | 70 | 9 |
| 2002-03 | Div 3 | 46 | 9 | 14 | 23 | 62 | 92 | 41 | 24 |
| 2003-04 | Conf. | 42 | 20 | 14 | 8 | 67 | 42 | 74 | 3 |

## DID YOU KNOW ?

Midland League champions at the first time of asking in 1937–38 and Welsh Cup winners after a replay against Swansea Town, Shrewsbury Town had the oddest of initial results. The first seven were: 2-1, 0-1, 11-0, 0-0, 6-0, 0-1, 0-1!

# SOUTHAMPTON FA Premiership

## FOUNDATION

Formed largely by players from the Deanery FC, which had been established by school teachers in 1880. Most of the founders were connected with the young men's association of St Mary's Church. At the inaugural meeting held in November 1885 the club was named Southampton St Mary's and the church's curate was elected president.

***The Friends Provident St Mary's Stadium, Britannia Road, Southampton SO14 5FP.***

***Telephone:*** 0870 220 0000.

***Fax:*** (02380) 727 727.

***Ticket Office:*** 0870 777 1000.

***Website:*** www.saintsfc.co.uk

***Email:*** sfc@saintsfc.co.uk

***Ground Capacity:*** 32,689.

***Record Attendance:*** 32,104 v Liverpool, FA Premier League, 18 January 2003.

***Pitch Measurements:*** 112yd × 74yd.

***Chairman:*** Rupert Lowe.

***Vice-chairman:*** Brian Hunt.

***Managing Director:*** Andrew Cowen.

***Secretary:*** Liz Coley.

***Manager:*** Paul Sturrock.

***Assistant Managers:*** Steve Wigley and Dennis Rofe.

***Physio:*** Jim Joyce.

***Colours:*** Red and white striped shirts, black shorts, red and white stockings.

***Change Colours:*** Sky blue shirts, navy shorts, navy socks.

***Year Formed:*** 1885.

***Turned Professional:*** 1894.

***Ltd Co.:*** 1897.

***Previous Name:*** 1885, Southampton St Mary's; 1897, Southampton.

***Club Nickname:*** 'The Saints'.

***Previous Grounds:*** 1885, Antelope Ground; 1897, County Cricket Ground; 1898, The Dell; 2001, St Mary's.

***First Football League Game:*** 28 August 1920, Division 3, v Gillingham (a) D 1–1 – Allen; Parker, Titmuss; Shelley, Campbell, Turner; Barratt, Dominy (1), Rawlings, Moore, Foxall.

***Record League Victory:*** 9–3 v Wolverhampton W, Division 2, 18 September 1965 – Godfrey; Jones, Williams; Walker, Knapp, Huxford; Paine (2), O'Brien (1), Melia, Chivers (4), Sydenham (2).

## HONOURS

*Football League:* Division 1 – Runners-up 1983–84; Division 2 – Runners-up 1965–66, 1977–78; Division 3 (S) – Champions 1921–22; Runners-up 1920–21; Division 3 – Champions 1959–60.

*FA Cup:* Winners 1976; Runners-up 1900, 1902, 2003.

*Football League Cup:* Runners-up 1979.

*Zenith Data Systems Cup:* Runners-up 1992.

***European Competitions:*** *European Fairs Cup:* 1969–70. *UEFA Cup:* 1971–72, 1981–82, 1982–83, 1984–85, 2003–04. *European Cup-Winners' Cup:* 1976–77.

## SKY SPORTS FACT FILE

When Southampton achieved promotion for the first time in 1965–66, it was due to a revival in the second half of the season having dropped to seventh by December following a lively start. Only one defeat was suffered after the turn of the year.

***Record Cup Victory:*** 7–1 v Ipswich T, FA Cup 3rd rd, 7 January 1961 – Reynolds; Davies, Traynor; Conner, Page, Huxford; Paine (1), O'Brien (3 incl. 1p), Reeves, Mulgrew (2), Penk (1).

***Record Defeat:*** 0–8 v Tottenham H, Division 2, 28 March 1936. 0–8 v Everton, Division 1, 20 November 1971.

***Most League Points (2 for a win):*** 61, Division 3 (S), 1921–22 and Division 3, 1959–60.

***Most League Points (3 for a win):*** 77, Division 1, 1983–84.

***Most League Goals:*** 112, Division 3 (S), 1957–58.

***Highest League Scorer in Season:*** Derek Reeves, 39, Division 3, 1959–60.

***Most League Goals in Total Aggregate:*** Mike Channon, 185, 1966–77, 1979–82.

***Most League Goals in One Match:*** 5, Charlie Wayman v Leicester C, Division 2, 23 October 1948.

***Most Capped Player:*** Peter Shilton, 49 (125), England.

***Most League Appearances:*** Terry Paine, 713, 1956–74.

***Youngest League Player:*** Danny Wallace, 16 years 313 days v Manchester U, 29 November 1980.

***Record Transfer Fee Received:*** £8,000,000 from Tottenham H for Dean Richards, October 2001.

***Record Transfer Fee Paid:*** £4,000,000 to Derby Co for Rory Delap, July 2001.

***Football League Record:*** 1920 Original Member of Division 3; 1921–22 Division 3 (S); 1922–53 Division 2; 1953–58 Division 3 (S); 1958–60 Division 3; 1960–66 Division 2; 1966–74 Division 1; 1974–78 Division 2; 1978–92 Division 1; 1992– FA Premier League.

## MANAGERS

Cecil Knight 1894–95
*(Secretary-Manager)*
Charles Robson 1895–97
E. Arnfield 1897–1911
*(Secretary-Manager)*
*(continued as Secretary)*
George Swift 1911–12
Ernest Arnfield 1912–19
Jimmy McIntyre 1919–24
Arthur Chadwick 1925–31
George Kay 1931–36
George Gross 1936–37
Tom Parker 1937–43
*J. R. Sarjantson stepped down from the board to act as Secretary-Manager 1943–47 with the next two listed being team Managers during this period*
Arthur Dominy 1943–46
Bill Dodgin Snr 1946–49
Sid Cann 1949–51
George Roughton 1952–55
Ted Bates 1955–73
Lawrie McMenemy 1973–85
Chris Nicholl 1985–91
Ian Branfoot 1991–94
Alan Ball 1994–95
Dave Merrington 1995–96
Graeme Souness 1996–97
Dave Jones 1997–2000
Glenn Hoddle 2000–01
Stuart Gray 2001
Gordon Strachan 2001–04
Paul Sturrock March 2004–

## LATEST SEQUENCES

***Longest Sequence of League Wins:*** 6, 3.3.1992 – 4.4.1992.

***Longest Sequence of League Defeats:*** 5, 16.8.1998 – 12.9.1998.

***Longest Sequence of League Draws:*** 7, 28.12.1994 – 11.2.1995.

***Longest Sequence of Unbeaten League Matches:*** 19, 5.9.1921 – 31.12.1921.

***Longest Sequence Without a League Win:*** 20, 30.8.1969 – 27.12.1969.

***Successive Scoring Runs:*** 24 from 5.9.1966.

***Successive Non-scoring Runs:*** 5 from 1.9.1937.

## TEN YEAR LEAGUE RECORD

| | | *P* | *W* | *D* | *L* | *F* | *A* | *Pts* | *Pos* |
|---|---|---|---|---|---|---|---|---|---|
| 1994-95 | PR Lge | 42 | 12 | 18 | 12 | 61 | 63 | 54 | 10 |
| 1995-96 | PR Lge | 38 | 9 | 11 | 18 | 34 | 52 | 38 | 17 |
| 1996-97 | PR Lge | 38 | 10 | 11 | 17 | 50 | 56 | 41 | 16 |
| 1997-98 | PR Lge | 38 | 14 | 6 | 18 | 50 | 55 | 48 | 12 |
| 1998-99 | PR Lge | 38 | 11 | 8 | 19 | 37 | 64 | 41 | 17 |
| 1999-2000 | PR Lge | 38 | 12 | 8 | 18 | 45 | 62 | 44 | 15 |
| 2000-01 | PR Lge | 38 | 14 | 10 | 14 | 40 | 48 | 52 | 10 |
| 2001-02 | PR Lge | 38 | 12 | 9 | 17 | 46 | 54 | 45 | 11 |
| 2002-03 | PR Lge | 38 | 13 | 13 | 12 | 43 | 46 | 52 | 8 |
| 2003-04 | PR Lge | 38 | 12 | 11 | 15 | 44 | 45 | 47 | 12 |

## DID YOU KNOW ?

Southampton had the distinction of knocking-out FA Cup holders Tottenham Hotspur after a three match marathon FA Cup tie in 1901–02. Following a 1-1 draw at White Hart Lane and 2-2 at The Dell after extra time, Saints won 2-1 at Elm Park.

## SOUTHAMPTON 2003–04 LEAGUE RECORD

| Match No. | Date | Venue | Opponents | Result | | H/T Score | Lg. Pos. | Goalscorers | Attendance |
|---|---|---|---|---|---|---|---|---|---|
| 1 | Aug 16 | A | Leicester C | D | 2-2 | 0-2 | — | Phillips [76], Beattie [80] | 31,621 |
| 2 | 23 | H | Birmingham C | D | 0-0 | 0-0 | 12 | | 31,656 |
| 3 | 26 | A | Leeds U | D | 0-0 | 0-0 | — | | 34,721 |
| 4 | 31 | H | Manchester U | W | 1-0 | 0-0 | 8 | Beattie [88] | 32,066 |
| 5 | Sept 13 | H | Wolverhampton W | W | 2-0 | 1-0 | 6 | Beattie 2 (1 pen) [37 (p), 52] | 31,711 |
| 6 | 20 | A | Tottenham H | W | 3-1 | 2-0 | 4 | Beattie 2 [3, 43], Gardner (og) [60] | 35,758 |
| 7 | 27 | H | Middlesbrough | L | 0-1 | 0-1 | 6 | | 30,772 |
| 8 | Oct 4 | A | Newcastle U | L | 0-1 | 0-1 | 7 | | 52,127 |
| 9 | 19 | A | Everton | D | 0-0 | 0-0 | 7 | | 35,775 |
| 10 | 25 | H | Blackburn R | W | 2-0 | 0-0 | 6 | Beattie [59], Griffit [87] | 31,620 |
| 11 | Nov 1 | H | Manchester C | L | 0-2 | 0-1 | 9 | | 31,952 |
| 12 | 8 | A | Bolton W | D | 0-0 | 0-0 | 9 | | 25,619 |
| 13 | 22 | H | Chelsea | L | 0-1 | 0-0 | 10 | | 32,149 |
| 14 | 29 | A | Aston Villa | L | 0-1 | 0-1 | 12 | | 31,285 |
| 15 | Dec 7 | H | Charlton Ath | W | 3-2 | 2-0 | 8 | Svensson M [6], Ormerod 2 [45, 86] | 30,513 |
| 16 | 13 | A | Liverpool | W | 2-1 | 1-0 | 6 | Ormerod [2], Svensson M [64] | 41,762 |
| 17 | 21 | H | Portsmouth | W | 3-0 | 1-0 | 4 | Schemmel (og) [34], Pahars [67], Beattie [90] | 31,697 |
| 18 | 26 | A | Fulham | L | 0-2 | 0-1 | 7 | | 15,640 |
| 19 | 29 | H | Arsenal | L | 0-1 | 0-1 | — | | 32,151 |
| 20 | Jan 7 | H | Leicester C | D | 0-0 | 0-0 | — | | 31,053 |
| 21 | 10 | A | Birmingham C | L | 1-2 | 1-1 | 9 | Ormerod [6] | 29,071 |
| 22 | 17 | H | Leeds U | W | 2-1 | 2-0 | 8 | Ormerod [36], Phillips [43] | 31,976 |
| 23 | 31 | A | Manchester U | L | 2-3 | 1-2 | 10 | Phillips 2 [38, 53] | 67,758 |
| 24 | Feb 7 | H | Fulham | D | 0-0 | 0-0 | 11 | | 31,820 |
| 25 | 10 | A | Arsenal | L | 0-2 | 0-1 | — | | 38,007 |
| 26 | 21 | H | Everton | D | 3-3 | 0-2 | 12 | Phillips [58], Beattie (pen) [82], Fernandes [90] | 31,875 |
| 27 | 28 | A | Blackburn R | D | 1-1 | 1-0 | 12 | Phillips [5] | 21,970 |
| 28 | Mar 14 | H | Liverpool | W | 2-0 | 0-0 | 11 | Beattie [51], Phillips [85] | 32,056 |
| 29 | 21 | A | Portsmouth | L | 0-1 | 0-0 | 12 | | 20,140 |
| 30 | 27 | H | Tottenham H | W | 1-0 | 0-0 | 10 | Delap [64] | 31,973 |
| 31 | Apr 3 | A | Wolverhampton W | W | 4-1 | 1-0 | 9 | Beattie [25], Lundekvam [58], Phillips 2 [89, 90] | 29,106 |
| 32 | 12 | A | Middlesbrough | L | 1-3 | 0-2 | 11 | Beattie [70] | 30,768 |
| 33 | 17 | A | Manchester C | W | 3-1 | 1-0 | 9 | Beattie [34], Phillips 2 [55, 81] | 47,152 |
| 34 | 24 | H | Bolton W | L | 1-2 | 1-0 | 11 | Pahars [21] | 31,712 |
| 35 | May 1 | A | Chelsea | L | 0-4 | 0-0 | 11 | | 41,321 |
| 36 | 8 | H | Aston Villa | D | 1-1 | 1-1 | 12 | Phillips [45] | 32,054 |
| 37 | 12 | H | Newcastle U | D | 3-3 | 2-2 | — | Beattie [19], Bramble (og) [39], Griffit [88] | 31,815 |
| 38 | 15 | A | Charlton Ath | L | 1-2 | 0-1 | 12 | Prutton [64] | 26,598 |

**Final League Position: 12**

### GOALSCORERS

*League (44):* Beattie 14 (2 pens), Phillips 12, Ormerod 5, Griffit 2, Pahars 2, Svensson M 2, Delap 1, Fernandes 1, Lundekvam 1, Prutton 1, own goals 3.
*Carling Cup (5):* Beattie 3 (1 pen), Le Saux 1, Ormerod 1.
*FA Cup (0).*
*UEFA Cup (1):* Phillips 1.

| Jones P 8 | Dodd J 27 + 1 | Le Saux G 19 | Delap R 26 + 1 | Lundekvam C 31 | Svensson M 26 | Telfer P 33 + 4 | Oakley M 7 | Beattie J 32 + 5 | Svensson A 17 + 13 | McCann N 9 + 9 | Higginbotham D 24 + 3 | Fernandes F 21 + 6 | Phillips K 28 + 6 | Tessem J 1 + 2 | Prutton D 22 + 5 | Ormerod B 14 + 8 | Marsden C 9 + 4 | Niemi A 28 | Griffit L 2 + 3 | Delgado A — + 4 | Pahars M 6 + 8 | Baird C 1 + 3 | Hall F 7 + 4 | Kenton D 3 + 4 | Crainey S 5 | Folly Y 9 | Cranie M 1 | Blayney A 2 | *Match No.* |
|---|---|---|---|---|---|---|---|---|---|---|---|---|---|---|---|---|---|---|---|---|---|---|---|---|---|---|---|---|---|
| 1 | 2 | 3 | 4 | 5[1] | 6 | 7[2] | 8 | 9 | 10[3] | 11 | 12 | 13 | 14 | | | | | | | | | | | | | | | | 1 |
| 1 | 2 | 3 | 4[2] | 5 | 6 | 12 | 8 | 9 | 13 | 11[3] | | 7[1] | 10 | 14 | | | | | | | | | | | | | | | 2 |
| 1 | 2 | 3 | 4[1] | 5 | 6 | 12 | 8 | 9 | | 13 | | 7 | 10[3] | | 11[2] | 14 | | | | | | | | | | | | | 3 |
| 1 | 2 | 3 | | 5 | 6 | 4 | 8 | 9 | 12 | 11[3] | | 7[1] | 10[2] | | | 13 | 14 | | | | | | | | | | | | 4 |
| 1 | 2 | 3 | | 5 | 6 | 4 | 8 | 9 | 12 | 13 | | 7[1] | 10 | | | | 11[2] | | | | | | | | | | | | 5 |
| 1 | 2 | 3 | | 5 | 6 | 4 | 8 | 9 | 12 | | | 7[1] | 10 | | 13 | | 11[2] | | | | | | | | | | | | 6 |
| 1 | 2[1] | 3 | | 5 | 6 | 4 | 8 | 9 | 12 | 13 | | 7[3] | 10■ | | | 14 | 11[2] | | | | | | | | | | | | 7 |
| | 2[2] | | | 5 | 6 | 4 | | 9 | 12 | 11[1] | 3 | 7[3] | 10 | | 13 | 14 | 8 | 1 | | | | | | | | | | | 8 |
| | 2 | | 8 | 5 | 6 | 4 | | 9 | 11 | | 3 | 7[1] | | | 12 | 10 | | 1 | | | | | | | | | | | 9 |
| | 2 | 3 | 8 | 5 | 6 | 4 | | 9[1] | 7 | 11 | | | | 10[2] | | | 12 | 1 | 13 | | | | | | | | | | 10 |
| 1 | 2[1] | 3 | 4 | 5 | 6 | 12 | | 9 | 8 | 13 | | 7[2] | 10[3] | | | 14 | 11 | | | | | | | | | | | | 11 |
| | 2 | 3 | 4 | 5 | 6■ | 7 | | 9 | 8 | | 12 | | 10[1] | | | | 11 | 1 | | | | | | | | | | | 12 |
| | | 3 | 4 | 5 | | 2 | | | 12 | | 6 | 7 | 10 | | 13 | 9[3] | 8[1] | 1 | 11[2] | 14 | | | | | | | | | 13 |
| | 12 | | 4[1] | 5 | 6 | 2 | | 9 | 8[2] | 11[3] | 3 | | 10 | | 7 | | 13 | 1 | | | 14 | | | | | | | | 14 |
| | 2 | | 4 | 5 | 6 | 7 | | 9 | | | 3 | | 12 | | 11 | 10 | | 1 | | | 8[1] | | | | | | | | 15 |
| | 2 | | 4 | 5[2] | 6 | 7 | | 9[3] | | | 3 | 12 | | | 11 | 10 | 13 | 1 | | 14 | 8[1] | | | | | | | | 16 |
| | 2 | | | 5 | 6 | 7 | | 9 | | 12 | 3 | | 13 | | 11 | 10[2] | 4[3] | 1 | | | 8[1] | 14 | | | | | | | 17 |
| | 2 | | | 5 | 6 | 4 | | 9 | | 11[2] | 3 | | 12 | | 7 | 10[1] | 8 | 1 | | 13 | | | | | | | | | 18 |
| | | | 4 | | 6 | 7[1] | | 9 | | 12 | 3 | | 10 | | 11 | 13 | | 1 | 8[2] | | | 2[3] | 5 | 14 | | | | | 19 |
| | 2 | | 12 | 5[1] | 6 | 4 | | 9 | 8 | 13 | 3 | 7[2] | 10[3] | | 11 | | | 1 | | 14 | | | | | | | | | 20 |
| | 2 | | 4[3] | | 6 | | | 9 | 8 | 13 | 3 | 7[2] | 12 | | 11■ | 10[1] | | 1 | | | 14 | | 5 | | | | | | 21 |
| | 2 | | 4 | | 6 | 13 | | 12 | 8 | | 3 | 7[2] | 10[1] | | 11 | 9 | | 1 | | | | | 5[3] | 14 | | | | | 22 |
| | 2 | 3[3] | 4 | | | 7 | | 12 | 8 | | 6 | 11[1] | 10 | | | 9[2] | | 1 | | | 13 | | 5 | 14 | | | | | 23 |
| | 2 | 3 | 4 | | 6 | 7 | | 12 | 11 | | 5 | | 10 | | | 9[1] | | 1 | | | 8 | | | | | | | | 24 |
| | | 11[3] | 4 | | 6 | 7 | | 13 | 8[1] | | 5 | | 10 | | | 9 | | 1 | | | 14 | 12[2] | | 2 | 3 | | | | 25 |
| | 2 | 11 | 4 | 5[2] | 6 | 7[3] | | 12 | | | 3 | 13 | 10 | | 8 | 9[1] | | 1 | | | 14 | | | | | | | | 26 |
| | 2 | 3 | 4 | 5 | 6 | 8 | | 9 | | 12 | | 7[1] | 10[2] | | 11 | | | 1 | | | 13 | | | | | | | | 27 |
| | 2 | 3[1] | 4 | 5 | 6 | 7 | | 9 | 13 | 11[2] | 12 | | 10[3] | 14 | 8 | | | 1 | | | | | | | | | | | 28 |
| | 2 | | 4 | 5 | | 7 | | 9 | 8[2] | 11[3] | 6 | 12 | 10 | | 13 | | | 1 | | | 14 | | | | 3[1] | | | | 29 |
| | 3 | | 4 | 5 | | 2 | | 9 | 12 | | 6 | 7[1] | 10[2] | | 11 | 13 | | 1 | | | | | | | | 8 | | | 30 |
| | 3[2] | | 4 | 5 | | 2 | | 9 | 12 | | 6 | 7[1] | 10 | | 11 | | | 1 | | | | | 13 | | | 8 | | | 31 |
| | | | 4[1] | 5 | | 2 | | 9 | 12 | | 6 | 7[2] | 10 | | 11 | | | 1 | | | 13 | | | | 3 | 8 | | | 32 |
| | | 3 | 4 | 5 | | 2 | | 9[2] | 12 | | 6 | | 10 | | 11 | | | 1 | | | 8[1] | | 13 | | | 7 | | | 33 |
| | | 3[3] | 4[2] | 5 | | 2 | | 9 | 13 | | 6 | 12 | 10 | | 11 | | | 1 | | | 7[1] | | 14 | | | 8 | | | 34 |
| | | | | 5 | | 2 | | 9 | 11[2] | | 6 | 12 | 10 | | 7 | 13 | | 1 | | | | | 14 | 4[3] | | 8 | 3[1] | | 35 |
| | | | | 5 | | 2 | | 9 | 8 | | 3 | 7 | 10 | | 11 | | | 1 | | | | | 6 | | | 4 | | | 36 |
| | | | | 5[3] | | 2 | | 9 | 8 | | | 7[2] | 12 | | 11 | 10[1] | | | 13 | | | | 6 | 14 | 3 | 4 | | 1 | 37 |
| | | | | | | 2 | | 9 | 8[2] | | | 7[1] | | | 11 | 10 | | | 12 | | | 13 | 6 | 5 | 3 | 4 | | 1 | 38 |

**Carling Cup**

| | | | |
|---|---|---|---|
| Third Round | Bristol C | (a) | 3-0 |
| Fourth Round | Portsmouth | (h) | 2-0 |
| Fifth Round | Bolton W | (a) | 0-1 |

**FA Cup**

| | | | |
|---|---|---|---|
| Third Round | Newcastle U | (h) | 0-3 |

**UEFA Cup**

| | | | |
|---|---|---|---|
| First Round | Steaua | (h) | 1-1 |
| | | (a) | 0-1 |

# SOUTHEND UNITED FL Championship 2

## FOUNDATION

The leading club in Southend around the turn of the century was Southend Athletic, but they were an amateur concern. Southend United was a more ambitious professional club when they were founded in 1906, employing Bob Jack as secretary-manager and immediately joining the Second Division of the Southern League.

***Roots Hall, Victoria Avenue, Southend-on-Sea, Essex SS2 6NQ.***

***Telephone:*** 0870 174 2000.

***Fax:*** (01702) 304 124.

***Ticket Office:*** 0870 174 2002.

***Website:*** www.southendunited.co.uk

***Email:*** info@southend-united.co.uk

***Ground Capacity:*** 12,268.

***Record Attendance:*** 31,090 v Liverpool, FA Cup 3rd rd, 10 January 1979.

***Pitch Measurements:*** 110yd × 74yd.

***Vice-chairman:*** Geoffrey King.

***Secretary:*** Helen Giles.

***Manager:*** Steve Tilson.

***Head Coach:*** Paul Brush.

***Physio:*** John Stannard.

***Club Nickname:*** 'The Blues' or 'The Shrimpers'.

***Colours:*** All navy with white trim.

***Change Colours:*** All white with black trim.

***Year Formed:*** 1906.

***Turned Professional:*** 1906.

***Ltd Co.:*** 1919.

***Previous Grounds:*** 1906, Roots Hall, Prittlewell; 1920, Kursaal; 1934, Southend Stadium; 1955, Roots Hall Football Ground.

***First Football League Game:*** 28 August 1920, Division 3, v Brighton & HA (a) W 2–0 – Capper; Reid, Newton; Wileman, Henderson, Martin; Nicholls, Nuttall, Fairclough (2), Myers, Dorsett.

***Record League Victory:*** 9–2 v Newport Co, Division 3 (S), 5 September 1936 – McKenzie; Nelson, Everest (1); Deacon, Turner, Carr; Bolan, Lane (1), Goddard (4), Dickinson (2), Oswald (1).

***Record Cup Victory:*** 10–1 v Golders Green, FA Cup 1st rd, 24 November 1934 – Moore; Morfitt, Kelly; Mackay, Joe Wilson, Carr (1); Lane (1), Johnson (5), Cheesmuir (2), Deacon (1), Oswald. 10–1 v Brentwood, FA Cup 2nd rd, 7 December 1968 – Roberts; Bentley, Birks; McMillan (1) Beesley, Kurila; Clayton, Chisnall, Moore (4), Best (5), Hamilton. 10–1 v Aldershot, Leyland Daf Cup Prel rd, 6 November 1990 – Sansome; Austin, Powell, Cornwell, Prior (1), Tilson (3), Cawley, Butler, Ansah (1), Benjamin (1), Angell (4).

## HONOURS

*Football League:* Division 1 best season: 13th, 1994–95. Division 3 – Runners-up 1990–91; Division 4 – Champions 1980–81; Runners-up 1971–72, 1977–78.

*FA Cup:* best season: old 3rd rd, 1921; 5th rd, 1926, 1952, 1976, 1993.

*Football League Cup:* never past 3rd rd.

*LDV Vans Trophy:* Runners-up 2004.

## SKY SPORTS FACT FILE

In 1931–32 Southend United finished a creditable third behind Fulham and Reading. They did particularly well against the Craven Cottage team drawing 1-1 away and winning 4-1 at the Kursaal, the start of an unbeaten run to the season's end of 14 games.

***Record Defeat:*** 1–9 v Brighton & HA, Division 3, 27 November 1965.

***Most League Points (2 for a win):*** 67, Division 4, 1980–81.

***Most League Points (3 for a win):*** 85, Division 3, 1990–91.

***Most League Goals:*** 92, Division 3 (S), 1950–51.

***Highest League Scorer in Season:*** Jim Shankly, 31, 1928–29; Sammy McCrory, 1957–58, both in Division 3 (S).

***Most League Goals in Total Aggregate:*** Roy Hollis, 122, 1953–60.

***Most League Goals in One Match:*** 5, Jim Shankly v Merthyr T, Division 3S, 1 March 1930.

***Most Capped Player:*** George Mackenzie, 9, Eire.

***Most League Appearances:*** Sandy Anderson, 452, 1950–63.

***Youngest League Player:*** Phil O'Connor, 16 years 76 days v Lincoln C, 26 December 1969.

***Record Transfer Fee Received:*** £3,570,000 from Nottingham F for Stan Collymore, June 1993.

***Record Transfer Fee Paid:*** £750,000 to Crystal Palace for Stan Collymore, November 1992.

***Football League Record:*** 1920 Original Member of Division 3; 1921–58 Division 3 (S); 1958–66 Division 3; 1966–72 Division 4; 1972–76 Division 3; 1976–78 Division 4; 1978–80 Division 3; 1980–81 Division 4; 1981–84 Division 3; 1984–87 Division 4; 1987–89 Division 3; 1989–90 Division 4; 1990–91 Division 3; 1991–92 Division 2; 1992–97 Division 1; 1997–98 Division 2; 1998–2004 Division 3; 2004– FL2.

## MANAGERS

Bob Jack 1906–10
George Molyneux 1910–11
O. M. Howard 1911–12
Joe Bradshaw 1912–19
Ned Liddell 1919–20
Tom Mather 1920–21
Ted Birnie 1921–34
David Jack 1934–40
Harry Warren 1946–56
Eddie Perry 1956–60
Frank Broome 1960
Ted Fenton 1961–65
Alvan Williams 1965–67
Ernie Shepherd 1967–69
Geoff Hudson 1969–70
Arthur Rowley 1970–76
Dave Smith 1976–83
Peter Morris 1983–84
Bobby Moore 1984–86
Dave Webb 1986–87
Dick Bate 1987
Paul Clark 1987–88
Dave Webb *(General Manager)* 1988–92
Colin Murphy 1992–93
Barry Fry 1993
Peter Taylor 1993–95
Steve Thompson 1995
Ronnie Whelan 1995–97
Alvin Martin 1997–99
Alan Little 1999–2000
David Webb 2000–01
Rob Newman 2001–03
Steve Wignall 2003–04
Steve Tilson May 2004–

## LATEST SEQUENCES

***Longest Sequence of League Wins:*** 7, 27.4.1990 – 18.9.1990.

***Longest Sequence of League Defeats:*** 6, 29.8.1987 – 19.9.1987.

***Longest Sequence of League Draws:*** 6, 30.1.1982 – 19.2.1982.

***Longest Sequence of Unbeaten League Matches:*** 16, 20.2.1932 – 29.8.1932.

***Longest Sequence Without a League Win:*** 17, 31.12.1983 – 14.4.1984.

***Successive Scoring Runs:*** 24 from 23.3.1929.

***Successive Non-scoring Runs:*** 6 from 28.10.1933.

## TEN YEAR LEAGUE RECORD

| | | P | W | D | L | F | A | Pts | Pos |
|---|---|---|---|---|---|---|---|---|---|
| 1994-95 | Div 1 | 46 | 18 | 8 | 20 | 54 | 73 | 62 | 13 |
| 1995-96 | Div 1 | 46 | 15 | 14 | 17 | 52 | 61 | 59 | 14 |
| 1996-97 | Div 1 | 46 | 8 | 15 | 23 | 42 | 86 | 39 | 24 |
| 1997-98 | Div 2 | 46 | 11 | 10 | 25 | 47 | 79 | 43 | 24 |
| 1998-99 | Div 3 | 46 | 14 | 12 | 20 | 52 | 58 | 54 | 18 |
| 1999-2000 | Div 3 | 46 | 15 | 11 | 20 | 53 | 61 | 56 | 16 |
| 2000-01 | Div 3 | 46 | 15 | 18 | 13 | 55 | 53 | 63 | 11 |
| 2001-02 | Div 3 | 46 | 15 | 13 | 18 | 51 | 54 | 58 | 12 |
| 2002-03 | Div 3 | 46 | 17 | 3 | 26 | 47 | 59 | 54 | 17 |
| 2003-04 | Div 3 | 46 | 14 | 12 | 20 | 51 | 63 | 54 | 17 |

## DID YOU KNOW?

Moving from the Greyhound Stadium to Roots Hall in 1955, Southend United began with a 3-1 win over Norwich City watched by a crowd of 17,700, the average being 10,028. But for indifferent form late on a higher final position than fourth would have been possible.

## SOUTHEND UNITED 2003–04 LEAGUE RECORD

| Match No. | Date | Venue | Opponents | Result | H/T Score | Lg. Pos. | Goalscorers | Attendance |
|---|---|---|---|---|---|---|---|---|
| 1 | Aug 9 | H | Cheltenham T | W 2-0 | 1-0 | — | Gower 2 (1 pen) [33, 90 (p)] | 4403 |
| 2 | 16 | A | Doncaster R | L 0-2 | 0-1 | 12 | | 5592 |
| 3 | 23 | H | Mansfield T | L 0-3 | 0-1 | 16 | | 3837 |
| 4 | 26 | A | York C | L 0-2 | 0-1 | — | | 4202 |
| 5 | 30 | H | Bury | W 1-0 | 0-0 | 19 | Constantine [89] | 3172 |
| 6 | Sept 6 | A | Oxford U | L 0-2 | 0-1 | 21 | | 5567 |
| 7 | 13 | A | Hull C | L 2-3 | 1-1 | 22 | Constantine [3], Bramble [82] | 12,545 |
| 8 | 16 | H | Lincoln C | L 0-2 | 0-1 | — | | 2874 |
| 9 | 20 | H | Carlisle U | D 2-2 | 2-0 | 23 | McSweeney [22], Constantine [23] | 4620 |
| 10 | 27 | A | Scunthorpe U | D 1-1 | 0-1 | 22 | Constantine [69] | 3390 |
| 11 | 30 | A | Darlington | D 0-0 | 0-0 | — | | 4369 |
| 12 | Oct 4 | H | Huddersfield T | L 1-2 | 1-1 | 23 | Odunsi [43] | 4205 |
| 13 | 11 | A | Kidderminster H | W 2-1 | 1-1 | 22 | Warren [44], Bramble [90] | 2429 |
| 14 | 18 | H | Leyton Orient | L 1-2 | 0-1 | 23 | Constantine [90] | 6077 |
| 15 | 21 | H | Boston U | L 0-2 | 0-0 | — | | 2463 |
| 16 | 25 | A | Macclesfield T | W 2-1 | 0-0 | 22 | Constantine [51], Smith (pen) [59] | 1821 |
| 17 | Nov 1 | H | Northampton T | L 0-1 | 0-0 | 22 | | 5085 |
| 18 | 15 | A | Yeovil T | L 0-4 | 0-3 | 23 | | 5248 |
| 19 | 22 | H | Rochdale | W 4-0 | 2-0 | 21 | Bramble 2 [34, 36], Corbett (pen) [67], Constantine [90] | 3169 |
| 20 | 29 | A | Torquay U | L 0-3 | 0-1 | 22 | | 2631 |
| 21 | Dec 13 | A | Swansea C | W 3-2 | 2-1 | 22 | Constantine [17], Gower [45], Warren [90] | 5439 |
| 22 | 20 | H | Bristol R | L 0-1 | 0-1 | 22 | | 3771 |
| 23 | 26 | A | Cambridge U | W 1-0 | 1-0 | 22 | Constantine [38] | 5368 |
| 24 | 28 | H | Oxford U | L 0-1 | 0-0 | 22 | | 6449 |
| 25 | Jan 9 | A | Cheltenham T | D 1-1 | 0-0 | — | Broughton [70] | 4451 |
| 26 | 17 | H | Doncaster R | L 0-2 | 0-2 | 22 | | 4308 |
| 27 | 24 | A | Mansfield T | L 0-1 | 0-1 | 22 | | 4292 |
| 28 | 27 | H | York C | D 0-0 | 0-0 | — | | 2943 |
| 29 | Feb 7 | H | Cambridge U | W 1-0 | 1-0 | 22 | Dudfield [43] | 4289 |
| 30 | 14 | H | Kidderminster H | W 3-0 | 1-0 | 20 | Constantine 2 (2 pens) [6, 54], Hinton (og) [79] | 3716 |
| 31 | 21 | A | Leyton Orient | L 1-2 | 1-0 | 23 | Dudfield [45] | 6119 |
| 32 | 24 | A | Bury | D 1-1 | 1-0 | — | Constantine [27] | 1670 |
| 33 | 28 | H | Macclesfield T | W 1-0 | 0-0 | 19 | Dudfield [83] | 4107 |
| 34 | Mar 3 | A | Boston U | W 2-0 | 1-0 | — | Bentley [6], Jenkins [65] | 2780 |
| 35 | 6 | A | Bristol R | D 1-1 | 0-1 | 18 | Gower [81] | 5625 |
| 36 | 13 | H | Swansea C | D 1-1 | 0-0 | 19 | Dudfield [66] | 4753 |
| 37 | 16 | A | Lincoln C | D 2-2 | 2-0 | — | Constantine 2 [30, 36] | 3943 |
| 38 | 27 | A | Carlisle U | W 2-1 | 0-0 | 17 | Constantine 2 (1 pen) [50, 77 (p)] | 6173 |
| 39 | Apr 2 | H | Scunthorpe U | W 4-2 | 3-1 | — | Constantine 2 [26, 86], Broughton [28], Cort [40] | 4976 |
| 40 | 10 | A | Huddersfield T | L 0-1 | 0-1 | 14 | | 10,680 |
| 41 | 12 | H | Darlington | W 3-2 | 0-2 | 12 | Bentley [46], Constantine (pen) [73], Gower [85] | 5132 |
| 42 | 17 | A | Northampton T | D 2-2 | 2-1 | 13 | Constantine (pen) [16], Reid (og) [45] | 5919 |
| 43 | 20 | H | Hull C | D 2-2 | 2-1 | — | Gower [34], Maher [45] | 5389 |
| 44 | 24 | H | Yeovil T | L 0-2 | 0-2 | 14 | | 5676 |
| 45 | May 1 | A | Rochdale | D 1-1 | 0-0 | 14 | Constantine [48] | 3591 |
| 46 | 8 | H | Torquay U | L 1-2 | 1-2 | 17 | Dudfield [17] | 8894 |

**Final League Position: 17**

### GOALSCORERS

*League (51):* Constantine 21 (5 pens), Gower 6 (1 pen), Dudfield 5, Bramble 4, Bentley 2, Broughton 2, Warren 2, Corbett 1 (pen), Cort 1, Jenkins 1, Maher 1, McSweeney 1, Odunsi 1, Smith 1 (pen), own goals 2.
*Carling Cup (2):* Broughton 1, Maher 1.
*FA Cup (8):* Smith 3, Bramble 2, Gower 2, Corbett 1.
*LDV Vans Trophy (15):* Broughton 5, Constantine 4, Bramble 2, Clark 1, Corbett 1, Gower 1, Kightly 1.

| Emberson C 6 | Jupp D 39 + 1 | McSweeney D 16 + 5 | Maher K 42 | Cort L 46 | Warren M 27 + 5 | Gower M 40 | Odunsi L 12 | Broughton D 27 + 8 | Husbands M 3 + 6 | Corbett J 13 + 4 | Bramble T 16 + 18 | Nightingale L — + 4 | Stuart J 23 + 3 | Wilson C 11 + 3 | Constantine L 40 + 3 | Kightly M 2 + 9 | Robinson R 2 | Smith J 16 + 2 | Jenkins N 7 + 9 | Petterson A 1 | Flahavan D 37 | Fullarton J 7 | Hunt L 23 + 3 | Clark S 2 + 4 | Tilson S — + 1 | Bentley M 15 + 6 | Dudfield L 13 | Pettefer C 11 | Nicolau N 9 | Match No. |
|---|---|---|---|---|---|---|---|---|---|---|---|---|---|---|---|---|---|---|---|---|---|---|---|---|---|---|---|---|---|---|
| 1 | 2 | 3 | 4 | 5 | 6 | 7 | 8 | 9 | $10^{1}$ | 11 | 12 | | | | | | | | | | | | | | | | | | | 1 |
| 1 | 2 | $3^{1}$ | 4 | 5 | 6 | 7 | 8 | 9 | $10^{2}$ | 11 | 12 | 13 | | | | | | | | | | | | | | | | | | 2 |
| 1 | 2 | | 4 | 5 | 6 | 7 | $8^{2}$ | 9 | $10^{3}$ | $11^{1}$ | | 12 | 3 | 13 | 14 | | | | | | | | | | | | | | | 3 |
| 1 | 2 | 4 | 11 | 5 | 6 | $7^{2}$ | 8 | 9 | | 12 | | | $3^{1}$ | | 10 | 13 | | | | | | | | | | | | | | 4 |
| 1 | 2 | 3 | 4 | 5 | 6 | 7 | 8 | $9^{1}$ | | 11 | | 12 | | | 10 | | | | | | | | | | | | | | | 5 |
| 1 | 2 | 3 | 4 | 5 | 6 | 7 | 8 | 9 | | 11 | | 12 | | | $10^{1}$ | | | | | | | | | | | | | | | 6 |
| | $2^{2}$ | 3■ | 4 | 5 | 6 | 7 | 8 | 9 | | $11^{3}$ | 12 | | 13 | | $10^{1}$ | | 1 | 14 | | | | | | | | | | | | 7 |
| | $2^{3}$ | 3 | 4 | 5 | 6 | 11 | 8 | $9^{2}$ | | 12 | 10 | | | | 13 | | 1 | $7^{1}$ | 14 | | | | | | | | | | | 8 |
| | $2^{2}$ | 3 | 4 | 5 | 6 | 7 | 8 | 12 | | 11 | $9^{1}$ | | 13 | | 10 | | | | | 1 | | | | | | | | | | 9 |
| | 2 | | 4 | 5 | $6^{2}$ | 7 | 8 | | | $11^{1}$ | 12 | | 3 | | 9 | | | | 13 | | 1 | 10 | | | | | | | | 10 |
| | 2 | | 4 | 5 | 6 | 7 | 8 | $9^{1}$ | | | 12 | | 3 | | 10 | | | | | | 1 | 11 | | | | | | | | 11 |
| | 2 | | 4 | 5 | 6 | 11 | $8^{2}$ | $9^{1}$ | | | 12 | | 3 | | 10 | | | 13 | | | 1 | 7 | | | | | | | | 12 |
| | 2 | 12 | 4 | 5 | $6^{1}$ | 11 | | $9^{2}$ | | | 13 | | 3 | | 10 | | | 8 | | | 1 | 7 | | | | | | | | 13 |
| | 2 | 12 | 4 | 5 | $6^{1}$ | 11 | | 13 | | | $9^{2}$ | | 3 | | 10 | 14 | | $8^{3}$ | | | 1 | 7 | | | | | | | | 14 |
| | 2 | $6^{2}$ | 4 | 5 | | 11 | | $9^{1}$ | 13 | | 12 | | 3 | | 10 | 14 | | $8^{3}$ | | | 1 | 7 | | | | | | | | 15 |
| | 2 | 6 | 4 | 5 | | 7 | | 12 | | 13 | $9^{2}$ | | 3 | | $10^{1}$ | | | 8 | 11 | | 1 | | | | | | | | | 16 |
| | $2^{1}$ | 12 | 4■ | 5 | | 7 | | | 13 | 11 | 9 | | | | $10^{2}$ | | | 8 | 3 | | 1 | | 6 | | | | | | | 17 |
| | 12 | 2 | | 5 | 13 | 7 | | $9^{3}$ | 14 | $8^{1}$ | 10 | | | $11^{2}$ | | | | 4 | 3■ | | 1 | | 6 | | | | | | | 18 |
| | | 2 | 4 | 5 | | $7^{1}$ | | 12 | | 10 | $9^{2}$ | | 3 | | 13 | | | 8 | 11 | | 1 | | 6 | | | | | | | 19 |
| | | 2 | 4 | 5 | | $11^{2}$ | | $9^{1}$ | 12 | | 10 | | | 3 | $7^{3}$ | 14 | | 8 | | | 1 | | 6 | 13 | | | | | | 20 |
| | | 2■ | 4 | 5 | 13 | 11■ | | 12 | | | $9^{1}$ | | | 3 | $10^{2}$ | $7^{3}$ | | 8■ | 14 | | 1 | | 6 | | | | | | | 21 |
| | | $2^{3}$ | 4 | 5 | 12 | 11 | | 13 | 14 | | 9 | | | 3 | 10 | $7^{2}$ | | 8 | | | 1 | | $6^{1}$ | | | | | | | 22 |
| | | 2 | 4 | 5 | | 7 | | | | | 9 | | 12 | 11 | 10 | | | 8 | $3^{1}$ | | 1 | | 6 | | | | | | | 23 |
| | 2 | | 4 | 5 | | | | 9■ | | | | | $3^{2}$ | $7^{1}$ | 10 | 12 | | | 11 | | 1 | 8 | 6 | | 13 | | | | | 24 |
| | 2 | | 4 | 5 | 12 | $7^{1}$ | | 9 | | | | | 3 | | 10 | 13 | | 8 | $11^{2}$ | | 1 | | 6 | | | | | | | 25 |
| | 2 | | | 5 | 4 | 11 | | | | | $9^{2}$ | | 3 | | 10 | 13 | | 8 | | | 1 | | $6^{1}$ | 12 | | 7 | | | | 26 |
| | 2 | | 4 | 5 | 6 | 11 | | 9 | | | | | $3^{1}$ | | 10 | 12 | | $8^{2}$ | | | 1 | | | 7 | | 13 | | | | 27 |
| | 2 | | 4 | 5 | $6^{1}$ | 11 | | 9 | | | | | 3 | 12 | 10 | 13 | | | | | 1 | | | $7^{2}$ | | 8 | | | | 28 |
| | 2 | | 4 | 5 | 6 | 11 | | $9^{1}$ | | | 12 | | 3 | | $7^{2}$ | | | $8^{3}$ | | | 1 | | | 13 | | 14 | 10 | | | 29 |
| | 2 | | 4 | 5 | 6 | 11 | | $9^{2}$ | | | 13 | | 3 | | $7^{3}$ | | | | | | 1 | | 12 | | | 14 | 10 | $8^{1}$ | | 30 |
| | | 13 | 4 | 5 | 6 | $11^{3}$ | | $9^{1}$ | | | 12 | | 3 | | 7 | | | | | | 1 | | $2^{2}$ | | | 14 | 10 | 8 | | 31 |
| | 2 | | 4 | 5 | 6 | $11^{1}$ | | | | | | | 3 | | 10 | | | | | | 1 | | 8 | | | 12 | 9 | 7 | | 32 |
| | 2 | | 4 | 5 | 6 | 11 | | | | | | | $3^{1}$ | 12 | 10 | | | | | | 1 | | $8^{2}$ | | | 13 | 9 | 7 | | 33 |
| | 2 | 13 | 4 | 5 | | $11^{3}$ | | | | | 12 | | | 3 | $10^{1}$ | | | | 14 | | 1 | | 6 | | | $8^{2}$ | 9 | 7 | | 34 |
| | 2 | | 4 | 5 | | 11 | | 13 | | | 12 | | | $3^{1}$ | 10 | | | | | | 1 | | 6 | | | 8 | 9 | $7^{2}$ | | 35 |
| | 2 | | 4 | 5 | | | | 9 | | | 12 | | | $3^{1}$ | 7 | | | | | | 1 | | 6 | | | 8 | 10 | 11 | | 36 |
| | 2 | | 4 | 5 | 12 | | | $9^{2}$ | | | 13 | | | 3 | 7 | | | | | | 1 | | 6 | | | 8 | $10^{1}$ | 11 | | 37 |
| | 2 | | 4 | 5 | 6 | $11^{1}$ | | 9 | | | | | | | 10 | | | | 12 | | 1 | | | | | 8 | | 7 | 3 | 38 |
| | 2 | | 4 | 5 | 6 | 11 | | $9^{1}$ | | | 12 | | | | 10 | | | | | | 1 | | 13 | | | $8^{2}$ | | 7 | 3 | 39 |
| | 2 | | | 5 | 6 | 11 | | 9 | | | 12 | | | | 10 | | | | | | 1 | | 4 | | | 8 | | $7^{1}$ | 3 | 40 |
| | 2 | | | 5 | 6 | 11 | | 9 | | | 10 | | | | 7 | | | | | | 1 | | 4 | | | 8 | | | 3 | 41 |
| | 2 | | 4 | 5 | | 11 | | | | | $9^{1}$ | | 3 | | 10 | | | | 12 | | 1 | | 7 | | | 8 | | | 6 | 42 |
| | 2 | | 4 | 5 | | 11 | | | | | | | 6 | | 10 | | | | 12 | | 1 | | 7 | | | 8 | $9^{1}$ | | 3 | 43 |
| | 2 | | 4 | 5 | | | | | | $11^{2}$ | 12 | | 6 | | 10 | | | | | | 1 | | $7^{1}$ | 13 | | 8 | 9 | | 3 | 44 |
| | 2 | | 4 | 5 | $6^{1}$ | | | | 13 | $11^{2}$ | 10 | | | | 7 | | | | 14 | | 1 | | 12 | | | 8 | $9^{3}$ | | 3 | 45 |
| | $2^{1}$ | | 4 | 5 | | | | 12 | | 14 | 10 | | | 11 | 7 | | | | 13 | | 1 | | 6 | | | $8^{3}$ | 9 | | $3^{2}$ | 46 |

**Carling Cup**

| | | | |
|---|---|---|---|
| First Round | Swindon T | (h) | 2-3 |

**FA Cup**

| | | | |
|---|---|---|---|
| First Round | Canvey Island | (h) | 1-1 |
| | | (a) | 3-2 |
| Second Round | Lincoln C | (h) | 3-0 |
| Third Round | Scarborough | (h) | 1-1 |
| | | (a) | 0-1 |

**LDV Vans Trophy**

| | | | |
|---|---|---|---|
| First Round | Bristol R | (h) | 2-1 |
| Second Round | Swansea C | (a) | 2-1 |
| Quarter-Final | Luton T | (h) | 3-0 |
| Semi-Final | QPR | (h) | 4-0 |
| Southern Final | Colchester U | (a) | 3-2 |
| | | (h) | 1-1 |
| Final | Blackpool | | 0-2 |
| *(at Millennium Stadium)* | | | |

# STOCKPORT COUNTY FL Championship 1

## FOUNDATION

Formed at a meeting held at Wellington Road South by members of Wycliffe Congregational Chapel in 1883, they called themselves Heaton Norris Rovers until changing to Stockport County in 1890, a year before joining the Football Combination.

***Edgeley Park, Hardcastle Road, Edgeley, Stockport, Cheshire SK3 9DD.***

***Telephone:*** (0161) 286 8888.

***Fax:*** (0161) 286 8900.

***Ticket Office:*** (0161) 286 8888.

***Website:*** www.stockportcounty.com

***Ground Capacity:*** 10,817.

***Record Attendance:*** 27,833 v Liverpool, FA Cup 5th rd, 11 February 1950.

***Pitch Measurements:*** 111yd × 72yd.

***Chairman:*** Mike Baker.

***Chief Executive:*** Niels De Vos.

***Secretary:*** Gary Glendenning.

***Manager:*** Sammy McIlroy.

***Assistant Manager:*** Mark Lillis.

***Physio:*** Rodger Wylde.

***Colours:*** All blue.

***Change Colours:*** All white.

***Year Formed:*** 1883.

***Turned Professional:*** 1891.

***Ltd Co.:*** 1908.

***Previous Names:*** 1883, Heaton Norris Rovers; 1888, Heaton Norris; 1890, Stockport County.

***Club Nicknames:*** 'County' or 'Hatters'.

***Previous Grounds:*** 1883 Heaton Norris Recreation Ground; 1884 Heaton Norris Wanderers Cricket Ground; 1885 Chorlton's Farm, Chorlton's Lane; 1886 Heaton Norris Cricket Ground; 1887 Wilkes' Field, Belmont Street; 1889 Nursery Inn, Green Lane; 1902 Edgeley Park.

***First Football League Game:*** 1 September 1900, Division 2, v Leicester Fosse (a) D 2–2 – Moores; Earp, Wainwright; Pickford, Limond, Harvey; Stansfield, Smith (1), Patterson, Foster, Betteley (1).

***Record League Victory:*** 13–0 v Halifax T, Division 3 (N), 6 January 1934 – McGann; Vincent (1p), Jenkinson; Robinson, Stevens, Len Jones; Foulkes (1), Hill (3), Lythgoe (2), Stevenson (2), Downes (4).

***Record Cup Victory:*** 5–0 v Lincoln C, FA Cup 1st rd, 11 November 1995 – Edwards; Connelly, Todd, Bennett, Flynn, Gannon (Dinning), Beaumont, Oliver, Ware, Eckhardt (3), Armstrong (1) (Mike), Chalk, (1 og).

## HONOURS

*Football League:* Division 1 best season: 8th, 1997–98; Division 2 – Runners-up 1996–97; Division 3 (N) – Champions 1921–22, 1936–37; Runners-up 1928–29, 1929-30, 1996–97; Division 4 – Champions 1966–67; Runners-up 1990–91.

*FA Cup:* best season: 5th rd, 1935, 1950, 2001.

*Football League Cup:* Semi-final 1997.

*Autoglass Trophy:* Runners-up 1992, 1993.

## SKY SPORTS FACT FILE

The 1929–30 season was unusual in Third Division (North) terms because though leaders Port Vale finished four points above Stockport County, there was then a gap of 13 before third place. Frank Newton was top County scorer with 36 League goals.

***Record Defeat:*** 1–8 v Chesterfield, Division 2, 19 April 1902.

***Most League Points (2 for a win):*** 64, Division 4, 1966–67.

***Most League Points (3 for a win):*** 85, Division 2, 1993–94.

***Most League Goals:*** 115, Division 3 (N), 1933–34.

***Highest League Scorer in Season:*** Alf Lythgoe, 46, Division 3 (N), 1933–34.

***Most League Goals in Total Aggregate:*** Jack Connor, 132, 1951–56.

***Most League Goals in One Match:*** 5, Joe Smith v Southport, Division 3N, 7 January 1928; 5, Joe Smith v Lincoln C, Division 3N, 15 September 1928; 5, Frank Newton v Nelson, Division 3N, 21 September 1929; 5, Alf Lythgoe v Southport, Division 3N, 25 August 1934; 5, Billy McNaughton v Mansfield T, Division 3N, 14 December 1935; 5, Jack Connor v Workington, Division 3N, 8 November 1952; 5, Jack Connor v Carlisle U, Division 3N, 7 April 1956.

***Most Capped Player:*** Jarkko Wiss, 9 (36), Finland.

***Most League Appearances:*** Andy Thorpe, 489, 1978–86, 1988–92.

***Youngest League Player:*** Jimmy Collier, 16 years 227 days v Bristol R, 8 April 1969.

***Record Transfer Fee Received:*** £1,600,000 from Middlesbrough for Alun Armstrong, February 1998.

***Record Transfer Fee Paid:*** £800,000 to Nottingham F for Ian Moore, July 1998.

***Football League Record:*** 1900 Elected to Division 2; 1904 Failed re-election; 1905–21 Division 2; 1921–22 Division 3 (N); 1922–26 Division 2; 1926–37 Division 3 (N); 1937–38 Division 2; 1938–58 Division 3 (N); 1958–59 Division 3; 1959–67 Division 4; 1967–70 Division 3; 1970–91 Division 4; 1991–92 Division 3; 1992–97 Division 2; 1997–2002 Division 1; 2002–04 Division 2; 2004– FL1.

## LATEST SEQUENCES

***Longest Sequence of League Wins:*** 8, 26.12.1927 – 28.1.1928.

***Longest Sequence of League Defeats:*** 10, 24.11.2001 – 13.01.2002

***Longest Sequence of League Draws:*** 7, 17.3.1989 – 14.4.1989.

***Longest Sequence of Unbeaten League Matches:*** 18, 28.1.1933 – 28.8.1933.

***Longest Sequence Without a League Win:*** 19, 28.12.1999 – 22.4.2000.

***Successive Scoring Runs:*** 24 from 8.9.1928.

***Successive Non-scoring Runs:*** 7 from 10.3.1923.

## MANAGERS

Fred Stewart 1894–1911
Harry Lewis 1911–14
David Ashworth 1914–19
Albert Williams 1919–24
Fred Scotchbrook 1924–26
Lincoln Hyde 1926–31
Andrew Wilson 1932–33
Fred Westgarth 1934–36
Bob Kelly 1936–38
George Hunt 1938–39
Bob Marshall 1939–49
Andy Beattie 1949–52
Dick Duckworth 1952–56
Billy Moir 1956–60
Reg Flewin 1960–63
Trevor Porteous 1963–65
Bert Trautmann *(General Manager)* 1965–66
Eddie Quigley *(Team Manager)* 1965–66
Jimmy Meadows 1966–69
Wally Galbraith 1969–70
Matt Woods 1970–71
Brian Doyle 1972–74
Jimmy Meadows 1974–75
Roy Chapman 1975–76
Eddie Quigley 1976–77
Alan Thompson 1977–78
Mike Summerbee 1978–79
Jimmy McGuigan 1979–82
Eric Webster 1982–85
Colin Murphy 1985
Les Chapman 1985–86
Jimmy Melia 1986
Colin Murphy 1986–87
Asa Hartford 1987–89
Danny Bergara 1989–95
Dave Jones 1995–97
Gary Megson 1997–99
Andy Kilner 1999–2001
Carlton Palmer 2001–03
Sammy McIlroy October 2003–

## TEN YEAR LEAGUE RECORD

| | | P | W | D | L | F | A | Pts | Pos |
|---|---|---|---|---|---|---|---|---|---|
| 1994-95 | Div 2 | 46 | 19 | 8 | 19 | 63 | 60 | 65 | 11 |
| 1995-96 | Div 2 | 46 | 19 | 13 | 14 | 61 | 47 | 70 | 9 |
| 1996-97 | Div 2 | 46 | 23 | 13 | 10 | 59 | 41 | 82 | 2 |
| 1997-98 | Div 1 | 46 | 19 | 8 | 19 | 71 | 69 | 65 | 8 |
| 1998-99 | Div 1 | 46 | 12 | 17 | 17 | 49 | 60 | 53 | 16 |
| 1999-2000 | Div 1 | 46 | 13 | 15 | 18 | 55 | 67 | 54 | 17 |
| 2000-01 | Div 1 | 46 | 11 | 18 | 17 | 58 | 65 | 51 | 19 |
| 2001-02 | Div 1 | 46 | 6 | 8 | 32 | 42 | 102 | 26 | 24 |
| 2002-03 | Div 2 | 46 | 15 | 10 | 21 | 65 | 70 | 55 | 14 |
| 2003-04 | Div 2 | 46 | 11 | 19 | 16 | 62 | 70 | 52 | 19 |

## DID YOU KNOW ?

Bob Murray held the Stockport County appearance record for nearly thirty years. A Scottish-born half-back he turned out 495 times in the League – 226 of them consecutively – and did not miss an FA Cup tie in 11 years from 1952 to 1963.

## STOCKPORT COUNTY 2003–04 LEAGUE RECORD

| Match No. | Date | Venue | Opponents | Result | | H/T Score | Lg. Pos. | Goalscorers | Attendance |
|---|---|---|---|---|---|---|---|---|---|
| 1 | Aug 9 | A | Wycombe W | L | 0-1 | 0-1 | — | | 4826 |
| 2 | 16 | H | Luton T | L | 1-2 | 0-1 | 21 | Jones R $^{72}$ | 4566 |
| 3 | 23 | A | Plymouth Arg | L | 1-3 | 1-3 | 22 | Beckett $^{43}$ | 7594 |
| 4 | 25 | H | Tranmere R | D | 1-1 | 0-1 | 22 | Beckett $^{90}$ | 4886 |
| 5 | 30 | A | Peterborough U | W | 2-1 | 1-0 | 22 | Beckett $^{38}$, Jones R $^{58}$ | 4395 |
| 6 | Sept 6 | H | Port Vale | D | 2-2 | 2-0 | 20 | Beckett $^{2}$, Ellison $^{40}$ | 5316 |
| 7 | 13 | A | Sheffield W | D | 2-2 | 0-2 | 20 | Wilbraham 2 $^{46, 74}$ | 22,535 |
| 8 | 16 | H | Hartlepool U | L | 1-2 | 1-1 | — | Wilbraham $^{43}$ | 4021 |
| 9 | 20 | H | Blackpool | L | 1-3 | 1-0 | 21 | Lambert $^{27}$ | 5420 |
| 10 | 27 | A | Rushden & D | D | 2-2 | 1-1 | 21 | Barlow 2 $^{6, 54}$ | 4048 |
| 11 | 30 | A | Oldham Ath | L | 0-2 | 0-1 | — | | 7015 |
| 12 | Oct 4 | H | Chesterfield | D | 0-0 | 0-0 | 22 | | 4764 |
| 13 | 11 | A | Swindon T | W | 2-1 | 0-1 | 20 | Barlow $^{51}$, Wilbraham $^{87}$ | 7060 |
| 14 | 18 | H | Notts Co | D | 2-2 | 0-0 | 21 | Wilbraham $^{47}$, Goodwin $^{89}$ | 4727 |
| 15 | 21 | H | Colchester U | L | 1-3 | 0-2 | — | Goodwin (pen) $^{58}$ | 3683 |
| 16 | 25 | A | Brighton & HA | W | 1-0 | 0-0 | 20 | Wilbraham $^{79}$ | 6171 |
| 17 | Nov 1 | H | QPR | L | 1-2 | 0-2 | 21 | Williams C $^{85}$ | 5461 |
| 18 | 15 | A | Grimsby T | D | 1-1 | 0-0 | 21 | Clare $^{67}$ | 4014 |
| 19 | 22 | H | Bournemouth | W | 3-2 | 2-0 | 21 | Wilbraham $^{3}$, Lambert (pen) $^{41}$, Barlow $^{81}$ | 4622 |
| 20 | 29 | A | Barnsley | D | 3-3 | 2-1 | 21 | Goodwin $^{33}$, Welsh $^{36}$, Lambert $^{80}$ | 9047 |
| 21 | Dec 13 | H | Brentford | D | 1-1 | 0-0 | 20 | Barlow $^{82}$ | 4081 |
| 22 | 20 | A | Bristol C | L | 0-1 | 0-0 | 21 | | 10,478 |
| 23 | 26 | H | Wrexham | L | 0-1 | 0-0 | 21 | | 6256 |
| 24 | 28 | A | Port Vale | D | 2-2 | 2-2 | 21 | Barlow $^{6}$, Lynch $^{29}$ | 6237 |
| 25 | Jan 10 | H | Wycombe W | W | 2-0 | 2-0 | 21 | Lambert (pen) $^{9}$, Lynch $^{43}$ | 4406 |
| 26 | 17 | A | Luton T | D | 2-2 | 1-1 | 21 | Lynch $^{18}$, McLachlan $^{72}$ | 5920 |
| 27 | 24 | H | Plymouth Arg | L | 0-2 | 0-1 | 21 | | 6608 |
| 28 | 27 | A | Tranmere R | L | 2-3 | 1-1 | — | Griffin $^{34}$, McLachlan $^{73}$ | 7137 |
| 29 | 31 | H | Peterborough U | D | 2-2 | 2-2 | 22 | Platt (og) $^{12}$, Lambert $^{26}$ | 4653 |
| 30 | Feb 7 | A | Wrexham | D | 0-0 | 0-0 | 22 | | 5046 |
| 31 | 14 | H | Swindon T | L | 2-4 | 1-3 | 22 | Robertson $^{21}$, Barlow $^{50}$ | 4833 |
| 32 | 21 | A | Notts Co | L | 1-4 | 0-2 | 22 | Byrne $^{58}$ | 5618 |
| 33 | 28 | H | Brighton & HA | D | 1-1 | 1-0 | 23 | McLachlan $^{41}$ | 5038 |
| 34 | Mar 2 | A | Colchester U | L | 1-2 | 0-0 | — | Lambert $^{46}$ | 2513 |
| 35 | 6 | H | Bristol C | W | 2-0 | 1-0 | 23 | Goodwin $^{11}$, Williams C $^{88}$ | 5050 |
| 36 | 13 | A | Brentford | W | 2-0 | 0-0 | 22 | Lambert (pen) $^{56}$, Williams C $^{85}$ | 6615 |
| 37 | 16 | A | Hartlepool U | D | 2-2 | 2-1 | — | Lambert (pen) $^{20}$, Daly $^{21}$ | 4674 |
| 38 | 20 | H | Sheffield W | W | 1-0 | 1-0 | 21 | Lambert $^{25}$ | 8011 |
| 39 | 27 | A | Blackpool | D | 1-1 | 0-0 | 22 | Wilbraham $^{74}$ | 7604 |
| 40 | Apr 3 | H | Rushden & D | W | 2-1 | 0-0 | 20 | Lambert 2 (1 pen) $^{68, 88 (p)}$ | 4717 |
| 41 | 10 | A | Chesterfield | W | 3-0 | 2-0 | 17 | Lambert $^{5}$, Daly $^{37}$, Jackman $^{53}$ | 5901 |
| 42 | 12 | H | Oldham Ath | D | 1-1 | 1-1 | 18 | Clare $^{33}$ | 8617 |
| 43 | 17 | A | QPR | D | 1-1 | 0-1 | 20 | Clare $^{58}$ | 15,162 |
| 44 | 24 | H | Grimsby T | W | 2-1 | 2-0 | 17 | Daly $^{4}$, Jackman $^{10}$ | 5924 |
| 45 | May 1 | A | Bournemouth | D | 0-0 | 0-0 | 17 | | 7541 |
| 46 | 8 | H | Barnsley | L | 2-3 | 0-2 | 19 | Morrison $^{58}$, Barlow $^{90}$ | 6581 |

**Final League Position: 19**

### GOALSCORERS

*League (62):* Lambert 12 (5 pens), Barlow 8, Wilbraham 8, Beckett 4, Goodwin 4 (1 pen), Clare 3, Daly 3, Lynch 3, McLachlan 3, Williams C 3, Jackman 2, Jones R 2, Byrne 1, Ellison 1, Griffin 1, Morrison 1, Robertson 1, Welsh 1, own goal 1.
*Carling Cup (1):* Barlow 1.
*FA Cup (1):* Goodwin 1 (pen).
*LDV Vans Trophy (7):* Barlow 3, Goodwin 1 (pen), Lambert 1, Morrison 1, Williams C 1.

| Colgan N 14 + 1 | Goodwin J 29 + 5 | Pemberton M 5 + 1 | McLachlan F 14 + 6 | Clare R 36 | Jones R 14 + 2 | Gibb A 23 + 3 | Lambert R 39 + 1 | Wilbraham A 32 + 9 | Beckett L 6 + 2 | Ellison K 10 + 4 | Barlow S 15 + 15 | Hardiker J 38 + 1 | Morrison O 11 + 11 | Collins W — + 2 | Daly J 19 + 6 | Welsh A 24 + 10 | Lescott A 12 + 2 | Challinor D 14 + 3 | Spencer J 15 | Smith S 3 + 3 | Williams C 4 + 12 | Heath M 8 | Jackman D 27 | Myhill B 2 | Lynch S 9 | Griffin D 15 | Robertson M 9 + 3 | Williams Anthony 15 | Cartwright L 14 + 1 | Walton D 7 | Byrne M 1 | Adams D 12 | Williams Ashley 10 | *Match No.* |
|---|---|---|---|---|---|---|---|---|---|---|---|---|---|---|---|---|---|---|---|---|---|---|---|---|---|---|---|---|---|---|---|---|---|---|
| 1 | 2 | 3 | 4 | 5 | 6 | 7[1] | 8 | 9 | 10 | 11 | 12 | | | | | | | | | | | | | | | | | | | | | | | 1 |
| 1 | 2 | | 4[1] | 5 | 6 | | 8 | 9[3] | | 11[2] | 10 | 3 | 7 | 12 | 13 | 14 | | | | | | | | | | | | | | | | | | 2 |
| 1 | 2 | | 4[1] | 5 | 6[3] | 7 | | 9[2] | 10 | 11 | | 3 | | 12 | 13 | | 8 | 14 | | | | | | | | | | | | | | | | 3 |
| 1 | 2 | | | 5 | 6 | 12 | | | 10■ | 11[1] | | 3 | 7[2] | | 9 | 13 | 8 | 4 | | | | | | | | | | | | | | | | 4 |
| 1 | 2 | | | 5 | 6 | 7[1] | | | 10 | 11[2] | | 3 | 12 | | 9 | 13 | 8 | 4 | | | | | | | | | | | | | | | | 5 |
| | 2■ | | | 5 | 6 | 7 | | 12 | 10[1] | 11[2] | | 3 | | | 9 | | 8 | 4 | 1 | 13 | | | | | | | | | | | | | | 6 |
| 1 | 12 | | | 5 | 6 | 13 | 8 | 14 | | 3[2] | | 2 | 11[1] | | 9[3] | | 7 | 4 | | | 10 | | | | | | | | | | | | | 7 |
| 1 | 3 | | | 5 | 11[3] | 2 | 8[2] | 9 | | | | 6 | | | 12 | 13 | 7 | 4 | | 14 | 10[1] | | | | | | | | | | | | | 8 |
| 1 | | | 11[1] | 5 | | 2 | 8[2] | 9 | | | | 6 | 12 | | 10 | 3 | 7 | 4 | | 13 | | | | | | | | | | | | | | 9 |
| 1 | | | 12 | | 6 | | 7 | 9[2] | | | 8 | 5 | 11[1] | | 13 | 3 | 4 | 10 | | 2 | | | | | | | | | | | | | | 10 |
| 1 | 14 | | 12 | | 6[3] | | 8 | 9 | | | 10 | 5 | 11 | | 13■ | 3[2] | 7[1] | 4 | | 2 | | | | | | | | | | | | | | 11 |
| 1 | 6 | | | | 5 | 12 | | 9 | | 13 | 10 | 2 | 7[2] | | | 11[1] | 8 | 4 | | 3 | | | | | | | | | | | | | | 12 |
| | 3 | 11 | | 5 | 6 | 7 | | 9 | | 8 | 10[1] | 2 | | | | | | 4 | 1 | | 12 | | | | | | | | | | | | | 13 |
| | 3 | | | 5 | 6[2] | 7 | 12 | 9 | | 11 | 10 | 2 | | | | 13 | 8[1] | 4 | 1 | | | | | | | | | | | | | | | 14 |
| 1 | 3 | 6 | | 5 | | 7[2] | 8 | 9 | | 11[1] | 10[3] | 2 | 13 | | | 12 | | 4 | | | 14 | | | | | | | | | | | | | 15 |
| | 4 | 3 | | 5 | | | 8 | 9 | | | 12 | 2 | 7 | | 10[1] | 11 | | | 1 | | | 6 | | | | | | | | | | | | 16 |
| | 4 | | | 6 | | | 8 | 9 | | | 10 | 2 | 7[1] | | | 11 | | | 1 | | 12 | 5 | 3 | | | | | | | | | | | 17 |
| 15 | 4 | | | 6 | | 7 | 8 | 9 | | | 12 | 2 | 13 | | 10[1] | 11[2] | | | 1[G] | | | 5 | 3 | | | | | | | | | | | 18 |
| | | 13 | | 6 | | 7 | 8 | 9 | | | 14 | 2 | | | | 11[1] | 4[2] | 12 | | | 10[3] | 5 | 3 | 1 | | | | | | | | | | 19 |
| | 4 | | | 6[1] | | 7 | 8 | 9 | | | | 2 | 14 | | | 11[3] | 13 | 12 | | | 10[2] | 5 | 3 | 1 | | | | | | | | | | 20 |
| 1 | 6 | | | | | 7[1] | 8 | 9 | | | 13 | 2 | 12 | | | 11 | | 4 | | | | 5 | 3 | | 10[2] | | | | | | | | | 21 |
| 1 | 4[1] | | | 6 | | 7 | 8 | 9[2] | | | 14 | 2 | | | 13 | 11 | 12 | | | | | 5 | 3 | | 10[3] | | | | | | | | | 22 |
| | | 7[1] | 4 | 6 | | 3 | 8 | 9[2] | | | 13 | 2 | 12 | | | 11[3] | | | 1 | | 14 | 5 | | | 10 | | | | | | | | | 23 |
| | | | 6 | 5 | | 2 | 8 | 12 | | 13 | 9[1] | 3 | 7[2] | | | 11 | | 4 | 1 | | | | | | 10 | | | | | | | | | 24 |
| | | | 6 | 5 | | 7 | 8 | 12 | | | 9[1] | 2 | | | | 11 | | | 1 | | | | 3 | | 10 | 4 | | | | | | | | 25 |
| | | | 6 | 5 | | 7[1] | 8 | 13 | | | 9 | 2 | 12 | | | 11 | | | 1 | | | | 3 | | 10[2] | 4 | | | | | | | | 26 |
| | | | 6 | 5[2] | | 7 | 8 | 14 | | | 12 | 2 | 13 | | | 9 | | | 1 | | | | 11 | | 10[3] | 3 | 4[1] | | | | | | | 27 |
| | 4 | | 7[1] | | | 11[2] | 8 | | | 13 | 12 | 2 | | | | 9 | | | | | | | 3 | | 10 | 6 | 5 | 1 | | | | | | 28 |
| | | | 6 | | | 11 | 8 | 13 | | | 12 | 2 | | | | 9[2] | | | | | | | 3 | | 10 | 4 | 5[1] | 1 | 7 | | | | | 29 |
| | 12 | | 6[1] | | | | 10 | 9 | | | | 2 | 13 | | | 11[2] | | | | | | | 3 | | | 4 | 8 | 1 | 7 | 5 | | | | 30 |
| | | | | | | 7 | 8 | 9 | | | 10[2] | 2 | 12 | | | 11[1] | | | | | 13 | | 3 | | | 4 | 6 | 1 | | 5 | | | | 31 |
| | | | 12 | | | 7 | 8 | 13 | | | 10[2] | 2[3] | | | | 11 | | | 1 | | | | 3 | | | 4 | 6[1] | | 14 | 5 | 9 | | | 32 |
| | | | 8[1] | 6 | | | 10 | | | | 12 | | | | 9 | 11 | | | | | | | 3 | | | 2 | 4 | 1 | 7 | 5 | | | | 33 |
| | 12 | | 8[2] | 6 | | | 10 | 13 | | 14 | | | | | 9 | 11[3] | | | | | | | 3 | | | 2 | 4[1] | 1 | 7 | 5 | | | | 34 |
| | 4 | | | 6 | | | 8 | 9 | | | 10[1] | | | | | | | | | | 12 | | 3 | | | 2 | | 1 | 7 | 5 | | 11 | | 35 |
| | 11[1] | | 12 | 6 | | | 8 | 9 | | | 10[3] | | | | | 13 | | | | | 14 | | 3[2] | | | 4 | | 1 | 7 | 5 | | 2 | | 36 |
| | 8 | | | 6 | 13 | | 11 | 9 | | | | | | | 10 | 12 | | | 1 | | | | 3[1] | | | 4 | | | 7[2] | | | 2 | 5 | 37 |
| | 8[1] | | 12 | 6 | | | 11 | 9 | | | 13 | | | | 10[2] | | | | | | | | 3 | | | 4 | | 1 | 7 | | | 2 | 5 | 38 |
| | 11 | | | 6 | | | 8 | 9 | | | | 12 | | | 10[3] | 13 | | | | | 14 | | 3[2] | | | 4[1] | | 1 | 7 | | | 2 | 5 | 39 |
| | 4 | | | 6 | | | 8 | 9[1] | | | 12 | 2 | | | 10 | 11[2] | | | | | 13 | | | | | | | 1 | 7 | | | 3 | 5 | 40 |
| | 4 | | | 6 | | | 8[2] | 9[1] | | | 12 | 2 | | | 10 | | | | | | 14 | | 11[3] | | | | 13 | 1 | 7 | | | 3 | 5 | 41 |
| | 4[2] | | | 6 | | | 8 | 9 | | | | 2 | | | 10 | 12 | | | | | | | 11[1] | | | | 13 | 1 | 7 | | | 3 | 5 | 42 |
| | 4[1] | | | 6 | | | 8 | 9 | | | | 2 | | | 10 | | | | | | | | 11 | | | | 12 | 1 | 7 | | | 3 | 5 | 43 |
| | 13 | | | 6 | | | 8 | 9 | 12 | | | 2 | | | 10[1] | | | | | | 14 | | 11 | | | | 4[2] | 1 | 7[3] | | | 3 | 5 | 44 |
| | 4 | | | 6[1] | 12 | | 8 | 9 | 13 | | | 2 | 7[3] | | 10[2] | | | | 1 | | 14 | | 11 | | | | | | | | | 3 | 5 | 45 |
| | 4[1] | | 13 | | 6 | | 8 | | 9[2] | | 12 | 2 | 7 | | 10 | | | | 1 | | | | 11 | | | | | | | | | 3 | 5 | 46 |

**Carling Cup**

| | | | |
|---|---|---|---|
| First Round | Lincoln C | (a) | 1-0 |
| Second Round | Everton | (a) | 0-3 |

**LDV Vans Trophy**

| | | | |
|---|---|---|---|
| First Round | Mansfield T | (a) | 2-1 |
| Second Round | Wrexham | (h) | 5-4 |
| Quarter-Final | Blackpool | (h) | 0-1 |

**FA Cup**

| | | | |
|---|---|---|---|
| First Round | Stevenage B | (a) | 1-2 |

# STOKE CITY FL Championship

## FOUNDATION

The date of the formation of this club has long been in doubt. The year 1863 was claimed, but more recent research by Wade Martin has uncovered nothing earlier than 1868, when a couple of Old Carthusians, who were apprentices at the local works of the old North Staffordshire Railway Company, met with some others from that works, to form Stoke Ramblers. It should also be noted that the old Stoke club went bankrupt in 1908 when a new club was formed.

***Britannia Stadium, Stanley Matthews Way, Stoke-on-Trent, Staffs ST4 4EG.***

***Telephone:*** (01782) 592 222.

***Fax:*** (01782) 592 221.

***Ticket Office:*** (01782) 592 204.

***Website:*** www.stokecityfc.com

***Email:*** info@stokecityfc.com

***Ground Capacity:*** 28,212.

***Record Attendance:*** 51,380 v Arsenal, Division 1, 29 March 1937.

***Pitch Measurements:*** 116yd × 70yd.

***Chairman:*** Gunnar Thor Gislason.

***Vice-chairman:*** Stefan Geir Thorisson.

***Chief Executive:*** Jonathan Fuller.

***Secretary:*** Diane Richardson.

***Manager:*** Tony Pulis.

***Assistant Manager:*** Lindsay Parsons.

***Physio:*** Dave Watson.

## HONOURS

*Football League:* Division 1 best season: 4th, 1935–36, 1946–47; Division 2 – Champions 1932–33, 1962–63, 1992–93; Runners-up 1921–22; Promoted 1978–79 (3rd), Promoted from Division 2 (play-offs) 2001–02; Division 3 (N) – Champions 1926–27.

*FA Cup:* Semi-finals 1899, 1971, 1972.

*Football League Cup:* Winners 1972.

*Autoglass Trophy:* Winners: 1992.

*Auto Windscreens Shield:* Winners: 2000.

***European Competitions:*** *UEFA Cup:* 1972–73, 1974–75.

***Colours:*** Red and white striped shirts, white shorts, white stockings.

***Change Colours:*** Silver shirts and shorts with blue side panels, blue stockings with silver stripe.

***Year Formed:*** 1863 *(*see Foundation*). ***Turned Professional:*** 1885. ***Ltd Co.:*** 1908.

***Previous Names:*** 1868, Stoke Ramblers; 1870, Stoke; 1925, Stoke City.

***Club Nickname:*** 'The Potters'.

***Previous Grounds:*** 1875, Sweeting's Field; 1878, Victoria Ground (previously known as the Athletic Club Ground); 1997, Britannia Stadium.

***First Football League Game:*** 8 September 1888, Football League, v WBA (h) L 0–2 – Rowley; Clare, Underwood; Ramsey, Shutt, Smith; Sayer, McSkimming, Staton, Edge, Tunnicliffe.

***Record League Victory:*** 10–3 v WBA, Division 1, 4 February 1937 – Doug Westland; Brigham, Harbot; Tutin, Turner (1p), Kirton; Matthews, Antonio (2), Freddie Steele (5), Jimmy Westland, Johnson (2).

## SKY SPORTS FACT FILE

An incidental fact about the record 10-3 League victory of Stoke City in 1937 is that two players made their debut, goalkeeper Doug Westland and full-back Jimmy Harbot whose outing proved to be his only one in Stoke's senior colours.

***Record Cup Victory:*** 7–1 v Burnley, FA Cup 2nd rd (replay), 20 February 1896 – Clawley; Clare, Eccles; Turner, Grewe, Robertson; Willie Maxwell, Dickson, A. Maxwell (3), Hyslop (4), Schofield.

***Record Defeat:*** 0–10 v Preston NE, Division 1, 14 September 1889.

***Most League Points (2 for a win):*** 63, Division 3 (N), 1926–27.

***Most League Points (3 for a win):*** 93, Division 2, 1992–93.

***Most League Goals:*** 92, Division 3 (N), 1926–27.

***Highest League Scorer in Season:*** Freddie Steele, 33, Division 1, 1936–37.

***Most League Goals in Total Aggregate:*** Freddie Steele, 142, 1934–49.

***Most League Goals in One Match:*** 7, Neville Coleman v Lincoln C, Division 2, 23 February 1957.

***Most Capped Player:*** Gordon Banks, 36 (73), England.

***Most League Appearances:*** Eric Skeels, 506, 1958–76.

***Youngest League Player:*** Peter Bullock, 16 years 163 days v Swansea C, 19 April 1958.

***Record Transfer Fee Received:*** £2,750,000 from QPR for Mike Sheron, July 1997.

***Record Transfer Fee Paid:*** £600,000 to Orgryte for Brynjar Gunnarsson, December 1999.

***Football League Record:*** 1888 Founder Member of Football League; 1890 Not re-elected; 1891 Re-elected; relegated in 1907, and after one year in Division 2, resigned for financial reasons; 1919 re-elected to Division 2; 1922–23 Division 1; 1923–26 Division 2; 1926–27 Division 3 (N); 1927–33 Division 2; 1933–53 Division 1; 1953–63 Division 2; 1963–77 Division 1; 1977–79 Division 2; 1979–85 Division 1; 1985–90 Division 2; 1990–92 Division 3; 1992–93 Division 2; 1993–98 Division 1; 1998–2002 Division 2; 2002–04 Division 1; 2004– FLC.

## MANAGERS

Tom Slaney 1874–83
*(Secretary-Manager)*
Walter Cox 1883–84
*(Secretary-Manager)*
Harry Lockett 1884–90
Joseph Bradshaw 1890–92
Arthur Reeves 1892–95
William Rowley 1895–97
H. D. Austerberry 1897–1908
A. J. Barker 1908–14
Peter Hodge 1914–15
Joe Schofield 1915–19
Arthur Shallcross 1919–23
John 'Jock' Rutherford 1923
Tom Mather 1923–35
Bob McGrory 1935–52
Frank Taylor 1952–60
Tony Waddington 1960–77
George Eastham 1977–78
Alan A'Court 1978
Alan Durban 1978–81
Richie Barker 1981–83
Bill Asprey 1984–85
Mick Mills 1985–89
Alan Ball 1989–91
Lou Macari 1991–93
Joe Jordan 1993–94
Lou Macari 1994–97
Chic Bates 1997–98
Chris Kamara 1998
Brian Little 1998–99
Gary Megson 1999
Gudjon Thordarson 1999–2002
Steve Cotterill 2002
Tony Pulis November 2002–

## LATEST SEQUENCES

***Longest Sequence of League Wins:*** 8, 30.3.1895 – 21.9.1895.

***Longest Sequence of League Defeats:*** 11, 6.4.1985 – 17.8.1985.

***Longest Sequence of League Draws:*** 5, 21.3.1987 – 11.4.1987.

***Longest Sequence of Unbeaten League Matches:*** 25, 5.9.1992 – 20.2.1993.

***Longest Sequence Without a League Win:*** 17, 22.4.1989 – 14.10.1989.

***Successive Scoring Runs:*** 21 from 24.12.1921.

***Successive Non-scoring Runs:*** 8 from 29.12.1984.

## TEN YEAR LEAGUE RECORD

| | | *P* | *W* | *D* | *L* | *F* | *A* | *Pts* | *Pos* |
|---|---|---|---|---|---|---|---|---|---|
| 1994-95 | Div 1 | 46 | 16 | 15 | 15 | 50 | 53 | 63 | 11 |
| 1995-96 | Div 1 | 46 | 20 | 13 | 13 | 60 | 49 | 73 | 4 |
| 1996-97 | Div 1 | 46 | 18 | 10 | 18 | 51 | 57 | 64 | 12 |
| 1997-98 | Div 1 | 46 | 11 | 13 | 22 | 44 | 74 | 46 | 23 |
| 1998-99 | Div 2 | 46 | 21 | 6 | 19 | 59 | 63 | 69 | 8 |
| 1999-2000 | Div 2 | 46 | 23 | 13 | 10 | 68 | 42 | 82 | 6 |
| 2000-01 | Div 2 | 46 | 21 | 14 | 11 | 74 | 49 | 77 | 5 |
| 2001-02 | Div 2 | 46 | 23 | 11 | 12 | 67 | 40 | 80 | 5 |
| 2002-03 | Div 1 | 46 | 12 | 14 | 20 | 45 | 69 | 50 | 21 |
| 2003-04 | Div 1 | 46 | 18 | 12 | 16 | 58 | 55 | 66 | 11 |

## DID YOU KNOW ?

Though their final position was fourth in 1946–47, Stoke City were only two points behind the champions Liverpool. It was also the season in which Stanley Matthews refused to play in the reserves at one point and left for Blackpool in April.

## STOKE CITY 2003–04 LEAGUE RECORD

| *Match No.* | *Date* | *Venue* | *Opponents* | *Result* | | *H/T Score* | *Lg. Pos.* | *Goalscorers* | *Attendance* |
|---|---|---|---|---|---|---|---|---|---|
| 1 | Aug 9 | A | Derby Co | W | 3-0 | 2-0 | — | Noel-Williams [15], Greenacre [20], Neal [90] | 21,517 |
| 2 | 16 | H | Wimbledon | W | 2-1 | 1-0 | 1 | Asaba (pen) [26], Thomas [90] | 12,550 |
| 3 | 23 | A | Walsall | D | 1-1 | 1-0 | 3 | Asaba [33] | 9033 |
| 4 | 26 | H | Millwall | D | 0-0 | 0-0 | — | | 13,087 |
| 5 | 30 | A | Preston NE | L | 0-1 | 0-1 | 10 | | 12,965 |
| 6 | Sept 6 | H | Burnley | L | 1-2 | 0-2 | 13 | Asaba [53] | 14,867 |
| 7 | 13 | A | Coventry C | L | 2-4 | 1-2 | 15 | Asaba [45], Thomas [78] | 13,982 |
| 8 | 16 | H | Sunderland | W | 3-1 | 0-0 | — | Noel-Williams [24], Russell 2 [37, 39] | 15,005 |
| 9 | 20 | H | Norwich C | D | 1-1 | 1-0 | 11 | Noel-Williams [36] | 10,672 |
| 10 | 27 | A | WBA | L | 0-1 | 0-0 | 14 | | 24,297 |
| 11 | 30 | A | Rotherham U | L | 0-3 | 0-1 | — | | 5450 |
| 12 | Oct 4 | H | Nottingham F | W | 2-1 | 2-0 | 13 | Thomas [6], Asaba [31] | 13,755 |
| 13 | 14 | A | Wigan Ath | L | 1-2 | 1-0 | — | Noel-Williams [40] | 7678 |
| 14 | 18 | A | Ipswich T | L | 0-1 | 0-1 | 17 | | 22,122 |
| 15 | 25 | H | Crewe Alex | D | 1-1 | 0-0 | 18 | Greenacre [90] | 17,569 |
| 16 | Nov 1 | H | Sheffield U | D | 2-2 | 2-0 | 19 | Noel-Williams [4], Akinbiyi [18] | 14,217 |
| 17 | 8 | A | Cardiff C | L | 1-3 | 0-1 | 19 | Commons [59] | 15,227 |
| 18 | 22 | H | Bradford C | W | 1-0 | 1-0 | 19 | Eustace [11] | 11,661 |
| 19 | 25 | H | Crystal Palace | L | 0-1 | 0-1 | — | | 10,277 |
| 20 | 29 | A | Gillingham | L | 1-3 | 0-2 | 21 | Eustace [77] | 7888 |
| 21 | Dec 6 | H | Cardiff C | L | 2-3 | 1-2 | 22 | Eustace [38], Akinbiyi [74] | 12,208 |
| 22 | 9 | A | West Ham U | W | 1-0 | 1-0 | — | Richardson [33] | 24,365 |
| 23 | 13 | H | Reading | W | 3-0 | 2-0 | 19 | Hoekstra 3 (1 pen) [18, 26, 87 (p)] | 11,212 |
| 24 | 20 | A | Watford | W | 3-1 | 1-1 | 16 | Taggart [15], Akinbiyi 2 [55, 72] | 13,732 |
| 25 | 26 | H | Preston NE | D | 1-1 | 0-0 | 16 | Eustace (pen) [90] | 20,126 |
| 26 | 28 | A | Burnley | W | 1-0 | 0-0 | 14 | Akinbiyi [52] | 12,812 |
| 27 | Jan 10 | H | Derby Co | W | 2-1 | 1-1 | 13 | Akinbiyi [29], Taggart [53] | 16,402 |
| 28 | 17 | A | Wimbledon | W | 1-0 | 0-0 | 12 | Noel-Williams [54] | 3623 |
| 29 | 31 | H | Walsall | W | 3-2 | 2-2 | 12 | Russell [8], Asaba 2 [37, 56] | 18,035 |
| 30 | Feb 7 | A | Millwall | D | 1-1 | 1-1 | 13 | Clarke [4] | 9034 |
| 31 | 14 | A | Crystal Palace | L | 3-6 | 2-4 | 13 | Eustace [6], Clarke [44], Asaba (pen) [83] | 16,715 |
| 32 | 21 | H | Wigan Ath | D | 1-1 | 1-0 | 13 | Akinbiyi [45] | 14,927 |
| 33 | Mar 2 | H | Ipswich T | W | 2-0 | 1-0 | — | Hoekstra (pen) [37], Akinbiyi [68] | 11,435 |
| 34 | 6 | H | Watford | W | 3-1 | 3-1 | 12 | Akinbiyi 2 [18, 43], Noel-Williams [20] | 13,108 |
| 35 | 13 | A | Reading | D | 0-0 | 0-0 | 13 | | 14,132 |
| 36 | 16 | A | Sunderland | D | 1-1 | 1-0 | — | Svard [13] | 24,510 |
| 37 | 23 | A | Crewe Alex | L | 0-2 | 0-1 | — | | 10,014 |
| 38 | 27 | A | Norwich C | L | 0-1 | 0-1 | 14 | | 23,565 |
| 39 | Apr 3 | H | Coventry C | W | 1-0 | 1-0 | 13 | Commons [41] | 12,855 |
| 40 | 10 | A | Nottingham F | D | 0-0 | 0-0 | 14 | | 28,758 |
| 41 | 12 | H | Rotherham U | L | 0-2 | 0-1 | 14 | | 11,978 |
| 42 | 17 | A | Sheffield U | W | 1-0 | 1-0 | 12 | Clarke [45] | 19,372 |
| 43 | 24 | H | West Ham U | L | 0-2 | 0-1 | 13 | | 18,227 |
| 44 | May 1 | A | Bradford C | W | 2-0 | 1-0 | 13 | Noel-Williams 2 [2, 46] | 10,147 |
| 45 | 4 | H | WBA | W | 4-1 | 1-0 | — | Russell [45], Commons 2 [62, 73], Noel-Williams [86] | 18,352 |
| 46 | 9 | H | Gillingham | D | 0-0 | 0-0 | 11 | | 19,240 |

**Final League Position: 11**

### GOALSCORERS

*League (58):* Akinbiyi 10, Noel-Williams 10, Asaba 8 (2 pens), Eustace 5 (1 pen), Commons 4, Hoekstra 4 (2 pens), Russell 4, Clarke 3, Thomas 3, Greenacre 2, Taggart 2, Neal 1, Richardson 1, Svard 1.
*Carling Cup (2):* Goodfellow 1, Iwelumo 1.
*FA Cup (1):* Eustace 1.

| De Goey E 37 | Thomas W 39 | Clarke C 41 + 1 | Andrews K 16 | Hall M 34 + 1 | Marteinsson P 3 | Russell D 46 | Noel-Williams G 40 + 2 | Asaba C 26 + 11 | Greenacre C 8 + 5 | Eustace J 26 | Iwelumo C 3 + 6 | Neal L 6 + 13 | Cutler N 9 + 4 | Goodfellow M — + 4 | Commons K 14 + 19 | Williams P 16 + 3 | Henry K 14 + 6 | Akinbiyi A 23 + 7 | Halls J 34 | Hill C 9 + 3 | Owen G 1 + 2 | Hoekstra P 20 + 4 | Richardson F 6 | Johnson R 3 + 4 | Taggart G 21 | Svard S 9 + 4 | Wilson B — + 2 | Wilkinson A 1 + 2 | Gunnarsson B 1 + 2 | Palmer J — + 3 | *Match No.* |
|---|---|---|---|---|---|---|---|---|---|---|---|---|---|---|---|---|---|---|---|---|---|---|---|---|---|---|---|---|---|---|---|
| $1^{G}$ | 2 | 3 | 4 | 5 | 6 | 7 | $8^{1}$ | 9 | $10^{2}$ | 11 | 12 | 13 | 15 | | | | | | | | | | | | | | | | | | 1 |
| | 2 | 3 | 4 | 5 | $6^{1}$ | 7 | 8 | 9 | $10^{2}$ | 11 | | | 1 | 12 | 13 | | | | | | | | | | | | | | | | 2 |
| 1 | 2 | 11 | 4 | 3 | $6^{1}$ | 7 | 10 | $9^{2}$ | | 8 | | | | | 12 | 5 | 13 | | | | | | | | | | | | | | 3 |
| 1 | 2 | 3 | 4 | 6 | | 7 | 8 | 9 | $10^{1}$ | 11 | | | | | 12 | 5 | | | | | | | | | | | | | | | 4 |
| 1 | 2 | 11 | 4 | 3 | | 7 | 8 | 9 | $10^{2}$ | $6^{1}$ | 12 | 14 | | 13 | | $5^{3}$ | | | | | | | | | | | | | | | 5 |
| 1 | 2 | 11 | 4 | 3 | | 7 | 8 | $9^{\blacksquare}$ | $10^{2}$ | 6 | 12 | | | 13 | | $5^{1}$ | | | | | | | | | | | | | | | 6 |
| 1 | 2 | 11 | 4 | 3 | | 7 | 8 | 9 | $10^{1}$ | 6 | 12 | 13 | | | | $5^{2}$ | | | | | | | | | | | | | | | 7 |
| 1 | 4 | 11 | 6 | 3 | | 2 | $8^{2}$ | 9 | $10^{1}$ | 7 | | 12 | | | | 5 | | 13 | | | | | | | | | | | | | 8 |
| 1 | 2 | 11 | 4 | $3^{3}$ | | 7 | 8 | | $10^{1}$ | 6 | 12 | 13 | | | 14 | 5 | | $9^{2}$ | | | | | | | | | | | | | 9 |
| 1 | $4^{3}$ | $3^{1}$ | 7 | $6^{\blacksquare}$ | | 2 | 8 | | | $11^{\blacksquare}$ | $9^{2}$ | 12 | | | 14 | 5 | 10 | 13 | | | | | | | | | | | | | 10 |
| 1 | 2 | | 4 | 3 | | 7 | 10 | | | $6^{1}$ | $9^{3}$ | 12 | | 13 | 11 | 5 | $8^{2}$ | 14 | | | | | | | | | | | | | 11 |
| 1 | $5^{1}$ | 3 | 4 | 6 | | 2 | 10 | 9 | | 8 | | 12 | | | $11^{2}$ | | | 13 | 7 | | | | | | | | | | | | 12 |
| 1 | | 3 | | | | 7 | 8 | 9 | | | | 10 | | | 11 | 5 | $4^{1}$ | 12 | 2 | $6^{2}$ | 13 | | | | | | | | | | 13 |
| | | $3^{1}$ | 4 | | | 11 | 10 | 9 | 12 | | | | 1 | | 13 | 5 | 7 | $8^{2}$ | 2 | $6^{3}$ | 14 | | | | | | | | | | 14 |
| 1 | | $3^{3}$ | 4 | | | 7 | 8 | 9 | 12 | | | 13 | | | 14 | 5 | $11^{2}$ | $10^{1}$ | 2 | 6 | | | | | | | | | | | 15 |
| 1 | $2^{\blacksquare}$ | | 4 | 5 | | 7 | 10 | | 12 | | | | | | $11^{3}$ | 13 | 8 | 9 | $3^{1}$ | $6^{2}$ | | 14 | | | | | | | | | 16 |
| 1 | 5 | | $4^{1}$ | 3 | | $11^{2}$ | 10 | | 12 | 8 | | 13 | | | 7 | | | 9 | | 6 | | | 2 | | | | | | | | 17 |
| 1 | | 13 | | 3 | | 7 | 10 | 12 | | 4 | | $8^{3}$ | | | $11^{2}$ | | | $9^{1}$ | 6 | 5 | | 14 | 2 | | | | | | | | 18 |
| 1 | 4 | | | 3 | | 7 | $10^{2}$ | 13 | | 6 | 12 | | | | 14 | | | $9^{1}$ | 2 | 5 | | 11 | $8^{3}$ | | | | | | | | 19 |
| 1 | | 3 | | 5 | | 8 | | 9 | | 6 | $10^{1}$ | | | | 13 | | | 12 | 2 | $4^{3}$ | | $11^{2}$ | 7 | 14 | | | | | | | 20 |
| 1 | 5 | 3 | | | | 7 | $10^{3}$ | 9 | 12 | 4 | | | | | 13 | | | 14 | 6 | | | 11 | $2^{1}$ | $8^{2}$ | | | | | | | 21 |
| 1 | 2 | 3 | | 5 | | 7 | $10^{2}$ | 12 | | 4 | | | | | | | | $9^{1}$ | 11 | | | | 8 | 13 | 6 | | | | | | 22 |
| 1 | 4 | 3 | | 13 | | 8 | 10 | 12 | | $7^{3}$ | | 6 | | | | | | $9^{1}$ | 2 | | | $11^{2}$ | | 14 | 5 | | | | | | 23 |
| 1 | 4 | 11 | | 3 | | 8 | 10 | 12 | | $6^{2}$ | | 13 | | | | | | $9^{1}$ | $2^{\blacksquare}$ | | | $7^{3}$ | | 14 | 5 | | | | | | 24 |
| 1 | 4 | 3 | | | | 7 | $10^{1}$ | 12 | | 6 | | $8^{2}$ | | | 13 | | | 9 | 2 | | | 11 | | | 5 | | | | | | 25 |
| $1^{G}$ | 4 | 11 | | $3^{\blacksquare}$ | | 7 | 10 | | | 6 | | | 15 | | $12^{2}$ | | 13 | 9 | 2 | | | | | 8 | $5^{1}$ | | | | | | 26 |
| 1 | 4 | 3 | | | | 8 | 10 | 12 | | 6 | | $7^{3}$ | | | 13 | | | $9^{1}$ | 2 | | | $11^{2}$ | | | 5 | 14 | | | | | 27 |
| 1 | 4 | 3 | | | | 7 | 10 | 12 | | 6 | | | | | 13 | | | $9^{1}$ | 2 | | | $11^{2}$ | | $8^{\blacksquare}$ | 5 | | | | | | 28 |
| | | 3 | | | | 7 | 10 | 9 | | | | $6^{3}$ | 1 | | 12 | 4 | | | $2^{2}$ | | | $11^{1}$ | | | 5 | 8 | 13 | 14 | | | 29 |
| 1 | 4 | 3 | | 11 | | 8 | 10 | 9 | | | | | | | | 5 | | | 2 | | | 7 | | | | 6 | | | | | 30 |
| 1 | 4 | 11 | | $3^{2}$ | | 8 | 12 | 9 | | $6^{1}$ | | | | | 13 | 5 | | 10 | 2 | | | | | | | 7 | | | | | 31 |
| | 4 | $3^{1}$ | | | | 7 | $8^{3}$ | 9 | | 6 | | | 1 | | 13 | 5 | | 10 | 2 | 12 | | $11^{2}$ | | | | 14 | | | | | 32 |
| 1 | 4 | 11 | | 3 | | 6 | $10^{3}$ | 14 | | | | | | | | 12 | | 9 | 2 | | | $7^{1}$ | | | 5 | $8^{2}$ | 13 | | | | 33 |
| $1^{G}$ | 4 | 11 | | 3 | | 6 | 10 | 12 | | | | | 15 | | | | 13 | $9^{1}$ | 2 | | | $7^{2}$ | | | 5 | 8 | | | | | 34 |
| 1 | 4 | 11 | | 3 | | 6 | $10^{1}$ | 12 | | | | | | | | | 13 | 9 | 2 | | | 7 | | | 5 | $8^{2}$ | | | | | 35 |
| 1 | 4 | 11 | | 3 | | 6 | | 9 | | | | | | | | | 12 | 10 | 2 | | | $7^{1}$ | | | 5 | 8 | | | | | 36 |
| 1 | 4 | 11 | | 3 | | 6 | | 9 | | | | | | | 13 | | | 10 | 2 | | | $7^{2}$ | | | 5 | $8^{1}$ | | | 12 | | 37 |
| 1 | 4 | 3 | | | | 8 | | 9 | | | | | | | 13 | | 7 | 10 | 2 | | | $11^{1}$ | | | 5 | | | 12 | $6^{2}$ | | 38 |
| $1^{G}$ | 4 | 11 | | 3 | | 6 | 12 | 9 | | | | | 15 | | 8 | | 7 | $10^{1}$ | 2 | | | | | | 5 | | | | | | 39 |
| | 4 | 11 | | 3 | | 6 | 10 | 9 | | | | | 1 | | 8 | | 7 | | 2 | | | | | | 5 | | | | | | 40 |
| | 4 | 11 | | 3 | | 6 | $10^{3}$ | 9 | | | | | 1 | | 8 | | 13 | | 2 | 12 | | $7^{2}$ | | | $5^{1}$ | | | | | 14 | 41 |
| | 4 | 11 | | 3 | | 6 | 10 | 9 | | | | | 1 | | $8^{1}$ | | 7 | | 2 | | | 12 | | | 5 | | | | | | 42 |
| | 4 | 11 | | $3^{3}$ | | $9^{1}$ | 10 | | | | | | 1 | | 8 | | 6 | | 2 | | | $7^{2}$ | | | 5 | 13 | | | 12 | 14 | 43 |
| 1 | 4 | 11 | | 3 | | 6 | 9 | | | | | | | | $10^{3}$ | | 8 | | 2 | 13 | | $7^{1}$ | | | $5^{2}$ | 12 | | | | 14 | 44 |
| | | 11 | | | | 6 | 9 | | | | | 13 | 1 | | 10 | 12 | 7 | | 2 | $5^{1}$ | 4 | | | | | $8^{2}$ | | 3 | | | 45 |
| 1 | 4 | 11 | | 3 | | 6 | 10 | 9 | | | | 13 | | | $8^{1}$ | | $7^{2}$ | | 2 | | | 12 | | | 5 | | | | | | 46 |

**Carling Cup**

| | | | |
|---|---|---|---|
| First Round | Rochdale | (h) | 2-1 |
| Second Round | Gillingham | (h) | 0-2 |

**FA Cup**

| | | | |
|---|---|---|---|
| Third Round | Wimbledon | (a) | 1-1 |
| | | (h) | 0-1 |

# SUNDERLAND FL Championship

## FOUNDATION

A Scottish schoolmaster named James Allan, working at Hendon Board School, took the initiative in the foundation of Sunderland in 1879 when they were formed as The Sunderland and District Teachers' Association FC at a meeting in the Adults School, Norfolk Street. Due to financial difficulties, they quickly allowed members from outside the teaching profession and so became Sunderland AFC in October 1880.

***Stadium of Light, Sunderland, Tyne and Wear SR5 1SU.***

***Telephone:*** (0191) 551 5000.

***Fax:*** (0191) 551 5123.

***Ticket Office:*** (0191) 551 5151.

***Website:*** www.safc.com

***Ground Capacity:*** 49,000.

***Record Attendance:*** Stadium of Light: 48,353 v Liverpool, FA Premier League, 13 April 2002. FA Premier League figure (46,062). Roker Park: 75,118 v Derby Co, FA Cup 6th rd replay, 8 March 1933.

***Pitch Measurements:*** 105m × 68m.

***Chairman:*** Bob Murray CBE.

***Vice-chairman:*** John Fickling.

***Secretary:*** Jane Purdon.

***Manager:*** Mick McCarthy.

***Assistant Manager:*** Ian Evans.

***Physio:*** Pete Friar.

***Colours:*** Red and white striped shirts, black shorts, black stockings.

***Change Colours:*** All white with red and black piping.

***Year Formed:*** 1879.

***Turned Professional:*** 1886.

***Ltd Co.:*** 1906.

***Previous Name:*** 1879, Sunderland and District Teacher's AFC; 1880, Sunderland.

***Previous Grounds:*** 1879, Blue House Field, Hendon; 1882, Groves Field, Ashbrooke; 1883, Horatio Street; 1884, Abbs Field, Fulwell; 1886, Newcastle Road; 1898, Roker Park; 1997, Stadium of Light.

***First Football League Game:*** 13 September 1890, Football League, v Burnley (h) L 2–3 – Kirtley; Porteous, Oliver; Wilson, Auld, Gibson; Spence (1), Miller, Campbell (1), Scott, D. Hannah.

***Record League Victory:*** 9–1 v Newcastle U (a), Division 1, 5 December 1908 – Roose; Forster, Melton; Daykin, Thomson, Low; Mordue (1), Hogg (3), Brown, Holley (3), Bridgett (2).

## HONOURS

*Football League:* Division 1 – Champions 1891–92, 1892–93, 1894–95, 1901–02, 1912–13, 1935–36, 1995–96, 1998–99; Runners-up 1893–94, 1897–98, 1900–01, 1922–23, 1934–35; Division 2 – Champions 1975–76; Runners-up 1963–64, 1979–80; 1989–90 (play-offs). Division 3 – Champions 1987–88.

*FA Cup:* Winners 1937, 1973; Runners-up 1913, 1992.

*Football League Cup:* Runners-up 1985.

***European Competitions:*** *European Cup-Winners' Cup:* 1973–74.

## SKY SPORTS FACT FILE

From September 1890 until December 1893, Sunderland were unbeaten at home during a sequence of 44 matches. In 1892–93 they won the First Division by 11 points from Preston North End. Though equalled, this remained the best margin until 1984–85.

***Record Cup Victory:*** 11–1 v Fairfield, FA Cup 1st rd, 2 February 1895 – Doig; McNeill, Johnston; Dunlop, McCreadie (1), Wilson; Gillespie (1), Millar (5), Campbell, Hannah (3), Scott (1).

***Record Defeat:*** 0–8 v Sheff Wed, Division 1, 26 December 1911. 0–8 v West Ham U, Division 1, 19 October 1968. 0–8 v Watford, Division 1, 25 September 1982.

***Most League Points (2 for a win):*** 61, Division 2, 1963–64.

***Most League Points (3 for a win):*** 105, Division 1, 1998–99 (Football League Record).

***Most League Goals:*** 109, Division 1, 1935–36.

***Highest League Scorer in Season:*** Dave Halliday, 43, Division 1, 1928–29.

***Most League Goals in Total Aggregate:*** Charlie Buchan, 209, 1911–25.

***Most League Goals in One Match:*** 5, Charlie Buchan v Liverpool, Division 1, 7 December 1919; 5, Bobby Gurney v Bolton W, Division 1, 7 December 1935; 5, Dominic Sharkey v Norwich C, Division 2, 20 February 1962.

***Most Capped Player:*** Charlie Hurley, 38 (40), Republic of Ireland.

***Most League Appearances:*** Jim Montgomery, 537, 1962–77.

***Youngest League Player:*** Derek Forster, 15 years 184 days v Leicester C, 22 August 1964.

***Record Transfer Fee Received:*** £5,600,000 from Leeds U for Michael Bridges, July 1999.

***Record Transfer Fee Paid:*** £8,000,000 to Rangers for Tore Andre Flo, August 2002.

***Football League Record:*** 1890 Elected to Division 1; 1958–64 Division 2; 1964–70 Division 1; 1970–76 Division 2; 1976–77 Division 1; 1977–80 Division 2; 1980–85 Division 1; 1985–87 Division 2; 1987–88 Division 3; 1988–90 Division 2; 1990–91 Division 1; 1991–92 Division 2; 1992–96 Division 1; 1996–97 FA Premier League; 1997–99 Division 1; 1999–2003 FA Premier League; 2003–04 Division 1; 2004– FLC.

## MANAGERS

Tom Watson 1888–96
Bob Campbell 1896–99
Alex Mackie 1899–1905
Bob Kyle 1905–28
Johnny Cochrane 1928–39
Bill Murray 1939–57
Alan Brown 1957–64
George Hardwick 1964–65
Ian McColl 1965–68
Alan Brown 1968–72
Bob Stokoe 1972–76
Jimmy Adamson 1976–78
Ken Knighton 1979–81
Alan Durban 1981–84
Len Ashurst 1984–85
Lawrie McMenemy 1985–87
Denis Smith 1987–91
Malcolm Crosby 1992–93
Terry Butcher 1993
Mick Buxton 1993–95
Peter Reid 1995–2002
Howard Wilkinson 2002–03
Mick McCarthy March 2003–

## LATEST SEQUENCES

***Longest Sequence of League Wins:*** 13, 14.11.1891 – 2.4.1892.

***Longest Sequence of League Defeats:*** 17, 18.1.2003 – 16.8.2003.

***Longest Sequence of League Draws:*** 6, 26.3.1949 – 19.4.1949.

***Longest Sequence of Unbeaten League Matches:*** 19, 3.5.1998 – 14.11.1998.

***Longest Sequence Without a League Win:*** 22, 21.12.2002 – 16.8.2003.

***Successive Scoring Runs:*** 29 from 8.11.1997

***Successive Non-scoring Runs:*** 10 from 27.11.1976.

## TEN YEAR LEAGUE RECORD

| | | *P* | *W* | *D* | *L* | *F* | *A* | *Pts* | *Pos* |
|---|---|---|---|---|---|---|---|---|---|
| 1994-95 | Div 1 | 46 | 12 | 18 | 16 | 41 | 45 | 54 | 20 |
| 1995-96 | Div 1 | 46 | 22 | 17 | 7 | 59 | 33 | 83 | 1 |
| 1996-97 | PR Lge | 38 | 10 | 10 | 18 | 35 | 53 | 40 | 18 |
| 1997-98 | Div 1 | 46 | 26 | 12 | 8 | 86 | 50 | 90 | 3 |
| 1998-99 | Div 1 | 46 | 31 | 12 | 3 | 91 | 28 | 105 | 1 |
| 1999-2000 | PR Lge | 38 | 16 | 10 | 12 | 57 | 56 | 58 | 7 |
| 2000-01 | PR Lge | 38 | 15 | 12 | 11 | 46 | 41 | 57 | 7 |
| 2001-02 | PR Lge | 38 | 10 | 10 | 18 | 29 | 51 | 40 | 17 |
| 2002-03 | PR Lge | 38 | 4 | 7 | 27 | 21 | 65 | 19 | 20 |
| 2003-04 | Div 1 | 46 | 22 | 13 | 11 | 62 | 45 | 79 | 3 |

## DID YOU KNOW ?

Jimmy Richardson scored four goals in each of two first round FA Cup ties in 1911–12 against Clapton Orient (6-0) and 1912–13 (9-0) when Chatham were the opponents. A Scot, he left for Ayr United because his wife could not settle in the area.

## SUNDERLAND 2003–04 LEAGUE RECORD

| Match No. | Date | Venue | Opponents | Result | | H/T Score | Lg. Pos. | Goalscorers | Attendance |
|---|---|---|---|---|---|---|---|---|---|
| 1 | Aug 9 | A | Nottingham F | L | 0-2 | 0-2 | — | | 23,729 |
| 2 | 16 | H | Millwall | L | 0-1 | 0-1 | 23 | | 24,877 |
| 3 | 23 | A | Preston NE | W | 2-0 | 2-0 | 17 | Thornton [4], Stewart [41] | 14,018 |
| 4 | 25 | H | Watford | W | 2-0 | 1-0 | 7 | Stewart (pen) [40], Wright [67] | 23,600 |
| 5 | 30 | A | Bradford C | W | 4-0 | 3-0 | 7 | Breen [10], Stewart [15], Arca [31], Thornton [76] | 14,116 |
| 6 | Sept 13 | H | Crystal Palace | W | 2-1 | 0-0 | 4 | Kyle [46], Stewart (pen) [90] | 27,324 |
| 7 | 16 | A | Stoke C | L | 1-3 | 0-0 | — | Kyle [54] | 15,005 |
| 8 | 20 | A | Derby Co | D | 1-1 | 0-0 | 9 | Poom [90] | 22,535 |
| 9 | 27 | H | Reading | W | 2-0 | 2-0 | 5 | Arca [28], Oster [32] | 22,420 |
| 10 | 30 | H | Ipswich T | W | 3-2 | 1-1 | — | Breen [44], Oster [49], Kyle [85] | 24,840 |
| 11 | Oct 4 | A | Sheffield U | W | 1-0 | 0-0 | 4 | Kyle [68] | 27,008 |
| 12 | 14 | H | Cardiff C | D | 0-0 | 0-0 | — | | 26,835 |
| 13 | 18 | H | Walsall | W | 1-0 | 1-0 | 4 | Stewart [42] | 36,278 |
| 14 | 21 | H | Rotherham U | D | 0-0 | 0-0 | — | | 24,506 |
| 15 | 25 | A | Norwich C | L | 0-1 | 0-1 | 5 | | 16,427 |
| 16 | Nov 1 | A | WBA | D | 0-0 | 0-0 | 5 | | 26,135 |
| 17 | 4 | A | Gillingham | W | 3-1 | 1-1 | — | Downing [45], Oster [58], Stewart [72] | 9066 |
| 18 | 8 | H | Coventry C | D | 0-0 | 0-0 | 5 | | 27,247 |
| 19 | 22 | A | Crewe Alex | L | 0-3 | 0-0 | 5 | | 9807 |
| 20 | 29 | H | Burnley | D | 1-1 | 1-0 | 8 | Kyle [39] | 29,852 |
| 21 | Dec 2 | H | Wigan Ath | D | 1-1 | 0-0 | — | Downing (pen) [82] | 22,167 |
| 22 | 8 | A | Coventry C | D | 1-1 | 1-1 | — | Downing [8] | 12,913 |
| 23 | 13 | A | West Ham U | L | 2-3 | 2-0 | 10 | McAteer [4], Oster [30] | 30,329 |
| 24 | 20 | H | Wimbledon | W | 2-1 | 1-1 | 8 | Stewart (pen) [27], Proctor [90] | 22,334 |
| 25 | 26 | H | Bradford C | W | 3-0 | 1-0 | 5 | McAteer [44], Smith [67], Kyle [82] | 29,639 |
| 26 | 28 | A | Rotherham U | W | 2-0 | 2-0 | 4 | Stewart 2 (1 pen) [30, 41 (p)] | 11,455 |
| 27 | Jan 10 | H | Nottingham F | W | 1-0 | 1-0 | 4 | Arca [38] | 26,340 |
| 28 | 17 | A | Millwall | L | 1-2 | 1-1 | 4 | Stewart [30] | 13,048 |
| 29 | Feb 7 | A | Watford | D | 2-2 | 0-1 | 6 | Stewart [76], Byfield [86] | 16,798 |
| 30 | 21 | A | Cardiff C | L | 0-4 | 0-2 | 7 | | 17,337 |
| 31 | Mar 3 | A | Walsall | W | 3-1 | 1-0 | — | Arca [18], Kyle [54], Stewart [81] | 7185 |
| 32 | 10 | H | Preston NE | D | 3-3 | 1-1 | — | Mears (og) [25], Thornton [70], Stewart (pen) [84] | 27,181 |
| 33 | 13 | H | West Ham U | W | 2-0 | 0-0 | 7 | Kyle [61], Whitley [76] | 29,533 |
| 34 | 16 | H | Stoke C | D | 1-1 | 0-1 | — | Byfield [69] | 24,510 |
| 35 | 20 | A | Reading | W | 2-0 | 0-0 | 6 | Byfield [73], Smith [74] | 18,019 |
| 36 | 23 | H | Gillingham | W | 2-1 | 1-1 | — | Thornton [11], Byfield [53] | 23,262 |
| 37 | 27 | H | Derby Co | W | 2-1 | 1-0 | 3 | Oster [31], Smith [50] | 30,838 |
| 38 | Apr 6 | A | Wimbledon | W | 2-1 | 1-0 | — | Stewart [45], Byfield [73] | 4800 |
| 39 | 9 | H | Sheffield U | W | 3-0 | 1-0 | — | Smith [7], Breen [65], Kyle [90] | 27,472 |
| 40 | 12 | A | Ipswich T | L | 0-1 | 0-1 | 3 | | 26,801 |
| 41 | 18 | H | WBA | L | 0-1 | 0-0 | 3 | | 32,201 |
| 42 | 21 | A | Crystal Palace | L | 0-3 | 0-1 | — | | 18,291 |
| 43 | 24 | A | Wigan Ath | D | 0-0 | 0-0 | 3 | | 11,380 |
| 44 | May 1 | H | Crewe Alex | D | 1-1 | 1-0 | 4 | Whitley [25] | 25,311 |
| 45 | 4 | H | Norwich C | W | 1-0 | 1-0 | — | Robinson [44] | 35,174 |
| 46 | 9 | A | Burnley | W | 2-1 | 1-1 | 3 | Breen [37], Kyle [66] | 18,852 |

**Final League Position: 3**

### GOALSCORERS

*League (62):* Stewart 14 (5 pens), Kyle 10, Byfield 5, Oster 5, Arca 4, Breen 4, Smith 4, Thornton 4, Downing 3 (1 pen), McAteer 2, Whitley 2, Poom 1, Proctor 1, Robinson 1, Wright 1, own goal 1.
*Carling Cup (4):* Kyle 3, own goal 1.
*FA Cup (7):* Smith 4, Arca 2, Kyle 1.
*Play-Offs (4):* Kyle 2, Stewart 2 (1 pen).

| Poom M 43 | Wright S 20 + 2 | McCartney G 40 + 1 | McAteer J 18 | Babb P 22 | Bjorklund J 19 + 6 | Oster J 35 + 3 | Thirlwell P 21 + 8 | Kyle K 36 + 8 | Proctor M 4 + 13 | Kilbane K 5 | Butler T 7 + 5 | Stewart M 28 + 12 | Breen G 32 | Clark B 2 + 3 | Piper M 4 + 5 | Thornton S 14 + 8 | Gray M — + 1 | Arca J 31 | Healy C 16 + 4 | Williams D 24 + 5 | James C 1 | Smith T 22 + 13 | Whitley J 33 | Quinn A 5 + 1 | Downing S 7 | Black C — + 1 | Cooper K — + 1 | Byfield D 8 + 9 | Cooper C — + 3 | Robinson C 6 + 1 | Myhre T 3 + 1 | *Match No.* |
|---|---|---|---|---|---|---|---|---|---|---|---|---|---|---|---|---|---|---|---|---|---|---|---|---|---|---|---|---|---|---|---|---|
| 1 | 2 | 3 | 4 | 5 | 6 | 7[1] | 8 | 9 | 10[2] | 11 | 12 | 13 | | | | | | | | | | | | | | | | | | | | 1 |
| 1 | 2 | 3 | | | | 12 | 4 | 9 | 10[2] | 11[3] | | 13 | 5 | 6 | 7[1] | 8 | 14 | | | | | | | | | | | | | | | 2 |
| 1 | 2 | 12 | | | | | 4 | 9 | 13 | 11 | | 10[2] | 5 | 6[1] | 7[3] | 8 | | 3 | 14 | | | | | | | | | | | | | 3 |
| 1 | 2 | 6 | | | | 7 | 8 | 9 | 12 | 11[2] | | 10[1] | 5 | | | 4 | | 3 | 13 | | | | | | | | | | | | | 4 |
| 1 | 2 | 6 | | | | 7[3] | 4 | 9[2] | 13 | 11[1] | 12 | 10 | 5 | | | 8 | | 3 | 14 | | | | | | | | | | | | | 5 |
| 1 | | 6 | 7[3] | | | 12 | 4 | 9 | 13 | | 11[2] | 10 | 5 | | | 8 | | 3 | 14 | 2[1] | | | | | | | | | | | | 6 |
| 1 | | 6 | | | 12 | 7 | 4 | 9 | | | 13 | 10 | 5[1] | | | 8■ | | 3 | 11 | | 2[2] | | | | | | | | | | | 7 |
| 1 | | 6 | | | 5 | 7 | 4 | 9 | | | 11[1] | 10 | | | | 12 | | 3 | 8 | 2 | | | | | | | | | | | | 8 |
| 1 | | 6 | | | | 7 | 4[1] | 9 | 13 | | 11[3] | 10[2] | 5 | | | 12 | | 3 | 8 | 2 | | 14 | | | | | | | | | | 9 |
| 1 | | 6 | | | 12 | 7[1] | | 9 | 13 | | 11[3] | 10[2] | 5 | | | | | 3 | 4 | 2 | | 14 | 8 | | | | | | | | | 10 |
| 1 | | 6 | | | 12 | 7 | | 9 | | | 11[2] | 10[1] | 5 | | | 13 | | 3■ | 4 | 2 | | | 8 | | | | | | | | | 11 |
| 1 | | 6 | | | | 7[1] | | 9 | 12 | | 11[3] | 10[2] | 5 | | | 13 | | 3 | 4 | 2 | | 14 | 8 | | | | | | | | | 12 |
| 1 | | 3 | | | 6 | 7 | | 9 | | | | 10 | 5 | 12 | | | | | 4 | 2[1] | | 13 | 8 | 11[2] | | | | | | | | 13 |
| 1 | | 6 | | | | 7 | | 9 | 12 | | | 10[1] | 5 | | | 13 | | 3 | 4 | 2 | | 11[2] | 8 | | | | | | | | | 14 |
| 1 | | 6 | | | | 7■ | | 9 | 12 | | | 10 | 5 | | | | | 3 | 4 | 2[2] | | 11[1] | 8 | 13 | | | | | | | | 15 |
| 1 | | 6 | | | | 7 | 12 | 9 | | | | 10[2] | 5 | | | | | 3 | 4 | 2 | | 13 | 8 | | 11[1] | | | | | | | 16 |
| 1 | | 6 | | | | 7 | | 9[1] | | | | 10 | 5 | | | | | 3 | 4 | 2 | | 12 | 8 | | 11 | | | | | | | 17 |
| 1 | | 6 | | | 12 | | 13 | 9[3] | | | | 10 | 5[1] | | | | | 3 | 4 | 2 | | 14 | 8 | 11[2] | 7 | | | | | | | 18 |
| 1 | 2 | 6 | | | 5 | | | | 12 | | | 10[2] | | | | | | 3 | 4 | | | 9 | 8 | 7[1] | 11 | 13 | | | | | | 19 |
| 1 | | 6 | | | 5 | | 12 | 9[3] | 10[2] | | | 13 | | | | | | 3 | 4 | 2 | | 14 | 8 | 11[1] | 7 | | | | | | | 20 |
| 1 | 12 | 6 | | | 5 | 7 | 13 | 9 | 10[1] | | | | | | | | | 3■ | 4[2] | 2[3] | | 14 | 8 | | 11 | | | | | | | 21 |
| 1 | 14 | 6 | | | 5 | | 13 | 9[3] | | | | 12 | | | | | | 3 | 4[2] | 2 | | 10 | 8 | 7[1] | 11 | | | | | | | 22 |
| 1 | 2 | 6 | 7[1] | | 5 | 11 | 4 | 12 | | | 13 | 10 | | | | | | 3 | | | | 9[2] | 8 | | | | | | | | | 23 |
| 1 | 2 | 3 | 7 | 5 | 6 | 11 | 4 | 12■ | 14 | | 13 | 10[3] | | | | | | | | | | 9[1] | 8[2] | | | | | | | | | 24 |
| 1 | 2 | 3[3] | 7 | 5 | 6 | 11 | 4[1] | 12 | 13 | | | 10[2] | | | | | | | | 14 | | 9 | 8 | | | | | | | | | 25 |
| 1 | 2 | 6 | 7 | 5 | 4 | 11 | | 12 | | | | 10 | | | | | | 3 | | | | 9[1] | 8 | | | | | | | | | 26 |
| 1 | 2 | 6 | 7 | 5 | 4 | | | 12 | 13 | | 11[1] | 10[2] | | | | | | 3 | | 14 | | 9[3] | 8 | | | | | | | | | 27 |
| 1 | 2 | 3 | 4 | 5 | 6 | 7 | | 9[1] | | | | 10 | | | | | | | | | | 11 | 8 | | | | 12 | | | | | 28 |
| 1 | 2 | 3 | 7 | 5 | 6 | | 4[2] | 9 | | | | 12 | | | | | | 11 | | | | 10[1] | 8 | | | | | 13 | | | | 29 |
| 1 | 2 | 3 | 4[1] | | 6■ | 7 | 12 | 9[3] | | | | 10[2] | 5 | | | | | 11 | | | | 13 | 8 | | | | | 14 | | | | 30 |
| 1 | | 6 | 4 | 5 | | 7[1] | 11 | 9[2] | | | | 12 | | | | | | 3 | | 2 | | 10 | 8 | | | | | 13 | | | | 31 |
| 1 | 2 | 3 | 7 | 6 | | 11[2] | 4 | 9[1] | | | | 12 | 5 | | | 13 | | | | | | 10[3] | 8■ | | | | | 14 | | | | 32 |
| 1 | 2 | 3 | | 6 | | 7[1] | 4 | 9 | | | | | 5 | | 12 | 11[2] | | | | 13 | | 10[3] | 8 | | | | | 14 | | | | 33 |
| 1 | 2 | 3 | | 6 | | 7 | 4 | 9 | | | | | 5 | | 12 | 11 | | | | | | 10[2] | 8[1] | | | | | 13 | | | | 34 |
| 1 | 2 | 3 | | 6 | | 7 | 4 | 9[1] | | | | | 5 | | 13 | 11[2] | | | | | | 12 | 8■ | | | | | 10[3] | 14 | | | 35 |
| 1 | 2[1] | 3 | | 6 | | 7 | 4 | 9[2] | | | | | 5 | | | 11[3] | | | | 12 | | 13 | 8 | | | | | 10 | 14 | | | 36 |
| 1 | | 3 | 8 | 6 | | 7 | 4 | | | | | 12 | 5 | | 13 | | | 11[3] | | 2 | | 9[2] | | | | | | 10[1] | 14 | | | 37 |
| 1 | | 3 | | | 6 | | 8 | 9 | | | | 10[2] | 5 | | 7[1] | 12 | | 11 | | 2 | | | | | | | | 13 | | 4 | | 38 |
| | | | 7[1] | 6 | | 11[2] | 12 | 13 | | | | 14 | 5 | | | 8 | | 3 | | 2 | | 10[3] | | | | | | 9 | | 4 | 1 | 39 |
| | | | 7 | 6 | | 11[2] | 12 | 9 | | | | 13 | 5 | | 14 | 8 | | 3 | | 2[1] | | | | | | | | 10 | | 4[3] | 1 | 40 |
| 1 | | 3[1] | | 6 | 12 | 7[2] | | 13 | | | | | 5 | | | | | 11 | | 2 | | 9 | 8 | | | | | 10 | | 4 | | 41 |
| 1■ | | | 4 | 6 | | 12 | | 9 | | | | 13 | 5 | | 7[1] | | | 3 | | 2 | | 11[G] | 8 | | | | | 10[2] | | | 15 | 42 |
| 1 | 2[1] | | 4 | 3 | 6 | 7 | | 9 | | | | 10[2] | 5 | | | | | | | 12 | | 11[3] | 8 | | | | | 13 | | 14 | | 43 |
| 1 | | 3 | 4 | 6 | 12 | 7 | | 9 | | | | 10[2] | 5[1] | | | 14 | | | | 2 | | 11[3] | 8 | | | | | 13 | | | | 44 |
| 1 | | 2 | | 6 | 3 | 7[2] | | 9 | | | | 10[1] | 5 | 13 | | 11 | | | | | | 12 | 8 | | | | | | | 4 | | 45 |
| | | | | 6 | 3 | 7 | | 12 | | | | 13 | 5 | 14 | | 11[3] | | | | 2 | | 9[2] | 8 | | | | | 10[1] | | 4 | 1 | 46 |

**Carling Cup**

| | | | |
|---|---|---|---|
| First Round | Mansfield T | (a) | 2-1 |
| Second Round | Huddersfield T | (h) | 2-4 |

**Play-Offs**

| | | | |
|---|---|---|---|
| Semi-Final | Crystal Palace | (a) | 2-3 |
| | | (h) | 2-1 |

**FA Cup**

| | | | |
|---|---|---|---|
| Third Round | Hartlepool U | (h) | 1-0 |
| Fourth Round | Ipswich T | (a) | 2-1 |
| Fifth Round | Birmingham C | (h) | 1-1 |
| | | (a) | 2-0 |
| Sixth Round | Sheffield U | (h) | 1-0 |
| Semi-Final *(at Old Trafford)* | Millwall | | 0-1 |

# SWANSEA CITY — FL Championship 2

## FOUNDATION

The earliest Association Football in Wales was played in the Northern part of the country and no international took place in the South until 1894, when a local paper still thought it necessary to publish an outline of the rules and an illustration of the pitch markings. There had been an earlier Swansea club, but this has no connection with Swansea Town (now City) formed at a public meeting in June 1912.

***Vetch Field, Swansea SA1 3SU.***

***Telephone:*** (01792) 633 400.

***Fax:*** (01792) 646 120.

***Ticket Office:*** (01792) 633 425.

***Website:*** www.swanseacity.net

***Email:*** dawn@swanseacityfc.co.uk

***Ground Capacity:*** 11,131.

***Record Attendance:*** 32,796 v Arsenal, FA Cup 4th rd, 17 February 1968.

***Pitch Measurements:*** 112yd × 74yd.

***Chairman:*** Huw Jenkins.

***Vice-chairman:*** Leigh Dineen.

***Secretary:*** Jackie Rockey.

***Manager:*** Kenny Jackett.

***Physio:*** Richard Evans.

***Colours:*** All white.

***Change Colours:*** All black.

***Year Formed:*** 1912.

***Turned Professional:*** 1912.

***Ltd Co.:*** 1912.

***Previous Name:*** Swansea Town until February 1970.

***Club Nicknames:*** 'The Swans', 'The Jacks'.

***First Football League Game:*** 28 August 1920, Division 3, v Portsmouth (a) L 0–3 – Crumley; Robson, Evans; Smith, Holdsworth, Williams; Hole, I. Jones, Edmundson, Rigsby, Spottiswood.

***Record League Victory:*** 8–0 v Hartlepool U, Division 4, 1 April 1978 – Barber; Evans, Bartley, Lally (1) (Morris), May, Bruton, Kevin Moore, Robbie James (3 incl. 1p), Curtis (3), Toshack (1), Chappell.

***Record Cup Victory:*** 12–0 v Sliema W (Malta), ECWC 1st rd 1st leg, 15 September 1982 – Davies; Marustik, Hadziabdic (1), Irwin (1), Kennedy, Rajkovic (1), Loveridge (2) (Leighton James), Robbie James, Charles (2), Stevenson (1), Latchford (1) (Walsh (3)).

## HONOURS

*Football League:* Division 1 best season: 6th, 1981–82; Division 2 – Promoted 1980–81 (3rd); Division 3 (S) – Champions 1924–25, 1948–49; Division 3 – Champions 1999–2000; Promoted 1978–79 (3rd); Division 4 – Promoted 1969–70 (3rd), 1977–78 (3rd), 1987–88 (play-offs).

*FA Cup:* Semi-finals 1926, 1964.

*Football League Cup:* best season: 4th rd, 1965, 1977.

*Welsh Cup:* Winners 10 times; Runners-up 8 times.

*Autoglass Trophy:* Winners 1994.

***European Competitions:*** *European Cup-Winners' Cup:* 1961–62, 1966–67, 1981–82, 1982–83, 1983–84, 1989–90, 1991–92.

## SKY SPORTS FACT FILE

As champions of Division Three (South) in 1948–49, the then Swansea Town had an outstanding home record dropping just one point, a 2-2 draw with Southend United. On travel the Swans were less impressive with seven of each possible result.

***Record Defeat:*** 0–8 v Liverpool, FA Cup 3rd rd, 9 January 1990. 0–8 v Monaco, ECWC, 1st rd 2nd leg, 1 October 1991.

***Most League Points (2 for a win):*** 62, Division 3 (S), 1948–49.

***Most League Points (3 for a win):*** 85, Division 3, 1999–2000.

***Most League Goals:*** 90, Division 2, 1956–57.

***Highest League Scorer in Season:*** Cyril Pearce, 35, Division 2, 1931–32.

***Most League Goals in Total Aggregate:*** Ivor Allchurch, 166, 1949–58, 1965–68.

***Most League Goals in One Match:*** 5, Jack Fowler v Charlton Ath, Division 3S, 27 December 1924.

***Most Capped Player:*** Ivor Allchurch, 42 (68), Wales.

***Most League Appearances:*** Wilfred Milne, 585, 1919–37.

***Youngest League Player:*** Nigel Dalling, 15 years 289 days v Southport, 6 December 1974.

***Record Transfer Fee Received:*** £400,000 from Bristol C for Steve Torpey, August 1997.

***Record Transfer Fee Paid:*** £340,000 to Liverpool for Colin Irwin, August 1981.

***Football League Record:*** 1920 Original Member of Division 3; 1921–25 Division 3 (S); 1925–47 Division 2; 1947–49 Division 3 (S); 1949–65 Division 2; 1965–67 Division 3; 1967–70 Division 4; 1970–73 Division 3; 1973–78 Division 4; 1978–79 Division 3; 1979–81 Division 2; 1981–83 Division 1; 1983–84 Division 2; 1984–86 Division 3; 1986–88 Division 4; 1988–92 Division 3; 1992–96 Division 2; 1996–2000 Division 3; 2000–01 Division 2; 2001–04 Division 3; 2004– FL2.

## MANAGERS

Walter Whittaker 1912–14
William Bartlett 1914–15
Joe Bradshaw 1919–26
Jimmy Thomson 1927–31
Neil Harris 1934–39
Haydn Green 1939–47
Bill McCandless 1947–55
Ron Burgess 1955–58
Trevor Morris 1958–65
Glyn Davies 1965–66
Billy Lucas 1967–69
Roy Bentley 1969–72
Harry Gregg 1972–75
Harry Griffiths 1975–77
John Toshack 1978–83
*(resigned October re-appointed in December) 1983–84*
Colin Appleton 1984
John Bond 1984–85
Tommy Hutchison 1985–86
Terry Yorath 1986–89
Ian Evans 1989–90
Terry Yorath 1990–91
Frank Burrows 1991–95
Bobby Smith 1995
Kevin Cullis 1996
Jan Molby 1996–97
Micky Adams 1997
Alan Cork 1997–98
John Hollins 1998–2001
Colin Addison 2001–02
Nick Cusack 2002
Brian Flynn 2002–04
Kenny Jackett April 2004–

## LATEST SEQUENCES

***Longest Sequence of League Wins:*** 9, 27.11.1999 – 22.01.2000.

***Longest Sequence of League Defeats:*** 9, 26.1.1991 – 19.3.1991.

***Longest Sequence of League Draws:*** 5, 5.1.1993 – 5.2.1993.

***Longest Sequence of Unbeaten League Matches:*** 19, 19.10.1970 – 9.3.1971.

***Longest Sequence Without a League Win:*** 15, 25.3.1989 – 2.9.1989.

***Successive Scoring Runs:*** 27 from 28.8.1947.

***Successive Non-scoring Runs:*** 6 from 6.2.1996.

## TEN YEAR LEAGUE RECORD

| | | *P* | *W* | *D* | *L* | *F* | *A* | *Pts* | *Pos* |
|---|---|---|---|---|---|---|---|---|---|
| 1994-95 | Div 2 | 46 | 19 | 14 | 13 | 57 | 45 | 71 | 10 |
| 1995-96 | Div 2 | 46 | 11 | 14 | 21 | 43 | 79 | 47 | 22 |
| 1996-97 | Div 3 | 46 | 21 | 8 | 17 | 62 | 58 | 71 | 5 |
| 1997-98 | Div 3 | 46 | 13 | 11 | 22 | 49 | 62 | 50 | 20 |
| 1998-99 | Div 3 | 46 | 19 | 14 | 13 | 56 | 48 | 71 | 7 |
| 1999-2000 | Div 3 | 46 | 24 | 13 | 9 | 51 | 30 | 85 | 1 |
| 2000-01 | Div 2 | 46 | 8 | 13 | 25 | 47 | 73 | 37 | 23 |
| 2001-02 | Div 3 | 46 | 13 | 12 | 21 | 53 | 77 | 51 | 20 |
| 2002-03 | Div 3 | 46 | 12 | 13 | 21 | 48 | 65 | 49 | 21 |
| 2003-04 | Div 3 | 46 | 15 | 14 | 17 | 58 | 61 | 59 | 10 |

## DID YOU KNOW ?

Sheffield-born schoolboy international Len Thompson was a goalscoring inside-left with Swansea Town in the 1920s. He scored the club's first hat-trick in the FA Cup proper on 8 January 1927 in a 4-1 win over Bury. Transferred to Arsenal for £4,000.

## SWANSEA CITY 2003–04 LEAGUE RECORD

| Match No. | Date | Venue | Opponents | Result | | H/T Score | Lg. Pos. | Goalscorers | Attendance |
|---|---|---|---|---|---|---|---|---|---|
| 1 | Aug 9 | H | Bury | W | 4-2 | 1-1 | — | Maylett 3 [5, 79, 90], Trundle [82] | 8826 |
| 2 | 16 | A | Cheltenham T | W | 4-3 | 1-2 | 3 | Thomas [37], Trundle 3 [63, 79, 90] | 4660 |
| 3 | 22 | H | Boston U | W | 3-0 | 0-0 | — | Trundle [49], Nugent [53], Robinson [87] | 9041 |
| 4 | 25 | A | Oxford U | L | 0-3 | 0-0 | 2 | | 6725 |
| 5 | 30 | H | Mansfield T | W | 4-1 | 1-1 | 1 | Durkan [16], Robinson [58], Trundle (pen) [70], Nugent [71] | 6991 |
| 6 | Sept 6 | A | Yeovil T | L | 0-2 | 0-1 | 2 | | 6656 |
| 7 | 13 | A | Scunthorpe U | D | 2-2 | 1-1 | 4 | Trundle 2 [7, 63] | 3510 |
| 8 | 16 | H | Macclesfield T | W | 3-0 | 2-0 | — | Britton [33], Duffy [45], Robinson [49] | 6641 |
| 9 | 20 | H | Huddersfield T | W | 2-0 | 1-0 | 1 | Trundle [33], Nugent [84] | 8048 |
| 10 | 27 | A | Carlisle U | W | 2-1 | 0-1 | 1 | Trundle (pen) [50], Wilson [55] | 4854 |
| 11 | 30 | A | Hull C | L | 0-1 | 0-1 | — | | 20,903 |
| 12 | Oct 4 | H | Lincoln C | D | 2-2 | 1-2 | 3 | Robinson [17], Futcher (og) [74] | 7914 |
| 13 | 11 | A | Leyton Orient | W | 2-1 | 2-0 | 3 | Trundle [9], Nugent [15] | 4393 |
| 14 | 18 | H | Kidderminster H | D | 0-0 | 0-0 | 3 | | 6825 |
| 15 | 21 | H | Cambridge U | L | 0-2 | 0-1 | — | | 6211 |
| 16 | 25 | A | Rochdale | W | 1-0 | 1-0 | 4 | Wilson [16] | 2646 |
| 17 | Nov 1 | H | Bristol R | D | 0-0 | 0-0 | 5 | | 7536 |
| 18 | 17 | A | Northampton T | L | 1-2 | 0-1 | — | Britton [48] | 4010 |
| 19 | 22 | H | Darlington | W | 1-0 | 1-0 | 6 | Trundle [41] | 5651 |
| 20 | 29 | A | York C | D | 0-0 | 0-0 | 6 | | 3209 |
| 21 | Dec 13 | H | Southend U | L | 2-3 | 1-2 | 6 | Thomas 2 [14, 90] | 5439 |
| 22 | 19 | A | Doncaster R | L | 1-3 | 0-2 | — | Robinson [74] | 6566 |
| 23 | 26 | A | Torquay U | D | 0-0 | 0-0 | 7 | | 4447 |
| 24 | 28 | H | Yeovil T | W | 3-2 | 1-0 | 6 | Trundle 2 (1 pen) [29 (p), 90], Connolly [67] | 9800 |
| 25 | Jan 6 | H | Oxford U | D | 0-0 | 0-0 | — | | 8896 |
| 26 | 10 | A | Bury | L | 0-2 | 0-0 | 8 | | 2799 |
| 27 | 17 | H | Cheltenham T | D | 0-0 | 0-0 | 9 | | 6474 |
| 28 | Feb 7 | H | Torquay U | L | 1-2 | 0-1 | 9 | Nugent [81] | 7323 |
| 29 | 18 | A | Boston U | D | 1-1 | 1-0 | — | Britton [14] | 2573 |
| 30 | 21 | A | Kidderminster H | L | 0-2 | 0-0 | 11 | | 3407 |
| 31 | 24 | H | Leyton Orient | W | 2-1 | 1-1 | — | Trundle [12], Tate [81] | 4727 |
| 32 | Mar 2 | A | Cambridge U | W | 1-0 | 1-0 | — | Iriekpen [5] | 2713 |
| 33 | 5 | H | Doncaster R | D | 1-1 | 1-0 | — | Roberts [39] | 8045 |
| 34 | 9 | H | Rochdale | D | 1-1 | 0-1 | — | Maylett [78] | 5819 |
| 35 | 13 | A | Southend U | D | 1-1 | 0-0 | 10 | Nugent [62] | 4753 |
| 36 | 16 | A | Macclesfield T | L | 1-2 | 0-1 | — | Maylett [74] | 1513 |
| 37 | 20 | H | Scunthorpe U | W | 4-2 | 1-1 | 10 | Robinson (pen) [41], Nugent [47], Connor 2 [61, 70] | 4400 |
| 38 | 23 | A | Mansfield T | D | 1-1 | 1-0 | — | Robinson [31] | 4058 |
| 39 | 27 | A | Huddersfield T | L | 0-3 | 0-0 | 10 | | 11,250 |
| 40 | Apr 3 | H | Carlisle U | L | 1-2 | 1-1 | 10 | Connor [15] | 5238 |
| 41 | 10 | A | Lincoln C | L | 1-2 | 1-0 | 10 | Rees [43] | 5455 |
| 42 | 12 | H | Hull C | L | 2-3 | 1-1 | 10 | Robinson [45], Trundle [83] | 5993 |
| 43 | 17 | A | Bristol R | L | 1-2 | 1-1 | 10 | Connor [8] | 7843 |
| 44 | 24 | H | Northampton T | L | 0-2 | 0-2 | 11 | | 4985 |
| 45 | May 1 | A | Darlington | W | 2-1 | 0-0 | 11 | Connor [50], Nugent [80] | 5487 |
| 46 | 8 | H | York C | D | 0-0 | 0-0 | 10 | | 6806 |

**Final League Position: 10**

### GOALSCORERS

*League (58):* Trundle 16 (3 pens), Nugent 8, Robinson 8 (1 pen), Connor 5, Maylett 5, Britton 3, Thomas 3, Wilson 2, Connolly 1, Duffy 1, Durkan 1, Iriekpen 1, Rees 1, Roberts 1, Tate 1, own goal 1.
*Carling Cup (1):* Connolly 1.
*FA Cup (10):* Trundle 5, Nugent 2, Robinson 2, Durkan 1.
*LDV Vans Trophy (1):* Nardiello 1.

| Murphy B 11 | Jones S 16 + 8 | Hylton L 10 + 1 | Britton L 42 | O'Leary K 28 + 6 | Johnrose L 21 + 4 | Martinez R 24 + 3 | Connolly K 4 + 6 | Thomas J 8 + 8 | Trundle L 29 + 2 | Maylett B 26 + 7 | Nugent K 31 + 8 | Jenkins L 8 + 3 | Coates J 14 + 13 | Robinson A 34 + 3 | Durkan K 11 + 4 | Iriekpen E 33 + 1 | Freestone R 35 + 2 | Duffy R 16 + 2 | Corbisierso A 1 + 4 | Howard M 25 | Wilson M 12 | Pritchard M 1 + 3 | Tate A 25 + 1 | Nardiello D 3 + 1 | Byrne S 9 | Roberts S 8 + 4 | Connor P 12 | Maxwell L 1 + 2 | Fieldwick L 4 + 1 | Rewbury J 1 + 1 | Rees M 3 | *Match No.* |
|---|---|---|---|---|---|---|---|---|---|---|---|---|---|---|---|---|---|---|---|---|---|---|---|---|---|---|---|---|---|---|---|---|
| 1 | 2 | 3 | 4 | 5 | 6 | 7 | 8 | $9^{1}$ | 10 | 11 | 12 | | | | | | | | | | | | | | | | | | | | | 1 |
| 1 | 12 | 3 | 4 | 5 | 6 | 7 | | $9^{2}$ | 10 | 11 | 13 | $2^{1}$ | $8^{3}$ | 14 | | | | | | | | | | | | | | | | | | 2 |
| 1 | 8 | 3 | 4 | 5 | 6 | $7^{1}$ | | | 10 | $11^{2}$ | 9 | 2 | | 12 | 13 | | | | | | | | | | | | | | | | | 3 |
| 1 | 2 | $3^{1}$ | 4 | 5 | $8^{2}$ | | | | 10 | 11 | 9 | 12 | 13 | 7 | | 6 | | | | | | | | | | | | | | | | 4 |
| | $7^{2}$ | 3 | 4 | 5 | | | | 12 | 10 | | 9 | $2^{1}$ | | $8^{3}$ | 11 | 6 | 1 | 13 | 14 | | | | | | | | | | | | | 5 |
| | 12 | | 4 | $5^{1}$ | | | | | 10 | 11 | 9 | $2^{3}$ | | 8 | $7^{2}$ | 6 | 1 | 14 | 13 | 3 | | | | | | | | | | | | 6 |
| | | $5^{1}$ | 4 | 12 | | | | | 10 | 7 | 9 | | | 8 | | 6■ | 1 | 2 | | 3 | 11 | | | | | | | | | | | 7 |
| | | | 4 | 5 | 12 | | | | 10 | $7^{2}$ | 9 | | | 8 | 13 | 6 | 1 | $2^{1}$ | | 3 | 11 | | | | | | | | | | | 8 |
| | | | 4 | 5 | 12 | | 13 | | 10 | $7^{3}$ | 9 | | | $8^{2}$ | 14 | 6 | 1 | $2^{1}$ | | 3 | 11 | | | | | | | | | | | 9 |
| | | | 4 | 5 | 6 | | | | 10 | | 9 | 12 | | 8 | 7 | | 1 | $2^{1}$ | | 3 | 11 | | | | | | | | | | | 10 |
| | | | 4 | 5 | 7 | | | | 10 | | 9 | | | 8 | | 6 | 1 | 2■ | | 3 | 11 | | | | | | | | | | | 11 |
| | | | 4 | 5 | 7 | | | | 10 | | 9 | 12 | | 8 | | 6 | 1 | $2^{1}$ | | 3 | 11 | | | | | | | | | | | 12 |
| | | | 4 | 5 | 7 | | | | $10^{1}$ | | 9 | | 12 | 8 | | 6 | 1 | 2 | | 3 | 11 | | | | | | | | | | | 13 |
| | | | 4 | 5 | $8^{1}$ | 12 | | | | 7 | 9 | 2 | | 10 | | 6 | 1 | | | 3 | 11 | | | | | | | | | | | 14 |
| | | | 4 | | 5 | 12 | | | | $7^{2}$ | 9 | 2 | $8^{1}$ | | 13 | 6 | 1 | | | 3 | 11 | 10 | | | | | | | | | | 15 |
| | | | 4 | | | 8 | | | | | 9 | 2 | 12 | | $7^{1}$ | 6 | 1 | | | 3 | 11 | | 5 | 10 | | | | | | | | 16 |
| | | | $4^{1}$ | | 12 | | | | | | 9 | 2 | 13 | $8^{2}$ | 7 | 6 | 1 | | | 3 | 11 | | 5 | 10 | | | | | | | | 17 |
| | | | 4 | 13 | 12 | | | | 10 | | 9 | | | 8 | $7^{3}$ | 6 | 1 | $2^{1}$ | | $3^{2}$ | 11 | | 5 | 14 | | | | | | | | 18 |
| | | | 4 | 12 | 11 | | | | 10 | | 13 | | 14 | 8 | $7^{3}$ | 6 | 1 | $2^{1}$ | | 3 | | | 5 | $9^{2}$ | | | | | | | | 19 |
| | 12 | | 4 | | 11 | | | 14 | 10■ | | $9^{3}$ | | 13 | 8 | $7^{2}$ | 6 | 1 | $2^{1}$ | | 3 | | | 5 | | | | | | | | | 20 |
| | 12 | | 4 | | 11 | | | 10 | | | 9 | | 13 | 8 | 7 | 6 | 1 | $2^{1}$ | | $3^{2}$ | | 14 | $5^{3}$ | | | | | | | | | 21 |
| | | | | 12 | 4 | | 14 | 10 | | 13 | 9 | | $11^{3}$ | 8 | $7^{2}$ | 6 | 1 | 2 | | 3 | | | $5^{1}$ | | | | | | | | | 22 |
| | | | 4 | | 11 | | $9^{1}$ | 10 | | 7 | 12 | | | 8 | | 6 | 1 | 2 | | 3 | | | 5 | | | | | | | | | 23 |
| | | 3 | $4^{1}$ | | 11 | | 13 | $9^{2}$ | 10 | 7 | | | 12 | 8 | | 6 | 1 | 2 | | | | | 5 | | | | | | | | | 24 |
| | | 12 | 4 | 5 | 11 | | 13 | | 10 | 7 | $9^{2}$ | | | 8 | | 6 | 1 | 2 | | $3^{1}$ | | | | | | | | | | | | 25 |
| | 3 | | 4 | 5 | $11^{1}$ | 12 | 14 | 13 | $10^{2}$ | | 9 | | | 8 | $7^{3}$ | 6 | 1 | 2■ | | | | | | | | | | | | | | 26 |
| | 3 | | 4 | 2 | $5^{2}$ | 8 | 11 | 12 | 10 | 7 | $9^{1}$ | | 13 | | | 6 | 1 | | | | | | | | | | | | | | | 27 |
| | | | | 5 | | 8 | $4^{1}$ | $10^{3}$ | | 7 | 9 | | 12 | 11 | | $6^{2}$ | 1 | | | 3 | | 14 | 13 | | 2 | | | | | | | 28 |
| | 12 | 3 | 4 | $6^{1}$ | | 8 | | | 10 | 7 | 9 | | | 11 | | | 1 | | | | | | 5 | | 2 | | | | | | | 29 |
| | 6 | 3 | 4 | | | 8 | | | 10 | $7^{1}$ | 9 | | 12 | 11 | | | 1 | | | | | | 5 | | 2 | | | | | | | 30 |
| | 13 | 3 | 4 | | | 8 | | | $10^{1}$ | $7^{3}$ | 12 | | 11 | 9 | | 6 | 1 | | | | | | 5 | | $2^{2}$ | 14 | | | | | | 31 |
| 1 | 2 | | 4 | 12 | | 8 | | 14 | | 13 | $9^{3}$ | | 10 | 11 | | 6 | | | | 3 | | | $5^{1}$ | | | $7^{2}$ | | | | | | 32 |
| 1 | | | 4 | 2 | | 8 | | 13 | | 12 | $9^{2}$ | | 10 | $11^{1}$ | | 6 | | | | 3 | | | 5 | | | 7 | | | | | | 33 |
| 1 | 13 | | 4 | $2^{2}$ | | 8 | | $9^{3}$ | | 12 | | | $11^{1}$ | 10 | | 6 | | | | 3 | | 14 | 5 | | | 7 | | | | | | 34 |
| 1■ | | | 4 | | 11 | 8 | | | | 12 | $9^{G}$ | | $3^{2}$ | 13 | | 6 | 15 | | | | | | 5 | | 2 | $7^{1}$ | 10 | | | | | 35 |
| 1 | 13 | | 4 | | 3 | 8 | | | | 12 | 9 | | | 11 | | $6^{2}$ | | | | | | | 5 | | 2■ | $7^{1}$ | 10 | | | | | 36 |
| | 6 | | 4 | | | 8 | | | 12 | 13 | $9^{1}$ | | 14 | $11^{2}$ | | | 1 | | | $3^{3}$ | | | 5 | | 2 | 7 | 10 | | | | | 37 |
| | 6 | | 4 | 12 | | 8 | | | | 11 | | | $7^{1}$ | 10 | | | 1 | | | 3 | | | 5 | | 2 | | 9 | | | | | 38 |
| | 6 | | 4 | 3 | | 8 | | 12 | | | | | $7^{2}$ | $10^{1}$ | | | 1 | | | | | | 5 | | 2 | $11^{3}$ | 9 | 13 | 14 | | | 39 |
| | 6 | | 4 | 2 | | 8 | | 13 | 10 | 7 | 12 | | | | | | 1 | | | | | | 5 | | | $11^{2}$ | $9^{1}$ | | 3 | | | 40 |
| | $2^{2}$ | | | 5 | | 8 | | | 10 | 7 | | | 11 | | | | 1 | | 12 | | | | | | | | 9 | $4^{1}$ | 3 | 13 | 6 | 41 |
| | | | | 2 | | 8 | | | 10 | $7^{2}$ | | | 12 | 11 | | | 1 | | $4^{3}$ | | | | | | | 13 | 9 | 14 | $5^{1}$ | 3 | 6 | 42 |
| | | | 4 | 2 | | 8 | | | $10^{2}$ | 7 | 13 | | | $11^{3}$ | | 12 | 1 | | | | | | 5 | | | 14 | 9 | | $3^{1}$ | | 6 | 43 |
| 1 | $3^{2}$ | | 4 | 2 | | 8 | 12 | | 10 | 7 | | | 11 | | | $6^{1}$ | | | 13 | | | | 5 | | | | 9 | | | | | 44 |
| 1G | 2 | | 4 | 3 | | 8 | | | $10^{1}$ | 7 | 12 | | 11 | | | 6 | 15 | | | | | | 5 | | | | 9 | | | | | 45 |
| | 2 | | 4 | 3 | | 8 | | | 12 | $7^{2}$ | $10^{1}$ | | 11 | | | 6 | 1 | | | | | | 5 | | | 13 | 9 | | | | | 46 |

**Carling Cup**
First Round — Bristol C — (a) — 1-4

**LDV Vans Trophy**
Second Round — Southend U — (h) — 1-2

**FA Cup**
First Round — Rushden & D — (h) — 3-0
Second Round — Stevenage B — (h) — 2-1
Third Round — Macclesfield T — (h) — 2-1
Fourth Round — Preston NE — (h) — 2-1
Fifth Round — Tranmere R — (a) — 1-2

# SWINDON TOWN FL Championship 1

## FOUNDATION

It is generally accepted that Swindon Town came into being in 1881, although there is no firm evidence that the club's founder, Rev. William Pitt, captain of the Spartans (an offshoot of a cricket club) changed his club's name to Swindon Town before 1883, when the Spartans amalgamated with St Mark's Young Men's Friendly Society.

***County Ground, County Road, Swindon SN1 2ED.***

***Telephone:*** 0870 443 1969.

***Fax:*** (01793) 333 703.

***Ticket Office:*** 0870 443 1894.

***Website:*** www.swindontownfc.co.uk

***Email:*** enquiries@swindontownfc.co.uk

***Ground Capacity:*** 14,540.

***Record Attendance:*** 32,000 v Arsenal, FA Cup 3rd rd, 15 January 1972.

***Pitch Measurements:*** 110yd × 70yd.

***Chairman:*** Willie Carson.

***Chief Executive:*** Mark Devlin.

***Secretary:*** Linda Birrell.

***Manager:*** Andy King.

***Assistant Manager:*** Malcolm Crosby.

***Physio:*** Dick Mackey.

***Colours:*** Red shirts, white shorts, red stockings with white turnover.

***Change Colours:*** Blue shirts and shorts with white trim, blue stockings with white turnover.

***Year Formed:*** 1881* (*see Foundation*).

***Turned Professional:*** 1894.

***Ltd Co.:*** 1894.

***Club Nickname:*** 'Robins'.

***Previous Ground:*** 1881, The Croft; 1896, County Ground.

***First Football League Game:*** 28 August 1920, Division 3, v Luton T (h) W 9–1 – Nash; Kay, Macconachie; Langford, Hawley, Wareing; Jefferson (1), Fleming (4), Rogers, Batty (2), Davies (1), (1 og).

***Record League Victory:*** 9–1 v Luton T, Division 3 (S), 28 August 1920 – Nash; Kay, Macconachie; Langford, Hawley, Wareing; Jefferson (1), Fleming (4), Rogers, Batty (2), Davies (1), (1 og).

## HONOURS

*FA Premier League:* best season: 22nd 1993–94; Division 1 – 1992–93 (play-offs).

*Football League:* Division 2 – Champions 1995–96; Division 3 – Runners-up 1962–63, 1968–69; Division 4 – Champions 1985–86 (with record 102 points).

*FA Cup:* Semi-finals 1910, 1912.

*Football League Cup:* Winners 1969.

*Anglo-Italian Cup:* Winners 1970.

## SKY SPORTS FACT FILE

Grenville Morris was a teenage debutant for the fledgling Swindon Town in 1897. Top scorer in successive seasons, he had to be sold to Nottingham Forest where the inside-forward enjoyed a lengthy career and 21 international caps for Wales.

***Record Cup Victory:*** 10–1 v Farnham U Breweries (away), FA Cup 1st rd (replay), 28 November 1925 – Nash; Dickenson, Weston, Archer, Bew, Adey; Denyer (2), Wall (1), Richardson (4), Johnson (3), Davies.

***Record Defeat:*** 1–10 v Manchester C, FA Cup 4th rd (replay), 25 January 1930.

***Most League Points (2 for a win):*** 64, Division 3, 1968–69.

***Most League Points (3 for a win):*** 102, Division 4, 1985–86.

***Most League Goals:*** 100, Division 3 (S), 1926–27.

***Highest League Scorer in Season:*** Harry Morris, 47, Division 3 (S), 1926–27.

***Most League Goals in Total Aggregate:*** Harry Morris, 216, 1926–33.

***Most League Goals in One Match:*** 5, Harry Morris v QPR, Division 3S, 18 December 1926; 5, Harry Morris v Norwich C, Division 3S, 26 April 1930; 5, Keith East v Mansfield T, Division 3, 20 November 1965.

***Most Capped Player:*** Rod Thomas, 30 (50), Wales.

***Most League Appearances:*** John Trollope, 770, 1960–80.

***Youngest League Player:*** Paul Rideout, 16 years 107 days v Hull C, 29 November 1980.

***Record Transfer Fee Received:*** £1,500,000 from Manchester C for Kevin Horlock, January 1997.

***Record Transfer Fee Paid:*** £800,000 to West Ham U for Joey Beauchamp, August 1994.

***Football League Record:*** 1920 Original Member of Division 3; 1921–58 Division 3 (S); 1958–63 Division 3; 1963–65 Division 2; 1965–69 Division 3; 1969–74 Division 2; 1974–82 Division 3; 1982–86 Division 4; 1986–87 Division 3; 1987–92 Division 2; 1992–93 Division 1; 1993–94 FA Premier League; 1994–95 Division 1; 1995–96 Division 2; 1996–2000 Division 1; 2000–04 Division 2; 2004– FL1.

## MANAGERS

Sam Allen 1902–33
Ted Vizard 1933–39
Neil Harris 1939–41
Louis Page 1945–53
Maurice Lindley 1953–55
Bert Head 1956–65
Danny Williams 1965–69
Fred Ford 1969–71
Dave Mackay 1971–72
Les Allen 1972–74
Danny Williams 1974–78
Bobby Smith 1978–80
John Trollope 1980–83
Ken Beamish 1983–84
Lou Macari 1984–89
Ossie Ardiles 1989–91
Glenn Hoddle 1991–93
John Gorman 1993–94
Steve McMahon 1994–99
Jimmy Quinn 1999–2000
Colin Todd 2000
Andy King 2000–01
Roy Evans 2001
Andy King January 2002–

## LATEST SEQUENCES

***Longest Sequence of League Wins:*** 8, 12.1.1986 – 15.3.1986.

***Longest Sequence of League Defeats:*** 6, 2.5.1993 – 25.8.1993.

***Longest Sequence of League Draws:*** 6, 22.11.1991 – 28.12.1991.

***Longest Sequence of Unbeaten League Matches:*** 22, 12.1.1986 – 23.8.86.

***Longest Sequence Without a League Win:*** 19, 30.10.1999 – 4.3.2000.

***Successive Scoring Runs:*** 31 from 17.4.1926.

***Successive Non-scoring Runs:*** 5 from 16.11.1963.

## TEN YEAR LEAGUE RECORD

| | | P | W | D | L | F | A | Pts | Pos |
|---|---|---|---|---|---|---|---|---|---|
| 1994-95 | Div 1 | 46 | 12 | 12 | 22 | 54 | 73 | 48 | 21 |
| 1995-96 | Div 2 | 46 | 25 | 17 | 4 | 71 | 34 | 92 | 1 |
| 1996-97 | Div 1 | 46 | 15 | 9 | 22 | 52 | 71 | 54 | 19 |
| 1997-98 | Div 1 | 46 | 14 | 10 | 22 | 42 | 73 | 52 | 18 |
| 1998-99 | Div 1 | 46 | 13 | 11 | 22 | 59 | 81 | 50 | 17 |
| 1999-2000 | Div 1 | 46 | 8 | 12 | 26 | 38 | 77 | 36 | 24 |
| 2000-01 | Div 2 | 46 | 13 | 13 | 20 | 47 | 65 | 52 | 20 |
| 2001-02 | Div 2 | 46 | 15 | 14 | 17 | 46 | 56 | 59 | 13 |
| 2002-03 | Div 2 | 46 | 16 | 12 | 18 | 59 | 63 | 60 | 10 |
| 2003-04 | Div 2 | 46 | 20 | 13 | 13 | 76 | 58 | 73 | 5 |

## DID YOU KNOW ?

Record breaking Swindon Town marksman Harry Morris scored in six successive FA Cup matches for the club from 1927 over two seasons. In fact his contribution during this period was ten of 13 in six games. He later played for Clapton Orient.

## SWINDON TOWN 2003–04 LEAGUE RECORD

| Match No. | Date | Venue | Opponents | Result | H/T Score | Lg. Pos. | Goalscorers | Attendance |
|---|---|---|---|---|---|---|---|---|
| 1 | Aug 9 | H | Sheffield W | L 2-3 | 1-3 | — | Miglioranzi [31], Igoe [57] | 10,573 |
| 2 | 15 | A | Colchester U | W 1-0 | 0-0 | — | Mooney [87] | 3339 |
| 3 | 23 | H | Notts Co | W 4-0 | 2-0 | 6 | Hewlett [8], Mooney [10], Parkin [47], Igoe [50] | 5758 |
| 4 | 25 | A | Bournemouth | D 2-2 | 2-1 | 7 | Mooney [18], Robinson S [35] | 6606 |
| 5 | 30 | H | Blackpool | D 2-2 | 2-2 | 8 | Mooney 2 [8, 30] | 6219 |
| 6 | Sept 6 | A | Brighton & HA | D 2-2 | 1-1 | 10 | Parkin 2 [14, 67] | 6534 |
| 7 | 13 | H | Wrexham | W 1-0 | 0-0 | 6 | Gurney [79] | 8160 |
| 8 | 16 | A | Grimsby T | W 2-1 | 0-1 | — | Gurney [53], Mooney [65] | 3535 |
| 9 | 20 | A | Barnsley | D 1-1 | 1-0 | 4 | Parkin [20] | 9006 |
| 10 | 27 | H | Peterborough U | W 2-0 | 0-0 | 2 | Parkin [84], Milner [90] | 6767 |
| 11 | Oct 1 | H | Luton T | D 2-2 | 1-0 | — | Milner [8], Howard [89] | 7573 |
| 12 | 4 | A | Bristol C | L 1-2 | 1-0 | 7 | Mooney [34] | 14,294 |
| 13 | 11 | H | Stockport Co | L 1-2 | 1-0 | 10 | Mooney [45] | 7060 |
| 14 | 18 | A | Chesterfield | L 0-3 | 0-2 | 12 | | 3506 |
| 15 | 21 | A | Tranmere R | L 0-1 | 0-0 | — | | 6675 |
| 16 | 25 | H | Port Vale | D 0-0 | 0-0 | 14 | | 5313 |
| 17 | Nov 1 | H | Wycombe W | W 2-0 | 1-0 | 10 | Burton [11], Miglioranzi [67] | 5681 |
| 18 | 15 | A | Oldham Ath | W 1-0 | 0-0 | 10 | Parkin [61] | 5282 |
| 19 | 22 | H | QPR | D 1-1 | 1-0 | 9 | Parkin [39] | 10,021 |
| 20 | 29 | A | Hartlepool U | L 0-2 | 0-1 | 13 | | 4493 |
| 21 | Dec 13 | H | Plymouth Arg | L 2-3 | 0-1 | 14 | Fallon [80], Parkin [89] | 9374 |
| 22 | 20 | A | Brentford | W 2-0 | 0-0 | 11 | Howard [66], Parkin [82] | 5077 |
| 23 | 26 | A | Rushden & D | L 0-2 | 0-1 | 14 | | 4845 |
| 24 | 28 | H | Brighton & HA | W 2-1 | 1-0 | 12 | Parkin [45], Miglioranzi [66] | 9269 |
| 25 | Jan 3 | H | Bournemouth | W 2-1 | 1-1 | 6 | Mooney 2 [15, 80] | 7158 |
| 26 | 10 | A | Sheffield W | D 1-1 | 0-0 | 7 | Mooney [52] | 22,751 |
| 27 | 17 | H | Colchester U | W 2-0 | 1-0 | 6 | Parkin [15], Mooney [46] | 6014 |
| 28 | 24 | A | Notts Co | W 2-1 | 1-0 | 4 | Howard [35], Mooney [86] | 6663 |
| 29 | 31 | A | Blackpool | D 2-2 | 0-1 | 6 | Parkin [48], Gurney [83] | 6463 |
| 30 | Feb 7 | H | Rushden & D | W 4-2 | 2-0 | 4 | Mooney [9], Gurney (pen) [17], Duke [76], Hunter (og) [90] | 7023 |
| 31 | 14 | A | Stockport Co | W 4-2 | 3-1 | 4 | Mooney 2 [4, 90], Howard [16], Nicholas [18] | 4833 |
| 32 | 21 | H | Chesterfield | W 2-0 | 1-0 | 4 | O'Hanlon [33], Parkin [86] | 6814 |
| 33 | Mar 3 | H | Tranmere R | W 2-0 | 1-0 | — | Parkin 2 [31, 82] | 6928 |
| 34 | 6 | H | Brentford | W 2-1 | 1-1 | 4 | Gurney [14], Igoe [82] | 7649 |
| 35 | 13 | A | Plymouth Arg | L 1-2 | 0-1 | 4 | Mooney [90] | 16,080 |
| 36 | 17 | H | Grimsby T | W 2-0 | 2-0 | — | Mooney 2 [34, 45] | 6954 |
| 37 | 20 | A | Wrexham | L 2-3 | 0-1 | 5 | Igoe [49], O'Hanlon [77] | 3384 |
| 38 | 27 | H | Barnsley | D 1-1 | 1-1 | 4 | Parkin [8] | 7305 |
| 39 | 30 | A | Port Vale | D 3-3 | 0-2 | — | Parkin [63], Hewlett [68], Fallon [83] | 5702 |
| 40 | Apr 3 | A | Peterborough U | L 2-4 | 1-2 | 5 | Heywood [4], Parkin [63] | 4745 |
| 41 | 10 | H | Bristol C | D 1-1 | 0-1 | 5 | Fallon [74] | 14,540 |
| 42 | 12 | A | Luton T | W 3-0 | 3-0 | 4 | Fallon 2 [3, 21], Hewlett [44] | 7008 |
| 43 | 17 | A | Wycombe W | W 3-0 | 1-0 | 4 | Miglioranzi [7], Parkin [52], Gurney (pen) [75] | 5769 |
| 44 | 24 | H | Oldham Ath | L 1-2 | 0-1 | 4 | Fallon [79] | 8506 |
| 45 | May 1 | A | QPR | L 0-1 | 0-1 | 5 | | 18,396 |
| 46 | 8 | H | Hartlepool U | D 1-1 | 1-0 | 5 | Igoe [7] | 11,627 |

**Final League Position: 5**

### GOALSCORERS

*League (76):* Mooney 19, Parkin 19, Fallon 6, Gurney 6 (2 pens), Igoe 5, Howard 4, Miglioranzi 4, Hewlett 3, Milner 2, O'Hanlon 2, Burton 1, Duke 1, Heywood 1, Nicholas 1, Robinson S 1, own goal 1.
*Carling Cup (5):* Parkin 3, Gurney 1, Mooney 1.
*FA Cup (1):* Gurney 1 (pen).
*LDV Vans Trophy (1):* Robinson S 1.
*Play-Offs (2):* Fallon 1, Parkin 1.

| Griemink B 5 + 1 | Duke D 35 + 7 | Robinson S 20 + 2 | Gurney A 42 | Viveash A 14 + 1 | Heywood M 39 + 1 | Miglioranzi S 34 + 1 | Igoe S 33 + 3 | Mooney T 41 + 4 | Parkin S 38 + 2 | Hewlett M 43 | Stevenson J 1 + 4 | Howard B 21 + 14 | Smith G — + 7 | Evans R 41 | Ifil J 16 | Milner J 6 | Reeves A 17 + 10 | Herring I 1 | Ruster S — + 2 | Burton D 4 | Nicholas A 28 + 3 | Lewis J 4 | Garrard L — + 1 | Fallon R 6 + 13 | O'Hanlon S 17 + 2 | Match No. |
|---|---|---|---|---|---|---|---|---|---|---|---|---|---|---|---|---|---|---|---|---|---|---|---|---|---|---|
| 1 | 2 | 3 | 4 | 5 | 6 | 7 | $8^{1}$ | 9 | 10 | $11^{2}$ | 12 | 13 | | | | | | | | | | | | | | 1 |
| 1 | 2 | 3 | 4 | 5 | 6 | 7 | 8 | 9 | 10 | 11 | | | | | | | | | | | | | | | | 2 |
| 1 | $2^{3}$ | $3^{2}$ | 4 | 5 | 6 | 7 | 8■ | $9^{1}$ | 10 | 11 | 12 | 13 | 14 | | | | | | | | | | | | | 3 |
| 1 | 2 | 3 | 4 | 5 | 6 | 7 | 8 | 9 | 10 | 11 | | | | | | | | | | | | | | | | 4 |
| | 2 | $3^{2}$ | 4 | 5 | 6 | $7^{1}$ | 8 | 9 | 10 | 11 | | 13 | 12 | 1 | | | | | | | | | | | | 5 |
| | $3^{1}$ | | 2 | 5 | 6 | 7 | | 9 | 10 | 11 | | | | 1 | 4 | 8 | 12 | | | | | | | | | 6 |
| | 3 | | 2 | 5 | 6 | 7 | | 9 | 10 | 11 | | | | 1 | 4 | $8^{1}$ | 12 | | | | | | | | | 7 |
| | 3 | | 2 | 5 | 6 | 7 | | 9 | 10 | 11 | | | | 1 | 4 | 8 | | | | | | | | | | 8 |
| | $3^{3}$ | | 2 | $5^{2}$ | 6 | 7 | 12 | 9 | 10 | 11 | | 14 | | 1 | 4 | $8^{1}$ | 13 | | | | | | | | | 9 |
| | | | 3 | 5 | 6 | 2 | $7^{1}$ | 9 | 10 | 11 | | 12 | | 1 | 4 | 8 | | | | | | | | | | 10 |
| | $3^{2}$ | 12 | 2 | 5 | 6 | 7■ | $8^{3}$ | 9 | | $11^{1}$ | | 14 | | 1 | 4 | 10 | 13 | | | | | | | | | 11 |
| | 3 | | 4 | 5 | 6 | $7^{1}$ | $8^{3}$ | 9 | | 11 | 14 | 10 | $12^{2}$ | 1 | | | 13 | 2 | | | | | | | | 12 |
| | 3 | 10 | 2 | 4 | 6 | | $8^{2}$ | 9 | | 11 | $7^{1}$ | 12 | | 1 | | | 5 | | 13 | | | | | | | 13 |
| | 3 | 7 | 2 | $4^{1}$ | 6 | | | 9 | | 11 | | $8^{2}$ | | 1 | | | 5 | | 12 | 10 | 13 | | | | | 14 |
| 15 | 3 | 7 | 2 | | 6 | | | 9 | | $11^{2}$ | | $8^{1}$ | 12 | $1^{6}$ | | | 5 | | | 10 | | 4 | 13 | | | 15 |
| | $3^{1}$ | 4 | | | 6 | 7 | | 9 | | 11 | 13 | 12 | | 1 | | | 5 | | | $10^{2}$ | 8 | 2 | | | | 16 |
| | $2^{2}$ | 3 | 4 | | 6 | 7 | | 9 | 12 | 11 | | 14 | | 1 | | | 13 | | | $10^{1}$ | 5 | $8^{3}$ | | | | 17 |
| | 3 | $8^{1}$ | 2 | | 6■ | 7 | | 9 | $10^{2}$ | 11 | | | | 1 | 5 | | 12 | | | | | 4 | | 13 | | 18 |
| | 3 | $2^{3}$ | 4 | | 6 | 7 | | $9^{2}$ | 10 | 11 | | $8^{1}$ | | 1 | 5 | | 12 | | | | 14 | | | 13 | | 19 |
| | 3 | 2 | 4 | | | $7^{1}$ | | 9 | 10 | 11 | | | | 1 | 6 | | 5 | | | | 8 | | | 12 | | 20 |
| | $3^{1}$ | 2■ | 4 | | 6 | 7 | $8^{2}$ | 9 | 10 | $11^{3}$ | | 12 | | 1 | 5 | | | | | | 14 | | | 13 | | 21 |
| | 13 | 4 | 2 | | $5^{1}$ | 7 | $8^{2}$ | 9 | 10 | | | 11 | | 1 | 6 | | 12 | | | | 3 | | | | | 22 |
| | 12 | 4 | 2 | | | 7 | $8^{2}$ | 13 | 10 | | | $3^{1}$ | | 1 | 6 | | 5 | | | | 11 | | | 9■ | | 23 |
| | | | 3 | | | 7 | 8 | 9 | 10 | 11 | | 4 | | 1 | 6 | | 5 | | | | 2 | | | | | 24 |
| | 12 | 13 | 2 | | | 7 | $8^{2}$ | 9 | 10 | 11 | | $3^{1}$ | | 1 | 6 | | 5 | | | | 4 | | | | | 25 |
| | 12 | $7^{2}$ | 4 | | 13 | | 8 | 9 | 10 | 11 | | $3^{1}$ | | 1 | 6 | | 5 | | | | 2 | | | | | 26 |
| | 3 | 7 | | | 5 | | 8 | 9 | 10 | 11 | | 4 | | 1 | 6 | | | | | | 2 | | | | | 27 |
| | 3 | $7^{2}$ | | | 4 | | 8 | 9 | 10 | 11 | | $6^{1}$ | 12 | 1 | | | 5 | | | | 2 | | | | 13 | 28 |
| | $3^{1}$ | $7^{3}$ | 2 | | 6 | | 8 | 9 | 10 | 11 | | 12 | | 1 | | | $5^{2}$ | | | | 4 | | | 13 | 14 | 29 |
| | 3 | | 4 | | 6 | 12 | $8^{1}$ | $9^{2}$ | 10 | 11 | | | | 1 | | | 5 | | | | 7 | | | 13 | 2 | 30 |
| | $3^{1}$ | | 4 | | 6 | 7 | 12 | 9 | 10 | 11 | | $8^{2}$ | 13 | 1 | | | | | | | 5 | | | | 2 | 31 |
| | | | 5 | | 6 | 7 | 8 | 9 | 10 | 11 | | 4 | | 1 | | | | | | | 3 | | | | 2 | 32 |
| | | | 4 | | 5 | 7 | 8 | 9 | 10 | 11 | | 6 | | 1 | | | | | | | 3 | | | | 2 | 33 |
| | 13 | | 4 | | 5 | $7^{2}$ | 8 | 9 | 10 | 11 | | 6 | | 1 | | | | | | | $3^{1}$ | | | 12 | 2 | 34 |
| | 12 | | 4■ | | 6 | | 8 | 9 | 10 | 11 | | 7 | | 1 | | | $5^{1}$ | | | | $3^{2}$ | | | 13 | 2 | 35 |
| | 3 | | 4 | | 5 | | 7 | 9 | 10 | 11 | | 6■ | | 1 | | | | | | | 8 | | | | 2 | 36 |
| | 3 | | 4 | | 5 | | 7 | 9 | 10 | 11 | | $6^{1}$ | | 1 | | | | | | | 8 | | | 12 | 2 | 37 |
| | 12 | | | | 6 | 7 | 8 | $9^{2}$ | 10 | 11 | | $4^{1}$ | | 1 | | | 5 | | | | 3 | | | 13 | 2 | 38 |
| | $3^{1}$ | | 4 | | 6 | 7 | $8^{2}$ | 9 | 10 | 11 | | 12 | | 1 | | | | | | | 5 | | | 13 | 2 | 39 |
| 1 | 11 | | 4 | | 6 | 7 | 8 | 9 | 10 | | | | | | | | 5 | | | | 3 | | | 12 | $2^{1}$ | 40 |
| | 3 | | 4 | | 5 | 6 | 7 | 9 | 10 | 11 | | | | 1 | | | | | | | $8^{1}$ | | | 12 | 2 | 41 |
| | 3 | | 4 | | 6 | 7 | 8 | 12 | $10^{1}$ | 11 | | | | 1 | | | | | | | 5 | | | 9 | 2 | 42 |
| | $3^{2}$ | | 4 | 12 | 6 | 7 | 8 | 14 | $10^{3}$ | 11 | | 13 | | 1 | | | | | | | 5 | | | 9 | $2^{1}$ | 43 |
| | 3 | | 4 | | 6 | 7 | 12 | 9 | 13 | $11^{3}$ | | $8^{1}$ | | 1 | | | 14 | | | | $5^{2}$ | | | 10 | 2 | 44 |
| | 3 | | 4 | | | $7^{2}$ | $8^{1}$ | 12 | 10 | 11 | | 13 | 14 | 1 | | | 5 | | | | $6^{3}$ | | | 9 | 2 | 45 |
| | 3 | | 4 | | | | 8 | | 10 | 11 | | 7 | | 1 | | | 5 | | | | 6 | | | 9 | 2 | 46 |

**Carling Cup**

| | | | |
|---|---|---|---|
| First Round | Southend U | (a) | 3-2 |
| Second Round | Leeds U | (a) | 2-2 |

**LDV Vans Trophy**

| | | | |
|---|---|---|---|
| First Round | Boston U | (a) | 1-2 |

**FA Cup**

| | | | |
|---|---|---|---|
| First Round | Wycombe W | (a) | 1-4 |

**Play-Offs**

| | | | |
|---|---|---|---|
| Semi-Final | Brighton & HA | (h) | 0-1 |
| | | (a) | 2-1 |

# TORQUAY UNITED FL Championship 1

## FOUNDATION

The idea of establishing a Torquay club was agreed by old boys of Torquay College and Torbay College, while sitting in Princess Gardens listening to the band. A proper meeting was subsequently held at Tor Abbey Hotel at which officers were elected. This was on 1 May 1899 and the club's first competition was the Eastern League (later known as the East Devon League). As an amateur club it played at Teignmouth Road, Torquay Recreation Ground and Cricket Field Road before settling down for four years at Torquay Cricket Ground where the rugby club now plays. They became Torquay United in 1921 after merging with Babbacombe FC.

***Plainmoor Ground, Torquay, Devon TQ1 3PS.***

***Telephone:*** (01803) 328 666.

***Fax:*** (01803) 323 976.

***Ticket Office:*** (01803) 328 666.

***Website:*** www.torquayunited.com

***Email:*** gullsfc@freeuk.com

***Ground Capacity:*** 6,269.

***Record Attendance:*** 21,908 v Huddersfield T, FA Cup 4th rd, 29 January 1955.

***Pitch Measurements:*** 110yd × 74yd.

***Chairman:*** Michael Bateson.

***Vice-chairman:*** Mervyn Benney.

***Secretary:*** Heather Kindeleit-Badcock.

***Manager:*** Leroy Rosenior.

***Physio:*** Norman Medhurst.

***Colours:*** Yellow shirts, blue shorts, yellow stockings.

***Change Colours:*** White shirts, white shorts with pale blue trim.

***Year Formed:*** 1899.

***Turned Professional:*** 1921.

***Ltd Co.:*** 1921.

***Previous Name:*** 1910, Torquay Town; 1921, Torquay United.

***Club Nickname:*** 'The Gulls'.

***Previous Grounds:*** 1899, Teignmouth Road; 1900, Torquay Recreation Ground; 1904, Cricket Field Road; 1906, Torquay Cricket Ground; 1910, Plainmoor Ground.

***First Football League Game:*** 27 August 1927, Division 3 (S), v Exeter C (h) D 1–1 – Millsom; Cook, Smith; Wellock, Wragg, Connor, Mackey, Turner (1), Jones, McGovern, Thomson.

## HONOURS

*Football League:* Division 3 – Promoted 2003–04 (3rd); Division 3 (S) – Runners-up 1956–57; Division 4 – Promoted 1959–60 (3rd), 1965–66 (3rd), 1990–91 (play-offs).

*FA Cup:* best season: 4th rd, 1949, 1955, 1971, 1983, 1990.

*Football League Cup:* never past 3rd rd.

*Sherpa Van Trophy:* Runners-up 1989.

## SKY SPORTS FACT FILE

The struggle for promotion in 1956–57 went down to the wire. On 1 May Torquay United a point ahead needed a win at Crystal Palace to go up. But while this ended goalless, Alf Ramsey's Ipswich Town won 2-0 at Southampton to take it on goal average.

***Record League Victory:*** 9–0 v Swindon T, Division 3 (S), 8 March 1952 – George Webber; Topping, Ralph Calland; Brown, Eric Webber, Towers; Shaw (1), Marchant (1), Northcott (2), Collins (3), Edds (2).

***Record Cup Victory:*** 7–1 v Northampton T, FA Cup 1st rd, 14 November 1959 – Gill; Penford, Downs; Bettany, George Northcott, Rawson; Baxter, Cox, Tommy Northcott (1), Bond (3), Pym (3).

***Record Defeat:*** 2–10 v Fulham, Division 3 (S), 7 September 1931. 2–10 v Luton T, Division 3 (S), 2 September 1933.

***Most League Points (2 for a win):*** 60, Division 4, 1959–60.

***Most League Points (3 for a win):*** 81, Division 3, 2003–04.

***Most League Goals:*** 89, Division 3 (S), 1956–57.

***Highest League Scorer in Season:*** Sammy Collins, 40, Division 3 (S), 1955–56.

***Most League Goals in Total Aggregate:*** Sammy Collins, 204, 1948–58.

***Most League Goals in One Match:*** 5, Robin Stubbs v Newport Co, Division 4, 19 October 1963.

***Most Capped Player:*** Rodney Jack, St Vincent.

***Most League Appearances:*** Dennis Lewis, 443, 1947–59.

***Youngest League Player:*** David Byng, 16 years 36 days v Walsall, 14 August 1993.

***Record Transfer Fee Received:*** £500,000 from Crewe Alex for Rodney Jack, July 1998.

***Record Transfer Fee Paid:*** £70,000 to Barry T for Eifion Williams, March 1999.

***Football League Record:*** 1927 Elected to Division 3 (S); 1958–60 Division 4; 1960–62 Division 3; 1962–66 Division 4; 1966–72 Division 3; 1972–91 Division 4; 1991–2004 Division 3; 2004– FL1.

## MANAGERS

Percy Mackrill 1927–29
A. H. Hoskins 1929
*(Secretary-Manager)*
Frank Womack 1929–32
Frank Brown 1932–38
Alf Steward 1938–40
Billy Butler 1945–46
Jack Butler 1946–47
John McNeil 1947–50
Bob John 1950
Alex Massie 1950–51
Eric Webber 1951–65
Frank O'Farrell 1965–68
Alan Brown 1969–71
Jack Edwards 1971–73
Malcolm Musgrove 1973–76
Mike Green 1977–81
Frank O'Farrell 1981–82
*(continued as General Manager to 1983)*
Bruce Rioch 1982–84
Dave Webb 1984–85
John Sims 1985
Stuart Morgan 1985–87
Cyril Knowles 1987–89
Dave Smith 1989–91
John Impey 1991–92
Ivan Golac 1992
Paul Compton 1992–93
Don O'Riordan 1993–95
Eddie May 1995–96
Kevin Hodges *(Head Coach)* 1996–98
Wes Saunders 1998–2001
Roy McFarland 2001–02
Leroy Rosenior June 2002–

## LATEST SEQUENCES

***Longest Sequence of League Wins:*** 8, 24.1.1998 – 3.3.1998.

***Longest Sequence of League Defeats:*** 8, 30.9.1995 – 18.11.1995.

***Longest Sequence of League Draws:*** 8, 25.10.1969 – 13.12.1969.

***Longest Sequence of Unbeaten League Matches:*** 15, 5.5.1990 – 3.11.1990.

***Longest Sequence Without a League Win:*** 17, 5.3.1938 – 10.9.1938.

***Successive Scoring Runs:*** 19 from 3.10.1953.

***Successive Non-scoring Runs:*** 7 from 8.1.1972.

## TEN YEAR LEAGUE RECORD

| | | P | W | D | L | F | A | Pts | Pos |
|---|---|---|---|---|---|---|---|---|---|
| 1994-95 | Div 3 | 42 | 14 | 13 | 15 | 54 | 57 | 55 | 13 |
| 1995-96 | Div 3 | 46 | 5 | 14 | 27 | 30 | 84 | 29 | 24 |
| 1996-97 | Div 3 | 46 | 13 | 11 | 22 | 46 | 62 | 50 | 21 |
| 1997-98 | Div 3 | 46 | 21 | 11 | 14 | 68 | 59 | 74 | 5 |
| 1998-99 | Div 3 | 46 | 12 | 17 | 17 | 47 | 58 | 53 | 20 |
| 1999-2000 | Div 3 | 46 | 19 | 12 | 15 | 62 | 52 | 69 | 9 |
| 2000-01 | Div 3 | 46 | 12 | 13 | 21 | 52 | 77 | 49 | 21 |
| 2001-02 | Div 3 | 46 | 12 | 15 | 19 | 46 | 63 | 51 | 19 |
| 2002-03 | Div 3 | 46 | 16 | 18 | 12 | 71 | 71 | 66 | 9 |
| 2003-04 | Div 3 | 46 | 23 | 12 | 11 | 68 | 44 | 81 | 3 |

## DID YOU KNOW ?

In 1989–90 Carl Airey equalled Sammy Collins record of scoring in seven successive League games for Torquay United and might well have beaten it in the following match on 14 November had he been allowed to take a penalty kick against Gillingham.

## TORQUAY UNITED 2003–04 LEAGUE RECORD

| Match No. | Date | Venue | Opponents | Result | | H/T Score | Lg. Pos. | Goalscorers | Atten-dance |
|---|---|---|---|---|---|---|---|---|---|
| 1 | Aug 9 | A | Northampton T | W | 1-0 | 0-0 | — | Fowler[62] | 5675 |
| 2 | 16 | H | Lincoln C | W | 1-0 | 0-0 | 7 | Hockley[89] | 2920 |
| 3 | 23 | A | Macclesfield T | D | 1-1 | 0-1 | 6 | Wills[55] | 1970 |
| 4 | 25 | H | Rochdale | L | 1-3 | 0-0 | 7 | Graham[75] | 3003 |
| 5 | 30 | A | Scunthorpe U | L | 1-2 | 1-0 | 12 | Gritton[15] | 3080 |
| 6 | Sept 6 | H | Leyton Orient | W | 2-1 | 0-0 | 9 | Graham 2[54, 73] | 2362 |
| 7 | 13 | A | Cambridge U | D | 1-1 | 1-1 | 10 | Osei-Kuffour[36] | 3723 |
| 8 | 16 | H | Bristol R | W | 2-1 | 2-0 | — | Graham[31], Taylor[45] | 3691 |
| 9 | 20 | H | Darlington | D | 2-2 | 2-1 | 6 | Woods[11], Graham[36] | 2420 |
| 10 | 27 | A | Yeovil T | W | 2-0 | 1-0 | 4 | Graham[15], Osei-Kuffour[67] | 7718 |
| 11 | Oct 1 | A | Oxford U | L | 0-1 | 0-0 | — | | 5479 |
| 12 | 4 | H | Bury | W | 3-1 | 1-1 | 5 | Graham[26], Osei-Kuffour[46], Russell[85] | 2732 |
| 13 | 11 | A | Huddersfield T | L | 0-1 | 0-0 | 7 | | 9117 |
| 14 | 18 | H | Hull C | D | 1-1 | 1-0 | 8 | Graham[7] | 3720 |
| 15 | 21 | H | Mansfield T | W | 1-0 | 1-0 | — | Hockley[35] | 2773 |
| 16 | 25 | A | Boston U | L | 0-4 | 0-1 | 8 | | 2431 |
| 17 | Nov 1 | A | Doncaster R | L | 0-1 | 0-1 | 10 | | 6863 |
| 18 | 15 | H | Cheltenham T | W | 3-1 | 0-0 | 9 | Graham 2[51, 68], Russell[86] | 2653 |
| 19 | 22 | A | Kidderminster H | W | 2-1 | 1-1 | 8 | Wills 2[7, 58] | 2725 |
| 20 | 29 | H | Southend U | W | 3-0 | 1-0 | 7 | Bedeau[45], Hockley[52], Graham[54] | 2631 |
| 21 | Dec 13 | H | York C | D | 1-1 | 0-0 | 7 | Parkin (og)[57] | 2564 |
| 22 | 20 | A | Carlisle U | L | 0-2 | 0-1 | 7 | | 3600 |
| 23 | 26 | H | Swansea C | D | 0-0 | 0-0 | 8 | | 4447 |
| 24 | 28 | A | Leyton Orient | D | 0-0 | 0-0 | 8 | | 4288 |
| 25 | Jan 3 | A | Rochdale | L | 0-1 | 0-1 | 9 | | 2559 |
| 26 | 10 | H | Northampton T | W | 3-1 | 2-0 | 9 | Osei-Kuffour[12], Canoville[40], Taylor[78] | 2585 |
| 27 | 17 | A | Lincoln C | W | 3-1 | 1-1 | 8 | Fowler[10], Hill[56], Osei-Kuffour[89] | 3873 |
| 28 | 24 | H | Macclesfield T | W | 4-1 | 3-1 | 8 | Hill[8], Graham[33], Taylor[41], Gritton[87] | 2770 |
| 29 | Feb 7 | A | Swansea C | W | 2-1 | 1-0 | 6 | Graham[18], Osei-Kuffour[85] | 7323 |
| 30 | 14 | H | Huddersfield T | L | 0-1 | 0-0 | 7 | | 3821 |
| 31 | 21 | A | Hull C | W | 1-0 | 1-0 | 7 | Gritton[45] | 15,222 |
| 32 | 24 | H | Scunthorpe U | W | 1-0 | 1-0 | — | Hockley[13] | 2561 |
| 33 | 28 | H | Boston U | W | 2-0 | 1-0 | 4 | Graham[27], Woods (pen)[57] | 3000 |
| 34 | Mar 6 | H | Carlisle U | W | 4-1 | 2-0 | 5 | Hill 2[4, 21], Graham[52], Woods (pen)[63] | 3366 |
| 35 | 13 | A | York C | D | 0-0 | 0-0 | 5 | | 3150 |
| 36 | 16 | A | Bristol R | D | 2-2 | 2-1 | — | Osei-Kuffour 2[5, 17] | 6461 |
| 37 | 20 | H | Cambridge U | W | 3-0 | 2-0 | 3 | Hockley[22], Graham 2[39, 50] | 2975 |
| 38 | 27 | A | Darlington | D | 1-1 | 0-1 | 4 | Graham[66] | 4317 |
| 39 | 30 | A | Mansfield T | L | 1-2 | 1-2 | — | Gritton[17] | 4552 |
| 40 | Apr 3 | H | Yeovil T | D | 2-2 | 1-2 | 4 | Taylor[44], Woods[59] | 6156 |
| 41 | 9 | A | Bury | L | 1-2 | 1-1 | — | Graham[30] | 2770 |
| 42 | 12 | H | Oxford U | W | 3-0 | 1-0 | 4 | Wanless (og)[33], Hazell[63], Graham[75] | 5114 |
| 43 | 17 | H | Doncaster R | W | 1-0 | 1-0 | 4 | Hill[38] | 5808 |
| 44 | 24 | A | Cheltenham T | W | 3-1 | 1-0 | 4 | Osei-Kuffour 2[18, 78], Woods[65] | 4900 |
| 45 | May 1 | H | Kidderminster H | D | 1-1 | 1-0 | — | Graham[42] | 5515 |
| 46 | 8 | A | Southend U | W | 2-1 | 2-1 | 3 | Woods[3], Graham[11] | 8894 |

**Final League Position: 3**

## GOALSCORERS

*League (68):* Graham 22, Osei-Kuffour 10, Woods 6 (2 pens), Hill 5, Hockley 5, Gritton 4, Taylor 4, Wills 3, Fowler 2, Russell 2, Bedeau 1, Canoville 1, Hazell 1, own goals 2.
*Carling Cup (1):* Graham 1.
*FA Cup (1):* Benefield 1.
*LDV Vans Trophy (2):* Benefield 1, Wills 1.

| Van Heusden A 25 | Woozley D 4 + 6 | Hankin S 1 | Hockley M 44 + 1 | Taylor C 43 | Woods S 46 | Russell A 42 + 1 | Canoville L 32 + 1 | Osei-Kuffour J 33 + 8 | Fowler J 24 + 7 | Hill K 42 + 3 | Graham D 41 + 4 | Wills K 7 + 16 | Gritton M 17 + 14 | Benefield J 3 + 12 | Killoughery G — + 3 | Bedeau A 13 + 11 | McGlinchey B 34 | Williamson M 9 + 2 | Broad J 4 + 10 | Dearden K 21 + 1 | Bond K — + 1 | Hazell R 12 + 7 | Bernard N — + 1 | Rosenior L 9 + 1 | McMahon D — + 1 | *Match No.* |
|---|---|---|---|---|---|---|---|---|---|---|---|---|---|---|---|---|---|---|---|---|---|---|---|---|---|---|
| 1 | 2 | 3 | 4 | 5 | 6 | 7 | 8 | $9^1$ | 10 | $11^2$ | 12 | 13 | | | | | | | | | | | | | | 1 |
| 1 | $3^2$ | | 4 | 5 | 6 | 7 | 2 | $9^3$ | $8^1$ | 11 | 10 | 12 | 13 | 14 | | | | | | | | | | | | 2 |
| 1 | | | 4 | 5 | 6 | 7 | 2 | $9^2$ | $8^1$ | 3 | 11 | 12 | 10 | 13 | | | | | | | | | | | | 3 |
| 1 | | | 4■ | 5 | 6 | 7 | $2^1$ | 13 | 12 | $3^3$ | 9 | 11 | 10 | $8^2$ | 14 | | | | | | | | | | | 4 |
| 1 | | | 2 | 5 | 6 | $8^1$ | | 9 | $4^3$ | 3 | 12 | 11 | 10 | 13 | 14 | $7^2$ | | | | | | | | | | 5 |
| 1 | | | 4 | 5■ | 6 | 8 | 2 | | $11^2$ | 3 | 12 | $9^1$ | 10 | 13 | | 7 | | | | | | | | | | 6 |
| 1 | | | | 5 | 6 | 8 | 2 | $7^1$ | 4 | 11 | 9 | 12 | 10 | | | | 3 | | | | | | | | | 7 |
| 1 | | | 4 | 5 | 6 | 7 | 2 | 10 | $8^1$ | 11 | $9^2$ | 12 | | | | | 3 | 13 | | | | | | | | 8 |
| 1 | | | 4 | | 6 | 7 | $2^3$ | 11 | $8^2$ | 3 | 9 | 12 | $10^1$ | 13 | 14 | | | 5 | | | | | | | | 9 |
| 1 | | | 4 | | 6 | 7 | $2^1$ | 10 | 8 | 11 | 9 | | | | | | 3 | 5 | 12 | | | | | | | 10 |
| 1 | | | 2 | | 6 | 7 | | $10^1$ | 4 | 11 | 9 | 12 | | 13 | | | 3 | 5 | $8^2$ | | | | | | | 11 |
| 1 | | | 2 | 4 | 6 | 7 | | 10 | 8 | 11 | 9 | | | | | | 3 | 5 | | | | | | | | 12 |
| | | | 2 | 4 | 6 | 7 | | 10 | $8^1$ | 11 | 9 | | | 12 | | | 3 | 5 | | 1 | | | | | | 13 |
| | | | 2 | 4 | 6 | 7 | | $10^2$ | 8 | 12 | $9^3$ | 13 | | | | $11^1$ | 3 | 5 | 14 | 1 | | | | | | 14 |
| | | | 2 | 4 | 6 | 7 | | 10 | $8^3$ | 12 | $9^2$ | | | 13 | | $11^1$ | 3 | 5 | 14 | 1 | | | | | | 15 |
| | | | 2 | 4 | 6 | $7^3$ | | 10 | $8^1$ | 11 | $9^2$ | | | 12 | | | 3 | 5 | 13 | 1 | 14 | | | | | 16 |
| | | | 2 | 4 | 6 | 7 | | $10^2$ | $8^1$ | 11 | 9 | 12 | | 13 | | | 3 | 5 | | 1 | | | | | | 17 |
| $1^6$ | | | 4 | 5 | 6 | 8 | 2 | | | 11 | 9 | 12 | | $10^1$ | | $7^2$ | 3 | 13 | | 15 | | | | | | 18 |
| 1 | | | 8 | 5 | 6 | 7 | $2^1$ | | | 11 | $9^2$ | 10 | | 13 | | 12 | 3 | | | | | 4 | | | | 19 |
| 1 | | | 4 | 5 | 6 | $8^2$ | $2^3$ | | | 11 | $9^1$ | 10 | | 12 | | 7 | 3 | | 13 | | | 14 | | | | 20 |
| 1 | | | 4 | 5 | 6 | 8 | $2^3$ | 12 | | | 9 | $10^1$ | | $11^2$ | | 7 | 3 | | 13 | | | | 14 | | | 21 |
| 1 | | | 4 | 5 | 6 | 8 | 2 | 13 | | 3 | 9 | $10^1$ | 12 | | | 7■ | | | $11^2$ | | | | | | | 22 |
| 1 | | | 12 | 5 | 6 | 8 | 2 | 11 | $4^1$ | 3 | 9 | 13 | $10^2$ | | | 7 | | | | | | | | | | 23 |
| 1 | 6 | | 4 | 5 | 8 | 13 | $2^1$ | 12 | | 3 | 9 | | | | | 7 | | | $10^2$ | | | 11 | | | | 24 |
| 1 | $6^2$ | | 4 | 5 | 8 | 7 | 2 | 12 | 13 | 3 | 9 | 14 | $10^3$ | | | | | | | | | $11^1$ | | | | 25 |
| | | | 4 | 5 | 6 | 7 | 2 | 9 | $8^2$ | 11 | | 12 | $10^1$ | | | | | | 13 | 1 | | 3 | | | | 26 |
| | | | 4 | 5 | 6 | 7 | 2 | 9 | $8^2$ | 11 | 12 | | $10^1$ | | | | 3 | | | 1 | | 13 | | | | 27 |
| | | | 4 | 5 | 6 | 7 | | $10^2$ | $8^1$ | 11 | $9^3$ | | 13 | | | 12 | 3 | | 14 | 1 | | 2 | | | | 28 |
| | | | 4 | 5 | 6 | 7 | 2 | 12 | $8^2$ | 11 | $9^3$ | | $10^1$ | | | 13 | 3 | | | 1 | | 14 | | | | 29 |
| | | | 4 | 5 | 6 | 7 | 2 | 10 | $8^2$ | 11 | 9 | | 12 | | | 13 | $3^1$ | | | 1 | | | | | | 30 |
| | | | 4 | 5 | 6 | 7 | 2 | $10^1$ | $8^2$ | 11 | $9^3$ | | 12 | | | 13 | 3 | | | 1 | | 14 | | | | 31 |
| | 14 | | 4 | 5 | 6 | 7 | 2 | | $8^2$ | 11 | $9^3$ | 12 | $10^1$ | | | 13 | 3 | | | 1 | | | | | | 32 |
| | | | 4 | 5 | 6 | $7^2$ | $2^3$ | 10 | | 11 | $9^1$ | | 12 | | | 8 | 3 | | 13 | 1 | | 14 | | | | 33 |
| | 12 | | 4 | $5^1$ | 6 | 8 | 2 | $10^2$ | | $11^3$ | 9 | | 13 | | | 7 | 3 | | 14 | 1 | | | | | | 34 |
| | | | 4 | 5 | 6 | | 2 | $10^1$ | | 11 | 9 | | 12 | | | | 3 | | 8 | 1 | | 7 | | | | 35 |
| | 12 | | 4 | 5 | 6 | | $2^2$ | 10 | | 11 | 9 | 13 | $8^1$ | | | | 3 | | | 1 | | 7 | | | | 36 |
| | | | 4 | 5 | 6 | | 2 | 10 | 12 | $11^3$ | $9^2$ | 13 | 8 | | | | 3 | | | 1 | | 14 | | $7^1$ | | 37 |
| | | | 4 | 5 | 6 | 8 | 2 | $10^1$ | | 11 | 9 | | 12 | | | 13 | 3 | | | 1 | | | | $7^2$ | | 38 |
| | | | $4^1$ | 5 | 6 | 8 | 2 | 13 | | $11^2$ | 9 | | 10 | | | 12 | 3 | | | 1 | | | | 7 | | 39 |
| | | | 4 | 5 | 6 | 8 | 2 | 12 | | $11^2$ | 9 | | $10^3$ | | | $7^1$ | 3 | | | 1 | | | | 13 | 14 | 40 |
| | | | 4 | 5 | 6 | 8 | $2^3$ | 11 | | 12 | 9 | | 10 | | | 13 | $3^1$ | | | 1 | | 14 | | $7^2$ | | 41 |
| 1 | 14 | | 4 | 5 | 6 | 8 | | 10 | 12 | 11 | $9^2$ | | 13 | | | | $3^3$ | | | | | 2 | | $7^1$ | | 42 |
| 1 | 14 | | 4 | 5 | 6 | 8 | | $10^2$ | 12 | 11 | $9^3$ | | 13 | | | | 3 | | | | | 2 | | $7^1$ | | 43 |
| 1 | | | 4 | 5 | 6 | 8 | | $10^3$ | 12 | 11 | $9^2$ | | 14 | | | 13 | 3 | | | | | 2 | | $7^1$ | | 44 |
| 1 | | | $4^2$ | 5 | 6 | 8 | 12 | 10 | 14 | 11 | 9 | | 13 | | | | $3^1$ | | | | | 2 | | $7^3$ | | 45 |
| 1 | 14 | | 4 | 5 | 6 | 8 | | $10^2$ | | 11 | $9^3$ | | 13 | | | 12 | 3 | | | | | 2 | | $7^1$ | | 46 |

**Carling Cup**
First Round Crystal Palace (h) 1-1

**LDV Vans Trophy**
First Round Peterborough U (a) 2-3

**FA Cup**
First Round Burton Alb (h) 1-2

# TOTTENHAM HOTSPUR FA Premiership

## FOUNDATION

The Hotspur Football Club was formed from an older cricket club in 1882. Most of the founders were old boys of St John's Presbyterian School and Tottenham Grammar School. The Casey brothers were well to the fore as the family provided the club's first goalposts (painted blue and white) and their first ball. They soon adopted the local YMCA as their meeting place, but after a couple of moves settled at the Red House, which is still their headquarters, although now known simply as 748 High Road.

***Bill Nicholson Way, 748 High Road, Tottenham, London N17 0AP.***

***Telephone:*** (020) 8365 5000.

***Fax:*** (020) 8365 5175.

***Ticket Office:*** 0870 420 5000.

***Website:*** www.spurs.co.uk

***Email:*** email@spurs.co.uk

***Ground Capacity:*** 36,252.

***Record Attendance:*** 75,038 v Sunderland, FA Cup 6th rd. 5 March 1938.

***Pitch Measurements:*** 110yd × 73yd.

***Chairman:*** Daniel Levy.

***Secretary:*** John Alexander.

***Sporting Director:*** Frank Arnesen.

***Manager:*** Jacques Santini.

***Assistant Manager:*** Martin Jol.

***Colours:*** White shirts, navy shorts, white stockings.

***Change Colours:*** Navy shirts, white shorts, navy stockings.

***Year Formed:*** 1882.

***Turned Professional:*** 1895.

***Ltd Co.:*** 1898.

***Previous Name:*** 1882–84, Hotspur Football Club.

***Club Nickname:*** 'Spurs'.

***Previous Grounds:*** 1882, Tottenham Marshes; 1888, Northumberland Park; 1899, White Hart Lane.

***First Football League Game:*** 1 September 1908, Division 2, v Wolverhampton W (h) W 3–0 – Hewitson; Coquet, Burton; Morris (1), D. Steel, Darnell; Walton, Woodward (2), Macfarlane, R. Steel, Middlemiss.

***Record League Victory:*** 9–0 v Bristol R, Division 2, 22 October 1977 – Daines; Naylor, Holmes, Hoddle (1), McAllister, Perryman, Pratt, McNab, Moores (3), Lee (4), Taylor (1).

## HONOURS

*Football League:* Division 1 – Champions 1950–51, 1960–61; Runners-up 1921–22, 1951–52, 1956–57, 1962–63; Division 2 – Champions 1919–20, 1949–50; Runners-up 1908–09, 1932–33; Promoted 1977–78 (3rd).

*FA Cup:* Winners 1901 (as non-League club), 1921, 1961, 1962, 1967, 1981, 1982, 1991; Runners-up 1987.

*Football League Cup:* Winners 1971, 1973, 1999; Runners-up 1982, 2002.

***European Competitions:*** *European Cup:* 1961–62. *European Cup-Winners' Cup:* 1962–63 (winners), 1963–64, 1967–68, 1981–82, 1982–83, 1991–92. *UEFA Cup:* 1971–72 (winners), 1972–73, 1973–74 (runners-up), 1983–84 (winners), 1984–85, 1999–2000. *Intertoto Cup:* 1995.

## SKY SPORTS FACT FILE

On two occasions Tottenham Hotspur have been involved in 5-5 draws. The first on 19 September 1925 was against Huddersfield Town who were on course for a third League title. The second was on 19 March 1966 against Aston Villa after leading 5-1.

***Record Cup Victory:*** 13–2 v Crewe Alex, FA Cup 4th rd (replay), 3 February 1960 – Brown; Hills, Henry; Blanchflower, Norman, Mackay; White, Harmer (1), Smith (4), Allen (5), Jones (3 incl. 1p).

***Record Defeat:*** 0–8 v Cologne, UEFA Intertoto Cup, 22 July 1995.

***Most League Points (2 for a win):*** 70, Division 2, 1919–20.

***Most League Points (3 for a win):*** 77, Division 1, 1984–85.

***Most League Goals:*** 115, Division 1, 1960–61.

***Highest League Scorer in Season:*** Jimmy Greaves, 37, Division 1, 1962–63.

***Most League Goals in Total Aggregate:*** Jimmy Greaves, 220, 1961–70.

***Most League Goals in One Match:*** 5, Ted Harper v Reading, Division 2, 30 August 1930; 5, Alf Stokes v Birmingham C, Division 1, 18 September 1957; 5, Bobby Smith v Aston Villa, Division 1, 29 March 1958.

***Most Capped Player:*** Pat Jennings, 74 (119), Northern Ireland.

***Most League Appearances:*** Steve Perryman, 655, 1969–86.

***Youngest League Player:*** Ally Dick, 16 years 301 days v Manchester C, 20 February 1982.

***Record Transfer Fee Received:*** £5,500,000 from Lazio for Paul Gascoigne, May 1992.

***Record Transfer Fee Paid:*** £11,000,000 to Dynamo Kiev for Sergei Rebrov, May 2000.

***Football League Record:*** 1908 Elected to Division 2; 1909–15 Division 1; 1919–20 Division 2; 1920–28 Division 1; 1928–33 Division 2; 1933–35 Division 1; 1935–50 Division 2; 1950–77 Division 1; 1977–78 Division 2; 1978–92 Division 1; 1992– FA Premier League.

## MANAGERS

Frank Brettell 1898–99
John Cameron 1899–1906
Fred Kirkham 1907–08
Peter McWilliam 1912–27
Billy Minter 1927–29
Percy Smith 1930–35
Jack Tresadern 1935–38
Peter McWilliam 1938–42
Arthur Turner 1942–46
Joe Hulme 1946–49
Arthur Rowe 1949–55
Jimmy Anderson 1955–58
Bill Nicholson 1958–74
Terry Neill 1974–76
Keith Burkinshaw 1976–84
Peter Shreeves 1984–86
David Pleat 1986–87
Terry Venables 1987–91
Peter Shreeves 1991–92
Ossie Ardiles 1993–94
Gerry Francis 1994–97
Christian Gross *(Head Coach)* 1997–98
George Graham 1998–2001
Glenn Hoddle 2001–03
David Pleat (*Caretaker*) 2003–04
Jacques Santini June 2004–

## LATEST SEQUENCES

***Longest Sequence of League Wins:*** 13, 23.4.1960 – 1.10.1960.

***Longest Sequence of League Defeats:*** 7, 1.1.1994 – 27.2.1994.

***Longest Sequence of League Draws:*** 6, 9.1.1999 – 27.2.1999.

***Longest Sequence of Unbeaten League Matches:*** 22, 31.8.1949 – 31.12.1949.

***Longest Sequence Without a League Win:*** 16, 29.12.1934 – 13.4.1935.

***Successive Scoring Runs:*** 32 from 24.2.1962

***Successive Non-scoring Runs:*** 6 from 28.12.1985

## TEN YEAR LEAGUE RECORD

| | | *P* | *W* | *D* | *L* | *F* | *A* | *Pts* | *Pos* |
|---|---|---|---|---|---|---|---|---|---|
| 1994-95 | PR Lge | 42 | 16 | 14 | 12 | 66 | 58 | 62 | 7 |
| 1995-96 | PR Lge | 38 | 16 | 13 | 9 | 50 | 38 | 61 | 8 |
| 1996-97 | PR Lge | 38 | 13 | 7 | 18 | 44 | 51 | 46 | 10 |
| 1997-98 | PR Lge | 38 | 11 | 11 | 16 | 44 | 56 | 44 | 14 |
| 1998-99 | PR Lge | 38 | 11 | 14 | 13 | 47 | 50 | 47 | 11 |
| 1999-2000 | PR Lge | 38 | 15 | 8 | 15 | 57 | 49 | 53 | 10 |
| 2000-01 | PR Lge | 38 | 13 | 10 | 15 | 47 | 54 | 49 | 12 |
| 2001-02 | PR Lge | 38 | 14 | 8 | 16 | 49 | 53 | 50 | 9 |
| 2002-03 | PR Lge | 38 | 14 | 8 | 16 | 51 | 62 | 50 | 10 |
| 2003-04 | PR Lge | 38 | 13 | 6 | 19 | 47 | 57 | 45 | 14 |

## DID YOU KNOW ?

Tottenham Hotspur made a splendid start to their Second Division championship winning season in 1919–20, remaining unbeaten in the opening 12 games, dropping just one point. In fact during the campaign they lost only 14 points overall.

## TOTTENHAM HOTSPUR 2003–04 LEAGUE RECORD

| Match No. | Date | Venue | Opponents | Result | | H/T Score | Lg. Pos. | Goalscorers | Attendance |
|---|---|---|---|---|---|---|---|---|---|
| 1 | Aug 16 | A | Birmingham C | L | 0-1 | 0-1 | — | | 29,358 |
| 2 | 23 | H | Leeds U | W | 2-1 | 1-1 | 10 | Taricco [41], Kanoute [71] | 34,350 |
| 3 | 27 | A | Liverpool | D | 0-0 | 0-0 | — | | 43,778 |
| 4 | 30 | H | Fulham | L | 0-3 | 0-1 | 15 | | 33,421 |
| 5 | Sept 13 | A | Chelsea | L | 2-4 | 1-2 | 16 | Kanoute 2 [25, 27] | 41,165 |
| 6 | 20 | H | Southampton | L | 1-3 | 0-2 | 18 | Kanoute [62] | 35,758 |
| 7 | 28 | A | Manchester C | D | 0-0 | 0-0 | 17 | | 46,842 |
| 8 | Oct 4 | H | Everton | W | 3-0 | 1-0 | 13 | Kanoute [43], Poyet [46], Keane [49] | 36,103 |
| 9 | 19 | A | Leicester C | W | 2-1 | 0-1 | 11 | Mabizela [79], Kanoute [90] | 31,521 |
| 10 | 26 | H | Middlesbrough | D | 0-0 | 0-0 | 12 | | 32,641 |
| 11 | Nov 1 | H | Bolton W | L | 0-1 | 0-0 | 12 | | 35,191 |
| 12 | 8 | A | Arsenal | L | 1-2 | 1-0 | 13 | Anderton [5] | 38,101 |
| 13 | 23 | H | Aston Villa | W | 2-1 | 0-0 | 12 | Ricketts [78], Keane [81] | 33,140 |
| 14 | 29 | A | Blackburn R | L | 0-1 | 0-0 | 15 | | 22,802 |
| 15 | Dec 6 | H | Wolverhampton W | W | 5-2 | 1-1 | 12 | Keane 3 [29, 75, 83], Kanoute [50], Dalmat [90] | 34,820 |
| 16 | 13 | A | Newcastle U | L | 0-4 | 0-1 | 13 | | 52,138 |
| 17 | 21 | H | Manchester U | L | 1-2 | 0-2 | 15 | Poyet [63] | 35,910 |
| 18 | 26 | A | Portsmouth | L | 0-2 | 0-0 | 17 | | 20,010 |
| 19 | 28 | H | Charlton Ath | L | 0-1 | 0-0 | 18 | | 34,534 |
| 20 | Jan 7 | H | Birmingham C | W | 4-1 | 3-0 | — | Dalmat 2 [10, 24], Davies [39], Keane [79] | 30,025 |
| 21 | 10 | A | Leeds U | W | 1-0 | 0-0 | 13 | Keane [56] | 35,365 |
| 22 | 17 | H | Liverpool | W | 2-1 | 1-0 | 11 | Keane (pen) [25], Postiga [54] | 36,104 |
| 23 | 31 | A | Fulham | L | 1-2 | 1-1 | 13 | Keane (pen) [18] | 17,024 |
| 24 | Feb 7 | H | Portsmouth | W | 4-3 | 2-1 | 12 | Defoe [13], Keane 2 [42, 79], Poyet [89] | 36,107 |
| 25 | 11 | A | Charlton Ath | W | 4-2 | 2-0 | — | Davies [10], Defoe [43], King [46], Jackson [85] | 26,645 |
| 26 | 22 | H | Leicester C | D | 4-4 | 3-1 | 10 | Brown [7], Defoe 2 [14, 89], Keane [28] | 35,218 |
| 27 | Mar 9 | A | Middlesbrough | L | 0-1 | 0-0 | — | | 31,789 |
| 28 | 14 | H | Newcastle U | W | 1-0 | 0-0 | 10 | O'Brien (og) [86] | 36,088 |
| 29 | 20 | A | Manchester U | L | 0-3 | 0-1 | 11 | | 67,644 |
| 30 | 27 | A | Southampton | L | 0-1 | 0-0 | 12 | | 31,973 |
| 31 | Apr 3 | H | Chelsea | L | 0-1 | 0-1 | 12 | | 36,101 |
| 32 | 9 | A | Everton | L | 1-3 | 0-3 | — | Carr [75] | 38,086 |
| 33 | 12 | H | Manchester C | D | 1-1 | 0-1 | 13 | Defoe [52] | 35,282 |
| 34 | 17 | A | Bolton W | L | 0-2 | 0-1 | 14 | | 26,440 |
| 35 | 25 | H | Arsenal | D | 2-2 | 0-2 | 16 | Redknapp [62], Keane (pen) [90] | 36,097 |
| 36 | May 2 | A | Aston Villa | L | 0-1 | 0-1 | 16 | | 42,573 |
| 37 | 8 | H | Blackburn R | W | 1-0 | 1-0 | 15 | Defoe [18] | 35,687 |
| 38 | 15 | A | Wolverhampton W | W | 2-0 | 1-0 | 14 | Keane [34], Defoe [57] | 29,389 |

**Final League Position: 14**

### GOALSCORERS

*League (47):* Keane 14 (3 pens), Defoe 7, Kanoute 7, Dalmat 3, Poyet 3, Davies 2, Anderton 1, Brown 1, Carr 1, Jackson 1, King 1, Mabizela 1, Postiga 1, Redknapp 1, Ricketts 1, Taricco 1, own goal 1.
*Carling Cup (8):* Anderton 2, Kanoute 2, Keane 1, Postiga 1, Ricketts 1, Zamora 1.
*FA Cup (7):* Kanoute 3, Doherty 1, Keane 1, King 1, Ziege 1.

| Keller K 38 | Carr S 32 | Taricco M 31 + 1 | Gardner A 33 | Doherty G 16 + 1 | Bunjevcevic G 3 + 4 | Davies S 17 | Redknapp J 14 + 3 | Keane R 31 + 3 | Postiga H 9 + 10 | Ricketts R 12 + 12 | Marney D 1 + 2 | Zamora B 6 + 10 | Kanoute F 19 + 8 | Richards D 23 | King L 28 + 1 | Anderton D 16 + 4 | Konchesky P 10 + 2 | Dalmat S 12 + 10 | Poyet G 12 + 8 | Mabizela M — + 6 | Blondel J — + 1 | Jackson J 9 + 2 | Kelly S 7 + 4 | Brown M 17 | Ziege C 7 + 1 | Defoe J 14 + 1 | Yeates M 1 | Match No. |
|---|---|---|---|---|---|---|---|---|---|---|---|---|---|---|---|---|---|---|---|---|---|---|---|---|---|---|---|---|
| 1 | 2 | $3^{1}$ | 4 | 5 | 6 | 7 | 8 | 9 | $10^{2}$ | 11 | 12 | 13 | | | | | | | | | | | | | | | | 1 |
| 1 | 2 | $3^{1}$ | 4 | | | 7 | 8 | | 10 | 11 | 12 | $9^{2}$ | 13 | 5 | 6 | | | | | | | | | | | | | 2 |
| 1 | 2 | 3 | 4 | | | 7 | 8 | | $9^{1}$ | 11 | | $10^{2}$ | 13 | 5 | 6 | 12 | | | | | | | | | | | | 3 |
| 1 | 2 | 3 | 4 | | | $7^{2}$ | 8 | | 10 | 11 | | 12 | 9 | 5 | $6^{1}$ | 13 | | | | | | | | | | | | 4 |
| 1 | 2 | $3^{2}$ | 4 | | 14 | | 8 | | | 11 | | 10 | 9 | 5 | $6^{3}$ | $7^{1}$ | 13 | 12 | | | | | | | | | | 5 |
| 1 | 2 | 3 | 4 | | $6^{2}$ | | 8 | 12 | 13 | 11 | | $10^{1}$ | 9 | 5 | | 14 | | $7^{3}$ | | | | | | | | | | 6 |
| 1 | 2 | 3 | 4 | | $6^{1}$ | | | 9 | | 12 | | | 10 | 5 | | 7 | $11^{2}$ | 13 | 8 | | | | | | | | | 7 |
| 1 | 2 | $3^{2}$ | 4 | | | | | 9 | 12 | 11 | | | $10^{1}$ | 5 | | 7 | 8 | 13 | 6 | | | | | | | | | 8 |
| 1 | 2 | 3 | | 5 | | | | 9 | | $11^{2}$ | | 12 | 10 | 6 | | 7 | $8^{1}$ | 13 | $4^{3}$ | 14 | | | | | | | | 9 |
| 1 | 2 | 3 | 4 | | | | | 9 | 12 | 13 | | $10^{1}$ | | 5 | 14 | 7 | $11^{2}$ | 8 | $6^{3}$ | | | | | | | | | 10 |
| 1 | 2 | $3^{3}$ | | 6 | | | | 9 | 12 | | | 10 | | 5 | $4^{2}$ | 7 | 11 | | $8^{1}$ | 13 | 14 | | | | | | | 11 |
| 1 | 2 | 3 | 4 | | | | | 9 | $10^{2}$ | 12 | | 13 | | 5 | 6 | 7 | $11^{3}$ | $8^{1}$ | | 14 | | | | | | | | 12 |
| 1 | 2 | 3 | 4 | | | | | 9 | $10^{2}$ | 12 | | 13 | | 5 | 6 | 7 | $11^{1}$ | 8 | | | | | | | | | | 13 |
| 1 | 2 | 3 | 4 | | | | | 9 | $10^{2}$ | 12 | | 13 | | 5 | 6 | 7 | $11^{1}$ | $8^{3}$ | | 14 | | | | | | | | 14 |
| 1 | 2 | 3 | 4 | | | | | 9 | | $11^{2}$ | | | 10 | 5 | 6 | 7 | 13 | 12 | $8^{1}$ | | | | | | | | | 15 |
| 1 | 2 | 3 | 4 | | | | | 9 | 13 | | | | $10^{2}$ | 5 | 6 | 7 | $11^{1}$ | 12 | $8^{3}$ | 14 | | | | | | | | 16 |
| 1 | 2 | $3^{1}$ | 4 | | | | | 9 | 13 | 12 | | | 10 | 5 | 6 | $7^{3}$ | 11 | $8^{2}$ | 14 | | | | | | | | | 17 |
| 1 | 2 | 3 | 4 | | | | | 9 | 14 | 12 | | 13 | $10^{2}$ | 5 | 6 | | | $8^{1}$ | $11^{3}$ | | | 7 | | | | | | 18 |
| 1 | | $3^{3}$ | 4 | | | | | 9 | 13 | $7^{1}$ | | 12 | 10 | 5 | 6 | | | | $8^{2}$ | 14 | | 11 | 2 | | | | | 19 |
| 1 | 2 | | | 5 | | 11 | | 9 | 13 | 12 | | | $10^{2}$ | | 6 | $7^{3}$ | | $8^{1}$ | 4 | | | 3 | 14 | | | | | 20 |
| 1 | 2 | 3 | 4 | 5 | | 11 | | 9 | | | | | 10 | | 6 | $7^{1}$ | | 8 | 12 | | | | | | | | | 21 |
| 1 | 2 | 3 | 4 | 5 | | 11 | | 9 | $10^{1}$ | | | 12 | | | | 7 | | $8^{2}$ | | | | 13 | | 6 | | | | 22 |
| 1 | 2 | | 4 | 5 | | 11 | | 9 | $10^{1}$ | | | 12 | | | 6 | | | 8 | | | | | | 7 | 3 | | | 23 |
| 1 | 2 | | 4 | | | 11 | | 9 | | 12 | | | | 5 | 6 | | | $8^{1}$ | 13 | | | 3 | | 7 | | $10^{2}$ | | 24 |
| 1 | 2 | 3 | | 4 | | 11 | | 9 | | | | | | 5 | 6 | | | | 12 | | | 8 | | 7 | | $10^{1}$ | | 25 |
| 1 | 2 | 3 | | 4 | | 7 | | 9 | | | | | 12 | 5 | 6 | 13 | | | | | | $11^{2}$ | | $8^{1}$ | | 10 | | 26 |
| 1 | 2 | 3 | 4 | | | | | 9 | 12 | | | | | 5 | 6 | $7^{1}$ | | 14 | 13 | | | $11^{3}$ | | $8^{2}$ | | 10 | | 27 |
| 1 | 2 | 3 | 4 | 5 | | | 13 | 9 | | | | | $8^{2}$ | | 6 | | | 12 | | | | | | 7 | $11^{1}$ | 10 | | 28 |
| 1 | 2 | $3^{1}$ | 4 | 5 | | | 14 | 9 | | | $7^{3}$ | | 13 | | 6 | | | 12 | | | | | | 8 | 11 | $10^{2}$ | | 29 |
| 1 | 2 | | 4 | 5 | | | 13 | 9 | | | | | 7 | | 6 | | | 12 | | | | $11^{2}$ | 14 | $8^{1}$ | $3^{3}$ | 10 | | 30 |
| 1 | 2 | $3^{3}$ | 4 | 5 | | | $8^{2}$ | 9 | | | | | 12 | | 6 | | | | | | | 13 | 14 | 7 | $11^{1}$ | 10 | | 31 |
| 1 | 2▮ | | 4 | 5 | 14 | $7^{2}$ | $8^{3}$ | 9 | | 13 | | | 12 | | | | | | | | | | 11 | 6 | $3^{1}$ | 10 | | 32 |
| 1 | $2^{3}$ | $3^{2}$ | 4 | 5 | 13 | 11 | 8 | 12 | | | | | 9 | | | | | | $7^{1}$ | | | | 14 | 6 | | 10 | | 33 |
| 1 | | 12 | 4 | 5 | | $11^{3}$ | $8^{2}$ | 13 | | 14 | | | 9 | | 3 | | | | $7^{1}$ | | | | 2 | 6 | | 10 | | 34 |
| 1 | | $3^{2}$ | 4 | | 13 | 7 | 8 | 9 | | | | | 10 | | 5 | | | | 12 | | | $11^{3}$ | $2^{1}$ | 6 | | 14 | | 35 |
| 1 | | 3 | 4 | 13 | | 11 | 7 | 9 | | 12 | | | $8^{2}$ | 5 | | | | | | | | | $2^{1}$ | 6 | | 10 | | 36 |
| 1 | | $3^{1}$ | 4 | | | 11 | $7^{2}$ | 9 | | $8^{3}$ | | | 14 | | 5 | | | | 13 | | | | 2 | 6 | 12 | 10 | | 37 |
| 1 | | | 4 | | | | 8 | $9^{2}$ | | $11^{1}$ | | | 12 | | 5 | | | | 13 | | | | 2 | 6 | 3 | 10 | 7 | 38 |

**Carling Cup**

| | | | |
|---|---|---|---|
| Second Round | Coventry C | (a) | 3-0 |
| Third Round | West Ham U | (h) | 1-0 |
| Fourth Round | Manchester C | (h) | 3-1 |
| Fifth Round | Middlesbrough | (h) | 1-1 |

**FA Cup**

| | | | |
|---|---|---|---|
| Third Round | Crystal Palace | (h) | 3-0 |
| Fourth Round | Manchester C | (a) | 1-1 |
| | | (h) | 3-4 |

# TRANMERE ROVERS FL Championship 1

## FOUNDATION

Formed in 1884 as Belmont they adopted their present title the following year and eventually joined their first league, the West Lancashire League in 1889–90, the same year as their first success in the Wirral Challenge Cup. The club almost folded in 1899–1900 when all the players left en bloc to join a rival club, but they survived the crisis and went from strength to strength winning the 'Combination' title in 1907–08 and the Lancashire Combination in 1913–14. They joined the Football League in 1921 from the Central League.

***Prenton Park, Prenton Road West, Birkenhead, Wirral CH42 9PY.***

***Telephone:*** (0151) 609 3333.

***Fax:*** (0151) 609 0606.

***Ticket Office:*** (0151) 609 3322.

***Website:*** www.tranmererovers.co.uk

***Email:*** customerservice@tranmererovers.co.uk

***Ground Capacity:*** 16,500.

***Record Attendance:*** 24,424 v Stoke C, FA Cup 4th rd, 5 February 1972.

***Pitch Measurements:*** 110yd × 70yd.

***Chairperson:*** Lorraine Rogers.

***Chief Executive/Secretary:*** Mick Horton.

***Manager:*** Brian Little.

***Physio:*** Les Parry.

***Colours:*** All white.

***Change Colours:*** TBA.

***Year Formed:*** 1884.

***Turned Professional:*** 1912.

***Ltd Co.:*** 1920.

***Previous Name:*** 1884, Belmont AFC; 1885, Tranmere Rovers.

***Club Nickname:*** 'The Rovers'.

***Previous Grounds:*** 1884, Steeles Field; 1887, Ravenshaws Field/Old Prenton Park; 1912, Prenton Park.

***First Football League Game:*** 27 August 1921, Division 3 (N), v Crewe Alex (h) W 4–1 – Bradshaw; Grainger, Stuart (1); Campbell, Milnes (1), Heslop; Moreton, Groves (1), Hyam, Ford (1), Hughes.

***Record League Victory:*** 13–4 v Oldham Ath, Division 3 (N), 26 December 1935 – Gray; Platt, Fairhurst; McLaren, Newton, Spencer; Eden, MacDonald (1), Bell (9), Woodward (2), Urmson (1).

## HONOURS

*Football League* Division 1 best season: 4th, 1992–93; Promoted from Division 3 1990–91 (play-offs); Division 3 (N) – Champions 1937–38; Promotion to 3rd Division: 1966–67, 1975–76; Division 4 – Runners-up 1988–89.

*FA Cup:* best season: 6th rd, 2000, 2001, 2004.

*Football League Cup:* Runners-up, 2000.

*Welsh Cup:* Winners 1935; Runners-up 1934.

*Leyland Daf Cup:* Winners 1990; Runners-up 1991.

## SKY SPORTS FACT FILE

In consecutive seasons 1934–35 and 1935–36 Tranmere Rovers remained unbeaten from the opening day until completing eight and nine matches respectively and finishing sixth and third. They had to wait until 1937–38 before taking the section title.

***Record Cup Victory:*** 13–0 v Oswestry U, FA Cup 2nd prel rd, 10 October 1914 – Ashcroft; Stevenson, Bullough, Hancock, Taylor, Holden (1), Moreton (1), Cunningham (2), Smith (5), Leck (3), Gould (1).

***Record Defeat:*** 1–9 v Tottenham H, FA Cup 3rd rd (replay), 14 January 1953.

***Most League Points (2 for a win):*** 60, Division 4, 1964–65.

***Most League Points (3 for a win):*** 80, Division 4, 1988–89; Division 3, 1989–90; Division 2, 2002–03.

***Most League Goals:*** 111, Division 3 (N), 1930–31.

***Highest League Scorer in Season:*** Bunny Bell, 35, Division 3 (N), 1933–34.

***Most League Goals in Total Aggregate:*** Ian Muir, 142, 1985–95.

***Most League Goals in One Match:*** 9, Bunny Bell v Oldham Ath, Division 3N, 26 December 1935.

***Most Capped Player:*** John Aldridge, 30 (69), Republic of Ireland.

***Most League Appearances:*** Harold Bell, 595, 1946–64 (incl. League record 401 consecutive appearances).

***Youngest League Player:*** Iain Hume, 16 years 167 days v Swindon T, 15 April 2000.

***Record Transfer Fee Received:*** £3,300,000 from Everton for Steve Simonsen, September 1998.

***Record Transfer Fee Paid:*** £450,000 to Aston Villa for Shaun Teale, August 1995.

***Football League Record:*** 1921 Original Member of Division 3 (N): 1938–39 Division 2; 1946–58 Division 3 (N); 1958–61 Division 3; 1961–67 Division 4; 1967–75 Division 3; 1975–76 Division 4; 1976–79 Division 3; 1979–89 Division 4; 1989–91 Division 3; 1991–92 Division 2; 1992–2001 Division 1; 2001–04 Division 2; 2004– FL1.

## MANAGERS

Bert Cooke 1912–35
Jackie Carr 1935–36
Jim Knowles 1936–39
Bill Ridding 1939–45
Ernie Blackburn 1946–55
Noel Kelly 1955–57
Peter Farrell 1957–60
Walter Galbraith 1961
Dave Russell 1961–69
Jackie Wright 1969–72
Ron Yeats 1972–75
John King 1975–80
Bryan Hamilton 1980–85
Frank Worthington 1985–87
Ronnie Moore 1987
John King 1987–96
John Aldridge 1996–2001
Dave Watson 2001–02
Ray Mathias 2002–03
Brian Little October 2003–

## LATEST SEQUENCES

***Longest Sequence of League Wins:*** 9, 9.2.1990 – 19.3.1990.

***Longest Sequence of League Defeats:*** 8, 29.10.1938 – 17.12.1938.

***Longest Sequence of League Draws:*** 5, 26.12.1997 – 31.1.1998.

***Longest Sequence of Unbeaten League Matches:*** 18, 16.3.1970 – 4.9.1970.

***Longest Sequence Without a League Win:*** 16, 8.11.1969 – 14.3.1970.

***Successive Scoring Runs:*** 32 from 24.2.1934.

***Successive Non-scoring Runs:*** 7 from 20.12.1997.

## TEN YEAR LEAGUE RECORD

| | | P | W | D | L | F | A | Pts | Pos |
|---|---|---|---|---|---|---|---|---|---|
| 1994-95 | Div 1 | 46 | 22 | 10 | 14 | 67 | 58 | 76 | 5 |
| 1995-96 | Div 1 | 46 | 14 | 17 | 15 | 64 | 60 | 59 | 13 |
| 1996-97 | Div 1 | 46 | 17 | 14 | 15 | 63 | 56 | 65 | 11 |
| 1997-98 | Div 1 | 46 | 14 | 14 | 18 | 54 | 57 | 56 | 14 |
| 1998-99 | Div 1 | 46 | 12 | 20 | 14 | 63 | 61 | 56 | 15 |
| 1999-2000 | Div 1 | 46 | 15 | 12 | 19 | 57 | 68 | 57 | 13 |
| 2000-01 | Div 1 | 46 | 9 | 11 | 26 | 46 | 77 | 38 | 24 |
| 2001-02 | Div 2 | 46 | 16 | 15 | 15 | 63 | 60 | 63 | 12 |
| 2002-03 | Div 2 | 46 | 23 | 11 | 12 | 66 | 57 | 80 | 7 |
| 2003-04 | Div 2 | 46 | 17 | 16 | 13 | 59 | 56 | 67 | 8 |

## DID YOU KNOW ?

On Christmas Day 1931 Farewell Watts gave a seasonal greeting to Rochdale with five goals in a 9-1 Tranmere Rovers win at Prenton Park. The following day he managed just one goal in a 6-3 victory in the return fixture.

## TRANMERE ROVERS 2003–04 LEAGUE RECORD

| Match No. | Date | Venue | Opponents | Result | H/T Score | Lg. Pos. | Goalscorers | Attendance |
|---|---|---|---|---|---|---|---|---|
| 1 | Aug 9 | H | Brentford | W 4-1 | 2-0 | — | Jones [23], Nicholson 2 (1 pen) [39, 81 (p)], Haworth [76] | 7307 |
| 2 | 16 | A | Hartlepool U | D 0-0 | 0-0 | 4 | | 5357 |
| 3 | 23 | H | Rushden & D | L 1-2 | 0-2 | 13 | Jones [69] | 7374 |
| 4 | 25 | A | Stockport Co | D 1-1 | 1-0 | 15 | Dadi [45] | 4886 |
| 5 | 30 | H | Colchester U | D 1-1 | 1-1 | 14 | Jones [14] | 6745 |
| 6 | Sept 6 | A | Sheffield W | L 0-2 | 0-0 | 16 | | 21,705 |
| 7 | 13 | H | Peterborough U | D 0-0 | 0-0 | 17 | | 6726 |
| 8 | 16 | A | Bristol C | L 0-2 | 0-0 | — | | 9365 |
| 9 | 20 | A | Notts Co | D 2-2 | 1-1 | 20 | Haworth 2 [7, 56] | 4215 |
| 10 | 27 | H | Wrexham | L 1-2 | 1-0 | 20 | Haworth [19] | 8230 |
| 11 | 30 | H | Wycombe W | W 2-1 | 1-0 | — | Dadi [41], Senda (og) [82] | 6847 |
| 12 | Oct 6 | A | Luton T | L 1-3 | 0-1 | — | Dagnall [54] | 5002 |
| 13 | 11 | A | Plymouth Arg | L 0-6 | 0-3 | 21 | | 7610 |
| 14 | 18 | H | Oldham Ath | W 2-1 | 0-1 | 19 | Hume [70], Roberts [79] | 8202 |
| 15 | 21 | H | Swindon T | W 1-0 | 0-0 | — | Jones [90] | 6675 |
| 16 | 25 | A | QPR | D 1-1 | 1-0 | 19 | Haworth [5] | 12,937 |
| 17 | Nov 1 | H | Bournemouth | D 1-1 | 1-0 | 19 | Allen [32] | 7123 |
| 18 | 15 | A | Barnsley | L 0-2 | 0-1 | 19 | | 9663 |
| 19 | 22 | H | Port Vale | W 1-0 | 0-0 | 19 | Hume [68] | 7081 |
| 20 | 29 | A | Grimsby T | W 1-0 | 0-0 | 18 | Jones [72] | 4406 |
| 21 | Dec 13 | A | Chesterfield | D 2-2 | 1-2 | 18 | Dadi 2 [1, 54] | 3123 |
| 22 | 20 | H | Brighton & HA | W 1-0 | 0-0 | 15 | Taylor (pen) [81] | 7616 |
| 23 | 26 | A | Blackpool | L 1-2 | 0-1 | 15 | Haworth [82] | 8340 |
| 24 | 28 | H | Sheffield W | D 2-2 | 0-2 | 15 | Jones [76], Taylor (pen) [85] | 9645 |
| 25 | Jan 10 | A | Brentford | D 2-2 | 1-1 | 16 | Dadi 2 [9, 60] | 4105 |
| 26 | 17 | H | Hartlepool U | D 0-0 | 0-0 | 17 | | 7418 |
| 27 | 27 | H | Stockport Co | W 3-2 | 1-1 | — | Taylor 2 (2 pens) [5, 87], Goodwin (og) [65] | 7137 |
| 28 | 31 | A | Colchester U | D 1-1 | 1-0 | 16 | Dadi [27] | 3099 |
| 29 | Feb 7 | H | Blackpool | D 1-1 | 0-1 | 15 | Hume [74] | 7919 |
| 30 | 17 | H | Plymouth Arg | W 3-0 | 2-0 | — | Dadi 2 [19, 52], Hume [23] | 7948 |
| 31 | 21 | A | Oldham Ath | D 1-1 | 0-0 | 13 | Dadi [87] | 6916 |
| 32 | 24 | A | Rushden & D | L 1-2 | 0-0 | — | Harrison [55] | 3074 |
| 33 | Mar 3 | A | Swindon T | L 0-2 | 0-1 | — | | 6928 |
| 34 | 10 | A | Brighton & HA | L 0-3 | 0-3 | — | | 5994 |
| 35 | 13 | H | Chesterfield | L 2-3 | 0-1 | 16 | Hume 2 [63, 73] | 7370 |
| 36 | 20 | A | Peterborough U | D 0-0 | 0-0 | 17 | | 4185 |
| 37 | 24 | H | Bristol C | W 1-0 | 0-0 | — | Dadi [82] | 6712 |
| 38 | 27 | H | Notts Co | W 4-0 | 2-0 | 15 | Dadi 2 (1 pen) [7, 15 (p)], Hume 2 [69, 74] | 7308 |
| 39 | Apr 3 | A | Wrexham | W 1-0 | 0-0 | 13 | Sharps [78] | 4496 |
| 40 | 6 | H | QPR | D 0-0 | 0-0 | — | | 7699 |
| 41 | 10 | H | Luton T | W 1-0 | 1-0 | 11 | Jones [30] | 7937 |
| 42 | 12 | A | Wycombe W | W 2-1 | 2-0 | 11 | Dadi 2 [11, 45] | 5256 |
| 43 | 17 | A | Bournemouth | W 5-1 | 1-0 | 10 | Jones 2 [42, 58], Harrison [51], Hall [56], Beresford [81] | 7063 |
| 44 | 24 | H | Barnsley | W 2-0 | 0-0 | 9 | Hume [62], Taylor [88] | 7612 |
| 45 | May 1 | A | Port Vale | L 1-2 | 1-1 | 10 | Hall [24] | 6806 |
| 46 | 8 | H | Grimsby T | W 2-1 | 0-1 | 8 | Hume [57], Dadi [61] | 10,301 |

**Final League Position: 8**

### GOALSCORERS

*League (59):* Dadi 16 (1 pen), Hume 10, Jones 9, Haworth 6, Taylor 5 (4 pens), Hall 2, Harrison 2, Nicholson 2 (1 pen), Allen 1, Beresford 1, Dagnall 1, Roberts 1, Sharps 1, own goals 2.
*Carling Cup (1):* Dadi 1.
*FA Cup (11):* Hume 3, Dadi 2, Jones 2, Mellon 2 (1 pen), Haworth 1, Taylor 1 (pen).
*LDV Vans Trophy (2):* Hume 1, Nicholson 1.

| Achterberg J 45 | Connelly S 33 + 4 | Roberts G 44 | Sharps I 25 + 2 | Allen G 40 + 1 | Taylor R 21 + 9 | Hume I 32 + 8 | Mellon M 39 + 4 | Haworth S 21 + 1 | Jones G 36 + 6 | Nicholson S 9 + 7 | Dadi E 29 + 9 | Navarro A 9 + 10 | Hay A 3 + 16 | Loran T 26 + 2 | Dagnall C 5 + 5 | Gray K 2 | Harrison D 32 | Linwood P 18 + 2 | Jennings S 1 + 3 | Beresford D 13 + 12 | Ashton N — + 1 | Goodison I 12 | Howarth R 1 | Onuora I 1 + 2 | Hall P 9 | *Match No.* |
|---|---|---|---|---|---|---|---|---|---|---|---|---|---|---|---|---|---|---|---|---|---|---|---|---|---|---|
| 1 | 2 | 3 | 4 | 5 | 6 | $7^1$ | $8^2$ | 9 | 10 | $11^3$ | 12 | 13 | 14 | | | | | | | | | | | | | 1 |
| 1 | 2 | 3 | 4 | 5 | 6 | 7 | 8 | 9 | 10 | $11^1$ | 12 | | | | | | | | | | | | | | | 2 |
| 1 | 2 | 3 | 4 | 5 | $6^1$ | 7 | 8 | 9 | 10 | $11^2$ | 13 | | 12 | | | | | | | | | | | | | 3 |
| 1 | 2 | 3 | 4 | 5 | 12 | $7^1$ | 8 | 9 | 6 | 11 | 10 | | | | | | | | | | | | | | | 4 |
| 1 | 2 | 3 | 4 | 5 | | 7 | $8^1$ | 9 | 6 | $11^2$ | 10■ | 12 | 13 | | | | | | | | | | | | | 5 |
| 1 | 2 | 3 | 4 | 5 | 12 | 8 | 13 | 9 | 6 | | $10^1$ | 14 | $11^3$ | $7^2$ | | | | | | | | | | | | 6 |
| 1 | 2 | 3 | 4 | 5 | $6^3$ | 10 | 12 | 9 | 8 | | | $11^2$ | 13 | $7^1$ | 14 | | | | | | | | | | | 7 |
| 1 | 2 | 3 | 4 | 5■ | $7^1$ | | 12 | 9 | 8 | $11^2$ | | 13 | | 6 | 10 | | | | | | | | | | | 8 |
| 1 | 2 | 3 | 4 | 5 | 7 | | | 9 | 8 | 11 | | | 12 | 6 | $10^1$ | | | | | | | | | | | 9 |
| 1 | 2 | 3 | | 5 | 12 | $7^1$ | $8^2$ | 9 | 11 | 13 | $10^3$ | | | 6 | 14 | 4 | | | | | | | | | | 10 |
| 1 | 2 | 3 | | | 6 | 12 | 8 | 9 | | 11 | $10^1$ | | | 4 | 7 | | 5 | | | | | | | | | 11 |
| 1 | 2 | 3 | | 12 | $4^1$ | 7 | 8 | 9 | | $11^2$ | | | 13 | 6 | 10 | | 5 | | | | | | | | | 12 |
| 1 | 2 | 3 | | 5 | $6^1$ | | 8 | 9 | 13 | | 12 | 14 | | 4 | $10^2$ | 7 | $11^3$ | | | | | | | | | 13 |
| 1 | 2 | 3 | | 5 | | $10^2$ | $8^1$ | 9 | | | 12 | 7 | | 6 | | | 11 | 4 | 13 | | | | | | | 14 |
| 1 | $2^3$ | 3 | | 5 | | 10 | $8^2$ | $9^1$ | 12 | | 13 | 11 | | 6 | | | 4 | 7 | 14 | | | | | | | 15 |
| 1 | 2 | 3 | | 5 | | $10^3$ | 12 | 9 | 8 | | 13 | 11 | | 6 | | | $7^2$ | $4^1$ | 14 | | | | | | | 16 |
| 1 | | 3 | 12 | 5 | 2 | 10 | 8 | | 13 | | $9^1$ | $11^2$ | | 6 | | | 7 | 4 | | | | | | | | 17 |
| 1 | 2 | 3 | 5 | | 12 | $10^2$ | 8 | 9 | 13 | | 14 | | | 6 | | | $7^1$ | 4 | | $11^3$ | | | | | | 18 |
| 1 | 2 | 3 | | 5 | | 7 | 8 | $9^2$ | 12 | | $10^1$ | | | 6 | | | 11 | 4 | | 13 | | | | | | 19 |
| 1 | 2 | 3 | | 5 | | | 8 | $9^1$ | 11 | | 10 | 12 | | 6 | | | 7 | 4 | | | | | | | | 20 |
| 1 | 2 | 3 | 12 | 5 | 13 | | 8 | | 10 | | $9^1$ | | | $6^3$ | | | 11■ | 4 | $7^2$ | 14 | | | | | | 21 |
| 1 | 2 | 3 | | 5 | 13 | $10^3$ | 8 | | 11 | | $9^1$ | | 12 | $6^2$ | | | 7 | 4 | | 14 | | | | | | 22 |
| 1 | 2 | 3 | 6 | 5 | 7 | | 8 | 12 | 10 | | $9^1$ | | 13 | | | | | $4^2$ | | 11 | | | | | | 23 |
| 1 | 2 | 3 | 6 | 5 | 12 | $7^2$ | 8 | 9 | 11 | | | | $10^1$ | | 13 | | | $4^3$ | | 14 | | | | | | 24 |
| 1 | 2 | 3 | | 5 | | $10^1$ | 8 | $9^2$ | 6 | | 7 | | 12 | | 13 | | | 4 | | $11^3$ | 14 | | | | | 25 |
| 1 | 12 | 3 | $6^1$ | 5 | 4 | 10 | 8 | | 11 | | $9^3$ | $7^2$ | 14 | | | | 2 | | | 13 | | | | | | 26 |
| 1 | 2 | $3^2$ | | 5 | 4 | 10 | 8 | | 6 | | $9^3$ | 12 | | | 14 | | 7 | 13 | | $11^1$ | | | | | | 27 |
| 1 | 2 | 3 | | 5 | 4 | $10^3$ | 8■ | | 6 | | $9^2$ | 12 | 13 | | | | 7 | 14 | | $11^1$ | | | | | | 28 |
| 1 | 2 | 3 | | 5 | 4 | 10 | 8 | | 6 | | 9 | 11 | | | | | 7 | | | | | | | | | 29 |
| 1 | 2 | 3 | | 5 | | $10^1$ | 8 | | 6 | 13 | 9 | | 12 | | | | 7 | 4 | | $11^2$ | | | | | | 30 |
| 1 | | 3 | | 5 | 6 | 10 | | | $8^2$ | 12 | $9^1$ | 11 | 13 | | | | 7 | 4 | | 14 | | $2^3$ | | | | 31 |
| 1 | | 3 | | $5^1$ | 6 | 10 | 8 | | 13 | 12 | 9 | | | | | | 7 | 4 | | $11^2$ | | 2 | | | | 32 |
| | 2 | 3 | | | | 12 | 8 | | 11 | | 10 | 13 | | $6^3$ | | | $7^2$ | 4 | | 14 | | 5 | 1 | $9^1$ | | 33 |
| 1 | 2 | 3 | 6 | | $5^1$ | 7 | 8 | | | 12 | $9^2$ | 11 | 10 | | | | | 4 | | | | | | 13 | | 34 |
| 1 | | 3 | 6 | 5 | 2 | 10 | 8 | | 11 | 12 | $9^3$ | | | 13 | | | $7^2$ | $4^1$ | | 14 | | | | | | 35 |
| 1 | 2 | 3 | | 5 | $4^1$ | 9 | 8 | | 10 | | | | | | | | 7 | | | 11 | | 6 | | 12 | | 36 |
| 1 | | | 4 | 5 | | $9^1$ | 8 | | 6 | | 10 | | 12 | 2 | | | 7 | | | 11 | | 3 | | | | 37 |
| 1 | | | 4 | 5 | | 12 | $8^2$ | | 10 | 14 | $9^1$ | 13 | | 2 | | | 6 | | | $11^3$ | | 3 | | | 7 | 38 |
| 1 | 13 | 3 | 6 | 5 | | 12 | 8 | | 10 | | $9^1$ | | | 2 | | | 4 | | | $11^2$ | | | | | 7 | 39 |
| 1 | | 3 | 6 | 5 | | 12 | 8 | | 10 | | 9 | | | 2 | | | 11 | | | | | 4 | | | $7^1$ | 40 |
| 1 | | 11 | 4 | 5 | | 12 | 8 | | 10 | | $9^1$ | | | 2 | | | 6 | | | 13 | | 3 | | | $7^2$ | 41 |
| 1 | 12 | $3^3$ | 4 | 5 | | 13 | 8 | | 10 | | 9 | | | $2^1$ | | | 11 | | | 14 | | 6 | | | $7^2$ | 42 |
| 1 | 12 | 3 | 4 | 5 | | 13 | 8 | | $10^2$ | | $9^3$ | | | $2^1$ | | | 11 | | | 14 | | 6 | | | 7 | 43 |
| 1 | 2 | 11 | 4 | 5 | 12 | 9 | 8 | | $10^2$ | | | | 13 | | | | 6 | | | 14 | | $3^3$ | | | $7^1$ | 44 |
| 1 | 2 | 3 | 4 | 5 | 12 | $9^3$ | $8^2$ | | 10 | | | | 14 | 13 | | | 6 | | | 11 | | | | | $7^1$ | 45 |
| 1 | | 3 | 4■ | | 6 | 9 | | | 10 | | 12 | | | 2 | | | 8 | | | $11^1$ | | 5 | | | 7 | 46 |

**Carling Cup**

| | | | |
|---|---|---|---|
| First Round | Bury | (h) | 1-0 |
| Second Round | Nottingham F | (h) | 0-0 |

**LDV Vans Trophy**

| | | | |
|---|---|---|---|
| First Round | Blackpool | (a) | 2-3 |

**FA Cup**

| | | | |
|---|---|---|---|
| First Round | Chesterfield | (h) | 3-2 |
| Second Round | Hornchurch | (a) | 1-0 |
| Third Round | Bolton W | (h) | 1-1 |
| | | (a) | 2-1 |
| Fourth Round | Luton T | (a) | 1-0 |
| Fifth Round | Swansea C | (h) | 2-1 |
| Sixth Round | Millwall | (a) | 0-0 |
| | | (h) | 1-2 |

# WALSALL FL Championship 1

## FOUNDATION

Two of the leading clubs around Walsall in the 1880s were Walsall Swifts (formed 1877) and Walsall Town (formed 1879). The Swifts were winners of the Birmingham Senior Cup in 1881, while the Town reached the 4th round (5th round modern equivalent) of the FA Cup in 1883. These clubs amalgamated as Walsall Town Swifts in 1888, becoming simply Walsall in 1895.

***Bescot Stadium, Bescot Crescent, Walsall WS1 4SA.***

***Telephone:*** (01922) 622 791.

***Fax:*** (01922) 613 202.

***Ticket Office:*** 0870 442 0111/0222.

***Website:*** www.saddlers.co.uk

***Email:*** info@walsallfc.co.uk

***Ground Capacity:*** 11,200.

***Record Attendance:*** 11,037 v Wolverhampton W, Division 1, 11 January 2003.

***Pitch Measurements:*** 110yd × 73yd.

***Chairman:*** Mike Lloyd.

***Chief Executive/Secretary:*** Roy Whalley.

***Manager:*** Paul Merson.

***Physio:*** John Whitney.

***Colours:*** Red shirts and shorts with black and white trim, red stockings.

***Change Colours:*** White shirts with navy blue side panel, navy shorts with white and blue side panel, navy stockings.

***Year Formed:*** 1888.

***Turned Professional:*** 1888.

***Ltd Co.:*** 1921.

***Previous Names:*** Walsall Swifts (founded 1877) and Walsall Town (founded 1879) amalgamated in 1888 and were known as Walsall Town Swifts until 1895.

***Club Nickname:*** 'The Saddlers'.

***Previous Grounds:*** 1888, Fellows Park; 1990, Bescot Stadium.

***First Football League Game:*** 3 September 1892, Division 2, v Darwen (h) L 1–2 – Hawkins; Withington, Pinches; Robinson, Whitrick, Forsyth; Marshall, Holmes, Turner, Gray (1), Pangbourn.

***Record League Victory:*** 10–0 v Darwen, Division 2, 4 March 1899 – Tennent; E. Peers (1), Davies; Hickinbotham, Jenkyns, Taggart; Dean (3), Vail (2), Aston (4), Martin, Griffin.

***Record Cup Victory:*** 7–0 v Macclesfield T (a), FA Cup 2nd rd, 6 December 1997 – Walker; Evans, Marsh, Viveash (1), Ryder, Peron, Boli (2 incl. 1p) (Ricketts), Porter (2), Keates, Watson (Platt), Hodge (2 incl. 1p).

## HONOURS

*Football League:* Division 2: Runners-up, 1998–99, Promoted to Division 1 – 2000–01 (play-offs); Division 3 – Runners-up 1960–61, 1994–95; Division 4 – Champions 1959–60; Runners-up 1979–80.

*FA Cup:* best season: 5th rd, 1939, 1975, 1978, 1987, 2002, 2003 and last 16 1889.

*Football League Cup:* Semi-final 1984.

## SKY SPORTS FACT FILE

On 19 April 1960 a 2-2 draw against Notts County started Walsall on a run of 26 unbeaten home League games. They were undefeated there in 1960–61, winning promotion for a second successive time and the sequence ended in September 1961.

***Record Defeat:*** 0–12 v Small Heath, 17 December 1892. 0–12 v Darwen, 26 December 1896, both Division 2.

***Most League Points (2 for a win):*** 65, Division 4, 1959–60.

***Most League Points (3 for a win):*** 87, Division 2, 1998–99.

***Most League Goals:*** 102, Division 4, 1959–60.

***Highest League Scorer in Season:*** Gilbert Alsop, 40, Division 3 (N), 1933–34 and 1934–35.

***Most League Goals in Total Aggregate:*** Tony Richards, 184, 1954–63; Colin Taylor, 184, 1958–63, 1964–68, 1969–73.

***Most League Goals in One Match:*** 5, Gilbert Alsop v Carlisle U, Division 3N, 2 February 1935; 5, Bill Evans v Mansfield T, Division 3N, 5 October 1935; 5, Johnny Devlin v Torquay U, Division 3S, 1 September 1949.

***Most Capped Player:*** Mick Kearns, 15 (18), Republic of Ireland.

***Most League Appearances:*** Colin Harrison, 467, 1964–82.

***Youngest League Player:*** Geoff Morris, 16 years 218 days v Scunthorpe U, 14 September 1965.

***Record Transfer Fee Received:*** £600,000 from West Ham U for David Kelly, July 1988.

***Record Transfer Fee Paid:*** £175,000 to Birmingham C for Alan Buckley, June 1979.

***Football League Record:*** 1892 Elected to Division 2; 1895 Failed re-election; 1896–1901 Division 2; 1901 Failed re-election; 1921 Original Member of Division 3 (N); 1927–31 Division 3 (S); 1931–36 Division 3 (N); 1936–58 Division 3 (S); 1958–60 Division 4; 1960–61 Division 3; 1961–63 Division 2; 1963–79 Division 3; 1979–80 Division 4; 1980–88 Division 3; 1988–89 Division 2; 1989–90 Division 3; 1990–92 Division 4; 1992–95 Division 3; 1995–99 Division 2; 1999–2000 Division 1; 2000–01 Division 2; 2001–04 Division 1; 2004– FL1.

## LATEST SEQUENCES

***Longest Sequence of League Wins:*** 7, 10.10.1959 – 21.11.1959.

***Longest Sequence of League Defeats:*** 15, 29.10.1988 – 4.2.1989.

***Longest Sequence of League Draws:*** 5, 7.5.1988 – 17.9.1988.

***Longest Sequence of Unbeaten League Matches:*** 21, 6.11.1979 – 22.3.1980.

***Longest Sequence Without a League Win:*** 18, 15.10.1988 – 4.2.1989.

***Successive Scoring Runs:*** 27 from 9.2.1928.

***Successive Non-scoring Runs:*** 5 from 8.10.1927.

## MANAGERS

H. Smallwood 1888–91 *(Secretary-Manager)*
A. G. Burton 1891–93
J. H. Robinson 1893–95
C. H. Ailso 1895–96 *(Secretary-Manager)*
A. E. Parsloe 1896–97 *(Secretary-Manager)*
L. Ford 1897–98 *(Secretary-Manager)*
G. Hughes 1898–99 *(Secretary-Manager)*
L. Ford 1899–1901 *(Secretary-Manager)*
J. E. Shutt 1908–13 *(Secretary-Manager)*
Haydn Price 1914–20
Joe Burchell 1920–26
David Ashworth 1926–27
Jack Torrance 1927–28
James Kerr 1928–29
Sid Scholey 1929–30
Peter O'Rourke 1930–32
Bill Slade 1932–34
Andy Wilson 1934–37
Tommy Lowes 1937–44
Harry Hibbs 1944–51
Tony McPhee 1951
Brough Fletcher 1952–53
Major Frank Buckley 1953–55
John Love 1955–57
Billy Moore 1957–64
Alf Wood 1964
Reg Shaw 1964–68
Dick Graham 1968
Ron Lewin 1968–69
Billy Moore 1969–72
John Smith 1972–73
Doug Fraser 1973–77
Dave Mackay 1977–78
Alan Ashman 1978
Frank Sibley 1979
Alan Buckley 1979–86
Neil Martin *(Joint Manager with Buckley)* 1981–82
Tommy Coakley 1986–88
John Barnwell 1989–90
Kenny Hibbitt 1990–94
Chris Nicholl 1994–97
Jan Sorensen 1997–98
Ray Graydon 1998–2002
Colin Lee 2002–04
Paul Merson May 2004–

## TEN YEAR LEAGUE RECORD

| | | P | W | D | L | F | A | Pts | Pos |
|---|---|---|---|---|---|---|---|---|---|
| 1994-95 | Div 3 | 42 | 24 | 11 | 7 | 75 | 40 | 83 | 2 |
| 1995-96 | Div 2 | 46 | 19 | 12 | 15 | 60 | 45 | 69 | 11 |
| 1996-97 | Div 2 | 46 | 19 | 10 | 17 | 54 | 53 | 67 | 12 |
| 1997-98 | Div 2 | 46 | 14 | 12 | 20 | 43 | 52 | 54 | 19 |
| 1998-99 | Div 2 | 46 | 26 | 9 | 11 | 63 | 47 | 87 | 2 |
| 1999-2000 | Div 1 | 46 | 11 | 13 | 22 | 52 | 77 | 46 | 22 |
| 2000-01 | Div 2 | 46 | 23 | 12 | 11 | 79 | 50 | 81 | 4 |
| 2001-02 | Div 1 | 46 | 13 | 12 | 21 | 51 | 71 | 51 | 18 |
| 2002-03 | Div 1 | 46 | 15 | 9 | 22 | 57 | 69 | 54 | 17 |
| 2003-04 | Div 1 | 46 | 13 | 12 | 21 | 45 | 65 | 51 | 22 |

## DID YOU KNOW ?

Though short of the club's record victory, Walsall defeated Southport 8-0 on 21 November 1959. On a previous occasion the Saddlers had reached eight goals against Mansfield Town on 19 January 1933, who replied once.

## WALSALL 2003–04 LEAGUE RECORD

| Match No. | Date | Venue | Opponents | Result | H/T Score | Lg. Pos. | Goalscorers | Attendance |
|---|---|---|---|---|---|---|---|---|
| 1 | Aug 9 | H | WBA | W 4-1 | 3-0 | — | Merson 2 [18, 39], Leitao [45], Corica [57] | 11,030 |
| 2 | 16 | A | Coventry C | D 0-0 | 0-0 | 5 | | 15,377 |
| 3 | 23 | H | Stoke C | D 1-1 | 0-1 | 6 | Merson [85] | 9033 |
| 4 | 25 | A | Crewe Alex | L 0-1 | 0-0 | 8 | | 7026 |
| 5 | 30 | H | Cardiff C | D 1-1 | 0-0 | 14 | Leitao [51] | 8974 |
| 6 | Sept 13 | H | Derby Co | L 0-1 | 0-0 | 17 | | 8726 |
| 7 | 16 | A | Ipswich T | L 1-2 | 1-1 | — | Birch [29] | 20,912 |
| 8 | 20 | A | Millwall | L 1-2 | 1-1 | 21 | Corica (pen) [7] | 9262 |
| 9 | 27 | H | Preston NE | W 2-1 | 0-0 | 19 | Emblen [50], Samways [59] | 6981 |
| 10 | 29 | H | Gillingham | W 2-1 | 1-0 | — | Matias [35], Hessenthaler (og) [84] | 6395 |
| 11 | Oct 4 | A | Burnley | L 1-3 | 1-1 | 19 | Merson [24] | 10,532 |
| 12 | 14 | A | Watford | D 1-1 | 1-0 | — | Osborn [40] | 12,231 |
| 13 | 18 | A | Sunderland | L 0-1 | 0-1 | 19 | | 36,278 |
| 14 | 21 | A | Reading | W 1-0 | 1-0 | — | Samways [4] | 11,225 |
| 15 | 25 | H | Wigan Ath | W 2-0 | 0-0 | 14 | Wrack 2 [50, 66] | 7041 |
| 16 | Nov 1 | H | Norwich C | L 1-3 | 1-0 | 16 | Birch [10] | 8331 |
| 17 | 4 | H | Nottingham F | W 4-1 | 2-1 | — | Wrack 2 [30, 64], Osborn [36], Birch [86] | 7321 |
| 18 | 8 | A | Bradford C | D 1-1 | 1-1 | 14 | Wrack [35] | 9629 |
| 19 | 22 | H | Crystal Palace | D 0-0 | 0-0 | 14 | | 6910 |
| 20 | 29 | A | Rotherham U | L 0-2 | 0-0 | 17 | | 6101 |
| 21 | Dec 6 | H | Bradford C | W 1-0 | 0-0 | 15 | Birch [77] | 6876 |
| 22 | 9 | A | Sheffield U | L 0-2 | 0-1 | — | | 18,602 |
| 23 | 13 | A | Wimbledon | W 1-0 | 0-0 | 13 | Emblen [72] | 3315 |
| 24 | 20 | H | West Ham U | D 1-1 | 0-1 | 14 | Leitao [69] | 9272 |
| 25 | 26 | A | Cardiff C | W 1-0 | 0-0 | 13 | Emblen [70] | 17,531 |
| 26 | 28 | H | Reading | D 1-1 | 1-0 | 13 | Leitao [30] | 8089 |
| 27 | Jan 9 | A | WBA | L 0-2 | 0-0 | — | | 24,558 |
| 28 | 17 | H | Coventry C | L 1-6 | 1-1 | 16 | Wrack [45] | 8264 |
| 29 | 31 | A | Stoke C | L 2-3 | 2-2 | 17 | Leitao [14], Taylor [42] | 18,035 |
| 30 | Feb 7 | H | Crewe Alex | D 1-1 | 1-0 | 17 | Leitao [27] | 6871 |
| 31 | 14 | A | Nottingham F | D 3-3 | 3-1 | 17 | Leitao [5], Lawrence [24], Wales [39] | 25,012 |
| 32 | 21 | H | Watford | L 0-1 | 0-1 | 18 | | 6684 |
| 33 | 28 | A | Wigan Ath | L 0-1 | 0-0 | 19 | | 7593 |
| 34 | Mar 3 | H | Sunderland | L 1-3 | 0-1 | — | Emblen [53] | 7185 |
| 35 | 6 | A | West Ham U | D 0-0 | 0-0 | 21 | | 33,177 |
| 36 | 13 | H | Wimbledon | W 1-0 | 1-0 | 18 | Emblen [27] | 6889 |
| 37 | 16 | H | Ipswich T | L 1-3 | 0-0 | — | Andrews [88] | 6562 |
| 38 | 20 | A | Preston NE | W 2-1 | 1-0 | 16 | Fryatt [2], Wright [65] | 11,551 |
| 39 | 27 | H | Millwall | D 1-1 | 0-0 | 18 | Andrews [78] | 6486 |
| 40 | Apr 3 | A | Derby Co | W 1-0 | 0-0 | 17 | Bradbury (pen) [86] | 23,574 |
| 41 | 10 | H | Burnley | L 0-1 | 0-0 | 17 | | 7769 |
| 42 | 12 | A | Gillingham | L 0-3 | 0-1 | 19 | | 8244 |
| 43 | 17 | A | Norwich C | L 0-5 | 0-2 | 20 | | 23,558 |
| 44 | 24 | H | Sheffield U | L 0-1 | 0-0 | 22 | | 7873 |
| 45 | May 1 | A | Crystal Palace | L 0-1 | 0-0 | 22 | | 21,518 |
| 46 | 9 | H | Rotherham U | W 3-2 | 0-0 | 22 | Osborn [49], Wright [69], Ritchie [90] | 11,049 |

**Final League Position: 22**

### GOALSCORERS

*League (45):* Leitao 7, Wrack 6, Emblen 5, Birch 4, Merson 4, Osborn 3, Andrews 2, Corica 2 (1 pen), Samways 2, Wright 2, Bradbury 1 (pen), Fryatt 1, Lawrence 1, Matias 1, Ritchie 1, Taylor 1, Wales 1, own goal 1.
*Carling Cup (3):* Merson 2, Leitao 1.
*FA Cup (1):* Leitao 1.

| Walker J 43 | Bazeley D 35 + 4 | Aranalde Z 29 + 7 | Emblen N 27 + 12 | Roper I 33 | Hay D 14 + 2 | Osborn S 39 + 4 | Merson P 31 + 3 | Leitao J 29 + 10 | Corica S 17 + 2 | Samways V 29 | Wrack D 23 + 4 | Oakes S 1 + 4 | Birch G 25 + 10 | Matias P 6 + 9 | Ritchie P 33 | Lawrence J 8 + 9 | Burton D 2 + 1 | Baird C 10 | O'Neil G 7 | Fryatt M 4 + 7 | Vincent J 12 | Dinning T 2 + 3 | Petterson A 3 | Wright M 3 + 8 | Carbon M 7 + 1 | Taylor K 5 + 6 | Wales G 5 + 2 | Bennett J — + 1 | Andrews K 10 | Burley C 5 | Bradbury L 7 + 1 | McSporran J 2 + 4 | Match No. |
|---|---|---|---|---|---|---|---|---|---|---|---|---|---|---|---|---|---|---|---|---|---|---|---|---|---|---|---|---|---|---|---|---|---|
| 1 | 2 | 3 | 4 | $5^1$ | 6 | 7 | $8^2$ | $9^3$ | 10 | 11 | 12 | 13 | 14 | | | | | | | | | | | | | | | | | | | | 1 |
| 1 | $2^1$ | 3 | 4 | 5 | 6 | 7 | 8 | $9^2$ | 10 | 11 | 12 | | 13 | | | | | | | | | | | | | | | | | | | | 2 |
| 1 | 2 | 3 | $4^3$ | 5 | 6 | $7^1$ | 8 | 9 | $10^2$ | 11■ | | 12 | 13 | 14 | | | | | | | | | | | | | | | | | | | 3 |
| 1 | 2 | 3 | 12 | $5^2$ | 6 | $7^1$ | 8 | $9^3$ | | 11 | 13 | | 14 | 10 | 4 | | | | | | | | | | | | | | | | | | 4 |
| 1 | 2 | 3■ | | 5 | 6 | 7 | 8 | $9^1$ | 10 | 11 | | | 12 | | 4 | | | | | | | | | | | | | | | | | | 5 |
| 1 | $2^2$ | | 12 | 5 | 6 | $7^1$ | 8 | 9 | | | 3 | 14 | | 13 | 4 | $11^3$ | 10 | | | | | | | | | | | | | | | | 6 |
| 1 | 2 | | 12 | $5^1$ | 6 | $7^3$ | 8 | 13 | 10 | 11 | 3 | | $9^2$ | | 4 | 14 | | | | | | | | | | | | | | | | | 7 |
| 1 | 2 | | 12 | | $6^2$ | 5 | | $9^1$ | 7 | 11 | $3^3$ | 13 | 10 | | 4■ | 14 | 8 | | | | | | | | | | | | | | | | 8 |
| 1 | | 3 | 5 | | | 12 | $8^3$ | $9^2$ | | $11^1$ | | | 13 | 7 | 6 | 10 | 14 | 2 | 4 | | | | | | | | | | | | | | 9 |
| 1 | 12 | 3 | 5 | | | 13 | $8^3$ | 9 | | $11^2$ | | | 14 | $7^1$ | 6 | 10 | | 2 | 4 | | | | | | | | | | | | | | 10 |
| 1 | | 3 | 5 | | 6 | | 8 | 9 | | 11 | | | 12 | $7^1$ | | 10 | | 2 | 4 | | | | | | | | | | | | | | 11 |
| 1 | 12 | 3 | | | 6 | 7 | 8 | 9 | | | | | 13 | | 4 | 11 | | 2 | $10^1$ | $5^2$ | | | | | | | | | | | | | 12 |
| 1 | 7 | | 12 | | 6 | 8 | | $9^2$ | 13 | | | | 10 | | 5 | 4 | | 2■ | $11^1$ | | 3 | | | | | | | | | | | | 13 |
| 1 | | | $4^2$ | 5 | 12 | $7^3$ | | | | $11^1$ | 9 | | 10 | 13 | 6 | 14 | | 2 | 8 | | 3 | | | | | | | | | | | | 14 |
| 1 | | | | $5^1$ | 12 | 7 | 8 | 13 | | $11^3$ | 9 | | $10^2$ | | 6 | 14 | | 2 | 4 | | 3 | | | | | | | | | | | | 15 |
| 1 | 2 | | 14 | 5 | | 4 | 8 | 12 | 13 | $11^3$ | 9 | | 10 | | 6■ | $7^2$ | | | | | $3^1$ | | | | | | | | | | | | 16 |
| 1 | | 13 | 12 | 5 | | $4^1$ | 8 | | 7 | $11^2$ | 9 | | 10 | | 6 | | | 2 | | | 3 | | | | | | | | | | | | 17 |
| 1 | | 12 | | | 5 | | $8^2$ | 13 | 7 | 11 | 9 | | 10 | | 6 | 4 | | 2 | | | $3^1$ | | | | | | | | | | | | 18 |
| 1 | | 12 | | 5 | 6 | $4^3$ | $8^1$ | 13 | 7 | 11 | 9 | | $10^2$ | | | | | 2■ | | | 3 | 14 | | | | | | | | | | | 19 |
| 1 | 13 | | $4^2$ | 5 | 6 | 12 | 8 | 14 | $7^3$ | 11 | $2^1$ | | 9 | | | | | | | | 3 | 10 | | | | | | | | | | | 20 |
| 1 | 2 | 14 | 13 | 5 | | 4 | 8 | 12 | $11^3$ | | 7 | | $9^2$ | | 6 | | | | | | 3 | $10^1$ | | | | | | | | | | | 21 |
| 1 | 2 | | | 5 | | 4 | 8 | 12 | $10^1$ | 11 | 7 | | 9 | | 6 | | | | | | 3 | | | | | | | | | | | | 22 |
| 1 | 2 | 13 | 12 | 5 | | 4 | | $9^3$ | $8^1$ | 11 | 7 | | 10 | | 6 | | | | | | $3^2$ | 14 | | | | | | | | | | | 23 |
| 1 | 2 | 3 | 12 | 5 | | $4^2$ | 8 | $9^1$ | | 11 | 7 | | 10 | | 6 | | | | | | | 13 | | | | | | | | | | | 24 |
| 1 | 2 | 3 | 8 | 5 | | 4 | | 9 | | $11^1$ | 7 | | 10 | | 6 | 12 | | | | | | | | | | | | | | | | | 25 |
| 1 | 2 | 3 | 8 | 5 | | $4^2$ | 12 | 9 | | $11^1$ | 7 | | 10 | | 6 | 13 | | | | | | | | | | | | | | | | | 26 |
| 1 | 2 | 12 | 13 | 5 | | $4^1$ | 8 | 9 | | 11 | 7 | | 10 | | $6^2$ | | | | | | 3 | | | | | | | | | | | | 27 |
| | 2 | 3 | 6 | 5 | | 4 | $8^1$ | | | | 7 | 10■ | 9 | $11^2$ | | 12 | | | | | | | 1 | 13 | | | | | | | | | 28 |
| | 2 | 3 | | | | | 8 | 9 | | $11^1$ | 7 | | 10 | | 6 | 12 | | | | | | | 1 | | 5 | $4^2$ | 13 | | | | | | 29 |
| | 2 | 3 | 13 | 5 | | 4 | | $9^1$ | | 11 | 7 | | 8 | 12 | 6 | | | | | | | | 1 | | | | $10^2$ | | | | | | 30 |
| 1 | 2 | 3 | 4 | $5^3$ | | 7 | | 9 | | 11 | | | $10^2$ | 12 | | 14 | | | | | | | | 13 | 6 | | $8^1$ | | | | | | 31 |
| 1 | 2 | 3 | 4 | | | $7^2$ | | 9 | | $11^3$ | | | $10^1$ | 12 | 6 | | | | | | | | | 13 | 5 | 14 | 8 | | | | | | 32 |
| 1 | 2 | 3 | 7 | | | 8 | | 9 | $11^1$ | | | | 13 | 12 | 6 | | | | | | | | | | $5^3$ | 4 | $10^2$ | 14 | | | | | 33 |
| 1 | 2 | 3 | 5 | | | 4 | | 9 | $8^1$ | $11^3$ | $7^2$ | | | 12 | 6 | | | | | 14 | | | | 13 | | | 10 | | | | | | 34 |
| 1 | 2 | 3 | 6 | 5 | | 4 | | 9 | | $11^1$ | | | $10^2$ | 7 | | | | | | 13 | | | | | | 8 | 12 | | | | | | 35 |
| 1 | 2 | 3 | 4 | 5 | | 8 | 12 | $9^1$ | | | | | $10^3$ | 13 | 6 | | | | | 14 | | | | | | $7^2$ | | | 11 | | | | 36 |
| 1 | 2 | 3 | 4 | 5 | | 7 | $8^1$ | | $9^2$ | | | | 10 | | 6 | | | | | 12 | | | | | | 13 | | | 11 | | | | 37 |
| 1 | 12 | 3 | $10^2$ | 5 | | 13 | 8 | | | | | | | | 6 | | | | | $9^3$ | | | | 2 | $4^1$ | 14 | | | 11 | 7 | | | 38 |
| 1 | 2 | 3 | 6 | 5 | | 4 | 8 | | | | | | | | | | | | | $9^1$ | | | | | | | | | 11 | 7 | 10 | 12 | 39 |
| 1 | 2 | 3 | 6 | 5 | | 4 | $8^1$ | $9^2$ | | | | | | | | | | | | | | | | 12 | | | | | 11 | 7 | 10 | 13 | 40 |
| 1 | 2 | 3 | 6 | $5^1$ | | 4 | $8^3$ | 9 | | | | | | | | | | | | | | | | 13 | 12 | | | | 11 | $7^2$ | 10 | 14 | 41 |
| 1 | 2 | 3 | $6^3$ | | | 4 | $8^1$ | 12 | 9 | | | | | | | | | | | | | | | 7 | 5 | 13 | | | $11^2$ | | 10 | 14 | 42 |
| 1 | 2 | 3 | 6 | | | $8^2$ | 12 | $9^3$ | | | | | | | 4 | | | | | 13 | | | | | 5 | 14 | | | | 7 | $10^1$ | 11 | 43 |
| 1 | 2 | | 4 | 5 | | $10^2$ | 8 | | | | 12 | | | | 6 | | | | | 9 | | | | 13 | | $3^1$ | | | 7 | | 14 | $11^3$ | 44 |
| 1 | $2^2$ | 3 | 8 | 5 | | 4 | | 12 | | | $9^3$ | | | | 6 | | | | | 13 | | | | 7 | | 14 | | | 11 | | $10^1$ | | 45 |
| 1 | $2^1$ | 12 | 3 | 5 | | 4■ | 8 | $9^3$ | | | 7 | | | | 6 | | | | | 14 | | | | 13 | | | | | 11 | | $10^2$ | | 46 |

| **Carling Cup** | | | |
|---|---|---|---|
| First Round | Carlisle U | (h) | 2-1 |
| Second Round | Bolton W | (a) | 1-3 |

| **FA Cup** | | | |
|---|---|---|---|
| Third Round | Millwall | (a) | 1-2 |

# WATFORD — FL Championship

## FOUNDATION

The club was formed as Watford Rovers in 1881. The name was changed to West Herts in 1893 and then the name Watford was adopted after rival club Watford St Mary's was absorbed in 1898.

***Vicarage Road Stadium, Vicarage Road, Watford WD18 0ER.***

***Telephone:*** 0870 111 1881.

***Fax:*** (01923) 496 001.

***Ticket Office:*** 0870 111 1881.

***Website:*** www.watfordfc.com

***Email:*** yourvoice@watfordfc.com

***Ground Capacity:*** 21,800.

***Record Attendance:*** 34,099 v Manchester U, FA Cup 4th rd (replay), 3 February 1969.

***Pitch Measurements:*** 113yd × 73yd.

***Chairman/Chief Executive:*** Graham Simpson.

***Vice-chairman:*** Jimmy Russo.

***Secretary:*** Cathy Alexander.

***Manager:*** Ray Lewington.

***Assistant Manager:*** Terry Burton.

***Physio:*** Luke Anthony.

***Colours:*** Yellow shirts, black shorts, black stockings.

***Change Colours:*** Navy blue shirts with sky blue trim, navy blue shorts, navy blue stockings.

***Year Formed:*** 1881.

***Turned Professional:*** 1897.

***Ltd Co.:*** 1909.

***Club Nickname:*** 'The Hornets'.

***Previous Names:*** 1881, Watford Rovers; 1893, West Herts; 1898, Watford.

***Previous Grounds:*** 1883, Vicarage Meadow, Rose and Crown Meadow; 1889, Colney Butts; 1890, Cassio Road; 1922, Vicarage Road.

***First Football League Game:*** 28 August 1920, Division 3, v QPR (a) W 2–1 – Williams; Horseman, F. Gregory; Bacon, Toone, Wilkinson; Bassett, Ronald (1), Hoddinott, White (1), Waterall.

***Record League Victory:*** 8–0 v Sunderland, Division 1, 25 September 1982 – Sherwood; Rice, Rostron, Taylor, Terry, Bolton, Callaghan (2), Blissett (4), Jenkins (2), Jackett, Barnes.

***Record Cup Victory:*** 10–1 v Lowestoft T, FA Cup 1st rd, 27 November 1926 – Yates; Prior, Fletcher (1); F. Smith, 'Bert' Smith, Strain; Stephenson, Warner (3), Edmonds (3), Swan (1), Daniels (1), (1 og).

## HONOURS

*Football League:* Division 1 – Runners-up 1982–83, promoted from Division 1 1998–99 (play-offs); Division 2 – Champions 1997–98; Runners-up 1981–82; Division 3 – Champions 1968–69; Runners-up 1978–79; Division 4 – Champions 1977–78; Promoted 1959–60 (4th).

*FA Cup:* Runners-up 1984, semi-finals 1970, 1984, 1987, 2003.

*Football League Cup:* Semi-final 1979.

***European Competitions:*** *UEFA Cup:* 1983–84.

## SKY SPORTS FACT FILE

George James, who had had England trials in 1925 during his West Bromwich Albion days, scored seven goals for Watford during their 1930–31 FA Cup run to the fifth round. He registered in four consecutive matches.

***Record Defeat:*** 0–10 v Wolverhampton W, FA Cup 1st rd (replay), 24 January 1912.

***Most League Points (2 for a win):*** 71, Division 4, 1977–78.

***Most League Points (3 for a win):*** 88, Division 2, 1997–98.

***Most League Goals:*** 92, Division 4, 1959–60.

***Highest League Scorer in Season:*** Cliff Holton, 42, Division 4, 1959–60.

***Most League Goals in Total Aggregate:*** Luther Blissett, 148, 1976–83, 1984–88, 1991–92.

***Most League Goals in One Match:*** 5, Eddie Mummery v Newport Co, Division 3S, 5 January 1924.

***Most Capped Player:*** John Barnes, 31 (79), England and Kenny Jackett, 31, Wales.

***Most League Appearances:*** Luther Blissett, 415, 1976–83, 1984–88, 1991–92.

***Youngest League Player:*** Keith Mercer, 16 years 125 days v Tranmere R, 16 February 1973.

***Record Transfer Fee Received:*** £2,300,000 from Chelsea for Paul Furlong, May 1994.

***Record Transfer Fee Paid:*** £2,250,000 to Tottenham H for Allan Nielsen, August 2000.

***Football League Record:*** 1920 Original Member of Division 3; 1921–58 Division 3 (S); 1958–60 Division 4; 1960–69 Division 3; 1969–72 Division 2; 1972–75 Division 3; 1975–78 Division 4; 1978–79 Division 3; 1979–82 Division 2; 1982–88 Division 1; 1988–92 Division 2; 1992–96 Division 1; 1996–98 Division 2; 1998–99 Division 1; 1999–2000 FA Premier League; 2000–04 Division 1; 2004– FLC.

## MANAGERS

John Goodall 1903–10
Harry Kent 1910–26
Fred Pagnam 1926–29
Neil McBain 1929–37
Bill Findlay 1938–47
Jack Bray 1947–48
Eddie Hapgood 1948–50
Ron Gray 1950–51
Haydn Green 1951–52
Len Goulden 1952–55
*(General Manager to 1956)*
Johnny Paton 1955–56
Neil McBain 1956–59
Ron Burgess 1959–63
Bill McGarry 1963–64
Ken Furphy 1964–71
George Kirby 1971–73
Mike Keen 1973–77
Graham Taylor 1977–87
Dave Bassett 1987–88
Steve Harrison 1988–90
Colin Lee 1990
Steve Perryman 1990–93
Glenn Roeder 1993–96
Kenny Jackett 1996–97
Graham Taylor 1997–2001
Gianluca Vialli 2001–02
Ray Lewington July 2002–

## LATEST SEQUENCES

***Longest Sequence of League Wins:*** 7, 28.8.2000 – 14.10.2000.

***Longest Sequence of League Defeats:*** 9, 26.12.1972 – 27.2.1973.

***Longest Sequence of League Draws:*** 7, 30.11.1996 – 27.1.1997.

***Longest Sequence of Unbeaten League Matches:*** 22, 1.10.1996 – 1.3.1997.

***Longest Sequence Without a League Win:*** 19, 27.11.1971 – 8.4.1972.

***Successive Scoring Runs:*** 22 from 20.8.1985.

***Successive Non-scoring Runs:*** 7 from 18.12.1971.

## TEN YEAR LEAGUE RECORD

| | | P | W | D | L | F | A | Pts | Pos |
|---|---|---|---|---|---|---|---|---|---|
| 1994-95 | Div 1 | 46 | 19 | 13 | 14 | 52 | 46 | 70 | 7 |
| 1995-96 | Div 1 | 46 | 10 | 18 | 18 | 62 | 70 | 48 | 23 |
| 1996-97 | Div 2 | 46 | 16 | 19 | 11 | 45 | 38 | 67 | 13 |
| 1997-98 | Div 2 | 46 | 24 | 16 | 6 | 67 | 41 | 88 | 1 |
| 1998-99 | Div 1 | 46 | 21 | 14 | 11 | 65 | 56 | 77 | 5 |
| 1999-2000 | PR Lge | 38 | 6 | 6 | 26 | 35 | 77 | 24 | 20 |
| 2000-01 | Div 1 | 46 | 20 | 9 | 17 | 76 | 67 | 69 | 9 |
| 2001-02 | Div 1 | 46 | 16 | 11 | 19 | 62 | 56 | 59 | 14 |
| 2002-03 | Div 1 | 46 | 17 | 9 | 20 | 54 | 70 | 60 | 13 |
| 2003-04 | Div 1 | 46 | 15 | 12 | 19 | 54 | 68 | 57 | 16 |

## DID YOU KNOW ?

In their 1968–69 championship-winning season, Watford achieved more wins (27) than previously, suffered fewer defeats (9) and conceded fewer goals (34). The 74 goals scored was not their best effort but equalled the previous season when sixth.

## WATFORD 2003–04 LEAGUE RECORD

| Match No. | Date | Venue | Opponents | Result | | H/T Score | Lg. Pos. | Goalscorers | Attendance |
|---|---|---|---|---|---|---|---|---|---|
| 1 | Aug 16 | A | Crystal Palace | L | 0-1 | 0-1 | 22 | | 15,333 |
| 2 | 23 | H | WBA | L | 0-1 | 0-0 | 23 | | 15,023 |
| 3 | 25 | A | Sunderland | L | 0-2 | 0-1 | 24 | | 23,600 |
| 4 | 30 | H | Gillingham | D | 2-2 | 1-0 | 23 | Helguson [7], Webber [54] | 12,793 |
| 5 | Sept 13 | H | Millwall | W | 3-1 | 2-1 | 20 | Dyer [8], Cox (pen) [45], Young [90] | 11,305 |
| 6 | 17 | A | Derby Co | L | 2-3 | 1-1 | — | Gayle [38], Young [81] | 18,459 |
| 7 | 20 | A | Wigan Ath | L | 0-1 | 0-1 | 23 | | 9211 |
| 8 | 27 | H | Ipswich T | L | 1-2 | 0-0 | 23 | Fitzgerald [49] | 15,350 |
| 9 | 30 | H | Burnley | D | 1-1 | 1-0 | — | Fitzgerald [45] | 11,573 |
| 10 | Oct 4 | A | Crewe Alex | W | 1-0 | 0-0 | 23 | Webber [61] | 7055 |
| 11 | 14 | H | Walsall | D | 1-1 | 0-1 | — | Baird (og) [61] | 12,231 |
| 12 | 18 | H | Bradford C | W | 1-0 | 0-0 | 21 | Fitzgerald [61] | 10,381 |
| 13 | 21 | H | Coventry C | D | 1-1 | 0-0 | — | Fitzgerald [83] | 13,487 |
| 14 | 25 | A | Wimbledon | W | 3-1 | 2-0 | 17 | Devlin [22], Webber [33], Fitzgerald [67] | 6115 |
| 15 | 28 | A | Cardiff C | L | 0-3 | 0-1 | — | | 14,011 |
| 16 | Nov 1 | H | Rotherham U | W | 1-0 | 0-0 | 17 | Webber [47] | 18,067 |
| 17 | 4 | A | Preston NE | L | 1-2 | 0-0 | — | Webber [64] | 11,152 |
| 18 | 8 | A | Nottingham F | D | 1-1 | 0-0 | 17 | Cook [84] | 21,229 |
| 19 | 15 | A | Norwich C | W | 2-1 | 1-0 | 15 | Fitzgerald [24], Cox (pen) [81] | 16,420 |
| 20 | 22 | H | West Ham U | D | 0-0 | 0-0 | 15 | | 20,950 |
| 21 | 29 | A | Reading | L | 1-2 | 0-0 | 18 | Cook [60] | 14,521 |
| 22 | Dec 6 | H | Nottingham F | D | 1-1 | 0-0 | 19 | Fitzgerald [73] | 14,988 |
| 23 | 13 | A | Sheffield U | D | 2-2 | 0-0 | 20 | Smith [64], Helguson [67] | 18,637 |
| 24 | 20 | H | Stoke C | L | 1-3 | 1-1 | 21 | Helguson [4] | 13,732 |
| 25 | 26 | A | Gillingham | L | 0-1 | 0-0 | 21 | | 8971 |
| 26 | 28 | H | Cardiff C | W | 2-1 | 0-0 | 19 | Fitzgerald [61], Cook [88] | 15,512 |
| 27 | Jan 10 | A | Coventry C | D | 0-0 | 0-0 | 19 | | 12,226 |
| 28 | 17 | H | Crystal Palace | L | 1-5 | 0-3 | 20 | Helguson (pen) [58] | 15,017 |
| 29 | 31 | A | WBA | L | 1-3 | 0-1 | 20 | Fitzgerald [77] | 23,958 |
| 30 | Feb 7 | H | Sunderland | D | 2-2 | 1-0 | 20 | Mahon [7], Cox (pen) [68] | 16,798 |
| 31 | 14 | H | Preston NE | W | 2-0 | 1-0 | 20 | Bouazza [36], Devlin [80] | 12,675 |
| 32 | 21 | A | Walsall | W | 1-0 | 1-0 | 19 | Cook [15] | 6684 |
| 33 | 28 | H | Wimbledon | W | 4-0 | 2-0 | 17 | Cook [5], Cox (pen) [39], Smith [63], Ardley [77] | 15,323 |
| 34 | Mar 6 | A | Stoke C | L | 1-3 | 1-3 | 17 | Helguson [36] | 13,108 |
| 35 | 9 | A | Bradford C | L | 0-2 | 0-2 | — | | 17,143 |
| 36 | 13 | H | Sheffield U | L | 0-2 | 0-1 | 20 | | 13,861 |
| 37 | 16 | H | Derby Co | W | 2-1 | 1-1 | — | Helguson [19], Mahon [53] | 13,931 |
| 38 | 20 | A | Ipswich T | L | 1-4 | 1-2 | 18 | Fitzgerald [45] | 23,524 |
| 39 | 27 | H | Wigan Ath | D | 1-1 | 1-1 | 20 | Helguson [24] | 13,382 |
| 40 | Apr 10 | H | Crewe Alex | W | 2-1 | 1-0 | 18 | Hyde [31], Wright (og) [62] | 18,041 |
| 41 | 12 | A | Burnley | W | 3-2 | 1-1 | 17 | Devlin (pen) [39], Helguson [55], Cook [84] | 11,413 |
| 42 | 17 | A | Rotherham U | D | 1-1 | 1-1 | 17 | Dyer [24] | 7221 |
| 43 | 20 | A | Millwall | W | 2-1 | 0-1 | — | Dyer [53], Cook [71] | 10,263 |
| 44 | 24 | H | Norwich C | L | 1-2 | 0-1 | 16 | Blizzard [78] | 19,290 |
| 45 | May 1 | A | West Ham U | L | 0-4 | 0-2 | 17 | | 34,685 |
| 46 | 9 | H | Reading | W | 1-0 | 1-0 | 16 | Young [43] | 17,979 |

**Final League Position: 16**

## GOALSCORERS

*League (54):* Fitzgerald 10, Helguson 8 (1 pen), Cook 7, Webber 5, Cox 4 (4 pens), Devlin 3 (1 pen), Dyer 3, Young 3, Mahon 2, Smith 2, Ardley 1, Blizzard 1, Bouazza 1, Gayle 1, Hyde 1, own goals 2.
*Carling Cup (1):* Fitzgerald 1.
*FA Cup (2):* Helguson 1, Mahon 1.

| Chamberlain A 20 + 1 | Doyley L 7 + 2 | Robinson P 10 | Cox N 35 | Gayle M 32 | Mahon G 32 | Ardley N 35 + 3 | Hyde M 28 + 5 | Webber D 24 + 3 | Dyer B 18 + 14 | Helguson H 20 + 2 | Fitzgerald S 28 + 16 | Hand J 16 + 6 | Cook L 20 + 21 | Dyche S 22 + 3 | McNamee A — + 2 | Devlin P 39 | Young A — + 5 | Fisken G — + 1 | Kelly S 13 | Vernazza P 17 + 12 | Ifil J 9 + 1 | Pidgeley L 26 + 1 | Smith J 16 + 1 | Brown W 12 | Bouazza H 6 + 3 | Mayo P 12 | Baird C 8 | Blizzard D 1 + 1 | Match No. |
|---|---|---|---|---|---|---|---|---|---|---|---|---|---|---|---|---|---|---|---|---|---|---|---|---|---|---|---|---|---|
| 1 | $2^{1}$ | 3 | 4 | 5 | 6 | 7 | $8^{2}$ | $9^{3}$ | 10 | 11 | 12 | 13 | 14 | | | | | | | | | | | | | | | | 1 |
| 1 | 2 | 3 | 4 | 5 | 6 | $7^{1}$ | $8^{2}$ | $9^{3}$ | 10 | 11 | 12 | 13 | 14 | | | | | | | | | | | | | | | | 2 |
| 1 | $2^{2}$ | 3 | 4 | 5 | 6 | | 8 | $9^{1}$ | 10 | 11 | 12 | $7^{3}$ | | 13 | 14 | | | | | | | | | | | | | | 3 |
| 1 | | 3 | 4 | 5 | 6 | 2■ | $8^{1}$ | 9 | $7^{2}$ | 10 | 13 | 12 | $11^{3}$ | | 14 | | | | | | | | | | | | | | 4 |
| 1 | | 3 | 2 | 5 | 6 | | | 9 | $10^{1}$ | | 12 | 8 | $11^{2}$ | 4 | | 7 | 13 | | | | | | | | | | | | 5 |
| 1 | | 3 | 2 | 5 | 6 | 12 | | $9^{1}$ | 10 | | 13 | $8^{2}$ | $11^{3}$ | 4 | | 7■ | 14 | | | | | | | | | | | | 6 |
| 1 | | 3 | 2 | 5 | 6 | | | 9 | $10^{1}$ | | 12 | $8^{3}$ | $11^{2}$ | 4 | | 7 | 13 | 14 | | | | | | | | | | | 7 |
| 1 | | 3 | 5 | | $6^{1}$ | 8 | | 9 | 12 | | 10 | 13 | $11^{2}$ | 4 | | 7 | | | 2 | | | | | | | | | | 8 |
| 1 | | 3 | 4 | 5 | 6 | 7 | | 9 | $10^{1}$ | | 11 | 12 | | | | | | | 2 | 8■ | | | | | | | | | 9 |
| 1■ | | 3 | 4 | 5 | $6^{1}$ | 7 | | $9^{2}$ | $11^{6}$ | | 10 | 12 | | | | | | | 2 | 8 | 13 | 15 | | | | | | | 10 |
| 1 | 2 | | 4 | 5 | | 8 | 12 | 9 | $10^{2}$ | | 11 | $6^{1}$ | | | | 7 | 13 | | 3 | | | | | | | | | | 11 |
| | | | 4 | $5^{2}$ | | 8 | $6^{3}$ | 9 | 12 | | $10^{1}$ | | 14 | 13 | | 7 | | | 2 | 11 | | 1 | 3 | | | | | | 12 |
| | | | 4 | | | 7 | | 9 | | | 10 | $6^{1}$ | 12 | 5 | | 11 | | | 2 | 8 | | 1 | 3 | | | | | | 13 |
| | | | 4 | 5 | | 7 | | $9^{1}$ | 12 | | $10^{2}$ | 6 | 13 | | | 11 | | | 2 | 8 | | 1 | 3 | | | | | | 14 |
| | | | 4 | 5 | | 7 | | $9^{3}$ | 12 | | $10^{2}$ | $6^{1}$ | 14 | 13 | | 11 | | | 2 | 8 | | 1 | | 3 | | | | | 15 |
| | | | 4 | 5 | | 7 | | $9^{1}$ | 12 | | 10 | $6^{2}$ | 13 | | | 11 | | | 2 | 8 | | 1 | | 3 | | | | | 16 |
| | | | 4 | 5 | | 7 | | $9^{2}$ | 12 | | $10^{1}$ | 6 | 13 | | | 11 | | | 2 | 8 | | 1 | | 3 | | | | | 17 |
| | | | 4 | 5 | | $7^{1}$ | 8 | 9 | | | 10 | | 12 | | | 11 | | | 2 | 6 | | 1 | | 3 | | | | | 18 |
| | | | 4 | 5 | | 7 | | 9 | | | 10 | 6 | $11^{1}$ | | | | | | 2 | 8 | | 1 | 12 | 3 | | | | | 19 |
| | | | 4 | 5 | | 7 | 8 | 9 | | | 10 | | | | | 11 | | | | 6 | | 1 | 2 | 3 | | | | | 20 |
| | | | 4 | 5 | | 7 | $8^{1}$ | $9^{2}$ | 12 | | 10 | | 13 | | | 11 | | | | 6 | | 1 | 2 | 3 | | | | | 21 |
| | | | 4 | | | $7^{2}$ | | $9^{1}$ | | 12 | 10 | 8 | 13 | 5 | | 11 | | | | 6 | | 1 | 2 | 3 | | | | | 22 |
| 15 | | | 4 | 5 | | 7 | 12 | | | $9^{1}$ | $10^{2}$ | $6^{6}$ | 13 | | | 11 | | | | 8 | | 1■ | 2 | 3 | | | | | 23 |
| | | | 4 | 5 | | 7 | 12 | | 13 | 9 | $10^{2}$ | $6^{3}$ | 14 | | | 11 | | | 2 | 8 | | 1 | | $3^{1}$ | | | | | 24 |
| | | | 4 | 5 | 2 | 7 | 13 | $9^{1}$ | 12 | 10 | | $6^{2}$ | 14 | | | 11 | | | | $8^{3}$ | | 1 | | 3 | | | | | 25 |
| 1 | | | 4 | 5 | 8 | 2 | 6 | 12 | | 9 | $10^{1}$ | | $11^{2}$ | | | 7 | | | | 13 | | | 3 | | | | | | 26 |
| | | | 4 | 5 | 11 | 2 | 6 | $9^{1}$ | 10 | | 12 | | 13 | | | 7 | | | | $8^{2}$ | | 1 | 3 | | | | | | 27 |
| | 14 | | 4■ | 5 | 8 | 2 | 12 | | 13 | 9 | $10^{2}$ | $6^{1}$ | $11^{3}$ | | | 7 | | | | | | 1 | 3 | | | | | | 28 |
| | | | | 5 | 6 | $7^{1}$ | 8 | | $10^{2}$ | 9■ | 13 | | 14 | 4 | | $11^{3}$ | | | | 12 | | 1 | 3 | 2 | | | | | 29 |
| | | | 2 | | 6 | $7^{1}$ | 8 | | | 9 | $10^{2}$ | | 12 | 5 | | $11^{3}$ | | | | 13 | 4 | 1 | 3 | | 14 | | | | 30 |
| | | | 2 | | 6 | 7 | 8 | | 12 | | 10 | | 13 | 5 | | $11^{1}$ | | | | | 4 | 1 | 3 | | $9^{2}$ | | | | 31 |
| | | | 2 | | 6 | 7 | 8 | | | | $10^{1}$ | | 11 | 5 | | 9 | | | | 12 | 4 | 1 | 3 | | | | | | 32 |
| | | | 2 | | 6 | 7 | 8 | | 12 | | $10^{2}$ | | $11^{1}$ | 5 | | 9 | | | | 13 | 4 | 1 | 3 | | | | | | 33 |
| | 13 | | $2^{1}$ | | 6 | 7 | 8 | | | 10 | 14 | | $11^{3}$ | 5 | | 9 | | | | 12 | 4 | 1 | $3^{2}$ | | | | | | 34 |
| | 2 | | | | 6 | $7^{3}$ | 8 | | $10^{1}$ | $9^{2}$ | 13 | | 12 | 5 | | 11 | | | | 14 | 4 | 1 | | | | 3 | | | 35 |
| | $2^{1}$ | | | | 6 | 7 | 8 | 12 | 13 | $9^{2}$ | $10^{3}$ | | 14 | 5 | | 11 | | | | | 4 | 1 | | | | 3 | | | 36 |
| | | | | | 6 | 2 | 8 | | | 9 | 10 | | $11^{1}$ | 5 | | 7 | | | | 12 | 4 | 1 | | | | 3 | | | 37 |
| | | | | | 6 | $7^{2}$ | 8 | 12 | | 9 | $10^{1}$ | | 13 | 5 | | 11 | | | | | 4 | 1 | | | | 3 | 2 | | 38 |
| 1 | | | | 5 | $6^{1}$ | 12 | 8 | | | 9 | $10^{2}$ | | 11 | 4 | | 7 | | | | | | | | | 13 | 3 | 2 | | 39 |
| 1 | | | | 5 | 6 | | 8 | | | 9 | $10^{1}$ | | 11 | 4 | | 7 | | | | | | | | | 12 | 3 | 2 | | 40 |
| 1 | | | | 5 | 6 | | 8 | | 13 | $9^{2}$ | | | $11^{1}$ | 4 | | 7 | | | | 12 | | | | | 10 | 3 | 2 | | 41 |
| 1 | | | | 5 | 6 | | 8 | | $10^{1}$ | | 12 | | $11^{2}$ | 4 | | 7 | | | | 13 | | | | | 9 | 3 | 2 | | 42 |
| 1 | | | | 5 | 6 | 12 | 8 | | 10 | | 13 | | $11^{1}$ | 4 | | 7 | | | | | | | | | $9^{2}$ | 3 | 2 | | 43 |
| 1 | | | | 5 | 6 | | $8^{2}$ | | 10 | | 12 | | 11 | 4 | | 7 | | | | | | | | | $9^{1}$ | 3 | 2 | 13 | 44 |
| 1 | | | 5 | | 6 | | $8^{1}$ | | 10 | 13 | 12 | | $11^{3}$ | | | 7 | | | | 14 | | | | | $9^{2}$ | 3 | 2 | 4 | 45 |
| 1 | 5 | | 4 | | $6^{2}$ | 2 | 8 | | 10 | $9^{1}$ | 12 | | $11^{3}$ | | | 7 | 14 | | | 13 | | | | | | 3 | | | 46 |

**Carling Cup**

| | | | |
|---|---|---|---|
| First Round | Bournemouth | (h) | 1-0 |
| Second Round | Bristol C | (a) | 0-1 |

**FA Cup**

| | | | |
|---|---|---|---|
| Third Round | Chelsea | (h) | 2-2 |
| | | (a) | 0-4 |

# WEST BROMWICH ALBION FA Premiership

## FOUNDATION

There is a well known story that when employees of Salter's Spring Works in West Bromwich decided to form a football club, they had to send someone to the nearby Association Football stronghold of Wednesbury to purchase a football. A weekly subscription of 2d (less than 1p) was imposed and the name of the new club was West Bromwich Strollers.

***The Hawthorns, West Bromwich, West Midlands B71 4LF.***

***Telephone:*** (0121) 525 8888

***Fax:*** (0121) 524 3461.

***Ticket Office:*** (0121) 525 888.

***Website:*** www.wbafc.co.uk

***Email:*** enquiries@wbafc.co.uk

***Ground Capacity:*** 28,000.

***Record Attendance:*** 64,815 v Arsenal, FA Cup 6th rd, 6 March 1937.

***Pitch Measurements:*** 115yd × 72yd.

***Chairman:*** Jeremy Peace.

***Secretary:*** Dr John J. Evans BA, PHD.

***Manager:*** Gary Megson.

***Assistant Manager:*** Frank Burrows.

***Physio:*** Nick Worth.

***Colours:*** Navy blue and white striped shirts, white shorts, navy blue stockings.

***Change Colours:*** Yellow and green striped shirts, green shorts, yellow stockings.

***Year Formed:*** 1878.

***Turned Professional:*** 1885.

***Ltd Co.:*** 1892.

***Plc:*** 1996.

***Previous Name:*** 1878, West Bromwich Strollers; 1881, West Bromwich Albion.

***Club Nicknames:*** 'Throstles', 'Baggies', 'Albion'.

***Previous Grounds:*** 1878, Coopers Hill; 1879, Dartmouth Park; 1881, Bunns Field, Walsall Street; 1882, Four Acres (Dartmouth Cricket Club); 1885, Stoney Lane; 1900, The Hawthorns.

***First Football League Game:*** 8 September 1888, Football League, v Stoke (a) W 2–0 – Roberts; J. Horton, Green; E. Horton, Perry, Bayliss; Bassett, Woodhall (1), Hendry, Pearson, Wilson (1).

***Record League Victory:*** 12–0 v Darwen, Division 1, 4 April 1892 – Reader; J. Horton, McCulloch; Reynolds (2), Perry, Groves; Bassett (3), McLeod, Nicholls (1), Pearson (4), Geddes (1), (1 og).

## HONOURS

*Football League:* Division 1 – Champions 1919–20; Runners-up 1924–25, 1953–54, 2001–02, 2003–04; Division 2 – Champions 1901–02, 1910–11; Runners-up 1930–31, 1948–49; Promoted to Division 1 1975–76 (3rd); 1992–93 (play-offs); Promoted to FA Premier League 2001–02.

*FA Cup:* Winners 1888, 1892, 1931, 1954, 1968; Runners-up 1886, 1887, 1895, 1912, 1935.

*Football League Cup:* Winners 1966; Runners-up 1967, 1970.

***European Competitions:*** *European Cup-Winners' Cup:* 1968–69. *European Fairs Cup:* 1966–67. *UEFA Cup:* 1978–79, 1979–80, 1981–82.

## SKY SPORTS FACT FILE

Ray Treacy was twice a debutant goalscorer for West Bromwich Albion. His first such achievement was on 8 October 1966 against Sunderland, the second on 25 September 1976 when they met Derby County. Meantime he had played for three other clubs.

***Record Cup Victory:*** 10–1 v Chatham (away), FA Cup 3rd rd, 2 March 1889 – Roberts; J. Horton, Green; Timmins (1), Charles Perry, E. Horton; Bassett (2), Perry (1), Bayliss (2), Pearson, Wilson (3), (1 og).

***Record Defeat:*** 3–10 v Stoke C, Division 1, 4 February 1937.

***Most League Points (2 for a win):*** 60, Division 1, 1919–20.

***Most League Points (3 for a win):*** 89, Division 1, 2001–02.

***Most League Goals:*** 105, Division 2, 1929–30.

***Highest League Scorer in Season:*** William 'Ginger' Richardson, 39, Division 1, 1935–36.

***Most League Goals in Total Aggregate:*** Tony Brown, 218, 1963–79.

***Most League Goals in One Match:*** 6, Jimmy Cookson v Blackpool, Division 2, 17 September 1927.

***Most Capped Player:*** Stuart Williams, 33 (43), Wales.

***Most League Appearances:*** Tony Brown, 574, 1963–80.

***Youngest League Player:*** Charlie Wilson, 16 years 73 days v Oldham Ath, 1 October 1921.

***Record Transfer Fee Received:*** £5,000,001 from Coventry C for Lee Hughes, July 2001.

***Record Transfer Fee Paid:*** £2,700,000 to FC Copenhagen for Martin Albrechtsen, June 2004.

***Football League Record:*** 1888 Founder Member of Football League; 1901–02 Division 2; 1902–04 Division 1; 1904–11 Division 2; 1911–27 Division 1; 1927–31 Division 2; 1931–38 Division 1; 1938–49 Division 2; 1949–73 Division 1; 1973–76 Division 2; 1976–86 Division 1; 1986–91 Division 2; 1991–92 Division 3; 1992–93 Division 2; 1993–2002 Division 1; 2002–03 FA Premier League; 2003–04 Division 1; 2004– FA Premier League.

## MANAGERS

Louis Ford 1890–92
*(Secretary-Manager)*
Henry Jackson 1892–94
*(Secretary-Manager)*
Edward Stephenson 1894–95
*(Secretary-Manager)*
Clement Keys 1895–96
*(Secretary-Manager)*
Frank Heaven 1896–1902
*(Secretary-Manager)*
Fred Everiss 1902–48
Jack Smith 1948–52
Jesse Carver 1952
Vic Buckingham 1953–59
Gordon Clark 1959–61
Archie Macaulay 1961–63
Jimmy Hagan 1963–67
Alan Ashman 1967–71
Don Howe 1971–75
Johnny Giles 1975–77
Ronnie Allen 1977
Ron Atkinson 1978–81
Ronnie Allen 1981–82
Ron Wylie 1982–84
Johnny Giles 1984–85
Ron Saunders 1986–87
Ron Atkinson 1987–88
Brian Talbot 1988–91
Bobby Gould 1991–92
Ossie Ardiles 1992–93
Keith Burkinshaw 1993–94
Alan Buckley 1994–97
Ray Harford 1997
Denis Smith 1997–2000
Brian Little 2000
Gary Megson March 2000–

## LATEST SEQUENCES

***Longest Sequence of League Wins:*** 11, 5.4.1930 – 8.9.1930.

***Longest Sequence of League Defeats:*** 11, 28.10.1995 – 26.12.1995.

***Longest Sequence of League Draws:*** 5, 30.8.1999 – 3.10.1999.

***Longest Sequence of Unbeaten League Matches:*** 17, 7.9.1957 – 7.12.1957.

***Longest Sequence Without a League Win:*** 14, 28.10.1995 – 3.2.1996.

***Successive Scoring Runs:*** 36 from 26.4.1958.

***Successive Non-scoring Runs:*** 4 from 15.2.1913.

## TEN YEAR LEAGUE RECORD

| | | P | W | D | L | F | A | Pts | Pos |
|---|---|---|---|---|---|---|---|---|---|
| 1994-95 | Div 1 | 46 | 16 | 10 | 20 | 51 | 57 | 58 | 19 |
| 1995-96 | Div 1 | 46 | 16 | 12 | 18 | 60 | 68 | 60 | 11 |
| 1996-97 | Div 1 | 46 | 14 | 15 | 17 | 68 | 72 | 57 | 16 |
| 1997-98 | Div 1 | 46 | 16 | 12 | 17 | 50 | 56 | 61 | 10 |
| 1998-99 | Div 1 | 46 | 16 | 11 | 19 | 69 | 76 | 59 | 12 |
| 1999-2000 | Div 1 | 46 | 10 | 19 | 17 | 43 | 60 | 49 | 21 |
| 2000-01 | Div 1 | 46 | 21 | 11 | 14 | 60 | 52 | 74 | 6 |
| 2001-02 | Div 1 | 46 | 27 | 8 | 11 | 61 | 29 | 89 | 2 |
| 2002-03 | PR Lge | 38 | 6 | 8 | 24 | 29 | 65 | 26 | 19 |
| 2003-04 | Div 1 | 46 | 25 | 11 | 10 | 64 | 42 | 86 | 2 |

## DID YOU KNOW ?

West Bromwich Albion fans saw eleven goals on floodlights-opening day, 29 October 1957 against CSKA Moscow. With 52,805 watching, Albion won 6-5 with Derek Kevan (2), Ronnie Allen (penalty), Bobby Robson, Frank Griffin and Don Howe scoring.

## WEST BROMWICH ALBION 2003–04 LEAGUE RECORD

| *Match No.* | *Date* | *Venue* | *Opponents* | *Result* | *H/T Score* | *Lg. Pos.* | *Goalscorers* | *Attendance* |
|---|---|---|---|---|---|---|---|---|
| 1 | Aug 9 | A | Walsall | L 1-4 | 0-3 | — | Koumas [70] | 11,030 |
| 2 | 16 | H | Burnley | W 4-1 | 1-1 | 10 | Sakiri [31], Hulse [59], Hughes 2 [88, 89] | 22,489 |
| 3 | 23 | A | Watford | W 1-0 | 0-0 | 5 | Hughes [56] | 15,023 |
| 4 | 25 | H | Preston NE | W 1-0 | 1-0 | 2 | Hughes (pen) [45] | 24,402 |
| 5 | 30 | A | Derby Co | W 1-0 | 0-0 | 1 | Hulse [76] | 21,499 |
| 6 | Sept 13 | H | Ipswich T | W 4-1 | 1-0 | 1 | Gaardsoe [11], Hulse 2 [16, 57], Diallo (og) [86] | 24,954 |
| 7 | 16 | A | Wigan Ath | L 0-1 | 0-1 | — | | 12,874 |
| 8 | 20 | A | Crystal Palace | D 2-2 | 0-0 | 3 | Hulse [52], Koumas [89] | 17,477 |
| 9 | 27 | H | Stoke C | W 1-0 | 0-0 | 3 | Dobie [59] | 24,297 |
| 10 | 30 | H | Millwall | W 2-1 | 2-1 | — | Koumas [5], Dobie [24] | 22,909 |
| 11 | Oct 4 | A | Gillingham | W 2-0 | 2-0 | 1 | Dobie [26], Clement [29] | 8883 |
| 12 | 14 | H | Sheffield U | L 0-2 | 0-2 | — | | 27,195 |
| 13 | 18 | H | Norwich C | W 1-0 | 1-0 | 2 | Koumas [35] | 24,966 |
| 14 | 21 | H | Wimbledon | L 0-1 | 0-0 | — | | 22,048 |
| 15 | 25 | A | Rotherham U | W 3-0 | 1-0 | 1 | Barker S (og) [30], Hulse 2 [49, 65] | 7815 |
| 16 | Nov 1 | H | Sunderland | D 0-0 | 0-0 | 2 | | 26,135 |
| 17 | 8 | A | West Ham U | W 4-3 | 2-3 | 1 | Hulse 2 [25, 40], Deane (og) [66], Hughes [77] | 30,359 |
| 18 | 22 | H | Reading | D 0-0 | 0-0 | 1 | | 22,839 |
| 19 | 25 | A | Cardiff C | D 1-1 | 0-0 | — | Koumas [49] | 17,678 |
| 20 | 29 | A | Nottingham F | W 3-0 | 2-0 | 1 | Koumas 2 [38, 90], Louis-Jean (og) [44] | 27,331 |
| 21 | Dec 6 | H | West Ham U | D 1-1 | 0-0 | 1 | Mullins (og) [80] | 26,194 |
| 22 | 9 | A | Bradford C | W 1-0 | 0-0 | — | Dobie [88] | 11,198 |
| 23 | 13 | H | Crewe Alex | D 2-2 | 1-2 | 1 | Haas [7], Gregan [72] | 22,825 |
| 24 | 20 | A | Coventry C | L 0-1 | 0-0 | 2 | | 17,616 |
| 25 | 26 | H | Derby Co | D 1-1 | 0-0 | 2 | Gaardsoe [90] | 26,412 |
| 26 | 30 | A | Wimbledon | D 0-0 | 0-0 | — | | 6376 |
| 27 | Jan 9 | H | Walsall | W 2-0 | 0-0 | — | Koumas [62], Horsfield [72] | 24,558 |
| 28 | 17 | A | Burnley | D 1-1 | 0-0 | 2 | Horsfield [73] | 13,106 |
| 29 | 31 | H | Watford | W 3-1 | 1-0 | 2 | Horsfield 2 [41, 66], Hughes [61] | 23,958 |
| 30 | Feb 7 | A | Preston NE | L 0-3 | 0-1 | 2 | | 16,569 |
| 31 | 14 | H | Cardiff C | W 2-1 | 0-0 | 2 | Clement [55], Hughes [85] | 25,196 |
| 32 | 21 | A | Sheffield U | W 2-1 | 0-0 | 2 | Moore [70], Gaardsoe [85] | 24,805 |
| 33 | 28 | H | Rotherham U | L 0-1 | 0-0 | 2 | | 24,104 |
| 34 | Mar 2 | A | Norwich C | D 0-0 | 0-0 | — | | 23,223 |
| 35 | 6 | H | Coventry C | W 3-0 | 1-0 | 2 | Horsfield [23], Hulse [52], Kinsella [78] | 25,414 |
| 36 | 13 | A | Crewe Alex | W 2-1 | 0-0 | 2 | Johnson [69], Hughes [73] | 8335 |
| 37 | 16 | H | Wigan Ath | W 2-1 | 0-0 | — | Hughes (pen) [77], Gaardsoe [90] | 26,215 |
| 38 | 27 | H | Crystal Palace | W 2-0 | 0-0 | 2 | Moore [81], Dyer [86] | 24,990 |
| 39 | Apr 4 | A | Ipswich T | W 3-2 | 0-1 | 2 | Koumas [71], Dyer [73], Horsfield [90] | 24,608 |
| 40 | 10 | H | Gillingham | W 1-0 | 1-0 | 2 | Hughes [78] | 24,524 |
| 41 | 12 | A | Millwall | D 1-1 | 0-1 | 2 | Johnson [55] | 13,304 |
| 42 | 18 | A | Sunderland | W 1-0 | 0-0 | 2 | Koumas [90] | 32,201 |
| 43 | 24 | H | Bradford C | W 2-0 | 0-0 | 2 | Horsfield [55], Hughes [60] | 26,143 |
| 44 | May 1 | A | Reading | L 0-1 | 0-0 | 2 | | 20,619 |
| 45 | 4 | A | Stoke C | L 1-4 | 0-1 | — | Dobie [50] | 18,352 |
| 46 | 9 | H | Nottingham F | L 0-2 | 0-1 | 2 | | 26,821 |

**Final League Position: 2**

## GOALSCORERS

*League (64):* Hughes 11 (2 pens), Hulse 10, Koumas 10, Horsfield 7, Dobie 5, Gaardsoe 4, Clement 2, Dyer 2, Johnson 2, Moore 2, Gregan 1, Haas 1, Kinsella 1, Sakiri 1, own goals 5.
*Carling Cup (10):* Hulse 3, Dobie 2, Haas 2, Clement 1, Hughes 1, own goal 1.
*FA Cup (0).*

| Hoult R 44 | Haas B 36 | Clement N 25 + 10 | Sigurdsson L 5 | Gregan S 40 + 3 | Volmer J 10 + 5 | O'Connor J 27 + 3 | Johnson A 33 + 5 | Hulse R 29 + 4 | Dichio D 5 + 6 | Koumas J 37 + 5 | Wallwork R 4 + 1 | Sakiri A 6 + 19 | Dobie S 14 + 17 | Gaardsoe T 45 | Hughes L 21 + 11 | Gilchrist P 16 + 1 | N'Dour A 2 | Berthe S 2 + 1 | Robinson P 29 + 1 | Chambers J 14 + 3 | Moore D 20 + 2 | Horsfield G 20 | Dyer L 2 + 15 | Kinsella M 15 + 3 | Facey D 2 + 7 | Skoubo M — + 2 | Murphy J 2 + 1 | *Match No.* |
|---|---|---|---|---|---|---|---|---|---|---|---|---|---|---|---|---|---|---|---|---|---|---|---|---|---|---|---|---|
| 1 | 2 | 3 | 4[1] | 5 | 6 | 7 | 8 | 9 | 10[3] | 11 | 12[2] | 13 | 14 | | | | | | | | | | | | | | | 1 |
| 1 | 2 | 3 | | | 6 | 7 | 12 | 9 | | 11[3] | | 8[1] | 10[2] | 5 | 13 | 14 | | | | 4 | | | | | | | | 2 |
| 1 | 2 | 3 | | 8 | 6 | 7 | 11 | 9[1] | 12 | 13 | | | 14 | 5 | 10[3] | | | | | 4[2] | | | | | | | | 3 |
| 1 | 2 | 3 | | 4 | 6[2] | 7 | 14 | 12 | 9[1] | 11 | | 8[3] | 13 | 5 | 10 | | | | | | | | | | | | | 4 |
| 1 | 2 | 3 | 4 | 7 | 6 | 8[1] | 13 | 9 | | 11[2] | | 12 | 14 | 5 | 10[3] | | | | | | | | | | | | | 5 |
| 1 | 2 | 3 | 4 | 7 | 6 | 8[1] | 12 | 9 | | 11[2] | | 13 | 14 | 5 | 10[3] | | | | | | | | | | | | | 6 |
| 1 | 2 | 3 | 4 | 7 | 6[1] | 8 | 12 | 9[2] | 13 | 11 | | 10[3] | | 5 | 14 | | | | | | | | | | | | | 7 |
| 1 | 2 | | 4[1] | 7 | | 12 | 8 | 9[2] | 13 | 11 | | | 14 | 5 | 10[3] | 6 | 3 | | | | | | | | | | | 8 |
| 1 | 2 | 3 | | 4[1] | | 7 | 8■ | 9 | | 11 | | 12 | 10 | 5 | | 6 | | | | | | | | | | | | 9 |
| 1 | 2 | 3 | | 4 | | 7 | 8 | 9 | 12 | 11[2] | | | 10[1] | 5 | | 6 | | 13 | | | | | | | | | | 10 |
| 1 | 2 | 3 | | 7 | 12 | 8 | 11 | 9[2] | | | | | 10 | 5 | 13 | 6[1] | | 4 | | | | | | | | | | 11 |
| 1 | 2 | 3 | | 7[2] | | 8 | | 9[3] | 12 | 11 | | 13 | 10 | 5 | 14 | 6 | | 4[1] | | | | | | | | | | 12 |
| 1 | 2 | | | 4 | 12 | 8 | | 9[3] | | 11 | 7[1] | 13 | 10[2] | 5 | 14 | 6 | | | 3 | | | | | | | | | 13 |
| 1 | 2 | 12 | | 4 | | 8 | | 9 | | 11 | 7[2] | 13 | 10[3] | 5 | 14 | 6 | | | 3[1] | | | | | | | | | 14 |
| 1 | 2 | 12 | | 4 | | 7[1] | 8 | 9 | | 11[2] | | 13 | 14 | 5 | 10[3] | 6 | | | 3 | | | | | | | | | 15 |
| 1 | 2 | 12 | | 4 | | 7[3] | 8 | 9[1] | | 11 | | 14 | 13 | 5 | 10[2] | 6 | | | 3 | | | | | | | | | 16 |
| 1 | 2 | 12 | | 4 | | 7[2] | 8 | 9 | | 11 | | 13 | 10[3] | 5 | 14 | 6 | | | 3[1] | | | | | | | | | 17 |
| 1 | 2 | 12 | | 4 | | 7[2] | 8 | 9 | 10[3] | 11 | | 13 | | 5 | 14 | 6 | | | 3[1] | | | | | | | | | 18 |
| 1 | 2 | | | 4 | | 7 | 8 | 9 | 13 | 11 | | 12[2] | 10[1] | 5 | | 6 | | | 3 | | | | | | | | | 19 |
| 1 | 2[1] | | | 4 | | 7 | 8 | 9 | 10 | 11[2] | | | | 5 | | 6 | | | 3 | 12 | 13 | | | | | | | 20 |
| 1 | 2 | 3 | | 4 | | 7 | 8 | 9 | 10[2] | 11[3] | | 14 | 13 | 5 | | 6[1] | | | 12 | | | | | | | | | 21 |
| 1 | 2 | | | | 12 | 7 | 8 | 9[3] | | 11 | | 13 | 10 | 5 | 14 | 6[2] | | | 3 | | 4[1] | | | | | | | 22 |
| 1 | 2 | | | 4 | 6 | 7[1] | 8 | 9 | | 11 | | 12 | 10[2] | 5 | 13 | | | | 3 | | | | | | | | | 23 |
| 1 | 2 | | | 4 | 6 | 7 | | 9[1] | | 11 | 8[2] | | 12 | 5 | | | | | 3 | | 13 | 10 | | | | | | 24 |
| 1 | 2 | | | 4 | | 7[1] | 8 | 12 | | 11 | | 14 | 13 | 5 | 10[3] | 6 | | | 3 | | | 9[2] | | | | | | 25 |
| 1 | | 3 | | | 6 | 12 | 8[1] | 9[2] | | 11 | 7 | | 13 | 5 | | | | | | 2 | 4 | 10 | | | | | | 26 |
| 1 | 2 | 11 | | 4 | | 12 | | 13 | | 7[1] | | 8[3] | 10[2] | 5 | | | | | 3 | | 6 | 9 | 14 | | | | | 27 |
| 1 | 2[1] | 11 | | 4 | | | 8 | 9■ | | | | | | 5 | | | | | 3 | 7 | 6[2] | 10 | 12 | 13 | | | | 28 |
| 1 | 2 | 11 | | 4 | | | 8[1] | | | | | | | 5 | 10[3] | | | | 3 | 12 | 6 | 9 | 13 | 7[2] | 14 | | | 29 |
| 1 | 2 | 11[1] | | 4 | | | 8 | | | 12 | | | | 5 | 10[3] | | | | 3 | | 6 | 9 | 13 | 7[2] | | 14 | | 30 |
| | 2 | 11 | | 12 | | | 8 | | | 7[1] | | | | 5 | 10[2] | | | | 3 | 13 | 6 | 9 | 14 | 4[3] | | | 1 | 31 |
| | 2 | 11 | | 12 | 13 | | 8 | | | 7 | | | | 5 | 10[3] | | 3[1] | | | | 6 | 9 | | 4[2] | 14 | | 1 | 32 |
| 1 | 2 | 11 | | 13 | 12 | | 8 | | | 7 | | | | 5 | 10[3] | | | | 3[1] | | 6 | 9 | | 4[2] | 14 | | | 33 |
| 1 | 2 | 12 | | 4 | | | 8 | | | 7 | | | 13 | 5 | | | | | 3 | 11 | | 9 | | 6[1] | 10[2] | | | 34 |
| 1 | | | | 4 | | | 8 | 9[3] | | 11[1] | | | | 5 | | | | | 3 | 2 | 6 | 10[2] | 12 | 7 | 14 | 13 | | 35 |
| 1 | 2 | 12 | | 4 | | | 8 | 9[2] | | 11[1] | | | | 5 | 13 | | | | 3 | | 6 | 10 | 14 | 7[3] | | | | 36 |
| 1 | 2 | 11 | | 4[2] | | | 8 | | | 7[1] | | | | 5 | 10 | | | | 3 | | 6 | 9[3] | 13 | 12 | 14 | | | 37 |
| 1 | | | | 4 | | | 8 | 9[3] | | 12 | | 11[1] | | 5 | 10 | | | | 3 | 2 | 6 | | 13 | 7[2] | 14 | | | 38 |
| 1[6] | | | | 4 | | | 8 | | | 12 | | 11[1] | | 5 | 10 | | | | 3 | 2 | 6 | 9 | 13 | 7[2] | | | 15 | 39 |
| 1 | | 12 | | 4 | | | 8 | | | 11[1] | | | | 5 | 10 | | | | 3 | 2 | 6 | 9 | 13 | 7[2] | | | | 40 |
| 1 | | 3 | | 4 | | 7[1] | 8 | | | 11■ | | | 12 | 5■ | | | | | | 2 | 6 | 9[2] | 14 | 13 | 10[3] | | | 41 |
| 1 | | 11 | | 4 | | | 8 | 13 | | 12 | | | 10[3] | 5 | | | | | 3 | 2 | 6[1] | 9[2] | 14 | 7 | | | | 42 |
| 1 | | 11[2] | | 4 | | | 8 | | | 7 | | | 12 | 5 | 10 | | | | 3 | 2 | | 9[1] | 13 | 6[3] | 14 | | | 43 |
| 1 | | 12 | | 4 | | 7 | | | | | | 14 | 13 | 5 | 10[3] | | | | 3[1] | 2 | 6 | 9[2] | 11 | 8 | | | | 44 |
| 1 | 2 | 12 | | 4 | | | | | | 11■ | | 13 | 9 | 5 | 10[2] | | | | 3 | | 6 | | 8 | 7[1] | | | | 45 |
| 1 | | 11 | | 4 | | 8[2] | | 9[1] | | 7 | | 13 | 12 | 5 | 10 | | | | 3[3] | 2 | 6 | | 14 | | | | | 46 |

**Carling Cup**

| | | | |
|---|---|---|---|
| First Round | Brentford | (h) | 4-0 |
| Second Round | Hartlepool U | (a) | 2-1 |
| Third Round | Newcastle U | (a) | 2-1 |
| Fourth Round | Manchester U | (h) | 2-0 |
| Fifth Round | Arsenal | (h) | 0-2 |

**FA Cup**

| | | | |
|---|---|---|---|
| Third Round | Nottingham F | (a) | 0-1 |

# WEST HAM UNITED FL Championship

## FOUNDATION

Thames Iron Works FC was formed by employees of this famous shipbuilding company in 1895 and entered the FA Cup in their initial season at Chatham and the London League in their second. The committee wanted to introduce professional players, so Thames Iron Works was wound up in June 1900 and relaunched a month later as West Ham United.

***The Boleyn Ground, Green Street, Upton Park, London E13 9AZ.***

***Telephone:*** (020) 8548 2748.

***Fax:*** (020) 8548 2758.

***Ticket Office:*** 0870 112 2700.

***Website:*** www.whufc.co.uk

***Ground Capacity:*** 35,056.

***Record Attendance:*** 42,322 v Tottenham H, Division 1, 17 October 1970.

***Pitch Measurements:*** 112yd × 72yd.

***Chairman:*** Terence Brown FCIS, AII, FCCA.

***Vice-chairman:*** Martin Cearns ACIB.

***Chief Executive:*** Paul Aldridge.

***Secretary:*** Peter Barnes.

***Manager:*** Alan Pardew.

***Assistant Manager:*** Peter Grant.

***Physio:*** John Green.

***Colours:*** Claret shirts with sky blue sleeves, white shorts, white stockings.

***Change Colours:*** Sky blue shirts with claret collars and thin claret chevrons, sky blue shorts with claret stripe, sky blue stockings.

***Year Formed:*** 1895.

***Turned Professional:*** 1900.

***Ltd Co.:*** 1900.

***Previous Name:*** Thames Iron Works FC, 1895–1900.

***Club Nicknames:*** 'The Hammers', 'The Irons'.

***Previous Grounds:*** 1895, Memorial Recreation Ground, Canning Town; 1904, Boleyn Ground.

***First Football League Game:*** 30 August 1919, Division 2, v Lincoln C (h) D 1–1 – Hufton; Cope, Lee; Lane, Fenwick, McCrae; D. Smith, Moyes (1), Puddefoot, Morris, Bradshaw.

## HONOURS

*Football League:* Division 1 best season: 3rd, 1985–86; Division 2 – Champions 1957–58, 1980–81; Runners-up 1922–23, 1990–91.

*FA Cup:* Winners 1964, 1975, 1980; Runners-up 1923.

*Football League Cup:* Runners-up 1966, 1981.

***European Competitions:*** *European Cup-Winners' Cup:* 1964–65 (winners), 1965–66, 1975–76 (runners-up), 1980–81. *UEFA Cup:* 1999–2000. *Intertoto Cup:* 1999 (winners).

## SKY SPORTS FACT FILE

West Ham United achieved the notable feat of drawing 5-5 away from home on two occasions. On 10 December 1960 they did so at Newcastle United while a week and six years later to the day, they enacted a repeat performance at Chelsea.

**MANAGERS**

Syd King 1902–32
Charlie Paynter 1932–50
Ted Fenton 1950–61
Ron Greenwood 1961–74
*(continued as General Manager to 1977)*
John Lyall 1974–89
Lou Macari 1989–90
Billy Bonds 1990–94
Harry Redknapp 1994–2001
Glenn Roeder 2001–03
Alan Pardew October 2003–

***Record League Victory:*** 8–0 v Rotherham U, Division 2, 8 March 1958 – Gregory; Bond, Wright; Malcolm, Brown, Lansdowne; Grice, Smith (2), Keeble (2), Dick (4), Musgrove. 8–0 v Sunderland, Division 1, 19 October 1968 – Ferguson; Bonds, Charles; Peters, Stephenson, Moore (1); Redknapp, Boyce, Brooking (1), Hurst (6), Sissons.

***Record Cup Victory:*** 10–0 v Bury, League Cup 2nd rd (2nd leg), 25 October 1983 – Parkes; Stewart (1), Walford, Bonds (Orr), Martin (1), Devonshire (2), Allen, Cottee (4), Swindlehurst, Brooking (2), Pike.

***Record Defeat:*** 2–8 v Blackburn R, Division 1, 26 December 1963.

***Most League Points (2 for a win):*** 66, Division 2, 1980–81.

***Most League Points (3 for a win):*** 88, Division 1, 1992–93.

***Most League Goals:*** 101, Division 2, 1957–58.

***Highest League Scorer in Season:*** Vic Watson, 42, Division 1, 1929–30.

***Most League Goals in Total Aggregate:*** Vic Watson, 298, 1920–35.

***Most League Goals in One Match:*** 6, Vic Watson v Leeds U, Division 1, 9 February 1929; 6, Geoff Hurst v Sunderland, Division 1, 19 October 1968.

***Most Capped Player:*** Bobby Moore, 108, England.

***Most League Appearances:*** Billy Bonds, 663, 1967–88.

***Youngest League Player:*** Neil Finn, 17 years 3 days v Manchester C, 1 January 1996.

***Record Transfer Fee Received:*** £18,000,000 from Leeds U for Rio Ferdinand, November 2000.

***Record Transfer Fee Paid:*** £5,000,000 to Sunderland for Don Hutchison, August 2001 and £5,000,000 to Sparta Prague for Tomas Repka, September 2001.

***Football League Record:*** 1919 Elected to Division 2; 1923–32 Division 1; 1932–58 Division 2; 1958–78 Division 1; 1978–81 Division 2; 1981–89 Division 1; 1989–91 Division 2; 1991–93 Division 1; 1993–2003 FA Premier League; 2003–04 Division 1; 2004– FLC.

## LATEST SEQUENCES

***Longest Sequence of League Wins:*** 9, 19.10.1985 – 14.12.1985.

***Longest Sequence of League Defeats:*** 9, 28.3.1932 – 29.8.1932.

***Longest Sequence of League Draws:*** 5, 15.10.2003 – 1.11.2003.

***Longest Sequence of Unbeaten League Matches:*** 27, 27.12.80 – 10.10.81.

***Longest Sequence Without a League Win:*** 17, 31.1.1976 – 21.8.1976.

***Successive Scoring Runs:*** 27 from 5.10.1957.

***Successive Non-scoring Runs:*** 5 from 1.5.1971.

**TEN YEAR LEAGUE RECORD**

| | | P | W | D | L | F | A | Pts | Pos |
|---|---|---|---|---|---|---|---|---|---|
| 1994-95 | PR Lge | 42 | 13 | 11 | 18 | 44 | 48 | 50 | 14 |
| 1995-96 | PR Lge | 38 | 14 | 9 | 15 | 43 | 52 | 51 | 10 |
| 1996-97 | PR Lge | 38 | 10 | 12 | 16 | 39 | 48 | 42 | 14 |
| 1997-98 | PR Lge | 38 | 16 | 8 | 14 | 56 | 57 | 56 | 8 |
| 1998-99 | PR Lge | 38 | 16 | 9 | 13 | 46 | 53 | 57 | 5 |
| 1999-2000 | PR Lge | 38 | 15 | 10 | 13 | 52 | 53 | 55 | 9 |
| 2000-01 | PR Lge | 38 | 10 | 12 | 16 | 45 | 50 | 42 | 15 |
| 2001-02 | PR Lge | 38 | 15 | 8 | 15 | 48 | 57 | 53 | 7 |
| 2002-03 | PR Lge | 38 | 10 | 12 | 16 | 42 | 59 | 42 | 18 |
| 2003-04 | Div 1 | 46 | 19 | 17 | 10 | 67 | 45 | 74 | 4 |

**DID YOU KNOW ?**

As a mark of respect for the late Bobby Moore, West Ham United retired the No.6 shirt for the home game against Wolverhampton Wanderers on 6 March 1993. Ian Bishop wore No.12 instead and the Hammers won 3-1.

## WEST HAM UNITED 2003–04 LEAGUE RECORD

| Match No. | Date | Venue | Opponents | Result | | H/T Score | Lg. Pos. | Goalscorers | Attendance |
|---|---|---|---|---|---|---|---|---|---|
| 1 | Aug 9 | A | Preston NE | W | 2-1 | 1-1 | — | Defoe [5], Connolly [69] | 18,246 |
| 2 | 16 | H | Sheffield U | D | 0-0 | 0-0 | 8 | | 28,972 |
| 3 | 23 | A | Rotherham U | L | 0-1 | 0-1 | 12 | | 8739 |
| 4 | 26 | H | Bradford C | W | 1-0 | 1-0 | — | Defoe [32] | 30,370 |
| 5 | 30 | A | Ipswich T | W | 2-1 | 1-0 | 6 | Defoe [21], Connolly [47] | 29,679 |
| 6 | Sept 13 | H | Reading | W | 1-0 | 1-0 | 3 | Dailly [17] | 32,634 |
| 7 | 16 | A | Crewe Alex | W | 3-0 | 0-0 | — | Connolly 2 [18, 21], Etherington [25] | 9575 |
| 8 | 20 | A | Gillingham | L | 0-2 | 0-0 | 4 | | 11,418 |
| 9 | 28 | H | Millwall | D | 1-1 | 1-0 | 7 | Connolly [24] | 31,626 |
| 10 | Oct 1 | H | Crystal Palace | W | 3-0 | 2-0 | — | Defoe [19], Mellor 2 [32, 56] | 31,861 |
| 11 | 4 | A | Derby Co | W | 1-0 | 0-0 | 3 | Hutchison [90] | 22,810 |
| 12 | 15 | H | Norwich C | D | 1-1 | 1-0 | — | Edworthy (og) [6] | 31,308 |
| 13 | 18 | H | Burnley | D | 2-2 | 1-1 | 5 | Connolly [20], Hutchison [86] | 31,474 |
| 14 | 22 | H | Nottingham F | D | 1-1 | 0-1 | — | Defoe [56] | 29,544 |
| 15 | 25 | A | Cardiff C | D | 0-0 | 0-0 | 6 | | 19,202 |
| 16 | Nov 1 | A | Coventry C | D | 1-1 | 1-1 | 6 | Defoe [15] | 19,126 |
| 17 | 8 | H | WBA | L | 3-4 | 3-2 | 6 | Defoe [1], Deane 2 [10, 18] | 30,359 |
| 18 | 22 | A | Watford | D | 0-0 | 0-0 | 9 | | 20,950 |
| 19 | 25 | A | Wimbledon | D | 1-1 | 0-0 | — | Deane [51] | 8118 |
| 20 | 29 | H | Wigan Ath | W | 4-0 | 2-0 | 7 | Horlock [4], Jarrett (og) [17], Harewood 2 (1 pen) [55 (p), 75] | 34,375 |
| 21 | Dec 6 | A | WBA | D | 1-1 | 0-0 | 8 | Deane [68] | 26,194 |
| 22 | 9 | H | Stoke C | L | 0-1 | 0-1 | — | | 24,365 |
| 23 | 13 | H | Sunderland | W | 3-2 | 0-2 | 6 | Defoe 2 [55, 61], Pearce [80] | 30,329 |
| 24 | 20 | A | Walsall | D | 1-1 | 1-0 | 6 | Harewood [10] | 9272 |
| 25 | 26 | H | Ipswich T | L | 1-2 | 0-0 | 8 | Defoe [49] | 35,021 |
| 26 | 28 | A | Nottingham F | W | 2-0 | 1-0 | 7 | Harewood [7], Defoe [84] | 27,491 |
| 27 | Jan 10 | H | Preston NE | L | 1-2 | 1-0 | 8 | Connolly [19] | 28,777 |
| 28 | 17 | A | Sheffield U | D | 3-3 | 3-1 | 8 | Carrick [19], Harley [22], Harewood [37] | 22,787 |
| 29 | 31 | H | Rotherham U | W | 2-1 | 1-1 | 7 | Deane [15], Dailly [59] | 34,483 |
| 30 | Feb 7 | A | Bradford C | W | 2-1 | 0-1 | 5 | Zamora [65], Harewood [78] | 13,078 |
| 31 | 21 | A | Norwich C | D | 1-1 | 0-0 | 5 | Harewood [61] | 23,940 |
| 32 | 28 | H | Cardiff C | W | 1-0 | 0-0 | 6 | Zamora [73] | 31,858 |
| 33 | Mar 2 | A | Burnley | D | 1-1 | 1-1 | — | Connolly (pen) [36] | 12,440 |
| 34 | 6 | H | Walsall | D | 0-0 | 0-0 | 5 | | 33,177 |
| 35 | 9 | H | Wimbledon | W | 5-0 | 2-0 | — | Etherington 3 [37, 49, 70], Zamora [39], Reo-Coker [62] | 29,818 |
| 36 | 13 | A | Sunderland | L | 0-2 | 0-0 | 5 | | 29,533 |
| 37 | 17 | H | Crewe Alex | W | 4-2 | 4-0 | — | Harewood 2 [6, 20], Reo-Coker [35], McAnuff [41] | 31,158 |
| 38 | 21 | A | Millwall | L | 1-4 | 0-1 | 5 | Harewood (pen) [49] | 14,055 |
| 39 | 27 | H | Gillingham | W | 2-1 | 1-1 | 4 | Zamora [3], Etherington [76] | 34,551 |
| 40 | Apr 3 | A | Reading | L | 0-2 | 0-1 | 4 | | 21,718 |
| 41 | 10 | H | Derby Co | D | 0-0 | 0-0 | 6 | | 28,207 |
| 42 | 12 | A | Crystal Palace | L | 0-1 | 0-0 | 8 | | 23,977 |
| 43 | 17 | H | Coventry C | W | 2-0 | 1-0 | 6 | Zamora [37], Connolly (pen) [71] | 27,890 |
| 44 | 24 | A | Stoke C | W | 2-0 | 1-0 | 5 | Connolly [39], Harewood [59] | 18,227 |
| 45 | May 1 | H | Watford | W | 4-0 | 2-0 | 3 | Hutchison 2 [17, 44], Harewood 2 (1 pen) [63 (p), 90] | 34,685 |
| 46 | 9 | A | Wigan Ath | D | 1-1 | 0-1 | 4 | Deane [90] | 20,069 |

**Final League Position: 4**

### GOALSCORERS

*League (67):* Harewood 13 (3 pens), Defoe 11, Connolly 10 (2 pens), Deane 6, Etherington 5, Zamora 5, Hutchison 4, Dailly 2, Mellor 2, Reo-Coker 2, Carrick 1, Harley 1, Horlock 1, McAnuff 1, Pearce 1, own goals 2.
*Carling Cup (6):* Defoe 4 (1 pen), Connolly 2.
*FA Cup (5):* Connolly 2, Deane 1, Harewood 1, Mullins 1.
*Play-Offs (2):* Dailly 1, Etherington 1.

| James D 27 | Ferdinand A 9 + 11 | Brevett R 2 | Hutchison D 10 + 14 | Repka T 40 | Dailly C 43 | Garcia R 2 + 5 | Lee R 12 + 4 | Mellor N 8 + 8 | Defoe J 19 | Etherington M 34 + 1 | Sofiane Y — + 1 | Connolly D 37 + 2 | Pearce I 24 | Horlock K 23 + 4 | Noble D — + 3 | Carrick M 34 + 1 | Kilgallon M 1 + 2 | Quinn W 22 | Alexandersson N 5 + 3 | Mullins H 27 | Stockdale R 5 + 2 | Deane B 9 + 17 | Harewood M 28 | Cohen C 1 + 6 | Bywater S 17 | Harley J 15 | Melville A 11 + 3 | Reo-Coker N 13 + 2 | Nowland A 2 + 9 | McAnuff J 4 + 8 | Zamora B 15 + 2 | Carole S — + 1 | Srnicek P 2 + 1 | Lomas S 5 | Match No. |
|---|---|---|---|---|---|---|---|---|---|---|---|---|---|---|---|---|---|---|---|---|---|---|---|---|---|---|---|---|---|---|---|---|---|---|---|
| 1 | 2 | 3 | 4 | 5 | 6 | $7^{1}$ | 8 | $9^{2}$ | 10 | 11 | 12 | 13 | | | | | | | | | | | | | | | | | | | | | | | 1 |
| 1 | | $3^{1}$ | 4 | 5 | 2 | $12^{2}$ | $7^{3}$ | 13 | 10 | 11 | | 9 | 6 | 8 | 14 | | | | | | | | | | | | | | | | | | | | 2 |
| 1 | $2^{1}$ | | $4^{3}$ | 5 | 6 | 12 | 8 | 13 | 10 | 11 | | $9^{2}$ | 3 | 7 | | 14 | | | | | | | | | | | | | | | | | | | 3 |
| 1 | | | 12 | 5 | 6 | | $2^{1}$ | 9 | 10 | 11 | | 8 | 4 | 3 | | 7 | | | | | | | | | | | | | | | | | | | 4 |
| 1 | | | 12 | 2 | 5 | | | $9^{1}$ | 10 | 11 | | 8 | 6 | 4 | | 7 | 3 | | | | | | | | | | | | | | | | | | 5 |
| 1 | $2^{2}$ | | | 5 | 6 | | 7 | $9^{1}$ | 10 | 12 | | 8 | 4 | 11 | | | | 3 | 13 | | | | | | | | | | | | | | | | 6 |
| 1 | 12 | | | 2 | 5 | | 7 | | 10 | $11^{1}$ | | 9 | 6 | 4 | 13 | | 14 | $3^{3}$ | $8^{2}$ | | | | | | | | | | | | | | | | 7 |
| 1 | 12 | | | 2 | 5 | | 7 | | 10■ | 11 | | 9 | 6 | $4^{2}$ | 13 | | | 3 | $8^{1}$ | | | | | | | | | | | | | | | | 8 |
| 1 | 12 | | | 2 | 5 | | 7 | $9^{2}$ | 10 | 11 | | 8 | $6^{1}$ | 4 | | | | 3 | 13 | | | | | | | | | | | | | | | | 9 |
| 1 | 12 | | | 2 | 5 | | $7^{1}$ | $9^{3}$ | 10 | 11 | | 8 | 6 | 4 | | | 13 | $3^{2}$ | 14 | | | | | | | | | | | | | | | | 10 |
| 1 | | | 12 | 2 | 5 | | 13 | $9^{1}$ | | 11 | | 10 | 6 | 4 | | $8^{2}$ | | 3 | 7 | | | | | | | | | | | | | | | | 11 |
| 1 | 12 | | 13 | 2 | 5 | $10^{2}$ | 14 | 9 | | $11^{1}$ | | | 6 | $4^{3}$ | | 8 | | 3 | 7 | | | | | | | | | | | | | | | | 12 |
| 1 | | | 12 | 2 | 5 | | 4 | 13 | 10 | 11 | | 9 | 6 | | | 8 | | $3^{2}$ | $7^{1}$ | | | | | | | | | | | | | | | | 13 |
| 1 | 12 | | 4 | 2 | 5 | | $7^{1}$ | 13 | 10 | 11 | | $9^{2}$ | | | | 8 | | 3 | | 6 | | | | | | | | | | | | | | | 14 |
| 1 | 14 | | 7 | 4 | 5 | | 12 | $13^{3}$ | 10 | 11 | | $9^{2}$ | | | | 8 | | 3 | | $6^{1}$ | 2 | | | | | | | | | | | | | | 15 |
| 1 | | | | 2 | 5 | 12 | $7^{1}$ | | 10 | 11 | | | 6 | 4 | | | | 3 | | 8 | | 9 | | | | | | | | | | | | | 16 |
| 1 | | | 7 | 2 | 5 | | 12 | | 10■ | 11 | | | 6 | | | 8 | | $3^{1}$ | | 4 | | 9 | | | | | | | | | | | | | 17 |
| 1 | | | 8 | 2 | 5 | 12 | | | | | | 9 | 6 | 4 | | 11 | | 3 | | 7 | | $10^{1}$ | | | | | | | | | | | | | 18 |
| 1 | | | 12 | 2 | 5 | | | | | | | 8 | 6 | 4 | | 11 | | 3 | | 7 | | $10^{1}$ | 9 | | | | | | | | | | | | 19 |
| 1 | 12 | | 14 | $2^{1}$ | 5 | 13 | | | | | | $8^{3}$ | 6 | $4^{2}$ | | 11 | | 3 | | 7 | | 10 | 9 | | | | | | | | | | | | 20 |
| 1 | | | 13 | 4 | 5 | | | | | | | 8 | 6 | 12 | | 11 | | 3 | | 7 | $2^{1}$ | $10^{2}$ | 9 | | | | | | | | | | | | 21 |
| 1 | | | 13 | $4^{1}$ | 5 | | | | | | | 8 | 6 | 12 | | 11 | | 3 | | 7 | 2 | $10^{2}$ | 9 | | | | | | | | | | | | 22 |
| 1 | | | 12 | 2 | 5 | | | | 10 | $11^{3}$ | | 8 | 6 | 4 | | | | $3^{1}$ | | 7 | | 13 | $9^{2}$ | 14 | | | | | | | | | | | 23 |
| 1 | | | 12 | 2 | | | | | 10■ | 11 | | $8^{1}$ | 6 | 4 | | 7 | | 3 | | 5 | | 13 | $9^{2}$ | | | | | | | | | | | | 24 |
| 1 | | | 13 | 2 | | | | 12 | 10 | 11 | | $8^{2}$ | 6 | $4^{3}$ | | 7 | | $3^{1}$ | | 5 | 14 | | 9 | | | | | | | | | | | | 25 |
| 1 | 12 | | | 2 | | | | | 10 | 11 | | $8^{2}$ | 6 | 13 | | 7 | | 3 | | 5 | $4^{1}$ | | 9 | | | | | | | | | | | | 26 |
| 1 | 13 | | $8^{3}$ | | 5 | | | 12 | | 11 | | 10 | 6 | | | 7 | | $3^{2}$ | | 4 | $2^{1}$ | 14 | 9 | | | | | | | | | | | | 27 |
| | 2 | | | | 5 | | | 12 | | $11^{1}$ | | 10 | | $8^{3}$ | | 7 | | | | 4 | 13 | 14 | $9^{2}$ | | 1 | 3 | 6 | | | | | | | | 28 |
| | | | | 2 | 5 | | | | | 11 | | 8 | | | | 7 | | | | 4 | | $10^{1}$ | $9^{2}$ | | 1 | 3 | 12 | 6 | 13 | | | | | | 29 |
| | | | | 4 | 5 | | | | | | | $8^{1}$ | | | | 7 | | | | 2 | | $10^{2}$ | 9 | | 1 | 3 | 12 | 6 | 14 | $11^{3}$ | 13 | | | | 30 |
| | | | | 5 | 6 | | | | | 11■ | | $8^{2}$ | | | | 7 | | | | 2 | | 12 | 9 | | 1 | 3 | | 4 | 13 | | $10^{1}$ | | | | 31 |
| | | | | 5 | 6 | | | | | 11 | | $8^{1}$ | | | | 7 | | | | 2 | | 12 | $9^{2}$ | | 1 | 3 | | 4 | 13 | 14 | $10^{3}$ | | | | 32 |
| | | | | 5 | 6 | | | | | $11^{2}$ | | $8^{1}$ | | | | 7 | | | | 2 | | 12 | $9^{3}$ | | 1 | 3 | | 4 | 13 | 14 | 10 | | | | 33 |
| | | | | 5 | 6 | | | | | | | $8^{1}$ | | | | 7 | | | | $2^{2}$ | | 12 | 9 | | 1 | 3 | 13 | 4 | $11^{3}$ | 14 | 10 | | | | 34 |
| | 12 | | | 2 | 6 | | | | | 11 | | 8 | | | | $7^{2}$ | | | | | | | 9 | | 1 | $3^{1}$ | 5 | 4 | 13 | 14 | $10^{3}$ | | | | 35 |
| | | | | 2 | 6 | | | | | $11^{2}$ | | | | 13 | | 7 | | | | | | 12 | $9^{3}$ | | 1 | 3 | 5 | 4 | 14 | $8^{1}$ | 10 | | | | 36 |
| | | | | 2 | 6 | | | | | | | | | 8 | | 7 | | | | | | 12 | 9 | 13 | 1 | 3 | 5 | $4^{2}$ | | $11^{3}$ | $10^{1}$ | 14 | | | 37 |
| | | | | 2 | 6 | | | | | $11^{6}$ | | | | $8^{1}$ | | 7 | | | | | | 12 | $9^{2}$ | | 1■ | 3 | 5 | 4 | | 13 | 10 | | 15 | | 38 |
| | | | | 2 | 6 | | | | | 11 | | $8^{2}$ | | | | 7 | | | | | | 12 | 9 | | 1 | 3 | 5 | $4^{1}$ | 13 | | 10 | | | | 39 |
| | | | 13 | 2 | 6 | | | | | 11 | | $8^{1}$ | | | | 7 | | | | | | 12 | $9^{3}$ | | 1 | 3 | $5^{2}$ | 4 | 14 | | 10 | | | | 40 |
| | | | | 2 | 6 | | | | | | | 8 | | | | 7 | | | | 5 | | 12 | $9^{3}$ | $11^{2}$ | | 3 | | 13 | | 14 | $10^{1}$ | | 1 | 4 | 41 |
| | 2 | | | 5 | 6 | | | | | | | 10■ | | 11 | | | | | | 7 | | 12 | 9 | 14 | | $3^{3}$ | | $4^{1}$ | | $8^{2}$ | 13 | | 1 | | 42 |
| | 2 | | | | 6 | | | | | | | 8 | | 3 | | | | | | 7 | | 12 | $9^{2}$ | 14 | 1 | | 5 | | $11^{3}$ | 13 | $10^{1}$ | | | 4 | 43 |
| | 2 | | 12 | | 6 | | | | | $11^{2}$ | | $8^{1}$ | | | | 7 | | | | 4 | | | 9 | 13 | 1 | | 5 | | | | 10 | | | 3 | 44 |
| | 2 | | 8 | | 6 | | | | | $11^{1}$ | | | | | | 7 | | | | 4 | | | 9 | 12 | 1 | | 5 | | | 13 | $10^{2}$ | | | 3 | 45 |
| | 2 | | $8^{1}$ | | 6 | | | | | $11^{3}$ | | 12 | | | | 7 | | | | 4 | | 13 | 9 | | 1 | | 5 | 14 | | | $10^{2}$ | | | 3 | 46 |

**Carling Cup**

| | | | |
|---|---|---|---|
| First Round | Rushden & D | (h) | 3-1 |
| Second Round | Cardiff C | (a) | 3-2 |
| Third Round | Tottenham H | (a) | 0-1 |

**FA Cup**

| | | | |
|---|---|---|---|
| Third Round | Wigan Ath | (a) | 2-1 |
| Fourth Round | Wolverhampton W | (a) | 3-1 |
| Fifth Round | Fulham | (a) | 0-0 |
| | | (h) | 0-3 |

**Play-Offs**

| | | | |
|---|---|---|---|
| Semi-Final | Ipswich T | (a) | 0-1 |
| | | (h) | 2-0 |
| Final *(at Millennium Stadium)* | Crystal Palace | | 0-1 |

# WIGAN ATHLETIC FL Championship

## FOUNDATION

Following the demise of Wigan Borough and their resignation from the Football League in 1931, a public meeting was called in Wigan at the Queen's Hall in May 1932 at which a new club, Wigan Athletic, was founded in the hope of carrying on in the Football League. With this in mind, they bought Springfield Park for £2,250, but failed to gain admission to the Football League until 46 years later.

***JJB Stadium, Wigan WN5 0UZ.***

***Telephone:*** (01942) 774 000.

***Fax:*** (01942) 770 477.

***Ticket Office:*** 0870 112 2552.

***Website:*** www.wiganathletic.tv

***Email:*** latics@jjbstadium.co.uk

***Ground Capacity:*** 25,000.

***Record Attendance:*** 27,526 v Hereford U, 12 December 1953.

***Pitch Measurements:*** 115yd × 75yd.

***Chairman:*** David Whelan.

***Chief Executive:*** Brenda Spencer.

***Secretary:*** Stuart Hayton.

***Manager:*** Paul Jewell.

***Assistant Manager:*** Chris Hutchings.

***Physio:*** Alex Cribley.

***Colours:*** Blue shirts, blue shorts, white stockings.

***Change Colours:*** All black with gold trim.

***Year Formed:*** 1932.

***Club Nickname:*** 'The Latics'.

***First Football League Game:*** 19 August 1978, Division 4, v Hereford U (a) D 0–0 – Brown; Hinnigan, Gore, Gillibrand, Ward, Davids, Corrigan, Purdie, Houghton, Wilkie, Wright.

***Record League Victory:*** 7–1 v Scarborough, Division 3, 11 March 1997 – Butler L, Butler J, Sharp (Morgan), Greenall, McGibbon (Biggins (1)), Martinez (1), Diaz (2), Jones (Lancashire (1)), Lowe (2), Rogers, Kilford.

***Record Cup Victory:*** 6–0 v Carlisle U (away), FA Cup 1st rd, 24 November 1934 – Caunce; Robinson, Talbot; Paterson, Watson, Tufnell; Armes (2), Robson (1), Roberts (2), Felton, Scott (1).

***Record Defeat:*** 1–6 v Bristol R, Division 3, 3 March 1990.

## HONOURS

*Football League:* Division 2 Champions, 2002–03; Division 3 Champions, 1996–97; Division 4 – Promoted (3rd) 1981–82.

*FA Cup:* best season: 6th rd, 1987.

*Football League Cup:* best season: 5th rd, 2003.

*Freight Rover Trophy:* Winners 1985.

*Auto Windscreens Shield:* Winners 1999.

## SKY SPORTS FACT FILE

Wigan Athletic reached the fifth round of the FA Cup for the first time after defeating Norwich City 1-0 on 31 January 1987, their opponents being members of the First Division at the time. The only goal came in the 78th minute from Paul Jewell.

***Most League Points (2 for a win):*** 55, Division 4, 1978–79 and 1979–80.

***Most League Points (3 for a win):*** 100, Division 2, 2002–03.

***Most League Goals:*** 84, Division 3, 1996–97.

***Highest League Scorer in Season:*** Graeme Jones, 31, Division 3, 1996–97.

***Most League Goals in Total Aggregate:*** Andy Liddell, 70, 1998–2004.

***Most League Goals in One Match:*** Not more than three goals by one player.

***Most Capped Player:*** Roy Carroll, 9 (14), Northern Ireland.

***Most League Appearances:*** Kevin Langley, 317, 1981–86, 1990–94.

***Youngest League Player:*** Steve Nugent, 16 years 132 days v Leyton Orient, 16 September 1989.

***Record Transfer Fee Received:*** £3,000,000 from Manchester U for Roy Carroll, July 2001

***Record Transfer Fee Paid:*** £1,400,000 to WBA for Jason Roberts, January 2004.

***Football League Record:*** 1978 Elected to Division 4; 1982–92 Division 3; 1992–93 Division 2; 1993–97 Division 3; 1997–2003 Division 2; 2003–04 Division 1; 2004– FLC.

## LATEST SEQUENCES

***Longest Sequence of League Wins:*** 11, 2.11.2002 – 18.1.2003.

***Longest Sequence of League Defeats:*** 7, 6.4.1993 – 4.5.1993.

***Longest Sequence of League Draws:*** 6, 11.12.2001 – 5.1.2002.

***Longest Sequence of Unbeaten League Matches:*** 25, 8.5.1999 – 3.1.2000.

***Longest Sequence Without a League Win:*** 14, 9.5.1989 – 17.10.1989.

***Successive Scoring Runs:*** 24 from 27.4.1996.

***Successive Non-scoring Runs:*** 4 from 15.4.1995.

## MANAGERS

Charlie Spencer 1932–37
Jimmy Milne 1946–47
Bob Pryde 1949–52
Ted Goodier 1952–54
Walter Crook 1954–55
Ron Suart 1955–56
Billy Cooke 1956
Sam Barkas 1957
Trevor Hitchen 1957–58
Malcolm Barrass 1958–59
Jimmy Shirley 1959
Pat Murphy 1959–60
Allenby Chilton 1960
Johnny Ball 1961–63
Allan Brown 1963–66
Alf Craig 1966–67
Harry Leyland 1967–68
Alan Saunders 1968
Ian McNeill 1968–70
Gordon Milne 1970–72
Les Rigby 1972–74
Brian Tiler 1974–76
Ian McNeill 1976–81
Larry Lloyd 1981–83
Harry McNally 1983–85
Bryan Hamilton 1985–86
Ray Mathias 1986–89
Bryan Hamilton 1989–93
Dave Philpotts 1993
Kenny Swain 1993–94
Graham Barrow 1994–95
John Deehan 1995–98
Ray Mathias 1998–99
John Benson 1999–2000
Bruce Rioch 2000–01
Steve Bruce 2001
Paul Jewell June 2001–

## TEN YEAR LEAGUE RECORD

| | | *P* | *W* | *D* | *L* | *F* | *A* | *Pts* | *Pos* |
|---|---|---|---|---|---|---|---|---|---|
| 1994-95 | Div 3 | 42 | 14 | 10 | 18 | 53 | 60 | 52 | 14 |
| 1995-96 | Div 3 | 46 | 20 | 10 | 16 | 62 | 56 | 70 | 10 |
| 1996-97 | Div 3 | 46 | 26 | 9 | 11 | 84 | 51 | 87 | 1 |
| 1997-98 | Div 2 | 46 | 17 | 11 | 18 | 64 | 66 | 62 | 11 |
| 1998-99 | Div 2 | 46 | 22 | 10 | 14 | 75 | 48 | 76 | 6 |
| 1999-2000 | Div 2 | 46 | 22 | 17 | 7 | 72 | 38 | 83 | 4 |
| 2000-01 | Div 2 | 46 | 19 | 18 | 9 | 53 | 42 | 75 | 6 |
| 2001-02 | Div 2 | 46 | 16 | 16 | 14 | 66 | 51 | 64 | 10 |
| 2002-03 | Div 2 | 46 | 29 | 13 | 4 | 68 | 25 | 100 | 1 |
| 2003-04 | Div 1 | 46 | 18 | 17 | 11 | 60 | 45 | 71 | 7 |

## DID YOU KNOW ?

Jack Roberts scored 46 goals in 42 Cheshire League matches in the 1934–35 season as well as 20 more in cup games for Wigan Athletic. Shortly after the start of the following season he was transferred to Port Vale.

## WIGAN ATHLETIC 2003–04 LEAGUE RECORD

| Match No. | Date | Venue | Opponents | Result | | H/T Score | Lg. Pos. | Goalscorers | Attendance |
|---|---|---|---|---|---|---|---|---|---|
| 1 | Aug 9 | A | Millwall | L | 0-2 | 0-0 | — | | 10,898 |
| 2 | 16 | H | Preston NE | D | 1-1 | 0-0 | 18 | McCulloch [89] | 12,073 |
| 3 | 23 | A | Burnley | W | 2-0 | 1-0 | 11 | Kennedy [13], Ellington [77] | 13,231 |
| 4 | 26 | H | Ipswich T | W | 1-0 | 0-0 | — | Ellington [57] | 8292 |
| 5 | 30 | A | Rotherham U | W | 3-0 | 0-0 | 4 | Jarrett [53], Ellington [59], Roberts N [72] | 6660 |
| 6 | Sept 13 | A | Wimbledon | W | 4-2 | 3-1 | 2 | Bullard [21], Liddell [29], Horsfield [33], Ellington [55] | 1054 |
| 7 | 16 | H | WBA | W | 1-0 | 1-0 | — | Horsfield [45] | 12,874 |
| 8 | 20 | H | Watford | W | 1-0 | 1-0 | 1 | McCulloch [11] | 9211 |
| 9 | 27 | A | Coventry C | D | 1-1 | 0-0 | 2 | Jackson [90] | 14,862 |
| 10 | 30 | A | Cardiff C | D | 0-0 | 0-0 | — | | 15,143 |
| 11 | Oct 4 | H | Norwich C | D | 1-1 | 1-0 | 5 | Liddell [24] | 9346 |
| 12 | 11 | A | Derby Co | D | 2-2 | 2-1 | 3 | Liddell 2 [4, 31] | 19,151 |
| 13 | 14 | H | Stoke C | W | 2-1 | 0-1 | — | Horsfield 2 [56, 69] | 7678 |
| 14 | 18 | H | Gillingham | W | 1-0 | 0-0 | 1 | Liddell (pen) [55] | 6696 |
| 15 | 21 | H | Sheffield U | D | 1-1 | 1-0 | — | Horsfield [4] | 12,032 |
| 16 | 25 | A | Walsall | L | 0-2 | 0-0 | 2 | | 7041 |
| 17 | Nov 1 | H | Crystal Palace | W | 5-0 | 2-0 | 1 | Liddell 2 (1 pen) [10, 50 (p)], Horsfield [31], Ellington 2 [56, 69] | 6796 |
| 18 | 8 | A | Reading | L | 0-1 | 0-0 | 4 | | 13,819 |
| 19 | 22 | H | Nottingham F | D | 2-2 | 1-0 | 3 | Ellington [44], Liddell [71] | 10,403 |
| 20 | 29 | A | West Ham U | L | 0-4 | 0-2 | 5 | | 34,375 |
| 21 | Dec 2 | A | Sunderland | D | 1-1 | 0-0 | — | De Vos [70] | 22,167 |
| 22 | 6 | H | Reading | L | 0-2 | 0-0 | 6 | | 7512 |
| 23 | 13 | H | Bradford C | W | 1-0 | 0-0 | 5 | Horsfield [85] | 7256 |
| 24 | 20 | A | Crewe Alex | W | 3-2 | 2-2 | 4 | McCulloch [8], De Vos [20], Bullard [80] | 7873 |
| 25 | 26 | H | Rotherham U | L | 1-2 | 0-0 | 6 | Ellington [90] | 9235 |
| 26 | 28 | A | Sheffield U | D | 1-1 | 1-1 | 6 | Ellington [24] | 26,056 |
| 27 | Jan 10 | H | Millwall | D | 0-0 | 0-0 | 7 | | 7047 |
| 28 | 17 | A | Preston NE | W | 4-2 | 2-1 | 6 | Roberts J [1], Ellington 2 [45, 80], Teale [71] | 19,161 |
| 29 | 31 | H | Burnley | D | 0-0 | 0-0 | 6 | | 11,147 |
| 30 | Feb 7 | A | Ipswich T | W | 3-1 | 2-0 | 3 | Roberts J [18], Ellington [33], Teale [53] | 22,093 |
| 31 | 14 | H | Derby Co | W | 2-0 | 1-0 | 3 | Ellington [45], McCulloch [78] | 9146 |
| 32 | 21 | A | Stoke C | D | 1-1 | 0-1 | 3 | Ellington [84] | 14,927 |
| 33 | 28 | H | Walsall | W | 1-0 | 0-0 | 3 | Ellington [81] | 7593 |
| 34 | Mar 6 | H | Crewe Alex | L | 2-3 | 2-2 | 3 | McCulloch 2 [30, 36] | 8367 |
| 35 | 13 | A | Bradford C | D | 0-0 | 0-0 | 3 | | 11,744 |
| 36 | 16 | A | WBA | L | 1-2 | 0-0 | — | Liddell (pen) [73] | 26,215 |
| 37 | 20 | H | Coventry C | W | 2-1 | 2-0 | 4 | Roberts J 2 [16, 22] | 8784 |
| 38 | 27 | A | Watford | D | 1-1 | 1-1 | 7 | Roberts J [13] | 13,382 |
| 39 | Apr 3 | H | Wimbledon | L | 0-1 | 0-1 | 8 | | 7622 |
| 40 | 6 | A | Gillingham | W | 3-0 | 2-0 | — | Ellington [33], Roberts J [42], Mahon [67] | 7410 |
| 41 | 9 | A | Norwich C | L | 0-2 | 0-0 | — | | 23,446 |
| 42 | 13 | H | Cardiff C | W | 3-0 | 1-0 | — | Roberts J 2 [36, 58], Ellington [54] | 8052 |
| 43 | 17 | A | Crystal Palace | D | 1-1 | 1-0 | 5 | Ellington [45] | 18,799 |
| 44 | 24 | H | Sunderland | D | 0-0 | 0-0 | 6 | | 11,380 |
| 45 | May 1 | A | Nottingham F | L | 0-1 | 0-0 | 7 | | 29,172 |
| 46 | 9 | H | West Ham U | D | 1-1 | 1-0 | 7 | Roberts N [34] | 20,069 |

**Final League Position: 7**

### GOALSCORERS

*League (60):* Ellington 18, Liddell 9 (3 pens), Roberts J 8, Horsfield 7, McCulloch 6, Bullard 2, De Vos 2, Roberts N 2, Teale 2, Jackson 1, Jarrett 1, Kennedy 1, Mahon 1.
*Carling Cup (4):* Bullard 1, Ellington 1, Jarrett 1, McCulloch 1.
*FA Cup (1):* own goal 1.

| Filan J 45 | Eaden N 46 | McMillan S 13 + 2 | Dinning T 11 + 2 | De Vos J 25 + 2 | Jackson M 23 + 1 | Teale G 15 + 13 | Bullard J 46 | Roberts N 9 + 19 | Liddell A 35 + 5 | McCulloch L 31 + 10 | Mitchell P 1 + 11 | Breckin I 43 + 2 | Jarrett J 33 + 8 | Kennedy P 10 + 2 | Burchill M 1 + 3 | Ellington N 43 + 1 | Horsfield G 16 | Baines L 23 + 3 | Walsh G 1 + 2 | Lawrence J — + 4 | Rogers A 5 | Flynn M 1 + 7 | Roberts J 14 | Mahon A 13 + 1 | Farrelly G 3 + 4 | *Match No.* |
|---|---|---|---|---|---|---|---|---|---|---|---|---|---|---|---|---|---|---|---|---|---|---|---|---|---|---|
| 1 | 2 | 3 | $4^1$ | $5^2$ | 6 | $7^3$ | 8 | 9 | 10 | 11 | 12 | 13 | 14 | | | | | | | | | | | | | 1 |
| 1 | 2 | 3 | | | 6 | 12 | 8 | $9^1$ | 7 | 10 | 13 | 5 | 4 | $11^2$ | | | | | | | | | | | | 2 |
| 1 | 2 | $3^2$ | | | 6 | | 8 | 12 | 7 | $10^1$ | 13 | 5 | 4 | 11 | $9^3$ | 14 | | | | | | | | | | 3 |
| 1 | 2 | $3^1$ | 12 | | 6 | | 8 | 9 | 7 | | 13 | 5 | 4 | $11^2$ | 14 | $10^3$ | | | | | | | | | | 4 |
| 1 | 2 | | 12 | | 6 | | $8^1$ | 10 | 7 | 11 | | 5 | 4 | 3 | 13 | $9^2$ | | | | | | | | | | 5 |
| 1 | 2 | | | | 6 | | 8 | | 7 | 11 | 12 | 5 | $4^1$ | 3 | 13 | $9^2$ | 10 | | | | | | | | | 6 |
| 1 | 2 | | 4 | | 6 | 12 | 8 | 13 | 7 | 11 | | 5 | | 3 | | $9^1$ | $10^2$ | | | | | | | | | 7 |
| 1 | 2 | | 4 | | 6 | 12 | 8 | 13 | $7^1$ | 11 | | 5 | | 3 | | 9 | $10^2$ | | | | | | | | | 8 |
| 1 | 2 | | 4 | | 6 | | 8 | 12 | $7^3$ | $11^2$ | 14 | 5 | 13 | 3■ | | 9 | $10^1$ | | | | | | | | | 9 |
| 1 | 2 | 3 | 4 | | 6 | 12 | 8 | 13 | $7^1$ | | | 5 | | 11 | | $9^2$ | 10 | | | | | | | | | 10 |
| 1 | 2 | 3 | $4^2$ | | 6 | 12 | 8 | | 7 | | | 5 | 13 | $11^1$ | | 9 | 10 | | | | | | | | | 11 |
| 1 | 2 | 3 | $4^2$ | | 6 | 12 | 8 | | 7 | $11^1$ | | 5 | 13 | | | 9 | 10 | | | | | | | | | 12 |
| 1 | 2 | 3 | 4 | | 6 | | 8 | 12 | 7 | 11 | | 5 | | | | $9^1$ | 10 | | | | | | | | | 13 |
| 1 | 2 | 3 | $4^1$ | | 6 | | 8 | 13 | 7 | $11^3$ | | 5 | 12 | 14 | | $9^2$ | 10 | | | | | | | | | 14 |
| 1 | 2 | 3 | $4^1$ | | 6 | | $8^3$ | 13 | 7 | 11 | 14 | 5 | 12 | | | $9^2$ | 10 | | | | | | | | | 15 |
| 1 | 2 | 3 | $4^3$ | | 6 | 12 | 8 | 13 | 7 | 11 | | 5 | 14 | | | $9^1$ | $10^2$ | | | | | | | | | 16 |
| 1 | 2 | $3^3$ | | | 6 | 12 | 8 | 13 | 7 | $11^1$ | | 5 | 4 | | | 9 | $10^2$ | 14 | | | | | | | | 17 |
| 1■ | 2 | | | | 6 | 13 | 8 | 12 | 7 | $11^2$ | | 5 | 4 | | | $9^6$ | 10 | $3^1$ | 15 | | | | | | | 18 |
| 1 | 2 | | | | 6 | | 8 | | 7 | 11 | | 5 | 4 | | | 9 | 10 | 3 | | | | | | | | 19 |
| 1 | 2 | | | 12 | 6■ | | 8 | 13 | $7^3$ | 11■ | | 5 | 4 | | | 9 | $10^2$ | $3^1$ | | 14 | | | | | | 20 |
| 1 | 2 | | | 12■ | $6^1$ | 13 | 8 | $10^2$ | 7 | 11 | | 5 | $4^3$ | | | 9 | | | | 14 | 3 | | | | | 21 |
| 1 | 2 | | | 6 | | 7 | 8 | 12 | 10 | 11 | | 5 | $4^1$ | | | 9 | | | | | 3 | | | | | 22 |
| 1 | $2^2$ | | | 6 | | 11 | $8^1$ | | 7 | | | 5 | 4 | | | 9 | 10 | | | 13 | 3 | 12 | | | | 23 |
| 1 | 2 | | | 6 | | 7 | 8 | | $10^2$ | 11 | 5 | | 4 | | | 9 | | 12 | | 13 | $3^1$ | | | | | 24 |
| 1 | 2 | | | 6 | | 7 | 8 | 12 | | 10 | | 5 | 4 | 13 | | 9 | | $3^1$ | | | | $11^2$ | | | | 25 |
| 1 | 2 | | | 6 | | 7 | 8 | 10 | | 11 | | 5 | 4 | | | 9 | | 3 | | | | | | | | 26 |
| 1 | $2^3$ | | | 6 | | 7 | 8 | 10 | | $11^1$ | 14 | 5 | 4 | | | 9 | | 13 | | | $3^2$ | 12 | | | | 27 |
| 1 | 2 | | | 6 | | 7 | 8 | 12 | | $11^2$ | | 5 | 4 | | | $9^1$ | | 3 | | | | 13 | 10 | | | 28 |
| 1 | 2 | | | 6 | | 7 | 8 | | 12 | $11^1$ | | 5 | 4 | | | 9 | | 3 | | | | | 10 | | | 29 |
| 1 | 2 | 13 | | 6 | | 7 | 8 | | | 12 | | 5 | $4^1$ | | | $9^2$ | | 3■ | | | | | 10 | 11 | | 30 |
| 1 | 2 | | | 6 | | 7 | 8 | | 12 | 13 | | 5 | $4^3$ | | | $9^1$ | | 3 | | | | 14 | $10^2$ | 11 | | 31 |
| 1 | 2 | 3 | | 6 | | $7^1$ | 8 | | 12 | 13 | | 5 | $4^2$ | | | 9 | | | | | | | 10■ | 11 | | 32 |
| 1 | 2 | | | 6 | | | $8^1$ | | 7 | 12 | 13 | 5 | 4 | | | $9^2$ | | 3 | | | | | 10 | 11 | | 33 |
| 1 | 2 | | | 6■ | 12 | | 8 | 13 | 7 | 10 | 14 | 5 | $4^3$ | | | $9^2$ | | $3^1$ | | | | | | 11 | | 34 |
| 1 | 2 | | | 6 | | | 8 | 13 | $7^1$ | 10 | | 5 | 4 | | | 9 | | 3 | | | | 12 | | | $11^2$ | 35 |
| 1■ | 2 | | | 6 | | | 8 | $10^6$ | $7^1$ | 11 | | 5 | 4 | | | 9 | | 3 | 15 | | | 12 | | | | 36 |
| 1 | 2 | | | | 6 | | 8 | | $7^1$ | 11 | | 5 | 4 | | | 9 | | 3 | | | | 12 | 10 | | | 37 |
| 1 | 2 | | | 6 | $5^1$ | | 8 | | 7 | 11 | | 12 | 4 | | | $9^2$ | | 3 | | | | | 10 | 13 | | 38 |
| | 2 | | | 6 | | | $8^2$ | | 7 | 12 | | 5 | 4 | | | 9 | | 3 | 1 | | | | $10^1$ | 11 | 13 | 39 |
| 1 | 2 | | | 6 | | | $8^3$ | 13 | 7 | 12 | | 5 | 4 | | | $9^2$ | | 3 | | | | | $10^1$ | 11 | 14 | 40 |
| 1 | 2 | | | 6 | | 13 | 8 | | $7^1$ | 12 | | 5 | $4^3$ | | | 9 | | 3 | | | | | 10 | $11^2$ | 14 | 41 |
| 1 | 2 | | | 6 | | 12 | $8^3$ | | $7^1$ | 13 | | 5 | 4 | | | $9^2$ | | 3 | | | | | 10 | 11 | 14 | 42 |
| 1 | 2 | | | 6 | | 12 | 8 | | $7^1$ | 13 | 14 | 5 | 4■ | | | 9 | | $3^3$ | | | | | 10■ | $11^2$ | | 43 |
| 1 | 2 | | | 6 | | 7 | 8 | | | 12 | | 5 | 4 | | | 9 | | 3 | | | | | 10 | $11^1$ | | 44 |
| 1 | 2 | | | 6 | | 7 | 4 | 13 | 12 | $10^2$ | | 5 | | | | 9 | | 3 | | | | | | $11^1$ | 8 | 45 |
| 1 | 2 | 14 | | 6 | | 7 | 4 | $10^2$ | 13 | | | 5 | 12 | | | 9 | | 3 | | | | | | $11^3$ | $8^1$ | 46 |

**Carling Cup**

| | | | |
|---|---|---|---|
| First Round | Hull C | (h) | 2-0 |
| Second Round | Fulham | (h) | 1-0 |
| Third Round | Middlesbrough | (h) | 1-2 |

**FA Cup**

| | | | |
|---|---|---|---|
| Third Round | West Ham U | (h) | 1-2 |

# WIMBLEDON (Now Milton Keynes Dons FC)

## FL Championship 1

### FOUNDATION

Old boys from Central School formed this club as Wimbledon Old Centrals in 1889. Their earliest successes were in the Clapham League before switching to the Southern Suburban League in 1902.

***The National Hockey Stadium, Silbury Boulevard, Central Milton Keynes, Buckinghamshire MK9 1FA.***

***Telephone:*** (01908) 607 090.

***Fax:*** (01908) 209 449.

***Ticket Office:*** (01908) 609 000.

***Website:*** www.mkdons.com

***Email:*** info@mkdons.com

***Ground Capacity:*** 8,630.

***Record Attendance:*** 30,115 v Manchester U, FA Premier League, 9 May 1993.

***Pitch Measurements:*** 110yd × 74yd.

***Chairman:*** Pete Winkelman.

***Deputy Chairman:*** Peter Lloyd-Cooper.

***Secretary:*** Steve Rooke.

***Manager:*** Stuart Murdoch.

***Assistant Manager:*** Jimmy Gilligan.

***Physio:*** Tony Flynn.

***Colours:*** All white with gold trim.

***Change Colours:*** All red with gold and black trim.

***Year Formed:*** 1889.

***Turned Professional:*** 1964.

***Ltd Co.:*** 1964.

***Previous Names:*** Wimbledon Old Centrals, 1899–1905; Wimbledon 1905–2004.

***Previous Grounds:*** 1899, Plough Lane; 1991, Selhurst Park.

***Club Nicknames:*** 'The Dons', 'The Crazy Gang'.

***First Football League Game:*** 20 August 1977, Division 4, v Halifax T (h) D 3–3 – Guy; Bryant (1), Galvin, Donaldson, Aitken, Davies, Galliers, Smith, Connell (1), Holmes, Leslie (1).

### HONOURS

*FA Premier League*: best season: 6th, 1993–94.

*Football League:* Division 3 – Runners-up 1983–84; Division 4 – Champions 1982–83.

*FA Cup:* Winners 1988.

*Football League Cup:* Semi-final 1996–97, 1998–99.

*League Group Cup:* Runners-up 1982.

*Amateur Cup:* Winners 1963; Runners-up 1935, 1947.

***European Competitions:*** *Intertoto Cup:* 1995.

### SKY SPORTS FACT FILE

Centre-forward William 'Doc' Dowden scored for Wimbledon against Fulham in an FA Cup tie in December 1930. Shortly afterwards he was invited to play for Fulham and scored in his only outing for them at Watford, then returned to the Dons.

***Record League Victory:*** 6–0 v Newport Co, Division 3, 3 September 1983 – Beasant; Peters, Winterburn, Galliers, Morris, Hatter, Evans (2), Ketteridge (1), Cork (3 incl. 1p), Downes, Hodges (Driver).

***Record Cup Victory:*** 7–2 v Windsor & Eton, FA Cup 1st rd, 22 November 1980 – Beasant; Jones, Armstrong, Galliers, Mick Smith (2), Cunningham (1), Ketteridge, Hodges, Leslie, Cork (1), Hubbick (3).

***Record Defeat:*** 0–8 v Everton, League Cup 2nd rd, 29 August 1978.

***Most League Points (2 for a win):*** 61, Division 4, 1978–79.

***Most League Points (3 for a win):*** 98, Division 4, 1982–83.

***Most League Goals:*** 97, Division 3, 1983–84.

***Highest League Scorer in Season:*** Alan Cork, 29, 1983–84.

***Most League Goals in Total Aggregate:*** Alan Cork, 145, 1977–92.

***Most League Goals in One Match:*** 4, Alan Cork v Torquay U, Division 4, 28 February 1979.

***Most Capped Player:*** Kenny Cunningham, 40 (57), Republic of Ireland.

***Most League Appearances:*** Alan Cork, 430, 1977–92.

***Youngest League Player:*** Kevin Gage, 17 years 15 days v Bury, 2 May 1981.

***Record Transfer Fee Received:*** £7,000,000 from Newcastle U for Carl Cort, July 2000.

***Record Transfer Fee Paid:*** £7,500,000 to West Ham U for John Hartson, January 1999.

***Football League Record:*** 1977 Elected to Division 4; 1979–80 Division 3; 1980–81 Division 4; 1981–82 Division 3; 1982–83 Division 4; 1983–84 Division 3; 1984–86 Division 2; 1986–92 Division 1; 1992–2000 FA Premier League; 2000–04 Division 1; 2004– FL1.

## MANAGERS

Les Henley 1955–71
Mike Everitt 1971–73
Dick Graham 1973–74
Allen Batsford 1974–78
Dario Gradi 1978–81
Dave Bassett 1981–87
Bobby Gould 1987–90
Ray Harford 1990–91
Peter Withe 1991
Joe Kinnear 1992–99
Egil Olsen 1999–2000
Terry Burton 2000–02
Stuart Murdoch June 2002–

## LATEST SEQUENCES

***Longest Sequence of League Wins:*** 7, 4.9.1996 – 19.10.1996.

***Longest Sequence of League Defeats:*** 14, 19.3.2000 – 28.8.2000.

***Longest Sequence of League Draws:*** 4, 24.4.2001 – 6.5.2001.

***Longest Sequence of Unbeaten League Matches:*** 22, 15.1.1983 – 14.5.1983.

***Longest Sequence Without a League Win:*** 14, 19.3.2000 – 28.8.2000.

***Successive Scoring Runs:*** 23 from 18.2.1984.

***Successive Non-scoring Runs:*** 5 from 13.4.1995.

## TEN YEAR LEAGUE RECORD

| | | *P* | *W* | *D* | *L* | *F* | *A* | *Pts* | *Pos* |
|---|---|---|---|---|---|---|---|---|---|
| 1994-95 | PR Lge | 42 | 15 | 11 | 16 | 48 | 65 | 56 | 9 |
| 1995-96 | PR Lge | 38 | 10 | 11 | 17 | 55 | 70 | 41 | 14 |
| 1996-97 | PR Lge | 38 | 15 | 11 | 12 | 49 | 46 | 56 | 8 |
| 1997-98 | PR Lge | 38 | 10 | 14 | 14 | 34 | 46 | 44 | 15 |
| 1998-99 | PR Lge | 38 | 10 | 12 | 16 | 40 | 63 | 42 | 16 |
| 1999-2000 | PR Lge | 38 | 7 | 12 | 19 | 46 | 74 | 33 | 18 |
| 2000-01 | Div 1 | 46 | 17 | 18 | 11 | 71 | 50 | 69 | 8 |
| 2001-02 | Div 1 | 46 | 18 | 13 | 15 | 63 | 57 | 67 | 9 |
| 2002-03 | Div 1 | 46 | 18 | 11 | 17 | 76 | 73 | 65 | 10 |
| 2003-04 | Div 1 | 46 | 8 | 5 | 33 | 41 | 89 | 29 | 24 |

## DID YOU KNOW ?

Despite disappointment at the events of 2003–04 for Wimbledon, they did succeed in recording three outstanding away wins against promotion hopefuls, 1-0 at West Bromwich Albion, 3-0 at Reading and 1-0 at Wigan Athletic.

## WIMBLEDON 2003–04 LEAGUE RECORD

| Match No. | Date | Venue | Opponents | Result | | H/T Score | Lg. Pos. | Goalscorers | Attendance |
|---|---|---|---|---|---|---|---|---|---|
| 1 | Aug 9 | H | Crewe Alex | W | 3-1 | 1-1 | — | Agyemang [15], Tapp [54], Reo-Coker [62] | 1145 |
| 2 | 16 | A | Stoke C | L | 1-2 | 0-1 | 9 | Agyemang [55] | 12,550 |
| 3 | 23 | H | Crystal Palace | L | 1-3 | 1-0 | 16 | Reo-Coker [34] | 6113 |
| 4 | 26 | A | Norwich C | L | 2-3 | 0-2 | — | Holdsworth [84], Leigertwood [90] | 16,082 |
| 5 | 30 | H | Reading | L | 0-3 | 0-1 | 20 | | 2066 |
| 6 | Sept 13 | H | Wigan Ath | L | 2-4 | 1-3 | 23 | Agyemang [34], McAnuff [48] | 1054 |
| 7 | 16 | A | Millwall | L | 0-2 | 0-1 | — | | 7855 |
| 8 | 20 | A | Ipswich T | L | 1-4 | 1-2 | 24 | Agyemang [45] | 23,428 |
| 9 | 27 | H | Burnley | D | 2-2 | 0-2 | 24 | Holdsworth [66], Agyemang [71] | 5639 |
| 10 | 30 | H | Sheffield U | L | 1-2 | 0-0 | — | Nowland [49] | 6016 |
| 11 | Oct 4 | A | Preston NE | L | 0-1 | 0-1 | 24 | | 13,801 |
| 12 | 15 | A | Coventry C | L | 0-1 | 0-0 | — | | 10,872 |
| 13 | 18 | A | Nottingham F | L | 0-6 | 0-3 | 24 | | 23,520 |
| 14 | 21 | A | WBA | W | 1-0 | 0-0 | — | McAnuff [79] | 22,048 |
| 15 | 25 | H | Watford | L | 1-3 | 0-2 | 24 | Leigertwood [49] | 6115 |
| 16 | Nov 1 | H | Bradford C | W | 2-1 | 0-1 | 24 | Agyemang [62], Reo-Coker [66] | 3334 |
| 17 | 8 | A | Rotherham U | L | 1-3 | 0-2 | 24 | Nowland [68] | 5777 |
| 18 | 15 | A | Gillingham | W | 2-1 | 1-1 | 24 | Nowland [22], Agyemang [66] | 9041 |
| 19 | 22 | H | Cardiff C | L | 0-1 | 0-1 | 24 | | 5056 |
| 20 | 25 | H | West Ham U | D | 1-1 | 0-0 | — | McAnuff [63] | 8118 |
| 21 | 29 | A | Derby Co | L | 1-3 | 1-1 | 24 | Reo-Coker [20] | 22,025 |
| 22 | Dec 6 | H | Rotherham U | L | 1-2 | 0-1 | 24 | Holdsworth (pen) [78] | 3061 |
| 23 | 13 | H | Walsall | L | 0-1 | 0-0 | 24 | | 3315 |
| 24 | 20 | A | Sunderland | L | 1-2 | 1-1 | 24 | Thirlwell (og) [45] | 22,334 |
| 25 | 26 | A | Reading | W | 3-0 | 2-0 | 24 | Small [9], Lewington [23], McAnuff [81] | 14,486 |
| 26 | 30 | H | WBA | D | 0-0 | 0-0 | — | | 6376 |
| 27 | Jan 10 | A | Crewe Alex | L | 0-1 | 0-0 | 24 | | 6234 |
| 28 | 17 | H | Stoke C | L | 0-1 | 0-0 | 24 | | 3623 |
| 29 | 31 | A | Crystal Palace | L | 1-3 | 0-1 | 24 | McAnuff [50] | 20,552 |
| 30 | Feb 7 | H | Norwich C | L | 0-1 | 0-1 | 24 | | 7368 |
| 31 | 21 | H | Coventry C | L | 0-3 | 0-2 | 24 | | 5905 |
| 32 | 28 | A | Watford | L | 0-4 | 0-2 | 24 | | 15,323 |
| 33 | Mar 2 | H | Nottingham F | L | 0-1 | 0-1 | — | | 6317 |
| 34 | 9 | A | West Ham U | L | 0-5 | 0-2 | — | | 29,818 |
| 35 | 13 | A | Walsall | L | 0-1 | 0-1 | 24 | | 6889 |
| 36 | 24 | H | Millwall | L | 0-1 | 0-1 | — | | 3037 |
| 37 | 27 | H | Ipswich T | L | 1-2 | 0-0 | 24 | Smith [77] | 6389 |
| 38 | Apr 3 | A | Wigan Ath | W | 1-0 | 1-0 | 24 | Chorley [5] | 7622 |
| 39 | 6 | H | Sunderland | L | 1-2 | 0-1 | — | Kamara [67] | 4800 |
| 40 | 10 | H | Preston NE | D | 3-3 | 1-2 | 24 | Gray 2 [6, 90], Chorley [65] | 2866 |
| 41 | 12 | A | Sheffield U | L | 1-2 | 1-0 | 24 | Gray (pen) [44] | 19,391 |
| 42 | 17 | A | Bradford C | W | 3-2 | 2-0 | 24 | Kamara [5], Smith [32], Gray [50] | 9011 |
| 43 | 20 | A | Burnley | L | 0-2 | 0-2 | — | | 13,555 |
| 44 | 24 | H | Gillingham | L | 1-2 | 0-0 | 24 | Smith [52] | 5049 |
| 45 | May 1 | A | Cardiff C | D | 1-1 | 0-0 | 24 | Williams [83] | 15,337 |
| 46 | 9 | H | Derby Co | W | 1-0 | 1-0 | 24 | Darlington [25] | 6509 |

**Final League Position: 24**

**GOALSCORERS**

*League (41):* Agyemang 7, McAnuff 5, Gray 4 (1 pen), Reo-Coker 4, Holdsworth 3 (1 pen), Nowland 3, Smith 3, Chorley 2, Kamara 2, Leigertwood 2, Darlington 1, Lewington 1, Small 1, Tapp 1, Williams 1, own goal 1.
*Carling Cup (0).*
*FA Cup (2):* Nowland 2.

| Banks S 24 | Darlington J 40+1 | Hawkins P 16+2 | Holloway D 8+5 | Chorley B 33+2 | Leigertwood M 27 | Gordon M 8+10 | Tapp A 12+2 | Agyemang P 23+3 | Nowland A 24+1 | Reo-Coker N 25 | Kamara M 15+12 | Holdsworth D 14+14 | Gier R 24+1 | McAnuff J 25+2 | Heald P 10 | McDonald S —+2 | Morgan L 2+1 | Jarrett A 3+6 | Gray W 20+13 | Small W 23+4 | Herzig N 18+1 | Lewington D 28 | Worgan L —+3 | Harding B 10+5 | McKoy N 1+2 | Mackie J 8+5 | Williams M 11 | Campbell-Ryce J 3+1 | Barton W 5 | Bevan S 10 | Oyedele S 9 | Puncheon J 6+2 | Ntimban-Zeh H 9+1 | Smith G 10+1 | Martin D 2 | Match No. |
|---|---|---|---|---|---|---|---|---|---|---|---|---|---|---|---|---|---|---|---|---|---|---|---|---|---|---|---|---|---|---|---|---|---|---|---|---|
| 1 | 2 | 3 | 4 | 5 | 6 | $7^{1}$ | 8 | $9^{2}$ | 10 | 11 | 12 | 13 | | | | | | | | | | | | | | | | | | | | | | | | 1 |
| 1 | 2 | | 12 | 5 | 6 | $7^{2}$ | 8 | 9 | $4^{1}$ | 11 | | 10 | 3 | 13 | | | | | | | | | | | | | | | | | | | | | | 2 |
| | $2^{2}$ | | | 5 | 6 | $11^{1}$ | 4 | 9 | 7 | 8 | | 10 | 3 | 12 | 1 | 13 | | | | | | | | | | | | | | | | | | | | 3 |
| 1 | 2 | 3■ | | 5 | 6 | 12 | 7 | $9^{3}$ | $10^{2}$ | 11 | | 13 | 4 | $8^{1}$ | | 14 | | | | | | | | | | | | | | | | | | | | 4 |
| 1 | 2 | 3 | 12 | 5 | 6 | 13 | 7 | $9^{2}$ | $10^{3}$ | 11 | | 14 | $4^{1}$ | 8 | | | | | | | | | | | | | | | | | | | | | | 5 |
| 1 | | | 2 | $5^{2}$ | 6 | | $3^{3}$ | $9^{1}$ | 10 | 11 | 13 | 12 | 4 | 7 | | | 8 | 14 | | | | | | | | | | | | | | | | | | 6 |
| 1 | 2 | | | 12 | $6^{1}$ | | $4^{3}$ | 9 | 10 | 11 | 3 | 13 | 5 | 8 | | | $7^{2}$ | 14 | | | | | | | | | | | | | | | | | | 7 |
| 1 | 2 | | 12 | | 6 | 13 | $4^{2}$ | 9 | 7 | 11 | $3^{1}$ | 14 | 5 | 8 | | | | $10^{3}$ | | | | | | | | | | | | | | | | | | 8 |
| | 2 | | 3 | 12 | 6 | 13 | | 9 | 7 | 11 | | $10^{3}$ | $5^{1}$ | 4 | 1 | | | $8^{2}$ | 14 | | | | | | | | | | | | | | | | | 9 |
| | 2 | | 3 | | 6 | $7^{2}$ | | 9 | 8 | 11 | 12 | $10^{1}$ | 5 | 4 | 1 | | | | 13 | | | | | | | | | | | | | | | | | 10 |
| | 2 | | 3■ | | 6 | $7^{1}$ | | $9^{3}$ | 8 | 11 | 12 | $10^{2}$ | 5 | 4 | 1 | | 13 | | 14 | | | | | | | | | | | | | | | | | 11 |
| | 2 | | 3■ | | 6 | $7^{2}$ | | 9 | 8 | 11 | | $10^{1}$ | 5 | 4 | 1 | | | | 12 | 13 | | | | | | | | | | | | | | | | 12 |
| | 2 | 12 | | 4 | 6 | | | $9^{2}$ | $8^{1}$ | 11 | 3 | | 5 | 7 | 1 | | | | 10 | 13 | | | | | | | | | | | | | | | | 13 |
| | | 3 | | 4 | 6 | | 9 | 12 | | 11 | $2^{2}$ | $10^{1}$ | 13 | 7 | 1 | | | | | 8 | 5 | | | | | | | | | | | | | | | 14 |
| | 12 | $3^{1}$ | | $4^{2}$ | 6 | | | $9^{3}$ | 13 | 11 | 2 | 10 | | 7 | 1 | | | | 14 | 8 | 5 | | | | | | | | | | | | | | | 15 |
| | 2 | | | 4 | 6 | | 9 | 12 | | 11 | | $10^{1}$ | | 7 | $1^{G}$ | | | | | 8 | 5 | 3 | 15 | | | | | | | | | | | | | 16 |
| | 2 | | | | 6 | $11^{1}$ | | 9 | 10 | | | | | 7 | $1^{G}$ | | | | 12 | 8 | 5 | 3 | 15■ | 4 | | | | | | | | | | | | 17 |
| 1 | 2 | | | 4 | 6 | | | 9 | 10 | 11 | | 12 | | | | | | | | 8 | 5 | 3 | | $7^{1}$ | | | | | | | | | | | | 18 |
| 1 | 2 | | | $4^{1}$ | 6 | | | 9 | 10 | 11 | | 12 | | 7 | | | | | 13 | $8^{2}$ | 5 | 3 | | | | | | | | | | | | | | 19 |
| 1 | 2 | | 12 | 4 | 6 | | | $9^{2}$ | 10 | $11^{1}$ | | 13 | | 7 | | | | | 14 | $8^{3}$ | 5 | 3 | | | | | | | | | | | | | | 20 |
| 1 | 2 | | 14 | 4 | 6 | | | $9^{1}$ | 10 | 11 | | 12 | | 7 | | | | | 13 | $8^{3}$ | $5^{2}$ | 3 | | | | | | | | | | | | | | 21 |
| 1 | 2 | | | $4^{1}$ | 6 | | | 12 | 8 | 11 | | 9 | | 7 | | | | | 10 | | 5 | 3 | | | | | | | | | | | | | | 22 |
| 1 | 11 | | 2 | | 5 | 12 | $4^{2}$ | 9 | 8 | | | | 6 | 7 | | | | | $10^{1}$ | | | 3 | | | 13 | | | | | | | | | | | 23 |
| 1 | 2 | | $5^{2}$ | 4 | | | 12 | 9 | 8 | 11 | | $10^{1}$ | 6 | 7 | | | | | | 13 | | 3 | | | | | | | | | | | | | | 24 |
| 1 | 2 | | | | 6 | | | 9 | 8 | 11 | | | 5 | 7 | | | | | 12 | 4 | | 3 | | | | $10^{1}$ | | | | | | | | | | 25 |
| 1 | 2 | | | | 6 | | | 9 | 10 | 11 | | | 5 | 4 | | | | | 12 | 8 | | 3 | | | | $7^{1}$ | | | | | | | | | | 26 |
| 1 | 2 | | | | 6 | 13 | 14 | | 7 | $11^{3}$ | | 12 | 5 | 4 | | | | | $9^{1}$ | 8 | | 3 | | | | $10^{2}$ | | | | | | | | | | 27 |
| 1 | 2 | | | 4 | 6 | | $8^{1}$ | | | | 14 | $9^{3}$ | 5 | 7 | | | | | $10^{2}$ | 11 | | 3 | | 12 | | 13 | | | | | | | | | | 28 |
| 1 | $2^{1}$ | $11^{3}$ | | 4 | | | | | | | 12 | $9^{2}$ | 6 | 7 | | | | | 13 | 8 | 5 | 3 | | | 14 | 10 | | | | | | | | | | 29 |
| 1■ | | | | 4 | | 12 | | | | | 2 | $9^{1}$ | 6 | | | | | | $10^{2}$ | 11 | | 3 | 15 | 8 | | 13 | 5■ | $7^{G}$ | | | | | | | | 30 |
| 1 | 2 | 8 | | 4 | | 14 | | | | | | 12 | 6 | | | | | | 13 | $11^{3}$ | 5 | 3■ | | | $10^{2}$ | $9^{1}$ | | 7 | | | | | | | | 31 |
| 1 | 2 | 3 | | 4 | | $11^{2}$ | | | | | 13 | | 6 | | | | | 12 | 10 | | | 9 | | $8^{1}$ | | 14 | | $7^{3}$ | 5 | | | | | | | 32 |
| 1 | 2 | 6 | | 8 | | | | | | | 11 | | | | | | | 13 | 9 | $10^{3}$ | 12 | $3^{1}$ | | $7^{2}$ | | | 5 | 14 | 4 | | | | | | | 33 |
| 1 | 2 | 3 | | 11 | | 12 | | | | | 10 | | 6 | | | | | 13 | $9^{1}$ | | 5 | | | 7 | | | 4 | | $8^{2}$ | | | | | | | 34 |
| | 2 | 3 | | 11 | | 12 | | | | | $10^{1}$ | | $6^{3}$ | | | | | 13 | | | 5 | | | $7^{2}$ | | | 4 | | 8 | 1 | 9 | 14 | | | | 35 |
| | 7 | 3 | | 6 | | | | | | | 12 | | | | | | | $4^{3}$ | 9 | | $10^{2}$ | | | | | 13 | 5 | | $8^{1}$ | 1 | 2 | 11 | | 14 | | 36 |
| | 7 | $6^{3}$ | | 4 | | | | | | | 13 | | | | | | | | $9^{1}$ | | | 3 | | 12 | | $10^{2}$ | 5 | | | 1 | 2 | 11 | 14 | 8 | | 37 |
| | 7 | | | 4 | | | | | | | 12 | | | | | | | | $9^{1}$ | | | 3 | | | | 10 | 5 | | | 1 | 2 | 11 | 6 | 8 | | 38 |
| | 7 | | | 4 | | | | | | | 13 | | | | | | | | 9 | 12 | | 3 | | | | $10^{2}$ | 5 | | | 1 | $2^{1}$ | 11 | 6 | 8 | | 39 |
| | 7 | 12 | | 4 | | | | | | | 14 | | | | | | | | 9 | $10^{2}$ | | 3 | | 13 | | | 5 | | | 1 | $2^{1}$ | $11^{3}$ | 6 | 8 | | 40 |
| | 7 | 2 | | 4 | | | | | | | 11 | | | | | | | | 9 | 10 | 5 | 3 | | | | | | | | 1 | | | 6 | 8 | | 41 |
| | 7 | 2 | | | | | | | | | $11^{1}$ | 12 | | | | | | | 9 | 10 | 5 | 3 | | 4 | | | | | | 1 | | | 6 | 8 | | 42 |
| | | 2 | | | | | | | | | 7 | | | | | | | | 9 | 10 | 5 | 3 | | 4 | | | | | | | | 11 | 6 | 8 | 1 | 43 |
| | | | | 4 | | | | | | | 11 | | | | | | | | 9 | 10 | 5 | $3^{2}$ | | $7^{1}$ | | 12 | | | | | 2 | 13 | 6 | 8 | 1 | 44 |
| | 7 | | | 4 | | | | | | | $11^{1}$ | | | | | | | | 9 | 10 | | 3 | | 12 | | | 5 | | | 1 | 2 | | 6 | 8 | | 45 |
| | 7 | | | 4 | | | | | | | $11^{1}$ | 12 | | | | | | | 9 | 10 | | 3 | | 13 | | | 5 | | | 1 | 2 | | 6 | $8^{2}$ | | 46 |

**Carling Cup**
First Round — Wycombe W — (a) 0-2

**FA Cup**
Third Round — Stoke C — (h) 1-1
(a) 1-0
Fourth Round — Birmingham C — (a) 0-1

# WOLVERHAMPTON WANDERERS FL Championship

## FOUNDATION

Enthusiasts of the game at St Luke's School, Blakenhall formed a club in 1877. In the same neighbourhood a cricket club called Blakenhall Wanderers had a football section. Several St Luke's footballers played cricket for them and shortly before the start of the 1879–80 season the two amalgamated and Wolverhampton Wanderers FC was brought into being.

***Molineux, Waterloo Road, Wolverhampton WV1 4QR.***

***Telephone:*** 0870 442 0123.

***Fax:*** (01902) 687 006.

***Ticket Office:*** 0870 442 0123.

***Website:*** wolves.co.uk

***Email:*** info@wolves.co.uk

***Ground Capacity:*** 28,666.

***Record Attendance:*** 61,315 v Liverpool, FA Cup 5th rd, 11 February 1939.

***Pitch Measurements:*** 110yd × 75yd.

***Chairman:*** Rick Hayward.

***Vice-chairman:*** Derek Harrington CBE.

***Chief Executive:*** Jez Moxey.

***Secretary:*** Richard Skirrow.

***Manager:*** Dave Jones.

***Coach:*** Stuart Gray.

***Physio:*** Barry Holmes.

***Colours:*** Gold and black.

***Change Colours:*** All blue.

***Year Formed:*** 1877* (*see Foundation*).

***Turned Professional:*** 1888.

***Ltd Co.:*** 1923 (but current club is WWFC (1986) Ltd).

***Previous Names:*** 1879, St Luke's combined with Wanderers Cricket Club to become Wolverhampton Wanderers (1923) Ltd. New limited companies followed in 1982 and 1986 (current).

***Club Nickname:*** 'Wolves'.

***Previous Grounds:*** 1877, Windmill Field; 1879, John Harper's Field; 1881, Dudley Road; 1889, Molineux.

***First Football League Game:*** 8 September 1888, Football League, v Aston Villa (h) D 1–1 – Baynton; Baugh, Mason; Fletcher, Allen, Lowder; Hunter, Cooper, Anderson, White, Cannon, (1 og).

***Record League Victory:*** 10–1 v Leicester C, Division 1, 15 April 1938 – Sidlow; Morris, Dowen; Galley, Cullis, Gardiner; Maguire (1), Horace Wright, Westcott (4), Jones (1), Dorsett (4).

## HONOURS

*Football League:* Division 1 – Champions 1953–54, 1957–58, 1958–59; Runners-up 1937–38, 1938–39, 1949–50, 1954–55, 1959–60; 2002–03 (play-offs). Division 2 – Champions 1931–32, 1976–77; Runners-up 1966–67, 1982–83; Division 3 (N) – Champions 1923–24; Division 3 – Champions 1988–89; Division 4 – Champions 1987–88.

*FA Cup:* Winners 1893, 1908, 1949, 1960; Runners-up 1889, 1896, 1921, 1939.

*Football League Cup:* Winners 1974, 1980.

*Texaco Cup:* Winners 1971.

*Sherpa Van Trophy:* Winners 1988.

***European Competitions:*** *European Cup:* 1958–59, 1959–60. *European Cup-Winners' Cup:* 1960–61. *UEFA Cup:* 1971–72 (runners-up), 1973–74, 1974–75, 1980–81.

## SKY SPORTS FACT FILE

In 1923–24 as Division Three (North) champions, Wolverhampton Wanderers conceded only 27 goals. Goalkeeper Noel George had 23 clean sheets. Oddly enough Wigan Borough managed a 3-3 draw against them, the most let in during one game.

***Record Cup Victory:*** 14–0 v Crosswell's Brewery, FA Cup 2nd rd, 13 November 1886 – I. Griffiths; Baugh, Mason; Pearson, Allen (1), Lowder; Hunter (4), Knight (2), Brodie (4), B. Griffiths (2), Wood. Plus one goal 'scrambled through'.

***Record Defeat:*** 1–10 v Newton Heath, Division 1, 15 October 1892.

***Most League Points (2 for a win):*** 64, Division 1, 1957–58.

***Most League Points (3 for a win):*** 92, Division 3, 1988–89.

***Most League Goals:*** 115, Division 2, 1931–32.

***Highest League Scorer in Season:*** Dennis Westcott, 38, Division 1, 1946–47.

***Most League Goals in Total Aggregate:*** Steve Bull, 250, 1986–99.

***Most League Goals in One Match:*** 5, Joe Butcher v Accrington, Division 1, 19 November 1892; 5, Tom Phillipson v Barnsley, Division 2, 26 April 1926; 5, Tom Phillipson v Bradford C, Division 2, 25 December 1926; 5, Billy Hartill v Notts Co, Division 2, 12 October 1929; 5, Billy Hartill v Aston Villa, Division 1, 3 September 1934.

***Most Capped Player:*** Billy Wright, 105, England (70 consecutive).

***Most League Appearances:*** Derek Parkin, 501, 1967–82.

***Youngest League Player:*** Jimmy Mullen, 16 years 43 days v Leeds U, 18 February 1939.

***Record Transfer Fee Received:*** £6,000,000 from Coventry C for Robbie Keane, August 1999.

***Record Transfer Fee Paid:*** £3,500,000 to Bristol C for Ade Akinbiyi, September 1999.

## MANAGERS

George Worrall 1877–85
*(Secretary-Manager)*
John Addenbrooke 1885–1922
George Jobey 1922–24
Albert Hoskins 1924–26
*(had been Secretary since 1922)*
Fred Scotchbrook 1926–27
Major Frank Buckley 1927–44
Ted Vizard 1944–48
Stan Cullis 1948–64
Andy Beattie 1964–65
Ronnie Allen 1966–68
Bill McGarry 1968–76
Sammy Chung 1976–78
John Barnwell 1978–81
Ian Greaves 1982
Graham Hawkins 1982–84
Tommy Docherty 1984–85
Bill McGarry 1985
Sammy Chapman 1985–86
Brian Little 1986
Graham Turner 1986–94
Graham Taylor 1994–95
Mark McGhee 1995–98
Colin Lee 1998–2000
Dave Jones January 2001–

***Football League Record:*** 1888 Founder Member of Football League: 1906–23 Division 2; 1923–24 Division 3 (N); 1924–32 Division 2; 1932–65 Division 1; 1965–67 Division 2; 1967–76 Division 1; 1976–77 Division 2; 1977–82 Division 1; 1982–83 Division 2; 1983–84 Division 1; 1984–85 Division 2; 1985–86 Division 3; 1986–88 Division 4; 1988–89 Division 3; 1989–92 Division 2; 1992–2003 Division 1; 2003–04 FA Premier League; 2004– FLC.

## LATEST SEQUENCES

***Longest Sequence of League Wins:*** 8, 15.10.1988 – 26.11.1988.

***Longest Sequence of League Defeats:*** 8, 5.12.1981 – 13.2.1982.

***Longest Sequence of League Draws:*** 6, 22.4.1995 – 20.8.1995.

***Longest Sequence of Unbeaten League Matches:*** 20, 24.11.1923 – 5.4.1924.

***Longest Sequence Without a League Win:*** 19, 1.12.1984 – 6.4.1985.

***Successive Scoring Runs:*** 41 from 20.12.1958.

***Successive Non-scoring Runs:*** 7 from 2.2.1985.

## TEN YEAR LEAGUE RECORD

| | | P | W | D | L | F | A | Pts | Pos |
|---|---|---|---|---|---|---|---|---|---|
| 1994-95 | Div 1 | 46 | 21 | 13 | 12 | 77 | 61 | 76 | 4 |
| 1995-96 | Div 1 | 46 | 13 | 16 | 17 | 56 | 62 | 55 | 20 |
| 1996-97 | Div 1 | 46 | 22 | 10 | 14 | 68 | 51 | 76 | 3 |
| 1997-98 | Div 1 | 46 | 18 | 11 | 17 | 57 | 53 | 65 | 9 |
| 1998-99 | Div 1 | 46 | 19 | 16 | 11 | 64 | 43 | 73 | 7 |
| 1999-2000 | Div 1 | 46 | 21 | 11 | 14 | 64 | 48 | 74 | 7 |
| 2000-01 | Div 1 | 46 | 14 | 13 | 19 | 45 | 48 | 55 | 12 |
| 2001-02 | Div 1 | 46 | 25 | 11 | 10 | 76 | 43 | 86 | 3 |
| 2002-03 | Div 1 | 46 | 20 | 16 | 10 | 81 | 44 | 76 | 5 |
| 2003-04 | PR Lge | 38 | 7 | 12 | 19 | 38 | 77 | 33 | 20 |

## DID YOU KNOW?

Wolverhampton Wanderers playing as Los Angeles Wolves won the 14 match International Soccer Tournament in the USA in 1967. In the final they defeated Aberdeen 6-5 with Davy Burnside scoring a hat-trick for the winners.

## WOLVERHAMPTON WANDERERS 2003–04 LEAGUE RECORD

| *Match No.* | *Date* | *Venue* | *Opponents* | *Result* | *H/T Score* | *Lg. Pos.* | *Goalscorers* | *Atten-dance* |
|---|---|---|---|---|---|---|---|---|
| 1 | Aug 16 | A | Blackburn R | L 1-5 | 0-2 | — | Iversen [71] | 26,270 |
| 2 | 23 | H | Charlton Ath | L 0-4 | 0-4 | 20 | | 27,327 |
| 3 | 27 | A | Manchester U | L 0-1 | 0-1 | — | | 67,648 |
| 4 | 30 | H | Portsmouth | D 0-0 | 0-0 | 20 | | 28,680 |
| 5 | Sept 13 | A | Southampton | L 0-2 | 0-1 | 20 | | 31,711 |
| 6 | 20 | H | Chelsea | L 0-5 | 0-2 | 20 | | 29,208 |
| 7 | 27 | A | Bolton W | D 1-1 | 1-0 | 20 | Rae [30] | 27,043 |
| 8 | Oct 4 | H | Manchester C | W 1-0 | 0-0 | 20 | Cameron [75] | 29,386 |
| 9 | 18 | A | Fulham | D 0-0 | 0-0 | 19 | | 17,031 |
| 10 | 25 | H | Leicester C | W 4-3 | 0-3 | 15 | Cameron 2 (1 pen) [52, 60 (p)], Rae [68], Camara [86] | 28,578 |
| 11 | Nov 1 | A | Middlesbrough | L 0-2 | 0-0 | 17 | | 30,303 |
| 12 | 8 | H | Birmingham C | D 1-1 | 0-0 | 18 | Iversen [66] | 28,831 |
| 13 | 22 | A | Everton | L 0-2 | 0-2 | 19 | | 40,190 |
| 14 | 29 | H | Newcastle U | D 1-1 | 1-1 | 19 | Blake [27] | 29,344 |
| 15 | Dec 6 | A | Tottenham H | L 2-5 | 1-1 | 20 | Ince [30], Rae [84] | 34,820 |
| 16 | 14 | A | Aston Villa | L 2-3 | 1-2 | 20 | Rae [36], Kennedy [80] | 36,964 |
| 17 | 26 | A | Arsenal | L 0-3 | 0-2 | 20 | | 38,003 |
| 18 | 28 | H | Leeds U | W 3-1 | 1-1 | 20 | Smith (og) [18], Iversen 2 [48, 90] | 29,139 |
| 19 | Jan 7 | H | Blackburn R | D 2-2 | 0-1 | — | Butler [63], Rae [72] | 27,393 |
| 20 | 10 | A | Charlton Ath | L 0-2 | 0-1 | 20 | | 26,123 |
| 21 | 17 | H | Manchester U | W 1-0 | 0-0 | 19 | Miller [67] | 29,396 |
| 22 | 21 | H | Liverpool | D 1-1 | 0-1 | — | Miller [90] | 29,380 |
| 23 | 31 | A | Portsmouth | D 0-0 | 0-0 | 19 | | 20,116 |
| 24 | Feb 7 | H | Arsenal | L 1-3 | 1-1 | 19 | Ganea [26] | 29,392 |
| 25 | 10 | A | Leeds U | L 1-4 | 1-2 | — | Ganea [21] | 36,867 |
| 26 | 21 | H | Fulham | W 2-1 | 1-0 | 18 | Ince [20], Cort [51] | 28,424 |
| 27 | 28 | A | Leicester C | D 0-0 | 0-0 | 18 | | 31,768 |
| 28 | Mar 14 | H | Aston Villa | L 0-4 | 0-3 | 19 | | 29,386 |
| 29 | 20 | A | Liverpool | L 0-1 | 0-0 | 19 | | 43,795 |
| 30 | 27 | A | Chelsea | L 2-5 | 1-1 | 20 | Camara [23], Craddock [57] | 41,215 |
| 31 | Apr 3 | H | Southampton | L 1-4 | 0-1 | 20 | Camara [72] | 29,106 |
| 32 | 10 | A | Manchester C | D 3-3 | 2-2 | 20 | Kennedy [14], Cort [22], Camara [78] | 47,248 |
| 33 | 12 | H | Bolton W | L 1-2 | 1-1 | 20 | Camara [44] | 28,695 |
| 34 | 17 | H | Middlesbrough | W 2-0 | 1-0 | 20 | Cort [28], Camara [62] | 27,975 |
| 35 | 25 | A | Birmingham C | D 2-2 | 1-2 | 20 | Cameron [6], Cort [75] | 29,494 |
| 36 | May 1 | H | Everton | W 2-1 | 0-1 | 18 | Camara [55], Cort [84] | 29,395 |
| 37 | 9 | A | Newcastle U | D 1-1 | 0-1 | 19 | Ganea [70] | 52,139 |
| 38 | 15 | H | Tottenham H | L 0-2 | 0-1 | 20 | | 29,389 |

**Final League Position: 20**

## GOALSCORERS

*League (38):* Camara 7, Cort 5, Rae 5, Cameron 4 (1 pen), Iversen 4, Ganea 3, Ince 2, Kennedy 2, Miller 2, Blake 1, Butler 1, Craddock 1, own goal 1.
*Carling Cup (5):* Rae 2, Craddock 1, Gudjonsson 1, Miller 1.
*FA Cup (4):* Miller 2, Ganea 1, Rae 1.

| Murray M 1 | Irwin D 30 + 2 | Naylor L 37 + 1 | Ince P 32 | Butler P 37 | Craddock J 31 + 1 | Newton S 20 + 8 | Cameron C 25 + 5 | Sturridge D 2 + 3 | Iversen S 11 + 5 | Silas J 2 + 7 | Camara H 29 + 1 | Luzhny O 4 + 2 | Blake N 10 + 3 | Oakes M 21 | Rae A 27 + 6 | Cooper K — + 1 | Gudjonsson J 5 + 6 | Kennedy M 28 + 3 | Kachloul H — + 4 | Miller K 17 + 8 | Clyde M 6 + 3 | Andrews K 1 | Ganea V 6 + 10 | Jones P 16 | Cort C 13 + 3 | Okoronkwo I 7 | *Match No.* |
|---|---|---|---|---|---|---|---|---|---|---|---|---|---|---|---|---|---|---|---|---|---|---|---|---|---|---|---|
| 1 | 2 | 3 | 4 | 5 | 6 | $7^{1}$ | 8 | $9^{2}$ | 10 | $11^{3}$ | 12 | 13 | 14 | | | | | | | | | | | | | | 1 |
| | 2 | 3 | 4 | 5 | 6 | 7 | $8^{2}$ | 12 | $10^{1}$ | $11^{3}$ | | | 9 | 1 | 13 | 14 | | | | | | | | | | | 2 |
| | 2 | 3 | 4 | 5 | 6 | $7^{1}$ | 8 | | | 12 | 11 | | 9 | 1 | 10 | | | | | | | | | | | | 3 |
| | 2 | 3 | 4 | 5 | 6 | 7 | 11 | | | | 10 | | 9 | 1 | $8^{1}$ | | 12 | | | | | | | | | | 4 |
| | 2 | 3 | 4 | 5 | 6 | $7^{1}$ | $10^{3}$ | | 13 | 12 | | | 9 | 1 | $8^{2}$ | | 14 | 11 | | | | | | | | | 5 |
| | 2 | 3 | 4 | 5 | 6 | $7^{1}$ | 12 | | 9 | 13 | 10 | | | 1 | | | $8^{2}$ | 11 | | | | | | | | | 6 |
| | 2 | 3 | 4 | 5 | 6 | $7^{1}$ | 8 | | $9^{2}$ | | | | | 1 | 10 | | | 11 | 12 | 13 | | | | | | | 7 |
| | 2 | 3 | 4 | 5 | 6 | 12 | 10 | | | | $11^{2}$ | | 9 | 1 | 8 | | | | 13 | $7^{1}$ | | | | | | | 8 |
| | 2 | 3 | | 5 | 6 | | 8 | | | | 11 | | 9 | 1 | 7 | | 4 | 12 | | $10^{1}$ | | | | | | | 9 |
| | 2 | 3 | | 5 | 6 | 12 | 8 | | | | 11 | | 9 | 1 | 7 | | $4^{1}$ | | 13 | $10^{2}$ | | | | | | | 10 |
| | 2 | 3 | 4 | 5 | 6 | | | | 9 | 12 | 11 | | | 1 | 8■ | | $7^{1}$ | 13 | | $10^{2}$ | | | | | | | 11 |
| | $2^{2}$ | 3 | 4 | 5 | 6 | 12 | | | 9 | | 7 | | | 1 | 8 | | | 11 | | $10^{1}$ | 13 | | | | | | 12 |
| | 2 | 3 | 4 | 5 | 6 | $7^{1}$ | | | $9^{2}$ | | 10 | | 13 | 1 | $8^{3}$ | | 14 | 11 | | 12 | | | | | | | 13 |
| | 2 | 3 | | 5 | 6 | | | | | | 10 | | 9 | 1 | 8 | | 7 | $11^{1}$ | | 12 | | 4 | | | | | 14 |
| | 2 | 3 | 4 | 5 | 6 | | 8 | 13 | | | 10 | | $9^{2}$ | 1 | $7^{1}$ | | | 11 | | 12 | | | | | | | 15 |
| | $3^{1}$ | 12 | 4 | 5 | 6 | | $8^{3}$ | $9^{2}$ | | 14 | 10 | 2 | | 1 | 7 | | | 11 | | 13 | | | | | | | 16 |
| | | 3 | 4 | 5 | 6 | 12 | 7 | 13 | | | $10^{2}$ | 2 | | 1 | 8 | | | 11 | | $9^{1}$ | | | | | | | 17 |
| | | 3 | 4 | 5 | 6 | $7^{1}$ | 8 | | 9 | | 11 | 2 | | 1 | | | | | 12 | 10 | | | | | | | 18 |
| | 2 | 3 | | 5 | 6 | $7^{2}$ | 4 | | $9^{1}$ | | 10 | | 12 | 1 | 8 | | 13 | 11 | | | | | | | | | 19 |
| | 2 | $3^{2}$ | 4 | | 6 | $7^{3}$ | $10^{1}$ | | | | 11 | 13 | 9 | 1 | 8 | | | 12 | | | 5 | | 14 | | | | 20 |
| | 2 | 3 | 4 | 5 | 6 | 7 | | | $9^{1}$ | | | | | 1 | 8 | | | 11 | | 10 | | | 12 | | | | 21 |
| | 2 | 3 | 4 | 5 | 6 | $7^{1}$ | 12 | | $9^{3}$ | 13 | | | | 1 | 8 | | | $11^{2}$ | | 10 | | | 14 | | | | 22 |
| | 2 | 3 | 4 | 5 | 6 | | 7 | | 12 | | | | | | 8 | | | 11 | | $10^{2}$ | | | 13 | 1 | $9^{1}$ | | 23 |
| | 2 | 3 | | 5 | 6 | | 4 | | 12 | | | | | | 8 | | | 11 | | 7 | | | 9 | 1 | $10^{1}$ | | 24 |
| | 2 | 3 | | 5 | 6 | | 4 | | 12 | 13 | | | | | 8 | | | 11 | | $7^{2}$ | | | 9 | 1 | $10^{1}$ | | 25 |
| | | 3 | 4 | 5 | 6 | | 12 | | | | 7 | | | | 8 | | | 11 | | $10^{2}$ | 2 | | 13 | 1 | $9^{1}$ | | 26 |
| | $2^{2}$ | 3 | 4 | 5 | 6 | 12 | | | | | $7^{1}$ | | | | 8 | | | 11 | | $10^{3}$ | 13 | | 14 | 1 | 9 | | 27 |
| | $2^{1}$ | 3 | 4 | 5 | 6 | | | | 13 | | 7 | | | | 8 | | | 11 | | | 12 | | 9 | 1 | $10^{2}$ | | 28 |
| | | 3 | 4 | 5 | 6 | 12 | | | | | 7 | | | | 8 | | | $11^{2}$ | | 10 | 2 | | $9^{1}$ | 1 | 13 | | 29 |
| | | 3 | 4 | 5 | 6 | 13 | 12 | | | | 10 | | | | $8^{1}$ | | | $11^{2}$ | | $7^{3}$ | 2 | | 9 | 1 | 14 | | 30 |
| | $2^{1}$ | 3 | 4 | 5 | 6 | 13 | 12 | | | | 7 | | | | 8 | | | 11 | | $10^{2}$ | | | $9^{3}$ | 1 | 14 | | 31 |
| | 12 | 3 | 4 | 5 | | $7^{3}$ | 8 | | | | $10^{2}$ | | | | | | 14 | 11 | | 13 | $2^{1}$ | | | 1 | 9 | 6 | 32 |
| | $2^{1}$ | 3 | 4 | 5 | | 7 | 8 | | | | 10 | | | | | | | 11 | | 12 | | | | 1 | 9 | 6 | 33 |
| | 12 | 3 | 4 | 5 | | $7^{2}$ | 8 | | | | 10 | | | | 13 | | | 11 | | | $2^{1}$ | | | 1 | 9 | 6 | 34 |
| | | 3 | 4 | 5 | | 7 | $8^{2}$ | | | | 10 | $2^{3}$ | | | 12 | | | $11^{1}$ | | 13 | | | 14 | 1 | 9 | 6 | 35 |
| | $2^{2}$ | 3 | 4 | 5 | | 7 | $8^{1}$ | | | | 10 | | | | 12 | | | 11 | | | | | 13 | 1 | 9 | 6 | 36 |
| | $2^{3}$ | $3^{1}$ | 4 | 5 | | 7 | $8^{2}$ | | | | 10 | | | | 12 | | 13 | 11 | | | | | 14 | 1 | 9 | 6 | 37 |
| | $2^{1}$ | $3^{2}$ | 4■ | 5 | 12 | $7^{3}$ | 8 | | | | 10 | | | | 13 | | | 11 | | | | | 14 | 1 | 9 | 6 | 38 |

**Carling Cup**

| | | | |
|---|---|---|---|
| Second Round | Darlington | (h) | 2-0 |
| Third Round | Burnley | (h) | 2-0 |
| Fourth Round | Arsenal | (a) | 1-5 |

**FA Cup**

| | | | |
|---|---|---|---|
| Third Round | Kidderminster H | (a) | 1-1 |
| | | (h) | 2-0 |
| Fourth Round | West Ham U | (h) | 1-3 |

# WREXHAM FL Championship 1

## FOUNDATION

The club was formed on 28 September 1872 by members of Wrexham Cricket Club, so they could continue playing a sport during the winter months. This meeting was held at the Turf Hotel, which although rebuilt since, still stands at one corner of the present ground. Their first game was a few weeks later and matches often included 17 players on either side! By 1875 team formations were reduced to 11 men and a year later the club was among the founder members of the Cambrian Football Association, which quickly changed its title to the Football Association of Wales.

***Racecourse Ground, Mold Road, Wrexham LL11 2AH.***

***Telephone:*** (01978) 262 129.

***Fax:*** (01978) 357 821.

***Ticket Office:*** (01978) 366 388.

***Website:*** www.wrexhamafc.co.uk

***Email:*** geraint@wrexhamafc.co.uk

***Ground Capacity:*** 15,500.

***Record Attendance:*** 34,445 v Manchester U, FA Cup 4th rd, 26 January 1957.

***Pitch Measurements:*** 111yd × 71yd.

***Chairman:*** Alex Hamilton.

***Secretary:*** Bill Wingrove.

***Manager:*** Denis Smith.

***Assistant Manager:*** Kevin Russell.

***Physio:*** Mel Pejic.

***Colours:*** Red shirts, white shorts, red stockings.

***Change Colours:*** Black shirts, white shorts, black stockings.

***Year Formed:*** 1872 (oldest club in Wales).

***Turned Professional:*** 1912.

***Ltd Co.:*** 1912.

***Club Nickname:*** 'Red Dragons'.

***Previous Grounds:*** 1872, Racecourse Ground; 1883, Rhosddu Recreation Ground; 1887, Racecourse Ground.

***First Football League Game:*** 27 August 1921, Division 3 (N), v Hartlepools U (h) L 0–2 – Godding; Ellis, Simpson; Matthias, Foster, Griffiths; Burton, Goode, Cotton, Edwards, Lloyd.

***Record League Victory:*** 10–1 v Hartlepool U, Division 4, 3 March 1962 – Keelan; Peter Jones, McGavan; Tecwyn Jones, Fox, Ken Barnes; Ron Barnes (3), Bennion (1), Davies (3), Ambler (3), Ron Roberts.

## HONOURS

*Football League:* Division 3 – Champions 1977–78; Runners-up 1992–93; Promoted (3rd) 2002–03; Division 3 (N) – Runners-up 1932–33; Division 4 – Runners-up 1969–70.

*FA Cup:* best season: 6th rd, 1974, 1978, 1997.

*Football League Cup:* best season: 5th rd, 1961, 1978.

*Welsh Cup:* Winners 22 times (joint record); Runners-up 22 times (record).

*FAW Premier Cup:* Winners 1998, 2000, 2001, 2003.

***European Competition:*** *European Cup-Winners' Cup:* 1972–73, 1975–76, 1978–79, 1979–80, 1984–85, 1986–87, 1990–91, 1995–96.

## SKY SPORTS FACT FILE

In 1926–27 either Cecil Smith, James Smith or both scored for Wrexham in 13 successive League games in a season in which they finished 13th. Cecil Smith himself scored 13 Division Three (North) goals in total.

**_Record Cup Victory:_** 11–1 v New Brighton, Football League Northern Section Cup 1st rd, 3 January 1934 – Foster; Alfred Jones, Hamilton, Bulling, McMahon, Lawrence, Bryant (3), Findlay (1), Bamford (5), Snow, Waller (1), (o.g. 1).

**_Record Defeat:_** 0–9 v Brentford, Division 3, 15 October 1963.

**_Most League Points (2 for a win):_** 61, Division 4, 1969–70 and Division 3, 1977–78.

**_Most League Points (3 for a win):_** 84, Division 3, 2002–03.

**_Most League Goals:_** 106, Division 3 (N), 1932–33.

**_Highest League Scorer in Season:_** Tom Bamford, 44, Division 3 (N), 1933–34.

**_Most League Goals in Total Aggregate:_** Tom Bamford, 175, 1928–34.

**_Most League Goals in One Match:_** 5, Tom Bamford v Carlisle U, Division 3N, 17 March 1934; 5, Lee Jones v Cambridge U, Division 2, 6 April 2002.

**_Most Capped Player:_** Joey Jones, 29 (72), Wales.

**_Most League Appearances:_** Arfon Griffiths, 592, 1959–61, 1962–79.

**_Youngest League Player:_** Ken Roberts, 15 years 158 days v Bradford PA, 1 September 1951.

**_Record Transfer Fee Received:_** £800,000 from Birmingham C for Bryan Hughes, March 1997.

**_Record Transfer Fee Paid:_** £210,000 to Liverpool for Joey Jones, October 1978.

**_Football League Record:_** 1921 Original Member of Division 3 (N); 1958–60 Division 3; 1960–62 Division 4; 1962–64 Division 3; 1964–70 Division 4; 1970–78 Division 3; 1978–82 Division 2; 1982–83 Division 3; 1983–92 Division 4; 1992–93 Division 3; 1993–2002 Division 2; 2002–03 Division 3; 2003–04 Division 2; 2004– FL1.

## MANAGERS

Selection Committee 1872–1924
Charlie Hewitt 1924–25
Selection Committee 1925–29
Jack Baynes 1929–31
Ernest Blackburn 1932–37
James Logan 1937–38
Arthur Cowell 1938
Tom Morgan 1938–42
Tom Williams 1942–49
Les McDowell 1949–50
Peter Jackson 1950–55
Cliff Lloyd 1955–57
John Love 1957–59
Cliff Lloyd 1959–60
Billy Morris 1960–61
Ken Barnes 1961–65
Billy Morris 1965
Jack Rowley 1966–67
Alvan Williams 1967–68
John Neal 1968–77
Arfon Griffiths 1977–81
Mel Sutton 1981–82
Bobby Roberts 1982–85
Dixie McNeil 1985–89
Brian Flynn 1989–2001
Denis Smith October 2001–

## LATEST SEQUENCES

**_Longest Sequence of League Wins:_** 8, 5.4.2003 – 3.5.2003.

**_Longest Sequence of League Defeats:_** 9, 2.10.1963 – 30.10.1963.

**_Longest Sequence of League Draws:_** 6, 12.11.1999 – 26.12.1999.

**_Longest Sequence of Unbeaten League Matches:_** 18, 8.3.2003 – 25.8.2003.

**_Longest Sequence Without a League Win:_** 16, 25.9.1999 – 3.1.2000.

**_Successive Scoring Runs:_** 25 from 5.5.1928.

**_Successive Non-scoring Runs:_** 6 from 12.9.1973.

## TEN YEAR LEAGUE RECORD

| | | *P* | *W* | *D* | *L* | *F* | *A* | *Pts* | *Pos* |
|---|---|---|---|---|---|---|---|---|---|
| 1994-95 | Div 2 | 46 | 16 | 15 | 15 | 65 | 64 | 63 | 13 |
| 1995-96 | Div 2 | 46 | 18 | 16 | 12 | 76 | 55 | 70 | 8 |
| 1996-97 | Div 2 | 46 | 17 | 18 | 11 | 54 | 50 | 69 | 8 |
| 1997-98 | Div 2 | 46 | 18 | 16 | 12 | 55 | 51 | 70 | 7 |
| 1998-99 | Div 2 | 46 | 13 | 14 | 19 | 43 | 62 | 53 | 17 |
| 1999-2000 | Div 2 | 46 | 17 | 11 | 18 | 52 | 61 | 62 | 11 |
| 2000-01 | Div 2 | 46 | 17 | 12 | 17 | 65 | 71 | 63 | 10 |
| 2001-02 | Div 2 | 46 | 11 | 10 | 25 | 56 | 89 | 43 | 23 |
| 2002-03 | Div 3 | 46 | 23 | 15 | 8 | 84 | 50 | 84 | 3 |
| 2003-04 | Div 2 | 46 | 17 | 9 | 20 | 50 | 60 | 60 | 13 |

## DID YOU KNOW?

Manchester City product Jack Boothway arrived from Crewe Alexandra and made his Wrexham debut on 2 November 1946. In only 28 League and Cup matches for the club he scored 25 goals. His League tally alone there yielded 55 in 95 matches.

## WREXHAM 2003–04 LEAGUE RECORD

| Match No. | Date | Venue | Opponents | Result | | H/T Score | Lg. Pos. | Goalscorers | Attendance |
|---|---|---|---|---|---|---|---|---|---|
| 1 | Aug 9 | H | Chesterfield | D | 0-0 | 0-0 | — | | 5688 |
| 2 | 16 | A | Notts Co | W | 1-0 | 0-0 | 8 | Sam [66] | 4768 |
| 3 | 23 | H | Brentford | W | 1-0 | 1-0 | 4 | Lawrence [19] | 4048 |
| 4 | 25 | A | Sheffield W | W | 3-2 | 1-1 | 2 | Lawrence [40], Llewellyn [53], Edwards C [64] | 24,478 |
| 5 | 30 | H | Bournemouth | L | 0-1 | 0-1 | 5 | | 4929 |
| 6 | Sept 13 | A | Swindon T | L | 0-1 | 0-0 | 10 | | 8160 |
| 7 | 16 | H | QPR | L | 0-2 | 0-1 | — | | 4539 |
| 8 | 20 | H | Plymouth Arg | D | 2-2 | 2-1 | 14 | Lawrence [28], Jones L (pen) [42] | 3945 |
| 9 | 27 | A | Tranmere R | W | 2-1 | 0-1 | 13 | Jones L [64], Holmes [65] | 8230 |
| 10 | 30 | A | Hartlepool U | L | 0-2 | 0-2 | — | | 4677 |
| 11 | Oct 4 | H | Port Vale | W | 2-1 | 1-1 | 13 | Jones L 2 (1 pen) [33, 78 (p)] | 5822 |
| 12 | 18 | H | Bristol C | D | 0-0 | 0-0 | 14 | | 4405 |
| 13 | 21 | H | Oldham Ath | W | 4-0 | 2-0 | — | Jones L [32], Edwards C [41], Lawrence [50], Jones M [89] | 3963 |
| 14 | 25 | A | Rushden & D | W | 3-2 | 2-0 | 9 | Edwards C [10], Ferguson [35], Sam [56] | 4117 |
| 15 | 28 | A | Barnsley | L | 1-2 | 0-1 | — | Holmes [74] | 8916 |
| 16 | 31 | H | Colchester U | L | 0-1 | 0-1 | — | | 4269 |
| 17 | Nov 11 | A | Blackpool | W | 1-0 | 0-0 | — | Lawrence [74] | 4864 |
| 18 | 15 | A | Luton T | L | 2-3 | 2-1 | 11 | Sam [19], Boyce (og) [43] | 5505 |
| 19 | 22 | H | Wycombe W | D | 0-0 | 0-0 | 11 | | 3208 |
| 20 | 29 | A | Brighton & HA | L | 0-2 | 0-1 | 14 | | 5642 |
| 21 | Dec 13 | H | Peterborough U | W | 2-0 | 0-0 | 11 | Carey [67], Sam [76] | 3035 |
| 22 | 26 | A | Stockport Co | W | 1-0 | 0-0 | 8 | Barrett [88] | 6256 |
| 23 | 28 | H | Blackpool | W | 4-2 | 4-2 | 6 | Llewellyn 2 [15, 21], Sam 2 [33, 44] | 6171 |
| 24 | Jan 3 | H | Sheffield W | L | 1-2 | 0-1 | 7 | Carey [49] | 8497 |
| 25 | 10 | A | Chesterfield | L | 1-2 | 0-0 | 9 | Armstrong [77] | 3585 |
| 26 | 17 | H | Notts Co | L | 0-1 | 0-1 | 10 | | 4212 |
| 27 | 20 | A | Grimsby T | W | 3-1 | 2-0 | — | Llewellyn [19], Thomas [24], Armstrong [63] | 3572 |
| 28 | 24 | A | Brentford | W | 1-0 | 0-0 | 5 | Armstrong [58] | 4567 |
| 29 | Feb 7 | H | Stockport Co | D | 0-0 | 0-0 | 8 | | 5046 |
| 30 | 14 | H | Barnsley | W | 1-0 | 1-0 | 6 | Llewellyn [24] | 4086 |
| 31 | 21 | A | Bristol C | L | 0-1 | 0-1 | 9 | | 13,871 |
| 32 | 24 | A | Bournemouth | L | 0-6 | 0-2 | — | | 5899 |
| 33 | 28 | H | Rushden & D | D | 1-1 | 1-1 | 10 | Edwards C [20] | 3680 |
| 34 | Mar 6 | H | Grimsby T | W | 3-0 | 3-0 | 10 | Crowell [34], Armstrong 2 [36, 37] | 3127 |
| 35 | 13 | A | Peterborough U | L | 1-6 | 1-2 | 10 | Llewellyn [21] | 4323 |
| 36 | 16 | A | QPR | L | 0-2 | 0-0 | — | | 13,363 |
| 37 | 20 | H | Swindon T | W | 3-2 | 1-0 | 10 | Llewellyn [25], Edwards C [54], Thomas [68] | 3384 |
| 38 | 27 | A | Plymouth Arg | D | 0-0 | 0-0 | 10 | | 12,275 |
| 39 | Apr 3 | H | Tranmere R | L | 0-1 | 0-0 | 11 | | 4496 |
| 40 | 10 | A | Port Vale | L | 0-1 | 0-0 | 13 | | 5892 |
| 41 | 12 | H | Hartlepool U | L | 1-2 | 0-1 | 14 | Barrett [71] | 3786 |
| 42 | 17 | A | Colchester U | L | 1-3 | 1-2 | 14 | Sam [18] | 3077 |
| 43 | 20 | A | Oldham Ath | D | 1-1 | 1-1 | — | Sam [19] | 5646 |
| 44 | 24 | H | Luton T | W | 2-1 | 1-0 | 14 | Sam 2 [35, 62] | 3239 |
| 45 | May 1 | A | Wycombe W | D | 1-1 | 0-0 | 12 | Llewellyn [80] | 4684 |
| 46 | 8 | H | Brighton & HA | L | 0-2 | 0-1 | 13 | | 4542 |

**Final League Position: 13**

## GOALSCORERS

*League (50):* Sam 10, Llewellyn 8, Armstrong 5, Edwards C 5, Jones L 5 (2 pens), Lawrence 5, Barrett 2, Carey 2, Holmes 2, Thomas 2, Crowell 1, Ferguson 1, Jones M 1, own goal 1.
*Carling Cup (0).*
*FA Cup (1):* Armstrong 1.
*LDV Vans Trophy (8):* Jones L 3 (1 pen), Sam 2 (1 pen), Armstrong 1, Holmes 1, Jones M 1.

| Dibble A 35 | Edwards C 42 | Edwards P 40 + 1 | Lawrence D 45 | Pejic S 20 + 1 | Carey B 32 + 2 | Whitley J 34 + 2 | Ferguson D 39 | Armstrong C 19 + 7 | Llewellyn C 46 | Thomas S 31 + 9 | Holmes S 3 + 10 | Jones L 13 + 9 | Crowell M 9 + 6 | Barrett P 19 + 8 | Sam H 24 + 13 | Jones M — + 13 | Morgan C 14 + 4 | One A 2 + 1 | Roberts S 24 + 3 | Whitfield P — + 2 | Ingham M 11 | Spender S 3 + 3 | Mackin L 1 | *Match No.* |
|---|---|---|---|---|---|---|---|---|---|---|---|---|---|---|---|---|---|---|---|---|---|---|---|---|
| 1 | 2 | $3^1$ | 4 | 5 | 6 | 7 | 8 | $9^2$ | 10 | $11^3$ | 12 | 13 | 14 | | | | | | | | | | | 1 |
| 1 | 2 | $3^1$ | 4 | 5 | 6 | $7^2$ | 8 | $9^3$ | 10 | 11 | 12 | | | 13 | 14 | | | | | | | | | 2 |
| 1 | 2 | 3 | 4 | 5 | 6 | | 8 | | 10 | $11^1$ | | | 12 | 7 | $9^2$ | 13 | | | | | | | | 3 |
| 1 | 2 | $3^1$ | 4 | 5 | 6 | | 8 | | 10 | 11 | 12 | | | 7 | $9^2$ | 13 | | | | | | | | 4 |
| 1 | 2 | 3 | 4 | 5 | | | 8 | | 10 | 11 | | | | 7 | $9^1$ | 12 | 6 | | | | | | | 5 |
| 1 | 2 | 3 | 4 | 5 | 6 | 7 | 8 | | 10 | 11 | | $9^1$ | | | $12^2$ | | | 13 | | | | | | 6 |
| 1 | 2 | $3^1$ | 4 | 5 | $6^3$ | 7 | 8 | | 10 | | 12 | 9 | | | 13 | | 14 | $11^2$ | | | | | | 7 |
| 1 | 2 | $3^2$ | 4 | 5 | 6 | $7^1$ | 8 | | 10 | 12 | 13 | 9 | | | 14 | | | $11^3$ | | | | | | 8 |
| 1 | 2 | $3^1$ | 4 | 5 | 6 | 7 | 8 | | 10 | 11 | 12 | $9^2$ | | | 13 | | | | | | | | | 9 |
| 1 | $2^2$ | 12 | 4 | $5^3$ | 6 | 7 | 8 | | 10 | 11 | $3^1$ | 9 | | | 13 | | | | 14 | | | | | 10 |
| $1^G$ | 2 | 3 | 4 | | 6 | 7 | 8 | | 10 | 12 | | $9^1$ | | | $11^2$ | 13 | | | 5 | 15 | | | | 11 |
| 1 | $2^1$ | 3 | 4 | | $6^3$ | 7 | 8 | | $11^2$ | 12 | | 9 | | | 10 | 13 | 14 | | 5 | | | | | 12 |
| 1 | 2 | 3 | 4 | | | 7 | $8^1$ | | 11 | 12 | | $9^2$ | | | 10 | 13 | 6 | | 5 | | | | | 13 |
| 1 | 2 | 3 | 4 | | 12 | 7 | 8 | | 11 | 13 | | $9^2$ | | | 10 | | $6^1$ | | 5 | | | | | 14 |
| 1 | 2 | $3^1$ | 4 | | 6 | $7^2$ | 8 | | 11 | 14 | 12 | 9 | | | $10^3$ | 13 | | | 5 | | | | | 15 |
| 1 | 2 | | $4^2$ | | 6 | 7 | 8 | 12 | $11^1$ | 13 | 3 | 9 | | | 10 | | | | 5 | | | | | 16 |
| 1 | 2 | | 4 | 5 | 6 | 7 | 8 | | 9 | 3 | | 12 | | 11 | $10^1$ | | | | | | | | | 17 |
| 1 | 2 | | 4 | 5 | 6 | | 8■ | 12 | $9^1$ | $3^2$ | | | 7 | 11 | 10 | 13 | | | | | | | | 18 |
| 1 | 2 | 3 | 4 | 5 | 6 | 7 | 8 | 12 | 9 | | | | | $11^2$ | $10^1$ | 13 | | | | | | | | 19 |
| 1 | 2 | 3 | 4 | 5 | $6^2$ | 7 | | $9^1$ | $8^3$ | 14 | | 12 | | 11 | 10 | | | | 13 | | | | | 20 |
| 1 | 2 | 3 | 4 | 5 | 6 | 7 | | | 10 | $8^2$ | | $9^1$ | 13 | 11 | 12 | | | | | | | | | 21 |
| 1 | 2 | 3 | 4 | 5 | 6 | 7 | | | 10 | 8 | | | | 11 | 9 | | | | | | | | | 22 |
| 1 | 2 | 3 | 4 | | 13 | 12 | 8 | | 10 | 7 | | | | 11 | 9 | | $6^2$ | | $5^1$ | | | | | 23 |
| 1 | 2 | 3 | 4 | $5^1$ | 6 | 7 | 8 | 13 | 10 | $12^2$ | | | | 11 | $9^3$ | 14 | | | | | | | | 24 |
| 1 | 2 | 3 | 4 | | 5 | 7 | 8 | 12 | 10 | | | | | $11^1$ | 9 | | 6 | | | | | | | 25 |
| 1 | 2 | 3 | 4 | | 5 | 13 | 8 | 14 | $10^3$ | 7 | | | | $11^2$ | 9 | | $6^1$ | | 12 | | | | | 26 |
| 1 | 2 | $3^2$ | 4 | | 6 | 7 | 8 | 9 | 10 | $11^1$ | 13 | | | 12 | | | | | 5 | | | | | 27 |
| 1 | 2 | 3 | 4 | | 6 | 7 | 8 | 9 | 10 | 11 | | | | | | | | | 5 | | | | | 28 |
| 1 | 2 | 3 | 4 | | 6 | 7 | 8 | 9 | 10 | $11^1$ | | | | | 12 | | | | 5 | | | | | 29 |
| 1 | 2 | 3 | 4■ | 13 | | 7 | 8 | $9^1$ | 10 | $11^2$ | | | | 12 | | | 6 | | 5 | | | | | 30 |
| 1 | 2 | $3^1$ | 4 | | 6 | 7 | 8 | 9 | 10 | $11^2$ | | 12 | | | 13 | | | | 5 | | | | | 31 |
| 1 | 2 | | 4 | | $6^1$ | 7 | 8 | 9 | 11 | $3^2$ | 14 | $10^3$ | | 12 | | | 13 | | 5■ | | | | | 32 |
| 1 | 2 | 3 | | 6 | 4 | 7 | | 9 | 10 | | | 12 | 8 | | $11^1$ | | | | 5 | | | | | 33 |
| 1 | 2 | 3 | 4 | 5 | | 7 | 8 | 9 | $10^2$ | | | | $11^1$ | 12 | 13 | | 6 | | | | | | | 34 |
| $1^G$ | 2 | 3 | 4 | 5 | | 7 | 8 | 9 | 10 | | | | $11^2$ | 12 | 13 | | $6^1$ | | | 15 | | | | 35 |
| | 2 | 3 | 4 | | 5 | $7^2$ | 8 | 9 | $10^1$ | 11 | | 12 | 13 | | | | | | 6 | | 1 | | | 36 |
| | 2 | 3 | 4 | | 5 | $7^1$ | 8 | 9 | 10 | 11 | | | 12 | | | | | | 6 | | 1 | | | 37 |
| | 2 | 3 | 4 | | | | 8■ | $9^1$ | 10 | $7^2$ | | | | 11 | 12 | | 6■ | | 5 | | 1 | 13 | | 38 |
| | $2^2$ | 3■ | 4 | | 5 | | 8 | 9 | 10 | 7 | | | 13 | $11^1$ | | 12 | | | 6 | | 1 | | | 39 |
| | 2 | 3 | 4 | | | 8 | | 9 | 10 | $7^2$ | 13 | 12 | 6 | $11^1$ | | | | | $5^3$ | | 1 | 14 | | 40 |
| | $2^3$ | 3 | 4 | | | $8^1$ | | 9 | 10 | 7 | | 12 | $6^2$ | 11 | 13 | | 5 | | | | 1 | 14 | | 41 |
| | | | 4 | | | | | $9^1$ | 10 | 7 | 2 | 12 | $6^2$ | 11 | 8 | 13 | 3 | | 5 | | 1 | | | 42 |
| | | 3 | 4 | | | | 8 | | 10 | 11 | | | $7^1$ | 12 | 9 | | 6 | | 5 | | 1 | 2 | | 43 |
| | | 3 | 4 | | | | 8 | | 10 | 7 | | | $6^1$ | 11 | 9 | 12 | | | 5 | | 1 | 2 | | 44 |
| | | 3 | 4 | | | | 8 | | 10 | 11 | | | | | 9 | | 6 | | 5 | | 1 | 2 | 7 | 45 |
| | 2 | 3 | 4 | | $5^3$ | $7^1$ | 8 | 12 | 10 | $11^2$ | | | | 13 | 9 | | 14 | | 6 | | 1 | | | 46 |

| | | | |
|---|---|---|---|
| **Carling Cup** | | | |
| First Round | Crewe Alex | (a) | 0-2 |
| **LDV Vans Trophy** | | | |
| First Round | Morecambe | (h) | 4-1 |
| Second Round | Stockport Co | (a) | 4-5 |

| | | | |
|---|---|---|---|
| **FA Cup** | | | |
| First Round | Yeovil T | (a) | 1-4 |

# WYCOMBE WANDERERS FL Championship 2

## FOUNDATION

In 1887 a group of young furniture trade workers called a meeting at the Steam Engine public house with the aim of forming a football club and entering junior football. It is thought that they were named after the famous FA Cup winners, The Wanderers who had visited the town in 1877 for a tie with the original High Wycombe club. It is also possible that they played informally before their formation, although there is no proof of this.

***Adams Park, Hillbottom Road, Sands, High Wycombe HP12 4HJ.***

***Telephone:*** (01494) 472 100.

***Fax:*** (01494) 527 633.

***Ticket Office:*** (01494) 441 118.

***Ground Capacity:*** 10,000.

***Record Attendance:*** 9,650 v Wimbledon, FA Cup 5th rd, 17 February 2001.

***Pitch Measurements:*** 115yd × 75yd.

***Chairman:*** Ivor L. Beeks.

***Vice-chairman:*** Brian Kane.

***Secretary:*** Keith J. Allen.

***Manager:*** Tony Adams.

***Assistant Manager:*** Peter Cawley.

***Physio:*** Shay Connolly.

***Colours:*** Sky blue and navy quartered shirts, navy shorts, sky blue stockings.

***Change Colours:*** All yellow.

***Year Formed:*** 1887.

***Turned Professional:*** 1974.

***Club Nicknames:*** 'Chairboys' (after High Wycombe's tradition of furniture making), 'The Blues'.

***Previous Grounds:*** 1887, The Rye; 1893, Spring Meadow; 1895, Loakes Park; 1899, Daws Hill Park; 1901, Loakes Park; 1990, Adams Park.

***First Football League Game:*** 14 August 1993, Division 3 v Carlisle U (a) D 2–2: Hyde; Cousins, Horton (Langford), Kerr, Crossley, Ryan, Carroll, Stapleton, Thompson, Scott, Guppy (1) (Hutchinson), (1 og).

***Record League Victory:*** 5–0 v Burnley, Division 2, 15 April 1997 – Parkin; Cousins, Bell, Kavanagh, McCarthy, Forsyth, Carroll (2p) (Simpson), Scott (Farrell), Stallard (1), McGavin (1) (Read (1)), Brown.

## HONOURS

*Football League:* Division 2 best season: 6th, 1994–95. Division 3 1993–94 (play-offs).

*FA Amateur Cup:* Winners 1931.

*FA Trophy:* Winners 1991, 1993.

*GM Vauxhall Conference:* Winners 1992–93.

*FA Cup:* semi-final 2001.

*Football League Cup:* never beyond 2nd rd.

## SKY SPORTS FACT FILE

Kenny Swain proved something of a talisman for Wycombe Wanderers albeit over a brief period. A right-winger spotted in college football, he made six appearances in an unbeaten run at the end of the 1972–73 season before being snapped up by Chelsea.

***Record Cup Victory:*** 5–0 v Hitchin T (a), FA Cup 2nd rd, 3 December 1994 – Hyde; Cousins, Brown, Crossley, Evans, Ryan (1), Carroll, Bell (1), Thompson, Garner (3) (Hemmings), Stapleton (Langford).

***Record Defeat:*** 0–5 v Walsall, Auto Windscreens Shield 1st rd, 7 November 1995.

***Most League Points (3 for a win):*** 78, Division 2, 1994–95.

***Most League Goals:*** 67, Division 3, 1993–94.

***Highest League Goalscorer in Season:*** Sean Devine, 23, 1999–2000.

***Most League Goals in Total Aggregate:*** Dave Carroll, 41, 1993–2002.

***Most League Goals in One Match:*** 3, Miguel Desouza v Bradford C, Division 2, 26 March 1996; 3, Mark Stallard v Walsall, Division 2, 21 October 1997; 3, Sean Devine v Reading, Division 2, 2 October 1999; 3, Sean Divine v Bury, Division 2, 26 February 2000.

***Most Capped Player:*** Mark Rogers, 7, Canada.

***Most League Appearances:*** Steve Brown, 371, 1994–2004.

***Youngest League Player:*** Roger Johnson, 17 years 8 days v Cambridge U, 6 May 2000.

***Record Transfer Fee Received:*** £375,000 from Swindon T for Keith Scott, November 1993.

***Record Transfer Fee Paid:*** £220,000 to Barnet for Sean Devine, 15 April 1999.

***Football League Record:*** Promoted to Division 3 from GM Vauxhall Conference in 1993; 1993–94 Division 3; 1994–2004 Division 2; 2004– FL2.

## MANAGERS

First coach appointed 1951.
*Prior to Brian Lee's appointment in 1969 the team was selected by a Match Committee which met every Monday evening.*
James McCormack 1951–52
Sid Cann 1952–61
Graham Adams 1961–62
Don Welsh 1962–64
Barry Darvill 1964–68
Brian Lee 1969–76
Ted Powell 1976–77
John Reardon 1977–78
Andy Williams 1978–80
Mike Keen 1980–84
Paul Bence 1984–86
Alan Gane 1986–87
Peter Suddaby 1987–88
Jim Kelman 1988–90
Martin O'Neill 1990–95
Alan Smith 1995–96
John Gregory 1996–98
Neil Smillie 1998–99
Lawrie Sanchez 1999–2003
Tony Adams November 2003–

## LATEST SEQUENCES

***Longest Sequence of League Wins:*** 4, 26.2.1994 – 19.3.1994.

***Longest Sequence of League Defeats:*** 4, 2.1.1999 – 30.1.1999.

***Longest Sequence of League Draws:*** 5, 24.1.2004 – 21.2.2004

***Longest Sequence of Unbeaten League Matches:*** 14, 29.8.1995 – 18.11.1995.

***Longest Sequence Without a League Win:*** 13, 16.8.2003 – 18.10.2003 and 10.1.2004 – 20.3.2004.

***Successive Scoring Runs:*** 11 from 29.3.1994

***Successive Non-scoring Runs:*** 5 from 15.10.1996

## TEN YEAR LEAGUE RECORD

| | | P | W | D | L | F | A | Pts | Pos |
|---|---|---|---|---|---|---|---|---|---|
| 1994-95 | Div 2 | 46 | 21 | 15 | 10 | 60 | 46 | 78 | 6 |
| 1995-96 | Div 2 | 46 | 15 | 15 | 16 | 63 | 59 | 60 | 12 |
| 1996-97 | Div 2 | 46 | 15 | 10 | 21 | 51 | 56 | 55 | 18 |
| 1997-98 | Div 2 | 46 | 14 | 18 | 14 | 51 | 53 | 60 | 14 |
| 1998-99 | Div 2 | 46 | 13 | 12 | 21 | 52 | 58 | 51 | 19 |
| 1999-2000 | Div 2 | 46 | 16 | 13 | 17 | 56 | 53 | 61 | 12 |
| 2000-01 | Div 2 | 46 | 15 | 14 | 17 | 46 | 53 | 59 | 13 |
| 2001-02 | Div 2 | 46 | 17 | 13 | 16 | 58 | 64 | 64 | 11 |
| 2002-03 | Div 2 | 46 | 13 | 13 | 20 | 59 | 66 | 52 | 18 |
| 2003-04 | Div 2 | 46 | 6 | 19 | 21 | 50 | 75 | 37 | 24 |

## DID YOU KNOW ?

In 1919–20 Wycombe Wanderers scored in each of their 27 League and Cup matches. Champions of the Spartan League they dropped only three points, scored 129 goals in all competitions and retained their title the following season.

## WYCOMBE WANDERERS 2003–04 LEAGUE RECORD

| Match No. | Date | Venue | Opponents | Result | | H/T Score | Lg. Pos. | Goalscorers | Atten-dance |
|---|---|---|---|---|---|---|---|---|---|
| 1 | Aug 9 | H | Stockport Co | W | 1-0 | 1-0 | — | Mapes [16] | 4826 |
| 2 | 16 | A | Blackpool | L | 2-3 | 2-2 | 13 | Patterson [24], Currie [31] | 5960 |
| 3 | 23 | H | Chesterfield | D | 3-3 | 2-2 | 15 | Currie [4], McSporran [20], Patterson [61] | 4529 |
| 4 | 25 | A | Grimsby T | L | 1-3 | 0-1 | 18 | Mapes [90] | 4512 |
| 5 | Sept 1 | H | Sheffield W | L | 1-2 | 1-2 | — | McSporran [42] | 6444 |
| 6 | 6 | A | Rushden & D | L | 0-2 | 0-1 | 21 | | 4192 |
| 7 | 13 | A | QPR | D | 0-0 | 0-0 | 22 | | 13,618 |
| 8 | 16 | H | Colchester U | L | 1-2 | 0-2 | — | Currie (pen) [51] | 4401 |
| 9 | 20 | H | Oldham Ath | L | 2-5 | 0-3 | 23 | Bell 2 [49, 76] | 4725 |
| 10 | 27 | A | Port Vale | D | 1-1 | 0-1 | 22 | Mapes [64] | 6822 |
| 11 | 30 | A | Tranmere R | L | 1-2 | 0-1 | — | Bell [78] | 6847 |
| 12 | Oct 4 | H | Plymouth Arg | D | 0-0 | 0-0 | 23 | | 5708 |
| 13 | 11 | A | Luton T | L | 1-3 | 0-0 | 23 | Brown (pen) [49] | 5695 |
| 14 | 18 | H | Barnsley | L | 1-2 | 0-2 | 24 | Thomson [68] | 4446 |
| 15 | 21 | H | Bristol C | W | 3-0 | 1-0 | — | Holligan 2 [40, 70], McSporran [90] | 4613 |
| 16 | 25 | A | Hartlepool U | D | 1-1 | 1-1 | 23 | Currie [3] | 5153 |
| 17 | Nov 1 | A | Swindon T | L | 0-2 | 0-1 | 24 | | 5681 |
| 18 | 15 | H | Brentford | L | 1-2 | 0-1 | 24 | McSporran [65] | 6445 |
| 19 | 22 | A | Wrexham | D | 0-0 | 0-0 | 24 | | 3208 |
| 20 | 29 | H | Peterborough U | L | 1-2 | 0-1 | 24 | Currie [62] | 4669 |
| 21 | Dec 13 | A | Notts Co | D | 1-1 | 1-0 | 24 | Simpson [45] | 5014 |
| 22 | 20 | H | Bournemouth | W | 2-0 | 1-0 | 23 | Ryan [45], Moore [75] | 5205 |
| 23 | 26 | A | Brighton & HA | L | 0-4 | 0-2 | 24 | | 6141 |
| 24 | 28 | H | Rushden & D | L | 0-2 | 0-2 | 24 | | 5421 |
| 25 | Jan 3 | H | Grimsby T | W | 4-1 | 2-1 | 24 | Moore 3 [5, 52, 90], McSporran [28] | 4519 |
| 26 | 10 | A | Stockport Co | L | 0-2 | 0-2 | 24 | | 4406 |
| 27 | 17 | H | Blackpool | L | 0-3 | 0-2 | 24 | | 4834 |
| 28 | 24 | A | Chesterfield | D | 2-2 | 1-0 | 24 | Tyson [8], Nethercott [51] | 3576 |
| 29 | 30 | A | Sheffield W | D | 1-1 | 1-0 | — | Simpemba [2] | 19,596 |
| 30 | Feb 7 | H | Brighton & HA | D | 1-1 | 1-1 | 24 | Tyson [45] | 6567 |
| 31 | 14 | H | Luton T | D | 0-0 | 0-0 | 24 | | 6407 |
| 32 | 21 | A | Barnsley | D | 0-0 | 0-0 | 24 | | 8507 |
| 33 | 28 | H | Hartlepool U | L | 3-4 | 2-3 | 24 | Simpemba [8], McSporran [23], Tyson [64] | 4731 |
| 34 | Mar 2 | A | Bristol C | D | 1-1 | 0-0 | — | McSporran [72] | 12,291 |
| 35 | 6 | A | Bournemouth | L | 0-1 | 0-1 | 24 | | 7311 |
| 36 | 13 | H | Notts Co | D | 1-1 | 0-1 | 24 | Tyson [78] | 5125 |
| 37 | 16 | A | Colchester U | D | 1-1 | 1-1 | — | Simpson [38] | 3092 |
| 38 | 20 | H | QPR | D | 2-2 | 2-0 | 24 | Bloomfield [27], Faulconbridge [30] | 7634 |
| 39 | 27 | A | Oldham Ath | W | 3-2 | 2-2 | 24 | Tyson 2 [23, 42], Faulconbridge [88] | 5758 |
| 40 | Apr 3 | H | Port Vale | W | 2-1 | 1-1 | 24 | Currie 2 (1 pen) [42 (p), 74] | 4738 |
| 41 | 10 | A | Plymouth Arg | L | 1-2 | 1-1 | 24 | Tyson [5] | 14,806 |
| 42 | 12 | H | Tranmere R | L | 1-2 | 0-2 | 24 | Johnson [88] | 5256 |
| 43 | 17 | H | Swindon T | L | 0-3 | 0-1 | 24 | | 5769 |
| 44 | 24 | A | Brentford | D | 1-1 | 0-0 | 24 | Tyson [54] | 7145 |
| 45 | May 1 | H | Wrexham | D | 1-1 | 0-0 | 24 | Johnson [79] | 4684 |
| 46 | 8 | A | Peterborough U | D | 1-1 | 0-0 | 24 | Tyson [90] | 6398 |

**Final League Position: 24**

## GOALSCORERS

*League (50):* Tyson 9, Currie 7 (2 pens), McSporran 7, Moore 4, Bell 3, Mapes 3, Faulconbridge 2, Holligan 2, Johnson 2, Patterson 2, Simpemba 2, Simpson 2, Bloomfield 1, Brown 1 (pen), Nethercott 1, Ryan 1, Thomson 1.
*Carling Cup (2):* Harris 2.
*FA Cup (7):* McSporran 3, Currie 2, Holligan 1, Thomson 1.
*LDV Vans Trophy (5):* McSporran 2, Branston 1, Johnson 1, Thomson 1.

| Williams S 19 / Henderson W 3 | Senda D 37+3 | Vinnicombe C 36 | Mapes C 10+5 | Rogers M 15 | Johnson R 28 | Currie D 42 | Simpson M 38 | Harris R 6+4 / Hole S —+1 | Patterson S 3+1 | McSporran J 29+4 | Oliver L —+2 | Bulman D 30+8 | Harding B —+2 | Onuora I 6 | Dixon J 2+6 | Dell S 3+1 | Talia F 17 | Cook L 1+4 | Roberts S 5+11 | Brown S 18+7 | Holligan G 8+5 | Ryan K 10+7 | Branston G 9 | Bell A 3+8 | Thomson A 11 | Simpemba I 17+2 | Marshall S 8 | Faulconbridge C 11+5 | Taylor S 6 | Moore L 6 | Reilly A 5 | Bloomfield M 10+2 | Nethercott S 22 | Tyson N 21 | Bevan S 5 | Philo M 4+8 | Worgan L 2 | *Match No.* |
|---|---|---|---|---|---|---|---|---|---|---|---|---|---|---|---|---|---|---|---|---|---|---|---|---|---|---|---|---|---|---|---|---|---|---|---|---|---|---|
| 1 | 2 | 3 | 4 | 5$^{1}$ | 6 | 7$^{2}$ | 8 | 9 | 10$^{3}$ | 11 | 12 | 13 | 14 ||||||||||||||||||||||||| 1 |
| 1 | 2$^{3}$ | 3 | 4$^{1}$ | 5 | 6 | 7 | 8 | 9$^{2}$ | 10 | 11 | 14 | 12 | 13 ||||||||||||||||||||||||| 2 |
| 1 | 12 | 3 | 4$^{2}$ | 5 | 6 | 7 | 8 || 14 | 11$^{1}$ || 13 || 9 | 10$^{3}$ | 2 |||||||||||||||||||||| 3 |
|| 12 | 3 | 13 | 5 | 6 | 7 | 8$^{2}$ || 10$^{1}$ | 11$^{3}$ || 4 || 9 | 14 | 2 | 1 ||||||||||||||||||||| 4 |
|| 12 | 3$^{3}$ | 4 | 5 | 6 | 7 | 8 | 9 || 11$^{2}$ |||| 10 | 13 | 2$^{1}$ | 1 | 14 |||||||||||||||||||| 5 |
|| 2 | 3■ || 5$^{1}$ | 6 | 7 | 8 | 9 || 11$^{2}$ || 4 || 10$^{3}$ ||| 1■ || 12 | 14 | 13 ||||||||||||||||| 6 |
|| 2 | 3 || 5 | 6 | 7 | 8 | 9$^{1}$ || 11$^{3}$ || 4 || 10$^{2}$ | 12 || 1 |||| 13 | 14 |||||||||||||||| 7 |
|| 2 | 3 || 5$^{1}$ | 6■ | 7 | 8 | 9$^{3}$ || 11 || 4 || 10$^{2}$ ||| 1 || 12■ || 13 | 14 |||||||||||||||| 8 |
| 1 |||| 5$^{1}$ | 6 | 11 | 8 ||| 12 || 7$^{3}$ |||| 14 || 13 || 3 | 10 | 2$^{2}$ | 4 | 9 |||||||||||||| 9 |
|| 2 | 3 | 4$^{1}$ ||| 11 | 8 | 13 |||| 7 ||||| 1 | 12 | 9$^{3}$ || 10$^{2}$ || 5 | 14 | 6 ||||||||||||| 10 |
|| 2 | 3 | 9$^{1}$ ||| 7$^{2}$ | 8 | 12 |||| 4 ||||| 1 | 11$^{3}$ ||| 10 | 13 | 5 | 14 | 6 ||||||||||||| 11 |
|| 2 | 3 |||| 7 | 8 | 12 |||| 4 ||||| 1 | 13 || 11$^{2}$ | 10$^{3}$ | 6$^{1}$ | 9 | 14 | 5 ||||||||||||| 12 |
|| 2 | 3 | 12 ||| 7$^{1}$ | 8 | 13 |||| 4 ||||| 1 ||| 11 | 10$^{2}$ | 9$^{3}$ | 5 | 14 | 6 ||||||||||||| 13 |
|| 2 | 3 |||| 7$^{2}$ | 8 ||| 12 || 4 ||||| 1 || 14 | 11 | 13 | 10$^{1}$ | 5 | 9$^{3}$ | 6 ||||||||||||| 14 |
|| 2 | 3 |||| 7 | 8 ||| 9 || 4 ||||| 1 || 12 | 11$^{1}$ | 10 || 5 || 6 ||||||||||||| 15 |
|| 2 | 3 |||| 7 | 8 ||| 9 || 4 ||||| 1 || 12 | 11$^{1}$ | 10$^{2}$ | 13 | 5 || 6 ||||||||||||| 16 |
|| 2 | 3 |||| 7$^{3}$ | 8 ||| 9 || 4 ||||| 1 || 12 | 11$^{1}$ | 10$^{2}$ | 14 | 5 | 13 | 6 ||||||||||||| 17 |
|| 2 | 3 ||| 6 | 7 | 8 ||| 9 || 4 ||||| 1 || 10 | 12 || 11$^{1}$ ||| 5 ||||||||||||| 18 |
|| 2 | 3 | 10$^{1}$ ||| 7 |||| 9 || 12 ||||| 1 || 11$^{2}$ | 8 ||||| 6 | 4 | 5 | 13 |||||||||| 19 |
|| 2 | 3 |||| 7 |||| 9$^{2}$ ||||||| 1 || 10 | 11$^{1}$ | 12 | 8 ||| 6 | 4 | 5 | 13 |||||||||| 20 |
| 1 || 3 | 10$^{1}$ | 2 | 6 | 7 | 8 ||| 11 || 4$^{3}$ ||| 13 ||||||| 12 |||||| 14 | 5 | 9$^{2}$ |||||||| 21 |
| 1 || 3 || 2 | 6 | 7 | 8 ||| 11$^{1}$ || 12 |||||||||| 4 || 13 |||| 10 | 5 | 9$^{2}$ |||||||| 22 |
| 1 || 3$^{1}$ || 2■ | 6■ | 7 | 8 ||| 11 || 12 ||||||| 13 ||| 4$^{2}$ |||| 14 || 10$^{3}$ | 5 | 9 |||||||| 23 |
| 1 | 2 || 8$^{1}$ ||||||| 11 || 12 ||||||| 13 ||| 6 || 14 || 4 || 10 | 5 | 9$^{2}$ | 3 | 7$^{3}$ |||||| 24 |
| 1 |||||| 7 | 8 ||| 11 || 4 ||||||| 12 ||||||| 3 | 5 || 2 | 9 ||| 6 | 10$^{1}$ |||| 25 |
| 1 |||||| 7$^{2}$ | 8$^{1}$ ||| 11 || 4 ||||||| 14 | 12 || 13 || 10$^{3}$ || 3 | 5 || 2 | 9 ||| 6 ||||| 26 |
|| 2 ||||| 7 |||||| 4 ||||||| 9 ||| 8$^{1}$ || 12 || 3 | 5 | 10$^{2}$ |||| 13 | 6 | 11 | 1 ||| 27 |
|| 2 ||||| 7$^{1}$ | 8 ||| 9 || 4 ||||||| 12 ||||||| 11 | 5 |||| 6 || 3 | 10 | 1 ||| 28 |
|| 2 ||||| 7 | 8 ||| 9 || 4 |||||||| 12 |||||| 11$^{1}$ | 5 |||| 3 || 6 | 10 | 1 ||| 29 |
|| 2 ||||| 7 | 8 ||| 9 || 4 |||||||| 11 ||||||| 5 |||| 3 || 6 | 10 | 1 ||| 30 |
|| 2 | 3 ||| 5 | 7 | 8 ||| 9 || 4 |||||||| 11 ||||||||||||| 6 | 10 | 1 ||| 31 |
|| 2 | 3 ||| 5 | 7 | 8 ||| 9$^{1}$ || 4 ||||| 1 ||| 11 ||||||||||||| 6 | 10 || 12 || 32 |
| 1 | 2 | 3 |||| 7 | 8 ||| 9 || 4$^{1}$ |||||||| 11$^{2}$ |||||| 5$^{3}$ || 12 |||| 13 | 6 | 10 || 14 || 33 |
| 1 | 2 | 3 ||| 5 | 7$^{2}$ |||| 9 || 4 |||||||| 11 |||||| 12 |||||| 8$^{1}$ | 6 | 10 || 13 || 34 |
| 1 | 2 | 3 ||| 5 | 7$^{1}$ |||| 12 || 4 |||||||| 11$^{2}$ |||||| 8 || 13 ||||| 6 | 10 || 9 || 35 |
| 1 | 2 | 3 ||| 5 | 7 | 8 ||| 11$^{1}$ || 4 |||||||||||||||| 9 ||||| 6 | 10 || 12 || 36 |
| 1 | 2 | 3 ||| 5 | 7 | 8 ||| 11 |||||||||||||||||| 9 |||| 4 | 6 | 10 |||| 37 |
| 1 | 2 | 3 || 4$^{1}$ | 5 | 7$^{3}$ | 8 ||| 12 |||||||||| 13 |||||||| 9$^{2}$ |||| 11 | 6 | 10 || 14 || 38 |
| 1 | 2 | 3 || 4 | 5 | 7 | 8 ||||||||||||||||||||| 9 |||| 11 | 6 | 10 |||| 39 |
| 1 | 2 | 3 ||| 5 | 7 | 8 ||||||||||||||||||| 4 || 9 |||| 11 | 6 | 10 |||| 40 |
| 1$^{6}$ | 2 | 3 ||| 5 | 7 | 8 ||||| 13 |||||||| 12 |||||| 4 || 9$^{1}$ |||| 11$^{2}$ | 6 | 10 || 15 || 41 |
|| 2 | 3$^{2}$ | 13 || 5 | 7 | 8 ||||| 4 ||| 12 ||||||||||| 11 || 9$^{3}$ ||||| 6 | 10$^{1}$ || 14 | 1 | 42 |
|| 2 || 13 | 3$^{1}$ | 5 | 7$^{3}$ | 8 ||||| 4$^{2}$ ||| 9 ||||| 12 |||||| 11 ||||||| 6 | 10 || 14 | 1 | 43 |
| 1 | 2 | 3 ||| 5 || 8 ||||||||||||| 4 |||||| 11 |||||| 7 | 6 | 10 || 9 || 44 |
| 1 | 2 | 3 | 12 || 5 ||||||| 4$^{1}$ |||||||| 8 |||||| 11 |||||| 7 | 6 | 10 || 9 || 45 |
| 1 | 2 || 4$^{1}$ || 5 ||| 13 ||||||| 12 ||||| 8 |||||| 11$^{2}$ ||||| 3 | 7 | 6 | 10 || 9 || 46 |

**Carling Cup**
First Round Wimbledon (h) 2-0
Second Round Aston Villa (h) 0-5

**LDV Vans Trophy**
First Round Cambridge U (h) 1-0
Second Round Plymouth Arg (a) 2-2
Quarter-Final Colchester U (h) 2-3

**FA Cup**
First Round Swindon T (h) 4-1
Second Round Mansfield T (h) 1-1
(a) 2-3

# YEOVIL TOWN FL Championship 2

## FOUNDATION

One of the prime movers of Yeovil football was Ernest J. Sercombe. His association with the club began in 1895 as a playing member of Yeovil Casuals, of which team he became vice-captain and in his last season 1899–1900, he was chosen to play for Somerset against Devon. Upon the reorganisation of the club, he became secretary of the old Yeovil Town FC and with the amalgamation with Petters United in 1914, he continued to serve until his resignation in 1930.

***Huish Park, Lufton Way, Yeovil, Somerset BA22 8YF.***

***Telephone:*** (01935) 423 662.

***Fax:*** (01935) 473 956.

***Ticket Office:*** (01935) 847 888.

***Website:*** www.ytfc.net

***Email:*** jcotton@ytfc.co.uk

***Ground Capacity:*** 9,564.

***Record Attendance:*** 8,612 v Arsenal, F.A. Cup 3rd rd, 2 January 1993 (16,318 v Sunderland at Huish).

***Chairman/Chief Executive:*** John R. Fry.

***Secretary:*** Jean Cotton

***Manager:*** Gary Johnson.

***Assistant Manager:*** Steve Thompson.

***Physio:*** Tony Farmer.

***Colours:*** Green and white hooped shirts, white shorts, white stockings.

***Change Colours:*** Red and black striped shirts, black shorts, black stockings.

***Year formed:*** 1895.

***Turned Professional:*** 1921.

***Ltd Co.:*** 1923.

## HONOURS

*FA Cup:* 5th rd 1949.

*League Cup:* 1st rd 2004.

*Conference:* Champions 2002–03.

*Southern League:* Champions 1954–55, 1963–64, 1970–71; Runners-up: 1923–24, 1931–32, 1934–35, 1969–70, 1972–73.

*Southern League Cup:* Winners 1948–49, 1954–55, 1960–61, 1965–66; Runners-up: 1946–47, 1955–56.

*Isthmian League*: Winners 1987–88; Runners-up: 1985–86, 1986–87, 1996–97.

*AC Delco Cup:* Winners 1987–88.

*Bob Lord Trophy:* Winners 1989–90.

*FA Trophy:* Winners 2002.

*London Combination:* Runners-up 1930–31, 1932–33.

## SKY SPORTS FACT FILE

In 1931–32 Yeovil Town scored an incredible 225 goals in all competitions including 81 away from home. The club also reached the second round of the FA Cup for the first time and later transferred 12 players to Football League clubs.

***Club Nickname:*** "Glovers".

***Previous names:*** 1895 Yeovil; 1907 Yeovil Town; 1914 Yeovil & Petters United; 1946 Yeovil Town.

***Previous grounds:*** Pen Mill Ground 1895–1921; Huish 1921–1990; Huish Park 1990.

***Record League Victory:*** 10–0 v Kidderminster H, Southern League, 27 December 1955. 10–0 v Bedford T, Southern League, 4 March 1961.

***Record Cup Victory:*** 12–1 v Westbury United, FA Cup 1st qual rd, 1923–24.

## MANAGERS

*(since 1990)*
Clive Whitehead
Steve Rutter
Brian Hall
Graham Roberts
Colin Lippiatt
Steve Thompson
Dave Webb
Gary Johnson June 2001–

***Record Defeat:*** 0–8 v Manchester United, FA Cup 5th rd, 12 February 1949.

***Most League Goals:*** Dave Taylor, 285, Southern League 1960–69.

***Highest League Scorer in Season:*** Dave Taylor, 59, Southern League 1960–61 (in all competitions Cecil Pemberton, 69, 1931–32).

***Most League Appearances:*** Len Harris, 691, 1958–1972.

***Record Transfer Fee Received:*** £75,000 from Bristol C for Mark Shail.

***Record Transfer Fee Paid:*** £25,000 to Hereford U for Michael McIndoe, February 2001.

***Football League Record:*** 2003 Promoted to Division 3 from Conference; 2003–04 Division 3; 2004– FL2

## LATEST SEQUENCES

***Longest Sequence of League Wins:*** 4, 6.9.2003 – 20.9.2003.

***Longest Sequence of Unbeaten League Matches:*** 5, 15.11.2003 – 20.12.2003.

***Longest Sequence Without a League Win:*** 5, 16.3.2004 – 17.4.2004.

***Successive Scoring Runs:*** 6 from 12.4.2004 – continuing.

## TEN YEAR LEAGUE RECORD

| | | *P* | *W* | *D* | *L* | *F* | *A* | *Pts* | *Pos* |
|---|---|---|---|---|---|---|---|---|---|
| 1994–95 | Conf. | 42 | 8 | 14 | 20 | 50 | 71 | 37* | 22 |
| 1995–96 | Isth. | 42 | 23 | 11 | 8 | 83 | 51 | 80 | 4 |
| 1996–97 | Isth. | 42 | 31 | 8 | 3 | 83 | 34 | 101 | 1 |
| 1997–98 | Conf. | 42 | 17 | 8 | 17 | 73 | 63 | 59 | 11 |
| 1998–99 | Conf. | 42 | 20 | 11 | 11 | 68 | 54 | 71 | 5 |
| 1999–2000 | Conf. | 42 | 18 | 10 | 14 | 60 | 63 | 64 | 7 |
| 2000–01 | Conf. | 42 | 24 | 8 | 10 | 73 | 50 | 80 | 2 |
| 2001–02 | Conf. | 42 | 19 | 13 | 10 | 66 | 53 | 70 | 3 |
| 2002–03 | Conf. | 42 | 28 | 11 | 3 | 100 | 37 | 95 | 1 |
| 2003-04 | Div 3 | 46 | 23 | 5 | 18 | 70 | 57 | 74 | 8 |

*1 point deducted.

## DID YOU KNOW ?

Famed FA Cup fighters, Yeovil Town had their earliest success against a Football League team in 1924–25 when after eliminating Westbury, Warminster and Taunton, they met Bournemouth. Taking a shock 3-0 lead they survived a comeback to win 3-2.

## YEOVIL TOWN 2003–04 LEAGUE RECORD

| Match No. | Date | Venue | Opponents | Result | H/T Score | Lg. Pos. | Goalscorers | Attendance |
|---|---|---|---|---|---|---|---|---|
| 1 | Aug 9 | A | Rochdale | W 3-1 | 1-1 | — | Gall 2 [26, 67], Johnson [55] | 4611 |
| 2 | 16 | H | Carlisle U | W 3-0 | 2-0 | 1 | Gall 2 [4, 18], Jackson [79] | 6347 |
| 3 | 23 | A | Leyton Orient | L 0-2 | 0-1 | 7 | | 4431 |
| 4 | 25 | H | Northampton T | L 0-2 | 0-2 | 8 | | 6105 |
| 5 | 30 | A | Macclesfield T | L 1-4 | 0-2 | 18 | Lockwood [63] | 2221 |
| 6 | Sept 6 | H | Swansea C | W 2-0 | 1-0 | 12 | Stansfield [39], Jackson [56] | 6656 |
| 7 | 13 | H | York C | W 3-0 | 2-0 | 5 | Jackson [21], Pluck [34], Stansfield [90] | 5653 |
| 8 | 16 | A | Doncaster R | W 1-0 | 1-0 | — | Williams [35] | 4716 |
| 9 | 20 | A | Mansfield T | W 1-0 | 1-0 | 3 | Jackson [42] | 5270 |
| 10 | 27 | H | Torquay U | L 0-2 | 0-1 | 5 | | 7718 |
| 11 | 30 | H | Boston U | W 2-0 | 2-0 | — | Williams (pen) [21], Lockwood [38] | 5093 |
| 12 | Oct 4 | A | Cheltenham T | L 1-3 | 1-2 | 6 | Gall [40] | 4960 |
| 13 | 11 | A | Oxford U | L 0-1 | 0-1 | 8 | | 6301 |
| 14 | 18 | H | Darlington | W 1-0 | 1-0 | 6 | Williams (pen) [5] | 4892 |
| 15 | 21 | H | Huddersfield T | W 2-1 | 1-1 | — | Skiverton [4], Johnson [51] | 5274 |
| 16 | 25 | A | Cambridge U | W 4-1 | 1-1 | 5 | Edwards 2 [16, 59], Gall [61], Way [87] | 4072 |
| 17 | Nov 1 | A | Bury | L 1-2 | 1-1 | 6 | Edwards [31] | 3086 |
| 18 | 15 | H | Southend U | W 4-0 | 3-0 | 5 | Elam [33], Way [40], Johnson 2 (1 pen) [43, 56 (p)] | 5248 |
| 19 | 22 | A | Hull C | D 0-0 | 0-0 | 5 | | 14,367 |
| 20 | 29 | H | Lincoln C | W 3-1 | 0-0 | 5 | Pluck [54], Stansfield [85], Gosling [90] | 4867 |
| 21 | Dec 13 | A | Bristol R | W 1-0 | 1-0 | 4 | Crittenden [43] | 9812 |
| 22 | 20 | H | Scunthorpe U | W 2-1 | 0-1 | 3 | Jackson [71], Lindegaard [82] | 5714 |
| 23 | 26 | H | Kidderminster H | L 1-2 | 0-1 | 5 | Gall [58] | 5640 |
| 24 | 28 | A | Swansea C | L 2-3 | 0-1 | 5 | Williams [73], Gall [89] | 9800 |
| 25 | Jan 10 | H | Rochdale | W 1-0 | 1-0 | 5 | Williams [13] | 5806 |
| 26 | 17 | A | Carlisle U | L 0-2 | 0-1 | 5 | | 5455 |
| 27 | 24 | H | Leyton Orient | L 1-2 | 0-2 | 6 | Crittenden [76] | 6299 |
| 28 | 31 | H | Macclesfield T | D 2-2 | 1-2 | 6 | Edwards [30], Way [60] | 5257 |
| 29 | Feb 3 | A | Northampton T | L 0-2 | 0-0 | — | | 4363 |
| 30 | 7 | A | Kidderminster H | W 1-0 | 0-0 | 5 | Williams [64] | 3255 |
| 31 | 14 | H | Oxford U | W 1-0 | 1-0 | 5 | Bishop [29] | 7404 |
| 32 | 21 | A | Darlington | L 2-3 | 1-2 | 6 | Johnson [22], Lockwood [90] | 4500 |
| 33 | 28 | H | Cambridge U | W 4-1 | 3-1 | 6 | Williams (pen) [18], Bishop [19], Stansfield [27], Pluck [48] | 5694 |
| 34 | Mar 2 | A | Huddersfield T | L 1-3 | 0-1 | — | Way [78] | 9395 |
| 35 | 6 | A | Scunthorpe U | L 0-3 | 0-2 | 7 | | 3355 |
| 36 | 13 | H | Bristol R | W 4-0 | 2-0 | 7 | Lockwood [16], El Kholti [43], Williams [49], Pluck [72] | 8726 |
| 37 | 16 | H | Doncaster R | L 0-1 | 0-0 | — | | 7587 |
| 38 | 27 | H | Mansfield T | D 1-1 | 0-0 | 8 | Skiverton [61] | 6002 |
| 39 | Apr 3 | A | Torquay U | D 2-2 | 2-1 | 8 | Way [17], Edwards [27] | 6156 |
| 40 | 10 | H | Cheltenham T | D 0-0 | 0-0 | 9 | | 6613 |
| 41 | 12 | A | Boston U | L 2-3 | 1-2 | 9 | Weatherstone [4], Stansfield [51] | 2848 |
| 42 | 17 | H | Bury | W 2-1 | 0-1 | 9 | Rodrigues D 2 [55, 59] | 5172 |
| 43 | 20 | A | York C | W 2-1 | 0-1 | — | Terry [46], Lindegaard [70] | 2802 |
| 44 | 24 | A | Southend U | W 2-0 | 2-0 | 7 | Rodrigues D 2 [21, 32] | 5676 |
| 45 | May 1 | H | Hull C | L 1-2 | 0-1 | 8 | Rodrigues H [64] | 8760 |
| 46 | 8 | A | Lincoln C | W 3-2 | 0-0 | 8 | Stansfield [47], Edwards [71], Williams [89] | 8154 |

**Final League Position: 8**

### GOALSCORERS

*League (70):* Williams 9 (3 pens), Gall 8, Edwards 6, Stansfield 6, Jackson 5, Johnson 5 (1 pen), Way 5, Lockwood 4, Pluck 4, Rodrigues D 4, Bishop 2, Crittenden 2, Lindegaard 2, Skiverton 2, El Kholti 1, Elam 1, Gosling 1, Rodrigues H 1, Terry 1, Weatherstone 1.
*Carling Cup (1):* own goal 1.
*FA Cup (9):* Williams 3 (1 pen), Edwards 2, Pluck 2, Crittenden 1, Gall 1.
*LDV Vans Trophy (4):* Edwards 2, Gall 1, Williams 1 (pen).

| Weale C 35 | Williams G 42 | Crittenden N 20 + 9 | Lockwood A 43 | O'Brien R 13 | Pluck C 36 | Gosling J 4 + 8 | Way D 38 + 1 | Jackson K 19 + 11 | Gall K 39 + 4 | Johnson L 45 | Lindegaard A 12 + 11 | Rodrigues H 23 + 11 | El Kholti A 19 + 4 | Stansfield A 7 + 25 | Terry P 22 + 12 | Bull R 7 | Edwards J 17 + 10 | Skiverton T 25 + 1 | Elam L 6 + 6 | Reed S 3 + 2 | Weatherstone S 11 + 4 | Giles C — + 1 | Bishop A 4 + 1 | Collis S 11 | Matthews L 2 + 2 | Rodrigues D 3 + 1 | Talbott N — + 1 | Match No. |
|---|---|---|---|---|---|---|---|---|---|---|---|---|---|---|---|---|---|---|---|---|---|---|---|---|---|---|---|---|
| 1 | $2^{1}$ | 3 | 4 | 5 | $6^{2}$ | $7^{3}$ | 8 | 9 | 10 | 11 | 12 | 13 | 14 | | | | | | | | | | | | | | | 1 |
| 1 | $2^{1}$ | 3 | 4 | 5 | 6 | $7^{2}$ | 8 | $9^{3}$ | 10 | 11 | 12 | | 13 | 14 | | | | | | | | | | | | | | 2 |
| 1 | 11 | $3^{3}$ | 4 | $5^{2}$ | 6 | $2^{1}$ | 7 | 9 | 10 | 8 | | 13 | 12 | | 14 | | | | | | | | | | | | | 3 |
| 1 | 2 | | 4 | 5 | $6^{1}$ | | 8 | $9^{3}$ | 10 | 11 | $7^{2}$ | 12 | 3 | 14 | 13 | | | | | | | | | | | | | 4 |
| 1 | 2 | | 4 | 5 | 6 | | 8 | 9 | 10 | 11 | 12 | | $3^{1}$ | 13 | $7^{2}$ | | | | | | | | | | | | | 5 |
| 1 | 7 | $3^{1}$ | 4 | 5 | 6 | 12 | 8 | $9^{2}$ | | 11 | | | | $10^{3}$ | 13 | 2 | 14 | | | | | | | | | | | 6 |
| 1 | 2 | 3 | 4 | 5 | 6 | 12 | 8 | $9^{2}$ | $10^{3}$ | 11 | | | | 14 | | $7^{1}$ | 13 | | | | | | | | | | | 7 |
| 1 | 2 | $3^{2}$ | 4 | 5 | 6 | | 8 | $9^{1}$ | 10 | 11 | | 14 | | 12 | 13 | $7^{3}$ | | | | | | | | | | | | 8 |
| 1 | 2 | $3^{1}$ | 4 | $5^{1}$ | 6 | 12 | 8 | $9^{3}$ | $10^{2}$ | 11 | | | | 13 | 14 | 7 | | | | | | | | | | | | 9 |
| 1 | 2 | 3 | 4 | 5 | $6^{3}$ | 12 | 8 | $9^{2}$ | 10 | 11 | | 14 | | 13 | | $7^{1}$ | | | | | | | | | | | | 10 |
| 1 | 2 | | 4 | 5 | | | 8 | $9^{2}$ | 10 | 11 | | 6 | $3^{1}$ | | 12 | 7 | 13 | | | | | | | | | | | 11 |
| 1 | 2 | | 4 | 5 | | 12 | 8 | $9^{3}$ | 10 | 11 | | $6^{2}$ | 3 | | 13 | $7^{1}$ | 14 | | | | | | | | | | | 12 |
| 1 | 2 | 3 | 4 | $5^{2}$ | 6 | | $8^{1}$ | 9 | $10^{3}$ | 11 | | 13 | | | 12 | | 14 | 7 | | | | | | | | | | 13 |
| 1 | 2 | 12 | 4 | | 6 | | $8^{1}$ | | 10 | 11 | | $5^{2}$ | 3 | 14 | 13 | | $9^{3}$ | 7 | | | | | | | | | | 14 |
| 1 | 2 | 12 | 4 | | 6 | | 8 | 13 | 10 | 11 | | 5 | $3^{1}$ | | 14 | | $9^{2}$ | $7^{3}$ | | | | | | | | | | 15 |
| 1 | 2 | 12 | 4 | | 6 | | 8 | 13 | $10^{3}$ | 11 | | 5 | $3^{1}$ | 14 | | | $9^{2}$ | 7 | | | | | | | | | | 16 |
| 1 | $2^{3}$ | | 4 | | 6 | | 8 | 12 | 10 | 11 | | | $3^{2}$ | 13 | 7 | | $9^{1}$ | | 14 | 5■ | | | | | | | | 17 |
| 1 | | 3 | 4 | | 6 | 13 | 8 | 12 | 10 | 11 | | | | 14 | $2^{3}$ | | $9^{1}$ | 5 | $7^{2}$ | | | | | | | | | 18 |
| 1 | 2 | $3^{3}$ | 4 | | 6 | 13 | | 12 | 10 | 11 | | $5^{2}$ | | | 8 | | $9^{1}$ | 7 | 14 | | | | | | | | | 19 |
| 1 | 2 | 12 | 4 | | 6 | 13 | | $9^{2}$ | $10^{3}$ | 11 | | 5 | | 14 | 8 | | | 7 | $3^{1}$ | | | | | | | | | 20 |
| 1 | 2 | 3 | 4 | | 6 | | | $9^{2}$ | $10^{1}$ | 11 | | 5 | | 12 | 8 | | 13■ | 7 | | | | | | | | | | 21 |
| 1 | | 3 | | | $6^{1}$ | $11^{3}$ | | 12 | 10 | | 2 | 5 | | 13 | 8 | | $9^{2}$ | 4 | 7 | 14 | | | | | | | | 22 |
| 1 | 2 | $3^{3}$ | $4^{1}$ | | 6 | | | $9^{2}$ | 10 | 11 | | 5 | | 13 | 8 | | 12 | 7 | 14 | | | | | | | | | 23 |
| 1 | 2 | $3^{3}$ | $4^{1}$ | | 6 | | 12 | 13 | 10 | 11 | 14 | 5 | | $9^{2}$ | 8 | | | 7 | | | | | | | | | | 24 |
| 1 | 2 | 3 | 4 | | | | 8 | 12 | $9^{2}$ | 11 | | 5 | | 13 | 10 | | | 6 | $7^{1}$ | | | | | | | | | 25 |
| 1 | | | | | 6 | | 8 | | 10 | 11 | | 5 | $12^{2}$ | 13 | 2 | | 9 | 4 | 7 | $3^{1}$ | | | | | | | | 26 |
| 1 | 2 | 12 | 4 | | 6 | | 8 | | 10 | 11 | | | | | $7^{2}$ | | 13 | 5 | $3^{1}$ | | 9 | | | | | | | 27 |
| 1 | 2 | | 4 | | $6^{2}$ | | 8 | | $10^{3}$ | 11 | 13 | 12 | | | 7 | | 9 | 5 | | | $3^{1}$ | 14 | | | | | | 28 |
| 1 | 2 | | 4 | | | | 8 | | $10^{1}$ | 11 | 6 | 5 | 3 | 12 | $7^{2}$ | | 9 | | | | 13 | | | | | | | 29 |
| 1 | 2 | $3^{1}$ | 4 | | | | 8 | | 13 | 11 | 7 | 5 | 6 | | | | $9^{3}$ | | $12^{2}$ | | 10 | | 14 | | | | | 30 |
| 1 | 2 | | 4 | | | | 8 | | $10^{1}$ | 11 | 13 | 5 | 3 | 12 | 6 | | | | | | $7^{2}$ | | 9 | | | | | 31 |
| 1 | 2 | | 4 | | | | 8 | | $10^{2}$ | 11 | 13 | 5 | 3 | 12 | 6■ | | | | 14 | | $7^{3}$ | | $9^{1}$ | | | | | 32 |
| 1 | 2 | | 4 | | 5 | | 8 | | 12 | 11 | 13 | | 3 | $10^{2}$ | | | | 6 | | | 7 | | $9^{1}$ | | | | | 33 |
| 1 | 2 | | 4 | | $5^{2}$ | | 8 | 12 | | 11 | 14 | 13 | 3 | 10 | $6^{3}$ | | | | | | 7 | | $9^{1}$ | | | | | 34 |
| 1 | 2 | | 4 | | | | 8 | 12 | 13 | 11 | 7 | $5^{1}$ | 3 | $10^{3}$ | | | | | 14 | 6 | $9^{2}$ | | | | | | | 35 |
| | 2 | | 4 | | 5 | | 8 | 9 | 10 | 11 | $7^{2}$ | 12 | $3^{3}$ | | 13 | | | $6^{1}$ | | | 14 | | | 1 | | | | 36 |
| | 2 | | 4 | | 5 | | 8 | 9 | $10^{1}$ | 11 | 7 | | 3 | 12 | | | | 6 | | | | | | 1 | | | | 37 |
| | 2 | | 4 | | 5 | | 8 | $9^{3}$ | $10^{1}$ | 11 | 13 | | 3 | 12 | | | | $6^{2}$ | | | 7 | | | 1 | 14 | | | 38 |
| | 2■ | $3^{1}$ | | | 5 | | 8 | | 12 | 11 | | | 6 | 13 | 7 | | $9^{2}$ | 4 | | | | | | 1 | 10 | | | 39 |
| | 2 | 3 | $4^{2}$ | | $5^{1}$ | | 8 | | 10 | 11 | 6 | 12 | | | | | $9^{3}$ | 7 | | 13 | | | | 1 | 14 | | | 40 |
| | 2 | 12 | 4 | | | | $8^{1}$ | | | 11 | | 5 | | 9 | 3 | | 13 | 6 | | | 7 | | | 1 | $10^{2}$ | | | 41 |
| | | 3 | 4 | | 5 | | | | $10^{3}$ | 11 | 12 | $6^{1}$ | | $8^{2}$ | 2 | | 9 | 7 | | | | | | 1 | | 13 | 14 | 42 |
| | 2 | 12 | 4 | | 5 | | | 13 | 8 | 11 | 7 | 14 | | | 3 | | $9^{2}$ | $6^{3}$ | | | | | | 1 | | $10^{1}$ | | 43 |
| | 2 | 12 | 4 | | 5 | | $8^{3}$ | | 7 | 11 | 3 | 6 | | 13 | | | $9^{1}$ | | | | 14 | | | 1 | | $10^{2}$ | | 44 |
| | 2 | | 4 | | $5^{1}$ | | 8 | | 7 | 11 | 3 | 6 | | | 13 | | $9^{2}$ | 12 | | | 14 | | | 1 | | $10^{3}$ | | 45 |
| | 2 | 12 | $4^{1}$ | | | | 8 | | $10^{3}$ | 11 | 3 | 6 | | 13 | 7 | | 14 | 5 | | | $9^{2}$ | | | 1 | | | | 46 |

**Carling Cup**

| | | | |
|---|---|---|---|
| First Round | Luton T | (a) | 1-4 |

**LDV Vans Trophy**

| | | | |
|---|---|---|---|
| First Round | Bournemouth | (h) | 2-0 |
| Second Round | Colchester U | (h) | 2-2 |

**FA Cup**

| | | | |
|---|---|---|---|
| First Round | Wrexham | (h) | 4-1 |
| Second Round | Barnet | (h) | 5-1 |
| Third Round | Liverpool | (h) | 0-2 |

# YORK CITY Conference National

## FOUNDATION

Although there was a York City club formed in 1903 by a soccer enthusiast from Darlington, this has no connection with the modern club because it went out of existence during World War I. Unlike many others of that period who restarted in 1919, York City did not re-form until 1922 and the tendency now is to ignore the modern club's pre-1922 existence.

***Bootham Crescent, York YO30 7AQ.***

***Telephone:*** (01904) 624 447.

***Fax:*** (01904) 631 457.

***Ticket Office:*** (01904) 624 447 (ext 2).

***Email:*** keith.usher@ycfc.net

***Ground Capacity:*** 9,496.

***Record Attendance:*** 28,123 v Huddersfield T, FA Cup 6th rd, 5 March 1938.

***Pitch Measurements:*** 115yd × 74yd.

***Chairman:*** Steve Beck.

***Chief Executive:*** Keith Usher.

***Manager:*** Chris Brass.

***Assistant Manager:*** Lee Nogan.

***Physio:*** Jeff Miller.

***Colours:*** Red shirts, navy shorts, navy stockings.

***Change Colours:*** Light blue shirts, navy shorts, navy stockings.

***Year Formed:*** 1922.

***Turned Professional:*** 1922.

***Ltd Co.:*** 1922.

***Club Nickname:*** 'Minstermen'.

***Previous Grounds:*** 1922, Fulfordgate; 1932, Bootham Crescent.

***First Football League Game:*** 31 August 1929, Division 3 (N), v Wigan Borough (a) W 2–0 – Farmery; Archibald, Johnson; Beck, Davis, Thompson; Evans, Gardner, Cowie (1), Smailes, Stockill (1).

***Record League Victory:*** 9–1 v Southport, Division 3 (N), 2 February 1957 – Forgan; Phillips, Howe; Brown (1), Cairney, Mollatt; Hill, Bottom (4 incl. 1p), Wilkinson (2), Wragg (1), Fenton (1).

***Record Cup Victory:*** 6–0 v South Shields (away), FA Cup 1st rd, 16 November 1968 – Widdowson; Baker (1p), Richardson; Carr, Jackson, Burrows; Taylor, Ross (3), MacDougall (2), Hodgson, Boyer.

***Record Defeat:*** 0–12 v Chester, Division 3 (N), 1 February 1936.

## HONOURS

*Football League:* Division 3 – Promoted 1973–74 (3rd); Division 4 – Champions 1983–84. 1992–93 (play-offs).

*FA Cup:* Semi-finals 1955, when in Division 3.

*Football League Cup:* best season: 5th rd, 1962.

## SKY SPORTS FACT FILE

After a disappointing spell with Bristol Rovers, Maurice 'Mick' Dando transferred to York City in 1933–34 and in two seasons scored 46 League goals before moving on to Chesterfield where he spearheaded that club's successful promotion season.

***Most League Points (2 for a win):*** 62, Division 4, 1964–65.

***Most League Points (3 for a win):*** 101, Division 4, 1983–84.

***Most League Goals:*** 96, Division 4, 1983–84.

***Highest League Scorer in Season:*** Bill Fenton, 31, Division 3 (N), 1951–52; Arthur Bottom, 31, Division 3 (N), 1954–55 and 1955–56.

***Most League Goals in Total Aggregate:*** Norman Wilkinson, 125, 1954–66.

***Most League Goals in One Match:*** 5, Alf Patrick v Rotherham U, Division 3N, 20 November 1948.

***Most Capped Player:*** Peter Scott, 7 (10), Northern Ireland.

***Most League Appearances:*** Barry Jackson, 481, 1958–70.

***Youngest League Player:*** Reg Stockill, 15 years 281 days v Wigan Borough, 31 August 1929.

***Record Transfer Fee Received:*** £1,000,000 from Manchester U for Jonathan Greening, March 1998.

***Record Transfer Fee Paid:*** £140,000 to Burnley for Adrian Randall, December 1995.

***Football League Record:*** 1929 Elected to Division 3 (N); 1958–59 Division 4; 1959–60 Division 3; 1960–65 Division 4; 1965–66 Division 3; 1966–71 Division 4; 1971–74 Division 3; 1974–76 Division 2; 1976–77 Division 3; 1977–84 Division 4; 1984–88 Division 3; 1988–92 Division 4; 1992–93 Division 3; 1993–99 Division 2; 1999–04 Division 3; 2004– Conference.

## MANAGERS

Bill Sherrington 1924–60
*(was Secretary for most of this time but virtually Secretary-Manager for a long pre-war spell)*
John Collier 1929–36
Tom Mitchell 1936–50
Dick Duckworth 1950–52
Charlie Spencer 1952–53
Jimmy McCormick 1953–54
Sam Bartram 1956–60
Tom Lockie 1960–67
Joe Shaw 1967–68
Tom Johnston 1968–75
Wilf McGuinness 1975–77
Charlie Wright 1977–80
Barry Lyons 1980–81
Denis Smith 1982–87
Bobby Saxton 1987–88
John Bird 1988–91
John Ward 1991–93
Alan Little 1993–99
Neil Thompson 1999–2000
Terry Dolan 2000–03
Chris Brass June 2003–

## LATEST SEQUENCES

***Longest Sequence of League Wins:*** 7, 31.10.1964 – 26.12.1964.

***Longest Sequence of League Defeats:*** 8, 14.11.1966 – 31.12.1966.

***Longest Sequence of League Draws:*** 6, 26.12.1992 – 22.1.1993.

***Longest Sequence of Unbeaten League Matches:*** 21, 10.9.1973 – 12.1.1974.

***Longest Sequence Without a League Win:*** 20, 17.1.2004 – continuing.

***Successive Scoring Runs:*** 24 from 3.3.1984.

***Successive Non-scoring Runs:*** 7 from 28.8.1972.

## TEN YEAR LEAGUE RECORD

| | | P | W | D | L | F | A | Pts | Pos |
|---|---|---|---|---|---|---|---|---|---|
| 1994-95 | Div 2 | 46 | 21 | 9 | 16 | 67 | 51 | 72 | 9 |
| 1995-96 | Div 2 | 46 | 13 | 13 | 20 | 58 | 73 | 52 | 20 |
| 1996-97 | Div 2 | 46 | 13 | 13 | 20 | 47 | 68 | 52 | 20 |
| 1997-98 | Div 2 | 46 | 14 | 17 | 15 | 52 | 58 | 59 | 16 |
| 1998-99 | Div 2 | 46 | 13 | 11 | 22 | 56 | 80 | 50 | 21 |
| 1999-2000 | Div 3 | 46 | 12 | 16 | 18 | 39 | 53 | 52 | 20 |
| 2000-01 | Div 3 | 46 | 13 | 13 | 20 | 42 | 63 | 52 | 17 |
| 2001-02 | Div 3 | 46 | 16 | 9 | 21 | 54 | 67 | 57 | 14 |
| 2002-03 | Div 3 | 46 | 17 | 15 | 14 | 52 | 53 | 66 | 10 |
| 2003-04 | Div 3 | 46 | 10 | 14 | 22 | 35 | 66 | 44 | 24 |

## DID YOU KNOW?

Local goalscoring favourite Reg Baines had three top-scoring spells with York City: in 1931–32 with 28 League goals, 29 the following season, returning in 1937–38 to lead again with 24. Part-timer of many clubs he was foreman in a chocolate factory.

## YORK CITY 2003–04 LEAGUE RECORD

| *Match No.* | *Date* | *Venue* | *Opponents* | *Result* | | *H/T Score* | *Lg. Pos.* | *Goalscorers* | *Attendance* |
|---|---|---|---|---|---|---|---|---|---|
| 1 | Aug 9 | A | Carlisle U | W | 2-1 | 2-1 | — | Bullock 2, Nogan 13 | 7261 |
| 2 | 16 | H | Northampton T | W | 1-0 | 1-0 | 6 | Nogan 44 | 3870 |
| 3 | 23 | A | Huddersfield T | W | 1-0 | 1-0 | 2 | Bullock 17 | 9850 |
| 4 | 26 | H | Southend U | W | 2-0 | 1-0 | — | Hope 36, George 49 | 4202 |
| 5 | 30 | A | Lincoln C | L | 0-3 | 0-1 | 2 | | 3892 |
| 6 | Sept 6 | H | Rochdale | L | 1-2 | 0-2 | 3 | Wilford 73 | 3982 |
| 7 | 13 | A | Yeovil T | L | 0-3 | 0-2 | 6 | | 5653 |
| 8 | 16 | H | Darlington | D | 1-1 | 1-1 | — | George 16 | 3867 |
| 9 | 20 | H | Bristol R | W | 2-1 | 2-1 | 5 | Bullock 14, Wilford 34 | 3968 |
| 10 | 27 | A | Macclesfield T | D | 0-0 | 0-0 | 8 | | 2311 |
| 11 | 30 | A | Bury | L | 0-2 | 0-1 | — | | 2282 |
| 12 | Oct 4 | H | Cambridge U | W | 2-0 | 1-0 | 7 | Bullock 5, Brackstone 64 | 3481 |
| 13 | 11 | A | Mansfield T | L | 0-2 | 0-1 | 10 | | 4914 |
| 14 | 18 | H | Boston U | D | 1-1 | 1-0 | 10 | Parkin 45 | 3190 |
| 15 | 21 | H | Oxford U | D | 2-2 | 1-1 | — | Nogan 37, Hope 63 | 3022 |
| 16 | 25 | A | Scunthorpe U | D | 0-0 | 0-0 | 10 | | 3807 |
| 17 | Nov 1 | A | Cheltenham T | D | 1-1 | 0-0 | 11 | Parkin 77 | 3431 |
| 18 | 15 | H | Doncaster R | W | 1-0 | 0-0 | 10 | Dunning (pen) 60 | 5942 |
| 19 | 22 | A | Leyton Orient | D | 2-2 | 0-2 | 12 | Edmondson 59, Brackstone 64 | 3593 |
| 20 | 29 | H | Swansea C | D | 0-0 | 0-0 | 11 | | 3209 |
| 21 | Dec 6 | A | Darlington | L | 0-3 | 0-2 | 11 | | 4115 |
| 22 | 13 | A | Torquay U | D | 1-1 | 0-0 | 11 | Nogan 47 | 2564 |
| 23 | 21 | H | Kidderminster H | W | 1-0 | 0-0 | 9 | Bullock 52 | 2973 |
| 24 | 26 | H | Hull C | L | 0-2 | 0-0 | 9 | | 7923 |
| 25 | 28 | A | Rochdale | W | 2-1 | 1-0 | 10 | Nogan 2 28, 76 | 2764 |
| 26 | Jan 10 | H | Carlisle U | W | 2-0 | 1-0 | 10 | Brass 29, Cooper 49 | 4804 |
| 27 | 17 | A | Northampton T | L | 1-2 | 0-2 | 10 | Bullock 90 | 5003 |
| 28 | 25 | H | Huddersfield T | L | 0-2 | 0-0 | 10 | | 6969 |
| 29 | 27 | A | Southend U | D | 0-0 | 0-0 | — | | 2943 |
| 30 | Feb 7 | A | Hull C | L | 1-2 | 0-0 | 11 | Nogan 66 | 19,099 |
| 31 | 14 | H | Mansfield T | L | 1-2 | 0-1 | 12 | Nogan 66 | 4068 |
| 32 | 17 | H | Lincoln C | L | 1-4 | 0-1 | — | Bullock 83 | 3396 |
| 33 | 21 | A | Boston U | L | 0-2 | 0-0 | 13 | | 2490 |
| 34 | Mar 3 | A | Oxford U | D | 0-0 | 0-0 | — | | 5091 |
| 35 | 6 | A | Kidderminster H | L | 1-4 | 1-3 | 16 | Cooper 41 | 2569 |
| 36 | 9 | H | Scunthorpe U | L | 1-3 | 0-2 | — | Bell 76 | 2676 |
| 37 | 13 | H | Torquay U | D | 0-0 | 0-0 | 16 | | 3150 |
| 38 | 27 | A | Bristol R | L | 0-3 | 0-2 | 21 | | 6723 |
| 39 | Apr 4 | H | Macclesfield T | L | 0-2 | 0-2 | 23 | | 3855 |
| 40 | 9 | A | Cambridge U | L | 0-2 | 0-1 | — | | 5120 |
| 41 | 13 | H | Bury | D | 1-1 | 1-1 | — | George 24 | 3111 |
| 42 | 17 | H | Cheltenham T | L | 0-2 | 0-0 | 23 | | 3221 |
| 43 | 20 | H | Yeovil T | L | 1-2 | 1-0 | — | Dunning 8 | 2802 |
| 44 | 24 | A | Doncaster R | L | 1-3 | 0-2 | 24 | Dunning 49 | 7843 |
| 45 | May 1 | H | Leyton Orient | L | 1-2 | 1-2 | 24 | Wise 5 | 3462 |
| 46 | 8 | A | Swansea C | D | 0-0 | 0-0 | 24 | | 6806 |

**Final League Position: 24**

## GOALSCORERS

*League (35):* Nogan 8, Bullock 7, Dunning 3 (1 pen), George 3, Brackstone 2, Cooper 2, Hope 2, Parkin 2, Wilford 2, Bell 1, Brass 1, Edmondson 1, Wise 1.
*Carling Cup (1):* Morris 1.
*FA Cup (1):* Nogan 1.
*LDV Vans Trophy (1):* Dunning 1 (pen).

| Ovendale M 41 | Edmondson D 26 + 1 | Merris D 42 + 2 | Wise S 18 + 1 | Brass C 39 | Hope R 36 | Ward M 27 + 4 | Dunning D 42 | Nogan L 38 + 1 | Bullock L 34 + 1 | Fox C 2 + 3 | Wood L 21 + 5 | Cooper R 26 + 11 | George L 14 + 8 | Stewart B 2 + 8 | Downes S 4 + 2 | Brackstone S 4 + 5 | Parkin J 9 + 6 | Wilford A 4 + 2 | Crowe D 2 + 3 | Smith C 26 + 2 | Dove C 1 | Browne G 2 + 4 | Shaw J 5 + 3 | Coad M — + 3 | Davies S 6 + 2 | Walker J 7 + 2 | Yalcin L 5 + 10 | Dickman J 2 | Bell A 3 + 7 | Porter C 5 | Offiong R 2 + 2 | Newby J 6 + 1 | Law G 2 + 2 | Arthur A 2 + 1 | Ashcroft K 1 + 1 | Haw R — + 1 | Match No. |
|---|---|---|---|---|---|---|---|---|---|---|---|---|---|---|---|---|---|---|---|---|---|---|---|---|---|---|---|---|---|---|---|---|---|---|---|---|---|
| 1 | 2 | 3 | 4 | 5■ | $6^1$ | 7 | 8 | 9 | 10 | $11^2$ | 12 | 13 | | | | | | | | | | | | | | | | | | | | | | | | | 1 |
| 1 | 2 | 3 | 4 | 5 | $6^1$ | 7 | 8 | $9^3$ | 10 | | 12 | 13 | $11^2$ | 14 | | | | | | | | | | | | | | | | | | | | | | | 2 |
| 1 | 2 | 3 | $4^1$ | | 6 | 7 | 8 | 9 | 11 | | 5 | 12 | $10^2$ | 13 | | | | | | | | | | | | | | | | | | | | | | | 3 |
| 1 | 2 | 3 | | | 6 | 7 | 8 | 9 | $11^3$ | | 5 | $4^2$ | $10^1$ | 12 | 13 | 14 | | | | | | | | | | | | | | | | | | | | | 4 |
| 1 | $2^3$ | 3 | | | 6 | 7 | 8■ | $9^2$ | 11 | | 5 | 4 | $10^1$ | 12 | 14 | | 13 | | | | | | | | | | | | | | | | | | | | 5 |
| 1 | | 3 | 4■ | 5 | 6 | $7^2$ | 8 | 9 | 11 | | | 12 | $10^3$ | | $2^1$ | 13 | | 14 | | | | | | | | | | | | | | | | | | | 6 |
| 1 | | 3 | 4 | 5 | $6^3$ | 7 | | $9^2$ | 11 | | 8 | 13 | 12 | 14 | 2 | | | $10^1$ | | | | | | | | | | | | | | | | | | | 7 |
| 1 | | 3 | 4 | 5 | | 7 | 8 | | 11 | | 6 | 12 | 10 | 13 | $2^1$ | | | $9^2$ | | | | | | | | | | | | | | | | | | | 8 |
| 1 | | 3 | | 5 | 6 | 7 | 8 | | 11 | | 4 | 2 | $10^1$ | 12 | | | | 9 | | | | | | | | | | | | | | | | | | | 9 |
| 1 | | 3 | | 5 | 6 | 7 | 8 | | 11 | | 4 | 2 | 10 | | | | | $9^1$ | 12 | | | | | | | | | | | | | | | | | | 10 |
| 1 | | 3 | | $5^3$ | 6 | 7 | 8 | | 9 | $11^2$ | 4 | 2 | $10^1$ | 12 | | | | | 13 | 14 | | | | | | | | | | | | | | | | | 11 |
| 1 | | 3 | | 5 | 6 | 7 | 8 | $9^2$ | $11^3$ | | 4 | 2 | 12 | | | 13 | | 14 | $10^1$ | | | | | | | | | | | | | | | | | | 12 |
| 1 | | 3 | 12 | $5^1$ | 6 | 7 | 8 | 9 | | | 4 | 2 | 13 | | | | 14 | | $10^2$ | | $11^3$ | | | | | | | | | | | | | | | | 13 |
| 1 | | 3 | | 5 | 6 | 7 | 8 | $9^1$ | $11^2$ | | | 2 | 12 | | | | 10 | | 13 | 4 | | | | | | | | | | | | | | | | | 14 |
| 1 | | $3^2$ | | 5 | 6 | 7 | 8 | 9 | 11 | | 13 | 2 | 12 | | | | $10^1$ | | | 4 | | | | | | | | | | | | | | | | | 15 |
| 1 | 2 | 3 | | 5 | 6 | 7 | 8 | $9^1$ | 11 | | | | 12 | | | | 10■ | | | 4 | | | | | | | | | | | | | | | | | 16 |
| 1 | 2 | 3 | | 5 | 6 | 7 | | 9 | 11 | | 12 | 8 | | | | | $10^1$ | | | 4 | | | | | | | | | | | | | | | | | 17 |
| 1 | 2 | 3 | | 5 | 4 | | 8 | 9 | 7 | | | | | | | 11 | | | | 6 | | $10^1$ | 12 | | | | | | | | | | | | | | 18 |
| 1 | 2 | 3 | | 5 | 4 | | 8 | 9 | 7 | | | | | | | 11 | | | | 6 | | $10^1$ | 12 | | | | | | | | | | | | | | 19 |
| 1 | 2 | 3 | | 5 | 4■ | | 8 | 9 | 7 | | | | | | | 11 | | | | 6 | | 12 | $10^1$ | | | | | | | | | | | | | | 20 |
| 1 | 2 | 3 | | 5 | | | 8 | $9^3$ | 7 | | | 4 | | | | $11^2$ | 12 | | | 6 | | 14 | $10^1$ | 13 | | | | | | | | | | | | | 21 |
| 1 | 2 | 3 | | 5 | | | 8 | $9^1$ | 7 | | | 11 | | | | | 4 | | | 6 | | 12 | 10 | | | | | | | | | | | | | | 22 |
| 1 | 2 | 3 | | 5 | | | 8 | 9 | 11 | | | 7 | | | | | 4 | | | 6 | | | 10 | | | | | | | | | | | | | | 23 |
| 1 | 2 | $3^3$ | | 5 | | 12 | 8 | $9^2$ | 11 | | | $7^1$ | | | | | 4 | | | 6 | | 13 | 10 | | 14 | | | | | | | | | | | | 24 |
| 1 | 2 | 3 | | 5 | 4 | 7 | 8 | $9^2$ | 10 | | | $11^1$ | | | | 12 | | | | 6 | | | 13 | | | | | | | | | | | | | | 25 |
| 1 | 2 | 3 | | 5 | 4 | $7^2$ | 8 | $9^3$ | $10^1$ | | | 11 | | | | | 12 | | | 6 | | | | | | 13 | 14 | | | | | | | | | | 26 |
| 1 | | 3 | | 5 | 4 | $7^1$ | 8 | $9^3$ | 10 | 12 | | 2 | | | | 13 | 6 | | | | | | | | | $11^2$ | 14 | | | | | | | | | | 27 |
| 1 | 2 | 3 | | 5 | 4 | 7 | 8 | $9^1$ | 10 | | | 11 | | | | | | | | 6 | | | | | | | 12 | | | | | | | | | | 28 |
| 1 | 2 | 3 | | 5 | 4 | 7 | 8 | 12 | $11^3$ | 13 | | | | | | | $10^1$ | | | 6 | | | | | | $9^2$ | 14 | | | | | | | | | | 29 |
| 1 | 2 | 3 | | 5 | 4 | $7^1$ | 8 | $9^2$ | 10 | | | | | | | | 12 | | | 6 | | | | | | 11 | 13 | | | | | | | | | | 30 |
| 1 | 12 | 3 | | 5 | 4 | $7^3$ | 8 | 9 | 13 | 14 | | $2^1$ | | | | | | | | 6 | | | | | | 11 | $10^2$ | | | | | | | | | | 31 |
| 1 | 2 | $3^1$ | | 5 | 4 | 13 | 8 | 9 | 7 | | | 14 | | | | | 12 | | | | | | | | 6 | $11^2$ | $10^3$ | | | | | | | | | | 32 |
| 1 | | 12 | | 5■ | 4 | | 8 | 9 | 11 | | | 2 | | | 7 | | | | | 6 | | | | | $3^1$ | 13 | $10^2$ | | | | | | | | | | 33 |
| 1 | | 3 | 4 | 5 | | 7 | | $9^3$ | 10 | | 6 | 13 | | | | | | | | 12 | | | | | $2^1$ | 11 | | $8^2$ | 14 | | | | | | | | 34 |
| 1 | | 3 | 4 | | | $7^2$ | | $9^3$ | 10 | | 6 | 12 | | | | | | | | 5 | | | | | 2 | 11 | 13 | $8^1$ | 14 | | | | | | | | 35 |
| 1 | $2^2$ | 3 | 5 | | | $7^1$ | 8 | $9^3$ | 10 | | 6 | 11 | | | | | | | | | | | | 13 | 4 | | 12 | | 14 | | | | | | | | 36 |
| | | 3 | 5 | | 4 | | 8 | 9 | | | 2 | 7 | | | | | | | | 6 | | | | | | | 12 | | 11 | 1 | $10^1$ | | | | | | 37 |
| | | 3 | 5 | | 4 | | 8 | $9^2$ | | | 7 | 2 | | | | | | | | 6 | | | | 14 | | | 13 | | $11^1$ | 1 | $10^3$ | 12 | | | | | 38 |
| | | $3^3$ | 6 | 5 | 4 | | 8 | 9 | | | | $7^1$ | | | | | | | | | | | | | 2 | | 12 | | $11^2$ | 1 | 13 | 10 | 14 | | | | 39 |
| 1 | 2 | 3 | 11 | 5 | 4■ | | 8 | $9^2$ | | | 12 | $7^1$ | 14 | | | | | | | 6 | | | | | | | | | | | 13 | $10^3$ | | | | | 40 |
| 1 | 2 | | $3^1$ | 5 | 4 | 12 | 8 | 9 | | | 7 | | 11 | | | | | | | 6 | | | | | | | | | | | | 10 | | | | | 41 |
| 1■ | 2 | | 3 | $5^1$ | 4 | 12 | 8 | $9^2$ | | | 7 | 13 | $11^3$ | | | | | | | 6 | | | | | | | | | 14 | | | 10 | | | | | 42 |
| 1 | 2 | 12 | 7 | $5^1$ | 4 | | 8 | $9^2$ | | | $11^3$ | 13 | 3 | | | | | | | 6 | | | | | | | | | 14 | | | 10 | | | | | 43 |
| 1 | $2^1$ | $3^3$ | 4 | 5 | | | 8 | | | | 11 | 7 | $9^2$ | | | | | | | 6 | | | | | | | | | 13 | | | 10 | 12 | 14 | | | 44 |
| | | $3^1$ | 4 | 5 | | | 8 | | | | 6 | | $10^2$ | 11 | | | | | | | | | | | 12 | | 9 | | 13 | 1 | | | 2 | $7^3$ | 14 | | 45 |
| | | 3 | | 5 | 4 | | 8 | | | | 6 | | 12 | 7 | | | | | | | | | | | | | 9 | | | 1 | | | 2 | $11^1$ | $10^2$ | 13 | 46 |

**Carling Cup**
First Round — Rotherham U — (a) — 1-2

**LDV Vans Trophy**
First Round — Halifax T — (a) — 1-2

**FA Cup**
First Round — Barnsley — (h) — 1-2

# ENGLISH LEAGUE PLAYERS DIRECTORY

*Free transfer, †Non-contract, ‡Registration cancelled, §Trainee/Scholar/Schoolboy
#Players over age 24, out of contract but who have been made an offer of re-engagement.
*Players listed refer to the retain and transfer list May 2003.*

*Players are listed alphabetically on pages 565–570.*
The number alongside each player corresponds to the team number heading. (Aaritalo, Mika 2 = team 2 (Aston Villa))

## ARSENAL (1)

**ALIADIERE, Jeremie (F)** 14 1
H: 6 0 W: 11 00 b.Rambouillet 30-3-83
*Source:* Scholarship.

| | | | | | |
|---|---|---|---|---|---|
| 1999–2000 | Arsenal | 0 | 0 | | |
| 2000–01 | Arsenal | 0 | 0 | | |
| 2001–02 | Arsenal | 1 | 0 | | |
| 2002–03 | Arsenal | 3 | 1 | | |
| 2003–04 | Arsenal | 10 | 0 | **14** | **1** |

**BAILEY, Alex* (D)** 0 0
H: 5 9 W: 10 07 b.Newham 21-9-83
*Source:* Scholar. *Honours:* England Youth.

| | | | |
|---|---|---|---|
| 2001–02 | Arsenal | 0 | 0 |
| 2002–03 | Arsenal | 0 | 0 |
| 2003–04 | Arsenal | 0 | 0 |

**BENTLEY, David (F)** 1 0
H: 5 10 W: 11 02 b.Peterborough 27-8-84
*Source:* Scholar. *Honours:* England Youth, Under-20, Under-21.

| | | | | | |
|---|---|---|---|---|---|
| 2001–02 | Arsenal | 0 | 0 | | |
| 2002–03 | Arsenal | 0 | 0 | | |
| 2003–04 | Arsenal | 1 | 0 | **1** | **0** |

**BERGKAMP, Dennis (F)** 499 191
H: 6 0 W: 12 10 b.Amsterdam 18-5-69
*Honours:* Holland 79 full caps, 36 goals.

| | | | | | |
|---|---|---|---|---|---|
| 1986–87 | Ajax | 14 | 2 | | |
| 1987–88 | Ajax | 25 | 5 | | |
| 1988–89 | Ajax | 30 | 13 | | |
| 1989–90 | Ajax | 25 | 8 | | |
| 1990–91 | Ajax | 33 | 25 | | |
| 1991–92 | Ajax | 30 | 24 | | |
| 1992–93 | Ajax | 28 | 26 | **185** | **103** |
| 1993–94 | Internazionale | 31 | 8 | | |
| 1994–95 | Internazionale | 21 | 3 | **52** | **11** |
| 1995–96 | Arsenal | 33 | 11 | | |
| 1996–97 | Arsenal | 29 | 12 | | |
| 1997–98 | Arsenal | 28 | 16 | | |
| 1998–99 | Arsenal | 29 | 12 | | |
| 1999–2000 | Arsenal | 28 | 6 | | |
| 2000–01 | Arsenal | 25 | 3 | | |
| 2001–02 | Arsenal | 33 | 9 | | |
| 2002–03 | Arsenal | 29 | 4 | | |
| 2003–04 | Arsenal | 28 | 4 | **262** | **77** |

**BIRCHALL, Adam (F)** 0 0
H: 5 7 W: 11 08 b.Maidstone 2-12-84
*Source:* Trainee. *Honours:* Wales Under-21.

| | | | |
|---|---|---|---|
| 2002–03 | Arsenal | 0 | 0 |
| 2003–04 | Arsenal | 0 | 0 |

**BRADLEY, Stephen* (M)** 0 0
H: 5 8 W: 9 07 b.Dublin 19-11-84
*Source:* Scholar.

| | | | |
|---|---|---|---|
| 2001–02 | Arsenal | 0 | 0 |
| 2002–03 | Arsenal | 0 | 0 |
| 2003–04 | Arsenal | 0 | 0 |

**CAMPBELL, Sol (D)** 354 15
H: 6 2 W: 15 07 b.Newham 18-9-74
*Source:* Trainee. *Honours:* England Youth, Under-21, 62 full caps, 1 goal.

| | | | | | |
|---|---|---|---|---|---|
| 1992–93 | Tottenham H | 1 | 1 | | |
| 1993–94 | Tottenham H | 34 | 0 | | |
| 1994–95 | Tottenham H | 30 | 0 | | |
| 1995–96 | Tottenham H | 31 | 1 | | |
| 1996–97 | Tottenham H | 38 | 0 | | |
| 1997–98 | Tottenham H | 34 | 0 | | |
| 1998–99 | Tottenham H | 37 | 6 | | |
| 1999–2000 | Tottenham H | 29 | 0 | | |
| 2000–01 | Tottenham H | 21 | 2 | **255** | **10** |
| 2001–02 | Arsenal | 31 | 2 | | |
| 2002–03 | Arsenal | 33 | 2 | | |
| 2003–04 | Arsenal | 35 | 1 | **99** | **5** |

**CHILVERS, Liam* (D)** 54 1
H: 6 0 W: 12 04 b.Chelmsford 6-11-81
*Source:* Scholar.

| | | | | | |
|---|---|---|---|---|---|
| 2000–01 | Arsenal | 0 | 0 | | |
| 2000–01 | *Northampton T* | 7 | 0 | **7** | **0** |
| 2001–02 | Arsenal | 0 | 0 | | |
| 2001–02 | *Notts Co* | 9 | 1 | **9** | **1** |
| 2002–03 | Arsenal | 0 | 0 | | |
| 2002–03 | *Colchester U* | 6 | 0 | | |
| 2003–04 | Arsenal | 0 | 0 | | |
| 2003–04 | *Colchester U* | 32 | 0 | **38** | **0** |

**CLICHY, Gael (D)** 12 0
H: 5 9 W: 10 04 b.Toulouse 26-7-85

| | | | | | |
|---|---|---|---|---|---|
| 2003–04 | Arsenal | 12 | 0 | **12** | **0** |

**COLE, Ashley (D)** 124 7
H: 5 8 W: 10 05 b.Stepney 20-12-80
*Source:* Trainee. *Honours:* England Youth, Under-21, 30 full caps.

| | | | | | |
|---|---|---|---|---|---|
| 1998–99 | Arsenal | 0 | 0 | | |
| 1999–2000 | Arsenal | 1 | 0 | | |
| 1999–2000 | *Crystal Palace* | 14 | 1 | **14** | **1** |
| 2000–01 | Arsenal | 17 | 3 | | |
| 2001–02 | Arsenal | 29 | 2 | | |
| 2002–03 | Arsenal | 31 | 1 | | |
| 2003–04 | Arsenal | 32 | 0 | **110** | **6** |

**CREGG, Patrick (M)** 0 0
H: 5 9 W: 10 04 b.Dublin 21-2-86
*Source:* Trainee.

| | | | |
|---|---|---|---|
| 2002–03 | Arsenal | 0 | 0 |
| 2003–04 | Arsenal | 0 | 0 |

**CYGAN, Pascal (D)** 215 10
H: 6 4 W: 13 12 b.Lens 19-4-74
*Source:* Wasquehal.

| | | | | | |
|---|---|---|---|---|---|
| 1995–96 | Lille | 27 | 0 | | |
| 1996–97 | Lille | 14 | 0 | | |
| 1997–98 | Lille | 26 | 3 | | |
| 1998–99 | Lille | 21 | 1 | | |
| 1999–2000 | Lille | 33 | 2 | | |
| 2000–01 | Lille | 29 | 2 | | |
| 2001–02 | Lille | 29 | 1 | **179** | **9** |
| 2002–03 | Arsenal | 18 | 1 | | |
| 2003–04 | Arsenal | 18 | 0 | **36** | **1** |

**EDU (M)** 95 5
H: 6 1 W: 12 06 b.Sao Paulo 15-5-78
*Honours:* Brazil 4 full caps.

| | | | | | |
|---|---|---|---|---|---|
| 1998 | Corinthians | 1 | 0 | | |
| 1999 | Corinthians | 19 | 0 | | |
| 2000 | Corinthians | 8 | 0 | **28** | **0** |
| 2000–01 | Arsenal | 5 | 0 | | |
| 2001–02 | Arsenal | 14 | 1 | | |
| 2002–03 | Arsenal | 18 | 2 | | |
| 2003–04 | Arsenal | 30 | 2 | **67** | **5** |

**FABREGAS, Francesc (M)** 0 0
H: 5 9 W: 10 09 b.Arenys de Mar 4-5-87
*Source:* Barcelona.

| | | | |
|---|---|---|---|
| 2003–04 | Arsenal | 0 | 0 |

**FOWLER, Jordan (M)** 0 0
H: 5 9 W: 11 00 b.Barking 1-10-84
*Source:* Trainee.

| | | | |
|---|---|---|---|
| 2002–03 | Arsenal | 0 | 0 |
| 2003–04 | Arsenal | 0 | 0 |

**GARRY, Ryan (D)** 1 0
H: 6 2 W: 13 00 b.Hornchurch 29-9-83
*Source:* Scholar. *Honours:* England Youth, Under-20.

| | | | | | |
|---|---|---|---|---|---|
| 2001–02 | Arsenal | 0 | 0 | | |
| 2002–03 | Arsenal | 1 | 0 | | |
| 2003–04 | Arsenal | 0 | 0 | **1** | **0** |

**HENRY, Thierry (F)** 294 135
H: 6 2 W: 13 05 b.Paris 17-8-77
*Honours:* France 63 full caps, 27 goals.

| | | | | | |
|---|---|---|---|---|---|
| 1994–95 | Monaco | 8 | 3 | | |
| 1995–96 | Monaco | 18 | 3 | | |
| 1996–97 | Monaco | 36 | 9 | | |
| 1997–98 | Monaco | 30 | 4 | | |
| 1998–99 | Monaco | 13 | 1 | **105** | **20** |
| 1998–99 | Juventus | 16 | 3 | **16** | **3** |
| 1999–2000 | Arsenal | 31 | 17 | | |
| 2000–01 | Arsenal | 35 | 17 | | |
| 2001–02 | Arsenal | 33 | 24 | | |
| 2002–03 | Arsenal | 37 | 24 | | |
| 2003–04 | Arsenal | 37 | 30 | **173** | **112** |

**HOJSTED, Ingi (M)** 0 0
H: 5 9 W: 9 10 b.Torshavn 12-12-85
*Source:* Trainee.

| | | | |
|---|---|---|---|
| 2002–03 | Arsenal | 0 | 0 |
| 2003–04 | Arsenal | 0 | 0 |

**HOLLOWAY, Craig* (G)** 0 0
b.Blackheath 10-8-84
*Source:* Trainee.

| | | | |
|---|---|---|---|
| 2002–03 | Arsenal | 0 | 0 |
| 2003–04 | Arsenal | 0 | 0 |

**HOYTE, Justin (D)** 2 0
H: 5 11 W: 11 00 b.Waltham Forest 20-11-84
*Source:* Scholar. *Honours:* England Youth, Under-20, Under-21.

| | | | | | |
|---|---|---|---|---|---|
| 2002–03 | Arsenal | 1 | 0 | | |
| 2003–04 | Arsenal | 1 | 0 | **2** | **0** |

**JEFFERS, Francis (F)** 89 22
H: 5 10 W: 11 02 b.Liverpool 25-1-81
*Source:* Trainee. *Honours:* England Schools, Youth, Under-21, 1 full cap, 1 goal.

| | | | | | |
|---|---|---|---|---|---|
| 1997–98 | Everton | 1 | 0 | | |
| 1998–99 | Everton | 15 | 6 | | |
| 1999–2000 | Everton | 21 | 6 | | |
| 2000–01 | Everton | 12 | 6 | | |
| 2001–02 | Arsenal | 6 | 2 | | |
| 2002–03 | Arsenal | 16 | 2 | | |
| 2003–04 | Arsenal | 0 | 0 | **22** | **4** |
| 2003–04 | *Everton* | 18 | 0 | **67** | **18** |

**JORDAN, Michael (G)** 0 0
H: 6 2 W: 13 02 b.Enfield 7-4-86
*Source:* Scholar.

| | | | |
|---|---|---|---|
| 2003–04 | Arsenal | 0 | 0 |

**JUAN‡ (D)** 3 0
H: 5 6 W: 9 07 b.Sao Paulo 6-2-82
*Source:* Sao Paulo.

| | | | | | |
|---|---|---|---|---|---|
| 2001–02 | Arsenal | 0 | 0 | | |
| 2002–03 | Arsenal | 0 | 0 | | |
| 2003–04 | Arsenal | 0 | 0 | | |
| 2003–04 | *Millwall* | 3 | 0 | **3** | **0** |

**KANU, Nwankwo* (F)** 245 71
H: 6 5 W: 12 01 b.Owerri 1-8-76
*Honours:* Nigeria 39 full caps, 6 goals.

| | | | | | |
|---|---|---|---|---|---|
| 1991–92 | Federation Works | 30 | 9 | **30** | **9** |
| 1992–93 | Iwanyanwu | 30 | 6 | **30** | **6** |
| 1993–94 | Ajax | 6 | 2 | | |
| 1994–95 | Ajax | 18 | 10 | | |
| 1995–96 | Ajax | 30 | 13 | **54** | **25** |
| 1996–97 | Internazionale | 0 | 0 | | |
| 1997–98 | Internazionale | 11 | 1 | | |
| 1998–99 | Internazionale | 1 | 0 | **12** | **1** |
| 1998–99 | Arsenal | 12 | 6 | | |
| 1999–2000 | Arsenal | 31 | 12 | | |
| 2000–01 | Arsenal | 27 | 3 | | |
| 2001–02 | Arsenal | 23 | 3 | | |
| 2002–03 | Arsenal | 16 | 5 | | |
| 2003–04 | Arsenal | 10 | 1 | **119** | **30** |

**KARBASSIYON, Daniel (F)** 0 0
H: 5 8 W: 11 07 b.Virginia 10-8-84
*Source:* Roanoke Star.

| | | | |
|---|---|---|---|
| 2003–04 | Arsenal | 0 | 0 |

**KEOWN, Martin* (D) 563 8**

H: 6 1 W: 12 04 b.Oxford 24-7-66

*Source:* Apprentice. *Honours:* England Youth, Under-21, B, 43 full caps, 2 goals.

| | | | | | |
|---|---|---|---|---|---|
| 1983–84 | Arsenal | 0 | 0 | | |
| 1984–85 | Arsenal | 0 | 0 | | |
| 1984–85 | *Brighton & HA* | 16 | 0 | | |
| 1985–86 | Arsenal | 22 | 0 | | |
| 1985–86 | *Brighton & HA* | 7 | 1 | **23** | **1** |
| 1986–87 | Aston Villa | 36 | 0 | | |
| 1987–88 | Aston Villa | 42 | 3 | | |
| 1988–89 | Aston Villa | 34 | 0 | **112** | **3** |
| 1989–90 | Everton | 20 | 0 | | |
| 1990–91 | Everton | 24 | 0 | | |
| 1991–92 | Everton | 39 | 0 | | |
| 1992–93 | Everton | 13 | 0 | **96** | **0** |
| 1992–93 | Arsenal | 16 | 0 | | |
| 1993–94 | Arsenal | 33 | 0 | | |
| 1994–95 | Arsenal | 31 | 1 | | |
| 1995–96 | Arsenal | 34 | 0 | | |
| 1996–97 | Arsenal | 33 | 1 | | |
| 1997–98 | Arsenal | 18 | 0 | | |
| 1998–99 | Arsenal | 34 | 1 | | |
| 1999–2000 | Arsenal | 27 | 1 | | |
| 2000–01 | Arsenal | 28 | 0 | | |
| 2001–02 | Arsenal | 22 | 0 | | |
| 2002–03 | Arsenal | 24 | 0 | | |
| 2003–04 | Arsenal | 10 | 0 | **332** | **4** |

**LARSSON, Sebastian (M) 0 0**

H: 5 10 W: 11 00 b.Eskiltuna 6-6-85

*Source:* Trainee.

| | | | |
|---|---|---|---|
| 2002–03 | Arsenal | 0 | 0 |
| 2003–04 | Arsenal | 0 | 0 |

**LAUREN, Etame-Mayer (D) 247 23**

H: 5 11 W: 11 07 b.Londi Kribi 19-1-77

*Honours:* Cameroon 25 full caps, 1 goal.

| | | | | | |
|---|---|---|---|---|---|
| 1995–96 | Utrera | 30 | 5 | **30** | **5** |
| 1996–97 | Sevilla B | 17 | 3 | **17** | **3** |
| 1997–98 | Levante | 34 | 6 | **34** | **6** |
| 1998–99 | Mallorca | 32 | 1 | | |
| 1999–2000 | Mallorca | 30 | 3 | **62** | **4** |
| 2000–01 | Arsenal | 18 | 2 | | |
| 2001–02 | Arsenal | 27 | 2 | | |
| 2002–03 | Arsenal | 27 | 1 | | |
| 2003–04 | Arsenal | 32 | 0 | **104** | **5** |

**LEHMANN, Jens (G) 372 2**

H: 6 4 W: 13 05 b.Essen 10-11-69

*Honours:* Germany 18 full caps.

| | | | | | |
|---|---|---|---|---|---|
| 1991–92 | Schalke | 37 | 0 | | |
| 1992–93 | Schalke | 8 | 0 | | |
| 1993–94 | Schalke | 21 | 0 | | |
| 1994–95 | Schalke | 34 | 1 | | |
| 1995–96 | Schalke | 32 | 0 | | |
| 1996–97 | Schalke | 34 | 0 | | |
| 1997–98 | Schalke | 34 | 1 | **200** | **2** |
| 1998–99 | AC Milan | 5 | 0 | **5** | **0** |
| 1998–99 | Borussia Dortmund | 13 | 0 | | |
| 1999–2000 | Borussia Dortmund | 31 | 0 | | |
| 2000–01 | Borussia Dortmund | 31 | 0 | | |
| 2001–02 | Borussia Dortmund | 30 | 0 | | |
| 2002–03 | Borussia Dortmund | 24 | 0 | **129** | **0** |
| 2003–04 | Arsenal | 38 | 0 | **38** | **0** |

**LJUNGBERG, Frederik (M) 226 45**

H: 5 9 W: 11 00 b.Vittsjo 16-4-77

*Honours:* Sweden 44 full caps, 4 goals.

| | | | | | |
|---|---|---|---|---|---|
| 1994 | Halmstad | 1 | 0 | | |
| 1995 | Halmstad | 16 | 1 | | |
| 1996 | Halmstad | 20 | 2 | | |
| 1997 | Halmstad | 24 | 5 | | |
| 1998 | Halmstad | 18 | 2 | **79** | **10** |
| 1998–99 | Arsenal | 16 | 1 | | |
| 1999–2000 | Arsenal | 26 | 6 | | |
| 2000–01 | Arsenal | 30 | 6 | | |
| 2001–02 | Arsenal | 25 | 12 | | |
| 2002–03 | Arsenal | 20 | 6 | | |
| 2003–04 | Arsenal | 30 | 4 | **147** | **35** |

**NICOLAU, Nicky* (D) 9 0**

H: 5 8 W: 10 08 b.Camden 12-10-83

*Source:* Trainee.

| | | | | | |
|---|---|---|---|---|---|
| 2002–03 | Arsenal | 0 | 0 | | |
| 2003–04 | Arsenal | 0 | 0 | | |
| 2003–04 | *Southend U* | 9 | 0 | **9** | **0** |

**O'DONNELL, Steven (M) 0 0**

H: 5 9 W: 11 02 b.Galway 15-1-86

*Source:* Trainee.

| | | | |
|---|---|---|---|
| 2002–03 | Arsenal | 0 | 0 |
| 2003–04 | Arsenal | 0 | 0 |

**OWUSU-ABEYIE, Quincy (F) 0 0**

H: 5 11 W: 11 10 b.Amsterdam 15-4-86

| | | | |
|---|---|---|---|
| 2003–04 | Arsenal | 0 | 0 |

**PAPADOPOULOS, Michal‡ (F) 13 1**

H: 6 0 W: 12 06 b.Czech Republic 14-4-85

| | | | | | |
|---|---|---|---|---|---|
| 2001–02 | Banik Ostrava | 1 | 0 | | |
| 2002–03 | Banik Ostrava | 12 | 1 | **13** | **1** |
| 2003–04 | Arsenal | 0 | 0 | | |

**PARLOUR, Ray (M) 339 22**

H: 5 10 W: 12 13 b.Romford 7-3-73

*Source:* Trainee. *Honours:* England Under-21, B, 10 full caps.

| | | | | | |
|---|---|---|---|---|---|
| 1990–91 | Arsenal | 0 | 0 | | |
| 1991–92 | Arsenal | 6 | 1 | | |
| 1992–93 | Arsenal | 21 | 1 | | |
| 1993–94 | Arsenal | 27 | 2 | | |
| 1994–95 | Arsenal | 30 | 0 | | |
| 1995–96 | Arsenal | 22 | 0 | | |
| 1996–97 | Arsenal | 30 | 2 | | |
| 1997–98 | Arsenal | 34 | 5 | | |
| 1998–99 | Arsenal | 35 | 6 | | |
| 1999–2000 | Arsenal | 30 | 1 | | |
| 2000–01 | Arsenal | 33 | 4 | | |
| 2001–02 | Arsenal | 27 | 0 | | |
| 2002–03 | Arsenal | 19 | 0 | | |
| 2003–04 | Arsenal | 25 | 0 | **339** | **22** |

**PAULINHO* (M) 0 0**

H: 5 7 W: 10 04 b.Sao Paulo 2-3-83

*Source:* Sao Paulo.

| | | | |
|---|---|---|---|
| 2001–02 | Arsenal | 0 | 0 |
| 2002–03 | Arsenal | 0 | 0 |
| 2003–04 | Arsenal | 0 | 0 |

**PENNANT, Jermaine (M) 62 7**

H: 5 9 W: 10 06 b.Nottingham 15-1-83

*Honours:* England Schools, Youth, England Under-21.

| | | | | | |
|---|---|---|---|---|---|
| 1998–99 | Notts Co | 0 | 0 | | |
| 1998–99 | Arsenal | 0 | 0 | | |
| 1999–2000 | Arsenal | 0 | 0 | | |
| 2000–01 | Arsenal | 0 | 0 | | |
| 2001–02 | Arsenal | 0 | 0 | | |
| 2001–02 | *Watford* | 9 | 2 | | |
| 2002–03 | Arsenal | 5 | 3 | | |
| 2002–03 | *Watford* | 12 | 0 | **21** | **2** |
| 2003–04 | Arsenal | 0 | 0 | **5** | **3** |
| 2003–04 | *Leeds U* | 36 | 2 | **36** | **2** |

**PIRES, Robert (M) 351 92**

H: 6 1 W: 12 09 b.Reims 29-10-73

*Honours:* France 74 full caps, 14 goals.

| | | | | | |
|---|---|---|---|---|---|
| 1992–93 | Metz | 2 | 0 | | |
| 1993–94 | Metz | 24 | 1 | | |
| 1994–95 | Metz | 35 | 9 | | |
| 1995–96 | Metz | 38 | 11 | | |
| 1996–97 | Metz | 32 | 11 | | |
| 1997–98 | Metz | 31 | 11 | **162** | **43** |
| 1998–99 | Marseille | 34 | 6 | | |
| 1999–2000 | Marseille | 32 | 2 | **66** | **8** |
| 2000–01 | Arsenal | 33 | 4 | | |
| 2001–02 | Arsenal | 28 | 9 | | |
| 2002–03 | Arsenal | 26 | 14 | | |
| 2003–04 | Arsenal | 36 | 14 | **123** | **41** |

**PROBETS, Ashley* (D) 0 0**

b.Bexley 13-12-84

| | | | |
|---|---|---|---|
| 2003–04 | Arsenal | 0 | 0 |

**REYES, Jose Antonio (F) 130 25**

H: 5 9 W: 12 01 b.Utrera 1-9-83

*Honours:* Spain 3 full caps, 2 goals.

| | | | | | |
|---|---|---|---|---|---|
| 1999–2000 | Sevilla B | 32 | 1 | | |
| 1999–2000 | Sevilla | 1 | 0 | | |
| 2000–01 | Sevilla B | 0 | 0 | **32** | **1** |
| 2000–01 | Sevilla | 1 | 0 | | |
| 2001–02 | Sevilla | 29 | 8 | | |
| 2002–03 | Sevilla | 34 | 9 | | |
| 2003–04 | Sevilla | 20 | 5 | **85** | **22** |
| 2003–04 | Arsenal | 13 | 2 | **13** | **2** |

**SENDEROS, Philippe (D) 26 3**

H: 6 1 W: 13 10 b.Geneva 14-2-85

| | | | | | |
|---|---|---|---|---|---|
| 2001–02 | Servette | 3 | 0 | | |
| 2002–03 | Servette | 23 | 3 | **26** | **3** |
| 2003–04 | Arsenal | 0 | 0 | | |

**SHAABAN, Rami* (G) 144 0**

H: 6 4 W: 14 02 b.Sweden 30-6-75

| | | | | | |
|---|---|---|---|---|---|
| 1994 | Saltsjobadens | 26 | 0 | | |
| 1995 | Saltsjobadens | 13 | 0 | **39** | **0** |
| 1995–96 | Zamalek | 4 | 0 | **4** | **0** |
| 1995–96 | Thadodosman | 5 | 0 | **5** | **0** |
| 1997 | Nacka | 2 | 0 | | |
| 1998 | Nacka | 20 | 0 | | |
| 1999 | Nacka | 26 | 0 | **48** | **0** |
| 2000 | Djurgaarden | 29 | 0 | | |
| 2001 | Djurgaarden | 5 | 0 | | |
| 2002 | Djurgaarden | 6 | 0 | **40** | **0** |
| 2002–03 | Arsenal | 3 | 0 | | |
| 2003–04 | Arsenal | 0 | 0 | **3** | **0** |
| 2003–04 | *West Ham U* | 0 | 0 | | |

**SHIELS, Dean (F) 0 0**

H: 5 11 W: 9 10 b.Magherfelt 1-2-85

*Source:* Trainee.

| | | | |
|---|---|---|---|
| 2002–03 | Arsenal | 0 | 0 |
| 2003–04 | Arsenal | 0 | 0 |

**SILVA, Gilberto (M) 94 7**

H: 6 3 W: 12 04 b.Lagoa da Prata 7-10-76

*Honours:* Brazil 27 full caps, 3 goals.

| | | | | | |
|---|---|---|---|---|---|
| 2000 | Atletico Mineiro | 1 | 0 | | |
| 2001 | Atletico Mineiro | 26 | 3 | **27** | **3** |
| 2002–03 | Arsenal | 35 | 0 | | |
| 2003–04 | Arsenal | 32 | 4 | **67** | **4** |

**SIMEK, Franklin (D) 0 0**

H: 6 0 W: 11 06 b.St Louis 13-10-84

*Source:* Trainee.

| | | | |
|---|---|---|---|
| 2002–03 | Arsenal | 0 | 0 |
| 2003–04 | Arsenal | 0 | 0 |

**SKULASON, Olafur-Ingi (M) 0 0**

H: 6 0 W: 12 04 b.Reykjavik 1-4-83

*Honours:* Iceland Under 21, 1 full cap.

*Source:* Fylkir.

| | | | |
|---|---|---|---|
| 2001–02 | Arsenal | 0 | 0 |
| 2002–03 | Arsenal | 0 | 0 |
| 2003–04 | Arsenal | 0 | 0 |

**SPICER, John (M) 0 0**

H: 5 11 W: 11 08 b.Romford 13-9-83

*Source:* Scholar. *Honours:* England Youth, Under-20.

| | | | |
|---|---|---|---|
| 2001–02 | Arsenal | 0 | 0 |
| 2002–03 | Arsenal | 0 | 0 |
| 2003–04 | Arsenal | 0 | 0 |

**STACK, Graham (G) 0 0**

H: 6 2 W: 13 02 b.Hampstead 26-9-81

*Honours:* Eire Under-21.

| | | | |
|---|---|---|---|
| 2000–01 | Arsenal | 0 | 0 |
| 2001–02 | Arsenal | 0 | 0 |
| 2002–03 | Arsenal | 0 | 0 |
| 2003–04 | Arsenal | 0 | 0 |

**STEPANOVS, Igor* (D) 166 13**

H: 6 4 W: 13 05 b.Ogre 21-1-76

*Honours:* Latvia 71 full caps, 3 goals.

| | | | | | |
|---|---|---|---|---|---|
| 1994 | Interskonto | 20 | 2 | **20** | **2** |
| 1995 | Skonto Riga | 23 | 1 | | |
| 1996 | Skonto Riga | 22 | 2 | | |
| 1997 | Skonto Riga | 22 | 2 | | |
| 1998 | Skonto Riga | 24 | 0 | | |
| 1999 | Skonto Riga | 20 | 4 | | |
| 2000 | Skonto Riga | 18 | 2 | **129** | **11** |
| 2000–01 | Arsenal | 9 | 0 | | |
| 2001–02 | Arsenal | 6 | 0 | | |
| 2002–03 | Arsenal | 2 | 0 | | |
| 2003–04 | Arsenal | 0 | 0 | **17** | **0** |

**SVARD, Sebastian (M) 13 1**

H: 6 0 W: 12 06 b.Hvidovre 15-1-83

| | | | | | |
|---|---|---|---|---|---|
| 2000–01 | Arsenal | 0 | 0 | | |
| 2001–02 | Arsenal | 0 | 0 | | |
| 2002–03 | Arsenal | 0 | 0 | | |
| 2003–04 | Arsenal | 0 | 0 | | |
| 2003–04 | *Stoke C* | 13 | 1 | **13** | **1** |

**TAVLARIDIS, Efstathios (D) 69 1**

H: 6 2 W: 12 11 b.Serres 25-1-80

| | | | | | |
|---|---|---|---|---|---|
| 1996–97 | Iraklis | 0 | 0 | | |
| 1997–98 | Iraklis | 2 | 0 | | |
| 1998–99 | Iraklis | 12 | 1 | | |
| 1999–2000 | Iraklis | 23 | 0 | | |
| 2000–01 | Iraklis | 27 | 0 | **64** | **1** |
| 2001–02 | Arsenal | 0 | 0 | | |
| 2002–03 | Arsenal | 1 | 0 | | |
| 2002–03 | *Portsmouth* | 4 | 0 | **4** | **0** |
| 2003–04 | Arsenal | 0 | 0 | **1** | **0** |

**TAYLOR, Stuart (G)** **38** **0**
H: 6 5 W: 14 03 b.Romford 28-11-80
*Source:* Trainee. *Honours:* FA Schools, England Youth, Under-21.

| | | | | | |
|---|---|---|---|---|---|
| 1998–99 | Arsenal | 0 | 0 | | |
| 1999–2000 | Arsenal | 0 | 0 | | |
| 1999–2000 | *Bristol R* | 4 | 0 | **4** | **0** |
| 2000–01 | Arsenal | 0 | 0 | | |
| 2000–01 | *Crystal Palace* | 10 | 0 | **10** | **0** |
| 2000–01 | *Peterborough U* | 6 | 0 | **6** | **0** |
| 2001–02 | Arsenal | 10 | 0 | | |
| 2002–03 | Arsenal | 8 | 0 | | |
| 2003–04 | Arsenal | 0 | 0 | **18** | **0** |

**TOURE, Kolo (D)** **63** **3**
H: 5 10 W: 13 08 b.Ivory Coast 19-3-81
*Source:* ASEC Mimosas. *Honours:* Ivory Coast full caps.

| | | | | | |
|---|---|---|---|---|---|
| 2001–02 | Arsenal | 0 | 0 | | |
| 2002–03 | Arsenal | 26 | 2 | | |
| 2003–04 | Arsenal | 37 | 1 | **63** | **3** |

**VAN BRONCKHORST, Giovanni (M)** **229** **39**
H: 5 9 W: 11 03 b.Rotterdam 5-2-75
*Source:* LMO, SC Feyenoord.
*Honours:* Holland 41 full caps, 3 goals.

| | | | | | |
|---|---|---|---|---|---|
| 1993–94 | Feyenoord | 0 | 0 | | |
| 1993–94 | RKC | 12 | 2 | **12** | **2** |
| 1994–95 | Feyenoord | 10 | 1 | | |
| 1995–96 | Feyenoord | 27 | 9 | | |
| 1996–97 | Feyenoord | 34 | 4 | | |
| 1997–98 | Feyenoord | 32 | 8 | **103** | **22** |
| 1998–99 | Rangers | 35 | 7 | | |
| 1999–2000 | Rangers | 27 | 4 | | |
| 2000–01 | Rangers | 11 | 2 | | |
| 2000–01 | Rangers | 0 | 0 | **73** | **13** |
| 2001–02 | Arsenal | 21 | 1 | | |
| 2002–03 | Arsenal | 20 | 1 | | |
| 2003–04 | Arsenal | 0 | 0 | **41** | **2** |

**VIEIRA, Patrick (M)** **298** **24**
H: 6 4 W: 13 09 b.Dakar 23-6-76
*Honours:* France Under-21, 72 full caps, 4 goals.

| | | | | | |
|---|---|---|---|---|---|
| 1993–94 | Cannes | 5 | 0 | | |
| 1994–95 | Cannes | 31 | 2 | | |
| 1995–96 | Cannes | 13 | 0 | **49** | **2** |
| 1995–96 | AC Milan | 2 | 0 | **2** | **0** |
| 1996–97 | Arsenal | 31 | 2 | | |
| 1997–98 | Arsenal | 33 | 2 | | |
| 1998–99 | Arsenal | 34 | 3 | | |
| 1999–2000 | Arsenal | 30 | 2 | | |
| 2000–01 | Arsenal | 30 | 5 | | |
| 2001–02 | Arsenal | 36 | 2 | | |
| 2002–03 | Arsenal | 24 | 3 | | |
| 2003–04 | Arsenal | 29 | 3 | **247** | **22** |

**WILTORD, Sylvain* (F)** **330** **89**
H: 5 9 W: 12 04 b.Neuilly-sur-Mame 10-5-74
*Honours:* France 65 full caps, 22 goals.

| | | | | | |
|---|---|---|---|---|---|
| 1991–92 | Rennes | 0 | 0 | | |
| 1992–93 | Rennes | 2 | 0 | | |
| 1993–94 | Rennes | 26 | 8 | | |
| 1994–95 | La Coruna | 0 | 0 | | |
| 1994–95 | Rennes | 25 | 5 | | |
| 1995–96 | Rennes | 37 | 15 | | |
| 1996–97 | Rennes | 35 | 5 | **125** | **33** |
| 1997–98 | Bordeaux | 34 | 10 | | |
| 1998–99 | Bordeaux | 33 | 2 | | |
| 1999–2000 | Bordeaux | 32 | 13 | **99** | **25** |
| 2000–01 | Arsenal | 27 | 8 | | |
| 2001–02 | Arsenal | 33 | 10 | | |
| 2002–03 | Arsenal | 34 | 10 | | |
| 2003–04 | Arsenal | 12 | 3 | **106** | **31** |

**Scholars**
Abduklkadir, Issa; Clohessy, Sean D; Djourou-Gbadjere, Johan Danon; Fabregas Soler, Francesc; Gilbert, Kerrea K; Hislop, Matthew H; Howard, Mark S; Jordan, Michael W; Kanu, Samuel; Owusu-Abeyie, Quincy J; Samuel, Aaron D; Smith, Ryan M; Spaul, Daniel C; Webb, Luke A; Wright, Christopher W

## ASTON VILLA (2)

**AARITALO, Mika (F)** **0** **0**
H: 6 1 W: 12 13 b.Taivassalo 25-7-85
*Source:* TPS Turku.

| | | | | | |
|---|---|---|---|---|---|
| 2002–03 | Aston Villa | 0 | 0 | | |
| 2003–04 | Aston Villa | 0 | 0 | | |

**ALLBACK, Marcus (F)** **306** **120**
H: 5 9 W: 12 00 b.Stockholm 5-7-73
*Honours:* Sweden 42 full caps, 20 goals.

| | | | | | |
|---|---|---|---|---|---|
| 1992 | Orgryte | 24 | 10 | | |
| 1993 | Orgryte | 20 | 4 | | |
| 1994 | Orgryte | 25 | 19 | | |
| 1995 | Orgryte | 22 | 4 | | |
| 1996 | Orgryte | 24 | 8 | | |
| 1997 | Orgryte | 24 | 9 | | |
| 1997–98 | Lyngby | 4 | 1 | **4** | **1** |
| 1997–98 | Bari | 16 | 0 | **16** | **0** |
| 1998 | Orgryte | 12 | 3 | | |
| 1999 | Orgryte | 26 | 15 | | |
| 2000 | Orgryte | 26 | 16 | **203** | **88** |
| 2000–01 | Heerenveen | 16 | 10 | | |
| 2001–02 | Heerenveen | 32 | 15 | **48** | **25** |
| 2002–03 | Aston Villa | 20 | 5 | | |
| 2003–04 | Aston Villa | 15 | 1 | **35** | **6** |

**ALPAY, Ozalan‡ (D)** **258** **14**
H: 6 2 W: 14 00 b.Izmir 29-5-73
*Source:* Soma Linyit. *Honours:* Turkey 84 full caps, 4 goals.

| | | | | | |
|---|---|---|---|---|---|
| 1992–93 | Altay | 23 | 1 | **23** | **1** |
| 1993–94 | Besiktas | 10 | 0 | | |
| 1994–95 | Besiktas | 29 | 3 | | |
| 1995–96 | Besiktas | 31 | 2 | | |
| 1996–97 | Besiktas | 25 | 3 | | |
| 1997–98 | Besiktas | 26 | 1 | | |
| 1998–99 | Besiktas | 27 | 0 | **148** | **9** |
| 1999–2000 | Fenerbahce | 29 | 3 | **29** | **3** |
| 2000–01 | Aston Villa | 33 | 0 | | |
| 2001–02 | Aston Villa | 14 | 0 | | |
| 2002–03 | Aston Villa | 5 | 0 | | |
| 2003–04 | Aston Villa | 6 | 1 | **58** | **1** |

**ANGEL, Juan Pablo (F)** **177** **75**
H: 6 0 W: 12 10 b.Medellin 24-10-75
*Source:* Nacional. *Honours:* Colombia 24 caps, 7 goals.

| | | | | | |
|---|---|---|---|---|---|
| 1997–98 | River Plate | 12 | 2 | | |
| 1998–99 | River Plate | 27 | 11 | | |
| 1999–2000 | River Plate | 34 | 19 | | |
| 2000–01 | River Plate | 18 | 13 | **91** | **45** |
| 2000–01 | Aston Villa | 9 | 1 | | |
| 2001–02 | Aston Villa | 29 | 12 | | |
| 2002–03 | Aston Villa | 15 | 1 | | |
| 2003–04 | Aston Villa | 33 | 16 | **86** | **30** |

**BALABAN, Bosko‡ (F)** **153** **50**
H: 5 10 W: 11 10 b.Rijeka 15-10-78
*Honours:* Croatia 13 full caps, 6 goals.

| | | | | | |
|---|---|---|---|---|---|
| 1995–96 | Rijeka | 2 | 0 | | |
| 1996–97 | Rijeka | 17 | 1 | | |
| 1997–98 | Rijeka | 26 | 1 | | |
| 1998–99 | Rijeka | 23 | 4 | | |
| 1999–2000 | Rijeka | 29 | 15 | **97** | **21** |
| 2000–01 | Dynamo Zagreb | 25 | 14 | | |
| 2001–02 | Aston Villa | 8 | 0 | | |
| 2002–03 | Aston Villa | 0 | 0 | | |
| 2002–03 | Dynamo Zagreb | 23 | 15 | **48** | **29** |
| 2003–04 | Aston Villa | 0 | 0 | **8** | **0** |

**BARRY, Gareth (D)** **185** **9**
H: 5 11 W: 12 06 b.Hastings 23-2-81
*Source:* Trainee. *Honours:* England Youth, Under-21, 8 full caps.

| | | | | | |
|---|---|---|---|---|---|
| 1997–98 | Aston Villa | 2 | 0 | | |
| 1998–99 | Aston Villa | 32 | 2 | | |
| 1999–2000 | Aston Villa | 30 | 1 | | |
| 2000–01 | Aston Villa | 30 | 0 | | |
| 2001–02 | Aston Villa | 20 | 0 | | |
| 2002–03 | Aston Villa | 35 | 3 | | |
| 2003–04 | Aston Villa | 36 | 3 | **185** | **9** |

**BRAZIL, Alan (M)** **0** **0**
H: 5 7 W: 12 02 b.Edinburgh 5-7-85
*Source:* Trainee.

| | | | | | |
|---|---|---|---|---|---|
| 2002–03 | Aston Villa | 0 | 0 | | |
| 2003–04 | Aston Villa | 0 | 0 | | |

**BRIDGES, Stuart (D)** **0** **0**
H: 5 9 W: 11 09 b.Oxford 6-1-86
*Source:* Trainee. *Honours:* FA Schools, England Youth.

| | | | | | |
|---|---|---|---|---|---|
| 2002–03 | Aston Villa | 0 | 0 | | |
| 2003–04 | Aston Villa | 0 | 0 | | |

**CAHILL, Gary (D)** **0** **0**
H: 6 2 W: 12 06 b.Sheffield 19-12-85
*Source:* Trainee.

| | | | | | |
|---|---|---|---|---|---|
| 2003–04 | Aston Villa | 0 | 0 | | |

**COOKE, Stephen (M)** **13** **0**
H: 5 7 W: 9 00 b.Walsall 15-2-83
*Honours:* England Youth, Under-20.

| | | | | | |
|---|---|---|---|---|---|
| 1999–2000 | Aston Villa | 0 | 0 | | |
| 2000–01 | Aston Villa | 0 | 0 | | |
| 2001–02 | Aston Villa | 0 | 0 | | |
| 2001–02 | *Bournemouth* | 7 | 0 | | |
| 2002–03 | Aston Villa | 3 | 0 | | |
| 2003–04 | Aston Villa | 0 | 0 | **3** | **0** |
| 2003–04 | *Bournemouth* | 3 | 0 | **10** | **0** |

**CORMELL, Scott* (M)** **0** **0**
H: 5 7 W: 9 11 b.Birmingham 29-10-84
*Source:* Scholar.

| | | | | | |
|---|---|---|---|---|---|
| 2003–04 | Aston Villa | 0 | 0 | | |

**CROUCH, Peter (F)** **131** **38**
H: 6 7 W: 11 12 b.Macclesfield 30-1-81
*Source:* Trainee. *Honours:* England Youth, Under-20, Under-21.

| | | | | | |
|---|---|---|---|---|---|
| 1998–99 | Tottenham H | 0 | 0 | | |
| 1999–2000 | Tottenham H | 0 | 0 | | |
| 2000–01 | QPR | 42 | 10 | **42** | **10** |
| 2001–02 | Portsmouth | 37 | 18 | **37** | **18** |
| 2001–02 | Aston Villa | 7 | 2 | | |
| 2002–03 | Aston Villa | 14 | 0 | | |
| 2003–04 | Aston Villa | 16 | 4 | **37** | **6** |
| 2003–04 | *Norwich C* | 15 | 4 | **15** | **4** |

**DAVIS, Steven (M)** **0** **0**
H: 5 7 W: 9 07 b.Ballymena 1-1-85
*Source:* Scholar. *Honours:* Northern Ireland Under-21.

| | | | | | |
|---|---|---|---|---|---|
| 2001–02 | Aston Villa | 0 | 0 | | |
| 2002–03 | Aston Villa | 0 | 0 | | |
| 2003–04 | Aston Villa | 0 | 0 | | |

**DE LA CRUZ, Ulises (D)** **132** **12**
H: 5 8 W: 12 10 b.Bolivar 8-2-74
*Source:* Cruzeiro. *Honours:* Ecuador 67 full caps, 3 goals.

| | | | | | |
|---|---|---|---|---|---|
| 1999 | LDU Quito | 22 | 4 | | |
| 1999 | LDU Quito | 0 | 0 | | |
| 2000 | LDU Quito | 30 | 5 | **52** | **9** |
| 2001–02 | Hibernian | 32 | 2 | **32** | **2** |
| 2002–03 | Aston Villa | 20 | 1 | | |
| 2003–04 | Aston Villa | 28 | 0 | **48** | **1** |

**DELANEY, Mark (D)** **144** **1**
H: 6 1 W: 11 07 b.Haverfordwest 13-5-76
*Source:* Carmarthen T. *Honours:* Wales 26 full caps.

| | | | | | |
|---|---|---|---|---|---|
| 1998–99 | Cardiff C | 28 | 0 | **28** | **0** |
| 1998–99 | Aston Villa | 2 | 0 | | |
| 1999–2000 | Aston Villa | 28 | 1 | | |
| 2000–01 | Aston Villa | 19 | 0 | | |
| 2001–02 | Aston Villa | 30 | 0 | | |
| 2002–03 | Aston Villa | 12 | 0 | | |
| 2003–04 | Aston Villa | 25 | 0 | **116** | **1** |

**DUBLIN, Dion* (F)** **473** **165**
H: 6 2 W: 12 04 b.Leicester 22-4-69
*Source:* Oakham U. *Honours:* England 4 full caps.

| | | | | | |
|---|---|---|---|---|---|
| 1987–88 | Norwich C | 0 | 0 | | |
| 1988–89 | Cambridge U | 21 | 6 | | |
| 1989–90 | Cambridge U | 46 | 15 | | |
| 1990–91 | Cambridge U | 46 | 16 | | |
| 1991–92 | Cambridge U | 43 | 15 | **156** | **52** |
| 1992–93 | Manchester U | 7 | 1 | | |
| 1993–94 | Manchester U | 5 | 1 | **12** | **2** |
| 1994–95 | Coventry C | 31 | 13 | | |
| 1995–96 | Coventry C | 34 | 14 | | |
| 1996–97 | Coventry C | 34 | 13 | | |
| 1997–98 | Coventry C | 36 | 18 | | |
| 1998–99 | Coventry C | 10 | 3 | **145** | **61** |
| 1998–99 | Aston Villa | 24 | 11 | | |
| 1999–2000 | Aston Villa | 26 | 12 | | |
| 2000–01 | Aston Villa | 33 | 8 | | |
| 2001–02 | Aston Villa | 21 | 4 | | |
| 2001–02 | *Millwall* | 5 | 2 | **5** | **2** |

| | | | | | |
|---|---|---|---|---|---|
| 2002–03 | Aston Villa | 28 | 10 | | |
| 2003–04 | Aston Villa | 23 | 3 | **155** | **48** |

**EDWARDS, Rob (D)** **26 2**

H: 6 1 W: 11 10 b.Telford 25-12-82

*Source:* Trainee. *Honours:* Wales 6 full caps.

| | | | | | |
|---|---|---|---|---|---|
| 1999–2000 | Aston Villa | 0 | 0 | | |
| 2000–01 | Aston Villa | 0 | 0 | | |
| 2001–02 | Aston Villa | 0 | 0 | | |
| 2002–03 | Aston Villa | 8 | 0 | | |
| 2003–04 | Aston Villa | 0 | 0 | **8** | **0** |
| 2003–04 | *Crystal Palace* | 7 | 1 | **7** | **1** |
| 2003–04 | *Derby Co* | 11 | 1 | **11** | **1** |

**ENNIS, Pierre‡ (D)** **0 0**

H: 5 10 W: 12 03 b.Dublin 25-2-84

*Source:* Scholar.

| | | | | | |
|---|---|---|---|---|---|
| 2000–01 | Aston Villa | 0 | 0 | | |
| 2001–02 | Aston Villa | 0 | 0 | | |
| 2002–03 | Aston Villa | 0 | 0 | | |
| 2003–04 | Aston Villa | 0 | 0 | | |

**FOLEY-SHERIDAN, Steven (M)** **0 0**

H: 5 4 W: 9 02 b.Dublin 10-2-86

*Source:* Trainee.

| | | | | | |
|---|---|---|---|---|---|
| 2002–03 | Aston Villa | 0 | 0 | | |
| 2003–04 | Aston Villa | 0 | 0 | | |

**GRANT, Lee (M)** **0 0**

H: 6 2 W: 12 02 b.York 31-12-85

*Source:* Trainee.

| | | | | | |
|---|---|---|---|---|---|
| 2003–04 | Aston Villa | 0 | 0 | | |

**HADJI, Mustapha‡ (M)** **303 50**

H: 5 11 W: 11 12 b.Ifrane 16-11-71

*Honours:* Morocco 60 full caps.

| | | | | | |
|---|---|---|---|---|---|
| 1992–93 | Nancy | 32 | 6 | | |
| 1993–94 | Nancy | 37 | 11 | | |
| 1994–95 | Nancy | 28 | 3 | | |
| 1995–96 | Nancy | 42 | 11 | **139** | **31** |
| 1996–97 | Sporting | 27 | 3 | | |
| 1997–98 | Sporting | 9 | 0 | **36** | **3** |
| 1997–98 | La Coruna | 10 | 0 | | |
| 1998–99 | La Coruna | 21 | 2 | **31** | **2** |
| 1999–2000 | Coventry C | 33 | 6 | | |
| 2000–01 | Coventry C | 29 | 6 | **62** | **12** |
| 2001–02 | Aston Villa | 23 | 2 | | |
| 2002–03 | Aston Villa | 11 | 0 | | |
| 2003–04 | Aston Villa | 1 | 0 | **35** | **2** |

**HENDERSON, Wayne (G)** **3 0**

H: 5 11 W: 12 02 b.Dublin 16-9-83

*Source:* Scholar. *Honours:* Eire Under-21.

| | | | | | |
|---|---|---|---|---|---|
| 2000–01 | Aston Villa | 0 | 0 | | |
| 2001–02 | Aston Villa | 0 | 0 | | |
| 2002–03 | Aston Villa | 0 | 0 | | |
| 2003–04 | Aston Villa | 0 | 0 | | |
| 2003–04 | *Wycombe W* | 3 | 0 | **3** | **0** |

**HENDRIE, Lee (M)** **205 21**

H: 5 10 W: 11 00 b.Birmingham 18-5-77

*Source:* Trainee. *Honours:* England Youth, Under-21, B, 1 full cap.

| | | | | | |
|---|---|---|---|---|---|
| 1993–94 | Aston Villa | 0 | 0 | | |
| 1994–95 | Aston Villa | 0 | 0 | | |
| 1995–96 | Aston Villa | 3 | 0 | | |
| 1996–97 | Aston Villa | 4 | 0 | | |
| 1997–98 | Aston Villa | 17 | 3 | | |
| 1998–99 | Aston Villa | 32 | 3 | | |
| 1999–2000 | Aston Villa | 29 | 1 | | |
| 2000–01 | Aston Villa | 32 | 6 | | |
| 2001–02 | Aston Villa | 29 | 2 | | |
| 2002–03 | Aston Villa | 27 | 4 | | |
| 2003–04 | Aston Villa | 32 | 2 | **205** | **21** |

**HITZLSPERGER, Thomas (M)** **76 6**

H: 6 0 W: 11 12 b.Germany 5-4-82

*Source:* Bayern Munich. *Honours:* Germany Under-21.

| | | | | | |
|---|---|---|---|---|---|
| 2000–01 | Aston Villa | 1 | 0 | | |
| 2001–02 | *Chesterfield* | 5 | 0 | **5** | **0** |
| 2001–02 | Aston Villa | 12 | 1 | | |
| 2002–03 | Aston Villa | 26 | 2 | | |
| 2003–04 | Aston Villa | 32 | 3 | **71** | **6** |

**HYNES, Peter* (F)** **9 1**

H: 5 9 W: 11 12 b.Dublin 28-11-83

*Source:* Trainee.

| | | | | | |
|---|---|---|---|---|---|
| 2000–01 | Aston Villa | 0 | 0 | | |
| 2001–02 | Aston Villa | 0 | 0 | | |
| 2002–03 | Aston Villa | 0 | 0 | | |
| 2003–04 | Aston Villa | 0 | 0 | | |
| 2003–04 | *Doncaster R* | 5 | 1 | **5** | **1** |
| 2003–04 | *Cheltenham T* | 4 | 0 | **4** | **0** |

**JOHNSEN, Ronny* (D)** **224 20**

H: 6 2 W: 13 00 b.Sandefjord 10-6-69

*Honours:* Norway 61 full caps, 3 goals.

| | | | | | |
|---|---|---|---|---|---|
| 1992 | Lyn | 12 | 1 | | |
| 1993 | Lyn | 19 | 6 | **31** | **7** |
| 1994 | Lillestrom | 10 | 3 | | |
| 1995 | Lillestrom | 13 | 1 | **23** | **4** |
| 1995–96 | Besiktas | 22 | 1 | **22** | **1** |
| 1996–97 | Manchester U | 31 | 0 | | |
| 1997–98 | Manchester U | 22 | 2 | | |
| 1998–99 | Manchester U | 22 | 3 | | |
| 1999–2000 | Manchester U | 3 | 0 | | |
| 2000–01 | Manchester U | 11 | 1 | | |
| 2001–02 | Manchester U | 10 | 1 | **99** | **7** |
| 2002–03 | Aston Villa | 26 | 0 | | |
| 2003–04 | Aston Villa | 23 | 1 | **49** | **1** |

**KACHLOUL, Hassan* (M)** **249 48**

H: 6 1 W: 12 01 b.Agadir 19-2-73

*Honours:* Morocco 12 full caps.

| | | | | | |
|---|---|---|---|---|---|
| 1992–93 | Nimes | 17 | 1 | | |
| 1993–94 | Nimes | 37 | 17 | | |
| 1994–95 | Nimes | 32 | 8 | **86** | **26** |
| 1995–96 | Dunkerque | 28 | 6 | **28** | **6** |
| 1996–97 | Metz | 7 | 0 | **7** | **0** |
| 1997–98 | St Etienne | 16 | 0 | **16** | **0** |
| 1998–99 | Southampton | 22 | 5 | | |
| 1999–2000 | Southampton | 32 | 5 | | |
| 2000–01 | Southampton | 32 | 4 | **86** | **14** |
| 2001–02 | Aston Villa | 22 | 2 | | |
| 2002–03 | Aston Villa | 0 | 0 | | |
| 2003–04 | Aston Villa | 0 | 0 | **22** | **2** |
| 2003–04 | *Wolverhampton W* | 4 | 0 | **4** | **0** |

**KOUMAN, Amadou (F)** **0 0**

H: 5 9 W: 11 00 b.Marcory 14-4-86

*Source:* Trainee.

| | | | | | |
|---|---|---|---|---|---|
| 2002–03 | Aston Villa | 0 | 0 | | |
| 2003–04 | Aston Villa | 0 | 0 | | |

**MARSHALL, Colin* (M)** **0 0**

H: 5 8 W: 11 01 b.Glasgow 25-10-84

*Source:* Scholar.

| | | | | | |
|---|---|---|---|---|---|
| 2003–04 | Aston Villa | 0 | 0 | | |

**MASALIN, Jon (G)** **0 0**

H: 6 2 W: 14 06 b.Helsinki 29-1-86

| | | | | | |
|---|---|---|---|---|---|
| 2002–03 | Aston Villa | 0 | 0 | | |
| 2003–04 | Aston Villa | 0 | 0 | | |

**McCANN, Gavin (M)** **155 8**

H: 5 11 W: 11 00 b.Blackpool 10-1-78

*Source:* Trainee. *Honours:* England 1 full cap.

| | | | | | |
|---|---|---|---|---|---|
| 1995–96 | Everton | 0 | 0 | | |
| 1996–97 | Everton | 0 | 0 | | |
| 1997–98 | Everton | 11 | 0 | | |
| 1998–99 | Everton | 0 | 0 | **11** | **0** |
| 1998–99 | Sunderland | 11 | 0 | | |
| 1999–2000 | Sunderland | 24 | 4 | | |
| 2000–01 | Sunderland | 22 | 3 | | |
| 2001–02 | Sunderland | 29 | 0 | | |
| 2002–03 | Sunderland | 30 | 1 | **116** | **8** |
| 2003–04 | Aston Villa | 28 | 0 | **28** | **0** |

**MELLBERG, Olof (D)** **265 2**

H: 6 1 W: 12 10 b.Amncharad 3-9-77

*Honours:* Sweden 47 full caps, 1 goal.

| | | | | | |
|---|---|---|---|---|---|
| 1996 | Degerfors | 22 | 0 | | |
| 1997 | Degerfors | 25 | 0 | **47** | **0** |
| 1998 | AIK Stockholm | 17 | 0 | **17** | **0** |
| 1998–99 | Santander | 25 | 0 | | |
| 1999–2000 | Santander | 37 | 0 | | |
| 2000–01 | Santander | 36 | 0 | **98** | **0** |
| 2001–02 | Aston Villa | 32 | 0 | | |
| 2002–03 | Aston Villa | 38 | 1 | | |
| 2003–04 | Aston Villa | 33 | 1 | **103** | **2** |

**MOORE, Luke (F)** **13 4**

H: 5 11 W: 11 13 b.Birmingham 13-2-86

*Source:* Trainee. *Honours:* FA Schools, England Youth.

| | | | | | |
|---|---|---|---|---|---|
| 2002–03 | Aston Villa | 0 | 0 | | |
| 2003–04 | Aston Villa | 7 | 0 | **7** | **0** |
| 2003–04 | *Wycombe W* | 6 | 4 | **6** | **4** |

**MOORE, Stefan (F)** **23 2**

H: 5 10 W: 10 12 b.Birmingham 28-9-83

*Source:* Scholar. *Honours:* England Youth.

| | | | | | |
|---|---|---|---|---|---|
| 2000–01 | Aston Villa | 0 | 0 | | |
| 2001–02 | Aston Villa | 0 | 0 | | |
| 2001–02 | *Chesterfield* | 2 | 0 | **2** | **0** |
| 2002–03 | Aston Villa | 13 | 1 | | |
| 2003–04 | Aston Villa | 8 | 1 | **21** | **2** |

**MULCAHY, Kevin (D)** **0 0**

H: 5 10 W: 11 00 b.Cork 2-3-86

*Source:* Trainee.

| | | | | | |
|---|---|---|---|---|---|
| 2002–03 | Aston Villa | 0 | 0 | | |
| 2003–04 | Aston Villa | 0 | 0 | | |

**NIX, Kyle (F)** **0 0**

H: 5 6 W: 9 10 b.Sydney 21-1-86

*Source:* Manchester U Trainee. *Honours:* FA Schools, England Youth.

| | | | | | |
|---|---|---|---|---|---|
| 2002–03 | Aston Villa | 0 | 0 | | |
| 2003–04 | Aston Villa | 0 | 0 | | |

**O'CONNOR, James (D)** **0 0**

H: 5 10 W: 12 05 b.Birmingham 20-11-84

*Source:* Scholar.

| | | | | | |
|---|---|---|---|---|---|
| 2003–04 | Aston Villa | 0 | 0 | | |

**PECORA, Anthony* (G)** **0 0**

H: 6 2 W: 13 09 b.Hull 26-6-85

*Source:* Scholar.

| | | | | | |
|---|---|---|---|---|---|
| 2003–04 | Aston Villa | 0 | 0 | | |

**POSTMA, Stefan (G)** **108 0**

H: 6 4 W: 15 04 b.Utrecht 6-10-76

| | | | | | |
|---|---|---|---|---|---|
| 1995–96 | Utrecht | 5 | 0 | | |
| 1996–97 | Utrecht | 12 | 0 | | |
| 1997–98 | Utrecht | 13 | 0 | | |
| 1998–99 | Utrecht | 1 | 0 | | |
| 1999–2000 | Utrecht | 2 | 0 | **33** | **0** |
| 2000–01 | De Graafschap | 34 | 0 | | |
| 2001–02 | De Graafschap | 33 | 0 | **67** | **0** |
| 2002–03 | Aston Villa | 6 | 0 | | |
| 2003–04 | Aston Villa | 2 | 0 | **8** | **0** |

**RIDGEWELL, Liam (D)** **16 0**

H: 5 10 W: 10 03 b.London 21-7-84

*Source:* Scholar. *Honours:* England Youth, Under-21.

| | | | | | |
|---|---|---|---|---|---|
| 2001–02 | Aston Villa | 0 | 0 | | |
| 2002–03 | Aston Villa | 0 | 0 | | |
| 2002–03 | *Bournemouth* | 5 | 0 | **5** | **0** |
| 2003–04 | Aston Villa | 11 | 0 | **11** | **0** |

**SAMUEL, J Lloyd (D)** **119 2**

H: 5 11 W: 11 04 b.Trinidad 29-3-81

*Source:* Charlton Ath Trainee. *Honours:* England Youth, Under-20, Under-21.

| | | | | | |
|---|---|---|---|---|---|
| 1998–99 | Aston Villa | 0 | 0 | | |
| 1999–2000 | Aston Villa | 9 | 0 | | |
| 2000–01 | Aston Villa | 3 | 0 | | |
| 2001–02 | *Gillingham* | 8 | 0 | **8** | **0** |
| 2001–02 | Aston Villa | 23 | 0 | | |
| 2002–03 | Aston Villa | 38 | 0 | | |
| 2003–04 | Aston Villa | 38 | 2 | **111** | **2** |

**SCULLION, David* (F)** **8 2**

H: 5 8 W: 10 03 b.Craigavon 27-4-84

| | | | | | |
|---|---|---|---|---|---|
| 2000–01 | Portadown | 8 | 2 | **8** | **2** |
| 2001–02 | Aston Villa | 0 | 0 | | |
| 2002–03 | Aston Villa | 0 | 0 | | |
| 2003–04 | Aston Villa | 0 | 0 | | |

**SOLANO, Nolberto (M)** **289 66**

H: 5 9 W: 11 06 b.Callao 12-12-74

*Honours:* Peru 65 full caps, 14 goals.

| | | | | | |
|---|---|---|---|---|---|
| 1994–95 | Sporting Cristal | 38 | 12 | | |
| 1995–96 | Sporting Cristal | 26 | 13 | | |
| 1996–97 | Sporting Cristal | 11 | 7 | **75** | **32** |
| 1997–98 | Boca Juniors | 32 | 5 | **32** | **5** |
| 1998–99 | Newcastle U | 29 | 6 | | |
| 1999–2000 | Newcastle U | 30 | 3 | | |
| 2000–01 | Newcastle U | 33 | 6 | | |
| 2001–02 | Newcastle U | 37 | 7 | | |
| 2002–03 | Newcastle U | 31 | 7 | | |
| 2003–04 | Newcastle U | 12 | 0 | **172** | **29** |
| 2003–04 | Aston Villa | 10 | 0 | **10** | **0** |

**SORENSEN, Thomas (G)** **209 0**

H: 6 4 W: 13 10 b.Fredericia 12-6-76

*Source:* Odense. *Honours:* Denmark 40 full caps.

| | | | | | |
|---|---|---|---|---|---|
| 1998–99 | Sunderland | 45 | 0 | | |
| 1999–2000 | Sunderland | 37 | 0 | | |
| 2000–01 | Sunderland | 34 | 0 | | |
| 2001–02 | Sunderland | 34 | 0 | | |
| 2002–03 | Sunderland | 21 | 0 | **171** | **0** |
| 2003–04 | Aston Villa | 38 | 0 | **38** | **0** |

**VASSELL, Darius (F)** **141 33**

H: 5 7 W: 12 00 b.Birmingham 13-6-80

*Source:* Trainee. *Honours:* England Youth, Under-21, 22 full caps, 6 goals.

| | | | | | |
|---|---|---|---|---|---|
| 1998–99 | Aston Villa | 6 | 0 | | |

| | | | | | |
|---|---|---|---|---|---|
| 1999–2000 | Aston Villa | 11 | 0 | | |
| 2000–01 | Aston Villa | 23 | 4 | | |
| 2001–02 | Aston Villa | 36 | 12 | | |
| 2002–03 | Aston Villa | 33 | 8 | | |
| 2003–04 | Aston Villa | 32 | 9 | **141** | **33** |

**WARD, Jamie (M)** **0 0**
H: 5 5 W: 9 04 b.Birmingham 12-5-86
*Source:* Scholar.

| | | | | | |
|---|---|---|---|---|---|
| 2003–04 | Aston Villa | 0 | 0 | | |

**WHITTINGHAM, Peter (D)** **36 0**
H: 5 10 W: 9 13 b.Nuneaton 8-9-84
*Source:* Trainee. *Honours:* England Youth, Under-21.

| | | | | | |
|---|---|---|---|---|---|
| 2002–03 | Aston Villa | 4 | 0 | | |
| 2003–04 | Aston Villa | 32 | 0 | **36** | **0** |

**Scholars**
Agbonlohor, Gabriel; Edkins, Ashley M; Gardner, Craig; Green, Paul M; Morgan, Oluwaseyi; Olejnik, Robert; Paul, Shane R; Troest, Magnus; Tshimanga, Christian K; Tuohy, Michael; Williams, Sam

## BARNSLEY (3)

**ALCOCK, Danny† (G)** **1 0**
H: 5 11 W: 11 03 b.Staffordshire 15-2-84
*Source:* Scholar.

| | | | | | |
|---|---|---|---|---|---|
| 2001–02 | Stoke C | 0 | 0 | | |
| 2002–03 | Stoke C | 0 | 0 | | |
| 2003–04 | Barnsley | 1 | 0 | **1** | **0** |

**ATKINSON, Robert§ (M)** **1 0**
H: 6 1 W: 12 00 b.Beverley 29-4-87
*Source:* Scholar.

| | | | | | |
|---|---|---|---|---|---|
| 2003–04 | Barnsley | 1 | 0 | **1** | **0** |

**AUSTIN, Neil (D)** **71 0**
H: 5 11 W: 11 09 b.Barnsley 26-4-83
*Source:* Trainee. *Honours:* England Youth, Under-20.

| | | | | | |
|---|---|---|---|---|---|
| 1999–2000 | Barnsley | 0 | 0 | | |
| 2000–01 | Barnsley | 0 | 0 | | |
| 2001–02 | Barnsley | 0 | 0 | | |
| 2002–03 | Barnsley | 34 | 0 | | |
| 2003–04 | Barnsley | 37 | 0 | **71** | **0** |

**BAKER, Tom§ (F)** **1 0**
H: 5 5 W: 9 00 b.Salford 28-3-85
*Source:* Scholar.

| | | | | | |
|---|---|---|---|---|---|
| 2003–04 | Barnsley | 1 | 0 | **1** | **0** |

**BERESFORD, Marlon (G)** **369 0**
H: 6 1 W: 13 01 b.Lincoln 2-9-69
*Source:* Trainee.

| | | | | | |
|---|---|---|---|---|---|
| 1987–88 | Sheffield W | 0 | 0 | | |
| 1988–89 | Sheffield W | 0 | 0 | | |
| 1989–90 | Sheffield W | 0 | 0 | | |
| 1989–90 | *Bury* | 1 | 0 | **1** | **0** |
| 1989–90 | *Ipswich T* | 0 | 0 | | |
| 1990–91 | Sheffield W | 0 | 0 | | |
| 1990–91 | *Northampton T* | 13 | 0 | | |
| 1990–91 | *Crewe Alex* | 3 | 0 | **3** | **0** |
| 1991–92 | Sheffield W | 0 | 0 | | |
| 1991–92 | *Northampton T* | 15 | 0 | **28** | **0** |
| 1992–93 | Burnley | 44 | 0 | | |
| 1993–94 | Burnley | 46 | 0 | | |
| 1994–95 | Burnley | 40 | 0 | | |
| 1995–96 | Burnley | 36 | 0 | | |
| 1996–97 | Burnley | 40 | 0 | | |
| 1997–98 | Burnley | 34 | 0 | | |
| 1997–98 | Middlesbrough | 3 | 0 | | |
| 1998–99 | Middlesbrough | 4 | 0 | | |
| 1999–2000 | Middlesbrough | 1 | 0 | | |
| 2000–01 | Middlesbrough | 1 | 0 | | |
| 2000–01 | *Sheffield W* | 4 | 0 | **4** | **0** |
| 2001–02 | Middlesbrough | 1 | 0 | **10** | **0** |
| 2001–02 | *Wolverhampton W* | 0 | 0 | | |
| 2001–02 | *Burnley* | 13 | 0 | | |
| 2002–03 | York C | 6 | 0 | **6** | **0** |
| 2002–03 | Burnley | 34 | 0 | | |
| 2003–04 | Burnley | 0 | 0 | **287** | **0** |
| 2003–04 | Bradford C | 5 | 0 | **5** | **0** |
| 2003–04 | Luton T | 11 | 0 | **11** | **0** |
| 2003–04 | Barnsley | 14 | 0 | **14** | **0** |

**BETSY, Kevin (M)** **116 16**
H: 6 1 W: 12 00 b.Seychelles 20-3-78
*Source:* Woking.

| | | | | | |
|---|---|---|---|---|---|
| 1998–99 | Fulham | 7 | 1 | | |
| 1999–2000 | Fulham | 2 | 0 | | |
| 1999–2000 | *Bournemouth* | 5 | 0 | **5** | **0** |
| 1999–2000 | *Hull C* | 2 | 0 | **2** | **0** |
| 2000–01 | Fulham | 5 | 0 | | |
| 2001–02 | Fulham | 1 | 0 | **15** | **1** |
| 2001–02 | Barnsley | 10 | 0 | | |
| 2002–03 | Barnsley | 39 | 5 | | |
| 2003–04 | Barnsley | 45 | 10 | **94** | **15** |

**BOULDING, Mick (F)** **152 39**
H: 5 8 W: 11 05 b.Sheffield 8-2-76

| | | | | | |
|---|---|---|---|---|---|
| 1999–2000 | Mansfield T | 33 | 6 | | |
| 2000–01 | Mansfield T | 33 | 6 | | |
| 2001–02 | Mansfield T | 0 | 0 | **66** | **12** |
| 2001–02 | Grimsby T | 35 | 11 | | |
| 2002–03 | Aston Villa | 0 | 0 | | |
| 2002–03 | *Sheffield U* | 6 | 0 | **6** | **0** |
| 2002–03 | Grimsby T | 12 | 4 | | |
| 2003–04 | Grimsby T | 27 | 12 | **74** | **27** |
| 2003–04 | Barnsley | 6 | 0 | **6** | **0** |

**BURNS, Jacob# (M)** **110 9**
H: 5 6 W: 11 08 b.Sydney 21-1-78
*Honours:* Australia Under-23, 2 full caps.

| | | | | | |
|---|---|---|---|---|---|
| 1996–97 | Sydney U | 5 | 0 | | |
| 1997–98 | Sydney U | 25 | 2 | | |
| 1998–99 | Sydney U | 27 | 3 | **57** | **5** |
| 1999–2000 | Parramatta Power | 25 | 3 | **25** | **3** |
| 2000–01 | Leeds U | 4 | 0 | | |
| 2001–02 | Leeds U | 0 | 0 | | |
| 2002–03 | Leeds U | 2 | 0 | | |
| 2003–04 | Leeds U | 0 | 0 | **6** | **0** |
| 2003–04 | Barnsley | 22 | 1 | **22** | **1** |

**CROOKS, Lee* (M)** **146 2**
H: 6 2 W: 13 01 b.Wakefield 14-1-78
*Source:* Trainee. *Honours:* England Youth.

| | | | | | |
|---|---|---|---|---|---|
| 1994–95 | Manchester C | 0 | 0 | | |
| 1995–96 | Manchester C | 0 | 0 | | |
| 1996–97 | Manchester C | 15 | 0 | | |
| 1997–98 | Manchester C | 5 | 0 | | |
| 1998–99 | Manchester C | 34 | 1 | | |
| 1999–2000 | Manchester C | 20 | 1 | | |
| 2000–01 | Manchester C | 2 | 0 | **76** | **2** |
| 2000–01 | *Northampton T* | 3 | 0 | **3** | **0** |
| 2000–01 | Barnsley | 0 | 0 | | |
| 2001–02 | Barnsley | 26 | 0 | | |
| 2002–03 | Barnsley | 18 | 0 | | |
| 2003–04 | Barnsley | 23 | 0 | **67** | **0** |

**DIXON, Kevin‡ (M)** **3 0**
H: 5 8 W: 12 08 b.Easington 27-6-80
*Source:* Trainee. *Honours:* England Youth.

| | | | | | |
|---|---|---|---|---|---|
| 1997–98 | Leeds U | 0 | 0 | | |
| 1998–99 | Leeds U | 0 | 0 | | |
| 1999–2000 | Leeds U | 0 | 0 | | |
| 1999–2000 | *York C* | 3 | 0 | **3** | **0** |
| 2000–01 | Leeds U | 0 | 0 | | |
| 2001–02 | Barnsley | 0 | 0 | | |
| 2002–03 | Barnsley | 0 | 0 | | |
| 2003–04 | Barnsley | 0 | 0 | | |

**GALLIMORE, Tony* (D)** **444 13**
H: 5 11 W: 11 01 b.Crewe 21-2-72
*Source:* Trainee.

| | | | | | |
|---|---|---|---|---|---|
| 1989–90 | Stoke C | 1 | 0 | | |
| 1990–91 | Stoke C | 7 | 0 | | |
| 1991–92 | Stoke C | 3 | 0 | | |
| 1991–92 | *Carlisle U* | 16 | 0 | | |
| 1992–93 | Stoke C | 0 | 0 | **11** | **0** |
| 1992–93 | *Carlisle U* | 8 | 1 | | |
| 1993–94 | Carlisle U | 40 | 1 | | |
| 1994–95 | Carlisle U | 40 | 5 | | |
| 1995–96 | Carlisle U | 36 | 2 | **140** | **9** |
| 1995–96 | Grimsby T | 10 | 1 | | |
| 1996–97 | Grimsby T | 42 | 1 | | |
| 1997–98 | Grimsby T | 35 | 2 | | |
| 1998–99 | Grimsby T | 43 | 0 | | |
| 1999–2000 | Grimsby T | 39 | 0 | | |
| 2000–01 | Grimsby T | 28 | 0 | | |
| 2001–02 | Grimsby T | 38 | 0 | | |
| 2002–03 | Grimsby T | 38 | 0 | **273** | **4** |
| 2003–04 | Barnsley | 20 | 0 | **20** | **0** |

**GIBBS, Paul‡ (D)** **215 17**
H: 5 11 W: 11 07 b.Great Yarmouth 26-10-72
*Source:* Diss T.

| | | | | | |
|---|---|---|---|---|---|
| 1994–95 | Colchester U | 9 | 0 | | |
| 1995–96 | Colchester U | 24 | 3 | | |
| 1996–97 | Colchester U | 20 | 0 | **53** | **3** |
| 1997–98 | Torquay U | 41 | 7 | **41** | **7** |
| 1998–99 | Plymouth Arg | 27 | 3 | | |
| 1999–2000 | Plymouth Arg | 7 | 0 | **34** | **3** |
| 2000–01 | Brentford | 27 | 1 | | |
| 2001–02 | Brentford | 27 | 2 | **54** | **3** |
| 2001–02 | Barnsley | 4 | 0 | | |
| 2002–03 | Barnsley | 26 | 1 | | |
| 2003–04 | Barnsley | 3 | 0 | **33** | **1** |

**GORRE, Dean* (M)** **316 51**
H: 5 8 W: 11 04 b.Surinam 10-9-70

| | | | | | |
|---|---|---|---|---|---|
| 1991–92 | SVV/Dordrecht | 32 | 8 | **32** | **8** |
| 1992–93 | Feyenoord | 25 | 2 | | |
| 1993–94 | Feyenoord | 12 | 3 | | |
| 1994–95 | Feyenoord | 5 | 1 | **42** | **6** |
| 1994–95 | Groningen | 12 | 3 | | |
| 1995–96 | Groningen | 34 | 4 | | |
| 1996–97 | Groningen | 34 | 11 | **80** | **18** |
| 1997–98 | Ajax | 21 | 3 | | |
| 1998–99 | Ajax | 14 | 1 | **35** | **4** |
| 1999–2000 | Huddersfield T | 28 | 4 | | |
| 2000–01 | Huddersfield T | 34 | 2 | **62** | **6** |
| 2001–02 | Barnsley | 19 | 2 | | |
| 2002–03 | Barnsley | 27 | 0 | | |
| 2003–04 | Barnsley | 19 | 7 | **65** | **9** |

**HANDYSIDE, Peter* (D)** **296 4**
H: 6 1 W: 12 03 b.Dumfries 31-7-74
*Source:* Trainee. *Honours:* Scotland Under-21.

| | | | | | |
|---|---|---|---|---|---|
| 1992–93 | Grimsby T | 11 | 0 | | |
| 1993–94 | Grimsby T | 13 | 0 | | |
| 1994–95 | Grimsby T | 35 | 0 | | |
| 1995–96 | Grimsby T | 30 | 0 | | |
| 1996–97 | Grimsby T | 9 | 1 | | |
| 1997–98 | Grimsby T | 42 | 0 | | |
| 1998–99 | Grimsby T | 31 | 2 | | |
| 1999–2000 | Grimsby T | 0 | 0 | | |
| 2000–01 | Grimsby T | 19 | 1 | **190** | **4** |
| 2001–02 | Stoke C | 34 | 0 | | |
| 2002–03 | Stoke C | 44 | 0 | **78** | **0** |
| 2003–04 | Barnsley | 28 | 0 | **28** | **0** |

**HAYWARD, Steve* (M)** **279 23**
H: 6 0 W: 12 05 b.Walsall 8-9-71
*Source:* Trainee. *Honours:* England Youth.

| | | | | | |
|---|---|---|---|---|---|
| 1988–89 | Derby Co | 0 | 0 | | |
| 1989–90 | Derby Co | 3 | 0 | | |
| 1990–91 | Derby Co | 1 | 0 | | |
| 1991–92 | Derby Co | 7 | 0 | | |
| 1992–93 | Derby Co | 7 | 1 | | |
| 1993–94 | Derby Co | 5 | 0 | | |
| 1994–95 | Derby Co | 3 | 0 | **26** | **1** |
| 1994–95 | Carlisle U | 9 | 2 | | |
| 1995–96 | Carlisle U | 38 | 4 | | |
| 1996–97 | Carlisle U | 43 | 7 | **90** | **13** |
| 1997–98 | Fulham | 35 | 4 | | |
| 1998–99 | Fulham | 42 | 3 | | |
| 1999–2000 | Fulham | 37 | 0 | | |
| 2000–01 | Fulham | 1 | 0 | **115** | **7** |
| 2000–01 | Barnsley | 10 | 1 | | |
| 2001–02 | Barnsley | 0 | 0 | | |
| 2002–03 | Barnsley | 6 | 0 | | |
| 2003–04 | Barnsley | 32 | 1 | **48** | **2** |

**IRELAND, Craig* (D)** **206 10**
H: 6 3 W: 13 09 b.Dundee 29-11-75
*Source:* Aberdeen Lads.

| | | | | | |
|---|---|---|---|---|---|
| 1994–95 | Aberdeen | 0 | 0 | | |
| 1995–96 | Aberdeen | 0 | 0 | | |
| 1995–96 | Dunfermline Ath | 10 | 0 | | |
| 1996–97 | Dunfermline Ath | 9 | 1 | | |
| 1997–98 | Dunfermline Ath | 12 | 1 | | |
| 1998–99 | Dunfermline Ath | 23 | 0 | | |
| 1999–2000 | Dunfermline Ath | 3 | 0 | **57** | **2** |
| 1999–2000 | Dundee | 14 | 1 | **14** | **1** |
| 2000–01 | Airdrieonians | 12 | 2 | **12** | **2** |
| 2000–01 | *Notts Co* | 16 | 0 | | |
| 2001–02 | Notts Co | 27 | 1 | | |
| 2002–03 | Notts Co | 37 | 1 | **80** | **2** |
| 2003–04 | Barnsley | 43 | 3 | **43** | **3** |

**JACK, Darren† (M)** **3 0**
H: 6 3 W: 13 03 b.Norwich 9-9-83

| | | | | | |
|---|---|---|---|---|---|
| 2000–01 | Ross Co | 0 | 0 | | |
| 2001–02 | Ross Co | 1 | 0 | **1** | **0** |
| 2002–03 | Motherwell | 2 | 0 | **2** | **0** |
| 2003–04 | Barnsley | 0 | 0 | | |

**JONES, Griff* (F)** **2 0**
H: 5 8 W: 12 02 b.Liverpool 22-6-84
*Source:* Scholar.

| | | | | | |
|---|---|---|---|---|---|
| 2002–03 | Barnsley | 2 | 0 | | |
| 2003–04 | Barnsley | 0 | 0 | **2** | **0** |

**KAY, Antony (M)** **67 3**
H: 5 11 W: 11 08 b.Barnsley 21-10-82
*Source:* Trainee. *Honours:* England Youth.
1999–2000 Barnsley 0 0
2000–01 Barnsley 7 0
2001–02 Barnsley 1 0
2002–03 Barnsley 16 0
2003–04 Barnsley 43 3 **67 3**

**LAIGHT, Ryan§ (D)** **0 0**
H: 6 0 W: 11 09 b.Barnsley 16-11-85
*Source:* Scholar.
2002–03 Barnsley 0 0
2003–04 Barnsley 0 0

**LUMSDON, Chris (M)** **109 14**
H: 5 11 W: 10 03 b.Newcastle 15-12-79
*Source:* Trainee.
1997–98 Sunderland 1 0
1998–99 Sunderland 0 0
1999–2000 Sunderland 1 0
1999–2000 *Blackpool* 6 1 **6 1**
2000–01 Sunderland 0 0
2000–01 *Crewe Alex* 16 0 **16 0**
2001–02 Sunderland 0 0 **2 0**
2001–02 Barnsley 32 7
2002–03 Barnsley 25 3
2003–04 Barnsley 28 3 **85 13**

**MONK, Garry* (D)** **61 0**
H: 6 0 W: 12 01 b.Bedford 6-3-79
*Source:* Trainee.
1995–96 Torquay U 5 0
1996–97 Southampton 0 0
1997–98 Southampton 0 0
1998–99 Southampton 4 0
1998–99 *Torquay U* 6 0 **11 0**
1999–2000 Southampton 2 0
1999–2000 *Stockport Co* 2 0 **2 0**
2000–01 Southampton 2 0
2000–01 *Oxford U* 5 0 **5 0**
2001–02 Southampton 2 0
2002–03 Southampton 1 0
2002–03 *Sheffield W* 15 0 **15 0**
2003–04 Southampton 0 0 **11 0**
2003–04 Barnsley 17 0 **17 0**

**NEIL, Alex* (M)** **137 9**
H: 5 8 W: 11 05 b.Bellshill 9-6-81
*Source:* Dunfermline Ath.
1999–2000 Airdrieonians 16 5 **16 5**
2000–01 Barnsley 32 0
2001–02 Barnsley 25 2
2002–03 Barnsley 33 0
2003–04 Barnsley 31 2 **121 4**

**O'CALLAGHAN, Brian* (D)** **75 1**
H: 6 1 W: 12 01 b.Limerick 24-2-81
*Source:* Pike Rovers.
1998–99 Barnsley 0 0
1999–2000 Barnsley 0 0
2000–01 Barnsley 26 0
2001–02 Barnsley 6 0
2002–03 Barnsley 14 1
2003–04 Barnsley 29 0 **75 1**

**SCOTHERN, Ashley§ (F)** **1 0**
H: 6 0 W: 11 00 b.Pontefract 11-9-84
*Source:* Scholar. *Honours:* England Youth.
2001–02 Barnsley 1 0
2002–03 Barnsley 0 0
2003–04 Barnsley 0 0 **1 0**

**SHUKER, Chris (M)** **56 3**
H: 5 5 W: 9 03 b.Liverpool 9-5-82
*Source:* Scholarship.
1999–2000 Manchester C 0 0
2000–01 Manchester C 0 0
2000–01 *Macclesfield T* 9 1 **9 1**
2001–02 Manchester C 2 0
2002–03 Manchester C 3 0
2002–03 *Walsall* 5 0 **5 0**
2003–04 Manchester C 0 0 **5 0**
2003–04 *Rochdale* 14 1 **14 1**
2003–04 *Hartlepool U* 14 1 **14 1**
2003–04 Barnsley 9 0 **9 0**

**STALLARD, Mark (F)** **343 107**
H: 6 0 W: 13 09 b.Derby 24-10-74
*Source:* Trainee.
1991–92 Derby Co 3 0
1992–93 Derby Co 5 0
1993–94 Derby Co 0 0
1994–95 Derby Co 16 2
1994–95 *Fulham* 4 3 **4 3**
1995–96 Derby Co 3 0 **27 2**
1995–96 Bradford C 21 9
1996–97 Bradford C 22 1 **43 10**
1996–97 *Preston NE* 4 1 **4 1**
1996–97 Wycombe W 12 4
1997–98 Wycombe W 43 17
1998–99 Wycombe W 15 2 **70 23**
1998–99 Notts Co 14 4
1999–2000 Notts Co 36 14
2000–01 Notts Co 42 17
2001–02 Notts Co 26 4
2002–03 Notts Co 45 24
2003–04 Notts Co 22 4 **185 67**
2003–04 Barnsley 10 1 **10 1**

**TONGE, Dale§ (M)** **1 0**
H: 5 10 W: 10 06 b.Doncaster 7-5-85
*Source:* Scholar.
2003–04 Barnsley 1 0 **1 0**

**WILLIAMS, Robbie§ (D)** **12 1**
H: 5 10 W: 11 13 b.Pontefract 2-10-84
*Source:* Scholar.
2002–03 Barnsley 8 0
2003–04 Barnsley 4 1 **12 1**

**WROE, Nicky§ (M)** **3 1**
H: 5 11 W: 11 13 b.Sheffield 28-9-85
*Source:* Scholar.
2002–03 Barnsley 1 0
2003–04 Barnsley 2 1 **3 1**

**Scholars**
Atkinson, Robert G; Baker, Thomas; Batley, Richard N; Farmery, Ian J; Flinders, Scott; Greaves, Sean; Harban, Thomas; Heslop, Simon J; Jarman, Nathan G; Joynes, Nathan; Laight, Ryan; Scothern, Ashley; Shackleton, Marc; Tonge, Dale; Williams, Robert I; Wordsworth, Dean; Wroe, Nicholas

**Non Contract**
Alcock, Daniel J; Jack, Darren

## BIRMINGHAM C (4)

**ALLEN, Mark‡ (M)** **0 0**
b.Birmingham 23-5-84
*Source:* Trainee.
2003–04 Birmingham C 0 0

**BARROWMAN, Andrew (F)** **5 1**
H: 5 11 W: 11 06 b.Wishaw 27-11-84
*Source:* Scholar. *Honours:* Scotland Youth.
2001–02 Birmingham C 0 0
2002–03 Birmingham C 0 0
2003–04 Birmingham C 1 0 **1 0**
2003–04 *Crewe Alex* 4 1 **4 1**

**BENNETT, Ian (G)** **359 0**
H: 6 0 W: 13 01 b.Worksop 10-10-71
*Source:* Newcastle U Trainee.
1991–92 Peterborough U 7 0
1992–93 Peterborough U 46 0
1993–94 Peterborough U 19 0 **72 0**
1993–94 Birmingham C 22 0
1994–95 Birmingham C 46 0
1995–96 Birmingham C 24 0
1996–97 Birmingham C 40 0
1997–98 Birmingham C 45 0
1998–99 Birmingham C 10 0
1999–2000 Birmingham C 21 0
2000–01 Birmingham C 45 0
2001–02 Birmingham C 18 0
2002–03 Birmingham C 10 0
2003–04 Birmingham C 6 0 **287 0**

**CARTER, Darren (M)** **30 1**
H: 6 2 W: 12 11 b.Solihull 18-12-83
*Source:* Scholar. *Honours:* England Youth, Under-20.
2001–02 Birmingham C 13 1
2002–03 Birmingham C 12 0
2003–04 Birmingham C 5 0 **30 1**

**CISSE, Aliou (M)** **102 2**
H: 5 9 W: 12 02 b.Zinguichor 24-3-76
*Honours:* Senegal 23 full caps, 1 goal.
1994–95 Lille 6 0
1995–96 Lille 0 0
1996–97 Lille 0 0 **6 0**
From Sedan
1998–99 Paris St Germain 8 0
1999–2000 Paris St Germain 25 1
2000–01 Paris St Germain 10 0 **43 1**
2001–02 Montpellier 17 1 **17 1**
2002–03 Birmingham C 21 0
2003–04 Birmingham C 15 0 **36 0**

**CLAPHAM, Jamie (M)** **260 10**
H: 5 9 W: 11 09 b.Lincoln 7-12-75
*Source:* Trainee.
1994–95 Tottenham H 0 0
1995–96 Tottenham H 0 0
1996–97 Tottenham H 1 0
1996–97 *Leyton Orient* 6 0 **6 0**
1996–97 *Bristol R* 5 0 **5 0**
1997–98 Tottenham H 0 0 **1 0**
1997–98 Ipswich T 22 0
1998–99 Ipswich T 46 3
1999–2000 Ipswich T 46 2
2000–01 Ipswich T 35 2
2001–02 Ipswich T 32 2
2002–03 Ipswich T 26 1 **207 10**
2002–03 Birmingham C 16 0
2003–04 Birmingham C 25 0 **41 0**

**CLEMENCE, Stephen (M)** **140 6**
H: 6 0 W: 12 09 b.Liverpool 31-3-78
*Source:* Trainee. *Honours:* England Schools, Youth, Under-21.
1994–95 Tottenham H 0 0
1995–96 Tottenham H 0 0
1996–97 Tottenham H 0 0
1997–98 Tottenham H 17 0
1998–99 Tottenham H 18 0
1999–2000 Tottenham H 20 1
2000–01 Tottenham H 29 1
2001–02 Tottenham H 6 0
2002–03 Tottenham H 0 0 **90 2**
2002–03 Birmingham C 15 2
2003–04 Birmingham C 35 2 **50 4**

**CUNNINGHAM, Kenny (D)** **453 1**
H: 5 11 W: 12 07 b.Dublin 28-6-71
*Source:* Tolka R. *Honours:* Eire Under-21, B, 57 full caps.
1989–90 Millwall 5 0
1990–91 Millwall 23 0
1991–92 Millwall 17 0
1992–93 Millwall 37 0
1993–94 Millwall 39 1
1994–95 Millwall 15 0 **136 1**
1994–95 Wimbledon 28 0
1995–96 Wimbledon 33 0
1996–97 Wimbledon 36 0
1997–98 Wimbledon 32 0
1998–99 Wimbledon 35 0
1999–2000 Wimbledon 37 0
2000–01 Wimbledon 15 0
2001–02 Wimbledon 34 0 **250 0**
2002–03 Birmingham C 31 0
2003–04 Birmingham C 36 0 **67 0**

**DUGARRY, Christophe‡ (F)** **362 60**
H: 6 1 W: 12 10 b.Bordeaux 24-3-72
*Honours:* France 55 full caps, 8 goals.
1988–89 Bordeaux 2 0
1989–90 Bordeaux 0 0
1990–91 Bordeaux 32 3
1991–92 Bordeaux 27 4
1992–93 Bordeaux 35 6
1993–94 Bordeaux 35 8
1994–95 Bordeaux 32 9
1995–96 Bordeaux 24 2
1996–97 AC Milan 21 5 **21 5**
1997–98 Barcelona 7 0 **7 0**
1997–98 Marseille 9 1
1998–99 Marseille 28 4
1999–2000 Marseille 15 3 **52 8**
1999–2000 Bordeaux 12 3
2000–01 Bordeaux 22 5
2001–02 Bordeaux 18 1
2002–03 Bordeaux 13 0 **252 41**
2002–03 Birmingham C 16 5
2003–04 Birmingham C 14 1 **30 6**

**DUNN, David (M)** **157 32**
H: 5 9 W: 12 03 b.Blackburn 27-12-79
*Source:* Trainee. *Honours:* England Youth, Under-21, 1 full cap.
1997–98 Blackburn R 0 0
1998–99 Blackburn R 15 1

| | | | | | |
|---|---|---|---|---|---|
| 1999–2000 | Blackburn R | 22 | 2 | | |
| 2000–01 | Blackburn R | 42 | 12 | | |
| 2001–02 | Blackburn R | 29 | 7 | | |
| 2002–03 | Blackburn R | 28 | 8 | **136** | **30** |
| 2003–04 | Birmingham C | 21 | 2 | **21** | **2** |

**FIGUEROA, Luciano (F)** **58** **35**
H: 6 0 W: 12 02 b.Argentina 19-5-81
*Honours:* Argentina 1 full cap.

| | | | | | |
|---|---|---|---|---|---|
| 2001–02 | Rosario Central | 20 | 8 | | |
| 2002–03 | Rosario Central | 37 | 27 | **57** | **35** |
| 2003–04 | Birmingham C | 1 | 0 | **1** | **0** |

**GRAINGER, Martin (D)** **380** **44**
H: 5 10 W: 12 11 b.Enfield 23-8-72
*Source:* Trainee.

| | | | | | |
|---|---|---|---|---|---|
| 1989–90 | Colchester U | 7 | 2 | | |
| 1990–91 | Colchester U | 0 | 0 | | |
| 1991–92 | Colchester U | 0 | 0 | | |
| 1992–93 | Colchester U | 31 | 3 | | |
| 1993–94 | Colchester U | 8 | 2 | **46** | **7** |
| 1993–94 | Brentford | 31 | 2 | | |
| 1994–95 | Brentford | 37 | 7 | | |
| 1995–96 | Brentford | 33 | 3 | **101** | **12** |
| 1995–96 | Birmingham C | 8 | 0 | | |
| 1996–97 | Birmingham C | 23 | 3 | | |
| 1997–98 | Birmingham C | 33 | 2 | | |
| 1998–99 | Birmingham C | 40 | 4 | | |
| 1999–2000 | Birmingham C | 34 | 5 | | |
| 2000–01 | Birmingham C | 35 | 6 | | |
| 2001–02 | Birmingham C | 40 | 4 | | |
| 2002–03 | Birmingham C | 9 | 0 | | |
| 2003–04 | Birmingham C | 4 | 1 | **226** | **25** |
| 2003–04 | *Coventry C* | 7 | 0 | **7** | **0** |

**HUGHES, Bryan* (M)** **342** **46**
H: 5 9 W: 11 03 b.Liverpool 19-6-76
*Source:* Trainee.

| | | | | | |
|---|---|---|---|---|---|
| 1993–94 | Wrexham | 11 | 0 | | |
| 1994–95 | Wrexham | 38 | 9 | | |
| 1995–96 | Wrexham | 22 | 0 | | |
| 1996–97 | Wrexham | 23 | 3 | **94** | **12** |
| 1996–97 | Birmingham C | 11 | 0 | | |
| 1997–98 | Birmingham C | 40 | 5 | | |
| 1998–99 | Birmingham C | 28 | 3 | | |
| 1999–2000 | Birmingham C | 45 | 10 | | |
| 2000–01 | Birmingham C | 45 | 4 | | |
| 2001–02 | Birmingham C | 31 | 7 | | |
| 2002–03 | Birmingham C | 22 | 2 | | |
| 2003–04 | Birmingham C | 26 | 3 | **248** | **34** |

**JOHN, Stern (F)** **201** **78**
H: 6 0 W: 12 11 b.Trinidad 30-10-76
*Honours:* Trinidad & Tobago 16 full caps, 8 goals.

| | | | | | |
|---|---|---|---|---|---|
| 1998 | Columbus Crew | 27 | 26 | | |
| 1999 | Columbus Crew | 28 | 18 | **55** | **44** |
| 1999–2000 | Nottingham F | 17 | 3 | | |
| 2000–01 | Nottingham F | 29 | 2 | | |
| 2001–02 | Nottingham F | 26 | 13 | **72** | **18** |
| 2001–02 | Birmingham C | 15 | 7 | | |
| 2002–03 | Birmingham C | 30 | 5 | | |
| 2003–04 | Birmingham C | 29 | 4 | **74** | **16** |

**JOHNSON, Damien (M)** **139** **6**
H: 5 9 W: 11 09 b.Lisburn 18-11-78
*Source:* Trainee. *Honours:* Northern Ireland Youth, Under-21, 30 full caps.

| | | | | | |
|---|---|---|---|---|---|
| 1995–96 | Blackburn R | 0 | 0 | | |
| 1996–97 | Blackburn R | 0 | 0 | | |
| 1997–98 | Blackburn R | 0 | 0 | | |
| 1997–98 | *Nottingham F* | 6 | 0 | **6** | **0** |
| 1998–99 | Blackburn R | 21 | 1 | | |
| 1999–2000 | Blackburn R | 16 | 1 | | |
| 2000–01 | Blackburn R | 16 | 0 | | |
| 2001–02 | Blackburn R | 7 | 1 | **60** | **3** |
| 2001–02 | Birmingham C | 8 | 1 | | |
| 2002–03 | Birmingham C | 30 | 1 | | |
| 2003–04 | Birmingham C | 35 | 1 | **73** | **3** |

**KILKENNY, Neil (M)** **0** **0**
H: 5 8 W: 10 08 b.Middlesex 19-12-85
*Source:* Arsenal Trainee. *Honours:* England Youth.

| | | | | | |
|---|---|---|---|---|---|
| 2003–04 | Birmingham C | 0 | 0 | | |

**KIROVSKI, Jovan‡ (F)** **104** **10**
H: 6 1 W: 12 01 b.Escondido 18-3-76
*Source:* San Diego Nomads. *Honours:* USA 62 full caps, 9 goals.

| | | | | | |
|---|---|---|---|---|---|
| 1994–95 | Manchester U | 0 | 0 | | |
| 1995–96 | Borussia Dortmund | 0 | 0 | | |
| 1996–97 | Borussia Dortmund | 7 | 1 | | |
| 1997–98 | Borussia Dortmund | 13 | 0 | | |
| 1998–99 | Fortuna Cologne | 20 | 2 | **20** | **2** |
| 1999–2000 | Borussia Dortmund | 0 | 0 | **20** | **1** |
| 2000–01 | Sporting Lisbon | 5 | 0 | **5** | **0** |
| 2001–02 | Crystal Palace | 36 | 5 | **36** | **5** |
| 2002–03 | Birmingham C | 17 | 2 | | |
| 2003–04 | Birmingham C | 6 | 0 | **23** | **2** |

**LAZARIDIS, Stan (M)** **296** **16**
H: 5 9 W: 11 12 b.Perth 16-8-72
*Honours:* Australia Youth, Under-23, 53 full caps.

| | | | | | |
|---|---|---|---|---|---|
| 1992–93 | Adelaide Sharks | 28 | 2 | | |
| 1993–94 | Adelaide Sharks | 23 | 3 | | |
| 1994–95 | Adelaide Sharks | 22 | 0 | **73** | **5** |
| 1995–96 | West Ham U | 4 | 0 | | |
| 1996–97 | West Ham U | 22 | 1 | | |
| 1997–98 | West Ham U | 28 | 2 | | |
| 1998–99 | West Ham U | 15 | 0 | **69** | **3** |
| 1999–2000 | Birmingham C | 31 | 2 | | |
| 2000–01 | Birmingham C | 31 | 2 | | |
| 2001–02 | Birmingham C | 32 | 0 | | |
| 2002–03 | *Portsmouth* | 0 | 0 | | |
| 2002–03 | Birmingham C | 30 | 2 | | |
| 2003–04 | Birmingham C | 30 | 2 | **154** | **8** |

**MORRISON, Clinton (F)** **217** **72**
H: 6 1 W: 11 13 b.Tooting 14-5-79
*Source:* Trainee. *Honours:* Eire 21 full caps, 5 goals.

| | | | | | |
|---|---|---|---|---|---|
| 1996–97 | Crystal Palace | 0 | 0 | | |
| 1997–98 | Crystal Palace | 1 | 1 | | |
| 1998–99 | Crystal Palace | 37 | 12 | | |
| 1999–2000 | Crystal Palace | 29 | 13 | | |
| 2000–01 | Crystal Palace | 45 | 14 | | |
| 2001–02 | Crystal Palace | 45 | 22 | **157** | **62** |
| 2002–03 | Birmingham C | 28 | 6 | | |
| 2003–04 | Birmingham C | 32 | 4 | **60** | **10** |

**OJI, Samuel (D)** **0** **0**
b.Westminster 9-10-85

| | | | | | |
|---|---|---|---|---|---|
| 2003–04 | Birmingham C | 0 | 0 | | |

**PURSE, Darren (D)** **282** **17**
H: 6 2 W: 13 01 b.Stepney 14-2-76
*Source:* Trainee. *Honours:* England Under-21.

| | | | | | |
|---|---|---|---|---|---|
| 1993–94 | Leyton Orient | 5 | 0 | | |
| 1994–95 | Leyton Orient | 38 | 3 | | |
| 1995–96 | Leyton Orient | 12 | 0 | **55** | **3** |
| 1996–97 | Oxford U | 31 | 1 | | |
| 1997–98 | Oxford U | 28 | 4 | **59** | **5** |
| 1997–98 | Birmingham C | 8 | 0 | | |
| 1998–99 | Birmingham C | 20 | 0 | | |
| 1999–2000 | Birmingham C | 38 | 2 | | |
| 2000–01 | Birmingham C | 37 | 3 | | |
| 2001–02 | Birmingham C | 36 | 3 | | |
| 2002–03 | Birmingham C | 20 | 1 | | |
| 2003–04 | Birmingham C | 9 | 0 | **168** | **9** |

**SADLER, Matthew (D)** **9** **0**
H: 5 11 W: 11 08 b.Birmingham 26-2-85
*Source:* Scholar. *Honours:* England Youth.

| | | | | | |
|---|---|---|---|---|---|
| 2001–02 | Birmingham C | 0 | 0 | | |
| 2002–03 | Birmingham C | 2 | 0 | | |
| 2003–04 | Birmingham C | 0 | 0 | **2** | **0** |
| 2003–04 | *Northampton T* | 7 | 0 | **7** | **0** |

**SAVAGE, Robbie (M)** **313** **25**
H: 5 11 W: 11 00 b.Wrexham 18-10-74
*Source:* Trainee. *Honours:* Wales Schools, Youth, Under-21, 35 full caps, 2 goals.

| | | | | | |
|---|---|---|---|---|---|
| 1993–94 | Manchester U | 0 | 0 | | |
| 1994–95 | Crewe Alex | 6 | 2 | | |
| 1995–96 | Crewe Alex | 30 | 7 | | |
| 1996–97 | Crewe Alex | 41 | 1 | **77** | **10** |
| 1997–98 | Leicester C | 35 | 2 | | |
| 1998–99 | Leicester C | 34 | 1 | | |
| 1999–2000 | Leicester C | 35 | 1 | | |
| 2000–01 | Leicester C | 33 | 4 | | |
| 2001–02 | Leicester C | 35 | 0 | **172** | **8** |
| 2002–03 | Birmingham C | 33 | 4 | | |
| 2003–04 | Birmingham C | 31 | 3 | **64** | **7** |

**TAYLOR, Maik (G)** **306** **0**
H: 6 4 W: 14 02 b.Hildeshein 4-9-71
*Source:* Farnborough T. *Honours:* Northern Ireland Under-21, B, 38 full caps.

| | | | | | |
|---|---|---|---|---|---|
| 1995–96 | Barnet | 45 | 0 | | |
| 1996–97 | Barnet | 25 | 0 | **70** | **0** |
| 1996–97 | Southampton | 18 | 0 | | |
| 1997–98 | Southampton | 0 | 0 | **18** | **0** |
| 1997–98 | Fulham | 28 | 0 | | |
| 1998–99 | Fulham | 46 | 0 | | |
| 1999–2000 | Fulham | 46 | 0 | | |
| 2000–01 | Fulham | 44 | 0 | | |
| 2001–02 | Fulham | 1 | 0 | | |
| 2002–03 | Fulham | 19 | 0 | | |
| 2003–04 | Fulham | 0 | 0 | **184** | **0** |
| 2003–04 | Birmingham C | 34 | 0 | **34** | **0** |

**TAYLOR, Martin (D)** **111** **6**
H: 6 4 W: 15 00 b.Ashington 9-11-79
*Source:* Trainee. *Honours:* England Youth, Under-21.

| | | | | | |
|---|---|---|---|---|---|
| 1997–98 | Blackburn R | 0 | 0 | | |
| 1998–99 | Blackburn R | 3 | 0 | | |
| 1999–2000 | Blackburn R | 6 | 0 | | |
| 1999–2000 | *Darlington* | 4 | 0 | **4** | **0** |
| 1999–2000 | *Stockport Co* | 7 | 0 | **7** | **0** |
| 2000–01 | Blackburn R | 16 | 3 | | |
| 2001–02 | Blackburn R | 19 | 0 | | |
| 2002–03 | Blackburn R | 33 | 2 | | |
| 2003–04 | Blackburn R | 11 | 0 | **88** | **5** |
| 2003–04 | Birmingham C | 12 | 1 | **12** | **1** |

**TEBILY, Oliver (D)** **103** **1**
H: 6 0 W: 13 05 b.Abidjan 19-12-75
*Source:* Chateauroux. *Honours:* Ivory Coast full caps.

| | | | | | |
|---|---|---|---|---|---|
| 1997–98 | Chateauroux | 11 | 1 | **11** | **1** |
| 1998–99 | Sheffield U | 8 | 0 | **8** | **0** |
| 1999–2000 | Celtic | 23 | 0 | | |
| 2000–01 | Celtic | 4 | 0 | | |
| 2001–02 | Celtic | 11 | 0 | **38** | **0** |
| 2001–02 | Birmingham C | 7 | 0 | | |
| 2002–03 | Birmingham C | 12 | 0 | | |
| 2003–04 | Birmingham C | 27 | 0 | **46** | **0** |

**UPSON, Matthew (D)** **101** **0**
H: 6 1 W: 11 04 b.Hartismere 18-4-79
*Source:* Trainee. *Honours:* England Youth, Under-21, 6 full caps.

| | | | | | |
|---|---|---|---|---|---|
| 1995–96 | Luton T | 0 | 0 | | |
| 1996–97 | Luton T | 1 | 0 | **1** | **0** |
| 1996–97 | Arsenal | 0 | 0 | | |
| 1997–98 | Arsenal | 5 | 0 | | |
| 1998–99 | Arsenal | 5 | 0 | | |
| 1999–2000 | Arsenal | 8 | 0 | | |
| 2000–01 | Arsenal | 2 | 0 | | |
| 2000–01 | *Nottingham F* | 1 | 0 | **1** | **0** |
| 2000–01 | *Crystal Palace* | 7 | 0 | **7** | **0** |
| 2001–02 | Arsenal | 14 | 0 | | |
| 2002–03 | Arsenal | 0 | 0 | **34** | **0** |
| 2002–03 | *Reading* | 14 | 0 | **14** | **0** |
| 2002–03 | Birmingham C | 14 | 0 | | |
| 2003–04 | Birmingham C | 30 | 0 | **44** | **0** |

**VAESEN, Nico (G)** **255** **0**
H: 6 3 W: 12 13 b.Hasselt 28-9-69
*Source:* Tongeren.

| | | | | | |
|---|---|---|---|---|---|
| 1993–94 | CS Brugge | 13 | 0 | | |
| 1994–95 | CS Brugge | 3 | 0 | **16** | **0** |
| 1995–96 | Aalst | 20 | 0 | | |
| 1996–97 | Aalst | 0 | 0 | | |
| 1997–98 | Aalst | 14 | 0 | **34** | **0** |
| 1998–99 | Huddersfield T | 43 | 0 | | |
| 1999–2000 | Huddersfield T | 46 | 0 | | |
| 2000–01 | Huddersfield T | 45 | 0 | **134** | **0** |
| 2001–02 | Birmingham C | 23 | 0 | | |
| 2002–03 | Birmingham C | 27 | 0 | | |
| 2003–04 | Birmingham C | 0 | 0 | **50** | **0** |
| 2003–04 | *Gillingham* | 5 | 0 | **5** | **0** |
| 2003–04 | *Bradford C* | 6 | 0 | **6** | **0** |
| 2003–04 | *Crystal Palace* | 10 | 0 | **10** | **0** |

**WILLIAMS, Tom‡ (M)** **92** **4**
H: 6 0 W: 11 13 b.Carshalton 8-7-80
*Source:* Walton & Hersham.

| | | | | | |
|---|---|---|---|---|---|
| 1999–2000 | West Ham U | 0 | 0 | | |
| 2000–01 | West Ham U | 0 | 0 | | |
| 2000–01 | *Peterborough U* | 2 | 0 | | |
| 2001–02 | Peterborough U | 34 | 2 | | |
| 2001–02 | Birmingham C | 4 | 0 | | |
| 2002–03 | Birmingham C | 0 | 0 | | |
| 2002–03 | *QPR* | 26 | 1 | | |
| 2003–04 | Birmingham C | 0 | 0 | **4** | **0** |
| 2003–04 | *QPR* | 5 | 0 | **31** | **1** |
| 2003–04 | *Peterborough U* | 21 | 1 | **57** | **3** |

**Scholars**
Alsop, Sam; Bagnall, Andrew B; Birley, Matthew M; Blake, James; Cottrill, Christopher; Courtney, Duane; Curtis, Dean;

Dormand, James; Doyle, Colin; Hall, Asa P; Hamilton, Davion; Howland, David; Legzdins, Adam R; Luckett, Stephen P; Motteram, Carl; Painter, Marcos; Parratt, Tom; Reynolds, Liam; Till, Peter

## BLACKBURN R (5)

**AMORUSO, Lorenzo (D)** **210 17**
H: 6 2 W: 13 10 b.Palese 28-6-71

| | | | | | |
|---|---|---|---|---|---|
| 1988–89 | Bari | 3 | 0 | | |
| 1989–90 | Bari | 3 | 0 | | |
| 1990–91 | Bari | 5 | 1 | | |
| 1991–92 | Bari | 0 | 0 | | |
| 1991–92 | Mantova | 13 | 1 | **13** | **1** |
| 1992–93 | Bari | 0 | 0 | | |
| 1992–93 | Pescavo | 19 | 1 | **19** | **1** |
| 1993–94 | Bari | 37 | 3 | | |
| 1994–95 | Bari | 27 | 4 | **75** | **8** |
| 1995–96 | Fiorentina | 31 | 2 | | |
| 1996–97 | Fiorentina | 23 | 1 | **54** | **3** |
| 1997–98 | Rangers | 4 | 0 | | |
| 1998–99 | Rangers | 33 | 1 | | |
| 1999–2000 | Rangers | 0 | 0 | | |
| 2000–01 | Rangers | 0 | 0 | | |
| 2001–02 | Rangers | 0 | 0 | **37** | **1** |
| 2003–04 | Blackburn R | 12 | 3 | **12** | **3** |

**ANDRESEN, Martin‡ (M)** **205 49**
H: 5 11 W: 11 04 b.Norway 2-2-77
*Honours:* Norway 12 full caps, 1 goal.

| | | | | | |
|---|---|---|---|---|---|
| 1996 | Moss | 24 | 7 | **24** | **7** |
| 1997 | Viking | 26 | 8 | **26** | **8** |
| 1998 | Stabaek | 25 | 8 | | |
| 1999 | Stabaek | 22 | 8 | | |
| 1999–2000 | Wimbledon | 14 | 1 | | |
| 2000 | Molde | 9 | 1 | **9** | **1** |
| 2001 | Stabaek | 24 | 8 | | |
| 2002 | Stabaek | 25 | 1 | | |
| 2001–02 | Wimbledon | 0 | 0 | **14** | **1** |
| 2003 | Stabaek | 25 | 7 | **121** | **32** |
| 2003–04 | Blackburn R | 11 | 0 | **11** | **0** |

**BAGGIO, Dino‡ (M)** **360 32**
H: 6 1 W: 11 04 b.Campo San Piero 24-7-71
*Honours:* Italy 60 full caps, 7 goals.

| | | | | | |
|---|---|---|---|---|---|
| 1988–89 | Torino | 31 | 6 | | |
| 1989–90 | Torino | 3 | 0 | | |
| 1990–91 | Torino | 25 | 2 | **59** | **8** |
| 1991–92 | Internazionale | 27 | 1 | **27** | **1** |
| 1992–93 | Juventus | 32 | 1 | | |
| 1993–94 | Juventus | 17 | 0 | **49** | **1** |
| 1994–95 | Parma | 31 | 6 | | |
| 1995–96 | Parma | 28 | 4 | | |
| 1996–97 | Parma | 31 | 2 | | |
| 1997–98 | Parma | 29 | 6 | | |
| 1998–99 | Parma | 29 | 2 | | |
| 1999–2000 | Parma | 24 | 0 | | |
| 2000–01 | Parma | 0 | 0 | **172** | **20** |
| 2000–01 | Lazio | 25 | 1 | | |
| 2001–02 | Lazio | 15 | 0 | | |
| 2002–03 | Lazio | 4 | 0 | **44** | **1** |
| 2003–04 | Blackburn R | 9 | 1 | **9** | **1** |

**BLACK, Ian (M)** **0 0**
b.Edinburgh 14-3-85
*Source:* Trainee.

| | | | | | |
|---|---|---|---|---|---|
| 2002–03 | Blackburn R | 0 | 0 | | |
| 2003–04 | Blackburn R | 0 | 0 | | |

**BRUCE, Alex (D)** **0 0**
b.Norwich 28-9-84
*Source:* Trainee.

| | | | | | |
|---|---|---|---|---|---|
| 2002–03 | Blackburn R | 0 | 0 | | |
| 2003–04 | Blackburn R | 0 | 0 | | |

**COLE, Andy (F)** **403 198**
H: 5 11 W: 12 02 b.Nottingham 15-10-71
*Source:* Trainee. *Honours:* England Schools, Youth, Under-21, B, 15 full caps, 1 goal. Football League.

| | | | | | |
|---|---|---|---|---|---|
| 1989–90 | Arsenal | 0 | 0 | | |
| 1990–91 | Arsenal | 1 | 0 | | |
| 1991–92 | Arsenal | 0 | 0 | **1** | **0** |
| 1991–92 | *Fulham* | 13 | 3 | **13** | **3** |
| 1991–92 | *Bristol C* | 12 | 8 | | |
| 1992–93 | Bristol C | 29 | 12 | **41** | **20** |
| 1992–93 | Newcastle U | 12 | 12 | | |
| 1993–94 | Newcastle U | 40 | 34 | | |
| 1994–95 | Newcastle U | 18 | 9 | **70** | **55** |
| 1994–95 | Manchester U | 18 | 12 | | |
| 1995–96 | Manchester U | 34 | 11 | | |
| 1996–97 | Manchester U | 20 | 6 | | |
| 1997–98 | Manchester U | 33 | 15 | | |
| 1998–99 | Manchester U | 32 | 17 | | |
| 1999–2000 | Manchester U | 28 | 19 | | |
| 2000–01 | Manchester U | 19 | 9 | | |
| 2001–02 | Manchester U | 11 | 4 | **195** | **93** |
| 2001–02 | Blackburn R | 15 | 9 | | |
| 2002–03 | Blackburn R | 34 | 7 | | |
| 2003–04 | Blackburn R | 34 | 11 | **83** | **27** |

**CUMMING, Stuart* (D)** **0 0**
b.Aberdeen 30-1-85

| | | | | | |
|---|---|---|---|---|---|
| 2001–02 | Blackburn R | 0 | 0 | | |
| 2002–03 | Blackburn R | 0 | 0 | | |
| 2003–04 | Blackburn R | 0 | 0 | | |

**DANNS, Neil (M)** **24 3**
H: 5 9 W: 11 02 b.Liverpool 23-11-82
*Source:* Scholar.

| | | | | | |
|---|---|---|---|---|---|
| 2000–01 | Blackburn R | 0 | 0 | | |
| 2001–02 | Blackburn R | 0 | 0 | | |
| 2002–03 | Blackburn R | 2 | 0 | | |
| 2003–04 | Blackpool | 12 | 2 | **12** | **2** |
| 2003–04 | Blackburn R | 1 | 0 | **3** | **0** |
| 2003–04 | *Hartlepool U* | 9 | 1 | **9** | **1** |

**DERBYSHIRE, Matt (F)** **0 0**
b.Blackburn 14-4-86
*Source:* Great Harwood T.

| | | | | | |
|---|---|---|---|---|---|
| 2003–04 | Blackburn R | 0 | 0 | | |

**DONNELLY, Ciaran (M)** **9 0**
b.Blackpool 2-4-84
*Source:* Scholar. *Honours:* England Youth.

| | | | | | |
|---|---|---|---|---|---|
| 2001–02 | Blackburn R | 0 | 0 | | |
| 2002–03 | Blackburn R | 0 | 0 | | |
| 2003–04 | *Blackpool* | 9 | 0 | **9** | **0** |

**DOUGLAS, Jonathan (M)** **38 5**
H: 6 0 W: 12 07 b.Clones 22-11-81
*Source:* Trainee. *Honours:* Eire Under-21, 2 full caps.

| | | | | | |
|---|---|---|---|---|---|
| 1999–2000 | Blackburn R | 0 | 0 | | |
| 2000–01 | Blackburn R | 0 | 0 | | |
| 2001–02 | Blackburn R | 0 | 0 | | |
| 2002–03 | Blackburn R | 1 | 0 | | |
| 2002–03 | *Chesterfield* | 7 | 1 | **7** | **1** |
| 2003–04 | Blackpool | 16 | 3 | **16** | **3** |
| 2003–04 | Blackburn R | 14 | 1 | **15** | **1** |

**DRENCH, Steven (G)** **0 0**
b.Salford 11-9-85
*Source:* Trainee.

| | | | | | |
|---|---|---|---|---|---|
| 2002–03 | Blackburn R | 0 | 0 | | |
| 2003–04 | Blackburn R | 0 | 0 | | |

**EMERTON, Brett (M)** **223 29**
H: 6 1 W: 13 05 b.Bankstown 22-2-79
*Honours:* Australia Youth, Under-20, Under-23, 31 full caps, 7 goals.

| | | | | | |
|---|---|---|---|---|---|
| 1996–97 | Sydney Olympic | 18 | 2 | | |
| 1997–98 | Sydney Olympic | 24 | 3 | | |
| 1998–99 | Sydney Olympic | 21 | 2 | | |
| 1999–2000 | Sydney Olympic | 31 | 9 | **94** | **16** |
| 2000–01 | Feyenoord | 28 | 2 | | |
| 2001–02 | Feyenoord | 31 | 6 | | |
| 2002–03 | Feyenoord | 33 | 3 | **92** | **11** |
| 2003–04 | Blackburn R | 37 | 2 | **37** | **2** |

**ENCKELMAN, Peter (G)** **133 0**
H: 6 2 W: 12 05 b.Turku 10-3-77
*Source:* TPS Turku. *Honours:* Finland 6 full caps.

| | | | | | |
|---|---|---|---|---|---|
| 1995 | TPS Turku | 6 | 0 | | |
| 1996 | TPS Turku | 24 | 0 | | |
| 1997 | TPS Turku | 25 | 0 | | |
| 1998 | TPS Turku | 24 | 0 | **79** | **0** |
| 1998–99 | Aston Villa | 0 | 0 | | |
| 1999–2000 | Aston Villa | 10 | 0 | | |
| 2000–01 | Aston Villa | 0 | 0 | | |
| 2001–02 | Aston Villa | 9 | 0 | | |
| 2002–03 | Aston Villa | 33 | 0 | | |
| 2003–04 | Aston Villa | 0 | 0 | **52** | **0** |
| 2003–04 | Blackburn R | 2 | 0 | **2** | **0** |

**FERGUSON, Barry (M)** **183 25**
H: 5 7 W: 9 10 b.Glasgow 2-2-78
*Source:* Rangers SABC. *Honours:* Scotland Under-21, 21 full caps, 2 goals.

| | | | | | |
|---|---|---|---|---|---|
| 1994–95 | Rangers | 0 | 0 | | |
| 1995–96 | Rangers | 0 | 0 | | |
| 1996–97 | Rangers | 1 | 0 | | |
| 1997–98 | Rangers | 7 | 0 | | |
| 1998–99 | Rangers | 23 | 1 | | |
| 1999–2000 | Rangers | 31 | 4 | | |
| 2000–01 | Rangers | 30 | 2 | | |
| 2001–02 | Rangers | 22 | 1 | | |
| 2002–03 | Rangers | 36 | 16 | | |
| 2003–04 | Rangers | 3 | 0 | **168** | **24** |
| 2003–04 | Blackburn R | 15 | 1 | **15** | **1** |

**FITZGERALD, John (D)** **0 0**
b.Dublin 2-10-84
*Source:* Scholar.

| | | | | | |
|---|---|---|---|---|---|
| 2000–01 | Blackburn R | 0 | 0 | | |
| 2001–02 | Blackburn R | 0 | 0 | | |
| 2002–03 | Blackburn R | 0 | 0 | | |
| 2003–04 | Blackburn R | 0 | 0 | | |

**FLITCROFT, Garry (M)** **352 27**
H: 6 0 W: 11 08 b.Bolton 6-11-72
*Source:* Trainee. *Honours:* England Schools, Under-21.

| | | | | | |
|---|---|---|---|---|---|
| 1991–92 | Manchester C | 0 | 0 | | |
| 1991–92 | *Bury* | 12 | 0 | **12** | **0** |
| 1992–93 | Manchester C | 32 | 5 | | |
| 1993–94 | Manchester C | 21 | 3 | | |
| 1994–95 | Manchester C | 37 | 5 | | |
| 1995–96 | Manchester C | 25 | 0 | **115** | **13** |
| 1995–96 | Blackburn R | 3 | 0 | | |
| 1996–97 | Blackburn R | 28 | 3 | | |
| 1997–98 | Blackburn R | 33 | 0 | | |
| 1998–99 | Blackburn R | 8 | 2 | | |
| 1999–2000 | Blackburn R | 19 | 0 | | |
| 2000–01 | Blackburn R | 41 | 3 | | |
| 2001–02 | Blackburn R | 29 | 1 | | |
| 2002–03 | Blackburn R | 33 | 2 | | |
| 2003–04 | Blackburn R | 31 | 3 | **225** | **14** |

**FRIEDEL, Brad (G)** **199 1**
H: 6 3 W: 14 00 b.Lakewood 18-5-71
*Honours:* USA 82 full caps.

| | | | | | |
|---|---|---|---|---|---|
| 1996 | Columbus Crew | 9 | 0 | | |
| 1997 | Columbus Crew | 29 | 0 | **38** | **0** |
| 1997–98 | Liverpool | 11 | 0 | | |
| 1998–99 | Liverpool | 12 | 0 | | |
| 1999–2000 | Liverpool | 2 | 0 | | |
| 2000–01 | Liverpool | 0 | 0 | **25** | **0** |
| 2000–01 | Blackburn R | 27 | 0 | | |
| 2001–02 | Blackburn R | 36 | 0 | | |
| 2002–03 | Blackburn R | 37 | 0 | | |
| 2003–04 | Blackburn R | 36 | 1 | **136** | **1** |

**GALLAGHER, Paul (F)** **27 3**
H: 6 1 W: 12 00 b.Glasgow 9-8-84
*Source:* Trainee. *Honours:* Scotland Under-21, 1 full cap.

| | | | | | |
|---|---|---|---|---|---|
| 2002–03 | Blackburn R | 1 | 0 | | |
| 2003–04 | Blackburn R | 26 | 3 | **27** | **3** |

**GRABBI, Corrado‡ (F)** **224 78**
H: 5 11 W: 12 13 b.Turin 29-7-75

| | | | | | |
|---|---|---|---|---|---|
| 1993–94 | Spartta Novara | 31 | 8 | **31** | **8** |
| 1994–95 | Juventus | 2 | 1 | **2** | **1** |
| 1995–96 | Lucchese | 8 | 1 | **8** | **1** |
| 1995–96 | Chievo | 18 | 2 | **18** | **2** |
| 1996–97 | Modena | 31 | 15 | | |
| 1997–98 | Modena | 27 | 14 | **58** | **29** |
| 1998–99 | Ternana | 14 | 2 | | |
| 1999–2000 | Ravenna | 29 | 13 | **29** | **13** |
| 2000–01 | Ternana | 34 | 20 | **48** | **22** |
| 2001–02 | Blackburn R | 14 | 1 | | |
| 2002–03 | Blackburn R | 11 | 1 | | |
| 2003–04 | Blackburn R | 5 | 0 | **30** | **2** |

**GRAY, Michael (D)** **377 16**
H: 5 9 W: 10 07 b.Sunderland 3-8-74
*Source:* Trainee. *Honours:* England 3 full caps.

| | | | | | |
|---|---|---|---|---|---|
| 1992–93 | Sunderland | 27 | 2 | | |
| 1993–94 | Sunderland | 22 | 1 | | |
| 1994–95 | Sunderland | 16 | 0 | | |
| 1995–96 | Sunderland | 46 | 4 | | |
| 1996–97 | Sunderland | 34 | 3 | | |
| 1997–98 | Sunderland | 44 | 2 | | |
| 1998–99 | Sunderland | 37 | 2 | | |
| 1999–2000 | Sunderland | 33 | 0 | | |
| 2000–01 | Sunderland | 36 | 1 | | |
| 2001–02 | Sunderland | 35 | 0 | | |
| 2002–03 | Sunderland | 32 | 1 | | |
| 2003–04 | Sunderland | 1 | 0 | **363** | **16** |
| 2003–04 | Blackburn R | 14 | 0 | **14** | **0** |

**GRESKO, Vratislav (M)** **155 6**
H: 6 0 W: 11 05 b.Bratislava 24-7-77
*Honours:* Slovakia 19 full caps.
1995–96 Dukla Banska 1 0
1996–97 Dukla Banska 7 0 **8 0**
1997–98 Internazionale 22 0
1998–99 Internazionale 29 5
1999–2000 Leverkusen 9 0
2000–01 Leverkusen 7 0 **16 0**
2000–01 Internazionale 18 0
2001–02 Internazionale 23 0 **92 5**
2002–03 Parma 5 0 **5 0**
2002–03 Blackburn R 10 0
2003–04 Blackburn R 24 1 **34 1**

**HARKINS, Gary (M)** **3 0**
H: 6 2 W: 12 10 b.Greenock 2-1-85
*Source:* Trainee.
2003–04 Blackburn R 0 0
2003–04 *Huddersfield T* 3 0 **3 0**

**JANSEN, Matt (F)** **219 63**
H: 5 11 W: 11 03 b.Carlisle 20-10-77
*Source:* Trainee. *Honours:* England Under-21.
1995–96 Carlisle U 0 0
1996–97 Carlisle U 19 1
1997–98 Carlisle U 23 9 **42 10**
1997–98 Crystal Palace 8 3
1998–99 Crystal Palace 18 7 **26 10**
1998–99 Blackburn R 11 2
1999–2000 Blackburn R 30 4
2000–01 Blackburn R 40 23
2001–02 Blackburn R 35 10
2002–03 Blackburn R 7 0
2002–03 *Coventry C* 9 2 **9 2**
2003–04 Blackburn R 19 2 **142 41**

**JOHANSSON, Nils-Eric (D)** **74 0**
H: 6 2 W: 13 03 b.Stockholm 13-1-80
*Source:* Viksjo, Brommapojkana. *Honours:* Sweden 4 full caps.
1998 AIK Stockholm 0 0
1998–99 Bayern Munich 2 0
1999–2000 Bayern Munich 0 0
2000–01 Bayern Munich 0 0 **2 0**
2001–02 Nuremberg 8 0 **8 0**
2001–02 Blackburn R 20 0
2002–03 Blackburn R 30 0
2003–04 Blackburn R 14 0 **64 0**

**JOHNSON, Jemal (F)** **0 0**
b.New Jersey 3-5-84
2001–02 Blackburn R 0 0
2002–03 Blackburn R 0 0
2003–04 Blackburn R 0 0

**KEBE, Yahia‡ (M)** **0 0**
b.Mali 11-7-85
*Source:* Trainee.
2002–03 Blackburn R 0 0
2003–04 Blackburn R 0 0

**McEVELEY, James (D)** **13 0**
H: 6 1 W: 12 11 b.Liverpool 11-2-85
*Source:* Trainee. *Honours:* England Under-20, Under-21.
2002–03 Blackburn R 9 0
2003–04 Blackburn R 0 0 **9 0**
2003–04 *Burnley* 4 0 **4 0**

**McKAY, Ross* (F)** **0 0**
b.North Shields 21-9-84
*Source:* Trainee.
2002–03 Blackburn R 0 0
2003–04 Blackburn R 0 0

**MORGAN, Alan (M)** **5 1**
H: 6 0 W: 12 06 b.Edinburgh 27-11-83
*Source:* Scholar.
2000–01 Blackburn R 0 0
2001–02 Blackburn R 0 0
2002–03 Blackburn R 0 0
2003–04 Blackburn R 0 0
2003–04 *Darlington* 5 1 **5 1**

**NEILL, Lucas (M)** **249 16**
H: 6 0 W: 12 03 b.Sydney 9-3-78
*Source:* NSW Soccer Academy. *Honours:* Australia Under-20, Under-23, 7 full caps.
1995–96 Millwall 13 0
1996–97 Millwall 39 3
1997–98 Millwall 6 0
1998–99 Millwall 35 6
1999–2000 Millwall 31 1
2000–01 Millwall 24 2
2001–02 Millwall 4 1 **152 13**
2001–02 Blackburn R 31 1
2002–03 Blackburn R 34 0
2003–04 Blackburn R 32 2 **97 3**

**NELSON, Adam* (M)** **0 0**
b.Edinburgh 24-7-84
*Source:* Trainee.
2002–03 Blackburn R 0 0
2003–04 Blackburn R 0 0

**PEERS, Gavin (D)** **0 0**
b.Dublin 10-11-85
*Source:* Trainee.
2002–03 Blackburn R 0 0
2003–04 Blackburn R 0 0

**PELZER, Sebastian‡ (D)** **0 0**
H: 5 11 W: 12 08 b.Trier 24-9-80
2002–03 Blackburn R 0 0
2003–04 Blackburn R 0 0

**REID, Andrew (M)** **0 0**
b.Kilmarnock 26-9-85
2002–03 Blackburn R 0 0
2003–04 Blackburn R 0 0

**REID, Steven (M)** **155 18**
H: 6 0 W: 12 07 b.Kingston 10-3-81
*Source:* Trainee. *Honours:* England Youth. Eire 13 full caps, 2 goals.
1997–98 Millwall 1 0
1998–99 Millwall 25 0
1999–2000 Millwall 21 0
2000–01 Millwall 37 7
2001–02 Millwall 35 5
2002–03 Millwall 20 6 **139 18**
2003–04 Blackburn R 16 0 **16 0**

**RENTON, Keiron* (G)** **0 0**
b.Edinburgh 13-2-84
*Source:* Scholar.
2001–02 Blackburn R 0 0
2002–03 Blackburn R 0 0
2003–04 Blackburn R 0 0

**SAKALI, Abdeltareck (F)** **0 0**
b.Torcy 25-4-86
*Source:* Trainee.
2002–03 Blackburn R 0 0
2003–04 Blackburn R 0 0

**SHORT, Craig (D)** **528 29**
H: 6 3 W: 14 06 b.Bridlington 25-6-68
*Source:* Pickering T. *Honours:* England Schools.
1987–88 Scarborough 21 2
1988–89 Scarborough 42 5 **63 7**
1989–90 Notts Co 44 2
1990–91 Notts Co 0 0
1990–91 Notts Co 43 0
1991–92 Notts Co 38 3
1992–93 Notts Co 3 1 **128 6**
1992–93 Derby Co 38 3
1993–94 Derby Co 43 3
1994–95 Derby Co 37 3 **118 9**
1995–96 Everton 23 2
1996–97 Everton 23 2
1997–98 Everton 31 0
1998–99 Everton 22 0 **99 4**
1999–2000 Blackburn R 17 0
2000–01 Blackburn R 35 1
2001–02 Blackburn R 22 0
2002–03 Blackburn R 27 1
2003–04 Blackburn R 19 1 **120 3**

**STEAD, Jon (M)** **81 28**
H: 6 3 W: 12 02 b.Huddersfield 7-4-83
*Source:* Scholar. *Honours:* England Under-21.
2001–02 Huddersfield T 0 0
2002–03 Huddersfield T 42 6
2003–04 Huddersfield T 26 16 **68 22**
2003–04 Blackburn R 13 6 **13 6**

**TAYLOR, Michael* (M)** **12 0**
b.Liverpool 21-11-82
*Source:* Scholarship.
1999–2000 Blackburn R 0 0
2000–01 Blackburn R 0 0
2001–02 Blackburn R 0 0
2002–03 Blackburn R 0 0
2002–03 *Carlisle U* 10 0 **10 0**
2002–03 *Rochdale* 2 0 **2 0**
2003–04 Blackburn R 0 0

**THOMPSON, David (M)** **158 25**
H: 5 7 W: 10 00 b.Birkenhead 12-9-77
*Source:* Trainee. *Honours:* England Youth, Under-21.
1994–95 Liverpool 0 0
1995–96 Liverpool 0 0
1996–97 Liverpool 2 0
1997–98 Liverpool 5 1
1997–98 *Swindon T* 10 0 **10 0**
1998–99 Liverpool 14 1
1999–2000 Liverpool 27 3 **48 5**
2000–01 Coventry C 25 3
2001–02 Coventry C 37 12
2002–03 Coventry C 4 0 **66 15**
2002–03 Blackburn R 23 4
2003–04 Blackburn R 11 1 **34 5**

**TODD, Andy (D)** **195 7**
H: 5 11 W: 13 04 b.Derby 21-9-74
*Source:* Trainee.
1991–92 Middlesbrough 0 0
1992–93 Middlesbrough 0 0
1993–94 Middlesbrough 3 0
1994–95 Middlesbrough 5 0 **8 0**
1994–95 *Swindon T* 13 0 **13 0**
1995–96 Bolton W 12 2
1996–97 Bolton W 15 0
1997–98 Bolton W 25 0
1998–99 Bolton W 20 0
1999–2000 Bolton W 12 0 **84 2**
1999–2000 Charlton Ath 12 0
2000–01 Charlton Ath 23 1
2001–02 Charlton Ath 5 0 **40 1**
2001–02 *Grimsby T* 12 3 **12 3**
2002–03 Blackburn R 12 1
2003–04 Blackburn R 19 0 **31 1**
2003–04 *Burnley* 7 0 **7 0**

**TUGAY, Kerimoglu (M)** **423 43**
H: 5 9 W: 11 00 b.Istanbul 24-8-70
*Honours:* Turkey 92 full caps, 2 goals.
1988–89 Galatasaray 16 0
1989–90 Galatasaray 23 0
1990–91 Galatasaray 12 0
1991–92 Galatasaray 26 3
1992–93 Galatasaray 25 6
1993–94 Galatasaray 25 12
1994–95 Galatasaray 23 1
1995–96 Galatasaray 30 3
1996–97 Galatasaray 33 4
1997–98 Galatasaray 30 2
1998–99 Galatasaray 22 2
1999–2000 Galatasaray 10 1 **275 34**
1999–2000 Rangers 16 1
2000–01 Rangers 26 3 **42 4**
2001–02 Blackburn R 33 3
2002–03 Blackburn R 37 1
2003–04 Blackburn R 36 1 **106 5**

**WATT, Jerome (M)** **0 0**
b.Preston 20-10-84
*Source:* Scholar. *Honours:* England Youth.
2001–02 Blackburn R 0 0
2002–03 Blackburn R 0 0
2003–04 Blackburn R 0 0

**WEAVER, Paul (M)** **0 0**
b.Irvine 27-2-86
*Source:* Trainee.
2002–03 Blackburn R 0 0
2003–04 Blackburn R 0 0

**YELLDELL, David (G)** **0 0**
b.Stuttgart 1-10-81
2003–04 Blackburn R 0 0

**YORKE, Dwight (F)** **383 133**
H: 5 10 W: 12 04 b.Canaan 3-11-71
*Source:* St Clair's, Tobago. *Honours:* Trinidad & Tobago full caps.
1989–90 Aston Villa 2 0
1990–91 Aston Villa 18 2
1991–92 Aston Villa 32 11
1992–93 Aston Villa 27 6
1993–94 Aston Villa 12 2
1994–95 Aston Villa 37 6
1995–96 Aston Villa 35 17
1996–97 Aston Villa 37 17

1997–98 Aston Villa 30 12
1998–99 Aston Villa 1 0 **231 73**
1998–99 Manchester U 32 18
1999–2000 Manchester U 32 20
2000–01 Manchester U 22 9
2001–02 Manchester U 10 1 **96 48**
2002–03 Blackburn R 33 8
2003–04 Blackburn R 23 4 **56 12**

**Scholars**
Abdillahi, Omar A; Barker, Keith H D; Barr, Craig J; Byrom, Joel A; Corvino, Peter; Gautron, Michael; Johnson, William D; Jones, Luke J; Kane, Anthony M; Misbah, Zaki P; Peter, Sergio M; Rowntree, Gari R; Stopforth, Gary; Taylor, Andrew; Walsh, Clark; Welch, Ralph L

## BLACKPOOL (6)

**BARNES, Phil* (G) 143 0**
H: 6 1 W: 11 01 b.Sheffield 2-3-79
*Source:* Trainee.
1996–97 Rotherham U 2 0 **2 0**
1997–98 Blackpool 1 0
1998–99 Blackpool 1 0
1999–2000 Blackpool 12 0
2000–01 Blackpool 34 0
2001–02 Blackpool 30 0
2002–03 Blackpool 44 0
2003–04 Blackpool 19 0 **141 0**

**BLINKHORN, Matthew (F) 22 3**
H: 6 0 W: 10 10 b.Blackpool 2-3-85
*Source:* Scholar.
2001–02 Blackpool 3 0
2002–03 Blackpool 7 2
2003–04 Blackpool 12 1 **22 3**

**BULLOCK, Martin (M) 316 9**
H: 5 5 W: 10 07 b.Derby 5-3-75
*Source:* Eastwood T. *Honours:* England Under-21.
1993–94 Barnsley 0 0
1994–95 Barnsley 29 0
1995–96 Barnsley 41 1
1996–97 Barnsley 28 0
1997–98 Barnsley 33 0
1998–99 Barnsley 32 2
1999–2000 Barnsley 4 0
1999–2000 *Port Vale* 6 1 **6 1**
2000–01 Barnsley 18 1
2001–02 Barnsley 0 0 **185 4**
2001–02 Blackpool 43 2
2002–03 Blackpool 38 1
2003–04 Blackpool 44 1 **125 4**

**BURNS, Jamie (M) 18 0**
H: 5 9 W: 10 11 b.Blackpool 6-3-84
*Source:* Scholar.
2002–03 Blackpool 7 0
2003–04 Blackpool 11 0 **18 0**

**CLANCY, Sean§ (M) 2 0**
H: 5 8 W: 9 12 b.Liverpool 16-9-87
*Source:* School.
2003–04 Blackpool 2 0 **2 0**

**COID, Danny (D) 166 9**
H: 5 11 W: 11 07 b.Liverpool 3-10-81
*Source:* Trainee.
1998–99 Blackpool 1 0
1999–2000 Blackpool 21 1
2000–01 Blackpool 46 1
2001–02 Blackpool 27 3
2002–03 Blackpool 36 1
2003–04 Blackpool 35 3 **166 9**

**DAVIS, Steve (D) 503 64**
H: 6 2 W: 14 07 b.Hexham 30-10-68
*Source:* Trainee.
1987–88 Southampton 0 0
1988–89 Southampton 0 0
1989–90 Southampton 4 0
1989–90 *Burnley* 9 0
1990–91 Southampton 3 0 **7 0**
1990–91 *Notts Co* 2 0 **2 0**
1991–92 Burnley 40 6
1992–93 Burnley 37 2
1993–94 Burnley 42 7
1994–95 Burnley 43 7
1995–96 Luton T 36 2
1996–97 Luton T 44 8
1997–98 Luton T 38 5
1998–99 Luton T 20 6 **138 21**
1998–99 Burnley 19 3
1999–2000 Burnley 42 7
2000–01 Burnley 44 5
2001–02 Burnley 23 1
2002–03 Burnley 28 4 **327 42**
2003–04 Blackpool 29 1 **29 1**

**DOUGHTY, Philip§ (M) 0 0**
H: 6 2 W: 13 02 b.Blackpool 6-9-86
2003–04 Blackpool 0 0

**EDGE, Lewis§ (G) 1 0**
H: 6 1 W: 12 10 b.Lancaster 12-1-87
*Source:* Scholar.
2003–04 Blackpool 1 0 **1 0**

**ELLIOTT, Steve# (D) 101 1**
H: 6 2 W: 14 08 b.Derby 29-10-78
*Source:* Trainee.
1996–97 Derby Co 0 0
1997–98 Derby Co 3 0
1998–99 Derby Co 11 0
1999–2000 Derby Co 20 0
2000–01 Derby Co 6 0
2001–02 Derby Co 6 0
2002–03 Derby Co 23 1
2003–04 Derby Co 4 0 **73 1**
2003–04 Blackpool 28 0 **28 0**

**EVANS, Gareth (D) 59 0**
H: 6 0 W: 11 11 b.Leeds 15-2-81
*Source:* Trainee. *Honours:* England Youth.
1997–98 Leeds U 0 0
1998–99 Leeds U 0 0
1999–2000 Leeds U 0 0
2000–01 Leeds U 1 0 **1 0**
2001–02 Huddersfield T 35 0
2002–03 Huddersfield T 0 0 **35 0**
2003–04 Blackpool 23 0 **23 0**

**FLYNN, Mike (D) 648 25**
H: 6 0 W: 11 00 b.Oldham 23-2-69
*Source:* Trainee.
1986–87 Oldham Ath 0 0
1987–88 Oldham Ath 31 1
1988–89 Oldham Ath 9 0 **40 1**
1988–89 Norwich C 0 0
1989–90 Norwich C 0 0
1989–90 Preston NE 23 1
1990–91 Preston NE 35 1
1991–92 Preston NE 43 3
1992–93 Preston NE 35 2 **136 7**
1992–93 Stockport Co 10 0
1993–94 Stockport Co 46 1
1994–95 Stockport Co 43 2
1995–96 Stockport Co 46 6
1996–97 Stockport Co 46 2
1997–98 Stockport Co 34 1
1998–99 Stockport Co 46 1
1999–2000 Stockport Co 46 1
2000–01 Stockport Co 44 0
2001–02 Stockport Co 26 2 **387 16**
2001–02 *Stoke C* 13 0 **13 0**
2001–02 Barnsley 7 0
2002–03 Barnsley 14 0 **21 0**
2002–03 Blackpool 21 0
2003–04 Blackpool 30 1 **51 1**

**GRAYSON, Simon# (D) 385 9**
H: 6 0 W: 13 07 b.Ripon 16-12-69
*Source:* Trainee.
1987–88 Leeds U 2 0
1988–89 Leeds U 0 0
1989–90 Leeds U 0 0
1990–91 Leeds U 0 0
1991–92 Leeds U 0 0 **2 0**
1991–92 Leicester C 13 0
1992–93 Leicester C 24 1
1993–94 Leicester C 40 1
1994–95 Leicester C 34 0
1995–96 Leicester C 41 2
1996–97 Leicester C 36 0 **188 4**
1997–98 Aston Villa 33 0
1998–99 Aston Villa 15 0 **48 0**
1999–2000 Blackburn R 34 0
2000–01 Blackburn R 0 0
2000–01 *Sheffield W* 5 0 **5 0**
2000–01 *Stockport Co* 13 0 **13 0**
2001–02 Blackburn R 0 0 **34 0**
2001–02 *Notts Co* 10 1 **10 1**
2001–02 *Bradford C* 7 0 **7 0**
2002–03 Blackpool 45 3
2003–04 Blackpool 33 1 **78 4**

**HERZIG, Denny (M) 0 0**
b.Pobneck 13-11-84
2001–02 Wimbledon 0 0
2002–03 Wimbledon 0 0
2002–03 Blackpool 0 0
2003–04 Blackpool 0 0

**HESSEY, Sean* (D) 61 1**
H: 6 0 W: 12 03 b.Liverpool 19-9-78
*Source:* Liverpool Trainee.
1997–98 Wigan Ath 0 0
1997–98 Leeds U 0 0
1997–98 Huddersfield T 1 0
1998–99 Huddersfield T 10 0 **11 0**
1999–2000 Kilmarnock 11 0
2000–01 Kilmarnock 6 0
2001–02 Kilmarnock 15 0
2002–03 Kilmarnock 5 0
2003–04 Kilmarnock 7 1 **44 1**
2003–04 Blackpool 6 0 **6 0**

**HILTON, Kirk* (D) 14 1**
H: 5 7 W: 10 01 b.Flixton 2-4-81
*Source:* Trainee.
1999–2000 Manchester U 0 0
2000–01 Manchester U 0 0
2001–02 Manchester U 0 0
2002–03 Manchester U 0 0
2003–04 Blackpool 14 1 **14 1**

**JASZCZUN, Tommy* (D) 122 0**
H: 5 10 W: 10 10 b.Kettering 16-9-77
*Source:* Trainee.
1996–97 Aston Villa 0 0
1997–98 Aston Villa 0 0
1998–99 Aston Villa 0 0
1999–2000 Aston Villa 0 0
1999–2000 Blackpool 19 0
2000–01 Blackpool 35 0
2001–02 Blackpool 40 0
2002–03 Blackpool 21 0
2003–04 Blackpool 7 0 **122 0**

**JONES, Lee (G) 178 0**
H: 6 3 W: 14 04 b.Pontypridd 9-8-70
*Source:* Porth.
1993–94 Swansea C 0 0
1994–95 Swansea C 2 0
1995–96 Swansea C 1 0
1995–96 *Crewe Alex* 0 0
1996–97 Swansea C 1 0
1997–98 Swansea C 2 0 **6 0**
1997–98 Bristol R 8 0
1998–99 Bristol R 32 0
1999–2000 Bristol R 36 0 **76 0**
2000–01 Stockport Co 27 0
2001–02 Stockport Co 24 0
2002–03 Stockport Co 24 0
2003–04 Stockport Co 0 0 **75 0**
2003–04 Blackpool 21 0 **21 0**

**MANGAN, Andrew§ (M) 2 0**
H: 5 9 W: 10 03 b.Liverpool 30-8-86
*Source:* Scholar.
2003–04 Blackpool 2 0 **2 0**

**McMAHON, Steve (M) 18 0**
H: 5 9 W: 10 05 b.Southport 31-7-84
*Source:* Scholar.
2002–03 Blackpool 6 0
2003–04 Blackpool 12 0 **18 0**

**McNULTY, Stephen† (D) 0 0**
b.Liverpool 26-9-83
*Source:* Scholar.
2001–02 Liverpool 0 0
2002–03 Liverpool 0 0
2003–04 Blackpool 0 0

**MURPHY, John (F) 290 86**
H: 6 2 W: 14 00 b.Whiston 18-10-76
*Source:* Trainee.
1994–95 Chester C 5 0
1995–96 Chester C 18 3
1996–97 Chester C 11 1
1997–98 Chester C 27 4
1998–99 Chester C 42 12 **103 20**
1999–2000 Blackpool 39 10

| | | | | | |
|---|---|---|---|---|---|
| 2000–01 | Blackpool | 46 | 18 | | |
| 2001–02 | Blackpool | 37 | 13 | | |
| 2002–03 | Blackpool | 35 | 16 | | |
| 2003–04 | Blackpool | 30 | 9 | **187** | **66** |

**RICHARDSON, Leam (D) 82 0**
H: 5 7 W: 11 04 b.Leeds 19-11-79
*Source:* Trainee.

| | | | | | |
|---|---|---|---|---|---|
| 1997–98 | Blackburn R | 0 | 0 | | |
| 1998–99 | Blackburn R | 0 | 0 | | |
| 1999–2000 | Blackburn R | 0 | 0 | | |
| 2000–01 | Bolton W | 12 | 0 | | |
| 2001–02 | Bolton W | 1 | 0 | | |
| 2001–02 | *Notts Co* | 21 | 0 | **21** | **0** |
| 2002–03 | Bolton W | 0 | 0 | **13** | **0** |
| 2002–03 | *Blackpool* | 20 | 0 | | |
| 2003–04 | Blackpool | 28 | 0 | **48** | **0** |

**SHERON, Mike# (F) 455 121**
H: 5 10 W: 11 13 b.St Helens 11-1-72
*Source:* Trainee. *Honours:* England Under-21.

| | | | | | |
|---|---|---|---|---|---|
| 1990–91 | Manchester C | 0 | 0 | | |
| 1990–91 | *Bury* | 5 | 1 | **5** | **1** |
| 1991–92 | Manchester C | 29 | 7 | | |
| 1992–93 | Manchester C | 38 | 11 | | |
| 1993–94 | Manchester C | 33 | 6 | **100** | **24** |
| 1994–95 | Norwich C | 21 | 1 | | |
| 1995–96 | Norwich C | 7 | 1 | **28** | **2** |
| 1995–96 | Stoke C | 28 | 15 | | |
| 1996–97 | Stoke C | 41 | 19 | **69** | **34** |
| 1997–98 | QPR | 40 | 11 | | |
| 1998–99 | QPR | 23 | 8 | **63** | **19** |
| 1998–99 | Barnsley | 15 | 2 | | |
| 1999–2000 | Barnsley | 36 | 9 | | |
| 2000–01 | Barnsley | 34 | 1 | | |
| 2001–02 | Barnsley | 33 | 12 | | |
| 2002–03 | Barnsley | 34 | 9 | **152** | **33** |
| 2003–04 | Blackpool | 38 | 8 | **38** | **8** |

**SOUTHERN, Keith (M) 66 3**
H: 5 10 W: 12 06 b.Gateshead 24-4-81
*Source:* Trainee.

| | | | | | |
|---|---|---|---|---|---|
| 1998–99 | Everton | 0 | 0 | | |
| 1999–2000 | Everton | 0 | 0 | | |
| 2000–01 | Everton | 0 | 0 | | |
| 2001–02 | Everton | 0 | 0 | | |
| 2002–03 | Everton | 0 | 0 | | |
| 2002–03 | Blackpool | 38 | 1 | | |
| 2003–04 | Blackpool | 28 | 2 | **66** | **3** |

**TAYLOR, Scott (F) 283 57**
H: 5 10 W: 11 04 b.Chertsey 5-5-76
*Source:* Staines T.

| | | | | | |
|---|---|---|---|---|---|
| 1994–95 | Millwall | 6 | 0 | | |
| 1995–96 | Millwall | 22 | 0 | **28** | **0** |
| 1995–96 | Bolton W | 1 | 0 | | |
| 1996–97 | Bolton W | 11 | 1 | | |
| 1997–98 | Bolton W | 0 | 0 | | |
| 1997–98 | *Rotherham U* | 10 | 3 | **10** | **3** |
| 1997–98 | *Blackpool* | 5 | 1 | | |
| 1998–99 | Bolton W | 0 | 0 | **12** | **1** |
| 1998–99 | Tranmere R | 36 | 9 | | |
| 1999–2000 | Tranmere R | 35 | 3 | | |
| 2000–01 | Tranmere R | 37 | 5 | **108** | **17** |
| 2001–02 | Stockport Co | 28 | 4 | **28** | **4** |
| 2001–02 | Blackpool | 17 | 2 | | |
| 2002–03 | Blackpool | 44 | 13 | | |
| 2003–04 | Blackpool | 31 | 16 | **97** | **32** |

**WELLENS, Richard (M) 160 13**
H: 5 9 W: 11 06 b.Manchester 26-3-80
*Source:* Trainee. *Honours:* England Youth.

| | | | | | |
|---|---|---|---|---|---|
| 1996–97 | Manchester U | 0 | 0 | | |
| 1997–98 | Manchester U | 0 | 0 | | |
| 1998–99 | Manchester U | 0 | 0 | | |
| 1999–2000 | Manchester U | 0 | 0 | | |
| 1999–2000 | Blackpool | 8 | 0 | | |
| 2000–01 | Blackpool | 36 | 8 | | |
| 2001–02 | Blackpool | 36 | 1 | | |
| 2002–03 | Blackpool | 39 | 1 | | |
| 2003–04 | Blackpool | 41 | 3 | **160** | **13** |

**WILES, Simon (M) 4 0**
H: 5 11 W: 11 04 b.Preston 22-4-85
*Source:* Scholar.

| | | | | | |
|---|---|---|---|---|---|
| 2003–04 | Blackpool | 4 | 0 | **4** | **0** |

**Scholars**
Bagdagi, Cabbar; Brown, Kevin P J; Doughty, Philip M; Edge, Lewis J S; Fenech, Jonathan; Gilston, Matthew; Lawlor, Sean P; Mangan, Andrew F; McInally, Garry; Paterson, Sean P; Russell, Mark P; Swan, Mark L; Whittaker, Daniel S

## BOLTON W (7)

**BA, Ibrahim* (M) 253 16**
H: 5 10 W: 11 09 b.Dakar 12-11-73
*Honours:* France 8 full caps.

| | | | | | |
|---|---|---|---|---|---|
| 1991–92 | Le Havre | 1 | 0 | | |
| 1992–93 | Le Havre | 28 | 0 | | |
| 1993–94 | Le Havre | 33 | 3 | | |
| 1994–95 | Le Havre | 33 | 3 | | |
| 1995–96 | Le Havre | 33 | 2 | **128** | **8** |
| 1996–97 | Bordeaux | 35 | 6 | **35** | **6** |
| 1997–98 | AC Milan | 31 | 1 | | |
| 1998–99 | AC Milan | 15 | 0 | | |
| 1999–2000 | AC Milan | 0 | 0 | | |
| 1999–2000 | Perugia | 16 | 1 | **16** | **1** |
| 2000–01 | AC Milan | 5 | 0 | | |
| 2001–02 | Marseille | 9 | 0 | **9** | **0** |
| 2001–02 | AC Milan | 2 | 0 | | |
| 2002–03 | AC Milan | 3 | 0 | **56** | **1** |
| 2003–04 | Bolton W | 9 | 0 | **9** | **0** |

**BARNESS, Anthony (D) 227 4**
H: 5 10 W: 12 11 b.Lewisham 25-2-73
*Source:* Trainee.

| | | | | | |
|---|---|---|---|---|---|
| 1990–91 | Charlton Ath | 0 | 0 | | |
| 1991–92 | Charlton Ath | 22 | 1 | | |
| 1992–93 | Charlton Ath | 5 | 0 | | |
| 1992–93 | Chelsea | 2 | 0 | | |
| 1993–94 | Chelsea | 0 | 0 | | |
| 1993–94 | *Middlesbrough* | 0 | 0 | | |
| 1994–95 | Chelsea | 12 | 0 | | |
| 1995–96 | Chelsea | 0 | 0 | **14** | **0** |
| 1995–96 | *Southend U* | 5 | 0 | **5** | **0** |
| 1996–97 | Charlton Ath | 45 | 2 | | |
| 1997–98 | Charlton Ath | 29 | 1 | | |
| 1998–99 | Charlton Ath | 3 | 0 | | |
| 1999–2000 | Charlton Ath | 19 | 0 | **123** | **4** |
| 2000–01 | Bolton W | 20 | 0 | | |
| 2001–02 | Bolton W | 25 | 0 | | |
| 2002–03 | Bolton W | 25 | 0 | | |
| 2003–04 | Bolton W | 15 | 0 | **85** | **0** |

**BON, Jeremy‡ (G) 0 0**
b.Begles 21-10-84
*Source:* Bordeaux.

| | | | | | |
|---|---|---|---|---|---|
| 2001–02 | Bolton W | 0 | 0 | | |
| 2002–03 | Bolton W | 0 | 0 | | |
| 2003–04 | Bolton W | 0 | 0 | | |

**CAMPO, Ivan (D) 238 13**
H: 6 1 W: 12 12 b.San Sebastian 21-2-74
*Honours:* Spain 4 full caps.

| | | | | | |
|---|---|---|---|---|---|
| 1993–94 | Alaves | 11 | 1 | | |
| 1994–95 | Alaves | 23 | 1 | | |
| 1995–96 | Alaves | 11 | 0 | **45** | **2** |
| 1995–96 | Valladolid | 24 | 2 | **24** | **2** |
| 1996–97 | Valencia | 7 | 1 | **7** | **1** |
| 1997–98 | Mallorca | 33 | 1 | **33** | **1** |
| 1998–99 | Real Madrid | 27 | 1 | | |
| 1999–2000 | Real Madrid | 20 | 0 | | |
| 2000–01 | Real Madrid | 10 | 0 | | |
| 2001–02 | Real Madrid | 3 | 0 | **60** | **1** |
| 2002–03 | Bolton W | 31 | 2 | | |
| 2003–04 | Bolton W | 38 | 4 | **69** | **6** |

**CHARLTON, Simon (D) 430 3**
H: 5 8 W: 11 04 b.Huddersfield 25-10-71
*Source:* Trainee. *Honours:* FA Schools.

| | | | | | |
|---|---|---|---|---|---|
| 1989–90 | Huddersfield T | 3 | 0 | | |
| 1990–91 | Huddersfield T | 30 | 0 | | |
| 1991–92 | Huddersfield T | 45 | 0 | | |
| 1992–93 | Huddersfield T | 46 | 1 | **124** | **1** |
| 1993–94 | Southampton | 33 | 1 | | |
| 1994–95 | Southampton | 25 | 1 | | |
| 1995–96 | Southampton | 26 | 0 | | |
| 1996–97 | Southampton | 27 | 0 | | |
| 1997–98 | Southampton | 3 | 0 | **114** | **2** |
| 1998–99 | Birmingham C | 28 | 0 | | |
| 1997–98 | Birmingham C | 24 | 0 | | |
| 1999–2000 | Birmingham C | 20 | 0 | **72** | **0** |
| 2000–01 | Bolton W | 22 | 0 | | |
| 2001–02 | Bolton W | 36 | 0 | | |
| 2002–03 | Bolton W | 31 | 0 | | |
| 2003–04 | Bolton W | 31 | 0 | **120** | **0** |

**COMYN-PLATT, Charlie§ (D) 0 0**
b.Manchester 2-10-85
*Source:* Scholar.

| | | | | | |
|---|---|---|---|---|---|
| 2003–04 | Bolton W | 0 | 0 | | |

**DAVIES, Kevin (F) 306 54**
H: 6 1 W: 13 11 b.Sheffield 26-3-77
*Source:* Trainee. *Honours:* England Youth, Under-21.

| | | | | | |
|---|---|---|---|---|---|
| 1993–94 | Chesterfield | 24 | 4 | | |
| 1994–95 | Chesterfield | 41 | 11 | | |
| 1995–96 | Chesterfield | 30 | 4 | | |
| 1996–97 | Chesterfield | 34 | 3 | **129** | **22** |
| 1996–97 | Southampton | 0 | 0 | | |
| 1997–98 | Southampton | 25 | 9 | | |
| 1998–99 | Blackburn R | 21 | 1 | | |
| 1999–2000 | Blackburn R | 2 | 0 | **23** | **1** |
| 1999–2000 | Southampton | 23 | 6 | | |
| 2000–01 | Southampton | 27 | 1 | | |
| 2001–02 | Southampton | 23 | 2 | | |
| 2002–03 | Southampton | 9 | 1 | **107** | **19** |
| 2002–03 | *Millwall* | 9 | 3 | **9** | **3** |
| 2003–04 | Bolton W | 38 | 9 | **38** | **9** |

**DJORKAEFF, Youri* (M) 523 184**
H: 5 10 W: 11 02 b.Lyon 9-3-68
*Honours:* France 82 full caps, 28 goals.

| | | | | | |
|---|---|---|---|---|---|
| 1984–85 | Grenoble | 2 | 0 | | |
| 1985–86 | Grenoble | 6 | 0 | | |
| 1986–87 | Grenoble | 26 | 4 | | |
| 1987–88 | Grenoble | 19 | 8 | | |
| 1988–89 | Grenoble | 25 | 11 | | |
| 1989–90 | Grenoble | 3 | 0 | **81** | **23** |
| 1989–90 | Strasbourg | 28 | 21 | | |
| 1990–91 | Strasbourg | 7 | 4 | **35** | **25** |
| 1990–91 | Monaco | 20 | 5 | | |
| 1991–92 | Monaco | 35 | 9 | | |
| 1992–93 | Monaco | 32 | 12 | | |
| 1993–94 | Monaco | 35 | 20 | | |
| 1994–95 | Monaco | 33 | 14 | **155** | **60** |
| 1995–96 | Paris St Germain | 35 | 13 | **35** | **13** |
| 1996–97 | Internazionale | 33 | 14 | | |
| 1997–98 | Internazionale | 29 | 8 | | |
| 1998–99 | Internazionale | 25 | 8 | **87** | **30** |
| 1999–2000 | Kaiserslautern | 25 | 11 | | |
| 2000–01 | Kaiserslautern | 26 | 3 | | |
| 2001–02 | Kaiserslautern | 4 | 0 | **55** | **14** |
| 2001–02 | Bolton W | 12 | 4 | | |
| 2002–03 | Bolton W | 36 | 7 | | |
| 2003–04 | Bolton W | 27 | 8 | **75** | **19** |

**EMERSON* (D) 152 3**
H: 6 2 W: 13 04 b.Porto Alegre 30-3-72
*Source:* Benfica.

| | | | | | |
|---|---|---|---|---|---|
| 1997–98 | Sheffield W | 6 | 0 | | |
| 1998–99 | Sheffield W | 38 | 1 | | |
| 1999–2000 | Sheffield W | 17 | 0 | **61** | **1** |
| 1999–2000 | Chelsea | 20 | 0 | | |
| 2000–01 | Chelsea | 1 | 0 | **21** | **0** |
| 2000–01 | Sunderland | 31 | 1 | | |
| 2001–02 | Sunderland | 12 | 1 | | |
| 2002–03 | Sunderland | 1 | 0 | | |
| 2003–04 | Sunderland | 0 | 0 | **44** | **2** |
| 2003–04 | Bolton W | 26 | 0 | **26** | **0** |

**FORSCHELET, Gerald* (M) 0 0**
H: 6 1 W: 13 05 b.Papeete 19-9-81
*Source:* Cannes.

| | | | | | |
|---|---|---|---|---|---|
| 2001–02 | Bolton W | 0 | 0 | | |
| 2002–03 | Bolton W | 0 | 0 | | |
| 2003–04 | Bolton W | 0 | 0 | | |

**FRANDSEN, Per* (M) 485 88**
H: 6 1 W: 12 06 b.Copenhagen 6-2-70
*Honours:* Denmark 23 full caps.

| | | | | | |
|---|---|---|---|---|---|
| 1990 | B 1903 | 25 | 15 | **25** | **15** |
| 1990–91 | Lille | 19 | 4 | | |
| 1991–92 | Lille | 27 | 8 | | |
| 1992–93 | Lille | 32 | 3 | | |
| 1993–94 | Lille | 31 | 4 | **109** | **19** |
| 1994–95 | FC Copenhagen | 29 | 12 | | |
| 1995–96 | FC Copenhagen | 26 | 7 | **55** | **19** |
| 1996–97 | Bolton W | 41 | 5 | | |
| 1997–98 | Bolton W | 38 | 2 | | |
| 1998–99 | Bolton W | 44 | 8 | | |
| 1999–2000 | Bolton W | 7 | 2 | | |
| 1999–2000 | Blackburn R | 31 | 5 | **31** | **5** |
| 2000–01 | Bolton W | 39 | 7 | | |
| 2001–02 | Bolton W | 29 | 3 | | |
| 2002–03 | Bolton W | 34 | 2 | | |
| 2003–04 | Bolton W | 33 | 1 | **265** | **30** |

**GARDNER, Ricardo (M)** **176 15**
H: 5 9 W: 11 00 b.St Andrews 25-9-78
*Source:* Harbour View. *Honours:* Jamaica 54 full caps, 5 goals.

| | | | | | |
|---|---|---|---|---|---|
| 1998–99 | Bolton W | 30 | 2 | | |
| 1999–2000 | Bolton W | 29 | 5 | | |
| 2000–01 | Bolton W | 32 | 3 | | |
| 2001–02 | Bolton W | 31 | 3 | | |
| 2002–03 | Bolton W | 32 | 2 | | |
| 2003–04 | Bolton W | 22 | 0 | **176** | **15** |

**GIANNAKOPOULOS, Stelios (F)** **337 98**
H: 5 8 W: 11 00 b.Athens 12-7-74
*Honours:* Greece 41 full caps, 6 goals.

| | | | | | |
|---|---|---|---|---|---|
| 1992–93 | Ethnikos | 32 | 6 | **32** | **6** |
| 1993–94 | Paniliakos | 26 | 9 | | |
| 1994–95 | Paniliakos | 31 | 10 | | |
| 1995–96 | Paniliakos | 27 | 7 | **84** | **26** |
| 1996–97 | Olympiakos | 31 | 7 | | |
| 1997–98 | Olympiakos | 31 | 3 | | |
| 1998–99 | Olympiakos | 23 | 7 | | |
| 1999–2000 | Olympiakos | 29 | 10 | | |
| 2000–01 | Olympiakos | 26 | 11 | | |
| 2001–02 | Olympiakos | 21 | 11 | | |
| 2002–03 | Olympiakos | 29 | 15 | **190** | **64** |
| 2003–04 | Bolton W | 31 | 2 | **31** | **2** |

**HOWEY, Steve* (D)** **301 18**
H: 6 2 W: 13 05 b.Sunderland 26-10-71
*Source:* Trainee. *Honours:* England 4 full caps.

| | | | | | |
|---|---|---|---|---|---|
| 1988–89 | Newcastle U | 1 | 0 | | |
| 1989–90 | Newcastle U | 0 | 0 | | |
| 1990–91 | Newcastle U | 11 | 0 | | |
| 1991–92 | Newcastle U | 21 | 1 | | |
| 1992–93 | Newcastle U | 41 | 2 | | |
| 1993–94 | Newcastle U | 14 | 0 | | |
| 1994–95 | Newcastle U | 30 | 1 | | |
| 1995–96 | Newcastle U | 28 | 1 | | |
| 1996–97 | Newcastle U | 8 | 1 | | |
| 1997–98 | Newcastle U | 14 | 0 | | |
| 1998–99 | Newcastle U | 14 | 0 | | |
| 1999–2000 | Newcastle U | 9 | 0 | **191** | **6** |
| 2000–01 | Manchester C | 36 | 6 | | |
| 2001–02 | Manchester C | 34 | 3 | | |
| 2002–03 | Manchester C | 24 | 2 | **94** | **11** |
| 2003–04 | Leicester C | 13 | 1 | **13** | **1** |
| 2003–04 | Bolton W | 3 | 0 | **3** | **0** |

**HUNT, Nicky (D)** **32 1**
H: 6 0 W: 11 00 b.Westhoughton 3-9-83
*Source:* Scholar. *Honours:* England Under-21.

| | | | | | |
|---|---|---|---|---|---|
| 2000–01 | Bolton W | 1 | 0 | | |
| 2001–02 | Bolton W | 0 | 0 | | |
| 2002–03 | Bolton W | 0 | 0 | | |
| 2003–04 | Bolton W | 31 | 1 | **32** | **1** |

**JAASKELAINEN, Jussi (G)** **323 0**
H: 6 4 W: 12 10 b.Mikkeli 19-4-75
*Honours:* Finland 17 full caps.

| | | | | | |
|---|---|---|---|---|---|
| 1992 | MP | 6 | 0 | | |
| 1993 | MP | 6 | 0 | | |
| 1994 | MP | 26 | 0 | | |
| 1995 | MP | 26 | 0 | **64** | **0** |
| 1996 | VPS | 27 | 0 | | |
| 1997 | VPS | 27 | 0 | **54** | **0** |
| 1997–98 | Bolton W | 0 | 0 | | |
| 1998–99 | Bolton W | 34 | 0 | | |
| 1999–2000 | Bolton W | 34 | 0 | | |
| 2000–01 | Bolton W | 27 | 0 | | |
| 2001–02 | Bolton W | 34 | 0 | | |
| 2002–03 | Bolton W | 38 | 0 | | |
| 2003–04 | Bolton W | 38 | 0 | **205** | **0** |

**JARDEL, Mario (F)** **233 218**
H: 6 2 W: 13 03 b.Fortaleza 18-9-73
*Honours:* Brazil 7 full caps, 1 goal.

| | | | | | |
|---|---|---|---|---|---|
| 1993 | Vasco da Gama | 2 | 0 | | |
| 1994 | Vasco da Gama | 13 | 3 | **15** | **3** |
| 1995 | Gremio | 13 | 10 | **13** | **10** |
| 1996–97 | Porto | 31 | 30 | | |
| 1997–98 | Porto | 30 | 26 | | |
| 1998–99 | Porto | 32 | 36 | | |
| 1999–2000 | Porto | 32 | 38 | **125** | **130** |
| 2000–01 | Galatasaray | 24 | 22 | **24** | **22** |
| 2001–02 | Marseille | 0 | 0 | | |
| 2001–02 | Sporting Lisbon | 30 | 42 | | |
| 2002–03 | Sporting Lisbon | 19 | 11 | **49** | **53** |
| 2003–04 | Bolton W | 7 | 0 | **7** | **0** |

**JAVI MORENO‡ (F)** **217 74**
H: 5 11 W: 12 04 b.Silla 10-9-74
*Honours:* Spain 5 full caps.

| | | | | | |
|---|---|---|---|---|---|
| 1995–96 | Barcelona C | 19 | 9 | **19** | **9** |
| 1996–97 | Barcelona B | 10 | 5 | | |
| 1996–97 | Cordoba | 0 | 0 | | |
| 1997–98 | Barcelona B | 0 | 0 | **10** | **5** |
| 1997–98 | Yeciano | 16 | 6 | **16** | **6** |
| 1997–98 | Alaves | 10 | 1 | | |
| 1998–99 | Numancia | 38 | 18 | **38** | **18** |
| 1999–2000 | Alaves | 37 | 7 | | |
| 2000–01 | Alaves | 34 | 21 | **81** | **29** |
| 2001–02 | AC Milan | 16 | 2 | **16** | **2** |
| 2002–03 | Atletico Madrid | 24 | 5 | | |
| 2003–04 | Atletico Madrid | 5 | 0 | **29** | **5** |
| 2003–04 | Bolton W | 8 | 0 | **8** | **0** |

**LAVILLE, Florent (D)** **220 2**
H: 6 2 W: 13 12 b.Valence 7-8-83

| | | | | | |
|---|---|---|---|---|---|
| 1993–94 | Lyon | 8 | 0 | | |
| 1994–95 | Lyon | 28 | 0 | | |
| 1995–96 | Lyon | 28 | 0 | | |
| 1996–97 | Lyon | 27 | 1 | | |
| 1997–98 | Lyon | 29 | 0 | | |
| 1998–99 | Lyon | 29 | 0 | | |
| 1999–2000 | Lyon | 29 | 0 | | |
| 2000–01 | Lyon | 9 | 0 | | |
| 2001–02 | Lyon | 13 | 0 | | |
| 2002–03 | Lyon | 5 | 1 | **205** | **2** |
| 2002–03 | Bolton W | 10 | 0 | | |
| 2003–04 | Bolton W | 5 | 0 | **15** | **0** |

**LIVESEY, Danny (D)** **26 0**
H: 6 3 W: 12 10 b.Salford 31-12-84
*Source:* Trainee.

| | | | | | |
|---|---|---|---|---|---|
| 2002–03 | Bolton W | 2 | 0 | | |
| 2003–04 | Bolton W | 0 | 0 | **2** | **0** |
| 2003–04 | *Notts Co* | 11 | 0 | **11** | **0** |
| 2003–04 | *Rochdale* | 13 | 0 | **13** | **0** |

**N'GOTTY, Bruno (D)** **449 24**
H: 6 2 W: 13 05 b.Lyon 10-6-71
*Honours:* France 6 full caps.

| | | | | | |
|---|---|---|---|---|---|
| 1989–90 | Lyon | 27 | 0 | | |
| 1990–91 | Lyon | 37 | 2 | | |
| 1991–92 | Lyon | 36 | 1 | | |
| 1992–93 | Lyon | 36 | 3 | | |
| 1993–94 | Lyon | 36 | 3 | | |
| 1994–95 | Lyon | 35 | 3 | **207** | **12** |
| 1995–96 | Paris St Germain | 24 | 1 | | |
| 1996–97 | Paris St Germain | 30 | 4 | | |
| 1997–98 | Paris St Germain | 26 | 2 | **80** | **7** |
| 1998–99 | AC Milan | 25 | 1 | | |
| 1999–2000 | AC Milan | 9 | 0 | **34** | **1** |
| 1999–2000 | Venezia | 16 | 0 | **16** | **0** |
| 2000–01 | Marseille | 30 | 0 | **30** | **0** |
| 2001–02 | Bolton W | 26 | 1 | | |
| 2002–03 | Bolton W | 23 | 1 | | |
| 2003–04 | Bolton W | 33 | 2 | **82** | **4** |

**NDIWA, Lord Kangana* (D)** **5 0**
H: 6 3 W: 13 03 b.Maquella-dozombo 28-2-84
*Source:* Djurgaarden. *Honours:* DR Congo full caps, Sweden Youth.

| | | | | | |
|---|---|---|---|---|---|
| 2003–04 | Bolton W | 0 | 0 | | |
| 2003–04 | *Oldham Ath* | 4 | 0 | **4** | **0** |
| 2003–04 | *Rochdale* | 1 | 0 | **1** | **0** |

**NOLAN, Kevin (M)** **140 19**
H: 6 0 W: 14 00 b.Liverpool 24-6-82
*Source:* Scholar. *Honours:* England Youth, Under-20, Under-21.

| | | | | | |
|---|---|---|---|---|---|
| 1999–2000 | Bolton W | 4 | 0 | | |
| 2000–01 | Bolton W | 31 | 1 | | |
| 2001–02 | Bolton W | 35 | 8 | | |
| 2002–03 | Bolton W | 33 | 1 | | |
| 2003–04 | Bolton W | 37 | 9 | **140** | **19** |

**OKOCHA, Jay-Jay* (M)** **302 66**
H: 5 7 W: 11 02 b.Enugu 14-8-73
*Source:* Enugu Rangers, Neunkirchen.
*Honours:* Nigeria 65 full caps, 12 goals.

| | | | | | |
|---|---|---|---|---|---|
| 1992–93 | Eintracht Frankfurt | 20 | 2 | | |
| 1993–94 | Eintracht Frankfurt | 19 | 2 | | |
| 1994–95 | Eintracht Frankfurt | 27 | 6 | | |
| 1995–96 | Eintracht Frankfurt | 24 | 7 | **90** | **17** |
| 1996–97 | Fenerbahce | 33 | 16 | | |
| 1997–98 | Fenerbahce | 30 | 14 | **63** | **30** |
| 1998–99 | Paris St Germain | 25 | 4 | | |
| 1999–2000 | Paris St Germain | 23 | 2 | | |
| 2000–01 | Paris St Germain | 15 | 2 | | |
| 2001–02 | Paris St Germain | 20 | 4 | **83** | **12** |
| 2002–03 | Bolton W | 31 | 7 | | |
| 2003–04 | Bolton W | 35 | 0 | **66** | **7** |

**PEDERSEN, Henrik (F)** **199 76**
H: 6 0 W: 12 05 b.Jutland 10-6-75
*Honours:* Denmark 2 full caps.

| | | | | | |
|---|---|---|---|---|---|
| 1995–96 | Silkeborg | 12 | 4 | | |
| 1996–97 | Silkeborg | 2 | 0 | | |
| 1997–98 | Silkeborg | 15 | 9 | | |
| 1998–99 | Silkeborg | 33 | 16 | | |
| 1999–2000 | Silkeborg | 28 | 13 | | |
| 2000–01 | Silkeborg | 32 | 20 | **122** | **62** |
| 2001–02 | Bolton W | 11 | 0 | | |
| 2002–03 | Bolton W | 33 | 7 | | |
| 2003–04 | Bolton W | 33 | 7 | **77** | **14** |

**PEZZAROSSI-GARCIA, Dwight* (F)** **0 0**
H: 6 7 W: 14 05 b.Guatemala City 4-7-79
*Source:* Comunicaciones.

| | | | | | |
|---|---|---|---|---|---|
| 2003–04 | Bolton W | 0 | 0 | | |

**POOLE, Kevin* (G)** **299 0**
H: 5 11 W: 12 06 b.Bromsgrove 21-7-63
*Source:* Apprentice.

| | | | | | |
|---|---|---|---|---|---|
| 1981–82 | Aston Villa | 0 | 0 | | |
| 1982–83 | Aston Villa | 0 | 0 | | |
| 1983–84 | Aston Villa | 0 | 0 | | |
| 1984–85 | Aston Villa | 7 | 0 | | |
| 1984–85 | *Northampton T* | 3 | 0 | **3** | **0** |
| 1985–86 | Aston Villa | 11 | 0 | | |
| 1986–87 | Aston Villa | 10 | 0 | **28** | **0** |
| 1987–88 | Middlesbrough | 1 | 0 | | |
| 1988–89 | Middlesbrough | 12 | 0 | | |
| 1989–90 | Middlesbrough | 21 | 0 | | |
| 1990–91 | Middlesbrough | 0 | 0 | **34** | **0** |
| 1990–91 | *Hartlepool U* | 12 | 0 | **12** | **0** |
| 1991–92 | Leicester C | 42 | 0 | | |
| 1992–93 | Leicester C | 19 | 0 | | |
| 1993–94 | Leicester C | 14 | 0 | | |
| 1994–95 | Leicester C | 36 | 0 | | |
| 1995–96 | Leicester C | 45 | 0 | | |
| 1996–97 | Leicester C | 7 | 0 | **163** | **0** |
| 1997–98 | Birmingham C | 1 | 0 | | |
| 1998–99 | Birmingham C | 36 | 0 | | |
| 1999–2000 | Birmingham C | 18 | 0 | | |
| 2000–01 | Birmingham C | 1 | 0 | | |
| 2001–02 | Birmingham C | 0 | 0 | **56** | **0** |
| 2001–02 | Bolton W | 3 | 0 | | |
| 2002–03 | Bolton W | 0 | 0 | | |
| 2003–04 | Bolton W | 0 | 0 | **3** | **0** |

**RICKETTS, Donovan (G)** **0 0**
H: 6 1 W: 11 05 b.St James 6-7-77
*Source:* Village U.

| | | | | | |
|---|---|---|---|---|---|
| 2003–04 | Bolton W | 0 | 0 | | |

**SHAKES, Ricky§ (M)** **0 0**
H: 5 10 W: 12 00 b.Brixton 26-1-85
*Source:* Scholar.

| | | | | | |
|---|---|---|---|---|---|
| 2003–04 | Bolton W | 0 | 0 | | |

**THACH, Duong (F)** **0 0**
b.Minh Hai 9-12-85
*Source:* Trainee.

| | | | | | |
|---|---|---|---|---|---|
| 2003–04 | Bolton W | 0 | 0 | | |

**VAZ TE, Ricardo§ (F)** **1 0**
H: 6 2 W: 12 07 b.Lisbon 1-10-86
*Source:* Trainee.

| | | | | | |
|---|---|---|---|---|---|
| 2003–04 | Bolton W | 1 | 0 | **1** | **0** |

**Scholars**
Ashton Samuel S; Buval, Bedi B; Comyn-Platt, Charlie; Gibb, Jamie A; Gillan, Michael A; Hill, Bradley; Howarth, Christopher; Knowles, Craig J; Kribib, Reda; Moran, Martin R; O'Brien, Joseph M; Powell, Rhys; Shakes, Ricky U; Talbot, Jason C; Vaz Te, Ricardo J; Whitehead, Dale A

## BOSTON U (8)

**ANGEL, Mark* (F)** **162 12**
H: 5 8 W: 11 02 b.Newcastle 23-8-75
*Source:* Trainee.

| | | | | | |
|---|---|---|---|---|---|
| 1993–94 | Sunderland | 0 | 0 | | |
| 1994–95 | Sunderland | 0 | 0 | | |
| 1995–96 | Oxford U | 27 | 1 | | |
| 1996–97 | Oxford U | 24 | 2 | | |
| 1997–98 | Oxford U | 22 | 1 | **73** | **4** |

1998–99 WBA 22 1
1999–2000 WBA 3 0 **25 1**
2000–01 Darlington 5 0 **5 0**
2000–01 *Q of S* 5 1 **5 1**
2002–03 Boston U 31 5
2003–04 Boston U 23 1 **54 6**

**BALMER, Stuart* (D) 417 21**
H: 6 1 W: 12 06 b.Falkirk 20-9-69
*Source:* Celtic BC. *Honours:* Scotland Schools, Youth.
1987–88 Celtic 0 0
1988–89 Celtic 0 0
1989–90 Celtic 0 0
1990–91 Charlton Ath 24 0
1991–92 Charlton Ath 18 0
1992–93 Charlton Ath 45 2
1993–94 Charlton Ath 31 1
1994–95 Charlton Ath 29 2
1995–96 Charlton Ath 32 1
1996–97 Charlton Ath 32 2
1997–98 Charlton Ath 16 0
1998–99 Charlton Ath 0 0 **227 8**
1998–99 Wigan Ath 36 1
1999–2000 Wigan Ath 41 2
2000–01 Wigan Ath 24 1 **101 4**
2001–02 Oldham Ath 36 6
2002–03 Oldham Ath 0 0 **36 6**
2002–03 *Scunthorpe U* 6 0 **6 0**
2002–03 Boston U 21 0
2003–04 Boston U 26 3 **47 3**

**BASTOCK, Paul# (G) 104 0**
H: 5 8 W: 10 00 b.Leamington 19-5-70
*Source:* Trainee.
1986–87 Coventry C 0 0
1987–88 Cambridge U 10 0
1988–89 Cambridge U 2 0 **12 0**
From Fisher, Kettering
2002–03 Boston U 46 0
2003–04 Boston U 46 0 **92 0**

**BEEVERS, Lee (D) 41 2**
H: 6 1 W: 13 00 b.Doncaster 4-12-83
*Source:* Scholar.
2000–01 Ipswich T 0 0
2001–02 Ipswich T 0 0
2002–03 Ipswich T 0 0
2002–03 *Boston U* 1 0
2003–04 Boston U 40 2 **41 2**

**BENNETT, Tom# (M) 382 16**
H: 5 11 W: 11 08 b.Falkirk 12-12-69
*Source:* Trainee.
1987–88 Aston Villa 0 0
1988–89 Wolverhampton W 2 0
1989–90 Wolverhampton W 30 0
1990–91 Wolverhampton W 26 0
1991–92 Wolverhampton W 38 2
1992–93 Wolverhampton W 1 0
1993–94 Wolverhampton W 10 0
1994–95 Wolverhampton W 8 0 **115 2**
1995–96 Stockport Co 24 1
1996–97 Stockport Co 43 3
1997–98 Stockport Co 27 1
1998–99 Stockport Co 7 0
1999–2000 Stockport Co 9 0 **110 5**
1999–2000 *Walsall* 11 3
2000–01 Walsall 38 5
2001–02 Walsall 40 0 **89 8**
2002–03 Boston U 33 0
2003–04 Boston U 35 1 **68 1**

**BROUGH, Scott† (M) 46 3**
H: 5 5 W: 9 11 b.Doncaster 10-2-83
2000–01 Scunthorpe U 4 0
2001–02 Scunthorpe U 19 1
2002–03 Scunthorpe U 23 2 **46 3**
2003–04 Boston U 0 0

**BROWN, Jermaine* (F) 5 0**
H: 5 11 W: 11 00 b.Lambeth 12-1-83
*Source:* Scholar.
2001–02 Arsenal 0 0
2002–03 Arsenal 0 0
2003–04 Arsenal 0 0
2003–04 Boston U 5 0 **5 0**

**CHAPMAN, Ben* (D) 95 0**
H: 5 6 W: 11 05 b.Scunthorpe 2-3-79
*Source:* Trainee.
1997–98 Grimsby T 0 0
1998–99 Grimsby T 1 0
1999–2000 Grimsby T 1 0
2000–01 Grimsby T 2 0
2001–02 Grimsby T 17 0 **21 0**
2002–03 Boston U 37 0
2003–04 Boston U 37 0 **74 0**

**CLARKE, Ryan (D) 4 0**
H: 5 11 W: 12 04 b.Sutton Coldfield 22-1-84
*Source:* Scholar.
2003–04 Boston U 4 0 **4 0**

**CROPPER, Dean* (F) 55 4**
H: 6 2 W: 13 11 b.Chesterfield 5-1-83
*Source:* Sheffield W Scholar.
2002–03 Lincoln C 29 3
2003–04 Lincoln C 21 0 **50 3**
2003–04 Boston U 5 1 **5 1**

**CROUDSON, Steve* (G) 10 0**
H: 6 0 W: 11 12 b.Grimsby 14-9-79
*Source:* Trainee.
1998–99 Grimsby T 2 0
1999–2000 Grimsby T 3 0
2000–01 Grimsby T 0 0
2001–02 *Scunthorpe U* 4 0 **4 0**
2001–02 Grimsby T 1 0
2002–03 Grimsby T 0 0 **6 0**
2003–04 Boston U 0 0

**DOUGLAS, Stuart* (F) 217 26**
H: 5 9 W: 12 05 b.London 9-4-78
*Source:* Trainee.
1995–96 Luton T 8 1
1996–97 Luton T 9 0
1997–98 Luton T 17 1
1998–99 Luton T 42 9
1999–2000 Luton T 40 3
2000–01 Luton T 21 4
2001–02 Luton T 9 0 **146 18**
2001–02 *Oxford U* 4 0 **4 0**
2001–02 *Rushden & D* 9 0 **9 0**
2002–03 Boston U 29 7
2003–04 Boston U 29 1 **58 8**

**ELLENDER, Paul# (D) 68 4**
H: 6 1 W: 12 07 b.Scunthorpe 21-10-74
*Source:* Trainee.
1992–93 Scunthorpe U 0 0
1993–94 Scunthorpe U 0 0
From Altrincham, Scarborough
2002–03 Boston U 26 0
2003–04 Boston U 42 4 **68 4**

**GREAVES, Mark# (D) 240 11**
H: 6 1 W: 13 00 b.Hull 22-1-75
*Source:* Brigg Town.
1996–97 Hull C 30 2
1997–98 Hull C 25 2
1998–99 Hull C 25 0
1999–2000 Hull C 38 3
2000–01 Hull C 30 2
2001–02 Hull C 26 1
2002–03 Hull C 3 0 **177 10**
2002–03 Boston U 26 1
2003–04 Boston U 37 0 **63 1**

**HIGGINS, Alex‡ (M) 14 0**
H: 5 9 W: 11 04 b.Sheffield 22-7-81
*Source:* Trainee. *Honours:* England Schools.
1998–99 Sheffield W 0 0
1999–2000 Sheffield W 0 0
2000–01 Sheffield W 0 0
2000–01 QPR 1 0 **1 0**
From Chester C, Stalybridge C
2002–03 Boston
2003–04 Boston U 0 0 **13 0**

**HOCKING, Matt* (D) 221 5**
H: 6 0 W: 12 09 b.Boston 30-1-78
*Source:* Trainee.
1995–96 Sheffield U 0 0
1996–97 Sheffield U 0 0
1997–98 Sheffield U 0 0
1997–98 Hull C 31 1
1998–99 Hull C 26 1 **57 2**
1998–99 *York C* 6 0
1999–2000 York C 32 2
2000–01 York C 26 0
2001–02 York C 33 0 **97 2**
2002–03 Boston U 45 1
2003–04 Boston U 22 0 **67 1**

**HOLLAND, Chris (M) 199 2**
H: 5 9 W: 12 13 b.Clitheroe 11-9-75
*Source:* Trainee. *Honours:* England Youth, Under-21.
1993–94 Preston NE 1 0 **1 0**
1993–94 Newcastle U 3 0
1994–95 Newcastle U 0 0
1995–96 Newcastle U 0 0
1996–97 Newcastle U 0 0 **3 0**
1996–97 Birmingham C 32 0
1997–98 Birmingham C 10 0
1998–99 Birmingham C 14 0
1999–2000 Birmingham C 14 0 **70 0**
1999–2000 Huddersfield T 17 1
2000–01 Huddersfield T 29 0
2001–02 Huddersfield T 37 1
2002–03 Huddersfield T 34 0
2003–04 Huddersfield T 3 0 **120 2**
2003–04 Boston U 5 0 **5 0**

**HURST, Kevan (F) 7 1**
H: 6 0 W: 11 07 b.Chesterfield 27-8-85
*Source:* Sheffield U Scholar.
2003–04 Boston U 7 1 **7 1**

**JONES, Graeme* (F) 286 86**
H: 6 1 W: 13 06 b.Gateshead 13-3-70
*Source:* Bridlington T.
1993–94 Doncaster R 28 4
1994–95 Doncaster R 32 12
1995–96 Doncaster R 32 10 **92 26**
1996–97 Wigan Ath 40 31
1997–98 Wigan Ath 33 9
1998–99 Wigan Ath 20 3
1999–2000 Wigan Ath 3 1 **96 44**
1999–2000 St Johnstone 19 3
2000–01 St Johnstone 9 3
2001–02 St Johnstone 13 1 **41 7**
2002–03 Southend U 21 2 **21 2**
2002–03 Boston U 3 1
2003–04 Boston U 33 6 **36 7**

**MELTON, Steve (M) 93 4**
H: 5 11 W: 12 03 b.Lincoln 3-10-78
*Source:* Trainee.
1995–96 Nottingham F 0 0
1996–97 Nottingham F 0 0
1997–98 Nottingham F 0 0
1998–99 Nottingham F 1 0
1999–2000 Nottingham F 2 0 **3 0**
1999–2000 Stoke C 5 0 **5 0**
2000–01 Brighton & HA 28 1
2001–02 Brighton & HA 10 1
2002–03 Brighton & HA 8 1 **46 3**
2002–03 Hull C 25 0
2003–04 Hull C 5 0 **30 0**
2003–04 Boston U 9 1 **9 1**

**NOBLE, David (M) 32 3**
H: 6 0 W: 12 04 b.Hitchin 2-2-82
*Source:* Scholar. *Honours:* England Youth, Under-20. Scotland Under-21.
2000–01 Arsenal 0 0
2001–02 Arsenal 0 0
2001–02 *Watford* 15 1 **15 1**
2002–03 Arsenal 0 0
2002–03 West Ham U 0 0
2003–04 West Ham U 3 0 **3 0**
2003–04 Boston U 14 2 **14 2**

**RODWELL, Jim† (D) 12 0**
H: 6 1 W: 14 02 b.Lincoln 20-11-70
*Source:* Halesowen T.
2001–02 Rushden & D 9 0 **9 0**
2002–03 Boston U 3 0
2003–04 Boston U 0 0 **3 0**

**RUSK, Simon (M) 37 2**
H: 5 11 W: 12 08 b.Peterborough 17-12-81
*Source:* Peterborough U.
2002–03 Boston U 18 2
2003–04 Boston U 19 0 **37 2**

**STRONG, Greg (D) 161 9**
H: 6 2 W: 11 12 b.Bolton 5-9-75
*Source:* Trainee. *Honours:* England Schools, Youth.
1992–93 Wigan Ath 0 0
1993–94 Wigan Ath 18 1
1994–95 Wigan Ath 17 2 **35 3**
1995–96 Bolton W 1 0
1996–97 Bolton W 0 0

| | | | | | |
|---|---|---|---|---|---|
| 1997–98 | Bolton W | 0 | 0 | | |
| 1997–98 | *Blackpool* | 11 | 1 | **11** | **1** |
| 1998–99 | Bolton W | 5 | 1 | | |
| 1998–99 | *Stoke C* | 5 | 1 | **5** | **1** |
| 1999–2000 | Bolton W | 6 | 0 | **12** | **1** |
| 1999–2000 | *Motherwell* | 10 | 0 | | |
| 2000–01 | Motherwell | 32 | 1 | | |
| 2001–02 | Motherwell | 32 | 2 | **74** | **3** |
| 2002–03 | Hull C | 3 | 0 | | |
| 2002–03 | *Cheltenham T* | 4 | 0 | **4** | **0** |
| 2002–03 | *Scunthorpe U* | 7 | 0 | **7** | **0** |
| 2003–04 | Hull C | 0 | 0 | **3** | **0** |
| 2003–04 | *Bury* | 10 | 0 | **10** | **0** |
| 2003–04 | Boston U | 0 | 0 | | |

**SUTCH, Daryl* (D) 327 10**
H: 5 11 W: 12 02 b.Lowestoft 11-9-71
*Source:* Trainee. *Honours:* England Youth, Under-21.

| | | | | | |
|---|---|---|---|---|---|
| 1989–90 | Norwich C | 0 | 0 | | |
| 1990–91 | Norwich C | 4 | 0 | | |
| 1991–92 | Norwich C | 9 | 0 | | |
| 1992–93 | Norwich C | 22 | 2 | | |
| 1993–94 | Norwich C | 3 | 0 | | |
| 1994–95 | Norwich C | 30 | 1 | | |
| 1995–96 | Norwich C | 13 | 0 | | |
| 1996–97 | Norwich C | 44 | 3 | | |
| 1997–98 | Norwich C | 40 | 1 | | |
| 1998–99 | Norwich C | 36 | 0 | | |
| 1999–2000 | Norwich C | 45 | 2 | | |
| 2000–01 | Norwich C | 40 | 0 | | |
| 2001–02 | Norwich C | 19 | 0 | | |
| 2002–03 | Norwich C | 0 | 0 | **305** | **9** |
| 2002–03 | Southend U | 16 | 1 | **16** | **1** |
| 2003–04 | Boston U | 6 | 0 | **6** | **0** |

**THOMAS, Danny (F) 70 5**
H: 5 7 W: 10 10 b.Leamington Spa 1-5-81
*Source:* Trainee.

| | | | | | |
|---|---|---|---|---|---|
| 1997–98 | Nottingham F | 0 | 0 | | |
| 1997–98 | Leicester C | 0 | 0 | | |
| 1998–99 | Leicester C | 0 | 0 | | |
| 1999–2000 | Leicester C | 3 | 0 | | |
| 2000–01 | Leicester C | 0 | 0 | | |
| 2001–02 | Leicester C | 0 | 0 | **3** | **0** |
| 2001–02 | Bournemouth | 12 | 0 | | |
| 2002–03 | Bournemouth | 37 | 2 | | |
| 2003–04 | Bournemouth | 10 | 0 | **59** | **2** |
| 2003–04 | Boston U | 8 | 3 | **8** | **3** |

**THOMPSON, Lee (M) 50 9**
H: 5 7 W: 10 10 b.Sheffield 25-3-83
*Honours:* England Schools.

| | | | | | |
|---|---|---|---|---|---|
| 2000–01 | Sheffield U | 0 | 0 | | |
| 2001–02 | Sheffield U | 0 | 0 | | |
| 2002–03 | Sheffield U | 0 | 0 | | |
| 2002–03 | Boston U | 15 | 4 | | |
| 2003–04 | Boston U | 35 | 5 | **50** | **9** |

**THOMPSON, Neil† (D) 404 47**
H: 6 0 W: 13 08 b.Beverley 2-10-63
*Source:* Nottingham F Apprentice.

| | | | | | |
|---|---|---|---|---|---|
| 1981–82 | Hull C | 23 | 0 | | |
| 1982–83 | Hull C | 8 | 0 | **31** | **0** |
| From Scarborough | | | | | |
| 1987–88 | Scarborough | 41 | 6 | | |
| 1988–89 | Scarborough | 46 | 9 | **87** | **15** |
| 1989–90 | Ipswich T | 45 | 3 | | |
| 1990–91 | Ipswich T | 38 | 6 | | |
| 1991–92 | Ipswich T | 45 | 6 | | |
| 1992–93 | Ipswich T | 31 | 3 | | |
| 1993–94 | Ipswich T | 32 | 0 | | |
| 1994–95 | Ipswich T | 10 | 0 | | |
| 1995–96 | Ipswich T | 5 | 1 | **206** | **19** |
| 1996–97 | Barnsley | 24 | 5 | | |
| 1997–98 | Barnsley | 3 | 0 | **27** | **5** |
| 1997–98 | *Oldham Ath* | 8 | 0 | **8** | **0** |
| 1997–98 | York C | 12 | 2 | | |
| 1998–99 | York C | 24 | 6 | | |
| 1999–2000 | York C | 6 | 0 | **42** | **8** |
| From Scarborough. | | | | | |
| 2002–03 | Boston U | 3 | 0 | | |
| 2003–04 | Boston U | 0 | 0 | **3** | **0** |

**Non Contract**
Brough, Scott; Raynor, Paul J; Rodwell, James R; Thompson, Neil

## BOURNEMOUTH (9)

**BROADHURST, Karl# (D) 129 2**
H: 6 1 W: 11 07 b.Portsmouth 18-3-80
*Source:* Trainee.

| | | | | | |
|---|---|---|---|---|---|
| 1998–99 | Bournemouth | 0 | 0 | | |
| 1999–2000 | Bournemouth | 16 | 0 | | |
| 2000–01 | Bournemouth | 30 | 0 | | |
| 2001–02 | Bournemouth | 23 | 0 | | |
| 2002–03 | Bournemouth | 21 | 1 | | |
| 2003–04 | Bournemouth | 39 | 1 | **129** | **2** |

**BROWNING, Marcus (M) 377 22**
H: 6 1 W: 12 12 b.Bristol 22-4-71
*Source:* Trainee. *Honours:* Wales 5 full caps.

| | | | | | |
|---|---|---|---|---|---|
| 1989–90 | Bristol R | 1 | 0 | | |
| 1990–91 | Bristol R | 0 | 0 | | |
| 1991–92 | Bristol R | 11 | 0 | | |
| 1992–93 | Bristol R | 19 | 1 | | |
| 1992–93 | *Hereford U* | 7 | 5 | **7** | **5** |
| 1993–94 | Bristol R | 31 | 4 | | |
| 1994–95 | Bristol R | 41 | 2 | | |
| 1995–96 | Bristol R | 45 | 4 | | |
| 1996–97 | Bristol R | 26 | 2 | **174** | **13** |
| 1996–97 | Huddersfield T | 13 | 0 | | |
| 1997–98 | Huddersfield T | 14 | 0 | | |
| 1998–99 | Huddersfield T | 6 | 0 | **33** | **0** |
| 1998–99 | Gillingham | 4 | 0 | | |
| 1999–2000 | Gillingham | 1 | 0 | | |
| 2000–01 | Gillingham | 31 | 0 | | |
| 2001–02 | Gillingham | 42 | 3 | **78** | **3** |
| 2002–03 | Bournemouth | 43 | 1 | | |
| 2003–04 | Bournemouth | 42 | 0 | **85** | **1** |

**CONNELL, Alan (F) 20 6**
H: 6 0 W: 10 10 b.London 5-2-83
*Source:* Ipswich T Trainee.

| | | | | | |
|---|---|---|---|---|---|
| 2002–03 | Bournemouth | 13 | 6 | | |
| 2003–04 | Bournemouth | 7 | 0 | **20** | **6** |

**CUMMINGS, Warren (D) 89 3**
H: 5 9 W: 11 08 b.Aberdeen 15-10-80
*Source:* Trainee. *Honours:* Scotland Under-21, 1 full cap.

| | | | | | |
|---|---|---|---|---|---|
| 1999–2000 | Chelsea | 0 | 0 | | |
| 2000–01 | Chelsea | 0 | 0 | | |
| 2000–01 | *Bournemouth* | 10 | 1 | | |
| 2000–01 | *WBA* | 3 | 0 | | |
| 2001–02 | Chelsea | 0 | 0 | | |
| 2001–02 | *WBA* | 14 | 0 | **17** | **0** |
| 2002–03 | Chelsea | 0 | 0 | | |
| 2002–03 | Bournemouth | 20 | 0 | | |
| 2003–04 | Bournemouth | 42 | 2 | **72** | **3** |

**ELLIOTT, Wade# (M) 177 27**
H: 5 10 W: 11 01 b.Southampton 14-12-78

| | | | | | |
|---|---|---|---|---|---|
| 1999–2000 | Bournemouth | 12 | 3 | | |
| 2000–01 | Bournemouth | 36 | 9 | | |
| 2001–02 | Bournemouth | 46 | 8 | | |
| 2002–03 | Bournemouth | 44 | 4 | | |
| 2003–04 | Bournemouth | 39 | 3 | **177** | **27** |

**FEENEY, Warren (F) 108 36**
H: 5 10 W: 11 05 b.Belfast 17-1-81
*Source:* Trainee. *Honours:* Northern Ireland Schools, Youth, Under-21, 3 full caps.

| | | | | | |
|---|---|---|---|---|---|
| 1997–98 | Leeds U | 0 | 0 | | |
| 1998–99 | Leeds U | 0 | 0 | | |
| 1999–2000 | Leeds U | 0 | 0 | | |
| 2000–01 | Leeds U | 0 | 0 | | |
| 2000–01 | *Bournemouth* | 10 | 4 | | |
| 2001–02 | Bournemouth | 37 | 13 | | |
| 2002–03 | Bournemouth | 21 | 7 | | |
| 2003–04 | Bournemouth | 40 | 12 | **108** | **36** |

**FLETCHER, Carl (M) 187 17**
H: 5 10 W: 11 07 b.Camberley 7-4-80
*Source:* Trainee. *Honours:* Wales 4 full caps.

| | | | | | |
|---|---|---|---|---|---|
| 1997–98 | Bournemouth | 1 | 0 | | |
| 1998–99 | Bournemouth | 1 | 0 | | |
| 1999–2000 | Bournemouth | 25 | 3 | | |
| 2000–01 | Bournemouth | 43 | 6 | | |
| 2001–02 | Bournemouth | 35 | 5 | | |
| 2002–03 | Bournemouth | 42 | 1 | | |
| 2003–04 | Bournemouth | 40 | 2 | **187** | **17** |

**FLETCHER, Steve# (F) 421 78**
H: 6 2 W: 14 09 b.Hartlepool 26-7-72
*Source:* Trainee.

| | | | | | |
|---|---|---|---|---|---|
| 1990–91 | Hartlepool U | 14 | 2 | | |
| 1991–92 | Hartlepool U | 18 | 2 | **32** | **4** |
| 1992–93 | Bournemouth | 31 | 4 | | |
| 1993–94 | Bournemouth | 36 | 6 | | |
| 1994–95 | Bournemouth | 40 | 6 | | |
| 1995–96 | Bournemouth | 7 | 1 | | |
| 1996–97 | Bournemouth | 35 | 7 | | |
| 1997–98 | Bournemouth | 42 | 12 | | |
| 1998–99 | Bournemouth | 39 | 8 | | |
| 1999–2000 | Bournemouth | 36 | 7 | | |
| 2000–01 | Bournemouth | 45 | 9 | | |
| 2001–02 | Bournemouth | 2 | 0 | | |
| 2002–03 | Bournemouth | 35 | 5 | | |
| 2003–04 | Bournemouth | 41 | 9 | **389** | **74** |

**HAYTER, James# (F) 231 45**
H: 5 9 W: 10 13 b.Newport (IW) 9-4-79
*Source:* Trainee.

| | | | | | |
|---|---|---|---|---|---|
| 1996–97 | Bournemouth | 2 | 0 | | |
| 1997–98 | Bournemouth | 5 | 0 | | |
| 1998–99 | Bournemouth | 20 | 2 | | |
| 1999–2000 | Bournemouth | 31 | 2 | | |
| 2000–01 | Bournemouth | 40 | 11 | | |
| 2001–02 | Bournemouth | 44 | 7 | | |
| 2002–03 | Bournemouth | 45 | 9 | | |
| 2003–04 | Bournemouth | 44 | 14 | **231** | **45** |

**HOLMES, Derek (F) 138 28**
H: 6 2 W: 13 07 b.Lanark 18-10-78
*Source:* Royal Albert.

| | | | | | |
|---|---|---|---|---|---|
| 1995–96 | Hearts | 0 | 0 | | |
| 1996–97 | Hearts | 1 | 0 | | |
| 1997–98 | Hearts | 1 | 1 | | |
| 1997–98 | Cowdenbeath | 13 | 5 | **13** | **5** |
| 1998–99 | Hearts | 6 | 0 | **8** | **1** |
| 1999–2000 | Ross Co | 25 | 8 | | |
| 2000–01 | Ross Co | 0 | 0 | **25** | **8** |
| 2001–02 | Bournemouth | 37 | 9 | | |
| 2002–03 | Bournemouth | 29 | 3 | | |
| 2003–04 | Bournemouth | 26 | 2 | **92** | **14** |

**MAHER, Shaun# (D) 134 5**
H: 6 1 W: 13 02 b.Dublin 20-6-78
*Source:* Bohemians.

| | | | | | |
|---|---|---|---|---|---|
| 1996–97 | Bohemians | 2 | 0 | | |
| 1997–98 | Fulham | 0 | 0 | | |
| 1997–98 | Bohemians | 11 | 0 | | |
| 1998–99 | Bohemians | 25 | 1 | | |
| 1999–2000 | Bohemians | 28 | 1 | | |
| 2000–01 | Bohemians | 0 | 0 | **66** | **2** |
| 2001–02 | Bournemouth | 31 | 0 | | |
| 2002–03 | Bournemouth | 8 | 2 | | |
| 2003–04 | Bournemouth | 29 | 1 | **68** | **3** |

**MOSS, Neil (G) 135 0**
H: 6 2 W: 13 10 b.New Milton 10-5-75
*Source:* Trainee.

| | | | | | |
|---|---|---|---|---|---|
| 1992–93 | Bournemouth | 1 | 0 | | |
| 1993–94 | Bournemouth | 6 | 0 | | |
| 1994–95 | Bournemouth | 8 | 0 | | |
| 1995–96 | Bournemouth | 7 | 0 | | |
| 1995–96 | Southampton | 0 | 0 | | |
| 1996–97 | Southampton | 3 | 0 | | |
| 1997–98 | Southampton | 0 | 0 | | |
| 1997–98 | *Gillingham* | 10 | 0 | **10** | **0** |
| 1998–99 | Southampton | 7 | 0 | | |
| 1999–2000 | Southampton | 9 | 0 | | |
| 2000–01 | Southampton | 3 | 0 | | |
| 2001–02 | Southampton | 2 | 0 | | |
| 2002–03 | Southampton | 0 | 0 | **24** | **0** |
| 2002–03 | Bournemouth | 33 | 0 | | |
| 2003–04 | Bournemouth | 46 | 0 | **101** | **0** |

**O'CONNOR, Gareth# (F) 158 15**
H: 5 10 W: 11 00 b.Dublin 10-11-78
*Source:* Bohemians.

| | | | | | |
|---|---|---|---|---|---|
| 1998–99 | Shamrock R | 8 | 0 | **8** | **0** |
| 1999–2000 | Bohemians | 22 | 4 | **22** | **4** |
| 2000–01 | Bournemouth | 22 | 1 | | |
| 2001–02 | Bournemouth | 28 | 0 | | |
| 2002–03 | Bournemouth | 41 | 8 | | |
| 2003–04 | Bournemouth | 37 | 2 | **128** | **11** |

**PURCHES, Stephen# (M) 161 8**
H: 5 11 W: 11 09 b.Ilford 14-1-80
*Source:* Trainee.

| | | | | | |
|---|---|---|---|---|---|
| 1998–99 | West Ham U | 0 | 0 | | |
| 1999–2000 | West Ham U | 0 | 0 | | |
| 2000–01 | Bournemouth | 34 | 0 | | |
| 2001–02 | Bournemouth | 41 | 2 | | |
| 2002–03 | Bournemouth | 44 | 3 | | |
| 2003–04 | Bournemouth | 42 | 3 | **161** | **8** |

**STEWART, Gareth (G)** **84 0**

H: 6 0 W: 12 08 b.Preston 3-2-80

*Source:* Trainee. *Honours:* England Schools, Youth.

| | | | | | |
|---|---|---|---|---|---|
| 1996–97 | Blackburn R | 0 | 0 | | |
| 1997–98 | Blackburn R | 0 | 0 | | |
| 1998–99 | Blackburn R | 0 | 0 | | |
| 1999–2000 | Bournemouth | 3 | 0 | | |
| 2000–01 | Bournemouth | 35 | 0 | | |
| 2001–02 | Bournemouth | 45 | 0 | | |
| 2002–03 | Bournemouth | 1 | 0 | | |
| 2003–04 | Bournemouth | 0 | 0 | **84** | **0** |

**STOCK, Brian (M)** **78 7**

H: 5 11 W: 11 02 b.Winchester 24-12-81

*Source:* Trainee. *Honours:* Wales Under-21.

| | | | | | |
|---|---|---|---|---|---|
| 1999–2000 | Bournemouth | 5 | 0 | | |
| 2000–01 | Bournemouth | 1 | 0 | | |
| 2001–02 | Bournemouth | 26 | 2 | | |
| 2002–03 | Bournemouth | 27 | 2 | | |
| 2003–04 | Bournemouth | 19 | 3 | **78** | **7** |

**TINDALL, Jason (M)** **160 6**

H: 6 1 W: 12 13 b.Stepney 15-11-77

*Source:* Trainee.

| | | | | | |
|---|---|---|---|---|---|
| 1996–97 | Charlton Ath | 0 | 0 | | |
| 1997–98 | Charlton Ath | 0 | 0 | | |
| 1998–99 | Bournemouth | 17 | 1 | | |
| 1999–2000 | Bournemouth | 8 | 0 | | |
| 2000–01 | Bournemouth | 45 | 1 | | |
| 2001–02 | Bournemouth | 44 | 3 | | |
| 2002–03 | Bournemouth | 27 | 1 | | |
| 2003–04 | Bournemouth | 19 | 0 | **160** | **6** |

**YOUNG, Neil# (D)** **302 4**

H: 5 9 W: 12 00 b.Harlow 31-8-73

*Source:* Trainee.

| | | | | | |
|---|---|---|---|---|---|
| 1991–92 | Tottenham H | 0 | 0 | | |
| 1992–93 | Tottenham H | 0 | 0 | | |
| 1993–94 | Tottenham H | 0 | 0 | | |
| 1994–95 | Bournemouth | 32 | 0 | | |
| 1995–96 | Bournemouth | 41 | 0 | | |
| 1996–97 | Bournemouth | 44 | 0 | | |
| 1997–98 | Bournemouth | 44 | 2 | | |
| 1998–99 | Bournemouth | 44 | 1 | | |
| 1999–2000 | Bournemouth | 37 | 0 | | |
| 2000–01 | Bournemouth | 7 | 0 | | |
| 2001–02 | Bournemouth | 11 | 0 | | |
| 2002–03 | Bournemouth | 32 | 1 | | |
| 2003–04 | Bournemouth | 10 | 0 | **302** | **4** |

**Non Contract**

Saadi, Fawzi; Tubbs, Matthew S

## BRADFORD C (10)

**ATHERTON, Peter (D)** **565 13**

H: 5 11 W: 13 12 b.Wigan 6-4-70

*Source:* Trainee. *Honours:* England Schools, Under-21.

| | | | | | |
|---|---|---|---|---|---|
| 1987–88 | Wigan Ath | 16 | 0 | | |
| 1988–89 | Wigan Ath | 40 | 1 | | |
| 1989–90 | Wigan Ath | 46 | 0 | | |
| 1990–91 | Wigan Ath | 46 | 0 | | |
| 1991–92 | Wigan Ath | 1 | 0 | **149** | **1** |
| 1991–92 | Coventry C | 35 | 0 | | |
| 1992–93 | Coventry C | 39 | 0 | | |
| 1993–94 | Coventry C | 40 | 0 | **114** | **0** |
| 1994–95 | Sheffield W | 41 | 1 | | |
| 1995–96 | Sheffield W | 36 | 0 | | |
| 1996–97 | Sheffield W | 37 | 2 | | |
| 1997–98 | Sheffield W | 27 | 3 | | |
| 1998–99 | Sheffield W | 38 | 2 | | |
| 1999–2000 | Sheffield W | 35 | 1 | **214** | **9** |
| 2000–01 | Bradford C | 25 | 0 | | |
| 2000–01 | *Birmingham C* | 10 | 0 | **10** | **0** |
| 2001–02 | Bradford C | 1 | 0 | | |
| 2002–03 | Bradford C | 25 | 1 | | |
| 2003–04 | Bradford C | 27 | 2 | **78** | **3** |

**BANNISTER, Patrick‡ (M)** **0 0**

H: 5 10 W: 11 00 b.Walsall 3-12-83

*Source:* Scholar.

| | | | | | |
|---|---|---|---|---|---|
| 2000–01 | Derby Co | 0 | 0 | | |
| 2001–02 | Derby Co | 0 | 0 | | |
| 2002–03 | Derby Co | 0 | 0 | | |
| 2003–04 | Bradford C | 0 | 0 | | |

**BOWER, Mark (D)** **100 4**

H: 5 10 W: 11 00 b.Bradford 23-1-80

*Source:* Trainee.

| | | | | | |
|---|---|---|---|---|---|
| 1997–98 | Bradford C | 3 | 0 | | |
| 1998–99 | Bradford C | 0 | 0 | | |
| 1999–2000 | Bradford C | 0 | 0 | | |
| 1999–2000 | *York C* | 15 | 1 | | |
| 2000–01 | Bradford C | 0 | 0 | | |
| 2000–01 | *York C* | 21 | 1 | **36** | **2** |
| 2001–02 | Bradford C | 10 | 2 | | |
| 2002–03 | Bradford C | 37 | 0 | | |
| 2003–04 | Bradford C | 14 | 0 | **64** | **2** |

**BRANCH, Michael (F)** **159 22**

H: 5 10 W: 11 07 b.Liverpool 18-10-78

*Source:* Trainee. *Honours:* England Schools, Youth, Under-21.

| | | | | | |
|---|---|---|---|---|---|
| 1995–96 | Everton | 3 | 0 | | |
| 1996–97 | Everton | 25 | 3 | | |
| 1997–98 | Everton | 6 | 0 | | |
| 1998–99 | Everton | 7 | 0 | | |
| 1998–99 | *Manchester C* | 4 | 0 | **4** | **0** |
| 1999–2000 | Everton | 0 | 0 | **41** | **3** |
| 2000–01 | Wolverhampton W | 38 | 4 | | |
| 1999–2000 | Wolverhampton W | 27 | 6 | | |
| 2001–02 | Wolverhampton W | 7 | 0 | | |
| 2001–02 | *Reading* | 2 | 0 | **2** | **0** |
| 2002–03 | Wolverhampton W | 0 | 0 | **72** | **10** |
| 2002–03 | *Hull C* | 7 | 3 | **7** | **3** |
| 2003–04 | Bradford C | 33 | 6 | **33** | **6** |

**CADAMARTERI, Danny (F)** **150 19**

H: 5 9 W: 12 10 b.Bradford 12-10-79

*Source:* Trainee. *Honours:* England Youth, Under-21.

| | | | | | |
|---|---|---|---|---|---|
| 1996–97 | Everton | 1 | 0 | | |
| 1997–98 | Everton | 26 | 4 | | |
| 1998–99 | Everton | 30 | 4 | | |
| 1999–2000 | Everton | 17 | 1 | | |
| 1999–2000 | *Fulham* | 5 | 1 | **5** | **1** |
| 2000–01 | Everton | 16 | 4 | | |
| 2001–02 | Everton | 3 | 0 | **93** | **13** |
| 2001–02 | Bradford C | 14 | 2 | | |
| 2002–03 | Bradford C | 20 | 0 | | |
| 2003–04 | Bradford C | 18 | 3 | **52** | **5** |

**COMBE, Alan (G)** **247 0**

H: 6 1 W: 12 05 b.Edinburgh 3-4-74

*Source:* Kelty Hearts.

| | | | | | |
|---|---|---|---|---|---|
| 1992–93 | Cowdenbeath | 18 | 0 | **18** | **0** |
| 1993–94 | St Mirren | 16 | 0 | | |
| 1994–95 | St Mirren | 21 | 0 | | |
| 1995–96 | St Mirren | 21 | 0 | | |
| 1996–97 | St Mirren | 36 | 0 | | |
| 1997–98 | St Mirren | 30 | 0 | **124** | **0** |
| 1998–99 | Dundee U | 10 | 0 | | |
| 1999–2000 | Dundee U | 35 | 0 | | |
| 2000–01 | Dundee U | 23 | 0 | | |
| 2001–02 | Dundee U | 0 | 0 | **68** | **0** |
| 2001–02 | Bradford C | 16 | 0 | | |
| 2002–03 | Bradford C | 0 | 0 | | |
| 2003–04 | Bradford C | 21 | 0 | **37** | **0** |

**CORNWALL, Luke (F)** **20 5**

H: 5 10 W: 12 01 b.Lambeth 23-7-80

*Source:* Trainee.

| | | | | | |
|---|---|---|---|---|---|
| 1998–99 | Fulham | 4 | 1 | | |
| 1999–2000 | Fulham | 0 | 0 | | |
| 2000–01 | Fulham | 0 | 0 | | |
| 2000–01 | *Grimsby T* | 10 | 4 | **10** | **4** |
| 2001–02 | Fulham | 0 | 0 | | |
| 2002–03 | Fulham | 0 | 0 | **4** | **1** |
| 2002–03 | *Lincoln C* | 3 | 0 | **3** | **0** |
| 2003–04 | Bradford C | 3 | 0 | **3** | **0** |

**DAVIES, Clint* (G)** **2 0**

H: 6 3 W: 12 07 b.Perth 24-4-83

*Source:* Scholar. *Honours:* Australia Under-23.

| | | | | | |
|---|---|---|---|---|---|
| 2002–03 | Birmingham C | 0 | 0 | | |
| 2003–04 | Bradford C | 2 | 0 | **2** | **0** |

**EDDS, Gareth (D)** **53 1**

H: 5 11 W: 11 01 b.Sydney 3-2-81

*Source:* Trainee. *Honours:* Australia Under-20, Under-23.

| | | | | | |
|---|---|---|---|---|---|
| 1997–98 | Nottingham F | 0 | 0 | | |
| 1998–99 | Nottingham F | 0 | 0 | | |
| 1999–2000 | Nottingham F | 2 | 0 | | |
| 2000–01 | Nottingham F | 13 | 1 | | |
| 2001–02 | Nottingham F | 1 | 0 | **16** | **1** |

| | | | | | |
|---|---|---|---|---|---|
| 2002–03 | Swindon T | 14 | 0 | **14** | **0** |
| 2003–04 | Bradford C | 23 | 0 | **23** | **0** |

**EMANUEL, Lewis (D)** **66 2**

H: 5 8 W: 12 01 b.Bradford 14-10-83

*Source:* Scholar. *Honours:* England Youth.

| | | | | | |
|---|---|---|---|---|---|
| 2001–02 | Bradford C | 9 | 0 | | |
| 2002–03 | Bradford C | 29 | 0 | | |
| 2003–04 | Bradford C | 28 | 2 | **66** | **2** |

**FOLKES, Peter (D)** **0 0**

H: 5 11 W: 12 08 b.Birmingham 16-11-84

*Source:* Bristol C Scholar.

| | | | | | |
|---|---|---|---|---|---|
| 2003–04 | Bradford C | 0 | 0 | | |

**FORREST, Danny (M)** **30 3**

H: 5 10 W: 11 07 b.Keighley 23-10-84

*Source:* Trainee. *Honours:* England Youth.

| | | | | | |
|---|---|---|---|---|---|
| 2002–03 | Bradford C | 17 | 3 | | |
| 2003–04 | Bradford C | 13 | 0 | **30** | **3** |

**GAVIN, Jason (D)** **89 1**

H: 6 0 W: 11 13 b.Dublin 14-3-80

*Source:* Trainee. *Honours:* Eire Under-21.

| | | | | | |
|---|---|---|---|---|---|
| 1996–97 | Middlesbrough | 0 | 0 | | |
| 1997–98 | Middlesbrough | 0 | 0 | | |
| 1998–99 | Middlesbrough | 2 | 0 | | |
| 1999–2000 | Middlesbrough | 6 | 0 | | |
| 2000–01 | Middlesbrough | 14 | 0 | | |
| 2001–02 | Middlesbrough | 9 | 0 | | |
| 2002–03 | Middlesbrough | 0 | 0 | **31** | **0** |
| 2002–03 | *Grimsby T* | 10 | 0 | **10** | **0** |
| 2002–03 | *Huddersfield T* | 10 | 1 | **10** | **1** |
| 2003–04 | Bradford C | 38 | 0 | **38** | **0** |

**HECKINGBOTTOM, Paul (D)** **207 6**

H: 6 0 W: 12 05 b.Barnsley 17-7-77

*Source:* Manchester U Trainee.

| | | | | | |
|---|---|---|---|---|---|
| 1995–96 | Sunderland | 0 | 0 | | |
| 1996–97 | Sunderland | 0 | 0 | | |
| 1997–98 | Sunderland | 0 | 0 | | |
| 1997–98 | *Scarborough* | 29 | 0 | **29** | **0** |
| 1998–99 | Sunderland | 0 | 0 | | |
| 1998–99 | *Hartlepool U* | 5 | 1 | **5** | **1** |
| 1998–99 | *Darlington* | 10 | 0 | | |
| 1999–2000 | Darlington | 45 | 1 | | |
| 2000–01 | Darlington | 18 | 1 | | |
| 2001–02 | Darlington | 42 | 3 | **115** | **5** |
| 2002–03 | Norwich C | 15 | 0 | **15** | **0** |
| 2003–04 | Bradford C | 43 | 0 | **43** | **0** |

**JACOBS, Wayne (D)** **481 18**

H: 5 9 W: 11 02 b.Sheffield 3-2-69

*Source:* Apprentice.

| | | | | | |
|---|---|---|---|---|---|
| 1986–87 | Sheffield W | 0 | 0 | | |
| 1987–88 | Sheffield W | 6 | 0 | **6** | **0** |
| 1987–88 | Hull C | 6 | 0 | | |
| 1988–89 | Hull C | 33 | 0 | | |
| 1989–90 | Hull C | 46 | 3 | | |
| 1990–91 | Hull C | 19 | 1 | | |
| 1991–92 | Hull C | 25 | 0 | | |
| 1992–93 | Hull C | 0 | 0 | **129** | **4** |
| 1993–94 | Rotherham U | 42 | 2 | **42** | **2** |
| 1994–95 | Bradford C | 38 | 1 | | |
| 1995–96 | Bradford C | 28 | 0 | | |
| 1996–97 | Bradford C | 39 | 3 | | |
| 1997–98 | Bradford C | 36 | 2 | | |
| 1998–99 | Bradford C | 44 | 3 | | |
| 1999–2000 | Bradford C | 24 | 0 | | |
| 2000–01 | Bradford C | 21 | 2 | | |
| 2001–02 | Bradford C | 38 | 1 | | |
| 2002–03 | Bradford C | 23 | 0 | | |
| 2003–04 | Bradford C | 13 | 0 | **304** | **12** |

**KEARNEY, Tom (M)** **26 0**

H: 5 11 W: 10 08 b.Liverpool 7-10-81

*Source:* Trainee.

| | | | | | |
|---|---|---|---|---|---|
| 1999–2000 | Everton | 0 | 0 | | |
| 2000–01 | Everton | 0 | 0 | | |
| 2001–02 | Everton | 0 | 0 | | |
| 2001–02 | Bradford C | 5 | 0 | | |
| 2002–03 | Bradford C | 4 | 0 | | |
| 2003–04 | Bradford C | 17 | 0 | **26** | **0** |

**MUIRHEAD, Ben* (M)** **36 2**

H: 5 9 W: 11 02 b.Doncaster 5-1-83

*Source:* Trainee. *Honours:* England Youth.

| | | | | | |
|---|---|---|---|---|---|
| 1999–2000 | Manchester U | 0 | 0 | | |
| 2000–01 | Manchester U | 0 | 0 | | |
| 2001–02 | Manchester U | 0 | 0 | | |
| 2002–03 | Manchester U | 0 | 0 | | |
| 2002–03 | Bradford C | 8 | 0 | | |
| 2003–04 | Bradford C | 28 | 2 | **36** | **2** |

**O'MALLEY, Aaron‡ (G)** **0 0**
H: 5 11 W: 13 01 b.Bromsgrove 21-3-85

| | | | | | |
|---|---|---|---|---|---|
| 2003–04 | Bradford C | 0 | 0 | | |

**PASTON, Mark (G)** **13 0**
H: 6 5 W: 14 03 b.Hastings, NZ 13-12-76
*Source:* Napier City R. *Honours:* New Zealand 7 full caps.

| | | | | | |
|---|---|---|---|---|---|
| 2003–04 | Bradford C | 13 | 0 | **13** | **0** |

**PENFORD, Thomas§ (M)** **7 0**
H: 5 10 W: 11 03 b.Leeds 5-1-85
*Source:* Scholar.

| | | | | | |
|---|---|---|---|---|---|
| 2002–03 | Bradford C | 3 | 0 | | |
| 2003–04 | Bradford C | 4 | 0 | **7** | **0** |

**SANASY, Kevin§ (M)** **6 1**
H: 5 8 W: 10 05 b.Leeds 2-11-84
*Source:* Scholar.

| | | | | | |
|---|---|---|---|---|---|
| 2002–03 | Bradford C | 1 | 0 | | |
| 2003–04 | Bradford C | 5 | 1 | **6** | **1** |

**STANDING, Michael (M)** **30 2**
H: 5 10 W: 10 05 b.Shoreham 20-3-81
*Source:* Trainee. *Honours:* England Schools.

| | | | | | |
|---|---|---|---|---|---|
| 1997–98 | Aston Villa | 0 | 0 | | |
| 1998–99 | Aston Villa | 0 | 0 | | |
| 1999–2000 | Aston Villa | 0 | 0 | | |
| 2000–01 | Aston Villa | 0 | 0 | | |
| 2001–02 | Aston Villa | 0 | 0 | | |
| 2001–02 | Bradford C | 0 | 0 | | |
| 2002–03 | Bradford C | 24 | 2 | | |
| 2003–04 | Bradford C | 6 | 0 | **30** | **2** |

**SUMMERBEE, Nicky (M)** **429 23**
H: 5 11 W: 12 08 b.Altrincham 26-8-71
*Source:* Trainee. *Honours:* England Under-21.

| | | | | | |
|---|---|---|---|---|---|
| 1989–90 | Swindon T | 1 | 0 | | |
| 1990–91 | Swindon T | 7 | 0 | | |
| 1991–92 | Swindon T | 27 | 0 | | |
| 1992–93 | Swindon T | 39 | 3 | | |
| 1993–94 | Swindon T | 38 | 3 | **112** | **6** |
| 1994–95 | Manchester C | 41 | 1 | | |
| 1995–96 | Manchester C | 37 | 1 | | |
| 1996–97 | Manchester C | 44 | 4 | | |
| 1997–98 | Manchester C | 9 | 0 | | |
| 1997–98 | Sunderland | 25 | 3 | | |
| 1998–99 | Sunderland | 36 | 3 | | |
| 1999–2000 | Sunderland | 32 | 1 | | |
| 2000–01 | Sunderland | 0 | 0 | **93** | **7** |
| 2000–01 | Bolton W | 12 | 1 | **12** | **1** |
| 2001–02 | Manchester C | 0 | 0 | **131** | **6** |
| 2001–02 | Nottingham F | 17 | 2 | **17** | **2** |
| 2002–03 | Leicester C | 29 | 0 | **29** | **0** |
| 2003–04 | Bradford C | 35 | 1 | **35** | **1** |

**WETHERALL, David (D)** **328 18**
H: 6 3 W: 13 12 b.Sheffield 14-3-71
*Source:* School. *Honours:* England Schools.

| | | | | | |
|---|---|---|---|---|---|
| 1989–90 | Sheffield W | 0 | 0 | | |
| 1990–91 | Sheffield W | 0 | 0 | | |
| 1991–92 | Leeds U | 1 | 0 | | |
| 1992–93 | Leeds U | 13 | 1 | | |
| 1993–94 | Leeds U | 32 | 1 | | |
| 1994–95 | Leeds U | 38 | 3 | | |
| 1995–96 | Leeds U | 34 | 4 | | |
| 1996–97 | Leeds U | 29 | 0 | | |
| 1997–98 | Leeds U | 34 | 3 | | |
| 1998–99 | Leeds U | 21 | 0 | **202** | **12** |
| 1999–2000 | Bradford C | 38 | 2 | | |
| 2000–01 | Bradford C | 18 | 1 | | |
| 2001–02 | Bradford C | 19 | 2 | | |
| 2002–03 | Bradford C | 17 | 0 | | |
| 2003–04 | Bradford C | 34 | 1 | **126** | **6** |

**WINDASS, Dean (F)** **451 124**
H: 5 10 W: 12 03 b.North Ferriby 1-4-69
*Source:* N Ferriby U.

| | | | | | |
|---|---|---|---|---|---|
| 1991–92 | Hull C | 32 | 6 | | |
| 1992–93 | Hull C | 41 | 7 | | |
| 1993–94 | Hull C | 43 | 23 | | |
| 1994–95 | Hull C | 44 | 17 | | |
| 1995–96 | Hull C | 16 | 4 | **176** | **57** |
| 1995–96 | Aberdeen | 20 | 6 | | |
| 1996–97 | Aberdeen | 29 | 10 | | |
| 1997–98 | Aberdeen | 24 | 5 | **73** | **21** |
| 1998–99 | Oxford U | 33 | 15 | **33** | **15** |
| 1998–99 | Bradford C | 12 | 3 | | |
| 1999–2000 | Bradford C | 38 | 10 | | |
| 2000–01 | Bradford C | 24 | 3 | | |
| 2000–01 | Middlesbrough | 8 | 2 | | |
| 2001–02 | Middlesbrough | 27 | 1 | | |
| 2001–02 | *Sheffield W* | 2 | 0 | **2** | **0** |
| 2002–03 | Middlesbrough | 2 | 0 | **37** | **3** |
| 2002–03 | Sheffield U | 20 | 6 | **20** | **6** |
| 2003–04 | Bradford C | 36 | 6 | **110** | **22** |

**WOLLEASTON, Robert (F)** **32 1**
H: 5 11 W: 11 09 b.Perivale 21-12-79
*Source:* Trainee.

| | | | | | |
|---|---|---|---|---|---|
| 1998–99 | Chelsea | 0 | 0 | | |
| 1999–2000 | Chelsea | 1 | 0 | | |
| 1999–2000 | *Bristol R* | 4 | 0 | **4** | **0** |
| 2000–01 | Chelsea | 0 | 0 | | |
| 2000–01 | *Portsmouth* | 6 | 0 | **6** | **0** |
| 2001–02 | Chelsea | 0 | 0 | | |
| 2001–02 | *Northampton T* | 7 | 0 | **7** | **0** |
| 2002–03 | Chelsea | 0 | 0 | **1** | **0** |
| 2003–04 | Bradford C | 14 | 1 | **14** | **1** |

**Scholars**
Beach, Nicholas; Bentham, Craig M; Clifford, Sean; Colbeck, Philip J; Denton, Sam; Denvers, Paul J; Doherty, Anthony P J; Ekoku, Daniel C; Ellis, Daniel L; Flynn, Liam D; Forrest, Daniel P H; Keehan, Kevin F A; Penford, Thomas J; Richardson, Luke C; Sanasy, Kevin R; Swift, John M; Wright, Jake M

**Non Contract**
Rhodes, Andrew C

**Players who do not hold a current contract but their registration has been retained by the club**
Holmes, Richard; Hutton, Peter; Tomlinson, Paul

## BRENTFORD (11)

**ALLEN-PAGE, Danny‡ (M)** **0 0**
H: 5 8 W: 10 13 b.London 30-10-83
*Source:* Trainee.

| | | | | | |
|---|---|---|---|---|---|
| 2002–03 | Brentford | 0 | 0 | | |
| 2003–04 | Brentford | 0 | 0 | | |

**BEADLE, Peter‡ (F)** **344 80**
H: 6 1 W: 15 10 b.Lambeth 13-5-72
*Source:* Trainee.

| | | | | | |
|---|---|---|---|---|---|
| 1988–89 | Gillingham | 2 | 0 | | |
| 1989–90 | Gillingham | 10 | 2 | | |
| 1990–91 | Gillingham | 22 | 7 | | |
| 1991–92 | Gillingham | 33 | 5 | **67** | **14** |
| 1992–93 | Tottenham H | 0 | 0 | | |
| 1992–93 | *Bournemouth* | 9 | 2 | **9** | **2** |
| 1993–94 | Tottenham H | 0 | 0 | | |
| 1993–94 | *Southend U* | 8 | 1 | **8** | **1** |
| 1994–95 | Tottenham H | 0 | 0 | | |
| 1994–95 | Watford | 20 | 1 | | |
| 1995–96 | Watford | 3 | 0 | **23** | **1** |
| 1995–96 | Bristol R | 27 | 12 | | |
| 1996–97 | Bristol R | 42 | 12 | | |
| 1997–98 | Bristol R | 40 | 15 | **109** | **39** |
| 1998–99 | Port Vale | 23 | 6 | **23** | **6** |
| 1998–99 | Notts Co | 14 | 3 | | |
| 1999–2000 | Notts Co | 8 | 0 | **22** | **3** |
| 1999–2000 | Bristol C | 25 | 6 | | |
| 2000–01 | Bristol C | 33 | 4 | | |
| 2001–02 | Bristol C | 0 | 0 | | |
| 2002–03 | Bristol C | 24 | 4 | **82** | **14** |
| 2003–04 | Brentford | 1 | 0 | **1** | **0** |

**BLACKMAN, Lloyd* (F)** **4 0**
H: 5 10 W: 12 03 b.London 24-9-83
*Source:* Trainee.

| | | | | | |
|---|---|---|---|---|---|
| 2002–03 | Brentford | 1 | 0 | | |
| 2003–04 | Brentford | 3 | 0 | **4** | **0** |

**BULL, Ronnie* (D)** **77 0**
H: 5 7 W: 11 01 b.Hackney 26-12-80
*Source:* Trainee.

| | | | | | |
|---|---|---|---|---|---|
| 1998–99 | Millwall | 1 | 0 | | |
| 1999–2000 | Millwall | 9 | 0 | | |
| 2000–01 | Millwall | 2 | 0 | | |
| 2001–02 | Millwall | 26 | 0 | | |
| 2002–03 | Millwall | 12 | 0 | | |
| 2003–04 | Millwall | 0 | 0 | **50** | **0** |
| 2003–04 | *Yeovil T* | 7 | 0 | **7** | **0** |
| 2003–04 | Brentford | 20 | 0 | **20** | **0** |

**DOBSON, Michael (D)** **153 2**
H: 5 11 W: 12 04 b.Isleworth 9-4-81
*Source:* Trainee.

| | | | | | |
|---|---|---|---|---|---|
| 1999–2000 | Brentford | 0 | 0 | | |
| 2000–01 | Brentford | 26 | 0 | | |
| 2001–02 | Brentford | 39 | 0 | | |
| 2002–03 | Brentford | 46 | 1 | | |
| 2003–04 | Brentford | 42 | 1 | **153** | **2** |

**EVANS, Stephen* (M)** **58 5**
H: 6 1 W: 11 06 b.Caerphilly 25-9-80
*Source:* Trainee. *Honours:* Wales Youth, Under-21.

| | | | | | |
|---|---|---|---|---|---|
| 1998–99 | Crystal Palace | 4 | 0 | | |
| 1999–2000 | Crystal Palace | 1 | 0 | | |
| 2000–01 | Crystal Palace | 1 | 0 | | |
| 2001–02 | Crystal Palace | 0 | 0 | **6** | **0** |
| 2001–02 | *Swansea C* | 4 | 0 | **4** | **0** |
| 2001–02 | Brentford | 0 | 0 | | |
| 2002–03 | Brentford | 23 | 3 | | |
| 2003–04 | Brentford | 25 | 2 | **48** | **5** |

**FIELDWICK, Lee* (D)** **17 0**
H: 5 11 W: 11 08 b.Croydon 6-9-82
*Source:* Trainee.

| | | | | | |
|---|---|---|---|---|---|
| 2001–02 | Brentford | 0 | 0 | | |
| 2002–03 | Brentford | 7 | 0 | | |
| 2003–04 | Brentford | 5 | 0 | **12** | **0** |
| 2003–04 | *Swansea C* | 5 | 0 | **5** | **0** |

**FRAMPTON, Andrew# (D)** **59 0**
H: 5 11 W: 10 10 b.Wimbledon 3-9-79
*Source:* Trainee.

| | | | | | |
|---|---|---|---|---|---|
| 1998–99 | Crystal Palace | 6 | 0 | | |
| 1999–2000 | Crystal Palace | 9 | 0 | | |
| 2000–01 | Crystal Palace | 10 | 0 | | |
| 2001–02 | Crystal Palace | 2 | 0 | | |
| 2002–03 | Crystal Palace | 1 | 0 | **28** | **0** |
| 2002–03 | Brentford | 15 | 0 | | |
| 2003–04 | Brentford | 16 | 0 | **31** | **0** |

**HARROLD, Matt (F)** **13 2**
H: 6 1 W: 11 10 b.Leyton 24-7-84
*Source:* Harlow T.

| | | | | | |
|---|---|---|---|---|---|
| 2003–04 | Brentford | 13 | 2 | **13** | **2** |

**HUGHES, Stephen* (F)** **12 0**
H: 6 1 W: 12 10 b.London 26-1-84
*Source:* Trainee.

| | | | | | |
|---|---|---|---|---|---|
| 2002–03 | Brentford | 3 | 0 | | |
| 2003–04 | Brentford | 9 | 0 | **12** | **0** |

**HUNT, Steve (M)** **120 22**
H: 5 7 W: 12 06 b.Port Laoise 1-8-80
*Source:* Trainee.

| | | | | | |
|---|---|---|---|---|---|
| 1999–2000 | Crystal Palace | 3 | 0 | | |
| 2000–01 | Crystal Palace | 0 | 0 | **3** | **0** |
| 2001–02 | Brentford | 35 | 4 | | |
| 2002–03 | Brentford | 42 | 7 | | |
| 2003–04 | Brentford | 40 | 11 | **117** | **22** |

**HUTCHINSON, Eddie (M)** **75 5**
H: 6 1 W: 12 07 b.Kingston 23-2-82
*Source:* Sutton U.

| | | | | | |
|---|---|---|---|---|---|
| 2000–01 | Brentford | 7 | 0 | | |
| 2001–02 | Brentford | 9 | 0 | | |
| 2002–03 | Brentford | 23 | 0 | | |
| 2003–04 | Brentford | 36 | 5 | **75** | **5** |

**JULIAN, Alan (G)** **16 0**
H: 6 2 W: 13 07 b.Ashford 11-3-83
*Source:* Trainee. *Honours:* Northern Ireland Youth.

| | | | | | |
|---|---|---|---|---|---|
| 2001–02 | Brentford | 0 | 0 | | |
| 2002–03 | Brentford | 3 | 0 | | |
| 2003–04 | Brentford | 13 | 0 | **16** | **0** |

**NELSON, Stuart (G)** **9 0**
H: 6 1 W: 12 12 b.Stroud 17-9-81
*Source:* Doncaster R, Hucknall T.

| | | | | | |
|---|---|---|---|---|---|
| 2003–04 | Brentford | 9 | 0 | **9** | **0** |

**O'CONNOR, Kevin (F)** **130 7**
H: 5 11 W: 12 00 b.Blackburn 24-2-82
*Source:* Trainee. *Honours:* Eire Under-21.

| | | | | | |
|---|---|---|---|---|---|
| 1999–2000 | Brentford | 6 | 0 | | |
| 2000–01 | Brentford | 11 | 1 | | |
| 2001–02 | Brentford | 25 | 0 | | |
| 2002–03 | Brentford | 45 | 5 | | |
| 2003–04 | Brentford | 43 | 1 | **130** | **7** |

**OLUGBODI, Jide‡ (M)** **2 0**
H: 5 11 W: 11 09 b.Lagos 29-11-77
*Source:* Lustenau.

| | | | | | |
|---|---|---|---|---|---|
| 2003–04 | Brentford | 2 | 0 | **2** | **0** |

**PETERS, Mark‡ (F)** **20** **1**
H: 5 8 W: 10 10 b.Frimley 4-10-83
*Source:* Scholar.

| | | | | | |
|---|---|---|---|---|---|
| 2000–01 | Southampton | 0 | 0 | | |
| 2001–02 | Southampton | 0 | 0 | | |
| 2001–02 | Brentford | 0 | 0 | | |
| 2002–03 | Brentford | 11 | 1 | | |
| 2003–04 | Brentford | 9 | 0 | **20** | **1** |

**RHODES, Alex (F)** **3** **1**
H: 5 9 W: 10 04 b.Cambridge 23-1-82
*Source:* Newmarket T.

| | | | | | |
|---|---|---|---|---|---|
| 2003–04 | Brentford | 3 | 1 | **3** | **1** |

**SMITH, Jay (M)** **46** **0**
H: 5 11 W: 11 07 b.Hammersmith 29-12-81
*Source:* Trainee.

| | | | | | |
|---|---|---|---|---|---|
| 2000–01 | Brentford | 3 | 0 | | |
| 2001–02 | Brentford | 0 | 0 | | |
| 2002–03 | Brentford | 26 | 0 | | |
| 2003–04 | Brentford | 17 | 0 | **46** | **0** |

**SOMNER, Matt (D)** **82** **1**
H: 6 0 W: 13 00 b.Isleworth 8-12-82
*Source:* Trainee. *Honours:* Wales Under-21.

| | | | | | |
|---|---|---|---|---|---|
| 2000–01 | Brentford | 3 | 0 | | |
| 2001–02 | Brentford | 0 | 0 | | |
| 2002–03 | Brentford | 40 | 1 | | |
| 2003–04 | Brentford | 39 | 0 | **82** | **1** |

**SONKO, Ibrahima (D)** **80** **8**
H: 6 3 W: 13 07 b.Bignola 22-1-81

| | | | | | |
|---|---|---|---|---|---|
| 2002–03 | Brentford | 37 | 5 | | |
| 2003–04 | Brentford | 43 | 3 | **80** | **8** |

**TABB, Jay (M)** **46** **9**
H: 5 5 W: 9 07 b.Tooting 21-2-84
*Source:* Trainee. *Honours:* Eire Under-21.

| | | | | | |
|---|---|---|---|---|---|
| 2000–01 | Brentford | 2 | 0 | | |
| 2001–02 | Brentford | 3 | 0 | | |
| 2002–03 | Brentford | 5 | 0 | | |
| 2003–04 | Brentford | 36 | 9 | **46** | **9** |

**TALBOT, Stuart (M)** **271** **20**
H: 6 0 W: 13 12 b.Birmingham 14-6-73
*Source:* Doncaster R, Moor Green.

| | | | | | |
|---|---|---|---|---|---|
| 1994–95 | Port Vale | 2 | 0 | | |
| 1995–96 | Port Vale | 20 | 0 | | |
| 1996–97 | Port Vale | 34 | 4 | | |
| 1997–98 | Port Vale | 42 | 6 | | |
| 1998–99 | Port Vale | 33 | 0 | | |
| 1999–2000 | Port Vale | 6 | 0 | **137** | **10** |
| 2000–01 | Rotherham U | 38 | 5 | | |
| 2001–02 | Rotherham U | 38 | 1 | | |
| 2002–03 | Rotherham U | 15 | 1 | | |
| 2002–03 | *Shrewsbury T* | 5 | 0 | **5** | **0** |
| 2003–04 | Rotherham U | 23 | 1 | **114** | **8** |
| 2003–04 | Brentford | 15 | 2 | **15** | **2** |

**THOMAS, Daniel* (M)** **0** **0**
b.Shrewsbury 16-6-84
*Source:* Trainee.

| | | | | | |
|---|---|---|---|---|---|
| 2002–03 | Brentford | 0 | 0 | | |
| 2003–04 | Brentford | 0 | 0 | | |

**TRAYNOR, Robert‡ (M)** **2** **0**
H: 5 9 W: 12 02 b.Burnham 1-11-83
*Source:* Trainee.

| | | | | | |
|---|---|---|---|---|---|
| 2002–03 | Brentford | 2 | 0 | | |
| 2003–04 | Brentford | 0 | 0 | **2** | **0** |

**VIANDER, Jani‡ (G)** **157** **0**
H: 6 4 W: 13 04 b.Tuusula 18-8-75
*Honours:* Finland 11 full caps.

| | | | | | |
|---|---|---|---|---|---|
| 1994 | FinnPa | 25 | 0 | | |
| 1995 | FinnPa | 14 | 0 | **39** | **0** |
| 1995 | Ilves | 6 | 0 | **6** | **0** |
| 1996 | Jaro | 27 | 0 | **27** | **0** |
| 1997 | Jazz | 2 | 0 | **2** | **0** |
| From Kortrijk | | | | | |
| 1998 | HJK Helsinki | 8 | 0 | | |
| 1999 | HJK Helsinki | 27 | 0 | | |
| 2000 | HJK Helsinki | 32 | 0 | | |
| 2001 | HJK Helsinki | 16 | 0 | **83** | **0** |
| 2001–02 | Stoke C | 0 | 0 | | |
| 2002–03 | Stoke C | 0 | 0 | | |
| 2003–04 | Plymouth Arg | 0 | 0 | | |
| 2003–04 | Brentford | 0 | 0 | | |

**WELLS, Dean‡ (D)** **1** **0**
H: 6 1 W: 13 02 b.Isleworth 25-3-85
*Source:* Scholar.

| | | | | | |
|---|---|---|---|---|---|
| 2003–04 | Brentford | 1 | 0 | **1** | **0** |

**Scholars**
Gauci Dominique V; Hillier, Sean; Lake, Ryan M; Lennie, Joshua; Marchena, Barry J; Masters, Clark J; Matharu, Harpal; McNamara, Steven; Moleski, George K; Morrison, James; Muldowney, Luke, J; Palmer, Jamie; Paterson, Matthew J; Peters, Ryan V; Scotchford, Mark N; Steele, Aaron D; Weight, Scott A

**Non Contract**
Stannard, James

## BRIGHTON & HA (12)

**BECK, Dan (F)** **1** **0**
H: 5 10 W: 10 06 b.Worthing 14-11-83
*Source:* Scholar.

| | | | | | |
|---|---|---|---|---|---|
| 2003–04 | Brighton & HA | 1 | 0 | **1** | **0** |

**BLACKWELL, Dean# (D)** **233** **3**
H: 6 1 W: 12 09 b.Camden 5-12-69
*Source:* Trainee. *Honours:* England Under-21.

| | | | | | |
|---|---|---|---|---|---|
| 1988–89 | Wimbledon | 0 | 0 | | |
| 1989–90 | Wimbledon | 3 | 0 | | |
| 1989–90 | *Plymouth Arg* | 7 | 0 | **7** | **0** |
| 1990–91 | Wimbledon | 35 | 0 | | |
| 1991–92 | Wimbledon | 4 | 1 | | |
| 1992–93 | Wimbledon | 24 | 0 | | |
| 1993–94 | Wimbledon | 18 | 0 | | |
| 1994–95 | Wimbledon | 0 | 0 | | |
| 1995–96 | Wimbledon | 8 | 0 | | |
| 1996–97 | Wimbledon | 27 | 0 | | |
| 1997–98 | Wimbledon | 35 | 0 | | |
| 1998–99 | Wimbledon | 28 | 0 | | |
| 1999–2000 | Wimbledon | 17 | 0 | | |
| 2000–01 | Wimbledon | 6 | 0 | | |
| 2001–02 | Wimbledon | 0 | 0 | | |
| 2002–03 | Wimbledon | 0 | 0 | **205** | **1** |
| 2002–03 | Brighton & HA | 21 | 2 | | |
| 2003–04 | Brighton & HA | 0 | 0 | **21** | **2** |

**BUTTERS, Guy# (D)** **416** **30**
H: 6 1 W: 15 05 b.Hillingdon 30-10-69
*Source:* Trainee. *Honours:* England Under-21.

| | | | | | |
|---|---|---|---|---|---|
| 1988–89 | Tottenham H | 28 | 1 | | |
| 1989–90 | Tottenham H | 7 | 0 | **35** | **1** |
| 1989–90 | *Southend U* | 16 | 3 | **16** | **3** |
| 1990–91 | Portsmouth | 23 | 0 | | |
| 1991–92 | Portsmouth | 33 | 2 | | |
| 1992–93 | Portsmouth | 15 | 1 | | |
| 1993–94 | Portsmouth | 15 | 1 | | |
| 1994–95 | Portsmouth | 24 | 0 | | |
| 1994–95 | *Oxford U* | 3 | 1 | **3** | **1** |
| 1995–96 | Portsmouth | 37 | 2 | | |
| 1996–97 | Portsmouth | 7 | 0 | **154** | **6** |
| 1996–97 | Gillingham | 30 | 0 | | |
| 1997–98 | Gillingham | 31 | 7 | | |
| 1998–99 | Gillingham | 23 | 3 | | |
| 1999–2000 | Gillingham | 40 | 2 | | |
| 2000–01 | Gillingham | 12 | 3 | | |
| 2001–02 | Gillingham | 23 | 1 | **159** | **16** |
| 2002–03 | Brighton & HA | 6 | 0 | | |
| 2003–04 | Brighton & HA | 43 | 3 | **49** | **3** |

**CARPENTER, Richard (M)** **428** **28**
H: 6 0 W: 13 03 b.Sheppey 30-9-72
*Source:* Trainee.

| | | | | | |
|---|---|---|---|---|---|
| 1990–91 | Gillingham | 9 | 1 | | |
| 1991–92 | Gillingham | 3 | 0 | | |
| 1992–93 | Gillingham | 28 | 0 | | |
| 1993–94 | Gillingham | 40 | 3 | | |
| 1994–95 | Gillingham | 29 | 0 | | |
| 1995–96 | Gillingham | 12 | 0 | | |
| 1996–97 | Gillingham | 1 | 0 | **122** | **4** |
| 1996–97 | Fulham | 34 | 5 | | |
| 1997–98 | Fulham | 24 | 2 | **58** | **7** |
| 1998–99 | Cardiff C | 42 | 1 | | |
| 1999–2000 | Cardiff C | 33 | 1 | **75** | **2** |
| 2000–01 | Brighton & HA | 42 | 6 | | |
| 2001–02 | Brighton & HA | 45 | 3 | | |
| 2002–03 | Brighton & HA | 44 | 2 | | |
| 2003–04 | Brighton & HA | 42 | 4 | **173** | **15** |

**CULLIP, Danny (D)** **264** **9**
H: 6 0 W: 12 12 b.Ascot 17-9-76
*Source:* Trainee.

| | | | | | |
|---|---|---|---|---|---|
| 1995–96 | Oxford U | 0 | 0 | | |
| 1996–97 | Fulham | 29 | 1 | | |
| 1997–98 | Fulham | 21 | 1 | **50** | **2** |
| 1997–98 | Brentford | 13 | 0 | | |
| 1998–99 | Brentford | 2 | 0 | | |
| 1999–2000 | Brentford | 0 | 0 | **15** | **0** |
| 1999–2000 | Brighton & HA | 33 | 2 | | |
| 2000–01 | Brighton & HA | 38 | 2 | | |
| 2001–02 | Brighton & HA | 44 | 0 | | |
| 2002–03 | Brighton & HA | 44 | 2 | | |
| 2003–04 | Brighton & HA | 40 | 1 | **199** | **7** |

**EL-ABD, Adam (D)** **11** **0**
H: 5 10 W: 13 05 b.Brighton 11-9-84
*Source:* Scholar.

| | | | | | |
|---|---|---|---|---|---|
| 2003–04 | Brighton & HA | 11 | 0 | **11** | **0** |

**HAMMOND, Dean (M)** **12** **0**
H: 6 1 W: 11 02 b.Hastings 7-3-83
*Source:* Scholar.

| | | | | | |
|---|---|---|---|---|---|
| 2002–03 | Brighton & HA | 4 | 0 | | |
| 2003–04 | Brighton & HA | 0 | 0 | **4** | **0** |
| 2003–04 | *Leyton Orient* | 8 | 0 | **8** | **0** |

**HARDING, Daniel (D)** **24** **0**
H: 6 0 W: 11 11 b.Gloucester 23-12-83
*Source:* Scholar.

| | | | | | |
|---|---|---|---|---|---|
| 2002–03 | Brighton & HA | 1 | 0 | | |
| 2003–04 | Brighton & HA | 23 | 0 | **24** | **0** |

**HART, Gary (F)** **249** **39**
H: 5 9 W: 12 07 b.Harlow 21-9-76
*Source:* Stansted.

| | | | | | |
|---|---|---|---|---|---|
| 1998–99 | Brighton & HA | 44 | 12 | | |
| 1999–2000 | Brighton & HA | 43 | 9 | | |
| 2000–01 | Brighton & HA | 45 | 7 | | |
| 2001–02 | Brighton & HA | 39 | 4 | | |
| 2002–03 | Brighton & HA | 36 | 4 | | |
| 2003–04 | Brighton & HA | 42 | 3 | **249** | **39** |

**HINSHELWOOD, Adam (D)** **24** **0**
H: 5 11 W: 13 00 b.Oxford 8-1-84
*Source:* Scholar.

| | | | | | |
|---|---|---|---|---|---|
| 2002–03 | Brighton & HA | 7 | 0 | | |
| 2003–04 | Brighton & HA | 17 | 0 | **24** | **0** |

**IWELUMO, Chris# (F)** **163** **27**
H: 6 3 W: 15 03 b.Coatbridge 1-8-78

| | | | | | |
|---|---|---|---|---|---|
| 1996–97 | St Mirren | 14 | 0 | | |
| 1997–98 | St Mirren | 12 | 0 | **26** | **0** |
| 1998–99 | Aarhus Fremad | 27 | 4 | **27** | **4** |
| 1999–2000 | Stoke C | 3 | 0 | | |
| 2000–01 | Stoke C | 2 | 1 | | |
| 2000–01 | *York C* | 12 | 2 | **12** | **2** |
| 2000–01 | *Cheltenham T* | 4 | 1 | **4** | **1** |
| 2001–02 | Stoke C | 38 | 10 | | |
| 2002–03 | Stoke C | 32 | 5 | | |
| 2003–04 | Stoke C | 9 | 0 | **84** | **16** |
| 2003–04 | Brighton & HA | 10 | 4 | **10** | **4** |

**JONES, Nathan# (M)** **248** **9**
H: 5 6 W: 10 06 b.Rhondda 28-5-73
*Source:* Cardiff C Trainee, Maesteg Park, Ton Pentre, Merthyr T.

| | | | | | |
|---|---|---|---|---|---|
| 1995–96 | Luton T | 0 | 0 | | |
| Badajoz, Numaicia | | | | | |
| 1997–98 | Southend U | 39 | 0 | | |
| 1998–99 | Southend U | 17 | 0 | | |
| 1998–99 | *Scarborough* | 9 | 0 | **9** | **0** |
| 1999–2000 | Southend U | 43 | 2 | **99** | **2** |
| 2000–01 | Brighton & HA | 40 | 4 | | |
| 2001–02 | Brighton & HA | 36 | 2 | | |
| 2002–03 | Brighton & HA | 28 | 1 | | |
| 2003–04 | Brighton & HA | 36 | 0 | **140** | **7** |

**JONES, Stuart† (G)** **35** **0**
H: 6 1 W: 14 05 b.Bristol 24-10-77
*Source:* Weston-Super-Mare.

| | | | | | |
|---|---|---|---|---|---|
| 1997–98 | Sheffield W | 0 | 0 | | |
| 1998–99 | Sheffield W | 0 | 0 | | |
| 1998–99 | *Crewe Alex* | 0 | 0 | | |
| 1999–2000 | Sheffield W | 0 | 0 | | |
| 1999–2000 | Torquay U | 16 | 0 | | |
| 2000–01 | Torquay U | 16 | 0 | | |
| 2001–02 | Torquay U | 0 | 0 | | |
| 2002–03 | Torquay U | 0 | 0 | | |
| 2003–04 | Torquay U | 0 | 0 | **32** | **0** |
| Fr Weston Super Mare | | | | | |
| 2003–04 | Brighton & HA | 3 | 0 | **3** | **0** |

**KNIGHT, Leon (F) 110 44**
H: 5 5 W: 10 02 b.Hackney 16-9-82
*Source:* Trainee. *Honours:* England Youth, Under-20.

| | | | | | |
|---|---|---|---|---|---|
| 1999–2000 | Chelsea | 0 | 0 | | |
| 2000–01 | Chelsea | 0 | 0 | | |
| 2000–01 | *QPR* | 11 | 0 | **11** | **0** |
| 2001–02 | Chelsea | 0 | 0 | | |
| 2001–02 | *Huddersfield T* | 31 | 16 | **31** | **16** |
| 2002–03 | Chelsea | 0 | 0 | | |
| 2002–03 | *Sheffield W* | 24 | 3 | **24** | **3** |
| 2003–04 | Chelsea | 0 | 0 | | |
| 2003–04 | Brighton & HA | 44 | 25 | **44** | **25** |

**KUIPERS, Michels (G) 108 0**
H: 6 2 W: 15 00 b.Amsterdam 26-6-74

| | | | | | |
|---|---|---|---|---|---|
| 1998–99 | Bristol R | 1 | 0 | | |
| 1999–2000 | Bristol R | 0 | 0 | **1** | **0** |
| 2000–01 | Brighton & HA | 34 | 0 | | |
| 2001–02 | Brighton & HA | 39 | 0 | | |
| 2002–03 | Brighton & HA | 21 | 0 | | |
| 2003–04 | Brighton & HA | 10 | 0 | **104** | **0** |
| 2003–04 | *Hull C* | 3 | 0 | **3** | **0** |

**LEE, David# (M) 64 9**
H: 5 11 W: 12 12 b.Basildon 28-3-80
*Source:* Trainee.

| | | | | | |
|---|---|---|---|---|---|
| 1998–99 | Tottenham H | 0 | 0 | | |
| 1999–2000 | Tottenham H | 0 | 0 | | |
| 2000–01 | Southend U | 42 | 8 | **42** | **8** |
| 2001–02 | Hull C | 11 | 1 | **11** | **1** |
| 2001–02 | Brighton & HA | 2 | 0 | | |
| 2002–03 | Brighton & HA | 0 | 0 | | |
| 2002–03 | *Bristol R* | 5 | 0 | **5** | **0** |
| 2003–04 | Brighton & HA | 4 | 0 | **6** | **0** |

**MARNEY, Daniel‡ (F) 32 0**
H: 5 9 W: 10 10 b.Sidcup 2-10-81
*Source:* Scholar.

| | | | | | |
|---|---|---|---|---|---|
| 2001–02 | Brighton & HA | 0 | 0 | | |
| 2002–03 | Brighton & HA | 12 | 0 | | |
| 2002–03 | *Southend U* | 17 | 0 | **17** | **0** |
| 2003–04 | Brighton & HA | 3 | 0 | **15** | **0** |

**MAYO, Kerry (D) 276 10**
H: 5 9 W: 13 10 b.Cuckfield 21-9-77
*Source:* Trainee.

| | | | | | |
|---|---|---|---|---|---|
| 1996–97 | Brighton & HA | 24 | 0 | | |
| 1997–98 | Brighton & HA | 44 | 6 | | |
| 1998–99 | Brighton & HA | 25 | 1 | | |
| 1999–2000 | Brighton & HA | 31 | 1 | | |
| 2000–01 | Brighton & HA | 45 | 1 | | |
| 2001–02 | Brighton & HA | 33 | 0 | | |
| 2002–03 | Brighton & HA | 41 | 1 | | |
| 2003–04 | Brighton & HA | 33 | 0 | **276** | **10** |

**McARTHUR, Duncan (M) 3 0**
H: 5 9 W: 12 06 b.Brighton 6-5-81
*Source:* Trainee.

| | | | | | |
|---|---|---|---|---|---|
| 1998–99 | Brighton & HA | 3 | 0 | | |
| 1999–2000 | Brighton & HA | 0 | 0 | | |
| 2000–01 | Brighton & HA | 0 | 0 | | |
| 2001–02 | Brighton & HA | 0 | 0 | | |
| 2002–03 | Brighton & HA | 0 | 0 | | |
| 2003–04 | Brighton & HA | 0 | 0 | **3** | **0** |

**McPHEE, Christopher (F) 37 4**
H: 6 0 W: 11 11 b.Eastbourne 20-3-83
*Source:* Scholarship.

| | | | | | |
|---|---|---|---|---|---|
| 1999–2000 | Brighton & HA | 4 | 0 | | |
| 2000–01 | Brighton & HA | 0 | 0 | | |
| 2001–02 | Brighton & HA | 2 | 0 | | |
| 2002–03 | Brighton & HA | 2 | 0 | | |
| 2003–04 | Brighton & HA | 29 | 4 | **37** | **4** |

**OATWAY, Charlie# (M) 331 8**
H: 5 7 W: 11 11 b.Hammersmith 28-11-73
*Source:* Yeading.

| | | | | | |
|---|---|---|---|---|---|
| 1994–95 | Cardiff C | 30 | 0 | | |
| 1995–96 | Cardiff C | 2 | 0 | **32** | **0** |
| 1995–96 | Torquay U | 24 | 0 | | |
| 1996–97 | Torquay U | 41 | 1 | | |
| 1997–98 | Torquay U | 2 | 0 | **67** | **1** |
| 1997–98 | Brentford | 33 | 0 | | |
| 1998–99 | Brentford | 24 | 0 | **57** | **0** |
| 1998–99 | *Lincoln C* | 3 | 0 | **3** | **0** |
| 1999–2000 | Brighton & HA | 42 | 4 | | |
| 2000–01 | Brighton & HA | 38 | 0 | | |
| 2001–02 | Brighton & HA | 32 | 1 | | |
| 2002–03 | Brighton & HA | 29 | 1 | | |
| 2003–04 | Brighton & HA | 31 | 1 | **172** | **7** |

**PETHICK, Robbie‡ (D) 316 5**
H: 5 11 W: 12 02 b.Tavistock 8-9-70
*Source:* Weymouth.

| | | | | | |
|---|---|---|---|---|---|
| 1993–94 | Portsmouth | 18 | 0 | | |
| 1994–95 | Portsmouth | 44 | 1 | | |
| 1995–96 | Portsmouth | 38 | 0 | | |
| 1996–97 | Portsmouth | 35 | 0 | | |
| 1997–98 | Portsmouth | 44 | 2 | | |
| 1998–99 | Portsmouth | 10 | 0 | **189** | **3** |
| 1998–99 | Bristol R | 9 | 0 | | |
| 1999–2000 | Bristol R | 41 | 2 | | |
| 2000–01 | Bristol R | 13 | 0 | **63** | **2** |
| 2001–02 | Brighton & HA | 24 | 0 | | |
| 2002–03 | Brighton & HA | 26 | 0 | | |
| 2003–04 | Brighton & HA | 14 | 0 | **64** | **0** |

**PIERCY, John# (M) 36 4**
H: 5 9 W: 13 00 b.Forest Gate 18-9-79
*Source:* Trainee. *Honours:* England Youth.

| | | | | | |
|---|---|---|---|---|---|
| 1998–99 | Tottenham H | 0 | 0 | | |
| 1999–2000 | Tottenham H | 3 | 0 | | |
| 2000–01 | Tottenham H | 5 | 0 | | |
| 2001–02 | Tottenham H | 0 | 0 | | |
| 2002–03 | Tottenham H | 0 | 0 | **8** | **0** |
| 2002–03 | Brighton & HA | 4 | 0 | | |
| 2003–04 | Brighton & HA | 24 | 4 | **28** | **4** |

**PITCHER, Geoff* (M) 24 2**
H: 5 7 W: 11 11 b.Sutton 15-8-75
*Source:* Millwall Trainee.

| | | | | | |
|---|---|---|---|---|---|
| 1994–95 | Watford | 4 | 1 | | |
| 1995–96 | Watford | 9 | 1 | **13** | **2** |
| From Kingstonian. | | | | | |
| 1996–97 | Colchester U | 1 | 0 | **1** | **0** |
| From Kingstonian. | | | | | |
| 2001–02 | Brighton & HA | 10 | 0 | | |
| 2002–03 | Brighton & HA | 0 | 0 | | |
| 2003–04 | Brighton & HA | 0 | 0 | **10** | **0** |

**REID, Paul† (M) 111 17**
H: 5 8 W: 12 09 b.Sydney 6-7-79
*Honours:* Australia Under-20.

| | | | | | |
|---|---|---|---|---|---|
| 1998–99 | Wollongong Wolves | 22 | 2 | | |
| 1999–2000 | Wollongong Wolves | 31 | 3 | | |
| 2000–01 | Wollongong Wolves | 30 | 7 | | |
| 2001–02 | Wollongong Wolves | 15 | 3 | **98** | **15** |
| 2002–03 | Bradford C | 8 | 2 | | |
| 2003–04 | Bradford C | 0 | 0 | **8** | **2** |
| 2003–04 | Brighton & HA | 5 | 0 | **5** | **0** |

**ROBERTS, Ben (G) 109 0**
H: 6 2 W: 13 05 b.Bishop Auckland 22-6-75
*Source:* Trainee. *Honours:* England Under-21.

| | | | | | |
|---|---|---|---|---|---|
| 1992–93 | Middlesbrough | 0 | 0 | | |
| 1993–94 | Middlesbrough | 0 | 0 | | |
| 1994–95 | Middlesbrough | 0 | 0 | | |
| 1995–96 | Middlesbrough | 0 | 0 | | |
| 1995–96 | *Hartlepool U* | 4 | 0 | **4** | **0** |
| 1995–96 | *Wycombe W* | 15 | 0 | **15** | **0** |
| 1996–97 | Middlesbrough | 10 | 0 | | |
| 1996–97 | *Bradford C* | 2 | 0 | **2** | **0** |
| 1997–98 | Middlesbrough | 6 | 0 | | |
| 1998–99 | Middlesbrough | 0 | 0 | | |
| 1998–99 | *Millwall* | 11 | 0 | **11** | **0** |
| 1999–2000 | Middlesbrough | 0 | 0 | **16** | **0** |
| 1999–2000 | *Luton T* | 14 | 0 | | |
| 2000–01 | Charlton Ath | 0 | 0 | | |
| 2001–02 | Charlton Ath | 0 | 0 | | |
| 2001–02 | *Reading* | 6 | 0 | **6** | **0** |
| 2002–03 | Charlton Ath | 1 | 0 | **1** | **0** |
| 2002–03 | *Luton T* | 5 | 0 | **19** | **0** |
| 2002–03 | *Brighton & HA* | 3 | 0 | | |
| 2003–04 | Brighton & HA | 32 | 0 | **35** | **0** |

**ROBINSON, Jake (F) 9 0**
H: 5 7 W: 10 10 b.Brighton 23-10-86
*Source:* Scholar.

| | | | | | |
|---|---|---|---|---|---|
| 2003–04 | Brighton & HA | 9 | 0 | **9** | **0** |

**RODGER, Simon# (M) 325 14**
H: 5 9 W: 11 05 b.Shoreham 3-10-71
*Source:* Trainee.

| | | | | | |
|---|---|---|---|---|---|
| 1989–90 | Crystal Palace | 0 | 0 | | |
| 1990–91 | Crystal Palace | 0 | 0 | | |
| 1991–92 | Crystal Palace | 22 | 0 | | |
| 1992–93 | Crystal Palace | 23 | 2 | | |
| 1993–94 | Crystal Palace | 42 | 3 | | |
| 1994–95 | Crystal Palace | 4 | 0 | | |
| 1995–96 | Crystal Palace | 24 | 0 | | |
| 1996–97 | Crystal Palace | 11 | 0 | | |
| 1996–97 | *Manchester C* | 8 | 1 | **8** | **1** |
| 1996–97 | *Stoke C* | 5 | 0 | **5** | **0** |
| 1997–98 | Crystal Palace | 29 | 2 | | |
| 1998–99 | Crystal Palace | 18 | 1 | | |
| 1999–2000 | Crystal Palace | 34 | 2 | | |
| 2000–01 | Crystal Palace | 33 | 0 | | |
| 2001–02 | Crystal Palace | 36 | 1 | **276** | **11** |
| From Woking. | | | | | |
| 2002–03 | Brighton & HA | 29 | 2 | | |
| 2003–04 | Brighton & HA | 7 | 0 | **36** | **2** |

**VIRGO, Adam (D) 46 1**
H: 6 2 W: 13 12 b.Brighton 25-1-83

| | | | | | |
|---|---|---|---|---|---|
| 2000–01 | Brighton & HA | 6 | 0 | | |
| 2001–02 | Brighton & HA | 6 | 0 | | |
| 2002–03 | Brighton & HA | 3 | 0 | | |
| 2002–03 | *Exeter C* | 9 | 0 | **9** | **0** |
| 2003–04 | Brighton & HA | 22 | 1 | **37** | **1** |

**WATSON, Paul (D) 342 20**
H: 5 8 W: 11 04 b.Hastings 4-1-75
*Source:* Trainee.

| | | | | | |
|---|---|---|---|---|---|
| 1992–93 | Gillingham | 1 | 0 | | |
| 1993–94 | Gillingham | 14 | 0 | | |
| 1994–95 | Gillingham | 39 | 2 | | |
| 1995–96 | Gillingham | 8 | 0 | **62** | **2** |
| 1996–97 | Fulham | 44 | 3 | | |
| 1997–98 | Fulham | 6 | 1 | **50** | **4** |
| 1997–98 | Brentford | 25 | 0 | | |
| 1998–99 | Brentford | 12 | 0 | **37** | **0** |
| 1999–2000 | Brighton & HA | 42 | 4 | | |
| 2000–01 | Brighton & HA | 46 | 5 | | |
| 2001–02 | Brighton & HA | 45 | 5 | | |
| 2002–03 | Brighton & HA | 45 | 0 | | |
| 2003–04 | Brighton & HA | 15 | 0 | **193** | **14** |

**WILKINSON, Shaun‡ (M) 18 0**
H: 5 6 W: 10 08 b.Portsmouth 12-9-81
*Source:* Scholarship.

| | | | | | |
|---|---|---|---|---|---|
| 1999–2000 | Brighton & HA | 2 | 0 | | |
| 2000–01 | Brighton & HA | 1 | 0 | | |
| 2001–02 | Brighton & HA | 0 | 0 | | |
| 2002–03 | Brighton & HA | 12 | 0 | | |
| 2002–03 | *Chesterfield* | 1 | 0 | **1** | **0** |
| 2003–04 | Brighton & HA | 2 | 0 | **17** | **0** |

**WINDSOR, Mark* (M) 0 0**
b.Brighton 18-2-85
*Source:* Scholar.

| | | | | | |
|---|---|---|---|---|---|
| 2003–04 | Brighton & HA | 0 | 0 | | |

**Scholars**
Breach, Christopher B; Budd; Darren L; Carey, Lee J; Cox, Dean A E; Elphick, Gary; Fillery, Ben M; May, Christopher; May, Stephen J; Mountford, Adam T; Piper, Matthew T; Rents, Samuel D; Watson, Ben C

**Non Contract**
Jones, Stuart, C; Keeley, John H; Reid, Paul J

**Players who do not hold a current contract but their registration has been retained by the club**
McArthur, Duncan E

## BRISTOL C (13)

**AMANKWAAH, Kevin (D) 67 1**
H: 6 0 W: 12 12 b.London 19-5-82
*Source:* Scholar. *Honours:* England Youth.

| | | | | | |
|---|---|---|---|---|---|
| 1999–2000 | Bristol C | 5 | 0 | | |
| 2000–01 | Bristol C | 14 | 0 | | |
| 2001–02 | Bristol C | 24 | 1 | | |
| 2002–03 | Bristol C | 1 | 0 | | |
| 2002–03 | *Torquay U* | 6 | 0 | **6** | **0** |
| 2003–04 | Bristol C | 5 | 0 | **49** | **1** |
| 2003–04 | *Cheltenham T* | 12 | 0 | **12** | **0** |

**ANYINSAH, Joseph (M) 0 0**
b.Bristol 8-10-84
*Source:* Scholar.

| | | | | | |
|---|---|---|---|---|---|
| 2001–02 | Bristol C | 0 | 0 | | |
| 2002–03 | Bristol C | 0 | 0 | | |
| 2003–04 | Bristol C | 0 | 0 | | |

**BELL, Mickey# (D) 532 49**
H: 5 7 W: 12 09 b.Newcastle 15-11-71
*Source:* Trainee.

| | | | | | |
|---|---|---|---|---|---|
| 1989–90 | Northampton T | 6 | 0 | | |
| 1990–91 | Northampton T | 28 | 0 | | |

| | | | | | |
|---|---|---|---|---|---|
| 1991–92 | Northampton T | 30 | 4 | | |
| 1992–93 | Northampton T | 39 | 5 | | |
| 1993–94 | Northampton T | 38 | 0 | | |
| 1994–95 | Northampton T | 12 | 1 | **153** | **10** |
| 1994–95 | Wycombe W | 31 | 3 | | |
| 1995–96 | Wycombe W | 41 | 1 | | |
| 1996–97 | Wycombe W | 46 | 2 | **118** | **6** |
| 1997–98 | Bristol C | 44 | 10 | | |
| 1998–99 | Bristol C | 33 | 5 | | |
| 1999–2000 | Bristol C | 36 | 5 | | |
| 2000–01 | Bristol C | 41 | 4 | | |
| 2001–02 | Bristol C | 42 | 7 | | |
| 2002–03 | Bristol C | 38 | 2 | | |
| 2003–04 | Bristol C | 27 | 0 | **261** | **33** |

**BROWN, Aaron (M)** **165 13**
H: 5 11 W: 12 13 b.Bristol 14-3-80
*Source:* Trainee. *Honours:* England Schools.

| | | | | | |
|---|---|---|---|---|---|
| 1997–98 | Bristol C | 0 | 0 | | |
| 1998–99 | Bristol C | 14 | 0 | | |
| 1999–2000 | Bristol C | 13 | 2 | | |
| 1999–2000 | *Exeter C* | 5 | 1 | **5** | **1** |
| 2000–01 | Bristol C | 35 | 2 | | |
| 2001–02 | Bristol C | 36 | 1 | | |
| 2002–03 | Bristol C | 32 | 2 | | |
| 2003–04 | Bristol C | 30 | 5 | **160** | **12** |

**BROWN, Marvin* (F)** **38 2**
H: 5 9 W: 11 12 b.Bristol 6-7-83
*Honours:* England Youth.

| | | | | | |
|---|---|---|---|---|---|
| 1999–2000 | Bristol C | 2 | 0 | | |
| 2000–01 | Bristol C | 5 | 0 | | |
| 2001–02 | Bristol C | 10 | 0 | | |
| 2002–03 | Bristol C | 0 | 0 | | |
| 2002–03 | *Torquay U* | 4 | 0 | **4** | **0** |
| 2002–03 | *Cheltenham T* | 15 | 2 | **15** | **2** |
| 2003–04 | Bristol C | 2 | 0 | **19** | **0** |

**BROWN, Scott* (G)** **0 0**
H: 6 2 W: 13 01 b.Wolverhampton 26-4-85
*Source:* Wolverhampton W Trainee.
From Welshpool T

| | | | | | |
|---|---|---|---|---|---|
| 2003–04 | Bristol C | 0 | 0 | | |

**BURNELL, Joe (D)** **131 1**
H: 5 8 W: 12 00 b.Bristol 10-10-80
*Source:* Trainee.

| | | | | | |
|---|---|---|---|---|---|
| 1999–2000 | Bristol C | 17 | 0 | | |
| 2000–01 | Bristol C | 23 | 0 | | |
| 2001–02 | Bristol C | 30 | 0 | | |
| 2002–03 | Bristol C | 44 | 0 | | |
| 2003–04 | Bristol C | 17 | 1 | **131** | **1** |

**BUTLER, Tony (D)** **412 8**
H: 6 1 W: 13 07 b.Stockport 28-9-72
*Source:* Trainee.

| | | | | | |
|---|---|---|---|---|---|
| 1990–91 | Gillingham | 6 | 0 | | |
| 1991–92 | Gillingham | 5 | 0 | | |
| 1992–93 | Gillingham | 41 | 0 | | |
| 1993–94 | Gillingham | 27 | 1 | | |
| 1994–95 | Gillingham | 33 | 2 | | |
| 1995–96 | Gillingham | 36 | 2 | **148** | **5** |
| 1996–97 | Blackpool | 42 | 0 | | |
| 1997–98 | Blackpool | 37 | 0 | | |
| 1998–99 | Blackpool | 20 | 0 | **99** | **0** |
| 1998–99 | Port Vale | 4 | 0 | | |
| 1999–2000 | Port Vale | 15 | 0 | **19** | **0** |
| 1999–2000 | WBA | 7 | 0 | | |
| 2000–01 | WBA | 44 | 1 | | |
| 2001–02 | WBA | 19 | 0 | | |
| 2002–03 | WBA | 0 | 0 | **70** | **1** |
| 2002–03 | Bristol C | 38 | 1 | | |
| 2003–04 | Bristol C | 38 | 1 | **76** | **2** |

**CAREY, Louis# (D)** **312 5**
H: 5 9 W: 12 09 b.Bristol 20-1-77
*Source:* Trainee. *Honours:* Scotland Under-21.

| | | | | | |
|---|---|---|---|---|---|
| 1995–96 | Bristol C | 23 | 0 | | |
| 1996–97 | Bristol C | 42 | 0 | | |
| 1997–98 | Bristol C | 38 | 0 | | |
| 1998–99 | Bristol C | 41 | 0 | | |
| 1999–2000 | Bristol C | 22 | 0 | | |
| 2000–01 | Bristol C | 46 | 3 | | |
| 2001–02 | Bristol C | 35 | 0 | | |
| 2002–03 | Bristol C | 24 | 1 | | |
| 2003–04 | Bristol C | 41 | 1 | **312** | **5** |

**CASKEY, Darren† (M)** **354 50**
H: 5 8 W: 12 04 b.Basildon 21-8-74
*Source:* Trainee. *Honours:* England Schools, Youth.

| | | | | | |
|---|---|---|---|---|---|
| 1991–92 | Tottenham H | 0 | 0 | | |
| 1992–93 | Tottenham H | 0 | 0 | | |
| 1993–94 | Tottenham H | 25 | 4 | | |
| 1994–95 | Tottenham H | 4 | 0 | | |
| 1995–96 | Tottenham H | 3 | 0 | **32** | **4** |
| 1995–96 | *Watford* | 6 | 1 | **6** | **1** |
| 1995–96 | Reading | 15 | 2 | | |
| 1996–97 | Reading | 35 | 0 | | |
| 1997–98 | Reading | 23 | 0 | | |
| 1998–99 | Reading | 42 | 7 | | |
| 1999–2000 | Reading | 44 | 17 | | |
| 2000–01 | Reading | 43 | 9 | **202** | **35** |
| 2001–02 | Notts Co | 42 | 5 | | |
| 2002–03 | Notts Co | 39 | 3 | | |
| 2003–04 | Notts Co | 33 | 2 | **114** | **10** |
| 2003–04 | Bristol C | 0 | 0 | | |

**CLIST, Simon‡ (M)** **82 8**
H: 5 8 W: 11 05 b.Bournemouth 13-6-81
*Source:* Tottenham H Trainee.

| | | | | | |
|---|---|---|---|---|---|
| 1999–2000 | Bristol C | 9 | 0 | | |
| 2000–01 | Bristol C | 38 | 4 | | |
| 2001–02 | Bristol C | 20 | 1 | | |
| 2002–03 | Bristol C | 3 | 1 | | |
| 2002–03 | *Torquay U* | 11 | 2 | **11** | **2** |
| 2003–04 | Bristol C | 1 | 0 | **71** | **6** |

**COLES, Daniel (D)** **110 4**
H: 6 0 W: 13 05 b.Bristol 31-10-81
*Source:* Scholarship.

| | | | | | |
|---|---|---|---|---|---|
| 1999–2000 | Bristol C | 1 | 0 | | |
| 2000–01 | Bristol C | 2 | 0 | | |
| 2001–02 | Bristol C | 23 | 0 | | |
| 2002–03 | Bristol C | 39 | 2 | | |
| 2003–04 | Bristol C | 45 | 2 | **110** | **4** |

**DOHERTY, Tom (M)** **159 6**
H: 5 7 W: 11 12 b.Bristol 17-3-79
*Source:* Trainee. *Honours:* Northern Ireland 5 full caps.

| | | | | | |
|---|---|---|---|---|---|
| 1997–98 | Bristol C | 30 | 2 | | |
| 1998–99 | Bristol C | 23 | 1 | | |
| 1999–2000 | Bristol C | 1 | 0 | | |
| 2000–01 | Bristol C | 0 | 0 | | |
| 2001–02 | Bristol C | 34 | 1 | | |
| 2002–03 | Bristol C | 38 | 0 | | |
| 2003–04 | Bristol C | 33 | 2 | **159** | **6** |

**FORTUNE, Clayton (D)** **17 0**
H: 6 0 W: 14 04 b.Forest Gate 10-11-82
*Source:* Tottenham H Scholar.

| | | | | | |
|---|---|---|---|---|---|
| 2000–01 | Bristol C | 0 | 0 | | |
| 2001–02 | Bristol C | 1 | 0 | | |
| 2002–03 | Bristol C | 10 | 0 | | |
| 2003–04 | Bristol C | 6 | 0 | **17** | **0** |

**GOODFELLOW, Marc (F)** **69 10**
H: 5 10 W: 11 00 b.Swadlincote 20-9-81

| | | | | | |
|---|---|---|---|---|---|
| 1998–99 | Stoke C | 0 | 0 | | |
| 1999–2000 | Stoke C | 0 | 0 | | |
| 2000–01 | Stoke C | 7 | 0 | | |
| 2001–02 | Stoke C | 23 | 5 | | |
| 2002–03 | Stoke C | 20 | 1 | | |
| 2003–04 | Stoke C | 4 | 0 | **54** | **6** |
| 2003–04 | Bristol C | 15 | 4 | **15** | **4** |

**HAWKINS, Darren (M)** **0 0**
H: 5 10 W: 11 09 b.Bristol 25-4-84
*Source:* Scholar.

| | | | | | |
|---|---|---|---|---|---|
| 2003–04 | Bristol C | 0 | 0 | | |

**HILL, Matt (D)** **175 6**
H: 5 7 W: 11 13 b.Bristol 26-3-81
*Source:* Trainee.

| | | | | | |
|---|---|---|---|---|---|
| 1998–99 | Bristol C | 3 | 0 | | |
| 1999–2000 | Bristol C | 14 | 0 | | |
| 2000–01 | Bristol C | 34 | 0 | | |
| 2001–02 | Bristol C | 40 | 1 | | |
| 2002–03 | Bristol C | 42 | 3 | | |
| 2003–04 | Bristol C | 42 | 2 | **175** | **6** |

**HULBERT, Robin‡ (M)** **75 0**
H: 5 8 W: 11 10 b.Plymouth 14-3-80
*Source:* Trainee. *Honours:* England Youth.

| | | | | | |
|---|---|---|---|---|---|
| 1997–98 | Swindon T | 1 | 0 | | |
| 1997–98 | *Newcastle U* | 0 | 0 | | |
| 1998–99 | Swindon T | 16 | 0 | | |
| 1999–2000 | Swindon T | 12 | 0 | **29** | **0** |
| 1999–2000 | Bristol C | 2 | 0 | | |
| 2000–01 | Bristol C | 19 | 0 | | |
| 2001–02 | Bristol C | 11 | 0 | | |
| 2002–03 | Bristol C | 7 | 0 | | |
| 2002–03 | *Shrewsbury T* | 7 | 0 | **7** | **0** |
| 2003–04 | Bristol C | 0 | 0 | **39** | **0** |

**JONES, Darren‡ (D)** **16 1**
H: 6 0 W: 14 12 b.Newport 28-8-83
*Source:* Scholar. *Honours:* Wales Schools, Youth.

| | | | | | |
|---|---|---|---|---|---|
| 2000–01 | Bristol C | 0 | 0 | | |
| 2001–02 | Bristol C | 2 | 0 | | |
| 2002–03 | Bristol C | 0 | 0 | | |
| 2003–04 | Bristol C | 0 | 0 | **2** | **0** |
| 2003–04 | *Cheltenham T* | 14 | 1 | **14** | **1** |

**LITA, Leroy (F)** **41 7**
H: 5 7 W: 11 12 b.Congo 28-12-84
*Source:* Scholar.

| | | | | | |
|---|---|---|---|---|---|
| 2002–03 | Bristol C | 15 | 2 | | |
| 2003–04 | Bristol C | 26 | 5 | **41** | **7** |

**LOXTON, Craig (M)** **0 0**
b.Bath 14-9-84
*Source:* Scholar.

| | | | | | |
|---|---|---|---|---|---|
| 2001–02 | Bristol C | 0 | 0 | | |
| 2002–03 | Bristol C | 0 | 0 | | |
| 2003–04 | Bristol C | 0 | 0 | | |

**MATTHEWS, Lee* (F)** **75 10**
H: 5 11 W: 14 08 b.Middlesbrough 16-1-79
*Source:* Trainee. *Honours:* England Youth.

| | | | | | |
|---|---|---|---|---|---|
| 1995–96 | Leeds U | 0 | 0 | | |
| 1996–97 | Leeds U | 0 | 0 | | |
| 1997–98 | Leeds U | 3 | 0 | | |
| 1998–99 | Leeds U | 0 | 0 | | |
| 1998–99 | *Notts Co* | 5 | 0 | **5** | **0** |
| 1999–2000 | Leeds U | 0 | 0 | | |
| 1999–2000 | *Gillingham* | 5 | 0 | **5** | **0** |
| 2000–01 | Leeds U | 0 | 0 | **3** | **0** |
| 2000–01 | Bristol C | 6 | 3 | | |
| 2001–02 | Bristol C | 22 | 3 | | |
| 2002–03 | Bristol C | 7 | 1 | | |
| 2003–04 | Bristol C | 8 | 2 | **43** | **9** |
| 2003–04 | *Darlington* | 6 | 1 | **6** | **1** |
| 2003–04 | *Bristol R* | 9 | 0 | **9** | **0** |
| 2003–04 | *Yeovil T* | 4 | 0 | **4** | **0** |

**MERCER, Billy* (G)** **282 0**
H: 6 1 W: 13 02 b.Liverpool 22-5-69
*Source:* Trainee.

| | | | | | |
|---|---|---|---|---|---|
| 1987–88 | Liverpool | 0 | 0 | | |
| 1988–89 | Liverpool | 0 | 0 | | |
| 1988–89 | Rotherham U | 0 | 0 | | |
| 1989–90 | Rotherham U | 2 | 0 | | |
| 1990–91 | Rotherham U | 13 | 0 | | |
| 1991–92 | Rotherham U | 35 | 0 | | |
| 1992–93 | Rotherham U | 36 | 0 | | |
| 1993–94 | Rotherham U | 17 | 0 | | |
| 1994–95 | Rotherham U | 1 | 0 | **104** | **0** |
| 1994–95 | Sheffield U | 3 | 0 | | |
| 1994–95 | *Nottingham F* | 0 | 0 | | |
| 1995–96 | Sheffield U | 1 | 0 | **4** | **0** |
| 1995–96 | Chesterfield | 34 | 0 | | |
| 1996–97 | Chesterfield | 35 | 0 | | |
| 1997–98 | Chesterfield | 36 | 0 | | |
| 1998–99 | Chesterfield | 44 | 0 | | |
| 1999–2000 | Chesterfield | 0 | 0 | **149** | **0** |
| 1999–2000 | Bristol C | 25 | 0 | | |
| 2000–01 | Bristol C | 0 | 0 | | |
| 2001–02 | Bristol C | 0 | 0 | | |
| 2002–03 | Bristol C | 0 | 0 | | |
| 2003–04 | Bristol C | 0 | 0 | **25** | **0** |

**MILLER, Lee (F)** **103 36**
H: 6 2 W: 11 07 b.Lanark 15-3-83
*Source:* Form S.

| | | | | | |
|---|---|---|---|---|---|
| 2000–01 | Falkirk | 0 | 0 | | |
| 2001–02 | Falkirk | 27 | 11 | | |
| 2002–03 | Falkirk | 34 | 17 | **61** | **28** |
| 2003–04 | Bristol C | 42 | 8 | **42** | **8** |

**MURRAY, Scott (M)** **268 51**
H: 5 7 W: 11 02 b.Aberdeen 26-5-74
*Source:* Fraserburgh. *Honours:* Scotland B.

| | | | | | |
|---|---|---|---|---|---|
| 1993–94 | Aston Villa | 0 | 0 | | |
| 1994–95 | Aston Villa | 0 | 0 | | |
| 1995–96 | Aston Villa | 3 | 0 | | |
| 1996–97 | Aston Villa | 1 | 0 | | |
| 1997–98 | Aston Villa | 0 | 0 | **4** | **0** |
| 1997–98 | Bristol C | 23 | 0 | | |
| 1998–99 | Bristol C | 32 | 3 | | |

| | | | | | |
|---|---|---|---|---|---|
| 1999–2000 | Bristol C | 41 | 6 | | |
| 2000–01 | Bristol C | 46 | 10 | | |
| 2001–02 | Bristol C | 37 | 8 | | |
| 2002–03 | Bristol C | 45 | 19 | | |
| 2003–04 | Reading | 34 | 5 | **34** | **5** |
| 2003–04 | Bristol C | 6 | 0 | **230** | **46** |

**PEACOCK, Lee# (F) 317 94**
H: 6 0 W: 13 13 b.Paisley 9-10-76
*Source:* Trainee. *Honours:* Scotland Youth, Under-21.

| | | | | | |
|---|---|---|---|---|---|
| 1993–94 | Carlisle U | 1 | 0 | | |
| 1994–95 | Carlisle U | 7 | 0 | | |
| 1995–96 | Carlisle U | 22 | 2 | | |
| 1996–97 | Carlisle U | 44 | 9 | | |
| 1997–98 | Carlisle U | 2 | 0 | **76** | **11** |
| 1997–98 | Mansfield T | 32 | 5 | | |
| 1998–99 | Mansfield T | 45 | 17 | | |
| 1999–2000 | Mansfield T | 12 | 7 | **89** | **29** |
| 1999–2000 | Manchester C | 8 | 0 | **8** | **0** |
| 2000–01 | Bristol C | 35 | 13 | | |
| 2001–02 | Bristol C | 31 | 15 | | |
| 2002–03 | Bristol C | 37 | 12 | | |
| 2003–04 | Bristol C | 41 | 14 | **144** | **54** |

**PHILLIPS, Steve (G) 192 0**
H: 6 0 W: 13 06 b.Bath 6-5-78
*Source:* Paulton R.

| | | | | | |
|---|---|---|---|---|---|
| 1996–97 | Bristol C | 0 | 0 | | |
| 1997–98 | Bristol C | 0 | 0 | | |
| 1998–99 | Bristol C | 15 | 0 | | |
| 1999–2000 | Bristol C | 21 | 0 | | |
| 2000–01 | Bristol C | 42 | 0 | | |
| 2001–02 | Bristol C | 22 | 0 | | |
| 2002–03 | Bristol C | 46 | 0 | | |
| 2003–04 | Bristol C | 46 | 0 | **192** | **0** |

**ROBERTS, Chris# (F) 188 41**
H: 5 9 W: 13 02 b.Cardiff 22-10-79
*Source:* Trainee. *Honours:* Wales Youth, Under-21.

| | | | | | |
|---|---|---|---|---|---|
| 1997–98 | Cardiff C | 11 | 3 | | |
| 1998–99 | Cardiff C | 4 | 0 | | |
| 1999–2000 | Cardiff C | 8 | 0 | **23** | **3** |
| 2000–01 | Exeter C | 42 | 8 | | |
| 2001–02 | Exeter C | 37 | 11 | **79** | **19** |
| 2001–02 | Bristol C | 4 | 0 | | |
| 2002–03 | Bristol C | 44 | 13 | | |
| 2003–04 | Bristol C | 38 | 6 | **86** | **19** |

**ROUGIER, Tony* (F) 269 27**
H: 6 0 W: 14 11 b.Trinidad 17-7-71
*Source:* Trinity Pros. *Honours:* Trinidad & Tobago full caps.

| | | | | | |
|---|---|---|---|---|---|
| 1994–95 | Raith R | 4 | 0 | | |
| 1995–96 | Raith R | 22 | 1 | | |
| 1996–97 | Raith R | 30 | 1 | **56** | **2** |
| 1997–98 | Hibernian | 20 | 3 | | |
| 1998–99 | Hibernian | 15 | 1 | **35** | **4** |
| 1998–99 | Port Vale | 13 | 0 | | |
| 1999–2000 | Port Vale | 38 | 8 | **51** | **8** |
| 2000–01 | Reading | 31 | 2 | | |
| 2001–02 | Reading | 33 | 1 | | |
| 2002–03 | Reading | 20 | 3 | **84** | **6** |
| 2002–03 | *Brighton & HA* | 6 | 2 | **6** | **2** |
| 2003–04 | Brentford | 31 | 4 | **31** | **4** |
| 2003–04 | Bristol C | 6 | 1 | **6** | **1** |

**SIMPSON, Sekani (M) 0 0**
H: 5 10 W: 11 10 b.Bristol 11-3-84
*Source:* Scholar.

| | | | | | |
|---|---|---|---|---|---|
| 2003–04 | Bristol C | 0 | 0 | | |

**STOWELL, Mike# (G) 453 0**
H: 6 2 W: 14 01 b.Preston 19-4-65
*Source:* Leyland Motors.

| | | | | | |
|---|---|---|---|---|---|
| 1984–85 | Preston NE | 0 | 0 | | |
| 1985–86 | Preston NE | 0 | 0 | | |
| 1985–86 | Everton | 0 | 0 | | |
| 1986–87 | Everton | 0 | 0 | | |
| 1987–88 | *Chester C* | 14 | 0 | **14** | **0** |
| 1987–88 | *York C* | 6 | 0 | **6** | **0** |
| 1987–88 | *Manchester C* | 14 | 0 | **14** | **0** |
| 1988–89 | Everton | 0 | 0 | | |
| 1988–89 | *Port Vale* | 7 | 0 | **7** | **0** |
| 1988–89 | *Wolverhampton W* | 7 | 0 | | |
| 1989–90 | Everton | 0 | 0 | | |
| 1989–90 | *Preston NE* | 2 | 0 | **2** | **0** |
| 1990–91 | Wolverhampton W | 39 | 0 | | |
| 1991–92 | Wolverhampton W | 46 | 0 | | |
| 1992–93 | Wolverhampton W | 26 | 0 | | |
| 1993–94 | Wolverhampton W | 46 | 0 | | |
| 1994–95 | Wolverhampton W | 37 | 0 | | |
| 1995–96 | Wolverhampton W | 38 | 0 | | |
| 1996–97 | Wolverhampton W | 46 | 0 | | |
| 1997–98 | Wolverhampton W | 35 | 0 | | |
| 1998–99 | Wolverhampton W | 46 | 0 | | |
| 1999–2000 | Wolverhampton W | 18 | 0 | | |
| 2000–01 | Wolverhampton W | 1 | 0 | **385** | **0** |
| 2001–02 | Bristol C | 25 | 0 | | |
| 2002–03 | Bristol C | 0 | 0 | | |
| 2003–04 | Bristol C | 0 | 0 | **25** | **0** |

**TINNION, Brian (M) 613 59**
H: 6 0 W: 13 05 b.Stanley 23-3-68
*Source:* Apprentice.

| | | | | | |
|---|---|---|---|---|---|
| 1985–86 | Newcastle U | 0 | 0 | | |
| 1986–87 | Newcastle U | 3 | 0 | | |
| 1987–88 | Newcastle U | 16 | 1 | | |
| 1988–89 | Newcastle U | 13 | 1 | **32** | **2** |
| 1988–89 | Bradford C | 14 | 1 | | |
| 1989–90 | Bradford C | 37 | 5 | | |
| 1990–91 | Bradford C | 41 | 5 | | |
| 1991–92 | Bradford C | 26 | 8 | | |
| 1992–93 | Bradford C | 27 | 3 | **145** | **22** |
| 1992–93 | Bristol C | 11 | 2 | | |
| 1993–94 | Bristol C | 41 | 5 | | |
| 1994–95 | Bristol C | 35 | 2 | | |
| 1995–96 | Bristol C | 30 | 3 | | |
| 1996–97 | Bristol C | 32 | 1 | | |
| 1997–98 | Bristol C | 44 | 3 | | |
| 1998–99 | Bristol C | 35 | 1 | | |
| 1999–2000 | Bristol C | 43 | 3 | | |
| 2000–01 | Bristol C | 42 | 1 | | |
| 2001–02 | Bristol C | 38 | 3 | | |
| 2002–03 | Bristol C | 40 | 9 | | |
| 2003–04 | Bristol C | 45 | 2 | **436** | **35** |

**WILKSHIRE, Luke (M) 58 2**
H: 5 10 W: 11 00 b.Wollongong 2-10-81
*Honours:* Australia Under-20, Under-23.

| | | | | | |
|---|---|---|---|---|---|
| 1998–99 | Middlesbrough | 0 | 0 | | |
| 1999–2000 | Middlesbrough | 0 | 0 | | |
| 2000–01 | Middlesbrough | 0 | 0 | | |
| 2001–02 | Middlesbrough | 7 | 0 | | |
| 2002–03 | Middlesbrough | 14 | 0 | **21** | **0** |
| 2003–04 | Bristol C | 37 | 2 | **37** | **2** |

**WOODMAN, Craig (D) 39 0**
H: 5 8 W: 11 00 b.Tiverton 22-12-82
*Source:* Trainee.

| | | | | | |
|---|---|---|---|---|---|
| 1999–2000 | Bristol C | 0 | 0 | | |
| 2000–01 | Bristol C | 2 | 0 | | |
| 2001–02 | Bristol C | 6 | 0 | | |
| 2002–03 | Bristol C | 10 | 0 | | |
| 2003–04 | Bristol C | 21 | 0 | **39** | **0** |

**Scholars**
Allward, Jack; Aubrey, Matthew D; Bailey, Sam; Barnes, Oliver J P; Benyon, Elliot P; Best, Nathan P; Clayton, Jonathan J; Davies, Christopher J; Denton, Matthew T; Flurry, Joe T; Harley, Ryan; Hart, Callum L; Hart, David T J; Hodgson, Dean A; Jacobs, Thomas; Lamb, Shaun A; Long, Joe; Lukeman, Daniel M; Mackay, Michael D; Monelle, Grant; Osman, Thomas C; Pearce, Sam; Pollinger, Jordan; Rivers, Sean F; Skuse, Cole; Smart, Robert P; Stabler, James N; Titcombe, Lee B; Turnor, James M; Wring, Daniel R

## BRISTOL R (14)

**AGOGO, Junior (F) 61 13**
H: 5 10 W: 11 07 b.Accra 1-8-79
*Source:* Willesden.

| | | | | | |
|---|---|---|---|---|---|
| 1996–97 | Sheffield W | 0 | 0 | | |
| 1997–98 | Sheffield W | 1 | 0 | | |
| 1998–99 | Sheffield W | 1 | 0 | | |
| 1999–2000 | Sheffield W | 0 | 0 | **2** | **0** |
| 1999–2000 | *Oldham Ath* | 2 | 0 | **2** | **0** |
| 1999–2000 | *Chester C* | 10 | 6 | **10** | **6** |
| 1999–2000 | *Chesterfield* | 4 | 0 | **4** | **0** |
| 1999–2000 | *Lincoln C* | 3 | 1 | **3** | **1** |
| From Colorado R, San Jose E. | | | | | |
| 2001–02 | QPR | 2 | 0 | **2** | **0** |
| 2002–03 | Barnet | 0 | 0 | | |
| 2003–04 | Bristol R | 38 | 6 | **38** | **6** |

**ANDERSON, Ijah (D) 260 4**
H: 5 8 W: 10 06 b.Hackney 30-12-75
*Source:* Tottenham H Trainee.

| | | | | | |
|---|---|---|---|---|---|
| 1994–95 | Southend U | 0 | 0 | | |
| 1995–96 | Brentford | 25 | 2 | | |
| 1996–97 | Brentford | 46 | 1 | | |
| 1997–98 | Brentford | 17 | 0 | | |
| 1998–99 | Brentford | 38 | 1 | | |
| 1999–2000 | Brentford | 31 | 0 | | |
| 2000–01 | Brentford | 1 | 0 | | |
| 2001–02 | Brentford | 35 | 0 | | |
| 2002–03 | Brentford | 9 | 0 | **202** | **4** |
| 2002–03 | *Wycombe W* | 5 | 0 | **5** | **0** |
| 2002–03 | Bristol R | 14 | 0 | | |
| 2003–04 | Bristol R | 39 | 0 | **53** | **0** |

**ANDERSON, John (D) 297 32**
H: 6 2 W: 12 02 b.Greenock 2-10-72
*Source:* Gourock YAC.

| | | | | | |
|---|---|---|---|---|---|
| 1993–94 | Morton | 19 | 2 | | |
| 1994–95 | Morton | 30 | 3 | | |
| 1995–96 | Morton | 30 | 4 | | |
| 1996–97 | Morton | 31 | 4 | | |
| 1997–98 | Morton | 33 | 4 | | |
| 1998–99 | Morton | 33 | 6 | | |
| 1999–2000 | Morton | 29 | 5 | **205** | **28** |
| 2000–01 | Livingston | 30 | 3 | | |
| 2001–02 | Livingston | 11 | 0 | **41** | **3** |
| 2002–03 | Hull C | 43 | 1 | | |
| 2003–04 | Hull C | 0 | 0 | **43** | **1** |
| 2003–04 | Bristol R | 8 | 0 | **8** | **0** |

**ARNDALE, Neil† (D) 5 0**
H: 5 7 W: 10 07 b.Bristol 26-4-84
*Source:* Scholar. *Honours:* England Youth.

| | | | | | |
|---|---|---|---|---|---|
| 2001–02 | Bristol R | 1 | 0 | | |
| 2002–03 | Bristol R | 1 | 0 | | |
| 2003–04 | Bristol R | 3 | 0 | **5** | **0** |

**AUSTIN, Kevin (D) 306 5**
H: 6 0 W: 14 00 b.Hackney 12-2-73
*Source:* Saffron Walden. *Honours:* Trinidad & Tobago 1 full cap.

| | | | | | |
|---|---|---|---|---|---|
| 1993–94 | Leyton Orient | 30 | 0 | | |
| 1994–95 | Leyton Orient | 39 | 2 | | |
| 1995–96 | Leyton Orient | 40 | 1 | **109** | **3** |
| 1996–97 | Lincoln C | 44 | 1 | | |
| 1997–98 | Lincoln C | 46 | 0 | | |
| 1998–99 | Lincoln C | 39 | 1 | **129** | **2** |
| 1999–2000 | Barnsley | 3 | 0 | | |
| 2000–01 | Barnsley | 0 | 0 | **3** | **0** |
| 2000–01 | *Brentford* | 3 | 0 | **3** | **0** |
| 2001–02 | Cambridge U | 6 | 0 | **6** | **0** |
| 2002–03 | Bristol R | 33 | 0 | | |
| 2003–04 | Bristol R | 23 | 0 | **56** | **0** |

**BARRETT, Adam* (D) 179 9**
H: 5 10 W: 12 00 b.Dagenham 29-11-79
*Source:* Leyton Orient Trainee.

| | | | | | |
|---|---|---|---|---|---|
| 1998–99 | Plymouth Arg | 1 | 0 | | |
| 1999–2000 | Plymouth Arg | 42 | 3 | | |
| 2000–01 | Plymouth Arg | 9 | 0 | **52** | **3** |
| 2000–01 | Mansfield T | 8 | 1 | | |
| 2001–02 | Mansfield T | 29 | 0 | **37** | **1** |
| 2002–03 | Bristol R | 45 | 1 | | |
| 2003–04 | Bristol R | 45 | 4 | **90** | **5** |

**BELL, Leon‡ (M) 12 0**
H: 5 7 W: 9 07 b.Hitchin 19-12-80
*Source:* Trainee.

| | | | | | |
|---|---|---|---|---|---|
| 1999–2000 | Barnet | 1 | 0 | | |
| 2000–01 | Barnet | 11 | 0 | | |
| 2001–02 | Barnet | 0 | 0 | | |
| 2002–03 | Barnet | 0 | 0 | **12** | **0** |
| 2003–04 | Bristol R | 0 | 0 | | |

**BOXALL, Danny* (D) 157 1**
H: 5 8 W: 11 05 b.Croydon 24-8-77
*Source:* Trainee. *Honours:* Eire Under-21.

| | | | | | |
|---|---|---|---|---|---|
| 1994–95 | Crystal Palace | 0 | 0 | | |
| 1995–96 | Crystal Palace | 1 | 0 | | |
| 1996–97 | Crystal Palace | 6 | 0 | | |
| 1997–98 | Crystal Palace | 1 | 0 | **8** | **0** |
| 1997–98 | *Oldham Ath* | 18 | 0 | **18** | **0** |
| 1998–99 | Brentford | 38 | 1 | | |
| 1999–2000 | Brentford | 25 | 0 | | |
| 2000–01 | Brentford | 0 | 0 | | |
| 2001–02 | Brentford | 5 | 0 | **68** | **1** |
| 2002–03 | Bristol R | 39 | 0 | | |
| 2003–04 | Bristol R | 24 | 0 | **63** | **0** |

**BRYANT, Simon (M)** **87** **2**
H: 5 11 W: 13 04 b.Bristol 22-11-82
*Source:* Scholarship. *Honours:* England Youth.

| | | | | | |
|---|---|---|---|---|---|
| 1999–2000 | Bristol R | 15 | 0 | | |
| 2000–01 | Bristol R | 30 | 1 | | |
| 2001–02 | Bristol R | 8 | 0 | | |
| 2002–03 | Bristol R | 22 | 1 | | |
| 2003–04 | Bristol R | 12 | 0 | **87** | **2** |

**CARLISLE, Wayne* (M)** **128** **19**
H: 6 0 W: 11 06 b.Lisburn 9-9-79
*Source:* Trainee. *Honours:* Northern Ireland Schools, Youth, Under-21.

| | | | | | |
|---|---|---|---|---|---|
| 1996–97 | Crystal Palace | 0 | 0 | | |
| 1997–98 | Crystal Palace | 0 | 0 | | |
| 1998–99 | Crystal Palace | 6 | 0 | | |
| 1999–2000 | Crystal Palace | 26 | 3 | | |
| 2000–01 | Crystal Palace | 14 | 0 | | |
| 2001–02 | Crystal Palace | 0 | 0 | **46** | **3** |
| 2001–02 | *Swindon T* | 11 | 2 | **11** | **2** |
| 2001–02 | Bristol R | 5 | 0 | | |
| 2002–03 | Bristol R | 41 | 7 | | |
| 2003–04 | Bristol R | 25 | 7 | **71** | **14** |

**CLARKE, Ryan (G)** **5** **0**
H: 6 3 W: 13 00 b.Bristol 30-4-82
*Source:* Scholar.

| | | | | | |
|---|---|---|---|---|---|
| 2001–02 | Bristol R | 1 | 0 | | |
| 2002–03 | Bristol R | 2 | 0 | | |
| 2003–04 | Bristol R | 2 | 0 | **5** | **0** |

**EDWARDS, Christian (D)** **246** **8**
H: 6 2 W: 12 08 b.Caerphilly 23-11-75
*Source:* Trainee. *Honours:* Wales Under-21, B, 1 full cap.

| | | | | | |
|---|---|---|---|---|---|
| 1994–95 | Swansea C | 9 | 0 | | |
| 1995–96 | Swansea C | 38 | 2 | | |
| 1996–97 | Swansea C | 36 | 0 | | |
| 1997–98 | Swansea C | 32 | 2 | **115** | **4** |
| 1997–98 | Nottingham F | 0 | 0 | | |
| 1998–99 | Nottingham F | 12 | 0 | | |
| 1998–99 | *Bristol C* | 3 | 0 | **3** | **0** |
| 1999–2000 | Nottingham F | 0 | 0 | | |
| 1999–2000 | *Oxford U* | 5 | 1 | | |
| 2000–01 | Nottingham F | 36 | 3 | | |
| 2001–02 | Nottingham F | 6 | 0 | | |
| 2001–02 | *Crystal Palace* | 9 | 0 | **9** | **0** |
| 2002–03 | Nottingham F | 0 | 0 | **54** | **3** |
| 2002–03 | *Tranmere R* | 12 | 0 | **12** | **0** |
| 2002–03 | *Oxford U* | 6 | 0 | **11** | **1** |
| 2003–04 | Bristol R | 42 | 0 | **42** | **0** |

**GIBB, Ali (M)** **304** **6**
H: 5 9 W: 11 07 b.Salisbury 17-2-76
*Source:* Trainee.

| | | | | | |
|---|---|---|---|---|---|
| 1994–95 | Norwich C | 0 | 0 | | |
| 1995–96 | Norwich C | 0 | 0 | | |
| 1995–96 | Northampton T | 23 | 2 | | |
| 1996–97 | Northampton T | 18 | 1 | | |
| 1997–98 | Northampton T | 35 | 1 | | |
| 1998–99 | Northampton T | 41 | 0 | | |
| 1999–2000 | Northampton T | 14 | 0 | **131** | **4** |
| 1999–2000 | Stockport Co | 14 | 0 | | |
| 2000–01 | Stockport Co | 39 | 0 | | |
| 2001–02 | Stockport Co | 41 | 0 | | |
| 2002–03 | Stockport Co | 45 | 1 | | |
| 2003–04 | Stockport Co | 26 | 0 | **165** | **1** |
| 2003–04 | Bristol R | 8 | 1 | **8** | **1** |

**GILROY, David‡ (F)** **19** **0**
H: 5 11 W: 11 05 b.Yeovil 23-10-82
*Source:* Scholar.

| | | | | | |
|---|---|---|---|---|---|
| 2001–02 | Bristol R | 4 | 0 | | |
| 2002–03 | Bristol R | 11 | 0 | | |
| 2003–04 | Bristol R | 4 | 0 | **19** | **0** |

**GREAVES, Danny† (G)** **0** **0**
H: 6 2 W: 12 06 b.Bristol 7-12-83

| | | | | | |
|---|---|---|---|---|---|
| 2003–04 | Bristol R | 0 | 0 | | |

**HALDANE, Lewis (F)** **27** **5**
H: 6 0 W: 11 03 b.Trowbridge 13-3-85
*Source:* Scholar.

| | | | | | |
|---|---|---|---|---|---|
| 2003–04 | Bristol R | 27 | 5 | **27** | **5** |

**HENRIKSEN, Bo* (F)** **204** **64**
H: 5 10 W: 11 00 b.Roskilde 7-2-75

| | | | | | |
|---|---|---|---|---|---|
| 1995–96 | Odense | 10 | 3 | | |
| 1996–97 | Odense | 23 | 8 | **33** | **11** |
| 1997–98 | Aarhus | 0 | 0 | | |
| 1997–98 | Herfolge | 15 | 6 | | |
| 1998–99 | Herfolge | 23 | 6 | | |
| 1999–2000 | Herfolge | 10 | 1 | | |
| 2000–01 | Herfolge | 21 | 1 | | |
| 2000–01 | *Frem* | 4 | 3 | **4** | **3** |
| 2001–02 | Herfolge | 10 | 6 | **79** | **20** |
| 2001–02 | Kidderminster H | 25 | 8 | | |
| 2002–03 | Kidderminster H | 37 | 20 | | |
| 2003–04 | Kidderminster H | 22 | 2 | **84** | **30** |
| 2003–04 | Bristol R | 4 | 0 | **4** | **0** |

**HOBBS, Shane§ (M)** **2** **0**
H: 5 7 W: 10 07 b.Bristol 30-4-85
*Source:* Scholar.

| | | | | | |
|---|---|---|---|---|---|
| 2003–04 | Bristol R | 2 | 0 | **2** | **0** |

**HODGES, Lee* (M)** **187** **23**
H: 5 5 W: 10 02 b.Plaistow 2-3-78
*Source:* Trainee. *Honours:* England Schools.

| | | | | | |
|---|---|---|---|---|---|
| 1994–95 | West Ham U | 0 | 0 | | |
| 1995–96 | West Ham U | 0 | 0 | | |
| 1996–97 | West Ham U | 0 | 0 | | |
| 1996–97 | *Exeter C* | 17 | 0 | **17** | **0** |
| 1996–97 | *Leyton Orient* | 3 | 0 | **3** | **0** |
| 1997–98 | West Ham U | 2 | 0 | | |
| 1997–98 | *Plymouth Arg* | 9 | 0 | **9** | **0** |
| 1998–99 | West Ham U | 1 | 0 | **3** | **0** |
| 1998–99 | *Ipswich T* | 4 | 0 | **4** | **0** |
| 1998–99 | *Southend U* | 10 | 1 | **10** | **1** |
| 1999–2000 | Scunthorpe U | 40 | 6 | | |
| 2000–01 | Scunthorpe U | 38 | 8 | | |
| 2001–02 | Scunthorpe U | 35 | 6 | **113** | **20** |
| 2002–03 | Rochdale | 7 | 0 | **7** | **0** |
| 2002–03 | *Bristol R* | 8 | 0 | | |
| 2003–04 | Bristol R | 13 | 2 | **21** | **2** |

**HYDE, Graham* (M)** **300** **16**
H: 5 7 W: 11 07 b.Doncaster 10-11-70
*Source:* Trainee.

| | | | | | |
|---|---|---|---|---|---|
| 1988–89 | Sheffield W | 0 | 0 | | |
| 1989–90 | Sheffield W | 0 | 0 | | |
| 1990–91 | Sheffield W | 0 | 0 | | |
| 1991–92 | Sheffield W | 13 | 0 | | |
| 1992–93 | Sheffield W | 20 | 1 | | |
| 1993–94 | Sheffield W | 36 | 1 | | |
| 1994–95 | Sheffield W | 35 | 5 | | |
| 1995–96 | Sheffield W | 26 | 1 | | |
| 1996–97 | Sheffield W | 19 | 2 | | |
| 1997–98 | Sheffield W | 22 | 1 | | |
| 1998–99 | Sheffield W | 1 | 0 | **172** | **11** |
| 1998–99 | Birmingham C | 13 | 0 | | |
| 1999–2000 | Birmingham C | 31 | 1 | | |
| 2000–01 | Birmingham C | 3 | 0 | | |
| 2001–02 | Birmingham C | 5 | 0 | | |
| 2001–02 | *Chesterfield* | 9 | 1 | **9** | **1** |
| 2002–03 | Birmingham C | 0 | 0 | **52** | **1** |
| 2002–03 | *Peterborough U* | 9 | 0 | **9** | **0** |
| 2002–03 | Bristol R | 21 | 1 | | |
| 2003–04 | Bristol R | 37 | 2 | **58** | **3** |

**MILLER, Kevin (G)** **586** **0**
H: 6 1 W: 13 00 b.Falmouth 15-3-69
*Source:* Newquay.

| | | | | | |
|---|---|---|---|---|---|
| 1988–89 | Exeter C | 3 | 0 | | |
| 1989–90 | Exeter C | 28 | 0 | | |
| 1990–91 | Exeter C | 46 | 0 | | |
| 1991–92 | Exeter C | 42 | 0 | | |
| 1992–93 | Exeter C | 44 | 0 | | |
| 1993–94 | Birmingham C | 24 | 0 | **24** | **0** |
| 1994–95 | Watford | 44 | 0 | | |
| 1995–96 | Watford | 42 | 0 | | |
| 1996–97 | Watford | 42 | 0 | **128** | **0** |
| 1997–98 | Crystal Palace | 38 | 0 | | |
| 1998–99 | Crystal Palace | 28 | 0 | | |
| 1999–2000 | Crystal Palace | 0 | 0 | **66** | **0** |
| 1999–2000 | Barnsley | 41 | 0 | | |
| 2000–01 | Barnsley | 46 | 0 | | |
| 2001–02 | Barnsley | 28 | 0 | **115** | **0** |
| 2002–03 | Exeter C | 46 | 0 | **209** | **0** |
| 2003–04 | Bristol R | 44 | 0 | **44** | **0** |

**PARKER, Sonny (D)** **30** **1**
H: 5 11 W: 11 11 b.Middlesbrough 28-2-83
*Source:* Trainee. *Honours:* England Youth.

| | | | | | |
|---|---|---|---|---|---|
| 1999–2000 | Birmingham C | 0 | 0 | | |
| 2000–01 | Birmingham C | 0 | 0 | | |
| 2001–02 | Birmingham C | 0 | 0 | | |
| 2002–03 | Birmingham C | 0 | 0 | | |
| 2002–03 | Bristol R | 15 | 0 | | |
| 2003–04 | Bristol R | 15 | 1 | **30** | **1** |

**QUINN, Robert* (M)** **240** **8**
H: 5 11 W: 11 02 b.Sidcup 8-11-76
*Source:* Trainee.

| | | | | | |
|---|---|---|---|---|---|
| 1994–95 | Crystal Palace | 0 | 0 | | |
| 1995–96 | Crystal Palace | 1 | 0 | | |
| 1996–97 | Crystal Palace | 21 | 1 | | |
| 1997–98 | Crystal Palace | 1 | 0 | **23** | **1** |
| 1998–99 | Brentford | 43 | 2 | | |
| 1999–2000 | Brentford | 44 | 0 | | |
| 2000–01 | Brentford | 22 | 0 | **109** | **2** |
| 2000–01 | Oxford U | 13 | 2 | | |
| 2001–02 | Oxford U | 16 | 0 | **29** | **2** |
| 2002–03 | Bristol R | 44 | 2 | | |
| 2003–04 | Bristol R | 35 | 1 | **79** | **3** |

**RAMMELL, Andy* (F)** **409** **111**
H: 6 1 W: 13 12 b.Nuneaton 10-2-67
*Source:* Atherstone U.

| | | | | | |
|---|---|---|---|---|---|
| 1989–90 | Manchester U | 0 | 0 | | |
| 1990–91 | Barnsley | 40 | 12 | | |
| 1991–92 | Barnsley | 37 | 8 | | |
| 1992–93 | Barnsley | 30 | 7 | | |
| 1993–94 | Barnsley | 34 | 6 | | |
| 1994–95 | Barnsley | 24 | 7 | | |
| 1995–96 | Barnsley | 20 | 4 | **185** | **44** |
| 1995–96 | Southend U | 7 | 2 | | |
| 1996–97 | Southend U | 36 | 9 | | |
| 1997–98 | Southend U | 26 | 2 | **69** | **13** |
| 1998–99 | Walsall | 39 | 18 | | |
| 1999–2000 | Walsall | 30 | 5 | | |
| 2000–01 | Walsall | 0 | 0 | **69** | **23** |
| 2000–01 | Wycombe W | 26 | 10 | | |
| 2001–02 | Wycombe W | 27 | 11 | | |
| 2002–03 | Wycombe W | 21 | 4 | **74** | **25** |
| 2002–03 | Bristol R | 7 | 4 | | |
| 2003–04 | Bristol R | 5 | 2 | **12** | **6** |

**SAVAGE, David (M)** **368** **31**
H: 6 2 W: 12 07 b.Dublin 30-7-73
*Source:* Longford T. *Honours:* Eire Under-21, 5 full caps.

| | | | | | |
|---|---|---|---|---|---|
| 1994–95 | Millwall | 37 | 2 | | |
| 1995–96 | Millwall | 27 | 0 | | |
| 1996–97 | Millwall | 35 | 3 | | |
| 1997–98 | Millwall | 31 | 1 | | |
| 1998–99 | Millwall | 2 | 0 | **132** | **6** |
| 1998–99 | Northampton T | 27 | 5 | | |
| 1999–2000 | Northampton T | 43 | 5 | | |
| 2000–01 | Northampton T | 43 | 8 | **113** | **18** |
| 2001–02 | Oxford U | 42 | 1 | | |
| 2002–03 | Oxford U | 43 | 4 | **85** | **5** |
| 2003–04 | Bristol R | 38 | 2 | **38** | **2** |

**STREET, Kevin‡ (M)** **150** **11**
H: 5 10 W: 11 02 b.Crewe 25-11-77
*Source:* Trainee.

| | | | | | |
|---|---|---|---|---|---|
| 1996–97 | Crewe Alex | 0 | 0 | | |
| 1997–98 | Crewe Alex | 32 | 4 | | |
| 1998–99 | Crewe Alex | 23 | 2 | | |
| 1999–2000 | Crewe Alex | 28 | 1 | | |
| 2000–01 | Crewe Alex | 23 | 1 | | |
| 2001–02 | *Luton T* | 2 | 0 | **2** | **0** |
| 2001–02 | Crewe Alex | 9 | 1 | | |
| 2002–03 | Crewe Alex | 0 | 0 | **115** | **9** |
| From Northwich Vic. | | | | | |
| 2002–03 | Bristol R | 20 | 1 | | |
| 2003–04 | Bristol R | 13 | 1 | **33** | **2** |

**TAIT, Paul* (F)** **144** **25**
H: 6 1 W: 11 10 b.Newcastle 24-10-74
*Source:* Trainee.

| | | | | | |
|---|---|---|---|---|---|
| 1993–94 | Everton | 0 | 0 | | |
| 1994–95 | Wigan Ath | 5 | 0 | | |
| 1995–96 | Wigan Ath | 0 | 0 | **5** | **0** |
| From Northwich Vic. | | | | | |
| 1999–2000 | Crewe Alex | 33 | 6 | | |
| 2000–01 | Crewe Alex | 18 | 0 | | |
| 2001–02 | *Hull C* | 2 | 0 | **2** | **0** |
| 2001–02 | Crewe Alex | 12 | 0 | **63** | **6** |
| 2002–03 | Bristol R | 41 | 7 | | |
| 2003–04 | Bristol R | 33 | 12 | **74** | **19** |

**THORPE, Lee (F)** **275** **71**
H: 6 1 W: 12 07 b.Wolverhampton 14-12-75
*Source:* Trainee.

| | | | | | |
|---|---|---|---|---|---|
| 1993–94 | Blackpool | 1 | 0 | | |
| 1994–95 | Blackpool | 1 | 0 | | |
| 1995–96 | Blackpool | 1 | 0 | | |
| 1996–97 | Blackpool | 9 | 0 | **12** | **0** |
| 1997–98 | Lincoln C | 44 | 14 | | |

| | | | | | |
|---|---|---|---|---|---|
| 1998–99 | Lincoln C | 38 | 8 | | |
| 1999–2000 | Lincoln C | 42 | 16 | | |
| 2000–01 | Lincoln C | 31 | 7 | | |
| 2001–02 | Lincoln C | 37 | 13 | **192** | **58** |
| 2001–02 | Leyton Orient | 0 | 0 | | |
| 2002–03 | Leyton Orient | 38 | 8 | | |
| 2003–04 | Leyton Orient | 17 | 4 | **55** | **12** |
| 2003–04 | *Grimsby T* | 6 | 0 | **6** | **0** |
| 2003–04 | Bristol R | 10 | 1 | **10** | **1** |

**U'DDIN, Anwar* (D)** **19 1**
H: 5 11 W: 11 10 b.Whitechapel 1-11-81
*Source:* West Ham U Scholar.

| | | | | | |
|---|---|---|---|---|---|
| 2001–02 | West Ham U | 0 | 0 | | |
| 2001–02 | Sheffield W | 0 | 0 | | |
| 2002–03 | Bristol R | 18 | 1 | | |
| 2003–04 | Bristol R | 1 | 0 | **19** | **1** |

**WILLIAMS, Danny* (M)** **156 12**
H: 6 1 W: 13 06 b.Wrexham 12-7-79
*Source:* Trainee. *Honours:* Wales Under-21.

| | | | | | |
|---|---|---|---|---|---|
| 1996–97 | Liverpool | 0 | 0 | | |
| 1997–98 | Liverpool | 0 | 0 | | |
| 1998–99 | Liverpool | 0 | 0 | | |
| 1998–99 | Wrexham | 0 | 0 | | |
| 1999–2000 | Wrexham | 24 | 1 | | |
| 2000–01 | Wrexham | 15 | 2 | **39** | **3** |
| 2001–02 | Kidderminster H | 38 | 1 | | |
| 2002–03 | Kidderminster H | 45 | 2 | | |
| 2003–04 | Kidderminster H | 28 | 5 | **111** | **8** |
| 2003–04 | Bristol R | 6 | 1 | **6** | **1** |

**WILLIAMS, Ryan (M)** **177 19**
H: 5 5 W: 11 04 b.Sutton-in-Ashfield 31-8-78
*Source:* Trainee. *Honours:* England Youth.

| | | | | | |
|---|---|---|---|---|---|
| 1995–96 | Mansfield T | 10 | 3 | | |
| 1996–97 | Mansfield T | 16 | 0 | **26** | **3** |
| 1997–98 | Tranmere R | 0 | 0 | | |
| 1998–99 | Tranmere R | 5 | 0 | | |
| 1999–2000 | Tranmere R | 0 | 0 | **5** | **0** |
| 1999–2000 | Chesterfield | 30 | 5 | | |
| 2000–01 | Chesterfield | 45 | 8 | **75** | **13** |
| 2001–02 | Hull C | 29 | 2 | | |
| 2002–03 | Hull C | 23 | 0 | | |
| 2003–04 | Hull C | 0 | 0 | **52** | **2** |
| 2003–04 | Bristol R | 19 | 1 | **19** | **1** |

**Scholars**
Duharty, Marcus; Guibarra, Daniel G; Hill, Matthew P; Hobbs, Shane M; Jones, Samuel M; Nestor, Christopher J; O'Neill, Darren; Price, Graham; Webb, Victor; Weisberg, Ryan P; Wilson, Dene

**Non Contract**
Arndale, Neil D; Greaves, Daniel G; Jinadu, Tobi

**Players who do not hold a current contract but their registration has been retained by the club**
Pierre, Nigel N

## BURNLEY (15)

**ABBEY, Nathan‡ (G)** **106 0**
H: 6 0 W: 11 03 b.Islington 11-7-78
*Source:* Trainee.

| | | | | | |
|---|---|---|---|---|---|
| 1995–96 | Luton T | 0 | 0 | | |
| 1996–97 | Luton T | 0 | 0 | | |
| 1997–98 | Luton T | 0 | 0 | | |
| 1998–99 | Luton T | 2 | 0 | | |
| 1999–2000 | Luton T | 33 | 0 | | |
| 2000–01 | Luton T | 20 | 0 | | |
| 2001–02 | Chesterfield | 46 | 0 | **46** | **0** |
| 2002–03 | Northampton T | 5 | 0 | **5** | **0** |
| 2003–04 | Luton T | 0 | 0 | **55** | **0** |
| 2003–04 | Macclesfield T | 0 | 0 | | |
| 2003–04 | Ipswich T | 0 | 0 | | |
| 2003–04 | Burnley | 0 | 0 | | |

**BLAKE, Robbie (F)** **328 94**
H: 5 9 W: 11 00 b.Middlesbrough 4-3-76
*Source:* Trainee.

| | | | | | |
|---|---|---|---|---|---|
| 1994–95 | Darlington | 9 | 0 | | |
| 1995–96 | Darlington | 29 | 11 | | |
| 1996–97 | Darlington | 30 | 10 | **68** | **21** |
| 1996–97 | Bradford C | 5 | 0 | | |
| 1997–98 | Bradford C | 34 | 8 | | |
| 1998–99 | Bradford C | 39 | 16 | | |
| 1999–2000 | Bradford C | 28 | 2 | | |
| 2000–01 | Bradford C | 21 | 4 | | |
| 2000–01 | *Nottingham F* | 11 | 1 | **11** | **1** |
| 2001–02 | Bradford C | 26 | 10 | **153** | **40** |
| 2001–02 | Burnley | 10 | 0 | | |
| 2002–03 | Burnley | 41 | 13 | | |
| 2003–04 | Burnley | 45 | 19 | **96** | **32** |

**BRANCH, Graham (D)** **302 26**
H: 6 2 W: 12 02 b.Liverpool 12-2-72
*Source:* Heswall.

| | | | | | |
|---|---|---|---|---|---|
| 1991–92 | Tranmere R | 4 | 0 | | |
| 1992–93 | Tranmere R | 3 | 0 | | |
| 1992–93 | *Bury* | 4 | 1 | **4** | **1** |
| 1993–94 | Tranmere R | 13 | 0 | | |
| 1994–95 | Tranmere R | 1 | 0 | | |
| 1995–96 | Tranmere R | 21 | 2 | | |
| 1996–97 | Tranmere R | 35 | 5 | | |
| 1997–98 | Tranmere R | 25 | 3 | **102** | **10** |
| 1997–98 | *Wigan Ath* | 3 | 0 | **3** | **0** |
| 1998–99 | Stockport Co | 14 | 3 | **14** | **3** |
| 1998–99 | Burnley | 20 | 1 | | |
| 1999–2000 | Burnley | 44 | 3 | | |
| 2000–01 | Burnley | 35 | 5 | | |
| 2001–02 | Burnley | 10 | 0 | | |
| 2002–03 | Burnley | 32 | 0 | | |
| 2003–04 | Burnley | 38 | 3 | **179** | **12** |

**CAMARA, Mo (D)** **207 2**
H: 5 11 W: 11 09 b.Conakry 25-6-75

| | | | | | |
|---|---|---|---|---|---|
| 1993–94 | Beauvais | 19 | 0 | | |
| 1994–95 | Beauvais | 0 | 0 | | |
| 1995–96 | Troyes | 13 | 0 | **13** | **0** |
| 1996–97 | Beauvais | 35 | 0 | **54** | **0** |
| 1997–98 | Le Havre | 14 | 0 | | |
| 1998–99 | Lille | 34 | 2 | **34** | **2** |
| 1999–2000 | Le Havre | 2 | 0 | **16** | **0** |
| 2000–01 | Wolverhampton W | 18 | 0 | | |
| 2001–02 | Wolverhampton W | 27 | 0 | | |
| 2002–03 | Wolverhampton W | 0 | 0 | **45** | **0** |
| 2003–04 | Burnley | 45 | 0 | **45** | **0** |

**CHAPLOW, Richard (M)** **44 5**
H: 5 9 W: 9 0 b.Accrington 2-2-85
*Source:* Scholar. *Honours:* England Youth, Under-21.

| | | | | | |
|---|---|---|---|---|---|
| 2002–03 | Burnley | 5 | 0 | | |
| 2003–04 | Burnley | 39 | 5 | **44** | **5** |

**GRANT, Tony (M)** **198 4**
H: 5 11 W: 10 10 b.Liverpool 14-11-74
*Source:* Trainee. *Honours:* England Under-21.

| | | | | | |
|---|---|---|---|---|---|
| 1993–94 | Everton | 0 | 0 | | |
| 1994–95 | Everton | 5 | 0 | | |
| 1995–96 | Everton | 13 | 1 | | |
| 1995–96 | *Swindon T* | 3 | 1 | **3** | **1** |
| 1996–97 | Everton | 18 | 0 | | |
| 1997–98 | Everton | 7 | 1 | | |
| 1998–99 | Everton | 16 | 0 | | |
| 1999–2000 | Everton | 2 | 0 | **61** | **2** |
| 1999–2000 | *Tranmere R* | 9 | 0 | **9** | **0** |
| 1999–2000 | Manchester C | 8 | 0 | | |
| 2000–01 | Manchester C | 10 | 0 | | |
| 2000–01 | *WBA* | 5 | 0 | **5** | **0** |
| 2001–02 | Manchester C | 3 | 0 | **21** | **0** |
| 2001–02 | Burnley | 28 | 0 | | |
| 2002–03 | Burnley | 34 | 1 | | |
| 2003–04 | Burnley | 37 | 0 | **99** | **1** |

**JENSEN, Brian (G)** **93 0**
H: 6 4 W: 12 04 b.Copenhagen 8-6-75

| | | | | | |
|---|---|---|---|---|---|
| 1997–98 | AZ | 0 | 0 | | |
| 1998–99 | AZ | 1 | 0 | **1** | **0** |
| 1999–2000 | WBA | 12 | 0 | | |
| 2000–01 | WBA | 33 | 0 | | |
| 2001–02 | WBA | 1 | 0 | | |
| 2002–03 | WBA | 0 | 0 | **46** | **0** |
| 2003–04 | Burnley | 46 | 0 | **46** | **0** |

**JOHNROSE, Lenny (M)** **430 49**
H: 5 10 W: 12 06 b.Preston 29-11-69
*Source:* Trainee.

| | | | | | |
|---|---|---|---|---|---|
| 1987–88 | Blackburn R | 1 | 0 | | |
| 1988–89 | Blackburn R | 0 | 0 | | |
| 1989–90 | Blackburn R | 8 | 3 | | |
| 1990–91 | Blackburn R | 26 | 7 | | |
| 1991–92 | Blackburn R | 7 | 1 | **42** | **11** |
| 1991–92 | *Preston NE* | 3 | 1 | **3** | **1** |
| 1991–92 | Hartlepool U | 15 | 2 | | |
| 1992–93 | Hartlepool U | 38 | 6 | | |
| 1993–94 | Hartlepool U | 13 | 3 | **66** | **11** |
| 1993–94 | Bury | 14 | 0 | | |
| 1994–95 | Bury | 26 | 4 | | |
| 1995–96 | Bury | 34 | 6 | | |
| 1996–97 | Bury | 43 | 4 | | |
| 1997–98 | Bury | 44 | 3 | | |
| 1998–99 | Bury | 27 | 2 | | |
| 1998–99 | Burnley | 12 | 1 | | |
| 1999–2000 | Burnley | 35 | 2 | | |
| 2000–01 | Burnley | 19 | 1 | | |
| 2001–02 | Burnley | 6 | 0 | | |
| 2002–03 | Burnley | 6 | 0 | | |
| 2002–03 | Bury | 6 | 0 | **194** | **19** |
| 2002–03 | Swansea C | 15 | 3 | | |
| 2003–04 | Swansea C | 25 | 0 | **40** | **3** |
| 2003–04 | Burnley | 7 | 0 | **85** | **4** |

**LITTLE, Glen* (M)** **262 35**
H: 6 3 W: 13 00 b.Wimbledon 15-10-75
*Source:* Trainee.

| | | | | | |
|---|---|---|---|---|---|
| 1994–95 | Crystal Palace | 0 | 0 | | |
| 1995–96 | Crystal Palace | 0 | 0 | | |
| 1996–97 | Glentoran | 6 | 2 | **6** | **2** |
| 1996–97 | Burnley | 9 | 0 | | |
| 1997–98 | Burnley | 24 | 4 | | |
| 1998–99 | Burnley | 34 | 5 | | |
| 1999–2000 | Burnley | 41 | 3 | | |
| 2000–01 | Burnley | 34 | 3 | | |
| 2001–02 | Burnley | 37 | 9 | | |
| 2002–03 | Burnley | 33 | 5 | | |
| 2002–03 | *Reading* | 6 | 1 | **6** | **1** |
| 2003–04 | Burnley | 34 | 3 | **246** | **32** |
| 2003–04 | *Bolton W* | 4 | 0 | **4** | **0** |

**MAY, David# (D)** **244 13**
H: 6 0 W: 12 10 b.Oldham 24-6-70
*Source:* Trainee.

| | | | | | |
|---|---|---|---|---|---|
| 1988–89 | Blackburn R | 1 | 0 | | |
| 1989–90 | Blackburn R | 17 | 0 | | |
| 1990–91 | Blackburn R | 19 | 1 | | |
| 1991–92 | Blackburn R | 12 | 0 | | |
| 1992–93 | Blackburn R | 34 | 1 | | |
| 1993–94 | Blackburn R | 40 | 1 | **123** | **3** |
| 1994–95 | Manchester U | 19 | 2 | | |
| 1995–96 | Manchester U | 16 | 1 | | |
| 1996–97 | Manchester U | 29 | 3 | | |
| 1997–98 | Manchester U | 9 | 0 | | |
| 1998–99 | Manchester U | 6 | 0 | | |
| 1999–2000 | Manchester U | 1 | 0 | | |
| 1999–2000 | *Huddersfield T* | 1 | 0 | **1** | **0** |
| 2000–01 | Manchester U | 2 | 0 | | |
| 2001–02 | Manchester U | 2 | 0 | | |
| 2002–03 | Manchester U | 1 | 0 | **85** | **6** |
| 2003–04 | Burnley | 35 | 4 | **35** | **4** |

**McGREGOR, Mark# (D)** **298 13**
H: 5 10 W: 11 05 b.Chester 16-2-77
*Source:* Trainee.

| | | | | | |
|---|---|---|---|---|---|
| 1994–95 | Wrexham | 1 | 0 | | |
| 1995–96 | Wrexham | 32 | 1 | | |
| 1996–97 | Wrexham | 38 | 1 | | |
| 1997–98 | Wrexham | 42 | 2 | | |
| 1998–99 | Wrexham | 43 | 1 | | |
| 1999–2000 | Wrexham | 45 | 1 | | |
| 2000–01 | Wrexham | 43 | 5 | | |
| 2001–02 | Wrexham | 0 | 0 | **244** | **11** |
| 2001–02 | Burnley | 1 | 0 | | |
| 2002–03 | Burnley | 30 | 1 | | |
| 2003–04 | Burnley | 23 | 1 | **54** | **2** |

**MOORE, Alan* (M)** **192 18**
H: 5 10 W: 12 00 b.Dublin 25-11-74
*Source:* Rivermount. *Honours:* Eire Under-21, 8 full caps.

| | | | | | |
|---|---|---|---|---|---|
| 1991–92 | Middlesbrough | 0 | 0 | | |
| 1992–93 | Middlesbrough | 2 | 0 | | |
| 1993–94 | Middlesbrough | 42 | 10 | | |
| 1994–95 | Middlesbrough | 37 | 4 | | |
| 1995–96 | Middlesbrough | 12 | 0 | | |
| 1996–97 | Middlesbrough | 17 | 0 | | |
| 1997–98 | Middlesbrough | 4 | 0 | | |
| 1998–99 | Middlesbrough | 4 | 0 | | |
| 1998–99 | *Barnsley* | 5 | 0 | **5** | **0** |
| 1999–2000 | Middlesbrough | 0 | 0 | | |
| 2000–01 | Middlesbrough | 0 | 0 | **118** | **14** |
| 2001–02 | Burnley | 29 | 3 | | |
| 2002–03 | Burnley | 27 | 1 | | |
| 2003–04 | Burnley | 13 | 0 | **69** | **4** |

**MOORE, Ian (F) 330 66**
H: 5 11 W: 12 02 b.Birkenhead 26-8-76
*Source:* Trainee. *Honours:* England Youth, Under-21.

| | | | | | |
|---|---|---|---|---|---|
| 1994–95 | Tranmere R | 1 | 0 | | |
| 1995–96 | Tranmere R | 36 | 9 | | |
| 1996–97 | Tranmere R | 21 | 3 | **58** | **12** |
| 1996–97 | *Bradford C* | 6 | 0 | **6** | **0** |
| 1996–97 | Nottingham F | 5 | 0 | | |
| 1997–98 | Nottingham F | 10 | 1 | **15** | **1** |
| 1997–98 | *West Ham U* | 1 | 0 | **1** | **0** |
| 1998–99 | Stockport Co | 38 | 3 | | |
| 1999–2000 | Stockport Co | 38 | 10 | | |
| 2000–01 | Stockport Co | 17 | 7 | **93** | **20** |
| 2000–01 | Burnley | 27 | 5 | | |
| 2001–02 | Burnley | 46 | 11 | | |
| 2002–03 | Burnley | 44 | 8 | | |
| 2003–04 | Burnley | 40 | 9 | **157** | **33** |

**O'NEILL, Matt (F) 11 0**
H: 5 11 W: 10 00 b.Accrington 25-6-84
*Source:* Scholar.

| | | | | | |
|---|---|---|---|---|---|
| 2002–03 | Burnley | 7 | 0 | | |
| 2003–04 | Burnley | 4 | 0 | **11** | **0** |

**PILKINGTON, Joel (M) 1 0**
H: 5 8 W: 10 04 b.Accrington 1-8-84
*Source:* Scholar.

| | | | | | |
|---|---|---|---|---|---|
| 2003–04 | Burnley | 1 | 0 | **1** | **0** |

**RICHARD, Fabrice‡ (M) 0 0**
b.Saintes 16-8-73

| | | | | | |
|---|---|---|---|---|---|
| 2003–04 | Burnley | 0 | 0 | | |

**ROCHE, Lee (D) 67 1**
H: 5 10 W: 10 11 b.Bolton 28-10-80
*Source:* Trainee. *Honours:* England Youth, Under-21.

| | | | | | |
|---|---|---|---|---|---|
| 1998–99 | Manchester U | 0 | 0 | | |
| 1999–2000 | Manchester U | 0 | 0 | | |
| 2000–01 | Manchester U | 0 | 0 | | |
| 2000–01 | *Wrexham* | 41 | 0 | **41** | **0** |
| 2001–02 | Manchester U | 0 | 0 | | |
| 2002–03 | Manchester U | 1 | 0 | **1** | **0** |
| 2003–04 | Burnley | 25 | 1 | **25** | **1** |

**SCOTT, Paul§ (D) 2 0**
H: 5 10 W: 11 10 b.Burnley 29-1-85
*Source:* Scholar.

| | | | | | |
|---|---|---|---|---|---|
| 2003–04 | Burnley | 2 | 0 | **2** | **0** |

**TOWNSEND, Ryan§ (M) 1 0**
H: 6 0 W: 12 05 b.Tameside 2-9-85
*Source:* Scholar.

| | | | | | |
|---|---|---|---|---|---|
| 2003–04 | Burnley | 1 | 0 | **1** | **0** |

**WELLER, Paul# (M) 252 11**
H: 5 8 W: 11 02 b.Brighton 6-3-75
*Source:* Trainee.

| | | | | | |
|---|---|---|---|---|---|
| 1993–94 | Burnley | 0 | 0 | | |
| 1994–95 | Burnley | 0 | 0 | | |
| 1995–96 | Burnley | 25 | 1 | | |
| 1996–97 | Burnley | 31 | 2 | | |
| 1997–98 | Burnley | 39 | 2 | | |
| 1998–99 | Burnley | 1 | 0 | | |
| 1999–2000 | Burnley | 7 | 1 | | |
| 2000–01 | Burnley | 44 | 3 | | |
| 2001–02 | Burnley | 38 | 2 | | |
| 2002–03 | Burnley | 34 | 0 | | |
| 2003–04 | Burnley | 33 | 0 | **252** | **11** |

**WEST, Dean# (D) 387 33**
H: 5 10 W: 11 07 b.Leeds 5-12-72
*Source:* Leeds U Schoolboy.

| | | | | | |
|---|---|---|---|---|---|
| 1990–91 | Lincoln C | 1 | 1 | | |
| 1991–92 | Lincoln C | 32 | 3 | | |
| 1992–93 | Lincoln C | 19 | 3 | | |
| 1993–94 | Lincoln C | 18 | 6 | | |
| 1994–95 | Lincoln C | 41 | 6 | | |
| 1995–96 | Lincoln C | 8 | 1 | **119** | **20** |
| 1995–96 | Bury | 37 | 1 | | |
| 1996–97 | Bury | 46 | 4 | | |
| 1997–98 | Bury | 4 | 0 | | |
| 1998–99 | Bury | 23 | 3 | **110** | **8** |
| 1999–2000 | Burnley | 34 | 0 | | |
| 2000–01 | Burnley | 7 | 0 | | |
| 2001–02 | Burnley | 44 | 0 | | |
| 2002–03 | Burnley | 41 | 4 | | |
| 2003–04 | Burnley | 32 | 1 | **158** | **5** |

**Scholars**
Avery, Darrell L; Blakey, Sean; Booth, Joseph A; Carpenter, Rhys E; Hale, Michael A; Ince, Thomas A; Jones, Colin A; Pitham, Daniel J; Pugh, Marc A; Scott, Paul D; Taylor, Alexander R; Townsend, Ryan M G; Trotman, Neal A

## BURY (16)

**BARRASS, Matt† (D) 75 2**
H: 5 10 W: 12 05 b.Bury 28-2-80
*Source:* Trainee.

| | | | | | |
|---|---|---|---|---|---|
| 1999–2000 | Bury | 25 | 1 | | |
| 2000–01 | Bury | 5 | 0 | | |
| 2001–02 | Bury | 7 | 0 | | |
| 2002–03 | Bury | 16 | 0 | | |
| 2003–04 | Bury | 22 | 1 | **75** | **2** |

**CARTLEDGE, Jon§ (D) 11 1**
H: 6 2 W: 13 00 b.Carshalton 27-11-84
*Source:* Scholar.

| | | | | | |
|---|---|---|---|---|---|
| 2003–04 | Bury | 11 | 1 | **11** | **1** |

**CHARNOCK, Phil‡ (M) 182 9**
H: 5 11 W: 13 01 b.Southport 14-2-75
*Source:* Trainee.

| | | | | | |
|---|---|---|---|---|---|
| 1992–93 | Liverpool | 0 | 0 | | |
| 1993–94 | Liverpool | 0 | 0 | | |
| 1994–95 | Liverpool | 0 | 0 | | |
| 1995–96 | Liverpool | 0 | 0 | | |
| 1995–96 | *Blackpool* | 4 | 0 | **4** | **0** |
| 1996–97 | Liverpool | 0 | 0 | | |
| 1996–97 | Crewe Alex | 32 | 1 | | |
| 1997–98 | Crewe Alex | 33 | 3 | | |
| 1998–99 | Crewe Alex | 44 | 2 | | |
| 1999–2000 | Crewe Alex | 16 | 1 | | |
| 2000–01 | Crewe Alex | 9 | 0 | | |
| 2001–02 | Crewe Alex | 23 | 1 | **157** | **8** |
| 2002–03 | Port Vale | 18 | 1 | **18** | **1** |
| 2003–04 | Bury | 3 | 0 | **3** | **0** |

**CLEGG, George‡ (F) 78 9**
H: 5 10 W: 12 00 b.Manchester 16-11-80
*Source:* Trainee.

| | | | | | |
|---|---|---|---|---|---|
| 1999–2000 | Manchester U | 0 | 0 | | |
| 2000–01 | Manchester U | 0 | 0 | | |
| 2000–01 | *Wycombe W* | 10 | 0 | **10** | **0** |
| 2001–02 | Bury | 31 | 4 | | |
| 2002–03 | Bury | 31 | 5 | | |
| 2003–04 | Bury | 6 | 0 | **68** | **9** |

**CONNELL, Lee* (D) 58 9**
H: 6 1 W: 13 01 b.Bury 24-6-81
*Source:* Trainee.

| | | | | | |
|---|---|---|---|---|---|
| 1999–2000 | Bury | 2 | 0 | | |
| 2000–01 | Bury | 1 | 1 | | |
| 2001–02 | Bury | 13 | 0 | | |
| 2002–03 | Bury | 14 | 2 | | |
| 2003–04 | Bury | 28 | 6 | **58** | **9** |

**DUNFIELD, Terry (M) 60 4**
H: 5 11 W: 12 04 b.Vancouver 20-2-82
*Source:* Trainee. *Honours:* Canada Under-23, England Youth.

| | | | | | |
|---|---|---|---|---|---|
| 1998–99 | Manchester C | 0 | 0 | | |
| 1999–2000 | Manchester C | 0 | 0 | | |
| 2000–01 | Manchester C | 1 | 0 | | |
| 2001–02 | Manchester C | 0 | 0 | | |
| 2002–03 | Manchester C | 0 | 0 | **1** | **0** |
| 2002–03 | Bury | 29 | 2 | | |
| 2003–04 | Bury | 30 | 2 | **59** | **4** |

**DUXBURY, Lee (M) 596 66**
H: 5 10 W: 10 09 b.Keighley 7-10-69
*Source:* Trainee.

| | | | | | |
|---|---|---|---|---|---|
| 1988–89 | Bradford C | 1 | 0 | | |
| 1989–90 | Bradford C | 12 | 1 | | |
| 1989–90 | *Rochdale* | 10 | 0 | **10** | **0** |
| 1990–91 | Bradford C | 45 | 5 | | |
| 1991–92 | Bradford C | 46 | 5 | | |
| 1992–93 | Bradford C | 42 | 5 | | |
| 1993–94 | Bradford C | 43 | 9 | | |
| 1994–95 | Bradford C | 20 | 0 | | |
| 1994–95 | Huddersfield T | 26 | 2 | | |
| 1995–96 | Huddersfield T | 3 | 0 | **29** | **2** |
| 1995–96 | Bradford C | 30 | 4 | | |
| 1996–97 | Bradford C | 33 | 3 | **272** | **32** |
| 1996–97 | Oldham Ath | 12 | 1 | | |
| 1997–98 | Oldham Ath | 38 | 5 | | |
| 1998–99 | Oldham Ath | 41 | 6 | | |
| 1999–2000 | Oldham Ath | 43 | 4 | | |
| 2000–01 | Oldham Ath | 40 | 8 | | |
| 2001–02 | Oldham Ath | 40 | 4 | | |
| 2002–03 | Oldham Ath | 34 | 4 | **248** | **32** |
| 2003–04 | Bury | 37 | 0 | **37** | **0** |

**FLITCROFT, David† (M) 369 24**
H: 5 11 W: 14 05 b.Bolton 14-1-74
*Source:* Trainee.

| | | | | | |
|---|---|---|---|---|---|
| 1991–92 | Preston NE | 0 | 0 | | |
| 1992–93 | Preston NE | 8 | 2 | | |
| 1993–94 | Preston NE | 0 | 0 | **8** | **2** |
| 1993–94 | *Lincoln C* | 2 | 0 | **2** | **0** |
| 1993–94 | Chester C | 8 | 1 | | |
| 1994–95 | Chester C | 32 | 0 | | |
| 1995–96 | Chester C | 9 | 1 | | |
| 1996–97 | Chester C | 32 | 6 | | |
| 1997–98 | Chester C | 44 | 4 | | |
| 1998–99 | Chester C | 42 | 6 | **167** | **18** |
| 1999–2000 | Rochdale | 43 | 2 | | |
| 2000–01 | Rochdale | 41 | 0 | | |
| 2001–02 | Rochdale | 35 | 0 | | |
| 2002–03 | Rochdale | 41 | 2 | **160** | **4** |
| 2003–04 | Macclesfield T | 15 | 0 | **15** | **0** |
| 2003–04 | Bury | 17 | 0 | **17** | **0** |

**FORREST, Martyn‡ (M) 106 2**
H: 5 9 W: 11 07 b.Bury 2-1-79

| | | | | | |
|---|---|---|---|---|---|
| 1997–98 | Bury | 0 | 0 | | |
| 1998–99 | Bury | 1 | 0 | | |
| 1999–2000 | Bury | 15 | 0 | | |
| 2000–01 | Bury | 27 | 0 | | |
| 2001–02 | Bury | 34 | 1 | | |
| 2002–03 | Bury | 29 | 1 | | |
| 2003–04 | Bury | 0 | 0 | **106** | **2** |

**GARNER, Glyn (G) 99 0**
H: 6 2 W: 13 04 b.Pontypool 9-12-76
*Source:* Llanelli.

| | | | | | |
|---|---|---|---|---|---|
| 2000–01 | Bury | 0 | 0 | | |
| 2001–02 | Bury | 7 | 0 | | |
| 2002–03 | Bury | 46 | 0 | | |
| 2003–04 | Bury | 46 | 0 | **99** | **0** |

**GUNBY, Stephen‡ (M) 6 0**
H: 5 11 W: 13 03 b.Lincoln 14-4-84
*Source:* Scholar.

| | | | | | |
|---|---|---|---|---|---|
| 2001–02 | Bury | 1 | 0 | | |
| 2002–03 | Bury | 0 | 0 | | |
| 2003–04 | Bury | 5 | 0 | **6** | **0** |

**KENNEDY, Tom (D) 27 0**
H: 5 10 W: 11 01 b.Bury 24-6-85
*Source:* Scholar.

| | | | | | |
|---|---|---|---|---|---|
| 2002–03 | Bury | 0 | 0 | | |
| 2003–04 | Bury | 27 | 0 | **27** | **0** |

**NUGENT, Dave (F) 62 7**
H: 5 11 W: 12 00 b.Liverpool 2-5-85
*Source:* Scholar.

| | | | | | |
|---|---|---|---|---|---|
| 2001–02 | Bury | 5 | 0 | | |
| 2002–03 | Bury | 31 | 4 | | |
| 2003–04 | Bury | 26 | 3 | **62** | **7** |

**O'SHAUGHNESSY, Paul* (M) 45 1**
H: 5 10 W: 11 10 b.Bury 3-10-81
*Source:* Scholar.

| | | | | | |
|---|---|---|---|---|---|
| 2001–02 | Bury | 2 | 0 | | |
| 2002–03 | Bury | 16 | 0 | | |
| 2003–04 | Bury | 27 | 1 | **45** | **1** |

**PORTER, Chris (F) 39 9**
H: 6 1 W: 12 08 b.Wigan 12-12-83

| | | | | | |
|---|---|---|---|---|---|
| 2002–03 | Bury | 2 | 0 | | |
| 2003–04 | Bury | 37 | 9 | **39** | **9** |

**RICKERS, Paul† (M) 272 20**
H: 5 11 W: 12 04 b.Pontefract 9-5-75
*Source:* Trainee.

| | | | | | |
|---|---|---|---|---|---|
| 1993–94 | Oldham Ath | 0 | 0 | | |
| 1994–95 | Oldham Ath | 4 | 1 | | |
| 1995–96 | Oldham Ath | 23 | 0 | | |
| 1996–97 | Oldham Ath | 46 | 4 | | |
| 1997–98 | Oldham Ath | 40 | 4 | | |
| 1998–99 | Oldham Ath | 45 | 4 | | |
| 1999–2000 | Oldham Ath | 41 | 3 | | |
| 2000–01 | Oldham Ath | 38 | 2 | | |
| 2001–02 | Oldham Ath | 24 | 2 | **261** | **20** |
| 2002–03 | Northampton T | 11 | 0 | | |
| 2003–04 | Northampton T | 0 | 0 | **11** | **0** |
| 2003–04 | Bury | 0 | 0 | | |

**SEDDON, Gareth# (F) 79 17**
H: 5 9 W: 12 04 b.Burnley 23-5-80
*Source:* Atherstone U.

| | | | | | |
|---|---|---|---|---|---|
| 2001–02 | Bury | 35 | 6 | | |

| | | | | | |
|---|---|---|---|---|---|
| 2002–03 | Bury | 4 | 0 | | |
| 2003–04 | Bury | 40 | 11 | **79** | **17** |

**SOLLY, Lewis* (G)** **0 0**
H: 6 1 W: 13 00 b.Kent 5-1-84
*Source:* Scholar.

| | | | | | |
|---|---|---|---|---|---|
| 2003–04 | Bury | 0 | 0 | | |

**SWAILES, Danny (D)** **144 12**
H: 6 3 W: 13 03 b.Bolton 1-4-79
*Source:* Trainee.

| | | | | | |
|---|---|---|---|---|---|
| 1997–98 | Bury | 0 | 0 | | |
| 1998–99 | Bury | 0 | 0 | | |
| 1999–2000 | Bury | 24 | 3 | | |
| 2000–01 | Bury | 11 | 0 | | |
| 2001–02 | Bury | 28 | 1 | | |
| 2002–03 | Bury | 39 | 3 | | |
| 2003–04 | Bury | 42 | 5 | **144** | **12** |

**THOMPSON, Justin‡ (D)** **1 0**
H: 6 2 W: 13 10 b.Prince Rupert 9-1-81

| | | | | | |
|---|---|---|---|---|---|
| 2003–04 | Bury | 1 | 0 | **1** | **0** |

**THORNLEY, Ben‡ (M)** **171 11**
H: 5 9 W: 11 08 b.Bury 21-4-75
*Source:* Trainee. *Honours:* England Schools, Under-21.

| | | | | | |
|---|---|---|---|---|---|
| 1992–93 | Manchester U | 0 | 0 | | |
| 1993–94 | Manchester U | 1 | 0 | | |
| 1994–95 | Manchester U | 0 | 0 | | |
| 1995–96 | Manchester U | 1 | 0 | | |
| 1995–96 | *Stockport Co* | 10 | 1 | **10** | **1** |
| 1995–96 | *Huddersfield T* | 12 | 2 | | |
| 1996–97 | Manchester U | 2 | 0 | | |
| 1997–98 | Manchester U | 5 | 0 | **9** | **0** |
| 1998–99 | Huddersfield T | 35 | 4 | | |
| 1999–2000 | Huddersfield T | 28 | 1 | | |
| 2000–01 | Huddersfield T | 36 | 0 | **111** | **7** |
| 2001–02 | Aberdeen | 24 | 3 | **24** | **3** |
| 2002–03 | Blackpool | 12 | 0 | **12** | **0** |
| 2003–04 | Bury | 5 | 0 | **5** | **0** |

**UNSWORTH, Lee# (D)** **238 5**
H: 5 11 W: 11 09 b.Eccles 25-2-73
*Source:* Ashton U.

| | | | | | |
|---|---|---|---|---|---|
| 1994–95 | Crewe Alex | 0 | 0 | | |
| 1995–96 | Crewe Alex | 29 | 0 | | |
| 1996–97 | Crewe Alex | 29 | 0 | | |
| 1997–98 | Crewe Alex | 36 | 0 | | |
| 1998–99 | Crewe Alex | 24 | 0 | | |
| 1999–2000 | Crewe Alex | 8 | 0 | **126** | **0** |
| 2000–01 | Bury | 15 | 0 | | |
| 2001–02 | Bury | 35 | 1 | | |
| 2002–03 | Bury | 35 | 2 | | |
| 2003–04 | Bury | 27 | 2 | **112** | **5** |

**WHALEY, Simon (F)** **12 1**
H: 5 10 W: 11 11 b.Bolton 7-6-85
*Source:* Scholar.

| | | | | | |
|---|---|---|---|---|---|
| 2002–03 | Bury | 2 | 0 | | |
| 2003–04 | Bury | 10 | 1 | **12** | **1** |

**WOODTHORPE, Colin# (D)** **470 12**
H: 6 0 W: 11 08 b.Ellesmere Pt 13-1-69
*Source:* Apprentice.

| | | | | | |
|---|---|---|---|---|---|
| 1986–87 | Chester C | 30 | 2 | | |
| 1987–88 | Chester C | 35 | 0 | | |
| 1988–89 | Chester C | 44 | 3 | | |
| 1989–90 | Chester C | 46 | 1 | **155** | **6** |
| 1990–91 | Norwich C | 1 | 0 | | |
| 1991–92 | Norwich C | 15 | 1 | | |
| 1992–93 | Norwich C | 7 | 0 | | |
| 1993–94 | Norwich C | 20 | 0 | **43** | **1** |
| 1994–95 | Aberdeen | 14 | 0 | | |
| 1995–96 | Aberdeen | 15 | 1 | | |
| 1996–97 | Aberdeen | 19 | 0 | **48** | **1** |
| 1997–98 | Stockport Co | 32 | 1 | | |
| 1998–99 | Stockport Co | 37 | 2 | | |
| 1999–2000 | Stockport Co | 26 | 0 | | |
| 2000–01 | Stockport Co | 24 | 1 | | |
| 2001–02 | Stockport Co | 34 | 0 | | |
| 2002–03 | Stockport Co | 0 | 0 | **153** | **4** |
| 2002–03 | Bury | 32 | 0 | | |
| 2003–04 | Bury | 39 | 0 | **71** | **0** |

**Scholars**
Adams, Nicolas W; Barrow, James G; Bernard, Ryan A L; Buchanan, David T H; Cartledge, Jon; Collinge, Peter J; Douglas-Pringle, Daniel F; Hitchen, Russell G; Horrocks, Luke A; Kazim-Richards, Colin; Maden, Steven A; Maloney, Ryan S; McDonald, Karl; Roscoe, Shaun M; Turner, Milton

**Non Contract**
Barrass, Matthew R; Flitcroft, David J; Rickers, Paul S

## CAMBRIDGE U (17)

**ANGUS, Stevland (D)** **130 1**
H: 6 0 W: 12 00 b.Essex 16-9-80
*Source:* Trainee.

| | | | | | |
|---|---|---|---|---|---|
| 1999–2000 | West Ham U | 0 | 0 | | |
| 2000–01 | West Ham U | 0 | 0 | | |
| 2000–01 | *Bournemouth* | 9 | 0 | **9** | **0** |
| 2001–02 | Cambridge U | 41 | 0 | | |
| 2002–03 | Cambridge U | 40 | 0 | | |
| 2003–04 | Cambridge U | 40 | 1 | **121** | **1** |

**BIMSON, Stuart (D)** **235 4**
H: 5 11 W: 11 12 b.Liverpool 29-9-69
*Source:* Macclesfield T.

| | | | | | |
|---|---|---|---|---|---|
| 1994–95 | Bury | 19 | 0 | | |
| 1995–96 | Bury | 16 | 0 | | |
| 1996–97 | Bury | 1 | 0 | **36** | **0** |
| 1996–97 | Lincoln C | 15 | 1 | | |
| 1997–98 | Lincoln C | 12 | 0 | | |
| 1998–99 | Lincoln C | 31 | 2 | | |
| 1999–2000 | Lincoln C | 20 | 0 | | |
| 2000–01 | Lincoln C | 20 | 0 | | |
| 2001–02 | Lincoln C | 35 | 0 | | |
| 2002–03 | Lincoln C | 42 | 1 | **175** | **4** |
| 2003–04 | Cambridge U | 24 | 0 | **24** | **0** |

**BRENNAN, Martin (G)** **1 0**
H: 6 1 W: 12 00 b.Whipps Cross 14-9-82

| | | | | | |
|---|---|---|---|---|---|
| 2000–01 | Charlton Ath | 0 | 0 | | |
| 2001–02 | Charlton Ath | 0 | 0 | | |
| 2002–03 | Cambridge U | 1 | 0 | | |
| 2003–04 | Cambridge U | 0 | 0 | **1** | **0** |

**BRIDGES, David (M)** **45 5**
H: 6 0 W: 12 00 b.Huntingdon 22-9-82
*Source:* Scholar.

| | | | | | |
|---|---|---|---|---|---|
| 2001–02 | Cambridge U | 7 | 1 | | |
| 2002–03 | Cambridge U | 17 | 2 | | |
| 2003–04 | Cambridge U | 21 | 2 | **45** | **5** |

**CHILLINGWORTH, Daniel (F)** **63 10**
H: 6 0 W: 12 06 b.Cambridge 13-9-81
*Source:* Scholarship.

| | | | | | |
|---|---|---|---|---|---|
| 1999–2000 | Cambridge U | 3 | 0 | | |
| 2000–01 | Cambridge U | 1 | 0 | | |
| 2001–02 | *Darlington* | 4 | 1 | **4** | **1** |
| 2001–02 | Cambridge U | 12 | 2 | | |
| 2002–03 | Cambridge U | 30 | 0 | | |
| 2003–04 | Cambridge U | 13 | 7 | **59** | **9** |

**CLARKE, Chris* (D)** **98 3**
H: 6 4 W: 12 04 b.Leeds 18-12-80
*Source:* Wolverhampton W Trainee.

| | | | | | |
|---|---|---|---|---|---|
| 1999–2000 | Halifax T | 1 | 0 | | |
| 2000–01 | Halifax T | 26 | 1 | | |
| 2001–02 | Halifax T | 24 | 0 | **51** | **1** |
| 2001–02 | Blackpool | 11 | 0 | | |
| 2002–03 | Blackpool | 17 | 1 | | |
| 2003–04 | Blackpool | 18 | 1 | **46** | **2** |
| 2003–04 | Cambridge U | 1 | 0 | **1** | **0** |

**DANIELS, David§ (M)** **1 0**
H: 5 8 W: 10 10 b.Bedford 14-9-85
*Source:* Scholar.

| | | | | | |
|---|---|---|---|---|---|
| 2003–04 | Cambridge U | 1 | 0 | **1** | **0** |

**DUNCAN, Andy# (D)** **200 5**
H: 5 11 W: 14 03 b.Hexham 20-10-77
*Source:* Trainee. *Honours:* England Schools.

| | | | | | |
|---|---|---|---|---|---|
| 1996–97 | Manchester U | 0 | 0 | | |
| 1997–98 | Manchester U | 0 | 0 | | |
| 1997–98 | Cambridge U | 19 | 0 | | |
| 1998–99 | Cambridge U | 45 | 1 | | |
| 1999–2000 | Cambridge U | 13 | 1 | | |
| 2000–01 | Cambridge U | 39 | 1 | | |
| 2001–02 | Cambridge U | 24 | 0 | | |
| 2002–03 | Cambridge U | 23 | 0 | | |
| 2003–04 | Cambridge U | 37 | 2 | **200** | **5** |

**DUTTON, Brian* (F)** **3 0**
H: 5 11 W: 12 00 b.Malton 12-4-85
*Source:* Pickering T.

| | | | | | |
|---|---|---|---|---|---|
| 2003–04 | Cambridge U | 3 | 0 | **3** | **0** |

**FLEMING, Terry* (M)** **381 15**
H: 5 9 W: 10 01 b.Marston Green 1-5-73
*Source:* Trainee.

| | | | | | |
|---|---|---|---|---|---|
| 1990–91 | Coventry C | 2 | 0 | | |
| 1991–92 | Coventry C | 0 | 0 | | |
| 1992–93 | Coventry C | 11 | 0 | **13** | **0** |
| 1993–94 | Northampton T | 31 | 1 | **31** | **1** |
| 1994–95 | Preston NE | 27 | 2 | | |
| 1995–96 | Preston NE | 5 | 0 | **32** | **2** |
| 1995–96 | Lincoln C | 22 | 0 | | |
| 1996–97 | Lincoln C | 37 | 0 | | |
| 1997–98 | Lincoln C | 40 | 3 | | |
| 1998–99 | Lincoln C | 43 | 0 | | |
| 1999–2000 | Lincoln C | 41 | 5 | **183** | **8** |
| 2000–01 | Plymouth Arg | 17 | 0 | **17** | **0** |
| 2000–01 | Cambridge U | 10 | 1 | | |
| 2001–02 | Cambridge U | 34 | 0 | | |
| 2002–03 | Cambridge U | 43 | 2 | | |
| 2003–04 | Cambridge U | 18 | 1 | **105** | **4** |

**FULLER, Ashley§ (M)** **1 0**
H: 5 9 W: 10 10 b.Bedford 14-11-86
*Source:* Scholar.

| | | | | | |
|---|---|---|---|---|---|
| 2003–04 | Cambridge U | 1 | 0 | **1** | **0** |

**GLEESON, Dan (M)** **7 0**
H: 6 3 W: 13 02 b.Cambridge 17-2-85
*Source:* Scholar.

| | | | | | |
|---|---|---|---|---|---|
| 2003–04 | Cambridge U | 7 | 0 | **7** | **0** |

**GOODHIND, Warren# (D)** **170 3**
H: 5 11 W: 11 02 b.Johannesburg 16-8-77
*Source:* Trainee.

| | | | | | |
|---|---|---|---|---|---|
| 1996–97 | Barnet | 3 | 0 | | |
| 1997–98 | Barnet | 35 | 1 | | |
| 1998–99 | Barnet | 15 | 1 | | |
| 1999–2000 | Barnet | 9 | 0 | | |
| 2000–01 | Barnet | 31 | 1 | | |
| 2001–02 | Barnet | 0 | 0 | **93** | **3** |
| 2001–02 | Cambridge U | 14 | 0 | | |
| 2002–03 | Cambridge U | 37 | 0 | | |
| 2003–04 | Cambridge U | 26 | 0 | **77** | **0** |

**GUTTRIDGE, Luke (M)** **120 17**
H: 5 5 W: 8 06 b.Barnstaple 27-3-82
*Source:* Trainee.

| | | | | | |
|---|---|---|---|---|---|
| 1999–2000 | Torquay U | 1 | 0 | | |
| 2000–01 | Torquay U | 0 | 0 | **1** | **0** |
| 2000–01 | Cambridge U | 1 | 1 | | |
| 2001–02 | Cambridge U | 29 | 2 | | |
| 2002–03 | Cambridge U | 43 | 3 | | |
| 2003–04 | Cambridge U | 46 | 11 | **119** | **17** |

**HEATHCOTE, Jon‡ (M)** **2 0**
H: 5 10 W: 11 02 b.Camberley 10-11-83
*Source:* Scholar.

| | | | | | |
|---|---|---|---|---|---|
| 2002–03 | Cambridge U | 2 | 0 | | |
| 2003–04 | Cambridge U | 0 | 0 | **2** | **0** |

**KELLY, Gavin† (G)** **0 0**
H: 6 0 W: 13 07 b.Hammersmith 3-6-81
*Source:* Trainee.

| | | | | | |
|---|---|---|---|---|---|
| 1999–2000 | Tottenham H | 0 | 0 | | |
| 2000–01 | Tottenham H | 0 | 0 | | |
| 2001–02 | Tottenham H | 0 | 0 | | |
| 2002–03 | Tottenham H | 0 | 0 | | |
| 2003–04 | Cambridge U | 0 | 0 | | |

**LOCKETT, Ryan§ (F)** **2 0**
H: 5 10 W: 11 08 b.Cambridge 11-11-86
*Source:* Scholar.

| | | | | | |
|---|---|---|---|---|---|
| 2003–04 | Cambridge U | 2 | 0 | **2** | **0** |

**MARSHALL, Shaun (G)** **154 0**
H: 6 1 W: 13 03 b.Fakenham 3-10-78
*Source:* Trainee.

| | | | | | |
|---|---|---|---|---|---|
| 1996–97 | Cambridge U | 1 | 0 | | |
| 1997–98 | Cambridge U | 2 | 0 | | |
| 1998–99 | Cambridge U | 19 | 0 | | |
| 1999–2000 | Cambridge U | 24 | 0 | | |
| 2000–01 | Cambridge U | 11 | 0 | | |
| 2001–02 | Cambridge U | 7 | 0 | | |
| 2002–03 | Cambridge U | 45 | 0 | | |
| 2003–04 | Cambridge U | 45 | 0 | **154** | **0** |

**MURRAY, Fred (D)** **88 0**
H: 5 10 W: 11 12 b.Tipperary 22-5-82
*Source:* Trainee.

| | | | | | |
|---|---|---|---|---|---|
| 1998–99 | Blackburn R | 0 | 0 | | |
| 1999–2000 | Blackburn R | 0 | 0 | | |
| 2000–01 | Blackburn R | 0 | 0 | | |
| 2001–02 | Blackburn R | 0 | 0 | | |
| 2001–02 | Cambridge U | 21 | 0 | | |

| | | | | | |
|---|---|---|---|---|---|
| 2002–03 | Cambridge U | 29 | 0 | | |
| 2003–04 | Cambridge U | 38 | 0 | 88 | 0 |

**NACCA, Franco (D)** **26 0**
H: 5 6 W: 10 00 b.Venezuela 9-11-82
*Source:* Scholar.

| | | | | | |
|---|---|---|---|---|---|
| 2000–01 | Cambridge U | 0 | 0 | | |
| 2001–02 | Cambridge U | 0 | 0 | | |
| 2002–03 | Cambridge U | 17 | 0 | | |
| 2003–04 | Cambridge U | 9 | 0 | 26 | 0 |

**OPARA, Lloyd‡ (F)** **16 1**
H: 6 1 W: 13 00 b.Edmonton 6-1-84
*Source:* Scholar.

| | | | | | |
|---|---|---|---|---|---|
| 2001–02 | Colchester U | 1 | 0 | | |
| 2002–03 | Colchester U | 5 | 0 | 6 | 0 |
| 2002–03 | Cambridge U | 2 | 0 | | |
| 2003–04 | Cambridge U | 8 | 1 | 10 | 1 |

**PRILASNIG, Gilbert* (M)** **0 0**
H: 6 0 W: 12 00 b.Austria 4-4-73
*Source:* Aris Salonika.

| | | | | | |
|---|---|---|---|---|---|
| 2003–04 | Cambridge U | 0 | 0 | | |

**QUINTON, Darren§ (M)** **1 0**
H: 5 8 W: 9 11 b.Romford 28-4-86
*Source:* Scholar.

| | | | | | |
|---|---|---|---|---|---|
| 2003–04 | Cambridge U | 1 | 0 | 1 | 0 |

**REVELL, Alex* (F)** **57 5**
H: 6 3 W: 13 00 b.Cambridge 7-7-83
*Source:* Scholar.

| | | | | | |
|---|---|---|---|---|---|
| 2000–01 | Cambridge U | 4 | 0 | | |
| 2001–02 | Cambridge U | 24 | 2 | | |
| 2002–03 | Cambridge U | 9 | 0 | | |
| 2003–04 | Cambridge U | 20 | 3 | 57 | 5 |

**ROBINSON, Matthew† (M)** **3 0**
H: 5 10 W: 11 06 b.Ipswich 22-3-84
*Source:* Scholar.

| | | | | | |
|---|---|---|---|---|---|
| 2003–04 | Ipswich T | 0 | 0 | | |
| 2003–04 | Bournemouth | 0 | 0 | | |
| 2003–04 | Cambridge U | 3 | 0 | 3 | 0 |

**RUDDY, John§ (G)** **1 0**
H: 6 4 W: 15 04 b.St Ives 24-10-86
*Source:* Scholar.

| | | | | | |
|---|---|---|---|---|---|
| 2003–04 | Cambridge U | 1 | 0 | 1 | 0 |

**SMITH, Stephen§ (M)** **2 0**
H: 5 8 W: 11 07 b.Harlow 19-9-86
*Source:* Scholar.

| | | | | | |
|---|---|---|---|---|---|
| 2003–04 | Cambridge U | 2 | 0 | 2 | 0 |

**TANN, Adam (D)** **85 3**
H: 6 0 W: 11 05 b.Fakenham 12-5-82
*Source:* Scholar. *Honours:* England Youth.

| | | | | | |
|---|---|---|---|---|---|
| 1999–2000 | Cambridge U | 0 | 0 | | |
| 2000–01 | Cambridge U | 1 | 0 | | |
| 2001–02 | Cambridge U | 25 | 0 | | |
| 2002–03 | Cambridge U | 25 | 1 | | |
| 2003–04 | Cambridge U | 34 | 2 | 85 | 3 |

**TUDOR, Shane (M)** **96 15**
H: 5 7 W: 11 00 b.Wolverhampton 10-2-82
*Source:* Trainee.

| | | | | | |
|---|---|---|---|---|---|
| 1999–2000 | Wolverhampton W | 0 | 0 | | |
| 2000–01 | Wolverhampton W | 1 | 0 | | |
| 2001–02 | Wolverhampton W | 0 | 0 | 1 | 0 |
| 2001–02 | Cambridge U | 32 | 3 | | |
| 2002–03 | Cambridge U | 27 | 9 | | |
| 2003–04 | Cambridge U | 36 | 3 | 95 | 15 |

**TURNER, John (F)** **37 4**
H: 5 10 W: 11 00 b.Harrow 12-2-86
*Source:* Scholar.

| | | | | | |
|---|---|---|---|---|---|
| 2002–03 | Cambridge U | 1 | 1 | | |
| 2003–04 | Cambridge U | 36 | 3 | 37 | 4 |

**VENUS, Mark‡ (D)** **521 24**
H: 6 0 W: 13 02 b.Hartlepool 6-4-67

| | | | | | |
|---|---|---|---|---|---|
| 1984–85 | Hartlepool U | 4 | 0 | 4 | 0 |
| 1985–86 | Leicester C | 1 | 0 | | |
| 1986–87 | Leicester C | 39 | 0 | | |
| 1987–88 | Leicester C | 21 | 1 | 61 | 1 |
| 1987–88 | Wolverhampton W | 4 | 0 | | |
| 1988–89 | Wolverhampton W | 35 | 0 | | |
| 1989–90 | Wolverhampton W | 44 | 2 | | |
| 1990–91 | Wolverhampton W | 6 | 0 | | |
| 1991–92 | Wolverhampton W | 46 | 1 | | |
| 1992–93 | Wolverhampton W | 12 | 0 | | |
| 1993–94 | Wolverhampton W | 39 | 1 | | |
| 1994–95 | Wolverhampton W | 39 | 3 | | |
| 1995–96 | Wolverhampton W | 22 | 0 | | |
| 1996–97 | Wolverhampton W | 40 | 0 | 287 | 7 |
| 1997–98 | Ipswich T | 14 | 1 | | |
| 1998–99 | Ipswich T | 44 | 9 | | |
| 1999–2000 | Ipswich T | 28 | 2 | | |
| 2000–01 | Ipswich T | 25 | 3 | | |
| 2001–02 | Ipswich T | 29 | 1 | | |
| 2002–03 | Ipswich T | 8 | 0 | 148 | 16 |
| 2003–04 | Cambridge U | 21 | 0 | 21 | 0 |

**WALKER, Justin# (M)** **279 12**
H: 5 11 W: 12 04 b.Nottingham 6-9-75
*Source:* Trainee. *Honours:* England Schools, Youth.

| | | | | | |
|---|---|---|---|---|---|
| 1992–93 | Nottingham F | 0 | 0 | | |
| 1993–94 | Nottingham F | 0 | 0 | | |
| 1994–95 | Nottingham F | 0 | 0 | | |
| 1995–96 | Nottingham F | 0 | 0 | | |
| 1996–97 | Nottingham F | 0 | 0 | | |
| 1996–97 | Scunthorpe U | 9 | 0 | | |
| 1997–98 | Scunthorpe U | 40 | 1 | | |
| 1998–99 | Scunthorpe U | 41 | 1 | | |
| 1999–2000 | Scunthorpe U | 42 | 0 | 132 | 2 |
| 2000–01 | Lincoln C | 45 | 1 | | |
| 2001–02 | Lincoln C | 31 | 3 | 76 | 4 |
| 2002–03 | Exeter C | 39 | 5 | 39 | 5 |
| 2003–04 | Cambridge U | 23 | 1 | 23 | 1 |
| 2003–04 | *York C* | 9 | 0 | 9 | 0 |

**WEBB, Daniel (F)** **88 8**
H: 6 1 W: 11 08 b.Poole 2-7-83

| | | | | | |
|---|---|---|---|---|---|
| 2000–01 | Southend U | 15 | 1 | | |
| 2001–02 | Southend U | 16 | 2 | | |
| 2001–02 | *Brighton & HA* | 12 | 1 | | |
| 2002–03 | Southend U | 0 | 0 | 31 | 3 |
| 2002–03 | *Brighton & HA* | 3 | 0 | 15 | 1 |
| 2002–03 | Hull C | 12 | 0 | | |
| 2002–03 | *Lincoln C* | 5 | 1 | 5 | 1 |
| 2003–04 | Hull C | 4 | 0 | 16 | 0 |
| 2003–04 | Cambridge U | 21 | 3 | 21 | 3 |

**Scholars**
Beech, Thomas P E; Daniels, David W; Davies, Adam G; Eastall, Duane E; Fuller, Ashley J; Hammond, Daniel J; Lockett, Ryan D C W; Meddows, Leigh J; Quinton, Darren J; Ruddy, John T G; Smith, James T; Smith, Stephen M, Stone, Brady T

**Non Contract**
Kelly, Gavin R; Pritchett, James K; Robbins, Nicholas E; Robinson, Matthew A; Turner, Steven T

**Players who do not hold a current contract but their registration has been retained by the club**
Millership, Jamie C; Okay, Erhan

## CARDIFF C (18)

**ALEXANDER, Neil (G)** **219 0**
H: 6 1 W: 11 07 b.Edinburgh 10-3-78
*Source:* Edina Hibs. *Honours:* Scotland Under-21.

| | | | | | |
|---|---|---|---|---|---|
| 1996–97 | Stenhousemuir | 12 | 0 | | |
| 1997–98 | Stenhousemuir | 36 | 0 | 48 | 0 |
| 1998–99 | Livingston | 21 | 0 | | |
| 1999–2000 | Livingston | 13 | 0 | | |
| 2000–01 | Livingston | 26 | 0 | 60 | 0 |
| 2001–02 | Cardiff C | 46 | 0 | | |
| 2002–03 | Cardiff C | 40 | 0 | | |
| 2003–04 | Cardiff C | 25 | 0 | 111 | 0 |

**ANTHONY, Byron (D)** **0 0**
H: 6 1 W: 11 00 b.Newport 20-9-84
*Source:* Scholar.

| | | | | | |
|---|---|---|---|---|---|
| 2003–04 | Cardiff C | 0 | 0 | | |

**BARKER, Chris (D)** **192 3**
H: 6 2 W: 11 08 b.Sheffield 2-3-80
*Source:* Alfreton.

| | | | | | |
|---|---|---|---|---|---|
| 1998–99 | Barnsley | 0 | 0 | | |
| 1999–2000 | Barnsley | 29 | 0 | | |
| 2000–01 | Barnsley | 40 | 0 | | |
| 2001–02 | Barnsley | 44 | 3 | 113 | 3 |
| 2002–03 | Cardiff C | 40 | 0 | | |
| 2003–04 | Cardiff C | 39 | 0 | 79 | 0 |

**BOLAND, Willie (M)** **236 3**
H: 5 9 W: 11 02 b.Ennis 6-8-75
*Source:* Trainee. *Honours:* Eire Youth, Under-21.

| | | | | | |
|---|---|---|---|---|---|
| 1992–93 | Coventry C | 1 | 0 | | |
| 1993–94 | Coventry C | 27 | 0 | | |
| 1994–95 | Coventry C | 12 | 0 | | |
| 1995–96 | Coventry C | 3 | 0 | | |
| 1996–97 | Coventry C | 1 | 0 | | |
| 1997–98 | Coventry C | 19 | 0 | | |
| 1998–99 | Coventry C | 0 | 0 | 63 | 0 |
| 1999–2000 | Cardiff C | 28 | 1 | | |
| 2000–01 | Cardiff C | 25 | 1 | | |
| 2001–02 | Cardiff C | 42 | 1 | | |
| 2002–03 | Cardiff C | 41 | 0 | | |
| 2003–04 | Cardiff C | 37 | 0 | 173 | 3 |

**BOWEN, Jason‡ (M)** **324 68**
H: 5 6 W: 8 10 b.Merthyr 24-8-72
*Source:* Trainee. *Honours:* Wales Schools, Youth, Under-21, 2 full caps.

| | | | | | |
|---|---|---|---|---|---|
| 1990–91 | Swansea C | 3 | 0 | | |
| 1991–92 | Swansea C | 11 | 0 | | |
| 1992–93 | Swansea C | 38 | 10 | | |
| 1993–94 | Swansea C | 41 | 11 | | |
| 1994–95 | Swansea C | 31 | 5 | 124 | 26 |
| 1995–96 | Birmingham C | 23 | 4 | | |
| 1996–97 | Birmingham C | 25 | 3 | | |
| 1997–98 | Birmingham C | 0 | 0 | 48 | 7 |
| 1997–98 | *Southampton* | 3 | 0 | 3 | 0 |
| 1997–98 | Reading | 14 | 1 | | |
| 1998–99 | Reading | 1 | 0 | 15 | 1 |
| 1998–99 | Cardiff C | 17 | 2 | | |
| 1999–2000 | Cardiff C | 39 | 12 | | |
| 2000–01 | Cardiff C | 40 | 12 | | |
| 2001–02 | Cardiff C | 25 | 5 | | |
| 2002–03 | Cardiff C | 11 | 3 | | |
| 2003–04 | Cardiff C | 2 | 0 | 134 | 34 |

**CAMPBELL, Andy (F)** **134 19**
H: 5 11 W: 11 07 b.Middlesbrough 18-4-79
*Source:* Trainee. *Honours:* England Youth, Under-21.

| | | | | | |
|---|---|---|---|---|---|
| 1995–96 | Middlesbrough | 2 | 0 | | |
| 1996–97 | Middlesbrough | 3 | 0 | | |
| 1997–98 | Middlesbrough | 7 | 0 | | |
| 1998–99 | Middlesbrough | 8 | 0 | | |
| 1998–99 | *Sheffield U* | 11 | 3 | 11 | 3 |
| 1999–2000 | Middlesbrough | 25 | 4 | | |
| 2000–01 | Middlesbrough | 7 | 0 | | |
| 2000–01 | *Bolton W* | 6 | 0 | 6 | 0 |
| 2001–02 | Middlesbrough | 4 | 0 | 56 | 4 |
| 2001–02 | Cardiff C | 8 | 7 | | |
| 2002–03 | Cardiff C | 28 | 3 | | |
| 2003–04 | Cardiff C | 25 | 2 | 61 | 12 |

**COLLINS, James (D)** **32 2**
H: 6 2 W: 13 00 b.Newport 23-8-83
*Source:* Scholar. *Honours:* Wales Youth, Under-21, 2 full caps.

| | | | | | |
|---|---|---|---|---|---|
| 2000–01 | Cardiff C | 3 | 0 | | |
| 2001–02 | Cardiff C | 7 | 1 | | |
| 2002–03 | Cardiff C | 2 | 0 | | |
| 2003–04 | Cardiff C | 20 | 1 | 32 | 2 |

**CROFT, Gary# (D)** **301 8**
H: 5 9 W: 11 08 b.Burton-on-Trent 17-2-74
*Source:* Trainee. *Honours:* England Under-21.

| | | | | | |
|---|---|---|---|---|---|
| 1990–91 | Grimsby T | 1 | 0 | | |
| 1991–92 | Grimsby T | 0 | 0 | | |
| 1992–93 | Grimsby T | 32 | 0 | | |
| 1993–94 | Grimsby T | 36 | 1 | | |
| 1994–95 | Grimsby T | 44 | 1 | | |
| 1995–96 | Grimsby T | 36 | 1 | 149 | 3 |
| 1995–96 | Blackburn R | 0 | 0 | | |
| 1996–97 | Blackburn R | 5 | 0 | | |
| 1997–98 | Blackburn R | 23 | 1 | | |
| 1998–99 | Blackburn R | 12 | 0 | | |
| 1999–2000 | Blackburn R | 0 | 0 | 40 | 1 |
| 1999–2000 | Ipswich T | 21 | 1 | | |
| 2000–01 | Ipswich T | 8 | 0 | | |
| 2001–02 | Ipswich T | 0 | 0 | 29 | 1 |
| 2001–02 | *Wigan Ath* | 7 | 0 | 7 | 0 |
| 2001–02 | *Cardiff C* | 6 | 1 | | |
| 2002–03 | Cardiff C | 43 | 1 | | |
| 2003–04 | Cardiff C | 27 | 1 | 76 | 3 |

**EARNSHAW, Robert (F)** **177 86**
H: 5 6 W: 9 09 b.Zambia 6-4-81
*Source:* Trainee. *Honours:* Wales Youth, Under-21, 13 full caps, 7 goals.

| | | | | | |
|---|---|---|---|---|---|
| 1997–98 | Cardiff C | 5 | 0 | | |
| 1998–99 | Cardiff C | 5 | 1 | | |
| 1998–99 | *Middlesbrough* | 0 | 0 | | |
| 1999–2000 | Cardiff C | 6 | 1 | | |
| 1999–2000 | *Morton* | 3 | 2 | 3 | 2 |

| | | | | | |
|---|---|---|---|---|---|
| 2000–01 | Cardiff C | 36 | 19 | | |
| 2001–02 | Cardiff C | 30 | 11 | | |
| 2002–03 | Cardiff C | 46 | 31 | | |
| 2003–04 | Cardiff C | 46 | 21 | **174** | **84** |

**FISH, Nicky (M)** **0** **0**
H: 5 10 W: 11 04 b.Cardiff 15-9-84
*Source:* Scholar.

| | | | | | |
|---|---|---|---|---|---|
| 2001–02 | Cardiff C | 0 | 0 | | |
| 2002–03 | Cardiff C | 0 | 0 | | |
| 2003–04 | Cardiff C | 0 | 0 | | |

**FLEETWOOD, Stuart (F)** **2** **0**
H: 5 10 W: 11 08 b.Gloucester 23-4-86
*Source:* Scholar. *Honours:* Wales Youth.

| | | | | | |
|---|---|---|---|---|---|
| 2003–04 | Cardiff C | 2 | 0 | **2** | **0** |

**GABBIDON, Daniel (D)** **172** **9**
H: 6 0 W: 11 02 b.Cwmbran 8-8-79
*Source:* Trainee. *Honours:* Wales Youth, Under-21, 12 full caps.

| | | | | | |
|---|---|---|---|---|---|
| 1998–99 | WBA | 2 | 0 | | |
| 1999–2000 | WBA | 18 | 0 | | |
| 2000–01 | WBA | 0 | 0 | **20** | **0** |
| 2000–01 | Cardiff C | 43 | 3 | | |
| 2001–02 | Cardiff C | 44 | 3 | | |
| 2002–03 | Cardiff C | 24 | 0 | | |
| 2003–04 | Cardiff C | 41 | 3 | **152** | **9** |

**GORDON, Gavin* (F)** **193** **43**
H: 6 1 W: 12 00 b.Manchester 24-6-79
*Source:* Trainee.

| | | | | | |
|---|---|---|---|---|---|
| 1995–96 | Hull C | 13 | 3 | | |
| 1996–97 | Hull C | 20 | 4 | | |
| 1997–98 | Hull C | 5 | 2 | **38** | **9** |
| 1997–98 | Lincoln C | 13 | 3 | | |
| 1998–99 | Lincoln C | 27 | 5 | | |
| 1999–2000 | Lincoln C | 41 | 11 | | |
| 2000–01 | Lincoln C | 18 | 9 | **99** | **28** |
| 2000–01 | Cardiff C | 10 | 1 | | |
| 2001–02 | Cardiff C | 15 | 1 | | |
| 2002–03 | Cardiff C | 10 | 2 | | |
| 2002–03 | *Oxford U* | 6 | 1 | **6** | **1** |
| 2003–04 | Cardiff C | 15 | 1 | **50** | **5** |

**HUGGINS, Kirk (D)** **0** **0**
H: 5 11 W: 11 03 b.Cardiff 4-6-85
*Source:* Scholar.

| | | | | | |
|---|---|---|---|---|---|
| 2002–03 | Cardiff C | 0 | 0 | | |
| 2003–04 | Cardiff C | 0 | 0 | | |

**INGRAM, Richard (F)** **0** **0**
H: 5 9 W: 10 08 b.Merthyr 15-2-85
*Source:* Scholar.

| | | | | | |
|---|---|---|---|---|---|
| 2001–02 | Cardiff C | 0 | 0 | | |
| 2002–03 | Cardiff C | 0 | 0 | | |
| 2003–04 | Cardiff C | 0 | 0 | | |

**KAVANAGH, Graham (M)** **360** **63**
H: 5 10 W: 12 08 b.Dublin 2-12-73
*Source:* Home Farm. *Honours:* Eire Under-21, 5 full caps, 1 goal.

| | | | | | |
|---|---|---|---|---|---|
| 1991–92 | Middlesbrough | 0 | 0 | | |
| 1992–93 | Middlesbrough | 10 | 0 | | |
| 1993–94 | Middlesbrough | 11 | 2 | | |
| 1993–94 | *Darlington* | 5 | 0 | **5** | **0** |
| 1994–95 | Middlesbrough | 7 | 0 | | |
| 1995–96 | Middlesbrough | 7 | 1 | | |
| 1996–97 | Middlesbrough | 0 | 0 | **35** | **3** |
| 1996–97 | Stoke C | 38 | 4 | | |
| 1997–98 | Stoke C | 44 | 5 | | |
| 1998–99 | Stoke C | 36 | 11 | | |
| 1999–2000 | Stoke C | 45 | 7 | | |
| 2000–01 | Stoke C | 43 | 8 | **206** | **35** |
| 2001–02 | Cardiff C | 43 | 13 | | |
| 2002–03 | Cardiff C | 44 | 5 | | |
| 2003–04 | Cardiff C | 27 | 7 | **114** | **25** |

**LANGLEY, Richard (M)** **177** **24**
H: 5 10 W: 11 04 b.Harlesden 27-12-79
*Source:* Trainee. *Honours:* England Youth. Jamaica 17 full caps.

| | | | | | |
|---|---|---|---|---|---|
| 1996–97 | QPR | 0 | 0 | | |
| 1997–98 | QPR | 0 | 0 | | |
| 1998–99 | QPR | 8 | 1 | | |
| 1999–2000 | QPR | 41 | 3 | | |
| 2000–01 | QPR | 26 | 1 | | |
| 2001–02 | QPR | 18 | 3 | | |
| 2002–03 | QPR | 39 | 9 | | |
| 2003–04 | QPR | 1 | 1 | **133** | **18** |
| 2003–04 | Cardiff C | 44 | 6 | **44** | **6** |

**LEE-BARRETT, Arran (G)** **0** **0**
H: 6 2 W: 12 10 b.Ipswich 28-2-84
*Source:* Norwich C Scholar.

| | | | | | |
|---|---|---|---|---|---|
| 2002–03 | Cardiff C | 0 | 0 | | |
| 2003–04 | Cardiff C | 0 | 0 | | |

**LEE, Alan (F)** **167** **44**
H: 6 2 W: 13 09 b.Galway 21-8-78
*Source:* Trainee. *Honours:* Eire Under-21, 7 full caps.

| | | | | | |
|---|---|---|---|---|---|
| 1995–96 | Aston Villa | 0 | 0 | | |
| 1996–97 | Aston Villa | 0 | 0 | | |
| 1997–98 | Aston Villa | 0 | 0 | | |
| 1998–99 | Aston Villa | 0 | 0 | | |
| 1998–99 | *Torquay U* | 7 | 2 | **7** | **2** |
| 1998–99 | *Port Vale* | 11 | 2 | **11** | **2** |
| 1999–2000 | Burnley | 15 | 0 | | |
| 2000–01 | Burnley | 0 | 0 | **15** | **0** |
| 2000–01 | Rotherham U | 31 | 13 | | |
| 2001–02 | Rotherham U | 38 | 9 | | |
| 2002–03 | Rotherham U | 41 | 15 | | |
| 2003–04 | Rotherham U | 1 | 0 | **111** | **37** |
| 2003–04 | Cardiff C | 23 | 3 | **23** | **3** |

**MARGETSON, Martyn# (G)** **162** **0**
H: 6 0 W: 13 12 b.West Neath 8-9-71
*Source:* Trainee. *Honours:* Wales Schools, Youth, Under-21, B, 1 full cap.

| | | | | | |
|---|---|---|---|---|---|
| 1990–91 | Manchester C | 2 | 0 | | |
| 1991–92 | Manchester C | 3 | 0 | | |
| 1992–93 | Manchester C | 1 | 0 | | |
| 1993–94 | Manchester C | 0 | 0 | | |
| 1993–94 | *Bristol R* | 3 | 0 | **3** | **0** |
| 1993–94 | *Bolton W* | 0 | 0 | | |
| 1994–95 | Manchester C | 0 | 0 | | |
| 1994–95 | *Luton T* | 0 | 0 | | |
| 1995–96 | Manchester C | 0 | 0 | | |
| 1996–97 | Manchester C | 17 | 0 | | |
| 1997–98 | Manchester C | 28 | 0 | **51** | **0** |
| 1998–99 | Southend U | 32 | 0 | **32** | **0** |
| 1999–2000 | Huddersfield T | 0 | 0 | | |
| 2000–01 | Huddersfield T | 2 | 0 | | |
| 2001–02 | Huddersfield T | 46 | 0 | **48** | **0** |
| 2002–03 | Cardiff C | 6 | 0 | | |
| 2003–04 | Cardiff C | 22 | 0 | **28** | **0** |

**PARKINS, Michael (M)** **0** **0**
H: 5 8 W: 11 02 b.Cardiff 12-1-85
*Source:* Scholar.

| | | | | | |
|---|---|---|---|---|---|
| 2001–02 | Cardiff C | 0 | 0 | | |
| 2002–03 | Cardiff C | 0 | 0 | | |
| 2003–04 | Cardiff C | 0 | 0 | | |

**PARRY, Paul (M)** **17** **1**
H: 5 11 W: 11 12 b.Newport 19-8-80
*Source:* Hereford U. *Honours:* Wales 3 full caps, 1 goal.

| | | | | | |
|---|---|---|---|---|---|
| 2003–04 | Cardiff C | 17 | 1 | **17** | **1** |

**PRIOR, Spencer* (D)** **438** **11**
H: 6 3 W: 13 00 b.Rochford 22-4-71
*Source:* Trainee.

| | | | | | |
|---|---|---|---|---|---|
| 1988–89 | Southend U | 14 | 1 | | |
| 1989–90 | Southend U | 15 | 1 | | |
| 1990–91 | Southend U | 19 | 0 | | |
| 1991–92 | Southend U | 42 | 1 | | |
| 1992–93 | Southend U | 45 | 0 | **135** | **3** |
| 1993–94 | Norwich C | 13 | 0 | | |
| 1994–95 | Norwich C | 17 | 0 | | |
| 1995–96 | Norwich C | 44 | 1 | **74** | **1** |
| 1996–97 | Leicester C | 34 | 0 | | |
| 1997–98 | Leicester C | 30 | 0 | **64** | **0** |
| 1998–99 | Derby Co | 34 | 1 | | |
| 1999–2000 | Derby Co | 20 | 0 | **54** | **1** |
| 1999–2000 | Manchester C | 9 | 3 | | |
| 2000–01 | Manchester C | 21 | 1 | **30** | **4** |
| 2001–02 | Cardiff C | 37 | 2 | | |
| 2002–03 | Cardiff C | 37 | 0 | | |
| 2003–04 | Cardiff C | 7 | 0 | **81** | **2** |

**ROBINSON, John (M)** **428** **43**
H: 5 10 W: 11 07 b.Bulawayo 29-8-71
*Source:* Apprentice. *Honours:* Wales Under-21, 30 full caps, 3 goals.

| | | | | | |
|---|---|---|---|---|---|
| 1989–90 | Brighton & HA | 5 | 0 | | |
| 1990–91 | Brighton & HA | 15 | 0 | | |
| 1991–92 | Brighton & HA | 36 | 6 | | |
| 1992–93 | Brighton & HA | 6 | 0 | **62** | **6** |
| 1992–93 | Charlton Ath | 15 | 2 | | |
| 1993–94 | Charlton Ath | 27 | 1 | | |
| 1994–95 | Charlton Ath | 21 | 3 | | |
| 1995–96 | Charlton Ath | 44 | 6 | | |
| 1996–97 | Charlton Ath | 42 | 3 | | |
| 1997–98 | Charlton Ath | 38 | 8 | | |
| 1998–99 | Charlton Ath | 30 | 2 | | |
| 1999–2000 | Charlton Ath | 45 | 7 | | |
| 2000–01 | Charlton Ath | 29 | 2 | | |
| 2001–02 | Charlton Ath | 28 | 1 | | |
| 2002–03 | Charlton Ath | 13 | 0 | **332** | **35** |
| 2003–04 | Cardiff C | 34 | 2 | **34** | **2** |

**THOMAS, Danny (F)** **0** **0**
H: 5 5 W: 10 10 b.Caerphilly 13-5-85
*Source:* Scholar.

| | | | | | |
|---|---|---|---|---|---|
| 2002–03 | Cardiff C | 0 | 0 | | |
| 2003–04 | Cardiff C | 0 | 0 | | |

**THORNE, Peter (F)** **341** **126**
H: 6 0 W: 12 10 b.Manchester 21-6-73
*Source:* Trainee.

| | | | | | |
|---|---|---|---|---|---|
| 1991–92 | Blackburn R | 0 | 0 | | |
| 1992–93 | Blackburn R | 0 | 0 | | |
| 1993–94 | Blackburn R | 0 | 0 | | |
| 1993–94 | *Wigan Ath* | 11 | 0 | **11** | **0** |
| 1994–95 | Blackburn R | 0 | 0 | | |
| 1994–95 | Swindon T | 20 | 9 | | |
| 1995–96 | Swindon T | 26 | 10 | | |
| 1996–97 | Swindon T | 31 | 8 | **77** | **27** |
| 1997–98 | Stoke C | 36 | 12 | | |
| 1998–99 | Stoke C | 34 | 9 | | |
| 1999–2000 | Stoke C | 45 | 24 | | |
| 2000–01 | Stoke C | 38 | 16 | | |
| 2001–02 | Stoke C | 5 | 4 | **158** | **65** |
| 2001–02 | Cardiff C | 26 | 8 | | |
| 2002–03 | Cardiff C | 46 | 13 | | |
| 2003–04 | Cardiff C | 23 | 13 | **95** | **34** |

**VIDMAR, Tony (D)** **383** **29**
H: 6 1 W: 12 10 b.Adelaide 15-4-69
*Honours:* Australia Schools, Under-23, 63 full caps, 2 goals.

| | | | | | |
|---|---|---|---|---|---|
| 1989 | Adelaide City | 11 | 1 | | |
| 1989–90 | Adelaide City | 27 | 4 | | |
| 1990–91 | Adelaide City | 27 | 3 | | |
| 1991–92 | Adelaide City | 24 | 1 | | |
| 1992–93 | Adelaide City | 9 | 0 | | |
| 1992–93 | Ekeren | 9 | 1 | **9** | **1** |
| 1993–94 | Adelaide City | 27 | 4 | | |
| 1994–95 | Adelaide City | 24 | 1 | **149** | **14** |
| 1995–96 | NAC | 30 | 2 | | |
| 1996–97 | NAC | 31 | 2 | **61** | **4** |
| 1997–98 | Rangers | 12 | 0 | | |
| 1998–99 | Rangers | 28 | 1 | | |
| 1999–2000 | Rangers | 27 | 6 | | |
| 2000–01 | Rangers | 15 | 1 | | |
| 2001–02 | Rangers | 25 | 1 | **107** | **9** |
| 2002–03 | Middlesbrough | 12 | 0 | **12** | **0** |
| 2003–04 | Cardiff C | 45 | 1 | **45** | **1** |

**WESTON, Rhys (D)** **128** **2**
H: 6 1 W: 12 03 b.Kingston 27-10-80
*Source:* Trainee. *Honours:* Wales Schools, Youth, Under-21, 6 full caps.

| | | | | | |
|---|---|---|---|---|---|
| 1999–2000 | Arsenal | 1 | 0 | | |
| 2000–01 | Arsenal | 0 | 0 | **1** | **0** |
| 2000–01 | Cardiff C | 28 | 0 | | |
| 2001–02 | Cardiff C | 37 | 0 | | |
| 2002–03 | Cardiff C | 38 | 2 | | |
| 2003–04 | Cardiff C | 24 | 0 | **127** | **2** |

**WHALLEY, Gareth (M)** **331** **14**
H: 5 10 W: 11 00 b.Manchester 19-12-73
*Source:* Trainee.

| | | | | | |
|---|---|---|---|---|---|
| 1992–93 | Crewe Alex | 25 | 1 | | |
| 1993–94 | Crewe Alex | 15 | 1 | | |
| 1994–95 | Crewe Alex | 40 | 1 | | |
| 1995–96 | Crewe Alex | 44 | 2 | | |
| 1996–97 | Crewe Alex | 38 | 3 | | |
| 1997–98 | Crewe Alex | 18 | 1 | | |
| 1998–99 | Bradford C | 45 | 2 | | |
| 1999–2000 | Bradford C | 16 | 1 | | |
| 2000–01 | Bradford C | 19 | 0 | | |
| 2001–02 | Bradford C | 23 | 0 | **103** | **3** |
| 2001–02 | *Crewe Alex* | 7 | 0 | **187** | **9** |
| 2002–03 | Cardiff C | 19 | 0 | | |
| 2003–04 | Cardiff C | 22 | 2 | **41** | **2** |

**YOUNG, Scott‡ (D)** **277** **22**
H: 6 1 W: 12 00 b.Tonypandy 14-1-76
*Source:* Trainee. *Honours:* Wales Under-21, B.

| | | | | | |
|---|---|---|---|---|---|
| 1993–94 | Cardiff C | 6 | 0 | | |
| 1994–95 | Cardiff C | 22 | 0 | | |

| | | | | | |
|---|---|---|---|---|---|
| 1995–96 | Cardiff C | 41 | 0 | | |
| 1996–97 | Cardiff C | 32 | 1 | | |
| 1997–98 | Cardiff C | 31 | 3 | | |
| 1998–99 | Cardiff C | 33 | 1 | | |
| 1999–2000 | Cardiff C | 22 | 2 | | |
| 2000–01 | Cardiff C | 45 | 10 | | |
| 2001–02 | Cardiff C | 33 | 4 | | |
| 2002–03 | Cardiff C | 12 | 1 | | |
| 2003–04 | Cardiff C | 0 | 0 | **277** | **22** |

**Scholars**
Attard, Craig A; Bailey, John; Brimble, Daniel; Cronin, Sean A; Hartley, Michael; Hayward, Michael; Jacobson, Joseph M; Jenkins, Lloyd A; Khalil, Tareq; Kift, Jonathan; Ledley, Joseph C; Morgan, Ryan R; Parslow, Daniel; Taylor, Anthony P

**Non Contract**
Jerome, Cameron

## CARLISLE U (19)

**ANDREWS, Lee (D)** **99 0**
H: 5 11 W: 12 00 b.Carlisle 23-4-83
*Source:* Scholar.

| | | | | | |
|---|---|---|---|---|---|
| 2001–02 | Carlisle U | 39 | 0 | | |
| 2002–03 | Carlisle U | 15 | 0 | | |
| 2002–03 | *Rochdale* | 8 | 0 | **8** | **0** |
| 2003–04 | Carlisle U | 37 | 0 | **91** | **0** |

**ARNISON, Paul (D)** **103 4**
H: 5 9 W: 10 12 b.Hartlepool 18-9-77
*Source:* Trainee.

| | | | | | |
|---|---|---|---|---|---|
| 1995–96 | Newcastle U | 0 | 0 | | |
| 1996–97 | Newcastle U | 0 | 0 | | |
| 1997–98 | Newcastle U | 0 | 0 | | |
| 1998–99 | Newcastle U | 0 | 0 | | |
| 1999–2000 | Newcastle U | 0 | 0 | | |
| 1999–2000 | Hartlepool U | 8 | 1 | | |
| 2000–01 | Hartlepool U | 27 | 1 | | |
| 2001–02 | Hartlepool U | 19 | 0 | | |
| 2002–03 | Hartlepool U | 19 | 1 | | |
| 2003–04 | Hartlepool U | 4 | 0 | **77** | **3** |
| 2003–04 | Carlisle U | 26 | 1 | **26** | **1** |

**BALDACCHINO, Ryan‡ (M)** **23 0**
H: 5 10 W: 11 08 b.Leicester 13-1-81
*Source:* Trainee.

| | | | | | |
|---|---|---|---|---|---|
| 1998–99 | Blackburn R | 0 | 0 | | |
| 1999–2000 | Blackburn R | 0 | 0 | | |
| 2000–01 | Blackburn R | 0 | 0 | | |
| 2000–01 | Bolton W | 0 | 0 | | |
| 2001–02 | Bolton W | 0 | 0 | | |
| 2002–03 | Carlisle U | 22 | 0 | | |
| 2003–04 | Carlisle U | 1 | 0 | **23** | **0** |

**BILLY, Chris (M)** **435 25**
H: 6 0 W: 12 13 b.Huddersfield 2-1-73
*Source:* Trainee.

| | | | | | |
|---|---|---|---|---|---|
| 1991–92 | Huddersfield T | 10 | 2 | | |
| 1992–93 | Huddersfield T | 13 | 0 | | |
| 1993–94 | Huddersfield T | 34 | 0 | | |
| 1994–95 | Huddersfield T | 37 | 2 | **94** | **4** |
| 1995–96 | Plymouth Arg | 32 | 4 | | |
| 1996–97 | Plymouth Arg | 45 | 3 | | |
| 1997–98 | Plymouth Arg | 41 | 2 | **118** | **9** |
| 1998–99 | Notts Co | 6 | 0 | **6** | **0** |
| 1998–99 | Bury | 37 | 0 | | |
| 1999–2000 | Bury | 36 | 4 | | |
| 2000–01 | Bury | 46 | 0 | | |
| 2001–02 | Bury | 21 | 3 | | |
| 2002–03 | Bury | 38 | 4 | **178** | **11** |
| 2003–04 | Carlisle U | 39 | 1 | **39** | **1** |

**BIRCH, Mark‡ (D)** **112 1**
H: 5 11 W: 12 08 b.Stoke 5-1-77
*Source:* Trainee.

| | | | | | |
|---|---|---|---|---|---|
| 1997–98 | Stoke C | 0 | 0 | | |

From Northwich V.

| | | | | | |
|---|---|---|---|---|---|
| 2000–01 | Carlisle U | 44 | 0 | | |
| 2001–02 | Carlisle U | 42 | 0 | | |
| 2002–03 | Carlisle U | 24 | 1 | | |
| 2003–04 | Carlisle U | 2 | 0 | **112** | **1** |

**BOYD, Mark* (M)** **51 4**
H: 5 9 W: 12 03 b.Carlisle 22-10-81
*Source:* Trainee.

| | | | | | |
|---|---|---|---|---|---|
| 1998–99 | Newcastle U | 0 | 0 | | |
| 1999–2000 | Newcastle U | 0 | 0 | | |
| 2000–01 | Newcastle U | 0 | 0 | | |
| 2001–02 | Newcastle U | 0 | 0 | | |
| 2002–03 | Port Vale | 20 | 3 | | |
| 2003–04 | Port Vale | 22 | 0 | **42** | **3** |
| 2003–04 | Carlisle U | 9 | 1 | **9** | **1** |

**BYRNE, Dessie‡ (D)** **39 0**
H: 5 10 W: 12 00 b.Dublin 10-4-81
*Source:* Trainee.

| | | | | | |
|---|---|---|---|---|---|
| 1998–99 | Stockport Co | 2 | 0 | **2** | **0** |
| 1999–2000 | Sr Patrick's Ath | 11 | 0 | **11** | **0** |
| 2000–01 | Wimbledon | 0 | 0 | | |
| 2001–02 | *Cambridge U* | 4 | 0 | **4** | **0** |
| 2001–02 | Wimbledon | 1 | 0 | | |
| 2002–03 | Wimbledon | 0 | 0 | **1** | **0** |
| 2002–03 | Carlisle U | 10 | 0 | | |
| 2003–04 | Carlisle U | 11 | 0 | **21** | **0** |

**BYRNE, Robert‡ (G)** **0 0**
b.Dublin 3-4-85
*Source:* Scholar.

| | | | | | |
|---|---|---|---|---|---|
| 2003–04 | Carlisle U | 0 | 0 | | |

**COWAN, Tom (D)** **352 17**
H: 5 6 W: 11 10 b.Bellshill 28-8-69
*Source:* Netherdale BC.

| | | | | | |
|---|---|---|---|---|---|
| 1988–89 | Clyde | 16 | 2 | **16** | **2** |
| 1988–89 | Rangers | 4 | 0 | | |
| 1989–90 | Rangers | 3 | 0 | | |
| 1990–91 | Rangers | 5 | 0 | **12** | **0** |
| 1991–92 | Sheffield U | 20 | 0 | | |
| 1992–93 | Sheffield U | 21 | 0 | | |
| 1993–94 | Sheffield U | 4 | 0 | **45** | **0** |
| 1993–94 | *Stoke C* | 14 | 0 | **14** | **0** |
| 1993–94 | *Huddersfield T* | 10 | 0 | | |
| 1994–95 | Huddersfield T | 37 | 2 | | |
| 1995–96 | Huddersfield T | 43 | 2 | | |
| 1996–97 | Huddersfield T | 42 | 4 | | |
| 1997–98 | Huddersfield T | 0 | 0 | | |
| 1998–99 | Huddersfield T | 5 | 0 | **137** | **8** |
| 1998–99 | Burnley | 12 | 1 | | |
| 1999–2000 | Burnley | 8 | 0 | **20** | **1** |
| 1999–2000 | *Cambridge U* | 4 | 0 | | |
| 2000–01 | Cambridge U | 41 | 2 | | |
| 2001–02 | Cambridge U | 5 | 1 | **50** | **3** |
| 2001–02 | *Peterborough U* | 5 | 1 | **5** | **1** |
| 2002–03 | York C | 33 | 1 | **33** | **1** |
| 2003–04 | Carlisle U | 20 | 1 | **20** | **1** |

**DILLON, Dan§ (M)** **1 0**
H: 5 9 W: 10 07 b.Huntingdon 6-9-86

| | | | | | |
|---|---|---|---|---|---|
| 2002–03 | Carlisle U | 1 | 0 | | |
| 2003–04 | Carlisle U | 0 | 0 | **1** | **0** |

**DUFFIELD, Peter* (F)** **386 129**
H: 5 7 W: 10 13 b.Middlesbrough 4-2-69
*Source:* Apprentice.

| | | | | | |
|---|---|---|---|---|---|
| 1986–87 | Middlesbrough | 0 | 0 | | |
| 1987–88 | Sheffield U | 11 | 1 | | |
| 1987–88 | *Halifax T* | 12 | 6 | **12** | **6** |
| 1988–89 | Sheffield U | 38 | 11 | | |
| 1989–90 | Sheffield U | 5 | 2 | | |
| 1990–91 | Sheffield U | 2 | 0 | | |
| 1990–91 | *Rotherham U* | 17 | 4 | **17** | **4** |
| 1991–92 | Sheffield U | 2 | 0 | | |
| 1992–93 | Sheffield U | 0 | 0 | | |
| 1992–93 | *Blackpool* | 5 | 1 | **5** | **1** |
| 1992–93 | *Bournemouth* | 0 | 0 | | |
| 1992–93 | *Stockport Co* | 7 | 4 | **7** | **4** |
| 1992–93 | *Crewe Alex* | 2 | 0 | **2** | **0** |
| 1993–94 | Sheffield U | 0 | 0 | **58** | **14** |
| 1993–94 | Hamilton A | 36 | 19 | | |
| 1994–95 | Hamilton A | 36 | 20 | **72** | **39** |
| 1995–96 | Airdrieonians | 24 | 6 | **24** | **6** |
| 1995–96 | Raith R | 9 | 5 | | |
| 1996–97 | Raith R | 33 | 5 | | |
| 1997–98 | Raith R | 0 | 0 | | |
| 1998–99 | Raith R | 0 | 0 | **42** | **10** |
| 1998–99 | Darlington | 14 | 2 | | |
| 1999–2000 | Darlington | 33 | 12 | **47** | **14** |
| 2000–01 | York C | 6 | 3 | | |
| 2001–02 | York C | 11 | 3 | | |
| 2002–03 | York C | 28 | 13 | **45** | **19** |
| 2002–03 | Boston U | 16 | 4 | | |
| 2003–04 | Boston U | 29 | 5 | **45** | **9** |
| 2003–04 | Carlisle U | 10 | 3 | **10** | **3** |

**FARRELL, Craig (F)** **63 18**
H: 6 0 W: 12 06 b.Middlesbrough 5-12-82
*Source:* Trainee.

| | | | | | |
|---|---|---|---|---|---|
| 1999–2000 | Leeds U | 0 | 0 | | |
| 2000–01 | Leeds U | 0 | 0 | | |
| 2001–02 | Leeds U | 0 | 0 | | |
| 2002–03 | Leeds U | 0 | 0 | | |
| 2002–03 | Carlisle U | 33 | 11 | | |
| 2003–04 | Carlisle U | 30 | 7 | **63** | **18** |

**FORAN, Richie* (F)** **123 36**
H: 6 1 W: 13 00 b.Dublin 16-6-80

| | | | | | |
|---|---|---|---|---|---|
| 2000–01 | Shelbourne | 28 | 11 | **28** | **11** |
| 2001–02 | Carlisle U | 37 | 14 | | |
| 2002–03 | Carlisle U | 31 | 7 | | |
| 2003–04 | Carlisle U | 23 | 4 | **91** | **25** |
| 2003–04 | *Oxford U* | 4 | 0 | **4** | **0** |

**GLENNON, Matty (G)** **141 0**
H: 6 2 W: 14 08 b.Stockport 8-10-78
*Source:* Trainee.

| | | | | | |
|---|---|---|---|---|---|
| 1997–98 | Bolton W | 0 | 0 | | |
| 1998–99 | Bolton W | 0 | 0 | | |
| 1999–2000 | Bolton W | 0 | 0 | | |
| 1999–2000 | *Port Vale* | 0 | 0 | | |
| 1999–2000 | *Stockport Co* | 0 | 0 | | |
| 2000–01 | Bolton W | 0 | 0 | | |
| 2000–01 | *Bristol R* | 1 | 0 | **1** | **0** |
| 2000–01 | *Carlisle U* | 29 | 0 | | |
| 2001–02 | Hull C | 26 | 0 | | |
| 2002–03 | Hull C | 9 | 0 | **35** | **0** |
| 2002–03 | Carlisle U | 32 | 0 | | |
| 2003–04 | Carlisle U | 44 | 0 | **105** | **0** |

**GRAY, Kevin (D)** **409 13**
H: 6 0 W: 13 00 b.Sheffield 7-1-72
*Source:* Trainee.

| | | | | | |
|---|---|---|---|---|---|
| 1988–89 | Mansfield T | 1 | 0 | | |
| 1989–90 | Mansfield T | 16 | 0 | | |
| 1990–91 | Mansfield T | 31 | 1 | | |
| 1991–92 | Mansfield T | 18 | 0 | | |
| 1992–93 | Mansfield T | 33 | 0 | | |
| 1993–94 | Mansfield T | 42 | 2 | **141** | **3** |
| 1994–95 | Huddersfield T | 5 | 0 | | |
| 1995–96 | Huddersfield T | 38 | 0 | | |
| 1996–97 | Huddersfield T | 39 | 1 | | |
| 1997–98 | Huddersfield T | 35 | 1 | | |
| 1998–99 | Huddersfield T | 34 | 1 | | |
| 1999–2000 | Huddersfield T | 18 | 2 | | |
| 2000–01 | *Stockport Co* | 1 | 0 | **1** | **0** |
| 2000–01 | Huddersfield T | 17 | 0 | | |
| 2001–02 | Huddersfield T | 44 | 1 | **230** | **6** |
| 2002–03 | Tranmere R | 10 | 1 | | |
| 2003–04 | Tranmere R | 2 | 0 | **12** | **1** |
| 2003–04 | Carlisle U | 25 | 3 | **25** | **3** |

**HENDERSON, Kevin‡ (F)** **164 32**
H: 5 11 W: 13 02 b.Ashington 8-6-74
*Source:* Morpeth Town.

| | | | | | |
|---|---|---|---|---|---|
| 1997–98 | Burnley | 7 | 0 | | |
| 1998–99 | Burnley | 7 | 1 | **14** | **1** |
| 1999–2000 | Hartlepool U | 35 | 8 | | |
| 2000–01 | Hartlepool U | 40 | 17 | | |
| 2001–02 | Hartlepool U | 23 | 2 | | |
| 2002–03 | Hartlepool U | 30 | 2 | | |
| 2003–04 | Hartlepool U | 3 | 0 | **131** | **29** |
| 2003–04 | Carlisle U | 19 | 2 | **19** | **2** |

**JACK, Michael (M)** **42 0**
H: 5 10 W: 11 08 b.Carlisle 2-10-82
*Source:* Trainee.

| | | | | | |
|---|---|---|---|---|---|
| 2001–02 | Carlisle U | 32 | 0 | | |
| 2002–03 | Carlisle U | 7 | 0 | | |
| 2003–04 | Carlisle U | 3 | 0 | **42** | **0** |

**KEEN, Peter (G)** **68 1**
H: 6 0 W: 13 00 b.Middlesbrough 16-11-76
*Source:* Trainee.

| | | | | | |
|---|---|---|---|---|---|
| 1995–96 | Newcastle U | 0 | 0 | | |
| 1996–97 | Newcastle U | 0 | 0 | | |
| 1997–98 | Newcastle U | 0 | 0 | | |
| 1998–99 | Newcastle U | 0 | 0 | | |
| 1999–2000 | Carlisle U | 6 | 0 | | |
| 2000–01 | Carlisle U | 3 | 1 | | |
| 2000–01 | *Darlington* | 7 | 0 | **7** | **0** |
| 2001–02 | Carlisle U | 36 | 0 | | |
| 2002–03 | Carlisle U | 13 | 0 | | |
| 2003–04 | Carlisle U | 3 | 0 | **61** | **1** |

**KELLY, Darren (D)** **42 2**
H: 6 0 W: 13 00 b.Derry 30-6-79
*Source:* Derry C.

| | | | | | |
|---|---|---|---|---|---|
| 2002–03 | Carlisle U | 32 | 1 | | |
| 2003–04 | Carlisle U | 10 | 1 | **42** | **2** |

**LIVINGSTONE, Steve‡ (F)** **362 58**
H: 6 1 W: 15 03 b.Middlesbrough 8-9-68
*Source:* Trainee.

| | | | | | |
|---|---|---|---|---|---|
| 1986–87 | Coventry C | 3 | 0 | | |

1987–88 Coventry C 4 0
1988–89 Coventry C 1 0
1989–90 Coventry C 13 3
1990–91 Coventry C 10 2 **31 5**
1990–91 Blackburn R 18 9
1991–92 Blackburn R 10 1
1992–93 Blackburn R 2 0 **30 10**
1992–93 Chelsea 1 0
1993–94 Chelsea 0 0 **1 0**
1993–94 *Port Vale* 5 0 **5 0**
1993–94 Grimsby T 27 3
1994–95 Grimsby T 34 8
1995–96 Grimsby T 38 11
1996–97 Grimsby T 32 6
1997–98 Grimsby T 41 5
1998–99 Grimsby T 23 0
1999–2000 Grimsby T 29 0
2000–01 Grimsby T 32 7
2001–02 Grimsby T 3 0
2002–03 Grimsby T 30 3 **289 43**
2003–04 Carlisle U 6 0 **6 0**

**LYNN, David‡ (D) 0 0**
b.Carlisle 18-1-85
*Source:* Scholar.
2003–04 Carlisle U 0 0

**MADDISON, Lee‡ (D) 268 2**
H: 5 11 W: 12 10 b.Bristol 5-10-72
*Source:* Trainee.
1991–92 Bristol R 10 0
1992–93 Bristol R 12 0
1993–94 Bristol R 37 0
1994–95 Bristol R 14 0
1995–96 Bristol R 0 0 **73 0**
1995–96 Northampton T 21 0
1996–97 Northampton T 34 0 **55 0**
1997–98 Dundee 24 1
1998–99 Dundee 21 0
1999–2000 Dundee 20 0
2000–01 Dundee 0 0 **65 1**
2000–01 Carlisle U 34 0
2001–02 Carlisle U 7 0
2001–02 *Oxford U* 11 0 **11 0**
2002–03 Carlisle U 21 1
2003–04 Carlisle U 2 0 **64 1**

**McDONAGH, Will (M) 63 4**
H: 6 0 W: 12 06 b.Dublin 14-3-83
*Source:* Bohemians.
2001–02 Carlisle U 12 1
2002–03 Carlisle U 24 2
2003–04 Carlisle U 27 1 **63 4**

**McGILL, Brendan (M) 106 12**
H: 5 7 W: 11 00 b.Dublin 22-3-81
1998–99 Sunderland 0 0
1999–2000 Sunderland 0 0
2000–01 Sunderland 0 0
2001–02 Sunderland 0 0
2001–02 *Carlisle U* 28 2
2002–03 Sunderland 0 0
2002–03 Carlisle U 34 3
2003–04 Carlisle U 44 7 **106 12**

**MOLLOY, David§ (M) 7 0**
H: 5 11 W: 11 01 b.Newcastle 29-8-86
*Source:* Scholar.
2003–04 Carlisle U 7 0 **7 0**

**MURPHY, Peter (D) 136 4**
H: 5 11 W: 12 06 b.Dublin 27-10-80
*Source:* Trainee. *Honours:* Eire Under-21.
1998–99 Blackburn R 0 0
1999–2000 Blackburn R 0 0
2000–01 Blackburn R 0 0
2000–01 *Halifax T* 21 1 **21 1**
2001–02 Blackburn R 0 0
2001–02 Carlisle U 40 0
2002–03 Carlisle U 40 2
2003–04 Carlisle U 35 1 **115 3**

**PREECE, Andy# (F) 488 118**
H: 6 2 W: 13 06 b.Evesham 27-3-67
*Source:* Evesham U.
1988–89 Northampton T 1 0 **1 0**
From Worcester C
1989–90 Wrexham 7 1
1990–91 Wrexham 34 4
1991–92 Wrexham 10 2 **51 7**
1991–92 Stockport Co 25 13
1992–93 Stockport Co 29 8
1993–94 Stockport Co 43 21 **97 42**
1994–95 Crystal Palace 20 4 **20 4**
1995–96 Blackpool 41 14
1996–97 Blackpool 41 10
1997–98 Blackpool 44 11 **126 35**
1998–99 Bury 39 3
1999–2000 Bury 43 12
2000–01 Bury 30 2
2001–02 Bury 13 1
2002–03 Bury 29 4
2003–04 Bury 14 5 **168 27**
2003–04 Carlisle U 25 3 **25 3**

**RAVEN, Paul (D) 384 22**
H: 6 1 W: 13 02 b.Salisbury 28-7-70
*Source:* School. *Honours:* England Schools, Youth.
1987–88 Doncaster R 17 3
1988–89 Doncaster R 35 1
1988–89 WBA 3 0
1989–90 WBA 7 0
1990–91 WBA 13 0
1991–92 WBA 7 1
1991–92 *Doncaster R* 7 0 **59 4**
1992–93 WBA 44 7
1993–94 WBA 34 1
1994–95 WBA 31 0
1995–96 WBA 40 4
1996–97 WBA 33 1
1997–98 WBA 8 0
1998–99 WBA 7 0
1998–99 *Rotherham U* 11 2 **11 2**
1999–2000 WBA 32 1 **259 15**
2000–01 Grimsby T 15 0
2001–02 Grimsby T 9 0
2002–03 Grimsby T 7 0 **31 0**
2002–03 Carlisle U 11 0
2003–04 Carlisle U 13 1 **24 1**

**REED, Michael* (M) 0 0**
b.Carlisle 4-5-85
*Source:* Scholar.
2003–04 Carlisle U 0 0

**RUNDLE, Adam (M) 61 1**
H: 5 8 W: 11 00 b.Durham 8-7-84
*Source:* Scholar.
2001–02 Darlington 12 0
2002–03 Darlington 5 0 **17 0**
2002–03 Carlisle U 21 1
2003–04 Carlisle U 23 0 **44 1**

**SHELLEY, Brian (D) 66 1**
H: 6 0 W: 13 00 b.Dublin 15-11-81
*Source:* Bohemians. *Honours:* Eire Under-21.
2002–03 Carlisle U 35 1
2003–04 Carlisle U 31 0 **66 1**

**SIMPSON, Paul# (M) 662 150**
H: 5 7 W: 12 03 b.Carlisle 26-7-66
*Source:* Apprentice. *Honours:* England Youth, Under-21.
1982–83 Manchester C 3 0
1983–84 Manchester C 0 0
1984–85 Manchester C 10 6
1985–86 Manchester C 37 8
1986–87 Manchester C 32 3
1987–88 Manchester C 38 1
1988–89 Manchester C 1 0 **121 18**
1988–89 Oxford U 25 8
1989–90 Oxford U 42 9
1990–91 Oxford U 46 17
1991–92 Oxford U 31 9 **144 43**
1991–92 Derby Co 16 7
1992–93 Derby Co 35 12
1993–94 Derby Co 34 9
1994–95 Derby Co 42 8
1995–96 Derby Co 39 10
1996–97 Derby Co 19 2
1996–97 *Sheffield U* 6 0 **6 0**
1997–98 Derby Co 1 0 **186 48**
1997–98 Wolverhampton W 28 4
1998–99 Wolverhampton W 11 2
1998–99 *Walsall* 10 1 **10 1**
1999–2000 Wolverhampton W 13 0
2000–01 Wolverhampton W 0 0 **52 6**
2000–01 Blackpool 44 12
2001–02 Blackpool 32 1 **76 13**
2001–02 Rochdale 7 5
2002–03 Rochdale 35 10 **42 15**
2003–04 Carlisle U 25 6 **25 6**

**SLAVEN, John‡ (F) 3 0**
H: 5 10 W: 11 00 b.Edinburgh 8-10-85
2001–02 Carlisle U 2 0
2002–03 Carlisle U 1 0
2003–04 Carlisle U 0 0 **3 0**

**SUMMERBELL, Mark (M) 106 2**
H: 5 9 W: 11 06 b.Durham 30-10-76
*Source:* Trainee.
1995–96 Middlesbrough 1 0
1996–97 Middlesbrough 2 0
1997–98 Middlesbrough 11 0
1998–99 Middlesbrough 11 0
1999–2000 Middlesbrough 19 0
2000–01 Middlesbrough 7 1
2001–02 Middlesbrough 0 0
2001–02 *Bristol C* 5 0 **5 0**
2001–02 *Portsmouth* 5 0 **5 0**
2002–03 Middlesbrough 0 0 **51 1**
2002–03 Carlisle U 39 1
2003–04 Carlisle U 6 0 **45 1**

**WAKE, Brian‡ (F) 43 9**
H: 6 0 W: 12 00 b.Stockton 13-8-82
*Source:* Tow Law T.
2001–02 Carlisle U 0 0
2002–03 Carlisle U 28 9
2003–04 Carlisle U 15 0 **43 9**

**Scholars**
Cawson, Peter J; Dillon, Daniel M; Doherty, Matthew; Ferris, Peter; Gardiner, Paul S; Molloy, David; Thompson, Neil

**Non Contract**
Dalton, Neil J

## CHARLTON ATH (20)

**BARTLETT, Shaun (F) 216 59**
H: 6 0 W: 12 06 b.Cape Town 31-10-72
*Honours:* Cape Town Spurs. South Africa 66 full caps, 27 goals.
1996 Colorado Rapids 26 8
1996–97 Amazulu 0 0
1997 New York/New Jersey M 13 2 **13 2**
1997 Colorado Rapids 10 1 **36 9**
1998 Cape Town Spurs 18 8 **18 8**
1998–99 Zurich 27 13
1999–2000 Zurich 20 2
2000–01 Zurich 20 8 **67 23**
2000–01 Charlton Ath 18 7
2001–02 Charlton Ath 14 1
2002–03 Charlton Ath 31 4
2003–04 Charlton Ath 19 5 **82 17**

**CAMPBELL-RYCE, Jamal (F) 24 2**
H: 5 7 W: 11 10 b.Lambeth 6-4-83
*Source:* Scholar. *Honours:* Jamaica 1 full cap.
2002–03 Charlton Ath 1 0
2002–03 *Leyton Orient* 17 2 **17 2**
2003–04 Charlton Ath 2 0 **3 0**
2003–04 *Wimbledon* 4 0 **4 0**

**DEANE, Adrian* (M) 0 0**
H: 5 10 W: 10 00 b.London 24-2-83
2001–02 Charlton Ath 0 0
2002–03 Charlton Ath 0 0
2003–04 Charlton Ath 0 0

**DI CANIO, Paolo* (F) 438 100**
H: 5 9 W: 11 09 b.Rome 9-7-68
*Source:* Milan AC.
1985–86 Lazio 0 0
1986–87 Ternana 27 2 **27 2**
1987–88 Lazio 0 0
1988–89 Lazio 30 1
1989–90 Lazio 24 3 **54 4**
1990–91 Juventus 23 3
1991–92 Juventus 24 0
1992–93 Juventus 31 3
1993–94 Napoli 26 5 **26 5**
1994–95 Juventus 0 0 **78 6**
1994–95 AC Milan 15 1
1995–96 AC Milan 22 5 **37 6**
1996–97 Celtic 26 12 **26 12**
1997–98 Sheffield W 35 12
1998–99 Sheffield W 6 3 **41 15**
1998–99 West Ham U 13 3
1999–2000 West Ham U 30 16

| | | | | | |
|---|---|---|---|---|---|
| 2000–01 | West Ham U | 31 | 9 | | |
| 2001–02 | West Ham U | 26 | 9 | | |
| 2002–03 | West Ham U | 18 | 9 | **118** | **46** |
| 2003–04 | Charlton Ath | 31 | 4 | **31** | **4** |

**EUELL, Jason (F)** **244** **72**

H: 5 11 W: 11 13 b.Lambeth 6-2-77

*Source:* Trainee. *Honours:* England Youth, Under-21.

| | | | | | |
|---|---|---|---|---|---|
| 1995–96 | Wimbledon | 9 | 2 | | |
| 1996–97 | Wimbledon | 7 | 2 | | |
| 1997–98 | Wimbledon | 19 | 4 | | |
| 1998–99 | Wimbledon | 33 | 10 | | |
| 1999–2000 | Wimbledon | 37 | 4 | | |
| 2000–01 | Wimbledon | 36 | 19 | **141** | **41** |
| 2001–02 | Charlton Ath | 36 | 11 | | |
| 2002–03 | Charlton Ath | 36 | 10 | | |
| 2003–04 | Charlton Ath | 31 | 10 | **103** | **31** |

**FISH, Mark (D)** **343** **14**

H: 6 4 W: 12 11 b.Cape Town 14-3-74

*Source:* Arcadia Shepherds. *Honours:* South Africa 62 full caps, 2 goals.

| | | | | | |
|---|---|---|---|---|---|
| 1992 | Jomo Cosmos | 14 | 1 | | |
| 1993 | Jomo Cosmos | 41 | 1 | **55** | **2** |
| 1994 | Orlando Pirates | 37 | 5 | | |
| 1995 | Orlando Pirates | 38 | 1 | **75** | **6** |
| 1996–97 | Lazio | 15 | 1 | **15** | **1** |
| 1997–98 | Bolton W | 22 | 2 | | |
| 1998–99 | Bolton W | 36 | 1 | | |
| 1999–2000 | Bolton W | 31 | 0 | | |
| 2000–01 | Bolton W | 14 | 0 | **103** | **3** |
| 2000–01 | Charlton Ath | 24 | 1 | | |
| 2001–02 | Charlton Ath | 25 | 0 | | |
| 2002–03 | Charlton Ath | 23 | 1 | | |
| 2003–04 | Charlton Ath | 23 | 0 | **95** | **2** |

**FORTUNE, Jon (D)** **91** **3**

H: 6 2 W: 12 12 b.Islington 23-8-80

*Source:* Trainee.

| | | | | | |
|---|---|---|---|---|---|
| 1998–99 | Charlton Ath | 0 | 0 | | |
| 1999–2000 | Charlton Ath | 0 | 0 | | |
| 1999–2000 | *Mansfield T* | 4 | 0 | | |
| 2000–01 | Charlton Ath | 0 | 0 | | |
| 2000–01 | *Mansfield T* | 14 | 0 | **18** | **0** |
| 2001–02 | Charlton Ath | 19 | 0 | | |
| 2002–03 | Charlton Ath | 26 | 1 | | |
| 2003–04 | Charlton Ath | 28 | 2 | **73** | **3** |

**HOLLAND, Matt (M)** **401** **62**

H: 5 10 W: 12 03 b.Bury 11-4-74

*Source:* Trainee. *Honours:* Eire 43 full caps, 5 goals.

| | | | | | |
|---|---|---|---|---|---|
| 1992–93 | West Ham U | 0 | 0 | | |
| 1993–94 | West Ham U | 0 | 0 | | |
| 1994–95 | West Ham U | 0 | 0 | | |
| 1994–95 | Bournemouth | 16 | 1 | | |
| 1995–96 | Bournemouth | 43 | 10 | | |
| 1996–97 | Bournemouth | 45 | 7 | **104** | **18** |
| 1997–98 | Ipswich T | 46 | 10 | | |
| 1998–99 | Ipswich T | 46 | 5 | | |
| 1999–2000 | Ipswich T | 46 | 10 | | |
| 2000–01 | Ipswich T | 38 | 3 | | |
| 2001–02 | Ipswich T | 38 | 3 | | |
| 2002–03 | Ipswich T | 45 | 7 | **259** | **38** |
| 2003–04 | Charlton Ath | 38 | 6 | **38** | **6** |

**HREIDARSSON, Hermann (D)** **303** **18**

H: 6 3 W: 12 12 b.Reykjavik 11-7-74

*Honours:* Iceland 52 full caps, 3 goals.

| | | | | | |
|---|---|---|---|---|---|
| 1993 | IBV | 2 | 0 | | |
| 1994 | IBV | 18 | 2 | | |
| 1995 | IBV | 18 | 1 | | |
| 1996 | IBV | 17 | 2 | | |
| 1997 | IBV | 11 | 0 | **66** | **5** |
| 1997–98 | Crystal Palace | 30 | 2 | | |
| 1998–99 | Crystal Palace | 7 | 0 | **37** | **2** |
| 1998–99 | Brentford | 33 | 4 | | |
| 1999–2000 | Brentford | 8 | 2 | **41** | **6** |
| 1999–2000 | Wimbledon | 24 | 1 | **24** | **1** |
| 2000–01 | Ipswich T | 36 | 1 | | |
| 2001–02 | Ipswich T | 38 | 1 | | |
| 2002–03 | Ipswich T | 28 | 0 | **102** | **2** |
| 2002–03 | Charlton Ath | 0 | 0 | | |
| 2003–04 | Charlton Ath | 33 | 2 | **33** | **2** |

**HUGHES, Stephen* (M)** **96** **5**

H: 6 0 W: 12 12 b.Wokingham 18-9-76

*Source:* Trainee. *Honours:* England Schools, Youth, Under-21.

| | | | | | |
|---|---|---|---|---|---|
| 1994–95 | Arsenal | 1 | 0 | | |
| 1995–96 | Arsenal | 1 | 0 | | |
| 1996–97 | Arsenal | 14 | 1 | | |
| 1997–98 | Arsenal | 17 | 2 | | |
| 1998–99 | Arsenal | 14 | 1 | | |
| 1999–2000 | Fulham | 3 | 0 | **3** | **0** |
| 1999–2000 | Arsenal | 2 | 0 | **49** | **4** |
| 1999–2000 | Everton | 11 | 1 | | |
| 2000–01 | Everton | 18 | 0 | **29** | **1** |
| 2001–02 | Watford | 15 | 0 | | |
| 2002–03 | Watford | 0 | 0 | **15** | **0** |
| 2003–04 | Charlton Ath | 0 | 0 | | |

**JENSEN, Claus (M)** **274** **38**

H: 5 11 W: 12 00 b.Nykobing 29-4-77

*Source:* Stubbekobing, Nykobing. *Honours:* Denmark Under-21, 33 full caps, 5 goals.

| | | | | | |
|---|---|---|---|---|---|
| 1995–96 | Naestved | 4 | 0 | **4** | **0** |
| 1996–97 | Lyngby | 31 | 3 | | |
| 1997–98 | Lyngby | 31 | 11 | **62** | **14** |
| 1998–99 | Bolton W | 44 | 2 | | |
| 1999–2000 | Bolton W | 42 | 6 | **86** | **8** |
| 2000–01 | Charlton Ath | 38 | 5 | | |
| 2001–02 | Charlton Ath | 18 | 1 | | |
| 2002–03 | Charlton Ath | 35 | 6 | | |
| 2003–04 | Charlton Ath | 31 | 4 | **122** | **16** |

**JOHANSSON, Jonatan (F)** **206** **52**

H: 6 2 W: 12 08 b.Stockholm 16-8-75

*Source:* Flora Tallinn. *Honours:* Finland 55 full caps, 10 goals.

| | | | | | |
|---|---|---|---|---|---|
| 1995 | TPS Turku | 9 | 0 | | |
| 1996 | TPS Turku | 23 | 6 | **32** | **6** |
| 1996–97 | Flora Tallinn | 9 | 9 | **9** | **9** |
| 1997–98 | Rangers | 6 | 0 | | |
| 1998–99 | Rangers | 25 | 8 | | |
| 1999–2000 | Rangers | 16 | 6 | **47** | **14** |
| 2000–01 | Charlton Ath | 31 | 11 | | |
| 2001–02 | Charlton Ath | 30 | 5 | | |
| 2002–03 | Charlton Ath | 31 | 3 | | |
| 2003–04 | Charlton Ath | 26 | 4 | **118** | **23** |

**KIELY, Dean (G)** **530** **0**

H: 6 1 W: 13 10 b.Salford 10-10-70

*Source:* WBA School. *Honours:* England Schools, FA Schools, Youth, Eire 8 full caps.

| | | | | | |
|---|---|---|---|---|---|
| 1987–88 | Coventry C | 0 | 0 | | |
| 1988–89 | Coventry C | 0 | 0 | | |
| 1989–90 | Coventry C | 0 | 0 | | |
| 1989–90 | *Ipswich T* | 0 | 0 | | |
| 1989–90 | *York C* | 0 | 0 | | |
| 1990–91 | York C | 17 | 0 | | |
| 1991–92 | York C | 21 | 0 | | |
| 1992–93 | York C | 40 | 0 | | |
| 1993–94 | York C | 46 | 0 | | |
| 1994–95 | York C | 46 | 0 | | |
| 1995–96 | York C | 40 | 0 | **210** | **0** |
| 1996–97 | Bury | 46 | 0 | | |
| 1997–98 | Bury | 46 | 0 | | |
| 1998–99 | Bury | 45 | 0 | **137** | **0** |
| 1999–2000 | Charlton Ath | 45 | 0 | | |
| 2000–01 | Charlton Ath | 25 | 0 | | |
| 2001–02 | Charlton Ath | 38 | 0 | | |
| 2002–03 | Charlton Ath | 38 | 0 | | |
| 2003–04 | Charlton Ath | 37 | 0 | **183** | **0** |

**KISHISHEV, Radostin (D)** **290** **19**

H: 5 11 W: 12 03 b.Bourgas 30-7-74

*Honours:* Bulgaria 50 full caps.

| | | | | | |
|---|---|---|---|---|---|
| 1991–92 | Chernomorets | 6 | 1 | | |
| 1992–93 | Chernomorets | 23 | 2 | | |
| 1993–94 | Chernomorets | 23 | 1 | **52** | **4** |
| 1994–95 | Neftochimik | 14 | 0 | | |
| 1995–96 | Neftochimik | 30 | 0 | | |
| 1996–97 | Neftochimik | 30 | 6 | | |
| 1997–98 | Neftochimik | 1 | 0 | **75** | **6** |
| 1997–98 | Bursaspor | 20 | 3 | **20** | **3** |
| 1997–98 | Litets Lovech | 5 | 0 | **5** | **0** |
| 1998–99 | Litets Lovech | 26 | 2 | | |
| 1999–2000 | Litets Lovech | 15 | 2 | **41** | **4** |
| 2000–01 | Charlton Ath | 27 | 0 | | |
| 2001–02 | Charlton Ath | 3 | 0 | | |
| 2002–03 | Charlton Ath | 34 | 2 | | |
| 2003–04 | Charlton Ath | 33 | 0 | **97** | **2** |

**KONCHESKY, Paul (D)** **133** **4**

H: 5 10 W: 11 07 b.Barking 15-5-81

*Source:* Trainee. *Honours:* England Youth, Under-20, Under-21, 1 full cap.

| | | | | | |
|---|---|---|---|---|---|
| 1997–98 | Charlton Ath | 3 | 0 | | |
| 1998–99 | Charlton Ath | 2 | 0 | | |
| 1999–2000 | Charlton Ath | 8 | 0 | | |
| 2000–01 | Charlton Ath | 23 | 0 | | |
| 2001–02 | Charlton Ath | 34 | 1 | | |
| 2002–03 | Charlton Ath | 30 | 3 | | |
| 2003–04 | Charlton Ath | 21 | 0 | **121** | **4** |
| 2003–04 | *Tottenham H* | 12 | 0 | **12** | **0** |

**LEITE, Sergio* (G)** **0** **0**

H: 6 0 W: 12 00 b.Oporto 16-8-79

| | | | | | |
|---|---|---|---|---|---|
| 2003–04 | Charlton Ath | 0 | 0 | | |

**LISBIE, Kevin (F)** **135** **19**

H: 5 10 W: 11 06 b.Hackney 17-10-78

*Source:* Trainee. *Honours:* England Youth. Jamaica 6 full caps.

| | | | | | |
|---|---|---|---|---|---|
| 1996–97 | Charlton Ath | 25 | 1 | | |
| 1997–98 | Charlton Ath | 17 | 1 | | |
| 1998–99 | Charlton Ath | 1 | 0 | | |
| 1998–99 | *Gillingham* | 7 | 4 | **7** | **4** |
| 1999–2000 | Charlton Ath | 0 | 0 | | |
| 1999–2000 | *Reading* | 2 | 0 | **2** | **0** |
| 2000–01 | Charlton Ath | 18 | 0 | | |
| 2000–01 | *QPR* | 2 | 0 | **2** | **0** |
| 2001–02 | Charlton Ath | 22 | 5 | | |
| 2002–03 | Charlton Ath | 32 | 4 | | |
| 2003–04 | Charlton Ath | 9 | 4 | **124** | **15** |

**LONG, Stacy (F)** **0** **0**

H: 5 8 W: 10 00 b.Bromley 11-1-85

*Source:* Scholar. *Honours:* England Youth.

| | | | | | |
|---|---|---|---|---|---|
| 2001–02 | Charlton Ath | 0 | 0 | | |
| 2002–03 | Charlton Ath | 0 | 0 | | |
| 2003–04 | Charlton Ath | 0 | 0 | | |

**McCAFFERTY, Neil (M)** **6** **0**

H: 5 7 W: 10 00 b.Derry 19-7-84

*Source:* Scholar.

| | | | | | |
|---|---|---|---|---|---|
| 2001–02 | Charlton Ath | 0 | 0 | | |
| 2002–03 | Charlton Ath | 0 | 0 | | |
| 2003–04 | Charlton Ath | 0 | 0 | | |
| 2003–04 | *Cambridge U* | 6 | 0 | **6** | **0** |

**PERRY, Chris (D)** **316** **6**

H: 5 8 W: 10 12 b.Carshalton 26-4-73

*Source:* Trainee.

| | | | | | |
|---|---|---|---|---|---|
| 1991–92 | Wimbledon | 0 | 0 | | |
| 1992–93 | Wimbledon | 0 | 0 | | |
| 1993–94 | Wimbledon | 2 | 0 | | |
| 1994–95 | Wimbledon | 22 | 0 | | |
| 1995–96 | Wimbledon | 37 | 0 | | |
| 1996–97 | Wimbledon | 37 | 1 | | |
| 1997–98 | Wimbledon | 35 | 1 | | |
| 1998–99 | Wimbledon | 34 | 0 | **167** | **2** |
| 1999–2000 | Tottenham H | 37 | 1 | | |
| 2000–01 | Tottenham H | 32 | 1 | | |
| 2001–02 | Tottenham H | 33 | 0 | | |
| 2002–03 | Tottenham H | 18 | 1 | | |
| 2003–04 | Tottenham H | 0 | 0 | **120** | **3** |
| 2003–04 | Charlton Ath | 29 | 1 | **29** | **1** |

**POWELL, Chris (D)** **553** **5**

H: 5 11 W: 11 12 b.Lambeth 8-9-69

*Source:* Trainee. *Honours:* England 5 full caps.

| | | | | | |
|---|---|---|---|---|---|
| 1987–88 | Crystal Palace | 0 | 0 | | |
| 1988–89 | Crystal Palace | 3 | 0 | | |
| 1989–90 | Crystal Palace | 0 | 0 | **3** | **0** |
| 1989–90 | *Aldershot* | 11 | 0 | **11** | **0** |
| 1990–91 | Southend U | 45 | 1 | | |
| 1991–92 | Southend U | 44 | 0 | | |
| 1992–93 | Southend U | 42 | 2 | | |
| 1993–94 | Southend U | 46 | 0 | | |
| 1994–95 | Southend U | 44 | 0 | | |
| 1995–96 | Southend U | 27 | 0 | **248** | **3** |
| 1995–96 | Derby Co | 19 | 0 | | |
| 1996–97 | Derby Co | 35 | 0 | | |
| 1997–98 | Derby Co | 37 | 1 | **91** | **1** |
| 1998–99 | Charlton Ath | 38 | 0 | | |
| 1999–2000 | Charlton Ath | 40 | 0 | | |
| 2000–01 | Charlton Ath | 33 | 0 | | |
| 2001–02 | Charlton Ath | 36 | 1 | | |
| 2002–03 | Charlton Ath | 37 | 0 | | |
| 2003–04 | Charlton Ath | 16 | 0 | **200** | **1** |

**RACHUBKA, Paul (G)** **30** **0**

H: 6 1 W: 13 01 b.San Luis Opispo 21-5-81

*Source:* Trainee. *Honours:* England Youth.

| | | | | | |
|---|---|---|---|---|---|
| 1999–2000 | Manchester U | 0 | 0 | | |
| 2000–01 | Manchester U | 1 | 0 | | |
| 2001–02 | Manchester U | 0 | 0 | **1** | **0** |
| 2001–02 | *Oldham Ath* | 16 | 0 | **16** | **0** |
| 2001–02 | Charlton Ath | 0 | 0 | | |
| 2002–03 | Charlton Ath | 0 | 0 | | |

| | | | | | |
|---|---|---|---|---|---|
| 2003–04 | Charlton Ath | 0 | 0 | | |
| 2003–04 | *Huddersfield T* | 13 | 0 | 13 | 0 |

**ROWETT, Gary (D) 338 20**
H: 6 0 W: 13 00 b.Bromsgrove 6-3-74
*Source:* Trainee.

| | | | | | |
|---|---|---|---|---|---|
| 1991–92 | Cambridge U | 13 | 2 | | |
| 1992–93 | Cambridge U | 21 | 2 | | |
| 1993–94 | Cambridge U | 29 | 5 | 63 | 9 |
| 1993–94 | Everton | 2 | 0 | | |
| 1994–95 | Everton | 2 | 0 | 4 | 0 |
| 1994–95 | *Blackpool* | 17 | 0 | 17 | 0 |
| 1995–96 | Derby Co | 35 | 0 | | |
| 1996–97 | Derby Co | 35 | 1 | | |
| 1997–98 | Derby Co | 35 | 1 | | |
| 1998–99 | Derby Co | 0 | 0 | 105 | 2 |
| 1998–99 | Birmingham C | 42 | 5 | | |
| 1999–2000 | Birmingham C | 45 | 1 | 87 | 6 |
| 2000–01 | Leicester C | 38 | 2 | | |
| 2001–02 | Leicester C | 11 | 0 | 49 | 2 |
| 2001–02 | Charlton Ath | 0 | 0 | | |
| 2002–03 | Charlton Ath | 12 | 1 | | |
| 2003–04 | Charlton Ath | 1 | 0 | 13 | 1 |

**ROYCE, Simon (G) 199 0**
H: 6 1 W: 13 09 b.Forest Gate 9-9-71
*Source:* Heybridge Swifts.

| | | | | | |
|---|---|---|---|---|---|
| 1991–92 | Southend U | 1 | 0 | | |
| 1992–93 | Southend U | 3 | 0 | | |
| 1993–94 | Southend U | 6 | 0 | | |
| 1994–95 | Southend U | 13 | 0 | | |
| 1995–96 | Southend U | 46 | 0 | | |
| 1996–97 | Southend U | 43 | 0 | | |
| 1997–98 | Southend U | 37 | 0 | 149 | 0 |
| 1998–99 | Charlton Ath | 8 | 0 | | |
| 1999–2000 | Charlton Ath | 0 | 0 | | |
| 2000–01 | Leicester C | 19 | 0 | | |
| 2001–02 | Leicester C | 0 | 0 | | |
| 2001–02 | *Brighton & HA* | 6 | 0 | 6 | 0 |
| 2001–02 | *Manchester C* | 0 | 0 | | |
| 2002–03 | Leicester C | 0 | 0 | 19 | 0 |
| 2002–03 | *QPR* | 16 | 0 | 16 | 0 |
| 2003–04 | Charlton Ath | 1 | 0 | 9 | 0 |

**RUFUS, Richard (D) 288 12**
H: 6 1 W: 12 12 b.Lewisham 12-1-75
*Source:* Trainee. *Honours:* England Under-21.

| | | | | | |
|---|---|---|---|---|---|
| 1993–94 | Charlton Ath | 0 | 0 | | |
| 1994–95 | Charlton Ath | 28 | 0 | | |
| 1995–96 | Charlton Ath | 41 | 0 | | |
| 1996–97 | Charlton Ath | 34 | 0 | | |
| 1997–98 | Charlton Ath | 42 | 0 | | |
| 1998–99 | Charlton Ath | 27 | 1 | | |
| 1999–2000 | Charlton Ath | 44 | 6 | | |
| 2000–01 | Charlton Ath | 32 | 2 | | |
| 2001–02 | Charlton Ath | 10 | 1 | | |
| 2002–03 | Charlton Ath | 30 | 2 | | |
| 2003–04 | Charlton Ath | 0 | 0 | 288 | 12 |

**SAM, Lloyd (F) 10 0**
H: 5 8 W: 10 00 b.Leeds 27-9-84
*Honours:* England Youth.

| | | | | | |
|---|---|---|---|---|---|
| 2002–03 | Charlton Ath | 0 | 0 | | |
| 2003–04 | Charlton Ath | 0 | 0 | | |
| 2003–04 | *Leyton Orient* | 10 | 0 | 10 | 0 |

**SANKOFA, Osei (D) 1 0**
H: 6 0 W: 12 04 b.London 19-3-85
*Source:* Scholar. *Honours:* England Youth.

| | | | | | |
|---|---|---|---|---|---|
| 2002–03 | Charlton Ath | 1 | 0 | | |
| 2003–04 | Charlton Ath | 0 | 0 | 1 | 0 |

**STUART, Graham (M) 420 69**
H: 5 9 W: 12 01 b.Tooting 24-10-70
*Source:* Trainee. *Honours:* FA Schools, England Under-21.

| | | | | | |
|---|---|---|---|---|---|
| 1989–90 | Chelsea | 2 | 1 | | |
| 1990–91 | Chelsea | 19 | 4 | | |
| 1991–92 | Chelsea | 27 | 0 | | |
| 1992–93 | Chelsea | 39 | 9 | 87 | 14 |
| 1993–94 | Everton | 30 | 3 | | |
| 1994–95 | Everton | 28 | 3 | | |
| 1995–96 | Everton | 29 | 9 | | |
| 1996–97 | Everton | 35 | 5 | | |
| 1997–98 | Everton | 14 | 2 | 136 | 22 |
| 1997–98 | Sheffield U | 28 | 5 | | |
| 1998–99 | Sheffield U | 25 | 6 | 53 | 11 |
| 1998–99 | Charlton Ath | 9 | 4 | | |
| 1999–2000 | Charlton Ath | 37 | 7 | | |
| 2000–01 | Charlton Ath | 35 | 5 | | |
| 2001–02 | Charlton Ath | 31 | 3 | | |
| 2002–03 | Charlton Ath | 4 | 0 | | |
| 2003–04 | Charlton Ath | 28 | 3 | 144 | 22 |

**THOMAS, Jerome (M) 11 3**
H: 5 10 W: 11 10 b.Brent 23-3-83
*Source:* Scholar. *Honours:* England Youth, Under-20.

| | | | | | |
|---|---|---|---|---|---|
| 2001–02 | Arsenal | 0 | 0 | | |
| 2001–02 | *QPR* | 4 | 1 | | |
| 2002–03 | Arsenal | 0 | 0 | | |
| 2002–03 | *QPR* | 6 | 2 | 10 | 3 |
| 2003–04 | Arsenal | 0 | 0 | | |
| 2003–04 | Charlton Ath | 1 | 0 | 1 | 0 |

**TUCKER, Stephen‡ (M) 0 0**
H: 5 9 W: 11 10 b.Dublin 9-9-85
*Source:* Trainee.

| | | | | | |
|---|---|---|---|---|---|
| 2003–04 | Charlton Ath | 0 | 0 | | |

**TURNER, Michael (D) 7 1**
H: 6 4 W: 12 06 b.Lewisham 9-11-83
*Source:* Scholar.

| | | | | | |
|---|---|---|---|---|---|
| 2001–02 | Charlton Ath | 0 | 0 | | |
| 2002–03 | Charlton Ath | 0 | 0 | | |
| 2002–03 | *Leyton Orient* | 7 | 1 | 7 | 1 |
| 2003–04 | Charlton Ath | 0 | 0 | | |

**VARNEY, Alex (F) 0 0**
b.Farnborough 27-12-84
*Source:* Trainee.

| | | | | | |
|---|---|---|---|---|---|
| 2003–04 | Charlton Ath | 0 | 0 | | |

**YOUNG, Luke (D) 148 0**
H: 6 0 W: 12 04 b.Harlow 19-7-79
*Source:* Trainee. *Honours:* England Youth, Under-21.

| | | | | | |
|---|---|---|---|---|---|
| 1997–98 | Tottenham H | 0 | 0 | | |
| 1998–99 | Tottenham H | 15 | 0 | | |
| 1999–2000 | Tottenham H | 20 | 0 | | |
| 2000–01 | Tottenham H | 23 | 0 | 58 | 0 |
| 2001–02 | Charlton Ath | 34 | 0 | | |
| 2002–03 | Charlton Ath | 32 | 0 | | |
| 2003–04 | Charlton Ath | 24 | 0 | 90 | 0 |

**Scholars**
Ashton, Nathan W; Cottrell, Adam S; Elliot, Robert; Evans, David M; Fuller, Barry M; Gross, Adam C; Phillips, Daniel; Randolph, Darren E; Ricketts, Mark J; Thanda, Lekeladio B; Wilson, Wayne

## CHELSEA (21)

**AMBROSIO, Marco (G) 136 0**
H: 6 1 W: 13 04 b.Brescia 30-5-73

| | | | | | |
|---|---|---|---|---|---|
| 1991–92 | Lumezzane | 2 | 0 | 2 | 0 |
| 1992–93 | Atalanta | 0 | 0 | | |
| 1993–94 | Pisa | 9 | 0 | 9 | 0 |
| 1993–94 | Atalanta | 0 | 0 | | |
| 1994–95 | Prato | 15 | 0 | | |
| 1995–96 | Atalanta | 0 | 0 | | |
| 1995–96 | Ravenna | 10 | 0 | 10 | 0 |
| 1996–97 | Prato | 34 | 0 | 49 | 0 |
| 1997–98 | Sampdoria | 3 | 0 | | |
| 1998–99 | Sampdoria | 7 | 0 | | |
| 1999–2000 | Sampdoria | 0 | 0 | 10 | 0 |
| 1999–2000 | Lucchese | 13 | 0 | | |
| 2000–01 | Lucchese | 33 | 0 | 46 | 0 |
| 2001–02 | Chievo | 2 | 0 | 2 | 0 |
| 2003–04 | Chelsea | 8 | 0 | 8 | 0 |

**BABAYARO, Celestine (D) 203 13**
H: 5 9 W: 12 01 b.Kaduna 29-8-78
*Source:* Plateau U. *Honours:* Nigeria 26 full caps.

| | | | | | |
|---|---|---|---|---|---|
| 1994–95 | Anderlecht | 22 | 0 | | |
| 1995–96 | Anderlecht | 28 | 5 | | |
| 1996–97 | Anderlecht | 25 | 3 | 75 | 8 |
| 1997–98 | Chelsea | 8 | 0 | | |
| 1998–99 | Chelsea | 28 | 3 | | |
| 1999–2000 | Chelsea | 25 | 0 | | |
| 2000–01 | Chelsea | 24 | 0 | | |
| 2001–02 | Chelsea | 18 | 0 | | |
| 2002–03 | Chelsea | 19 | 1 | | |
| 2003–04 | Chelsea | 6 | 1 | 128 | 5 |

**BOGARDE, Winston* (D) 201 26**
H: 6 3 W: 15 04 b.Rotterdam 22-10-70
*Honours:* Holland 20 full caps.

| | | | | | |
|---|---|---|---|---|---|
| 1988–89 | SVV | 9 | 1 | | |
| 1989–90 | SVV | 2 | 0 | | |
| 1989–90 | Excelsior | 10 | 1 | 10 | 1 |
| 1990–91 | SVV | 0 | 0 | 11 | 1 |
| 1991–92 | Sparta | 0 | 0 | | |
| 1992–93 | Sparta | 32 | 3 | | |
| 1993–94 | Sparta | 33 | 11 | 65 | 14 |
| 1994–95 | Ajax | 13 | 0 | | |
| 1995–96 | Ajax | 33 | 2 | | |
| 1996–97 | Ajax | 16 | 4 | 62 | 6 |
| 1997–98 | AC Milan | 3 | 0 | 3 | 0 |
| 1997–98 | Barcelona | 19 | 2 | | |
| 1998–99 | Barcelona | 1 | 0 | | |
| 1999–2000 | Barcelona | 21 | 2 | 41 | 4 |
| 2000–01 | Chelsea | 9 | 0 | | |
| 2001–02 | Chelsea | 0 | 0 | | |
| 2002–03 | Chelsea | 0 | 0 | | |
| 2003–04 | Chelsea | 0 | 0 | 9 | 0 |

**BOUSSOUFA, Mbark* (F) 0 0**
H: 5 6 W: 8 10 b.Amsterdam 15-8-84

| | | | | | |
|---|---|---|---|---|---|
| 2002–03 | Chelsea | 0 | 0 | | |
| 2003–04 | Chelsea | 0 | 0 | | |

**BRIDGE, Wayne (D) 185 3**
H: 5 10 W: 12 08 b.Southampton 5-8-80
*Source:* Trainee. *Honours:* England Youth, Under-21, 17 full caps, 1 goal.

| | | | | | |
|---|---|---|---|---|---|
| 1997–98 | Southampton | 0 | 0 | | |
| 1998–99 | Southampton | 23 | 0 | | |
| 1999–2000 | Southampton | 19 | 1 | | |
| 2000–01 | Southampton | 38 | 0 | | |
| 2001–02 | Southampton | 38 | 0 | | |
| 2002–03 | Southampton | 34 | 1 | 152 | 2 |
| 2003–04 | Chelsea | 33 | 1 | 33 | 1 |

**COLE, Carlton (F) 44 9**
H: 6 3 W: 13 10 b.Croydon 12-10-83
*Source:* Scholar. *Honours:* England Youth, Under-20, Under-21.

| | | | | | |
|---|---|---|---|---|---|
| 2000–01 | Chelsea | 0 | 0 | | |
| 2001–02 | Chelsea | 3 | 1 | | |
| 2002–03 | Chelsea | 13 | 3 | | |
| 2002–03 | *Wolverhampton W* | 7 | 1 | 7 | 1 |
| 2003–04 | Chelsea | 0 | 0 | 16 | 4 |
| 2003–04 | *Charlton Ath* | 21 | 4 | 21 | 4 |

**COLE, Joe (M) 161 11**
H: 5 9 W: 11 13 b.Islington 8-11-81
*Source:* Trainee. *Honours:* England Schools, Youth, Under-21, 17 full caps, 2 goals.

| | | | | | |
|---|---|---|---|---|---|
| 1998–99 | West Ham U | 8 | 0 | | |
| 1999–2000 | West Ham U | 22 | 1 | | |
| 2000–01 | West Ham U | 30 | 5 | | |
| 2001–02 | West Ham U | 30 | 0 | | |
| 2002–03 | West Ham U | 36 | 4 | 126 | 10 |
| 2003–04 | Chelsea | 35 | 1 | 35 | 1 |

**CRESPO, Hernan (F) 271 141**
H: 6 0 W: 12 13 b.Florida 5-7-75
*Honours:* Argentina 46 full caps, 26 goals.

| | | | | | |
|---|---|---|---|---|---|
| 1993–94 | River Plate | 25 | 13 | | |
| 1994–95 | River Plate | 18 | 5 | | |
| 1995–96 | River Plate | 21 | 5 | 64 | 23 |
| 1996–97 | Parma | 27 | 12 | | |
| 1997–98 | Parma | 25 | 12 | | |
| 1998–99 | Parma | 30 | 16 | | |
| 1999–2000 | Parma | 34 | 22 | 116 | 62 |
| 2000–01 | Lazio | 32 | 26 | | |
| 2001–02 | Lazio | 22 | 13 | 54 | 39 |
| 2002–03 | Internazionale | 18 | 7 | 18 | 7 |
| 2003–04 | Chelsea | 19 | 10 | 19 | 10 |

**CUDICINI, Carlo (G) 198 0**
H: 6 1 W: 12 06 b.Milan 6-9-73

| | | | | | |
|---|---|---|---|---|---|
| 1991–92 | AC Milan | 0 | 0 | | |
| 1992–93 | AC Milan | 0 | 0 | | |
| 1993–94 | Como | 6 | 0 | 6 | 0 |
| 1994–95 | AC Milan | 0 | 0 | | |
| 1995–96 | AC Milan | 0 | 0 | | |
| 1995–96 | Prato | 30 | 0 | 30 | 0 |
| 1996–97 | Lazio | 1 | 0 | 1 | 0 |
| 1997–98 | Castel di Sangro | 14 | 0 | | |
| 1998–99 | Castel di Sangro | 32 | 0 | 46 | 0 |
| 1999–2000 | Chelsea | 1 | 0 | | |
| 2000–01 | Chelsea | 24 | 0 | | |
| 2001–02 | Chelsea | 28 | 0 | | |
| 2002–03 | Chelsea | 36 | 0 | | |
| 2003–04 | Chelsea | 26 | 0 | 115 | 0 |

**DE ARAUJO, Gustavo‡ (D) 0 0**
b.Curitiba 8-8-84

| | | | | | |
|---|---|---|---|---|---|
| 2003–04 | Chelsea | 0 | 0 | | |

**DE LUCAS, Enrique‡ (M) 189 41**
H: 5 8 W: 11 11 b.LHospitalet Llobregat 17-8-78

| | | | | | |
|---|---|---|---|---|---|
| 1996–97 | Espanyol B | 27 | 5 | | |
| 1997–98 | Espanyol B | 28 | 13 | | |
| 1997–98 | Espanyol | 1 | 1 | | |
| 1998–99 | Espanyol B | 13 | 5 | **68** | **23** |
| 1998–99 | Espanyol | 20 | 6 | | |
| 1999–2000 | Espanyol | 30 | 4 | | |
| 2000–01 | Espanyol | 8 | 0 | | |
| 2000–01 | Paris St Germain | 4 | 0 | **4** | **0** |
| 2001–02 | Espanyol | 33 | 7 | **92** | **18** |
| 2002–03 | Chelsea | 25 | 0 | | |
| 2003–04 | Chelsea | 0 | 0 | **25** | **0** |

**DESAILLY, Marcel (D) 505 17**
H: 6 0 W: 13 05 b.Accra 7-9-68
*Honours:* France 116 full caps, 3 goals.

| | | | | | |
|---|---|---|---|---|---|
| 1986–87 | Nantes | 15 | 0 | | |
| 1987–88 | Nantes | 11 | 0 | | |
| 1988–89 | Nantes | 36 | 1 | | |
| 1989–90 | Nantes | 36 | 1 | | |
| 1990–91 | Nantes | 34 | 1 | | |
| 1991–92 | Nantes | 32 | 2 | **164** | **5** |
| 1992–93 | Marseille | 31 | 1 | | |
| 1993–94 | Marseille | 15 | 0 | **46** | **1** |
| 1993–94 | AC Milan | 21 | 1 | | |
| 1994–95 | AC Milan | 22 | 1 | | |
| 1995–96 | AC Milan | 32 | 2 | | |
| 1996–97 | AC Milan | 29 | 1 | | |
| 1997–98 | AC Milan | 33 | 0 | **137** | **5** |
| 1998–99 | Chelsea | 31 | 0 | | |
| 1999–2000 | Chelsea | 23 | 1 | | |
| 2000–01 | Chelsea | 34 | 2 | | |
| 2001–02 | Chelsea | 24 | 1 | | |
| 2002–03 | Chelsea | 31 | 2 | | |
| 2003–04 | Chelsea | 15 | 0 | **158** | **6** |

**DI CESARE, Valerio (D) 0 0**
H: 6 0 W: 12 11 b.Rome 23-5-83

| | | | | | |
|---|---|---|---|---|---|
| 2000–01 | Chelsea | 0 | 0 | | |
| 2001–02 | Chelsea | 0 | 0 | | |
| 2002–03 | Chelsea | 0 | 0 | | |
| 2003–04 | Chelsea | 0 | 0 | | |

**DUFF, Damien (F) 207 32**
H: 5 9 W: 12 02 b.Ballyboden 2-3-79
*Source:* Lourdes Celtic. *Honours:* Eire Youth, 43 full caps, 6 goals.

| | | | | | |
|---|---|---|---|---|---|
| 1995–96 | Blackburn R | 0 | 0 | | |
| 1996–97 | Blackburn R | 1 | 0 | | |
| 1997–98 | Blackburn R | 26 | 4 | | |
| 1998–99 | Blackburn R | 28 | 1 | | |
| 1999–2000 | Blackburn R | 39 | 5 | | |
| 2000–01 | Blackburn R | 32 | 1 | | |
| 2001–02 | Blackburn R | 32 | 7 | | |
| 2002–03 | Blackburn R | 26 | 9 | **184** | **27** |
| 2003–04 | Chelsea | 23 | 5 | **23** | **5** |

**FORSSELL, Mikael (F) 149 46**
H: 6 0 W: 13 08 b.Steinfurt 15-3-81
*Honours:* Finland 29 full caps, 10 goals.

| | | | | | |
|---|---|---|---|---|---|
| 1997 | HJK Helsinki | 1 | 0 | | |
| 1998 | HJK Helsinki | 16 | 1 | **17** | **1** |
| 1998–99 | Chelsea | 10 | 1 | | |
| 1999–2000 | Chelsea | 0 | 0 | | |
| 1999–2000 | *Crystal Palace* | 13 | 3 | | |
| 2000–01 | Chelsea | 0 | 0 | | |
| 2000–01 | *Crystal Palace* | 39 | 13 | **52** | **16** |
| 2001–02 | Chelsea | 22 | 4 | | |
| 2002–03 | *Moenchengladbach* | 16 | 7 | **16** | **7** |
| 2002–03 | Chelsea | 0 | 0 | | |
| 2003–04 | Chelsea | 0 | 0 | **32** | **5** |
| 2003–04 | *Birmingham C* | 32 | 17 | **32** | **17** |

**GALLACCIO, Michele (F) 0 0**
H: 5 9 W: 10 12 b.Rome 3-3-86
*Source:* Lazio.

| | | | | | |
|---|---|---|---|---|---|
| 2002–03 | Chelsea | 0 | 0 | | |
| 2003–04 | Chelsea | 0 | 0 | | |

**GALLAS, William (D) 200 7**
H: 6 0 W: 12 02 b.Asnieres 17-8-77
*Honours:* France 20 caps.

| | | | | | |
|---|---|---|---|---|---|
| 1996–97 | Caen | 18 | 0 | **18** | **0** |
| 1997–98 | Marseille | 3 | 0 | | |
| 1998–99 | Marseille | 30 | 0 | | |
| 1999–2000 | Marseille | 22 | 0 | | |
| 2000–01 | Marseille | 30 | 2 | **85** | **2** |
| 2001–02 | Chelsea | 30 | 1 | | |
| 2002–03 | Chelsea | 38 | 4 | | |
| 2003–04 | Chelsea | 29 | 0 | **97** | **5** |

**GEREMI (M) 166 17**
H: 5 9 W: 13 03 b.Bafoussam 20-12-78
*Source:* Racing Bafousam. *Honours:* Cameroon 60 full caps.

| | | | | | |
|---|---|---|---|---|---|
| 1997 | Cerro Porteno | 6 | 0 | **6** | **0** |
| 1997–98 | Genclerbirligi | 28 | 4 | | |
| 1998–99 | Genclerbirligi | 29 | 5 | **57** | **9** |
| 1999–2000 | Real Madrid | 20 | 0 | | |
| 2000–01 | Real Madrid | 16 | 0 | | |
| 2001–02 | Real Madrid | 9 | 0 | **45** | **0** |
| 2002–03 | Middlesbrough | 33 | 7 | **33** | **7** |
| 2003–04 | Chelsea | 25 | 1 | **25** | **1** |

**GRONKJAER, Jesper (M) 230 28**
H: 6 2 W: 12 11 b.Nuuk 12-8-77
*Honours:* Denmark 49 full caps, 5 goals.

| | | | | | |
|---|---|---|---|---|---|
| 1995–96 | Aalborg | 29 | 3 | | |
| 1996–97 | Aalborg | 28 | 1 | | |
| 1997–98 | Aalborg | 29 | 6 | **86** | **10** |
| 1998–99 | Ajax | 25 | 8 | | |
| 1999–2000 | Ajax | 25 | 3 | | |
| 2000–01 | Ajax | 6 | 0 | **56** | **11** |
| 2000–01 | Chelsea | 14 | 1 | | |
| 2001–02 | Chelsea | 13 | 0 | | |
| 2002–03 | Chelsea | 30 | 4 | | |
| 2003–04 | Chelsea | 31 | 2 | **88** | **7** |

**GUDJOHNSEN, Eidur (F) 214 68**
H: 6 1 W: 14 01 b.Reykjavik 15-9-78
*Honours:* Iceland Youth, 27 full caps, 9 goals.

| | | | | | |
|---|---|---|---|---|---|
| 1994–95 | Valur | 17 | 7 | **17** | **7** |
| 1995–96 | PSV Eindhoven | 13 | 3 | | |
| 1996–97 | PSV Eindhoven | 0 | 0 | **13** | **3** |
| 1998 | KR | 6 | 0 | **6** | **0** |
| 1998–99 | Bolton W | 14 | 5 | | |
| 1999–2000 | Bolton W | 41 | 13 | **55** | **18** |
| 2000–01 | Chelsea | 30 | 10 | | |
| 2001–02 | Chelsea | 32 | 14 | | |
| 2002–03 | Chelsea | 35 | 10 | | |
| 2003–04 | Chelsea | 26 | 6 | **123** | **40** |

**HASSELBAINK, Jimmy Floyd (F) 299 159**
H: 5 10 W: 13 11 b.Paramaribo 27-3-72
*Honours:* Holland 23 full caps, 9 goals.

| | | | | | |
|---|---|---|---|---|---|
| 1995–96 | Campomairorense | 31 | 12 | **31** | **12** |
| 1996–97 | Boavista | 29 | 20 | **29** | **20** |
| 1997–98 | Leeds U | 33 | 16 | | |
| 1998–99 | Leeds U | 36 | 18 | **69** | **34** |
| 1999–2000 | Atletico Madrid | 34 | 24 | **34** | **24** |
| 2000–01 | Chelsea | 35 | 23 | | |
| 2001–02 | Chelsea | 35 | 23 | | |
| 2002–03 | Chelsea | 36 | 11 | | |
| 2003–04 | Chelsea | 30 | 12 | **136** | **69** |

**HOLLANDS, Danny (M) 0 0**
H: 6 0 W: 10 02 b.Ashford 6-11-85
*Source:* Trainee.

| | | | | | |
|---|---|---|---|---|---|
| 2003–04 | Chelsea | 0 | 0 | | |

**HUTH, Robert (D) 19 0**
H: 6 3 W: 13 12 b.Berlin 18-8-84

| | | | | | |
|---|---|---|---|---|---|
| 2001–02 | Chelsea | 1 | 0 | | |
| 2002–03 | Chelsea | 2 | 0 | | |
| 2003–04 | Chelsea | 16 | 0 | **19** | **0** |

**JEFFREYS, Danny* (M) 0 0**
H: 5 7 W: 9 12 b.Hammersmith 21-1-85
*Source:* Scholar. *Honours:* England Youth.

| | | | | | |
|---|---|---|---|---|---|
| 2001–02 | Chelsea | 0 | 0 | | |
| 2002–03 | Chelsea | 0 | 0 | | |
| 2003–04 | Chelsea | 0 | 0 | | |

**JOHNSON, Glen (D) 42 3**
H: 5 11 W: 12 11 b.Greenwich 23-8-84
*Source:* Scholar. *Honours:* England Youth, Under-20, Under-21, 1 full cap.

| | | | | | |
|---|---|---|---|---|---|
| 2001–02 | West Ham U | 0 | 0 | | |
| 2002–03 | West Ham U | 15 | 0 | **15** | **0** |
| 2002–03 | *Millwall* | 8 | 0 | **8** | **0** |
| 2003–04 | Chelsea | 19 | 3 | **19** | **3** |

**KEENAN, Joe (M) 2 0**
H: 5 8 W: 10 03 b.Southampton 14-10-82
*Source:* Trainee. *Honours:* England Youth, Under-20.

| | | | | | |
|---|---|---|---|---|---|
| 1999–2000 | Chelsea | 0 | 0 | | |
| 2000–01 | Chelsea | 0 | 0 | | |
| 2001–02 | Chelsea | 1 | 0 | | |
| 2002–03 | Chelsea | 1 | 0 | | |
| 2003–04 | Chelsea | 0 | 0 | **2** | **0** |

**KITAMIRIKE, Joel* (D) 22 0**
H: 5 11 W: 12 11 b.Kampala 5-4-84
*Source:* Scholar. *Honours:* England Youth.

| | | | | | |
|---|---|---|---|---|---|
| 2000–01 | Chelsea | 0 | 0 | | |
| 2001–02 | Chelsea | 0 | 0 | | |
| 2002–03 | Chelsea | 0 | 0 | | |
| 2003–04 | Chelsea | 0 | 0 | | |
| 2003–04 | *Brentford* | 22 | 0 | **22** | **0** |

**KNEISSL, Sebastian (F) 0 0**
H: 6 0 W: 13 03 b.Lindelfels 13-1-83

| | | | | | |
|---|---|---|---|---|---|
| 2000–01 | Chelsea | 0 | 0 | | |
| 2001–02 | Chelsea | 0 | 0 | | |
| 2002–03 | Chelsea | 0 | 0 | | |
| 2003–04 | Chelsea | 0 | 0 | | |

**LAMPARD, Frank (M) 270 45**
H: 6 0 W: 13 12 b.Romford 20-6-78
*Source:* Trainee. *Honours:* England Youth, Under-21, B, 23 full caps, 5 goals.

| | | | | | |
|---|---|---|---|---|---|
| 1994–95 | West Ham U | 0 | 0 | | |
| 1995–96 | West Ham U | 2 | 0 | | |
| 1995–96 | *Swansea C* | 9 | 1 | **9** | **1** |
| 1996–97 | West Ham U | 13 | 0 | | |
| 1997–98 | West Ham U | 31 | 4 | | |
| 1998–99 | West Ham U | 38 | 5 | | |
| 1999–2000 | West Ham U | 34 | 7 | | |
| 2000–01 | West Ham U | 30 | 7 | **148** | **23** |
| 2001–02 | Chelsea | 37 | 5 | | |
| 2002–03 | Chelsea | 38 | 6 | | |
| 2003–04 | Chelsea | 38 | 10 | **113** | **21** |

**MACHO, Jurgen (G) 22 0**
H: 6 3 W: 13 05 b.Vienna 24-8-77
*Source:* Honda Havelka, First Vienna.

| | | | | | |
|---|---|---|---|---|---|
| 2000–01 | Sunderland | 5 | 0 | | |
| 2001–02 | Sunderland | 4 | 0 | | |
| 2002–03 | Sunderland | 13 | 0 | **22** | **0** |
| 2003–04 | Chelsea | 0 | 0 | | |

**MAKALAMBAY, Yves (G) 0 0**
H: 6 5 W: 14 09 b.Brussels 31-1-86

| | | | | | |
|---|---|---|---|---|---|
| 2003–04 | Chelsea | 0 | 0 | | |

**MAKELELE, Claude (M) 396 16**
H: 5 7 W: 10 08 b.Kinshasa 18-2-73
*Source:* Brest. *Honours:* France 34 full caps.

| | | | | | |
|---|---|---|---|---|---|
| 1992–93 | Nantes | 34 | 1 | | |
| 1993–94 | Nantes | 30 | 0 | | |
| 1994–95 | Nantes | 36 | 3 | | |
| 1995–96 | Nantes | 33 | 0 | | |
| 1996–97 | Nantes | 36 | 5 | **169** | **9** |
| 1997–98 | Marseille | 33 | 4 | **33** | **4** |
| 1998–99 | Celta Vigo | 36 | 2 | | |
| 1999–2000 | Celta Vigo | 34 | 1 | **70** | **3** |
| 2000–01 | Real Madrid | 33 | 0 | | |
| 2001–02 | Real Madrid | 32 | 0 | | |
| 2002–03 | Real Madrid | 29 | 0 | **94** | **0** |
| 2003–04 | Chelsea | 30 | 0 | **30** | **0** |

**McKINLAY, Kevin (F) 0 0**
H: 5 11 W: 11 01 b.Stirling 28-2-86
*Source:* Trainee.

| | | | | | |
|---|---|---|---|---|---|
| 2003–04 | Chelsea | 0 | 0 | | |

**MELCHIOT, Mario* (D) 203 5**
H: 6 2 W: 12 08 b.Amsterdam 4-11-76
*Honours:* Holland 11 full caps.

| | | | | | |
|---|---|---|---|---|---|
| 1996–97 | Ajax | 23 | 0 | | |
| 1997–98 | Ajax | 26 | 0 | | |
| 1998–99 | Ajax | 24 | 1 | **73** | **1** |
| 1999–2000 | Chelsea | 5 | 0 | | |
| 2000–01 | Chelsea | 31 | 0 | | |
| 2001–02 | Chelsea | 37 | 2 | | |
| 2002–03 | Chelsea | 34 | 0 | | |
| 2003–04 | Chelsea | 23 | 2 | **130** | **4** |

**MORAIS, Filipe (M) 0 0**
H: 5 8 W: 11 07 b.Lisbon 21-11-85
*Source:* Trainee.

| | | | | | |
|---|---|---|---|---|---|
| 2003–04 | Chelsea | 0 | 0 | | |

**MUTU, Adrian (F) 197 73**
H: 5 11 W: 11 11 b.Calinesti 8-1-79
*Honours:* Romania 32 full caps, 8 goals.

| | | | | | |
|---|---|---|---|---|---|
| 1996–97 | Arges | 5 | 0 | | |
| 1997–98 | Arges | 21 | 4 | | |
| 1998–99 | Arges | 15 | 7 | **41** | **11** |
| 1998–99 | Dinamo Bucharest | 15 | 4 | | |
| 1999–2000 | Dinamo Bucharest | 18 | 18 | **33** | **22** |
| 1999–2000 | Internazionale | 10 | 0 | **10** | **0** |
| 2000–01 | Verona | 25 | 4 | | |
| 2001–02 | Verona | 32 | 12 | **57** | **16** |

| | | | | | |
|---|---|---|---|---|---|
| 2002–03 | Parma | 31 | 18 | **31** | **18** |
| 2003–04 | Chelsea | 25 | 6 | **25** | **6** |

**NICOLAS, Alexis (M)** **2 0**
H: 5 8 W: 9 13 b.Westminster 13-2-83
*Source:* Scholar.

| | | | | | |
|---|---|---|---|---|---|
| 2000–01 | Aston Villa | 0 | 0 | | |
| 2001–02 | Aston Villa | 0 | 0 | | |
| 2001–02 | Chelsea | 0 | 0 | | |
| 2002–03 | Chelsea | 0 | 0 | | |
| 2003–04 | Chelsea | 2 | 0 | **2** | **0** |

**OLIVEIRA, Filipe (F)** **4 0**
H: 5 10 W: 11 11 b.Braga 27-5-84

| | | | | | |
|---|---|---|---|---|---|
| 2001–02 | Chelsea | 0 | 0 | | |
| 2002–03 | Chelsea | 3 | 0 | | |
| 2003–04 | Chelsea | 1 | 0 | **4** | **0** |

**PARKER, Scott (M)** **145 11**
H: 5 9 W: 10 10 b.Lambeth 13-10-80
*Source:* Trainee. *Honours:* England Schools, Youth, Under-21, 2 full caps.

| | | | | | |
|---|---|---|---|---|---|
| 1997–98 | Charlton Ath | 3 | 0 | | |
| 1998–99 | Charlton Ath | 4 | 0 | | |
| 1999–2000 | Charlton Ath | 15 | 1 | | |
| 2000–01 | Charlton Ath | 20 | 1 | | |
| 2000–01 | *Norwich C* | 6 | 1 | **6** | **1** |
| 2001–02 | Charlton Ath | 38 | 1 | | |
| 2002–03 | Charlton Ath | 28 | 4 | | |
| 2003–04 | Charlton Ath | 20 | 2 | **128** | **9** |
| 2003–04 | Chelsea | 11 | 1 | **11** | **1** |

**PETIT, Emmanuel* (M)** **385 16**
H: 6 1 W: 13 05 b.Dieppe 22-9-70
*Source:* ES Arques. *Honours:* France 63 full caps, 6 goals.

| | | | | | |
|---|---|---|---|---|---|
| 1988–89 | Monaco | 9 | 0 | | |
| 1989–90 | Monaco | 28 | 0 | | |
| 1990–91 | Monaco | 27 | 1 | | |
| 1991–92 | Monaco | 28 | 0 | | |
| 1992–93 | Monaco | 25 | 1 | | |
| 1993–94 | Monaco | 28 | 0 | | |
| 1994–95 | Monaco | 25 | 1 | | |
| 1995–96 | Monaco | 23 | 1 | | |
| 1996–97 | Monaco | 29 | 0 | **222** | **4** |
| 1997–98 | Arsenal | 32 | 2 | | |
| 1998–99 | Arsenal | 27 | 4 | | |
| 1999–2000 | Arsenal | 26 | 3 | **85** | **9** |
| 2000–01 | Barcelona | 23 | 1 | **23** | **1** |
| 2001–02 | Chelsea | 27 | 1 | | |
| 2002–03 | Chelsea | 24 | 1 | | |
| 2003–04 | Chelsea | 4 | 0 | **55** | **2** |

**PIDGELEY, Lenny (G)** **27 0**
H: 6 3 W: 13 05 b.Isleworth 7-2-84
*Source:* Scholar. *Honours:* England Under-20.

| | | | | | |
|---|---|---|---|---|---|
| 2003–04 | Chelsea | 0 | 0 | | |
| 2003–04 | *Watford* | 27 | 0 | **27** | **0** |

**ROCASTLE, Craig (M)** **7 0**
H: 6 1 W: 12 13 b.Lewisham 17-8-81
*Source:* Kingstonian.

| | | | | | |
|---|---|---|---|---|---|
| 2003–04 | Chelsea | 0 | 0 | | |
| 2003–04 | *Barnsley* | 5 | 0 | **5** | **0** |
| 2003–04 | *Lincoln C* | 2 | 0 | **2** | **0** |

**SMERTIN, Alexei (M)** **373 27**
H: 5 9 W: 10 08 b.Barnaul 1-5-75
*Honours:* Russia 42 full caps.

| | | | | | |
|---|---|---|---|---|---|
| 1992 | Dynamo Barnaul | 18 | 2 | | |
| 1993 | Dynamo Barnaul | 24 | 0 | **42** | **2** |
| 1994 | Zarya | 49 | 2 | | |
| 1995 | Zarya | 37 | 7 | | |
| 1996 | Zarya | 34 | 4 | | |
| 1997 | Zarya | 13 | 0 | **133** | **13** |
| 1997 | Uralan | 23 | 0 | | |
| 1998 | Uralan | 26 | 3 | **49** | **3** |
| 1999 | Lokomotiv Moscow | 29 | 6 | | |
| 2000 | Lokomotiv Moscow | 10 | 1 | **39** | **7** |
| 2000–01 | Bordeaux | 23 | 0 | | |
| 2001–02 | Bordeaux | 28 | 0 | | |
| 2002–03 | Bordeaux | 33 | 2 | **84** | **2** |
| 2003–04 | Chelsea | 0 | 0 | | |
| 2003–04 | *Portsmouth* | 26 | 0 | **26** | **0** |

**SMITH, Dean (D)** **0 0**
H: 5 10 W: 9 11 b.Islington 13-8-86
*Source:* Trainee.

| | | | | | |
|---|---|---|---|---|---|
| 2003–04 | Chelsea | 0 | 0 | | |

**STANIC, Mario (M)** **324 88**
H: 6 2 W: 13 11 b.Sarajevo 10-4-72
*Honours:* Croatia 49 full caps, 7 goals.

| | | | | | |
|---|---|---|---|---|---|
| 1988–89 | Zeljeznicar | 14 | 0 | | |
| 1989–90 | Zeljeznicar | 14 | 0 | | |
| 1990–91 | Zeljeznicar | 28 | 1 | | |
| 1991–92 | Zeljeznicar | 21 | 11 | **77** | **12** |
| 1992–93 | Croatia Zagreb | 26 | 11 | **26** | **11** |
| 1993–94 | Gijon | 34 | 7 | **34** | **7** |
| 1994–95 | Benfica | 14 | 5 | **14** | **5** |
| 1995–96 | FC Brugge | 30 | 20 | | |
| 1996–97 | FC Brugge | 7 | 7 | **37** | **27** |
| 1996–97 | Parma | 13 | 3 | | |
| 1997–98 | Parma | 23 | 4 | | |
| 1998–99 | Parma | 18 | 7 | | |
| 1999–2000 | Parma | 23 | 5 | **77** | **19** |
| 2000–01 | Chelsea | 12 | 2 | | |
| 2001–02 | Chelsea | 27 | 1 | | |
| 2002–03 | Chelsea | 18 | 4 | | |
| 2003–04 | Chelsea | 2 | 0 | **59** | **7** |

**SULLIVAN, Neil (G)** **250 0**
H: 6 3 W: 15 04 b.Sutton 24-2-70
*Source:* Trainee. *Honours:* Scotland 28 full caps.

| | | | | | |
|---|---|---|---|---|---|
| 1988–89 | Wimbledon | 0 | 0 | | |
| 1989–90 | Wimbledon | 0 | 0 | | |
| 1990–91 | Wimbledon | 1 | 0 | | |
| 1991–92 | Wimbledon | 1 | 0 | | |
| 1991–92 | *Crystal Palace* | 1 | 0 | **1** | **0** |
| 1992–93 | Wimbledon | 1 | 0 | | |
| 1993–94 | Wimbledon | 2 | 0 | | |
| 1994–95 | Wimbledon | 11 | 0 | | |
| 1995–96 | Wimbledon | 16 | 0 | | |
| 1996–97 | Wimbledon | 36 | 0 | | |
| 1997–98 | Wimbledon | 38 | 0 | | |
| 1998–99 | Wimbledon | 38 | 0 | | |
| 1999–2000 | Wimbledon | 37 | 0 | **181** | **0** |
| 2000–01 | Tottenham H | 35 | 0 | | |
| 2001–02 | Tottenham H | 29 | 0 | | |
| 2002–03 | Tottenham H | 0 | 0 | **64** | **0** |
| 2003–04 | Chelsea | 4 | 0 | **4** | **0** |

**TERRY, John (D)** **120 7**
H: 6 1 W: 13 12 b.Barking 7-12-80
*Source:* Trainee. *Honours:* England Under-21, 11 full caps.

| | | | | | |
|---|---|---|---|---|---|
| 1997–98 | Chelsea | 0 | 0 | | |
| 1998–99 | Chelsea | 2 | 0 | | |
| 1999–2000 | Chelsea | 4 | 0 | | |
| 1999–2000 | *Nottingham F* | 6 | 0 | **6** | **0** |
| 2000–01 | Chelsea | 22 | 1 | | |
| 2001–02 | Chelsea | 33 | 1 | | |
| 2002–03 | Chelsea | 20 | 3 | | |
| 2003–04 | Chelsea | 33 | 2 | **114** | **7** |

**TILLEN, Sam (D)** **0 0**
H: 5 9 W: 10 12 b.Reading 16-4-85
*Source:* Trainee. *Honours:* England Youth.

| | | | | | |
|---|---|---|---|---|---|
| 2002–03 | Chelsea | 0 | 0 | | |
| 2003–04 | Chelsea | 0 | 0 | | |

**VERON, Juan Sebastian (F)** **275 38**
H: 5 11 W: 12 04 b.La Plata 9-3-75
*Honours:* Argentina 56 full caps, 9 goals.

| | | | | | |
|---|---|---|---|---|---|
| 1993–94 | Estudiantes | 7 | 0 | | |
| 1994–95 | Estudiantes | 38 | 5 | | |
| 1995–96 | Estudiantes | 15 | 2 | **60** | **7** |
| 1995–96 | Boca Juniors | 17 | 4 | **17** | **4** |
| 1996–97 | Sampdoria | 32 | 5 | | |
| 1997–98 | Sampdoria | 29 | 2 | **61** | **7** |
| 1998–99 | Parma | 26 | 1 | **26** | **1** |
| 1999–2000 | Lazio | 31 | 8 | | |
| 2000–01 | Lazio | 22 | 3 | **53** | **11** |
| 2001–02 | Manchester U | 26 | 5 | | |
| 2002–03 | Manchester U | 25 | 2 | **51** | **7** |
| 2003–04 | Chelsea | 7 | 1 | **7** | **1** |

**WATT, Steven (D)** **0 0**
H: 6 3 W: 13 12 b.Aberdeen 1-5-85
*Source:* Trainee.

| | | | | | |
|---|---|---|---|---|---|
| 2002–03 | Chelsea | 0 | 0 | | |
| 2003–04 | Chelsea | 0 | 0 | | |

**WOODARDS, Danny (F)** **0 0**
H: 5 11 W: 11 01 b.Forest Gate 7-10-83
*Source:* Trainee.

| | | | | | |
|---|---|---|---|---|---|
| 2003–04 | Chelsea | 0 | 0 | | |

**ZENDEN, Boudewijn (M)** **249 34**
H: 5 8 W: 11 11 b.Maastricht 15-8-76
*Honours:* Holland 53 full caps, 7 goals.

| | | | | | |
|---|---|---|---|---|---|
| 1994–95 | PSV Eindhoven | 27 | 5 | | |
| 1995–96 | PSV Eindhoven | 25 | 7 | | |
| 1996–97 | PSV Eindhoven | 34 | 8 | | |
| 1997–98 | PSV Eindhoven | 25 | 3 | **111** | **23** |
| 1998–99 | Barcelona | 25 | 0 | | |
| 1999–2000 | Barcelona | 29 | 2 | | |
| 2000–01 | Barcelona | 10 | 1 | **64** | **3** |
| 2001–02 | Chelsea | 22 | 3 | | |
| 2002–03 | Chelsea | 21 | 1 | | |
| 2003–04 | Chelsea | 0 | 0 | **43** | **4** |
| 2003–04 | *Middlesbrough* | 31 | 4 | **31** | **4** |

**Scholars**
Brand, Edward C; Grant, Anthony P S A; Hudell, Ben J C; Pettigrew, Adrian R J; Smith, James D; Tillen, Joseph E; Younghusband, James J; Younghusband, Philip J

## CHELTENHAM T (22)

**BIRD, David (M)** **38 0**
H: 5 9 W: 12 00 b.Gloucester 26-12-84
*Source:* Cinderford T.

| | | | | | |
|---|---|---|---|---|---|
| 2001–02 | Cheltenham T | 0 | 0 | | |
| 2002–03 | Cheltenham T | 14 | 0 | | |
| 2003–04 | Cheltenham T | 24 | 0 | **38** | **0** |

**BOOK, Steve* (G)** **172 0**
H: 5 11 W: 11 08 b.Bournemouth 7-7-69

| | | | | | |
|---|---|---|---|---|---|
| 1997–98 | Brighton & HA | 0 | 0 | | |
| 1998–99 | Lincoln C | 0 | 0 | | |
| From Forest Green R. | | | | | |
| 1999–2000 | Cheltenham T | 46 | 0 | | |
| 2000–01 | Cheltenham T | 46 | 0 | | |
| 2001–02 | Cheltenham T | 39 | 0 | | |
| 2002–03 | Cheltenham T | 36 | 0 | | |
| 2003–04 | Cheltenham T | 5 | 0 | **172** | **0** |

**BRAYSON, Paul* (F)** **187 33**
H: 5 4 W: 10 10 b.Newcastle 16-9-77
*Source:* Trainee. *Honours:* England Youth.

| | | | | | |
|---|---|---|---|---|---|
| 1995–96 | Newcastle U | 0 | 0 | | |
| 1996–97 | Newcastle U | 0 | 0 | | |
| 1996–97 | *Swansea C* | 11 | 5 | **11** | **5** |
| 1997–98 | Newcastle U | 0 | 0 | | |
| 1997–98 | Reading | 6 | 1 | | |
| 1998–99 | Reading | 28 | 0 | | |
| 1999–2000 | Reading | 7 | 0 | **41** | **1** |
| 1999–2000 | *Cardiff C* | 9 | 1 | | |
| 2000–01 | Cardiff C | 40 | 15 | | |
| 2001–02 | Cardiff C | 35 | 3 | **84** | **19** |
| 2002–03 | Cheltenham T | 20 | 1 | | |
| 2003–04 | Cheltenham T | 31 | 7 | **51** | **8** |

**BROUGH, John# (D)** **218 10**
H: 6 0 W: 12 10 b.Ilkeston 8-1-73

| | | | | | |
|---|---|---|---|---|---|
| 1991–92 | Notts Co | 0 | 0 | | |
| 1992–93 | Shrewsbury T | 14 | 1 | | |
| 1993–94 | Shrewsbury T | 2 | 0 | **16** | **1** |
| From Telford U. | | | | | |
| 1994–95 | Hereford U | 18 | 1 | | |
| 1995–96 | Hereford U | 22 | 1 | | |
| 1996–97 | Hereford U | 39 | 1 | **79** | **3** |
| 1999–2000 | Cheltenham T | 37 | 2 | | |
| 2000–01 | Cheltenham T | 10 | 0 | | |
| 2001–02 | Cheltenham T | 21 | 1 | | |
| 2002–03 | Cheltenham T | 29 | 1 | | |
| 2003–04 | Cheltenham T | 26 | 2 | **123** | **6** |

**BUTTERY, Luke* (D)** **0 0**
H: 5 10 W: 10 12 b.Wegberg 12-2-85

| | | | | | |
|---|---|---|---|---|---|
| 2002–03 | Cheltenham T | 0 | 0 | | |
| 2003–04 | Cheltenham T | 0 | 0 | | |

**CLEVERLEY, Ben* (M)** **8 0**
H: 5 9 W: 10 00 b.Bristol 12-9-81
*Source:* Scholar.

| | | | | | |
|---|---|---|---|---|---|
| 2001–02 | Bristol C | 0 | 0 | | |
| 2002–03 | Bristol C | 0 | 0 | | |
| 2003–04 | Cheltenham T | 8 | 0 | **8** | **0** |

**CORBETT, Luke (F)** **1 0**
H: 6 0 W: 11 06 b.Worcester 10-8-84

| | | | | | |
|---|---|---|---|---|---|
| 2002–03 | Cheltenham T | 0 | 0 | | |
| 2003–04 | Cheltenham T | 1 | 0 | **1** | **0** |

**COZIC, Bertrand‡ (M)** **7 1**
H: 5 10 W: 12 06 b.Quimper 18-5-78
*Source:* Team Bath.

| | | | | | |
|---|---|---|---|---|---|
| 2003–04 | Cheltenham T | 7 | 1 | **7** | **1** |

**DEVANEY, Martin (M)** **165 28**
H: 5 11 W: 12 00 b.Cheltenham 1-6-80
*Source:* Trainee.

| | | | | | |
|---|---|---|---|---|---|
| 1997–98 | Coventry C | 0 | 0 | | |
| 1998–99 | Coventry C | 0 | 0 | | |

| | | | | | |
|---|---|---|---|---|---|
| 1999–2000 | Cheltenham T | 26 | 6 | | |
| 2000–01 | Cheltenham T | 34 | 10 | | |
| 2001–02 | Cheltenham T | 25 | 1 | | |
| 2002–03 | Cheltenham T | 40 | 6 | | |
| 2003–04 | Cheltenham T | 40 | 5 | **165** | **28** |

**DOBSON, Craig* (M)** **2 0**
H: 5 7 W: 10 06 b.Chingford 23-1-84
*Source:* Crystal Palace scholar. *Honours:* Jamaica 1 full cap.

| | | | | | |
|---|---|---|---|---|---|
| 2003–04 | Cheltenham T | 2 | 0 | **2** | **0** |

**DUFF, Michael (D)** **201 12**
H: 6 1 W: 12 05 b.Belfast 11-1-78
*Source:* Trainee. *Honours:* Northern Ireland 3 full caps.

| | | | | | |
|---|---|---|---|---|---|
| 1999–2000 | Cheltenham T | 31 | 2 | | |
| 2000–01 | Cheltenham T | 39 | 5 | | |
| 2001–02 | Cheltenham T | 45 | 3 | | |
| 2002–03 | Cheltenham T | 44 | 2 | | |
| 2003–04 | Cheltenham T | 42 | 0 | **201** | **12** |

**DUFF, Shane (D)** **33 1**
H: 6 1 W: 12 10 b.Wroughton 2-4-82
*Honours:* Northern Ireland Under-21.

| | | | | | |
|---|---|---|---|---|---|
| 2000–01 | Cheltenham T | 0 | 0 | | |
| 2001–02 | Cheltenham T | 0 | 0 | | |
| 2002–03 | Cheltenham T | 18 | 0 | | |
| 2003–04 | Cheltenham T | 15 | 1 | **33** | **1** |

**FINNIGAN, John (M)** **225 7**
H: 5 8 W: 10 09 b.Wakefield 29-3-76
*Source:* Trainee.

| | | | | | |
|---|---|---|---|---|---|
| 1992–93 | Nottingham F | 0 | 0 | | |
| 1993–94 | Nottingham F | 0 | 0 | | |
| 1994–95 | Nottingham F | 0 | 0 | | |
| 1995–96 | Nottingham F | 0 | 0 | | |
| 1996–97 | Nottingham F | 0 | 0 | | |
| 1997–98 | Nottingham F | 0 | 0 | | |
| 1997–98 | *Lincoln C* | 6 | 0 | | |
| 1998–99 | Lincoln C | 37 | 1 | | |
| 1999–2000 | Lincoln C | 37 | 2 | | |
| 2000–01 | Lincoln C | 40 | 0 | | |
| 2001–02 | Lincoln C | 23 | 0 | **143** | **3** |
| 2001–02 | Cheltenham T | 12 | 2 | | |
| 2002–03 | Cheltenham T | 37 | 1 | | |
| 2003–04 | Cheltenham T | 33 | 1 | **82** | **4** |

**FORSYTH, Richard* (M)** **243 25**
H: 5 11 W: 12 04 b.Dudley 3-10-70
*Source:* Kidderminster H.

| | | | | | |
|---|---|---|---|---|---|
| 1995–96 | Birmingham C | 26 | 2 | **26** | **2** |
| 1996–97 | Stoke C | 40 | 8 | | |
| 1997–98 | Stoke C | 37 | 7 | | |
| 1998–99 | Stoke C | 18 | 2 | **95** | **17** |
| 1999–2000 | Blackpool | 13 | 0 | **13** | **0** |
| 2000–01 | Peterborough U | 30 | 2 | | |
| 2001–02 | Peterborough U | 32 | 0 | | |
| 2002–03 | Peterborough U | 8 | 0 | **70** | **2** |
| 2002–03 | Cheltenham T | 12 | 2 | | |
| 2003–04 | Cheltenham T | 27 | 2 | **39** | **4** |

**FYFE, Graham (D)** **32 1**
H: 5 6 W: 10 06 b.Dundee 7-12-82

| | | | | | |
|---|---|---|---|---|---|
| 2001–02 | Celtic | 0 | 0 | | |
| 2002–03 | Raith R | 12 | 1 | **12** | **1** |
| 2003–04 | Cheltenham T | 20 | 0 | **20** | **0** |

**GILL, Jeremy† (D)** **108 0**
H: 5 11 W: 12 00 b.Clevedon 8-9-70
*Source:* Yeovil T.

| | | | | | |
|---|---|---|---|---|---|
| 1997–98 | Birmingham C | 3 | 0 | | |
| 1998–99 | Birmingham C | 3 | 0 | | |
| 1999–2000 | Birmingham C | 11 | 0 | | |
| 2000–01 | Birmingham C | 29 | 0 | | |
| 2001–02 | Birmingham C | 14 | 0 | | |
| 2002–03 | Birmingham C | 0 | 0 | **60** | **0** |
| 2002–03 | Northampton T | 41 | 0 | | |
| 2003–04 | Northampton T | 0 | 0 | **41** | **0** |
| 2003–04 | Cheltenham T | 7 | 0 | **7** | **0** |

**GRIFFIN, Anthony* (D)** **102 1**
H: 5 11 W: 11 02 b.Bournemouth 22-3-79
*Source:* Trainee.

| | | | | | |
|---|---|---|---|---|---|
| 1997–98 | Bournemouth | 0 | 0 | | |
| 1998–99 | Bournemouth | 6 | 0 | **6** | **0** |
| 1999–2000 | Cheltenham T | 24 | 0 | | |
| 2000–01 | Cheltenham T | 22 | 1 | | |
| 2001–02 | Cheltenham T | 24 | 0 | | |
| 2002–03 | Cheltenham T | 11 | 0 | | |
| 2003–04 | Cheltenham T | 15 | 0 | **96** | **1** |

**HIGGS, Shane (G)** **64 0**
H: 6 3 W: 14 06 b.Oxford 13-5-77
*Source:* Trainee.

| | | | | | |
|---|---|---|---|---|---|
| 1994–95 | Bristol R | 0 | 0 | | |
| 1995–96 | Bristol R | 0 | 0 | | |
| 1996–97 | Bristol R | 2 | 0 | | |
| 1997–98 | Bristol R | 8 | 0 | **10** | **0** |

From Worcester C.

| | | | | | |
|---|---|---|---|---|---|
| 1999–2000 | Cheltenham T | 0 | 0 | | |
| 2000–01 | Cheltenham T | 1 | 0 | | |
| 2001–02 | Cheltenham T | 1 | 0 | | |
| 2002–03 | Cheltenham T | 10 | 0 | | |
| 2003–04 | Cheltenham T | 42 | 0 | **54** | **0** |

**HOWELLS, Lee* (M)** **121 6**
H: 5 11 W: 11 12 b.Fremantle 14-10-68
*Source:* Apprentice.

| | | | | | |
|---|---|---|---|---|---|
| 1986–87 | Bristol R | 0 | 0 | | |

From Brisbane Lions.

| | | | | | |
|---|---|---|---|---|---|
| 1999–2000 | Cheltenham T | 45 | 3 | | |
| 2000–01 | Cheltenham T | 36 | 1 | | |
| 2001–02 | Cheltenham T | 31 | 2 | | |
| 2002–03 | Cheltenham T | 0 | 0 | | |
| 2003–04 | Cheltenham T | 9 | 0 | **121** | **6** |

**McCANN, Grant (M)** **106 17**
H: 5 10 W: 11 00 b.Belfast 14-4-80
*Source:* Trainee. *Honours:* Northern Ireland Youth, Under-21, 9 full caps.

| | | | | | |
|---|---|---|---|---|---|
| 1998–99 | West Ham U | 0 | 0 | | |
| 1999–2000 | West Ham U | 0 | 0 | | |
| 2000–01 | West Ham U | 1 | 0 | | |
| 2000–01 | *Notts Co* | 2 | 0 | **2** | **0** |
| 2000–01 | *Cheltenham T* | 30 | 3 | | |
| 2001–02 | West Ham U | 3 | 0 | | |
| 2002–03 | West Ham U | 0 | 0 | **4** | **0** |
| 2002–03 | Cheltenham T | 27 | 6 | | |
| 2003–04 | Cheltenham T | 43 | 8 | **100** | **17** |

**ODEJAYI, Kayode (F)** **36 5**
H: 6 2 W: 12 02 b.Ibadon 21-2-82
*Source:* Scholarship.

| | | | | | |
|---|---|---|---|---|---|
| 1999–2000 | Bristol C | 3 | 0 | | |
| 2000–01 | Bristol C | 3 | 0 | | |
| 2001–02 | Bristol C | 0 | 0 | | |
| 2002–03 | Bristol C | 0 | 0 | **6** | **0** |
| 2003–04 | Cheltenham T | 30 | 5 | **30** | **5** |

**SPENCER, Damien (F)** **85 16**
H: 6 1 W: 14 00 b.Ascot 19-9-81
*Source:* Scholarship.

| | | | | | |
|---|---|---|---|---|---|
| 1999–2000 | Bristol C | 9 | 1 | | |
| 2000–01 | Bristol C | 4 | 0 | | |
| 2000–01 | *Exeter C* | 6 | 0 | **6** | **0** |
| 2001–02 | Bristol C | 0 | 0 | **13** | **1** |
| 2002–03 | Cheltenham T | 30 | 6 | | |
| 2003–04 | Cheltenham T | 36 | 9 | **66** | **15** |

**TAYLOR, Bob* (F)** **577 200**
H: 5 10 W: 12 04 b.Easington 3-2-67
*Source:* Horden CW.

| | | | | | |
|---|---|---|---|---|---|
| 1985–86 | Leeds U | 2 | 0 | | |
| 1986–87 | Leeds U | 2 | 0 | | |
| 1987–88 | Leeds U | 32 | 9 | | |
| 1988–89 | Leeds U | 6 | 0 | **42** | **9** |
| 1988–89 | Bristol C | 12 | 8 | | |
| 1989–90 | Bristol C | 37 | 27 | | |
| 1990–91 | Bristol C | 39 | 11 | | |
| 1991–92 | Bristol C | 18 | 4 | **106** | **50** |
| 1991–92 | WBA | 19 | 8 | | |
| 1992–93 | WBA | 46 | 30 | | |
| 1993–94 | WBA | 42 | 18 | | |
| 1994–95 | WBA | 42 | 11 | | |
| 1995–96 | WBA | 42 | 17 | | |
| 1996–97 | WBA | 32 | 10 | | |
| 1997–98 | WBA | 15 | 2 | | |
| 1997–98 | *Bolton W* | 12 | 3 | | |
| 1998–99 | Bolton W | 38 | 15 | | |
| 1999–2000 | Bolton W | 27 | 3 | **77** | **21** |
| 1999–2000 | WBA | 8 | 5 | | |
| 2000–01 | WBA | 40 | 5 | | |
| 2001–02 | WBA | 34 | 7 | | |
| 2002–03 | WBA | 4 | 0 | **324** | **113** |
| 2003–04 | Cheltenham T | 28 | 7 | **28** | **7** |

**VICTORY, Jamie (D)** **200 17**
H: 5 10 W: 12 13 b.Hackney 14-11-75
*Source:* Trainee.

| | | | | | |
|---|---|---|---|---|---|
| 1994–95 | West Ham U | 0 | 0 | | |
| 1995–96 | Bournemouth | 16 | 1 | | |
| 1996–97 | Bournemouth | 0 | 0 | **16** | **1** |
| 1999–2000 | Cheltenham T | 46 | 4 | | |
| 2000–01 | Cheltenham T | 3 | 1 | | |
| 2001–02 | Cheltenham T | 46 | 7 | | |
| 2002–03 | Cheltenham T | 45 | 2 | | |
| 2003–04 | Cheltenham T | 44 | 2 | **184** | **16** |

**WALKER, Richard‡ (D)** **141 5**
H: 5 10 W: 12 00 b.Nottingham 9-11-71
*Source:* Trainee.

| | | | | | |
|---|---|---|---|---|---|
| 1991–92 | Notts Co | 0 | 0 | | |
| 1992–93 | Notts Co | 12 | 3 | | |
| 1993–94 | Notts Co | 21 | 1 | | |
| 1994–95 | Notts Co | 7 | 0 | | |
| 1994–95 | *Mansfield T* | 4 | 0 | **4** | **0** |
| 1995–96 | Notts Co | 11 | 0 | | |
| 1996–97 | Notts Co | 16 | 0 | **67** | **4** |

From Hereford U.

| | | | | | |
|---|---|---|---|---|---|
| 1999–2000 | Cheltenham T | 7 | 0 | | |
| 2000–01 | Cheltenham T | 36 | 0 | | |
| 2001–02 | Cheltenham T | 12 | 1 | | |
| 2002–03 | Cheltenham T | 15 | 0 | | |
| 2003–04 | Cheltenham T | 0 | 0 | **70** | **1** |

**WILSON, Brian (D)** **20 0**
H: 5 10 W: 11 00 b.Manchester 9-5-83
*Source:* Scholar.

| | | | | | |
|---|---|---|---|---|---|
| 2001–02 | Stoke C | 1 | 0 | | |
| 2002–03 | Stoke C | 3 | 0 | | |
| 2003–04 | Stoke C | 2 | 0 | **6** | **0** |
| 2003–04 | Cheltenham T | 14 | 0 | **14** | **0** |

**Scholars**
Bridges, Daniel M; Connolly, Adam J; Cook, Steven D; Crotty, Richard J; Davis, Lee M; Henry, Leon; Lewis, Greg W; Mazurek, Daniel; Thompson, Daniel P; Warren, Thomas W; Whittington, Michael J; Wylde, Michael J

**Non Contract**
Gill, Jeremy M; Humphries, Craig R

## CHESTERFIELD (23)

**ALLOTT, Mark# (M)** **248 37**
H: 5 10 W: 12 00 b.Manchester 3-10-77
*Source:* Trainee.

| | | | | | |
|---|---|---|---|---|---|
| 1995–96 | Oldham Ath | 0 | 0 | | |
| 1996–97 | Oldham Ath | 5 | 1 | | |
| 1997–98 | Oldham Ath | 22 | 2 | | |
| 1998–99 | Oldham Ath | 41 | 7 | | |
| 1999–2000 | Oldham Ath | 32 | 10 | | |
| 2000–01 | Oldham Ath | 39 | 7 | | |
| 2001–02 | Oldham Ath | 15 | 4 | **154** | **31** |
| 2001–02 | Chesterfield | 21 | 4 | | |
| 2002–03 | Chesterfield | 33 | 0 | | |
| 2003–04 | Chesterfield | 40 | 2 | **94** | **6** |

**BLATHERWICK, Steve# (D)** **213 5**
H: 6 2 W: 14 00 b.Nottingham 20-9-73
*Source:* Notts Co.

| | | | | | |
|---|---|---|---|---|---|
| 1992–93 | Nottingham F | 0 | 0 | | |
| 1993–94 | Nottingham F | 3 | 0 | | |
| 1993–94 | *Wycombe W* | 2 | 0 | **2** | **0** |
| 1994–95 | Nottingham F | 0 | 0 | | |
| 1995–96 | Nottingham F | 0 | 0 | | |
| 1995–96 | *Hereford U* | 10 | 1 | **10** | **1** |
| 1996–97 | Nottingham F | 7 | 0 | **10** | **0** |
| 1996–97 | *Reading* | 7 | 0 | **7** | **0** |
| 1997–98 | Burnley | 21 | 0 | | |
| 1998–99 | Burnley | 3 | 0 | **24** | **0** |
| 1998–99 | Chesterfield | 14 | 1 | | |
| 1999–2000 | Chesterfield | 36 | 0 | | |
| 2000–01 | Chesterfield | 38 | 1 | | |
| 2001–02 | Chesterfield | 5 | 0 | | |
| 2002–03 | Chesterfield | 31 | 0 | | |
| 2003–04 | Chesterfield | 36 | 2 | **160** | **4** |

**BRANDON, Chris# (M)** **150 19**
H: 5 8 W: 11 00 b.Bradford 7-4-76
*Source:* Bradford PA.

| | | | | | |
|---|---|---|---|---|---|
| 1999–2000 | Torquay U | 42 | 5 | | |
| 2000–01 | Torquay U | 2 | 0 | | |
| 2001–02 | Torquay U | 27 | 3 | **71** | **8** |
| 2002–03 | Chesterfield | 36 | 7 | | |
| 2003–04 | Chesterfield | 43 | 4 | **79** | **11** |

**BURT, Jamie‡ (F)** **45 9**
H: 5 10 W: 12 00 b.Ashington 29-9-79
*Source:* Whitby T.

| | | | | | |
|---|---|---|---|---|---|
| 2001–02 | Chesterfield | 24 | 7 | | |
| 2002–03 | Chesterfield | 16 | 1 | | |
| 2002–03 | *Carlisle U* | 4 | 1 | **4** | **1** |
| 2003–04 | Chesterfield | 1 | 0 | **41** | **8** |

**DAVIES, Gareth (M)** **62 1**
H: 6 0 W: 12 05 b.Chesterfield 4-2-83
*Source:* Trainee.

| | | | | | |
|---|---|---|---|---|---|
| 2001–02 | Chesterfield | 0 | 0 | | |
| 2002–03 | Chesterfield | 34 | 1 | | |
| 2003–04 | Chesterfield | 28 | 0 | **62** | **1** |

**DAWSON, Kevin (D)** **66 1**
H: 5 11 W: 13 00 b.Northallerton 18-6-81
*Source:* Trainee.

| | | | | | |
|---|---|---|---|---|---|
| 1998–99 | Nottingham F | 0 | 0 | | |
| 1999–2000 | Nottingham F | 7 | 0 | | |
| 2000–01 | Nottingham F | 1 | 0 | | |
| 2000–01 | *Barnet* | 5 | 0 | **5** | **0** |
| 2001–02 | Nottingham F | 3 | 0 | **11** | **0** |
| 2002–03 | Chesterfield | 26 | 1 | | |
| 2003–04 | Chesterfield | 24 | 0 | **50** | **1** |

**DE BOLLA, Mark (F)** **8 1**
H: 5 7 W: 11 09 b.London 1-1-83
*Source:* Trainee.

| | | | | | |
|---|---|---|---|---|---|
| 1999–2000 | Aston Villa | 0 | 0 | | |
| 2000–01 | Charlton Ath | 0 | 0 | | |
| 2001–02 | Charlton Ath | 0 | 0 | | |
| 2002–03 | Charlton Ath | 0 | 0 | | |
| 2003–04 | Charlton Ath | 0 | 0 | | |
| 2003–04 | Chesterfield | 8 | 1 | **8** | **1** |

**EVATT, Ian (M)** **88 5**
H: 6 3 W: 14 00 b.Coventry 19-11-81
*Source:* Trainee.

| | | | | | |
|---|---|---|---|---|---|
| 1998–99 | Derby Co | 0 | 0 | | |
| 1999–2000 | Derby Co | 0 | 0 | | |
| 2000–01 | Derby Co | 1 | 0 | | |
| 2001–02 | *Northampton T* | 11 | 0 | **11** | **0** |
| 2001–02 | Derby Co | 3 | 0 | | |
| 2002–03 | Derby Co | 30 | 0 | **34** | **0** |
| 2003–04 | Chesterfield | 43 | 5 | **43** | **5** |

**FOLAN, Caleb (F)** **27 1**
H: 6 2 W: 14 00 b.Leeds 26-10-82
*Source:* Trainee.

| | | | | | |
|---|---|---|---|---|---|
| 1999–2000 | Leeds U | 0 | 0 | | |
| 2000–01 | Leeds U | 0 | 0 | | |
| 2001–02 | Leeds U | 0 | 0 | | |
| 2001–02 | *Rushden & D* | 6 | 0 | **6** | **0** |
| 2001–02 | *Hull C* | 1 | 0 | **1** | **0** |
| 2002–03 | Leeds U | 0 | 0 | | |
| 2002–03 | Chesterfield | 13 | 1 | | |
| 2003–04 | Chesterfield | 7 | 0 | **20** | **1** |

**FULLARTON, Jamie† (M)** **218 5**
H: 5 10 W: 10 06 b.Bellshill 20-7-75

| | | | | | |
|---|---|---|---|---|---|
| 1991–92 | St Mirren | 1 | 0 | | |
| 1992–93 | St Mirren | 25 | 0 | | |
| 1993–94 | St Mirren | 37 | 0 | | |
| 1994–95 | St Mirren | 17 | 1 | | |
| 1995–96 | St Mirren | 22 | 2 | **102** | **3** |
| 1996–97 | Bastia | 17 | 0 | **17** | **0** |
| 1997–98 | Crystal Palace | 25 | 1 | | |
| 1998–99 | Crystal Palace | 7 | 0 | | |
| 1998–99 | *Bolton W* | 1 | 0 | **1** | **0** |
| 1999–2000 | Crystal Palace | 13 | 0 | | |
| 2000–01 | Crystal Palace | 2 | 0 | **47** | **1** |
| 2000–01 | Dundee U | 5 | 0 | | |
| 2001–02 | Dundee U | 11 | 0 | **16** | **0** |
| 2002–03 | Brentford | 27 | 1 | **27** | **1** |
| 2003–04 | Southend U | 7 | 0 | **7** | **0** |
| 2003–04 | Chesterfield | 1 | 0 | **1** | **0** |

**HOWSON, Stuart* (D)** **69 4**
H: 6 1 W: 13 05 b.Chorley 30-9-81
*Source:* Trainee.

| | | | | | |
|---|---|---|---|---|---|
| 1999–2000 | Blackburn R | 0 | 0 | | |
| 2000–01 | Blackburn R | 0 | 0 | | |
| 2000–01 | Northern Spirit | 14 | 1 | **14** | **1** |
| 2001–02 | Blackburn R | 0 | 0 | | |
| 2001–02 | Chesterfield | 13 | 1 | | |
| 2002–03 | Chesterfield | 33 | 2 | | |
| 2003–04 | Chesterfield | 9 | 0 | **55** | **3** |

**HUDSON, Mark (M)** **79 6**
H: 5 11 W: 11 08 b.Bishop Auckland 24-10-80
*Source:* Trainee.

| | | | | | |
|---|---|---|---|---|---|
| 1999–2000 | Middlesbrough | 0 | 0 | | |
| 2000–01 | Middlesbrough | 3 | 0 | | |
| 2001–02 | Middlesbrough | 2 | 0 | | |
| 2002–03 | Middlesbrough | 0 | 0 | **5** | **0** |
| 2002–03 | *Carlisle U* | 15 | 1 | **15** | **1** |
| 2002–03 | Chesterfield | 24 | 3 | | |
| 2003–04 | Chesterfield | 35 | 2 | **59** | **5** |

**HURST, Glynn# (F)** **185 66**
H: 5 10 W: 11 07 b.Barnsley 17-1-76
*Source:* Tottenham H Trainee.

| | | | | | |
|---|---|---|---|---|---|
| 1994–95 | Barnsley | 2 | 0 | | |
| 1995–96 | Barnsley | 5 | 0 | | |
| 1995–96 | *Swansea C* | 2 | 1 | **2** | **1** |
| 1996–97 | Barnsley | 1 | 0 | **8** | **0** |
| 1996–97 | *Mansfield T* | 6 | 0 | **6** | **0** |
| 1998–99 | Ayr U | 34 | 18 | | |
| 1999–2000 | Ayr U | 25 | 14 | **59** | **32** |
| 2000–01 | Stockport Co | 11 | 0 | | |
| 2001–02 | Stockport Co | 15 | 4 | **26** | **4** |
| 2001–02 | Chesterfield | 23 | 9 | | |
| 2002–03 | Chesterfield | 32 | 7 | | |
| 2003–04 | Chesterfield | 29 | 13 | **84** | **29** |

**INNES, Mark# (M)** **128 3**
H: 5 10 W: 12 02 b.Bellshill 27-9-78
*Source:* Trainee.

| | | | | | |
|---|---|---|---|---|---|
| 1995–96 | Oldham Ath | 0 | 0 | | |
| 1996–97 | Oldham Ath | 0 | 0 | | |
| 1997–98 | Oldham Ath | 4 | 0 | | |
| 1998–99 | Oldham Ath | 13 | 1 | | |
| 1999–2000 | Oldham Ath | 21 | 0 | | |
| 2000–01 | Oldham Ath | 30 | 0 | | |
| 2001–02 | Oldham Ath | 5 | 0 | **73** | **1** |
| 2001–02 | Chesterfield | 23 | 2 | | |
| 2002–03 | Chesterfield | 10 | 0 | | |
| 2003–04 | Chesterfield | 22 | 0 | **55** | **2** |

**MITCHELL, Jez‡ (F)** **0 0**
H: 6 0 W: 12 00 b.Chesterfield 5-10-84
*Source:* trainee.

| | | | |
|---|---|---|---|
| 2003–04 | Chesterfield | 0 | 0 |

**MUGGLETON, Carl# (G)** **354 0**
H: 6 2 W: 13 08 b.Leicester 13-9-68
*Source:* Apprentice. *Honours:* England Under-21.

| | | | | | |
|---|---|---|---|---|---|
| 1986–87 | Leicester C | 0 | 0 | | |
| 1987–88 | Leicester C | 0 | 0 | | |
| 1987–88 | *Chesterfield* | 17 | 0 | | |
| 1987–88 | *Blackpool* | 2 | 0 | **2** | **0** |
| 1988–89 | Leicester C | 3 | 0 | | |
| 1988–89 | *Hartlepool U* | 8 | 0 | **8** | **0** |
| 1989–90 | Leicester C | 0 | 0 | | |
| 1989–90 | *Stockport Co* | 4 | 0 | **4** | **0** |
| 1990–91 | Leicester C | 22 | 0 | | |
| 1990–91 | *Liverpool* | 0 | 0 | | |
| 1991–92 | Leicester C | 4 | 0 | | |
| 1992–93 | Leicester C | 17 | 0 | | |
| 1993–94 | Leicester C | 0 | 0 | **46** | **0** |
| 1993–94 | *Stoke C* | 6 | 0 | | |
| 1993–94 | *Sheffield U* | 0 | 0 | | |
| 1993–94 | Celtic | 12 | 0 | **12** | **0** |
| 1994–95 | Stoke C | 24 | 0 | | |
| 1995–96 | Stoke C | 6 | 0 | | |
| 1995–96 | *Rotherham U* | 6 | 0 | **6** | **0** |
| 1995–96 | *Sheffield U* | 1 | 0 | **1** | **0** |
| 1996–97 | Stoke C | 33 | 0 | | |
| 1997–98 | Stoke C | 34 | 0 | | |
| 1998–99 | Stoke C | 40 | 0 | | |
| 1999–2000 | Stoke C | 0 | 0 | | |
| 1999–2000 | *Mansfield T* | 9 | 0 | **9** | **0** |
| 1999–2000 | *Chesterfield* | 5 | 0 | | |
| 2000–01 | Stoke C | 12 | 0 | **155** | **0** |
| 2000–01 | *Cardiff C* | 6 | 0 | **6** | **0** |
| 2001–02 | Cheltenham T | 7 | 0 | **7** | **0** |
| 2001–02 | *Bradford C* | 4 | 0 | **4** | **0** |
| 2002–03 | Chesterfield | 26 | 0 | | |
| 2003–04 | Chesterfield | 46 | 0 | **94** | **0** |

**N'TOYA, Tcham (F)** **6 0**
H: 5 10 W: 12 10 b.Kinshasa 3-11-83

| | | | | | |
|---|---|---|---|---|---|
| 2003–04 | Chesterfield | 6 | 0 | **6** | **0** |

**NIVEN, Derek (M)** **23 1**
H: 6 1 W: 11 02 b.Falkirk 12-12-83
*Source:* Stenhousemuir.

| | | | | | |
|---|---|---|---|---|---|
| 2000–01 | Raith R | 1 | 0 | **1** | **0** |
| 2001–02 | Bolton W | 0 | 0 | | |
| 2002–03 | Bolton W | 0 | 0 | | |
| 2003–04 | Bolton W | 0 | 0 | | |
| 2003–04 | Chesterfield | 22 | 1 | **22** | **1** |

**O'HALLORAN, Matt† (M)** **16 1**
H: 5 10 W: 11 06 b.Buxton 14-5-81
*Source:* Trainee.

| | | | | | |
|---|---|---|---|---|---|
| 2002–03 | Derby Co | 0 | 0 | | |
| 2003–04 | Oldham Ath | 13 | 1 | **13** | **1** |
| 2003–04 | Chesterfield | 3 | 0 | **3** | **0** |

**O'HARE, Alan (D)** **81 1**
H: 6 1 W: 12 04 b.Drogheda 31-7-82
*Source:* Scholar.

| | | | | | |
|---|---|---|---|---|---|
| 2001–02 | Bolton W | 0 | 0 | | |
| 2001–02 | *Chesterfield* | 19 | 0 | | |
| 2002–03 | Bolton W | 0 | 0 | | |
| 2002–03 | Chesterfield | 22 | 0 | | |
| 2003–04 | Chesterfield | 40 | 1 | **81** | **1** |

**REEVES, David* (F)** **616 168**
H: 6 1 W: 13 08 b.Birkenhead 19-11-67
*Source:* Heswall.

| | | | | | |
|---|---|---|---|---|---|
| 1986–87 | Sheffield W | 0 | 0 | | |
| 1986–87 | *Scunthorpe U* | 4 | 2 | | |
| 1987–88 | Sheffield W | 0 | 0 | | |
| 1987–88 | *Scunthorpe U* | 6 | 4 | **10** | **6** |
| 1987–88 | *Burnley* | 16 | 8 | **16** | **8** |
| 1988–89 | Sheffield W | 17 | 2 | **17** | **2** |
| 1989–90 | Bolton W | 41 | 10 | | |
| 1990–91 | Bolton W | 44 | 10 | | |
| 1991–92 | Bolton W | 35 | 8 | | |
| 1992–93 | Bolton W | 14 | 1 | **134** | **29** |
| 1992–93 | Notts Co | 9 | 2 | | |
| 1993–94 | Notts Co | 4 | 0 | **13** | **2** |
| 1993–94 | Carlisle U | 34 | 11 | | |
| 1994–95 | Carlisle U | 42 | 21 | | |
| 1995–96 | Carlisle U | 43 | 13 | | |
| 1996–97 | Carlisle U | 8 | 3 | **127** | **48** |
| 1996–97 | Preston NE | 34 | 11 | | |
| 1997–98 | Preston NE | 13 | 1 | **47** | **12** |
| 1997–98 | Chesterfield | 26 | 5 | | |
| 1998–99 | Chesterfield | 40 | 10 | | |
| 1999–2000 | Chesterfield | 43 | 14 | | |
| 2000–01 | Chesterfield | 37 | 13 | | |
| 2001–02 | Chesterfield | 22 | 4 | | |
| 2001–02 | Oldham Ath | 13 | 3 | | |
| 2002–03 | Oldham Ath | 0 | 0 | **13** | **3** |
| 2002–03 | Chesterfield | 40 | 8 | | |
| 2003–04 | Chesterfield | 31 | 4 | **239** | **58** |

**RICHARDSON, Lee J* (M)** **402 38**
H: 5 11 W: 12 02 b.Halifax 12-3-69
*Source:* Trainee.

| | | | | | |
|---|---|---|---|---|---|
| 1986–87 | Halifax T | 1 | 0 | | |
| 1987–88 | Halifax T | 30 | 1 | | |
| 1988–89 | Halifax T | 25 | 1 | **56** | **2** |
| 1988–89 | Watford | 9 | 0 | | |
| 1989–90 | Watford | 32 | 1 | **41** | **1** |
| 1990–91 | Blackburn R | 38 | 2 | | |
| 1991–92 | Blackburn R | 24 | 1 | | |
| 1992–93 | Blackburn R | 0 | 0 | **62** | **3** |
| 1992–93 | Aberdeen | 29 | 2 | | |
| 1993–94 | Aberdeen | 35 | 4 | **64** | **6** |
| 1994–95 | Oldham Ath | 30 | 6 | | |
| 1995–96 | Oldham Ath | 27 | 11 | | |
| 1996–97 | Oldham Ath | 31 | 4 | | |
| 1997–98 | Oldham Ath | 0 | 0 | **88** | **21** |
| 1997–98 | *Stockport Co* | 6 | 0 | **6** | **0** |
| 1997–98 | Huddersfield T | 21 | 3 | | |
| 1998–99 | Huddersfield T | 15 | 0 | | |
| 1999–2000 | Huddersfield T | 0 | 0 | **36** | **3** |
| 1999–2000 | *Bury* | 5 | 1 | **5** | **1** |
| 1999–2000 | Livingston | 0 | 0 | | |
| 2000–01 | Chesterfield | 30 | 0 | | |
| 2001–02 | Chesterfield | 14 | 1 | | |
| 2002–03 | Chesterfield | 0 | 0 | | |
| 2003–04 | Chesterfield | 0 | 0 | **44** | **1** |

**RICHMOND, Andy (G)** **7 0**
H: 6 3 W: 12 10 b.Chesterfield 9-1-83
*Source:* Scholar.

| | | | | | |
|---|---|---|---|---|---|
| 2002–03 | Chesterfield | 7 | 0 | | |
| 2003–04 | Chesterfield | 0 | 0 | **7** | **0** |

**ROBINSON, Marvin (F)** **53 9**
H: 6 0 W: 13 05 b.Crewe 11-4-80
*Source:* Trainee.

| | | | | | |
|---|---|---|---|---|---|
| 1998–99 | Derby Co | 1 | 0 | | |
| 1999–2000 | Derby Co | 8 | 0 | | |
| 2000–01 | Derby Co | 0 | 0 | | |
| 2000–01 | *Stoke C* | 3 | 1 | **3** | **1** |
| 2001–02 | Derby Co | 2 | 1 | | |
| 2002–03 | Derby Co | 1 | 0 | **12** | **1** |
| 2002–03 | *Tranmere R* | 6 | 1 | **6** | **1** |
| 2003–04 | Chesterfield | 32 | 6 | **32** | **6** |

**RUSHBURY, Andy‡ (M)** **40 1**
H: 5 9 W: 11 04 b.Carlisle 7-3-83
*Source:* Scholar.

| | | | |
|---|---|---|---|
| 2000–01 | Chesterfield | 2 | 0 |
| 2001–02 | Chesterfield | 3 | 0 |

2002–03 Chesterfield 30 0
2003–04 Chesterfield 5 1 **40 1**

**SEARLE, Damon‡ (D) 493 9**
H: 5 9 W: 12 00 b.Cardiff 26-10-71
*Source:* Trainee. *Honours:* Wales Schools, Youth, Under-21, B.
1990–91 Cardiff C 35 0
1991–92 Cardiff C 42 1
1992–93 Cardiff C 42 1
1993–94 Cardiff C 42 0
1994–95 Cardiff C 32 0
1995–96 Cardiff C 41 1 **234 3**
1996–97 Stockport Co 10 0
1997–98 Stockport Co 31 0 **41 0**
1998–99 Carlisle U 45 2
1999–2000 Carlisle U 21 1 **66 3**
1999–2000 *Rochdale* 14 0 **14 0**
2000–01 Southend U 46 1
2001–02 Southend U 43 1
2002–03 Southend U 44 1 **133 3**
2003–04 Chesterfield 5 0 **5 0**

**SMITH, Adam§ (M) 3 0**
b.Huddersfield 20-2-85
*Source:* Scholar.
2003–04 Chesterfield 3 0 **3 0**

**SMITH, Mark‡ (M) 0 0**
H: 5 10 W: 10 06 b.Nottingham 4-11-83
*Source:* Scholar.
2003–04 Chesterfield 0 0

**UHLENBEEK, Gus‡ (D) 326 9**
H: 5 10 W: 12 00 b.Paramaribo 20-8-70
1990–91 Ajax 2 0
1991–92 Ajax 0 0 **2 0**
1992–93 Cambuur 24 0
1993–94 Cambuur 15 0 **39 0**
1994–95 TOPS SV 22 3 **22 3**
1995–96 Ipswich T 40 4
1996–97 Ipswich T 38 0
1997–98 Ipswich T 11 0 **89 4**
1998–99 Fulham 23 1
1999–2000 Fulham 16 0 **39 1**
2000–01 Sheffield U 31 0
2001–02 Sheffield U 20 0 **51 0**
2001–02 *Walsall* 5 0 **5 0**
2002–03 Bradford C 42 1 **42 1**
2003–04 Chesterfield 37 0 **37 0**

**WARNE, Stephen (M) 3 0**
H: 5 10 W: 12 00 b.Sutton-in-Ashfield 27-2-84
*Source:* Scholar.
2002–03 Chesterfield 3 0
2003–04 Chesterfield 0 0 **3 0**

**Scholars**
Bunn, Michael A; Cancellara, Ryan A; Cressey, Ben; Di Gregorio, Adrian; Donnelly, Jamie N E; Fox, Michael J S N; Foyle, Ashley P; Jenkinson, Simon; Jubb, Anthony; Lancaster, Samuel J; Lockwood, Daniel R; Lowry, Jamie; Mitchell, Adam T; Smith, Nathan A; Wharton, Lee; Wright, Simon

**Non Contract**
Fullarton, Jamie; O'Halloran, Matthew V

## COLCHESTER U (24)

**ANDREWS, Wayne (F) 118 32**
H: 5 10 W: 11 02 b.Paddington 25-11-77
*Source:* Trainee.
1995–96 Watford 1 0
1996–97 Watford 25 4
1997–98 Watford 2 0
1998–99 Watford 0 0 **28 4**
1998–99 *Cambridge U* 2 0 **2 0**
1998–99 *Peterborough U* 10 5 **10 5**
From Chesham U
2001–02 Oldham Ath 0 0
2002–03 Oldham Ath 37 11 **37 11**
2003–04 Colchester U 41 12 **41 12**

**BALDWIN, Pat (D) 23 0**
H: 6 2 W: 11 07 b.London 12-11-82
*Source:* Chelsea Academy.
2002–03 Colchester U 19 0
2003–04 Colchester U 4 0 **23 0**

**BOWRY, Bobby# (M) 285 8**
H: 5 8 W: 10 08 b.Hampstead 19-5-71
*Honours:* St. Kitts & Nevis full caps.
1990–91 QPR 0 0
From Carshalton Ath
1991–92 Crystal Palace 0 0
1992–93 Crystal Palace 11 1
1993–94 Crystal Palace 21 0
1994–95 Crystal Palace 18 0 **50 1**
1995–96 Millwall 38 2
1996–97 Millwall 28 1
1997–98 Millwall 43 2
1998–99 Millwall 25 0
1999–2000 Millwall 5 0
2000–01 Millwall 1 0 **140 5**
2001–02 Colchester U 36 1
2002–03 Colchester U 35 1
2003–04 Colchester U 24 0 **95 2**

**BROWN, Simon* (G) 143 0**
H: 6 2 W: 15 00 b.Chelmsford 3-12-76
*Source:* Trainee.
1995–96 Tottenham H 0 0
1996–97 Tottenham H 0 0
1997–98 Tottenham H 0 0
1997–98 *Lincoln C* 1 0 **1 0**
1998–99 Tottenham H 0 0
1998–99 *Fulham* 0 0
1999–2000 Colchester U 38 0
2000–01 Colchester U 18 0
2001–02 Colchester U 19 0
2002–03 Colchester U 27 0
2003–04 Colchester U 40 0 **142 0**

**CADE, Jamie (F) 25 2**
H: 5 8 W: 10 10 b.Durham 15-1-84
*Source:* Scholar. *Honours:* England Youth.
2001–02 Middlesbrough 0 0
2002–03 Middlesbrough 0 0
2003–04 Middlesbrough 0 0
2003–04 *Chesterfield* 10 2 **10 2**
2003–04 Colchester U 15 0 **15 0**

**COOTE, Adrian‡ (F) 94 8**
H: 6 2 W: 13 00 b.Gt Yarmouth 30-9-78
*Source:* Trainee. *Honours:* Northern Ireland Under-21, B, 6 full caps.
1997–98 Norwich C 23 2
1998–99 Norwich C 6 0
1999–2000 Norwich C 11 1
2000–01 Norwich C 14 0
2001–02 Norwich C 0 0 **54 3**
2001–02 Colchester U 19 4
2002–03 Colchester U 16 0
2002–03 *Bristol R* 5 1 **5 1**
2003–04 Colchester U 0 0 **35 4**

**DUGUID, Karl (M) 270 37**
H: 5 11 W: 11 06 b.Hitchin 21-3-78
*Source:* Trainee.
1995–96 Colchester U 16 1
1996–97 Colchester U 20 3
1997–98 Colchester U 21 3
1998–99 Colchester U 33 4
1999–2000 Colchester U 41 12
2000–01 Colchester U 41 5
2001–02 Colchester U 41 4
2002–03 Colchester U 27 3
2003–04 Colchester U 30 2 **270 37**

**FAGAN, Craig (F) 44 10**
H: 5 11 W: 11 08 b.Birmingham 11-12-82
*Source:* Scholar.
2001–02 Birmingham C 0 0
2002–03 Birmingham C 1 0
2002–03 *Bristol C* 6 1 **6 1**
2003–04 Birmingham C 0 0 **1 0**
2003–04 Colchester U 37 9 **37 9**

**FITZGERALD, Scott* (D) 326 2**
H: 6 1 W: 13 00 b.Westminster 13-8-69
*Source:* Trainee. *Honours:* Eire Under-21, B.
1988–89 Wimbledon 0 0
1989–90 Wimbledon 1 0
1990–91 Wimbledon 0 0
1991–92 Wimbledon 36 1
1992–93 Wimbledon 20 0
1993–94 Wimbledon 28 0
1994–95 Wimbledon 17 0
1995–96 Wimbledon 4 0
1995–96 *Sheffield U* 6 0 **6 0**
1996–97 Wimbledon 0 0 **106 1**
1996–97 *Millwall* 7 0
1997–98 Millwall 18 0
1998–99 Millwall 32 1
1999–2000 Millwall 31 0
2000–01 Millwall 1 0 **89 1**
2000–01 Colchester U 30 0
2001–02 Colchester U 37 0
2002–03 Colchester U 26 0
2003–04 Colchester U 23 0 **116 0**
2003–04 *Brentford* 9 0 **9 0**

**GERKEN, Dean§ (G) 1 0**
H: 6 3 W: 13 00 b.Southend-on-Sea 22-5-85
*Source:* Scholar.
2003–04 Colchester U 1 0 **1 0**

**HADLAND, Phil‡ (F) 50 4**
H: 5 9 W: 11 05 b.Warrington 20-10-80
*Source:* Trainee.
1999–2000 Reading 0 0
2000–01 Rochdale 32 2 **32 2**
2001–02 *Carlisle U* 4 1 **4 1**
2001–02 Leyton Orient 5 1 **5 1**
2001–02 Brighton & HA 2 0 **2 0**
2002–03 Darlington 6 0 **6 0**
2003–04 Colchester U 1 0 **1 0**

**HALFORD, Greg (D) 19 4**
H: 6 3 W: 13 10 b.Chelmsford 8-12-84
*Source:* Scholar.
2002–03 Colchester U 1 0
2003–04 Colchester U 18 4 **19 4**

**IZZET, Kem (M) 135 15**
H: 5 8 W: 10 05 b.Mile End 29-9-80
*Source:* Trainee.
1998–99 Charlton Ath 0 0
1999–2000 Charlton Ath 0 0
2000–01 Charlton Ath 0 0
2000–01 Colchester U 6 1
2001–02 Colchester U 40 3
2002–03 Colchester U 45 8
2003–04 Colchester U 44 3 **135 15**

**JOHNSON, Gavin‡ (M) 349 23**
H: 5 11 W: 11 12 b.Stowmarket 10-10-70
*Source:* Trainee.
1988–89 Ipswich T 4 0
1989–90 Ipswich T 6 0
1990–91 Ipswich T 7 0
1991–92 Ipswich T 42 5
1992–93 Ipswich T 40 5
1993–94 Ipswich T 16 1
1994–95 Ipswich T 17 0 **132 11**
1995–96 Luton T 5 0 **5 0**
1995–96 Wigan Ath 27 3
1996–97 Wigan Ath 37 3
1997–98 Wigan Ath 20 2 **84 8**
1998–99 Dunfermline Ath 18 0 **18 0**
1999–2000 Colchester U 27 0
2000–01 Colchester U 37 2
2001–02 Colchester U 20 1
2002–03 Colchester U 8 0
2003–04 Colchester U 18 1 **110 4**

**KEITH, Joe (D) 177 19**
H: 5 7 W: 10 06 b.London 1-10-78
*Source:* Trainee.
1997–98 West Ham U 0 0
1998–99 West Ham U 0 0
1999–2000 Colchester U 45 1
2000–01 Colchester U 27 3
2001–02 Colchester U 41 4
2002–03 Colchester U 36 9
2003–04 Colchester U 28 2 **177 19**

**McGLEISH, Scott* (F) 364 95**
H: 5 9 W: 11 09 b.Barnet 10-2-74
*Source:* Edgware T.
1994–95 Charlton Ath 6 0 **6 0**
1994–95 *Leyton Orient* 6 1
1995–96 Peterborough U 12 0
1995–96 *Colchester U* 15 6
1996–97 Peterborough U 1 0 **13 0**
1996–97 *Cambridge U* 10 7 **10 7**
1996–97 Leyton Orient 28 7
1997–98 Leyton Orient 8 0 **42 8**
1997–98 Barnet 37 13
1998–99 Barnet 36 8
1999–2000 Barnet 42 10

| | | | | | |
|---|---|---|---|---|---|
| 2000–01 | Barnet | 19 | 5 | **134** | **36** |
| 2000–01 | Colchester U | 21 | 5 | | |
| 2001–02 | Colchester U | 46 | 15 | | |
| 2002–03 | Colchester U | 43 | 8 | | |
| 2003–04 | Colchester U | 34 | 10 | **159** | **44** |

**McKINNEY, Richard* (G) 27 0**
H: 6 2 W: 13 06 b.Ballymoney 18-5-79
*Source:* Ballymena U.

| | | | | | |
|---|---|---|---|---|---|
| 1999–2000 | Manchester C | 0 | 0 | | |
| 2000–01 | Manchester C | 0 | 0 | | |
| 2001–02 | Swindon T | 1 | 0 | **1** | **0** |
| 2002–03 | Colchester U | 21 | 0 | | |
| 2003–04 | Colchester U | 5 | 0 | **26** | **0** |

**MYERS, Andy* (D) 202 5**
H: 5 8 W: 11 00 b.Hounslow 3-11-73
*Source:* Trainee. *Honours:* England Schools, Youth, Under-21.

| | | | | | |
|---|---|---|---|---|---|
| 1990–91 | Chelsea | 3 | 0 | | |
| 1991–92 | Chelsea | 11 | 1 | | |
| 1992–93 | Chelsea | 3 | 0 | | |
| 1993–94 | Chelsea | 6 | 0 | | |
| 1994–95 | Chelsea | 10 | 0 | | |
| 1995–96 | Chelsea | 20 | 0 | | |
| 1996–97 | Chelsea | 18 | 1 | | |
| 1997–98 | Chelsea | 12 | 0 | | |
| 1998–99 | Chelsea | 1 | 0 | **84** | **2** |
| 1999–2000 | Bradford C | 13 | 0 | | |
| 1999–2000 | *Portsmouth* | 8 | 0 | **8** | **0** |
| 2000–01 | Bradford C | 20 | 1 | | |
| 2001–02 | Bradford C | 32 | 2 | | |
| 2002–03 | Bradford C | 24 | 0 | **89** | **3** |
| 2003–04 | Colchester U | 21 | 0 | **21** | **0** |

**PARKINSON, Phil (M) 507 25**
H: 6 0 W: 12 09 b.Chorley 1-12-67
*Source:* Apprentice.

| | | | | | |
|---|---|---|---|---|---|
| 1985–86 | Southampton | 0 | 0 | | |
| 1986–87 | Southampton | 0 | 0 | | |
| 1987–88 | Southampton | 0 | 0 | | |
| 1987–88 | Bury | 8 | 1 | | |
| 1988–89 | Bury | 39 | 0 | | |
| 1989–90 | Bury | 22 | 2 | | |
| 1990–91 | Bury | 44 | 2 | | |
| 1991–92 | Bury | 32 | 0 | **145** | **5** |
| 1992–93 | Reading | 39 | 4 | | |
| 1993–94 | Reading | 42 | 3 | | |
| 1994–95 | Reading | 31 | 0 | | |
| 1995–96 | Reading | 42 | 0 | | |
| 1996–97 | Reading | 24 | 1 | | |
| 1997–98 | Reading | 37 | 0 | | |
| 1998–99 | Reading | 42 | 5 | | |
| 1999–2000 | Reading | 22 | 1 | | |
| 2000–01 | Reading | 44 | 4 | | |
| 2001–02 | Reading | 33 | 2 | | |
| 2002–03 | Reading | 6 | 0 | **362** | **20** |
| 2003–04 | Colchester U | 0 | 0 | | |

**PINAULT, Thomas* (M) 133 5**
H: 5 9 W: 11 03 b.Grasse 4-12-81
*Source:* Cannes.

| | | | | | |
|---|---|---|---|---|---|
| 1999–2000 | Colchester U | 4 | 0 | | |
| 2000–01 | Colchester U | 5 | 1 | | |
| 2001–02 | Colchester U | 42 | 0 | | |
| 2002–03 | Colchester U | 42 | 4 | | |
| 2003–04 | Colchester U | 40 | 0 | **133** | **5** |

**STOCKLEY, Sam# (D) 300 3**
H: 6 0 W: 12 08 b.Tiverton 5-9-77
*Source:* Trainee.

| | | | | | |
|---|---|---|---|---|---|
| 1996–97 | Southampton | 0 | 0 | | |
| 1996–97 | Barnet | 21 | 0 | | |
| 1997–98 | Barnet | 41 | 0 | | |
| 1998–99 | Barnet | 41 | 0 | | |
| 1999–2000 | Barnet | 34 | 1 | | |
| 2000–01 | Barnet | 45 | 1 | **182** | **2** |
| 2001–02 | Oxford U | 41 | 0 | | |
| 2002–03 | Oxford U | 0 | 0 | **41** | **0** |
| 2002–03 | Colchester U | 33 | 1 | | |
| 2003–04 | Colchester U | 44 | 0 | **77** | **1** |

**WHITE, Alan* (D) 223 7**
H: 6 2 W: 13 04 b.Darlington 22-3-76
*Source:* Derby Co Schoolboy.

| | | | | | |
|---|---|---|---|---|---|
| 1994–95 | Middlesbrough | 0 | 0 | | |
| 1995–96 | Middlesbrough | 0 | 0 | | |
| 1996–97 | Middlesbrough | 0 | 0 | | |
| 1997–98 | Middlesbrough | 0 | 0 | | |
| 1997–98 | Luton T | 28 | 1 | | |
| 1998–99 | Luton T | 33 | 1 | | |
| 1999–2000 | Luton T | 19 | 1 | **80** | **3** |

| | | | | | |
|---|---|---|---|---|---|
| 1999–2000 | *Colchester U* | 4 | 0 | | |
| 2000–01 | Colchester U | 32 | 0 | | |
| 2001–02 | Colchester U | 33 | 3 | | |
| 2002–03 | Colchester U | 41 | 0 | | |
| 2003–04 | Colchester U | 33 | 1 | **143** | **4** |

**Scholars**
Artun, Ergun C; Coleman, Liam P; Cousins, Mark; Crouch, Ross A; Driver, Sherdan; Edwards, Dwayne W; Gerken, Dean J; Guy, Jamie L; Harrop, Angelo; Irving, Daniel J; Johnston, Craig J; King, Robert J; Moxom, Charlie; Pond, Russell; Richards, Garry; Toney, Tristan; White, John A

**Players who do not hold a current contract but their registration has been retained by the club**
Launders, Brian T

## COVENTRY C (25)

**ADEBOLA, Dele (F) 328 78**
H: 6 3 W: 15 00 b.Lagos 23-6-75
*Source:* Trainee.

| | | | | | |
|---|---|---|---|---|---|
| 1992–93 | Crewe Alex | 6 | 0 | | |
| 1993–94 | Crewe Alex | 0 | 0 | | |
| 1994–95 | Crewe Alex | 30 | 8 | | |
| 1995–96 | Crewe Alex | 29 | 8 | | |
| 1996–97 | Crewe Alex | 32 | 16 | | |
| 1997–98 | Crewe Alex | 27 | 7 | **124** | **39** |
| 1997–98 | Birmingham C | 17 | 7 | | |
| 1998–99 | Birmingham C | 39 | 13 | | |
| 1999–2000 | Birmingham C | 42 | 5 | | |
| 2000–01 | Birmingham C | 31 | 6 | | |
| 2001–02 | Birmingham C | 0 | 0 | **129** | **31** |
| 2001–02 | *Oldham Ath* | 5 | 0 | **5** | **0** |
| 2002–03 | Crystal Palace | 39 | 5 | **39** | **5** |
| 2003–04 | Coventry C | 28 | 2 | **28** | **2** |
| 2003–04 | *Burnley* | 3 | 1 | **3** | **1** |

**ARPHEXAD, Pegguy* (G) 37 0**
H: 6 2 W: 13 07 b.Abymes 18-5-73
*Source:* Brest.

| | | | | | |
|---|---|---|---|---|---|
| 1994–95 | Lens | 0 | 0 | | |
| 1995–96 | Lens | 3 | 0 | | |
| 1996–97 | Lens | 0 | 0 | **3** | **0** |
| 1997–98 | Leicester C | 6 | 0 | | |
| 1998–99 | Leicester C | 4 | 0 | | |
| 1999–2000 | Leicester C | 11 | 0 | **21** | **0** |
| 2000–01 | Liverpool | 0 | 0 | | |
| 2001–02 | *Stockport Co* | 3 | 0 | **3** | **0** |
| 2001–02 | Liverpool | 2 | 0 | | |
| 2002–03 | Liverpool | 0 | 0 | **2** | **0** |
| 2003–04 | Coventry C | 5 | 0 | **5** | **0** |
| 2003–04 | *Notts Co* | 3 | 0 | **3** | **0** |

**BARRETT, Graham (F) 87 7**
H: 5 10 W: 11 07 b.Dublin 6-10-81
*Source:* Trainee. *Honours:* Eire Schools, Youth, Under-21, 5 full cap, 2 goals.

| | | | | | |
|---|---|---|---|---|---|
| 1998–99 | Arsenal | 0 | 0 | | |
| 1999–2000 | Arsenal | 2 | 0 | | |
| 2000–01 | Arsenal | 0 | 0 | | |
| 2000–01 | *Bristol R* | 1 | 0 | **1** | **0** |
| 2001–02 | Arsenal | 0 | 0 | | |
| 2001–02 | *Crewe Alex* | 3 | 0 | **3** | **0** |
| 2001–02 | *Colchester U* | 20 | 4 | **20** | **4** |
| 2002–03 | Arsenal | 0 | 0 | **2** | **0** |
| 2002–03 | *Brighton & HA* | 30 | 1 | **30** | **1** |
| 2003–04 | Coventry C | 31 | 2 | **31** | **2** |

**BATES, Tom (M) 1 0**
H: 5 10 W: 12 00 b.Coventry 31-10-85

| | | | | | |
|---|---|---|---|---|---|
| 2002–03 | Coventry C | 1 | 0 | | |
| 2003–04 | Coventry C | 0 | 0 | **1** | **0** |

**BRISCOE, Michael* (D) 0 0**
H: 5 11 W: 12 00 b.Northampton 4-7-83

| | | | | | |
|---|---|---|---|---|---|
| 2002–03 | Coventry C | 0 | 0 | | |
| 2003–04 | Coventry C | 0 | 0 | | |

**BRUSH, Richard (G) 0 0**
H: 6 1 W: 12 00 b.Birmingham 26-11-84
*Source:* Scholar.

| | | | | | |
|---|---|---|---|---|---|
| 2002–03 | Coventry C | 0 | 0 | | |
| 2003–04 | Coventry C | 0 | 0 | | |

**COONEY, Sean (D) 1 0**
H: 6 3 W: 13 00 b.Perth 31-10-83
*Source:* Scholar.

| | | | | | |
|---|---|---|---|---|---|
| 2002–03 | Coventry C | 1 | 0 | | |
| 2003–04 | Coventry C | 0 | 0 | **1** | **0** |

**DAHL, Andreas* (M) 0 0**
H: 5 11 W: 12 10 b.Sweden 6-6-84
*Source:* IFK Hassleholm.

| | | | | | |
|---|---|---|---|---|---|
| 2001–02 | Coventry C | 0 | 0 | | |
| 2002–03 | Coventry C | 0 | 0 | | |
| 2003–04 | Coventry C | 0 | 0 | | |

**DAVENPORT, Calum (D) 69 3**
H: 6 4 W: 14 00 b.Bedford 1-1-83
*Source:* Trainee. *Honours:* England Youth, Under-20.

| | | | | | |
|---|---|---|---|---|---|
| 1999–2000 | Coventry C | 0 | 0 | | |
| 2000–01 | Coventry C | 1 | 0 | | |
| 2001–02 | Coventry C | 3 | 0 | | |
| 2002–03 | Coventry C | 32 | 3 | | |
| 2003–04 | Coventry C | 33 | 0 | **69** | **3** |

**DELOUMEAUX, Eric (D) 138 7**
H: 5 10 W: 11 13 b.Montbeliard 12-5-73

| | | | | | |
|---|---|---|---|---|---|
| 1999–2000 | Le Havre | 28 | 0 | | |
| 2000–01 | Le Havre | 25 | 2 | **53** | **2** |
| 2001–02 | Motherwell | 23 | 0 | **23** | **0** |
| 2002–03 | Aberdeen | 32 | 2 | | |
| 2002–03 | Aberdeen | 11 | 2 | **43** | **4** |
| 2003–04 | Coventry C | 19 | 1 | **19** | **1** |

**DOYLE, Micky (M) 40 5**
H: 5 8 W: 11 00 b.Dublin 8-7-81
*Source:* Celtic. *Honours:* Eire 1 full cap.

| | | | | | |
|---|---|---|---|---|---|
| 2003–04 | Coventry C | 40 | 5 | **40** | **5** |

**GIDDINGS, Stuart§ (D) 1 0**
H: 6 0 W: 11 08 b.Coventry 27-3-86
*Source:* Scholar. *Honours:* England Youth.

| | | | | | |
|---|---|---|---|---|---|
| 2003–04 | Coventry C | 1 | 0 | **1** | **0** |

**GORDON, Dean* (D) 309 27**
H: 5 11 W: 13 08 b.Thornton Heath 10-2-73
*Source:* Trainee. *Honours:* England Under-21.

| | | | | | |
|---|---|---|---|---|---|
| 1991–92 | Crystal Palace | 4 | 0 | | |
| 1992–93 | Crystal Palace | 10 | 0 | | |
| 1993–94 | Crystal Palace | 45 | 5 | | |
| 1994–95 | Crystal Palace | 41 | 2 | | |
| 1995–96 | Crystal Palace | 34 | 8 | | |
| 1996–97 | Crystal Palace | 30 | 3 | | |
| 1997–98 | Crystal Palace | 37 | 2 | **201** | **20** |
| 1998–99 | Middlesbrough | 38 | 3 | | |
| 1999–2000 | Middlesbrough | 4 | 0 | | |
| 2000–01 | Middlesbrough | 20 | 1 | | |
| 2001–02 | Middlesbrough | 1 | 0 | **63** | **4** |
| 2001–02 | *Cardiff C* | 7 | 2 | **7** | **2** |
| 2002–03 | Coventry C | 30 | 1 | | |
| 2003–04 | Coventry C | 5 | 0 | **35** | **1** |
| 2003–04 | *Reading* | 3 | 0 | **3** | **0** |

**GUDJONSSON, Bjarni# (M) 189 29**
H: 5 8 W: 11 02 b.Reykjavik 26-2-79
*Honours:* Iceland Under-21, 12 full caps, 1 goal.

| | | | | | |
|---|---|---|---|---|---|
| 1995 | IA Akranes | 2 | 0 | | |
| 1996 | IA Akranes | 17 | 13 | | |
| 1997 | IA Akranes | 6 | 2 | **25** | **15** |
| 1997–98 | Newcastle U | 0 | 0 | | |
| 1998–99 | Newcastle U | 0 | 0 | | |
| 1999–2000 | Genk | 14 | 0 | **14** | **0** |
| 1999–2000 | Stoke C | 8 | 1 | | |
| 2000–01 | Stoke C | 42 | 6 | | |
| 2001–02 | Stoke C | 46 | 3 | | |
| 2002–03 | Stoke C | 36 | 1 | **132** | **11** |
| 2003–04 | Coventry C | 18 | 3 | **18** | **3** |

**HIGGINS, Ruaidhri* (M) 0 0**
H: 5 10 W: 12 00 b.Derry 23-10-84
*Source:* Scholar.

| | | | | | |
|---|---|---|---|---|---|
| 2001–02 | Coventry C | 0 | 0 | | |
| 2002–03 | Coventry C | 0 | 0 | | |
| 2003–04 | Coventry C | 0 | 0 | | |

**JEPHCOTT, Avun* (F) 1 0**
H: 6 2 W: 14 00 b.Coventry 16-10-83
*Source:* Scholar.

| | | | | | |
|---|---|---|---|---|---|
| 2002–03 | Coventry C | 1 | 0 | | |
| 2003–04 | Coventry C | 0 | 0 | **1** | **0** |

**JOACHIM, Julian* (F)** **296 75**
H: 5 6 W: 12 00 b.Boston 20-9-74
*Source:* Trainee. *Honours:* England Youth, Under-21.

| | | | | | |
|---|---|---|---|---|---|
| 1992–93 | Leicester C | 26 | 10 | | |
| 1993–94 | Leicester C | 36 | 11 | | |
| 1994–95 | Leicester C | 15 | 3 | | |
| 1995–96 | Leicester C | 22 | 1 | **99** | **25** |
| 1995–96 | Aston Villa | 11 | 1 | | |
| 1996–97 | Aston Villa | 15 | 3 | | |
| 1997–98 | Aston Villa | 26 | 8 | | |
| 1998–99 | Aston Villa | 36 | 14 | | |
| 1999–2000 | Aston Villa | 33 | 6 | | |
| 2000–01 | Aston Villa | 20 | 7 | **141** | **39** |
| 2001–02 | Coventry C | 16 | 1 | | |
| 2002–03 | Coventry C | 11 | 2 | | |
| 2003–04 | Coventry C | 29 | 8 | **56** | **11** |

**JORGENSEN, Claus (M)** **162 26**
H: 5 11 W: 11 00 b.Holstebro 27-4-76
*Source:* Resen-Humlum, Struer BK, Holstebro, Aarhus, AC Horsens.

| | | | | | |
|---|---|---|---|---|---|
| 1999–2000 | Bournemouth | 44 | 6 | | |
| 2000–01 | Bournemouth | 43 | 8 | | |
| 2001–02 | Bradford C | 18 | 1 | | |
| 2002–03 | Bradford C | 32 | 11 | **50** | **12** |
| 2003–04 | Coventry C | 8 | 0 | **8** | **0** |
| 2003–04 | *Bournemouth* | 17 | 0 | **104** | **14** |

**LOWE, Onandi* (F)** **97 51**
H: 6 3 W: 14 12 b.Kingston, Jamaica 2-12-74
*Honours:* Jamaica full caps.

| | | | | | |
|---|---|---|---|---|---|
| 2000–01 | Port Vale | 5 | 1 | **5** | **1** |
| From Kansas City W. | | | | | |
| 2001–02 | Rushden & D | 25 | 19 | | |
| 2002–03 | Rushden & D | 39 | 15 | | |
| 2003–04 | Rushden & D | 26 | 15 | **90** | **49** |
| 2003–04 | Coventry C | 2 | 1 | **2** | **1** |

**MACKEY, Ben§ (M)** **3 0**
H: 5 8 W: 11 09 b.Leamington 27-10-86

| | | | | | |
|---|---|---|---|---|---|
| 2002–03 | Coventry C | 3 | 0 | | |
| 2003–04 | Coventry C | 0 | 0 | **3** | **0** |

**MANSOURI, Yazid‡ (M)** **148 2**
H: 5 8 W: 10 08 b.Revin 25-2-78
*Source:* Tingueux. *Honours:* Algeria full caps.

| | | | | | |
|---|---|---|---|---|---|
| 1997–98 | Le Havre | 10 | 0 | | |
| 1998–99 | Le Havre | 17 | 0 | | |
| 1999–2000 | Le Havre | 29 | 0 | | |
| 2000–01 | Le Havre | 21 | 0 | | |
| 2001–02 | Le Havre | 29 | 2 | | |
| 2002–03 | Le Havre | 28 | 0 | **134** | **2** |
| 2003–04 | Coventry C | 14 | 0 | **14** | **0** |

**McALLISTER, Gary† (M)** **720 119**
H: 6 1 W: 11 11 b.Motherwell 25-12-64
*Source:* Fir Park BC. *Honours:* Scotland Under-21, B, 57 full caps, 5 goals.

| | | | | | |
|---|---|---|---|---|---|
| 1981–82 | Motherwell | 1 | 0 | | |
| 1982–83 | Motherwell | 1 | 0 | | |
| 1983–84 | Motherwell | 21 | 0 | | |
| 1984–85 | Motherwell | 35 | 6 | | |
| 1985–86 | Motherwell | 1 | 0 | **59** | **6** |
| 1985–86 | Leicester C | 31 | 7 | | |
| 1986–87 | Leicester C | 39 | 10 | | |
| 1987–88 | Leicester C | 42 | 9 | | |
| 1988–89 | Leicester C | 46 | 11 | | |
| 1989–90 | Leicester C | 43 | 10 | **201** | **47** |
| 1990–91 | Leeds U | 38 | 2 | | |
| 1991–92 | Leeds U | 42 | 5 | | |
| 1992–93 | Leeds U | 32 | 5 | | |
| 1993–94 | Leeds U | 42 | 8 | | |
| 1994–95 | Leeds U | 41 | 6 | | |
| 1995–96 | Leeds U | 36 | 5 | **231** | **31** |
| 1996–97 | Coventry C | 38 | 6 | | |
| 1997–98 | Coventry C | 14 | 0 | | |
| 1998–99 | Coventry C | 29 | 3 | | |
| 1999–2000 | Coventry C | 38 | 11 | | |
| 2000–01 | Liverpool | 30 | 5 | | |
| 2001–02 | Liverpool | 25 | 0 | **55** | **5** |
| 2002–03 | Coventry C | 41 | 7 | | |
| 2003–04 | Coventry C | 14 | 3 | **174** | **30** |

**McSHEFFREY, Gary (F)** **83 26**
H: 5 8 W: 10 06 b.Coventry 13-8-82
*Source:* Trainee. *Honours:* England Youth, Under-20.

| | | | | | |
|---|---|---|---|---|---|
| 1998–99 | Coventry C | 1 | 0 | | |
| 1999–2000 | Coventry C | 3 | 0 | | |
| 2000–01 | Coventry C | 0 | 0 | | |
| 2001–02 | *Stockport Co* | 5 | 1 | **5** | **1** |
| 2001–02 | Coventry C | 8 | 1 | | |
| 2002–03 | Coventry C | 29 | 4 | | |
| 2003–04 | Coventry C | 19 | 11 | **60** | **16** |
| 2003–04 | *Luton T* | 18 | 9 | **18** | **9** |

**MORRELL, Andy (F)** **140 49**
H: 5 11 W: 11 06 b.Doncaster 28-9-74
*Source:* Newcastle Blue Star.

| | | | | | |
|---|---|---|---|---|---|
| 1998–99 | Wrexham | 7 | 0 | | |
| 1999–2000 | Wrexham | 13 | 1 | | |
| 2000–01 | Wrexham | 20 | 3 | | |
| 2001–02 | Wrexham | 25 | 2 | | |
| 2002–03 | Wrexham | 45 | 34 | **110** | **40** |
| 2003–04 | Coventry C | 30 | 9 | **30** | **9** |

**MUNN, Stephen (D)** **0 0**
H: 5 10 W: 12 00 b.Belfast 28-4-86
*Source:* Scholar.

| | | | | | |
|---|---|---|---|---|---|
| 2003–04 | Coventry C | 0 | 0 | | |

**NOON, Mark‡ (M)** **2 0**
H: 5 10 W: 12 00 b.Leamington Spa 23-9-83
*Source:* Scholar.

| | | | | | |
|---|---|---|---|---|---|
| 2001–02 | Coventry C | 0 | 0 | | |
| 2002–03 | Coventry C | 2 | 0 | | |
| 2003–04 | Coventry C | 0 | 0 | **2** | **0** |

**O'DONOVAN, Roy (F)** **0 0**
H: 5 10 W: 11 07 b.Cork 10-8-85
*Source:* Scholar.

| | | | | | |
|---|---|---|---|---|---|
| 2002–03 | Coventry C | 0 | 0 | | |
| 2003–04 | Coventry C | 0 | 0 | | |

**O'NEILL, Keith‡ (M)** **122 9**
H: 6 1 W: 13 03 b.Dublin 16-12-76
*Source:* Trainee. *Honours:* Eire 13 full caps, 4 goals.

| | | | | | |
|---|---|---|---|---|---|
| 1994–95 | Norwich C | 1 | 0 | | |
| 1995–96 | Norwich C | 19 | 1 | | |
| 1996–97 | Norwich C | 26 | 6 | | |
| 1997–98 | Norwich C | 9 | 1 | | |
| 1998–99 | Norwich C | 18 | 1 | **73** | **9** |
| 1998–99 | Middlesbrough | 6 | 0 | | |
| 1999–2000 | Middlesbrough | 16 | 0 | | |
| 2000–01 | Middlesbrough | 15 | 0 | **37** | **0** |
| 2001–02 | Coventry C | 11 | 0 | | |
| 2002–03 | Coventry C | 0 | 0 | | |
| 2003–04 | Coventry C | 1 | 0 | **12** | **0** |

**OSBOURNE, Isaac (M)** **2 0**
H: 5 9 W: 11 11 b.Birmingham 22-6-86
*Source:* Scholar.

| | | | | | |
|---|---|---|---|---|---|
| 2002–03 | Coventry C | 2 | 0 | | |
| 2003–04 | Coventry C | 0 | 0 | **2** | **0** |

**PEAD, Craig (M)** **42 3**
H: 5 9 W: 11 06 b.Bromsgrove 15-9-81
*Source:* Trainee. *Honours:* England Youth, Under-20.

| | | | | | |
|---|---|---|---|---|---|
| 1998–99 | Coventry C | 0 | 0 | | |
| 1999–2000 | Coventry C | 0 | 0 | | |
| 2000–01 | Coventry C | 0 | 0 | | |
| 2001–02 | Coventry C | 1 | 0 | | |
| 2002–03 | Coventry C | 24 | 2 | | |
| 2003–04 | Coventry C | 17 | 1 | **42** | **3** |

**QUINN, Barry* (M)** **93 0**
H: 6 0 W: 12 02 b.Dublin 9-5-79
*Source:* Trainee. *Honours:* Eire Under-21, 4 full caps.

| | | | | | |
|---|---|---|---|---|---|
| 1996–97 | Coventry C | 0 | 0 | | |
| 1997–98 | Coventry C | 0 | 0 | | |
| 1998–99 | Coventry C | 7 | 0 | | |
| 1999–2000 | Coventry C | 11 | 0 | | |
| 2000–01 | Coventry C | 25 | 0 | | |
| 2001–02 | Coventry C | 22 | 0 | | |
| 2002–03 | Coventry C | 18 | 0 | | |
| 2003–04 | Coventry C | 0 | 0 | **83** | **0** |
| 2003–04 | *Rushden & D* | 4 | 0 | **4** | **0** |
| 2003–04 | *Oxford U* | 6 | 0 | **6** | **0** |

**SAFRI, Youseff (M)** **91 1**
H: 5 8 W: 10 12 b.Casablanca 13-1-77
*Source:* Raja. *Honours:* Morocco full caps.

| | | | | | |
|---|---|---|---|---|---|
| 2001–02 | Coventry C | 33 | 1 | | |
| 2002–03 | Coventry C | 27 | 0 | | |
| 2003–04 | Coventry C | 31 | 0 | **91** | **1** |

**SHAW, Richard# (D)** **470 4**
H: 5 9 W: 12 08 b.Brentford 11-9-68
*Source:* Apprentice.

| | | | | | |
|---|---|---|---|---|---|
| 1986–87 | Crystal Palace | 0 | 0 | | |
| 1987–88 | Crystal Palace | 3 | 0 | | |
| 1988–89 | Crystal Palace | 14 | 0 | | |
| 1989–90 | Crystal Palace | 21 | 0 | | |
| 1989–90 | *Hull C* | 4 | 0 | **4** | **0** |
| 1990–91 | Crystal Palace | 36 | 1 | | |
| 1991–92 | Crystal Palace | 10 | 0 | | |
| 1992–93 | Crystal Palace | 33 | 0 | | |
| 1993–94 | Crystal Palace | 34 | 2 | | |
| 1994–95 | Crystal Palace | 41 | 0 | | |
| 1995–96 | Crystal Palace | 15 | 0 | **207** | **3** |
| 1995–96 | Coventry C | 21 | 0 | | |
| 1996–97 | Coventry C | 35 | 0 | | |
| 1997–98 | Coventry C | 33 | 0 | | |
| 1998–99 | Coventry C | 37 | 0 | | |
| 1999–2000 | Coventry C | 29 | 0 | | |
| 2000–01 | Coventry C | 24 | 0 | | |
| 2001–02 | Coventry C | 32 | 0 | | |
| 2002–03 | Coventry C | 29 | 0 | | |
| 2003–04 | Coventry C | 19 | 1 | **259** | **1** |

**SHEARER, Scott (G)** **79 0**
H: 6 3 W: 14 08 b.Glasgow 15-2-81
*Source:* Tower Hearts. *Honours:* Scotland B.

| | | | | | |
|---|---|---|---|---|---|
| 2000–01 | Albion R | 3 | 0 | | |
| 2001–02 | Albion R | 10 | 0 | | |
| 2002–03 | Albion R | 36 | 0 | **49** | **0** |
| 2003–04 | Coventry C | 30 | 0 | **30** | **0** |

**STANFORD, Eddie‡ (M)** **1 0**
H: 5 7 W: 10 05 b.Blackburn 4-2-85
*Source:* Scholar.

| | | | | | |
|---|---|---|---|---|---|
| 2002–03 | Coventry C | 1 | 0 | | |
| 2003–04 | Coventry C | 0 | 0 | **1** | **0** |

**STAUNTON, Steve (D)** **439 20**
H: 6 0 W: 12 12 b.Dundalk 19-1-69
*Source:* Dundalk. *Honours:* Eire Under-21, 102 full caps, 7 goals.

| | | | | | |
|---|---|---|---|---|---|
| 1986–87 | Liverpool | 0 | 0 | | |
| 1987–88 | Liverpool | 0 | 0 | | |
| 1987–88 | *Bradford C* | 8 | 0 | **8** | **0** |
| 1988–89 | Liverpool | 21 | 0 | | |
| 1989–90 | Liverpool | 20 | 0 | | |
| 1990–91 | Liverpool | 24 | 0 | | |
| 1991–92 | Aston Villa | 37 | 4 | | |
| 1992–93 | Aston Villa | 42 | 2 | | |
| 1993–94 | Aston Villa | 24 | 2 | | |
| 1994–95 | Aston Villa | 35 | 5 | | |
| 1995–96 | Aston Villa | 13 | 0 | | |
| 1996–97 | Aston Villa | 30 | 2 | | |
| 1997–98 | Aston Villa | 27 | 1 | | |
| 1998–99 | Liverpool | 31 | 0 | | |
| 1999–2000 | Liverpool | 12 | 0 | | |
| 2000–01 | Liverpool | 1 | 0 | **109** | **0** |
| 2000–01 | *Crystal Palace* | 6 | 1 | **6** | **1** |
| 2000–01 | Aston Villa | 14 | 0 | | |
| 2001–02 | Aston Villa | 33 | 0 | | |
| 2002–03 | Aston Villa | 26 | 0 | | |
| 2003–04 | Aston Villa | 0 | 0 | **281** | **16** |
| 2003–04 | Coventry C | 35 | 3 | **35** | **3** |

**SUFFO, Patrick (F)** **93 16**
H: 5 9 W: 13 05 b.Ebolowa 17-1-78
*Source:* Tonnerre Yaounde. *Honours:* Cameroon full caps.

| | | | | | |
|---|---|---|---|---|---|
| 1995–96 | Nantes | 0 | 0 | | |
| 1996–97 | Barcelona | 0 | 0 | | |
| 1997–98 | Nantes | 4 | 0 | | |
| 1998–99 | Nantes | 21 | 4 | | |
| 1999–2000 | Nantes | 5 | 0 | **30** | **4** |
| 2000–01 | Sheffield U | 16 | 1 | | |
| 2001–02 | Sheffield U | 20 | 4 | | |
| 2002–03 | Sheffield U | 0 | 0 | **36** | **5** |
| 2003–04 | Coventry C | 27 | 7 | **27** | **7** |

**THORNTON, Kevin (M)** **0 0**
H: 5 7 W: 11 00 b.Drogheda 9-7-86
*Source:* Scholar.

| | | | | | |
|---|---|---|---|---|---|
| 2003–04 | Coventry C | 0 | 0 | | |

**TUFFEY, Jonathan (G)** **0 0**
b.Newry 20-1-87
*Source:* Scholar.

| | | | | | |
|---|---|---|---|---|---|
| 2003–04 | Coventry C | 0 | 0 | | |

**WARD, Gavin* (G)** **271 0**
H: 6 3 W: 12 12 b.Sutton Coldfield 30-6-70
*Source:* Aston Villa Trainee.

| | | | | | |
|---|---|---|---|---|---|
| 1988–89 | Shrewsbury T | 0 | 0 | | |
| 1989–90 | WBA | 0 | 0 | | |
| 1989–90 | Cardiff C | 2 | 0 | | |
| 1990–91 | Cardiff C | 1 | 0 | | |
| 1991–92 | Cardiff C | 24 | 0 | | |
| 1992–93 | Cardiff C | 32 | 0 | **59** | **0** |
| 1993–94 | Leicester C | 32 | 0 | | |
| 1994–95 | Leicester C | 6 | 0 | **38** | **0** |
| 1995–96 | Bradford C | 36 | 0 | **36** | **0** |
| 1995–96 | Bolton W | 5 | 0 | | |
| 1996–97 | Bolton W | 11 | 0 | | |
| 1997–98 | Bolton W | 6 | 0 | | |
| 1998–99 | Bolton W | 0 | 0 | **22** | **0** |
| 1998–99 | *Burnley* | 17 | 0 | **17** | **0** |
| 1998–99 | Stoke C | 6 | 0 | | |
| 1999–2000 | Stoke C | 46 | 0 | | |
| 2000–01 | Stoke C | 17 | 0 | | |
| 2001–02 | Stoke C | 10 | 0 | **79** | **0** |
| 2002–03 | Walsall | 7 | 0 | **7** | **0** |
| 2003–04 | Coventry C | 12 | 0 | **12** | **0** |
| 2003–04 | *Barnsley* | 1 | 0 | **1** | **0** |

**WHING, Andrew (D)** **42 1**
H: 6 0 W: 12 00 b.Birmingham 20-9-84
*Source:* Scholar.

| | | | | | |
|---|---|---|---|---|---|
| 2002–03 | Coventry C | 14 | 0 | | |
| 2003–04 | Coventry C | 28 | 1 | **42** | **1** |

**YAZDANI, Hussain* (M)** **0 0**
H: 5 9 W: 11 00 b.Dublin 6-1-85
*Source:* Scholar.

| | | | |
|---|---|---|---|
| 2001–02 | Coventry C | 0 | 0 |
| 2002–03 | Coventry C | 0 | 0 |
| 2003–04 | Coventry C | 0 | 0 |

**Scholars**
Davis Liam L; Giddings, Stuart J; Goodman, Mark I; Hall, Andrew; Lynch, Ryan P; Mackey, Ben M; Newbold, Blake; Nicell, Liam; Oddy, Robert J; Ogarro, Azariah A; O'Toole, Gary T; Partridge, Timothy P; Wall, Stuart

**Non Contract**
McAllister, Gary

## CREWE ALEX (26)

**ASHTON, Dean (F)** **135 43**
H: 6 2 W: 12 08 b.Crewe 24-11-83
*Source:* Schoolboy. *Honours:* England Youth, Under-20, Under-21.

| | | | | | |
|---|---|---|---|---|---|
| 2000–01 | Crewe Alex | 21 | 8 | | |
| 2001–02 | Crewe Alex | 31 | 7 | | |
| 2002–03 | Crewe Alex | 39 | 9 | | |
| 2003–04 | Crewe Alex | 44 | 19 | **135** | **43** |

**BANKOLE, Ademola* (G)** **59 0**
H: 6 3 W: 14 00 b.Lagos 9-9-69
*Source:* Leyton Orient.

| | | | | | |
|---|---|---|---|---|---|
| 1996–97 | Crewe Alex | 3 | 0 | | |
| 1997–98 | Crewe Alex | 3 | 0 | | |
| 1998–99 | QPR | 0 | 0 | | |
| 1998–99 | *Grimsby T* | 0 | 0 | | |
| 1999–2000 | QPR | 1 | 0 | **1** | **0** |
| 1999–2000 | *Bradford C* | 0 | 0 | | |
| 2000–01 | Crewe Alex | 21 | 0 | | |
| 2001–02 | Crewe Alex | 28 | 0 | | |
| 2002–03 | Crewe Alex | 3 | 0 | | |
| 2003–04 | Crewe Alex | 0 | 0 | **58** | **0** |

**BELL, Lee (M)** **20 1**
H: 5 11 W: 11 00 b.Crewe 26-1-83
*Source:* Scholar.

| | | | | | |
|---|---|---|---|---|---|
| 2000–01 | Crewe Alex | 0 | 0 | | |
| 2001–02 | Crewe Alex | 0 | 0 | | |
| 2002–03 | Crewe Alex | 17 | 1 | | |
| 2003–04 | Crewe Alex | 3 | 0 | **20** | **1** |

**BETTS, Tom‡ (D)** **0 0**
H: 6 0 W: 12 00 b.Stone 3-12-82
*Source:* Scholar.

| | | | |
|---|---|---|---|
| 2000–01 | Crewe Alex | 0 | 0 |
| 2001–02 | Crewe Alex | 0 | 0 |
| 2002–03 | Crewe Alex | 0 | 0 |
| 2003–04 | Crewe Alex | 0 | 0 |

**BRAMMER, Dave# (M)** **297 19**
H: 5 11 W: 12 00 b.Bromborough 28-2-75
*Source:* Trainee.

| | | | | | |
|---|---|---|---|---|---|
| 1992–93 | Wrexham | 2 | 0 | | |
| 1993–94 | Wrexham | 22 | 2 | | |
| 1994–95 | Wrexham | 14 | 1 | | |
| 1995–96 | Wrexham | 11 | 2 | | |
| 1996–97 | Wrexham | 21 | 1 | | |
| 1997–98 | Wrexham | 33 | 4 | | |
| 1998–99 | Wrexham | 34 | 2 | **137** | **12** |
| 1998–99 | Port Vale | 9 | 0 | | |
| 1999–2000 | Port Vale | 29 | 0 | | |
| 2000–01 | Port Vale | 35 | 3 | **73** | **3** |
| 2001–02 | Crewe Alex | 30 | 2 | | |
| 2002–03 | Crewe Alex | 41 | 1 | | |
| 2003–04 | Crewe Alex | 16 | 1 | **87** | **4** |

**COCHRANE, Justin (M)** **40 0**
H: 5 11 W: 11 07 b.Hackney 26-1-82
*Source:* Scholarship.

| | | | | | |
|---|---|---|---|---|---|
| 1999–2000 | QPR | 0 | 0 | | |
| 2000–01 | QPR | 1 | 0 | | |
| 2001–02 | QPR | 0 | 0 | | |
| 2002–03 | QPR | 0 | 0 | **1** | **0** |
| From Hayes. | | | | | |
| 2003–04 | Crewe Alex | 39 | 0 | **39** | **0** |

**EDWARDS, Paul (F)** **12 0**
H: 6 0 W: 11 07 b.Derby 10-11-82
*Source:* Scholar.

| | | | | | |
|---|---|---|---|---|---|
| 2000–01 | Crewe Alex | 0 | 0 | | |
| 2001–02 | Crewe Alex | 0 | 0 | | |
| 2002–03 | Crewe Alex | 2 | 0 | | |
| 2003–04 | Crewe Alex | 10 | 0 | **12** | **0** |

**FOSTER, Stephen (D)** **145 11**
H: 6 0 W: 11 05 b.Warrington 10-9-80
*Source:* Trainee. *Honours:* England Schools.

| | | | | | |
|---|---|---|---|---|---|
| 1998–99 | Crewe Alex | 1 | 0 | | |
| 1999–2000 | Crewe Alex | 0 | 0 | | |
| 2000–01 | Crewe Alex | 30 | 0 | | |
| 2001–02 | Crewe Alex | 34 | 5 | | |
| 2002–03 | Crewe Alex | 35 | 4 | | |
| 2003–04 | Crewe Alex | 45 | 2 | **145** | **11** |

**FROST, Carl‡ (F)** **0 0**
H: 5 9 W: 10 07 b.Chester 19-7-83
*Source:* Scholar.

| | | | |
|---|---|---|---|
| 2000–01 | Crewe Alex | 0 | 0 |
| 2001–02 | Crewe Alex | 0 | 0 |
| 2002–03 | Crewe Alex | 0 | 0 |
| 2003–04 | Crewe Alex | 0 | 0 |

**GARNER, Matt‡ (D)** **0 0**
H: 6 0 W: 11 07 b.Warrington 9-4-84
*Source:* Scholar.

| | | | |
|---|---|---|---|
| 2003–04 | Crewe Alex | 0 | 0 |

**HIGDON, Michael (M)** **10 1**
H: 6 1 W: 11 05 b.Liverpool 2-9-83
*Source:* School.

| | | | | | |
|---|---|---|---|---|---|
| 2000–01 | Crewe Alex | 0 | 0 | | |
| 2001–02 | Crewe Alex | 0 | 0 | | |
| 2002–03 | Crewe Alex | 0 | 0 | | |
| 2003–04 | Crewe Alex | 10 | 1 | **10** | **1** |

**INCE, Clayton (G)** **100 0**
H: 6 3 W: 13 00 b.Trinidad 13-7-72
*Source:* Defence Force. *Honours:* Trinidad & Tobago 34 full caps.

| | | | | | |
|---|---|---|---|---|---|
| 1999–2000 | Crewe Alex | 1 | 0 | | |
| 2000–01 | Crewe Alex | 1 | 0 | | |
| 2001–02 | Crewe Alex | 19 | 0 | | |
| 2002–03 | Crewe Alex | 43 | 0 | | |
| 2003–04 | Crewe Alex | 36 | 0 | **100** | **0** |

**JEFFS, Ian‡ (F)** **0 0**
H: 5 7 W: 10 00 b.Chester 12-10-82
*Source:* Scholar.

| | | | |
|---|---|---|---|
| 2000–01 | Crewe Alex | 0 | 0 |
| 2001–02 | Crewe Alex | 0 | 0 |
| 2002–03 | Crewe Alex | 0 | 0 |
| 2003–04 | Crewe Alex | 0 | 0 |

**JONES, Billy§ (M)** **27 1**
H: 5 11 W: 13 00 b.Shrewsbury 24-3-87
*Source:* Scholar. *Honours:* England Youth.

| | | | | | |
|---|---|---|---|---|---|
| 2003–04 | Crewe Alex | 27 | 1 | **27** | **1** |

**JONES, Steve (F)** **91 25**
H: 5 10 W: 10 05 b.Derry 25-10-76
*Source:* Leigh RMI. *Honours:* Northern Ireland 11 full caps, 1 goals.

| | | | | | |
|---|---|---|---|---|---|
| 2001–02 | *Rochdale* | 9 | 1 | **9** | **1** |
| 2001–02 | Crewe Alex | 6 | 0 | | |
| 2002–03 | Crewe Alex | 31 | 9 | | |
| 2003–04 | Crewe Alex | 45 | 15 | **82** | **24** |

**LUNT, Kenny (M)** **284 26**
H: 5 10 W: 10 05 b.Runcorn 20-11-79
*Source:* Trainee. *Honours:* England Schools, Youth.

| | | | | | |
|---|---|---|---|---|---|
| 1997–98 | Crewe Alex | 41 | 2 | | |
| 1998–99 | Crewe Alex | 18 | 1 | | |
| 1999–2000 | Crewe Alex | 43 | 3 | | |
| 2000–01 | Crewe Alex | 46 | 1 | | |
| 2001–02 | Crewe Alex | 45 | 5 | | |
| 2002–03 | Crewe Alex | 46 | 7 | | |
| 2003–04 | Crewe Alex | 45 | 7 | **284** | **26** |

**McCREADY, Chris (D)** **31 0**
H: 6 1 W: 12 05 b.Chester 5-9-81
*Source:* Scholar.

| | | | | | |
|---|---|---|---|---|---|
| 2000–01 | Crewe Alex | 0 | 0 | | |
| 2001–02 | Crewe Alex | 1 | 0 | | |
| 2002–03 | Crewe Alex | 8 | 0 | | |
| 2003–04 | Crewe Alex | 22 | 0 | **31** | **0** |

**MORRIS, Alex (M)** **0 0**
H: 6 0 W: 11 08 b.Stoke 5-10-82
*Source:* Scholar.

| | | | |
|---|---|---|---|
| 2000–01 | Crewe Alex | 0 | 0 |
| 2001–02 | Crewe Alex | 0 | 0 |
| 2002–03 | Crewe Alex | 0 | 0 |
| 2003–04 | Crewe Alex | 0 | 0 |

**MOSES, Adi (D)** **241 4**
H: 5 11 W: 13 01 b.Doncaster 4-5-75
*Source:* School. *Honours:* England Under-21.

| | | | | | |
|---|---|---|---|---|---|
| 1993–94 | Barnsley | 0 | 0 | | |
| 1994–95 | Barnsley | 4 | 0 | | |
| 1995–96 | Barnsley | 24 | 1 | | |
| 1996–97 | Barnsley | 28 | 2 | | |
| 1997–98 | Barnsley | 35 | 0 | | |
| 1998–99 | Barnsley | 34 | 0 | | |
| 1999–2000 | Barnsley | 12 | 0 | | |
| 2000–01 | Barnsley | 14 | 0 | **151** | **3** |
| 2000–01 | Huddersfield T | 12 | 0 | | |
| 2001–02 | Huddersfield T | 17 | 0 | | |
| 2002–03 | Huddersfield T | 40 | 1 | **69** | **1** |
| 2003–04 | Crewe Alex | 21 | 0 | **21** | **0** |

**PLATT, Matthew (F)** **0 0**
H: 6 0 W: 11 03 b.Crewe 15-10-83
*Source:* Scholar.

| | | | |
|---|---|---|---|
| 2002–03 | Crewe Alex | 0 | 0 |
| 2003–04 | Crewe Alex | 0 | 0 |

**RIX, Ben (M)** **70 2**
H: 5 9 W: 11 05 b.Wolverhampton 11-12-82
*Source:* Scholar.

| | | | | | |
|---|---|---|---|---|---|
| 2000–01 | Crewe Alex | 0 | 0 | | |
| 2001–02 | Crewe Alex | 21 | 0 | | |
| 2002–03 | Crewe Alex | 23 | 0 | | |
| 2003–04 | Crewe Alex | 26 | 2 | **70** | **2** |

**ROBERTS, Gary§ (M)** **0 0**
H: 5 8 W: 10 05 b.Chester 4-2-87
*Source:* Scholar. *Honours:* England Youth.

| | | | |
|---|---|---|---|
| 2003–04 | Crewe Alex | 0 | 0 |

**ROBERTS, Mark (D)** **2 0**
H: 6 1 W: 12 00 b.Northwich 16-10-83
*Source:* Scholar.

| | | | | | |
|---|---|---|---|---|---|
| 2002–03 | Crewe Alex | 0 | 0 | | |
| 2003–04 | Crewe Alex | 2 | 0 | **2** | **0** |

**ROBINSON, James (F)** **10 1**
H: 5 10 W: 11 03 b.Whiston 18-9-82
*Source:* Scholar.

| | | | | | |
|---|---|---|---|---|---|
| 2001–02 | Crewe Alex | 0 | 0 | | |
| 2002–03 | Crewe Alex | 1 | 0 | | |
| 2003–04 | Crewe Alex | 9 | 1 | **10** | **1** |

**SMART, Allan* (F)** **183 41**
H: 6 2 W: 12 04 b.Perth 8-7-74

| | | | | | |
|---|---|---|---|---|---|
| 1994–95 | Caledonian Th | 4 | 0 | **4** | **0** |
| 1994–95 | Preston NE | 19 | 6 | | |
| 1995–96 | Preston NE | 2 | 0 | | |
| 1995–96 | *Carlisle U* | 4 | 0 | | |
| 1996–97 | Preston NE | 0 | 0 | **21** | **6** |
| 1996–97 | *Northampton T* | 1 | 0 | **1** | **0** |
| 1996–97 | Carlisle U | 28 | 10 | | |
| 1997–98 | Carlisle U | 16 | 6 | **48** | **16** |
| 1998–99 | Watford | 35 | 7 | | |
| 1999–2000 | Watford | 14 | 5 | | |
| 2000–01 | Watford | 8 | 0 | | |

| | | | | | |
|---|---|---|---|---|---|
| 2001–02 | Watford | 0 | 0 | **57** | **12** |
| 2001–02 | *Hibernian* | 5 | 1 | **5** | **1** |
| 2001–02 | *Stoke C* | 2 | 0 | **2** | **0** |
| 2001–02 | Oldham Ath | 21 | 6 | **21** | **6** |
| 2002–03 | Dundee U | 18 | 0 | **18** | **0** |
| 2003–04 | Crewe Alex | 6 | 0 | **6** | **0** |

**SORVEL, Neil (M)** **299** **17**
H: 6 0 W: 12 03 b.Widnes 2-3-73
*Source:* Trainee.

| | | | | | |
|---|---|---|---|---|---|
| 1991–92 | Crewe Alex | 9 | 0 | | |
| 1992–93 | Crewe Alex | 0 | 0 | | |
| 1997–98 | Macclesfield T | 45 | 3 | | |
| 1998–99 | Macclesfield T | 41 | 4 | **86** | **7** |
| 1999–2000 | Crewe Alex | 46 | 6 | | |
| 2000–01 | Crewe Alex | 46 | 1 | | |
| 2001–02 | Crewe Alex | 38 | 0 | | |
| 2002–03 | Crewe Alex | 43 | 3 | | |
| 2003–04 | Crewe Alex | 31 | 0 | **213** | **10** |

**TOMLINSON, Stuart (G)** **2** **0**
H: 6 1 W: 11 02 b.Chester 10-5-85
*Source:* Scholar.

| | | | | | |
|---|---|---|---|---|---|
| 2002–03 | Crewe Alex | 1 | 0 | | |
| 2003–04 | Crewe Alex | 1 | 0 | **2** | **0** |

**TONKIN, Anthony (D)** **50** **0**
H: 5 11 W: 12 02 b.Cornwall 19-1-80
*Source:* Yeovil T.

| | | | | | |
|---|---|---|---|---|---|
| 2002–03 | Stockport Co | 24 | 0 | | |
| 2003–04 | Stockport Co | 0 | 0 | **24** | **0** |
| 2003–04 | Crewe Alex | 26 | 0 | **26** | **0** |

**VARNEY, Luke (F)** **8** **1**
H: 5 11 W: 11 00 b.Leicester 28-9-82
*Source:* Quorn.

| | | | | | |
|---|---|---|---|---|---|
| 2002–03 | Crewe Alex | 0 | 0 | | |
| 2003–04 | Crewe Alex | 8 | 1 | **8** | **1** |

**VAUGHAN, David (M)** **77** **3**
H: 5 7 W: 11 00 b.St Asaph 18-2-83
*Source:* Scholar. *Honours:* Wales Under-21, 2 full caps.

| | | | | | |
|---|---|---|---|---|---|
| 2000–01 | Crewe Alex | 1 | 0 | | |
| 2001–02 | Crewe Alex | 13 | 0 | | |
| 2002–03 | Crewe Alex | 32 | 3 | | |
| 2003–04 | Crewe Alex | 31 | 0 | **77** | **3** |

**WALKER, Richard (D)** **59** **3**
H: 6 2 W: 12 08 b.Stafford 17-9-80
*Source:* Brook House.

| | | | | | |
|---|---|---|---|---|---|
| 1999–2000 | Crewe Alex | 0 | 0 | | |
| 2000–01 | Crewe Alex | 3 | 0 | | |
| 2001–02 | Crewe Alex | 1 | 0 | | |
| 2002–03 | Crewe Alex | 35 | 2 | | |
| 2003–04 | Crewe Alex | 20 | 1 | **59** | **3** |

**WILSON, Kyle (F)** **0** **0**
H: 5 10 W: 11 05 b.Wirrall 14-11-85
*Source:* Scholar. *Honours:* England Youth.

| | | | | | |
|---|---|---|---|---|---|
| 2003–04 | Crewe Alex | 0 | 0 | | |

**WRIGHT, David (D)** **211** **3**
H: 5 11 W: 11 00 b.Warrington 1-5-80
*Source:* Trainee. *Honours:* England Youth.

| | | | | | |
|---|---|---|---|---|---|
| 1997–98 | Crewe Alex | 3 | 0 | | |
| 1998–99 | Crewe Alex | 20 | 1 | | |
| 1999–2000 | Crewe Alex | 45 | 0 | | |
| 2000–01 | Crewe Alex | 42 | 0 | | |
| 2001–02 | Crewe Alex | 30 | 0 | | |
| 2002–03 | Crewe Alex | 31 | 1 | | |
| 2003–04 | Crewe Alex | 40 | 1 | **211** | **3** |

**YATES, Adam* (D)** **0** **0**
H: 5 10 W: 10 07 b.Stoke 28-5-83
*Source:* Scholar.

| | | | | | |
|---|---|---|---|---|---|
| 2000–01 | Crewe Alex | 0 | 0 | | |
| 2001–02 | Crewe Alex | 0 | 0 | | |
| 2002–03 | Crewe Alex | 0 | 0 | | |
| 2003–04 | Crewe Alex | 0 | 0 | | |

**Scholars**
Austin, Ryan; Ball, Craig; Bignot, Paul J; Bond, Andrew M; Brown, Alexander J A; Carrington, Mark R; Clark, James; Collymore, Lee J; Coo, Cavell S; Fletcher, James E; Hawthorne, Robert; Hogg, Christopher J; Holroyd, Christopher; Howard, Adam; Jones, Billy; Lee, Jamie A; Lloyd, Robert F; Maynard, Nicholas D; McGowan, Lloyd Edwin; Oates, Michael L; Roberts, Gary S; Sutton, Ritchie A; Warlow, Adam T; White, Christopher J; Williams, Owain F

## CRYSTAL PALACE (27)

**BERTHELIN, Cedric (G)** **35** **0**
H: 6 4 W: 15 00 b.Courrieres 25-12-76

| | | | | | |
|---|---|---|---|---|---|
| 2002–03 | Luton T | 9 | 0 | **9** | **0** |
| 2002–03 | Crystal Palace | 9 | 0 | | |
| 2003–04 | Crystal Palace | 17 | 0 | **26** | **0** |

**BLACK, Tommy (M)** **136** **11**
H: 5 7 W: 11 10 b.Chigwell 26-11-79
*Source:* Trainee.

| | | | | | |
|---|---|---|---|---|---|
| 1998–99 | Arsenal | 0 | 0 | | |
| 1999–2000 | Arsenal | 1 | 0 | **1** | **0** |
| 1999–2000 | *Carlisle U* | 5 | 1 | **5** | **1** |
| 1999–2000 | *Bristol C* | 4 | 0 | **4** | **0** |
| 2000–01 | Crystal Palace | 40 | 4 | | |
| 2001–02 | Crystal Palace | 25 | 0 | | |
| 2002–03 | Crystal Palace | 36 | 6 | | |
| 2003–04 | Crystal Palace | 25 | 0 | **126** | **10** |

**BORROWDALE, Gary (D)** **36** **0**
H: 6 0 W: 12 01 b.Sutton 16-7-85
*Source:* Scholar. *Honours:* England Youth.

| | | | | | |
|---|---|---|---|---|---|
| 2002–03 | Crystal Palace | 13 | 0 | | |
| 2003–04 | Crystal Palace | 23 | 0 | **36** | **0** |

**BUTTERFIELD, Danny (D)** **215** **8**
H: 5 10 W: 11 06 b.Boston 21-11-79
*Source:* Trainee. *Honours:* England Youth.

| | | | | | |
|---|---|---|---|---|---|
| 1997–98 | Grimsby T | 7 | 0 | | |
| 1998–99 | Grimsby T | 12 | 0 | | |
| 1999–2000 | Grimsby T | 29 | 0 | | |
| 2000–01 | Grimsby T | 30 | 1 | | |
| 2001–02 | Grimsby T | 46 | 2 | **124** | **3** |
| 2002–03 | Crystal Palace | 46 | 1 | | |
| 2003–04 | Crystal Palace | 45 | 4 | **91** | **5** |

**CLARKE, Matt (G)** **212** **0**
H: 6 4 W: 13 08 b.Sheffield 3-11-73
*Source:* Trainee.

| | | | | | |
|---|---|---|---|---|---|
| 1992–93 | Rotherham U | 9 | 0 | | |
| 1993–94 | Rotherham U | 30 | 0 | | |
| 1994–95 | Rotherham U | 45 | 0 | | |
| 1995–96 | Rotherham U | 40 | 0 | **124** | **0** |
| 1996–97 | Sheffield W | 1 | 0 | | |
| 1997–98 | Sheffield W | 3 | 0 | | |
| 1998–99 | Sheffield W | 0 | 0 | **4** | **0** |
| 1999–2000 | Bradford C | 21 | 0 | | |
| 2000–01 | Bradford C | 17 | 0 | | |
| 2000–01 | *Bolton W* | 8 | 0 | **8** | **0** |
| 2001–02 | Bradford C | 0 | 0 | **38** | **0** |
| 2001–02 | *Fulham* | 0 | 0 | | |
| 2001–02 | Crystal Palace | 28 | 0 | | |
| 2002–03 | Crystal Palace | 6 | 0 | | |
| 2003–04 | Crystal Palace | 4 | 0 | **38** | **0** |

**CRONIN, Lance (G)** **0** **0**
H: 6 1 W: 13 04 b.Brighton 11-9-85
*Source:* Scholar.

| | | | | | |
|---|---|---|---|---|---|
| 2002–03 | Crystal Palace | 0 | 0 | | |
| 2003–04 | Crystal Palace | 0 | 0 | | |

**DERRY, Shaun (M)** **276** **8**
H: 5 10 W: 13 02 b.Nottingham 6-12-77
*Source:* Trainee.

| | | | | | |
|---|---|---|---|---|---|
| 1995–96 | Notts Co | 12 | 0 | | |
| 1996–97 | Notts Co | 39 | 2 | | |
| 1997–98 | Notts Co | 28 | 2 | **79** | **4** |
| 1997–98 | Sheffield U | 12 | 0 | | |
| 1998–99 | Sheffield U | 26 | 0 | | |
| 1999–2000 | Sheffield U | 34 | 0 | **72** | **0** |
| 1999–2000 | Portsmouth | 9 | 1 | | |
| 2000–01 | Portsmouth | 28 | 0 | | |
| 2001–02 | Portsmouth | 12 | 0 | **49** | **1** |
| 2002–03 | Crystal Palace | 39 | 1 | | |
| 2003–04 | Crystal Palace | 37 | 2 | **76** | **3** |

**FLEMING, Curtis* (D)** **317** **3**
H: 5 10 W: 12 09 b.Manchester 8-10-68
*Source:* St Patrick's Ath. *Honours:* Eire Youth, Under-21, B, 10 full caps.

| | | | | | |
|---|---|---|---|---|---|
| 1991–92 | Middlesbrough | 28 | 0 | | |
| 1992–93 | Middlesbrough | 24 | 0 | | |
| 1993–94 | Middlesbrough | 40 | 0 | | |
| 1994–95 | Middlesbrough | 21 | 0 | | |
| 1995–96 | Middlesbrough | 13 | 1 | | |
| 1996–97 | Middlesbrough | 30 | 0 | | |
| 1997–98 | Middlesbrough | 31 | 1 | | |
| 1998–99 | Middlesbrough | 14 | 1 | | |
| 1999–2000 | Middlesbrough | 27 | 0 | | |
| 2000–01 | Middlesbrough | 30 | 0 | | |
| 2001–02 | Middlesbrough | 8 | 0 | **266** | **3** |
| 2001–02 | *Birmingham C* | 6 | 0 | **6** | **0** |
| 2001–02 | Crystal Palace | 17 | 0 | | |
| 2002–03 | Crystal Palace | 11 | 0 | | |
| 2003–04 | Crystal Palace | 17 | 0 | **45** | **0** |

**FREEDMAN, Dougie (F)** **366** **139**
H: 5 9 W: 12 05 b.Glasgow 21-1-74
*Source:* Trainee. *Honours:* Scotland Schools, Under-21, B, 2 full caps, 1 goal.

| | | | | | |
|---|---|---|---|---|---|
| 1991–92 | QPR | 0 | 0 | | |
| 1992–93 | QPR | 0 | 0 | | |
| 1993–94 | QPR | 0 | 0 | | |
| 1994–95 | Barnet | 42 | 24 | | |
| 1995–96 | Barnet | 5 | 3 | **47** | **27** |
| 1995–96 | Crystal Palace | 39 | 20 | | |
| 1996–97 | Crystal Palace | 44 | 11 | | |
| 1997–98 | Crystal Palace | 7 | 0 | | |
| 1997–98 | Wolverhampton W | 29 | 10 | **29** | **10** |
| 1998–99 | Nottingham F | 31 | 9 | | |
| 1999–2000 | Nottingham F | 34 | 9 | | |
| 2000–01 | Nottingham F | 5 | 0 | **70** | **18** |
| 2000–01 | Crystal Palace | 26 | 11 | | |
| 2001–02 | Crystal Palace | 40 | 20 | | |
| 2002–03 | Crystal Palace | 29 | 9 | | |
| 2003–04 | Crystal Palace | 35 | 13 | **220** | **84** |

**GRANVILLE, Danny (D)** **274** **16**
H: 6 0 W: 12 00 b.Islington 19-1-75
*Source:* Trainee. *Honours:* England Under-21.

| | | | | | |
|---|---|---|---|---|---|
| 1993–94 | Cambridge U | 11 | 5 | | |
| 1994–95 | Cambridge U | 16 | 2 | | |
| 1995–96 | Cambridge U | 35 | 0 | | |
| 1996–97 | Cambridge U | 37 | 0 | **99** | **7** |
| 1996–97 | Chelsea | 5 | 0 | | |
| 1997–98 | Chelsea | 13 | 0 | **18** | **0** |
| 1998–99 | Leeds U | 9 | 0 | | |
| 1999–2000 | Leeds U | 0 | 0 | **9** | **0** |
| 1999–2000 | Manchester C | 35 | 2 | | |
| 2000–01 | Manchester C | 19 | 0 | | |
| 2000–01 | *Norwich C* | 6 | 0 | **6** | **0** |
| 2001–02 | Manchester C | 16 | 1 | **70** | **3** |
| 2001–02 | Crystal Palace | 16 | 0 | | |
| 2002–03 | Crystal Palace | 35 | 3 | | |
| 2003–04 | Crystal Palace | 21 | 3 | **72** | **6** |

**GRAY, Julian# (M)** **135** **10**
H: 6 1 W: 11 08 b.Lewisham 21-9-79
*Source:* Trainee.

| | | | | | |
|---|---|---|---|---|---|
| 1998–99 | Arsenal | 0 | 0 | | |
| 1999–2000 | Arsenal | 1 | 0 | **1** | **0** |
| 2000–01 | Crystal Palace | 23 | 1 | | |
| 2001–02 | Crystal Palace | 43 | 2 | | |
| 2002–03 | Crystal Palace | 35 | 5 | | |
| 2003–04 | Crystal Palace | 24 | 2 | **125** | **10** |
| 2003–04 | *Cardiff C* | 9 | 0 | **9** | **0** |

**HEEROO, Gavin* (M)** **1** **0**
H: 5 11 W: 11 07 b.Harringey 2-9-84
*Honours:* Mauritius full caps.

| | | | | | |
|---|---|---|---|---|---|
| 2001–02 | Crystal Palace | 0 | 0 | | |
| 2002–03 | Crystal Palace | 0 | 0 | | |
| 2003–04 | Crystal Palace | 1 | 0 | **1** | **0** |

**HUGHES, Michael# (M)** **344** **31**
H: 5 6 W: 10 08 b.Larne 2-8-71
*Source:* Carrick R. *Honours:* Northern Ireland Schools, Youth, Under-21, Under-23, 69 full caps, 5 goals.

| | | | | | |
|---|---|---|---|---|---|
| 1988–89 | Manchester C | 1 | 0 | | |
| 1989–90 | Manchester C | 0 | 0 | | |
| 1990–91 | Manchester C | 1 | 0 | | |
| 1991–92 | Manchester C | 24 | 1 | **26** | **1** |
| 1992–93 | Strasbourg | 36 | 2 | | |
| 1993–94 | Strasbourg | 34 | 7 | | |
| 1994–95 | Strasbourg | 13 | 0 | **83** | **9** |
| 1994–95 | *West Ham U* | 17 | 2 | | |
| 1995–96 | *West Ham U* | 28 | 0 | | |
| 1996–97 | West Ham U | 33 | 3 | | |
| 1997–98 | West Ham U | 5 | 0 | **83** | **5** |
| 1997–98 | Wimbledon | 29 | 4 | | |
| 1998–99 | Wimbledon | 30 | 2 | | |
| 1999–2000 | Wimbledon | 20 | 2 | | |
| 2000–01 | Wimbledon | 10 | 1 | | |
| 2001–02 | Wimbledon | 26 | 4 | | |
| 2001–02 | *Birmingham C* | 3 | 0 | **3** | **0** |
| 2002–03 | Wimbledon | 0 | 0 | **115** | **13** |
| 2003–04 | Crystal Palace | 34 | 3 | **34** | **3** |

**JOHNSON, Andrew (F) 153 46**
H: 5 7 W: 10 09 b.Bedford 10-2-81
*Source:* Trainee. *Honours:* England Youth, Under-20.

| | | | | | |
|---|---|---|---|---|---|
| 1997–98 | Birmingham C | 0 | 0 | | |
| 1998–99 | Birmingham C | 4 | 0 | | |
| 1999–2000 | Birmingham C | 22 | 1 | | |
| 2000–01 | Birmingham C | 34 | 4 | | |
| 2001–02 | Birmingham C | 23 | 3 | **83** | **8** |
| 2002–03 | Crystal Palace | 28 | 11 | | |
| 2003–04 | Crystal Palace | 42 | 27 | **70** | **38** |

**LEIGERTWOOD, Mikele (D) 76 2**
H: 6 1 W: 11 04 b.Enfield 12-11-82
*Source:* Scholar.

| | | | | | |
|---|---|---|---|---|---|
| 2001–02 | Wimbledon | 1 | 0 | | |
| 2001–02 | *Leyton Orient* | 8 | 0 | **8** | **0** |
| 2002–03 | Wimbledon | 28 | 0 | | |
| 2003–04 | Wimbledon | 27 | 2 | **56** | **2** |
| 2003–04 | Crystal Palace | 12 | 0 | **12** | **0** |

**POPOVIC, Tony# (D) 339 34**
H: 6 5 W: 13 01 b.Australia 7-4-73
*Honours:* Australia Youth, Under-20, Under-23, 43 full caps, 7 goals.

| | | | | | |
|---|---|---|---|---|---|
| 1989–90 | Sydney U | 13 | 0 | | |
| 1990–91 | Sydney U | 17 | 1 | | |
| 1991–92 | Sydney U | 20 | 1 | | |
| 1992–93 | Sydney U | 24 | 2 | | |
| 1993–94 | Sydney U | 27 | 2 | | |
| 1994–95 | Sydney U | 25 | 3 | | |
| 1995–96 | Sydney U | 29 | 4 | | |
| 1995–96 | Wolverhampton W | 0 | 0 | | |
| 1996–97 | Wolverhampton W | 0 | 0 | | |
| 1996–97 | Sydney U | 7 | 2 | **162** | **15** |
| 1997 | Sanfrecce | 11 | 0 | | |
| 1998 | Sanfrecce | 25 | 4 | | |
| 1999 | Sanfrecce | 23 | 6 | | |
| 2000 | Sanfrecce | 21 | 3 | | |
| 2001 | Sanfrecce | 7 | 0 | **87** | **13** |
| 2001–02 | Crystal Palace | 20 | 2 | | |
| 2002–03 | Crystal Palace | 36 | 3 | | |
| 2003–04 | Crystal Palace | 34 | 1 | **90** | **6** |

**POWELL, Darren (D) 177 7**
H: 6 4 W: 13 03 b.Hammersmith 10-3-76
*Source:* Hampton.

| | | | | | |
|---|---|---|---|---|---|
| 1998–99 | Brentford | 33 | 2 | | |
| 1999–2000 | Brentford | 36 | 2 | | |
| 2000–01 | Brentford | 18 | 1 | | |
| 2001–02 | Brentford | 41 | 1 | **128** | **6** |
| 2002–03 | Crystal Palace | 39 | 1 | | |
| 2003–04 | Crystal Palace | 10 | 0 | **49** | **1** |

**RIIHILAHTI, Aki# (M) 135 12**
H: 5 11 W: 12 06 b.Helsinki 9-9-76
*Honours:* Finland 51 full caps, 8 goals.

| | | | | | |
|---|---|---|---|---|---|
| 1999 | Valerenga | 25 | 5 | **25** | **5** |
| 2000–01 | Crystal Palace | 9 | 1 | | |
| 2001–02 | Crystal Palace | 45 | 5 | | |
| 2002–03 | Crystal Palace | 25 | 1 | | |
| 2003–04 | Crystal Palace | 31 | 0 | **110** | **7** |

**ROUTLEDGE, Wayne (F) 72 10**
H: 5 6 W: 10 07 b.Eltham 7-1-85
*Source:* Scholar. *Honours:* England Youth.

| | | | | | |
|---|---|---|---|---|---|
| 2001–02 | Crystal Palace | 2 | 0 | | |
| 2002–03 | Crystal Palace | 26 | 4 | | |
| 2003–04 | Crystal Palace | 44 | 6 | **72** | **10** |

**SHIPPERLEY, Neil (F) 395 109**
H: 6 0 W: 13 00 b.Chatham 30-10-74
*Source:* Trainee. *Honours:* England Under-21.

| | | | | | |
|---|---|---|---|---|---|
| 1992–93 | Chelsea | 3 | 1 | | |
| 1993–94 | Chelsea | 24 | 4 | | |
| 1994–95 | Chelsea | 10 | 2 | **37** | **7** |
| 1994–95 | *Watford* | 6 | 1 | **6** | **1** |
| 1994–95 | Southampton | 19 | 4 | | |
| 1995–96 | Southampton | 37 | 7 | | |
| 1996–97 | Southampton | 10 | 1 | **66** | **12** |
| 1996–97 | Crystal Palace | 32 | 12 | | |
| 1997–98 | Crystal Palace | 26 | 7 | | |
| 1998–99 | Crystal Palace | 3 | 1 | | |
| 1998–99 | Nottingham F | 20 | 1 | **20** | **1** |
| 1999–2000 | Barnsley | 39 | 13 | | |
| 2000–01 | Barnsley | 39 | 14 | **78** | **27** |
| 2001–02 | Wimbledon | 41 | 12 | | |
| 2002–03 | Wimbledon | 46 | 20 | **87** | **32** |
| 2003–04 | Crystal Palace | 40 | 9 | **101** | **29** |

**SMITH, Jamie* (D) 245 5**
H: 5 8 W: 11 02 b.Birmingham 17-9-74
*Source:* Trainee.

| | | | | | |
|---|---|---|---|---|---|
| 1993–94 | Wolverhampton W | 0 | 0 | | |
| 1994–95 | Wolverhampton W | 25 | 0 | | |
| 1995–96 | Wolverhampton W | 13 | 0 | | |
| 1996–97 | Wolverhampton W | 38 | 0 | | |
| 1997–98 | Wolverhampton W | 11 | 0 | **87** | **0** |
| 1997–98 | Crystal Palace | 18 | 0 | | |
| 1998–99 | Crystal Palace | 26 | 0 | | |
| 1998–99 | *Fulham* | 9 | 1 | **9** | **1** |
| 1999–2000 | Crystal Palace | 27 | 0 | | |
| 2000–01 | Crystal Palace | 29 | 0 | | |
| 2001–02 | Crystal Palace | 32 | 4 | | |
| 2002–03 | Crystal Palace | 2 | 0 | | |
| 2003–04 | Crystal Palace | 15 | 0 | **149** | **4** |

**SOARES, Tom§ (M) 3 0**
H: 6 0 W: 11 04 b.Reading 10-7-86
*Source:* Scholar.

| | | | | | |
|---|---|---|---|---|---|
| 2003–04 | Crystal Palace | 3 | 0 | **3** | **0** |

**SUREY, Ben* (M) 0 0**
H: 5 10 W: 11 02 b.Camberley 18-12-82
*Source:* Scholar.

| | | | |
|---|---|---|---|
| 2002–03 | Crystal Palace | 0 | 0 |
| 2003–04 | Crystal Palace | 0 | 0 |

**SYMONS, Kit# (D) 436 27**
H: 6 1 W: 13 00 b.Basingstoke 8-3-71
*Source:* Trainee. *Honours:* Wales Youth, Under-21, B, 37 full caps, 2 goals.

| | | | | | |
|---|---|---|---|---|---|
| 1988–89 | Portsmouth | 2 | 0 | | |
| 1989–90 | Portsmouth | 1 | 0 | | |
| 1990–91 | Portsmouth | 1 | 0 | | |
| 1991–92 | Portsmouth | 46 | 1 | | |
| 1992–93 | Portsmouth | 41 | 2 | | |
| 1993–94 | Portsmouth | 29 | 3 | | |
| 1994–95 | Portsmouth | 40 | 4 | | |
| 1995–96 | Portsmouth | 1 | 0 | **161** | **10** |
| 1995–96 | Manchester C | 38 | 2 | | |
| 1996–97 | Manchester C | 44 | 0 | | |
| 1997–98 | Manchester C | 42 | 2 | **124** | **4** |
| 1998–99 | Fulham | 45 | 11 | | |
| 1999–2000 | Fulham | 29 | 2 | | |
| 2000–01 | Fulham | 24 | 0 | | |
| 2001–02 | Fulham | 4 | 0 | **102** | **13** |
| 2001–02 | Crystal Palace | 9 | 0 | | |
| 2002–03 | Crystal Palace | 25 | 0 | | |
| 2003–04 | Crystal Palace | 15 | 0 | **49** | **0** |

**TOGWELL, Sam§ (D) 1 0**
H: 5 11 W: 12 04 b.Beaconsfield 14-10-84
*Source:* Scholar.

| | | | | | |
|---|---|---|---|---|---|
| 2002–03 | Crystal Palace | 1 | 0 | | |
| 2003–04 | Crystal Palace | 0 | 0 | **1** | **0** |

**WATSON, Ben§ (M) 21 1**
H: 5 10 W: 10 11 b.London 9-7-85
*Source:* Scholar.

| | | | | | |
|---|---|---|---|---|---|
| 2002–03 | Crystal Palace | 5 | 0 | | |
| 2003–04 | Crystal Palace | 16 | 1 | **21** | **1** |

**WILLIAMS, Gareth (F) 25 9**
H: 5 10 W: 11 13 b.Germiston 10-9-82
*Source:* Scholar. *Honours:* Wales Under-21.

| | | | | | |
|---|---|---|---|---|---|
| 2002–03 | Crystal Palace | 5 | 0 | | |
| 2002–03 | *Colchester U* | 8 | 6 | | |
| 2003–04 | Crystal Palace | 0 | 0 | **5** | **0** |
| 2003–04 | *Cambridge U* | 4 | 1 | **4** | **1** |
| 2003–04 | *Bournemouth* | 1 | 0 | **1** | **0** |
| 2003–04 | *Colchester U* | 7 | 2 | **15** | **8** |

**Scholars**
Bashkal, Kerem; Berry, Tyrone M; Conroy, Jay; Dolan, Ricci J; El-Salahi, Karim; Fray, Arron; Gibson, James D; Hay, Adam; Nabil, Tariq; Prigent, Gary R D; Simpson, Nathaniel; Smith, Anton L; Soares, Thomas J; Togwell, Samuel; Watson, Ben: Wilson, Glenn M

**Non Contract**
McCormack, Andrew

## DARLINGTON (28)

**ALEXANDER, John§ (F) 4 0**
H: 5 11 W: 12 00 b.Middlesbrough 24-9-85

| | | | | | |
|---|---|---|---|---|---|
| 2002–03 | Darlington | 1 | 0 | | |
| 2003–04 | Darlington | 3 | 0 | **4** | **0** |

**ARTUN, Erdem‡ (D) 0 0**
b.London 11-11-82
*Source:* Trainee.

| | | | |
|---|---|---|---|
| 1999–2000 | Ipswich T | 0 | 0 |
| 2000–01 | Ipswich T | 0 | 0 |
| 2001–02 | Ipswich T | 0 | 0 |
| 2002–03 | Ipswich T | 0 | 0 |
| 2003–04 | Darlington | 0 | 0 |

**BOSSY, Fabien‡ (D) 67 0**
H: 6 2 W: 12 06 b.Marseille 1-10-77
*Source:* Montpellier, Academica.

| | | | | | |
|---|---|---|---|---|---|
| 2000–01 | Clydebank | 14 | 0 | | |
| 2001–02 | Clydebank | 30 | 0 | **44** | **0** |
| 2002–03 | Ayr U | 2 | 0 | **2** | **0** |
| 2002–03 | Clyde | 15 | 0 | **15** | **0** |
| 2003–04 | Darlington | 6 | 0 | **6** | **0** |

**CLARK, Ian# (M) 278 44**
H: 5 11 W: 11 07 b.Stockton 23-10-74
*Source:* Stockton.

| | | | | | |
|---|---|---|---|---|---|
| 1995–96 | Doncaster R | 23 | 1 | | |
| 1996–97 | Doncaster R | 20 | 2 | | |
| 1997–98 | Doncaster R | 2 | 0 | **45** | **3** |
| 1997–98 | Hartlepool U | 24 | 7 | | |
| 1998–99 | Hartlepool U | 39 | 2 | | |
| 1999–2000 | Hartlepool U | 44 | 6 | | |
| 2000–01 | Hartlepool U | 24 | 0 | | |
| 2001–02 | Hartlepool U | 7 | 2 | **138** | **17** |
| 2001–02 | Darlington | 28 | 13 | | |
| 2002–03 | Darlington | 33 | 7 | | |
| 2003–04 | Darlington | 34 | 4 | **95** | **24** |

**CLARKE, Matthew (D) 152 9**
H: 6 3 W: 13 00 b.Leeds 18-12-80
*Source:* Wolverhampton W Trainee.

| | | | | | |
|---|---|---|---|---|---|
| 1999–2000 | Halifax T | 19 | 0 | | |
| 2000–01 | Halifax T | 19 | 1 | | |
| 2001–02 | Halifax T | 31 | 1 | **69** | **2** |
| 2002–03 | Darlington | 38 | 3 | | |
| 2003–04 | Darlington | 45 | 4 | **83** | **7** |

**CLOSE, Brian (D) 20 1**
H: 5 10 W: 12 00 b.Belfast 27-1-82
*Honours:* Northern Ireland Under-21.

| | | | | | |
|---|---|---|---|---|---|
| 1999–2000 | Middlesbrough | 0 | 0 | | |
| 2000–01 | Middlesbrough | 0 | 0 | | |
| 2001–02 | Middlesbrough | 0 | 0 | | |
| 2002–03 | Middlesbrough | 0 | 0 | | |
| 2002–03 | *Chesterfield* | 8 | 1 | **8** | **1** |
| 2003–04 | Middlesbrough | 0 | 0 | | |
| 2003–04 | Darlington | 12 | 0 | **12** | **0** |

**COGHLAN, Michael§ (M) 3 0**
H: 5 10 W: 11 00 b.Sunderland 15-1-85
*Source:* Scholar.

| | | | | | |
|---|---|---|---|---|---|
| 2003–04 | Darlington | 3 | 0 | **3** | **0** |

**COLLETT, Andy* (G) 234 0**
H: 6 0 W: 12 05 b.Middlesbrough 28-10-73
*Source:* Trainee.

| | | | | | |
|---|---|---|---|---|---|
| 1991–92 | Middlesbrough | 0 | 0 | | |
| 1992–93 | Middlesbrough | 2 | 0 | | |
| 1993–94 | Middlesbrough | 0 | 0 | | |
| 1994–95 | Middlesbrough | 0 | 0 | **2** | **0** |
| 1994–95 | Bristol R | 4 | 0 | | |
| 1995–96 | Bristol R | 26 | 0 | | |
| 1996–97 | Bristol R | 44 | 0 | | |
| 1997–98 | Bristol R | 30 | 0 | | |
| 1998–99 | Bristol R | 3 | 0 | **107** | **0** |
| 1999–2000 | Darlington | 13 | 0 | | |
| 2000–01 | Darlington | 37 | 0 | | |
| 2001–02 | Darlington | 28 | 0 | | |
| 2002–03 | Darlington | 38 | 0 | | |
| 2003–04 | Darlington | 9 | 0 | **125** | **0** |

**CONLON, Barry* (F) 243 67**
H: 6 3 W: 14 00 b.Drogheda 1-10-78
*Source:* QPR Trainee. *Honours:* Eire Under-21.

| | | | | | |
|---|---|---|---|---|---|
| 1997–98 | Manchester C | 7 | 0 | | |
| 1997–98 | *Plymouth Arg* | 13 | 2 | **13** | **2** |
| 1998–99 | Manchester C | 0 | 0 | **7** | **0** |
| 1998–99 | Southend U | 34 | 7 | **34** | **7** |
| 1999–2000 | York C | 40 | 11 | | |
| 2000–01 | York C | 8 | 0 | **48** | **11** |
| 2000–01 | *Colchester U* | 26 | 8 | **26** | **8** |
| 2001–02 | Darlington | 35 | 10 | | |
| 2002–03 | Darlington | 41 | 15 | | |
| 2003–04 | Darlington | 39 | 14 | **115** | **39** |

**CONVERY, Mark (M)** 53 3
H: 5 6 W: 10 05 b.Newcastle 29-5-81
*Source:* Trainee.

| | | | | | |
|---|---|---|---|---|---|
| 1998–99 | Sunderland | 0 | 0 | | |
| 1999–2000 | Sunderland | 0 | 0 | | |
| 2000–01 | Sunderland | 0 | 0 | | |
| 2000–01 | Darlington | 11 | 0 | | |
| 2001–02 | Darlington | 17 | 1 | | |
| 2002–03 | Darlington | 0 | 0 | | |
| 2003–04 | Darlington | 25 | 2 | **53** | **3** |

**HUGHES, Chris (M)** 30 2
H: 5 11 W: 10 10 b.Sunderland 5-3-84
*Source:* Scholar.

| | | | | | |
|---|---|---|---|---|---|
| 2003–04 | Darlington | 30 | 2 | **30** | **2** |

**HUTCHINSON, Jonathan (D)** 43 0
H: 5 11 W: 11 11 b.Middlesbrough 2-4-82
*Source:* Scholar.

| | | | | | |
|---|---|---|---|---|---|
| 2000–01 | Birmingham C | 0 | 0 | | |
| 2001–02 | Birmingham C | 3 | 0 | | |
| 2002–03 | Birmingham C | 1 | 0 | **4** | **0** |
| 2003–04 | Darlington | 39 | 0 | **39** | **0** |

**KELTIE, Clark (M)** 62 4
H: 5 11 W: 11 08 b.Newcastle 31-8-83
*Source:* Shildon.

| | | | | | |
|---|---|---|---|---|---|
| 2001–02 | Darlington | 1 | 0 | | |
| 2002–03 | Darlington | 30 | 3 | | |
| 2003–04 | Darlington | 31 | 1 | **62** | **4** |

**KILTY, Mark‡ (D)** 23 1
H: 5 11 W: 12 05 b.Sunderland 24-6-81
*Source:* Trainee.

| | | | | | |
|---|---|---|---|---|---|
| 1998–99 | Darlington | 2 | 0 | | |
| 1999–2000 | Darlington | 2 | 0 | | |
| 2000–01 | Darlington | 18 | 1 | | |
| 2001–02 | Darlington | 1 | 0 | | |
| 2002–03 | Darlington | 0 | 0 | | |
| 2003–04 | Darlington | 0 | 0 | **23** | **1** |

**LIDDLE, Craig# (D)** 290 16
H: 5 11 W: 12 03 b.Chester-le-Street 21-10-71
*Source:* Blyth Spartans.

| | | | | | |
|---|---|---|---|---|---|
| 1994–95 | Middlesbrough | 1 | 0 | | |
| 1995–96 | Middlesbrough | 13 | 0 | | |
| 1996–97 | Middlesbrough | 5 | 0 | | |
| 1997–98 | Middlesbrough | 6 | 0 | **25** | **0** |
| 1997–98 | *Darlington* | 15 | 0 | | |
| 1998–99 | Darlington | 44 | 3 | | |
| 1999–2000 | Darlington | 45 | 1 | | |
| 2000–01 | Darlington | 45 | 2 | | |
| 2001–02 | Darlington | 31 | 2 | | |
| 2002–03 | Darlington | 42 | 4 | | |
| 2003–04 | Darlington | 43 | 4 | **265** | **16** |

**MADDISON, Neil# (M)** 325 27
H: 5 10 W: 12 00 b.Darlington 2-10-69
*Source:* Trainee.

| | | | | | |
|---|---|---|---|---|---|
| 1987–88 | Southampton | 0 | 0 | | |
| 1988–89 | Southampton | 5 | 2 | | |
| 1989–90 | Southampton | 2 | 0 | | |
| 1990–91 | Southampton | 4 | 0 | | |
| 1991–92 | Southampton | 6 | 0 | | |
| 1992–93 | Southampton | 37 | 4 | | |
| 1993–94 | Southampton | 41 | 7 | | |
| 1994–95 | Southampton | 35 | 3 | | |
| 1995–96 | Southampton | 15 | 1 | | |
| 1996–97 | Southampton | 18 | 1 | | |
| 1997–98 | Southampton | 6 | 1 | **169** | **19** |
| 1997–98 | Middlesbrough | 22 | 4 | | |
| 1998–99 | Middlesbrough | 21 | 0 | | |
| 1999–2000 | Middlesbrough | 13 | 0 | | |
| 2000–01 | Middlesbrough | 0 | 0 | **56** | **4** |
| 2000–01 | *Barnsley* | 3 | 0 | **3** | **0** |
| 2000–01 | *Bristol C* | 7 | 1 | **7** | **1** |
| 2001–02 | Darlington | 30 | 1 | | |
| 2002–03 | Darlington | 28 | 1 | | |
| 2003–04 | Darlington | 32 | 1 | **90** | **3** |

**MASON, Chris§ (M)** 1 0
H: 6 0 W: 12 00 b.Newton Aycliffe 26-6-86
*Source:* Scholar.

| | | | | | |
|---|---|---|---|---|---|
| 2003–04 | Darlington | 1 | 0 | **1** | **0** |

**McGURK, David (D)** 43 4
H: 6 0 W: 11 10 b.Middlesbrough 30-9-82
*Source:* Scholar.

| | | | | | |
|---|---|---|---|---|---|
| 2001–02 | Darlington | 12 | 0 | | |
| 2002–03 | Darlington | 4 | 0 | | |
| 2003–04 | Darlington | 27 | 4 | **43** | **4** |

**MELLANBY, Danny‡ (F)** 44 8
H: 5 10 W: 11 05 b.Bishop Auckland 17-7-79
*Source:* Bishop Auckland.

| | | | | | |
|---|---|---|---|---|---|
| 2001–02 | Darlington | 24 | 4 | | |
| 2002–03 | Darlington | 13 | 4 | | |
| 2003–04 | Darlington | 7 | 0 | **44** | **8** |

**NICHOLLS, Ashley (M)** 83 7
H: 5 11 W: 11 11 b.Suffolk 30-10-81
*Source:* Ipswich W. *Honours:* England Schools.

| | | | | | |
|---|---|---|---|---|---|
| 2000–01 | Ipswich T | 0 | 0 | | |
| 2001–02 | Ipswich T | 0 | 0 | | |
| 2002–03 | Darlington | 41 | 6 | | |
| 2003–04 | Darlington | 26 | 0 | **67** | **6** |
| 2003–04 | *Cambridge U* | 16 | 1 | **16** | **1** |

**PEARSON, Gary* (D)** 48 3
H: 6 0 W: 12 00 b.Easington 7-12-76
*Source:* Trainee.

| | | | | | |
|---|---|---|---|---|---|
| 1995–96 | Sheffield U | 0 | 0 | | |
| 1996–97 | Sheffield U | 0 | 0 | | |
| 1997–98 | Sheffield U | 0 | 0 | | |
| 1998–99 | Sheffield U | 0 | 0 | | |
| From Durham C. | | | | | |
| 2001–02 | Darlington | 9 | 1 | | |
| 2002–03 | Darlington | 21 | 1 | | |
| 2003–04 | Darlington | 18 | 1 | **48** | **3** |

**PRICE, Mike (G)** 36 0
H: 6 3 W: 13 10 b.Ashington 3-4-83
*Source:* Scholar.

| | | | | | |
|---|---|---|---|---|---|
| 2000–01 | Leicester C | 0 | 0 | | |
| 2001–02 | Leicester C | 0 | 0 | | |
| 2002–03 | Leicester C | 0 | 0 | | |
| 2003–04 | Darlington | 36 | 0 | **36** | **0** |

**ROBSON, Glen‡ (F)** 16 0
H: 5 10 W: 10 04 b.Sunderland 25-9-77
*Source:* Murton.

| | | | | | |
|---|---|---|---|---|---|
| 1996–97 | Rochdale | 3 | 0 | | |
| 1997–98 | Rochdale | 7 | 0 | | |
| 1998–99 | Rochdale | 0 | 0 | | |
| 1999–2000 | Rochdale | 0 | 0 | | |
| 2000–01 | Rochdale | 0 | 0 | | |
| 2001–02 | Rochdale | 0 | 0 | **10** | **0** |
| 2003–04 | Darlington | 6 | 0 | **6** | **0** |

**RUSSELL, Craig† (F)** 278 41
H: 5 10 W: 12 06 b.Jarrow 4-2-74
*Source:* Trainee.

| | | | | | |
|---|---|---|---|---|---|
| 1991–92 | Sunderland | 4 | 0 | | |
| 1992–93 | Sunderland | 0 | 0 | | |
| 1993–94 | Sunderland | 35 | 9 | | |
| 1994–95 | Sunderland | 38 | 5 | | |
| 1995–96 | Sunderland | 41 | 13 | | |
| 1996–97 | Sunderland | 29 | 4 | | |
| 1997–98 | Sunderland | 3 | 0 | **150** | **31** |
| 1997–98 | Manchester C | 24 | 1 | | |
| 1998–99 | Manchester C | 7 | 1 | | |
| 1998–99 | *Tranmere R* | 4 | 0 | **4** | **0** |
| 1998–99 | *Port Vale* | 8 | 1 | **8** | **1** |
| 1999–2000 | Manchester C | 0 | 0 | **31** | **2** |
| 1999–2000 | *Darlington* | 12 | 2 | | |
| 1999–2000 | *Oxford U* | 6 | 0 | **6** | **0** |
| 1999–2000 | *St Johnstone* | 1 | 1 | | |
| 2000–01 | St Johnstone | 13 | 1 | | |
| 2001–02 | St Johnstone | 14 | 1 | | |
| 2002–03 | St Johnstone | 8 | 0 | **36** | **3** |
| 2002–03 | Carlisle U | 13 | 1 | | |
| 2003–04 | Carlisle U | 6 | 0 | **19** | **1** |
| 2003–04 | Darlington | 12 | 1 | **24** | **3** |

**SHEERAN, Mark‡ (F)** 32 6
H: 6 0 W: 11 10 b.Newcastle 9-9-82
*Source:* Scholar.

| | | | | | |
|---|---|---|---|---|---|
| 2001–02 | Darlington | 22 | 6 | | |
| 2002–03 | Darlington | 4 | 0 | | |
| 2003–04 | Darlington | 6 | 0 | **32** | **6** |

**VALENTINE, Ryan (D)** 83 3
H: 5 10 W: 11 05 b.Wrexham 19-8-82
*Source:* Trainee. *Honours:* Wales Under-21.

| | | | | | |
|---|---|---|---|---|---|
| 1999–2000 | Everton | 0 | 0 | | |
| 2000–01 | Everton | 0 | 0 | | |
| 2001–02 | Everton | 0 | 0 | | |
| 2002–03 | Darlington | 43 | 1 | | |
| 2003–04 | Darlington | 40 | 2 | **83** | **3** |

**WAINWRIGHT, Neil# (M)** 146 19
H: 6 0 W: 12 00 b.Warrington 4-11-77
*Source:* Trainee.

| | | | | | |
|---|---|---|---|---|---|
| 1996–97 | Wrexham | 0 | 0 | | |
| 1997–98 | Wrexham | 11 | 3 | **11** | **3** |
| 1998–99 | Sunderland | 2 | 0 | | |
| 1999–2000 | Sunderland | 0 | 0 | | |
| 1999–2000 | *Darlington* | 17 | 4 | | |
| 2000–01 | Sunderland | 0 | 0 | | |
| 2000–01 | *Halifax T* | 13 | 0 | **13** | **0** |
| 2001–02 | Sunderland | 0 | 0 | **2** | **0** |
| 2001–02 | Darlington | 35 | 4 | | |
| 2002–03 | Darlington | 33 | 1 | | |
| 2003–04 | Darlington | 35 | 7 | **120** | **16** |

**Scholars**
Addison, Richard C; Alexander, John D; Barwick, Martin; Bond, Michael; Coghlan, Michael J; Gibson, Andrew J; Graham, Stephen T; Hartley, Liam J M; Mason, Christopher; Matthewson, Graeme T; McLeod, Mark; Mendum, Dale S; Molyneux, Daniel T; Morley, Steven; Norton, Jack D; Parkin, Gavin R; Smith, Martin M; Summers, Benjamin J

**Non Contract**
Russell, Craig S

## DERBY CO (29)

**BOERTIEN, Paul (D)** 127 3
H: 5 11 W: 11 11 b.Carlisle 21-1-79
*Source:* Trainee.

| | | | | | |
|---|---|---|---|---|---|
| 1996–97 | Carlisle U | 0 | 0 | | |
| 1997–98 | Carlisle U | 9 | 0 | | |
| 1998–99 | Carlisle U | 8 | 1 | **17** | **1** |
| 1998–99 | Derby Co | 1 | 0 | | |
| 1999–2000 | Derby Co | 2 | 0 | | |
| 1999–2000 | *Crewe Alex* | 2 | 0 | **2** | **0** |
| 2000–01 | Derby Co | 8 | 1 | | |
| 2001–02 | Derby Co | 32 | 0 | | |
| 2002–03 | Derby Co | 42 | 1 | | |
| 2003–04 | Derby Co | 18 | 0 | **103** | **2** |
| 2003–04 | *Notts Co* | 5 | 0 | **5** | **0** |

**BOLDER, Adam (M)** 102 7
H: 6 3 W: 11 13 b.Hull 25-10-80
*Source:* Trainee.

| | | | | | |
|---|---|---|---|---|---|
| 1998–99 | Hull C | 1 | 0 | | |
| 1999–2000 | Hull C | 19 | 0 | **20** | **0** |
| 1999–2000 | Derby Co | 0 | 0 | | |
| 2000–01 | Derby Co | 2 | 0 | | |
| 2001–02 | Derby Co | 11 | 0 | | |
| 2002–03 | Derby Co | 45 | 6 | | |
| 2003–04 | Derby Co | 24 | 1 | **82** | **7** |

**CAMP, Lee (G)** 13 0
H: 5 11 W: 11 11 b.Derby 22-8-84
*Source:* Scholar. *Honours:* England Youth, Under-20.

| | | | | | |
|---|---|---|---|---|---|
| 2002–03 | Derby Co | 1 | 0 | | |
| 2003–04 | Derby Co | 0 | 0 | **1** | **0** |
| 2003–04 | *QPR* | 12 | 0 | **12** | **0** |

**COSTA, Candido* (M)** 34 1
H: 5 7 W: 11 06 b.Sao Joao da Madeira 30-4-81

| | | | | | |
|---|---|---|---|---|---|
| 2003–04 | Derby Co | 34 | 1 | **34** | **1** |

**DOYLE, Nathan (M)** 2 0
H: 5 11 W: 11 11 b.Derby 12-1-87
*Source:* Scholar. *Honours:* England Youth.

| | | | | | |
|---|---|---|---|---|---|
| 2003–04 | Derby Co | 2 | 0 | **2** | **0** |

**GRANT, Lee (G)** 65 0
H: 6 2 W: 13 00 b.Watford 27-1-83
*Source:* Scholar. *Honours:* England Youth, Under-21.

| | | | | | |
|---|---|---|---|---|---|
| 2000–01 | Derby Co | 0 | 0 | | |
| 2001–02 | Derby Co | 0 | 0 | | |
| 2002–03 | Derby Co | 29 | 0 | | |
| 2003–04 | Derby Co | 36 | 0 | **65** | **0** |

**HOLMES, Lee§ (M)** 25 2
H: 5 7 W: 10 06 b.Mansfield 2-4-87
*Honours:* FA Schools, England Youth.

| | | | | | |
|---|---|---|---|---|---|
| 2002–03 | Derby Co | 2 | 0 | | |
| 2003–04 | Derby Co | 23 | 2 | **25** | **2** |

**HUDDLESTONE, Tom (D) 43 0**
H: 6 3 W: 14 12 b.Nottingham 28-12-86
*Honours:* England Youth.

| | | | | | |
|---|---|---|---|---|---|
| 2003–04 | Derby Co | 43 | 0 | **43** | **0** |

**HUNT, Lewis (D) 37 0**
H: 5 11 W: 12 08 b.Birmingham 25-8-82
*Source:* Scholar.

| | | | | | |
|---|---|---|---|---|---|
| 2000–01 | Derby Co | 0 | 0 | | |
| 2001–02 | Derby Co | 0 | 0 | | |
| 2002–03 | Derby Co | 10 | 0 | | |
| 2003–04 | Derby Co | 1 | 0 | **11** | **0** |
| 2003–04 | *Southend U* | 26 | 0 | **26** | **0** |

**JACKSON, Richard# (D) 90 0**
H: 5 8 W: 11 02 b.Whitby 18-4-80
*Source:* Trainee.

| | | | | | |
|---|---|---|---|---|---|
| 1997–98 | Scarborough | 2 | 0 | | |
| 1998–99 | Scarborough | 20 | 0 | **22** | **0** |
| 1998–99 | Derby Co | 0 | 0 | | |
| 1999–2000 | Derby Co | 2 | 0 | | |
| 2000–01 | Derby Co | 2 | 0 | | |
| 2001–02 | Derby Co | 7 | 0 | | |
| 2002–03 | Derby Co | 21 | 0 | | |
| 2003–04 | Derby Co | 36 | 0 | **68** | **0** |

**JOHNSON, Michael (D) 408 14**
H: 5 11 W: 12 08 b.Nottingham 4-7-73
*Source:* Trainee. *Honours:* Jamaica 14 full caps.

| | | | | | |
|---|---|---|---|---|---|
| 1991–92 | Notts Co | 5 | 0 | | |
| 1992–93 | Notts Co | 37 | 0 | | |
| 1993–94 | Notts Co | 34 | 0 | | |
| 1994–95 | Notts Co | 31 | 0 | | |
| 1995–96 | Notts Co | 0 | 0 | **107** | **0** |
| 1995–96 | Birmingham C | 33 | 0 | | |
| 1996–97 | Birmingham C | 35 | 0 | | |
| 1997–98 | Birmingham C | 38 | 3 | | |
| 1998–99 | Birmingham C | 45 | 5 | | |
| 1999–2000 | Birmingham C | 34 | 2 | | |
| 2000–01 | Birmingham C | 39 | 2 | | |
| 2001–02 | Birmingham C | 32 | 1 | | |
| 2002–03 | Birmingham C | 6 | 0 | | |
| 2003–04 | Birmingham C | 0 | 0 | **262** | **13** |
| 2003–04 | Derby Co | 39 | 1 | **39** | **1** |

**JUNIOR# (F) 48 19**
H: 6 0 W: 13 00 b.Brazil 20-7-76
*Source:* Trezze.

| | | | | | |
|---|---|---|---|---|---|
| 2002–03 | Walsall | 36 | 15 | **36** | **15** |
| 2003–04 | Derby Co | 12 | 4 | **12** | **4** |

**KENNA, Jeff (D) 370 9**
H: 5 11 W: 12 04 b.Dublin 27-8-70
*Source:* Trainee. *Honours:* Eire Youth, Under-21, B, 27 full caps.

| | | | | | |
|---|---|---|---|---|---|
| 1988–89 | Southampton | 0 | 0 | | |
| 1989–90 | Southampton | 0 | 0 | | |
| 1990–91 | Southampton | 2 | 0 | | |
| 1991–92 | Southampton | 14 | 0 | | |
| 1992–93 | Southampton | 29 | 2 | | |
| 1993–94 | Southampton | 41 | 2 | | |
| 1994–95 | Southampton | 28 | 0 | **114** | **4** |
| 1994–95 | Blackburn R | 9 | 1 | | |
| 1995–96 | Blackburn R | 32 | 0 | | |
| 1996–97 | Blackburn R | 37 | 0 | | |
| 1997–98 | Blackburn R | 37 | 0 | | |
| 1998–99 | Blackburn R | 23 | 0 | | |
| 1999–2000 | Blackburn R | 11 | 0 | | |
| 2000–01 | Blackburn R | 6 | 0 | | |
| 2000–01 | *Tranmere R* | 11 | 0 | **11** | **0** |
| 2001–02 | Blackburn R | 0 | 0 | **155** | **1** |
| 2001–02 | *Wigan Ath* | 6 | 1 | **6** | **1** |
| 2001–02 | Birmingham C | 21 | 0 | | |
| 2002–03 | Birmingham C | 37 | 1 | | |
| 2003–04 | Birmingham C | 17 | 2 | **75** | **3** |
| 2003–04 | Derby Co | 9 | 0 | **9** | **0** |

**KONJIC, Muhamed (D) 300 16**
H: 6 3 W: 13 00 b.Bosnia 14-5-70
*Honours:* Bosnia 38 full caps, 3 goals.

| | | | | | |
|---|---|---|---|---|---|
| 1990–91 | Tuzla | 3 | 0 | | |
| 1991–92 | Tuzla | 5 | 0 | **8** | **0** |
| 1992–93 | Belisce | 18 | 0 | **18** | **0** |
| 1993–94 | Zagreb | 29 | 3 | | |
| 1994–95 | Zagreb | 19 | 1 | | |
| 1995–96 | Zagreb | 15 | 1 | **63** | **5** |
| 1996–97 | Zurich | 29 | 2 | | |
| 1997–98 | Zurich | 7 | 3 | **36** | **5** |
| 1997–98 | Monaco | 19 | 0 | | |
| 1998–99 | Monaco | 18 | 2 | **37** | **2** |
| 1998–99 | Coventry C | 4 | 0 | | |
| 1999–2000 | Coventry C | 4 | 0 | | |
| 2000–01 | Coventry C | 8 | 0 | | |
| 2001–02 | Coventry C | 38 | 2 | | |
| 2002–03 | Coventry C | 42 | 0 | | |
| 2003–04 | Coventry C | 42 | 2 | **138** | **4** |
| 2003–04 | Derby Co | 0 | 0 | | |

**LABARTHE, Gianfranco (F) 6 0**
H: 5 10 W: 10 07 b.Lima 20-9-84
*Source:* Sport Boys.

| | | | | | |
|---|---|---|---|---|---|
| 2002–03 | Huddersfield T | 3 | 0 | **3** | **0** |
| 2003–04 | Derby Co | 3 | 0 | **3** | **0** |

**MANEL* (F) 16 3**
H: 6 1 W: 13 12 b.Barcelona 3-11-73
*Source:* Espanyol.

| | | | | | |
|---|---|---|---|---|---|
| 2003–04 | Derby Co | 16 | 3 | **16** | **3** |

**MAWENE, Youl# (D) 61 1**
H: 6 1 W: 13 05 b.Caen 16-7-79

| | | | | | |
|---|---|---|---|---|---|
| 1999–2000 | Lens | 6 | 0 | **6** | **0** |
| 2000–01 | Derby Co | 8 | 0 | | |
| 2001–02 | Derby Co | 17 | 1 | | |
| 2002–03 | Derby Co | 0 | 0 | | |
| 2003–04 | Derby Co | 30 | 0 | **55** | **1** |

**McLEOD, Izale (F) 46 4**
H: 6 0 W: 11 02 b.Perry Bar 15-10-84
*Source:* Scholar.

| | | | | | |
|---|---|---|---|---|---|
| 2002–03 | Derby Co | 29 | 3 | | |
| 2003–04 | Derby Co | 10 | 1 | **39** | **4** |
| 2003–04 | *Sheffield U* | 7 | 0 | **7** | **0** |

**MILLS, Pablo (D) 35 0**
H: 6 0 W: 11 06 b.Birmingham 27-5-84
*Source:* Trainee. *Honours:* England Youth.

| | | | | | |
|---|---|---|---|---|---|
| 2002–03 | Derby Co | 16 | 0 | | |
| 2003–04 | Derby Co | 19 | 0 | **35** | **0** |

**MOLLOY, Barry‡ (M) 0 0**
H: 5 9 W: 11 00 b.Derry 28-11-83
*Source:* Trainee.

| | | | | | |
|---|---|---|---|---|---|
| 2002–03 | Derby Co | 0 | 0 | | |
| 2003–04 | Derby Co | 0 | 0 | | |

**OAKES, Andy (G) 62 0**
H: 6 3 W: 12 04 b.Crewe 11-1-77

| | | | | | |
|---|---|---|---|---|---|
| 1995–96 | Bury | 0 | 0 | | |
| 1996–97 | Bury | 0 | 0 | | |
| 1997–98 | Bury | 0 | 0 | | |
| From Winsford U. | | | | | |
| 1998–99 | Hull C | 19 | 0 | **19** | **0** |
| 1999–2000 | Derby Co | 0 | 0 | | |
| 1999–2000 | *Port Vale* | 0 | 0 | | |
| 2000–01 | Derby Co | 6 | 0 | | |
| 2001–02 | Derby Co | 20 | 0 | | |
| 2002–03 | Derby Co | 7 | 0 | | |
| 2003–04 | Derby Co | 10 | 0 | **43** | **0** |

**PALMER, Chris* (D) 0 0**
H: 5 6 W: 11 00 b.Derby 16-10-83
*Source:* Scholar.

| | | | | | |
|---|---|---|---|---|---|
| 2003–04 | Derby Co | 0 | 0 | | |

**PESCHISOLIDO, Paul (F) 363 102**
H: 5 7 W: 11 08 b.Canada 25-5-71
*Source:* Toronto Blizzard. *Honours:* Canada 51 full caps, 10 goals.

| | | | | | |
|---|---|---|---|---|---|
| 1992–93 | Birmingham C | 19 | 7 | | |
| 1993–94 | Birmingham C | 24 | 9 | | |
| 1994–95 | Stoke C | 40 | 13 | | |
| 1995–96 | Stoke C | 26 | 6 | **66** | **19** |
| 1995–96 | Birmingham C | 9 | 1 | **52** | **17** |
| 1996–97 | WBA | 37 | 15 | | |
| 1997–98 | WBA | 8 | 3 | **45** | **18** |
| 1997–98 | Fulham | 32 | 13 | | |
| 1998–99 | Fulham | 33 | 7 | | |
| 1999–2000 | Fulham | 30 | 4 | | |
| 2000–01 | Fulham | 0 | 0 | **95** | **24** |
| 2000–01 | *QPR* | 5 | 1 | **5** | **1** |
| 2000–01 | *Sheffield U* | 5 | 2 | | |
| 2000–01 | *Norwich C* | 5 | 0 | **5** | **0** |
| 2001–02 | Sheffield U | 29 | 6 | | |
| 2002–03 | Sheffield U | 23 | 3 | | |
| 2003–04 | Sheffield U | 27 | 8 | **84** | **19** |
| 2003–04 | Derby Co | 11 | 4 | **11** | **4** |

**REICH, Marco (F) 156 9**
H: 6 0 W: 11 13 b.Meiserheim 30-12-77
*Honours:* Germany 1 full cap.

| | | | | | |
|---|---|---|---|---|---|
| 1996–97 | Kaiserslautern | 0 | 0 | | |
| 1997–98 | Kaiserslautern | 31 | 1 | | |
| 1998–99 | Kaiserslautern | 27 | 3 | | |
| 1999–2000 | Kaiserslautern | 28 | 2 | | |
| 2000–01 | Kaiserslautern | 18 | 2 | **104** | **8** |
| 2001–02 | Cologne | 24 | 0 | **24** | **0** |
| 2002–03 | Werder Bremen | 15 | 0 | **15** | **0** |
| 2003–04 | Derby Co | 13 | 1 | **13** | **1** |

**TAYLOR, Ian# (M) 372 68**
H: 6 0 W: 12 00 b.Birmingham 4-6-68
*Source:* Moor Green.

| | | | | | |
|---|---|---|---|---|---|
| 1992–93 | Port Vale | 41 | 15 | | |
| 1993–94 | Port Vale | 42 | 13 | **83** | **28** |
| 1994–95 | Sheffield W | 14 | 1 | **14** | **1** |
| 1994–95 | Aston Villa | 22 | 1 | | |
| 1995–96 | Aston Villa | 25 | 3 | | |
| 1996–97 | Aston Villa | 34 | 2 | | |
| 1997–98 | Aston Villa | 32 | 6 | | |
| 1998–99 | Aston Villa | 33 | 4 | | |
| 1999–2000 | Aston Villa | 29 | 5 | | |
| 2000–01 | Aston Villa | 29 | 4 | | |
| 2001–02 | Aston Villa | 16 | 3 | | |
| 2002–03 | Aston Villa | 13 | 0 | **233** | **28** |
| 2003–04 | Derby Co | 42 | 11 | **42** | **11** |

**TUDGAY, Marcus (F) 37 6**
H: 5 10 W: 12 02 b.Worthing 3-2-83
*Source:* Trainee.

| | | | | | |
|---|---|---|---|---|---|
| 2002–03 | Derby Co | 8 | 0 | | |
| 2003–04 | Derby Co | 29 | 6 | **37** | **6** |

**TURNER, James* (D) 0 0**
H: 5 11 W: 11 04 b.Derby 4-10-83
*Source:* Scholar.

| | | | | | |
|---|---|---|---|---|---|
| 2003–04 | Derby Co | 0 | 0 | | |

**TWIGG, Gary (F) 17 0**
H: 6 0 W: 11 02 b.Glasgow 19-3-84
*Source:* Scholar.

| | | | | | |
|---|---|---|---|---|---|
| 2000–01 | Derby Co | 0 | 0 | | |
| 2001–02 | Derby Co | 1 | 0 | | |
| 2002–03 | Derby Co | 8 | 0 | | |
| 2003–04 | Derby Co | 0 | 0 | **9** | **0** |
| 2003–04 | *Bristol R* | 8 | 0 | **8** | **0** |

**VALAKARI, Simo‡ (M) 198 8**
H: 5 11 W: 12 08 b.Helsinki 28-4-73
*Honours:* Finland 32 full caps.

| | | | | | |
|---|---|---|---|---|---|
| 1995 | Finn PA | 22 | 3 | | |
| 1996 | Finn PA | 26 | 2 | **48** | **5** |
| 1996–97 | Motherwell | 11 | 0 | | |
| 1997–98 | Motherwell | 28 | 0 | | |
| 1998–99 | Motherwell | 35 | 0 | | |
| 1999–2000 | Motherwell | 30 | 0 | **104** | **0** |
| 2000–01 | Derby Co | 11 | 1 | | |
| 2001–02 | Derby Co | 9 | 0 | | |
| 2002–03 | Derby Co | 6 | 2 | | |
| 2003–04 | Derby Co | 20 | 0 | **46** | **3** |

**VINCENT, Jamie (D) 264 9**
H: 5 10 W: 11 09 b.London 18-6-75
*Source:* Trainee.

| | | | | | |
|---|---|---|---|---|---|
| 1993–94 | Crystal Palace | 0 | 0 | | |
| 1994–95 | Crystal Palace | 0 | 0 | | |
| 1994–95 | *Bournemouth* | 8 | 0 | | |
| 1995–96 | Crystal Palace | 25 | 0 | | |
| 1996–97 | Crystal Palace | 0 | 0 | **25** | **0** |
| 1996–97 | Bournemouth | 29 | 0 | | |
| 1997–98 | Bournemouth | 44 | 3 | | |
| 1998–99 | Bournemouth | 32 | 2 | **113** | **5** |
| 1998–99 | Huddersfield T | 7 | 0 | | |
| 1999–2000 | Huddersfield T | 36 | 2 | | |
| 2000–01 | Huddersfield T | 16 | 0 | **59** | **2** |
| 2000–01 | Portsmouth | 14 | 0 | | |
| 2001–02 | Portsmouth | 34 | 1 | | |
| 2002–03 | Portsmouth | 0 | 0 | | |
| 2003–04 | Portsmouth | 0 | 0 | **48** | **1** |
| 2003–04 | *Walsall* | 12 | 0 | **12** | **0** |
| 2003–04 | Derby Co | 7 | 1 | **7** | **1** |

**WALTON, David (D) 295 13**
H: 6 2 W: 13 00 b.Bellingham 10-4-73
*Source:* Trainee.

| | | | | | |
|---|---|---|---|---|---|
| 1991–92 | Sheffield U | 0 | 0 | | |
| 1992–93 | Sheffield U | 0 | 0 | | |
| 1993–94 | Sheffield U | 0 | 0 | | |
| 1993–94 | Shrewsbury T | 27 | 5 | | |
| 1994–95 | Shrewsbury T | 36 | 3 | | |
| 1995–96 | Shrewsbury T | 35 | 0 | | |
| 1996–97 | Shrewsbury T | 24 | 1 | | |
| 1997–98 | Shrewsbury T | 6 | 1 | **128** | **10** |
| 1997–98 | Crewe Alex | 27 | 0 | | |
| 1998–99 | Crewe Alex | 38 | 1 | | |
| 1999–2000 | Crewe Alex | 11 | 0 | | |
| 2000–01 | Crewe Alex | 20 | 0 | | |
| 2001–02 | Crewe Alex | 31 | 1 | | |

2002–03 Crewe Alex 28 1 **155 3**
2003–04 Derby Co 5 0 **5 0**
2003–04 *Stockport Co* 7 0 **7 0**

**WECKSTROM, Kristoffer (F) 0 0**
H: 5 9 W: 11 04 b.Helsinki 26-5-83
*Source:* IFK Mariehamn.
2000–01 Derby Co 0 0
2001–02 Derby Co 0 0
2002–03 Derby Co 0 0
2003–04 Derby Co 0 0

**WHELAN, Noel‡ (F) 274 51**
H: 6 2 W: 12 03 b.Leeds 30-12-74
*Source:* Trainee. *Honours:* England Under-21.
1992–93 Leeds U 1 0
1993–94 Leeds U 16 0
1994–95 Leeds U 23 7
1995–96 Leeds U 8 0 **48 7**
1995–96 Coventry C 21 8
1996–97 Coventry C 35 6
1997–98 Coventry C 21 6
1998–99 Coventry C 31 10
1999–2000 Coventry C 26 1 **134 31**
2000–01 Middlesbrough 27 1
2001–02 Middlesbrough 19 4
2002–03 Middlesbrough 15 1 **61 6**
2002–03 *Crystal Palace* 8 3 **8 3**
2003–04 Millwall 15 4 **15 4**
2003–04 Derby Co 8 0 **8 0**

**ZAVAGNO, Luciano (D) 113 4**
H: 5 11 W: 11 07 b.Rosario 6-8-77
1997–98 Strasbourg 5 0
1998–99 Strasbourg 9 1 **14 1**
1999–2000 Troyes 26 0
2000–01 Troyes 13 0
2001–02 Troyes 8 0 **47 0**
2001–02 Derby Co 26 0
2002–03 Derby Co 9 2
2003–04 Derby Co 17 1 **52 3**

**Scholars**
Bradshaw Luke P; Cassidy, David; Deans, Christopher; Gibson-Cain, Stephen; Hamilton, Lewis E; Holmes, Lee D; Kemp, Thomas J R; Kirby, Benjamin; Kuduzovic, Fahrudin; MacAuley, Kyle D; Martin, Daniel A; Richardson, Liam; Sheard, Carl G; Short, John J M; Turner, Christopher J C; Wilkinson, Alistair B; Wilson, Lee T

**Non Contract**
Taylor, Thomas M

## DONCASTER R (30)

**AKINFENWA, Adebayo* (F) 36 9**
H: 5 11 W: 13 07 b.London 10-5-82
2001 Atlantas 19 4
2002 Atlantas 4 1 **23 5**
From Barry T
2003–04 Boston U 3 0 **3 0**
2003–04 Leyton Orient 1 0 **1 0**
2003–04 Rushden & D 0 0
2003–04 Doncaster R 9 4 **9 4**

**ALBRIGHTON, Mark (D) 28 3**
H: 6 1 W: 12 07 b.Nuneaton 6-3-76
*Source:* Atherstone U, Nuneaton B, Telford U.
2003–04 Doncaster R 28 3 **28 3**

**BARNES, Paul‡ (F) 397 140**
H: 5 11 W: 13 07 b.Leicester 16-11-67
*Source:* Apprentice.
1985–86 Notts Co 14 4
1986–87 Notts Co 0 0
1987–88 Notts Co 11 2
1988–89 Notts Co 15 7
1989–90 Notts Co 13 1 **53 14**
1989–90 Stoke C 5 0
1990–91 Stoke C 6 0
1990–91 *Chesterfield* 1 0 **1 0**
1991–92 Stoke C 13 3 **24 3**
1992–93 York C 40 21
1993–94 York C 42 24
1994–95 York C 36 16
1995–96 York C 30 15 **148 76**
1995–96 Birmingham C 15 7
1996–97 Birmingham C 0 0 **15 7**
1996–97 Burnley 40 24
1997–98 Burnley 25 6 **65 30**
1997–98 Huddersfield T 15 1
1998–99 Huddersfield T 15 1 **30 2**
1998–99 Bury 8 0
1999–2000 Bury 30 4
2000–01 Bury 16 4
2001–02 Bury 0 0 **54 8**
2003–04 Doncaster R 7 0 **7 0**

**BEECH, Chris (D) 112 2**
H: 5 10 W: 11 12 b.Congleton 5-11-75
*Source:* Trainee. *Honours:* England Schools, Youth.
1992–93 Manchester C 0 0
1993–94 Manchester C 0 0
1994–95 Manchester C 0 0
1995–96 Manchester C 0 0
1996–97 Manchester C 0 0
1997–98 Cardiff C 46 1 **46 1**
1998–99 Rotherham U 24 0
1999–2000 Rotherham U 6 0
2000–01 Rotherham U 15 0
2001–02 Rotherham U 8 1
2002–03 Rotherham U 2 0 **55 1**
2003–04 Doncaster R 11 0 **11 0**

**BLACK, Chris‡ (M) 4 0**
H: 6 0 W: 12 00 b.Ashington 7-9-82
*Source:* Scholar.
2000–01 Sunderland 0 0
2001–02 Sunderland 0 0
2002–03 Sunderland 2 0
2003–04 Sunderland 1 0 **3 0**
2003–04 Doncaster R 1 0 **1 0**

**BLUNDELL, Greg (F) 44 18**
H: 5 9 W: 12 02 b.Liverpool 1-1-76
*Source:* Tranmere R Trainee, Vauxhall M, Northwich Vic.
2003–04 Doncaster R 44 18 **44 18**

**BLUNT, Jason‡ (M) 6 0**
H: 5 9 W: 10 10 b.Penzance 16-8-77
*Source:* Trainee. *Honours:* England Youth.
1994–95 Leeds U 0 0
1995–96 Leeds U 3 0
1996–97 Leeds U 1 0
1997–98 Leeds U 0 0 **4 0**
1998–99 Blackpool 2 0
1999–2000 Blackpool 0 0
2000–01 Blackpool 0 0
2001–02 Blackpool 0 0 **2 0**
From Scarborough
2003–04 Doncaster R 0 0

**BURTON, Steve* (F) 14 0**
H: 6 1 W: 13 07 b.Doncaster 9-10-83
*Source:* Trainee.
2002–03 Ipswich T 0 0
2002–03 *Boston U* 8 0 **8 0**
2003–04 Doncaster R 6 0 **6 0**

**COLLIN, Adam* (G) 0 0**
H: 6 2 W: 12 00 b.Carlisle 9-12-84
*Source:* Trainee.
2003–04 Newcastle U 0 0
2003–04 *Oldham Ath* 0 0
2003–04 Doncaster R 0 0

**CRAIG, Bryan‡ (M) 0 0**
H: 5 6 W: 10 00 b.Irvine 19-4-85
*Source:* Trainee.
2003–04 Doncaster R 0 0

**DICKMAN, Chris‡ (M) 0 0**
H: 5 9 W: 11 02 b.Rotherham 22-12-84
*Source:* Trainee.
2003–04 Doncaster R 0 0

**DOOLAN, John (M) 304 17**
H: 6 1 W: 13 00 b.Liverpool 7-5-74
*Source:* Trainee.
1992–93 Everton 0 0
1993–94 Everton 0 0
1994–95 Mansfield T 24 1
1995–96 Mansfield T 42 2
1996–97 Mansfield T 41 6
1997–98 Mansfield T 24 1 **131 10**
1997–98 Barnet 17 0
1998–99 Barnet 42 2
1999–2000 Barnet 44 2
2000–01 Barnet 31 3
2001–02 Barnet 0 0
2002–03 Barnet 0 0 **134 7**
2003–04 Doncaster R 39 0 **39 0**

**DRURY, Martin‡ (D) 0 0**
H: 5 9 W: 11 00 b.Huddersfield 10-4-86
*Source:* Trainee.
2003–04 Doncaster R 0 0

**FORTUNE-WEST, Leo (F) 287 83**
H: 6 3 W: 13 10 b.Stratford 9-4-71
*Source:* Tiptree, Dagenham, Dartford, Bishops Stortford, Stevenage Bor.
1995–96 Gillingham 40 12
1996–97 Gillingham 7 2
1996–97 *Leyton Orient* 5 0 **5 0**
1997–98 Gillingham 20 4 **67 18**
1998–99 Lincoln C 9 1 **9 1**
1998–99 Brentford 11 0 **11 0**
1998–99 Rotherham U 20 12
1999–2000 Rotherham U 39 17
2000–01 Rotherham U 5 1 **64 30**
2000–01 Cardiff C 37 12
2001–02 Cardiff C 36 9
2002–03 Cardiff C 19 2 **92 23**
2003–04 Doncaster R 39 11 **39 11**

**FOSTER, Steve (D) 246 8**
H: 6 1 W: 12 00 b.Mansfield 3-12-74
*Source:* Trainee.
1993–94 Mansfield T 5 0 **5 0**
From Telford U, Woking
1997–98 Bristol R 34 0
1998–99 Bristol R 43 1
1999–2000 Bristol R 43 1
2000–01 Bristol R 44 4
2001–02 Bristol R 33 1
2002–03 Bristol R 0 0 **197 7**
2003–04 Doncaster R 44 1 **44 1**

**FRAZER, Adam‡ (D) 0 0**
H: 5 11 W: 12 00 b.Dewsbury 31-12-84
*Source:* Trainee.
2003–04 Doncaster R 0 0

**GILL, Robert (F) 1 0**
H: 5 11 W: 11 00 b.Nottingham 10-2-82
*Source:* Nottingham F Trainee.
2003–04 Doncaster R 1 0 **1 0**

**GREEN, Paul (M) 43 8**
H: 5 10 W: 11 07 b.Pontefract 10-4-83
*Source:* Trainee.
2003–04 Doncaster R 43 8 **43 8**

**JACKSON, Ben (M) 0 0**
2003–04 Doncaster R 0 0

**JACKSON, Justin‡ (F) 49 5**
H: 6 0 W: 11 06 b.Nottingham 10-12-74
*Source:* Woking.
1997–98 Notts Co 15 1
1998–99 Notts Co 10 0 **25 1**
1998–99 *Rotherham U* 2 1 **2 1**
1998–99 Halifax T 16 3
1999–2000 Halifax T 1 0
2000–01 Halifax T 0 0 **17 3**
2001–02 Rushden & D 5 0
2002–03 Rushden & D 0 0 **5 0**
2003–04 Doncaster R 0 0

**MALONEY, Jon (M) 1 0**
H: 6 0 W: 11 12 b.Leeds 3-3-85
*Source:* Trainee.
2003–04 Doncaster R 1 0 **1 0**

**MARPLES, Simon (D) 16 0**
H: 5 10 W: 11 00 b.Sheffield 30-7-75
*Source:* Stocksbridge Park Steels.
2003–04 Doncaster R 16 0 **16 0**

**McGRATH, John (M) 14 0**
H: 5 10 W: 10 04 b.Limerick 27-3-80
*Source:* Belvedere. *Honours:* Eire Under-21.
1999–2000 Aston Villa 0 0
2000–01 Aston Villa 3 0
2001–02 Aston Villa 0 0
2002–03 Aston Villa 0 0 **3 0**
2003–04 Doncaster R 11 0 **11 0**

**McINDOE, Michael (M) 84 10**
H: 5 8 W: 11 00 b.Edinburgh 2-12-79
*Honours:* Scotland B.
*Source:* Trainee.
1997–98 Luton T 0 0
1998–99 Luton T 22 0

1999–2000 Luton T 17 0 **39 0**
Fr Hereford, Yeovil
2003–04 Doncaster R 45 10 **45 10**

**MORLEY, Dave (D) 163 6**
H: 6 2 W: 12 07 b.St Helens 25-9-77
*Source:* Trainee.
1995–96 Manchester C 0 0
1996–97 Manchester C 0 0
1997–98 Manchester C 3 1
1997–98 *Ayr U* 4 0 **4 0**
1998–99 Manchester C 0 0 **3 1**
1998–99 Southend U 27 0
1999–2000 Southend U 32 0
2000–01 Southend U 17 0 **76 0**
2000–01 Carlisle U 23 1
2001–02 Carlisle U 18 0 **41 1**
2001–02 Oxford U 18 3 **18 3**
2003–04 Doncaster R 21 1 **21 1**

**MULLIGAN, David (D) 79 2**
H: 5 8 W: 9 13 b.Fazakerley 24-3-82
*Source:* Scholar. *Honours:* New Zealand Youth, Under-23, 6 full caps.
2000–01 Barnsley 0 0
2001–02 Barnsley 28 0
2002–03 Barnsley 33 1
2003–04 Barnsley 4 0 **65 1**
2003–04 Doncaster R 14 1 **14 1**

**O'BRIEN, Rob* (M) 1 0**
H: 5 10 W: 11 00 b.Leeds 28-11-83
*Source:* Leeds U.
2003–04 Doncaster R 1 0 **1 0**

**PATERSON, Jamie* (M) 217 38**
H: 5 5 W: 10 07 b.Dumfries 26-4-73
*Source:* Trainee.
1990–91 Halifax T 6 1
1991–92 Halifax T 15 2
1992–93 Halifax T 23 2
1993–94 Halifax T 42 13
1994–95 Falkirk 4 0 **4 0**
1995–96 Scunthorpe U 26 2
1996–97 Scunthorpe U 29 0
1997–98 Scunthorpe U 0 0 **55 2**
1998–99 Halifax T 24 10
1999–2000 Halifax T 40 7 **150 35**
2003–04 Doncaster R 8 1 **8 1**

**PRICE, Jamie (D) 19 0**
H: 5 9 W: 11 00 b.Normanton 27-10-81
*Source:* Trainee.
2003–04 Doncaster R 19 0 **19 0**

**RAVENHILL, Ricky (M) 36 3**
H: 5 10 W: 11 03 b.Doncaster 16-1-81
*Source:* Barnsley Trainee.
2003–04 Doncaster R 36 3 **36 3**

**RICHARDSON, Barry‡ (G) 307 0**
H: 6 1 W: 12 01 b.Willington Quay 5-8-69
*Source:* Trainee.
1987–88 Sunderland 0 0
1988–89 Scunthorpe U 0 0
1989–90 Scarborough 24 0
1990–91 Scarborough 6 0 **30 0**
1991–92 Northampton T 27 0
1992–93 Northampton T 42 0
1993–94 Northampton T 27 0 **96 0**
1994–95 Preston NE 17 0
1995–96 Preston NE 3 0 **20 0**
1995–96 Lincoln C 34 0
1996–97 Lincoln C 36 0
1997–98 Lincoln C 26 0
1998–99 Lincoln C 13 0
1999–2000 Lincoln C 22 0
1999–2000 *Mansfield T* 6 0 **6 0**
1999–2000 *Sheffield W* 0 0
2000–01 Lincoln C 0 0 **131 0**
From Doncaster R.
2001–02 Halifax T 24 0 **24 0**
From Gainsborough T
2003–04 Doncaster R 0 0

**RIGOGLIOSO, Adriano (M) 17 0**
H: 6 1 W: 12 07 b.Liverpool 28-5-79
*Source:* Morecambe.
2003–04 Doncaster R 17 0 **17 0**

**RYAN, Tim (D) 72 2**
H: 5 10 W: 11 00 b.Stockport 10-12-74
*Source:* Trainee.
1992–93 Scunthorpe U 1 0
1993–94 Scunthorpe U 1 0
1994–95 Scunthorpe U 0 0 **2 0**
From Buxton.
1996–97 Doncaster R 28 0
From Southport
2003–04 Doncaster R 42 2 **70 2**

**TIERNEY, Fran (M) 140 18**
H: 5 10 W: 12 07 b.Liverpool 10-9-75
*Source:* Trainee.
1992–93 Crewe Alex 1 0
1993–94 Crewe Alex 8 1
1994–95 Crewe Alex 20 4
1995–96 Crewe Alex 22 2
1996–97 Crewe Alex 32 3
1997–98 Crewe Alex 4 0
1998–99 Crewe Alex 0 0 **87 10**
1998–99 Notts Co 20 3
1999–2000 Notts Co 13 1 **33 4**
From Witton Alb
2000–01 Exeter C 7 1 **7 1**
2003–04 Doncaster R 13 3 **13 3**

**WARRINGTON, Andy (G) 107 0**
H: 6 3 W: 12 13 b.Sheffield 10-6-76
*Source:* Trainee.
1994–95 York C 0 0
1995–96 York C 6 0
1996–97 York C 27 0
1997–98 York C 17 0
1998–99 York C 11 0 **61 0**
2003–04 Doncaster R 46 0 **46 0**

**WHITMAN, Tristam‡ (F) 0 0**
H: 5 7 W: 11 00 b.Nottingham 9-6-80
*Source:* Arnold T.
2003–04 Doncaster R 0 0

## EVERTON (31)

**ALEXANDERSSON, Niclas‡ (M) 338 50**
H: 5 9 W: 11 08 b.Halmstad 29-12-71
*Honours:* Sweden 68 full caps, 7 goals.
1989 Halmstad 4 0
1990 Halmstad 22 2
1991 Halmstad 16 3
1992 Halmstad 27 7
1993 Halmstad 25 4
1994 Halmstad 25 4
1995 Halmstad 26 5 **145 25**
1996 IFK Gothenburg 26 7
1997 IFK Gothenburg 26 6 **52 13**
1997–98 Sheffield W 6 0
1998–99 Sheffield W 32 3
1999–2000 Sheffield W 37 5 **75 8**
2000–01 Everton 20 2
2001–02 Everton 31 2
2002–03 Everton 7 0
2003–04 Everton 0 0 **58 4**
2003–04 *West Ham U* 8 0 **8 0**

**BROWN, Scott* (M) 0 0**
H: 5 7 W: 10 03 b.Chester 8-5-85
*Source:* Scholar. *Honours:* England Youth.
2001–02 Everton 0 0
2002–03 Everton 0 0
2003–04 Everton 0 0

**CAMPBELL, Kevin (F) 429 142**
H: 6 0 W: 13 13 b.Lambeth 4-2-70
*Source:* Trainee. *Honours:* England Under-21, B.
1987–88 Arsenal 1 0
1988–89 Arsenal 0 0
1988–89 *Leyton Orient* 16 9 **16 9**
1989–90 Arsenal 15 2
1989–90 *Leicester C* 11 5 **11 5**
1990–91 Arsenal 22 9
1991–92 Arsenal 31 13
1992–93 Arsenal 37 4
1993–94 Arsenal 37 14
1994–95 Arsenal 23 4 **166 46**
1995–96 Nottingham F 21 3
1996–97 Nottingham F 17 6
1997–98 Nottingham F 42 23 **80 32**
1998–99 Trabzonspor 17 5 **17 5**
1998–99 Everton 8 9
1999–2000 Everton 26 12
2000–01 Everton 29 9
2001–02 Everton 23 4
2002–03 Everton 36 10
2003–04 Everton 17 1 **139 45**

**CARSLEY, Lee (M) 284 25**
H: 5 10 W: 12 04 b.Birmingham 28-2-74
*Source:* Trainee. *Honours:* Eire 29 full caps.
1992–93 Derby Co 0 0
1993–94 Derby Co 0 0
1994–95 Derby Co 23 2
1995–96 Derby Co 35 1
1996–97 Derby Co 24 0
1997–98 Derby Co 34 1
1998–99 Derby Co 22 1 **138 5**
1998–99 Blackburn R 8 0
1999–2000 Blackburn R 30 10
2000–01 Blackburn R 8 0 **46 10**
2000–01 Coventry C 21 2
2001–02 Coventry C 26 2 **47 4**
2001–02 Everton 8 1
2002–03 Everton 24 3
2003–04 Everton 21 2 **53 6**

**CHADWICK, Nick (F) 34 7**
H: 5 11 W: 10 09 b.Stoke 26-10-82
1999–2000 Everton 0 0
2000–01 Everton 0 0
2001–02 Everton 9 3
2002–03 Everton 1 0
2002–03 *Derby Co* 6 0 **6 0**
2003–04 Everton 3 0 **13 3**
2003–04 *Millwall* 15 4 **15 4**

**CLARKE, Peter (D) 43 4**
H: 6 0 W: 12 00 b.Southport 3-1-82
*Source:* Trainee. *Honours:* England Youth, Under-20, Under-21.
1998–99 Everton 0 0
1999–2000 Everton 0 0
2000–01 Everton 1 0
2001–02 Everton 7 0
2002–03 Everton 0 0
2002–03 *Blackpool* 16 3 **16 3**
2002–03 *Port Vale* 13 1 **13 1**
2003–04 Everton 1 0 **9 0**
2003–04 *Coventry C* 5 0 **5 0**

**FERGUSON, Duncan (F) 298 92**
H: 6 4 W: 13 07 b.Stirling 27-12-71
*Source:* Carse T. *Honours:* Scotland Schools, Youth, Under-21, B, 7 full caps.
1990–91 Dundee U 9 1
1991–92 Dundee U 38 15
1992–93 Dundee U 30 12 **77 28**
1993–94 Rangers 10 1
1994–95 Rangers 4 1 **14 2**
1994–95 Everton 23 7
1995–96 Everton 18 5
1996–97 Everton 33 10
1997–98 Everton 29 11
1998–99 Everton 13 4
1998–99 Newcastle U 7 2
1999–2000 Newcastle U 23 6 **30 8**
2000–01 Everton 12 6
2001–02 Everton 22 6
2002–03 Everton 7 0
2003–04 Everton 20 5 **177 54**

**GARSIDE, Craig* (D) 0 0**
H: 5 11 W: 13 00 b.Chester 11-1-85
*Source:* Scholar.
2001–02 Everton 0 0
2002–03 Everton 0 0
2003–04 Everton 0 0

**GEMMILL, Scot* (M) 349 27**
H: 5 10 W: 11 08 b.Paisley 2-1-71
*Source:* School. *Honours:* Scotland Under-21, B, 26 full caps, 1 goal.
1989–90 Nottingham F 0 0
1990–91 Nottingham F 4 0
1991–92 Nottingham F 39 8
1992–93 Nottingham F 33 1
1993–94 Nottingham F 31 8
1994–95 Nottingham F 19 1
1995–96 Nottingham F 31 1
1996–97 Nottingham F 24 0
1997–98 Nottingham F 44 2
1998–99 Nottingham F 20 0 **245 21**
1998–99 Everton 7 1
1999–2000 Everton 14 1
2000–01 Everton 28 2
2001–02 Everton 32 1

| | | | | | |
|---|---|---|---|---|---|
| 2002–03 | Everton | 16 | 0 | | |
| 2003–04 | Everton | 0 | 0 | **97** | **5** |
| 2003–04 | *Preston NE* | 7 | 1 | **7** | **1** |

**GERRARD, Paul* (G) 254 1**
H: 6 2 W: 13 11 b.Heywood 22-1-73
*Source:* Trainee. *Honours:* England Under-21.

| | | | | | |
|---|---|---|---|---|---|
| 1991–92 | Oldham Ath | 0 | 0 | | |
| 1992–93 | Oldham Ath | 25 | 0 | | |
| 1993–94 | Oldham Ath | 16 | 0 | | |
| 1994–95 | Oldham Ath | 42 | 0 | | |
| 1995–96 | Oldham Ath | 36 | 1 | **119** | **1** |
| 1996–97 | Everton | 5 | 0 | | |
| 1997–98 | Everton | 4 | 0 | | |
| 1998–99 | Everton | 0 | 0 | | |
| 1998–99 | *Oxford U* | 16 | 0 | **16** | **0** |
| 1999–2000 | Everton | 34 | 0 | | |
| 2000–01 | Everton | 32 | 0 | | |
| 2001–02 | Everton | 13 | 0 | | |
| 2002–03 | Everton | 2 | 0 | | |
| 2002–03 | *Ipswich T* | 5 | 0 | **5** | **0** |
| 2003–04 | Everton | 0 | 0 | **90** | **0** |
| 2003–04 | *Sheffield U* | 16 | 0 | **16** | **0** |
| 2003–04 | *Nottingham F* | 8 | 0 | **8** | **0** |

**GRAVESEN, Thomas (M) 252 23**
H: 5 9 W: 13 06 b.Vejle 11-3-76
*Honours:* Denmark 47 full caps, 5 goals.

| | | | | | |
|---|---|---|---|---|---|
| 1995–96 | Vejle | 28 | 2 | | |
| 1996–97 | Vejle | 30 | 8 | **58** | **10** |
| 1997–98 | Hamburg | 26 | 2 | | |
| 1998–99 | Hamburg | 22 | 3 | | |
| 1999–2000 | Hamburg | 26 | 1 | **74** | **6** |
| 2000–01 | Everton | 32 | 2 | | |
| 2001–02 | Everton | 25 | 2 | | |
| 2002–03 | Everton | 33 | 1 | | |
| 2003–04 | Everton | 30 | 2 | **120** | **7** |

**HIBBERT, Tony (D) 62 0**
H: 5 9 W: 11 05 b.Liverpool 20-2-81
*Source:* Trainee.

| | | | | | |
|---|---|---|---|---|---|
| 1998–99 | Everton | 0 | 0 | | |
| 1999–2000 | Everton | 0 | 0 | | |
| 2000–01 | Everton | 3 | 0 | | |
| 2001–02 | Everton | 10 | 0 | | |
| 2002–03 | Everton | 24 | 0 | | |
| 2003–04 | Everton | 25 | 0 | **62** | **0** |

**KILBANE, Kevin (M) 296 29**
H: 6 1 W: 13 05 b.Preston 1-2-77
*Source:* Trainee. *Honours:* Eire Under-21, 53 full caps, 4 goals.

| | | | | | |
|---|---|---|---|---|---|
| 1993–94 | Preston NE | 0 | 0 | | |
| 1994–95 | Preston NE | 0 | 0 | | |
| 1995–96 | Preston NE | 11 | 1 | | |
| 1996–97 | Preston NE | 36 | 2 | **47** | **3** |
| 1997–98 | WBA | 43 | 4 | | |
| 1998–99 | WBA | 44 | 6 | | |
| 1999–2000 | WBA | 19 | 5 | **106** | **15** |
| 1999–2000 | Sunderland | 20 | 1 | | |
| 2000–01 | Sunderland | 30 | 4 | | |
| 2001–02 | Sunderland | 28 | 2 | | |
| 2002–03 | Sunderland | 30 | 1 | | |
| 2003–04 | Sunderland | 5 | 0 | **113** | **8** |
| 2003–04 | Everton | 30 | 3 | **30** | **3** |

**LI TIE (M) 34 0**
H: 6 0 W: 11 10 b.China 18-9-77
*Source:* Liaoning Bodao. *Honours:* China 79 full caps, 5 goals.

| | | | | | |
|---|---|---|---|---|---|
| 2002–03 | Everton | 29 | 0 | | |
| 2003–04 | Everton | 5 | 0 | **34** | **0** |

**LINDEROTH, Tobias (M) 165 13**
H: 5 10 W: 11 08 b.Marseille 21-4-79
*Honours:* Sweden 39 full caps, 1 goal.

| | | | | | |
|---|---|---|---|---|---|
| 1996 | Elfsborg | 10 | 0 | | |
| 1997 | Elfsborg | 25 | 1 | | |
| 1998 | Elfsborg | 22 | 3 | **57** | **4** |
| 1999 | Stabaek | 23 | 3 | | |
| 2000 | Stabaek | 24 | 4 | | |
| 2001 | Stabaek | 21 | 2 | **68** | **9** |
| 2001–02 | Everton | 8 | 0 | | |
| 2002–03 | Everton | 5 | 0 | | |
| 2003–04 | Everton | 27 | 0 | **40** | **0** |

**MARTYN, Nigel (G) 614 0**
H: 6 1 W: 15 11 b.St Austell 11-8-66
*Source:* St Blazey. *Honours:* England Under-21, B, 23 full caps.

| | | | | | |
|---|---|---|---|---|---|
| 1987–88 | Bristol R | 39 | 0 | | |
| 1988–89 | Bristol R | 46 | 0 | | |
| 1989–90 | Bristol R | 16 | 0 | **101** | **0** |
| 1989–90 | Crystal Palace | 25 | 0 | | |
| 1990–91 | Crystal Palace | 38 | 0 | | |
| 1991–92 | Crystal Palace | 38 | 0 | | |
| 1992–93 | Crystal Palace | 42 | 0 | | |
| 1993–94 | Crystal Palace | 46 | 0 | | |
| 1994–95 | Crystal Palace | 37 | 0 | | |
| 1995–96 | Crystal Palace | 46 | 0 | **272** | **0** |
| 1996–97 | Leeds U | 37 | 0 | | |
| 1997–98 | Leeds U | 37 | 0 | | |
| 1998–99 | Leeds U | 34 | 0 | | |
| 1999–2000 | Leeds U | 38 | 0 | | |
| 2000–01 | Leeds U | 23 | 0 | | |
| 2001–02 | Leeds U | 38 | 0 | | |
| 2002–03 | Leeds U | 0 | 0 | | |
| 2003–04 | Leeds U | 0 | 0 | **207** | **0** |
| 2003–04 | Everton | 34 | 0 | **34** | **0** |

**McFADDEN, James (M) 86 26**
H: 6 0 W: 12 11 b.Glasgow 14-4-83
*Honours:* Scotland 14 full caps, 4 goals.

| | | | | | |
|---|---|---|---|---|---|
| 2000–01 | Motherwell | 6 | 0 | | |
| 2001–02 | Motherwell | 24 | 10 | | |
| 2002–03 | Motherwell | 30 | 13 | | |
| 2003–04 | Motherwell | 3 | 3 | **63** | **26** |
| 2003–04 | Everton | 23 | 0 | **23** | **0** |

**MOOGAN, Alan* (M) 0 0**
b.Liverpool 22-2-84
*Source:* Scholar. *Honours:* England Youth.

| | | | | | |
|---|---|---|---|---|---|
| 2000–01 | Everton | 0 | 0 | | |
| 2001–02 | Everton | 0 | 0 | | |
| 2002–03 | Everton | 0 | 0 | | |
| 2003–04 | Everton | 0 | 0 | | |

**MOOGAN, Brian* (D) 0 0**
b.Liverpool 22-2-84
*Source:* Scholar.

| | | | | | |
|---|---|---|---|---|---|
| 2001–02 | Everton | 0 | 0 | | |
| 2002–03 | Everton | 0 | 0 | | |
| 2003–04 | Everton | 0 | 0 | | |

**NAYSMITH, Gary (D) 198 8**
H: 5 9 W: 12 01 b.Edinburgh 16-11-78
*Source:* Whitehill Welfare Colts. *Honours:* Scotland Schools, Under-21, 22 full caps, 1 goal.

| | | | | | |
|---|---|---|---|---|---|
| 1995–96 | Hearts | 1 | 0 | | |
| 1996–97 | Hearts | 10 | 0 | | |
| 1997–98 | Hearts | 16 | 2 | | |
| 1998–99 | Hearts | 26 | 0 | | |
| 1999–2000 | Hearts | 35 | 1 | | |
| 2000–01 | Hearts | 9 | 0 | **97** | **3** |
| 2000–01 | Everton | 20 | 2 | | |
| 2001–02 | Everton | 24 | 0 | | |
| 2002–03 | Everton | 28 | 1 | | |
| 2003–04 | Everton | 29 | 2 | **101** | **5** |

**NYARKO, Alex (M) 199 16**
H: 6 0 W: 13 00 b.Accra 15-10-73
*Source:* Asanti Kotoko, Deawe Youngsters. *Honours:* Ghana full caps.

| | | | | | |
|---|---|---|---|---|---|
| 1994–95 | Sportul | 0 | 0 | | |
| 1995–96 | Basle | 26 | 3 | | |
| 1996–97 | Basle | 29 | 5 | **55** | **8** |
| 1997–98 | Karlsruhe | 22 | 1 | **22** | **1** |
| 1998–99 | Lens | 24 | 3 | | |
| 1999–2000 | Lens | 21 | 1 | **45** | **4** |
| 2000–01 | Everton | 22 | 1 | | |
| 2001–02 | Everton | 0 | 0 | | |
| 2001–02 | Monaco | 26 | 2 | **26** | **2** |
| 2002–03 | Paris St Germain | 18 | 0 | **18** | **0** |
| 2003–04 | Everton | 11 | 0 | **33** | **1** |

**OSMAN, Leon (F) 35 5**
H: 5 8 W: 10 09 b.Billinge 17-5-81
*Source:* Trainee. *Honours:* England Schools, Youth.

| | | | | | |
|---|---|---|---|---|---|
| 1998–99 | Everton | 0 | 0 | | |
| 1999–2000 | Everton | 0 | 0 | | |
| 2000–01 | Everton | 0 | 0 | | |
| 2001–02 | Everton | 0 | 0 | | |
| 2002–03 | Everton | 2 | 0 | | |
| 2002–03 | *Carlisle U* | 12 | 1 | **12** | **1** |
| 2003–04 | Everton | 4 | 1 | **6** | **1** |
| 2003–04 | *Derby Co* | 17 | 3 | **17** | **3** |

**PASCUCCI, Patrizio (F) 0 0**
H: 5 9 W: 12 04 b.L'Aquila 25-11-85

| | | | | | |
|---|---|---|---|---|---|
| 2003–04 | Everton | 0 | 0 | | |

**PISTONE, Alessandro (D) 214 8**
H: 5 11 W: 11 08 b.Milan 27-7-75

| | | | | | |
|---|---|---|---|---|---|
| 1992–93 | Vicenza | 0 | 0 | | |
| 1993–94 | Solbiatese | 20 | 1 | **20** | **1** |
| 1994–95 | Crevalcore | 29 | 4 | **29** | **4** |
| 1995–96 | Vicenza | 6 | 0 | **6** | **0** |
| 1995–96 | Internazionale | 19 | 1 | | |
| 1996–97 | Internazionale | 26 | 0 | **45** | **1** |
| 1997–98 | Newcastle U | 28 | 0 | | |
| 1998–99 | Newcastle U | 3 | 0 | | |
| 1999–2000 | Newcastle U | 15 | 1 | **46** | **1** |
| 2000–01 | Everton | 7 | 0 | | |
| 2001–02 | Everton | 25 | 1 | | |
| 2002–03 | Everton | 15 | 0 | | |
| 2003–04 | Everton | 21 | 0 | **68** | **1** |

**RADZINSKI, Tomasz (F) 273 119**
H: 5 7 W: 11 10 b.Poznan 14-12-73
*Source:* Toronto Rockets, St Catherines Roma. *Honours:* Canada 22 full caps, 7 goals.

| | | | | | |
|---|---|---|---|---|---|
| 1994–95 | Ekeren | 28 | 6 | | |
| 1995–96 | Ekeren | 22 | 9 | | |
| 1996–97 | Ekeren | 23 | 8 | | |
| 1997–98 | Ekeren | 31 | 19 | **104** | **42** |
| 1998–99 | Anderlecht | 22 | 15 | | |
| 1999–2000 | Anderlecht | 25 | 14 | | |
| 2000–01 | Anderlecht | 31 | 23 | **78** | **52** |
| 2001–02 | Everton | 27 | 6 | | |
| 2002–03 | Everton | 30 | 11 | | |
| 2003–04 | Everton | 34 | 8 | **91** | **25** |

**ROONEY, Wayne (F) 67 15**
H: 5 10 W: 12 04 b.Liverpool 24-10-85
*Source:* Scholar. *Honours:* FA Schools, England Youth, 17 full caps, 9 goals.

| | | | | | |
|---|---|---|---|---|---|
| 2002–03 | Everton | 33 | 6 | | |
| 2003–04 | Everton | 34 | 9 | **67** | **15** |

**SCHUMACHER, Steven* (M) 4 0**
H: 5 10 W: 11 00 b.Liverpool 30-4-84
*Source:* Scholar. *Honours:* England Youth.

| | | | | | |
|---|---|---|---|---|---|
| 2000–01 | Everton | 0 | 0 | | |
| 2001–02 | Everton | 0 | 0 | | |
| 2002–03 | Everton | 0 | 0 | | |
| 2003–04 | Everton | 0 | 0 | | |
| 2003–04 | *Carlisle U* | 4 | 0 | **4** | **0** |

**SIMONSEN, Steve* (G) 65 0**
H: 6 2 W: 14 00 b.South Shields 3-4-79
*Source:* Trainee. *Honours:* England Youth, Under-21.

| | | | | | |
|---|---|---|---|---|---|
| 1996–97 | Tranmere R | 0 | 0 | | |
| 1997–98 | Tranmere R | 30 | 0 | | |
| 1998–99 | Tranmere R | 5 | 0 | **35** | **0** |
| 1998–99 | Everton | 0 | 0 | | |
| 1999–2000 | Everton | 1 | 0 | | |
| 2000–01 | Everton | 1 | 0 | | |
| 2001–02 | Everton | 25 | 0 | | |
| 2002–03 | Everton | 2 | 0 | | |
| 2003–04 | Everton | 1 | 0 | **30** | **0** |

**STUBBS, Alan (D) 401 14**
H: 6 2 W: 13 12 b.Kirkby 6-10-71
*Source:* Trainee.

| | | | | | |
|---|---|---|---|---|---|
| 1990–91 | Bolton W | 23 | 0 | | |
| 1991–92 | Bolton W | 32 | 1 | | |
| 1992–93 | Bolton W | 42 | 2 | | |
| 1993–94 | Bolton W | 41 | 1 | | |
| 1994–95 | Bolton W | 39 | 1 | | |
| 1995–96 | Bolton W | 25 | 4 | **202** | **9** |
| 1996–97 | Celtic | 20 | 0 | | |
| 1997–98 | Celtic | 29 | 1 | | |
| 1998–99 | Celtic | 23 | 1 | | |
| 1999–2000 | Celtic | 23 | 0 | | |
| 2000–01 | Celtic | 11 | 1 | **106** | **3** |
| 2001–02 | Everton | 31 | 2 | | |
| 2002–03 | Everton | 35 | 0 | | |
| 2003–04 | Everton | 27 | 0 | **93** | **2** |

**SYMES, Michael* (F) 4 1**
H: 6 3 W: 12 04 b.Gt Yarmouth 31-10-83
*Source:* Scholar.

| | | | | | |
|---|---|---|---|---|---|
| 2001–02 | Everton | 0 | 0 | | |
| 2002–03 | Everton | 0 | 0 | | |
| 2003–04 | Everton | 0 | 0 | | |
| 2003–04 | *Crewe Alex* | 4 | 1 | **4** | **1** |

**TURNER, Iain (G) 0 0**
H: 6 3 W: 12 10 b.Stirling 26-1-84
*Source:* Trainee.

| | | | | | |
|---|---|---|---|---|---|
| 2002–03 | Everton | 0 | 0 | | |
| 2003–04 | Everton | 0 | 0 | | |

**UNSWORTH, Dave (D) 336 36**
H: 6 1 W: 15 02 b.Chorley 16-10-73
*Source:* Trainee. *Honours:* England Youth, Under-21, 1 full cap.

| | | | | | |
|---|---|---|---|---|---|
| 1991–92 | Everton | 2 | 1 | | |
| 1992–93 | Everton | 3 | 0 | | |
| 1993–94 | Everton | 8 | 0 | | |
| 1994–95 | Everton | 38 | 3 | | |
| 1995–96 | Everton | 31 | 2 | | |
| 1996–97 | Everton | 34 | 5 | | |
| 1997–98 | West Ham U | 32 | 2 | **32** | **2** |
| 1998–99 | Aston Villa | 0 | 0 | | |
| 1998–99 | Everton | 34 | 1 | | |
| 1999–2000 | Everton | 33 | 6 | | |
| 2000–01 | Everton | 29 | 5 | | |
| 2001–02 | Everton | 33 | 3 | | |
| 2002–03 | Everton | 33 | 5 | | |
| 2003–04 | Everton | 26 | 3 | **304** | **34** |

**WATSON, Steve (D) 350 26**
H: 6 0 W: 12 07 b.North Shields 1-4-74
*Source:* Trainee. *Honours:* England Youth, Under-21, B.

| | | | | | |
|---|---|---|---|---|---|
| 1990–91 | Newcastle U | 24 | 0 | | |
| 1991–92 | Newcastle U | 28 | 1 | | |
| 1992–93 | Newcastle U | 2 | 0 | | |
| 1993–94 | Newcastle U | 32 | 2 | | |
| 1994–95 | Newcastle U | 27 | 4 | | |
| 1995–96 | Newcastle U | 23 | 3 | | |
| 1996–97 | Newcastle U | 36 | 1 | | |
| 1997–98 | Newcastle U | 29 | 1 | | |
| 1998–99 | Newcastle U | 7 | 0 | **208** | **12** |
| 1998–99 | Aston Villa | 27 | 0 | | |
| 1999–2000 | Aston Villa | 14 | 0 | **41** | **0** |
| 2000–01 | Everton | 34 | 0 | | |
| 2001–02 | Everton | 25 | 4 | | |
| 2002–03 | Everton | 18 | 5 | | |
| 2003–04 | Everton | 24 | 5 | **101** | **14** |

**WEIR, David (D) 388 23**
H: 6 5 W: 14 03 b.Falkirk 10-5-70
*Source:* Celtic BC. *Honours:* Scotland 37 full caps, 1 goal.

| | | | | | |
|---|---|---|---|---|---|
| 1992–93 | Falkirk | 30 | 1 | | |
| 1993–94 | Falkirk | 37 | 3 | | |
| 1994–95 | Falkirk | 32 | 1 | | |
| 1995–96 | Falkirk | 34 | 3 | **133** | **8** |
| 1996–97 | Hearts | 34 | 6 | | |
| 1997–98 | Hearts | 35 | 1 | | |
| 1998–99 | Hearts | 23 | 1 | **92** | **8** |
| 1998–99 | Everton | 14 | 0 | | |
| 1999–2000 | Everton | 35 | 2 | | |
| 2000–01 | Everton | 37 | 1 | | |
| 2001–02 | Everton | 36 | 4 | | |
| 2002–03 | Everton | 31 | 0 | | |
| 2003–04 | Everton | 10 | 0 | **163** | **7** |

**WRIGHT, Richard (G) 289 0**
H: 6 2 W: 14 04 b.Ipswich 5-11-77
*Source:* Trainee. *Honours:* England Schools, Youth, Under-21, 2 full caps.

| | | | | | |
|---|---|---|---|---|---|
| 1994–95 | Ipswich T | 3 | 0 | | |
| 1995–96 | Ipswich T | 23 | 0 | | |
| 1996–97 | Ipswich T | 40 | 0 | | |
| 1997–98 | Ipswich T | 46 | 0 | | |
| 1998–99 | Ipswich T | 46 | 0 | | |
| 1999–2000 | Ipswich T | 46 | 0 | | |
| 2000–01 | Ipswich T | 36 | 0 | **240** | **0** |
| 2001–02 | Arsenal | 12 | 0 | **12** | **0** |
| 2002–03 | Everton | 33 | 0 | | |
| 2003–04 | Everton | 4 | 0 | **37** | **0** |

**YOBO, Joseph (D) 123 4**
H: 6 1 W: 13 00 b.Kano 6-9-80
*Source:* Mechelen. *Honours:* Nigeria full caps.

| | | | | | |
|---|---|---|---|---|---|
| 1998–99 | Standard Liege | 0 | 0 | | |
| 1999–2000 | Standard Liege | 18 | 0 | | |
| 2000–01 | Standard Liege | 30 | 2 | **48** | **2** |
| 2001–02 | Marseille | 23 | 0 | **23** | **0** |
| 2002–03 | Everton | 24 | 0 | | |
| 2003–04 | Everton | 28 | 2 | **52** | **2** |

**Scholars**
Boyle, Patrick J G; Fowler, Andrew; Fox, Daniel; Gallagher, Craig; Gerard, Anthony; Harris, James W; Hopkins, Paul D; Hughes, Mark A; Martland, Damon G; Potter, James; Seargeant, Christian M; Wilson, Laurence T; Wright, Sean G; Wynne, Stephen

# FULHAM (32)

**BAKER, Nicholas (G) 0 0**
b.London 18-12-84

| | | | | | |
|---|---|---|---|---|---|
| 2003–04 | Fulham | 0 | 0 | | |

**BEASANT, Dave* (G) 773 0**
H: 6 4 W: 14 04 b.Willesden 20-3-59
*Source:* Edgware T. *Honours:* England B, 2 full caps.

| | | | | | |
|---|---|---|---|---|---|
| 1979–80 | Wimbledon | 2 | 0 | | |
| 1980–81 | Wimbledon | 34 | 0 | | |
| 1981–82 | Wimbledon | 46 | 0 | | |
| 1982–83 | Wimbledon | 46 | 0 | | |
| 1983–84 | Wimbledon | 46 | 0 | | |
| 1984–85 | Wimbledon | 42 | 0 | | |
| 1985–86 | Wimbledon | 42 | 0 | | |
| 1986–87 | Wimbledon | 42 | 0 | | |
| 1987–88 | Wimbledon | 40 | 0 | **340** | **0** |
| 1988–89 | Newcastle U | 20 | 0 | **20** | **0** |
| 1988–89 | Chelsea | 22 | 0 | | |
| 1989–90 | Chelsea | 38 | 0 | | |
| 1990–91 | Chelsea | 35 | 0 | | |
| 1991–92 | Chelsea | 21 | 0 | | |
| 1992–93 | Chelsea | 17 | 0 | | |
| 1992–93 | *Grimsby T* | 6 | 0 | **6** | **0** |
| 1992–93 | *Wolverhampton W* | 4 | 0 | **4** | **0** |
| 1993–94 | Chelsea | 0 | 0 | **133** | **0** |
| 1993–94 | Southampton | 25 | 0 | | |
| 1994–95 | Southampton | 13 | 0 | | |
| 1995–96 | Southampton | 36 | 0 | | |
| 1996–97 | Southampton | 14 | 0 | | |
| 1997–98 | Southampton | 0 | 0 | **88** | **0** |
| 1997–98 | Nottingham F | 41 | 0 | | |
| 1998–99 | Nottingham F | 26 | 0 | | |
| 1999–2000 | Nottingham F | 27 | 0 | | |
| 2000–01 | Nottingham F | 45 | 0 | **139** | **0** |
| 2001–02 | Portsmouth | 27 | 0 | **27** | **0** |
| 2002–03 | Bradford C | 0 | 0 | | |
| 2002–03 | Wigan Ath | 0 | 0 | | |
| 2002–03 | Brighton & HA | 16 | 0 | **16** | **0** |
| 2003–04 | Fulham | 0 | 0 | | |

**BOA MORTE, Luis (F) 163 31**
H: 5 10 W: 11 10 b.Lisbon 4-8-77
*Source:* Sporting Lisbon, Lourihanense (loan). *Honours:* Portugal Under-21, 13 full caps, 1 goal.

| | | | | | |
|---|---|---|---|---|---|
| 1997–98 | Arsenal | 15 | 0 | | |
| 1998–99 | Arsenal | 8 | 0 | | |
| 1999–2000 | Arsenal | 2 | 0 | **25** | **0** |
| 1999–2000 | Southampton | 14 | 1 | | |
| 2000–01 | Southampton | 0 | 0 | **14** | **1** |
| 2000–01 | *Fulham* | 39 | 18 | | |
| 2001–02 | Fulham | 23 | 1 | | |
| 2002–03 | Fulham | 29 | 2 | | |
| 2003–04 | Fulham | 33 | 9 | **124** | **30** |

**BOCANEGRA, Carlos (D) 102 5**
H: 6 0 W: 12 04 b.Alta Loma 25-5-79
*Honours:* USA 25 full caps.

| | | | | | |
|---|---|---|---|---|---|
| 2000 | Chicago Fire | 27 | 1 | | |
| 2001 | Chicago Fire | 15 | 1 | | |
| 2002 | Chicago Fire | 26 | 2 | | |
| 2003 | Chicago Fire | 19 | 1 | **87** | **5** |
| 2003–04 | Fulham | 15 | 0 | **15** | **0** |

**BONNISSEL, Jerome (D) 283 1**
H: 5 8 W: 11 11 b.Montpellier 16-4-73

| | | | | | |
|---|---|---|---|---|---|
| 1992–93 | Montpellier | 18 | 0 | | |
| 1993–94 | Montpellier | 32 | 1 | | |
| 1994–95 | Montpellier | 37 | 0 | | |
| 1995–96 | Montpellier | 32 | 0 | **119** | **1** |
| 1996–97 | La Coruna | 20 | 0 | | |
| 1997–98 | La Coruna | 27 | 0 | | |
| 1998–99 | La Coruna | 16 | 0 | **63** | **0** |
| 1999–2000 | Bordeaux | 26 | 0 | | |
| 2000–01 | Bordeaux | 31 | 0 | | |
| 2001–02 | Bordeaux | 13 | 0 | | |
| 2002–03 | Bordeaux | 12 | 0 | **82** | **0** |
| 2002–03 | Rangers | 3 | 0 | **3** | **0** |
| 2003–04 | Fulham | 16 | 0 | **16** | **0** |

**BUARI, Malik (M) 3 0**
H: 5 11 W: 11 11 b.Accra 21-1-84
*Source:* Trainee.

| | | | | | |
|---|---|---|---|---|---|
| 2003–04 | Fulham | 3 | 0 | **3** | **0** |

**CLARK, Lee (M) 400 58**
H: 5 8 W: 11 10 b.Wallsend 27-10-72
*Source:* Trainee. *Honours:* England Schools, Youth, Under-21.

| | | | | | |
|---|---|---|---|---|---|
| 1989–90 | Newcastle U | 0 | 0 | | |
| 1990–91 | Newcastle U | 19 | 2 | | |
| 1991–92 | Newcastle U | 29 | 5 | | |
| 1992–93 | Newcastle U | 46 | 9 | | |
| 1993–94 | Newcastle U | 29 | 2 | | |
| 1994–95 | Newcastle U | 19 | 1 | | |
| 1995–96 | Newcastle U | 28 | 2 | | |
| 1996–97 | Newcastle U | 25 | 2 | **195** | **23** |
| 1997–98 | Sunderland | 46 | 13 | | |
| 1998–99 | Sunderland | 27 | 3 | **73** | **16** |
| 1999–2000 | Fulham | 42 | 8 | | |
| 2000–01 | Fulham | 45 | 7 | | |
| 2001–02 | Fulham | 9 | 0 | | |
| 2002–03 | Fulham | 11 | 2 | | |
| 2003–04 | Fulham | 25 | 2 | **132** | **19** |

**COLLINS, Matthew (M) 0 0**
b.Merthyr 31-3-86
*Source:* Trainee.

| | | | | | |
|---|---|---|---|---|---|
| 2002–03 | Fulham | 0 | 0 | | |
| 2003–04 | Fulham | 0 | 0 | | |

**CROSSLEY, Mark (G) 352 0**
H: 6 0 W: 15 09 b.Barnsley 16-6-69
*Source:* Trainee. *Honours:* England Under-21, Wales B, 7 full caps.

| | | | | | |
|---|---|---|---|---|---|
| 1987–88 | Nottingham F | 0 | 0 | | |
| 1988–89 | Nottingham F | 2 | 0 | | |
| 1989–90 | Nottingham F | 8 | 0 | | |
| 1989–90 | *Manchester U* | 0 | 0 | | |
| 1990–91 | Nottingham F | 38 | 0 | | |
| 1991–92 | Nottingham F | 36 | 0 | | |
| 1992–93 | Nottingham F | 37 | 0 | | |
| 1993–94 | Nottingham F | 37 | 0 | | |
| 1994–95 | Nottingham F | 42 | 0 | | |
| 1995–96 | Nottingham F | 38 | 0 | | |
| 1996–97 | Nottingham F | 33 | 0 | | |
| 1997–98 | Nottingham F | 0 | 0 | | |
| 1997–98 | *Millwall* | 13 | 0 | **13** | **0** |
| 1998–99 | Nottingham F | 12 | 0 | | |
| 1999–2000 | Nottingham F | 20 | 0 | **303** | **0** |
| 2000–01 | Middlesbrough | 5 | 0 | | |
| 2001–02 | Middlesbrough | 18 | 0 | | |
| 2002–03 | Middlesbrough | 0 | 0 | **23** | **0** |
| 2002–03 | *Stoke C* | 12 | 0 | **12** | **0** |
| 2003–04 | Fulham | 1 | 0 | **1** | **0** |

**DAVIS, Sean (M) 155 14**
H: 5 9 W: 12 09 b.Clapham 20-9-79
*Source:* Trainee. *Honours:* England Under-21.

| | | | | | |
|---|---|---|---|---|---|
| 1996–97 | Fulham | 1 | 0 | | |
| 1997–98 | Fulham | 0 | 0 | | |
| 1998–99 | Fulham | 6 | 0 | | |
| 1999–2000 | Fulham | 26 | 0 | | |
| 2000–01 | Fulham | 40 | 6 | | |
| 2001–02 | Fulham | 30 | 0 | | |
| 2002–03 | Fulham | 28 | 3 | | |
| 2003–04 | Fulham | 24 | 5 | **155** | **14** |

**DAVIS, Tom* (M) 0 0**
H: 5 9 W: 11 07 b.Bromley 17-2-84

| | | | | | |
|---|---|---|---|---|---|
| 2003–04 | Fulham | 0 | 0 | | |

**DJETOU, Martin‡ (M) 273 8**
H: 5 11 W: 12 06 b.Brogohla 15-12-74
*Honours:* France 6 full caps.

| | | | | | |
|---|---|---|---|---|---|
| 1992–93 | Strasbourg | 28 | 0 | | |
| 1993–94 | Strasbourg | 4 | 0 | | |
| 1994–95 | Strasbourg | 21 | 0 | | |
| 1995–96 | Strasbourg | 30 | 1 | **83** | **1** |
| 1996–97 | Monaco | 26 | 0 | | |
| 1997–98 | Monaco | 24 | 3 | | |
| 1998–99 | Monaco | 15 | 0 | | |
| 1999–2000 | Monaco | 22 | 0 | | |
| 2000–01 | Monaco | 29 | 1 | **116** | **4** |
| 2001–02 | Parma | 23 | 2 | **23** | **2** |
| 2002–03 | Fulham | 25 | 1 | | |
| 2003–04 | Fulham | 26 | 0 | **51** | **1** |

**DOHERTY, Sean* (M) 1 0**
H: 5 8 W: 10 00 b.Basingstoke 10-5-85
*Source:* Scholar. *Honours:* England Youth, Under-20.

| | | | | | |
|---|---|---|---|---|---|
| 2001–02 | Fulham | 0 | 0 | | |
| 2002–03 | Fulham | 0 | 0 | | |

| | | | | | |
|---|---|---|---|---|---|
| 2003–04 | Fulham | 0 | 0 | | |
| 2003–04 | *Blackpool* | 1 | 0 | **1** | **0** |

**FAZACKERLEY, Loui* (M) 0 0**
b.Winchester 24-7-84

| | | | | | |
|---|---|---|---|---|---|
| 2002–03 | Fulham | 0 | 0 | | |
| 2003–04 | Fulham | 0 | 0 | | |

**FLITNEY, Ross (G) 3 0**
H: 6 1 W: 11 11 b.Hitchin 1-6-84
*Source:* Scholar.

| | | | | | |
|---|---|---|---|---|---|
| 2003–04 | Fulham | 0 | 0 | | |
| 2003–04 | *Brighton & HA* | 3 | 0 | **3** | **0** |

**FONTAINE, Liam (D) 0 0**
b.Beckenham 7-1-86
*Source:* Trainee.

| | | | | | |
|---|---|---|---|---|---|
| 2003–04 | Fulham | 0 | 0 | | |

**GOMA, Alain (D) 317 5**
H: 6 0 W: 13 05 b.Sault 15-10-72
*Honours:* France 2 full caps.

| | | | | | |
|---|---|---|---|---|---|
| 1990–91 | Auxerre | 1 | 0 | | |
| 1991–92 | Auxerre | 1 | 0 | | |
| 1992–93 | Auxerre | 15 | 1 | | |
| 1993–94 | Auxerre | 33 | 0 | | |
| 1994–95 | Auxerre | 28 | 0 | | |
| 1995–96 | Auxerre | 32 | 0 | | |
| 1996–97 | Auxerre | 34 | 2 | | |
| 1997–98 | Auxerre | 22 | 1 | **166** | **4** |
| 1998–99 | Paris St Germain | 30 | 0 | **30** | **0** |
| 1999–2000 | Newcastle U | 14 | 0 | | |
| 2000–01 | Newcastle U | 19 | 1 | **33** | **1** |
| 2000–01 | Fulham | 3 | 0 | | |
| 2001–02 | Fulham | 33 | 0 | | |
| 2002–03 | Fulham | 29 | 0 | | |
| 2003–04 | Fulham | 23 | 0 | **88** | **0** |

**GREEN, Adam (D) 4 0**
H: 5 9 W: 10 11 b.Hillingdon 12-1-84
*Source:* Scholar.

| | | | | | |
|---|---|---|---|---|---|
| 2003–04 | Fulham | 4 | 0 | **4** | **0** |

**HAMMOND, Elvis (F) 21 0**
H: 5 10 W: 11 06 b.Accra 6-10-80
*Source:* Trainee.

| | | | | | |
|---|---|---|---|---|---|
| 1999–2000 | Fulham | 0 | 0 | | |
| 2000–01 | Fulham | 0 | 0 | | |
| 2001–02 | Fulham | 0 | 0 | | |
| 2001–02 | *Bristol R* | 7 | 0 | **7** | **0** |
| 2002–03 | Fulham | 10 | 0 | | |
| 2003–04 | Fulham | 0 | 0 | **10** | **0** |
| 2003–04 | *Norwich C* | 4 | 0 | **4** | **0** |

**HARLEY, Jon (D) 90 7**
H: 5 9 W: 11 05 b.Maidstone 26-9-79
*Source:* Trainee. *Honours:* England Under-21.

| | | | | | |
|---|---|---|---|---|---|
| 1996–97 | Chelsea | 0 | 0 | | |
| 1997–98 | Chelsea | 3 | 0 | | |
| 1998–99 | Chelsea | 0 | 0 | | |
| 1999–2000 | Chelsea | 17 | 2 | | |
| 2000–01 | Chelsea | 10 | 0 | **30** | **2** |
| 2000–01 | *Wimbledon* | 6 | 2 | **6** | **2** |
| 2001–02 | Fulham | 10 | 0 | | |
| 2002–03 | Fulham | 11 | 1 | | |
| 2002–03 | *Sheffield U* | 9 | 1 | | |
| 2003–04 | Fulham | 4 | 0 | **25** | **1** |
| 2003–04 | *Sheffield U* | 5 | 0 | **14** | **1** |
| 2003–04 | *West Ham U* | 15 | 1 | **15** | **1** |

**HAYLES, Barry* (F) 237 76**
H: 5 10 W: 12 11 b.Lambeth 17-5-72
*Source:* Stevenage Bor. *Honours:* Jamaica 10 full caps.

| | | | | | |
|---|---|---|---|---|---|
| 1997–98 | Bristol R | 45 | 23 | | |
| 1998–99 | Bristol R | 17 | 9 | **62** | **32** |
| 1998–99 | Fulham | 30 | 8 | | |
| 1999–2000 | Fulham | 35 | 5 | | |
| 2000–01 | Fulham | 35 | 18 | | |
| 2001–02 | Fulham | 35 | 8 | | |
| 2002–03 | Fulham | 14 | 1 | | |
| 2003–04 | Fulham | 26 | 4 | **175** | **44** |

**HERRERA, Martin (G) 135 0**
H: 6 0 W: 12 06 b.Argentina 13-9-70

| | | | | | |
|---|---|---|---|---|---|
| 1997–98 | Toluca | 5 | 0 | **5** | **0** |
| 1998–99 | Ferro Carril | 34 | 0 | **34** | **0** |
| 1999–2000 | Alaves | 38 | 0 | | |
| 2000–01 | Alaves | 36 | 0 | | |
| 2001–02 | Alaves | 20 | 0 | **94** | **0** |
| 2002–03 | Fulham | 2 | 0 | | |
| 2003–04 | Fulham | 0 | 0 | **2** | **0** |

**HUDSON, Mark (D) 29 0**
H: 6 3 W: 12 06 b.Guildford 30-3-82
*Source:* Trainee.

| | | | | | |
|---|---|---|---|---|---|
| 1998–99 | Fulham | 0 | 0 | | |
| 1999–2000 | Fulham | 0 | 0 | | |
| 2000–01 | Fulham | 0 | 0 | | |
| 2001–02 | Fulham | 0 | 0 | | |
| 2002–03 | Fulham | 0 | 0 | | |
| 2003–04 | Fulham | 0 | 0 | | |
| 2003–04 | *Oldham Ath* | 15 | 0 | **15** | **0** |
| 2003–04 | *Crystal Palace* | 14 | 0 | **14** | **0** |

**INAMOTO, Junichi‡ (M) 159 20**
H: 5 11 W: 11 11 b.Osaka 18-9-79
*Honours:* Japan 50 full caps, 4 goals.

| | | | | | |
|---|---|---|---|---|---|
| 1997 | Gamba Osaka | 27 | 3 | | |
| 1998 | Gamba Osaka | 28 | 6 | | |
| 1999 | Gamba Osaka | 22 | 1 | | |
| 2000 | Gamba Osaka | 28 | 4 | | |
| 2001 | Gamba Osaka | 13 | 2 | **118** | **16** |
| 2001–02 | Arsenal | 0 | 0 | | |
| 2002–03 | Fulham | 19 | 2 | | |
| 2003–04 | Fulham | 22 | 2 | **41** | **4** |

**JOHN, Collins (F) 43 15**
H: 6 0 W: 12 11 b.Zwandru 17-10-85

| | | | | | |
|---|---|---|---|---|---|
| 2002–03 | Twente | 17 | 2 | | |
| 2003–04 | Twente | 18 | 9 | **35** | **11** |
| 2003–04 | Fulham | 8 | 4 | **8** | **4** |

**KNIGHT, Zat (D) 66 0**
H: 6 6 W: 14 06 b.Solihull 2-5-80
*Honours:* England Under-21.

| | | | | | |
|---|---|---|---|---|---|
| 1998–99 | Fulham | 0 | 0 | | |
| 1999–2000 | Fulham | 0 | 0 | | |
| 1999–2000 | *Peterborough U* | 8 | 0 | **8** | **0** |
| 2000–01 | Fulham | 0 | 0 | | |
| 2001–02 | Fulham | 10 | 0 | | |
| 2002–03 | Fulham | 17 | 0 | | |
| 2003–04 | Fulham | 31 | 0 | **58** | **0** |

**LAWLESS, Alex (F) 0 0**
b.Llwynupion 26-3-85

| | | | | | |
|---|---|---|---|---|---|
| 2003–04 | Fulham | 0 | 0 | | |

**LEACOCK, Dean (D) 4 0**
H: 6 2 W: 12 04 b.Croydon 10-6-84
*Source:* Trainee. *Honours:* England Youth, Under-20.

| | | | | | |
|---|---|---|---|---|---|
| 2002–03 | Fulham | 0 | 0 | | |
| 2003–04 | Fulham | 4 | 0 | **4** | **0** |

**LEGWINSKI, Sylvain (M) 274 22**
H: 6 1 W: 11 10 b.Clermont-Ferrand 6-10-73

| | | | | | |
|---|---|---|---|---|---|
| 1992–93 | Monaco | 2 | 0 | | |
| 1993–94 | Monaco | 0 | 0 | | |
| 1994–95 | Monaco | 21 | 1 | | |
| 1995–96 | Monaco | 29 | 2 | | |
| 1996–97 | Monaco | 37 | 9 | | |
| 1997–98 | Monaco | 22 | 0 | | |
| 1998–99 | Monaco | 14 | 1 | **125** | **13** |
| 1999–2000 | Bordeaux | 13 | 1 | | |
| 2000–01 | Bordeaux | 32 | 1 | | |
| 2001–02 | Bordeaux | 4 | 0 | **49** | **2** |
| 2001–02 | Fulham | 33 | 3 | | |
| 2002–03 | Fulham | 35 | 4 | | |
| 2003–04 | Fulham | 32 | 0 | **100** | **7** |

**MALBRANQUE, Steed (M) 189 25**
H: 5 8 W: 11 10 b.Mouscron 6-1-80

| | | | | | |
|---|---|---|---|---|---|
| 1997–98 | Lyon | 2 | 0 | | |
| 1998–99 | Lyon | 21 | 0 | | |
| 1999–2000 | Lyon | 28 | 3 | | |
| 2000–01 | Lyon | 26 | 2 | **77** | **5** |
| 2001–02 | Fulham | 37 | 8 | | |
| 2002–03 | Fulham | 37 | 6 | | |
| 2003–04 | Fulham | 38 | 6 | **112** | **20** |

**MARLET, Steve (F) 193 48**
H: 5 11 W: 11 10 b.Pithiviers 10-1-74
*Honours:* France 23 full caps, 6 goals.

| | | | | | |
|---|---|---|---|---|---|
| 1996–97 | Auxerre | 24 | 3 | | |
| 1997–98 | Auxerre | 18 | 6 | | |
| 1998–99 | Auxerre | 32 | 7 | | |
| 1999–2000 | Auxerre | 33 | 9 | **107** | **25** |
| 2000–01 | Lyon | 31 | 12 | **31** | **12** |
| 2001–02 | Fulham | 26 | 6 | | |
| 2002–03 | Fulham | 28 | 4 | | |
| 2003–04 | Fulham | 1 | 1 | **55** | **11** |

**McBRIDE, Brian (F) 206 72**
H: 6 1 W: 12 06 b.USA 17-8-72
*Source:* St Louis Univ. *Honours:* USA 76 full caps, 23 goals.

| | | | | | |
|---|---|---|---|---|---|
| 1994–95 | Wolfsburg | 12 | 1 | **12** | **1** |
| 1996 | Columbus Crew | 28 | 17 | | |
| 1997 | Columbus Crew | 13 | 6 | | |
| 1998 | Columbus Crew | 24 | 10 | | |
| 1999 | Columbus Crew | 25 | 5 | | |
| 2000 | Columbus Crew | 18 | 6 | | |
| 2000–01 | Preston NE | 9 | 1 | **9** | **1** |
| 2001 | Columbus Crew | 15 | 1 | | |
| 2002 | Columbus Crew | 14 | 5 | | |
| 2002–03 | Everton | 8 | 4 | **8** | **4** |
| 2003 | Columbus Crew | 24 | 12 | **161** | **62** |
| 2003–04 | Fulham | 16 | 4 | **16** | **4** |

**McDERMOTT, Neale (M) 0 0**
H: 5 9 W: 10 11 b.Newcastle 8-3-85
*Source:* Scholar. *Honours:* England Youth.

| | | | | | |
|---|---|---|---|---|---|
| 2001–02 | Newcastle U | 0 | 0 | | |
| 2002–03 | Newcastle U | 0 | 0 | | |
| 2002–03 | Fulham | 0 | 0 | | |
| 2003–04 | Fulham | 0 | 0 | | |

**NOBLE, Stuart (F) 0 0**
H: 6 0 W: 12 09 b.Edinburgh 14-10-83
*Source:* Trainee.

| | | | | | |
|---|---|---|---|---|---|
| 2002–03 | Fulham | 0 | 0 | | |
| 2003–04 | Fulham | 0 | 0 | | |

**OUADDOU, Abdes (D) 68 0**
H: 6 4 W: 12 03 b.Ksar-Askour 1-11-78
*Honours:* Morocco full caps.

| | | | | | |
|---|---|---|---|---|---|
| 1999–2000 | Nancy | 16 | 0 | | |
| 2000–01 | Nancy | 31 | 0 | **47** | **0** |
| 2001–02 | Fulham | 8 | 0 | | |
| 2002–03 | Fulham | 13 | 0 | | |
| 2003–04 | Fulham | 0 | 0 | **21** | **0** |

**PEARCE, Ian (D) 221 11**
H: 6 3 W: 14 04 b.Bury St Edmunds 7-5-74
*Source:* School. *Honours:* England Youth, Under-21.

| | | | | | |
|---|---|---|---|---|---|
| 1990–91 | Chelsea | 1 | 0 | | |
| 1991–92 | Chelsea | 2 | 0 | | |
| 1992–93 | Chelsea | 1 | 0 | | |
| 1993–94 | Chelsea | 0 | 0 | **4** | **0** |
| 1993–94 | Blackburn R | 5 | 1 | | |
| 1994–95 | Blackburn R | 28 | 0 | | |
| 1995–96 | Blackburn R | 12 | 1 | | |
| 1996–97 | Blackburn R | 12 | 0 | | |
| 1997–98 | Blackburn R | 5 | 0 | **62** | **2** |
| 1997–98 | West Ham U | 30 | 1 | | |
| 1998–99 | West Ham U | 33 | 2 | | |
| 1999–2000 | West Ham U | 1 | 0 | | |
| 2000–01 | West Ham U | 15 | 1 | | |
| 2001–02 | West Ham U | 9 | 2 | | |
| 2002–03 | West Ham U | 30 | 2 | | |
| 2003–04 | West Ham U | 24 | 1 | **142** | **9** |
| 2003–04 | Fulham | 13 | 0 | **13** | **0** |

**PEMBRIDGE, Mark (M) 385 51**
H: 5 7 W: 11 09 b.Merthyr 29-11-70
*Source:* Trainee. *Honours:* Wales Schools, Under-21, B, 51 full caps, 6 goals.

| | | | | | |
|---|---|---|---|---|---|
| 1989–90 | Luton T | 0 | 0 | | |
| 1990–91 | Luton T | 18 | 1 | | |
| 1991–92 | Luton T | 42 | 5 | **60** | **6** |
| 1992–93 | Derby Co | 42 | 8 | | |
| 1993–94 | Derby Co | 41 | 11 | | |
| 1994–95 | Derby Co | 27 | 9 | **110** | **28** |
| 1995–96 | Sheffield W | 25 | 1 | | |
| 1996–97 | Sheffield W | 34 | 6 | | |
| 1997–98 | Sheffield W | 34 | 4 | **93** | **11** |
| 1998–99 | Benfica | 19 | 1 | **19** | **1** |
| 1999–2000 | Everton | 31 | 2 | | |
| 2000–01 | Everton | 21 | 0 | | |
| 2001–02 | Everton | 14 | 1 | | |
| 2002–03 | Everton | 21 | 1 | | |
| 2003–04 | Everton | 4 | 0 | **91** | **4** |
| 2003–04 | Fulham | 12 | 1 | **12** | **1** |

**PRATLEY, Darren (F) 1 0**
H: 6 0 W: 10 13 b.Barking 22-4-85
*Source:* Scholar.

| | | | | | |
|---|---|---|---|---|---|
| 2001–02 | Fulham | 0 | 0 | | |
| 2002–03 | Fulham | 0 | 0 | | |
| 2003–04 | Fulham | 1 | 0 | **1** | **0** |

**REHMAN, Zesh (M)** **12 2**
H: 6 2 W: 12 09 b.Birmingham 14-10-83
*Source:* Scholar. *Honours:* England Youth.

| | | | | | |
|---|---|---|---|---|---|
| 2001–02 | Fulham | 0 | 0 | | |
| 2002–03 | Fulham | 0 | 0 | | |
| 2003–04 | Fulham | 1 | 0 | **1** | **0** |
| 2003–04 | *Brighton & HA* | 11 | 2 | **11** | **2** |

**ROSENIOR, Liam (M)** **32 2**
H: 5 9 W: 11 05 b.Wandsworth 9-7-84
*Source:* Scholar.

| | | | | | |
|---|---|---|---|---|---|
| 2001–02 | Bristol C | 1 | 0 | | |
| 2002–03 | Bristol C | 21 | 2 | | |
| 2003–04 | Bristol C | 0 | 0 | **22** | **2** |
| 2003–04 | Fulham | 0 | 0 | | |
| 2003–04 | *Torquay U* | 10 | 0 | **10** | **0** |

**SAVA, Facundo (F)** **276 79**
H: 6 1 W: 13 03 b.Ituzaingo 7-3-74

| | | | | | |
|---|---|---|---|---|---|
| 1993–94 | Ferro Carril | 27 | 3 | | |
| 1994–95 | Ferro Carril | 18 | 0 | | |
| 1995–96 | Ferro Carril | 34 | 4 | | |
| 1996–97 | Ferro Carril | 1 | 0 | **80** | **7** |
| 1996–97 | Boca Juniors | 7 | 0 | **7** | **0** |
| 1997–98 | Gimnasia | 32 | 8 | | |
| 1998–99 | Gimnasia | 28 | 10 | | |
| 1999–2000 | Gimnasia | 35 | 12 | | |
| 2000–01 | Gimnasia | 34 | 13 | | |
| 2001–02 | Gimnasia | 34 | 23 | **163** | **66** |
| 2002–03 | Fulham | 20 | 5 | | |
| 2003–04 | Fulham | 6 | 1 | **26** | **6** |

**STOLCERS, Andrejs* (M)** **135 36**
H: 5 11 W: 11 00 b.Latvia 8-7-74
*Honours:* Latvia 79 full caps, 7 goals.

| | | | | | |
|---|---|---|---|---|---|
| 1996 | Skonto Riga | 26 | 6 | | |
| 1997 | Skonto Riga | 23 | 9 | **49** | **15** |
| 1997–98 | Shakhtjar Donetsk | 13 | 4 | | |
| 1998–99 | Shakhtjar Donetsk | 21 | 6 | | |
| 1999–2000 | Shakhtjar Donetsk | 15 | 4 | **49** | **14** |
| 2000 | Spartak Moscow | 12 | 5 | **12** | **5** |
| 2000–01 | Fulham | 15 | 2 | | |
| 2001–02 | Fulham | 5 | 0 | | |
| 2002–03 | Fulham | 5 | 0 | | |
| 2003–04 | Fulham | 0 | 0 | **25** | **2** |

**TIMLIN, Michael (M)** **0 0**
b.London 19-3-85
*Source:* Trainee.

| | | | | | |
|---|---|---|---|---|---|
| 2002–03 | Fulham | 0 | 0 | | |
| 2003–04 | Fulham | 0 | 0 | | |

**VAN DER SAR, Edwin (G)** **385 1**
H: 6 5 W: 14 08 b.Voorhout 29-10-70
*Honours:* Holland 89 full caps.

| | | | | | |
|---|---|---|---|---|---|
| 1990–91 | Ajax | 9 | 0 | | |
| 1991–92 | Ajax | 0 | 0 | | |
| 1992–93 | Ajax | 19 | 0 | | |
| 1993–94 | Ajax | 32 | 0 | | |
| 1994–95 | Ajax | 33 | 0 | | |
| 1995–96 | Ajax | 33 | 0 | | |
| 1996–97 | Ajax | 33 | 0 | | |
| 1997–98 | Ajax | 33 | 1 | **192** | **1** |
| 1998–99 | Juventus | 34 | 0 | | |
| 1999–2000 | Juventus | 32 | 0 | | |
| 2000–01 | Juventus | 34 | 0 | **100** | **0** |
| 2001–02 | Fulham | 37 | 0 | | |
| 2002–03 | Fulham | 19 | 0 | | |
| 2003–04 | Fulham | 37 | 0 | **93** | **0** |

**VOLZ, Moritz (D)** **43 1**
H: 5 10 W: 12 06 b.Siegen 21-1-83
*Source:* Schalke.

| | | | | | |
|---|---|---|---|---|---|
| 1999–2000 | Arsenal | 0 | 0 | | |
| 2000–01 | Arsenal | 0 | 0 | | |
| 2001–02 | Arsenal | 0 | 0 | | |
| 2002–03 | Arsenal | 0 | 0 | | |
| 2002–03 | *Wimbledon* | 10 | 1 | **10** | **1** |
| 2003–04 | Arsenal | 0 | 0 | | |
| 2003–04 | Fulham | 33 | 0 | **33** | **0** |

**WATKINS, Robert (D)** **0 0**
b.Carshalton 14-10-85
*Source:* Trainee.

| | | | | | |
|---|---|---|---|---|---|
| 2003–04 | Fulham | 0 | 0 | | |

**Scholars**
Bagley, Nicholas; Davidson, Mark; James, Christopher; Kouadio, Ismael; Legate, Callum J; Mabbutt, Gary D; Milsom, Robert S; Nowacki, Aaron M

## GILLINGHAM (33)

**AGYEMANG, Patrick (F)** **153 26**
H: 6 1 W: 12 00 b.Walthamstow 20-9-80
*Source:* Trainee.

| | | | | | |
|---|---|---|---|---|---|
| 1998–99 | Wimbledon | 0 | 0 | | |
| 1999–2000 | Wimbledon | 0 | 0 | | |
| 1999–2000 | *Brentford* | 12 | 0 | **12** | **0** |
| 2000–01 | Wimbledon | 29 | 4 | | |
| 2001–02 | Wimbledon | 33 | 4 | | |
| 2002–03 | Wimbledon | 33 | 5 | | |
| 2003–04 | Wimbledon | 26 | 7 | **121** | **20** |
| 2003–04 | Gillingham | 20 | 6 | **20** | **6** |

**ASHBY, Barry (D)** **486 14**
H: 6 2 W: 14 05 b.Park Royal 2-11-70
*Source:* Trainee.

| | | | | | |
|---|---|---|---|---|---|
| 1988–89 | Watford | 0 | 0 | | |
| 1989–90 | Watford | 18 | 1 | | |
| 1990–91 | Watford | 23 | 0 | | |
| 1991–92 | Watford | 21 | 0 | | |
| 1992–93 | Watford | 35 | 0 | | |
| 1993–94 | Watford | 17 | 2 | **114** | **3** |
| 1993–94 | Brentford | 8 | 1 | | |
| 1994–95 | Brentford | 40 | 1 | | |
| 1995–96 | Brentford | 33 | 1 | | |
| 1996–97 | Brentford | 40 | 1 | **121** | **4** |
| 1997–98 | Gillingham | 43 | 0 | | |
| 1998–99 | Gillingham | 38 | 1 | | |
| 1999–2000 | Gillingham | 41 | 3 | | |
| 2000–01 | Gillingham | 40 | 1 | | |
| 2001–02 | Gillingham | 28 | 1 | | |
| 2002–03 | Gillingham | 38 | 0 | | |
| 2003–04 | Gillingham | 23 | 1 | **251** | **7** |

**AWUAH, Jones (F)** **4 0**
H: 5 11 W: 11 06 b.Ghana 10-7-83
*Source:* Scholar.

| | | | | | |
|---|---|---|---|---|---|
| 2002–03 | Gillingham | 4 | 0 | | |
| 2003–04 | Gillingham | 0 | 0 | **4** | **0** |

**BANKS, Steve (G)** **313 0**
H: 6 0 W: 13 12 b.Hillingdon 9-2-72
*Source:* Trainee.

| | | | | | |
|---|---|---|---|---|---|
| 1991–92 | West Ham U | 0 | 0 | | |
| 1992–93 | West Ham U | 0 | 0 | | |
| 1993–94 | Gillingham | 29 | 0 | | |
| 1994–95 | Gillingham | 38 | 0 | | |
| 1995–96 | Blackpool | 24 | 0 | | |
| 1996–97 | Blackpool | 46 | 0 | | |
| 1997–98 | Blackpool | 45 | 0 | | |
| 1998–99 | Blackpool | 35 | 0 | **150** | **0** |
| 1998–99 | Bolton W | 9 | 0 | | |
| 1999–2000 | Bolton W | 2 | 0 | | |
| 2000–01 | Bolton W | 9 | 0 | | |
| 2001–02 | Bolton W | 1 | 0 | | |
| 2001–02 | *Rochdale* | 15 | 0 | **15** | **0** |
| 2002–03 | Bolton W | 0 | 0 | **21** | **0** |
| 2002–03 | *Bradford C* | 9 | 0 | **9** | **0** |
| 2002–03 | Stoke C | 14 | 0 | **14** | **0** |
| 2003–04 | Wimbledon | 24 | 0 | **24** | **0** |
| 2003–04 | Gillingham | 13 | 0 | **80** | **0** |

**BARTRAM, Vince‡ (G)** **356 0**
H: 6 3 W: 15 05 b.Birmingham 7-8-68
*Source:* Local.

| | | | | | |
|---|---|---|---|---|---|
| 1985–86 | Wolverhampton W | 0 | 0 | | |
| 1986–87 | Wolverhampton W | 1 | 0 | | |
| 1987–88 | Wolverhampton W | 0 | 0 | | |
| 1988–89 | Wolverhampton W | 0 | 0 | | |
| 1989–90 | Wolverhampton W | 0 | 0 | | |
| 1989–90 | *Blackpool* | 9 | 0 | **9** | **0** |
| 1990–91 | Wolverhampton W | 4 | 0 | | |
| 1990–91 | *WBA* | 0 | 0 | | |
| 1991–92 | Bournemouth | 46 | 0 | | |
| 1992–93 | Bournemouth | 45 | 0 | | |
| 1993–94 | Bournemouth | 41 | 0 | **132** | **0** |
| 1994–95 | Arsenal | 11 | 0 | | |
| 1995–96 | Arsenal | 0 | 0 | | |
| 1996–97 | Arsenal | 0 | 0 | | |
| 1996–97 | *Wolverhampton W* | 0 | 0 | **5** | **0** |
| 1997–98 | Arsenal | 0 | 0 | **11** | **0** |
| 1997–98 | *Huddersfield T* | 12 | 0 | **12** | **0** |
| 1997–98 | Gillingham | 9 | 0 | | |
| 1998–99 | Gillingham | 44 | 0 | | |
| 1999–2000 | Gillingham | 43 | 0 | | |
| 2000–01 | Gillingham | 46 | 0 | | |
| 2001–02 | Gillingham | 36 | 0 | | |
| 2002–03 | Gillingham | 8 | 0 | | |
| 2003–04 | Gillingham | 1 | 0 | **187** | **0** |

**BECKWITH, Dean (D)** **0 0**
H: 6 3 W: 13 04 b.Southwark 18-9-83
*Source:* Scholar.

| | | | | | |
|---|---|---|---|---|---|
| 2003–04 | Gillingham | 0 | 0 | | |

**BOSSU, Bertrand (G)** **4 0**
H: 6 7 W: 14 00 b.Calais 14-10-80

| | | | | | |
|---|---|---|---|---|---|
| 1999–2000 | Barnet | 0 | 0 | | |
| 2000–01 | Barnet | 0 | 0 | | |
| 2001–02 | Barnet | 0 | 0 | | |
| 2002–03 | Barnet | 0 | 0 | | |
| From Hayes. | | | | | |
| 2003–04 | Gillingham | 4 | 0 | **4** | **0** |

**BROWN, Jason (G)** **71 0**
H: 6 0 W: 15 12 b.Southwark 18-5-82
*Source:* Charlton Ath Scholar. *Honours:* Wales Under-21.

| | | | | | |
|---|---|---|---|---|---|
| 2000–01 | Gillingham | 0 | 0 | | |
| 2001–02 | Gillingham | 10 | 0 | | |
| 2002–03 | Gillingham | 39 | 0 | | |
| 2003–04 | Gillingham | 22 | 0 | **71** | **0** |

**COX, Ian (D)** **335 21**
H: 6 1 W: 12 07 b.Croydon 25-3-71
*Source:* Carshalton Ath. *Honours:* Trinidad & Tobago 5 full caps.

| | | | | | |
|---|---|---|---|---|---|
| 1993–94 | Crystal Palace | 0 | 0 | | |
| 1994–95 | Crystal Palace | 11 | 0 | | |
| 1995–96 | Crystal Palace | 4 | 0 | **15** | **0** |
| 1995–96 | Bournemouth | 8 | 0 | | |
| 1996–97 | Bournemouth | 44 | 8 | | |
| 1997–98 | Bournemouth | 46 | 3 | | |
| 1998–99 | Bournemouth | 46 | 5 | | |
| 1999–2000 | Bournemouth | 28 | 0 | **172** | **16** |
| 1999–2000 | Burnley | 17 | 1 | | |
| 2000–01 | Burnley | 38 | 1 | | |
| 2001–02 | Burnley | 34 | 2 | | |
| 2002–03 | Burnley | 26 | 1 | **115** | **5** |
| 2003–04 | Gillingham | 33 | 0 | **33** | **0** |

**CROFTS, Andrew (F)** **9 0**
H: 5 10 W: 11 08 b.Chatham 29-5-84
*Source:* Trainee.

| | | | | | |
|---|---|---|---|---|---|
| 2000–01 | Gillingham | 1 | 0 | | |
| 2001–02 | Gillingham | 0 | 0 | | |
| 2002–03 | Gillingham | 0 | 0 | | |
| 2003–04 | Gillingham | 8 | 0 | **9** | **0** |

**EDUSEI, Akwasi§ (M)** **2 0**
H: 5 9 W: 11 00 b.London 12-9-86

| | | | | | |
|---|---|---|---|---|---|
| 2002–03 | Gillingham | 2 | 0 | | |
| 2003–04 | Gillingham | 0 | 0 | **2** | **0** |

**HENDERSON, Darius (F)** **85 13**
H: 6 2 W: 13 02 b.Doncaster 7-9-81
*Source:* Trainee.

| | | | | | |
|---|---|---|---|---|---|
| 1999–2000 | Reading | 6 | 0 | | |
| 2000–01 | Reading | 4 | 0 | | |
| 2001–02 | Reading | 38 | 7 | | |
| 2002–03 | Reading | 22 | 4 | | |
| 2003–04 | Reading | 1 | 0 | **71** | **11** |
| 2003–04 | *Brighton & HA* | 10 | 2 | **10** | **2** |
| 2003–04 | Gillingham | 4 | 0 | **4** | **0** |

**HESSENTHALER, Andy (M)** **465 30**
H: 5 8 W: 11 05 b.Gravesend 17-6-65
*Source:* Dartford, Redbridge Forest.

| | | | | | |
|---|---|---|---|---|---|
| 1991–92 | Watford | 35 | 1 | | |
| 1992–93 | Watford | 45 | 3 | | |
| 1993–94 | Watford | 42 | 5 | | |
| 1994–95 | Watford | 43 | 2 | | |
| 1995–96 | Watford | 30 | 0 | **195** | **11** |
| 1996–97 | Gillingham | 38 | 2 | | |
| 1997–98 | Gillingham | 42 | 0 | | |
| 1998–99 | Gillingham | 39 | 7 | | |
| 1999–2000 | Gillingham | 42 | 5 | | |
| 2000–01 | Gillingham | 23 | 2 | | |
| 2001–02 | Gillingham | 17 | 0 | | |
| 2002–03 | Gillingham | 33 | 1 | | |
| 2003–04 | Gillingham | 36 | 2 | **270** | **19** |

**HILLS, John (D)** **212 19**
H: 5 8 W: 12 04 b.St Annes-on-Sea 21-4-78
*Source:* Trainee.

| | | | | | |
|---|---|---|---|---|---|
| 1995–96 | Blackpool | 0 | 0 | | |
| 1995–96 | Everton | 0 | 0 | | |
| 1996–97 | Everton | 3 | 0 | | |
| 1996–97 | *Swansea C* | 11 | 0 | | |
| 1997–98 | Everton | 0 | 0 | **3** | **0** |
| 1997–98 | *Swansea C* | 7 | 1 | **18** | **1** |

1997–98 Blackpool 19 1
1998–99 Blackpool 28 1
1999–2000 Blackpool 33 2
2000–01 Blackpool 18 2
2001–02 Blackpool 37 5
2002–03 Blackpool 27 5 **162 16**
2003–04 Gillingham 29 2 **29 2**

**HOPE, Chris (D) 462 29**
H: 6 1 W: 12 11 b.Sheffield 14-11-72
*Source:* Darlington.
1991–92 Nottingham F 0 0
1992–93 Nottingham F 0 0
1993–94 Scunthorpe U 41 0
1994–95 Scunthorpe U 24 0
1995–96 Scunthorpe U 40 3
1996–97 Scunthorpe U 46 3
1997–98 Scunthorpe U 46 5
1998–99 Scunthorpe U 46 5
1999–2000 Scunthorpe U 44 3 **287 19**
2000–01 Gillingham 46 2
2001–02 Gillingham 46 4
2002–03 Gillingham 46 1
2003–04 Gillingham 37 3 **175 10**

**JAMES, Kevin‡ (F) 49 4**
H: 5 8 W: 12 00 b.Southwark 3-1-80
*Source:* Trainee.
1998–99 Charlton Ath 0 0
1999–2000 Charlton Ath 0 0
2000–01 Gillingham 7 0
2001–02 Gillingham 10 0
2002–03 Gillingham 15 3
2003–04 Gillingham 17 1 **49 4**

**JARVIS, Matthew§ (M) 10 0**
H: 5 8 W: 11 07 b.Middlesbrough 22-5-86
*Source:* Scholar.
2003–04 Gillingham 10 0 **10 0**

**JOHNSON, Leon (D) 86 3**
H: 6 1 W: 12 10 b.London 10-5-81
*Source:* Scholarship.
1999–2000 Southend U 0 0
2000–01 Southend U 20 1
2001–02 Southend U 28 2 **48 3**
2002–03 Gillingham 18 0
2003–04 Gillingham 20 0 **38 0**

**JOHNSON, Tommy (F) 344 111**
H: 6 0 W: 13 01 b.Newcastle 15-1-71
*Source:* Trainee. *Honours:* England Under-21.
1988–89 Notts Co 10 4
1989–90 Notts Co 40 18
1990–91 Notts Co 37 16
1991–92 Notts Co 31 9 **118 47**
1991–92 Derby Co 12 2
1992–93 Derby Co 35 8
1993–94 Derby Co 37 13
1994–95 Derby Co 14 7 **98 30**
1994–95 Aston Villa 14 4
1995–96 Aston Villa 23 5
1996–97 Aston Villa 20 4 **57 13**
1996–97 Celtic 4 1
1997–98 Celtic 2 0
1998–99 Celtic 3 3
1999–2000 Celtic 10 9
1999–2000 *Everton* 3 0 **3 0**
2000–01 Celtic 0 0
2001–02 Celtic 0 0 **19 13**
2001–02 Sheffield W 8 3 **8 3**
2002–03 Gillingham 26 2
2003–04 Gillingham 15 3 **41 5**

**NOSWORTHY, Nayron (D) 137 5**
H: 6 1 W: 13 00 b.Brixton 11-10-80
*Source:* Trainee.
1998–99 Gillingham 3 0
1999–2000 Gillingham 29 1
2000–01 Gillingham 10 0
2001–02 Gillingham 29 0
2002–03 Gillingham 39 2
2003–04 Gillingham 27 2 **137 5**

**PERPETUINI, David* (M) 102 6**
H: 5 9 W: 12 01 b.Hitchin 26-9-79
*Source:* Trainee.
1997–98 Watford 0 0
1998–99 Watford 1 0
1999–2000 Watford 13 1
2000–01 Watford 5 0 **19 1**
2001–02 Gillingham 34 1
2002–03 Gillingham 29 2
2003–04 Gillingham 20 2 **83 5**

**PHILLIPS, Michael‡ (M) 1 0**
H: 5 10 W: 10 00 b.Camberwell 22-1-83
*Source:* Trainee.
2000–01 Gillingham 1 0
2001–02 Gillingham 0 0
2002–03 Gillingham 0 0
2003–04 Gillingham 0 0 **1 0**

**POUTON, Alan (M) 230 19**
H: 6 0 W: 12 10 b.Newcastle 1-2-77
*Source:* Newcastle U Trainee.
1995–96 Oxford U 0 0
1995–96 York C 0 0
1996–97 York C 22 1
1997–98 York C 41 5
1998–99 York C 27 1
1999–2000 York C 0 0 **90 7**
1999–2000 Grimsby T 35 1
2000–01 Grimsby T 21 1
2001–02 Grimsby T 35 5
2002–03 Grimsby T 25 5
2003–04 Grimsby T 5 0 **121 12**
2003–04 Gillingham 19 0 **19 0**

**ROSE, Richard (D) 35 0**
H: 6 2 W: 11 10 b.Pembury 8-9-82
*Source:* Trainee.
2000–01 Gillingham 4 0
2001–02 Gillingham 3 0
2002–03 Gillingham 2 0
2002–03 *Bristol R* 9 0 **9 0**
2003–04 Gillingham 17 0 **26 0**

**SAUNDERS, Mark (M) 241 26**
H: 6 1 W: 13 02 b.Reading 23-7-71
*Source:* Tiverton.
1995–96 Plymouth Arg 10 1
1996–97 Plymouth Arg 25 3
1997–98 Plymouth Arg 37 7 **72 11**
1998–99 Gillingham 34 4
1999–2000 Gillingham 26 1
2000–01 Gillingham 35 5
2001–02 Gillingham 19 1
2002–03 Gillingham 34 3
2003–04 Gillingham 21 1 **169 15**

**SIDIBE, Mamady (F) 102 15**
H: 6 4 W: 14 03 b.Mali 18-12-79
*Source:* CA Paris. *Honours:* Mali 7 full caps.
2001–02 Swansea C 31 7 **31 7**
2002–03 Gillingham 30 3
2003–04 Gillingham 41 5 **71 8**

**SMITH, Paul (M) 480 30**
H: 6 0 W: 13 13 b.East Ham 18-9-71
*Source:* Trainee.
1989–90 Southend U 10 1
1990–91 Southend U 2 0
1991–92 Southend U 0 0
1992–93 Southend U 8 0 **20 1**
1993–94 Brentford 32 3
1994–95 Brentford 35 3
1995–96 Brentford 46 4
1996–97 Brentford 46 1 **159 11**
1997–98 Gillingham 46 3
1998–99 Gillingham 45 6
1999–2000 Gillingham 44 1
2000–01 Gillingham 42 3
2001–02 Gillingham 46 2
2002–03 Gillingham 45 3
2003–04 Gillingham 33 0 **301 18**

**SOUTHALL, Nicky (M) 450 48**
H: 5 11 W: 12 07 b.Stockton 28-1-72
*Source:* Trainee.
1990–91 Hartlepool U 0 0
1991–92 Hartlepool U 22 3
1992–93 Hartlepool U 39 6
1993–94 Hartlepool U 40 9
1994–95 Hartlepool U 37 6 **138 24**
1995–96 Grimsby T 33 2
1996–97 Grimsby T 34 3
1997–98 Grimsby T 5 0 **72 5**
1997–98 Gillingham 23 2
1998–99 Gillingham 42 4
1999–2000 Gillingham 45 9
2000–01 Gillingham 44 2
2001–02 Bolton W 18 1
2002–03 Bolton W 0 0 **18 1**
2002–03 *Norwich C* 9 0 **9 0**
2002–03 Gillingham 24 1
2003–04 Gillingham 35 0 **213 18**

**SPILLER, Danny (M) 50 6**
H: 5 9 W: 10 12 b.Maidstone 10-10-81
*Source:* Trainee.
2000–01 Gillingham 0 0
2001–02 Gillingham 1 0
2002–03 Gillingham 10 0
2003–04 Gillingham 39 6 **50 6**

**WALES, Gary# (F) 109 26**
H: 5 10 W: 11 02 b.East Calder 4-1-79
*Source:* Links U.
1997–98 Hamilton A 3 0
1998–99 Hamilton A 30 11 **33 11**
1999–2000 Hearts 24 6
2000–01 Hearts 7 1
2001–02 Hearts 32 6
2003–04 Hearts 0 0 **63 13**
2003–04 *Walsall* 7 1 **7 1**
2003–04 Gillingham 6 1 **6 1**

**WALLACE, Rod‡ (F) 472 152**
H: 5 7 W: 11 00 b.Lewisham 2-10-69
*Source:* Trainee. *Honours:* England Under-21, B.
1987–88 Southampton 15 1
1988–89 Southampton 38 12
1989–90 Southampton 38 18
1990–91 Southampton 37 14 **128 45**
1991–92 Leeds U 34 11
1992–93 Leeds U 32 7
1993–94 Leeds U 37 17
1994–95 Leeds U 32 4
1995–96 Leeds U 24 1
1996–97 Leeds U 22 3
1997–98 Leeds U 31 10 **212 53**
1998–99 Rangers 34 18
1999–2000 Rangers 28 16
2000–01 Rangers 15 5 **77 39**
2001–02 Bolton W 19 3 **19 3**
2002–03 Gillingham 22 11
2003–04 Gillingham 14 1 **36 12**

**Scholars**
Boorman, Richard J; Carew, Ashley; Dumas, Ashley D F; Fobi-Edusei, Akwasi; Green, Mark; Howell, Luke A; Jarvis, Matthew T; Knowles, Daniel; Lawson, Danny J L; Marsden, Darren M; Solomon, Leon; Vella, Daniel M T; Wallis, Jonathan

## GRIMSBY T (34)

**ANDERSON, Iain (M) 247 35**
H: 5 8 W: 9 07 b.Glasgow 23-7-77
*Source:* X-Form. *Honours:* Scotland Under-21.
1994–95 Dundee 10 1
1995–96 Dundee 17 0
1996–97 Dundee 35 5
1997–98 Dundee 36 6
1998–99 Dundee 28 3 **126 15**
1999–2000 Toulouse 3 0 **3 0**
1999–2000 Preston NE 12 2
2000–01 Preston NE 31 6
2001–02 Preston NE 31 5
2002–03 Preston NE 8 0 **82 13**
2002–03 *Tranmere R* 7 2 **7 2**
2003–04 Grimsby T 29 5 **29 5**

**ANTOINE-CURIER, Mickael (F) 38 7**
H: 6 0 W: 12 00 b.Orsay 5-3-83
2000–01 Preston NE 0 0
2001–02 Nottingham F 0 0
2002–03 Nottingham F 0 0
2002–03 *Brentford* 11 3 **11 3**
2003–04 Burnley 0 0
2003–04 Oldham Ath 8 2 **8 2**
2003–04 Kidderminster H 1 0 **1 0**
2003–04 Rochdale 8 1 **8 1**
2003–04 Sheffield W 1 0 **1 0**
2003–04 Notts Co 4 1 **4 1**
2003–04 Grimsby T 5 0 **5 0**

**BARNARD, Darren* (D) 344 49**
H: 5 9 W: 13 00 b.Rinteln 30-11-71
*Source:* Wokingham T. *Honours:* England Schools, Wales 22 full caps.

| | | | | | |
|---|---|---|---|---|---|
| 1990–91 | Chelsea | 0 | 0 | | |
| 1991–92 | Chelsea | 4 | 0 | | |
| 1992–93 | Chelsea | 13 | 1 | | |
| 1993–94 | Chelsea | 12 | 1 | | |
| 1994–95 | Chelsea | 0 | 0 | | |
| 1994–95 | *Reading* | 4 | 0 | **4** | **0** |
| 1995–96 | Chelsea | 0 | 0 | **29** | **2** |
| 1995–96 | Bristol C | 34 | 4 | | |
| 1996–97 | Bristol C | 44 | 11 | **78** | **15** |
| 1997–98 | Barnsley | 35 | 2 | | |
| 1998–99 | Barnsley | 26 | 4 | | |
| 1999–2000 | Barnsley | 41 | 13 | | |
| 2000–01 | Barnsley | 30 | 2 | | |
| 2001–02 | Barnsley | 38 | 7 | **170** | **28** |
| 2002–03 | Grimsby T | 29 | 2 | | |
| 2003–04 | Grimsby T | 34 | 2 | **63** | **4** |

**BOLDER, Chris* (M) 19 0**
H: 5 11 W: 12 00 b.Hull 19-8-82
*Source:* Hull C Scholar.

| | | | | | |
|---|---|---|---|---|---|
| 2001–02 | Grimsby T | 0 | 0 | | |
| 2002–03 | Grimsby T | 12 | 0 | | |
| 2003–04 | Grimsby T | 7 | 0 | **19** | **0** |

**CAMPBELL, Stuart* (M) 194 12**
H: 5 10 W: 12 00 b.Corby 9-12-77
*Source:* Trainee. *Honours:* Scotland Under-21.

| | | | | | |
|---|---|---|---|---|---|
| 1996–97 | Leicester C | 10 | 0 | | |
| 1997–98 | Leicester C | 11 | 0 | | |
| 1998–99 | Leicester C | 12 | 0 | | |
| 1999–2000 | Leicester C | 4 | 0 | | |
| 1999–2000 | *Birmingham C* | 2 | 0 | **2** | **0** |
| 2000–01 | Leicester C | 0 | 0 | **37** | **0** |
| 2000–01 | *Grimsby T* | 38 | 2 | | |
| 2001–02 | Grimsby T | 33 | 3 | | |
| 2002–03 | Grimsby T | 45 | 6 | | |
| 2003–04 | Grimsby T | 39 | 1 | **155** | **12** |

**CAS, Marcel‡ (M) 150 16**
H: 6 1 W: 12 08 b.Breda 30-4-72

| | | | | | |
|---|---|---|---|---|---|
| 1997–98 | RBC | 27 | 3 | | |
| 1998–99 | RBC | 9 | 1 | | |
| 1999–2000 | RBC | 30 | 2 | **66** | **6** |
| 2001–02 | Notts Co | 40 | 6 | | |
| 2002–03 | Notts Co | 18 | 2 | **58** | **8** |
| 2002–03 | Sheffield U | 6 | 0 | **6** | **0** |
| 2003–04 | Grimsby T | 20 | 2 | **20** | **2** |

**COLDICOTT, Stacy (M) 299 6**
H: 5 8 W: 12 08 b.Worcester 29-4-74
*Source:* Trainee.

| | | | | | |
|---|---|---|---|---|---|
| 1991–92 | WBA | 0 | 0 | | |
| 1992–93 | WBA | 14 | 0 | | |
| 1993–94 | WBA | 5 | 0 | | |
| 1994–95 | WBA | 11 | 0 | | |
| 1995–96 | WBA | 33 | 0 | | |
| 1996–97 | WBA | 19 | 3 | | |
| 1996–97 | *Cardiff C* | 6 | 0 | **6** | **0** |
| 1997–98 | WBA | 22 | 0 | **104** | **3** |
| 1998–99 | Grimsby T | 37 | 0 | | |
| 1999–2000 | Grimsby T | 44 | 2 | | |
| 2000–01 | Grimsby T | 37 | 1 | | |
| 2001–02 | Grimsby T | 26 | 0 | | |
| 2002–03 | Grimsby T | 31 | 0 | | |
| 2003–04 | Grimsby T | 14 | 0 | **189** | **3** |

**CRANE, Tony (D) 86 7**
H: 6 5 W: 12 05 b.Liverpool 8-9-82
*Source:* Trainee. *Honours:* England Youth.

| | | | | | |
|---|---|---|---|---|---|
| 1999–2000 | Sheffield W | 0 | 0 | | |
| 2000–01 | Sheffield W | 15 | 2 | | |
| 2001–02 | Sheffield W | 15 | 0 | | |
| 2002–03 | Sheffield W | 19 | 2 | **49** | **4** |
| 2003–04 | Grimsby T | 37 | 3 | **37** | **3** |

**CROWE, Jason (D) 135 5**
H: 5 9 W: 10 09 b.Sidcup 30-9-78
*Source:* Trainee. *Honours:* England Schools, Youth.

| | | | | | |
|---|---|---|---|---|---|
| 1995–96 | Arsenal | 0 | 0 | | |
| 1996–97 | Arsenal | 0 | 0 | | |
| 1997–98 | Arsenal | 0 | 0 | | |
| 1998–99 | Arsenal | 0 | 0 | | |
| 1998–99 | *Crystal Palace* | 8 | 0 | **8** | **0** |
| 1999–2000 | Portsmouth | 25 | 0 | | |
| 2000–01 | Portsmouth | 23 | 0 | | |
| 2000–01 | *Brentford* | 9 | 0 | **9** | **0** |
| 2001–02 | Portsmouth | 22 | 1 | | |
| 2002–03 | Portsmouth | 16 | 4 | **86** | **5** |
| 2003–04 | Grimsby T | 32 | 0 | **32** | **0** |

**DAVISON, Aidan (G) 253 0**
H: 6 1 W: 13 12 b.Sedgefield 11-5-68
*Source:* Billingham Synthonia. *Honours:* Northern Ireland B, 3 full caps.

| | | | | | |
|---|---|---|---|---|---|
| 1987–88 | Notts Co | 0 | 0 | | |
| 1988–89 | Notts Co | 1 | 0 | | |
| 1989–90 | Notts Co | 0 | 0 | **1** | **0** |
| 1989–90 | *Leyton Orient* | 0 | 0 | | |
| 1989–90 | Bury | 0 | 0 | | |
| 1989–90 | *Chester C* | 0 | 0 | | |
| 1990–91 | Bury | 0 | 0 | | |
| 1990–91 | *Blackpool* | 0 | 0 | | |
| 1991–92 | Millwall | 33 | 0 | | |
| 1992–93 | Millwall | 1 | 0 | **34** | **0** |
| 1993–94 | Bolton W | 31 | 0 | | |
| 1994–95 | Bolton W | 4 | 0 | | |
| 1995–96 | Bolton W | 2 | 0 | | |
| 1996–97 | Bolton W | 0 | 0 | **37** | **0** |
| 1996–97 | *Ipswich T* | 0 | 0 | | |
| 1996–97 | *Hull C* | 9 | 0 | **9** | **0** |
| 1996–97 | Bradford C | 10 | 0 | | |
| 1997–98 | Grimsby T | 42 | 0 | | |
| 1998–99 | Grimsby T | 35 | 0 | | |
| 1999–2000 | Grimsby T | 0 | 0 | | |
| 1999–2000 | Sheffield U | 2 | 0 | **2** | **0** |
| 1999–2000 | Bradford C | 6 | 0 | | |
| 2000–01 | Bradford C | 2 | 0 | | |
| 2001–02 | Bradford C | 9 | 0 | | |
| 2002–03 | Bradford C | 34 | 0 | **61** | **0** |
| 2003–04 | Grimsby T | 32 | 0 | **109** | **0** |

**EDWARDS, Mike* (D) 216 7**
H: 6 0 W: 12 10 b.North Ferriby 25-4-80
*Source:* Trainee.

| | | | | | |
|---|---|---|---|---|---|
| 1997–98 | Hull C | 21 | 0 | | |
| 1998–99 | Hull C | 30 | 0 | | |
| 1999–2000 | Hull C | 40 | 1 | | |
| 2000–01 | Hull C | 42 | 4 | | |
| 2001–02 | Hull C | 39 | 1 | | |
| 2002–03 | Hull C | 6 | 0 | **178** | **6** |
| 2002–03 | Colchester U | 5 | 0 | **5** | **0** |
| 2003–04 | Grimsby T | 33 | 1 | **33** | **1** |

**FORD, Simon* (D) 78 4**
H: 6 1 W: 12 04 b.Lincoln 17-11-81
*Source:* Charlton Ath scholar.

| | | | | | |
|---|---|---|---|---|---|
| 2001–02 | Grimsby T | 13 | 1 | | |
| 2002–03 | Grimsby T | 39 | 2 | | |
| 2003–04 | Grimsby T | 26 | 1 | **78** | **4** |

**HAMILTON, Des‡ (M) 181 6**
H: 5 11 W: 14 00 b.Bradford 15-8-76
*Source:* Trainee. *Honours:* England Under-21.

| | | | | | |
|---|---|---|---|---|---|
| 1993–94 | Bradford C | 2 | 1 | | |
| 1994–95 | Bradford C | 30 | 1 | | |
| 1995–96 | Bradford C | 24 | 3 | | |
| 1996–97 | Bradford C | 32 | 0 | **88** | **5** |
| 1996–97 | Newcastle U | 0 | 0 | | |
| 1997–98 | Newcastle U | 12 | 0 | | |
| 1998–99 | Newcastle U | 0 | 0 | | |
| 1998–99 | *Sheffield U* | 6 | 0 | **6** | **0** |
| 1998–99 | *Huddersfield T* | 10 | 1 | **10** | **1** |
| 1999–2000 | Newcastle U | 0 | 0 | | |
| 1999–2000 | *Norwich C* | 7 | 0 | **7** | **0** |
| 2000–01 | Newcastle U | 0 | 0 | **12** | **0** |
| 2000–01 | *Tranmere R* | 6 | 0 | **6** | **0** |
| 2001–02 | Cardiff C | 19 | 0 | | |
| 2002–03 | Cardiff C | 6 | 0 | **25** | **0** |
| 2003–04 | Grimsby T | 27 | 0 | **27** | **0** |

**HOCKLESS, Graham (M) 14 2**
H: 5 7 W: 10 02 b.Hull 20-10-82

| | | | | | |
|---|---|---|---|---|---|
| 2001–02 | Grimsby T | 0 | 0 | | |
| 2002–03 | Grimsby T | 1 | 0 | | |
| 2003–04 | Grimsby T | 13 | 2 | **14** | **2** |

**HUGHES, Bradley‡ (G) 0 0**
H: 5 11 W: 12 06 b.Hemel Hempstead 24-3-84
*Source:* Scholar.

| | | | | | |
|---|---|---|---|---|---|
| 2003–04 | Grimsby T | 0 | 0 | | |

**JEVONS, Phil* (F) 95 21**
H: 5 10 W: 12 00 b.Liverpool 1-8-79
*Source:* Trainee.

| | | | | | |
|---|---|---|---|---|---|
| 1996–97 | Everton | 0 | 0 | | |
| 1997–98 | Everton | 0 | 0 | | |
| 1998–99 | Everton | 1 | 0 | | |
| 1999–2000 | Everton | 3 | 0 | | |
| 2000–01 | Everton | 4 | 0 | **8** | **0** |
| 2001–02 | Grimsby T | 31 | 6 | | |
| 2002–03 | Grimsby T | 3 | 0 | | |
| 2002–03 | *Hull C* | 24 | 3 | **24** | **3** |
| 2003–04 | Grimsby T | 29 | 12 | **63** | **18** |

**LAWRENCE, Jamie# (M) 262 18**
H: 5 9 W: 12 10 b.Balham 8-3-70
*Source:* Cowes. *Honours:* Jamaica 19 full caps.

| | | | | | |
|---|---|---|---|---|---|
| 1993–94 | Sunderland | 4 | 0 | **4** | **0** |
| 1993–94 | Doncaster R | 9 | 1 | | |
| 1994–95 | Doncaster R | 16 | 2 | **25** | **3** |
| 1994–95 | Leicester C | 17 | 1 | | |
| 1995–96 | Leicester C | 15 | 0 | | |
| 1996–97 | Leicester C | 15 | 0 | **47** | **1** |
| 1997–98 | Bradford C | 43 | 3 | | |
| 1998–99 | Bradford C | 35 | 2 | | |
| 1999–2000 | Bradford C | 23 | 3 | | |
| 2000–01 | Bradford C | 17 | 1 | | |
| 2001–02 | Bradford C | 21 | 2 | | |
| 2002–03 | Bradford C | 16 | 1 | **155** | **12** |
| 2002–03 | Walsall | 5 | 0 | | |
| 2003–04 | Walsall | 17 | 1 | **22** | **1** |
| 2003–04 | *Wigan Ath* | 4 | 0 | **4** | **0** |
| 2003–04 | Grimsby T | 5 | 1 | **5** | **1** |

**MANSARAM, Darren (F) 65 5**
H: 6 1 W: 11 02 b.Doncaster 25-6-84
*Source:* Scholar.

| | | | | | |
|---|---|---|---|---|---|
| 2002–03 | Grimsby T | 34 | 2 | | |
| 2003–04 | Grimsby T | 31 | 3 | **65** | **5** |

**McDERMOTT, John (D) 553 7**
H: 5 7 W: 10 13 b.Middlesbrough 3-2-69
*Source:* Trainee.

| | | | | | |
|---|---|---|---|---|---|
| 1986–87 | Grimsby T | 13 | 0 | | |
| 1987–88 | Grimsby T | 28 | 0 | | |
| 1988–89 | Grimsby T | 38 | 1 | | |
| 1989–90 | Grimsby T | 39 | 0 | | |
| 1990–91 | Grimsby T | 43 | 0 | | |
| 1991–92 | Grimsby T | 39 | 1 | | |
| 1992–93 | Grimsby T | 38 | 2 | | |
| 1993–94 | Grimsby T | 26 | 0 | | |
| 1994–95 | Grimsby T | 12 | 0 | | |
| 1995–96 | Grimsby T | 28 | 1 | | |
| 1996–97 | Grimsby T | 29 | 1 | | |
| 1997–98 | Grimsby T | 41 | 1 | | |
| 1998–99 | Grimsby T | 37 | 0 | | |
| 1999–2000 | Grimsby T | 26 | 0 | | |
| 2000–01 | Grimsby T | 36 | 0 | | |
| 2001–02 | Grimsby T | 24 | 0 | | |
| 2002–03 | Grimsby T | 35 | 0 | | |
| 2003–04 | Grimsby T | 21 | 0 | **553** | **7** |

**NIMMO, Liam§ (F) 2 0**
H: 6 0 W: 11 05 b.Boston 28-12-84
*Source:* Scholar.

| | | | | | |
|---|---|---|---|---|---|
| 2003–04 | Grimsby T | 2 | 0 | **2** | **0** |

**PARKER, Wesley§ (D) 9 0**
H: 5 8 W: 10 05 b.Boston 7-12-83
*Source:* Scholar.

| | | | | | |
|---|---|---|---|---|---|
| 2002–03 | Grimsby T | 5 | 0 | | |
| 2003–04 | Grimsby T | 4 | 0 | **9** | **0** |

**PETTINGER, Andrew* (G) 3 0**
H: 6 0 W: 12 02 b.Doncaster 21-4-84
*Source:* Scunthorpe U.

| | | | | | |
|---|---|---|---|---|---|
| 2000–01 | Everton | 0 | 0 | | |
| 2001–02 | Everton | 0 | 0 | | |
| 2002–03 | Everton | 0 | 0 | | |
| 2002–03 | Grimsby T | 0 | 0 | | |
| 2003–04 | Grimsby T | 3 | 0 | **3** | **0** |

**RANKIN, Isiah# (F) 137 27**
H: 5 10 W: 11 00 b.London 22-5-78
*Source:* Trainee.

| | | | | | |
|---|---|---|---|---|---|
| 1995–96 | Arsenal | 0 | 0 | | |
| 1996–97 | Arsenal | 0 | 0 | | |
| 1997–98 | Arsenal | 1 | 0 | **1** | **0** |
| 1997–98 | *Colchester U* | 11 | 5 | **11** | **5** |
| 1998–99 | Bradford C | 27 | 4 | | |
| 1999–2000 | Bradford C | 9 | 0 | | |
| 1999–2000 | *Birmingham C* | 13 | 4 | **13** | **4** |
| 2000–01 | Bradford C | 1 | 0 | **37** | **4** |
| 2000–01 | *Bolton W* | 16 | 2 | **16** | **2** |
| 2000–01 | Barnsley | 9 | 1 | | |
| 2001–02 | Barnsley | 9 | 1 | | |
| 2002–03 | Barnsley | 9 | 1 | | |

2003–04 Barnsley 20 5 **47 8**
2003–04 Grimsby T 12 4 **12 4**

**ROWAN, Jonathan* (F) 52 6**
H: 5 10 W: 11 06 b.Grimsby 29-11-81
2000–01 Grimsby T 5 0
2001–02 Grimsby T 24 4
2002–03 Grimsby T 9 0
2003–04 Grimsby T 14 2 **52 6**

**SOAMES, David§ (F) 20 1**
H: 5 5 W: 10 08 b.Grimsby 10-2-84
*Source:* Scholar.
2002–03 Grimsby T 10 1
2003–04 Grimsby T 10 0 **20 1**

**THORRINGTON, John‡ (M) 70 7**
H: 5 8 W: 10 06 b.Johannesburg 10-7-79
*Source:* US College. *Honours:* USA 1 full cap.
1997–98 Manchester U 0 0
1998–99 Manchester U 0 0
1999–2000 Manchester U 0 0
2000–01 Huddersfield T 0 0
2001–02 Huddersfield T 31 6
2002–03 Huddersfield T 31 1
2003–04 Huddersfield T 5 0 **67 7**
2003–04 Grimsby T 3 0 **3 0**

**WARD, Iain* (D) 12 0**
H: 6 0 W: 10 10 b.Cleethorpes 13-5-83
2000–01 Grimsby T 0 0
2001–02 Grimsby T 1 0
2002–03 Grimsby T 11 0
2003–04 Grimsby T 0 0 **12 0**

**WARHURST, Paul† (M) 329 17**
H: 6 0 W: 13 00 b.Stockport 26-9-69
*Source:* Trainee. *Honours:* England Under-21.
1987–88 Manchester C 0 0
1988–89 Oldham Ath 4 0
1989–90 Oldham Ath 30 1
1990–91 Oldham Ath 33 1 **67 2**
1991–92 Sheffield W 33 0
1992–93 Sheffield W 29 6
1993–94 Sheffield W 4 0 **66 6**
1993–94 Blackburn R 9 0
1994–95 Blackburn R 27 2
1995–96 Blackburn R 10 0
1996–97 Blackburn R 11 2 **57 4**
1997–98 Crystal Palace 22 3
1998–99 Crystal Palace 5 1 **27 4**
1998–99 Bolton W 20 0
1999–2000 Bolton W 19 0
2000–01 Bolton W 20 0
2001–02 Bolton W 25 0
2002–03 Bolton W 7 0 **91 0**
2002–03 *Stoke C* 5 1 **5 1**
2003–04 Chesterfield 4 0 **4 0**
2003–04 Barnsley 4 0 **4 0**
2003–04 Carlisle U 1 0 **1 0**
2003–04 Grimsby T 7 0 **7 0**

**WHEELER, Kirk (D) 0 0**
H: 6 0 W: 12 01 b.Grimsby 13-6-84
2002–03 Grimsby T 0 0
2003–04 Grimsby T 0 0

**YOUNG, Greg (D) 18 0**
H: 6 2 W: 12 05 b.Doncaster 25-4-83
2002–03 Grimsby T 1 0
2003–04 Grimsby T 17 0 **18 0**

**Scholars**
Ashton, Paul A; Carchedi, Giovanni R; Chamberlain, Miles H; Davey, James A; Haseley, Ashley; Hegarty, Nicholas I; Hildred, Ashley; Howard, Ben A C; Huckett, Paul M; Hyam, Christopher; Lightowler, Joseph; Morfitt, Adrian J; Newton, Mark; Nimmo, Liam; Parker, Liam S; Parker, Wesley; Richardson, Oliver W; Smith, Michael G; Soames, David M; Stares, Matthew; Ward, Andrew S

**Non Contract**
Warhurst, Paul

## HARTLEPOOL U (35)

**BARRON, Micky (D) 271 3**
H: 5 11 W: 11 10 b.Lumley 22-12-74
*Source:* Trainee.
1992–93 Middlesbrough 0 0
1993–94 Middlesbrough 2 0
1994–95 Middlesbrough 0 0
1995–96 Middlesbrough 1 0
1996–97 Middlesbrough 0 0 **3 0**
1996–97 *Hartlepool U* 16 0
1997–98 Hartlepool U 33 0
1998–99 Hartlepool U 38 1
1999–2000 Hartlepool U 40 0
2000–01 Hartlepool U 28 0
2001–02 Hartlepool U 39 1
2002–03 Hartlepool U 42 0
2003–04 Hartlepool U 32 1 **268 3**

**BASS, Jon‡ (D) 102 1**
H: 6 0 W: 12 02 b.Weston-Super-Mare 1-1-76
*Source:* Trainee. *Honours:* England Schools.
1994–95 Birmingham C 0 0
1995–96 Birmingham C 5 0
1996–97 Birmingham C 13 0
1996–97 *Carlisle U* 3 0 **3 0**
1997–98 Birmingham C 30 0
1998–99 Birmingham C 11 0
1999–2000 Birmingham C 8 0
1999–2000 *Gillingham* 7 0 **7 0**
2000–01 Birmingham C 1 0 **68 0**
2001–02 Hartlepool U 20 1
2002–03 Hartlepool U 4 0
2003–04 Hartlepool U 0 0 **24 1**

**BOYD, Adam (F) 92 31**
H: 5 9 W: 10 12 b.Hartlepool 25-5-82
*Source:* Scholarship.
1999–2000 Hartlepool U 4 1
2000–01 Hartlepool U 5 0
2001–02 Hartlepool U 29 9
2002–03 Hartlepool U 22 5
2003–04 Hartlepool U 18 12 **78 27**
2003–04 *Boston U* 14 4 **14 4**

**BRACKSTONE, John (D) 6 0**
H: 5 11 W: 10 08 b.Hartlepool 9-2-85
*Source:* Scholar.
2003–04 Hartlepool U 6 0 **6 0**

**CARSON, Stephen (M) 36 1**
H: 5 10 W: 12 00 b.Ballymoney 6-10-80
2000–01 Rangers 2 0 **2 0**
2001–02 Dundee U 13 0
2002–03 Dundee U 7 0 **20 0**
2003–04 Barnsley 11 1 **11 1**
2003–04 Hartlepool U 3 0 **3 0**

**CLARKE, Darrell# (M) 272 43**
H: 5 10 W: 11 06 b.Mansfield 16-12-77
*Source:* Trainee.
1995–96 Mansfield T 3 0
1996–97 Mansfield T 19 2
1997–98 Mansfield T 35 4
1998–99 Mansfield T 33 5
1999–2000 Mansfield T 39 7
2000–01 Mansfield T 32 6 **161 24**
2001–02 Hartlepool U 33 7
2002–03 Hartlepool U 45 7
2003–04 Hartlepool U 33 5 **111 19**

**CRADDOCK, Darren§ (M) 10 0**
H: 6 0 W: 12 02 b.Bishop Auckland 23-2-85
*Source:* Scholar.
2003–04 Hartlepool U 10 0 **10 0**

**EASTER, Jermaine‡ (F) 42 4**
H: 5 10 W: 12 03 b.Cardiff 15-1-82
*Source:* Trainee. *Honours:* Wales Youth.
2000–01 Wolverhampton W 0 0
2000–01 Hartlepool U 4 0
2001–02 Hartlepool U 12 2
2002–03 Hartlepool U 8 0
2003–04 Hartlepool U 3 0 **27 2**
2003–04 *Cambridge U* 15 2 **15 2**

**FOLEY, David§ (F) 1 0**
H: 5 4 W: 8 09 b.South Shields 12-5-87
*Source:* Scholar.
2003–04 Hartlepool U 1 0 **1 0**

**GABBIADINI, Marco‡ (F) 659 222**
H: 5 10 W: 13 04 b.Nottingham 20-1-68
*Source:* Apprentice. *Honours:* England Under-21, B.
1984–85 York C 1 0
1985–86 York C 22 4
1986–87 York C 29 9
1987–88 York C 8 1
1987–88 Sunderland 35 21
1988–89 Sunderland 36 18
1989–90 Sunderland 46 21
1990–91 Sunderland 31 9
1991–92 Sunderland 9 5 **157 74**
1991–92 Crystal Palace 15 5 **15 5**
1991–92 Derby Co 20 6
1992–93 Derby Co 44 9
1993–94 Derby Co 39 13
1994–95 Derby Co 32 11
1995–96 Derby Co 39 11
1996–97 Derby Co 14 0 **188 50**
1996–97 *Birmingham C* 2 0 **2 0**
1996–97 *Oxford U* 5 1 **5 1**
1997–98 Stoke C 8 0 **8 0**
1997–98 York C 7 1 **67 15**
1998–99 Darlington 40 23
1999–2000 Darlington 42 24 **82 47**
2000–01 Northampton T 44 6
2001–02 Northampton T 35 7
2002–03 Northampton T 41 12 **120 25**
2003–04 Hartlepool U 15 5 **15 5**

**HUMPHREYS, Richie (M) 227 30**
H: 5 11 W: 12 07 b.Sheffield 30-11-77
*Source:* Trainee. *Honours:* England Youth, Under-21.
1995–96 Sheffield W 5 0
1996–97 Sheffield W 29 3
1997–98 Sheffield W 7 0
1998–99 Sheffield W 19 1
1999–2000 Sheffield W 0 0
1999–2000 *Scunthorpe U* 6 2 **6 2**
1999–2000 *Cardiff C* 9 2 **9 2**
2000–01 Sheffield W 7 0 **67 4**
2000–01 Cambridge U 7 3 **7 3**
2001–02 Hartlepool U 46 5
2002–03 Hartlepool U 46 11
2003–04 Hartlepool U 46 3 **138 19**

**ISTEAD, Steven§ (F) 37 1**
H: 5 8 W: 11 06 b.South Shields 23-4-86
*Source:* Scholar.
2002–03 Hartlepool U 6 0
2003–04 Hartlepool U 31 1 **37 1**

**JORDAN, Andy (D) 21 0**
H: 6 2 W: 13 05 b.Manchester 14-12-79
*Source:* Trainee. *Honours:* Scotland Under-21.
1997–98 Bristol C 0 0
1998–99 Bristol C 1 0
1999–2000 Bristol C 8 0
2000–01 Bristol C 2 0 **11 0**
2000–01 Cardiff C 5 0
2001–02 Cardiff C 0 0
2002–03 Cardiff C 0 0 **5 0**
2003–04 Hartlepool U 5 0 **5 0**

**KONSTANTOPOULOS, Dimitrios (G) 0 0**
H: 6 4 W: 14 02 b.Salonika 29-11-78
2003–04 Hartlepool U 0 0

**McCANN, Ryan (M) 22 3**
H: 5 8 W: 11 03 b.Bellshill 15-9-82
1999–2000 Celtic 1 0
2000–01 Celtic 0 0
2001–02 Celtic 0 0
2002–03 Celtic 0 0 **1 0**
2002–03 St Johnstone 17 3 **17 3**
2003–04 Hartlepool U 4 0 **4 0**

**NELSON, Michael (D) 112 11**
H: 6 2 W: 13 03 b.Gateshead 15-3-82
2000–01 Bury 2 1
2001–02 Bury 31 2
2002–03 Bury 39 5 **72 8**
2003–04 Hartlepool U 40 3 **40 3**

**PORTER, Joel (F) 135 38**
H: 5 9 W: 11 13 b.Adelaide 25-12-78
*Honours:* Australia 4 full caps, 5 goals.
1998–99 West Adelaide 20 3 **20 3**
2000–01 Melbourne Knights 30 12

| | | | | | |
|---|---|---|---|---|---|
| 2001–02 | Melbourne Knights | 26 | 12 | **56** | **24** |
| 2002–03 | Sydney Olympic | 32 | 8 | **32** | **8** |
| 2003–04 | Hartlepool U | 27 | 3 | **27** | **3** |

**PROVETT, Jim (G)** **45 0**
H: 6 0 W: 13 04 b.Stockton 22-12-82
*Source:* Trainee.

| | | | | | |
|---|---|---|---|---|---|
| 1999–2000 | Hartlepool U | 0 | 0 | | |
| 2000–01 | Hartlepool U | 0 | 0 | | |
| 2001–02 | Hartlepool U | 0 | 0 | | |
| 2002–03 | Hartlepool U | 0 | 0 | | |
| 2003–04 | Hartlepool U | 45 | 0 | **45** | **0** |

**ROBERTSON, Hugh (D)** **196 22**
H: 5 9 W: 13 11 b.Aberdeen 19-3-75
*Source:* Lewis U. *Honours:* Scotland Under-21.

| | | | | | |
|---|---|---|---|---|---|
| 1993–94 | Aberdeen | 8 | 0 | | |
| 1994–95 | Aberdeen | 3 | 2 | | |
| 1995–96 | Aberdeen | 11 | 0 | | |
| 1996–97 | Aberdeen | 0 | 0 | **22** | **2** |
| 1996–97 | Dundee | 15 | 1 | | |
| 1997–98 | Dundee | 0 | 0 | | |
| 1997–98 | *Brechin C* | 7 | 0 | **7** | **0** |
| 1998–99 | Dundee | 10 | 0 | | |
| 1998–99 | Inverness C | 12 | 1 | **12** | **1** |
| 1999–2000 | Dundee | 0 | 0 | | |
| 2000–01 | Dundee | 0 | 0 | **25** | **1** |
| 2000–01 | Ayr U | 8 | 1 | **8** | **1** |
| 2000–01 | Ross Co | 16 | 1 | | |
| 2001–02 | Ross Co | 36 | 6 | | |
| 2002–03 | Ross Co | 32 | 4 | | |
| 2003–04 | Ross Co | 20 | 2 | **104** | **13** |
| 2003–04 | Hartlepool U | 18 | 4 | **18** | **4** |

**ROBINSON, Mark* (D)** **85 0**
H: 5 9 W: 11 00 b.Guisborough 24-7-81
*Source:* Trainee.

| | | | | | |
|---|---|---|---|---|---|
| 1999–2000 | Hartlepool U | 0 | 0 | | |
| 2000–01 | Hartlepool U | 6 | 0 | | |
| 2001–02 | Hartlepool U | 37 | 0 | | |
| 2002–03 | Hartlepool U | 38 | 0 | | |
| 2003–04 | Hartlepool U | 4 | 0 | **85** | **0** |

**ROBINSON, Paul# (F)** **104 13**
H: 5 11 W: 11 00 b.Sunderland 20-11-78
*Source:* Trainee.

| | | | | | |
|---|---|---|---|---|---|
| 1995–96 | Darlington | 4 | 0 | | |
| 1996–97 | Darlington | 3 | 0 | | |
| 1997–98 | Darlington | 19 | 3 | **26** | **3** |
| 1997–98 | Newcastle U | 0 | 0 | | |
| 1998–99 | Newcastle U | 0 | 0 | | |
| 1999–2000 | Newcastle U | 11 | 0 | **11** | **0** |
| 2000–01 | Wimbledon | 2 | 0 | | |
| 2000–01 | *Burnley* | 4 | 0 | **4** | **0** |
| 2001–02 | Wimbledon | 1 | 0 | **3** | **0** |
| 2001–02 | *Grimsby T* | 5 | 0 | | |
| 2002–03 | Grimsby T | 12 | 1 | **17** | **1** |
| 2002–03 | *Carlisle U* | 5 | 1 | **5** | **1** |
| 2002–03 | Blackpool | 7 | 1 | **7** | **1** |
| 2003–04 | Hartlepool U | 31 | 7 | **31** | **7** |

**ROBSON, Matty (D)** **23 1**
H: 5 9 W: 11 02 b.Durham 23-1-85
*Source:* Scholar.

| | | | | | |
|---|---|---|---|---|---|
| 2002–03 | Hartlepool U | 0 | 0 | | |
| 2003–04 | Hartlepool U | 23 | 1 | **23** | **1** |

**STRACHAN, Gavin (M)** **67 5**
H: 5 10 W: 11 07 b.Aberdeen 23-12-78
*Source:* Trainee. *Honours:* Scotland Youth, Under-21.

| | | | | | |
|---|---|---|---|---|---|
| 1996–97 | Coventry C | 0 | 0 | | |
| 1997–98 | Coventry C | 9 | 0 | | |
| 1998–99 | Coventry C | 0 | 0 | | |
| 1998–99 | *Dundee* | 6 | 0 | **6** | **0** |
| 1999–2000 | Coventry C | 3 | 0 | | |
| 2000–01 | Coventry C | 2 | 0 | | |
| 2001–02 | Coventry C | 1 | 0 | | |
| 2002–03 | Coventry C | 1 | 0 | **16** | **0** |
| 2002–03 | *Peterborough U* | 2 | 0 | **2** | **0** |
| 2002–03 | Southend U | 7 | 0 | **7** | **0** |
| 2003–04 | Hartlepool U | 36 | 5 | **36** | **5** |

**SWEENEY, Anthony (M)** **17 1**
H: 6 0 W: 11 07 b.Stockton 5-9-83
*Source:* Scholar.

| | | | | | |
|---|---|---|---|---|---|
| 2001–02 | Hartlepool U | 2 | 0 | | |
| 2002–03 | Hartlepool U | 4 | 0 | | |
| 2003–04 | Hartlepool U | 11 | 1 | **17** | **1** |

**TINKLER, Mark (M)** **328 40**
H: 6 2 W: 12 00 b.Bishop Auckland 24-10-74
*Source:* Trainee. *Honours:* England Schools, Youth.

| | | | | | |
|---|---|---|---|---|---|
| 1991–92 | Leeds U | 0 | 0 | | |
| 1992–93 | Leeds U | 7 | 0 | | |
| 1993–94 | Leeds U | 3 | 0 | | |
| 1994–95 | Leeds U | 3 | 0 | | |
| 1995–96 | Leeds U | 9 | 0 | | |
| 1996–97 | Leeds U | 3 | 0 | **25** | **0** |
| 1996–97 | York C | 9 | 1 | | |
| 1997–98 | York C | 44 | 5 | | |
| 1998–99 | York C | 37 | 2 | | |
| 1999–2000 | York C | 0 | 0 | **90** | **8** |
| 1999–2000 | Southend U | 41 | 0 | | |
| 2000–01 | Southend U | 15 | 1 | **56** | **1** |
| 2000–01 | Hartlepool U | 28 | 3 | | |
| 2001–02 | Hartlepool U | 40 | 9 | | |
| 2002–03 | Hartlepool U | 45 | 13 | | |
| 2003–04 | Hartlepool U | 44 | 6 | **157** | **31** |

**VAN DOMMELLE, Adam‡ (D)** **0 0**
H: 6 0 W: 12 10 b.Adelaide 5-9-84

| | | | | | |
|---|---|---|---|---|---|
| 2003–04 | Hartlepool U | 0 | 0 | | |

**WALKER, Scott‡ (D)** **177 15**
H: 6 1 W: 13 09 b.Glasgow 5-3-75

| | | | | | |
|---|---|---|---|---|---|
| 1997–98 | E Stirling | 17 | 0 | | |
| 1998–99 | E Stirling | 25 | 4 | **42** | **4** |
| 1999–2000 | St Mirren | 33 | 4 | | |
| 2000–01 | St Mirren | 30 | 2 | | |
| 2001–02 | St Mirren | 34 | 3 | | |
| 2002–03 | Dunfermline Ath | 20 | 2 | **20** | **2** |
| 2003–04 | St Mirren | 1 | 0 | **98** | **9** |
| 2003–04 | Alloa | 11 | 0 | **11** | **0** |
| 2003–04 | Hartlepool U | 6 | 0 | **6** | **0** |

**WESTWOOD, Chris (D)** **217 4**
H: 5 11 W: 12 10 b.Dudley 13-2-77
*Source:* Trainee.

| | | | | | |
|---|---|---|---|---|---|
| 1995–96 | Wolverhampton W | 0 | 0 | | |
| 1996–97 | Wolverhampton W | 0 | 0 | | |
| 1997–98 | Wolverhampton W | 4 | 1 | | |
| 1998–99 | Wolverhampton W | 0 | 0 | **4** | **1** |
| 1998–99 | Hartlepool U | 4 | 0 | | |
| 1999–2000 | Hartlepool U | 37 | 0 | | |
| 2000–01 | Hartlepool U | 46 | 1 | | |
| 2001–02 | Hartlepool U | 35 | 1 | | |
| 2002–03 | Hartlepool U | 46 | 1 | | |
| 2003–04 | Hartlepool U | 45 | 0 | **213** | **3** |

**WILKINSON, Jack§ (M)** **4 2**
H: 5 8 W: 10 08 b.Beverley 12-9-85
*Source:* Scholar.

| | | | | | |
|---|---|---|---|---|---|
| 2003–04 | Hartlepool U | 4 | 2 | **4** | **2** |

**WILLIAMS, Anthony* (G)** **172 0**
H: 6 2 W: 13 08 b.Ogwr 20-9-77
*Source:* Trainee. *Honours:* Wales Youth, Under-21.

| | | | | | |
|---|---|---|---|---|---|
| 1996–97 | Blackburn R | 0 | 0 | | |
| 1997–98 | Blackburn R | 0 | 0 | | |
| 1997–98 | *QPR* | 0 | 0 | | |
| 1998–99 | Blackburn R | 0 | 0 | | |
| 1998–99 | *Macclesfield T* | 4 | 0 | | |
| 1998–99 | *Huddersfield T* | 0 | 0 | | |
| 1998–99 | *Bristol R* | 9 | 0 | **9** | **0** |
| 1999–2000 | Blackburn R | 0 | 0 | | |
| 1999–2000 | *Gillingham* | 2 | 0 | **2** | **0** |
| 1999–2000 | *Macclesfield T* | 11 | 0 | **15** | **0** |
| 2000–01 | Hartlepool U | 41 | 0 | | |
| 2001–02 | Hartlepool U | 43 | 0 | | |
| 2002–03 | Hartlepool U | 46 | 0 | | |
| 2003–04 | Hartlepool U | 1 | 0 | **131** | **0** |
| 2003–04 | *Swansea C* | 0 | 0 | | |
| 2003–04 | *Stockport Co* | 15 | 0 | **15** | **0** |

**WILLIAMS, Eifion (F)** **205 56**
H: 5 11 W: 11 02 b.Bangor 15-11-75
*Source:* Barry T. *Honours:* Wales B.

| | | | | | |
|---|---|---|---|---|---|
| 1998–99 | Torquay U | 7 | 5 | | |
| 1999–2000 | Torquay U | 42 | 9 | | |
| 2000–01 | Torquay U | 37 | 9 | | |
| 2001–02 | Torquay U | 25 | 1 | **111** | **24** |
| 2001–02 | Hartlepool U | 8 | 4 | | |
| 2002–03 | Hartlepool U | 45 | 15 | | |
| 2003–04 | Hartlepool U | 41 | 13 | **94** | **32** |

**Scholars**
Appleby, Andrew; Craddock, Darren; Duncan, Kevin M; Foley, David J; Fox, Daniel J; Istead, Steven B; Low, Maurice G; Maidens, Michael D; Muckles, Neil; Richards, Karl D; Turnbull, Philip; Turnbull, Stephen; Watts, Andrew; Wilkinson, Jack L; Wilkinson, Neil S; Winter, James H

## HUDDERSFIELD T (36)

**ABBOTT, Pawel (F)** **55 17**
H: 5 7 W: 11 07 b.York 5-5-82
*Source:* LKS Lodz.

| | | | | | |
|---|---|---|---|---|---|
| 2000–01 | Preston NE | 0 | 0 | | |
| 2001–02 | Preston NE | 0 | 0 | | |
| 2002–03 | Preston NE | 16 | 4 | | |
| 2002–03 | *Bury* | 17 | 6 | **17** | **6** |
| 2003–04 | Preston NE | 9 | 2 | **25** | **6** |
| 2003–04 | Huddersfield T | 13 | 5 | **13** | **5** |

**AHMED, Adnan (M)** **1 0**
H: 5 10 W: 11 12 b.Burnley 7-6-84
*Source:* Scholar.

| | | | | | |
|---|---|---|---|---|---|
| 2003–04 | Huddersfield T | 1 | 0 | **1** | **0** |

**BOOTH, Andy (F)** **374 115**
H: 6 1 W: 13 00 b.Huddersfield 6-12-73
*Source:* Trainee. *Honours:* England Under-21.

| | | | | | |
|---|---|---|---|---|---|
| 1991–92 | Huddersfield T | 3 | 0 | | |
| 1992–93 | Huddersfield T | 5 | 2 | | |
| 1993–94 | Huddersfield T | 26 | 10 | | |
| 1994–95 | Huddersfield T | 46 | 26 | | |
| 1995–96 | Huddersfield T | 43 | 16 | | |
| 1996–97 | Sheffield W | 35 | 10 | | |
| 1997–98 | Sheffield W | 23 | 7 | | |
| 1998–99 | Sheffield W | 34 | 6 | | |
| 1999–2000 | Sheffield W | 23 | 2 | | |
| 2000–01 | Sheffield W | 18 | 3 | **133** | **28** |
| 2000–01 | *Tottenham H* | 4 | 0 | **4** | **0** |
| 2000–01 | Huddersfield T | 8 | 3 | | |
| 2001–02 | Huddersfield T | 36 | 11 | | |
| 2002–03 | Huddersfield T | 33 | 6 | | |
| 2003–04 | Huddersfield T | 37 | 13 | **237** | **87** |

**BOOTY, Martyn# (D)** **327 8**
H: 5 8 W: 11 02 b.Kirby Muxloe 30-5-71
*Source:* Trainee.

| | | | | | |
|---|---|---|---|---|---|
| 1991–92 | Coventry C | 3 | 0 | | |
| 1992–93 | Coventry C | 0 | 0 | | |
| 1993–94 | Coventry C | 2 | 0 | **5** | **0** |
| 1993–94 | Crewe Alex | 31 | 1 | | |
| 1994–95 | Crewe Alex | 44 | 2 | | |
| 1995–96 | Crewe Alex | 21 | 2 | **96** | **5** |
| 1995–96 | Reading | 17 | 1 | | |
| 1996–97 | Reading | 14 | 0 | | |
| 1997–98 | Reading | 25 | 0 | | |
| 1998–99 | Reading | 8 | 0 | **64** | **1** |
| 1998–99 | Southend U | 20 | 0 | | |
| 1999–2000 | Southend U | 28 | 0 | | |
| 2000–01 | Southend U | 32 | 0 | **80** | **0** |
| 2001–02 | Chesterfield | 40 | 2 | | |
| 2002–03 | Chesterfield | 38 | 0 | **78** | **2** |
| 2003–04 | Huddersfield T | 4 | 0 | **4** | **0** |

**BROWN, Nat (F)** **59 0**
H: 6 2 W: 12 05 b.Sheffield 15-6-81
*Source:* Trainee.

| | | | | | |
|---|---|---|---|---|---|
| 1999–2000 | Huddersfield T | 0 | 0 | | |
| 2000–01 | Huddersfield T | 0 | 0 | | |
| 2001–02 | Huddersfield T | 0 | 0 | | |
| 2002–03 | Huddersfield T | 38 | 0 | | |
| 2003–04 | Huddersfield T | 21 | 0 | **59** | **0** |

**CARSS, Tony (M)** **252 11**
H: 5 11 W: 11 13 b.Alnwick 31-3-76
*Source:* Bradford C Trainee.

| | | | | | |
|---|---|---|---|---|---|
| 1994–95 | Blackburn R | 0 | 0 | | |
| 1995–96 | Darlington | 28 | 2 | | |
| 1996–97 | Darlington | 29 | 0 | **57** | **2** |
| 1997–98 | Cardiff C | 42 | 1 | **42** | **1** |
| 1998–99 | Chesterfield | 4 | 0 | | |
| 1999–2000 | Chesterfield | 31 | 1 | **35** | **1** |
| 2000–01 | Carlisle U | 7 | 0 | **7** | **0** |
| 2000–01 | Oldham Ath | 35 | 2 | | |
| 2001–02 | Oldham Ath | 14 | 1 | | |
| 2002–03 | Oldham Ath | 26 | 2 | **75** | **5** |
| 2003–04 | Huddersfield T | 36 | 2 | **36** | **2** |

**CLARKE, Nathan (D)** **65 2**
H: 6 2 W: 12 00 b.Halifax 30-11-83
*Source:* Scholar.

| | | | | | |
|---|---|---|---|---|---|
| 2001–02 | Huddersfield T | 36 | 1 | | |

| | | | | | |
|---|---|---|---|---|---|
| 2002–03 | Huddersfield T | 3 | 0 | | |
| 2003–04 | Huddersfield T | 26 | 1 | **65** | **2** |

**EDWARDS, Rob# (D)** **404 66**
H: 5 8 W: 12 01 b.Manchester 23-2-70
*Source:* Trainee.

| | | | | | |
|---|---|---|---|---|---|
| 1987–88 | Crewe Alex | 6 | 1 | | |
| 1988–89 | Crewe Alex | 4 | 0 | | |
| 1989–90 | Crewe Alex | 4 | 0 | | |
| 1990–91 | Crewe Alex | 29 | 11 | | |
| 1991–92 | Crewe Alex | 28 | 6 | | |
| 1992–93 | Crewe Alex | 23 | 7 | | |
| 1993–94 | Crewe Alex | 12 | 2 | | |
| 1994–95 | Crewe Alex | 17 | 2 | | |
| 1995–96 | Crewe Alex | 32 | 15 | **155** | **44** |
| 1995–96 | Huddersfield T | 13 | 7 | | |
| 1996–97 | Huddersfield T | 33 | 3 | | |
| 1997–98 | Huddersfield T | 38 | 1 | | |
| 1998–99 | Huddersfield T | 45 | 2 | | |
| 1999–2000 | Huddersfield T | 9 | 1 | | |
| 2000–01 | Huddersfield T | 0 | 0 | | |
| 2000–01 | Chesterfield | 34 | 4 | | |
| 2001–02 | Chesterfield | 31 | 1 | | |
| 2002–03 | Chesterfield | 29 | 2 | **94** | **7** |
| 2003–04 | Huddersfield T | 17 | 1 | **155** | **15** |

**FOWLER, Lee (M)** **43 0**
H: 5 7 W: 10 00 b.Cardiff 10-6-83
*Source:* Scholar. *Honours:* Wales Under-21.

| | | | | | |
|---|---|---|---|---|---|
| 2000–01 | Coventry C | 0 | 0 | | |
| 2001–02 | Coventry C | 13 | 0 | | |
| 2002–03 | Coventry C | 1 | 0 | | |
| 2003–04 | Coventry C | 0 | 0 | **14** | **0** |
| 2003–04 | Huddersfield T | 29 | 0 | **29** | **0** |

**GRAY, Ian (G)** **151 0**
H: 6 2 W: 13 13 b.Manchester 25-2-75
*Source:* Trainee.

| | | | | | |
|---|---|---|---|---|---|
| 1993–94 | Oldham Ath | 0 | 0 | | |
| 1994–95 | Oldham Ath | 0 | 0 | | |
| 1994–95 | *Rochdale* | 12 | 0 | | |
| 1995–96 | Rochdale | 20 | 0 | | |
| 1996–97 | Rochdale | 46 | 0 | **78** | **0** |
| 1997–98 | Stockport Co | 3 | 0 | | |
| 1998–99 | Stockport Co | 3 | 0 | | |
| 1999–2000 | Stockport Co | 10 | 0 | **16** | **0** |
| 2000–01 | Rotherham U | 33 | 0 | | |
| 2001–02 | Rotherham U | 1 | 0 | | |
| 2002–03 | Rotherham U | 6 | 0 | **40** | **0** |
| 2003–04 | Huddersfield T | 17 | 0 | **17** | **0** |

**HOLDSWORTH, Andy (D)** **36 0**
H: 5 9 W: 11 02 b.Pontefract 29-1-84
*Source:* Scholar.

| | | | | | |
|---|---|---|---|---|---|
| 2003–04 | Huddersfield T | 36 | 0 | **36** | **0** |

**HUGHES, Ian# (D)** **348 5**
H: 5 11 W: 12 00 b.Bangor 2-8-74
*Source:* Trainee. *Honours:* Wales Youth, Under-21.

| | | | | | |
|---|---|---|---|---|---|
| 1991–92 | Bury | 17 | 0 | | |
| 1992–93 | Bury | 15 | 0 | | |
| 1992–93 | Bury | 15 | 0 | | |
| 1993–94 | Bury | 38 | 0 | | |
| 1994–95 | Bury | 23 | 1 | | |
| 1995–96 | Bury | 32 | 0 | | |
| 1996–97 | Bury | 22 | 0 | | |
| 1997–98 | Bury | 13 | 0 | **175** | **1** |
| 1997–98 | Blackpool | 21 | 0 | | |
| 1998–99 | Blackpool | 33 | 1 | | |
| 1999–2000 | Blackpool | 34 | 0 | | |
| 2000–01 | Blackpool | 34 | 1 | | |
| 2001–02 | Blackpool | 20 | 1 | | |
| 2002–03 | Blackpool | 18 | 0 | **160** | **3** |
| 2003–04 | Huddersfield T | 13 | 1 | **13** | **1** |

**LLOYD, Anthony (D)** **31 3**
H: 5 7 W: 11 00 b.Taunton 14-3-84
*Source:* Scholar.

| | | | | | |
|---|---|---|---|---|---|
| 2003–04 | Huddersfield T | 31 | 3 | **31** | **3** |

**MACARI, Paul‡ (F)** **14 0**
H: 5 8 W: 12 06 b.Manchester 23-8-76
*Source:* Trainee.

| | | | | | |
|---|---|---|---|---|---|
| 1993–94 | Stoke C | 0 | 0 | | |
| 1994–95 | Stoke C | 0 | 0 | | |
| 1995–96 | Stoke C | 0 | 0 | | |
| 1996–97 | Stoke C | 0 | 0 | | |
| 1997–98 | Stoke C | 3 | 0 | **3** | **0** |
| 1998–99 | Sheffield U | 0 | 0 | | |
| 1999–2000 | Sheffield U | 0 | 0 | | |
| 2000–01 | Huddersfield T | 0 | 0 | | |
| 2001–02 | Huddersfield T | 6 | 0 | | |
| 2002–03 | Huddersfield T | 5 | 0 | | |
| 2003–04 | Huddersfield T | 0 | 0 | **11** | **0** |

**MATTIS, Dwayne‡ (M)** **69 2**
H: 6 1 W: 11 12 b.Huddersfield 31-7-81
*Source:* Trainee. *Honours:* Eire Under-21.

| | | | | | |
|---|---|---|---|---|---|
| 1998–99 | Huddersfield T | 2 | 0 | | |
| 1999–2000 | Huddersfield T | 0 | 0 | | |
| 2000–01 | Huddersfield T | 0 | 0 | | |
| 2001–02 | Huddersfield T | 29 | 1 | | |
| 2002–03 | Huddersfield T | 33 | 1 | | |
| 2003–04 | Huddersfield T | 5 | 0 | **69** | **2** |

**McALISKEY, John§ (F)** **8 4**
H: 6 5 W: 12 07 b.Huddersfield 2-9-84
*Source:* Scholar.

| | | | | | |
|---|---|---|---|---|---|
| 2003–04 | Huddersfield T | 8 | 4 | **8** | **4** |

**McCOMBE, John§ (M)** **1 0**
H: 6 2 W: 12 10 b.Pontefract 7-5-85
*Source:* Scholar.

| | | | | | |
|---|---|---|---|---|---|
| 2002–03 | Huddersfield T | 1 | 0 | | |
| 2003–04 | Huddersfield T | 0 | 0 | **1** | **0** |

**MIRFIN, David (M)** **22 2**
H: 6 2 W: 14 05 b.Sheffield 18-4-85
*Source:* Scholar.

| | | | | | |
|---|---|---|---|---|---|
| 2002–03 | Huddersfield T | 1 | 0 | | |
| 2003–04 | Huddersfield T | 21 | 2 | **22** | **2** |

**NEWBY, Jon (F)** **150 21**
H: 5 11 W: 11 00 b.Warrington 28-11-78
*Source:* Trainee.

| | | | | | |
|---|---|---|---|---|---|
| 1998–99 | Liverpool | 0 | 0 | | |
| 1999–2000 | Liverpool | 1 | 0 | | |
| 1999–2000 | *Crewe Alex* | 6 | 0 | **6** | **0** |
| 2000–01 | Liverpool | 0 | 0 | **1** | **0** |
| 2000–01 | *Sheffield U* | 13 | 0 | **13** | **0** |
| 2000–01 | Bury | 17 | 5 | | |
| 2001–02 | Bury | 46 | 6 | | |
| 2002–03 | Bury | 46 | 10 | **109** | **21** |
| 2003–04 | Huddersfield T | 14 | 0 | **14** | **0** |
| 2003–04 | *York C* | 7 | 0 | **7** | **0** |

**ONUORA, Iffy* (F)** **452 116**
H: 6 2 W: 13 13 b.Glasgow 28-7-67
*Source:* British Univ.

| | | | | | |
|---|---|---|---|---|---|
| 1989–90 | Huddersfield T | 20 | 3 | | |
| 1990–91 | Huddersfield T | 43 | 7 | | |
| 1991–92 | Huddersfield T | 41 | 8 | | |
| 1992–93 | Huddersfield T | 39 | 6 | | |
| 1993–94 | Huddersfield T | 22 | 6 | | |
| 1994–95 | Mansfield T | 14 | 7 | | |
| 1995–96 | Mansfield T | 14 | 1 | **28** | **8** |
| 1996–97 | Gillingham | 40 | 21 | | |
| 1997–98 | Gillingham | 22 | 2 | | |
| 1997–98 | Swindon T | 6 | 1 | | |
| 1998–99 | Swindon T | 43 | 20 | | |
| 1999–2000 | Swindon T | 24 | 4 | **73** | **25** |
| 1999–2000 | Gillingham | 22 | 6 | | |
| 2000–01 | Gillingham | 31 | 9 | | |
| 2001–02 | Gillingham | 33 | 11 | **148** | **49** |
| 2002–03 | Sheffield U | 7 | 1 | | |
| 2003–04 | Sheffield U | 0 | 0 | **7** | **1** |
| 2003–04 | *Wycombe W* | 6 | 0 | **6** | **0** |
| 2003–04 | *Grimsby T* | 19 | 3 | **19** | **3** |
| 2003–04 | Tranmere R | 3 | 0 | **3** | **0** |
| 2003–04 | Huddersfield T | 3 | 0 | **168** | **30** |

**SCHOFIELD, Danny (F)** **114 18**
H: 5 11 W: 12 00 b.Doncaster 10-4-80
*Source:* Brodsworth.

| | | | | | |
|---|---|---|---|---|---|
| 1998–99 | Huddersfield T | 1 | 0 | | |
| 1999–2000 | Huddersfield T | 2 | 0 | | |
| 2000–01 | Huddersfield T | 1 | 0 | | |
| 2001–02 | Huddersfield T | 40 | 8 | | |
| 2002–03 | Huddersfield T | 30 | 2 | | |
| 2003–04 | Huddersfield T | 40 | 8 | **114** | **18** |

**SCOTT, Paul# (D)** **32 2**
H: 5 11 W: 12 00 b.Wakefield 5-11-79
*Source:* Trainee.

| | | | | | |
|---|---|---|---|---|---|
| 1998–99 | Huddersfield T | 0 | 0 | | |
| 1999–2000 | Huddersfield T | 0 | 0 | | |
| 2000–01 | Huddersfield T | 0 | 0 | | |
| 2001–02 | Huddersfield T | 0 | 0 | | |
| 2002–03 | Huddersfield T | 13 | 0 | | |
| 2003–04 | Huddersfield T | 19 | 2 | **32** | **2** |

**SENIOR, Philip (G)** **34 0**
H: 5 11 W: 11 00 b.Huddersfield 30-10-82
*Source:* Trainee.

| | | | | | |
|---|---|---|---|---|---|
| 1999–2000 | Huddersfield T | 0 | 0 | | |
| 2000–01 | Huddersfield T | 0 | 0 | | |
| 2001–02 | Huddersfield T | 0 | 0 | | |
| 2002–03 | Huddersfield T | 18 | 0 | | |
| 2003–04 | Huddersfield T | 16 | 0 | **34** | **0** |

**SODJE, Efe (D)** **232 13**
H: 6 1 W: 12 00 b.Greenwich 5-10-72
*Source:* Delta Steel Pioneer, Stevenage Bor.
*Honours:* Nigeria 10 full caps, 1 goal.

| | | | | | |
|---|---|---|---|---|---|
| 1997–98 | Macclesfield T | 41 | 3 | | |
| 1998–99 | Macclesfield T | 42 | 3 | **83** | **6** |
| 1999–2000 | Luton T | 9 | 0 | **9** | **0** |
| 1999–2000 | Colchester U | 3 | 0 | **3** | **0** |
| 2000–01 | Crewe Alex | 32 | 0 | | |
| 2001–02 | Crewe Alex | 36 | 2 | | |
| 2002–03 | Crewe Alex | 30 | 1 | **98** | **3** |
| 2003–04 | Huddersfield T | 39 | 4 | **39** | **4** |

**THOMPSON, Tyrone (F)** **3 0**
H: 5 10 W: 11 00 b.Sheffield 8-5-82
*Source:* Scholar.

| | | | | | |
|---|---|---|---|---|---|
| 2000–01 | Sheffield U | 0 | 0 | | |
| 2001–02 | Sheffield U | 0 | 0 | | |
| 2002–03 | Sheffield U | 0 | 0 | | |
| 2002–03 | *Lincoln C* | 1 | 0 | **1** | **0** |
| 2003–04 | Sheffield U | 0 | 0 | | |
| 2003–04 | Huddersfield T | 2 | 0 | **2** | **0** |

**WASHINGTON, Joe‡ (M)** **0 0**
H: 5 8 W: 11 06 b.Huddersfield 4-10-83
*Source:* Scholar.

| | | | | | |
|---|---|---|---|---|---|
| 2003–04 | Huddersfield T | 0 | 0 | | |

**WORTHINGTON, Jon (M)** **61 3**
H: 5 9 W: 11 05 b.Dewsbury 16-4-83
*Source:* Scholar.

| | | | | | |
|---|---|---|---|---|---|
| 2001–02 | Huddersfield T | 0 | 0 | | |
| 2002–03 | Huddersfield T | 22 | 0 | | |
| 2003–04 | Huddersfield T | 39 | 3 | **61** | **3** |

**YATES, Steve (D)** **491 10**
H: 5 11 W: 12 00 b.Bristol 29-1-70
*Source:* Trainee.

| | | | | | |
|---|---|---|---|---|---|
| 1986–87 | Bristol R | 2 | 0 | | |
| 1987–88 | Bristol R | 0 | 0 | | |
| 1988–89 | Bristol R | 35 | 0 | | |
| 1989–90 | Bristol R | 42 | 0 | | |
| 1990–91 | Bristol R | 34 | 0 | | |
| 1991–92 | Bristol R | 39 | 0 | | |
| 1992–93 | Bristol R | 44 | 0 | | |
| 1993–94 | Bristol R | 1 | 0 | **197** | **0** |
| 1993–94 | QPR | 29 | 0 | | |
| 1994–95 | QPR | 23 | 1 | | |
| 1995–96 | QPR | 30 | 0 | | |
| 1996–97 | QPR | 16 | 1 | | |
| 1997–98 | QPR | 30 | 0 | | |
| 1998–99 | QPR | 6 | 0 | **134** | **2** |
| 1999–2000 | Tranmere R | 33 | 2 | | |
| 2000–01 | Tranmere R | 43 | 2 | | |
| 2001–02 | Tranmere R | 37 | 3 | **113** | **7** |
| 2002–03 | Sheffield U | 12 | 0 | **12** | **0** |
| 2003–04 | Huddersfield T | 35 | 1 | **35** | **1** |

**Scholars**
Caulfield, Luke P; Collins, Michael A; Draper, Thomas; Evans, Christopher D; Giles, Jacob D; Hand, James F; Hardy, Aaron; Huxall, Gavin T; Kerridge, Matthew D; McAliskey, John J; McCombe, John P; Shaw, Joseph M; Sheridan, Mark; Walls, David E; Walsh, Joseph J; Young, Matthew G

**Non Contract**
Martin, Lee B

## HULL C (37)

**ALLSOPP, Danny (F)** **218 71**
H: 6 1 W: 14 00 b.Melbourne 10-8-78
*Honours:* Australia Youth, Under-20, Under-23.

| | | | | | |
|---|---|---|---|---|---|
| 1995–96 | South Melbourne | 14 | 1 | | |
| 1996–97 | South Melbourne | 6 | 1 | **20** | **2** |
| 1997–98 | Carlton | 16 | 3 | **16** | **3** |
| 1998–99 | Manchester C | 24 | 4 | | |
| 1999–2000 | Manchester C | 4 | 0 | | |
| 1999–2000 | *Notts Co* | 3 | 1 | | |
| 1999–2000 | *Wrexham* | 3 | 4 | **3** | **4** |
| 2000–01 | Manchester C | 1 | 0 | **29** | **4** |
| 2000–01 | *Bristol R* | 6 | 0 | **6** | **0** |
| 2000–01 | Notts Co | 29 | 13 | | |

| | | | | | |
|---|---|---|---|---|---|
| 2001–02 | Notts Co | 43 | 19 | | |
| 2002–03 | Notts Co | 33 | 10 | **108** | **43** |
| 2002–03 | Hull C | 0 | 0 | | |
| 2003–04 | Hull C | 36 | 15 | **36** | **15** |

**APPLEBY, Ritchie‡ (M)** **148** **15**
H: 5 9 W: 11 04 b.Stockton 18-9-75
*Source:* Trainee. *Honours:* England Youth.

| | | | | | |
|---|---|---|---|---|---|
| 1993–94 | Newcastle U | 0 | 0 | | |
| 1994–95 | Newcastle U | 0 | 0 | | |
| 1994–95 | *Darlington* | 0 | 0 | | |
| 1995–96 | Ipswich T | 3 | 0 | **3** | **0** |
| 1996–97 | Swansea C | 11 | 1 | | |
| 1997–98 | Swansea C | 35 | 3 | | |
| 1998–99 | Swansea C | 39 | 3 | | |
| 1999–2000 | Swansea C | 20 | 4 | | |
| 2000–01 | Swansea C | 5 | 0 | | |
| 2001–02 | Swansea C | 10 | 0 | **120** | **11** |
| 2001–02 | Kidderminster H | 19 | 4 | | |
| 2002–03 | Kidderminster H | 0 | 0 | **19** | **4** |
| 2002–03 | Hull C | 6 | 0 | | |
| 2003–04 | Hull C | 0 | 0 | **6** | **0** |

**ASHBEE, Ian (M)** **274** **14**
H: 6 1 W: 13 07 b.Birmingham 6-9-76
*Source:* Trainee. *Honours:* England Youth.

| | | | | | |
|---|---|---|---|---|---|
| 1994–95 | Derby Co | 1 | 0 | | |
| 1995–96 | Derby Co | 0 | 0 | | |
| 1996–97 | Derby Co | 0 | 0 | **1** | **0** |
| 1996–97 | Cambridge U | 18 | 0 | | |
| 1997–98 | Cambridge U | 27 | 1 | | |
| 1998–99 | Cambridge U | 31 | 4 | | |
| 1999–2000 | Cambridge U | 45 | 1 | | |
| 2000–01 | Cambridge U | 44 | 3 | | |
| 2001–02 | Cambridge U | 38 | 2 | **203** | **11** |
| 2002–03 | Hull C | 31 | 1 | | |
| 2003–04 | Hull C | 39 | 2 | **70** | **3** |

**BURGESS, Ben (F)** **149** **59**
H: 6 3 W: 14 13 b.Buxton 9-11-81
*Source:* Trainee. *Honours:* Eire Under-21.

| | | | | | |
|---|---|---|---|---|---|
| 1998–99 | Blackburn R | 0 | 0 | | |
| 1999–2000 | Blackburn R | 2 | 0 | | |
| 2000–01 | Blackburn R | 0 | 0 | | |
| 2000–01 | Northern Spirit | 27 | 16 | **27** | **16** |
| 2001–02 | Blackburn R | 0 | 0 | **2** | **0** |
| 2001–02 | *Brentford* | 43 | 17 | **43** | **17** |
| 2002–03 | Stockport Co | 19 | 4 | **19** | **4** |
| 2002–03 | *Oldham Ath* | 7 | 0 | **7** | **0** |
| 2002–03 | Hull C | 7 | 4 | | |
| 2003–04 | Hull C | 44 | 18 | **51** | **22** |

**DAWSON, Andy (D)** **228** **11**
H: 5 9 W: 11 12 b.Northallerton 20-10-78
*Source:* Trainee.

| | | | | | |
|---|---|---|---|---|---|
| 1995–96 | Nottingham F | 0 | 0 | | |
| 1996–97 | Nottingham F | 0 | 0 | | |
| 1997–98 | Nottingham F | 0 | 0 | | |
| 1998–99 | Nottingham F | 0 | 0 | | |
| 1998–99 | Scunthorpe U | 24 | 0 | | |
| 1999–2000 | Scunthorpe U | 43 | 2 | | |
| 2000–01 | Scunthorpe U | 41 | 4 | | |
| 2001–02 | Scunthorpe U | 44 | 0 | | |
| 2002–03 | Scunthorpe U | 43 | 2 | **195** | **8** |
| 2003–04 | Hull C | 33 | 3 | **33** | **3** |

**DELANEY, Damien (D)** **105** **4**
H: 6 3 W: 13 10 b.Cork 20-7-81
*Source:* Cork C.

| | | | | | |
|---|---|---|---|---|---|
| 2000–01 | Leicester C | 5 | 0 | | |
| 2001–02 | Leicester C | 3 | 0 | | |
| 2001–02 | *Stockport Co* | 12 | 1 | **12** | **1** |
| 2001–02 | *Huddersfield T* | 2 | 0 | **2** | **0** |
| 2002–03 | Leicester C | 0 | 0 | **8** | **0** |
| 2002–03 | *Mansfield T* | 7 | 0 | **7** | **0** |
| 2002–03 | Hull C | 30 | 1 | | |
| 2003–04 | Hull C | 46 | 2 | **76** | **3** |

**DONALDSON, Clayton (F)** **2** **0**
H: 6 1 W: 11 07 b.Bradford 7-2-84
*Source:* Scholar.

| | | | | | |
|---|---|---|---|---|---|
| 2002–03 | Hull C | 2 | 0 | | |
| 2003–04 | Hull C | 0 | 0 | **2** | **0** |

**ELLIOTT, Stuart (M)** **244** **75**
H: 5 10 W: 11 09 b.Belfast 23-7-78
*Honours:* Northern Ireland Under-21, 20 full caps, 2 goals.

| | | | | | |
|---|---|---|---|---|---|
| 1994–95 | Glentoran | 0 | 0 | | |
| 1995–96 | Glentoran | 1 | 0 | | |
| 1996–97 | Glentoran | 8 | 1 | | |
| 1997–98 | Glentoran | 22 | 5 | | |
| 1998–99 | Glentoran | 31 | 7 | | |
| 1999–2000 | Glentoran | 34 | 16 | **96** | **29** |
| 2000–01 | Motherwell | 33 | 10 | | |
| 2001–02 | Motherwell | 37 | 10 | **70** | **20** |
| 2002–03 | Hull C | 36 | 12 | | |
| 2003–04 | Hull C | 42 | 14 | **78** | **26** |

**FETTIS, Alan (G)** **312** **2**
H: 6 1 W: 11 04 b.Newtownards 1-2-71
*Source:* Ards. *Honours:* Northern Ireland Schools, Youth, B, 25 full caps.

| | | | | | |
|---|---|---|---|---|---|
| 1991–92 | Hull C | 43 | 0 | | |
| 1992–93 | Hull C | 20 | 0 | | |
| 1993–94 | Hull C | 37 | 0 | | |
| 1994–95 | Hull C | 28 | 2 | | |
| 1995–96 | Hull C | 7 | 0 | | |
| 1995–96 | *WBA* | 3 | 0 | **3** | **0** |
| 1996–97 | Nottingham F | 4 | 0 | | |
| 1997–98 | Nottingham F | 0 | 0 | **4** | **0** |
| 1997–98 | Blackburn R | 8 | 0 | | |
| 1998–99 | Blackburn R | 2 | 0 | | |
| 1999–2000 | Blackburn R | 1 | 0 | **11** | **0** |
| 1999–2000 | *Leicester C* | 0 | 0 | | |
| 1999–2000 | York C | 13 | 0 | | |
| 2000–01 | York C | 46 | 0 | | |
| 2001–02 | York C | 45 | 0 | | |
| 2002–03 | York C | 21 | 0 | **125** | **0** |
| 2002–03 | Hull C | 17 | 0 | | |
| 2003–04 | Hull C | 3 | 0 | **155** | **2** |
| 2003–04 | *Sheffield U* | 3 | 0 | **3** | **0** |
| 2003–04 | *Grimsby T* | 11 | 0 | **11** | **0** |

**FORRESTER, Jamie (F)** **324** **96**
H: 5 6 W: 11 00 b.Bradford 1-11-74
*Source:* Auxerre. *Honours:* England Schools, Youth.

| | | | | | |
|---|---|---|---|---|---|
| 1992–93 | Leeds U | 6 | 0 | | |
| 1993–94 | Leeds U | 3 | 0 | | |
| 1994–95 | Leeds U | 0 | 0 | | |
| 1994–95 | *Southend U* | 5 | 0 | **5** | **0** |
| 1994–95 | *Grimsby T* | 9 | 1 | | |
| 1995–96 | Leeds U | 0 | 0 | **9** | **0** |
| 1995–96 | Grimsby T | 28 | 5 | | |
| 1996–97 | Grimsby T | 13 | 1 | **50** | **7** |
| 1996–97 | Scunthorpe U | 10 | 6 | | |
| 1997–98 | Scunthorpe U | 45 | 11 | | |
| 1998–99 | Scunthorpe U | 46 | 20 | **101** | **37** |
| 1999–2000 | Utrecht | 1 | 0 | **1** | **0** |
| 1999–2000 | Walsall | 5 | 0 | **5** | **0** |
| 1999–2000 | *Northampton T* | 10 | 6 | | |
| 2000–01 | Northampton T | 43 | 17 | | |
| 2001–02 | Northampton T | 43 | 17 | | |
| 2002–03 | Northampton T | 25 | 5 | **121** | **45** |
| 2002–03 | Hull C | 11 | 3 | | |
| 2003–04 | Hull C | 21 | 4 | **32** | **7** |

**FRANCE, Ryan (M)** **28** **2**
H: 5 11 W: 11 11 b.Sheffield 13-12-80
*Source:* Alfreton T.

| | | | | | |
|---|---|---|---|---|---|
| 2003–04 | Hull C | 28 | 2 | **28** | **2** |

**FRY, Russell (M)** **0** **0**
H: 6 0 W: 11 13 b.Hull 4-12-85
*Source:* Scholar.

| | | | | | |
|---|---|---|---|---|---|
| 2002–03 | Hull C | 0 | 0 | | |
| 2003–04 | Hull C | 0 | 0 | | |

**GREEN, Stuart (M)** **96** **17**
H: 5 10 W: 11 00 b.Carlisle 15-6-81
*Source:* Trainee.

| | | | | | |
|---|---|---|---|---|---|
| 1999–2000 | Newcastle U | 0 | 0 | | |
| 2000–01 | Newcastle U | 0 | 0 | | |
| 2001–02 | Newcastle U | 0 | 0 | | |
| 2001–02 | *Carlisle U* | 16 | 3 | | |
| 2002–03 | Newcastle U | 0 | 0 | | |
| 2002–03 | Hull C | 28 | 6 | | |
| 2002–03 | *Carlisle U* | 10 | 2 | **26** | **5** |
| 2003–04 | Hull C | 42 | 6 | **70** | **12** |

**HINDS, Richard (D)** **94** **1**
H: 6 2 W: 12 02 b.Sheffield 22-8-80
*Source:* Schoolboy.

| | | | | | |
|---|---|---|---|---|---|
| 1998–99 | Tranmere R | 2 | 0 | | |
| 1999–2000 | Tranmere R | 6 | 0 | | |
| 2000–01 | Tranmere R | 29 | 0 | | |
| 2001–02 | Tranmere R | 10 | 0 | | |
| 2002–03 | Tranmere R | 8 | 0 | **55** | **0** |
| 2003–04 | Hull C | 39 | 1 | **39** | **1** |

**HOLT, Andy* (M)** **211** **13**
H: 6 1 W: 12 06 b.Stockport 21-5-78
*Source:* Trainee.

| | | | | | |
|---|---|---|---|---|---|
| 1996–97 | Oldham Ath | 1 | 0 | | |
| 1997–98 | Oldham Ath | 14 | 1 | | |
| 1998–99 | Oldham Ath | 43 | 5 | | |
| 1999–2000 | Oldham Ath | 46 | 3 | | |
| 2000–01 | Oldham Ath | 20 | 1 | **124** | **10** |
| 2000–01 | *Hull C* | 10 | 2 | | |
| 2001–02 | Hull C | 30 | 0 | | |
| 2002–03 | Hull C | 6 | 0 | | |
| 2002–03 | *Barnsley* | 7 | 0 | **7** | **0** |
| 2002–03 | *Shrewsbury T* | 9 | 0 | **9** | **0** |
| 2003–04 | Hull C | 25 | 1 | **71** | **3** |

**JOSEPH, Marc (D)** **269** **3**
H: 6 2 W: 10 07 b.Leicester 10-11-76
*Source:* Trainee.

| | | | | | |
|---|---|---|---|---|---|
| 1995–96 | Cambridge U | 12 | 0 | | |
| 1996–97 | Cambridge U | 8 | 0 | | |
| 1997–98 | Cambridge U | 41 | 0 | | |
| 1998–99 | Cambridge U | 29 | 0 | | |
| 1999–2000 | Cambridge U | 33 | 0 | | |
| 2000–01 | Cambridge U | 30 | 0 | **153** | **0** |
| 2001–02 | Peterborough U | 44 | 2 | | |
| 2002–03 | Peterborough U | 17 | 0 | **61** | **2** |
| 2002–03 | Hull C | 23 | 0 | | |
| 2003–04 | Hull C | 32 | 1 | **55** | **1** |

**MUSSELWHITE, Paul* (G)** **539** **0**
H: 6 2 W: 14 02 b.Portsmouth 22-12-68
*Source:* Apprentice.

| | | | | | |
|---|---|---|---|---|---|
| 1987–88 | Portsmouth | 0 | 0 | | |
| 1988–89 | Scunthorpe U | 41 | 0 | | |
| 1989–90 | Scunthorpe U | 29 | 0 | | |
| 1990–91 | Scunthorpe U | 38 | 0 | | |
| 1991–92 | Scunthorpe U | 24 | 0 | **132** | **0** |
| 1992–93 | Port Vale | 41 | 0 | | |
| 1993–94 | Port Vale | 46 | 0 | | |
| 1994–95 | Port Vale | 44 | 0 | | |
| 1995–96 | Port Vale | 39 | 0 | | |
| 1996–97 | Port Vale | 33 | 0 | | |
| 1997–98 | Port Vale | 41 | 0 | | |
| 1998–99 | Port Vale | 38 | 0 | | |
| 1999–2000 | Port Vale | 30 | 0 | **312** | **0** |
| 2000–01 | Sheffield W | 0 | 0 | | |
| 2000–01 | Hull C | 37 | 0 | | |
| 2001–02 | Hull C | 20 | 0 | | |
| 2002–03 | Hull C | 20 | 0 | | |
| 2003–04 | Hull C | 18 | 0 | **95** | **0** |

**MYHILL, Boaz (G)** **42** **0**
H: 6 3 W: 14 06 b.California 9-11-82
*Source:* Scholar. *Honours:* England Youth, Under-20.

| | | | | | |
|---|---|---|---|---|---|
| 2000–01 | Aston Villa | 0 | 0 | | |
| 2001–02 | Aston Villa | 0 | 0 | | |
| 2001–02 | *Stoke C* | 0 | 0 | | |
| 2002–03 | Aston Villa | 0 | 0 | | |
| 2002–03 | *Bristol C* | 0 | 0 | | |
| 2002–03 | *Bradford C* | 2 | 0 | **2** | **0** |
| 2003–04 | Aston Villa | 0 | 0 | | |
| 2003–04 | *Macclesfield T* | 15 | 0 | **15** | **0** |
| 2003–04 | *Stockport Co* | 2 | 0 | **2** | **0** |
| 2003–04 | Hull C | 23 | 0 | **23** | **0** |

**PEAT, Nathan (D)** **8** **0**
H: 5 9 W: 10 09 b.Hull 19-9-82
*Source:* Scholar.

| | | | | | |
|---|---|---|---|---|---|
| 2002–03 | Hull C | 1 | 0 | | |
| 2003–04 | Hull C | 1 | 0 | **2** | **0** |
| 2003–04 | *Cambridge U* | 6 | 0 | **6** | **0** |

**PRICE, Jason (M)** **241** **38**
H: 6 2 W: 11 05 b.Pontypridd 12-4-77
*Source:* Aberaman Ath. *Honours:* Wales Under-21.

| | | | | | |
|---|---|---|---|---|---|
| 1995–96 | Swansea C | 0 | 0 | | |
| 1996–97 | Swansea C | 2 | 0 | | |
| 1997–98 | Swansea C | 34 | 3 | | |
| 1998–99 | Swansea C | 28 | 4 | | |
| 1999–2000 | Swansea C | 39 | 6 | | |
| 2000–01 | Swansea C | 41 | 4 | **144** | **17** |
| 2001–02 | Brentford | 15 | 1 | **15** | **1** |
| 2001–02 | Tranmere R | 24 | 7 | | |
| 2002–03 | Tranmere R | 25 | 4 | **49** | **11** |
| 2003–04 | Hull C | 33 | 9 | **33** | **9** |

**REGAN, Carl‡ (D) 75 0**
H: 6 0 W: 11 03 b.Liverpool 14-1-80
*Source:* Trainee. *Honours:* England Youth.

| | | | | | |
|---|---|---|---|---|---|
| 1997–98 | Everton | 0 | 0 | | |
| 1998–99 | Everton | 0 | 0 | | |
| 1999–2000 | Everton | 0 | 0 | | |
| 2000–01 | Barnsley | 27 | 0 | | |
| 2001–02 | Barnsley | 10 | 0 | | |
| 2002–03 | Barnsley | 0 | 0 | **37** | **0** |
| 2002–03 | Hull C | 38 | 0 | | |
| 2003–04 | Hull C | 0 | 0 | **38** | **0** |

**RUSSELL, Simon§ (M) 1 0**
b.Beverley 19-3-85
*Source:* Scholar.

| | | | | | |
|---|---|---|---|---|---|
| 2002–03 | Hull C | 1 | 0 | | |
| 2003–04 | Hull C | 0 | 0 | **1** | **0** |

**THELWELL, Alton (D) 44 1**
H: 5 10 W: 12 02 b.Holloway 5-9-80
*Source:* Trainee.

| | | | | | |
|---|---|---|---|---|---|
| 1998–99 | Tottenham H | 0 | 0 | | |
| 1999–2000 | Tottenham H | 0 | 0 | | |
| 2000–01 | Tottenham H | 16 | 0 | | |
| 2001–02 | Tottenham H | 2 | 0 | | |
| 2002–03 | Tottenham H | 0 | 0 | **18** | **0** |
| 2003–04 | Hull C | 26 | 1 | **26** | **1** |

**WALTERS, Jonathan (F) 39 6**
H: 6 0 W: 12 06 b.Wirral 20-9-83
*Source:* Blackburn R Scholar. *Honours:* Eire Under-21.

| | | | | | |
|---|---|---|---|---|---|
| 2001–02 | Bolton W | 0 | 0 | | |
| 2002–03 | Bolton W | 4 | 0 | | |
| 2002–03 | *Hull C* | 11 | 5 | | |
| 2003–04 | Bolton W | 0 | 0 | **4** | **0** |
| 2003–04 | Crewe Alex | 0 | 0 | | |
| 2003–04 | *Barnsley* | 8 | 0 | **8** | **0** |
| 2003–04 | Hull C | 16 | 1 | **27** | **6** |

**WHITTLE, Justin# (D) 272 3**
H: 6 1 W: 12 12 b.Derby 18-3-71
*Source:* Celtic.

| | | | | | |
|---|---|---|---|---|---|
| 1994–95 | Stoke C | 0 | 0 | | |
| 1995–96 | Stoke C | 8 | 0 | | |
| 1996–97 | Stoke C | 37 | 0 | | |
| 1997–98 | Stoke C | 20 | 0 | | |
| 1998–99 | Stoke C | 14 | 1 | **79** | **1** |
| 1998–99 | Hull C | 24 | 1 | | |
| 1999–2000 | Hull C | 38 | 0 | | |
| 2000–01 | Hull C | 38 | 0 | | |
| 2001–02 | Hull C | 36 | 0 | | |
| 2002–03 | Hull C | 39 | 1 | | |
| 2003–04 | Hull C | 18 | 0 | **193** | **2** |

**WISEMAN, Scott (M) 2 0**
H: 6 0 W: 11 06 b.Hull 9-10-85
*Source:* Scholar.

| | | | | | |
|---|---|---|---|---|---|
| 2003–04 | Hull C | 2 | 0 | **2** | **0** |

**Scholars**
Allanson, Ashley G; Beattie, Thomas E; Benson, Alistair D; Byron, Michael J; Cattermole, Liam K L; Cooper, Michael J N; Harvey, Daniel; Hudson, Christopher J; Matthews, Thomas M; O'Neill, Edward; Russell, Simon C; Tomlinson, James; Turnbull, Peter E

**Non Contract**
Butler, Stephen

**Players who do not hold a current contract but their registration has been retained by the club**
Johnson, Julian

## IPSWICH T (38)

**ABIDALLAH, Nabil‡ (M) 3 0**
H: 5 7 W: 9 00 b.Amsterdam 5-8-82

| | | | | | |
|---|---|---|---|---|---|
| 2000–01 | Ipswich T | 2 | 0 | | |
| 2001–02 | Ipswich T | 0 | 0 | | |
| 2002–03 | Ipswich T | 0 | 0 | | |
| 2003–04 | Ipswich T | 0 | 0 | **2** | **0** |
| 2003–04 | *Northampton T* | 1 | 0 | **1** | **0** |

**ARMSTRONG, Alun* (F) 279 72**
H: 6 0 W: 13 08 b.Gateshead 22-2-75
*Source:* School.

| | | | | | |
|---|---|---|---|---|---|
| 1993–94 | Newcastle U | 0 | 0 | | |
| 1994–95 | Stockport Co | 45 | 14 | | |
| 1995–96 | Stockport Co | 46 | 13 | | |
| 1996–97 | Stockport Co | 39 | 9 | | |
| 1997–98 | Stockport Co | 29 | 12 | **159** | **48** |
| 1997–98 | Middlesbrough | 11 | 7 | | |
| 1998–99 | Middlesbrough | 6 | 1 | | |
| 1999–2000 | Middlesbrough | 12 | 1 | | |
| 1999–2000 | *Huddersfield T* | 6 | 0 | **6** | **0** |
| 2000–01 | Middlesbrough | 0 | 0 | **29** | **9** |
| 2000–01 | Ipswich T | 21 | 7 | | |
| 2001–02 | Ipswich T | 32 | 4 | | |
| 2002–03 | Ipswich T | 19 | 1 | | |
| 2003–04 | Ipswich T | 7 | 2 | **79** | **14** |
| 2003–04 | *Bradford C* | 6 | 1 | **6** | **1** |

**ATAY, Adem (F) 0 0**

| | | | | | |
|---|---|---|---|---|---|
| 2003–04 | Ipswich T | 0 | 0 | | |

**BARRON, Scott (D) 0 0**
*Source:* Scholar.

| | | | | | |
|---|---|---|---|---|---|
| 2003–04 | Ipswich T | 0 | 0 | | |

**BART-WILLIAMS, Chris* (M) 422 52**
H: 5 11 W: 11 06 b.Freetown 16-6-74
*Source:* Trainee. *Honours:* England Youth, Under-21.

| | | | | | |
|---|---|---|---|---|---|
| 1990–91 | Leyton Orient | 21 | 2 | | |
| 1991–92 | Leyton Orient | 15 | 0 | **36** | **2** |
| 1991–92 | Sheffield W | 15 | 0 | | |
| 1992–93 | Sheffield W | 34 | 6 | | |
| 1993–94 | Sheffield W | 37 | 8 | | |
| 1994–95 | Sheffield W | 38 | 2 | **124** | **16** |
| 1995–96 | Nottingham F | 33 | 0 | | |
| 1996–97 | Nottingham F | 16 | 1 | | |
| 1997–98 | Nottingham F | 33 | 4 | | |
| 1998–99 | Nottingham F | 24 | 3 | | |
| 1999–2000 | Nottingham F | 38 | 5 | | |
| 2000–01 | Nottingham F | 46 | 14 | | |
| 2001–02 | Nottingham F | 17 | 3 | **207** | **30** |
| 2001–02 | Charlton Ath | 16 | 1 | | |
| 2002–03 | Charlton Ath | 13 | 1 | | |
| 2003–04 | Charlton Ath | 0 | 0 | **29** | **2** |
| 2003–04 | Ipswich T | 26 | 2 | **26** | **2** |

**BENT, Darren (F) 77 29**
H: 5 11 W: 11 07 b.Tooting 6-2-84
*Source:* Scholar. *Honours:* England Youth, Under-21.

| | | | | | |
|---|---|---|---|---|---|
| 2001–02 | Ipswich T | 5 | 1 | | |
| 2002–03 | Ipswich T | 35 | 12 | | |
| 2003–04 | Ipswich T | 37 | 16 | **77** | **29** |

**BENT, Marcus (F) 300 72**
H: 6 2 W: 12 04 b.Hammersmith 19-5-78
*Source:* Trainee. *Honours:* England Under-21.

| | | | | | |
|---|---|---|---|---|---|
| 1995–96 | Brentford | 12 | 1 | | |
| 1996–97 | Brentford | 34 | 3 | | |
| 1997–98 | Brentford | 24 | 4 | **70** | **8** |
| 1997–98 | Crystal Palace | 16 | 5 | | |
| 1998–99 | Crystal Palace | 12 | 0 | **28** | **5** |
| 1998–99 | Port Vale | 15 | 0 | | |
| 1999–2000 | Port Vale | 8 | 1 | **23** | **1** |
| 1999–2000 | Sheffield U | 32 | 15 | | |
| 2000–01 | Sheffield U | 16 | 5 | **48** | **20** |
| 2000–01 | Blackburn R | 28 | 8 | | |
| 2001–02 | Blackburn R | 9 | 0 | **37** | **8** |
| 2001–02 | Ipswich T | 25 | 9 | | |
| 2002–03 | Ipswich T | 32 | 11 | | |
| 2003–04 | Ipswich T | 4 | 1 | **61** | **21** |
| 2003–04 | *Leicester C* | 33 | 9 | **33** | **9** |

**BOWDITCH, Dean (F) 21 4**
H: 5 11 W: 10 08 b.Hertfordshire 15-6-86
*Source:* Trainee. *Honours:* FA Schools, England Youth.

| | | | | | |
|---|---|---|---|---|---|
| 2002–03 | Ipswich T | 5 | 0 | | |
| 2003–04 | Ipswich T | 16 | 4 | **21** | **4** |

**COLLINS, Aidan (D) 1 0**
H: 6 3 W: 13 09 b.Harlow 18-10-86

| | | | | | |
|---|---|---|---|---|---|
| 2002–03 | Ipswich T | 1 | 0 | | |
| 2003–04 | Ipswich T | 0 | 0 | **1** | **0** |

**COUNAGO, Pablo (F) 129 33**
H: 5 11 W: 11 06 b.Pontevedra 9-8-79

| | | | | | |
|---|---|---|---|---|---|
| 1998–99 | Numancia | 13 | 1 | **13** | **1** |
| 1998–99 | Celta Vigo | 1 | 0 | | |
| 1999–2000 | Huelva | 26 | 4 | **26** | **4** |
| 2000–01 | Celta Vigo | 8 | 0 | **9** | **0** |
| 2001–02 | Ipswich T | 13 | 0 | | |
| 2002–03 | Ipswich T | 39 | 17 | | |
| 2003–04 | Ipswich T | 29 | 11 | **81** | **28** |

**DAVIS, Kelvin (G) 272 0**
H: 6 1 W: 14 00 b.Bedford 29-9-76
*Source:* Trainee. *Honours:* England Youth, Under-21.

| | | | | | |
|---|---|---|---|---|---|
| 1993–94 | Luton T | 1 | 0 | | |
| 1994–95 | Luton T | 9 | 0 | | |
| 1994–95 | *Torquay U* | 2 | 0 | **2** | **0** |
| 1995–96 | Luton T | 6 | 0 | | |
| 1996–97 | Luton T | 0 | 0 | | |
| 1997–98 | Luton T | 32 | 0 | | |
| 1997–98 | *Hartlepool U* | 2 | 0 | **2** | **0** |
| 1998–99 | Luton T | 44 | 0 | **92** | **0** |
| 1999–2000 | Wimbledon | 0 | 0 | | |
| 2000–01 | Wimbledon | 45 | 0 | | |
| 2001–02 | Wimbledon | 40 | 0 | | |
| 2002–03 | Wimbledon | 46 | 0 | **131** | **0** |
| 2003–04 | Ipswich T | 45 | 0 | **45** | **0** |

**DIALLO, Drissa (D) 33 1**
H: 6 0 W: 11 08 b.Nouadhibou 4-1-73
*Honours:* Guinea full caps.

| | | | | | |
|---|---|---|---|---|---|
| 2002–03 | Burnley | 14 | 1 | **14** | **1** |
| 2003–04 | Ipswich T | 19 | 0 | **19** | **0** |

**HOGG, Chris (D) 10 0**
H: 6 0 W: 12 07 b.Middlesbrough 12-3-85
*Source:* Trainee. *Honours:* England Youth.

| | | | | | |
|---|---|---|---|---|---|
| 2002–03 | Ipswich T | 0 | 0 | | |
| 2003–04 | Ipswich T | 0 | 0 | | |
| 2003–04 | *Boston U* | 10 | 0 | **10** | **0** |

**KUQI, Shefki (F) 257 69**
H: 6 2 W: 13 10 b.Kosovo 10-11-76
*Source:* Trepka, Miki. *Honours:* Albania 8 full caps, 1 goal; Finland 34 full caps, 4 goals.

| | | | | | |
|---|---|---|---|---|---|
| 1995 | MP | 24 | 3 | | |
| 1996 | MP | 26 | 7 | **50** | **10** |
| 1997 | HJK Helsinki | 25 | 6 | | |
| 1998 | HJK Helsinki | 22 | 1 | | |
| 1999 | HJK Helsinki | 25 | 11 | **72** | **18** |
| From Jokerit | | | | | |
| 2000–01 | Stockport Co | 17 | 6 | | |
| 2001–02 | Stockport Co | 18 | 5 | **35** | **11** |
| 2001–02 | Sheffield W | 17 | 6 | | |
| 2002–03 | Sheffield W | 40 | 8 | | |
| 2003–04 | Sheffield W | 7 | 5 | **64** | **19** |
| 2003–04 | Ipswich T | 36 | 11 | **36** | **11** |

**MAGILTON, Jim# (M) 507 60**
H: 6 0 W: 13 10 b.Belfast 6-5-69
*Source:* Apprentice. *Honours:* Northern Ireland Schools, Youth, Under-21, Under-23, 52 full caps, 5 goals. Football League.

| | | | | | |
|---|---|---|---|---|---|
| 1986–87 | Liverpool | 0 | 0 | | |
| 1987–88 | Liverpool | 0 | 0 | | |
| 1988–89 | Liverpool | 0 | 0 | | |
| 1989–90 | Liverpool | 0 | 0 | | |
| 1990–91 | Liverpool | 0 | 0 | | |
| 1990–91 | Oxford U | 37 | 6 | | |
| 1991–92 | Oxford U | 44 | 12 | | |
| 1992–93 | Oxford U | 40 | 11 | | |
| 1993–94 | Oxford U | 29 | 5 | **150** | **34** |
| 1993–94 | Southampton | 15 | 0 | | |
| 1994–95 | Southampton | 42 | 6 | | |
| 1995–96 | Southampton | 31 | 3 | | |
| 1996–97 | Southampton | 37 | 4 | | |
| 1997–98 | Southampton | 5 | 0 | **130** | **13** |
| 1997–98 | Sheffield W | 21 | 1 | | |
| 1998–99 | Sheffield W | 6 | 0 | **27** | **1** |
| 1998–99 | Ipswich T | 19 | 3 | | |
| 1999–2000 | Ipswich T | 38 | 4 | | |
| 2000–01 | Ipswich T | 33 | 1 | | |
| 2001–02 | Ipswich T | 24 | 0 | | |
| 2002–03 | Ipswich T | 40 | 3 | | |
| 2003–04 | Ipswich T | 46 | 1 | **200** | **12** |

**MAKIN, Chris# (D) 336 7**
H: 5 10 W: 11 02 b.Manchester 8-5-73
*Source:* Trainee. *Honours:* England Schools, Under-21.

| | | | | | |
|---|---|---|---|---|---|
| 1991–92 | Oldham Ath | 0 | 0 | | |
| 1992–93 | Oldham Ath | 0 | 0 | | |
| 1992–93 | *Wigan Ath* | 15 | 2 | **15** | **2** |
| 1993–94 | Oldham Ath | 27 | 1 | | |
| 1994–95 | Oldham Ath | 28 | 1 | | |
| 1995–96 | Oldham Ath | 39 | 2 | **94** | **4** |
| 1996–97 | Marseille | 29 | 0 | **29** | **0** |
| 1997–98 | Sunderland | 25 | 0 | | |
| 1998–99 | Sunderland | 38 | 0 | | |
| 1999–2000 | Sunderland | 34 | 1 | | |
| 2000–01 | Sunderland | 23 | 0 | **120** | **1** |

| | | | | | |
|---|---|---|---|---|---|
| 2000–01 | Ipswich T | 10 | 0 | | |
| 2001–02 | Ipswich T | 30 | 0 | | |
| 2002–03 | Ipswich T | 33 | 0 | | |
| 2003–04 | Ipswich T | 5 | 0 | **78** | **0** |

**McGREAL, John# (D)** **318** **5**

H: 5 11 W: 13 00 b.Birkenhead 2-6-72

*Source:* Trainee.

| | | | | | |
|---|---|---|---|---|---|
| 1990–91 | Tranmere R | 3 | 0 | | |
| 1991–92 | Tranmere R | 0 | 0 | | |
| 1992–93 | Tranmere R | 0 | 0 | | |
| 1993–94 | Tranmere R | 15 | 1 | | |
| 1994–95 | Tranmere R | 43 | 0 | | |
| 1995–96 | Tranmere R | 32 | 0 | | |
| 1996–97 | Tranmere R | 24 | 0 | | |
| 1997–98 | Tranmere R | 42 | 0 | | |
| 1998–99 | Tranmere R | 36 | 0 | **195** | **1** |
| 1999–2000 | Ipswich T | 34 | 0 | | |
| 2000–01 | Ipswich T | 28 | 1 | | |
| 2001–02 | Ipswich T | 27 | 1 | | |
| 2002–03 | Ipswich T | 16 | 1 | | |
| 2003–04 | Ipswich T | 18 | 1 | **123** | **4** |

**MILLER, Tommy (M)** **209** **52**

H: 6 1 W: 11 12 b.Shotton Colliery 8-1-79

*Source:* Trainee.

| | | | | | |
|---|---|---|---|---|---|
| 1997–98 | Hartlepool U | 13 | 1 | | |
| 1998–99 | Hartlepool U | 34 | 4 | | |
| 1999–2000 | Hartlepool U | 44 | 14 | | |
| 2000–01 | Hartlepool U | 46 | 16 | | |
| 2001–02 | Hartlepool U | 0 | 0 | **137** | **35** |
| 2001–02 | Ipswich T | 8 | 0 | | |
| 2002–03 | Ipswich T | 30 | 6 | | |
| 2003–04 | Ipswich T | 34 | 11 | **72** | **17** |

**MITCHELL, Scott (M)** **2** **0**

H: 5 11 W: 12 00 b.Ely 2-9-85

*Source:* Scholar.

| | | | | | |
|---|---|---|---|---|---|
| 2003–04 | Ipswich T | 2 | 0 | **2** | **0** |

**MORROW, Sam‡ (F)** **2** **0**

H: 6 0 W: 12 10 b.Derry 3-3-85

*Source:* Trainee. *Honours:* Northern Ireland Youth.

| | | | | | |
|---|---|---|---|---|---|
| 2002–03 | Ipswich T | 0 | 0 | | |
| 2003–04 | Ipswich T | 0 | 0 | | |
| 2003–04 | *Boston U* | 2 | 0 | **2** | **0** |

**MURRAY, Antonio (M)** **1** **0**

H: 5 9 W: 11 00 b.Cambridge 15-9-84

*Source:* Scholar.

| | | | | | |
|---|---|---|---|---|---|
| 2002–03 | Ipswich T | 1 | 0 | | |
| 2003–04 | Ipswich T | 0 | 0 | **1** | **0** |

**NASH, Gerard (D)** **1** **0**

H: 6 1 W: 11 08 b.Dublin 11-7-86

*Source:* Scholar. *Honours:* Eire Youth.

| | | | | | |
|---|---|---|---|---|---|
| 2003–04 | Ipswich T | 1 | 0 | **1** | **0** |

**NAYLOR, Richard# (F)** **192** **28**

H: 6 1 W: 13 07 b.Leeds 28-2-77

*Source:* Trainee.

| | | | | | |
|---|---|---|---|---|---|
| 1995–96 | Ipswich T | 0 | 0 | | |
| 1996–97 | Ipswich T | 27 | 4 | | |
| 1997–98 | Ipswich T | 5 | 2 | | |
| 1998–99 | Ipswich T | 30 | 5 | | |
| 1999–2000 | Ipswich T | 36 | 8 | | |
| 2000–01 | Ipswich T | 13 | 1 | | |
| 2001–02 | Ipswich T | 14 | 1 | | |
| 2001–02 | *Millwall* | 3 | 0 | **3** | **0** |
| 2001–02 | *Barnsley* | 8 | 0 | **8** | **0** |
| 2002–03 | Ipswich T | 17 | 2 | | |
| 2003–04 | Ipswich T | 39 | 5 | **181** | **28** |

**PATTEN, Ben (D)** **0** **0**

H: 6 1 W: 12 00 b.London 16-2-86

*Source:* Ford U.

| | | | | | |
|---|---|---|---|---|---|
| 2003–04 | Ipswich T | 0 | 0 | | |

**PRICE, Lewis (G)** **1** **0**

H: 6 3 W: 13 06 b.Bournemouth 19-7-84

*Source:* Southampton Academy. *Honours:* Wales Youth.

| | | | | | |
|---|---|---|---|---|---|
| 2002–03 | Ipswich T | 0 | 0 | | |
| 2003–04 | Ipswich T | 1 | 0 | **1** | **0** |

**REUSER, Martijn (M)** **189** **34**

H: 5 7 W: 12 10 b.Amsterdam 1-2-75

*Honours:* Holland 1 full cap.

| | | | | | |
|---|---|---|---|---|---|
| 1993–94 | Ajax | 2 | 0 | | |
| 1994–95 | Ajax | 2 | 0 | | |
| 1995–96 | Ajax | 18 | 3 | | |
| 1996–97 | Ajax | 19 | 3 | | |
| 1997–98 | Ajax | 1 | 0 | **42** | **6** |
| 1997–98 | Vitesse | 24 | 6 | | |
| 1998–99 | Vitesse | 32 | 8 | **56** | **14** |
| 1999–2000 | Ipswich T | 8 | 2 | | |
| 2000–01 | Ipswich T | 26 | 6 | | |
| 2001–02 | Ipswich T | 24 | 1 | | |
| 2002–03 | Ipswich T | 16 | 2 | | |
| 2003–04 | Ipswich T | 17 | 3 | **91** | **14** |

**RICHARDS, Matt (D)** **57** **1**

H: 5 8 W: 10 10 b.Harlow 26-12-84

*Source:* Scholar.

| | | | | | |
|---|---|---|---|---|---|
| 2001–02 | Ipswich T | 0 | 0 | | |
| 2002–03 | Ipswich T | 13 | 0 | | |
| 2003–04 | Ipswich T | 44 | 1 | **57** | **1** |

**SANTOS, Georges (M)** **176** **10**

H: 6 3 W: 14 00 b.Marseille 15-8-70

*Source:* Toulon.

| | | | | | |
|---|---|---|---|---|---|
| 1998–99 | Tranmere R | 37 | 1 | | |
| 1999–2000 | Tranmere R | 10 | 1 | **47** | **2** |
| 1999–2000 | WBA | 8 | 0 | **8** | **0** |
| 2000–01 | Sheffield U | 31 | 4 | | |
| 2001–02 | Sheffield U | 30 | 2 | **61** | **6** |
| 2002–03 | Grimsby T | 26 | 1 | **26** | **1** |
| 2003–04 | Ipswich T | 34 | 1 | **34** | **1** |

**SOBERS, Jerome (D)** **0** **0**

H: 6 2 W: 13 05 b.London 18-4-86

| | | | | | |
|---|---|---|---|---|---|
| 2003–04 | Ipswich T | 0 | 0 | | |

**WESTLAKE, Ian (M)** **43** **6**

H: 5 11 W: 11 00 b.Clacton 10-11-83

*Source:* Scholar.

| | | | | | |
|---|---|---|---|---|---|
| 2002–03 | Ipswich T | 4 | 0 | | |
| 2003–04 | Ipswich T | 39 | 6 | **43** | **6** |

**WILNIS, Fabian# (D)** **413** **9**

H: 5 8 W: 12 06 b.Paramaribo 23-8-70

*Source:* Het Noorden, NOC, De Zwervers, Sparta.

| | | | | | |
|---|---|---|---|---|---|
| 1990–91 | NAC | 7 | 3 | | |
| 1991–92 | NAC | 30 | 0 | | |
| 1992–93 | NAC | 32 | 0 | | |
| 1993–94 | NAC | 34 | 0 | | |
| 1994–95 | NAC | 31 | 0 | **134** | **3** |
| 1995–96 | De Graafschap | 32 | 0 | | |
| 1996–97 | De Graafschap | 23 | 0 | | |
| 1997–98 | De Graafschap | 33 | 1 | | |
| 1998–99 | De Graafschap | 19 | 0 | **107** | **1** |
| 1998–99 | Ipswich T | 18 | 1 | | |
| 1999–2000 | Ipswich T | 35 | 0 | | |
| 2000–01 | Ipswich T | 29 | 2 | | |
| 2001–02 | Ipswich T | 14 | 0 | | |
| 2002–03 | Ipswich T | 35 | 2 | | |
| 2003–04 | Ipswich T | 41 | 0 | **172** | **5** |

**WRIGHT, Jermaine# (M)** **266** **15**

H: 5 10 W: 12 07 b.Greenwich 21-10-75

*Source:* Trainee. *Honours:* England Youth.

| | | | | | |
|---|---|---|---|---|---|
| 1992–93 | Millwall | 0 | 0 | | |
| 1993–94 | Millwall | 0 | 0 | | |
| 1994–95 | Millwall | 0 | 0 | | |
| 1994–95 | Wolverhampton W | 6 | 0 | | |
| 1995–96 | Wolverhampton W | 7 | 0 | | |
| 1995–96 | *Doncaster R* | 13 | 0 | **13** | **0** |
| 1996–97 | Wolverhampton W | 3 | 0 | | |
| 1997–98 | Wolverhampton W | 4 | 0 | **20** | **0** |
| 1997–98 | Crewe Alex | 5 | 0 | | |
| 1998–99 | Crewe Alex | 44 | 5 | **49** | **5** |
| 1999–2000 | Ipswich T | 34 | 1 | | |
| 2000–01 | Ipswich T | 37 | 2 | | |
| 2001–02 | Ipswich T | 29 | 1 | | |
| 2002–03 | Ipswich T | 39 | 1 | | |
| 2003–04 | Ipswich T | 45 | 5 | **184** | **10** |

**Scholars**

Beveridge, Fraser; Boardley, Stuart J; Craig, Liam; Flack, Daniel; Hammond, Blair M V; Kamara, Alfred; Krause, James R; Lordan, Cathal T; Manning, Liam; O'Connor, Gerard; Okay, Erkan; Peat, Scott M; Reid, Craig K; Smith, Marc A; Supple, Shane; Synnott, Michael A R

## KIDDERMINSTER H (39)

**AYRES, Lee‡ (D)** **35** **2**

H: 6 2 W: 12 06 b.Birmingham 28-8-82

| | | | | | |
|---|---|---|---|---|---|
| 2001–02 | Kidderminster H | 6 | 0 | | |
| 2002–03 | Kidderminster H | 29 | 2 | | |
| 2003–04 | Kidderminster H | 0 | 0 | **35** | **2** |

**BENNETT, Dean# (M)** **155** **16**

H: 6 0 W: 12 00 b.Wolverhampton 13-12-77

| | | | | | |
|---|---|---|---|---|---|
| 1996–97 | WBA | 1 | 0 | | |
| 1997–98 | WBA | 0 | 0 | **1** | **0** |

From Bromsgrove R

| | | | | | |
|---|---|---|---|---|---|
| 2000–01 | Kidderminster H | 42 | 4 | | |
| 2001–02 | Kidderminster H | 42 | 8 | | |
| 2002–03 | Kidderminster H | 32 | 1 | | |
| 2003–04 | Kidderminster H | 38 | 3 | **154** | **16** |

**BETTS, Robert‡ (D)** **37** **2**

H: 5 10 W: 11 00 b.Doncaster 21-12-81

*Source:* School.

| | | | | | |
|---|---|---|---|---|---|
| 1997–98 | Doncaster R | 3 | 0 | **3** | **0** |
| 1998–99 | Coventry C | 0 | 0 | | |
| 1999–2000 | Coventry C | 2 | 0 | | |
| 2000–01 | Coventry C | 1 | 0 | | |
| 2000–01 | *Plymouth Arg* | 4 | 0 | **4** | **0** |
| 2001–02 | *Lincoln C* | 3 | 0 | **3** | **0** |
| 2001–02 | Coventry C | 9 | 0 | | |
| 2002–03 | Coventry C | 1 | 0 | **13** | **0** |
| 2003–04 | Rochdale | 5 | 2 | **5** | **2** |
| 2003–04 | Kidderminster H | 9 | 0 | **9** | **0** |

**BROCK, Stuart* (G)** **135** **0**

H: 6 1 W: 14 00 b.Sandwell 26-9-76

*Source:* Trainee.

| | | | | | |
|---|---|---|---|---|---|
| 1994–95 | Aston Villa | 0 | 0 | | |
| 1995–96 | Aston Villa | 0 | 0 | | |
| 1996–97 | Aston Villa | 0 | 0 | | |
| 1996–97 | Northampton T | 0 | 0 | | |
| 1997–98 | Northampton T | 0 | 0 | | |
| 1998–99 | Northampton T | 0 | 0 | | |
| 1999–2000 | Northampton T | 0 | 0 | | |
| 2000–01 | Kidderminster H | 21 | 0 | | |
| 2001–02 | Kidderminster H | 42 | 0 | | |
| 2002–03 | Kidderminster H | 35 | 0 | | |
| 2003–04 | Kidderminster H | 37 | 0 | **135** | **0** |

**BURTON, Steven (D)** **23** **0**

H: 6 1 W: 11 05 b.Hull 10-10-82

*Source:* Scholar.

| | | | | | |
|---|---|---|---|---|---|
| 2002–03 | Hull C | 11 | 0 | | |
| 2003–04 | Hull C | 0 | 0 | **11** | **0** |
| 2003–04 | Kidderminster H | 12 | 0 | **12** | **0** |

**CHRISTIANSEN, Jesper (F)** **48** **4**

H: 6 3 W: 13 06 b.Denmark 18-6-80

| | | | | | |
|---|---|---|---|---|---|
| 2002–03 | Odense | 26 | 3 | | |
| 2003–04 | Odense | 1 | 0 | **27** | **3** |
| 2003–04 | Kidderminster H | 21 | 1 | **21** | **1** |

**COLEMAN, Kenny* (D)** **25** **0**

H: 6 0 W: 13 07 b.Cork 20-9-82

*Source:* Scholar.

| | | | | | |
|---|---|---|---|---|---|
| 2000–01 | Wolverhampton W | 0 | 0 | | |
| 2001–02 | Wolverhampton W | 0 | 0 | | |
| 2002–03 | Wolverhampton W | 0 | 0 | | |
| 2002–03 | *Kidderminster H* | 15 | 0 | | |
| 2003–04 | Kidderminster H | 10 | 0 | **25** | **0** |

**DANBY, John (G)** **11** **0**

H: 6 2 W: 14 06 b.Stoke 20-9-83

| | | | | | |
|---|---|---|---|---|---|
| 2001–02 | Kidderminster H | 2 | 0 | | |
| 2002–03 | Kidderminster H | 0 | 0 | | |
| 2003–04 | Kidderminster H | 9 | 0 | **11** | **0** |

**FLYNN, Sean‡ (M)** **387** **28**

H: 5 8 W: 11 09 b.Birmingham 13-3-68

*Source:* Halesowen T.

| | | | | | |
|---|---|---|---|---|---|
| 1991–92 | Coventry C | 22 | 2 | | |
| 1992–93 | Coventry C | 7 | 0 | | |
| 1993–94 | Coventry C | 36 | 3 | | |
| 1994–95 | Coventry C | 32 | 4 | **97** | **9** |
| 1995–96 | Derby Co | 42 | 2 | | |
| 1996–97 | Derby Co | 17 | 1 | **59** | **3** |
| 1996–97 | *Stoke C* | 5 | 0 | **5** | **0** |
| 1997–98 | WBA | 35 | 2 | | |
| 1998–99 | WBA | 38 | 2 | | |
| 1999–2000 | WBA | 36 | 4 | **109** | **8** |
| 2000–01 | Tranmere R | 35 | 1 | | |
| 2001–02 | Tranmere R | 31 | 5 | **66** | **6** |
| 2002–03 | Kidderminster H | 45 | 2 | | |
| 2003–04 | Kidderminster H | 6 | 0 | **51** | **2** |

**GADSBY, Matt* (D)** **89** **2**

H: 6 1 W: 11 12 b.Sutton Coldfield 6-9-79

*Source:* Trainee.

| | | | | | |
|---|---|---|---|---|---|
| 1997–98 | Walsall | 1 | 0 | | |
| 1998–99 | Walsall | 6 | 0 | | |
| 1999–2000 | Walsall | 3 | 0 | | |
| 2000–01 | Walsall | 5 | 0 | | |

| | | | | | |
|---|---|---|---|---|---|
| 2001–02 | Walsall | 22 | 0 | | |
| 2002–03 | Walsall | 0 | 0 | **37** | **0** |
| 2002–03 | Mansfield T | 20 | 0 | **20** | **0** |
| 2003–04 | Kidderminster H | 32 | 2 | **32** | **2** |

**HATSWELL, Wayne (D)** **80 2**
H: 6 0 W: 13 10 b.Swindon 8-2-75
*Source:* Forest Green R.

| | | | | | |
|---|---|---|---|---|---|
| 2000–01 | Oxford U | 27 | 0 | | |
| 2001–02 | Oxford U | 21 | 0 | | |
| 2002–03 | Oxford U | 0 | 0 | **48** | **0** |
| From Chester C. | | | | | |
| 2003–04 | Kidderminster H | 32 | 2 | **32** | **2** |

**HEATH, Nick‡ (M)** **1 0**
H: 5 9 W: 11 00 b.Sutton Coldfield 2-1-85

| | | | | | |
|---|---|---|---|---|---|
| 2002–03 | Kidderminster H | 1 | 0 | | |
| 2003–04 | Kidderminster H | 0 | 0 | **1** | **0** |

**HINTON, Craig# (D)** **173 3**
H: 6 0 W: 12 06 b.Wolverhampton 26-11-77
*Source:* Trainee.

| | | | | | |
|---|---|---|---|---|---|
| 1996–97 | Birmingham C | 0 | 0 | | |
| 1997–98 | Birmingham C | 0 | 0 | | |
| 2000–01 | Kidderminster H | 46 | 2 | | |
| 2001–02 | Kidderminster H | 41 | 0 | | |
| 2002–03 | Kidderminster H | 44 | 0 | | |
| 2003–04 | Kidderminster H | 42 | 1 | **173** | **3** |

**JENKINS, Lee (M)** **176 3**
H: 5 9 W: 11 00 b.Pontypool 28-6-79
*Source:* Trainee. *Honours:* Wales Schools, Youth, Under-21.

| | | | | | |
|---|---|---|---|---|---|
| 1996–97 | Swansea C | 23 | 2 | | |
| 1997–98 | Swansea C | 21 | 0 | | |
| 1998–99 | Swansea C | 12 | 0 | | |
| 1999–2000 | Swansea C | 16 | 0 | | |
| 2000–01 | Swansea C | 39 | 0 | | |
| 2001–02 | Swansea C | 15 | 1 | | |
| 2002–03 | Swansea C | 32 | 0 | | |
| 2003–04 | Swansea C | 11 | 0 | **169** | **3** |
| 2003–04 | Kidderminster H | 7 | 0 | **7** | **0** |

**KEATES, Dean (M)** **217 15**
H: 5 6 W: 10 10 b.Walsall 30-6-78
*Source:* Trainee.

| | | | | | |
|---|---|---|---|---|---|
| 1996–97 | Walsall | 2 | 0 | | |
| 1997–98 | Walsall | 33 | 1 | | |
| 1998–99 | Walsall | 43 | 2 | | |
| 1999–2000 | Walsall | 35 | 1 | | |
| 2000–01 | Walsall | 33 | 4 | | |
| 2001–02 | Walsall | 13 | 1 | **159** | **9** |
| 2002–03 | Hull C | 36 | 4 | | |
| 2003–04 | Hull C | 14 | 0 | **50** | **4** |
| 2003–04 | Kidderminster H | 8 | 2 | **8** | **2** |

**LEWIS, Matt‡ (F)** **8 0**
H: 6 2 W: 12 02 b.Coventry 20-3-84
*Source:* Marconi.

| | | | | | |
|---|---|---|---|---|---|
| 2001–02 | Kidderminster H | 2 | 0 | | |
| 2002–03 | Kidderminster H | 2 | 0 | | |
| 2003–04 | Kidderminster H | 4 | 0 | **8** | **0** |

**McHALE, Chris (D)** **1 0**
H: 6 0 W: 12 00 b.Birmingham 4-11-82

| | | | | | |
|---|---|---|---|---|---|
| 2003–04 | Kidderminster H | 1 | 0 | **1** | **0** |

**MURRAY, Adam (M)** **94 10**
H: 5 9 W: 11 11 b.Birmingham 30-9-81
*Source:* Trainee. *Honours:* England Youth, Under-20.

| | | | | | |
|---|---|---|---|---|---|
| 1998–99 | Derby Co | 4 | 0 | | |
| 1999–2000 | Derby Co | 8 | 0 | | |
| 2000–01 | Derby Co | 14 | 0 | | |
| 2001–02 | Derby Co | 6 | 0 | | |
| 2001–02 | *Mansfield T* | 13 | 7 | **13** | **7** |
| 2002–03 | Derby Co | 24 | 0 | | |
| 2003–04 | Derby Co | 0 | 0 | **56** | **0** |
| 2003–04 | Kidderminster H | 22 | 3 | **22** | **3** |
| From Burton Alb. | | | | | |
| 2003–04 | Notts Co | 3 | 0 | **3** | **0** |

**PARRISH, Sean* (M)** **289 40**
H: 5 10 W: 12 00 b.Wrexham 14-3-72
*Source:* Trainee.

| | | | | | |
|---|---|---|---|---|---|
| 1989–90 | Shrewsbury T | 2 | 0 | | |
| 1990–91 | Shrewsbury T | 1 | 0 | **3** | **0** |
| From Telford U | | | | | |
| 1994–95 | Doncaster R | 25 | 3 | | |
| 1995–96 | Doncaster R | 41 | 5 | **66** | **8** |
| 1996–97 | Northampton T | 39 | 8 | | |
| 1997–98 | Northampton T | 12 | 1 | | |
| 1998–99 | Northampton T | 33 | 1 | | |
| 1999–2000 | Northampton T | 25 | 3 | **109** | **13** |
| 2000–01 | Chesterfield | 35 | 10 | | |
| 2001–02 | Chesterfield | 20 | 1 | **55** | **11** |
| 2002–03 | Kidderminster H | 29 | 5 | | |
| 2003–04 | Kidderminster H | 27 | 3 | **56** | **8** |

**RICKARDS, Scott (F)** **13 1**
H: 5 9 W: 12 00 b.Birmingham 3-11-81
*Source:* Tamworth.

| | | | | | |
|---|---|---|---|---|---|
| 2003–04 | Kidderminster H | 13 | 1 | **13** | **1** |

**SALL, Abdou† (D)** **39 2**
H: 6 3 W: 14 00 b.Senegal 1-11-80
*Source:* Toulouse.

| | | | | | |
|---|---|---|---|---|---|
| 2001–02 | Kidderminster H | 27 | 2 | | |
| 2002–03 | Kidderminster H | 4 | 0 | | |
| 2002–03 | *Oxford U* | 1 | 0 | **1** | **0** |
| 2003–04 | Kidderminster H | 7 | 0 | **38** | **2** |

**SHILTON, Sam‡ (M)** **143 12**
H: 5 11 W: 13 00 b.Nottingham 21-7-78
*Source:* School.

| | | | | | |
|---|---|---|---|---|---|
| 1994–95 | Plymouth Arg | 2 | 0 | | |
| 1995–96 | Plymouth Arg | 1 | 0 | **3** | **0** |
| 1995–96 | Coventry C | 0 | 0 | | |
| 1996–97 | Coventry C | 0 | 0 | | |
| 1997–98 | Coventry C | 2 | 0 | | |
| 1998–99 | Coventry C | 5 | 0 | | |
| 1999–2000 | Coventry C | 0 | 0 | **7** | **0** |
| 1999–2000 | Hartlepool U | 21 | 3 | | |
| 2000–01 | Hartlepool U | 33 | 4 | **54** | **7** |
| 2001–02 | Kidderminster H | 24 | 0 | | |
| 2002–03 | Kidderminster H | 41 | 5 | | |
| 2003–04 | Kidderminster H | 14 | 0 | **79** | **5** |

**SMITH, Adie‡ (D)** **122 8**
H: 5 10 W: 12 02 b.Birmingham 11-8-73
*Source:* Bromsgrove R.

| | | | | | |
|---|---|---|---|---|---|
| 2000–01 | Kidderminster H | 34 | 5 | | |
| 2001–02 | Kidderminster H | 36 | 2 | | |
| 2002–03 | Kidderminster H | 30 | 1 | | |
| 2003–04 | Kidderminster H | 22 | 0 | **122** | **8** |

**STAMPS, Scott* (D)** **271 6**
H: 5 10 W: 12 03 b.Edgbaston 20-3-75
*Source:* Trainee.

| | | | | | |
|---|---|---|---|---|---|
| 1992–93 | Torquay U | 2 | 0 | | |
| 1993–94 | Torquay U | 6 | 0 | | |
| 1994–95 | Torquay U | 25 | 1 | | |
| 1995–96 | Torquay U | 23 | 1 | | |
| 1996–97 | Torquay U | 30 | 3 | **86** | **5** |
| 1996–97 | Colchester U | 8 | 0 | | |
| 1997–98 | Colchester U | 27 | 1 | | |
| 1998–99 | Colchester U | 21 | 0 | **56** | **1** |
| 2000–01 | Kidderminster H | 34 | 0 | | |
| 2001–02 | Kidderminster H | 37 | 0 | | |
| 2002–03 | Kidderminster H | 23 | 0 | | |
| 2003–04 | Kidderminster H | 35 | 0 | **129** | **0** |

**WARD, Graham‡ (M)** **21 0**
H: 5 8 W: 11 09 b.Dublin 25-2-83
*Source:* Scholar. *Honours:* Eire Under-21.

| | | | | | |
|---|---|---|---|---|---|
| 2000–01 | Wolverhampton W | 0 | 0 | | |
| 2001–02 | Wolverhampton W | 0 | 0 | | |
| 2002–03 | Wolverhampton W | 0 | 0 | | |
| 2003–04 | Kidderminster H | 21 | 0 | **21** | **0** |

**WILLIAMS, John† (F)** **452 71**
H: 6 1 W: 13 12 b.Birmingham 11-5-68
*Source:* Cradley T.

| | | | | | |
|---|---|---|---|---|---|
| 1991–92 | Swansea C | 39 | 11 | | |
| 1992–93 | Coventry C | 41 | 8 | | |
| 1993–94 | Coventry C | 32 | 3 | | |
| 1994–95 | Coventry C | 7 | 0 | | |
| 1994–95 | *Notts Co* | 5 | 2 | **5** | **2** |
| 1994–95 | *Stoke C* | 4 | 0 | **4** | **0** |
| 1994–95 | *Swansea C* | 7 | 2 | | |
| 1995–96 | Coventry C | 0 | 0 | **80** | **11** |
| 1995–96 | Wycombe W | 29 | 8 | | |
| 1996–97 | Wycombe W | 19 | 1 | **48** | **9** |
| 1996–97 | Hereford U | 11 | 3 | **11** | **3** |
| 1997–98 | Walsall | 1 | 0 | **1** | **0** |
| 1997–98 | Exeter C | 36 | 4 | **36** | **4** |
| 1998–99 | Cardiff C | 43 | 12 | | |
| 1999–2000 | Cardiff C | 0 | 0 | **43** | **12** |
| 1999–2000 | York C | 36 | 3 | | |
| 2000–01 | York C | 6 | 0 | **42** | **3** |
| 2000–01 | Darlington | 24 | 5 | **24** | **5** |
| 2001–02 | Swansea C | 41 | 4 | | |
| 2002–03 | Swansea C | 27 | 1 | **114** | **18** |
| 2003–04 | Kidderminster H | 44 | 4 | **44** | **4** |

**WILLIS, Adam* (D)** **114 2**
H: 6 1 W: 12 02 b.Nuneaton 21-9-76
*Source:* Trainee.

| | | | | | |
|---|---|---|---|---|---|
| 1995–96 | Coventry C | 0 | 0 | | |
| 1996–97 | Coventry C | 0 | 0 | | |
| 1997–98 | Coventry C | 0 | 0 | | |
| 1997–98 | Swindon T | 0 | 0 | | |
| 1998–99 | Swindon T | 11 | 0 | | |
| 1998–99 | *Mansfield T* | 10 | 0 | **10** | **0** |
| 1999–2000 | Swindon T | 23 | 0 | | |
| 2000–01 | Swindon T | 21 | 0 | | |
| 2001–02 | Swindon T | 22 | 1 | | |
| 2002–03 | Swindon T | 15 | 0 | **92** | **1** |
| 2003–04 | Kidderminster H | 12 | 1 | **12** | **1** |

**YATES, Mark‡ (M)** **328 32**
H: 5 11 W: 13 08 b.Birmingham 24-1-70

| | | | | | |
|---|---|---|---|---|---|
| 1987–88 | Birmingham C | 3 | 0 | | |
| 1988–89 | Birmingham C | 20 | 3 | | |
| 1989–90 | Birmingham C | 20 | 2 | | |
| 1990–91 | Birmingham C | 9 | 1 | | |
| 1991–92 | Birmingham C | 2 | 0 | **54** | **6** |
| 1991–92 | Burnley | 17 | 1 | | |
| 1992–93 | Burnley | 1 | 0 | **18** | **1** |
| 1992–93 | *Lincoln C* | 14 | 0 | **14** | **0** |
| 1993–94 | Doncaster R | 34 | 4 | **34** | **4** |
| From Kidderminster H | | | | | |
| 1999–2000 | Cheltenham T | 46 | 2 | | |
| 2000–01 | Cheltenham T | 45 | 6 | | |
| 2001–02 | Cheltenham T | 45 | 7 | | |
| 2002–03 | Cheltenham T | 37 | 2 | | |
| 2003–04 | Cheltenham T | 21 | 2 | **194** | **19** |
| 2003–04 | Kidderminster H | 14 | 2 | **14** | **2** |

**Non Contract**
Sall, Abdou H; Williams, John N

## LEEDS U (40)

**ALLAWAY, Shaun‡ (G)** **0 0**
H: 6 2 W: 13 00 b.Reading 16-2-83
*Source:* Trainee. *Honours:* England Youth, Under-20.

| | | | |
|---|---|---|---|
| 1999–2000 | Reading | 0 | 0 |
| 1999–2000 | Leeds U | 0 | 0 |
| 2000–01 | Leeds U | 0 | 0 |
| 2001–02 | Leeds U | 0 | 0 |
| 2002–03 | *Grimsby T* | 0 | 0 |
| 2002–03 | Leeds U | 0 | 0 |
| 2003–04 | Leeds U | 0 | 0 |
| 2003–04 | *Walsall* | 0 | 0 |

**ARMSTRONG, Chris* (F)** **0 0**
H: 6 1 W: 13 09 b.Durham 8-11-84
*Source:* Scholar.

| | | | |
|---|---|---|---|
| 2001–02 | Leeds U | 0 | 0 |
| 2002–03 | Leeds U | 0 | 0 |
| 2003–04 | Leeds U | 0 | 0 |

**BAKKE, Eirik (M)** **205 25**
H: 6 2 W: 13 03 b.Sogndal 13-9-77
*Honours:* Norway 25 full caps.

| | | | | | |
|---|---|---|---|---|---|
| 1994 | Sogndal | 5 | 0 | | |
| 1995 | Sogndal | 0 | 0 | | |
| 1996 | Sogndal | 19 | 8 | | |
| 1997 | Sogndal | 25 | 4 | | |
| 1998 | Sogndal | 19 | 2 | | |
| 1999 | Sogndal | 8 | 3 | **76** | **17** |
| 1999–2000 | Leeds U | 29 | 2 | | |
| 2000–01 | Leeds U | 29 | 2 | | |
| 2001–02 | Leeds U | 27 | 2 | | |
| 2002–03 | Leeds U | 34 | 1 | | |
| 2003–04 | Leeds U | 10 | 1 | **129** | **8** |

**BARMBY, Nick (M)** **308 53**
H: 5 7 W: 10 09 b.Hull 11-2-74
*Source:* Trainee. *Honours:* England Schools, Youth, Under-21, B, 23 full caps, 4 goals.

| | | | | | |
|---|---|---|---|---|---|
| 1991–92 | Tottenham H | 0 | 0 | | |
| 1992–93 | Tottenham H | 22 | 6 | | |
| 1993–94 | Tottenham H | 27 | 5 | | |
| 1994–95 | Tottenham H | 38 | 9 | **87** | **20** |
| 1995–96 | Middlesbrough | 32 | 7 | | |
| 1996–97 | Middlesbrough | 10 | 1 | **42** | **8** |
| 1996–97 | Everton | 25 | 4 | | |
| 1997–98 | Everton | 30 | 2 | | |
| 1998–99 | Everton | 24 | 3 | | |
| 1999–2000 | Everton | 37 | 9 | **116** | **18** |
| 2000–01 | Liverpool | 26 | 2 | | |

| | | | | | |
|---|---|---|---|---|---|
| 2001–02 | Liverpool | 6 | 0 | **32** | **2** |
| 2002–03 | Leeds U | 19 | 4 | | |
| 2003–04 | *Nottingham F* | 6 | 1 | **6** | **1** |
| 2003–04 | Leeds U | 6 | 0 | **25** | **4** |

**BATTY, David* (M) 438 8**
H: 5 8 W: 12 01 b.Leeds 2-12-68
*Source:* Trainee. *Honours:* England Under-21, B, 42 full caps.

| | | | | | |
|---|---|---|---|---|---|
| 1987–88 | Leeds U | 23 | 1 | | |
| 1988–89 | Leeds U | 30 | 0 | | |
| 1989–90 | Leeds U | 42 | 0 | | |
| 1990–91 | Leeds U | 37 | 0 | | |
| 1991–92 | Leeds U | 40 | 2 | | |
| 1992–93 | Leeds U | 30 | 1 | | |
| 1993–94 | Leeds U | 9 | 0 | | |
| 1993–94 | Blackburn R | 26 | 0 | | |
| 1994–95 | Blackburn R | 5 | 0 | | |
| 1995–96 | Blackburn R | 23 | 1 | **54** | **1** |
| 1995–96 | Newcastle U | 11 | 1 | | |
| 1996–97 | Newcastle U | 32 | 1 | | |
| 1997–98 | Newcastle U | 32 | 1 | | |
| 1998–99 | Newcastle U | 8 | 0 | **83** | **3** |
| 1998–99 | Leeds U | 10 | 0 | | |
| 1999–2000 | Leeds U | 16 | 0 | | |
| 2000–01 | Leeds U | 16 | 0 | | |
| 2001–02 | Leeds U | 36 | 0 | | |
| 2002–03 | Leeds U | 0 | 0 | | |
| 2003–04 | Leeds U | 12 | 0 | **301** | **4** |

**BOWLER, Justin (F) 0 0**
H: 5 8 W: 11 02 b.Leeds 26-6-86
*Source:* Trainee.

| | | | |
|---|---|---|---|
| 2003–04 | Leeds U | 0 | 0 |

**BRIDGES, Michael* (F) 141 35**
H: 6 0 W: 12 04 b.North Shields 5-8-78
*Source:* Trainee. *Honours:* England Schools, Youth, Under-21.

| | | | | | |
|---|---|---|---|---|---|
| 1995–96 | Sunderland | 15 | 4 | | |
| 1996–97 | Sunderland | 25 | 3 | | |
| 1997–98 | Sunderland | 9 | 1 | | |
| 1998–99 | Sunderland | 30 | 8 | **79** | **16** |
| 1999–2000 | Leeds U | 34 | 19 | | |
| 2000–01 | Leeds U | 7 | 0 | | |
| 2001–02 | Leeds U | 0 | 0 | | |
| 2002–03 | Leeds U | 5 | 0 | | |
| 2003–04 | Leeds U | 10 | 0 | **56** | **19** |
| 2003–04 | *Newcastle U* | 6 | 0 | **6** | **0** |

**BYRNE, Luke‡ (M) 0 0**
H: 5 7 W: 10 06 b.Castle Bar 2-9-85
*Source:* Scholar.

| | | | |
|---|---|---|---|
| 2002–03 | Leeds U | 0 | 0 |
| 2003–04 | Leeds U | 0 | 0 |

**CAMARA, Zoumana‡ (D) 126 4**
H: 5 10 W: 12 11 b.Colombes 3-4-79
*Honours:* France 1 full cap.

| | | | | | |
|---|---|---|---|---|---|
| 1996–97 | St Etienne | 6 | 0 | | |
| 1997–98 | St Etienne | 26 | 1 | **32** | **1** |
| 1998–99 | Internazionale | 0 | 0 | | |
| 1998–99 | Empoli | 12 | 0 | **12** | **0** |
| 1999–2000 | Internazionale | 0 | 0 | | |
| 1999–2000 | Bastia | 27 | 1 | **27** | **1** |
| 2000–01 | Marseille | 31 | 1 | | |
| 2001–02 | Marseille | 11 | 0 | **42** | **1** |
| 2003–04 | Leeds U | 13 | 1 | **13** | **1** |

**CARSON, Scott (G) 3 0**
H: 6 3 W: 13 09 b.Whitehaven 3-9-85
*Source:* Scholar. *Honours:* England Youth, Under-21.

| | | | | | |
|---|---|---|---|---|---|
| 2002–03 | Leeds U | 0 | 0 | | |
| 2003–04 | Leeds U | 3 | 0 | **3** | **0** |

**CHAPUIS, Cyril‡ (F) 78 17**
H: 6 0 W: 12 04 b.Lyon 21-3-79

| | | | | | |
|---|---|---|---|---|---|
| 1998–99 | Niort | 2 | 0 | | |
| 1999–2000 | Niort | 22 | 4 | **24** | **4** |
| 2000–01 | Rennes | 32 | 10 | | |
| 2001–02 | Rennes | 12 | 3 | **44** | **13** |
| 2001–02 | Marseille | 9 | 0 | **9** | **0** |
| 2003–04 | Leeds U | 1 | 0 | **1** | **0** |

**CONSTABLE, Robert (D) 0 0**
H: 6 0 W: 11 13 b.Pontefract 26-1-86
*Source:* Trainee.

| | | | |
|---|---|---|---|
| 2002–03 | Leeds U | 0 | 0 |
| 2003–04 | Leeds U | 0 | 0 |

**CORR, Barry (F) 0 0**
H: 6 4 W: 12 05 b.Co Wicklow 2-4-85
*Source:* Scholar.

| | | | |
|---|---|---|---|
| 2001–02 | Leeds U | 0 | 0 |
| 2002–03 | Leeds U | 0 | 0 |
| 2003–04 | Leeds U | 0 | 0 |

**COUSINS, Andrew (M) 0 0**
H: 5 8 W: 11 02 b.Dublin 30-1-85
*Source:* Scholar.

| | | | |
|---|---|---|---|
| 2001–02 | Leeds U | 0 | 0 |
| 2002–03 | Leeds U | 0 | 0 |
| 2003–04 | Leeds U | 0 | 0 |

**COYLES, William (G) 0 0**
H: 6 0 W: 11 12 b.Co Antrim 20-12-84
*Source:* Scholar.

| | | | |
|---|---|---|---|
| 2001–02 | Leeds U | 0 | 0 |
| 2002–03 | Leeds U | 0 | 0 |
| 2003–04 | Leeds U | 0 | 0 |

**CRONIN, Kevin (D) 0 0**
H: 6 0 W: 11 11 b.Dublin 18-5-85
*Source:* Scholar.

| | | | |
|---|---|---|---|
| 2001–02 | Leeds U | 0 | 0 |
| 2002–03 | Leeds U | 0 | 0 |
| 2003–04 | Leeds U | 0 | 0 |

**DOMI, Didier‡ (D) 142 3**
H: 5 10 W: 12 01 b.Sarcelles 2-5-78

| | | | | | |
|---|---|---|---|---|---|
| 1995–96 | Paris St Germain | 1 | 0 | | |
| 1996–97 | Paris St Germain | 12 | 0 | | |
| 1997–98 | Paris St Germain | 27 | 0 | | |
| 1998–99 | Paris St Germain | 8 | 0 | | |
| 1998–99 | Newcastle U | 14 | 0 | | |
| 1999–2000 | Newcastle U | 27 | 3 | | |
| 2000–01 | Newcastle U | 14 | 0 | **55** | **3** |
| 2000–01 | Paris St Germain | 8 | 0 | | |
| 2001–02 | Paris St Germain | 10 | 0 | | |
| 2002–03 | Paris St Germain | 9 | 0 | **75** | **0** |
| 2003–04 | Leeds U | 12 | 0 | **12** | **0** |

**DUBERRY, Michael (D) 147 5**
H: 6 1 W: 14 09 b.Enfield 14-10-75
*Source:* Trainee. *Honours:* England Under-21.

| | | | | | |
|---|---|---|---|---|---|
| 1993–94 | Chelsea | 1 | 0 | | |
| 1994–95 | Chelsea | 0 | 0 | | |
| 1995–96 | Chelsea | 22 | 0 | | |
| 1995–96 | *Bournemouth* | 7 | 0 | **7** | **0** |
| 1996–97 | Chelsea | 15 | 1 | | |
| 1997–98 | Chelsea | 23 | 0 | | |
| 1998–99 | Chelsea | 25 | 0 | **86** | **1** |
| 1999–2000 | Leeds U | 13 | 1 | | |
| 2000–01 | Leeds U | 5 | 0 | | |
| 2001–02 | Leeds U | 3 | 0 | | |
| 2002–03 | Leeds U | 14 | 0 | | |
| 2003–04 | Leeds U | 19 | 3 | **54** | **4** |

**EDWARDS, Stewart (D) 0 0**
H: 6 0 W: 12 01 b.Swansea 1-10-84
*Source:* Scholar.

| | | | |
|---|---|---|---|
| 2001–02 | Leeds U | 0 | 0 |
| 2002–03 | Leeds U | 0 | 0 |
| 2003–04 | Leeds U | 0 | 0 |

**FARREN, Larry‡ (D) 0 0**
H: 6 0 W: 12 08 b.Donegal 29-7-83
*Source:* Scholar.

| | | | |
|---|---|---|---|
| 2000–01 | Leeds U | 0 | 0 |
| 2001–02 | Leeds U | 0 | 0 |
| 2002–03 | Leeds U | 0 | 0 |
| 2003–04 | Leeds U | 0 | 0 |

**GRAY, Nicholas (M) 0 0**
H: 6 1 W: 10 06 b.Harrogate 17-10-85
*Source:* Trainee.

| | | | |
|---|---|---|---|
| 2002–03 | Leeds U | 0 | 0 |
| 2003–04 | Leeds U | 0 | 0 |

**HARTE, Ian (D) 213 28**
H: 5 11 W: 12 06 b.Drogheda 31-8-77
*Source:* Trainee. *Honours:* Eire 56 full caps, 9 goals.

| | | | | | |
|---|---|---|---|---|---|
| 1995–96 | Leeds U | 4 | 0 | | |
| 1996–97 | Leeds U | 14 | 2 | | |
| 1997–98 | Leeds U | 12 | 0 | | |
| 1998–99 | Leeds U | 35 | 4 | | |
| 1999–2000 | Leeds U | 33 | 6 | | |
| 2000–01 | Leeds U | 29 | 7 | | |
| 2001–02 | Leeds U | 36 | 5 | | |
| 2002–03 | Leeds U | 27 | 3 | | |
| 2003–04 | Leeds U | 23 | 1 | **213** | **28** |

**JOHNSON, Seth (M) 214 11**
H: 5 10 W: 12 06 b.Birmingham 12-3-79
*Source:* Trainee. *Honours:* England Youth, Under-21, 1 full cap.

| | | | | | |
|---|---|---|---|---|---|
| 1996–97 | Crewe Alex | 11 | 1 | | |
| 1997–98 | Crewe Alex | 40 | 1 | | |
| 1998–99 | Crewe Alex | 42 | 4 | **93** | **6** |
| 1999–2000 | Derby Co | 36 | 1 | | |
| 2000–01 | Derby Co | 30 | 1 | | |
| 2001–02 | Derby Co | 7 | 0 | **73** | **2** |
| 2001–02 | Leeds U | 14 | 0 | | |
| 2002–03 | Leeds U | 9 | 1 | | |
| 2003–04 | Leeds U | 25 | 2 | **48** | **3** |

**JOHNSON, Simon (F) 25 3**
H: 5 10 W: 12 06 b.West Bromwich 9-3-83
*Source:* Scholar. *Honours:* England Youth, Under-20.

| | | | | | |
|---|---|---|---|---|---|
| 2000–01 | Leeds U | 0 | 0 | | |
| 2001–02 | Leeds U | 0 | 0 | | |
| 2002–03 | Leeds U | 4 | 0 | | |
| 2002–03 | *Hull C* | 12 | 2 | **12** | **2** |
| 2003–04 | Leeds U | 5 | 0 | **9** | **0** |
| 2003–04 | *Blackpool* | 4 | 1 | **4** | **1** |

**JONES, Chris (M) 0 0**
H: 5 8 W: 8 11 b.Bangor 9-10-85
*Source:* Trainee.

| | | | |
|---|---|---|---|
| 2002–03 | Leeds U | 0 | 0 |
| 2003–04 | Leeds U | 0 | 0 |

**KEEGAN, Paul (M) 2 0**
H: 5 11 W: 12 00 b.Dublin 5-7-84
*Source:* Scholar. *Honours:* Eire Under-21.

| | | | | | |
|---|---|---|---|---|---|
| 2000–01 | Leeds U | 0 | 0 | | |
| 2001–02 | Leeds U | 0 | 0 | | |
| 2002–03 | Leeds U | 0 | 0 | | |
| 2003–04 | Leeds U | 0 | 0 | | |
| 2003–04 | *Scunthorpe U* | 2 | 0 | **2** | **0** |

**KELLY, Gary (D) 327 2**
H: 5 10 W: 11 06 b.Drogheda 9-7-74
*Source:* Home Farm. *Honours:* Eire Youth, 52 full caps, 2 goals.

| | | | | | |
|---|---|---|---|---|---|
| 1991–92 | Leeds U | 2 | 0 | | |
| 1992–93 | Leeds U | 0 | 0 | | |
| 1993–94 | Leeds U | 42 | 0 | | |
| 1994–95 | Leeds U | 42 | 0 | | |
| 1995–96 | Leeds U | 34 | 0 | | |
| 1996–97 | Leeds U | 36 | 2 | | |
| 1997–98 | Leeds U | 34 | 0 | | |
| 1998–99 | Leeds U | 0 | 0 | | |
| 1999–2000 | Leeds U | 31 | 0 | | |
| 2000–01 | Leeds U | 24 | 0 | | |
| 2001–02 | Leeds U | 20 | 0 | | |
| 2002–03 | Leeds U | 25 | 0 | | |
| 2003–04 | Leeds U | 37 | 0 | **327** | **2** |

**KEOGH, Andrew (F) 0 0**
H: 6 0 W: 11 07 b.Dublin 16-5-86
*Source:* Scholar.

| | | | |
|---|---|---|---|
| 2003–04 | Leeds U | 0 | 0 |

**KEYES, Edward (D) 0 0**
H: 5 9 W: 10 10 b.Dublin 2-5-85
*Source:* Scholar.

| | | | |
|---|---|---|---|
| 2001–02 | Leeds U | 0 | 0 |
| 2002–03 | Leeds U | 0 | 0 |
| 2003–04 | Leeds U | 0 | 0 |

**KILGALLON, Matthew (D) 13 2**
H: 6 1 W: 12 02 b.York 8-1-84
*Source:* Scholar. *Honours:* England Youth, Under-20, Under-21.

| | | | | | |
|---|---|---|---|---|---|
| 2000–01 | Leeds U | 0 | 0 | | |
| 2001–02 | Leeds U | 0 | 0 | | |
| 2002–03 | Leeds U | 2 | 0 | | |
| 2003–04 | Leeds U | 8 | 2 | **10** | **2** |
| 2003–04 | *West Ham U* | 3 | 0 | **3** | **0** |

**KRIEF, Domonique‡ (D) 0 0**
H: 5 9 W: 10 06 b.Leeds 15-9-83
*Source:* Scholar.

| | | | |
|---|---|---|---|
| 2000–01 | Leeds U | 0 | 0 |
| 2001–02 | Leeds U | 0 | 0 |
| 2002–03 | Leeds U | 0 | 0 |
| 2003–04 | Leeds U | 0 | 0 |

**LEISTER, Brenton (D) 0 0**
H: 5 11 W: 11 12 b.Leeds 3-9-85
*Source:* Scholar.

| | | | |
|---|---|---|---|
| 2002–03 | Leeds U | 0 | 0 |
| 2003–04 | Leeds U | 0 | 0 |

**LENNON, Aaron§ (F)** **11 0**
H: 5 5 W: 9 12 b.Leeds 16-4-87
*Source:* Trainee.

| | | | | | |
|---|---|---|---|---|---|
| 2003–04 | Leeds U | 11 | 0 | **11** | **0** |

**MATTEO, Dominic (D)** **243 3**
H: 6 1 W: 13 08 b.Dumfries 28-4-74
*Source:* Trainee. *Honours:* England Youth, Under-21, B, Scotland 6 full caps.

| | | | | | |
|---|---|---|---|---|---|
| 1992–93 | Liverpool | 0 | 0 | | |
| 1993–94 | Liverpool | 11 | 0 | | |
| 1994–95 | Liverpool | 7 | 0 | | |
| 1994–95 | *Sunderland* | 1 | 0 | **1** | **0** |
| 1995–96 | Liverpool | 5 | 0 | | |
| 1996–97 | Liverpool | 26 | 0 | | |
| 1997–98 | Liverpool | 26 | 0 | | |
| 1998–99 | Liverpool | 20 | 1 | | |
| 1999–2000 | Liverpool | 32 | 0 | | |
| 2000–01 | Liverpool | 0 | 0 | **127** | **1** |
| 2000–01 | Leeds U | 30 | 0 | | |
| 2001–02 | Leeds U | 32 | 0 | | |
| 2002–03 | Leeds U | 20 | 0 | | |
| 2003–04 | Leeds U | 33 | 2 | **115** | **2** |

**McDAID, Sean (D)** **0 0**
H: 5 8 W: 10 07 b.Harrogate 6-3-86
*Source:* Trainee.

| | | | | | |
|---|---|---|---|---|---|
| 2002–03 | Leeds U | 0 | 0 | | |
| 2003–04 | Leeds U | 0 | 0 | | |

**McKEOWN, Steven§ (F)** **0 0**
H: 5 10 W: 10 08 b.Paisley 3-6-87
*Source:* Livingston.

| | | | | | |
|---|---|---|---|---|---|
| 2003–04 | Leeds U | 0 | 0 | | |

**McMASTER, Jamie (M)** **12 2**
H: 5 11 W: 12 00 b.Sydney 29-11-82
*Source:* NSW Academy. *Honours:* England Youth, Under-20.

| | | | | | |
|---|---|---|---|---|---|
| 1999–2000 | Leeds U | 0 | 0 | | |
| 2000–01 | Leeds U | 0 | 0 | | |
| 2001–02 | Leeds U | 0 | 0 | | |
| 2002–03 | Leeds U | 4 | 0 | | |
| 2002–03 | *Coventry C* | 2 | 0 | **2** | **0** |
| 2003–04 | Leeds U | 0 | 0 | **4** | **0** |
| 2003–04 | *Chesterfield* | 6 | 2 | **6** | **2** |

**McPHAIL, Stephen (M)** **95 3**
H: 5 9 W: 12 02 b.London 9-12-79
*Source:* Trainee. *Honours:* Eire Under-21, 10 full caps, 1 goal.

| | | | | | |
|---|---|---|---|---|---|
| 1996–97 | Leeds U | 0 | 0 | | |
| 1997–98 | Leeds U | 4 | 0 | | |
| 1998–99 | Leeds U | 17 | 0 | | |
| 1999–2000 | Leeds U | 24 | 2 | | |
| 2000–01 | Leeds U | 7 | 0 | | |
| 2001–02 | Leeds U | 1 | 0 | | |
| 2001–02 | *Millwall* | 3 | 0 | **3** | **0** |
| 2002–03 | Leeds U | 13 | 0 | | |
| 2003–04 | Leeds U | 12 | 1 | **78** | **3** |
| 2003–04 | *Nottingham F* | 14 | 0 | **14** | **0** |

**McSTAY, Henry (D)** **0 0**
H: 6 0 W: 11 11 b.Co Armagh 6-3-85
*Source:* Scholar.

| | | | | | |
|---|---|---|---|---|---|
| 2001–02 | Leeds U | 0 | 0 | | |
| 2002–03 | Leeds U | 0 | 0 | | |
| 2003–04 | Leeds U | 0 | 0 | | |

**MILLS, Danny (D)** **240 6**
H: 5 11 W: 12 06 b.Norwich 18-5-77
*Source:* Trainee. *Honours:* England Youth, Under-21, 19 full caps.

| | | | | | |
|---|---|---|---|---|---|
| 1994–95 | Norwich C | 0 | 0 | | |
| 1995–96 | Norwich C | 14 | 0 | | |
| 1996–97 | Norwich C | 32 | 0 | | |
| 1997–98 | Norwich C | 20 | 0 | **66** | **0** |
| 1997–98 | Charlton Ath | 9 | 1 | | |
| 1998–99 | Charlton Ath | 36 | 2 | **45** | **3** |
| 1999–2000 | Leeds U | 17 | 1 | | |
| 2000–01 | Leeds U | 23 | 0 | | |
| 2001–02 | Leeds U | 28 | 1 | | |
| 2002–03 | Leeds U | 33 | 1 | | |
| 2003–04 | Leeds U | 0 | 0 | **101** | **3** |
| 2003–04 | *Middlesbrough* | 28 | 0 | **28** | **0** |

**MILNER, James (F)** **54 7**
H: 5 9 W: 11 00 b.Leeds 4-1-86
*Source:* Trainee. *Honours:* FA Schools, England Youth, Under-20, Under-21.

| | | | | | |
|---|---|---|---|---|---|
| 2002–03 | Leeds U | 18 | 2 | | |
| 2003–04 | Leeds U | 30 | 3 | **48** | **5** |
| 2003–04 | *Swindon T* | 6 | 2 | **6** | **2** |

**MILOSEVIC, Danny‡ (G)** **33 0**
H: 6 2 W: 14 08 b.Carlton 26-6-78
*Honours:* Australia Under-20, Under-23.

| | | | | | |
|---|---|---|---|---|---|
| 1995–96 | Canberra Cosmos | 3 | 0 | | |
| 1996–97 | Canberra Cosmos | 11 | 0 | **14** | **0** |
| 1997–98 | Arminia Bielefeld | 0 | 0 | | |
| 1997–98 | Prussen Munster | 0 | 0 | | |
| 1998–99 | Perth Glory | 17 | 0 | **17** | **0** |
| 1999–2000 | Leeds U | 0 | 0 | | |
| 2000–01 | Leeds U | 0 | 0 | | |
| 2001–02 | Leeds U | 0 | 0 | | |
| 2001–02 | *Wolverhampton W* | 0 | 0 | | |
| 2002–03 | Leeds U | 0 | 0 | | |
| 2002–03 | *Plymouth Arg* | 1 | 0 | **1** | **0** |
| 2002–03 | *Crewe Alex* | 1 | 0 | **1** | **0** |
| 2003–04 | Leeds U | 0 | 0 | | |

**MORRIS, Ian§ (F)** **0 0**
H: 6 0 W: 11 02 b.Dublin 27-2-87
*Source:* Scholar.

| | | | | | |
|---|---|---|---|---|---|
| 2003–04 | Leeds U | 0 | 0 | | |

**OLEMBE, Salomon‡ (M)** **123 7**
H: 5 7 W: 10 04 b.Yaounde 8-12-80
*Honours:* Cameroon full caps.

| | | | | | |
|---|---|---|---|---|---|
| 1997–98 | Nantes | 9 | 0 | | |
| 1998–99 | Nantes | 29 | 1 | | |
| 1999–2000 | Nantes | 22 | 2 | | |
| 2000–01 | Nantes | 30 | 4 | | |
| 2001–02 | Nantes | 13 | 0 | **103** | **7** |
| 2001–02 | Marseille | 8 | 0 | | |
| 2002–03 | Marseille | 0 | 0 | **8** | **0** |
| 2003–04 | Leeds U | 12 | 0 | **12** | **0** |

**RADEBE, Lucas (D)** **197 0**
H: 6 0 W: 11 10 b.Johannesburg 12-4-69
*Source:* Kaizer Chiefs. *Honours:* South Africa 70 full caps, 2 goals.

| | | | | | |
|---|---|---|---|---|---|
| 1994–95 | Leeds U | 12 | 0 | | |
| 1995–96 | Leeds U | 13 | 0 | | |
| 1996–97 | Leeds U | 32 | 0 | | |
| 1997–98 | Leeds U | 27 | 0 | | |
| 1998–99 | Leeds U | 29 | 0 | | |
| 1999–2000 | Leeds U | 31 | 0 | | |
| 2000–01 | Leeds U | 20 | 0 | | |
| 2001–02 | Leeds U | 0 | 0 | | |
| 2002–03 | Leeds U | 19 | 0 | | |
| 2003–04 | Leeds U | 14 | 0 | **197** | **0** |

**REEVES, Damian (F)** **0 0**
H: 5 9 W: 11 09 b.Doncaster 18-12-85
*Source:* Trainee.

| | | | | | |
|---|---|---|---|---|---|
| 2002–03 | Leeds U | 0 | 0 | | |
| 2003–04 | Leeds U | 0 | 0 | | |

**RICHARDSON, Frazer (D)** **17 1**
H: 5 11 W: 11 08 b.Rotherham 29-10-82
*Source:* Trainee. *Honours:* England Youth, Under-20.

| | | | | | |
|---|---|---|---|---|---|
| 1999–2000 | Leeds U | 0 | 0 | | |
| 2000–01 | Leeds U | 0 | 0 | | |
| 2001–02 | Leeds U | 0 | 0 | | |
| 2002–03 | Leeds U | 0 | 0 | | |
| 2002–03 | *Stoke C* | 7 | 0 | | |
| 2003–04 | Leeds U | 4 | 0 | **4** | **0** |
| 2003–04 | *Stoke C* | 6 | 1 | **13** | **1** |

**ROQUE JUNIOR, Jose‡ (D)** **114 2**
H: 6 1 W: 12 11 b.Santa Rita do Sapucal 31-8-76
*Honours:* Brazil 33 full caps.

| | | | | | |
|---|---|---|---|---|---|
| 1995 | Palmeiras | 1 | 0 | | |
| 1996 | Palmeiras | 12 | 0 | | |
| 1997 | Palmeiras | 28 | 1 | | |
| 1998 | Palmeiras | 8 | 0 | | |
| 1999 | Palmeiras | 16 | 1 | **65** | **2** |
| 2000–01 | AC Milan | 22 | 0 | | |
| 2001–02 | AC Milan | 18 | 0 | | |
| 2002–03 | AC Milan | 4 | 0 | **44** | **0** |
| 2003–04 | Leeds U | 5 | 0 | **5** | **0** |

**SAKHO, Lamine‡ (F)** **182 38**
H: 5 11 W: 11 08 b.Louga 28-9-77
*Source:* Crocodiles.

| | | | | | |
|---|---|---|---|---|---|
| 1997–98 | Nimes | 28 | 1 | | |
| 1998–99 | Nimes | 34 | 8 | **62** | **9** |
| 1999–2000 | Lens | 23 | 8 | | |
| 2000–01 | Lens | 23 | 6 | | |
| 2001–02 | Lens | 16 | 4 | **62** | **18** |
| 2001–02 | Marseille | 12 | 5 | | |
| 2002–03 | Marseille | 29 | 5 | **41** | **10** |
| 2003–04 | Leeds U | 17 | 1 | **17** | **1** |

**SHIELDS, Robbie (M)** **0 0**
H: 5 6 W: 9 13 b.Dublin 1-5-84
*Source:* Scholar.

| | | | | | |
|---|---|---|---|---|---|
| 2000–01 | Leeds U | 0 | 0 | | |
| 2001–02 | Leeds U | 0 | 0 | | |
| 2002–03 | Leeds U | 0 | 0 | | |
| 2003–04 | Leeds U | 0 | 0 | | |

**SINGH, Harpal (F)** **46 4**
H: 5 7 W: 10 02 b.Bradford 15-9-81
*Source:* Trainee.

| | | | | | |
|---|---|---|---|---|---|
| 1998–99 | Leeds U | 0 | 0 | | |
| 1999–2000 | Leeds U | 0 | 0 | | |
| 2000–01 | Leeds U | 0 | 0 | | |
| 2001–02 | Leeds U | 0 | 0 | | |
| 2001–02 | *Bury* | 12 | 2 | | |
| 2001–02 | *Bristol C* | 3 | 0 | **3** | **0** |
| 2002–03 | Leeds U | 0 | 0 | | |
| 2002–03 | *Bradford C* | 3 | 0 | **3** | **0** |
| 2003–04 | Leeds U | 0 | 0 | | |
| 2003–04 | *Bury* | 28 | 2 | **40** | **4** |

**SMITH, Alan (F)** **172 38**
H: 5 10 W: 12 01 b.Leeds 28-10-80
*Source:* Trainee. *Honours:* England Youth, Under-21, 8 full caps, 1 goal.

| | | | | | |
|---|---|---|---|---|---|
| 1997–98 | Leeds U | 0 | 0 | | |
| 1998–99 | Leeds U | 22 | 7 | | |
| 1999–2000 | Leeds U | 26 | 4 | | |
| 2000–01 | Leeds U | 33 | 11 | | |
| 2001–02 | Leeds U | 23 | 4 | | |
| 2002–03 | Leeds U | 33 | 3 | | |
| 2003–04 | Leeds U | 35 | 9 | **172** | **38** |

**SMITH, Kevin§ (F)** **0 0**
H: 5 11 W: 11 02 b.Edinburgh 20-3-87
*Source:* Scholar.

| | | | | | |
|---|---|---|---|---|---|
| 2003–04 | Leeds U | 0 | 0 | | |

**STIENS, Craig‡ (F)** **3 0**
H: 5 8 W: 13 01 b.Swansea 31-7-84
*Source:* Scholar.

| | | | | | |
|---|---|---|---|---|---|
| 2000–01 | Leeds U | 0 | 0 | | |
| 2001–02 | Leeds U | 0 | 0 | | |
| 2002–03 | Leeds U | 0 | 0 | | |
| 2002–03 | *Swansea C* | 3 | 0 | **3** | **0** |
| 2003–04 | Leeds U | 0 | 0 | | |

**TYRRELL, Derek (D)** **0 0**
H: 6 1 W: 12 00 b.Dublin 14-4-85
*Source:* Scholar.

| | | | | | |
|---|---|---|---|---|---|
| 2001–02 | Leeds U | 0 | 0 | | |
| 2002–03 | Leeds U | 0 | 0 | | |
| 2003–04 | Leeds U | 0 | 0 | | |

**VIDUKA, Mark (F)** **299 169**
H: 6 2 W: 15 05 b.Melbourne 9-10-75
*Honours:* Australia Under-20, Under-23, 23 full caps, 3 goals.

| | | | | | |
|---|---|---|---|---|---|
| 1992–93 | Melbourne Knights | 4 | 2 | | |
| 1993–94 | Melbourne Knights | 20 | 17 | | |
| 1994–95 | Melbourne Knights | 24 | 21 | **48** | **40** |
| 1995–96 | Croatia Zagreb | 27 | 12 | | |
| 1996–97 | Croatia Zagreb | 25 | 18 | | |
| 1997–98 | Croatia Zagreb | 25 | 8 | | |
| 1998–99 | Croatia Zagreb | 7 | 2 | **84** | **40** |
| 1998–99 | Celtic | 9 | 5 | | |
| 1999–2000 | Celtic | 28 | 25 | **37** | **30** |
| 2000–01 | Leeds U | 34 | 17 | | |
| 2001–02 | Leeds U | 33 | 11 | | |
| 2002–03 | Leeds U | 33 | 20 | | |
| 2003–04 | Leeds U | 30 | 11 | **130** | **59** |

**WILBERFORCE, Mark§ (G)** **0 0**
H: 5 10 W: 11 07 b.Hull 30-1-87
*Source:* Scholar.

| | | | | | |
|---|---|---|---|---|---|
| 2003–04 | Leeds U | 0 | 0 | | |

**WILCOX, Jason* (M)** **350 35**
H: 6 0 W: 11 11 b.Bolton 15-7-71
*Source:* Trainee. *Honours:* England B, 3 full caps.

| | | | | | |
|---|---|---|---|---|---|
| 1989–90 | Blackburn R | 1 | 0 | | |
| 1990–91 | Blackburn R | 18 | 0 | | |
| 1991–92 | Blackburn R | 38 | 4 | | |
| 1992–93 | Blackburn R | 33 | 4 | | |
| 1993–94 | Blackburn R | 33 | 6 | | |
| 1994–95 | Blackburn R | 27 | 5 | | |
| 1995–96 | Blackburn R | 10 | 3 | | |
| 1996–97 | Blackburn R | 28 | 2 | | |
| 1997–98 | Blackburn R | 31 | 4 | | |
| 1998–99 | Blackburn R | 30 | 3 | | |
| 1999–2000 | Blackburn R | 20 | 0 | **269** | **31** |

| | | | | | |
|---|---|---|---|---|---|
| 1999–2000 | Leeds U | 20 | 3 | | |
| 2000–01 | Leeds U | 17 | 0 | | |
| 2001–02 | Leeds U | 13 | 0 | | |
| 2002–03 | Leeds U | 25 | 1 | | |
| 2003–04 | Leeds U | 6 | 0 | **81** | **4** |

**WINTER, Jamie (M)** **0 0**
H: 5 10 W: 11 11 b.Dundee 4-8-85
*Source:* Scholar.

| | | | |
|---|---|---|---|
| 2002–03 | Leeds U | 0 | 0 |
| 2003–04 | Leeds U | 0 | 0 |

**WOODS, Martin (M)** **0 0**
H: 5 11 W: 11 11 b.Bellshill 1-1-86
*Source:* Trainee.

| | | | |
|---|---|---|---|
| 2002–03 | Leeds U | 0 | 0 |
| 2003–04 | Leeds U | 0 | 0 |

**Scholars**
Lennon, Aaron; McKeown, Steven; Morris, Ian; Smith, Kevin J; Wilberforce, Mark J

## LEICESTER C (41)

**BENJAMIN, Trevor (F)** **229 53**
H: 6 2 W: 14 04 b.Kettering 8-2-79
*Source:* Trainee. *Honours:* England Under-21, Jamaica 2 full caps.

| | | | | | |
|---|---|---|---|---|---|
| 1995–96 | Cambridge U | 5 | 0 | | |
| 1996–97 | Cambridge U | 7 | 1 | | |
| 1997–98 | Cambridge U | 25 | 4 | | |
| 1998–99 | Cambridge U | 42 | 10 | | |
| 1999–2000 | Cambridge U | 44 | 20 | **123** | **35** |
| 2000–01 | Leicester C | 21 | 1 | | |
| 2001–02 | Leicester C | 11 | 0 | | |
| 2001–02 | *Crystal Palace* | 6 | 1 | **6** | **1** |
| 2001–02 | *Norwich C* | 6 | 0 | **6** | **0** |
| 2001–02 | *WBA* | 3 | 1 | **3** | **1** |
| 2002–03 | Leicester C | 35 | 8 | | |
| 2003–04 | Leicester C | 4 | 0 | **71** | **9** |
| 2003–04 | *Gillingham* | 4 | 1 | **4** | **1** |
| 2003–04 | *Rushden & D* | 6 | 1 | **6** | **1** |
| 2003–04 | *Brighton & HA* | 10 | 5 | **10** | **5** |

**BROOKER, Paul (M)** **204 19**
H: 5 8 W: 10 06 b.Hammersmith 25-11-76
*Source:* Trainee.

| | | | | | |
|---|---|---|---|---|---|
| 1995–96 | Fulham | 20 | 2 | | |
| 1996–97 | Fulham | 26 | 2 | | |
| 1997–98 | Fulham | 9 | 0 | | |
| 1998–99 | Fulham | 1 | 0 | | |
| 1999–2000 | Fulham | 0 | 0 | **56** | **4** |
| 1999–2000 | *Brighton & HA* | 15 | 2 | | |
| 2000–01 | Brighton & HA | 41 | 3 | | |
| 2001–02 | Brighton & HA | 41 | 4 | | |
| 2002–03 | Brighton & HA | 37 | 6 | **134** | **15** |
| 2003–04 | Leicester C | 3 | 0 | **3** | **0** |
| 2003–04 | *Reading* | 11 | 0 | **11** | **0** |

**CANERO, Peter (D)** **124 10**
H: 5 9 W: 11 04 b.Glasgow 18-1-81
*Honours:* Scotland 1 full cap.

| | | | | | |
|---|---|---|---|---|---|
| 1999–2000 | Kilmarnock | 11 | 0 | | |
| 2000–01 | Kilmarnock | 28 | 1 | | |
| 2001–02 | Kilmarnock | 32 | 1 | | |
| 2002–03 | Kilmarnock | 33 | 6 | | |
| 2003–04 | Kilmarnock | 13 | 2 | **117** | **10** |
| 2003–04 | Leicester C | 7 | 0 | **7** | **0** |

**COYNE, Danny (G)** **296 0**
H: 6 0 W: 13 04 b.Prestatyn 27-8-73
*Source:* Trainee. *Honours:* Wales Schools, Youth, Under-21, B, 5 full caps.

| | | | | | |
|---|---|---|---|---|---|
| 1991–92 | Tranmere R | 0 | 0 | | |
| 1992–93 | Tranmere R | 1 | 0 | | |
| 1993–94 | Tranmere R | 5 | 0 | | |
| 1994–95 | Tranmere R | 5 | 0 | | |
| 1995–96 | Tranmere R | 46 | 0 | | |
| 1996–97 | Tranmere R | 21 | 0 | | |
| 1997–98 | Tranmere R | 16 | 0 | | |
| 1998–99 | Tranmere R | 17 | 0 | **111** | **0** |
| 1999–2000 | Grimsby T | 44 | 0 | | |
| 2000–01 | Grimsby T | 46 | 0 | | |
| 2001–02 | Grimsby T | 45 | 0 | | |
| 2002–03 | Grimsby T | 46 | 0 | **181** | **0** |
| 2003–04 | Leicester C | 4 | 0 | **4** | **0** |

**DABIZAS, Nikos (D)** **252 18**
H: 6 1 W: 12 07 b.Amindeo 3-8-73
*Honours:* Greece 67 full caps.

| | | | | | |
|---|---|---|---|---|---|
| 1994–95 | Olympiakos | 26 | 2 | | |
| 1995–96 | Olympiakos | 27 | 1 | | |
| 1996–97 | Olympiakos | 31 | 0 | | |
| 1997–98 | Olympiakos | 20 | 5 | **104** | **8** |
| 1997–98 | Newcastle U | 11 | 1 | | |
| 1998–99 | Newcastle U | 30 | 3 | | |
| 1999–2000 | Newcastle U | 29 | 3 | | |
| 2000–01 | Newcastle U | 9 | 0 | | |
| 2001–02 | Newcastle U | 35 | 3 | | |
| 2002–03 | Newcastle U | 16 | 0 | | |
| 2003–04 | Newcastle U | 0 | 0 | **130** | **10** |
| 2003–04 | Leicester C | 18 | 0 | **18** | **0** |

**DAVIDSON, Callum* (D)** **210 7**
H: 5 10 W: 12 10 b.Stirling 25-6-76
*Source:* 'S' Form. *Honours:* Scotland Under-21, 17 full caps.

| | | | | | |
|---|---|---|---|---|---|
| 1994–95 | St Johnstone | 7 | 1 | | |
| 1995–96 | St Johnstone | 2 | 0 | | |
| 1996–97 | St Johnstone | 20 | 2 | | |
| 1997–98 | St Johnstone | 15 | 1 | **44** | **4** |
| 1997–98 | Blackburn R | 1 | 0 | | |
| 1998–99 | Blackburn R | 34 | 1 | | |
| 1999–2000 | Blackburn R | 30 | 0 | **65** | **1** |
| 2000–01 | Leicester C | 28 | 1 | | |
| 2001–02 | Leicester C | 30 | 0 | | |
| 2002–03 | Leicester C | 30 | 1 | | |
| 2003–04 | Leicester C | 13 | 0 | **101** | **2** |

**DAWSON, Stephen (D)** **0 0**
H: 5 9 W: 11 02 b.Dublin 4-12-85
*Source:* Scholar.

| | | | |
|---|---|---|---|
| 2003–04 | Leicester C | 0 | 0 |

**DICKOV, Paul (F)** **289 74**
H: 5 6 W: 10 06 b.Livingston 1-11-72
*Source:* Trainee. *Honours:* Scotland Schools, Youth, Under-21, 8 full caps, 1 goal.

| | | | | | |
|---|---|---|---|---|---|
| 1992–93 | Arsenal | 3 | 2 | | |
| 1993–94 | Arsenal | 1 | 0 | | |
| 1993–94 | *Luton T* | 15 | 1 | **15** | **1** |
| 1993–94 | *Brighton & HA* | 8 | 5 | **8** | **5** |
| 1994–95 | Arsenal | 9 | 0 | | |
| 1995–96 | Arsenal | 7 | 1 | | |
| 1996–97 | Arsenal | 1 | 0 | **21** | **3** |
| 1996–97 | Manchester C | 29 | 5 | | |
| 1997–98 | Manchester C | 30 | 9 | | |
| 1998–99 | Manchester C | 35 | 10 | | |
| 1999–2000 | Manchester C | 34 | 5 | | |
| 2000–01 | Manchester C | 21 | 4 | | |
| 2001–02 | Manchester C | 7 | 0 | **156** | **33** |
| 2001–02 | Leicester C | 12 | 4 | | |
| 2002–03 | Leicester C | 42 | 17 | | |
| 2003–04 | Leicester C | 35 | 11 | **89** | **32** |

**DOYLE, Jamie‡ (M)** **0 0**
H: 5 8 W: 10 01 b.Glasgow 23-5-85
*Source:* Trainee.

| | | | |
|---|---|---|---|
| 2002–03 | Leicester C | 0 | 0 |
| 2003–04 | Leicester C | 0 | 0 |

**ELLIOTT, Matt (D)** **586 70**
H: 6 3 W: 14 12 b.Wandsworth 1-11-68
*Source:* Epsom & Ewell. *Honours:* Scotland 18 full caps, 1 goal.

| | | | | | |
|---|---|---|---|---|---|
| 1988–89 | Charlton Ath | 0 | 0 | | |
| 1988–89 | Torquay U | 13 | 2 | | |
| 1989–90 | Torquay U | 33 | 2 | | |
| 1990–91 | Torquay U | 45 | 6 | | |
| 1991–92 | Torquay U | 33 | 5 | **124** | **15** |
| 1991–92 | *Scunthorpe U* | 8 | 1 | | |
| 1992–93 | Scunthorpe U | 39 | 6 | | |
| 1993–94 | Scunthorpe U | 14 | 1 | **61** | **8** |
| 1993–94 | Oxford U | 32 | 5 | | |
| 1994–95 | Oxford U | 45 | 4 | | |
| 1995–96 | Oxford U | 45 | 8 | | |
| 1996–97 | Oxford U | 26 | 4 | **148** | **21** |
| 1996–97 | Leicester C | 16 | 4 | | |
| 1997–98 | Leicester C | 37 | 7 | | |
| 1998–99 | Leicester C | 37 | 2 | | |
| 1999–2000 | Leicester C | 37 | 6 | | |
| 2000–01 | Leicester C | 34 | 2 | | |
| 2001–02 | Leicester C | 31 | 0 | | |
| 2002–03 | Leicester C | 44 | 5 | | |
| 2003–04 | Leicester C | 7 | 0 | **243** | **26** |
| 2003–04 | *Ipswich T* | 10 | 0 | **10** | **0** |

**FERDINAND, Les* (F)** **419 182**
H: 5 11 W: 14 12 b.Paddington 8-12-66
*Source:* Hayes. *Honours:* England B, 17 full caps, 5 goals.

| | | | | | |
|---|---|---|---|---|---|
| 1986–87 | QPR | 2 | 0 | | |
| 1987–88 | QPR | 1 | 0 | | |
| 1987–88 | *Brentford* | 3 | 0 | **3** | **0** |
| 1988–89 | QPR | 0 | 0 | | |
| 1988–89 | *Besiktas* | 24 | 14 | **24** | **14** |
| 1989–90 | QPR | 9 | 2 | | |
| 1990–91 | QPR | 18 | 8 | | |
| 1991–92 | QPR | 23 | 10 | | |
| 1992–93 | QPR | 37 | 20 | | |
| 1993–94 | QPR | 36 | 16 | | |
| 1994–95 | QPR | 37 | 24 | **163** | **80** |
| 1995–96 | Newcastle U | 37 | 25 | | |
| 1996–97 | Newcastle U | 31 | 16 | **68** | **41** |
| 1997–98 | Tottenham H | 21 | 5 | | |
| 1998–99 | Tottenham H | 24 | 5 | | |
| 1999–2000 | Tottenham H | 9 | 2 | | |
| 2000–01 | Tottenham H | 28 | 10 | | |
| 2001–02 | Tottenham H | 25 | 9 | | |
| 2002–03 | Tottenham H | 11 | 2 | **118** | **33** |
| 2002–03 | West Ham U | 14 | 2 | **14** | **2** |
| 2003–04 | Leicester C | 29 | 12 | **29** | **12** |

**FREUND, Steffen* (M)** **324 9**
H: 5 10 W: 12 08 b.Brandenburg 19-1-70
*Source:* Motor Sud, Stahl Brandenburg. *Honours:* Germany 21 full caps.

| | | | | | |
|---|---|---|---|---|---|
| 1989–90 | Brandenburg | 9 | 0 | | |
| 1990–91 | Brandenburg | 22 | 0 | **31** | **0** |
| 1991–92 | Schalke | 33 | 1 | | |
| 1992–93 | Schalke | 20 | 2 | **53** | **3** |
| 1993–94 | Borussia Dortmund | 19 | 0 | | |
| 1994–95 | Borussia Dortmund | 28 | 2 | | |
| 1995–96 | Borussia Dortmund | 30 | 2 | | |
| 1996–97 | Borussia Dortmund | 2 | 0 | | |
| 1997–98 | Borussia Dortmund | 25 | 2 | | |
| 1998–99 | Borussia Dortmund | 13 | 0 | **117** | **6** |
| 1998–99 | Tottenham H | 17 | 0 | | |
| 1999–2000 | Tottenham H | 27 | 0 | | |
| 2000–01 | Tottenham H | 21 | 0 | | |
| 2001–02 | Tottenham H | 20 | 0 | | |
| 2002–03 | Tottenham H | 17 | 0 | **102** | **0** |
| 2003–04 | Kaiserslautern | 7 | 0 | **7** | **0** |
| 2003–04 | Leicester C | 14 | 0 | **14** | **0** |

**GILLESPIE, Keith (M)** **260 21**
H: 5 10 W: 11 10 b.Larne 18-2-75
*Source:* Trainee. *Honours:* Northern Ireland Schools, Youth, Under-21, 55 full caps, 1 goal.

| | | | | | |
|---|---|---|---|---|---|
| 1992–93 | Manchester U | 0 | 0 | | |
| 1993–94 | Manchester U | 0 | 0 | | |
| 1993–94 | *Wigan Ath* | 8 | 4 | | |
| 1994–95 | Manchester U | 9 | 1 | **9** | **1** |
| 1994–95 | Newcastle U | 17 | 2 | | |
| 1995–96 | Newcastle U | 28 | 4 | | |
| 1996–97 | Newcastle U | 32 | 1 | | |
| 1997–98 | Newcastle U | 29 | 4 | | |
| 1998–99 | Newcastle U | 7 | 0 | **113** | **11** |
| 1998–99 | Blackburn R | 16 | 1 | | |
| 1999–2000 | Blackburn R | 22 | 2 | | |
| 2000–01 | Blackburn R | 18 | 0 | | |
| 2000–01 | *Wigan Ath* | 5 | 0 | **13** | **4** |
| 2001–02 | Blackburn R | 32 | 2 | | |
| 2002–03 | Blackburn R | 25 | 0 | **113** | **5** |
| 2003–04 | Leicester C | 12 | 0 | **12** | **0** |

**GUPPY, Steve* (M)** **307 29**
H: 5 11 W: 11 11 b.Winchester 29-3-69
*Source:* Southampton. *Honours:* England Under-21, B, 1 full cap.

| | | | | | |
|---|---|---|---|---|---|
| 1993–94 | Wycombe W | 41 | 8 | **41** | **8** |
| 1994–95 | Newcastle U | 0 | 0 | | |
| 1994–95 | Port Vale | 27 | 2 | | |
| 1995–96 | Port Vale | 44 | 4 | | |
| 1996–97 | Port Vale | 34 | 6 | **105** | **12** |
| 1996–97 | Leicester C | 13 | 0 | | |
| 1997–98 | Leicester C | 37 | 2 | | |
| 1998–99 | Leicester C | 38 | 4 | | |
| 1999–2000 | Leicester C | 30 | 2 | | |
| 2000–01 | Leicester C | 28 | 1 | | |
| 2001–02 | Leicester C | 0 | 0 | | |
| 2003–04 | Leicester C | 15 | 0 | **161** | **9** |

**HEATH, Matthew (D)** **37 3**
H: 6 4 W: 13 08 b.Leicester 1-11-81
*Source:* Scholar.

| | | | | | |
|---|---|---|---|---|---|
| 2000–01 | Leicester C | 0 | 0 | | |
| 2001–02 | Leicester C | 5 | 0 | | |
| 2002–03 | Leicester C | 11 | 3 | | |
| 2003–04 | Leicester C | 13 | 0 | **29** | **3** |
| 2003–04 | *Stockport Co* | 8 | 0 | **8** | **0** |

**HIGNETT, Craig (M)** 445 116
H: 5 9 W: 12 06 b.Whiston 12-1-70
*Source:* Liverpool Trainee.

| | | | | | |
|---|---|---|---|---|---|
| 1987–88 | Crewe Alex | 0 | 0 | | |
| 1988–89 | Crewe Alex | 1 | 0 | | |
| 1989–90 | Crewe Alex | 35 | 8 | | |
| 1990–91 | Crewe Alex | 38 | 13 | | |
| 1991–92 | Crewe Alex | 33 | 13 | | |
| 1992–93 | Crewe Alex | 14 | 8 | | |
| 1992–93 | Middlesbrough | 21 | 4 | | |
| 1993–94 | Middlesbrough | 29 | 5 | | |
| 1994–95 | Middlesbrough | 26 | 8 | | |
| 1995–96 | Middlesbrough | 22 | 5 | | |
| 1996–97 | Middlesbrough | 22 | 4 | | |
| 1997–98 | Middlesbrough | 36 | 7 | **156** | **33** |
| 1998–99 | Aberdeen | 13 | 2 | **13** | **2** |
| 1998–99 | Barnsley | 24 | 9 | | |
| 1999–2000 | Barnsley | 42 | 19 | **66** | **28** |
| 2000–01 | Blackburn R | 30 | 3 | | |
| 2001–02 | Blackburn R | 20 | 4 | | |
| 2002–03 | Blackburn R | 3 | 1 | **53** | **8** |
| 2002–03 | *Coventry C* | 8 | 2 | **8** | **2** |
| 2003–04 | Leicester C | 13 | 1 | **13** | **1** |
| 2003–04 | *Crewe Alex* | 15 | 0 | **136** | **42** |

**IMPEY, Andrew* (D)** 382 15
H: 5 8 W: 11 10 b.Hammersmith 30-9-71
*Source:* Yeading. *Honours:* England Under-21.

| | | | | | |
|---|---|---|---|---|---|
| 1990–91 | QPR | 0 | 0 | | |
| 1991–92 | QPR | 13 | 0 | | |
| 1992–93 | QPR | 40 | 2 | | |
| 1993–94 | QPR | 33 | 3 | | |
| 1994–95 | QPR | 40 | 3 | | |
| 1995–96 | QPR | 29 | 3 | | |
| 1996–97 | QPR | 32 | 2 | **187** | **13** |
| 1997–98 | West Ham U | 19 | 0 | | |
| 1998–99 | West Ham U | 8 | 0 | **27** | **0** |
| 1998–99 | Leicester C | 18 | 0 | | |
| 1999–2000 | Leicester C | 29 | 1 | | |
| 2000–01 | Leicester C | 33 | 0 | | |
| 2001–02 | Leicester C | 27 | 0 | | |
| 2002–03 | Leicester C | 32 | 0 | | |
| 2003–04 | Leicester C | 13 | 0 | **152** | **1** |
| 2003–04 | *Nottingham F* | 16 | 1 | **16** | **1** |

**IZZET, Muzzy* (M)** 269 38
H: 5 10 W: 10 13 b.Mile End 31-10-74
*Source:* Trainee. *Honours:* Turkey 8 full caps.

| | | | | | |
|---|---|---|---|---|---|
| 1993–94 | Chelsea | 0 | 0 | | |
| 1994–95 | Chelsea | 0 | 0 | | |
| 1995–96 | Chelsea | 0 | 0 | | |
| 1995–96 | *Leicester C* | 9 | 1 | | |
| 1996–97 | Leicester C | 35 | 3 | | |
| 1997–98 | Leicester C | 36 | 4 | | |
| 1998–99 | Leicester C | 31 | 5 | | |
| 1999–2000 | Leicester C | 32 | 8 | | |
| 2000–01 | Leicester C | 27 | 7 | | |
| 2001–02 | Leicester C | 31 | 4 | | |
| 2002–03 | Leicester C | 38 | 4 | | |
| 2003–04 | Leicester C | 30 | 2 | **269** | **38** |

**JONES, Matthew (M)** 50 1
H: 5 11 W: 12 10 b.Llanelli 1-9-80
*Source:* Trainee. *Honours:* Wales Youth, Under-21, B, 13 full caps.

| | | | | | |
|---|---|---|---|---|---|
| 1997–98 | Leeds U | 0 | 0 | | |
| 1998–99 | Leeds U | 8 | 0 | | |
| 1999–2000 | Leeds U | 11 | 0 | | |
| 2000–01 | Leeds U | 4 | 0 | **23** | **0** |
| 2000–01 | Leicester C | 11 | 0 | | |
| 2001–02 | Leicester C | 10 | 1 | | |
| 2002–03 | Leicester C | 6 | 0 | | |
| 2003–04 | Leicester C | 0 | 0 | **27** | **1** |

**LARVIN, Kevin‡ (F)** 0 0
H: 5 10 W: 11 02 b.Hull 4-9-84
*Source:* Trainee.

| | | | |
|---|---|---|---|
| 2002–03 | Leicester C | 0 | 0 |
| 2003–04 | Leicester C | 0 | 0 |

**LEWIS, Junior* (M)** 136 13
H: 6 5 W: 12 10 b.Wembley 9-10-73
*Source:* Trainee.

| | | | | | |
|---|---|---|---|---|---|
| 1992–93 | Fulham | 6 | 0 | **6** | **0** |
| From Dover, Hendon | | | | | |
| 1999–2000 | Gillingham | 42 | 6 | | |
| 2000–01 | Gillingham | 17 | 2 | **59** | **8** |
| 2000–01 | Leicester C | 15 | 0 | | |
| 2001–02 | Leicester C | 6 | 0 | | |
| 2001–02 | *Brighton & HA* | 15 | 3 | **15** | **3** |
| 2002–03 | Leicester C | 9 | 1 | | |
| 2002–03 | *Swindon T* | 9 | 0 | | |
| 2003–04 | Leicester C | 0 | 0 | **30** | **1** |
| 2003–04 | *Swindon T* | 4 | 0 | **13** | **0** |
| 2003–04 | *Hull C* | 13 | 1 | **13** | **1** |

**LOGAN, Conrad (G)** 0 0
H: 6 0 W: 14 04 b.Letterkenny 18-4-86
*Source:* Scholar.

| | | | |
|---|---|---|---|
| 2003–04 | Leicester C | 0 | 0 |

**McANALLEN, Conor (D)** 0 0
H: 5 11 W: 9 13 b.Craigavon 3-1-86
*Source:* Scholar.

| | | | |
|---|---|---|---|
| 2003–04 | Leicester C | 0 | 0 |

**McGAVIGAN, Ryan (M)** 0 0
H: 5 9 W: 11 02 b.County Donegal 31-3-86
*Source:* Scholar.

| | | | |
|---|---|---|---|
| 2003–04 | Leicester C | 0 | 0 |

**McKINLAY, Billy* (M)** 384 27
H: 5 8 W: 11 06 b.Glasgow 22-4-69
*Source:* Hamilton Th. *Honours:* Scotland Under-21, B, 29 full caps, 4 goals.

| | | | | | |
|---|---|---|---|---|---|
| 1986–87 | Dundee U | 3 | 0 | | |
| 1987–88 | Dundee U | 12 | 1 | | |
| 1988–89 | Dundee U | 30 | 1 | | |
| 1989–90 | Dundee U | 13 | 0 | | |
| 1990–91 | Dundee U | 34 | 2 | | |
| 1991–92 | Dundee U | 22 | 1 | | |
| 1992–93 | Dundee U | 37 | 1 | | |
| 1993–94 | Dundee U | 39 | 9 | | |
| 1994–95 | Dundee U | 27 | 4 | | |
| 1995–96 | Dundee U | 5 | 4 | **222** | **23** |
| 1995–96 | Blackburn R | 19 | 2 | | |
| 1996–97 | Blackburn R | 25 | 1 | | |
| 1997–98 | Blackburn R | 30 | 0 | | |
| 1998–99 | Blackburn R | 16 | 0 | | |
| 1999–2000 | Blackburn R | 0 | 0 | | |
| 2000–01 | Blackburn R | 0 | 0 | **90** | **3** |
| 2000–01 | *Leicester C* | 0 | 0 | | |
| 2000–01 | Bradford C | 11 | 0 | **11** | **0** |
| 2001–02 | Preston NE | 0 | 0 | | |
| 2001–02 | Clydebank | 8 | 0 | **8** | **0** |
| 2002–03 | Leicester C | 37 | 1 | | |
| 2003–04 | Leicester C | 16 | 0 | **53** | **1** |

**MORRIS, Lee (F)** 122 24
H: 5 9 W: 11 02 b.Driffield 30-4-80
*Source:* Trainee. *Honours:* England Youth.

| | | | | | |
|---|---|---|---|---|---|
| 1997–98 | Sheffield U | 5 | 0 | | |
| 1998–99 | Sheffield U | 20 | 6 | | |
| 1999–2000 | Sheffield U | 1 | 0 | **26** | **6** |
| 1999–2000 | Derby Co | 3 | 0 | | |
| 2000–01 | Derby Co | 20 | 0 | | |
| 2000–01 | *Huddersfield T* | 5 | 1 | **5** | **1** |
| 2001–02 | Derby Co | 15 | 4 | | |
| 2002–03 | Derby Co | 30 | 8 | | |
| 2003–04 | Derby Co | 23 | 5 | **91** | **17** |
| 2003–04 | Leicester C | 0 | 0 | | |

**MURPHY, Paul* (G)** 0 0
H: 6 0 W: 12 06 b.Dundalk 28-3-85
*Source:* Trainee.

| | | | |
|---|---|---|---|
| 2002–03 | Leicester C | 0 | 0 |
| 2003–04 | Leicester C | 0 | 0 |

**NALIS, Lilian (M)** 268 20
H: 6 1 W: 13 03 b.Nogent sur Marne 29-9-71

| | | | | | |
|---|---|---|---|---|---|
| 1992–93 | Auxerre | 0 | 0 | | |
| 1993–94 | Caen | 16 | 0 | | |
| 1994–95 | Caen | 4 | 0 | **20** | **0** |
| 1995–96 | Laval | 42 | 4 | | |
| 1996–97 | Laval | 39 | 8 | **81** | **12** |
| 1997–98 | Guingamp | 30 | 0 | **30** | **0** |
| 1998–99 | Le Havre | 27 | 3 | **27** | **3** |
| 1999–2000 | Bastia | 28 | 1 | | |
| 2000–01 | Bastia | 28 | 1 | | |
| 2001–02 | Bastia | 26 | 2 | **82** | **4** |
| 2002–03 | Chievo | 8 | 0 | **8** | **0** |
| 2003–04 | Leicester C | 20 | 1 | **20** | **1** |

**O'GRADY, Christopher§ (M)** 1 0
b.Nottingham 25-1-86
*Source:* Trainee. *Honours:* England Youth.

| | | | | | |
|---|---|---|---|---|---|
| 2002–03 | Leicester C | 1 | 0 | | |
| 2003–04 | Leicester C | 0 | 0 | **1** | **0** |

**PEARMAIN, Dominic (F)** 0 0
H: 5 9 W: 10 03 b.Peterborough 2-9-84
*Source:* Scholar.

| | | | |
|---|---|---|---|
| 2003–04 | Leicester C | 0 | 0 |

**PETRESCU, Tomi (F)** 1 0
H: 5 9 W: 10 05 b.Jyvaskyla 24-7-86
*Source:* Scholar.

| | | | | | |
|---|---|---|---|---|---|
| 2002–03 | Leicester C | 1 | 0 | | |
| 2003–04 | Leicester C | 0 | 0 | **1** | **0** |

**POWELL, Liam (D)** 0 0
H: 5 10 W: 12 06 b.Cardiff 18-9-85
*Source:* Scholar. *Honours:* Wales Under-21.

| | | | |
|---|---|---|---|
| 2003–04 | Leicester C | 0 | 0 |

**PRIET, Nicolas* (D)** 0 0
H: 6 3 W: 12 12 b.Villeurbanne 31-1-83

| | | | |
|---|---|---|---|
| 2003–04 | Leicester C | 0 | 0 |

**ROGERS, Alan* (D)** 273 18
H: 5 9 W: 12 10 b.Liverpool 3-1-77
*Source:* Trainee.

| | | | | | |
|---|---|---|---|---|---|
| 1995–96 | Tranmere R | 26 | 2 | | |
| 1996–97 | Tranmere R | 31 | 0 | **57** | **2** |
| 1997–98 | Nottingham F | 46 | 1 | | |
| 1998–99 | Nottingham F | 34 | 3 | | |
| 1999–2000 | Nottingham F | 37 | 9 | | |
| 2000–01 | Nottingham F | 17 | 3 | | |
| 2001–02 | Nottingham F | 3 | 0 | | |
| 2001–02 | Leicester C | 13 | 0 | | |
| 2002–03 | Leicester C | 41 | 0 | | |
| 2003–04 | Leicester C | 8 | 0 | **62** | **0** |
| 2003–04 | *Wigan Ath* | 5 | 0 | **5** | **0** |
| 2003–04 | *Nottingham F* | 12 | 0 | **149** | **16** |

**SCIMECA, Riccardo (M)** 253 10
H: 6 1 W: 13 04 b.Leamington Spa 13-6-75
*Source:* Trainee. *Honours:* England Under-21, B.

| | | | | | |
|---|---|---|---|---|---|
| 1993–94 | Aston Villa | 0 | 0 | | |
| 1994–95 | Aston Villa | 0 | 0 | | |
| 1995–96 | Aston Villa | 17 | 0 | | |
| 1996–97 | Aston Villa | 17 | 0 | | |
| 1997–98 | Aston Villa | 21 | 0 | | |
| 1998–99 | Aston Villa | 18 | 2 | **73** | **2** |
| 1999–2000 | Nottingham F | 38 | 0 | | |
| 2000–01 | Nottingham F | 36 | 4 | | |
| 2001–02 | Nottingham F | 37 | 0 | | |
| 2002–03 | Nottingham F | 40 | 3 | **151** | **7** |
| 2003–04 | Leicester C | 29 | 1 | **29** | **1** |

**SCOWCROFT, James (F)** 304 67
H: 6 1 W: 14 07 b.Bury St Edmunds 15-11-75
*Source:* Trainee. *Honours:* England Under-21.

| | | | | | |
|---|---|---|---|---|---|
| 1994–95 | Ipswich T | 0 | 0 | | |
| 1995–96 | Ipswich T | 23 | 2 | | |
| 1996–97 | Ipswich T | 41 | 9 | | |
| 1997–98 | Ipswich T | 31 | 6 | | |
| 1998–99 | Ipswich T | 32 | 13 | | |
| 1999–2000 | Ipswich T | 41 | 13 | | |
| 2000–01 | Ipswich T | 34 | 4 | **202** | **47** |
| 2001–02 | Leicester C | 24 | 5 | | |
| 2002–03 | Leicester C | 43 | 10 | | |
| 2003–04 | Leicester C | 35 | 5 | **102** | **20** |

**SINCLAIR, Frank* (D)** 339 11
H: 5 9 W: 12 03 b.Lambeth 3-12-71
*Source:* Trainee. *Honours:* Jamaica 24 full caps, 1 goal.

| | | | | | |
|---|---|---|---|---|---|
| 1989–90 | Chelsea | 0 | 0 | | |
| 1990–91 | Chelsea | 4 | 0 | | |
| 1991–92 | Chelsea | 8 | 1 | | |
| 1991–92 | *WBA* | 6 | 1 | **6** | **1** |
| 1992–93 | Chelsea | 32 | 0 | | |
| 1993–94 | Chelsea | 35 | 0 | | |
| 1994–95 | Chelsea | 35 | 3 | | |
| 1995–96 | Chelsea | 13 | 1 | | |
| 1996–97 | Chelsea | 20 | 1 | | |
| 1997–98 | Chelsea | 22 | 1 | **169** | **7** |
| 1998–99 | Leicester C | 31 | 1 | | |
| 1999–2000 | Leicester C | 34 | 0 | | |
| 2000–01 | Leicester C | 17 | 0 | | |
| 2001–02 | Leicester C | 35 | 0 | | |
| 2002–03 | Leicester C | 33 | 1 | | |
| 2003–04 | Leicester C | 14 | 1 | **164** | **3** |

**STEWART, Jordan (D)** 79 5
H: 5 11 W: 12 06 b.Birmingham 3-3-82
*Source:* Trainee. *Honours:* England Youth, Under-21.

| | | | | | |
|---|---|---|---|---|---|
| 1999–2000 | Leicester C | 1 | 0 | | |
| 1999–2000 | *Bristol R* | 4 | 0 | **4** | **0** |
| 2000–01 | Leicester C | 0 | 0 | | |
| 2001–02 | Leicester C | 12 | 0 | | |

| | | | | | |
|---|---|---|---|---|---|
| 2002–03 | Leicester C | 37 | 4 | | |
| 2003–04 | Leicester C | 25 | 1 | **75** | **5** |

**THATCHER, Ben (D)** **241** **2**
H: 5 10 W: 12 07 b.Swindon 30-11-75
*Source:* Trainee. *Honours:* England Youth, Under-21, Wales 3 full caps.

| | | | | | |
|---|---|---|---|---|---|
| 1992–93 | Millwall | 0 | 0 | | |
| 1993–94 | Millwall | 8 | 0 | | |
| 1994–95 | Millwall | 40 | 1 | | |
| 1995–96 | Millwall | 42 | 0 | **90** | **1** |
| 1996–97 | Wimbledon | 9 | 0 | | |
| 1997–98 | Wimbledon | 26 | 0 | | |
| 1998–99 | Wimbledon | 31 | 0 | | |
| 1999–2000 | Wimbledon | 20 | 0 | **86** | **0** |
| 2000–01 | Tottenham H | 12 | 0 | | |
| 2001–02 | Tottenham H | 12 | 0 | | |
| 2002–03 | Tottenham H | 12 | 0 | **36** | **0** |
| 2003–04 | Leicester C | 29 | 1 | **29** | **1** |

**WALKER, Ian (G)** **379** **0**
H: 6 2 W: 13 03 b.Watford 31-10-71
*Source:* Trainee. *Honours:* England Youth, Under-21, B, 4 full caps.

| | | | | | |
|---|---|---|---|---|---|
| 1989–90 | Tottenham H | 0 | 0 | | |
| 1990–91 | Tottenham H | 1 | 0 | | |
| 1990–91 | *Oxford U* | 2 | 0 | **2** | **0** |
| 1990–91 | *Ipswich T* | 0 | 0 | | |
| 1991–92 | Tottenham H | 18 | 0 | | |
| 1992–93 | Tottenham H | 17 | 0 | | |
| 1993–94 | Tottenham H | 11 | 0 | | |
| 1994–95 | Tottenham H | 41 | 0 | | |
| 1995–96 | Tottenham H | 38 | 0 | | |
| 1996–97 | Tottenham H | 37 | 0 | | |
| 1997–98 | Tottenham H | 29 | 0 | | |
| 1998–99 | Tottenham H | 25 | 0 | | |
| 1999–2000 | Tottenham H | 38 | 0 | | |
| 2000–01 | Tottenham H | 4 | 0 | **259** | **0** |
| 2001–02 | Leicester C | 35 | 0 | | |
| 2002–03 | Leicester C | 46 | 0 | | |
| 2003–04 | Leicester C | 37 | 0 | **118** | **0** |

**WILLIAMSON, Tom (M)** **1** **0**
H: 5 9 W: 10 04 b.Leicester 24-12-84
*Source:* Scholar.

| | | | | | |
|---|---|---|---|---|---|
| 2001–02 | Leicester C | 1 | 0 | | |
| 2002–03 | Leicester C | 0 | 0 | | |
| 2003–04 | Leicester C | 0 | 0 | **1** | **0** |

**WRIGHT, Tommy (F)** **39** **5**
H: 6 0 W: 12 02 b.Leicester 28-9-84
*Source:* Scholar. *Honours:* England Youth, Under-20.

| | | | | | |
|---|---|---|---|---|---|
| 2001–02 | Leicester C | 1 | 0 | | |
| 2002–03 | Leicester C | 13 | 2 | | |
| 2003–04 | Leicester C | 0 | 0 | **14** | **2** |
| 2003–04 | *Brentford* | 25 | 3 | **25** | **3** |

**Scholars**
Butcher, Aarran S; Dodds, Louis B; Gondal, Usman I; Graham, James A; O'Grady, Christopher J; Porter, Levi R; Sheehan, Alan; Smedley, Jay; Stearman, Richard J; Wesolowski, James

## LEYTON ORIENT (42)

**ALEXANDER, Gary (F)** **203** **63**
H: 6 0 W: 13 01 b.Lambeth 15-8-79
*Source:* Trainee.

| | | | | | |
|---|---|---|---|---|---|
| 1998–99 | West Ham U | 0 | 0 | | |
| 1999–2000 | West Ham U | 0 | 0 | | |
| 1999–2000 | *Exeter C* | 37 | 16 | **37** | **16** |
| 2000–01 | Swindon T | 37 | 7 | **37** | **7** |
| 2001–02 | Hull C | 43 | 17 | | |
| 2002–03 | Hull C | 25 | 6 | **68** | **23** |
| 2002–03 | Leyton Orient | 17 | 2 | | |
| 2003–04 | Leyton Orient | 44 | 15 | **61** | **17** |

**BARNARD, Donny (D)** **62** **0**
H: 5 10 W: 11 05 b.Forest Gate 1-7-84

| | | | | | |
|---|---|---|---|---|---|
| 2001–02 | Leyton Orient | 10 | 0 | | |
| 2002–03 | Leyton Orient | 29 | 0 | | |
| 2003–04 | Leyton Orient | 23 | 0 | **62** | **0** |

**BRAZIER, Matt* (M)** **171** **10**
H: 5 10 W: 10 10 b.Whipps Cross 2-7-76
*Source:* Trainee.

| | | | | | |
|---|---|---|---|---|---|
| 1994–95 | QPR | 0 | 0 | | |
| 1995–96 | QPR | 11 | 0 | | |
| 1996–97 | QPR | 27 | 2 | | |
| 1997–98 | QPR | 11 | 0 | **49** | **2** |
| 1997–98 | Fulham | 7 | 1 | | |
| 1998–99 | Fulham | 2 | 0 | **9** | **1** |
| 1998–99 | *Cardiff C* | 11 | 2 | | |
| 1999–2000 | Cardiff C | 30 | 1 | | |
| 2000–01 | Cardiff C | 26 | 2 | | |
| 2001–02 | Cardiff C | 0 | 0 | **67** | **5** |
| 2001–02 | Leyton Orient | 8 | 0 | | |
| 2002–03 | Leyton Orient | 33 | 1 | | |
| 2003–04 | Leyton Orient | 5 | 1 | **46** | **2** |

**DOWNER, Simon* (D)** **79** **0**
H: 6 1 W: 13 02 b.Romford 19-10-81
*Source:* Trainee.

| | | | | | |
|---|---|---|---|---|---|
| 1998–99 | Leyton Orient | 1 | 0 | | |
| 1999–2000 | Leyton Orient | 24 | 0 | | |
| 2000–01 | Leyton Orient | 31 | 0 | | |
| 2001–02 | Leyton Orient | 12 | 0 | | |
| 2002–03 | Leyton Orient | 8 | 0 | | |
| 2003–04 | Leyton Orient | 3 | 0 | **79** | **0** |

**DUNCAN, Derek§ (M)** **1** **0**
H: 5 9 W: 10 12 b.Newham 23-4-87
*Source:* Scholar.

| | | | | | |
|---|---|---|---|---|---|
| 2003–04 | Leyton Orient | 1 | 0 | **1** | **0** |

**EBDON, Marcus‡ (M)** **353** **28**
H: 5 10 W: 11 02 b.Pontypool 17-10-70
*Source:* Trainee. *Honours:* Wales Youth, Under-21.

| | | | | | |
|---|---|---|---|---|---|
| 1988–89 | Everton | 0 | 0 | | |
| 1989–90 | Everton | 0 | 0 | | |
| 1990–91 | Everton | 0 | 0 | | |
| 1991–92 | Peterborough U | 15 | 2 | | |
| 1992–93 | Peterborough U | 28 | 4 | | |
| 1993–94 | Peterborough U | 10 | 0 | | |
| 1994–95 | Peterborough U | 35 | 6 | | |
| 1995–96 | Peterborough U | 39 | 2 | | |
| 1996–97 | Peterborough U | 20 | 1 | **147** | **15** |
| 1996–97 | Chesterfield | 12 | 1 | | |
| 1997–98 | Chesterfield | 33 | 2 | | |
| 1998–99 | Chesterfield | 40 | 1 | | |
| 1999–2000 | Chesterfield | 11 | 0 | | |
| 2000–01 | Chesterfield | 41 | 3 | | |
| 2001–02 | Chesterfield | 31 | 2 | | |
| 2002–03 | Chesterfield | 24 | 4 | **192** | **13** |
| 2003–04 | Leyton Orient | 14 | 0 | **14** | **0** |

**FORBES, Boniek‡ (F)** **13** **0**
H: 5 10 W: 11 00 b.Guinea Bissau 30-9-83
*Source:* Scholar.

| | | | | | |
|---|---|---|---|---|---|
| 2002–03 | Leyton Orient | 3 | 0 | | |
| 2003–04 | Leyton Orient | 10 | 0 | **13** | **0** |

**HARNWELL, Jamie‡ (M)** **149** **19**
H: 6 3 W: 12 00 b.Australia 21-7-77

| | | | | | |
|---|---|---|---|---|---|
| 1998–99 | Perth Glory | 23 | 1 | | |
| 1999–2000 | Perth Glory | 31 | 4 | | |
| 2000–01 | Perth Glory | 28 | 6 | | |
| 2001–02 | Perth Glory | 23 | 4 | | |
| 2002–03 | Perth Glory | 29 | 3 | | |
| 2003–04 | Perth Glory | 12 | 1 | **146** | **19** |
| 2003–04 | Leyton Orient | 3 | 0 | **3** | **0** |

**HARRISON, Lee (G)** **235** **0**
H: 6 2 W: 13 03 b.Billericay 12-9-71
*Source:* Trainee.

| | | | | | |
|---|---|---|---|---|---|
| 1990–91 | Charlton Ath | 0 | 0 | | |
| 1991–92 | Charlton Ath | 0 | 0 | | |
| 1991–92 | *Fulham* | 0 | 0 | | |
| 1991–92 | *Gillingham* | 2 | 0 | **2** | **0** |
| 1992–93 | Charlton Ath | 0 | 0 | | |
| 1992–93 | *Fulham* | 0 | 0 | | |
| 1993–94 | Fulham | 0 | 0 | | |
| 1994–95 | Fulham | 7 | 0 | | |
| 1995–96 | Fulham | 5 | 0 | **12** | **0** |
| 1996–97 | Barnet | 21 | 0 | | |
| 1997–98 | Barnet | 46 | 0 | | |
| 1998–99 | Barnet | 43 | 0 | | |
| 1999–2000 | Barnet | 43 | 0 | | |
| 2000–01 | Barnet | 30 | 0 | | |
| 2001–02 | Barnet | 0 | 0 | **183** | **0** |
| 2002–03 | Peterborough U | 12 | 0 | **12** | **0** |
| 2002–03 | Leyton Orient | 6 | 0 | | |
| 2003–04 | Leyton Orient | 20 | 0 | **26** | **0** |

**HUNT, David (D)** **40** **1**
H: 5 11 W: 11 09 b.Dulwich 10-9-82
*Source:* Scholar.

| | | | | | |
|---|---|---|---|---|---|
| 2002–03 | Crystal Palace | 2 | 0 | **2** | **0** |
| 2003–04 | Leyton Orient | 38 | 1 | **38** | **1** |

**IBEHRE, Jabo (F)** **96** **15**
H: 6 2 W: 13 00 b.Islington 28-1-83
*Source:* Trainee.

| | | | | | |
|---|---|---|---|---|---|
| 1999–2000 | Leyton Orient | 3 | 0 | | |
| 2000–01 | Leyton Orient | 5 | 2 | | |
| 2001–02 | Leyton Orient | 28 | 4 | | |
| 2002–03 | Leyton Orient | 25 | 5 | | |
| 2003–04 | Leyton Orient | 35 | 4 | **96** | **15** |

**JONES, Billy (D)** **72** **0**
H: 6 1 W: 11 04 b.Chatham 26-3-83
*Source:* Trainee.

| | | | | | |
|---|---|---|---|---|---|
| 2000–01 | Leyton Orient | 1 | 0 | | |
| 2001–02 | Leyton Orient | 16 | 0 | | |
| 2002–03 | Leyton Orient | 24 | 0 | | |
| 2003–04 | Leyton Orient | 31 | 0 | **72** | **0** |

**JOSEPH, Matt* (D)** **383** **8**
H: 5 5 W: 10 07 b.Bethnal Green 30-9-72
*Source:* Trainee. *Honours:* Barbados 2 full caps.

| | | | | | |
|---|---|---|---|---|---|
| 1991–92 | Arsenal | 0 | 0 | | |
| 1992–93 | Gillingham | 0 | 0 | | |
| 1993–94 | Cambridge U | 27 | 2 | | |
| 1994–95 | Cambridge U | 39 | 2 | | |
| 1995–96 | Cambridge U | 42 | 2 | | |
| 1996–97 | Cambridge U | 44 | 0 | | |
| 1997–98 | Cambridge U | 7 | 0 | **159** | **6** |
| 1997–98 | Leyton Orient | 14 | 1 | | |
| 1998–99 | Leyton Orient | 34 | 0 | | |
| 1999–2000 | Leyton Orient | 41 | 0 | | |
| 2000–01 | Leyton Orient | 44 | 0 | | |
| 2001–02 | Leyton Orient | 30 | 1 | | |
| 2002–03 | Leyton Orient | 37 | 0 | | |
| 2003–04 | Leyton Orient | 24 | 0 | **224** | **2** |

**LOCKWOOD, Matt (D)** **265** **26**
H: 5 10 W: 11 07 b.Rochford 17-10-76
*Source:* Trainee.

| | | | | | |
|---|---|---|---|---|---|
| 1994–95 | QPR | 0 | 0 | | |
| 1995–96 | QPR | 0 | 0 | | |
| 1996–97 | Bristol R | 39 | 1 | | |
| 1997–98 | Bristol R | 24 | 0 | **63** | **1** |
| 1998–99 | Leyton Orient | 37 | 3 | | |
| 1999–2000 | Leyton Orient | 41 | 6 | | |
| 2000–01 | Leyton Orient | 32 | 7 | | |
| 2001–02 | Leyton Orient | 24 | 2 | | |
| 2002–03 | Leyton Orient | 43 | 5 | | |
| 2003–04 | Leyton Orient | 25 | 2 | **202** | **25** |

**MACKIE, John (D)** **91** **4**
H: 6 1 W: 13 00 b.London 5-7-76
*Source:* Sutton U.

| | | | | | |
|---|---|---|---|---|---|
| 1999–2000 | Reading | 0 | 0 | | |
| 2000–01 | Reading | 10 | 0 | | |
| 2001–02 | Reading | 27 | 2 | | |
| 2002–03 | Reading | 25 | 0 | | |
| 2003–04 | Reading | 9 | 1 | **71** | **3** |
| 2003–04 | Leyton Orient | 20 | 1 | **20** | **1** |

**McGHEE, Dave‡ (D)** **232** **15**
H: 6 0 W: 13 07 b.Worthing 19-6-76
*Source:* Trainee.

| | | | | | |
|---|---|---|---|---|---|
| 1994–95 | Brentford | 7 | 1 | | |
| 1995–96 | Brentford | 36 | 5 | | |
| 1996–97 | Brentford | 45 | 1 | | |
| 1997–98 | Brentford | 29 | 1 | | |
| 1998–99 | Brentford | 0 | 0 | **117** | **8** |
| From Stevenage Bor. | | | | | |
| 1999–2000 | Leyton Orient | 23 | 1 | | |
| 2000–01 | Leyton Orient | 39 | 3 | | |
| 2001–02 | Leyton Orient | 40 | 2 | | |
| 2002–03 | Leyton Orient | 3 | 0 | | |
| 2003–04 | Leyton Orient | 10 | 1 | **115** | **7** |

**MILLER, Justin (D)** **53** **2**
H: 6 0 W: 11 04 b.Johannesburg 16-12-80
*Source:* Academy.

| | | | | | |
|---|---|---|---|---|---|
| 1999–2000 | Ipswich T | 0 | 0 | | |
| 2000–01 | Ipswich T | 0 | 0 | | |
| 2001–02 | Ipswich T | 0 | 0 | | |
| 2002–03 | Ipswich T | 0 | 0 | | |
| 2002–03 | Leyton Orient | 19 | 0 | | |
| 2003–04 | Leyton Orient | 34 | 2 | **53** | **2** |

**MORRIS, Glenn (G)** **52** **0**
H: 5 11 W: 11 00 b.Woolwich 20-12-83
*Source:* Scholar.

| | | | | | |
|---|---|---|---|---|---|
| 2001–02 | Leyton Orient | 2 | 0 | | |
| 2002–03 | Leyton Orient | 23 | 0 | | |
| 2003–04 | Leyton Orient | 27 | 0 | **52** | **0** |

**NEWEY, Tom (D)** **47 3**
H: 5 10 W: 11 00 b.Sheffield 31-10-82
*Source:* Scholar.

| | | | | | |
|---|---|---|---|---|---|
| 2000–01 | Leeds U | 0 | 0 | | |
| 2001–02 | Leeds U | 0 | 0 | | |
| 2002–03 | Leeds U | 0 | 0 | | |
| 2002–03 | *Cambridge U* | 6 | 0 | **6** | **0** |
| 2002–03 | *Darlington* | 7 | 1 | **7** | **1** |
| 2003–04 | Leyton Orient | 34 | 2 | **34** | **2** |

**PETERS, Mark# (D)** **233 12**
H: 6 0 W: 13 04 b.St Asaph 6-7-72
*Source:* Trainee. *Honours:* Wales Under-21.

| | | | | | |
|---|---|---|---|---|---|
| 1991–92 | Manchester C | 0 | 0 | | |
| 1992–93 | Norwich C | 0 | 0 | | |
| 1993–94 | Peterborough U | 19 | 0 | | |
| 1994–95 | Peterborough U | 0 | 0 | **19** | **0** |
| 1994–95 | Mansfield T | 26 | 4 | | |
| 1995–96 | Mansfield T | 21 | 2 | | |
| 1996–97 | Mansfield T | 0 | 0 | | |
| 1997–98 | Mansfield T | 24 | 2 | | |
| 1998–99 | Mansfield T | 37 | 1 | **108** | **9** |
| 2001–02 | Rushden & D | 40 | 0 | | |
| 2002–03 | Rushden & D | 27 | 1 | | |
| 2003–04 | Rushden & D | 0 | 0 | **67** | **1** |
| 2003–04 | Leyton Orient | 39 | 2 | **39** | **2** |

**PURSER, Wayne (F)** **66 11**
H: 5 8 W: 12 05 b.Basildon 13-4-80
*Source:* Trainee.

| | | | | | |
|---|---|---|---|---|---|
| 1996–97 | QPR | 0 | 0 | | |
| 1997–98 | QPR | 0 | 0 | | |
| 1998–99 | QPR | 0 | 0 | | |
| 1999–2000 | QPR | 0 | 0 | | |
| 2000–01 | Barnet | 18 | 3 | | |
| 2001–02 | Barnet | 0 | 0 | | |
| 2002–03 | Barnet | 0 | 0 | **18** | **3** |
| 2002–03 | Leyton Orient | 7 | 3 | | |
| 2003–04 | Leyton Orient | 41 | 5 | **48** | **8** |

**SAAH, Brian§ (M)** **6 0**
H: 6 1 W: 11 00 b.Hornchurch 16-12-86
*Source:* Scholar.

| | | | | | |
|---|---|---|---|---|---|
| 2003–04 | Leyton Orient | 6 | 0 | **6** | **0** |

**SCOTT, Andy (F)** **309 62**
H: 6 1 W: 12 04 b.Epsom 2-8-72
*Source:* Sutton U.

| | | | | | |
|---|---|---|---|---|---|
| 1992–93 | Sheffield U | 2 | 1 | | |
| 1993–94 | Sheffield U | 15 | 0 | | |
| 1994–95 | Sheffield U | 37 | 4 | | |
| 1995–96 | Sheffield U | 7 | 0 | | |
| 1996–97 | Sheffield U | 8 | 1 | | |
| 1996–97 | *Chesterfield* | 5 | 3 | **5** | **3** |
| 1996–97 | *Bury* | 8 | 0 | **8** | **0** |
| 1997–98 | Sheffield U | 6 | 0 | **75** | **6** |
| 1997–98 | Brentford | 26 | 5 | | |
| 1998–99 | Brentford | 34 | 7 | | |
| 1999–2000 | Brentford | 36 | 3 | | |
| 2000–01 | Brentford | 22 | 13 | **118** | **28** |
| 2000–01 | Oxford U | 21 | 5 | | |
| 2001–02 | Oxford U | 30 | 8 | | |
| 2002–03 | Oxford U | 38 | 11 | | |
| 2003–04 | Oxford U | 6 | 0 | **95** | **24** |
| 2003–04 | Leyton Orient | 8 | 1 | **8** | **1** |

**STEPHENS, Kevin‡ (D)** **4 0**
H: 5 10 W: 12 05 b.Enfield 28-7-84
*Source:* Scholar.

| | | | | | |
|---|---|---|---|---|---|
| 2002–03 | Leyton Orient | 3 | 0 | | |
| 2003–04 | Leyton Orient | 1 | 0 | **4** | **0** |

**TATE, Chris* (F)** **142 27**
H: 6 0 W: 12 08 b.York 27-12-77
*Source:* York C Trainee.

| | | | | | |
|---|---|---|---|---|---|
| 1996–97 | Sunderland | 0 | 0 | | |
| 1997–98 | Scarborough | 24 | 1 | | |
| 1998–99 | Scarborough | 25 | 12 | **49** | **13** |
| 1999–2000 | Halifax T | 18 | 4 | **18** | **4** |
| From Scarborough. | | | | | |
| 2000–01 | Leyton Orient | 22 | 3 | | |
| 2001–02 | Leyton Orient | 7 | 0 | | |
| 2002–03 | Leyton Orient | 23 | 6 | | |
| 2003–04 | Leyton Orient | 23 | 1 | **75** | **10** |

**TONER, Ciaran* (M)** **64 2**
H: 5 10 W: 12 10 b.Craigavon 30-6-81
*Source:* Trainee. *Honours:* Northern Ireland Under-21, 2 full caps.

| | | | | | |
|---|---|---|---|---|---|
| 1999–2000 | Tottenham H | 0 | 0 | | |
| 2000–01 | Tottenham H | 0 | 0 | | |
| 2001–02 | Tottenham H | 0 | 0 | | |
| 2001–02 | *Peterborough U* | 6 | 0 | **6** | **0** |
| 2001–02 | Bristol R | 6 | 0 | **6** | **0** |
| 2001–02 | Leyton Orient | 0 | 0 | | |
| 2002–03 | Leyton Orient | 25 | 1 | | |
| 2003–04 | Leyton Orient | 27 | 1 | **52** | **2** |

**ZAKUANI, Gaby§ (M)** **11 2**
H: 6 1 W: 10 10 b.Zaire 31-5-86
*Source:* Scholar.

| | | | | | |
|---|---|---|---|---|---|
| 2002–03 | Leyton Orient | 1 | 0 | | |
| 2003–04 | Leyton Orient | 10 | 2 | **11** | **2** |

**Scholars**
Butler, Graeme K M; Delpesh O'Cearuill, Joseph; Duncan, Derek H J; Echanomi, Efe; Game, Matthew; Glozier, Daniel; Holder, Philip; Jones, Paul; Laxton, Thomas; Palmer, Aiden; Rodden, James C; Saah, Brian E; Tiffin, Gregory; Toku, Prince K; Wareham, Ross; Williams, Andre; Zakuani, Gabriel

## LINCOLN C (43)

**BAILEY, Mark# (D)** **165 2**
H: 5 8 W: 10 12 b.Stoke 12-8-76
*Source:* Trainee.

| | | | | | |
|---|---|---|---|---|---|
| 1994–95 | Stoke C | 0 | 0 | | |
| 1995–96 | Stoke C | 0 | 0 | | |
| 1996–97 | Stoke C | 0 | 0 | | |
| 1996–97 | Rochdale | 15 | 0 | | |
| 1997–98 | Rochdale | 33 | 0 | | |
| 1998–99 | Rochdale | 19 | 1 | | |
| 1999–2000 | Rochdale | 0 | 0 | | |
| 2000–01 | Rochdale | 0 | 0 | **67** | **1** |
| From Northwich Vic. | | | | | |
| 2001–02 | Lincoln C | 18 | 0 | | |
| 2002–03 | Lincoln C | 45 | 0 | | |
| 2003–04 | Lincoln C | 35 | 1 | **98** | **1** |

**BLOOMER, Matt# (D)** **60 1**
H: 6 1 W: 13 11 b.Cleethorpes 3-11-78
*Source:* Trainee.

| | | | | | |
|---|---|---|---|---|---|
| 1997–98 | Grimsby T | 0 | 0 | | |
| 1998–99 | Grimsby T | 4 | 0 | | |
| 1999–2000 | Grimsby T | 2 | 0 | | |
| 2000–01 | Grimsby T | 6 | 0 | | |
| 2001–02 | Grimsby T | 0 | 0 | **12** | **0** |
| 2001–02 | Hull C | 3 | 0 | | |
| 2001–02 | *Lincoln C* | 5 | 0 | | |
| 2002–03 | Hull C | 0 | 0 | **3** | **0** |
| 2002–03 | Lincoln C | 13 | 1 | | |
| 2003–04 | Lincoln C | 27 | 0 | **45** | **1** |

**BUTCHER, Richard (M)** **58 9**
H: 6 0 W: 12 12 b.Northampton 22-1-81
*Source:* Kettering T.

| | | | | | |
|---|---|---|---|---|---|
| 2002–03 | Lincoln C | 26 | 3 | | |
| 2003–04 | Lincoln C | 32 | 6 | **58** | **9** |

**CAMM, Mark‡ (D)** **32 0**
H: 5 7 W: 11 05 b.Mansfield 1-10-80
*Source:* Trainee.

| | | | | | |
|---|---|---|---|---|---|
| 1999–2000 | Sheffield U | 0 | 0 | | |
| 2000–01 | Lincoln C | 3 | 0 | | |
| 2001–02 | Lincoln C | 16 | 0 | | |
| 2002–03 | Lincoln C | 13 | 0 | | |
| 2003–04 | Lincoln C | 0 | 0 | **32** | **0** |

**CORNELLY, Chris# (F)** **16 0**
H: 5 7 W: 11 07 b.Huddersfield 7-7-76
*Source:* Leigh RMI, Ashton U.

| | | | | | |
|---|---|---|---|---|---|
| 2002–03 | Lincoln C | 16 | 0 | | |
| 2003–04 | Lincoln C | 0 | 0 | **16** | **0** |

**COULSON, David‡ (D)** **0 0**
H: 6 1 W: 12 10 b.Durham 21-3-84

| | | | | | |
|---|---|---|---|---|---|
| 2001–02 | Barnsley | 0 | 0 | | |
| 2002–03 | Barnsley | 0 | 0 | | |
| 2003–04 | Lincoln C | 0 | 0 | | |

**DAVIES, Chris‡ (D)** **0 0**
H: 5 10 W: 11 10 b.Rotherham 8-4-84
*Source:* Scholar.

| | | | | | |
|---|---|---|---|---|---|
| 2003–04 | Lincoln C | 0 | 0 | | |

**FLETCHER, Gary (F)** **68 17**
H: 5 11 W: 12 06 b.Liverpool 4-6-81
*Source:* Northwich Vic. *Honours:* England Schools.

| | | | | | |
|---|---|---|---|---|---|
| 2000–01 | Hull C | 5 | 0 | **5** | **0** |
| 2001–02 | Leyton Orient | 9 | 0 | | |
| 2002–03 | Leyton Orient | 12 | 1 | **21** | **1** |
| 2003–04 | Lincoln C | 42 | 16 | **42** | **16** |

**FRECKLINGTON, Lee§ (M)** **0 0**
H: 5 8 W: 11 00 b.Lincoln 8-9-85
*Source:* Scholar.

| | | | | | |
|---|---|---|---|---|---|
| 2003–04 | Lincoln C | 0 | 0 | | |

**FUTCHER, Ben (D)** **96 10**
H: 6 7 W: 12 05 b.Bradford 20-2-81
*Source:* Trainee.

| | | | | | |
|---|---|---|---|---|---|
| 1999–2000 | Oldham Ath | 5 | 0 | | |
| 2000–01 | Oldham Ath | 5 | 0 | | |
| 2001–02 | Oldham Ath | 0 | 0 | **10** | **0** |
| From Stalybridge C, Doncaster R | | | | | |
| 2002–03 | Lincoln | | | | |
| 2003–04 | Lincoln C | 43 | 2 | **86** | **10** |

**GAIN, Peter (M)** **187 21**
H: 6 0 W: 11 07 b.Hammersmith 2-11-76
*Source:* Trainee.

| | | | | | |
|---|---|---|---|---|---|
| 1995–96 | Tottenham H | 0 | 0 | | |
| 1996–97 | Tottenham H | 0 | 0 | | |
| 1997–98 | Tottenham H | 0 | 0 | | |
| 1998–99 | Tottenham H | 0 | 0 | | |
| 1998–99 | Lincoln C | 4 | 0 | | |
| 1999–2000 | Lincoln C | 32 | 2 | | |
| 2000–01 | Lincoln C | 24 | 5 | | |
| 2001–02 | Lincoln C | 42 | 2 | | |
| 2002–03 | Lincoln C | 43 | 5 | | |
| 2003–04 | Lincoln C | 42 | 7 | **187** | **21** |

**GEORGE, Kevin* (M)** **0 0**
H: 5 11 W: 12 04 b.London 21-11-82
*Source:* Scholar.

| | | | | | |
|---|---|---|---|---|---|
| 2000–01 | Charlton Ath | 0 | 0 | | |
| 2001–02 | Charlton Ath | 0 | 0 | | |
| 2002–03 | Grimsby T | 0 | 0 | | |
| 2003–04 | Lincoln C | 0 | 0 | | |

**GREEN, Francis (F)** **143 21**
H: 5 9 W: 11 04 b.Derby 23-4-80
*Source:* Ilkeston T.

| | | | | | |
|---|---|---|---|---|---|
| 1997–98 | Peterborough U | 4 | 1 | | |
| 1998–99 | Peterborough U | 7 | 1 | | |
| 1999–2000 | Peterborough U | 20 | 1 | | |
| 2000–01 | Peterborough U | 32 | 6 | | |
| 2001–02 | Peterborough U | 23 | 3 | | |
| 2002–03 | Peterborough U | 19 | 2 | | |
| 2003–04 | Peterborough U | 3 | 0 | **108** | **14** |
| 2003–04 | Lincoln C | 35 | 7 | **35** | **7** |

**HORRIGAN, Darren* (G)** **1 0**
H: 6 4 W: 13 07 b.Middlesbrough 2-6-83
*Source:* Scholar.

| | | | | | |
|---|---|---|---|---|---|
| 2001–02 | Lincoln C | 1 | 0 | | |
| 2002–03 | Lincoln C | 0 | 0 | | |
| 2003–04 | Lincoln C | 0 | 0 | **1** | **0** |

**LIBURD, Richard* (D)** **306 13**
H: 5 9 W: 11 08 b.Nottingham 26-9-73
*Source:* Forest Ath.

| | | | | | |
|---|---|---|---|---|---|
| 1992–93 | Middlesbrough | 0 | 0 | | |
| 1993–94 | Middlesbrough | 41 | 1 | **41** | **1** |
| 1994–95 | Bradford C | 9 | 1 | | |
| 1995–96 | Bradford C | 33 | 1 | | |
| 1996–97 | Bradford C | 36 | 1 | | |
| 1997–98 | Bradford C | 0 | 0 | **78** | **3** |
| 1997–98 | Carlisle U | 9 | 0 | **9** | **0** |
| 1998–99 | Notts Co | 35 | 1 | | |
| 1999–2000 | Notts Co | 31 | 1 | | |
| 2000–01 | Notts Co | 31 | 3 | | |
| 2001–02 | Notts Co | 25 | 2 | | |
| 2002–03 | Notts Co | 32 | 2 | **154** | **9** |
| 2003–04 | Lincoln C | 24 | 0 | **24** | **0** |

**LOGAN, Richard (D)** **228 21**
H: 6 0 W: 12 08 b.Barnsley 24-5-69
*Source:* Gainsborough T.

| | | | | | |
|---|---|---|---|---|---|
| 1993–94 | Huddersfield T | 16 | 0 | | |
| 1994–95 | Huddersfield T | 27 | 1 | | |
| 1995–96 | Huddersfield T | 2 | 0 | **45** | **1** |
| 1995–96 | Plymouth Arg | 31 | 4 | | |
| 1996–97 | Plymouth Arg | 28 | 4 | | |
| 1997–98 | Plymouth Arg | 27 | 4 | **86** | **12** |
| 1998–99 | Scunthorpe U | 41 | 6 | | |
| 1999–2000 | Scunthorpe U | 39 | 1 | **80** | **7** |
| 2000–01 | Lincoln C | 5 | 0 | | |
| 2001–02 | Lincoln C | 2 | 0 | | |
| 2002–03 | Lincoln C | 10 | 1 | | |
| 2003–04 | Lincoln C | 0 | 0 | **17** | **1** |

**MARRIOTT, Alan (G)** **183 0**
H: 6 0 W: 12 04 b.Bedford 3-9-78
*Source:* Trainee.

| | | | | | |
|---|---|---|---|---|---|
| 1997–98 | Tottenham H | 0 | 0 | | |

1998–99 Tottenham H 0 0
1999–2000 Lincoln C 18 0
2000–01 Lincoln C 30 0
2001–02 Lincoln C 43 0
2002–03 Lincoln C 46 0
2003–04 Lincoln C 46 0 **183 0**

**MAY, Rory* (F) 5 0**
H: 6 4 W: 12 07 b.Birmingham 25-11-84
*Honours:* Coventry C Scholar.
2003–04 Lincoln C 5 0 **5 0**

**McCOMBE, Jamie (D) 71 1**
H: 6 5 W: 12 05 b.Pontefract 1-1-83
*Source:* Scholar.
2001–02 Scunthorpe U 17 0
2002–03 Scunthorpe U 31 1
2003–04 Scunthorpe U 15 0 **63 1**
2003–04 Lincoln C 8 0 **8 0**

**McNAMARA, Niall* (F) 14 0**
H: 6 1 W: 12 07 b.Limerick 26-1-82
*Source:* Trainee.
1998–99 Nottingham F 0 0
1999–2000 Nottingham F 0 0
2000–01 Nottingham F 0 0
2001–02 Notts Co 4 0
2002–03 Notts Co 0 0 **4 0**
From Belper T.
2003–04 Lincoln C 10 0 **10 0**

**MORGAN, Paul (D) 120 1**
H: 6 0 W: 11 05 b.Belfast 23-10-78
*Source:* Trainee. *Honours:* Northern Ireland Under-21.
1997–98 Preston NE 0 0
1998–99 Preston NE 0 0
1999–2000 Preston NE 0 0
2000–01 Preston NE 0 0
2001–02 Lincoln C 34 1
2002–03 Lincoln C 45 0
2003–04 Lincoln C 41 0 **120 1**

**PEARCE, Allan* (F) 19 1**
H: 5 10 W: 11 05 b.Wellington 7-4-83
*Source:* Barnsley Scholar. *Honours:* New Zealand Youth, Under-20, Under-23.
2002–03 Lincoln C 16 1
2003–04 Lincoln C 3 0 **19 1**

**REMY, Ellis‡ (M) 1 0**
H: 6 2 W: 13 00 b.London 13-2-84
2001–02 Wimbledon 0 0
2002–03 Wimbledon 0 0
2003–04 Lincoln C 1 0 **1 0**

**RICHARDSON, Marcus# (F) 120 25**
H: 6 3 W: 12 05 b.Reading 31-8-77
*Source:* Harrow B.
2000–01 Cambridge U 10 2
2001–02 Cambridge U 6 0 **16 2**
2001–02 Torquay U 30 6
2002–03 Torquay U 9 2 **39 8**
2002–03 Hartlepool U 24 5
2003–04 Hartlepool U 3 0 **27 5**
2003–04 Lincoln C 38 10 **38 10**

**SANDWITH, Kevin (D) 6 0**
H: 5 11 W: 12 05 b.Workington 30-4-78
*Source:* Trainee.
1996–97 Carlisle U 0 0
1997–98 Carlisle U 3 0
1998–99 Carlisle U 0 0 **3 0**
From Halifax T
2003–04 Lincoln C 3 0 **3 0**

**SEDGEMORE, Ben* (M) 304 17**
H: 5 10 W: 12 13 b.Wolverhampton 5-8-75
*Source:* Trainee. *Honours:* England Schools.
1993–94 Birmingham C 0 0
1994–95 Birmingham C 0 0
1994–95 *Northampton T* 1 0 **1 0**
1995–96 Birmingham C 0 0
1995–96 *Mansfield T* 9 0
1995–96 Peterborough U 17 0
1996–97 Peterborough U 0 0 **17 0**
1996–97 Mansfield T 39 4
1997–98 Mansfield T 28 2 **76 6**
1997–98 Macclesfield T 5 0
1998–99 Macclesfield T 35 2
1999–2000 Macclesfield T 35 1
2000–01 Macclesfield T 27 3 **102 6**
2000–01 Lincoln C 10 1
2001–02 Lincoln C 43 2
2002–03 Lincoln C 28 2
2003–04 Lincoln C 27 0 **108 5**

**SMITH, Paul‡ (M) 157 19**
H: 5 10 W: 11 11 b.Hastings 25-1-76
*Source:* Hastings T.
1994–95 Nottingham F 0 0
1995–96 Nottingham F 0 0
1996–97 Nottingham F 0 0
1997–98 Nottingham F 0 0
1997–98 *Lincoln C* 17 3
1998–99 Lincoln C 28 2
1999–2000 Lincoln C 27 5
2000–01 Lincoln C 40 7
2001–02 Lincoln C 8 0
2002–03 Lincoln C 37 2
2003–04 Lincoln C 0 0 **157 19**

**WATTLEY, David* (M) 3 0**
H: 5 11 W: 11 08 b.Enfield 5-9-83
*Source:* School.
2000–01 QPR 0 0
2001–02 QPR 0 0
2002–03 QPR 0 0
2003–04 Lincoln C 3 0 **3 0**

**WEAVER, Simon# (D) 85 3**
H: 6 1 W: 10 07 b.Doncaster 20-12-77
*Source:* Trainee.
1996–97 Sheffield W 0 0
1996–97 *Doncaster R* 2 0 **2 0**
1997–98 Sheffield W 0 0
From Ilkeston T, Nuneaton B
2002–03 Lincoln
2003–04 Lincoln C 39 0 **83 3**

**WILFORD, Aaron* (F) 11 3**
H: 6 2 W: 14 02 b.Scarborough 14-1-82
*Source:* Harrogate College.
1999–2000 Middlesbrough 0 0
2000–01 Middlesbrough 0 0
2001–02 Middlesbrough 0 0
2002–03 Middlesbrough 0 0
From Whitby T.
2003–04 York C 6 2 **6 2**
2003–04 Lincoln C 5 1 **5 1**

**WILLIS, Scott* (M) 34 3**
H: 5 9 W: 11 07 b.Liverpool 20-2-82
*Source:* Wigan Ath Trainee.
1999–2000 Mansfield T 0 0
2000–01 Mansfield T 0 0
2001–02 Carlisle U 1 0 **1 0**
2002–03 Lincoln C 30 3
2003–04 Lincoln C 3 0 **33 3**

**YEO, Simon# (M) 78 16**
H: 5 10 W: 11 08 b.Stockport 20-10-73
*Source:* Hyde U.
2002–03 Lincoln C 37 5
2003–04 Lincoln C 41 11 **78 16**

**Scholars**
Bell, Jonathan; Cooke, Tomas F; Duffy, Ayden; Fisher, Daniel; Frecklington, Lee C; Gordon, Christopher; Holtham, Adam D; Jones, Gareth; Kerley, Adam L; Langley, Ricky; Mettam, Leon; Ryan, Oliver; Scaife, Nicky L; Smith, Samuel A H; Stant, Craig P A; Trout, Charlie J S; Wilkinson, Thomas

**Non Contract**
Draper, Matthew C

## LIVERPOOL (44)

**BABBEL, Markus (D) 309 16**
H: 6 0 W: 13 03 b.Munich 8-9-72
*Honours:* Germany 51 full caps, 1 goal.
1991–92 Bayern Munich 12 0
1992–93 Hamburg 27 1
1993–94 Hamburg 33 0 **60 1**
1994–95 Bayern Munich 26 2
1995–96 Bayern Munich 30 2
1996–97 Bayern Munich 31 2
1997–98 Bayern Munich 30 1
1998–99 Bayern Munich 27 1
1999–2000 Bayern Munich 26 1 **182 9**
2000–01 Liverpool 38 3
2001–02 Liverpool 2 0
2002–03 Liverpool 2 0
2003–04 Liverpool 0 0 **42 3**
2003–04 *Blackburn R* 25 3 **25 3**

**BAROS, Milan (F) 101 21**
H: 6 0 W: 13 02 b.Valasske Mezirici 28-10-81
*Honours:* Czech Republic 30 full caps, 21 goals.
1998–99 Banik Ostrava 6 0
1999–2000 Banik Ostrava 29 6
2000–01 Banik Ostrava 26 5 **61 11**
2001–02 Liverpool 0 0
2002–03 Liverpool 27 9
2003–04 Liverpool 13 1 **40 10**

**BISCAN, Igor (M) 132 12**
H: 6 3 W: 12 08 b.Zagreb 4-5-78
*Honours:* Croatia 15 full caps, 1 goal.
1997–98 Samobor 12 1 **12 1**
1997–98 Dynamo Zagreb 5 0
1998–99 Dynamo Zagreb 19 2
1998–99 Dynamo Zagreb 0 0
1999–2000 Dynamo Zagreb 29 6
2000–01 Dynamo Zagreb 14 3 **67 11**
2000–01 Liverpool 13 0
2001–02 Liverpool 5 0
2002–03 Liverpool 6 0
2003–04 Liverpool 29 0 **53 0**

**CARRAGHER, Jamie (M) 216 2**
H: 6 1 W: 12 05 b.Liverpool 28-1-78
*Source:* Trainee. *Honours:* England Youth, Under-21, B, 12 full caps.
1995–96 Liverpool 0 0
1996–97 Liverpool 2 1
1997–98 Liverpool 20 0
1998–99 Liverpool 34 1
1999–2000 Liverpool 36 0
2000–01 Liverpool 34 0
2001–02 Liverpool 33 0
2002–03 Liverpool 35 0
2003–04 Liverpool 22 0 **216 2**

**CHEYROU, Bruno (M) 126 30**
H: 6 1 W: 13 03 b.Suresnes 10-5-78
*Source:* Lens, Racing. *Honours:* France 2 full caps.
1998–99 Lille 20 6
1999–2000 Lille 21 5
2000–01 Lille 27 6
2001–02 Lille 27 11 **95 28**
2002–03 Liverpool 19 0
2003–04 Liverpool 12 2 **31 2**

**DIAO, Salif (M) 106 1**
H: 6 1 W: 13 03 b.Kedougou 10-2-77
*Honours:* Senegal 29 full caps, 3 goals.
1996–97 Epinal 2 0 **2 0**
1996–97 Monaco 0 0
1997–98 Monaco 12 0
1998–99 Monaco 14 0
1999–2000 Monaco 1 0 **27 0**
2000–01 Sedan 26 0
2001–02 Sedan 22 0 **48 0**
2002–03 Liverpool 26 1
2003–04 Liverpool 3 0 **29 1**

**DIARRA, Alou (D) 25 0**
H: 6 2 W: 12 07 b.Villepinte 15-7-81
*Source:* Louhans, Bayern Munich.
2002–03 Le Havre 25 0 **25 0**
2003–04 Liverpool 0 0

**DIOUF, El Hadji (F) 152 22**
H: 5 9 W: 12 03 b.Dakar 15-1-81
*Honours:* Senegal 31 full caps, 13 goals.
1998–99 Sochaux 15 0 **15 0**
1999–2000 Rennes 28 1 **28 1**
2000–01 Lens 28 8
2001–02 Lens 26 10 **54 18**
2002–03 Liverpool 29 3
2003–04 Liverpool 26 0 **55 3**

**DUDEK, Jerzy (G) 246 0**
H: 6 2 W: 12 08 b.Ribnek 23-3-73
*Source:* GKS Tychy. *Honours:* Poland 41 full caps.
1995–96 Sokol Tychy 15 0 **15 0**
1996–97 Feyenoord 0 0
1997–98 Feyenoord 34 0
1998–99 Feyenoord 34 0
1999–2000 Feyenoord 34 0
2000–01 Feyenoord 34 0 **136 0**

| | | | | | |
|---|---|---|---|---|---|
| 2001–02 | Liverpool | 35 | 0 | | |
| 2002–03 | Liverpool | 30 | 0 | | |
| 2003–04 | Liverpool | 30 | 0 | 95 | 0 |

**FINNAN, Steve (M) 306 14**
H: 6 0 W: 12 09 b.Limerick 24-4-76
*Source:* Welling U. *Honours:* Eire 28 full caps, 1 goal.

| | | | | | |
|---|---|---|---|---|---|
| 1995–96 | Birmingham C | 12 | 1 | | |
| 1995–96 | *Notts Co* | 17 | 2 | | |
| 1996–97 | Birmingham C | 3 | 0 | 15 | 1 |
| 1996–97 | Notts Co | 23 | 0 | | |
| 1997–98 | Notts Co | 44 | 5 | | |
| 1998–99 | Notts Co | 13 | 0 | 97 | 7 |
| 1998–99 | Fulham | 22 | 2 | | |
| 1999–2000 | Fulham | 35 | 2 | | |
| 2000–01 | Fulham | 45 | 2 | | |
| 2001–02 | Fulham | 38 | 0 | | |
| 2002–03 | Fulham | 32 | 0 | 172 | 6 |
| 2003–04 | Liverpool | 22 | 0 | 22 | 0 |

**FOLEY-SHERIDAN, Michael* (M) 0 0**
H: 5 6 W: 11 01 b.Dublin 9-3-83

| | | | | | |
|---|---|---|---|---|---|
| 1999–2000 | Liverpool | 0 | 0 | | |
| 2000–01 | Liverpool | 0 | 0 | | |
| 2001–02 | Liverpool | 0 | 0 | | |
| 2002–03 | Liverpool | 0 | 0 | | |
| 2003–04 | Liverpool | 0 | 0 | | |

**FOY, Robert (F) 0 0**
b.Edinburgh 29-10-85
*Source:* Trainee.

| | | | | | |
|---|---|---|---|---|---|
| 2002–03 | Liverpool | 0 | 0 | | |
| 2003–04 | Liverpool | 0 | 0 | | |

**GERRARD, Steven (M) 170 20**
H: 6 1 W: 12 03 b.Whiston 30-5-80
*Source:* Trainee. *Honours:* England Youth, Under-21, 28 full caps, 4 goals.

| | | | | | |
|---|---|---|---|---|---|
| 1997–98 | Liverpool | 0 | 0 | | |
| 1998–99 | Liverpool | 12 | 0 | | |
| 1999–2000 | Liverpool | 29 | 1 | | |
| 2000–01 | Liverpool | 33 | 7 | | |
| 2001–02 | Liverpool | 28 | 3 | | |
| 2002–03 | Liverpool | 34 | 5 | | |
| 2003–04 | Liverpool | 34 | 4 | 170 | 20 |

**HAMANN, Dietmar (M) 272 18**
H: 6 2 W: 12 01 b.Waldasson 27-8-73
*Source:* Wacker Munich. *Honours:* Germany 57 full caps, 5 goals.

| | | | | | |
|---|---|---|---|---|---|
| 1993–94 | Bayern Munich | 5 | 1 | | |
| 1994–95 | Bayern Munich | 30 | 0 | | |
| 1995–96 | Bayern Munich | 20 | 2 | | |
| 1996–97 | Bayern Munich | 22 | 1 | | |
| 1997–98 | Bayern Munich | 28 | 2 | 105 | 6 |
| 1998–99 | Newcastle U | 23 | 4 | 23 | 4 |
| 1999–2000 | Liverpool | 28 | 1 | | |
| 2000–01 | Liverpool | 30 | 2 | | |
| 2001–02 | Liverpool | 31 | 1 | | |
| 2002–03 | Liverpool | 30 | 2 | | |
| 2003–04 | Liverpool | 25 | 2 | 144 | 8 |

**HARRISON, Paul (G) 0 0**
b.Liverpool 18-12-84
*Source:* Scholar.

| | | | | | |
|---|---|---|---|---|---|
| 2003–04 | Liverpool | 0 | 0 | | |

**HENCHOZ, Stephane (D) 345 3**
H: 6 1 W: 12 13 b.Billens 7-9-74
*Source:* Bulle. *Honours:* Switzerland 68 full caps.

| | | | | | |
|---|---|---|---|---|---|
| 1992–93 | Neuchatel Xamax | 35 | 0 | | |
| 1993–94 | Neuchatel Xamax | 21 | 1 | | |
| 1994–95 | Neuchatel Xamax | 35 | 0 | 91 | 1 |
| 1995–96 | Hamburg | 31 | 2 | | |
| 1996–97 | Hamburg | 18 | 0 | 49 | 2 |
| 1997–98 | Blackburn R | 36 | 0 | | |
| 1998–99 | Blackburn R | 34 | 0 | 70 | 0 |
| 1999–2000 | Liverpool | 29 | 0 | | |
| 2000–01 | Liverpool | 32 | 0 | | |
| 2001–02 | Liverpool | 37 | 0 | | |
| 2002–03 | Liverpool | 19 | 0 | | |
| 2003–04 | Liverpool | 18 | 0 | 135 | 0 |

**HESKEY, Emile (F) 304 79**
H: 6 1 W: 14 04 b.Leicester 11-1-78
*Source:* Trainee. *Honours:* England Youth, Under-21, B, 43 full caps, 5 goals.

| | | | | | |
|---|---|---|---|---|---|
| 1994–95 | Leicester C | 1 | 0 | | |
| 1995–96 | Leicester C | 30 | 7 | | |
| 1996–97 | Leicester C | 35 | 10 | | |
| 1997–98 | Leicester C | 35 | 10 | | |
| 1998–99 | Leicester C | 30 | 6 | | |
| 1999–2000 | Leicester C | 23 | 7 | 154 | 40 |
| 1999–2000 | Liverpool | 12 | 3 | | |
| 2000–01 | Liverpool | 36 | 14 | | |
| 2001–02 | Liverpool | 35 | 9 | | |
| 2002–03 | Liverpool | 32 | 6 | | |
| 2003–04 | Liverpool | 35 | 7 | 150 | 39 |

**HYYPIA, Sami (D) 347 21**
H: 6 4 W: 13 11 b.Porvoo 7-10-73
*Source:* KuMu. *Honours:* Finland 61 full caps, 4 goals.

| | | | | | |
|---|---|---|---|---|---|
| 1993 | MyPa 47 | 12 | 0 | | |
| 1994 | MyPa 47 | 25 | 0 | | |
| 1995 | MyPa 47 | 26 | 3 | 63 | 3 |
| 1995–96 | Willem II | 14 | 0 | | |
| 1996–97 | Willem II | 30 | 1 | | |
| 1997–98 | Willem II | 30 | 0 | | |
| 1998–99 | Willem II | 26 | 2 | 100 | 3 |
| 1999–2000 | Liverpool | 38 | 2 | | |
| 2000–01 | Liverpool | 35 | 3 | | |
| 2001–02 | Liverpool | 37 | 3 | | |
| 2002–03 | Liverpool | 36 | 3 | | |
| 2003–04 | Liverpool | 38 | 4 | 184 | 15 |

**KEWELL, Harry (M) 217 52**
H: 5 11 W: 13 00 b.Sydney 22-9-78
*Source:* NSW Soccer Academy. *Honours:* Australia Youth, Under-20, 15 full caps, 5 goals.

| | | | | | |
|---|---|---|---|---|---|
| 1995–96 | Leeds U | 2 | 0 | | |
| 1996–97 | Leeds U | 1 | 0 | | |
| 1997–98 | Leeds U | 29 | 5 | | |
| 1998–99 | Leeds U | 38 | 6 | | |
| 1999–2000 | Leeds U | 36 | 10 | | |
| 2000–01 | Leeds U | 17 | 2 | | |
| 2001–02 | Leeds U | 27 | 8 | | |
| 2002–03 | Leeds U | 31 | 14 | 181 | 45 |
| 2003–04 | Liverpool | 36 | 7 | 36 | 7 |

**KIRKLAND, Christopher (G) 39 0**
H: 6 6 W: 14 12 b.Leicester 2-5-81
*Source:* Trainee. *Honours:* England Youth, Under-21.

| | | | | | |
|---|---|---|---|---|---|
| 1997–98 | Coventry C | 0 | 0 | | |
| 1998–99 | Coventry C | 0 | 0 | | |
| 1999–2000 | Coventry C | 0 | 0 | | |
| 2000–01 | Coventry C | 23 | 0 | | |
| 2001–02 | Coventry C | 1 | 0 | 24 | 0 |
| 2001–02 | Liverpool | 1 | 0 | | |
| 2002–03 | Liverpool | 8 | 0 | | |
| 2003–04 | Liverpool | 6 | 0 | 15 | 0 |

**LE TALLEC, Anthony (M) 67 7**
H: 6 0 W: 11 07 b.Hennebont 3-10-84

| | | | | | |
|---|---|---|---|---|---|
| 2001–02 | Le Havre | 24 | 5 | | |
| 2002–03 | Le Havre | 30 | 2 | 54 | 7 |
| 2003–04 | Liverpool | 13 | 0 | 13 | 0 |

**LUZI-BERNARDI, Patrice (G) 1 0**
H: 6 2 W: 14 01 b.Ajaccio 8-7-80
*Source:* Monaco.

| | | | | | |
|---|---|---|---|---|---|
| 2002–03 | Liverpool | 0 | 0 | | |
| 2003–04 | Liverpool | 1 | 0 | 1 | 0 |

**MANNIX, David (M) 0 0**
b.Crewe 24-9-85
*Source:* Trainee.

| | | | | | |
|---|---|---|---|---|---|
| 2003–04 | Liverpool | 0 | 0 | | |

**MASSIE, Jason§ (M) 0 0**
b.Whiston 13-9-84
*Honours:* England Youth.

| | | | | | |
|---|---|---|---|---|---|
| 2001–02 | Liverpool | 0 | 0 | | |
| 2002–03 | Liverpool | 0 | 0 | | |
| 2003–04 | Liverpool | 0 | 0 | | |

**MEDJANI, Carl (D) 0 0**
H: 6 0 W: 13 00 b.Lyon 15-5-85

| | | | | | |
|---|---|---|---|---|---|
| 2003–04 | Liverpool | 0 | 0 | | |

**MELLOR, Neil (F) 19 2**
H: 6 0 W: 13 07 b.Manchester 4-11-82
*Source:* Scholar.

| | | | | | |
|---|---|---|---|---|---|
| 2001–02 | Liverpool | 0 | 0 | | |
| 2002–03 | Liverpool | 3 | 0 | | |
| 2003–04 | Liverpool | 0 | 0 | 3 | 0 |
| 2003–04 | *West Ham U* | 16 | 2 | 16 | 2 |

**MURPHY, Danny (M) 320 53**
H: 5 9 W: 12 08 b.Chester 18-3-77
*Source:* Trainee. *Honours:* England Schools, Youth, Under-21, 9 full caps, 1 goal.

| | | | | | |
|---|---|---|---|---|---|
| 1993–94 | Crewe Alex | 12 | 2 | | |
| 1994–95 | Crewe Alex | 35 | 5 | | |
| 1995–96 | Crewe Alex | 42 | 10 | | |
| 1996–97 | Crewe Alex | 45 | 10 | | |
| 1997–98 | Liverpool | 16 | 0 | | |
| 1998–99 | Liverpool | 1 | 0 | | |
| 1998–99 | *Crewe Alex* | 16 | 1 | 150 | 28 |
| 1999–2000 | Liverpool | 23 | 3 | | |
| 2000–01 | Liverpool | 27 | 4 | | |
| 2001–02 | Liverpool | 36 | 6 | | |
| 2002–03 | Liverpool | 36 | 7 | | |
| 2003–04 | Liverpool | 31 | 5 | 170 | 25 |

**OTSEMOBOR, John (D) 14 3**
H: 5 10 W: 12 07 b.Liverpool 23-3-83
*Source:* Trainee. *Honours:* England Youth, Under-20.

| | | | | | |
|---|---|---|---|---|---|
| 1999–2000 | Liverpool | 0 | 0 | | |
| 2000–01 | Liverpool | 0 | 0 | | |
| 2001–02 | Liverpool | 0 | 0 | | |
| 2002–03 | Liverpool | 0 | 0 | | |
| 2002–03 | *Hull C* | 9 | 3 | 9 | 3 |
| 2003–04 | Liverpool | 4 | 0 | 4 | 0 |
| 2003–04 | *Bolton W* | 1 | 0 | 1 | 0 |

**OWEN, Michael (F) 216 118**
H: 5 8 W: 10 13 b.Chester 14-12-79
*Source:* Trainee. *Honours:* England Schools, Youth, Under-21, 60 full caps, 26 goals.

| | | | | | |
|---|---|---|---|---|---|
| 1996–97 | Liverpool | 2 | 1 | | |
| 1997–98 | Liverpool | 36 | 18 | | |
| 1998–99 | Liverpool | 30 | 18 | | |
| 1999–2000 | Liverpool | 27 | 11 | | |
| 2000–01 | Liverpool | 28 | 16 | | |
| 2001–02 | Liverpool | 29 | 19 | | |
| 2002–03 | Liverpool | 35 | 19 | | |
| 2003–04 | Liverpool | 29 | 16 | 216 | 118 |

**PARTRIDGE, Richie* (M) 33 5**
H: 5 8 W: 10 07 b.Dublin 12-9-80
*Source:* Trainee. *Honours:* Eire Under-21.

| | | | | | |
|---|---|---|---|---|---|
| 1998–99 | Liverpool | 0 | 0 | | |
| 1999–2000 | Liverpool | 0 | 0 | | |
| 2000–01 | Liverpool | 0 | 0 | | |
| 2000–01 | *Bristol R* | 6 | 1 | 6 | 1 |
| 2001–02 | Liverpool | 0 | 0 | | |
| 2002–03 | Liverpool | 0 | 0 | | |
| 2002–03 | *Coventry C* | 27 | 4 | 27 | 4 |
| 2003–04 | Liverpool | 0 | 0 | | |

**POTTER, Darren (M) 0 0**
H: 6 1 W: 11 05 b.Liverpool 21-12-84
*Source:* Scholar.

| | | | | | |
|---|---|---|---|---|---|
| 2001–02 | Liverpool | 0 | 0 | | |
| 2002–03 | Liverpool | 0 | 0 | | |
| 2003–04 | Liverpool | 0 | 0 | | |

**RAVEN, David (D) 0 0**
b.Wirral 10-3-85
*Source:* Scholar. *Honours:* England Youth.

| | | | | | |
|---|---|---|---|---|---|
| 2001–02 | Liverpool | 0 | 0 | | |
| 2002–03 | Liverpool | 0 | 0 | | |
| 2003–04 | Liverpool | 0 | 0 | | |

**RIISE, John Arne (M) 147 17**
H: 6 1 W: 12 08 b.Molde 24-9-80
*Honours:* Norway 35 full caps, 5 goals.

| | | | | | |
|---|---|---|---|---|---|
| 1998–99 | Monaco | 7 | 0 | | |
| 1999–2000 | Monaco | 21 | 1 | | |
| 2000–01 | Monaco | 16 | 3 | 44 | 4 |
| 2001–02 | Liverpool | 38 | 7 | | |
| 2002–03 | Liverpool | 37 | 6 | | |
| 2003–04 | Liverpool | 28 | 0 | 103 | 13 |

**SINAMA-PONGOLLE, Florent (F) 26 4**
H: 5 7 W: 12 02 b.Saint-Pierre 20-10-84

| | | | | | |
|---|---|---|---|---|---|
| 2001–02 | Le Havre | 11 | 2 | | |
| 2002–03 | Le Havre | 0 | 0 | 11 | 2 |
| 2003–04 | Liverpool | 15 | 2 | 15 | 2 |

**SJOLUND, Danny‡ (F) 0 0**
H: 5 11 W: 12 00 b.Mariehamn 22-4-83

| | | | | | |
|---|---|---|---|---|---|
| 1999–2000 | West Ham U | 0 | 0 | | |
| 2000–01 | West Ham U | 0 | 0 | | |
| 2000–01 | Liverpool | 0 | 0 | | |
| 2001–02 | Liverpool | 0 | 0 | | |
| 2002–03 | Liverpool | 0 | 0 | | |
| 2003–04 | Liverpool | 0 | 0 | | |

**SMICER, Vladimir (M) 283 52**
H: 5 10 W: 12 02 b.Degin 24-5-73
*Honours:* Czechoslovakia 1 full cap, Czech Republic 72 full caps, 25 goals.

| | | | | | |
|---|---|---|---|---|---|
| 1992–93 | Slavia Prague | 21 | 8 | | |
| 1993–94 | Slavia Prague | 17 | 6 | | |

| | | | | | |
|---|---|---|---|---|---|
| 1994–95 | Slavia Prague | 15 | 3 | | |
| 1995–96 | Slavia Prague | 28 | 9 | **81** | **26** |
| 1996–97 | Lens | 33 | 5 | | |
| 1997–98 | Lens | 28 | 7 | | |
| 1998–99 | Lens | 30 | 4 | **91** | **16** |
| 1999–2000 | Liverpool | 21 | 1 | | |
| 2000–01 | Liverpool | 27 | 2 | | |
| 2001–02 | Liverpool | 22 | 4 | | |
| 2002–03 | Liverpool | 21 | 0 | | |
| 2003–04 | Liverpool | 20 | 3 | **111** | **10** |

**SMYTH, Mark (M) 0 0**

b.Liverpool 9-1-85

*Source:* Scholar. *Honours:* England Youth.

| | | | | | |
|---|---|---|---|---|---|
| 2001–02 | Liverpool | 0 | 0 | | |
| 2002–03 | Liverpool | 0 | 0 | | |
| 2003–04 | Liverpool | 0 | 0 | | |

**TRAORE, Djimi (D) 66 0**

H: 6 1 W: 12 06 b.Saint-Ouen 1-3-80

*Source:* Laval.

| | | | | | |
|---|---|---|---|---|---|
| 1998–99 | Liverpool | 0 | 0 | | |
| 1999–2000 | Liverpool | 0 | 0 | | |
| 2000–01 | Liverpool | 8 | 0 | | |
| 2001–02 | Liverpool | 0 | 0 | | |
| 2001–02 | Lens | 19 | 0 | **19** | **0** |
| 2002–03 | Liverpool | 32 | 0 | | |
| 2003–04 | Liverpool | 7 | 0 | **47** | **0** |

**VAUGHAN, Stephen‡ (D) 0 0**

b.Liverpool 22-1-85

*Source:* Scholar.

| | | | | | |
|---|---|---|---|---|---|
| 2001–02 | Liverpool | 0 | 0 | | |
| 2002–03 | Liverpool | 0 | 0 | | |
| 2003–04 | Liverpool | 0 | 0 | | |

**VIGNAL, Gregory (D) 26 0**

H: 5 11 W: 12 03 b.Montpellier 19-7-81

| | | | | | |
|---|---|---|---|---|---|
| 2000–01 | Liverpool | 6 | 0 | | |
| 2001–02 | Liverpool | 4 | 0 | | |
| 2002–03 | Liverpool | 1 | 0 | | |
| 2002–03 | Bastia | 15 | 0 | **15** | **0** |
| 2003–04 | Liverpool | 0 | 0 | **11** | **0** |

**WARNOCK, Stephen (M) 56 4**

H: 5 7 W: 12 01 b.Ormskirk 12-12-81

*Source:* Trainee. *Honours:* England Schools, Youth.

| | | | | | |
|---|---|---|---|---|---|
| 1998–99 | Liverpool | 0 | 0 | | |
| 1999–2000 | Liverpool | 0 | 0 | | |
| 2000–01 | Liverpool | 0 | 0 | | |
| 2001–02 | Liverpool | 0 | 0 | | |
| 2002–03 | Liverpool | 0 | 0 | | |
| 2002–03 | *Bradford C* | 12 | 1 | **12** | **1** |
| 2003–04 | Liverpool | 0 | 0 | | |
| 2003–04 | *Coventry C* | 44 | 3 | **44** | **3** |

**WELSH, John (M) 1 0**

H: 5 7 W: 11 06 b.Liverpool 10-1-84

*Source:* Scholar. *Honours:* England Youth, Under-20, Under-21.

| | | | | | |
|---|---|---|---|---|---|
| 2000–01 | Liverpool | 0 | 0 | | |
| 2001–02 | Liverpool | 0 | 0 | | |
| 2002–03 | Liverpool | 0 | 0 | | |
| 2003–04 | Liverpool | 1 | 0 | **1** | **0** |

**WHITBREAD, Zak (D) 0 0**

H: 6 2 W: 11 06 b.Houston 4-3-84

| | | | | | |
|---|---|---|---|---|---|
| 2002–03 | Liverpool | 0 | 0 | | |
| 2003–04 | Liverpool | 0 | 0 | | |

**WILKIE, Ryan (M) 0 0**

b.Glasgow 11-12-85

*Source:* Trainee.

| | | | | | |
|---|---|---|---|---|---|
| 2002–03 | Liverpool | 0 | 0 | | |
| 2003–04 | Liverpool | 0 | 0 | | |

**WILLIS, Paul (M) 0 0**

*Source:* Trainee.

| | | | | | |
|---|---|---|---|---|---|
| 2003–04 | Liverpool | 0 | 0 | | |

**WRIGHT, Andrew§ (M) 0 0**

b.Southport 15-1-85

*Source:* Scholar.

| | | | | | |
|---|---|---|---|---|---|
| 2001–02 | Liverpool | 0 | 0 | | |
| 2002–03 | Liverpool | 0 | 0 | | |
| 2003–04 | Liverpool | 0 | 0 | | |

**XAVIER, Abel‡ (D) 242 7**

H: 6 3 W: 12 07 b.Mozambique 30-11-72

*Honours:* Portugal 19 full caps, 2 goals.

| | | | | | |
|---|---|---|---|---|---|
| 1990–91 | Amadora | 22 | 0 | | |
| 1991–92 | Amadora | 21 | 0 | | |
| 1992–93 | Amadora | 0 | 0 | **43** | **0** |
| 1993–94 | Benfica | 24 | 1 | | |
| 1994–95 | Benfica | 22 | 3 | **46** | **4** |
| 1995–96 | Bari | 8 | 0 | **8** | **0** |
| 1996–97 | Oviedo | 27 | 0 | | |
| 1997–98 | Oviedo | 31 | 0 | **58** | **0** |
| 1998–99 | PSV Eindhoven | 19 | 2 | **19** | **2** |
| 1999–2000 | Everton | 20 | 0 | | |
| 2000–01 | Everton | 11 | 0 | | |
| 2001–02 | Everton | 12 | 0 | **43** | **0** |
| 2001–02 | Liverpool | 10 | 1 | | |
| 2002–03 | Liverpool | 4 | 0 | | |
| 2002–03 | Galatasaray | 11 | 0 | **11** | **0** |
| 2003–04 | Liverpool | 0 | 0 | **14** | **1** |

**Scholars**

Butler, Christopher W; Flynn, Adam J; Gillespie, Steven; Guthrie, Danny S; Hitchen, Adam R; Kelly, John P; Lancaster, Paul; Massie, Jason D; Noon, Karl A; O'Donnell, Daniel; Peltier, Lee A; Platt, Conal J; Roberts, Mark R; Smith, Daniel P; Townley, Philip P; Woods, Calum J; Wright, Andrew D

## LUTON T (45)

**BARNETT, Leon§ (D) 0 0**

H: 6 0 W: 11 04 b.Stevenage 30-11-85

*Source:* Scholar.

| | | | | | |
|---|---|---|---|---|---|
| 2003–04 | Luton T | 0 | 0 | | |

**BAYLISS, Dave (D) 223 9**

H: 6 0 W: 12 11 b.Liverpool 8-6-76

*Source:* Trainee.

| | | | | | |
|---|---|---|---|---|---|
| 1994–95 | Rochdale | 1 | 0 | | |
| 1995–96 | Rochdale | 28 | 0 | | |
| 1996–97 | Rochdale | 24 | 0 | | |
| 1997–98 | Rochdale | 29 | 2 | | |
| 1998–99 | Rochdale | 25 | 1 | | |
| 1999–2000 | Rochdale | 29 | 3 | | |
| 2000–01 | Rochdale | 41 | 3 | | |
| 2001–02 | Rochdale | 9 | 0 | **186** | **9** |
| 2001–02 | Luton T | 18 | 0 | | |
| 2002–03 | Luton T | 13 | 0 | | |
| 2003–04 | Luton T | 6 | 0 | **37** | **0** |

**BECKWITH, Rob§ (G) 17 0**

H: 6 2 W: 13 05 b.London 12-9-84

*Source:* Scholar.

| | | | | | |
|---|---|---|---|---|---|
| 2002–03 | Luton T | 4 | 0 | | |
| 2003–04 | Luton T | 13 | 0 | **17** | **0** |

**BOYCE, Emmerson# (D) 186 8**

H: 6 0 W: 11 13 b.Aylesbury 24-9-79

*Source:* Trainee.

| | | | | | |
|---|---|---|---|---|---|
| 1997–98 | Luton T | 0 | 0 | | |
| 1998–99 | Luton T | 1 | 0 | | |
| 1999–2000 | Luton T | 30 | 1 | | |
| 2000–01 | Luton T | 42 | 3 | | |
| 2001–02 | Luton T | 37 | 0 | | |
| 2002–03 | Luton T | 34 | 0 | | |
| 2003–04 | Luton T | 42 | 4 | **186** | **8** |

**BRILL, Dean§ (G) 5 0**

H: 6 2 W: 12 05 b.Luton 2-12-85

*Source:* Scholar.

| | | | | | |
|---|---|---|---|---|---|
| 2003–04 | Luton T | 5 | 0 | **5** | **0** |

**BRKOVIC, Ahmet# (M) 158 13**

H: 5 8 W: 11 10 b.Dubrovnik 23-9-74

*Source:* Dubrovnik.

| | | | | | |
|---|---|---|---|---|---|
| 1999–2000 | Leyton Orient | 29 | 5 | | |
| 2000–01 | Leyton Orient | 40 | 3 | | |
| 2001–02 | Leyton Orient | 0 | 0 | **69** | **8** |
| 2001–02 | Luton T | 21 | 1 | | |
| 2002–03 | Luton T | 36 | 3 | | |
| 2003–04 | Luton T | 32 | 1 | **89** | **5** |

**COYNE, Chris# (D) 144 6**

H: 6 2 W: 13 12 b.Brisbane 20-12-78

*Source:* Perth SC. *Honours:* Australia Youth, Under-23.

| | | | | | |
|---|---|---|---|---|---|
| 1995–96 | West Ham U | 0 | 0 | | |
| 1996–97 | West Ham U | 0 | 0 | | |
| 1997–98 | West Ham U | 0 | 0 | | |
| 1998–99 | West Ham U | 1 | 0 | **1** | **0** |
| 1998–99 | *Brentford* | 7 | 0 | **7** | **0** |
| 1998–99 | *Southend U* | 1 | 0 | **1** | **0** |
| 1999–2000 | Dundee | 2 | 0 | | |
| 2000–01 | Dundee | 18 | 0 | **20** | **0** |
| 2001–02 | Luton T | 31 | 3 | | |
| 2002–03 | Luton T | 40 | 1 | | |
| 2003–04 | Luton T | 44 | 2 | **115** | **6** |

**DAVIES, Curtis§ (D) 6 0**

H: 6 1 W: 11 13 b.London 15-3-85

*Source:* Scholar.

| | | | | | |
|---|---|---|---|---|---|
| 2003–04 | Luton T | 6 | 0 | **6** | **0** |

**DAVIS, Sol (D) 187 0**

H: 5 8 W: 11 12 b.Cheltenham 4-9-79

*Source:* Trainee.

| | | | | | |
|---|---|---|---|---|---|
| 1997–98 | Swindon T | 6 | 0 | | |
| 1998–99 | Swindon T | 25 | 0 | | |
| 1999–2000 | Swindon T | 29 | 0 | | |
| 2000–01 | Swindon T | 36 | 0 | | |
| 2001–02 | Swindon T | 21 | 0 | | |
| 2002–03 | Swindon T | 0 | 0 | **117** | **0** |
| 2002–03 | Luton T | 34 | 0 | | |
| 2003–04 | Luton T | 36 | 0 | **70** | **0** |

**DEENEY, David§ (D) 0 0**

H: 5 9 W: 10 06 b.Bulawayo 12-1-87

*Source:* Scholar.

| | | | | | |
|---|---|---|---|---|---|
| 2003–04 | Luton T | 0 | 0 | | |

**FOLEY, Kevin (M) 35 1**

H: 5 10 W: 11 03 b.London 1-11-84

*Source:* Scholar. *Honours:* Eire Under-21.

| | | | | | |
|---|---|---|---|---|---|
| 2002–03 | Luton T | 2 | 0 | | |
| 2003–04 | Luton T | 33 | 1 | **35** | **1** |

**FORBES, Adrian# (M) 184 22**

H: 5 7 W: 12 02 b.Greenford 23-1-79

*Source:* Trainee. *Honours:* England Youth.

| | | | | | |
|---|---|---|---|---|---|
| 1996–97 | Norwich C | 10 | 0 | | |
| 1997–98 | Norwich C | 33 | 4 | | |
| 1998–99 | Norwich C | 15 | 0 | | |
| 1999–2000 | Norwich C | 25 | 1 | | |
| 2000–01 | Norwich C | 29 | 3 | **112** | **8** |
| 2001–02 | Luton T | 40 | 4 | | |
| 2002–03 | Luton T | 5 | 1 | | |
| 2003–04 | Luton T | 27 | 9 | **72** | **14** |

**HILLIER, Ian (D) 56 1**

H: 6 1 W: 12 01 b.Neath 26-12-79

*Source:* Trainee. *Honours:* Wales Schools, Youth, Under-21.

| | | | | | |
|---|---|---|---|---|---|
| 1998–99 | Tottenham H | 0 | 0 | | |
| 1999–2000 | Tottenham H | 0 | 0 | | |
| 2000–01 | Tottenham H | 0 | 0 | | |
| 2001–02 | Tottenham H | 0 | 0 | | |
| 2001–02 | Luton T | 23 | 1 | | |
| 2002–03 | Luton T | 22 | 0 | | |
| 2003–04 | Luton T | 11 | 0 | **56** | **1** |

**HOLMES, Peter (M) 58 6**

H: 5 11 W: 11 08 b.Bishop Auckland 18-11-80

*Source:* Trainee. *Honours:* England Schools.

| | | | | | |
|---|---|---|---|---|---|
| 1997–98 | Sheffield W | 0 | 0 | | |
| 1998–99 | Sheffield W | 0 | 0 | | |
| 1999–2000 | Sheffield W | 0 | 0 | | |
| 2000–01 | Luton T | 18 | 1 | | |
| 2001–02 | Luton T | 7 | 1 | | |
| 2002–03 | Luton T | 17 | 1 | | |
| 2003–04 | Luton T | 16 | 3 | **58** | **6** |

**HOWARD, Steve (F) 357 108**

H: 6 3 W: 15 00 b.Durham 10-5-76

*Source:* Tow Law T.

| | | | | | |
|---|---|---|---|---|---|
| 1995–96 | Hartlepool U | 39 | 7 | | |
| 1996–97 | Hartlepool U | 32 | 8 | | |
| 1997–98 | Hartlepool U | 43 | 7 | | |
| 1998–99 | Hartlepool U | 28 | 5 | **142** | **27** |
| 1998–99 | Northampton T | 12 | 0 | | |
| 1999–2000 | Northampton T | 41 | 10 | | |
| 2000–01 | Northampton T | 33 | 8 | **86** | **18** |
| 2000–01 | Luton T | 12 | 3 | | |
| 2001–02 | Luton T | 42 | 24 | | |
| 2002–03 | Luton T | 41 | 22 | | |
| 2003–04 | Luton T | 34 | 14 | **129** | **63** |

**HUGHES, Paul# (M) 111 9**

H: 6 0 W: 12 05 b.Hammersmith 17-4-76

*Source:* Trainee. *Honours:* England Schools.

| | | | | | |
|---|---|---|---|---|---|
| 1994–95 | Chelsea | 0 | 0 | | |
| 1995–96 | Chelsea | 0 | 0 | | |
| 1996–97 | Chelsea | 12 | 2 | | |
| 1997–98 | Chelsea | 9 | 0 | | |
| 1998–99 | Chelsea | 0 | 0 | | |
| 1998–99 | *Stockport Co* | 7 | 0 | **7** | **0** |
| 1998–99 | *Norwich C* | 4 | 1 | **4** | **1** |
| 1999–2000 | Chelsea | 0 | 0 | **21** | **2** |
| 1999–2000 | *Crewe Alex* | 0 | 0 | | |
| 1999–2000 | Southampton | 0 | 0 | | |
| 2000–01 | Southampton | 0 | 0 | | |

2001–02 Southampton 0 0
2001–02 Luton T 22 2
2002–03 Luton T 35 3
2003–04 Luton T 22 1 79 6

**HYLDGAARD, Morten* (G) 50 0**
H: 6 6 W: 14 00 b.Herning 26-1-78
*Source:* Ikast.
1999–2000 Coventry C 0 0
1999–2000 *Scunthorpe U* 5 0 5 0
2000–01 Coventry C 0 0
2000–01 *Grimsby T* 0 0
2001–02 Coventry C 0 0
2002–03 Coventry C 27 0 27 0
2003–04 Luton T 18 0 18 0

**JUDGE, Matthew§ (F) 2 0**
H: 6 0 W: 11 07 b.Barking 18-1-85
*Source:* Scholar. *Honours:* Eire Youth.
2002–03 Luton T 1 0
2003–04 Luton T 1 0 2 0

**KEANE, Keith§ (M) 15 1**
H: 5 9 W: 11 01 b.Luton 20-11-86
*Source:* Scholar.
2003–04 Luton T 15 1 15 1

**LEARY, Michael (M) 14 2**
H: 5 11 W: 11 10 b.Ealing 17-4-83
*Source:* Scholar.
2001–02 Luton T 0 0
2002–03 Luton T 0 0
2003–04 Luton T 14 2 14 2

**MANSELL, Lee (M) 46 8**
H: 5 9 W: 11 00 b.Gloucester 28-10-82
*Source:* Scholar.
2000–01 Luton T 18 5
2001–02 Luton T 11 1
2002–03 Luton T 1 0
2003–04 Luton T 16 2 46 8

**NEILSON, Alan (D) 184 4**
H: 5 11 W: 12 12 b.Wegburg 26-9-72
*Source:* Trainee. *Honours:* Wales Under-21, B, 5 full caps.
1990–91 Newcastle U 3 0
1991–92 Newcastle U 16 1
1992–93 Newcastle U 3 0
1993–94 Newcastle U 14 0
1994–95 Newcastle U 6 0 42 1
1995–96 Southampton 18 0
1996–97 Southampton 29 0
1997–98 Southampton 8 0 55 0
1997–98 Fulham 17 0
1998–99 Fulham 4 1
1999–2000 Fulham 5 1
2000–01 Fulham 3 0
2001–02 Fulham 0 0 29 2
2001–02 *Grimsby T* 10 0 10 0
2001–02 Luton T 8 0
2002–03 Luton T 26 0
2003–04 Luton T 14 1 48 1

**NICHOLLS, Kevin (M) 143 16**
H: 5 10 W: 12 04 b.Newham 2-1-79
*Source:* Trainee. *Honours:* England Youth.
1995–96 Charlton Ath 0 0
1996–97 Charlton Ath 6 1
1997–98 Charlton Ath 6 0
1998–99 Charlton Ath 0 0 12 1
1998–99 *Brighton & HA* 4 1 4 1
1999–2000 Wigan Ath 8 0
2000–01 Wigan Ath 20 0 28 0
2001–02 Luton T 42 7
2002–03 Luton T 36 5
2003–04 Luton T 21 2 99 14

**O'LEARY, Stephen§ (M) 5 1**
H: 5 10 W: 11 08 b.London 12-2-85
*Source:* Scholar. *Honours:* Eire Youth.
2003–04 Luton T 5 1 5 1

**OKAI, Parys§ (M) 0 0**
H: 5 9 W: 11 05 b.London 23-11-84
*Source:* Scholar.
2003–04 Luton T 0 0

**PERRETT, Russell# (D) 167 10**
H: 6 1 W: 12 04 b.Barton-on-Sea 18-6-73
*Source:* AFC Lymington.
1995–96 Portsmouth 9 0
1996–97 Portsmouth 32 1
1997–98 Portsmouth 16 1
1998–99 Portsmouth 15 0 72 2
1999–2000 Cardiff C 27 1
2000–01 Cardiff C 2 0 29 1
2001–02 Luton T 40 3
2002–03 Luton T 20 2
2003–04 Luton T 6 2 66 7

**ROBINSON, Steve# (M) 335 56**
H: 5 9 W: 11 02 b.Lisburn 10-12-74
*Source:* Trainee. *Honours:* Northern Ireland Schools, Youth, Under-21, B, 5 full caps.
1992–93 Tottenham H 0 0
1993–94 Tottenham H 2 0
1994–95 Tottenham H 0 0 2 0
1994–95 *Leyton Orient* 0 0
1994–95 Bournemouth 32 5
1995–96 Bournemouth 41 7
1996–97 Bournemouth 40 7
1997–98 Bournemouth 45 10
1998–99 Bournemouth 42 13
1999–2000 Bournemouth 40 9 240 51
2000–01 Preston NE 22 1
2001–02 Preston NE 2 0 24 1
2001–02 *Bristol C* 6 1 6 1
2002–03 Luton T 29 1
2003–04 Luton T 34 2 63 3

**SHOWUNMI, Enoch (F) 26 7**
H: 6 3 W: 14 10 b.London 21-4-82
*Source:* Willesden Constantine.
2003–04 Luton T 26 7 26 7

**SPRING, Matthew* (M) 250 25**
H: 6 0 W: 12 06 b.Harlow 17-11-79
*Source:* Trainee.
1997–98 Luton T 12 0
1998–99 Luton T 45 3
1999–2000 Luton T 45 6
2000–01 Luton T 41 4
2001–02 Luton T 42 6
2002–03 Luton T 41 5
2003–04 Luton T 24 1 250 25

**UNDERWOOD, Paul (M) 111 1**
H: 5 11 W: 12 11 b.Wimbledon 16-8-73
*Source:* Enfield.
2001–02 Rushden & D 40 0
2002–03 Rushden & D 40 1
2003–04 Rushden & D 30 0 110 1
2003–04 Luton T 1 0 1 0

**Scholars**
Barnett, Leon P; Beckwith, Robert; Brill, Dean M; Davies, Curtis; Deeney, David R; Howell, Max; Judge, Matthew P; Keane, Keith F; Maitland, Luke E M; Mansell, Richard J; Mountford, Niki W; Okai, Parys; O'Leary, Stephen; Ridgway, Mark S D

# MACCLESFIELD T (46)

**ABBEY, George* (D) 100 1**
H: 5 9 W: 10 08 b.Port Harcourt 20-10-78
*Source:* Sharks. *Honours:* Nigeria 10 full caps.
1999–2000 Macclesfield T 18 0
2000–01 Macclesfield T 18 0
2001–02 Macclesfield T 17 0
2002–03 Macclesfield T 22 1
2003–04 Macclesfield T 25 0 100 1

**ASKEY, John† (F) 181 31**
H: 6 0 W: 12 01 b.Stoke 4-11-64
*Source:* Port Vale.
1997–98 Macclesfield T 39 6
1998–99 Macclesfield T 38 4
1999–2000 Macclesfield T 40 15
2000–01 Macclesfield T 37 3
2001–02 Macclesfield T 18 1
2002–03 Macclesfield T 9 2
2003–04 Macclesfield T 0 0 181 31

**BRACKENRIDGE, Steve (M) 9 2**
H: 5 10 W: 10 08 b.Rochdale 31-7-84
*Source:* Scholar.
2002–03 Macclesfield T 2 0
2003–04 Macclesfield T 7 2 9 2

**CARR, Michael (D) 11 0**
H: 5 9 W: 11 04 b.Crewe 6-12-83
*Source:* Scholar.
2002–03 Macclesfield T 4 0
2003–04 Macclesfield T 7 0 11 0

**CARRAGHER, Matt (D) 331 1**
H: 5 9 W: 10 07 b.Liverpool 14-1-76
*Source:* Trainee.
1993–94 Wigan Ath 32 0
1994–95 Wigan Ath 41 0
1995–96 Wigan Ath 28 0
1996–97 Wigan Ath 18 0 119 0
1997–98 Port Vale 26 0
1998–99 Port Vale 10 0
1999–2000 Port Vale 37 1
2000–01 Port Vale 45 0
2001–02 Port Vale 41 0
2002–03 Port Vale 35 0
2003–04 Port Vale 0 0 194 1
2003–04 Macclesfield T 18 0 18 0

**CARRUTHERS, Martin (F) 393 110**
H: 5 11 W: 11 10 b.Nottingham 7-8-72
*Source:* Trainee.
1990–91 Aston Villa 0 0
1991–92 Aston Villa 3 0
1992–93 Aston Villa 1 0 4 0
1992–93 *Hull C* 13 6 13 6
1993–94 Stoke C 34 5
1994–95 Stoke C 32 5
1995–96 Stoke C 24 3
1996–97 Stoke C 1 0 91 13
1996–97 Peterborough U 14 4
1997–98 Peterborough U 39 15
1998–99 Peterborough U 14 2 67 21
1998–99 *York C* 6 0 6 0
1998–99 Darlington 11 2
1999–2000 Darlington 6 0 17 2
1999–2000 Southend U 38 19
2000–01 Southend U 32 7 70 26
2000–01 Scunthorpe U 8 1
2001–02 Scunthorpe U 33 13
2002–03 Scunthorpe U 45 20 86 34
2003–04 Macclesfield T 39 8 39 8

**HADDRELL, Matt‡ (D) 14 1**
H: 6 2 W: 14 00 b.Staffordshire 19-3-81
2002–03 Macclesfield T 4 0
2003–04 Macclesfield T 10 1 14 1

**HARSLEY, Paul# (M) 248 20**
H: 5 8 W: 11 05 b.Scunthorpe 29-5-78
*Source:* Trainee.
1996–97 Grimsby T 0 0
1997–98 Scunthorpe U 15 1
1998–99 Scunthorpe U 34 0
1999–2000 Scunthorpe U 46 3
2000–01 Scunthorpe U 33 1 128 5
2001–02 Halifax T 45 11 45 11
2002–03 Northampton T 45 2
2003–04 Northampton T 14 0 59 2
2003–04 Macclesfield T 16 2 16 2

**HITCHEN, Steve‡ (D) 151 1**
H: 5 8 W: 11 07 b.Salford 28-11-76
*Source:* Trainee.
1995–96 Blackburn R 0 0
1996–97 Blackburn R 0 0
1997–98 Macclesfield T 2 0
1998–99 Macclesfield T 35 0
1999–2000 Macclesfield T 5 0
2000–01 Macclesfield T 37 0
2001–02 Macclesfield T 30 1
2002–03 Macclesfield T 33 0
2003–04 Macclesfield T 9 0 151 1

**LITTLE, Colin‡ (F) 228 39**
H: 5 10 W: 12 00 b.Wythenshaw 4-11-72
*Source:* Hyde U.
1995–96 Crewe Alex 12 1
1996–97 Crewe Alex 17 0
1997–98 Crewe Alex 40 13
1998–99 Crewe Alex 37 10
1999–2000 Crewe Alex 37 4
2000–01 Crewe Alex 27 4
2001–02 Crewe Alex 17 1
2002–03 Crewe Alex 6 0 193 33
2002–03 *Mansfield T* 5 0 5 0
2002–03 *Macclesfield T* 6 1
2003–04 Macclesfield T 24 5 30 6

**MACAULEY, Steve‡ (D) 315 27**
H: 6 1 W: 12 00 b.Lytham 4-3-69
*Source:* Fleetwood T.
1991–92 Crewe Alex 9 1
1992–93 Crewe Alex 25 3

| | | | | | |
|---|---|---|---|---|---|
| 1993–94 | Crewe Alex | 17 | 3 | | |
| 1994–95 | Crewe Alex | 43 | 4 | | |
| 1995–96 | Crewe Alex | 29 | 7 | | |
| 1996–97 | Crewe Alex | 42 | 2 | | |
| 1997–98 | Crewe Alex | 0 | 0 | | |
| 1998–99 | Crewe Alex | 20 | 1 | | |
| 1999–2000 | Crewe Alex | 37 | 4 | | |
| 2000–01 | Crewe Alex | 30 | 1 | | |
| 2001–02 | Crewe Alex | 9 | 0 | **261** | **26** |
| 2001–02 | *Macclesfield T* | 12 | 0 | | |
| 2002–03 | Rochdale | 6 | 0 | **6** | **0** |
| 2002–03 | Macclesfield T | 20 | 1 | | |
| 2003–04 | Macclesfield T | 16 | 0 | **48** | **1** |

**MILES, John (F)** **43** **11**
H: 5 10 W: 10 08 b.Fazackerley 28-9-81
*Source:* Trainee.

| | | | | | |
|---|---|---|---|---|---|
| 1998–99 | Liverpool | 0 | 0 | | |
| 1999–2000 | Liverpool | 0 | 0 | | |
| 2000–01 | Liverpool | 0 | 0 | | |
| 2001–02 | Liverpool | 0 | 0 | | |
| 2001–02 | Stoke C | 1 | 0 | **1** | **0** |
| 2002–03 | Crewe Alex | 5 | 1 | **5** | **1** |
| 2002–03 | Macclesfield T | 8 | 4 | | |
| 2003–04 | Macclesfield T | 29 | 6 | **37** | **10** |

**MISKELLY, David† (G)** **20** **0**
H: 6 0 W: 12 02 b.Ards 3-9-79
*Source:* Trainee. *Honours:* Northern Ireland Youth, Under-21.

| | | | | | |
|---|---|---|---|---|---|
| 1997–98 | Oldham Ath | 0 | 0 | | |
| 1998–99 | Oldham Ath | 1 | 0 | | |
| 1999–2000 | Oldham Ath | 2 | 0 | | |
| 2000–01 | Oldham Ath | 2 | 0 | | |
| 2001–02 | Oldham Ath | 4 | 0 | | |
| 2002–03 | Oldham Ath | 11 | 0 | **20** | **0** |
| 2003–04 | Macclesfield T | 0 | 0 | | |

**MUNROE, Karl* (D)** **120** **1**
H: 6 0 W: 10 08 b.Manchester 23-9-79
*Source:* Trainee.

| | | | | | |
|---|---|---|---|---|---|
| 1997–98 | Swansea C | 1 | 0 | | |
| 1998–99 | Swansea C | 0 | 0 | | |
| 1999–2000 | Swansea C | 0 | 0 | **1** | **0** |
| 1999–2000 | Macclesfield T | 5 | 0 | | |
| 2000–01 | Macclesfield T | 23 | 1 | | |
| 2001–02 | Macclesfield T | 30 | 0 | | |
| 2002–03 | Macclesfield T | 25 | 0 | | |
| 2003–04 | Macclesfield T | 36 | 0 | **119** | **1** |

**OLSEN, James† (D)** **6** **0**
H: 5 10 W: 12 00 b.Bootle 23-10-81
*Source:* Liverpool scholar.

| | | | | | |
|---|---|---|---|---|---|
| 2000–01 | Tranmere R | 1 | 0 | | |
| 2001–02 | Tranmere R | 0 | 0 | | |
| 2002–03 | Tranmere R | 3 | 0 | | |
| 2003–04 | Tranmere R | 0 | 0 | **4** | **0** |
| 2003–04 | Macclesfield T | 2 | 0 | **2** | **0** |

**PARKIN, Jonathan (F)** **97** **15**
H: 6 4 W: 13 07 b.Barnsley 30-12-81
*Source:* Scholarship.

| | | | | | |
|---|---|---|---|---|---|
| 1998–99 | Barnsley | 2 | 0 | | |
| 1999–2000 | Barnsley | 0 | 0 | | |
| 2000–01 | Barnsley | 4 | 0 | | |
| 2001–02 | Barnsley | 4 | 0 | **10** | **0** |
| 2001–02 | *Hartlepool U* | 1 | 0 | **1** | **0** |
| 2001–02 | York C | 18 | 2 | | |
| 2002–03 | York C | 41 | 10 | | |
| 2003–04 | York C | 15 | 2 | **74** | **14** |
| 2003–04 | Macclesfield T | 12 | 1 | **12** | **1** |

**PAYNE, Steve (D)** **241** **10**
H: 5 11 W: 12 00 b.Castleford 1-8-75
*Source:* Trainee.

| | | | | | |
|---|---|---|---|---|---|
| 1993–94 | Huddersfield T | 0 | 0 | | |
| 1994–95 | Huddersfield T | 0 | 0 | | |
| 1995–96 | Huddersfield T | 0 | 0 | | |
| 1996–97 | Huddersfield T | 0 | 0 | | |
| 1997–98 | Macclesfield T | 39 | 0 | | |
| 1998–99 | Macclesfield T | 38 | 2 | | |
| 1999–2000 | Chesterfield | 18 | 3 | | |
| 2000–01 | Chesterfield | 35 | 1 | | |
| 2001–02 | Chesterfield | 44 | 1 | | |
| 2002–03 | Chesterfield | 34 | 2 | | |
| 2003–04 | Chesterfield | 20 | 1 | **151** | **8** |
| 2003–04 | Macclesfield T | 13 | 0 | **90** | **2** |

**POTTER, Graham (D)** **274** **10**
H: 6 1 W: 11 12 b.Solihull 20-5-75
*Source:* Trainee. *Honours:* England Youth, Under-21.

| | | | | | |
|---|---|---|---|---|---|
| 1992–93 | Birmingham C | 18 | 2 | | |
| 1993–94 | Birmingham C | 7 | 0 | **25** | **2** |
| 1993–94 | *Wycombe W* | 3 | 0 | **3** | **0** |
| 1993–94 | Stoke C | 3 | 0 | | |
| 1994–95 | Stoke C | 1 | 0 | | |
| 1995–96 | Stoke C | 41 | 1 | **45** | **1** |
| 1996–97 | Southampton | 8 | 0 | **8** | **0** |
| 1996–97 | WBA | 6 | 0 | | |
| 1997–98 | WBA | 5 | 0 | | |
| 1997–98 | *Northampton T* | 4 | 0 | **4** | **0** |
| 1998–99 | WBA | 22 | 0 | | |
| 1999–2000 | WBA | 10 | 0 | **43** | **0** |
| 1999–2000 | *Reading* | 4 | 0 | **4** | **0** |
| 2000–01 | York C | 38 | 2 | | |
| 2001–02 | York C | 37 | 2 | | |
| 2002–03 | York C | 39 | 1 | **114** | **5** |
| 2003–04 | Boston U | 12 | 0 | **12** | **0** |
| 2003–04 | Macclesfield T | 16 | 2 | **16** | **2** |

**PRIEST, Chris* (M)** **317** **39**
H: 5 9 W: 12 00 b.Leigh 18-10-73
*Source:* Trainee.

| | | | | | |
|---|---|---|---|---|---|
| 1992–93 | Everton | 0 | 0 | | |
| 1993–94 | Everton | 0 | 0 | | |
| 1994–95 | Everton | 0 | 0 | | |
| 1994–95 | Chester C | 24 | 1 | | |
| 1995–96 | Chester C | 39 | 13 | | |
| 1996–97 | Chester C | 32 | 2 | | |
| 1997–98 | Chester C | 37 | 6 | | |
| 1998–99 | Chester C | 35 | 4 | **167** | **26** |
| 1999–2000 | Macclesfield T | 36 | 4 | | |
| 2000–01 | Macclesfield T | 15 | 4 | | |
| 2001–02 | Macclesfield T | 33 | 1 | | |
| 2002–03 | Macclesfield T | 37 | 2 | | |
| 2003–04 | Macclesfield T | 29 | 2 | **150** | **13** |

**ROBINSON, Neil‡ (F)** **11** **0**
H: 6 0 W: 12 12 b.Liverpool 18-11-79
*Source:* Prescot Cables.

| | | | | | |
|---|---|---|---|---|---|
| 2002–03 | Macclesfield T | 10 | 0 | | |
| 2003–04 | Macclesfield T | 1 | 0 | **11** | **0** |

**ROSS, Neil (F)** **28** **2**
H: 6 1 W: 12 02 b.West Bromwich 10-8-82
*Source:* Birmingham C Trainee, Leeds U Trainee.

| | | | | | |
|---|---|---|---|---|---|
| 1999–2000 | Leeds U | 0 | 0 | | |
| 1999–2000 | Stockport Co | 2 | 0 | | |
| 2000–01 | Stockport Co | 0 | 0 | | |
| 2001–02 | *Bristol R* | 5 | 0 | **5** | **0** |
| 2001–02 | Stockport Co | 3 | 1 | | |
| 2002–03 | Stockport Co | 4 | 1 | **9** | **2** |
| 2002–03 | Macclesfield T | 8 | 0 | | |
| 2003–04 | Macclesfield T | 6 | 0 | **14** | **0** |

**SMITH, David‡ (M)** **308** **5**
H: 5 10 W: 11 12 b.Liverpool 26-12-70
*Source:* Trainee.

| | | | | | |
|---|---|---|---|---|---|
| 1989–90 | Norwich C | 1 | 0 | | |
| 1990–91 | Norwich C | 3 | 0 | | |
| 1991–92 | Norwich C | 1 | 0 | | |
| 1992–93 | Norwich C | 6 | 0 | | |
| 1993–94 | Norwich C | 7 | 0 | **18** | **0** |
| 1994–95 | Oxford U | 42 | 0 | | |
| 1995–96 | Oxford U | 45 | 1 | | |
| 1996–97 | Oxford U | 45 | 0 | | |
| 1997–98 | Oxford U | 44 | 1 | | |
| 1998–99 | Oxford U | 22 | 0 | **198** | **2** |
| 1998–99 | Stockport Co | 17 | 1 | | |
| 1999–2000 | Stockport Co | 9 | 1 | | |
| 2000–01 | Stockport Co | 34 | 1 | | |
| 2001–02 | Stockport Co | 11 | 0 | **71** | **3** |
| 2001–02 | *Macclesfield T* | 8 | 0 | | |
| 2002–03 | Macclesfield T | 3 | 0 | | |
| 2003–04 | Macclesfield T | 10 | 0 | **21** | **0** |

**TIPTON, Matt# (F)** **199** **44**
H: 5 10 W: 11 02 b.Bangor 29-6-80
*Source:* Trainee. *Honours:* Wales Youth, Under-21.

| | | | | | |
|---|---|---|---|---|---|
| 1997–98 | Oldham Ath | 3 | 0 | | |
| 1998–99 | Oldham Ath | 28 | 2 | | |
| 1999–2000 | Oldham Ath | 29 | 3 | | |
| 2000–01 | Oldham Ath | 30 | 5 | | |
| 2001–02 | Oldham Ath | 22 | 5 | **112** | **15** |
| 2001–02 | Macclesfield T | 13 | 3 | | |
| 2002–03 | Macclesfield T | 36 | 10 | | |
| 2003–04 | Macclesfield T | 38 | 16 | **87** | **29** |

**VAN BLERK, Jason‡ (D)** **381** **22**
H: 6 0 W: 13 00 b.Sydney 16-3-68
*Honours:* Australia Under-20, 27 full caps, 1 goal.

| | | | | | |
|---|---|---|---|---|---|
| 1989 | Blackdown City | 24 | 3 | **24** | **3** |
| 1989–90 | Leichhardt | 25 | 1 | | |
| 1990–91 | St Truiden | 23 | 2 | **23** | **2** |
| 1991–92 | Leichhardt | 14 | 4 | **39** | **5** |
| 1992–93 | Go Ahead | 18 | 1 | | |
| 1993–94 | Go Ahead | 30 | 4 | **48** | **5** |
| 1994–95 | Millwall | 27 | 1 | | |
| 1995–96 | Millwall | 42 | 1 | | |
| 1996–97 | Millwall | 4 | 0 | **73** | **2** |
| 1997–98 | Manchester C | 19 | 0 | **19** | **0** |
| 1997–98 | WBA | 8 | 0 | | |
| 1998–99 | WBA | 30 | 0 | | |
| 1999–2000 | WBA | 35 | 1 | | |
| 2000–01 | WBA | 36 | 2 | **109** | **3** |
| 2001–02 | Stockport Co | 13 | 0 | **13** | **0** |
| 2001–02 | Hull C | 10 | 1 | **10** | **1** |
| 2002–03 | Shrewsbury T | 23 | 1 | **23** | **1** |
| 2003–04 | Mansfield T | 0 | 0 | | |
| 2003–04 | Macclesfield T | 0 | 0 | | |

**WELCH, Michael (D)** **83** **3**
H: 6 3 W: 11 13 b.Crewe 11-1-82
*Source:* Barnsley Scholar.

| | | | | | |
|---|---|---|---|---|---|
| 2001–02 | Macclesfield T | 6 | 0 | | |
| 2002–03 | Macclesfield T | 39 | 3 | | |
| 2003–04 | Macclesfield T | 38 | 0 | **83** | **3** |

**WHITAKER, Danny (M)** **93** **17**
H: 5 10 W: 11 00 b.Manchester 14-11-80

| | | | | | |
|---|---|---|---|---|---|
| 2000–01 | Macclesfield T | 0 | 0 | | |
| 2001–02 | Macclesfield T | 16 | 2 | | |
| 2002–03 | Macclesfield T | 41 | 10 | | |
| 2003–04 | Macclesfield T | 36 | 5 | **93** | **17** |

**WIDDRINGTON, Tommy# (M)** **343** **24**
H: 5 10 W: 11 12 b.Newcastle 1-10-71
*Source:* Trainee.

| | | | | | |
|---|---|---|---|---|---|
| 1989–90 | Southampton | 0 | 0 | | |
| 1990–91 | Southampton | 0 | 0 | | |
| 1991–92 | Southampton | 3 | 0 | | |
| 1991–92 | *Wigan Ath* | 6 | 0 | **6** | **0** |
| 1992–93 | Southampton | 12 | 0 | | |
| 1993–94 | Southampton | 11 | 1 | | |
| 1994–95 | Southampton | 28 | 0 | | |
| 1995–96 | Southampton | 21 | 2 | **75** | **3** |
| 1996–97 | Grimsby T | 42 | 4 | | |
| 1997–98 | Grimsby T | 21 | 3 | | |
| 1998–99 | Grimsby T | 26 | 1 | **89** | **8** |
| 1998–99 | *Port Vale* | 9 | 1 | | |
| 1999–2000 | Port Vale | 38 | 5 | | |
| 2000–01 | Port Vale | 35 | 2 | **82** | **8** |
| 2001–02 | Hartlepool U | 24 | 2 | | |
| 2002–03 | Hartlepool U | 32 | 3 | **56** | **5** |
| 2003–04 | Macclesfield T | 35 | 0 | **35** | **0** |

**WILSON, Steve (G)** **296** **0**
H: 5 10 W: 10 07 b.Hull 24-4-74
*Source:* Trainee.

| | | | | | |
|---|---|---|---|---|---|
| 1990–91 | Hull C | 2 | 0 | | |
| 1991–92 | Hull C | 3 | 0 | | |
| 1992–93 | Hull C | 26 | 0 | | |
| 1993–94 | Hull C | 9 | 0 | | |
| 1994–95 | Hull C | 20 | 0 | | |
| 1995–96 | Hull C | 19 | 0 | | |
| 1996–97 | Hull C | 15 | 0 | | |
| 1997–98 | Hull C | 37 | 0 | | |
| 1998–99 | Hull C | 23 | 0 | | |
| 1999–2000 | Hull C | 27 | 0 | | |
| 2000–01 | Hull C | 0 | 0 | **181** | **0** |
| 2000–01 | *Macclesfield T* | 1 | 0 | | |
| 2001–02 | Macclesfield T | 38 | 0 | | |
| 2002–03 | Macclesfield T | 44 | 0 | | |
| 2003–04 | Macclesfield T | 32 | 0 | **115** | **0** |

**Scholars**
Byrne, Michael B; Campbell, John R; Cropper, Wayne E; Deasy, Timothy; Drummond, Philip A; Goodeve, Jordan; Matranga, Aiden L; McDonald, Marvin M; Owens, Stephen P; Reid, Izak G; Swann, Paul M; Teague, Andrew H; Vernon, Karl M

**Non Contract**
Askey, John C; Miskelly, David T; Olsen, James P

**Players who do not hold a current contract but their registration has been retained by the club**
Bayliss, Richard L

# MANCHESTER C (47)

**ANELKA, Nicolas (F)** **223 70**
H: 6 1 W: 13 03 b.Versailles 14-3-79
*Honours:* France Youth, Under-21, 28 full caps, 6 goals.

| | | | | | |
|---|---|---|---|---|---|
| 1995–96 | Paris St Germain | 2 | 0 | | |
| 1996–97 | Paris St Germain | 8 | 1 | | |
| 1996–97 | Arsenal | 4 | 0 | | |
| 1997–98 | Arsenal | 26 | 6 | | |
| 1998–99 | Arsenal | 35 | 17 | **65** | **23** |
| 1999–2000 | Real Madrid | 19 | 2 | **19** | **2** |
| 2000–01 | Paris St Germain | 27 | 8 | | |
| 2001–02 | Paris St Germain | 12 | 2 | **49** | **11** |
| 2001–02 | Liverpool | 20 | 4 | **20** | **4** |
| 2002–03 | Manchester C | 38 | 14 | | |
| 2003–04 | Manchester C | 32 | 16 | **70** | **30** |

**ARASON, Arni* (G)** **105 0**
H: 6 2 W: 13 05 b.Reykjavik 7-5-75
*Honours:* Iceland 33 full caps.

| | | | | | |
|---|---|---|---|---|---|
| 1994 | IA Akranes | 1 | 0 | | |
| 1995 | IA Akranes | 3 | 0 | | |
| 1996 | IA Akranes | 2 | 0 | **6** | **0** |
| 1997 | Stjarnan | 18 | 0 | **18** | **0** |
| 1998 | Rosenborg | 3 | 0 | | |
| 1999 | Rosenborg | 6 | 0 | | |
| 2000 | Rosenborg | 22 | 0 | | |
| 2001 | Rosenborg | 24 | 0 | | |
| 2002 | Rosenborg | 24 | 0 | | |
| 2003 | Rosenborg | 2 | 0 | **81** | **0** |
| 2003–04 | Manchester C | 0 | 0 | | |

**BARTON, Joey (M)** **35 2**
H: 5 11 W: 11 09 b.Huyton 2-9-82
*Source:* Scholar. *Honours:* England Under-21.

| | | | | | |
|---|---|---|---|---|---|
| 2001–02 | Manchester C | 0 | 0 | | |
| 2002–03 | Manchester C | 7 | 1 | | |
| 2003–04 | Manchester C | 28 | 1 | **35** | **2** |

**BENNETT, Ian (M)** **0 0**
b.Rochdale 24-2-86
*Source:* Trainee.

| | | | | | |
|---|---|---|---|---|---|
| 2003–04 | Manchester C | 0 | 0 | | |

**BERMINGHAM, Karl (M)** **0 0**
b.Dublin 6-10-85
*Source:* Scholar.

| | | | | | |
|---|---|---|---|---|---|
| 2002–03 | Manchester C | 0 | 0 | | |
| 2003–04 | Manchester C | 0 | 0 | | |

**BISCHOFF, Mikkel (D)** **11 0**
H: 6 3 W: 13 11 b.Denmark 3-2-82

| | | | | | |
|---|---|---|---|---|---|
| 2001–02 | AB Copenhagen | 10 | 0 | **10** | **0** |
| 2002–03 | Manchester C | 1 | 0 | | |
| 2003–04 | Manchester C | 0 | 0 | **1** | **0** |

**BOSVELT, Paul (M)** **406 79**
H: 6 0 W: 13 00 b.Doetinchem 26-3-70
*Honours:* Holland 24 full caps.

| | | | | | |
|---|---|---|---|---|---|
| 1989–90 | Go Ahead | 32 | 2 | | |
| 1990–91 | Go Ahead | 26 | 8 | | |
| 1991–92 | Go Ahead | 27 | 4 | | |
| 1992–93 | Go Ahead | 22 | 4 | | |
| 1993–94 | Go Ahead | 32 | 9 | **139** | **27** |
| 1994–95 | Twente | 33 | 7 | | |
| 1995–96 | Twente | 32 | 7 | | |
| 1996–97 | Twente | 31 | 7 | **96** | **21** |
| 1997–98 | Feyenoord | 30 | 4 | | |
| 1998–99 | Feyenoord | 33 | 4 | | |
| 1999–2000 | Feyenoord | 32 | 8 | | |
| 2000–01 | Feyenoord | 20 | 8 | | |
| 2001–02 | Feyenoord | 31 | 7 | **146** | **31** |
| 2003–04 | Manchester C | 25 | 0 | **25** | **0** |

**CROFT, Lee (F)** **0 0**
b.Wigan 21-6-85
*Source:* Scholar. *Honours:* England Youth, Under-20.

| | | | | | |
|---|---|---|---|---|---|
| 2002–03 | Manchester C | 0 | 0 | | |
| 2003–04 | Manchester C | 0 | 0 | | |

**D'LARYEA, Jonathan (M)** **0 0**
b.Manchester 3-9-85
*Source:* Trainee.

| | | | | | |
|---|---|---|---|---|---|
| 2003–04 | Manchester C | 0 | 0 | | |

**D'LARYEA, Nathan (D)** **0 0**
b.Manchester 3-9-85
*Source:* Trainee.

| | | | | | |
|---|---|---|---|---|---|
| 2003–04 | Manchester C | 0 | 0 | | |

**DISTIN, Sylvain (D)** **187 6**
H: 6 3 W: 14 08 b.Bagnolet 16-12-77

| | | | | | |
|---|---|---|---|---|---|
| 1998–99 | Tours | 26 | 3 | **26** | **3** |
| 1999–2000 | Gueugnon | 33 | 1 | **33** | **1** |
| 2000–01 | Paris St Germain | 28 | 0 | **28** | **0** |
| 2001–02 | Newcastle U | 28 | 0 | **28** | **0** |
| 2002–03 | Manchester C | 34 | 0 | | |
| 2003–04 | Manchester C | 38 | 2 | **72** | **2** |

**DUNNE, Richard (D)** **182 1**
H: 6 2 W: 15 12 b.Dublin 21-9-79
*Source:* Trainee. *Honours:* Eire Under-21, 20 full caps, 4 goals.

| | | | | | |
|---|---|---|---|---|---|
| 1996–97 | Everton | 7 | 0 | | |
| 1997–98 | Everton | 3 | 0 | | |
| 1998–99 | Everton | 16 | 0 | | |
| 1999–2000 | Everton | 31 | 0 | | |
| 2000–01 | Everton | 3 | 0 | **60** | **0** |
| 2000–01 | Manchester C | 25 | 0 | | |
| 2001–02 | Manchester C | 43 | 1 | | |
| 2002–03 | Manchester C | 25 | 0 | | |
| 2003–04 | Manchester C | 29 | 0 | **122** | **1** |

**ELLEGAARD, Kevin Stuhr (G)** **4 0**
H: 6 5 W: 14 06 b.Charlottenlund 23-5-83
*Source:* Farum.

| | | | | | |
|---|---|---|---|---|---|
| 2001–02 | Manchester C | 0 | 0 | | |
| 2002–03 | Manchester C | 0 | 0 | | |
| 2003–04 | Manchester C | 4 | 0 | **4** | **0** |

**ELLIOTT, Stephen (F)** **2 0**
H: 5 7 W: 11 06 b.Dublin 6-1-84
*Source:* School. *Honours:* Eire Under-21.

| | | | | | |
|---|---|---|---|---|---|
| 2000–01 | Manchester C | 0 | 0 | | |
| 2001–02 | Manchester C | 0 | 0 | | |
| 2002–03 | Manchester C | 0 | 0 | | |
| 2003–04 | Manchester C | 2 | 0 | **2** | **0** |

**FLOOD, Willo (M)** **6 0**
H: 5 6 W: 9 11 b.Dublin 10-4-85
*Honours:* Eire Under-21.

| | | | | | |
|---|---|---|---|---|---|
| 2001–02 | Manchester C | 0 | 0 | | |
| 2002–03 | Manchester C | 0 | 0 | | |
| 2003–04 | Manchester C | 0 | 0 | | |
| 2003–04 | *Rochdale* | 6 | 0 | **6** | **0** |

**FOWLER, Robbie (F)** **310 143**
H: 5 10 W: 12 05 b.Liverpool 9-4-75
*Source:* Trainee. *Honours:* England Youth, B, Under-21, 26 full caps, 7 goals.

| | | | | | |
|---|---|---|---|---|---|
| 1991–92 | Liverpool | 0 | 0 | | |
| 1992–93 | Liverpool | 0 | 0 | | |
| 1993–94 | Liverpool | 28 | 12 | | |
| 1994–95 | Liverpool | 42 | 25 | | |
| 1995–96 | Liverpool | 38 | 28 | | |
| 1996–97 | Liverpool | 32 | 18 | | |
| 1997–98 | Liverpool | 20 | 9 | | |
| 1998–99 | Liverpool | 25 | 14 | | |
| 1999–2000 | Liverpool | 14 | 3 | | |
| 2000–01 | Liverpool | 27 | 8 | | |
| 2001–02 | Liverpool | 10 | 3 | **236** | **120** |
| 2001–02 | Leeds U | 22 | 12 | | |
| 2002–03 | Leeds U | 8 | 2 | **30** | **14** |
| 2002–03 | Manchester C | 13 | 2 | | |
| 2003–04 | Manchester C | 31 | 7 | **44** | **9** |

**JAMES, David (G)** **478 0**
H: 6 5 W: 14 02 b.Welwyn 1-8-70
*Source:* Trainee. *Honours:* England Youth, Under-21, B, 28 full caps.

| | | | | | |
|---|---|---|---|---|---|
| 1988–89 | Watford | 0 | 0 | | |
| 1989–90 | Watford | 0 | 0 | | |
| 1990–91 | Watford | 46 | 0 | | |
| 1991–92 | Watford | 43 | 0 | **89** | **0** |
| 1992–93 | Liverpool | 29 | 0 | | |
| 1993–94 | Liverpool | 14 | 0 | | |
| 1994–95 | Liverpool | 42 | 0 | | |
| 1995–96 | Liverpool | 38 | 0 | | |
| 1996–97 | Liverpool | 38 | 0 | | |
| 1997–98 | Liverpool | 27 | 0 | | |
| 1998–99 | Liverpool | 26 | 0 | **214** | **0** |
| 1999–2000 | Aston Villa | 29 | 0 | | |
| 2000–01 | Aston Villa | 38 | 0 | **67** | **0** |
| 2001–02 | West Ham U | 26 | 0 | | |
| 2002–03 | West Ham U | 38 | 0 | | |
| 2003–04 | West Ham U | 27 | 0 | **91** | **0** |
| 2003–04 | Manchester C | 17 | 0 | **17** | **0** |

**JIHAI, Sun (D)** **91 3**
H: 5 9 W: 12 02 b.Dalian 30-9-77
*Source:* Dalian Wanda. *Honours:* China 62 full caps, 8 goals.

| | | | | | |
|---|---|---|---|---|---|
| 1998–99 | Crystal Palace | 23 | 0 | **23** | **0** |
| From Dalian Wanda. | | | | | |
| 2001–02 | Manchester C | 7 | 0 | | |
| 2002–03 | Manchester C | 28 | 2 | | |
| 2003–04 | Manchester C | 33 | 1 | **68** | **3** |

**JORDAN, Stephen (D)** **14 0**
H: 6 1 W: 11 13 b.Warrington 6-3-82
*Source:* Scholarship.

| | | | | | |
|---|---|---|---|---|---|
| 1998–99 | Manchester C | 0 | 0 | | |
| 1999–2000 | Manchester C | 0 | 0 | | |
| 2000–01 | Manchester C | 0 | 0 | | |
| 2001–02 | Manchester C | 0 | 0 | | |
| 2002–03 | Manchester C | 1 | 0 | | |
| 2002–03 | *Cambridge U* | 11 | 0 | **11** | **0** |
| 2003–04 | Manchester C | 2 | 0 | **3** | **0** |

**LAIRD, Marc (M)** **0 0**
b.Edinburgh 23-1-86
*Source:* Trainee.

| | | | | | |
|---|---|---|---|---|---|
| 2003–04 | Manchester C | 0 | 0 | | |

**MACKEN, Jon (F)** **212 69**
H: 5 11 W: 13 13 b.Manchester 7-9-77
*Source:* Trainee. *Honours:* England Youth.

| | | | | | |
|---|---|---|---|---|---|
| 1996–97 | Manchester U | 0 | 0 | | |
| 1997–98 | Preston NE | 29 | 6 | | |
| 1998–99 | Preston NE | 42 | 8 | | |
| 1999–2000 | Preston NE | 44 | 22 | | |
| 2000–01 | Preston NE | 38 | 19 | | |
| 2001–02 | Preston NE | 31 | 8 | **184** | **63** |
| 2001–02 | Manchester C | 8 | 5 | | |
| 2002–03 | Manchester C | 5 | 0 | | |
| 2003–04 | Manchester C | 15 | 1 | **28** | **6** |

**MATTHEWS, James (M)** **0 0**
b.Dublin 2-2-85
*Source:* Scholar.

| | | | | | |
|---|---|---|---|---|---|
| 2002–03 | Manchester C | 0 | 0 | | |
| 2003–04 | Manchester C | 0 | 0 | | |

**McCARTHY, Patrick (D)** **18 0**
H: 6 2 W: 13 07 b.Dublin 31-5-83
*Source:* Scholar. *Honours:* Eire Under-21.

| | | | | | |
|---|---|---|---|---|---|
| 2000–01 | Manchester C | 0 | 0 | | |
| 2001–02 | Manchester C | 0 | 0 | | |
| 2002–03 | Manchester C | 0 | 0 | | |
| 2002–03 | *Boston U* | 12 | 0 | **12** | **0** |
| 2002–03 | *Notts Co* | 6 | 0 | **6** | **0** |
| 2003–04 | Manchester C | 0 | 0 | | |

**McDOWALL, Ryan‡ (M)** **0 0**
b.Knowsley 30-3-84
*Source:* School.

| | | | | | |
|---|---|---|---|---|---|
| 2000–01 | Manchester C | 0 | 0 | | |
| 2001–02 | Manchester C | 0 | 0 | | |
| 2002–03 | Manchester C | 0 | 0 | | |
| 2003–04 | Manchester C | 0 | 0 | | |

**McMANAMAN, Steve (M)** **386 54**
H: 6 1 W: 11 11 b.Liverpool 11-2-72
*Source:* School. *Honours:* England Youth, Under-21, 24 full caps.

| | | | | | |
|---|---|---|---|---|---|
| 1989–90 | Liverpool | 0 | 0 | | |
| 1990–91 | Liverpool | 2 | 0 | | |
| 1991–92 | Liverpool | 30 | 5 | | |
| 1992–93 | Liverpool | 31 | 4 | | |
| 1993–94 | Liverpool | 30 | 2 | | |
| 1994–95 | Liverpool | 40 | 7 | | |
| 1995–96 | Liverpool | 38 | 6 | | |
| 1996–97 | Liverpool | 37 | 7 | | |
| 1997–98 | Liverpool | 36 | 11 | | |
| 1998–99 | Liverpool | 28 | 4 | **272** | **46** |
| 1999–2000 | Real Madrid | 28 | 3 | | |
| 2000–01 | Real Madrid | 26 | 2 | | |
| 2001–02 | Real Madrid | 23 | 2 | | |
| 2002–03 | Real Madrid | 15 | 1 | **92** | **8** |
| 2003–04 | Manchester C | 22 | 0 | **22** | **0** |

**MURPHY, Paul (D)** **0 0**
b.Wexford 12-4-85
*Source:* Scholar.

| | | | | | |
|---|---|---|---|---|---|
| 2002–03 | Manchester C | 0 | 0 | | |
| 2003–04 | Manchester C | 0 | 0 | | |

**NEGOUAI, Christian (M)** **50 7**
H: 6 4 W: 14 01 b.Fort-de-France 20-1-75

| | | | | | |
|---|---|---|---|---|---|
| 1999–2000 | Charleroi | 9 | 0 | | |
| 2000–01 | Charleroi | 26 | 4 | | |
| 2001–02 | Charleroi | 10 | 2 | **45** | **6** |

| | | | | | |
|---|---|---|---|---|---|
| 2001–02 | Manchester C | 5 | 1 | | |
| 2002–03 | Manchester C | 0 | 0 | | |
| 2003–04 | Manchester C | 0 | 0 | **5** | **1** |

**PEARSON, Sean (M) 0 0**
b.Manchester 7-3-85

| | | | | | |
|---|---|---|---|---|---|
| 2002–03 | Manchester C | 0 | 0 | | |
| 2003–04 | Manchester C | 0 | 0 | | |

**PROFFITT, Darrly (M) 0 0**
b.Stoke 2-5-85
*Source:* Scholar. *Honours:* England Youth.

| | | | | | |
|---|---|---|---|---|---|
| 2002–03 | Manchester C | 0 | 0 | | |
| 2003–04 | Manchester C | 0 | 0 | | |
| 2003–04 | *Coventry C* | 0 | 0 | | |

**REYNA, Claudio (M) 167 18**
H: 5 9 W: 11 08 b.New Jersey 20-7-73
*Source:* Union County SC, Univ Virginia.
*Honours:* USA 102 full caps, 8 goals.

| | | | | | |
|---|---|---|---|---|---|
| 1996–97 | Leverkusen | 5 | 0 | **5** | **0** |
| 1997–98 | Wolfsburg | 28 | 4 | | |
| 1998–99 | Wolfsburg | 20 | 2 | **48** | **6** |
| 1998–99 | Rangers | 6 | 0 | | |
| 1999–2000 | Rangers | 29 | 5 | | |
| 2000–01 | Rangers | 18 | 2 | | |
| 2001–02 | Rangers | 10 | 1 | **63** | **8** |
| 2001–02 | Sunderland | 17 | 3 | | |
| 2002–03 | Sunderland | 11 | 0 | | |
| 2003–04 | Sunderland | 0 | 0 | **28** | **3** |
| 2003–04 | Manchester C | 23 | 1 | **23** | **1** |

**SCHMEICHEL, Kasper§ (G) 0 0**
H: 6 0 W: 12 00 b.Denmark 5-11-86
*Source:* Scholar.

| | | | | | |
|---|---|---|---|---|---|
| 2003–04 | Manchester C | 0 | 0 | | |

**SEAMAN, David‡ (G) 731 0**
H: 6 4 W: 15 06 b.Rotherham 19-9-63
*Source:* Apprentice. *Honours:* England Under-21, B, 75 full caps.

| | | | | | |
|---|---|---|---|---|---|
| 1981–82 | Leeds U | 0 | 0 | | |
| 1982–83 | Peterborough U | 38 | 0 | | |
| 1983–84 | Peterborough U | 45 | 0 | | |
| 1984–85 | Peterborough U | 8 | 0 | **91** | **0** |
| 1984–85 | Birmingham C | 33 | 0 | | |
| 1985–86 | Birmingham C | 42 | 0 | **75** | **0** |
| 1986–87 | QPR | 41 | 0 | | |
| 1987–88 | QPR | 32 | 0 | | |
| 1988–89 | QPR | 35 | 0 | | |
| 1989–90 | QPR | 33 | 0 | **141** | **0** |
| 1990–91 | Arsenal | 38 | 0 | | |
| 1991–92 | Arsenal | 42 | 0 | | |
| 1992–93 | Arsenal | 39 | 0 | | |
| 1993–94 | Arsenal | 39 | 0 | | |
| 1994–95 | Arsenal | 31 | 0 | | |
| 1995–96 | Arsenal | 38 | 0 | | |
| 1996–97 | Arsenal | 22 | 0 | | |
| 1997–98 | Arsenal | 31 | 0 | | |
| 1998–99 | Arsenal | 32 | 0 | | |
| 1999–2000 | Arsenal | 24 | 0 | | |
| 2000–01 | Arsenal | 24 | 0 | | |
| 2001–02 | Arsenal | 17 | 0 | | |
| 2002–03 | Arsenal | 28 | 0 | **405** | **0** |
| 2003–04 | Manchester C | 19 | 0 | **19** | **0** |

**SIBIERSKI, Antoine (M) 293 66**
H: 6 2 W: 12 04 b.Lille 5-8-74

| | | | | | |
|---|---|---|---|---|---|
| 1992–93 | Lille | 6 | 0 | | |
| 1993–94 | Lille | 22 | 1 | | |
| 1994–95 | Lille | 36 | 7 | | |
| 1995–96 | Lille | 33 | 9 | **97** | **17** |
| 1996–97 | Auxerre | 30 | 7 | | |
| 1997–98 | Auxerre | 12 | 1 | **42** | **8** |
| 1998–99 | Nantes | 4 | 0 | | |
| 1999–2000 | Nantes | 28 | 13 | **32** | **13** |
| 2000–01 | Lens | 27 | 5 | | |
| 2001–02 | Lens | 25 | 6 | | |
| 2002–03 | Lens | 37 | 12 | **89** | **23** |
| 2003–04 | Manchester C | 33 | 5 | **33** | **5** |

**SINCLAIR, Trevor (M) 485 69**
H: 5 9 W: 13 05 b.Dulwich 2-3-73
*Source:* Trainee. *Honours:* England Youth, Under-21, B, 12 full caps.

| | | | | | |
|---|---|---|---|---|---|
| 1989–90 | Blackpool | 9 | 0 | | |
| 1990–91 | Blackpool | 31 | 1 | | |
| 1991–92 | Blackpool | 27 | 3 | | |
| 1992–93 | Blackpool | 45 | 11 | **112** | **15** |
| 1993–94 | QPR | 32 | 4 | | |
| 1994–95 | QPR | 33 | 4 | | |
| 1995–96 | QPR | 37 | 2 | | |
| 1996–97 | QPR | 39 | 3 | | |
| 1997–98 | QPR | 26 | 3 | **167** | **16** |
| 1997–98 | West Ham U | 14 | 7 | | |
| 1998–99 | West Ham U | 36 | 7 | | |
| 1999–2000 | West Ham U | 36 | 7 | | |
| 2000–01 | West Ham U | 19 | 3 | | |
| 2001–02 | West Ham U | 34 | 5 | | |
| 2002–03 | West Ham U | 38 | 8 | **177** | **37** |
| 2003–04 | Manchester C | 29 | 1 | **29** | **1** |

**SLACK, Leyton‡ (M) 0 0**
b.Glasgow 25-7-85
*Source:* Scholar.

| | | | | | |
|---|---|---|---|---|---|
| 2002–03 | Manchester C | 0 | 0 | | |
| 2003–04 | Manchester C | 0 | 0 | | |

**SOMMEIL, David (D) 291 5**
H: 5 10 W: 12 12 b.Ponte-a-Pitre 10-8-74

| | | | | | |
|---|---|---|---|---|---|
| 1993–94 | Caen | 1 | 0 | | |
| 1994–95 | Caen | 25 | 0 | | |
| 1995–96 | Caen | 30 | 0 | | |
| 1996–97 | Caen | 25 | 0 | | |
| 1997–98 | Caen | 38 | 1 | **119** | **1** |
| 1998–99- | Rennes | 33 | 0 | | |
| 1999–2000 | Rennes | 30 | 1 | **63** | **1** |
| 2000–01 | Bordeaux | 29 | 0 | | |
| 2001–02 | Bordeaux | 31 | 0 | | |
| 2002–03 | Bordeaux | 17 | 1 | **77** | **1** |
| 2002–03 | Manchester C | 14 | 1 | | |
| 2003–04 | Manchester C | 18 | 1 | **32** | **2** |

**TANDY, Jamie (M) 0 0**
b.Manchester 1-9-84
*Source:* Scholar.

| | | | | | |
|---|---|---|---|---|---|
| 2002–03 | Manchester C | 0 | 0 | | |
| 2003–04 | Manchester C | 0 | 0 | | |

**TARNAT, Michael* (D) 369 30**
H: 5 11 W: 13 04 b.Hilden 27-10-69
*Honours:* Germany 19 full caps.

| | | | | | |
|---|---|---|---|---|---|
| 1990–91 | Duisburg | 33 | 4 | | |
| 1991–92 | Duisburg | 34 | 0 | | |
| 1992–93 | Duisburg | 43 | 7 | | |
| 1993–94 | Duisburg | 24 | 1 | **134** | **12** |
| 1994–95 | Karlsruhe | 24 | 3 | | |
| 1995–96 | Karlsruhe | 30 | 2 | | |
| 1996–97 | Karlsruhe | 27 | 2 | **81** | **7** |
| 1997–98 | Bayern Munich | 32 | 5 | | |
| 1998–99 | Bayern Munich | 20 | 1 | | |
| 1999–2000 | Bayern Munich | 26 | 1 | | |
| 2000–01 | Bayern Munich | 23 | 1 | | |
| 2001–02 | Bayern Munich | 10 | 0 | | |
| 2002–03 | Bayern Munich | 11 | 0 | **122** | **8** |
| 2003–04 | Manchester C | 32 | 3 | **32** | **3** |

**TIATTO, Danny* (M) 209 8**
H: 5 7 W: 11 11 b.Melbourne 22-5-73
*Honours:* Australia Under-23, 21 full caps, 1 goal.

| | | | | | |
|---|---|---|---|---|---|
| 1994–95 | Melbourne Knights | 25 | 3 | | |
| 1995–96 | Melbourne Knights | 18 | 0 | **43** | **3** |
| 1996–97 | Salernitana | 11 | 1 | **11** | **1** |
| 1997–98 | Stoke C | 15 | 1 | **15** | **1** |
| From Baden | | | | | |
| 1998–99 | Manchester C | 17 | 0 | | |
| 1999–2000 | Manchester C | 35 | 0 | | |
| 2000–01 | Manchester C | 33 | 2 | | |
| 2001–02 | Manchester C | 37 | 1 | | |
| 2002–03 | Manchester C | 13 | 0 | | |
| 2003–04 | Manchester C | 5 | 0 | **140** | **3** |

**TIMMS, Ashley (M) 0 0**
b.Manchester 6-11-85
*Source:* Scholar.

| | | | | | |
|---|---|---|---|---|---|
| 2002–03 | Manchester C | 0 | 0 | | |
| 2003–04 | Manchester C | 0 | 0 | | |

**VAN BUYTEN, Daniel‡ (D) 139 18**
H: 6 5 W: 13 10 b.Chimay 7-2-78
*Honours:* Belgium 21 full caps, 1 goal.

| | | | | | |
|---|---|---|---|---|---|
| 1997–98 | Charleroi | 0 | 0 | | |
| 1998–99 | Charleroi | 19 | 1 | **19** | **1** |
| 1999–2000 | Standard Liege | 28 | 3 | | |
| 2000–01 | Standard Liege | 29 | 4 | **57** | **7** |
| 2001–02 | Marseille | 23 | 2 | | |
| 2002–03 | Marseille | 35 | 8 | **58** | **10** |
| 2003–04 | Manchester C | 5 | 0 | **5** | **0** |

**VUOSO, Vicente (D) 65 8**
H: 5 9 W: 12 05 b.Mar del Plata 3-11-81

| | | | | | |
|---|---|---|---|---|---|
| 2000–01 | Independiente | 29 | 7 | | |
| 2001–02 | Independiente | 36 | 1 | **65** | **8** |
| 2002–03 | Manchester C | 0 | 0 | | |
| 2003–04 | Manchester C | 0 | 0 | | |

**WANCHOPE, Paulo (F) 171 62**
H: 6 3 W: 13 10 b.Heredia 31-7-76
*Source:* Herediano. *Honours:* Costa Rica 53 full caps, 37 goals.

| | | | | | |
|---|---|---|---|---|---|
| 1996–97 | Derby Co | 5 | 1 | | |
| 1997–98 | Derby Co | 32 | 13 | | |
| 1998–99 | Derby Co | 35 | 9 | **72** | **23** |
| 1999–2000 | West Ham U | 35 | 12 | **35** | **12** |
| 2000–01 | Manchester C | 27 | 9 | | |
| 2001–02 | Manchester C | 15 | 12 | | |
| 2002–03 | Manchester C | 0 | 0 | | |
| 2003–04 | Manchester C | 22 | 6 | **64** | **27** |

**WEAVER, Nick (G) 147 0**
H: 6 4 W: 14 07 b.Sheffield 2-3-79
*Source:* Trainee. *Honours:* England Under-21.

| | | | | | |
|---|---|---|---|---|---|
| 1995–96 | Mansfield T | 1 | 0 | | |
| 1996–97 | Mansfield T | 0 | 0 | **1** | **0** |
| 1996–97 | Manchester C | 0 | 0 | | |
| 1997–98 | Manchester C | 0 | 0 | | |
| 1998–99 | Manchester C | 45 | 0 | | |
| 1999–2000 | Manchester C | 45 | 0 | | |
| 2000–01 | Manchester C | 31 | 0 | | |
| 2001–02 | Manchester C | 25 | 0 | | |
| 2002–03 | Manchester C | 0 | 0 | | |
| 2003–04 | Manchester C | 0 | 0 | **146** | **0** |

**WESTWOOD, Keiren* (G) 0 0**
b.Manchester 23-10-84

| | | | | | |
|---|---|---|---|---|---|
| 2001–02 | Manchester C | 0 | 0 | | |
| 2002–03 | Manchester C | 0 | 0 | | |
| 2003–04 | Manchester C | 0 | 0 | | |
| 2003–04 | *Oldham Ath* | 0 | 0 | | |

**WHELAN, Glenn* (D) 13 0**
H: 6 0 W: 12 09 b.Dublin 13-1-84
*Source:* Scholar. *Honours:* Eire Under-21.

| | | | | | |
|---|---|---|---|---|---|
| 2000–01 | Manchester C | 0 | 0 | | |
| 2001–02 | Manchester C | 0 | 0 | | |
| 2002–03 | Manchester C | 0 | 0 | | |
| 2003–04 | Manchester C | 0 | 0 | | |
| 2003–04 | *Bury* | 13 | 0 | **13** | **0** |

**WIEKENS, Gerard* (D) 215 11**
H: 5 9 W: 13 10 b.Tolhuiswyk 25-2-73

| | | | | | |
|---|---|---|---|---|---|
| 1996–97 | Veendam | 33 | 1 | **33** | **1** |
| 1997–98 | Manchester C | 37 | 5 | | |
| 1998–99 | Manchester C | 42 | 2 | | |
| 1999–2000 | Manchester C | 34 | 1 | | |
| 2000–01 | Manchester C | 34 | 2 | | |
| 2001–02 | Manchester C | 29 | 1 | | |
| 2002–03 | Manchester C | 6 | 0 | | |
| 2003–04 | Manchester C | 0 | 0 | **182** | **10** |

**WRIGHT-PHILLIPS, Bradley (M) 0 0**
b.Lewisham 12-3-85
*Source:* Scholar.

| | | | | | |
|---|---|---|---|---|---|
| 2002–03 | Manchester C | 0 | 0 | | |
| 2003–04 | Manchester C | 0 | 0 | | |

**WRIGHT-PHILLIPS, Shaun (M) 119 16**
H: 5 5 W: 9 12 b.London 25-10-81
*Honours:* England Under-21.

| | | | | | |
|---|---|---|---|---|---|
| 1998–99 | Manchester C | 0 | 0 | | |
| 1999–2000 | Manchester C | 4 | 0 | | |
| 2000–01 | Manchester C | 15 | 0 | | |
| 2001–02 | Manchester C | 35 | 8 | | |
| 2002–03 | Manchester C | 31 | 1 | | |
| 2003–04 | Manchester C | 34 | 7 | **119** | **16** |

**Scholars**
Collins, Paul J; Grant, Tyrone; Grimes, Ashley J; Ireland, Stephen J; Logan, Carlos S; Miller, Ishmael A; Onuoha, Chinedum; Schmeichel, Kasper P; Ward, Michael V; Warrender, Daniel J

## MANCHESTER U (48)

**BARDSLEY, Phillip (D) 0 0**
H: 5 11 W: 11 08 b.Salford 28-6-85
*Source:* Trainee.

| | | | | | |
|---|---|---|---|---|---|
| 2003–04 | Manchester U | 0 | 0 | | |

**BARTHEZ, Fabien (G) 367 0**
H: 5 11 W: 12 08 b.Lavelanet 28-6-71
*Honours:* France 70 full caps.

| | | | | | |
|---|---|---|---|---|---|
| 1991–92 | Toulouse | 26 | 0 | **26** | **0** |
| 1992–93 | Marseille | 30 | 0 | | |
| 1993–94 | Marseille | 37 | 0 | | |
| 1994–95 | Marseille | 39 | 0 | **106** | **0** |

1995–96 Monaco 21 0
1996–97 Monaco 36 0
1997–98 Monaco 30 0
1998–99 Monaco 32 0
1999–2000 Monaco 24 0 **143 0**
2000–01 Manchester U 30 0
2001–02 Manchester U 32 0
2002–03 Manchester U 30 0
2003–04 Manchester U 0 0 **92 0**

**BELLION, David (F) 34 3**
H: 6 0 W: 11 09 b.Sevres 27-11-82
*Source:* Cannes.
2001–02 Sunderland 9 0
2002–03 Sunderland 11 1 **20 1**
2003–04 Manchester U 14 2 **14 2**

**BROWN, Wes (D) 100 0**
H: 6 1 W: 13 11 b.Manchester 13-10-79
*Source:* Trainee. *Honours:* England Schools, Youth, Under-21, 7 full caps.
1996–97 Manchester U 0 0
1997–98 Manchester U 2 0
1998–99 Manchester U 14 0
1999–2000 Manchester U 0 0
2000–01 Manchester U 28 0
2001–02 Manchester U 17 0
2002–03 Manchester U 22 0
2003–04 Manchester U 17 0 **100 0**

**BUTT, Nicky (M) 270 21**
H: 5 10 W: 11 11 b.Manchester 21-1-75
*Source:* Trainee. *Honours:* England Schools, Youth, Under-21, 35 full caps.
1992–93 Manchester U 1 0
1993–94 Manchester U 1 0
1994–95 Manchester U 22 1
1995–96 Manchester U 32 2
1996–97 Manchester U 26 5
1997–98 Manchester U 33 3
1998–99 Manchester U 31 2
1999–2000 Manchester U 32 3
2000–01 Manchester U 28 3
2001–02 Manchester U 25 1
2002–03 Manchester U 18 0
2003–04 Manchester U 21 1 **270 21**

**BYRNE, Danny‡ (F) 2 0**
H: 5 9 W: 10 06 b.Frimley 30-11-84
*Source:* Trainee.
2003–04 Manchester U 0 0
2003–04 *Hartlepool U* 2 0 **2 0**

**CALLISTE, Ramon (F) 0 0**
H: 5 10 W: 11 06 b.Cardiff 16-12-85
*Source:* Trainee.
2003–04 Manchester U 0 0

**CARROLL, Roy (G) 204 0**
H: 6 2 W: 13 12 b.Enniskillen 30-9-77
*Source:* Trainee. *Honours:* Northern Ireland Youth, Under-21, 14 full caps.
1995–96 Hull C 23 0
1996–97 Hull C 23 0 **46 0**
1996–97 Wigan Ath 0 0
1997–98 Wigan Ath 29 0
1998–99 Wigan Ath 43 0
1999–2000 Wigan Ath 34 0
2000–01 Wigan Ath 29 0 **135 0**
2001–02 Manchester U 7 0
2002–03 Manchester U 10 0
2003–04 Manchester U 6 0 **23 0**

**CHADWICK, Luke (F) 76 8**
H: 5 11 W: 11 08 b.Cambridge 18-11-80
*Source:* Trainee. *Honours:* England Youth, Under-21.
1998–99 Manchester U 0 0
1999–2000 Manchester U 0 0
2000–01 Manchester U 16 2
2001–02 Manchester U 8 0
2002–03 Manchester U 1 0
2002–03 *Reading* 15 1 **15 1**
2003–04 Manchester U 0 0 **25 2**
2003–04 *Burnley* 36 5 **36 5**

**COLLETT, Ben (D) 0 0**
H: 5 8 W: 10 00 b.Bury 11-9-84
*Source:* Trainee.
2003–04 Manchester U 0 0

**COOPER, Kenny (F) 0 0**
H: 6 3 W: 14 01 b.Baltimore 21-10-84
2003–04 Manchester U 0 0

**DJEMBA-DJEMBA, Eric (M) 57 1**
H: 5 9 W: 11 13 b.Douala 4-5-81
*Source:* Kadji Sport, UCB Douala. *Honours:* Cameroon full caps.
2001–02 Nantes 14 0
2002–03 Nantes 28 1 **42 1**
2003–04 Manchester U 15 0 **15 0**

**DJORDJIC, Bojan (F) 6 0**
H: 5 10 W: 11 01 b.Belgrade 6-2-82
1998–99 Manchester U 0 0
1999–2000 Manchester U 0 0
2000–01 Manchester U 1 0
2001–02 Manchester U 0 0
2001–02 *Sheffield W* 5 0 **5 0**
2002–03 Manchester U 0 0
2003–04 Manchester U 0 0 **1 0**

**EAGLES, Chris (M) 0 0**
H: 6 0 W: 10 08 b.Hemel Hempstead 19-11-85
*Source:* Trainee. *Honours:* England Youth.
2003–04 Manchester U 0 0

**FERDINAND, Rio (D) 239 4**
H: 6 2 W: 13 12 b.Peckham 7-11-78
*Source:* Trainee. *Honours:* England Youth, Under-21, 33 full caps, 1 goal.
1995–96 West Ham U 1 0
1996–97 West Ham U 15 2
1996–97 *Bournemouth* 10 0 **10 0**
1997–98 West Ham U 35 0
1998–99 West Ham U 31 0
1999–2000 West Ham U 33 0
2000–01 West Ham U 12 0 **127 2**
2000–01 Leeds U 23 2
2001–02 Leeds U 31 0 **54 2**
2002–03 Manchester U 28 0
2003–04 Manchester U 20 0 **48 0**

**FLETCHER, Darren (M) 22 0**
H: 6 0 W: 13 01 b.Edinburgh 1-2-84
*Source:* Scholar. *Honours:* Scotland Under-21, 8 full caps, 2 goals.
2000–01 Manchester U 0 0
2001–02 Manchester U 0 0
2002–03 Manchester U 0 0
2003–04 Manchester U 22 0 **22 0**

**FORLAN, Diego (F) 139 46**
H: 5 8 W: 11 11 b.Montevideo 19-5-79
*Honours:* Uruguay 13 full caps, 7 goals.
1998–99 Independiente 2 0
1999–2000 Independiente 24 7
2000–01 Independiente 36 18
2001–02 Independiente 15 11 **77 36**
2001–02 Manchester U 13 0
2002–03 Manchester U 25 6
2003–04 Manchester U 24 4 **62 10**

**FORTUNE, Quinton (F) 155 13**
H: 5 9 W: 11 09 b.Cape Town 21-5-77
*Source:* Kaizer Chiefs, Tottenham H schoolboy. *Honours:* South Africa 43 full caps, 1 goal.
1995–96 Mallorca 8 1 **8 1**
1995–96 Atletico Madrid 3 0
1996–97 Atletico Madrid B 30 2
1996–97 Atletico Madrid 2 0
1997–98 Atletico Madrid B 31 1
1997–98 Atletico Madrid 0 0
1998–99 Atletico Madrid 2 0
1998–99 Atletico Madrid B 20 4 **7 0**
1999–2000 Manchester U 6 2
2000–01 Manchester U 7 2
2001–02 Manchester U 14 1
2002–03 Manchester U 9 0
2003–04 Manchester U 23 0 **59 5**

**FOX, David (M) 0 0**
H: 5 9 W: 12 02 b.Stoke 13-12-83
*Source:* Scholar. *Honours:* England Youth, Under-20.
2000–01 Manchester U 0 0
2001–02 Manchester U 0 0
2002–03 Manchester U 0 0
2003–04 Manchester U 0 0

**GIGGS, Ryan (F) 415 86**
H: 5 11 W: 11 00 b.Cardiff 29-11-73
*Source:* School. *Honours:* England Schools, Wales Youth, Under-21, 48 full caps, 8 goals.
1990–91 Manchester U 2 1
1991–92 Manchester U 38 4
1992–93 Manchester U 41 9
1993–94 Manchester U 38 13
1994–95 Manchester U 29 1
1995–96 Manchester U 33 11
1996–97 Manchester U 26 3
1997–98 Manchester U 29 8
1998–99 Manchester U 24 3
1999–2000 Manchester U 30 6
2000–01 Manchester U 31 5
2001–02 Manchester U 25 7
2002–03 Manchester U 36 8
2003–04 Manchester U 33 7 **415 86**

**HEATH, Colin (F) 0 0**
H: 6 0 W: 13 01 b.Chesterfield 31-12-83
*Source:* Scholar.
2000–01 Manchester U 0 0
2001–02 Manchester U 0 0
2002–03 Manchester U 0 0
2003–04 Manchester U 0 0

**HEATON, Tom (G) 0 0**
H: 6 1 W: 13 06 b.Chester 15-4-86
*Source:* Trainee. *Honours:* England Youth.
2003–04 Manchester U 0 0

**HOWARD, Tim (G) 117 0**
H: 6 3 W: 14 12 b.North Brunswick 6-3-79
*Honours:* USA 10 full caps.
1998 NY/NJ MetroStars 1 0
1999 NY/NJ MetroStars 9 0
2000 NY/NJ MetroStars 9 0
2001 NY/NJ MetroStars 26 0
2002 NY/NJ MetroStars 27 0
2003 NY/NJ MetroStars 13 0 **85 0**
2003–04 Manchester U 32 0 **32 0**

**JOHNSON, Eddie (F) 0 0**
H: 5 10 W: 13 05 b.Chester 20-9-84
*Source:* Scholar. *Honours:* England Youth, Under-20.
2001–02 Manchester U 0 0
2002–03 Manchester U 0 0
2003–04 Manchester U 0 0

**JONES, David (M) 0 0**
H: 5 11 W: 10 00 b.Southport 4-11-84
*Source:* Trainee. *Honours:* England Youth, Under-21.
2003–04 Manchester U 0 0

**JOWSEY, James* (G) 0 0**
H: 6 0 W: 12 04 b.Scarborough 24-11-83
*Source:* Scholar.
2000–01 Manchester U 0 0
2001–02 Manchester U 0 0
2002–03 Manchester U 0 0
2003–04 Manchester U 0 0

**KEANE, Roy (M) 404 54**
H: 5 11 W: 11 10 b.Cork 10-8-71
*Source:* Cobh Ramb. *Honours:* Eire Youth, Under-21, 59 full caps, 9 goals.
1990–91 Nottingham F 35 8
1991–92 Nottingham F 39 8
1992–93 Nottingham F 40 6 **114 22**
1993–94 Manchester U 37 5
1994–95 Manchester U 25 2
1995–96 Manchester U 29 6
1996–97 Manchester U 21 2
1997–98 Manchester U 9 2
1998–99 Manchester U 35 2
1999–2000 Manchester U 29 5
2000–01 Manchester U 28 2
2001–02 Manchester U 28 3
2002–03 Manchester U 21 0
2003–04 Manchester U 28 3 **290 32**

**KLEBERSON, Jose (M) 112 14**
H: 5 9 W: 10 00 b.Urai 19-6-79
*Honours:* Brazil 21 full caps, 2 goals.
1999 Atletico PR 14 1
2000 Atletico PR 24 4
2001 Atletico PR 29 3
2002 Atletico PR 21 4
2003 Atletico PR 12 0 **100 12**
2003–04 Manchester U 12 2 **12 2**

**LAWRENCE, Lee (D) 0 0**
H: 5 7 W: 9 02 b.Boston 1-12-84
*Source:* Trainee.
2002–03 Manchester U 0 0
2003–04 Manchester U 0 0

**LYNCH, Mark (D)** **20 0**

H: 5 11 W: 11 03 b.Manchester 2-9-81

*Source:* Trainee.

| | | | | | |
|---|---|---|---|---|---|
| 1999–2000 | Manchester U | 0 | 0 | | |
| 2000–01 | Manchester U | 0 | 0 | | |
| 2001–02 | Manchester U | 0 | 0 | | |
| 2001–02 | *St Johnstone* | 20 | 0 | **20** | **0** |
| 2002–03 | Manchester U | 0 | 0 | | |
| 2003–04 | Manchester U | 0 | 0 | | |

**McSHANE, Paul (D)** **0 0**

H: 5 11 W: 11 05 b.Wicklow 6-1-86

*Source:* Trainee.

| | | | | | |
|---|---|---|---|---|---|
| 2002–03 | Manchester U | 0 | 0 | | |
| 2003–04 | Manchester U | 0 | 0 | | |

**NARDIELLO, Daniel (F)** **20 7**

H: 5 11 W: 11 06 b.Coventry 22-10-82

*Source:* Trainee.

| | | | | | |
|---|---|---|---|---|---|
| 1999–2000 | Manchester U | 0 | 0 | | |
| 2000–01 | Manchester U | 0 | 0 | | |
| 2001–02 | Manchester U | 0 | 0 | | |
| 2002–03 | Manchester U | 0 | 0 | | |
| 2003–04 | Manchester U | 0 | 0 | | |
| 2003–04 | *Swansea C* | 4 | 0 | **4** | **0** |
| 2003–04 | *Barnsley* | 16 | 7 | **16** | **7** |

**NEUMAYR, Marcus (M)** **0 0**

H: 5 11 W: 11 05 b.Aschaffenburg 26-3-86

*Source:* Scholar.

| | | | | | |
|---|---|---|---|---|---|
| 2003–04 | Manchester U | 0 | 0 | | |

**NEVILLE, Gary (D)** **293 5**

H: 5 11 W: 12 04 b.Bury 18-2-75

*Source:* Trainee. *Honours:* England Youth, 67 full caps.

| | | | | | |
|---|---|---|---|---|---|
| 1992–93 | Manchester U | 0 | 0 | | |
| 1993–94 | Manchester U | 1 | 0 | | |
| 1994–95 | Manchester U | 18 | 0 | | |
| 1995–96 | Manchester U | 31 | 0 | | |
| 1996–97 | Manchester U | 31 | 1 | | |
| 1997–98 | Manchester U | 34 | 0 | | |
| 1998–99 | Manchester U | 34 | 1 | | |
| 1999–2000 | Manchester U | 22 | 0 | | |
| 2000–01 | Manchester U | 32 | 1 | | |
| 2001–02 | Manchester U | 34 | 0 | | |
| 2002–03 | Manchester U | 26 | 0 | | |
| 2003–04 | Manchester U | 30 | 2 | **293** | **5** |

**NEVILLE, Phil (D)** **244 5**

H: 5 11 W: 12 00 b.Bury 21-1-77

*Source:* Trainee. *Honours:* England Schools, Youth, Under-21, 50 full caps.

| | | | | | |
|---|---|---|---|---|---|
| 1994–95 | Manchester U | 2 | 0 | | |
| 1995–96 | Manchester U | 24 | 0 | | |
| 1996–97 | Manchester U | 18 | 0 | | |
| 1997–98 | Manchester U | 30 | 1 | | |
| 1998–99 | Manchester U | 28 | 0 | | |
| 1999–2000 | Manchester U | 29 | 0 | | |
| 2000–01 | Manchester U | 29 | 1 | | |
| 2001–02 | Manchester U | 28 | 2 | | |
| 2002–03 | Manchester U | 25 | 1 | | |
| 2003–04 | Manchester U | 31 | 0 | **244** | **5** |

**O'SHEA, John (D)** **84 3**

H: 6 3 W: 12 10 b.Waterford 30-4-81

*Source:* Waterford. *Honours:* Eire Under-21, 14 full caps, 1 goal.

| | | | | | |
|---|---|---|---|---|---|
| 1998–99 | Manchester U | 0 | 0 | | |
| 1999–2000 | Manchester U | 0 | 0 | | |
| 1999–2000 | *Bournemouth* | 10 | 1 | **10** | **1** |
| 2000–01 | Manchester U | 0 | 0 | | |
| 2001–02 | Manchester U | 9 | 0 | | |
| 2002–03 | Manchester U | 32 | 0 | | |
| 2003–04 | Manchester U | 33 | 2 | **74** | **2** |

**POOLE, David (F)** **0 0**

H: 5 8 W: 12 00 b.Manchester 12-11-84

*Source:* Trainee.

| | | | | | |
|---|---|---|---|---|---|
| 2002–03 | Manchester U | 0 | 0 | | |
| 2003–04 | Manchester U | 0 | 0 | | |

**PORT, Graeme (M)** **0 0**

H: 5 10 W: 10 12 b.York 13-4-86

*Source:* Trainee.

| | | | | | |
|---|---|---|---|---|---|
| 2003–04 | Manchester U | 0 | 0 | | |

**PUGH, Danny (D)** **1 0**

H: 6 0 W: 12 10 b.Manchester 19-10-82

*Source:* Scholar.

| | | | | | |
|---|---|---|---|---|---|
| 2000–01 | Manchester U | 0 | 0 | | |
| 2001–02 | Manchester U | 0 | 0 | | |
| 2002–03 | Manchester U | 1 | 0 | | |
| 2003–04 | Manchester U | 0 | 0 | **1** | **0** |

**RICARDO (G)** **119 0**

H: 6 2 W: 13 12 b.Madrid 31-12-71

*Honours:* Spain 1 full cap.

| | | | | | |
|---|---|---|---|---|---|
| 1994–95 | Atletico Madrid B | 29 | 0 | | |
| 1995–96 | Atletico Madrid | 0 | 0 | | |
| 1996–97 | Atletico Madrid | 1 | 0 | | |
| 1997–98 | Atletico Madrid B | 35 | 0 | **1** | **0** |
| 1998–99 | Valladolid | 0 | 0 | | |
| 1999–2000 | Valladolid | 3 | 0 | | |
| 2000–01 | Valladolid | 12 | 0 | | |
| 2001–02 | Valladolid | 38 | 0 | **53** | **0** |
| 2002–03 | Manchester U | 1 | 0 | | |
| 2003–04 | Manchester U | 0 | 0 | **1** | **0** |

**RICHARDSON, Kieran (M)** **2 0**

H: 5 8 W: 11 00 b.Greenwich 21-10-84

*Source:* Scholar.

| | | | | | |
|---|---|---|---|---|---|
| 2002–03 | Manchester U | 2 | 0 | | |
| 2003–04 | Manchester U | 0 | 0 | **2** | **0** |

**RONALDO, Cristiano (F)** **54 7**

H: 6 1 W: 12 04 b.Funchal 5-2-85

*Honours:* Portugal 13 full caps, 2 goals.

| | | | | | |
|---|---|---|---|---|---|
| 2002–03 | Sporting Lisbon | 25 | 3 | **25** | **3** |
| 2003–04 | Manchester U | 29 | 4 | **29** | **4** |

**SAHA, Louis (F)** **187 66**

H: 6 1 W: 12 06 b.Paris 8-8-78

*Honours:* France 5 full caps, 2 goals.

| | | | | | |
|---|---|---|---|---|---|
| 1997–98 | Metz | 21 | 1 | | |
| 1998–99 | Metz | 3 | 0 | | |
| 1998–99 | Newcastle U | 11 | 1 | **11** | **1** |
| 1999–2000 | Metz | 23 | 4 | **47** | **5** |
| 2000–01 | Fulham | 43 | 27 | | |
| 2001–02 | Fulham | 36 | 8 | | |
| 2002–03 | Fulham | 17 | 5 | | |
| 2003–04 | Fulham | 21 | 13 | **117** | **53** |
| 2003–04 | Manchester U | 12 | 7 | **12** | **7** |

**SCHOLES, Paul (M)** **288 78**

H: 5 7 W: 11 00 b.Salford 16-11-74

*Source:* Trainee. *Honours:* England Youth, 66 full caps, 14 goals.

| | | | | | |
|---|---|---|---|---|---|
| 1992–93 | Manchester U | 0 | 0 | | |
| 1993–94 | Manchester U | 0 | 0 | | |
| 1994–95 | Manchester U | 17 | 5 | | |
| 1995–96 | Manchester U | 26 | 10 | | |
| 1996–97 | Manchester U | 24 | 3 | | |
| 1997–98 | Manchester U | 31 | 8 | | |
| 1998–99 | Manchester U | 31 | 6 | | |
| 1999–2000 | Manchester U | 31 | 9 | | |
| 2000–01 | Manchester U | 32 | 6 | | |
| 2001–02 | Manchester U | 35 | 8 | | |
| 2002–03 | Manchester U | 33 | 14 | | |
| 2003–04 | Manchester U | 28 | 9 | **288** | **78** |

**SILVESTRE, Mikael (D)** **231 3**

H: 6 0 W: 13 01 b.Chambray les Tours 9-8-77

*Honours:* France 34 full caps, 2 goals.

| | | | | | |
|---|---|---|---|---|---|
| 1995–96 | Rennes | 1 | 0 | | |
| 1996–97 | Rennes | 16 | 0 | | |
| 1997–98 | Rennes | 32 | 0 | **49** | **0** |
| 1998–99 | Internazionale | 18 | 1 | **18** | **1** |
| 1999–2000 | Manchester U | 31 | 0 | | |
| 2000–01 | Manchester U | 30 | 1 | | |
| 2001–02 | Manchester U | 35 | 0 | | |
| 2002–03 | Manchester U | 34 | 1 | | |
| 2003–04 | Manchester U | 34 | 0 | **164** | **2** |

**SIMS, Lee‡ (D)** **0 0**

H: 5 9 W: 10 08 b.Manchester 6-9-84

*Source:* Trainee.

| | | | | | |
|---|---|---|---|---|---|
| 2002–03 | Manchester U | 0 | 0 | | |
| 2003–04 | Manchester U | 0 | 0 | | |

**SOLSKJAER, Ole Gunnar (F)** **255 115**

H: 5 10 W: 11 11 b.Kristiansund 26-2-73

*Honours:* Norway Under-21, 62 full caps, 21 goals.

| | | | | | |
|---|---|---|---|---|---|
| 1995 | Molde | 26 | 20 | | |
| 1996 | Molde | 16 | 11 | **42** | **31** |
| 1996–97 | Manchester U | 33 | 18 | | |
| 1997–98 | Manchester U | 22 | 6 | | |
| 1998–99 | Manchester U | 19 | 12 | | |
| 1999–2000 | Manchester U | 28 | 12 | | |
| 2000–01 | Manchester U | 31 | 10 | | |
| 2001–02 | Manchester U | 30 | 17 | | |
| 2002–03 | Manchester U | 37 | 9 | | |
| 2003–04 | Manchester U | 13 | 0 | **213** | **84** |

**SPECTOR, Jonathan (D)** **0 0**

H: 6 0 W: 12 08 b.Arlington Heights 1-3-86

| | | | | | |
|---|---|---|---|---|---|
| 2003–04 | Manchester U | 0 | 0 | | |

**STEELE, Luke (G)** **2 0**

H: 6 2 W: 12 00 b.Peterborough 24-9-84

*Source:* Scholar. *Honours:* England Youth.

| | | | | | |
|---|---|---|---|---|---|
| 2001–02 | Peterborough U | 2 | 0 | **2** | **0** |
| 2001–02 | Manchester U | 0 | 0 | | |
| 2002–03 | Manchester U | 0 | 0 | | |
| 2003–04 | Manchester U | 0 | 0 | | |

**STEWART, Michael (M)** **20 0**

H: 5 11 W: 11 11 b.Edinburgh 26-2-81

*Source:* Trainee. *Honours:* Scotland Schools, Under-21, 3 full caps.

| | | | | | |
|---|---|---|---|---|---|
| 1997–98 | Manchester U | 0 | 0 | | |
| 1998–99 | Manchester U | 0 | 0 | | |
| 1999–2000 | Manchester U | 0 | 0 | | |
| 2000–01 | Manchester U | 3 | 0 | | |
| 2001–02 | Manchester U | 3 | 0 | | |
| 2002–03 | Manchester U | 1 | 0 | | |
| 2003–04 | Manchester U | 0 | 0 | **7** | **0** |
| 2003–04 | *Nottingham F* | 13 | 0 | **13** | **0** |

**TIERNEY, Paul (D)** **19 1**

H: 5 10 W: 12 05 b.Salford 15-9-82

*Source:* Scholar. *Honours:* Eire Under-21.

| | | | | | |
|---|---|---|---|---|---|
| 2000–01 | Manchester U | 0 | 0 | | |
| 2001–02 | Manchester U | 0 | 0 | | |
| 2002–03 | Manchester U | 0 | 0 | | |
| 2002–03 | *Crewe Alex* | 17 | 1 | **17** | **1** |
| 2003–04 | Manchester U | 0 | 0 | | |
| 2003–04 | *Colchester U* | 2 | 0 | **2** | **0** |

**TIMM, Mads (F)** **0 0**

H: 5 9 W: 12 10 b.Odense 31-10-84

*Source:* Scholar.

| | | | | | |
|---|---|---|---|---|---|
| 2001–02 | Manchester U | 0 | 0 | | |
| 2002–03 | Manchester U | 0 | 0 | | |
| 2003–04 | Manchester U | 0 | 0 | | |

**VAN NISTELROOY, Ruud (F)** **265 160**

H: 6 2 W: 12 13 b.Oss 1-7-76

*Source:* Nooit Gedacht, Margriet. *Honours:* Holland 38 full caps, 18 goals.

| | | | | | |
|---|---|---|---|---|---|
| 1993–94 | Den Bosch | 2 | 0 | | |
| 1994–95 | Den Bosch | 15 | 3 | | |
| 1995–96 | Den Bosch | 21 | 2 | | |
| 1996–97 | Den Bosch | 31 | 12 | **69** | **17** |
| 1997–98 | Heerenveen | 31 | 13 | **31** | **13** |
| 1998–99 | PSV Eindhoven | 34 | 31 | | |
| 1999–2000 | PSV Eindhoven | 23 | 29 | | |
| 2000–01 | PSV Eindhoven | 10 | 2 | **67** | **62** |
| 2001–02 | Manchester U | 32 | 23 | | |
| 2002–03 | Manchester U | 34 | 25 | | |
| 2003–04 | Manchester U | 32 | 20 | **98** | **68** |

**WILLIAMS, Ben* (G)** **24 0**

H: 6 0 W: 13 01 b.Manchester 27-8-82

*Source:* Scholar. *Honours:* England Schools.

| | | | | | |
|---|---|---|---|---|---|
| 2001–02 | Manchester U | 0 | 0 | | |
| 2002–03 | Manchester U | 0 | 0 | | |
| 2002–03 | *Coventry C* | 0 | 0 | | |
| 2002–03 | *Chesterfield* | 14 | 0 | **14** | **0** |
| 2003–04 | Manchester U | 0 | 0 | | |
| 2003–04 | *Crewe Alex* | 10 | 0 | **10** | **0** |

**WOOD, Neil* (M)** **13 2**

H: 5 10 W: 13 02 b.Manchester 4-1-83

*Source:* Trainee. *Honours:* England Youth.

| | | | | | |
|---|---|---|---|---|---|
| 1999–2000 | Manchester U | 0 | 0 | | |
| 2000–01 | Manchester U | 0 | 0 | | |
| 2001–02 | Manchester U | 0 | 0 | | |
| 2002–03 | Manchester U | 0 | 0 | | |
| 2003–04 | Manchester U | 0 | 0 | | |
| 2003–04 | *Peterborough U* | 3 | 1 | **3** | **1** |
| 2003–04 | *Burnley* | 10 | 1 | **10** | **1** |

**Scholars**

Ebanks-Blake, Sylvan; Eckersley, Adam J; Hogg, Steven R; Howard, Mark J; Jones, Richard G; Lee, Thomas E; Marsh, Philip; Martin, Lee R; Moran, Kyle M; N'Galula, Floribert; Picken, Philip J; Puustinen, Jami P; Simpson, Daniel P

## MANSFIELD T (49)

**ARTELL, Dave (D) 91 8**
H: 6 2 W: 13 00 b.Rotherham 22-11-80
*Source:* Trainee.

| | | | | | |
|---|---|---|---|---|---|
| 1999–2000 | Rotherham U | 1 | 0 | | |
| 2000–01 | Rotherham U | 36 | 4 | | |
| 2001–02 | Rotherham U | 0 | 0 | | |
| 2002–03 | Rotherham U | 0 | 0 | **37** | **4** |
| 2002–03 | *Shrewsbury T* | 28 | 1 | **28** | **1** |
| 2003–04 | Mansfield T | 26 | 3 | **26** | **3** |

**BEARDSLEY, Chris* (F) 20 1**
H: 6 0 W: 12 00 b.Derby 28-2-84
*Source:* Scholar.

| | | | | | |
|---|---|---|---|---|---|
| 2002–03 | Mansfield T | 5 | 0 | | |
| 2003–04 | Mansfield T | 15 | 1 | **20** | **1** |

**BUXTON, Jake (D) 12 1**
H: 6 1 W: 12 13 b.Sutton-in-Ashfield 4-3-85
*Source:* Scholar.

| | | | | | |
|---|---|---|---|---|---|
| 2002–03 | Mansfield T | 3 | 0 | | |
| 2003–04 | Mansfield T | 9 | 1 | **12** | **1** |

**CHRISTIE, Iyseden* (F) 216 56**
H: 5 10 W: 12 02 b.Coventry 14-11-76
*Source:* Trainee.

| | | | | | |
|---|---|---|---|---|---|
| 1994–95 | Coventry C | 0 | 0 | | |
| 1995–96 | Coventry C | 1 | 0 | | |
| 1996–97 | Coventry C | 0 | 0 | **1** | **0** |
| 1996–97 | *Bournemouth* | 4 | 0 | **4** | **0** |
| 1996–97 | *Mansfield T* | 8 | 0 | | |
| 1997–98 | Mansfield T | 39 | 10 | | |
| 1998–99 | Mansfield T | 42 | 8 | | |
| 1999–2000 | Leyton Orient | 36 | 7 | | |
| 2000–01 | Leyton Orient | 7 | 2 | | |
| 2001–02 | Leyton Orient | 15 | 3 | **58** | **12** |
| 2002–03 | Mansfield T | 37 | 18 | | |
| 2003–04 | Mansfield T | 27 | 8 | **153** | **44** |

**CLARKE, Jamie* (D) 34 1**
H: 6 2 W: 12 09 b.Sunderland 18-9-82
*Source:* Scholar.

| | | | | | |
|---|---|---|---|---|---|
| 2001–02 | Mansfield T | 1 | 0 | | |
| 2002–03 | Mansfield T | 21 | 1 | | |
| 2003–04 | Mansfield T | 12 | 0 | **34** | **1** |

**CORDEN, Wayne (M) 234 33**
H: 5 10 W: 11 08 b.Leek 1-11-75
*Source:* Trainee.

| | | | | | |
|---|---|---|---|---|---|
| 1994–95 | Port Vale | 1 | 0 | | |
| 1995–96 | Port Vale | 2 | 0 | | |
| 1996–97 | Port Vale | 12 | 0 | | |
| 1997–98 | Port Vale | 33 | 1 | | |
| 1998–99 | Port Vale | 16 | 0 | | |
| 1999–2000 | Port Vale | 2 | 0 | **66** | **1** |
| 2000–01 | Mansfield T | 34 | 3 | | |
| 2001–02 | Mansfield T | 46 | 8 | | |
| 2002–03 | Mansfield T | 44 | 13 | | |
| 2003–04 | Mansfield T | 44 | 8 | **168** | **32** |

**CURLE, Keith† (D) 705 34**
H: 6 0 W: 12 07 b.Bristol 14-11-63
*Source:* Apprentice. *Honours:* England B, 3 full caps.

| | | | | | |
|---|---|---|---|---|---|
| 1981–82 | Bristol R | 20 | 2 | | |
| 1982–83 | Bristol R | 12 | 2 | | |
| 1983–84 | Bristol R | 0 | 0 | **32** | **4** |
| 1983–84 | Torquay U | 16 | 5 | **16** | **5** |
| 1983–84 | Bristol C | 6 | 0 | | |
| 1984–85 | Bristol C | 40 | 0 | | |
| 1985–86 | Bristol C | 44 | 1 | | |
| 1986–87 | Bristol C | 28 | 0 | | |
| 1987–88 | Bristol C | 3 | 0 | **121** | **1** |
| 1987–88 | Reading | 30 | 0 | | |
| 1988–89 | Reading | 10 | 0 | **40** | **0** |
| 1988–89 | Wimbledon | 18 | 0 | | |
| 1989–90 | Wimbledon | 38 | 2 | | |
| 1990–91 | Wimbledon | 37 | 1 | **93** | **3** |
| 1991–92 | Manchester C | 40 | 5 | | |
| 1992–93 | Manchester C | 39 | 3 | | |
| 1993–94 | Manchester C | 29 | 1 | | |
| 1994–95 | Manchester C | 31 | 2 | | |
| 1995–96 | Manchester C | 32 | 0 | **171** | **11** |
| 1996–97 | Wolverhampton W | 21 | 2 | | |
| 1997–98 | Wolverhampton W | 40 | 1 | | |
| 1998–99 | Wolverhampton W | 44 | 4 | | |
| 1999–2000 | Wolverhampton W | 45 | 2 | **150** | **9** |
| 2000–01 | Sheffield U | 25 | 0 | | |
| 2001–02 | Sheffield U | 32 | 1 | **57** | **1** |
| 2002–03 | Barnsley | 11 | 0 | **11** | **0** |
| 2002–03 | Mansfield T | 14 | 0 | | |
| 2003–04 | Mansfield T | 0 | 0 | **14** | **0** |

**CURLE, Thomas§ (M) 1 0**
H: 5 10 W: 10 00 b.Bristol 3-3-86
*Source:* Scholar.

| | | | | | |
|---|---|---|---|---|---|
| 2003–04 | Mansfield T | 1 | 0 | **1** | **0** |

**CURTIS, Tom# (M) 326 12**
H: 5 10 W: 12 00 b.Exeter 1-3-73
*Source:* School.

| | | | | | |
|---|---|---|---|---|---|
| 1991–92 | Derby Co | 0 | 0 | | |
| 1992–93 | Derby Co | 0 | 0 | | |
| 1993–94 | Chesterfield | 36 | 3 | | |
| 1994–95 | Chesterfield | 40 | 2 | | |
| 1995–96 | Chesterfield | 46 | 0 | | |
| 1996–97 | Chesterfield | 40 | 3 | | |
| 1997–98 | Chesterfield | 36 | 1 | | |
| 1998–99 | Chesterfield | 24 | 3 | | |
| 1999–2000 | Chesterfield | 18 | 0 | **240** | **12** |
| 2000–01 | Portsmouth | 4 | 0 | | |
| 2001–02 | Portsmouth | 9 | 0 | | |
| 2001–02 | *Walsall* | 4 | 0 | **4** | **0** |
| 2002–03 | Portsmouth | 0 | 0 | **13** | **0** |
| 2002–03 | *Tranmere R* | 8 | 0 | **8** | **0** |
| 2002–03 | Mansfield T | 23 | 0 | | |
| 2003–04 | Mansfield T | 38 | 0 | **61** | **0** |

**D'JAFFO, Laurent* (F) 213 43**
H: 6 0 W: 14 00 b.Aquitane 5-11-70
*Honours:* Benin full caps.

| | | | | | |
|---|---|---|---|---|---|
| 1991–92 | Montpellier | 11 | 2 | | |
| 1992–93 | Montpellier | 5 | 0 | | |
| 1993–94 | Montpellier | 12 | 1 | | |
| 1994–95 | Montpellier | 8 | 0 | **36** | **3** |
| From Niort | | | | | |
| 1997–98 | Ayr U | 24 | 10 | **24** | **10** |
| 1998–99 | Bury | 37 | 8 | **37** | **8** |
| 1999–2000 | Stockport Co | 21 | 7 | **21** | **7** |
| 1999–2000 | Sheffield U | 15 | 1 | | |
| 2000–01 | Sheffield U | 22 | 5 | | |
| 2001–02 | Sheffield U | 32 | 5 | **69** | **11** |
| 2002–03 | Aberdeen | 18 | 3 | **18** | **3** |
| 2003–04 | Mansfield T | 8 | 1 | **8** | **1** |

**DAY, Rhys (D) 73 7**
H: 6 2 W: 12 08 b.Bridgend 31-8-82
*Source:* Scholarship. *Honours:* Wales Under-21.

| | | | | | |
|---|---|---|---|---|---|
| 1999–2000 | Manchester C | 0 | 0 | | |
| 2000–01 | Manchester C | 0 | 0 | | |
| 2001–02 | Manchester C | 0 | 0 | | |
| 2001–02 | *Blackpool* | 9 | 0 | **9** | **0** |
| 2002–03 | Manchester C | 0 | 0 | | |
| 2002–03 | Mansfield T | 23 | 1 | | |
| 2003–04 | Mansfield T | 41 | 6 | **64** | **7** |

**DIMECH, Luke# (D) 20 1**
H: 5 11 W: 13 04 b.Malta 11-1-77
*Source:* Shamrock R. *Honours:* Malta 28 full caps.

| | | | | | |
|---|---|---|---|---|---|
| 2003–04 | Mansfield T | 20 | 1 | **20** | **1** |

**DISLEY, Craig (M) 141 16**
H: 5 10 W: 11 00 b.Worksop 24-8-81
*Source:* Trainee.

| | | | | | |
|---|---|---|---|---|---|
| 1999–2000 | Mansfield T | 5 | 0 | | |
| 2000–01 | Mansfield T | 24 | 0 | | |
| 2001–02 | Mansfield T | 36 | 7 | | |
| 2002–03 | Mansfield T | 42 | 4 | | |
| 2003–04 | Mansfield T | 34 | 5 | **141** | **16** |

**EATON, Adam# (D) 37 0**
H: 5 10 W: 11 08 b.Liverpool 2-5-80
*Source:* Trainee.

| | | | | | |
|---|---|---|---|---|---|
| 1997–98 | Everton | 0 | 0 | | |
| 1998–99 | Everton | 0 | 0 | | |
| 1999–2000 | Preston NE | 0 | 0 | | |
| 2000–01 | Preston NE | 1 | 0 | | |
| 2001–02 | Preston NE | 12 | 0 | | |
| 2002–03 | Preston NE | 1 | 0 | **14** | **0** |
| 2002–03 | Mansfield T | 20 | 0 | | |
| 2003–04 | Mansfield T | 3 | 0 | **23** | **0** |

**HANKEY, Dean§ (M) 1 0**
H: 5 8 W: 10 10 b.Sutton-in-Ashfield 23-8-86
*Source:* Scholar.

| | | | | | |
|---|---|---|---|---|---|
| 2002–03 | Mansfield T | 1 | 0 | | |
| 2003–04 | Mansfield T | 0 | 0 | **1** | **0** |

**HASSELL, Bobby# (D) 160 3**
H: 5 9 W: 12 06 b.Derby 4-6-80
*Source:* Trainee.

| | | | | | |
|---|---|---|---|---|---|
| 1997–98 | Mansfield T | 9 | 0 | | |
| 1998–99 | Mansfield T | 3 | 0 | | |
| 1999–2000 | Mansfield T | 11 | 1 | | |
| 2000–01 | Mansfield T | 40 | 1 | | |
| 2001–02 | Mansfield T | 43 | 1 | | |
| 2002–03 | Mansfield T | 20 | 0 | | |
| 2003–04 | Mansfield T | 34 | 0 | **160** | **3** |

**HURST, Mark§ (D) 1 0**
H: 5 11 W: 11 08 b.Mansfield 18-2-85
*Source:* Scholar.

| | | | | | |
|---|---|---|---|---|---|
| 2002–03 | Mansfield T | 1 | 0 | | |
| 2003–04 | Mansfield T | 0 | 0 | **1** | **0** |

**JOHN-BAPTISTE, Alex (D) 21 0**
H: 5 11 W: 11 07 b.Sutton-in-Ashfield 31-1-86
*Source:* Scholar.

| | | | | | |
|---|---|---|---|---|---|
| 2002–03 | Mansfield T | 4 | 0 | | |
| 2003–04 | Mansfield T | 17 | 0 | **21** | **0** |

**JONES, Andy§ (M) 1 0**
H: 5 8 W: 11 07 b.Sutton-in-Ashfield 12-2-86
*Source:* Scholar.

| | | | | | |
|---|---|---|---|---|---|
| 2002–03 | Mansfield T | 1 | 0 | | |
| 2003–04 | Mansfield T | 0 | 0 | **1** | **0** |

**LARKIN, Colin (F) 95 20**
H: 5 9 W: 10 02 b.Dundalk 27-4-82
*Source:* Trainee.

| | | | | | |
|---|---|---|---|---|---|
| 1998–99 | Wolverhampton W | 0 | 0 | | |
| 1999–2000 | Wolverhampton W | 1 | 0 | | |
| 2000–01 | Wolverhampton W | 2 | 0 | | |
| 2001–02 | Wolverhampton W | 0 | 0 | **3** | **0** |
| 2001–02 | *Kidderminster H* | 33 | 6 | **33** | **6** |
| 2002–03 | Mansfield T | 22 | 7 | | |
| 2003–04 | Mansfield T | 37 | 7 | **59** | **14** |

**LAWRENCE, Liam (M) 136 34**
H: 5 10 W: 11 03 b.Retford 14-12-81
*Source:* Trainee.

| | | | | | |
|---|---|---|---|---|---|
| 1999–2000 | Mansfield T | 2 | 0 | | |
| 2000–01 | Mansfield T | 18 | 4 | | |
| 2001–02 | Mansfield T | 32 | 2 | | |
| 2002–03 | Mansfield T | 43 | 10 | | |
| 2003–04 | Mansfield T | 41 | 18 | **136** | **34** |

**MACKENZIE, Neil# (M) 167 9**
H: 6 2 W: 12 05 b.Birmingham 15-4-76
*Source:* WBA schoolboy.

| | | | | | |
|---|---|---|---|---|---|
| 1996–97 | Stoke C | 22 | 1 | | |
| 1997–98 | Stoke C | 12 | 0 | | |
| 1998–99 | Stoke C | 6 | 0 | | |
| 1998–99 | *Cambridge U* | 4 | 1 | | |
| 1999–2000 | Stoke C | 2 | 0 | **42** | **1** |
| 1999–2000 | Cambridge U | 22 | 0 | | |
| 2000–01 | Cambridge U | 6 | 0 | **32** | **1** |
| 2000–01 | Kidderminster H | 23 | 3 | **23** | **3** |
| 2001–02 | Blackpool | 14 | 1 | **14** | **1** |
| 2002–03 | Mansfield T | 24 | 1 | | |
| 2003–04 | Mansfield T | 32 | 2 | **56** | **3** |

**MENDES, Junior# (F) 102 23**
H: 5 10 W: 11 0 b.Balham 15-9-76
*Source:* Trainee.

| | | | | | |
|---|---|---|---|---|---|
| 1995–96 | Chelsea | 0 | 0 | | |
| 1996–97 | Chelsea | 0 | 0 | | |
| 1997–98 | Chelsea | 0 | 0 | | |
| 1998–99 | St Mirren | 22 | 4 | | |
| 1998–99 | *Carlisle U* | 6 | 1 | | |
| 1999–2000 | Carlisle U | 0 | 0 | | |
| 2000–01 | Carlisle U | 0 | 0 | **6** | **1** |
| 2001–02 | Rushden & D | 0 | 0 | | |
| 2002–03 | St Mirren | 17 | 6 | **39** | **10** |
| 2002–03 | Mansfield T | 18 | 1 | | |
| 2003–04 | Mansfield T | 39 | 11 | **57** | **12** |

**MITCHELL, Craig* (F) 16 1**
H: 6 1 W: 12 02 b.Mansfield 6-5-85
*Source:* Scholar.

| | | | | | |
|---|---|---|---|---|---|
| 2002–03 | Mansfield T | 15 | 1 | | |
| 2003–04 | Mansfield T | 1 | 0 | **16** | **1** |

**MULLIGAN, Lance‡ (M) 1 0**
H: 5 7 W: 11 06 b.Sutton-in-Ashfield 21-10-85
*Source:* Scholar.

| | | | | | |
|---|---|---|---|---|---|
| 2003–04 | Mansfield T | 1 | 0 | **1** | **0** |

**PILKINGTON, Kevin (G) 177 0**
H: 6 2 W: 12 10 b.Hitchin 8-3-74
*Source:* Trainee. *Honours:* England Schools.

| | | | | | |
|---|---|---|---|---|---|
| 1992–93 | Manchester U | 0 | 0 | | |
| 1993–94 | Manchester U | 0 | 0 | | |

| | | | | | |
|---|---|---|---|---|---|
| 1994–95 | Manchester U | 1 | 0 | | |
| 1995–96 | Manchester U | 3 | 0 | | |
| 1995–96 | *Rochdale* | 6 | 0 | **6** | **0** |
| 1996–97 | Manchester U | 0 | 0 | | |
| 1996–97 | *Rotherham U* | 17 | 0 | **17** | **0** |
| 1997–98 | Manchester U | 2 | 0 | | |
| 1998–99 | Manchester U | 0 | 0 | **6** | **0** |
| 1998–99 | Port Vale | 8 | 0 | | |
| 1999–2000 | Port Vale | 15 | 0 | **23** | **0** |
| 2000–01 | Macclesfield T | 0 | 0 | | |
| 2000–01 | Wigan Ath | 0 | 0 | | |
| 2000–01 | Mansfield T | 2 | 0 | | |
| 2001–02 | Mansfield T | 45 | 0 | | |
| 2002–03 | Mansfield T | 32 | 0 | | |
| 2003–04 | Mansfield T | 46 | 0 | **125** | **0** |

**VAUGHAN, Tony* (D) 223 8**
H: 6 1 W: 11 02 b.Manchester 11-10-75
*Source:* Trainee. *Honours:* England Schools.

| | | | | | |
|---|---|---|---|---|---|
| 1994–95 | Ipswich T | 10 | 0 | | |
| 1995–96 | Ipswich T | 25 | 1 | | |
| 1996–97 | Ipswich T | 32 | 2 | **67** | **3** |
| 1997–98 | Manchester C | 19 | 1 | | |
| 1998–99 | Manchester C | 38 | 1 | | |
| 1999–2000 | Manchester C | 1 | 0 | **58** | **2** |
| 1999–2000 | *Cardiff C* | 14 | 0 | **14** | **0** |
| 1999–2000 | Nottingham F | 10 | 0 | | |
| 2000–01 | Nottingham F | 25 | 1 | | |
| 2001–02 | Nottingham F | 8 | 0 | | |
| 2001–02 | *Scunthorpe U* | 5 | 0 | **5** | **0** |
| 2002–03 | Nottingham F | 0 | 0 | **43** | **1** |
| 2002–03 | *Mansfield T* | 4 | 0 | | |
| 2003–04 | Mansfield T | 32 | 2 | **36** | **2** |

**WHITE, Andy* (F) 83 11**
H: 6 4 W: 14 03 b.Derby 6-11-81
*Source:* Hucknall T.

| | | | | | |
|---|---|---|---|---|---|
| 2000–01 | Mansfield T | 4 | 0 | | |
| 2001–02 | Mansfield T | 22 | 4 | | |
| 2002–03 | Mansfield T | 28 | 6 | | |
| 2002–03 | *Crewe Alex* | 2 | 0 | **2** | **0** |
| 2003–04 | Mansfield T | 14 | 0 | **68** | **10** |
| 2003–04 | *Boston U* | 6 | 0 | **6** | **0** |
| 2003–04 | *Kidderminster H* | 7 | 1 | **7** | **1** |

**WHITE, Jason (G) 1 0**
H: 6 2 W: 12 01 b.Mansfield 28-1-83
*Source:* Trainee.

| | | | | | |
|---|---|---|---|---|---|
| 2002–03 | Mansfield T | 1 | 0 | | |
| 2003–04 | Mansfield T | 0 | 0 | **1** | **0** |

**WILLIAMSON, Lee (M) 140 3**
H: 5 10 W: 10 04 b.Derby 7-6-82
*Source:* Trainee.

| | | | | | |
|---|---|---|---|---|---|
| 1999–2000 | Mansfield T | 4 | 0 | | |
| 2000–01 | Mansfield T | 15 | 0 | | |
| 2001–02 | Mansfield T | 46 | 3 | | |
| 2002–03 | Mansfield T | 40 | 0 | | |
| 2003–04 | Mansfield T | 35 | 0 | **140** | **3** |

**Scholars**
Brown, Anton A; Carter, Mark; Coates, James A; Curle, Thomas K; Davies, Andrew P; Hankey, Dean A; Heron, Daniel C; Holmes, Adam L; Hurst, Mark; Jones, Andrew S; Lloyd, Callum; Parks, Ryan C; Rennalls, Alton; Ryalls, Peter; Sangra, Gavinder S; Wood, Christopher H; Zaccaria, Haydon G

**Non Contract**
Curle, Keith

## MIDDLESBROUGH (50)

**BATES, Matthew§ (D) 0 0**
H: 5 10 W: 12 03 b.Stockton 10-12-86
*Source:* Scholar. *Honours:* England Youth.

| | | | | | |
|---|---|---|---|---|---|
| 2003–04 | Middlesbrough | 0 | 0 | | |

**BOATENG, George (M) 290 10**
H: 5 9 W: 12 06 b.Nkawkaw 5-9-75
*Honours:* Holland 2 full caps.

| | | | | | |
|---|---|---|---|---|---|
| 1994–95 | Excelsior | 9 | 0 | **9** | **0** |
| 1995–96 | Feyenoord | 24 | 1 | | |
| 1996–97 | Feyenoord | 26 | 0 | | |
| 1997–98 | Feyenoord | 18 | 0 | **68** | **1** |
| 1997–98 | Coventry C | 14 | 1 | | |
| 1998–99 | Coventry C | 33 | 4 | **47** | **5** |
| 1999–2000 | Aston Villa | 33 | 2 | | |
| 2000–01 | Aston Villa | 33 | 1 | | |
| 2001–02 | Aston Villa | 37 | 1 | **103** | **4** |
| 2002–03 | Middlesbrough | 28 | 0 | | |
| 2003–04 | Middlesbrough | 35 | 0 | **63** | **0** |

**CHRISTIE, Malcolm (F) 138 35**
H: 6 0 W: 12 06 b.Peterborough 11-4-79
*Source:* Nuneaton B. *Honours:* England Under-21.

| | | | | | |
|---|---|---|---|---|---|
| 1998–99 | Derby Co | 2 | 0 | | |
| 1999–2000 | Derby Co | 21 | 5 | | |
| 2000–01 | Derby Co | 34 | 8 | | |
| 2001–02 | Derby Co | 35 | 9 | | |
| 2002–03 | Derby Co | 24 | 8 | **116** | **30** |
| 2002–03 | Middlesbrough | 12 | 4 | | |
| 2003–04 | Middlesbrough | 10 | 1 | **22** | **5** |

**COOPER, Colin (D) 590 37**
H: 5 11 W: 11 11 b.Sedgefield 28-2-67
*Honours:* England Under-21, 2 full caps.

| | | | | | |
|---|---|---|---|---|---|
| 1984–85 | Middlesbrough | 0 | 0 | | |
| 1985–86 | Middlesbrough | 11 | 0 | | |
| 1986–87 | Middlesbrough | 46 | 0 | | |
| 1987–88 | Middlesbrough | 43 | 2 | | |
| 1988–89 | Middlesbrough | 35 | 2 | | |
| 1989–90 | Middlesbrough | 21 | 2 | | |
| 1990–91 | Middlesbrough | 32 | 0 | | |
| 1991–92 | Millwall | 36 | 2 | | |
| 1992–93 | Millwall | 41 | 4 | **77** | **6** |
| 1993–94 | Nottingham F | 37 | 7 | | |
| 1994–95 | Nottingham F | 35 | 1 | | |
| 1995–96 | Nottingham F | 37 | 5 | | |
| 1996–97 | Nottingham F | 36 | 2 | | |
| 1997–98 | Nottingham F | 35 | 5 | | |
| 1998–99 | Nottingham F | 0 | 0 | **180** | **20** |
| 1998–99 | Middlesbrough | 32 | 1 | | |
| 1999–2000 | Middlesbrough | 26 | 0 | | |
| 2000–01 | Middlesbrough | 27 | 2 | | |
| 2001–02 | Middlesbrough | 18 | 2 | | |
| 2002–03 | Middlesbrough | 20 | 0 | | |
| 2003–04 | Middlesbrough | 19 | 0 | **330** | **11** |
| 2003–04 | *Sunderland* | 3 | 0 | **3** | **0** |

**DAVIES, Andrew (D) 11 0**
H: 6 3 W: 14 08 b.Stockton 17-12-84
*Source:* Scholar. *Honours:* England Youth, Under-20, Under-21.

| | | | | | |
|---|---|---|---|---|---|
| 2002–03 | Middlesbrough | 1 | 0 | | |
| 2003–04 | Middlesbrough | 10 | 0 | **11** | **0** |

**DORIVA‡ (M) 207 10**
H: 5 7 W: 11 04 b.Mirasol 28-5-72
*Honours:* Brazil 12 full caps.

| | | | | | |
|---|---|---|---|---|---|
| 1993 | Sao Paulo | 12 | 0 | | |
| 1994 | Sao Paulo | 15 | 0 | **27** | **0** |
| 1995 | Atletico Mineiro | 11 | 1 | | |
| 1996 | Atletico Mineiro | 24 | 0 | | |
| 1997 | Atletico Mineiro | 24 | 0 | **59** | **1** |
| 1997–98 | Porto | 13 | 1 | | |
| 1998–99 | Porto | 17 | 4 | **30** | **5** |
| 1999–2000 | Sampdoria | 31 | 3 | **31** | **3** |
| 2000–01 | Celta Vigo | 17 | 1 | | |
| 2001–02 | Celta Vigo | 14 | 0 | | |
| 2002–03 | Celta Vigo | 3 | 0 | **34** | **1** |
| 2002–03 | Middlesbrough | 5 | 0 | | |
| 2003–04 | Middlesbrough | 21 | 0 | **26** | **0** |

**DOVE, Craig* (M) 1 0**
H: 5 8 W: 11 00 b.Hartlepool 16-8-83
*Source:* Scholar. *Honours:* England Youth, Under-20.

| | | | | | |
|---|---|---|---|---|---|
| 2000–01 | Middlesbrough | 0 | 0 | | |
| 2001–02 | Middlesbrough | 0 | 0 | | |
| 2002–03 | Middlesbrough | 0 | 0 | | |
| 2003–04 | Middlesbrough | 0 | 0 | | |
| 2003–04 | *York C* | 1 | 0 | **1** | **0** |

**DOWNING, Stewart (M) 32 3**
H: 5 11 W: 10 04 b.Middlesbrough 22-7-84
*Source:* Scholar. *Honours:* England Youth, Under-21.

| | | | | | |
|---|---|---|---|---|---|
| 2001–02 | Middlesbrough | 3 | 0 | | |
| 2002–03 | Middlesbrough | 2 | 0 | | |
| 2003–04 | Middlesbrough | 20 | 0 | **25** | **0** |
| 2003–04 | *Sunderland* | 7 | 3 | **7** | **3** |

**EHIOGU, Ugo (D) 337 19**
H: 6 2 W: 14 10 b.Hackney 3-11-72
*Source:* Trainee. *Honours:* England Under-21, B, 4 full caps, 1 goal.

| | | | | | |
|---|---|---|---|---|---|
| 1990–91 | WBA | 2 | 0 | **2** | **0** |
| 1991–92 | Aston Villa | 8 | 0 | | |
| 1992–93 | Aston Villa | 4 | 0 | | |
| 1993–94 | Aston Villa | 17 | 0 | | |
| 1994–95 | Aston Villa | 39 | 3 | | |
| 1995–96 | Aston Villa | 36 | 1 | | |
| 1996–97 | Aston Villa | 38 | 3 | | |
| 1997–98 | Aston Villa | 37 | 2 | | |
| 1998–99 | Aston Villa | 25 | 2 | | |
| 1999–2000 | Aston Villa | 31 | 1 | | |
| 2000–01 | Aston Villa | 2 | 0 | **237** | **12** |
| 2000–01 | Middlesbrough | 21 | 3 | | |
| 2001–02 | Middlesbrough | 29 | 1 | | |
| 2002–03 | Middlesbrough | 32 | 3 | | |
| 2003–04 | Middlesbrough | 16 | 0 | **98** | **7** |

**GRAHAM, Danny (F) 9 2**
H: 5 11 W: 12 05 b.Gateshead 12-8-85
*Source:* Trainee.

| | | | | | |
|---|---|---|---|---|---|
| 2003–04 | Middlesbrough | 0 | 0 | | |
| 2003–04 | *Darlington* | 9 | 2 | **9** | **2** |

**GREENING, Jonathan (M) 138 6**
H: 6 0 W: 11 08 b.Scarborough 2-1-79
*Source:* Trainee. *Honours:* England Youth, Under-21.

| | | | | | |
|---|---|---|---|---|---|
| 1996–97 | York C | 5 | 0 | | |
| 1997–98 | York C | 20 | 2 | **25** | **2** |
| 1997–98 | Manchester U | 0 | 0 | | |
| 1998–99 | Manchester U | 3 | 0 | | |
| 1999–2000 | Manchester U | 4 | 0 | | |
| 2000–01 | Manchester U | 7 | 0 | **14** | **0** |
| 2001–02 | Middlesbrough | 36 | 1 | | |
| 2002–03 | Middlesbrough | 38 | 2 | | |
| 2003–04 | Middlesbrough | 25 | 1 | **99** | **4** |

**GULLIVER, Phil* (D) 22 0**
H: 6 2 W: 13 10 b.Bishop Auckland 12-9-82
*Source:* Scholar.

| | | | | | |
|---|---|---|---|---|---|
| 2000–01 | Middlesbrough | 0 | 0 | | |
| 2001–02 | Middlesbrough | 0 | 0 | | |
| 2002–03 | Middlesbrough | 0 | 0 | | |
| 2002–03 | *Blackpool* | 3 | 0 | **3** | **0** |
| 2002–03 | *Carlisle U* | 1 | 0 | **1** | **0** |
| 2002–03 | *Bournemouth* | 6 | 0 | **6** | **0** |
| 2003–04 | Middlesbrough | 0 | 0 | | |
| 2003–04 | *Bury* | 10 | 0 | **10** | **0** |
| 2003–04 | *Scunthorpe U* | 2 | 0 | **2** | **0** |

**JOB, Joseph-Desire (F) 133 27**
H: 5 11 W: 11 00 b.Venissieux 1-12-77
*Honours:* Cameroon 43 full caps, 6 goals.

| | | | | | |
|---|---|---|---|---|---|
| 1997–98 | Lyon | 22 | 5 | | |
| 1998–99 | Lyon | 19 | 6 | **41** | **11** |
| 1999–2000 | Lens | 24 | 4 | **24** | **4** |
| 2000–01 | Middlesbrough | 12 | 3 | | |
| 2001–02 | Middlesbrough | 4 | 0 | | |
| 2002–03 | Middlesbrough | 28 | 4 | | |
| 2003–04 | Middlesbrough | 24 | 5 | **68** | **12** |

**JOHNSTON, Allan* (M) 264 39**
H: 5 10 W: 11 04 b.Glasgow 14-12-73
*Source:* Tynecastle BC. *Honours:* Scotland Under-21, B, 18 full caps, 2 goals.

| | | | | | |
|---|---|---|---|---|---|
| 1991–92 | Hearts | 0 | 0 | | |
| 1992–93 | Hearts | 2 | 1 | | |
| 1993–94 | Hearts | 28 | 1 | | |
| 1994–95 | Hearts | 21 | 1 | | |
| 1995–96 | Hearts | 33 | 9 | **84** | **12** |
| 1996–97 | Rennes | 23 | 2 | **23** | **2** |
| 1996–97 | Sunderland | 6 | 1 | | |
| 1997–98 | Sunderland | 40 | 11 | | |
| 1998–99 | Sunderland | 40 | 7 | **86** | **19** |
| 1999–2000 | Rangers | 0 | 0 | | |
| 1999–2000 | *Birmingham C* | 9 | 0 | **9** | **0** |
| 1999–2000 | Bolton W | 19 | 3 | **19** | **3** |
| 2000–01 | Rangers | 13 | 0 | | |
| 2001–02 | Rangers | 1 | 0 | **14** | **0** |
| 2001–02 | Middlesbrough | 17 | 1 | | |
| 2002–03 | Middlesbrough | 0 | 0 | | |
| 2002–03 | *Sheffield W* | 12 | 2 | **12** | **2** |
| 2003–04 | Middlesbrough | 0 | 0 | **17** | **1** |

**JONES, Brad (G) 7 0**
H: 6 3 W: 12 01 b.Armadale 19-3-82
*Source:* Trainee. *Honours:* Australia Under-20, Under-23.

| | | | | | |
|---|---|---|---|---|---|
| 1998–99 | Middlesbrough | 0 | 0 | | |
| 1999–2000 | Middlesbrough | 0 | 0 | | |
| 2000–01 | Middlesbrough | 0 | 0 | | |
| 2001–02 | Middlesbrough | 0 | 0 | | |
| 2002–03 | Middlesbrough | 0 | 0 | | |
| 2002–03 | *Stockport Co* | 1 | 0 | **1** | **0** |
| 2003–04 | Middlesbrough | 1 | 0 | **1** | **0** |

| | | | | | |
|---|---|---|---|---|---|
| 2003–04 | *Blackpool* | 5 | 0 | **5** | **0** |
| 2003–04 | *Rotherham U* | 0 | 0 | | |

**JUNINHO (F)** **267 53**
H: 5 5 W: 9 10 b.Sao Paulo 22-2-73
*Source:* Juventus, Corinthians, Ituano, Sao Paulo. *Honours:* Brazil 50 full caps, 5 goals.

| | | | | | |
|---|---|---|---|---|---|
| 1993 | Sao Paulo | 16 | 1 | | |
| 1994 | Sao Paulo | 19 | 0 | | |
| 1995 | Sao Paulo | 9 | 0 | **44** | **1** |
| 1995–96 | Middlesbrough | 21 | 2 | | |
| 1996–97 | Middlesbrough | 35 | 12 | | |
| 1997–98 | Atletico Madrid | 23 | 6 | | |
| 1998–99 | Atletico Madrid | 32 | 8 | **55** | **14** |
| 1999–2000 | Middlesbrough | 28 | 4 | | |
| 2000 | Vasco da Gama | 28 | 5 | | |
| 2001 | Vasco da Gama | 15 | 4 | **43** | **9** |
| 2002–03 | Middlesbrough | 10 | 3 | | |
| 2003–04 | Middlesbrough | 31 | 8 | **125** | **29** |

**LIDDLE, Gary (D)** **0 0**
b.Middlesbrough 15-6-86
*Source:* Trainee. *Honours:* England Youth.

| | | | | | |
|---|---|---|---|---|---|
| 2003–04 | Middlesbrough | 0 | 0 | | |

**MACCARONE, Massimo (F)** **92 31**
H: 5 10 W: 12 05 b.Galliate 6-9-79
*Honours:* Italy 2 full caps.

| | | | | | |
|---|---|---|---|---|---|
| 2000–01 | Empoli | 35 | 16 | | |
| 2001–02 | Empoli | 0 | 0 | **35** | **16** |
| 2002–03 | Middlesbrough | 34 | 9 | | |
| 2003–04 | Middlesbrough | 23 | 6 | **57** | **15** |

**MARINELLI, Carlos‡ (M)** **43 3**
H: 5 8 W: 11 06 b.Buenos Aires 14-3-82
*Source:* Boca Juniors.

| | | | | | |
|---|---|---|---|---|---|
| 1999–2000 | Middlesbrough | 2 | 0 | | |
| 2000–01 | Middlesbrough | 13 | 0 | | |
| 2001–02 | Middlesbrough | 20 | 2 | | |
| 2002–03 | Middlesbrough | 7 | 0 | | |
| 2003–04 | Middlesbrough | 1 | 1 | **43** | **3** |

**McMAHON, Anthony (D)** **0 0**
H: 5 10 W: 11 04 b.Bishop Auckland 24-3-86
*Source:* Scholar. *Honours:* England Youth.

| | | | | | |
|---|---|---|---|---|---|
| 2003–04 | Middlesbrough | 0 | 0 | | |

**MENDIETA, Gaizka‡ (M)** **378 50**
H: 5 9 W: 11 02 b.Bilbao 27-3-74
*Honours:* Spain 40 full caps 8 goals.

| | | | | | |
|---|---|---|---|---|---|
| 1991–92 | Castellon | 16 | 0 | **16** | **0** |
| 1992–93 | Valencia B | 31 | 2 | | |
| 1992–93 | Valencia | 2 | 0 | | |
| 1993–94 | Valencia B | 17 | 0 | **48** | **2** |
| 1993–94 | Valencia | 20 | 0 | | |
| 1994–95 | Valencia | 13 | 1 | | |
| 1995–96 | Valencia | 34 | 0 | | |
| 1996–97 | Valencia | 29 | 1 | | |
| 1997–98 | Valencia | 30 | 10 | | |
| 1998–99 | Valencia | 38 | 7 | | |
| 1999–2000 | Valencia | 33 | 13 | | |
| 2000–01 | Valencia | 31 | 10 | **230** | **42** |
| 2001–02 | Lazio | 20 | 0 | **20** | **0** |
| 2002–03 | Barcelona | 33 | 4 | **33** | **4** |
| 2003–04 | Middlesbrough | 31 | 2 | **31** | **2** |

**MORRISON, James (M)** **1 0**
H: 5 10 W: 10 06 b.Darlington 25-5-86
*Source:* Trainee. *Honours:* England Youth.

| | | | | | |
|---|---|---|---|---|---|
| 2003–04 | Middlesbrough | 1 | 0 | **1** | **0** |

**MURPHY, David* (D)** **23 2**
H: 6 1 W: 12 03 b.Hartlepool 1-3-84
*Source:* Scholar. *Honours:* England Youth.

| | | | | | |
|---|---|---|---|---|---|
| 2001–02 | Middlesbrough | 5 | 0 | | |
| 2002–03 | Middlesbrough | 8 | 0 | | |
| 2003–04 | Middlesbrough | 0 | 0 | **13** | **0** |
| 2003–04 | *Barnsley* | 10 | 2 | **10** | **2** |

**NASH, Carlo (G)** **149 0**
H: 6 3 W: 15 03 b.Bolton 13-9-73
*Source:* Clitheroe.

| | | | | | |
|---|---|---|---|---|---|
| 1996–97 | Crystal Palace | 21 | 0 | | |
| 1997–98 | Crystal Palace | 0 | 0 | **21** | **0** |
| 1998–99 | Stockport Co | 43 | 0 | | |
| 1999–2000 | Stockport Co | 38 | 0 | | |
| 2000–01 | Stockport Co | 8 | 0 | **89** | **0** |
| 2000–01 | Manchester C | 6 | 0 | | |
| 2001–02 | Manchester C | 23 | 0 | | |
| 2002–03 | Manchester C | 9 | 0 | **38** | **0** |
| 2003–04 | Middlesbrough | 1 | 0 | **1** | **0** |

**NEMETH, Szilard (F)** **237 103**
H: 5 11 W: 11 04 b.Komarno 8-8-77
*Honours:* Slovakia 44 full caps, 17 goals.

| | | | | | |
|---|---|---|---|---|---|
| 1994–95 | Slovan Bratislava | 3 | 0 | | |
| 1995–96 | Slovan Bratislava | 28 | 12 | | |
| 1996–97 | Slovan Bratislava | 30 | 13 | **61** | **25** |
| 1997–98 | Kosice | 18 | 12 | | |
| 1998–99 | Kosice | 19 | 8 | **37** | **20** |
| 1999–2000 | Inter Bratislava | 26 | 16 | | |
| 2000–01 | Inter Bratislava | 32 | 23 | **58** | **39** |
| 2001–02 | Middlesbrough | 21 | 3 | | |
| 2002–03 | Middlesbrough | 28 | 7 | | |
| 2003–04 | Middlesbrough | 32 | 9 | **81** | **19** |

**NORDGREN, Niklas‡ (M)** **0 0**
b.Sweden 1-4-85
*Source:* Trainee.

| | | | | | |
|---|---|---|---|---|---|
| 2002–03 | Middlesbrough | 0 | 0 | | |
| 2003–04 | Middlesbrough | 0 | 0 | | |

**PARNABY, Stuart (M)** **40 0**
H: 5 11 W: 11 00 b.Durham City 19-7-82
*Source:* Trainee. *Honours:* England Youth, Under-20, Under-21.

| | | | | | |
|---|---|---|---|---|---|
| 1999–2000 | Middlesbrough | 0 | 0 | | |
| 2000–01 | Middlesbrough | 0 | 0 | | |
| 2000–01 | *Halifax T* | 6 | 0 | **6** | **0** |
| 2001–02 | Middlesbrough | 0 | 0 | | |
| 2002–03 | Middlesbrough | 21 | 0 | | |
| 2003–04 | Middlesbrough | 13 | 0 | **34** | **0** |

**PEACOCK, Anthony (M)** **0 0**
b.Middlesbrough 6-9-85
*Source:* Trainee.

| | | | | | |
|---|---|---|---|---|---|
| 2003–04 | Middlesbrough | 0 | 0 | | |

**QUEUDRUE, Franck (D)** **132 5**
H: 6 1 W: 12 01 b.Paris 27-8-78
*Source:* Meaux.

| | | | | | |
|---|---|---|---|---|---|
| 1999–2000 | Lens | 16 | 1 | | |
| 2000–01 | Lens | 24 | 1 | | |
| 2001–02 | Lens | 2 | 0 | **42** | **2** |
| 2001–02 | Middlesbrough | 28 | 2 | | |
| 2002–03 | Middlesbrough | 31 | 1 | | |
| 2003–04 | Middlesbrough | 31 | 0 | **90** | **3** |

**RICARDINHO‡ (M)** **152 23**
H: 5 9 W: 11 02 b.Sao Paulo 23-5-76
*Honours:* Brazil 4 full caps.

| | | | | | |
|---|---|---|---|---|---|
| 1994 | Parana | 0 | 0 | | |
| 1995 | Parana | 13 | 0 | | |
| 1996 | Parana | 15 | 1 | **28** | **1** |
| 1997–98 | Bordeaux | 18 | 1 | **18** | **1** |
| 1998 | Corinthians | 22 | 2 | | |
| 1999 | Corinthians | 26 | 7 | | |
| 2000 | Corinthians | 20 | 2 | | |
| 2001 | Corinthians | 21 | 7 | **89** | **18** |
| 2002 | Sao Paulo | 17 | 3 | **17** | **3** |
| 2003–04 | Middlesbrough | 0 | 0 | | |

**RICKETTS, Michael (F)** **206 54**
H: 6 2 W: 15 00 b.Birmingham 4-12-78
*Source:* Trainee. *Honours:* England 1 full cap.

| | | | | | |
|---|---|---|---|---|---|
| 1995–96 | Walsall | 1 | 1 | | |
| 1996–97 | Walsall | 11 | 1 | | |
| 1997–98 | Walsall | 24 | 1 | | |
| 1998–99 | Walsall | 8 | 0 | | |
| 1999–2000 | Walsall | 32 | 11 | **76** | **14** |
| 2000–01 | Bolton W | 39 | 19 | | |
| 2001–02 | Bolton W | 37 | 12 | | |
| 2002–03 | Bolton W | 22 | 6 | **98** | **37** |
| 2002–03 | Middlesbrough | 9 | 1 | | |
| 2003–04 | Middlesbrough | 23 | 2 | **32** | **3** |

**RIGGOTT, Chris (D)** **113 7**
H: 6 2 W: 13 09 b.Derby 1-9-80
*Source:* Trainee. *Honours:* England Youth, Under-21.

| | | | | | |
|---|---|---|---|---|---|
| 1998–99 | Derby Co | 0 | 0 | | |
| 1999–2000 | Derby Co | 1 | 0 | | |
| 2000–01 | Derby Co | 31 | 3 | | |
| 2001–02 | Derby Co | 37 | 0 | | |
| 2002–03 | Derby Co | 22 | 2 | **91** | **5** |
| 2002–03 | Middlesbrough | 5 | 2 | | |
| 2003–04 | Middlesbrough | 17 | 0 | **22** | **2** |

**RUSSELL, Sam* (G)** **11 0**
H: 6 0 W: 11 00 b.Middlesbrough 4-10-82
*Source:* Scholar.

| | | | | | |
|---|---|---|---|---|---|
| 2000–01 | Middlesbrough | 0 | 0 | | |
| 2001–02 | Middlesbrough | 0 | 0 | | |
| 2002–03 | Middlesbrough | 0 | 0 | | |
| 2002–03 | *Darlington* | 1 | 0 | **1** | **0** |
| 2003–04 | Middlesbrough | 0 | 0 | | |
| 2003–04 | *Scunthorpe U* | 10 | 0 | **10** | **0** |

**SCHWARZER, Mark (G)** **316 0**
H: 6 4 W: 14 07 b.Sydney 6-10-72
*Honours:* Australia Youth, Under-20, 25 full caps.

| | | | | | |
|---|---|---|---|---|---|
| 1990–91 | Marconi Stallions | 1 | 0 | | |
| 1991–92 | Marconi Stallions | 9 | 0 | | |
| 1992–93 | Marconi Stallions | 23 | 0 | | |
| 1993–94 | Marconi Stallions | 25 | 0 | **58** | **0** |
| 1994–95 | Dynamo Dresden | 2 | 0 | **2** | **0** |
| 1995–96 | Kaiserslautern | 4 | 0 | | |
| 1996–97 | Kaiserslautern | 0 | 0 | **4** | **0** |
| 1996–97 | Bradford C | 13 | 0 | **13** | **0** |
| 1996–97 | Middlesbrough | 7 | 0 | | |
| 1997–98 | Middlesbrough | 35 | 0 | | |
| 1998–99 | Middlesbrough | 34 | 0 | | |
| 1999–2000 | Middlesbrough | 37 | 0 | | |
| 2000–01 | Middlesbrough | 31 | 0 | | |
| 2001–02 | Middlesbrough | 21 | 0 | | |
| 2002–03 | Middlesbrough | 38 | 0 | | |
| 2003–04 | Middlesbrough | 36 | 0 | **239** | **0** |

**SMITH, Gary* (M)** **11 3**
H: 5 8 W: 10 08 b.Middlesbrough 30-1-84
*Source:* Trainee.

| | | | | | |
|---|---|---|---|---|---|
| 2002–03 | Middlesbrough | 0 | 0 | | |
| 2003–04 | Middlesbrough | 0 | 0 | | |
| 2003–04 | *Wimbledon* | 11 | 3 | **11** | **3** |

**SOUTHGATE, Gareth (D)** **443 26**
H: 6 0 W: 12 03 b.Watford 3-9-70
*Source:* Trainee. *Honours:* England 57 full caps, 2 goals.

| | | | | | |
|---|---|---|---|---|---|
| 1988–89 | Crystal Palace | 0 | 0 | | |
| 1989–90 | Crystal Palace | 0 | 0 | | |
| 1990–91 | Crystal Palace | 1 | 0 | | |
| 1991–92 | Crystal Palace | 30 | 0 | | |
| 1992–93 | Crystal Palace | 33 | 3 | | |
| 1993–94 | Crystal Palace | 46 | 9 | | |
| 1994–95 | Crystal Palace | 42 | 3 | **152** | **15** |
| 1995–96 | Aston Villa | 31 | 1 | | |
| 1996–97 | Aston Villa | 28 | 1 | | |
| 1997–98 | Aston Villa | 32 | 0 | | |
| 1998–99 | Aston Villa | 38 | 1 | | |
| 1999–2000 | Aston Villa | 31 | 2 | | |
| 2000–01 | Aston Villa | 31 | 2 | **191** | **7** |
| 2001–02 | Middlesbrough | 37 | 1 | | |
| 2002–03 | Middlesbrough | 36 | 2 | | |
| 2003–04 | Middlesbrough | 27 | 1 | **100** | **4** |

**STOCKDALE, Robbie (D)** **104 3**
H: 6 0 W: 12 03 b.Middlesbrough 30-11-79
*Source:* Trainee. *Honours:* England Under-21, Scotland 5 full caps.

| | | | | | |
|---|---|---|---|---|---|
| 1997–98 | Middlesbrough | 1 | 0 | | |
| 1998–99 | Middlesbrough | 19 | 0 | | |
| 1999–2000 | Middlesbrough | 11 | 1 | | |
| 2000–01 | Middlesbrough | 0 | 0 | | |
| 2000–01 | *Sheffield W* | 6 | 0 | **6** | **0** |
| 2001–02 | Middlesbrough | 28 | 1 | | |
| 2002–03 | Middlesbrough | 14 | 0 | | |
| 2003–04 | Middlesbrough | 2 | 0 | **75** | **2** |
| 2003–04 | *West Ham U* | 7 | 0 | **7** | **0** |
| 2003–04 | *Rotherham U* | 16 | 1 | **16** | **1** |

**TAYLOR, Andrew (D)** **0 0**
H: 5 10 W: 11 04 b.Hartlepool 1-8-86
*Source:* Trainee. *Honours:* England Youth, Under-20.

| | | | | | |
|---|---|---|---|---|---|
| 2003–04 | Middlesbrough | 0 | 0 | | |

**TURNBULL, Ross (G)** **4 0**
H: 6 4 W: 15 00 b.Bishop Auckland 4-1-85
*Source:* Trainee. *Honours:* England Youth.

| | | | | | |
|---|---|---|---|---|---|
| 2002–03 | Middlesbrough | 0 | 0 | | |
| 2003–04 | Middlesbrough | 0 | 0 | | |
| 2003–04 | *Darlington* | 1 | 0 | **1** | **0** |
| 2003–04 | *Barnsley* | 3 | 0 | **3** | **0** |

**WILSON, Mark (M)** **51 6**
H: 5 10 W: 12 07 b.Scunthorpe 9-2-79
*Source:* Trainee. *Honours:* England Schools, Under-21.

| | | | | | |
|---|---|---|---|---|---|
| 1995–96 | Manchester U | 0 | 0 | | |
| 1996–97 | Manchester U | 0 | 0 | | |
| 1997–98 | Manchester U | 0 | 0 | | |
| 1997–98 | *Wrexham* | 13 | 4 | **13** | **4** |
| 1998–99 | Manchester U | 0 | 0 | | |
| 1999–2000 | Manchester U | 3 | 0 | | |
| 2000–01 | Manchester U | 0 | 0 | **3** | **0** |

| | | | | | |
|---|---|---|---|---|---|
| 2001–02 | Middlesbrough | 10 | 0 | | |
| 2002–03 | Middlesbrough | 6 | 0 | | |
| 2002–03 | *Stoke C* | 4 | 0 | **4** | **0** |
| 2003–04 | Middlesbrough | 0 | 0 | **16** | **0** |
| 2003–04 | *Swansea C* | 12 | 2 | **12** | **2** |
| 2003–04 | *Sheffield W* | 3 | 0 | **3** | **0** |

**Scholars**

Bates, Matthew D; Craddock, Thomas; Johnson, Adam; Kennedy, Jason B; Knight, David S; Mulligan, Nathan M; Reed, Danny S; Roberts, Dale; Wheater, David J

## MILLWALL (51)

**ASHIKODI, Moses‡ (M) 5 0**

H: 6 0 W: 11 09 b.Lagos 27-6-87

*Honours:* FA Schools, England Youth.

| | | | | | |
|---|---|---|---|---|---|
| 2002–03 | Millwall | 5 | 0 | | |
| 2003–04 | Millwall | 0 | 0 | **5** | **0** |

**BRANIFF, Kevin (F) 32 1**

H: 5 11 W: 10 03 b.Belfast 4-3-83

*Source:* Scholarship. *Honours:* Northern Ireland Schools, Youth, Under-21.

| | | | | | |
|---|---|---|---|---|---|
| 1999–2000 | Millwall | 0 | 0 | | |
| 2000–01 | Millwall | 5 | 0 | | |
| 2001–02 | Millwall | 1 | 0 | | |
| 2002–03 | Millwall | 10 | 0 | | |
| 2003–04 | Millwall | 16 | 1 | **32** | **1** |

**CAHILL, Tim (M) 217 52**

H: 5 10 W: 10 12 b.Sydney 6-12-79

*Source:* Sydney U. *Honours:* Australia 4 full caps, 6 goals.

| | | | | | |
|---|---|---|---|---|---|
| 1997–98 | Millwall | 1 | 0 | | |
| 1998–99 | Millwall | 36 | 6 | | |
| 1999–2000 | Millwall | 45 | 12 | | |
| 2000–01 | Millwall | 41 | 9 | | |
| 2001–02 | Millwall | 43 | 13 | | |
| 2002–03 | Millwall | 11 | 3 | | |
| 2003–04 | Millwall | 40 | 9 | **217** | **52** |

**CLANCY, Tim (M) 0 0**

H: 5 11 W: 10 11 b.Trim 8-6-84

| | | | | | |
|---|---|---|---|---|---|
| 2002–03 | Millwall | 0 | 0 | | |
| 2003–04 | Millwall | 0 | 0 | | |

**COGAN, Barry (F) 3 0**

H: 5 9 W: 9 0 b.Sligo 4-11-84

*Source:* Scholar. *Honours:* Eire Under-21.

| | | | | | |
|---|---|---|---|---|---|
| 2001–02 | Millwall | 0 | 0 | | |
| 2002–03 | Millwall | 0 | 0 | | |
| 2003–04 | Millwall | 3 | 0 | **3** | **0** |

**CRAIG, Tony (D) 11 1**

H: 6 0 W: 10 03 b.Greenwich 20-4-85

*Source:* Scholar.

| | | | | | |
|---|---|---|---|---|---|
| 2002–03 | Millwall | 2 | 1 | | |
| 2003–04 | Millwall | 9 | 0 | **11** | **1** |

**DICHIO, Danny (F) 251 56**

H: 6 4 W: 13 10 b.Hammersmith 19-10-74

*Source:* Trainee. *Honours:* England Schools, Under-21.

| | | | | | |
|---|---|---|---|---|---|
| 1993–94 | QPR | 0 | 0 | | |
| 1993–94 | *Barnet* | 9 | 2 | **9** | **2** |
| 1994–95 | QPR | 9 | 3 | | |
| 1995–96 | QPR | 29 | 10 | | |
| 1996–97 | QPR | 37 | 7 | **75** | **20** |
| 1997–98 | Sampdoria | 0 | 0 | | |
| 1997–98 | Lecce | 4 | 1 | **4** | **1** |
| 1997–98 | Sunderland | 13 | 0 | | |
| 1998–99 | Sunderland | 36 | 10 | | |
| 1999–2000 | Sunderland | 12 | 0 | | |
| 2000–01 | Sunderland | 15 | 1 | | |
| 2001–02 | Sunderland | 0 | 0 | **76** | **11** |
| 2001–02 | WBA | 27 | 9 | | |
| 2002–03 | WBA | 28 | 5 | | |
| 2003–04 | WBA | 11 | 0 | **66** | **14** |
| 2003–04 | *Derby Co* | 6 | 1 | **6** | **1** |
| 2003–04 | Millwall | 15 | 7 | **15** | **7** |

**DOLAN, Joe (D) 49 3**

H: 6 3 W: 13 02 b.Harrow 27-5-80

*Source:* Chelsea Trainee. *Honours:* Northern Ireland Youth, Under-21.

| | | | | | |
|---|---|---|---|---|---|
| 1998–99 | Millwall | 9 | 1 | | |
| 1999–2000 | Millwall | 17 | 1 | | |
| 2000–01 | Millwall | 20 | 1 | | |
| 2001–02 | Millwall | 0 | 0 | | |
| 2002–03 | Millwall | 2 | 0 | | |
| 2003–04 | Millwall | 1 | 0 | **49** | **3** |

**DONOVAN, James (M) 0 0**

H: 6 2 W: 13 12 b.Sidcup 11-9-84

*Source:* Scholar.

| | | | | | |
|---|---|---|---|---|---|
| 2003–04 | Millwall | 0 | 0 | | |

**DUNNE, Alan (D) 13 0**

H: 5 10 W: 10 13 b.Dublin 23-8-82

| | | | | | |
|---|---|---|---|---|---|
| 1999–2000 | Millwall | 0 | 0 | | |
| 2000–01 | Millwall | 0 | 0 | | |
| 2001–02 | Millwall | 1 | 0 | | |
| 2002–03 | Millwall | 4 | 0 | | |
| 2003–04 | Millwall | 8 | 0 | **13** | **0** |

**ELLIOTT, Marvin (M) 22 0**

H: 6 0 W: 12 02 b.Wandsworth 15-9-84

*Source:* Scholar.

| | | | | | |
|---|---|---|---|---|---|
| 2001–02 | Millwall | 0 | 0 | | |
| 2002–03 | Millwall | 1 | 0 | | |
| 2003–04 | Millwall | 21 | 0 | **22** | **0** |

**FOFANA, Aboubacar* (M) 16 0**

H: 6 0 W: 12 04 b.Paris 4-10-82

*Source:* Juventus.

| | | | | | |
|---|---|---|---|---|---|
| 2003–04 | Millwall | 16 | 0 | **16** | **0** |

**GUERET, Willy# (G) 14 0**

H: 6 1 W: 13 05 b.Saint Claude 3-8-73

| | | | | | |
|---|---|---|---|---|---|
| 2000–01 | Millwall | 11 | 0 | | |
| 2001–02 | Millwall | 1 | 0 | | |
| 2002–03 | Millwall | 0 | 0 | | |
| 2003–04 | Millwall | 2 | 0 | **14** | **0** |

**HARRIS, Neil (F) 221 92**

H: 5 11 W: 12 01 b.Orsett 12-7-77

*Source:* Cambridge C.

| | | | | | |
|---|---|---|---|---|---|
| 1997–98 | Millwall | 3 | 0 | | |
| 1998–99 | Millwall | 39 | 15 | | |
| 1999–2000 | Millwall | 38 | 25 | | |
| 2000–01 | Millwall | 42 | 27 | | |
| 2001–02 | Millwall | 21 | 4 | | |
| 2002–03 | Millwall | 40 | 12 | | |
| 2003–04 | Millwall | 38 | 9 | **221** | **92** |

**HEALY, Joe (M) 0 0**

| | | | | | |
|---|---|---|---|---|---|
| 2003–04 | Millwall | 0 | 0 | | |

**HEARN, Charley (M) 18 0**

H: 5 11 W: 11 13 b.Ashford 5-11-83

*Source:* School.

| | | | | | |
|---|---|---|---|---|---|
| 2000–01 | Millwall | 0 | 0 | | |
| 2001–02 | Millwall | 2 | 0 | | |
| 2002–03 | Millwall | 9 | 0 | | |
| 2003–04 | Millwall | 7 | 0 | **18** | **0** |

**IFILL, Paul (M) 212 36**

H: 6 0 W: 12 01 b.Brighton 20-10-79

*Source:* Trainee. *Honours:* Barbados full caps.

| | | | | | |
|---|---|---|---|---|---|
| 1998–99 | Millwall | 15 | 1 | | |
| 1999–2000 | Millwall | 44 | 11 | | |
| 2000–01 | Millwall | 35 | 6 | | |
| 2001–02 | Millwall | 40 | 4 | | |
| 2002–03 | Millwall | 45 | 6 | | |
| 2003–04 | Millwall | 33 | 8 | **212** | **36** |

**LAWRENCE, Matthew (D) 287 5**

H: 6 0 W: 12 07 b.Northampton 19-6-74

*Source:* Grays Ath. *Honours:* England Schools.

| | | | | | |
|---|---|---|---|---|---|
| 1995–96 | Wycombe W | 3 | 0 | | |
| 1996–97 | Wycombe W | 13 | 1 | | |
| 1996–97 | Fulham | 15 | 0 | | |
| 1997–98 | Fulham | 43 | 0 | | |
| 1998–99 | Fulham | 1 | 0 | **59** | **0** |
| 1998–99 | Wycombe W | 34 | 2 | | |
| 1999–2000 | Wycombe W | 29 | 2 | **79** | **5** |
| 1999–2000 | Millwall | 9 | 0 | | |
| 2000–01 | Millwall | 45 | 0 | | |
| 2001–02 | Millwall | 26 | 0 | | |
| 2002–03 | Millwall | 33 | 0 | | |
| 2003–04 | Millwall | 36 | 0 | **149** | **0** |

**LIVERMORE, David (M) 191 8**

H: 5 11 W: 12 07 b.Edmonton 20-5-80

*Source:* Trainee.

| | | | | | |
|---|---|---|---|---|---|
| 1998–99 | Arsenal | 0 | 0 | | |
| 1999–2000 | Millwall | 32 | 2 | | |
| 2000–01 | Millwall | 39 | 3 | | |
| 2001–02 | Millwall | 43 | 0 | | |
| 2002–03 | Millwall | 41 | 2 | | |
| 2003–04 | Millwall | 36 | 1 | **191** | **8** |

**MARSHALL, Andy# (G) 280 0**

H: 6 2 W: 13 07 b.Bury 14-4-75

*Source:* Trainee. *Honours:* England Under-21.

| | | | | | |
|---|---|---|---|---|---|
| 1993–94 | Norwich C | 0 | 0 | | |
| 1994–95 | Norwich C | 21 | 0 | | |
| 1995–96 | Norwich C | 3 | 0 | | |
| 1996–97 | Norwich C | 7 | 0 | | |
| 1996–97 | *Bournemouth* | 11 | 0 | **11** | **0** |
| 1996–97 | *Gillingham* | 5 | 0 | **5** | **0** |
| 1997–98 | Norwich C | 42 | 0 | | |
| 1998–99 | Norwich C | 37 | 0 | | |
| 1999–2000 | Norwich C | 44 | 0 | | |
| 2000–01 | Norwich C | 41 | 0 | **195** | **0** |
| 2001–02 | Ipswich T | 13 | 0 | | |
| 2002–03 | Ipswich T | 40 | 0 | | |
| 2003–04 | Ipswich T | 0 | 0 | **53** | **0** |
| 2003–04 | Millwall | 16 | 0 | **16** | **0** |

**MASTERSON, Terence (G) 0 0**

H: 6 2 W: 11 04 b.Dublin 5-6-86

*Source:* Scholar.

| | | | | | |
|---|---|---|---|---|---|
| 2003–04 | Millwall | 0 | 0 | | |

**MAY, Ben (F) 57 8**

H: 6 1 W: 12 12 b.Gravesend 10-3-84

| | | | | | |
|---|---|---|---|---|---|
| 2000–01 | Millwall | 0 | 0 | | |
| 2001–02 | Millwall | 0 | 0 | | |
| 2002–03 | Millwall | 10 | 1 | | |
| 2002–03 | *Colchester U* | 6 | 0 | **6** | **0** |
| 2003–04 | Millwall | 0 | 0 | **10** | **1** |
| 2003–04 | *Brentford* | 41 | 7 | **41** | **7** |

**McCAMMON, Mark (F) 101 12**

H: 6 3 W: 15 02 b.Barnet 7-8-78

*Source:* Cambridge C.

| | | | | | |
|---|---|---|---|---|---|
| 1997–98 | Cambridge U | 2 | 0 | | |
| 1998–99 | Cambridge U | 2 | 0 | **4** | **0** |
| 1998–99 | Charlton Ath | 0 | 0 | | |
| 1999–2000 | Charlton Ath | 4 | 0 | **4** | **0** |
| 1999–2000 | *Swindon T* | 4 | 0 | **4** | **0** |
| 2000–01 | Brentford | 24 | 3 | | |
| 2001–02 | Brentford | 14 | 0 | | |
| 2002–03 | Brentford | 37 | 7 | **75** | **10** |
| 2002–03 | Millwall | 7 | 2 | | |
| 2003–04 | Millwall | 7 | 0 | **14** | **2** |

**McCARTNEY, David‡ (G) 0 0**

H: 5 11 W: 11 03 b.Essex 6-4-84

*Source:* Scholar.

| | | | | | |
|---|---|---|---|---|---|
| 2003–04 | Millwall | 0 | 0 | | |

**MUSCAT, Kevin (D) 360 22**

H: 5 11 W: 11 07 b.Crawley 7-8-73

*Honours:* Australia Under-20, Under-23, 40 full caps, 10 goals.

| | | | | | |
|---|---|---|---|---|---|
| 1989–90 | Sunshine | 9 | 0 | | |
| 1990–91 | Sunshine | 0 | 0 | **9** | **0** |
| 1991–92 | Heidelberg | 18 | 0 | **18** | **0** |
| 1992–93 | South Melbourne | 17 | 0 | | |
| 1993–94 | South Melbourne | 24 | 2 | | |
| 1994–95 | South Melbourne | 20 | 3 | | |
| 1995–96 | South Melbourne | 12 | 1 | **73** | **6** |
| 1996–97 | Crystal Palace | 44 | 2 | | |
| 1997–98 | Crystal Palace | 9 | 0 | **53** | **2** |
| 1997–98 | Wolverhampton W | 24 | 3 | | |
| 1998–99 | Wolverhampton W | 37 | 4 | | |
| 1999–2000 | Wolverhampton W | 45 | 4 | | |
| 2000–01 | Wolverhampton W | 37 | 3 | | |
| 2001–02 | Wolverhampton W | 37 | 0 | | |
| 2002–03 | Wolverhampton W | 0 | 0 | **180** | **14** |
| 2003–04 | Millwall | 27 | 0 | **27** | **0** |

**PEETERS, Bob (F) 273 74**

H: 6 5 W: 13 12 b.Lier 28-1-72

*Source:* Ternesse. *Honours:* Belgium 2 full caps.

| | | | | | |
|---|---|---|---|---|---|
| 1992–93 | Lierse | 12 | 0 | | |
| 1993–94 | Lierse | 17 | 0 | | |
| 1994–95 | Lierse | 26 | 8 | | |
| 1995–96 | Lierse | 29 | 7 | | |
| 1996–97 | Lierse | 34 | 7 | **118** | **22** |
| 1997–98 | Roda | 30 | 11 | | |
| 1998–99 | Roda | 33 | 13 | | |
| 1999–2000 | Roda | 30 | 15 | **93** | **39** |
| 2000–01 | Vitesse | 32 | 8 | | |
| 2001–02 | Vitesse | 10 | 2 | **42** | **10** |
| 2003–04 | Millwall | 20 | 3 | **20** | **3** |

**PHILLIPS, Mark (D) 8 0**

H: 6 2 W: 11 00 b.Lambeth 27-1-82

*Source:* Scholarship.

| | | | | | |
|---|---|---|---|---|---|
| 1999–2000 | Millwall | 0 | 0 | | |

| | | | | | |
|---|---|---|---|---|---|
| 2000–01 | Millwall | 0 | 0 | | |
| 2001–02 | Millwall | 1 | 0 | | |
| 2002–03 | Millwall | 7 | 0 | | |
| 2003–04 | Millwall | 0 | 0 | **8** | **0** |

**QUIGLEY, Mark (M) 1 0**
H: 5 10 W: 11 07 b.Dublin 27-10-85
*Source:* Scholar. *Honours:* Eire Youth.

| | | | | | |
|---|---|---|---|---|---|
| 2002–03 | Millwall | 0 | 0 | | |
| 2003–04 | Millwall | 1 | 0 | **1** | **0** |

**REES, Matt (D) 3 1**
H: 6 2 W: 12 00 b.Swansea 2-9-82
*Source:* Trainee. *Honours:* Wales Under-21.

| | | | | | |
|---|---|---|---|---|---|
| 1999–2000 | Millwall | 0 | 0 | | |
| 2000–01 | Millwall | 0 | 0 | | |
| 2001–02 | Millwall | 0 | 0 | | |
| 2002–03 | Millwall | 0 | 0 | | |
| 2003–04 | Millwall | 0 | 0 | | |
| 2003–04 | *Swansea C* | 3 | 1 | **3** | **1** |

**ROBERTS, Andy (M) 418 16**
H: 5 11 W: 14 05 b.Dartford 20-3-74
*Source:* Trainee. *Honours:* England Under-21.

| | | | | | |
|---|---|---|---|---|---|
| 1991–92 | Millwall | 7 | 0 | | |
| 1992–93 | Millwall | 45 | 0 | | |
| 1993–94 | Millwall | 42 | 2 | | |
| 1994–95 | Millwall | 44 | 3 | | |
| 1995–96 | Crystal Palace | 38 | 0 | | |
| 1996–97 | Crystal Palace | 45 | 2 | | |
| 1997–98 | Crystal Palace | 25 | 0 | **108** | **2** |
| 1997–98 | Wimbledon | 12 | 1 | | |
| 1998–99 | Wimbledon | 28 | 2 | | |
| 1999–2000 | Wimbledon | 16 | 0 | | |
| 2000–01 | Wimbledon | 27 | 2 | | |
| 2001–02 | Wimbledon | 18 | 1 | **101** | **6** |
| 2001–02 | *Norwich C* | 5 | 0 | **5** | **0** |
| 2002–03 | Millwall | 33 | 2 | | |
| 2003–04 | Millwall | 33 | 1 | **204** | **8** |

**ROBINSON, Anton (M) 0 0**
b.London 17-2-86
*Source:* Scholar.

| | | | | | |
|---|---|---|---|---|---|
| 2003–04 | Millwall | 0 | 0 | | |

**ROBINSON, Paul (D) 23 0**
H: 6 1 W: 11 08 b.Barnet 7-1-82
*Source:* Scholar.

| | | | | | |
|---|---|---|---|---|---|
| 2000–01 | Millwall | 0 | 0 | | |
| 2001–02 | Millwall | 0 | 0 | | |
| 2002–03 | Millwall | 14 | 0 | | |
| 2003–04 | Millwall | 9 | 0 | **23** | **0** |

**ROBINSON, Trevor (M) 1 0**
H: 5 9 W: 12 11 b.Jamaica 20-9-84
*Source:* Scholar.

| | | | | | |
|---|---|---|---|---|---|
| 2003–04 | Millwall | 1 | 0 | **1** | **0** |

**ROSE, Jason (D) 0 0**
H: 6 1 W: 10 13 b.Sidcup 28-1-85
*Source:* Scholar.

| | | | | | |
|---|---|---|---|---|---|
| 2003–04 | Millwall | 0 | 0 | | |

**RYAN, Robbie# (D) 241 2**
H: 5 10 W: 12 05 b.Dublin 16-5-77
*Source:* Belvedere. *Honours:* Eire Youth, Under-21.

| | | | | | |
|---|---|---|---|---|---|
| 1994–95 | Huddersfield T | 0 | 0 | | |
| 1995–96 | Huddersfield T | 0 | 0 | | |
| 1996–97 | Huddersfield T | 5 | 0 | | |
| 1997–98 | Huddersfield T | 10 | 0 | **15** | **0** |
| 1997–98 | Millwall | 16 | 0 | | |
| 1998–99 | Millwall | 26 | 0 | | |
| 1999–2000 | Millwall | 34 | 0 | | |
| 2000–01 | Millwall | 42 | 0 | | |
| 2001–02 | Millwall | 37 | 0 | | |
| 2002–03 | Millwall | 41 | 2 | | |
| 2003–04 | Millwall | 30 | 0 | **226** | **2** |

**SADLIER, Richard‡ (F) 145 34**
H: 6 2 W: 13 02 b.Dublin 14-1-79
*Source:* Belvedere. *Honours:* Eire Youth, Under-21, 1 full cap.

| | | | | | |
|---|---|---|---|---|---|
| 1996–97 | Millwall | 10 | 0 | | |
| 1997–98 | Millwall | 4 | 3 | | |
| 1998–99 | Millwall | 31 | 5 | | |
| 1999–2000 | Millwall | 27 | 5 | | |
| 2000–01 | Millwall | 29 | 6 | | |
| 2001–02 | Millwall | 37 | 14 | | |
| 2002–03 | Millwall | 5 | 1 | | |
| 2003–04 | Millwall | 2 | 0 | **145** | **34** |

**SAMBA, Cherno* (M) 0 0**
H: 5 10 W: 10 01 b.Gambia 10-1-85
*Source:* Scholar. *Honours:* England Youth.

| | | | | | |
|---|---|---|---|---|---|
| 2001–02 | Millwall | 0 | 0 | | |
| 2002–03 | Millwall | 0 | 0 | | |
| 2003–04 | Millwall | 0 | 0 | | |

**SUTTON, John (F) 12 1**
H: 6 0 W: 14 02 b.Norwich 26-12-83
*Source:* Scholar. *Honours:* England Youth.

| | | | | | |
|---|---|---|---|---|---|
| 2001–02 | Tottenham H | 0 | 0 | | |
| 2002–03 | Tottenham H | 0 | 0 | | |
| 2002–03 | *Carlisle U* | 7 | 1 | **7** | **1** |
| 2002–03 | Swindon T | 1 | 0 | **1** | **0** |
| 2003–04 | Millwall | 4 | 0 | **4** | **0** |

**SWEENEY, Peter (F) 35 3**
H: 6 0 W: 12 01 b.Glasgow 25-9-84
*Source:* Scholar.

| | | | | | |
|---|---|---|---|---|---|
| 2001–02 | Millwall | 1 | 0 | | |
| 2002–03 | Millwall | 5 | 1 | | |
| 2003–04 | Millwall | 29 | 2 | **35** | **3** |

**TIESSE, Alex* (M) 0 0**
H: 5 7 W: 9 11 b.Ivory Coast 15-8-85
*Source:* Scholar.

| | | | | | |
|---|---|---|---|---|---|
| 2002–03 | Millwall | 0 | 0 | | |
| 2003–04 | Millwall | 0 | 0 | | |

**WARD, Darren (D) 172 6**
H: 6 4 W: 11 04 b.Kenton 13-9-78
*Source:* Trainee.

| | | | | | |
|---|---|---|---|---|---|
| 1995–96 | Watford | 1 | 0 | | |
| 1996–97 | Watford | 7 | 0 | | |
| 1997–98 | Watford | 0 | 0 | | |
| 1998–99 | Watford | 1 | 0 | | |
| 1999–2000 | Watford | 9 | 1 | | |
| 1999–2000 | *QPR* | 14 | 0 | **14** | **0** |
| 2000–01 | Watford | 40 | 1 | | |
| 2001–02 | Watford | 1 | 0 | **59** | **2** |
| 2001–02 | Millwall | 14 | 0 | | |
| 2002–03 | Millwall | 39 | 1 | | |
| 2003–04 | Millwall | 46 | 3 | **99** | **4** |

**WARNER, Tony# (G) 211 0**
H: 6 4 W: 15 00 b.Liverpool 11-5-74
*Source:* School.

| | | | | | |
|---|---|---|---|---|---|
| 1993–94 | Liverpool | 0 | 0 | | |
| 1994–95 | Liverpool | 0 | 0 | | |
| 1995–96 | Liverpool | 0 | 0 | | |
| 1996–97 | Liverpool | 0 | 0 | | |
| 1997–98 | Liverpool | 0 | 0 | | |
| 1997–98 | *Swindon T* | 2 | 0 | **2** | **0** |
| 1998–99 | Liverpool | 0 | 0 | | |
| 1998–99 | *Celtic* | 3 | 0 | **3** | **0** |
| 1998–99 | *Aberdeen* | 6 | 0 | **6** | **0** |
| 1999–2000 | Millwall | 45 | 0 | | |
| 2000–01 | Millwall | 35 | 0 | | |
| 2001–02 | Millwall | 46 | 0 | | |
| 2002–03 | Millwall | 46 | 0 | | |
| 2003–04 | Millwall | 28 | 0 | **200** | **0** |

**WESTON, Curtis (M) 1 0**
H: 5 11 W: 11 09 b.Greenwich 24-1-87
*Source:* Scholar.

| | | | | | |
|---|---|---|---|---|---|
| 2003–04 | Millwall | 1 | 0 | **1** | **0** |

**WISE, Dennis (M) 544 85**
H: 5 6 W: 10 10 b.Kensington 16-12-66
*Source:* Southampton Apprentice. *Honours:* England Under-21, B, 21 full caps, 1 goal.

| | | | | | |
|---|---|---|---|---|---|
| 1984–85 | Wimbledon | 1 | 0 | | |
| 1985–86 | Wimbledon | 4 | 0 | | |
| 1986–87 | Wimbledon | 28 | 4 | | |
| 1987–88 | Wimbledon | 30 | 10 | | |
| 1988–89 | Wimbledon | 37 | 5 | | |
| 1989–90 | Wimbledon | 35 | 8 | **135** | **27** |
| 1990–91 | Chelsea | 33 | 10 | | |
| 1991–92 | Chelsea | 38 | 10 | | |
| 1992–93 | Chelsea | 27 | 3 | | |
| 1993–94 | Chelsea | 35 | 4 | | |
| 1994–95 | Chelsea | 19 | 6 | | |
| 1995–96 | Chelsea | 35 | 7 | | |
| 1996–97 | Chelsea | 31 | 3 | | |
| 1997–98 | Chelsea | 26 | 3 | | |
| 1998–99 | Chelsea | 22 | 0 | | |
| 1999–2000 | Chelsea | 30 | 4 | | |
| 2000–01 | Chelsea | 36 | 3 | **332** | **53** |
| 2001–02 | Leicester C | 17 | 1 | | |
| 2002–03 | Leicester C | 0 | 0 | **17** | **1** |
| 2002–03 | Millwall | 29 | 3 | | |
| 2003–04 | Millwall | 31 | 1 | **60** | **4** |

**Scholars**
Brooks, Alan M; Cant, Steven; Elliott, Jason; Harris, Daniel R; Hart, Edward M; Hendry, William M; Kelch, Keith P; McDonnell, Joseph E; Pooley, Dean; Williams, Marvin T

## NEWCASTLE U (52)

**ACUNA, Clarence‡ (M) 217 25**
H: 5 10 W: 12 00 b.Rancagua 8-2-75
*Honours:* Chile 58 full caps, 3 goals.

| | | | | | |
|---|---|---|---|---|---|
| 1994 | O'Higgins | 28 | 2 | | |
| 1995 | O'Higgins | 26 | 3 | | |
| 1996 | O'Higgins | 27 | 3 | **81** | **8** |
| 1997 | Univ de Chile | 27 | 3 | | |
| 1998 | Univ de Chile | 27 | 3 | | |
| 1999 | Univ de Chile | 36 | 5 | **90** | **11** |
| 2000–01 | Newcastle U | 26 | 3 | | |
| 2001–02 | Newcastle U | 16 | 3 | | |
| 2002–03 | Newcastle U | 4 | 0 | | |
| 2003–04 | Newcastle U | 0 | 0 | **46** | **6** |

**AMBROSE, Darren (M) 55 10**
H: 5 11 W: 10 05 b.Harlow 29-2-84
*Source:* Scholar. *Honours:* England Youth, Under-21.

| | | | | | |
|---|---|---|---|---|---|
| 2001–02 | Ipswich T | 1 | 0 | | |
| 2002–03 | Ipswich T | 29 | 8 | **30** | **8** |
| 2002–03 | Newcastle U | 1 | 0 | | |
| 2003–04 | Newcastle U | 24 | 2 | **25** | **2** |

**AMEOBI, Foluwashola (F) 89 14**
H: 6 3 W: 12 03 b.Zaria 12-10-81
*Source:* Trainee. *Honours:* England Under-21.

| | | | | | |
|---|---|---|---|---|---|
| 1998–99 | Newcastle U | 0 | 0 | | |
| 1999–2000 | Newcastle U | 0 | 0 | | |
| 2000–01 | Newcastle U | 20 | 2 | | |
| 2001–02 | Newcastle U | 15 | 0 | | |
| 2002–03 | Newcastle U | 28 | 5 | | |
| 2003–04 | Newcastle U | 26 | 7 | **89** | **14** |

**BELLAMY, Craig (F) 190 58**
H: 5 10 W: 11 00 b.Cardiff 13-7-79
*Source:* Trainee. *Honours:* Wales Schools, Youth, Under-21, 25 full caps, 6 goals.

| | | | | | |
|---|---|---|---|---|---|
| 1996–97 | Norwich C | 3 | 0 | | |
| 1997–98 | Norwich C | 36 | 13 | | |
| 1998–99 | Norwich C | 40 | 17 | | |
| 1999–2000 | Norwich C | 4 | 2 | | |
| 2000–01 | Norwich C | 1 | 0 | **84** | **32** |
| 2000–01 | Coventry C | 34 | 6 | **34** | **6** |
| 2001–02 | Newcastle U | 27 | 9 | | |
| 2002–03 | Newcastle U | 29 | 7 | | |
| 2003–04 | Newcastle U | 16 | 4 | **72** | **20** |

**BERNARD, Olivier (D) 91 8**
H: 5 7 W: 10 11 b.Paris 14-10-79

| | | | | | |
|---|---|---|---|---|---|
| 2000–01 | Newcastle U | 0 | 0 | | |
| 2000–01 | *Darlington* | 10 | 2 | **10** | **2** |
| 2001–02 | Newcastle U | 16 | 3 | | |
| 2002–03 | Newcastle U | 30 | 2 | | |
| 2003–04 | Newcastle U | 35 | 1 | **81** | **6** |

**BOWYER, Lee (M) 283 48**
H: 5 8 W: 10 04 b.London 3-1-77
*Source:* Trainee. *Honours:* England Youth, Under-21, 1 full cap.

| | | | | | |
|---|---|---|---|---|---|
| 1993–94 | Charlton Ath | 0 | 0 | | |
| 1994–95 | Charlton Ath | 5 | 0 | | |
| 1995–96 | Charlton Ath | 41 | 8 | **46** | **8** |
| 1996–97 | Leeds U | 32 | 4 | | |
| 1997–98 | Leeds U | 25 | 3 | | |
| 1998–99 | Leeds U | 35 | 9 | | |
| 1999–2000 | Leeds U | 33 | 5 | | |
| 2000–01 | Leeds U | 38 | 9 | | |
| 2001–02 | Leeds U | 25 | 5 | | |
| 2002–03 | Leeds U | 15 | 3 | **203** | **38** |
| 2002–03 | West Ham U | 10 | 0 | **10** | **0** |
| 2003–04 | Newcastle U | 24 | 2 | **24** | **2** |

**BRAMBLE, Titus (D) 95 1**
H: 6 2 W: 14 10 b.Ipswich 31-7-81
*Source:* Trainee. *Honours:* England Under-21.

| | | | | | |
|---|---|---|---|---|---|
| 1998–99 | Ipswich T | 4 | 0 | | |
| 1999–2000 | Ipswich T | 0 | 0 | | |
| 1999–2000 | *Colchester U* | 2 | 0 | **2** | **0** |
| 2000–01 | Ipswich T | 26 | 1 | | |
| 2001–02 | Ipswich T | 18 | 0 | **48** | **1** |

| | | | | | |
|---|---|---|---|---|---|
| 2002–03 | Newcastle U | 16 | 0 | | |
| 2003–04 | Newcastle U | 29 | 0 | **45** | **0** |

**BRENNAN, Stephen (D) 0 0**
H: 5 8 W: 11 10 b.Dublin 26-3-83
*Honours:* Eire Under-21.

| | | | | | |
|---|---|---|---|---|---|
| 1999–2000 | Newcastle U | 0 | 0 | | |
| 2000–01 | Newcastle U | 0 | 0 | | |
| 2001–02 | Newcastle U | 0 | 0 | | |
| 2002–03 | Newcastle U | 0 | 0 | | |
| 2003–04 | Newcastle U | 0 | 0 | | |

**BRITTAIN, Martin (M) 1 0**
H: 5 8 W: 10 07 b.Newcastle 29-12-84
*Source:* Trainee.

| | | | | | |
|---|---|---|---|---|---|
| 2003–04 | Newcastle U | 1 | 0 | **1** | **0** |

**CAIG, Tony (G) 289 0**
H: 6 0 W: 13 04 b.Whitehaven 11-4-74
*Source:* Trainee.

| | | | | | |
|---|---|---|---|---|---|
| 1992–93 | Carlisle U | 1 | 0 | | |
| 1993–94 | Carlisle U | 20 | 0 | | |
| 1994–95 | Carlisle U | 40 | 0 | | |
| 1995–96 | Carlisle U | 33 | 0 | | |
| 1996–97 | Carlisle U | 46 | 0 | | |
| 1997–98 | Carlisle U | 46 | 0 | | |
| 1998–99 | Carlisle U | 37 | 0 | **223** | **0** |
| 1998–99 | Blackpool | 10 | 0 | | |
| 1999–2000 | Blackpool | 33 | 0 | | |
| 2000–01 | Blackpool | 6 | 0 | **49** | **0** |
| 2000–01 | Charlton Ath | 1 | 0 | **1** | **0** |
| 2001–02 | Hibernian | 8 | 0 | | |
| 2002–03 | Hibernian | 5 | 0 | **13** | **0** |
| 2002–03 | Newcastle U | 0 | 0 | | |
| 2003–04 | Newcastle U | 0 | 0 | | |
| 2003–04 | *Barnsley* | 3 | 0 | **3** | **0** |

**CALDWELL, Gary‡ (D) 60 0**
H: 5 11 W: 11 10 b.Stirling 12-4-82
*Source:* Trainee. *Honours:* Scotland Under-21, 8 full caps, 1 goal.

| | | | | | |
|---|---|---|---|---|---|
| 1998–99 | Newcastle U | 0 | 0 | | |
| 1999–2000 | Newcastle U | 0 | 0 | | |
| 2000–01 | Newcastle U | 0 | 0 | | |
| 2001–02 | Newcastle U | 0 | 0 | | |
| 2001–02 | *Darlington* | 4 | 0 | **4** | **0** |
| 2001–02 | *Hibernian* | 11 | 0 | **11** | **0** |
| 2002–03 | Newcastle U | 0 | 0 | | |
| 2002–03 | *Coventry C* | 36 | 0 | **36** | **0** |
| 2003–04 | Newcastle U | 0 | 0 | | |
| 2003–04 | *Derby Co* | 9 | 0 | **9** | **0** |

**CALDWELL, Steven* (D) 56 2**
H: 6 0 W: 11 05 b.Stirling 12-9-80
*Source:* Trainee. *Honours:* Scotland Youth, Under-21, 4 full caps.

| | | | | | |
|---|---|---|---|---|---|
| 1997–98 | Newcastle U | 0 | 0 | | |
| 1998–99 | Newcastle U | 0 | 0 | | |
| 1999–2000 | Newcastle U | 0 | 0 | | |
| 2000–01 | Newcastle U | 9 | 0 | | |
| 2001–02 | Newcastle U | 0 | 0 | | |
| 2001–02 | *Blackpool* | 6 | 0 | **6** | **0** |
| 2001–02 | *Bradford C* | 9 | 0 | **9** | **0** |
| 2002–03 | Newcastle U | 14 | 1 | | |
| 2003–04 | Newcastle U | 5 | 0 | **28** | **1** |
| 2003–04 | *Leeds U* | 13 | 1 | **13** | **1** |

**CHOPRA, Michael (F) 17 5**
H: 5 8 W: 9 06 b.Newcastle 23-12-83
*Source:* Scholar. *Honours:* England Youth, Under-20, Under-21.

| | | | | | |
|---|---|---|---|---|---|
| 2000–01 | Newcastle U | 0 | 0 | | |
| 2001–02 | Newcastle U | 0 | 0 | | |
| 2002–03 | Newcastle U | 1 | 0 | | |
| 2002–03 | *Watford* | 5 | 5 | **5** | **5** |
| 2003–04 | Newcastle U | 6 | 0 | **7** | **0** |
| 2003–04 | *Nottingham F* | 5 | 0 | **5** | **0** |

**DYER, Kieron (M) 225 23**
H: 5 7 W: 9 07 b.Ipswich 29-12-78
*Source:* Trainee. *Honours:* England Youth, Under-21, B, 23 full caps.

| | | | | | |
|---|---|---|---|---|---|
| 1996–97 | Ipswich T | 13 | 0 | | |
| 1997–98 | Ipswich T | 41 | 4 | | |
| 1998–99 | Ipswich T | 37 | 5 | **91** | **9** |
| 1999–2000 | Newcastle U | 30 | 3 | | |
| 2000–01 | Newcastle U | 26 | 5 | | |
| 2001–02 | Newcastle U | 18 | 3 | | |
| 2002–03 | Newcastle U | 35 | 2 | | |
| 2003–04 | Newcastle U | 25 | 1 | **134** | **14** |

**ELLIOTT, Robbie (D) 194 15**
H: 5 8 W: 12 03 b.Gosforth 25-12-73
*Source:* Trainee. *Honours:* England Under-21.

| | | | | | |
|---|---|---|---|---|---|
| 1990–91 | Newcastle U | 6 | 0 | | |
| 1991–92 | Newcastle U | 9 | 0 | | |
| 1992–93 | Newcastle U | 0 | 0 | | |
| 1993–94 | Newcastle U | 15 | 0 | | |
| 1994–95 | Newcastle U | 14 | 2 | | |
| 1995–96 | Newcastle U | 6 | 0 | | |
| 1996–97 | Newcastle U | 29 | 7 | | |
| 1997–98 | Bolton W | 4 | 0 | | |
| 1998–99 | Bolton W | 22 | 0 | | |
| 1999–2000 | Bolton W | 27 | 3 | | |
| 2000–01 | Bolton W | 33 | 2 | **86** | **5** |
| 2001–02 | Newcastle U | 27 | 1 | | |
| 2002–03 | Newcastle U | 2 | 0 | | |
| 2003–04 | Newcastle U | 0 | 0 | **108** | **10** |

**FERRELL, Andrew* (M) 0 0**
b.Newcastle 9-1-84
*Source:* Trainee.

| | | | | | |
|---|---|---|---|---|---|
| 2002–03 | Newcastle U | 0 | 0 | | |
| 2003–04 | Newcastle U | 0 | 0 | | |

**GATE, Kris (D) 0 0**
H: 5 7 W: 10 03 b.Newcastle 1-1-85
*Source:* Trainee.

| | | | | | |
|---|---|---|---|---|---|
| 2003–04 | Newcastle U | 0 | 0 | | |

**GAVILAN, Diego‡ (D) 7 1**
H: 5 8 W: 10 07 b.Asuncion 1-3-80
*Source:* Cerro Porteno. *Honours:* Paraguay 23 full caps.

| | | | | | |
|---|---|---|---|---|---|
| 1999–2000 | Newcastle U | 6 | 1 | | |
| 2000–01 | Newcastle U | 1 | 0 | | |
| 2001–02 | Newcastle U | 0 | 0 | | |
| 2002–03 | Newcastle U | 0 | 0 | | |
| 2003–04 | Newcastle U | 0 | 0 | **7** | **1** |

**GIVEN, Shay (G) 241 0**
H: 6 0 W: 13 04 b.Lifford 20-4-76
*Source:* Celtic. *Honours:* Eire Under-21, 60 full caps.

| | | | | | |
|---|---|---|---|---|---|
| 1994–95 | Blackburn R | 0 | 0 | | |
| 1994–95 | *Swindon T* | 0 | 0 | | |
| 1995–96 | Blackburn R | 0 | 0 | | |
| 1995–96 | *Swindon T* | 5 | 0 | **5** | **0** |
| 1995–96 | *Sunderland* | 17 | 0 | **17** | **0** |
| 1996–97 | Blackburn R | 2 | 0 | **2** | **0** |
| 1997–98 | Newcastle U | 24 | 0 | | |
| 1998–99 | Newcastle U | 31 | 0 | | |
| 1999–2000 | Newcastle U | 14 | 0 | | |
| 2000–01 | Newcastle U | 34 | 0 | | |
| 2001–02 | Newcastle U | 38 | 0 | | |
| 2002–03 | Newcastle U | 38 | 0 | | |
| 2003–04 | Newcastle U | 38 | 0 | **217** | **0** |

**GRIFFIN, Andy* (D) 133 4**
H: 5 9 W: 10 10 b.Billinge 7-3-79
*Source:* Trainee. *Honours:* England Youth, Under-21.

| | | | | | |
|---|---|---|---|---|---|
| 1996–97 | Stoke C | 34 | 1 | | |
| 1997–98 | Stoke C | 23 | 1 | **57** | **2** |
| 1997–98 | Newcastle U | 4 | 0 | | |
| 1998–99 | Newcastle U | 14 | 0 | | |
| 1999–2000 | Newcastle U | 3 | 1 | | |
| 2000–01 | Newcastle U | 19 | 0 | | |
| 2001–02 | Newcastle U | 4 | 0 | | |
| 2002–03 | Newcastle U | 27 | 1 | | |
| 2003–04 | Newcastle U | 5 | 0 | **76** | **2** |

**GUY, Lewis (F) 0 0**
H: 5 10 W: 10 08 b.Penrith 27-8-85
*Source:* Trainee. *Honours:* England Youth.

| | | | | | |
|---|---|---|---|---|---|
| 2002–03 | Newcastle U | 0 | 0 | | |
| 2003–04 | Newcastle U | 0 | 0 | | |

**HARPER, Steve (G) 71 0**
H: 6 2 W: 13 00 b.Easington 14-3-75
*Source:* Seaham Red Star.

| | | | | | |
|---|---|---|---|---|---|
| 1993–94 | Newcastle U | 0 | 0 | | |
| 1994–95 | Newcastle U | 0 | 0 | | |
| 1995–96 | Newcastle U | 0 | 0 | | |
| 1995–96 | *Bradford C* | 1 | 0 | **1** | **0** |
| 1996–97 | Newcastle U | 0 | 0 | | |
| 1996–97 | *Stockport Co* | 0 | 0 | | |
| 1997–98 | Newcastle U | 0 | 0 | | |
| 1997–98 | *Hartlepool U* | 15 | 0 | **15** | **0** |
| 1997–98 | *Huddersfield T* | 24 | 0 | **24** | **0** |
| 1998–99 | Newcastle U | 8 | 0 | | |
| 1999–2000 | Newcastle U | 18 | 0 | | |
| 2000–01 | Newcastle U | 5 | 0 | | |
| 2001–02 | Newcastle U | 0 | 0 | | |
| 2002–03 | Newcastle U | 0 | 0 | | |
| 2003–04 | Newcastle U | 0 | 0 | **31** | **0** |

**HUGHES, Aaron (D) 183 3**
H: 6 1 W: 11 02 b.Cookstown 8-11-79
*Source:* Trainee. *Honours:* Northern Ireland Youth, B, 35 full caps.

| | | | | | |
|---|---|---|---|---|---|
| 1996–97 | Newcastle U | 0 | 0 | | |
| 1997–98 | Newcastle U | 4 | 0 | | |
| 1998–99 | Newcastle U | 14 | 0 | | |
| 1999–2000 | Newcastle U | 27 | 2 | | |
| 2000–01 | Newcastle U | 35 | 0 | | |
| 2001–02 | Newcastle U | 34 | 0 | | |
| 2002–03 | Newcastle U | 35 | 1 | | |
| 2003–04 | Newcastle U | 34 | 0 | **183** | **3** |

**JENAS, Jermaine (M) 104 12**
H: 5 10 W: 12 00 b.Nottingham 18-2-83
*Source:* Scholar. *Honours:* England Youth, Under-21, 6 full caps.

| | | | | | |
|---|---|---|---|---|---|
| 1999–2000 | Nottingham F | 0 | 0 | | |
| 2000–01 | Nottingham F | 1 | 0 | | |
| 2001–02 | Nottingham F | 28 | 4 | **29** | **4** |
| 2001–02 | Newcastle U | 12 | 0 | | |
| 2002–03 | Newcastle U | 32 | 6 | | |
| 2003–04 | Newcastle U | 31 | 2 | **75** | **8** |

**KERR, Brian* (M) 21 0**
H: 5 10 W: 10 11 b.Motherwell 12-10-81
*Source:* Trainee. *Honours:* Scotland Schools, Youth, Under-21, 2 full caps.

| | | | | | |
|---|---|---|---|---|---|
| 1998–99 | Newcastle U | 0 | 0 | | |
| 1999–2000 | Newcastle U | 0 | 0 | | |
| 2000–01 | Newcastle U | 1 | 0 | | |
| 2001–02 | Newcastle U | 0 | 0 | | |
| 2002–03 | Newcastle U | 8 | 0 | | |
| 2002–03 | *Coventry C* | 3 | 0 | | |
| 2003–04 | Newcastle U | 0 | 0 | **9** | **0** |
| 2003–04 | *Coventry C* | 9 | 0 | **12** | **0** |

**LUA-LUA, Lomano (F) 135 24**
H: 5 8 W: 12 00 b.Kinshasa 28-12-80
*Honours:* DR Congo 4 full caps.

| | | | | | |
|---|---|---|---|---|---|
| 1998–99 | Colchester U | 13 | 1 | | |
| 1999–2000 | Colchester U | 41 | 12 | | |
| 2000–01 | Colchester U | 7 | 2 | **61** | **15** |
| 2000–01 | Newcastle U | 21 | 0 | | |
| 2001–02 | Newcastle U | 20 | 3 | | |
| 2002–03 | Newcastle U | 11 | 2 | | |
| 2003–04 | Newcastle U | 7 | 0 | **59** | **5** |
| 2003–04 | *Portsmouth* | 15 | 4 | **15** | **4** |

**McCLEN, Jamie (M) 14 0**
H: 5 8 W: 10 07 b.Newcastle 13-5-79
*Source:* Trainee.

| | | | | | |
|---|---|---|---|---|---|
| 1997–98 | Newcastle U | 0 | 0 | | |
| 1998–99 | Newcastle U | 1 | 0 | | |
| 1999–2000 | Newcastle U | 9 | 0 | | |
| 2000–01 | Newcastle U | 0 | 0 | | |
| 2001–02 | Newcastle U | 3 | 0 | | |
| 2002–03 | Newcastle U | 1 | 0 | | |
| 2003–04 | Newcastle U | 0 | 0 | **14** | **0** |

**NORTON, Lee‡ (M) 0 0**
b.Newcastle 1-8-84
*Source:* Trainee.

| | | | | | |
|---|---|---|---|---|---|
| 2002–03 | Newcastle U | 0 | 0 | | |
| 2003–04 | Newcastle U | 0 | 0 | | |

**O'BRIEN, Alan (M) 0 0**
H: 5 9 W: 11 00 b.Dublin 20-2-85
*Source:* Scholar.

| | | | | | |
|---|---|---|---|---|---|
| 2001–02 | Newcastle U | 0 | 0 | | |
| 2002–03 | Newcastle U | 0 | 0 | | |
| 2003–04 | Newcastle U | 0 | 0 | | |

**O'BRIEN, Andy (D) 230 7**
H: 6 3 W: 11 05 b.Harrogate 29-6-79
*Source:* Trainee. *Honours:* England Youth, Under-21, Eire Under-21, 13 full caps.

| | | | | | |
|---|---|---|---|---|---|
| 1996–97 | Bradford C | 22 | 2 | | |
| 1997–98 | Bradford C | 26 | 0 | | |
| 1998–99 | Bradford C | 31 | 0 | | |
| 1999–2000 | Bradford C | 36 | 1 | | |
| 2000–01 | Bradford C | 18 | 0 | **133** | **3** |
| 2000–01 | Newcastle U | 9 | 1 | | |
| 2001–02 | Newcastle U | 34 | 2 | | |
| 2002–03 | Newcastle U | 26 | 0 | | |
| 2003–04 | Newcastle U | 28 | 1 | **97** | **4** |

**OFFIONG, Richard (F)** **20 2**
H: 5 11 W: 12 00 b.South Shields 17-12-83
*Source:* Scholar. *Honours:* England Youth, Under-20.

| | | | | | |
|---|---|---|---|---|---|
| 2001–02 | Newcastle U | 0 | 0 | | |
| 2002–03 | Newcastle U | 0 | 0 | | |
| 2002–03 | *Darlington* | 7 | 2 | **7** | **2** |
| 2002–03 | *Motherwell* | 9 | 0 | **9** | **0** |
| 2003–04 | Newcastle U | 0 | 0 | | |
| 2003–04 | *York C* | 4 | 0 | **4** | **0** |

**ORR, Bradley* (M)** **4 0**
H: 6 0 W: 11 11 b.Liverpool 1-11-82
*Source:* Scholar.

| | | | | | |
|---|---|---|---|---|---|
| 2001–02 | Newcastle U | 0 | 0 | | |
| 2002–03 | Newcastle U | 0 | 0 | | |
| 2003–04 | Newcastle U | 0 | 0 | | |
| 2003–04 | *Burnley* | 4 | 0 | **4** | **0** |

**RAMAGE, Peter (D)** **0 0**
H: 6 1 W: 11 13 b.Ashington 22-11-83
*Source:* Trainee.

| | | | | | |
|---|---|---|---|---|---|
| 2003–04 | Newcastle U | 0 | 0 | | |

**ROBERT, Laurent (M)** **283 61**
H: 5 8 W: 10 13 b.Saint-Benoit 21-5-75
*Honours:* France 9 full caps, 1 goal.

| | | | | | |
|---|---|---|---|---|---|
| 1994–95 | Montpellier | 7 | 0 | | |
| 1995–96 | Montpellier | 21 | 5 | | |
| 1996–97 | Nancy | 38 | 1 | **38** | **1** |
| 1997–98 | Montpellier | 26 | 2 | | |
| 1998–99 | Montpellier | 32 | 11 | **86** | **18** |
| 1999–2000 | Paris St Germain | 28 | 9 | | |
| 2000–01 | Paris St Germain | 32 | 14 | | |
| 2001–02 | Paris St Germain | 1 | 0 | **61** | **23** |
| 2001–02 | Newcastle U | 36 | 8 | | |
| 2002–03 | Newcastle U | 27 | 5 | | |
| 2003–04 | Newcastle U | 35 | 6 | **98** | **19** |

**SHEARER, Alan (F)** **499 266**
H: 6 0 W: 12 06 b.Newcastle 13-8-70
*Source:* Trainee. *Honours:* England Youth, Under-21, B, 63 full caps, 30 goals.

| | | | | | |
|---|---|---|---|---|---|
| 1987–88 | Southampton | 5 | 3 | | |
| 1988–89 | Southampton | 10 | 0 | | |
| 1989–90 | Southampton | 26 | 3 | | |
| 1990–91 | Southampton | 36 | 4 | | |
| 1991–92 | Southampton | 41 | 13 | **118** | **23** |
| 1992–93 | Blackburn R | 21 | 16 | | |
| 1993–94 | Blackburn R | 40 | 31 | | |
| 1994–95 | Blackburn R | 42 | 34 | | |
| 1995–96 | Blackburn R | 35 | 31 | **138** | **112** |
| 1996–97 | Newcastle U | 31 | 25 | | |
| 1997–98 | Newcastle U | 17 | 2 | | |
| 1998–99 | Newcastle U | 30 | 14 | | |
| 1999–2000 | Newcastle U | 37 | 23 | | |
| 2000–01 | Newcastle U | 19 | 5 | | |
| 2001–02 | Newcastle U | 37 | 23 | | |
| 2002–03 | Newcastle U | 35 | 17 | | |
| 2003–04 | Newcastle U | 37 | 22 | **243** | **131** |

**SPEED, Gary (M)** **519 84**
H: 5 10 W: 10 12 b.Deeside 8-9-69
*Source:* Trainee. *Honours:* Wales Youth, Under-21, 80 full caps, 6 goals.

| | | | | | |
|---|---|---|---|---|---|
| 1988–89 | Leeds U | 1 | 0 | | |
| 1989–90 | Leeds U | 25 | 3 | | |
| 1990–91 | Leeds U | 38 | 7 | | |
| 1991–92 | Leeds U | 41 | 7 | | |
| 1992–93 | Leeds U | 39 | 7 | | |
| 1993–94 | Leeds U | 36 | 10 | | |
| 1994–95 | Leeds U | 39 | 3 | | |
| 1995–96 | Leeds U | 29 | 2 | **248** | **39** |
| 1996–97 | Everton | 37 | 9 | | |
| 1997–98 | Everton | 21 | 7 | **58** | **16** |
| 1997–98 | Newcastle U | 13 | 1 | | |
| 1998–99 | Newcastle U | 38 | 4 | | |
| 1999–2000 | Newcastle U | 36 | 9 | | |
| 2000–01 | Newcastle U | 35 | 5 | | |
| 2001–02 | Newcastle U | 29 | 5 | | |
| 2002–03 | Newcastle U | 24 | 2 | | |
| 2003–04 | Newcastle U | 38 | 3 | **213** | **29** |

**TAYLOR, Steven (D)** **7 0**
H: 6 1 W: 13 00 b.Greenwich 23-1-86
*Source:* Trainee. *Honours:* FA Schools, England Youth, Under-20, Under-21.

| | | | | | |
|---|---|---|---|---|---|
| 2002–03 | Newcastle U | 0 | 0 | | |
| 2003–04 | Newcastle U | 1 | 0 | **1** | **0** |
| 2003–04 | *Wycombe W* | 6 | 0 | **6** | **0** |

**VIANA, Hugo (M)** **65 3**
H: 5 9 W: 11 09 b.Barcelos 15-1-83
*Honours:* Portugal 12 full caps.

| | | | | | |
|---|---|---|---|---|---|
| 2001–02 | Sporting Lisbon | 26 | 1 | **26** | **1** |
| 2002–03 | Newcastle U | 23 | 2 | | |
| 2003–04 | Newcastle U | 16 | 0 | **39** | **2** |

**WOODGATE, Jonathan (D)** **132 4**
H: 6 2 W: 12 06 b.Middlesbrough 22-1-80
*Source:* Trainee. *Honours:* England Youth, Under-21, 5 full caps.

| | | | | | |
|---|---|---|---|---|---|
| 1996–97 | Leeds U | 0 | 0 | | |
| 1997–98 | Leeds U | 0 | 0 | | |
| 1998–99 | Leeds U | 25 | 2 | | |
| 1999–2000 | Leeds U | 34 | 1 | | |
| 2000–01 | Leeds U | 14 | 1 | | |
| 2001–02 | Leeds U | 13 | 0 | | |
| 2002–03 | Leeds U | 18 | 0 | **104** | **4** |
| 2002–03 | Newcastle U | 10 | 0 | | |
| 2003–04 | Newcastle U | 18 | 0 | **28** | **0** |

**ZOLA MAKONGO, Calvin* (F)** **25 5**
H: 6 1 W: 12 00 b.Kinshasha 31-12-84
*Source:* Scholar.

| | | | | | |
|---|---|---|---|---|---|
| 2001–02 | Newcastle U | 0 | 0 | | |
| 2002–03 | Newcastle U | 0 | 0 | | |
| 2003–04 | Newcastle U | 0 | 0 | | |
| 2003–04 | *Oldham Ath* | 25 | 5 | **25** | **5** |

**Scholars**
Atkin, Liam; Bartlett, Adam J; Bates, Guy L; Baxter, Craig M; Cave, Philip A; Edgar, David E; Farman, Christopher; Finnigan, Carl J; Howe, Daniel R; Marshall, Scott A; Pattison, Matthew; Shanks, Christopher; Smith, Benjamin J; Smylie, Daryl; Walton, Marc D; Webster, Benjamin G

## NORTHAMPTON T (53)

**AMOO, Ryan (M)** **1 0**
H: 5 10 W: 9 12 b.Leicester 11-10-83
*Source:* Scholar.

| | | | | | |
|---|---|---|---|---|---|
| 2001–02 | Aston Villa | 0 | 0 | | |
| 2002–03 | Aston Villa | 0 | 0 | | |
| 2003–04 | Aston Villa | 0 | 0 | | |
| 2003–04 | Northampton T | 1 | 0 | **1** | **0** |

**ASAMOAH, Derek (F)** **113 10**
H: 5 6 W: 10 12 b.Ghana 1-5-81
*Source:* Slough T.

| | | | | | |
|---|---|---|---|---|---|
| 2001–02 | Northampton T | 40 | 3 | | |
| 2002–03 | Northampton T | 42 | 4 | | |
| 2003–04 | Northampton T | 31 | 3 | **113** | **10** |

**BURGESS, Oliver‡ (M)** **19 1**
H: 5 10 W: 11 08 b.Bracknell 12-10-81
*Source:* Scholar.

| | | | | | |
|---|---|---|---|---|---|
| 2000–01 | QPR | 1 | 0 | | |
| 2001–02 | QPR | 4 | 1 | | |
| 2002–03 | QPR | 5 | 0 | **10** | **1** |
| 2003–04 | Northampton T | 9 | 0 | **9** | **0** |

**CARRUTHERS, Chris (D)** **73 1**
H: 5 10 W: 12 03 b.Kettering 19-8-83
*Source:* Scholar. *Honours:* England Under-20.

| | | | | | |
|---|---|---|---|---|---|
| 2000–01 | Northampton T | 3 | 0 | | |
| 2001–02 | Northampton T | 13 | 1 | | |
| 2002–03 | Northampton T | 33 | 0 | | |
| 2003–04 | Northampton T | 24 | 0 | **73** | **1** |

**CAVILL, Aaran‡ (M)** **1 0**
H: 5 11 W: 11 03 b.Bedford 5-3-84
*Source:* Scholar.

| | | | | | |
|---|---|---|---|---|---|
| 2001–02 | Northampton T | 1 | 0 | | |
| 2002–03 | Northampton T | 0 | 0 | | |
| 2003–04 | Northampton T | 0 | 0 | **1** | **0** |

**CHAMBERS, Luke (D)** **25 0**
H: 6 1 W: 11 13 b.Kettering 29-8-85
*Source:* Scholar.

| | | | | | |
|---|---|---|---|---|---|
| 2002–03 | Northampton T | 1 | 0 | | |
| 2003–04 | Northampton T | 24 | 0 | **25** | **0** |

**CLARK, Peter (D)** **160 4**
H: 6 1 W: 12 01 b.Romford 10-12-79
*Source:* Arsenal Trainee.

| | | | | | |
|---|---|---|---|---|---|
| 1998–99 | Carlisle U | 36 | 0 | | |
| 1999–2000 | Carlisle U | 43 | 1 | **79** | **1** |
| 2000–01 | Stockport Co | 37 | 2 | | |
| 2001–02 | Stockport Co | 14 | 0 | | |
| 2002–03 | Stockport Co | 21 | 1 | **72** | **3** |
| 2002–03 | *Mansfield T* | 3 | 0 | **3** | **0** |
| 2003–04 | Northampton T | 6 | 0 | **6** | **0** |

**CRACKNELL, Dean‡ (M)** **0 0**
H: 5 10 W: 12 04 b.Hitchin 12-10-83
*Source:* Scholar.

| | | | | | |
|---|---|---|---|---|---|
| 2003–04 | Northampton T | 0 | 0 | | |

**GALBRAITH, David† (M)** **0 0**
H: 5 8 W: 11 00 b.Luton 21-12-83
*Source:* Trainee.

| | | | | | |
|---|---|---|---|---|---|
| 2003–04 | Tottenham H | 0 | 0 | | |
| 2003–04 | Northampton T | 0 | 0 | | |

**HARGREAVES, Chris# (M)** **392 22**
H: 5 11 W: 13 02 b.Cleethorpes 12-5-72
*Source:* Trainee.

| | | | | | |
|---|---|---|---|---|---|
| 1989–90 | Grimsby T | 19 | 2 | | |
| 1990–91 | Grimsby T | 18 | 3 | | |
| 1991–92 | Grimsby T | 10 | 0 | | |
| 1992–93 | Grimsby T | 4 | 0 | | |
| 1992–93 | *Scarborough* | 3 | 0 | **3** | **0** |
| 1993–94 | Grimsby T | 0 | 0 | **51** | **5** |
| 1993–94 | Hull C | 28 | 0 | | |
| 1994–95 | Hull C | 21 | 0 | **49** | **0** |
| 1995–96 | WBA | 1 | 0 | **1** | **0** |
| 1995–96 | *Hereford U* | 17 | 2 | | |
| 1996–97 | Hereford U | 44 | 4 | | |
| 1997–98 | Hereford U | 0 | 0 | **61** | **6** |

From Hereford U.

| | | | | | |
|---|---|---|---|---|---|
| 1998–99 | Plymouth Arg | 32 | 2 | | |
| 1999–2000 | Plymouth Arg | 44 | 3 | **76** | **5** |
| 2000–01 | Northampton T | 31 | 0 | | |
| 2001–02 | Northampton T | 39 | 3 | | |
| 2002–03 | Northampton T | 39 | 0 | | |
| 2003–04 | Northampton T | 42 | 3 | **151** | **6** |

**HARPER, Lee# (G)** **192 0**
H: 6 1 W: 15 06 b.Chelsea 30-10-71
*Source:* Sittingbourne.

| | | | | | |
|---|---|---|---|---|---|
| 1994–95 | Arsenal | 0 | 0 | | |
| 1995–96 | Arsenal | 0 | 0 | | |
| 1996–97 | Arsenal | 1 | 0 | **1** | **0** |
| 1997–98 | QPR | 36 | 0 | | |
| 1998–99 | QPR | 15 | 0 | | |
| 1999–2000 | QPR | 38 | 0 | | |
| 2000–01 | QPR | 29 | 0 | **118** | **0** |
| 2001–02 | Walsall | 3 | 0 | **3** | **0** |
| 2002–03 | Northampton T | 31 | 0 | | |
| 2003–04 | Northampton T | 39 | 0 | **70** | **0** |

**HICKS, David (M)** **0 0**
*Source:* Tottenham H Scholar.

| | | | | | |
|---|---|---|---|---|---|
| 2003–04 | Northampton T | 0 | 0 | | |

**LINCOLN, Greg* (M)** **19 1**
H: 5 9 W: 10 13 b.Cheshunt 23-3-80
*Source:* Trainee. *Honours:* England Youth.

| | | | | | |
|---|---|---|---|---|---|
| 1998–99 | Arsenal | 0 | 0 | | |
| 1999–2000 | Arsenal | 0 | 0 | | |
| 2000–01 | Arsenal | 0 | 0 | | |
| 2001–02 | Torquay U | 0 | 0 | | |
| 2002–03 | Northampton T | 12 | 0 | | |
| 2003–04 | Northampton T | 7 | 1 | **19** | **1** |

**LOW, Josh (F)** **156 13**
H: 6 2 W: 14 03 b.Bristol 15-2-79
*Source:* Trainee. *Honours:* Wales Youth, Under-21.

| | | | | | |
|---|---|---|---|---|---|
| 1995–96 | Bristol R | 1 | 0 | | |
| 1996–97 | Bristol R | 3 | 0 | | |
| 1997–98 | Bristol R | 10 | 0 | | |
| 1998–99 | Bristol R | 8 | 0 | **22** | **0** |
| 1999–2000 | Leyton Orient | 5 | 1 | **5** | **1** |
| 1999–2000 | Cardiff C | 17 | 2 | | |
| 2000–01 | Cardiff C | 36 | 4 | | |
| 2001–02 | Cardiff C | 22 | 0 | | |
| 2002–03 | Cardiff C | 0 | 0 | **75** | **6** |
| 2002–03 | Oldham Ath | 21 | 3 | **21** | **3** |
| 2003–04 | Northampton T | 33 | 3 | **33** | **3** |

**LYTTLE, Des* (D)** **352 5**
H: 5 9 W: 12 13 b.Wolverhampton 24-9-71
*Source:* Worcester C.

| | | | | | |
|---|---|---|---|---|---|
| 1992–93 | Swansea C | 46 | 1 | **46** | **1** |
| 1993–94 | Nottingham F | 37 | 1 | | |
| 1994–95 | Nottingham F | 38 | 0 | | |
| 1995–96 | Nottingham F | 33 | 1 | | |
| 1996–97 | Nottingham F | 32 | 1 | | |
| 1997–98 | Nottingham F | 35 | 0 | | |
| 1998–99 | Nottingham F | 10 | 0 | **185** | **3** |
| 1998–99 | *Port Vale* | 7 | 0 | **7** | **0** |
| 1999–2000 | Watford | 11 | 0 | **11** | **0** |

| | | | | | |
|---|---|---|---|---|---|
| 1999–2000 | *WBA* | 9 | 0 | | |
| 2000–01 | WBA | 40 | 1 | | |
| 2001–02 | WBA | 23 | 0 | | |
| 2002–03 | WBA | 4 | 0 | | |
| 2003–04 | WBA | 0 | 0 | **76** | **1** |
| 2003–04 | Northampton T | 27 | 0 | **27** | **0** |

**MORISON, Steven (F)** **19 2**

H: 6 2 W: 13 07 b.Enfield 29-8-83

*Source:* Scholar.

| | | | | | |
|---|---|---|---|---|---|
| 2001–02 | Northampton T | 1 | 0 | | |
| 2002–03 | Northampton T | 13 | 1 | | |
| 2003–04 | Northampton T | 5 | 1 | **19** | **2** |

**REEVES, Martin (M)** **30 1**

H: 6 0 W: 12 01 b.Birmingham 7-9-81

*Source:* Scholar.

| | | | | | |
|---|---|---|---|---|---|
| 2000–01 | Leicester C | 0 | 0 | | |
| 2001–02 | Leicester C | 5 | 0 | | |
| 2002–03 | Leicester C | 3 | 0 | **8** | **0** |
| 2002–03 | *Hull C* | 8 | 1 | **8** | **1** |
| 2003–04 | Northampton T | 14 | 0 | **14** | **0** |

**REID, Paul (D)** **72 3**

H: 6 2 W: 12 05 b.Carlisle 18-2-82

*Source:* Trainee. *Honours:* England Youth, Under-20.

| | | | | | |
|---|---|---|---|---|---|
| 1998–99 | Carlisle U | 0 | 0 | | |
| 1999–2000 | Carlisle U | 19 | 0 | **19** | **0** |
| 2000–01 | Rangers | 0 | 0 | | |
| 2001–02 | Rangers | 0 | 0 | | |
| 2001–02 | *Preston NE* | 1 | 1 | **1** | **1** |
| 2002–03 | Rangers | 0 | 0 | | |
| 2002–03 | *Northampton T* | 19 | 0 | | |
| 2003–04 | Northampton T | 33 | 2 | **52** | **2** |

**RICHARDS, Marc (F)** **72 15**

H: 6 0 W: 13 04 b.Wolverhampton 8-7-82

*Source:* Trainee. *Honours:* England Youth, Under-20.

| | | | | | |
|---|---|---|---|---|---|
| 1999–2000 | Blackburn R | 0 | 0 | | |
| 2000–01 | Blackburn R | 0 | 0 | | |
| 2001–02 | Blackburn R | 0 | 0 | | |
| 2001–02 | *Crewe Alex* | 4 | 0 | **4** | **0** |
| 2001–02 | *Oldham Ath* | 5 | 0 | **5** | **0** |
| 2001–02 | *Halifax T* | 5 | 0 | **5** | **0** |
| 2002–03 | Blackburn R | 0 | 0 | | |
| 2002–03 | *Swansea C* | 17 | 7 | **17** | **7** |
| 2003–04 | Northampton T | 41 | 8 | **41** | **8** |

**SABIN, Eric# (F)** **124 18**

H: 6 1 W: 12 04 b.Sarcelles 22-1-75

| | | | | | |
|---|---|---|---|---|---|
| 2000–01 | Wasquehal | 28 | 3 | **28** | **3** |
| 2001–02 | Swindon T | 34 | 5 | | |
| 2002–03 | Swindon T | 39 | 4 | **73** | **9** |
| 2003–04 | QPR | 10 | 1 | **10** | **1** |
| 2003–04 | *Boston U* | 2 | 0 | **2** | **0** |
| 2003–04 | Northampton T | 11 | 5 | **11** | **5** |

**SAMPSON, Ian* (D)** **407 27**

H: 6 2 W: 13 07 b.Wakefield 14-11-68

*Source:* Goole T.

| | | | | | |
|---|---|---|---|---|---|
| 1990–91 | Sunderland | 0 | 0 | | |
| 1991–92 | Sunderland | 8 | 0 | | |
| 1992–93 | Sunderland | 5 | 1 | | |
| 1993–94 | Sunderland | 4 | 0 | **17** | **1** |
| 1993–94 | *Northampton T* | 8 | 0 | | |
| 1994–95 | Northampton T | 42 | 2 | | |
| 1995–96 | Northampton T | 33 | 4 | | |
| 1996–97 | Northampton T | 43 | 5 | | |
| 1997–98 | Northampton T | 39 | 3 | | |
| 1998–99 | Northampton T | 42 | 1 | | |
| 1999–2000 | Northampton T | 45 | 6 | | |
| 2000–01 | Northampton T | 41 | 2 | | |
| 2001–02 | Northampton T | 27 | 0 | | |
| 2002–03 | Northampton T | 33 | 1 | | |
| 2003–04 | Northampton T | 37 | 2 | **390** | **26** |

**SMITH, Martin (F)** **269 75**

H: 5 11 W: 12 07 b.Sunderland 13-11-74

*Source:* Trainee. *Honours:* England Schools, Under-21.

| | | | | | |
|---|---|---|---|---|---|
| 1992–93 | Sunderland | 0 | 0 | | |
| 1993–94 | Sunderland | 29 | 8 | | |
| 1994–95 | Sunderland | 35 | 10 | | |
| 1995–96 | Sunderland | 20 | 2 | | |
| 1996–97 | Sunderland | 11 | 0 | | |
| 1997–98 | Sunderland | 16 | 2 | | |
| 1998–99 | Sunderland | 8 | 3 | **119** | **25** |
| 1999–2000 | Sheffield U | 26 | 10 | **26** | **10** |
| 1999–2000 | Huddersfield T | 12 | 4 | | |
| 2000–01 | Huddersfield T | 30 | 8 | | |
| 2001–02 | Huddersfield T | 0 | 0 | | |
| 2002–03 | Huddersfield T | 38 | 17 | **80** | **29** |
| 2003–04 | Northampton T | 44 | 11 | **44** | **11** |

**SMITH, Tom‡ (D)** **0 0**

H: 6 1 W: 12 03 b.Sheffield 26-12-83

*Source:* Rotherham U Scholar.

| | | | | | |
|---|---|---|---|---|---|
| 2003–04 | Northampton T | 0 | 0 | | |

**TAYLOR, John† (F)** **524 152**

H: 6 2 W: 13 12 b.Norwich 24-10-64

*Source:* Local.

| | | | | | |
|---|---|---|---|---|---|
| 1982–83 | Colchester U | 0 | 0 | | |
| 1983–84 | Colchester U | 0 | 0 | | |
| 1984–85 | Colchester U | 0 | 0 | | |
| From Sudbury T | | | | | |
| 1988–89 | Cambridge U | 40 | 12 | | |
| 1989–90 | Cambridge U | 45 | 15 | | |
| 1990–91 | Cambridge U | 40 | 14 | | |
| 1991–92 | Cambridge U | 35 | 5 | | |
| 1991–92 | Bristol R | 8 | 7 | | |
| 1992–93 | Bristol R | 42 | 14 | | |
| 1993–94 | Bristol R | 45 | 23 | **95** | **44** |
| 1994–95 | Bradford C | 36 | 11 | **36** | **11** |
| 1994–95 | Luton T | 9 | 3 | | |
| 1995–96 | Luton T | 28 | 0 | | |
| 1996–97 | Luton T | 0 | 0 | **37** | **3** |
| 1996–97 | *Lincoln C* | 5 | 2 | **5** | **2** |
| 1996–97 | *Colchester U* | 8 | 5 | **8** | **5** |
| 1996–97 | Cambridge U | 21 | 4 | | |
| 1997–98 | Cambridge U | 34 | 10 | | |
| 1998–99 | Cambridge U | 40 | 17 | | |
| 1999–2000 | Cambridge U | 40 | 6 | | |
| 2000–01 | Cambridge U | 30 | 3 | | |
| 2001–02 | Cambridge U | 0 | 0 | | |
| 2002–03 | Cambridge U | 1 | 0 | | |
| 2003–04 | Cambridge U | 9 | 0 | **335** | **86** |
| 2003–04 | Northampton T | 8 | 1 | **8** | **1** |

**THOMPSON, Glyn* (G)** **36 0**

H: 6 2 W: 13 01 b.Telford 24-2-81

*Source:* Trainee.

| | | | | | |
|---|---|---|---|---|---|
| 1998–99 | Shrewsbury T | 1 | 0 | | |
| 1999–2000 | Shrewsbury T | 0 | 0 | | |
| 1999–2000 | Fulham | 0 | 0 | | |
| 1999–2000 | *Mansfield T* | 16 | 0 | **16** | **0** |
| 2000–01 | Fulham | 0 | 0 | | |
| 2000–01 | *Shrewsbury T* | 0 | 0 | **1** | **0** |
| 2001–02 | Fulham | 0 | 0 | | |
| 2002–03 | Fulham | 0 | 0 | | |
| 2002–03 | Northampton T | 11 | 0 | | |
| 2003–04 | Northampton T | 8 | 0 | **19** | **0** |

**TROLLOPE, Paul# (M)** **353 35**

H: 6 0 W: 11 13 b.Swindon 3-6-72

*Source:* Trainee. *Honours:* Wales B, 9 full caps.

| | | | | | |
|---|---|---|---|---|---|
| 1989–90 | Swindon T | 0 | 0 | | |
| 1990–91 | Swindon T | 0 | 0 | | |
| 1991–92 | Swindon T | 0 | 0 | | |
| 1991–92 | *Torquay U* | 10 | 0 | | |
| 1992–93 | Torquay U | 36 | 2 | | |
| 1993–94 | Torquay U | 42 | 10 | | |
| 1994–95 | Torquay U | 18 | 4 | **106** | **16** |
| 1994–95 | Derby Co | 24 | 4 | | |
| 1995–96 | Derby Co | 17 | 0 | | |
| 1996–97 | Derby Co | 14 | 1 | | |
| 1996–97 | *Grimsby T* | 7 | 1 | **7** | **1** |
| 1996–97 | *Crystal Palace* | 9 | 0 | **9** | **0** |
| 1997–98 | Derby Co | 10 | 0 | **65** | **5** |
| 1997–98 | Fulham | 24 | 3 | | |
| 1998–99 | Fulham | 20 | 2 | | |
| 1999–2000 | Fulham | 22 | 0 | | |
| 2000–01 | Fulham | 10 | 0 | | |
| 2001–02 | Fulham | 0 | 0 | **76** | **5** |
| 2001–02 | Coventry C | 6 | 0 | **6** | **0** |
| 2002–03 | Northampton T | 41 | 2 | | |
| 2003–04 | Northampton T | 43 | 6 | **84** | **8** |

**ULLATHORNE, Robert# (D)** **196 9**

H: 5 8 W: 11 03 b.Wakefield 11-10-71

*Source:* Trainee.

| | | | | | |
|---|---|---|---|---|---|
| 1989–90 | Norwich C | 0 | 0 | | |
| 1990–91 | Norwich C | 2 | 0 | | |
| 1991–92 | Norwich C | 20 | 3 | | |
| 1992–93 | Norwich C | 0 | 0 | | |
| 1993–94 | Norwich C | 16 | 2 | | |
| 1994–95 | Norwich C | 27 | 2 | | |
| 1995–96 | Norwich C | 29 | 0 | **94** | **7** |
| 1996–97 | Osasuna | 18 | 0 | **18** | **0** |
| 1996–97 | Leicester C | 0 | 0 | | |
| 1997–98 | Leicester C | 6 | 1 | | |
| 1998–99 | Leicester C | 25 | 0 | | |
| 1999–2000 | Leicester C | 0 | 0 | **31** | **1** |
| 2000–01 | Sheffield U | 14 | 0 | | |
| 2001–02 | Sheffield U | 14 | 0 | | |
| 2002–03 | Sheffield U | 12 | 0 | **40** | **0** |
| 2003–04 | Northampton T | 13 | 1 | **13** | **1** |

**WEAVER, Luke‡ (G)** **68 0**

H: 6 2 W: 14 13 b.Woolwich 26-6-79

*Source:* Trainee. *Honours:* England Schools, Youth.

| | | | | | |
|---|---|---|---|---|---|
| 1996–97 | Leyton Orient | 9 | 0 | | |
| 1996–97 | *West Ham U* | 0 | 0 | | |
| 1997–98 | Leyton Orient | 0 | 0 | **9** | **0** |
| 1997–98 | Sunderland | 0 | 0 | | |
| 1998–99 | Sunderland | 0 | 0 | | |
| 1998–99 | *Scarborough* | 6 | 0 | **6** | **0** |
| 1999–2000 | Sunderland | 0 | 0 | | |
| 1999–2000 | Carlisle U | 29 | 0 | | |
| 2000–01 | Carlisle U | 14 | 0 | | |
| 2001–02 | Carlisle U | 10 | 0 | | |
| 2002–03 | Carlisle U | 0 | 0 | **53** | **0** |
| 2003–04 | Northampton T | 0 | 0 | | |

**WESTWOOD, Ashley (D)** **213 16**

H: 6 0 W: 12 09 b.Bridgnorth 31-8-76

*Source:* Trainee. *Honours:* England Youth.

| | | | | | |
|---|---|---|---|---|---|
| 1994–95 | Manchester U | 0 | 0 | | |
| 1995–96 | Crewe Alex | 33 | 4 | | |
| 1996–97 | Crewe Alex | 44 | 2 | | |
| 1997–98 | Crewe Alex | 21 | 3 | **98** | **9** |
| 1998–99 | Bradford C | 19 | 2 | | |
| 1999–2000 | Bradford C | 5 | 0 | | |
| 2000–01 | Bradford C | 0 | 0 | **24** | **2** |
| 2000–01 | Sheffield W | 33 | 2 | | |
| 2001–02 | Sheffield W | 26 | 1 | | |
| 2002–03 | Sheffield W | 23 | 2 | **82** | **5** |
| 2003–04 | Northampton T | 9 | 0 | **9** | **0** |

**WILLMOTT, Chris (D)** **116 3**

H: 6 2 W: 13 08 b.Bedford 30-9-77

*Source:* Trainee.

| | | | | | |
|---|---|---|---|---|---|
| 1995–96 | Luton T | 0 | 0 | | |
| 1996–97 | Luton T | 0 | 0 | | |
| 1997–98 | Luton T | 0 | 0 | | |
| 1998–99 | Luton T | 14 | 0 | | |
| 1999–2000 | Wimbledon | 7 | 0 | | |
| 2000–01 | Wimbledon | 14 | 1 | | |
| 2001–02 | Wimbledon | 27 | 1 | | |
| 2002–03 | Wimbledon | 5 | 0 | **53** | **2** |
| 2002–03 | *Luton T* | 13 | 0 | **27** | **0** |
| 2003–04 | Northampton T | 36 | 1 | **36** | **1** |

**YOUNGS, Tom (F)** **167 43**

H: 5 9 W: 11 13 b.Bury St Edmunds 31-8-79

*Source:* Trainee.

| | | | | | |
|---|---|---|---|---|---|
| 1997–98 | Cambridge U | 4 | 0 | | |
| 1998–99 | Cambridge U | 10 | 0 | | |
| 1999–2000 | Cambridge U | 21 | 8 | | |
| 2000–01 | Cambridge U | 38 | 14 | | |
| 2001–02 | Cambridge U | 42 | 11 | | |
| 2002–03 | Cambridge U | 35 | 10 | **150** | **43** |
| 2002–03 | Northampton T | 5 | 0 | | |
| 2003–04 | Northampton T | 12 | 0 | **17** | **0** |

**Scholars**

Barradell, Adam L; Bridgeford, Adam; Bunn, Mark J; Carr, Daniel T; Danaher, Paul D; Davison, Mark; Doherty, Ryan S; Gearing, Matthew L; Graham, Luke W; Howard, Matthew A; Khan, Yakoob; Ngoyi Gregory

**Non Contract**

Galbraith, David J; Taylor, John P

## NORWICH C (54)

**ABBEY, Zema# (F)** **81 12**

H: 6 1 W: 12 10 b.Luton 17-4-77

*Source:* Arlesey, Baldock T, Hitchin T.

| | | | | | |
|---|---|---|---|---|---|
| 1999–2000 | Cambridge U | 8 | 0 | | |
| 2000–01 | Cambridge U | 14 | 5 | **22** | **5** |
| 2000–01 | Norwich C | 20 | 1 | | |
| 2001–02 | Norwich C | 6 | 1 | | |
| 2002–03 | Norwich C | 30 | 5 | | |
| 2003–04 | Norwich C | 3 | 0 | **59** | **7** |

**BRENNAN, Jim (D)** **195** **5**
H: 5 11 W: 13 00 b.Toronto 8-5-77
*Source:* Sora Lazio. *Honours:* Canada 36 full caps, 5 goals.

| | | | | | |
|---|---|---|---|---|---|
| 1994–95 | Bristol C | 0 | 0 | | |
| 1995–96 | Bristol C | 0 | 0 | | |
| 1996–97 | Bristol C | 8 | 0 | | |
| 1997–98 | Bristol C | 6 | 0 | | |
| 1998–99 | Bristol C | 29 | 1 | | |
| 1999–2000 | Bristol C | 12 | 2 | **55** | **3** |
| 1999–2000 | Nottingham F | 25 | 0 | | |
| 2000–01 | Nottingham F | 12 | 0 | | |
| 2000–01 | *Huddersfield T* | 2 | 0 | **2** | **0** |
| 2001–02 | Nottingham F | 41 | 0 | | |
| 2002–03 | Nottingham F | 45 | 1 | **123** | **1** |
| 2003–04 | Norwich C | 15 | 1 | **15** | **1** |

**BRIGGS, Keith (D)** **63** **2**
H: 6 0 W: 11 02 b.Glossop 11-12-81
*Source:* Trainee.

| | | | | | |
|---|---|---|---|---|---|
| 1999–2000 | Stockport Co | 7 | 1 | | |
| 2000–01 | Stockport Co | 0 | 0 | | |
| 2001–02 | Stockport Co | 32 | 0 | | |
| 2002–03 | Stockport Co | 19 | 1 | **58** | **2** |
| 2002–03 | Norwich C | 2 | 0 | | |
| 2003–04 | Norwich C | 3 | 0 | **5** | **0** |

**CRICHTON, Paul* (G)** **418** **0**
H: 6 1 W: 13 00 b.Pontefract 3-10-68
*Source:* Apprentice.

| | | | | | |
|---|---|---|---|---|---|
| 1986–87 | Nottingham F | 0 | 0 | | |
| 1986–87 | *Notts Co* | 5 | 0 | **5** | **0** |
| 1986–87 | *Darlington* | 5 | 0 | | |
| 1986–87 | *Peterborough U* | 4 | 0 | | |
| 1987–88 | Nottingham F | 0 | 0 | | |
| 1987–88 | *Darlington* | 3 | 0 | **8** | **0** |
| 1987–88 | *Swindon T* | 4 | 0 | **4** | **0** |
| 1987–88 | *Rotherham U* | 6 | 0 | **6** | **0** |
| 1988–89 | Nottingham F | 0 | 0 | | |
| 1988–89 | *Torquay U* | 13 | 0 | **13** | **0** |
| 1988–89 | Peterborough U | 31 | 0 | | |
| 1989–90 | Peterborough U | 16 | 0 | **51** | **0** |
| 1990–91 | Doncaster R | 20 | 0 | | |
| 1991–92 | Doncaster R | 16 | 0 | | |
| 1992–93 | Doncaster R | 41 | 0 | **77** | **0** |
| 1993–94 | Grimsby T | 46 | 0 | | |
| 1994–95 | Grimsby T | 43 | 0 | | |
| 1995–96 | Grimsby T | 44 | 0 | | |
| 1996–97 | Grimsby T | 0 | 0 | **133** | **0** |
| 1996–97 | WBA | 30 | 0 | | |
| 1997–98 | WBA | 2 | 0 | | |
| 1997–98 | *Aston Villa* | 0 | 0 | | |
| 1998–99 | WBA | 0 | 0 | **32** | **0** |
| 1998–99 | Burnley | 29 | 0 | | |
| 1999–2000 | Burnley | 46 | 0 | | |
| 2000–01 | Burnley | 8 | 0 | **83** | **0** |
| 2001–02 | Norwich C | 6 | 0 | | |
| 2002–03 | Norwich C | 0 | 0 | | |
| 2003–04 | Norwich C | 0 | 0 | **6** | **0** |

**DRURY, Adam (D)** **276** **4**
H: 5 10 W: 11 07 b.Cottenham 29-8-78
*Source:* Trainee.

| | | | | | |
|---|---|---|---|---|---|
| 1995–96 | Peterborough U | 1 | 0 | | |
| 1996–97 | Peterborough U | 5 | 1 | | |
| 1997–98 | Peterborough U | 31 | 0 | | |
| 1998–99 | Peterborough U | 40 | 0 | | |
| 1999–2000 | Peterborough U | 42 | 1 | | |
| 2000–01 | Peterborough U | 29 | 0 | **148** | **2** |
| 2000–01 | Norwich C | 6 | 0 | | |
| 2001–02 | Norwich C | 35 | 0 | | |
| 2002–03 | Norwich C | 45 | 2 | | |
| 2003–04 | Norwich C | 42 | 0 | **128** | **2** |

**EASTON, Clint‡ (M)** **114** **6**
H: 5 11 W: 11 00 b.Barking 1-10-77
*Source:* Trainee. *Honours:* England Youth.

| | | | | | |
|---|---|---|---|---|---|
| 1996–97 | Watford | 17 | 1 | | |
| 1997–98 | Watford | 12 | 0 | | |
| 1998–99 | Watford | 7 | 0 | | |
| 1999–2000 | Watford | 17 | 0 | | |
| 2000–01 | Watford | 11 | 0 | **64** | **1** |
| 2001–02 | Norwich C | 14 | 1 | | |
| 2002–03 | Norwich C | 26 | 2 | | |
| 2003–04 | Norwich C | 10 | 2 | **50** | **5** |

**EDWORTHY, Marc (D)** **336** **2**
H: 5 8 W: 10 03 b.Barnstaple 24-12-72
*Source:* Trainee.

| | | | | | |
|---|---|---|---|---|---|
| 1990–91 | Plymouth Arg | 0 | 0 | | |
| 1991–92 | Plymouth Arg | 15 | 0 | | |
| 1992–93 | Plymouth Arg | 15 | 0 | | |
| 1993–94 | Plymouth Arg | 12 | 0 | | |
| 1994–95 | Plymouth Arg | 27 | 1 | **69** | **1** |
| 1995–96 | Crystal Palace | 44 | 0 | | |
| 1996–97 | Crystal Palace | 45 | 0 | | |
| 1997–98 | Crystal Palace | 34 | 0 | | |
| 1998–99 | Crystal Palace | 3 | 0 | **126** | **0** |
| 1998–99 | Coventry C | 22 | 0 | | |
| 1999–2000 | Coventry C | 10 | 0 | | |
| 2000–01 | Coventry C | 24 | 1 | | |
| 2001–02 | Coventry C | 20 | 0 | **76** | **1** |
| 2002–03 | Wolverhampton W | 22 | 0 | **22** | **0** |
| 2003–04 | Norwich C | 43 | 0 | **43** | **0** |

**FLEMING, Craig (D)** **480** **11**
H: 5 11 W: 12 06 b.Halifax 6-10-71
*Source:* Trainee.

| | | | | | |
|---|---|---|---|---|---|
| 1988–89 | Halifax T | 1 | 0 | | |
| 1989–90 | Halifax T | 10 | 0 | | |
| 1990–91 | Halifax T | 46 | 0 | **57** | **0** |
| 1991–92 | Oldham Ath | 32 | 1 | | |
| 1992–93 | Oldham Ath | 24 | 0 | | |
| 1993–94 | Oldham Ath | 37 | 0 | | |
| 1994–95 | Oldham Ath | 5 | 0 | | |
| 1995–96 | Oldham Ath | 22 | 0 | | |
| 1996–97 | Oldham Ath | 44 | 0 | **164** | **1** |
| 1997–98 | Norwich C | 22 | 1 | | |
| 1998–99 | Norwich C | 37 | 3 | | |
| 1999–2000 | Norwich C | 39 | 3 | | |
| 2000–01 | Norwich C | 39 | 0 | | |
| 2001–02 | Norwich C | 46 | 0 | | |
| 2002–03 | Norwich C | 30 | 0 | | |
| 2003–04 | Norwich C | 46 | 3 | **259** | **10** |

**FRANCIS, Damien (M)** **138** **22**
H: 6 0 W: 11 08 b.Wandsworth 27-2-79
*Source:* Trainee. *Honours:* Jamaica 1 full cap.

| | | | | | |
|---|---|---|---|---|---|
| 1996–97 | Wimbledon | 0 | 0 | | |
| 1997–98 | Wimbledon | 2 | 0 | | |
| 1998–99 | Wimbledon | 0 | 0 | | |
| 1999–2000 | Wimbledon | 9 | 0 | | |
| 2000–01 | Wimbledon | 29 | 8 | | |
| 2001–02 | Wimbledon | 23 | 1 | | |
| 2002–03 | Wimbledon | 34 | 6 | **97** | **15** |
| 2003–04 | Norwich C | 41 | 7 | **41** | **7** |

**GREEN, Robert (G)** **143** **0**
H: 6 3 W: 13 01 b.Chertsey 18-1-80
*Source:* Trainee. *Honours:* England Youth.

| | | | | | |
|---|---|---|---|---|---|
| 1997–98 | Norwich C | 0 | 0 | | |
| 1998–99 | Norwich C | 2 | 0 | | |
| 1999–2000 | Norwich C | 3 | 0 | | |
| 2000–01 | Norwich C | 5 | 0 | | |
| 2001–02 | Norwich C | 41 | 0 | | |
| 2002–03 | Norwich C | 46 | 0 | | |
| 2003–04 | Norwich C | 46 | 0 | **143** | **0** |

**HENDERSON, Ian (F)** **39** **5**
H: 5 9 W: 10 12 b.Thetford 24-1-85
*Source:* Scholar. *Honours:* England Youth.

| | | | | | |
|---|---|---|---|---|---|
| 2002–03 | Norwich C | 20 | 1 | | |
| 2003–04 | Norwich C | 19 | 4 | **39** | **5** |

**HOLT, Gary (M)** **293** **12**
H: 6 0 W: 12 00 b.Irvine 9-3-73
*Source:* Celtic. *Honours:* Scotland 6 full caps, 1 goal.

| | | | | | |
|---|---|---|---|---|---|
| 1994–95 | Stoke C | 0 | 0 | | |
| 1995–96 | Kilmarnock | 26 | 0 | | |
| 1996–97 | Kilmarnock | 12 | 1 | | |
| 1997–98 | Kilmarnock | 27 | 2 | | |
| 1998–99 | Kilmarnock | 33 | 3 | | |
| 1999–2000 | Kilmarnock | 35 | 0 | | |
| 2000–01 | Kilmarnock | 19 | 3 | **152** | **9** |
| 2000–01 | Norwich C | 4 | 0 | | |
| 2001–02 | Norwich C | 46 | 2 | | |
| 2002–03 | Norwich C | 45 | 0 | | |
| 2003–04 | Norwich C | 46 | 1 | **141** | **3** |

**HUCKERBY, Darren (F)** **283** **79**
H: 5 10 W: 12 02 b.Nottingham 23-4-76
*Source:* Trainee. *Honours:* England Under-21, B.

| | | | | | |
|---|---|---|---|---|---|
| 1993–94 | Lincoln C | 6 | 1 | | |
| 1994–95 | Lincoln C | 6 | 2 | | |
| 1995–96 | Lincoln C | 16 | 2 | **28** | **5** |
| 1995–96 | Newcastle U | 1 | 0 | | |
| 1996–97 | Newcastle U | 0 | 0 | **1** | **0** |
| 1996–97 | *Millwall* | 6 | 3 | **6** | **3** |
| 1996–97 | Coventry C | 25 | 5 | | |
| 1997–98 | Coventry C | 34 | 14 | | |
| 1998–99 | Coventry C | 34 | 9 | | |
| 1999–2000 | Coventry C | 1 | 0 | **94** | **28** |
| 1999–2000 | Leeds U | 33 | 2 | | |
| 2000–01 | Leeds U | 7 | 0 | **40** | **2** |
| 2000–01 | Manchester C | 13 | 1 | | |
| 2001–02 | Manchester C | 40 | 20 | | |
| 2002–03 | Manchester C | 16 | 1 | | |
| 2002–03 | *Nottingham F* | 9 | 5 | **9** | **5** |
| 2003–04 | Manchester C | 0 | 0 | **69** | **22** |
| 2003–04 | Norwich C | 36 | 14 | **36** | **14** |

**JARVIS, Ryan (F)** **15** **1**
H: 6 0 W: 11 04 b.Fakenham 11-7-86
*Source:* Scholar. *Honours:* FA Schools, England Youth.

| | | | | | |
|---|---|---|---|---|---|
| 2002–03 | Norwich C | 3 | 0 | | |
| 2003–04 | Norwich C | 12 | 1 | **15** | **1** |

**MACKAY, Malky (D)** **319** **25**
H: 6 3 W: 13 02 b.Bellshill 19-2-72
*Source:* Queen's Park Youth. *Honours:* Scotland 3 full caps.

| | | | | | |
|---|---|---|---|---|---|
| 1990–91 | Queen's Park | 10 | 0 | | |
| 1991–92 | Queen's Park | 27 | 3 | | |
| 1992–93 | Queen's Park | 33 | 3 | **70** | **6** |
| 1993–94 | Celtic | 0 | 0 | | |
| 1994–95 | Celtic | 1 | 0 | | |
| 1995–96 | Celtic | 11 | 1 | | |
| 1996–97 | Celtic | 20 | 1 | | |
| 1997–98 | Celtic | 4 | 1 | | |
| 1998–99 | Celtic | 1 | 1 | **37** | **4** |
| 1998–99 | Norwich C | 27 | 1 | | |
| 1999–2000 | Norwich C | 21 | 0 | | |
| 2000–01 | Norwich C | 38 | 1 | | |
| 2001–02 | Norwich C | 44 | 3 | | |
| 2002–03 | Norwich C | 37 | 6 | | |
| 2003–04 | Norwich C | 45 | 4 | **212** | **15** |

**McKENZIE, Leon (F)** **210** **69**
H: 5 10 W: 10 03 b.Croydon 17-5-78
*Source:* Trainee.

| | | | | | |
|---|---|---|---|---|---|
| 1995–96 | Crystal Palace | 12 | 0 | | |
| 1996–97 | Crystal Palace | 21 | 2 | | |
| 1997–98 | Crystal Palace | 3 | 0 | | |
| 1997–98 | *Fulham* | 3 | 0 | **3** | **0** |
| 1998–99 | Crystal Palace | 16 | 1 | | |
| 1998–99 | *Peterborough U* | 14 | 8 | | |
| 1999–2000 | Crystal Palace | 25 | 4 | | |
| 2000–01 | Crystal Palace | 8 | 0 | **85** | **7** |
| 2000–01 | Peterborough U | 30 | 13 | | |
| 2001–02 | Peterborough U | 30 | 18 | | |
| 2002–03 | Peterborough U | 11 | 5 | | |
| 2003–04 | Peterborough U | 19 | 9 | **104** | **53** |
| 2003–04 | Norwich C | 18 | 9 | **18** | **9** |

**McVEIGH, Paul (F)** **145** **29**
H: 5 6 W: 10 11 b.Belfast 6-12-77
*Source:* Trainee. *Honours:* Northern Ireland Schools, Youth, Under-21, 16 full caps.

| | | | | | |
|---|---|---|---|---|---|
| 1995–96 | Tottenham H | 0 | 0 | | |
| 1996–97 | Tottenham H | 3 | 1 | | |
| 1997–98 | Tottenham H | 0 | 0 | | |
| 1998–99 | Tottenham H | 0 | 0 | | |
| 1999–2000 | Tottenham H | 0 | 0 | **3** | **1** |
| 1999–2000 | Norwich C | 1 | 0 | | |
| 2000–01 | Norwich C | 11 | 1 | | |
| 2001–02 | Norwich C | 42 | 8 | | |
| 2002–03 | Norwich C | 44 | 14 | | |
| 2003–04 | Norwich C | 44 | 5 | **142** | **28** |

**MULRYNE, Phil (M)** **152** **18**
H: 5 9 W: 11 01 b.Belfast 1-1-78
*Source:* Trainee. *Honours:* Northern Ireland Youth, Under-21, B, 25 full caps, 3 goals.

| | | | | | |
|---|---|---|---|---|---|
| 1994–95 | Manchester U | 0 | 0 | | |
| 1995–96 | Manchester U | 0 | 0 | | |
| 1996–97 | Manchester U | 0 | 0 | | |
| 1997–98 | Manchester U | 1 | 0 | | |
| 1998–99 | Manchester U | 0 | 0 | **1** | **0** |
| 1998–99 | Norwich C | 7 | 2 | | |
| 1999–2000 | Norwich C | 9 | 0 | | |
| 2000–01 | Norwich C | 28 | 1 | | |
| 2001–02 | Norwich C | 40 | 6 | | |
| 2002–03 | Norwich C | 33 | 6 | | |
| 2003–04 | Norwich C | 34 | 3 | **151** | **18** |

**NIELSEN, David‡ (F)** **206** **59**
H: 6 0 W: 11 12 b.Sonderborg 1-12-76

| | | | | | |
|---|---|---|---|---|---|
| 1996–97 | FC Copenhagen | 14 | 1 | | |
| 1997–98 | FC Copenhagen | 31 | 11 | | |
| 1998–99 | FC Copenhagen | 30 | 15 | | |
| 1999–2000 | FC Copenhagen | 26 | 8 | | |
| 2000–01 | FC Copenhagen | 7 | 1 | **108** | **36** |

| | | | | | |
|---|---|---|---|---|---|
| 2000–01 | Grimsby T | 17 | 5 | **17** | **5** |
| 2000–01 | Wimbledon | 11 | 2 | | |
| 2001–02 | Wimbledon | 12 | 2 | **23** | **4** |
| 2001–02 | Norwich C | 23 | 8 | | |
| 2002–03 | Norwich C | 33 | 6 | | |
| 2003–04 | Norwich C | 2 | 0 | **58** | **14** |

**NOTMAN, Alex‡ (F)** **66 4**
H: 5 7 W: 11 04 b.Edinburgh 10-12-79
*Source:* Trainee. *Honours:* Scotland Schools, Youth, Under-21.

| | | | | | |
|---|---|---|---|---|---|
| 1996–97 | Manchester U | 0 | 0 | | |
| 1997–98 | Manchester U | 0 | 0 | | |
| 1998–99 | Manchester U | 0 | 0 | | |
| 1998–99 | *Aberdeen* | 2 | 0 | **2** | **0** |
| 1999–2000 | Manchester U | 0 | 0 | | |
| 1999–2000 | *Sheffield U* | 10 | 3 | **10** | **3** |
| 2000–01 | Manchester U | 0 | 0 | | |
| 2000–01 | Norwich C | 15 | 1 | | |
| 2001–02 | Norwich C | 30 | 0 | | |
| 2002–03 | Norwich C | 8 | 0 | | |
| 2003–04 | Norwich C | 1 | 0 | **54** | **1** |

**RIVERS, Mark (F)** **277 53**
H: 5 10 W: 11 04 b.Crewe 26-11-75
*Source:* Trainee.

| | | | | | |
|---|---|---|---|---|---|
| 1993–94 | Crewe Alex | 0 | 0 | | |
| 1994–95 | Crewe Alex | 0 | 0 | | |
| 1995–96 | Crewe Alex | 33 | 10 | | |
| 1996–97 | Crewe Alex | 27 | 6 | | |
| 1997–98 | Crewe Alex | 35 | 6 | | |
| 1998–99 | Crewe Alex | 43 | 7 | | |
| 1999–2000 | Crewe Alex | 32 | 7 | | |
| 2000–01 | Crewe Alex | 33 | 7 | **203** | **43** |
| 2001–02 | Norwich C | 32 | 2 | | |
| 2002–03 | Norwich C | 30 | 4 | | |
| 2003–04 | Norwich C | 12 | 4 | **74** | **10** |

**ROBERTS, Iwan* (F)** **616 196**
H: 6 3 W: 13 00 b.Bangor 26-6-68
*Source:* Trainee. *Honours:* Wales Schools, Youth, B, 15 full caps.

| | | | | | |
|---|---|---|---|---|---|
| 1985–86 | Watford | 4 | 0 | | |
| 1986–87 | Watford | 3 | 1 | | |
| 1987–88 | Watford | 25 | 2 | | |
| 1988–89 | Watford | 22 | 6 | | |
| 1989–90 | Watford | 9 | 0 | **63** | **9** |
| 1990–91 | Huddersfield T | 44 | 13 | | |
| 1991–92 | Huddersfield T | 46 | 24 | | |
| 1992–93 | Huddersfield T | 37 | 9 | | |
| 1993–94 | Huddersfield T | 15 | 4 | **142** | **50** |
| 1993–94 | Leicester C | 26 | 13 | | |
| 1994–95 | Leicester C | 37 | 9 | | |
| 1995–96 | Leicester C | 37 | 19 | **100** | **41** |
| 1996–97 | Wolverhampton W | 33 | 12 | **33** | **12** |
| 1997–98 | Norwich C | 31 | 5 | | |
| 1998–99 | Norwich C | 45 | 19 | | |
| 1999–2000 | Norwich C | 44 | 17 | | |
| 2000–01 | Norwich C | 44 | 15 | | |
| 2001–02 | Norwich C | 30 | 13 | | |
| 2002–03 | Norwich C | 43 | 7 | | |
| 2003–04 | Norwich C | 41 | 8 | **278** | **84** |

**SHACKELL, Jason (D)** **8 0**
H: 6 3 W: 12 08 b.Hitchin 27-9-83
*Source:* Scholar.

| | | | | | |
|---|---|---|---|---|---|
| 2002–03 | Norwich C | 2 | 0 | | |
| 2003–04 | Norwich C | 6 | 0 | **8** | **0** |

**SINCLAIR, Dean‡ (M)** **2 0**
H: 5 10 W: 11 00 b.St Albans 17-12-84
*Source:* Scholar.

| | | | | | |
|---|---|---|---|---|---|
| 2002–03 | Norwich C | 2 | 0 | | |
| 2003–04 | Norwich C | 0 | 0 | **2** | **0** |

**SVENSSON, Mathias (F)** **205 53**
H: 6 1 W: 12 08 b.Boras 24-9-74
*Honours:* Sweden 3 full caps.

| | | | | | |
|---|---|---|---|---|---|
| 1996 | Elfsborg | 22 | 15 | **22** | **15** |
| 1996–97 | Portsmouth | 19 | 6 | | |
| 1997–98 | Portsmouth | 26 | 4 | **45** | **10** |
| 1998–99 | Innsbruck | 6 | 1 | **6** | **1** |
| 1998–99 | Crystal Palace | 8 | 1 | | |
| 1999–2000 | Crystal Palace | 24 | 9 | **32** | **10** |
| 1999–2000 | Charlton Ath | 18 | 2 | | |
| 2000–01 | Charlton Ath | 22 | 5 | | |
| 2001–02 | Charlton Ath | 12 | 0 | | |
| 2002–03 | Charlton Ath | 15 | 0 | | |
| 2003–04 | Charlton Ath | 3 | 0 | **70** | **7** |
| 2003–04 | *Derby Co* | 10 | 3 | **10** | **3** |
| 2003–04 | Norwich C | 20 | 7 | **20** | **7** |

**Scholars**
Batt, Damien A N; Blackburn, Lee C; Chick, David R; Clarke, Joshua K; Crane, Gregory W; Crow, Daniel S; Eagle, Robert J; Halliday, Matthew R; Herbert, Shane R; Howell, Nicholas; Howlett, Lee R K; Osborne, Aaron A; Osborne, Jake; Smith, Adam; Tyrie, David L; Watts, Matthew T; Willis, Oliver D

**Non Contract**
Palmer, Stuart J

## NOTTINGHAM F (55)

**BEAUMONT, James (M)** **0 0**
H: 5 7 W: 10 10 b.Stockton 11-11-84
*Source:* Scholar.

| | | | | | |
|---|---|---|---|---|---|
| 2001–02 | Newcastle U | 0 | 0 | | |
| 2002–03 | Newcastle U | 0 | 0 | | |
| 2003–04 | Nottingham F | 0 | 0 | | |

**BIGGINS, James (D)** **0 0**
H: 5 9 W: 11 13 b.Nottingham 6-6-85
*Source:* Scholar. *Honours:* England Youth.

| | | | | | |
|---|---|---|---|---|---|
| 2002–03 | Nottingham F | 0 | 0 | | |
| 2003–04 | Nottingham F | 0 | 0 | | |

**BODKIN, Matt* (F)** **0 0**
b.Chatham 16-9-83
*Source:* Scholar.

| | | | | | |
|---|---|---|---|---|---|
| 2002–03 | Nottingham F | 0 | 0 | | |
| 2003–04 | Nottingham F | 0 | 0 | | |

**BOPP, Eugene (M)** **47 4**
H: 5 11 W: 12 03 b.Kiev 5-9-83
*Source:* Bayern Munich.

| | | | | | |
|---|---|---|---|---|---|
| 2000–01 | Nottingham F | 0 | 0 | | |
| 2001–02 | Nottingham F | 19 | 1 | | |
| 2002–03 | Nottingham F | 13 | 2 | | |
| 2003–04 | Nottingham F | 15 | 1 | **47** | **4** |

**CASH, Brian (M)** **12 0**
H: 5 9 W: 11 01 b.Dublin 24-11-82
*Source:* Trainee. *Honours:* Eire Under-21.

| | | | | | |
|---|---|---|---|---|---|
| 1999–2000 | Nottingham F | 0 | 0 | | |
| 2000–01 | Nottingham F | 0 | 0 | | |
| 2001–02 | Nottingham F | 5 | 0 | | |
| 2002–03 | Nottingham F | 1 | 0 | | |
| 2002–03 | *Swansea C* | 5 | 0 | **5** | **0** |
| 2003–04 | Nottingham F | 1 | 0 | **7** | **0** |

**DAWSON, Michael (D)** **69 6**
H: 6 2 W: 12 02 b.Northallerton 18-11-83
*Source:* School. *Honours:* England Youth, Under-21.

| | | | | | |
|---|---|---|---|---|---|
| 2000–01 | Nottingham F | 0 | 0 | | |
| 2001–02 | Nottingham F | 1 | 0 | | |
| 2002–03 | Nottingham F | 38 | 5 | | |
| 2003–04 | Nottingham F | 30 | 1 | **69** | **6** |

**DOIG, Chris (D)** **65 1**
H: 6 2 W: 13 07 b.Dumfries 13-2-81
*Source:* Trainee. *Honours:* Scotland Schools, Youth, Under-21.

| | | | | | |
|---|---|---|---|---|---|
| 1997–98 | Nottingham F | 0 | 0 | | |
| 1998–99 | Nottingham F | 2 | 0 | | |
| 1999–2000 | Nottingham F | 11 | 0 | | |
| 2000–01 | Nottingham F | 15 | 0 | | |
| 2001–02 | Nottingham F | 8 | 1 | | |
| 2002–03 | Nottingham F | 10 | 0 | | |
| 2003–04 | Nottingham F | 10 | 0 | **56** | **1** |
| 2003–04 | *Northampton T* | 9 | 0 | **9** | **0** |

**ERVIN, Jim* (D)** **0 0**
b.Belfast 5-6-85
*Source:* Scholar.

| | | | | | |
|---|---|---|---|---|---|
| 2002–03 | Nottingham F | 0 | 0 | | |
| 2003–04 | Nottingham F | 0 | 0 | | |

**EVANS, Paul (M)** **388 63**
H: 5 8 W: 12 06 b.Oswestry 1-9-74
*Source:* Trainee. *Honours:* Wales Youth, Under-21, 2 full caps.

| | | | | | |
|---|---|---|---|---|---|
| 1991–92 | Shrewsbury T | 2 | 0 | | |
| 1992–93 | Shrewsbury T | 4 | 0 | | |
| 1993–94 | Shrewsbury T | 13 | 0 | | |
| 1994–95 | Shrewsbury T | 32 | 5 | | |
| 1995–96 | Shrewsbury T | 34 | 3 | | |
| 1996–97 | Shrewsbury T | 42 | 6 | | |
| 1997–98 | Shrewsbury T | 39 | 6 | | |
| 1998–99 | Shrewsbury T | 32 | 6 | **198** | **26** |
| 1998–99 | Brentford | 14 | 3 | | |
| 1999–2000 | Brentford | 33 | 7 | | |
| 2000–01 | Brentford | 43 | 7 | | |
| 2001–02 | Brentford | 40 | 14 | **130** | **31** |
| 2002–03 | Bradford C | 19 | 2 | | |
| 2002–03 | *Blackpool* | 10 | 1 | **10** | **1** |
| 2003–04 | Bradford C | 23 | 3 | **42** | **5** |
| 2003–04 | Nottingham F | 8 | 0 | **8** | **0** |

**FORMANN, Pascal* (G)** **0 0**
H: 6 1 W: 11 07 b.Werne 16-11-82

| | | | | | |
|---|---|---|---|---|---|
| 2000–01 | Nottingham F | 0 | 0 | | |
| 2001–02 | Nottingham F | 0 | 0 | | |
| 2002–03 | Nottingham F | 0 | 0 | | |
| 2003–04 | Nottingham F | 0 | 0 | | |

**GARDNER, Ross (M)** **2 0**
H: 5 8 W: 10 06 b.South Shields 15-12-85
*Source:* Scholar. *Honours:* England Youth.

| | | | | | |
|---|---|---|---|---|---|
| 2001–02 | Newcastle U | 0 | 0 | | |
| 2002–03 | Newcastle U | 0 | 0 | | |
| 2003–04 | Nottingham F | 2 | 0 | **2** | **0** |

**GROVES, Tom* (D)** **0 0**
b.Nottingham 18-7-85
*Source:* Scholar. *Honours:* England Youth.

| | | | | | |
|---|---|---|---|---|---|
| 2002–03 | Nottingham F | 0 | 0 | | |
| 2003–04 | Nottingham F | 0 | 0 | | |

**GUNNARSSON, Brynjar‡ (D)** **202 19**
H: 6 1 W: 12 01 b.Reykjavik 16-10-75
*Honours:* Iceland 39 full caps, 3 goals.

| | | | | | |
|---|---|---|---|---|---|
| 1995 | KR | 16 | 1 | | |
| 1996 | KR | 18 | 0 | | |
| 1997 | KR | 16 | 0 | **50** | **1** |
| 1998 | Moss | 5 | 2 | **5** | **2** |
| 1999–2000 | Stoke C | 22 | 1 | | |
| 2000–01 | Stoke C | 46 | 5 | | |
| 2001–02 | Stoke C | 23 | 5 | | |
| 2002–03 | Stoke C | 40 | 5 | | |
| 2003–04 | Nottingham F | 13 | 0 | **13** | **0** |
| 2003–04 | *Stoke C* | 3 | 0 | **134** | **16** |

**HAMILTON, Paul (D)** **0 0**
b.Belfast 28-10-86
*Source:* Scholar.

| | | | | | |
|---|---|---|---|---|---|
| 2003–04 | Nottingham F | 0 | 0 | | |

**HASKINS, Andy* (M)** **0 0**
b.York 30-4-84
*Source:* School. *Honours:* England Youth.

| | | | | | |
|---|---|---|---|---|---|
| 2000–01 | Nottingham F | 0 | 0 | | |
| 2001–02 | Nottingham F | 0 | 0 | | |
| 2002–03 | Nottingham F | 0 | 0 | | |
| 2003–04 | Nottingham F | 0 | 0 | | |

**JEFFREY, Richard* (F)** **0 0**
H: 5 9 W: 11 00 b.Derby 4-11-83
*Source:* Scholar.

| | | | | | |
|---|---|---|---|---|---|
| 2000–01 | Nottingham F | 0 | 0 | | |
| 2001–02 | Nottingham F | 0 | 0 | | |
| 2002–03 | Nottingham F | 0 | 0 | | |
| 2003–04 | Nottingham F | 0 | 0 | | |

**JESS, Eoin# (M)** **464 101**
H: 5 10 W: 11 09 b.Aberdeen 13-12-70
*Source:* Rangers 'S' Form. *Honours:* Scotland Under-21, B, 18 full caps, 2 goals.

| | | | | | |
|---|---|---|---|---|---|
| 1987–88 | Aberdeen | 0 | 0 | | |
| 1988–89 | Aberdeen | 2 | 0 | | |
| 1989–90 | Aberdeen | 11 | 3 | | |
| 1990–91 | Aberdeen | 27 | 13 | | |
| 1991–92 | Aberdeen | 39 | 12 | | |
| 1992–93 | Aberdeen | 31 | 12 | | |
| 1993–94 | Aberdeen | 41 | 6 | | |
| 1994–95 | Aberdeen | 25 | 1 | | |
| 1995–96 | Aberdeen | 25 | 3 | | |
| 1995–96 | Coventry C | 12 | 1 | | |
| 1996–97 | Coventry C | 27 | 0 | **39** | **1** |
| 1997–98 | Aberdeen | 34 | 9 | | |
| 1998–99 | Aberdeen | 36 | 14 | | |
| 1999–2000 | Aberdeen | 26 | 5 | | |
| 2000–01 | Aberdeen | 0 | 0 | **297** | **78** |
| 2000–01 | Bradford C | 17 | 3 | | |
| 2001–02 | Bradford C | 45 | 14 | **62** | **17** |
| 2002–03 | Nottingham F | 32 | 3 | | |
| 2003–04 | Nottingham F | 34 | 2 | **66** | **5** |

**JOHNSON, David (F)** **343 117**
H: 5 6 W: 12 00 b.Kingston, Jamaica 15-8-76
*Source:* Trainee. *Honours:* England Schools, B, Jamaica 4 full caps.

| | | | | | |
|---|---|---|---|---|---|
| 1994–95 | Manchester U | 0 | 0 | | |
| 1995–96 | Bury | 36 | 5 | | |

1996–97 Bury 44 8
1997–98 Bury 17 5 **97 18**
1997–98 Ipswich T 31 20
1998–99 Ipswich T 42 13
1999–2000 Ipswich T 44 22
2000–01 Ipswich T 14 0 **131 55**
2000–01 Nottingham F 19 2
2001–02 Nottingham F 22 3
2001–02 *Sheffield W* 7 2 **7 2**
2001–02 *Burnley* 8 5 **8 5**
2002–03 Nottingham F 42 25
2003–04 Nottingham F 17 7 **100 37**

**KING, Marlon (F) 178 59**
H: 6 0 W: 12 10 b.Dulwich 26-4-80
*Source:* Trainee. *Honours:* Jamaica 5 full caps.
1998–99 Barnet 22 6
1999–2000 Barnet 31 8 **53 14**
2000–01 Gillingham 38 15
2001–02 Gillingham 42 17
2002–03 Gillingham 10 4
2003–04 Gillingham 11 4 **101 40**
2003–04 Nottingham F 24 5 **24 5**

**KUBILSKIS, Alexis (F) 0 0**
b.Berchem 10-12-86
*Source:* Scholar.
2003–04 Nottingham F 0 0

**LORRIMER, Wayne‡ (M) 0 0**
b.Belfast 27-10-84
*Source:* Scholar.
2002–03 Nottingham F 0 0
2003–04 Nottingham F 0 0

**LOUIS-JEAN, Mathieu (D) 251 3**
H: 5 9 W: 11 03 b.Mont-St-Aignan 22-2-76
1993–94 Le Havre 7 0
1994–95 Le Havre 9 0
1995–96 Le Havre 15 0
1996–97 Le Havre 31 0
1997–98 Le Havre 16 0 **78 0**
1998–99 Nottingham F 16 0
1999–2000 Nottingham F 27 0
2000–01 Nottingham F 13 0
2001–02 Nottingham F 38 1
2002–03 Nottingham F 41 1
2003–04 Nottingham F 38 1 **173 3**

**LUKIC, John (G) 0 0**
b.Enfield 25-4-86
*Source:* Scholar.
2002–03 Nottingham F 0 0
2003–04 Nottingham F 0 0

**McCLEAN, Craig* (M) 0 0**
b.Belfast 6-7-85
*Source:* Scholar.
2002–03 Nottingham F 0 0
2003–04 Nottingham F 0 0

**MORGAN, Wes (D) 37 3**
H: 6 2 W: 14 00 b.Nottingham 21-1-84
*Source:* Scholar.
2002–03 Nottingham F 0 0
2002–03 *Kidderminster H* 5 1 **5 1**
2003–04 Nottingham F 32 2 **32 2**

**MUNSTER, Darren‡ (M) 0 0**
b.Belfast 27-10-85
*Source:* Scholar.
2003–04 Nottingham F 0 0

**OYEN, Davy‡ (D) 21 1**
H: 6 0 W: 12 02 b.Bilzen 17-7-75
*Honours:* Belgium 3 full caps.
1999–2000 Anderlecht 7 0
2000–01 Anderlecht 4 1
2001–02 Anderlecht 2 0
2002–03 Anderlecht 0 0 **13 1**
2002–03 Nottingham F 4 0
2003–04 Nottingham F 4 0 **8 0**

**PERCH, James (D) 0 0**
b.Mansfield 29-9-85
*Source:* Scholar.
2002–03 Nottingham F 0 0
2003–04 Nottingham F 0 0

**REID, Andy (F) 119 16**
H: 5 8 W: 11 02 b.Dublin 29-7-82
*Source:* Trainee. *Honours:* Eire Under-21, 7 full caps.
1999–2000 Nottingham F 0 0
2000–01 Nottingham F 14 2
2001–02 Nottingham F 29 0
2002–03 Nottingham F 30 1
2003–04 Nottingham F 46 13 **119 16**

**RIGBY, Andrew (M) 0 0**
b.Nottingham 19-1-87
2003–04 Nottingham F 0 0

**ROBERTS, Justyn (D) 0 0**
b.Lewisham 12-2-86
*Source:* Scholar.
2002–03 Nottingham F 0 0
2003–04 Nottingham F 0 0

**ROBERTSON, Gregor (D) 16 0**
H: 6 0 W: 12 04 b.Edinburgh 19-1-84
2000–01 Nottingham F 0 0
2001–02 Nottingham F 0 0
2002–03 Nottingham F 0 0
2003–04 Nottingham F 16 0 **16 0**

**ROCHE, Barry (G) 11 0**
H: 6 5 W: 14 00 b.Dublin 6-4-82
*Source:* Trainee.
1999–2000 Nottingham F 0 0
2000–01 Nottingham F 2 0
2001–02 Nottingham F 0 0
2002–03 Nottingham F 1 0
2003–04 Nottingham F 8 0 **11 0**

**SONNER, Danny* (M) 213 15**
H: 5 11 W: 12 08 b.Wigan 9-1-72
*Source:* Wigan Ath. *Honours:* Northern Ireland B, 12 full caps.
1990–91 Burnley 2 0
1991–92 Burnley 3 0
1992–93 Burnley 1 0 **6 0**
1992–93 *Bury* 5 3 **5 3**
From Erzgebirge Aue
1996–97 Ipswich T 29 2
1997–98 Ipswich T 23 1
1998–99 Ipswich T 4 0 **56 3**
1998–99 Sheffield W 26 3
1999–2000 Sheffield W 27 0 **53 3**
2000–01 Birmingham C 26 1
2001–02 Birmingham C 15 1 **41 2**
2002–03 Walsall 24 4 **24 4**
2003–04 Nottingham F 28 0 **28 0**

**STEVENSON, David‡ (G) 0 0**
b.Blackpool 20-9-84
*Source:* Trainee.
2002–03 Blackburn R 0 0
2002–03 Nottingham F 0 0
2003–04 Nottingham F 0 0

**TARKA, David (D) 45 1**
b.Perth 11-2-83
*Honours:* Australia Schools, Under-20, Under-23, 2 full caps.
2001–02 Perth Glory 17 0
2002–03 Perth Glory 28 1 **45 1**
2003–04 Nottingham F 0 0

**TAYLOR, Charlie (M) 0 0**
b.Lewisham 28-12-85
2002–03 Crystal Palace 0 0
2003–04 Nottingham F 0 0

**TAYLOR, Gareth (F) 333 96**
H: 6 2 W: 13 07 b.Weston-Super-Mare 25-2-73
*Source:* Southampton Trainee. *Honours:* Wales Under-21, 14 full caps, 1 goal.
1991–92 Bristol R 1 0
1992–93 Bristol R 0 0
1993–94 Bristol R 0 0
1994–95 Bristol R 39 12
1995–96 Bristol R 7 4 **47 16**
1995–96 Crystal Palace 20 1 **20 1**
1995–96 Sheffield U 10 2
1996–97 Sheffield U 34 12
1997–98 Sheffield U 28 10
1998–99 Sheffield U 12 1 **84 25**
1998–99 Manchester C 26 4
1999–2000 Manchester C 17 5
1999–2000 *Port Vale* 4 0 **4 0**
1999–2000 *QPR* 6 1 **6 1**
2000–01 Manchester C 0 0 **43 9**
2000–01 *Burnley* 15 4
2001–02 Burnley 40 16
2002–03 Burnley 40 16
2003–04 Burnley 0 0 **95 36**
2003–04 Nottingham F 34 8 **34 8**

**THOMPSON, John (D) 60 4**
H: 6 0 W: 12 01 b.Dublin 12-10-81
*Honours:* Eire Under-21, 1 full cap.
1999–2000 Nottingham F 0 0
2000–01 Nottingham F 0 0
2001–02 Nottingham F 8 0
2002–03 Nottingham F 20 3
2003–04 Nottingham F 32 1 **60 4**

**TYNAN, Scott* (G) 0 0**
b.Knowsley 27-11-83
*Source:* Wigan Ath Scholar.
2001–02 Nottingham F 0 0
2002–03 Nottingham F 0 0
2003–04 Nottingham F 0 0

**WALKER, Des* (D) 657 1**
H: 5 11 W: 11 13 b.Enfield 26-11-65
*Source:* Apprentice. *Honours:* England Under-21, 59 full caps.
1983–84 Nottingham F 4 0
1984–85 Nottingham F 3 0
1985–86 Nottingham F 39 0
1986–87 Nottingham F 41 0
1987–88 Nottingham F 35 0
1988–89 Nottingham F 34 0
1989–90 Nottingham F 38 0
1990–91 Nottingham F 37 0
1991–92 Nottingham F 33 1
1992–93 Sampdoria 30 0 **30 0**
1993–94 Sheffield W 42 0
1994–95 Sheffield W 38 0
1995–96 Sheffield W 36 0
1996–97 Sheffield W 36 0
1997–98 Sheffield W 38 0
1998–99 Sheffield W 37 0
1999–2000 Sheffield W 37 0
2000–01 Sheffield W 43 0 **307 0**
2001–02 Nottingham F 0 0
2002–03 Nottingham F 31 0
2003–04 Nottingham F 25 0 **320 1**

**WARD, Darren (G) 455 0**
H: 6 0 W: 13 02 b.Worksop 11-5-74
*Source:* Trainee. *Honours:* Wales Under-21, B, 5 full caps.
1992–93 Mansfield T 13 0
1993–94 Mansfield T 33 0
1994–95 Mansfield T 35 0 **81 0**
1995–96 Notts Co 46 0
1996–97 Notts Co 38 0
1997–98 Notts Co 44 0
1998–99 Notts Co 43 0
1999–2000 Notts Co 45 0
2000–01 Notts Co 35 0 **251 0**
2000–01 Nottingham F 0 0
2001–02 Nottingham F 46 0
2002–03 Nottingham F 45 0
2003–04 Nottingham F 32 0 **123 0**

**WEBB, Steven* (D) 0 0**
b.Macclesfield 13-9-84
*Source:* Academy.
2001–02 Nottingham F 0 0
2002–03 Nottingham F 0 0
2003–04 Nottingham F 0 0

**WEIR-DALEY, Spencer (F) 0 0**
b.Leicester 5-9-85
*Source:* Scholar.
2003–04 Nottingham F 0 0

**WESTCARR, Craig (F) 22 1**
H: 5 11 W: 11 04 b.Nottingham 29-1-85
*Source:* Scholar. *Honours:* England Youth.
2001–02 Nottingham F 8 0
2002–03 Nottingham F 11 1
2003–04 Nottingham F 3 0 **22 1**

**WILLIAMS, Gareth (M) 142 9**
H: 6 1 W: 12 03 b.Glasgow 16-12-81
*Source:* Trainee. *Honours:* Scotland Youth, Under-21, 5 full caps.
1998–99 Nottingham F 0 0
1999–2000 Nottingham F 2 0
2000–01 Nottingham F 17 0
2001–02 Nottingham F 44 0
2002–03 Nottingham F 40 3
2003–04 Nottingham F 39 6 **142 9**

**WILMET, Jonathan (F) 0 0**
b.Ottegnies 7-1-86
2003–04 Nottingham F 0 0

**Scholars**
Blair, Daniel J A; Deakin, Ian C G; France, Aaron J; Freyne, David P; Handbury, Ryan M; Hanson, Ricky D; Hawkins, Nicholas C; Hughes, Robert I; Hurren, Gavin D M; Litchfield, Sam; Morgan, Neil; Naughton, Cathal; Pittman, Jon P; Plummer, Michael J; Vickerton, Martin D

## NOTTS CO (56)

**BALDRY, Simon* (M)** 186 9
H: 5 11 W: 11 00 b.Huddersfield 12-2-76
*Source:* Trainee.

| | | | | | |
|---|---|---|---|---|---|
| 1993–94 | Huddersfield T | 10 | 2 | | |
| 1994–95 | Huddersfield T | 11 | 0 | | |
| 1995–96 | Huddersfield T | 14 | 0 | | |
| 1996–97 | Huddersfield T | 7 | 0 | | |
| 1997–98 | Huddersfield T | 11 | 1 | | |
| 1998–99 | Huddersfield T | 13 | 0 | | |
| 1998–99 | *Bury* | 5 | 0 | **5** | **0** |
| 1999–2000 | Huddersfield T | 19 | 1 | | |
| 2000–01 | Huddersfield T | 35 | 2 | | |
| 2001–02 | Huddersfield T | 4 | 0 | | |
| 2002–03 | Huddersfield T | 22 | 2 | **146** | **8** |
| 2003–04 | Notts Co | 35 | 1 | **35** | **1** |

**BARACLOUGH, Ian* (D)** 471 33
H: 6 1 W: 12 09 b.Leicester 4-12-70
*Source:* Trainee.

| | | | | | |
|---|---|---|---|---|---|
| 1988–89 | Leicester C | 0 | 0 | | |
| 1989–90 | Leicester C | 0 | 0 | | |
| 1989–90 | *Wigan Ath* | 9 | 2 | **9** | **2** |
| 1990–91 | Leicester C | 0 | 0 | | |
| 1990–91 | *Grimsby T* | 4 | 0 | | |
| 1991–92 | Grimsby T | 0 | 0 | | |
| 1992–93 | Grimsby T | 1 | 0 | **5** | **0** |
| 1992–93 | Lincoln C | 36 | 5 | | |
| 1993–94 | Lincoln C | 37 | 5 | **73** | **10** |
| 1994–95 | Mansfield T | 36 | 3 | | |
| 1995–96 | Mansfield T | 11 | 2 | **47** | **5** |
| 1995–96 | Notts Co | 35 | 2 | | |
| 1996–97 | Notts Co | 38 | 2 | | |
| 1997–98 | Notts Co | 38 | 6 | | |
| 1997–98 | QPR | 8 | 0 | | |
| 1998–99 | QPR | 43 | 1 | | |
| 1999–2000 | QPR | 45 | 0 | | |
| 2000–01 | QPR | 29 | 0 | **125** | **1** |
| 2001–02 | Notts Co | 33 | 3 | | |
| 2002–03 | Notts Co | 34 | 2 | | |
| 2003–04 | Notts Co | 34 | 0 | **212** | **15** |

**BARRAS, Tony* (D)** 442 29
H: 6 0 W: 12 04 b.Billingham 29-3-71
*Source:* Trainee.

| | | | | | |
|---|---|---|---|---|---|
| 1988–89 | Hartlepool U | 3 | 0 | | |
| 1989–90 | Hartlepool U | 9 | 0 | **12** | **0** |
| 1990–91 | Stockport Co | 40 | 0 | | |
| 1991–92 | Stockport Co | 42 | 5 | | |
| 1992–93 | Stockport Co | 14 | 0 | | |
| 1993–94 | Stockport Co | 3 | 0 | **99** | **5** |
| 1993–94 | *Rotherham U* | 5 | 1 | **5** | **1** |
| 1994–95 | York C | 31 | 1 | | |
| 1995–96 | York C | 32 | 3 | | |
| 1996–97 | York C | 46 | 1 | | |
| 1997–98 | York C | 38 | 6 | | |
| 1998–99 | York C | 24 | 0 | **171** | **11** |
| 1998–99 | Reading | 6 | 1 | **6** | **1** |
| 1999–2000 | Walsall | 24 | 4 | | |
| 2000–01 | Walsall | 36 | 1 | | |
| 2001–02 | Walsall | 26 | 4 | | |
| 2002–03 | Walsall | 19 | 0 | **105** | **9** |
| 2002–03 | *Plymouth Arg* | 4 | 0 | **4** | **0** |
| 2003–04 | Notts Co | 40 | 2 | **40** | **2** |

**BEWERS, Jon (D)** 4 0
H: 5 8 W: 9 13 b.Kettering 10-9-82
*Source:* Trainee. *Honours:* England Youth, Under-20.

| | | | | | |
|---|---|---|---|---|---|
| 1999–2000 | Aston Villa | 1 | 0 | | |
| 2000–01 | Aston Villa | 0 | 0 | | |
| 2001–02 | Aston Villa | 0 | 0 | | |
| 2002–03 | Aston Villa | 0 | 0 | | |
| 2003–04 | Aston Villa | 0 | 0 | **1** | **0** |
| 2003–04 | Notts Co | 3 | 0 | **3** | **0** |

**BOLLAND, Paul (M)** 144 5
H: 5 11 W: 12 05 b.Bradford 23-12-79
*Source:* Trainee.

| | | | | | |
|---|---|---|---|---|---|
| 1997–98 | Bradford C | 10 | 0 | | |
| 1998–99 | Bradford C | 2 | 0 | **12** | **0** |
| 1998–99 | Notts Co | 13 | 0 | | |
| 1999–2000 | Notts Co | 25 | 1 | | |
| 2000–01 | Notts Co | 7 | 0 | | |
| 2001–02 | Notts Co | 19 | 0 | | |
| 2002–03 | Notts Co | 29 | 3 | | |
| 2003–04 | Notts Co | 39 | 1 | **132** | **5** |

**BRIGGS, Mark (M)** 0 0
H: 6 0 W: 11 07 b.Wolverhampton 16-2-82
*Source:* Scholar.

| | | | | | |
|---|---|---|---|---|---|
| 2000–01 | WBA | 0 | 0 | | |
| 2001–02 | WBA | 0 | 0 | | |
| 2002–03 | WBA | 0 | 0 | | |
| 2003–04 | Notts Co | 0 | 0 | | |

**BROUGH, Michael‡ (M)** 89 2
H: 6 0 W: 12 05 b.Nottingham 1-8-81
*Source:* Trainee. *Honours:* Wales Under-21.

| | | | | | |
|---|---|---|---|---|---|
| 1999–2000 | Notts Co | 11 | 0 | | |
| 2000–01 | Notts Co | 16 | 1 | | |
| 2001–02 | Notts Co | 21 | 0 | | |
| 2002–03 | Notts Co | 31 | 1 | | |
| 2003–04 | Notts Co | 10 | 0 | **89** | **2** |

**DEENEY, Saul (G)** 10 0
H: 6 1 W: 12 07 b.Londonderry 12-3-83
*Source:* Scholar.

| | | | | | |
|---|---|---|---|---|---|
| 2000–01 | Notts Co | 0 | 0 | | |
| 2001–02 | Notts Co | 0 | 0 | | |
| 2002–03 | Notts Co | 7 | 0 | | |
| 2003–04 | Notts Co | 3 | 0 | **10** | **0** |

**FENTON, Nicky* (D)** 196 10
H: 6 0 W: 12 01 b.Preston 23-11-79
*Source:* Trainee. *Honours:* England Youth.

| | | | | | |
|---|---|---|---|---|---|
| 1996–97 | Manchester C | 0 | 0 | | |
| 1997–98 | Manchester C | 0 | 0 | | |
| 1998–99 | Manchester C | 15 | 0 | | |
| 1999–2000 | Manchester C | 0 | 0 | | |
| 1999–2000 | *Notts Co* | 13 | 1 | | |
| 1999–2000 | *Bournemouth* | 8 | 0 | | |
| 2000–01 | Manchester C | 0 | 0 | **15** | **0** |
| 2000–01 | *Bournemouth* | 5 | 0 | **13** | **0** |
| 2000–01 | Notts Co | 30 | 2 | | |
| 2001–02 | Notts Co | 42 | 3 | | |
| 2002–03 | Notts Co | 40 | 3 | | |
| 2003–04 | Notts Co | 43 | 1 | **168** | **10** |

**FRANCIS, Willis§ (M)** 13 0
H: 5 5 W: 10 10 b.Nottingham 26-7-85
*Source:* Scholar.

| | | | | | |
|---|---|---|---|---|---|
| 2002–03 | Notts Co | 10 | 0 | | |
| 2003–04 | Notts Co | 3 | 0 | **13** | **0** |

**FRIARS, Emmet (M)** 0 0

| | | | | | |
|---|---|---|---|---|---|
| 2003–04 | Notts Co | 0 | 0 | | |

**GARDEN, Stuart* (G)** 52 0
H: 6 0 W: 12 06 b.Dundee 10-2-72

| | | | | | |
|---|---|---|---|---|---|
| 2001–02 | Notts Co | 21 | 0 | | |
| 2002–03 | Notts Co | 18 | 0 | | |
| 2003–04 | Notts Co | 13 | 0 | **52** | **0** |

**HACKWORTH, Tony (F)** 54 1
H: 6 1 W: 13 03 b.Durham 19-5-80
*Source:* Trainee. *Honours:* England Youth.

| | | | | | |
|---|---|---|---|---|---|
| 1997–98 | Leeds U | 0 | 0 | | |
| 1998–99 | Leeds U | 0 | 0 | | |
| 1999–2000 | Leeds U | 0 | 0 | | |
| 2000–01 | Leeds U | 0 | 0 | | |
| 2001–02 | Notts Co | 33 | 1 | | |
| 2002–03 | Notts Co | 9 | 0 | | |
| 2003–04 | Notts Co | 12 | 0 | **54** | **1** |

**HARRAD, Shaun (M)** 13 0
H: 5 10 W: 12 04 b.Nottingham 11-12-84
*Source:* Scholar.

| | | | | | |
|---|---|---|---|---|---|
| 2002–03 | Notts Co | 5 | 0 | | |
| 2003–04 | Notts Co | 8 | 0 | **13** | **0** |

**HEFFERNAN, Paul (F)** 100 36
H: 5 10 W: 11 00 b.Dublin 29-12-81
*Source:* Newton.

| | | | | | |
|---|---|---|---|---|---|
| 1999–2000 | Notts Co | 2 | 0 | | |
| 2000–01 | Notts Co | 1 | 0 | | |
| 2001–02 | Notts Co | 23 | 6 | | |
| 2002–03 | Notts Co | 36 | 10 | | |
| 2003–04 | Notts Co | 38 | 20 | **100** | **36** |

**McFAUL, Shane (M)** 6 0
H: 6 1 W: 11 10 b.Dublin 23-5-86
*Source:* Scholar.

| | | | | | |
|---|---|---|---|---|---|
| 2003–04 | Notts Co | 6 | 0 | **6** | **0** |

**McGOLDRICK, David‡ (M)** 4 0
H: 6 1 W: 11 10 b.Nottingham 29-11-87

| | | | | | |
|---|---|---|---|---|---|
| 2003–04 | Notts Co | 4 | 0 | **4** | **0** |

**McHUGH, Frazer (M)** 37 0
H: 5 9 W: 12 05 b.Nottingham 14-7-81
*Source:* Trainee.

| | | | | | |
|---|---|---|---|---|---|
| 1998–99 | Swindon T | 1 | 0 | | |
| 1999–2000 | Swindon T | 14 | 0 | | |
| 2000–01 | Swindon T | 4 | 0 | | |
| 2001–02 | Swindon T | 0 | 0 | **19** | **0** |
| From Tamworth, Gainsborough T | | | | | |
| 2002–03 | Bradford | | | | |
| 2003–04 | Bradford C | 3 | 0 | **5** | **0** |
| 2003–04 | Notts Co | 13 | 0 | **13** | **0** |

**MILDENHALL, Steve (G)** 108 0
H: 6 5 W: 15 01 b.Swindon 13-5-78
*Source:* Trainee.

| | | | | | |
|---|---|---|---|---|---|
| 1996–97 | Swindon T | 1 | 0 | | |
| 1997–98 | Swindon T | 4 | 0 | | |
| 1998–99 | Swindon T | 0 | 0 | | |
| 1999–2000 | Swindon T | 5 | 0 | | |
| 2000–01 | Swindon T | 23 | 0 | **33** | **0** |
| 2001–02 | Notts Co | 26 | 0 | | |
| 2002–03 | Notts Co | 21 | 0 | | |
| 2003–04 | Notts Co | 28 | 0 | **75** | **0** |

**NICHOLSON, Kevin* (D)** 103 3
H: 5 8 W: 12 05 b.Derby 2-10-80
*Source:* Trainee. *Honours:* England Schools.

| | | | | | |
|---|---|---|---|---|---|
| 1997–98 | Sheffield W | 0 | 0 | | |
| 1998–99 | Sheffield W | 0 | 0 | | |
| 1999–2000 | Sheffield W | 0 | 0 | | |
| 2000–01 | Sheffield W | 1 | 0 | **1** | **0** |
| From Forest Green R | | | | | |
| 2000–01 | Northampton T | 7 | 0 | **7** | **0** |
| 2000–01 | Notts Co | 11 | 2 | | |
| 2001–02 | Notts Co | 24 | 1 | | |
| 2002–03 | Notts Co | 37 | 0 | | |
| 2003–04 | Notts Co | 23 | 0 | **95** | **3** |

**OAKES, Stefan (M)** 90 2
H: 6 1 W: 13 04 b.Leicester 6-9-78
*Source:* Trainee.

| | | | | | |
|---|---|---|---|---|---|
| 1997–98 | Leicester C | 0 | 0 | | |
| 1998–99 | Leicester C | 3 | 0 | | |
| 1999–2000 | Leicester C | 22 | 1 | | |
| 2000–01 | Leicester C | 13 | 0 | | |
| 2001–02 | Leicester C | 21 | 1 | | |
| 2002–03 | Leicester C | 5 | 0 | **64** | **2** |
| 2002–03 | *Crewe Alex* | 7 | 0 | **7** | **0** |
| 2003–04 | Walsall | 5 | 0 | **5** | **0** |
| 2003–04 | Notts Co | 14 | 0 | **14** | **0** |

**PIPE, David (M)** 39 1
H: 5 9 W: 12 01 b.Caerphilly 5-11-83
*Source:* Scholar. *Honours:* Wales Under-21, 1 full cap.

| | | | | | |
|---|---|---|---|---|---|
| 2000–01 | Coventry C | 0 | 0 | | |
| 2001–02 | Coventry C | 0 | 0 | | |
| 2002–03 | Coventry C | 21 | 1 | | |
| 2003–04 | Coventry C | 0 | 0 | **21** | **1** |
| 2003–04 | Notts Co | 18 | 0 | **18** | **0** |

**RHODES, Chris§ (M)** 1 0
H: 5 9 W: 10 12 b.Mansfield 9-1-87
*Source:* Scholar.

| | | | | | |
|---|---|---|---|---|---|
| 2003–04 | Notts Co | 1 | 0 | **1** | **0** |

**RICHARDSON, Ian (D)** 250 21
H: 5 10 W: 11 01 b.Barking 22-10-70
*Source:* Dagenham & Redbridge.

| | | | | | |
|---|---|---|---|---|---|
| 1995–96 | Birmingham C | 7 | 0 | **7** | **0** |
| 1995–96 | Notts Co | 15 | 0 | | |
| 1996–97 | Notts Co | 19 | 1 | | |
| 1997–98 | Notts Co | 30 | 2 | | |
| 1998–99 | Notts Co | 23 | 7 | | |
| 1999–2000 | Notts Co | 33 | 4 | | |
| 2000–01 | Notts Co | 25 | 1 | | |
| 2001–02 | Notts Co | 24 | 2 | | |
| 2002–03 | Notts Co | 34 | 1 | | |
| 2003–04 | Notts Co | 40 | 3 | **243** | **21** |

**RILEY, Paul* (D)** 28 3
H: 5 9 W: 10 07 b.Nottingham 29-9-82
*Source:* Scholar.

| | | | | | |
|---|---|---|---|---|---|
| 2001–02 | Notts Co | 6 | 0 | | |

2002–03 Notts Co 3 0
2003–04 Notts Co 19 3 **28 3**

**SCOFFHAM, Steve (F) 15 2**
H: 5 11 W: 11 04 b.Germany 12-7-83
*Source:* Gedling.
2003–04 Notts Co 15 2 **15 2**

**SCULLY, Tony‡ (M) 135 7**
H: 5 7 W: 11 06 b.Dublin 12-6-76
*Source:* Trainee. *Honours:* Eire Under-21.
1993–94 Crystal Palace 0 0
1994–95 Crystal Palace 0 0
1994–95 *Bournemouth* 10 0 **10 0**
1995–96 Crystal Palace 2 0
1995–96 *Cardiff C* 14 0 **14 0**
1996–97 Crystal Palace 1 0
1997–98 Crystal Palace 0 0 **3 0**
1997–98 Manchester C 9 0 **9 0**
1997–98 *Stoke C* 7 0 **7 0**
1997–98 QPR 7 0
1998–99 QPR 23 2
1999–2000 QPR 8 0
2000–01 QPR 2 0 **40 2**
2001–02 Cambridge U 25 2
2002–03 Cambridge U 6 0 **31 2**
2002–03 *Southend U* 8 0 **8 0**
2002–03 *Peterborough U* 3 0
2003–04 Peterborough U 0 0 **3 0**
From Dagenham & R
2003–04 Notts Co 10 3 **10 3**

**WILLIAMS, Matthew (F) 7 0**
H: 5 8 W: 9 11 b.St Asaph 5-11-82
*Honours:* Wales Under-21.
1999–2000 Manchester U 0 0
2000–01 Manchester U 0 0
2001–02 Manchester U 0 0
2002–03 Manchester U 0 0
2003–04 Manchester U 0 0
2003–04 Notts Co 7 0 **7 0**

**WILSON, Kelvin§ (M) 3 0**
H: 6 2 W: 12 03 b.Nottingham 3-9-85
*Source:* Scholar.
2003–04 Notts Co 3 0 **3 0**

**Scholars**
Appleby, Craig; Barcherini, Alessandro; Commons, Spencer J; Francis, Willis D; Hannigan, Thomas J; McIntyre, Edmond J J; Nurse, Kristopher F; Rhodes, Christopher K; Richardson, Ben; Sherlock, Marc; Smith, Gregory M; Taylor, Gareth; Wilson, Kelvin

## OLDHAM ATH (57)

**APPLEBY, Matty (M) 277 17**
H: 5 10 W: 11 04 b.Middlesbrough 16-4-72
*Source:* Trainee.
1989–90 Newcastle U 0 0
1990–91 Newcastle U 1 0
1991–92 Newcastle U 18 0
1992–93 Newcastle U 0 0
1993–94 Newcastle U 1 0 **20 0**
1993–94 *Darlington* 10 1
1994–95 Darlington 36 1
1995–96 Darlington 43 6 **89 8**
1996–97 Barnsley 35 0
1997–98 Barnsley 15 0
1998–99 Barnsley 34 0
1999–2000 Barnsley 36 5
2000–01 Barnsley 19 2
2001–02 Barnsley 0 0 **139 7**
2001–02 Oldham Ath 17 2
2002–03 Oldham Ath 12 0
2003–04 Oldham Ath 0 0 **29 2**

**BARLOW, Matty§ (M) 1 0**
H: 5 11 W: 10 02 b.Oldham 25-6-87
*Source:* Scholar.
2003–04 Oldham Ath 1 0 **1 0**

**BEHARALL, David (D) 77 3**
H: 6 0 W: 11 06 b.Newcastle 8-3-79
*Source:* Trainee.
1997–98 Newcastle U 0 0
1998–99 Newcastle U 4 0
1999–2000 Newcastle U 2 0
2000–01 Newcastle U 0 0 **6 0**
2001–02 Grimsby T 14 0 **14 0**
2001–02 Oldham Ath 18 1
2002–03 Oldham Ath 32 0
2003–04 Oldham Ath 7 2 **57 3**

**BONNER, Mark# (M) 329 17**
H: 5 10 W: 11 00 b.Ormskirk 7-6-74
*Source:* Trainee.
1991–92 Blackpool 3 0
1992–93 Blackpool 15 0
1993–94 Blackpool 40 7
1994–95 Blackpool 17 0
1995–96 Blackpool 42 3
1996–97 Blackpool 29 1
1997–98 Blackpool 32 3 **178 14**
1998–99 Cardiff C 25 1
1998–99 *Hull C* 1 1 **1 1**
1999–2000 Cardiff C 31 0
2000–01 Cardiff C 24 1
2001–02 Cardiff C 29 0
2002–03 Cardiff C 14 0
2003–04 Cardiff C 20 0 **143 2**
2003–04 Oldham Ath 7 0 **7 0**

**BOSHELL, Danny (M) 54 1**
H: 5 11 W: 11 08 b.Bradford 30-5-81
*Source:* Trainee.
1998–99 Oldham Ath 0 0
1999–2000 Oldham Ath 8 0
2000–01 Oldham Ath 18 1
2001–02 Oldham Ath 4 0
2002–03 Oldham Ath 2 0
2003–04 Oldham Ath 22 0 **54 1**

**CLEGG, Michael (D) 64 0**
H: 5 9 W: 11 07 b.Ashton-under-Lyne 3-7-77
*Source:* Trainee. *Honours:* England Under-21.
1995–96 Manchester U 0 0
1996–97 Manchester U 4 0
1997–98 Manchester U 3 0
1998–99 Manchester U 0 0
1999–2000 Manchester U 2 0
1999–2000 *Ipswich T* 3 0 **3 0**
1999–2000 *Wigan Ath* 6 0 **6 0**
2000–01 Manchester U 0 0
2001–02 Manchester U 0 0 **9 0**
2001–02 Oldham Ath 6 0
2002–03 Oldham Ath 8 0
2003–04 Oldham Ath 32 0 **46 0**

**COOKSEY, Ernie (M) 36 4**
H: 5 9 W: 11 04 b.Essex 17-9-78
*Source:* Crawley T.
2003–04 Oldham Ath 36 4 **36 4**

**CROWE, Dean‡ (F) 156 32**
H: 5 7 W: 11 08 b.Stockport 6-6-79
*Source:* Trainee.
1996–97 Stoke C 0 0
1997–98 Stoke C 16 4
1998–99 Stoke C 38 8
1999–2000 Stoke C 6 0
1999–2000 *Northampton T* 5 0 **5 0**
1999–2000 *Bury* 4 1
2000–01 Stoke C 0 0
2000–01 *Bury* 7 1 **11 2**
2001–02 Stoke C 0 0 **60 12**
2001–02 *Plymouth Arg* 1 0 **1 0**
2001–02 Luton T 34 15
2002–03 Luton T 27 2
2003–04 Luton T 8 0 **69 17**
2003–04 *York C* 5 0 **5 0**
2003–04 Oldham Ath 5 1 **5 1**

**EYRE, John (M) 329 78**
H: 6 0 W: 11 05 b.Hull 9-10-74
*Source:* Trainee.
1993–94 Oldham Ath 2 0
1994–95 Oldham Ath 8 1
1994–95 *Scunthorpe U* 9 8
1995–96 Scunthorpe U 39 10
1996–97 Scunthorpe U 42 8
1997–98 Scunthorpe U 42 10
1998–99 Scunthorpe U 41 15 **173 51**
1999–2000 Hull C 24 8
2000–01 Hull C 28 5 **52 13**
2001–02 Oldham Ath 20 5
2002–03 Oldham Ath 31 2
2003–04 Oldham Ath 43 6 **104 14**

**EYRES, David* (M) 585 122**
H: 5 11 W: 11 06 b.Liverpool 26-2-64
*Source:* Rhyl.
1989–90 Blackpool 35 7
1990–91 Blackpool 36 6
1991–92 Blackpool 41 9
1992–93 Blackpool 46 16 **158 38**
1993–94 Burnley 45 19
1994–95 Burnley 39 8
1995–96 Burnley 42 6
1996–97 Burnley 36 3
1997–98 Burnley 13 1 **175 37**
1997–98 Preston NE 28 4
1998–99 Preston NE 34 8
1999–2000 Preston NE 41 7
2000–01 Preston NE 5 0 **108 19**
2000–01 Oldham Ath 30 3
2001–02 Oldham Ath 45 9
2002–03 Oldham Ath 40 13
2003–04 Oldham Ath 29 3 **144 28**

**FLEMING, Craig§ (M) 1 0**
H: 5 10 W: 11 02 b.Stockport 1-12-84
*Source:* Scholar.
2003–04 Oldham Ath 1 0 **1 0**

**FORDE, Danny (D) 0 0**
H: 5 10 W: 11 07 b.Salford 26-10-87
*Source:* Scholar.
2003–04 Oldham Ath 0 0

**GRIFFIN, Adam (M) 27 1**
H: 5 7 W: 10 03 b.Manchester 26-8-84
*Source:* Scholar.
2001–02 Oldham Ath 1 0
2002–03 Oldham Ath 0 0
2003–04 Oldham Ath 26 1 **27 1**

**HAINING, Will (D) 61 4**
H: 6 0 W: 11 00 b.Glasgow 2-10-82
*Source:* Scholar.
2001–02 Oldham Ath 4 0
2002–03 Oldham Ath 26 2
2003–04 Oldham Ath 31 2 **61 4**

**HALL, Chris§ (D) 1 0**
H: 6 1 W: 11 04 b.Manchester 27-11-86
2003–04 Oldham Ath 1 0 **1 0**

**HALL, Danny (D) 33 1**
H: 6 0 W: 12 01 b.Tameside 14-11-83
*Source:* Scholar.
2002–03 Oldham Ath 2 0
2003–04 Oldham Ath 31 1 **33 1**

**HOLDEN, Dean (D) 81 9**
H: 6 1 W: 12 05 b.Salford 15-9-79
*Source:* Trainee. *Honours:* England Youth.
1997–98 Bolton W 0 0
1998–99 Bolton W 0 0
1999–2000 Bolton W 12 0
2000–01 Bolton W 1 1
2001–02 Bolton W 0 0 **13 1**
2001–02 *Oldham Ath* 23 2
2002–03 Oldham Ath 6 2
2003–04 Oldham Ath 39 4 **68 8**

**JOHNSON, Jermaine* (M) 32 5**
H: 5 11 W: 11 05 b.Kingston, Jamaica 25-6-80
*Source:* Tivoli Gardens. *Honours:* Jamaica full caps.
2001–02 Bolton W 10 0
2002–03 Bolton W 2 0
2003–04 Bolton W 0 0 **12 0**
2003–04 Oldham Ath 20 5 **20 5**

**KILLEN, Chris (F) 64 14**
H: 6 0 W: 11 05 b.Wellington 8-10-81
*Source:* Miramar R. *Honours:* New Zealand Under-20, Under-23, 16 full caps, 7 goals.
1998–99 Manchester C 0 0
1999–2000 Manchester C 0 0
2000–01 Manchester C 0 0
2000–01 *Wrexham* 12 3 **12 3**
2001–02 *Port Vale* 9 6 **9 6**
2001–02 Manchester C 3 0 **3 0**
2002–03 Oldham Ath 27 3
2003–04 Oldham Ath 13 2 **40 5**

**LOMAX, Kelvin§ (M) 1 0**
H: 5 11 W: 12 03 b.Bury 12-11-86
*Source:* Scholar.
2003–04 Oldham Ath 1 0 **1 0**

**MURRAY, Paul* (M)** **277 23**
H: 5 9 W: 10 08 b.Carlisle 31-8-76
*Source:* Trainee. *Honours:* England Youth, Under-21, B.

| | | | | | |
|---|---|---|---|---|---|
| 1993–94 | Carlisle U | 8 | 0 | | |
| 1994–95 | Carlisle U | 5 | 0 | | |
| 1995–96 | Carlisle U | 28 | 1 | **41** | **1** |
| 1995–96 | QPR | 1 | 0 | | |
| 1996–97 | QPR | 32 | 5 | | |
| 1997–98 | QPR | 32 | 1 | | |
| 1997–98 | QPR | 0 | 0 | | |
| 1998–99 | QPR | 39 | 1 | | |
| 1999–2000 | QPR | 30 | 0 | | |
| 2000–01 | QPR | 6 | 0 | **140** | **7** |
| 2001–02 | Southampton | 1 | 0 | **1** | **0** |
| 2001–02 | Oldham Ath | 24 | 5 | | |
| 2002–03 | Oldham Ath | 30 | 1 | | |
| 2003–04 | Oldham Ath | 41 | 9 | **95** | **15** |

**POGLIACOMI, Les* (G)** **188 0**
H: 6 4 W: 13 02 b.Sydney 3-5-76
*Honours:* Australia Schools, Under-20.

| | | | | | |
|---|---|---|---|---|---|
| 1994–95 | Marconi Stallions | 11 | 0 | | |
| 1995–96 | Marconi Stallions | 1 | 0 | | |
| 1996–97 | Marconi Stallions | 10 | 0 | **22** | **0** |
| 1997–98 | Adelaide City | 0 | 0 | | |
| 1998–99 | Wollongong Wolves | 22 | 0 | | |
| 1999–2000 | Wollongong Wolves | 34 | 0 | **56** | **0** |
| 2000–01 | Parramatta Power | 8 | 0 | | |
| 2001–02 | Parramatta Power | 19 | 0 | **27** | **0** |
| 2002–03 | Oldham Ath | 37 | 0 | | |
| 2003–04 | Oldham Ath | 46 | 0 | **83** | **0** |

**ROCA, Carlos§ (F)** **7 0**
H: 5 4 W: 10 07 b.Manchester 4-9-84
*Source:* Scholar.

| | | | | | |
|---|---|---|---|---|---|
| 2003–04 | Oldham Ath | 7 | 0 | **7** | **0** |

**SHERIDAN, Darren* (M)** **317 11**
H: 5 6 W: 10 10 b.Manchester 8-12-67
*Source:* Winsford U.

| | | | | | |
|---|---|---|---|---|---|
| 1993–94 | Barnsley | 3 | 0 | | |
| 1994–95 | Barnsley | 35 | 2 | | |
| 1995–96 | Barnsley | 41 | 0 | | |
| 1996–97 | Barnsley | 41 | 2 | | |
| 1997–98 | Barnsley | 26 | 0 | | |
| 1998–99 | Barnsley | 25 | 1 | **171** | **5** |
| 1999–2000 | Wigan Ath | 31 | 3 | | |
| 2000–01 | Wigan Ath | 27 | 0 | **58** | **3** |
| 2001–02 | Oldham Ath | 28 | 2 | | |
| 2002–03 | Oldham Ath | 33 | 1 | | |
| 2003–04 | Oldham Ath | 27 | 0 | **88** | **3** |

**SHERIDAN, John† (M)** **606 88**
H: 5 10 W: 11 12 b.Stretford 1-10-64
*Source:* Local. *Honours:* Eire Youth, Under-21, Under-23, B, 34 full caps, 5 goals.

| | | | | | |
|---|---|---|---|---|---|
| 1981–82 | Leeds U | 0 | 0 | | |
| 1982–83 | Leeds U | 27 | 2 | | |
| 1983–84 | Leeds U | 11 | 1 | | |
| 1984–85 | Leeds U | 42 | 6 | | |
| 1985–86 | Leeds U | 32 | 4 | | |
| 1986–87 | Leeds U | 40 | 15 | | |
| 1987–88 | Leeds U | 38 | 12 | | |
| 1988–89 | Leeds U | 40 | 7 | **230** | **47** |
| 1989–90 | Nottingham F | 0 | 0 | | |
| 1989–90 | Sheffield W | 27 | 2 | | |
| 1990–91 | Sheffield W | 46 | 10 | | |
| 1991–92 | Sheffield W | 24 | 6 | | |
| 1992–93 | Sheffield W | 25 | 3 | | |
| 1993–94 | Sheffield W | 20 | 3 | | |
| 1994–95 | Sheffield W | 36 | 1 | | |
| 1995–96 | Sheffield W | 17 | 0 | | |
| 1995–96 | *Birmingham C* | 2 | 0 | **2** | **0** |
| 1996–97 | Sheffield W | 2 | 0 | **197** | **25** |
| 1996–97 | Bolton W | 20 | 2 | | |
| 1997–98 | Bolton W | 12 | 0 | **32** | **2** |
| From Doncaster R | | | | | |
| 1998–99 | Oldham Ath | 30 | 2 | | |
| 1999–2000 | Oldham Ath | 36 | 1 | | |
| 2000–01 | Oldham Ath | 25 | 4 | | |
| 2001–02 | Oldham Ath | 27 | 2 | | |
| 2002–03 | Oldham Ath | 5 | 0 | | |
| 2003–04 | Oldham Ath | 22 | 5 | **145** | **14** |

**TIERNEY, Marc (D)** **2 0**
H: 5 11 W: 11 02 b.Manchester 7-9-86
*Source:* Trainee.

| | | | | | |
|---|---|---|---|---|---|
| 2003–04 | Oldham Ath | 2 | 0 | **2** | **0** |

**VERNON, Scott (F)** **53 13**
H: 6 0 W: 11 10 b.Manchester 8-7-84
*Source:* Scholar.

| | | | | | |
|---|---|---|---|---|---|
| 2002–03 | Oldham Ath | 8 | 1 | | |
| 2003–04 | Oldham Ath | 45 | 12 | **53** | **13** |

**WALKER, Rob§ (M)** **1 0**
H: 5 9 W: 11 00 b.Bolton 20-9-85
*Source:* Scholar.

| | | | | | |
|---|---|---|---|---|---|
| 2003–04 | Oldham Ath | 1 | 0 | **1** | **0** |

**WILKINSON, Wes (F)** **5 0**
H: 5 10 W: 11 01 b.Wythenshawe 1-5-84
*Source:* Nantwich T.

| | | | | | |
|---|---|---|---|---|---|
| 2003–04 | Oldham Ath | 5 | 0 | **5** | **0** |

**WOLFENDEN, Matthew§ (M)** **1 0**
H: 5 9 W: 11 01 b.Oldham 23-7-87
*Source:* Scholar.

| | | | | | |
|---|---|---|---|---|---|
| 2003–04 | Oldham Ath | 1 | 0 | **1** | **0** |

**Scholars**
Armstrong, Paul V; Barlow, Matthew J; Eardley, Ian S; Fleming, Craig M; Grange, Christopher D; Hall, Christopher M; Jacobs, Kyle K; Lever, Christopher D; Lomax, Kelvin; Roca, Carlos J; Taylor, Jason J; Treacy, Charles; Walker, Robert S; Winn, Ashley; Wolfenden, Matthew; Yates, Daniel T

**Non Contract**
Booth, Paul; Corry, Steven; Dowie, Iain; Sheridan, John J

## OXFORD U (58)

**ALEXIS, Michael (M)** **0 0**
H: 6 2 W: 12 02 b.Oxford 2-1-85

| | | | | | |
|---|---|---|---|---|---|
| 2001–02 | Oxford U | 0 | 0 | | |
| 2002–03 | Oxford U | 0 | 0 | | |
| 2003–04 | Oxford U | 0 | 0 | | |

**ALSOP, Julian (F)** **269 60**
H: 6 4 W: 15 02 b.Nuneaton 28-5-73
*Source:* Nuneaton, VS Rugby, RC Warwick, Tamworth, Halesowen T.

| | | | | | |
|---|---|---|---|---|---|
| 1996–97 | Bristol R | 16 | 3 | | |
| 1997–98 | Bristol R | 17 | 1 | **33** | **4** |
| 1997–98 | Swansea C | 12 | 3 | | |
| 1998–99 | Swansea C | 41 | 10 | | |
| 1999–2000 | Swansea C | 37 | 3 | **90** | **16** |
| 2000–01 | Cheltenham T | 39 | 5 | | |
| 2001–02 | Cheltenham T | 41 | 20 | | |
| 2002–03 | Cheltenham T | 37 | 10 | **117** | **35** |
| 2003–04 | Oxford U | 29 | 5 | **29** | **5** |

**ASHTON, Jon (D)** **45 0**
H: 6 2 W: 13 07 b.Nuneaton 4-10-82
*Source:* Scholar.

| | | | | | |
|---|---|---|---|---|---|
| 2000–01 | Leicester C | 0 | 0 | | |
| 2001–02 | Leicester C | 7 | 0 | | |
| 2002–03 | *Notts Co* | 4 | 0 | **4** | **0** |
| 2003–04 | Leicester C | 0 | 0 | **7** | **0** |
| 2003–04 | Oxford U | 34 | 0 | **34** | **0** |

**BASHAM, Steve (F)** **161 38**
H: 5 11 W: 12 01 b.Southampton 2-12-77
*Source:* Trainee.

| | | | | | |
|---|---|---|---|---|---|
| 1996–97 | Southampton | 6 | 0 | | |
| 1997–98 | Southampton | 9 | 0 | | |
| 1997–98 | *Wrexham* | 5 | 0 | **5** | **0** |
| 1998–99 | Southampton | 4 | 1 | **19** | **1** |
| 1998–99 | *Preston NE* | 17 | 10 | | |
| 1999–2000 | Preston NE | 24 | 2 | | |
| 2000–01 | Preston NE | 11 | 2 | | |
| 2001–02 | Preston NE | 16 | 1 | **68** | **15** |
| 2002–03 | Oxford U | 31 | 8 | | |
| 2003–04 | Oxford U | 38 | 14 | **69** | **22** |

**BOUND, Matt* (D)** **334 17**
H: 6 2 W: 14 06 b.Bradford-on-Avon 9-11-72
*Source:* Trainee.

| | | | | | |
|---|---|---|---|---|---|
| 1990–91 | Southampton | 1 | 0 | | |
| 1991–92 | Southampton | 0 | 0 | | |
| 1992–93 | Southampton | 3 | 0 | | |
| 1993–94 | Southampton | 1 | 0 | | |
| 1993–94 | *Hull C* | 7 | 1 | **7** | **1** |
| 1994–95 | Southampton | 0 | 0 | **5** | **0** |
| 1994–95 | Stockport Co | 14 | 0 | | |
| 1995–96 | Stockport Co | 26 | 5 | | |
| 1995–96 | *Lincoln C* | 4 | 0 | **4** | **0** |
| 1996–97 | Stockport Co | 4 | 0 | | |
| 1997–98 | Stockport Co | 0 | 0 | **44** | **5** |
| 1997–98 | Swansea C | 28 | 0 | | |
| 1998–99 | Swansea C | 45 | 2 | | |
| 1999–2000 | Swansea C | 43 | 2 | | |
| 2000–01 | Swansea C | 40 | 3 | | |
| 2001–02 | Swansea C | 18 | 2 | **174** | **9** |
| 2001–02 | Oxford U | 22 | 0 | | |
| 2002–03 | Oxford U | 41 | 1 | | |
| 2003–04 | Oxford U | 37 | 1 | **100** | **2** |

**BROOKS, Jamie (M)** **29 11**
H: 5 10 W: 10 08 b.Oxford 12-8-83
*Source:* Scholar.

| | | | | | |
|---|---|---|---|---|---|
| 2000–01 | Oxford U | 4 | 1 | | |
| 2001–02 | Oxford U | 25 | 10 | | |
| 2002–03 | Oxford U | 0 | 0 | | |
| 2003–04 | Oxford U | 0 | 0 | **29** | **11** |

**BROWN, Danny (M)** **65 3**
H: 6 0 W: 12 06 b.Bethnal Green 12-9-80
*Source:* Trainee.

| | | | | | |
|---|---|---|---|---|---|
| 1997–98 | Leyton Orient | 0 | 0 | | |
| 1998–99 | Leyton Orient | 0 | 0 | | |
| 1999–2000 | Barnet | 24 | 3 | | |
| 2000–01 | Barnet | 29 | 0 | | |
| 2001–02 | Barnet | 0 | 0 | | |
| 2002–03 | Barnet | 0 | 0 | **53** | **3** |
| 2003–04 | Oxford U | 12 | 0 | **12** | **0** |

**COX, Simon (G)** **5 0**
H: 6 1 W: 11 00 b.Clapham 23-3-84
*Source:* Scholar.

| | | | | | |
|---|---|---|---|---|---|
| 2003–04 | Oxford U | 5 | 0 | **5** | **0** |

**CROSBY, Andy# (D)** **456 24**
H: 6 2 W: 14 00 b.Rotherham 3-3-73
*Source:* Leeds U Trainee.

| | | | | | |
|---|---|---|---|---|---|
| 1991–92 | Doncaster R | 22 | 0 | | |
| 1992–93 | Doncaster R | 29 | 0 | | |
| 1993–94 | Doncaster R | 0 | 0 | **51** | **0** |
| 1993–94 | Darlington | 25 | 0 | | |
| 1994–95 | Darlington | 35 | 0 | | |
| 1995–96 | Darlington | 45 | 1 | | |
| 1996–97 | Darlington | 42 | 1 | | |
| 1997–98 | Darlington | 34 | 1 | **181** | **3** |
| 1998–99 | Chester C | 41 | 4 | **41** | **4** |
| 1999–2000 | Brighton & HA | 36 | 3 | | |
| 2000–01 | Brighton & HA | 34 | 2 | | |
| 2001–02 | Brighton & HA | 2 | 0 | **72** | **5** |
| 2001–02 | Oxford U | 23 | 1 | | |
| 2002–03 | Oxford U | 46 | 6 | | |
| 2003–04 | Oxford U | 42 | 5 | **111** | **12** |

**HACKETT, Chris (M)** **67 3**
H: 6 0 W: 11 09 b.Oxford 1-3-83
*Source:* Scholarship.

| | | | | | |
|---|---|---|---|---|---|
| 1999–2000 | Oxford U | 2 | 0 | | |
| 2000–01 | Oxford U | 16 | 2 | | |
| 2001–02 | Oxford U | 15 | 0 | | |
| 2002–03 | Oxford U | 12 | 0 | | |
| 2003–04 | Oxford U | 22 | 1 | **67** | **3** |

**HUNT, James# (M)** **271 12**
H: 6 0 W: 12 05 b.Derby 17-12-76
*Source:* Trainee.

| | | | | | |
|---|---|---|---|---|---|
| 1994–95 | Notts Co | 0 | 0 | | |
| 1995–96 | Notts Co | 10 | 1 | | |
| 1996–97 | Notts Co | 9 | 0 | **19** | **1** |
| 1997–98 | Northampton T | 21 | 0 | | |
| 1998–99 | Northampton T | 35 | 2 | | |
| 1999–2000 | Northampton T | 37 | 1 | | |
| 2000–01 | Northampton T | 41 | 1 | | |
| 2001–02 | Northampton T | 38 | 4 | **172** | **8** |
| 2002–03 | Oxford U | 39 | 1 | | |
| 2003–04 | Oxford U | 41 | 2 | **80** | **3** |

**JUDGE, Alan† (G)** **284 0**
H: 5 11 W: 11 06 b.Kingsbury 14-5-60
*Source:* Amateur.

| | | | | | |
|---|---|---|---|---|---|
| 1977–78 | Luton T | 0 | 0 | | |
| 1978–79 | Luton T | 0 | 0 | | |
| 1979–80 | Luton T | 1 | 0 | | |
| 1980–81 | Luton T | 2 | 0 | | |
| 1981–82 | Luton T | 4 | 0 | | |
| 1982–83 | Luton T | 4 | 0 | **11** | **0** |
| 1982–83 | *Reading* | 33 | 0 | | |
| 1983–84 | Reading | 41 | 0 | | |
| 1984–85 | Reading | 3 | 0 | **77** | **0** |
| 1984–85 | Oxford U | 0 | 0 | | |
| 1985–86 | Oxford U | 19 | 0 | | |

| | | | | | |
|---|---|---|---|---|---|
| 1985–86 | *Lincoln C* | 2 | 0 | **2** | **0** |
| 1986–87 | Oxford U | 9 | 0 | | |
| 1987–88 | Oxford U | 9 | 0 | | |
| 1987–88 | *Cardiff C* | 8 | 0 | **8** | **0** |
| 1988–89 | Oxford U | 20 | 0 | | |
| 1989–90 | Oxford U | 17 | 0 | | |
| 1990–91 | Oxford U | 6 | 0 | | |
| 1991–92 | Hereford U | 24 | 0 | | |
| 1992–93 | Hereford U | 42 | 0 | | |
| 1993–94 | Hereford U | 39 | 0 | **105** | **0** |
| 1994–95 | Chelsea | 0 | 0 | | |
| 2002–03 | Oxford U | 1 | 0 | | |
| From retirement | | | | | |
| 2002–03 | Swindon T | 0 | 0 | | |
| 2003–04 | Oxford U | 0 | 0 | **81** | **0** |

**LOUIS, Jefferson (F)** **55** **8**
H: 6 2 W: 14 13 b.Harrow 22-2-79
*Source:* Thame U.

| | | | | | |
|---|---|---|---|---|---|
| 2001–02 | Oxford U | 1 | 0 | | |
| 2002–03 | Oxford U | 34 | 6 | | |
| 2003–04 | Oxford U | 20 | 2 | **55** | **8** |

**McCARTHY, Paul* (D)** **428** **18**
H: 6 0 W: 13 10 b.Cork 4-8-71
*Source:* Trainee. *Honours:* Eire Youth, Under-21.

| | | | | | |
|---|---|---|---|---|---|
| 1989–90 | Brighton & HA | 3 | 0 | | |
| 1990–91 | Brighton & HA | 21 | 0 | | |
| 1991–92 | Brighton & HA | 20 | 0 | | |
| 1992–93 | Brighton & HA | 30 | 0 | | |
| 1993–94 | Brighton & HA | 37 | 3 | | |
| 1994–95 | Brighton & HA | 37 | 2 | | |
| 1995–96 | Brighton & HA | 33 | 1 | **181** | **6** |
| 1996–97 | Wycombe W | 40 | 0 | | |
| 1997–98 | Wycombe W | 31 | 1 | | |
| 1998–99 | Wycombe W | 29 | 1 | | |
| 1999–2000 | Wycombe W | 22 | 1 | | |
| 2000–01 | Wycombe W | 38 | 2 | | |
| 2001–02 | Wycombe W | 28 | 3 | | |
| 2002–03 | Wycombe W | 24 | 1 | **212** | **9** |
| 2002–03 | *Oxford U* | 6 | 1 | | |
| 2003–04 | Oxford U | 29 | 2 | **35** | **3** |

**McNIVEN, Scott# (D)** **307** **4**
H: 5 10 W: 12 07 b.Leeds 27-5-78
*Source:* Trainee. *Honours:* Scotland Youth, Under-21.

| | | | | | |
|---|---|---|---|---|---|
| 1994–95 | Oldham Ath | 1 | 0 | | |
| 1995–96 | Oldham Ath | 15 | 0 | | |
| 1996–97 | Oldham Ath | 12 | 0 | | |
| 1997–98 | Oldham Ath | 32 | 1 | | |
| 1998–99 | Oldham Ath | 37 | 1 | | |
| 1999–2000 | Oldham Ath | 45 | 1 | | |
| 2000–01 | Oldham Ath | 45 | 0 | | |
| 2001–02 | Oldham Ath | 35 | 0 | **222** | **3** |
| 2002–03 | Oxford U | 44 | 1 | | |
| 2003–04 | Oxford U | 41 | 0 | **85** | **1** |

**OLDFIELD, David* (F)** **551** **73**
H: 6 1 W: 13 02 b.Perth (Aus) 30-5-68
*Source:* Apprentice. *Honours:* England Under-21.

| | | | | | |
|---|---|---|---|---|---|
| 1986–87 | Luton T | 0 | 0 | | |
| 1987–88 | Luton T | 8 | 3 | | |
| 1988–89 | Luton T | 21 | 1 | | |
| 1988–89 | Manchester C | 11 | 3 | | |
| 1989–90 | Manchester C | 15 | 3 | **26** | **6** |
| 1989–90 | Leicester C | 20 | 5 | | |
| 1990–91 | Leicester C | 42 | 7 | | |
| 1991–92 | Leicester C | 41 | 4 | | |
| 1992–93 | Leicester C | 44 | 5 | | |
| 1993–94 | Leicester C | 27 | 4 | | |
| 1994–95 | Leicester C | 14 | 1 | **188** | **26** |
| 1994–95 | *Millwall* | 17 | 6 | **17** | **6** |
| 1995–96 | Luton T | 34 | 2 | | |
| 1996–97 | Luton T | 38 | 6 | | |
| 1997–98 | Luton T | 45 | 10 | **146** | **22** |
| 1998–99 | Stoke C | 46 | 6 | | |
| 1999–2000 | Stoke C | 19 | 1 | **65** | **7** |
| 1999–2000 | Peterborough U | 9 | 0 | | |
| 2000–01 | Peterborough U | 39 | 3 | | |
| 2001–02 | Peterborough U | 30 | 1 | **78** | **4** |
| 2002–03 | Oxford U | 28 | 2 | | |
| 2003–04 | Oxford U | 3 | 0 | **31** | **2** |

**OMOYINMI, Manny* (F)** **112** **16**
H: 5 6 W: 10 08 b.Nigeria 28-12-77
*Source:* Trainee. *Honours:* England Schools.

| | | | | | |
|---|---|---|---|---|---|
| 1994–95 | West Ham U | 0 | 0 | | |
| 1995–96 | West Ham U | 0 | 0 | | |
| 1996–97 | West Ham U | 1 | 0 | | |
| 1996–97 | *Bournemouth* | 7 | 0 | **7** | **0** |
| 1997–98 | West Ham U | 5 | 2 | | |
| 1997–98 | *Dundee U* | 4 | 0 | **4** | **0** |
| 1998–99 | West Ham U | 3 | 0 | | |
| 1998–99 | *Leyton Orient* | 4 | 1 | **4** | **1** |
| 1999–2000 | West Ham U | 0 | 0 | **9** | **2** |
| 1999–2000 | *Gillingham* | 9 | 3 | **9** | **3** |
| 1999–2000 | *Scunthorpe U* | 6 | 1 | **6** | **1** |
| 1999–2000 | *Barnet* | 6 | 0 | **6** | **0** |
| 2000–01 | Oxford U | 24 | 3 | | |
| 2001–02 | Oxford U | 23 | 3 | | |
| 2002–03 | Oxford U | 17 | 3 | | |
| 2003–04 | Oxford U | 3 | 0 | **67** | **9** |

**PITT, Courtney* (M)** **60** **3**
H: 5 7 W: 10 08 b.London 17-12-81
*Source:* Scholar.

| | | | | | |
|---|---|---|---|---|---|
| 2000–01 | Chelsea | 0 | 0 | | |
| 2001–02 | Portsmouth | 39 | 3 | | |
| 2002–03 | Portsmouth | 0 | 0 | | |
| 2003–04 | Portsmouth | 0 | 0 | **39** | **3** |
| 2003–04 | *Luton T* | 12 | 0 | **12** | **0** |
| 2003–04 | *Coventry C* | 1 | 0 | **1** | **0** |
| 2003–04 | Oxford U | 8 | 0 | **8** | **0** |

**POWELL, Paul† (D)** **178** **17**
H: 5 8 W: 11 13 b.Wallingford 30-6-78
*Source:* Trainee.

| | | | | | |
|---|---|---|---|---|---|
| 1995–96 | Oxford U | 3 | 0 | | |
| 1996–97 | Oxford U | 0 | 0 | | |
| 1997–98 | Oxford U | 21 | 1 | | |
| 1998–99 | Oxford U | 44 | 3 | | |
| 1999–2000 | Oxford U | 40 | 6 | | |
| 2000–01 | Oxford U | 20 | 1 | | |
| 2001–02 | Oxford U | 36 | 4 | | |
| 2002–03 | Oxford U | 14 | 2 | | |
| 2003–04 | Oxford U | 0 | 0 | **178** | **17** |

**RAWLE, Mark (F)** **109** **23**
H: 5 11 W: 12 02 b.Leicester 27-4-79
*Source:* Boston U.

| | | | | | |
|---|---|---|---|---|---|
| 2000–01 | Southend U | 14 | 1 | | |
| 2001–02 | Southend U | 30 | 5 | | |
| 2002–03 | Southend U | 34 | 9 | **78** | **15** |
| 2003–04 | Oxford U | 31 | 8 | **31** | **8** |

**ROBINSON, Matt# (D)** **230** **3**
H: 5 11 W: 11 09 b.Exeter 23-12-74
*Source:* Trainee.

| | | | | | |
|---|---|---|---|---|---|
| 1993–94 | Southampton | 0 | 0 | | |
| 1994–95 | Southampton | 1 | 0 | | |
| 1995–96 | Southampton | 5 | 0 | | |
| 1996–97 | Southampton | 7 | 0 | | |
| 1997–98 | Southampton | 1 | 0 | **14** | **0** |
| 1997–98 | Portsmouth | 15 | 0 | | |
| 1998–99 | Portsmouth | 29 | 1 | | |
| 1999–2000 | Portsmouth | 25 | 0 | **69** | **1** |
| 1999–2000 | Reading | 19 | 0 | | |
| 2000–01 | Reading | 32 | 0 | | |
| 2001–02 | Reading | 14 | 0 | **65** | **0** |
| 2002–03 | Oxford U | 42 | 1 | | |
| 2003–04 | Oxford U | 40 | 1 | **82** | **2** |

**STEELE, Lee* (F)** **199** **52**
H: 5 8 W: 12 05 b.Liverpool 2-12-73
*Source:* Bootle, Northwich V.

| | | | | | |
|---|---|---|---|---|---|
| 1997–98 | Shrewsbury T | 38 | 13 | | |
| 1998–99 | Shrewsbury T | 38 | 13 | | |
| 1999–2000 | Shrewsbury T | 37 | 11 | **113** | **37** |
| 2000–01 | Brighton & HA | 23 | 2 | | |
| 2001–02 | Brighton & HA | 37 | 9 | **60** | **11** |
| 2002–03 | Oxford U | 10 | 3 | | |
| 2003–04 | Oxford U | 16 | 1 | **26** | **4** |

**TOWNSLEY, Derek‡ (D)** **196** **34**
H: 6 5 W: 13 01 b.Carlisle 21-1-73
*Source:* Gretna.

| | | | | | |
|---|---|---|---|---|---|
| 1996–97 | Q of S | 31 | 2 | | |
| 1997–98 | Q of S | 29 | 6 | | |
| 1998–99 | Q of S | 27 | 10 | **87** | **18** |
| 1999–2000 | Motherwell | 25 | 1 | | |
| 2000–01 | Motherwell | 30 | 6 | **55** | **7** |
| 2001–02 | Hibernian | 18 | 5 | | |
| 2002–03 | Hibernian | 25 | 4 | **43** | **9** |
| 2003–04 | Oxford U | 11 | 0 | **11** | **0** |

**WALKER, Richard* (F)** **135** **27**
H: 6 0 W: 12 00 b.Sutton Coldfield 8-11-77
*Source:* Trainee.

| | | | | | |
|---|---|---|---|---|---|
| 1995–96 | Aston Villa | 0 | 0 | | |
| 1996–97 | Aston Villa | 0 | 0 | | |
| 1997–98 | Aston Villa | 1 | 0 | | |
| 1998–99 | Aston Villa | 0 | 0 | | |
| 1998–99 | *Cambridge U* | 21 | 3 | **21** | **3** |
| 1999–2000 | Aston Villa | 5 | 2 | | |
| 2000–01 | Aston Villa | 0 | 0 | | |
| 2000–01 | *Blackpool* | 18 | 3 | | |
| 2001–02 | Aston Villa | 0 | 0 | **6** | **2** |
| 2001–02 | *Wycombe W* | 12 | 3 | **12** | **3** |
| 2001–02 | Blackpool | 21 | 8 | | |
| 2002–03 | Blackpool | 32 | 4 | | |
| 2003–04 | Blackpool | 9 | 0 | **80** | **15** |
| 2003–04 | *Northampton T* | 12 | 4 | **12** | **4** |
| 2003–04 | Oxford U | 4 | 0 | **4** | **0** |

**WANLESS, Paul (M)** **362** **49**
H: 6 1 W: 14 08 b.Banbury 14-12-73
*Source:* Trainee.

| | | | | | |
|---|---|---|---|---|---|
| 1991–92 | Oxford U | 6 | 0 | | |
| 1992–93 | Oxford U | 7 | 0 | | |
| 1993–94 | Oxford U | 9 | 0 | | |
| 1994–95 | Oxford U | 10 | 0 | | |
| 1995–96 | Lincoln C | 8 | 0 | **8** | **0** |
| 1995–96 | *Cambridge U* | 14 | 1 | | |
| 1996–97 | Cambridge U | 30 | 3 | | |
| 1997–98 | Cambridge U | 42 | 8 | | |
| 1998–99 | Cambridge U | 45 | 8 | | |
| 1999–2000 | Cambridge U | 42 | 3 | | |
| 2000–01 | Cambridge U | 43 | 10 | | |
| 2001–02 | Cambridge U | 29 | 6 | | |
| 2002–03 | Cambridge U | 39 | 5 | **284** | **44** |
| 2003–04 | Oxford U | 38 | 5 | **70** | **5** |

**WATERMAN, David# (M)** **127** **1**
H: 5 11 W: 11 13 b.Guernsey 16-5-77
*Source:* Trainee. *Honours:* Northern Ireland Under-21.

| | | | | | |
|---|---|---|---|---|---|
| 1995–96 | Portsmouth | 0 | 0 | | |
| 1996–97 | Portsmouth | 4 | 0 | | |
| 1997–98 | Portsmouth | 15 | 0 | | |
| 1998–99 | Portsmouth | 10 | 0 | | |
| 1999–2000 | Portsmouth | 20 | 0 | | |
| 2000–01 | Portsmouth | 22 | 0 | | |
| 2001–02 | Portsmouth | 9 | 0 | **80** | **0** |
| 2001–02 | Oxford U | 5 | 0 | | |
| 2002–03 | Oxford U | 29 | 1 | | |
| 2003–04 | Oxford U | 13 | 0 | **47** | **1** |

**WHITEHEAD, Dean (M)** **122** **9**
H: 5 11 W: 12 07 b.Oxford 12-1-82
*Source:* Trainee.

| | | | | | |
|---|---|---|---|---|---|
| 1999–2000 | Oxford U | 0 | 0 | | |
| 2000–01 | Oxford U | 20 | 0 | | |
| 2001–02 | Oxford U | 40 | 1 | | |
| 2002–03 | Oxford U | 18 | 1 | | |
| 2003–04 | Oxford U | 44 | 7 | **122** | **9** |

**WINTERS, Tom (M)** **1** **0**
H: 5 9 W: 10 10 b.Banbury 11-12-85
*Source:* Scholar.

| | | | | | |
|---|---|---|---|---|---|
| 2003–04 | Oxford U | 1 | 0 | **1** | **0** |

**WOODMAN, Andy* (G)** **402** **0**
H: 6 3 W: 14 00 b.Camberwell 11-8-71
*Source:* Apprentice.

| | | | | | |
|---|---|---|---|---|---|
| 1989–90 | Crystal Palace | 0 | 0 | | |
| 1990–91 | Crystal Palace | 0 | 0 | | |
| 1991–92 | Crystal Palace | 0 | 0 | | |
| 1992–93 | Crystal Palace | 0 | 0 | | |
| 1993–94 | Crystal Palace | 0 | 0 | | |
| 1994–95 | Exeter C | 6 | 0 | **6** | **0** |
| 1994–95 | Northampton T | 10 | 0 | | |
| 1995–96 | Northampton T | 44 | 0 | | |
| 1996–97 | Northampton T | 45 | 0 | | |
| 1997–98 | Northampton T | 46 | 0 | | |
| 1998–99 | Northampton T | 18 | 0 | **163** | **0** |
| 1998–99 | Brentford | 22 | 0 | | |
| 1999–2000 | Brentford | 39 | 0 | | |
| 1999–2000 | *Peterborough U* | 0 | 0 | | |
| 2000–01 | Brentford | 0 | 0 | **61** | **0** |
| 2000–01 | *Southend U* | 17 | 0 | **17** | **0** |
| 2000–01 | Colchester U | 28 | 0 | | |
| 2001–02 | Colchester U | 26 | 0 | **54** | **0** |
| 2001–02 | Oxford U | 15 | 0 | | |
| 2002–03 | Oxford U | 45 | 0 | | |
| 2003–04 | Oxford U | 41 | 0 | **101** | **0** |

**Scholars**
Beechers, Billy J; Brandish, Matthew; Burton, Paul D; Carbon, Josias; Davies, Craig M; Garner, Adam R; Keeble, James T; Mackay, Angus R; O'Sullivan, Taurean J; Tweed,

James A; Tweed, Richard J; Winters, Thomas R

**Non Contract**
Judge, Alan G; Powell, Paul

## PETERBOROUGH U (59)

**ARBER, Mark# (D)** **194 20**
H: 6 1 W: 12 11 b.Johannesburg 8-10-77
*Source:* Trainee.

| | | | | | |
|---|---|---|---|---|---|
| 1995–96 | Tottenham H | 0 | 0 | | |
| 1996–97 | Tottenham H | 0 | 0 | | |
| 1997–98 | Tottenham H | 0 | 0 | | |
| 1998–99 | Tottenham H | 0 | 0 | | |
| 1998–99 | Barnet | 35 | 2 | | |
| 1999–2000 | Barnet | 45 | 6 | | |
| 2000–01 | Barnet | 45 | 7 | | |
| 2001–02 | Barnet | 0 | 0 | **125** | **15** |
| 2002–03 | Peterborough U | 25 | 2 | | |
| 2003–04 | Peterborough U | 44 | 3 | **69** | **5** |

**BURTON, Sagi# (D)** **182 4**
H: 6 2 W: 13 06 b.Birmingham 25-11-77
*Source:* Trainee. *Honours:* St Kitts & Nevis full caps.

| | | | | | |
|---|---|---|---|---|---|
| 1995–96 | Crystal Palace | 0 | 0 | | |
| 1996–97 | Crystal Palace | 0 | 0 | | |
| 1997–98 | Crystal Palace | 2 | 0 | | |
| 1998–99 | Crystal Palace | 23 | 1 | **25** | **1** |
| 1999–2000 | Colchester U | 9 | 0 | **9** | **0** |
| 1999–2000 | Sheffield U | 0 | 0 | | |
| 1999–2000 | Port Vale | 20 | 2 | | |
| 2000–01 | Port Vale | 29 | 0 | | |
| 2001–02 | Port Vale | 37 | 0 | **86** | **2** |
| 2002–03 | Crewe Alex | 1 | 0 | **1** | **0** |
| 2002–03 | Peterborough U | 31 | 0 | | |
| 2003–04 | Peterborough U | 30 | 1 | **61** | **1** |

**CLARKE, Andy (F)** **377 71**
H: 5 10 W: 11 07 b.Islington 22-7-67
*Source:* Barnet.

| | | | | | |
|---|---|---|---|---|---|
| 1990–91 | Wimbledon | 12 | 3 | | |
| 1991–92 | Wimbledon | 34 | 3 | | |
| 1992–93 | Wimbledon | 33 | 5 | | |
| 1993–94 | Wimbledon | 23 | 2 | | |
| 1994–95 | Wimbledon | 25 | 1 | | |
| 1995–96 | Wimbledon | 18 | 2 | | |
| 1996–97 | Wimbledon | 11 | 1 | | |
| 1997–98 | Wimbledon | 14 | 0 | | |
| 1998–99 | Wimbledon | 0 | 0 | **170** | **17** |
| 1998–99 | *Port Vale* | 6 | 0 | **6** | **0** |
| 1998–99 | *Northampton T* | 4 | 0 | **4** | **0** |
| 1998–99 | Peterborough U | 0 | 0 | | |
| 1999–2000 | Peterborough U | 37 | 15 | | |
| 2000–01 | Peterborough U | 42 | 9 | | |
| 2001–02 | Peterborough U | 28 | 5 | | |
| 2002–03 | Peterborough U | 45 | 16 | | |
| 2003–04 | Peterborough U | 45 | 9 | **197** | **54** |

**CLARKE, Lee† (F)** **2 0**
H: 5 11 W: 10 08 b.Peterborough 28-7-83
*Source:* Yaxley. *Honours:* Northern Ireland Under-21.

| | | | | | |
|---|---|---|---|---|---|
| 2001–02 | Peterborough U | 1 | 0 | | |
| 2002–03 | Peterborough U | 1 | 0 | | |
| 2003–04 | Peterborough U | 0 | 0 | **2** | **0** |

**COULSON, Mark (M)** **0 0**
b.Huntingdon 11-2-86
*Source:* Scholar.

| | | | | | |
|---|---|---|---|---|---|
| 2002–03 | Peterborough U | 0 | 0 | | |
| 2003–04 | Peterborough U | 0 | 0 | | |

**DAY, Jamie (M)** **0 0**
H: 5 9 W: 10 06 b.Wycombe 7-5-86
*Source:* Scholar.

| | | | | | |
|---|---|---|---|---|---|
| 2003–04 | Peterborough U | 0 | 0 | | |

**FARRELL, Dave (M)** **348 43**
H: 5 11 W: 11 08 b.Birmingham 11-11-71
*Source:* Redditch U.

| | | | | | |
|---|---|---|---|---|---|
| 1992–93 | Aston Villa | 2 | 0 | | |
| 1992–93 | *Scunthorpe U* | 5 | 1 | **5** | **1** |
| 1993–94 | Aston Villa | 4 | 0 | | |
| 1994–95 | Aston Villa | 0 | 0 | | |
| 1995–96 | Aston Villa | 0 | 0 | **6** | **0** |
| 1995–96 | Wycombe W | 33 | 7 | | |
| 1996–97 | Wycombe W | 27 | 1 | **60** | **8** |
| 1997–98 | Peterborough U | 42 | 6 | | |
| 1998–99 | Peterborough U | 37 | 4 | | |
| 1999–2000 | Peterborough U | 35 | 3 | | |
| 2000–01 | Peterborough U | 44 | 7 | | |
| 2001–02 | Peterborough U | 38 | 6 | | |
| 2002–03 | Peterborough U | 37 | 3 | | |
| 2003–04 | Peterborough U | 44 | 5 | **277** | **34** |

**FOTIADIS, Andrew (F)** **142 20**
H: 6 0 W: 12 13 b.Hitchin 6-9-77
*Source:* School. *Honours:* England Schools.

| | | | | | |
|---|---|---|---|---|---|
| 1996–97 | Luton T | 17 | 3 | | |
| 1997–98 | Luton T | 15 | 1 | | |
| 1998–99 | Luton T | 21 | 2 | | |
| 1999–2000 | Luton T | 23 | 2 | | |
| 2000–01 | Luton T | 22 | 3 | | |
| 2001–02 | Luton T | 8 | 1 | | |
| 2002–03 | Luton T | 17 | 6 | **123** | **18** |
| 2002–03 | Peterborough U | 11 | 2 | | |
| 2003–04 | Peterborough U | 8 | 0 | **19** | **2** |

**FRY, Adam† (M)** **0 0**
H: 5 8 W: 10 07 b.Luton 9-2-85
*Source:* Scholar.

| | | | | | |
|---|---|---|---|---|---|
| 2002–03 | Peterborough U | 0 | 0 | | |
| 2003–04 | Peterborough U | 0 | 0 | | |

**GILL, Matthew (M)** **151 5**
H: 5 11 W: 11 07 b.Cambridge 8-11-80
*Source:* Trainee.

| | | | | | |
|---|---|---|---|---|---|
| 1997–98 | Peterborough U | 2 | 0 | | |
| 1998–99 | Peterborough U | 26 | 0 | | |
| 1999–2000 | Peterborough U | 20 | 1 | | |
| 2000–01 | Peterborough U | 17 | 1 | | |
| 2001–02 | Peterborough U | 12 | 2 | | |
| 2002–03 | Peterborough U | 41 | 1 | | |
| 2003–04 | Peterborough U | 33 | 0 | **151** | **5** |

**JELLEYMAN, Gareth (D)** **87 0**
H: 5 10 W: 10 03 b.Holywell 14-11-80
*Source:* Trainee. *Honours:* Wales Youth, Under-21.

| | | | | | |
|---|---|---|---|---|---|
| 1998–99 | Peterborough U | 0 | 0 | | |
| 1999–2000 | Peterborough U | 20 | 0 | | |
| 2000–01 | Peterborough U | 8 | 0 | | |
| 2001–02 | Peterborough U | 10 | 0 | | |
| 2002–03 | Peterborough U | 32 | 0 | | |
| 2003–04 | Peterborough U | 17 | 0 | **87** | **0** |

**JENKINS, Steve (D)** **455 5**
H: 5 11 W: 12 12 b.Merthyr 16-7-72
*Source:* Trainee. *Honours:* Wales Youth, Under-21, 16 full caps.

| | | | | | |
|---|---|---|---|---|---|
| 1990–91 | Swansea C | 1 | 0 | | |
| 1991–92 | Swansea C | 34 | 0 | | |
| 1992–93 | Swansea C | 33 | 0 | | |
| 1993–94 | Swansea C | 40 | 1 | | |
| 1994–95 | Swansea C | 42 | 0 | | |
| 1995–96 | Swansea C | 15 | 0 | **165** | **1** |
| 1995–96 | Huddersfield T | 31 | 1 | | |
| 1996–97 | Huddersfield T | 33 | 0 | | |
| 1997–98 | Huddersfield T | 29 | 1 | | |
| 1998–99 | Huddersfield T | 36 | 1 | | |
| 1999–2000 | Huddersfield T | 33 | 0 | | |
| 2000–01 | Huddersfield T | 30 | 0 | | |
| 2000–01 | *Birmingham C* | 3 | 0 | **3** | **0** |
| 2001–02 | Huddersfield T | 40 | 1 | | |
| 2002–03 | Huddersfield T | 26 | 0 | **258** | **4** |
| 2002–03 | Cardiff C | 4 | 0 | **4** | **0** |
| 2003–04 | Notts Co | 17 | 0 | **17** | **0** |
| 2003–04 | Peterborough U | 8 | 0 | **8** | **0** |

**KANU, Chris (D)** **21 0**
H: 5 8 W: 11 04 b.Owerri 4-12-79
*Source:* TOP Oss. *Honours:* Nigeria full caps.

| | | | | | |
|---|---|---|---|---|---|
| 2003–04 | Peterborough U | 21 | 0 | **21** | **0** |

**LEGG, Andy# (M)** **537 56**
H: 5 8 W: 10 07 b.Neath 28-7-66
*Source:* Briton Ferry. *Honours:* Wales 6 full caps.

| | | | | | |
|---|---|---|---|---|---|
| 1988–89 | Swansea C | 6 | 0 | | |
| 1989–90 | Swansea C | 26 | 3 | | |
| 1990–91 | Swansea C | 39 | 5 | | |
| 1991–92 | Swansea C | 46 | 9 | | |
| 1992–93 | Swansea C | 46 | 12 | **163** | **29** |
| 1993–94 | Notts Co | 30 | 2 | | |
| 1994–95 | Notts Co | 34 | 3 | | |
| 1995–96 | Notts Co | 25 | 4 | **89** | **9** |
| 1995–96 | Birmingham C | 12 | 1 | | |
| 1996–97 | Birmingham C | 33 | 4 | | |
| 1997–98 | Birmingham C | 0 | 0 | **45** | **5** |
| 1997–98 | *Ipswich T* | 6 | 1 | **6** | **1** |
| 1997–98 | Reading | 10 | 0 | | |
| 1998–99 | Reading | 2 | 0 | **12** | **0** |
| 1998–99 | *Peterborough U* | 5 | 0 | | |
| 1998–99 | Cardiff C | 24 | 2 | | |
| 1999–2000 | Cardiff C | 42 | 2 | | |
| 2000–01 | Cardiff C | 39 | 3 | | |
| 2001–02 | Cardiff C | 35 | 2 | | |
| 2002–03 | Cardiff C | 35 | 3 | **175** | **12** |
| 2003–04 | Peterborough U | 42 | 0 | **47** | **0** |

**LOGAN, Richard (F)** **88 22**
H: 6 0 W: 12 05 b.Bury St Edmunds 4-1-82
*Source:* Trainee. *Honours:* England Youth.

| | | | | | |
|---|---|---|---|---|---|
| 1998–99 | Ipswich T | 2 | 0 | | |
| 1999–2000 | Ipswich T | 1 | 0 | | |
| 2000–01 | Ipswich T | 0 | 0 | | |
| 2000–01 | *Cambridge U* | 5 | 1 | **5** | **1** |
| 2001–02 | Ipswich T | 0 | 0 | | |
| 2001–02 | *Torquay U* | 16 | 4 | **16** | **4** |
| 2002–03 | Ipswich T | 0 | 0 | **3** | **0** |
| 2002–03 | Boston U | 27 | 10 | | |
| 2003–04 | Boston U | 8 | 0 | **35** | **10** |
| 2003–04 | Peterborough U | 29 | 7 | **29** | **7** |

**McSHANE, Luke (G)** **0 0**
H: 6 1 W: 10 09 b.Peterborough 6-11-85
*Source:* Scholar.

| | | | | | |
|---|---|---|---|---|---|
| 2003–04 | Peterborough U | 0 | 0 | | |

**NEWTON, Adam (M)** **108 6**
H: 5 10 W: 11 00 b.Ascot 4-12-80
*Source:* West Ham U Trainee. *Honours:* England Under-21. St Kitts & Nevis full caps.

| | | | | | |
|---|---|---|---|---|---|
| 1999–2000 | West Ham U | 2 | 0 | | |
| 1999–2000 | *Portsmouth* | 3 | 0 | **3** | **0** |
| 2000–01 | West Ham U | 0 | 0 | | |
| 2000–01 | *Notts Co* | 20 | 1 | **20** | **1** |
| 2001–02 | West Ham U | 0 | 0 | **2** | **0** |
| 2001–02 | *Leyton Orient* | 10 | 1 | **10** | **1** |
| 2002–03 | Peterborough U | 36 | 2 | | |
| 2003–04 | Peterborough U | 37 | 2 | **73** | **4** |

**NOLAN, Matt (F)** **1 0**
H: 6 0 W: 12 00 b.Hitchin 25-2-82
*Source:* Hitchin T.

| | | | | | |
|---|---|---|---|---|---|
| 2003–04 | Peterborough U | 1 | 0 | **1** | **0** |

**PEARCE, Dennis‡ (D)** **141 3**
H: 6 0 W: 11 07 b.Wolverhampton 10-9-74
*Source:* Trainee.

| | | | | | |
|---|---|---|---|---|---|
| 1993–94 | Aston Villa | 0 | 0 | | |
| 1994–95 | Aston Villa | 0 | 0 | | |
| 1995–96 | Wolverhampton W | 5 | 0 | | |
| 1996–97 | Wolverhampton W | 4 | 0 | **9** | **0** |
| 1997–98 | Notts Co | 38 | 2 | | |
| 1998–99 | Notts Co | 33 | 1 | | |
| 1999–2000 | Notts Co | 20 | 0 | | |
| 2000–01 | Notts Co | 27 | 0 | **118** | **3** |
| 2000–01 | Peterborough U | 0 | 0 | | |
| 2001–02 | Peterborough U | 9 | 0 | | |
| 2002–03 | Peterborough U | 2 | 0 | | |
| 2003–04 | Peterborough U | 3 | 0 | **14** | **0** |

**PLATT, Clive (F)** **238 39**
H: 6 4 W: 12 07 b.Wolverhampton 27-10-77
*Source:* Trainee.

| | | | | | |
|---|---|---|---|---|---|
| 1995–96 | Walsall | 4 | 2 | | |
| 1996–97 | Walsall | 1 | 0 | | |
| 1997–98 | Walsall | 20 | 1 | | |
| 1998–99 | Walsall | 7 | 1 | | |
| 1999–2000 | Walsall | 0 | 0 | **32** | **4** |
| 1999–2000 | Rochdale | 41 | 9 | | |
| 2000–01 | Rochdale | 43 | 8 | | |
| 2001–02 | Rochdale | 43 | 7 | | |
| 2002–03 | Rochdale | 42 | 6 | **169** | **30** |
| 2003–04 | Notts Co | 19 | 3 | **19** | **3** |
| 2003–04 | Peterborough U | 18 | 2 | **18** | **2** |

**PULLEN, James (G)** **20 0**
H: 6 2 W: 14 00 b.Chelmsford 18-3-82
*Source:* Heybridge S.

| | | | | | |
|---|---|---|---|---|---|
| 1999–2000 | Ipswich T | 0 | 0 | | |
| 2000–01 | Ipswich T | 0 | 0 | | |
| 2001–02 | Ipswich T | 0 | 0 | | |
| 2001–02 | *Blackpool* | 16 | 0 | **16** | **0** |
| 2002–03 | Ipswich T | 1 | 0 | | |
| 2003–04 | Ipswich T | 0 | 0 | **1** | **0** |
| 2003–04 | Peterborough U | 3 | 0 | **3** | **0** |

**REA, Simon (D)** **146 8**
H: 6 1 W: 13 00 b.Coventry 20-9-76
*Source:* Trainee.

| | | | | | |
|---|---|---|---|---|---|
| 1994–95 | Birmingham C | 0 | 0 | | |
| 1995–96 | Birmingham C | 1 | 0 | | |

1996–97 Birmingham C 0 0
1997–98 Birmingham C 0 0
1998–99 Birmingham C 0 0
1999–2000 Birmingham C 0 0 **1 0**
1999–2000 Peterborough U 14 1
2000–01 Peterborough U 36 2
2001–02 Peterborough U 30 1
2002–03 Peterborough U 37 3
2003–04 Peterborough U 28 1 **145 8**

**SCOTT, Richard‡ (M) 214 26**
H: 5 11 W: 12 08 b.Dudley 29-9-74
*Source:* Trainee.
1992–93 Birmingham C 1 0
1993–94 Birmingham C 6 0
1994–95 Birmingham C 5 0 **12 0**
1994–95 Shrewsbury T 8 1
1995–96 Shrewsbury T 36 6
1996–97 Shrewsbury T 27 1
1997–98 Shrewsbury T 34 10 **105 18**
1998–99 Peterborough U 27 4
1999–2000 Peterborough U 34 3
2000–01 Peterborough U 20 0
From Telford U, Stevenage B
2002–03 Peterborough
2003–04 Peterborough U 0 0 **97 8**

**SEMPLE, Ryan (M) 5 0**
H: 5 11 W: 10 11 b.Belfast 4-7-85
*Source:* Scholar.
2002–03 Peterborough U 3 0
2003–04 Peterborough U 2 0 **5 0**

**SHIELDS, Tony‡ (M) 124 3**
H: 5 8 W: 10 01 b.Derry 4-6-80
*Source:* Trainee.
1997–98 Peterborough U 1 0
1998–99 Peterborough U 9 0
1999–2000 Peterborough U 24 1
2000–01 Peterborough U 33 1
2001–02 Peterborough U 15 0
2002–03 Peterborough U 33 1
2003–04 Peterborough U 9 0 **124 3**

**SHOWLER, Paul (M) 186 33**
H: 5 10 W: 11 00 b.Doncaster 10-10-66
*Source:* Sheffield W, Sunderland, Colne Dynamoes, Altrincham.
1991–92 Barnet 39 7
1992–93 Barnet 32 5 **71 12**
1993–94 Bradford C 32 5
1994–95 Bradford C 23 2
1995–96 Bradford C 33 8 **88 15**
1996–97 Luton T 23 6
1997–98 Luton T 1 0
1998–99 Luton T 3 0 **27 6**
1999–2000 Peterborough U 0 0
2000–01 Peterborough U 0 0
2001–02 Peterborough U 0 0
2002–03 Peterborough U 0 0
2003–04 Peterborough U 0 0

**ST LEDGER-HALL, Sean (D) 3 0**
H: 6 0 W: 11 09 b.Solihull 28-12-84
*Source:* Scholar.
2002–03 Peterborough U 1 0
2003–04 Peterborough U 2 0 **3 0**

**THOMAS, Bradley‡ (D) 0 0**
H: 6 2 W: 13 02 b.Forest Green 29-3-84
*Source:* Scholar.
2003–04 Peterborough U 0 0

**THOMSON, Steve (M) 140 2**
H: 5 8 W: 10 04 b.Glasgow 23-1-78
*Source:* Trainee. *Honours:* Scotland Youth.
1995–96 Crystal Palace 0 0
1996–97 Crystal Palace 0 0
1997–98 Crystal Palace 0 0
1998–99 Crystal Palace 16 0
1999–2000 Crystal Palace 21 0
2000–01 Crystal Palace 18 0
2001–02 Crystal Palace 23 0
2002–03 Crystal Palace 27 1 **105 1**
2003–04 Peterborough U 35 1 **35 1**

**TOLLEY, Shane‡ (F) 0 0**
H: 5 7 W: 11 11 b.Barnstaple 18-2-85
*Source:* Scholar. *Honours:* England Youth.
2001–02 Peterborough U 0 0
2002–03 Peterborough U 0 0
2003–04 Peterborough U 0 0

**TYLER, Mark (G) 269 0**
H: 5 11 W: 12 00 b.Norwich 2-4-77
*Source:* Trainee. *Honours:* England Youth.
1994–95 Peterborough U 5 0
1995–96 Peterborough U 0 0
1996–97 Peterborough U 3 0
1997–98 Peterborough U 46 0
1998–99 Peterborough U 27 0
1999–2000 Peterborough U 32 0
2000–01 Peterborough U 40 0
2001–02 Peterborough U 44 0
2002–03 Peterborough U 29 0
2003–04 Peterborough U 43 0 **269 0**

**WILLOCK, Calum (F) 42 8**
H: 6 0 W: 12 09 b.London 29-10-81
*Source:* Scholar. *Honours:* England Schools.
*Honours*: St Kitts & Nevis full caps.
2000–01 Fulham 1 0
2001–02 Fulham 2 0
2002–03 Fulham 2 0
2002–03 *QPR* 3 0 **3 0**
2003–04 Fulham 0 0 **5 0**
2003–04 *Bristol R* 5 0 **5 0**
2003–04 Peterborough U 29 8 **29 8**

**WOODHOUSE, Curtis (M) 190 15**
H: 5 7 W: 12 02 b.Driffield 17-4-80
*Source:* Trainee. *Honours:* England Youth, Under-21.
1997–98 Sheffield U 9 0
1998–99 Sheffield U 33 3
1999–2000 Sheffield U 37 3
2000–01 Sheffield U 25 0 **104 6**
2000–01 Birmingham C 17 2
2001–02 Birmingham C 28 0
2002–03 Birmingham C 3 0
2002–03 *Rotherham U* 11 0 **11 0**
2003–04 Birmingham C 0 0 **48 2**
2003–04 Peterborough U 27 7 **27 7**

**Scholars**
Chapman, Simon M J; Kennedy, Luke D

**Non Contract**
Burnett, Wayne; Chatfield, Jonathan D; Clarke, Lee C; Fry, Adam G; Huke, Shane; Hutton, Rory N; Naisbitt, Daniel J; Thomas, Bradley M; Williams, Thomas A

## PLYMOUTH ARG (60)

**ADAMS, Steve (M) 137 6**
H: 6 0 W: 12 01 b.Plymouth 25-9-80
*Source:* Trainee.
1999–2000 Plymouth Arg 1 0
2000–01 Plymouth Arg 17 0
2001–02 Plymouth Arg 46 2
2002–03 Plymouth Arg 37 2
2003–04 Plymouth Arg 36 2 **137 6**

**ALJOFREE, Hasney (D) 110 5**
H: 6 0 W: 12 03 b.Manchester 11-7-78
*Source:* Trainee.
1996–97 Bolton W 0 0
1997–98 Bolton W 2 0
1998–98 Bolton W 4 0
1999–2000 Bolton W 8 0 **14 0**
2000–01 Dundee U 26 2
2001–02 Dundee U 27 2 **53 4**
2002–03 Plymouth Arg 19 1
2003–04 Plymouth Arg 24 0 **43 1**

**BASTOW, Darren (M) 42 3**
H: 5 11 W: 12 00 b.Torquay 22-12-81
*Source:* Trainee.
1998–99 Plymouth Arg 29 2
1999–2000 Plymouth Arg 13 1
2000–01 Plymouth Arg 0 0
2001–02 Plymouth Arg 0 0
2002–03 Plymouth Arg 0 0
2003–04 Plymouth Arg 0 0 **42 3**

**BENT, Jason* (M) 122 7**
H: 5 9 W: 11 11 b.Toronto 8-3-77
*Honours:* Canada 32 full caps.
1998 Colorado Rapids 14 0
1999 Colorado Rapids 20 0
2000 Colorado Rapids 24 2 **58 2**
2001–02 Plymouth Arg 21 3
2002–03 Plymouth Arg 25 1
2003–04 Plymouth Arg 18 1 **64 5**

**CAPALDI, Tony (M) 34 7**
H: 6 0 W: 12 00 b.Porsgrunn 12-8-81
*Source:* Trainee. *Honours:* Northern Ireland Under-21, 5 full caps.
1999–2000 Birmingham C 0 0
2000–01 Birmingham C 0 0
2001–02 Birmingham C 0 0
2002–03 Birmingham C 0 0
2002–03 Plymouth Arg 1 0
2003–04 Plymouth Arg 33 7 **34 7**

**CONNOLLY, Paul (D) 32 0**
H: 6 0 W: 11 01 b.Liverpool 29-9-83
*Source:* Scholar.
2000–01 Plymouth Arg 1 0
2001–02 Plymouth Arg 0 0
2002–03 Plymouth Arg 2 0
2003–04 Plymouth Arg 29 0 **32 0**

**COUGHLAN, Graham (D) 193 25**
H: 6 2 W: 13 04 b.Dublin 18-11-74
*Source:* Bray Wanderers.
1995–96 Blackburn R 0 0
1996–97 Blackburn R 0 0
1996–97 *Swindon T* 3 0 **3 0**
1997–98 Blackburn R 0 0
1998–99 Livingston 6 0
1999–2000 Livingston 29 0
2000–01 Livingston 21 2 **56 2**
2001–02 Plymouth Arg 46 11
2002–03 Plymouth Arg 42 5
2003–04 Plymouth Arg 46 7 **134 23**

**EVANS, Micky (F) 403 78**
H: 6 0 W: 13 04 b.Plymouth 1-1-73
*Source:* Trainee. *Honours:* Eire 1 full cap.
1990–91 Plymouth Arg 4 0
1991–92 Plymouth Arg 13 0
1992–93 Plymouth Arg 23 1
1992–93 *Blackburn R* 0 0
1993–94 Plymouth Arg 22 9
1994–95 Plymouth Arg 23 4
1995–96 Plymouth Arg 45 12
1996–97 Plymouth Arg 33 12
1996–97 Southampton 12 4
1997–98 Southampton 10 0 **22 4**
1997–98 WBA 10 1
1998–99 WBA 20 2
1999–2000 WBA 33 3
2000–01 WBA 0 0 **63 6**
2000–01 Bristol R 21 4 **21 4**
2000–01 Plymouth Arg 10 4
2001–02 Plymouth Arg 38 7
2002–03 Plymouth Arg 42 4
2003–04 Plymouth Arg 44 11 **297 64**

**FRIIO, David (M) 139 33**
H: 6 0 W: 11 05 b.Thionville 17-2-73
*Source:* Epinal, Nimes, ASOA Valence.
2000–01 Plymouth Arg 26 5
2001–02 Plymouth Arg 41 8
2002–03 Plymouth Arg 36 6
2003–04 Plymouth Arg 36 14 **139 33**

**GILBERT, Peter (D) 40 1**
H: 5 11 W: 12 13 b.Newcastle 31-7-83
*Source:* Scholar.
2001–02 Birmingham C 0 0
2002–03 Birmingham C 0 0
2003–04 Birmingham C 0 0
2003–04 Plymouth Arg 40 1 **40 1**

**HODGES, Lee# (M) 320 49**
H: 6 0 W: 12 01 b.Epping 4-9-73
*Source:* Trainee.
1991–92 Tottenham H 0 0
1992–93 Tottenham H 4 0
1992–93 *Plymouth Arg* 7 2
1993–94 Tottenham H 0 0 **4 0**
1993–94 *Wycombe W* 4 0 **4 0**
1994–95 Barnet 34 4
1995–96 Barnet 40 17
1996–97 Barnet 31 5 **105 26**
1997–98 Reading 24 6
1998–99 Reading 1 0
1999–2000 Reading 25 2
2000–01 Reading 29 2
2001–02 Reading 0 0 **79 10**
2001–02 Plymouth Arg 45 6
2002–03 Plymouth Arg 39 2
2003–04 Plymouth Arg 37 3 **128 13**

**KEITH, Marino# (F) 187 63**
H: 5 10 W: 12 13 b.Fraserburgh 16-12-74
*Source:* Fraserburgh.

| | | | | | |
|---|---|---|---|---|---|
| 1995–96 | Dundee U | 4 | 0 | | |
| 1996–97 | Dundee U | 0 | 0 | **4** | **0** |
| 1997–98 | Falkirk | 32 | 10 | | |
| 1998–99 | Falkirk | 29 | 17 | **61** | **27** |
| 1999–2000 | Livingston | 9 | 4 | | |
| 2000–01 | Livingston | 13 | 3 | **22** | **7** |
| 2001–02 | Plymouth Arg | 23 | 9 | | |
| 2002–03 | Plymouth Arg | 37 | 11 | | |
| 2003–04 | Plymouth Arg | 40 | 9 | **100** | **29** |

**LARRIEU, Romain (G) 109 0**
H: 6 2 W: 13 00 b.Mont-de-Marsan 31-8-76
*Source:* Montpellier, ASOA Valence.

| | | | | | |
|---|---|---|---|---|---|
| 2000–01 | Plymouth Arg | 15 | 0 | | |
| 2001–02 | Plymouth Arg | 45 | 0 | | |
| 2002–03 | Plymouth Arg | 43 | 0 | | |
| 2003–04 | Plymouth Arg | 6 | 0 | **109** | **0** |

**LOWNDES, Nathan (F) 143 27**
H: 5 10 W: 12 06 b.Salford 2-6-77
*Source:* Trainee.

| | | | | | |
|---|---|---|---|---|---|
| 1994–95 | Leeds U | 0 | 0 | | |
| 1995–96 | Leeds U | 0 | 0 | | |
| 1995–96 | Watford | 0 | 0 | | |
| 1996–97 | Watford | 3 | 0 | | |
| 1997–98 | Watford | 4 | 0 | **7** | **0** |
| 1998–99 | St Johnstone | 29 | 2 | | |
| 1999–2000 | St Johnstone | 25 | 10 | | |
| 2000–01 | St Johnstone | 10 | 2 | **64** | **14** |
| 2001–02 | Livingston | 21 | 3 | **21** | **3** |
| 2001–02 | *Rotherham U* | 2 | 0 | **2** | **0** |
| 2002–03 | Plymouth Arg | 16 | 2 | | |
| 2003–04 | Plymouth Arg | 33 | 8 | **49** | **10** |

**McCORMICK, Luke (G) 44 0**
H: 6 0 W: 13 12 b.Coventry 15-8-83
*Source:* Scholar.

| | | | | | |
|---|---|---|---|---|---|
| 2000–01 | Plymouth Arg | 1 | 0 | | |
| 2001–02 | Plymouth Arg | 0 | 0 | | |
| 2002–03 | Plymouth Arg | 3 | 0 | | |
| 2003–04 | Plymouth Arg | 40 | 0 | **44** | **0** |

**NORRIS, David (M) 84 12**
H: 5 7 W: 11 06 b.Peterborough 22-2-81
*Source:* Boston U.

| | | | | | |
|---|---|---|---|---|---|
| 1999–2000 | Bolton W | 0 | 0 | | |
| 2000–01 | Bolton W | 0 | 0 | | |
| 2001–02 | Bolton W | 0 | 0 | | |
| 2001–02 | *Hull C* | 6 | 1 | **6** | **1** |
| 2002–03 | Bolton W | 0 | 0 | | |
| 2002–03 | Plymouth Arg | 33 | 6 | | |
| 2003–04 | Plymouth Arg | 45 | 5 | **78** | **11** |

**PHILLIPS, Martin* (M) 218 16**
H: 5 11 W: 12 08 b.Exeter 13-3-76
*Source:* Trainee.

| | | | | | |
|---|---|---|---|---|---|
| 1992–93 | Exeter C | 6 | 0 | | |
| 1993–94 | Exeter C | 9 | 0 | | |
| 1994–95 | Exeter C | 24 | 2 | | |
| 1995–96 | Exeter C | 13 | 3 | | |
| 1995–96 | Manchester C | 11 | 0 | | |
| 1996–97 | Manchester C | 4 | 0 | | |
| 1997–98 | Manchester C | 0 | 0 | | |
| 1997–98 | *Scunthorpe U* | 3 | 0 | **3** | **0** |
| 1997–98 | *Exeter C* | 8 | 0 | **60** | **5** |
| 1998–99 | Manchester C | 0 | 0 | **15** | **0** |
| 1998–99 | Portsmouth | 17 | 1 | | |
| 1998–99 | *Bristol R* | 2 | 0 | **2** | **0** |
| 1999–2000 | Portsmouth | 7 | 0 | **24** | **1** |
| 2000–01 | Plymouth Arg | 42 | 1 | | |
| 2001–02 | Plymouth Arg | 39 | 6 | | |
| 2002–03 | Plymouth Arg | 24 | 2 | | |
| 2003–04 | Plymouth Arg | 9 | 1 | **114** | **10** |

**STONEBRIDGE, Ian (F) 171 38**
H: 6 0 W: 11 04 b.Lewisham 30-8-81
*Source:* Tottenham H Trainee. *Honours:* England Youth.

| | | | | | |
|---|---|---|---|---|---|
| 1999–2000 | Plymouth Arg | 31 | 9 | | |
| 2000–01 | Plymouth Arg | 31 | 11 | | |
| 2001–02 | Plymouth Arg | 42 | 8 | | |
| 2002–03 | Plymouth Arg | 37 | 5 | | |
| 2003–04 | Plymouth Arg | 30 | 5 | **171** | **38** |

**STURROCK, Blair (F) 90 8**
H: 6 0 W: 11 01 b.Dundee 25-8-81
*Source:* Dundee U.

| | | | | | |
|---|---|---|---|---|---|
| 2000–01 | Brechin C | 27 | 6 | **27** | **6** |
| 2001–02 | Plymouth Arg | 19 | 1 | | |
| 2002–03 | Plymouth Arg | 20 | 1 | | |
| 2003–04 | Plymouth Arg | 24 | 0 | **63** | **2** |

**VILLIS, Matt (D) 0 0**
b.Bridgwater 13-4-84

| | | | | | |
|---|---|---|---|---|---|
| 2002–03 | Plymouth Arg | 0 | 0 | | |
| 2003–04 | Plymouth Arg | 0 | 0 | | |

**WATKINS, Andrew‡ (F) 0 0**
b.Plymouth 3-4-85
*Source:* St Blazey.

| | | | | | |
|---|---|---|---|---|---|
| 2003–04 | Plymouth Arg | 0 | 0 | | |

**WORRELL, David (D) 134 0**
H: 5 11 W: 11 08 b.Dublin 12-1-78
*Source:* Trainee. *Honours:* Eire Youth, Under-21.

| | | | | | |
|---|---|---|---|---|---|
| 1994–95 | Blackburn R | 0 | 0 | | |
| 1995–96 | Blackburn R | 0 | 0 | | |
| 1996–97 | Blackburn R | 0 | 0 | | |
| 1997–98 | Blackburn R | 0 | 0 | | |
| 1998–99 | Blackburn R | 0 | 0 | | |
| 1998–99 | Dundee U | 4 | 0 | | |
| 1999–2000 | Dundee U | 13 | 0 | **17** | **0** |
| 2000–01 | Plymouth Arg | 14 | 0 | | |
| 2001–02 | Plymouth Arg | 42 | 0 | | |
| 2002–03 | Plymouth Arg | 43 | 0 | | |
| 2003–04 | Plymouth Arg | 18 | 0 | **117** | **0** |

**WOTTON, Paul (D) 279 29**
H: 5 11 W: 11 01 b.Plymouth 17-8-77
*Source:* Trainee.

| | | | | | |
|---|---|---|---|---|---|
| 1994–95 | Plymouth Arg | 7 | 0 | | |
| 1995–96 | Plymouth Arg | 1 | 0 | | |
| 1996–97 | Plymouth Arg | 9 | 1 | | |
| 1997–98 | Plymouth Arg | 34 | 1 | | |
| 1998–99 | Plymouth Arg | 36 | 1 | | |
| 1999–2000 | Plymouth Arg | 23 | 0 | | |
| 2000–01 | Plymouth Arg | 42 | 4 | | |
| 2001–02 | Plymouth Arg | 46 | 5 | | |
| 2002–03 | Plymouth Arg | 43 | 8 | | |
| 2003–04 | Plymouth Arg | 38 | 9 | **279** | **29** |

**YETTON, Stuart§ (M) 2 0**
H: 5 8 W: 10 03 b.Plymouth 27-7-85
*Source:* Scholar.

| | | | | | |
|---|---|---|---|---|---|
| 2002–03 | Plymouth Arg | 1 | 0 | | |
| 2003–04 | Plymouth Arg | 1 | 0 | **2** | **0** |

**Scholars**
Bulley, Daniel S A; Coxon, Lee D; Dickson, Ryan A; Entwisle, Thomas; Evans, Dean M; Fice, Ryan P; Guppy, Robert A; Hoyles, Jon G; Kerr, Scott S; Martin, Marcus A P; Nute, Brinton J; O'Sullivan, Wayne P; Parish, Darren L; Routledge, John J; Sawyer, Gary D; Schofield, Kenny S; Yetton, Stewart D

**Non Contract**
Chapman, Jason

**Players who do not hold a current contract but their registration has been retained by the club**
Bastow, Darren J

## PORT VALE (61)

**ARMSTRONG, Ian (M) 80 11**
H: 5 8 W: 10 04 b.Liverpool 16-11-81
*Source:* Trainee. *Honours:* England Schools, Youth.

| | | | | | |
|---|---|---|---|---|---|
| 1998–99 | Liverpool | 0 | 0 | | |
| 1999–2000 | Liverpool | 0 | 0 | | |
| 2000–01 | Liverpool | 0 | 0 | | |
| 2001–02 | Port Vale | 31 | 3 | | |
| 2002–03 | Port Vale | 29 | 7 | | |
| 2003–04 | Port Vale | 20 | 1 | **80** | **11** |

**BIRCHALL, Chris (F) 13 0**
H: 5 9 W: 13 02 b.Stafford 5-5-84
*Source:* Scholar.

| | | | | | |
|---|---|---|---|---|---|
| 2001–02 | Port Vale | 1 | 0 | | |
| 2002–03 | Port Vale | 2 | 0 | | |
| 2003–04 | Port Vale | 10 | 0 | **13** | **0** |

**BRAIN, Jonny (G) 32 0**
H: 6 3 W: 13 06 b.Carlisle 11-2-83

| | | | | | |
|---|---|---|---|---|---|
| 2003–04 | Port Vale | 32 | 0 | **32** | **0** |

**BRIDGE-WILKINSON, Marc# (M) 132 31**
H: 5 8 W: 11 09 b.Coventry 16-3-79
*Source:* Trainee.

| | | | | | |
|---|---|---|---|---|---|
| 1996–97 | Derby Co | 0 | 0 | | |
| 1997–98 | Derby Co | 0 | 0 | | |
| 1998–99 | Derby Co | 1 | 0 | | |
| 1998–99 | *Carlisle U* | 7 | 0 | **7** | **0** |
| 1999–2000 | Derby Co | 0 | 0 | **1** | **0** |
| 2000–01 | Port Vale | 42 | 9 | | |
| 2001–02 | Port Vale | 19 | 6 | | |
| 2002–03 | Port Vale | 31 | 9 | | |
| 2003–04 | Port Vale | 32 | 7 | **124** | **31** |

**BRIGHTWELL, Ian† (D) 443 18**
H: 5 10 W: 12 10 b.Lutterworth 9-4-68
*Source:* Congleton T. *Honours:* England Schools, Youth, Under-21.

| | | | | | |
|---|---|---|---|---|---|
| 1986–87 | Manchester C | 16 | 1 | | |
| 1987–88 | Manchester C | 33 | 5 | | |
| 1988–89 | Manchester C | 26 | 6 | | |
| 1989–90 | Manchester C | 28 | 2 | | |
| 1990–91 | Manchester C | 33 | 0 | | |
| 1991–92 | Manchester C | 40 | 1 | | |
| 1992–93 | Manchester C | 21 | 1 | | |
| 1993–94 | Manchester C | 7 | 0 | | |
| 1994–95 | Manchester C | 30 | 0 | | |
| 1995–96 | Manchester C | 29 | 0 | | |
| 1996–97 | Manchester C | 37 | 2 | | |
| 1997–98 | Manchester C | 21 | 0 | **321** | **18** |
| 1998–99 | Coventry C | 0 | 0 | | |
| 1999–2000 | Coventry C | 0 | 0 | | |
| 1999–2000 | Walsall | 10 | 0 | | |
| 2000–01 | Walsall | 44 | 0 | | |
| 2001–02 | Walsall | 27 | 0 | **81** | **0** |
| 2001–02 | Stoke C | 4 | 0 | **4** | **0** |
| 2002–03 | Port Vale | 35 | 0 | | |
| 2003–04 | Port Vale | 2 | 0 | **37** | **0** |

**BRISCO, Neil# (M) 118 2**
H: 6 0 W: 13 10 b.Billinge 26-1-78
*Source:* Trainee.

| | | | | | |
|---|---|---|---|---|---|
| 1996–97 | Manchester C | 0 | 0 | | |
| 1997–98 | Manchester C | 0 | 0 | | |
| 1998–99 | Port Vale | 1 | 0 | | |
| 1999–2000 | Port Vale | 12 | 0 | | |
| 2000–01 | Port Vale | 17 | 1 | | |
| 2001–02 | Port Vale | 37 | 0 | | |
| 2002–03 | Port Vale | 24 | 1 | | |
| 2003–04 | Port Vale | 27 | 0 | **118** | **2** |

**BROOKER, Stephen (F) 123 31**
H: 5 11 W: 13 10 b.Newport Pagnell 21-5-81
*Source:* Trainee.

| | | | | | |
|---|---|---|---|---|---|
| 1999–2000 | Watford | 1 | 0 | | |
| 2000–01 | Watford | 0 | 0 | **1** | **0** |
| 2000–01 | Port Vale | 23 | 9 | | |
| 2001–02 | Port Vale | 41 | 9 | | |
| 2002–03 | Port Vale | 26 | 5 | | |
| 2003–04 | Port Vale | 32 | 8 | **122** | **31** |

**BROWN, Ryan (D) 18 0**
H: 5 9 W: 11 04 b.Stoke 15-3-85
*Source:* Scholar.

| | | | | | |
|---|---|---|---|---|---|
| 2002–03 | Port Vale | 1 | 0 | | |
| 2003–04 | Port Vale | 17 | 0 | **18** | **0** |

**BURNS, Liam* (D) 118 0**
H: 6 2 W: 13 10 b.Belfast 30-10-78
*Source:* Trainee. *Honours:* Northern Ireland Youth, Under-21.

| | | | | | |
|---|---|---|---|---|---|
| 1997–98 | Port Vale | 1 | 0 | | |
| 1998–99 | Port Vale | 4 | 0 | | |
| 1999–2000 | Port Vale | 24 | 0 | | |
| 2000–01 | Port Vale | 13 | 0 | | |
| 2001–02 | Port Vale | 33 | 0 | | |
| 2002–03 | Port Vale | 16 | 0 | | |
| 2003–04 | Port Vale | 27 | 0 | **118** | **0** |

**COLLINS, Sam (D) 206 11**
H: 6 3 W: 13 12 b.Pontefract 5-6-77
*Source:* Trainee.

| | | | | | |
|---|---|---|---|---|---|
| 1994–95 | Huddersfield T | 0 | 0 | | |
| 1995–96 | Huddersfield T | 0 | 0 | | |
| 1996–97 | Huddersfield T | 4 | 0 | | |
| 1997–98 | Huddersfield T | 10 | 0 | | |
| 1998–99 | Huddersfield T | 23 | 0 | **37** | **0** |
| 1999–2000 | Bury | 19 | 0 | | |
| 2000–01 | Bury | 34 | 2 | | |
| 2001–02 | Bury | 29 | 0 | **82** | **2** |
| 2002–03 | Port Vale | 44 | 5 | | |
| 2003–04 | Port Vale | 43 | 4 | **87** | **9** |

**CUMMINS, Michael# (M)** **177 19**
H: 5 11 W: 13 02 b.Dublin 1-6-78
*Source:* Trainee. *Honours:* Eire Youth, Under-21.
1995–96 Middlesbrough 0 0
1996–97 Middlesbrough 0 0
1997–98 Middlesbrough 0 0
1998–99 Middlesbrough 1 0
1999–2000 Middlesbrough 1 0 **2 0**
1999–2000 Port Vale 12 1
2000–01 Port Vale 45 2
2001–02 Port Vale 46 8
2002–03 Port Vale 30 4
2003–04 Port Vale 42 4 **175 19**

**DELANY, Dean* (G)** **36 0**
H: 6 2 W: 13 06 b.Dublin 15-9-80
*Honours:* Eire Under-21.
1997–98 Everton 0 0
1998–99 Everton 0 0
1999–2000 Everton 0 0
2000–01 Port Vale 8 0
2001–02 Port Vale 4 0
2002–03 Port Vale 10 0
2003–04 *Macclesfield T* 0 0
2003–04 Port Vale 14 0 **36 0**

**ELDERSHAW, Simon (F)** **2 0**
H: 5 11 W: 11 02 b.Stoke 2-12-83
*Source:* Scholar.
2002–03 Port Vale 2 0
2003–04 Port Vale 0 0 **2 0**

**GOODLAD, Mark (G)** **124 0**
H: 6 2 W: 13 12 b.Barnsley 9-9-79
*Source:* Trainee.
1996–97 Nottingham F 0 0
1997–98 Nottingham F 0 0
1998–99 Nottingham F 0 0
1998–99 *Scarborough* 3 0 **3 0**
1999–2000 Nottingham F 0 0
1999–2000 Port Vale 1 0
2000–01 Port Vale 40 0
2001–02 Port Vale 43 0
2002–03 Port Vale 37 0
2003–04 Port Vale 0 0 **121 0**

**JAMES, Craig (D)** **19 1**
H: 6 2 W: 12 10 b.Middlesbrough 15-11-82
*Source:* Scholar.
2000–01 Sunderland 0 0
2001–02 Sunderland 0 0
2002–03 Sunderland 0 0
2003–04 Sunderland 1 0 **1 0**
2003–04 *Darlington* 10 1 **10 1**
2003–04 Port Vale 8 0 **8 0**

**LIPA, Andreas (M)** **30 2**
H: 6 2 W: 12 04 b.Vienna 26-4-71
*Source:* Xanthi. *Honours:* Austria 1 full cap.
2003–04 Port Vale 30 2 **30 2**

**LITTLEJOHN, Adrian* (M)** **395 71**
H: 5 10 W: 11 05 b.Wolverhampton 26-9-71
*Source:* WBA Trainee.
1989–90 Walsall 11 0
1990–91 Walsall 33 1 **44 1**
1991–92 Sheffield U 7 0
1992–93 Sheffield U 27 8
1993–94 Sheffield U 19 3
1994–95 Sheffield U 16 1
1995–96 Plymouth Arg 42 17
1996–97 Plymouth Arg 37 6
1997–98 Plymouth Arg 31 6 **110 29**
1997–98 Oldham Ath 5 3
1998–99 Oldham Ath 16 2 **21 5**
1998–99 Bury 20 1
1999–2000 Bury 42 9
2000–01 Bury 37 4 **99 14**
2001–02 Sheffield U 3 0
2002–03 Sheffield U 0 0 **72 12**
2002–03 Port Vale 13 3
2003–04 Port Vale 36 7 **49 10**

**McPHEE, Stephen (F)** **130 39**
H: 5 8 W: 12 02 b.Glasgow 5-6-81
*Honours:* Scotland Under-21.
1998–99 Coventry C 0 0
1999–2000 Coventry C 0 0
2000–01 Coventry C 0 0
2001–02 Port Vale 44 11
2002–03 Port Vale 40 3
2003–04 Port Vale 46 25 **130 39**

**PAYNTER, Billy (F)** **83 18**
H: 6 0 W: 13 02 b.Liverpool 13-7-84
*Source:* Schoolboy.
2000–01 Port Vale 1 0
2001–02 Port Vale 7 0
2002–03 Port Vale 31 5
2003–04 Port Vale 44 13 **83 18**

**PILKINGTON, George (D)** **51 1**
H: 5 11 W: 12 07 b.Rugeley 7-11-81
*Source:* Trainee. *Honours:* England Youth.
1998–99 Everton 0 0
1999–2000 Everton 0 0
2000–01 Everton 0 0
2001–02 Everton 0 0
2002–03 Everton 0 0
2002–03 *Exeter C* 7 0 **7 0**
2003–04 Port Vale 44 1 **44 1**

**REID, Levi (M)** **12 0**
H: 5 6 W: 11 12 b.Stafford 19-12-83
*Source:* Scholar.
2002–03 Port Vale 1 0
2003–04 Port Vale 11 0 **12 0**

**ROWLAND, Stephen (D)** **79 1**
H: 5 10 W: 12 00 b.Wrexham 2-11-81
*Source:* Scholar.
2001–02 Port Vale 25 1
2002–03 Port Vale 25 0
2003–04 Port Vale 29 0 **79 1**

**WALSH, Michael* (D)** **231 5**
H: 6 0 W: 13 07 b.Rotherham 5-8-77
*Source:* Trainee.
1994–95 Scunthorpe U 3 0
1995–96 Scunthorpe U 25 0
1996–97 Scunthorpe U 36 0
1997–98 Scunthorpe U 39 1 **103 1**
1998–99 Port Vale 19 1
1999–2000 Port Vale 12 1
2000–01 Port Vale 39 1
2001–02 Port Vale 28 0
2002–03 Port Vale 17 1
2003–04 Port Vale 13 0 **128 4**

**Scholars**
Anyon, Joseph; Booth, Edward A R; Brownfield, Dominic B; Cardle, Joseph; Doxey, Shaun G; Gowland, Matthew J; Hall, Mark R; Hibbert, David J; Holmes, Daniel C; Molloy, Joseph M; Orpe, Mark; Reid, Ishmale M; Robert, Owen T; Robinson, Simon
Winters, James M

**Non Contract**
Brightwell Ian R

## PORTSMOUTH (62)

**BARRETT, Neil (M)** **26 2**
H: 5 10 W: 11 00 b.Tooting 24-12-81
*Source:* Chelsea. *Honours:* England Schools.
2001–02 Portsmouth 26 2
2002–03 Portsmouth 0 0
2003–04 Portsmouth 0 0 **26 2**

**BERGER, Patrik (M)** **282 61**
H: 6 1 W: 13 00 b.Prague 10-11-73
*Honours:* Czechoslovakia 2 full caps.Czech Republic 44 full caps, 18 goals.
1991–92 Slavia Prague 20 3
1992–93 Slavia Prague 29 10
1993–94 Slavia Prague 12 4
1994–95 Slavia Prague 28 7 **89 24**
1995–96 Borussia Dortmund 25 4 **25 4**
1996–97 Liverpool 23 6
1997–98 Liverpool 22 3
1998–99 Liverpool 32 7
1999–2000 Liverpool 34 9
2000–01 Liverpool 14 2
2001–02 Liverpool 21 1
2002–03 Liverpool 2 0 **148 28**
2003–04 Portsmouth 20 5 **20 5**

**BERKOVIC, Eyal (M)** **331 59**
H: 5 9 W: 10 13 b.Haifa 2-4-72
*Honours:* Israel 77 full caps, 9 goals.
1992–93 Maccabi Haifa 32 7
1993–94 Maccabi Haifa 38 10
1994–95 Maccabi Haifa 29 5
1995–96 Maccabi Haifa 29 3 **128 25**
1996–97 Southampton 28 4 **28 4**
1997–98 West Ham U 35 7
1998–99 West Ham U 30 3 **65 10**
1999–2000 Celtic 28 9
2000–01 Celtic 4 1 **32 10**
2000–01 Blackburn R 11 2 **11 2**
2001–02 Manchester C 25 6
2002–03 Manchester C 27 1
2003–04 Manchester C 4 0 **56 7**
2003–04 Portsmouth 11 1 **11 1**

**BRADSHAW, Craig* (G)** **0 0**
b.Chertsey 31-7-84
*Source:* Scholar.
2001–02 Portsmouth 0 0
2002–03 Portsmouth 0 0
2003–04 Portsmouth 0 0

**BURCHILL, Mark (F)** **76 23**
H: 5 8 W: 11 09 b.Broxburn 18-8-80
*Source:* Celtic BC. *Honours:* Scotland Schools, Under-21, 6 full caps.
1997–98 Celtic 0 0
1998–99 Celtic 21 9
1999–2000 Celtic 0 0
2000–01 Celtic 2 1 **23 10**
2000–01 *Birmingham C* 13 4 **13 4**
2000–01 *Ipswich T* 7 1
2001–02 Ipswich T 0 0 **7 1**
2001–02 Portsmouth 6 4
2002–03 Portsmouth 18 4
2003–04 Portsmouth 0 0 **24 8**
2003–04 *Wigan Ath* 4 0 **4 0**
2003–04 *Sheffield W* 5 0 **5 0**

**BURTON, Deon* (F)** **230 44**
H: 5 9 W: 11 09 b.Reading 25-10-77
*Source:* Trainee. *Honours:* Jamaica 48 full caps, 8 goals.
1993–94 Portsmouth 2 0
1994–95 Portsmouth 7 2
1995–96 Portsmouth 32 7
1996–97 Portsmouth 21 1
1996–97 *Cardiff C* 5 2 **5 2**
1997–98 Derby Co 29 3
1998–99 Derby Co 21 9
1998–99 *Barnsley* 3 0 **3 0**
1999–2000 Derby Co 19 4
2000–01 Derby Co 32 5
2001–02 Derby Co 17 1
2001–02 *Stoke C* 12 2 **12 2**
2002–03 Derby Co 7 3 **125 25**
2002–03 Portsmouth 15 4
2003–04 Portsmouth 1 0 **78 14**
2003–04 *Walsall* 3 0 **3 0**
2003–04 *Swindon T* 4 1 **4 1**

**BUXTON, Lewis (D)** **77 0**
H: 6 1 W: 13 10 b.Newport (IW) 10-12-83
*Source:* School.
2000–01 Portsmouth 0 0
2001–02 Portsmouth 29 0
2002–03 Portsmouth 1 0
2002–03 *Exeter C* 4 0 **4 0**
2002–03 *Bournemouth* 17 0
2003–04 Portsmouth 0 0 **30 0**
2003–04 *Bournemouth* 26 0 **43 0**

**CASEY, Mark‡ (M)** **0 0**
b.Glasgow 9-10-82
2001–02 Portsmouth 0 0
2002–03 Portsmouth 0 0
2003–04 Portsmouth 0 0

**CLARK, Christopher (M)** **0 0**
b.Shoreham 9-6-84
*Source:* Scholar.
2002–03 Portsmouth 0 0
2003–04 Portsmouth 0 0

**COOPER, Shaun (D)** **16 0**
H: 5 10 W: 10 07 b.Isle of Wight 5-10-83
*Source:* School.
2000–01 Portsmouth 0 0
2001–02 Portsmouth 7 0
2002–03 Portsmouth 0 0
2003–04 Portsmouth 0 0 **7 0**
2003–04 *Leyton Orient* 9 0 **9 0**

**CURTIS, John (D) 135 2**
H: 5 10 W: 11 07 b.Nuneaton 3-9-78
*Source:* Trainee. *Honours:* England Schools, Youth, Under-21, B.

| | | | | | |
|---|---|---|---|---|---|
| 1995–96 | Manchester U | 0 | 0 | | |
| 1996–97 | Manchester U | 0 | 0 | | |
| 1997–98 | Manchester U | 8 | 0 | | |
| 1998–99 | Manchester U | 4 | 0 | | |
| 1999–2000 | Manchester U | 1 | 0 | **13** | **0** |
| 1999–2000 | *Barnsley* | 28 | 2 | **28** | **2** |
| 2000–01 | Blackburn R | 46 | 0 | | |
| 2001–02 | Blackburn R | 10 | 0 | | |
| 2002–03 | Blackburn R | 5 | 0 | **61** | **0** |
| 2002–03 | *Sheffield U* | 12 | 0 | **12** | **0** |
| 2003–04 | Leicester C | 15 | 0 | **15** | **0** |
| 2003–04 | Portsmouth | 6 | 0 | **6** | **0** |

**DE ZEEUW, Arjan (D) 440 20**
H: 6 0 W: 13 06 b.Castricum 16-4-70
*Source:* Vitesse 22.

| | | | | | |
|---|---|---|---|---|---|
| 1992–93 | Telstar | 30 | 1 | | |
| 1993–94 | Telstar | 31 | 2 | | |
| 1994–95 | Telstar | 29 | 1 | | |
| 1995–96 | Telstar | 12 | 1 | **102** | **5** |
| 1995–96 | Barnsley | 31 | 1 | | |
| 1996–97 | Barnsley | 43 | 2 | | |
| 1997–98 | Barnsley | 26 | 0 | | |
| 1998–99 | Barnsley | 38 | 4 | **138** | **7** |
| 1999–2000 | Wigan Ath | 39 | 3 | | |
| 2000–01 | Wigan Ath | 45 | 1 | | |
| 2001–02 | Wigan Ath | 42 | 2 | **126** | **6** |
| 2002–03 | Portsmouth | 38 | 1 | | |
| 2003–04 | Portsmouth | 36 | 1 | **74** | **2** |

**DUFFY, Richard (D) 19 1**
H: 5 10 W: 9 05 b.Swansea 30-8-85
*Source:* Scholar.

| | | | | | |
|---|---|---|---|---|---|
| 2002–03 | Swansea C | 0 | 0 | | |
| 2003–04 | Swansea C | 18 | 1 | **18** | **1** |
| 2003–04 | Portsmouth | 1 | 0 | **1** | **0** |

**FAYE, Amdy (M) 107 2**
H: 6 1 W: 12 04 b.Dakar 12-3-77
*Source:* Frejus.

| | | | | | |
|---|---|---|---|---|---|
| 1998–99 | Auxerre | 0 | 0 | | |
| 1999–2000 | Auxerre | 3 | 0 | | |
| 2000–01 | Auxerre | 23 | 0 | | |
| 2001–02 | Auxerre | 20 | 0 | | |
| 2002–03 | Auxerre | 34 | 2 | **80** | **2** |
| 2003–04 | Portsmouth | 27 | 0 | **27** | **0** |

**FOXE, Hayden (D) 95 7**
H: 6 3 W: 13 05 b.Sydney 23-6-77
*Honours:* Australia Youth, Under-20, Under-23, 11 full caps, 2 goals.

| | | | | | |
|---|---|---|---|---|---|
| 1997–98 | Arminia Bielefeld | 1 | 0 | **1** | **0** |
| 1998 | Sanfrecce | 15 | 3 | | |
| 1999 | Sanfrecce | 22 | 2 | **37** | **5** |
| 2000–01 | Mechelen | 4 | 0 | **4** | **0** |
| 2000–01 | West Ham U | 5 | 0 | | |
| 2001–02 | West Ham U | 6 | 0 | **11** | **0** |
| 2002–03 | Portsmouth | 32 | 1 | | |
| 2003–04 | Portsmouth | 10 | 1 | **42** | **2** |

**HARPER, Kevin (F) 265 26**
H: 5 6 W: 12 00 b.Oldham 15-1-76
*Source:* Hutcheson Vale BC. *Honours:* Scotland Schools, Under-21, B.

| | | | | | |
|---|---|---|---|---|---|
| 1993–94 | Hibernian | 2 | 0 | | |
| 1994–95 | Hibernian | 23 | 5 | | |
| 1995–96 | Hibernian | 16 | 3 | | |
| 1996–97 | Hibernian | 26 | 5 | | |
| 1997–98 | Hibernian | 27 | 1 | | |
| 1998–99 | Hibernian | 2 | 1 | **96** | **15** |
| 1998–99 | Derby Co | 27 | 1 | | |
| 1999–2000 | Derby Co | 5 | 0 | **32** | **1** |
| 1999–2000 | *Walsall* | 9 | 1 | **9** | **1** |
| 1999–2000 | Portsmouth | 12 | 2 | | |
| 2000–01 | Portsmouth | 24 | 2 | | |
| 2001–02 | Portsmouth | 39 | 1 | | |
| 2002–03 | Portsmouth | 37 | 4 | | |
| 2003–04 | Portsmouth | 7 | 0 | **119** | **9** |
| 2003–04 | *Norwich C* | 9 | 0 | **9** | **0** |

**HISLOP, Shaka (G) 338 0**
H: 6 4 W: 14 04 b.Hackney 22-2-69
*Source:* Howard Univ, USA. *Honours:* England Under-21. Trinidad & Tobago 15 full caps.

| | | | | | |
|---|---|---|---|---|---|
| 1992–93 | Reading | 12 | 0 | | |
| 1993–94 | Reading | 46 | 0 | | |
| 1994–95 | Reading | 46 | 0 | **104** | **0** |
| 1995–96 | Newcastle U | 24 | 0 | | |
| 1996–97 | Newcastle U | 16 | 0 | | |
| 1997–98 | Newcastle U | 13 | 0 | **53** | **0** |
| 1998–99 | West Ham U | 37 | 0 | | |
| 1999–2000 | West Ham U | 22 | 0 | | |
| 2000–01 | West Ham U | 34 | 0 | | |
| 2001–02 | West Ham U | 12 | 0 | **105** | **0** |
| 2002–03 | Portsmouth | 46 | 0 | | |
| 2003–04 | Portsmouth | 30 | 0 | **76** | **0** |

**HOWE, Eddie (D) 202 10**
H: 5 11 W: 11 07 b.Amersham 29-11-77
*Source:* Trainee.

| | | | | | |
|---|---|---|---|---|---|
| 1995–96 | Bournemouth | 5 | 0 | | |
| 1996–97 | Bournemouth | 13 | 0 | | |
| 1997–98 | Bournemouth | 40 | 1 | | |
| 1998–99 | Bournemouth | 45 | 2 | | |
| 1999–2000 | Bournemouth | 28 | 1 | | |
| 2000–01 | Bournemouth | 31 | 2 | | |
| 2001–02 | Bournemouth | 38 | 4 | **200** | **10** |
| 2001–02 | Portsmouth | 1 | 0 | | |
| 2002–03 | Portsmouth | 1 | 0 | | |
| 2003–04 | Portsmouth | 0 | 0 | **2** | **0** |
| 2003–04 | *Swindon T* | 0 | 0 | | |

**HUGHES, Richard (M) 160 15**
H: 6 0 W: 13 03 b.Glasgow 25-6-79
*Source:* Atalanta. *Honours:* Scotland Youth, Under-21, 2 full caps.

| | | | | | |
|---|---|---|---|---|---|
| 1997–98 | Arsenal | 0 | 0 | | |
| 1998–99 | Bournemouth | 44 | 2 | | |
| 1999–2000 | Bournemouth | 21 | 2 | | |
| 2000–01 | Bournemouth | 44 | 8 | | |
| 2001–02 | Bournemouth | 22 | 2 | **131** | **14** |
| 2002–03 | Portsmouth | 6 | 0 | | |
| 2002–03 | *Grimsby T* | 12 | 1 | **12** | **1** |
| 2003–04 | Portsmouth | 11 | 0 | **17** | **0** |

**HUNT, Warren* (F) 6 0**
H: 5 9 W: 10 07 b.Portsmouth 2-3-84
*Source:* Scholar.

| | | | | | |
|---|---|---|---|---|---|
| 2001–02 | Portsmouth | 0 | 0 | | |
| 2002–03 | Portsmouth | 0 | 0 | | |
| 2003–04 | Portsmouth | 0 | 0 | | |
| 2003–04 | *Leyton Orient* | 6 | 0 | **6** | **0** |

**MORNAR, Ivica (F) 236 67**
H: 6 2 W: 13 01 b.Split 12-1-74
*Honours:* Croatia 20 full caps, 1 goal.

| | | | | | |
|---|---|---|---|---|---|
| 1992–93 | Hajduk Split | 21 | 7 | | |
| 1993–94 | Hajduk Split | 27 | 8 | | |
| 1994–95 | Hajduk Split | 9 | 3 | | |
| 1995–96 | Hajduk Split | 1 | 0 | **58** | **18** |
| 1995–96 | Eintracht Frankfurt | 19 | 1 | **19** | **1** |
| 1996–97 | Sevilla | 11 | 2 | **11** | **2** |
| 1997–98 | Ourense | 28 | 8 | **28** | **8** |
| 1998–99 | Standard Liege | 15 | 3 | | |
| 1999–2000 | Standard Liege | 24 | 8 | | |
| 2000–01 | Standard Liege | 30 | 12 | **69** | **23** |
| 2001–02 | Anderlecht | 23 | 8 | | |
| 2002–03 | Anderlecht | 20 | 6 | **43** | **14** |
| 2003–04 | Portsmouth | 8 | 1 | **8** | **1** |

**O'NEIL, Gary (M) 85 7**
H: 5 10 W: 11 00 b.Beckenham 18-5-83
*Source:* Scholar. *Honours:* England Youth, Under-20.

| | | | | | |
|---|---|---|---|---|---|
| 1999–2000 | Portsmouth | 1 | 0 | | |
| 2000–01 | Portsmouth | 10 | 1 | | |
| 2001–02 | Portsmouth | 33 | 1 | | |
| 2002–03 | Portsmouth | 31 | 3 | | |
| 2003–04 | Portsmouth | 3 | 2 | **78** | **7** |
| 2003–04 | *Walsall* | 7 | 0 | **7** | **0** |

**OLSZAR, Sebastian* (F) 64 11**
H: 5 11 W: 11 09 b.Poland 10-12-81

| | | | | | |
|---|---|---|---|---|---|
| 2000–01 | Gornik Zabrze | 4 | 1 | | |
| 2001–02 | Gornik Zabrze | 26 | 5 | **30** | **6** |
| 2002–03 | Admira Modling | 29 | 5 | **29** | **5** |
| 2003–04 | Portsmouth | 0 | 0 | | |
| 2003–04 | *Coventry C* | 5 | 0 | **5** | **0** |

**PARKER, Terry* (M) 0 0**
b.Southampton 20-12-83
*Source:* Scholar.

| | | | | | |
|---|---|---|---|---|---|
| 2002–03 | Portsmouth | 0 | 0 | | |
| 2003–04 | Portsmouth | 0 | 0 | | |

**PASANEN, Petri‡ (D) 150 9**
H: 6 1 W: 12 11 b.Lahti 24-9-80
*Honours:* Finland 20 full caps, 1 goal.

| | | | | | |
|---|---|---|---|---|---|
| 1996 | Kuusysi | 2 | 0 | **2** | **0** |
| 1997 | Hameenlinna | 4 | 0 | | |
| 1997 | Pallo-Lahti | 15 | 0 | **15** | **0** |
| 1998 | Hameenlinna | 1 | 0 | **5** | **0** |
| 1998 | Lahti | 15 | 1 | | |
| 1999 | Lahti | 27 | 0 | | |
| 2000 | Lahti | 15 | 1 | **57** | **2** |
| 2000–01 | Ajax | 29 | 4 | | |
| 2001–02 | Ajax | 1 | 0 | | |
| 2002–03 | Ajax | 22 | 3 | | |
| 2003–04 | Ajax | 7 | 0 | **59** | **7** |
| 2003–04 | Portsmouth | 12 | 0 | **12** | **0** |

**PERICARD, Vincent de Paul (F) 38 9**
H: 6 1 W: 13 08 b.Efko 3-10-82
*Source:* Juventus.

| | | | | | |
|---|---|---|---|---|---|
| 2002–03 | Portsmouth | 32 | 9 | | |
| 2003–04 | Portsmouth | 6 | 0 | **38** | **9** |

**PETTEFER, Carl* (M) 45 1**
H: 5 7 W: 10 02 b.Taplow 22-3-81
*Source:* Trainee.

| | | | | | |
|---|---|---|---|---|---|
| 1998–99 | Portsmouth | 0 | 0 | | |
| 1999–2000 | Portsmouth | 0 | 0 | | |
| 2000–01 | Portsmouth | 1 | 0 | | |
| 2001–02 | Portsmouth | 2 | 0 | | |
| 2002–03 | Portsmouth | 0 | 0 | | |
| 2002–03 | *Exeter C* | 31 | 1 | **31** | **1** |
| 2003–04 | Portsmouth | 0 | 0 | **3** | **0** |
| 2003–04 | *Southend U* | 11 | 0 | **11** | **0** |

**PRIMUS, Linvoy (D) 332 10**
H: 5 10 W: 12 04 b.Forest Gate 14-9-73
*Source:* Trainee.

| | | | | | |
|---|---|---|---|---|---|
| 1992–93 | Charlton Ath | 4 | 0 | | |
| 1993–94 | Charlton Ath | 0 | 0 | **4** | **0** |
| 1994–95 | Barnet | 39 | 0 | | |
| 1995–96 | Barnet | 42 | 4 | | |
| 1996–97 | Barnet | 46 | 3 | **127** | **7** |
| 1997–98 | Reading | 36 | 1 | | |
| 1998–99 | Reading | 31 | 0 | | |
| 1999–2000 | Reading | 28 | 0 | **95** | **1** |
| 2000–01 | Portsmouth | 23 | 0 | | |
| 2001–02 | Portsmouth | 22 | 2 | | |
| 2002–03 | Portsmouth | 40 | 0 | | |
| 2003–04 | Portsmouth | 21 | 0 | **106** | **2** |

**PULIS, Anthony (M) 0 0**
b.Bristol 21-7-84
*Source:* Scholar.

| | | | | | |
|---|---|---|---|---|---|
| 2002–03 | Portsmouth | 0 | 0 | | |
| 2003–04 | Portsmouth | 0 | 0 | | |

**QUASHIE, Nigel (M) 230 18**
H: 5 9 W: 12 08 b.Nunhead 20-7-78
*Source:* Trainee. *Honours:* England Youth, Under-21, B, Scotland 2 full caps, 1 goal.

| | | | | | |
|---|---|---|---|---|---|
| 1995–96 | QPR | 11 | 0 | | |
| 1996–97 | QPR | 13 | 0 | | |
| 1997–98 | QPR | 33 | 3 | | |
| 1998–99 | QPR | 0 | 0 | **57** | **3** |
| 1998–99 | Nottingham F | 16 | 0 | | |
| 1999–2000 | Nottingham F | 28 | 2 | **44** | **2** |
| 2000–01 | Portsmouth | 31 | 5 | | |
| 2001–02 | Portsmouth | 35 | 2 | | |
| 2002–03 | Portsmouth | 42 | 5 | | |
| 2003–04 | Portsmouth | 21 | 1 | **129** | **13** |

**ROBINSON, Carl (M) 225 22**
H: 5 10 W: 12 10 b.Llandrindod Wells 13-10-76
*Source:* Trainee. *Honours:* Wales Youth, Under-21, B, 17 full caps.

| | | | | | |
|---|---|---|---|---|---|
| 1995–96 | Wolverhampton W | 0 | 0 | | |
| 1995–96 | *Shrewsbury T* | 4 | 0 | **4** | **0** |
| 1996–97 | Wolverhampton W | 2 | 0 | | |
| 1997–98 | Wolverhampton W | 32 | 3 | | |
| 1998–99 | Wolverhampton W | 34 | 8 | | |
| 1999–2000 | Wolverhampton W | 33 | 3 | | |
| 2000–01 | Wolverhampton W | 40 | 3 | | |
| 2001–02 | Wolverhampton W | 23 | 2 | **164** | **19** |
| 2002–03 | Portsmouth | 15 | 0 | | |
| 2002–03 | *Sheffield W* | 4 | 1 | **4** | **1** |
| 2002–03 | *Walsall* | 11 | 1 | **11** | **1** |
| 2003–04 | Portsmouth | 1 | 0 | **16** | **0** |
| 2003–04 | *Rotherham U* | 14 | 0 | **14** | **0** |
| 2003–04 | *Sheffield U* | 5 | 0 | **5** | **0** |
| 2003–04 | *Sunderland* | 7 | 1 | **7** | **1** |

**SCHEMMEL, Sebastian (D) 283 4**
H: 5 8 W: 11 13 b.Nancy 2-6-75

| | | | | | |
|---|---|---|---|---|---|
| 1993–94 | Nancy | 6 | 0 | | |
| 1994–95 | Nancy | 35 | 0 | | |
| 1995–96 | Nancy | 33 | 0 | | |
| 1996–97 | Nancy | 32 | 0 | | |

| | | | | | |
|---|---|---|---|---|---|
| 1997–98 | Nancy | 40 | 1 | **146** | **1** |
| 1998–99 | Metz | 20 | 1 | | |
| 1999–2000 | Metz | 21 | 1 | | |
| 2000–01 | Metz | 19 | 0 | **60** | **2** |
| 2000–01 | West Ham U | 12 | 0 | | |
| 2001–02 | West Ham U | 35 | 1 | | |
| 2002–03 | West Ham U | 16 | 0 | **63** | **1** |
| 2003–04 | Portsmouth | 14 | 0 | **14** | **0** |

**SHERINGHAM, Teddy* (F) 639 244**
H: 5 11 W: 12 05 b.Highams Park 2-4-66
*Source:* Apprentice. *Honours:* England Youth, 51 full caps, 11 goals.

| | | | | | |
|---|---|---|---|---|---|
| 1983–84 | Millwall | 7 | 1 | | |
| 1984–85 | Millwall | 0 | 0 | | |
| 1984–85 | *Aldershot* | 5 | 0 | **5** | **0** |
| 1985–86 | Millwall | 18 | 4 | | |
| 1986–87 | Millwall | 42 | 13 | | |
| 1987–88 | Millwall | 43 | 22 | | |
| 1988–89 | Millwall | 33 | 11 | | |
| 1989–90 | Millwall | 31 | 9 | | |
| 1990–91 | Millwall | 46 | 33 | **220** | **93** |
| 1991–92 | Nottingham F | 39 | 13 | | |
| 1992–93 | Nottingham F | 3 | 1 | **42** | **14** |
| 1992–93 | Tottenham H | 38 | 21 | | |
| 1993–94 | Tottenham H | 19 | 13 | | |
| 1994–95 | Tottenham H | 42 | 18 | | |
| 1995–96 | Tottenham H | 38 | 16 | | |
| 1996–97 | Tottenham H | 29 | 7 | | |
| 1997–98 | Manchester U | 31 | 9 | | |
| 1998–99 | Manchester U | 17 | 2 | | |
| 1999–2000 | Manchester U | 27 | 5 | | |
| 2000–01 | Manchester U | 29 | 15 | **104** | **31** |
| 2001–02 | Tottenham H | 34 | 10 | | |
| 2002–03 | Tottenham H | 36 | 12 | **236** | **97** |
| 2003–04 | Portsmouth | 32 | 9 | **32** | **9** |

**SHERWOOD, Tim* (M) 472 50**
H: 6 0 W: 12 08 b.St Albans 2-2-69
*Source:* Trainee. *Honours:* England Under-21, B, 3 full caps.

| | | | | | |
|---|---|---|---|---|---|
| 1986–87 | Watford | 0 | 0 | | |
| 1987–88 | Watford | 13 | 0 | | |
| 1988–89 | Watford | 19 | 2 | **32** | **2** |
| 1989–90 | Norwich C | 27 | 3 | | |
| 1990–91 | Norwich C | 37 | 7 | | |
| 1991–92 | Norwich C | 7 | 0 | **71** | **10** |
| 1991–92 | Blackburn R | 11 | 0 | | |
| 1992–93 | Blackburn R | 39 | 3 | | |
| 1993–94 | Blackburn R | 38 | 2 | | |
| 1994–95 | Blackburn R | 38 | 6 | | |
| 1995–96 | Blackburn R | 33 | 3 | | |
| 1996–97 | Blackburn R | 37 | 3 | | |
| 1997–98 | Blackburn R | 31 | 5 | | |
| 1998–99 | Blackburn R | 19 | 3 | **246** | **25** |
| 1998–99 | Tottenham H | 14 | 2 | | |
| 1999–2000 | Tottenham H | 27 | 8 | | |
| 2000–01 | Tottenham H | 33 | 2 | | |
| 2001–02 | Tottenham H | 19 | 0 | | |
| 2002–03 | Tottenham H | 0 | 0 | **93** | **12** |
| 2002–03 | Portsmouth | 17 | 1 | | |
| 2003–04 | Portsmouth | 13 | 0 | **30** | **1** |

**SILK, Gary (M) 0 0**
b.Newport (IW) 13-9-84
*Source:* Scholar.

| | | | | | |
|---|---|---|---|---|---|
| 2003–04 | Portsmouth | 0 | 0 | | |

**STEFANOVIC, Dejan (D) 238 20**
H: 6 2 W: 13 01 b.Belgrade 28-10-74
*Honours:* Serbia-Montenegro 23 full caps.

| | | | | | |
|---|---|---|---|---|---|
| 1992–93 | Red Star Belgrade | 14 | 0 | | |
| 1993–94 | Red Star Belgrade | 2 | 0 | | |
| 1994–95 | Red Star Belgrade | 30 | 9 | **46** | **9** |
| 1995–96 | Sheffield W | 6 | 0 | | |
| 1996–97 | Sheffield W | 29 | 2 | | |
| 1997–98 | Sheffield W | 20 | 2 | | |
| 1998–99 | Sheffield W | 11 | 0 | **66** | **4** |
| 1999–2000 | Perugia | 0 | 0 | | |
| 1999–2000 | OFK Belgrade | 0 | 0 | | |
| 1999–2000 | Vitesse | 14 | 0 | | |
| 2000–01 | Vitesse | 27 | 1 | | |
| 2001–02 | Vitesse | 25 | 3 | | |
| 2002–03 | Vitesse | 28 | 0 | **94** | **4** |
| 2003–04 | Portsmouth | 32 | 3 | **32** | **3** |

**STONE, Steve (F) 333 33**
H: 5 8 W: 12 07 b.Gateshead 20-8-71
*Source:* Trainee. *Honours:* England 9 full caps, 2 goals.

| | | | | | |
|---|---|---|---|---|---|
| 1989–90 | Nottingham F | 0 | 0 | | |
| 1990–91 | Nottingham F | 0 | 0 | | |
| 1991–92 | Nottingham F | 1 | 0 | | |
| 1992–93 | Nottingham F | 12 | 1 | | |
| 1993–94 | Nottingham F | 45 | 5 | | |
| 1994–95 | Nottingham F | 41 | 5 | | |
| 1995–96 | Nottingham F | 34 | 7 | | |
| 1996–97 | Nottingham F | 5 | 0 | | |
| 1997–98 | Nottingham F | 29 | 2 | | |
| 1998–99 | Nottingham F | 26 | 3 | **193** | **23** |
| 1998–99 | Aston Villa | 10 | 0 | | |
| 1999–2000 | Aston Villa | 24 | 1 | | |
| 2000–01 | Aston Villa | 34 | 2 | | |
| 2001–02 | Aston Villa | 22 | 1 | | |
| 2002–03 | Aston Villa | 0 | 0 | **90** | **4** |
| 2002–03 | Portsmouth | 18 | 4 | | |
| 2003–04 | Portsmouth | 32 | 2 | **50** | **6** |

**TARDIF, Chris* (G) 14 0**
H: 6 1 W: 12 07 b.Guernsey 10-9-79
*Source:* Trainee.

| | | | | | |
|---|---|---|---|---|---|
| 1998–99 | Portsmouth | 0 | 0 | | |
| 1999–2000 | Portsmouth | 0 | 0 | | |
| 2000–01 | Portsmouth | 4 | 0 | | |
| 2001–02 | Portsmouth | 1 | 0 | | |
| 2002–03 | Portsmouth | 0 | 0 | | |
| 2002–03 | *Bournemouth* | 9 | 0 | **9** | **0** |
| 2003–04 | Portsmouth | 0 | 0 | **5** | **0** |

**TAYLOR, Matthew (D) 194 23**
H: 5 11 W: 12 03 b.Oxford 27-11-81
*Source:* Trainee. *Honours:* England Under-21.

| | | | | | |
|---|---|---|---|---|---|
| 1998–99 | Luton T | 0 | 0 | | |
| 1999–2000 | Luton T | 41 | 4 | | |
| 2000–01 | Luton T | 45 | 1 | | |
| 2001–02 | Luton T | 43 | 11 | **129** | **16** |
| 2002–03 | Portsmouth | 35 | 7 | | |
| 2003–04 | Portsmouth | 30 | 0 | **65** | **7** |

**TODOROV, Svetoslav (F) 146 67**
H: 6 0 W: 12 02 b.Dobrich 30-8-78
*Honours:* Bulgaria 31 full caps, 4 goals.

| | | | | | |
|---|---|---|---|---|---|
| 1996–97 | Dobrudzha | 12 | 2 | **12** | **2** |
| 1997–98 | Litets Lovech | 19 | 9 | | |
| 1998–99 | Litets Lovech | 11 | 2 | | |
| 1999–2000 | Litets Lovech | 26 | 19 | | |
| 2000–01 | Litets Lovech | 15 | 7 | **71** | **37** |
| 2000–01 | West Ham U | 8 | 1 | | |
| 2001–02 | West Ham U | 6 | 0 | **14** | **1** |
| 2001–02 | Portsmouth | 3 | 1 | | |
| 2002–03 | Portsmouth | 45 | 26 | | |
| 2003–04 | Portsmouth | 1 | 0 | **49** | **27** |

**VINE, Rowan (F) 90 16**
H: 6 1 W: 11 12 b.Basingstoke 21-9-82
*Source:* Scholar.

| | | | | | |
|---|---|---|---|---|---|
| 2000–01 | Portsmouth | 2 | 0 | | |
| 2001–02 | Portsmouth | 11 | 0 | | |
| 2002–03 | Portsmouth | 0 | 0 | | |
| 2002–03 | *Brentford* | 42 | 10 | **42** | **10** |
| 2003–04 | Portsmouth | 0 | 0 | **13** | **0** |
| 2003–04 | *Colchester U* | 35 | 6 | **35** | **6** |

**WAPENAAR, Harald (G) 243 0**
H: 6 1 W: 13 07 b.Vlaardingen 10-4-70

| | | | | | |
|---|---|---|---|---|---|
| 1992–93 | Feyenoord | 0 | 0 | | |
| 1993–94 | RBC | 4 | 0 | **4** | **0** |
| 1994–95 | Helmond Sp | 20 | 0 | | |
| 1995–96 | Helmond Sp | 33 | 0 | | |
| 1996–97 | Helmond Sp | 28 | 0 | | |
| 1997–98 | Helmond Sp | 0 | 0 | **81** | **0** |
| 1997–98 | Utrecht | 21 | 0 | | |
| 1998–99 | Udinese | 2 | 0 | **2** | **0** |
| 1999–2000 | Utrecht | 33 | 0 | | |
| 2000–01 | Utrecht | 34 | 0 | | |
| 2001–02 | Utrecht | 33 | 0 | | |
| 2002–03 | Utrecht | 30 | 0 | **151** | **0** |
| 2003–04 | Portsmouth | 5 | 0 | **5** | **0** |

**YAKUBU, Ayegbeni (F) 110 45**
H: 6 0 W: 13 01 b.Nigeria 22-11-82
*Source:* Julius Berger. *Honours:* Nigeria full caps.

| | | | | | |
|---|---|---|---|---|---|
| 1999–2000 | Gil Vicente | 0 | 0 | | |
| 1999–2000 | Hapoel Kfar-Sava | 23 | 6 | **23** | **6** |
| 2000–01 | Maccabi Haifa | 14 | 3 | | |
| 2001–02 | Maccabi Haifa | 22 | 13 | **36** | **16** |
| 2002–03 | Portsmouth | 14 | 7 | | |
| 2003–04 | Portsmouth | 37 | 16 | **51** | **23** |

**ZIVKOVIC, Boris‡ (D) 235 11**
H: 6 0 W: 12 08 b.Zivinice 15-11-75
*Honours:* Croatia 38 full caps, 2 goals.

| | | | | | |
|---|---|---|---|---|---|
| 1994–95 | Marsonia | 13 | 0 | | |
| 1995–96 | Marsonia | 31 | 1 | **44** | **1** |
| 1996–97 | Dragovoljac | 29 | 1 | **29** | **1** |
| 1997–98 | Leverkusen | 16 | 1 | | |
| 1998–99 | Leverkusen | 22 | 2 | | |
| 1999–2000 | Leverkusen | 23 | 3 | | |
| 2000–01 | Leverkusen | 30 | 0 | | |
| 2001–02 | Leverkusen | 23 | 2 | | |
| 2002–03 | Leverkusen | 30 | 1 | **144** | **9** |
| 2003–04 | Portsmouth | 18 | 0 | **18** | **0** |

**Scholars**
Angus, Calum J; Brookes, Luke A; Day, Matthew J; Fordyce, Daryl T; Harris, Scott G; Horsted, Liam A; Keene, James D; Moore, Benjamin F C; Swayne, Kyle; Vongas, Michael G; Wilson, Marc D

**Non Contract**
Knight, Alan E

## PRESTON NE (63)

**ALEXANDER, Graham (D) 534 69**
H: 5 11 W: 12 02 b.Coventry 10-10-71
*Source:* Trainee. *Honours:* Scotland 14 full caps.

| | | | | | |
|---|---|---|---|---|---|
| 1989–90 | Scunthorpe U | 0 | 0 | | |
| 1990–91 | Scunthorpe U | 1 | 0 | | |
| 1991–92 | Scunthorpe U | 36 | 5 | | |
| 1992–93 | Scunthorpe U | 41 | 5 | | |
| 1993–94 | Scunthorpe U | 41 | 4 | | |
| 1994–95 | Scunthorpe U | 40 | 4 | **159** | **18** |
| 1995–96 | Luton T | 37 | 1 | | |
| 1996–97 | Luton T | 45 | 2 | | |
| 1997–98 | Luton T | 39 | 8 | | |
| 1998–99 | Luton T | 29 | 4 | **150** | **15** |
| 1998–99 | Preston NE | 10 | 0 | | |
| 1999–2000 | Preston NE | 46 | 6 | | |
| 2000–01 | Preston NE | 34 | 5 | | |
| 2001–02 | Preston NE | 45 | 6 | | |
| 2002–03 | Preston NE | 45 | 10 | | |
| 2003–04 | Preston NE | 45 | 9 | **225** | **36** |

**BAILEY, John‡ (M) 1 0**
H: 5 8 W: 10 05 b.Manchester 2-7-84
*Source:* Scholar. *Honours:* England Youth.

| | | | | | |
|---|---|---|---|---|---|
| 2001–02 | Preston NE | 0 | 0 | | |
| 2002–03 | Preston NE | 1 | 0 | | |
| 2003–04 | Preston NE | 0 | 0 | **1** | **0** |

**BRISCOE, Lee# (D) 191 9**
H: 5 11 W: 11 12 b.Pontefract 30-9-75
*Source:* Trainee. *Honours:* England Under-21.

| | | | | | |
|---|---|---|---|---|---|
| 1993–94 | Sheffield W | 1 | 0 | | |
| 1994–95 | Sheffield W | 6 | 0 | | |
| 1995–96 | Sheffield W | 26 | 0 | | |
| 1996–97 | Sheffield W | 6 | 0 | | |
| 1997–98 | Sheffield W | 7 | 0 | | |
| 1997–98 | *Manchester C* | 5 | 1 | **5** | **1** |
| 1998–99 | Sheffield W | 16 | 1 | | |
| 1999–2000 | Sheffield W | 16 | 0 | **78** | **1** |
| 2000–01 | Burnley | 29 | 0 | | |
| 2001–02 | Burnley | 44 | 5 | | |
| 2002–03 | Burnley | 33 | 2 | **106** | **7** |
| 2003–04 | Preston NE | 2 | 0 | **2** | **0** |

**BROOMES, Marlon# (D) 140 2**
H: 6 0 W: 12 12 b.Meriden 28-11-77
*Source:* Trainee. *Honours:* England Schools, Youth, Under-21.

| | | | | | |
|---|---|---|---|---|---|
| 1994–95 | Blackburn R | 0 | 0 | | |
| 1995–96 | Blackburn R | 0 | 0 | | |
| 1996–97 | Blackburn R | 0 | 0 | | |
| 1996–97 | *Swindon T* | 12 | 1 | **12** | **1** |
| 1997–98 | Blackburn R | 4 | 0 | | |
| 1998–99 | Blackburn R | 13 | 0 | | |
| 1999–2000 | Blackburn R | 13 | 1 | | |
| 2000–01 | Blackburn R | 1 | 0 | | |
| 2000–01 | *QPR* | 5 | 0 | **5** | **0** |
| 2001–02 | Blackburn R | 0 | 0 | **31** | **1** |
| 2001–02 | *Grimsby T* | 15 | 0 | **15** | **0** |
| 2001–02 | Sheffield W | 19 | 0 | **19** | **0** |
| 2002–03 | Preston NE | 28 | 0 | | |
| 2003–04 | Preston NE | 30 | 0 | **58** | **0** |

**CRESSWELL, Richard (F) 277 57**
H: 6 0 W: 11 08 b.Bridlington 20-9-77
*Source:* Trainee. *Honours:* England Under-21.

| | | | | | |
|---|---|---|---|---|---|
| 1995–96 | York C | 16 | 1 | | |
| 1996–97 | York C | 17 | 0 | | |
| 1996–97 | *Mansfield T* | 5 | 1 | **5** | **1** |
| 1997–98 | York C | 26 | 4 | | |
| 1998–99 | York C | 36 | 16 | **95** | **21** |
| 1998–99 | Sheffield W | 7 | 1 | | |
| 1999–2000 | Sheffield W | 20 | 1 | | |
| 2000–01 | Sheffield W | 4 | 0 | **31** | **2** |
| 2000–01 | Leicester C | 8 | 0 | **8** | **0** |
| 2000–01 | *Preston NE* | 11 | 2 | | |
| 2001–02 | Preston NE | 40 | 13 | | |
| 2002–03 | Preston NE | 42 | 16 | | |
| 2003–04 | Preston NE | 45 | 2 | **138** | **33** |

**DAVIS, Claude (D) 22 1**
H: 6 3 W: 14 04 b.Jamaica 6-3-79
*Source:* Portmore U. *Honours:* Jamaica full caps.

| | | | | | |
|---|---|---|---|---|---|
| 2003–04 | Preston NE | 22 | 1 | **22** | **1** |

**EDWARDS, Rob* (D) 433 14**
H: 6 0 W: 13 03 b.Carlisle 1-7-73
*Source:* Trainee. *Honours:* Wales Youth, Under-21, B, 4 full caps.

| | | | | | |
|---|---|---|---|---|---|
| 1989–90 | Carlisle U | 12 | 0 | | |
| 1990–91 | Carlisle U | 36 | 5 | **48** | **5** |
| 1990–91 | Bristol C | 0 | 0 | | |
| 1991–92 | Bristol C | 20 | 1 | | |
| 1992–93 | Bristol C | 18 | 0 | | |
| 1993–94 | Bristol C | 38 | 2 | | |
| 1994–95 | Bristol C | 30 | 0 | | |
| 1995–96 | Bristol C | 19 | 0 | | |
| 1996–97 | Bristol C | 31 | 0 | | |
| 1997–98 | Bristol C | 37 | 2 | | |
| 1998–99 | Bristol C | 23 | 0 | **216** | **5** |
| 1999–2000 | Preston NE | 41 | 2 | | |
| 2000–01 | Preston NE | 42 | 0 | | |
| 2001–02 | Preston NE | 36 | 2 | | |
| 2002–03 | Preston NE | 26 | 0 | | |
| 2003–04 | Preston NE | 24 | 0 | **169** | **4** |

**ELEBERT, David (D) 0 0**
b.Dublin 21-3-86
*Source:* Scholar.

| | | | | | |
|---|---|---|---|---|---|
| 2002–03 | Preston NE | 0 | 0 | | |
| 2003–04 | Preston NE | 0 | 0 | | |

**ETUHU, Dixon (M) 98 12**
H: 6 2 W: 13 00 b.Kano 8-6-82
*Source:* Scholarship.

| | | | | | |
|---|---|---|---|---|---|
| 1999–2000 | Manchester C | 0 | 0 | | |
| 2000–01 | Manchester C | 0 | 0 | | |
| 2001–02 | Manchester C | 12 | 0 | **12** | **0** |
| 2001–02 | Preston NE | 16 | 3 | | |
| 2002–03 | Preston NE | 39 | 6 | | |
| 2003–04 | Preston NE | 31 | 3 | **86** | **12** |

**FULLER, Ricardo (F) 91 34**
H: 6 3 W: 13 13 b.Kingston, Jamaica 31-10-79
*Source:* Tivoli Gardens. *Honours:* Jamaica full caps.

| | | | | | |
|---|---|---|---|---|---|
| 2000–01 | Crystal Palace | 8 | 0 | **8** | **0** |
| 2001–02 | Hearts | 27 | 8 | **27** | **8** |
| From Tivoli Gardens. | | | | | |
| 2002–03 | Preston NE | 18 | 9 | | |
| 2003–04 | Preston NE | 38 | 17 | **56** | **26** |

**GOULD, Jonathan (G) 210 0**
H: 6 1 W: 12 07 b.Paddington 18-7-68
*Source:* Clevedon T. *Honours:* Scotland B, 2 full caps..

| | | | | | |
|---|---|---|---|---|---|
| 1990–91 | Halifax T | 23 | 0 | | |
| 1991–92 | Halifax T | 9 | 0 | **32** | **0** |
| 1991–92 | WBA | 0 | 0 | | |
| 1992–93 | Coventry C | 9 | 0 | | |
| 1993–94 | Coventry C | 9 | 0 | | |
| 1994–95 | Coventry C | 7 | 0 | | |
| 1995–96 | Coventry C | 0 | 0 | **25** | **0** |
| 1995–96 | *Bradford C* | 9 | 0 | | |
| 1996–97 | Bradford C | 9 | 0 | **18** | **0** |
| 1996–97 | *Gillingham* | 3 | 0 | **3** | **0** |
| 1997–98 | Celtic | 35 | 0 | | |
| 1998–99 | Celtic | 28 | 0 | | |
| 1999–2000 | Celtic | 0 | 0 | | |
| 2000–01 | Celtic | 15 | 0 | | |
| 2001–02 | Celtic | 1 | 0 | | |
| 2002–03 | Celtic | 2 | 0 | **81** | **0** |
| 2002–03 | Preston NE | 14 | 0 | | |
| 2003–04 | Preston NE | 37 | 0 | **51** | **0** |

**HEALY, David (F) 158 44**
H: 5 8 W: 10 09 b.Downpatrick 5-8-79
*Source:* Trainee. *Honours:* Northern Ireland Schools, Youth, Under-21, B, 35 full caps, 14 goals.

| | | | | | |
|---|---|---|---|---|---|
| 1997–98 | Manchester U | 0 | 0 | | |
| 1998–99 | Manchester U | 0 | 0 | | |
| 1999–2000 | Manchester U | 0 | 0 | | |
| 1999–2000 | *Port Vale* | 16 | 3 | **16** | **3** |
| 2000–01 | Manchester U | 1 | 0 | **1** | **0** |
| 2000–01 | Preston NE | 22 | 9 | | |
| 2001–02 | Preston NE | 44 | 10 | | |
| 2002–03 | Preston NE | 24 | 5 | | |
| 2002–03 | *Norwich C* | 13 | 2 | **13** | **2** |
| 2003–04 | Preston NE | 38 | 15 | **128** | **39** |

**JACKSON, Mark§ (M) 1 0**
H: 5 11 W: 11 09 b.Preston 3-2-86
*Source:* Scholar.

| | | | | | |
|---|---|---|---|---|---|
| 2003–04 | Preston NE | 1 | 0 | **1** | **0** |

**JACKSON, Michael# (D) 381 26**
H: 6 0 W: 13 07 b.Chester 4-12-73
*Source:* Trainee.

| | | | | | |
|---|---|---|---|---|---|
| 1991–92 | Crewe Alex | 1 | 0 | | |
| 1992–93 | Crewe Alex | 4 | 0 | **5** | **0** |
| 1993–94 | Bury | 39 | 0 | | |
| 1994–95 | Bury | 24 | 2 | | |
| 1995–96 | Bury | 31 | 4 | | |
| 1996–97 | Bury | 31 | 3 | **125** | **9** |
| 1996–97 | Preston NE | 7 | 0 | | |
| 1997–98 | Preston NE | 40 | 2 | | |
| 1998–99 | Preston NE | 44 | 8 | | |
| 1999–2000 | Preston NE | 46 | 5 | | |
| 2000–01 | Preston NE | 30 | 1 | | |
| 2001–02 | Preston NE | 13 | 0 | | |
| 2002–03 | Preston NE | 22 | 1 | | |
| 2002–03 | *Tranmere R* | 6 | 0 | **6** | **0** |
| 2003–04 | Preston NE | 43 | 0 | **245** | **17** |

**KEANE, Michael (M) 64 5**
H: 5 4 W: 13 07 b.Dublin 29-12-82
*Source:* Scholar. *Honours:* Eire Under-21.

| | | | | | |
|---|---|---|---|---|---|
| 2000–01 | Preston NE | 2 | 0 | | |
| 2001–02 | Preston NE | 20 | 2 | | |
| 2002–03 | Preston NE | 5 | 0 | | |
| 2002–03 | *Grimsby T* | 7 | 2 | **7** | **2** |
| 2003–04 | Preston NE | 30 | 1 | **57** | **3** |

**KOUMANTARAKIS, George* (F) 163 53**
H: 6 3 W: 13 03 b.South Africa 27-3-74
*Source:* AmaZulu, Manning R, Supersport U. *Honours:* South Africa 12 full caps, 1 goal.

| | | | | | |
|---|---|---|---|---|---|
| 1997–98 | Supersport U | 35 | 14 | **35** | **14** |
| 1998–99 | Lucerne | 27 | 9 | **27** | **9** |
| 1999–2000 | Basle | 32 | 13 | | |
| 2000–01 | Basle | 13 | 3 | | |
| 2001–02 | Basle | 28 | 10 | | |
| 2002–03 | Basle | 11 | 0 | **84** | **26** |
| 2002–03 | Preston NE | 10 | 3 | | |
| 2003–04 | Preston NE | 7 | 1 | **17** | **4** |

**LANGMEAD, Kelvin (F) 11 1**
H: 6 1 W: 13 06 b.Coventry 23-3-85
*Source:* Scholar.

| | | | | | |
|---|---|---|---|---|---|
| 2003–04 | Preston NE | 0 | 0 | | |
| 2003–04 | *Carlisle U* | 11 | 1 | **11** | **1** |

**LEWIS, Eddie (M) 202 20**
H: 5 10 W: 11 03 b.Cerritos 17-5-74
*Honours:* USA 57 full caps, 5 goals.

| | | | | | |
|---|---|---|---|---|---|
| 1996 | San Jose Clash | 25 | 0 | | |
| 1997 | San Jose Clash | 29 | 2 | | |
| 1998 | San Jose Clash | 32 | 3 | | |
| 1999 | San Jose Clash | 29 | 4 | **115** | **9** |
| 1999–2000 | Fulham | 8 | 0 | | |
| 2000–01 | Fulham | 7 | 0 | | |
| 2001–02 | Fulham | 1 | 0 | **16** | **0** |
| 2002–03 | Preston NE | 38 | 5 | | |
| 2003–04 | Preston NE | 33 | 6 | **71** | **11** |

**LONERGAN, Andrew (G) 11 0**
H: 6 3 W: 12 02 b.Preston 19-10-83
*Source:* Scholar. *Honours:* England Youth, Under-20.

| | | | | | |
|---|---|---|---|---|---|
| 2000–01 | Preston NE | 1 | 0 | | |
| 2001–02 | Preston NE | 0 | 0 | | |
| 2002–03 | Preston NE | 0 | 0 | | |
| 2002–03 | *Darlington* | 2 | 0 | **2** | **0** |
| 2003–04 | Preston NE | 8 | 0 | **9** | **0** |

**LUCAS, David (G) 158 0**
H: 6 2 W: 13 03 b.Preston 23-11-77
*Source:* Trainee. *Honours:* England Youth.

| | | | | | |
|---|---|---|---|---|---|
| 1995–96 | Preston NE | 1 | 0 | | |
| 1995–96 | *Darlington* | 6 | 0 | | |
| 1996–97 | Preston NE | 2 | 0 | | |
| 1996–97 | *Darlington* | 7 | 0 | **13** | **0** |
| 1996–97 | *Scunthorpe U* | 6 | 0 | **6** | **0** |
| 1997–98 | Preston NE | 6 | 0 | | |
| 1998–99 | Preston NE | 31 | 0 | | |
| 1999–2000 | Preston NE | 6 | 0 | | |
| 2000–01 | Preston NE | 29 | 0 | | |
| 2001–02 | Preston NE | 24 | 0 | | |
| 2002–03 | Preston NE | 21 | 0 | | |
| 2003–04 | Preston NE | 2 | 0 | **122** | **0** |
| 2003–04 | *Sheffield W* | 17 | 0 | **17** | **0** |

**LUCKETTI, Chris (D) 502 16**
H: 6 0 W: 13 06 b.Littleborough 28-9-71
*Source:* Trainee.

| | | | | | |
|---|---|---|---|---|---|
| 1988–89 | Rochdale | 1 | 0 | | |
| 1989–90 | Rochdale | 0 | 0 | **1** | **0** |
| 1990–91 | Stockport Co | 0 | 0 | | |
| 1991–92 | Halifax T | 36 | 0 | | |
| 1992–93 | Halifax T | 42 | 2 | **78** | **2** |
| 1993–94 | Bury | 27 | 1 | | |
| 1994–95 | Bury | 39 | 3 | | |
| 1995–96 | Bury | 42 | 1 | | |
| 1996–97 | Bury | 38 | 0 | | |
| 1997–98 | Bury | 46 | 2 | | |
| 1998–99 | Bury | 43 | 1 | **235** | **8** |
| 1999–2000 | Huddersfield T | 26 | 0 | | |
| 2000–01 | Huddersfield T | 40 | 1 | | |
| 2001–02 | Huddersfield T | 2 | 0 | **68** | **1** |
| 2001–02 | Preston NE | 40 | 2 | | |
| 2002–03 | Preston NE | 43 | 2 | | |
| 2003–04 | Preston NE | 37 | 1 | **120** | **5** |

**LYNCH, Simon (F) 49 8**
H: 6 0 W: 11 00 b.Montreal 19-5-82
*Honours:* Scotland Under-21.

| | | | | | |
|---|---|---|---|---|---|
| 1999–2000 | Celtic | 2 | 1 | | |
| 2000–01 | Celtic | 0 | 0 | | |
| 2001–02 | Celtic | 1 | 2 | | |
| 2002–03 | Celtic | 1 | 0 | **4** | **3** |
| 2002–03 | Preston NE | 17 | 1 | | |
| 2003–04 | Preston NE | 19 | 1 | **36** | **2** |
| 2003–04 | *Stockport Co* | 9 | 3 | **9** | **3** |

**LYNG, Ciaran (M) 0 0**
*Source:* Scholar.

| | | | | | |
|---|---|---|---|---|---|
| 2003–04 | Preston NE | 0 | 0 | | |

**McCORMACK, Alan (M) 15 0**
H: 5 8 W: 11 05 b.Dublin 10-1-84

| | | | | | |
|---|---|---|---|---|---|
| 2002–03 | Preston NE | 0 | 0 | | |
| 2003–04 | Preston NE | 5 | 0 | **5** | **0** |
| 2003–04 | *Leyton Orient* | 10 | 0 | **10** | **0** |

**McKENNA, Paul (M) 232 21**
H: 5 7 W: 11 12 b.Eccleston 20-10-77
*Source:* Trainee.

| | | | | | |
|---|---|---|---|---|---|
| 1995–96 | Preston NE | 0 | 0 | | |
| 1996–97 | Preston NE | 5 | 1 | | |
| 1997–98 | Preston NE | 5 | 0 | | |
| 1998–99 | Preston NE | 36 | 0 | | |
| 1999–2000 | Preston NE | 24 | 2 | | |
| 2000–01 | Preston NE | 44 | 5 | | |
| 2001–02 | Preston NE | 38 | 4 | | |
| 2002–03 | Preston NE | 41 | 3 | | |
| 2003–04 | Preston NE | 39 | 6 | **232** | **21** |

**MEARS, Tyrone (M) 35 2**
H: 5 10 W: 11 09 b.Stockport 18-2-83

| | | | | | |
|---|---|---|---|---|---|
| 2000–01 | Manchester C | 0 | 0 | | |
| 2001–02 | Manchester C | 1 | 0 | **1** | **0** |
| 2002–03 | Preston NE | 22 | 1 | | |
| 2003–04 | Preston NE | 12 | 1 | **34** | **2** |

**O'NEIL, Brian (D) 265 13**
H: 6 1 W: 12 03 b.Paisley 6-9-72
*Source:* X Form. *Honours:* Scotland Schools, Youth, Under-21, 6 full caps.

| | | | | | |
|---|---|---|---|---|---|
| 1991–92 | Celtic | 28 | 1 | | |
| 1992–93 | Celtic | 17 | 3 | | |
| 1993–94 | Celtic | 28 | 2 | | |
| 1994–95 | Celtic | 26 | 0 | | |
| 1995–96 | Celtic | 5 | 0 | | |
| 1996–97 | Celtic | 16 | 2 | **120** | **8** |
| 1996–97 | *Nottingham F* | 5 | 0 | **5** | **0** |

1997–98 Aberdeen 29 1 **29 1**
1998–99 Wolfsburg 26 2
1999–2000 Wolfsburg 16 1
2000–01 Wolfsburg 8 0 **50 3**
2000–01 Derby Co 4 0
2001–02 Derby Co 10 0
2002–03 Derby Co 3 0 **17 0**
2002–03 Preston NE 15 0
2003–04 Preston NE 29 1 **44 1**

**O'NEILL, Joe (F) 23 3**
H: 6 0 W: 10 05 b.Blackburn 28-10-82
*Source:* Scholar.
2001–02 Preston NE 0 0
2002–03 Preston NE 0 0
2003–04 Preston NE 0 0
2003–04 *Bury* 23 3 **23 3**

**ONIBUJE, Fola* (F) 2 0**
H: 6 5 W: 14 09 b.Lagos 25-9-84
2002–03 Preston NE 0 0
2003–04 Preston NE 0 0
2003–04 *Huddersfield T* 2 0 **2 0**

**SKORA, Eric (M) 42 0**
H: 5 10 W: 11 00 b.Metz 20-8-81
2001–02 Preston NE 4 0
2002–03 Preston NE 36 0
2003–04 Preston NE 2 0 **42 0**

**SMITH, Jeff* (M) 20 2**
H: 5 10 W: 11 08 b.Middlesbrough 28-6-80
*Source:* Trainee.
1998–99 Hartlepool U 3 0
1999–2000 Hartlepool U 0 0 **3 0**
From Bishop Auckland
2000–01 Bolton W 1 0
2001–02 *Macclesfield T* 8 2 **8 2**
2001–02 Bolton W 1 0
2002–03 Bolton W 0 0
2003–04 Bolton W 0 0 **2 0**
2003–04 *Scunthorpe U* 1 0 **1 0**
2003–04 *Rochdale* 1 0 **1 0**
2003–04 Preston NE 5 0 **5 0**

**Scholars**
Armstrong, Kyle; Beattie, Warren S; Brown, Michael; Carvill, Paul G; Clampitt, Carl E; Curwen, George E; Jackson, Mark P; Kempson, Darran K; Kewley, Michael; Kitchen, Benjamin; Neal, Christopher M; Procter, David A K; Upson, Thomas N D

**Players who do not hold a current contract but their registration has been retained by the club**
Wilkinson, Craig R

## QPR (64)

**AINSWORTH, Gareth (M) 313 74**
H: 5 10 W: 12 05 b.Blackburn 10-5-73
*Source:* Blackburn R Trainee.
1991–92 Preston NE 5 0
1992–93 Cambridge U 4 1 **4 1**
1992–93 Preston NE 26 0
1993–94 Preston NE 38 11
1994–95 Preston NE 16 1
1995–96 Preston NE 2 0
1995–96 Lincoln C 31 12
1996–97 Lincoln C 46 22
1997–98 Lincoln C 6 3 **83 37**
1997–98 Port Vale 40 5
1998–99 Port Vale 15 5 **55 10**
1998–99 Wimbledon 8 0
1999–2000 Wimbledon 2 2
2000–01 Wimbledon 12 2
2001–02 Wimbledon 2 0
2001–02 *Preston NE* 5 1 **92 13**
2002–03 Wimbledon 12 2 **36 6**
2002–03 *Walsall* 5 1 **5 1**
2002–03 Cardiff C 9 0 **9 0**
2003–04 QPR 29 6 **29 6**

**BEAN, Marcus§ (M) 38 1**
H: 5 11 W: 11 06 b.Hammersmith 2-11-84
*Source:* Scholar.
2002–03 QPR 7 0
2003–04 QPR 31 1 **38 1**

**BIGNOT, Marcus (D) 249 4**
H: 5 7 W: 11 04 b.Birmingham 22-8-74
*Source:* Kidderminster H.
1997–98 Crewe Alex 42 0
1998–99 Crewe Alex 26 0
1999–2000 Crewe Alex 27 0 **95 0**
2000–01 Bristol R 26 1 **26 1**
2000–01 QPR 9 1
2001–02 QPR 45 0
2002–03 Rushden & D 33 0
2003–04 Rushden & D 35 2 **68 2**
2003–04 QPR 6 0 **60 1**

**BIRCHAM, Marc* (M) 178 7**
H: 5 11 W: 11 06 b.Hammersmith 11-5-78
*Source:* Trainee. *Honours:* Canada 17 full caps, 1 goal.
1996–97 Millwall 6 0
1997–98 Millwall 4 0
1998–99 Millwall 28 0
1999–2000 Millwall 22 1
2000–01 Millwall 20 2
2001–02 Millwall 24 0 **104 3**
2002–03 QPR 36 2
2003–04 QPR 38 2 **74 4**

**CARLISLE, Clarke* (D) 189 13**
H: 6 3 W: 12 07 b.Preston 14-10-79
*Source:* Trainee. *Honours:* England Under-21.
1997–98 Blackpool 11 2
1998–99 Blackpool 39 1
1999–2000 Blackpool 43 4 **93 7**
2000–01 QPR 27 3
2001–02 QPR 0 0
2002–03 QPR 36 2
2003–04 QPR 33 1 **96 6**

**CULKIN, Nick (G) 93 0**
H: 6 2 W: 13 07 b.York 6-7-78
*Source:* York C.
1995–96 Manchester U 0 0
1996–97 Manchester U 0 0
1997–98 Manchester U 0 0
1998–99 Manchester U 0 0
1999–2000 Manchester U 1 0
1999–2000 *Hull C* 4 0 **4 0**
2000–01 Manchester U 0 0
2000–01 *Bristol R* 45 0 **45 0**
2001–02 Manchester U 0 0 **1 0**
2001–02 *Livingston* 21 0 **21 0**
2002–03 QPR 17 0
2003–04 QPR 5 0 **22 0**

**CURETON, Jamie (F) 329 130**
H: 5 8 W: 12 08 b.Bristol 28-8-75
*Source:* Trainee. *Honours:* England Youth.
1992–93 Norwich C 0 0
1993–94 Norwich C 0 0
1994–95 Norwich C 17 4
1995–96 Norwich C 12 2
1995–96 *Bournemouth* 5 0 **5 0**
1996–97 Norwich C 0 0 **29 6**
1996–97 Bristol R 38 11
1997–98 Bristol R 43 13
1998–99 Bristol R 46 25
1999–2000 Bristol R 46 22
2000–01 Bristol R 1 1 **174 72**
2000–01 Reading 43 26
2001–02 Reading 38 15
2002–03 Reading 27 9 **108 50**
From Busan Icons.
2003–04 QPR 13 2 **13 2**

**DALY, Wesley§ (M) 9 0**
H: 5 9 W: 11 00 b.Hammersmith 7-3-84
*Source:* Scholar.
2001–02 QPR 1 0
2002–03 QPR 6 0
2003–04 QPR 2 0 **9 0**

**DAY, Chris (G) 106 0**
H: 6 2 W: 13 06 b.Whipps Cross 28-7-75
*Source:* Trainee. *Honours:* England Under-21.
1992–93 Tottenham H 0 0
1993–94 Tottenham H 0 0
1994–95 Tottenham H 0 0
1995–96 Tottenham H 0 0
1996–97 Crystal Palace 24 0 **24 0**
1997–98 Watford 0 0
1998–99 Watford 0 0
1999–2000 Watford 11 0
2000–01 Watford 0 0 **11 0**
2000–01 *Lincoln C* 14 0 **14 0**
2001–02 QPR 16 0
2002–03 QPR 12 0
2003–04 QPR 29 0 **57 0**

**EDGHILL, Richard# (D) 205 1**
H: 5 9 W: 12 01 b.Oldham 23-9-74
*Source:* Trainee. *Honours:* England Under-21.
1992–93 Manchester C 0 0
1993–94 Manchester C 22 0
1994–95 Manchester C 14 0
1995–96 Manchester C 13 0
1996–97 Manchester C 0 0
1997–98 Manchester C 36 0
1998–99 Manchester C 38 0
1999–2000 Manchester C 41 1
2000–01 Manchester C 6 0
2000–01 *Birmingham C* 3 0 **3 0**
2001–02 Manchester C 11 0 **181 1**
2002–03 Wigan Ath 0 0
2002–03 Sheffield U 1 0 **1 0**
2003–04 QPR 20 0 **20 0**

**FORBES, Terrell* (D) 114 0**
H: 6 0 W: 12 05 b.Southwark 17-8-81
*Source:* Trainee.
1999–2000 West Ham U 0 0
1999–2000 *Bournemouth* 3 0 **3 0**
2000–01 West Ham U 0 0
2001–02 QPR 43 0
2002–03 QPR 38 0
2003–04 QPR 30 0 **111 0**

**FURLONG, Paul* (F) 387 136**
H: 6 0 W: 13 11 b.London 1-10-68
*Source:* Enfield.
1991–92 Coventry C 37 4 **37 4**
1992–93 Watford 41 19
1993–94 Watford 38 18 **79 37**
1994–95 Chelsea 36 10
1995–96 Chelsea 28 3 **64 13**
1996–97 Birmingham C 43 10
1997–98 Birmingham C 25 15
1998–99 Birmingham C 29 13
1999–2000 Birmingham C 19 11
2000–01 Birmingham C 4 0
2000–01 *QPR* 3 1
2001–02 Birmingham C 11 1
2001–02 *Sheffield U* 4 2 **4 2**
2002–03 Birmingham C 0 0 **131 50**
2002–03 QPR 33 13
2003–04 QPR 36 16 **72 30**

**GALLEN, Kevin (F) 330 85**
H: 5 11 W: 13 05 b.Hammersmith 21-9-75
*Source:* Trainee. *Honours:* England Schools, Youth, Under-21.
1992–93 QPR 0 0
1993–94 QPR 0 0
1994–95 QPR 37 10
1995–96 QPR 30 8
1996–97 QPR 2 3
1997–98 QPR 27 3
1998–99 QPR 44 8
1999–2000 QPR 31 4
2000–01 Huddersfield T 38 10 **38 10**
2001–02 Barnsley 9 2 **9 2**
2001–02 QPR 25 7
2002–03 QPR 42 13
2003–04 QPR 45 17 **283 73**

**GNOHERE, Arthur (D) 127 8**
H: 6 0 W: 13 00 b.Yamoussoukro 20-11-78
2000–01 Caen 28 2 **28 2**
2001–02 Burnley 34 3
2002–03 Burnley 33 2
2003–04 Burnley 14 1 **81 6**
2003–04 QPR 18 0 **18 0**

**JOHNSON, Richard# (M) 266 21**
H: 5 10 W: 11 13 b.Kurri Kurri 27-4-74
*Source:* Trainee. *Honours:* Australia 1 full cap.
1991–92 Watford 2 0
1992–93 Watford 1 0
1993–94 Watford 27 0
1994–95 Watford 35 3
1995–96 Watford 20 1

| | | | | | |
|---|---|---|---|---|---|
| 1996–97 | Watford | 37 | 2 | | |
| 1997–98 | Watford | 42 | 7 | | |
| 1998–99 | Watford | 40 | 4 | | |
| 1999–2000 | Watford | 23 | 3 | | |
| 2000–01 | Watford | 3 | 0 | | |
| 2001–02 | Watford | 0 | 0 | | |
| 2002–03 | Watford | 12 | 0 | | |
| 2002–03 | *Northampton T* | 6 | 1 | **6** | **1** |
| 2003–04 | Watford | 0 | 0 | **242** | **20** |
| 2003–04 | Colchester U | 0 | 0 | | |
| 2003–04 | Stoke C | 7 | 0 | **7** | **0** |
| 2003–04 | QPR | 11 | 0 | **11** | **0** |

**McLEOD, Kevin (M)** **48 5**
H: 5 11 W: 12 00 b.Liverpool 12-9-80
*Source:* Trainee.

| | | | | | |
|---|---|---|---|---|---|
| 1998–99 | Everton | 0 | 0 | | |
| 1999–2000 | Everton | 0 | 0 | | |
| 2000–01 | Everton | 5 | 0 | | |
| 2001–02 | Everton | 0 | 0 | | |
| 2002–03 | Everton | 0 | 0 | | |
| 2002–03 | *QPR* | 8 | 2 | | |
| 2003–04 | Everton | 0 | 0 | **5** | **0** |
| 2003–04 | QPR | 35 | 3 | **43** | **5** |

**OLI, Dennis* (F)** **23 0**
H: 6 0 W: 12 00 b.Newham 28-1-84

| | | | | | |
|---|---|---|---|---|---|
| 2001–02 | QPR | 2 | 0 | | |
| 2002–03 | QPR | 18 | 0 | | |
| 2003–04 | QPR | 3 | 0 | **23** | **0** |

**PACQUETTE, Richard* (F)** **36 7**
H: 5 11 W: 13 12 b.Paddington 28-1-83
*Source:* Trainee.

| | | | | | |
|---|---|---|---|---|---|
| 1999–2000 | QPR | 0 | 0 | | |
| 2000–01 | QPR | 2 | 0 | | |
| 2001–02 | QPR | 16 | 2 | | |
| 2002–03 | QPR | 11 | 4 | | |
| 2003–04 | QPR | 2 | 0 | **31** | **6** |
| 2003–04 | *Mansfield T* | 5 | 1 | **5** | **1** |

**PADULA, Gino (D)** **86 4**
H: 5 9 W: 12 11 b.Buenos Aires 11-7-76
*Source:* Xerex.

| | | | | | |
|---|---|---|---|---|---|
| 1999–2000 | Bristol R | 0 | 0 | | |
| 1999–2000 | Walsall | 25 | 0 | **25** | **0** |
| 2000–01 | Wigan Ath | 4 | 0 | | |
| 2001–02 | Wigan Ath | 0 | 0 | **4** | **0** |
| 2002–03 | QPR | 21 | 1 | | |
| 2003–04 | QPR | 36 | 3 | **57** | **4** |

**PALMER, Steve* (D)** **473 19**
H: 6 1 W: 12 13 b.Brighton 31-3-68
*Source:* Cambridge Univ. *Honours:* England Schools.

| | | | | | |
|---|---|---|---|---|---|
| 1989–90 | Ipswich T | 5 | 0 | | |
| 1990–91 | Ipswich T | 23 | 1 | | |
| 1991–92 | Ipswich T | 23 | 0 | | |
| 1992–93 | Ipswich T | 7 | 0 | | |
| 1993–94 | Ipswich T | 36 | 1 | | |
| 1994–95 | Ipswich T | 12 | 0 | | |
| 1995–96 | Ipswich T | 5 | 0 | **111** | **2** |
| 1995–96 | Watford | 35 | 1 | | |
| 1996–97 | Watford | 41 | 2 | | |
| 1997–98 | Watford | 41 | 2 | | |
| 1998–99 | Watford | 41 | 2 | | |
| 1999–2000 | Watford | 38 | 0 | | |
| 2000–01 | Watford | 39 | 1 | **235** | **8** |
| 2001–02 | QPR | 46 | 4 | | |
| 2002–03 | QPR | 46 | 1 | | |
| 2003–04 | QPR | 35 | 4 | **127** | **9** |

**PERRY, Jack (M)** **0 0**
b.Islington 26-10-84

| | | | | | |
|---|---|---|---|---|---|
| 2003–04 | QPR | 0 | 0 | | |

**ROSE, Matthew* (D)** **193 6**
H: 5 11 W: 12 02 b.Dartford 24-9-75
*Source:* Trainee. *Honours:* England Under-21.

| | | | | | |
|---|---|---|---|---|---|
| 1994–95 | Arsenal | 0 | 0 | | |
| 1995–96 | Arsenal | 4 | 0 | | |
| 1996–97 | Arsenal | 1 | 0 | **5** | **0** |
| 1997–98 | QPR | 16 | 0 | | |
| 1998–99 | QPR | 29 | 0 | | |
| 1999–2000 | QPR | 29 | 1 | | |
| 2000–01 | QPR | 27 | 0 | | |
| 2001–02 | QPR | 39 | 3 | | |
| 2002–03 | QPR | 28 | 2 | | |
| 2003–04 | QPR | 20 | 0 | **188** | **6** |

**ROWLANDS, Martin (M)** **191 30**
H: 5 9 W: 10 10 b.Hammersmith 8-2-79
*Source:* Farnborough T. *Honours:* Eire Under-21, 3 full caps.

| | | | | | |
|---|---|---|---|---|---|
| 1998–99 | Brentford | 36 | 4 | | |
| 1999–2000 | Brentford | 40 | 6 | | |
| 2000–01 | Brentford | 32 | 2 | | |
| 2001–02 | Brentford | 23 | 7 | | |
| 2002–03 | Brentford | 18 | 1 | **149** | **20** |
| 2003–04 | QPR | 42 | 10 | **42** | **10** |

**SHITTU, Dan (D)** **107 11**
H: 6 2 W: 16 03 b.Lagos 2-9-80
*Honours:* Nigeria 1 full cap.

| | | | | | |
|---|---|---|---|---|---|
| 1999–2000 | Charlton Ath | 0 | 0 | | |
| 2000–01 | Charlton Ath | 0 | 0 | | |
| 2000–01 | *Blackpool* | 17 | 2 | **17** | **2** |
| 2001–02 | Charlton Ath | 0 | 0 | | |
| 2001–02 | QPR | 27 | 2 | | |
| 2002–03 | QPR | 43 | 7 | | |
| 2003–04 | QPR | 20 | 0 | **90** | **9** |

**THORPE, Tony (F)** **340 132**
H: 5 9 W: 12 01 b.Leicester 10-4-74
*Source:* Leicester C.

| | | | | | |
|---|---|---|---|---|---|
| 1992–93 | Luton T | 0 | 0 | | |
| 1993–94 | Luton T | 14 | 1 | | |
| 1994–95 | Luton T | 4 | 0 | | |
| 1995–96 | Luton T | 33 | 7 | | |
| 1996–97 | Luton T | 41 | 28 | | |
| 1997–98 | Luton T | 28 | 14 | | |
| 1997–98 | Fulham | 13 | 3 | **13** | **3** |
| 1998–99 | Bristol C | 16 | 2 | | |
| 1998–99 | *Reading* | 6 | 1 | **6** | **1** |
| 1998–99 | *Luton T* | 8 | 4 | | |
| 1999–2000 | Bristol C | 31 | 13 | | |
| 1999–2000 | *Luton T* | 4 | 1 | | |
| 2000–01 | Bristol C | 39 | 19 | | |
| 2001–02 | Bristol C | 42 | 16 | **128** | **50** |
| 2002–03 | Luton T | 30 | 13 | **162** | **68** |
| 2003–04 | QPR | 31 | 10 | **31** | **10** |

**WALSHE, Ben* (M)** **2 0**
H: 5 11 W: 12 12 b.Hammersmith 24-5-83
*Source:* Scholar.

| | | | | | |
|---|---|---|---|---|---|
| 2000–01 | QPR | 1 | 0 | | |
| 2001–02 | QPR | 0 | 0 | | |
| 2002–03 | QPR | 1 | 0 | | |
| 2003–04 | QPR | 0 | 0 | **2** | **0** |

**Scholars**
Barnett, Lee A; Bean, Marcus, T; Butler, Kerry, R J; Cole, Jake; Craig, Lee P; Daly, Wesley J P; Farr, Sonny J C; Fletcher, John C; Ifura, Marien M; Johnson, Ryan J; Judge, Andrew F; Lodge, Dean; Mills, Christopher I; Mulholland, Scott R; Murphy, Daniel S; Ramsey, Matthew J; Townsend, Luke A; Williams, Martyn

## READING (65)

**ASHDOWN, Jamie (G)** **34 0**
H: 6 1 W: 13 05 b.Reading 30-11-80

| | | | | | |
|---|---|---|---|---|---|
| 1999–2000 | Reading | 0 | 0 | | |
| 2000–01 | Reading | 1 | 0 | | |
| 2001–02 | Reading | 1 | 0 | | |
| 2001–02 | *Arsenal* | 0 | 0 | | |
| 2002–03 | Reading | 1 | 0 | | |
| 2002–03 | *Bournemouth* | 2 | 0 | **2** | **0** |
| 2003–04 | Reading | 10 | 0 | **13** | **0** |
| 2003–04 | *Rushden & D* | 19 | 0 | **19** | **0** |

**BOUCAUD, Andre* (M)** **14 1**
H: 5 10 W: 11 04 b.Enfield 9-10-84
*Source:* Scholar. *Honours:* Trinidad & Tobago 3 full caps.

| | | | | | |
|---|---|---|---|---|---|
| 2001–02 | Reading | 0 | 0 | | |
| 2002–03 | Reading | 0 | 0 | | |
| 2002–03 | *Peterborough U* | 6 | 0 | | |
| 2003–04 | Reading | 0 | 0 | | |
| 2003–04 | *Peterborough U* | 8 | 1 | **14** | **1** |

**BROWN, Steve (D)** **282 10**
H: 6 1 W: 13 10 b.Brighton 13-5-72
*Source:* Trainee.

| | | | | | |
|---|---|---|---|---|---|
| 1990–91 | Charlton Ath | 0 | 0 | | |
| 1991–92 | Charlton Ath | 1 | 0 | | |
| 1992–93 | Charlton Ath | 0 | 0 | | |
| 1993–94 | Charlton Ath | 19 | 0 | | |
| 1994–95 | Charlton Ath | 42 | 3 | | |
| 1995–96 | Charlton Ath | 19 | 0 | | |
| 1996–97 | Charlton Ath | 27 | 0 | | |
| 1997–98 | Charlton Ath | 34 | 2 | | |
| 1998–99 | Charlton Ath | 18 | 0 | | |
| 1999–2000 | Charlton Ath | 40 | 2 | | |
| 2000–01 | Charlton Ath | 25 | 0 | | |
| 2001–02 | Charlton Ath | 14 | 2 | | |
| 2002–03 | Charlton Ath | 3 | 0 | **242** | **9** |
| 2002–03 | Reading | 21 | 1 | | |
| 2003–04 | Reading | 19 | 0 | **40** | **1** |

**CAMPBELL, Darren (M)** **1 0**
H: 5 5 W: 10 00 b.Huntingdon 16-4-86
*Source:* Scholar. *Honours:* England Youth.

| | | | | | |
|---|---|---|---|---|---|
| 2002–03 | Reading | 1 | 0 | | |
| 2003–04 | Reading | 0 | 0 | **1** | **0** |

**CASTLE, Peter (D)** **1 0**
H: 6 0 W: 12 02 b.Southampton 12-3-87
*Source:* Scholar. *Honours:* FA Schools.

| | | | | | |
|---|---|---|---|---|---|
| 2002–03 | Reading | 1 | 0 | | |
| 2003–04 | Reading | 0 | 0 | **1** | **0** |

**DALEY, Omar‡ (M)** **6 0**
H: 5 10 W: 11 00 b.Jamaica 25-4-81
*Source:* Portmore U. *Honours:* Jamaica full caps.

| | | | | | |
|---|---|---|---|---|---|
| 2003–04 | Reading | 6 | 0 | **6** | **0** |

**FORSTER, Nicky (F)** **401 127**
H: 5 8 W: 11 05 b.Caterham 8-9-73
*Source:* Horley T. *Honours:* England Under-21.

| | | | | | |
|---|---|---|---|---|---|
| 1992–93 | Gillingham | 26 | 6 | | |
| 1993–94 | Gillingham | 41 | 18 | **67** | **24** |
| 1994–95 | Brentford | 46 | 24 | | |
| 1995–96 | Brentford | 38 | 5 | | |
| 1996–97 | Brentford | 25 | 10 | **109** | **39** |
| 1996–97 | Birmingham C | 7 | 3 | | |
| 1997–98 | Birmingham C | 28 | 3 | | |
| 1998–99 | Birmingham C | 33 | 5 | **68** | **11** |
| 1999–2000 | Reading | 36 | 10 | | |
| 2000–01 | Reading | 9 | 1 | | |
| 2001–02 | Reading | 42 | 19 | | |
| 2002–03 | Reading | 40 | 16 | | |
| 2003–04 | Reading | 30 | 7 | **157** | **53** |

**GAMBLE, Joe* (M)** **7 0**
H: 5 7 W: 11 00 b.Cork 14-1-82
*Source:* Cork C. *Honours:* Eire Under-21.

| | | | | | |
|---|---|---|---|---|---|
| 2000–01 | Reading | 1 | 0 | | |
| 2001–02 | Reading | 6 | 0 | | |
| 2002–03 | Reading | 0 | 0 | | |
| 2003–04 | Reading | 0 | 0 | **7** | **0** |

**GOATER, Shaun (F)** **503 206**
H: 6 1 W: 11 10 b.Bermuda 25-2-70
*Honours:* Bermuda 19 full caps.

| | | | | | |
|---|---|---|---|---|---|
| 1988–89 | Manchester U | 0 | 0 | | |
| 1989–90 | Manchester U | 0 | 0 | | |
| 1989–90 | Rotherham U | 12 | 2 | | |
| 1990–91 | Rotherham U | 22 | 2 | | |
| 1991–92 | Rotherham U | 24 | 9 | | |
| 1992–93 | Rotherham U | 23 | 7 | | |
| 1993–94 | Rotherham U | 39 | 13 | | |
| 1993–94 | *Notts Co* | 1 | 0 | **1** | **0** |
| 1994–95 | Rotherham U | 45 | 19 | | |
| 1995–96 | Rotherham U | 44 | 18 | **209** | **70** |
| 1996–97 | Bristol C | 42 | 23 | | |
| 1997–98 | Bristol C | 33 | 17 | **75** | **40** |
| 1997–98 | Manchester C | 7 | 3 | | |
| 1998–99 | Manchester C | 43 | 17 | | |
| 1999–2000 | Manchester C | 40 | 23 | | |
| 2000–01 | Manchester C | 26 | 6 | | |
| 2001–02 | Manchester C | 42 | 28 | | |
| 2002–03 | Manchester C | 26 | 7 | **184** | **84** |
| 2003–04 | Reading | 34 | 12 | **34** | **12** |

**HAHNEMANN, Marcus (G)** **156 0**
H: 6 3 W: 16 04 b.Seattle 15-6-72
*Honours:* USA 4 full caps.

| | | | | | |
|---|---|---|---|---|---|
| 1997 | Colorado Rapids | 25 | 0 | | |
| 1998 | Colorado Rapids | 28 | 0 | | |
| 1999 | Colorado Rapids | 13 | 0 | **66** | **0** |
| 1999–2000 | Fulham | 0 | 0 | | |
| 2000–01 | Fulham | 2 | 0 | | |
| 2001–02 | Fulham | 0 | 0 | **2** | **0** |
| 2001–02 | *Rochdale* | 5 | 0 | **5** | **0** |
| 2001–02 | *Reading* | 6 | 0 | | |
| 2002–03 | Reading | 41 | 0 | | |
| 2003–04 | Reading | 36 | 0 | **83** | **0** |

**HARPER, James (M)** **116 5**
H: 5 10 W: 11 02 b.Chelmsford 9-11-80
*Source:* Trainee.

| | | | | | |
|---|---|---|---|---|---|
| 1999–2000 | Arsenal | 0 | 0 | | |
| 2000–01 | Arsenal | 0 | 0 | | |
| 2000–01 | *Cardiff C* | 3 | 0 | **3** | **0** |
| 2000–01 | Reading | 12 | 1 | | |
| 2001–02 | Reading | 26 | 1 | | |
| 2002–03 | Reading | 36 | 2 | | |
| 2003–04 | Reading | 39 | 1 | **113** | **5** |

**HUGHES, Andy (M)** **268 36**
H: 5 11 W: 12 01 b.Stockport 2-1-78
*Source:* Trainee.

| | | | | | |
|---|---|---|---|---|---|
| 1995–96 | Oldham Ath | 15 | 1 | | |
| 1996–97 | Oldham Ath | 8 | 0 | | |
| 1997–98 | Oldham Ath | 10 | 0 | **33** | **1** |
| 1997–98 | Notts Co | 15 | 2 | | |
| 1998–99 | Notts Co | 30 | 3 | | |
| 1999–2000 | Notts Co | 35 | 7 | | |
| 2000–01 | Notts Co | 30 | 5 | **110** | **17** |
| 2001–02 | Reading | 39 | 6 | | |
| 2002–03 | Reading | 43 | 9 | | |
| 2003–04 | Reading | 43 | 3 | **125** | **18** |

**INGIMARSSON, Ivar (D)** **251 24**
H: 6 0 W: 12 07 b.Reykjavik 20-8-77
*Honours:* Iceland 12 full caps.

| | | | | | |
|---|---|---|---|---|---|
| 1995 | Valur | 12 | 0 | | |
| 1996 | Valur | 17 | 2 | | |
| 1997 | Valur | 16 | 3 | **45** | **5** |
| 1998 | IBV | 18 | 1 | | |
| 1999 | IBV | 18 | 4 | **36** | **5** |
| 1999–2000 | Torquay U | 4 | 1 | **4** | **1** |
| 1999–2000 | Brentford | 25 | 1 | | |
| 2000–01 | Brentford | 42 | 3 | | |
| 2001–02 | Brentford | 46 | 6 | **113** | **10** |
| 2002–03 | Wolverhampton W | 13 | 2 | | |
| 2002–03 | *Brighton & HA* | 15 | 0 | **15** | **0** |
| 2003–04 | Wolverhampton W | 0 | 0 | **13** | **2** |
| 2003–04 | Reading | 25 | 1 | **25** | **1** |

**JACK, Kelvin* (M)** **0 0**
*Source:* San Juan.

| | | | | | |
|---|---|---|---|---|---|
| 2003–04 | Reading | 0 | 0 | | |

**KITSON, Dave (F)** **119 45**
H: 6 3 W: 13 00 b.Hitchin 21-1-80
*Source:* Arlesey.

| | | | | | |
|---|---|---|---|---|---|
| 2000–01 | Cambridge U | 8 | 1 | | |
| 2001–02 | Cambridge U | 33 | 9 | | |
| 2002–03 | Cambridge U | 44 | 20 | | |
| 2003–04 | Cambridge U | 17 | 10 | **102** | **40** |
| 2003–04 | Reading | 17 | 5 | **17** | **5** |

**MORGAN, Dean (F)** **84 7**
H: 6 0 W: 12 02 b.Enfield 3-10-83
*Source:* Scholar.

| | | | | | |
|---|---|---|---|---|---|
| 2000–01 | Colchester U | 4 | 0 | | |
| 2001–02 | Colchester U | 30 | 0 | | |
| 2002–03 | Colchester U | 37 | 6 | | |
| 2003–04 | Colchester U | 0 | 0 | **71** | **6** |
| 2003–04 | Reading | 13 | 1 | **13** | **1** |

**MURTY, Graeme (D)** **291 8**
H: 5 10 W: 11 10 b.Saltburn 13-11-74
*Source:* Trainee. *Honours:* Scotland B, 1 full cap.

| | | | | | |
|---|---|---|---|---|---|
| 1992–93 | York C | 0 | 0 | | |
| 1993–94 | York C | 1 | 0 | | |
| 1994–95 | York C | 20 | 2 | | |
| 1995–96 | York C | 35 | 2 | | |
| 1996–97 | York C | 27 | 2 | | |
| 1997–98 | York C | 34 | 1 | **117** | **7** |
| 1998–99 | Reading | 9 | 0 | | |
| 1999–2000 | Reading | 17 | 0 | | |
| 2000–01 | Reading | 23 | 1 | | |
| 2001–02 | Reading | 43 | 0 | | |
| 2002–03 | Reading | 44 | 0 | | |
| 2003–04 | Reading | 38 | 0 | **174** | **1** |

**NEWMAN, Ricky# (D)** **312 10**
H: 5 10 W: 12 06 b.Guildford 5-8-70
*Source:* Trainee.

| | | | | | |
|---|---|---|---|---|---|
| 1987–88 | Crystal Palace | 0 | 0 | | |
| 1988–89 | Crystal Palace | 0 | 0 | | |
| 1989–90 | Crystal Palace | 0 | 0 | | |
| 1990–91 | Crystal Palace | 0 | 0 | | |
| 1991–92 | Crystal Palace | 0 | 0 | | |
| 1991–92 | *Maidstone U* | 10 | 1 | **10** | **1** |
| 1992–93 | Crystal Palace | 2 | 0 | | |
| 1993–94 | Crystal Palace | 11 | 0 | | |
| 1994–95 | Crystal Palace | 35 | 3 | **48** | **3** |
| 1995–96 | Millwall | 36 | 1 | | |
| 1996–97 | Millwall | 41 | 3 | | |
| 1997–98 | Millwall | 35 | 1 | | |
| 1998–99 | Millwall | 24 | 0 | | |
| 1999–2000 | Millwall | 14 | 0 | **150** | **5** |
| 1999–2000 | *Reading* | 7 | 1 | | |
| 2000–01 | Reading | 39 | 0 | | |
| 2001–02 | Reading | 0 | 0 | | |
| 2002–03 | Reading | 28 | 0 | | |
| 2003–04 | Reading | 30 | 0 | **104** | **1** |

**OWUSU, Lloyd (F)** **232 77**
H: 6 1 W: 13 07 b.Slough 12-12-76
*Source:* Slough T.

| | | | | | |
|---|---|---|---|---|---|
| 1998–99 | Brentford | 46 | 22 | | |
| 1999–2000 | Brentford | 41 | 12 | | |
| 2000–01 | Brentford | 33 | 10 | | |
| 2001–02 | Brentford | 44 | 20 | **164** | **64** |
| 2002–03 | Sheffield W | 32 | 4 | | |
| 2003–04 | Sheffield W | 20 | 5 | **52** | **9** |
| 2003–04 | Reading | 16 | 4 | **16** | **4** |

**RIFAT, Ahmet (D)** **0 0**
H: 6 3 W: 11 08 b.London 3-1-86
*Source:* Scholar. *Honours:* England Youth.

| | | | | | |
|---|---|---|---|---|---|
| 2002–03 | Reading | 0 | 0 | | |
| 2003–04 | Reading | 0 | 0 | | |

**SALAKO, John* (M)** **475 45**
H: 5 10 W: 12 08 b.Nigeria 11-2-69
*Source:* Trainee. *Honours:* England 5 full caps.

| | | | | | |
|---|---|---|---|---|---|
| 1986–87 | Crystal Palace | 4 | 0 | | |
| 1987–88 | Crystal Palace | 31 | 0 | | |
| 1988–89 | Crystal Palace | 28 | 0 | | |
| 1989–90 | Crystal Palace | 17 | 2 | | |
| 1989–90 | *Swansea C* | 13 | 3 | **13** | **3** |
| 1990–91 | Crystal Palace | 35 | 6 | | |
| 1991–92 | Crystal Palace | 10 | 2 | | |
| 1992–93 | Crystal Palace | 13 | 0 | | |
| 1993–94 | Crystal Palace | 38 | 8 | | |
| 1994–95 | Crystal Palace | 39 | 4 | **215** | **22** |
| 1995–96 | Coventry C | 37 | 3 | | |
| 1996–97 | Coventry C | 24 | 1 | | |
| 1997–98 | Coventry C | 11 | 0 | **72** | **4** |
| 1997–98 | Bolton W | 7 | 0 | **7** | **0** |
| 1998–99 | Fulham | 10 | 1 | | |
| 1999–2000 | Fulham | 0 | 0 | **10** | **1** |
| 1999–2000 | Charlton Ath | 27 | 2 | | |
| 2000–01 | Charlton Ath | 17 | 0 | | |
| 2001–02 | Charlton Ath | 3 | 0 | **47** | **2** |
| 2001–02 | Reading | 31 | 6 | | |
| 2002–03 | Reading | 43 | 4 | | |
| 2003–04 | Reading | 37 | 3 | **111** | **13** |

**SAVAGE, Bas (F)** **16 0**
H: 6 4 W: 13 08 b.London 7-1-82
*Source:* Walton & Hersham.

| | | | | | |
|---|---|---|---|---|---|
| 2001–02 | Reading | 1 | 0 | | |
| 2002–03 | Reading | 0 | 0 | | |
| 2003–04 | Reading | 15 | 0 | **16** | **0** |

**SHOREY, Nicky (D)** **125 4**
H: 5 9 W: 10 10 b.Romford 19-2-81
*Source:* Trainee.

| | | | | | |
|---|---|---|---|---|---|
| 1999–2000 | Leyton Orient | 7 | 0 | | |
| 2000–01 | Leyton Orient | 8 | 0 | **15** | **0** |
| 2000–01 | Reading | 0 | 0 | | |
| 2001–02 | Reading | 32 | 0 | | |
| 2002–03 | Reading | 43 | 2 | | |
| 2003–04 | Reading | 35 | 2 | **110** | **4** |

**SIDWELL, Steven (M)** **98 19**
H: 5 10 W: 11 00 b.Wandsworth 14-12-82
*Source:* Scholar. *Honours:* England Under-20, Under-21.

| | | | | | |
|---|---|---|---|---|---|
| 2001–02 | Arsenal | 0 | 0 | | |
| 2001–02 | *Brentford* | 30 | 4 | **30** | **4** |
| 2002–03 | Arsenal | 0 | 0 | | |
| 2002–03 | *Brighton & HA* | 12 | 5 | **12** | **5** |
| 2002–03 | Reading | 13 | 2 | | |
| 2003–04 | Reading | 43 | 8 | **56** | **10** |

**WATSON, Kevin* (M)** **261 10**
H: 6 0 W: 12 06 b.Hackney 3-1-74
*Source:* Trainee.

| | | | | | |
|---|---|---|---|---|---|
| 1991–92 | Tottenham H | 0 | 0 | | |
| 1992–93 | Tottenham H | 5 | 0 | | |
| 1993–94 | Tottenham H | 0 | 0 | | |
| 1993–94 | *Brentford* | 3 | 0 | **3** | **0** |
| 1994–95 | Tottenham H | 0 | 0 | | |
| 1994–95 | *Bristol C* | 2 | 0 | **2** | **0** |
| 1994–95 | *Barnet* | 13 | 0 | **13** | **0** |
| 1995–96 | Tottenham H | 0 | 0 | **5** | **0** |
| 1996–97 | Swindon T | 27 | 1 | | |
| 1997–98 | Swindon T | 18 | 0 | | |
| 1998–99 | Swindon T | 18 | 0 | **63** | **1** |
| 1999–2000 | Rotherham U | 44 | 1 | | |
| 2000–01 | Rotherham U | 46 | 5 | | |
| 2001–02 | Rotherham U | 19 | 1 | **109** | **7** |
| 2001–02 | Reading | 12 | 1 | | |
| 2002–03 | Reading | 32 | 1 | | |
| 2003–04 | Reading | 22 | 0 | **66** | **2** |

**WILLIAMS, Adrian (D)** **349 18**
H: 6 2 W: 13 02 b.Reading 16-8-71
*Source:* Trainee. *Honours:* Wales 13 full caps, 1 goal.

| | | | | | |
|---|---|---|---|---|---|
| 1988–89 | Reading | 8 | 0 | | |
| 1989–90 | Reading | 16 | 2 | | |
| 1990–91 | Reading | 7 | 0 | | |
| 1991–92 | Reading | 40 | 4 | | |
| 1992–93 | Reading | 31 | 4 | | |
| 1993–94 | Reading | 41 | 0 | | |
| 1994–95 | Reading | 22 | 1 | | |
| 1995–96 | Reading | 31 | 3 | | |
| 1996–97 | Wolverhampton W | 6 | 0 | | |
| 1997–98 | Wolverhampton W | 20 | 0 | | |
| 1998–99 | Wolverhampton W | 0 | 0 | | |
| 1999–2000 | Wolverhampton W | 1 | 0 | **27** | **0** |
| 1999–2000 | *Reading* | 15 | 1 | | |
| 2000–01 | Reading | 5 | 0 | | |
| 2001–02 | Reading | 35 | 1 | | |
| 2002–03 | Reading | 38 | 1 | | |
| 2003–04 | Reading | 33 | 1 | **322** | **18** |

**YOUNG, Jamie (G)** **1 0**
H: 5 11 W: 13 01 b.Brisbane 25-8-85
*Source:* Scholar. *Honours:* England Youth.

| | | | | | |
|---|---|---|---|---|---|
| 2003–04 | Reading | 1 | 0 | **1** | **0** |

**Scholars**
Bailey, Nathan; Bird, Leon; Bouton, Richard L M; Catney, Ryan; Clarke, Bradie J; Cox, Simon R; Crockford, Ryan W; Davies, Christopher; Fashanu, Andre; Hayes, Jonathan; Howell, Simieon; Middleton, Gary; Mullins, John C; Noto, Mario; Osano, Curtis; Rendell, Scott D; Soares, Louie; Stapleton, Darren A; Theophanides, Adam

## ROCHDALE (66)

**BEECH, Chris* (M)** **279 39**
H: 5 9 W: 12 02 b.Blackpool 16-9-74
*Source:* Trainee.

| | | | | | |
|---|---|---|---|---|---|
| 1992–93 | Blackpool | 1 | 0 | | |
| 1993–94 | Blackpool | 35 | 2 | | |
| 1994–95 | Blackpool | 28 | 2 | | |
| 1995–96 | Blackpool | 18 | 0 | **82** | **4** |
| 1996–97 | Hartlepool U | 42 | 7 | | |
| 1997–98 | Hartlepool U | 36 | 6 | | |
| 1998–99 | Hartlepool U | 16 | 9 | **94** | **22** |
| 1998–99 | Huddersfield T | 17 | 2 | | |
| 1999–2000 | Huddersfield T | 35 | 9 | | |
| 2000–01 | Huddersfield T | 10 | 0 | | |
| 2001–02 | Huddersfield T | 9 | 1 | **71** | **12** |
| 2002–03 | Rochdale | 18 | 1 | | |
| 2003–04 | Rochdale | 14 | 0 | **32** | **1** |

**BERTOS, Leo (M)** **52 10**
H: 5 10 W: 12 11 b.Wellington 20-12-81
*Honours:* New Zealand Under-23, 6 full caps.

| | | | | | |
|---|---|---|---|---|---|
| 2000–01 | Barnsley | 2 | 0 | | |
| 2001–02 | Barnsley | 4 | 0 | | |
| 2002–03 | Barnsley | 6 | 1 | **12** | **1** |
| 2003–04 | Rochdale | 40 | 9 | **40** | **9** |

**BURGESS, Daryl (D)** **428 12**
H: 6 0 W: 13 05 b.Birmingham 24-1-71
*Source:* Trainee.

| | | | | | |
|---|---|---|---|---|---|
| 1989–90 | WBA | 34 | 0 | | |
| 1990–91 | WBA | 25 | 0 | | |
| 1991–92 | WBA | 36 | 2 | | |
| 1992–93 | WBA | 18 | 1 | | |
| 1993–94 | WBA | 43 | 2 | | |
| 1994–95 | WBA | 22 | 0 | | |
| 1995–96 | WBA | 45 | 2 | | |
| 1996–97 | WBA | 33 | 1 | | |
| 1997–98 | WBA | 27 | 1 | | |
| 1998–99 | WBA | 20 | 0 | | |

| | | | | | |
|---|---|---|---|---|---|
| 1999–2000 | WBA | 26 | 1 | | |
| 2000–01 | WBA | 3 | 0 | **332** | **10** |
| 2001–02 | Northampton T | 36 | 1 | | |
| 2002–03 | Northampton T | 25 | 1 | **61** | **2** |
| 2003–04 | Rochdale | 35 | 0 | **35** | **0** |

**DOUGHTY, Matt (D)** **141 2**

H: 5 8 W: 11 00 b.Warrington 2-11-81

*Source:* Scholarship.

| | | | | | |
|---|---|---|---|---|---|
| 1999–2000 | Chester C | 33 | 1 | **33** | **1** |
| 2001–02 | Rochdale | 36 | 1 | | |
| 2002–03 | Rochdale | 41 | 0 | | |
| 2003–04 | Rochdale | 31 | 0 | **108** | **1** |

**DUFFY, Lee‡ (M)** **28 0**

H: 5 7 W: 8 08 b.Oldham 24-7-82

*Source:* Scholar.

| | | | | | |
|---|---|---|---|---|---|
| 2001–02 | Rochdale | 6 | 0 | | |
| 2002–03 | Rochdale | 22 | 0 | | |
| 2003–04 | Rochdale | 0 | 0 | **28** | **0** |

**EDWARDS, Neil# (G)** **387 0**

H: 5 9 W: 12 09 b.Aberdare 5-12-70

*Source:* Trainee.

| | | | | | |
|---|---|---|---|---|---|
| 1988–89 | Leeds U | 0 | 0 | | |
| 1989–90 | Leeds U | 0 | 0 | | |
| 1990–91 | Leeds U | 0 | 0 | | |
| 1990–91 | *Huddersfield T* | 0 | 0 | | |
| 1991–92 | Stockport Co | 39 | 0 | | |
| 1992–93 | Stockport Co | 35 | 0 | | |
| 1993–94 | Stockport Co | 26 | 0 | | |
| 1994–95 | Stockport Co | 19 | 0 | | |
| 1995–96 | Stockport Co | 45 | 0 | | |
| 1996–97 | Stockport Co | 0 | 0 | | |
| 1997–98 | Stockport Co | 0 | 0 | **164** | **0** |
| 1997–98 | Rochdale | 27 | 0 | | |
| 1998–99 | Rochdale | 45 | 0 | | |
| 1999–2000 | Rochdale | 40 | 0 | | |
| 2000–01 | Rochdale | 44 | 0 | | |
| 2001–02 | Rochdale | 7 | 0 | | |
| 2002–03 | Rochdale | 26 | 0 | | |
| 2003–04 | Rochdale | 34 | 0 | **223** | **0** |

**EVANS, Wayne# (D)** **402 4**

H: 5 11 W: 11 12 b.Abermule 25-8-71

*Source:* Welshpool.

| | | | | | |
|---|---|---|---|---|---|
| 1993–94 | Walsall | 41 | 0 | | |
| 1994–95 | Walsall | 36 | 0 | | |
| 1995–96 | Walsall | 24 | 0 | | |
| 1996–97 | Walsall | 28 | 0 | | |
| 1997–98 | Walsall | 43 | 1 | | |
| 1998–99 | Walsall | 11 | 0 | **183** | **1** |
| 1999–2000 | Rochdale | 46 | 1 | | |
| 2000–01 | Rochdale | 45 | 2 | | |
| 2001–02 | Rochdale | 43 | 0 | | |
| 2002–03 | Rochdale | 40 | 0 | | |
| 2003–04 | Rochdale | 45 | 0 | **219** | **3** |

**GILKS, Matthew (G)** **54 0**

H: 6 3 W: 13 05 b.Rochdale 4-6-82

*Source:* Scholar.

| | | | | | |
|---|---|---|---|---|---|
| 2000–01 | Rochdale | 3 | 0 | | |
| 2001–02 | Rochdale | 19 | 0 | | |
| 2002–03 | Rochdale | 20 | 0 | | |
| 2003–04 | Rochdale | 12 | 0 | **54** | **0** |

**GRAND, Simon* (D)** **40 2**

H: 6 2 W: 11 08 b.Chorley 23-2-84

*Source:* Scholar.

| | | | | | |
|---|---|---|---|---|---|
| 2002–03 | Rochdale | 23 | 2 | | |
| 2003–04 | Rochdale | 17 | 0 | **40** | **2** |

**GRIFFITHS, Gareth (D)** **269 17**

H: 6 4 W: 13 04 b.Winsford 10-4-70

*Source:* Rhyl.

| | | | | | |
|---|---|---|---|---|---|
| 1992–93 | Port Vale | 0 | 0 | | |
| 1993–94 | Port Vale | 4 | 2 | | |
| 1994–95 | Port Vale | 20 | 0 | | |
| 1995–96 | Port Vale | 41 | 2 | | |
| 1996–97 | Port Vale | 26 | 0 | | |
| 1997–98 | Port Vale | 3 | 0 | **94** | **4** |
| 1997–98 | *Shrewsbury T* | 6 | 0 | **6** | **0** |
| 1998–99 | Wigan Ath | 20 | 0 | | |
| 1999–2000 | Wigan Ath | 16 | 1 | | |
| 2000–01 | Wigan Ath | 17 | 1 | **53** | **2** |
| 2001–02 | Rochdale | 41 | 4 | | |
| 2002–03 | Rochdale | 42 | 6 | | |
| 2003–04 | Rochdale | 33 | 1 | **116** | **11** |

**HEALD, Greg (D)** **265 21**

H: 6 1 W: 12 10 b.Enfield 26-9-71

*Source:* Enfield. *Honours:* England Schools.

| | | | | | |
|---|---|---|---|---|---|
| 1994–95 | Peterborough U | 29 | 0 | | |
| 1995–96 | Peterborough U | 40 | 4 | | |
| 1996–97 | Peterborough U | 36 | 2 | **105** | **6** |
| 1997–98 | Barnet | 43 | 3 | | |
| 1998–99 | Barnet | 19 | 2 | | |
| 1999–2000 | Barnet | 40 | 5 | | |
| 2000–01 | Barnet | 39 | 3 | | |
| 2001–02 | Barnet | 0 | 0 | | |
| 2002–03 | Barnet | 0 | 0 | **141** | **13** |
| 2002–03 | Leyton Orient | 5 | 1 | | |
| 2003–04 | Leyton Orient | 4 | 0 | **9** | **1** |
| 2003–04 | Rochdale | 10 | 1 | **10** | **1** |

**HILL, Stephen* (D)** **11 0**

H: 5 11 W: 13 06 b.Prescot 12-11-82

*Source:* Scholar.

| | | | | | |
|---|---|---|---|---|---|
| 2002–03 | Rochdale | 10 | 0 | | |
| 2003–04 | Rochdale | 1 | 0 | **11** | **0** |

**HOLT, Grant (M)** **44 7**

H: 6 0 W: 12 06 b.Carlisle 12-4-81

*Source:* Workington.

| | | | | | |
|---|---|---|---|---|---|
| 1999–2000 | Halifax T | 4 | 0 | | |
| 2000–01 | Halifax T | 2 | 0 | **6** | **0** |
| From Sengkang,Barrow | | | | | |
| 2002–03 | Sheffield W | 7 | 1 | | |
| 2003–04 | Sheffield W | 17 | 2 | **24** | **3** |
| 2003–04 | Rochdale | 14 | 4 | **14** | **4** |

**JONES, Gary‡ (M)** **230 28**

H: 5 11 W: 12 06 b.Birkenhead 3-6-77

| | | | | | |
|---|---|---|---|---|---|
| 1997–98 | Swansea C | 8 | 0 | **8** | **0** |
| 1997–98 | Rochdale | 17 | 2 | | |
| 1998–99 | Rochdale | 20 | 0 | | |
| 1999–2000 | Rochdale | 39 | 7 | | |
| 2000–01 | Rochdale | 44 | 8 | | |
| 2001–02 | Rochdale | 20 | 5 | | |
| 2001–02 | Barnsley | 25 | 1 | | |
| 2002–03 | Barnsley | 31 | 1 | | |
| 2003–04 | Barnsley | 0 | 0 | **56** | **2** |
| 2003–04 | Rochdale | 26 | 4 | **166** | **26** |

**McCLARE, Sean* (M)** **137 7**

H: 5 9 W: 11 12 b.Rotherham 12-1-78

*Source:* Trainee. *Honours:* Eire Under-21.

| | | | | | |
|---|---|---|---|---|---|
| 1996–97 | Barnsley | 0 | 0 | | |
| 1997–98 | Barnsley | 0 | 0 | | |
| 1998–99 | Barnsley | 30 | 3 | | |
| 1999–2000 | Barnsley | 10 | 2 | | |
| 1999–2000 | *Rochdale* | 9 | 0 | | |
| 2000–01 | Barnsley | 10 | 1 | | |
| 2001–02 | Barnsley | 0 | 0 | **50** | **6** |
| 2001–02 | Port Vale | 23 | 1 | | |
| 2002–03 | Port Vale | 17 | 0 | **40** | **1** |
| 2003–04 | Rochdale | 38 | 0 | **47** | **0** |

**McCOURT, Patrick (M)** **73 8**

H: 6 0 W: 11 13 b.Derry 16-12-83

*Source:* Scholar. *Honours:* Northern Ireland Under-21, 1 full cap.

| | | | | | |
|---|---|---|---|---|---|
| 2001–02 | Rochdale | 23 | 4 | | |
| 2002–03 | Rochdale | 26 | 2 | | |
| 2003–04 | Rochdale | 24 | 2 | **73** | **8** |

**McEVILLY, Lee* (F)** **85 25**

H: 6 1 W: 14 12 b.Liverpool 15-4-82

*Source:* Burscough. *Honours:* Northern Ireland Under-21, 1 full cap.

| | | | | | |
|---|---|---|---|---|---|
| 2001–02 | Rochdale | 18 | 4 | | |
| 2002–03 | Rochdale | 37 | 15 | | |
| 2003–04 | Rochdale | 30 | 6 | **85** | **25** |

**PATTERSON, Rory§ (M)** **15 0**

H: 5 10 W: 10 13 b.Derry 16-7-84

*Source:* Scholar.

| | | | | | |
|---|---|---|---|---|---|
| 2002–03 | Rochdale | 8 | 0 | | |
| 2003–04 | Rochdale | 7 | 0 | **15** | **0** |

**REDFEARN, Neil† (M)** **790 157**

H: 5 11 W: 13 01 b.Dewsbury 20-6-65

*Source:* Nottingham F Apprentice.

| | | | | | |
|---|---|---|---|---|---|
| 1982–83 | Bolton W | 10 | 0 | | |
| 1983–84 | Bolton W | 25 | 1 | **35** | **1** |
| 1983–84 | *Lincoln C* | 10 | 1 | | |
| 1984–85 | Lincoln C | 45 | 4 | | |
| 1985–86 | Lincoln C | 45 | 8 | **100** | **13** |
| 1986–87 | Doncaster R | 46 | 14 | **46** | **14** |
| 1987–88 | Crystal Palace | 42 | 8 | | |
| 1988–89 | Crystal Palace | 15 | 2 | **57** | **10** |
| 1988–89 | Watford | 12 | 2 | | |
| 1989–90 | Watford | 12 | 1 | **24** | **3** |
| 1989–90 | Oldham Ath | 17 | 2 | | |
| 1990–91 | Oldham Ath | 45 | 14 | **62** | **16** |
| 1991–92 | Barnsley | 36 | 4 | | |
| 1992–93 | Barnsley | 46 | 3 | | |
| 1993–94 | Barnsley | 46 | 12 | | |
| 1994–95 | Barnsley | 39 | 11 | | |
| 1995–96 | Barnsley | 45 | 14 | | |
| 1996–97 | Barnsley | 43 | 17 | | |
| 1997–98 | Barnsley | 37 | 10 | **292** | **71** |
| 1998–99 | Charlton Ath | 30 | 3 | **30** | **3** |
| 1999–2000 | Bradford C | 17 | 1 | **17** | **1** |
| 1999–2000 | Wigan Ath | 12 | 6 | | |
| 2000–01 | Wigan Ath | 10 | 1 | **22** | **7** |
| 2000–01 | Halifax T | 12 | 0 | | |
| 2001–02 | Halifax T | 30 | 6 | **42** | **6** |
| 2002–03 | Boston U | 31 | 6 | | |
| 2003–04 | Boston U | 23 | 6 | **54** | **12** |
| 2003–04 | Rochdale | 9 | 0 | **9** | **0** |

**SIMPKINS, Mike (D)** **77 0**

H: 6 1 W: 13 03 b.Sheffield 28-11-78

*Source:* Trainee.

| | | | | | |
|---|---|---|---|---|---|
| 1997–98 | Sheffield W | 0 | 0 | | |
| 1997–98 | Chesterfield | 0 | 0 | | |
| 1998–99 | Chesterfield | 1 | 0 | | |
| 1999–2000 | Chesterfield | 9 | 0 | | |
| 2000–01 | Chesterfield | 16 | 0 | **26** | **0** |
| 2001–02 | Cardiff C | 17 | 0 | | |
| 2002–03 | Cardiff C | 0 | 0 | **17** | **0** |
| 2002–03 | *Exeter C* | 5 | 0 | **5** | **0** |
| 2002–03 | *Cheltenham T* | 2 | 0 | **2** | **0** |
| 2003–04 | Rochdale | 27 | 0 | **27** | **0** |

**SMITH, Shaun† (D)** **454 42**

H: 5 10 W: 11 00 b.Leeds 9-4-71

*Source:* Trainee.

| | | | | | |
|---|---|---|---|---|---|
| 1988–89 | Halifax T | 1 | 0 | | |
| 1989–90 | Halifax T | 6 | 0 | | |
| 1990–91 | Halifax T | 0 | 0 | **7** | **0** |
| 1991–92 | Crewe Alex | 10 | 0 | | |
| 1992–93 | Crewe Alex | 36 | 4 | | |
| 1993–94 | Crewe Alex | 37 | 7 | | |
| 1994–95 | Crewe Alex | 45 | 8 | | |
| 1995–96 | Crewe Alex | 29 | 1 | | |
| 1996–97 | Crewe Alex | 38 | 4 | | |
| 1997–98 | Crewe Alex | 43 | 6 | | |
| 1998–99 | Crewe Alex | 46 | 4 | | |
| 1999–2000 | Crewe Alex | 31 | 2 | | |
| 2000–01 | Crewe Alex | 45 | 4 | | |
| 2001–02 | Crewe Alex | 42 | 1 | **402** | **41** |
| 2002–03 | Hull C | 22 | 1 | | |
| 2003–04 | Hull C | 0 | 0 | **22** | **1** |
| 2003–04 | *Stockport Co* | 6 | 0 | **6** | **0** |
| 2003–04 | *Carlisle U* | 4 | 0 | **4** | **0** |
| 2003–04 | Rochdale | 13 | 0 | **13** | **0** |

**STRACHAN, Craig‡ (M)** **1 0**

H: 5 8 W: 10 06 b.Aberdeen 19-5-82

*Source:* Trainee.

| | | | | | |
|---|---|---|---|---|---|
| 1999–2000 | Coventry C | 0 | 0 | | |
| 2000–01 | Coventry C | 0 | 0 | | |
| 2001–02 | Coventry C | 0 | 0 | | |
| 2002–03 | Coventry C | 0 | 0 | | |
| 2003–04 | Rochdale | 1 | 0 | **1** | **0** |

**TOWNSON, Kevin (F)** **101 25**

H: 5 8 W: 11 01 b.Kirby 19-4-83

*Honours:* England Youth.

| | | | | | |
|---|---|---|---|---|---|
| 2000–01 | Rochdale | 3 | 0 | | |
| 2001–02 | Rochdale | 41 | 14 | | |
| 2002–03 | Rochdale | 24 | 1 | | |
| 2003–04 | Rochdale | 33 | 10 | **101** | **25** |

**WARNER, Scott (M)** **21 1**

H: 5 11 W: 12 02 b.Rochdale 3-12-83

*Source:* Scholar.

| | | | | | |
|---|---|---|---|---|---|
| 2002–03 | Rochdale | 7 | 0 | | |
| 2003–04 | Rochdale | 14 | 1 | **21** | **1** |

**Scholars**

Allen, Nicholas; Brown, Gary; Brown, Seamus A; Crowther, Dean; Doherty, Eoin; Gartside, Karl; Gibbins, Kevin P; Gibbons, Joseph; Hamilton, Kiel; Hartley, Daniel L; Keigher, Kevin M; Mann, James; Murray, Michael P; Patterson, Rory C; Semmens, Christopher

**Non Contract**

Redfearn, Neil D; Smith, Gareth S

## ROTHERHAM U (67)

**BARKER, Richard (F) 247 47**
H: 6 1 W: 13 12 b.Sheffield 30-5-75
*Source:* Trainee. *Honours:* England Schools.

| | | | | | |
|---|---|---|---|---|---|
| 1993–94 | Sheffield W | 0 | 0 | | |
| 1994–95 | Sheffield W | 0 | 0 | | |
| 1995–96 | Sheffield W | 0 | 0 | | |
| 1995–96 | *Doncaster R* | 6 | 0 | **6** | **0** |
| 1996–97 | Sheffield W | 0 | 0 | | |
| From Linfield | | | | | |
| 1997–98 | Brighton & HA | 17 | 2 | | |
| 1998–99 | Brighton & HA | 43 | 10 | **60** | **12** |
| 1999–2000 | Macclesfield T | 35 | 16 | | |
| 2000–01 | Macclesfield T | 23 | 7 | **58** | **23** |
| 2000–01 | Rotherham U | 19 | 1 | | |
| 2001–02 | Rotherham U | 35 | 3 | | |
| 2002–03 | Rotherham U | 37 | 7 | | |
| 2003–04 | Rotherham U | 32 | 1 | **123** | **12** |

**BARKER, Shaun (D) 47 2**
H: 6 2 W: 12 10 b.Nottingham 19-9-82
*Source:* Scholar.

| | | | | | |
|---|---|---|---|---|---|
| 2002–03 | Rotherham U | 11 | 0 | | |
| 2003–04 | Rotherham U | 36 | 2 | **47** | **2** |

**BAUDET, Julien* (M) 55 3**
H: 6 3 W: 15 03 b.St Martin D'heres 13-1-79
*Source:* Toulouse.

| | | | | | |
|---|---|---|---|---|---|
| 2001–02 | Oldham Ath | 20 | 1 | | |
| 2002–03 | Oldham Ath | 24 | 2 | **44** | **3** |
| 2003–04 | Rotherham U | 11 | 0 | **11** | **0** |

**BRANSTON, Guy* (D) 151 15**
H: 6 1 W: 15 02 b.Leicester 9-1-79
*Source:* Trainee.

| | | | | | |
|---|---|---|---|---|---|
| 1997–98 | Leicester C | 0 | 0 | | |
| 1997–98 | *Colchester U* | 12 | 1 | | |
| 1998–99 | Leicester C | 0 | 0 | | |
| 1998–99 | *Colchester U* | 1 | 0 | **13** | **1** |
| 1998–99 | *Plymouth Arg* | 7 | 1 | **7** | **1** |
| 1999–2000 | Leicester C | 0 | 0 | | |
| 1999–2000 | *Lincoln C* | 4 | 0 | **4** | **0** |
| 1999–2000 | Rotherham U | 30 | 4 | | |
| 2000–01 | Rotherham U | 41 | 6 | | |
| 2001–02 | Rotherham U | 10 | 1 | | |
| 2002–03 | Rotherham U | 15 | 2 | | |
| 2003–04 | Rotherham U | 8 | 0 | **104** | **13** |
| 2003–04 | *Wycombe W* | 9 | 0 | **9** | **0** |
| 2003–04 | *Peterborough U* | 14 | 0 | **14** | **0** |

**BUTLER, Martin (F) 317 96**
H: 5 11 W: 12 00 b.Wordsley 15-9-74
*Source:* Trainee.

| | | | | | |
|---|---|---|---|---|---|
| 1993–94 | Walsall | 15 | 3 | | |
| 1994–95 | Walsall | 8 | 0 | | |
| 1995–96 | Walsall | 28 | 4 | | |
| 1996–97 | Walsall | 23 | 1 | **74** | **8** |
| 1997–98 | Cambridge U | 31 | 10 | | |
| 1998–99 | Cambridge U | 46 | 17 | | |
| 1999–2000 | Cambridge U | 26 | 14 | **103** | **41** |
| 1999–2000 | Reading | 17 | 4 | | |
| 2000–01 | Reading | 45 | 24 | | |
| 2001–02 | Reading | 17 | 2 | | |
| 2002–03 | Reading | 21 | 2 | | |
| 2003–04 | Reading | 3 | 0 | **103** | **32** |
| 2003–04 | Rotherham U | 37 | 15 | **37** | **15** |

**DAWS, Nick# (M) 458 18**
H: 5 11 W: 13 11 b.Salford 15-3-70
*Source:* Altrincham.

| | | | | | |
|---|---|---|---|---|---|
| 1992–93 | Bury | 36 | 1 | | |
| 1993–94 | Bury | 37 | 1 | | |
| 1994–95 | Bury | 34 | 2 | | |
| 1995–96 | Bury | 37 | 1 | | |
| 1996–97 | Bury | 46 | 2 | | |
| 1997–98 | Bury | 46 | 2 | | |
| 1998–99 | Bury | 46 | 2 | | |
| 1999–2000 | Bury | 43 | 2 | | |
| 2000–01 | Bury | 44 | 3 | **369** | **16** |
| 2001–02 | Rotherham U | 35 | 1 | | |
| 2002–03 | Rotherham U | 33 | 1 | | |
| 2003–04 | Rotherham U | 4 | 0 | **72** | **2** |
| 2003–04 | Grimsby T | 17 | 0 | **17** | **0** |

**GARNER, Darren (M) 273 24**
H: 5 10 W: 12 05 b.Plymouth 10-12-71
*Source:* Trainee.

| | | | | | |
|---|---|---|---|---|---|
| 1988–89 | Plymouth Arg | 1 | 0 | | |
| 1989–90 | Plymouth Arg | 1 | 0 | | |
| 1990–91 | Plymouth Arg | 5 | 1 | | |
| 1991–92 | Plymouth Arg | 10 | 0 | | |
| 1992–93 | Plymouth Arg | 10 | 0 | | |
| 1993–94 | Plymouth Arg | 0 | 0 | **27** | **1** |
| From Dorchester T. | | | | | |
| 1995–96 | Rotherham U | 31 | 1 | | |
| 1996–97 | Rotherham U | 30 | 2 | | |
| 1997–98 | Rotherham U | 40 | 3 | | |
| 1998–99 | Rotherham U | 40 | 4 | | |
| 1999–2000 | Rotherham U | 35 | 9 | | |
| 2000–01 | Rotherham U | 31 | 1 | | |
| 2001–02 | Rotherham U | 0 | 0 | | |
| 2002–03 | Rotherham U | 26 | 3 | | |
| 2003–04 | Rotherham U | 13 | 0 | **246** | **23** |

**HOSKINS, Will§ (M) 4 2**
H: 5 11 W: 11 02 b.Nottingham 6-5-86
*Source:* Scholar. *Honours:* England Youth.

| | | | | | |
|---|---|---|---|---|---|
| 2003–04 | Rotherham U | 4 | 2 | **4** | **2** |

**HURST, Paul (D) 340 13**
H: 5 5 W: 10 02 b.Sheffield 25-9-74
*Source:* Trainee.

| | | | | | |
|---|---|---|---|---|---|
| 1993–94 | Rotherham U | 4 | 0 | | |
| 1994–95 | Rotherham U | 13 | 0 | | |
| 1995–96 | Rotherham U | 40 | 1 | | |
| 1996–97 | Rotherham U | 30 | 3 | | |
| 1997–98 | Rotherham U | 30 | 0 | | |
| 1998–99 | Rotherham U | 32 | 2 | | |
| 1999–2000 | Rotherham U | 30 | 2 | | |
| 2000–01 | Rotherham U | 44 | 3 | | |
| 2001–02 | Rotherham U | 45 | 0 | | |
| 2002–03 | Rotherham U | 44 | 1 | | |
| 2003–04 | Rotherham U | 28 | 1 | **340** | **13** |

**McINTOSH, Martin (D) 375 38**
H: 6 2 W: 13 00 b.East Kilbride 19-3-71
*Honours:* Scotland B.

| | | | | | |
|---|---|---|---|---|---|
| 1988–89 | St Mirren | 2 | 0 | | |
| 1989–90 | St Mirren | 2 | 0 | | |
| 1990–91 | St Mirren | 0 | 0 | **4** | **0** |
| 1991–92 | Clydebank | 28 | 5 | | |
| 1992–93 | Clydebank | 33 | 4 | | |
| 1993–94 | Clydebank | 4 | 1 | **65** | **10** |
| 1993–94 | Hamilton A | 13 | 2 | | |
| 1994–95 | Hamilton A | 30 | 2 | | |
| 1995–96 | Hamilton A | 23 | 1 | | |
| 1996–97 | Hamilton A | 33 | 7 | **99** | **12** |
| 1997–98 | Stockport Co | 38 | 2 | | |
| 1998–99 | Stockport Co | 41 | 3 | | |
| 1999–2000 | Stockport Co | 20 | 0 | **99** | **5** |
| 1999–2000 | Hibernian | 9 | 0 | | |
| 2000–01 | Hibernian | 0 | 0 | | |
| 2001–02 | Hibernian | 0 | 0 | **9** | **0** |
| 2001–02 | Rotherham U | 39 | 4 | | |
| 2002–03 | Rotherham U | 42 | 5 | | |
| 2003–04 | Rotherham U | 18 | 2 | **99** | **11** |

**MINTO, Scott# (D) 348 11**
H: 5 10 W: 12 02 b.Wirral 6-8-71
*Source:* Trainee. *Honours:* England Youth, Under-21.

| | | | | | |
|---|---|---|---|---|---|
| 1988–89 | Charlton Ath | 3 | 0 | | |
| 1989–90 | Charlton Ath | 23 | 2 | | |
| 1990–91 | Charlton Ath | 43 | 1 | | |
| 1991–92 | Charlton Ath | 33 | 1 | | |
| 1992–93 | Charlton Ath | 36 | 1 | | |
| 1993–94 | Charlton Ath | 42 | 2 | **180** | **7** |
| 1994–95 | Chelsea | 19 | 0 | | |
| 1995–96 | Chelsea | 10 | 0 | | |
| 1996–97 | Chelsea | 25 | 4 | **54** | **4** |
| 1997–98 | Benfica | 21 | 0 | | |
| 1998–99 | Benfica | 10 | 0 | **31** | **0** |
| 1998–99 | West Ham U | 15 | 0 | | |
| 1999–2000 | West Ham U | 18 | 0 | | |
| 2000–01 | West Ham U | 1 | 0 | | |
| 2001–02 | West Ham U | 5 | 0 | | |
| 2002–03 | West Ham U | 12 | 0 | **51** | **0** |
| 2003–04 | Rotherham U | 32 | 0 | **32** | **0** |

**MONKHOUSE, Andy (M) 102 6**
H: 6 2 W: 12 12 b.Leeds 23-10-80
*Source:* Trainee.

| | | | | | |
|---|---|---|---|---|---|
| 1998–99 | Rotherham U | 5 | 1 | | |
| 1999–2000 | Rotherham U | 0 | 0 | | |
| 2000–01 | Rotherham U | 12 | 0 | | |
| 2001–02 | Rotherham U | 38 | 2 | | |
| 2002–03 | Rotherham U | 20 | 0 | | |
| 2003–04 | Rotherham U | 27 | 3 | **102** | **6** |

**MONTGOMERY, Gary (G) 14 0**
H: 6 1 W: 14 01 b.Leamington Spa 8-10-82
*Source:* Scholar.

| | | | | | |
|---|---|---|---|---|---|
| 2000–01 | Coventry C | 0 | 0 | | |
| 2001–02 | Coventry C | 0 | 0 | | |
| 2001–02 | *Crewe Alex* | 0 | 0 | | |
| 2001–02 | *Kidderminster H* | 2 | 0 | **2** | **0** |
| 2002–03 | Coventry C | 8 | 0 | **8** | **0** |
| 2003–04 | Rotherham U | 4 | 0 | **4** | **0** |

**MORRIS, Jody‡ (M) 146 6**
H: 5 5 W: 10 05 b.Hammersmith 22-12-78
*Source:* Trainee. *Honours:* England Schools, Youth, Under-21.

| | | | | | |
|---|---|---|---|---|---|
| 1995–96 | Chelsea | 1 | 0 | | |
| 1996–97 | Chelsea | 12 | 0 | | |
| 1997–98 | Chelsea | 12 | 1 | | |
| 1998–99 | Chelsea | 18 | 1 | | |
| 1999–2000 | Chelsea | 30 | 3 | | |
| 2000–01 | Chelsea | 21 | 0 | | |
| 2001–02 | Chelsea | 5 | 0 | | |
| 2002–03 | Chelsea | 25 | 0 | **124** | **5** |
| 2003–04 | Leeds U | 12 | 0 | **12** | **0** |
| 2003–04 | Rotherham U | 10 | 1 | **10** | **1** |

**MULLIN, John# (M) 249 23**
H: 6 1 W: 12 10 b.Bury 11-8-75
*Source:* School.

| | | | | | |
|---|---|---|---|---|---|
| 1992–93 | Burnley | 0 | 0 | | |
| 1993–94 | Burnley | 6 | 1 | | |
| 1994–95 | Burnley | 12 | 1 | | |
| 1995–96 | Sunderland | 10 | 1 | | |
| 1996–97 | Sunderland | 10 | 1 | | |
| 1997–98 | Sunderland | 6 | 0 | | |
| 1997–98 | *Preston NE* | 7 | 0 | **7** | **0** |
| 1997–98 | *Burnley* | 6 | 0 | | |
| 1998–99 | Sunderland | 9 | 2 | **35** | **4** |
| 1999–2000 | Burnley | 37 | 5 | | |
| 2000–01 | Burnley | 36 | 3 | | |
| 2001–02 | Burnley | 4 | 0 | **101** | **10** |
| 2001–02 | Rotherham U | 34 | 2 | | |
| 2002–03 | Rotherham U | 34 | 3 | | |
| 2003–04 | Rotherham U | 38 | 4 | **106** | **9** |

**POLLITT, Mike (G) 417 0**
H: 6 4 W: 15 01 b.Farnworth 29-2-72
*Source:* Trainee.

| | | | | | |
|---|---|---|---|---|---|
| 1990–91 | Manchester U | 0 | 0 | | |
| 1990–91 | *Oldham Ath* | 0 | 0 | | |
| 1991–92 | Bury | 0 | 0 | | |
| 1992–93 | Lincoln C | 27 | 0 | | |
| 1993–94 | Lincoln C | 30 | 0 | **57** | **0** |
| 1994–95 | Darlington | 40 | 0 | | |
| 1995–96 | Darlington | 15 | 0 | **55** | **0** |
| 1995–96 | Notts Co | 0 | 0 | | |
| 1996–97 | Notts Co | 8 | 0 | | |
| 1997–98 | Notts Co | 2 | 0 | **10** | **0** |
| 1997–98 | *Oldham Ath* | 16 | 0 | **16** | **0** |
| 1997–98 | *Gillingham* | 6 | 0 | **6** | **0** |
| 1997–98 | *Brentford* | 5 | 0 | **5** | **0** |
| 1997–98 | Sunderland | 0 | 0 | | |
| 1998–99 | Rotherham U | 46 | 0 | | |
| 1999–2000 | Rotherham U | 46 | 0 | | |
| 2000–01 | Chesterfield | 46 | 0 | **46** | **0** |
| 2001–02 | Rotherham U | 46 | 0 | | |
| 2002–03 | Rotherham U | 41 | 0 | | |
| 2003–04 | Rotherham U | 43 | 0 | **222** | **0** |

**PROCTOR, Michael (F) 120 31**
H: 6 0 W: 11 08 b.Sunderland 3-10-80
*Source:* Trainee.

| | | | | | |
|---|---|---|---|---|---|
| 1997–98 | Sunderland | 0 | 0 | | |
| 1998–99 | Sunderland | 0 | 0 | | |
| 1999–2000 | Sunderland | 0 | 0 | | |
| 2000–01 | Sunderland | 0 | 0 | | |
| 2000–01 | *Halifax T* | 12 | 4 | **12** | **4** |
| 2001–02 | Sunderland | 0 | 0 | | |
| 2001–02 | *York C* | 41 | 14 | **41** | **14** |
| 2002–03 | Sunderland | 21 | 2 | | |
| 2002–03 | *Bradford C* | 12 | 4 | **12** | **4** |
| 2003–04 | Sunderland | 17 | 1 | **38** | **3** |
| 2003–04 | Rotherham U | 17 | 6 | **17** | **6** |

**SCOTT, Rob (D) 260 31**
H: 6 1 W: 12 08 b.Epsom 15-8-73
*Source:* Sutton U.

| | | | | | |
|---|---|---|---|---|---|
| 1993–94 | Sheffield U | 0 | 0 | | |
| 1994–95 | Sheffield U | 1 | 0 | | |
| 1994–95 | *Scarborough* | 8 | 3 | **8** | **3** |
| 1995–96 | Sheffield U | 5 | 1 | **6** | **1** |
| 1995–96 | *Northampton T* | 5 | 0 | **5** | **0** |

| | | | | | |
|---|---|---|---|---|---|
| 1995–96 | Fulham | 21 | 5 | | |
| 1996–97 | Fulham | 43 | 9 | | |
| 1997–98 | Fulham | 17 | 3 | | |
| 1998–99 | Fulham | 3 | 0 | **84** | **17** |
| 1998–99 | *Carlisle U* | 7 | 3 | **7** | **3** |
| 1998–99 | Rotherham U | 6 | 1 | | |
| 1999–2000 | Rotherham U | 34 | 1 | | |
| 2000–01 | Rotherham U | 39 | 2 | | |
| 2001–02 | Rotherham U | 38 | 3 | | |
| 2002–03 | Rotherham U | 23 | 0 | | |
| 2003–04 | Rotherham U | 10 | 0 | **150** | **7** |

**SEDGWICK, Chris (M)** **223 15**
H: 6 1 W: 12 05 b.Sheffield 28-4-80
*Source:* Trainee.

| | | | | | |
|---|---|---|---|---|---|
| 1997–98 | Rotherham U | 4 | 0 | | |
| 1998–99 | Rotherham U | 33 | 4 | | |
| 1999–2000 | Rotherham U | 38 | 5 | | |
| 2000–01 | Rotherham U | 21 | 2 | | |
| 2001–02 | Rotherham U | 44 | 1 | | |
| 2002–03 | Rotherham U | 43 | 1 | | |
| 2003–04 | Rotherham U | 40 | 2 | **223** | **15** |

**SWAILES, Chris (D)** **338 23**
H: 6 2 W: 13 00 b.Gateshead 19-10-70
*Source:* Ipswich T Trainee, Peterborough U, Boston U, Birmingham C, Bridlington T.

| | | | | | |
|---|---|---|---|---|---|
| 1993–94 | Doncaster R | 17 | 0 | | |
| 1994–95 | Doncaster R | 32 | 0 | **49** | **0** |
| 1995–96 | Ipswich T | 5 | 0 | | |
| 1996–97 | Ipswich T | 23 | 1 | | |
| 1997–98 | Ipswich T | 5 | 0 | **33** | **1** |
| 1997–98 | Bury | 13 | 1 | | |
| 1998–99 | Bury | 43 | 3 | | |
| 1999–2000 | Bury | 27 | 2 | | |
| 2000–01 | Bury | 43 | 4 | **126** | **10** |
| 2001–02 | Rotherham U | 44 | 6 | | |
| 2002–03 | Rotherham U | 43 | 3 | | |
| 2003–04 | Rotherham U | 43 | 3 | **130** | **12** |

**WARNE, Paul (F)** **242 30**
H: 5 10 W: 11 07 b.Norwich 8-5-73
*Source:* Wroxham.

| | | | | | |
|---|---|---|---|---|---|
| 1997–98 | Wigan Ath | 25 | 2 | | |
| 1998–99 | Wigan Ath | 11 | 1 | **36** | **3** |
| 1998–99 | Rotherham U | 19 | 8 | | |
| 1999–2000 | Rotherham U | 43 | 10 | | |
| 2000–01 | Rotherham U | 44 | 7 | | |
| 2001–02 | Rotherham U | 25 | 0 | | |
| 2002–03 | Rotherham U | 40 | 1 | | |
| 2003–04 | Rotherham U | 35 | 1 | **206** | **27** |

**Scholars**
Bradford, Benjamin; Clayton, Gareth N; Duncum, Samuel; Fells, Daniel D; Fletcher, Thomas M; Hoskins, William R; Jones, Andrew S; Kay, Liam J; Ludlam, Stuart J; Middlebrook, Andrew; Mudd, Craig R; Newsham, Marc A; Page, Nicholas A; Pritchard, Luke J; Waite, Jamie; Whittington, Lee S

## RUSHDEN & D (68)

**BELL JNR, David* (M)** **1 0**
H: 5 10 W: 11 01 b.Buncrana 13-5-85
*Source:* Institute.

| | | | | | |
|---|---|---|---|---|---|
| 2001–02 | Rushden & D | 1 | 0 | | |
| 2002–03 | Rushden & D | 0 | 0 | | |
| 2003–04 | Rushden & D | 0 | 0 | **1** | **0** |

**BELL, David (M)** **67 4**
H: 5 10 W: 12 01 b.Kettering 21-1-84
*Source:* Trainee.

| | | | | | |
|---|---|---|---|---|---|
| 2001–02 | Rushden & D | 0 | 0 | | |
| 2002–03 | Rushden & D | 30 | 3 | | |
| 2003–04 | Rushden & D | 37 | 1 | **67** | **4** |

**BURGESS, Andy (M)** **96 9**
H: 6 2 W: 11 12 b.Bedford 10-8-81

| | | | | | |
|---|---|---|---|---|---|
| 2001–02 | Rushden & D | 32 | 4 | | |
| 2002–03 | Rushden & D | 27 | 1 | | |
| 2003–04 | Rushden & D | 37 | 4 | **96** | **9** |

**DARBY, Duane‡ (F)** **318 85**
H: 5 11 W: 13 12 b.Birmingham 17-10-73
*Source:* Trainee.

| | | | | | |
|---|---|---|---|---|---|
| 1991–92 | Torquay U | 14 | 2 | | |
| 1992–93 | Torquay U | 34 | 12 | | |
| 1993–94 | Torquay U | 36 | 8 | | |
| 1994–95 | Torquay U | 24 | 4 | **108** | **26** |
| 1995–96 | Doncaster R | 17 | 4 | **17** | **4** |
| 1995–96 | Hull C | 8 | 1 | | |
| 1996–97 | Hull C | 41 | 13 | | |
| 1997–98 | Hull C | 29 | 13 | | |
| 1998–99 | Notts Co | 0 | 0 | | |
| 1998–99 | *Hull C* | 8 | 0 | **86** | **27** |
| 1999–2000 | Notts Co | 28 | 5 | | |
| 2000–01 | Notts Co | 0 | 0 | **28** | **5** |
| 2001–02 | Rushden & D | 30 | 7 | | |
| 2002–03 | Rushden & D | 37 | 14 | | |
| 2003–04 | Rushden & D | 12 | 2 | **79** | **23** |

**DEMPSTER, John (D)** **37 1**
H: 6 0 W: 12 05 b.Kettering 1-4-83
*Source:* Trainee. *Honours:* Scotland Youth, Under-21.

| | | | | | |
|---|---|---|---|---|---|
| 2001–02 | Rushden & D | 2 | 0 | | |
| 2002–03 | Rushden & D | 16 | 1 | | |
| 2003–04 | Rushden & D | 19 | 0 | **37** | **1** |

**DUFFY, Robert (F)** **28 1**
H: 6 1 W: 13 01 b.Swansea 2-12-82
*Honours:* Wales Under-18.

| | | | | | |
|---|---|---|---|---|---|
| 2001–02 | Rushden & D | 8 | 1 | | |
| 2002–03 | Rushden & D | 12 | 0 | | |
| 2003–04 | Rushden & D | 8 | 0 | **28** | **1** |

**EDWARDS, Andy* (D)** **494 20**
H: 6 2 W: 12 13 b.Epping 17-9-71
*Source:* Trainee.

| | | | | | |
|---|---|---|---|---|---|
| 1988–89 | Southend U | 1 | 0 | | |
| 1989–90 | Southend U | 8 | 0 | | |
| 1990–91 | Southend U | 2 | 1 | | |
| 1991–92 | Southend U | 9 | 0 | | |
| 1992–93 | Southend U | 41 | 0 | | |
| 1993–94 | Southend U | 42 | 1 | | |
| 1994–95 | Southend U | 44 | 3 | **147** | **5** |
| 1995–96 | Birmingham C | 37 | 1 | | |
| 1996–97 | Birmingham C | 3 | 0 | **40** | **1** |
| 1996–97 | Peterborough U | 25 | 0 | | |
| 1997–98 | Peterborough U | 46 | 2 | | |
| 1998–99 | Peterborough U | 41 | 2 | | |
| 1999–2000 | Peterborough U | 44 | 2 | | |
| 2000–01 | Peterborough U | 43 | 1 | | |
| 2001–02 | Peterborough U | 44 | 2 | | |
| 2002–03 | Peterborough U | 23 | 1 | **266** | **10** |
| 2002–03 | Rushden & D | 12 | 1 | | |
| 2003–04 | Rushden & D | 29 | 3 | **41** | **4** |

**EVANS, Paul‡ (G)** **9 0**
H: 6 4 W: 15 00 b.Newcastle, SA 28-12-73
*Source:* Witts Univ.

| | | | | | |
|---|---|---|---|---|---|
| 1995–96 | Leeds U | 0 | 0 | | |
| 1995–96 | *Crystal Palace* | 0 | 0 | | |
| 1996–97 | Leeds U | 0 | 0 | | |
| 1996–97 | *Bradford C* | 0 | 0 | | |
| From Jomo Cosmos. | | | | | |
| 2001–02 | Huddersfield T | 0 | 0 | | |
| 2002–03 | Sheffield W | 7 | 0 | **7** | **0** |
| 2003–04 | Rushden & D | 2 | 0 | **2** | **0** |

**GRAY, Stuart (M)** **165 15**
H: 5 10 W: 13 07 b.Harrogate 18-12-73
*Source:* Giffnock N. *Honours:* Scotland Under-21.

| | | | | | |
|---|---|---|---|---|---|
| 1992–93 | Celtic | 1 | 0 | | |
| 1993–94 | Celtic | 0 | 0 | | |
| 1994–95 | Celtic | 11 | 0 | | |
| 1995–96 | Celtic | 5 | 1 | | |
| 1996–97 | Celtic | 11 | 0 | | |
| 1997–98 | Celtic | 0 | 0 | **28** | **1** |
| 1997–98 | Reading | 7 | 0 | | |
| 1998–99 | Reading | 27 | 2 | | |
| 1999–2000 | Reading | 15 | 0 | | |
| 2000–01 | Reading | 3 | 0 | **52** | **2** |
| 2001–02 | Rushden & D | 12 | 0 | | |
| 2002–03 | Rushden & D | 38 | 7 | | |
| 2003–04 | Rushden & D | 35 | 5 | **85** | **12** |

**HANLON, Ritchie* (M)** **111 10**
H: 6 1 W: 13 09 b.Kenton 25-5-78
*Source:* Chelsea Trainee.

| | | | | | |
|---|---|---|---|---|---|
| 1996–97 | Southend U | 2 | 0 | | |
| 1997–98 | Southend U | 0 | 0 | **2** | **0** |
| From Rushden & D. | | | | | |
| 1998–99 | Peterborough U | 4 | 1 | | |
| From Welling U. | | | | | |
| 1999–2000 | Peterborough U | 16 | 1 | | |
| 2000–01 | Peterborough U | 26 | 1 | | |
| 2001–02 | Peterborough U | 1 | 0 | **47** | **3** |
| 2001–02 | Rushden & D | 35 | 6 | | |
| 2002–03 | Rushden & D | 0 | 0 | | |
| 2003–04 | Rushden & D | 27 | 1 | **62** | **7** |

**HUNTER, Barry# (D)** **286 16**
H: 6 4 W: 12 06 b.Coleraine 18-11-68
*Source:* Crusaders. *Honours:* Northern Ireland Youth, B, 15 full caps, 1 goal.

| | | | | | |
|---|---|---|---|---|---|
| 1993–94 | Wrexham | 23 | 1 | | |
| 1994–95 | Wrexham | 37 | 0 | | |
| 1995–96 | Wrexham | 31 | 3 | **91** | **4** |
| 1996–97 | Reading | 27 | 2 | | |
| 1997–98 | Reading | 0 | 0 | | |
| 1998–99 | Reading | 3 | 0 | | |
| 1998–99 | *Southend U* | 5 | 2 | **5** | **2** |
| 1999–2000 | Reading | 31 | 1 | | |
| 2000–01 | Reading | 23 | 1 | | |
| 2001–02 | Reading | 0 | 0 | **84** | **4** |
| 2001–02 | Rushden & D | 23 | 1 | | |
| 2002–03 | Rushden & D | 40 | 1 | | |
| 2003–04 | Rushden & D | 43 | 4 | **106** | **6** |

**JACK, Rodney (F)** **295 69**
H: 5 7 W: 10 05 b.Kingston, Jamaica 28-9-72
*Source:* Lambada. *Honours:* St Vincent full caps.

| | | | | | |
|---|---|---|---|---|---|
| 1995–96 | Torquay U | 14 | 2 | | |
| 1996–97 | Torquay U | 33 | 10 | | |
| 1997–98 | Torquay U | 40 | 12 | **87** | **24** |
| 1998–99 | Crewe Alex | 39 | 9 | | |
| 1999–2000 | Crewe Alex | 23 | 4 | | |
| 2000–01 | Crewe Alex | 30 | 4 | | |
| 2001–02 | Crewe Alex | 33 | 7 | | |
| 2002–03 | Crewe Alex | 38 | 9 | **163** | **33** |
| 2003–04 | Rushden & D | 45 | 12 | **45** | **12** |

**KELLY, Marcus† (M)** **8 0**
H: 5 7 W: 10 00 b.Ketteringham 16-3-86
*Source:* Juniors.

| | | | | | |
|---|---|---|---|---|---|
| 2003–04 | Rushden & D | 8 | 0 | **8** | **0** |

**KITSON, Paul‡ (F)** **302 78**
H: 6 0 W: 13 00 b.Murton 9-1-71
*Source:* Trainee. *Honours:* England Under-21.

| | | | | | |
|---|---|---|---|---|---|
| 1988–89 | Leicester C | 0 | 0 | | |
| 1989–90 | Leicester C | 13 | 0 | | |
| 1990–91 | Leicester C | 7 | 0 | | |
| 1991–92 | Leicester C | 30 | 6 | **50** | **6** |
| 1991–92 | Derby Co | 12 | 4 | | |
| 1992–93 | Derby Co | 44 | 17 | | |
| 1993–94 | Derby Co | 41 | 13 | | |
| 1994–95 | Derby Co | 8 | 2 | **105** | **36** |
| 1994–95 | Newcastle U | 26 | 8 | | |
| 1995–96 | Newcastle U | 7 | 2 | | |
| 1996–97 | Newcastle U | 3 | 0 | **36** | **10** |
| 1996–97 | West Ham U | 14 | 8 | | |
| 1997–98 | West Ham U | 13 | 4 | | |
| 1998–99 | West Ham U | 17 | 3 | | |
| 1999–2000 | West Ham U | 10 | 0 | | |
| 1999–2000 | *Charlton Ath* | 6 | 1 | **6** | **1** |
| 2000–01 | West Ham U | 2 | 0 | | |
| 2000–01 | *Crystal Palace* | 4 | 0 | **4** | **0** |
| 2001–02 | West Ham U | 7 | 3 | | |
| 2002–03 | West Ham U | 0 | 0 | **63** | **18** |
| 2002–03 | Brighton & HA | 10 | 2 | | |
| 2003–04 | Brighton & HA | 0 | 0 | **10** | **2** |
| 2003–04 | Rushden & D | 28 | 5 | **28** | **5** |

**MANANGU, Eric§ (M)** **1 0**
b.DR Congo 9-9-85
*Source:* Scholar.

| | | | | | |
|---|---|---|---|---|---|
| 2003–04 | Rushden & D | 1 | 0 | **1** | **0** |

**MILLS, Gary (M)** **69 1**
H: 5 9 W: 11 11 b.Sheppey 20-5-81

| | | | | | |
|---|---|---|---|---|---|
| 2001–02 | Rushden & D | 9 | 0 | | |
| 2002–03 | Rushden & D | 30 | 0 | | |
| 2003–04 | Rushden & D | 30 | 1 | **69** | **1** |

**NAYLOR, Stuart† (G)** **541 0**
H: 6 4 W: 13 12 b.Wetherby 6-12-62
*Source:* Yorkshire Amateur. *Honours:* England Youth, B.

| | | | | | |
|---|---|---|---|---|---|
| 1980–81 | Lincoln C | 0 | 0 | | |
| 1981–82 | Lincoln C | 3 | 0 | | |
| 1982–83 | Lincoln C | 1 | 0 | | |
| 1982–83 | *Peterborough U* | 8 | 0 | **8** | **0** |
| 1983–84 | Lincoln C | 0 | 0 | | |
| 1983–84 | *Crewe Alex* | 38 | 0 | | |
| 1984–85 | *Crewe Alex* | 17 | 0 | **55** | **0** |
| 1984–85 | Lincoln C | 25 | 0 | | |
| 1985–86 | Lincoln C | 20 | 0 | **49** | **0** |
| 1985–86 | WBA | 12 | 0 | | |

| | | | | | |
|---|---|---|---|---|---|
| 1986–87 | WBA | 42 | 0 | | |
| 1987–88 | WBA | 35 | 0 | | |
| 1988–89 | WBA | 44 | 0 | | |
| 1989–90 | WBA | 39 | 0 | | |
| 1990–91 | WBA | 28 | 0 | | |
| 1991–92 | WBA | 34 | 0 | | |
| 1992–93 | WBA | 32 | 0 | | |
| 1993–94 | WBA | 20 | 0 | | |
| 1994–95 | WBA | 42 | 0 | | |
| 1995–96 | WBA | 27 | 0 | **355** | **0** |
| 1996–97 | Bristol C | 35 | 0 | | |
| 1997–98 | Bristol C | 2 | 0 | | |
| 1998–99 | Bristol C | 0 | 0 | **37** | **0** |
| 1998–99 | *Mansfield T* | 6 | 0 | **6** | **0** |
| 1998–99 | Walsall | 0 | 0 | | |
| 1999–2000 | Exeter C | 31 | 0 | | |
| 2000–01 | Exeter C | 0 | 0 | **31** | **0** |
| 2001–02 | Rushden & D | 0 | 0 | | |
| 2002–03 | Rushden & D | 0 | 0 | | |
| 2003–04 | Rushden & D | 0 | 0 | | |

**OKUONGHAE, Magnus§ (F)** **1 0**
H: 6 3 W: 13 04 b.Nigeria 16-2-86
*Source:* Scholar.

| | | | | | |
|---|---|---|---|---|---|
| 2003–04 | Rushden & D | 1 | 0 | **1** | **0** |

**ROGET, Leo* (D)** **198 8**
H: 6 1 W: 12 02 b.Ilford 1-8-77
*Source:* Trainee.

| | | | | | |
|---|---|---|---|---|---|
| 1995–96 | Southend U | 8 | 1 | | |
| 1996–97 | Southend U | 25 | 0 | | |
| 1997–98 | Southend U | 11 | 0 | | |
| 1998–99 | Southend U | 14 | 0 | | |
| 1999–2000 | Southend U | 36 | 2 | | |
| 2000–01 | Southend U | 26 | 4 | **120** | **7** |
| 2000–01 | Stockport Co | 9 | 0 | | |
| 2001–02 | Stockport Co | 22 | 1 | **31** | **1** |
| 2001–02 | *Reading* | 1 | 0 | **1** | **0** |
| 2002–03 | Brentford | 14 | 0 | | |
| 2003–04 | Brentford | 15 | 0 | **29** | **0** |
| 2003–04 | Rushden & D | 17 | 0 | **17** | **0** |

**SAMBROOK, Andrew (D)** **62 0**
H: 5 10 W: 11 09 b.Chatham 13-7-79
*Source:* Trainee.

| | | | | | |
|---|---|---|---|---|---|
| 1996–97 | Gillingham | 1 | 0 | | |
| 1997–98 | Gillingham | 0 | 0 | | |
| 1998–99 | Gillingham | 0 | 0 | **1** | **0** |
| 2001–02 | Rushden & D | 26 | 0 | | |
| 2002–03 | Rushden & D | 15 | 0 | | |
| 2003–04 | Rushden & D | 20 | 0 | **61** | **0** |

**STORY, Owen§ (M)** **5 0**
H: 5 11 W: 10 10 b.Burton 3-8-84
*Source:* Scholar.

| | | | | | |
|---|---|---|---|---|---|
| 2003–04 | Rushden & D | 5 | 0 | **5** | **0** |

**TALBOT, Daniel (M)** **23 1**
H: 5 9 W: 11 00 b.Enfield 30-1-84

| | | | | | |
|---|---|---|---|---|---|
| 2001–02 | Rushden & D | 3 | 0 | | |
| 2002–03 | Rushden & D | 13 | 0 | | |
| 2003–04 | Rushden & D | 7 | 1 | **23** | **1** |

**TURLEY, Billy (G)** **154 0**
H: 6 3 W: 15 11 b.Wolverhampton 15-7-73
*Source:* Evesham U.

| | | | | | |
|---|---|---|---|---|---|
| 1995–96 | Northampton T | 2 | 0 | | |
| 1996–97 | Northampton T | 1 | 0 | | |
| 1997–98 | Northampton T | 0 | 0 | | |
| 1997–98 | *Leyton Orient* | 14 | 0 | **14** | **0** |
| 1998–99 | Northampton T | 25 | 0 | **28** | **0** |
| 2001–02 | Rushden & D | 43 | 0 | | |
| 2002–03 | Rushden & D | 44 | 0 | | |
| 2003–04 | Rushden & D | 25 | 0 | **112** | **0** |

**WARDLEY, Stuart* (M)** **144 24**
H: 5 11 W: 13 12 b.Cambridge 10-9-75
*Source:* Saffron Walden T.

| | | | | | |
|---|---|---|---|---|---|
| 1999–2000 | QPR | 43 | 11 | | |
| 2000–01 | QPR | 34 | 3 | | |
| 2001–02 | QPR | 10 | 0 | **87** | **14** |
| 2001–02 | Rushden & D | 18 | 4 | | |
| 2002–03 | Rushden & D | 39 | 6 | | |
| 2003–04 | Rushden & D | 0 | 0 | **57** | **10** |

**Scholars**
Burndam, Eugene Raymond; Clark, Ricky J; Daniels, Karl; Gahan, Stephen; Jackson, Simeon A; Josephs, Ricardo R; Manangu, Eric M; Okuonghae, Magnus; Shaw, Thomas W; Story, Owen G; Taylor, Jason L; Wark, Scott A

**Non Contract**
Kelly, Marcus P; Naylor, Stuart W

## SCUNTHORPE U (69)

**BARWICK, Terry (M)** **46 1**
H: 5 11 W: 10 12 b.Doncaster 11-1-83
*Source:* Scholarship.

| | | | | | |
|---|---|---|---|---|---|
| 1999–2000 | Scunthorpe U | 1 | 0 | | |
| 2000–01 | Scunthorpe U | 0 | 0 | | |
| 2001–02 | Scunthorpe U | 10 | 0 | | |
| 2002–03 | Scunthorpe U | 5 | 0 | | |
| 2003–04 | Scunthorpe U | 30 | 1 | **46** | **1** |

**BEAGRIE, Peter# (M)** **595 83**
H: 5 8 W: 12 04 b.Middlesbrough 28-11-65
*Source:* Local. *Honours:* England Under-21, B.

| | | | | | |
|---|---|---|---|---|---|
| 1983–84 | Middlesbrough | 0 | 0 | | |
| 1984–85 | Middlesbrough | 7 | 1 | | |
| 1985–86 | Middlesbrough | 26 | 1 | **33** | **2** |
| 1986–87 | Sheffield U | 41 | 9 | | |
| 1987–88 | Sheffield U | 43 | 2 | **84** | **11** |
| 1988–89 | Stoke C | 41 | 7 | | |
| 1989–90 | Stoke C | 13 | 0 | **54** | **7** |
| 1989–90 | Everton | 19 | 0 | | |
| 1990–91 | Everton | 17 | 2 | | |
| 1991–92 | Everton | 27 | 3 | | |
| 1991–92 | *Sunderland* | 5 | 1 | **5** | **1** |
| 1992–93 | Everton | 22 | 3 | | |
| 1993–94 | Everton | 29 | 3 | | |
| 1993–94 | Manchester C | 9 | 1 | | |
| 1994–95 | Manchester C | 37 | 2 | | |
| 1995–96 | Manchester C | 5 | 0 | | |
| 1996–97 | Manchester C | 1 | 0 | **52** | **3** |
| 1997–98 | Bradford C | 34 | 0 | | |
| 1997–98 | *Everton* | 6 | 0 | **120** | **11** |
| 1998–99 | Bradford C | 43 | 12 | | |
| 1999–2000 | Bradford C | 35 | 7 | | |
| 2000–01 | Bradford C | 19 | 1 | **131** | **20** |
| 2000–01 | Wigan Ath | 10 | 1 | **10** | **1** |
| 2001–02 | Scunthorpe U | 40 | 11 | | |
| 2002–03 | Scunthorpe U | 34 | 5 | | |
| 2003–04 | Scunthorpe U | 32 | 11 | **106** | **27** |

**BUTLER, Andy (D)** **35 2**
H: 6 0 W: 13 06 b.Doncaster 4-11-83
*Source:* Scholar.

| | | | | | |
|---|---|---|---|---|---|
| 2003–04 | Scunthorpe U | 35 | 2 | **35** | **2** |

**BYRNE, Cliff (D)** **52 1**
H: 6 0 W: 12 11 b.Dublin 27-4-82
*Honours:* Eire Under-21.

| | | | | | |
|---|---|---|---|---|---|
| 1999–2000 | Sunderland | 0 | 0 | | |
| 2000–01 | Sunderland | 0 | 0 | | |
| 2001–02 | Sunderland | 0 | 0 | | |
| 2002–03 | Sunderland | 0 | 0 | | |
| 2002–03 | *Scunthorpe U* | 13 | 0 | | |
| 2003–04 | Scunthorpe U | 39 | 1 | **52** | **1** |

**CALVO-GARCIA, Alex* (M)** **233 32**
H: 5 9 W: 12 03 b.Ordizia 1-1-72
*Source:* Eibar.

| | | | | | |
|---|---|---|---|---|---|
| 1996–97 | Scunthorpe U | 13 | 1 | | |
| 1997–98 | Scunthorpe U | 44 | 6 | | |
| 1998–99 | Scunthorpe U | 43 | 9 | | |
| 1999–2000 | Scunthorpe U | 18 | 1 | | |
| 2000–01 | Scunthorpe U | 34 | 4 | | |
| 2001–02 | Scunthorpe U | 34 | 6 | | |
| 2002–03 | Scunthorpe U | 35 | 3 | | |
| 2003–04 | Scunthorpe U | 12 | 2 | **233** | **32** |

**EVANS, Tom (G)** **227 0**
H: 6 1 W: 13 11 b.Doncaster 31-12-76
*Source:* Trainee. *Honours:* Northern Ireland Youth.

| | | | | | |
|---|---|---|---|---|---|
| 1995–96 | Sheffield U | 0 | 0 | | |
| 1996–97 | Crystal Palace | 0 | 0 | | |
| 1996–97 | *Coventry C* | 0 | 0 | | |
| 1997–98 | Scunthorpe U | 5 | 0 | | |
| 1998–99 | Scunthorpe U | 24 | 0 | | |
| 1999–2000 | Scunthorpe U | 28 | 0 | | |
| 2000–01 | Scunthorpe U | 46 | 0 | | |
| 2001–02 | Scunthorpe U | 42 | 0 | | |
| 2002–03 | Scunthorpe U | 46 | 0 | | |
| 2003–04 | Scunthorpe U | 36 | 0 | **227** | **0** |

**FEATHERSTONE, Lee (M)** **31 0**
H: 6 0 W: 12 08 b.Chesterfield 20-7-83
*Source:* Scholar.

| | | | | | |
|---|---|---|---|---|---|
| 2001–02 | Sheffield U | 0 | 0 | | |
| 2002–03 | Sheffield U | 0 | 0 | | |
| 2002–03 | Scunthorpe U | 20 | 0 | | |
| 2003–04 | Scunthorpe U | 11 | 0 | **31** | **0** |

**GRAVES, Wayne (M)** **135 6**
H: 5 8 W: 11 01 b.Scunthorpe 18-9-80
*Source:* Trainee.

| | | | | | |
|---|---|---|---|---|---|
| 1997–98 | Scunthorpe U | 3 | 0 | | |
| 1998–99 | Scunthorpe U | 0 | 0 | | |
| 1999–2000 | Scunthorpe U | 19 | 0 | | |
| 2000–01 | Scunthorpe U | 34 | 2 | | |
| 2001–02 | Scunthorpe U | 17 | 3 | | |
| 2002–03 | Scunthorpe U | 41 | 1 | | |
| 2003–04 | Scunthorpe U | 21 | 0 | **135** | **6** |

**GROVES, Paul† (M)** **627 101**
H: 5 11 W: 13 04 b.Derby 28-2-66
*Source:* Burton Alb.

| | | | | | |
|---|---|---|---|---|---|
| 1987–88 | Leicester C | 1 | 1 | | |
| 1988–89 | Leicester C | 15 | 0 | | |
| 1989–90 | Leicester C | 0 | 0 | **16** | **1** |
| 1989–90 | *Lincoln C* | 8 | 1 | **8** | **1** |
| 1989–90 | Blackpool | 19 | 1 | | |
| 1990–91 | Blackpool | 46 | 11 | | |
| 1991–92 | Blackpool | 42 | 9 | **107** | **21** |
| 1992–93 | Grimsby T | 46 | 12 | | |
| 1993–94 | Grimsby T | 46 | 11 | | |
| 1994–95 | Grimsby T | 46 | 5 | | |
| 1995–96 | Grimsby T | 46 | 10 | | |
| 1996–97 | WBA | 29 | 4 | **29** | **4** |
| 1997–98 | Grimsby T | 46 | 7 | | |
| 1998–99 | Grimsby T | 46 | 14 | | |
| 1999–2000 | Grimsby T | 43 | 3 | | |
| 2000–01 | Grimsby T | 45 | 4 | | |
| 2001–02 | Grimsby T | 43 | 2 | | |
| 2002–03 | Grimsby T | 36 | 3 | | |
| 2003–04 | Grimsby T | 11 | 0 | **454** | **71** |
| 2003–04 | Scunthorpe U | 13 | 3 | **13** | **3** |

**HAYES, Paul (F)** **53 10**
H: 6 0 W: 12 12 b.Dagenham 20-9-83
*Source:* Norwich C Scholar.

| | | | | | |
|---|---|---|---|---|---|
| 2002–03 | Scunthorpe U | 18 | 8 | | |
| 2003–04 | Scunthorpe U | 35 | 2 | **53** | **10** |

**HUNT, Jon§ (M)** **1 0**
H: 5 10 W: 12 04 b.Leeds 11-9-84
*Source:* Scholar.

| | | | | | |
|---|---|---|---|---|---|
| 2003–04 | Scunthorpe U | 1 | 0 | **1** | **0** |

**JACKSON, Mark (D)** **158 4**
H: 6 0 W: 12 02 b.Leeds 30-9-77
*Source:* Trainee. *Honours:* England Youth.

| | | | | | |
|---|---|---|---|---|---|
| 1995–96 | Leeds U | 1 | 0 | | |
| 1996–97 | Leeds U | 17 | 0 | | |
| 1997–98 | Leeds U | 1 | 0 | | |
| 1998–99 | Leeds U | 0 | 0 | | |
| 1998–99 | *Huddersfield T* | 5 | 0 | **5** | **0** |
| 1999–2000 | Leeds U | 0 | 0 | **19** | **0** |
| 1999–2000 | *Barnsley* | 1 | 0 | **1** | **0** |
| 1999–2000 | Scunthorpe U | 6 | 0 | | |
| 2000–01 | Scunthorpe U | 32 | 1 | | |
| 2001–02 | Scunthorpe U | 45 | 3 | | |
| 2002–03 | Scunthorpe U | 33 | 0 | | |
| 2003–04 | Scunthorpe U | 17 | 0 | **133** | **4** |

**KELL, Richard† (M)** **55 6**
H: 6 1 W: 11 02 b.Bishop Auckland 15-9-79
*Source:* Trainee.

| | | | | | |
|---|---|---|---|---|---|
| 1998–99 | Middlesbrough | 0 | 0 | | |
| 1999–2000 | Middlesbrough | 0 | 0 | | |
| 2000–01 | Middlesbrough | 0 | 0 | | |
| 2000–01 | Torquay U | 15 | 3 | | |
| 2001–02 | Torquay U | 0 | 0 | **15** | **3** |
| 2001–02 | Scunthorpe U | 16 | 1 | | |
| 2002–03 | Scunthorpe U | 0 | 0 | | |
| 2003–04 | Scunthorpe U | 24 | 2 | **40** | **3** |

**KILFORD, Ian* (M)** **268 35**
H: 5 10 W: 11 10 b.Bristol 6-10-73
*Source:* Trainee.

| | | | | | |
|---|---|---|---|---|---|
| 1991–92 | Nottingham F | 0 | 0 | | |
| 1992–93 | Nottingham F | 0 | 0 | | |
| 1993–94 | Nottingham F | 1 | 0 | **1** | **0** |
| 1993–94 | *Wigan Ath* | 8 | 3 | | |
| 1994–95 | Wigan Ath | 35 | 5 | | |
| 1995–96 | Wigan Ath | 25 | 3 | | |
| 1996–97 | Wigan Ath | 35 | 8 | | |
| 1997–98 | Wigan Ath | 30 | 10 | | |
| 1998–99 | Wigan Ath | 23 | 0 | | |
| 1999–2000 | Wigan Ath | 21 | 1 | | |
| 2000–01 | Wigan Ath | 24 | 2 | | |
| 2001–02 | Wigan Ath | 20 | 0 | **221** | **32** |
| 2002–03 | Bury | 0 | 0 | | |

| | | | | | |
|---|---|---|---|---|---|
| 2002–03 | Scunthorpe U | 28 | 3 | | |
| 2003–04 | Scunthorpe U | 18 | 0 | **46** | **3** |

**MACLEAN, Steve (F) 45 23**
H: 5 10 W: 11 01 b.Edinburgh 23-8-82
*Honours:* Scotland Under-21.

| | | | | | |
|---|---|---|---|---|---|
| 2002–03 | Rangers | 3 | 0 | **3** | **0** |
| 2003–04 | Scunthorpe U | 42 | 23 | **42** | **23** |

**PARTON, Andy (F) 12 0**
H: 5 10 W: 12 00 b.Doncaster 29-9-83
*Source:* Scholar.

| | | | | | |
|---|---|---|---|---|---|
| 2001–02 | Scunthorpe U | 1 | 0 | | |
| 2002–03 | Scunthorpe U | 8 | 0 | | |
| 2003–04 | Scunthorpe U | 3 | 0 | **12** | **0** |

**RIDLEY, Lee (D) 35 1**
H: 5 9 W: 11 11 b.Scunthorpe 5-12-81
*Source:* Scholar.

| | | | | | |
|---|---|---|---|---|---|
| 2000–01 | Scunthorpe U | 2 | 0 | | |
| 2001–02 | Scunthorpe U | 4 | 0 | | |
| 2002–03 | Scunthorpe U | 11 | 0 | | |
| 2003–04 | Scunthorpe U | 18 | 1 | **35** | **1** |

**SHARP, Kevin (D) 289 12**
H: 5 9 W: 11 11 b.Ontario 19-9-74
*Source:* Auxerre. *Honours:* England Schools, Youth.

| | | | | | |
|---|---|---|---|---|---|
| 1992–93 | Leeds U | 4 | 0 | | |
| 1993–94 | Leeds U | 10 | 0 | | |
| 1994–95 | Leeds U | 2 | 0 | | |
| 1995–96 | Leeds U | 1 | 0 | **17** | **0** |
| 1995–96 | Wigan Ath | 20 | 6 | | |
| 1996–97 | Wigan Ath | 35 | 2 | | |
| 1997–98 | Wigan Ath | 38 | 0 | | |
| 1998–99 | Wigan Ath | 31 | 2 | | |
| 1999–2000 | Wigan Ath | 21 | 0 | | |
| 2000–01 | Wigan Ath | 31 | 0 | | |
| 2001–02 | Wigan Ath | 2 | 0 | **178** | **10** |
| 2001–02 | Wrexham | 15 | 0 | **15** | **0** |
| 2002–03 | Huddersfield T | 39 | 0 | **39** | **0** |
| 2003–04 | Scunthorpe U | 40 | 2 | **40** | **2** |

**SPARROW, Matt (M) 126 17**
H: 5 11 W: 10 10 b.London 3-10-81
*Source:* Scholarship.

| | | | | | |
|---|---|---|---|---|---|
| 1999–2000 | Scunthorpe U | 11 | 0 | | |
| 2000–01 | Scunthorpe U | 11 | 4 | | |
| 2001–02 | Scunthorpe U | 24 | 1 | | |
| 2002–03 | Scunthorpe U | 42 | 9 | | |
| 2003–04 | Scunthorpe U | 38 | 3 | **126** | **17** |

**STANTON, Nathan (D) 194 0**
H: 5 9 W: 12 06 b.Nottingham 6-5-81
*Source:* Trainee. *Honours:* England Youth.

| | | | | | |
|---|---|---|---|---|---|
| 1997–98 | Scunthorpe U | 1 | 0 | | |
| 1998–99 | Scunthorpe U | 4 | 0 | | |
| 1999–2000 | Scunthorpe U | 34 | 0 | | |
| 2000–01 | Scunthorpe U | 38 | 0 | | |
| 2001–02 | Scunthorpe U | 42 | 0 | | |
| 2002–03 | Scunthorpe U | 42 | 0 | | |
| 2003–04 | Scunthorpe U | 33 | 0 | **194** | **0** |

**TAYLOR, Cleveland (M) 23 3**
H: 5 8 W: 11 08 b.Leicester 9-9-83
*Source:* Scholar.

| | | | | | |
|---|---|---|---|---|---|
| 2001–02 | Bolton W | 0 | 0 | | |
| 2002–03 | Bolton W | 0 | 0 | | |
| 2002–03 | *Exeter C* | 3 | 0 | **3** | **0** |
| 2003–04 | Bolton W | 0 | 0 | | |
| 2003–04 | Scunthorpe U | 20 | 3 | **20** | **3** |

**TORPEY, Steve# (F) 506 125**
H: 6 3 W: 13 06 b.Islington 8-12-70
*Source:* Trainee.

| | | | | | |
|---|---|---|---|---|---|
| 1988–89 | Millwall | 0 | 0 | | |
| 1989–90 | Millwall | 7 | 0 | | |
| 1990–91 | Millwall | 0 | 0 | **7** | **0** |
| 1990–91 | Bradford C | 29 | 7 | | |
| 1991–92 | Bradford C | 43 | 10 | | |
| 1992–93 | Bradford C | 24 | 5 | **96** | **22** |
| 1993–94 | Swansea C | 40 | 9 | | |
| 1994–95 | Swansea C | 41 | 11 | | |
| 1995–96 | Swansea C | 42 | 15 | | |
| 1996–97 | Swansea C | 39 | 9 | **162** | **44** |
| 1997–98 | Bristol C | 29 | 8 | | |
| 1998–99 | Bristol C | 21 | 4 | | |
| 1998–99 | *Notts Co* | 6 | 1 | **6** | **1** |
| 1999–2000 | Bristol C | 20 | 1 | **70** | **13** |
| 1999–2000 | Scunthorpe U | 15 | 1 | | |
| 2000–01 | Scunthorpe U | 40 | 10 | | |
| 2001–02 | Scunthorpe U | 39 | 13 | | |
| 2002–03 | Scunthorpe U | 28 | 10 | | |
| 2003–04 | Scunthorpe U | 43 | 11 | **165** | **45** |

**WILLIAMS, Marcus§ (M) 1 0**
H: 5 8 W: 10 09 b.Doncaster 8-4-86
*Source:* Scholar.

| | | | | | |
|---|---|---|---|---|---|
| 2003–04 | Scunthorpe U | 1 | 0 | **1** | **0** |

**Scholars**
Brown, Andrew D; Capp, Adam; Ford, Jason A; Hunt, Jonathan M; Johnston Bradley D; Lillis, Joshua M; Morley, Craig C; Penn, Russell; Priestley, Adam; Ridout, Aaron J; Rose, Shane C; Smith, Robert James; Twibey, Dean K; Williams, Marcus V

**Non Contract**
Groves, Paul; Kell, Richard

## SHEFFIELD U (70)

**ALLISON, Wayne (F) 637 150**
H: 6 1 W: 15 07 b.Huddersfield 16-10-68
*Source:* Trainee.

| | | | | | |
|---|---|---|---|---|---|
| 1986–87 | Halifax T | 8 | 4 | | |
| 1987–88 | Halifax T | 35 | 4 | | |
| 1988–89 | Halifax T | 41 | 15 | **84** | **23** |
| 1989–90 | Watford | 7 | 0 | **7** | **0** |
| 1990–91 | Bristol C | 37 | 6 | | |
| 1991–92 | Bristol C | 43 | 10 | | |
| 1992–93 | Bristol C | 39 | 4 | | |
| 1993–94 | Bristol C | 39 | 15 | | |
| 1994–95 | Bristol C | 37 | 13 | **195** | **48** |
| 1995–96 | Swindon T | 44 | 17 | | |
| 1996–97 | Swindon T | 41 | 11 | | |
| 1997–98 | Swindon T | 16 | 3 | **101** | **31** |
| 1997–98 | Huddersfield T | 27 | 6 | | |
| 1998–99 | Huddersfield T | 44 | 9 | | |
| 1999–2000 | Huddersfield T | 3 | 0 | **74** | **15** |
| 1999–2000 | Tranmere R | 40 | 16 | | |
| 2000–01 | Tranmere R | 36 | 6 | | |
| 2001–02 | Tranmere R | 27 | 4 | **103** | **26** |
| 2002–03 | Sheffield U | 34 | 6 | | |
| 2003–04 | Sheffield U | 39 | 1 | **73** | **7** |

**ARMSTRONG, Chris (D) 110 3**
H: 5 9 W: 11 00 b.Newcastle 5-8-82
*Source:* Scholar. *Honours:* England Under-20.

| | | | | | |
|---|---|---|---|---|---|
| 2000–01 | Bury | 22 | 1 | | |
| 2001–02 | Bury | 11 | 0 | **33** | **1** |
| 2001–02 | Oldham Ath | 32 | 0 | | |
| 2002–03 | Oldham Ath | 33 | 1 | **65** | **1** |
| 2003–04 | Sheffield U | 12 | 1 | **12** | **1** |

**BAXTER, Lee† (G) 1 0**
H: 6 1 W: 13 06 b.Helsingborg 17-7-76
*Source:* Malmo.

| | | | | | |
|---|---|---|---|---|---|
| 2003–04 | Sheffield U | 1 | 0 | **1** | **0** |

**BOUSSATTA, Dries‡ (M) 6 0**
H: 5 8 W: 10 06 b.Amsterdam 23-12-72
*Source:* Excelsior. *Honours:* Holland 3 full caps.

| | | | | | |
|---|---|---|---|---|---|
| 2001–02 | Sheffield U | 0 | 0 | | |
| 2002–03 | Sheffield U | 0 | 0 | | |
| 2003–04 | Sheffield U | 6 | 0 | **6** | **0** |

**BRITTON, Andrew (G) 0 0**
H: 6 1 W: 13 07 b.California 26-5-85

| | | | | | |
|---|---|---|---|---|---|
| 2003–04 | Sheffield U | 0 | 0 | | |

**CRYAN, Colin* (D) 5 0**
H: 5 11 W: 13 00 b.Kildare 23-3-81
*Source:* Scholar. *Honours:* Eire Under-21.

| | | | | | |
|---|---|---|---|---|---|
| 1999–2000 | Sheffield U | 0 | 0 | | |
| 2000–01 | Sheffield U | 1 | 0 | | |
| 2001–02 | Sheffield U | 1 | 0 | | |
| 2002–03 | Sheffield U | 2 | 0 | | |
| 2003–04 | Sheffield U | 1 | 0 | **5** | **0** |

**FORTE, Jonathan (M) 7 0**
H: 6 0 W: 12 02 b.Sheffield 25-7-86
*Source:* Scholar. *Honours:* England Youth.

| | | | | | |
|---|---|---|---|---|---|
| 2003–04 | Sheffield U | 7 | 0 | **7** | **0** |

**FRANCIS, Simon (D) 60 1**
H: 6 0 W: 12 06 b.Nottingham 16-2-85
*Source:* Scholar. *Honours:* England Youth.

| | | | | | |
|---|---|---|---|---|---|
| 2002–03 | Bradford C | 25 | 1 | | |
| 2003–04 | Bradford C | 30 | 0 | **55** | **1** |
| 2003–04 | Sheffield U | 5 | 0 | **5** | **0** |

**GRAY, Andy (M) 192 31**
H: 6 2 W: 13 00 b.Harrogate 15-11-77
*Source:* Trainee. *Honours:* Scotland Youth, 2 full caps.

| | | | | | |
|---|---|---|---|---|---|
| 1995–96 | Leeds U | 15 | 0 | | |
| 1996–97 | Leeds U | 7 | 0 | | |
| 1997–98 | Leeds U | 0 | 0 | | |
| 1997–98 | *Bury* | 6 | 1 | **6** | **1** |
| 1998–99 | Leeds U | 0 | 0 | **22** | **0** |
| 1998–99 | Nottingham F | 8 | 0 | | |
| 1998–99 | *Preston NE* | 5 | 0 | **5** | **0** |
| 1998–99 | *Oldham Ath* | 4 | 0 | **4** | **0** |
| 1999–2000 | Nottingham F | 22 | 0 | | |
| 2000–01 | Nottingham F | 18 | 0 | | |
| 2001–02 | Nottingham F | 16 | 1 | **64** | **1** |
| 2002–03 | Bradford C | 44 | 15 | | |
| 2003–04 | Bradford C | 33 | 5 | **77** | **20** |
| 2003–04 | Sheffield U | 14 | 9 | **14** | **9** |

**ILIC, Sasa* (G) 84 0**
H: 6 4 W: 14 12 b.Melbourne 18-7-72
*Source:* Partizan Belgrade, Radnicki, Ringwood, Daewoo Royals, St Leonards Stamcroft. *Honours:* Yugoslavia 1 full cap.

| | | | | | |
|---|---|---|---|---|---|
| 1997–98 | Charlton Ath | 14 | 0 | | |
| 1998–99 | Charlton Ath | 23 | 0 | | |
| 1999–2000 | Charlton Ath | 1 | 0 | | |
| 1999–2000 | *West Ham U* | 1 | 0 | **1** | **0** |
| 2000–01 | Charlton Ath | 13 | 0 | | |
| 2001–02 | Charlton Ath | 0 | 0 | **51** | **0** |
| 2001–02 | *Portsmouth* | 7 | 0 | | |
| 2002–03 | Portsmouth | 0 | 0 | **7** | **0** |
| 2003–04 | Barnsley | 25 | 0 | **25** | **0** |
| 2003–04 | Sheffield U | 0 | 0 | | |

**JAGIELKA, Phil (M) 124 6**
H: 5 11 W: 13 05 b.Manchester 17-8-82
*Source:* Scholar. *Honours:* England Youth, Under-20, Under-21.

| | | | | | |
|---|---|---|---|---|---|
| 1999–2000 | Sheffield U | 1 | 0 | | |
| 2000–01 | Sheffield U | 15 | 0 | | |
| 2001–02 | Sheffield U | 23 | 3 | | |
| 2002–03 | Sheffield U | 42 | 0 | | |
| 2003–04 | Sheffield U | 43 | 3 | **124** | **6** |

**JAGIELKA, Steve* (F) 165 17**
H: 5 8 W: 11 03 b.Manchester 10-3-78
*Source:* Trainee.

| | | | | | |
|---|---|---|---|---|---|
| 1996–97 | Stoke C | 0 | 0 | | |
| 1997–98 | Shrewsbury T | 16 | 1 | | |
| 1998–99 | Shrewsbury T | 31 | 1 | | |
| 1999–2000 | Shrewsbury T | 33 | 1 | | |
| 2000–01 | Shrewsbury T | 31 | 6 | | |
| 2001–02 | Shrewsbury T | 31 | 5 | | |
| 2002–03 | Shrewsbury T | 23 | 3 | | |
| 2003–04 | Shrewsbury T | 0 | 0 | **165** | **17** |
| 2003–04 | Sheffield U | 0 | 0 | | |

**JAVARY, Jean-Philippe‡ (M) 44 1**
H: 6 0 W: 12 07 b.Montpellier 10-1-78

| | | | | | |
|---|---|---|---|---|---|
| 1995–96 | Montpellier | 3 | 0 | | |
| 1996–97 | Montpellier | 7 | 0 | | |
| 1997–98 | Montpellier | 0 | 0 | **10** | **0** |
| 1998–99 | Espanyol | 0 | 0 | | |
| 1999–2000 | Raith R | 11 | 0 | **11** | **0** |
| 2000–01 | Brentford | 6 | 0 | **6** | **0** |
| 2000–01 | Plymouth Arg | 4 | 0 | | |
| 2001–02 | Plymouth Arg | 0 | 0 | **4** | **0** |
| 2001–02 | Sheffield U | 7 | 1 | | |
| 2002–03 | Sheffield U | 6 | 0 | | |
| 2003–04 | Sheffield U | 0 | 0 | **13** | **1** |

**KABBA, Steven (F) 52 14**
H: 5 10 W: 11 12 b.Lambeth 7-3-81
*Source:* Trainee.

| | | | | | |
|---|---|---|---|---|---|
| 1999–2000 | Crystal Palace | 1 | 0 | | |
| 2000–01 | Crystal Palace | 1 | 0 | | |
| 2001–02 | Crystal Palace | 4 | 0 | | |
| 2001–02 | *Luton T* | 3 | 0 | **3** | **0** |
| 2002–03 | Crystal Palace | 4 | 1 | **10** | **1** |
| 2002–03 | *Grimsby T* | 13 | 6 | **13** | **6** |
| 2002–03 | Sheffield U | 25 | 7 | | |
| 2003–04 | Sheffield U | 1 | 0 | **26** | **7** |

**KENNY, Paddy (G) 205 0**
H: 6 0 W: 15 00 b.Halifax 17-5-78
*Source:* Bradford PA. *Honours:* Eire 2 full caps.

| | | | | | |
|---|---|---|---|---|---|
| 1998–99 | Bury | 0 | 0 | | |
| 1999–2000 | Bury | 46 | 0 | | |
| 2000–01 | Bury | 46 | 0 | | |
| 2001–02 | Bury | 41 | 0 | | |

| | | | | | |
|---|---|---|---|---|---|
| 2002–03 | Bury | 0 | 0 | **133** | **0** |
| 2002–03 | Sheffield U | 45 | 0 | | |
| 2003–04 | Sheffield U | 27 | 0 | **72** | **0** |

**KOZLUK, Rob (D)** **188 2**
H: 5 8 W: 11 08 b.Sutton-in-Ashfield 5-7-77
*Source:* Trainee. *Honours:* England Under-21.

| | | | | | |
|---|---|---|---|---|---|
| 1995–96 | Derby Co | 0 | 0 | | |
| 1996–97 | Derby Co | 0 | 0 | | |
| 1997–98 | Derby Co | 9 | 0 | | |
| 1998–99 | Derby Co | 7 | 0 | **16** | **0** |
| 1998–99 | Sheffield U | 10 | 0 | | |
| 1999–2000 | Sheffield U | 39 | 0 | | |
| 2000–01 | Sheffield U | 27 | 0 | | |
| 2000–01 | *Huddersfield T* | 14 | 0 | **14** | **0** |
| 2001–02 | Sheffield U | 8 | 0 | | |
| 2002–03 | Sheffield U | 32 | 1 | | |
| 2003–04 | Sheffield U | 42 | 1 | **158** | **2** |

**LESTER, Jack (F)** **275 51**
H: 5 11 W: 11 00 b.Sheffield 8-10-75
*Source:* Trainee. *Honours:* England Schools.

| | | | | | |
|---|---|---|---|---|---|
| 1994–95 | Grimsby T | 7 | 0 | | |
| 1995–96 | Grimsby T | 5 | 0 | | |
| 1996–97 | Grimsby T | 22 | 5 | | |
| 1996–97 | *Doncaster R* | 11 | 1 | **11** | **1** |
| 1997–98 | Grimsby T | 40 | 4 | | |
| 1998–99 | Grimsby T | 33 | 4 | | |
| 1999–2000 | Grimsby T | 26 | 4 | **133** | **17** |
| 1999–2000 | Nottingham F | 15 | 2 | | |
| 2000–01 | Nottingham F | 19 | 7 | | |
| 2001–02 | Nottingham F | 32 | 5 | | |
| 2002–03 | Nottingham F | 33 | 7 | **99** | **21** |
| 2003–04 | Sheffield U | 32 | 12 | **32** | **12** |

**McCALL, Stuart (M)** **763 67**
H: 5 8 W: 10 02 b.Leeds 10-6-64
*Source:* Apprentice. *Honours:* Scotland Under-21, 40 full caps, 1 goal.

| | | | | | |
|---|---|---|---|---|---|
| 1982–83 | Bradford C | 28 | 4 | | |
| 1983–84 | Bradford C | 46 | 5 | | |
| 1984–85 | Bradford C | 46 | 8 | | |
| 1985–86 | Bradford C | 38 | 4 | | |
| 1986–87 | Bradford C | 36 | 7 | | |
| 1987–88 | Bradford C | 44 | 9 | | |
| 1988–89 | Everton | 33 | 0 | | |
| 1989–90 | Everton | 37 | 3 | | |
| 1990–91 | Everton | 33 | 3 | **103** | **6** |
| 1991–92 | Rangers | 36 | 1 | | |
| 1992–93 | Rangers | 36 | 5 | | |
| 1993–94 | Rangers | 34 | 3 | | |
| 1994–95 | Rangers | 30 | 2 | | |
| 1995–96 | Rangers | 21 | 3 | | |
| 1996–97 | Rangers | 7 | 0 | | |
| 1997–98 | Rangers | 30 | 0 | **194** | **14** |
| 1998–99 | Bradford C | 43 | 3 | | |
| 1999–2000 | Bradford C | 34 | 1 | | |
| 2000–01 | Bradford C | 37 | 1 | | |
| 2001–02 | Bradford C | 43 | 3 | **395** | **45** |
| 2002–03 | Sheffield U | 34 | 0 | | |
| 2003–04 | Sheffield U | 37 | 2 | **71** | **2** |

**MONTGOMERY, Nick (M)** **117 5**
H: 5 9 W: 12 06 b.Leeds 28-10-81
*Source:* Scholar. *Honours:* Scotland Under-21.

| | | | | | |
|---|---|---|---|---|---|
| 2000–01 | Sheffield U | 27 | 0 | | |
| 2001–02 | Sheffield U | 31 | 2 | | |
| 2002–03 | Sheffield U | 23 | 0 | | |
| 2003–04 | Sheffield U | 36 | 3 | **117** | **5** |

**MORGAN, Chris (M)** **217 8**
H: 6 1 W: 12 09 b.Barnsley 9-11-77
*Source:* Trainee.

| | | | | | |
|---|---|---|---|---|---|
| 1996–97 | Barnsley | 0 | 0 | | |
| 1997–98 | Barnsley | 11 | 0 | | |
| 1998–99 | Barnsley | 19 | 0 | | |
| 1999–2000 | Barnsley | 37 | 0 | | |
| 2000–01 | Barnsley | 40 | 1 | | |
| 2001–02 | Barnsley | 42 | 4 | | |
| 2002–03 | Barnsley | 36 | 2 | **185** | **7** |
| 2003–04 | Sheffield U | 32 | 1 | **32** | **1** |

**NDLOVU, Peter (F)** **425 88**
H: 5 7 W: 10 02 b.Bulawayo 25-2-73
*Source:* Highlanders. *Honours:* Zimbabwe full caps.

| | | | | | |
|---|---|---|---|---|---|
| 1991–92 | Coventry C | 23 | 2 | | |
| 1992–93 | Coventry C | 32 | 7 | | |
| 1993–94 | Coventry C | 40 | 11 | | |
| 1994–95 | Coventry C | 30 | 11 | | |
| 1995–96 | Coventry C | 32 | 5 | | |
| 1996–97 | Coventry C | 20 | 1 | **177** | **37** |
| 1997–98 | Birmingham C | 39 | 9 | | |
| 1998–99 | Birmingham C | 43 | 10 | | |
| 1999–2000 | Birmingham C | 13 | 1 | | |
| 2000–01 | Birmingham C | 12 | 2 | **107** | **22** |
| 2000–01 | *Huddersfield T* | 6 | 4 | **6** | **4** |
| 2000–01 | Sheffield U | 15 | 4 | | |
| 2001–02 | Sheffield U | 45 | 4 | | |
| 2002–03 | Sheffield U | 39 | 8 | | |
| 2003–04 | Sheffield U | 36 | 9 | **135** | **25** |

**PAGE, Robert (D)** **323 3**
H: 5 11 W: 13 12 b.Tylorstown 3-9-74
*Source:* Trainee. *Honours:* Wales Schools, Youth, Under-21, B, 33 full caps.

| | | | | | |
|---|---|---|---|---|---|
| 1992–93 | Watford | 0 | 0 | | |
| 1993–94 | Watford | 4 | 0 | | |
| 1994–95 | Watford | 5 | 0 | | |
| 1995–96 | Watford | 19 | 0 | | |
| 1996–97 | Watford | 36 | 0 | | |
| 1997–98 | Watford | 41 | 0 | | |
| 1998–99 | Watford | 39 | 0 | | |
| 1999–2000 | Watford | 36 | 1 | | |
| 2000–01 | Watford | 36 | 1 | | |
| 2001–02 | Watford | 0 | 0 | **216** | **2** |
| 2001–02 | Sheffield U | 43 | 0 | | |
| 2002–03 | Sheffield U | 34 | 0 | | |
| 2003–04 | Sheffield U | 30 | 1 | **107** | **1** |

**PARKINSON, Andy (F)** **185 21**
H: 5 8 W: 10 12 b.Liverpool 27-5-79
*Source:* Liverpool Trainee.

| | | | | | |
|---|---|---|---|---|---|
| 1996–97 | Tranmere R | 0 | 0 | | |
| 1997–98 | Tranmere R | 18 | 1 | | |
| 1998–99 | Tranmere R | 29 | 2 | | |
| 1999–2000 | Tranmere R | 37 | 7 | | |
| 2000–01 | Tranmere R | 39 | 6 | | |
| 2001–02 | Tranmere R | 31 | 2 | | |
| 2002–03 | Tranmere R | 10 | 0 | **164** | **18** |
| 2003–04 | Sheffield U | 7 | 0 | **7** | **0** |
| 2003–04 | *Notts Co* | 14 | 3 | **14** | **3** |

**RANKINE, Mark* (M)** **548 33**
H: 5 10 W: 11 01 b.Doncaster 30-9-69
*Source:* Trainee.

| | | | | | |
|---|---|---|---|---|---|
| 1987–88 | Doncaster R | 18 | 2 | | |
| 1988–89 | Doncaster R | 46 | 11 | | |
| 1989–90 | Doncaster R | 36 | 2 | | |
| 1990–91 | Doncaster R | 40 | 2 | | |
| 1991–92 | Doncaster R | 24 | 3 | **164** | **20** |
| 1991–92 | Wolverhampton W | 15 | 1 | | |
| 1992–93 | Wolverhampton W | 27 | 0 | | |
| 1993–94 | Wolverhampton W | 31 | 0 | | |
| 1994–95 | Wolverhampton W | 27 | 0 | | |
| 1995–96 | Wolverhampton W | 32 | 0 | | |
| 1996–97 | Wolverhampton W | 0 | 0 | **132** | **1** |
| 1996–97 | Preston NE | 23 | 0 | | |
| 1997–98 | Preston NE | 35 | 1 | | |
| 1998–99 | Preston NE | 42 | 3 | | |
| 1999–2000 | Preston NE | 44 | 0 | | |
| 2000–01 | Preston NE | 44 | 4 | | |
| 2001–02 | Preston NE | 26 | 4 | | |
| 2002–03 | Preston NE | 19 | 0 | **233** | **12** |
| 2002–03 | *Sheffield U* | 6 | 0 | | |
| 2003–04 | Sheffield U | 13 | 0 | **19** | **0** |

**ROGERS, Kristian* (G)** **40 0**
H: 6 0 W: 11 12 b.Chester 2-10-80
*Honours:* England Schools.

| | | | | | |
|---|---|---|---|---|---|
| 1999–2000 | Wrexham | 1 | 0 | | |
| 2000–01 | Wrexham | 5 | 0 | | |
| 2001–02 | Wrexham | 27 | 0 | | |
| 2002–03 | Wrexham | 7 | 0 | **40** | **0** |
| 2003–04 | Sheffield U | 0 | 0 | | |
| 2003–04 | *Macclesfield T* | 0 | 0 | | |

**SCOTT, Ben‡ (G)** **0 0**
H: 6 0 W: 12 04 b.Doncaster 16-11-83
*Source:* Schoolboy.

| | | | | | |
|---|---|---|---|---|---|
| 2001–02 | Sheffield U | 0 | 0 | | |
| 2002–03 | Sheffield U | 0 | 0 | | |
| 2003–04 | Sheffield U | 0 | 0 | | |

**SESTANOVICH, Ashley (M)** **2 0**
H: 6 3 W: 13 00 b.London 18-9-81
*Source:* Hampton & Richmond B.

| | | | | | |
|---|---|---|---|---|---|
| 2002–03 | Sheffield U | 0 | 0 | | |
| 2003–04 | Sheffield U | 2 | 0 | **2** | **0** |

**SHAW, Paul (F)** **296 64**
H: 5 11 W: 13 03 b.Burnham 4-9-73
*Source:* Trainee.

| | | | | | |
|---|---|---|---|---|---|
| 1991–92 | Arsenal | 0 | 0 | | |
| 1992–93 | Arsenal | 0 | 0 | | |
| 1993–94 | Arsenal | 0 | 0 | | |
| 1994–95 | Arsenal | 1 | 0 | | |
| 1994–95 | *Burnley* | 9 | 4 | **9** | **4** |
| 1995–96 | Arsenal | 3 | 0 | | |
| 1995–96 | *Cardiff C* | 6 | 0 | **6** | **0** |
| 1995–96 | *Peterborough U* | 12 | 5 | **12** | **5** |
| 1996–97 | Arsenal | 8 | 2 | | |
| 1997–98 | Arsenal | 0 | 0 | **12** | **2** |
| 1997–98 | Millwall | 40 | 11 | | |
| 1998–99 | Millwall | 34 | 10 | | |
| 1999–2000 | Millwall | 35 | 5 | **109** | **26** |
| 2000–01 | Gillingham | 33 | 1 | | |
| 2001–02 | Gillingham | 37 | 7 | | |
| 2002–03 | Gillingham | 44 | 12 | | |
| 2003–04 | Gillingham | 21 | 6 | **135** | **26** |
| 2003–04 | Sheffield U | 13 | 1 | **13** | **1** |

**TANSLEY, Anthony‡ (M)** **0 0**
H: 5 11 W: 12 00 b.Derby 17-1-84
*Source:* Scholar.

| | | | | | |
|---|---|---|---|---|---|
| 2002–03 | Sheffield U | 0 | 0 | | |
| 2003–04 | Sheffield U | 0 | 0 | | |

**TEN HEUVEL, Laurens‡ (F)** **24 0**
H: 6 2 W: 12 03 b.Duivendrecht 6-6-76
*Source:* Den Bosch.

| | | | | | |
|---|---|---|---|---|---|
| 1995–96 | Den Bosch | 3 | 0 | **3** | **0** |
| 1995–96 | Barnsley | 2 | 0 | | |
| 1996–97 | Barnsley | 3 | 0 | | |
| 1997–98 | Barnsley | 2 | 0 | **7** | **0** |
| 1997–98 | *Northampton T* | 0 | 0 | | |

From First Vienna, DCG.

| | | | | | |
|---|---|---|---|---|---|
| 2001–02 | Telstar | 0 | 0 | | |
| 2002–03 | Sheffield U | 5 | 0 | | |
| 2002–03 | *Bradford C* | 5 | 0 | **5** | **0** |
| 2003–04 | Sheffield U | 0 | 0 | **5** | **0** |
| 2003–04 | *Grimsby T* | 4 | 0 | **4** | **0** |

**TONGE, Michael (M)** **122 13**
H: 6 0 W: 13 02 b.Manchester 7-4-83
*Source:* Scholar. *Honours:* England Under-20, Under-21.

| | | | | | |
|---|---|---|---|---|---|
| 2000–01 | Sheffield U | 2 | 0 | | |
| 2001–02 | Sheffield U | 30 | 3 | | |
| 2002–03 | Sheffield U | 44 | 6 | | |
| 2003–04 | Sheffield U | 46 | 4 | **122** | **13** |

**WARD, Ashley (F)** **378 109**
H: 6 1 W: 11 07 b.Manchester 24-11-70
*Source:* Trainee.

| | | | | | |
|---|---|---|---|---|---|
| 1989–90 | Manchester C | 1 | 0 | | |
| 1990–91 | Manchester C | 0 | 0 | **1** | **0** |
| 1990–91 | *Wrexham* | 4 | 2 | **4** | **2** |
| 1991–92 | Leicester C | 10 | 0 | | |
| 1992–93 | Leicester C | 0 | 0 | **10** | **0** |
| 1992–93 | *Blackpool* | 2 | 1 | **2** | **1** |
| 1992–93 | Crewe Alex | 20 | 4 | | |
| 1993–94 | Crewe Alex | 25 | 13 | | |
| 1994–95 | Crewe Alex | 16 | 8 | **61** | **25** |
| 1994–95 | Norwich C | 25 | 8 | | |
| 1995–96 | Norwich C | 28 | 10 | **53** | **18** |
| 1995–96 | Derby Co | 7 | 1 | | |
| 1996–97 | Derby Co | 30 | 8 | | |
| 1997–98 | Derby Co | 3 | 0 | **40** | **9** |
| 1997–98 | Barnsley | 29 | 8 | | |
| 1998–99 | Barnsley | 17 | 12 | **46** | **20** |
| 1998–99 | Blackburn R | 17 | 5 | | |
| 1999–2000 | Blackburn R | 37 | 8 | **54** | **13** |
| 2000–01 | Bradford C | 33 | 4 | | |
| 2001–02 | Bradford C | 27 | 10 | | |
| 2002–03 | Bradford C | 24 | 3 | **84** | **17** |
| 2003–04 | Sheffield U | 23 | 4 | **23** | **4** |

**WHITLOW, Mike* (D)** **373 15**
H: 6 0 W: 12 13 b.Northwich 13-1-68
*Source:* Witton Alb.

| | | | | | |
|---|---|---|---|---|---|
| 1988–89 | Leeds U | 20 | 1 | | |
| 1989–90 | Leeds U | 29 | 1 | | |
| 1990–91 | Leeds U | 18 | 1 | | |
| 1991–92 | Leeds U | 10 | 1 | **77** | **4** |
| 1991–92 | Leicester C | 5 | 0 | | |
| 1992–93 | Leicester C | 24 | 1 | | |
| 1993–94 | Leicester C | 31 | 2 | | |
| 1994–95 | Leicester C | 28 | 2 | | |
| 1995–96 | Leicester C | 42 | 3 | | |
| 1996–97 | Leicester C | 17 | 0 | | |
| 1997–98 | Leicester C | 0 | 0 | **147** | **8** |
| 1997–98 | Bolton W | 13 | 0 | | |
| 1998–99 | Bolton W | 28 | 0 | | |
| 1999–2000 | Bolton W | 37 | 1 | | |

| | | | | | |
|---|---|---|---|---|---|
| 2000–01 | Bolton W | 8 | 1 | | |
| 2001–02 | Bolton W | 29 | 0 | | |
| 2002–03 | Bolton W | 17 | 0 | **132** | **2** |
| 2003–04 | Sheffield U | 17 | 1 | **17** | **1** |

**WOOD, Danny* (M)** **0** **0**
H: 5 8 W: 10 12 b.Sheffield 17-2-84
*Source:* Scholar.

| | | | | | |
|---|---|---|---|---|---|
| 2003–04 | Sheffield U | 0 | 0 | | |

**WRIGHT, Alan (D)** **455** **7**
H: 5 4 W: 9 09 b.Ashton-under-Lyme 28-9-71
*Source:* Trainee. *Honours:* England Schools, Youth, Under-21.

| | | | | | |
|---|---|---|---|---|---|
| 1987–88 | Blackpool | 1 | 0 | | |
| 1988–89 | Blackpool | 16 | 0 | | |
| 1989–90 | Blackpool | 24 | 0 | | |
| 1990–91 | Blackpool | 45 | 0 | | |
| 1991–92 | Blackpool | 12 | 0 | **98** | **0** |
| 1991–92 | Blackburn R | 33 | 1 | | |
| 1992–93 | Blackburn R | 24 | 0 | | |
| 1993–94 | Blackburn R | 12 | 0 | | |
| 1994–95 | Blackburn R | 5 | 0 | **74** | **1** |
| 1994–95 | Aston Villa | 8 | 0 | | |
| 1995–96 | Aston Villa | 38 | 2 | | |
| 1996–97 | Aston Villa | 38 | 1 | | |
| 1997–98 | Aston Villa | 37 | 0 | | |
| 1998–99 | Aston Villa | 38 | 0 | | |
| 1999–2000 | Aston Villa | 32 | 1 | | |
| 2000–01 | Aston Villa | 36 | 1 | | |
| 2001–02 | Aston Villa | 23 | 0 | | |
| 2002–03 | Aston Villa | 10 | 0 | **260** | **5** |
| 2003–04 | Middlesbrough | 2 | 0 | **2** | **0** |
| 2003–04 | Sheffield U | 21 | 1 | **21** | **1** |

**Scholars**
Ashmore, James C; Beanes, Rory; Binnion, Travis; Coupe, Christopher C; Ellis, Nicky; Forte, Jonathan R J; Gyaki, Ryan; Harper, Adrian; Hill, Benjamin F; Horwood, Evan D; Lindley, Thomas; Marrison, Colin I; McGuinness, Craig; Platel, Daniel; Robertson, Christopher; Roma, Dominic M; Ross, Ian; Sharp, Billy L; Speight, Jake C; Starosta, Ben M

**Non Contract**
Baxter, Lee S

## SHEFFIELD W (71)

**ARMSTRONG, Craig (M)** **234** **7**
H: 5 11 W: 12 09 b.South Shields 23-5-75
*Source:* Trainee.

| | | | | | |
|---|---|---|---|---|---|
| 1992–93 | Nottingham F | 0 | 0 | | |
| 1993–94 | Nottingham F | 0 | 0 | | |
| 1994–95 | Nottingham F | 0 | 0 | | |
| 1994–95 | *Burnley* | 4 | 0 | **4** | **0** |
| 1995–96 | Nottingham F | 0 | 0 | | |
| 1995–96 | *Bristol R* | 14 | 0 | **14** | **0** |
| 1996–97 | Nottingham F | 0 | 0 | | |
| 1996–97 | *Gillingham* | 10 | 0 | **10** | **0** |
| 1996–97 | *Watford* | 15 | 0 | **15** | **0** |
| 1997–98 | Nottingham F | 18 | 0 | | |
| 1998–99 | Nottingham F | 22 | 0 | **40** | **0** |
| 1998–99 | Huddersfield T | 13 | 1 | | |
| 1999–2000 | Huddersfield T | 39 | 0 | | |
| 2000–01 | Huddersfield T | 44 | 3 | | |
| 2001–02 | Huddersfield T | 11 | 1 | **107** | **5** |
| 2001–02 | Sheffield W | 8 | 0 | | |
| 2002–03 | Sheffield W | 17 | 1 | | |
| 2003–04 | Sheffield W | 10 | 0 | **35** | **1** |
| 2003–04 | *Grimsby T* | 9 | 1 | **9** | **1** |

**BARRY-MURPHY, Brian* (D)** **174** **3**
H: 6 1 W: 13 01 b.Cork 27-7-78
*Honours:* Eire Under-21.

| | | | | | |
|---|---|---|---|---|---|
| 1995–96 | Cork City | 13 | 0 | | |
| 1996–97 | Cork City | 25 | 0 | | |
| 1997–98 | Cork City | 15 | 1 | | |
| 1998–99 | Cork City | 27 | 1 | **80** | **2** |
| 1999–2000 | Preston NE | 1 | 0 | | |
| 2000–01 | Preston NE | 14 | 0 | | |
| 2001–02 | Preston NE | 4 | 0 | | |
| 2001–02 | *Southend U* | 8 | 1 | **8** | **1** |
| 2002–03 | Preston NE | 2 | 0 | **21** | **0** |
| 2002–03 | *Hartlepool U* | 7 | 0 | **7** | **0** |
| 2002–03 | Sheffield W | 17 | 0 | | |
| 2003–04 | Sheffield W | 41 | 0 | **58** | **0** |

**BESWETHERICK, John* (D)** **164** **0**
H: 6 0 W: 12 07 b.Liverpool 15-1-78
*Source:* Trainee.

| | | | | | |
|---|---|---|---|---|---|
| 1996–97 | Plymouth Arg | 0 | 0 | | |
| 1997–98 | Plymouth Arg | 2 | 0 | | |
| 1998–99 | Plymouth Arg | 22 | 0 | | |
| 1999–2000 | Plymouth Arg | 45 | 0 | | |
| 2000–01 | Plymouth Arg | 45 | 0 | | |
| 2001–02 | Plymouth Arg | 32 | 0 | **146** | **0** |
| 2002–03 | Sheffield W | 6 | 0 | | |
| 2002–03 | *Swindon T* | 3 | 0 | **3** | **0** |
| 2003–04 | Sheffield W | 5 | 0 | **11** | **0** |
| 2003–04 | *Macclesfield T* | 4 | 0 | **4** | **0** |

**BROMBY, Leigh* (D)** **115** **3**
H: 6 2 W: 12 07 b.Dewsbury 2-6-80
*Honours:* England Schools.

| | | | | | |
|---|---|---|---|---|---|
| 1998–99 | Sheffield W | 0 | 0 | | |
| 1999–2000 | Sheffield W | 0 | 0 | | |
| 1999–2000 | *Mansfield T* | 10 | 1 | **10** | **1** |
| 2000–01 | Sheffield W | 18 | 0 | | |
| 2001–02 | Sheffield W | 26 | 1 | | |
| 2002–03 | Sheffield W | 27 | 0 | | |
| 2002–03 | *Norwich C* | 5 | 0 | **5** | **0** |
| 2003–04 | Sheffield W | 29 | 1 | **100** | **2** |

**BRUNT, Chris (M)** **9** **2**
H: 6 1 W: 12 13 b.Belfast 14-12-84
*Source:* Trainee. *Honours:* Northern Ireland Under-23.

| | | | | | |
|---|---|---|---|---|---|
| 2002–03 | Middlesbrough | 0 | 0 | | |
| 2003–04 | Middlesbrough | 0 | 0 | | |
| 2003–04 | Sheffield W | 9 | 2 | **9** | **2** |

**CARR, Chris (D)** **2** **0**
H: 5 11 W: 12 06 b.Newcastle 14-12-84
*Source:* Trainee.

| | | | | | |
|---|---|---|---|---|---|
| 2003–04 | Newcastle U | 0 | 0 | | |
| 2003–04 | Sheffield W | 2 | 0 | **2** | **0** |

**COOKE, Terry* (M)** **136** **12**
H: 5 7 W: 10 12 b.Marston Green 5-8-76
*Source:* Trainee. *Honours:* England Youth, Under-21.

| | | | | | |
|---|---|---|---|---|---|
| 1994–95 | Manchester U | 0 | 0 | | |
| 1995–96 | Manchester U | 4 | 0 | | |
| 1995–96 | *Sunderland* | 6 | 0 | **6** | **0** |
| 1996–97 | Manchester U | 0 | 0 | | |
| 1996–97 | *Birmingham C* | 4 | 0 | **4** | **0** |
| 1997–98 | Manchester U | 0 | 0 | | |
| 1998–99 | Manchester U | 0 | 0 | **4** | **0** |
| 1998–99 | *Wrexham* | 10 | 0 | **10** | **0** |
| 1998–99 | Manchester C | 21 | 7 | | |
| 1999–2000 | Manchester C | 13 | 0 | | |
| 1999–2000 | *Wigan Ath* | 10 | 1 | **10** | **1** |
| 2000–01 | Manchester C | 0 | 0 | | |
| 2000–01 | *Sheffield W* | 17 | 1 | | |
| 2001–02 | Manchester C | 0 | 0 | **34** | **7** |
| 2001–02 | Grimsby T | 3 | 1 | | |
| 2002–03 | Grimsby T | 25 | 0 | **28** | **1** |
| 2003–04 | Sheffield W | 23 | 2 | **40** | **3** |

**EVANS, Richard (M)** **10** **1**
H: 5 10 W: 12 09 b.Cardiff 19-6-83
*Source:* Scholar.

| | | | | | |
|---|---|---|---|---|---|
| 2002–03 | Birmingham C | 0 | 0 | | |
| 2002–03 | Sheffield W | 4 | 1 | | |
| 2003–04 | Sheffield W | 6 | 0 | **10** | **1** |

**GEARY, Derek* (D)** **104** **0**
H: 5 6 W: 11 00 b.Dublin 19-6-80

| | | | | | |
|---|---|---|---|---|---|
| 1997–98 | Sheffield W | 0 | 0 | | |
| 1998–99 | Sheffield W | 0 | 0 | | |
| 1999–2000 | Sheffield W | 0 | 0 | | |
| 2000–01 | Sheffield W | 5 | 0 | | |
| 2001–02 | Sheffield W | 32 | 0 | | |
| 2002–03 | Sheffield W | 26 | 0 | | |
| 2003–04 | Sheffield W | 41 | 0 | **104** | **0** |

**HAMSHAW, Matthew (M)** **54** **1**
H: 5 9 W: 12 08 b.Rotherham 1-1-82
*Source:* Trainee. *Honours:* England Youth, Under-20.

| | | | | | |
|---|---|---|---|---|---|
| 1998–99 | Sheffield W | 0 | 0 | | |
| 1999–2000 | Sheffield W | 0 | 0 | | |
| 2000–01 | Sheffield W | 18 | 0 | | |
| 2001–02 | Sheffield W | 21 | 0 | | |
| 2002–03 | Sheffield W | 15 | 1 | | |
| 2003–04 | Sheffield W | 0 | 0 | **54** | **1** |

**HASLAM, Steven* (D)** **144** **2**
H: 5 11 W: 11 08 b.Sheffield 6-9-79
*Source:* Trainee. *Honours:* England Schools, Youth.

| | | | | | |
|---|---|---|---|---|---|
| 1996–97 | Sheffield W | 0 | 0 | | |
| 1997–98 | Sheffield W | 0 | 0 | | |
| 1998–99 | Sheffield W | 2 | 0 | | |
| 1999–2000 | Sheffield W | 23 | 0 | | |
| 2000–01 | Sheffield W | 27 | 1 | | |
| 2001–02 | Sheffield W | 41 | 0 | | |
| 2002–03 | Sheffield W | 26 | 1 | | |
| 2003–04 | Sheffield W | 25 | 0 | **144** | **2** |

**LEE, Graeme (D)** **249** **22**
H: 6 2 W: 13 09 b.Middlesbrough 31-5-78
*Source:* Trainee.

| | | | | | |
|---|---|---|---|---|---|
| 1995–96 | Hartlepool U | 6 | 0 | | |
| 1996–97 | Hartlepool U | 24 | 0 | | |
| 1997–98 | Hartlepool U | 37 | 3 | | |
| 1998–99 | Hartlepool U | 24 | 3 | | |
| 1999–2000 | Hartlepool U | 38 | 7 | | |
| 2000–01 | Hartlepool U | 6 | 0 | | |
| 2001–02 | Hartlepool U | 39 | 4 | | |
| 2002–03 | Hartlepool U | 45 | 2 | **219** | **19** |
| 2003–04 | Sheffield W | 30 | 3 | **30** | **3** |

**McLAREN, Paul* (M)** **263** **12**
H: 6 1 W: 13 05 b.High Wycombe 17-11-76
*Source:* Trainee.

| | | | | | |
|---|---|---|---|---|---|
| 1993–94 | Luton T | 1 | 0 | | |
| 1994–95 | Luton T | 0 | 0 | | |
| 1995–96 | Luton T | 12 | 1 | | |
| 1996–97 | Luton T | 24 | 0 | | |
| 1997–98 | Luton T | 43 | 0 | | |
| 1998–99 | Luton T | 23 | 0 | | |
| 1999–2000 | Luton T | 29 | 1 | | |
| 2000–01 | Luton T | 35 | 2 | **167** | **4** |
| 2001–02 | Sheffield W | 35 | 2 | | |
| 2002–03 | Sheffield W | 36 | 4 | | |
| 2003–04 | Sheffield W | 25 | 2 | **96** | **8** |

**McMAHON, Lewis§ (M)** **10** **0**
H: 5 9 W: 10 12 b.Doncaster 2-5-85
*Source:* Scholar.

| | | | | | |
|---|---|---|---|---|---|
| 2003–04 | Sheffield W | 10 | 0 | **10** | **0** |

**MUSTOE, Robbie* (M)** **487** **36**
H: 6 0 W: 12 03 b.Oxford 28-8-68

| | | | | | |
|---|---|---|---|---|---|
| 1986–87 | Oxford U | 3 | 0 | | |
| 1987–88 | Oxford U | 17 | 0 | | |
| 1988–89 | Oxford U | 33 | 3 | | |
| 1989–90 | Oxford U | 38 | 7 | **91** | **10** |
| 1990–91 | Middlesbrough | 41 | 4 | | |
| 1991–92 | Middlesbrough | 30 | 2 | | |
| 1992–93 | Middlesbrough | 23 | 1 | | |
| 1993–94 | Middlesbrough | 38 | 2 | | |
| 1994–95 | Middlesbrough | 27 | 3 | | |
| 1995–96 | Middlesbrough | 21 | 1 | | |
| 1996–97 | Middlesbrough | 31 | 3 | | |
| 1997–98 | Middlesbrough | 32 | 3 | | |
| 1998–99 | Middlesbrough | 33 | 4 | | |
| 1999–2000 | Middlesbrough | 28 | 0 | | |
| 2000–01 | Middlesbrough | 25 | 0 | | |
| 2001–02 | Middlesbrough | 36 | 2 | **365** | **25** |
| 2002–03 | Charlton Ath | 6 | 0 | **6** | **0** |
| 2003–04 | Sheffield W | 25 | 1 | **25** | **1** |

**N'DUMBU NSUNGU, Guylain (M)** **24** **9**
H: 6 1 W: 12 08 b.Kinshasa 26-12-82
*Source:* Amiens.

| | | | | | |
|---|---|---|---|---|---|
| 2003–04 | Sheffield W | 24 | 9 | **24** | **9** |

**NIXON, Eric† (G)** **524** **0**
H: 6 4 W: 15 07 b.Manchester 4-10-62
*Source:* Curzon Ashton.

| | | | | | |
|---|---|---|---|---|---|
| 1983–84 | Manchester C | 0 | 0 | | |
| 1984–85 | Manchester C | 0 | 0 | | |
| 1985–86 | Manchester C | 28 | 0 | | |
| 1986–87 | Manchester C | 5 | 0 | | |
| 1986–87 | *Wolverhampton W* | 16 | 0 | **16** | **0** |
| 1986–87 | *Bradford C* | 3 | 0 | | |
| 1986–87 | *Southampton* | 4 | 0 | **4** | **0** |
| 1986–87 | *Carlisle U* | 16 | 0 | **16** | **0** |
| 1987–88 | Manchester C | 25 | 0 | **58** | **0** |
| 1987–88 | *Tranmere R* | 8 | 0 | | |
| 1988–89 | Tranmere R | 45 | 0 | | |
| 1989–90 | Tranmere R | 46 | 0 | | |
| 1990–91 | Tranmere R | 43 | 0 | | |
| 1991–92 | Tranmere R | 46 | 0 | | |
| 1992–93 | Tranmere R | 45 | 0 | | |
| 1993–94 | Tranmere R | 42 | 0 | | |

| | | | | | |
|---|---|---|---|---|---|
| 1994–95 | Tranmere R | 41 | 0 | | |
| 1995–96 | Tranmere R | 0 | 0 | | |
| 1995–96 | *Blackpool* | 20 | 0 | **20** | **0** |
| 1996–97 | Tranmere R | 25 | 0 | | |
| 1996–97 | *Bradford C* | 12 | 0 | **15** | **0** |
| 1997–98 | Stockport Co | 43 | 0 | | |
| 1998–99 | Stockport Co | 0 | 0 | **43** | **0** |
| 1998–99 | Wigan Ath | 3 | 0 | **3** | **0** |
| 1999–2000 | Tranmere R | 2 | 0 | | |
| 2000–01 | Tranmere R | 0 | 0 | | |
| 2001–02 | Kidderminster H | 2 | 0 | **2** | **0** |
| 2001–02 | Tranmere R | 1 | 0 | | |
| 2002–03 | Tranmere R | 2 | 0 | **346** | **0** |
| 2003–04 | Sheffield W | 1 | 0 | **1** | **0** |

**OLSEN, Kim (F)** **10 0**
H: 6 4 W: 13 07 b.Herning 11-2-79
*Source:* Midtjylland.

| | | | | | |
|---|---|---|---|---|---|
| 2003–04 | Sheffield W | 10 | 0 | **10** | **0** |

**POULTER, Robert§ (G)** **0 0**
H: 5 11 W: 12 07 b.Sheffield 2-2-86
*Source:* Scholar.

| | | | | | |
|---|---|---|---|---|---|
| 2003–04 | Sheffield W | 0 | 0 | | |

**PRESSMAN, Kevin* (G)** **408 0**
H: 6 1 W: 15 05 b.Fareham 6-11-67
*Source:* Apprentice. *Honours:* England Schools, Youth, Under-21, B.

| | | | | | |
|---|---|---|---|---|---|
| 1985–86 | Sheffield W | 0 | 0 | | |
| 1986–87 | Sheffield W | 0 | 0 | | |
| 1987–88 | Sheffield W | 11 | 0 | | |
| 1988–89 | Sheffield W | 9 | 0 | | |
| 1989–90 | Sheffield W | 15 | 0 | | |
| 1990–91 | Sheffield W | 23 | 0 | | |
| 1991–92 | Sheffield W | 1 | 0 | | |
| 1991–92 | *Stoke C* | 4 | 0 | **4** | **0** |
| 1992–93 | Sheffield W | 3 | 0 | | |
| 1993–94 | Sheffield W | 32 | 0 | | |
| 1994–95 | Sheffield W | 34 | 0 | | |
| 1995–96 | Sheffield W | 30 | 0 | | |
| 1996–97 | Sheffield W | 38 | 0 | | |
| 1997–98 | Sheffield W | 36 | 0 | | |
| 1998–99 | Sheffield W | 15 | 0 | | |
| 1999–2000 | Sheffield W | 19 | 0 | | |
| 2000–01 | Sheffield W | 39 | 0 | | |
| 2001–02 | Sheffield W | 40 | 0 | | |
| 2002–03 | Sheffield W | 38 | 0 | | |
| 2003–04 | *WBA* | 0 | 0 | | |
| 2003–04 | Sheffield W | 21 | 0 | **404** | **0** |

**PROUDLOCK, Adam (F)** **118 22**
H: 6 0 W: 14 07 b.Wellington 9-5-81
*Source:* Trainee.

| | | | | | |
|---|---|---|---|---|---|
| 1999–2000 | Wolverhampton W | 0 | 0 | | |
| 2000–01 | *Clyde* | 4 | 4 | **4** | **4** |
| 2000–01 | Wolverhampton W | 35 | 8 | | |
| 2001–02 | Wolverhampton W | 19 | 3 | | |
| 2001–02 | *Nottingham F* | 3 | 0 | **3** | **0** |
| 2002–03 | Wolverhampton W | 17 | 2 | | |
| 2002–03 | *Tranmere R* | 5 | 0 | **5** | **0** |
| 2002–03 | *Sheffield W* | 5 | 2 | | |
| 2003–04 | Wolverhampton W | 0 | 0 | **71** | **13** |
| 2003–04 | Sheffield W | 30 | 3 | **35** | **5** |

**QUINN, Alan* (M)** **163 16**
H: 5 10 W: 11 04 b.Dublin 13-6-79
*Source:* Cherry Orchard. *Honours:* Eire Under-21, 4 full caps.

| | | | | | |
|---|---|---|---|---|---|
| 1997–98 | Sheffield W | 1 | 0 | | |
| 1998–99 | Sheffield W | 1 | 0 | | |
| 1999–2000 | Sheffield W | 19 | 3 | | |
| 2000–01 | Sheffield W | 37 | 2 | | |
| 2001–02 | Sheffield W | 38 | 2 | | |
| 2002–03 | Sheffield W | 37 | 5 | | |
| 2003–04 | Sheffield W | 24 | 4 | **157** | **16** |
| 2003–04 | *Sunderland* | 6 | 0 | **6** | **0** |

**ROBINS, Mark* (F)** **347 100**
H: 5 8 W: 12 00 b.Ashton-under-Lyne 22-12-69
*Source:* Apprentice. *Honours:* England Under-21.

| | | | | | |
|---|---|---|---|---|---|
| 1986–87 | Manchester U | 0 | 0 | | |
| 1987–88 | Manchester U | 0 | 0 | | |
| 1988–89 | Manchester U | 10 | 0 | | |
| 1989–90 | Manchester U | 17 | 7 | | |
| 1990–91 | Manchester U | 19 | 4 | | |
| 1991–92 | Manchester U | 2 | 0 | **48** | **11** |
| 1992–93 | Norwich C | 37 | 15 | | |
| 1993–94 | Norwich C | 13 | 1 | | |
| 1994–95 | Norwich C | 17 | 4 | **67** | **20** |
| 1994–95 | Leicester C | 17 | 5 | | |
| 1995–96 | Leicester C | 31 | 6 | | |
| 1996–97 | Leicester C | 8 | 1 | | |
| 1997–98 | Leicester C | 0 | 0 | **56** | **12** |
| 1997–98 | *Reading* | 5 | 0 | **5** | **0** |

From Panionios.

| | | | | | |
|---|---|---|---|---|---|
| 1998–99 | Manchester C | 2 | 0 | **2** | **0** |
| 1999–2000 | Walsall | 40 | 6 | **40** | **6** |
| 2000–01 | Rotherham U | 42 | 24 | | |
| 2001–02 | Rotherham U | 41 | 15 | | |
| 2002–03 | Rotherham U | 16 | 5 | | |
| 2002–03 | *Bristol C* | 6 | 4 | **6** | **4** |
| 2003–04 | Rotherham U | 9 | 0 | **108** | **44** |
| 2003–04 | Sheffield W | 15 | 3 | **15** | **3** |

**SHAW, Jon (F)** **23 2**
H: 6 0 W: 12 12 b.Sheffield 10-11-83
*Source:* Scholar.

| | | | | | |
|---|---|---|---|---|---|
| 2002–03 | Sheffield W | 1 | 0 | | |
| 2003–04 | Sheffield W | 14 | 2 | **15** | **2** |
| 2003–04 | *York C* | 8 | 0 | **8** | **0** |

**SHAW, Matthew‡ (F)** **0 0**
H: 6 1 W: 11 09 b.Blackpool 17-5-84

| | | | | | |
|---|---|---|---|---|---|
| 2001–02 | Sheffield W | 0 | 0 | | |
| 2002–03 | Sheffield W | 0 | 0 | | |
| 2003–04 | Sheffield W | 0 | 0 | | |

**SMITH, Dean* (D)** **553 54**
H: 6 1 W: 13 06 b.West Bromwich 19-3-71
*Source:* Trainee.

| | | | | | |
|---|---|---|---|---|---|
| 1988–89 | Walsall | 15 | 0 | | |
| 1989–90 | Walsall | 7 | 0 | | |
| 1990–91 | Walsall | 33 | 0 | | |
| 1991–92 | Walsall | 9 | 0 | | |
| 1992–93 | Walsall | 42 | 1 | | |
| 1993–94 | Walsall | 36 | 1 | **142** | **2** |
| 1994–95 | Hereford U | 35 | 3 | | |
| 1995–96 | Hereford U | 40 | 8 | | |
| 1996–97 | Hereford U | 42 | 8 | **117** | **19** |
| 1997–98 | Leyton Orient | 43 | 9 | | |
| 1998–99 | Leyton Orient | 37 | 9 | | |
| 1999–2000 | Leyton Orient | 44 | 4 | | |
| 2000–01 | Leyton Orient | 43 | 5 | | |
| 2001–02 | Leyton Orient | 45 | 2 | | |
| 2002–03 | Leyton Orient | 27 | 3 | **239** | **32** |
| 2002–03 | Sheffield W | 14 | 0 | | |
| 2003–04 | Sheffield W | 41 | 1 | **55** | **1** |

**SMITH, Paul (M)** **190 11**
H: 6 1 W: 13 06 b.Easington 22-1-76
*Source:* Trainee.

| | | | | | |
|---|---|---|---|---|---|
| 1993–94 | Burnley | 1 | 0 | | |
| 1994–95 | Burnley | 0 | 0 | | |
| 1995–96 | Burnley | 10 | 0 | | |
| 1996–97 | Burnley | 37 | 4 | | |
| 1997–98 | Burnley | 14 | 0 | | |
| 1998–99 | Burnley | 12 | 0 | | |
| 1999–2000 | Burnley | 24 | 0 | | |
| 2000–01 | Burnley | 14 | 1 | **112** | **5** |
| 2000–01 | *Oldham Ath* | 4 | 0 | **4** | **0** |
| 2001–02 | Torquay U | 0 | 0 | | |
| 2001–02 | Hartlepool U | 31 | 4 | | |
| 2002–03 | Hartlepool U | 24 | 0 | **55** | **4** |
| 2003–04 | Sheffield W | 19 | 2 | **19** | **2** |

**STRINGER, Chris* (G)** **9 0**
H: 6 2 W: 14 00 b.Grimsby 16-6-83
*Source:* Scholar.

| | | | | | |
|---|---|---|---|---|---|
| 2000–01 | Sheffield W | 5 | 0 | | |
| 2001–02 | Sheffield W | 1 | 0 | | |
| 2002–03 | Sheffield W | 3 | 0 | | |
| 2003–04 | Sheffield W | 0 | 0 | **9** | **0** |

**TIDMAN, Ola (G)** **33 0**
H: 6 2 W: 12 08 b.Malmo 11-5-79

| | | | | | |
|---|---|---|---|---|---|
| 2001–02 | La Louviere | 6 | 0 | **6** | **0** |
| 2002–03 | Stockport Co | 18 | 0 | **18** | **0** |
| 2003–04 | Sheffield W | 9 | 0 | **9** | **0** |

**WILSON, Laurie§ (M)** **0 0**
H: 5 10 W: 11 00 b.Brighton 5-12-84
*Source:* Scholar. *Honours:* Northern Ireland Youth.

| | | | | | |
|---|---|---|---|---|---|
| 2003–04 | Sheffield W | 0 | 0 | | |

**WOOD, Richard (D)** **15 1**
H: 6 3 W: 12 01 b.Ossett 5-7-85
*Source:* Scholar.

| | | | | | |
|---|---|---|---|---|---|
| 2002–03 | Sheffield W | 3 | 1 | | |
| 2003–04 | Sheffield W | 12 | 0 | **15** | **1** |

**Scholars**
Callaghan, Aaron C; Douglas, Ian M; Foster, Luke J; Greenwood, Ross M; Lowe, Scott; Mason, Greg; McAllister, Sean B; McArdle, Rory A; McMahon, Lewis J; Needham, Liam P; Ogden, Adam J; Orlik, Marcus J; Poulter, Robert J; Stone, Keeron J; Wilson, Laurie J

**Non Contract**
Nixon, Eric W

## SOUTHAMPTON (72)

**ANDERSON, Stuart (M)** **0 0**
b.Banff 22-4-86
*Source:* Scholar.

| | | | | | |
|---|---|---|---|---|---|
| 2003–04 | Southampton | 0 | 0 | | |

**BAIRD, Chris (D)** **25 0**
H: 5 10 W: 11 11 b.Ballymoney 25-2-82
*Source:* Scholar. *Honours:* Northern Ireland Under-21, 11 full caps.

| | | | | | |
|---|---|---|---|---|---|
| 2000–01 | Southampton | 0 | 0 | | |
| 2001–02 | Southampton | 0 | 0 | | |
| 2002–03 | Southampton | 3 | 0 | | |
| 2003–04 | Southampton | 4 | 0 | **7** | **0** |
| 2003–04 | *Walsall* | 10 | 0 | **10** | **0** |
| 2003–04 | *Watford* | 8 | 0 | **8** | **0** |

**BEATTIE, James (F)** **197 65**
H: 6 1 W: 13 06 b.Lancaster 27-2-78
*Source:* Trainee. *Honours:* England Under-21, 5 full caps.

| | | | | | |
|---|---|---|---|---|---|
| 1994–95 | Blackburn R | 0 | 0 | | |
| 1995–96 | Blackburn R | 0 | 0 | | |
| 1996–97 | Blackburn R | 1 | 0 | | |
| 1997–98 | Blackburn R | 3 | 0 | **4** | **0** |
| 1998–99 | Southampton | 35 | 5 | | |
| 1999–2000 | Southampton | 18 | 0 | | |
| 2000–01 | Southampton | 37 | 11 | | |
| 2001–02 | Southampton | 28 | 12 | | |
| 2002–03 | Southampton | 38 | 23 | | |
| 2003–04 | Southampton | 37 | 14 | **193** | **65** |

**BLAYNEY, Alan (G)** **6 0**
H: 6 2 W: 13 12 b.Belfast 9-10-81
*Source:* Scholar. *Honours:* Northern Ireland Under-21.

| | | | | | |
|---|---|---|---|---|---|
| 2001–02 | Southampton | 0 | 0 | | |
| 2002–03 | Southampton | 0 | 0 | | |
| 2002–03 | *Stockport Co* | 2 | 0 | **2** | **0** |
| 2002–03 | *Bournemouth* | 2 | 0 | **2** | **0** |
| 2003–04 | Southampton | 2 | 0 | **2** | **0** |

**CHRISTENSEN, Matthew‡ (M)** **0 0**
H: 5 9 W: 10 09 b.Brisbane 8-6-86
*Source:* Trainee. *Honours:* Australia Youth.

| | | | | | |
|---|---|---|---|---|---|
| 2003–04 | Southampton | 0 | 0 | | |

**CRAINEY, Stephen (D)** **46 0**
H: 5 9 W: 9 11 b.Glasgow 22-6-81
*Honours:* Scotland 6 full caps.

| | | | | | |
|---|---|---|---|---|---|
| 1999–2000 | Celtic | 9 | 0 | | |
| 2000–01 | Celtic | 2 | 0 | | |
| 2001–02 | Celtic | 15 | 0 | | |
| 2002–03 | Celtic | 13 | 0 | **39** | **0** |
| 2003–04 | Celtic | 2 | 0 | **41** | **0** |
| 2003–04 | Southampton | 5 | 0 | **5** | **0** |

**CRANIE, Martin§ (M)** **1 0**
H: 6 0 W: 12 04 b.Yeovil 23-9-86
*Source:* Scholar. *Honours:* England Youth, Under-20.

| | | | | | |
|---|---|---|---|---|---|
| 2003–04 | Southampton | 1 | 0 | **1** | **0** |

**DAVIES, Arron (M)** **4 0**
H: 5 9 W: 10 00 b.Cardiff 22-6-84
*Source:* Trainee.

| | | | | | |
|---|---|---|---|---|---|
| 2002–03 | Southampton | 0 | 0 | | |
| 2003–04 | Southampton | 0 | 0 | | |
| 2003–04 | *Barnsley* | 4 | 0 | **4** | **0** |

**DELAP, Rory (M)** **247 21**
H: 6 3 W: 13 00 b.Sutton Coldfield 6-7-76
*Source:* Trainee. *Honours:* Eire 11 full caps.

| | | | | | |
|---|---|---|---|---|---|
| 1992–93 | Carlisle U | 1 | 0 | | |
| 1993–94 | Carlisle U | 1 | 0 | | |
| 1994–95 | Carlisle U | 3 | 0 | | |
| 1995–96 | Carlisle U | 19 | 3 | | |
| 1996–97 | Carlisle U | 32 | 4 | | |
| 1997–98 | Carlisle U | 9 | 0 | **65** | **7** |
| 1997–98 | Derby Co | 13 | 0 | | |
| 1998–99 | Derby Co | 23 | 0 | | |
| 1999–2000 | Derby Co | 34 | 8 | | |
| 2000–01 | Derby Co | 33 | 3 | **103** | **11** |
| 2001–02 | Southampton | 28 | 2 | | |
| 2002–03 | Southampton | 24 | 0 | | |
| 2003–04 | Southampton | 27 | 1 | **79** | **3** |

**DELGADO, Agustin (F) 165 73**
H: 6 3 W: 13 08 b.Ibarra 23-12-74
*Honours:* Ecuador 54 full caps, 22 goals.

| | | | | | |
|---|---|---|---|---|---|
| 1996 | Nacional | 30 | 18 | **30** | **18** |
| 1997 | Barcelona | 25 | 12 | | |
| 1998 | Barcelona | 9 | 3 | **34** | **15** |
| 1998–99 | Cruz Azul | 8 | 2 | **8** | **2** |
| 1998–99 | Necaxa | 15 | 5 | | |
| 1999–2000 | Necaxa | 33 | 25 | | |
| 2000–01 | Necaxa | 34 | 8 | **82** | **38** |
| 2001–02 | Southampton | 1 | 0 | | |
| 2002–03 | Southampton | 6 | 0 | | |
| 2003–04 | Southampton | 4 | 0 | **11** | **0** |

**DODD, Jason (D) 393 9**
H: 5 10 W: 12 11 b.Bath 2-11-70
*Source:* Bath C. *Honours:* England Under-21.

| | | | | | |
|---|---|---|---|---|---|
| 1988–89 | Southampton | 0 | 0 | | |
| 1989–90 | Southampton | 22 | 0 | | |
| 1990–91 | Southampton | 19 | 0 | | |
| 1991–92 | Southampton | 28 | 0 | | |
| 1992–93 | Southampton | 30 | 1 | | |
| 1993–94 | Southampton | 10 | 0 | | |
| 1994–95 | Southampton | 26 | 2 | | |
| 1995–96 | Southampton | 37 | 2 | | |
| 1996–97 | Southampton | 23 | 1 | | |
| 1997–98 | Southampton | 36 | 1 | | |
| 1998–99 | Southampton | 28 | 1 | | |
| 1999–2000 | Southampton | 31 | 0 | | |
| 2000–01 | Southampton | 31 | 1 | | |
| 2001–02 | Southampton | 29 | 0 | | |
| 2002–03 | Southampton | 15 | 0 | | |
| 2003–04 | Southampton | 28 | 0 | **393** | **9** |

**DRAPER, Mark‡ (M) 405 53**
H: 5 10 W: 12 02 b.Long Eaton 11-11-70
*Source:* Trainee. *Honours:* England Under-21.

| | | | | | |
|---|---|---|---|---|---|
| 1988–89 | Notts Co | 20 | 3 | | |
| 1989–90 | Notts Co | 34 | 3 | | |
| 1990–91 | Notts Co | 45 | 9 | | |
| 1991–92 | Notts Co | 35 | 1 | | |
| 1992–93 | Notts Co | 44 | 11 | | |
| 1993–94 | Notts Co | 44 | 13 | **222** | **40** |
| 1994–95 | Leicester C | 39 | 5 | **39** | **5** |
| 1995–96 | Aston Villa | 36 | 2 | | |
| 1996–97 | Aston Villa | 29 | 0 | | |
| 1997–98 | Aston Villa | 31 | 3 | | |
| 1998–99 | Aston Villa | 23 | 2 | | |
| 1999–2000 | Aston Villa | 1 | 0 | **120** | **7** |
| 2000–01 | Southampton | 22 | 1 | | |
| 2001–02 | Southampton | 2 | 0 | | |
| 2002–03 | Southampton | 0 | 0 | | |
| 2003–04 | Southampton | 0 | 0 | **24** | **1** |

**FERNANDES, Fabrice (M) 145 11**
H: 5 8 W: 10 07 b.Aubervilliers 29-10-79

| | | | | | |
|---|---|---|---|---|---|
| 1998–99 | Rennes | 15 | 2 | | |
| 1999–2000 | Rennes | 17 | 1 | | |
| 2000–01 | Fulham | 29 | 2 | **29** | **2** |
| 2000–01 | Rangers | 4 | 1 | **4** | **1** |
| 2001–02 | Marseille | 4 | 0 | **4** | **0** |
| 2001–02 | Southampton | 11 | 1 | | |
| 2001–02 | Rennes | 1 | 0 | **33** | **3** |
| 2002–03 | Southampton | 37 | 3 | | |
| 2003–04 | Southampton | 27 | 1 | **75** | **5** |

**FOLLY, Yoann (M) 9 0**
H: 5 11 W: 11 00 b.Togo 6-6-85
*Source:* St Etienne.

| | | | | | |
|---|---|---|---|---|---|
| 2003–04 | Southampton | 9 | 0 | **9** | **0** |

**GILLETT, Simon (M) 0 0**
H: 5 5 W: 11 06 b.London 6-11-85
*Source:* Trainee.

| | | | |
|---|---|---|---|
| 2003–04 | Southampton | 0 | 0 |

**GLEESON, Jamie* (F) 0 0**
H: 6 0 W: 12 03 b.Poole 15-1-85
*Source:* Trainee.

| | | | |
|---|---|---|---|
| 2002–03 | Southampton | 0 | 0 |
| 2003–04 | Southampton | 0 | 0 |

**GREEN, Michael‡ (D) 0 0**
H: 5 9 W: 11 04 b.Gloucester 18-12-84
*Source:* Trainee.

| | | | |
|---|---|---|---|
| 2002–03 | Southampton | 0 | 0 |
| 2003–04 | Southampton | 0 | 0 |

**GRIFFIT, Leandre (F) 5 2**
H: 5 11 W: 11 01 b.Maubeuge 21-5-84
*Source:* Amiens.

| | | | | | |
|---|---|---|---|---|---|
| 2003–04 | Southampton | 5 | 2 | **5** | **2** |

**HALL, Fitz (D) 55 5**
H: 6 2 W: 12 07 b.Leytonstone 20-12-80
*Source:* Barnet Trainee, Chesham U.

| | | | | | |
|---|---|---|---|---|---|
| 2001–02 | Oldham Ath | 4 | 1 | | |
| 2002–03 | Oldham Ath | 40 | 4 | **44** | **5** |
| 2003–04 | Southampton | 11 | 0 | **11** | **0** |

**HIGGINBOTHAM, Danny (D) 126 3**
H: 6 2 W: 12 03 b.Manchester 29-12-78
*Source:* Trainee.

| | | | | | |
|---|---|---|---|---|---|
| 1997–98 | Manchester U | 1 | 0 | | |
| 1998–99 | Manchester U | 0 | 0 | | |
| 1999–2000 | Manchester U | 3 | 0 | **4** | **0** |
| 2000–01 | Derby Co | 26 | 0 | | |
| 2001–02 | Derby Co | 37 | 1 | | |
| 2002–03 | Derby Co | 23 | 2 | **86** | **3** |
| 2002–03 | Southampton | 9 | 0 | | |
| 2003–04 | Southampton | 27 | 0 | **36** | **0** |

**JONES, Richard* (M) 0 0**
H: 5 10 W: 10 01 b.Swansea 6-1-85
*Source:* Scholar. *Honours:* Wales Youth.

| | | | |
|---|---|---|---|
| 2001–02 | Southampton | 0 | 0 |
| 2002–03 | Southampton | 0 | 0 |
| 2003–04 | Southampton | 0 | 0 |
| 2003–04 | *Swansea C* | 0 | 0 |

**KENTON, Darren (D) 165 9**
H: 5 10 W: 12 06 b.Wandsworth 13-9-78
*Source:* Trainee.

| | | | | | |
|---|---|---|---|---|---|
| 1997–98 | Norwich C | 11 | 0 | | |
| 1998–99 | Norwich C | 22 | 1 | | |
| 1999–2000 | Norwich C | 26 | 1 | | |
| 2000–01 | Norwich C | 29 | 2 | | |
| 2001–02 | Norwich C | 33 | 4 | | |
| 2002–03 | Norwich C | 37 | 1 | **158** | **9** |
| 2002–03 | Southampton | 0 | 0 | | |
| 2003–04 | Southampton | 7 | 0 | **7** | **0** |

**LE SAUX, Graeme (D) 378 19**
H: 5 9 W: 11 07 b.Jersey 17-10-68
*Source:* St Pauls. *Honours:* England Under-21, B, 36 full caps, 1 goal.

| | | | | | |
|---|---|---|---|---|---|
| 1987–88 | Chelsea | 0 | 0 | | |
| 1988–89 | Chelsea | 1 | 0 | | |
| 1989–90 | Chelsea | 7 | 1 | | |
| 1990–91 | Chelsea | 28 | 4 | | |
| 1991–92 | Chelsea | 40 | 3 | | |
| 1992–93 | Chelsea | 14 | 0 | | |
| 1992–93 | Blackburn R | 9 | 0 | | |
| 1993–94 | Blackburn R | 41 | 2 | | |
| 1994–95 | Blackburn R | 39 | 3 | | |
| 1995–96 | Blackburn R | 14 | 1 | | |
| 1996–97 | Blackburn R | 26 | 1 | **129** | **7** |
| 1997–98 | Chelsea | 26 | 1 | | |
| 1998–99 | Chelsea | 31 | 0 | | |
| 1999–2000 | Chelsea | 8 | 0 | | |
| 2000–01 | Chelsea | 20 | 0 | | |
| 2001–02 | Chelsea | 27 | 1 | | |
| 2002–03 | Chelsea | 28 | 2 | **230** | **12** |
| 2003–04 | Southampton | 19 | 0 | **19** | **0** |

**LUCAS, Jay* (F) 7 0**
H: 6 1 W: 13 03 b.Wollongong 14-1-85
*Source:* Scholar. *Honours:* Australia Youth, Under-20, Under-23.

| | | | | | |
|---|---|---|---|---|---|
| 2000–01 | Wollongong Wolves | 7 | 0 | **7** | **0** |
| 2001–02 | Southampton | 0 | 0 | | |
| 2002–03 | Southampton | 0 | 0 | | |
| 2003–04 | Southampton | 0 | 0 | | |

**LUNDEKVAM, Claus (D) 309 2**
H: 6 3 W: 13 05 b.Austevoll 22-2-73
*Honours:* Norway 28 full caps, 1 goal.

| | | | | | |
|---|---|---|---|---|---|
| 1993 | Brann | 3 | 0 | | |
| 1994 | Brann | 20 | 0 | | |
| 1995 | Brann | 14 | 0 | | |
| 1996 | Brann | 16 | 1 | **53** | **1** |
| 1996–97 | Southampton | 29 | 0 | | |
| 1997–98 | Southampton | 31 | 0 | | |
| 1998–99 | Southampton | 33 | 0 | | |
| 1999–2000 | Southampton | 27 | 0 | | |
| 2000–01 | Southampton | 38 | 0 | | |
| 2001–02 | Southampton | 34 | 0 | | |
| 2002–03 | Southampton | 33 | 0 | | |
| 2003–04 | Southampton | 31 | 1 | **256** | **1** |

**MARSDEN, Chris‡ (M) 408 22**
H: 5 11 W: 12 08 b.Sheffield 3-1-69
*Source:* Trainee.

| | | | | | |
|---|---|---|---|---|---|
| 1986–87 | Sheffield U | 0 | 0 | | |
| 1987–88 | Sheffield U | 16 | 1 | **16** | **1** |
| 1988–89 | Huddersfield T | 14 | 1 | | |
| 1989–90 | Huddersfield T | 32 | 2 | | |
| 1990–91 | Huddersfield T | 43 | 5 | | |
| 1991–92 | Huddersfield T | 23 | 1 | | |
| 1992–93 | Huddersfield T | 7 | 0 | | |
| 1993–94 | Huddersfield T | 2 | 0 | **121** | **9** |
| 1993–94 | *Coventry C* | 7 | 0 | **7** | **0** |
| 1993–94 | Wolverhampton W | 8 | 0 | | |
| 1994–95 | Wolverhampton W | 0 | 0 | **8** | **0** |
| 1994–95 | Notts Co | 7 | 0 | | |
| 1995–96 | Notts Co | 3 | 0 | **10** | **0** |
| 1995–96 | Stockport Co | 20 | 1 | | |
| 1996–97 | Stockport Co | 35 | 2 | | |
| 1997–98 | Stockport Co | 10 | 0 | **65** | **3** |
| 1997–98 | Birmingham C | 32 | 1 | | |
| 1998–99 | Birmingham C | 20 | 2 | **52** | **3** |
| 1998–99 | Southampton | 14 | 2 | | |
| 1999–2000 | Southampton | 21 | 0 | | |
| 2000–01 | Southampton | 23 | 0 | | |
| 2001–02 | Southampton | 28 | 3 | | |
| 2002–03 | Southampton | 30 | 1 | | |
| 2003–04 | Southampton | 13 | 0 | **129** | **6** |

**McCANN, Neil (M) 283 42**
H: 5 10 W: 10 00 b.Greenock 11-8-74
*Source:* Port Glasgow BC. *Honours:* Scotland Under-21, B, 22 full caps, 3 goals.

| | | | | | |
|---|---|---|---|---|---|
| 1992–93 | Dundee | 3 | 0 | | |
| 1993–94 | Dundee | 22 | 1 | | |
| 1994–95 | Dundee | 32 | 2 | | |
| 1995–96 | Dundee | 22 | 2 | **79** | **5** |
| 1996–97 | Hearts | 30 | 5 | | |
| 1997–98 | Hearts | 35 | 10 | | |
| 1998–99 | Hearts | 8 | 3 | **73** | **18** |
| 1998–99 | Rangers | 19 | 5 | | |
| 1999–2000 | Rangers | 30 | 3 | | |
| 2000–01 | Rangers | 21 | 3 | | |
| 2001–02 | Rangers | 25 | 7 | | |
| 2002–03 | Rangers | 18 | 1 | **113** | **19** |
| 2003–04 | Southampton | 18 | 0 | **18** | **0** |

**McDONALD, Chris (D) 0 0**
H: 6 1 W: 13 00 b.Wycombe 28-12-85
*Source:* Trainee.

| | | | |
|---|---|---|---|
| 2002–03 | Southampton | 0 | 0 |
| 2003–04 | Southampton | 0 | 0 |

**NIEMI, Antti (G) 304 0**
H: 6 1 W: 13 00 b.Oulu 31-5-72
*Honours:* Finland 61 full caps.

| | | | | | |
|---|---|---|---|---|---|
| 1991 | HJK Helsinki | 2 | 0 | | |
| 1992 | HJK Helsinki | 28 | 0 | | |
| 1993 | HJK Helsinki | 24 | 0 | | |
| 1994 | HJK Helsinki | 24 | 0 | | |
| 1995 | HJK Helsinki | 24 | 0 | **102** | **0** |
| 1995–96 | FC Copenhagen | 17 | 0 | | |
| 1996–97 | FC Copenhagen | 30 | 0 | **47** | **0** |
| 1997–98 | Rangers | 5 | 0 | | |
| 1998–99 | Rangers | 7 | 0 | | |
| 1999–2000 | Rangers | 1 | 0 | **13** | **0** |
| 1999–2000 | Hearts | 17 | 0 | | |
| 2000–01 | Hearts | 37 | 0 | | |
| 2001–02 | Hearts | 32 | 0 | | |
| 2002–03 | Hearts | 3 | 0 | **89** | **0** |
| 2002–03 | Southampton | 25 | 0 | | |
| 2003–04 | Southampton | 28 | 0 | **53** | **0** |

**OAKLEY, Matthew (M) 225 11**
H: 5 10 W: 12 06 b.Peterborough 17-8-77
*Source:* Trainee. *Honours:* England Under-21.

| | | | | | |
|---|---|---|---|---|---|
| 1994–95 | Southampton | 1 | 0 | | |
| 1995–96 | Southampton | 10 | 0 | | |
| 1996–97 | Southampton | 28 | 3 | | |
| 1997–98 | Southampton | 33 | 1 | | |
| 1998–99 | Southampton | 22 | 2 | | |
| 1999–2000 | Southampton | 31 | 3 | | |
| 2000–01 | Southampton | 35 | 1 | | |
| 2001–02 | Southampton | 27 | 1 | | |
| 2002–03 | Southampton | 31 | 0 | | |
| 2003–04 | Southampton | 7 | 0 | **225** | **11** |

**ORMEROD, Brett (F) 199 56**
H: 5 11 W: 11 12 b.Blackburn 18-10-76
*Source:* Blackburn R Trainee, Accrington S.

| | | | | | |
|---|---|---|---|---|---|
| 1996–97 | Blackpool | 4 | 0 | | |
| 1997–98 | Blackpool | 9 | 2 | | |
| 1998–99 | Blackpool | 40 | 8 | | |
| 1999–2000 | Blackpool | 13 | 5 | | |
| 2000–01 | Blackpool | 41 | 17 | | |
| 2001–02 | Blackpool | 21 | 13 | **128** | **45** |

| | | | | | |
|---|---|---|---|---|---|
| 2001–02 | Southampton | 18 | 1 | | |
| 2002–03 | Southampton | 31 | 5 | | |
| 2003–04 | Southampton | 22 | 5 | **71** | **11** |

**PAHARS, Marian (F)** **247** **93**
H: 5 8 W: 10 08 b.Latvia 5-8-76
*Honours:* Latvia 63 full caps, 15 goals.

| | | | | | |
|---|---|---|---|---|---|
| 1994 | Pardaugava Riga | 17 | 3 | **17** | **3** |
| 1995 | Skonto/Metals Riga | 16 | 4 | **16** | **4** |
| 1995 | Skonto Riga | 9 | 8 | | |
| 1996 | Skonto Riga | 28 | 12 | | |
| 1997 | Skonto Riga | 22 | 5 | | |
| 1998 | Skonto Riga | 26 | 19 | **85** | **44** |
| 1998–99 | Southampton | 6 | 3 | | |
| 1999–2000 | Southampton | 33 | 13 | | |
| 2000–01 | Southampton | 31 | 9 | | |
| 2001–02 | Southampton | 36 | 14 | | |
| 2002–03 | Southampton | 9 | 1 | | |
| 2003–04 | Southampton | 14 | 2 | **129** | **42** |

**PHILLIPS, Kevin (F)** **301** **149**
H: 5 7 W: 11 05 b.Hitchin 25-7-73
*Source:* Baldock T. *Honours:* England B, 8 full caps.

| | | | | | |
|---|---|---|---|---|---|
| 1994–95 | Watford | 16 | 9 | | |
| 1995–96 | Watford | 27 | 11 | | |
| 1996–97 | Watford | 16 | 4 | **59** | **24** |
| 1997–98 | Sunderland | 43 | 29 | | |
| 1998–99 | Sunderland | 26 | 23 | | |
| 1999–2000 | Sunderland | 36 | 30 | | |
| 2000–01 | Sunderland | 34 | 14 | | |
| 2001–02 | Sunderland | 37 | 11 | | |
| 2002–03 | Sunderland | 32 | 6 | **208** | **113** |
| 2003–04 | Southampton | 34 | 12 | **34** | **12** |

**POKE, Michael (G)** **0** **0**
H: 6 1 W: 13 02 b.Spelthorne 21-11-85
*Source:* Trainee.

| | | | | | |
|---|---|---|---|---|---|
| 2003–04 | Southampton | 0 | 0 | | |

**PRUTTON, David (M)** **182** **8**
H: 5 10 W: 12 03 b.Hull 12-9-81
*Source:* Trainee. *Honours:* England Youth, Under-21.

| | | | | | |
|---|---|---|---|---|---|
| 1998–99 | Nottingham F | 0 | 0 | | |
| 1999–2000 | Nottingham F | 34 | 2 | | |
| 2000–01 | Nottingham F | 42 | 1 | | |
| 2001–02 | Nottingham F | 43 | 3 | | |
| 2002–03 | Nottingham F | 24 | 1 | **143** | **7** |
| 2002–03 | Southampton | 12 | 0 | | |
| 2003–04 | Southampton | 27 | 1 | **39** | **1** |

**ROCHE, Jermaine* (F)** **0** **0**
H: 5 8 W: 9 00 b.High Wycombe 4-9-85
*Source:* Trainee.

| | | | | | |
|---|---|---|---|---|---|
| 2002–03 | Southampton | 0 | 0 | | |
| 2003–04 | Southampton | 0 | 0 | | |

**SMITH, Paul (G)** **87** **0**
H: 6 4 W: 14 02 b.Epsom 17-12-79

| | | | | | |
|---|---|---|---|---|---|
| 1998–99 | Charlton Ath | 0 | 0 | | |
| 1998–99 | *Brentford* | 0 | 0 | | |
| 1999–2000 | Charlton Ath | 0 | 0 | | |
| From Carshalton Ath. | | | | | |
| 2000–01 | Brentford | 2 | 0 | | |
| 2001–02 | Brentford | 18 | 0 | | |
| 2002–03 | Brentford | 43 | 0 | | |
| 2003–04 | Brentford | 24 | 0 | **87** | **0** |
| 2003–04 | Southampton | 0 | 0 | | |

**SURMAN, Andrew (M)** **0** **0**
H: 5 10 W: 11 05 b.Johannesburg 20-8-86
*Source:* Trainee.

| | | | | | |
|---|---|---|---|---|---|
| 2003–04 | Southampton | 0 | 0 | | |

**SVENSSON, Anders (M)** **254** **44**
H: 5 10 W: 12 10 b.Gothenburg 17-7-76
*Honours:* Sweden 50 full caps, 10 goals.

| | | | | | |
|---|---|---|---|---|---|
| 1992 | Hestrafors | 2 | 0 | **2** | **0** |
| 1993 | Elfsborg | 0 | 0 | | |
| 1994 | Elfsborg | 1 | 0 | | |
| 1995 | Elfsborg | 26 | 3 | | |
| 1996 | Elfsborg | 24 | 9 | | |
| 1997 | Elfsborg | 26 | 3 | | |
| 1998 | Elfsborg | 26 | 5 | | |
| 1999 | Elfsborg | 20 | 3 | | |
| 2000 | Elfsborg | 24 | 10 | | |
| 2001 | Elfsborg | 8 | 5 | **155** | **38** |
| 2001–02 | Southampton | 34 | 4 | | |
| 2002–03 | Southampton | 33 | 2 | | |
| 2003–04 | Southampton | 30 | 0 | **97** | **6** |

**SVENSSON, Michael (D)** **238** **11**
H: 6 2 W: 13 07 b.Sweden 25-11-75
*Honours:* Sweden 25 full caps.

| | | | | | |
|---|---|---|---|---|---|
| 1992 | Skillingaryds | 21 | 0 | **21** | **0** |
| 1993 | Varnamo | 20 | 0 | | |
| 1994 | Varnamo | 20 | 0 | | |
| 1995 | Varnamo | 17 | 1 | | |
| 1996 | Varnamo | 0 | 0 | **57** | **1** |
| 1997 | Halmstad | 0 | 0 | | |
| 1998 | Halmstad | 14 | 2 | | |
| 1999 | Halmstad | 20 | 0 | | |
| 2000 | Halmstad | 25 | 2 | | |
| 2001 | Halmstad | 18 | 1 | **77** | **5** |
| 2001–02 | Troyes | 23 | 1 | **23** | **1** |
| 2002–03 | Southampton | 34 | 2 | | |
| 2003–04 | Southampton | 26 | 2 | **60** | **4** |

**TELFER, Paul (M)** **433** **26**
H: 5 10 W: 11 13 b.Edinburgh 21-10-71
*Source:* Trainee. *Honours:* Scotland Under-21, B, 1 full cap.

| | | | | | |
|---|---|---|---|---|---|
| 1988–89 | Luton T | 0 | 0 | | |
| 1989–90 | Luton T | 0 | 0 | | |
| 1990–91 | Luton T | 1 | 0 | | |
| 1991–92 | Luton T | 20 | 1 | | |
| 1992–93 | Luton T | 32 | 2 | | |
| 1993–94 | Luton T | 45 | 7 | | |
| 1994–95 | Luton T | 46 | 9 | **144** | **19** |
| 1995–96 | Coventry C | 31 | 1 | | |
| 1996–97 | Coventry C | 34 | 0 | | |
| 1997–98 | Coventry C | 33 | 3 | | |
| 1998–99 | Coventry C | 32 | 2 | | |
| 1999–2000 | Coventry C | 30 | 0 | | |
| 2000–01 | Coventry C | 31 | 0 | | |
| 2001–02 | Coventry C | 0 | 0 | **191** | **6** |
| 2001–02 | Southampton | 28 | 1 | | |
| 2002–03 | Southampton | 33 | 0 | | |
| 2003–04 | Southampton | 37 | 0 | **98** | **1** |

**TESSEM, Jo (M)** **210** **49**
H: 6 2 W: 13 01 b.Orlandet 28-2-72
*Honours:* Norway 9 full caps.

| | | | | | |
|---|---|---|---|---|---|
| 1996 | Lyn | 22 | 15 | | |
| 1997 | Lyn | 26 | 8 | **48** | **23** |
| 1998 | Molde | 26 | 8 | | |
| 1999 | Molde | 26 | 6 | **52** | **14** |
| 1999–2000 | Southampton | 25 | 4 | | |
| 2000–01 | Southampton | 33 | 4 | | |
| 2001–02 | Southampton | 22 | 2 | | |
| 2002–03 | Southampton | 27 | 2 | | |
| 2003–04 | Southampton | 3 | 0 | **110** | **12** |

**WILLIAMS, Gareth* (G)** **0** **0**
H: 6 1 W: 12 05 b.Pontypool 18-3-85
*Source:* Scholar.

| | | | | | |
|---|---|---|---|---|---|
| 2001–02 | Southampton | 0 | 0 | | |
| 2002–03 | Southampton | 0 | 0 | | |
| 2003–04 | Southampton | 0 | 0 | | |

**WILLIAMSON, Mike (D)** **14** **0**
H: 6 4 W: 13 03 b.Stoke 8-11-83
*Source:* Trainee.

| | | | | | |
|---|---|---|---|---|---|
| 2001–02 | Torquay U | 3 | 0 | | |
| 2001–02 | Southampton | 0 | 0 | | |
| 2002–03 | Southampton | 0 | 0 | | |
| 2003–04 | Southampton | 0 | 0 | | |
| 2003–04 | *Torquay U* | 11 | 0 | **14** | **0** |
| 2003–04 | *Doncaster R* | 0 | 0 | | |

**Scholars**
Anaclet, Edward B O; Best, Leon J B; Blackstock, Dexter A; Cranie, Martin J; Critchell, Kyle A R; Da Assuncao Condesso, Feliciano P; McNeil, Andrew D; Mills, Matthew C; Richards, Craig; Sparv, Tim S; Wallis-Tayler, Sebastian N

## SOUTHEND U (73)

**BENTLEY, Mark (M)** **21** **2**
H: 6 2 W: 13 00 b.Hertford 7-1-78

| | | | | | |
|---|---|---|---|---|---|
| 2003–04 | Southend U | 21 | 2 | **21** | **2** |

**BRAMBLE, Tesfaye (F)** **119** **28**
H: 6 2 W: 13 13 b.Ipswich 20-7-80
*Source:* Cambridge C.

| | | | | | |
|---|---|---|---|---|---|
| 2000–01 | Southend U | 16 | 6 | | |
| 2001–02 | Southend U | 35 | 9 | | |
| 2002–03 | Southend U | 34 | 9 | | |
| 2003–04 | Southend U | 34 | 4 | **119** | **28** |

**BROUGHTON, Drewe (F)** **178** **30**
H: 6 2 W: 13 06 b.Hitchin 25-10-78
*Source:* Trainee.

| | | | | | |
|---|---|---|---|---|---|
| 1996–97 | Norwich C | 8 | 1 | | |
| 1997–98 | Norwich C | 1 | 0 | | |
| 1997–98 | *Wigan Ath* | 4 | 0 | **4** | **0** |
| 1998–99 | Norwich C | 0 | 0 | **9** | **1** |
| 1998–99 | Brentford | 1 | 0 | **1** | **0** |
| 1998–99 | Peterborough U | 25 | 7 | | |
| 1999–2000 | Peterborough U | 10 | 1 | | |
| 2000–01 | Peterborough U | 0 | 0 | **35** | **8** |
| 2000–01 | Kidderminster H | 19 | 7 | | |
| 2001–02 | Kidderminster H | 38 | 8 | | |
| 2002–03 | Kidderminster H | 37 | 4 | **94** | **19** |
| 2003–04 | Southend U | 35 | 2 | **35** | **2** |

**BYRNE, Paul (M)** **125** **11**
H: 5 11 W: 13 00 b.Dublin 30-6-72
*Source:* Trainee. *Honours:* Eire Youth.

| | | | | | |
|---|---|---|---|---|---|
| 1989–90 | Oxford U | 3 | 0 | | |
| 1990–91 | Oxford U | 2 | 0 | | |
| 1991–92 | Oxford U | 1 | 0 | **6** | **0** |
| From Bangor | | | | | |
| 1993–94 | Celtic | 22 | 2 | | |
| 1994–95 | Celtic | 6 | 2 | **28** | **4** |
| 1994–95 | *Brighton & HA* | 8 | 1 | **8** | **1** |
| 1995–96 | Southend U | 41 | 5 | | |
| 1996–97 | Southend U | 32 | 1 | | |
| 1997–98 | Southend U | 10 | 0 | | |
| 1998–99 | Southend U | 0 | 0 | | |
| 1999–2000 | Southend U | 0 | 0 | | |
| 2000–01 | Southend U | 0 | 0 | | |
| 2001–02 | Southend U | 0 | 0 | | |
| 2002–03 | Southend U | 0 | 0 | | |
| 2003–04 | Southend U | 0 | 0 | **83** | **6** |

**CLARK, Anthony§ (M)** **2** **0**
H: 5 10 W: 8 10 b.Camden 5-10-84
*Source:* Scholar.

| | | | | | |
|---|---|---|---|---|---|
| 2001–02 | Southend U | 2 | 0 | | |
| 2002–03 | Southend U | 0 | 0 | | |
| 2003–04 | Southend U | 0 | 0 | **2** | **0** |

**CLARK, Steve* (M)** **55** **1**
H: 5 11 W: 12 04 b.Mile End 10-2-82
*Source:* Scholar.

| | | | | | |
|---|---|---|---|---|---|
| 2001–02 | West Ham U | 0 | 0 | | |
| 2001–02 | Southend U | 12 | 1 | | |
| 2002–03 | Southend U | 33 | 0 | | |
| 2003–04 | Southend U | 6 | 0 | **51** | **1** |
| 2003–04 | *Macclesfield T* | 4 | 0 | **4** | **0** |

**CONSTANTINE, Leon# (F)** **73** **24**
H: 6 3 W: 12 00 b.Hackney 24-2-78
*Source:* Edgware T.

| | | | | | |
|---|---|---|---|---|---|
| 2000–01 | Millwall | 1 | 0 | | |
| 2001–02 | Millwall | 0 | 0 | **1** | **0** |
| 2001–02 | *Leyton Orient* | 10 | 3 | **10** | **3** |
| 2001–02 | *Partick T* | 2 | 0 | **2** | **0** |
| 2002–03 | Brentford | 17 | 0 | **17** | **0** |
| 2003–04 | Southend U | 43 | 21 | **43** | **21** |

**CORBETT, Jimmy* (M)** **43** **5**
H: 5 9 W: 11 08 b.Hackney 6-7-80
*Source:* Trainee.

| | | | | | |
|---|---|---|---|---|---|
| 1997–98 | Gillingham | 16 | 2 | **16** | **2** |
| 1998–99 | Blackburn R | 0 | 0 | | |
| 1999–2000 | Blackburn R | 0 | 0 | | |
| 2000–01 | Blackburn R | 0 | 0 | | |
| 2001–02 | Blackburn R | 0 | 0 | | |
| 2002–03 | Blackburn R | 0 | 0 | | |
| 2002–03 | *Darlington* | 10 | 2 | **10** | **2** |
| 2003–04 | Southend U | 17 | 1 | **17** | **1** |

**CORT, Leon# (D)** **137** **11**
H: 6 4 W: 12 07 b.Southwark 11-9-79
*Source:* Dulwich H.

| | | | | | |
|---|---|---|---|---|---|
| 1997–98 | Millwall | 0 | 0 | | |
| 1998–99 | Millwall | 0 | 0 | | |
| 1999–2000 | Millwall | 0 | 0 | | |
| 2000–01 | Millwall | 0 | 0 | | |
| 2001–02 | Southend U | 45 | 4 | | |
| 2002–03 | Southend U | 46 | 6 | | |
| 2003–04 | Southend U | 46 | 1 | **137** | **11** |

**DUDFIELD, Lawrie (F)** **120** **25**
H: 6 1 W: 13 09 b.Southwark 7-5-80
*Source:* Kettering T.

| | | | | | |
|---|---|---|---|---|---|
| 1997–98 | Leicester C | 0 | 0 | | |
| 1998–99 | Leicester C | 0 | 0 | | |
| 1999–2000 | Leicester C | 2 | 0 | | |
| 2000–01 | Leicester C | 0 | 0 | **2** | **0** |

| | | | | | |
|---|---|---|---|---|---|
| 2000–01 | *Lincoln C* | 3 | 0 | **3** | **0** |
| 2000–01 | *Chesterfield* | 14 | 3 | **14** | **3** |
| 2001–02 | Hull C | 38 | 12 | | |
| 2002–03 | Hull C | 21 | 1 | **59** | **13** |
| 2002–03 | Northampton T | 10 | 1 | | |
| 2003–04 | Northampton T | 19 | 3 | **29** | **4** |
| 2003–04 | Southend U | 13 | 5 | **13** | **5** |

**EMBERSON, Carl‡ (G) 259 0**
H: 6 2 W: 14 02 b.Epsom 13-7-73
*Source:* Trainee.

| | | | | | |
|---|---|---|---|---|---|
| 1991–92 | Millwall | 0 | 0 | | |
| 1992–93 | Millwall | 0 | 0 | | |
| 1992–93 | *Colchester U* | 13 | 0 | | |
| 1993–94 | Millwall | 0 | 0 | | |
| 1994–95 | Colchester U | 20 | 0 | | |
| 1995–96 | Colchester U | 41 | 0 | | |
| 1996–97 | Colchester U | 35 | 0 | | |
| 1997–98 | Colchester U | 46 | 0 | | |
| 1998–99 | Colchester U | 37 | 0 | **192** | **0** |
| 1999–2000 | Walsall | 5 | 0 | | |
| 2000–01 | Walsall | 3 | 0 | **8** | **0** |
| 2001–02 | Luton T | 33 | 0 | | |
| 2002–03 | Luton T | 20 | 0 | **53** | **0** |
| 2003–04 | Southend U | 6 | 0 | **6** | **0** |

**FLAHAVAN, Darryl# (G) 148 0**
H: 5 11 W: 12 06 b.Southampton 28-11-78
*Source:* Trainee.
From Woking.

| | | | | | |
|---|---|---|---|---|---|
| 2000–01 | Southend U | 29 | 0 | | |
| 2001–02 | Southend U | 41 | 0 | | |
| 2002–03 | Southend U | 41 | 0 | | |
| 2003–04 | Southend U | 37 | 0 | **148** | **0** |

**GOWER, Mark (M) 63 8**
H: 5 8 W: 12 02 b.Edmonton 5-10-78
*Source:* Trainee. *Honours:* England Schools, Youth.

| | | | | | |
|---|---|---|---|---|---|
| 1996–97 | Tottenham H | 0 | 0 | | |
| 1997–98 | Tottenham H | 0 | 0 | | |
| 1998–99 | Tottenham H | 0 | 0 | | |
| 1998–99 | *Motherwell* | 9 | 1 | **9** | **1** |
| 1999–2000 | Tottenham H | 0 | 0 | | |
| 2000–01 | Tottenham H | 0 | 0 | | |
| 2000–01 | Barnet | 14 | 1 | | |
| 2001–02 | Barnet | 0 | 0 | | |
| 2002–03 | Barnet | 0 | 0 | **14** | **1** |
| 2003–04 | Southend U | 40 | 6 | **40** | **6** |

**HUSBANDS, Michael (F) 9 0**
H: 5 8 W: 10 10 b.Birmingham 13-11-83
*Source:* Scholar.

| | | | | | |
|---|---|---|---|---|---|
| 2001–02 | Aston Villa | 0 | 0 | | |
| 2002–03 | Aston Villa | 0 | 0 | | |
| 2003–04 | Southend U | 9 | 0 | **9** | **0** |

**JENKINS, Neil* (M) 50 8**
H: 5 6 W: 10 05 b.Carshalton 6-1-82
*Source:* Scholar. *Honours:* England Youth, Under-20.

| | | | | | |
|---|---|---|---|---|---|
| 2000–01 | Wimbledon | 0 | 0 | | |
| 2001–02 | Wimbledon | 0 | 0 | | |
| 2002–03 | Southend U | 34 | 7 | | |
| 2003–04 | Southend U | 16 | 1 | **50** | **8** |

**JUPP, Duncan (D) 188 2**
H: 6 1 W: 12 12 b.Guildford 25-1-75
*Source:* Trainee. *Honours:* Scotland Under-21.

| | | | | | |
|---|---|---|---|---|---|
| 1992–93 | Fulham | 3 | 0 | | |
| 1993–94 | Fulham | 30 | 0 | | |
| 1994–95 | Fulham | 36 | 2 | | |
| 1995–96 | Fulham | 36 | 0 | **105** | **2** |
| 1996–97 | Wimbledon | 6 | 0 | | |
| 1997–98 | Wimbledon | 3 | 0 | | |
| 1998–99 | Wimbledon | 6 | 0 | | |
| 1999–2000 | Wimbledon | 9 | 0 | | |
| 2000–01 | Wimbledon | 4 | 0 | | |
| 2001–02 | Wimbledon | 2 | 0 | | |
| 2002–03 | Wimbledon | 0 | 0 | **30** | **0** |
| 2002–03 | *Notts Co* | 8 | 0 | **8** | **0** |
| 2002–03 | Luton T | 5 | 0 | **5** | **0** |
| 2003–04 | Southend U | 40 | 0 | **40** | **0** |

**KIGHTLY, Michael (F) 12 0**
H: 5 10 W: 10 00 b.Basildon 24-1-86
*Source:* Scholar.

| | | | | | |
|---|---|---|---|---|---|
| 2002–03 | Southend U | 1 | 0 | | |
| 2003–04 | Southend U | 11 | 0 | **12** | **0** |

**MAHER, Kevin# (M) 237 15**
H: 6 0 W: 13 01 b.Ilford 17-10-76
*Source:* Trainee.

| | | | | | |
|---|---|---|---|---|---|
| 1995–96 | Tottenham H | 0 | 0 | | |
| 1996–97 | Tottenham H | 0 | 0 | | |
| 1997–98 | Tottenham H | 0 | 0 | | |
| 1997–98 | Southend U | 18 | 1 | | |
| 1998–99 | Southend U | 34 | 4 | | |
| 1999–2000 | Southend U | 24 | 0 | | |
| 2000–01 | Southend U | 41 | 2 | | |
| 2001–02 | Southend U | 36 | 5 | | |
| 2002–03 | Southend U | 42 | 2 | | |
| 2003–04 | Southend U | 42 | 1 | **237** | **15** |

**McSWEENEY, Dave* (D) 70 1**
H: 5 9 W: 11 11 b.Basildon 28-12-81
*Source:* Scholar.

| | | | | | |
|---|---|---|---|---|---|
| 2000–01 | Southend U | 11 | 0 | | |
| 2001–02 | Southend U | 21 | 0 | | |
| 2002–03 | Southend U | 17 | 0 | | |
| 2003–04 | Southend U | 21 | 1 | **70** | **1** |

**NIGHTINGALE, Luke‡ (F) 52 4**
H: 5 11 W: 12 03 b.Portsmouth 22-12-80
*Source:* Trainee.

| | | | | | |
|---|---|---|---|---|---|
| 1998–99 | Portsmouth | 19 | 3 | | |
| 1999–2000 | Portsmouth | 7 | 0 | | |
| 2000–01 | Portsmouth | 19 | 1 | | |
| 2001–02 | Portsmouth | 0 | 0 | | |
| 2002–03 | Portsmouth | 0 | 0 | **45** | **4** |
| 2002–03 | *Swindon T* | 3 | 0 | **3** | **0** |
| 2003–04 | Southend U | 4 | 0 | **4** | **0** |

**ODUNSI, Leke* (M) 35 1**
H: 5 9 W: 11 09 b.Walworth 5-12-80
*Source:* Trainee.

| | | | | | |
|---|---|---|---|---|---|
| 1998–99 | Millwall | 3 | 0 | | |
| 1999–2000 | Millwall | 4 | 0 | | |
| 2000–01 | Millwall | 8 | 0 | | |
| 2001–02 | Millwall | 2 | 0 | | |
| 2002–03 | Millwall | 0 | 0 | **17** | **0** |
| 2002–03 | *Colchester U* | 6 | 0 | **6** | **0** |
| 2003–04 | Southend U | 12 | 1 | **12** | **1** |

**ROBINSON, Ryan* (G) 2 0**
H: 6 2 W: 13 04 b.Tebay 13-10-82
*Source:* Scholar.

| | | | | | |
|---|---|---|---|---|---|
| 2001–02 | Blackburn R | 0 | 0 | | |
| 2002–03 | Blackburn R | 0 | 0 | | |
| 2003–04 | Southend U | 2 | 0 | **2** | **0** |

**SMITH, Jay (M) 49 6**
H: 5 7 W: 10 11 b.London 24-9-81
*Source:* Scholar.

| | | | | | |
|---|---|---|---|---|---|
| 2000–01 | Aston Villa | 0 | 0 | | |
| 2001–02 | Aston Villa | 0 | 0 | | |
| 2002–03 | Aston Villa | 0 | 0 | | |
| 2002–03 | Southend U | 31 | 5 | | |
| 2003–04 | Southend U | 18 | 1 | **49** | **6** |

**STUART, Jamie* (D) 182 4**
H: 5 10 W: 12 06 b.Southwark 15-10-76
*Source:* Trainee. *Honours:* England Youth, Under-21.

| | | | | | |
|---|---|---|---|---|---|
| 1994–95 | Charlton Ath | 12 | 0 | | |
| 1995–96 | Charlton Ath | 27 | 2 | | |
| 1996–97 | Charlton Ath | 10 | 1 | | |
| 1997–98 | Charlton Ath | 1 | 0 | **50** | **3** |
| 1998–99 | Millwall | 35 | 0 | | |
| 1999–2000 | Millwall | 9 | 0 | | |
| 2000–01 | Millwall | 1 | 0 | | |
| 2001–02 | Millwall | 0 | 0 | **45** | **0** |
| 2001–02 | Bury | 24 | 1 | | |
| 2002–03 | Bury | 37 | 0 | **61** | **1** |
| 2003–04 | Southend U | 26 | 0 | **26** | **0** |

**TILSON, Steve† (M) 245 26**
H: 5 11 W: 13 00 b.Wickford 27-7-66
*Source:* Burnham Ramb.

| | | | | | |
|---|---|---|---|---|---|
| 1988–89 | Southend U | 16 | 2 | | |
| 1989–90 | Southend U | 16 | 0 | | |
| 1990–91 | Southend U | 38 | 8 | | |
| 1991–92 | Southend U | 46 | 7 | | |
| 1992–93 | Southend U | 31 | 3 | | |
| 1993–94 | Southend U | 10 | 0 | | |
| 1993–94 | *Brentford* | 2 | 0 | **2** | **0** |
| 1994–95 | Southend U | 26 | 2 | | |
| 1995–96 | Southend U | 28 | 3 | | |
| 1996–97 | Southend U | 28 | 1 | | |
| 1997–98 | Southend U | 0 | 0 | | |
| 1998–99 | Southend U | 0 | 0 | | |

From Canvey Island

| | | | | | |
|---|---|---|---|---|---|
| 2002–03 | Southend U | 3 | 0 | | |
| 2003–04 | Southend U | 1 | 0 | **243** | **26** |

**WARREN, Mark# (D) 292 8**
H: 6 0 W: 12 12 b.Hackney 12-11-74
*Source:* Trainee.

| | | | | | |
|---|---|---|---|---|---|
| 1991–92 | Leyton Orient | 1 | 0 | | |
| 1992–93 | Leyton Orient | 14 | 0 | | |
| 1993–94 | Leyton Orient | 6 | 0 | | |
| 1993–94 | *West Ham U* | 0 | 0 | | |
| 1994–95 | Leyton Orient | 31 | 3 | | |
| 1995–96 | Leyton Orient | 22 | 1 | | |
| 1996–97 | Leyton Orient | 27 | 1 | | |
| 1997–98 | Leyton Orient | 41 | 0 | | |
| 1998–99 | Leyton Orient | 10 | 0 | **152** | **5** |
| 1998–99 | *Oxford U* | 4 | 0 | **4** | **0** |
| 1998–99 | Notts Co | 18 | 0 | | |
| 1999–2000 | Notts Co | 33 | 1 | | |
| 2000–01 | Notts Co | 16 | 0 | | |
| 2001–02 | Notts Co | 17 | 0 | **84** | **1** |
| 2002–03 | Colchester U | 20 | 0 | **20** | **0** |
| 2003–04 | Southend U | 32 | 2 | **32** | **2** |

**WILSON, Che# (D) 111 0**
H: 5 9 W: 12 01 b.Ely 17-1-79
*Source:* Trainee.

| | | | | | |
|---|---|---|---|---|---|
| 1997–98 | Norwich C | 0 | 0 | | |
| 1998–99 | Norwich C | 17 | 0 | | |
| 1999–2000 | Norwich C | 5 | 0 | **22** | **0** |
| 2000–01 | Bristol R | 37 | 0 | | |
| 2001–02 | Bristol R | 38 | 0 | | |
| 2002–03 | Bristol R | 0 | 0 | **75** | **0** |

From Cambridge C.

| | | | | | |
|---|---|---|---|---|---|
| 2003–04 | Southend U | 14 | 0 | **14** | **0** |

**Scholars**
Anderson, Philip A; Bourne, Steven P; Bryan, David; Byrne, Thomas M; Clark, Anthony C; Gray, Jamie; Husnu, Kurt; Ilett, Joseph P; Kawu-Zinga, Flory; Lawson, James P; Moore, Luke; Morgan, Nick T; Plummer, Daryl O; Price, Benjamin M; Skelton, Nicholas J; Williams, Stuart

**Non Contract**
Tilson, Stephen B

**Players who do not hold a current contract but their registration has been retained by the club**
Byrne, Paul P

## STOCKPORT CO (74)

**ADAMS, Danny (D) 160 1**
H: 5 8 W: 13 09 b.Manchester 3-1-76
*Source:* Altrincham.

| | | | | | |
|---|---|---|---|---|---|
| 2000–01 | Macclesfield T | 37 | 0 | | |
| 2001–02 | Macclesfield T | 39 | 0 | | |
| 2002–03 | Macclesfield T | 45 | 1 | | |
| 2003–04 | Macclesfield T | 27 | 0 | **148** | **1** |
| 2003–04 | Stockport Co | 12 | 0 | **12** | **0** |

**BAGULEY, Jamie* (M) 0 0**
H: 5 10 W: 10 08 b.Salford 12-12-84
*Source:* Scholar.

| | | | | | |
|---|---|---|---|---|---|
| 2003–04 | Stockport Co | 0 | 0 | | |

**BAILEY, Matt (F) 0 0**
H: 6 4 W: 11 06 b.Crewe 12-3-86
*Source:* Nantwich T.

| | | | | | |
|---|---|---|---|---|---|
| 2003–04 | Stockport Co | 0 | 0 | | |

**BARLOW, Stuart# (F) 371 108**
H: 5 10 W: 11 00 b.Liverpool 16-7-68
*Source:* School.

| | | | | | |
|---|---|---|---|---|---|
| 1990–91 | Everton | 2 | 0 | | |
| 1991–92 | Everton | 7 | 0 | | |
| 1991–92 | *Rotherham U* | 0 | 0 | | |
| 1992–93 | Everton | 26 | 5 | | |
| 1993–94 | Everton | 22 | 3 | | |
| 1994–95 | Everton | 11 | 2 | | |
| 1995–96 | Everton | 3 | 0 | **71** | **10** |
| 1995–96 | Oldham Ath | 26 | 7 | | |
| 1996–97 | Oldham Ath | 35 | 12 | | |
| 1997–98 | Oldham Ath | 32 | 12 | **93** | **31** |
| 1997–98 | Wigan Ath | 9 | 3 | | |
| 1998–99 | Wigan Ath | 41 | 19 | | |
| 1999–2000 | Wigan Ath | 33 | 18 | **83** | **40** |
| 2000–01 | Tranmere R | 27 | 2 | | |
| 2001–02 | Tranmere R | 38 | 14 | | |

| | | | | | |
|---|---|---|---|---|---|
| 2002–03 | Tranmere R | 29 | 3 | **94** | **19** |
| 2003–04 | Stockport Co | 30 | 8 | **30** | **8** |

**BECKETT, Luke (F) 205 85**
H: 5 11 W: 11 06 b.Sheffield 25-11-76
*Source:* Trainee.

| | | | | | |
|---|---|---|---|---|---|
| 1995–96 | Barnsley | 0 | 0 | | |
| 1996–97 | Barnsley | 0 | 0 | | |
| 1997–98 | Barnsley | 0 | 0 | | |
| 1998–99 | Chester C | 28 | 11 | | |
| 1999–2000 | Chester C | 46 | 14 | **74** | **25** |
| 2000–01 | Chesterfield | 41 | 16 | | |
| 2001–02 | Chesterfield | 21 | 6 | **62** | **22** |
| 2001–02 | Stockport Co | 19 | 7 | | |
| 2002–03 | Stockport Co | 42 | 27 | | |
| 2003–04 | Stockport Co | 8 | 4 | **69** | **38** |

**BUCHAN, Jamie‡ (M) 129 5**
H: 5 10 W: 10 10 b.Manchester 3-4-77
*Source:* Stonehaven. *Honours:* Scotland Under-21.

| | | | | | |
|---|---|---|---|---|---|
| 1995–96 | Aberdeen | 4 | 1 | | |
| 1996–97 | Aberdeen | 14 | 0 | | |
| 1997–98 | Aberdeen | 10 | 0 | | |
| 1998–99 | Aberdeen | 23 | 2 | | |
| 1999–2000 | Aberdeen | 8 | 0 | **59** | **3** |
| 2000–01 | Dundee U | 35 | 1 | | |
| 2001–02 | Dundee U | 7 | 0 | **42** | **1** |
| 2002–03 | Partick T | 28 | 1 | **28** | **1** |
| 2003–04 | Stockport Co | 0 | 0 | | |

**BYRNE, Michael‡ (F) 1 1**
H: 5 10 W: 11 06 b.Ashton-under-Lyne 14-5-85
*Source:* Bolton W Trainee.

| | | | | | |
|---|---|---|---|---|---|
| 2003–04 | Cardiff C | 0 | 0 | | |
| 2003–04 | Stockport Co | 1 | 1 | **1** | **1** |

**CARTWRIGHT, Lee (M) 412 22**
H: 5 8 W: 11 00 b.Rawtenstall 19-9-72
*Source:* Trainee.

| | | | | | |
|---|---|---|---|---|---|
| 1990–91 | Preston NE | 14 | 1 | | |
| 1991–92 | Preston NE | 33 | 3 | | |
| 1992–93 | Preston NE | 34 | 3 | | |
| 1993–94 | Preston NE | 39 | 1 | | |
| 1994–95 | Preston NE | 36 | 1 | | |
| 1995–96 | Preston NE | 26 | 3 | | |
| 1996–97 | Preston NE | 14 | 1 | | |
| 1997–98 | Preston NE | 36 | 2 | | |
| 1998–99 | Preston NE | 27 | 4 | | |
| 1999–2000 | Preston NE | 30 | 1 | | |
| 2000–01 | Preston NE | 38 | 0 | | |
| 2001–02 | Preston NE | 36 | 1 | | |
| 2002–03 | Preston NE | 22 | 1 | | |
| 2003–04 | Preston NE | 12 | 0 | **397** | **22** |
| 2003–04 | Stockport Co | 15 | 0 | **15** | **0** |

**CHALLINOR, Dave (D) 236 7**
H: 6 1 W: 12 06 b.Chester 2-10-75
*Source:* Brombrough Pool. *Honours:* England Schools.

| | | | | | |
|---|---|---|---|---|---|
| 1994–95 | Tranmere R | 0 | 0 | | |
| 1995–96 | Tranmere R | 0 | 0 | | |
| 1996–97 | Tranmere R | 5 | 0 | | |
| 1997–98 | Tranmere R | 32 | 1 | | |
| 1998–99 | Tranmere R | 34 | 2 | | |
| 1999–2000 | Tranmere R | 41 | 3 | | |
| 2000–01 | Tranmere R | 22 | 0 | | |
| 2001–02 | Tranmere R | 6 | 0 | **140** | **6** |
| 2001–02 | Stockport Co | 18 | 0 | | |
| 2002–03 | Stockport Co | 46 | 1 | | |
| 2003–04 | Stockport Co | 17 | 0 | **81** | **1** |
| 2003–04 | *Bury* | 15 | 0 | **15** | **0** |

**CLARE, Rob (D) 117 3**
H: 6 1 W: 11 07 b.Belper 28-2-83
*Source:* Trainee. *Honours:* England Under-20.

| | | | | | |
|---|---|---|---|---|---|
| 1999–2000 | Stockport Co | 0 | 0 | | |
| 2000–01 | Stockport Co | 22 | 0 | | |
| 2001–02 | Stockport Co | 23 | 0 | | |
| 2002–03 | Stockport Co | 36 | 0 | | |
| 2003–04 | Stockport Co | 36 | 3 | **117** | **3** |

**COLLINS, Wayne† (M) 228 24**
H: 5 11 W: 12 02 b.Manchester 4-3-69
*Source:* Winsford U.

| | | | | | |
|---|---|---|---|---|---|
| 1993–94 | Crewe Alex | 35 | 2 | | |
| 1994–95 | Crewe Alex | 40 | 11 | | |
| 1995–96 | Crewe Alex | 42 | 1 | | |
| 1996–97 | Sheffield W | 12 | 1 | | |
| 1997–98 | Sheffield W | 19 | 5 | **31** | **6** |
| 1997–98 | Fulham | 13 | 1 | | |
| 1998–99 | Fulham | 21 | 2 | | |
| 1999–2000 | Fulham | 19 | 1 | | |
| 2000–01 | Fulham | 5 | 0 | **58** | **4** |
| 2001–02 | Crewe Alex | 20 | 0 | | |
| 2002–03 | Crewe Alex | 0 | 0 | **137** | **14** |
| 2003–04 | Stockport Co | 2 | 0 | **2** | **0** |

**DALY, Jon (F) 84 12**
H: 6 1 W: 12 04 b.Dublin 8-1-83
*Source:* Trainee. *Honours:* Eire Under-21.

| | | | | | |
|---|---|---|---|---|---|
| 1999–2000 | Stockport Co | 4 | 0 | | |
| 2000–01 | Stockport Co | 0 | 0 | | |
| 2001–02 | Stockport Co | 13 | 1 | | |
| 2002–03 | Stockport Co | 35 | 7 | | |
| 2003–04 | Stockport Co | 25 | 3 | **77** | **11** |
| 2003–04 | *Bury* | 7 | 1 | **7** | **1** |

**ELLISON, Kevin* (M) 60 2**
H: 6 1 W: 12 08 b.Liverpool 23-2-79
*Source:* Altrincham.

| | | | | | |
|---|---|---|---|---|---|
| 2000–01 | Leicester C | 1 | 0 | | |
| 2001–02 | Leicester C | 0 | 0 | **1** | **0** |
| 2001–02 | Stockport Co | 11 | 0 | | |
| 2002–03 | Stockport Co | 23 | 1 | | |
| 2003–04 | Stockport Co | 14 | 1 | **48** | **2** |
| 2003–04 | *Lincoln C* | 11 | 0 | **11** | **0** |

**GOODWIN, Jim (D) 67 7**
H: 5 9 W: 12 02 b.Waterford 20-11-81
*Source:* Tramore. *Honours:* Eire Under-21, 1 full cap.

| | | | | | |
|---|---|---|---|---|---|
| 2001–02 | Celtic | 0 | 0 | | |
| 2002–03 | Stockport Co | 33 | 3 | | |
| 2003–04 | Stockport Co | 34 | 4 | **67** | **7** |

**GRIFFIN, Danny (D) 216 9**
H: 5 10 W: 10 12 b.Belfast 10-8-77
*Source:* St Andrews, Belfast. *Honours:* Northern Ireland Under-21, 29 full caps, 1 goal.

| | | | | | |
|---|---|---|---|---|---|
| 1993–94 | St Johnstone | 0 | 0 | | |
| 1994–95 | St Johnstone | 3 | 0 | | |
| 1995–96 | St Johnstone | 31 | 1 | | |
| 1996–97 | St Johnstone | 29 | 1 | | |
| 1997–98 | St Johnstone | 13 | 0 | | |
| 1998–99 | St Johnstone | 19 | 1 | | |
| 1999–2000 | St Johnstone | 29 | 1 | **124** | **4** |
| 2000–01 | Dundee U | 18 | 1 | | |
| 2001–02 | Dundee U | 29 | 2 | | |
| 2002–03 | Dundee U | 17 | 1 | | |
| 2003–04 | Dundee U | 13 | 0 | **77** | **4** |
| 2003–04 | Stockport Co | 15 | 1 | **15** | **1** |

**HARDIKER, John (D) 74 3**
H: 6 0 W: 11 04 b.Preston 17-2-82
*Source:* Morecambe.

| | | | | | |
|---|---|---|---|---|---|
| 2001–02 | Stockport Co | 12 | 3 | | |
| 2002–03 | Stockport Co | 23 | 0 | | |
| 2003–04 | Stockport Co | 39 | 0 | **74** | **3** |

**HOLT, David* (F) 1 0**
H: 5 8 W: 10 06 b.Gorton 18-11-84
*Source:* Trainee.

| | | | | | |
|---|---|---|---|---|---|
| 2001–02 | Stockport Co | 1 | 0 | | |
| 2002–03 | Stockport Co | 0 | 0 | | |
| 2003–04 | Stockport Co | 0 | 0 | **1** | **0** |

**JACKMAN, Danny (D) 34 3**
H: 5 4 W: 9 08 b.Worcester 3-1-83
*Source:* Scholar.

| | | | | | |
|---|---|---|---|---|---|
| 2000–01 | Aston Villa | 0 | 0 | | |
| 2001–02 | Aston Villa | 0 | 0 | | |
| 2001–02 | *Cambridge U* | 7 | 1 | **7** | **1** |
| 2002–03 | Aston Villa | 0 | 0 | | |
| 2003–04 | Aston Villa | 0 | 0 | | |
| 2003–04 | Stockport Co | 27 | 2 | **27** | **2** |

**JONES, Rob (D) 17 2**
H: 6 7 W: 12 02 b.Stockton 30-11-79
*Source:* Gateshead.

| | | | | | |
|---|---|---|---|---|---|
| 2002–03 | Stockport Co | 0 | 0 | | |
| 2003–04 | Stockport Co | 16 | 2 | **16** | **2** |
| 2003–04 | *Macclesfield T* | 1 | 0 | **1** | **0** |

**LAMBERT, Ricky (M) 116 22**
H: 5 10 W: 11 02 b.Liverpool 16-2-82
*Source:* Trainee.

| | | | | | |
|---|---|---|---|---|---|
| 1999–2000 | Blackpool | 3 | 0 | | |
| 2000–01 | Blackpool | 0 | 0 | **3** | **0** |
| 2000–01 | Macclesfield T | 9 | 0 | | |
| 2001–02 | Macclesfield T | 35 | 8 | **44** | **8** |
| 2001–02 | Stockport Co | 0 | 0 | | |
| 2002–03 | Stockport Co | 29 | 2 | | |
| 2003–04 | Stockport Co | 40 | 12 | **69** | **14** |

**LESCOTT, Aaron (M) 122 1**
H: 5 8 W: 10 09 b.Birmingham 2-12-78
*Source:* Trainee. *Honours:* England Schools.

| | | | | | |
|---|---|---|---|---|---|
| 1996–97 | Aston Villa | 0 | 0 | | |
| 1997–98 | Aston Villa | 0 | 0 | | |
| 1998–99 | Aston Villa | 0 | 0 | | |
| 1999–2000 | Aston Villa | 0 | 0 | | |
| 1999–2000 | *Lincoln C* | 5 | 0 | **5** | **0** |
| 2000–01 | Aston Villa | 0 | 0 | | |
| 2000–01 | Sheffield W | 30 | 0 | | |
| 2001–02 | Sheffield W | 7 | 0 | **37** | **0** |
| 2001–02 | Stockport Co | 17 | 0 | | |
| 2002–03 | Stockport Co | 41 | 1 | | |
| 2003–04 | Stockport Co | 14 | 0 | **72** | **1** |
| 2003–04 | *Bristol R* | 8 | 0 | **8** | **0** |

**LORD, Alex* (D) 0 0**
H: 6 1 W: 10 12 b.Astley 3-12-84
*Source:* Scholar.

| | | | | | |
|---|---|---|---|---|---|
| 2003–04 | Stockport Co | 0 | 0 | | |

**McLACHLAN, Fraser (M) 53 4**
H: 5 11 W: 12 06 b.Knutsford 9-11-82
*Source:* Scholar.

| | | | | | |
|---|---|---|---|---|---|
| 2001–02 | Stockport Co | 11 | 1 | | |
| 2002–03 | Stockport Co | 22 | 0 | | |
| 2003–04 | Stockport Co | 20 | 3 | **53** | **4** |

**MORRISON, Owen (M) 88 9**
H: 5 8 W: 11 12 b.Derry 8-12-81
*Source:* Trainee. *Honours:* Northern Ireland Schools, Youth, Under-21.

| | | | | | |
|---|---|---|---|---|---|
| 1998–99 | Sheffield W | 1 | 0 | | |
| 1999–2000 | Sheffield W | 0 | 0 | | |
| 2000–01 | Sheffield W | 30 | 6 | | |
| 2001–02 | Sheffield W | 24 | 2 | | |
| 2002–03 | Sheffield W | 1 | 0 | **56** | **8** |
| 2002–03 | *Hull C* | 2 | 0 | **2** | **0** |
| 2002–03 | Sheffield U | 8 | 0 | **8** | **0** |
| 2003–04 | Stockport Co | 22 | 1 | **22** | **1** |

**PEMBERTON, Martin (M) 133 7**
H: 5 11 W: 12 06 b.Bradford 1-2-76
*Source:* Trainee.

| | | | | | |
|---|---|---|---|---|---|
| 1994–95 | Oldham Ath | 0 | 0 | | |
| 1995–96 | Oldham Ath | 2 | 0 | | |
| 1996–97 | Oldham Ath | 3 | 0 | **5** | **0** |
| 1996–97 | Doncaster R | 9 | 1 | | |
| 1997–98 | Doncaster R | 26 | 1 | **35** | **2** |
| 1997–98 | Scunthorpe U | 6 | 0 | **6** | **0** |
| 1998–99 | Hartlepool U | 4 | 0 | | |
| 1999–2000 | Hartlepool U | 0 | 0 | **4** | **0** |
| From Bradford PA. | | | | | |
| 2000–01 | Mansfield T | 18 | 1 | | |
| 2001–02 | Mansfield T | 38 | 4 | **56** | **5** |
| 2001–02 | Stockport Co | 0 | 0 | | |
| 2002–03 | Stockport Co | 20 | 0 | | |
| 2003–04 | Stockport Co | 6 | 0 | **26** | **0** |
| 2003–04 | *Rochdale* | 1 | 0 | **1** | **0** |

**REILLY, Philip (M) 0 0**

| | | | | | |
|---|---|---|---|---|---|
| 2003–04 | Stockport Co | 0 | 0 | | |

**ROBERTSON, Mark# (M) 137 5**
H: 5 9 W: 12 04 b.Sydney 6-4-77
*Honours:* Australia Schools, Under-20, Under-23, 1 full cap.

| | | | | | |
|---|---|---|---|---|---|
| 1994–95 | Marconi Stallions | 8 | 0 | | |
| 1996–97 | Marconi Stallions | 15 | 0 | **23** | **0** |
| 1997–98 | Burnley | 11 | 0 | | |
| 1998–99 | Burnley | 24 | 1 | | |
| 1999–2000 | Burnley | 1 | 0 | **36** | **1** |
| 1999–2000 | Wollongong Wolves | 12 | 0 | **12** | **0** |
| 2000–01 | Dundee | 4 | 0 | | |
| 2000–01 | Swindon T | 10 | 1 | **10** | **1** |
| 2001–02 | Dundee | 16 | 0 | | |
| 2002–03 | Dundee | 5 | 0 | **25** | **0** |
| 2002–03 | St Johnstone | 10 | 1 | | |
| 2003–04 | St Johnstone | 9 | 1 | **19** | **2** |
| 2003–04 | Stockport Co | 12 | 1 | **12** | **1** |

**SPENCER, James (G) 18 0**
H: 6 5 W: 15 02 b.Stockport 11-4-85
*Source:* Trainee.

| | | | | | |
|---|---|---|---|---|---|
| 2001–02 | Stockport Co | 2 | 0 | | |
| 2002–03 | Stockport Co | 1 | 0 | | |
| 2003–04 | Stockport Co | 15 | 0 | **18** | **0** |

**WELSH, Andy (M) 68 5**
H: 5 8 W: 9 08 b.Manchester 24-11-83
*Source:* Scholar.

| | | | | | |
|---|---|---|---|---|---|
| 2001–02 | Stockport Co | 15 | 0 | | |
| 2002–03 | Stockport Co | 13 | 2 | | |

| | | | | | |
|---|---|---|---|---|---|
| 2002–03 | *Macclesfield T* | 6 | 2 | 6 | 2 |
| 2003–04 | Stockport Co | 34 | 1 | 62 | 3 |

**WILBRAHAM, Aaron (F)** **172 35**
H: 6 3 W: 12 04 b.Knutsford 21-10-79
*Source:* Trainee.

| | | | | | |
|---|---|---|---|---|---|
| 1997–98 | Stockport Co | 7 | 1 | | |
| 1998–99 | Stockport Co | 26 | 0 | | |
| 1999–2000 | Stockport Co | 26 | 4 | | |
| 2000–01 | Stockport Co | 36 | 12 | | |
| 2001–02 | Stockport Co | 21 | 3 | | |
| 2002–03 | Stockport Co | 15 | 7 | | |
| 2003–04 | Stockport Co | 41 | 8 | 172 | 35 |

**WILLIAMS, Ashley (D)** **10 0**
H: 6 0 W: 11 02 b.Wolverhampton 23-8-84
*Source:* Hednesford T.

| | | | | | |
|---|---|---|---|---|---|
| 2003–04 | Stockport Co | 10 | 0 | 10 | 0 |

**WILLIAMS, Chris (F)** **22 3**
H: 5 8 W: 9 06 b.Manchester 2-2-85
*Source:* Scholar.

| | | | | | |
|---|---|---|---|---|---|
| 2001–02 | Stockport Co | 5 | 0 | | |
| 2002–03 | Stockport Co | 1 | 0 | | |
| 2003–04 | Stockport Co | 16 | 3 | 22 | 3 |

**Non Contract**
Collins, Wayne

## STOKE C (75)

**AKINBIYI, Ade (F)** **323 100**
H: 6 1 W: 12 08 b.Hackney 10-10-74
*Source:* Trainee. *Honours:* Nigeria full caps.

| | | | | | |
|---|---|---|---|---|---|
| 1992–93 | Norwich C | 0 | 0 | | |
| 1993–94 | Norwich C | 2 | 0 | | |
| 1993–94 | *Hereford U* | 4 | 2 | 4 | 2 |
| 1994–95 | Norwich C | 13 | 0 | | |
| 1994–95 | *Brighton & HA* | 7 | 4 | 7 | 4 |
| 1995–96 | Norwich C | 22 | 3 | | |
| 1996–97 | Norwich C | 12 | 0 | 49 | 3 |
| 1996–97 | Gillingham | 19 | 7 | | |
| 1997–98 | Gillingham | 44 | 21 | 63 | 28 |
| 1998–99 | Bristol C | 44 | 19 | | |
| 1999–2000 | Bristol C | 3 | 2 | 47 | 21 |
| 1999–2000 | Wolverhampton W | 37 | 16 | 37 | 16 |
| 2000–01 | Leicester C | 37 | 9 | | |
| 2001–02 | Leicester C | 21 | 2 | 58 | 11 |
| 2001–02 | Crystal Palace | 14 | 2 | | |
| 2002–03 | Crystal Palace | 10 | 1 | | |
| 2002–03 | *Stoke C* | 4 | 2 | | |
| 2003–04 | Crystal Palace | 0 | 0 | 24 | 3 |
| 2003–04 | Stoke C | 30 | 10 | 34 | 12 |

**ASABA, Carl (F)** **280 102**
H: 6 2 W: 14 02 b.London 28-1-73
*Source:* Dulwich Hamlet.

| | | | | | |
|---|---|---|---|---|---|
| 1994–95 | Brentford | 0 | 0 | | |
| 1994–95 | *Colchester U* | 12 | 2 | 12 | 2 |
| 1995–96 | Brentford | 10 | 2 | | |
| 1996–97 | Brentford | 44 | 23 | 54 | 25 |
| 1997–98 | Reading | 32 | 8 | | |
| 1998–99 | Reading | 1 | 0 | 33 | 8 |
| 1998–99 | Gillingham | 41 | 20 | | |
| 1999–2000 | Gillingham | 11 | 6 | | |
| 2000–01 | Gillingham | 25 | 10 | 77 | 36 |
| 2000–01 | Sheffield U | 10 | 5 | | |
| 2001–02 | Sheffield U | 29 | 7 | | |
| 2002–03 | Sheffield U | 28 | 11 | 67 | 23 |
| 2003–04 | Stoke C | 37 | 8 | 37 | 8 |

**CARTWRIGHT, Shaun (M)** **0 0**
b.Stoke-on-Trent 15-4-86
*Source:* Scholar.

| | | | | | |
|---|---|---|---|---|---|
| 2002–03 | Stoke C | 0 | 0 | | |
| 2003–04 | Stoke C | 0 | 0 | | |

**CLARKE, Clive (D)** **181 8**
H: 6 0 W: 12 02 b.Dublin 14-1-80
*Source:* Trainee. *Honours:* Eire Under-21, 2 full caps.

| | | | | | |
|---|---|---|---|---|---|
| 1996–97 | Stoke C | 0 | 0 | | |
| 1997–98 | Stoke C | 0 | 0 | | |
| 1998–99 | Stoke C | 2 | 0 | | |
| 1999–2000 | Stoke C | 42 | 1 | | |
| 2000–01 | Stoke C | 21 | 0 | | |
| 2001–02 | Stoke C | 43 | 1 | | |
| 2002–03 | Stoke C | 31 | 3 | | |
| 2003–04 | Stoke C | 42 | 3 | 181 | 8 |

**COMMONS, Kris (D)** **41 5**
H: 5 6 W: 9 08 b.Nottingham 30-8-83
*Source:* Scholar.

| | | | | | |
|---|---|---|---|---|---|
| 2000–01 | Stoke C | 0 | 0 | | |
| 2001–02 | Stoke C | 0 | 0 | | |
| 2002–03 | Stoke C | 8 | 1 | | |
| 2003–04 | Stoke C | 33 | 4 | 41 | 5 |

**CUTLER, Neil# (G)** **123 0**
H: 6 3 W: 12 00 b.Birmingham 3-9-76
*Source:* Trainee. *Honours:* England Schools, Youth.

| | | | | | |
|---|---|---|---|---|---|
| 1993–94 | WBA | 0 | 0 | | |
| 1994–95 | WBA | 0 | 0 | | |
| 1995–96 | WBA | 0 | 0 | | |
| 1995–96 | *Coventry C* | 0 | 0 | | |
| 1995–96 | *Chester C* | 1 | 0 | | |
| 1996–97 | Crewe Alex | 0 | 0 | | |
| 1996–97 | *Chester C* | 5 | 0 | | |
| 1997–98 | Crewe Alex | 0 | 0 | | |
| 1998–99 | Chester C | 23 | 0 | | |
| 1999–2000 | Chester C | 0 | 0 | 29 | 0 |
| 1999–2000 | Aston Villa | 1 | 0 | | |
| 2000–01 | Aston Villa | 0 | 0 | | |
| 2000–01 | *Oxford U* | 11 | 0 | 11 | 0 |
| 2001–02 | Aston Villa | 0 | 0 | 1 | 0 |
| 2001–02 | Stoke C | 36 | 0 | | |
| 2002–03 | Stoke C | 20 | 0 | | |
| 2002–03 | *Swansea C* | 13 | 0 | 13 | 0 |
| 2003–04 | Stoke C | 13 | 0 | 69 | 0 |

**DE GOEY, Ed (G)** **506 0**
H: 6 6 W: 14 05 b.Gouda 20-12-66
*Honours:* Holland 31 full caps.

| | | | | | |
|---|---|---|---|---|---|
| 1985–86 | Sparta | 12 | 0 | | |
| 1986–87 | Sparta | 34 | 0 | | |
| 1987–88 | Sparta | 34 | 0 | | |
| 1988–89 | Sparta | 31 | 0 | | |
| 1989–90 | Sparta | 34 | 0 | 145 | 0 |
| 1990–91 | Feyenoord | 34 | 0 | | |
| 1991–92 | Feyenoord | 34 | 0 | | |
| 1992–93 | Feyenoord | 33 | 0 | | |
| 1993–94 | Feyenoord | 34 | 0 | | |
| 1994–95 | Feyenoord | 32 | 0 | | |
| 1995–96 | Feyenoord | 34 | 0 | 201 | 0 |
| 1997–98 | Chelsea | 28 | 0 | | |
| 1998–99 | Chelsea | 35 | 0 | | |
| 1999–2000 | Chelsea | 37 | 0 | | |
| 2000–01 | Chelsea | 15 | 0 | | |
| 2001–02 | Chelsea | 6 | 0 | | |
| 2002–03 | Chelsea | 2 | 0 | 123 | 0 |
| 2003–04 | Stoke C | 37 | 0 | 37 | 0 |

**EUSTACE, John (M)** **124 13**
H: 5 11 W: 11 12 b.Solihull 3-11-79
*Source:* Trainee.

| | | | | | |
|---|---|---|---|---|---|
| 1996–97 | Coventry C | 0 | 0 | | |
| 1997–98 | Coventry C | 0 | 0 | | |
| 1998–99 | Coventry C | 0 | 0 | | |
| 1998–99 | Dundee U | 11 | 1 | 11 | 1 |
| 1999–2000 | Coventry C | 16 | 1 | | |
| 2000–01 | Coventry C | 32 | 2 | | |
| 2001–02 | Coventry C | 6 | 0 | | |
| 2002–03 | Coventry C | 32 | 4 | 86 | 7 |
| 2002–03 | *Middlesbrough* | 1 | 0 | 1 | 0 |
| 2003–04 | Stoke C | 26 | 5 | 26 | 5 |

**FOSTER, Ben (G)** **0 0**
H: 6 2 W: 12 06 b.Leamington Spa 3-4-83
*Source:* Racing Club Warwick.

| | | | | | |
|---|---|---|---|---|---|
| 2000–01 | Stoke C | 0 | 0 | | |
| 2001–02 | Stoke C | 0 | 0 | | |
| 2002–03 | Stoke C | 0 | 0 | | |
| 2003–04 | Stoke C | 0 | 0 | | |

**GREENACRE, Chris (F)** **199 60**
H: 5 11 W: 12 08 b.Halifax 23-12-77
*Source:* Trainee.

| | | | | | |
|---|---|---|---|---|---|
| 1995–96 | Manchester C | 0 | 0 | | |
| 1996–97 | Manchester C | 4 | 0 | | |
| 1997–98 | Manchester C | 3 | 1 | | |
| 1997–98 | *Cardiff C* | 11 | 2 | 11 | 2 |
| 1997–98 | *Blackpool* | 4 | 0 | 4 | 0 |
| 1998–99 | Manchester C | 1 | 0 | | |
| 1998–99 | *Scarborough* | 12 | 2 | 12 | 2 |
| 1999–2000 | Manchester C | 0 | 0 | 8 | 1 |
| 1999–2000 | Mansfield T | 31 | 9 | | |
| 2000–01 | Mansfield T | 46 | 19 | | |
| 2001–02 | Mansfield T | 44 | 21 | 121 | 49 |
| 2002–03 | Stoke C | 30 | 4 | | |
| 2003–04 | Stoke C | 13 | 2 | 43 | 6 |

**HALL, Laurence* (F)** **0 0**
H: 6 0 W: 12 00 b.Nottingham 26-3-84
*Source:* Scholar.

| | | | | | |
|---|---|---|---|---|---|
| 2001–02 | Stoke C | 0 | 0 | | |
| 2002–03 | Stoke C | 0 | 0 | | |
| 2003–04 | Stoke C | 0 | 0 | | |

**HALL, Marcus (D)** **192 2**
H: 6 1 W: 12 02 b.Coventry 24-3-76
*Source:* Trainee. *Honours:* England Under-21, B.

| | | | | | |
|---|---|---|---|---|---|
| 1994–95 | Coventry C | 5 | 0 | | |
| 1995–96 | Coventry C | 25 | 0 | | |
| 1996–97 | Coventry C | 13 | 0 | | |
| 1997–98 | Coventry C | 25 | 1 | | |
| 1998–99 | Coventry C | 5 | 0 | | |
| 1999–2000 | Coventry C | 9 | 0 | | |
| 2000–01 | Coventry C | 21 | 0 | | |
| 2001–02 | Coventry C | 29 | 1 | 132 | 2 |
| 2002–03 | Nottingham F | 1 | 0 | 1 | 0 |
| 2002–03 | Stoke C | 24 | 0 | | |
| 2003–04 | Stoke C | 35 | 0 | 59 | 0 |

**HALLS, John (D)** **40 0**
H: 6 0 W: 11 00 b.Islington 14-2-82
*Source:* Scholar. *Honours:* England Youth, Under-20.

| | | | | | |
|---|---|---|---|---|---|
| 2000–01 | Arsenal | 0 | 0 | | |
| 2001–02 | Arsenal | 0 | 0 | | |
| 2001–02 | *Colchester U* | 6 | 0 | 6 | 0 |
| 2002–03 | Arsenal | 0 | 0 | | |
| 2003–04 | Arsenal | 0 | 0 | | |
| 2003–04 | Stoke C | 34 | 0 | 34 | 0 |

**HENRY, Karl (M)** **71 2**
H: 6 0 W: 11 04 b.Wolverhampton 26-11-82
*Source:* Trainee. *Honours:* England Youth, Under-20.

| | | | | | |
|---|---|---|---|---|---|
| 1999–2000 | Stoke C | 0 | 0 | | |
| 2000–01 | Stoke C | 0 | 0 | | |
| 2001–02 | Stoke C | 24 | 0 | | |
| 2002–03 | Stoke C | 18 | 1 | | |
| 2003–04 | Stoke C | 20 | 0 | 62 | 1 |
| 2003–04 | *Cheltenham T* | 9 | 1 | 9 | 1 |

**HILL, Clint (D)** **169 17**
H: 6 0 W: 12 00 b.Liverpool 19-10-78
*Source:* Trainee.

| | | | | | |
|---|---|---|---|---|---|
| 1997–98 | Tranmere R | 14 | 0 | | |
| 1998–99 | Tranmere R | 33 | 4 | | |
| 1999–2000 | Tranmere R | 29 | 5 | | |
| 2000–01 | Tranmere R | 34 | 5 | | |
| 2001–02 | Tranmere R | 30 | 2 | 140 | 16 |
| 2002–03 | Oldham Ath | 17 | 1 | 17 | 1 |
| 2003–04 | Stoke C | 12 | 0 | 12 | 0 |

**HOEKSTRA, Peter‡ (M)** **250 47**
H: 6 3 W: 12 03 b.Asser 4-4-73
*Source:* ACV. *Honours:* Holland 5 full caps.

| | | | | | |
|---|---|---|---|---|---|
| 1991–92 | PSV Eindhoven | 14 | 3 | | |
| 1992–93 | PSV Eindhoven | 19 | 0 | | |
| 1993–94 | PSV Eindhoven | 23 | 6 | | |
| 1994–95 | PSV Eindhoven | 19 | 6 | | |
| 1995–96 | PSV Eindhoven | 15 | 6 | 90 | 21 |
| 1995–96 | Ajax | 16 | 5 | | |
| 1996–97 | Ajax | 8 | 0 | | |
| 1997–98 | Ajax | 23 | 3 | | |
| 1998–99 | Ajax | 21 | 6 | | |
| 1999–2000 | Ajax | 0 | 0 | 68 | 14 |
| 2000–01 | Groningen | 14 | 1 | 14 | 1 |
| 2001–02 | Stoke C | 24 | 3 | | |
| 2002–03 | Stoke C | 30 | 4 | | |
| 2003–04 | Stoke C | 24 | 4 | 78 | 11 |

**HUTCHINSON, Ryan‡ (M)** **0 0**
b.Manchester 8-9-83
*Source:* Scholar.

| | | | | | |
|---|---|---|---|---|---|
| 2003–04 | Stoke C | 0 | 0 | | |

**MARTEINSSON, Petur‡ (M)** **183 10**
H: 6 1 W: 12 02 b.Reykjavik 14-7-73
*Honours:* Iceland 27 full caps, 1 goal.

| | | | | | |
|---|---|---|---|---|---|
| 1994 | Fram | 16 | 0 | | |
| 1995 | Fram | 16 | 0 | 32 | 0 |
| 1996 | Hammarby | 23 | 0 | | |
| 1997 | Hammarby | 23 | 2 | | |
| 1998 | Hammarby | 24 | 2 | | |
| 1999 | Hammarby | 0 | 0 | 70 | 4 |

| | | | | | |
|---|---|---|---|---|---|
| 1999 | Stabaek | 18 | 0 | | |
| 2000 | Stabaek | 21 | 2 | | |
| 2001 | Stabaek | 24 | 2 | **63** | **4** |
| 2001–02 | Stoke C | 3 | 0 | | |
| 2002–03 | Stoke C | 12 | 2 | | |
| 2003–04 | Stoke C | 3 | 0 | **18** | **2** |

**NEAL, Lewis (M)** **47** **1**
H: 5 10 W: 10 11 b.Leicester 14-7-81

| | | | | | |
|---|---|---|---|---|---|
| 1998–99 | Stoke C | 0 | 0 | | |
| 1999–2000 | Stoke C | 0 | 0 | | |
| 2000–01 | Stoke C | 1 | 0 | | |
| 2001–02 | Stoke C | 11 | 0 | | |
| 2002–03 | Stoke C | 16 | 0 | | |
| 2003–04 | Stoke C | 19 | 1 | **47** | **1** |

**NOEL-WILLIAMS, Gifton (F)** **211** **43**
H: 6 1 W: 14 00 b.Islington 21-1-80
*Source:* Trainee. *Honours:* England Youth.

| | | | | | |
|---|---|---|---|---|---|
| 1996–97 | Watford | 25 | 2 | | |
| 1997–98 | Watford | 38 | 7 | | |
| 1998–99 | Watford | 26 | 10 | | |
| 1999–2000 | Watford | 3 | 0 | | |
| 2000–01 | Watford | 32 | 8 | | |
| 2001–02 | Watford | 29 | 6 | | |
| 2002–03 | Watford | 16 | 0 | **169** | **33** |
| 2003–04 | Stoke C | 42 | 10 | **42** | **10** |

**OWEN, Gareth (D)** **18** **1**
H: 6 1 W: 11 07 b.Stoke 21-9-82
*Source:* Scholar. *Honours:* Wales Youth.

| | | | | | |
|---|---|---|---|---|---|
| 2001–02 | Stoke C | 0 | 0 | | |
| 2002–03 | Stoke C | 0 | 0 | | |
| 2003–04 | Stoke C | 3 | 0 | **3** | **0** |
| 2003–04 | *Oldham Ath* | 15 | 1 | **15** | **1** |

**PALMER, Jermaine (F)** **3** **0**
H: 6 0 W: 11 03 b.Nottingham 28-8-86
*Source:* Scholar.

| | | | | | |
|---|---|---|---|---|---|
| 2003–04 | Stoke C | 3 | 0 | **3** | **0** |

**RUSSELL, Darel (M)** **178** **11**
H: 6 0 W: 12 01 b.Mile End 22-10-80
*Source:* Trainee. *Honours:* England Youth.

| | | | | | |
|---|---|---|---|---|---|
| 1997–98 | Norwich C | 1 | 0 | | |
| 1998–99 | Norwich C | 13 | 1 | | |
| 1999–2000 | Norwich C | 33 | 4 | | |
| 2000–01 | Norwich C | 41 | 2 | | |
| 2001–02 | Norwich C | 23 | 0 | | |
| 2002–03 | Norwich C | 21 | 0 | **132** | **7** |
| 2003–04 | Stoke C | 46 | 4 | **46** | **4** |

**TAGGART, Gerry# (D)** **431** **32**
H: 6 2 W: 14 07 b.Belfast 18-10-70
*Source:* Trainee. *Honours:* Northern Ireland Schools, Youth, Under-23, 51 full caps, 7 goals.

| | | | | | |
|---|---|---|---|---|---|
| 1988–89 | Manchester C | 11 | 1 | | |
| 1989–90 | Manchester C | 1 | 0 | **12** | **1** |
| 1989–90 | Barnsley | 21 | 2 | | |
| 1990–91 | Barnsley | 30 | 2 | | |
| 1991–92 | Barnsley | 38 | 3 | | |
| 1992–93 | Barnsley | 44 | 4 | | |
| 1993–94 | Barnsley | 38 | 2 | | |
| 1994–95 | Barnsley | 41 | 3 | **212** | **16** |
| 1995–96 | Bolton W | 11 | 1 | | |
| 1996–97 | Bolton W | 43 | 3 | | |
| 1997–98 | Bolton W | 15 | 0 | **69** | **4** |
| 1998–99 | Leicester C | 15 | 0 | | |
| 1999–2000 | Leicester C | 31 | 6 | | |
| 2000–01 | Leicester C | 24 | 2 | | |
| 2001–02 | Leicester C | 1 | 0 | | |
| 2002–03 | Leicester C | 37 | 1 | | |
| 2003–04 | Leicester C | 9 | 0 | **117** | **9** |
| 2003–04 | Stoke C | 21 | 2 | **21** | **2** |

**THOMAS, Wayne (D)** **277** **10**
H: 6 0 W: 11 02 b.Gloucester 17-5-79
*Source:* Trainee.

| | | | | | |
|---|---|---|---|---|---|
| 1995–96 | Torquay U | 6 | 0 | | |
| 1996–97 | Torquay U | 12 | 0 | | |
| 1997–98 | Torquay U | 21 | 1 | | |
| 1998–99 | Torquay U | 44 | 1 | | |
| 1999–2000 | Torquay U | 40 | 3 | **123** | **5** |
| 2000–01 | Stoke C | 34 | 0 | | |
| 2001–02 | Stoke C | 40 | 2 | | |
| 2002–03 | Stoke C | 41 | 0 | | |
| 2003–04 | Stoke C | 39 | 3 | **154** | **5** |

**WILKINSON, Andy (D)** **3** **0**
H: 5 11 W: 11 00 b.Stone 6-8-84
*Source:* Scholar.

| | | | | | |
|---|---|---|---|---|---|
| 2001–02 | Stoke C | 0 | 0 | | |
| 2002–03 | Stoke C | 0 | 0 | | |
| 2003–04 | Stoke C | 3 | 0 | **3** | **0** |

**WILLIAMS, Paul (D)** **390** **31**
H: 6 0 W: 14 04 b.Burton 26-3-71
*Source:* Trainee. *Honours:* England Under-21.

| | | | | | |
|---|---|---|---|---|---|
| 1989–90 | Derby Co | 10 | 1 | | |
| 1989–90 | *Lincoln C* | 3 | 0 | **3** | **0** |
| 1990–91 | Derby Co | 19 | 4 | | |
| 1991–92 | Derby Co | 41 | 13 | | |
| 1992–93 | Derby Co | 19 | 4 | | |
| 1993–94 | Derby Co | 34 | 1 | | |
| 1994–95 | Derby Co | 37 | 3 | **160** | **26** |
| 1995–96 | Coventry C | 32 | 2 | | |
| 1996–97 | Coventry C | 32 | 2 | | |
| 1997–98 | Coventry C | 20 | 0 | | |
| 1998–99 | Coventry C | 22 | 0 | | |
| 1999–2000 | Coventry C | 28 | 1 | | |
| 2000–01 | Coventry C | 30 | 0 | | |
| 2001–02 | Coventry C | 5 | 0 | **169** | **5** |
| 2001–02 | Southampton | 28 | 0 | | |
| 2002–03 | Southampton | 11 | 0 | | |
| 2003–04 | Southampton | 0 | 0 | **39** | **0** |
| 2003–04 | Stoke C | 19 | 0 | **19** | **0** |

**Scholars**
Armstrong, Matthew; Baptist, Adam R; Denny, Jay; Dickinson, Carl M; Duggan, Robert; Graves, Eric; Hughes, Daniel T; Humphreys, Shaun J; Jones, Steven D; Keogh, Richard J; Musgrove, Scott B; Palmer, Jermaine, A C; Paterson, Martin A; Sanna, Christopher M; Smith, Daniel R; Swift, Christopher; Swift, Matthew M; Teague, Wayne R; Tortoishell, Paul J; Warwick, Michael

**Players who do not hold a current contract but their registration has been retained by the club**
Beardsley, Gary J; Robinson, Martin P

## SUNDERLAND (76)

**ALNWICK, Ben (G)** **0** **0**
H: 6 0 W: 12 09 b.Sunderland 1-1-87
*Source:* Scholar. *Honours:* England Youth.

| | | | | | |
|---|---|---|---|---|---|
| 2003–04 | Sunderland | 0 | 0 | | |

**ARCA, Julio (D)** **129** **8**
H: 5 9 W: 11 00 b.Quilmes 31-1-81

| | | | | | |
|---|---|---|---|---|---|
| 1999–2000 | Argentinos Juniors | 19 | 0 | | |
| 2000–01 | Argentinos Juniors | 17 | 1 | **36** | **1** |
| 2000–01 | Sunderland | 27 | 2 | | |
| 2001–02 | Sunderland | 22 | 1 | | |
| 2002–03 | Sunderland | 13 | 0 | | |
| 2003–04 | Sunderland | 31 | 4 | **93** | **7** |

**BABB, Phil* (D)** **348** **18**
H: 6 0 W: 13 00 b.Lambeth 30-11-70
*Source:* Trainee. *Honours:* Eire B, 35 full caps.

| | | | | | |
|---|---|---|---|---|---|
| 1988–89 | Millwall | 0 | 0 | | |
| 1989–90 | Millwall | 0 | 0 | | |
| 1990–91 | Bradford C | 34 | 10 | | |
| 1991–92 | Bradford C | 46 | 4 | **80** | **14** |
| 1992–93 | Coventry C | 34 | 0 | | |
| 1993–94 | Coventry C | 40 | 3 | | |
| 1994–95 | Coventry C | 3 | 0 | **77** | **3** |
| 1994–95 | Liverpool | 34 | 0 | | |
| 1995–96 | Liverpool | 28 | 0 | | |
| 1996–97 | Liverpool | 22 | 1 | | |
| 1997–98 | Liverpool | 19 | 0 | | |
| 1998–99 | Liverpool | 25 | 0 | | |
| 1999–2000 | Liverpool | 0 | 0 | **128** | **1** |
| 1999–2000 | *Tranmere R* | 4 | 0 | **4** | **0** |
| 2000–01 | Sporting Lisbon | 11 | 0 | | |
| 2001–02 | Sporting Lisbon | 0 | 0 | **11** | **0** |
| 2002–03 | Sunderland | 26 | 0 | | |
| 2003–04 | Sunderland | 22 | 0 | **48** | **0** |

**BELL, Ryan (D)** **0** **0**
H: 6 3 W: 12 08 b.Ashington 30-3-86
*Source:* Trainee.

| | | | | | |
|---|---|---|---|---|---|
| 2003–04 | Sunderland | 0 | 0 | | |

**BJORKLUND, Joachim* (D)** **332** **1**
H: 5 11 W: 12 08 b.Vaxjo 15-3-71
*Honours:* Sweden 78 full caps.

| | | | | | |
|---|---|---|---|---|---|
| 1988 | Osters | 6 | 0 | | |
| 1989 | Osters | 0 | 0 | **6** | **0** |
| 1990 | Brann | 21 | 0 | | |
| 1991 | Brann | 22 | 0 | | |
| 1992 | Brann | 13 | 0 | **56** | **0** |
| 1993 | IFK Gothenburg | 19 | 0 | | |
| 1994 | IFK Gothenburg | 16 | 0 | | |
| 1995 | IFK Gothenburg | 11 | 0 | **46** | **0** |
| 1995–96 | Vicenza | 33 | 0 | **33** | **0** |
| 1996–97 | Rangers | 28 | 0 | | |
| 1997–98 | Rangers | 31 | 0 | **59** | **0** |
| 1998–99 | Valencia | 24 | 1 | | |
| 1999–2000 | Valencia | 23 | 0 | | |
| 2000–01 | Valencia | 10 | 0 | **57** | **1** |
| 2001–02 | Venezia | 18 | 0 | **18** | **0** |
| 2001–02 | Sunderland | 12 | 0 | | |
| 2002–03 | Sunderland | 20 | 0 | | |
| 2003–04 | Sunderland | 25 | 0 | **57** | **0** |

**BREEN, Gary (D)** **371** **9**
H: 6 2 W: 11 12 b.London 12-12-73
*Source:* Charlton Ath. *Honours:* Eire Under-21, 60 full caps, 6 goals.

| | | | | | |
|---|---|---|---|---|---|
| 1991–92 | Maidstone U | 19 | 0 | **19** | **0** |
| 1992–93 | Gillingham | 29 | 0 | | |
| 1993–94 | Gillingham | 22 | 0 | **51** | **0** |
| 1994–95 | Peterborough U | 44 | 1 | | |
| 1995–96 | Peterborough U | 25 | 0 | **69** | **1** |
| 1995–96 | Birmingham C | 18 | 1 | | |
| 1996–97 | Birmingham C | 22 | 1 | **40** | **2** |
| 1996–97 | Coventry C | 9 | 0 | | |
| 1997–98 | Coventry C | 30 | 1 | | |
| 1998–99 | Coventry C | 25 | 0 | | |
| 1999–2000 | Coventry C | 21 | 0 | | |
| 2000–01 | Coventry C | 31 | 1 | | |
| 2001–02 | Coventry C | 30 | 0 | **146** | **2** |
| 2002–03 | West Ham U | 14 | 0 | **14** | **0** |
| 2003–04 | Sunderland | 32 | 4 | **32** | **4** |

**BROWN, Chris (F)** **22** **10**
H: 6 1 W: 13 04 b.Doncaster 11-12-84
*Source:* Trainee. *Honours:* England Youth.

| | | | | | |
|---|---|---|---|---|---|
| 2002–03 | Sunderland | 0 | 0 | | |
| 2003–04 | Sunderland | 0 | 0 | | |
| 2003–04 | *Doncaster R* | 22 | 10 | **22** | **10** |

**BUTLER, Thomas (M)** **39** **0**
H: 5 7 W: 10 06 b.Dublin 25-4-81
*Source:* Trainee. *Honours:* Eire Under-21, 2 full caps.

| | | | | | |
|---|---|---|---|---|---|
| 1998–99 | Sunderland | 0 | 0 | | |
| 1999–2000 | Sunderland | 1 | 0 | | |
| 2000–01 | Sunderland | 4 | 0 | | |
| 2000–01 | *Darlington* | 8 | 0 | **8** | **0** |
| 2001–02 | Sunderland | 7 | 0 | | |
| 2002–03 | Sunderland | 7 | 0 | | |
| 2003–04 | Sunderland | 12 | 0 | **31** | **0** |

**BYFIELD, Darren# (F)** **187** **42**
H: 5 11 W: 12 00 b.Sutton Coldfield 29-9-76
*Source:* Trainee. *Honours:* Jamaica 7 full caps.

| | | | | | |
|---|---|---|---|---|---|
| 1993–94 | Aston Villa | 0 | 0 | | |
| 1994–95 | Aston Villa | 0 | 0 | | |
| 1995–96 | Aston Villa | 0 | 0 | | |
| 1996–97 | Aston Villa | 0 | 0 | | |
| 1997–98 | Aston Villa | 7 | 0 | | |
| 1998–99 | Aston Villa | 0 | 0 | | |
| 1998–99 | *Preston NE* | 5 | 1 | **5** | **1** |
| 1999–2000 | Aston Villa | 0 | 0 | **7** | **0** |
| 1999–2000 | *Northampton T* | 6 | 1 | **6** | **1** |
| 1999–2000 | *Cambridge U* | 4 | 0 | **4** | **0** |
| 1999–2000 | *Blackpool* | 3 | 0 | **3** | **0** |
| 2000–01 | Walsall | 40 | 9 | | |
| 2001–02 | Walsall | 37 | 4 | **77** | **13** |
| 2001–02 | Rotherham U | 3 | 2 | | |
| 2002–03 | Rotherham U | 37 | 13 | | |
| 2003–04 | Rotherham U | 28 | 7 | **68** | **22** |
| 2003–04 | Sunderland | 17 | 5 | **17** | **5** |

**CLARK, Ben (D)** **6** **0**
H: 6 2 W: 12 03 b.Shotley Bridge 24-1-83
*Source:* Manchester U Trainee. *Honours:* England Youth, Under-20.

| | | | | | |
|---|---|---|---|---|---|
| 2000–01 | Sunderland | 0 | 0 | | |
| 2001–02 | Sunderland | 0 | 0 | | |
| 2002–03 | Sunderland | 1 | 0 | | |
| 2003–04 | Sunderland | 5 | 0 | **6** | **0** |

**COLLINS, Patrick* (D)** 0 0

H: 6 2 W: 12 08 b.Newcastle 4-2-85

*Source:* Scholar. *Honours:* England Youth.

| | | | | | |
|---|---|---|---|---|---|
| 2001–02 | Sunderland | 0 | 0 | | |
| 2002–03 | Sunderland | 0 | 0 | | |
| 2003–04 | Sunderland | 0 | 0 | | |

**DICKMAN, Jonjo (M)** 3 0

H: 5 8 W: 10 05 b.Hexham 22-9-81

| | | | | | |
|---|---|---|---|---|---|
| 1998–99 | Sunderland | 0 | 0 | | |
| 1999–2000 | Sunderland | 0 | 0 | | |
| 2000–01 | Sunderland | 0 | 0 | | |
| 2001–02 | Sunderland | 0 | 0 | | |
| 2002–03 | Sunderland | 1 | 0 | | |
| 2003–04 | Sunderland | 0 | 0 | 1 | 0 |
| 2003–04 | *York C* | 2 | 0 | 2 | 0 |

**DODDS, Lewis (M)** 0 0

H: 5 8 W: 10 07 b.Spennymoor 14-12-85

*Source:* Trainee. *Honours:* England Youth.

| | | | | | |
|---|---|---|---|---|---|
| 2002–03 | Sunderland | 0 | 0 | | |
| 2003–04 | Sunderland | 0 | 0 | | |

**FLYNN, Niall (M)** 0 0

H: 5 7 W: 10 00 b.Dublin 22-1-86

*Source:* Trainee.

| | | | | | |
|---|---|---|---|---|---|
| 2002–03 | Sunderland | 0 | 0 | | |
| 2003–04 | Sunderland | 0 | 0 | | |

**GEORGE, Lee‡ (F)** 0 0

H: 5 10 W: 10 00 b.Ashington 20-4-85

*Source:* Trainee.

| | | | | | |
|---|---|---|---|---|---|
| 2002–03 | Sunderland | 0 | 0 | | |
| 2003–04 | Sunderland | 0 | 0 | | |

**HEALY, Colin (M)** 65 3

H: 5 11 W: 11 00 b.Cork 14-3-80

*Source:* Wilton U. *Honours:* Eire 13 full caps, 1 goal.

| | | | | | |
|---|---|---|---|---|---|
| 1998–99 | Celtic | 3 | 0 | | |
| 1999–2000 | Celtic | 10 | 1 | | |
| 2000–01 | Celtic | 11 | 0 | | |
| 2001–02 | Celtic | 4 | 0 | | |
| 2001–02 | *Coventry C* | 17 | 2 | 17 | 2 |
| 2002–03 | Celtic | 0 | 0 | 28 | 1 |
| 2003–04 | Sunderland | 20 | 0 | 20 | 0 |

**HUNTLEY, Rob‡ (M)** 0 0

H: 5 8 W: 10 00 b.Easington 27-9-84

| | | | | | |
|---|---|---|---|---|---|
| 2002–03 | Sunderland | 0 | 0 | | |
| 2003–04 | Sunderland | 0 | 0 | | |

**INGHAM, Michael (G)** 56 0

H: 6 4 W: 13 10 b.Preston 9-9-80

*Source:* Malachians. *Honours:* Northern Ireland Under-21.

| | | | | | |
|---|---|---|---|---|---|
| 1998–99 | Cliftonville | 18 | 0 | 18 | 0 |
| 1999–2000 | Sunderland | 0 | 0 | | |
| 1999–2000 | *Carlisle U* | 7 | 0 | 7 | 0 |
| 2000–01 | Sunderland | 0 | 0 | | |
| 2001–02 | Sunderland | 0 | 0 | | |
| 2001–02 | *Stoke C* | 0 | 0 | | |
| 2002–03 | Sunderland | 0 | 0 | | |
| 2002–03 | *Darlington* | 3 | 0 | 3 | 0 |
| 2002–03 | *York C* | 17 | 0 | 17 | 0 |
| 2003–04 | Sunderland | 0 | 0 | | |
| 2003–04 | *Wrexham* | 11 | 0 | 11 | 0 |

**KINGSBERRY, Chris (M)** 0 0

H: 5 5 W: 7 00 b.Lisburn 10-9-85

*Source:* Trainee.

| | | | | | |
|---|---|---|---|---|---|
| 2002–03 | Sunderland | 0 | 0 | | |
| 2003–04 | Sunderland | 0 | 0 | | |

**KYLE, Kevin (F)** 85 11

H: 6 3 W: 13 00 b.Stranraer 7-6-81

*Honours:* Scotland Under-21, 9 full caps, 1 goal.

| | | | | | |
|---|---|---|---|---|---|
| 1998–99 | Sunderland | 0 | 0 | | |
| 1999–2000 | Sunderland | 0 | 0 | | |
| 2000–01 | Sunderland | 3 | 0 | | |
| 2000–01 | *Huddersfield T* | 4 | 0 | 4 | 0 |
| 2000–01 | *Darlington* | 5 | 1 | 5 | 1 |
| 2000–01 | *Rochdale* | 6 | 0 | 6 | 0 |
| 2001–02 | Sunderland | 6 | 0 | | |
| 2002–03 | Sunderland | 17 | 0 | | |
| 2003–04 | Sunderland | 44 | 10 | 70 | 10 |

**LEADBITTER, Grant (M)** 0 0

H: 5 9 W: 10 03 b.Sunderland 7-1-86

*Source:* Trainee. *Honours:* FA Schools, England Youth.

| | | | | | |
|---|---|---|---|---|---|
| 2002–03 | Sunderland | 0 | 0 | | |
| 2003–04 | Sunderland | 0 | 0 | | |

**McATEER, Jason* (M)** 339 20

H: 5 10 W: 12 04 b.Birkenhead 18-6-71

*Source:* Marine. *Honours:* Eire B, 52 full caps, 3 goals.

| | | | | | |
|---|---|---|---|---|---|
| 1991–92 | Bolton W | 0 | 0 | | |
| 1992–93 | Bolton W | 21 | 0 | | |
| 1993–94 | Bolton W | 46 | 3 | | |
| 1994–95 | Bolton W | 43 | 5 | | |
| 1995–96 | Bolton W | 4 | 0 | 114 | 8 |
| 1995–96 | Liverpool | 29 | 0 | | |
| 1996–97 | Liverpool | 37 | 1 | | |
| 1997–98 | Liverpool | 21 | 2 | | |
| 1998–99 | Liverpool | 13 | 0 | 100 | 3 |
| 1998–99 | Blackburn R | 13 | 1 | | |
| 1999–2000 | Blackburn R | 28 | 2 | | |
| 2000–01 | Blackburn R | 27 | 1 | | |
| 2001–02 | Blackburn R | 4 | 0 | 72 | 4 |
| 2001–02 | Sunderland | 26 | 2 | | |
| 2002–03 | Sunderland | 9 | 1 | | |
| 2003–04 | Sunderland | 18 | 2 | 53 | 5 |

**McCARTNEY, George (D)** 85 0

H: 5 11 W: 10 10 b.Belfast 29-4-81

*Source:* Trainee. *Honours:* Northern Ireland Schools, Youth, Under-21, 16 full caps, 1 goal.

| | | | | | |
|---|---|---|---|---|---|
| 1998–99 | Sunderland | 0 | 0 | | |
| 1999–2000 | Sunderland | 0 | 0 | | |
| 2000–01 | Sunderland | 2 | 0 | | |
| 2001–02 | Sunderland | 18 | 0 | | |
| 2002–03 | Sunderland | 24 | 0 | | |
| 2003–04 | Sunderland | 41 | 0 | 85 | 0 |

**McLEAN, Euan (G)** 0 0

H: 6 3 W: 13 07 b.Kilmarnock 9-1-86

*Source:* Trainee.

| | | | | | |
|---|---|---|---|---|---|
| 2003–04 | Sunderland | 0 | 0 | | |

**MEDINA, Nicolas (M)** 47 1

H: 5 9 W: 10 04 b.Buenos Aires 17-2-82

| | | | | | |
|---|---|---|---|---|---|
| 1999–2000 | Argentinos Jun | 26 | 0 | | |
| 2000–01 | Argentinos Jun | 21 | 1 | 47 | 1 |
| 2001–02 | Sunderland | 0 | 0 | | |
| 2002–03 | Sunderland | 0 | 0 | | |
| 2003–04 | Sunderland | 0 | 0 | | |

**MYHRE, Thomas (G)** 225 0

H: 6 4 W: 13 12 b.Sarpsborg 16-10-73

*Honours:* Norway 33 full caps.

| | | | | | |
|---|---|---|---|---|---|
| 1993 | Viking | 22 | 0 | | |
| 1994 | Viking | 22 | 0 | | |
| 1995 | Viking | 24 | 0 | | |
| 1996 | Viking | 0 | 0 | | |
| 1997 | Viking | 26 | 0 | 94 | 0 |
| 1997–98 | Everton | 22 | 0 | | |
| 1998–99 | Everton | 38 | 0 | | |
| 1999–2000 | Everton | 4 | 0 | | |
| 1999–2000 | *Rangers* | 3 | 0 | 3 | 0 |
| 1999–2000 | *Birmingham C* | 7 | 0 | 7 | 0 |
| 2000–01 | Everton | 6 | 0 | | |
| 2000–01 | *Tranmere R* | 3 | 0 | 3 | 0 |
| 2000–01 | FC Copenhagen | 14 | 0 | 14 | 0 |
| 2001–02 | Everton | 0 | 0 | 70 | 0 |
| 2001–02 | Besiktas | 13 | 0 | 13 | 0 |
| 2002–03 | Sunderland | 2 | 0 | | |
| 2003–04 | Sunderland | 4 | 0 | 6 | 0 |
| 2003–04 | *Crystal Palace* | 15 | 0 | 15 | 0 |

**OSTER, John# (M)** 142 15

H: 5 9 W: 10 09 b.Boston 8-12-78

*Source:* Trainee. *Honours:* Wales Youth, Under-21, B, 11 full caps.

| | | | | | |
|---|---|---|---|---|---|
| 1996–97 | Grimsby T | 24 | 3 | | |
| 1997–98 | Everton | 31 | 1 | | |
| 1998–99 | Everton | 9 | 0 | 40 | 1 |
| 1999–2000 | Sunderland | 10 | 0 | | |
| 2000–01 | Sunderland | 8 | 0 | | |
| 2001–02 | Sunderland | 0 | 0 | | |
| 2001–02 | *Barnsley* | 2 | 0 | 2 | 0 |
| 2002–03 | Sunderland | 3 | 0 | | |
| 2002–03 | *Grimsby T* | 17 | 6 | 41 | 9 |
| 2003–04 | Sunderland | 38 | 5 | 59 | 5 |

**PEETERS, Tom‡ (M)** 33 1

H: 5 10 W: 11 00 b.Bornem 25-9-78

*Source:* Ekeren.

| | | | | | |
|---|---|---|---|---|---|
| 1999–2000 | Mechelen | 33 | 1 | 33 | 1 |
| 2000–01 | Sunderland | 0 | 0 | | |
| 2001–02 | Sunderland | 0 | 0 | | |
| 2002–03 | Sunderland | 0 | 0 | | |
| 2003–04 | Sunderland | 0 | 0 | | |

**PIPER, Matt (F)** 46 2

H: 6 0 W: 13 00 b.Leicester 29-9-81

*Source:* Trainee.

| | | | | | |
|---|---|---|---|---|---|
| 1999–2000 | Leicester C | 0 | 0 | | |
| 2000–01 | Leicester C | 0 | 0 | | |
| 2001–02 | *Mansfield T* | 8 | 1 | 8 | 1 |
| 2001–02 | Leicester C | 16 | 1 | | |
| 2002–03 | Leicester C | 0 | 0 | 16 | 1 |
| 2002–03 | Sunderland | 13 | 0 | | |
| 2003–04 | Sunderland | 9 | 0 | 22 | 0 |

**POOM, Mart (G)** 238 1

H: 6 4 W: 14 03 b.Tallinn 3-2-72

*Honours:* Estonia 98 full caps.

| | | | | | |
|---|---|---|---|---|---|
| 1992–93 | Flora Tallinn | 11 | 0 | | |
| 1993–94 | Flora Tallinn | 11 | 0 | | |
| 1994–95 | Portsmouth | 0 | 0 | | |
| 1995–96 | Portsmouth | 4 | 0 | | |
| 1995–96 | Flora Tallinn | 7 | 0 | | |
| 1996–97 | Portsmouth | 0 | 0 | 4 | 0 |
| 1996–97 | Flora Tallinn | 12 | 0 | 41 | 0 |
| 1996–97 | Derby Co | 4 | 0 | | |
| 1997–98 | Derby Co | 36 | 0 | | |
| 1998–99 | Derby Co | 17 | 0 | | |
| 1999–2000 | Derby Co | 28 | 0 | | |
| 2000–01 | Derby Co | 33 | 0 | | |
| 2001–02 | Derby Co | 15 | 0 | | |
| 2002–03 | Derby Co | 13 | 0 | 146 | 0 |
| 2002–03 | Sunderland | 4 | 0 | | |
| 2003–04 | Sunderland | 43 | 1 | 47 | 1 |

**RAMSDEN, Simon* (D)** 32 0

H: 6 0 W: 12 04 b.Bishop Auckland 17-12-81

*Source:* Scholar.

| | | | | | |
|---|---|---|---|---|---|
| 2000–01 | Sunderland | 0 | 0 | | |
| 2001–02 | Sunderland | 0 | 0 | | |
| 2002–03 | Sunderland | 0 | 0 | | |
| 2002–03 | *Notts Co* | 32 | 0 | 32 | 0 |
| 2003–04 | Sunderland | 0 | 0 | | |

**REDDY, Michael* (F)** 71 15

H: 6 1 W: 11 07 b.Graignamanagh 24-3-80

*Source:* Kilkenny C. *Honours:* Eire Under-21.

| | | | | | |
|---|---|---|---|---|---|
| 1999–2000 | Sunderland | 8 | 1 | | |
| 2000–01 | Sunderland | 2 | 0 | | |
| 2000–01 | *Swindon T* | 18 | 4 | 18 | 4 |
| 2001–02 | Sunderland | 0 | 0 | | |
| 2001–02 | *Hull C* | 5 | 4 | 5 | 4 |
| 2001–02 | *Barnsley* | 0 | 0 | | |
| 2002–03 | Sunderland | 0 | 0 | | |
| 2002–03 | *York C* | 11 | 2 | 11 | 2 |
| 2002–03 | *Sheffield W* | 15 | 3 | | |
| 2003–04 | Sunderland | 0 | 0 | 10 | 1 |
| 2003–04 | *Sheffield W* | 12 | 1 | 27 | 4 |

**ROSSITER, Mark* (D)** 0 0

H: 5 10 W: 12 04 b.Sligo 27-5-83

*Source:* Scholar. *Honours:* Eire Under-21.

| | | | | | |
|---|---|---|---|---|---|
| 2000–01 | Sunderland | 0 | 0 | | |
| 2001–02 | Sunderland | 0 | 0 | | |
| 2002–03 | Sunderland | 0 | 0 | | |
| 2003–04 | Sunderland | 0 | 0 | | |

**RYAN, Richie (M)** 2 0

H: 5 10 W: 10 07 b.Kilkenny 6-1-85

*Source:* Scholar.

| | | | | | |
|---|---|---|---|---|---|
| 2001–02 | Sunderland | 0 | 0 | | |
| 2002–03 | Sunderland | 2 | 0 | | |
| 2003–04 | Sunderland | 0 | 0 | 2 | 0 |

**SCOTT, Chris‡ (D)** 0 0

H: 5 9 W: 11 05 b.South Shields 11-1-85

*Source:* Trainee.

| | | | | | |
|---|---|---|---|---|---|
| 2002–03 | Sunderland | 0 | 0 | | |
| 2003–04 | Sunderland | 0 | 0 | | |

**SMITH, Daniel (D)** 0 0

H: 5 10 W: 10 08 b.Sunderland 5-10-86

*Source:* Scholar.

| | | | | | |
|---|---|---|---|---|---|
| 2003–04 | Sunderland | 0 | 0 | | |

**SMITH, Tommy# (F)** 184 37

H: 5 9 W: 10 00 b.Hemel Hempstead 22-5-80

*Source:* Trainee. *Honours:* England Youth, Under-21

| | | | | | |
|---|---|---|---|---|---|
| 1997–98 | Watford | 1 | 0 | | |
| 1998–99 | Watford | 8 | 2 | | |
| 1999–2000 | Watford | 22 | 2 | | |
| 2000–01 | Watford | 43 | 11 | | |
| 2001–02 | Watford | 40 | 11 | | |
| 2002–03 | Watford | 35 | 7 | | |

| | | | | | |
|---|---|---|---|---|---|
| 2003–04 | Watford | 0 | 0 | **149** | **33** |
| 2003–04 | Sunderland | 35 | 4 | **35** | **4** |

**STEWART, Marcus (F)** **438 157**
H: 5 10 W: 11 08 b.Bristol 7-11-72
*Source:* Trainee. *Honours:* England Schools, Football League.

| | | | | | |
|---|---|---|---|---|---|
| 1991–92 | Bristol R | 33 | 5 | | |
| 1992–93 | Bristol R | 38 | 11 | | |
| 1993–94 | Bristol R | 29 | 5 | | |
| 1994–95 | Bristol R | 27 | 15 | | |
| 1995–96 | Bristol R | 44 | 21 | **171** | **57** |
| 1996–97 | Huddersfield T | 20 | 7 | | |
| 1997–98 | Huddersfield T | 41 | 15 | | |
| 1998–99 | Huddersfield T | 43 | 22 | | |
| 1999–2000 | Huddersfield T | 29 | 14 | **133** | **58** |
| 1999–2000 | Ipswich T | 10 | 2 | | |
| 2000–01 | Ipswich T | 34 | 19 | | |
| 2001–02 | Ipswich T | 28 | 6 | | |
| 2002–03 | Ipswich T | 3 | 0 | **75** | **27** |
| 2002–03 | Sunderland | 19 | 1 | | |
| 2003–04 | Sunderland | 40 | 14 | **59** | **15** |

**TAYLOR, Sean (D)** **0 0**
H: 5 7 W: 10 07 b.Amble 9-12-85
*Source:* Trainee.

| | | | | | |
|---|---|---|---|---|---|
| 2002–03 | Sunderland | 0 | 0 | | |
| 2003–04 | Sunderland | 0 | 0 | | |

**TEGGART, Neil (F)** **15 0**
H: 6 2 W: 12 01 b.Downpatrick 16-9-84
*Source:* Scholar. *Honours:* Northern Ireland Youth.

| | | | | | |
|---|---|---|---|---|---|
| 2001–02 | Sunderland | 0 | 0 | | |
| 2002–03 | Sunderland | 0 | 0 | | |
| 2003–04 | Sunderland | 0 | 0 | | |
| 2003–04 | *Darlington* | 15 | 0 | **15** | **0** |

**THIRLWELL, Paul* (M)** **89 0**
H: 6 2 W: 12 02 b.Springwell 13-2-79
*Source:* Trainee. *Honours:* England Under-21.

| | | | | | |
|---|---|---|---|---|---|
| 1996–97 | Sunderland | 0 | 0 | | |
| 1997–98 | Sunderland | 0 | 0 | | |
| 1998–99 | Sunderland | 2 | 0 | | |
| 1999–2000 | Sunderland | 8 | 0 | | |
| 1999–2000 | *Swindon T* | 12 | 0 | **12** | **0** |
| 2000–01 | Sunderland | 5 | 0 | | |
| 2001–02 | Sunderland | 14 | 0 | | |
| 2002–03 | Sunderland | 19 | 0 | | |
| 2003–04 | Sunderland | 29 | 0 | **77** | **0** |

**THORNTON, Sean (M)** **47 6**
H: 5 11 W: 12 03 b.Drogheda 18-5-83
*Source:* Scholar. *Honours:* Eire Under-21.

| | | | | | |
|---|---|---|---|---|---|
| 2001–02 | Tranmere R | 11 | 1 | **11** | **1** |
| 2002–03 | Sunderland | 11 | 1 | | |
| 2002–03 | *Blackpool* | 3 | 0 | **3** | **0** |
| 2003–04 | Sunderland | 22 | 4 | **33** | **5** |

**WHITLEY, Jeff# (M)** **183 12**
H: 5 8 W: 11 00 b.Zambia 28-1-79
*Source:* Trainee. *Honours:* Northern Ireland Under-21, B, 12 full caps, 1 goal.

| | | | | | |
|---|---|---|---|---|---|
| 1995–96 | Manchester C | 0 | 0 | | |
| 1996–97 | Manchester C | 23 | 1 | | |
| 1997–98 | Manchester C | 17 | 1 | | |
| 1998–99 | Manchester C | 8 | 1 | | |
| 1998–99 | *Wrexham* | 9 | 2 | **9** | **2** |
| 1999–2000 | Manchester C | 42 | 4 | | |
| 2000–01 | Manchester C | 31 | 1 | | |
| 2001–02 | Manchester C | 2 | 0 | | |
| 2001–02 | *Notts Co* | 6 | 0 | | |
| 2002–03 | Manchester C | 0 | 0 | **123** | **8** |
| 2002–03 | *Notts Co* | 12 | 0 | **18** | **0** |
| 2003–04 | Sunderland | 33 | 2 | **33** | **2** |

**WILLIAMS, Darren (D)** **218 4**
H: 5 11 W: 12 00 b.Middlebrough 28-4-77
*Source:* Trainee. *Honours:* England Under-21, B.

| | | | | | |
|---|---|---|---|---|---|
| 1994–95 | York C | 1 | 0 | | |
| 1995–96 | York C | 18 | 0 | | |
| 1996–97 | York C | 1 | 0 | **20** | **0** |
| 1996–97 | Sunderland | 11 | 2 | | |
| 1997–98 | Sunderland | 36 | 2 | | |
| 1998–99 | Sunderland | 25 | 0 | | |
| 1999–2000 | Sunderland | 25 | 0 | | |
| 2000–01 | Sunderland | 28 | 0 | | |
| 2001–02 | Sunderland | 28 | 0 | | |
| 2002–03 | Sunderland | 16 | 0 | | |
| 2003–04 | Sunderland | 29 | 0 | **198** | **4** |

**WRIGHT, Stephen (D)** **85 1**
H: 6 0 W: 12 08 b.Liverpool 8-2-80
*Source:* Trainee. *Honours:* England Youth, Under-21.

| | | | | | |
|---|---|---|---|---|---|
| 1997–98 | Liverpool | 0 | 0 | | |
| 1998–99 | Liverpool | 0 | 0 | | |
| 1999–2000 | Liverpool | 0 | 0 | | |
| 1999–2000 | *Crewe Alex* | 23 | 0 | **23** | **0** |
| 2000–01 | Liverpool | 2 | 0 | | |
| 2001–02 | Liverpool | 12 | 0 | **14** | **0** |
| 2002–03 | Sunderland | 26 | 0 | | |
| 2003–04 | Sunderland | 22 | 1 | **48** | **1** |

**Scholars**
Christensen, Ben; Clarkson, Robert J; Graham, Ian P; Martin, Jay B; Smith, Adam; Toft, John; Wanless, Robert J

## SWANSEA C (77)

**BRITTON, Leon (M)** **67 3**
H: 5 6 W: 10 00 b.Merton 16-9-82
*Source:* Trainee. *Honours:* England Youth.

| | | | | | |
|---|---|---|---|---|---|
| 1999–2000 | West Ham U | 0 | 0 | | |
| 2000–01 | West Ham U | 0 | 0 | | |
| 2001–02 | West Ham U | 0 | 0 | | |
| 2002–03 | West Ham U | 0 | 0 | | |
| 2002–03 | *Swansea C* | 25 | 0 | | |
| 2003–04 | Swansea C | 42 | 3 | **67** | **3** |

**COATES, Jonathan* (M)** **280 23**
H: 5 8 W: 10 04 b.Swansea 27-6-75
*Source:* Trainee. *Honours:* Wales Youth, B, Under-21.

| | | | | | |
|---|---|---|---|---|---|
| 1993–94 | Swansea C | 4 | 1 | | |
| 1994–95 | Swansea C | 5 | 0 | | |
| 1995–96 | Swansea C | 18 | 0 | | |
| 1996–97 | Swansea C | 40 | 3 | | |
| 1997–98 | Swansea C | 44 | 7 | | |
| 1998–99 | Swansea C | 33 | 0 | | |
| 1999–2000 | Swansea C | 42 | 6 | | |
| 2000–01 | Swansea C | 19 | 1 | | |
| 2001–02 | Swansea C | 45 | 5 | | |
| 2001–02 | Cheltenham T | 0 | 0 | | |
| From Woking. | | | | | |
| 2002–03 | Swansea C | 3 | 0 | | |
| 2003–04 | Swansea C | 27 | 0 | **280** | **23** |

**CONNOLLY, Karl* (M)** **440 101**
H: 5 9 W: 11 08 b.Prescot 9-2-70
*Source:* Napoli (Liverpool Sunday League).

| | | | | | |
|---|---|---|---|---|---|
| 1990–91 | Wrexham | 0 | 0 | | |
| 1991–92 | Wrexham | 36 | 8 | | |
| 1992–93 | Wrexham | 42 | 9 | | |
| 1993–94 | Wrexham | 39 | 2 | | |
| 1994–95 | Wrexham | 45 | 10 | | |
| 1995–96 | Wrexham | 46 | 18 | | |
| 1996–97 | Wrexham | 30 | 14 | | |
| 1997–98 | Wrexham | 35 | 7 | | |
| 1998–99 | Wrexham | 44 | 11 | | |
| 1999–2000 | Wrexham | 41 | 9 | **358** | **88** |
| 2000–01 | QPR | 23 | 4 | | |
| 2001–02 | QPR | 33 | 4 | | |
| 2002–03 | QPR | 16 | 4 | **72** | **12** |
| 2003–04 | Swansea C | 10 | 1 | **10** | **1** |

**CONNOR, Paul (F)** **160 45**
H: 6 2 W: 11 08 b.Bishop Auckland 12-1-79
*Source:* Trainee.

| | | | | | |
|---|---|---|---|---|---|
| 1996–97 | Middlesbrough | 0 | 0 | | |
| 1997–98 | Middlesbrough | 0 | 0 | | |
| 1997–98 | *Hartlepool U* | 5 | 0 | **5** | **0** |
| 1998–99 | Middlesbrough | 0 | 0 | | |
| 1998–99 | *Stoke C* | 3 | 2 | | |
| 1999–2000 | Stoke C | 26 | 5 | | |
| 2000–01 | Stoke C | 7 | 0 | **36** | **7** |
| 2000–01 | *Cambridge U* | 13 | 5 | **13** | **5** |
| 2000–01 | Rochdale | 14 | 10 | | |
| 2001–02 | Rochdale | 17 | 1 | | |
| 2002–03 | Rochdale | 39 | 12 | | |
| 2003–04 | Rochdale | 24 | 5 | **94** | **28** |
| 2003–04 | Swansea C | 12 | 5 | **12** | **5** |

**CORBISIERSO, Antonio§ (M)** **5 0**
H: 5 8 W: 11 04 b.Reading 17-11-84
*Source:* Scholar.

| | | | | | |
|---|---|---|---|---|---|
| 2003–04 | Swansea C | 5 | 0 | **5** | **0** |

**DAVIS, Earl‡ (D)** **0 0**
H: 6 1 W: 13 02 b.Manchester 17-5-83
*Source:* Scholar.

| | | | | | |
|---|---|---|---|---|---|
| 2002–03 | Burnley | 0 | 0 | | |
| 2003–04 | Swansea C | 0 | 0 | | |

**DURKAN, Kieron‡ (M)** **275 22**
H: 5 11 W: 10 05 b.Chester 1-12-73
*Source:* Trainee. *Honours:* Eire Under-21.

| | | | | | |
|---|---|---|---|---|---|
| 1991–92 | Wrexham | 1 | 0 | | |
| 1992–93 | Wrexham | 1 | 0 | | |
| 1993–94 | Wrexham | 10 | 1 | | |
| 1994–95 | Wrexham | 30 | 2 | | |
| 1995–96 | Wrexham | 8 | 0 | **50** | **3** |
| 1995–96 | Stockport Co | 16 | 0 | | |
| 1996–97 | Stockport Co | 41 | 3 | | |
| 1997–98 | Stockport Co | 7 | 1 | **64** | **4** |
| 1997–98 | Macclesfield T | 4 | 0 | | |
| 1998–99 | Macclesfield T | 26 | 3 | | |
| 1999–2000 | Macclesfield T | 42 | 6 | | |
| 2000–01 | Macclesfield T | 31 | 4 | **103** | **13** |
| 2000–01 | *York C* | 7 | 0 | **7** | **0** |
| 2001–02 | Rochdale | 30 | 1 | | |
| 2002–03 | Rochdale | 0 | 0 | **30** | **1** |
| 2002–03 | Swansea C | 6 | 0 | | |
| 2003–04 | Swansea C | 15 | 1 | **21** | **1** |

**FREESTONE, Roger* (G)** **629 3**
H: 6 3 W: 13 00 b.Newport 19-8-68
*Source:* Trainee. *Honours:* Wales Schools, Youth, Under-21, 1 full cap.

| | | | | | |
|---|---|---|---|---|---|
| 1986–87 | Newport Co | 13 | 0 | **13** | **0** |
| 1986–87 | Chelsea | 6 | 0 | | |
| 1987–88 | Chelsea | 15 | 0 | | |
| 1988–89 | Chelsea | 21 | 0 | | |
| 1989–90 | Chelsea | 0 | 0 | | |
| 1989–90 | *Swansea C* | 14 | 0 | | |
| 1989–90 | *Hereford U* | 8 | 0 | **8** | **0** |
| 1990–91 | Chelsea | 0 | 0 | **42** | **0** |
| 1991–92 | Swansea C | 42 | 0 | | |
| 1992–93 | Swansea C | 46 | 0 | | |
| 1993–94 | Swansea C | 46 | 0 | | |
| 1994–95 | Swansea C | 45 | 1 | | |
| 1995–96 | Swansea C | 45 | 2 | | |
| 1996–97 | Swansea C | 45 | 0 | | |
| 1997–98 | Swansea C | 43 | 0 | | |
| 1998–99 | Swansea C | 38 | 0 | | |
| 1999–2000 | Swansea C | 46 | 0 | | |
| 2000–01 | Swansea C | 43 | 0 | | |
| 2001–02 | Swansea C | 43 | 0 | | |
| 2002–03 | Swansea C | 33 | 0 | | |
| 2003–04 | Swansea C | 37 | 0 | **566** | **3** |

**HOWARD, Mike* (D)** **228 2**
H: 5 6 W: 10 07 b.Birkenhead 2-12-78
*Source:* Tranmere R Trainee.

| | | | | | |
|---|---|---|---|---|---|
| 1997–98 | Swansea C | 3 | 0 | | |
| 1998–99 | Swansea C | 39 | 1 | | |
| 1999–2000 | Swansea C | 40 | 0 | | |
| 2000–01 | Swansea C | 41 | 0 | | |
| 2001–02 | Swansea C | 42 | 1 | | |
| 2002–03 | Swansea C | 38 | 0 | | |
| 2003–04 | Swansea C | 25 | 0 | **228** | **2** |

**HYLTON, Leon (D)** **19 0**
H: 5 9 W: 11 00 b.Birmingham 27-1-83
*Honours:* England Youth, Under-20.

| | | | | | |
|---|---|---|---|---|---|
| 1999–2000 | Aston Villa | 0 | 0 | | |
| 2000–01 | Aston Villa | 0 | 0 | | |
| 2001–02 | Aston Villa | 0 | 0 | | |
| 2002–03 | Aston Villa | 0 | 0 | | |
| 2002–03 | *Swansea C* | 8 | 0 | | |
| 2003–04 | Swansea C | 11 | 0 | **19** | **0** |

**IRIEKPEN, Ezomo (D)** **52 3**
H: 6 1 W: 12 02 b.East London 14-5-82
*Source:* Trainee. *Honours:* England Youth.

| | | | | | |
|---|---|---|---|---|---|
| 1998–99 | West Ham U | 0 | 0 | | |
| 1999–2000 | West Ham U | 0 | 0 | | |
| 2000–01 | West Ham U | 0 | 0 | | |
| 2001–02 | West Ham U | 0 | 0 | | |
| 2002–03 | West Ham U | 0 | 0 | | |
| 2002–03 | *Leyton Orient* | 5 | 1 | **5** | **1** |
| 2002–03 | *Cambridge U* | 13 | 1 | **13** | **1** |
| 2003–04 | Swansea C | 34 | 1 | **34** | **1** |

**JONES, Stuart (D)** **30 0**
H: 6 0 W: 11 08 b.Aberystwyth 14-3-84
*Source:* Scholar. *Honours:* Wales Youth.

| | | | | | |
|---|---|---|---|---|---|
| 2002–03 | Swansea C | 6 | 0 | | |
| 2003–04 | Swansea C | 24 | 0 | **30** | **0** |

**MARTINEZ, Roberto (M)** 256 19
H: 5 9 W: 12 02 b.Balaguer 13-7-73
*Source:* Balaguer.
1995–96 Wigan Ath 42 9
1996–97 Wigan Ath 43 4
1997–98 Wigan Ath 33 1
1998–99 Wigan Ath 10 0
1999–2000 Wigan Ath 25 3
2000–01 Wigan Ath 34 0 **187 17**
2001–02 Motherwell 17 0 **17 0**
2002–03 Walsall 6 0 **6 0**
2002–03 Swansea C 19 2
2003–04 Swansea C 27 0 **46 2**

**MAXWELL, Leyton‡ (M)** 57 3
H: 5 8 W: 11 00 b.Rhyl 3-10-79
*Source:* Trainee. *Honours:* Wales Youth, Under-21.
1997–98 Liverpool 0 0
1998–99 Liverpool 0 0
1999–2000 Liverpool 0 0
2000–01 Liverpool 0 0
2000–01 *Stockport Co* 20 2 **20 2**
2001–02 Cardiff C 17 1
2002–03 Cardiff C 16 0
2003–04 Cardiff C 1 0 **34 1**
2003–04 Swansea C 3 0 **3 0**

**MAYLETT, Brad (M)** 84 5
H: 5 10 W: 10 04 b.Manchester 24-12-80
*Source:* Trainee.
1998–99 Burnley 17 0
1999–2000 Burnley 0 0
2000–01 Burnley 12 0
2001–02 Burnley 10 0
2002–03 Burnley 6 0 **45 0**
2002–03 *Swansea C* 6 0
2003–04 Swansea C 33 5 **39 5**

**MUMFORD, Andrew* (M)** 62 6
H: 6 1 W: 12 03 b.Neath 18-6-81
*Source:* Llanelli. *Honours:* Wales Schools, Youth, Under-21.
2000–01 Swansea C 6 0
2001–02 Swansea C 32 5
2002–03 Swansea C 24 1
2003–04 Swansea C 0 0 **62 6**

**MURPHY, Brian (G)** 12 0
H: 6 0 W: 13 00 b.Waterford 7-5-83
*Honours:* Eire Under-21.
2000–01 Manchester C 0 0
2001–02 Manchester C 0 0
2002–03 Manchester C 0 0
2002–03 *Oldham Ath* 0 0
2002–03 *Peterborough U* 1 0 **1 0**
From Waterford
2003–04 Swansea C 11 0 **11 0**

**NUGENT, Kevin* (F)** 476 112
H: 6 1 W: 13 03 b.Edmonton 10-4-69
*Source:* Trainee. *Honours:* Eire Youth.
1987–88 Leyton Orient 11 3
1988–89 Leyton Orient 3 0
1989–90 Leyton Orient 11 0
1990–91 Leyton Orient 33 5
1991–92 Leyton Orient 36 12
1991–92 Plymouth Arg 4 0
1992–93 Plymouth Arg 45 11
1993–94 Plymouth Arg 39 14
1994–95 Plymouth Arg 37 7
1995–96 Plymouth Arg 6 0 **131 32**
1995–96 Bristol C 34 8
1996–97 Bristol C 36 6 **70 14**
1997–98 Cardiff C 4 0
1998–99 Cardiff C 41 15
1999–2000 Cardiff C 39 10
2000–01 Cardiff C 14 4
2001–02 Cardiff C 1 0 **99 29**
2001–02 Leyton Orient 9 1
2002–03 Leyton Orient 19 3 **122 24**
2002–03 Swansea C 15 5
2003–04 Swansea C 39 8 **54 13**

**O'LEARY, Kristian# (D)** 203 7
H: 6 0 W: 12 09 b.Port Talbot 30-8-77
*Source:* Trainee. *Honours:* Wales Youth.
1995–96 Swansea C 1 0
1996–97 Swansea C 12 1
1997–98 Swansea C 29 0
1998–99 Swansea C 19 2
1999–2000 Swansea C 20 0
2000–01 Swansea C 24 2
2001–02 Swansea C 31 2
2002–03 Swansea C 33 0
2003–04 Swansea C 34 0 **203 7**

**PRITCHARD, Mark (F)** 4 0
H: 5 10 W: 12 04 b.Tredegar 23-11-85
2003–04 Swansea C 4 0 **4 0**

**REWBURY, Jamie§ (D)** 2 0
H: 6 2 W: 12 01 b.Wattstown 15-2-86
*Source:* Scholar. *Honours:* Wales Youth.
2003–04 Swansea C 2 0 **2 0**

**ROBERTS, Stuart* (F)** 174 19
H: 5 6 W: 9 08 b.Carmarthen 22-7-80
*Source:* Trainee. *Honours:* Wales Under-21.
1998–99 Swansea C 32 3
1999–2000 Swansea C 11 1
2000–01 Swansea C 36 5
2001–02 Swansea C 13 5
2001–02 Wycombe W 26 0
2002–03 Wycombe W 28 4
2003–04 Wycombe W 16 0 **70 4**
2003–04 Swansea C 12 1 **104 15**

**ROBINSON, Andy (M)** 37 8
H: 5 8 W: 11 04 b.Birkenhead 3-11-79
*Source:* Cammell Laird.
2002–03 Tranmere R 0 0
2003–04 Swansea C 37 8 **37 8**

**SMITH, Jason‡ (D)** 142 8
H: 6 3 W: 14 00 b.Bromsgrove 6-9-74
*Source:* Tiverton. *Honours:* England Schools.
1993–94 Coventry C 0 0
1994–95 Coventry C 0 0
1995–96 Coventry C 0 0
1996–97 Coventry C 0 0
1997–98 Coventry C 0 0
From Tiverton T
1998–99 Swansea C 42 4
1999–2000 Swansea C 43 1
2000–01 Swansea C 22 0
2001–02 Swansea C 8 0
2002–03 Swansea C 27 3
2003–04 Swansea C 0 0 **142 8**

**TATE, Alan (D)** 53 1
H: 6 1 W: 13 05 b.Easington 2-9-82
*Source:* Scholar.
2000–01 Manchester U 0 0
2001–02 Manchester U 0 0
2002–03 Manchester U 0 0
2002–03 *Swansea C* 27 0
2003–04 Manchester U 0 0
2003–04 Swansea C 26 1 **53 1**

**THOMAS, James (F)** 88 21
H: 6 0 W: 13 05 b.Swansea 16-1-79
*Source:* Trainee. *Honours:* Wales Under-21.
1996–97 Blackburn R 0 0
1997–98 Blackburn R 0 0
1997–98 *WBA* 3 0 **3 0**
1998–99 Blackburn R 0 0
1999–2000 Blackburn R 0 0
1999–2000 *Blackpool* 9 2 **9 2**
2000–01 Blackburn R 4 1
2000–01 *Sheffield U* 10 1 **10 1**
2001–02 Blackburn R 0 0 **4 1**
2001–02 *Bristol R* 7 1 **7 1**
2002–03 Swansea C 39 13
2003–04 Swansea C 16 3 **55 16**

**TRUNDLE, Lee (F)** 125 43
H: 6 0 W: 13 03 b.Liverpool 10-10-76
*Source:* Rhyl.
2000–01 Wrexham 14 8
2001–02 Wrexham 36 8
2002–03 Wrexham 44 11 **94 27**
2003–04 Swansea C 31 16 **31 16**

**Scholars**
Bond, Chad D; Corbisiero, Antonio; Davies, Kevin R; Evans, Steven M; Harrington, Luke; Harrison, Ryan-Lee; Pritchard, Mark O; Rewbury, Jamie; Roberts, Matthew N; Surman, Lee B

## SWINDON T (78)

**BAMPTON, David§ (M)** 3 0
H: 5 8 W: 11 02 b.Swindon 5-5-85
2002–03 Swindon T 3 0
2003–04 Swindon T 0 0 **3 0**

**DUKE, David# (M)** 160 6
H: 5 10 W: 11 03 b.Inverness 7-11-78
*Source:* Redby CA.
1997–98 Sunderland 0 0
1998–99 Sunderland 0 0
1999–2000 Sunderland 0 0
2000–01 Swindon T 32 1
2001–02 Swindon T 42 2
2002–03 Swindon T 44 2
2003–04 Swindon T 42 1 **160 6**

**EVANS, Rhys (G)** 63 0
H: 6 1 W: 12 02 b.Swindon 27-1-82
*Source:* Trainee. *Honours:* England Schools, Youth, Under-20, Under-21.
1998–99 Chelsea 0 0
1999–2000 Chelsea 0 0
1999–2000 *Bristol R* 4 0 **4 0**
2000–01 Chelsea 0 0
2001–02 Chelsea 0 0
2001–02 *QPR* 11 0 **11 0**
2002–03 Chelsea 0 0
2002–03 *Leyton Orient* 7 0 **7 0**
2003–04 Swindon T 41 0 **41 0**

**FALLON, Rory (F)** 82 17
H: 6 2 W: 11 10 b.Gisbourne 20-3-82
*Source:* North Shore U. *Honours:* England Youth.
1998–99 Barnsley 0 0
1999–2000 Barnsley 0 0
2000–01 Barnsley 1 0
2001–02 Barnsley 9 0
2001–02 *Shrewsbury T* 11 0 **11 0**
2002–03 Barnsley 26 7
2003–04 Barnsley 16 4 **52 11**
2003–04 Swindon T 19 6 **19 6**

**GARRARD, Luke† (M)** 2 0
H: 5 10 W: 11 09 b.Barnet 22-9-85
2002–03 Swindon T 1 0
2003–04 Swindon T 1 0 **2 0**

**GRIEMINK, Bart* (G)** 202 0
H: 6 4 W: 15 04 b.Holland 29-3-72
*Source:* WKE.
1995–96 Birmingham C 20 0
1996–97 Birmingham C 0 0 **20 0**
1996–97 *Barnsley* 0 0
1996–97 Peterborough U 27 0
1997–98 Peterborough U 0 0
1998–99 Peterborough U 17 0
1999–2000 Peterborough U 14 0 **58 0**
1999–2000 *Swindon T* 4 0
2000–01 Swindon T 25 0
2001–02 Swindon T 45 0
2002–03 Swindon T 44 0
2003–04 Swindon T 6 0 **124 0**

**GURNEY, Andy (D)** 365 42
H: 5 10 W: 11 06 b.Bristol 25-1-74
*Source:* Trainee.
1992–93 Bristol R 0 0
1993–94 Bristol R 3 0
1994–95 Bristol R 38 1
1995–96 Bristol R 43 6
1996–97 Bristol R 24 2 **108 9**
1997–98 Torquay U 44 9
1998–99 Torquay U 20 1 **64 10**
1998–99 Reading 8 0
1999–2000 Reading 38 2
2000–01 Reading 21 1 **67 3**
2001–02 Swindon T 43 6
2002–03 Swindon T 41 8
2003–04 Swindon T 42 6 **126 20**

**HERRING, Ian‡ (M)** 6 0
H: 6 1 W: 11 12 b.Swindon 14-2-84
*Source:* Scholar.
2001–02 Swindon T 1 0
2002–03 Swindon T 4 0
2003–04 Swindon T 1 0 **6 0**

**HEWLETT, Matt (M) 277 14**
H: 6 2 W: 11 03 b.Bristol 25-2-76
*Source:* Trainee. *Honours:* England Youth.

| | | | | | |
|---|---|---|---|---|---|
| 1993–94 | Bristol C | 12 | 0 | | |
| 1994–95 | Bristol C | 1 | 0 | | |
| 1995–96 | Bristol C | 27 | 2 | | |
| 1996–97 | Bristol C | 36 | 2 | | |
| 1997–98 | Bristol C | 34 | 4 | | |
| 1998–99 | Bristol C | 10 | 1 | | |
| 1998–99 | *Burnley* | 2 | 0 | **2** | **0** |
| 1999–2000 | Bristol C | 7 | 0 | **127** | **9** |
| 2000–01 | Swindon T | 26 | 0 | | |
| 2001–02 | Swindon T | 39 | 1 | | |
| 2002–03 | Swindon T | 40 | 1 | | |
| 2003–04 | Swindon T | 43 | 3 | **148** | **5** |

**HEYWOOD, Matthew (D) 164 7**
H: 6 2 W: 14 00 b.Chatham 26-8-79
*Source:* Trainee.

| | | | | | |
|---|---|---|---|---|---|
| 1998–99 | Burnley | 13 | 0 | | |
| 1999–2000 | Burnley | 0 | 0 | | |
| 2000–01 | Burnley | 0 | 0 | **13** | **0** |
| 2000–01 | Swindon T | 21 | 2 | | |
| 2001–02 | Swindon T | 44 | 3 | | |
| 2002–03 | Swindon T | 46 | 1 | | |
| 2003–04 | Swindon T | 40 | 1 | **151** | **7** |

**HOWARD, Brian (M) 35 4**
H: 5 8 W: 11 05 b.Winchester 23-1-83
*Source:* Trainee. *Honours:* England Youth, Under-20.

| | | | | | |
|---|---|---|---|---|---|
| 1999–2000 | Southampton | 0 | 0 | | |
| 2000–01 | Southampton | 0 | 0 | | |
| 2001–02 | Southampton | 0 | 0 | | |
| 2002–03 | Southampton | 0 | 0 | | |
| 2003–04 | Swindon T | 35 | 4 | **35** | **4** |

**IGOE, Sammy (M) 285 23**
H: 5 6 W: 10 00 b.Staines 30-9-75
*Source:* Trainee.

| | | | | | |
|---|---|---|---|---|---|
| 1993–94 | Portsmouth | 0 | 0 | | |
| 1994–95 | Portsmouth | 1 | 0 | | |
| 1995–96 | Portsmouth | 22 | 0 | | |
| 1996–97 | Portsmouth | 40 | 2 | | |
| 1997–98 | Portsmouth | 31 | 3 | | |
| 1998–99 | Portsmouth | 40 | 5 | | |
| 1999–2000 | Portsmouth | 26 | 1 | **160** | **11** |
| 1999–2000 | Reading | 6 | 0 | | |
| 2000–01 | Reading | 31 | 6 | | |
| 2001–02 | Reading | 35 | 1 | | |
| 2002–03 | Reading | 15 | 0 | **87** | **7** |
| 2002–03 | *Luton T* | 2 | 0 | **2** | **0** |
| 2003–04 | Swindon T | 36 | 5 | **36** | **5** |

**MARTIN, Ben* (D) 0 0**
H: 6 7 W: 15 00 b.Harpenden 15-11-82
*Source:* Aylesbury U.

| | | | | | |
|---|---|---|---|---|---|
| 2003–04 | Swindon T | 0 | 0 | | |
| 2003–04 | *Lincoln C* | 0 | 0 | | |

**MIGLIORANZI, Stefani# (M) 111 9**
H: 6 0 W: 11 12 b.Pacos de Caldas 20-9-77
*Source:* St Johns Univ.

| | | | | | |
|---|---|---|---|---|---|
| 1998–99 | Portsmouth | 7 | 0 | | |
| 1999–2000 | Portsmouth | 13 | 2 | | |
| 2000–01 | Portsmouth | 12 | 0 | | |
| 2001–02 | Portsmouth | 3 | 0 | **35** | **2** |
| 2002–03 | Swindon T | 41 | 3 | | |
| 2003–04 | Swindon T | 35 | 4 | **76** | **7** |

**MOONEY, Tommy# (F) 473 130**
H: 5 10 W: 12 06 b.Billingham 11-8-71
*Source:* Trainee.

| | | | | | |
|---|---|---|---|---|---|
| 1989–90 | Aston Villa | 0 | 0 | | |
| 1990–91 | Scarborough | 27 | 13 | | |
| 1991–92 | Scarborough | 40 | 8 | | |
| 1992–93 | Scarborough | 40 | 9 | **107** | **30** |
| 1993–94 | Southend U | 14 | 5 | **14** | **5** |
| 1993–94 | *Watford* | 10 | 2 | | |
| 1994–95 | Watford | 29 | 3 | | |
| 1995–96 | Watford | 42 | 6 | | |
| 1996–97 | Watford | 37 | 13 | | |
| 1997–98 | Watford | 45 | 6 | | |
| 1998–99 | Watford | 36 | 9 | | |
| 1999–2000 | Watford | 12 | 2 | | |
| 2000–01 | Watford | 39 | 19 | **250** | **60** |
| 2001–02 | Birmingham C | 33 | 13 | | |
| 2002–03 | Birmingham C | 1 | 0 | **34** | **13** |
| 2002–03 | *Stoke C* | 12 | 3 | **12** | **3** |
| 2002–03 | *Sheffield U* | 3 | 0 | **3** | **0** |
| 2002–03 | *Derby Co* | 8 | 0 | **8** | **0** |
| 2003–04 | Swindon T | 45 | 19 | **45** | **19** |

**MURPHY, Danny‡ (D) 23 0**
H: 5 6 W: 10 04 b.London 4-12-82
*Source:* Trainee.

| | | | | | |
|---|---|---|---|---|---|
| 1999–2000 | QPR | 0 | 0 | | |
| 2000–01 | QPR | 0 | 0 | | |
| 2001–02 | QPR | 12 | 0 | | |
| 2002–03 | QPR | 11 | 0 | **23** | **0** |
| 2003–04 | Swindon T | 0 | 0 | | |

**NICHOLAS, Andrew (D) 31 1**
H: 6 0 W: 12 10 b.Liverpool 10-10-83
*Honours:* Liverpool Trainee.

| | | | | | |
|---|---|---|---|---|---|
| 2003–04 | Swindon T | 31 | 1 | **31** | **1** |

**O'HANLON, Sean (D) 19 2**
H: 6 1 W: 12 05 b.Southport 2-1-83
*Honours:* England Youth, Under-20.

| | | | | | |
|---|---|---|---|---|---|
| 1999–2000 | Everton | 0 | 0 | | |
| 2000–01 | Everton | 0 | 0 | | |
| 2001–02 | Everton | 0 | 0 | | |
| 2002–03 | Everton | 0 | 0 | | |
| 2003–04 | Everton | 0 | 0 | | |
| 2003–04 | Swindon T | 19 | 2 | **19** | **2** |

**PARKIN, Sam (F) 145 56**
H: 6 2 W: 13 00 b.Roehampton 14-3-81
*Honours:* England Schools.

| | | | | | |
|---|---|---|---|---|---|
| 1998–99 | Chelsea | 0 | 0 | | |
| 1999–2000 | Chelsea | 0 | 0 | | |
| 2000–01 | Chelsea | 0 | 0 | | |
| 2000–01 | *Millwall* | 7 | 4 | **7** | **4** |
| 2000–01 | *Wycombe W* | 8 | 1 | **8** | **1** |
| 2000–01 | *Oldham Ath* | 7 | 3 | **7** | **3** |
| 2001–02 | Chelsea | 0 | 0 | | |
| 2001–02 | *Northampton T* | 40 | 4 | **40** | **4** |
| 2002–03 | Swindon T | 43 | 25 | | |
| 2003–04 | Swindon T | 40 | 19 | **83** | **44** |

**POOK, Michael§ (M) 0 0**
H: 5 11 W: 11 10 b.Swindon 22-10-85
*Source:* Scholar.

| | | | | | |
|---|---|---|---|---|---|
| 2003–04 | Swindon T | 0 | 0 | | |

**REEVES, Alan# (D) 435 26**
H: 6 0 W: 12 00 b.Birkenhead 19-11-67
*Source:* Heswall.

| | | | | | |
|---|---|---|---|---|---|
| 1988–89 | Norwich C | 0 | 0 | | |
| 1988–89 | *Gillingham* | 18 | 0 | **18** | **0** |
| 1989–90 | Chester C | 30 | 2 | | |
| 1990–91 | Chester C | 10 | 0 | **40** | **2** |
| 1991–92 | Rochdale | 34 | 3 | | |
| 1992–93 | Rochdale | 41 | 3 | | |
| 1993–94 | Rochdale | 41 | 3 | | |
| 1994–95 | Rochdale | 5 | 0 | **121** | **9** |
| 1994–95 | Wimbledon | 31 | 3 | | |
| 1995–96 | Wimbledon | 24 | 1 | | |
| 1996–97 | Wimbledon | 2 | 0 | | |
| 1997–98 | Wimbledon | 0 | 0 | **57** | **4** |
| 1998–99 | Swindon T | 24 | 2 | | |
| 1999–2000 | Swindon T | 43 | 1 | | |
| 2000–01 | Swindon T | 44 | 3 | | |
| 2001–02 | Swindon T | 25 | 2 | | |
| 2002–03 | Swindon T | 36 | 3 | | |
| 2003–04 | Swindon T | 27 | 0 | **199** | **11** |

**ROBINSON, Steve# (M) 210 5**
H: 5 9 W: 11 03 b.Nottingham 17-1-75
*Source:* Trainee.

| | | | | | |
|---|---|---|---|---|---|
| 1993–94 | Birmingham C | 0 | 0 | | |
| 1994–95 | Birmingham C | 6 | 0 | | |
| 1995–96 | Birmingham C | 0 | 0 | | |
| 1995–96 | *Peterborough U* | 5 | 0 | **5** | **0** |
| 1996–97 | Birmingham C | 9 | 0 | | |
| 1997–98 | Birmingham C | 25 | 0 | | |
| 1998–99 | Birmingham C | 31 | 0 | | |
| 1999–2000 | Birmingham C | 6 | 0 | | |
| 2000–01 | Birmingham C | 4 | 0 | **81** | **0** |
| 2000–01 | Swindon T | 18 | 2 | | |
| 2001–02 | Swindon T | 40 | 0 | | |
| 2002–03 | Swindon T | 44 | 2 | | |
| 2003–04 | Swindon T | 22 | 1 | **124** | **5** |

**RUSTER, Sebastien‡ (M) 2 0**
H: 5 10 W: 12 03 b.Marseille 6-9-82

| | | | | | |
|---|---|---|---|---|---|
| 2003–04 | Swindon T | 2 | 0 | **2** | **0** |

**SMITH, Grant (M) 33 1**
H: 6 1 W: 12 07 b.Irvine 5-5-80

| | | | | | |
|---|---|---|---|---|---|
| 1998–99 | Reading | 0 | 0 | | |
| 1999–2000 | Reading | 0 | 0 | | |
| 2000–01 | Reading | 0 | 0 | | |
| 2001–02 | *Halifax T* | 11 | 0 | **11** | **0** |
| 2001–02 | Sheffield U | 7 | 0 | | |
| 2002–03 | Sheffield U | 3 | 0 | **10** | **0** |
| 2002–03 | *Plymouth Arg* | 5 | 1 | **5** | **1** |
| 2003–04 | Swindon T | 7 | 0 | **7** | **0** |

**STEVENSON, Jon* (F) 17 2**
H: 5 6 W: 11 11 b.Leicester 13-10-82
*Source:* Scholar.

| | | | | | |
|---|---|---|---|---|---|
| 2000–01 | Leicester C | 0 | 0 | | |
| 2001–02 | Leicester C | 6 | 1 | | |
| 2002–03 | Leicester C | 6 | 1 | **12** | **2** |
| 2003–04 | Swindon T | 5 | 0 | **5** | **0** |

**TAYLOR, Chris§ (D) 4 0**
H: 5 8 W: 10 05 b.Swindon 30-10-85
*Source:* Scholar.

| | | | | | |
|---|---|---|---|---|---|
| 2002–03 | Swindon T | 4 | 0 | | |
| 2003–04 | Swindon T | 0 | 0 | **4** | **0** |

**VIVEASH, Adrian (D) 365 19**
H: 6 2 W: 12 13 b.Swindon 30-9-69
*Source:* Trainee.

| | | | | | |
|---|---|---|---|---|---|
| 1988–89 | Swindon T | 0 | 0 | | |
| 1989–90 | Swindon T | 0 | 0 | | |
| 1990–91 | Swindon T | 25 | 1 | | |
| 1991–92 | Swindon T | 10 | 0 | | |
| 1992–93 | Swindon T | 5 | 0 | | |
| 1992–93 | *Reading* | 5 | 0 | | |
| 1993–94 | Swindon T | 0 | 0 | | |
| 1994–95 | Swindon T | 14 | 1 | | |
| 1994–95 | *Reading* | 6 | 0 | | |
| 1995–96 | Swindon T | 0 | 0 | | |
| 1995–96 | *Barnsley* | 2 | 1 | **2** | **1** |
| 1995–96 | Walsall | 31 | 0 | | |
| 1996–97 | Walsall | 46 | 9 | | |
| 1997–98 | Walsall | 42 | 3 | | |
| 1998–99 | Walsall | 40 | 0 | | |
| 1999–2000 | Walsall | 43 | 1 | **202** | **13** |
| 2000–01 | Reading | 40 | 2 | | |
| 2001–02 | Reading | 18 | 1 | | |
| 2002–03 | Reading | 5 | 0 | **74** | **3** |
| 2002–03 | *Oxford U* | 11 | 0 | **11** | **0** |
| 2003–04 | Swindon T | 15 | 0 | **69** | **2** |
| 2003–04 | *Kidderminster H* | 7 | 0 | **7** | **0** |

**YOUNG, Alan‡ (F) 29 1**
H: 5 6 W: 10 00 b.Swindon 12-8-83
*Source:* Scholar. *Honours:* England Youth.

| | | | | | |
|---|---|---|---|---|---|
| 2000–01 | Swindon T | 4 | 0 | | |
| 2001–02 | Swindon T | 14 | 1 | | |
| 2002–03 | Swindon T | 11 | 0 | | |
| 2003–04 | Swindon T | 0 | 0 | **29** | **1** |

**Scholars**
Bampton, David P; Bulman, Matthew K; Hambidge, James H; Henry, Leigh C D; Holgate, Ashan B S; Lapham, Kyle; Lewis, Lance W; McKay, Justyn A; Oliver, Ian A; Pook, Michael D; Smith, Steven A; Stroud, David A; Taylor, Christopher J; Taylor, Daniel S

**Non Contract**
Garrard, Luke E

## TORQUAY U (79)

**BEDEAU, Anthony (F) 242 47**
H: 5 10 W: 11 00 b.Hammersmith 24-3-79
*Source:* Trainee. *Honours:* Grenada full caps.

| | | | | | |
|---|---|---|---|---|---|
| 1995–96 | Torquay U | 4 | 0 | | |
| 1996–97 | Torquay U | 8 | 1 | | |
| 1997–98 | Torquay U | 34 | 5 | | |
| 1998–99 | Torquay U | 36 | 9 | | |
| 1999–2000 | Torquay U | 38 | 16 | | |
| 2000–01 | Torquay U | 34 | 5 | | |
| 2001–02 | Torquay U | 21 | 4 | | |
| 2001–02 | *Barnsley* | 3 | 0 | **3** | **0** |
| 2002–03 | Torquay U | 40 | 6 | | |
| 2003–04 | Torquay U | 24 | 1 | **239** | **47** |

**BENEFIELD, Jimmy* (F) 32 0**
H: 5 10 W: 11 02 b.Torbay 6-5-83
*Source:* Scholar.

| | | | | | |
|---|---|---|---|---|---|
| 2000–01 | Torquay U | 1 | 0 | | |
| 2001–02 | Torquay U | 8 | 0 | | |
| 2002–03 | Torquay U | 8 | 0 | | |
| 2003–04 | Torquay U | 15 | 0 | **32** | **0** |

**BERNARD, Narada‡ (D) 30 0**
H: 5 7 W: 10 05 b.Bristol 30-1-81
*Source:* Trainee. *Honours:* Jamaica 1 full cap.
1999–2000 Arsenal 0 0
2000–01 Bournemouth 14 0
2001–02 Bournemouth 8 0
2002–03 Bournemouth 7 0
2003–04 Bournemouth 0 0 **29 0**
From Woking.
2003–04 Torquay U 1 0 **1 0**

**BOND, Kain (F) 2 0**
H: 5 9 W: 10 10 b.Torquay 19-6-85
*Source:* Scholar.
2002–03 Torquay U 1 0
2003–04 Torquay U 1 0 **2 0**

**BROAD, Joseph† (M) 26 0**
H: 5 11 W: 12 07 b.Bristol 24-8-82
*Source:* Trainee.
2000–01 Plymouth Arg 0 0
2001–02 Plymouth Arg 7 0
2002–03 Plymouth Arg 5 0
2003–04 Plymouth Arg 0 0 **12 0**
2003–04 Torquay U 14 0 **14 0**

**BURGESS, Luke* (M) 0 0**
H: 5 10 W: 10 00 b.Torbay 26-9-84
*Source:* Trainee.
2003–04 Torquay U 0 0

**CAMARA, Ben‡ (F) 2 0**
H: 6 2 W: 12 05 b.Bonn 20-8-84
*Source:* Trainee.
2002–03 Torquay U 2 0
2003–04 Torquay U 0 0 **2 0**

**CANOVILLE, Lee (M) 83 2**
H: 6 1 W: 11 03 b.Ealing 14-3-81
*Source:* Trainee. *Honours:* FA Schools, England Youth.
1998–99 Arsenal 0 0
1999–2000 Arsenal 0 0
2000–01 Arsenal 0 0
2000–01 *Northampton T* 2 0 **2 0**
2001–02 Torquay U 12 1
2002–03 Torquay U 36 0
2003–04 Torquay U 33 1 **81 2**

**DEARDEN, Kevin# (G) 433 0**
H: 5 11 W: 13 04 b.Luton 8-3-70
*Source:* Trainee.
1988–89 Tottenham H 0 0
1988–89 *Cambridge U* 15 0 **15 0**
1989–90 Tottenham H 0 0
1989–90 *Hartlepool U* 10 0 **10 0**
1989–90 *Oxford U* 0 0
1989–90 *Swindon T* 1 0 **1 0**
1990–91 Tottenham H 0 0
1990–91 *Peterborough U* 7 0 **7 0**
1990–91 *Hull C* 3 0 **3 0**
1991–92 Tottenham H 0 0
1991–92 *Rochdale* 2 0 **2 0**
1991–92 *Birmingham C* 12 0 **12 0**
1992–93 Tottenham H 1 0
1992–93 *Portsmouth* 0 0
1993–94 Tottenham H 0 0 **1 0**
1993–94 Brentford 35 0
1994–95 Brentford 43 0
1995–96 Brentford 41 0
1996–97 Brentford 44 0
1997–98 Brentford 35 0
1998–99 Brentford 7 0 **205 0**
1998–99 *Barnet* 1 0 **1 0**
1998–99 *Huddersfield T* 0 0
1999–2000 Wrexham 45 0
2000–01 Wrexham 36 0 **81 0**
2001–02 Torquay U 46 0
2002–03 Torquay U 27 0
2003–04 Torquay U 22 0 **95 0**

**FOWLER, Jason (M) 255 21**
H: 6 3 W: 11 12 b.Bristol 20-8-74
*Source:* Trainee.
1992–93 Bristol C 1 0
1993–94 Bristol C 1 0
1994–95 Bristol C 13 0
1995–96 Bristol C 10 0 **25 0**
1996–97 Cardiff C 37 5
1997–98 Cardiff C 38 5
1998–99 Cardiff C 37 3
1999–2000 Cardiff C 28 1
2000–01 Cardiff C 5 0
2001–02 Cardiff C 0 0 **145 14**
2001–02 Torquay U 14 1
2002–03 Torquay U 40 4
2003–04 Torquay U 31 2 **85 7**

**GRAHAM, David (F) 144 49**
H: 5 10 W: 11 05 b.Edinburgh 6-10-78
*Source:* Rangers SABC. *Honours:* Scotland Under-21.
1995–96 Rangers 0 0
1996–97 Rangers 0 0
1997–98 Rangers 0 0
1998–99 Rangers 3 0 **3 0**
1998–99 Dunfermline Ath 21 2
1999–2000 Dunfermline Ath 0 0
2000–01 Dunfermline Ath 0 0 **21 2**
2000–01 Torquay U 5 2
2001–02 Torquay U 36 8
2002–03 Torquay U 34 15
2003–04 Torquay U 45 22 **120 47**

**GRITTON, Martin (F) 118 24**
H: 6 1 W: 12 07 b.Glasgow 1-6-78
*Source:* Porthleven.
1998–99 Plymouth Arg 2 0
1999–2000 Plymouth Arg 30 6
2000–01 Plymouth Arg 10 1
2001–02 Plymouth Arg 2 0
2002–03 Plymouth Arg 0 0 **44 7**
2002–03 Torquay U 43 13
2003–04 Torquay U 31 4 **74 17**

**HANKIN, Sean‡ (D) 48 1**
H: 5 11 W: 12 04 b.Camberley 28-2-81
*Source:* Trainee.
1999–2000 Crystal Palace 1 0
2000–01 Crystal Palace 0 0
2001–02 Crystal Palace 0 0 **1 0**
2001–02 Torquay U 27 0
2002–03 Torquay U 19 1
2003–04 Torquay U 1 0 **47 1**

**HAZELL, Reuben# (D) 126 3**
H: 5 11 W: 12 00 b.Birmingham 24-4-79
*Source:* Trainee.
1996–97 Aston Villa 0 0
1997–98 Aston Villa 0 0
1998–99 Aston Villa 0 0
1999–2000 Tranmere R 23 1
2000–01 Tranmere R 13 0
2001–02 Tranmere R 6 0 **42 1**
2001–02 Torquay U 19 0
2002–03 Torquay U 46 1
2003–04 Torquay U 19 1 **84 2**

**HILL, Kevin# (M) 287 34**
H: 5 8 W: 10 03 b.Exeter 6-3-76
*Source:* Torrington.
1997–98 Torquay U 37 7
1998–99 Torquay U 35 5
1999–2000 Torquay U 43 2
2000–01 Torquay U 44 9
2001–02 Torquay U 44 2
2002–03 Torquay U 39 4
2003–04 Torquay U 45 5 **287 34**

**HOCKLEY, Matthew (D) 103 8**
H: 5 10 W: 11 07 b.Paignton 5-6-82
*Source:* Trainee.
2000–01 Torquay U 6 1
2001–02 Torquay U 12 0
2002–03 Torquay U 40 2
2003–04 Torquay U 45 5 **103 8**

**KILLOUGHERY, Graham‡ (M) 6 0**
H: 5 10 W: 11 07 b.London 22-7-84
*Source:* Trainee.
2002–03 Torquay U 3 0
2003–04 Torquay U 3 0 **6 0**

**McGLINCHEY, Brian (D) 131 4**
H: 5 9 W: 12 00 b.Derry 26-10-77
*Source:* Trainee. *Honours:* Northern Ireland Youth, Under-21, B.
1995–96 Manchester C 0 0
1996–97 Manchester C 0 0
1997–98 Manchester C 0 0
1998–99 Port Vale 15 1 **15 1**
1999–2000 Gillingham 13 1
2000–01 Gillingham 1 0 **14 1**
2000–01 Plymouth Arg 20 0
2001–02 Plymouth Arg 29 1
2002–03 Plymouth Arg 19 1
2003–04 Plymouth Arg 0 0 **68 2**
2003–04 Torquay U 34 0 **34 0**

**ORCHARD, Steven‡ (M) 0 0**
b.Tiverton 18-2-85
2003–04 Torquay U 0 0

**OSEI-KUFFOUR, Jo (F) 82 17**
H: 5 7 W: 10 06 b.Edmonton 17-11-81
*Source:* Scholar.
2000–01 Arsenal 0 0
2001–02 Arsenal 0 0
2001–02 *Swindon T* 11 2 **11 2**
2002–03 Torquay U 30 5
2003–04 Torquay U 41 10 **71 15**

**RUSSELL, Alex (M) 298 40**
H: 5 9 W: 11 07 b.Crosby 17-3-73
*Source:* Burscough.
1994–95 Rochdale 7 1
1995–96 Rochdale 25 0
1996–97 Rochdale 39 9
1997–98 Rochdale 31 4 **102 14**
1998–99 Cambridge U 37 6
1999–2000 Cambridge U 15 0
2000–01 Cambridge U 29 2 **81 8**
2001–02 Torquay U 33 7
2002–03 Torquay U 39 9
2003–04 Torquay U 43 2 **115 18**

**TAYLOR, Craig (D) 191 13**
H: 6 1 W: 13 02 b.Plymouth 24-1-74
*Source:* Dorchester T.
1996–97 Swindon T 0 0
1997–98 Swindon T 32 2
1998–99 Swindon T 21 0
1998–99 *Plymouth Arg* 6 1
1999–2000 Swindon T 2 0 **55 2**
1999–2000 Plymouth Arg 41 3
2000–01 Plymouth Arg 39 3
2001–02 Plymouth Arg 1 0
2002–03 Plymouth Arg 1 0 **88 7**
2002–03 *Torquay U* 5 0
2003–04 Torquay U 43 4 **48 4**

**VAN HEUSDEN, Arjan (G) 199 0**
H: 6 3 W: 14 07 b.Alphen 11-12-72
*Source:* Noordwijk.
1994–95 Port Vale 2 0
1995–96 Port Vale 7 0
1996–97 Port Vale 13 0
1997–98 Port Vale 5 0 **27 0**
1997–98 *Oxford U* 11 0 **11 0**
1998–99 Cambridge U 27 0
1999–2000 Cambridge U 15 0 **42 0**
2000–01 Exeter C 41 0
2001–02 Exeter C 33 0 **74 0**
2002–03 Mansfield T 5 0 **5 0**
2002–03 Torquay U 15 0
2003–04 Torquay U 25 0 **40 0**

**WILLS, Kevin* (M) 75 5**
H: 5 8 W: 10 07 b.Torbay 15-10-80
*Source:* Trainee.
1998–99 Plymouth Arg 2 0
1999–2000 Plymouth Arg 2 0
2000–01 Plymouth Arg 10 1
2001–02 Plymouth Arg 18 0
2002–03 Plymouth Arg 0 0 **32 1**
2002–03 Torquay U 20 1
2003–04 Torquay U 23 3 **43 4**

**WOODS, Steve† (D) 157 8**
H: 5 11 W: 12 03 b.Northwich 15-12-76
*Source:* Trainee.
1995–96 Stoke C 0 0
1996–97 Stoke C 0 0
1997–98 Stoke C 1 0
1997–98 *Plymouth Arg* 5 0 **5 0**
1998–99 Stoke C 33 0 **34 0**
1999–2000 Chesterfield 25 0
2000–01 Chesterfield 0 0 **25 0**
2001–02 Torquay U 38 2
2002–03 Torquay U 9 0
2003–04 Torquay U 46 6 **93 8**

**WOOZLEY, David# (D) 108 3**
H: 6 0 W: 12 10 b.Ascot 6-12-79
*Source:* Trainee.
1997–98 Crystal Palace 0 0
1998–99 Crystal Palace 7 0
1999–2000 Crystal Palace 23 0

| | | | | | |
|---|---|---|---|---|---|
| 2000–01 | Crystal Palace | 0 | 0 | | |
| 2000–01 | *Bournemouth* | 6 | 0 | **6** | **0** |
| 2001–02 | Crystal Palace | 0 | 0 | **30** | **0** |
| 2001–02 | Torquay U | 16 | 0 | | |
| 2002–03 | Torquay U | 46 | 3 | | |
| 2003–04 | Torquay U | 10 | 0 | **72** | **3** |

**Non Contract**

Broad, Joseph R; Hancox, Richard C; Woods, Stephen J

## TOTTENHAM H (80)

**ACIMOVIC, Milenko‡ (M) 153 41**

H: 6 2 W: 12 08 b.Ljubljana 15-2-77

*Honours:* Slovenia 52 full caps, 10 goals.

| | | | | | |
|---|---|---|---|---|---|
| 1996–97 | Olimpija | 18 | 3 | | |
| 1997–98 | Olimpija | 16 | 4 | **34** | **7** |
| 1997–98 | Red Star Belgrade | 9 | 1 | | |
| 1998–99 | Red Star Belgrade | 22 | 8 | | |
| 1999–2000 | Red Star Belgrade | 21 | 4 | | |
| 2000–01 | Red Star Belgrade | 28 | 14 | | |
| 2001–02 | Red Star Belgrade | 22 | 7 | **102** | **34** |
| 2001–02 | Tottenham H | 0 | 0 | | |
| 2002–03 | Tottenham H | 17 | 0 | | |
| 2003–04 | Tottenham H | 0 | 0 | **17** | **0** |

**ANDERTON, Darren* (M) 361 41**

H: 6 1 W: 12 11 b.Southampton 3-3-72

*Source:* Trainee. *Honours:* England Youth, Under-21, B, 30 full caps, 7 goals.

| | | | | | |
|---|---|---|---|---|---|
| 1989–90 | Portsmouth | 0 | 0 | | |
| 1990–91 | Portsmouth | 20 | 0 | | |
| 1991–92 | Portsmouth | 42 | 7 | **62** | **7** |
| 1992–93 | Tottenham H | 34 | 6 | | |
| 1993–94 | Tottenham H | 37 | 6 | | |
| 1994–95 | Tottenham H | 37 | 5 | | |
| 1995–96 | Tottenham H | 8 | 2 | | |
| 1996–97 | Tottenham H | 16 | 3 | | |
| 1997–98 | Tottenham H | 15 | 0 | | |
| 1998–99 | Tottenham H | 32 | 3 | | |
| 1999–2000 | Tottenham H | 22 | 3 | | |
| 2000–01 | Tottenham H | 23 | 2 | | |
| 2001–02 | Tottenham H | 35 | 3 | | |
| 2002–03 | Tottenham H | 20 | 0 | | |
| 2003–04 | Tottenham H | 20 | 1 | **299** | **34** |

**BARNARD, Lee (F) 3 0**

H: 5 10 W: 10 10 b.Romford 18-7-84

*Source:* Trainee.

| | | | | | |
|---|---|---|---|---|---|
| 2002–03 | Tottenham H | 0 | 0 | | |
| 2002–03 | *Exeter C* | 3 | 0 | **3** | **0** |
| 2003–04 | Tottenham H | 0 | 0 | | |

**BLACK, Jonathan‡ (M) 0 0**

b.Larne 7-5-85

*Source:* Trainee. *Honours:* Northern Ireland Under-21.

| | | | | | |
|---|---|---|---|---|---|
| 2002–03 | Tottenham H | 0 | 0 | | |
| 2003–04 | Tottenham H | 0 | 0 | | |

**BLONDEL, Jonathan‡ (M) 20 0**

H: 5 8 W: 10 12 b.Ypres 3-4-84

*Honours:* Belgium 3 full caps.

| | | | | | |
|---|---|---|---|---|---|
| 2001–02 | Mouscron | 18 | 0 | **18** | **0** |
| 2002–03 | Tottenham H | 1 | 0 | | |
| 2003–04 | Tottenham H | 1 | 0 | **2** | **0** |

**BOWDITCH, Ben‡ (D) 0 0**

H: 5 9 W: 11 07 b.Harlow 19-2-84

*Source:* Scholar. *Honours:* England Youth, Under-20.

| | | | | | |
|---|---|---|---|---|---|
| 2000–01 | Tottenham H | 0 | 0 | | |
| 2001–02 | Tottenham H | 0 | 0 | | |
| 2002–03 | Tottenham H | 0 | 0 | | |
| 2003–04 | Tottenham H | 0 | 0 | | |

**BROWN, Michael R (M) 267 31**

H: 5 9 W: 12 04 b.Hartlepool 25-1-77

*Source:* Trainee. *Honours:* England Under-21.

| | | | | | |
|---|---|---|---|---|---|
| 1994–95 | Manchester C | 0 | 0 | | |
| 1995–96 | Manchester C | 21 | 0 | | |
| 1996–97 | Manchester C | 11 | 0 | | |
| 1996–97 | *Hartlepool U* | 6 | 1 | **6** | **1** |
| 1997–98 | Manchester C | 26 | 0 | | |
| 1998–99 | Manchester C | 31 | 2 | | |
| 1999–2000 | Manchester C | 0 | 0 | **89** | **2** |
| 1999–2000 | *Portsmouth* | 4 | 0 | **4** | **0** |
| 1999–2000 | Sheffield U | 24 | 3 | | |
| 2000–01 | Sheffield U | 36 | 1 | | |
| 2001–02 | Sheffield U | 36 | 5 | | |
| 2002–03 | Sheffield U | 40 | 16 | | |
| 2003–04 | Sheffield U | 15 | 2 | **151** | **27** |
| 2003–04 | Tottenham H | 17 | 1 | **17** | **1** |

**BUNJEVCEVIC, Goran (D) 233 21**

H: 6 3 W: 12 02 b.Karlovac 17-2-73

*Honours:* Serbia-Montenegro 17 full caps.

| | | | | | |
|---|---|---|---|---|---|
| 1994–95 | Rad | 17 | 0 | | |
| 1995–96 | Rad | 13 | 2 | | |
| 1996–97 | Rad | 30 | 3 | **60** | **5** |
| 1997–98 | Red Star Belgrade | 30 | 5 | | |
| 1998–99 | Red Star Belgrade | 22 | 4 | | |
| 1999–2000 | Red Star Belgrade | 40 | 7 | | |
| 2000–01 | Red Star Belgrade | 33 | 0 | **125** | **16** |
| 2001–02 | Tottenham H | 6 | 0 | | |
| 2002–03 | Tottenham H | 35 | 0 | | |
| 2003–04 | Tottenham H | 7 | 0 | **48** | **0** |

**BURCH, Rob (G) 0 0**

H: 6 2 W: 12 13 b.Yeovil 8-10-83

*Source:* Trainee. *Honours:* England Under-20.

| | | | | | |
|---|---|---|---|---|---|
| 2002–03 | Tottenham H | 0 | 0 | | |
| 2003–04 | Tottenham H | 0 | 0 | | |

**CARR, Stephen (D) 226 7**

H: 5 9 W: 12 04 b.Dublin 29-8-76

*Source:* Trainee. *Honours:* Eire Under-21, 30 full caps.

| | | | | | |
|---|---|---|---|---|---|
| 1993–94 | Tottenham H | 1 | 0 | | |
| 1994–95 | Tottenham H | 0 | 0 | | |
| 1995–96 | Tottenham H | 0 | 0 | | |
| 1996–97 | Tottenham H | 26 | 0 | | |
| 1997–98 | Tottenham H | 38 | 0 | | |
| 1998–99 | Tottenham H | 37 | 0 | | |
| 1999–2000 | Tottenham H | 34 | 3 | | |
| 2000–01 | Tottenham H | 28 | 3 | | |
| 2001–02 | Tottenham H | 0 | 0 | | |
| 2002–03 | Tottenham H | 30 | 0 | | |
| 2003–04 | Tottenham H | 32 | 1 | **226** | **7** |

**DALMAT, Stephane‡ (M) 157 12**

H: 6 1 W: 12 08 b.Joue-les-Tours 16-2-79

| | | | | | |
|---|---|---|---|---|---|
| 1997–98 | Chateauroux | 29 | 1 | **29** | **1** |
| 1998–99 | Lens | 25 | 3 | **25** | **3** |
| 1999–2000 | Marseille | 29 | 1 | **29** | **1** |
| 2000–01 | Paris St Germain | 19 | 1 | **19** | **1** |
| 2000–01 | Internazionale | 17 | 2 | | |
| 2001–02 | Internazionale | 16 | 1 | | |
| 2002–03 | Internazionale | 0 | 0 | **33** | **3** |
| 2003–04 | Tottenham H | 22 | 3 | **22** | **3** |

**DAVIES, Simon (M) 165 19**

H: 5 10 W: 11 07 b.Haverfordwest 23-10-79

*Source:* Trainee. *Honours:* Wales Youth, Under-21, B, 19 full caps, 4 goals.

| | | | | | |
|---|---|---|---|---|---|
| 1997–98 | Peterborough U | 6 | 0 | | |
| 1998–99 | Peterborough U | 43 | 4 | | |
| 1999–2000 | Peterborough U | 16 | 2 | **65** | **6** |
| 1999–2000 | Tottenham H | 3 | 0 | | |
| 2000–01 | Tottenham H | 13 | 2 | | |
| 2001–02 | Tottenham H | 31 | 4 | | |
| 2002–03 | Tottenham H | 36 | 5 | | |
| 2003–04 | Tottenham H | 17 | 2 | **100** | **13** |

**DEFOE, Jermain (F) 137 54**

H: 5 7 W: 10 04 b.Beckton 7-10-82

*Source:* Charlton Ath. *Honours:* England Youth, Under-21, 2 full caps.

| | | | | | |
|---|---|---|---|---|---|
| 1999–2000 | West Ham U | 0 | 0 | | |
| 2000–01 | West Ham U | 1 | 0 | | |
| 2000–01 | *Bournemouth* | 29 | 18 | **29** | **18** |
| 2001–02 | West Ham U | 35 | 10 | | |
| 2002–03 | West Ham U | 38 | 8 | | |
| 2003–04 | West Ham U | 19 | 11 | **93** | **29** |
| 2003–04 | Tottenham H | 15 | 7 | **15** | **7** |

**DOHERTY, Gary (D) 133 16**

H: 6 2 W: 13 01 b.Carndonagh 31-1-80

*Source:* Trainee. *Honours:* Eire Under-21, 26 full caps, 4 goals.

| | | | | | |
|---|---|---|---|---|---|
| 1997–98 | Luton T | 10 | 0 | | |
| 1998–99 | Luton T | 20 | 6 | | |
| 1999–2000 | Luton T | 40 | 6 | **70** | **12** |
| 1999–2000 | Tottenham H | 2 | 0 | | |
| 2000–01 | Tottenham H | 22 | 3 | | |
| 2001–02 | Tottenham H | 7 | 0 | | |
| 2002–03 | Tottenham H | 15 | 1 | | |
| 2003–04 | Tottenham H | 17 | 0 | **63** | **4** |

**EYRE, Nicky (G) 0 0**

b.Braintree 7-9-85

*Source:* Trainee.

| | | | | | |
|---|---|---|---|---|---|
| 2002–03 | Tottenham H | 0 | 0 | | |
| 2003–04 | Tottenham H | 0 | 0 | | |

**FOSTER, Danny* (D) 0 0**

b.Enfield 23-9-84

*Source:* Trainee.

| | | | | | |
|---|---|---|---|---|---|
| 2002–03 | Tottenham H | 0 | 0 | | |
| 2003–04 | Tottenham H | 0 | 0 | | |

**GARDNER, Anthony (D) 109 5**

H: 6 3 W: 14 00 b.Stafford 19-9-80

*Source:* Trainee. *Honours:* England Under-21, 1 full cap.

| | | | | | |
|---|---|---|---|---|---|
| 1998–99 | Port Vale | 15 | 1 | | |
| 1999–2000 | Port Vale | 26 | 3 | **41** | **4** |
| 1999–2000 | Tottenham H | 0 | 0 | | |
| 2000–01 | Tottenham H | 8 | 0 | | |
| 2001–02 | Tottenham H | 15 | 0 | | |
| 2002–03 | Tottenham H | 12 | 1 | | |
| 2003–04 | Tottenham H | 33 | 0 | **68** | **1** |

**HENRY, Ronnie‡ (D) 3 0**

H: 5 11 W: 11 10 b.Hemel Hempstead 2-1-84

*Source:* Trainee.

| | | | | | |
|---|---|---|---|---|---|
| 2002–03 | Tottenham H | 0 | 0 | | |
| 2002–03 | *Southend U* | 3 | 0 | **3** | **0** |
| 2003–04 | Tottenham H | 0 | 0 | | |

**HIRSCHFELD, Lars* (G) 7 0**

H: 6 4 W: 13 08 b.Edmonton 17-10-78

*Honours:* Canada 16 full caps.

| | | | | | |
|---|---|---|---|---|---|
| 2002–03 | Tottenham H | 0 | 0 | | |
| 2002–03 | *Luton T* | 5 | 0 | **5** | **0** |
| 2003–04 | Tottenham H | 0 | 0 | | |
| 2003–04 | *Gillingham* | 2 | 0 | **2** | **0** |

**HUGHES, Mark (M) 0 0**

H: 5 10 W: 12 04 b.Dungannon 16-9-83

*Source:* Scholar. *Honours:* Northern Ireland Under-21.

| | | | | | |
|---|---|---|---|---|---|
| 2001–02 | Tottenham H | 0 | 0 | | |
| 2002–03 | Tottenham H | 0 | 0 | | |
| 2003–04 | Tottenham H | 0 | 0 | | |

**JACKSON, Johnnie (M) 37 4**

H: 6 1 W: 12 00 b.Camden 15-8-82

*Source:* Trainee. *Honours:* England Youth, Under-20.

| | | | | | |
|---|---|---|---|---|---|
| 1999–2000 | Tottenham H | 0 | 0 | | |
| 2000–01 | Tottenham H | 0 | 0 | | |
| 2001–02 | Tottenham H | 0 | 0 | | |
| 2002–03 | Tottenham H | 0 | 0 | | |
| 2002–03 | *Swindon T* | 13 | 1 | **13** | **1** |
| 2002–03 | *Colchester U* | 8 | 0 | **8** | **0** |
| 2003–04 | Tottenham H | 11 | 1 | **11** | **1** |
| 2003–04 | *Coventry C* | 5 | 2 | **5** | **2** |

**JALAL, Shwan* (G) 0 0**

H: 6 2 W: 14 02 b.Baghdad 14-8-83

*Source:* Hastings T.

| | | | | | |
|---|---|---|---|---|---|
| 2001–02 | Tottenham H | 0 | 0 | | |
| 2002–03 | Tottenham H | 0 | 0 | | |
| 2003–04 | Tottenham H | 0 | 0 | | |

**KANOUTE, Frederic (F) 151 45**

H: 6 3 W: 13 08 b.Ste. Foy-Les-Lyon 2-9-77

*Honours:* Mali 5 full caps, 4 goals.

| | | | | | |
|---|---|---|---|---|---|
| 1997–98 | Lyon | 18 | 6 | | |
| 1998–99 | Lyon | 9 | 2 | | |
| 1999–2000 | Lyon | 13 | 1 | **40** | **9** |
| 1999–2000 | West Ham U | 8 | 2 | | |
| 2000–01 | West Ham U | 32 | 11 | | |
| 2001–02 | West Ham U | 27 | 11 | | |
| 2002–03 | West Ham U | 17 | 5 | **84** | **29** |
| 2003–04 | Tottenham H | 27 | 7 | **27** | **7** |

**KEANE, Robbie (F) 219 76**

H: 5 9 W: 12 06 b.Dublin 8-7-80

*Source:* Trainee. *Honours:* Eire 52 full caps, 20 goals.

| | | | | | |
|---|---|---|---|---|---|
| 1997–98 | Wolverhampton W | 38 | 11 | | |
| 1998–99 | Wolverhampton W | 33 | 11 | | |
| 1999–2000 | Wolverhampton W | 2 | 2 | **73** | **24** |
| 1999–2000 | Coventry C | 31 | 12 | **31** | **12** |
| 2000–01 | Internazionale | 6 | 0 | **6** | **0** |
| 2000–01 | Leeds U | 18 | 9 | | |
| 2001–02 | Leeds U | 25 | 3 | | |
| 2002–03 | Leeds U | 3 | 1 | **46** | **13** |
| 2002–03 | Tottenham H | 29 | 13 | | |
| 2003–04 | Tottenham H | 34 | 14 | **63** | **27** |

**KELLER, Kasey (G)** **411 0**
H: 6 1 W: 13 08 b.Washington 27-11-69
*Source:* Portland Univ. *Honours:* USA 70 full caps.

| | | | | | |
|---|---|---|---|---|---|
| 1991–92 | Millwall | 1 | 0 | | |
| 1992–93 | Millwall | 45 | 0 | | |
| 1993–94 | Millwall | 44 | 0 | | |
| 1994–95 | Millwall | 44 | 0 | | |
| 1995–96 | Millwall | 42 | 0 | **176** | **0** |
| 1996–97 | Leicester C | 31 | 0 | | |
| 1997–98 | Leicester C | 32 | 0 | | |
| 1998–99 | Leicester C | 36 | 0 | **99** | **0** |
| 1999–2000 | Rayo Vallecano | 28 | 0 | | |
| 2000–01 | Rayo Vallecano | 23 | 0 | **51** | **0** |
| 2001–02 | Tottenham H | 9 | 0 | | |
| 2002–03 | Tottenham H | 38 | 0 | | |
| 2003–04 | Tottenham H | 38 | 0 | **85** | **0** |

**KELLY, Stephen (D)** **41 0**
H: 6 1 W: 12 01 b.Dublin 6-9-83
*Honours:* Eire Under-21.

| | | | | | |
|---|---|---|---|---|---|
| 2000–01 | Tottenham H | 0 | 0 | | |
| 2001–02 | Tottenham H | 0 | 0 | | |
| 2002–03 | Tottenham H | 0 | 0 | | |
| 2002–03 | *Southend U* | 10 | 0 | **10** | **0** |
| 2002–03 | *QPR* | 7 | 0 | **7** | **0** |
| 2003–04 | Tottenham H | 11 | 0 | **11** | **0** |
| 2003–04 | *Watford* | 13 | 0 | **13** | **0** |

**KING, Ledley (D)** **108 2**
H: 6 2 W: 14 05 b.Bow 12-10-80
*Source:* Trainee. *Honours:* England Youth, Under-21, 7 full caps, 1 goal.

| | | | | | |
|---|---|---|---|---|---|
| 1998–99 | Tottenham H | 1 | 0 | | |
| 1999–2000 | Tottenham H | 3 | 0 | | |
| 2000–01 | Tottenham H | 18 | 1 | | |
| 2001–02 | Tottenham H | 32 | 0 | | |
| 2002–03 | Tottenham H | 25 | 0 | | |
| 2003–04 | Tottenham H | 29 | 1 | **108** | **2** |

**MABIZELA, Mbulelo (D)** **6 1**
H: 5 10 W: 12 06 b.Pietermaritzburg 16-9-80
*Source:* Orlando P. *Honours:* South Africa 31 full caps.

| | | | | | |
|---|---|---|---|---|---|
| 2003–04 | Tottenham H | 6 | 1 | **6** | **1** |

**MALCOLM, Michael (F)** **0 0**
b.Harrow 13-10-85
*Source:* Trainee. *Honours:* England Youth.

| | | | | | |
|---|---|---|---|---|---|
| 2002–03 | Tottenham H | 0 | 0 | | |
| 2003–04 | Tottenham H | 0 | 0 | | |

**MARNEY, Dean (D)** **14 0**
H: 5 9 W: 11 04 b.Barking 31-1-84
*Source:* Scholar.

| | | | | | |
|---|---|---|---|---|---|
| 2002–03 | Tottenham H | 0 | 0 | | |
| 2002–03 | *Swindon T* | 9 | 0 | **9** | **0** |
| 2003–04 | Tottenham H | 3 | 0 | **3** | **0** |
| 2003–04 | *QPR* | 2 | 0 | **2** | **0** |

**McKENNA, Kieran (M)** **0 0**
b.London 14-5-86
*Source:* Academy.

| | | | | | |
|---|---|---|---|---|---|
| 2003–04 | Tottenham H | 0 | 0 | | |

**McKIE, Marcel (D)** **0 0**
b.Edmonton 22-9-84
*Source:* Scholar. *Honours:* England Youth.

| | | | | | |
|---|---|---|---|---|---|
| 2001–02 | Tottenham H | 0 | 0 | | |
| 2002–03 | Tottenham H | 0 | 0 | | |
| 2003–04 | Tottenham H | 0 | 0 | | |

**O'DONOGHUE, Paul (D)** **0 0**
H: 6 1 W: 13 10 b.Lewisham 14-12-83
*Source:* Scholar.

| | | | | | |
|---|---|---|---|---|---|
| 2001–02 | Tottenham H | 0 | 0 | | |
| 2002–03 | Tottenham H | 0 | 0 | | |
| 2003–04 | Tottenham H | 0 | 0 | | |

**POSTIGA, Helder (F)** **77 23**
H: 5 11 W: 11 00 b.Povoa de Varzim 2-8-82
*Honours:* Portugal 9 full caps, 4 goals.

| | | | | | |
|---|---|---|---|---|---|
| 2001–02 | Porto | 27 | 9 | | |
| 2002–03 | Porto | 31 | 13 | **58** | **22** |
| 2003–04 | Tottenham H | 19 | 1 | **19** | **1** |

**POYET, Gustavo* (M)** **426 117**
H: 6 2 W: 13 00 b.Montevideo 15-11-67
*Source:* River Plate, Grenoble, Bella Vista. *Honours:* Uruguay 25 full caps, 3 goals.

| | | | | | |
|---|---|---|---|---|---|
| 1990–91 | Zaragoza | 31 | 7 | | |
| 1991–92 | Zaragoza | 33 | 3 | | |
| 1992–93 | Zaragoza | 33 | 6 | | |
| 1993–94 | Zaragoza | 34 | 11 | | |
| 1994–95 | Zaragoza | 34 | 11 | | |
| 1995–96 | Zaragoza | 36 | 11 | | |
| 1996–97 | Zaragoza | 38 | 14 | **239** | **63** |
| 1997–98 | Chelsea | 14 | 4 | | |
| 1998–99 | Chelsea | 28 | 11 | | |
| 1999–2000 | Chelsea | 33 | 10 | | |
| 2000–01 | Chelsea | 30 | 11 | **105** | **36** |
| 2001–02 | Tottenham H | 34 | 10 | | |
| 2002–03 | Tottenham H | 28 | 5 | | |
| 2003–04 | Tottenham H | 20 | 3 | **82** | **18** |

**PRICE, Owen (F)** **0 0**
b.London 20-10-85

| | | | | | |
|---|---|---|---|---|---|
| 2003–04 | Tottenham H | 0 | 0 | | |

**REBROV, Sergei (F)** **288 117**
H: 5 8 W: 11 00 b.Gorlovka 3-6-74
*Honours:* Ukraine 52 full caps, 13 goals.

| | | | | | |
|---|---|---|---|---|---|
| 1991 | Shakhtor Donetsk | 7 | 2 | | |
| 1991–92 | Shakhtor Donetsk | 19 | 10 | **26** | **12** |
| 1992–93 | Dynamo Kiev | 23 | 5 | | |
| 1993–94 | Dynamo Kiev | 10 | 2 | | |
| 1994–95 | Dynamo Kiev | 25 | 8 | | |
| 1995–96 | Dynamo Kiev | 31 | 9 | | |
| 1996–97 | Dynamo Kiev | 30 | 20 | | |
| 1997–98 | Dynamo Kiev | 29 | 22 | | |
| 1998–99 | Dynamo Kiev | 22 | 9 | | |
| 1999–2000 | Dynamo Kiev | 20 | 18 | **190** | **93** |
| 2000–01 | Tottenham H | 29 | 9 | | |
| 2001–02 | Tottenham H | 30 | 1 | | |
| 2002–03 | Tottenham H | 0 | 0 | **59** | **10** |
| 2002–03 | *Fenerbahce* | 13 | 2 | **13** | **2** |

**REDKNAPP, Jamie (M)** **284 34**
H: 6 0 W: 13 03 b.Barton-on-Sea 25-6-73
*Source:* Tottenham H Schoolboy, Bournemouth Trainee. *Honours:* England Schools, Youth, B, Under-21, 17 full caps, 1 goal.

| | | | | | |
|---|---|---|---|---|---|
| 1989–90 | Bournemouth | 4 | 0 | | |
| 1990–91 | Bournemouth | 9 | 0 | **13** | **0** |
| 1990–91 | Liverpool | 0 | 0 | | |
| 1991–92 | Liverpool | 6 | 1 | | |
| 1992–93 | Liverpool | 29 | 2 | | |
| 1993–94 | Liverpool | 35 | 4 | | |
| 1994–95 | Liverpool | 41 | 3 | | |
| 1995–96 | Liverpool | 23 | 3 | | |
| 1996–97 | Liverpool | 23 | 2 | | |
| 1997–98 | Liverpool | 20 | 3 | | |
| 1998–99 | Liverpool | 34 | 8 | | |
| 1999–2000 | Liverpool | 22 | 3 | | |
| 2000–01 | Liverpool | 0 | 0 | | |
| 2001–02 | Liverpool | 4 | 1 | **237** | **30** |
| 2001–02 | Tottenham H | 0 | 0 | | |
| 2002–03 | Tottenham H | 17 | 3 | | |
| 2003–04 | Tottenham H | 17 | 1 | **34** | **4** |

**RICHARDS, Dean (D)** **348 18**
H: 6 2 W: 13 01 b.Bradford 9-6-74
*Source:* Trainee. *Honours:* England Under-21.

| | | | | | |
|---|---|---|---|---|---|
| 1991–92 | Bradford C | 7 | 1 | | |
| 1992–93 | Bradford C | 3 | 0 | | |
| 1993–94 | Bradford C | 46 | 2 | | |
| 1994–95 | Bradford C | 30 | 1 | **86** | **4** |
| 1994–95 | *Wolverhampton W* | 10 | 2 | | |
| 1995–96 | Wolverhampton W | 37 | 1 | | |
| 1996–97 | Wolverhampton W | 21 | 1 | | |
| 1997–98 | Wolverhampton W | 13 | 0 | | |
| 1998–99 | Wolverhampton W | 41 | 3 | **122** | **7** |
| 1999–2000 | Southampton | 35 | 2 | | |
| 2000–01 | Southampton | 28 | 1 | | |
| 2001–02 | Southampton | 4 | 0 | **67** | **3** |
| 2001–02 | Tottenham H | 24 | 2 | | |
| 2002–03 | Tottenham H | 26 | 2 | | |
| 2003–04 | Tottenham H | 23 | 0 | **73** | **4** |

**RICKETTS, Rohan (M)** **24 1**
H: 5 8 W: 11 05 b.Clapham 22-12-82
*Source:* Scholar. *Honours:* England Youth, Under-20.

| | | | | | |
|---|---|---|---|---|---|
| 2001–02 | Arsenal | 0 | 0 | | |
| 2002–03 | Tottenham H | 0 | 0 | | |
| 2003–04 | Tottenham H | 24 | 1 | **24** | **1** |

**ROBINSON, Paul (G)** **95 0**
H: 6 4 W: 15 07 b.Beverley 15-10-79
*Source:* Trainee. *Honours:* England Under-21, 5 full caps.

| | | | | | |
|---|---|---|---|---|---|
| 1996–97 | Leeds U | 0 | 0 | | |
| 1997–98 | Leeds U | 0 | 0 | | |
| 1998–99 | Leeds U | 5 | 0 | | |
| 1999–2000 | Leeds U | 0 | 0 | | |
| 2000–01 | Leeds U | 16 | 0 | | |
| 2001–02 | Leeds U | 0 | 0 | | |
| 2002–03 | Leeds U | 38 | 0 | | |
| 2003–04 | Leeds U | 36 | 0 | **95** | **0** |
| 2003–04 | Tottenham H | 0 | 0 | | |

**SLABBER, Jamie (F)** **1 0**
H: 6 2 W: 11 10 b.Enfield 31-12-84
*Source:* Scholar. *Honours:* England Youth.

| | | | | | |
|---|---|---|---|---|---|
| 2001–02 | Tottenham H | 0 | 0 | | |
| 2002–03 | Tottenham H | 1 | 0 | | |
| 2003–04 | Tottenham H | 0 | 0 | **1** | **0** |

**TARICCO, Mauricio (D)** **288 6**
H: 5 8 W: 11 07 b.Buenos Aires 10-3-73
*Honours:* Argentina Under-23.

| | | | | | |
|---|---|---|---|---|---|
| 1993–94 | Argentinos Juniors | 21 | 0 | **21** | **0** |
| 1994–95 | Ipswich T | 0 | 0 | | |
| 1995–96 | Ipswich T | 39 | 0 | | |
| 1996–97 | Ipswich T | 41 | 3 | | |
| 1997–98 | Ipswich T | 41 | 0 | | |
| 1998–99 | Ipswich T | 16 | 1 | **137** | **4** |
| 1998–99 | Tottenham H | 13 | 0 | | |
| 1999–2000 | Tottenham H | 29 | 0 | | |
| 2000–01 | Tottenham H | 5 | 0 | | |
| 2001–02 | Tottenham H | 30 | 0 | | |
| 2002–03 | Tottenham H | 21 | 1 | | |
| 2003–04 | Tottenham H | 32 | 1 | **130** | **2** |

**TODA, Kazuyuki‡ (M)** **167 7**
H: 5 10 W: 10 11 b.Tokyo 30-12-77
*Honours:* Japan 15 full caps, 1 goal.

| | | | | | |
|---|---|---|---|---|---|
| 1994 | Shimizu S-Pulse | 0 | 0 | | |
| 1995 | Shimizu S-Pulse | 0 | 0 | | |
| 1996 | Shimizu S-Pulse | 5 | 0 | | |
| 1997 | Shimizu S-Pulse | 20 | 5 | | |
| 1998 | Shimizu S-Pulse | 34 | 0 | | |
| 1999 | Shimizu S-Pulse | 28 | 0 | | |
| 2000 | Shimizu S-Pulse | 27 | 1 | | |
| 2001 | Shimizu S-Pulse | 27 | 0 | | |
| 2002 | Shimizu S-Pulse | 22 | 1 | **163** | **7** |
| 2002–03 | Tottenham H | 4 | 0 | | |
| 2003–04 | Tottenham H | 0 | 0 | **4** | **0** |

**WATSON, Joe‡ (M)** **0 0**
b.London 3-10-85
*Source:* Trainee.

| | | | | | |
|---|---|---|---|---|---|
| 2003–04 | Tottenham H | 0 | 0 | | |

**YEATES, Mark (F)** **10 0**
H: 5 9 W: 10 07 b.Dublin 11-1-85
*Source:* Trainee. *Honours:* Eire Under-21.

| | | | | | |
|---|---|---|---|---|---|
| 2002–03 | Tottenham H | 0 | 0 | | |
| 2003–04 | Tottenham H | 1 | 0 | **1** | **0** |
| 2003–04 | *Brighton & HA* | 9 | 0 | **9** | **0** |

**ZIEGE, Christian* (D)** **303 59**
H: 6 1 W: 12 13 b.Berlin 1-2-72
*Honours:* Germany 72 full caps, 9 goals.

| | | | | | |
|---|---|---|---|---|---|
| 1990–91 | Bayern Munich | 13 | 1 | | |
| 1991–92 | Bayern Munich | 26 | 2 | | |
| 1992–93 | Bayern Munich | 28 | 9 | | |
| 1993–94 | Bayern Munich | 29 | 3 | | |
| 1994–95 | Bayern Munich | 29 | 10 | | |
| 1995–96 | Bayern Munich | 20 | 9 | | |
| 1996–97 | Bayern Munich | 27 | 7 | **172** | **41** |
| 1997–98 | AC Milan | 22 | 2 | | |
| 1998–99 | AC Milan | 17 | 2 | **39** | **4** |
| 1999–2000 | Middlesbrough | 29 | 6 | | |
| 2000–01 | Middlesbrough | 0 | 0 | **29** | **6** |
| 2000–01 | Liverpool | 16 | 1 | **16** | **1** |
| 2001–02 | Tottenham H | 27 | 5 | | |
| 2002–03 | Tottenham H | 12 | 2 | | |
| 2003–04 | Tottenham H | 8 | 0 | **47** | **7** |

**Scholars**
Barcham, Andrew; Daniels, Charlie; Forecast, Tommy S; Ifil, Philip N; Lee, Charlie; Mascarenhas, Brian A; O'Hara, Jamie D; Stevens, Danny R; Thyer, Scott M; Welch, Thomas C; Wright, Mark C E

## TRANMERE R (81)

**ACHTERBERG, John (G)** **224 0**
H: 6 1 W: 13 00 b.Utrecht 8-7-71
*Source:* VV RUC, Utrecht.

| | | | | | |
|---|---|---|---|---|---|
| 1993–94 | NAC | 1 | 0 | | |

| | | | | | |
|---|---|---|---|---|---|
| 1994–95 | NAC | 2 | 0 | | |
| 1995–96 | NAC | 6 | 0 | **9** | **0** |
| 1996–97 | Eindhoven | 32 | 0 | **32** | **0** |

From Utrecht.

| | | | | | |
|---|---|---|---|---|---|
| 1998–99 | Tranmere R | 24 | 0 | | |
| 1999–2000 | Tranmere R | 26 | 0 | | |
| 2000–01 | Tranmere R | 25 | 0 | | |
| 2001–02 | Tranmere R | 25 | 0 | | |
| 2002–03 | Tranmere R | 38 | 0 | | |
| 2003–04 | Tranmere R | 45 | 0 | **183** | **0** |

**ALLEN, Graham‡ (D) 206 10**

H: 6 1 W: 12 00 b.Bolton 8-4-77

*Source:* Trainee. *Honours:* England Youth.

| | | | | | |
|---|---|---|---|---|---|
| 1994–95 | Everton | 0 | 0 | | |
| 1995–96 | Everton | 0 | 0 | | |
| 1996–97 | Everton | 1 | 0 | | |
| 1997–98 | Everton | 5 | 0 | | |
| 1998–99 | Everton | 0 | 0 | **6** | **0** |
| 1998–99 | Tranmere R | 41 | 5 | | |
| 1999–2000 | Tranmere R | 24 | 0 | | |
| 2000–01 | Tranmere R | 22 | 0 | | |
| 2001–02 | Tranmere R | 31 | 1 | | |
| 2002–03 | Tranmere R | 41 | 3 | | |
| 2003–04 | Tranmere R | 41 | 1 | **200** | **10** |

**ASHTON, Neil (M) 1 0**

H: 5 10 W: 11 12 b.Liverpool 15-1-85

*Source:* Scholar.

| | | | | | |
|---|---|---|---|---|---|
| 2002–03 | Tranmere R | 0 | 0 | | |
| 2003–04 | Tranmere R | 1 | 0 | **1** | **0** |

**BERESFORD, David# (F) 201 7**

H: 5 8 W: 10 09 b.Middleton 11-11-76

*Source:* Trainee. *Honours:* England Schools, Youth.

| | | | | | |
|---|---|---|---|---|---|
| 1993–94 | Oldham Ath | 1 | 0 | | |
| 1994–95 | Oldham Ath | 2 | 0 | | |
| 1995–96 | Oldham Ath | 28 | 2 | | |
| 1995–96 | *Swansea C* | 6 | 0 | **6** | **0** |
| 1996–97 | Oldham Ath | 33 | 0 | **64** | **2** |
| 1996–97 | Huddersfield T | 6 | 1 | | |
| 1997–98 | Huddersfield T | 8 | 0 | | |
| 1998–99 | Huddersfield T | 19 | 2 | | |
| 1999–2000 | Huddersfield T | 0 | 0 | | |
| 1999–2000 | *Preston NE* | 4 | 0 | **4** | **0** |
| 2000–01 | Huddersfield T | 2 | 0 | **35** | **3** |
| 2000–01 | *Port Vale* | 4 | 0 | **4** | **0** |
| 2001–02 | Hull C | 41 | 1 | **41** | **1** |
| 2002–03 | Plymouth Arg | 16 | 0 | | |
| 2003–04 | Plymouth Arg | 1 | 0 | **17** | **0** |
| 2003–04 | *Macclesfield T* | 5 | 0 | **5** | **0** |
| 2003–04 | Tranmere R | 25 | 1 | **25** | **1** |

**CONNELLY, Sean‡ (D) 386 6**

H: 5 10 W: 11 10 b.Sheffield 26-6-70

*Source:* Hallam.

| | | | | | |
|---|---|---|---|---|---|
| 1991–92 | Stockport Co | 0 | 0 | | |
| 1992–93 | Stockport Co | 7 | 0 | | |
| 1993–94 | Stockport Co | 32 | 0 | | |
| 1994–95 | Stockport Co | 39 | 0 | | |
| 1995–96 | Stockport Co | 43 | 0 | | |
| 1996–97 | Stockport Co | 45 | 0 | | |
| 1997–98 | Stockport Co | 45 | 2 | | |
| 1998–99 | Stockport Co | 35 | 1 | | |
| 1999–2000 | Stockport Co | 43 | 3 | | |
| 2000–01 | Stockport Co | 13 | 0 | **302** | **6** |
| 2000–01 | *Wolverhampton W* | 6 | 0 | | |
| 2001–02 | Wolverhampton W | 8 | 0 | | |
| 2002–03 | Wolverhampton W | 0 | 0 | **14** | **0** |
| 2002–03 | Tranmere R | 33 | 0 | | |
| 2003–04 | Tranmere R | 37 | 0 | **70** | **0** |

**DADI, Eugene# (F) 144 33**

H: 6 2 W: 12 11 b.Abidjan 20-8-73

| | | | | | |
|---|---|---|---|---|---|
| 1997–98 | Linz | 19 | 4 | | |
| 1998–99 | Linz | 20 | 3 | | |
| 1999–2000 | Linz | 13 | 3 | **52** | **10** |
| 2000–01 | Toulouse | 3 | 0 | **3** | **0** |
| 2001–02 | Aberdeen | 28 | 4 | **28** | **4** |
| 2002–03 | Livingston | 23 | 3 | **23** | **3** |
| 2003–04 | Tranmere R | 38 | 16 | **38** | **16** |

**DAGNALL, Chris (F) 10 1**

H: 5 8 W: 12 09 b.Liverpool 15-4-86

*Source:* Scholar.

| | | | | | |
|---|---|---|---|---|---|
| 2003–04 | Tranmere R | 10 | 1 | **10** | **1** |

**GOODISON, Ian# (D) 82 1**

H: 6 1 W: 12 06 b.St James, Jamaica 21-11-72

*Source:* Olympic Gardens. *Honours:* Jamaica full caps.

| | | | | | |
|---|---|---|---|---|---|
| 1999–2000 | Hull C | 18 | 0 | | |
| 2000–01 | Hull C | 36 | 1 | | |
| 2001–02 | Hull C | 16 | 0 | | |
| 2002–03 | Hull C | 0 | 0 | **70** | **1** |

From Seba U.

| | | | | | |
|---|---|---|---|---|---|
| 2003–04 | Tranmere R | 12 | 0 | **12** | **0** |

**HALL, Paul# (M) 479 77**

H: 5 8 W: 12 06 b.Manchester 3-7-72

*Source:* Trainee. *Honours:* Jamaica 41 full caps, 9 goals.

| | | | | | |
|---|---|---|---|---|---|
| 1989–90 | Torquay U | 10 | 0 | | |
| 1990–91 | Torquay U | 17 | 0 | | |
| 1991–92 | Torquay U | 38 | 1 | | |
| 1992–93 | Torquay U | 28 | 0 | **93** | **1** |
| 1992–93 | Portsmouth | 0 | 0 | | |
| 1993–94 | Portsmouth | 28 | 4 | | |
| 1994–95 | Portsmouth | 43 | 5 | | |
| 1995–96 | Portsmouth | 46 | 10 | | |
| 1996–97 | Portsmouth | 42 | 13 | | |
| 1997–98 | Portsmouth | 29 | 5 | **188** | **37** |
| 1998–99 | Coventry C | 9 | 0 | | |
| 1998–99 | *Bury* | 7 | 0 | **7** | **0** |
| 1999–2000 | Coventry C | 1 | 0 | **10** | **0** |
| 1999–2000 | *Sheffield U* | 4 | 1 | **4** | **1** |
| 1999–2000 | *WBA* | 4 | 0 | **4** | **0** |
| 1999–2000 | Walsall | 10 | 4 | | |
| 2000–01 | Walsall | 42 | 6 | | |
| 2001–02 | Walsall | 0 | 0 | **52** | **10** |
| 2001–02 | Rushden & D | 34 | 8 | | |
| 2002–03 | Rushden & D | 45 | 16 | | |
| 2003–04 | Rushden & D | 33 | 2 | **112** | **26** |
| 2003–04 | Tranmere R | 9 | 2 | **9** | **2** |

**HARRISON, Danny (M) 45 2**

H: 5 11 W: 12 04 b.Liverpool 4-11-82

*Source:* Scholar.

| | | | | | |
|---|---|---|---|---|---|
| 2001–02 | Tranmere R | 1 | 0 | | |
| 2002–03 | Tranmere R | 12 | 0 | | |
| 2003–04 | Tranmere R | 32 | 2 | **45** | **2** |

**HAWORTH, Simon# (F) 241 84**

H: 6 1 W: 13 08 b.Cardiff 30-3-77

*Source:* Trainee. *Honours:* Wales Youth, Under-21, B, 5 full caps.

| | | | | | |
|---|---|---|---|---|---|
| 1995–96 | Cardiff C | 13 | 0 | | |
| 1996–97 | Cardiff C | 24 | 9 | **37** | **9** |
| 1997–98 | Coventry C | 10 | 0 | | |
| 1998–99 | Coventry C | 1 | 0 | **11** | **0** |
| 1998–99 | Wigan Ath | 20 | 10 | | |
| 1999–2000 | Wigan Ath | 40 | 13 | | |
| 2000–01 | Wigan Ath | 30 | 11 | | |
| 2001–02 | Wigan Ath | 27 | 10 | **117** | **44** |
| 2001–02 | Tranmere R | 12 | 5 | | |
| 2002–03 | Tranmere R | 42 | 20 | | |
| 2003–04 | Tranmere R | 22 | 6 | **76** | **31** |

**HAY, Alex‡ (F) 41 3**

H: 5 10 W: 11 05 b.Birkenhead 14-10-81

*Source:* Scholarship.

| | | | | | |
|---|---|---|---|---|---|
| 1999–2000 | Tranmere R | 0 | 0 | | |
| 2000–01 | Tranmere R | 0 | 0 | | |
| 2001–02 | Tranmere R | 3 | 0 | | |
| 2002–03 | Tranmere R | 19 | 3 | | |
| 2003–04 | Tranmere R | 19 | 0 | **41** | **3** |

**HOWARTH, Russell (G) 12 0**

H: 6 2 W: 14 05 b.York 27-3-82

*Source:* Scholar. *Honours:* England Youth, Under-20.

| | | | | | |
|---|---|---|---|---|---|
| 1999–2000 | York C | 6 | 0 | | |
| 2000–01 | York C | 0 | 0 | | |
| 2001–02 | York C | 2 | 0 | | |
| 2002–03 | York C | 0 | 0 | **8** | **0** |
| 2002–03 | Tranmere R | 3 | 0 | | |
| 2003–04 | Tranmere R | 1 | 0 | **4** | **0** |

**HUME, Iain (F) 102 16**

H: 5 7 W: 11 02 b.Brampton 31-10-83

*Honours:* Canada 6 full caps.

| | | | | | |
|---|---|---|---|---|---|
| 1999–2000 | Tranmere R | 3 | 0 | | |
| 2000–01 | Tranmere R | 10 | 0 | | |
| 2001–02 | Tranmere R | 14 | 0 | | |
| 2002–03 | Tranmere R | 35 | 6 | | |
| 2003–04 | Tranmere R | 40 | 10 | **102** | **16** |

**JENNINGS, Steven (M) 4 0**

H: 5 7 W: 11 07 b.Liverpool 28-10-84

*Source:* Scholar.

| | | | | | |
|---|---|---|---|---|---|
| 2002–03 | Tranmere R | 0 | 0 | | |
| 2003–04 | Tranmere R | 4 | 0 | **4** | **0** |

**JONES, Gary (M) 296 45**

H: 6 3 W: 14 00 b.Chester 10-5-75

*Source:* Trainee.

| | | | | | |
|---|---|---|---|---|---|
| 1993–94 | Tranmere R | 6 | 2 | | |
| 1994–95 | Tranmere R | 19 | 3 | | |
| 1995–96 | Tranmere R | 23 | 1 | | |
| 1996–97 | Tranmere R | 30 | 6 | | |
| 1997–98 | Tranmere R | 43 | 8 | | |
| 1998–99 | Tranmere R | 26 | 5 | | |
| 1999–2000 | Tranmere R | 31 | 3 | | |
| 2000–01 | Nottingham F | 31 | 1 | | |
| 2001–02 | Nottingham F | 5 | 1 | | |
| 2002–03 | Nottingham F | 0 | 0 | **36** | **2** |
| 2002–03 | Tranmere R | 40 | 6 | | |
| 2003–04 | Tranmere R | 42 | 9 | **260** | **43** |

**LINWOOD, Paul (D) 20 0**

H: 6 2 W: 12 08 b.Birkenhead 24-10-83

*Source:* Scholar.

| | | | | | |
|---|---|---|---|---|---|
| 2001–02 | Tranmere R | 0 | 0 | | |
| 2002–03 | Tranmere R | 0 | 0 | | |
| 2003–04 | Tranmere R | 20 | 0 | **20** | **0** |

**LORAN, Tyrone (D) 45 0**

H: 6 2 W: 13 11 b.Amsterdam 29-6-81

| | | | | | |
|---|---|---|---|---|---|
| 2002–03 | Manchester C | 0 | 0 | | |
| 2002–03 | Tranmere R | 17 | 0 | | |
| 2003–04 | Tranmere R | 28 | 0 | **45** | **0** |

**McGUIRE, Jamie‡ (M) 0 0**

H: 5 7 W: 11 01 b.Birkenhead 13-11-83

*Source:* Scholar.

| | | | | | |
|---|---|---|---|---|---|
| 2001–02 | Tranmere R | 0 | 0 | | |
| 2002–03 | Tranmere R | 0 | 0 | | |
| 2003–04 | Tranmere R | 0 | 0 | | |

**MELLON, Micky* (M) 462 32**

H: 5 10 W: 12 11 b.Paisley 18-3-72

*Source:* Trainee.

| | | | | | |
|---|---|---|---|---|---|
| 1989–90 | Bristol C | 9 | 0 | | |
| 1990–91 | Bristol C | 0 | 0 | | |
| 1991–92 | Bristol C | 16 | 0 | | |
| 1992–93 | Bristol C | 10 | 1 | **35** | **1** |
| 1992–93 | WBA | 17 | 3 | | |
| 1993–94 | WBA | 21 | 2 | | |
| 1994–95 | WBA | 7 | 1 | **45** | **6** |
| 1994–95 | Blackpool | 26 | 4 | | |
| 1995–96 | Blackpool | 45 | 6 | | |
| 1996–97 | Blackpool | 43 | 4 | | |
| 1997–98 | Blackpool | 10 | 0 | **124** | **14** |
| 1997–98 | Tranmere R | 33 | 2 | | |
| 1998–99 | Tranmere R | 24 | 1 | | |
| 1998–99 | Burnley | 20 | 2 | | |
| 1999–2000 | Burnley | 42 | 3 | | |
| 2000–01 | Burnley | 22 | 0 | **84** | **5** |
| 2000–01 | Tranmere R | 13 | 1 | | |
| 2001–02 | Tranmere R | 27 | 1 | | |
| 2002–03 | Tranmere R | 34 | 1 | | |
| 2003–04 | Tranmere R | 43 | 0 | **174** | **6** |

**NAVARRO, Alan (D) 60 2**

H: 5 10 W: 11 07 b.Liverpool 31-5-81

*Source:* Trainee.

| | | | | | |
|---|---|---|---|---|---|
| 1998–99 | Liverpool | 0 | 0 | | |
| 1999–2000 | Liverpool | 0 | 0 | | |
| 2000–01 | Liverpool | 0 | 0 | | |
| 2000–01 | *Crewe Alex* | 8 | 1 | | |
| 2001–02 | Liverpool | 0 | 0 | | |
| 2001–02 | *Crewe Alex* | 7 | 0 | **15** | **1** |
| 2001–02 | Tranmere R | 21 | 1 | | |
| 2002–03 | Tranmere R | 5 | 0 | | |
| 2003–04 | Tranmere R | 19 | 0 | **45** | **1** |

**NICHOLSON, Shane‡ (D) 439 19**

H: 5 10 W: 12 02 b.Newark 3-6-70

*Source:* Trainee.

| | | | | | |
|---|---|---|---|---|---|
| 1986–87 | Lincoln C | 7 | 0 | | |
| 1987–88 | Lincoln C | 0 | 0 | | |
| 1988–89 | Lincoln C | 34 | 1 | | |
| 1989–90 | Lincoln C | 23 | 0 | | |
| 1990–91 | Lincoln C | 40 | 4 | | |
| 1991–92 | Lincoln C | 29 | 1 | **133** | **6** |
| 1991–92 | Derby Co | 0 | 0 | | |
| 1992–93 | Derby Co | 17 | 0 | | |
| 1993–94 | Derby Co | 22 | 1 | | |
| 1994–95 | Derby Co | 15 | 0 | | |

1995–96 Derby Co 20 0 74 1
1995–96 WBA 18 0
1996–97 WBA 18 0
1997–98 WBA 16 0 52 0
1998–99 Chesterfield 24 0 24 0
1999–2000 Stockport Co 42 1
2000–01 Stockport Co 35 2 77 3
2001–02 Sheffield U 25 3 25 3
2002–03 Tranmere R 38 4
2003–04 Tranmere R 16 2 54 6

**PALETHORPE, Philip (G)** 0 0
b.Liverpool 17-9-86
*Source:* Scholar.
2003–04 Tranmere R 0 0

**ROBERTS, Gareth# (D)** 197 8
H: 5 8 W: 11 00 b.Wrexham 6-2-78
*Source:* Trainee. *Honours:* Wales Under-21, B, 6 full caps.
1995–96 Liverpool 0 0
1996–97 Liverpool 0 0
1997–98 Liverpool 0 0
1998–99 Liverpool 0 0
1999–2000 Tranmere R 37 1
2000–01 Tranmere R 34 0
2001–02 Tranmere R 45 2
2002–03 Tranmere R 37 4
2003–04 Tranmere R 44 1 197 8

**ROBINSON, Paul (F)** 0 0
H: 6 0 W: 12 00 b.Newcastle 25-5-83
*Source:* Scholar.
2002–03 Tranmere R 0 0
2003–04 Tranmere R 0 0

**SHARPS, Ian (D)** 87 4
H: 6 3 W: 13 05 b.Warrington 23-10-80
*Source:* Trainee.
1998–99 Tranmere R 1 0
1999–2000 Tranmere R 0 0
2000–01 Tranmere R 0 0
2001–02 Tranmere R 29 0
2002–03 Tranmere R 30 3
2003–04 Tranmere R 27 1 87 4

**TAYLOR, Ryan (D)** 55 6
H: 5 8 W: 10 04 b.Liverpool 19-8-84
*Source:* Scholar. *Honours:* England Youth.
2001–02 Tranmere R 0 0
2002–03 Tranmere R 25 1
2003–04 Tranmere R 30 5 55 6

**TREMARCO, Carl (M)** 0 0
H: 5 11 W: 12 03 b.Liverpool 11-10-85
*Source:* Scholar.
2003–04 Tranmere R 0 0

**Scholars**
Brown, Paul; Carroll, Thomas; Dickinson, Adam C; Fowler, Joseph A; Griffiths, Alan T; Hooper, Gareth P; James, Oliver D; Jones, Michael D; Martin, Paul A; Pinch, Gary; Quadrio, James J; Scott, Gerard; Vaughan, James

**Non Contract**
Hayton, Andrew D

## WALSALL (82)

**ARANALDE, Zigor (D)** 165 5
H: 6 1 W: 13 03 b.Ibarra 28-2-73
*Source:* Logrones.
2000–01 Walsall 45 0
2001–02 Walsall 45 2
2002–03 Walsall 39 3
2003–04 Walsall 36 0 165 5

**BAZELEY, Darren# (D)** 392 25
H: 5 11 W: 11 09 b.Northampton 5-10-72
*Source:* Trainee. *Honours:* England Under-21.
1989–90 Watford 1 0
1990–91 Watford 7 0
1991–92 Watford 34 6
1992–93 Watford 22 1
1993–94 Watford 10 1
1994–95 Watford 28 4
1995–96 Watford 41 1
1996–97 Watford 41 3
1997–98 Watford 16 3
1998–99 Watford 40 2 240 21
1999–2000 Wolverhampton W 46 3
2000–01 Wolverhampton W 24 1
2001–02 Wolverhampton W 0 0 70 4
2002–03 Walsall 43 0
2003–04 Walsall 39 0 82 0

**BENNETT, Julian§ (M)** 1 0
H: 6 0 W: 12 07 b.Nottingham 17-12-84
*Source:* Scholar.
2003–04 Walsall 1 0 1 0

**BIRCH, Gary (F)** 87 9
H: 6 0 W: 12 03 b.Birmingham 8-10-81
*Source:* Trainee.
1998–99 Walsall 0 0
1999–2000 Walsall 0 0
2000–01 Walsall 0 0
2000–01 *Exeter C* 9 2
2001–02 *Exeter C* 15 0 24 2
2001–02 Walsall 1 0
2002–03 Walsall 19 1
2003–04 Walsall 35 4 55 5
2003–04 *Barnsley* 8 2 8 2

**BISHOP, Andy* (F)** 55 10
H: 6 0 W: 10 10 b.Stone 19-10-82
*Source:* Scholar.
2002–03 Walsall 0 0
2002–03 *Kidderminster H* 29 5
2003–04 *Kidderminster H* 11 2 40 7
2003–04 *Rochdale* 10 1 10 1
2003–04 *Yeovil T* 5 2 5 2

**BRADBURY, Lee† (F)** 272 68
H: 6 0 W: 13 10 b.Isle of Wight 3-7-75
*Source:* Cowes. *Honours:* England Under-21.
1995–96 Portsmouth 12 0
1995–96 *Exeter C* 14 5 14 5
1996–97 Portsmouth 42 15
1997–98 Manchester C 27 7
1998–99 Manchester C 13 3 40 10
1998–99 Crystal Palace 22 4
1998–99 *Birmingham C* 7 0 7 0
1999–2000 Crystal Palace 10 2 32 6
1999–2000 Portsmouth 35 10
2000–01 Portsmouth 39 10
2001–02 Portsmouth 22 7
2002–03 Portsmouth 3 1
2002–03 *Sheffield W* 11 3 11 3
2003–04 Portsmouth 0 0 153 43
2003–04 *Derby Co* 7 0 7 0
2003–04 Walsall 8 1 8 1

**BURLEY, Craig† (M)** 251 36
H: 6 1 W: 13 03 b.Ayr 24-9-71
*Source:* Trainee. *Honours:* Scotland Schools, Youth, Under-21, 46 full caps, 3 goals.
1989–90 Chelsea 0 0
1990–91 Chelsea 1 0
1991–92 Chelsea 8 0
1992–93 Chelsea 3 0
1993–94 Chelsea 23 3
1994–95 Chelsea 25 2
1995–96 Chelsea 22 0
1996–97 Chelsea 31 2 113 7
1997–98 Celtic 35 10
1998–99 Celtic 21 9
1999–2000 Celtic 0 0 56 19
1999–2000 Derby Co 18 5
2000–01 Derby Co 24 2
2001–02 Derby Co 11 0
2002–03 Derby Co 20 3
2003–04 Derby Co 0 0 73 10
2003–04 Preston NE 4 0 4 0
2003–04 Walsall 5 0 5 0

**CAINES, Gavin† (D)** 0 0
H: 6 1 W: 12 00 b.Birmingham 20-9-83
*Source:* Scholar.
2003–04 Walsall 0 0

**CARBON, Matt‡ (D)** 258 17
H: 6 2 W: 12 05 b.Nottingham 8-6-75
*Source:* Trainee. *Honours:* England Under-21.
1992–93 Lincoln C 1 0
1993–94 Lincoln C 9 0
1994–95 Lincoln C 33 7
1995–96 Lincoln C 26 3
1995–96 Derby Co 6 0
1996–97 Derby Co 10 0
1997–98 Derby Co 4 0 20 0
1997–98 WBA 16 1
1998–99 WBA 39 2
1999–2000 WBA 34 2
2000–01 WBA 24 0 113 5
2001–02 Walsall 22 1
2002–03 Walsall 25 1
2003–04 Walsall 8 0 55 2
2003–04 *Lincoln C* 1 0 70 10

**CORICA, Steve (M)** 335 44
H: 5 8 W: 10 10 b.Cairns 24-3-73
*Honours:* Australia Youth, Under-20, Under-23, 31 full caps, 5 goals.
1990–91 Marconi Stallions 17 0
1991–92 Marconi Stallions 17 2
1992–93 Marconi Stallions 27 4
1993–94 Marconi Stallions 24 5
1994–95 Marconi Stallions 18 3 103 14
1995–96 Leicester C 16 2 16 2
1995–96 Wolverhampton W 17 0
1996–97 Wolverhampton W 36 2
1997–98 Wolverhampton W 1 0
1998–99 Wolverhampton W 31 2
1999–2000 Wolverhampton W 15 1 100 5
2000 Sanfrecce 21 3
2001 Sanfrecce 22 11 43 14
2001–02 Walsall 13 3
2002–03 Walsall 41 4
2003–04 Walsall 19 2 73 9

**EMBLEN, Neil# (M)** 285 21
H: 6 1 W: 13 11 b.Bromley 19-6-71
*Source:* Tonbridge, Sittingbourne.
1993–94 Millwall 12 0 12 0
1994–95 Wolverhampton W 27 7
1995–96 Wolverhampton W 33 2
1996–97 Wolverhampton W 28 0
1997–98 Wolverhampton W 7 0
1997–98 Crystal Palace 13 0 13 0
1998–99 Wolverhampton W 33 2
1999–2000 Wolverhampton W 46 5
2000–01 Wolverhampton W 28 0 202 16
2001–02 Norwich C 2 0
2002–03 Norwich C 12 0 14 0
2002–03 Walsall 5 0
2003–04 Walsall 39 5 44 5

**FRYATT, Matty (F)** 21 2
H: 5 10 W: 11 00 b.Nuneaton 5-3-86
*Source:* Scholar.
2002–03 Walsall 0 0
2003–04 Walsall 11 1 11 1
2003–04 *Carlisle U* 10 1 10 1

**HAWLEY, Karl‡ (F)** 1 0
H: 5 8 W: 12 02 b.Walsall 6-12-81
*Source:* Scholar.
2000–01 Walsall 0 0
2001–02 Walsall 1 0
2002–03 Walsall 0 0
2003–04 Walsall 0 0 1 0

**HAY, Danny‡ (D)** 97 2
H: 6 4 W: 14 11 b.Auckland 15-5-75
*Source:* Waitakere, Central Utd. *Honours:* New Zealand 17 full caps.
1997–98 Perth Glory 24 1
1998–99 Perth Glory 24 1 48 2
1999–2000 Leeds U 0 0
2000–01 Leeds U 4 0
2001–02 Leeds U 0 0 4 0
2002–03 Walsall 29 0
2003–04 Walsall 16 0 45 0

**KERR, Aaron* (G)** 0 0
H: 6 2 W: 13 00 b.Carrickfergus 8-12-82
*Source:* Havant & W'ville.
2003–04 Walsall 0 0

**LEITAO, Jorge# (F)** 165 44
H: 5 11 W: 13 06 b.Oporto 14-1-74
*Source:* Feirense.
2000–01 Walsall 44 18
2001–02 Walsall 38 8
2002–03 Walsall 44 11
2003–04 Walsall 39 7 165 44

**MATIAS, Pedro* (M)** 186 27
H: 6 0 W: 12 00 b.Madrid 11-10-73
1998–99 Logrones 12 0 12 0
1998–99 Macclesfield T 22 2 22 2
1999–2000 Tranmere R 4 0 4 0
1999–2000 Walsall 33 6

| | | | | | |
|---|---|---|---|---|---|
| 2000–01 | Walsall | 40 | 9 | | |
| 2001–02 | Walsall | 30 | 5 | | |
| 2002–03 | Walsall | 23 | 3 | | |
| 2003–04 | Walsall | 15 | 1 | **141** | **24** |
| 2003–04 | *Blackpool* | 7 | 1 | **7** | **1** |

**McSPORRAN, Jermaine* (M) 164 30**

H: 5 10 W: 10 12 b.Manchester 1-1-77

*Source:* Oxford C.

| | | | | | |
|---|---|---|---|---|---|
| 1998–99 | Wycombe W | 26 | 4 | | |
| 1999–2000 | Wycombe W | 38 | 9 | | |
| 2000–01 | Wycombe W | 20 | 2 | | |
| 2001–02 | Wycombe W | 32 | 7 | | |
| 2002–03 | Wycombe W | 9 | 1 | | |
| 2003–04 | Wycombe W | 33 | 7 | **158** | **30** |
| 2003–04 | Walsall | 6 | 0 | **6** | **0** |

**MERSON, Paul (F) 578 123**

H: 6 0 W: 12 10 b.Harlesden 20-3-68

*Source:* Apprentice. *Honours:* England Youth, Under-21, B, 21 full caps, 3 goals.

| | | | | | |
|---|---|---|---|---|---|
| 1985–86 | Arsenal | 0 | 0 | | |
| 1986–87 | Arsenal | 7 | 3 | | |
| 1986–87 | *Brentford* | 7 | 0 | **7** | **0** |
| 1987–88 | Arsenal | 15 | 5 | | |
| 1988–89 | Arsenal | 37 | 10 | | |
| 1989–90 | Arsenal | 29 | 7 | | |
| 1990–91 | Arsenal | 37 | 13 | | |
| 1991–92 | Arsenal | 42 | 12 | | |
| 1992–93 | Arsenal | 33 | 6 | | |
| 1993–94 | Arsenal | 33 | 7 | | |
| 1994–95 | Arsenal | 24 | 4 | | |
| 1995–96 | Arsenal | 38 | 5 | | |
| 1996–97 | Arsenal | 32 | 6 | **327** | **78** |
| 1997–98 | Middlesbrough | 45 | 11 | | |
| 1998–99 | Middlesbrough | 3 | 0 | **48** | **11** |
| 1998–99 | Aston Villa | 26 | 5 | | |
| 1999–2000 | Aston Villa | 32 | 5 | | |
| 2000–01 | Aston Villa | 38 | 6 | | |
| 2001–02 | Aston Villa | 21 | 2 | **117** | **18** |
| 2002–03 | Portsmouth | 45 | 12 | **45** | **12** |
| 2003–04 | Walsall | 34 | 4 | **34** | **4** |

**OSBORN, Simon (M) 363 31**

H: 5 9 W: 11 04 b.New Addington 19-1-72

*Source:* Apprentice.

| | | | | | |
|---|---|---|---|---|---|
| 1989–90 | Crystal Palace | 0 | 0 | | |
| 1990–91 | Crystal Palace | 4 | 0 | | |
| 1991–92 | Crystal Palace | 14 | 2 | | |
| 1992–93 | Crystal Palace | 31 | 2 | | |
| 1993–94 | Crystal Palace | 6 | 1 | **55** | **5** |
| 1994–95 | Reading | 32 | 5 | **32** | **5** |
| 1995–96 | QPR | 9 | 1 | **9** | **1** |
| 1995–96 | Wolverhampton W | 21 | 2 | | |
| 1996–97 | Wolverhampton W | 35 | 5 | | |
| 1997–98 | Wolverhampton W | 24 | 2 | | |
| 1998–99 | Wolverhampton W | 37 | 2 | | |
| 1999–2000 | Wolverhampton W | 25 | 0 | | |
| 2000–01 | Wolverhampton W | 20 | 0 | **162** | **11** |
| 2000–01 | Tranmere R | 9 | 1 | **9** | **1** |
| 2001–02 | Port Vale | 7 | 0 | **7** | **0** |
| 2001–02 | Gillingham | 28 | 4 | | |
| 2002–03 | Gillingham | 18 | 1 | **46** | **5** |
| 2003–04 | Walsall | 43 | 3 | **43** | **3** |

**PETTERSON, Andy† (G) 156 0**

H: 6 2 W: 15 02 b.Fremantle 29-9-69

| | | | | | |
|---|---|---|---|---|---|
| 1988–89 | Luton T | 0 | 0 | | |
| 1988–89 | *Swindon T* | 0 | 0 | | |
| 1989–90 | Luton T | 0 | 0 | | |
| 1990–91 | Luton T | 0 | 0 | | |
| 1991–92 | Luton T | 0 | 0 | | |
| 1991–92 | *Ipswich T* | 0 | 0 | | |
| 1992–93 | Luton T | 14 | 0 | | |
| 1992–93 | *Ipswich T* | 1 | 0 | | |
| 1993–94 | Luton T | 5 | 0 | **19** | **0** |
| 1994–95 | Charlton Ath | 9 | 0 | | |
| 1994–95 | *Bradford C* | 3 | 0 | **3** | **0** |
| 1995–96 | Charlton Ath | 9 | 0 | | |
| 1995–96 | *Ipswich T* | 1 | 0 | **2** | **0** |
| 1995–96 | *Plymouth Arg* | 6 | 0 | **6** | **0** |
| 1995–96 | *Colchester U* | 5 | 0 | **5** | **0** |
| 1996–97 | Charlton Ath | 21 | 0 | | |
| 1997–98 | Charlton Ath | 23 | 0 | | |
| 1998–99 | Charlton Ath | 10 | 0 | **72** | **0** |
| 1998–99 | Portsmouth | 13 | 0 | | |
| 1999–2000 | Portsmouth | 17 | 0 | | |
| 1999–2000 | *Wolverhampton W* | 0 | 0 | | |
| 2000–01 | Portsmouth | 2 | 0 | | |
| 2000–01 | *Torquay U* | 6 | 0 | **6** | **0** |
| 2001–02 | Portsmouth | 0 | 0 | **32** | **0** |
| 2001–02 | WBA | 0 | 0 | | |
| 2002–03 | Bournemouth | 0 | 0 | | |
| 2002–03 | Brighton & HA | 7 | 0 | **7** | **0** |
| 2002–03 | Bournemouth | 0 | 0 | | |
| 2003–04 | Rushden & D | 0 | 0 | | |
| 2003–04 | Southend U | 1 | 0 | **1** | **0** |
| 2003–04 | Walsall | 3 | 0 | **3** | **0** |

**RITCHIE, Paul# (D) 219 5**

H: 5 11 W: 12 00 b.Kirkcaldy 21-8-75

*Source:* Links U. *Honours:* Scotland Schools, Under-21, B, 7 full caps, 1 goal.

| | | | | | |
|---|---|---|---|---|---|
| 1992–93 | Hearts | 0 | 0 | | |
| 1993–94 | Hearts | 0 | 0 | | |
| 1994–95 | Hearts | 0 | 0 | | |
| 1995–96 | Hearts | 28 | 1 | | |
| 1996–97 | Hearts | 28 | 1 | | |
| 1997–98 | Hearts | 34 | 0 | | |
| 1998–99 | Hearts | 29 | 1 | | |
| 1999–2000 | Hearts | 14 | 1 | **133** | **4** |
| 1999–2000 | Bolton W | 14 | 0 | **14** | **0** |
| 2000–01 | Manchester C | 12 | 0 | | |
| 2001–02 | Manchester C | 8 | 0 | | |
| 2002–03 | Manchester C | 0 | 0 | **20** | **0** |
| 2002–03 | *Portsmouth* | 12 | 0 | **12** | **0** |
| 2002–03 | *Derby Co* | 7 | 0 | **7** | **0** |
| 2003–04 | Walsall | 33 | 1 | **33** | **1** |

**ROPER, Ian (D) 228 2**

H: 6 2 W: 14 00 b.Nuneaton 20-6-77

*Source:* Trainee.

| | | | | | |
|---|---|---|---|---|---|
| 1994–95 | Walsall | 0 | 0 | | |
| 1995–96 | Walsall | 5 | 0 | | |
| 1996–97 | Walsall | 11 | 0 | | |
| 1997–98 | Walsall | 21 | 0 | | |
| 1998–99 | Walsall | 32 | 1 | | |
| 1999–2000 | Walsall | 34 | 1 | | |
| 2000–01 | Walsall | 25 | 0 | | |
| 2001–02 | Walsall | 27 | 0 | | |
| 2002–03 | Walsall | 40 | 0 | | |
| 2003–04 | Walsall | 33 | 0 | **228** | **2** |

**SAMWAYS, Vinny‡ (M) 462 21**

H: 5 8 W: 11 00 b.Bethnal Green 27-10-68

*Source:* Apprentice. *Honours:* England Youth, Under-21.

| | | | | | |
|---|---|---|---|---|---|
| 1985–86 | Tottenham H | 0 | 0 | | |
| 1986–87 | Tottenham H | 2 | 0 | | |
| 1987–88 | Tottenham H | 26 | 0 | | |
| 1988–89 | Tottenham H | 19 | 3 | | |
| 1989–90 | Tottenham H | 23 | 3 | | |
| 1990–91 | Tottenham H | 23 | 1 | | |
| 1991–92 | Tottenham H | 27 | 1 | | |
| 1992–93 | Tottenham H | 34 | 0 | | |
| 1993–94 | Tottenham H | 39 | 3 | **193** | **11** |
| 1994–95 | Everton | 19 | 1 | | |
| 1995–96 | Everton | 4 | 1 | | |
| 1995–96 | *Wolverhampton W* | 3 | 0 | **3** | **0** |
| 1995–96 | *Birmingham C* | 12 | 0 | **12** | **0** |
| 1996–97 | Las Palmas | 20 | 0 | | |
| 1997–98 | Las Palmas | 32 | 2 | | |
| 1998–99 | Las Palmas | 35 | 1 | | |
| 1999–2000 | Las Palmas | 38 | 2 | | |
| 2000–01 | Las Palmas | 31 | 0 | | |
| 2001–02 | Las Palmas | 33 | 1 | **189** | **6** |
| 2002–03 | Sevilla | 0 | 0 | | |
| 1997–98 | Everton | 0 | 0 | | |
| 1998–99 | Everton | 0 | 0 | **23** | **2** |
| 2002–03 | Walsall | 13 | 0 | | |
| 2003–04 | Walsall | 29 | 2 | **42** | **2** |

**SMITH, Nick* (M) 0 0**

H: 5 10 W: 10 08 b.Bloxwich 5-10-82

*Source:* Scholar.

| | | | | | |
|---|---|---|---|---|---|
| 2002–03 | Walsall | 0 | 0 | | |
| 2003–04 | Walsall | 0 | 0 | | |

**STANLEY, Craig‡ (M) 0 0**

H: 5 8 W: 10 08 b.Bedworth 3-3-83

*Source:* Scholar.

| | | | | | |
|---|---|---|---|---|---|
| 2002–03 | Walsall | 0 | 0 | | |
| 2003–04 | Walsall | 0 | 0 | | |

**TAYLOR, Kris (M) 11 1**

H: 5 9 W: 11 05 b.Stafford 12-1-84

*Source:* Scholar. *Honours:* England Youth.

| | | | | | |
|---|---|---|---|---|---|
| 2000–01 | Manchester U | 0 | 0 | | |
| 2001–02 | Manchester U | 0 | 0 | | |
| 2002–03 | Manchester U | 0 | 0 | | |
| 2002–03 | Walsall | 0 | 0 | | |
| 2003–04 | Walsall | 11 | 1 | **11** | **1** |

**WALKER, James# (G) 403 0**

H: 5 11 W: 13 04 b.Sutton-in-Ashfield 9-7-73

*Source:* Trainee.

| | | | | | |
|---|---|---|---|---|---|
| 1991–92 | Notts Co | 0 | 0 | | |
| 1992–93 | Notts Co | 0 | 0 | | |
| 1993–94 | Walsall | 31 | 0 | | |
| 1994–95 | Walsall | 4 | 0 | | |
| 1995–96 | Walsall | 26 | 0 | | |
| 1996–97 | Walsall | 36 | 0 | | |
| 1997–98 | Walsall | 46 | 0 | | |
| 1998–99 | Walsall | 46 | 0 | | |
| 1999–2000 | Walsall | 43 | 0 | | |
| 2000–01 | Walsall | 44 | 0 | | |
| 2001–02 | Walsall | 43 | 0 | | |
| 2002–03 | Walsall | 41 | 0 | | |
| 2003–04 | Walsall | 43 | 0 | **403** | **0** |

**WRACK, Darren (M) 274 39**

H: 5 9 W: 12 03 b.Cleethorpes 5-5-76

*Source:* Trainee.

| | | | | | |
|---|---|---|---|---|---|
| 1994–95 | Derby Co | 16 | 1 | | |
| 1995–96 | Derby Co | 10 | 0 | **26** | **1** |
| 1996–97 | Grimsby T | 12 | 1 | | |
| 1996–97 | *Shrewsbury T* | 4 | 0 | **4** | **0** |
| 1997–98 | Grimsby T | 1 | 0 | **13** | **1** |
| 1998–99 | Walsall | 46 | 13 | | |
| 1999–2000 | Walsall | 44 | 4 | | |
| 2000–01 | Walsall | 28 | 4 | | |
| 2001–02 | Walsall | 43 | 4 | | |
| 2002–03 | Walsall | 43 | 6 | | |
| 2003–04 | Walsall | 27 | 6 | **231** | **37** |

**WRIGHT, Mark (M) 20 2**

H: 5 11 W: 11 00 b.Wolverhampton 24-2-82

*Source:* Scholar.

| | | | | | |
|---|---|---|---|---|---|
| 2000–01 | Walsall | 4 | 0 | | |
| 2001–02 | Walsall | 0 | 0 | | |
| 2002–03 | Walsall | 5 | 0 | | |
| 2003–04 | Walsall | 11 | 2 | **20** | **2** |

**Scholars**

Atieno, Taiwo L; Bennett, Julian; Bowen, Eric G; Branch, Mark L; Churchill, Lewis A; Dann, Scott; Deakin, Graham L; Harkness, Jonathan; Harris, Andrew; Leaver, Shaun E W; Lloyd, Arron S D; Perry, Kyle B; Platt, Sean D; Taylor, Daryl S; Wheeler, B J; Willetts, Ryan J; Williams, Leroy D

**Non Contract**

Bradbury, Lee Michael; Burley, Craig W; Caines, Gavin L; Coleman, Dean S; Jamieson, Nathan; Lopez Soler, Mario; Petterson, Andrew K

## WATFORD (83)

**ARDLEY, Neal* (M) 326 21**

H: 5 10 W: 12 12 b.Epsom 1-9-72

*Source:* Trainee. *Honours:* England Under-21.

| | | | | | |
|---|---|---|---|---|---|
| 1990–91 | Wimbledon | 1 | 0 | | |
| 1991–92 | Wimbledon | 8 | 0 | | |
| 1992–93 | Wimbledon | 26 | 4 | | |
| 1993–94 | Wimbledon | 16 | 1 | | |
| 1994–95 | Wimbledon | 14 | 1 | | |
| 1995–96 | Wimbledon | 6 | 0 | | |
| 1996–97 | Wimbledon | 34 | 2 | | |
| 1997–98 | Wimbledon | 34 | 2 | | |
| 1998–99 | Wimbledon | 23 | 0 | | |
| 1999–2000 | Wimbledon | 17 | 2 | | |
| 2000–01 | Wimbledon | 37 | 3 | | |
| 2001–02 | Wimbledon | 29 | 3 | **245** | **18** |
| 2002–03 | Watford | 43 | 2 | | |
| 2003–04 | Watford | 38 | 1 | **81** | **3** |

**BLIZZARD, Dominic (M) 2 1**

H: 6 2 W: 13 05 b.High Wycombe 2-9-83

*Source:* Scholar.

| | | | | | |
|---|---|---|---|---|---|
| 2001–02 | Watford | 0 | 0 | | |
| 2002–03 | Watford | 0 | 0 | | |
| 2003–04 | Watford | 2 | 1 | **2** | **1** |

**BOUAZZA, Hameur§ (F) 9 1**

H: 5 10 W: 12 00 b.Evry 22-2-85

*Source:* Scholar.

| | | | | | |
|---|---|---|---|---|---|
| 2003–04 | Watford | 9 | 1 | **9** | **1** |

**BROWN, Wayne (D)** **117 6**
H: 6 1 W: 12 10 b.Barking 20-8-77
*Source:* Trainee.

| | | | | | |
|---|---|---|---|---|---|
| 1995–96 | Ipswich T | 0 | 0 | | |
| 1996–97 | Ipswich T | 0 | 0 | | |
| 1997–98 | Ipswich T | 1 | 0 | | |
| 1997–98 | *Colchester U* | 2 | 0 | | |
| 1998–99 | Ipswich T | 1 | 0 | | |
| 1999–2000 | Ipswich T | 25 | 0 | | |
| 2000–01 | Ipswich T | 4 | 0 | | |
| 2000–01 | *QPR* | 2 | 0 | **2** | **0** |
| 2001–02 | Ipswich T | 0 | 0 | | |
| 2001–02 | *Wimbledon* | 17 | 1 | **17** | **1** |
| 2001–02 | *Watford* | 11 | 3 | | |
| 2002–03 | Ipswich T | 9 | 0 | **40** | **0** |
| 2002–03 | Watford | 13 | 1 | | |
| 2003–04 | Watford | 12 | 0 | **36** | **4** |
| 2003–04 | *Gillingham* | 4 | 1 | **4** | **1** |
| 2003–04 | *Colchester U* | 16 | 0 | **18** | **0** |

**CHAMBERLAIN, Alec* (G)** **666 0**
H: 6 2 W: 14 00 b.March 20-6-64
*Source:* Ramsey T.

| | | | | | |
|---|---|---|---|---|---|
| 1981–82 | Ipswich T | 0 | 0 | | |
| 1982–83 | Colchester U | 0 | 0 | | |
| 1983–84 | Colchester U | 46 | 0 | | |
| 1984–85 | Colchester U | 46 | 0 | | |
| 1985–86 | Colchester U | 46 | 0 | | |
| 1986–87 | Colchester U | 46 | 0 | **184** | **0** |
| 1987–88 | Everton | 0 | 0 | | |
| 1987–88 | *Tranmere R* | 15 | 0 | **15** | **0** |
| 1988–89 | Luton T | 6 | 0 | | |
| 1989–90 | Luton T | 38 | 0 | | |
| 1990–91 | Luton T | 38 | 0 | | |
| 1991–92 | Luton T | 24 | 0 | | |
| 1992–93 | Luton T | 32 | 0 | **138** | **0** |
| 1992–93 | *Chelsea* | 0 | 0 | | |
| 1993–94 | Sunderland | 43 | 0 | | |
| 1994–95 | Sunderland | 18 | 0 | | |
| 1994–95 | *Liverpool* | 0 | 0 | | |
| 1995–96 | Sunderland | 29 | 0 | **90** | **0** |
| 1996–97 | Watford | 4 | 0 | | |
| 1997–98 | Watford | 46 | 0 | | |
| 1998–99 | Watford | 46 | 0 | | |
| 1999–2000 | Watford | 27 | 0 | | |
| 2000–01 | Watford | 21 | 0 | | |
| 2001–02 | Watford | 32 | 0 | | |
| 2002–03 | Watford | 42 | 0 | | |
| 2003–04 | Watford | 21 | 0 | **239** | **0** |

**COOK, Lee (M)** **79 9**
H: 5 8 W: 11 10 b.Hammersmith 3-8-82
*Source:* Aylesbury U.

| | | | | | |
|---|---|---|---|---|---|
| 1999–2000 | Watford | 0 | 0 | | |
| 2000–01 | Watford | 4 | 0 | | |
| 2001–02 | Watford | 10 | 0 | | |
| 2002–03 | Watford | 4 | 0 | | |
| 2002–03 | *York C* | 7 | 1 | **7** | **1** |
| 2002–03 | *QPR* | 13 | 1 | **13** | **1** |
| 2003–04 | Watford | 41 | 7 | **59** | **7** |

**COX, Neil (D)** **425 34**
H: 5 11 W: 13 08 b.Scunthorpe 8-10-71
*Source:* Trainee. *Honours:* England Under-21.

| | | | | | |
|---|---|---|---|---|---|
| 1989–90 | Scunthorpe U | 0 | 0 | | |
| 1990–91 | Scunthorpe U | 17 | 1 | **17** | **1** |
| 1990–91 | Aston Villa | 0 | 0 | | |
| 1991–92 | Aston Villa | 7 | 0 | | |
| 1992–93 | Aston Villa | 15 | 1 | | |
| 1993–94 | Aston Villa | 20 | 2 | **42** | **3** |
| 1994–95 | Middlesbrough | 40 | 1 | | |
| 1995–96 | Middlesbrough | 35 | 2 | | |
| 1996–97 | Middlesbrough | 31 | 0 | **106** | **3** |
| 1997–98 | Bolton W | 21 | 1 | | |
| 1998–99 | Bolton W | 44 | 4 | | |
| 1999–2000 | Bolton W | 15 | 2 | **80** | **7** |
| 1999–2000 | Watford | 21 | 0 | | |
| 2000–01 | Watford | 44 | 5 | | |
| 2001–02 | Watford | 40 | 2 | | |
| 2002–03 | Watford | 40 | 9 | | |
| 2003–04 | Watford | 35 | 4 | **180** | **20** |

**DEVLIN, Paul (M)** **455 84**
H: 5 7 W: 11 13 b.Birmingham 14-4-72
*Source:* Stafford R. *Honours:* Scotland 10 full caps.

| | | | | | |
|---|---|---|---|---|---|
| 1991–92 | Notts Co | 2 | 0 | | |
| 1992–93 | Notts Co | 32 | 3 | | |
| 1993–94 | Notts Co | 41 | 7 | | |
| 1994–95 | Notts Co | 40 | 9 | | |
| 1995–96 | Notts Co | 26 | 6 | | |
| 1995–96 | Birmingham C | 16 | 7 | | |
| 1996–97 | Birmingham C | 38 | 16 | | |
| 1997–98 | Birmingham C | 22 | 5 | | |
| 1997–98 | Sheffield U | 10 | 1 | | |
| 1998–99 | Sheffield U | 33 | 5 | | |
| 1998–99 | *Notts Co* | 5 | 0 | **146** | **25** |
| 1999–2000 | Sheffield U | 44 | 11 | | |
| 2000–01 | Sheffield U | 41 | 5 | | |
| 2001–02 | Sheffield U | 19 | 2 | **147** | **24** |
| 2001–02 | Birmingham C | 13 | 1 | | |
| 2002–03 | Birmingham C | 32 | 3 | | |
| 2003–04 | Birmingham C | 2 | 0 | **123** | **32** |
| 2003–04 | Watford | 39 | 3 | **39** | **3** |

**DOYLEY, Lloyd (D)** **51 0**
H: 5 10 W: 12 05 b.Whitechapel 1-12-82
*Source:* Scholar.

| | | | | | |
|---|---|---|---|---|---|
| 2000–01 | Watford | 0 | 0 | | |
| 2001–02 | Watford | 20 | 0 | | |
| 2002–03 | Watford | 22 | 0 | | |
| 2003–04 | Watford | 9 | 0 | **51** | **0** |

**DYCHE, Sean* (D)** **380 12**
H: 6 1 W: 13 12 b.Kettering 28-6-71
*Source:* Trainee.

| | | | | | |
|---|---|---|---|---|---|
| 1988–89 | Nottingham F | 0 | 0 | | |
| 1989–90 | Nottingham F | 0 | 0 | | |
| 1989–90 | Chesterfield | 22 | 2 | | |
| 1990–91 | Chesterfield | 28 | 2 | | |
| 1991–92 | Chesterfield | 42 | 3 | | |
| 1992–93 | Chesterfield | 20 | 1 | | |
| 1993–94 | Chesterfield | 20 | 0 | | |
| 1994–95 | Chesterfield | 22 | 0 | | |
| 1995–96 | Chesterfield | 41 | 0 | | |
| 1996–97 | Chesterfield | 36 | 0 | **231** | **8** |
| 1997–98 | Bristol C | 11 | 0 | | |
| 1998–99 | Bristol C | 6 | 0 | **17** | **0** |
| 1998–99 | *Luton T* | 14 | 1 | **14** | **1** |
| 1999–2000 | Millwall | 1 | 0 | | |
| 2000–01 | Millwall | 33 | 0 | | |
| 2001–02 | Millwall | 35 | 3 | **69** | **3** |
| 2002–03 | Watford | 24 | 0 | | |
| 2003–04 | Watford | 25 | 0 | **49** | **0** |

**DYER, Bruce (F)** **380 105**
H: 5 11 W: 12 11 b.Ilford 13-4-75
*Source:* Trainee. *Honours:* England Under-21.

| | | | | | |
|---|---|---|---|---|---|
| 1992–93 | Watford | 2 | 0 | | |
| 1993–94 | Watford | 29 | 6 | | |
| 1993–94 | Crystal Palace | 11 | 0 | | |
| 1994–95 | Crystal Palace | 16 | 1 | | |
| 1995–96 | Crystal Palace | 35 | 13 | | |
| 1996–97 | Crystal Palace | 43 | 17 | | |
| 1997–98 | Crystal Palace | 24 | 4 | | |
| 1998–99 | Crystal Palace | 6 | 2 | **135** | **37** |
| 1998–99 | Barnsley | 28 | 7 | | |
| 1999–2000 | Barnsley | 32 | 6 | | |
| 2000–01 | Barnsley | 38 | 15 | | |
| 2001–02 | Barnsley | 44 | 14 | | |
| 2002–03 | Barnsley | 40 | 17 | **182** | **59** |
| 2003–04 | Watford | 32 | 3 | **63** | **9** |

**FISKEN, Gary (M)** **22 1**
H: 5 11 W: 12 05 b.Watford 27-10-81
*Source:* Scholarship.

| | | | | | |
|---|---|---|---|---|---|
| 1999–2000 | Watford | 0 | 0 | | |
| 2000–01 | Watford | 0 | 0 | | |
| 2001–02 | Watford | 17 | 1 | | |
| 2002–03 | Watford | 4 | 0 | | |
| 2003–04 | Watford | 1 | 0 | **22** | **1** |

**FITZGERALD, Scott (F)** **48 11**
H: 5 11 W: 12 00 b.Hillingdon 18-11-79
*Source:* Northwood.

| | | | | | |
|---|---|---|---|---|---|
| 2002–03 | Watford | 4 | 1 | | |
| 2003–04 | Watford | 44 | 10 | **48** | **11** |

**GAYLE, Marcus (D)** **495 64**
H: 6 3 W: 14 03 b.Hammersmith 28-9-70
*Source:* Trainee. *Honours:* England Youth. Jamaica 14 full caps, 3 goals.

| | | | | | |
|---|---|---|---|---|---|
| 1988–89 | Brentford | 3 | 0 | | |
| 1989–90 | Brentford | 9 | 0 | | |
| 1990–91 | Brentford | 33 | 6 | | |
| 1991–92 | Brentford | 38 | 6 | | |
| 1992–93 | Brentford | 38 | 4 | | |
| 1993–94 | Brentford | 35 | 6 | **156** | **22** |
| 1993–94 | Wimbledon | 10 | 0 | | |
| 1994–95 | Wimbledon | 23 | 2 | | |
| 1995–96 | Wimbledon | 34 | 5 | | |
| 1996–97 | Wimbledon | 36 | 8 | | |
| 1997–98 | Wimbledon | 30 | 2 | | |
| 1998–99 | Wimbledon | 35 | 10 | | |
| 1999–2000 | Wimbledon | 36 | 7 | | |
| 2000–01 | Wimbledon | 32 | 3 | **236** | **37** |
| 2000–01 | Rangers | 4 | 0 | **4** | **0** |
| 2001–02 | Watford | 36 | 4 | | |
| 2002–03 | Watford | 31 | 0 | | |
| 2003–04 | Watford | 32 | 1 | **99** | **5** |

**GODFREY, Elliott* (F)** **1 0**
H: 5 8 W: 11 03 b.Toronto 22-2-83
*Source:* Scholar.

| | | | | | |
|---|---|---|---|---|---|
| 2000–01 | Watford | 0 | 0 | | |
| 2001–02 | Watford | 0 | 0 | | |
| 2002–03 | Watford | 1 | 0 | | |
| 2003–04 | Watford | 0 | 0 | **1** | **0** |

**GRAHAM, Steve* (G)** **0 0**
H: 6 2 W: 13 07 b.Hitchin 21-8-85
*Source:* Hitchin T.

| | | | | | |
|---|---|---|---|---|---|
| 2003–04 | Watford | 0 | 0 | | |

**HAND, Jamie (M)** **55 0**
H: 5 10 W: 12 13 b.Uxbridge 7-2-84
*Source:* Scholar. *Honours:* England Youth.

| | | | | | |
|---|---|---|---|---|---|
| 2001–02 | Watford | 10 | 0 | | |
| 2002–03 | Watford | 23 | 0 | | |
| 2003–04 | Watford | 22 | 0 | **55** | **0** |

**HELGUSON, Heidar (F)** **179 57**
H: 5 10 W: 12 09 b.Akureyri 22-8-77
*Source:* Throttur. *Honours:* Iceland 25 full caps, 2 goals.

| | | | | | |
|---|---|---|---|---|---|
| 1998 | Lillestrom | 19 | 2 | | |
| 1999 | Lillestrom | 25 | 16 | **44** | **18** |
| 1999–2000 | Watford | 16 | 6 | | |
| 2000–01 | Watford | 33 | 8 | | |
| 2001–02 | Watford | 34 | 6 | | |
| 2002–03 | Watford | 30 | 11 | | |
| 2003–04 | Watford | 22 | 8 | **135** | **39** |

**HERD, Ben (D)** **0 0**
H: 5 9 W: 10 12 b.Welwyn 21-6-85
*Source:* Scholar.

| | | | | | |
|---|---|---|---|---|---|
| 2002–03 | Watford | 0 | 0 | | |
| 2003–04 | Watford | 0 | 0 | | |

**HYDE, Micah* (M)** **360 37**
H: 5 10 W: 12 09 b.Newham 10-11-74
*Source:* Trainee. *Honours:* Jamaica 12 full caps.

| | | | | | |
|---|---|---|---|---|---|
| 1993–94 | Cambridge U | 18 | 2 | | |
| 1994–95 | Cambridge U | 27 | 0 | | |
| 1995–96 | Cambridge U | 24 | 4 | | |
| 1996–97 | Cambridge U | 38 | 7 | **107** | **13** |
| 1997–98 | Watford | 40 | 4 | | |
| 1998–99 | Watford | 44 | 2 | | |
| 1999–2000 | Watford | 34 | 3 | | |
| 2000–01 | Watford | 26 | 6 | | |
| 2001–02 | Watford | 39 | 4 | | |
| 2002–03 | Watford | 37 | 4 | | |
| 2003–04 | Watford | 33 | 1 | **253** | **24** |

**IFIL, Jerel (D)** **38 0**
H: 6 0 W: 13 01 b.London 27-6-82
*Source:* Academy.

| | | | | | |
|---|---|---|---|---|---|
| 1999–2000 | Watford | 0 | 0 | | |
| 2000–01 | Watford | 0 | 0 | | |
| 2001–02 | Watford | 0 | 0 | | |
| 2001–02 | *Huddersfield T* | 2 | 0 | **2** | **0** |
| 2002–03 | Watford | 1 | 0 | | |
| 2002–03 | *Swindon T* | 9 | 0 | | |
| 2003–04 | Watford | 10 | 0 | **11** | **0** |
| 2003–04 | *Swindon T* | 16 | 0 | **25** | **0** |

**KOO-BOOTHE, Nathan* (D)** **0 0**
H: 6 4 W: 14 03 b.London 18-7-84

| | | | | | |
|---|---|---|---|---|---|
| 2002–03 | Watford | 0 | 0 | | |
| 2003–04 | Watford | 0 | 0 | | |

**LEE, Richard (G)** **4 0**
H: 6 0 W: 13 03 b.Oxford 5-10-82
*Source:* Scholar. *Honours:* England Under-20.

| | | | | | |
|---|---|---|---|---|---|
| 2000–01 | Watford | 0 | 0 | | |
| 2001–02 | Watford | 0 | 0 | | |
| 2002–03 | Watford | 4 | 0 | | |
| 2003–04 | Watford | 0 | 0 | **4** | **0** |

**MAHON, Gavin (M)** **207 11**
H: 6 0 W: 13 00 b.Birmingham 2-1-77
*Source:* Trainee.

| | | | | | |
|---|---|---|---|---|---|
| 1995–96 | Wolverhampton W | 0 | 0 | | |

| | | | | | |
|---|---|---|---|---|---|
| 1996–97 | Hereford U | 11 | 1 | | |
| 1997–98 | Hereford U | 0 | 0 | | |
| 1998–99 | Hereford U | 0 | 0 | **11** | **1** |
| 1998–99 | Brentford | 29 | 4 | | |
| 1999–2000 | Brentford | 37 | 3 | | |
| 2000–01 | Brentford | 40 | 1 | | |
| 2001–02 | Brentford | 35 | 0 | **141** | **8** |
| 2001–02 | Watford | 6 | 0 | | |
| 2002–03 | Watford | 17 | 0 | | |
| 2003–04 | Watford | 32 | 2 | **55** | **2** |

**MAYO, Paul (D)** **118 6**
H: 5 11 W: 11 13 b.Lincoln 13-10-81
*Source:* Scholarship.

| | | | | | |
|---|---|---|---|---|---|
| 1999–2000 | Lincoln C | 19 | 0 | | |
| 2000–01 | Lincoln C | 27 | 0 | | |
| 2001–02 | Lincoln C | 14 | 0 | | |
| 2002–03 | Lincoln C | 15 | 0 | | |
| 2003–04 | Lincoln C | 31 | 6 | **106** | **6** |
| 2003–04 | Watford | 12 | 0 | **12** | **0** |

**McNAMEE, Anthony (M)** **32 1**
H: 5 6 W: 9 11 b.Lambeth 13-7-84
*Source:* Scholar. *Honours:* England Youth, Under-20.

| | | | | | |
|---|---|---|---|---|---|
| 2001–02 | Watford | 7 | 1 | | |
| 2002–03 | Watford | 23 | 0 | | |
| 2003–04 | Watford | 2 | 0 | **32** | **1** |

**NORVILLE, Jason (F)** **14 1**
H: 6 0 W: 11 07 b.Trinidad & Tobago 9-9-83
*Source:* Scholar.

| | | | | | |
|---|---|---|---|---|---|
| 2001–02 | Watford | 2 | 0 | | |
| 2002–03 | Watford | 12 | 1 | | |
| 2003–04 | Watford | 0 | 0 | **14** | **1** |

**PATTERSON, Simon* (F)** **4 2**
H: 6 5 W: 14 05 b.Northwick Park 4-9-82

| | | | | | |
|---|---|---|---|---|---|
| 2000–01 | Watford | 0 | 0 | | |
| 2001–02 | Watford | 0 | 0 | | |
| 2002–03 | Watford | 0 | 0 | | |
| 2003–04 | Watford | 0 | 0 | | |
| 2003–04 | *Wycombe W* | 4 | 2 | **4** | **2** |

**SMITH, Jack (D)** **18 2**
H: 5 10 W: 11 05 b.Hemel Hempstead 14-11-83
*Source:* Scholar.

| | | | | | |
|---|---|---|---|---|---|
| 2001–02 | Watford | 0 | 0 | | |
| 2002–03 | Watford | 1 | 0 | | |
| 2003–04 | Watford | 17 | 2 | **18** | **2** |

**SWONNELL, Sam* (M)** **2 0**
H: 5 9 W: 11 09 b.Brentwood 13-9-82
*Source:* Scholar.

| | | | | | |
|---|---|---|---|---|---|
| 2000–01 | Watford | 0 | 0 | | |
| 2001–02 | Watford | 0 | 0 | | |
| 2002–03 | Watford | 2 | 0 | | |
| 2003–04 | Watford | 0 | 0 | **2** | **0** |

**VERNAZZA, Paulo* (M)** **110 3**
H: 5 11 W: 12 03 b.Islington 1-11-79
*Source:* Trainee. *Honours:* England Youth, Under-21.

| | | | | | |
|---|---|---|---|---|---|
| 1997–98 | Arsenal | 1 | 0 | | |
| 1998–99 | Arsenal | 0 | 0 | | |
| 1998–99 | *Ipswich T* | 2 | 0 | **2** | **0** |
| 1999–2000 | Arsenal | 2 | 0 | | |
| 1999–2000 | *Portsmouth* | 7 | 0 | **7** | **0** |
| 2000–01 | Arsenal | 2 | 1 | **5** | **1** |
| 2000–01 | Watford | 23 | 2 | | |
| 2001–02 | Watford | 21 | 0 | | |
| 2002–03 | Watford | 23 | 0 | | |
| 2003–04 | Watford | 29 | 0 | **96** | **2** |

**WEBBER, Danny (F)** **48 9**
H: 5 8 W: 11 00 b.Manchester 28-12-81
*Source:* Trainee. *Honours:* England Youth, Under-20.

| | | | | | |
|---|---|---|---|---|---|
| 1998–99 | Manchester U | 0 | 0 | | |
| 1999–2000 | Manchester U | 0 | 0 | | |
| 2000–01 | Manchester U | 0 | 0 | | |
| 2001–02 | Manchester U | 0 | 0 | | |
| 2001–02 | *Port Vale* | 4 | 0 | **4** | **0** |
| 2001–02 | *Watford* | 5 | 2 | | |
| 2002–03 | Manchester U | 0 | 0 | | |
| 2002–03 | *Watford* | 12 | 2 | | |
| 2003–04 | Watford | 27 | 5 | **44** | **9** |

**YOUNG, Ashley (M)** **5 3**
H: 5 9 W: 9 13 b.Stevenage 9-7-85

| | | | | | |
|---|---|---|---|---|---|
| 2002–03 | Watford | 0 | 0 | | |
| 2003–04 | Watford | 5 | 3 | **5** | **3** |

**Scholars**
Ainon, Michael; Bouazza, Hameur; Catchpole, Lee A; Chapman, Andrew P; Chase, Christopher; Collins, James E; Cowen, Joseph W; Coyne, Paul; Dean, Peter A E; Diafutua, Gauthier; Diagouraga, Toumani; Gilligan, Ryan J; Grant, Joel V; Hammond, Benjamin I; Harrington, Leigh R; Horlock, Joseph; Kirk, Reece E; Mariappa, Adrian J; Martin, Robert; Mawer, Cameron

**Non Contract**
Hitchcock, Kevin

## WBA (84)

**ADAMS, Ross‡ (D)** **0 0**
H: 5 11 W: 12 04 b.Birmingham 11-3-83
*Source:* Scholar.

| | | | | | |
|---|---|---|---|---|---|
| 2001–02 | WBA | 0 | 0 | | |
| 2002–03 | WBA | 0 | 0 | | |
| 2003–04 | WBA | 0 | 0 | | |

**APPLETON, Michael* (M)** **162 15**
H: 5 8 W: 11 00 b.Salford 4-12-75
*Source:* Trainee.

| | | | | | |
|---|---|---|---|---|---|
| 1994–95 | Manchester U | 0 | 0 | | |
| 1995–96 | Manchester U | 0 | 0 | | |
| 1995–96 | *Lincoln C* | 4 | 0 | **4** | **0** |
| 1996–97 | Manchester U | 0 | 0 | | |
| 1996–97 | *Grimsby T* | 10 | 3 | **10** | **3** |
| 1997–98 | Preston NE | 38 | 2 | | |
| 1998–99 | Preston NE | 25 | 2 | | |
| 1999–2000 | Preston NE | 26 | 3 | | |
| 2000–01 | Preston NE | 26 | 5 | **115** | **12** |
| 2000–01 | WBA | 15 | 0 | | |
| 2001–02 | WBA | 18 | 0 | | |
| 2002–03 | WBA | 0 | 0 | | |
| 2003–04 | WBA | 0 | 0 | **33** | **0** |

**BERTHE, Sekou (D)** **23 0**
H: 6 3 W: 13 02 b.Bamoko 7-10-77
*Source:* Monaco. *Honours:* Mali full caps.

| | | | | | |
|---|---|---|---|---|---|
| 1999–2000 | Troyes | 10 | 0 | | |
| 2000–01 | Troyes | 6 | 0 | | |
| 2001–02 | Troyes | 4 | 0 | | |
| 2002–03 | Troyes | 0 | 0 | **20** | **0** |
| 2003–04 | WBA | 3 | 0 | **3** | **0** |

**BROWN, Simon (M)** **8 2**
H: 5 10 W: 11 00 b.West Bromwich 18-9-83
*Source:* Scholar.

| | | | | | |
|---|---|---|---|---|---|
| 2003–04 | WBA | 0 | 0 | | |
| 2003–04 | *Kidderminster H* | 8 | 2 | **8** | **2** |

**CHAMBERS, Adam (M)** **67 1**
H: 5 10 W: 11 12 b.Sandwell 20-11-80
*Source:* Trainee. *Honours:* England Youth.

| | | | | | |
|---|---|---|---|---|---|
| 1998–99 | WBA | 0 | 0 | | |
| 1999–2000 | WBA | 0 | 0 | | |
| 2000–01 | WBA | 11 | 1 | | |
| 2001–02 | WBA | 32 | 0 | | |
| 2002–03 | WBA | 13 | 0 | | |
| 2003–04 | WBA | 0 | 0 | **56** | **1** |
| 2003–04 | *Sheffield W* | 11 | 0 | **11** | **0** |

**CHAMBERS, James (D)** **73 0**
H: 5 10 W: 11 10 b.Sandwell 20-11-80
*Source:* Trainee. *Honours:* England Youth.

| | | | | | |
|---|---|---|---|---|---|
| 1998–99 | WBA | 0 | 0 | | |
| 1999–2000 | WBA | 12 | 0 | | |
| 2000–01 | WBA | 31 | 0 | | |
| 2001–02 | WBA | 5 | 0 | | |
| 2002–03 | WBA | 8 | 0 | | |
| 2003–04 | WBA | 17 | 0 | **73** | **0** |

**CLEMENT, Neil (D)** **193 17**
H: 6 0 W: 12 03 b.Reading 3-10-78
*Source:* Trainee. *Honours:* England Schools, Youth.

| | | | | | |
|---|---|---|---|---|---|
| 1995–96 | Chelsea | 0 | 0 | | |
| 1996–97 | Chelsea | 1 | 0 | | |
| 1997–98 | Chelsea | 0 | 0 | | |
| 1998–99 | Chelsea | 0 | 0 | | |
| 1998–99 | *Reading* | 11 | 1 | **11** | **1** |
| 1998–99 | *Preston NE* | 4 | 0 | **4** | **0** |
| 1999–2000 | Chelsea | 0 | 0 | **1** | **0** |
| 1999–2000 | *Brentford* | 8 | 0 | **8** | **0** |
| 1999–2000 | *WBA* | 8 | 0 | | |
| 2000–01 | WBA | 45 | 5 | | |
| 2001–02 | WBA | 45 | 6 | | |
| 2002–03 | WBA | 36 | 3 | | |
| 2003–04 | WBA | 35 | 2 | **169** | **16** |

**CRANE, Daniel* (G)** **0 0**
b.Birmingham 27-5-84
*Source:* Scholar.

| | | | | | |
|---|---|---|---|---|---|
| 2003–04 | WBA | 0 | 0 | | |

**DOBIE, Scott (F)** **247 44**
H: 6 1 W: 12 05 b.Workington 10-10-78
*Source:* Trainee. *Honours:* Scotland 6 full caps, 1 goal.

| | | | | | |
|---|---|---|---|---|---|
| 1996–97 | Carlisle U | 2 | 1 | | |
| 1997–98 | Carlisle U | 23 | 0 | | |
| 1998–99 | Carlisle U | 33 | 6 | | |
| 1998–99 | *Clydebank* | 6 | 0 | **6** | **0** |
| 1999–2000 | Carlisle U | 34 | 7 | | |
| 2000–01 | Carlisle U | 44 | 10 | **136** | **24** |
| 2001–02 | WBA | 43 | 10 | | |
| 2002–03 | WBA | 31 | 5 | | |
| 2003–04 | WBA | 31 | 5 | **105** | **20** |

**DYER, Lloyd (F)** **24 3**
H: 5 10 W: 11 04 b.Birmingham 13-9-82

| | | | | | |
|---|---|---|---|---|---|
| 2001–02 | WBA | 0 | 0 | | |
| 2002–03 | WBA | 0 | 0 | | |
| 2003–04 | WBA | 17 | 2 | **17** | **2** |
| 2003–04 | *Kidderminster H* | 7 | 1 | **7** | **1** |

**FACEY, Delroy* (F)** **114 22**
H: 6 0 W: 13 00 b.Huddersfield 22-4-80
*Source:* Trainee.

| | | | | | |
|---|---|---|---|---|---|
| 1996–97 | Huddersfield T | 3 | 0 | | |
| 1997–98 | Huddersfield T | 3 | 0 | | |
| 1998–99 | Huddersfield T | 20 | 3 | | |
| 1999–2000 | Huddersfield T | 2 | 0 | | |
| 2000–01 | Huddersfield T | 34 | 10 | | |
| 2001–02 | Huddersfield T | 13 | 2 | | |
| 2002–03 | Huddersfield T | 0 | 0 | **75** | **15** |
| 2002–03 | *Bradford C* | 6 | 1 | **6** | **1** |
| 2002–03 | Bolton W | 9 | 1 | | |
| 2003–04 | Bolton W | 1 | 0 | **10** | **1** |
| 2003–04 | *Burnley* | 14 | 5 | **14** | **5** |
| 2003–04 | WBA | 9 | 0 | **9** | **0** |

**GAARDSOE, Thomas (D)** **148 14**
H: 6 2 W: 12 08 b.Denmark 23-11-79
*Honours:* Denmark 1 full cap.

| | | | | | |
|---|---|---|---|---|---|
| 1996–97 | Aalborg | 1 | 0 | | |
| 1997–98 | Aalborg | 6 | 1 | | |
| 1998–99 | Aalborg | 17 | 2 | | |
| 1999–2000 | Aalborg | 18 | 2 | | |
| 2000–01 | Aalborg | 20 | 0 | **62** | **5** |
| 2001–02 | Ipswich T | 4 | 1 | | |
| 2002–03 | Ipswich T | 37 | 4 | **41** | **5** |
| 2003–04 | WBA | 45 | 4 | **45** | **4** |

**GILCHRIST, Phil* (D)** **398 11**
H: 5 11 W: 13 04 b.Stockton 25-8-73
*Source:* Trainee.

| | | | | | |
|---|---|---|---|---|---|
| 1990–91 | Nottingham F | 0 | 0 | | |
| 1991–92 | Middlesbrough | 0 | 0 | | |
| 1992–93 | Hartlepool U | 24 | 0 | | |
| 1993–94 | Hartlepool U | 35 | 0 | | |
| 1994–95 | Hartlepool U | 23 | 0 | **82** | **0** |
| 1994–95 | Oxford U | 18 | 1 | | |
| 1995–96 | Oxford U | 42 | 3 | | |
| 1996–97 | Oxford U | 38 | 2 | | |
| 1997–98 | Oxford U | 39 | 2 | | |
| 1998–99 | Oxford U | 39 | 2 | | |
| 1999–2000 | Oxford U | 1 | 0 | **177** | **10** |
| 1999–2000 | Leicester C | 27 | 1 | | |
| 2000–01 | Leicester C | 12 | 0 | **39** | **1** |
| 2000–01 | WBA | 8 | 0 | | |
| 2001–02 | WBA | 43 | 0 | | |
| 2002–03 | WBA | 22 | 0 | | |
| 2003–04 | WBA | 17 | 0 | **90** | **0** |
| 2003–04 | *Rotherham U* | 10 | 0 | **10** | **0** |

**GREGAN, Sean (M)** **427 18**
H: 6 2 W: 14 08 b.Guisborough 29-3-74
*Source:* Trainee.

| | | | | | |
|---|---|---|---|---|---|
| 1991–92 | Darlington | 17 | 0 | | |
| 1992–93 | Darlington | 17 | 1 | | |
| 1993–94 | Darlington | 23 | 1 | | |
| 1994–95 | Darlington | 25 | 2 | | |
| 1995–96 | Darlington | 38 | 0 | | |
| 1996–97 | Darlington | 16 | 0 | **136** | **4** |
| 1996–97 | Preston NE | 21 | 1 | | |
| 1997–98 | Preston NE | 35 | 2 | | |
| 1998–99 | Preston NE | 41 | 3 | | |
| 1999–2000 | Preston NE | 33 | 3 | | |

| | | | | | |
|---|---|---|---|---|---|
| 2000–01 | Preston NE | 41 | 2 | | |
| 2001–02 | Preston NE | 41 | 1 | **212** | **12** |
| 2002–03 | WBA | 36 | 1 | | |
| 2003–04 | WBA | 43 | 1 | **79** | **2** |

**HAAS, Bernt (D)** **223** **7**
H: 6 1 W: 12 08 b.Vienna 8-4-78
*Honours:* Switzerland 31 full caps, 3 goals.

| | | | | | |
|---|---|---|---|---|---|
| 1994–95 | Grasshoppers | 2 | 0 | | |
| 1995–96 | Grasshoppers | 20 | 0 | | |
| 1996–97 | Grasshoppers | 29 | 1 | | |
| 1997–98 | Grasshoppers | 27 | 2 | | |
| 1998–99 | Grasshoppers | 28 | 1 | | |
| 1999–2000 | Grasshoppers | 29 | 1 | | |
| 2000–01 | Grasshoppers | 25 | 1 | **160** | **6** |
| 2001–02 | Sunderland | 27 | 0 | | |
| 2002–03 | Sunderland | 0 | 0 | **27** | **0** |
| 2003–04 | WBA | 36 | 1 | **36** | **1** |

**HORSFIELD, Geoff (F)** **225** **67**
H: 5 10 W: 11 02 b.Barnsley 1-11-73

| | | | | | |
|---|---|---|---|---|---|
| 1992–93 | Scarborough | 6 | 1 | | |
| 1993–94 | Scarborough | 6 | 0 | **12** | **1** |
| From Witton Alb | | | | | |
| 1998–99 | Halifax T | 10 | 7 | **10** | **7** |
| 1998–99 | Fulham | 28 | 15 | | |
| 1999–2000 | Fulham | 31 | 7 | **59** | **22** |
| 2000–01 | Birmingham C | 34 | 7 | | |
| 2001–02 | Birmingham C | 40 | 11 | | |
| 2002–03 | Birmingham C | 31 | 5 | | |
| 2003–04 | Birmingham C | 3 | 0 | **108** | **23** |
| 2003–04 | Wigan Ath | 16 | 7 | **16** | **7** |
| 2003–04 | WBA | 20 | 7 | **20** | **7** |

**HOULT, Russell (G)** **333** **0**
H: 6 3 W: 14 09 b.Ashby 22-11-72
*Source:* Trainee.

| | | | | | |
|---|---|---|---|---|---|
| 1990–91 | Leicester C | 0 | 0 | | |
| 1991–92 | Leicester C | 0 | 0 | | |
| 1991–92 | *Lincoln C* | 2 | 0 | | |
| 1991–92 | *Blackpool* | 0 | 0 | | |
| 1992–93 | Leicester C | 10 | 0 | | |
| 1993–94 | Leicester C | 0 | 0 | | |
| 1993–94 | *Bolton W* | 4 | 0 | **4** | **0** |
| 1994–95 | Leicester C | 0 | 0 | **10** | **0** |
| 1994–95 | *Lincoln C* | 15 | 0 | **17** | **0** |
| 1994–95 | *Derby Co* | 15 | 0 | | |
| 1995–96 | Derby Co | 41 | 0 | | |
| 1996–97 | Derby Co | 32 | 0 | | |
| 1997–98 | Derby Co | 2 | 0 | | |
| 1998–99 | Derby Co | 23 | 0 | | |
| 1999–2000 | Derby Co | 10 | 0 | **123** | **0** |
| 1999–2000 | Portsmouth | 18 | 0 | | |
| 2000–01 | Portsmouth | 22 | 0 | **40** | **0** |
| 2000–01 | WBA | 13 | 0 | | |
| 2001–02 | WBA | 45 | 0 | | |
| 2002–03 | WBA | 37 | 0 | | |
| 2003–04 | WBA | 44 | 0 | **139** | **0** |

**HUGHES, Lee (F)** **253** **104**
H: 5 10 W: 12 00 b.Smethwick 22-5-76
*Source:* Kidderminster H.

| | | | | | |
|---|---|---|---|---|---|
| 1997–98 | WBA | 37 | 14 | | |
| 1998–99 | WBA | 42 | 31 | | |
| 1999–2000 | WBA | 36 | 12 | | |
| 2000–01 | WBA | 41 | 21 | | |
| 2001–02 | Coventry C | 38 | 14 | | |
| 2002–03 | Coventry C | 4 | 1 | **42** | **15** |
| 2002–03 | WBA | 23 | 0 | | |
| 2003–04 | WBA | 32 | 11 | **211** | **89** |

**HULSE, Rob (F)** **149** **56**
H: 6 1 W: 11 04 b.Crewe 25-10-79
*Source:* Trainee.

| | | | | | |
|---|---|---|---|---|---|
| 1998–99 | Crewe Alex | 0 | 0 | | |
| 1999–2000 | Crewe Alex | 4 | 1 | | |
| 2000–01 | Crewe Alex | 33 | 11 | | |
| 2001–02 | Crewe Alex | 41 | 12 | | |
| 2002–03 | Crewe Alex | 38 | 22 | **116** | **46** |
| 2003–04 | WBA | 33 | 10 | **33** | **10** |

**JOHNSON, Andy (M)** **287** **29**
H: 6 0 W: 13 00 b.Bristol 2-5-74
*Source:* Trainee. *Honours:* Wales 14 full caps.

| | | | | | |
|---|---|---|---|---|---|
| 1991–92 | Norwich C | 2 | 0 | | |
| 1992–93 | Norwich C | 2 | 1 | | |
| 1993–94 | Norwich C | 2 | 0 | | |
| 1994–95 | Norwich C | 7 | 0 | | |
| 1995–96 | Norwich C | 26 | 7 | | |
| 1996–97 | Norwich C | 27 | 5 | **66** | **13** |
| 1997–98 | Nottingham F | 34 | 4 | | |
| 1998–99 | Nottingham F | 28 | 0 | | |
| 1999–2000 | Nottingham F | 25 | 2 | | |
| 2000–01 | Nottingham F | 31 | 3 | | |
| 2001–02 | Nottingham F | 1 | 0 | **119** | **9** |
| 2001–02 | WBA | 32 | 4 | | |
| 2002–03 | WBA | 32 | 1 | | |
| 2003–04 | WBA | 38 | 2 | **102** | **7** |

**JORDAO‡ (M)** **250** **18**
H: 6 2 W: 12 08 b.Malanje 30-8-71

| | | | | | |
|---|---|---|---|---|---|
| 1990–91 | Amadora | 0 | 0 | | |
| 1991–92 | Amadora | 17 | 3 | | |
| 1992–93 | Amadora | 3 | 0 | | |
| 1993–94 | Campomaiorense | 9 | 0 | **9** | **0** |
| 1994–95 | Leca | 26 | 3 | **26** | **3** |
| 1995–96 | Amadora | 30 | 1 | | |
| 1996–97 | Amadora | 31 | 3 | **81** | **7** |
| 1997–98 | Benfica | 6 | 0 | **6** | **0** |
| 1997–98 | Braga | 14 | 1 | | |
| 1998–99 | Braga | 29 | 1 | | |
| 1999–2000 | Braga | 22 | 0 | **65** | **2** |
| 2000–01 | WBA | 35 | 1 | | |
| 2001–02 | WBA | 25 | 5 | | |
| 2002–03 | WBA | 3 | 0 | | |
| 2003–04 | WBA | 0 | 0 | **63** | **6** |

**KINSELLA, Mark* (M)** **427** **47**
H: 5 9 W: 11 00 b.Dublin 12-8-72
*Source:* Home Farm. *Honours:* Eire 48 full caps, 3 goals.

| | | | | | |
|---|---|---|---|---|---|
| 1989–90 | Colchester U | 6 | 0 | | |
| 1990–91 | Colchester U | 0 | 0 | | |
| 1991–92 | Colchester U | 0 | 0 | | |
| 1992–93 | Colchester U | 38 | 6 | | |
| 1993–94 | Colchester U | 42 | 8 | | |
| 1994–95 | Colchester U | 42 | 6 | | |
| 1995–96 | Colchester U | 45 | 5 | | |
| 1996–97 | Colchester U | 7 | 2 | **180** | **27** |
| 1996–97 | Charlton Ath | 37 | 6 | | |
| 1997–98 | Charlton Ath | 46 | 6 | | |
| 1998–99 | Charlton Ath | 38 | 2 | | |
| 1999–2000 | Charlton Ath | 38 | 3 | | |
| 2000–01 | Charlton Ath | 32 | 2 | | |
| 2001–02 | Charlton Ath | 17 | 0 | | |
| 2002–03 | Charlton Ath | 0 | 0 | **208** | **19** |
| 2002–03 | Aston Villa | 19 | 0 | | |
| 2003–04 | Aston Villa | 2 | 0 | **21** | **0** |
| 2003–04 | WBA | 18 | 1 | **18** | **1** |

**KOUMAS, Jason (M)** **201** **39**
H: 5 10 W: 11 02 b.Wrexham 25-9-79
*Source:* Trainee. *Honours:* Wales 9 full caps, 1 goal.

| | | | | | |
|---|---|---|---|---|---|
| 1997–98 | Tranmere R | 0 | 0 | | |
| 1998–99 | Tranmere R | 23 | 3 | | |
| 1999–2000 | Tranmere R | 23 | 2 | | |
| 2000–01 | Tranmere R | 39 | 10 | | |
| 2001–02 | Tranmere R | 38 | 8 | | |
| 2002–03 | Tranmere R | 4 | 2 | **127** | **25** |
| 2002–03 | WBA | 32 | 4 | | |
| 2003–04 | WBA | 42 | 10 | **74** | **14** |

**MARSHALL, Lee (M)** **182** **12**
H: 6 0 W: 11 10 b.Islington 21-1-79
*Source:* Enfield. *Honours:* England Under-21.

| | | | | | |
|---|---|---|---|---|---|
| 1996–97 | Norwich C | 0 | 0 | | |
| 1997–98 | Norwich C | 4 | 0 | | |
| 1998–99 | Norwich C | 44 | 3 | | |
| 1999–2000 | Norwich C | 33 | 5 | | |
| 2000–01 | Norwich C | 36 | 3 | **117** | **11** |
| 2000–01 | Leicester C | 9 | 0 | | |
| 2001–02 | Leicester C | 35 | 0 | | |
| 2002–03 | Leicester C | 1 | 0 | **45** | **0** |
| 2002–03 | WBA | 9 | 1 | | |
| 2003–04 | WBA | 0 | 0 | **9** | **1** |
| 2003–04 | *Hull C* | 11 | 0 | **11** | **0** |

**MIOTTO, Simon (G)** **14** **0**
H: 6 1 W: 13 03 b.Tasmania 5-9-69
*Source:* Riverside Olympic.

| | | | | | |
|---|---|---|---|---|---|
| 1994–95 | Blackpool | 0 | 0 | | |
| 1995–96 | Blackpool | 0 | 0 | | |
| 1996–97 | Blackpool | 0 | 0 | | |
| 1997–98 | Blackpool | 0 | 0 | | |
| 1998–99 | Hartlepool U | 5 | 0 | | |
| 1999–2000 | Hartlepool U | 0 | 0 | **5** | **0** |
| 2000–01 | Raith R | 0 | 0 | | |
| 2001–02 | Raith R | 9 | 0 | **9** | **0** |
| 2002–03 | St Johnstone | 0 | 0 | | |
| 2003–04 | WBA | 0 | 0 | | |

**MKANDAWIRE, Tamika* (D)** **0** **0**
H: 6 1 W: 12 03 b.Malawi 28-5-83
*Source:* Scholar.

| | | | | | |
|---|---|---|---|---|---|
| 2002–03 | WBA | 0 | 0 | | |
| 2003–04 | WBA | 0 | 0 | | |

**MOORE, Darren (D)** **383** **26**
H: 6 2 W: 15 07 b.Birmingham 22-4-74
*Source:* Trainee. *Honours:* Jamaica 3 full caps.

| | | | | | |
|---|---|---|---|---|---|
| 1991–92 | Torquay U | 5 | 1 | | |
| 1992–93 | Torquay U | 31 | 2 | | |
| 1993–94 | Torquay U | 37 | 2 | | |
| 1994–95 | Torquay U | 30 | 3 | **103** | **8** |
| 1995–96 | Doncaster R | 35 | 2 | | |
| 1996–97 | Doncaster R | 41 | 5 | **76** | **7** |
| 1997–98 | Bradford C | 18 | 0 | | |
| 1998–99 | Bradford C | 44 | 3 | | |
| 1999–2000 | Bradford C | 0 | 0 | **62** | **3** |
| 1999–2000 | Portsmouth | 25 | 1 | | |
| 2000–01 | Portsmouth | 32 | 1 | | |
| 2001–02 | Portsmouth | 2 | 0 | **59** | **2** |
| 2001–02 | WBA | 32 | 2 | | |
| 2002–03 | WBA | 29 | 2 | | |
| 2003–04 | WBA | 22 | 2 | **83** | **6** |

**MURPHY, Joe (G)** **68** **0**
H: 6 2 W: 13 06 b.Dublin 21-8-81
*Source:* Trainee. *Honours:* Eire Under-21, 1 full cap.

| | | | | | |
|---|---|---|---|---|---|
| 1999–2000 | Tranmere R | 21 | 0 | | |
| 2000–01 | Tranmere R | 20 | 0 | | |
| 2001–02 | Tranmere R | 22 | 0 | **63** | **0** |
| 2002–03 | WBA | 2 | 0 | | |
| 2003–04 | WBA | 3 | 0 | **5** | **0** |

**N'DOUR, Alassane* (D)** **2** **0**
H: 6 1 W: 12 05 b.Dakar 12-12-81
*Honours:* Senegal full caps.

| | | | | | |
|---|---|---|---|---|---|
| 2003–04 | WBA | 2 | 0 | **2** | **0** |

**O'CONNOR, James (M)** **206** **16**
H: 5 8 W: 11 06 b.Dublin 1-9-79
*Source:* Trainee. *Honours:* Eire Under-21.

| | | | | | |
|---|---|---|---|---|---|
| 1996–97 | Stoke C | 0 | 0 | | |
| 1997–98 | Stoke C | 0 | 0 | | |
| 1998–99 | Stoke C | 4 | 0 | | |
| 1999–2000 | Stoke C | 42 | 6 | | |
| 2000–01 | Stoke C | 44 | 8 | | |
| 2001–02 | Stoke C | 43 | 2 | | |
| 2002–03 | Stoke C | 43 | 0 | **176** | **16** |
| 2003–04 | WBA | 30 | 0 | **30** | **0** |

**ROBINSON, Paul (D)** **250** **8**
H: 5 9 W: 11 12 b.Watford 14-12-78
*Source:* Trainee. *Honours:* England Under-21.

| | | | | | |
|---|---|---|---|---|---|
| 1996–97 | Watford | 12 | 0 | | |
| 1997–98 | Watford | 22 | 2 | | |
| 1998–99 | Watford | 29 | 0 | | |
| 1999–2000 | Watford | 32 | 0 | | |
| 2000–01 | Watford | 39 | 0 | | |
| 2001–02 | Watford | 38 | 3 | | |
| 2002–03 | Watford | 37 | 3 | | |
| 2003–04 | Watford | 10 | 0 | **219** | **8** |
| 2003–04 | WBA | 31 | 0 | **31** | **0** |

**SAKIRI, Artim (M)** **25** **1**
H: 5 11 W: 12 00 b.Struga 23-9-73
*Source:* CSKA Sofia. *Honours:* Macedonia 61 full caps, 14 goals.

| | | | | | |
|---|---|---|---|---|---|
| 2003–04 | WBA | 25 | 1 | **25** | **1** |

**SIGURDSSON, Larus (D)** **316** **8**
H: 6 0 W: 11 00 b.Akureyri 4-6-73
*Source:* Thor. *Honours:* Iceland 42 full caps, 2 goals.

| | | | | | |
|---|---|---|---|---|---|
| 1994–95 | Stoke C | 23 | 1 | | |
| 1995–96 | Stoke C | 46 | 0 | | |
| 1996–97 | Stoke C | 45 | 0 | | |
| 1997–98 | Stoke C | 43 | 1 | | |
| 1998–99 | Stoke C | 38 | 4 | | |
| 1999–2000 | Stoke C | 5 | 1 | **200** | **7** |
| 1999–2000 | WBA | 27 | 0 | | |
| 2000–01 | WBA | 12 | 0 | | |
| 2001–02 | WBA | 43 | 1 | | |
| 2002–03 | WBA | 29 | 0 | | |
| 2003–04 | WBA | 5 | 0 | **116** | **1** |

**SKOUBO, Morten* (F)** **80** **27**
H: 6 3 W: 13 08 b.Holstebro 30-6-80
*Honours:* Denmark 1 full cap.

| | | | | | |
|---|---|---|---|---|---|
| 2000–01 | Midtjylland | 19 | 3 | | |
| 2001–02 | Midtjylland | 27 | 19 | | |
| 2002–03 | Midtjylland | 4 | 1 | **50** | **23** |
| 2002–03 | Moenchengladbach | 21 | 4 | | |
| 2003–04 | Moenchengladbach | 7 | 0 | **28** | **4** |
| 2003–04 | WBA | 2 | 0 | **2** | **0** |

**VOLMER, Joost* (D)** **219 19**
H: 6 2 W: 13 05 b.Enschede 7-3-74

| | | | | | |
|---|---|---|---|---|---|
| 1993–94 | Twente | 1 | 0 | | |
| 1994–95 | Twente | 8 | 0 | | |
| 1995–96 | Twente | 4 | 1 | **13** | **1** |
| 1995–96 | Helmond Sport | 11 | 1 | **11** | **1** |
| 1996–97 | VVV | 30 | 5 | **30** | **5** |
| 1997–98 | MVV | 32 | 2 | | |
| 1998–99 | MVV | 32 | 1 | **64** | **3** |
| 1999–2000 | Fortuna Sittard | 32 | 4 | | |
| 2000–01 | Fortuna Sittard | 31 | 3 | | |
| 2001–02 | Fortuna Sittard | 23 | 2 | **86** | **9** |
| 2003–04 | WBA | 15 | 0 | **15** | **0** |

**WALLWORK, Ronnie (M)** **75 5**
H: 5 10 W: 12 09 b.Manchester 10-9-77
*Source:* Trainee. *Honours:* England Youth.

| | | | | | |
|---|---|---|---|---|---|
| 1994–95 | Manchester U | 0 | 0 | | |
| 1995–96 | Manchester U | 0 | 0 | | |
| 1996–97 | Manchester U | 0 | 0 | | |
| 1997–98 | Manchester U | 1 | 0 | | |
| 1997–98 | *Carlisle U* | 10 | 1 | **10** | **1** |
| 1997–98 | *Stockport Co* | 7 | 0 | **7** | **0** |
| 1998–99 | Manchester U | 0 | 0 | | |
| 1999–2000 | Manchester U | 5 | 0 | | |
| 2000–01 | Manchester U | 12 | 0 | | |
| 2001–02 | Manchester U | 1 | 0 | **19** | **0** |
| 2002–03 | WBA | 27 | 0 | | |
| 2003–04 | WBA | 5 | 0 | **32** | **0** |
| 2003–04 | *Bradford C* | 7 | 4 | **7** | **4** |

**Scholars**
Attewell, Stuart J; Barnett, Thomas A; Clarke, Ross E; Cudworth, Jack R; Davies, Robert J; Elvins, Robert M; Hodgkiss, Jared; Holmes, James; Jones, Matthew R; McHugh, Cameron J; Midworth, Philip; Nightingale, Peter E; Paszkowec, Benjamin J; Patterson, Kyle J; Sherwood, Lee G; Smikle, Brian J; Tomlinson, Ezekiel J; Warmer, Thomas E

**Players who do not hold a current contract but their registration has been retained by the club**
Blake, Mosiah

## WEST HAM U (85)

**BREVETT, Rufus (D)** **449 5**
H: 5 8 W: 11 13 b.Derby 24-9-69
*Source:* Trainee.

| | | | | | |
|---|---|---|---|---|---|
| 1987–88 | Doncaster R | 17 | 0 | | |
| 1988–89 | Doncaster R | 23 | 0 | | |
| 1989–90 | Doncaster R | 42 | 0 | | |
| 1990–91 | Doncaster R | 27 | 3 | **109** | **3** |
| 1990–91 | QPR | 10 | 0 | | |
| 1991–92 | QPR | 7 | 0 | | |
| 1992–93 | QPR | 15 | 0 | | |
| 1993–94 | QPR | 7 | 0 | | |
| 1994–95 | QPR | 19 | 0 | | |
| 1995–96 | QPR | 27 | 1 | | |
| 1996–97 | QPR | 44 | 0 | | |
| 1997–98 | QPR | 23 | 0 | **152** | **1** |
| 1997–98 | Fulham | 11 | 0 | | |
| 1998–99 | Fulham | 45 | 1 | | |
| 1999–2000 | Fulham | 23 | 0 | | |
| 2000–01 | Fulham | 39 | 0 | | |
| 2001–02 | Fulham | 35 | 0 | | |
| 2002–03 | Fulham | 20 | 0 | **173** | **1** |
| 2002–03 | West Ham U | 13 | 0 | | |
| 2003–04 | West Ham U | 2 | 0 | **15** | **0** |

**BYRNE, Shaun* (D)** **13 0**
H: 5 9 W: 11 08 b.Taplow 21-1-81
*Source:* Trainee. *Honours:* Eire Under-21.

| | | | | | |
|---|---|---|---|---|---|
| 1999–2000 | West Ham U | 1 | 0 | | |
| 1999–2000 | *Bristol R* | 2 | 0 | **2** | **0** |
| 2000–01 | West Ham U | 0 | 0 | | |
| 2001–02 | West Ham U | 1 | 0 | | |
| 2002–03 | West Ham U | 0 | 0 | | |
| 2003–04 | West Ham U | 0 | 0 | **2** | **0** |
| 2003–04 | *Swansea C* | 9 | 0 | **9** | **0** |

**BYWATER, Steve (G)** **28 0**
H: 6 2 W: 12 00 b.Manchester 7-6-81
*Source:* Trainee. *Honours:* England Youth, Under-20, Under-21.

| | | | | | |
|---|---|---|---|---|---|
| 1997–98 | Rochdale | 0 | 0 | | |
| 1998–99 | West Ham U | 0 | 0 | | |
| 1999–2000 | West Ham U | 4 | 0 | | |
| 1999–2000 | *Wycombe W* | 2 | 0 | **2** | **0** |
| 1999–2000 | *Hull C* | 4 | 0 | **4** | **0** |
| 2000–01 | West Ham U | 1 | 0 | | |
| 2001–02 | West Ham U | 0 | 0 | | |
| 2001–02 | *Wolverhampton W* | 0 | 0 | | |
| 2001–02 | *Cardiff C* | 0 | 0 | | |
| 2002–03 | West Ham U | 0 | 0 | | |
| 2003–04 | West Ham U | 17 | 0 | **22** | **0** |

**CAMARA, Titi* (F)** **262 47**
H: 6 0 W: 13 00 b.Conakry 17-11-72
*Honours:* Guinea full caps.

| | | | | | |
|---|---|---|---|---|---|
| 1990–91 | St Etienne | 4 | 0 | | |
| 1991–92 | St Etienne | 15 | 3 | | |
| 1992–93 | St Etienne | 16 | 2 | | |
| 1993–94 | St Etienne | 26 | 4 | | |
| 1994–95 | St Etienne | 33 | 7 | **94** | **16** |
| 1995–96 | Lens | 36 | 8 | | |
| 1996–97 | Lens | 27 | 6 | **63** | **14** |
| 1997–98 | Marseille | 31 | 2 | | |
| 1998–99 | Marseille | 30 | 6 | **61** | **8** |
| 1999–2000 | Liverpool | 33 | 9 | | |
| 2000–01 | Liverpool | 0 | 0 | **33** | **9** |
| 2000–01 | West Ham U | 6 | 0 | | |
| 2001–02 | West Ham U | 1 | 0 | | |
| 2002–03 | West Ham U | 4 | 0 | | |
| 2003–04 | West Ham U | 0 | 0 | **11** | **0** |

**CAROLE, Sebastien* (M)** **1 0**
H: 5 6 W: 11 04 b.Pintoise 8-9-82
*Source:* Monaco.

| | | | | | |
|---|---|---|---|---|---|
| 2003–04 | West Ham U | 1 | 0 | **1** | **0** |

**CARRICK, Michael (M)** **144 8**
H: 6 1 W: 11 10 b.Wallsend 28-7-81
*Source:* Trainee. *Honours:* England Youth, Under-21, 2 full caps.

| | | | | | |
|---|---|---|---|---|---|
| 1998–99 | West Ham U | 0 | 0 | | |
| 1999–2000 | West Ham U | 8 | 1 | | |
| 1999–2000 | *Swindon T* | 6 | 2 | **6** | **2** |
| 1999–2000 | *Birmingham C* | 2 | 0 | **2** | **0** |
| 2000–01 | West Ham U | 33 | 1 | | |
| 2001–02 | West Ham U | 30 | 2 | | |
| 2002–03 | West Ham U | 30 | 1 | | |
| 2003–04 | West Ham U | 35 | 1 | **136** | **6** |

**COHEN, Chris (D)** **7 0**
H: 5 11 W: 10 11 b.Norwich 5-3-87
*Source:* Scholar. *Honours:* England Youth.

| | | | | | |
|---|---|---|---|---|---|
| 2003–04 | West Ham U | 7 | 0 | **7** | **0** |

**COLE, Mitchell (M)** **0 0**
b.London 6-10-85
*Source:* Trainee. *Honours:* England Youth.

| | | | | | |
|---|---|---|---|---|---|
| 2002–03 | West Ham U | 0 | 0 | | |
| 2003–04 | West Ham U | 0 | 0 | | |

**CONNOLLY, David (F)** **217 104**
H: 5 8 W: 10 09 b.Willesden 6-6-77
*Source:* Trainee. *Honours:* Eire 40 full caps, 9 goals.

| | | | | | |
|---|---|---|---|---|---|
| 1994–95 | Watford | 2 | 0 | | |
| 1995–96 | Watford | 11 | 8 | | |
| 1996–97 | Watford | 13 | 2 | **26** | **10** |
| 1997–98 | Feyenoord | 10 | 2 | | |
| 1998–99 | Wolverhampton W | 32 | 6 | **32** | **6** |
| 1999–2000 | Excelsior | 32 | 29 | **32** | **29** |
| 2000–01 | Feyenoord | 15 | 5 | **25** | **7** |
| 2001–02 | Wimbledon | 35 | 18 | | |
| 2002–03 | Wimbledon | 28 | 24 | **63** | **42** |
| 2003–04 | West Ham U | 39 | 10 | **39** | **10** |

**DAILLY, Christian (D)** **397 28**
H: 6 0 W: 12 10 b.Dundee 23-10-73
*Source:* 'S' Form. *Honours:* Scotland Schools, Youth, B, Under-21, 53 full caps, 4 goals.

| | | | | | |
|---|---|---|---|---|---|
| 1990–91 | Dundee U | 18 | 5 | | |
| 1991–92 | Dundee U | 8 | 0 | | |
| 1992–93 | Dundee U | 14 | 4 | | |
| 1993–94 | Dundee U | 38 | 4 | | |
| 1994–95 | Dundee U | 33 | 4 | | |
| 1995–96 | Dundee U | 30 | 1 | **141** | **18** |
| 1996–97 | Derby Co | 36 | 3 | | |
| 1997–98 | Derby Co | 30 | 1 | | |
| 1998–99 | Derby Co | 1 | 0 | **67** | **4** |
| 1998–99 | Blackburn R | 17 | 0 | | |
| 1999–2000 | Blackburn R | 43 | 4 | | |
| 2000–01 | Blackburn R | 10 | 0 | **70** | **4** |
| 2000–01 | West Ham U | 12 | 0 | | |
| 2001–02 | West Ham U | 38 | 0 | | |
| 2002–03 | West Ham U | 26 | 0 | | |
| 2003–04 | West Ham U | 43 | 2 | **119** | **2** |

**DEANE, Brian* (F)** **608 187**
H: 6 3 W: 14 05 b.Leeds 7-2-68
*Source:* Apprentice. *Honours:* England B, 3 full caps.

| | | | | | |
|---|---|---|---|---|---|
| 1985–86 | Doncaster R | 3 | 0 | | |
| 1986–87 | Doncaster R | 20 | 2 | | |
| 1987–88 | Doncaster R | 43 | 10 | **66** | **12** |
| 1988–89 | Sheffield U | 43 | 22 | | |
| 1989–90 | Sheffield U | 45 | 21 | | |
| 1990–91 | Sheffield U | 38 | 13 | | |
| 1991–92 | Sheffield U | 30 | 12 | | |
| 1992–93 | Sheffield U | 41 | 14 | | |
| 1993–94 | Leeds U | 41 | 11 | | |
| 1994–95 | Leeds U | 35 | 9 | | |
| 1995–96 | Leeds U | 34 | 7 | | |
| 1996–97 | Leeds U | 28 | 5 | **138** | **32** |
| 1997–98 | Sheffield U | 24 | 11 | **221** | **93** |
| 1997–98 | Benfica | 14 | 7 | | |
| 1998–99 | Benfica | 4 | 0 | **18** | **7** |
| 1998–99 | Middlesbrough | 26 | 6 | | |
| 1999–2000 | Middlesbrough | 29 | 9 | | |
| 2000–01 | Middlesbrough | 25 | 2 | | |
| 2001–02 | Middlesbrough | 7 | 1 | **87** | **18** |
| 2001–02 | Leicester C | 15 | 6 | | |
| 2002–03 | Leicester C | 32 | 13 | | |
| 2003–04 | Leicester C | 5 | 0 | **52** | **19** |
| 2003–04 | West Ham U | 26 | 6 | **26** | **6** |

**ETHERINGTON, Matthew (F)** **144 13**
H: 5 9 W: 10 12 b.Truro 14-8-81
*Source:* School. *Honours:* England Youth, Under-21.

| | | | | | |
|---|---|---|---|---|---|
| 1996–97 | Peterborough U | 1 | 0 | | |
| 1997–98 | Peterborough U | 2 | 0 | | |
| 1998–99 | Peterborough U | 29 | 3 | | |
| 1999–2000 | Peterborough U | 19 | 3 | **51** | **6** |
| 1999–2000 | Tottenham H | 5 | 0 | | |
| 2000–01 | Tottenham H | 6 | 0 | | |
| 2001–02 | *Bradford C* | 13 | 1 | **13** | **1** |
| 2001–02 | Tottenham H | 11 | 0 | | |
| 2002–03 | Tottenham H | 23 | 1 | **45** | **1** |
| 2003–04 | West Ham U | 35 | 5 | **35** | **5** |

**FERDINAND, Anton (D)** **20 0**
H: 6 0 W: 11 00 b.Peckham 18-2-85
*Source:* Trainee. *Honours:* England Youth.

| | | | | | |
|---|---|---|---|---|---|
| 2002–03 | West Ham U | 0 | 0 | | |
| 2003–04 | West Ham U | 20 | 0 | **20** | **0** |

**FORDE, David* (G)** **0 0**
H: 6 3 W: 13 06 b.Galway 20-12-79
*Source:* Barry T.

| | | | | | |
|---|---|---|---|---|---|
| 2001–02 | West Ham U | 0 | 0 | | |
| 2002–03 | West Ham U | 0 | 0 | | |
| 2003–04 | West Ham U | 0 | 0 | | |

**GARCIA, Richard (F)** **33 4**
H: 5 11 W: 12 00 b.Perth 9-4-81
*Source:* Trainee. *Honours:* Australia Under-23.

| | | | | | |
|---|---|---|---|---|---|
| 1998–99 | West Ham U | 0 | 0 | | |
| 1999–2000 | West Ham U | 0 | 0 | | |
| 2000–01 | West Ham U | 0 | 0 | | |
| 2000–01 | *Leyton Orient* | 18 | 4 | **18** | **4** |
| 2001–02 | West Ham U | 8 | 0 | | |
| 2002–03 | West Ham U | 0 | 0 | | |
| 2003–04 | West Ham U | 7 | 0 | **15** | **0** |

**HAREWOOD, Marlon (F)** **216 65**
H: 6 1 W: 13 07 b.Hampstead 25-8-79
*Source:* Trainee.

| | | | | | |
|---|---|---|---|---|---|
| 1996–97 | Nottingham F | 0 | 0 | | |
| 1997–98 | Nottingham F | 1 | 0 | | |
| 1998–99 | Nottingham F | 23 | 1 | | |
| 1998–99 | *Ipswich T* | 6 | 1 | **6** | **1** |
| 1999–2000 | Nottingham F | 34 | 4 | | |
| 2000–01 | Nottingham F | 33 | 3 | | |
| 2001–02 | Nottingham F | 28 | 11 | | |
| 2002–03 | Nottingham F | 44 | 20 | | |
| 2003–04 | Nottingham F | 19 | 12 | **182** | **51** |
| 2003–04 | West Ham U | 28 | 13 | **28** | **13** |

**HORLOCK, Kevin (M)** **394 60**
H: 6 0 W: 12 12 b.Erith 1-11-72
*Source:* Trainee. *Honours:* Northern Ireland B, 32 full caps.

| | | | | | |
|---|---|---|---|---|---|
| 1991–92 | West Ham U | 0 | 0 | | |
| 1992–93 | West Ham U | 0 | 0 | | |
| 1992–93 | Swindon T | 14 | 1 | | |
| 1993–94 | Swindon T | 38 | 0 | | |
| 1994–95 | Swindon T | 38 | 1 | | |

| | | | | | |
|---|---|---|---|---|---|
| 1995–96 | Swindon T | 45 | 12 | | |
| 1996–97 | Swindon T | 28 | 8 | **163** | **22** |
| 1996–97 | Manchester C | 18 | 4 | | |
| 1997–98 | Manchester C | 25 | 5 | | |
| 1998–99 | Manchester C | 37 | 9 | | |
| 1999–2000 | Manchester C | 38 | 10 | | |
| 2000–01 | Manchester C | 14 | 2 | | |
| 2001–02 | Manchester C | 42 | 7 | | |
| 2002–03 | Manchester C | 30 | 0 | **204** | **37** |
| 2003–04 | West Ham U | 27 | 1 | **27** | **1** |

**HUTCHISON, Don (M) 349 48**

H: 6 1 W: 11 08 b.Gateshead 9-5-71

*Source:* Trainee. *Honours:* Scotland B, 26 full caps, 6 goals.

| | | | | | |
|---|---|---|---|---|---|
| 1989–90 | Hartlepool U | 13 | 2 | | |
| 1990–91 | Hartlepool U | 11 | 0 | **24** | **2** |
| 1990–91 | Liverpool | 0 | 0 | | |
| 1991–92 | Liverpool | 3 | 0 | | |
| 1992–93 | Liverpool | 31 | 7 | | |
| 1993–94 | Liverpool | 11 | 0 | **45** | **7** |
| 1994–95 | West Ham U | 23 | 9 | | |
| 1995–96 | West Ham U | 12 | 2 | | |
| 1995–96 | Sheffield U | 19 | 2 | | |
| 1996–97 | Sheffield U | 41 | 3 | | |
| 1997–98 | Sheffield U | 18 | 0 | **78** | **5** |
| 1997–98 | Everton | 11 | 1 | | |
| 1998–99 | Everton | 33 | 3 | | |
| 1999–2000 | Everton | 31 | 6 | **75** | **10** |
| 2000–01 | Sunderland | 32 | 8 | | |
| 2001–02 | Sunderland | 2 | 0 | **34** | **8** |
| 2001–02 | West Ham U | 24 | 1 | | |
| 2002–03 | West Ham U | 10 | 0 | | |
| 2003–04 | West Ham U | 24 | 4 | **93** | **16** |

**LABANT, Vladimir* (D) 147 8**

H: 6 0 W: 13 00 b.Zilina 8-6-74

*Honours:* Slovakia 24 full caps, 2 goals.

| | | | | | |
|---|---|---|---|---|---|
| 1996–97 | Bystrica | 28 | 3 | **28** | **3** |
| 1997–98 | Slavia Prague | 23 | 0 | | |
| 1998–99 | Slavia Prague | 26 | 1 | **49** | **1** |
| 1999–2000 | Sparta Prague | 12 | 2 | | |
| 2000–01 | Sparta Prague | 24 | 1 | | |
| 2001–02 | Sparta Prague | 16 | 1 | **52** | **4** |
| 2001–02 | West Ham U | 12 | 0 | | |
| 2002–03 | West Ham U | 1 | 0 | | |
| 2002–03 | *Sparta Prague* | 5 | 0 | **5** | **0** |
| 2003–04 | West Ham U | 0 | 0 | **13** | **0** |

**LEE, Robert* (M) 665 105**

H: 5 10 W: 11 10 b.Plaistow 1-2-66

*Source:* Hornchurch. *Honours:* England Under-21, 21 full caps, 2 goals.

| | | | | | |
|---|---|---|---|---|---|
| 1983–84 | Charlton Ath | 11 | 4 | | |
| 1984–85 | Charlton Ath | 39 | 10 | | |
| 1985–86 | Charlton Ath | 35 | 8 | | |
| 1986–87 | Charlton Ath | 33 | 3 | | |
| 1987–88 | Charlton Ath | 23 | 2 | | |
| 1988–89 | Charlton Ath | 31 | 5 | | |
| 1989–90 | Charlton Ath | 37 | 1 | | |
| 1990–91 | Charlton Ath | 43 | 13 | | |
| 1991–92 | Charlton Ath | 39 | 12 | | |
| 1992–93 | Charlton Ath | 7 | 1 | **298** | **59** |
| 1992–93 | Newcastle U | 36 | 10 | | |
| 1993–94 | Newcastle U | 41 | 7 | | |
| 1994–95 | Newcastle U | 35 | 9 | | |
| 1995–96 | Newcastle U | 36 | 8 | | |
| 1996–97 | Newcastle U | 33 | 5 | | |
| 1997–98 | Newcastle U | 28 | 4 | | |
| 1998–99 | Newcastle U | 26 | 0 | | |
| 1999–2000 | Newcastle U | 30 | 0 | | |
| 2000–01 | Newcastle U | 22 | 0 | | |
| 2001–02 | Newcastle U | 16 | 1 | **303** | **44** |
| 2001–02 | Derby Co | 13 | 0 | | |
| 2002–03 | Derby Co | 35 | 2 | **48** | **2** |
| 2003–04 | West Ham U | 16 | 0 | **16** | **0** |

**LOMAS, Steve (M) 275 17**

H: 6 0 W: 12 08 b.Hanover 14-3-72

*Source:* Trainee. *Honours:* Northern Ireland Schools, Youth, B, 45 full caps, 3 goals.

| | | | | | |
|---|---|---|---|---|---|
| 1991–92 | Manchester C | 0 | 0 | | |
| 1992–93 | Manchester C | 0 | 0 | | |
| 1993–94 | Manchester C | 23 | 0 | | |
| 1994–95 | Manchester C | 20 | 2 | | |
| 1995–96 | Manchester C | 33 | 3 | | |
| 1996–97 | Manchester C | 35 | 3 | **111** | **8** |
| 1996–97 | West Ham U | 7 | 0 | | |
| 1997–98 | West Ham U | 33 | 2 | | |
| 1998–99 | West Ham U | 30 | 1 | | |
| 1999–2000 | West Ham U | 25 | 1 | | |
| 2000–01 | West Ham U | 20 | 1 | | |
| 2001–02 | West Ham U | 15 | 4 | | |
| 2002–03 | West Ham U | 29 | 0 | | |
| 2003–04 | West Ham U | 5 | 0 | **164** | **9** |

**McANUFF, Jobi (M) 108 14**

H: 5 9 W: 10 07 b.Edmonton 9-11-81

*Source:* Scholar. *Honours:* Jamaica 1 full cap.

| | | | | | |
|---|---|---|---|---|---|
| 2000–01 | Wimbledon | 0 | 0 | | |
| 2001–02 | Wimbledon | 38 | 4 | | |
| 2002–03 | Wimbledon | 31 | 4 | | |
| 2003–04 | Wimbledon | 27 | 5 | **96** | **13** |
| 2003–04 | West Ham U | 12 | 1 | **12** | **1** |

**McMAHON, Daryl* (M) 1 0**

H: 5 11 W: 12 02 b.Dublin 10-10-83

*Honours:* Eire Youth.

| | | | | | |
|---|---|---|---|---|---|
| 2000–01 | West Ham U | 0 | 0 | | |
| 2001–02 | West Ham U | 0 | 0 | | |
| 2002–03 | West Ham U | 0 | 0 | | |
| 2003–04 | West Ham U | 0 | 0 | | |
| 2003–04 | *Torquay U* | 1 | 0 | **1** | **0** |

**MELVILLE, Andy (D) 687 54**

H: 6 1 W: 12 13 b.Swansea 29-11-68

*Source:* School. *Honours:* Wales Under-21, B, 63 full caps, 3 goals.

| | | | | | |
|---|---|---|---|---|---|
| 1985–86 | Swansea C | 5 | 0 | | |
| 1986–87 | Swansea C | 42 | 3 | | |
| 1987–88 | Swansea C | 37 | 4 | | |
| 1988–89 | Swansea C | 45 | 10 | | |
| 1989–90 | Swansea C | 46 | 5 | **175** | **22** |
| 1990–91 | Oxford U | 46 | 3 | | |
| 1991–92 | Oxford U | 45 | 4 | | |
| 1992–93 | Oxford U | 44 | 6 | **135** | **13** |
| 1993–94 | Sunderland | 44 | 2 | | |
| 1994–95 | Sunderland | 36 | 3 | | |
| 1995–96 | Sunderland | 40 | 4 | | |
| 1996–97 | Sunderland | 30 | 2 | | |
| 1997–98 | Sunderland | 10 | 1 | | |
| 1997–98 | *Bradford C* | 6 | 1 | **6** | **1** |
| 1998–99 | Sunderland | 44 | 2 | **204** | **14** |
| 1999–2000 | Fulham | 40 | 3 | | |
| 2000–01 | Fulham | 43 | 1 | | |
| 2001–02 | Fulham | 35 | 0 | | |
| 2002–03 | Fulham | 26 | 0 | | |
| 2003–04 | Fulham | 9 | 0 | **153** | **4** |
| 2003–04 | West Ham U | 14 | 0 | **14** | **0** |

**MULLINS, Hayden (D) 249 18**

H: 6 0 W: 11 12 b.Reading 27-3-79

*Source:* Trainee. *Honours:* England Under-21.

| | | | | | |
|---|---|---|---|---|---|
| 1996–97 | Crystal Palace | 0 | 0 | | |
| 1997–98 | Crystal Palace | 0 | 0 | | |
| 1998–99 | Crystal Palace | 40 | 5 | | |
| 1999–2000 | Crystal Palace | 45 | 10 | | |
| 2000–01 | Crystal Palace | 41 | 1 | | |
| 2001–02 | Crystal Palace | 43 | 0 | | |
| 2002–03 | Crystal Palace | 43 | 2 | | |
| 2003–04 | Crystal Palace | 10 | 0 | **222** | **18** |
| 2003–04 | West Ham U | 27 | 0 | **27** | **0** |

**NOWLAND, Adam (M) 136 10**

H: 5 11 W: 11 06 b.Preston 6-7-81

*Source:* Trainee.

| | | | | | |
|---|---|---|---|---|---|
| 1997–98 | Blackpool | 1 | 0 | | |
| 1998–99 | Blackpool | 37 | 2 | | |
| 1999–2000 | Blackpool | 21 | 3 | | |
| 2000–01 | Blackpool | 10 | 0 | **69** | **5** |
| 2001–02 | Wimbledon | 7 | 0 | | |
| 2002–03 | Wimbledon | 24 | 2 | | |
| 2003–04 | Wimbledon | 25 | 3 | **56** | **5** |
| 2003–04 | West Ham U | 11 | 0 | **11** | **0** |

**PEARSON, Greg (F) 0 0**

b.Birmingham 3-4-85

*Source:* Trainee.

| | | | | | |
|---|---|---|---|---|---|
| 2003–04 | West Ham U | 0 | 0 | | |

**QUINN, Wayne* (D) 182 6**

H: 5 10 W: 11 12 b.Truro 19-11-76

*Source:* Trainee. *Honours:* England Under-21, B.

| | | | | | |
|---|---|---|---|---|---|
| 1994–95 | Sheffield U | 0 | 0 | | |
| 1995–96 | Sheffield U | 0 | 0 | | |
| 1996–97 | Sheffield U | 0 | 0 | | |
| 1997–98 | Sheffield U | 28 | 2 | | |
| 1998–99 | Sheffield U | 44 | 1 | | |
| 1999–2000 | Sheffield U | 43 | 1 | | |
| 2000–01 | Sheffield U | 24 | 2 | | |
| 2000–01 | Newcastle U | 15 | 0 | | |
| 2001–02 | Newcastle U | 0 | 0 | | |
| 2002–03 | Newcastle U | 0 | 0 | | |
| 2002–03 | *Sheffield U* | 6 | 0 | **145** | **6** |
| 2003–04 | Newcastle U | 0 | 0 | **15** | **0** |
| 2003–04 | West Ham U | 22 | 0 | **22** | **0** |

**REO-COKER, Nigel (M) 73 8**

H: 5 9 W: 12 03 b.Southwark 14-5-84

*Source:* Scholar. *Honours:* England Youth, Under-21.

| | | | | | |
|---|---|---|---|---|---|
| 2001–02 | Wimbledon | 1 | 0 | | |
| 2002–03 | Wimbledon | 32 | 2 | | |
| 2003–04 | Wimbledon | 25 | 4 | **58** | **6** |
| 2003–04 | West Ham U | 15 | 2 | **15** | **2** |

**REPKA, Tomas (D) 350 9**

H: 6 0 W: 12 04 b.Slavicin Zlin 2-1-74

*Honours:* Czechoslovakia 1 full cap.Czech Republic 46 full caps, 1 goal.

| | | | | | |
|---|---|---|---|---|---|
| 1991–92 | Banik Ostrava | 16 | 1 | | |
| 1992–93 | Banik Ostrava | 19 | 0 | | |
| 1993–94 | Banik Ostrava | 26 | 2 | | |
| 1994–95 | Banik Ostrava | 16 | 0 | **77** | **3** |
| 1995–96 | Sparta Prague | 29 | 3 | | |
| 1996–97 | Sparta Prague | 25 | 1 | | |
| 1997–98 | Sparta Prague | 28 | 2 | **82** | **6** |
| 1998–99 | Fiorentina | 31 | 0 | | |
| 1999–2000 | Fiorentina | 29 | 0 | | |
| 2000–01 | Fiorentina | 28 | 0 | **88** | **0** |
| 2001–02 | West Ham U | 31 | 0 | | |
| 2002–03 | West Ham U | 32 | 0 | | |
| 2003–04 | West Ham U | 40 | 0 | **103** | **0** |

**SOFIANE, Youssef (F) 1 0**

H: 5 8 W: 11 00 b.Lyon 8-7-84

| | | | | | |
|---|---|---|---|---|---|
| 2001–02 | Auxerre | 0 | 0 | | |
| 2002–03 | West Ham U | 0 | 0 | | |
| 2003–04 | West Ham U | 1 | 0 | **1** | **0** |

**SRNICEK, Pavel* (G) 237 0**

H: 6 2 W: 14 09 b.Bohumin 10-3-68

*Source:* Banik Ostrava. *Honours:* Czech Republic 49 full caps.

| | | | | | |
|---|---|---|---|---|---|
| 1990–91 | Newcastle U | 7 | 0 | | |
| 1991–92 | Newcastle U | 13 | 0 | | |
| 1992–93 | Newcastle U | 32 | 0 | | |
| 1993–94 | Newcastle U | 21 | 0 | | |
| 1994–95 | Newcastle U | 38 | 0 | | |
| 1995–96 | Newcastle U | 15 | 0 | | |
| 1996–97 | Newcastle U | 22 | 0 | | |
| 1997–98 | Newcastle U | 1 | 0 | **149** | **0** |
| 1998–99 | Banik Ostrava | 6 | 0 | **6** | **0** |
| 1998–99 | Sheffield W | 24 | 0 | | |
| 1999–2000 | Sheffield W | 20 | 0 | **44** | **0** |
| 2000–01 | Brescia | 26 | 0 | | |
| 2001–02 | Brescia | 1 | 0 | | |
| 2002–03 | Brescia | 5 | 0 | **32** | **0** |
| 2003–04 | Portsmouth | 3 | 0 | **3** | **0** |
| 2003–04 | West Ham U | 3 | 0 | **3** | **0** |

**WARD, Elliott (D) 0 0**

b.Harrow 19-1-85

*Source:* Scholar.

| | | | | | |
|---|---|---|---|---|---|
| 2001–02 | West Ham U | 0 | 0 | | |
| 2002–03 | West Ham U | 0 | 0 | | |
| 2003–04 | West Ham U | 0 | 0 | | |

**ZAMORA, Bobby (F) 162 81**

H: 5 11 W: 11 11 b.Barking 16-1-81

*Source:* Trainee. *Honours:* England Under-21.

| | | | | | |
|---|---|---|---|---|---|
| 1999–2000 | Bristol R | 4 | 0 | **4** | **0** |
| 1999–2000 | *Brighton & HA* | 6 | 6 | | |
| 2000–01 | Brighton & HA | 43 | 28 | | |
| 2001–02 | Brighton & HA | 41 | 28 | | |
| 2002–03 | Brighton & HA | 35 | 14 | **125** | **76** |
| 2003–04 | Tottenham H | 16 | 0 | **16** | **0** |
| 2003–04 | West Ham U | 17 | 5 | **17** | **5** |

**Scholars**

Akinsete, Ayo; Allen, Oliver T; Behcet, Darren N; Blewitt, Darren L; Brady, Darren J; Bunce, Daniel C; Carrick, Graeme; Collington, Marce D; Henry-Glasgow, Jemel De Freitas; Laws, Thomas S; Lumsden, Philip; McClenahan, Trent J; Noble, Mark J; Parrington, Liam W; Reed, Matthew J; Sealey, George B; Shaw, David I; Stokes, Tony R; Tattam, Brent S; Tucker, Ian M C; Wright, Sam A; Yao, Sosthene A

**Non Contract**

Keen, Kevin I; Miklosko, Ludek

## WIGAN ATH (86)

**BAINES, Leighton (D)** **32** **0**
H: 5 8 W: 11 10 b.Liverpool 11-12-84

| | | | | | |
|---|---|---|---|---|---|
| 2002–03 | Wigan Ath | 6 | 0 | | |
| 2003–04 | Wigan Ath | 26 | 0 | **32** | **0** |

**BRANNAN, Ged‡ (M)** **413** **36**
H: 6 0 W: 12 08 b.Liverpool 15-1-72
*Source:* Trainee.

| | | | | | |
|---|---|---|---|---|---|
| 1990–91 | Tranmere R | 18 | 1 | | |
| 1991–92 | Tranmere R | 18 | 1 | | |
| 1992–93 | Tranmere R | 38 | 1 | | |
| 1993–94 | Tranmere R | 45 | 9 | | |
| 1994–95 | Tranmere R | 41 | 2 | | |
| 1995–96 | Tranmere R | 44 | 0 | | |
| 1996–97 | Tranmere R | 34 | 6 | **238** | **20** |
| 1996–97 | Manchester C | 11 | 1 | | |
| 1997–98 | Manchester C | 32 | 3 | | |
| 1998–99 | Manchester C | 0 | 0 | **43** | **4** |
| 1998–99 | *Norwich C* | 11 | 1 | **11** | **1** |
| 1998–99 | Motherwell | 25 | 5 | | |
| 1999–2000 | Motherwell | 33 | 5 | **58** | **10** |
| 2000–01 | Wigan Ath | 13 | 0 | | |
| 2001–02 | Wigan Ath | 33 | 0 | | |
| 2002–03 | Wigan Ath | 6 | 0 | | |
| 2003–04 | Wigan Ath | 0 | 0 | **52** | **0** |
| 2003–04 | *Rochdale* | 11 | 1 | **11** | **1** |

**BRECKIN, Ian (D)** **398** **14**
H: 6 2 W: 13 05 b.Rotherham 24-2-75
*Source:* Trainee.

| | | | | | |
|---|---|---|---|---|---|
| 1993–94 | Rotherham U | 10 | 0 | | |
| 1994–95 | Rotherham U | 41 | 2 | | |
| 1995–96 | Rotherham U | 39 | 1 | | |
| 1996–97 | Rotherham U | 42 | 3 | **132** | **6** |
| 1997–98 | Chesterfield | 43 | 1 | | |
| 1998–99 | Chesterfield | 44 | 2 | | |
| 1999–2000 | Chesterfield | 38 | 1 | | |
| 2000–01 | Chesterfield | 45 | 3 | | |
| 2001–02 | Chesterfield | 42 | 1 | **212** | **8** |
| 2002–03 | Wigan Ath | 9 | 0 | | |
| 2003–04 | Wigan Ath | 45 | 0 | **54** | **0** |

**BULLARD, Jimmy (M)** **129** **14**
H: 5 10 W: 11 07 b.Newham 23-10-78
*Source:* Corinthian, Dartford, Gravesend & N.

| | | | | | |
|---|---|---|---|---|---|
| 1998–99 | West Ham U | 0 | 0 | | |
| 1999–2000 | West Ham U | 0 | 0 | | |
| 2000–01 | West Ham U | 0 | 0 | | |
| 2001–02 | Peterborough U | 40 | 8 | | |
| 2002–03 | Peterborough U | 26 | 3 | **66** | **11** |
| 2002–03 | Wigan Ath | 17 | 1 | | |
| 2003–04 | Wigan Ath | 46 | 2 | **63** | **3** |

**DE VOS, Jason# (D)** **227** **22**
H: 6 4 W: 14 10 b.London, Canada 2-1-74
*Source:* Montreal Impact. *Honours:* Canada 46 full caps.

| | | | | | |
|---|---|---|---|---|---|
| 1996–97 | Darlington | 8 | 0 | | |
| 1997–98 | Darlington | 24 | 3 | | |
| 1998–99 | Darlington | 12 | 2 | **44** | **5** |
| 1998–99 | Dundee U | 25 | 0 | | |
| 1999–2000 | Dundee U | 35 | 2 | | |
| 2000–01 | Dundee U | 33 | 0 | **93** | **2** |
| 2001–02 | Wigan Ath | 20 | 5 | | |
| 2002–03 | Wigan Ath | 43 | 8 | | |
| 2003–04 | Wigan Ath | 27 | 2 | **90** | **15** |

**DINNING, Tony (M)** **330** **46**
H: 6 0 W: 13 00 b.Wallsend 12-4-75
*Source:* Trainee.

| | | | | | |
|---|---|---|---|---|---|
| 1993–94 | Newcastle U | 0 | 0 | | |
| 1994–95 | Stockport Co | 40 | 1 | | |
| 1995–96 | Stockport Co | 10 | 1 | | |
| 1996–97 | Stockport Co | 20 | 2 | | |
| 1997–98 | Stockport Co | 30 | 4 | | |
| 1998–99 | Stockport Co | 41 | 5 | | |
| 1999–2000 | Stockport Co | 44 | 12 | | |
| 2000–01 | Stockport Co | 6 | 0 | **191** | **25** |
| 2000–01 | Wolverhampton W | 31 | 6 | | |
| 2001–02 | Wolverhampton W | 4 | 0 | **35** | **6** |
| 2001–02 | Wigan Ath | 33 | 5 | | |
| 2001–02 | *Stoke C* | 5 | 0 | **5** | **0** |
| 2002–03 | Wigan Ath | 38 | 7 | | |
| 2003–04 | Wigan Ath | 13 | 0 | **84** | **12** |
| 2003–04 | *Walsall* | 5 | 0 | **5** | **0** |
| 2003–04 | *Blackpool* | 10 | 3 | **10** | **3** |

**EADEN, Nicky (D)** **450** **13**
H: 5 9 W: 12 02 b.Sheffield 12-12-72
*Source:* Trainee.

| | | | | | |
|---|---|---|---|---|---|
| 1991–92 | Barnsley | 0 | 0 | | |
| 1992–93 | Barnsley | 2 | 0 | | |
| 1993–94 | Barnsley | 37 | 2 | | |
| 1994–95 | Barnsley | 45 | 1 | | |
| 1995–96 | Barnsley | 46 | 2 | | |
| 1996–97 | Barnsley | 46 | 3 | | |
| 1997–98 | Barnsley | 35 | 0 | | |
| 1998–99 | Barnsley | 40 | 1 | | |
| 1999–2000 | Barnsley | 42 | 1 | **293** | **10** |
| 2000–01 | Birmingham C | 45 | 2 | | |
| 2001–02 | Birmingham C | 29 | 1 | | |
| 2002–03 | Birmingham C | 0 | 0 | **74** | **3** |
| 2002–03 | Wigan Ath | 37 | 0 | | |
| 2003–04 | Wigan Ath | 46 | 0 | **83** | **0** |

**ELLINGTON, Nathan (F)** **205** **70**
H: 5 10 W: 13 01 b.Bradford 2-7-81
*Source:* Walton & Hersham.

| | | | | | |
|---|---|---|---|---|---|
| 1998–99 | Bristol R | 10 | 1 | | |
| 1999–2000 | Bristol R | 37 | 4 | | |
| 2000–01 | Bristol R | 42 | 15 | | |
| 2001–02 | Bristol R | 27 | 15 | **116** | **35** |
| 2001–02 | Wigan Ath | 3 | 2 | | |
| 2002–03 | Wigan Ath | 42 | 15 | | |
| 2003–04 | Wigan Ath | 44 | 18 | **89** | **35** |

**FARRELLY, Gareth# (M)** **162** **8**
H: 6 0 W: 12 07 b.Dublin 28-8-75
*Source:* Home Farm. *Honours:* Eire Under-21, 6 full caps.

| | | | | | |
|---|---|---|---|---|---|
| 1992–93 | Aston Villa | 0 | 0 | | |
| 1993–94 | Aston Villa | 0 | 0 | | |
| 1994–95 | Aston Villa | 0 | 0 | | |
| 1994–95 | *Rotherham U* | 10 | 2 | | |
| 1995–96 | Aston Villa | 5 | 0 | | |
| 1996–97 | Aston Villa | 3 | 0 | **8** | **0** |
| 1997–98 | Everton | 26 | 1 | | |
| 1998–99 | Everton | 1 | 0 | | |
| 1999–2000 | Everton | 0 | 0 | **27** | **1** |
| 1999–2000 | Bolton W | 11 | 1 | | |
| 2000–01 | Bolton W | 41 | 3 | | |
| 2001–02 | Bolton W | 18 | 0 | | |
| 2002–03 | Bolton W | 8 | 1 | | |
| 2002–03 | *Rotherham U* | 6 | 0 | **16** | **2** |
| 2003–04 | Bolton W | 0 | 0 | **78** | **5** |
| 2003–04 | *Burnley* | 12 | 0 | **12** | **0** |
| 2003–04 | *Bradford C* | 14 | 0 | **14** | **0** |
| 2003–04 | Wigan Ath | 7 | 0 | **7** | **0** |

**FILAN, John (G)** **343** **0**
H: 6 2 W: 14 06 b.Sydney 8-2-70
*Honours:* Australia Under-20, Under-23, 2 full caps.

| | | | | | |
|---|---|---|---|---|---|
| 1989–90 | St George | 26 | 0 | | |
| 1990–91 | St George | 26 | 0 | **52** | **0** |
| 1991–92 | Wollongong Wolves | 23 | 0 | | |
| 1992–93 | Wollongong Wolves | 6 | 0 | **29** | **0** |
| 1992–93 | Cambridge U | 6 | 0 | | |
| 1993–94 | Cambridge U | 46 | 0 | | |
| 1994–95 | Cambridge U | 16 | 0 | **68** | **0** |
| 1994–95 | *Nottingham F* | 0 | 0 | | |
| 1994–95 | Coventry C | 2 | 0 | | |
| 1995–96 | Coventry C | 13 | 0 | | |
| 1996–97 | Coventry C | 1 | 0 | **16** | **0** |
| 1997–98 | Blackburn R | 7 | 0 | | |
| 1998–99 | Blackburn R | 26 | 0 | | |
| 1999–2000 | Blackburn R | 16 | 0 | | |
| 2000–01 | Blackburn R | 13 | 0 | | |
| 2001–02 | Blackburn R | 0 | 0 | **62** | **0** |
| 2001–02 | Wigan Ath | 25 | 0 | | |
| 2002–03 | Wigan Ath | 46 | 0 | | |
| 2003–04 | Wigan Ath | 45 | 0 | **116** | **0** |

**FLYNN, Mike (M)** **25** **1**
H: 5 10 W: 12 10 b.Newport 17-10-80
*Source:* Barry T.

| | | | | | |
|---|---|---|---|---|---|
| 2002–03 | Wigan Ath | 17 | 1 | | |
| 2003–04 | Wigan Ath | 8 | 0 | **25** | **1** |

**JACKSON, Matt# (D)** **432** **12**
H: 6 1 W: 14 00 b.Leeds 19-10-71
*Source:* School. *Honours:* England Schools, Under-21.

| | | | | | |
|---|---|---|---|---|---|
| 1990–91 | Luton T | 0 | 0 | | |
| 1990–91 | *Preston NE* | 4 | 0 | **4** | **0** |
| 1991–92 | Luton T | 9 | 0 | **9** | **0** |
| 1991–92 | Everton | 30 | 1 | | |
| 1992–93 | Everton | 27 | 3 | | |
| 1993–94 | Everton | 38 | 0 | | |
| 1994–95 | Everton | 29 | 0 | | |
| 1995–96 | Everton | 14 | 0 | | |
| 1995–96 | *Charlton Ath* | 8 | 0 | **8** | **0** |
| 1996–97 | Everton | 0 | 0 | **138** | **4** |
| 1996–97 | *QPR* | 7 | 0 | **7** | **0** |
| 1996–97 | *Birmingham C* | 10 | 0 | **10** | **0** |
| 1996–97 | Norwich C | 19 | 2 | | |
| 1997–98 | Norwich C | 41 | 3 | | |
| 1998–99 | Norwich C | 37 | 1 | | |
| 1999–2000 | Norwich C | 38 | 0 | | |
| 2000–01 | Norwich C | 26 | 0 | | |
| 2001–02 | Norwich C | 0 | 0 | **161** | **6** |
| 2001–02 | Wigan Ath | 26 | 0 | | |
| 2002–03 | Wigan Ath | 45 | 1 | | |
| 2003–04 | Wigan Ath | 24 | 1 | **95** | **2** |

**JARRETT, Jason (M)** **146** **5**
H: 6 1 W: 13 01 b.Bury 14-9-79
*Source:* Trainee.

| | | | | | |
|---|---|---|---|---|---|
| 1998–99 | Blackpool | 2 | 0 | | |
| 1999–2000 | Blackpool | 0 | 0 | **2** | **0** |
| 1999–2000 | Wrexham | 1 | 0 | **1** | **0** |
| 2000–01 | Bury | 25 | 2 | | |
| 2001–02 | Bury | 37 | 2 | **62** | **4** |
| 2001–02 | Wigan Ath | 5 | 0 | | |
| 2002–03 | Wigan Ath | 35 | 0 | | |
| 2003–04 | Wigan Ath | 41 | 1 | **81** | **1** |

**KENNEDY, Peter* (M)** **207** **21**
H: 5 10 W: 11 11 b.Lisburn 10-9-73
*Source:* Portadown. *Honours:* Northern Ireland B, 20 full caps.

| | | | | | |
|---|---|---|---|---|---|
| 1996–97 | Notts Co | 22 | 0 | **22** | **0** |
| 1997–98 | Watford | 34 | 11 | | |
| 1998–99 | Watford | 46 | 6 | | |
| 1999–2000 | Watford | 18 | 1 | | |
| 2000–01 | Watford | 17 | 0 | **115** | **18** |
| 2001–02 | Wigan Ath | 31 | 0 | | |
| 2002–03 | Wigan Ath | 22 | 1 | | |
| 2003–04 | Wigan Ath | 12 | 1 | **65** | **2** |
| 2003–04 | *Derby Co* | 5 | 1 | **5** | **1** |

**LIDDELL, Andy# (F)** **415** **104**
H: 5 9 W: 11 07 b.Leeds 28-6-73
*Source:* Trainee. *Honours:* Scotland Under-21.

| | | | | | |
|---|---|---|---|---|---|
| 1990–91 | Barnsley | 0 | 0 | | |
| 1991–92 | Barnsley | 1 | 0 | | |
| 1992–93 | Barnsley | 21 | 2 | | |
| 1993–94 | Barnsley | 22 | 1 | | |
| 1994–95 | Barnsley | 39 | 13 | | |
| 1995–96 | Barnsley | 43 | 9 | | |
| 1996–97 | Barnsley | 38 | 8 | | |
| 1997–98 | Barnsley | 26 | 1 | | |
| 1998–99 | Barnsley | 8 | 0 | **198** | **34** |
| 1998–99 | Wigan Ath | 28 | 10 | | |
| 1999–2000 | Wigan Ath | 41 | 8 | | |
| 2000–01 | Wigan Ath | 37 | 9 | | |
| 2001–02 | Wigan Ath | 34 | 18 | | |
| 2002–03 | Wigan Ath | 37 | 16 | | |
| 2003–04 | Wigan Ath | 40 | 9 | **217** | **70** |

**MAHON, Alan (M)** **197** **18**
H: 5 8 W: 11 10 b.Dublin 4-4-78
*Source:* Crumplin U. *Honours:* Eire Under-21, 2 full caps.

| | | | | | |
|---|---|---|---|---|---|
| 1994–95 | Tranmere R | 0 | 0 | | |
| 1995–96 | Tranmere R | 2 | 0 | | |
| 1996–97 | Tranmere R | 25 | 2 | | |
| 1997–98 | Tranmere R | 18 | 1 | | |
| 1998–99 | Tranmere R | 39 | 6 | | |
| 1999–2000 | Tranmere R | 36 | 4 | **120** | **13** |
| 2000–01 | Sporting Lisbon | 1 | 0 | **1** | **0** |
| 2000–01 | Blackburn R | 18 | 0 | | |
| 2001–02 | Blackburn R | 13 | 1 | | |
| 2002–03 | Blackburn R | 2 | 0 | | |
| 2002–03 | *Cardiff C* | 15 | 2 | **15** | **2** |
| 2003–04 | Blackburn R | 3 | 0 | **36** | **1** |
| 2003–04 | *Ipswich T* | 11 | 1 | **11** | **1** |
| 2003–04 | Wigan Ath | 14 | 1 | **14** | **1** |

**McCULLOCH, Lee (F)** **245** **43**
H: 6 1 W: 13 00 b.Bellshill 14-5-78
*Source:* Cumbernauld U. *Honours:* Scotland Under-18, Under-21.

| | | | | | |
|---|---|---|---|---|---|
| 1995–96 | Motherwell | 1 | 0 | | |
| 1996–97 | Motherwell | 15 | 0 | | |
| 1997–98 | Motherwell | 25 | 2 | | |
| 1998–99 | Motherwell | 26 | 3 | | |
| 1999–2000 | Motherwell | 29 | 9 | | |

| | | | | | |
|---|---|---|---|---|---|
| 2000–01 | Motherwell | 26 | 8 | **122** | **22** |
| 2000–01 | Wigan Ath | 10 | 3 | | |
| 2001–02 | Wigan Ath | 34 | 6 | | |
| 2002–03 | Wigan Ath | 38 | 6 | | |
| 2003–04 | Wigan Ath | 41 | 6 | **123** | **21** |

**McMILLAN, Steve (D) 234 6**

H: 5 9 W: 11 12 b.Edinburgh 19-1-76

*Source:* Troon Juniors. *Honours:* Scotland Under-21.

| | | | | | |
|---|---|---|---|---|---|
| 1993–94 | Motherwell | 1 | 0 | | |
| 1994–95 | Motherwell | 3 | 0 | | |
| 1995–96 | Motherwell | 12 | 0 | | |
| 1996–97 | Motherwell | 16 | 0 | | |
| 1997–98 | Motherwell | 34 | 1 | | |
| 1998–99 | Motherwell | 30 | 2 | | |
| 1999–2000 | Motherwell | 31 | 3 | | |
| 2000–01 | Motherwell | 25 | 0 | **152** | **6** |
| 2000–01 | Wigan Ath | 6 | 0 | | |
| 2001–02 | Wigan Ath | 29 | 0 | | |
| 2002–03 | Wigan Ath | 32 | 0 | | |
| 2003–04 | Wigan Ath | 15 | 0 | **82** | **0** |

**MITCHELL, Paul (D) 74 0**

H: 5 9 W: 11 12 b.Manchester 26-8-81

*Source:* Trainee.

| | | | | | |
|---|---|---|---|---|---|
| 2000–01 | Wigan Ath | 1 | 0 | | |
| 2000–01 | *Halifax T* | 11 | 0 | **11** | **0** |
| 2001–02 | Wigan Ath | 23 | 0 | | |
| 2002–03 | Wigan Ath | 27 | 0 | | |
| 2003–04 | Wigan Ath | 12 | 0 | **63** | **0** |

**ROBERTS, Jason (F) 208 78**

H: 6 0 W: 12 06 b.Park Royal 25-1-78

*Source:* Hayes. *Honours:* Grenada 6 full caps.

| | | | | | |
|---|---|---|---|---|---|
| 1997–98 | Wolverhampton W | 0 | 0 | | |
| 1997–98 | *Torquay U* | 14 | 6 | **14** | **6** |
| 1997–98 | *Bristol C* | 3 | 1 | **3** | **1** |
| 1998–99 | Bristol R | 37 | 16 | | |
| 1999–2000 | Bristol R | 41 | 22 | **78** | **38** |
| 2000–01 | WBA | 43 | 14 | | |
| 2001–02 | WBA | 14 | 7 | | |
| 2002–03 | WBA | 32 | 3 | | |
| 2003–04 | WBA | 0 | 0 | **89** | **24** |
| 2003–04 | *Portsmouth* | 10 | 1 | **10** | **1** |
| 2003–04 | Wigan Ath | 14 | 8 | **14** | **8** |

**ROBERTS, Neil (F) 206 36**

H: 5 10 W: 12 08 b.Wrexham 7-4-78

*Source:* Trainee. *Honours:* Wales Youth, Under-21, B, 3 full caps.

| | | | | | |
|---|---|---|---|---|---|
| 1996–97 | Wrexham | 0 | 0 | | |
| 1997–98 | Wrexham | 34 | 8 | | |
| 1998–99 | Wrexham | 22 | 3 | | |
| 1999–2000 | Wrexham | 19 | 6 | **75** | **17** |
| 1999–2000 | Wigan Ath | 9 | 1 | | |
| 2000–01 | Wigan Ath | 34 | 6 | | |
| 2001–02 | *Hull C* | 6 | 0 | **6** | **0** |
| 2001–02 | Wigan Ath | 17 | 4 | | |
| 2002–03 | Wigan Ath | 37 | 6 | | |
| 2003–04 | Wigan Ath | 28 | 2 | **125** | **19** |

**SALISBURY, James (G) 0 0**

H: 6 1 W: 13 00 b.Preston 10-3-84

*Source:* Burnley Scholar.

| | | | | | |
|---|---|---|---|---|---|
| 2003–04 | Wigan Ath | 0 | 0 | | |

**TEALE, Gary (F) 233 26**

H: 5 11 W: 12 00 b.Glasgow 21-7-78

*Source:* Ayr U.

| | | | | | |
|---|---|---|---|---|---|
| 1996–97 | Clydebank | 33 | 6 | | |
| 1997–98 | Clydebank | 27 | 6 | **60** | **12** |
| 1998–99 | Ayr U | 23 | 4 | | |
| 1999–2000 | Ayr U | 32 | 0 | | |
| 2000–01 | Ayr U | 29 | 5 | **84** | **9** |
| 2001–02 | Wigan Ath | 23 | 1 | | |
| 2002–03 | Wigan Ath | 38 | 2 | | |
| 2003–04 | Wigan Ath | 28 | 2 | **89** | **5** |

**TRAYNOR, Greg§ (M) 1 0**

b.Salford 17-10-84

*Source:* Scholar.

| | | | | | |
|---|---|---|---|---|---|
| 2001–02 | Wigan Ath | 1 | 0 | | |
| 2002–03 | Wigan Ath | 0 | 0 | | |
| 2003–04 | Wigan Ath | 0 | 0 | **1** | **0** |

**VIEIRA, Magno (F) 10 2**

H: 5 9 W: 11 00 b.Brazil 13-2-85

| | | | | | |
|---|---|---|---|---|---|
| 2003–04 | Wigan Ath | 0 | 0 | | |
| 2003–04 | *Northampton T* | 10 | 2 | **10** | **2** |

**WALSH, Gary# (G) 241 0**

H: 6 3 W: 14 13 b.Wigan 21-3-68

*Source:* Apprentice. *Honours:* England Under-21.

| | | | | | |
|---|---|---|---|---|---|
| 1984–85 | Manchester U | 0 | 0 | | |
| 1985–86 | Manchester U | 0 | 0 | | |
| 1986–87 | Manchester U | 14 | 0 | | |
| 1987–88 | Manchester U | 16 | 0 | | |
| 1988–89 | Manchester U | 0 | 0 | | |
| 1988–89 | *Airdrieonians* | 3 | 0 | **3** | **0** |
| 1989–90 | Manchester U | 0 | 0 | | |
| 1990–91 | Manchester U | 5 | 0 | | |
| 1991–92 | Manchester U | 2 | 0 | | |
| 1992–93 | Manchester U | 0 | 0 | | |
| 1993–94 | Manchester U | 3 | 0 | | |
| 1993–94 | *Oldham Ath* | 6 | 0 | **6** | **0** |
| 1994–95 | Manchester U | 10 | 0 | **50** | **0** |
| 1995–96 | Middlesbrough | 32 | 0 | | |
| 1996–97 | Middlesbrough | 12 | 0 | | |
| 1997–98 | Middlesbrough | 0 | 0 | | |
| 1997–98 | Bradford C | 35 | 0 | | |
| 1998–99 | Bradford C | 46 | 0 | | |
| 1999–2000 | Bradford C | 11 | 0 | | |
| 2000–01 | Bradford C | 19 | 0 | | |
| 2000–01 | *Middlesbrough* | 3 | 0 | **47** | **0** |
| 2001–02 | Bradford C | 18 | 0 | | |
| 2002–03 | Bradford C | 3 | 0 | **132** | **0** |
| 2003–04 | Wigan Ath | 3 | 0 | **3** | **0** |

**YEOMANS, Ryan* (G) 0 0**

H: 6 0 W: 12 10 b.Blackpool 20-11-85

*Source:* Scholar.

| | | | | | |
|---|---|---|---|---|---|
| 2002–03 | Wigan Ath | 0 | 0 | | |
| 2003–04 | Wigan Ath | 0 | 0 | | |

**Scholars**

Dixon, Philip T; Edwards, Philip L; Foulkes, Michael G; Hazeldine, Michael J; Jones, Christopher; Joyce, Luke J; Kay, Robert P; Lee, Kevin; Lynch, Christopher; Middleton, Philip C; Moore, David L; Owens, Lee T; Perry-Acton, Benjamin; Roberts, Joseph; Thompson, Jonathan; Traynor, Greg

## WIMBLEDON (87)

### Now Milton Keynes Dons

**BARTON, Warren# (D) 447 14**

H: 6 3 W: 11 13 b.Islington 19-3-69

*Source:* Leytonstone/Ilford. *Honours:* England B, 3 full caps.

| | | | | | |
|---|---|---|---|---|---|
| 1989–90 | Maidstone U | 42 | 0 | **42** | **0** |
| 1990–91 | Wimbledon | 37 | 3 | | |
| 1991–92 | Wimbledon | 42 | 1 | | |
| 1992–93 | Wimbledon | 23 | 2 | | |
| 1993–94 | Wimbledon | 39 | 2 | | |
| 1994–95 | Wimbledon | 39 | 2 | | |
| 1995–96 | Newcastle U | 31 | 0 | | |
| 1996–97 | Newcastle U | 18 | 1 | | |
| 1997–98 | Newcastle U | 23 | 3 | | |
| 1998–99 | Newcastle U | 24 | 0 | | |
| 1999–2000 | Newcastle U | 34 | 0 | | |
| 2000–01 | Newcastle U | 29 | 0 | | |
| 2001–02 | Newcastle U | 5 | 0 | **164** | **4** |
| 2001–02 | Derby Co | 14 | 0 | | |
| 2002–03 | Derby Co | 39 | 0 | | |
| 2003–04 | Derby Co | 0 | 0 | **53** | **0** |
| 2003–04 | QPR | 3 | 0 | **3** | **0** |
| 2003–04 | Wimbledon | 5 | 0 | **185** | **10** |

**BEVAN, Scott# (G) 45 0**

H: 6 6 W: 15 10 b.Southampton 16-9-79

*Source:* Trainee.

| | | | | | |
|---|---|---|---|---|---|
| 1997–98 | Southampton | 0 | 0 | | |
| 1998–99 | Southampton | 0 | 0 | | |
| 1999–2000 | Southampton | 0 | 0 | | |
| 2000–01 | Southampton | 0 | 0 | | |
| 2001–02 | Southampton | 0 | 0 | | |
| 2001–02 | *Stoke C* | 0 | 0 | | |
| 2002–03 | Southampton | 0 | 0 | | |
| 2002–03 | *Huddersfield T* | 30 | 0 | **30** | **0** |
| 2003–04 | Southampton | 0 | 0 | | |
| 2003–04 | *Wycombe W* | 5 | 0 | **5** | **0** |
| 2003–04 | Wimbledon | 10 | 0 | **10** | **0** |

**CHORLEY, Ben (D) 47 2**

H: 6 3 W: 13 02 b.Sidcup 30-9-82

*Source:* Scholar.

| | | | | | |
|---|---|---|---|---|---|
| 2001–02 | Arsenal | 0 | 0 | | |
| 2002–03 | Arsenal | 0 | 0 | | |
| 2002–03 | *Brentford* | 2 | 0 | **2** | **0** |
| 2002–03 | Wimbledon | 10 | 0 | | |
| 2003–04 | Wimbledon | 35 | 2 | **45** | **2** |

**DARLINGTON, Jermaine* (D) 176 5**

H: 5 9 W: 13 00 b.Hackney 11-4-74

*Source:* Aylesbury U.

| | | | | | |
|---|---|---|---|---|---|
| 1998–99 | QPR | 4 | 0 | | |
| 1999–2000 | QPR | 34 | 2 | | |
| 2000–01 | QPR | 33 | 0 | **71** | **2** |
| 2001–02 | Wimbledon | 29 | 0 | | |
| 2002–03 | Wimbledon | 35 | 2 | | |
| 2003–04 | Wimbledon | 41 | 1 | **105** | **3** |

**GIER, Rob* (D) 71 0**

H: 5 9 W: 11 07 b.Ascot 6-1-80

*Source:* Trainee.

| | | | | | |
|---|---|---|---|---|---|
| 1998–99 | Wimbledon | 0 | 0 | | |
| 1999–2000 | Wimbledon | 0 | 0 | | |
| 2000–01 | Wimbledon | 14 | 0 | | |
| 2001–02 | Wimbledon | 3 | 0 | | |
| 2002–03 | Wimbledon | 29 | 0 | | |
| 2003–04 | Wimbledon | 25 | 0 | **71** | **0** |

**GORDON, Michael* (M) 19 0**

H: 5 6 W: 10 04 b.Wandsworth 11-10-84

*Source:* Arsenal Trainee.

| | | | | | |
|---|---|---|---|---|---|
| 2002–03 | Wimbledon | 1 | 0 | | |
| 2003–04 | Wimbledon | 18 | 0 | **19** | **0** |

**GORE, Shane‡ (G) 1 0**

H: 6 1 W: 12 01 b.Ashford 28-10-81

*Source:* Scholar.

| | | | | | |
|---|---|---|---|---|---|
| 2001–02 | Wimbledon | 1 | 0 | | |
| 2002–03 | Wimbledon | 0 | 0 | | |
| 2003–04 | Wimbledon | 0 | 0 | **1** | **0** |

**GRAY, Wayne* (F) 109 14**

H: 5 10 W: 12 07 b.South London 7-11-80

*Source:* Trainee.

| | | | | | |
|---|---|---|---|---|---|
| 1998–99 | Wimbledon | 0 | 0 | | |
| 1999–2000 | Wimbledon | 1 | 0 | | |
| 1999–2000 | *Swindon T* | 12 | 2 | **12** | **2** |
| 2000–01 | Wimbledon | 11 | 0 | | |
| 2000–01 | *Port Vale* | 3 | 0 | **3** | **0** |
| 2001–02 | Wimbledon | 0 | 0 | | |
| 2001–02 | *Leyton Orient* | 15 | 5 | **15** | **5** |
| 2001–02 | *Brighton & HA* | 4 | 1 | **4** | **1** |
| 2002–03 | Wimbledon | 30 | 2 | | |
| 2003–04 | Wimbledon | 33 | 4 | **75** | **6** |

**HARDING, Ben (M) 15 0**

H: 5 10 W: 11 02 b.Carshalton 6-9-84

*Source:* Scholar. *Honours:* England Youth.

| | | | | | |
|---|---|---|---|---|---|
| 2001–02 | Wimbledon | 0 | 0 | | |
| 2002–03 | Wimbledon | 0 | 0 | | |
| 2003–04 | Wimbledon | 15 | 0 | **15** | **0** |

**HAWKINS, Peter* (D) 134 0**

H: 6 0 W: 11 04 b.Maidstone 19-9-78

*Source:* Trainee.

| | | | | | |
|---|---|---|---|---|---|
| 1996–97 | Wimbledon | 0 | 0 | | |
| 1997–98 | Wimbledon | 0 | 0 | | |
| 1998–99 | Wimbledon | 0 | 0 | | |
| 1999–2000 | Wimbledon | 0 | 0 | | |
| 1999–2000 | *York C* | 14 | 0 | **14** | **0** |
| 2000–01 | Wimbledon | 30 | 0 | | |
| 2001–02 | Wimbledon | 29 | 0 | | |
| 2002–03 | Wimbledon | 43 | 0 | | |
| 2003–04 | Wimbledon | 18 | 0 | **120** | **0** |

**HEALD, Paul* (G) 223 0**

H: 6 2 W: 14 00 b.Wath-on-Dearne 20-9-68

*Source:* Trainee.

| | | | | | |
|---|---|---|---|---|---|
| 1987–88 | Sheffield U | 0 | 0 | | |
| 1988–89 | Sheffield U | 0 | 0 | | |
| 1988–89 | Leyton Orient | 28 | 0 | | |
| 1989–90 | Leyton Orient | 37 | 0 | | |
| 1990–91 | Leyton Orient | 38 | 0 | | |
| 1991–92 | Leyton Orient | 2 | 0 | | |
| 1991–92 | *Coventry C* | 2 | 0 | **2** | **0** |
| 1992–93 | Leyton Orient | 26 | 0 | | |
| 1992–93 | *Crystal Palace* | 0 | 0 | | |
| 1993–94 | Leyton Orient | 0 | 0 | | |
| 1993–94 | *Swindon T* | 2 | 0 | **2** | **0** |
| 1994–95 | Leyton Orient | 45 | 0 | **176** | **0** |
| 1995–96 | Wimbledon | 18 | 0 | | |
| 1996–97 | Wimbledon | 2 | 0 | | |

| | | | | | |
|---|---|---|---|---|---|
| 1997–98 | Wimbledon | 0 | 0 | | |
| 1998–99 | Wimbledon | 0 | 0 | | |
| 1999–2000 | Wimbledon | 1 | 0 | | |
| 2000–01 | Wimbledon | 3 | 0 | | |
| 2001–02 | Wimbledon | 4 | 0 | | |
| 2001–02 | *Sheffield W* | 5 | 0 | 5 | 0 |
| 2002–03 | Wimbledon | 0 | 0 | | |
| 2003–04 | Wimbledon | 10 | 0 | 38 | 0 |

**HERZIG, Nico (M)** **19 0**
H: 5 10 W: 11 00 b.Pobneck 10-12-83
*Source:* Carl Zeiss Jena.

| | | | | | |
|---|---|---|---|---|---|
| 2001–02 | Wimbledon | 0 | 0 | | |
| 2002–03 | Wimbledon | 0 | 0 | | |
| 2003–04 | Wimbledon | 19 | 0 | 19 | 0 |

**HOLDSWORTH, Dean* (F)** **527 163**
H: 5 11 W: 11 13 b.Walthamstow 8-11-68
*Source:* Trainee.

| | | | | | |
|---|---|---|---|---|---|
| 1986–87 | Watford | 2 | 0 | | |
| 1987–88 | *Carlisle U* | 4 | 1 | 4 | 1 |
| 1987–88 | *Port Vale* | 6 | 2 | 6 | 2 |
| 1988–89 | Watford | 10 | 2 | | |
| 1988–89 | *Swansea C* | 5 | 1 | 5 | 1 |
| 1988–89 | *Brentford* | 7 | 1 | | |
| 1989–90 | Watford | 4 | 1 | 16 | 3 |
| 1989–90 | Brentford | 39 | 24 | | |
| 1990–91 | Brentford | 30 | 5 | | |
| 1991–92 | Brentford | 41 | 24 | 117 | 54 |
| 1992–93 | Wimbledon | 36 | 19 | | |
| 1993–94 | Wimbledon | 42 | 17 | | |
| 1994–95 | Wimbledon | 28 | 7 | | |
| 1995–96 | Wimbledon | 33 | 10 | | |
| 1996–97 | Wimbledon | 25 | 5 | | |
| 1997–98 | Wimbledon | 5 | 0 | | |
| 1997–98 | Bolton W | 20 | 3 | | |
| 1998–99 | Bolton W | 32 | 12 | | |
| 1999–2000 | Bolton W | 35 | 11 | | |
| 2000–01 | Bolton W | 31 | 11 | | |
| 2001–02 | Bolton W | 31 | 2 | | |
| 2002–03 | Bolton W | 9 | 0 | 158 | 39 |
| 2002–03 | Coventry C | 17 | 0 | 17 | 0 |
| 2002–03 | Rushden & D | 7 | 2 | 7 | 2 |
| 2003–04 | Wimbledon | 28 | 3 | 197 | 61 |

**HOLLOWAY, Darren* (D)** **164 1**
H: 6 0 W: 12 05 b.Crook 3-10-77
*Source:* Trainee. *Honours:* England Under-21.

| | | | | | |
|---|---|---|---|---|---|
| 1995–96 | Sunderland | 0 | 0 | | |
| 1996–97 | Sunderland | 0 | 0 | | |
| 1997–98 | Sunderland | 32 | 0 | | |
| 1997–98 | *Carlisle U* | 5 | 0 | 5 | 0 |
| 1998–99 | Sunderland | 6 | 0 | | |
| 1999–2000 | Sunderland | 15 | 0 | | |
| 1999–2000 | *Bolton W* | 4 | 0 | 4 | 0 |
| 2000–01 | Sunderland | 5 | 0 | 58 | 0 |
| 2000–01 | Wimbledon | 31 | 0 | | |
| 2001–02 | Wimbledon | 32 | 0 | | |
| 2002–03 | Wimbledon | 16 | 0 | | |
| 2003–04 | Wimbledon | 13 | 0 | 92 | 0 |
| 2003–04 | *Scunthorpe U* | 5 | 1 | 5 | 1 |

**JARRETT, Albert* (M)** **9 0**
H: 5 11 W: 11 02 b.Sierra Leone 23-10-84
*Source:* Dulwich Hamlet.

| | | | | | |
|---|---|---|---|---|---|
| 2002–03 | Wimbledon | 0 | 0 | | |
| 2003–04 | Wimbledon | 9 | 0 | 9 | 0 |

**KAMARA, Malvin (M)** **29 2**
H: 5 11 W: 13 07 b.London 17-11-83
*Source:* Scholar.

| | | | | | |
|---|---|---|---|---|---|
| 2002–03 | Wimbledon | 2 | 0 | | |
| 2003–04 | Wimbledon | 27 | 2 | 29 | 2 |

**LEWINGTON, Dean (M)** **29 1**
H: 5 11 W: 11 02 b.London 18-5-84
*Source:* Scholar.

| | | | | | |
|---|---|---|---|---|---|
| 2002–03 | Wimbledon | 1 | 0 | | |
| 2003–04 | Wimbledon | 28 | 1 | 29 | 1 |

**MACKIE, Jamie (F)** **13 0**
H: 5 8 W: 11 02 b.London 22-9-85
*Source:* Leatherhead.

| | | | | | |
|---|---|---|---|---|---|
| 2003–04 | Wimbledon | 13 | 0 | 13 | 0 |

**MARTIN, David (G)** **2 0**
H: 6 1 W: 13 07 b.Romford 22-1-86
*Source:* Scholar. *Honours:* England Youth.

| | | | | | |
|---|---|---|---|---|---|
| 2003–04 | Wimbledon | 2 | 0 | 2 | 0 |

**McDONALD, Scott‡ (F)** **27 2**
H: 5 7 W: 12 07 b.Dandenorg 21-8-83
*Honours:* Australia Youth, Under-20, Under-23.

| | | | | | |
|---|---|---|---|---|---|
| 1998–99 | Eastern Pride | 3 | 0 | 3 | 0 |
| 1999–2000 | Southampton | 0 | 0 | | |
| 2000–01 | Southampton | 0 | 0 | | |
| 2001–02 | Southampton | 2 | 0 | | |
| 2002–03 | Southampton | 0 | 0 | 2 | 0 |
| 2002–03 | *Huddersfield T* | 13 | 1 | 13 | 1 |
| 2002–03 | Bournemouth | 7 | 1 | 7 | 1 |
| 2003–04 | Wimbledon | 2 | 0 | 2 | 0 |

**McKOY, Nick§ (M)** **3 0**
H: 6 0 W: 12 04 b.Newham 3-9-86

| | | | | | |
|---|---|---|---|---|---|
| 2003–04 | Wimbledon | 3 | 0 | 3 | 0 |

**MORGAN, Lionel‡ (F)** **30 2**
H: 6 0 W: 12 03 b.Tottenham 17-2-83
*Source:* Scholar. *Honours:* England Youth, Under-20.

| | | | | | |
|---|---|---|---|---|---|
| 2000–01 | Wimbledon | 5 | 0 | | |
| 2001–02 | Wimbledon | 11 | 1 | | |
| 2002–03 | Wimbledon | 11 | 1 | | |
| 2003–04 | Wimbledon | 3 | 0 | 30 | 2 |

**MOUTER, Ryan‡ (M)** **0 0**
H: 5 11 W: 11 01 b.Sunderland 2-7-85
*Source:* Redheugh BC.

| | | | | | |
|---|---|---|---|---|---|
| 2002–03 | Wimbledon | 0 | 0 | | |
| 2003–04 | Wimbledon | 0 | 0 | | |

**NTIMBAN-ZEH, Harry† (D)** **10 0**
H: 6 1 W: 12 07 b.France 26-9-73
*Source:* SC Espinho.

| | | | | | |
|---|---|---|---|---|---|
| 2003–04 | Wimbledon | 10 | 0 | 10 | 0 |

**OYEDELE, Shola§ (D)** **9 0**
H: 5 11 W: 12 07 b.Kano 14-9-84
*Source:* Scholar.

| | | | | | |
|---|---|---|---|---|---|
| 2003–04 | Wimbledon | 9 | 0 | 9 | 0 |

**PUNCHEON, Jason§ (D)** **8 0**
H: 5 8 W: 12 00 b.Croydon 26-6-86
*Source:* Scholar.

| | | | | | |
|---|---|---|---|---|---|
| 2003–04 | Wimbledon | 8 | 0 | 8 | 0 |

**SMALL, Wade (M)** **27 1**
H: 5 7 W: 11 07 b.Croydon 23-2-84
*Source:* Scholar.

| | | | | | |
|---|---|---|---|---|---|
| 2003–04 | Wimbledon | 27 | 1 | 27 | 1 |

**TAPP, Alex (M)** **38 3**
H: 5 8 W: 10 13 b.Redhill 7-6-82
*Source:* Trainee.

| | | | | | |
|---|---|---|---|---|---|
| 1999–2000 | Wimbledon | 0 | 0 | | |
| 2000–01 | Wimbledon | 0 | 0 | | |
| 2001–02 | Wimbledon | 0 | 0 | | |
| 2002–03 | Wimbledon | 24 | 2 | | |
| 2003–04 | Wimbledon | 14 | 1 | 38 | 3 |

**WILLIAMS, Mark# (D)** **384 24**
H: 6 0 W: 13 00 b.Stalybridge 28-9-70
*Source:* Newtown. *Honours:* Northern Ireland B, 30 full caps, 1 goal.

| | | | | | |
|---|---|---|---|---|---|
| 1991–92 | Shrewsbury T | 3 | 0 | | |
| 1992–93 | Shrewsbury T | 28 | 1 | | |
| 1993–94 | Shrewsbury T | 36 | 1 | | |
| 1994–95 | Shrewsbury T | 35 | 1 | 102 | 3 |
| 1995–96 | Chesterfield | 42 | 3 | | |
| 1996–97 | Chesterfield | 42 | 3 | | |
| 1997–98 | Chesterfield | 44 | 3 | | |
| 1998–99 | Chesterfield | 40 | 3 | 168 | 12 |
| 1999–2000 | Watford | 22 | 1 | 22 | 1 |
| 2000–01 | Wimbledon | 42 | 6 | | |
| 2001–02 | Wimbledon | 5 | 0 | | |
| 2002–03 | Wimbledon | 23 | 1 | | |
| 2002–03 | Stoke C | 6 | 0 | 6 | 0 |
| 2003 | Columbus Crew | 5 | 0 | 5 | 0 |
| 2003–04 | Wimbledon | 11 | 1 | 81 | 8 |

**WORGAN, Lee* (G)** **5 0**
H: 6 1 W: 13 10 b.Eastbourne 1-12-83
*Source:* Scholar. *Honours:* Wales Youth.

| | | | | | |
|---|---|---|---|---|---|
| 2003–04 | Wimbledon | 3 | 0 | 3 | 0 |
| 2003–04 | *Wycombe W* | 2 | 0 | 2 | 0 |

**Scholars**
Ahmed, Shahed; Boyce, Jerome; Carter, Thomas R; Crooks, Leon E G; Deacons, James T; Drake, James P D; E'Beyer, Mark E; Emery, Charles W; Ewart, Craig A; Holmes, Antony I; Jerwood, Ryan; Makofo, Serge; McKoy, Nicholas P; Morgan, Daniel F; Oyedele, Shola; Puncheon, Jason D I; Slater, Jamie R

**Non Contract**
Ntimban-Zeh, Harry D

## WOLVERHAMPTON W (88)

**ANDREWS, Keith (M)** **75 3**
H: 6 0 W: 13 05 b.Dublin 13-9-80
*Source:* Trainee.

| | | | | | |
|---|---|---|---|---|---|
| 1997–98 | Wolverhampton W | 0 | 0 | | |
| 1998–99 | Wolverhampton W | 0 | 0 | | |
| 1999–2000 | Wolverhampton W | 2 | 0 | | |
| 2000–01 | Wolverhampton W | 22 | 0 | | |
| 2000–01 | *Oxford U* | 4 | 1 | 4 | 1 |
| 2001–02 | Wolverhampton W | 11 | 0 | | |
| 2002–03 | Wolverhampton W | 9 | 0 | | |
| 2003–04 | Wolverhampton W | 1 | 0 | 45 | 0 |
| 2003–04 | *Stoke C* | 16 | 0 | 16 | 0 |
| 2003–04 | *Walsall* | 10 | 2 | 10 | 2 |

**BLAKE, Nathan* (F)** **436 144**
H: 5 11 W: 13 12 b.Cardiff 27-1-72
*Source:* Chelsea Trainee. *Honours:* Wales Youth, B, Under-21, 29 full caps, 4 goals.

| | | | | | |
|---|---|---|---|---|---|
| 1989–90 | Cardiff C | 6 | 0 | | |
| 1990–91 | Cardiff C | 40 | 4 | | |
| 1991–92 | Cardiff C | 31 | 6 | | |
| 1992–93 | Cardiff C | 34 | 11 | | |
| 1993–94 | Cardiff C | 20 | 14 | 131 | 35 |
| 1993–94 | Sheffield U | 12 | 5 | | |
| 1994–95 | Sheffield U | 35 | 17 | | |
| 1995–96 | Sheffield U | 22 | 12 | 69 | 34 |
| 1995–96 | Bolton W | 18 | 1 | | |
| 1996–97 | Bolton W | 42 | 19 | | |
| 1997–98 | Bolton W | 35 | 12 | | |
| 1998–99 | Bolton W | 12 | 6 | 107 | 38 |
| 1998–99 | Blackburn R | 11 | 3 | | |
| 1999–2000 | Blackburn R | 28 | 3 | | |
| 2000–01 | Blackburn R | 12 | 6 | | |
| 2001–02 | Blackburn R | 3 | 1 | 54 | 13 |
| 2001–02 | Wolverhampton W | 39 | 11 | | |
| 2002–03 | Wolverhampton W | 23 | 12 | | |
| 2003–04 | Wolverhampton W | 13 | 1 | 75 | 24 |

**BONNAR, Thomas (M)** **0 0**
b.Letterkenny 20-10-85
*Source:* Scholar.

| | | | | | |
|---|---|---|---|---|---|
| 2003–04 | Wolverhampton W | 0 | 0 | | |

**BUTLER, Paul* (D)** **445 20**
H: 6 0 W: 14 09 b.Manchester 2-11-72
*Source:* Trainee. *Honours:* Eire 1 full cap.

| | | | | | |
|---|---|---|---|---|---|
| 1990–91 | Rochdale | 2 | 0 | | |
| 1991–92 | Rochdale | 25 | 0 | | |
| 1992–93 | Rochdale | 16 | 2 | | |
| 1993–94 | Rochdale | 38 | 2 | | |
| 1994–95 | Rochdale | 39 | 3 | | |
| 1995–96 | Rochdale | 38 | 3 | 158 | 10 |
| 1996–97 | Bury | 41 | 2 | | |
| 1997–98 | Bury | 43 | 2 | 84 | 4 |
| 1998–99 | Sunderland | 44 | 2 | | |
| 1999–2000 | Sunderland | 32 | 1 | | |
| 2000–01 | Sunderland | 3 | 0 | 79 | 3 |
| 2000–01 | Wolverhampton W | 12 | 0 | | |
| 2001–02 | Wolverhampton W | 43 | 1 | | |
| 2002–03 | Wolverhampton W | 32 | 1 | | |
| 2003–04 | Wolverhampton W | 37 | 1 | 124 | 3 |

**CAMARA, Henri (F)** **132 49**
H: 5 9 W: 10 08 b.Dakar 10-5-77
*Honours:* Senegal full caps.

| | | | | | |
|---|---|---|---|---|---|
| 1999–2000 | Neuchatel Xamax | 20 | 12 | | |
| 2000–01 | Neuchatel Xamax | 12 | 5 | 32 | 17 |
| 2000–01 | Grasshoppers | 11 | 3 | 11 | 3 |
| 2001–02 | Sedan | 25 | 8 | | |
| 2002–03 | Sedan | 34 | 14 | 59 | 22 |
| 2003–04 | Wolverhampton W | 30 | 7 | 30 | 7 |

**CAMERON, Colin (M)** **381 84**
H: 5 8 W: 11 00 b.Kirkcaldy 23-10-72
*Source:* Lochore Welfare. *Honours:* Scotland B, 26 full caps, 2 goals.

| | | | | | |
|---|---|---|---|---|---|
| 1990–91 | Raith R | 0 | 0 | | |
| 1991–92 | *Sligo R* | 0 | 0 | | |
| 1992–93 | Raith R | 16 | 1 | | |
| 1993–94 | Raith R | 41 | 6 | | |
| 1994–95 | Raith R | 35 | 7 | | |
| 1995–96 | Raith R | 30 | 9 | 122 | 23 |
| 1995–96 | Hearts | 4 | 2 | | |
| 1996–97 | Hearts | 36 | 7 | | |
| 1997–98 | Hearts | 31 | 8 | | |

| | | | | | |
|---|---|---|---|---|---|
| 1998–99 | Hearts | 11 | 6 | | |
| 1999–2000 | Hearts | 32 | 8 | | |
| 2000–01 | Hearts | 37 | 12 | | |
| 2001–02 | Hearts | 4 | 3 | **155** | **46** |
| 2001–02 | Wolverhampton W | 41 | 4 | | |
| 2002–03 | Wolverhampton W | 33 | 7 | | |
| 2003–04 | Wolverhampton W | 30 | 4 | **104** | **15** |

**CLARKE, Leon (F)** **4** **0**
H: 6 2 W: 14 02 b.Birmingham 10-2-85
*Source:* Scholar.

| | | | | | |
|---|---|---|---|---|---|
| 2003–04 | Wolverhampton W | 0 | 0 | | |
| 2003–04 | *Kidderminster H* | 4 | 0 | **4** | **0** |

**CLINGAN, Sammy (M)** **0** **0**
H: 5 11 W: 11 06 b.Belfast 13-1-84
*Source:* Scholar. *Honours:* Northern Ireland Under-21.

| | | | | | |
|---|---|---|---|---|---|
| 2001–02 | Wolverhampton W | 0 | 0 | | |
| 2002–03 | Wolverhampton W | 0 | 0 | | |
| 2003–04 | Wolverhampton W | 0 | 0 | | |

**CLYDE, Mark (D)** **30** **0**
H: 6 2 W: 12 04 b.Limavady 27-12-82
*Source:* Scholar. *Honours:* Northern Ireland Under-21.

| | | | | | |
|---|---|---|---|---|---|
| 2001–02 | Wolverhampton W | 0 | 0 | | |
| 2002–03 | Wolverhampton W | 17 | 0 | | |
| 2002–03 | *Kidderminster H* | 4 | 0 | **4** | **0** |
| 2003–04 | Wolverhampton W | 9 | 0 | **26** | **0** |

**COOPER, Kevin (M)** **264** **37**
H: 5 8 W: 10 04 b.Derby 8-2-75
*Source:* Trainee.

| | | | | | |
|---|---|---|---|---|---|
| 1993–94 | Derby Co | 0 | 0 | | |
| 1994–95 | Derby Co | 1 | 0 | | |
| 1995–96 | Derby Co | 1 | 0 | | |
| 1996–97 | Derby Co | 0 | 0 | **2** | **0** |
| 1996–97 | *Stockport Co* | 12 | 3 | | |
| 1997–98 | Stockport Co | 38 | 8 | | |
| 1998–99 | Stockport Co | 38 | 1 | | |
| 1999–2000 | Stockport Co | 46 | 4 | | |
| 2000–01 | Stockport Co | 34 | 5 | **168** | **21** |
| 2000–01 | Wimbledon | 11 | 3 | | |
| 2001–02 | Wimbledon | 40 | 10 | **51** | **13** |
| 2001–02 | Wolverhampton W | 5 | 0 | | |
| 2002–03 | Wolverhampton W | 26 | 3 | | |
| 2003–04 | Wolverhampton W | 1 | 0 | **32** | **3** |
| 2003–04 | *Sunderland* | 1 | 0 | **1** | **0** |
| 2003–04 | *Norwich C* | 10 | 0 | **10** | **0** |

**CORT, Carl (F)** **117** **29**
H: 6 4 W: 12 07 b.Southwark 1-11-77
*Source:* Trainee. *Honours:* England Under-21.

| | | | | | |
|---|---|---|---|---|---|
| 1996–97 | Wimbledon | 1 | 0 | | |
| 1996–97 | *Lincoln C* | 6 | 1 | **6** | **1** |
| 1997–98 | Wimbledon | 22 | 4 | | |
| 1998–99 | Wimbledon | 16 | 3 | | |
| 1999–2000 | Wimbledon | 34 | 9 | **73** | **16** |
| 2000–01 | Newcastle U | 13 | 6 | | |
| 2001–02 | Newcastle U | 8 | 1 | | |
| 2002–03 | Newcastle U | 1 | 0 | | |
| 2003–04 | Newcastle U | 0 | 0 | **22** | **7** |
| 2003–04 | Wolverhampton W | 16 | 5 | **16** | **5** |

**CRADDOCK, Jody (D)** **333** **7**
H: 6 2 W: 12 00 b.Bromsgrove 25-7-75
*Source:* Christchurch.

| | | | | | |
|---|---|---|---|---|---|
| 1993–94 | Cambridge U | 20 | 0 | | |
| 1994–95 | Cambridge U | 38 | 0 | | |
| 1995–96 | Cambridge U | 46 | 3 | | |
| 1996–97 | Cambridge U | 41 | 1 | **145** | **4** |
| 1997–98 | Sunderland | 32 | 0 | | |
| 1998–99 | Sunderland | 6 | 0 | | |
| 1999–2000 | Sunderland | 19 | 0 | | |
| 1999–2000 | *Sheffield U* | 10 | 0 | **10** | **0** |
| 2000–01 | Sunderland | 34 | 0 | | |
| 2001–02 | Sunderland | 30 | 1 | | |
| 2002–03 | Sunderland | 25 | 1 | **146** | **2** |
| 2003–04 | Wolverhampton W | 32 | 1 | **32** | **1** |

**FLYNN, Patrick (M)** **0** **0**
b.Dublin 13-1-85
*Source:* Scholar.

| | | | | | |
|---|---|---|---|---|---|
| 2002–03 | Wolverhampton W | 0 | 0 | | |
| 2003–04 | Wolverhampton W | 0 | 0 | | |

**GANEA, Viorel* (F)** **267** **79**
H: 5 10 W: 12 06 b.Fagaras 10-8-73
*Honours:* Romania 44 full caps 18 goals.

| | | | | | |
|---|---|---|---|---|---|
| 1994–95 | Brasov | 30 | 0 | | |
| 1995–96 | Brasov | 20 | 4 | **50** | **4** |
| 1995–96 | Uni Craiova | 17 | 5 | | |
| 1996–97 | Uni Craiova | 19 | 6 | | |
| 1997–98 | Uni Craiova | 26 | 11 | **62** | **22** |
| 1998–99 | Rapid Bucharest | 16 | 11 | **16** | **11** |
| 1999–2000 | Stuttgart | 29 | 7 | | |
| 2000–01 | Stuttgart | 32 | 8 | | |
| 2001–02 | Stuttgart | 23 | 10 | | |
| 2002–03 | Stuttgart | 23 | 9 | **107** | **34** |
| 2003–04 | Bursa | 16 | 5 | **16** | **5** |
| 2003–04 | Wolverhampton W | 16 | 3 | **16** | **3** |

**GOBERN, Lewis (M)** **0** **0**
b.Birmingham 28-1-85
*Source:* Scholar.

| | | | | | |
|---|---|---|---|---|---|
| 2003–04 | Wolverhampton W | 0 | 0 | | |

**GUDJONSSON, Joey‡ (M)** **88** **11**
H: 5 8 W: 11 05 b.Akranes 25-5-80
*Honours:* Iceland 15 full caps, 1 goal.

| | | | | | |
|---|---|---|---|---|---|
| 1998–99 | Genk | 5 | 0 | **5** | **0** |
| 1999–2000 | MVV | 19 | 5 | **19** | **5** |
| 2000–01 | RKC | 31 | 4 | **31** | **4** |
| 2001–02 | Betis | 11 | 0 | **11** | **0** |
| 2002–03 | Aston Villa | 11 | 2 | **11** | **2** |
| 2003–04 | Wolverhampton W | 11 | 0 | **11** | **0** |

**INCE, Paul* (M)** **559** **65**
H: 5 10 W: 12 04 b.Ilford 21-10-67
*Source:* Trainee. *Honours:* England Youth, Under-21, B, 53 full caps, 2 goals.

| | | | | | |
|---|---|---|---|---|---|
| 1985–86 | West Ham U | 0 | 0 | | |
| 1986–87 | West Ham U | 10 | 1 | | |
| 1987–88 | West Ham U | 28 | 3 | | |
| 1988–89 | West Ham U | 33 | 3 | | |
| 1989–90 | West Ham U | 1 | 0 | **72** | **7** |
| 1989–90 | Manchester U | 26 | 0 | | |
| 1990–91 | Manchester U | 31 | 3 | | |
| 1991–92 | Manchester U | 33 | 3 | | |
| 1992–93 | Manchester U | 41 | 5 | | |
| 1993–94 | Manchester U | 39 | 8 | | |
| 1994–95 | Manchester U | 36 | 5 | **206** | **24** |
| 1995–96 | Internazionale | 30 | 3 | | |
| 1996–97 | Internazionale | 24 | 6 | **54** | **9** |
| 1997–98 | Liverpool | 31 | 8 | | |
| 1998–99 | Liverpool | 34 | 6 | **65** | **14** |
| 1999–2000 | Middlesbrough | 32 | 3 | | |
| 2000–01 | Middlesbrough | 30 | 2 | | |
| 2001–02 | Middlesbrough | 31 | 2 | **93** | **7** |
| 2002–03 | Wolverhampton W | 37 | 2 | | |
| 2003–04 | Wolverhampton W | 32 | 2 | **69** | **4** |

**IRWIN, Denis* (D)** **682** **29**
H: 5 8 W: 10 10 b.Cork 31-10-65
*Source:* Apprentice. *Honours:* Eire Schools, Youth, Under-21, B, 56 full caps, 4 goals.

| | | | | | |
|---|---|---|---|---|---|
| 1983–84 | Leeds U | 12 | 0 | | |
| 1984–85 | Leeds U | 41 | 1 | | |
| 1985–86 | Leeds U | 19 | 0 | **72** | **1** |
| 1986–87 | Oldham Ath | 41 | 1 | | |
| 1987–88 | Oldham Ath | 43 | 0 | | |
| 1988–89 | Oldham Ath | 41 | 2 | | |
| 1989–90 | Oldham Ath | 42 | 1 | **167** | **4** |
| 1990–91 | Manchester U | 34 | 0 | | |
| 1991–92 | Manchester U | 38 | 4 | | |
| 1992–93 | Manchester U | 40 | 5 | | |
| 1993–94 | Manchester U | 42 | 2 | | |
| 1994–95 | Manchester U | 40 | 2 | | |
| 1995–96 | Manchester U | 31 | 1 | | |
| 1996–97 | Manchester U | 31 | 1 | | |
| 1997–98 | Manchester U | 25 | 2 | | |
| 1998–99 | Manchester U | 29 | 2 | | |
| 1999–2000 | Manchester U | 25 | 3 | | |
| 2000–01 | Manchester U | 21 | 0 | | |
| 2001–02 | Manchester U | 12 | 0 | **368** | **22** |
| 2002–03 | Wolverhampton W | 43 | 2 | | |
| 2003–04 | Wolverhampton W | 32 | 0 | **75** | **2** |

**IVERSEN, Steffen* (F)** **184** **49**
H: 6 1 W: 12 07 b.Oslo 10-11-76
*Honours:* Norway 45 full caps, 9 goals.

| | | | | | |
|---|---|---|---|---|---|
| 1996 | Rosenborg | 25 | 10 | **25** | **10** |
| 1996–97 | Tottenham H | 16 | 6 | | |
| 1997–98 | Tottenham H | 13 | 0 | | |
| 1998–99 | Tottenham H | 27 | 8 | | |
| 1999–2000 | Tottenham H | 36 | 14 | | |
| 2000–01 | Tottenham H | 14 | 2 | | |
| 2001–02 | Tottenham H | 18 | 4 | | |
| 2002–03 | Tottenham H | 19 | 1 | **143** | **35** |
| 2003–04 | Wolverhampton W | 16 | 4 | **16** | **4** |

**JONES, Jimmi‡ (M)** **0** **0**
b.Wolverhampton 11-11-83
*Source:* Scholar.

| | | | | | |
|---|---|---|---|---|---|
| 2002–03 | Wolverhampton W | 0 | 0 | | |
| 2003–04 | Wolverhampton W | 0 | 0 | | |

**JONES, Paul (G)** **290** **0**
H: 6 3 W: 15 02 b.Chirk 18-4-67
*Source:* Bridgnorth, Kidderminster H.
*Honours:* Wales 38 full caps.

| | | | | | |
|---|---|---|---|---|---|
| 1991–92 | Wolverhampton W | 0 | 0 | | |
| 1992–93 | Wolverhampton W | 16 | 0 | | |
| 1993–94 | Wolverhampton W | 0 | 0 | | |
| 1994–95 | Wolverhampton W | 9 | 0 | | |
| 1995–96 | Wolverhampton W | 8 | 0 | | |
| 1996–97 | Stockport Co | 46 | 0 | **46** | **0** |
| 1997–98 | Southampton | 38 | 0 | | |
| 1998–99 | Southampton | 31 | 0 | | |
| 1999–2000 | Southampton | 31 | 0 | | |
| 2000–01 | Southampton | 35 | 0 | | |
| 2001–02 | Southampton | 36 | 0 | | |
| 2002–03 | Southampton | 14 | 0 | | |
| 2003–04 | Southampton | 8 | 0 | **193** | **0** |
| 2003–04 | *Liverpool* | 2 | 0 | **2** | **0** |
| 2003–04 | Wolverhampton W | 16 | 0 | **49** | **0** |

**KENNEDY, Mark (M)** **251** **29**
H: 5 11 W: 11 09 b.Dublin 15-5-76
*Source:* Belvedere, Trainee. *Honours:* Eire Under-21, 34 full caps, 3 goals.

| | | | | | |
|---|---|---|---|---|---|
| 1992–93 | Millwall | 1 | 0 | | |
| 1993–94 | Millwall | 12 | 4 | | |
| 1994–95 | Millwall | 30 | 5 | **43** | **9** |
| 1994–95 | Liverpool | 6 | 0 | | |
| 1995–96 | Liverpool | 4 | 0 | | |
| 1996–97 | Liverpool | 5 | 0 | | |
| 1997–98 | Liverpool | 1 | 0 | **16** | **0** |
| 1997–98 | *QPR* | 8 | 2 | **8** | **2** |
| 1997–98 | Wimbledon | 4 | 0 | | |
| 1998–99 | Wimbledon | 17 | 0 | **21** | **0** |
| 1999–2000 | Manchester C | 41 | 8 | | |
| 2000–01 | Manchester C | 25 | 0 | **66** | **8** |
| 2001–02 | Wolverhampton W | 35 | 5 | | |
| 2002–03 | Wolverhampton W | 31 | 3 | | |
| 2003–04 | Wolverhampton W | 31 | 2 | **97** | **10** |

**LESCOTT, Jolean (D)** **125** **8**
H: 6 2 W: 14 00 b.Birmingham 16-8-82
*Source:* Trainee. *Honours:* England Youth, Under-20, Under-21.

| | | | | | |
|---|---|---|---|---|---|
| 1999–2000 | Wolverhampton W | 0 | 0 | | |
| 2000–01 | Wolverhampton W | 37 | 2 | | |
| 2001–02 | Wolverhampton W | 44 | 5 | | |
| 2002–03 | Wolverhampton W | 44 | 1 | | |
| 2003–04 | Wolverhampton W | 0 | 0 | **125** | **8** |

**LUZHNY, Oleg* (D)** **321** **11**
H: 5 10 W: 12 01 b.Ukraine 5-8-68
*Honours:* USSR 8 full caps, Ukraine 52 full caps.

| | | | | | |
|---|---|---|---|---|---|
| 1989 | Dynamo Kiev | 27 | 0 | | |
| 1990 | Dynamo Kiev | 12 | 0 | | |
| 1991 | Dynamo Kiev | 28 | 0 | | |
| 1992–93 | Dynamo Kiev | 26 | 3 | | |
| 1993–94 | Dynamo Kiev | 34 | 1 | | |
| 1994–95 | Dynamo Kiev | 24 | 4 | | |
| 1995–96 | Dynamo Kiev | 24 | 1 | | |
| 1996–97 | Dynamo Kiev | 28 | 2 | | |
| 1997–98 | Dynamo Kiev | 16 | 0 | | |
| 1998–99 | Dynamo Kiev | 21 | 0 | **240** | **11** |
| 1999–2000 | Arsenal | 21 | 0 | | |
| 2000–01 | Arsenal | 19 | 0 | | |
| 2001–02 | Arsenal | 18 | 0 | | |
| 2002–03 | Arsenal | 17 | 0 | **75** | **0** |
| 2003–04 | Wolverhampton W | 6 | 0 | **6** | **0** |

**McGRANE, Ian‡ (M)** **0** **0**
H: 5 10 W: 12 00 b.Dublin 4-8-84
*Source:* Scholar.

| | | | | | |
|---|---|---|---|---|---|
| 2001–02 | Wolverhampton W | 0 | 0 | | |
| 2002–03 | Wolverhampton W | 0 | 0 | | |
| 2003–04 | Wolverhampton W | 0 | 0 | | |

**MELLIGAN, John (M)** **65** **13**
H: 5 9 W: 11 02 b.Dublin 11-2-82
*Source:* Trainee. *Honours:* Eire Under-21.

| | | | | | |
|---|---|---|---|---|---|
| 2000–01 | Wolverhampton W | 0 | 0 | | |
| 2001–02 | Wolverhampton W | 0 | 0 | | |
| 2001–02 | *Bournemouth* | 8 | 0 | **8** | **0** |
| 2002–03 | Wolverhampton W | 2 | 0 | | |
| 2002–03 | *Kidderminster H* | 29 | 10 | | |
| 2003–04 | Wolverhampton W | 0 | 0 | **2** | **0** |
| 2003–04 | *Kidderminster H* | 5 | 1 | **34** | **11** |
| 2003–04 | *Doncaster R* | 21 | 2 | **21** | **2** |

**MILLER, Kenny (F)** **163** **43**
H: 5 10 W: 11 04 b.Edinburgh 23-12-79
*Source:* Hutchison Vale. *Honours:* Scotland Under-21, 12 full caps, 2 goals.

| | | | | | |
|---|---|---|---|---|---|
| 1996–97 | Hibernian | 0 | 0 | | |

1997–98 Hibernian 7 0
1998–99 Hibernian 7 1
1999–2000 Hibernian 31 11 **45 12**
2000–01 Rangers 27 8
2001–02 Rangers 3 0 **30 8**
2001–02 Wolverhampton W 20 2
2002–03 Wolverhampton W 43 19
2003–04 Wolverhampton W 25 2 **88 23**

**MULLIGAN, Gary (M) 0 0**
b.Dublin 23-4-85
*Source:* Scholar.
2002–03 Wolverhampton W 0 0
2003–04 Wolverhampton W 0 0

**MURRAY, Matt (G) 41 0**
H: 6 4 W: 13 10 b.Solihull 2-5-81
*Source:* Trainee. *Honours:* England Youth, Under-21.
1997–98 Wolverhampton W 0 0
1998–99 Wolverhampton W 0 0
1999–2000 Wolverhampton W 0 0
2000–01 Wolverhampton W 0 0
2001–02 Wolverhampton W 0 0
2002–03 Wolverhampton W 40 0
2003–04 Wolverhampton W 1 0 **41 0**

**NAYLOR, Lee (D) 212 5**
H: 5 10 W: 12 00 b.Bloxwich 19-3-80
*Source:* Trainee. *Honours:* England Youth, Under-21.
1997–98 Wolverhampton W 16 0
1998–99 Wolverhampton W 23 1
1999–2000 Wolverhampton W 30 2
2000–01 Wolverhampton W 46 1
2001–02 Wolverhampton W 27 0
2002–03 Wolverhampton W 32 1
2003–04 Wolverhampton W 38 0 **212 5**

**NDAH, George* (F) 234 38**
H: 6 1 W: 12 06 b.Dulwich 23-12-74
*Source:* Trainee.
1992–93 Crystal Palace 13 0
1993–94 Crystal Palace 1 0
1994–95 Crystal Palace 12 1
1995–96 Crystal Palace 23 4
1995–96 *Bournemouth* 12 2 **12 2**
1996–97 Crystal Palace 26 3
1997–98 Crystal Palace 3 0 **78 8**
1997–98 *Gillingham* 4 0 **4 0**
1997–98 Swindon T 14 2
1998–99 Swindon T 41 11
1999–2000 Swindon T 12 1 **67 14**
1999–2000 Wolverhampton W 4 0
2000–01 Wolverhampton W 29 6
2001–02 Wolverhampton W 15 1
2002–03 Wolverhampton W 25 7
2003–04 Wolverhampton W 0 0 **73 14**

**NEWTON, Shaun (M) 346 31**
H: 5 8 W: 11 00 b.Camberwell 20-8-75
*Source:* Trainee. *Honours:* England Under-21.
1992–93 Charlton Ath 2 0
1993–94 Charlton Ath 19 2
1994–95 Charlton Ath 26 0
1995–96 Charlton Ath 41 5
1996–97 Charlton Ath 43 3
1997–98 Charlton Ath 41 5
1998–99 Charlton Ath 16 0
1999–2000 Charlton Ath 42 5
2000–01 Charlton Ath 10 0 **240 20**
2001–02 Wolverhampton W 45 8
2002–03 Wolverhampton W 33 3
2003–04 Wolverhampton W 28 0 **106 11**

**O'CONNOR, Kevin (M) 0 0**
b.Dublin 19-10-85
*Source:* Scholar. *Honours:* Eire Under-21.
2003–04 Wolverhampton W 0 0

**OAKES, Michael (G) 199 0**
H: 6 2 W: 14 00 b.Northwich 30-10-73
*Source:* Trainee. *Honours:* England Under-21.
1991–92 Aston Villa 0 0
1992–93 Aston Villa 0 0
1993–94 Aston Villa 0 0
1993–94 *Scarborough* 1 0 **1 0**
1993–94 *Tranmere R* 0 0
1994–95 Aston Villa 0 0
1995–96 Aston Villa 0 0
1996–97 Aston Villa 20 0
1997–98 Aston Villa 8 0
1998–99 Aston Villa 23 0
1999–2000 Aston Villa 0 0 **51 0**
1999–2000 Wolverhampton W 28 0
2000–01 Wolverhampton W 46 0
2001–02 Wolverhampton W 46 0
2002–03 Wolverhampton W 6 0
2003–04 Wolverhampton W 21 0 **147 0**

**OKORONKWO, Isaac* (D) 7 0**
H: 6 0 W: 11 09 b.Nbene 1-5-78
*Honours:* Nigeria full caps.
2003–04 Wolverhampton W 7 0 **7 0**

**RAE, Alex* (M) 522 110**
H: 5 10 W: 11 09 b.Glasgow 30-9-69
*Source:* Bishopbriggs. *Honours:* Scotland Under-21, B.
1987–88 Falkirk 12 0
1988–89 Falkirk 37 12
1989–90 Falkirk 34 8 **83 20**
1990–91 Millwall 39 10
1991–92 Millwall 38 11
1992–93 Millwall 30 6
1993–94 Millwall 36 13
1994–95 Millwall 38 10
1995–96 Millwall 37 13 **218 63**
1996–97 Sunderland 23 2
1997–98 Sunderland 29 3
1998–99 Sunderland 15 2
1999–2000 Sunderland 26 3
2000–01 Sunderland 18 2
2001–02 Sunderland 3 0 **114 12**
2001–02 Wolverhampton W 36 7
2002–03 Wolverhampton W 38 3
2003–04 Wolverhampton W 33 5 **107 15**

**SILAS, Jorge (M) 73 13**
H: 5 9 W: 11 03 b.Lisbon 1-9-76
*Honours:* Portugal 3 full caps.
2001–02 Uniao Leiria 32 5
2002–03 Uniao Leiria 32 8 **64 13**
2003–04 Wolverhampton W 9 0 **9 0**

**STURRIDGE, Dean (F) 297 94**
H: 5 8 W: 12 02 b.Birmingham 27-7-73
*Source:* Trainee.
1991–92 Derby Co 1 0
1992–93 Derby Co 10 0
1993–94 Derby Co 0 0
1994–95 Derby Co 12 1
1994–95 *Torquay U* 10 5 **10 5**
1995–96 Derby Co 39 20
1996–97 Derby Co 30 11
1997–98 Derby Co 30 9
1998–99 Derby Co 29 5
1999–2000 Derby Co 25 6
2000–01 Derby Co 14 1 **190 53**
2000–01 Leicester C 13 3
2001–02 Leicester C 9 3 **22 6**
2001–02 Wolverhampton W 27 20
2002–03 Wolverhampton W 39 10
2003–04 Wolverhampton W 5 0 **71 30**
2003–04 *Sheffield U* 4 0 **4 0**

**WALTERS, Marlon‡ (D) 0 0**
b.Birmingham 24-12-83
*Source:* Scholar.
2003–04 Wolverhampton W 0 0

**Scholars**
Cornes, Christopher; Hennessey, Wayne R; Ikeme, Carl; Jones, Daniel J; Lowe, Keith S; Lyons, Aidan C; Musson, Gareth L; Rafferty, Conor; Riley, Martin J; Stewart, Thomas; Townsend, Michael J; Welsh, Adam K

## WREXHAM (89)

**ARMSTRONG, Chris (F) 373 116**
H: 6 0 W: 13 03 b.Newcastle 19-6-71
*Source:* Llay Welfare. *Honours:* England B.
1988–89 Wrexham 0 0
1989–90 Wrexham 22 3
1990–91 Wrexham 38 10
1991–92 Wrexham 25 4
1992–93 Millwall 3 1 **28 5**
1992–93 Crystal Palace 35 15
1993–94 Crystal Palace 43 22
1994–95 Crystal Palace 40 8 **118 45**
1995–96 Tottenham H 36 15
1996–97 Tottenham H 12 5
1997–98 Tottenham H 19 5
1998–99 Tottenham H 34 7
1999–2000 Tottenham H 31 14
2000–01 Tottenham H 9 2
2001–02 Tottenham H 0 0 **141 48**
2002–03 Bolton W 0 0
2003–04 Wrexham 26 5 **86 18**

**BARRETT, Paul* (M) 120 5**
H: 5 10 W: 11 04 b.Newcastle 13-4-78
*Source:* Trainee.
1996–97 Newcastle U 0 0
1997–98 Newcastle U 0 0
1998–99 Newcastle U 0 0
1998–99 Wrexham 10 0
1999–2000 Wrexham 18 2
2000–01 Wrexham 24 0
2001–02 Wrexham 15 0
2002–03 Wrexham 26 1
2003–04 Wrexham 27 2 **120 5**

**CAREY, Brian# (D) 352 17**
H: 6 3 W: 13 02 b.Cork 31-5-68
*Source:* Cork C. *Honours:* Eire 3 full caps.
1989–90 Manchester U 0 0
1990–91 Manchester U 0 0
1990–91 *Wrexham* 3 0
1991–92 Manchester U 0 0
1991–92 *Wrexham* 13 1
1992–93 Manchester U 0 0
1993–94 Leicester C 27 0
1994–95 Leicester C 12 0
1995–96 Leicester C 19 1 **58 1**
1996–97 Wrexham 38 0
1997–98 Wrexham 43 1
1998–99 Wrexham 36 2
1999–2000 Wrexham 43 1
2000–01 Wrexham 33 3
2001–02 Wrexham 18 2
2002–03 Wrexham 33 4
2003–04 Wrexham 34 2 **294 16**

**CROWELL, Matt (M) 15 1**
H: 5 11 W: 11 00 b.Bridgend 3-7-84
*Source:* Scholar. *Honours:* Wales Under-21.
2001–02 Southampton 0 0
2002–03 Southampton 0 0
2003–04 Wrexham 15 1 **15 1**

**DIBBLE, Andy# (G) 379 0**
H: 6 4 W: 13 07 b.Cwmbran 8-5-65
*Source:* Apprentice. *Honours:* Wales Schools, Youth, Under-21, 3 full caps.
1981–82 Cardiff C 1 0
1982–83 Cardiff C 20 0
1983–84 Cardiff C 41 0 **62 0**
1984–85 Luton T 13 0
1985–86 Luton T 7 0
1985–86 *Sunderland* 12 0 **12 0**
1986–87 Luton T 1 0
1986–87 *Huddersfield T* 5 0 **5 0**
1987–88 Luton T 9 0
1988–89 Manchester C 38 0
1989–90 Manchester C 31 0
1990–91 Manchester C 3 0
1990–91 *Aberdeen* 5 0 **5 0**
1990–91 *Middlesbrough* 19 0
1991–92 Manchester C 2 0
1991–92 *Bolton W* 13 0 **13 0**
1991–92 *WBA* 9 0 **9 0**
1992–93 Manchester C 2 0
1992–93 *Oldham Ath* 0 0
1993–94 Manchester C 11 0
1994–95 Manchester C 15 0
1995–96 Manchester C 0 0
1996–97 Manchester C 13 0 **115 0**
1996–97 Rangers 7 0 **7 0**
1997–98 Luton T 1 0 **31 0**
1997–98 Middlesbrough 2 0
1998–99 Middlesbrough 0 0 **21 0**
From Altrincham
1998–99 Hartlepool U 0 0
1999–2000 Hartlepool U 6 0 **6 0**
1999–2000 *Carlisle U* 2 0 **2 0**
2000–01 Stockport Co 10 0
2001–02 Stockport Co 13 0 **23 0**
2002–03 Wrexham 33 0
2003–04 Wrexham 35 0 **68 0**

**EDWARDS, Carlos (M) 148 22**
H: 5 11 W: 11 01 b.Trinidad 24-10-78
*Honours:* Trinidad & Tobago 31 full caps.
2000–01 Wrexham 36 4
2001–02 Wrexham 26 5

| | | | | | |
|---|---|---|---|---|---|
| 2002–03 | Wrexham | 44 | 8 | | |
| 2003–04 | Wrexham | 42 | 5 | **148** | **22** |

**EDWARDS, Paul# (M)** **99** **4**

H: 5 11 W: 11 02 b.Manchester 1-1-80

*Source:* Altrincham.

| | | | | | |
|---|---|---|---|---|---|
| 2001–02 | Swindon T | 20 | 0 | **20** | **0** |
| 2002–03 | Wrexham | 38 | 4 | | |
| 2003–04 | Wrexham | 41 | 0 | **79** | **4** |

**FERGUSON, Darren (M)** **342** **23**

H: 6 0 W: 11 10 b.Glasgow 9-2-72

*Source:* Trainee. *Honours:* Scotland Youth, Under-21.

| | | | | | |
|---|---|---|---|---|---|
| 1990–91 | Manchester U | 5 | 0 | | |
| 1991–92 | Manchester U | 4 | 0 | | |
| 1992–93 | Manchester U | 15 | 0 | | |
| 1993–94 | Manchester U | 3 | 0 | **27** | **0** |
| 1993–94 | Wolverhampton W | 14 | 0 | | |
| 1994–95 | Wolverhampton W | 24 | 0 | | |
| 1995–96 | Wolverhampton W | 33 | 1 | | |
| 1996–97 | Wolverhampton W | 16 | 3 | | |
| 1997–98 | Wolverhampton W | 26 | 0 | | |
| 1998–99 | Wolverhampton W | 4 | 0 | | |
| 1999–2000 | Wolverhampton W | 0 | 0 | **117** | **4** |
| 1999–2000 | Wrexham | 37 | 4 | | |
| 2000–01 | Wrexham | 43 | 9 | | |
| 2001–02 | Wrexham | 38 | 3 | | |
| 2002–03 | Wrexham | 41 | 2 | | |
| 2003–04 | Wrexham | 39 | 1 | **198** | **19** |

**HOLMES, Shaun* (D)** **83** **2**

H: 5 9 W: 10 07 b.Derry 27-12-80

*Source:* Trainee. *Honours:* Northern Ireland Under-21, 1 full cap.

| | | | | | |
|---|---|---|---|---|---|
| 1997–98 | Manchester C | 0 | 0 | | |
| 1998–99 | Manchester C | 0 | 0 | | |
| 1999–2000 | Manchester C | 0 | 0 | | |
| 2000–01 | Manchester C | 0 | 0 | | |
| 2001–02 | Wrexham | 40 | 0 | | |
| 2002–03 | Wrexham | 30 | 0 | | |
| 2003–04 | Wrexham | 13 | 2 | **83** | **2** |

**JONES, Lee* (F)** **251** **55**

H: 5 8 W: 10 06 b.Wrexham 29-5-73

*Source:* Trainee. *Honours:* Wales Youth, Under-21, B, 2 full caps.

| | | | | | |
|---|---|---|---|---|---|
| 1990–91 | Wrexham | 18 | 5 | | |
| 1991–92 | Wrexham | 21 | 5 | | |
| 1991–92 | Liverpool | 0 | 0 | | |
| 1992–93 | Liverpool | 0 | 0 | | |
| 1993–94 | Liverpool | 0 | 0 | | |
| 1993–94 | *Crewe Alex* | 8 | 1 | **8** | **1** |
| 1994–95 | Liverpool | 1 | 0 | | |
| 1995–96 | Liverpool | 0 | 0 | | |
| 1995–96 | *Wrexham* | 20 | 9 | | |
| 1996–97 | Liverpool | 2 | 0 | **3** | **0** |
| 1996–97 | *Wrexham* | 6 | 0 | | |
| 1996–97 | *Tranmere R* | 8 | 5 | | |
| 1997–98 | Tranmere R | 34 | 9 | | |
| 1998–99 | Tranmere R | 30 | 2 | | |
| 1999–2000 | Tranmere R | 14 | 0 | **86** | **16** |
| 2000–01 | Barnsley | 27 | 5 | | |
| 2001–02 | Barnsley | 13 | 0 | **40** | **5** |
| From Oswestry T | | | | | |
| 2001–02 | Wrexham | 4 | 5 | | |
| 2002–03 | Wrexham | 23 | 4 | | |
| 2003–04 | Wrexham | 22 | 5 | **114** | **33** |

**JONES, Mark (M)** **14** **1**

H: 5 11 W: 10 12 b.Wrexham 15-8-83

*Source:* Scholar. *Honours:* Wales Under-21.

| | | | | | |
|---|---|---|---|---|---|
| 2002–03 | Wrexham | 1 | 0 | | |
| 2003–04 | Wrexham | 13 | 1 | **14** | **1** |

**LAWRENCE, Dennis# (D)** **112** **8**

H: 6 7 W: 11 13 b.Trinidad 1-8-74

*Source:* Defence Force. *Honours:* Trinidad & Tobago 40 full caps.

| | | | | | |
|---|---|---|---|---|---|
| 2000–01 | Wrexham | 3 | 0 | | |
| 2001–02 | Wrexham | 32 | 2 | | |
| 2002–03 | Wrexham | 32 | 1 | | |
| 2003–04 | Wrexham | 45 | 5 | **112** | **8** |

**LLEWELLYN, Chris (M)** **202** **28**

H: 6 0 W: 11 06 b.Merthyr 29-8-79

*Source:* Trainee. *Honours:* Wales Youth, Under-21, B, 4 full caps.

| | | | | | |
|---|---|---|---|---|---|
| 1996–97 | Norwich C | 0 | 0 | | |
| 1997–98 | Norwich C | 15 | 4 | | |
| 1998–99 | Norwich C | 31 | 2 | | |
| 1999–2000 | Norwich C | 36 | 3 | | |
| 2000–01 | Norwich C | 42 | 8 | | |
| 2001–02 | Norwich C | 13 | 0 | | |
| 2002–03 | Norwich C | 5 | 0 | **142** | **17** |
| 2002–03 | *Bristol R* | 14 | 3 | **14** | **3** |
| 2003–04 | Wrexham | 46 | 8 | **46** | **8** |

**MACKIN, Levi§ (M)** **1** **0**

H: 6 1 W: 12 00 b.Chester 4-4-86

*Source:* Scholar.

| | | | | | |
|---|---|---|---|---|---|
| 2003–04 | Wrexham | 1 | 0 | **1** | **0** |

**McNULTY, Jim§ (D)** **0** **0**

H: 6 1 W: 12 00 b.Liverpool 13-2-85

*Source:* Scholar.

| | | | | | |
|---|---|---|---|---|---|
| 2003–04 | Wrexham | 0 | 0 | | |

**MORGAN, Craig (D)** **26** **1**

H: 6 0 W: 11 12 b.St Asaph 18-6-85

*Source:* Scholar.

| | | | | | |
|---|---|---|---|---|---|
| 2001–02 | Wrexham | 2 | 0 | | |
| 2002–03 | Wrexham | 6 | 1 | | |
| 2003–04 | Wrexham | 18 | 0 | **26** | **1** |

**ONE, Armand‡ (F)** **41** **5**

H: 6 4 W: 14 00 b.Paris 15-3-83

*Source:* Nantes.

| | | | | | |
|---|---|---|---|---|---|
| 2001–02 | Cambridge U | 32 | 4 | | |
| 2002–03 | Cambridge U | 0 | 0 | **32** | **4** |
| 2002–03 | *Northampton T* | 6 | 1 | **6** | **1** |
| 2003–04 | Wrexham | 3 | 0 | **3** | **0** |

**PEJIC, Shaun (D)** **61** **0**

H: 6 0 W: 11 07 b.Hereford 16-11-82

*Honours:* Wales Under-21.

| | | | | | |
|---|---|---|---|---|---|
| 2000–01 | Wrexham | 1 | 0 | | |
| 2001–02 | Wrexham | 12 | 0 | | |
| 2002–03 | Wrexham | 27 | 0 | | |
| 2003–04 | Wrexham | 21 | 0 | **61** | **0** |

**ROBERTS, Steve (D)** **116** **3**

H: 6 2 W: 11 06 b.Wrexham 24-2-80

*Source:* Trainee. *Honours:* Wales Youth, Under-21.

| | | | | | |
|---|---|---|---|---|---|
| 1997–98 | Wrexham | 0 | 0 | | |
| 1998–99 | Wrexham | 0 | 0 | | |
| 1999–2000 | Wrexham | 19 | 0 | | |
| 2000–01 | Wrexham | 7 | 0 | | |
| 2001–02 | Wrexham | 24 | 1 | | |
| 2002–03 | Wrexham | 39 | 2 | | |
| 2003–04 | Wrexham | 27 | 0 | **116** | **3** |

**SAM, Hector (F)** **112** **26**

H: 5 9 W: 11 05 b.Trinidad 25-2-78

*Source:* San Juan Jabloteh. *Honours:* Trinidad & Tobago 15 full caps, 1 goal.

| | | | | | |
|---|---|---|---|---|---|
| 2000–01 | Wrexham | 20 | 6 | | |
| 2001–02 | Wrexham | 29 | 5 | | |
| 2002–03 | Wrexham | 26 | 5 | | |
| 2003–04 | Wrexham | 37 | 10 | **112** | **26** |

**SPENDER, Simon§ (D)** **6** **0**

H: 5 11 W: 11 00 b.Mold 15-11-85

*Source:* Scholar. *Honours:* Wales Youth.

| | | | | | |
|---|---|---|---|---|---|
| 2003–04 | Wrexham | 6 | 0 | **6** | **0** |

**THOMAS, Steve* (M)** **115** **7**

H: 5 10 W: 11 07 b.Hartlepool 23-6-79

*Source:* Trainee. *Honours:* Wales Youth, Under-21.

| | | | | | |
|---|---|---|---|---|---|
| 1997–98 | Wrexham | 0 | 0 | | |
| 1998–99 | Wrexham | 4 | 0 | | |
| 1999–2000 | Wrexham | 2 | 0 | | |
| 2000–01 | Wrexham | 6 | 0 | | |
| 2001–02 | Wrexham | 38 | 3 | | |
| 2002–03 | Wrexham | 25 | 2 | | |
| 2003–04 | Wrexham | 40 | 2 | **115** | **7** |

**WHITFIELD, Paul* (G)** **10** **0**

H: 6 0 W: 11 05 b.St Asaph 6-5-82

*Source:* Scholar. *Honours:* wales Under-21.

| | | | | | |
|---|---|---|---|---|---|
| 2001–02 | Wrexham | 0 | 0 | | |
| 2002–03 | Wrexham | 8 | 0 | | |
| 2003–04 | Wrexham | 2 | 0 | **10** | **0** |

**WHITLEY, Jim# (M)** **183** **2**

H: 5 9 W: 10 12 b.Zambia 14-4-75

*Source:* Trainee. *Honours:* Northern Ireland B, 3 full caps.

| | | | | | |
|---|---|---|---|---|---|
| 1993–94 | Manchester C | 0 | 0 | | |
| 1994–95 | Manchester C | 0 | 0 | | |
| 1995–96 | Manchester C | 0 | 0 | | |
| 1996–97 | Manchester C | 0 | 0 | | |
| 1997–98 | Manchester C | 19 | 0 | | |
| 1998–99 | Manchester C | 18 | 0 | | |
| 1999–2000 | Manchester C | 1 | 0 | | |
| 1999–2000 | *Blackpool* | 8 | 0 | **8** | **0** |
| 2000–01 | Manchester C | 0 | 0 | **38** | **0** |
| 2000–01 | *Norwich C* | 8 | 1 | **8** | **1** |
| 2000–01 | *Swindon T* | 2 | 0 | **2** | **0** |
| 2000–01 | *Northampton T* | 13 | 0 | **13** | **0** |
| 2000–01 | *Nottingham F* | 0 | 0 | | |
| 2001–02 | Wrexham | 34 | 0 | | |
| 2002–03 | Wrexham | 44 | 1 | | |
| 2003–04 | Wrexham | 36 | 0 | **114** | **1** |

**Scholars**

Anderson, Mark; Evans, Christopher W; Evans, Daniel; Gray, Philip M; Harris, Mark; Jones, Liam D; Leather, Wayne M; Mackin, Levi; McNulty, Jimmy; Parry, Christopher D; Quinn, Kieran F; Spencer, Andrew P; Spender, Simon; Williams, Kevin Williams, Michael P

## WYCOMBE W (90)

**BLOOMFIELD, Matt (M)** **12** **1**

H: 5 9 W: 11 00 b.Ipswich 8-2-84

*Source:* Scholar. *Honours:* England Youth, Under-20.

| | | | | | |
|---|---|---|---|---|---|
| 2001–02 | Ipswich T | 0 | 0 | | |
| 2002–03 | Ipswich T | 0 | 0 | | |
| 2003–04 | Ipswich T | 0 | 0 | | |
| 2003–04 | Wycombe W | 12 | 1 | **12** | **1** |

**BROWN, Steve* (M)** **529** **54**

H: 5 10 W: 11 12 b.Northampton 6-7-66

| | | | | | |
|---|---|---|---|---|---|
| 1985–86 | Northampton T | 0 | 0 | | |
| From Irthlingborough D | | | | | |
| 1989–90 | Northampton T | 21 | 1 | | |
| 1990–91 | Northampton T | 40 | 2 | | |
| 1991–92 | Northampton T | 35 | 3 | | |
| 1992–93 | Northampton T | 38 | 9 | | |
| 1993–94 | Northampton T | 24 | 4 | **158** | **19** |
| 1993–94 | Wycombe W | 9 | 2 | | |
| 1994–95 | Wycombe W | 40 | 1 | | |
| 1995–96 | Wycombe W | 38 | 0 | | |
| 1996–97 | Wycombe W | 34 | 5 | | |
| 1997–98 | Wycombe W | 40 | 3 | | |
| 1998–99 | Wycombe W | 38 | 3 | | |
| 1999–2000 | Wycombe W | 39 | 3 | | |
| 2000–01 | Wycombe W | 32 | 4 | | |
| 2001–02 | Wycombe W | 39 | 8 | | |
| 2002–03 | Wycombe W | 37 | 5 | | |
| 2003–04 | Wycombe W | 25 | 1 | **371** | **35** |

**BULMAN, Dannie* (M)** **202** **14**

H: 5 9 W: 11 12 b.Ashford 24-1-79

*Source:* Ashford T.

| | | | | | |
|---|---|---|---|---|---|
| 1998–99 | Wycombe W | 11 | 1 | | |
| 1999–2000 | Wycombe W | 29 | 1 | | |
| 2000–01 | Wycombe W | 36 | 4 | | |
| 2001–02 | Wycombe W | 46 | 5 | | |
| 2002–03 | Wycombe W | 42 | 3 | | |
| 2003–04 | Wycombe W | 38 | 0 | **202** | **14** |

**COOK, Lewis* (M)** **22** **0**

H: 5 7 W: 11 01 b.High Wycombe 28-12-83

*Source:* Scholar.

| | | | | | |
|---|---|---|---|---|---|
| 2002–03 | Wycombe W | 17 | 0 | | |
| 2003–04 | Wycombe W | 5 | 0 | **22** | **0** |

**CURRIE, Darren* (M)** **353** **43**

H: 5 10 W: 12 07 b.Hampstead 29-11-74

*Source:* Trainee.

| | | | | | |
|---|---|---|---|---|---|
| 1993–94 | West Ham U | 0 | 0 | | |
| 1994–95 | West Ham U | 0 | 0 | | |
| 1994–95 | *Shrewsbury T* | 17 | 2 | | |
| 1995–96 | West Ham U | 0 | 0 | | |
| 1995–96 | *Leyton Orient* | 10 | 0 | **10** | **0** |
| 1995–96 | Shrewsbury T | 13 | 2 | | |
| 1996–97 | Shrewsbury T | 37 | 2 | | |
| 1997–98 | Shrewsbury T | 16 | 4 | **83** | **10** |
| 1997–98 | Plymouth Arg | 7 | 0 | **7** | **0** |
| 1998–99 | Barnet | 38 | 4 | | |
| 1999–2000 | Barnet | 44 | 5 | | |
| 2000–01 | Barnet | 45 | 10 | **127** | **19** |
| 2001–02 | Wycombe W | 46 | 3 | | |
| 2002–03 | Wycombe W | 38 | 4 | | |
| 2003–04 | Wycombe W | 42 | 7 | **126** | **14** |

**DELL, Steven‡ (D)** **4** **0**

H: 5 10 W: 12 12 b.London 6-2-80

*Source:* Beaconsfield.

| | | | | | |
|---|---|---|---|---|---|
| 2003–04 | Wycombe W | 4 | 0 | **4** | **0** |

**DIXON, Jonny (F) 30 5**
H: 5 9 W: 11 01 b.Murcia 16-1-84
*Source:* Scholar.

| | | | | | |
|---|---|---|---|---|---|
| 2002–03 | Wycombe W | 22 | 5 | | |
| 2003–04 | Wycombe W | 8 | 0 | **30** | **5** |

**FAULCONBRIDGE, Craig (F) 184 40**
H: 6 1 W: 13 00 b.Nuneaton 20-4-78
*Source:* Trainee.

| | | | | | |
|---|---|---|---|---|---|
| 1996–97 | Coventry C | 0 | 0 | | |
| 1997–98 | Coventry C | 0 | 0 | | |
| 1997–98 | Dunfermline Ath | 7 | 1 | | |
| 1998–99 | Dunfermline Ath | 6 | 0 | **13** | **1** |
| 1998–99 | *Hull C* | 10 | 0 | **10** | **0** |
| 1999–2000 | Wrexham | 35 | 8 | | |
| 2000–01 | Wrexham | 39 | 10 | | |
| 2001–02 | Wrexham | 37 | 13 | **111** | **31** |
| 2002–03 | Wycombe W | 34 | 6 | | |
| 2003–04 | Wycombe W | 16 | 2 | **50** | **8** |

**HARDING, Billy (F) 2 0**
H: 6 0 W: 12 07 b.Carshalton 20-1-85
*Source:* Scholar.

| | | | | | |
|---|---|---|---|---|---|
| 2003–04 | Wycombe W | 2 | 0 | **2** | **0** |

**HARRIS, Richard* (F) 50 5**
H: 5 11 W: 10 09 b.Croydon 23-10-80
*Source:* Trainee.

| | | | | | |
|---|---|---|---|---|---|
| 1997–98 | Crystal Palace | 0 | 0 | | |
| 1998–99 | Crystal Palace | 1 | 0 | | |
| 1999–2000 | Crystal Palace | 6 | 0 | | |
| 2000–01 | Crystal Palace | 2 | 0 | | |
| 2001–02 | Crystal Palace | 0 | 0 | **9** | **0** |
| 2001–02 | *Mansfield T* | 6 | 0 | **6** | **0** |
| 2001–02 | Wycombe W | 3 | 0 | | |
| 2002–03 | Wycombe W | 22 | 5 | | |
| 2003–04 | Wycombe W | 10 | 0 | **35** | **5** |

**HOLE, Stuart (D) 1 0**
H: 6 0 W: 11 11 b.Oxford 17-7-85
*Source:* Scholar.

| | | | | | |
|---|---|---|---|---|---|
| 2003–04 | Wycombe W | 1 | 0 | **1** | **0** |

**HOLLIGAN, Gavin‡ (F) 48 8**
H: 5 10 W: 13 00 b.Lambeth 30-6-80
*Source:* Kingstonian.

| | | | | | |
|---|---|---|---|---|---|
| 1998–99 | West Ham U | 1 | 0 | | |
| 1999–2000 | West Ham U | 0 | 0 | | |
| 1999–2000 | *Leyton Orient* | 1 | 0 | **1** | **0** |
| 2000–01 | West Ham U | 0 | 0 | **1** | **0** |
| 2000–01 | *Exeter C* | 3 | 0 | **3** | **0** |
| 2001–02 | Wycombe W | 20 | 4 | | |
| 2002–03 | Wycombe W | 10 | 2 | | |
| 2003–04 | Wycombe W | 13 | 2 | **43** | **8** |

**JOHNSON, Roger (D) 70 6**
H: 6 3 W: 11 00 b.Ashford 28-4-83
*Source:* Trainee.

| | | | | | |
|---|---|---|---|---|---|
| 1999–2000 | Wycombe W | 1 | 0 | | |
| 2000–01 | Wycombe W | 1 | 0 | | |
| 2001–02 | Wycombe W | 7 | 1 | | |
| 2002–03 | Wycombe W | 33 | 3 | | |
| 2003–04 | Wycombe W | 28 | 2 | **70** | **6** |

**KELLY, John‡ (M) 0 0**
b.Edinburgh 26-4-85
*Source:* Scholar.

| | | | | | |
|---|---|---|---|---|---|
| 2003–04 | Wycombe W | 0 | 0 | | |

**MAPES, Charlie* (M) 15 3**
H: 5 10 W: 11 03 b.West Hampstead 4-7-82
*Source:* Berkhamsted T.

| | | | | | |
|---|---|---|---|---|---|
| 2003–04 | Wycombe W | 15 | 3 | **15** | **3** |

**MARSHALL, Scott* (D) 138 5**
H: 6 1 W: 12 05 b.Edinburgh 1-5-73
*Source:* Trainee. *Honours:* Scotland Youth, Under-21.

| | | | | | |
|---|---|---|---|---|---|
| 1992–93 | Arsenal | 2 | 0 | | |
| 1993–94 | Arsenal | 0 | 0 | | |
| 1993–94 | *Rotherham U* | 10 | 1 | **10** | **1** |
| 1993–94 | *Oxford U* | 0 | 0 | | |
| 1994–95 | Arsenal | 0 | 0 | | |
| 1994–95 | *Sheffield U* | 17 | 0 | **17** | **0** |
| 1995–96 | Arsenal | 11 | 1 | | |
| 1996–97 | Arsenal | 8 | 0 | | |
| 1997–98 | Arsenal | 3 | 0 | **24** | **1** |
| 1998–99 | Southampton | 2 | 0 | | |
| 1998–99 | Celtic | 2 | 0 | **2** | **0** |
| 1999–2000 | Southampton | 0 | 0 | **2** | **0** |
| 1999–2000 | Brentford | 22 | 2 | | |
| 2000–01 | Brentford | 29 | 0 | | |
| 2001–02 | Brentford | 0 | 0 | | |
| 2002–03 | Brentford | 24 | 1 | | |
| 2003–04 | Brentford | 0 | 0 | **75** | **3** |
| 2003–04 | Wycombe W | 8 | 0 | **8** | **0** |

**McCLURG, James* (M) 0 0**
b.Ascot 10-10-85

| | | | | | |
|---|---|---|---|---|---|
| 2002–03 | Wycombe W | 0 | 0 | | |
| 2003–04 | Wycombe W | 0 | 0 | | |

**NETHERCOTT, Stuart‡ (D) 307 12**
H: 6 0 W: 13 01 b.Ilford 21-3-73
*Source:* Trainee. *Honours:* England Under-21.

| | | | | | |
|---|---|---|---|---|---|
| 1991–92 | Tottenham H | 0 | 0 | | |
| 1991–92 | *Maidstone U* | 13 | 1 | **13** | **1** |
| 1991–92 | *Barnet* | 3 | 0 | **3** | **0** |
| 1992–93 | Tottenham H | 5 | 0 | | |
| 1993–94 | Tottenham H | 10 | 0 | | |
| 1994–95 | Tottenham H | 17 | 0 | | |
| 1995–96 | Tottenham H | 13 | 0 | | |
| 1996–97 | Tottenham H | 9 | 0 | | |
| 1997–98 | Tottenham H | 0 | 0 | **54** | **0** |
| 1997–98 | Millwall | 10 | 0 | | |
| 1998–99 | Millwall | 37 | 2 | | |
| 1999–2000 | Millwall | 37 | 0 | | |
| 2000–01 | Millwall | 35 | 2 | | |
| 2001–02 | Millwall | 46 | 3 | | |
| 2002–03 | Millwall | 36 | 2 | | |
| 2003–04 | Millwall | 14 | 1 | **215** | **10** |
| 2003–04 | Wycombe W | 22 | 1 | **22** | **1** |

**OLIVER, Luke‡ (D) 4 0**
H: 6 6 W: 14 05 b.Hammersmith 1-5-84

| | | | | | |
|---|---|---|---|---|---|
| 2002–03 | Wycombe W | 2 | 0 | | |
| 2003–04 | Wycombe W | 2 | 0 | **4** | **0** |

**PHILO, Mark (M) 12 0**
H: 5 11 W: 11 05 b.Bracknell 5-10-84
*Source:* Scholar.

| | | | | | |
|---|---|---|---|---|---|
| 2003–04 | Wycombe W | 12 | 0 | **12** | **0** |

**REILLY, Andy (D) 5 0**
H: 5 10 W: 12 08 b.Luton 26-10-85
*Source:* Scholar. *Honours:* Scotland Youth, Under-21.

| | | | | | |
|---|---|---|---|---|---|
| 2003–04 | Wycombe W | 5 | 0 | **5** | **0** |

**ROGERS, Mark‡ (D) 139 4**
H: 5 11 W: 12 12 b.Geulph 3-11-78
*Honours:* Canada 7 full caps.

| | | | | | |
|---|---|---|---|---|---|
| 1998–99 | Wycombe W | 0 | 0 | | |
| 1999–2000 | Wycombe W | 25 | 0 | | |
| 2000–01 | Wycombe W | 22 | 1 | | |
| 2001–02 | Wycombe W | 41 | 2 | | |
| 2002–03 | Wycombe W | 36 | 1 | | |
| 2003–04 | Wycombe W | 15 | 0 | **139** | **4** |

**RYAN, Keith (M) 313 27**
H: 5 10 W: 12 06 b.Northampton 25-6-70
*Source:* Berkhamsted T.

| | | | | | |
|---|---|---|---|---|---|
| 1993–94 | Wycombe W | 42 | 1 | | |
| 1994–95 | Wycombe W | 24 | 4 | | |
| 1995–96 | Wycombe W | 23 | 4 | | |
| 1996–97 | Wycombe W | 0 | 0 | | |
| 1997–98 | Wycombe W | 40 | 3 | | |
| 1998–99 | Wycombe W | 28 | 1 | | |
| 1999–2000 | Wycombe W | 38 | 6 | | |
| 2000–01 | Wycombe W | 30 | 4 | | |
| 2001–02 | Wycombe W | 35 | 1 | | |
| 2002–03 | Wycombe W | 36 | 2 | | |
| 2003–04 | Wycombe W | 17 | 1 | **313** | **27** |

**SENDA, Danny (D) 188 5**
H: 5 10 W: 10 02 b.Harrow 17-4-81
*Source:* Southampton Trainee. *Honours:* England Youth.

| | | | | | |
|---|---|---|---|---|---|
| 1998–99 | Wycombe W | 6 | 0 | | |
| 1999–2000 | Wycombe W | 27 | 1 | | |
| 2000–01 | Wycombe W | 31 | 2 | | |
| 2001–02 | Wycombe W | 43 | 0 | | |
| 2002–03 | Wycombe W | 41 | 2 | | |
| 2003–04 | Wycombe W | 40 | 0 | **188** | **5** |

**SIMPEMBA, Ian (M) 20 2**
H: 6 2 W: 12 08 b.Dublin 28-3-83
*Source:* Scholar.

| | | | | | |
|---|---|---|---|---|---|
| 2001–02 | Wycombe W | 0 | 0 | | |
| 2002–03 | Wycombe W | 1 | 0 | | |
| 2003–04 | Wycombe W | 19 | 2 | **20** | **2** |

**SIMPSON, Michael* (M) 346 19**
H: 5 8 W: 11 07 b.Nottingham 28-2-74
*Source:* Trainee.

| | | | | | |
|---|---|---|---|---|---|
| 1992–93 | Notts Co | 0 | 0 | | |
| 1993–94 | Notts Co | 6 | 1 | | |
| 1994–95 | Notts Co | 19 | 2 | | |
| 1995–96 | Notts Co | 23 | 0 | | |
| 1996–97 | Notts Co | 1 | 0 | **49** | **3** |
| 1996–97 | *Plymouth Arg* | 12 | 0 | **12** | **0** |
| 1996–97 | Wycombe W | 20 | 1 | | |
| 1997–98 | Wycombe W | 21 | 0 | | |
| 1998–99 | Wycombe W | 33 | 4 | | |
| 1999–2000 | Wycombe W | 43 | 0 | | |
| 2000–01 | Wycombe W | 45 | 3 | | |
| 2001–02 | Wycombe W | 43 | 1 | | |
| 2002–03 | Wycombe W | 42 | 5 | | |
| 2003–04 | Wycombe W | 38 | 2 | **285** | **16** |

**TALIA, Frank (G) 193 0**
H: 6 1 W: 13 06 b.Melbourne 20-7-72
*Honours:* Australia Schools, Under-20.

| | | | | | |
|---|---|---|---|---|---|
| 1990–91 | Sunshine | 11 | 0 | | |
| 1991–92 | Sunshine | 0 | 0 | **11** | **0** |
| 1992–93 | Blackburn R | 0 | 0 | | |
| 1992–93 | *Hartlepool U* | 14 | 0 | **14** | **0** |
| 1993–94 | Blackburn R | 0 | 0 | | |
| 1994–95 | Blackburn R | 0 | 0 | | |
| 1995–96 | Blackburn R | 0 | 0 | | |
| 1995–96 | Swindon T | 16 | 0 | | |
| 1996–97 | Swindon T | 15 | 0 | | |
| 1997–98 | Swindon T | 2 | 0 | | |
| 1998–99 | Swindon T | 43 | 0 | | |
| 1999–2000 | Swindon T | 31 | 0 | **107** | **0** |
| 2000–01 | Wolverhampton W | 0 | 0 | | |
| 2000–01 | Sheffield U | 6 | 0 | **6** | **0** |
| 2001–02 | Antwerp | 3 | 0 | **3** | **0** |
| 2001–02 | Reading | 0 | 0 | | |
| 2002–03 | Wycombe W | 35 | 0 | | |
| 2003–04 | Wycombe W | 17 | 0 | **52** | **0** |

**THOMSON, Andy* (D) 292 11**
H: 6 3 W: 14 03 b.Swindon 28-3-74
*Source:* Trainee.

| | | | | | |
|---|---|---|---|---|---|
| 1992–93 | Swindon T | 0 | 0 | | |
| 1993–94 | Swindon T | 1 | 0 | | |
| 1994–95 | Swindon T | 21 | 0 | | |
| 1995–96 | Swindon T | 0 | 0 | **22** | **0** |
| 1995–96 | Portsmouth | 16 | 0 | | |
| 1996–97 | Portsmouth | 28 | 1 | | |
| 1997–98 | Portsmouth | 35 | 2 | | |
| 1998–99 | Portsmouth | 14 | 0 | **93** | **3** |
| 1998–99 | Bristol R | 21 | 1 | | |
| 1999–2000 | Bristol R | 43 | 3 | | |
| 2000–01 | Bristol R | 32 | 1 | | |
| 2001–02 | Bristol R | 31 | 1 | **127** | **6** |
| 2001–02 | Wycombe W | 3 | 0 | | |
| 2002–03 | Wycombe W | 36 | 1 | | |
| 2003–04 | Wycombe W | 11 | 1 | **50** | **2** |

**TYSON, Nathan (F) 73 12**
H: 5 10 W: 10 02 b.Reading 4-5-82
*Source:* Trainee. *Honours:* England Under-20.

| | | | | | |
|---|---|---|---|---|---|
| 1999–2000 | Reading | 1 | 0 | | |
| 2000–01 | Reading | 0 | 0 | | |
| 2001–02 | Reading | 1 | 0 | | |
| 2001–02 | *Swansea C* | 11 | 1 | **11** | **1** |
| 2001–02 | *Cheltenham T* | 8 | 1 | **8** | **1** |
| 2002–03 | Reading | 23 | 1 | | |
| 2003–04 | Reading | 8 | 0 | **33** | **1** |
| 2003–04 | Wycombe W | 21 | 9 | **21** | **9** |

**VINNICOMBE, Chris* (D) 378 7**
H: 5 9 W: 10 12 b.Exeter 20-10-70
*Source:* Trainee. *Honours:* England Under-21.

| | | | | | |
|---|---|---|---|---|---|
| 1988–89 | Exeter C | 25 | 0 | | |
| 1989–90 | Exeter C | 14 | 1 | **39** | **1** |
| 1989–90 | Rangers | 7 | 0 | | |
| 1990–91 | Rangers | 10 | 1 | | |
| 1991–92 | Rangers | 2 | 0 | | |
| 1992–93 | Rangers | 0 | 0 | | |
| 1993–94 | Rangers | 4 | 0 | **23** | **1** |
| 1994–95 | Burnley | 29 | 1 | | |
| 1995–96 | Burnley | 35 | 2 | | |
| 1996–97 | Burnley | 8 | 0 | | |
| 1997–98 | Burnley | 23 | 0 | **95** | **3** |
| 1998–99 | Wycombe W | 41 | 0 | | |
| 1999–2000 | Wycombe W | 35 | 0 | | |
| 2000–01 | Wycombe W | 42 | 1 | | |
| 2001–02 | Wycombe W | 42 | 1 | | |
| 2002–03 | Wycombe W | 25 | 0 | | |
| 2003–04 | Wycombe W | 36 | 0 | **221** | **2** |

**WILLIAMS, Steve (G) 19 0**
H: 6 6 W: 13 10 b.Oxford 21-4-83
*Source:* Scholar.

| | | | | | |
|---|---|---|---|---|---|
| 2001–02 | Wycombe W | 0 | 0 | | |

2002–03 Wycombe W 0 0
2003–04 Wycombe W 19 0 **19 0**

**Scholars**
Boland, Mark L; Flower, Stephen; Fox, Matthew W; Gordon, Leon; Gott, Tom P; Gregory, Steven M; Grier, Liam A; Griffiths, Nathaniel R; Hole, Stuart M; Tungatt, Robert P; Warner, Matthew J

## YEOVIL T (91)

**COLLIS, Steve (G) 11 0**
H: 6 3 W: 12 05 b.Barnet 18-3-81
1999–2000 Barnet 0 0
2000–01 Nottingham F 0 0
2001–02 Nottingham F 0 0
2003–04 Yeovil T 11 0 **11 0**

**CRITTENDEN, Nick* (M) 33 2**
H: 5 10 W: 11 07 b.Bracknell 11-11-78
*Source:* Trainee.
1997–98 Chelsea 2 0
1998–99 Chelsea 0 0
1998–99 *Plymouth Arg* 2 0 **2 0**
1999–2000 Chelsea 0 0 **2 0**
2003–04 Yeovil T 29 2 **29 2**

**EDWARDS, Jake* (F) 38 8**
H: 6 1 W: 13 01 b.Prestwich 11-5-76
*Source:* James Maddison Uni.
1998–99 Wrexham 9 1
1999–2000 Wrexham 2 1 **11 2**
From Telford U.
2003–04 Yeovil T 27 6 **27 6**

**EL KHOLTI, Abdelhalim* (M) 23 1**
H: 5 10 W: 11 00 b.Annesse 17-10-80
*Source:* Raja.
2003–04 Yeovil T 23 1 **23 1**

**ELAM, Lee (M) 12 1**
H: 5 8 W: 10 12 b.Bradford 24-9-76
*Source:* Halifax T.
2003–04 Yeovil T 12 1 **12 1**

**GALL, Kevin (F) 93 13**
H: 5 9 W: 10 08 b.Merthyr 4-2-82
*Source:* Trainee. *Honours:* Wales Schools, Youth, Under-21.
1998–99 Newcastle U 0 0
1999–2000 Newcastle U 0 0
2000–01 Newcastle U 0 0
2000–01 Bristol R 10 2
2001–02 Bristol R 31 3
2002–03 Bristol R 9 0 **50 5**
2003–04 Yeovil T 43 8 **43 8**

**GILES, Chris‡ (F) 1 0**
H: 6 2 W: 13 00 b.Milborne Port 16-4-82
*Source:* Sherborne.
2003–04 Yeovil T 1 0 **1 0**

**GOSLING, Jamie* (M) 12 1**
H: 6 0 W: 10 06 b.Bath 21-3-82
*Source:* Bath C.
2003–04 Yeovil T 12 1 **12 1**

**JACKSON, Kirk‡ (F) 58 7**
H: 6 0 W: 13 00 b.Barnsley 16-10-76
*Source:* Sheffield W Trainee.
1996–97 Scunthorpe U 4 1 **4 1**
1997–98 Chesterfield 3 0 **3 0**
From Grantham T, Worksop
2001–02 Darlington 11 0 **21 1**
From Stevenage B.
2003–04 Yeovil T 30 5 **30 5**

**JOHNSON, Lee (M) 45 5**
H: 5 6 W: 10 07 b.Newmarket 7-6-81
*Source:* Trainee.
1998–99 Watford 0 0
1999–2000 Watford 0 0
2000–01 Brighton & HA 0 0
2000–01 Brentford 0 0
2001–02 Brentford 0 0
2003–04 Yeovil T 45 5 **45 5**

**LINDEGAARD, Andy (F) 23 2**
H: 5 8 W: 11 04 b.Taunton 10-9-80
*Source:* Westland Sp.
2003–04 Yeovil T 23 2 **23 2**

**LOCKWOOD, Adam (D) 43 4**
H: 6 0 W: 12 07 b.Wakefield 26-10-81
*Source:* Reading Trainee.
2003–04 Yeovil T 43 4 **43 4**

**O'BRIEN, Roy* (D) 14 0**
H: 6 0 W: 12 02 b.Cork 27-11-74
*Source:* Trainee.
1993–94 Arsenal 0 0
1994–95 Arsenal 0 0
1995–96 Arsenal 0 0
1996–97 Wigan Ath 0 0
1996–97 Bournemouth 1 0 **1 0**
From Dorchester T
2003–04 Yeovil T 13 0 **13 0**

**PLUCK, Colin (D) 41 4**
H: 6 0 W: 13 10 b.Edmonton 6-9-78
*Source:* Trainee.
1996–97 Watford 0 0
1997–98 Watford 1 0
1998–99 Watford 0 0 **1 0**
1999–2000 Morton 4 0 **4 0**
From Dover Ath
2003–04 Yeovil T 36 4 **36 4**

**REED, Steve (D) 5 0**
H: 5 8 W: 12 02 b.Barnstaple 18-6-85
*Source:* Juniors.
2003–04 Yeovil T 5 0 **5 0**

**RODRIGUES, Dani* (F) 34 5**
H: 6 0 W: 11 09 b.Madeira 3-3-80
*Source:* Farense.
1998–99 Bournemouth 5 0 **5 0**
1998–99 Southampton 0 0
1999–2000 Southampton 2 0
2000–01 Southampton 0 0
2000–01 *Bristol C* 4 0
2001–02 Southampton 0 0 **2 0**
2001–02 *Bristol C* 4 0 **8 0**
2002–03 Walsall 1 0 **1 0**
2002–03 Ionikos 14 1 **14 1**
2003–04 Yeovil T 4 4 **4 4**

**RODRIGUES, Hugo* (D) 34 1**
H: 6 8 W: 15 06 b.Santa Maria de Feira 22-11-79
*Source:* Pedras Rubras.
2003–04 Yeovil T 34 1 **34 1**

**SKIVERTON, Terry (D) 46 3**
H: 6 1 W: 13 06 b.Mile End 26-6-75
*Source:* Trainee.
1993–94 Chelsea 0 0
1994–95 Chelsea 0 0
1994–95 *Wycombe W* 10 0
1995–96 Chelsea 0 0
1995–96 Wycombe W 4 1
1996–97 Wycombe W 6 0 **20 1**
From Welling U
2003–04 Yeovil T 26 2 **26 2**

**STANSFIELD, Adam* (F) 32 6**
H: 5 11 W: 11 02 b.Plymouth 10-9-78
*Source:* Elmore.
2003–04 Yeovil T 32 6 **32 6**

**TALBOTT, Nathan* (D) 1 0**
H: 6 1 W: 13 00 b.Wolverhampton 21-10-84
*Source:* Wolverhampton W Scholar.
2003–04 Yeovil T 1 0 **1 0**

**TERRY, Paul (M) 34 1**
H: 5 10 W: 12 06 b.Barking 3-4-79
*Source:* Dagenham & R.
2003–04 Yeovil T 34 1 **34 1**

**WAY, Darren (M) 39 5**
H: 5 6 W: 10 00 b.Plymouth 21-11-79
*Source:* Norwich C Trainee.
2003–04 Yeovil T 39 5 **39 5**

**WEALE, Chris (G) 35 0**
H: 6 2 W: 13 03 b.Yeovil 9-2-82
*Source:* Juniors.
2003–04 Yeovil T 35 0 **35 0**

**WEATHERSTONE, Simon (F) 129 14**
H: 5 10 W: 12 00 b.Reading 26-1-80
*Source:* Trainee.
1996–97 Oxford U 1 0
1997–98 Oxford U 11 1
1998–99 Oxford U 12 1
1999–2000 Oxford U 21 1
2000–01 Oxford U 7 0 **52 3**
2002–03 Boston U 45 6
2003–04 Boston U 17 4 **62 10**
2003–04 Yeovil T 15 1 **15 1**

**WILLIAMS, Gavin (M) 42 9**
H: 5 10 W: 11 05 b.Merthyr 20-6-80
*Source:* Hereford U.
2003–04 Yeovil T 42 9 **42 9**

**Non Contract**
Sheffield, Jonathan; Thompson, Steven J

## YORK C (92)

**ARTHUR, Adam§ (M) 3 0**
H: 5 9 W: 11 00 b.Nottingham 27-10-85
*Source:* Scholar.
2003–04 York C 3 0 **3 0**

**ASHCROFT, Kane§ (M) 2 0**
H: 5 9 W: 11 11 b.Leeds 19-3-86
*Source:* Scholar.
2003–04 York C 2 0 **2 0**

**BELL, Andy‡ (F) 21 4**
H: 5 10 W: 12 06 b.Blackburn 12-2-84
*Source:* Scholar. *Honours:* England Youth.
2000–01 Blackburn R 0 0
2001–02 Blackburn R 0 0
2002–03 Blackburn R 0 0
2003–04 Wycombe W 11 3 **11 3**
2003–04 York C 10 1 **10 1**

**BRACKSTONE, Stephen‡ (M) 44 4**
H: 5 11 W: 11 03 b.Hartlepool 19-9-82
*Source:* Scholar. *Honours:* England Youth.
2000–01 Middlesbrough 0 0
2001–02 Middlesbrough 0 0
2001–02 York C 9 0
2002–03 York C 26 2
2003–04 York C 9 2 **44 4**

**BRASS, Chris (M) 277 6**
H: 5 10 W: 11 13 b.Easington 24-7-75
*Source:* Trainee.
1993–94 Burnley 0 0
1994–95 Burnley 5 0
1994–95 *Torquay U* 7 0 **7 0**
1995–96 Burnley 9 0
1996–97 Burnley 39 0
1997–98 Burnley 40 1
1998–99 Burnley 34 0
1999–2000 Burnley 7 0
2000–01 Burnley 0 0 **134 1**
2000–01 *Halifax T* 6 0 **6 0**
2000–01 York C 10 1
2001–02 York C 41 2
2002–03 York C 40 1
2003–04 York C 39 1 **130 5**

**BROWNE, Gary‡ (F) 6 0**
H: 5 10 W: 10 10 b.Dundonald 17-1-83
*Source:* Scholar. *Honours:* Northern Ireland Under-21.
2000–01 Manchester C 0 0
2001–02 Manchester C 0 0
2002–03 Manchester C 0 0
2003–04 Manchester C 0 0
From Whitby T.
2003–04 York C 6 0 **6 0**

**BULLOCK, Lee (M) 182 27**
H: 6 0 W: 13 00 b.Stockton 22-5-81
*Source:* Trainee.
1999–2000 York C 24 0
2000–01 York C 33 3
2001–02 York C 40 8
2002–03 York C 39 6
2003–04 York C 35 7 **171 24**
2003–04 *Cardiff C* 11 3 **11 3**

**COAD, Matthew§ (M) 3 0**
H: 5 8 W: 11 00 b.Darlington 25-9-84
*Source:* Scholar.
2003–04 York C 3 0 **3 0**

**COOPER, Richard‡ (M) 103 4**
H: 5 8 W: 11 06 b.Nottingham 27-9-79
*Source:* Trainee. *Honours:* England Schools, Youth.
1996–97 Nottingham F 0 0
1997–98 Nottingham F 0 0
1998–99 Nottingham F 0 0
1999–2000 Nottingham F 1 0
2000–01 Nottingham F 2 0 **3 0**

| | | | | | |
|---|---|---|---|---|---|
| 2000–01 | York C | 14 | 0 | | |
| 2001–02 | York C | 25 | 1 | | |
| 2002–03 | York C | 24 | 1 | | |
| 2003–04 | York C | 37 | 2 | **100** | **4** |

**DAVIES, Sean§ (M) 8 0**
H: 6 1 W: 12 08 b.Middlesbrough 1-6-85
*Source:* Scholar.

| | | | | | |
|---|---|---|---|---|---|
| 2003–04 | York C | 8 | 0 | **8** | **0** |

**DONOVAN, Kevin† (M) 411 45**
H: 5 10 W: 11 11 b.Halifax 17-12-71
*Source:* Trainee.

| | | | | | |
|---|---|---|---|---|---|
| 1989–90 | Huddersfield T | 1 | 0 | | |
| 1990–91 | Huddersfield T | 6 | 1 | | |
| 1991–92 | Huddersfield T | 10 | 0 | | |
| 1991–92 | *Halifax T* | 6 | 0 | **6** | **0** |
| 1992–93 | Huddersfield T | 3 | 0 | **20** | **1** |
| 1992–93 | WBA | 32 | 6 | | |
| 1993–94 | WBA | 37 | 8 | | |
| 1994–95 | WBA | 33 | 5 | | |
| 1995–96 | WBA | 34 | 0 | | |
| 1996–97 | WBA | 32 | 0 | **168** | **19** |
| 1997–98 | Grimsby T | 46 | 16 | | |
| 1998–99 | Grimsby T | 28 | 0 | | |
| 1999–2000 | Grimsby T | 41 | 3 | | |
| 2000–01 | Grimsby T | 41 | 5 | **156** | **24** |
| 2001–02 | Barnsley | 32 | 1 | | |
| 2002–03 | Barnsley | 22 | 0 | | |
| 2003–04 | Barnsley | 0 | 0 | **54** | **1** |
| 2003–04 | Rochdale | 7 | 0 | **7** | **0** |
| 2003–04 | York C | 0 | 0 | | |

**DOWNES, Steven* (D) 6 0**
H: 5 6 W: 9 12 b.Leeds 22-11-81

| | | | | | |
|---|---|---|---|---|---|
| 2002–03 | Grimsby T | 0 | 0 | | |
| 2003–04 | York C | 6 | 0 | **6** | **0** |

**DUNNING, Darren (M) 86 4**
H: 5 7 W: 11 12 b.Scarborough 8-1-81
*Source:* Trainee.

| | | | | | |
|---|---|---|---|---|---|
| 1998–99 | Blackburn R | 0 | 0 | | |
| 1999–2000 | Blackburn R | 0 | 0 | | |
| 2000–01 | Blackburn R | 1 | 0 | | |
| 2000–01 | *Bristol C* | 9 | 0 | **9** | **0** |
| 2001–02 | Blackburn R | 0 | 0 | | |
| 2001–02 | *Rochdale* | 5 | 0 | **5** | **0** |
| 2001–02 | *Blackpool* | 5 | 0 | **5** | **0** |
| 2002–03 | Blackburn R | 0 | 0 | **1** | **0** |
| 2002–03 | *Torquay U* | 7 | 1 | **7** | **1** |
| 2002–03 | *Macclesfield T* | 17 | 0 | **17** | **0** |
| 2003–04 | York C | 42 | 3 | **42** | **3** |

**EDMONDSON, Darren‡ (D) 386 15**
H: 6 0 W: 12 05 b.Ulverston 4-11-71
*Source:* Trainee.

| | | | | | |
|---|---|---|---|---|---|
| 1990–91 | Carlisle U | 31 | 0 | | |
| 1991–92 | Carlisle U | 27 | 2 | | |
| 1992–93 | Carlisle U | 34 | 0 | | |
| 1993–94 | Carlisle U | 22 | 3 | | |
| 1994–95 | Carlisle U | 38 | 2 | | |
| 1995–96 | Carlisle U | 42 | 1 | | |
| 1996–97 | Carlisle U | 20 | 1 | **214** | **9** |
| 1996–97 | Huddersfield T | 10 | 0 | | |
| 1997–98 | Huddersfield T | 19 | 0 | | |
| 1998–99 | Huddersfield T | 3 | 0 | | |
| 1998–99 | *Plymouth Arg* | 4 | 0 | **4** | **0** |
| 1999–2000 | Huddersfield T | 5 | 0 | **37** | **0** |
| 1999–2000 | York C | 7 | 0 | | |
| 2000–01 | York C | 23 | 0 | | |
| 2001–02 | York C | 36 | 0 | | |
| 2002–03 | York C | 38 | 5 | | |
| 2003–04 | York C | 27 | 1 | **131** | **6** |

**FOX, Christian‡ (M) 70 1**
H: 5 10 W: 11 08 b.Auchenbrae 11-4-81
*Source:* Trainee.

| | | | | | |
|---|---|---|---|---|---|
| 1999–2000 | York C | 34 | 1 | | |
| 2000–01 | York C | 8 | 0 | | |
| 2001–02 | York C | 12 | 0 | | |
| 2002–03 | York C | 11 | 0 | | |
| 2003–04 | York C | 5 | 0 | **70** | **1** |

**GEORGE, Liam‡ (F) 135 24**
H: 5 10 W: 11 05 b.Luton 2-2-79
*Source:* Trainee. *Honours:* Eire Under-21.

| | | | | | |
|---|---|---|---|---|---|
| 1996–97 | Luton T | 0 | 0 | | |
| 1997–98 | Luton T | 1 | 0 | | |
| 1998–99 | Luton T | 12 | 0 | | |
| 1999–2000 | Luton T | 42 | 13 | | |
| 2000–01 | Luton T | 43 | 7 | | |
| 2001–02 | Luton T | 4 | 0 | **102** | **20** |

From Stevenage B.

| | | | | | |
|---|---|---|---|---|---|
| 2002–03 | Bury | 8 | 1 | **8** | **1** |
| 2002–03 | Boston U | 3 | 0 | **3** | **0** |
| 2003–04 | York C | 22 | 3 | **22** | **3** |

**HAW, Robbie§ (M) 1 0**
H: 5 8 W: 10 10 b.York 10-10-86
*Source:* Scholar.

| | | | | | |
|---|---|---|---|---|---|
| 2003–04 | York C | 1 | 0 | **1** | **0** |

**HOPE, Richard# (D) 234 10**
H: 6 3 W: 13 13 b.Middlesbrough 22-6-78
*Source:* Trainee.

| | | | | | |
|---|---|---|---|---|---|
| 1995–96 | Blackburn R | 0 | 0 | | |
| 1996–97 | Blackburn R | 0 | 0 | | |
| 1996–97 | Darlington | 20 | 0 | | |
| 1997–98 | Darlington | 35 | 1 | | |
| 1998–99 | Darlington | 8 | 0 | **63** | **1** |
| 1998–99 | Northampton T | 19 | 0 | | |
| 1999–2000 | Northampton T | 17 | 0 | | |
| 2000–01 | Northampton T | 33 | 0 | | |
| 2001–02 | Northampton T | 43 | 6 | | |
| 2002–03 | Northampton T | 23 | 1 | **135** | **7** |
| 2003–04 | York C | 36 | 2 | **36** | **2** |

**LAW, Graeme§ (M) 4 0**
H: 5 10 W: 10 10 b.Kirkcaldy 6-10-84
*Source:* Scholar. *Honours:* Scotland Youth.

| | | | | | |
|---|---|---|---|---|---|
| 2003–04 | York C | 4 | 0 | **4** | **0** |

**MERRIS, Dave (D) 44 0**
H: 5 7 W: 10 06 b.Rotherham 13-10-80
*Source:* Harrogate T.

| | | | | | |
|---|---|---|---|---|---|
| 2003–04 | York C | 44 | 0 | **44** | **0** |

**NOGAN, Lee (F) 561 114**
H: 5 10 W: 11 08 b.Cardiff 21-5-69
*Source:* Apprentice. *Honours:* Wales Under-21, B, 2 full caps.

| | | | | | |
|---|---|---|---|---|---|
| 1986–87 | Oxford U | 0 | 0 | | |
| 1986–87 | *Brentford* | 11 | 2 | **11** | **2** |
| 1987–88 | Oxford U | 3 | 0 | | |
| 1987–88 | *Southend U* | 6 | 1 | | |
| 1988–89 | Oxford U | 3 | 0 | | |
| 1989–90 | Oxford U | 4 | 0 | | |
| 1990–91 | Oxford U | 32 | 5 | | |
| 1991–92 | Oxford U | 22 | 5 | **64** | **10** |
| 1991–92 | Watford | 23 | 5 | | |
| 1992–93 | Watford | 42 | 11 | | |
| 1993–94 | Watford | 26 | 3 | | |
| 1993–94 | *Southend U* | 5 | 0 | **11** | **1** |
| 1994–95 | Watford | 14 | 7 | **105** | **26** |
| 1994–95 | Reading | 20 | 10 | | |
| 1995–96 | Reading | 39 | 10 | | |
| 1996–97 | Reading | 32 | 6 | **91** | **26** |
| 1996–97 | *Notts Co* | 6 | 0 | **6** | **0** |
| 1997–98 | Grimsby T | 36 | 8 | | |
| 1998–99 | Grimsby T | 38 | 2 | **74** | **10** |
| 1999–2000 | Darlington | 31 | 2 | | |
| 2000–01 | Darlington | 18 | 4 | **49** | **6** |
| 2000–01 | *Luton T* | 7 | 1 | **7** | **1** |
| 2000–01 | York C | 16 | 6 | | |
| 2001–02 | York C | 42 | 13 | | |
| 2002–03 | York C | 46 | 5 | | |
| 2003–04 | York C | 39 | 8 | **143** | **32** |

**OVENDALE, Mark‡ (G) 181 0**
H: 6 2 W: 14 03 b.Leicester 22-11-73
*Source:* Wisbech T.

| | | | | | |
|---|---|---|---|---|---|
| 1994–95 | Northampton T | 6 | 0 | **6** | **0** |

From Barry T.

| | | | | | |
|---|---|---|---|---|---|
| 1997–98 | Bournemouth | 0 | 0 | | |
| 1998–99 | Bournemouth | 46 | 0 | | |
| 1999–2000 | Bournemouth | 43 | 0 | **89** | **0** |
| 2000–01 | Luton T | 26 | 0 | | |
| 2001–02 | Luton T | 13 | 0 | | |
| 2002–03 | Luton T | 6 | 0 | **45** | **0** |

From Barry T.

| | | | | | |
|---|---|---|---|---|---|
| 2003–04 | York C | 41 | 0 | **41** | **0** |

**PORTER, Chris (G) 15 0**
H: 6 2 W: 12 10 b.Middlesbrough 10-11-79
*Source:* Trainee.

| | | | | | |
|---|---|---|---|---|---|
| 1998–99 | Sunderland | 0 | 0 | | |
| 1999–2000 | Sunderland | 0 | 0 | | |
| 2000–01 | Darlington | 0 | 0 | | |
| 2000–01 | Hartlepool U | 0 | 0 | | |
| 2000–01 | Southend U | 0 | 0 | | |
| 2001–02 | Darlington | 7 | 0 | | |
| 2002–03 | Darlington | 3 | 0 | **10** | **0** |
| 2003–04 | York C | 5 | 0 | **5** | **0** |

**SMITH, Christopher‡ (D) 79 0**
H: 5 11 W: 12 10 b.Derby 30-6-81
*Source:* Trainee.

| | | | | | |
|---|---|---|---|---|---|
| 1999–2000 | Reading | 0 | 0 | | |
| 2000–01 | Reading | 0 | 0 | | |
| 2001–02 | York C | 15 | 0 | | |
| 2002–03 | York C | 36 | 0 | | |
| 2003–04 | York C | 28 | 0 | **79** | **0** |

**STEWART, Bryan§ (M) 10 0**
H: 5 11 W: 11 00 b.Stockton 13-9-85

| | | | | | |
|---|---|---|---|---|---|
| 2003–04 | York C | 10 | 0 | **10** | **0** |

**STOCKDALE, David§ (G) 1 0**
H: 6 3 W: 13 04 b.Leeds 20-9-85
*Source:* Scholar.

| | | | | | |
|---|---|---|---|---|---|
| 2002–03 | York C | 1 | 0 | | |
| 2003–04 | York C | 0 | 0 | **1** | **0** |

**WARD, Mitch‡ (M) 290 12**
H: 5 8 W: 11 12 b.Sheffield 19-6-71
*Source:* Trainee.

| | | | | | |
|---|---|---|---|---|---|
| 1989–90 | Sheffield U | 0 | 0 | | |
| 1990–91 | Sheffield U | 4 | 0 | | |
| 1990–91 | *Crewe Alex* | 4 | 1 | **4** | **1** |
| 1991–92 | Sheffield U | 6 | 2 | | |
| 1992–93 | Sheffield U | 26 | 0 | | |
| 1993–94 | Sheffield U | 22 | 1 | | |
| 1994–95 | Sheffield U | 14 | 2 | | |
| 1995–96 | Sheffield U | 42 | 1 | | |
| 1996–97 | Sheffield U | 34 | 4 | | |
| 1997–98 | Sheffield U | 6 | 1 | **154** | **11** |
| 1997–98 | Everton | 8 | 0 | | |
| 1998–99 | Everton | 6 | 0 | | |
| 1999–2000 | Everton | 10 | 0 | **24** | **0** |
| 2000–01 | Barnsley | 36 | 0 | | |
| 2001–02 | Barnsley | 15 | 0 | | |
| 2002–03 | Barnsley | 26 | 0 | **77** | **0** |
| 2003–04 | York C | 31 | 0 | **31** | **0** |

**WISE, Stuart* (D) 33 1**
H: 5 10 W: 13 13 b.Middlesbrough 4-4-84
*Source:* Scholar.

| | | | | | |
|---|---|---|---|---|---|
| 2001–02 | York C | 6 | 0 | | |
| 2002–03 | York C | 8 | 0 | | |
| 2003–04 | York C | 19 | 1 | **33** | **1** |

**WOOD, Leigh‡ (M) 64 0**
H: 5 11 W: 11 06 b.Selby 21-5-83
*Source:* Scholar.

| | | | | | |
|---|---|---|---|---|---|
| 2000–01 | York C | 5 | 0 | | |
| 2001–02 | York C | 14 | 0 | | |
| 2002–03 | York C | 19 | 0 | | |
| 2003–04 | York C | 26 | 0 | **64** | **0** |

**YALCIN, Levent§ (M) 20 0**
H: 6 0 W: 12 02 b.Middlesbrough 25-3-85
*Source:* Scholar.

| | | | | | |
|---|---|---|---|---|---|
| 2002–03 | York C | 5 | 0 | | |
| 2003–04 | York C | 15 | 0 | **20** | **0** |

**Scholars**
Anderson, Gary D; Arthur, Adam J; Ashcroft, Kane J; Baynes, Steven; Coad, Matthew P; Davies, Sean G; Green, Andrew; Haw, Robert A; Kamara, Nathan J; Law, Graeme; Lyon, Steven W; Mackenzie, Michael; Reid, Arran W; Staley, Michael R; Stewart, Bryan W; Stockdale, David A; Webster, Byron C; Yalcin, Levent

**Non Contract**
Donovan, Kevin

# ENGLISH LEAGUE PLAYERS – INDEX

# TRANSFERS 2003–04

| | *From* | *To* | *Fee in £* |
|---|---|---|---|
| **MAY 2003** | | | |
| 27 Loran, Tyrone | Manchester City | Tranmere Rovers | undisclosed |
| 19 Reid, Paul M. | Rangers | Northampton Town | 100,000 |
| **JUNE 2003** | | | |
| 14 Chaaban, Ali | Leatherhead | Farnborough Town | undisclosed |
| 11 Clark, Peter J. | Stockport County | Northampton Town | undisclosed |
| 30 Finnan, Stephen J. | Fulham | Liverpool | 3,500,000 |
| 17 Holland, Matthew R. | Ipswich Town | Charlton Athletic | 750,000 |
| 23 Maylett, Bradley | Burnley | Swansea City | Free |
| 6 Young, Ryan | Hucknall Town | Hednesford Town | undisclosed |
| **JULY 2003** | | | |
| 10 Agogo, Manuel | Barnet | Bristol Rovers | 110,000+ |
| 15 Aldridge, Paul A. | Berkhamsted Town | Chesham United | undisclosed |
| 12 Armstrong, Christopher | Oldham Athletic | Sheffield United | 100,000 |
| 21 Bridge, Wayne M. | Southampton | Chelsea | 7,000,000 |
| 15 Clifford, Peter A. | Berkhamsted Town | Chesham United | undisclosed |
| 19 Cochrane, Justin V. | Hayes | Crewe Alexandra | undisclosed |
| 4 Coyne, Daniel | Grimsby Town | Leicester City | Free |
| 26 Duff, Damien A. | Blackburn Rovers | Chelsea | 17,000,000 |
| 9 Dunn, David J.I. | Blackburn Rovers | Birmingham City | 5,500,000 |
| 21 Francis, Damien J. | Wimbledon | Norwich City | undisclosed |
| 15 Gower, Mark | Barnet | Southend United | 25,000 |
| 8 Grazioli, Giuliano | Bristol Rovers | Barnet | exch. |
| 14 Hall, Fitz | Oldham Athletic | Southampton | 250,000 |
| 22 Henry, Anthony F. | Folkestone Invicta | Welling United | undisclosed |
| 25 Hignett, Craig J. | Blackburn Rovers | Leicester City | Free |
| 22 Hill, Clinton S. | Oldham Athletic | Stoke City | 120,000 |
| 4 Howey, Stephen N. | Manchester City | Leicester City | 300,000 |
| 11 Hulse, Robert W. | Crewe Alexandra | West Bromwich Albion | 750,000 |
| 11 Hunt, David J. | Crystal Palace | Leyton Orient | undisclosed |
| 22 Johnson, Glen M.C. | West Ham United | Chelsea | 6,000,000 |
| 19 Kelly, Leon M. | Ilkeston Town | Worcester City | undisclosed |
| 9 Kewell, Harry | Leeds United | Liverpool | 5,000,000 |
| 21 Le Saux, Graeme P. | Chelsea | Southampton | 500,000 |
| 31 Low, Joshua D. | Oldham Athletic | Northampton Town | 165,000 |
| 31 McCann, Gavin P. | Sunderland | Aston Villa | 2,250,000 |
| 30 Miller, Lee A. | Falkirk | Bristol City | 300,000 |
| 9 Murray, Scott G. | Bristol City | Reading | 650,000 |
| 10 Nelson, Michael J. | Bury | Hartlepool United | 70,000 |
| 23 Paul, Trevor | Bishop's Stortford | Leyton | undisclosed |
| 30 Reid, Steven J. | Millwall | Blackburn Rovers | 1,800,000 |
| 24 Shipperley, Neil J. | Wimbledon | Crystal Palace | undisclosed |
| 22 Sinclair, Trevor | West Ham United | Manchester City | 2,500,000 |
| 15 Sippetts, Garry J. | Berkhamsted Town | Chesham United | undisclosed |
| 17 Talbot, Robert T. | Morecambe | Burton Albion | undisclosed |
| 17 Thatcher, Benjamin D. | Tottenham Hotspur | Leicester City | 300,000 |
| 16 Webber, Daniel V. | Manchester United | Watford | undisclosed |
| 22 Zamora, Robert L. | Brighton & Hove Albion | Tottenham Hotspur | 1,500,000 |

**TEMPORARY TRANSFERS**

15 Chadwick, Luke H. – Manchester United – Burnley
7 Davis, James R.W. – Manchester United – Watford
24 Knight, Leon L. – Chelsea – Brighton & Hove Albion
25 Patterson, Simon G. – Watford – Wycombe Wanderers
31 Stewart, Michael J. – Manchester United – Nottingham F
28 Davies, Clint A. – Bradford City – Halifax Town
10 Gilbert, Peter – Birmingham City – Plymouth Argyle
8 O'Neill, Joseph – Preston North End – Bury
29 Stanley, Craig – Walsall – Raith Rovers
31 Warnock, Stephen – Liverpool – Coventry City

| | | | |
|---|---|---|---|
| **AUGUST 2003** | | | |
| 26 Arphexad, Pegguy M. | Liverpool | Coventry City | Free |
| 11 Beaumont, James | Newcastle United | Nottingham Forest | undisclosed |
| 9 Blount, Mark | Burton Albion | Alfreton Town | undisclosed |
| 8 Britton, Leon J. | West Ham United | Swansea City | Free |
| 22 Bruce, Joseph M. | Hitchin Town | Grays Athletic | undisclosed |
| 29 Butler, Martin N. | Reading | Rotherham United | 150,000 |
| 6 Cole, Joseph J. | West Ham United | Chelsea | 6,600,000 |
| 8 Connolly, David J. | Wimbledon | West Ham United | 285,000 |
| 20 Cooksey, Ernest G. | Crawley Town | Oldham Athletic | undisclosed |
| 15 Craddock, Jody | Sunderland | Wolverhampton Wanderers | 1,750,000 |
| 14 Crossley, Mark G. | Middlesbrough | Fulham | 500,000 |
| 15 Curtis, John C.K. | Blackburn Rovers | Leicester City | Free |
| 8 Davis, Kelvin G. | Wimbledon | Ipswich Town | Free |
| 8 Etherington, Matthew | Tottenham Hotspur | West Ham United | 1,000,000 |
| 11 Gardner, Ross | Newcastle United | Nottingham Forest | undisclosed |
| 4 Goater, Shaun L. | Manchester City | Reading | 500,000 |
| 15 Godbold, Jamie T. | Lowestoft Town | Cambridge City | undisclosed |
| 8 Haas, Bernt | Sunderland | West Bromwich Albion | 400,000 |
| 18 Hendy, Scott | Mangotsfield United | Bath City | undisclosed |
| 21 Holyoak, Daniel | King's Lynn | Ilkeston Town | undisclosed |
| 15 Horlock, Kevin | Manchester City | West Ham United | 300,000 |
| 8 Hutchinson, Jonathan | Birmingham City | Darlington | Free |
| 8 Hylton, Leon D. | Aston Villa | Swansea City | Free |
| 15 Iversen, Steffen | Tottenham Hotspur | Wolverhampton Wanderers | Free |
| 15 Johnson, Michael O. | Birmingham City | Derby County | undisclosed |
| 6 Kanoute, Frederic | West Ham United | Tottenham Hotspur | 3,500,000 |

| | | | |
|---|---|---|---|
| 14 Kinch, Scott | Carshalton Athletic | Tooting & Mitcham United | undisclosed |
| 21 Knight, Leon L. | Chelsea | Brighton & Hove Albion | 100,000 |
| 15 Langley, Richard B.M. | Queens Park Rangers | Cardiff City | 250,000 |
| 15 Lee, Alan D. | Rotherham United | Cardiff City | 850,000 |
| 29 McCann, Ryan P. | Celtic | Hartlepool United | Free |
| 7 McIndoe, Michael | Yeovil Town | Doncaster Rovers | 50,000 |
| 22 McLeod, Kevin A. | Everton | Queens Park Rangers | undisclosed |
| 14 Nash, Carlo J. | Manchester City | Middlesbrough | 150,000 |
| 8 O'Connor, James K. | Stoke City | West Bromwich Albion | undisclosed |
| 15 Phillips, Kevin M. | Sunderland | Southampton | 3,250,000 |
| 15 Pluck, Lee K. | Barnet | Cambridge City | undisclosed |
| 29 Reyna, Claudio | Sunderland | Manchester City | 2,500,000 |
| 8 Russell, Darel F.R.G. | Norwich City | Stoke City | 125,000 |
| 14 Schemmel, Sebastien | West Ham United | Portsmouth | Free |
| 9 Sodje, Efetobore P. | Crewe Alexandra | Huddersfield Town | Free |
| 8 Sorensen, Thomas | Sunderland | Aston Villa | 2,225,000 |
| 22 Stamp, Darryn | Northampton Town | Chester City | undisclosed |
| 18 Steane, Ben | Bedworth United | Halesowen Town | undisclosed |
| 29 Sullivan, Neil | Tottenham Hotspur | Chelsea | 500,000 |
| 27 Taylor, Gareth K. | Burnley | Nottingham Forest | 500,000 |
| 29 Thome, Emerson A. | Sunderland | Bolton Wanderers | Free |
| 22 Thorpe, Anthony L. | Luton Town | Queens Park Rangers | 50,000 |
| 26 Tonkin, Anthony | Stockport County | Crewe Alexandra | 150,000 |
| 7 Veron, Juan S. | Manchester United | Chelsea | 12,500,000 |
| 7 Wanless, Paul S. | Cambridge United | Oxford United | Free |
| 7 Wilkshire, Luke | Middlesbrough | Bristol City | 250,000 |
| 5 Woolley, Barry | Ilkeston Town | Worcester City | undisclosed |
| 11 Wright, Peter D. | Burscough | Southport | undisclosed |

**TEMPORARY TRANSFERS**

16 Amankwaah, Kevin – Bristol City – Cheltenham Town
8 Ashton, Jonathan J. – Leicester City – Oxford United
29 Bailey, John A.K. – Preston North End – Hamilton A
15 Beck, Daniel G. – Brighton & HA – Bognor Regis Town
8 Boucaud, Andre – Reading – Peterborough United
21 Burchill, Mark J. – Portsmouth – Wigan Athletic
21 Callery, Alex J. – Worksop Town – Ilkeston Town
26 Chilvers, Liam C. – Arsenal – Colchester United
20 Cole, Carlton – Chelsea – Charlton Athletic
29 Collin, Adam J. – Newcastle United – Oldham Athletic
22 Corbett, Luke J. – Cheltenham Town – Chelmsford City
22 Donaldson, Clayton A. – Hull City – Scarborough
5 Fagan, Craig – Birmingham City – Colchester United
29 Forssell, Mikael K. – Chelsea – Birmingham City
16 Furness, Adam – Stevenage Borough – Aveley
29 Gerrard, Paul W. – Everton – Sheffield United
8 Gilroy, David M. – Bristol Rovers – Forest Green Rovers
14 Hammond, Elvis Z. – Fulham – Norwich City
22 Haworth, Robert J. – Hendon – Gravesend & Northfleet
25 Hudson, Mark A. – Fulham – Oldham Athletic
6 Jones, Bradley – Middlesbrough – Rotherham United
16 Jones, Jimmi-Lee – Wolverhampton W – Forest Green R
8 Jones, Mark A. – Hednesford Town – Bromsgrove Rovers
23 Kilgallon, Matthew – Leeds United – West Ham United
29 Kuipers, Michael – Brighton & Hove Albion – Hull City
6 MacLean, Steven – Rangers – Scunthorpe United
15 Marney, Daniel G. – Brighton & HA – Crawley Town
29 McCormack, Alan – Preston North End – Leyton Orient
18 McLeod, Kevin A. – Everton – Queens Park Rangers
23 McSheffrey, Gary – Coventry City – Luton Town
22 Mills, Daniel J. – Leeds United – Middlesbrough
8 Myhill, Glyn O. – Aston Villa – Macclesfield Town
20 Onuora, Ifem – Sheffield United – Wycombe Wanderers
20 Pennant, Jermaine – Arsenal – Leeds United
8 Pitt, Courtney L. – Portsmouth – Luton Town
2 Pullen, James – Ipswich Town – Dagenham & Redbridge
22 Ritchie, Paul M. – Manchester City – Walsall
22 Russell, Samuel I. – Middlesbrough – Scunthorpe United
18 Senior, Michael – Halifax Town – Ossett Town
7 Shuker, Christopher A. – Manchester City – Rochdale
27 Smertin, Alexei – Chelsea – Portsmouth
2 Strong, Greg – Hull City – Bury
8 Taylor, Maik S. – Fulham – Birmingham City
14 Thomas, Bradley M. – Peterborough United – Kettering T
8 Voltz, Moritz – Arsenal – Fulham
4 Williams, Thomas A. – Birmingham C – Queens Park R
30 Zenden, Boudewijn – Chelsea – Middlesbrough
9 Andrews, Keith J. – Wolverhampton Wanderers – Stoke City
27 Babbel, Markus – Liverpool – Blackburn Rovers
22 Baldacchino, Ryan L. – Carlisle United – Gretna
8 Bishop, Andrew J. – Walsall – Kidderminster Harriers
14 Bradbury, Lee M. – Portsmouth – Derby County
8 Caldwell, Gary – Newcastle United – Derby County
8 Cameron, David A. – Chester City – Halifax Town
14 Clarke, Lee – Peterborough United – Kettering Town
8 Colgan, Nick – Hibernian – Stockport County
28 Connell, Darren S. – Accrington Stanley – Burscough
7 Danns, Neil A. – Blackburn Rovers – Blackpool
7 Douglas, Jonathan – Blackburn Rovers – Blackpool
29 Flitney, Ross D. – Fulham – Brighton & Hove Albion
7 Fowler, Lee A. – Coventry City – Huddersfield Town
8 Gamble, Joseph F. – Reading – Barnet
7 Gill, Robert – Doncaster Rovers – Chester City
31 Gray, Michael – Sunderland – Celtic
29 Hawley, Karl L. – Walsall – Raith Rovers
8 Henderson, Darius A. – Reading – Brighton & Hove Albion
27 Jenkins, Rory A. – Stevenage Borough – Oxford City
25 Jones, Darren L. – Bristol City – Cheltenham Town
8 Jones, Lee – Stockport County – Blackpool
1 Juan, Maldonado D. – Arsenal – Millwall
14 Kirkwood, Scott – Crawley Town – Horsham
4 Louis, Jefferson L. – Oxford United – Woking
9 Manuella, Fiston – Aylesbury United – Aldershot Town
25 May, Ben S. – Millwall – Brentford
15 McKenzie, Michael – Kettering Town – Stamford
27 McPhail, Stephen J.P. – Leeds United – Nottingham Forest
7 Mellor, Neil A. – Liverpool – West Ham United
29 Murray, Adam D. – Derby County – Kidderminster Harriers
8 Ndiwa, Lord-Kangana – Bolton Wanderers – Oldham Ath
30 Pell, Robert A. – Worksop Town – Lancaster City
2 Pitcher, Geoffrey – Brighton & Hove Albion – Stevenage B
11 Price, Jamie B. – Doncaster Rovers – Halifax Town
22 Richardson, Marcus G. – Hartlepool United – Lincoln City
11 Robinson, Neil D. – Macclesfield Town – Leigh RMI
8 Scott, Benjamin T. – Sheffield United – Hereford United
15 Shipperley, James A. – Hayes – Wealdstone
7 Singh, Harpal – Leeds United – Bury
20 Stirling, Jude B. – Stevenage Borough – Hornchurch
22 Svensson, Mattias – Charlton Athletic – Derby County
8 Ten Heuvel, Laurens – Sheffield United – Grimsby Town
7 Vine, Rowan – Portsmouth – Colchester United
8 Walters, Jonathan R. – Bolton Wanderers – Crewe Alexandra
11 Willock, Calum – Fulham – Bristol Rovers
30 Zola Makongo, Calvin – Newcastle United – Oldham Athletic

**SEPTEMBER 2003**

| | | | |
|---|---|---|---|
| 15 Akinbiyi, Adeola P. | Crystal Palace | Stoke City | Free |
| 12 Ashton, Jonathan J. | Leicester City | Oxford United | Free |
| 17 Devlin, Paul J. | Birmingham City | Watford | 150,000 |
| 25 France, Ryan | Alfreton Town | Hull City | 15,000 |
| 25 Green, Francis J. | Peterborough United | Lincoln City | 7500 |
| 19 Haworth, Robert J. | Hendon | Gravesend & Northfleet | undisclosed |
| 9 Horsfield, Geoffrey M. | Birmingham City | Wigan Athletic | 1,000,000 |
| 5 Jones, Daniel R. | Worcester City | Halesowen Town | undisclosed |

| | | | |
|---|---|---|---|
| 3 Kerrigan, Daniel A. | Grays Athletic | Hornchurch | undisclosed |
| 2 Kilbane, Kevin D. | Sunderland | Everton | 750,000 |
| 1 Martyn, Antony N. | Leeds United | Everton | 500,000 |
| 19 Milsom, Paul J. | Bath City | Tiverton Town | undisclosed |
| 23 Nolan, Matthew L. | Hitchin Town | Peterborough United | undisclosed |
| 1 Pembridge, Mark | Everton | Fulham | 500,000 |
| 6 Proudlock, Adam D. | Wolverhampton Wanderers | Sheffield Wednesday | 150,000 |
| 17 Rawlins, Matthew | Chippenham Town | Yate Town | undisclosed |
| 5 Ritchie, Paul M. | Manchester City | Walsall | Free |
| 25 Smith, Thomas W. | Watford | Sunderland | undisclosed |
| 3 Sugden, Ryan S. | Burton Albion | Morecambe | undisclosed |

**TEMPORARY TRANSFERS**

2 Adams, Adrian – Forest Green Rovers – Bath City
27 Allen, Daniel T. – Forest Green Rovers – Evesham United
19 Ayres, Lee T. – Kidderminster Harriers – Tamworth
12 Bart-Williams, Christopher G. – Charlton Ath – Ipswich T
8 Beesley, Mark A. – Chester City – Southport
1 Bent, Marcus N. – Ipswich Town – Leicester City
23 Blackman, Lloyd J. – Brentford – Scarborough
12 Brannan, Gerard D. – Wigan Athletic – Rochdale
6 Brayley, Albert P. – Canvey Island – Heybridge Swifts
19 Brown, Wayne L. – Watford – Gillingham
17 Burton, Deon J. – Portsmouth – Walsall
19 Cavill, Aaran – Northampton Town – Bedford Town
26 Clark, Steven T. – Southend United – Macclesfield Town
27 Cooper, Adam – Nuneaton Borough – Solihull Borough
26 Crowe, Dean A. – Luton Town – York City
16 Davies, Darren J. – Dover Athletic – Molesey
11 De Bolla, Mark – Charlton Athletic – Chesterfield
24 Doherty, Sean A. – Fulham – Blackpool
12 Dolby, Christopher – Alfreton Town – Wakefield & Emley
1 Facey, Delroy M. – Bolton Wanderers – Burnley
1 Farrelly, Gareth – Bolton Wanderers – Burnley
23 Forde, David – West Ham United – Barnet
12 Gilroy, David M. – Bristol Rovers – Clevedon Town
5 Green, Dean – Farnborough Town – Staines Town
9 Hall, Laurence W.L. – Stoke City – Tiverton Town
22 Hardie, Brian – Kettering Town – Corby Town
12 Harper, Kevin P. – Portsmouth – Norwich City
5 Henderson, Darius A. – Reading – Brighton & Hove Albion
8 Henry, Solomon – Barnet – Berkhamsted Town
19 Horrigan, Darren C. – Lincoln City – Cambridge City
12 Huckerby, Darren C. – Manchester City – Norwich City
4 Ifil, Jerel C. – Watford – Swindon Town
26 Jones, Darren L. – Bristol City – Cheltenham Town
10 Kelly, James – Chester City – Scarborough
4 Kielty, Gerrard T. – Leigh RMI – Stalybridge Celtic
1 Konchesky, Paul M. – Charlton Athletic – Tottenham H
5 Lewis, Matthew T. – Kidderminster Harriers – Hinckley U
5 Livesey, Daniel – Bolton Wanderers – Notts County
11 Lucas, Adam – Leigh RMI – Burscough
15 Marney, Daniel G. – Brighton & Hove Albion – Crawley T
24 May, Ben S. – Millwall – Brentford
22 McCartney, David J. – Millwall – Egham Town
12 McGlinchey, Brian K. – Plymouth Argyle – Torquay U
12 McKenzie, Michael – Kettering Town – Stamford
17 McSheffrey, Gary – Coventry City – Luton Town
12 Muller, Adam P. – Worksop Town – Wakefield & Emley
19 Neill, Thomas E. – Farnborough Town – Bishop's Stortford
13 Omoyinmi, Emmanuel – Oxford United – Margate
19 Onuora, Ifem – Sheffield United – Grimsby Town
19 Penfold, Terry – Gravesend & Northfleet – Erith & B
16 Pidgeley, Leonard J. – Chelsea – Watford
6 Proudlock, Adam D. – Wolverhampton W – Sheffield W
29 Rehman, Zeshan – Fulham – Brighton & Hove Albion
8 Roache, Leigh P. – Barnet – Berkhamsted Town
19 Robinson, Carl P. – Portsmouth – Rotherham United
19 Ross, Neil J. – Macclesfield Town – Northwich Victoria
19 Russell, Samuel I. – Middlesbrough – Scunthorpe United
7 Shuker, Christopher A. – Manchester City – Rochdale
5 Smith, Gareth S. – Hull City – Stockport County
22 Svensson, Mattias – Charlton Athletic – Derby County
4 Todd, Andrew J.J. – Blackburn Rovers – Burnley
5 Walshe, Benjamin M. – Queens Park R – Gravesend & N
29 Whelan, Glenn D. – Manchester City – Bury
7 Whitman, Tristram – Doncaster Rovers – Tamworth
19 Williams, Benjamin W. – Manchester United – Altrincham
12 Wilson, Mark A. – Middlesbrough – Swansea City
12 Wright, Thomas A. – Leicester City – Brentford
11 Alexandersson, Niclas – Everton – West Ham United
17 Amankwaah, Kevin – Bristol City – Cheltenham Town
26 Baird, Christopher P. – Southampton – Walsall
15 Beck, Daniel G. – Brighton & HA – Bognor Regis Town
20 Benjamin, Trevor J. – Leicester City – Gillingham
9 Bishop, Andrew – Walsall – Kidderminster Harriers
7 Boucaud, Andre – Reading – Peterborough United
19 Branston, Guy P.B. – Rotherham United – Wycombe W
2 Brodie, Stephen E. – Chester City – Forest Green Rovers
4 Bull, Ronnie R. – Millwall – Yeovil Town
25 Cade, Jamie W. – Middlesbrough – Chesterfield
17 Charles, Anthony D. – Aldershot Town – Lewes
28 Connell, Darren S. – Accrington Stanley – Burscough
8 Crouch, Peter J. – Aston Villa – Norwich City
5 Davies, Christopher M. – Lincoln City – Stamford
19 Dawes, Nicholas J. – Rotherham United – Grimsby Town
12 Devlin, Paul J. – Birmingham City – Watford
15 Doig, Christopher R. – Nottingham Forest – Northampton T
5 Dyer, Lloyd R. – West Bromwich Albion – Kidderminster H
7 Fagan, Craig – Birmingham City – Colchester United
30 Flitney, Ross – Fulham – Brighton & Hove Albion
12 Forrest, Martyn W. – Bury – Leigh RMI
4 Gnohere, Arthur – Burnley – Queens Park Rangers
16 Green, Francis J. – Peterborough United – Lincoln City
13 Hammond, Dean J. – Brighton & Hove Albion – Aldershot T
16 Harley, Jon – Fulham – Sheffield United
19 Heath, Nicholas A. – Kidderminster Harriers – Solihull B
12 Henderson, Kevin M. – Hartlepool United – Carlisle United
18 Hogg, Anthony T. – Gravesend & N – Folkestone Invicta
8 Horsfield, Geoffrey M. – Birmingham City – Wigan Athletic
23 Hudson, Mark A. – Fulham – Oldham Athletic
1 Jeffers, Francis – Arsenal – Everton
1 Kachloul, Hassan – Aston Villa – Wolverhampton Wanderers
24 Kelly, Stephen M. – Tottenham Hotspur – Watford
19 Kitamirike, Joel D. – Chelsea – Brentford
26 Kuqi, Shefki – Sheffield Wednesday – Ipswich Town
1 Little, Glen M. – Burnley – Bolton Wanderers
24 Logan, Richard J. – Boston United – Peterborough United
9 Mahon, Alan J. – Blackburn Rovers – Ipswich Town
19 Martin, Ian – Leigh RMI – Rossendale United
1 McCarthy, David – Worksop Town – Altrincham
30 McCormack, Alan – Preston North End – Leyton Orient
6 McGregor, Marc R. – Tamworth – Chippenham Town
19 McNamara, Niall A. – Lincoln City – Alfreton Town
4 Milner, James P. – Leeds United – Swindon Town
2 Mumford, Andrew O. – Swansea City – Newport County
19 O'Brien, Robert L. – Doncaster Rovers – Gainsborough T
26 O'Neil, Gary P. – Portsmouth – Walsall
5 Owen, Gareth J. – Stoke City – Tiverton Town
1 Perry, Christopher J. – Tottenham Hotspur – Charlton Ath
19 Pitt, Courtney L. – Portsmouth – Luton Town
11 Quinn, Wayne R. – Newcastle United – West Ham United
23 Richardson, Marcus G. – Hartlepool United – Lincoln City
1 Roberts, Jason A.D. – West Bromwich Albion – Portsmouth
10 Robinson, Neil – Macclesfield Town – Leigh RMI
19 Russell, Matthew L. – Forest Green Rovers – Farsley Celtic
12 Sale, Mark D. – Tamworth – Hucknall Town
19 Simpemba, Ian F. – Wycombe Wanderers – Woking
16 Stephens, Kevin – Leyton Orient – Billericay Town
16 Tevendale, James R. – Hucknall Town – Leek Town
26 Twigg, Gary – Derby County – Burton Albion
2 Westhead, Mark – Stevenage Borough – Hyde United
11 White, Andrew – Mansfield Town – Boston United
9 Wilkinson, Shaun F. – Brighton & HA – Havant & W
15 Williamson, Michael J. – Southampton – Torquay United
12 Wood, Neil A. – Manchester United – Peterborough United

**OCTOBER 2003**

| | | | |
|---|---|---|---|
| 31 Dean, Brian C. | Leicester City | West Ham United | Free |
| 16 Hatswell, Wayne | Chester City | Kidderminster Harriers | 15,000 |
| 23 Ingimarsson, Ivar | Wolverhampton Wanderers | Reading | 100,000 |
| 17 Moore, Christian | Burton Albion | Telford United | undisclosed |
| 23 Mullins, Hayden I. | Crystal Palace | West Ham United | 600,000 |

| | | | |
|---|---|---|---|
| 14 Quinn, Wayne R. | Newcastle United | West Ham United | Free |
| 14 Robinson, Paul P. | Watford | West Bromwich Albion | 250,000 |
| 17 Szewczyk, Paul T. | Stafford Rangers | Bromsgrove Rovers | undisclosed |

**TEMPORARY TRANSFERS**

18 Abbott, Paul – Margate – Hitchin Town
31 Arnison, Paul S. – Hartlepool United – Carlisle United
13 Barrowman, Andrew – Birmingham City – Crewe Alexandra
3 Beckwith, Dean S. – Gillingham – Dagenham & Redbridge
3 Beresford, David – Plymouth Argyle – Macclesfield Town
21 Bouffong, Jonathon – Ford United – Berkhamsted Town
12 Brannan, Gerrard D. – Wigan Athletic – Rochdale
4 Brayley, Albert P. – Canvey Island – Heybridge Swifts
5 Bull, Ronnie R. – Millwall – Yeovil Town
24 Burton, Steven P.G. – Hull City – Kidderminster Harriers
30 Buxton, Lewis E. – Portsmouth – AFC Bournemouth
23 Callery, Alex J. – Worksop Town – Belper Town
14 Camm, Mark L. – Lincoln City – King's Lynn
24 Clancy, Timothy – Millwall – Weymouth
17 Cooper, Shaun D. – Portsmouth – Leyton Orient
31 Cryan, Colin – Sheffield United – Scarborough
17 Dichio, Daniele S.E. – West Bromwich Albion – Derby Co
29 Downing, Stewart – Middlesbrough – Sunderland
31 Elam, Lee P.G. – Halifax Town – Yeovil Town
31 Facey, Delroy M. – Bolton Wanderers – Burnley
31 Farrelly, Gareth – Bolton Wanderers – Burnley
11 Forde, David – West Ham United – Barnet
18 Furness, Adam – Stevenage Borough – Hitchin Town
1 Gilbert, Peter – Birmingham City – Plymouth Argyle
10 Gore, Shane S. – Wimbledon – St Albans City
10 Gulliver, Philip S. – Middlesbrough – Bury
17 Hammond, Dean J. – Brighton & HA – Leyton Orient
23 Hardie, Brian – Kettering Town – Corby Town
14 Heathcote, Jonathan – Cambridge United – Grays Athletic
13 Henderson, Kevin M. – Hartlepool United – Carlisle United
10 Hogg, Christopher – Ipswich Town – Boston United
24 Horrigan, Darren C. – Lincoln City – Ilkeston Town
31 Jackman, Daniel J. – Aston Villa – Stockport County
31 Jones, Robert W. – Stockport County – Macclesfield Town
22 Kelly, Stephen M. – Tottenham Hotspur – Watford
10 Kirkwood, Scott – Crawley Town – Fulham
6 Konchesky, Paul M. – Charlton Athletic – Tottenham H
21 Lewis, Karl J. – Leicester City – Swindon Town
24 Leworthy, Craig – Havant & Waterlooville – Fleet Town
9 Lovett, Jay – Farnborough Town – Lewes
31 Martin, Ben – Swindon Town – Lincoln City
31 McCombe, Jamie – Scunthorpe United – Halifax Town
12 McGlinchey, Brian K. – Plymouth Argyle – Torquay United
7 McGregor, Marc R. – Tamworth – Weston-Super-Mare
22 McSheffrey, Gary – Coventry City – Luton Town
9 Mitchell, Craig R. – Mansfield Town – Harrogate Town
31 Moore, Paul – Telford United – Hucknall Town
22 Mullins, Hayden I. – Crystal Palace – West Ham United
24 Myhre, Thomas – Sunderland – Crystal Palace
20 O'Brien, Robert L. – Doncaster Rovers – Gainsborough T
27 O'Neil, Gary – Portsmouth – Walsall
24 Pennant, Jermaine – Arsenal – Leeds United
15 Pidgeley, Leonard J. – Chelsea – Watford
31 Pullen, James – Ipswich Town – Peterborough United
3 Reddy, Michael – Sunderland – Sheffield Wednesday
4 Reynolds, Craig J. – Arlesey Town – St Albans City
19 Robinson, Carl P. – Portsmouth – Rotherham United
19 Russell, Matthew L. – Forest Green Rovers – Farsley Celtic
31 Schumacher, Steven T. – Everton – Carlisle United
18 Shields, Anthony G. – Peterborough United – Aldershot T
24 Stark, Paul – Eastbourne Borough – Burgess Hill Town
20 Surey, Ben – Crystal Palace – Basingstoke Town
12 Sykes, Alexander – Forest Green Rovers – Bath City
24 Tate, Alan – Manchester United – Swansea City
17 Vincent, Jamie R. – Portsmouth – Walsall
7 Walshe, Benjamin M. – Queens Park R – Gravesend & N
31 White, Andrew – Mansfield Town – Kidderminster Harriers
12 Whittaker, Andrew – Southport – Kendal Town
30 Williams, Gareth A. – Crystal Palace – Cambridge United
16 Williamson, Michael J. – Southampton – Torquay United
13 Willock, Calum D. – Fulham – Peterborough United
13 Wright, Thomas – Leicester City – Brentford
24 Allaway, Shaun – Leeds United – Walsall
27 Baird, Christopher P. – Southampton – Walsall
13 Bart-Williams, Christopher G. – Charlton Ath – Ipswich T
7 Bell, Lee – Crewe Alexandra – Shrewsbury Town
31 Blackman, Lloyd J. – Brentford – Chelmsford City
3 Brady, Matthew J. – Windsor & Eton – Mangotsfield United
20 Branston, Guy – Rotherham United – Wycombe Wanderers
3 Brown, Christopher – Sunderland – Doncaster Rovers
17 Burton, Deon J. – Portsmouth – Swindon Town
24 Buxton, Jake – Mansfield Town – Alfreton Town
26 Cade, Jamie W. – Middlesbrough – Chesterfield
18 Cameron, David A. – Chester City – Droylsden
24 Carbon, Matthew P. – Walsall – Lincoln City
21 Clarke, Simon N. – Chelmsford City – Ford United
24 Coulson, David W. – Lincoln City – Ilkeston Town
13 De Bolla, Mark – Charlton Athletic – Chesterfield
10 Dove, Craig – Middlesbrough – York City
23 Drysdale, Leon A. – Shrewbury Town – Nuneaton Borough
17 Evans, Louie – Gravesend & Northfleet – Bedford Town
8 Fagan, Craig – Birmingham City – Colchester United
7 Folkes, Peter A. – Bradford City – Farsley Celtic
17 Frost, Carl R. – Crewe Alexandra – Witton Albion
30 Gamble, Joseph – Reading – Barnet
2 Gnohere, Arthur – Burnley – Queens Park Rangers
13 Gray, Julian R. – Crystal Palace – Cardiff City
4 Halls, John – Arsenal – Stoke City
10 Hanney, Joseph – Tamworth – Rothwell Town
10 Harper, Kevin P. – Portsmouth – Norwich City
24 Heath, Matthew P. – Leicester City – Stockport County
26 Hogg, Anthony T. – Gravesend & N – Folkestone Invicta
17 Hooper, Ellis – Crawley Town – Carshalton Athletic
28 Hunt, Lewis J. – Derby County – Southend United
25 Jones, Darren L. – Bristol City – Cheltenham Town
21 Keegan, Paul A. – Leeds United – Scunthorpe United
31 Kennedy, Peter H.J. – Wigan Athletic – Derby County
20 Kitamirike, Joel D. – Chelsea – Brentford
17 Lee, David J.F. – Brighton & Hove Albion – Thurrock
8 Lewis, Matthew T. – Kidderminster H – Hinckley United
7 Livesey, Daniel – Bolton Wanderers – Notts County
1 Lucas, David A. – Preston North End – Sheffield Wednesday
21 McCartney, David J. – Millwall – Egham Town
2 McCormack, Alan – Preston North End – Leyton Orient
5 McGregor, Marc R. – Tamworth – Chippenham Town
17 McKenzie, Michael – Kettering Town – Stamford
3 Melligan, John J. – Wolverhampton W – Kidderminster H
2 Mkandawire, Tamika P. – West Bromwich A – Hereford U
10 Morgan, Alan W. – Blackburn Rovers – Darlington
31 Murray, Karl A. – Shrewsbury Town – Northwich Victoria
24 Nardiello, David A. – Manchester United – Swansea City
17 Omoyinmi, Emmanuel – Oxford United – Margate
17 Oshitola, Oloruntori O. – Grays Athletic – Kettering Town
6 Perry, Christopher J. – Tottenham Hotspur – Charlton Ath
3 Pitcher, Geoffrey – Brighton & Hove Albion – Woking
3 Quinn, Alan – Sheffield Wednesday – Sunderland
10 Rees, Matthew R. – Millwall – Aldershot Town
14 Roberts, Darren A. – Worksop Town – Belper Town
24 Robinson, Ryan – Southend United – Wivenhoe Town
22 Russell, Samuel I. – Middlesbrough – Scunthorpe United
31 Sestanovich, Ashley – Sheffield United – Scarborough
21 Smith, Gareth S. – Hull City – Carlisle United
23 Stockdale, Robert K. – Middlesbrough – West Ham United
21 Svensson, Matthias – Charlton Athletic – Derby County
23 Tardif, Christopher L. – Portsmouth – Havant & W
31 Traynor, Robert T. – Brentford – Chelmsford City
21 Walker, Richard M. – Blackpool – Northampton Town
13 Warne, Stephen J. – Chesterfield – Worksop Town
6 Whitman, Tristram – Doncaster Rovers – Tamworth
16 Wilkinson, Shaun F. – Brighton & HA – Havant & W
30 Williams, Ryan N. – Hull City – Bristol Rovers
31 Willis, Adam P. – Kidderminster Harriers – Burton Albion
31 Wright, Alan G. – Middlesbrough – Sheffield United
2 Zola Makongo, Calvin – Newcastle United – Oldham Athletic

**NOVEMBER 2003**

| | | | |
|---|---|---|---|
| 21 Baker, Carl P. | Prescot Cables | Southport | undisclosed |
| 27 Cade, Jamie W. | Middlesbrough | Colchester United | Free |
| 14 Corbett, Andrew | Nuneaton Borough | Burton Albion | undisclosed |
| 4 Davis, Craig A. | Bashley | Salisbury City | undisclosed |
| 14 Fallon, Rory M. | Barnsley | Swindon Town | 60,000 |
| 26 Harewood, Marlon A. | Nottingham Forest | West Ham United | 500,000 |
| 20 Heathcote, Jonathan | Cambridge United | Hornchurch | undisclosed |
| 6 Hendy, Scott | Bath City | Mangotsfield United | undisclosed |
| 27 King, Marlon F. | Gillingham | Nottingham Forest | 950,000 |

| | | | |
|---|---|---|---|
| 7 Lynch, Darren P. | Bedford Town | Aylesbury United | undisclosed |
| 10 McDonnell, Nicholas | St Albans City | Carshalton Athletic | undisclosed |
| 20 McFlynn, Terry M. | Margate | Morecambe | undisclosed |
| 28 Perry, Christopher J. | Tottenham Hotspur | Charlton Athletic | 100,000 |
| 27 Potts, Colin E. | Stalybridge Celtic | Northwich Victoria | undisclosed |
| 3 Price, Christopher | FC Runcorn Halton | Southport | undisclosed |
| 11 Rhodes, Alexander | Newmarket Town | Brentford | undisclosed |
| 6 Rigoglioso, Adriano | Morecambe | Doncaster Rovers | 20,000 |
| 28 Stanley, Jai F.F. | Moor Green | Worcester City | undisclosed |
| 14 Wright, Peter D. | Southport | Northwich Victoria | undisclosed |
| 19 Young, Philip N. | Vauxhall Motors | Northwich Victoria | undisclosed |

**TEMPORARY TRANSFERS**

24 Allaway, Shaun – Leeds United – Walsall
27 Arnison, Paul S. – Hartlepool United – Carlisle United
13 Bart-Williams, Christopher G. – Charlton Ath – Ipswich T
14 Benjamin, Trevor J. – Leicester City – Rushden & Diamonds
14 Bevan, Scott – Southampton – Woking
14 Boyd, Adam M. – Hartlepool United – Boston United
15 Brodie, Stephen E. – Chester City – Droylsden
24 Brown, Karl E. – Hednesford Town – Northwich Victoria
25 Burton, Steven P.G. – Hull City – Kidderminster Harriers
25 Byrne, Daniel T. – Manchester United – Hartlepool United
10 Camm, Mark – Lincoln City – Kings Lyn
26 Chadwick, Nicholas G. – Everton – Millwall
10 Clark, Dean W. – Woking – Lewes
21 Clarke, Simon N. – Chelmsford City – Ford United
10 Cropper, Dene J. – Lincoln City – Gainsborough Trinity
15 Cumberbatch, Mark – Barnet – Ashford Town
28 Danaher, Adam P. – Crawley Town – Camberley Town
20 Dinning, Tony – Wigan Athletic – Walsall
21 Drysdale, Leon A. – Shrewsbury Town – Nuneaton Borough
14 Elliott, Steven W. – Derby County – Blackpool
3 Fagan, Craig – Birmingham City – Colchester United
21 Formann, Pascal – Nottingham Forest – Grantham Town
17 Frost, Carl R. – Crewe Alexandra – Witton Albion
10 Gill, Robert – Doncaster Rovers – Dagenham & Redbridge
7 Haines, Danny – Tiverton Town – Mangotsfield United
2 Halls, John – Arsenal – Stoke City
8 Hanney, Joseph – Tamworth – Rothwell Town
7 Heath, Nicholas A. – Kidderminster H – Cinderford Town
28 Hudson, Mark A. – Fulham – Oldham Athletic
14 Ifil, Jerel C. – Watford – Swindon Town
21 Jackson, Johnnie – Tottenham Hotspur – Coventry City
28 Johnson, Jermaine – Bolton Wanderers – Oldham Athletic
4 Jones, Bradley – Middlesbrough – Blackpool
13 Jones, Gary R. – Barnsley – Rochdale
20 Kitamirike, Joel D. – Chelsea – Brentford
14 Larkin, Daniel – Folkestone Invicta – Chatham Town
14 Lindegaard, Andrew – Yeovil Town – Weymouth
20 Lock, Anthony – Grays Athletic – Ford United
26 Mahon, Alan – Blackburn Rovers – Ipswich Town
26 May, Ben S. – Millwall – Brentford
17 McGlinchey, Brian K. – Plymouth Argyle – Torquay United
21 McGuire, Jamie A. – Tranmere Rovers – Northwich Victoria
25 Meechan, Alexander T. – Dagenham & R – Forest Green R
2 Mkandawire, Tamika – West Bromwich A – Hereford U
14 Muller, Adam P. – Worksop Town – Wakefield & Emley
21 Myhre, Thomas – Sunderland – Crystal Palace
28 O'Brien, Robert L. – Doncaster Rovers – Gainsborough T
21 Onibuje, Folawiyo – Preston North End – Huddersfield T
20 Pennant, Jermaine – Arsenal – Leeds United
11 Pidgeley, Leonard J. – Chelsea – Watford
21 Potter, Graham S. – Boston United – Shrewsbury Town
21 Quinn, Alan – Sheffield Wednesday – Sunderland
14 Rehman, Zeshan – Fulham – Brighton & Hove Albion
14 Roberts, Darren A. – Worksop Town – Belper Town
20 Russell, Matthew L. – Forest Green Rovers – Farsley Celtic
21 Semple, Ryan D. – Peterborough United – Farnborough T
14 Shaw, Jon S. – Sheffield Wednesday – York City
10 Singh, Harpal – Leeds United – Bury
14 Smith, Gavin D. – Worksop Town – Bradford Park Avenue
24 Stark, Paul – Eastbourne Borough – Burgess Hill Town
17 Surey, Ben – Crystal Palace – Basingstoke Town
14 Turnbull, Ross – Middlesbrough – Darlington
21 Walker, Richard M. – Blackpool – Northampton Town
12 Walters, Jonathan R. – Bolton Wanderers – Barnsley
14 Westwood, Keiren – Manchester City – Oldham Athletic
14 Whittaker, Andrew – Southport – Kendal Town
21 Williams, Anthony S. – Hartlepool United – Swansea City
13 Wright, Thomas – Leicester City – Brentford
14 Yeates, Mark S. – Tottenham Hotspur – Brighton & HA
28 Allen, Mark A. – Birmingham City – Bromsgrove Rovers
14 Ashdown, Jamie L. – Reading – Rushden & Diamonds
3 Bell, Lee – Crewe Alexandra – Shrewsbury Town
1 Beresford, David – Plymouth Argyle – Macclesfield Town
20 Bishop, Andrew J. – Walsall – Rochdale
20 Bradbury, Lee M. – Portsmouth – Derby County
3 Brown, Christopher – Sunderland – Doncaster Rovers
24 Brush, Richard J. – Coventry City – Tamworth
1 Buttery, Luke – Cheltenham Town – Chippenham Town
21 Caines, Gavin L. – Walsall – Stafford Rangers
8 Chard, Anthony J. – Burgess Hill Town – Worthing
7 Chilvers, Liam C. – Arsenal – Colchester United
21 Clarke, Jamie C. – Grantham Town – Corby Town
14 Crofts, Andrew L. – Gillingham – Dover Athletic
21 Cryan, Colin – Sheffield United – Scarborough
21 Curtis, Wayne J. – Morecambe – Barrow
28 Delany, Dean – Port Vale – Macclesfield Town
30 Browning, Stewart – Middlesbrough – Sunderland
21 Edwards, Robert O. – Aston Villa – Crystal Palace
7 Enckelman, Peter – Aston Villa – Blackburn Rovers
28 Farrelly, Gareth – Bolton Wanderers – Bradford City
26 Forssell, Mikael K. – Chelsea – Birmingham City
10 Garnett, Shaun M. – Halifax Town – Morecambe
10 Gulliver, Philip S. – Middlesbrough – Bury
21 Hallows, Marcus P. – Chorley – Altrincham
16 Hammond, Dean – Brighton & Hove Albion – Leyton Orient
25 Harewood, Marlon A. – Nottingham F – West Ham United
25 Heath, Matthew P. – Leicester City – Stockport County
30 Hunt, Lewis J. – Derby County – Southend United
14 Jackson, James T.W. – Dagenham & Redbridge – Dover Ath
14 James, Craig P. – Sunderland – Darlington
1 Johnson, Paul M. – Staines Town – Chertsey Town
26 Jones, Darren L. – Bristol City – Forest Green Rovers
21 Kielty, Anthony – Hyde United – Kidsgrove Athletic
10 Konchesky, Paul M. – Charlton Athletic – Tottenham H
20 Lawrence, James H. – Walsall – Wigan Athletic
3 Livesey, Daniel – Bolton Wanderers – Notts County
20 Lynn, Charles D. – Carlisle United – Workington
18 Marshall, Andrew J. – Ipswich Town – Wolverhampton W
25 McCombe, Jamie – Scunthorpe United – Halifax Town
4 McGregor, Marc R. – Tamworth – Weston-Super-Mare
24 McSheffrey, Gary – Coventry City – Luton Town
17 Melligan, John J. – Wolverhampton W – Doncaster Rovers
21 Monk, Garry – Southampton – Barnsley
22 Myhill, Glyn O. – Aston Villa – Stockport County
29 Neill, Thomas E. – Farnborough Town – Chesham United
21 Oli, Dennis C. – Queens Park Rangers – Gravesend & N
14 Pell, Robert A. – Worksop Town – Wakefield & Emley
10 Perry, Christopher J. – Tottenham Hotspur – Charlton Ath
21 Piper, Leonard H. – Dagenham & Redbridge – Margate
28 Protheroe, Lee – Canvey Island – Gravesend & Northfleet
9 Rees, Matthew R. – Millwall – Aldershot Town
8 Richardson, Frazer – Leeds United – Stoke City
21 Roberts, Mark A. – Crewe Alexandra – Leek Town
21 Sadler, Matthew – Birmingham City – Northampton Town
28 Sestanovic, Ashley – Sheffield United – Scarborough
13 Sheeran, Mark J. – Darlington – Whitby Town
8 Smissen, Michael – Dover Athletic – Sittingbourne
28 Smith, Thomas – Northampton Town – Gainsborough Trinity
30 Stockdale, Robert K. – Middlesbrough – West Ham United
28 Tickle, David – Leigh RMI – Chorley
17 Vincent, Jamie R. – Portsmouth – Walsall
9 Walshe, Benjamin M. – Queens Park R – Gravesend & N
21 Watkins, Dale A. – Chelmsford City – Grantham Town
2 Whelan, Glenn D. – Manchester City – Bury
20 Wilkinson, Andrew G. – Stoke City – Telford United
16 Willock, Calum – Fulham – Peterborough United
15 Yates, Adam P. – Crewe Alexandra – Halifax Town
2 Zola, Makongo Calvin – Newcastle United – Oldham Athletic

**DECEMBER 2003**

| | | | |
|---|---|---|---|
| 12 Bart-Williams, Christopher G. | Charlton Athletic | Ipswich Town | Free |
| 24 Bloomfield, Matthew J. | Ipswich Town | Wycombe Wanderers | Free |
| 31 Brown, Michael R. | Sheffield United | Tottenham Hotspur | 500,000 |
| 9 Elam, Lee P.G. | Halifax Town | Yeovil Town | undisclosed |

| | | | |
|---|---|---|---|
| 5 Halls, John | Arsenal | Stoke City | undisclosed |
| 24 Harrington, Mark P. | Chippenham Town | Paulton Rovers | undisclosed |
| 18 Horsfield, Geoffrey M. | Wigan Athletic | West Bromwich Albion | 1,000,000 |
| 27 Huckerby, Darren C. | Manchester City | Norwich City | 750,000 |
| 31 Jackman, Daniel J. | Aston Villa | Stockport County | 70,000 |
| 12 Jenkins, Lee D. | Swansea City | Kidderminster Harriers | Free |
| 30 Kitson, David B. | Cambridge United | Reading | 150,000 |
| 2 Kuqi, Shefki | Sheffield Wednesday | Ipswich Town | Free |
| 4 Lewis, Matthew T. | Kidderminster Harriers | Hinckley United | 5000 |
| 18 Logan, Richard J. | Boston United | Peterborough United | Free |
| 15 McKenzie, Leon M. | Peterborough United | Norwich City | 325,000 |
| 12 Myhill, Glyn O. | Aston Villa | Hull City | 50,000 |
| 8 Robins, Mark G. | Rotherham United | Sheffield Wednesday | undisclosed |
| 19 Svensson, Matthias | Charlton Athletic | Norwich City | 50,000 |
| 29 Thomson, Peter | Southport | Lancaster City | undisclosed |
| 19 Voice, Scott H. | Hinckley United | Redditch United | undisclosed |
| 30 Williams, Ryan N. | Hull City | Bristol Rovers | Free |
| 18 Willock, Calum D. | Fulham | Peterborough United | 25,000 |

**TEMPORARY TRANSFERS**

29 Allen, Mark A. – Birmingham City – Bromsgrove Rovers
29 Arnison, Paul S. – Hartlepool United – Carlisle United
5 Baldwin, Patrick M. – Colchester United – St Albans City
5 Beckford, Jermaine – Wealdstone – Uxbridge
21 Bishop, Andrew – Walsall – Rochdale
5 Bonfield, Darren – Hemel Hempstead Town – Leighton T
6 Bowling, Ian – Worksop Town – Stalybridge Celtic
29 Brayley, Albert P. – Canvey Island – Heybridge Swifts
20 Brodie, Stephen E. – Chester City – Droylsden
3 Brown, Christopher – Sunderland – Doncaster Rovers
11 Bryant, Simon C. – Bristol Rovers – Tiverton Town
24 Burchill, Mark J. – Portsmouth – Sheffield Wednesday
22 Caines, Gavin L. – Walsall – Stafford Rangers
8 Causon, Stephen – Crawley Town – Eastbourne Borough
27 Chadwick, Nicholas G. – Everton – Millwall
19 Coulson, Mark D. – Peterborough United – Hitchin Town
14 Cumberbatch, Mark – Barnet – Ashford Town
19 Dell, Steven – Wycombe Wanderers – Eastbourne Borough
12 Duffy, Lee – Rochdale – Rossendale United
19 Easter, Jermaine M. – Hartlepool United – Spennymoor U
5 Enckelman, Peter – Aston Villa – Blackburn Rovers
12 Fitzpatrick, Ian M. – Shrewsbury Town – Leigh RMI
18 Fryatt, Matthew C. – Walsall – Carlisle United
10 Goodwin, Mark C. – Eastbourne Borough – Burgess Hill T
19 Green, Michael F. – Southampton – Chippenham Town
26 Hambley, Timothy J. – Welling United – Folkestone Invicta
12 Harris, Richard L.S. – Wycombe Wanderers – Woking
11 Hawkins, Darren M. – Bristol City – Bath City
7 Heath, Nicholas – Kidderminster Harriers – Cinderford T
12 Hogg, Christopher – Ipswich Town – Boston United
19 Holt, David A. – Stockport County – Altrincham
31 Hunt, Lewis J. – Derby County – Southend United
13 Hynes, Peter J. – Aston Villa – Doncaster Rovers
16 Jackson, James T.W. – Dagenham & R – Dover Ath
14 James, Craig P. – Sunderland – Darlington
13 Johnson, Simon A. – Leeds United – Blackpool
30 Jones, Darren L. – Bristol City – Forest Green Rovers
16 Kelly, Stephen M. – Tottenham Hotspur – Watford
15 Larkin, Daniel – Folkestone Invicta – Chatham Town
13 Lucas, David A. – Preston North End – Sheffield Wednesday
18 Lynn, Charles D. – Carlisle United – Workington
12 Martin, Simon – St Albans City – Cambridge City
23 McCafferty, Neil – Charlton Athletic – Cambridge United
19 McKenzie, Michael – Kettering Town – Corby Town
19 McShane, Luke – Peterborough United – Stamford
23 Monk, Garry – Southampton – Barnsley
5 Morison, Steve – Northampton Town – Bishop's Stortford
23 Mumford, Andrew O. – Swansea City – Aldershot Town
12 Niven, Derek – Bolton Wanderers – Chesterfield
29 O'Brien, Robert L. – Doncaster Rovers – Gainsborough T
22 Onibuje, Folawiyo – Preston North End – Huddersfield T
30 Pacquette, Richard – Queens Park R – Dagenham & R
24 Peat, Nathan N.M. – Hull City – Cambridge United
12 Pitcher, Geoffrey – Brighton & Hove Albion – Barnet
29 Protheroe, Lee – Canvey Island – Gravesend & Northfleet
7 Rees, Matthew R. – Millwall – Aldershot Town
15 Rehman, Zeshan – Fulham – Brighton & Hove Albion
31 Rickers, Paul S. – Northampton Town – Leigh RMI
19 Roberts, Darren A. – Worksop Town – Belper Town
8 Robins, Mark G. – Rotherham United – Sheffield W
23 Robinson, Neil D. – Macclesfield Town – Southport
24 Rushbury, Andrew J. – Chesterfield – Alfreton Town
19 Semple, Ryan D. – Peterborough United – Farnborough T
13 Shuker, Christopher A. – Manchester City – Hartlepool U
12 Smith, Gavin D. – Worksop Town – Bradford Park Avenue
6 Sollitt, Adam J. – Scarborough – Hucknall Town
30 Stockdale, Robert K. – Middlesbrough – West Ham United
14 Surey, Ben – Crystal Palace – Basingstoke Town
27 Armstrong, Alun – Ipswich Town – Bradford City
31 Ashdown, Jamie – Reading – Rushden & Diamonds
13 Baptiste, Alex – Mansfield Town – Tamworth
15 Benjamin, Trevor J. – Leicester City – Rushden & Diamonds
2 Blackman, Lloyd J. – Brentford – Chelmsford City
24 Bonsall, Scott M. – Harrogate Town – Stalybridge Celtic
15 Boyd, Adam M. – Hartlepool United – Boston United
19 Brennan, Dean J.G. – Stevenage Borough – Hendon
12 Brooks, Jamie P. – Oxford United – Maidenhead United
22 Brush, Richard J. – Coventry City – Tamworth
12 Budge, Kevin C. – Heybridge Swifts – Rothwell Town
31 Buxton, Lewis E. – Portsmouth – AFC Bournemouth
11 Camm, Mark – Lincoln City – King's Lynn
12 Cavill, Arran – Northampton Town – Aylesbury United
22 Corbett, Luke J. – Cheltenham Town – Weston-Super-Mare
16 Crofts, Andrew L. – Gillingham – Dover Athletic
30 Delany, Dean – Port Vale – Macclesfield Town
29 Dixon, Jonathan J. – Wycombe Wanderers – Crawley Town
1 Dyer, Kenneth – Dover Athletic – Chatham Town
15 Elliott, Steven W. – Derby County – Blackpool
5 Fettis, Alan – Hull City – Sheffield United
24 Flitney, Ross D. – Fulham – Brighton & Hove Albion
19 Furness, Adam – Stevenage Borough – Hertford Town
6 Green, Leon – Weymouth – Harrow Borough
6 Haines, Danny – Tiverton Town – Mangotsfield United
6 Hanney, Joseph – Tamworth – Rothwell Town
23 Harvey, Iain D. – Bath City – Yate Town
23 Heath, Matthew P. – Leicester City – Stockport County
9 Herring, Ian – Swindon Town – Chippenham Town
29 Holligan, Gavin V. – Wycombe Wanderers – Crawley Town
19 Huke, Shane – Peterborough United – Bedford Town
19 Hutton, Rory N. – Peterborough United – Hitchin Town
2 Jackman, Daniel J. – Aston Villa – Stockport County
21 Jackson, Johnnie – Tottenham Hotspur – Coventry City
29 Johnson, Jermaine – Bolton Wanderers – Oldham Athletic
3 Jones, Bradley – Middlesbrough – Blackpool
3 Jones, Robert W. – Stockport County – Macclesfield Town
16 Konchesky, Paul M. – Charlton Athletic – Tottenham H
24 Larvin, Kevin – Leicester City – Hinckley United
12 Lynch, Simon – Preston North End – Stockport County
17 Marshall, Andrew J. – Ipswich Town – Wolverhampton W
11 Matthews, Lee J. – Bristol City – Darlington
15 McEveley, James – Blackburn Rovers – Burnley
19 McNamee, Anthony – Watford – Barnet
29 Melligan, John J. – Wolverhampton Wanderers – Doncaster R
11 Moore, Luke I. – Aston Villa – Wycombe Wanderers
12 Morrow, Samuel – Ipswich Town – Boston United
30 Myhre, Thomas – Sunderland – Crystal Palace
13 Northmore, Ryan – Woking – Bath City
21 Oli, Dennis C. – Queens Park Rangers – Gravesend & N
23 Owusu, Lloyd M. – Sheffield Wednesday – Reading
12 Parton, Andrew – Scunthorpe United – Harrogate Town
20 Pennant, Jermaine – Arsenal – Leeds United
28 Pitt, Courtney L. – Portsmouth – Coventry City
5 Reece, Dominic M.A. – Farnborough Town – Halesowen T
19 Regan, Carl A. – Hull City – Chester City
8 Richardson, Marcus G. – Hartlepool United – Lincoln City
9 Roache, Lee P. – Barnet – Bishop's Stortford
21 Roberts, Mark A. – Crewe Alexandra – Leek Town
11 Robinson, Mark – Hartlepool United – Spennymoor United
30 Rogers, Alan – Leicester City – Wigan Athletic
23 Sadler, Matthew – Birmingham City – Northampton Town
14 Shaw, Jon S. – Sheffield Wednesday – York City
8 Smissen, Michael – Dover Athletic – Sittingbourne
19 Smith, Nicholas – Walsall – Tamworth
31 Stephens, Kevin – Leyton Orient – Hornchurch
12 Strouts, James G. – Gravesend & Northfleet – Welling United
9 Taggart, Gerald P. – Leicester City – Stoke City

19 Taylor, Jamie – Aldershot Town – Carshalton Athletic
31 Tevendale, James R. – Hucknall Town – Ilkeston Town
2 Traynor, Robert – Brentford – Chelmsford City
12 Uddin, Anwar – Bristol Rovers – Hereford United
31 Walters, Jonathan R. – Bolton Wanderers – Barnsley
5 Weaver, Luke D.S. – Northampton Town – Billericay Town
31 Westwood, Keiren – Manchester City – Oldham Athletic
22 Whellans, Robert – Harrogate Town – Radcliffe Borough
5 White, Robert – Nuneaton Borough – Corby Town
11 Wilford, Aron L. – York City – Worksop Town
1 Willis, Adam P. – Kidderminster Harriers – Burton Albion
13 Woodards, Bradley – Ford United – Barking & East Ham U
15 Yeates, Mark – Tottenham Hotspur – Brighton & Hove A
12 Taylor, Steven V. – Newcastle United – Wycombe Wanderers
12 Thomas, Bradley M. – Peterborough United – Aldershot T
24 Tynan, Scott J. – Nottingham Forest – Telford United
24 Vaesen, Nico – Birmingham City – Gillingham
22 Watkins, Dale A. – Chelmsford City – Kings Lynn
18 Webb, Daniel J. – Hull City – Cambridge United
23 Whelan, Glenn D. – Manchester City – Bury
31 White, Andrew – Mansfield Town – Kidderminster Harriers
27 Whitworth, Neil A. – Southport – Radcliffe Borough
31 Wilkinson, Andrew G. – Stoke City – Telford United
12 Wilson, Brian – Stoke City – Cheltenham Town
30 Wright, Thomas – Leicester City – Brentford

**JANUARY 2004**

| | | | |
|---|---|---|---|
| 13 Agyemang, Patrick | Wimbledon | Gillingham | 200,000 |
| 15 Bentley, Mark J. | Dagenham & Redbridge | Southend United | undisclosed |
| 9 Berkovic, Eyal | Manchester City | Portsmouth | Free |
| 28 Cort, Carl E.R. | Newcastle United | Wolverhampton Wanderers | 2,000,000 |
| 2 Dabizas, Nikos | Newcastle United | Leicester City | Free |
| 26 Duffy, Richard M. | Swansea City | Portsmouth | 300,000 |
| 23 Edwards, Darren M.P. | Mangotsfield United | Tiverton Town | undisclosed |
| 7 Enckelman, Peter | Aston Villa | Blackburn Rovers | 150,000 |
| 9 Goodfellow, Marc D. | Stoke City | Bristol City | 50,000 |
| 2 Henderson, Darius A. | Reading | Gillingham | 25,000 |
| 30 Holt, Grant | Sheffield Wednesday | Rochdale | undisclosed |
| 30 Howey, Stephen N. | Leicester City | Bolton Wanderers | Free |
| 9 Jackman, David J. | Aston Villa | Stockport County | 70,000 |
| 14 James, David B. | West Ham United | Manchester City | 1,300,000 |
| 29 Jones, Paul S. | Southampton | Wolverhampton Wanderers | 250,000 |
| 29 Melville, Andrew R. | Fulham | West Ham United | exch. |
| 23 Millar, James S. | Folkestone Invicta | Dover Athletic | undisclosed |
| 28 Nowland, Adam C. | Wimbledon | West Ham United | 75,000 |
| 30 Parker, Scott M. | Charlton Athletic | Chelsea | 10,000,000 |
| 23 Pearce, Ian A. | West Ham United | Fulham | 400,000 + exch. |
| 27 Pouton, Alan | Grimsby Town | Gillingham | 35,000 |
| 23 Reo-Coker, Nigel S.A. | Wimbledon | West Ham United | 575,000 |
| 12 Richardson, Marcus G. | Hartlepool United | Lincoln City | Free |
| 13 Roberts, Jason A.D. | West Bromwich Albion | Wigan Athletic | 2,000,000 |
| 31 Robertson, Hugh S. | Ross County | Hartlepool United | Free |
| 23 Saha, Louis | Fulham | Manchester United | 12,850,000 |
| 12 Shaw, Paul | Gillingham | Sheffield United | 75,000 |
| 27 Smith, Paul D. | Brentford | Southampton | 250,000 |
| 29 Solano, Todco N.A. | Newcastle United | Aston Villa | 1,500,000 |
| 30 Sutton, John W.M. | Raith Rovers | Millwall | 60,000 |
| 16 Vincent, Jamie R. | Portsmouth | Derby County | Free |
| 16 Volz, Moritz | Arsenal | Fulham | 2,200,000 |
| 23 Weatherstone, Simon | Boston United | Yeovil Town | 15,000 |
| 12 Wright, Alan G. | Middlesbrough | Sheffield United | Free |

**TEMPORARY TRANSFERS**

16 Abidallah, Nabil – Ipswich Town – Northampton Town
1 Allen, Daniel T. – Forest Green Rovers – Clevedon Town
2 Bannister, Patrick T. – Bradford City – Hednesford Town
5 Beckford, Jermaine – Wealdstone – Uxbridge
16 Beswetherick, Jonathan B. – Sheffield W – Macclesfield T
16 Bevan, Scott – Southampton – Wycombe Wanderers
29 Bonsall, Scott M. – Harrogate Town – Rossendale United
30 Boyd, Adam M. – Hartlepool United – Boston United
23 Brayley, Albert P. – Canvey Island – Hornchurch
7 Bull, Ronnie R. – Millwall – Brentford
16 Caig, Anthony – Newcastle United – Barnsley
16 Campbell, Jamie – Woking – Havant & Waterlooville
8 Coates, Steven – Ilkeston Town – Shepshed Dynamo
1 Connolly, Gary M. – Bashley – Havant & Waterlooville
6 Cooke, Stephen L. – Aston Villa – AFC Bournemouth
20 Corbett, Luke J. – Cheltenham Town – Weston-Super-Mare
15 Cumberbatch, Mark – Barnet – Ashford Town
17 Daws, Nicholas J. – Rotherham United – Grimsby Town
13 Dichio, Daniele S.E. – West Bromwich Albion – Millwall
16 Downey, Gareth – Scarborough – Spennymoor United
16 Edwards, Nathan M. – Chippenham T – Swindon Super
24 Essandoh, Roy K. – Bishop's Stortford – Gravesend & N
2 Fettis, Alan – Hull City – Sheffield United
9 Forbes, Dean – Bromley – Tonbridge Angels
23 Frost, Carl R. – Crewe Alexandra – Leek Town
23 Furness, Adam – Stevenage Borough – Braintree Town
17 Goodwin, Mark C. – Eastbourne Borough – Hastings United
7 Green, Leon – Weymouth – Harrow Borough
6 Haines, Danny – Tiverton Town – Mangotsfield United
26 Hambley, Timothy J. – Welling United – Folkestone Invicta
13 Harris, Richard – Wycombe Wanderers – Woking
11 Hawkins, Darren M. – Bristol City – Bath City
18 Holt, David – Stockport County – Altrincham
19 Hutton, Rory N. – Peterborough United – Hitchin Town
23 Jackson, Kirk S.S. – Yeovil Town – Dagenham & Redbridge
25 Jones, Darren L. – Bristol City – Forest Green Rovers
9 Jones, Paul S. – Southampton – Liverpool
1 Allaway, Shaun – Leeds United – Walsall
23 Bankole, Ademola – Crewe Alexandra – Barnet
15 Beardsley, Christopher K. – Mansfield Town – Worksop T
16 Benjamin, Trevor J. – Leicester City – Brighton & Hove A
30 Betts, Thomas G. – Crewe Alexandra – Vauxhall Motors
23 Boertien, Paul – Derby County – Notts County
23 Bowker, Terrence – Stalybridge Celtic – Radcliffe Borough
16 Bradley, John – Hornchurch – Boreham Wood
19 Brush, Richard J. – Coventry City – Tamworth
30 Byrne, Shaun R. – West Ham United – Swansea City
22 Caines, Gavin L. – Walsall – Stafford Rangers
9 Challinor, David P. – Stockport County – Bury
30 Cobb, Paul M. – East Thurrock United – Tilbury
23 Cook, Lewis L. – Wycombe Wanderers – Weymouth
6 Cooper, Kevin L. – Wolverhampton Wanderers – Sunderland
19 Coulsen, Mark D. – Peterborough United – Hitchin Town
2 Daly, Jonathan M. – Stockport County – Bury
20 Dell, Steven – Wycombe Wanderers – Eastbourne Borough
23 Dinning, Tony – Wigan Athletic – Blackpool
16 Duffy, Lee – Rochdale – Rossendale United
9 Edwards, Robert O. – Aston Villa – Derby County
30 Facey, Delroy M. – Bolton Wanderers – West Bromwich A
9 Foran, Richard – Carlisle United – Oxford United
17 Forbes, Scott – Canvey Island – Bishop's Stortford
19 Fryatt, Matthew C. – Walsall – Carlisle United
16 Glover, Simon D. – Dover Athletic – Ashford Town
30 Gradley, Patrick – Gravesend & Northfleet – Boreham Wood
16 Gulliver, Philip S. – Middlesbrough – Scunthorpe United
16 Hall, Laurence W.L. – Stoke City – Gresley Rovers
16 Harley, Jon – Fulham – West Ham United
26 Harvey, Iain D. – Bath City – Yate Town
13 Henry, Karl L.D. – Stoke City – Cheltenham Town
16 Hudson, Mark A. – Fulham – Crystal Palace
23 Hynes, Peter J. – Aston Villa – Cheltenham Town
15 Jephcott, Avun C. – Coventry City – Notts County
14 Jones, Gary R. – Barnsley – Rochdale
1 Jones, Robert W. – Stockport County – Macclesfield Town

23 Jorgensen, Claus B. – Coventry City – AFC Bournemouth
19 Lucas, David A. – Preston North End – Sheffield Wednesday
15 Lynn, Charles D. – Carlisle United – Workington
23 Marshall, Andrew J. – Ipswich Town – Millwall
31 Martin, Andrew – Hornchurch – East Thurrock United
3 Maynard, Tony D. – Hornchurch – Braintree Town
19 McEvilly, Lee R. – Rochdale – Accrington Stanley
7 McMaster, Jamie – Leeds United – Chesterfield
16 Melville, Andrew R. – Fulham – West Ham United
14 Mitchell, Craig R. – Mansfield Town – Northwich Victoria
19 Myhre, Thomas – Sunderland – Crystal Palace
8 Neill, Thomas E. – Farnborough Town – Chesham United
23 Niven, Derek – Bolton Wanderers – Chesterfield
23 O'Hanlon, Sean P. – Everton – Swindon Town
29 Orr, Bradley J. – Newcastle United – Burnley
16 Owen, Gareth J. – Stoke City – Oldham Athletic
6 Pacquette, Richard F. – Queens Park R – Dagenham & R
15 Parkinson, Andrew J. – Sheffield United – Notts County
25 Pears, Richard J. – Tiverton Town – Mangotsfield United
9 Pemberton, Martin C. – Stockport County – Rochdale
20 Pennant, Jermaine – Arsenal – Leeds United
15 Pipe, David R. – Coventry City – Notts County
18 Pouton, Alan – Grimsby Town – Gillingham
4 Pulman, Ian J. – Margate – Eastbourne Borough
29 Rachubka, Paul S. – Charlton Athletic – Burnley
23 Reece, Dominic M.A. – Farnborough T – Sutton Coldfield T
23 Roache, Lee P. – Barnet – Windsor & Eton
30 Robinson, Carl P. – Portsmouth – Sheffield United
26 Rushbury, Andrew J. – Chesterfield – Alfreton Town
2 Scott, Richard P. – Peterborough United – Stevenage B
16 Shaaban, Rami – Arsenal – West Ham United
23 Skora, Eric – Preston North End – Kilmarnock
24 Stark, Paul – Eastbourne Borough – Burgess Hill Town
16 Stowe, Christopher J. – Hampton & RB – Billericay Town
2 Sturridge, Dean C. – Wolverhampton W – Sheffield U
6 Taggart, Gerald P. – Leicester City – Stoke City
30 Tierney, Paul T. – Manchester United – Colchester United
27 Tucker, Anthony – Walton & Hersham – Hayes
2 Tyson, Nathan – Reading – Wycombe Wanderers
16 Vieira, Magno S. – Wigan Athletic – Northampton Town
8 Walker, Justin – Cambridge United – York City
21 Watkins, Dale A. – Chelmsford City – Kings Lynn
19 Webb, Daniel J. – Hull City – Cambridge United
23 Williams, Anthony S. – Hartlepool United – Stockport Co
16 Willis, Scott L. – Lincoln City – Northwich Victoria
22 Wilson, Mark A. – Middlesbrough – Sheffield Wednesday
13 Lever, Mark – Ilkeston Town – Ossett Town
13 Lynch, Simon – Preston North End – Stockport County
16 Marney, Dean E. – Tottenham Hotspur – Queens Park R
23 Marshall, Lee K. – West Bromwich Albion – Hull City
13 Matthews, Lee J. – Bristol City – Bristol Rovers
27 McCafferty, Neil – Charlton Athletic – Cambridge United
9 McGuire, Liam J. – Southport – Prescot Cables
3 McShane, Luke – Peterborough United – Stamford
23 Mings, Adrian – Chippenham Town – Gloucester City
21 Monk, Garry – Southampton – Barnsley
27 Nardiello, Daniel A. – Manchester United – Barnsley
2 Nethercott, Stuart – Millwall – Wycombe Wanderers
23 Nolan, Matthew L. – Peterborough United – Cambridge City
17 Omoyinmi, Emmanuel – Oxford United – Margate
26 Osman, Leon – Everton – Derby County
20 Owusu, Lloyd – Sheffield Wednesday – Reading
16 Palmer, Christopher L. – Derby County – Hereford United
23 Pattison, Matthew – Farnborough Town – Kingstonian
26 Peat, Nathan N.M. – Hull City – Cambridge United
30 Penfold, Terry – Gravesend & Northfleet – Chelmsford City
16 Pethick, Robert J. – Brighton & Hove Albion – Weymouth
31 Poate, Brett – Havant & Waterlooville – Bognor Regis Town
26 Protheroe, Lee – Canvey Island – Gravesend & Northfleet
9 Quinn, Barry S. – Coventry City – Rushden & Diamonds
30 Raw, Thomas D. – Scarborough – Chorley
23 Rees, Matthew R. – Millwall – Dagenham & Redbridge
30 Roberts, Mark A. – Crewe Alexandra – Vauxhall Motors
14 Rogers, Mark A. – Wycombe Wanderers – Stevenage B
15 Sam, Lloyd E. – Charlton Athletic – Leyton Orient
9 Semple, Ryan D. – Peterborough United – Farnborough T
12 Shuker, Christopher A. – Manchester City – Hartlepool U
16 Smith, Jeff – Bolton Wanderers – Scunthorpe United
2 St Ledger-Hall, Sean P. – Peterborough United – Stevenage B
12 Strouts, James G. – Gravesend & Northfleet – Welling United
1 Svard, Sebastian – Arsenal – Stoke City
16 Taylor, Cleveland – Bolton Wanderers – Scunthorpe United
30 Traynor, Robert T. – Brentford – Crawley Town
25 Tynan, Scott J. – Nottingham Forest – Telford United
14 Uddin, Anwar – Bristol Rovers – Hereford United
30 Wales, Gary – Heart of Midlothian – Walsall
22 Wallwork, Ronald – West Bromwich Albion – Bradford City
6 Weaver, Luke D.S. – Northampton Town – Billericay Town
7 White, Robert – Nuneaton Borough – Corby Town
2 Williams, Thomas A. – Birmingham City – Peterborough U
10 Wilson, Brian – Stoke City – Cheltenham Town
30 Wood, Neil A. – Manchester United – Burnley

**FEBRUARY 2004**

| | | | |
|---|---|---|---|
| 2 Arnison, Paul S. | Hartlepool United | Carlisle United | Free |
| 12 Boulding, Michael | Grimsby Town | Barnsley | 50,000 |
| 6 Byfield, Darren | Rotherham United | Sunderland | exch. |
| 2 Defoe, Jermain C. | West Ham United | Tottenham Hotspur | 7,000,000 + exch. |
| 27 Dichio, Daniele S.E. | West Bromwich Albion | Millwall | 200,000 |
| 2 Facey, Delroy M. | Bolton Wanderers | West Bromwich Albion | 100,000 |
| 19 Gnohere, Arthur | Burnley | Queens Park Rangers | Free |
| 2 Godbold, Jamie T. | Cambridge City | Lowestoft Town | undisclosed |
| 27 Gray, Andrew D. | Bradford City | Sheffield United | nominal |
| 13 Haddrell, Matt | Macclesfield Town | Leek Town | Free |
| 4 Haines, Danny | Tiverton Town | Mangotsfield United | undisclosed |
| 14 Keates, Dean S. | Hull City | Kidderminster Harriers | undisclosed |
| 2 Leigertwood, Mikele B. | Wimbledon | Crystal Palace | 150,000 |
| 6 Mahon, Alan | Blackburn Rovers | Wigan Athletic | Free |
| 4 McAnuff, Joel J.F.M. | Wimbledon | West Ham United | 300,000 |
| 2 Morris, Lee | Derby County | Leicester City | 120,000 |
| 2 Nelson, Stuart | Hucknall Town | Brentford | 10,000 |
| 20 Parkin, Jonathan | York City | Macclesfield Town | Free |
| 10 Proctor, Michael A. | Sunderland | Rotherham United | exch. |
| 27 Rayner, Terry R. | Maldon Town | AFC Sudbury | undisclosed |
| 17 Scoffham, Steven | Gedling Town | Notts County | undisclosed |
| 6 Smissen, Michael | Dover Athletic | Sittingbourne | undisclosed |
| 2 Stead, Jonathan | Huddersfield Town | Blackburn Rovers | 1,200,000 |
| 6 Tate, Alan | Manchester United | Swansea City | Free |
| 2 Taylor, Martin | Blackburn Rovers | Birmingham City | 1,250,000 |
| 2 Thomas, Jerome W. | Arsenal | Charlton Athletic | 100,000 |
| 5 Walters, Jonathan R. | Bolton Wanderers | Hull City | 50,000 |
| 26 Webb, Daniel J. | Hull City | Cambridge United | Free |
| 6 Wilkinson, Shaun F. | Havant & Waterlooville | Weymouth | undisclosed |

**TEMPORARY TRANSFERS**

7 Abbott, Paul – Margate – Braintree Town
13 Adams, Adrian – Forest Green Rovers – Bashley
24 Armstrong, Alun – Ipswich Town – Bradford City
6 Awuah, Jones – Gillingham – Dover Athletic
19 Baptiste, Liam D. – Waltham F – Barking & East Ham U
6 Bishop, Andrew J. – Walsall – Yeovil Town
7 Bradshaw, Craig R.J. – Portsmouth – Dorchester Town
2 Bridges, Michael – Leeds United – Newcastle United
27 Brooker, Paul – Leicester City – Reading
16 Abbott, Pawel T.H. – Preston North End – Huddersfield T
6 Allen, Daniel T. – Forest Green Rovers – Bashley
24 Armstrong, Craig S. – Sheffield Wednesday – Grimsby Town
6 Baptiste, Alex – Mansfield Town – Burton Albion
27 Barmby, Nicholas J. – Leeds United – Nottingham Forest
20 Bowker, Terrence – Stalybridge Celtic – Radcliffe Borough
25 Branston, Guy P.B. – Rotherham United – Peterborough U
13 Brodie, Stephen E. – Chester City – Leigh RMI
6 Brooks, Jamie P. – Oxford United – Tamworth

17 Brown, Wayne L. – Watford – Colchester United
27 Buttery, Luke – Cheltenham Town – Swindon Supermarine
6 Campbell-Ryce, Jamal J. – Charlton Athletic – Wimbledon
19 Chambers, Adam C. – West Bromwich Albion – Sheffield W
25 Clancy, Timothy – Millwall – Weymouth
7 Coates, Steven – Ilkeston Town – Shepshed Dynamo
24 Cook, James S. – Stevenage Borough – Bath City
2 Daly, Jonathan M. – Stockport County – Bury
23 Daws, Nicholas J. – Rotherham United – Grimsby Town
25 Dickman, Jonjo – Sunderland – York City
6 Donaldson, Clayton A. – Hull City – Halifax Town
5 Dudfield, Lawrie G. – Northampton Town – Southend United
6 Evans, Louie – Gravesend & Northfleet – King's Lynn
18 Forbes, Scott – Canvey Island – Bishop's Stortford
12 Frendo, John – Hendon – Ware
2 Fry, Adam G. – Peterborough United – Rothwell Town
21 Glover, Simon D. – Dover Athletic – Ashford Town
13 Grainger, Martin R. – Birmingham City – Coventry City
27 Groves, Paul – Grimsby Town – Scunthorpe United
17 Harley, Jon – Fulham – West Ham United
27 Hemmings, Anthony G. – Alfreton Town – Halesowen Town
20 Hignett, Craig J. – Leicester City – Crewe Alexandra
16 Holligan, Gavin V. – Wycombe Wanderers – Hornchurch
6 Howells, Lee – Cheltenham Town – Merthyr Tydfil
13 Impey, Andrew R. – Leicester City – Nottingham Forest
24 Jorgensen, Claus B. – Coventry City – AFC Bournemouth
27 Langmead, Kelvin S. – Preston North End – Carlisle United
19 Lever, Mark – Ilkeston Town – Ossett Town
2 Lindley, James E. – Tamworth – Hucknall Town
3 Lua-Lua, Lomano T. – Newcastle United – Portsmouth
20 Marney, Daniel G. – Brighton & Hove Albion – Crawley T
23 Marshall, Lee – West Bromwich Albion – Hull City
17 Matthews, Lee J. – Bristol City – Bristol Rovers
20 McEvilly, Lee – Rochdale – Accrington Stanley
9 McMaster, Jamie – Leeds United – Chesterfield
20 Moore, Neil – Nuneaton Borough – Stafford Rangers
6 Ndiwa, Kangana L. – Bolton Wanderers – Rochdale
11 Nicholls, Ashley – Darlington – Cambridge United
22 Nolan, Matthew L. – Peterborough United – Cambridge C
17 Oli, Dennis C. – Queens Park Rangers – Farnborough Town
10 Oshitola, Oloruntori – Grays Athletic – Great Wakering R
2 Otsemobor, John – Liverpool – Bolton Wanderers
20 Owusu, Lloyd M. – Sheffield Wednesday – Reading
6 Parsons, Phil – Woking – Walton & Hersham
29 Penfold, Terry – Gravesend & Northfleet – Chelmsford C
10 Pettefer, Carl J. – Portsmouth – Southend United
7 Pitcher, Geoffrey – Brighton & Hove Albion – Havant & W
13 Pressman, Kevin P. – Sheffield W – West Bromwich Albion
27 Proffitt, Darryl S. – Manchester City – Coventry City
9 Pulman, Ian J. – Margate – Eastbourne Borough
12 Rankin, Isiah – Barnsley – Grimsby Town
24 Roache, Lee P. – Barnet – Windsor & Eton
24 Roberts, Stuart I. – Wycombe Wanderers – Swansea City
19 Robinson, Neil D. – Macclesfield Town – Southport
13 Rogers, Alan – Leicester City – Nottingham Forest
22 Rushbury, Andrew J. – Chesterfield – Alfreton Town
20 Saxby, Gavin A. – Alfreton Town – Ilkeston Town
14 Smith, Gavin D. – Worksop Town – Ilkeston Town
20 Srnicek, Pavel – Portsmouth – West Ham United
12 Strouts, James G. – Gravesend & Northfleet – Welling U
16 Taylor, Cleveland – Bolton Wanderers – Scunthorpe United
6 Thorpe, Lee A. – Leyton Orient – Grimsby Town
6 Turner, Iain R. – Everton – Chester City
2 Tyson, Nathan – Reading – Wycombe Wanderers
16 Vieira, Magno S. – Wigan Athletic – Northampton Town
6 Walton, David L. – Derby County – Stockport County
14 White, Robert – Nuneaton Borough – Corby Town
22 Williams, Anthony S. – Hartlepool United – Stockport Co
20 Williams, Gareth A. – Crystal Palace – AFC Bournemouth
1 Williams, Thomas A. – Birmingham City – Peterborough U
2 Zayed, Eamon – Bray Wanderers – Crewe Alexandra
9 Bull, Ronnie R. – Millwall – Brentford
2 Caldwell, Stephen – Newcastle United – Leeds United
8 Challinor, David P. – Stockport County – Bury
7 Chopra, Rocky M. – Newcastle United – Nottingham Forest
13 Clarke, Peter M. – Everton – Coventry City
1 Connolly, Gary M. – Bashley – Havant & Waterlooville
27 Cumberbatch, Mark – Barnet – Wealdstone
13 Davies, Arron R. – Southampton – Barnsley
10 Dichio, Daniele S.E. – West Bromwich Albion – Millwall
27 Dinning, Tony – Wigan Athletic – Blackpool
12 Downey, Gareth – Scarborough – Spennymoor United
6 Easter, Jermaine M. – Hartlepool United – Cambridge United
10 Fettis, Alan – Hull City – Sheffield United
10 Foster, James I. – Chester City – Kidderminster Harriers
23 Frost, Carl R. – Crewe Alexandra – Leek Town
13 Giles, Christopher – Yeovil Town – Woking
19 Goodwin, Mark C. – Eastbourne Borough – Hastings United
27 Green, Michael F. – Southampton – Chippenham Town
27 Hambley, Timothy J. – Welling United – Folkestone Invicta
11 Hawkins, Darren M. – Bristol City – Bath City
10 Henry, Karl – Stoke City – Cheltenham Town
27 Hirschfeld, Lars – Tottenham Hotspur – Gillingham
27 Holloway, Darren – Wimbledon – Scunthorpe United
14 Hudson, Mark A. – Fulham – Crystal Palace
2 Johnson, Jermaine – Bolton Wanderers – Oldham Athletic
10 Keates, Dean S. – Hull City – Kidderminster Harriers
20 Lee, Kris – Thurrock – Heybridge Swifts
25 Lewis, Karl J. – Leicester City – Hull City
6 Livesey, Daniel – Bolton Wanderers – Rochdale
28 Lucas, Richard – Gainsborough Trin – Stocksbridge Park S
27 Marshall, Andrew J. – Ipswich Town – Millwall
28 Martin, Andrew – Hornchurch – East Thurrock United
20 McClements, Eddie – Gravesend & Northfleet – Dartford
6 McGuire, Liam J. – Southport – Prescot Cables
20 Mkandawire, Tamika P. – West Bromwich A – Hereford U
29 Nardiello, Daniel A. – Manchester United – Barnsley
3 Nethercott, Stuart – Millwall – Wycombe Wanderers
27 Noble, David J. – West Ham United – Boston United
23 O'Hanlon, Sean P. – Everton – Swindon Town
27 Omoyinmi, Emmanuel – Oxford United – Gravesend & N
23 Osman, Leon – Everton – Derby County
17 Owen, Gareth J. – Stoke City – Oldham Athletic
6 Pacquette, Richard F. – Queens Park Rangers – Mansfield T
27 Pearson, Gregory – West Ham United – Barnet
20 Pennant, Jermaine – Arsenal – Leeds United
17 Pipe, David R. – Coventry City – Notts County
13 Placid, Darren – Heybridge Swifts – Waltham Forest
6 Proctor, Michael A. – Sunderland – Rotherham United
27 Pullen, James D.C. – Peterborough United – Heybridge Swifts
20 Randall, Martin J. – Hendon – Ashford Town (Middlesex)
26 Reece, Dominic M.A. – Farnborough T – Sutton Coldfield T
27 Roberts, Mark A. – Crewe Alexandra – Vauxhall Motors
28 Robinson, Mark – Hartlepool United – Scarborough
13 Rocastle, Craig A. – Chelsea – Barnsley
16 Rogers, Mark A. – Wycombe Wanderers – Stevenage B
14 Sam, Lloyd – Charlton Athletic – Leyton Orient
10 Shuker, Christopher A. – Manchester C – Hartlepool U
4 Smith, Jeff – Bolton Wanderers – Rochdale
20 Stockdale, Robert K. – Middlesbrough – Rotherham United
6 Tansley, Anthony – Alfreton Town – Belper Town
6 Teggart, Neil – Sunderland – Darlington
29 Traynor, Robert – Brentford – Crawley Town
3 Tyson, Scott J. – Nottingham Forest – Telford United
13 Vaesen, Nico – Birmingham City – Bradford City
26 Wallwork, Ronald – West Bromwich Albion – Bradford City
19 White, Andrew – Mansfield Town – Burton Albion
13 Wilford, Aron L. – York City – Harrogate Town
20 Williams, Daniel I.L. – Kidderminster Harriers – Chester City
4 Williams, Lee – Grays Athletic – Hornchurch
26 Willis, Scott L. – Lincoln City – Hereford United

**MARCH 2004**

| | | | |
|---|---|---|---|
| 15 Abbott, Pawel T.H. | Preston North End | Huddersfield Town | undisclosed |
| 12 Adams, Daniel B. | Macclesfield Town | Stockport County | nominal |
| 25 Anderson, John | Hull City | Bristol Rovers | Free |
| 12 Banks, Steven | Wimbledon | Gillingham | Free |
| 25 Burton, Steven P.G. | Hull City | Kidderminster Harriers | Free |
| 25 Challis, Trevor M. | Telford United | Shrewsbury Town | undisclosed |
| 5 Close, Brian A. | Middlesbrough | Darlington | Free |
| 12 Connor, Paul | Rochdale | Swansea City | 35,000 |
| 19 Cook, Aaron | Bashley | Salisbury City | undisclosed |
| 26 Cropper, Dene J. | Lincoln City | Boston United | Free |
| 25 De Bolla, Mark | Charlton Athletic | Chesterfield | Free |
| 15 Dudfield, Lawrie G. | Northampton Town | Southend United | Free |
| 26 Evans, Paul S. | Bradford City | Nottingham Forest | undisclosed |
| 25 Fagan, Craig | Birmingham City | Colchester United | Free |
| 17 Francis, Simon C. | Bradford City | Sheffield United | 200,000 |

| | | | |
|---|---|---|---|
| 15 Heald, Gregory J. | Leyton Orient | Rochdale | Free |
| 25 Henriksen, Bo | Kidderminster Harriers | Bristol Rovers | Free |
| 18 Iwelumo, Chris | Stoke City | Brighton & Hove Albion | undisclosed |
| 25 Johnson, Jermaine | Bolton Wanderers | Oldham Athletic | Free |
| 2 Keates, Dean S. | Hull City | Kidderminster Harriers | undisclosed |
| 12 Manuella, Fiston | Farnborough Town | Crawley Town | undisclosed |
| 8 Mayo, Paul | Lincoln City | Watford | 100,000 |
| 4 McGuire, Liam J. | Southport | Prescot Cables | undisclosed |
| 25 McSporran, Jermaine | Wycombe Wanderers | Walsall | Free |
| 19 Melton, Stephen | Hull City | Boston United | Free |
| 9 Mings, Adrian | Chippenham Town | Weston-Super-Mare | undisclosed |
| 26 Murray, Scott G. | Reading | Bristol City | 500,000 |
| 11 Niven, Derek | Bolton Wanderers | Chesterfield | Free |
| 24 Noble, David J. | West Ham United | Boston United | Free |
| 25 O'Hanlon, Sean P. | Everton | Swindon Town | 150,000 |
| 25 Owusu, Lloyd M. | Sheffield Wednesday | Reading | undisclosed |
| 9 Patten, Ben | Ford United | Ipswich Town | undisclosed |
| 5 Payne, Stephen J. | Chesterfield | Macclesfield Town | Free |
| 12 Peschisolido, Paul P. | Sheffield United | Derby County | Free |
| 25 Rankin, Isaiah | Barnsley | Grimsby Town | undisclosed |
| 12 Sabin, Eric | Queens Park Rangers | Northampton Town | Free |
| 17 Shuker, Christopher A. | Manchester City | Barnsley | undisclosed |
| 4 Smith, Jeff | Bolton Wanderers | Preston North End | Free |
| 9 Sobers, Jerrome | Ford United | Ipswich Town | undisclosed |
| 22 Srnicek, Pavel | Portsmouth | West Ham United | Free |
| 12 Strong, Greg | Hull City | Boston United | Free |
| 5 Tait, Allan D. | Folkestone Invicta | Crawley Town | undisclosed |
| 16 Taylor, Cleveland K.W. | Bolton Wanderers | Scunthorpe United | Free |
| 31 Taylor, Maik S. | Fulham | Birmingham City | 1,500,000 |
| 19 Thomas, Danny J. | AFC Bournemouth | Boston United | Free |
| 12 Tyson, Nathan | Reading | Wycombe Wanderers | Free |
| 24 Wales, Gary | Heart of Midlothian | Walsall | Free |
| 19 Walker, Richard M. | Blackpool | Oxford United | undisclosed |
| 4 Wilkinson, Wesley | Nantwich Town | Oldham Athletic | undisclosed |
| 25 Williams, Daniel I.L. | Kidderminster Harriers | Bristol Rovers | Free |
| 31 Wilson, Brian | Stoke City | Cheltenham Town | undisclosed |

**TEMPORARY TRANSFERS**

5 Adams, Daniel B. – Macclesfield Town – Stockport County
17 Allen, Daniel T. – Forest Green Rovers – Taunton Town
25 Armstrong, Craig – Sheffield Wednesday – Grimsby Town
11 Ashcroft, Lee – Southport – Chorley
8 Bailey, Mathew J. – Stockport County – Altrincham
19 Baptiste, Liam D. – Waltham F – Barking & East Ham U
26 Bates, Tom – Coventry City – Bedworth United
31 Bixby, Robert – Hayes – Berkhamsted Town
25 Branston, Guy – Rotherham United – Peterborough United
31 Brooker, Paul – Leicester City – Reading
25 Brown, Simon A. – West Bromwich A – Kidderminster H
9 Bull, Ronnie R. – Millwall – Brentford
12 Camp, Lee M.J. – Derby County – Queens Park Rangers
19 Chadwick, Nicholas G. – Everton – Millwall
20 Chambers, Adam – West Bromwich Albion – Sheffield W
13 Coates, Steven – Ilkeston Town – Shepshed Dynamo
5 Coleano, Rudi A. – Farsley Celtic – Guiseley
31 Cook, James S. – Stevenage Borough – Bath City
12 Cooper, Colin T. – Middlesbrough – Sunderland
25 Cooper, Shaun D. – Portsmouth – Leyton Orient
5 De Bolla, Mark – Charlton Athletic – Chesterfield
19 Donovan, James – Millwall – Farnborough Town
13 Dudfield, Lawrie G. – Northampton Town – Southend U
4 Dunbavin, Ian S. – Shrewsbury Town – Morecambe
25 Elam, Lee P.G. – Yeovil Town – Chester City
12 Ellison, Kevin – Stockport County – Lincoln City
11 Fettis, Alan – Hull City – Grimsby Town
16 Fitzgerald, Scott B. – Colchester United – Brentford
15 Flood, William R. – Manchester City – Rochdale
11 Foster, James I. – Chester City – Kidderminster Harriers
16 Francis, Simon – Bradford City – Sheffield United
12 Gemmill, Scott – Everton – Preston North End
12 Gilchrist, Philip A. – West Bromwich A – Rotherham U
23 Gordon, Dean D. – Coventry City – Reading
22 Gourlay, William – Kettering Town – Corby Town
19 Graham, Daniel A.W. – Middlesbrough – Darlington
19 Gunnarsson, Brynjar B. – Nottingham Forest – Stoke City
19 Hardie, Brian – Kettering Town – Corby Town
30 Harris, Richard L.S. – Wycombe W – Maidenhead U
30 Hemmings, Anthony G. – Alfreton Town – Grantham Town
22 Hignett, Craig J. – Leicester City – Crewe Alexandra
25 Howe, Edward J.F. – Portsmouth – Swindon Town
25 Hunt, Warren D. – Portsmouth – Leyton Orient
15 Impey, Andrew R. – Leicester City – Nottingham Forest
16 Iwelumo, Chris – Stoke City – Brighton & Hove Albion
19 John, Jerome L. – Billericay Town – Great Wakering Rovers
17 Kerr, Brian – Newcastle United – Coventry City
6 Knight, Glen J. – Dagenham & Redbridge – Bromley
22 Lawrence, Lee A. – Manchester United – Shrewsbury Town
8 Livesey, Daniel – Bolton Wanderers – Rochdale
25 Adebola, Bamberdele O. – Coventry City – Burnley
13 Andrews, Keith J. – Wolverhampton Wanderers – Walsall
11 Arphexad, Pegguy M. – Coventry City – Notts County
8 Baguley, Jamie C. – Stockport County – Altrincham
16 Baird, Christopher P. – Southampton – Watford
24 Barnard, Lee J. – Tottenham Hotspur – Stevenage Borough
25 Birch, Gary S. – Walsall – Barnsley
25 Blackman, Lloyd J. – Brentford – Cambridge City
30 Britton, Andrew – Sheffield United – Bradford Park Avenue
25 Brown, Jermaine A.A. – Boston United – King's Lynn
19 Brown, Wayne L. – Watford – Colchester United
11 Bullock, Lee – York City – Cardiff City
25 Cartwright, Shaun – Stoke City – Leek Town
9 Challinor, David P. – Stockport County – Bury
25 Clarke, Leon M. – Wolverhampton W – Kidderminster H
15 Cobb, Paul M. – East Thurrock United – Tilbury
4 Connolly, Gary M. – Bashley – Havant & Waterlooville
27 Cook, Lewis L. – Wycombe Wanderers – Cambridge City
19 Cooper, Kevin – Wolverhampton Wanderers – Norwich City
12 Danns, Neil A. – Blackburn Rovers – Hartlepool United
24 Donnelly, Ciaran – Blackburn Rovers – Blackpool
5 Downer, Simon – Leyton Orient – Aldershot Town
9 Duffield, Peter – Boston United – Carlisle United
9 Easter, Jermaine – Hartlepool United – Cambridge United
16 Elliott, Matthew S. – Leicester City – Ipswich Town
25 Evans, Paul S. – Bradford City – Nottingham Forest
25 Fieldwick, Lee P. – Brentford – Swansea City
22 Fitzpatrick, Ian M. – Shrewsbury Town – Forest Green R
5 Foster, Benjamin – Stoke City – Stafford Rangers
19 Fotiadis, Andrew – Peterborough United – Heybridge Swifts
31 Furness, Adam – Stevenage Borough – Ware
25 Gerrard, Paul W. – Everton – Nottingham Forest
12 Gill, Robert – Doncaster Rovers – Burton Albion
19 Gosling, Jamie J. – Yeovil Town – Aldershot Town
31 Gradley, Patrick – Gravesend & Northfleet – Boreham Wood
19 Grainger, Martin R. – Birmingham City – Coventry City
11 Hackworth, Anthony – Notts County – Scarborough
25 Harkins, Gary – Blackburn Rovers – Huddersfield Town
5 Haworth, Robert J. – Gravesend & N – Maidenhead United
12 Henderson, Wayne – Aston Villa – Tamworth
23 Hill, Stephen B. – Rochdale – Morecambe
31 Hughes, Stephen T. – Brentford – Basingstoke Town
25 Hurst, Kevan – Sheffield United – Boston United
16 Ingham, Michael G. – Sunderland – Wrexham
19 James, Craig P. – Sunderland – Port Vale
25 Jorgensen, Claus B. – Coventry City – AFC Bournemouth
19 King, Jordan – Hereford United – Hednesford Town
29 Langmead, Kelvin S. – Preston North End – Carlisle United
25 Lescott, Aaron A. – Stockport County – Bristol Rovers
29 Lucas, Richard – Gainsborough T– Stocksbridge Park Steels

25 Matias, Pedro M.M. – Walsall – Blackpool
8 May, Rory J. – Lincoln City – Halifax Town
25 McClements, Eddie – Gravesend & Northfleet – Fisher Ath
24 McMahon, Daryl – West Ham United – Torquay United
12 Murphy, David P. – Middlesbrough – Barnsley
25 Newby, Jon P.R. – Huddersfield Town – York City
25 Nicolau, Nicky G. – Arsenal – Southend United
19 Northmore, Ryan – Woking – Yeovil Town
17 Olszar, Sebastian – Portsmouth – Coventry City
24 Osman, Leon – Everton – Derby County
19 Parker, Daniel – Worcester City – Evesham United
29 Pearson, Gregory – West Ham United – Barnet
12 Pettefer, Carl J. – Portsmouth – Southend United
19 Pitcher, Geoffrey – Brighton & Hove A – Farnborough T
25 Price, Michael D. – Scarborough – Leigh RMI
3 Quinn, Barry S. – Coventry City – Oxford United
5 Ralph, Andrew O. – Northwich Victoria – Stalybridge Celtic
25 Rees, Matthew R. – Millwall – Swansea City
5 Roberts, Darren A. – Worksop Town – Farsley Celtic
25 Robinson, Carl P. – Portsmouth – Sunderland
19 Rogers, Alan – Leicester City – Nottingham Forest
19 Rosenior, Liam J. – Fulham – Torquay United
3 Sabin, Eric – Queens Park Rangers – Boston United
4 Schumacher, Steven T. – Everton – Oldham Athletic
22 Smith, Gary S. – Middlesbrough – Wimbledon
31 Standen, Dean – Welling United – Erith & Belvedere
25 Surey, Ben D. – Crystal Palace – Gravesend & Northfleet
25 Talbot, Daniel B. – Rushden & Diamonds – Stevenage B
5 Teesdale, Richard – Hereford United – Moor Green
5 Thomas, Daniel K. – Brentford – Staines Town
16 Twigg, Gary – Derby County – Bristol Rovers
17 Uddin, Anwar – Bristol Rovers – Telford United
12 Venus, Mark – Cambridge United – Dagenham & R
17 Walker, Richard M. – Blackpool – Oxford United
29 Warne, Stephen J. – Chesterfield – Matlock Town
19 Williams, Benjamin P. – Manchester United – Crewe Alex
12 Williams, Gareth – Southampton – Tiverton Town
4 Williams, Thomas A. – Birmingham City – Peterborough U
25 Wilson, Brian – Stoke City – Cheltenham Town
20 Matthews, Lee J. – Bristol City – Yeovil Town
31 McCarthy, David – Worksop Town – Stalybridge Celtic
12 McLeod, Izale M. – Derby County – Sheffield United
29 McSweeney, David – Southend United – Welling United
5 Nethercott, Stuart – Millwall – Wycombe Wanderers
12 Nicholson, Kevin J. – Notts County – Scarborough
5 Noble, Stuart W. – Fulham – Woking
12 Offiong, Richard – Newcastle United – York City
29 Omoyinmi, Emmanuel – Oxford United – Gravesend & N
24 Owen, Gareth J. – Stoke City – Oldham Athletic
19 Parkinson, Andrew J. – Sheffield United – Notts County
20 Pennant, Jermaine – Arsenal – Leeds United
22 Pipe, David R. – Coventry City – Notts County
25 Platt, Matthew – Crewe Alexandra – Runcorn FC Halton
27 Pullen, James – Peterborough United – Heybridge Swifts
2 Rachubka, Paul S. – Charlton Athletic – Huddersfield Town
4 Raw, Thomas D. – Scarborough – Spennymoor United
4 Rioch, Gregor J. – Shrewsbury Town – Northwich Victoria
22 Roberts, Mark A. – Crewe Alexandra – Vauxhall Motors
25 Rocastle, Craig A. – Chelsea – Lincoln City
25 Rogers, Kristian R. – Sheffield United – Macclesfield Town
13 Ruffer, Carl J. – Chester City – Droylsden
5 Salisbury, James A. – Wigan Athletic – Leigh RMI
6 Simpson, Sekani – Bristol City – Forest Green Rovers
11 Smith, Mark – Chesterfield – Frickley Athletic
22 Stockdale, Robert K. – Middlesbrough – Rotherham United
24 Symes, Michael – Everton – Crewe Alexandra
8 Tansley, Anthony – Alfreton Town – Belper Town
7 Teggart, Neil – Sunderland – Darlington
8 Turner, Iain R. – Everton – Chester City
5 Tyson, Nathan – Reading – Wycombe Wanderers
18 Vaesen, Nico – Birmingham City – Crystal Palace
2 Viveash, Adrian L. – Swindon Town – Kidderminster Harriers
9 Walton, David L. – Derby County – Stockport County
19 Whitman, Tristram – Scarborough – Leigh RMI
22 Williams, Gareth A. – Crystal Palace – Colchester United
24 Williamson, Michael J. – Southampton – Doncaster Rovers
28 Willis, Scott L. – Lincoln City – Hereford United
1 Wood, Neil A. – Manchester United – Burnley

**APRIL 2004**

| | | | |
|---|---|---|---|
| 7 Bull, Ronnie R. | Millwall | Brentford | undisclosed |
| 24 Gilbert, Peter | Birmingham City | Plymouth Argyle | undisclosed |
| 6 James, Craig P. | Sunderland | Port Vale | undisclosed |

**TEMPORARY TRANSFERS**

10 Allen, Daniel T. – Forest Green Rovers – Taunton Town
8 Bailey, Matthew – Stockport County – Altrincham
25 Brown, Simon – West Bromwich Albion – Kidderminster H
16 Danns, Neil A. – Blackburn Rovers – Hartlepool United
5 Downer, Simon – Leyton Orient – Aldershot Town
16 Elliott, Matthew S. – Leicester City – Ipswich Town
13 Gilchrist, Philip A. – West Bromwich Albion – Rotherham U
20 Graham, Daniel A.W. – Middlesbrough – Darlington
22 Harkins, Gary – Blackburn Rovers – Huddersfield Town
20 Hignett, Craig J. – Leicester City – Crewe Alexandra
18 King, Jordan – Hereford United – Hednesford Town
8 Livesey, Daniel – Bolton Wanderers – Rochdale
16 Matthews, Lee J. – Bristol City – Yeovil Town
14 Nicholson, Kevin J. – Notts County – Scarborough
25 Pearson, Gregory – West Ham United – Barnet
4 Quinn, Barry S. – Coventry City – Oxford United
1 Reece, Dominic M.A. – Farnborough T – Sutton Coldfield T
5 Roberts, Darren A. – Worksop Town – Farsley Celtic
22 Smith, Gary S. – Middlesbrough – Wimbledon
4 Teesdale, Richard – Hereford United – Moor Green
15 Turnbull, Ross – Middlesbrough – Barnsley
29 Ward, Gavin J. – Coventry City – Barnsley
12 Worgan, Lee J. – Wimbledon – Wycombe Wanderers
8 Baguley, Jamie C. – Stockport County – Altrincham
19 Baird, Christopher P. – Southampton – Watford
13 Camp, Lee M.J. – Derby County – Queens Park Rangers
25 Donnelly, Ciaran – Blackburn Rovers – Blackpool
8 Easter, Jermaine – Hartlepool United – Cambridge United
13 Ellison, Kevin – Stockport County – Lincoln City
18 Gosling, Jamie J. – Yeovil Town – Aldershot Town
14 Hackworth, Anthony – Notts County – Scarborough
23 Henderson, Wayne – Aston Villa – Wycombe Wanderers
13 Hudson, Mark A. – Fulham – Crystal Palace
23 Lawrence, Lee A. – Manchester United – Shrewsbury Town
22 MacKenzie, Christopher – Telford United – Hereford United
7 Murphy, David P. – Middlesbrough – Barnsley
14 Northmore, Ryan – Woking – Yeovil Town
20 Pennant, Jermaine – Arsenal – Leeds United
4 Rachubka, Paul S. – Charlton Athletic – Huddersfield Town
1 Rioch, Gregor J. – Shrewsbury Town – Northwich Victoria
15 Rosenior, Liam – Fulham – Torquay United
16 Symes, Michael – Everton – Crewe Alexandra
3 Thomas, Daniel K. – Brentford – Staines Town
16 Twigg, Gary – Derby County – Bristol Rovers
13 Williams, Benjamin W. – Manchester United – Crewe Alex

**MAY 2004**

| | | | |
|---|---|---|---|
| 25 Lucas, David A. | Preston North End | Sheffield Wednesday | undisclosed |
| 27 Pugh, Daniel | Manchester United | Leeds United | undisclosed |
| 16 Robinson, Paul W. | Leeds United | Tottenham Hotspur | £1,500,000 |
| 24 Scimeca, Riccardo | Leicester City | West Bromwich Albion | |
| 26 Smith, Alan | Leeds United | Manchester United | 7,050,000 |

**TEMPORARY TRANSFERS**

2 Bradshaw, Craig R.J. – Portsmouth – Dorchester Town
4 Downer, Simon – Leyton Orient – Aldershot Town
6 Henderson, Wayne – Aston Villa – Wycombe Wanderers
10 Rachubka, Paul S. – Charlton Athletic – Huddersfield Town
6 Turnbull, Ross – Middlesbrough – Barnsley
13 Danns, Neil A. – Blackburn Rovers – Hartlepool United
11 Ellison, Kevin – Stockport County – Lincoln City
2 King, Jordan – Hereford United – Hednesford Town
7 Robinson, Carl P. – Portsmouth – Sunderland

# THE NEW FOREIGN LEGION 2003–04

| | From | To | Fee in £ |
|---|---|---|---|
| **MAY 2003** | | | |
| 15 Dugarry, Christophe | Bordeaux | Birmingham City | Free |
| 30 Neumayr, Markus M. | Eintracht Frankfurt | Manchester United | undisclosed |
| **JULY 2003** | | | |
| 9 Ambrosio, Marco | Chievo | Chelsea | Free |
| 15 Amoruso, Lorenzo | Rangers | Blackburn Rovers | 1,400,000 |
| 29 Bosvelt, Paul | Feyenoord | Manchester City | undisclosed |
| 22 Campo, Ivan R. | Real Madrid | Bolton Wanderers | free |
| 29 Djemba Djemba, Eric D. | Nantes | Manchester United | 3,500,000 |
| 21 Emerton, Brett | Feyenoord | Blackburn Rovers | 2,200,000 |
| 31 Folly, Yoann | St Etienne | Southampton | 250,000 |
| 16 Giannakopoulos, Stelios | Olympiakos | Bolton Wanderers | Free |
| 23 Griffit, Leandre | Amiens | Southampton | Free |
| 28 Doriva, Guidoni D. | Celta Vigo | Middlesbrough | Free |
| 22 Howard, Timothy M. | New York/New Jersey MetroStars | Manchester United | 2,300,000 |
| 15 Laville, Florent | Lyon | Bolton Wanderers | 500,000 |
| 18 Le Tallec, Anthony | Le Havre | Liverpool | undisclosed |
| 1 Makabu-Ma-Kalamby, Yves | PSV Eindhoven | Chelsea | Free |
| 16 Nalis, Lilian B.P. | Chievo | Leicester City | Free |
| 30 Okoronkwo, Isaac | Shakhtjor Donetsk | Wolverhampton Wanderers | Free |
| 18 Postiga, Helder M.M. | Porto | Tottenham Hotspur | 6,250,000 |
| 18 Senderos, Philippe | Servette | Arsenal | 2,500,000 |
| 21 Silas, Jorge M.F. | Uniao Leiria | Wolverhampton Wanderers | 1,000,000 |
| 18 Sinama-Pongolle, Florent | Le Havre | Liverpool | undisclosed |
| 30 Stefanovic, Dejan | Vitesse | Portsmouth | 1,850,000 |
| 9 Tarnat, Michael | Bayern Munich | Manchester City | Free |
| 11 Wapenaar, Harald | Utrecht | Portsmouth | Free |
| 22 Yelldell, David R. | Stuttgart Kickers | Blackburn Rovers | 100,000 |
| 10 Yobo, Joseph | Marseille | Everton | 3,500,000 |
| 17 Zivkovic, Boris | Leverkusen | Portsmouth | Free |
| **AUGUST 2003** | | | |
| 1 Bonnissel, Jerome | Rangers | Fulham | Free |
| 6 Camara, Henri | Sedan | Wolverhampton Wanderers | 1,500,000 |
| 1 Camara, Zoumana | Lens | Leeds United | loan |
| 6 Clichy, Gael | Cannes | Arsenal | 250,000 |
| 29 Crespo, Herman | Internazionale | Chelsea | 16,800,000 |
| 12 Domi, Didier | Paris St Germain | Leeds United | loan |
| 14 Faye, Andy M. | Auxerre | Portsmouth | 1,500,000 |
| 1 Figueroa, Luciano G. | Rosario Central | Birmingham City | 2,500,000 |
| 1 Geremi N.F.S. | Real Madrid | Chelsea | 6,900,000 |
| 7 Gresko, Vratislav | Parma | Blackburn Rovers | 1,200,000 |
| 29 Gudjonsson, Johannes K. | Betis | Wolverhampton Wanderers | loan |
| 15 Jardel, Mario D.A.R. | Sporting Lisbon | Bolton Wanderers | Free |
| 29 Karbassiyon, Danny | Roanoke Star | Arsenal | undisclosed |
| 13 Kleberson, Pereira J. | Atletico Paranaense | Manchester United | 5,930,000 |
| 5 Lehmann, Jens | Borussia Dortmund | Arsenal | 1,250,000 |
| 14 Leite, Sergio | Boavista | Charlton Athletic | Free |
| 26 Mabizela, Mbulelo O. | Orlando Pirates | Tottenham Hotspur | undisclosed |
| 30 McManaman, Steve | Real Madrid | Manchester City | Free |
| 29 Medjani, Carl | St Etienne | Liverpool | Free |
| 26 Mendieta-Zabala, Gaizka | Lazio | Middlesbrough | loan |
| 19 Mutu, Adrian | Parma | Chelsea | 15,800,000 |
| 31 Olembe, Salomon R.O. | Marseille | Leeds United | loan |
| 1 Pericard, Vincent D.P. | Juventus | Portsmouth | 400,000 |
| 14 Ronaldo, Cristiano Dos Santos A. | Sporting Lisbon | Manchester United | 12,240,000 |
| 14 Sakho, Lamine | Marseille | Leeds United | loan |
| 14 Schemmel, Sebastien | West Ham United | Portsmouth | Free |
| 7 Sibierski, Antoine | Lens | Manchester City | 700,000 |
| 26 Smertin, Alexei | Bordeaux | Chelsea | 3,800,000 |
| **SEPTEMBER 2003** | | | |
| 1 Baggio, Dino | Lazio | Blackburn Rovers | loan |
| 12 Ba, Ibrahim | AC Milan | Bolton Wanderers | Free |
| 3 Chapuis, Cyril S.T. | Marseille | Leeds United | loan |
| 1 Dalmat, Stephane | Internazionale | Tottenham Hotspur | loan |
| 1 Makelele, Claude | Real Madrid | Chelsea | 13,900,000 |
| 1 Papadopoulos, Michal | Banik Ostrava | Arsenal | loan |
| 1 Roque Junior, Jose V. | AC Milan | Leeds United | loan |
| 1 Srnicek, Pavel | Brescia | Portsmouth | Free |
| **OCTOBER 2003** | | | |
| 24 Fabregas, Cese | Barcelona | Arsenal | 2,250,000 |
| **JANUARY 2004** | | | |
| 31 Andresen, Martin | Stabaek | Blackburn Rovers | loan |
| 16 Arason, Arni G. | Rosenborg | Manchester City | Free |
| 14 Bocanegra, Carlos | Chicago Fire | Fulham | undisclosed |
| 31 John, Collins | Twente | Fulham | 600,000 |
| 31 Freund, Steffen | Kaiserslautern | Leicester City | loan |
| 1 Ganea, Viorel I. | Bursaspor | Wolverhampton Wanderers | loan |
| 27 McBride, Brian R. | Columbus Crewe | Fulham | 600,000 |
| 7 Moreno, Javi V. | Atletico Madrid | Bolton Wanderers | loan |
| 30 Mornar, Ivica | Anderlecht | Portsmouth | 400,000 |
| 30 Olszar, Sebastian | Admira Modling | Portsmouth | 100,000 |
| 5 Pasanen, Petri M. | Ajax | Portsmouth | loan |
| 30 Reyes, Jose Antonio | Sevilla | Arsenal | 17,600,000 |
| 1 Ricketts, Donovan | Village United | Bolton Wanderers | loan |
| 31 Van Buyten, Daniel | Marseille | Manchester City | loan |

# REFEREEING AND THE REFEREES

There have been over the last 12 months some extravagant and in some cases quite peculiar pronouncements from FIFA's hierarchy, which would have impacted on the Laws of the Game and how it would be played if implemented. These included making women players turn out in tight kit and making sure every match ended in a result. These have given rise to ribald and cynical pronouncements that if these had come to fruition the game would have lurched from 'tight drawers to no draws'. However both ideas have received short shrift and as a result, once again, there have been few substantive Law and Rule changes for the 2004–05 Season. The two principles of safety and protection have become the watchwords for the new period. Now the practise of taping rings, which has not been entirely satisfactory, has led to a direction that this shall be allowed only if it renders them entirely safe. Referees are thus instructed not just to carry out inspections on this aspect prior to every match but also on studs and blades on footwear. Another extension of the rule that bleeding players are required to leave the field has come with the prohibition of a returning player wearing blood-stained kit since that constitutes a danger to other participants. Incidentally so far as kit is concerned, the International Board has specified that use of a 'one-piece' playing suit is contrary to its Law on equipment.

One very big change, which has been allowed, is the reintroduction of artificial playing surfaces. This is because it has been felt that artificial surface technology has advanced so far as to be acceptable. Nevertheless these pitches must meet the requirements of the 'FIFA Quality concept for Artificial Turf' or the 'International Artificial Turf Standard' unless special dispensation is given by FIFA.

Unfortunately, for the England Manager and several others who have used International and other 'friendlies' to play different teams in each half, from now on Substitutes in these matches will be limited to six. The reason expressed being that it otherwise devalues the game.

On the disciplinary front a mandatory Law change has been introduced which follows a directive mentioned here last season but more often honoured in the breach than the performance. Now a player removing his/her jersey when celebrating a goal MUST be cautioned for unsporting behaviour. At long last this has been deemed an unnecessary and excessive form of celebration. Referees are also reminded that racist remarks made by players constitute a dismissal offence under the Law dealing with offensive insulting or abusive language.

Finally on the Laws, after the melting away of the golden goal last season, the silver goal has also lost its lustre. Apart from competition rules governing extra time and away goals, where those fail to find a winner, where it is necessary, it will be a return to the straight forward 'penalty shoot-out' if that can ever be straight forward. Witness some Referees allowing players to halt in their stride in taking penalties in EURO 2004 since that practise had been outlawed as far back as the mid 1950s.

An interesting requirement being introduced by the FA for the re-registration of Referees for 2004–05 is that they must complete the FA's Child Protection Distance Learning Course. For new Referees wanting to be registered they must complete the FA Child Protection and Best Practice Work Shop unless under 18, when the distance learning course will suffice. This will lead to a 3-year Child Protection Certificate.

There are now two vibrant Referees Bodies. They are the Referees Association – Website http://www.footballreferee.org and the Football Association Match Officials Association (FAMOA) – e-mail famoa@TheFA.com

The Year's most prestigious Refereeing appointment went to Markus Merk of Germany who refereed the EURO 2004 Final between the hosts Portugal and the winners Greece.

The current Select Group of Referees will be reduced to 19 for this Season. It results from there being one new Official in the Squad namely Mark Clattenburgh from Newcastle-upon-Tyne, but three top ones have been retired through age. These are Graham Barber, Jeff Winter, who was honoured with last term's FA Cup Final and the man lauded by many as the best Referee of his generation, Paul Durkin.

In addition there are 36 Assistant Referees on the Select List. The whole group is overseen by three men who carry-out the requirements of the Selection Board which is comprised of the Chief Executives of the FA, the Premier League and the Football League. Those three are General Manager Keith Hackett; National Group Manager Len Ashworth and FA Referee Manager Joe Guest.

The full compliment of both the Select Group and the remaining majority National List for the forthcoming season is set out below.

KEN GOLDMAN

# NATIONAL LIST OF REFEREES FOR SEASON 2003–04

**Indicates Select Group Referees*

Armstrong, P (Paul) Berkshire
Atkinson, M (Martin) W. Yorkshire
Barry, NS (Neale) N. Lincolnshire*
Bates, A (Tony) Staffordshire
Beeby, RJ (Richard) Northamptonshire
Bennett, SG (Steve) Kent*
Booth, RJ (Russell) Nottinghamshire
Boyeson, C (Carl) E. Yorkshire
Cable, LE (Lee) Surrey
Clattenburg, M (Mark) Tyne & Wear*
Cowburn, MG (Mark) Lancashire
Crossley, PT (Phil) Kent
Curson, B (Brian) Leicestershire
Danson, PS (Paul) Leicestershire
Dean, ML (Mike) Wirral*
Dowd, P (Phil) Staffordshire*
Drysdale, D (Darren) Lincolnshire
Dunn, SW (Steve) Gloucestershire*
D'Urso, AP (Andy) Essex*
Evans, EM (Eddie) Greater Manchester
Fletcher, M (Mick) Worcestershire
Foy, CJ (Chris) Merseyside*
Friend, KA (Kevin) Leicestershire
Gallagher, DJ (Dermot) Oxfordshire*
Graham, F (Fred) Essex
Hall, AR (Andy) W. Midlands
Halsey, MR (Mark) Lancashire*
Hegley, GK (Grant) Hertfordshire
Hill, KD (Keith) Hertfordshire
Ilderton, EL (Eddie) Tyne & Wear
Jones, MJ (Michael) Cheshire
Joslin, PJ (Phil) Nottinghamshire
Kaye, A (Alan) W. Yorkshire
Kettle, TM (Trevor) Berkshire
Knight, B (Barry) Kent*
Laws, G (Graham) Tyne & Wear
Leake, AR (Tony) Lancashire
Lewis, GJ (Gary) Haddenham, Cambridgeshire
Marriner, AM (Andre) W. Midlands
Mason, LS (Lee) Lancashire
Mathieson, SW (Scott) Cheshire
Melin, PW (Paul) Surrey
Messias, MD (Matt) W. Yorkshire*
Miller, NS (Nigel) Co. Durham
Oliver, CW (Clive) Northumberland
Olivier, RJ (Ray) W. Midlands
Parkes, TA (Trevor) W. Midlands
Penn, AM (Andy) W. Midlands
Penton, C (Clive) Sussex
Pike, MS (Mike) Cumbria
Poll, G (Graham) Hertfordshire*
Probert, LW (Lee) Gloucestershire
Prosser, PJ (Phil) W. Yorkshire
Rennie, UD (Uriah) S. Yorkshire*
Riley, MA (Mike) W. Yorkshire*
Robinson, JP (Paul) E. Yorkshire
Ross, JJ (Joe) London
Russell, MP (Mike) Hertfordshire
Ryan, M (Michael) Lancashire
Salisbury, G (Graham) Lancashire
Singh, J (Jarnall) Middlesex
Stroud, KP (Keith) Dorset
Styles, R (Rob) Hampshire*
Tanner, SJ (Steve) Somerset
Taylor, P (Paul) Hertfordshire
Thorpe, M (Mike) Suffolk
Tomlin, SG (Steve) E. Sussex
Walton, P (Peter) Northamptonshire*
Warren, MR (Mark) W. Midlands
Webb, HM (Howard) S. Yorkshire*
Webster, CH (Colin) Tyne & Wear
Wiley, AG (Alan) Staffordshire*
Williamson, IG (Iain) Berkshire
Woolmer, KA (Andy) Northamptonshire
Wright, KK (Kevin) Cambridgeshire

## ASSISTANT REFEREES

Ansell, I (Ian) – Devon
Appleby, ND (Norman) – Hertfordshire
Artis, SG (Stephen) – Norfolk
Astley, MA (Mark) – Greater Manchester
Aston, GA (Glenn) – W. Midlands
Atkins, G (Graeme) – W. Yorkshire
Babski, DS (Dave) – Lincolnshire
Baker, BD (Bernard) – Hampshire
Bannister, N (Nigel) – E. Yorkshire
Barker, CA (Craig) – W. Yorkshire
Barnes, K G (Kevin) – Wiltshire
Barnes, PW (Paul) – Cambridgeshire
Bassindale, C (Carl) – S. Yorkshire
Beadle, J (Jon) – Kent
Beale, GA (Guy) – Somerset
Beck, SP (Simon) – Essex
Beevor, R (Richard) – Norfolk
Bentley, I F (Ian) – Kent
Benton, DK (David) – S. Yorkshire
Birkett, DJ (Dave) – Lincolnshire
Bone, R (Ralph) – Kent
Bramley, P (Philip) – W. Yorkshire
Bratt, SJ (Steve) – W. Midlands
Brittain, GM (Gary) – S. Yorkshire
Brown, M (Mark) – E. Yorkshire
Brumwell, CA (Chris) – Cumbria
Bryan, DS (Dave) – Lincolnshire
Bull, M (Michael) – Essex
Buller, KR (Keith) – Somerset
Burton, R (Roy) – Staffordshire
Butler, AN (Andrew) – Lancashire
Cairns, MJ (Mike) – Northamptonshire
Canadine, P (Paul) – S. Yorkshire
Cann, DJ (Darren) – Norfolk
Carter, JE (John) – Tyne & Wear
Cassidy, MT (Martin) – Somerset
Castle, S (Steve) – W. Midlands
Chapman, A (Alison) – Berkshire
Chapman, GJ (Gary) – Gloucestershire
Chittenden, S (Steve) – Hertfordshire,
Clyde, AL (Alec) – S. Yorkshire
Cook, SJ (Steve) – Derbyshire
Cooke, SG (Stephen) – Nottinghamshire
Cooper MA (Mark) – West Midlands,
Cordy, JN (Jon) – S. Gloucestershire
Coulson, DH (Des) – N. Yorkshire
Creighton, SW (Steve) – Berkshire
Curry, PE (Paul) – Northumberland
Darlow, M (Martin) – Bedfordshire
Deadman, D (Darren) – Cambridgeshire
Desmond, RP (Bob) – Wiltshire
Devine, JP (Jim) – Cleveland
Dewfield, A (Adam) – Leicestershire
Dexter, MC (Martin) – Leicestershire
Dorr, SJ (Steve) – Worcestershire
Drew, S (Steve) – Tyne & Wear
Duncan, SAJ (Scott) – Tyne & Wear
Dunn, C (Carl) – Staffordshire
East, R (Roger) – Wiltshire
Eastwood, P (Peter) – Greater Manchester
Ebbage, M (Martin) – Hampshire
Evans, C (Craig) – Lincolnshire
Evans, IA (Ian) – W. Midlands
Evans, KG (Karl) – Greater Manchester
Evetts, GS (Gary) – Hertfordshire
Farries, J (John) – Oxfordshire
Faulkner, IL (Ian) – Merseyside
Flynn, J (John) – Wiltshire
Foster, D (Dave) – Tyne & Wear
Foulkes, GW (Gary) – Merseyside
Francis, CJ (Chris) – Cambridgeshire
Ganfield, RS (Ron) – Somerset
Garratt, AM (Andy) – W. Midlands
Gate, S (Stan) – Tyne & Wear
Gibbs, PN (Phil) – W. Midlands
Gosling, IJ (Ian) – Kent
Gould, R (Ray) – Staffordshire
Greaves, AJ (Alan) – S. Yorkshire
Green, AJ (Tony) – Leicestershire
Green, RC (Russell) – Gloucestershire
Grove, PJ (Peter) – W. Midlands
Haines, A (Andy) – Tyne & Wear
Halliday, A (Andy) – N. Yorkshire
Hambling, GS (Glenn) – Norfolk
Hancox, N (Neil) – W. Midlands
Harris, IR (Ian) – Cornwall
Harris, MA (Martin) – Lincolnshire
Harwood, CN (Colin) – Greater Manchester
Hawken, MA (Mike) – Cornwall
Hawkes, KJ (Kevin) – Gloucestershire
Hayto, JM (John) – Essex
Haywood, M (Mark) – W. Yorkshire
Hendley, AR (Andy) – W. Midlands
Hewitt, RT (Richard) – N. Yorkshire
Hilton, G (Gary) – Lancashire
Hine, DJ (David) – Worcestershire
Hogg, AS (Andy) – S. Yorkshire
Holbrook, JH (John) – Worcestershire
Holdsworth, RJ (Richard) – W. Yorkshire
Hollick, S (Simon) – Devon
Horton, AJ (Tony) – W. Midlands
Horwood, GD (Graham) – Bedfordshire
Howes, TP (Tim) – Norfolk
Hubbard, JR (Jim) – Leicestershire
Hutchinson, AD (Andrew) – Cheshire
Hutchinson, SM (Mark) – Nottinghamshire
Ingram, KR (Kevin) – W. Midlands
Ives, GL (Gary) – Essex
Ives, M (Mark) – Bedfordshire
James, RG (Ron) – Buckinghamshire
John, MA (Mark) – Surrey
Keane, PJ (Patrick) – W. Midlands
Kellett, DG (Gary) – W. Yorkshire
Kinseley, N (Nick) – Essex
Kirkup, PJ (Peter) – Northamptonshire
Knight, MT (Matthew) – Sussex
Law, GC (Geoff) – Leicestershire
Lee, R (Ray) – Essex
Lewis, RL (Robert) – Shropshire
Linington, JJ (James) – Isle of Wight
Lockhart, R (Bob) – Tyne & Wear
Lodge, JR (John) – Essex
Lomas, WD (Wayne) – S. Yorkshire
McCallum, DA (Dave) – Tyne & Wear
McCoy, MT (Michael) – Kent
McDermid, DS (Danny) – Hampshire
McDonough, M (Mick) – Tyne & Wear
McGee, A (Tony) – Merseyside
McIntosh, WA (Wayne) – Lincolnshire
McPherson, MW (Michael) – Cambridgeshire
Mackrell, EB (Eric) – Hampshire
Malone, B (Brendan) – Wiltshire
Martin, AJ (Andy) – Staffordshire
Martin, EAC (Edward) – Somerset
Martin, PC (Paul) – Northamptonshire
Martin, RW (Rob) – S. Yorkshire
Mason, T (Tony) – Kent
Massey, T (Trevor) – Cheshire
Matadar, M (Mo) – Lancashire
Mattocks, KJ (Kevin) – Lancashire
Mellor, G (Glyn) – Derbyshire
Mellor, GS (Gary) – S. Yorkshire
Merchant, K (Kevin) – Surrey
Miller, P (Patrick) – Bedfordshire
Morrison, DP (Des) – Derbyshire
Moss, J (Jonathon) – W. Yorkshire
Mullarkey, M (Mike) – Devon
Murphy, ME (Michael) – W. Midlands
Murphy, N (Nigel) – Nottinghamshire
Naylor, D (Dave) – Nottinghamshire
Nicholson, AR (Andy) – W. Yorkshire
Nicholson, PW (Paul) – Co. Durham
Nolan, I (Ian) – Lancashire
Norman, PV (Paul) – Dorset
Oliver, M (Michael) – Northumberland
Page, A (Andy) – Derbyshire
Palmer, R (Richard) – Somerset
Parker, AR (Alan) – Derbyshire
Parry, B (Brian) – Co. Durham
Pearce, JE (John) – Essex
Perlejewski, AJ (Andy) – Dorset
Phillips, D (David) – Sussex
Pickavance, SD (Stephen) – S. Yorkshire
Pike, K (Kevin) – Dorset
Pollard, TJ (Trevor) – Suffolk
Pollock, RM (Bob) – Merseyside
Powell, K (Ken) – Co. Durham
Procter-Green, SRM (Shaun) – Lincolnshire
Pryme, GD (Greg) – Essex
Ramsay, W (William) – W. Midlands
Rawcliffe, A (Allan) – Greater Manchester
Rayner, AE (Amy) – Leicestershire
Reeves, CL (Christopher) – E. Yorkshire
Richards, DC (Ceri) – Carmarthenshire
Richardson, D (David) – W. Yorkshire
Roberts, DJ (Danny) – Greater Manchester
Roberts, B (Bob) – Lancashire
Robinson, MG (Martin) – Co. Durham
Rubery, SP (Steve) – Essex
Russell, GR (Geoff) – Northamptonshire
Sainsbury, A (Andrew) – Wiltshire
Sarginson, CD (Christopher) – Staffordshire
Scarr, IK (Ian) – W. Midlands
Scholes, MS (Mark) – Buckinghamshire
Searle, IR (Ian) – Hertfordshire
Sharp, PR (Phil) – Hertfordshire
Sheffield, JA (Alan) – W. Midlands
Shoebridge, RL (Robert) – Derbyshire
Short, M (Michael) – S. Yorkshire
Short, ML (Martyn) – Lincolnshire
Sim, TJ (Tom) – Staffordshire
Simpson, GH (George) – N. Yorkshire
Simpson, P (Paul) – Co. Durham
Smallwood, W (William) – Cheshire
Smith, AN (Andrew) – W. Yorkshire
Smith, RH (Richard) – W. Midlands
Snartt, SP (Simon) – S. Gloucestershire
Steans, RJ (Rob) – Leicestershire
Stewart, M (Matt) – Essex
Stokes, JD (John) – Merseyside
Storrie, D (David) – W. Yorkshire
Stott, GT (Gary) – Greater Manchester
Stretton, GS (Guy) – Leicestershire
Sutton, GJ (Gary) – Lincolnshire
Swarbrick, ND (Neil) – Lancashire
Sygmuta, BC (Barry) – N. Yorkshire
Tarry, EJ (Eddie) – Greater Manchester
Tattan, JF (James) – Merseyside
Taylor, JT (Joe) – Lancashire
Thiarra, SS (Sukhdev) – Bedfordshire
Tiffin, R (Russell) – Co. Durham
Tilling, MR (Mark) – Cleveland
Tincknell, SW (Steve) – Hertfordshire
Tingey, M (Mike) – Buckinghamshire
Tomlinson, SD (Stephen) – Hampshire
Toms, WA (Wendy) – Dorset
Turner, A (Andrew) – Devon
Turner, GB (Glenn) – Derbyshire
Unsworth, D (David) – Lancashire
Varley, PC (Paul) – W. Yorkshire
Vaughan, RG (Roger) – Somerset
Wallace, G (Gary) – Tyne & Wear
Ward, GL (Gavin) – Kent
Waring, J (Jim) – Lancashire
Weaver, M (Mark) – W. Midlands
West, MG (Malcolm) – Cornwall
West, RJ (Richard) – E. Yorkshire
Whitby, D (Dave) – Merseyside
Whitestone, D (Dean) – Northamptonshire
Wilkinson, K (Keith) – Northumberland
Williams, MA (Andy) – Herefordshire
Wilson, SM (Stuart) – W. Yorkshire
Wood, PM (Paul) – Lancashire
Woodward, IJ (Irvine) – E. Sussex
Yates, NA (Neil) – Lancashire
Yeo, KG (Keith) – Essex
Yerby, MS (Martin) – Kent
Young, GR (Gary) – Bedfordshire

# THE THINGS THEY SAID . . .

**Harry Redknapp's radar concerning Portsmouth's foreign players being dropped:**
*"I knew they were saying – blah, blah blah, le b*****d manager, f***ing useless b*****d!"*

**Kevin Keegan musing on Manchester City:**
*"People will say that was typical City, which really annoys me. But that's typical City, I suppose."*

**Gordon Strachan going fourth while with Southampton:**
"I'm going home and I'm going to sit with a bottle of Coke, a packet of crisps and stare at the Teletext League Tables for three hours."

**Swindon Manager Andy King praising Leeds goalkeeper Paul Robinson:**
*"We have partly lost this game to an act of God. I can only remember three occasions in my lifetime that a goalkeeper has come up to score."*

**Sir Bobby Robson before Newcastle scored five in a European game:**
*"I said to our players, – you've got to think that you're not playing Breda, you've got to think that you're playing Barcelona."*

**Chelsea boss Claudio Ranieri watching the replay of the Champions League winner against Arsenal:**
*"It's crazy man."*

**Berti Vogts No. 2 at Scotland Tommy Burns:**
*"If I'd been in charge I would have done the same thing – used 40 players and seen what qualities they could bring."*

**Gerard Houllier the Liverpool manager on Steven Gerrard's performance and the team against Manchester United:**
*"Gerrard was awesome. He did everything and he is becoming a world-class player. When you win at Old Trafford it is always a great performance. I would like to dedicate it to the fans."*

**Fiona Bruce on BBC News:**
*"The funeral has been held of John Charles, known as the Silent Giant."*

**Sven Goran Eriksson on his away visits:**
*"I don't know how many times I have been to David Dein's house. I just hope I am not supposed to be the next Arsenal boss."*

**Martin O'Neill on his future:**
*"How many times can I say it? How many times do you want to ask the same thing? How many times do you want to be wrong?"*

**Mark Lawrenson in February on the seemingly impossible:**
*"Premiership leaders Arsenal are by far and away the best team in the country – but not even they will go through the season unbeaten."*

**Andy Townsend on a moot legal point:**
*"I'm not trying to defend Wayne Rooney – I'm making the case for him."*

**Jason McAteer on his Sunderland nickname of Trigger:**
*"I once bought a pizza and was asked if I wanted it sliced into four or eight. I said just four because I couldn't manage eight slices."*

**Artim Sakiri on the difference in football culture:**
*"Players in England swear all the time during matches. In Macedonia people say things like – I'm going to kill you."*

**Professor John McKenzie on annual losses at Leeds United:**
*"Leeds lived the dream and it turned out to be a bit of a nightmare."*

**Chris Waddle on a save by the Fulham goalkeeper:**
*"If that had gone in, I don't think Van der Sar would have saved it."*

**Steve Coppell wrestling with the points system:**
*"Only time will tell if this is a point gained or three dropped."*

**John Terry on the complexities of winning, drawing and losing:**
*"We didn't come here for a draw, or any other result."*

**Steve Wilson on BBC Two – the lost year:**
*"Trapattoni wasn't born the last time Wales beat Italy. Mind you, not many people were born in 1929."*

**Stuart Murdoch on life as manager of Wimbledon:**
*"I think about resigning about every 25 minutes and it seems like the last time we scored was in about 1066."*

**Gerard Houllier on defeat against Marseille:**
*"I have joked recently it is not players that get you the sack but referees – and that referee has dealt a bad blow to Liverpool Football Club."*

**Sir Bobby Robson unimpressed by Wales wanting Craig Bellamy:**
*"Craig was told to take two weeks' rest and he hasn't kicked a ball since. So it's ironic he's going off to play for Wales."*

**Claudio Ranieri on his Monaco faux-pas:**
*"It was without doubt the worst 45 minutes since I have been in charge of Chelsea. I take the blame. I made a mistake."*

**Jose Antonio Reyes on his own-goal debut for Arsenal:**
*"I am sorry for the fans and ask them to forgive me. For my first goal at the club to have a negative impact is distressing."*

**Louis Saha comparing his Manchester United colleague Ruud Van Nistelrooy with Arsenal's Thierry Henry:**
*"Ruud doesn't take much part in collective play … lacks big game experience … never scores from outside the 18-yard area and never takes free-kicks."*

**Sven Goran Eriksson on secret talks with Chelsea:**
*"I hope I am still as popular as I was before this happened."*

**David O'Leary on the vexed question of the vagaries of football:**
*"If we had taken our chances we would have won – at least."*

**Gordon Strachan in his Southampton programme notes concerning his quitting at the end of the season:**
*"You could hear the birds singing at the training ground as we came into work in the morning. It seems much duller now. The dark forces have taken over."*

**Sir Alex Ferguson on the excitement of the Champions League draw:**
*"It's a great draw. I was half expecting to get a Scottish team, but also not expecting it."*

**Malcolm Macdonald with grounds for confusion:**
*"I saw Arsenal play Leicester a couple of weeks ago at Filbert Street."*

**Stuttgart coach Felix Magath on good and bad being the same in Germany as England:**
*"In the two games, we don't think we've been the worst team. Although perhaps we've not been the best team."*

**Joe Cole on a video nasty:**
*"The closest I've been to the Champions League is on my Playstation."*

**Kevin Keegan on Steve McManaman, one-time at Liverpool:**
*"They compare Steve McManaman to Steve Heighway and he's nothing like him, but I can see why ... it's because he's a bit different."*

**Sir Bobby Robson criticising Laurent Robert against Leeds:**
*"I told him in Hebrew, Israeli, Spanish and any language you can think of that wingers don't pass the ball backwards."*

**Andy Roberts of Millwall on the problems of the North-South divide with his wife expecting:**
*"There's a good chance she would go into a hospital in Manchester – and I don't want a northern baby."*

**John Terry on being a true Brit at Chelsea:**
*"I think there will always be an English mentality to this club, no matter how many foreign signings the manager makes."*

**David Pleat, Director of Football at Tottenham Hotspur on the vacancy at White Hart Lane:**
*"The man we want has to fit a certain profile. Is he a top coach? Would the players respect him? Is he a nutcase?"*

**Jimmy Armfield on the squad system:**
*"All this permutating doesn't do players any good."*

**Neil Warnock after his players failed to "turn up" for the defeat against Derby County:**
*"I think we were still at the hotel, wondering whether the game was going to go ahead or not."*

**Alan Curbishley on losing Scott Parker to Chelsea:**
*"The bottom line is that Scott, from the moment he heard Chelsea were interested, hasn't wanted to play for us and has been totally not focused on what he was doing."*

**Claudio Ranieri on the subtleties of the English language:**
*"Chelsea are my arse and I want my arse to cross the line first – reply: your arse? – Not my arse! My horse!"*

**Graeme Souness on Blackburn Rovers throwing a comfortable lead against Bolton Wanderers:**
*"It was a real sickener. That was our season summed up – very good at things, very bad at things and occasionally just bad."*

**Paolo Di Canio arriving for training at Charlton carrying a large trifle:**
*"Buon giorno, guten morgen, lovely jubbly."*

**On Arsenal's unbeaten run in the Premier League – Charlie George:**
*"We thought winning the double in 1971 was something special but this team is taking the game to new heights. They'll conquer Europe next season."*

**Rio Ferdinand on his missing the drug test:**
*"I am absolutely devastated by this situation and I want to categorically state that I have never used drugs."*

**Leicester City manager Micky Adams on the plight of a relegated manager:**
*"I'll be here unless I get that vote of confidence."*

**Ronaldo the Real Madrid striker on his partnership with David Beckham:**
*"I can assure you that David and I will play together in the same side for many years to come. I will go wherever he goes."*

**Arsene Wenger the Arsenal manager commenting on the clutch of red cards collected by the club during his stewardship:**
*"For some, even if you hanged us it would not be enough."*

**Sir Alex Ferguson on the feud with Arsenal:**
*"We at Manchester United have to hope we win titles without any help."*

**Martin Allen the Barnet manager on Stalybridge motivating his players:**
*"I'd just like to thank Stalybridge players who shouted – southern softies, wait until you get up north in the tunnel – after the 2-2 draw at our place."*

**David Beckham paying tribute to the No. 1 referee Pierluigi Collina on his handling of the incident in the Turkey game:**
*"Collina kept his cool and kept me on the pitch."*

**Christian Panucci on why Italy failed to beat Denmark:**
*"The socks were the problem. The thread that they were made with was too rough."*

**Commentator Clive Tyldesley seconds before the Zidane equaliser for France against England:**
*"The England fans will be talking about their 1-0 win over France in Lisbon for many years to come."*

**David Beckham after Johan Vonlanthen beat Wayne Rooney's record as the youngest European Championship scorer:**
*"I'm sure it'll just make him even more determined to get it back against Portugal tonight."*

**Wayne Rooney summing up his impact on England's Euro 2004 performance:**
*"I scored a few goals, but I would have traded all of them for us winning the competition."*

**Jose Andrade, the Portuguese player responsible for Wayne Rooney's injury:**
*"I wish him all the best. I had an injury like this in the past and know how much it costs to recover."*

**Sven Goran Eriksson on the post-mortem verdict:**
*"Were there mistakes in selection? Absolutely not. I think those XI were the best and they will not change much before 2006."*

**Frank Lampard in the aftermath of the Portugal defeat:**
*"We've been a bit unlucky but we can't keep blaming it on that alone. We have got to look at other things."*

**One-time Southampton and England winger Terry Paine:**
*"Eriksson does this all the time, substituting offensive players with defensive ones."*

**Former FIFA referee David Elleray on Swiss referee Meier's decision to disallow Sol Campbell's goal against Portugal:**
*"Meier did not cheat but, in terms of the English game, he was wrong. But so, too, was Dick Jol the Dutch referee when he gave the dubious free kick at Old Trafford that allowed Beckham to score and send England to the World Cup finals in Japan."*

# THE FA CHARITY SHIELD WINNERS 1908–2003

| | | |
|---|---|---|
| 1908 | Manchester U v QPR | 4-0 after 1-1 draw |
| 1909 | Newcastle U v Northampton T | 2-0 |
| 1910 | Brighton v Aston Villa | 1-0 |
| 1911 | Manchester U v Swindon T | 8-4 |
| 1912 | Blackburn R v QPR | 2-1 |
| 1913 | Professionals v Amateurs | 7-2 |
| 1920 | WBA v Tottenham H | 2-0 |
| 1921 | Tottenham H v Burnley | 2-0 |
| 1922 | Huddersfield T v Liverpool | 1-0 |
| 1923 | Professionals v Amateurs | 2-0 |
| 1924 | Professionals v Amateurs | 3-1 |
| 1925 | Amateurs v Professionals | 6-1 |
| 1926 | Amateurs v Professionals | 6-3 |
| 1927 | Cardiff C v Corinthians | 2-1 |
| 1928 | Everton v Blackburn R | 2-1 |
| 1929 | Professionals v Amateurs | 3-0 |
| 1930 | Arsenal v Sheffield W | 2-1 |
| 1931 | Arsenal v WBA | 1-0 |
| 1932 | Everton v Newcastle U | 5-3 |
| 1933 | Arsenal v Everton | 3-0 |
| 1934 | Arsenal v Manchester C | 4-0 |
| 1935 | Sheffield W v Arsenal | 1-0 |
| 1936 | Sunderland v Arsenal | 2-1 |
| 1937 | Manchester C v Sunderland | 2-0 |
| 1938 | Arsenal v Preston NE | 2-1 |
| 1948 | Arsenal v Manchester U | 4-3 |
| 1949 | Portsmouth v Wolverhampton W | 1-1* |
| 1950 | World Cup Team v Canadian Touring Team | 4-2 |
| 1951 | Tottenham H v Newcastle U | 2-1 |
| 1952 | Manchester U v Newcastle U | 4-2 |
| 1953 | Arsenal v Blackpool | 3-1 |
| 1954 | Wolverhampton W v WBA | 4-4* |
| 1955 | Chelsea v Newcastle U | 3-0 |
| 1956 | Manchester U v Manchester C | 1-0 |
| 1957 | Manchester U v Aston Villa | 4-0 |
| 1958 | Bolton W v Wolverhampton W | 4-1 |
| 1959 | Wolverhampton W v Nottingham F | 3-1 |
| 1960 | Burnley v Wolverhampton W | 2-2* |
| 1961 | Tottenham H v FA XI | 3-2 |
| 1962 | Tottenham H v Ipswich T | 5-1 |
| 1963 | Everton v Manchester U | 4-0 |
| 1964 | Liverpool v West Ham U | 2-2* |
| 1965 | Manchester U v Liverpool | 2-2* |
| 1966 | Liverpool v Everton | 1-0 |
| 1967 | Manchester U v Tottenham H | 3-3* |
| 1968 | Manchester C v WBA | 6-1 |
| 1969 | Leeds U v Manchester C | 2-1 |
| 1970 | Everton v Chelsea | 2-1 |
| 1971 | Leicester C v Liverpool | 1-0 |
| 1972 | Manchester C v Aston Villa | 1-0 |
| 1973 | Burnley v Manchester C | 1-0 |
| 1974 | Liverpool† v Leeds U | 1-1 |
| 1975 | Derby Co v West Ham U | 2-0 |
| 1976 | Liverpool v Southampton | 1-0 |
| 1977 | Liverpool v Manchester U | 0-0* |
| 1978 | Nottingham F v Ipswich T | 5-0 |
| 1979 | Liverpool v Arsenal | 3-1 |
| 1980 | Liverpool v West Ham U | 1-0 |
| 1981 | Aston Villa v Tottenham H | 2-2* |
| 1982 | Liverpool v Tottenham H | 1-0 |
| 1983 | Manchester U v Liverpool | 2-0 |
| 1984 | Everton v Liverpool | 1-0 |
| 1985 | Everton v Manchester U | 2-0 |
| 1986 | Everton v Liverpool | 1-1* |
| 1987 | Everton v Coventry C | 1-0 |
| 1988 | Liverpool v Wimbledon | 2-1 |
| 1989 | Liverpool v Arsenal | 1-0 |
| 1990 | Liverpool v Manchester U | 1-1* |
| 1991 | Arsenal v Tottenham H | 0-0* |
| 1992 | Leeds U v Liverpool | 4-3 |
| 1993 | Manchester U† v Arsenal | 1-1 |
| 1994 | Manchester U v Blackburn R | 2-0 |
| 1995 | Everton v Blackburn R | 1-0 |
| 1996 | Manchester U v Newcastle U | 4-0 |
| 1997 | Manchester U† v Chelsea | 1-1 |
| 1998 | Arsenal v Manchester U | 3-0 |
| 1999 | Arsenal v Manchester U | 2-1 |
| 2000 | Chelsea v Manchester U | 2-0 |
| 2001 | Liverpool v Manchester U | 2-1 |
| 2002 | Arsenal v Liverpool | 1-0 |
| 2003 | Manchester U† v Arsenal | 1-1 |

** Each club retained shield for six months.* *† Won on penalties.*

## THE FA COMMUNITY SHIELD 2003

### Manchester U (1) 1, Arsenal (1) 1

At Millennium Stadium, 10 August 2003, attendance 59,293

*Manchester U:* Howard; Neville P (Forlan), Fortune (O'Shea), Ferdinand, Keane, Silvestre, Solskjaer, Butt (Djemba Djemba), Van Nistelrooy, Giggs, Scholes.

*Scorer:* Silvestre 15.

*Arsenal:* Lehmann; Lauren, Cole, Vieira, Campbell, Toure, Parlour (Wiltord), Silva (Edu), Henry (Pires), Bergkamp (Jeffers■), Ljungberg (Van Bronckhorst).

*Scorer:* Henry 20.

(Manchester U won 4-3 on penalties: Scholes (scored), Edu (scored), Ferdinand (scored), Van Bronckhorst (saved), Van Nistelrooy (saved), Wiltord (scored), Solskjaer (scored), Lauren (scored), Forlan (scored), Pires (saved).)

*Referee:* S. Bennett (Kent).

■ *Denotes player sent off.*

# ENGLISH LEAGUE HONOURS 1888 TO 2004

## FA PREMIER LEAGUE

*Maximum points: a 126; b 114.*

**Won or placed on goal average (ratio), goal difference or most goals scored.*
*††Not promoted after play-offs.*

| | First | Pts | Second | Pts | Third | Pts |
|---|---|---|---|---|---|---|
| 1992–93*a* | Manchester U | 84 | Aston Villa | 74 | Norwich C | 72 |
| 1993–94*a* | Manchester U | 92 | Blackburn R | 84 | Newcastle U | 77 |
| 1994–95*a* | Blackburn R | 89 | Manchester U | 88 | Nottingham F | 77 |
| 1995–96*a* | Manchester U | 82 | Newcastle U | 78 | Liverpool | 71 |
| 1996–97*b* | Manchester U | 75 | Newcastle U* | 68 | Arsenal* | 68 |
| 1997–98*b* | Arsenal | 78 | Manchester U | 77 | Liverpool | 65 |
| 1998–99*b* | Manchester U | 79 | Arsenal | 78 | Chelsea | 75 |
| 1999–2000*b* | Manchester U | 91 | Arsenal | 73 | Leeds U | 69 |
| 2000–01 | Manchester U | 80 | Arsenal | 70 | Liverpool | 69 |
| 2001–02 | Arsenal | 87 | Liverpool | 80 | Manchester U | 77 |
| 2002–03 | Manchester U | 83 | Arsenal | 78 | Newcastle U | 69 |
| 2003–04 | Arsenal | 90 | Chelsea | 79 | Manchester U | 75 |

## FIRST DIVISION

**MAXIMUM POINTS: 138**

| | | | | | | |
|---|---|---|---|---|---|---|
| 1992–93 | Newcastle U | 96 | West Ham U* | 88 | Portsmouth†† | 88 |
| 1993–94 | Crystal Palace | 90 | Nottingham F | 83 | Millwall†† | 74 |
| 1994–95 | Middlesbrough | 82 | Reading†† | 79 | Bolton W | 77 |
| 1995–96 | Sunderland | 83 | Derby Co | 79 | Crystal Palace†† | 75 |
| 1996–97 | Bolton W | 98 | Barnsley | 80 | Wolverhampton W†† | 76 |
| 1997–98 | Nottingham F | 94 | Middlesbrough | 91 | Sunderland†† | 90 |
| 1998–99 | Sunderland | 105 | Bradford C | 87 | Ipswich T†† | 86 |
| 1999–2000 | Charlton Ath | 91 | Manchester C | 89 | Ipswich T | 87 |
| 2000–01 | Fulham | 101 | Blackburn R | 91 | Bolton W | 87 |
| 2001–02 | Manchester C | 99 | WBA | 89 | Wolverhampton W†† | 86 |
| 2002–03 | Portsmouth | 98 | Leicester C | 92 | Sheffield U†† | 80 |
| 2003–04 | Norwich C | 94 | WBA | 86 | Sunderland†† | 79 |

## SECOND DIVISION

**MAXIMUM POINTS: 138**

| | | | | | | |
|---|---|---|---|---|---|---|
| 1992–93 | Stoke C | 93 | Bolton W | 90 | Port Vale†† | 89 |
| 1993–94 | Reading | 89 | Port Vale | 88 | Plymouth Arg*†† | 85 |
| 1994–95 | Birmingham C | 89 | Brentford†† | 85 | Crewe Alex†† | 83 |
| 1995–96 | Swindon T | 92 | Oxford U | 83 | Blackpool†† | 82 |
| 1996–97 | Bury | 84 | Stockport Co | 82 | Luton T†† | 78 |
| 1997–98 | Watford | 88 | Bristol C | 85 | Grimsby T | 72 |
| 1998–99 | Fulham | 101 | Walsall | 87 | Manchester C | 82 |
| 1999–2000 | Preston NE | 95 | Burnley | 88 | Gillingham | 85 |
| 2000–01 | Millwall | 93 | Rotherham U | 91 | Reading†† | 86 |
| 2001–02 | Brighton & HA | 90 | Reading | 84 | Brentford*†† | 83 |
| 2002–03 | Wigan Ath | 100 | Crewe Alex | 86 | Bristol C†† | 83 |
| 2003–04 | Plymouth Arg | 90 | QPR | 83 | Bristol C†† | 82 |

## THIRD DIVISION

**MAXIMUM POINTS: A 126; B 138.**

| | | | | | | |
|---|---|---|---|---|---|---|
| 1992–93*a* | Cardiff C | 83 | Wrexham | 80 | Barnet | 79 |
| 1993–94*a* | Shrewsbury T | 79 | Chester C | 74 | Crewe Alex | 73 |
| 1994–95*a* | Carlisle U | 91 | Walsall | 83 | Chesterfield | 81 |
| 1995–96*b* | Preston NE | 86 | Gillingham | 83 | Bury | 79 |
| 1996–97*b* | Wigan Ath* | 87 | Fulham | 87 | Carlisle U | 84 |
| 1997–98*b* | Notts Co | 99 | Macclesfield T | 82 | Lincoln C | 72 |
| 1998–99*b* | Brentford | 85 | Cambridge U | 81 | Cardiff C | 80 |
| 1999–2000*b* | Swansea C | 85 | Rotherham U | 84 | Northampton T | 82 |
| 2000–01 | Brighton & HA | 92 | Cardiff C | 82 | Chesterfield¶ | 80 |
| 2001–02 | Plymouth Arg | 102 | Luton T | 97 | Mansfield T | 79 |
| 2002–03 | Rushden & D | 87 | Hartlepool U | 85 | Wrexham | 84 |
| 2003–04 | Doncaster R | 92 | Hull C | 88 | Torquay U* | 81 |

*¶9pts deducted for irregularities.*

## FOOTBALL LEAGUE

***MAXIMUM POINTS: A 44; B 60***

| | First | Pts | Second | Pts | Third | Pts |
|---|---|---|---|---|---|---|
| 1888–89*a* | Preston NE | 40 | Aston Villa | 29 | Wolverhampton W | 28 |
| 1889–90*a* | Preston NE | 33 | Everton | 31 | Blackburn R | 27 |
| 1890–91*a* | Everton | 29 | Preston NE | 27 | Notts Co | 26 |
| 1891–92*b* | Sunderland | 42 | Preston NE | 37 | Bolton W | 36 |

## FIRST DIVISION to 1991–92

***MAXIMUM POINTS: A 44; B 52; C 60; D 68; E 76; F 84; G 126; H 120; K 114.***

| | | | | | | |
|---|---|---|---|---|---|---|
| 1892–93*c* | Sunderland | 48 | Preston NE | 37 | Everton | 36 |
| 1893–94*c* | Aston Villa | 44 | Sunderland | 38 | Derby Co | 36 |
| 1894–95*c* | Sunderland | 47 | Everton | 42 | Aston Villa | 39 |
| 1895–96*c* | Aston Villa | 45 | Derby Co | 41 | Everton | 39 |
| 1896–97*c* | Aston Villa | 47 | Sheffield U* | 36 | Derby Co | 36 |
| 1897–98*c* | Sheffield U | 42 | Sunderland | 37 | Wolverhampton W* | 35 |

| | *First* | *Pts* | *Second* | *Pts* | *Third* | *Pts* |
|---|---|---|---|---|---|---|
| 1898–99*d* | Aston Villa | 45 | Liverpool | 43 | Burnley | 39 |
| 1899–1900*d* | Aston Villa | 50 | Sheffield U | 48 | Sunderland | 41 |
| 1900–01*d* | Liverpool | 45 | Sunderland | 43 | Notts Co | 40 |
| 1901–02*d* | Sunderland | 44 | Everton | 41 | Newcastle U | 37 |
| 1902–03*d* | The Wednesday | 42 | Aston Villa* | 41 | Sunderland | 41 |
| 1903–04*d* | The Wednesday | 47 | Manchester C | 44 | Everton | 43 |
| 1904–05*d* | Newcastle U | 48 | Everton | 47 | Manchester C | 46 |
| 1905–06*e* | Liverpool | 51 | Preston NE | 47 | The Wednesday | 44 |
| 1906–07*e* | Newcastle U | 51 | Bristol C | 48 | Everton* | 45 |
| 1907–08*e* | Manchester U | 52 | Aston Villa* | 43 | Manchester C | 43 |
| 1908–09*e* | Newcastle U | 53 | Everton | 46 | Sunderland | 44 |
| 1909–10*e* | Aston Villa | 53 | Liverpool | 48 | Blackburn R* | 45 |
| 1910–11*e* | Manchester U | 52 | Aston Villa | 51 | Sunderland* | 45 |
| 1911–12*e* | Blackburn R | 49 | Everton | 46 | Newcastle U | 44 |
| 1912–13*e* | Sunderland | 54 | Aston Villa | 50 | Sheffield W | 49 |
| 1913–14*e* | Blackburn R | 51 | Aston Villa | 44 | Middlesbrough* | 43 |
| 1914–15*e* | Everton | 46 | Oldham Ath | 45 | Blackburn R* | 43 |
| 1919–20*f* | WBA | 60 | Burnley | 51 | Chelsea | 49 |
| 1920–21*f* | Burnley | 59 | Manchester C | 54 | Bolton W | 52 |
| 1921–22*f* | Liverpool | 57 | Tottenham H | 51 | Burnley | 49 |
| 1922–23*f* | Liverpool | 60 | Sunderland | 54 | Huddersfield T | 53 |
| 1923–24*f* | Huddersfield T* | 57 | Cardiff C | 57 | Sunderland | 53 |
| 1924–25*f* | Huddersfield T | 58 | WBA | 56 | Bolton W | 55 |
| 1925–26*f* | Huddersfield T | 57 | Arsenal | 52 | Sunderland | 48 |
| 1926–27*f* | Newcastle U | 56 | Huddersfield T | 51 | Sunderland | 49 |
| 1927–28*f* | Everton | 53 | Huddersfield T | 51 | Leicester C | 48 |
| 1928–29*f* | Sheffield W | 52 | Leicester C | 51 | Aston Villa | 50 |
| 1929–30*f* | Sheffield W | 60 | Derby Co | 50 | Manchester C* | 47 |
| 1930–31*f* | Arsenal | 66 | Aston Villa | 59 | Sheffield W | 52 |
| 1931–32*f* | Everton | 56 | Arsenal | 54 | Sheffield W | 50 |
| 1932–33*f* | Arsenal | 58 | Aston Villa | 54 | Sheffield W | 51 |
| 1933–34*f* | Arsenal | 59 | Huddersfield T | 56 | Tottenham H | 49 |
| 1934–35*f* | Arsenal | 58 | Sunderland | 54 | Sheffield W | 49 |
| 1935–36*f* | Sunderland | 56 | Derby Co* | 48 | Huddersfield T | 48 |
| 1936–37*f* | Manchester C | 57 | Charlton Ath | 54 | Arsenal | 52 |
| 1937–38*f* | Arsenal | 52 | Wolverhampton W | 51 | Preston NE | 49 |
| 1938–39*f* | Everton | 59 | Wolverhampton W | 55 | Charlton Ath | 50 |
| 1946–47*f* | Liverpool | 57 | Manchester U* | 56 | Wolverhampton W | 56 |
| 1947–48*f* | Arsenal | 59 | Manchester U* | 52 | Burnley | 52 |
| 1948–49*f* | Portsmouth | 58 | Manchester U* | 53 | Derby Co | 53 |
| 1949–50*f* | Portsmouth* | 53 | Wolverhampton W | 53 | Sunderland | 52 |
| 1950–51*f* | Tottenham H | 60 | Manchester U | 56 | Blackpool | 50 |
| 1951–52*f* | Manchester U | 57 | Tottenham H* | 53 | Arsenal | 53 |
| 1952–53*f* | Arsenal* | 54 | Preston NE | 54 | Wolverhampton W | 51 |
| 1953–54*f* | Wolverhampton W | 57 | WBA | 53 | Huddersfield T | 51 |
| 1954–55*f* | Chelsea | 52 | Wolverhampton W* | 48 | Portsmouth* | 48 |
| 1955–56*f* | Manchester U | 60 | Blackpool* | 49 | Wolverhampton W | 49 |
| 1956–57*f* | Manchester U | 64 | Tottenham H* | 56 | Preston NE | 56 |
| 1957–58*f* | Wolverhampton W | 64 | Preston NE | 59 | Tottenham H | 51 |
| 1958–59*f* | Wolverhampton W | 61 | Manchester U | 55 | Arsenal* | 50 |
| 1959–60*f* | Burnley | 55 | Wolverhampton W | 54 | Tottenham H | 53 |
| 1960–61*f* | Tottenham H | 66 | Sheffield W | 58 | Wolverhampton W | 57 |
| 1961–62*f* | Ipswich T | 56 | Burnley | 53 | Tottenham H | 52 |
| 1962–63*f* | Everton | 61 | Tottenham H | 55 | Burnley | 54 |
| 1963–64*f* | Liverpool | 57 | Manchester U | 53 | Everton | 52 |
| 1964–65*f* | Manchester U* | 61 | Leeds U | 61 | Chelsea | 56 |
| 1965–66*f* | Liverpool | 61 | Leeds U* | 55 | Burnley | 55 |
| 1966–67*f* | Manchester U | 60 | Nottingham F* | 56 | Tottenham H | 56 |
| 1967–68*f* | Manchester C | 58 | Manchester U | 56 | Liverpool | 55 |
| 1968–69*f* | Leeds U | 67 | Liverpool | 61 | Everton | 57 |
| 1969–70*f* | Everton | 66 | Leeds U | 57 | Chelsea | 55 |
| 1970–71*f* | Arsenal | 65 | Leeds U | 64 | Tottenham H* | 52 |
| 1971–72*f* | Derby Co | 58 | Leeds U* | 57 | Liverpool* | 57 |
| 1972–73*f* | Liverpool | 60 | Arsenal | 57 | Leeds U | 53 |
| 1973–74*f* | Leeds U | 62 | Liverpool | 57 | Derby Co | 48 |
| 1974–75*f* | Derby Co | 53 | Liverpool* | 51 | Ipswich T | 51 |
| 1975–76*f* | Liverpool | 60 | QPR | 59 | Manchester U | 56 |
| 1976–77*f* | Liverpool | 57 | Manchester C | 56 | Ipswich T | 52 |
| 1977–78*f* | Nottingham F | 64 | Liverpool | 57 | Everton | 55 |
| 1978–79*f* | Liverpool | 68 | Nottingham F | 60 | WBA | 59 |
| 1979–80*f* | Liverpool | 60 | Manchester U | 58 | Ipswich T | 52 |
| 1980–81*f* | Aston Villa | 60 | Ipswich T | 56 | Arsenal | 53 |
| 1981–82*g* | Liverpool | 87 | Ipswich T | 83 | Manchester U | 78 |
| 1982–83*g* | Liverpool | 82 | Watford | 71 | Manchester U | 70 |
| 1983–84*g* | Liverpool | 80 | Southampton | 77 | Nottingham F* | 74 |
| 1984–85*g* | Everton | 90 | Liverpool* | 77 | Tottenham H | 77 |
| 1985–86*g* | Liverpool | 88 | Everton | 86 | West Ham U | 84 |
| 1986–87*g* | Everton | 86 | Liverpool | 77 | Tottenham H | 71 |
| 1987–88*h* | Liverpool | 90 | Manchester U | 81 | Nottingham F | 73 |
| 1988–89*k* | Arsenal* | 76 | Liverpool | 76 | Nottingham F | 64 |
| 1989–90*k* | Liverpool | 79 | Aston Villa | 70 | Tottenham H | 63 |
| 1990–91*k* | Arsenal† | 83 | Liverpool | 76 | Crystal Palace | 69 |
| 1991–92*g* | Leeds U | 82 | Manchester U | 78 | Sheffield W | 75 |

*No official competition during 1915–19 and 1939–46; Regional Leagues operated.*
†2 pts deducted

## SECOND DIVISION to 1991–92

***MAXIMUM POINTS:** A 44; B 56; C 60; D 68; E 76; F 84; G 126; H 132; K 138.*

| | *First* | *Pts* | *Second* | *Pts* | *Third* | *Pts* |
|---|---|---|---|---|---|---|
| 1892–93*a* | Small Heath | 36 | Sheffield U | 35 | Darwen | 30 |
| 1893–94*b* | Liverpool | 50 | Small Heath | 42 | Notts Co | 39 |
| 1894–95*c* | Bury | 48 | Notts Co | 39 | Newton Heath* | 38 |
| 1895–96*c* | Liverpool* | 46 | Manchester C | 46 | Grimsby T* | 42 |
| 1896–97*c* | Notts Co | 42 | Newton Heath | 39 | Grimsby T | 38 |
| 1897–98*c* | Burnley | 48 | Newcastle U | 45 | Manchester C | 39 |
| 1898–99*d* | Manchester C | 52 | Glossop NE | 46 | Leicester Fosse | 45 |
| 1899–1900*d* | The Wednesday | 54 | Bolton W | 52 | Small Heath | 46 |
| 1900–01*d* | Grimsby T | 49 | Small Heath | 48 | Burnley | 44 |
| 1901–02*d* | WBA | 55 | Middlesbrough | 51 | Preston NE* | 42 |
| 1902–03*d* | Manchester C | 54 | Small Heath | 51 | Woolwich A | 48 |
| 1903–04*d* | Preston NE | 50 | Woolwich A | 49 | Manchester U | 48 |
| 1904–05*d* | Liverpool | 58 | Bolton W | 56 | Manchester U | 53 |
| 1905–06*e* | Bristol C | 66 | Manchester U | 62 | Chelsea | 53 |
| 1906–07*e* | Nottingham F | 60 | Chelsea | 57 | Leicester Fosse | 48 |
| 1907–08*e* | Bradford C | 54 | Leicester Fosse | 52 | Oldham Ath | 50 |
| 1908–09*e* | Bolton W | 52 | Tottenham H* | 51 | WBA | 51 |
| 1909–10*e* | Manchester C | 54 | Oldham Ath* | 53 | Hull C* | 53 |
| 1910–11*e* | WBA | 53 | Bolton W | 51 | Chelsea | 49 |
| 1911–12*e* | Derby Co* | 54 | Chelsea | 54 | Burnley | 52 |
| 1912–13*e* | Preston NE | 53 | Burnley | 50 | Birmingham | 46 |
| 1913–14*e* | Notts Co | 53 | Bradford PA* | 49 | Woolwich A | 49 |
| 1914–15*e* | Derby Co | 53 | Preston NE | 50 | Barnsley | 47 |
| 1919–20*f* | Tottenham H | 70 | Huddersfield T | 64 | Birmingham | 56 |
| 1920–21*f* | Birmingham* | 58 | Cardiff C | 58 | Bristol C | 51 |
| 1921–22*f* | Nottingham F | 56 | Stoke C* | 52 | Barnsley | 52 |
| 1922–23*f* | Notts Co | 53 | West Ham U* | 51 | Leicester C | 51 |
| 1923–24*f* | Leeds U | 54 | Bury* | 51 | Derby Co | 51 |
| 1924–25*f* | Leicester C | 59 | Manchester U | 57 | Derby Co | 55 |
| 1925–26*f* | Sheffield W | 60 | Derby Co | 57 | Chelsea | 52 |
| 1926–27*f* | Middlesbrough | 62 | Portsmouth* | 54 | Manchester C | 54 |
| 1927–28*f* | Manchester C | 59 | Leeds U | 57 | Chelsea | 54 |
| 1928–29*f* | Middlesbrough | 55 | Grimsby T | 53 | Bradford PA* | 48 |
| 1929–30*f* | Blackpool | 58 | Chelsea | 55 | Oldham Ath | 53 |
| 1930–31*f* | Everton | 61 | WBA | 54 | Tottenham H | 51 |
| 1931–32*f* | Wolverhampton W | 56 | Leeds U | 54 | Stoke C | 52 |
| 1932–33*f* | Stoke C | 56 | Tottenham H | 55 | Fulham | 50 |
| 1933–34*f* | Grimsby T | 59 | Preston NE | 52 | Bolton W* | 51 |
| 1934–35*f* | Brentford | 61 | Bolton W* | 56 | West Ham U | 56 |
| 1935–36*f* | Manchester U | 56 | Charlton Ath | 55 | Sheffield U* | 52 |
| 1936–37*f* | Leicester C | 56 | Blackpool | 55 | Bury | 52 |
| 1937–38*f* | Aston Villa | 57 | Manchester U* | 53 | Sheffield U | 53 |
| 1938–39*f* | Blackburn R | 55 | Sheffield U | 54 | Sheffield W | 53 |
| 1946–47*f* | Manchester C | 62 | Burnley | 58 | Birmingham C | 55 |
| 1947–48*f* | Birmingham C | 59 | Newcastle U | 56 | Southampton | 52 |
| 1948–49*f* | Fulham | 57 | WBA | 56 | Southampton | 55 |
| 1949–50*f* | Tottenham H | 61 | Sheffield W* | 52 | Sheffield U* | 52 |
| 1950–51*f* | Preston NE | 57 | Manchester C | 52 | Cardiff C | 50 |
| 1951–52*f* | Sheffield W | 53 | Cardiff C* | 51 | Birmingham C | 51 |
| 1952–53*f* | Sheffield U | 60 | Huddersfield T | 58 | Luton T | 52 |
| 1953–54*f* | Leicester C* | 56 | Everton | 56 | Blackburn R | 55 |
| 1954–55*f* | Birmingham C* | 54 | Luton T* | 54 | Rotherham U | 54 |
| 1955–56*f* | Sheffield W | 55 | Leeds U | 52 | Liverpool* | 48 |
| 1956–57*f* | Leicester C | 61 | Nottingham F | 54 | Liverpool | 53 |
| 1957–58*f* | West Ham U | 57 | Blackburn R | 56 | Charlton Ath | 55 |
| 1958–59*f* | Sheffield W | 62 | Fulham | 60 | Sheffield U* | 53 |
| 1959–60*f* | Aston Villa | 59 | Cardiff C | 58 | Liverpool* | 50 |
| 1960–61*f* | Ipswich T | 59 | Sheffield U | 58 | Liverpool | 52 |
| 1961–62*f* | Liverpool | 62 | Leyton Orient | 54 | Sunderland | 53 |
| 1962–63*f* | Stoke C | 53 | Chelsea* | 52 | Sunderland | 52 |
| 1963–64*f* | Leeds U | 63 | Sunderland | 61 | Preston NE | 56 |
| 1964–65*f* | Newcastle U | 57 | Northampton T | 56 | Bolton W | 50 |
| 1965–66*f* | Manchester C | 59 | Southampton | 54 | Coventry C | 53 |
| 1966–67*f* | Coventry C | 59 | Wolverhampton W | 58 | Carlisle U | 52 |
| 1967–68*f* | Ipswich T | 59 | QPR* | 58 | Blackpool | 58 |
| 1968–69*f* | Derby Co | 63 | Crystal Palace | 56 | Charlton Ath | 50 |
| 1969–70*f* | Huddersfield T | 60 | Blackpool | 53 | Leicester C | 51 |
| 1970–71*f* | Leicester C | 59 | Sheffield U | 56 | Cardiff C* | 53 |
| 1971–72*f* | Norwich C | 57 | Birmingham C | 56 | Millwall | 55 |
| 1972–73*f* | Burnley | 62 | QPR | 61 | Aston Villa | 50 |
| 1973–74*f* | Middlesbrough | 65 | Luton T | 50 | Carlisle U | 49 |
| 1974–75*f* | Manchester U | 61 | Aston Villa | 58 | Norwich C | 53 |
| 1975–76*f* | Sunderland | 56 | Bristol C* | 53 | WBA | 53 |
| 1976–77*f* | Wolverhampton W | 57 | Chelsea | 55 | Nottingham F | 52 |
| 1977–78*f* | Bolton W | 58 | Southampton | 57 | Tottenham H* | 56 |
| 1978–79*f* | Crystal Palace | 57 | Brighton & HA* | 56 | Stoke C | 56 |
| 1979–80*f* | Leicester C | 55 | Sunderland | 54 | Birmingham C* | 53 |
| 1980–81*f* | West Ham U | 66 | Notts Co | 53 | Swansea C* | 50 |
| 1981–82*g* | Luton T | 88 | Watford | 80 | Norwich C | 71 |
| 1982–83*g* | QPR | 85 | Wolverhampton W | 75 | Leicester C | 70 |
| 1983–84*g* | Chelsea* | 88 | Sheffield W | 88 | Newcastle U | 80 |

| | First | Pts | Second | Pts | Third | Pts |
|---|---|---|---|---|---|---|
| 1984–85g | Oxford U | 84 | Birmingham C | 82 | Manchester C | 74 |
| 1985–86g | Norwich C | 84 | Charlton Ath | 77 | Wimbledon | 76 |
| 1986–87g | Derby Co | 84 | Portsmouth | 78 | Oldham Ath†† | 75 |
| 1987–88h | Millwall | 82 | Aston Villa* | 78 | Middlesbrough | 78 |
| 1988–89k | Chelsea | 99 | Manchester C | 82 | Crystal Palace | 81 |
| 1989–90k | Leeds U* | 85 | Sheffield U | 85 | Newcastle U†† | 80 |
| 1990–91k | Oldham Ath | 88 | West Ham U | 87 | Sheffield W | 82 |
| 1991–92k | Ipswich T | 84 | Middlesbrough | 80 | Derby Co | 78 |

*No official competition during 1915–19 and 1939–46; Regional Leagues operated.*

## THIRD DIVISION to 1991–92

***MAXIMUM POINTS:* 92; 138 FROM 1981–82.**

| | First | Pts | Second | Pts | Third | Pts |
|---|---|---|---|---|---|---|
| 1958–59 | Plymouth Arg | 62 | Hull C | 61 | Brentford* | 57 |
| 1959–60 | Southampton | 61 | Norwich C | 59 | Shrewsbury T* | 52 |
| 1960–61 | Bury | 68 | Walsall | 62 | QPR | 60 |
| 1961–62 | Portsmouth | 65 | Grimsby T | 62 | Bournemouth* | 59 |
| 1962–63 | Northampton T | 62 | Swindon T | 58 | Port Vale | 54 |
| 1963–64 | Coventry C* | 60 | Crystal Palace | 60 | Watford | 58 |
| 1964–65 | Carlisle U | 60 | Bristol C* | 59 | Mansfield T | 59 |
| 1965–66 | Hull C | 69 | Millwall | 65 | QPR | 57 |
| 1966–67 | QPR | 67 | Middlesbrough | 55 | Watford | 54 |
| 1967–68 | Oxford U | 57 | Bury | 56 | Shrewsbury T | 55 |
| 1968–69 | Watford* | 64 | Swindon T | 64 | Luton T | 61 |
| 1969–70 | Orient | 62 | Luton T | 60 | Bristol R | 56 |
| 1970–71 | Preston NE | 61 | Fulham | 60 | Halifax T | 56 |
| 1971–72 | Aston Villa | 70 | Brighton & HA | 65 | Bournemouth* | 62 |
| 1972–73 | Bolton W | 61 | Notts Co | 57 | Blackburn R | 55 |
| 1973–74 | Oldham Ath | 62 | Bristol R* | 61 | York C | 61 |
| 1974–75 | Blackburn R | 60 | Plymouth Arg | 59 | Charlton Ath | 55 |
| 1975–76 | Hereford U | 63 | Cardiff C | 57 | Millwall | 56 |
| 1976–77 | Mansfield T | 64 | Brighton & HA | 61 | Crystal Palace* | 59 |
| 1977–78 | Wrexham | 61 | Cambridge U | 58 | Preston NE* | 56 |
| 1978–79 | Shrewsbury T | 61 | Watford* | 60 | Swansea C | 60 |
| 1979–80 | Grimsby T | 62 | Blackburn R | 59 | Sheffield W | 58 |
| 1980–81 | Rotherham U | 61 | Barnsley* | 59 | Charlton Ath | 59 |
| 1981–82 | Burnley* | 80 | Carlisle U | 80 | Fulham | 78 |
| 1982–83 | Portsmouth | 91 | Cardiff C | 86 | Huddersfield T | 82 |
| 1983–84 | Oxford U | 95 | Wimbledon | 87 | Sheffield U* | 83 |
| 1984–85 | Bradford C | 94 | Millwall | 90 | Hull C | 87 |
| 1985–86 | Reading | 94 | Plymouth Arg | 87 | Derby Co | 84 |
| 1986–87 | Bournemouth | 97 | Middlesbrough | 94 | Swindon T | 87 |
| 1987–88 | Sunderland | 93 | Brighton & HA | 84 | Walsall | 82 |
| 1988–89 | Wolverhampton W | 92 | Sheffield U* | 84 | Port Vale | 84 |
| 1989–90 | Bristol R | 93 | Bristol C | 91 | Notts Co | 87 |
| 1990–91 | Cambridge U | 86 | Southend U | 85 | Grimsby T* | 83 |
| 1991–92 | Brentford | 82 | Birmingham C | 81 | Huddersfield T | 78 |

## FOURTH DIVISION (1958–1992)

***MAXIMUM POINTS:* 92; 138 FROM 1981–82.**

| | First | Pts | Second | Pts | Third | Pts | Fourth | Pts |
|---|---|---|---|---|---|---|---|---|
| 1958–59 | Port Vale | 64 | Coventry C* | 60 | York C | 60 | Shrewsbury T | 58 |
| 1959–60 | Walsall | 65 | Notts Co* | 60 | Torquay U | 60 | Watford | 57 |
| 1960–61 | Peterborough U | 66 | Crystal Palace | 64 | Northampton T* | 60 | Bradford PA | 60 |
| 1961–62† | Millwall | 56 | Colchester U | 55 | Wrexham | 53 | Carlisle U | 52 |
| 1962–63 | Brentford | 62 | Oldham Ath* | 59 | Crewe Alex | 59 | Mansfield T* | 57 |
| 1963–64 | Gillingham* | 60 | Carlisle U | 60 | Workington | 59 | Exeter C | 58 |
| 1964–65 | Brighton & HA | 63 | Millwall* | 62 | York C | 62 | Oxford U | 61 |
| 1965–66 | Doncaster R* | 59 | Darlington | 59 | Torquay U | 58 | Colchester U* | 56 |
| 1966–67 | Stockport Co | 64 | Southport* | 59 | Barrow | 59 | Tranmere R | 58 |
| 1967–68 | Luton T | 66 | Barnsley | 61 | Hartlepools U | 60 | Crewe Alex | 58 |
| 1968–69 | Doncaster R | 59 | Halifax T | 57 | Rochdale* | 56 | Bradford C | 56 |
| 1969–70 | Chesterfield | 64 | Wrexham | 61 | Swansea C | 60 | Port Vale | 59 |
| 1970–71 | Notts Co | 69 | Bournemouth | 60 | Oldham Ath | 59 | York C | 56 |
| 1971–72 | Grimsby T | 63 | Southend U | 60 | Brentford | 59 | Scunthorpe U | 57 |
| 1972–73 | Southport | 62 | Hereford U | 58 | Cambridge U | 57 | Aldershot* | 56 |
| 1973–74 | Peterborough U | 65 | Gillingham | 62 | Colchester U | 60 | Bury | 59 |
| 1974–75 | Mansfield T | 68 | Shrewsbury T | 62 | Rotherham U | 59 | Chester* | 57 |
| 1975–76 | Lincoln C | 74 | Northampton T | 68 | Reading | 60 | Tranmere R | 58 |
| 1976–77 | Cambridge U | 65 | Exeter C | 62 | Colchester U* | 59 | Bradford C | 59 |
| 1977–78 | Watford | 71 | Southend U | 60 | Swansea C* | 56 | Brentford | 56 |
| 1978–79 | Reading | 65 | Grimsby T* | 61 | Wimbledon* | 61 | Barnsley | 61 |
| 1979–80 | Huddersfield T | 66 | Walsall | 64 | Newport Co | 61 | Portsmouth* | 60 |
| 1980–81 | Southend U | 67 | Lincoln C | 65 | Doncaster R | 56 | Wimbledon | 55 |
| 1981–82 | Sheffield U | 96 | Bradford C* | 91 | Wigan Ath | 91 | Bournemouth | 88 |
| 1982–83 | Wimbledon | 98 | Hull C | 90 | Port Vale | 88 | Scunthorpe U | 83 |
| 1983–84 | York C | 101 | Doncaster R | 85 | Reading* | 82 | Bristol C | 82 |
| 1984–85 | Chesterfield | 91 | Blackpool | 86 | Darlington | 85 | Bury | 84 |
| 1985–86 | Swindon T | 102 | Chester C | 84 | Mansfield T | 81 | Port Vale | 79 |
| 1986–87 | Northampton T | 99 | Preston NE | 90 | Southend U | 80 | Wolverhampton W†† | 79 |
| 1987–88 | Wolverhampton W | 90 | Cardiff C | 85 | Bolton W | 78 | Scunthorpe U†† | 77 |
| 1988–89 | Rotherham U | 82 | Tranmere R | 80 | Crewe Alex | 78 | Scunthorpe U†† | 77 |

| | *First* | *Pts* | *Second* | *Pts* | *Third* | *Pts* | *Fourth* | *Pts* |
|---|---|---|---|---|---|---|---|---|
| 1989–90 | Exeter C | 89 | Grimsby T | 79 | Southend U | 75 | Stockport Co†† | 74 |
| 1990–91 | Darlington | 83 | Stockport Co* | 82 | Hartlepool U | 82 | Peterborough U | 80 |
| 1991–92†* | Burnley | 83 | Rotherham U* | 77 | Mansfield T | 77 | Blackpool | 76 |

†*Maximum points:* 88 owing to Accrington Stanley's resignation.
†**Maximum points:* 126 owing to Aldershot being expelled (and only 23 teams started the competition).

## THIRD DIVISION—SOUTH (1920–1958)

**1920–21 SEASON AS THIRD DIVISION. *MAXIMUM POINTS: A* 84; *B* 92.**

| | *First* | *Pts* | *Second* | *Pts* | *Third* | *Pts* |
|---|---|---|---|---|---|---|
| 1920–21*a* | Crystal Palace | 59 | Southampton | 54 | QPR | 53 |
| 1921–22*a* | Southampton* | 61 | Plymouth Arg | 61 | Portsmouth | 53 |
| 1922–23*a* | Bristol C | 59 | Plymouth Arg* | 53 | Swansea T | 53 |
| 1923–24*a* | Portsmouth | 59 | Plymouth Arg | 55 | Millwall | 54 |
| 1924–25*a* | Swansea T | 57 | Plymouth Arg | 56 | Bristol C | 53 |
| 1925–26*a* | Reading | 57 | Plymouth Arg | 56 | Millwall | 53 |
| 1926–27*a* | Bristol C | 62 | Plymouth Arg | 60 | Millwall | 56 |
| 1927–28*a* | Millwall | 65 | Northampton T | 55 | Plymouth Arg | 53 |
| 1928–29*a* | Charlton Ath* | 54 | Crystal Palace | 54 | Northampton T* | 52 |
| 1929–30*a* | Plymouth Arg | 68 | Brentford | 61 | QPR | 51 |
| 1930–31*a* | Notts Co | 59 | Crystal Palace | 51 | Brentford | 50 |
| 1931–32*a* | Fulham | 57 | Reading | 55 | Southend U | 53 |
| 1932–33*a* | Brentford | 62 | Exeter C | 58 | Norwich C | 57 |
| 1933–34*a* | Norwich C | 61 | Coventry C* | 54 | Reading* | 54 |
| 1934–35*a* | Charlton Ath | 61 | Reading | 53 | Coventry C | 51 |
| 1935–36*a* | Coventry C | 57 | Luton T | 56 | Reading | 54 |
| 1936–37*a* | Luton T | 58 | Notts Co | 56 | Brighton & HA | 53 |
| 1937–38*a* | Millwall | 56 | Bristol C | 55 | QPR* | 53 |
| 1938–39*a* | Newport Co | 55 | Crystal Palace | 52 | Brighton & HA | 49 |
| 1939–46 | Competition cancelled owing to war. Regional Leagues operated. | | | | | |
| 1946–47*a* | Cardiff C | 66 | QPR | 57 | Bristol C | 51 |
| 1947–48*a* | QPR | 61 | Bournemouth | 57 | Walsall | 51 |
| 1948–49*a* | Swansea T | 62 | Reading | 55 | Bournemouth | 52 |
| 1949–50*a* | Notts Co | 58 | Northampton T* | 51 | Southend U | 51 |
| 1950–51*b* | Nottingham F | 70 | Norwich C | 64 | Reading* | 57 |
| 1951–52*b* | Plymouth Arg | 66 | Reading* | 61 | Norwich C | 61 |
| 1952–53*b* | Bristol R | 64 | Millwall* | 62 | Northampton T | 62 |
| 1953–54*b* | Ipswich T | 64 | Brighton & HA | 61 | Bristol C | 56 |
| 1954–55*b* | Bristol C | 70 | Leyton Orient | 61 | Southampton | 59 |
| 1955–56*b* | Leyton Orient | 66 | Brighton & HA | 65 | Ipswich T | 64 |
| 1956–57*b* | Ipswich T* | 59 | Torquay U | 59 | Colchester U | 58 |
| 1957–58*b* | Brighton & HA | 60 | Brentford* | 58 | Plymouth Arg | 58 |

## THIRD DIVISION—NORTH (1921–1958)

**MAXIMUM POINTS: A 76; B 84; C 80; D 92.**

| | *First* | *Pts* | *Second* | *Pts* | *Third* | *Pts* |
|---|---|---|---|---|---|---|
| 1921–22*a* | Stockport Co | 56 | Darlington* | 50 | Grimsby T | 50 |
| 1922–23*a* | Nelson | 51 | Bradford PA | 47 | Walsall | 46 |
| 1923–24*b* | Wolverhampton W | 63 | Rochdale | 62 | Chesterfield | 54 |
| 1924–25*b* | Darlington | 58 | Nelson* | 53 | New Brighton | 53 |
| 1925–26*b* | Grimsby T | 61 | Bradford PA | 60 | Rochdale | 59 |
| 1926–27*b* | Stoke C | 63 | Rochdale | 58 | Bradford PA | 55 |
| 1927–28*b* | Bradford PA | 63 | Lincoln C | 55 | Stockport Co | 54 |
| 1928–29*b* | Bradford C | 63 | Stockport Co | 62 | Wrexham | 52 |
| 1929–30*b* | Port Vale | 67 | Stockport Co | 63 | Darlington* | 50 |
| 1930–31*b* | Chesterfield | 58 | Lincoln C | 57 | Wrexham* | 54 |
| 1931–32*c* | Lincoln C* | 57 | Gateshead | 57 | Chester | 50 |
| 1932–33*b* | Hull C | 59 | Wrexham | 57 | Stockport Co | 54 |
| 1933–34*b* | Barnsley | 62 | Chesterfield | 61 | Stockport Co | 59 |
| 1934–35*b* | Doncaster R | 57 | Halifax T | 55 | Chester | 54 |
| 1935–36*b* | Chesterfield | 60 | Chester* | 55 | Tranmere R | 55 |
| 1936–37*b* | Stockport Co | 60 | Lincoln C | 57 | Chester | 53 |
| 1937–38*b* | Tranmere R | 56 | Doncaster R | 54 | Hull C | 53 |
| 1938–39*b* | Barnsley | 67 | Doncaster R | 56 | Bradford C | 52 |
| 1939–46 | Competition cancelled owing to war. Regional Leagues operated. | | | | | |
| 1946–47*b* | Doncaster R | 72 | Rotherham U | 60 | Chester | 56 |
| 1947–48*b* | Lincoln C | 60 | Rotherham U | 59 | Wrexham | 50 |
| 1948–49*b* | Hull C | 65 | Rotherham U | 62 | Doncaster R | 50 |
| 1949–50*b* | Doncaster R | 55 | Gateshead | 53 | Rochdale* | 51 |
| 1950–51*d* | Rotherham U | 71 | Mansfield T | 64 | Carlisle U | 62 |
| 1951–52*d* | Lincoln C | 69 | Grimsby T | 66 | Stockport Co | 59 |
| 1952–53*d* | Oldham Ath | 59 | Port Vale | 58 | Wrexham | 56 |
| 1953–54*d* | Port Vale | 69 | Barnsley | 58 | Scunthorpe U | 57 |
| 1954–55*d* | Barnsley | 65 | Accrington S | 61 | Scunthorpe U* | 58 |
| 1955–56*d* | Grimsby T | 68 | Derby Co | 63 | Accrington S | 59 |
| 1956–57*d* | Derby Co | 63 | Hartlepools U | 59 | Accrington S* | 58 |
| 1957–58*d* | Scunthorpe U | 66 | Accrington S | 59 | Bradford C | 57 |

## PROMOTED AFTER PLAY-OFFS

**(NOT ACCOUNTED FOR IN PREVIOUS SECTION)**

1986–87 Aldershot to Division 3.
1987–88 Swansea C to Division 3.
1988–89 Leyton Orient to Division 3.

1989–90 Sunderland to Division 1; Notts Co to Division 2; Cambridge U to Division 3.
1990–91 Notts Co to Division 1; Tranmere R to Division 2; Torquay U to Division 3.
1991–92 Blackburn R to Premier League; Peterborough U to Division 1.
1992–93 Swindon T to Premier League; WBA to Division 1; York C to Division 2.
1993–94 Leicester C to Premier League; Burnley to Division 1; Wycombe W to Division 2.
1994–95 Huddersfield T to Division 1.
1995–96 Leicester C to Premier League; Bradford C to Division 1; Plymouth Arg to Division 2.
1996–97 Crystal Palace to Premier League; Crewe Alex to Division 1; Northampton T to Division 2.
1997–98 Charlton Ath to Premier League; Colchester U to Division 2.
1998–99 Watford to Premier League; Scunthorpe U to Division 2.
1999–2000 Peterborough U to Division 2
2000–01 Walsall to Division 1; Blackpool to Division 2
2001–02 Birmingham C to Premier League; Stoke C to Division 1; Cheltenham T to Division 2
2002–03 Wolverhampton W to Premier League; Cardiff C to Division 1; Bournemouth to Division 2
2003–04 Crystal Palace to Premier League; Brighton & HA to Division 1; Huddersfield T to Division 2

## LEAGUE TITLE WINS

FA PREMIER LEAGUE – Manchester U 8, Arsenal 3, Blackburn R 1.

LEAGUE DIVISION 1 – Liverpool 18, Arsenal 10, Everton 9, Sunderland 8, Aston Villa 7, Manchester U 7, Newcastle U 5, Sheffield W 4, Huddersfield T 3, Leeds U 3, Manchester C 3, Portsmouth 3, Wolverhampton W 3, Blackburn R 2, Burnley 2, Derby Co 2, Nottingham F 2, Preston NE 2, Tottenham H 2; Bolton W, Charlton Ath, Chelsea, Crystal Palace, Fulham, Ipswich T, Middlesbrough, Norwich C, Sheffield U, WBA 1 each.

LEAGUE DIVISION 2 – Leicester C 6, Manchester C 6, Birmingham C (one as Small Heath) 5, Sheffield W 5, Derby Co 4, Liverpool 4, Preston NE 4, Ipswich T 3, Leeds U 3, Middlesbrough 3, Notts Co 3, Stoke C 3, Aston Villa 2, Bolton W 2, Burnley 2, Bury 2, Chelsea 2, Fulham 2, Grimsby T 2, Manchester U 2, Millwall 2, Norwich C 2, Nottingham F 2, Tottenham H 2, WBA 2, West Ham U 2, Wolverhampton W 2; Blackburn R, Blackpool, Bradford C, Brentford, Brighton & HA, Bristol C, Coventry C, Crystal Palace, Everton, Huddersfield T, Luton T, Newcastle U, QPR, Oldham Ath, Oxford U, Plymouth Arg, Reading, Sheffield U, Sunderland, Swindon T, Watford, Wigan Ath 1 each.

LEAGUE DIVISION 3 – Brentford 2, Carlisle U 2, Oxford U 2, Plymouth Arg 2, Portsmouth 2, Preston NE 2, Shrewsbury T 2; Aston Villa, Blackburn R, Bolton W, Bournemouth, Bradford C, Brighton & HA, Bristol R, Burnley, Bury, Cambridge U, Cardiff C, Coventry C, Doncaster R. Grimsby T, Hereford U, Hull C, Leyton Orient, Mansfield T, Northampton T, Notts Co, Oldham Ath, QPR, Reading, Rotherham U, Rushden & D Southampton, Sunderland, Swansea C, Watford, Wigan Ath, Wolverhampton W, Wrexham 1 each.

LEAGUE DIVISION 4 – Chesterfield 2, Doncaster R 2, Peterborough U 2; Brentford, Brighton & HA, Burnley, Cambridge U, Darlington, Exeter C, Gillingham, Grimsby T, Huddersfield T, Lincoln C, Luton T, Mansfield T, Millwall, Northampton T, Notts Co, Port Vale, Reading, Rotherham U, Sheffield U, Southend U, Southport, Stockport Co, Swindon T, Walsall, Watford, Wimbledon, Wolverhampton W, York C 1 each.

#### TO 1957–58

DIVISION 3 (South) – Bristol C 3, Charlton Ath 2, Ipswich T 2, Millwall 2, Notts Co 2, Plymouth Arg 2, Swansea T 2; Brentford, Brighton & HA, Bristol R, Cardiff C, Coventry C, Crystal Palace, Fulham, Leyton Orient, Luton T, Newport Co, Norwich C, Nottingham F, Portsmouth, QPR, Reading, Southampton 1 each.

DIVISION 3 (North) – Barnsley 3, Doncaster R 3, Lincoln C 3, Chesterfield 2, Grimsby T 2, Hull C 2, Port Vale 2, Stockport Co 2; Bradford C, Bradford PA, Darlington, Derby Co, Nelson, Oldham Ath, Rotherham U, Scunthorpe U, Stoke C, Tranmere R, Wolverhampton W 1 each.

## RELEGATED CLUBS

1891–92 League extended. Newton Heath, Sheffield W and Nottingham F admitted. *Second Division formed* including Darwen.
1892–93 In Test matches, Sheffield U and Darwen won promotion in place of Notts Co and Accrington S.
1893–94 In Tests, Liverpool and Small Heath won promotion. Newton Heath and Darwen relegated.
1894–95 After Tests, Bury promoted, Liverpool relegated.
1895–96 After Tests, Liverpool promoted, Small Heath relegated.
1896–97 After Tests, Notts Co promoted, Burnley relegated.
1897–98 Test system abolished after success of Stoke C and Burnley. League extended. Blackburn R and Newcastle U elected to First Division. *Automatic promotion and relegation introduced.*

#### FA PREMIER LEAGUE TO DIVISION 1

1992–93 Crystal Palace, Middlesbrough, Nottingham F
1993–94 Sheffield U, Oldham Ath, Swindon T
1994–95 Crystal Palace, Norwich C, Leicester C, Ipswich T
1995–96 Manchester C, QPR, Bolton W
1996–97 Sunderland, Middlesbrough, Nottingham F
1997–98 Bolton W, Barnsley, Crystal Palace
1998–99 Charlton Ath, Blackburn R, Nottingham F
1999–2000 Wimbledon, Sheffield W, Watford
2000–01 Manchester C, Coventry C, Bradford C
2001–02 Ipswich T, Derby Co, Leicester C
2002–03 West Ham U, WBA, Sunderland
2003–04 Leicester C, Leeds U, Wolverhampton W.

#### DIVISION 1 TO DIVISION 2

1898–99 Bolton W and Sheffield W
1899–1900 Burnley and Glossop
1900–01 Preston NE and WBA
1901–02 Small Heath and Manchester C
1902–03 Grimsby T and Bolton W
1903–04 Liverpool and WBA
1904–05 League extended. Bury and Notts Co, two bottom clubs in First Division, re-elected.
1905–06 Nottingham F and Wolverhampton W
1906–07 Derby Co and Stoke C
1907–08 Bolton W and Birmingham C
1908–09 Manchester C and Leicester Fosse
1909–10 Bolton W and Chelsea
1910–11 Bristol C and Nottingham F
1911–12 Preston NE and Bury
1912–13 Notts Co and Woolwich Arsenal
1913–14 Preston NE and Derby Co
1914–15 Tottenham H and Chelsea*
1919–20 Notts Co and Sheffield W
1920–21 Derby Co and Bradford PA
1921–22 Bradford C and Manchester U
1922–23 Stoke C and Oldham Ath
1923–24 Chelsea and Middlesbrough
1924–25 Preston NE and Nottingham F
1925–26 Manchester C and Notts Co
1926–27 Leeds U and WBA
1927–28 Tottenham H and Middlesbrough
1928–29 Bury and Cardiff C

1929–30 Burnley and Everton
1930–31 Leeds U and Manchester U
1931–32 Grimsby T and West Ham U
1932–33 Bolton W and Blackpool
1933–34 Newcastle U and Sheffield U
1934–35 Leicester C and Tottenham H
1935–36 Aston Villa and Blackburn R
1936–37 Manchester U and Sheffield W
1937–38 Manchester C and WBA
1938–39 Birmingham C and Leicester C
1946–47 Brentford and Leeds U
1947–48 Blackburn R and Grimsby T
1948–49 Preston NE and Sheffield U
1949–50 Manchester C and Birmingham C
1950–51 Sheffield W and Everton
1951–52 Huddersfield T and Fulham
1952–53 Stoke C and Derby Co
1953–54 Middlesbrough and Liverpool
1954–55 Leicester C and Sheffield W
1955–56 Huddersfield T and Sheffield U
1956–57 Charlton Ath and Cardiff C
1957–58 Sheffield W and Sunderland
1958–59 Portsmouth and Aston Villa
1959–60 Luton T and Leeds U
1960–61 Preston NE and Newcastle U
1961–62 Chelsea and Cardiff C
1962–63 Manchester C and Leyton Orient
1963–64 Bolton W and Ipswich T
1964–65 Wolverhampton W and Birmingham C
1965–66 Northampton T and Blackburn R
1966–67 Aston Villa and Blackpool
1967–68 Fulham and Sheffield U
1968–69 Leicester C and QPR
1969–70 Sunderland and Sheffield W
1970–71 Burnley and Blackpool
1971–72 Huddersfield T and Nottingham F
1972–73 Crystal Palace and WBA
1973–74 Southampton, Manchester U, Norwich C
1974–75 Luton T, Chelsea, Carlisle U
1975–76 Wolverhampton W, Burnley, Sheffield U
1976–77 Sunderland, Stoke C, Tottenham H
1977–78 West Ham U, Newcastle U, Leicester C
1978–79 QPR, Birmingham C, Chelsea
1979–80 Bristol C, Derby Co, Bolton W
1980–81 Norwich C, Leicester C, Crystal Palace
1981–82 Leeds U, Wolverhampton W, Middlesbrough
1982–83 Manchester C, Swansea C, Brighton & HA
1983–84 Birmingham C, Notts Co, Wolverhampton W
1984–85 Norwich C, Sunderland, Stoke C
1985–86 Ipswich T, Birmingham C, WBA
1986–87 Leicester C, Manchester C, Aston Villa
1987–88 Chelsea**, Portsmouth, Watford, Oxford U
1988–89 Middlesbrough, West Ham U, Newcastle U
1989–90 Sheffield W, Charlton Ath, Millwall
1990–91 Sunderland and Derby Co
1991–92 Luton T, Notts Co, West Ham U
1992–93 Brentford, Cambridge U, Bristol R
1993–94 Birmingham C, Oxford U, Peterborough U
1994–95 Swindon T, Burnley, Bristol C, Notts Co
1995–96 Millwall, Watford, Luton T
1996–97 Grimsby T, Oldham Ath, Southend U
1997–98 Manchester C, Stoke C, Reading
1998–99 Bury, Oxford U, Bristol C
1999–2000 Walsall, Port Vale, Swindon T
2000–01 Huddersfield T, QPR, Tranmere R
2001–02 Crewe Alex, Barnsley, Stockport Co
2002–03 Sheffield W, Brighton & HA, Grimsby T
2003–04 Walsall, Bradford C, Wimbledon

***Relegated after play-offs.*
**Subsequently re-elected to Division 1 when League was extended after the War.*

**DIVISION 2 TO DIVISION 3**

1920–21 Stockport Co
1921–22 Bradford PA and Bristol C
1922–23 Rotherham Co and Wolverhampton W
1923–24 Nelson and Bristol C
1924–25 Crystal Palace and Coventry C
1925–26 Stoke C and Stockport Co
1926–27 Darlington and Bradford C
1927–28 Fulham and South Shields
1928–29 Port Vale and Clapton Orient
1929–30 Hull C and Notts Co
1930–31 Reading and Cardiff C
1931–32 Barnsley and Bristol C
1932–33 Chesterfield and Charlton Ath
1933–34 Millwall and Lincoln C
1934–35 Oldham Ath and Notts Co
1935–36 Port Vale and Hull C
1936–37 Doncaster R and Bradford C
1937–38 Barnsley and Stockport Co
1938–39 Norwich C and Tranmere R
1946–47 Swansea T and Newport Co
1947–48 Doncaster R and Millwall
1948–49 Nottingham F and Lincoln C
1949–50 Plymouth Arg and Bradford PA
1950–51 Grimsby T and Chesterfield
1951–52 Coventry C and QPR
1952–53 Southampton and Barnsley
1953–54 Brentford and Oldham Ath
1954–55 Ipswich T and Derby Co
1955–56 Plymouth Arg and Hull C
1956–57 Port Vale and Bury
1957–58 Doncaster R and Notts Co
1958–59 Barnsley and Grimsby T
1959–60 Bristol C and Hull C
1960–61 Lincoln C and Portsmouth
1961–62 Brighton & HA and Bristol R
1962–63 Walsall and Luton T
1963–64 Grimsby T and Scunthorpe U
1964–65 Swindon T and Swansea T
1965–66 Middlesbrough and Leyton Orient
1966–67 Northampton T and Bury
1967–68 Plymouth Arg and Rotherham U
1968–69 Fulham and Bury
1969–70 Preston NE and Aston Villa
1970–71 Blackburn R and Bolton W
1971–72 Charlton Ath and Watford
1972–73 Huddersfield T and Brighton & HA
1973–74 Crystal Palace, Preston NE, Swindon T
1974–75 Millwall, Cardiff C, Sheffield W
1975–76 Oxford U, York C, Portsmouth
1976–77 Carlisle U, Plymouth Arg, Hereford U
1977–78 Blackpool, Mansfield T, Hull C
1978–79 Sheffield U, Millwall, Blackburn R
1979–80 Fulham, Burnley, Charlton Ath
1980–81 Preston NE, Bristol C, Bristol R
1981–82 Cardiff C, Wrexham, Orient
1982–83 Rotherham U, Burnley, Bolton W
1983–84 Derby Co, Swansea C, Cambridge U
1984–85 Notts Co, Cardiff C, Wolverhampton W
1985–86 Carlisle U, Middlesbrough, Fulham
1986–87 Sunderland**, Grimsby T, Brighton & HA
1987–88 Huddersfield T, Reading, Sheffield U**
1988–89 Shrewsbury T, Birmingham C, Walsall
1989–90 Bournemouth, Bradford C, Stoke C
1990–91 WBA and Hull C
1991–92 Plymouth Arg, Brighton & HA, Port Vale
1992–93 Preston NE, Mansfield T, Wigan Ath, Chester C
1993–94 Fulham, Exeter C, Hartlepool U, Barnet
1994–95 Cambridge U, Plymouth Arg, Cardiff C, Chester C, Leyton Orient
1995–96 Carlisle U, Swansea C, Brighton & HA, Hull C
1996–97 Peterborough U, Shrewsbury T, Rotherham U, Notts Co
1997–98 Brentford, Plymouth Arg, Carlisle U, Southend U
1998–99 York C, Northampton T, Lincoln C, Macclesfield T
1999–2000 Cardiff C, Blackpool, Scunthorpe U, Chesterfield
2000–01 Bristol R, Luton T, Swansea C, Oxford U
2001–02 Bournemouth, Bury, Wrexham, Cambridge U
2002–03 Cheltenham T, Huddersfield T, Mansfield T Northampton T
2003–04 Grimsby T, Rushden & D, Notts Co, Wycombe W

**DIVISION 3 TO DIVISION 4**

1958–59 Rochdale, Notts Co, Doncaster R, Stockport Co
1959–60 Accrington S, Wrexham, Mansfield T, York C
1960–61 Chesterfield, Colchester U, Bradford C, Tranmere R
1961–62 Newport Co, Brentford, Lincoln C, Torquay U
1962–63 Bradford PA, Brighton & HA, Carlisle U, Halifax T
1963–64 Millwall, Crewe Alex, Wrexham, Notts Co

1964–65 Luton T, Port Vale, Colchester U, Barnsley
1965–66 Southend U, Exeter C, Brentford, York C
1966–67 Doncaster R, Workington, Darlington, Swansea T
1967–68 Scunthorpe U, Colchester U, Grimsby T, Peterborough U (demoted)
1968–69 Oldham Ath, Crewe Alex, Hartlepool, Northampton T
1969–70 Bournemouth, Southport, Barrow, Stockport Co
1970–71 Reading, Bury, Doncaster R, Gillingham
1971–72 Mansfield T, Barnsley, Torquay U, Bradford C
1972–73 Rotherham U, Brentford, Swansea C, Scunthorpe U
1973–74 Cambridge U, Shrewsbury T, Southport, Rochdale
1974–75 Bournemouth, Tranmere R, Watford, Huddersfield T
1975–76 Aldershot, Colchester U, Southend U, Halifax T
1976–77 Reading, Northampton T, Grimsby T, York C
1977–78 Port Vale, Bradford C, Hereford U, Portsmouth
1978–79 Peterborough U, Walsall, Tranmere R, Lincoln C
1979–80 Bury, Southend U, Mansfield T, Wimbledon
1980–81 Sheffield U, Colchester U, Blackpool, Hull C
1981–82 Wimbledon, Swindon T, Bristol C, Chester
1982–83 Reading, Wrexham, Doncaster R, Chesterfield
1983–84 Scunthorpe U, Southend U, Port Vale, Exeter C
1984–85 Burnley, Orient, Preston NE, Cambridge U
1985–86 Lincoln C, Cardiff C, Wolverhampton W, Swansea C
1986–87 Bolton W**, Carlisle U, Darlington, Newport Co
1987–88 Doncaster R, York C, Grimsby T, Rotherham U**
1988–89 Southend U, Chesterfield, Gillingham, Aldershot
1989–90 Cardiff C, Northampton T, Blackpool, Walsall
1990–91 Crewe Alex, Rotherham U, Mansfield T
1991–92 Bury, Shrewsbury T, Torquay U, Darlington

*** Relegated after play-offs. N.B. Relegated clubs not featured in exact order of finishing.*

## APPLICATIONS FOR RE-ELECTION

### FOURTH DIVISION

**Eleven:** Hartlepool U.
**Seven:** Crewe Alex.
**Six:** Barrow (lost League place to Hereford U 1972), Halifax T, Rochdale, Southport (lost League place to Wigan Ath 1978), York C.
**Five:** Chester C, Darlington, Lincoln C, Stockport Co, Workington (lost League place to Wimbledon 1977).
**Four:** Bradford PA (lost League place to Cambridge U 1970), Newport Co, Northampton T.
**Three:** Doncaster R, Hereford U.
**Two:** Bradford C, Exeter C, Oldham Ath, Scunthorpe U, Torquay U.
**One:** Aldershot, Colchester U, Gateshead (lost League place to Peterborough U 1960), Grimsby T, Swansea C, Tranmere R, Wrexham, Blackpool, Cambridge U, Preston NE.
Accrington S resigned and Oxford U were elected 1962.
Port Vale were forced to re-apply following expulsion in 1968.
Aldershot expelled March 1992. Maidstone U resigned August 1992.

### THIRD DIVISIONS NORTH & SOUTH

**Seven:** Walsall.
**Six:** Exeter C, Halifax T, Newport Co.
**Five:** Accrington S, Barrow, Gillingham, New Brighton, Southport.
**Four:** Rochdale, Norwich C.
**Three:** Crystal Palace, Crewe Alex, Darlington, Hartlepool U, Merthyr T, Swindon T.
**Two:** Aberdare Ath, Aldershot, Ashington, Bournemouth, Brentford, Chester, Colchester U, Durham C, Millwall, Nelson, QPR, Rotherham U, Southend U, Tranmere R, Watford, Workington.
**One:** Bradford C, Bradford PA, Brighton & HA, Bristol R, Cardiff C, Carlisle U, Charlton Ath, Gateshead, Grimsby T, Mansfield T, Shrewsbury T, Torquay U, York C.

## LEAGUE STATUS FROM 1986–87

| | RELEGATED FROM LEAGUE | PROMOTED TO LEAGUE |
|---|---|---|
| 1986–87 | Lincoln C | Scarborough |
| 1987–88 | Newport Co | Lincoln C |
| 1988–89 | Darlington | Maidstone U |
| 1989–90 | Colchester U | Darlington |
| 1990–91 | — | Barnet |
| 1991–92 | — | Colchester U |
| 1992–93 | Halifax T | Wycombe W |
| 1993–94 | — | — |
| 1994–95 | — | — |
| 1995–96 | — | — |
| 1996–97 | Hereford U | Macclesfield T |
| 1997–98 | Doncaster R | Halifax T |
| 1998–99 | Scarborough | Cheltenham T |
| 1999–2000 | Chester C | Kidderminster H |
| 2000–01 | Barnet | Rushden & D |
| 2001–02 | Halifax T | Boston U |
| 2002–03 | Shrewsbury T, Exeter C | Yeovil T, Doncaster R |
| 2003–04 | Carlisle U, York C | Chester C, Shrewsbury T |

# FOOTBALL AWARDS 2004

## FOOTBALLER OF THE YEAR

The Football Writers' Association Sir Stanley Matthews Trophy for the Footballer of the Year went to Thierry Henry of Arsenal and France.

## THE PFA AWARDS 2004

Player of the Year: Thierry Henry, Arsenal and France.
Young Player of the Year: Scott Parker, Chelsea and England.
Merit Award: Dario Gradi (Crewe Alex).

## SCOTTISH FOOTBALL WRITERS ASSOCIATION 2004

Player of the Year: Jackie McNamara (Celtic)

## SCOTTISH PFA 'PLAYER OF THE YEAR' AWARDS 2004

Player of the year: Chris Sutton (Celtic)
First Division: Ian Harty (Clyde)
Second Division: Paul Tosh (Forfar Athletic)
Third Division: Michael Moore (Stranraer)
Young Player of the Year: Stephen Pearson (Celtic)

## EUROPEAN FOOTBALLER OF THE YEAR 2003

Thierry Henry, Arsenal and France.

## WORLD PLAYER OF THE YEAR 2003

Zinedine Zidane, Real Madrid and France.

## WOMEN'S PLAYER OF THE YEAR 2003

Birgit Prinz, Germany.

## WORLD TEAM OF THE YEAR 2003

Brazil.

## LMA MANAGER OF THE YEAR 2004

Arsène Wenger, Arsenal.

For the second season in succession Thierry Henry won both the PFA and Football Writers' Footballer of the Year awards. (Colorsport)

# LEAGUE ATTENDANCES SINCE 1946–47

| *Season* | *Matches* | *Total* | *Div. 1* | *Div. 2* | *Div. 3 (S)* | *Div. 3 (N)* |
|---|---|---|---|---|---|---|
| 1946–47 | 1848 | 35,604,606 | 15,005,316 | 11,071,572 | 5,664,004 | 3,863,714 |
| 1947–48 | 1848 | 40,259,130 | 16,732,341 | 12,286,350 | 6,653,610 | 4,586,829 |
| 1948–49 | 1848 | 41,271,414 | 17,914,667 | 11,353,237 | 6,998,429 | 5,005,081 |
| 1949–50 | 1848 | 40,517,865 | 17,278,625 | 11,694,158 | 7,104,155 | 4,440,927 |
| 1950–51 | 2028 | 39,584,967 | 16,679,454 | 10,780,580 | 7,367,884 | 4,757,109 |
| 1951–52 | 2028 | 39,015,866 | 16,110,322 | 11,066,189 | 6,958,927 | 4,880,428 |
| 1952–53 | 2028 | 37,149,966 | 16,050,278 | 9,686,654 | 6,704,299 | 4,708,735 |
| 1953–54 | 2028 | 36,174,590 | 16,154,915 | 9,510,053 | 6,311,508 | 4,198,114 |
| 1954–55 | 2028 | 34,133,103 | 15,087,221 | 8,988,794 | 5,996,017 | 4,051,071 |
| 1955–56 | 2028 | 33,150,809 | 14,108,961 | 9,080,002 | 5,692,479 | 4,269,367 |
| 1956–57 | 2028 | 32,744,405 | 13,803,037 | 8,718,162 | 5,622,189 | 4,601,017 |
| 1957–58 | 2028 | 33,562,208 | 14,468,652 | 8,663,712 | 6,097,183 | 4,332,661 |
| | | | | | *Div. 3* | *Div. 4* |
| 1958–59 | 2028 | 33,610,985 | 14,727,691 | 8,641,997 | 5,946,600 | 4,276,697 |
| 1959–60 | 2028 | 32,538,611 | 14,391,227 | 8,399,627 | 5,739,707 | 4,008,050 |
| 1960–61 | 2028 | 28,619,754 | 12,926,948 | 7,033,936 | 4,784,256 | 3,874,614 |
| 1961–62 | 2015 | 27,979,902 | 12,061,194 | 7,453,089 | 5,199,106 | 3,266,513 |
| 1962–63 | 2028 | 28,885,852 | 12,490,239 | 7,792,770 | 5,341,362 | 3,261,481 |
| 1963–64 | 2028 | 28,535,022 | 12,486,626 | 7,594,158 | 5,419,157 | 3,035,081 |
| 1964–65 | 2028 | 27,641,168 | 12,708,752 | 6,984,104 | 4,436,245 | 3,512,067 |
| 1965–66 | 2028 | 27,206,980 | 12,480,644 | 6,914,757 | 4,779,150 | 3,032,429 |
| 1966–67 | 2028 | 28,902,596 | 14,242,957 | 7,253,819 | 4,421,172 | 2,984,648 |
| 1967–68 | 2028 | 30,107,298 | 15,289,410 | 7,450,410 | 4,013,087 | 3,354,391 |
| 1968–69 | 2028 | 29,382,172 | 14,584,851 | 7,382,390 | 4,339,656 | 3,075,275 |
| 1969–70 | 2028 | 29,600,972 | 14,868,754 | 7,581,728 | 4,223,761 | 2,926,729 |
| 1970–71 | 2028 | 28,194,146 | 13,954,337 | 7,098,265 | 4,377,213 | 2,764,331 |
| 1971–72 | 2028 | 28,700,729 | 14,484,603 | 6,769,308 | 4,697,392 | 2,749,426 |
| 1972–73 | 2028 | 25,448,642 | 13,998,154 | 5,631,730 | 3,737,252 | 2,081,506 |
| 1973–74 | 2027 | 24,982,203 | 13,070,991 | 6,326,108 | 3,421,624 | 2,163,480 |
| 1974–75 | 2028 | 25,577,977 | 12,613,178 | 6,955,970 | 4,086,145 | 1,992,684 |
| 1975–76 | 2028 | 24,896,053 | 13,089,861 | 5,798,405 | 3,948,449 | 2,059,338 |
| 1976–77 | 2028 | 26,182,800 | 13,647,585 | 6,250,597 | 4,152,218 | 2,132,400 |
| 1977–78 | 2028 | 25,392,872 | 13,255,677 | 6,474,763 | 3,332,042 | 2,330,390 |
| 1978–79 | 2028 | 24,540,627 | 12,704,549 | 6,153,223 | 3,374,558 | 2,308,297 |
| 1979–80 | 2028 | 24,623,975 | 12,163,002 | 6,112,025 | 3,999,328 | 2,349,620 |
| 1980–81 | 2028 | 21,907,569 | 11,392,894 | 5,175,442 | 3,637,854 | 1,701,379 |
| 1981–82 | 2028 | 20,006,961 | 10,420,793 | 4,750,463 | 2,836,915 | 1,998,790 |
| 1982–83 | 2028 | 18,766,158 | 9,295,613 | 4,974,937 | 2,943,568 | 1,552,040 |
| 1983–84 | 2028 | 18,358,631 | 8,711,448 | 5,359,757 | 2,729,942 | 1,557,484 |
| 1984–85 | 2028 | 17,849,835 | 9,761,404 | 4,030,823 | 2,667,008 | 1,390,600 |
| 1985–86 | 2028 | 16,488,577 | 9,037,854 | 3,551,968 | 2,490,481 | 1,408,274 |
| 1986–87 | 2028 | 17,379,218 | 9,144,676 | 4,168,131 | 2,350,970 | 1,715,441 |
| 1987–88 | 2030 | 17,959,732 | 8,094,571 | 5,341,599 | 2,751,275 | 1,772,287 |
| 1988–89 | 2036 | 18,464,192 | 7,809,993 | 5,887,805 | 3,035,327 | 1,791,067 |
| 1989–90 | 2036 | 19,445,442 | 7,883,039 | 6,867,674 | 2,803,551 | 1,891,178 |
| 1990–91 | 2036 | 19,508,202 | 8,618,709 | 6,285,068 | 2,835,759 | 1,768,666 |
| 1991–92 | 2064* | 20,487,273 | 9,989,160 | 5,809,787 | 2,993,352 | 1,694,974 |
| | | *Total* | *FA Premier* | *Div. 1* | *Div. 2* | *Div. 3* |
| 1992–93 | 2028 | 20,657,327 | 9,759,809 | 5,874,017 | 3,483,073 | 1,540,428 |
| 1993–94 | 2028 | 21,683,381 | 10,644,551 | 6,487,104 | 2,972,702 | 1,579,024 |
| 1994–95 | 2028 | 21,856,020 | 11,213,168 | 6,044,293 | 3,037,752 | 1,560,807 |
| 1995–96 | 2036 | 21,844,416 | 10,469,107 | 6,566,349 | 2,843,652 | 1,965,308 |
| 1996–97 | 2036 | 22,783,163 | 10,804,762 | 6,931,539 | 3,195,223 | 1,851,639 |
| 1997–98 | 2036 | 24,692,608 | 11,092,106 | 8,330,018 | 3,503,264 | 1,767,220 |
| 1998–99 | 2036 | 25,435,542 | 11,620,326 | 7,543,369 | 4,169,697 | 2,102,150 |
| 1999-2000 | 2036 | 25,341,090 | 11,668,497 | 7,810,208 | 3,700,433 | 2,161,952 |
| 2000–01 | 2036 | 26,030,167 | 12,472,094 | 7,909,512 | 3,488,166 | 2,160,395 |
| 2001–02 | 2036 | 27,756,977 | 13,043,118 | 8,352,128 | 3,963,153 | 2,398,578 |
| 2002–03 | 2036 | 28,343,386 | 13,468,965 | 8,521,017 | 3,892,469 | 2,460,935 |
| 2003–04 | 2036 | 29,197,510 | 13,303,136 | 8,772,780 | 4,146,495 | 2,975,099 |

**Figures include matches played by Aldershot.*
*Football League official total for their three divisions in 2001–02 was 14,716,162.*

# ENGLISH LEAGUE ATTENDANCES 2003–04

## FA BARCLAYCARD PREMIERSHIP ATTENDANCES

| | *Average Gate* | | | *Season 2003/04* | |
|---|---|---|---|---|---|
| | 2002/03 | 2003/04 | +/–% | Highest | Lowest |
| Arsenal | 38,040 | 38,079 | +0.10 | 38,419 | 37,677 |
| Aston Villa | 35,081 | 36,622 | +4.21 | 42,573 | 28,625 |
| Birmingham City | 28,813 | 29,078 | +0.91 | 29,588 | 27,225 |
| Blackburn Rovers | 26,228 | 24,376 | –7.60 | 30,074 | 19,939 |
| Bolton Wanderers | 24,965 | 26,718 | +6.56 | 27,668 | 23,098 |
| Charlton Athletic | 26,235 | 26,278 | +0.16 | 26,752 | 25,184 |
| Chelsea | 39,799 | 41,272 | +3.57 | 41,932 | 40,491 |
| Everton | 38,468 | 38,837 | +0.95 | 40,228 | 35,775 |
| Fulham | 16,685 | 16,240 | –2.74 | 18,431 | 13,981 |
| Leeds United | 39,127 | 36,666 | –6.71 | 40,153 | 30,544 |
| Leicester City | 29,219 | 30,983 | +5.69 | 32,148 | 26,674 |
| Liverpool | 43,234 | 42,677 | –1.31 | 44,374 | 34,663 |
| Manchester City | 34,451 | 46,830 | +26.43 | 47,304 | 44,307 |
| Manchester United | 67,630 | 67,641 | +0.02 | 67,758 | 67,346 |
| Middlesbrough | 31,005 | 30,395 | –2.01 | 34,738 | 26,721 |
| Newcastle United | 51,920 | 51,966 | +0.09 | 52,165 | 50,104 |
| Portsmouth | 18,934 | 20,054 | +5.58 | 20,140 | 19,126 |
| Southampton | 30,680 | 31,717 | +3.27 | 32,151 | 30,513 |
| Tottenham Hotspur | 35,899 | 34,872 | –2.95 | 36,107 | 30,025 |
| Wolverhampton Wanderers | 25,745 | 28,864 | +10.81 | 29,396 | 27,327 |

| | |
|---|---|
| TOTAL ATTENDANCES: | 13,303,136 (380 games) |
| | Average 35,008 (–1.25%) |
| HIGHEST: | 67,758 Manchester United v Southampton |
| LOWEST: | 13,981 Fulham v Blackburn Rovers |
| HIGHEST AVERAGE: | 67,641 Mancheser United |
| LOWEST AVERAGE: | 16,240 Fulham |

## NATIONWIDE FOOTBALL LEAGUE: DIVISION ONE ATTENDANCES

| | *Average Gate* | | | *Season 2003/04* | |
|---|---|---|---|---|---|
| | 2002/03 | 2003/04 | +/–% | Highest | Lowest |
| Bradford City | 12,501 | 11,377 | –9.9 | 17,143 | 9,011 |
| Burnley | 13,977 | 12,541 | –11.5 | 18,852 | 9,473 |
| Cardiff City | 13,050 | 15,569 | +16.2 | 19,202 | 13,021 |
| Coventry City | 14,813 | 14,816 | +0.0 | 22,195 | 10,872 |
| Crewe Alexandra | 6,761 | 7,741 | +12.7 | 10,014 | 5,867 |
| Crystal Palace | 16,867 | 17,344 | +2.8 | 23,977 | 12,259 |
| Derby County | 25,470 | 22,200 | –14.7 | 32,390 | 18,459 |
| Gillingham | 8,082 | 8,517 | +5.1 | 11,418 | 6,923 |
| Ipswich Town | 25,455 | 24,520 | –3.8 | 30,152 | 20,912 |
| Millwall | 8,512 | 10,497 | +18.9 | 14,425 | 7,855 |
| Norwich City | 20,353 | 19,074 | –6.7 | 23,942 | 16,082 |
| Nottingham Forest | 24,437 | 24,759 | +1.3 | 29,172 | 20,168 |
| Preston North End | 13,853 | 14,150 | +2.1 | 19,161 | 11,152 |
| Reading | 16,011 | 15,095 | –6.1 | 21,718 | 10,543 |
| Rotherham United | 7,522 | 7,138 | –5.4 | 11,455 | 5,450 |
| Sheffield United | 18,113 | 21,646 | +16.3 | 27,008 | 17,396 |
| Stoke City | 14,588 | 14,425 | –1.1 | 20,126 | 10,277 |
| Sunderland | 39,698 | 27,119 | –46.4 | 36,278 | 22,167 |
| Walsall | 6,978 | 7,853 | +11.1 | 11,049 | 6,395 |
| Watford | 13,405 | 14,856 | +9.8 | 20,950 | 10,381 |
| West Bromwich Albion | 26,523 | 24,765 | –7.1 | 27,195 | 22,048 |
| West Ham United | 34,404 | 31,167 | –10.4 | 35,021 | 24,365 |
| Wigan Athletic | 7,288 | 9,505 | +23.3 | 20,069 | 6,696 |
| Wimbledon | 2,786 | 4,751 | +41.4 | 8,118 | 1,054 |

| | |
|---|---|
| TOTAL ATTENDANCES: | 8,772,780 (552 games) |
| | Average 15,893 (+2.9%) |
| HIGHEST: | 36,278 Sunderland v Walsall |
| LOWEST: | 1,054 Wimbledon v Wigan Athletic |
| HIGHEST AVERAGE: | 31,167 West Ham United |
| LOWEST AVERAGE: | 4,751 Wimbledon |

*Premiership attendance averages and highest crowd figures for 2003–04 are official. Other attendances unofficial.*

## NATIONWIDE FOOTBALL LEAGUE: DIVISION TWO ATTENDANCES

| | *Average Gate* | | | *Season 2003/04* | |
|---|---|---|---|---|---|
| | 2002/03 | 2003/04 | +/–% | Highest | Lowest |
| Barnsley | 9,758 | 9,620 | –1.4 | 20,438 | 7,547 |
| Blackpool | 6,991 | 6,326 | –10.5 | 8,340 | 4,617 |
| AFC Bournemouth | 5,829 | 6,913 | +15.7 | 8,909 | 5,837 |
| Brentford | 5,759 | 5,542 | –3.9 | 9,485 | 3,818 |
| Brighton & Hove Albion | 6,651 | 6,248 | –6.5 | 6,618 | 5,642 |
| Bristol City | 11,890 | 12,879 | +7.7 | 19,101 | 9,365 |
| Chesterfield | 4,108 | 4,331 | +5.1 | 7,695 | 3,123 |
| Colchester United | 3,387 | 3,536 | +4.2 | 5,083 | 2,513 |
| Grimsby Town | 5,884 | 4,730 | –24.4 | 6,856 | 3,143 |
| Hartlepool United | 4,943 | 5,419 | +8.8 | 7,448 | 4,135 |
| Luton Town | 6,747 | 6,339 | –6.4 | 8,499 | 5,002 |
| Notts County | 6,154 | 5,940 | –3.6 | 9,601 | 4,145 |
| Oldham Athletic | 6,699 | 6,566 | –2.0 | 13,007 | 4,990 |
| Peterborough United | 4,955 | 5,274 | +6.0 | 10,194 | 3,855 |
| Plymouth Argyle | 8,981 | 12,654 | +29.0 | 19,888 | 7,594 |
| Port Vale | 4,436 | 5,810 | +23.6 | 7,958 | 4,523 |
| Queens Park Rangers | 13,206 | 14,785 | +10.7 | 18,396 | 11,854 |
| Rushden & Diamonds | 4,330 | 4,457 | +2.8 | 5,823 | 3,074 |
| Sheffield Wednesday | 20,327 | 22,336 | +9.0 | 29,313 | 18,799 |
| Stockport County | 5,489 | 5,315 | –3.3 | 8,617 | 3,683 |
| Swindon Town | 5,440 | 7,925 | +31.4 | 14,540 | 5,313 |
| Tranmere Rovers | 7,877 | 7,606 | –3.6 | 10,301 | 6,675 |
| Wrexham | 4,263 | 4,440 | +4.0 | 8,497 | 3,035 |
| Wycombe Wanderers | 6,002 | 5,291 | –13.4 | 7,634 | 4,401 |

| | |
|---|---|
| TOTAL ATTENDANCES: | 4,146,495 (552 games) |
| | Average 7,512 (+6.1%) |
| HIGHEST: | 29,313 Sheffield Wednesday v Queens Park Rangers |
| LOWEST: | 2,513 Colchester United v Stockport County |
| HIGHEST AVERAGE: | 22,336 Sheffield Wednesday |
| LOWEST AVERAGE: | 3,536 Colchester United |

## NATIONWIDE FOOTBALL LEAGUE: DIVISION THREE ATTENDANCES

| | *Average Gate* | | | *Season 2003/04* | |
|---|---|---|---|---|---|
| | 2002/03 | 2003/04 | +/–% | Highest | Lowest |
| Boston United | 3,049 | 2,964 | –2.9 | 5,708 | 2,147 |
| Bristol Rovers | 6,934 | 7,142 | +2.9 | 9,812 | 5,333 |
| Bury | 3,226 | 2,892 | –11.5 | 4,591 | 1,670 |
| Cambridge United | 4,173 | 3,919 | –6.5 | 5,368 | 2,713 |
| Carlisle United | 4,776 | 5,617 | +15.0 | 9,524 | 3,437 |
| Cheltenham Town | 4,655 | 4,116 | –13.1 | 5,814 | 2,745 |
| Darlington | 3,312 | 5,023 | +34.1 | 11,600 | 2,920 |
| Doncaster Rovers | 3,540 | 6,939 | +49.0 | 9,720 | 4,716 |
| Huddersfield Town | 9,506 | 10,528 | +9.7 | 18,633 | 8,275 |
| Hull City | 12,843 | 16,847 | +23.8 | 23,495 | 11,308 |
| Kidderminster Harriers | 2,895 | 2,980 | +2.9 | 4,051 | 2,162 |
| Leyton Orient | 4,257 | 4,157 | –2.4 | 6,119 | 3,475 |
| Lincoln City | 3,924 | 4,910 | +20.1 | 8,154 | 3,441 |
| Macclesfield Town | 2,110 | 2,385 | +11.5 | 3,801 | 1,513 |
| Mansfield Town | 4,887 | 5,207 | +6.1 | 8,065 | 3,920 |
| Northampton Town | 5,211 | 5,306 | +1.8 | 7,160 | 4,010 |
| Oxford United | 5,862 | 6,296 | +6.9 | 9,477 | 4,962 |
| Rochdale | 2,740 | 3,277 | +16.4 | 4,942 | 2,049 |
| Scunthorpe United | 3,692 | 3,840 | +3.9 | 6,426 | 2,326 |
| Southend United | 3,951 | 4,535 | +12.9 | 8,894 | 2,463 |
| Swansea City | 5,160 | 6,853 | +24.7 | 9,800 | 4,400 |
| Torquay United | 3,132 | 3,460 | +9.5 | 6,156 | 2,362 |
| Yeovil Town | 4,741 | 6,197 | +23.5 | 8,760 | 4,867 |
| York City | 4,176 | 3,963 | –5.4 | 7,923 | 2,676 |

| | |
|---|---|
| TOTAL ATTENDANCES: | 2,975,099 (552 games) |
| | Average 5,390 (+17.3%) |
| HIGHEST: | 23,495 Hull City v Huddersfield Town |
| LOWEST: | 1,513 Macclesfield Town v Swansea City |
| HIGHEST AVERAGE: | 16,847 Hull City |
| LOWEST AVERAGE: | 2,385 Macclesfield Town |

# LEAGUE CUP FINALISTS 1961–2004

*Played as a two-leg final until 1966. All subsequent finals at Wembley until 2000, then at Millennium Stadium, Cardiff.*

| *Year* | *Winners* | *Runners-up* | *Score* |
|---|---|---|---|
| 1961 | Aston Villa | Rotherham U | 0-2, 3-0 (aet) |
| 1962 | Norwich C | Rochdale | 3-0, 1-0 |
| 1963 | Birmingham C | Aston Villa | 3-1, 0-0 |
| 1964 | Leicester C | Stoke C | 1-1, 3-2 |
| 1965 | Chelsea | Leicester C | 3-2, 0-0 |
| 1966 | WBA | West Ham U | 1-2, 4-1 |
| 1967 | QPR | WBA | 3-2 |
| 1968 | Leeds U | Arsenal | 1-0 |
| 1969 | Swindon T | Arsenal | 3-1 (aet) |
| 1970 | Manchester C | WBA | 2-1 (aet) |
| 1971 | Tottenham H | Aston Villa | 2-0 |
| 1972 | Stoke C | Chelsea | 2-1 |
| 1973 | Tottenham H | Norwich C | 1-0 |
| 1974 | Wolverhampton W | Manchester C | 2-1 |
| 1975 | Aston Villa | Norwich C | 1-0 |
| 1976 | Manchester C | Newcastle U | 2-1 |
| 1977 | Aston Villa | Everton | 0-0, 1-1 (aet), 3-2 (aet) |
| 1978 | Nottingham F | Liverpool | 0-0 (aet), 1-0 |
| 1979 | Nottingham F | Southampton | 3-2 |
| 1980 | Wolverhampton W | Nottingham F | 1-0 |
| 1981 | Liverpool | West Ham U | 1-1 (aet), 2-1 |

## MILK CUP

| | | | |
|---|---|---|---|
| 1982 | Liverpool | Tottenham H | 3-1 (aet) |
| 1983 | Liverpool | Manchester U | 2-1 (aet) |
| 1984 | Liverpool | Everton | 0-0 (aet), 1-0 |
| 1985 | Norwich C | Sunderland | 1-0 |
| 1986 | Oxford U | QPR | 3-0 |

## LITTLEWOODS CUP

| | | | |
|---|---|---|---|
| 1987 | Arsenal | Liverpool | 2-1 |
| 1988 | Luton T | Arsenal | 3-2 |
| 1989 | Nottingham F | Luton T | 3-1 |
| 1990 | Nottingham F | Oldham Ath | 1-0 |

## RUMBELOWS LEAGUE CUP

| | | | |
|---|---|---|---|
| 1991 | Sheffield W | Manchester U | 1-0 |
| 1992 | Manchester U | Nottingham F | 1-0 |

## COCA-COLA CUP

| | | | |
|---|---|---|---|
| 1993 | Arsenal | Sheffield W | 2-1 |
| 1994 | Aston Villa | Manchester U | 3-1 |
| 1995 | Liverpool | Bolton W | 2-1 |
| 1996 | Aston Villa | Leeds U | 3-0 |
| 1997 | Leicester C | Middlesbrough | 1-1 (aet), 1-0 (aet) |
| 1998 | Chelsea | Middlesbrough | 2-0 (aet) |

## WORTHINGTON CUP

| | | | |
|---|---|---|---|
| 1999 | Tottenham H | Leicester C | 1-0 |
| 2000 | Leicester C | Tranmere R | 2-1 |
| 2001 | Liverpool | Birmingham C | 1-1 (aet) |
| *Liverpool won 5-4 on penalties* | | | |
| 2002 | Blackburn R | Tottenham H | 2-1 |
| 2003 | Liverpool | Manchester U | 2-0 |

## CARLING CUP

| | | | |
|---|---|---|---|
| 2004 | Middlesbrough | Bolton W | 2-1 |

### LEAGUE CUP WINS

Liverpool 7, Aston Villa 5, Nottingham F 4, Leicester C 3, Tottenham H 3, Arsenal 2, Chelsea 2, Manchester C 2, Norwich C 2, Wolverhampton W 2, Birmingham C 1, Blackburn R 1, Leeds U 1, Luton T 1, Manchester U 1, Middlesbrough 1, Oxford U 1, QPR 1, Sheffield W 1, Stoke C 1, Swindon T 1, WBA 1.

### APPEARANCES IN FINALS

Liverpool 9, Aston Villa 7, Nottingham F 6, Arsenal 5, Leicester C 5, Manchester U 5, Tottenham H 5, Norwich C 4, Chelsea 3, Manchester C 3, Middlesbrough 3, WBA 3, Birmingham C 2, Bolton W 2, Everton 2, Leeds U 2, Luton T 2, QPR 2, Sheffield W 2, Stoke C 2, West Ham U 2, Wolverhampton W 2, Blackburn R 1, Newcastle U 1, Oldham Ath 1, Oxford U 1, Rochdale 1, Rotherham U 1, Southampton 1, Sunderland 1, Swindon T 1, Tranmere R 1.

### APPEARANCES IN SEMI-FINALS

Aston Villa 12, Liverpool 12, Arsenal 10, Tottenham H 10, Manchester U 8, Chelsea 7, West Ham U 7, Nottingham F 6, Leeds U 5, Leicester C 5, Manchester C 5, Middlesbrough 5, Norwich C 5, Birmingham C 4, Blackburn R 4, Bolton W 4, Sheffield W 4, WBA 4, Burnley 3, Crystal Palace 3, Everton 3, Ipswich T 3, QPR 3, Sunderland 3, Swindon T 3, Wolverhampton W 3, Bristol C 2, Coventry C 2, Luton T 2, Oxford U 2, Plymouth Arg 2, Southampton 2, Stoke C 2, Tranmere R 2, Wimbledon 2, Blackpool 1, Bury 1, Cardiff C 1, Carlisle U 1, Chester C 1, Derby Co 1, Huddersfield T 1, Newcastle U 1, Oldham Ath 1, Peterborough U 1, Rochdale 1, Rotherham U 1, Sheffield U 1, Shrewsbury T 1, Stockport Co 1, Walsall 1, Watford 1.

# CARLING CUP 2003–04

■ *Denotes player sent off.*

**FIRST ROUND**

Tuesday, 12 August 2003

**Barnsley (0) 1** *(Gorre 63 (pen))*
**Blackpool (2) 2** *(Taylor 5, 22)* 5378

*Barnsley:* Ilic; O'Callaghan, Gallimore, Kay, Handyside, Ireland (Austin), Gibbs (Rankin), Hayward (Lumsdon), Fallon, Gorre, Betsy.
*Blackpool:* Jones L; Hilton, Richardson, Flynn, Davis, Danns, Wellens (Grayson), Bullock, Sheron (Clarke), Taylor, Douglas.

**Bradford C (0) 0**
**Darlington (0) 0** 4077

*Bradford C:* Paston; Edds, Heckingbottom, Evans (Muirhead), Wetherall, Francis, Gray, Kearney, Windass, Branch (Wolleaston), Emanuel (Cornwall).
*Darlington:* Price; McGurk, Valentine, Liddle, Clarke (Clark), Bossy (Hughes), Keltie, Nicholls, Conlon, Robson, Maddison.
*aet; Darlington won 5-3 on penalties.*

**Bristol R (0) 0**
**Brighton & HA (0) 1** *(McPhee 49)* 5518

*Bristol R:* Miller; Boxall (Bryant), Anderson, Edwards, Barrett, Quinn, Carlisle, Savage, Tait, Agogo (Hodges) (Parker), Street.
*Brighton & HA:* Roberts; Watson, Mayo, Cullip, Hinshelwood, Jones N■, Rodger, Oatway (Carpenter), Knight, Hart, McPhee (Harding).

**Cambridge U (1) 1** *(Walker 28)*
**Gillingham (0) 2** *(Hills 73, Nosworthy 86)* 3044

*Cambridge U:* Marshall; Murray, Bimson, Tann, Angus, Venus, Tudor (Revell), Guttridge, Kitson, Chillingworth, Walker.
*Gillingham:* Brown; Southall, Hills, Hope, Ashby, Cox, Spiller (Hessenthaler), Saunders, Sidibe (Johnson T■), Nosworthy, Shaw (Perpetuini).

**Cardiff C (2) 4** *(Earnshaw 39, 40, 55, Campbell 56)*
**Leyton Orient (0) 1** *(Ibehre 75)* 4503

*Cardiff C:* Margetson; Vidmar, Barker, Collins, Gabbidon, Whalley, Bonner (Boland), Maxwell, Earnshaw (Fleetwood), Campbell, Bowen.
*Leyton Orient:* Harrison (Morris); Hunt, Lockwood, Ebdon, Miller, Jones, Purser, Newey, Alexander (Tate), Toner (Ibehre), Brazier.

**Cheltenham T (1) 1** *(McCann 4)*
**QPR (1) 2** *(Ainsworth 16, Langley 86)* 3697

*Cheltenham T:* Book; Griffin, Victory, Brough, Fyfe, Duff M, Bird (Cozic), Yates, Spencer, Odejayi (Devaney) (Brayson), McCann.
*QPR:* Day; Forbes, Padula, Palmer, Shittu, Carlisle, Langley, Ainsworth, Furlong■, Gallen (Sabin), Bircham.

**Chesterfield (0) 0**
**Burnley (0) 0** 2928

*Chesterfield:* Muggleton; O'Hare, Evatt, Dawson, Blatherwick (Davies), Payne, Brandon, Hudson, Reeves (Rushbury), Hurst, Allott.
*Burnley:* Jensen; Camara, Roche, Grant, Branch (West), Gnohere, Little, Weller, Moore A (Chaplow), Blake, Chadwick.
*aet; Burnley won 3-2 on penalties.*

**Colchester U (2) 2** *(Fagan 22, Pinault 40)*
**Plymouth Arg (1) 1** *(Evans 24)* 2367

*Colchester U:* Brown S; Stockley, Myers, Pinault, Fitzgerald, White, Duguid, Izzet, Fagan, McGleish, Keith.
*Plymouth Arg:* Larrieu; Worrell, Gilbert (Wotton), Adams (Friio), Aljofree (Stonebridge), Coughlan, Norris, Bent, Evans, Keith, Capaldi.

**Crewe Alex (0) 2** *(Ashton 54 (pen), Jones S 88)*
**Wrexham (0) 0** 3152

*Crewe Alex:* Ince; Wright, Vaughan, Brammer, Foster, Moses, Lunt, Cochrane, Ashton (McCready), Jones S, Rix.
*Wrexham:* Dibble; Edwards C, Edwards P, Lawrence, Pejic, Carey■, Whitley, Ferguson, Llewellyn, Jones L (Sam), Thomas (Crowell).

**Doncaster R (0) 3** *(Fortune-West 76, Barnes 81 (pen), Blundell 90)*
**Grimsby T (1) 2** *(Campbell 38, Anderson 67 (pen))* 6057

*Doncaster R:* Warrington; Marples, Beech (Barnes), Green, Ryan, Foster, Paterson (Tierney), Doolan (Ravenhill), Blundell, Fortune-West, McIndoe.
*Grimsby T:* Davison; Crowe, Barnard, Hamilton■, Ford, Crane, Cas■, Campbell, Boulding (Mansaram), Ten Heuvel (Groves), Anderson.

**Huddersfield T (0) 2** *(Stead 59, Thorrington 70)*
**Derby Co (1) 1** *(Taylor 41)* 6672

*Huddersfield T:* Gray; Sodje, Edwards, Fowler, Hughes, Yates, Thorrington, Schofield, Newby, Stead, Carss.
*Derby Co:* Grant; Jackson, Boertien, Caldwell (Morris), Mills (McLeod), Elliott, Valakari, Taylor, Candido Costa, Labarthe, Huddlestone.

**Lincoln C (0) 0**
**Stockport Co (0) 1** *(Barlow 87)* 2296

*Lincoln C:* Marriott; Bloomer, Mayo, Weaver, Morgan, Futcher, Butcher, Liburd (Yeo), May (Remy), McNamara (Pearce), Sedgemore.
*Stockport Co:* Colgan; Goodwin, Pemberton (Hardiker), McLachlan, Clare, Jones, Morrison, Lambert, Barlow, Beckett, Ellison (Welsh).

**Luton T (1) 4** *(Foley 25, Thorpe 56, Pitt 64, Howard 68)*
**Yeovil T (0) 1** *(Boyce 47 (og))* 4337

*Luton T:* Beckwith; Foley, Neilson (Davis), Spring, Boyce, Coyne, Pitt, Nicholls, Howard, Thorpe (Crowe) (Okai), Hughes.
*Yeovil T:* Weale; Lockwood, Crittenden (El Kholti), Gosling (Reed), O'Brien, Rodrigues (Lindegaard), Williams, Way, Jackson, Gall, Johnson.

**Macclesfield T (1) 1** *(Whitaker 45)*
**Sheffield U (1) 2** *(Lester 35, 87 (pen))* 2764

*Macclesfield T:* Myhill; Abbey (Hitchen), Adams, Welch, Haddrell (Tipton), Munroe, Little, Smith, Miles, Carruthers, Whitaker.
*Sheffield U:* Kenny; Jagielka, Kozluk, McCall, Page, Morgan, Ndlovu, Montgomery, Lester, Ward (Allison), Tonge.

**Millwall (0) 0**
**Oxford U (0) 1** *(Basham 59)* 4781

*Millwall:* Warner; Lawrence, Craig (Phillips), Cahill, Nethercott, Ward, Hearn (Dunne), Juan, Harris, Whelan (Braniff), Roberts.
*Oxford U:* Woodman; McNiven, Robinson, Crosby, Bound, Ashton, Whitehead, Wanless, Basham (Oldfield), Brown, Townsley.

**Northampton T (1) 1** *(Low 8)*
**Norwich C (0) 0** 5476

*Northampton T:* Thompson; Chambers, Clark, Trollope, Willmott, Reid, Low, Richards (Dudfield), Burgess, Smith, Reeves (Hargreaves).
*Norwich C:* Green; Edworthy, Drury, Fleming, Mackay, Holt, Rivers, Francis (Mulryne), Jarvis (Nielsen), Henderson (McVeigh), Easton.

**Port Vale (0) 0**
**Nottingham F (0) 0** 4950
*Port Vale:* Delany; Cummins, Lipa, Collins, Walsh, Pilkington, Brown, Littlejohn, McPhee, Brooker (Paynter), Bridge-Wilkinson.
*Nottingham F:* Ward; Biggins, Oyen (Doig), Morgan, Thompson, Sonner, Stewart■, Williams (Bopp), Johnson, Harewood, Reid.
*aet; Nottingham F won 3-2 on penalties.*

**Preston NE (0) 0**
**Notts Co (0) 0** 5016
*Preston NE:* Gould; Alexander, Edwards (Abbott), Etuhu, Lucketti, Jackson, Skora (Healy), Cartwright (Mears), Cresswell, Fuller, Keane.
*Notts Co:* Mildenhall; Jenkins, Nicholson, Richardson, Fenton, Barras, Brough (Bolland), Heffernan, Platt (Hackworth), Stallard, Baraclough.
*aet; Notts Co won 7-6 on penalties.*

**Rotherham U (2) 2** *(Swailes 2, Sedgwick 43)*
**York C (1) 1** *(Merris 33)* 2919
*Rotherham U:* Pollitt; Barker S, Minto, Monkhouse, Swailes, Branston, Sedgwick (Warne), Mullin, Lee, Byfield (Barker R), Talbot.
*York C:* Ovendale; Edmondson, Merris, Hope, Brass, Wood, Ward, Dunning, Nogan (Stewart), Bullock, Wise.

**Scunthorpe U (0) 2** *(Hayes 51, 57)*
**Oldham Ath (0) 1** *(Antoine-Curier 61)* 2366
*Scunthorpe U:* Evans; Stanton, Sharp, Kell (Calvo-Garcia), Jackson, Byrne, Sparrow■, Kilford (Graves), Hayes (McLean), Torpey, Beagrie.
*Oldham Ath:* Pogliacomi; Murray, Sheridan D■, Boshell■, Hall D, Haining, Tierney, Vernon (O'Halloran), Antoine-Curier (Sheridan J), Roca (Carney), Eyre.

**Southend U (2) 2** *(Maher 11, Broughton 38)*
**Swindon T (1) 3** *(Parkin 34, 48, Mooney 73)* 3385
*Southend U:* Emberson; Jupp, McSweeney, Maher, Cort, Warren, Gower, Odunsi, Broughton, Husbands, Corbett (Bramble).
*Swindon T:* Evans; Heywood, Robinson, Viveash, Reeves, Howard (Miglioranzi), Igoe, Stevenson (Mooney), Parkin, Smith (Duke), Hewlett.

**Torquay U (0) 1** *(Graham 61)*
**Crystal Palace (1) 1** *(Freedman 29)* 3366
*Torquay U:* Van Heusden; Woozley, Hankin, Hockley, Taylor, Woods, Russell, Canoville, Osei Kuffour (Benefield), Fowler (Graham), Hill (Wills).
*Crystal Palace:* Berthelin; Butterfield, Riihilahti (Watson), Symons (Black), Popovic■, Powell, Derry, Johnson, Freedman, Shipperley, Routledge (Smith).
*aet; Crystal Palace won 3-1 on penalties.*

**Tranmere R (0) 1** *(Dadi 89)*
**Bury (0) 0** 4272
*Tranmere R:* Achterberg; Connelly, Roberts, Sharps, Allen, Taylor, Hume, Mellon, Haworth, Jones, Nicholson (Dadi).
*Bury:* Garner; Unsworth, Woodthorpe, Clegg, Swailes, Strong, Duxbury, Connell (O'Neill), Porter (Preece), Nugent (Seddon), Singh.

**WBA (1) 4** *(Hulse 18, 76, Haas 74, Dobie 90)*
**Brentford (0) 0** 10,440
*WBA:* Hoult; Haas, Clement, Gregan, Gaardsoe, Volmer, Sakiri, O'Connor (Johnson), Hulse (Dobie), Dichio (Hughes), Koumas.
*Brentford:* Smith P■; Dobson, Somner, Sonko, Frampton, Hutchinson, Smith J, O'Connor (Blackman), Peters (Julian), Tabb, Hunt (Hughes).

**Walsall (1) 2** *(Merson 35, Leitao 49)*
**Carlisle U (1) 1** *(Russell 32)* 4665
*Walsall:* Walker; Bazeley, Aranalde, Emblen, Roper, Osborn, Wrack (Matias), Merson, Leitao, Corica, Samways.
*Carlisle U:* Glennon; Shelley, Maddison (Kelly), McDonagh, Andrews, Murphy, Baldacchino, Russell, Foran (Billy), Wake (Livingstone), Rundle.

**Watford (0) 1** *(Fitzgerald 108)*
**Bournemouth (0) 0** 9561
*Watford:* Chamberlain; Doyley, Mahon, Cox, Gayle, Johnson (Hand), Ardley (Cook), Helguson (Fitzgerald), Webber, Dyer, Hyde.
*Bournemouth:* Moss; Purches (Holmes), Cummings, Broadhurst, Fletcher C, Browning (Tindall), Elliott, O'Connor, Hayter, Fletcher S, Thomas (Feeney).
*aet.*

**Wigan Ath (1) 2** *(McCulloch 7, Jarrett 87)*
**Hull C (0) 0** 3295
*Wigan Ath:* Walsh; Eaden, McMillan, Jarrett, Breckin, Jackson, Liddell, Bullard, Roberts N, McCulloch, Kennedy (Mitchell).
*Hull C:* Fettis; Price (Melton), Delaney, Thelwell, Whittle, Hinds, Green, Ashbee, Allsopp, Burgess, Elliott (Keates).

**Wycombe W (1) 2** *(Harris 3, 57)*
**Wimbledon (0) 0** 1986
*Wycombe W:* Williams; Senda, Vinnicombe, Mapes, Rogers, Johnson, Currie, Simpson, Harris, Patterson, McSporran (Roberts).
*Wimbledon:* Banks; Darlington, Hawkins (Gier), Holloway (Holdsworth), Chorley, Leigertwood, Gordon, Tapp (Jarrett), Agyemang, Nowland, Reo-Coker.

### Wednesday, 13 August 2003

**Boston U (0) 1** *(Redfearn 69 (pen))*
**Reading (1) 3** *(Forster 16, 87, Sidwell 83)* 2055
*Boston U:* Bastock; Sutch (Logan), Chapman, Hocking, Greaves, Ellender, Potter (Redfearn), Bennett, Douglas, Duffield (Jones), Rusk.
*Reading:* Hahnemann; Harper, Shorey, Brown, Williams, Newman, Murray, Sidwell, Goater (Salako), Forster, Hughes.

**Bristol C (1) 4** *(Peacock 14, 108, Bell 96 (pen), Coles 103)*
**Swansea C (1) 1** *(Connolly 18)* 5807
*Bristol C:* Phillips; Carey, Hill, Burnell (Matthews), Butler, Coles, Wilkshire (Tinnion), Doherty, Peacock, Miller (Roberts), Bell.
*Swansea C:* Murphy; Jones, Hylton, Britton (Thomas), O'Leary, Johnrose, Durkan (Nugent), Martinez, Connolly (Coates), Trundle, Maylett■.
*aet.*

**Coventry C (0) 2** *(Barrett 63, Adebola 67)*
**Peterborough U (0) 0** 5280
*Coventry C:* Shearer; Whing, Pead (Pipe), Safri, Konjic (Jephcott), Warnock, Doyle, Barrett, Adebola, Suffo, Jorgensen (Morrell).
*Peterborough U:* Tyler; Gill, Legg, Arber, Rea (Farrell), Burton, Kanu, Shields, Clarke A, McKenzie (Green), Boucaud (Newton).

**Ipswich T (0) 1** *(Bowditch 91)*
**Kidderminster H (0) 0** 11,118
*Ipswich T:* Davis; Makin, Richards, Miller, Diallo, Santos, Magilton (Naylor), Reuser, Counago (Bent M) (Bowditch), Bent D, Wright.
*Kidderminster H:* Brock; Coleman, Shilton (Parrish), Stamps, Hinton, Willis, Bennett, Flynn, Ward, Williams J (Lewis), Williams D (Smith).
*aet.*

**Mansfield T (0) 1** *(Kyle 89 (og))*
**Sunderland (1) 2** *(Artell 18 (og), Kyle 90)* 5665
*Mansfield T:* Pilkington; Hassell, Clarke, Curtis (Day), Artell, Dimech, Lawrence, Williamson, Christie (White A), Mendes, Corden (MacKenzie).
*Sunderland:* Poom; Williams (Wright), Gray (Oster), Piper, Babb, Clark, Thornton, Whitley, Flo (Kyle), Stewart, Kilbane.

**Sheffield W (0) 2** *(Lee 50, Wood 115)*
**Hartlepool U (0) 2** *(Robinson P 56 (pen), Istead 104)* 13,410
*Sheffield W:* Tidman; Geary, Barry-Murphy, Armstrong (Cooke), Lee, Smith D, Evans, Quinn, Owusu (Holt), Kuqi, Wood.
*Hartlepool U:* Provett; Jordan, Strachan, Nelson, Westwood, Robson, Clarke (Henderson), Tinkler (Barron), Williams E (Istead), Robinson P, Humphreys.
*aet; Hartlepool U won 5-4 on penalties.*

**West Ham U (2) 3** *(Defoe 9, Connolly 14, 78)*
**Rushden & D (1) 1** *(Lowe 34)* 13,715
*West Ham U:* James; Ferdinand (Garcia), Brevett, Sofiane (Byrne), Repka, Dailly, Noble, Lee, Connolly, Defoe, Etherington.
*Rushden & D:* Turley; Bignot, Underwood, Bell, Hunter (Dempster), Edwards, Hall, Mills (Gray), Jack (Darby), Lowe, Burgess.

Tuesday, 19 August 2003

**Stoke C (1) 2** *(Iwelumo 13, Goodfellow 90)*
**Rochdale (0) 1** *(Townson 76)* 4687
*Stoke C:* De Goey; Thomas, Clarke, Henry, Hall, Eustace (Neal), Russell (Wilson), Wilkinson, Iwelumo, Greenacre (Commons), Goodfellow.
*Rochdale:* Gilks; Evans, Simpkins, Beech (Betts), Burgess, Grand, Bertos (Townson), McClare, Shuker, Connor, Doughty (McCourt).

## SECOND ROUND

Tuesday, 23 September 2003

**Blackpool (1) 1** *(Taylor 6)*
**Birmingham C (0) 0** 7370
*Blackpool:* Jones L; Grayson, Evans, Southern, Davis, Clarke, Wellens (Coid), Danns, Sheron (Murphy), Taylor (Bullock), Douglas.
*Birmingham C:* Taylor; Johnson, Clapham, Cunningham (Kirovski), Upson, Clemence, Dunn, Cisse (Figueroa), Morrison, John (Forssell), Lazaridis.

**Bristol C (0) 1** *(Miller 94)*
**Watford (0) 0** 5213
*Bristol C:* Phillips; Carey (Fortune), Bell, Doherty (Hulbert), Butler, Coles, Wilkshire, Tinnion (Matthews), Miller, Roberts, Brown A.
*Watford:* Chamberlain; Doyley, Robinson, Dyche, Cox, Mahon, Devlin, Young (Cook), Webber, Dyer, Fisken (Hyde) (Hand).
*aet.*

**Cardiff C (2) 2** *(Earnshaw 12, 25)*
**West Ham U (1) 3** *(Defoe 45 (pen), 64, 88)* 10,724
*Cardiff C:* Margetson; Weston, Barker, Boland, Gabbidon, Vidmar, Bowen (Campbell), Kavanagh, Earnshaw, Thorne (Gordon), Bonner.
*West Ham U:* James; Ferdinand, Quinn, Pearce, Repka, Dailly, Horlock, Mellor (Garcia), Connolly, Defoe, Etherington.

**Charlton Ath (1) 4** *(Parker 41, Lisbie 58, Di Canio 90, Jensen 95)*
**Luton T (2) 4** *(Foley 30, Bayliss 32, McSheffrey 78, Coyne 110)* 10,905
*Charlton Ath:* Kiely; Young, Powell (Euell), Holland, Fortune, Fish, Stuart (Johansson), Jensen, Lisbie (Campbell-Ryce), Di Canio, Parker.
*Luton T:* Beckwith; Boyce, Davis, Spring, Bayliss (Hillier), Coyne, Foley (Leary), Brkovic (Pitt), Howard, McSheffrey, Hughes.
*aet; Charlton Ath won 8-7 on penalties.*

**Crystal Palace (2) 2** *(Johnson 17 (pen), 25 (pen))*
**Doncaster R (0) 1** *(Blundell 47)* 4904
*Crystal Palace:* Berthelin; Butterfield, Borrowdale, Mullins (Fleming), Williams (Riihilahti), Powell, Derry, Watson, Johnson (Routledge), Shipperley, Hughes.
*Doncaster R:* Warrington; Price, Morley, Foster, Ryan, Ravenhill, McGrath (Barnes) (Paterson), Doolan, Blundell, Fortune-West, McIndoe.

**Hartlepool U (1) 1** *(Robinson P 45 (pen))*
**WBA (0) 2** *(Clement 61, Hulse 81)* 5265
*Hartlepool U:* Provett; Barron, Clarke (Istead), Nelson, Westwood■, Tinkler, Humphreys, Robinson P, Williams E, Gabbiadini (McCann), Strachan.
*WBA:* Hoult; Haas, N'Dour (Clement), Berthe, Gaardsoe, Gilchrist, O'Connor, Johnson, Hulse, Hughes (Dobie) (Dichio), Koumas.

**Leicester C (0) 1** *(Dickov 82 (pen))*
**Crewe Alex (0) 0** 27,675
*Leicester C:* Walker; Curtis, Sinclair, Scimeca, Howey, Brooker (Priet), Impey, Scowcroft (Izzet), Dickov, Deane (Stewart), Nalis.
*Crewe Alex:* Ince; Wright, Vaughan, Brammer, Foster, Walker, Lunt, Cochrane (Varney), Ashton, Edwards, Rix (Tonkin).

**Notts Co (2) 2** *(Baldry 2, Stallard 10 (pen))*
**Ipswich T (1) 1** *(Counago 6 (pen))* 4059
*Notts Co:* Mildenhall; Richardson, Nicholson, Jenkins (Riley), Fenton, Barras, Baldry, Caskey, Platt (Heffernan), Stallard, Baraclough.
*Ipswich T:* Davis; Wilnis, Richards (Armstrong), Naylor, Bowditch (Morrow), Santos, Magilton, Wright, Counago, Mahon (Bloomfield), Westlake.

**Portsmouth (3) 5** *(Sherwood 13, 83, Roberts 17, 60, Taylor 41)*
**Northampton T (0) 2** *(Hargreaves 77 (pen), Dudfield 90)* 11,130
*Portsmouth:* Wapenaar; Schemmel (Stone), Taylor, O'Neil, Primus, Foxe, Sherwood, Roberts, Pericard, Sheringham, Smertin.
*Northampton T:* Harper; Chambers, Carruthers, Trollope, Willmott (Sampson), Reid■, Harsley (Rickers), Richards (Burgess), Dudfield, Youngs, Hargreaves.

**Rotherham U (1) 1** *(Sedgwick 22)*
**Colchester U (0) 0** 2474
*Rotherham U:* Pollitt; Barker S, Minto, Robinson, Swailes, McIntosh, Sedgwick (Warne), Talbot (Robins), Butler, Byfield, Monkhouse (Hurst).
*Colchester U:* Brown S; Stockley, Keith (Coote), Baldwin (Hadland), White, Chilvers■, Izzet, Bowry (Pinault), Fagan, Vine, Duguid.

**Scunthorpe U (1) 2** *(McLean 32, Beagrie 85)*
**Burnley (2) 3** *(Chadwick 22, Blake 42, Moore I 77)* 2915
*Scunthorpe U:* Russell; Byrne, Sharp (Beagrie), McCombe, Butler, Kell, Sparrow, Featherstone, McLean (Hayes), Torpey, Barwick.
*Burnley:* Jensen; West, Camara, Weller, Todd, May, Chadwick, Blake, Moore I, Facey, Farrelly.

**Sheffield U (0) 0**
**QPR (2) 2** *(Rowlands 30, 45)* 9578
*Sheffield U:* Rogers; Kozluk, Armstrong, Parkinson (Hurst), Jagielka, Whitlow (Cryan), Rankine, Brown, Lester (Peschisolido), Allison, Tonge.
*QPR:* Day; Edghill, Padula, Rowlands (Ainsworth), Shittu, Forbes, Bircham, Bean, Furlong, Gallen, McLeod.

**Stoke C (0) 0**
**Gillingham (1) 2** *(Saunders 24, King 52)* 4607
*Stoke C:* Cutler; Russell, Hall■, Eustace, Williams, Hoekstra, Goodfellow (Commons), Noel-Williams (Iwelumo), Asaba (Akinbiyi), Neal, Clarke.
*Gillingham:* Brown; Nosworthy, Hills, Hope, Cox, Smith, Spiller (Crofts), Saunders, Sidibe, King (Johnson T), Perpetuini.

**Sunderland (1) 2** *(Kyle 25, 90)*
**Huddersfield T (2) 4** *(Carss 2, Stead 20, Holdsworth 54, Booth 87)* 13,516
*Sunderland:* Ingham; James, Clark■, Whitley, Bjorklund (Williams), McCartney, Oster (Leadbitter), Thornton, Kyle, Proctor (Stewart), Butler.
*Huddersfield T:* Gray; Schofield, Scott, Fowler, Yates, Mirfin, Worthington, Holdsworth, Booth (Brown), Stead, Carss.

**Tranmere R (0) 0**

**Nottingham F (0) 0** 4477

*Tranmere R:* Achterberg; Connelly, Roberts, Sharps, Allen, Loran, Hume (Dagnall), Mellon (Taylor), Haworth, Dadi, Jones.
*Nottingham F:* Ward; Louis-Jean, Morgan, Sonner, Thompson, Dawson, Robertson, McPhail (Stewart), Taylor (Jess), Harewood, Reid.
*aet; Nottingham F won 4-1 on penalties.*

**Wigan Ath (0) 1** *(Ellington 73)*

**Fulham (0) 0** 4874

*Wigan Ath:* Filan; Eaden, Kennedy, Dinning, Breckin, Jackson, Liddell, Bullard, Ellington, Horsfield (Roberts), McCulloch.
*Fulham:* Crossley; Leacock, Green, Pembridge, Djetou, Melville, Buari (Boa Morte), Inamoto (Rehman), Sava, Stolcers (Pratley), Legwinski.

**Wolverhampton W (1) 2** *(Rae 37, Gudjonsson 53)*

**Darlington (0) 0** 10,232

*Wolverhampton W:* Murray (Oakes); Luzhny, Naylor, Gudjonsson (Newton), Craddock, Okoronkwo, Cameron, Rae, Iversen, Silas, Kennedy (Clarke).
*Darlington:* Collett; McGurk, Valentine, Liddle, Hutchinson, Hughes, Keltie, Nicholls, Conlon, Clarke, Clark.

**Wycombe W (0) 0**

**Aston Villa (2) 5** *(Whittingham 14, Angel 31, 50 (pen), 55, Vassell 86 (pen))* 6072

*Wycombe W:* Williams; Senda, Vinnicombe, Thomson (Harris), Rogers, Johnson, Currie, Simpson, Bell (Cook), Holligan, Brown (Bulman).
*Aston Villa:* Sorensen; De la Cruz, Samuel, McCann, Dublin, Delaney, Hendrie (Ridgewell), Barry, Angel (Vassell), Allback (Moore S), Whittingham.

Wednesday, 24 September 2003

**Bolton W (1) 3** *(Jardel 15, 80, Nolan 69)*

**Walsall (0) 1** *(Merson 74)* 5229

*Bolton W:* Poole; Hunt, Charlton, Ba (Giannakopoulos), N'Gotty (Comyn-Platt), Barness, Nolan, Frandsen, Pedersen, Jardel, Okocha (Gardner).
*Walsall:* Walker; Bazeley, Aranalde, Osborn, Emblen, Ritchie, Lawrence, Merson, Burton (Birch), Corica (Fryatt), Samways.

**Coventry C (0) 0**

**Tottenham H (2) 3** *(Kanoute 13, Keane 23, Ricketts 65)* 15,474

*Coventry C:* Shearer; Shaw, Warnock, Mansouri, Konjic, Staunton, Morrell, Safri, Adebola, Suffo (Barrett), Doyle (Jorgensen).
*Tottenham H:* Keller; Carr, Taricco, Gardner, Richards, Bunjecevic, Anderton, Poyet, Keane (Postiga), Kanoute, Blondel (Ricketts).

**Everton (2) 3** *(Ferguson 26 (pen), 56, Chadwick 44)*

**Stockport Co (0) 0** 19,807

*Everton:* Martyn; Hibbert (Unsworth), Pistone, Carsley, Yobo (Clarke), Weir, Watson, Gravesen (Rooney), Chadwick, Ferguson, McFadden.
*Stockport Co:* Colgan; Smith, Hardiker, Challinor, Clare (Daly), Jones, Williams C (Barlow), Lambert, Wilbraham, Lescott, Welsh.

**Leeds U (0) 2** *(Harte 77, Robinson 90)*

**Swindon T (1) 2** *(Gurney 44, Parkin 74)* 29,211

*Leeds U:* Robinson; Kelly (Radebe), Harte, Batty, Camara, Roque Junior, Lennon, Olembe, Chapuis (Bridges), Smith, Wilcox (Domi).
*Swindon T:* Griemink■; Gurney, Duke, Smith (Herring), Reeves, Heywood, Miglioranzi, Igoe (Evans), Stevenson (Howard), Parkin, Hewlett.
*aet; Leeds U won 4-3 on penalties.*

**Middlesbrough (0) 1** *(Christie 94)*

**Brighton & HA (0) 0** 10,435

*Middlesbrough:* Schwarzer; Mills, Queudrue, Doriva, Cooper, Southgate (Riggott), Greening, Boateng, Nemeth, Ricketts (Juninho), Downing (Christie).
*Brighton & HA:* Kuipers; Hinshelwood, Mayo (Harding), Cullip, Butters, Carpenter, Hart (Robinson), Rodger (Pethick), Knight, McPhee, Jones N.
*aet.*

**Oxford U (0) 1** *(Louis 75)*

**Reading (0) 3** *(Salako 52, Forster 65, Harper 90)* 9870

*Oxford U:* Woodman; McNiven, Robinson, Crosby, Bound, Ashton, Townsley (Hackett), Hunt, Alsop (Louis), Rawle (Scott), Whitehead.
*Reading:* Hahnemann; Murty, Shorey, Brown, Williams, Newman, Murray (Daley), Hughes, Forster, Harper, Salako.

## THIRD ROUND

Tuesday, 28 October 2003

**Arsenal (1) 1** *(Aliadiere 11)*

**Rotherham U (0) 1** *(Byfield 90)* 27,451

*Arsenal:* Stack; Tavlaridis, Hoyte (Spicer), Edu, Clichy, Cygan, Fabregas Soler (Owusu-Abeyie), Aliadiere, Wiltord, Kanu, Thomas (Smith).
*Rotherham U:* Pollitt■; Barker S, Hurst, Robinson (Mullin), Swailes, McIntosh, Sedgwick (Montgomery), Talbot (Baudet), Barker R, Byfield, Warne.
*aet; Arsenal won 9-8 on penalties.*

**Blackpool (0) 1** *(Southern 88)*

**Crystal Palace (1) 3** *(Johnson 24, 87, Freedman 62 (pen))* 6010

*Blackpool:* Barnes■; Coid, Evans, Grayson, Davis, Clarke, Wellens (Sheron), Bullock (Southern), Murphy, Taylor, Douglas.
*Crystal Palace:* Myhre; Butterfield, Routledge, Symons, Smith (Borrowdale), Riihilahti, Derry, Johnson, Freedman, Shipperley, Hughes (Watson).

**Bolton W (1) 2** *(Giannakopoulos 25, Pedersen 66)*

**Gillingham (0) 0** 5258

*Bolton W:* Poole; Hunt, Barness, Campo, Emerson, Charlton, Giannakopoulos (Gardner), Ba (Okocha), Pedersen, Jardel, Nolan.
*Gillingham:* Brown; Nosworthy, Hills, Hope, Ashby, Cox, Southall, Hessenthaler (King) (James), Wallace, Shaw (Sidibe), Smith.

**Bristol C (0) 0**

**Southampton (1) 3** *(Beattie 31, Ormerod 67, Le Saux 89)* 17,408

*Bristol C:* Phillips; Coles, Amankwaah (Miller), Burnell, Butler, Hill, Wilkshire (Hulbert), Tinnion, Peacock, Roberts (Lita), Woodman.
*Southampton:* Niemi (Jones); Dodd, Le Saux, Delap (Telfer), Lundekvam, Svensson M, Fernandes (McCann), Svensson A, Beattie, Ormerod, Marsden.

**Leeds U (0) 2** *(Roque Junior 49, 114)*

**Manchester U (0) 3** *(Bellion 78, Forlan 108, Djemba-Djemba 117)* 37,546

*Leeds U:* Robinson; Kelly, Harte, Olembe (Lennon), Camara, Roque Junior, Sakho (Chapuis), Seth Johnson, Bridges (Domi), Smith, Milner.
*Manchester U:* Carroll; Neville P, Fortune, Neville G, Butt, O'Shea, Fletcher (Johnson), Djemba-Djemba, Forlan, Bellion, Richardson (Eagles).
*aet.*

**QPR (0) 0**

**Manchester C (1) 3** *(Wright-Phillips 22, 77, Macken 79)* 16,773

*QPR:* Day; Edghill, Padula, Carlisle, Forbes, Bircham, Ainsworth, Rowlands, Gallen, Pacquette (Sabin), McLeod.
*Manchester C:* Seaman; Jihai, Tarnat, Dunne, Distin, Barton, Wright-Phillips, Bosvelt, Anelka (Macken), Fowler (Siberski), Sinclair (Berkovic).

**Reading (0) 1** *(Forster 83)*
**Huddersfield T (0) 0** 11,892
*Reading:* Hahnemann; Newman, Shorey, Ingimarsson, Williams, Watson, Murray (Goater), Sidwell, Forster, Hughes, Salako.
*Huddersfield T:* Gray; Sodje, Schofield, Holdsworth (Brown), Yates, Clarke, Worthington, Fowler, Booth, Stead, Carss.

**Wolverhampton W (0) 2** *(Miller 48, Craddock 81)*
**Burnley (0) 0** 18,548
*Wolverhampton W:* Oakes; Luzhny, Naylor, Gudjonsson, Butler, Craddock, Silas, Ince (Rae), Iversen (Clarke), Miller, Camara.
*Burnley:* Jensen; West (Roche), Camara, Chaplow (Farrelly), Branch, Gnohere, Little, Blake, Moore I, Grant, Facey.

Wednesday, 29 October 2003

**Aston Villa (0) 1** *(Hitzlsperger 75)*
**Leicester C (0) 0** 26,729
*Aston Villa:* Sorensen; Delaney, Samuel, McCann, Johnsen, Mellberg (Dublin), De la Cruz (Allback), Barry, Angel, Vassell (Hitzlsperger), Whittingham.
*Leicester C:* Coyne; Impey, Stewart, McKinlay (Izzet), Howey, Sinclair, Brooker (Scowcroft), Hignett (Gillespie), Dickov, Deane, Nalis.

**Blackburn R (1) 3** *(Yorke 35, 90, Ferguson 81)*
**Liverpool (1) 4** *(Murphy 41 (pen), Heskey 49, 61, Kewell 79)* 16,918
*Blackburn R:* Friedel; Neill■, Gresko (Johansson), Babbel, Taylor, Tugay, Reid (Gallagher), Ferguson, Cole, Yorke, Thompson (Emerton).
*Liverpool:* Kirkland; Biscan, Traore, Le Tallec, Henchoz, Hyypia (Riise), Gerrard (Hamann), Murphy, Heskey, Sinama-Pongolle (Kewell), Diouf.

**Chelsea (2) 4** *(Hasselbaink 14, Gudjohnsen 36, 65 (pen), Cole J 87)*
**Notts Co (1) 2** *(Barras 27, Stallard 85)* 35,997
*Chelsea:* Ambrosio; Johnson, Babayaro, Veron, Melchiot, Huth, Gronkjaer (Cole J), Geremi, Hasselbaink (Stanic), Gudjohnsen, Duff.
*Notts Co:* Mildenhall; Jenkins, Richardson (Nicholson), Riley (Bolland), Fenton, Barras, Baldry, Caskey, Platt, Heffernan (Stallard), Baraclough.

**Everton (1) 1** *(Linderoth 42)*
**Charlton Ath (0) 0** 24,863
*Everton:* Martyn; Hibbert, Naysmith, Yobo, Weir, Linderoth, Nyarko (Stubbs), Gravesen (Li Tie), Ferguson, Rooney, McFadden (Radzinski).
*Charlton Ath:* Kiely; Kishishev, Hreidarsson, Holland (Campbell-Ryce), Perry, Fish (Fortune), Stuart (Svensson), Euell, Johansson, Jensen, Parker.

**Newcastle U (0) 1** *(Robert 65)*
**WBA (1) 2** *(Ameobi 29 (og), Hughes 101)* 46,932
*Newcastle U:* Harper; Griffin, Bernard, Solano (Ambrose), Bramble, Caldwell, Viana (Speed), Jenas, Lua-Lua, Ameobi, Robert (Shearer).
*WBA:* Hoult; Haas, Clement, Gregan, Gaardsoe, Gilchrist (Volmer), O'Connor, Sakiri (Wallwork), Hulse (Hughes), Dobie, Johnson.
*aet.*

**Nottingham F (1) 2** *(Bopp 42, 67)*
**Portsmouth (0) 4** *(Walker 57 (og), Yakubu 64, 108, Roberts 101)* 20,078
*Nottingham F:* Ward; Louis-Jean, Morgan, Sonner (Williams), Thompson, Walker (Robertson), Bopp, McPhail (Jess), Taylor, Harewood, Reid.
*Portsmouth:* Wapenaar; Schemmel, De Zeeuw, Sherwood, Foxe, Stefanovic (Yakubu), Stone, Quashie (Berger), Roberts, Sheringham (O'Neil), Taylor.
*aet.*

**Tottenham H (0) 1** *(Zamora 91)*
**West Ham U (0) 0** 36,053
*Tottenham H:* Keller; Carr, Ziege (Blondel), Gardner, Doherty, King, Konchesky, Dalmat (Mabizela), Keane, Zamora, Ricketts (Postiga).
*West Ham U:* James; Stockdale (Ferdinand), Quinn, Horlock (Mellor), Kilgallon, Dailly, Carrick, Lee (Garcia), Hutchison, Defoe, Etherington.
*aet.*

**Wigan Ath (0) 1** *(Bullard 75)*
**Middlesbrough (1) 2** *(Maccarone 36, Mendieta 66)* 8046
*Wigan Ath:* Walsh; Eaden, Baines, Jarrett, Breckin, Jackson, Liddell (Teale), Bullard, Roberts, McCulloch (Ellington), Kennedy (Flynn).
*Middlesbrough:* Schwarzer; Mills, Queudrue, Southgate, Riggott, Boateng, Mendieta (Zenden), Juninho, Ricketts (Doriva), Maccarone (Nemeth), Greening.

---

## FOURTH ROUND

Tuesday, 2 December 2003

**Arsenal (1) 5** *(Aliadiere 24, 71, Kanu 68, Wiltord 79, Fabregas Soler 88)*
**Wolverhampton W (0) 1** *(Rae 81)* 28,161
*Arsenal:* Stack; Tavlaridis, Hoyte (Skulason), Vieira, Simek, Clichy, Fabregas Soler, Bentley (Smith), Kanu, Aliadiere (Papadopoulos), Wiltord.
*Wolverhampton W:* Marshall; Naylor, Craddock, Andrews (Sturridge), Butler, Gudjonsson, Rae, Ince, Blake, Miller (Kennedy), Camara (Newton).

**Southampton (1) 2** *(Beattie 33, 90 (pen))*
**Portsmouth (0) 0** 29,201
*Southampton:* Niemi; Dodd, Higginbotham, Delap, Lundekvam, Svensson M, Fernandes, Telfer, Beattie, Ormerod (Delgado), Marsden (Prutton).
*Portsmouth:* Srnicek; Zivkovic (Foxe), Taylor, Faye (Sherwood), De Zeeuw■, Stefanovic, Stone, Smertin, Yakubu, Sheringham, Berger.

Wednesday, 3 December 2003

**Aston Villa (1) 3** *(Symons 22 (og), McCann 70, Angel 79)*
**Crystal Palace (0) 0** 24,258
*Aston Villa:* Sorensen; De la Cruz, Samuel, McCann, Dublin (Ridgewell), Mellberg, Moore S, Hitzlsperger, Angel, Vassell (Allback), Barry (Whittingham).
*Crystal Palace:* Berthelin; Borrowdale, Fleming (Riihilahti), Derry (Watson), Popovic, Symons, Butterfield, Black (Routledge), Freedman, Shipperley, Hughes.

**Liverpool (0) 2** *(Murphy 66, Smicer 88)*
**Bolton W (1) 3** *(Jardel 4, Okocha 79, Djorkaeff 90 (pen))* 33,185
*Liverpool:* Dudek; Otsemobor, Riise, Diao, Biscan, Traore (Gerrard), Diouf (Kewell), Murphy, Heskey, Le Tallec (Sinama-Pongolle), Smicer.
*Bolton W:* Poole; Barness, Gardner, Campo, N'Gotty (Charlton), Emerson, Ba, Jardel (Davies), Pedersen, Djorkaeff (Nolan), Okocha.

**Middlesbrough (0) 0**
**Everton (0) 0** 18,568
*Middlesbrough:* Schwarzer; Mills, Queudrue, Southgate, Riggott, Boateng, Greening, Mendieta, Nemeth (Ricketts), Maccarone, Zenden.
*Everton:* Martyn; Unsworth, Naysmith, Stubbs, Hibbert, Li Tie (Linderoth), Carsley, Gravesen, Rooney (Radzinski), Jeffers (Osman), McFadden.
*aet; Middlesbrough won 5-4 on penalties.*

**Reading (0) 0**
**Chelsea (0) 1** *(Hasselbaink 57)* 24,107
*Reading:* Hahnemann; Murty, Shorey, Ingimarsson, Mackie, Watson, Savage, Sidwell, Forster, Hughes (Murray), Salako (Tyson).
*Chelsea:* Sullivan; Johnson, Babayaro, Lampard, Terry, Desailly, Geremi, Cole J (Makelele), Hasselbaink (Stanic), Crespo, Gronkjaer (Mutu).

**Tottenham H (2) 3** *(Anderton 9, Postiga 30, Kanoute 90)*
**Manchester C (0) 1** *(Fowler 80)* 31,727
*Tottenham H:* Keller; Carr, Taricco, Gardner, Doherty, King, Anderton, Poyet (Dalmat), Keane, Postiga (Kanoute), Ricketts (Konchesky).
*Manchester C:* Ellegaard; Dunne, Tarnat (McManaman), Sommeil, Distin, Barton, Wright-Phillips, Reyna, Anelka, Fowler, Sinclair.

**WBA (1) 2** *(Haas 6, Dobie 56)*
**Manchester U (0) 0** 25,282
*WBA:* Hoult; Haas, Clement, Gregan, Gaardsoe, Gilchrist, O'Connor, Johnson, Hulse (Dobie), Dichio (Sakiri), Koumas (Chambers A).
*Manchester U:* Carroll; Bardsley, Pugh, O'Shea, Butt, Tierney, Ronaldo (Eagles), Fletcher, Bellion, Kleberson (Nardiello), Richardson.

## FIFTH ROUND

Tuesday, 16 December 2003

**Bolton W (0) 1** *(Pedersen 115)*
**Southampton (0) 0** 13,957
*Bolton W:* Poole; Hunt (Barness), Gardner, Campo, N'Gotty, Charlton, Giannakopoulos (Djorkaeff), Ba, Pedersen, Davies (Jardel), Okocha.
*Southampton:* Niemi; Dodd, Higginbotham, Delap, Hall, Svensson M, Telfer, Pahars (McCann), Delgado (Marsden), Ormerod, Prutton.
*aet.*

**WBA (0) 0**
**Arsenal (1) 2** *(Kanu 25, Aliadiere 57)* 20,369
*WBA:* Hoult; Haas, Clement, Gregan, Gaardsoe, Volmer (Gilchrist), O'Connor (Sakiri), Wallwork, Hulse, Dobie, Johnson (Hughes).
*Arsenal:* Stack; Lauren, Clichy, Edu, Keown, Tavlaridis, Wiltord, Parlour, Aliadiere (Fabregas Soler), Kanu, Bentley (Thomas).

Wednesday, 17 December 2003

**Aston Villa (1) 2** *(Angel 16, McCann 78)*
**Chelsea (0) 1** *(Cole J 69)* 30,414
*Aston Villa:* Sorensen; Delaney, Samuel, McCann, Johnsen, Mellberg, Hendrie (Hitzlsperger), Barry, Angel (Crouch), Vassell (Moore S), Whittingham.
*Chelsea:* Sullivan; Johnson (Crespo), Babayaro, Makelele (Lampard), Terry, Gallas, Melchiot, Geremi, Hasselbaink, Cole J, Duff (Gronkjaer).

**Tottenham H (1) 1** *(Anderton 2)*
**Middlesbrough (0) 1** *(Ricketts 86)* 25,307
*Tottenham H:* Keller; Carr, Taricco, Gardner, Richards (Doherty), King, Anderton (Poyet), Ricketts (Dalmat), Keane, Kanoute, Konchesky.
*Middlesbrough:* Schwarzer; Mills, Queudrue, Southgate, Cooper (Nemeth), Boateng, Mendieta, Juninho, Ricketts, Maccarone (Downing), Zenden.
*aet; Middlesbrough won 5-4 on penalties.*

## SEMI-FINAL FIRST LEG

Tuesday, 20 January 2004

**Arsenal (0) 0**
**Middlesbrough (0) 1** *(Juninho 53)* 31,070
*Arsenal:* Stack; Toure, Clichy, Edu, Keown, Cygan, Parlour, Silva, Kanu, Owusu-Abeyie (Thomas), Bentley (Smith).
*Middlesbrough:* Schwarzer; Mills, Queudrue, Riggott, Ehiogu, Doriva, Mendieta (Parnaby), Boateng, Maccarone (Job), Juninho, Zenden.

Wednesday, 21 January 2004

**Bolton W (3) 5** *(Okocha 2, 80, Nolan 9, Giannakopoulos 17, N'Gotty 74)*
**Aston Villa (1) 2** *(Angel 20, 56)* 16,302
*Bolton W:* Jaaskelainen; Hunt, Barness (Charlton), Campo, N'Gotty, Emerson, Giannakopoulos (Pedersen), Nolan, Davies, Djorkaeff (Ba), Okocha.
*Aston Villa:* Sorensen; Delaney, Samuel, McCann, Dublin, Mellberg (Johnsen), Hendrie, Barry (Hitzlsperger), Angel, Vassell (Allback), Whittingham.

## SEMI-FINAL SECOND LEG

Tuesday, 27 January 2004

**Aston Villa (1) 2** *(Hitzlsperger 10, Samuel 88)*
**Bolton W (0) 0** 36,883
*Aston Villa:* Sorensen; Delaney, Samuel, McCann■, Dublin, Mellberg, Hendrie (Whittingham), Hitzlsperger, Crouch, Vassell, Barry.
*Bolton W:* Jaaskelainen; Hunt, Charlton (Barness), Campo, N'Gotty, Emerson, Giannakopoulos, Frandsen (Javi Moreno), Davies, Djorkaeff (Pedersen), Ba.

Tuesday, 3 February 2004

**Middlesbrough (0) 2** *(Zenden 69, Reyes 85 (og))*
**Arsenal (0) 1** *(Edu 77)* 28,781
*Middlesbrough:* Schwarzer; Mills, Queudrue, Southgate, Riggott, Doriva, Greening (Parnaby), Mendieta, Maccarone (Job), Juninho, Zenden.
*Arsenal:* Stack; Toure, Cole, Vieira, Keown■, Cygan, Parlour, Edu, Reyes, Bentley, Clichy (Owusu-Abeyie).

## FINAL (AT MILLENNIUM STADIUM)

Sunday, 29 February 2004

**Middlesbrough (2) 2** *(Job 2, Zenden 7 (pen))*
**Bolton W (1) 1** *(Davies 21)* 72,634
*Middlesbrough:* Schwarzer; Mills, Queudrue, Southgate, Ehiogu, Doriva, Mendieta, Boateng, Job (Ricketts), Juninho, Zenden.
*Bolton W:* Jaaskelainen; Hunt (Giannakopoulos), Charlton, Campo, N'Gotty, Emerson, Nolan (Javi Moreno), Frandsen (Pedersen), Davies, Djorkaeff, Okocha.
*Referee:* M. Riley (W. Yorkshire).

# FOOTBALL LEAGUE COMPETITION ATTENDANCES

## LEAGUE CUP ATTENDANCES

| *Season* | *Attendances* | *Games* | *Average* |
|---|---|---|---|
| 1960–61 | 1,204,580 | 112 | 10,755 |
| 1961–62 | 1,030,534 | 104 | 9,909 |
| 1962–63 | 1,029,893 | 102 | 10,097 |
| 1963–64 | 945,265 | 104 | 9,089 |
| 1964–65 | 962,802 | 98 | 9,825 |
| 1965–66 | 1,205,876 | 106 | 11,376 |
| 1966–67 | 1,394,553 | 118 | 11,818 |
| 1967–68 | 1,671,326 | 110 | 15,194 |
| 1968–69 | 2,064,647 | 118 | 17,497 |
| 1969–70 | 2,299,819 | 122 | 18,851 |
| 1970–71 | 2,035,315 | 116 | 17,546 |
| 1971–72 | 2,397,154 | 123 | 19,489 |
| 1972–73 | 1,935,474 | 120 | 16,129 |
| 1973–74 | 1,722,629 | 132 | 13,050 |
| 1974–75 | 1,901,094 | 127 | 14,969 |
| 1975–76 | 1,841,735 | 140 | 13,155 |
| 1976–77 | 2,236,636 | 147 | 15,215 |
| 1977–78 | 2,038,295 | 148 | 13,772 |
| 1978–79 | 1,825,643 | 139 | 13,134 |
| 1979–80 | 2,322,866 | 169 | 13,745 |
| 1980–81 | 2,051,576 | 161 | 12,743 |
| 1981–82 | 1,880,682 | 161 | 11,681 |
| 1982–83 | 1,679,756 | 160 | 10,498 |
| 1983–84 | 1,900,491 | 168 | 11,312 |
| 1984–85 | 1,876,429 | 167 | 11,236 |
| 1985–86 | 1,579,916 | 163 | 9,693 |
| 1986–87 | 1,531,498 | 157 | 9,755 |
| 1987–88 | 1,539,253 | 158 | 9,742 |
| 1988–89 | 1,552,780 | 162 | 9,585 |
| 1989–90 | 1,836,916 | 168 | 10,934 |
| 1990–91 | 1,675,496 | 159 | 10,538 |
| 1991–92 | 1,622,337 | 164 | 9,892 |
| 1992–93 | 1,558,031 | 161 | 9,677 |
| 1993–94 | 1,744,120 | 163 | 10,700 |
| 1994–95 | 1,530,478 | 157 | 9,748 |
| 1995–96 | 1,776,060 | 162 | 10,963 |
| 1996–97 | 1,529,321 | 163 | 9,382 |
| 1997–98 | 1,484,297 | 153 | 9,701 |
| 1998–99 | 1,555,856 | 153 | 10,169 |
| 1999–2000 | 1,354,233 | 153 | 8,851 |
| 2000–01 | 1,501,304 | 154 | 9,749 |
| 2001–02 | 1,076,390 | 93 | 11,574 |
| 2002-03 | 1,242,478 | 92 | 13,505 |

## CARLING CUP 2003–04

| *Round* | *Aggregate* | *Games* | *Average* |
|---|---|---|---|
| One | 232,377 | 38 | 6,115 |
| Two | 301,680 | 26 | 11,603 |
| Three | 356,502 | 16 | 22,281 |
| Four | 214,489 | 8 | 26,811 |
| Five | 90,047 | 4 | 22,512 |
| Semi-finals | 112,036 | 4 | 28,009 |
| Final | 72,634 | 1 | 72,634 |
| Total | 1,267,729 | 93 | 13,631 |

## LDV VANS TROPHY 2003–04

| *Round* | *Aggregate* | *Games* | *Average* |
|---|---|---|---|
| One | 64,842 | 28 | 2,316 |
| Two | 87,168 | 18 | 4,843 |
| Area Quarter-finals | 23,339 | 8 | 2,917 |
| Area Semi-finals | 24,858 | 4 | 6,215 |
| Area finals | 43,876 | 4 | 10,969 |
| Final | 34,031 | 4 | 34,031 |
| Total | 247,121 | 61 | 4,051 |

# FA CUP ATTENDANCES 1967–2004

| | *1st Round* | *2nd Round* | *3rd Round* | *4th Round* | *5th Round* | *6th Round* | *Semi-finals & Final* | *Total* | *No. of matches* | *Average per match* |
|---|---|---|---|---|---|---|---|---|---|---|
| 2003–04 | 162,738 | 117,967 | 624,732 | 347,964 | 292,521 | 156,780 | 167,401 | 1,870,103 | 149 | 12,551 |
| 2002–03 | 189,905 | 104,103 | 577,494 | 404,599 | 242,483 | 156,244 | 175,498 | 1,850,326 | 150 | 12,336 |
| 2001–02 | 198,369 | 119,781 | 566,284 | 330,434 | 249,190 | 173,757 | 171,278 | 1,809,093 | 148 | 12,224 |
| 2000–01 | 171,689 | 122,061 | 577,204 | 398,241 | 256,899 | 100,663 | 177,778 | 1,804,535 | 151 | 11,951 |
| 1999–2000 | 181,485 | 127,728 | 514,030 | 374,795 | 182,511 | 105,443 | 214,921 | 1,700,913 | 158 | 10,765 |
| 1998–99 | 191,954 | 132,341 | 609,486 | 431,613 | 359,398 | 181,005 | 202,150 | 2,107,947 | 155 | 13,599 |
| 1997–98 | 204,803 | 130,261 | 629,127 | 455,557 | 341,290 | 192,651 | 172,007 | 2,125,696 | 165 | 12,883 |
| 1996–97 | 209,521 | 122,324 | 651,139 | 402,293 | 199,873 | 67,035 | 191,813 | 1,843,998 | 151 | 12,211 |
| 1995–96 | 185,538 | 115,669 | 748,997 | 391,218 | 274,055 | 174,142 | 156,500 | 2,046,199 | 167 | 12,252 |
| 1994–95 | 219,511 | 125,629 | 640,017 | 438,596 | 257,650 | 159,787 | 174,059 | 2,015,249 | 161 | 12,517 |
| 1993–94 | 190,683 | 118,031 | 691,064 | 430,234 | 172,196 | 134,705 | 228,233 | 1,965,146 | 159 | 12,359 |
| 1992–93 | 241,968 | 174,702 | 612,494 | 377,211 | 198,379 | 149,675 | 293,241 | 2,047,670 | 161 | 12,718 |
| 1991–92 | 231,940 | 117,078 | 586,014 | 372,576 | 270,537 | 155,603 | 201,592 | 1,935,340 | 160 | 12,095 |
| 1990–91 | 194,195 | 121,450 | 594,592 | 530,279 | 276,112 | 124,826 | 196,434 | 2,038,518 | 162 | 12,583 |
| 1989–90 | 209,542 | 133,483 | 683,047 | 412,483 | 351,423 | 123,065 | 277,420 | 2,190,463 | 170 | 12,885 |
| 1988–89 | 212,775 | 121,326 | 690,199 | 421,255 | 206,781 | 176,629 | 167,353 | 1,966,318 | 164 | 12,173 |
| 1987–88 | 204,411 | 104,561 | 720,121 | 443,133 | 281,461 | 119,313 | 177,585 | 2,050,585 | 155 | 13,229 |
| 1986–87 | 209,290 | 146,761 | 593,520 | 349,342 | 263,550 | 119,396 | 195,533 | 1,877,400 | 165 | 11,378 |
| 1985–86 | 171,142 | 130,034 | 486,838 | 495,526 | 311,833 | 184,262 | 192,316 | 1,971,951 | 168 | 11,738 |
| 1984–85 | 174,604 | 137,078 | 616,229 | 320,772 | 269,232 | 148,690 | 242,754 | 1,909,359 | 157 | 12,162 |
| 1983–84 | 192,276 | 151,647 | 625,965 | 417,298 | 181,832 | 185,382 | 187,000 | 1,941,400 | 166 | 11,695 |
| 1982–83 | 191,312 | 150,046 | 670,503 | 452,688 | 260,069 | 193,845 | 291,162 | 2,209,625 | 154 | 14,348 |
| 1981–82 | 236,220 | 127,300 | 513,185 | 356,987 | 203,334 | 124,308 | 279,621 | 1,840,955 | 160 | 11,506 |
| 1980–81 | 246,824 | 194,502 | 832,578 | 534,402 | 320,530 | 288,714 | 339,250 | 2,756,800 | 169 | 16,312 |
| 1979–80 | 267,121 | 204,759 | 804,701 | 507,725 | 364,039 | 157,530 | 355,541 | 2,661,416 | 163 | 16,328 |
| 1978–79 | 243,773 | 185,343 | 880,345 | 537,748 | 243,683 | 263,213 | 249,897 | 2,604,002 | 166 | 15,687 |
| 1977–78 | 258,248 | 178,930 | 881,406 | 540,164 | 400,751 | 137,059 | 198,020 | 2,594,578 | 160 | 16,216 |
| 1976–77 | 379,230 | 192,159 | 942,523 | 631,265 | 373,330 | 205,379 | 258,216 | 2,982,102 | 174 | 17,139 |
| 1975–76 | 255,533 | 178,099 | 867,880 | 573,843 | 471,925 | 206,851 | 205,810 | 2,759,941 | 161 | 17,142 |
| 1974–75 | 283,956 | 170,466 | 914,994 | 646,434 | 393,323 | 268,361 | 291,369 | 2,968,903 | 172 | 17,261 |
| 1973–74 | 214,236 | 125,295 | 840,142 | 747,909 | 346,012 | 233,307 | 273,051 | 2,779,952 | 167 | 16,646 |
| 1972–73 | 259,432 | 169,114 | 938,741 | 735,825 | 357,386 | 241,934 | 226,543 | 2,928,975 | 160 | 18,306 |
| 1971–72 | 277,726 | 236,127 | 986,094 | 711,399 | 486,378 | 230,292 | 248,546 | 3,158,562 | 160 | 19,741 |
| 1970–71 | 329,687 | 230,942 | 956,683 | 757,852 | 360,687 | 304,937 | 279,644 | 3,220,432 | 162 | 19,879 |
| 1969–70 | 345,229 | 195,102 | 925,930 | 651,374 | 319,893 | 198,537 | 390,700 | 3,026,765 | 170 | 17,805 |
| 1968–69 | 331,858 | 252,710 | 1,094,043 | 883,675 | 464,915 | 188,121 | 216,232 | 3,431,554 | 157 | 21,857 |
| 1967–68 | 322,121 | 236,195 | 1,229,519 | 771,284 | 563,779 | 240,095 | 223,831 | 3,586,824 | 160 | 22,418 |

# LDV VANS TROPHY 2003–04

▪ *Denotes player sent off.*

## NORTHERN SECTION FIRST ROUND

Tuesday, 14 October 2003

**Blackpool (3) 3** *(Murphy 16, 35, 43)*
**Tranmere R (0) 2** *(Nicholson 78, Hume 80)* 2838
*Blackpool:* Barnes; Richardson, Hilton, Flynn, Clarke, Danns, Bullock (Wiles), Burns (Grayson), Murphy, Sheron, Douglas (McMahon).
*Tranmere R:* Achterberg; Connelly, Roberts, Gray, Allen, Loran (Nicholson), Dadi (Hume), Mellon, Haworth, Linwood, Jones (Navarro).

**Carlisle U (1) 2** *(Rundle 36, Wake 89)*
**Rochdale (0) 0** 1828
*Carlisle U:* Glennon; Shelley, Byrne, Andrews, Livingstone, McDonagh, Billy, McGill, Foran (Farrell), Henderson (Wake), Rundle.
*Rochdale:* Edwards; Evans, Simpkins, Brannan, Griffiths, Grand, Bertos, McClare, Patterson (Antoine-Curier), Townson, Doughty (McCourt).

**Chester C (0) 0**
**Doncaster R (0) 1** *(Tierney 62)* 1141
*Chester C:* Brown; Collins, McIntyre, Harris, Guyett, Carey (Dogun▪), Brady, Twiss (Buckley), Rapley, Foster (Beesley), Heard.
*Doncaster R:* Richardson; Price, Albrighton, Morley (Maloney), Beech, Ravenhill, Tierney, Doolan, Gill (Fortune-West), Barnes, McIndoe.

**Chesterfield (2) 2** *(Cade 6, Robinson 15)*
**Macclesfield T (1) 1** *(Adams 16)* 1631
*Chesterfield:* Muggleton; Davies, O'Hare, Evatt (Allott), Blatherwick, Payne, Brandon, Hudson, Robinson (Reeves), Cade (Innes), De Bolla.
*Macclesfield T:* Wilson; Abbey, Adams (Priest), Welch (Miles), Macauley, Munroe, Widdrington, Flitcroft (Beresford), Tipton, Carruthers, Whitaker.

**Darlington (0) 1** *(Sheeran 81)*
**Hull C (2) 3** *(France 36, Forrester 45, Williams 82)* 1578
*Darlington:* Price; McGurk, Valentine, Liddle, Hutchinson, Bossy (Convery), Morgan, Nicholls (Coghlan), Clarke, Maddison, Clark (Sheeran).
*Hull C:* Fettis; Regan, Smith (Peat), France, Strong, Burton, Melton, Keates, Forrester (Donaldson), Webb, Williams.

**Halifax T (1) 2** *(Mallon 31, Quinn 79)*
**York C (0) 1** *(Dunning 70 (pen))* 1148
*Halifax T:* Cartwright; Hockenhull, Sandwith, Bushell, Quinn, Dudgeon▪, Mallon, Hudson, Killeen (Senior), Sagare (Tozer), Elam (Midgley).
*York C:* Ovendale; Cooper, Downer, Hope (Merris), Smith, Wise, Brackstone, Dunning, Parkin, Wilford (Nogan), Dove (George).

**Lincoln C (1) 3** *(Green 10, Richardson 72, Bailey 84)*
**Telford U (0) 1** *(Mills 54)* 1503
*Lincoln C:* Marriott; Bailey, Mayo, Weaver, Bloomer, Futcher, Frecklington (Sedgemore), Butcher (Willis), Fletcher (Yeo), Richardson, Green.
*Telford U:* MacKenzie; Clarke (Grant), Whitehead, Murphy, Green, Challis (Blackwood), Williams, Simpson, Mills, Naylor (Rowe), Ricketts.

**Mansfield T (0) 1** *(Day 59)*
**Stockport Co (1) 2** *(Barlow 11, 85)* 3718
*Mansfield T:* Pilkington; Buxton, Clarke, Williamson, Baptiste, Day, MacKenzie, Disley (Artell), Beardsley (White A), Larkin, Corden.
*Stockport Co:* Spencer; Hardiker, Goodwin, Challinor, Clare, Jones (McLachlan), Gibb, Ellison (Welsh), Wilbraham, Barlow, Pemberton.

**Oldham Ath (2) 3** *(Zola 6, Vernon 22, Boshell 71)*
**Hartlepool U (1) 3** *(Williams E 12, Clarke 59, 90)* 3575
*Oldham Ath:* Pogliacomi; Clegg, Sheridan D, Tierney, Hudson, Beharall, Murray (Holden), Boshell, Vernon, Zola (O'Halloran), Cooksey (Roca).
*Hartlepool U:* Williams A; Barron, Robinson M, Nelson, Westwood, Tinkler, Clarke, Humphreys, Williams E (Robinson P), Gabbiadini (Boyd), Strachan.
*aet; Oldham Ath won 5-3 on penalties.*

**Scarborough (0) 2** *(Senior 77, Kelly 89)*
**Port Vale (1) 1** *(McPhee 29)* 1003
*Scarborough:* Walker; Lyth (McSweeney), Baker, Kerr, Hotte, Price, Kelly, Senior, Marcelle, Blackman (Graydon), Gill.
*Port Vale:* Brain; Cummins, Armstrong (Boyd), Brightwell, Rowland, Pilkington, Brisco, Littlejohn, McPhee, Paynter, Bridge-Wilkinson.

**Scunthorpe U (0) 2** *(Jackson 75, Kell 89)*
**Shrewsbury T (1) 1** *(Lowe 18)* 1265
*Scunthorpe U:* Russell; Stanton, Sharp, Kell, Butler, Byrne (Jackson), Sparrow, Calvo-Garcia (Barwick), MacLean (Torpey), Hayes, Beagrie.
*Shrewsbury T:* Howie; Moss, Rioch, Tolley J, Tinson, Ridler, Bell, O'Connor, Watts (Cramb), Lowe, Aiston (Fitzpatrick).

**Wrexham (1) 4** *(Jones L 37, 51 (pen), 54, Sam 64 (pen))*
**Morecambe (0) 1** *(Morgan 72 (og))* 1078
*Wrexham:* Whitfield; Edwards C (Thomas), Edwards P, Lawrence, Roberts, Morgan, Whitley, Ferguson (Crowell), Jones L (Jones M), Sam, Llewellyn.
*Morecambe:* Mawson; Lane, Walmsley, Murphy▪, Swan, Perkins (McKearney), Thompson (Rogan), Collins, Rigoglioso, Sugden (Carlton), Howell.

Wednesday, 15 October 2003

**Notts Co (0) 0**
**Barnsley (0) 0** 1220
*Notts Co:* Mildenhall; Bolland, Nicholson, Livesey, Fenton (Barras), McFaul (Baraclough), Baldry, Brough (Caskey), Hackworth, Heffernan, Jenkins.
*Barnsley:* Ilic; Crooks, Gallimore, Kay, Handyside (Austin), Ireland, Betsy, Lumsdon, Fallon (Rankin), Gorre (Carson), O'Callaghan.
*aet; Barnsley won 4-2 on penalties.*

**Sheffield W (0) 1** *(Proudlock 71)*
**Grimsby T (1) 1** *(Mansaram 2)* 7323
*Sheffield W:* Pressman; Geary, Barry-Murphy, Bromby, Lee, Wood, Haslam, Reddy (Holt), Proudlock, N'Dumbu Nsungu (Shaw J), Beswetherick.
*Grimsby T:* Davison; Crowe, Barnard, Hamilton, Edwards, Ford (Young), Cas (Campbell), Daws, Mansaram (Boulding), Onuora, Anderson.
*aet; Sheffield W won 5-4 on penalties.*

## SOUTHERN SECTION FIRST ROUND

Monday, 13 October 2003

**Brighton & HA (1) 2** *(Knight 36, Robinson 88)*
**Forest Green R (0) 0** 3969
*Brighton & HA:* Kuipers; Watson, Mayo, Pethick, Butters, Carpenter, Hart, Rehman, Knight (Robinson), McPhee, Jones N (Harding).
*Forest Green R:* Perrin; Phillips, Searle, Foster, Ingram, Richardson, Kennedy (Rogers), Owers, Grayson, Moralee (Jones L), Stoker.

Tuesday, 14 October 2003

**Barnet (2) 3** *(Lopez 6, Henry 34 (pen), Hatch 104)*
**Brentford (0) 3** *(Tabb 52, 98, Hunt 85 (pen))* 1248
*Barnet:* Gore; Rooney, King, Baimass, Cumberbatch▪, Sylla (Hatch), Lopez, Hogg, Henry (Freeman), Roach, Taggart.

*Brentford:* Smith P; Dobson, Frampton (Smith J), Roget, Kitamirike, Evans, Rougier (Hutchinson), Tabb, May■, Olugbodi (O'Connor), Hunt.
*aet; Brentford won 3-1 on penalties.*

**Cheltenham T (1) 1** *(Devaney 18)*
**Colchester U (1) 3** *(Keith 41, Vine 65, 88)* 1324
*Cheltenham T:* Higgs; Bird (Odejayi), Victory, Finnigan, Duff S (Dobson), Fyfe, Cleverley, Yates, Taylor (Spencer), Devaney, McCann.
*Colchester U:* Brown S; Halford (Baldwin), Myers (Stockley), Pinault, Fitzgerald, Chilvers, Duguid, Bowry (Vine), Fagan, McGleish, Keith.

**Peterborough U (2) 3** *(Burton 18 (pen), Clarke A 31, Farrell 97)*
**Torquay U (2) 2** *(Wills 29, Benefield 38)* 1980
*Peterborough U:* Tyler; Kanu, Jelleyman, Woodhouse (Gill), St Ledger, Burton, Newton, Thomson, Clarke A, Willock (Fotiadis), Farrell.
*Torquay U:* Dearden; Hockley, Benefield, Taylor, Williamson, Woods, Russell, Broad, Bedeau (Osei-Kuffour), Fowler (Killoughery), Wills (Graham).
*aet; Peterborough U won on slow death.*

**Plymouth Arg (2) 4** *(Keith 10, Lowndes 45, 86, Gilbert 55)*
**Bristol C (0) 0** 4927
*Plymouth Arg:* McCormick; Worrell, Gilbert, Friio (Hodges), Aljofree, Wotton, Adams, Bent, Stonebridge (Sturrock), Lowndes, Keith (Capaldi).
*Bristol C:* Stowell; Carey, Woodman, Burnell (Matthews), Butler (Hill), Coles, Lita, Doherty, Peacock (Hulbert), Roberts, Brown A.

**QPR (1) 2** *(Pacquette 40, Gnohere 81)*
**Kidderminster H (0) 0** 3671
*QPR:* Culkin; Barton, Padula, Bean, Forbes, Gnohere, Rowlands, Pacquette (Thorpe), Sabin, Oli (Gallen), Bircham (Palmer).
*Kidderminster H:* Brock; Stamps, Shilton (Bennett), Coleman, Hinton, Smith, Melligan (Lewis), Gadsby (Parrish), Ward, Williams J, Williams D.

**Southend U (1) 2** *(Constantine 39, Gower 110)*
**Bristol R (1) 1** *(Haldane 36)* 1714
*Southend U:* Flahavan; Jupp, Jenkins, Maher, McSweeney, Stuart, Fullarton, Kightly (Husbands), Bramble (Broughton), Constantine, Gower.
*Bristol R:* Miller; Boxall (Uddin), Anderson, Edwards, Barrett, Quinn (Street), Carlisle, Hyde, Tait, Haldane (Rammell), Savage.
*aet.*

**Stevenage B (0) 0**
**Luton T (0) 1** *(Judge 90)* 1754
*Stevenage B:* Westhead; Warner, Travis, Gould (Flynn), Laker, Costello (Maamria), Wormull, Holloway, Battersby, Elding, Richards (Cook).
*Luton T:* Brill; Hillier, Davis (Deeney), Robinson, Barnett, Coyne, Leary, Mansell, Showunmi, Brkovic, Okai (Judge).

**Wycombe W (1) 1** *(Branston 20)*
**Cambridge U (0) 0** 977
*Wycombe W:* Talia; Senda, Vinnicombe, Bulman (Cook), Thomson, Johnson (Brown), Currie, Simpson, Branston, Bell, Ryan.
*Cambridge U:* Marshall; Tann, Bridges (Nacca), Duncan, Angus, Murray, Tudor, Guttridge, Opara (Turner), Taylor, Walker.

**Yeovil T (0) 2** *(Edwards 74, Williams 86 (pen))*
**Bournemouth (0) 0** 5035
*Yeovil T:* Collis; Williams, El Kholti (Gosling), Lockwood (Terry), Rodrigues, Pluck, Skiverton, Way, Edwards (Stansfield), Gall, Johnson.
*Bournemouth:* Stewart; Young (Hayter), Purches, Tindall, Fletcher C, Browning (Broadhurst), Elliott, O'Connor, Feeney, Holmes (Fletcher S), Thomas.

Wednesday, 15 October 2003

**Boston U (1) 2** *(Beevers 16, Akinfenwa 90)*
**Swindon T (1) 1** *(Robinson 31)* 1514
*Boston U:* Bastock; Hogg, Beevers, Hocking, Ellender, Bennett, Thompson L (Brough), Clarke, Weatherstone (Duffield), Akinfenwa, Angel.
*Swindon T:* Griemink; Herring, Nicholas, Viveash, Reeves, Ruster (Duke), Pook (Garrard), Robinson, Howard, Smith (Martin), Stevenson.

**Dagenham & R (0) 4** *(Bentley 49, 69, Scully 55, Braithwaite 66)*
**Leyton Orient (0) 1** *(Lockwood 76 (pen))* 1857
*Dagenham & R:* Roberts; Janney (McGowan), Mustafa, Vickers, Beckwith, Hill, Scully, Bentley, Braithwaite, Meechan (Shipp), Kimble.
*Leyton Orient:* Harrison; Hunt, Lockwood, Ebdon, Peters, McGhee, Purser, Forbes (Thorpe), Tate (Alexander), Ibehre, McCormack (Jones).

**Oxford U (0) 0**
**Rushden & D (1) 1** *(Gray 38 (pen))* 2510
*Oxford U:* Woodman; McNiven, Robinson, Bound (Omoyinmi), Crosby, Ashton, Townsley, Brown, Louis, Hackett, Waterman.
*Rushden & D:* Evans; Bignot (Sambrook), Underwood, Bell, Dempster, Edwards, Hanlon, Mills, Kitson (Story), Jack (Burgess), Gray.

Tuesday, 21 October 2003

**Hereford U (0) 2** *(Brown 46, Guinan 87)*
**Exeter C (0) 0** 1513
*Hereford U:* Baker; Green, Rose, King, Mkandawire, Teesdale, Williams (Craven), Parry, Guinan, Brown (Carey-Bertram), Pitman.
*Exeter C:* Rice; Duncan (Afful), Jeannin, Cronin, Gaia (Reed), Moxey, McConnell, Taylor, Flack, Canham, Sheldon.

## NORTHERN SECTION SECOND ROUND

Monday, 3 November 2003

**Bury (1) 2** *(Preece 6, Thompson 78)*
**Oldham Ath (0) 1** *(Vernon 90)* 3102
*Bury:* Garner; Thompson, Unsworth, Whelan, Swailes, Woodthorpe, Connell, Dunfield, Preece, O'Neill, Kennedy (Whaley).
*Oldham Ath:* Pogliacomi; Clegg, Sheridan D, Hall D, Beharall, Holden, O'Halloran (Roca), Boshell (Murray), Vernon, Zola, Eyre (Cooksey).

Tuesday, 4 November 2003

**Blackpool (0) 1** *(Sheron 83)*
**Doncaster R (0) 0** 2954
*Blackpool:* Jones B; Richardson, Evans, Southern, Flynn, Clarke, Wellens, Bullock, Sheron, Taylor, Coid (Burns).
*Doncaster R:* Richardson; Marples, Morley, Foster, Ryan, Green, McGrath, Ravenhill, Gill (Burton), Barnes, McIndoe.

**Carlisle U (2) 2** *(Schumacher 3, Wake 15)*
**Huddersfield T (0) 0** 1346
*Carlisle U:* Glennon; Shelley, Kelly, Schumacher (Russell), Livingstone (Jack), Andrews, Billy, McDonagh, Farrell, Wake, McGill.
*Huddersfield T:* Gray; Holdsworth, Scott, Mirfin (Sodje), Hughes, Holland, Worthington (Brown), Schofield, Booth, Stead, Lloyd.

**Hull C (0) 1** *(Webb 65)*
**Scunthorpe U (1) 3** *(Torpey 14, Sparrow 80, MacLean 90)* 6656
*Hull C:* Fettis; Joseph (Hinds), Peat, Strong, Whittle, Holt, Price (Donaldson), Melton, Webb, France (Fry), Keates.
*Scunthorpe U:* Evans; Jackson, Sharp, Barwick, Butler, Byrne, Sparrow, Kilford (Kell), MacLean, Torpey, Beagrie (Ridley).

**Lincoln C (1) 4** *(Fletcher 11, 95, Yeo 47, Mayo 85 (pen))*
**Chesterfield (1) 3** *(Brandon 34, 68, Warhurst 53)* 2395
*Lincoln C:* Marriott; Liburd, Mayo, Weaver, Bloomer, Futcher, Sedgemore (Frecklington), Butcher, Fletcher (Wattley), Yeo (May), Green.
*Chesterfield:* Richmond; Uhlenbeek, O'Hare, Howson (Allott), Blatherwick, Payne, Brandon, Hudson (Evatt), Reeves (Cade), Robinson, Warhurst.
*aet; Lincoln C won on slow death.*

**Scarborough (0) 0**
**Halifax T (0) 1** *(Midgley 64 (pen))* 699
*Scarborough:* Walker; Baker, Capper, Kerr, Redmile, Cryan, Kelly, Sestanovich (Senior), Quayle (Gill), Marcelle (Bachelor), Rose.
*Halifax T:* Cartwright; Hockenhull, Sandwith, Dudgeon, Quinn, Bushell, Mallon, Hudson, Lee, Sagare (Killeen), Midgley.

Wednesday, 5 November 2003

**Stockport Co (2) 5** *(Barlow 21, Lambert 39, Morrison 72, Williams C 78, Goodwin 98 (pen))*
**Wrexham (2) 4** *(Jones M 9, Holmes 42, Sam 48, Armstrong 61)* 1469
*Stockport Co:* Spencer; Hardiker, Jackman (Pemberton), Goodwin, Heath (Challinor), Clare, Lescott (Morrison), Lambert, Williams C, Barlow, Welsh.
*Wrexham:* Whitfield; Barrett, Holmes, Morgan, Pejic, Roberts (McNulty), Thomas, Jones M, Armstrong, Sam (Llewellyn), Crowell.
*aet; Stockport Co won on slow death.*

Wednesday, 12 November 2003

**Sheffield W (0) 1** *(Reddy 90)*
**Barnsley (0) 0** 13,575
*Sheffield W:* Pressman; Geary, Barry-Murphy, Lee (Cooke) (N'Dumbu Nsungu), Smith D, Bromby, Mustoe, McLaren (Haslam), Owusu, Proudlock, Reddy.
*Barnsley:* Ilic; O'Callaghan, Gallimore, Kay, Crooks, Ireland, Burns, Hayward (Lumsdon), Rankin, Betsy, Carson (Walters).

## SOUTHERN SECTION SECOND ROUND

Tuesday, 4 November 2003

**Brighton & HA (1) 3** *(Carpenter 23, McPhee 93, 105 (pen))*
**Boston U (0) 1** *(Duffield 81)* 4026
*Brighton & HA:* Roberts, Hinshelwood, Mayo, El-Abd, Butters, Carpenter, Hart (Piercy), Pethick, Knight (Marney), McPhee, Jones N.
*Boston U:* Bastock; Hogg (Chapman), Beevers, Hocking, Greaves (Sutch), Ellender, Clarke (Potter), Redfearn, Duffield, Weatherstone, Thompson L.
*aet; Brighton & HA won on slow death.*

**Hereford U (0) 1** *(Brown 87)*
**Northampton T (0) 1** *(Dudfield 75)* 1517
*Hereford U:* Baker; Green, Rose, Craven (Teesdale), Mkandawire, James, Smith (King), Purdey (Harrhy), Guinan, Brown, Pitman.
*Northampton T:* Harper; Lyttle, Carruthers, Chambers, Willmott, Harsley (Trollope), Low, Richards (Dudfield), Walker, Asamoah (Smith), Reeves.
*aet; Northampton T won 4-3 on penalties.*

**Peterborough U (1) 3** *(Logan 22, McKenzie 81, 86)*
**Brentford (1) 2** *(Dobson 37, Hunt 90 (pen))* 1821
*Peterborough U:* Tyler; Kanu, Jelleyman, Arber, Rea (Legg), Woodhouse, Willock (Newton), Thomson, Logan (Fotiadis), McKenzie, Farrell.
*Brentford:* Smith P; Dobson (Allen-Page), Somner (Olugbodi), Frampton, Kitamirike (Hughes), Evans, Smith J, O'Connor, Peters, Harrold, Hunt.

**Plymouth Arg (2) 2** *(Coughlan 22, Evans 34)*
**Wycombe W (2) 2** *(McSporran 8, 15)* 4298
*Plymouth Arg:* McCormick; Worrell, Gilbert, Friio, Wotton, Coughlan, Hodges (Capaldi), Bent, Stonebridge (Lowndes), Evans, Keith (Norris).
*Wycombe W:* Talia; Senda, Vinnicombe, Bulman, Branston■, Johnson (Brown), Currie (Thomson), Simpson, McSporran, Roberts, Mapes (Ryan).
*aet; Wycombe W won 4-2 on penalties.*

**QPR (1) 2** *(Padula 38, McLeod 82)*
**Dagenham & R (0) 1** *(Scully 87)* 4464
*QPR:* Culkin; Barton (Edghill), Padula, Palmer, Forbes, Carlisle, Ainsworth, Bean (Gallen), Sabin, Pacquette (Thorpe), McLeod.
*Dagenham & R:* Roberts; Mustafa, Vickers, Cole, Matthews (Kimble), Hill, Scully, Bentley, Janney (Piper C), Braithwaite, Bruce (Meechan).

**Rushden & D (1) 1** *(Jack 23)*
**Luton T (2) 2** *(Showunmi 7, Leary 18 (pen))* 2746
*Rushden & D:* Evans; Bignot, Underwood, Hanlon, Dempster, Edwards, Gray, Mills (Hall), Kitson, Jack, Burgess (Talbot).
*Luton T:* Brill; Hillier, Davis■, Crowe, Barnett, Keane, Leary, O'Leary (Davies), Showunmi, Mansell, Brkovic.

**Swansea C (0) 1** *(Nardiello 90)*
**Southend U (0) 2** *(Bramble 70, Corbett 78)* 2055
*Swansea C:* Murphy; Duffy, Howard, Jones S, Tate, Coates, Durkan, Jones R (Jenkins), Thomas (Trundle), Nardiello, Wilson.
*Southend U:* Flahavan; McSweeney, Wilson (Constantine), Maher, Cort, Hunt, Gower, Smith, Bramble (Broughton), Corbett, Jenkins.

**Yeovil T (1) 2** *(Edwards 11, Gall 66)*
**Colchester U (1) 2** *(Andrews 41, McGleish 77)* 3052
*Yeovil T:* Weale; Williams, Crittenden, Lockwood, Skiverton (Gosling), Pluck (Reed), Terry, Way, Edwards (Stansfield), Gall, Johnson.
*Colchester U:* Brown S; Stockley, Halford (McGleish), Pinault, Fitzgerald (Baldwin), White, Bowry (Johnson R), Fagan, Andrews, Vine, Keith.
*aet; Colchester U won 4-2 on penalties.*

## NORTHERN SECTION QUARTER-FINALS

Tuesday, 9 December 2003

**Bury (0) 0**
**Scunthorpe U (0) 1** *(Hayes 99)* 1246
*Bury:* Garner; Unsworth, Woodthorpe (Gunby), Barrass, Swailes, Thompson, Clegg, Dunfield, Porter (O'Neill), Preece (Nugent), Connell.
*Scunthorpe U:* Evans; Barwick (Graves), Sharp, Byrne, Butler, McCombe, Sparrow, Kell, MacLean (Hayes), Torpey, Beagrie (Featherstone).
*aet; Scunthorpe U won on slow death.*

**Carlisle U (0) 0**
**Sheffield W (1) 3** *(Lee 45, Robins 77, 84)* 2869
*Carlisle U:* Glennon; Shelley, Arnison, McDonagh, Andrews, Raven, Russell (Simpson), McGill, Foran, Henderson (Molloy), Billy.
*Sheffield W:* Pressman; Geary, Barry-Murphy, Haslam, Lee, Bromby, Wilson, N'Dumbu Nsungu (Beswetherick), Robins (Owusu), Holt (Proudlock), Reddy.

**Stockport Co (0) 0**
**Blackpool (0) 1** *(Blinkhorn 109)* 2337
*Stockport Co:* Myhill; Hardiker (Morrison), Jackman, Goodwin (Lescott), Heath, Challinor, Gibb, Lambert, Wilbraham, Williams C (Barlow), Welsh.
*Blackpool:* Jones B; Grayson, Richardson (McMahon), Southern (Davis), Flynn, Burns, Evans, Bullock, Sheron (Blinkhorn), Taylor, Elliott.
*aet.*

Tuesday, 16 December 2003

**Halifax T (1) 1** *(Sandwith 21)*
**Lincoln C (0) 0** 1162
*Halifax T:* Cartwright; Yates, Sandwith, Bushell (Hudson), Dudgeon, Colley, Mallon, Owen, Sagare, Farrell (Allan), Midgley (Hockenhull).

*Lincoln C:* Marriott; Bailey (Bloomer), Mayo, Butcher, Morgan, Futcher, Liburd (Sedgemore), McNamara (Pearce), Cropper, Yeo, Gain.

## SOUTHERN SECTION QUARTER-FINALS

Sunday, 7 December 2003

**QPR (2) 2** *(Palmer 18, Thorpe 23)*
**Brighton & HA (0) 1** *(McPhee 79)* 7535
*QPR:* Culkin; Forbes, Edghill (Rose), Palmer, Shittu, Carlisle, Ainsworth (Furlong), Bean, Gallen, Thorpe, Rowlands.
*Brighton & HA:* Roberts; El-Abd, Mayo, Pethick, Butters, Carpenter (McPhee), Rehman, Yeates, Knight, Lee (Hart), Harding (Jones N).

Tuesday, 9 December 2003

**Northampton T (0) 2** *(Low 52, Dudfield 100)*
**Peterborough U (0) 1** *(McKenzie 90)* 4290
*Northampton T:* Harper; Lyttle, Sadler, Lincoln (Dudfield), Willmott, Sampson, Low (Reid), Richards (Reeves), Walker, Smith, Hargreaves.
*Peterborough U:* Tyler; Gill, Jelleyman, Arber, Burton, Woodhouse, Newton, Thomson (Kanu), Clarke A (Logan), McKenzie, Farrell (Legg).
*aet; Northampton T won on slow death.*

**Southend U (2) 3** *(Constantine 2, Kightly 27, Broughton 84)*
**Luton T (0) 0** 2027
*Southend U:* Flahavan; McSweeney, Wilson, Maher, Cort, Hunt, Kightly (Husbands), Smith, Bramble (Broughton), Constantine, Gower (Clark).
*Luton T:* Beresford; Deeney (Leary), Davis, Spring, Hillier, Coyne, Mansell (Forbes), Robinson, Howard, Crowe (Showunmi), Holmes.

**Wycombe W (1) 2** *(Thomson 22, Johnson 69)*
**Colchester U (2) 3** *(McGleish 8, 33, Brown J 120)* 1873
*Wycombe W:* Williams; Reilly, Roberts (Faulconbridge), Thomson, Rogers, Johnson, Currie, Simpson, McSporran, Holligan, Simpemba.
*Colchester U:* Brown S; Stockley, Myers, Johnson G (Bowry) (Brown J), White, Chilvers, Duguid, Izzet, Andrews (Keith), McGleish, Vine.
*aet.*

## NORTHERN SECTION SEMI-FINALS

Tuesday, 20 January 2004

**Blackpool (2) 3** *(Sheron 24, Coid 45, Taylor 54)*
**Halifax T (2) 2** *(Killeen 19, Owen 34)* 4764
*Blackpool:* Jones L; Grayson, Hilton (Evans), McMahon, Davis, Elliott, Wellens (Burns), Bullock, Sheron (Flynn), Taylor, Coid.
*Halifax T:* Cartwright; Sandwith, Hockenhull, Monington, Colley, Owen, Mallon (Lee), Bushell, Killeen, Sagare (Farrell), Midgley (Quinn).

**Sheffield W (2) 4** *(Robins 7, 71, Proudlock 32, 49)*
**Scunthorpe U (0) 0** 10,236
*Sheffield W:* Lucas; Geary (McMahon), Barry-Murphy, Armstrong, Smith D, Haslam, N'Dumbu Nsungu, Smith P, Robins (Holt), Proudlock (Shaw J), Quinn.
*Scunthorpe U:* Evans; Stanton, Sharp, Barwick (Kell), Gulliver, Byrne, Sparrow, Kilford (Featherstone), Taylor (Hayes), Torpey, Graves.

## SOUTHERN SECTION SEMI-FINALS

Tuesday, 20 January 2004

**Northampton T (1) 2** *(Walker 14, 51)*
**Colchester U (0) 3** *(McGleish 61, 86, 95)* 4034
*Northampton T:* Harper; Lyttle, Carruthers, Sampson■, Willmott, Reid (Harsley), Trollope, Asamoah (Abidallah) (Richards), Walker, Smith, Hargreaves.
*Colchester U:* McKinney; Stockley, Keith, Pinault, White, Chilvers, Halford (McGleish), Izzet, Andrews, Fagan, Vine.
*aet; Colchester U won on slow death.*

**Southend U (1) 4** *(Constantine 12, Clark 67, Broughton 69, 79)*
**QPR (0) 0** 5824
*Southend U:* Flahavan; Jupp, Stuart (Wilson), Maher, Cort, Warren, Clark (Kightly), Smith, Broughton, Constantine, Gower (Jenkins).
*QPR:* Day; Forbes, Padula, Bircham (Palmer), Shittu, Carlisle, Rose, Rowlands, Furlong, Gallen (Oli), Marney (Sabin).

## NORTHERN FINAL FIRST LEG

Tuesday, 10 February 2004

**Blackpool (0) 1** *(Taylor 82)*
**Sheffield W (0) 0** 7482
*Blackpool:* Jones L; Richardson, Evans (Southern), Dinning, Flynn, Elliott, Wellens, Bullock (Blinkhorn), Sheron, Taylor, Coid.
*Sheffield W:* Tidman; Geary, Barry-Murphy, Bromby (Wood), Smith D, Haslam, N'Dumbu Nsungu, Smith P, Robins (Olsen), Proudlock, Armstrong.

## NORTHERN FINAL SECOND LEG

Wednesday, 25 February 2004

**Sheffield W (0) 0**
**Blackpool (2) 2** *(Sheron 20, Southern 31)* 21,390
*Sheffield W:* Tidman (Poulter); Haslam, Barry-Murphy, Bromby, Smith D, Wood, Chambers, Shaw J, Olsen, N'Dumbu Nsungu, Quinn.
*Blackpool:* Jones L; Grayson, Evans, Richardson, Flynn, Elliott, McMahon, Southern, Sheron (Bullock), Murphy (Blinkhorn), Dinning (Hessey).

## SOUTHERN FINAL FIRST LEG

Tuesday, 10 February 2004

**Colchester U (1) 2** *(Pinault 7, Andrews 75)*
**Southend U (2) 3** *(Constantine 17, Broughton 42, Bramble 68)* 5401
*Colchester U:* Brown S; Stockley, Tierney (Andrews), Pinault, White, Chilvers, Duguid, Izzet, Vine, McGleish, Keith.
*Southend U:* Flahavan; Jupp, Stuart, Maher, Cort, Warren, Constantine (Clark), Hunt (Wilson), Broughton■, Bramble (Pettefer), Gower.

## SOUTHERN FINAL SECOND LEG

Tuesday, 17 February 2004

**Southend U (1) 1** *(Broughton 45)*
**Colchester U (1) 1** *(Izzet 3)* 9603
*Southend U:* Flahavan; Jupp, Stuart, Maher, Cort, Warren, Constantine, Hunt, Broughton, Bramble, Gower (Pettefer).
*Colchester U:* Brown S; Stockley (Johnson G), Halford (Vine), Pinault, White, Chilvers (Brown W), Duguid, Izzet, Fagan, McGleish, Keith.

## FINAL (AT MILLENNIUM STADIUM)

Sunday, 21 March 2004

**Blackpool (1) 2** *(Murphy 2, Coid 55)*
**Southend U (0) 0** 34,031
*Blackpool:* Jones L; Grayson, Jaszczun, Dinning, Flynn, Elliott, Wellens (McMahon), Bullock (Richardson), Murphy, Sheron (Blinkhorn), Coid.
*Southend U:* Flahavan; Jupp, Wilson (Bramble), Maher, Cort, Warren, Pettefer, Hunt, Broughton, Constantine, Gower (Jenkins).
*Referee:* R. Pearson (Peterlee).

# FA CUP FINALS 1872–2004

| | | | |
|---|---|---|---|
| 1872 and 1874–92 | Kennington Oval | 1910 | Replay at Everton |
| 1873 | Lillie Bridge | 1911 | Replay at Old Trafford |
| 1886 | Replay at Derby (Racecourse Ground) | 1912 | Replay at Bramall Lane |
| | | 1915 | Old Trafford, Manchester |
| 1893 | Fallowfield, Manchester | 1920–22 | Stamford Bridge |
| 1894 | Everton | 1923 to 2000 | Wembley |
| 1895–1914 | Crystal Palace | 1970 | Replay at Old Trafford |
| 1901 | Replay at Bolton | 2001 to date | Millennium Stadium, Cardiff |

| *Year* | *Winners* | *Runners-up* | *Score* |
|---|---|---|---|
| 1872 | Wanderers | Royal Engineers | 1-0 |
| 1873 | Wanderers | Oxford University | 2-0 |
| 1874 | Oxford University | Royal Engineers | 2-0 |
| 1875 | Royal Engineers | Old Etonians | 2-0 (after 1-1 draw aet) |
| 1876 | Wanderers | Old Etonians | 3-0 (after 1-1 draw aet) |
| 1877 | Wanderers | Oxford University | 2-1 (aet) |
| 1878 | Wanderers* | Royal Engineers | 3-1 |
| 1879 | Old Etonians | Clapham R | 1-0 |
| 1880 | Clapham R | Oxford University | 1-0 |
| 1881 | Old Carthusians | Old Etonians | 3-0 |
| 1882 | Old Etonians | Blackburn R | 1-0 |
| 1883 | Blackburn Olympic | Old Etonians | 2-1 (aet) |
| 1884 | Blackburn R | Queen's Park, Glasgow | 2-1 |
| 1885 | Blackburn R | Queen's Park, Glasgow | 2-0 |
| 1886 | Blackburn R† | WBA | 2-0 (after 0-0 draw) |
| 1887 | Aston Villa | WBA | 2-0 |
| 1888 | WBA | Preston NE | 2-1 |
| 1889 | Preston NE | Wolverhampton W | 3-0 |
| 1890 | Blackburn R | Sheffield W | 6-1 |
| 1891 | Blackburn R | Notts Co | 3-1 |
| 1892 | WBA | Aston Villa | 3-0 |
| 1893 | Wolverhampton W | Everton | 1-0 |
| 1894 | Notts Co | Bolton W | 4-1 |
| 1895 | Aston Villa | WBA | 1-0 |
| 1896 | Sheffield W | Wolverhampton W | 2-1 |
| 1897 | Aston Villa | Everton | 3-2 |
| 1898 | Nottingham F | Derby Co | 3-1 |
| 1899 | Sheffield U | Derby Co | 4-1 |
| 1900 | Bury | Southampton | 4-0 |
| 1901 | Tottenham H | Sheffield U | 3-1 (after 2-2 draw) |
| 1902 | Sheffield U | Southampton | 2-1 (after 1-1 draw) |
| 1903 | Bury | Derby Co | 6-0 |
| 1904 | Manchester C | Bolton W | 1-0 |
| 1905 | Aston Villa | Newcastle U | 2-0 |
| 1906 | Everton | Newcastle U | 1-0 |
| 1907 | Sheffield W | Everton | 2-1 |
| 1908 | Wolverhampton W | Newcastle U | 3-1 |
| 1909 | Manchester U | Bristol C | 1-0 |
| 1910 | Newcastle U | Barnsley | 2-0 (after 1-1 draw) |
| 1911 | Bradford C | Newcastle U | 1-0 (after 0-0 draw) |
| 1912 | Barnsley | WBA | 1-0 (aet, after 0-0 draw) |
| 1913 | Aston Villa | Sunderland | 1-0 |
| 1914 | Burnley | Liverpool | 1-0 |
| 1915 | Sheffield U | Chelsea | 3-0 |
| 1920 | Aston Villa | Huddersfield T | 1-0 (aet) |
| 1921 | Tottenham H | Wolverhampton W | 1-0 |
| 1922 | Huddersfield T | Preston NE | 1-0 |
| 1923 | Bolton W | West Ham U | 2-0 |
| 1924 | Newcastle U | Aston Villa | 2-0 |
| 1925 | Sheffield U | Cardiff C | 1-0 |
| 1926 | Bolton W | Manchester C | 1-0 |
| 1927 | Cardiff C | Arsenal | 1-0 |
| 1928 | Blackburn R | Huddersfield T | 3-1 |
| 1929 | Bolton W | Portsmouth | 2-0 |
| 1930 | Arsenal | Huddersfield T | 2-0 |
| 1931 | WBA | Birmingham | 2-1 |
| 1932 | Newcastle U | Arsenal | 2-1 |
| 1933 | Everton | Manchester C | 3-0 |
| 1934 | Manchester C | Portsmouth | 2-1 |
| 1935 | Sheffield W | WBA | 4-2 |
| 1936 | Arsenal | Sheffield U | 1-0 |
| 1937 | Sunderland | Preston NE | 3-1 |
| 1938 | Preston NE | Huddersfield T | 1-0 (aet) |
| 1939 | Portsmouth | Wolverhampton W | 4-1 |
| 1946 | Derby Co | Charlton Ath | 4-1 (aet) |
| 1947 | Charlton Ath | Burnley | 1-0 (aet) |
| 1948 | Manchester U | Blackpool | 4-2 |
| 1949 | Wolverhampton W | Leicester C | 3-1 |
| 1950 | Arsenal | Liverpool | 2-0 |
| 1951 | Newcastle U | Blackpool | 2-0 |
| 1952 | Newcastle U | Arsenal | 1-0 |
| 1953 | Blackpool | Bolton W | 4-3 |
| 1954 | WBA | Preston NE | 3-2 |
| 1955 | Newcastle U | Manchester C | 3-1 |
| 1956 | Manchester C | Birmingham C | 3-1 |

| Year | Winners | Runners-up | Score |
|---|---|---|---|
| 1957 | Aston Villa | Manchester U | 2-1 |
| 1958 | Bolton W | Manchester U | 2-0 |
| 1959 | Nottingham F | Luton T | 2-1 |
| 1960 | Wolverhampton W | Blackburn R | 3-0 |
| 1961 | Tottenham H | Leicester C | 2-0 |
| 1962 | Tottenham H | Burnley | 3-1 |
| 1963 | Manchester U | Leicester C | 3-1 |
| 1964 | West Ham U | Preston NE | 3-2 |
| 1965 | Liverpool | Leeds U | 2-1 (aet) |
| 1966 | Everton | Sheffield W | 3-2 |
| 1967 | Tottenham H | Chelsea | 2-1 |
| 1968 | WBA | Everton | 1-0 (aet) |
| 1969 | Manchester C | Leicester C | 1-0 |
| 1970 | Chelsea | Leeds U | 2-1 (aet) |
| | *(after 2-2 draw,* | *after extra time)* | |
| 1971 | Arsenal | Liverpool | 2-1 (aet) |
| 1972 | Leeds U | Arsenal | 1-0 |
| 1973 | Sunderland | Leeds U | 1-0 |
| 1974 | Liverpool | Newcastle U | 3-0 |
| 1975 | West Ham U | Fulham | 2-0 |
| 1976 | Southampton | Manchester U | 1-0 |
| 1977 | Manchester U | Liverpool | 2-1 |
| 1978 | Ipswich T | Arsenal | 1-0 |
| 1979 | Arsenal | Manchester U | 3-2 |
| 1980 | West Ham U | Arsenal | 1-0 |
| 1981 | Tottenham H | Manchester C | 3-2 |
| | *(after 1-1 draw,* | *after extra time)* | |
| 1982 | Tottenham H | QPR | 1-0 |
| | *(after 1-1 draw,* | *after extra time)* | |
| 1983 | Manchester U | Brighton & HA | 4-0 |
| | *(after 2-2 draw,* | *after extra time)* | |
| 1984 | Everton | Watford | 2-0 |
| 1985 | Manchester U | Everton | 1-0 (aet) |
| 1986 | Liverpool | Everton | 3-1 |
| 1987 | Coventry C | Tottenham H | 3-2 (aet) |
| 1988 | Wimbledon | Liverpool | 1-0 |
| 1989 | Liverpool | Everton | 3-2 (aet) |
| 1990 | Manchester U | Crystal Palace | 1-0 |
| | *(after 3-3 draw,* | *after extra time)* | |
| 1991 | Tottenham H | Nottingham F | 2-1 (aet) |
| 1992 | Liverpool | Sunderland | 2-0 |
| 1993 | Arsenal | Sheffield W | 2-1 (aet) |
| | *(after 1-1 draw,* | *after extra time)* | |
| 1994 | Manchester U | Chelsea | 4-0 |
| 1995 | Everton | Manchester U | 1-0 |
| 1996 | Manchester U | Liverpool | 1-0 |
| 1997 | Chelsea | Middlesbrough | 2-0 |
| 1998 | Arsenal | Newcastle U | 2-0 |
| 1999 | Manchester U | Newcastle U | 2-0 |
| 2000 | Chelsea | Aston Villa | 1-0 |
| 2001 | Liverpool | Arsenal | 2-1 |
| 2002 | Arsenal | Chelsea | 2-0 |
| 2003 | Arsenal | Southampton | 1-0 |
| 2004 | Manchester U | Millwall | 3-0 |

* *Won outright, but restored to the Football Association.*
† *A special trophy was awarded for third consecutive win.*

## FA CUP WINS

Manchester U 11, Arsenal 9, Tottenham H 8, Aston Villa 7, Blackburn R 6, Liverpool 6, Newcastle U 6, Everton 5, The Wanderers 5, WBA 5, Bolton W 4, Manchester C 4, Sheffield U 4, Wolverhampton W 4, Chelsea 3, Sheffield W 3, West Ham U 3, Bury 2, Nottingham F 2, Old Etonians 2, Preston NE 2, Sunderland 2, Barnsley 1, Blackburn Olympic 1, Blackpool 1, Bradford C 1, Burnley 1, Cardiff C 1, Charlton Ath 1, Clapham R 1, Coventry C 1, Derby Co 1, Huddersfield T 1, Ipswich T 1, Leeds U 1, Notts Co 1, Old Carthusians 1, Oxford University 1, Portsmouth 1, Royal Engineers 1, Southampton 1, Wimbledon 1.

## APPEARANCES IN FINALS

Arsenal 16, Manchester U 16, Newcastle U 13, Everton 12, Liverpool 12, Newcastle U 12, Aston Villa 10, WBA 10, Tottenham H 9, Blackburn R 8, Manchester C 8, Wolverhampton W 8, Bolton W 7, Chelsea 7, Preston NE 7, Old Etonians 6, Sheffield U 6, Sheffield W 6, Huddersfield T 5, *The Wanderers 5, Derby Co 4, Leeds U 4, Leicester C 4, Oxford University 4, Royal Engineers 4, Southampton 4, Sunderland 4, West Ham U 4, Blackpool 3, Burnley 3, Nottingham F 3, Portsmouth 3, Barnsley 2, Birmingham C 2, *Bury 2, Cardiff C 2, Charlton Ath 2, Clapham R 2, Notts Co 2, Queen's Park (Glasgow) 2, *Blackburn Olympic 1, *Bradford C 1, Brighton & HA 1, Bristol C 1, *Coventry C 1, Crystal Palace 1, Fulham 1, *Ipswich T 1, Luton T 4, Middlesbrough 1, Millwall 1, *Old Carthusians 1, QPR 1, Watford 1, *Wimbledon 1.
* *Denotes undefeated.*

## APPEARANCES IN SEMI-FINALS

Arsenal 24, Everton 23, Manchester U 23, Liverpool 21, Aston Villa 19, WBA 19, Tottenham H 17, Blackburn R 16, Newcastle U 16, Sheffield W 16, Chelsea 15, Wolverhampton W 14, Bolton W 13, Derby Co 13, Sheffield U 13, Nottingham F 12, Sunderland 12, Southampton 11, Manchester C 10, Preston NE 10, Birmingham C 9, Burnley 8, Leeds U 8, Leicester C 8, Huddersfield T 7, Old Etonians 6, Fulham 6, Oxford University 6, West Ham U 6, Notts Co 5, Portsmouth 5, The Wanderers 5, Luton T 4, Millwall 4, Queen's Park (Glasgow) 4, Royal Engineers 4, Watford 4, Blackpool 3, Cardiff C 3, Clapham R 3, Crystal Palace (professional club) 3, Ipswich T 3, Norwich C 3, Old Carthusians 3, Oldham Ath 3, Stoke C 3, The Swifts 3, Barnsley 2, Blackburn Olympic 2, Bristol C 2, Bury 2, Charlton Ath 2, Grimsby T 2, Middlesbrough 2, Swansea T 2, Swindon T 2, Wimbledon 2, Bradford C 1, Brighton & HA 1, Cambridge University 1, Chesterfield 1, Coventry C 1, Crewe Alex 1, Crystal Palace (amateur club) 1, Darwen 1, Derby Junction 1, Glasgow R 1, Hull C 1, Marlow 1, Old Harrovians 1, Orient 1, Plymouth Arg 1, Port Vale 1, QPR 1, Reading 1, Shropshire W 1, Wycombe W 1, York C 1.

# THE FA CUP 2003–04

## PRELIMINARY AND QUALIFYING ROUNDS

### EXTRA PRELIMINARY ROUND

| | |
|---|---|
| Skelmersdale United v Glasshoughton Welfare | 7-2 |
| Brodsworth MW v Pickering Town | 0-1 |
| St Helens Town v Trafford | 0-2 |
| Garforth Town v Whickham | 0-3 |
| Holker Old Boys v Penrith | 1-0 |
| Colne v Mossley | 2-3 |
| Norton & Stockton Ancients v Evenwood Town | 0-2 |
| Ossett Albion v Alnwick Town | 5-2 |
| Washington Nissan v Jarrow Roofing Boldon CA | 1-2 |
| Shotton Comrades v Newcastle Blue Star | 1-4 |
| Dunston FB v Abbey Hey | 1-0 |
| Eccleshill United v Warrington Town | 1-2 |
| Oldham Town v Northallerton Town | 3-2 |
| Fleetwood Town v Darwen | 1-0 |
| Blackstones v Gedling Town | 1-4 |
| Holbech United v Staveley MW | 1-1, 2-3 |
| Carlton Town v Shirebrook Town | 0-3 |
| Lincoln Moorlands v Arnold Town | 1-0 |
| Nantwich Town v Stratford Town | 1-2 |
| Cradley Town v Daventry Town | 2-0 |
| Maldon Town v Holmer Green | 4-1 |
| Stotfold v London Colney | 1-2 |
| Wroxham v Halstead Town | 4-1 |
| Brentwood v Haringey Borough | 0-2 |
| Kingsbury Town v Stowmarket Town | 1-2 |
| Harpenden Town v Woodbridge Town | 6-1 |
| Needham Market v Norwich United | 0-3 |
| Romford v Bury Town | 0-2 |
| Tiptree United v Coggenhoe United | 0-1 |
| Northampton Spencer v Desborough Town | 2-2, 2-4 |
| Broxbourne Borough V&E v Yaxley | 0-2 |
| Mildenhall Town v Ilford | 2-1 |
| St Margaretsbury v Henley Town | 0-0, 3-0 |
| Bedford United & Valerio v Harefield United | 1-0 |
| Southend Manor v Buckingham Town | 1-1, 1-4 |
| Ruislip Manor v Ely City | 2-2, 2-0 |
| Hadleigh United v Wootton Blue Cross | 0-1 |
| Brackley Town v Hullbridge Sports | 2-1 |
| Royston Town v Ford Sports Daventry | 0-3 |
| Great Yarmouth Town v Southall Town | 4-1 |
| St Leonards v Arundel | 1-4 |
| Thatcham Town v Selsey | 6-0 |
| East Preston v Andover | 2-3 |
| Walton Casuals v Westfield | 5-0 |
| Brockenhurst v VCD Athletic | 2-3 |
| Wokingham Town v Chertsey Town | 2-0 |
| Chichester City United v Tunbridge Wells | 4-1 |
| Sandhurst Town v Camberley Town | 2-1 |
| Didcot Town v Ramsgate | 2-1 |
| Saltdean United v Cray Wanderers | 0-4 |
| Bedfont v Littlehampton Town | 4-0 |
| Horsham YMCA v Gosport Borough | 3-3, 0-1 |
| Eastbourne United v Lordswood | 1-0 |
| BAT Sports v Cobham | 3-1 |
| Carterton Town v Hungerford Town | 1-0 |
| Lancing v Whitehawk | 0-3 |
| AFC Totton v Erith Town | 3-0 |
| Reading Town v Lymington & New Milton | 1-2 |
| Barnstaple Town v Exmouth Town | 2-3 |
| Highworth Town v Shortwood United | 3-1 |
| Frome Town v Tuffley Rovers | 1-0 |
| Shepton Mallet v Falmouth Town | 0-1 |
| Minehead v Liskeard Athletic | 2-0 |
| Devizes Town v Christchurch | 0-4 |
| Chard Town v Paulton Rovers | 0-3 |

### PRELIMINARY ROUND

| | |
|---|---|
| Brigg Town v Billingham Town | 2-2, 0-1 |
| Maine Road v Ashington | 2-4 |
| Bishop Auckland v Flixton | 8-0 |
| Harrogate Railway w.o. v Hatfield Main removed. | |
| Armthorpe Welfare w.o. v Louth United removed. | |
| Chadderton v Holker Old Boys | 1-2 |
| Peterlee Newtown v Bridlington Town | 1-2 |
| Mossley v Curzon Ashton | 1-1, 3-2 |
| Bamber Bridge v Prescot Cables | 3-1 |
| Stocksbridge Park Steels v Squires Gate | 2-1 |
| Goole v Rossendale United | 2-4 |
| Witton Albion v Nelson | 4-1 |
| Thackley v Ossett Town | 0-1 |
| Skelmersdale United v Atherton LR | 3-0 |
| Pontefract Collieries v Clitheroe | 0-2 |
| Blackpool Mechanics v Colwyn Bay | 1-1, 1-3 |
| Crook Town v Guiseley | 2-3 |
| Tow Law Town v Salford City | 1-1, 3-4 |
| South Shields v Bedlington Terriers | 0-0, 1-4 |
| Willington v Consett | 0-5 |
| Fleetwood Town v Parkgate | 3-0 |
| Newcastle Blue Star v Dunston FB | 1-2 |
| Billingham Synthonia v Chorley | 1-1, 1-3 |
| Hyde United v Hallam | 6-1 |
| Liversedge v Gateshead | 3-1 |
| Guisborough Town v Kendal Town | 1-1, 2-2 |
| *Guisborough Town won 8-7 on penalties.* | |
| Tadcaster Albion v Winsford United | 0-4 |
| Great Harwood Town v North Ferriby United | 0-3 |
| Cheadle Town v Chester-Le-Street Town | 1-2 |
| Woodleigh Sports v Ramsbottom United | 1-1, 0-3 |
| Durham City v Rossington Main | 0-0, 1-0 |
| Horden CW v Brandon United | 0-1 |
| Esh Winning v Bacup Borough | 1-3 |
| Whickham v Hebburn Town | 2-2, 2-1 |
| Thornaby v Easington Colliery | 5-1 |
| Shildon v Workington | 2-1 |
| Selby Town v Washington | 0-0, 3-3 |
| *Selby Town won 5-4 on penalties.* | |
| Maltby Main v West Auckland Town | 1-0 |
| Sheffield v Jarrow Roofing Boldon CA | 1-0 |
| Pickering Town v Whitley Bay | 2-0 |
| Evenwood Town v Oldham Town | 3-5 |
| Hall Road Rangers v Trafford | 1-1, 1-3 |
| Marske United v Winterton Rangers | 3-0 |
| Warrington Town v Yorkshire Amateur | 1-0 |
| Prudhoe Town v Morpeth Town | 2-0 |
| Ossett Albion v Alsager Town | 2-1 |
| Seaham Red Star v Murton | 3-4 |
| Atherton Collieries v Farsley Celtic | 0-3 |
| Gresley Rovers v Buxton | 1-1, 0-4 |
| Stamford v Bourne Town | 2-0 |
| Shepshed Dynamo v Congleton Town | 0-1 |
| Shirebrook Town v Matlock Town | 2-1 |
| Grosvenor Park v Glapwell | 0-0, 0-2 |
| Quorn v Gedling Town | 0-1 |
| Studley v Rushall Olympic | 3-0 |
| Oadby Town v Stratford Town | 5-1 |
| Corby Town v Lincoln United | 2-1 |
| Bedworth United v Halesowen Town | 0-2 |
| Belper Town v Boston Town | 1-1, 1-0 |
| Mickleover Sports v Ludlow Town | 3-0 |
| Chasetown v Sutton Coldfield Town | 1-2 |
| Kidsgrove Athletic v Rugby United | 1-3 |
| Borrowash Victoria v Biddulph Victoria | 3-4 |
| Racing Club Warwick v Stafford Town | 0-1 |
| Rocester v Ilkeston Town | 1-1, 1-3 |
| Staveley MW v Sutton Town | 0-1 |
| Atherstone United removed v Pelsall Villa w.o. | |
| Eastwood Town v Deeping Rangers | 2-2, 2-1 |
| Lincoln Moorlands v Leek Town | 1-2 |
| Spalding United v Glossop North End | 3-0 |
| Stourport Swifts v Boldmere St Michaels | 1-0 |
| Cradley Town v Bromsgrove Rovers | 0-4 |
| Solihull Borough v Stone Dominoes | 3-0 |
| Leek CSOB v Redditch United | 2-3 |
| Barwell v Oldbury United | 3-1 |
| Newcastle Town v Willenhall Town | 3-0 |
| Stourbridge v Causeway United | 0-2 |
| Long Eaton United v Norton United | 0-0, 2-0 |
| Gorleston removed v Haverhill Rovers w.o. | |
| Burnham v Arlesey Town | 1-7 |
| Burnham Ramblers v Potters Bar Town | 4-1 |
| Dunstable Town w.o. v Saffron Walden Town removed. | |
| Leighton Town v Wootton Blue Cross | 3-1 |
| Tring Town removed v Mildenhall Town w.o. | |
| Sawbridgeworth Town v AFC Wallingford | 2-2, 0-2 |
| Newmarket Town v Wembley | 5-0 |
| Chalfont St Peter v Chesham United | 0-6 |
| Boreham Wood v Desborough Town | 2-1 |
| Ware v London Colney | 2-2, 1-0 |
| Enfield Town v Clacton Town | 2-1 |
| Norwich United v Leyton | 2-2, 1-2 |
| AFC Sudbury v Diss Town | 4-3 |
| Histon v Yeading | 7-0 |
| Hampton & Richmond Borough v Great Wakering Rovers | 3-0 |
| Harpenden Town v St Margaretsbury | 1-3 |
| Haringey Borough v Dereham Town | 1-3 |
| Barton Rovers v Rothwell Town | 2-2, 0-3 |
| Stewarts & Lloyds v Fakenham Town | 3-0 |
| Milton Keynes City removed v Tilbury w.o. | |
| Bedford United & Valerio v St Neots Town | 0-2 |
| Beaconsfield SYCOB v Ipswich Wanderers | 1-1, 1-2 |
| Wisbech Town v Aveley | 1-2 |

| | |
|---|---|
| Stowmarket Town v Waltham Forest | 0-2 |
| Stanway Rovers v Staines Town | 0-1 |
| Wivenhoe Town v Bowers United | 7-0 |
| Cheshunt v Harlow Town | 2-3 |
| Coggenhoe United v Maldon Town | 1-2 |
| Wingate & Finchley v Bury Town | 3-2 |
| Edgware Town v Clapton | 2-2, 1-0 |
| Stansted v Uxbridge | 0-7 |
| Great Yarmouth Town v Berkhamsted Town | 0-1 |
| Raunds Town v Hoddesdon Town | 1-0 |
| Buckingham Town v Ford Sports Daventry | 2-0 |
| Hertford Town v Lowestoft Town | 2-4 |
| Yaxley v Barking & East Ham United | 2-1 |
| Ruislip Manor v Soham Town Rangers | 1-4 |
| Enfield v Hemel Hempstead Town | 1-1, 3-2 |
| Wroxham v Banbury United | 6-1 |
| Flackwell Heath v Concord Rangers | 4-1 |
| Long Buckby v King's Lynn | 1-5 |
| Hanwell Town v East Thurrock United | 2-2, 3-6 |
| Witham Town v Marlow | 2-0 |
| Brook House v Wealdstone | 1-4 |
| Brackley Town v Harwich & Parkeston | 4-2 |
| Greenwich Borough v Maidstone United | 1-1, 0-1 |
| Hailsham Town v Cowes Sports | 0-1 |
| Chessington & Hook United v Merstham | 2-0 |
| Leatherhead v Moneyfields | 3-1 |
| Windsor & Eton v Metropolitan Police | 0-1 |
| Dartford v Bashley | 1-0 |
| Walton & Hersham v Walton Casuals | 0-2 |
| Three Bridges v Redhill | 1-1, 3-0 |
| Tonbridge Angels v BAT Sports | 4-0 |
| Fisher Athletic v Bedfont | 3-4 |
| Blackfield & Langley v Thamesmead Town | 1-3 |
| Abingdon United v Cove | 3-2 |
| Banstead Athletic v Winchester City | 0-2 |
| Arundel v Hassocks | 4-0 |
| Tooting & Mitcham United v Ashford Town (Mx) | 3-1 |
| Chipstead v Ringmer | 1-2 |
| Croydon v Hythe Town | 1-1, 1-1 |
| *Hythe Town won 5-4 on penalties.* | |
| Abingdon Town v Chichester City United | 3-1 |
| Whitchurch United v Withdean 2000 | 4-1 |
| Worthing v Ash United | 7-0 |
| Fleet Town v Epsom & Ewell | 1-0 |
| Slade Green v Hartley Wintney | 1-2 |
| Egham Town v Thame United | 1-8 |
| Sidlesham v Sittingbourne | 0-2 |
| AFC Totton v AFC Newbury | 3-1 |
| Didcot Town v Eastbourne Town | 4-1 |
| Ashford Town v Eastbourne United | 3-0 |
| Gosport Borough v Erith & Belvedere | 2-4 |
| Hastings United v Bracknell Town | 1-3 |
| Southwick v Burgess Hill Town | 1-4 |
| VCD Athletic v Eastleigh | 2-1 |
| Beckenham Town v Sandhurst Town | 2-5 |
| Slough Town v East Grinstead Town | 5-0 |
| Dulwich Hamlet v Folkestone Invicta | 1-3 |
| Wokingham Town v Deal Town | 0-1 |
| Dorking v Lewes | 3-5 |
| Hillingdon Borough v Corinthian Casuals | 2-0 |
| Wick v Whyteleafe | 0-5 |
| Oxford City v Farnham Town | 6-1 |
| Molesey v Godalming & Guilford | 1-2 |
| Croydon Athletic v Herne Bay | 2-1 |
| Bromley v North Leigh | 2-1 |
| Whitehawk v Lymington & New Milton | 0-2 |
| Thatcham Town v Alton Town | 1-2 |
| Whitstable Town v Raynes Park Vale | 1-3 |
| Cray Wanderers v Pagham | 4-0 |
| Peacehaven & Telscombe v Chessington United | 2-1 |
| Horsham v Newport (IW) | 1-2 |
| Carterton Town v Fareham Town | 1-2 |
| Chatham Town v Andover | 2-4 |
| Bitton v Christchurch | 3-4 |
| Bideford v Swindon Supermarine | 1-3 |
| Backwell United v Fairford Town | 2-0 |
| Bishop Sutton v Falmouth Town | 1-0 |
| Bridport v Street | 2-0 |
| Cinderford Town v Brislington | 1-3 |
| Melksham Town v Mangotsfield United | 0-4 |
| Evesham United v Hallen | 3-3, 1-2 |
| Taunton Town v Bournemouth | 1-1, 5-0 |
| St Blazey v Willand Rovers | 5-0 |
| Highworth Town v Portland United | 4-3 |
| Westbury United v Keynsham Town | 2-2, 5-2 |
| Minehead v Welton Rovers | 2-2, 1-2 |
| Bemerton Heath Harlequins v Torrington | 3-2 |
| Bristol Manor Farm v Gloucester City | 0-5 |
| Frome Town v Clevedon Town | 1-1, 3-2 |
| Porthleven v Team Bath | 0-4 |
| Salisbury City v Odd Down | 4-0 |
| Elmore v Wimborne Town | 1-3 |
| Downton v Exmouth Town | 3-4 |
| Yate Town v Cirencester Town | 1-2 |
| Paulton Rovers v Calne Town | 2-0 |
| Bridgwater Town v Corsham Town | 0-1 |
| Dawlish Town v Clevedon United | 1-2 |

**FIRST QUALIFYING ROUND**

| | |
|---|---|
| Witton Albion v Holker Old Boys | 7-0 |
| Stocksbridge Park Steels v Prudhoe Town | 6-1 |
| Mossley v Hyde United | 1-6 |
| Rossendale United v Harrogate Railway | 2-1 |
| Clitheroe v Brandon United | 0-1 |
| Maltby Main v Colwyn Bay | 4-2 |
| Winsford United v Marske United | 2-1 |
| Oldham Town v Liversedge | 3-2 |
| Ossett Albion v Ossett Town | 0-0, 3-1 |
| Durham City v Shildon | 0-2 |
| Ashington v Ramsbottom United | 3-1 |
| Thornaby v Guisborough Town | 1-2 |
| Armthorpe Welfare v Whickham | 0-0, 1-2 |
| Bamber Bridge v Bacup Borough | 2-0 |
| Guiseley v Trafford | 1-0 |
| Bishop Auckland v Pickering Town | 0-1 |
| Chester-Le-Street Town v Murton | 2-0 |
| Warrington Town v North Ferriby United | 6-1 |
| Chorley v Selby Town | 2-1 |
| Dunston FB v Billingham Town | 2-2, 1-0 |
| Farsley Celtic v Sheffield | 1-1, 3-1 |
| Bridlington Town v Salford City | 5-0 |
| Skelmersdale United v Consett | 2-0 |
| Fleetwood Town v Bedlington Terriers | 3-2 |
| Stourport Swifts v Rugby United | 0-3 |
| Oadby Town v Stamford | 0-2 |
| Barwell v Newcastle Town | 2-5 |
| Glapwell v Gedling Town | 1-2 |
| Shirebrook Town v Stafford Town | 2-0 |
| Studley v Bromsgrove Rovers | 0-1 |
| Solihull Borough v Redditch United | 0-3 |
| Long Eaton United v Ilkeston Town | 0-2 |
| Mickleover Sports v Eastwood Town | 0-0, 0-1 |
| Sutton Coldfield Town v Causeway United | 1-1, 3-0 |
| Pelsall Villa v Belper Town | 0-4 |
| Corby Town v Halesowen Town | 1-1, 2-3 |
| Spalding United v Sutton Town | 2-2, 5-0 |
| Congleton Town v Leek Town | 1-0 |
| Biddulph Victoria v Buxton | 1-1, 2-3 |
| Newmarket Town v Brackley Town | 6-1 |
| Hampton & Richmond Borough v Dunstable Town | 1-0 |
| Harlow Town v St Neots Town | 1-0 |
| Waltham Forest v Rothwell Town | 1-3 |
| Dereham Town v Tilbury | 1-4 |
| Aveley v Lowestoft Town | 1-2 |
| Wealdstone v Uxbridge | 0-1 |
| Leyton v Arlesey Town | 4-0 |
| Edgware Town v Enfield Town | 0-1 |
| Ware v Buckingham Town | 2-2, 1-2 |
| Wingate & Finchley v Raunds Town | 3-1 |
| Mildenhall Town v Histon | 1-6 |
| AFC Wallingford v Ipswich Wanderers | 2-0 |
| Berkhamsted Town v AFC Sudbury | 0-9 |
| Chesham United v Yaxley | 2-0 |
| Wroxham v Flackwell Heath | 2-2, 0-1 |
| East Thurrock United v Staines Town | 2-1 |
| Wivenhoe Town v Soham Town Rangers | 2-3 |
| Boreham Wood v Maldon Town | 2-1 |
| St Margaretsbury v Leighton Town | 2-2, 1-0 |
| Haverhill Rovers v Burnham Ramblers | 1-2 |
| King's Lynn v Stewarts & Lloyds | 2-2, 3-0 |
| Enfield v Witham Town | 4-0 |
| Whitchurch United v Tooting & Mitcham United | 0-3 |
| Raynes Park Vale v Folkestone Invicta | 0-2 |
| Lymington & New Milton v Erith & Belvedere | 1-0 |
| Cray Wanderers v Sandhurst Town | 4-1 |
| Deal Town v Leatherhead | 1-2 |
| Ashford Town v Bromley | 1-1, 0-1 |
| Tonbridge Angels v Lewes | 1-1, 1-2 |
| Hillingdon Borough v Oxford City | 1-1, 1-2 |
| Chessington & Hook United v Thamesmead Town | 1-4 |
| Slough Town v Godalming & Guildford | 2-0 |
| Metropolitan Police v Winchester City | 2-3 |
| Fareham Town v Newport (IW) | 1-2 |
| Hythe Town v Alton Town | 3-1 |
| Burgess Hill Town v Abingdon United | 2-1 |
| Thame United v VCD Athletic | 4-2 |
| Worthing v Walton Casuals | 4-1 |
| Dartford v Peacehaven & Telscombe | 3-0 |
| Sittingbourne v Whyteleafe | 1-0 |
| Andover v Arundel | 5-0 |
| Abingdon Town v Ringmer | 4-3 |
| Bracknell Town v Hartley Witney | 3-2 |
| Three Bridges v Fleet Town | 1-2 |
| Croydon Athletic v Bedfont | 7-1 |
| AFC Totton v Didcot Town | 1-3 |
| Maidstone United v Cowes Sports | 4-0 |

| | |
|---|---|
| Clevedon United v Frome Town | 4-1 |
| Paulton Rovers v Bemerton Heath Harlequins | 2-0 |
| Gloucester City v Team Bath | 0-0, 2-0 |
| Christchurch v Westbury United | 2-3 |
| Mangotsfield United v Bridport | 4-3 |
| Cirencester Town v Swindon Supermarine | 2-1 |
| Corsham Town v Brislington | 1-2 |
| Salisbury City v Taunton Town | 4-1 |
| Exmouth Town v St Blazey | 2-2, 3-3 |
| *Exmouth Town won 4-3 on penalties.* | |
| Hallen v Highworth Town | 1-2 |
| Backwell United v Wimborne Town | 1-4 |
| Welton Rovers v Bishop Sutton | 3-3, 0-1 |

**SECOND QUALIFYING ROUND**

| | |
|---|---|
| Frickley Athletic v Shildon | 0-0, 1-5 |
| Whitby Town v Winsford United | 3-0 |
| Runcorn FC Halton v Guiseley | 3-0 |
| Droylsden v Burscough | 2-2, 2-1 |
| Pickering Town v Ossett Albion | 0-1 |
| Vauxhall Motors v Southport | 3-1 |
| Dunston FB v Fleetwood Town | 1-1, 2-1 |
| Bridlington Town v Farsley Celtic | 2-2, 0-3 |
| Stocksbridge Park Steels v Brandon United | 3-2 |
| Ashton United v Hyde United | 1-1, 2-1 |
| Blyth Spartans v Bamber Bridge | 3-0 |
| Marine v Rossendale United | 3-1 |
| Chester-Le-Street Town v Bradford Park Avenue | 0-2 |
| Maltby Main v Ashington | 2-3 |
| Barrow v Harrogate Town | 2-0 |
| Lancaster City v Altrincham | 2-0 |
| Gainsborough Trinity v Skelmersdale United | 6-0 |
| Witton Albion v Wakefield & Emley | 0-1 |
| Guisborough Town v Stalybridge Celtic | 2-2, 1-3 |
| Chorley v Whickham | 5-0 |
| Radcliffe Borough v Oldham Town | 2-1 |
| Spennymoor United v Warrington Town | 0-2 |
| Gedling Town v Alfreton Town | 1-0 |
| Newcastle Town v Sutton Coldfield Town | 2-1 |
| Cambridge City v Ilkeston Town | 3-1 |
| Hednesford Town v Bromsgrove Rovers | 0-2 |
| Rothwell Town v Bedford Town | 0-1 |
| Stafford Rangers v Grantham Town | 1-2 |
| Redditch United v Shirebrook Town | 1-1, 2-2 |
| *Shirebrook Town won 4-1 on penalties.* | |
| Spalding United v Halesowen Town | 1-2 |
| Stamford v Kettering Town | 0-3 |
| Hucknall Town v Congleton Town | 1-1, 2-3 |
| Soham Town Rangers v Histon | 0-2 |
| Buxton v Belper Town | 1-0 |
| Nuneaton Borough v Worcester City | 1-0 |
| Worksop Town v King's Lynn | 2-2, 4-1 |
| Rugby United v Eastwood Town | 1-3 |
| Moor Green v Hinckley United | 1-2 |
| Basingstoke Town v Cray Wanderers | 1-0 |
| Sutton United v Bishop's Stortford | 0-0, 1-1 |
| *Bishop's Stortford won 5-3 on penalties.* | |
| Buckingham Town v Thurrock | 1-2 |
| Bromley v Dartford | 3-0 |
| Sittingbourne v East Thurrock United | 1-2 |
| Boreham Wood v Burgess Hill Town | 4-0 |
| Bracknell Town v Tilbury | 4-2 |
| Hendon v Enfield | 4-0 |
| Canvey Island v Uxbridge | 6-1 |
| Wingate & Finchley v Oxford City | 1-2 |
| Hampton & Richmond Borough v Kingstonian | 2-1 |
| Heybridge Swifts v Worthing | 3-3, 0-2 |
| Lowestoft Town v Lewes | 2-1 |
| Hythe Town v Maidstone United | 0-4 |
| Leyton v Leatherhead | 1-0 |
| Slough Town v Welling United | 1-1, 1-4 |
| Thame United v Thamesmead Town | 4-0 |
| Abingdon Town v Chesham United | 1-2 |
| Hornchurch v Billericay Town | 2-1 |
| Newmarket Town v Fleet Town | 3-0 |
| Braintree Town v Aylesbury United | 3-2 |
| St Albans City v Grays Athletic | 2-4 |
| Hayes v Tooting & Mitcham United | 4-2 |
| Enfield Town v Carshalton Athletic | 0-1 |
| Hitchin Town v Folkestone Invicta | 0-0, 0-3 |
| Ford United v Didcot Town | 3-1 |
| Croydon Athletic v AFC Wallingford | 2-0 |
| Northwood v AFC Sudbury | 2-4 |
| Dover Athletic v Maidenhead United | 4-0 |
| Burnham Ramblers v St Margaretsbury | 1-3 |
| Eastbourne Borough v Chelmsford City | 2-2, 2-0 |
| Harrow Borough v Flackwell Heath | 0-0, 1-0 |
| Harlow Town v Crawley Town | 0-4 |
| Newport County v Weymouth | 3-2 |
| Bognor Regis Town v Havant & Waterlooville | 0-4 |
| Newport (IW) v Tiverton Town | 2-1 |
| Weston-Super-Mare v Dorchester Town | 4-1 |
| Paulton Rovers v Bishop Sutton | 4-1 |
| Mangotsfield United v Wimborne Town | 3-0 |
| Brislington v Bath City | 0-2 |
| Salisbury City v Westbury United | 1-1, 2-1 |
| Chippenham Town v Winchester City | 2-1 |
| Gloucester City v Merthyr Tydfil | 2-0 |
| Lymington & New Milton v Clevedon United | 8-2 |
| Cirencester Town v Andover | 3-2 |
| Exmouth Town v Highworth Town | 0-1 |

**THIRD QUALIFYING ROUND**

| | |
|---|---|
| Ashton United v Barrow | 2-1 |
| Farsley Celtic v Worksop Town | 3-0 |
| Shirebrook Town v Shildon | 1-3 |
| Nuneaton Borough v Runcorn FC Halton | 1-1, 2-2 |
| *Runcorn FC Halton won 5-4 on penalties.* | |
| Ashington v Grantham Town | 1-3 |
| Gedling Town v Stalybridge Celtic | 0-1 |
| Eastwood Town v Stocksbridge Park Steels | 1-1, 2-3 |
| Newcastle Town v Ossett Albion | 1-1, 4-4 |
| *Ossett Albion won 3-0 on penalties.* | |
| Marine v Dunston FB | 1-2 |
| Blyth Spartans v Halesowen Town | 2-1 |
| Bradford Park Avenue v Vauxhall Motors | 1-1, 3-1 |
| Warrington Town v Whitby Town | 0-0, 1-2 |
| Wakefield & Emley v Hinckley United | 0-2 |
| Droylsden v Gainsborough Trinity | 0-2 |
| Buxton v Radcliffe Borough | 2-1 |
| Chorley v Lancaster City | 1-1, 0-1 |
| Congleton Town v Bromsgrove Rovers | 0-2 |
| Kettering Town v St Margaretsbury | 2-0 |
| Folkestone Invicta v Welling United | 1-1, 2-2 |
| *Welling United won 5-3 on penalties.* | |
| Bromley v Thurrock | 1-1, 0-3 |
| Histon v Newmarket Town | 0-0, 1-0 |
| Hornchurch v Carshalton Athletic | 5-0 |
| Canvey Island v Dover Athletic | 4-3 |
| Ford United v Worthing | 3-2 |
| Cambridge City v Lowestoft Town | 3-0 |
| Maidstone United v Bishop's Stortford | 1-1, 2-3 |
| Hayes v Boreham Wood | 1-1, 1-3 |
| East Thurrock United v AFC Sudbury | 1-1, 1-1 |
| *East Thurrock United won 4-2 on penalties.* | |
| Leyton v Bedford Town | 3-0 |
| Grays Athletic v Hendon | 3-0 |
| Braintree Town v Eastbourne Borough | 0-4 |
| Crawley Town v Croydon Athletic | 6-1 |
| Basingstoke Town v Bracknell Town | 0-0, 0-1 |
| Gloucester City v Chippenham Town | 4-3 |
| Thame United v Bath City | 3-0 |
| Oxford City v Cirencester Town | 0-3 |
| Havant & Waterlooville v Salisbury City | 3-4 |
| Newport (IW) v Harrow Borough | 2-2, 0-2 |
| Newport County v Mangotsfield United | 3-6 |
| Weston-Super-Mare v Chesham United | 1-1, 2-1 |
| Lymington & New Milton v Highworth Town | 2-0 |
| Paulton Rovers v Hampton & Richmond Borough | 2-1 |

**FOURTH QUALIFYING ROUND**

| | |
|---|---|
| Ossett Albion v Stalybridge Celtic | 0-1 |
| Dunston FB v Lancaster City | 0-1 |
| Ashton United v Grantham Town | 1-2 |
| Blyth Spartans v Chester City | 0-1 |
| Bromsgrove Rovers v Whitby Town | 2-2, 1-2 |
| Burton Albion v Buxton | 6-0 |
| Morecambe v Shrewsbury Town | 2-4 |
| Telford United v Tamworth | 3-3, 3-2 |
| Scarborough v Hinckley United | 3-1 |
| Farsley Celtic v Gainsborough Trinity | 1-1, 0-3 |
| Accrington Stanley v Leigh RMI | 2-0 |
| Northwich Victoria v Halifax Town | 1-0 |
| Runcorn FC Halton v Bradford Park Avenue | 0-1 |
| Shildon v Stocksbridge Park Steels | 6-0 |
| Leyton v Histon | 1-2 |
| Eastbourne Borough v Stevenage Borough | 2-2, 0-1 |
| Bracknell Town v Barnet | 0-3 |
| Thame United v Farnborough Town | 1-2 |
| Grays Athletic v Margate | 3-3, 3-3 |
| *Grays Athletic won 3-1 on penalties.* | |
| Welling United v Weston-Super-Mare | 2-3 |
| Boreham Wood v Kettering Town | 1-0 |
| Forest Green Rovers v Aldershot Town | 1-3 |
| Thurrock v Dagenham & Redbridge | 2-1 |
| Harrow Borough v Hereford United | 1-6 |
| Bishop's Stortford v Gloucester City | 2-0 |
| Salisbury City v Lymington & New Milton | 5-1 |
| Cambridge City v Ford United | 2-3 |
| Mangotsfield United v Canvey Island | 1-2 |
| Hornchurch v Paulton Rovers | 1-0 |
| East Thurrock United v Woking | 1-1, 0-2 |
| Cirencester Town v Crawley Town | 2-4 |
| Exeter City v Gravesend & Northfleet | 0-0, 3-3 |
| *Gravesend & Northfleet won 6-5 on penalties.* | |

# THE FA CUP 2003–04

## COMPETITION PROPER

▪ *Denotes player sent off.*

### FIRST ROUND

Friday, 7 November 2003

**Thurrock (0) 1** *(Bowes 80)*

**Luton T (1) 1** *(Boyce 39)* 1551

*Thurrock:* Gothard; Collis, Goodfellow, Heffer, Purdie, McFarlane, Akurang (Allen), Lee D, Lee K (Linger), Kandol, Bowes.
*Luton T:* Beresford; Hillier, Davis, Spring, Boyce, Coyne, Mansell (Leary), Robinson, Forbes (Crowe), Showunmi, Brkovic.

Saturday, 8 November 2003

**Barnet (2) 2** *(Gamble 4, Beadle 30)*

**Stalybride C (1) 2** *(Keeling 45, Eastwood 77 (pen))* 1736

*Barnet:* Gore; Rooney (Williams), King, Hendon, Plummer, Maddix, Lopez (Roach), Gamble, Grazioli, Beadle (Hatch), Yakubu.
*Stalybride C:* Dootson; German, Bowker, Pearce, Heald, Keeling, Kielty, Wharton, Foster, Eastwood, Mayers.

**Blackpool (2) 4** *(Taylor 12, 89, Coid 14, Burns 90)*

**Boreham Wood (0) 0** 3969

*Blackpool:* Barnes; Grayson, Jaszczun, Southern, Davis (Flynn), Clarke, Bullock, Taylor, Murphy, Sheron (Burns), Coid (McMahon).
*Boreham Wood:* Imber; Reeks (Duah), Moran, Braithwaite, Grime (James), Browne, Harvey, Palmer, Hakki (Williams), Winston, Baker.

**Bournemouth (1) 1** *(Elliott 37)*

**Bristol R (0) 0** 7200

*Bournemouth:* Moss; Purches, Cummings, Broadhurst, Fletcher C, Buxton, O'Connor (Tindall), Browning, Feeney (Hayter), Fletcher S, Elliott (Maher).
*Bristol R:* Miller; Parker, Austin▪, Edwards, Barrett, Quinn (Carlisle), Savage, Hyde, Williams, Rammell, Haldane (Gilroy).

**Brentford (1) 7** *(Harrold 45, 65, 86, Rougier 47, Purkiss 50 (og), Frampton 55, O'Connor 76)*

**Gainsborough T (0) 1** *(Smith 81)* 3041

*Brentford:* Smith P; Smith J, Somner, Sonko, Frampton, Hutchinson, Rougier (Hughes), O'Connor, Tabb (Olugbodi), Harrold, Hunt (Evans).
*Gainsborough T:* Norton; Purkiss, Timons, Reddington, Birley, Eshelby, Hurst (Adam), Staton, Smith, Ellington, Grant.

**Bury (0) 1** *(Porter 71)*

**Rochdale (1) 2** *(Bertos 27, Townson 50)* 5464

*Bury:* Garner; Unsworth, Singh, Gulliver, Duxbury, Woodthorpe, O'Shaughnessy, Whelan, Nugent (O'Neill), Preece, Connell (Porter).
*Rochdale:* Edwards (Gilks); Evans, Burgess, Brannan, Griffiths, Grand, Bertos, McClare, McEvilly, Townson (Antoine-Curier), McCourt (Doughty).

**Cheltenham T (1) 3** *(Spencer 6, Yates 48, Brayson 90)*

**Hull C (0) 1** *(Price 46)* 3624

*Cheltenham T:* Higgs; Bird, Howells, Finnigan, Brough, Duff M, Cleverley (Forsyth), Yates, Brayson, Spencer, McCann.
*Hull C:* Musselwhite; Joseph, Dawson, Ashbee, Whittle, Delaney, Price, Hinds (Elliott), Green, Burgess, Holt (Forrester).

**Chester C (0) 0**

**Gravesend & N (1) 1** *(Skinner 39 (pen))* 2251

*Chester C:* McCaldon; Collins, McIntyre, Carden, Bolland, Ruffer, Davies, Stamp, Clare (Rapley), Foster (Twiss), Heard (Brady).
*Gravesend & N:* Wilkerson; Perkins, Skinner, Lee, Moore, Duku, Owen, McKimm, Haworth, Pinnock, Walshe (Drury).

**Colchester U (1) 1** *(McGleish 38)*

**Oxford U (0) 0** 3672

*Colchester U:* Brown S; Stockley, Myers, Pinault, Chilvers, White, Duguid, Bowry, Fagan, McGleish, Vine.
*Oxford U:* Woodman; McNiven, Waterman, Bound, Crosby, Ashton, Whitehead, Wanless (Rawle), Basham (Louis), Alsop, Hunt (Hackett).

**Farnborough T (0) 0**

**Weston-Super-Mare (1) 1** *(Clark 5)* 936

*Farnborough T:* Osborn; Weatherstone, Opinel, Hutchings (Manuella), Charles▪, Burton, Hodgson, Beall, Charlery (Chaaban), Harkness (Clarke), Hayes.
*Weston-Super-Mare:* Jones; Rose, McKeever (Howell), Jarman, Clark, Benton, Slater (Davis), Jackson, Skinner, McGregor, French.

**Grantham T (1) 1** *(Wilkin K 4)*

**Leyton Orient (1) 2** *(Purser 17, Alexander 90)* 2792

*Grantham T:* Ziccardi▪; Wooding, Dakin, Gould, Fox, Wilson, Minett, Wilkin P, Kearns, Wilkin K, Collins.
*Leyton Orient:* Harrison; Joseph (Akinfenwa), Lockwood, McGhee, Peters, Hammond (Miller), Purser, Hunt▪, Alexander, Ibehre, Newey (Forbes).

**Grays Ath (0) 1** *(Griffiths 55)*

**Aldershot T (0) 2** *(D'Sane 73 (pen), 78)* 1500

*Grays Ath:* Capleton; Williams (Bradshaw), Robinson, Olayinka▪, Youds, Bruce, Marwa (Lunan), Carthy, Martin, Lock (Hayzelden), Griffiths.
*Aldershot T:* Barnard; Hooper, Sterling, Shields, Warburton, Rees, McLean (Charles), Miller, Sills, D'Sane, Chewins (Challinor).

**Grimsby T (0) 1** *(Boulding 80)*

**QPR (0) 0** 4144

*Grimsby T:* Davison; McDermott, Barnard, Hamilton, Edwards, Crane, Crowe, Campbell, Boulding, Onuora, Anderson (Cas).
*QPR:* Day; Forbes, Rowlands (Daly), Palmer, Carlisle, Bean, Ainsworth (Oli), Sabin, Gallen, Thorpe, McLeod.

**Hartlepool U (2) 4** *(Gabbiadini 25, 30, Humphreys 51, Brackstone 68)*

**Whitby T (0) 0** 5294

*Hartlepool U:* Provett; Barron (Craddock), Brackstone, Nelson, Westwood, Tinkler, Humphreys, Robinson P (Wilkinson), Williams E, Gabbiadini (Clarke), Strachan.
*Whitby T:* Clementson; Reed (Swales), Linighan, Hall, Obern (Ure), Williams, Robinson, Veart, Dixon, Browne, Ormerod (McTiernan).

**Kidderminster H (1) 2** *(Bennett 39, 84)*

**Northwich Vic (0) 1** *(Thompson 87)* 2052

*Kidderminster H:* Brock; Gadsby (Betts), Shilton, Smith, Hinton, Hatswell, Williams D, Bennett, Williams J (Lewis), White, Parrish (Henriksen).
*Northwich Vic:* Woods; Woodyatt, Brazier, Foran, Charnock, Black (Thompson), Norris, Murray, Devlin (Owen), Garvey, Allan.

**Lancaster C (1) 1** *(Hughes 35 (pen))*
**Cambridge U (1) 2** *(Kitson 16, Guttridge 90)* 1864
*Lancaster C:* Welsby; Kilbame, Sparrow, Scott, Uberschar, Clarkson, Mercer, Prince, Elderton, Hughes, Jones.
*Cambridge U:* Marshall; Goodhind, Bimson, Fleming, Angus, Duncan, Tudor, Guttridge, Kitson, Taylor (Tann), Nacca (Murray).

**Lincoln C (2) 3** *(Mayo 13 (pen), Bloomer 37, Yeo 60)*
**Brighton & HA (0) 1** *(McPhee 83)* 4425
*Lincoln C:* Marriott; Bloomer, Mayo, Weaver, Morgan, Futcher, Butcher, Green (McNamara), Fletcher, Yeo (May), Gain.
*Brighton & HA:* Kuipers; Hinshelwood, Mayo, Cullip, Butters, Carpenter, Hart, Pethick (Wilkinson), Knight, McPhee, Jones N (Piercy).

**Macclesfield T (1) 3** *(Carruthers 20, 61, Little 90)*
**Boston U (0) 0** 2059
*Macclesfield T:* Wilson; Abbey, Adams, Widdrington, Haddrell, Munroe, Little, Priest, Tipton, Carruthers, Whitaker.
*Boston U:* Bastock; Hogg (Douglas), Beevers, Greaves, Balmer (Hocking), Ellender, Thompson L, Redfearn, Duffield, Bennett, Potter (Sutch).

**Mansfield T (4) 6** *(MacKenzie 12, 43, 51, Mendes 15, Larkin 42, Curtis 78)*
**Bishop's Stortford (0) 0** 4679
*Mansfield T:* Pilkington; Hassell, Vaughan, Curtis, Artell (Disley), Day, Lawrence (Clarke), MacKenzie, Mendes, Larkin (Beardsley), Corden.
*Bishop's Stortford:* Desborough; Allman, Wiltshire (Lewis), Barnett, Gwillam■, Southam, Rainford, Beale, Essandoh, Renner (Bunn), McKeown (Parker).

**Northampton T (1) 3** *(Walker 37, Hargreaves 60, Asamoah 83)*
**Plymouth Arg (1) 2** *(Friio 32, Stonebridge 63)* 4385
*Northampton T:* Harper; Lyttle, Carruthers, Sampson, Willmott, Trollope, Low (Asamoah), Reeves (Dudfield), Walker, Smith, Hargreaves.
*Plymouth Arg:* McCormick; Worrell (Phillips), Gilbert (Lowndes), Friio, Wotton, Coughlan, Norris, Bent, Stonebridge, Evans, Keith (Hodges).

**Oldham Ath (2) 3** *(Zola 35, Cooksey 37, 78)*
**Carlisle U (0) 0** 4391
*Oldham Ath:* Pogliacomi; Clegg, Cooksey, Hall D, Beharall, Holden, Sheridan D (Boshell), Sheridan J (Hall C), Vernon, Zola (O'Halloran), Roca.
*Carlisle U:* Glennon (Keen); Shelley, Smith, Andrews, Schumacher, Jack (Henderson), McGill, McDonagh, Russell, Wake (Molloy), Farrell.

**Peterborough U (0) 2** *(Willock 53, Logan 58)*
**Hereford U (0) 0** 4479
*Peterborough U:* Tyler; Kanu (Gill), Jelleyman, Arber, Rea (Legg), Woodhouse, Newton (Scott), Thomson, Logan, Willock, Farrell.
*Hereford U:* Baker; Green, James, Mkandawire, Rose, Williams, Parry, Smith (Purdey), Guinan, Brown (Teesdale), Pitman.

**Port Vale (0) 2** *(McPhee 60, Burns 64)*
**Ford U (1) 2** *(Abraham 20, Fiddes 74)* 4016
*Port Vale:* Brain; Reid, Lipa, Collins, Burns, Pilkington, Birchall, Boyd, McPhee, Brooker (Bridge-Wilkinson), Littlejohn.
*Ford U:* Lunan; McLeod, Chandler, Perkins C, O'Sullivan, Cooper, Fiddes, Poole, Edwards, Abraham, Watson (Reinelt).

**Scarborough (0) 1** *(Rose 79)*
**Doncaster R (0) 0** 3497
*Scarborough:* Walker; Baker (Lyth), Capper, Kerr, Redmile, Cryan, Sestanovich, Kelly, Marcelle, Quayle, Rose.
*Doncaster R:* Warrington; Marples, Morley, Albrighton, Ryan, McGrath, Green, Doolan (Ravenhill), Blundell, Fortune-West (Barnes), McIndoe.

**Scunthorpe U (1) 2** *(Hayes 9, 90)*
**Shrewsbury T (0) 1** *(Quinn 87)* 3232
*Scunthorpe U:* Evans; Ridley, Sharp, Kell, Butler, Byrne, Sparrow, Barwick, MacLean (Hunt), Hayes, Beagrie.
*Shrewsbury T:* Howie; Moss, Rioch, Tolley J, Tinson, Ridler (Cramb), Street (Lowe), O'Connor, Rodgers, Quinn, Aiston.

**Stevenage B (2) 2** *(Maamria 29, 37)*
**Stockport Co (0) 1** *(Goodwin 69 (pen))* 2538
*Stevenage B:* Perez; Warner, Flynn, Bunce, Laker, Gould, Wormull (Holloway), Watson, Maamria, Elding (Baptiste), Travis (Brennan).
*Stockport Co:* Spencer; Hardiker, Pemberton, Challinor, Clare, Goodwin, Gibb, Lambert, Daly (Morrison), Barlow (Williams C), Welsh (Wilbraham).

**Swansea C (1) 3** *(Trundle 38, Nugent 58, Durkan 88)*
**Rushden & D (0) 0** 5031
*Swansea C:* Freestone; Duffy, Howard, Britton, O'Leary, Iriekpen, Durkan, Robinson (Coates), Nugent, Trundle (Thomas), Johnrose.
*Rushden & D:* Evans; Bignot, Underwood, Bell (Hall), Hunter, Edwards (Dempster), Gray, Mills, Darby, Jack, Burgess (Hanlon).

**Telford U (0) 3** *(Lavery 58, Ricketts 72, Murphy 90)*
**Crawley T (2) 2** *(Armstrong 8, Gregory 28)* 1581
*Telford U:* MacKenzie; Green, Challis, Whitehead, Simpson (Grant), Clarke, Ricketts, Blackwood (Lavery), Murphy, Naylor (Moore), Mills.
*Crawley T:* Anderson; Judge, Hemsley, Pullan, Payne (Ready), Harkin, Smith, Armstrong, Gregory, Vansittart (Forde), Dennis (MacDonald).

**Torquay U (0) 1** *(Benefield 55)*
**Burton Alb (1) 2** *(Woods 10 (og), Talbot 71)* 2790
*Torquay U:* Van Heusden; Canoville, Hazell, Hockley (Wills), Taylor, Woods, Russell, Fowler (Hill), Graham, Benefield, Bedeau.
*Burton Alb:* Duke; Willis, Webster, Chettle (Crosby), Kirkwood, Stride, Howard, Ducros, Clough, Anderson, Colkin (Talbot).

**Tranmere R (1) 3** *(Dadi 4, Hume 80, Mellon 87 (pen))*
**Chesterfield (0) 2** *(Davies 51, Evatt 83)* 5633
*Tranmere R:* Achterberg; Connelly, Roberts, Linwood, Allen, Loran, Harrison, Mellon, Haworth, Dadi (Jones), Hume (Nicholson).
*Chesterfield:* Muggleton; Davies, O'Hare, Dawson (Blatherwick), Evatt, Payne, Brandon, Warhurst, Robinson, Cade (Reeves), Allott.

**Woking (3) 3** *(Selley 23, 39 (pen), Sharpling 45)*
**Histon (1) 1** *(Cambridge A 2)* 2217
*Woking:* Bayes; Townsend (Canham), MacDonald, Boardman, Sharp, Sharpling, Smith, Selley, Nade, Haule, Foyewa.
*Histon:* Barber; Farrington, Hipperson, Vowden, Goddard, Cambridge A, Hanvier (Kennedy), Andrews, Barker, Rowe (Coburn), Cambridge I.

**Wycombe W (1) 4** *(Thomson 44, Currie 64, 85, McSporran 87)*
**Swindon T (0) 1** *(Gurney 71 (pen))* 4738
*Wycombe W:* Talia; Senda, Vinnicombe, Bulman, Thomson, Johnson, Currie, Simpson, McSporran, Roberts (Brown), Ryan (Mapes).
*Swindon T:* Evans; Gurney, Duke, Nicholas, Reeves (Ruster), Heywood, Miglioranzi, Robinson, Mooney, Parkin, Howard (Smith).

**Yeovil T (1) 4** *(Gall 39, Williams 46, Pluck 59, Edwards 66)*
**Wrexham (0) 1** *(Armstrong 88)* 5049
*Yeovil T:* Weale; Williams, Crittenden (El Kholti), Lockwood, Skiverton, Pluck, Terry, Way, Edwards (Jackson), Gall (Stansfield), Johnson.
*Wrexham:* Dibble; Edwards C, Holmes, Lawrence, Roberts, Carey (Morgan), Whitley, Ferguson, Sam, Jones L (Armstrong), Llewellyn (Thomas).

Sunday, 9 November 2003

**Accrington S (0) 1** *(Gouck 90)*
**Huddersfield T (0) 0** 3129
*Accrington S:* Kennedy; Cavanagh, Hollis, Halford (Smith), Williams, Cook (Gouck), Calcutt (Jackson), Proctor, James, Mullin, Prendergast.
*Huddersfield T:* Gray (Senior P); Sodje, Lloyd, Holdsworth, Scott (Brown), Clarke, Worthington■, Holland (Mattis), Booth, Stead, Schofield.

**Bradford PA (2) 2** *(Hayward 5, Coles 13 (og))*
**Bristol C (2) 5** *(Amankwaah 6, 8, Stansfield 55 (og), Wilkshire 67, Matthews 83)* 1945
*Bradford PA:* Boswell; Mitchell, Maxwell (Walsh), Serrant, Collins (Smith), Stansfield, Oleksewycz (Wright), Benn, Wood, Crossley, Hayward.
*Bristol C:* Phillips; Amankwaah, Woodman, Coles, Butler, Hill, Wilkshire (Clist), Burnell, Peacock, Roberts (Matthews), Brown A (Lita).

**Hornchurch (1) 2** *(West 43 (pen), John 61)*
**Darlington (0) 0** 2186
*Hornchurch:* Gay; Gooding, Kerrigan, Locke, West, Adedeji, Keeling, Sterling (Rowland), Opara, John (Allen), Graham.
*Darlington:* Price; McGurk, Morgan, Hughes, Pearson, Clarke, Keltie (Hutchinson), Maddison, Conlon, Clark, Nicholls (Wainwright).

**Notts Co (3) 7** *(Fenton 7, Platt 14, 18, Nicholson 64, Richardson 69, Barras 84, Heffernan 88)*
**Shildon (0) 2** *(Middleton 55, Barnes 63 (pen))* 4016
*Notts Co:* Mildenhall; Jenkins, Richardson, Riley (Nicholson), Fenton, Barras, Baldry (Brough), Caskey, Platt (Heffernan), Stallard, Baraclough.
*Shildon:* Jackson; Hainsworth (Owers), Walton (Reid), Bayles, Middleton, Liddle, Bolton (Richmond), Key, Barnes, Ellison, Emmerson.

**Sheffield W (1) 4** *(Proudlock 32 (pen), 46, 64, Owusu 70)*
**Salisbury C (0) 0** 11,419
*Sheffield W:* Pressman; Geary, Beswetherick, Lee, Smith D, Bromby, Mustoe (Haslam), McLaren, Owusu, Proudlock (Shaw J), Reddy (Cooke).
*Salisbury C:* Sawyer; Bartlett (Holmes), Thomas, Davies, Cooper (Purches), Cook, Turk, Funnell, Wallace, Strong (Crook), James.

**Southend U (1) 1** *(Gower 2)*
**Canvey Island (1) 1** *(Chenery 7)* 9234
*Southend U:* Flahavan; McSweeney, Jenkins, Maher (Husbands), Cort, Warren, Wilson, Smith, Bramble, Corbett, Gower.
*Canvey Island:* Potter; Midgley, Duffy, Chenery, Ward, Theobald, Kennedy, Gooden (Dobinson), Gregory, Boylan (McDougald), Minton.

**York C (1) 1** *(Nogan 36)*
**Barnsley (1) 2** *(Rankin 38, Betsy 82)* 5658
*York C:* Ovendale; Edmondson, Merris, Hope, Brass, Smith, Ward (Brackstone), Dunning (George), Nogan, Bullock, Cooper (Wilford).
*Barnsley:* Ilic; O'Callaghan, Gallimore, Kay, Handyside (Austin), Ireland, Burns, Hayward, Rankin, Betsy, Carson (Lumsdon).

## FIRST ROUND REPLAYS

Tuesday, 18 November 2003

**Luton T (1) 3** *(Forbes 39, 76, 87 (pen))*
**Thurrock (0) 1** *(Akurang 49)* 3667
*Luton T:* Beresford; Foley (Hillier), Barnett (Crowe), Spring, Boyce, Coyne, Mansell (Okai), Robinson, Forbes, Howard, Brkovic.
*Thurrock:* Gothard; Collis, Goodfellow, Heffer, McFarlane, Purdie, Linger, Howard (Lee K), Akurang, Kandol, Bowes.

**Stalybridge C (0) 0**
**Barnet (1) 2** *(Grazioli 27, 54)* 1549
*Stalybridge C:* Dootson; Pearce (Foster), Bowman (Smith■), Keeling, German, Bowker, Clegg, Heald, Mayers■, Potts, Eastwood.
*Barnet:* Gore; Rooney, King, Hendon, Plummer, Maddix■, Hogg (Lopez), Gamble, Grazioli (Williams), Strevens, Yakubu.

Wednesday, 19 November 2003

**Canvey Island (2) 2** *(Boylan 10, Minton 45)*
**Southend U (1) 3** *(Bramble 23, Smith 46, 90)* 2731
*Canvey Island:* Potter; Midgley, Duffy, Chenery, Ward, Theobald, Kennedy, Gooden (Dobinson), Gregory, Boylan, Minton.
*Southend U:* Flahavan; McSweeney, Stuart, Maher, Cort, Warren■, Gower, Smith, Bramble, Corbett, Jenkins.

**Ford U (0) 1** *(Poole 90)*
**Port Vale (1) 2** *(Paynter 38, Chandler 114 (og))* 1374
*Ford U:* Lunan; Halle, O'Sullivan (Reinelt) (Patten), Fiddes, Chandler, Perkins C, Edwards, Poole, Watson (Fenton), Abraham, Cooper.
*Port Vale:* Brain; Cummins, Reid, Collins, Burns, Pilkington, Boyd (Birchall), Brisco, McPhee, Paynter, Littlejohn (Armstrong■).
*aet.*

## SECOND ROUND

Friday, 5 December 2003

**Wycombe W (0) 1** *(Holligan 53)*
**Mansfield T (0) 1** *(Christie 61)* 3212
*Wycombe W:* Talia; Senda, Vinnicombe, Bulman, Marshall, Johnson, Currie, Simpemba, McSporran, Faulconbridge, Holligan (Roberts).
*Mansfield T:* Pilkington; Hassell, Vaughan, Williamson, Artell, Day, Lawrence, MacKenzie, Christie, Mendes, Disley (Larkin).

Saturday, 6 December 2003

**Bournemouth (0) 1** *(Browning 56)*
**Accrington S (1) 1** *(Mullin 9)* 7551
*Bournemouth:* Moss; Purches, Cummings, Broadhurst, Fletcher C, Browning, Elliott (Tindall), Stock, Feeney, Fletcher S, O'Connor.
*Accrington S:* Speare; Cavanagh, Halford, Smith (Howarth), Williams, Cook (Flitcroft), Proctor, Gouck (Armstrong), James, Mullin, Prendergast.

**Bristol C (0) 0**
**Barnsley (0) 0** 6741
*Bristol C:* Phillips; Carey, Woodman, Clist (Roberts), Coles, Hill, Wilkshire, Tinnion, Peacock (Matthews), Miller, Brown A.
*Barnsley:* Ilic; O'Callaghan, Gallimore, Monk, Ireland, Kay (Neil), Austin, Hayward, Betsy, Walters, Lumsdon.

**Cheltenham T (2) 3** *(McCann 18 (pen), 34, Taylor 60)*
**Leyton Orient (0) 1** *(Lockwood 69)* 3959
*Cheltenham T:* Higgs; Bird, Victory, Finnigan, Brough, Duff M (Duff S), Devaney, Yates, Taylor (Odejayi), Spencer, McCann.
*Leyton Orient:* Morris■; Joseph, Lockwood, Miller, Peters, Zakuani, Purser (Harrison), Hunt, Alexander, Thorpe, Newey (Ibehre).

**Colchester U (0) 1** *(Vine 83)*
**Aldershot T (0) 0** 4255
*Colchester U:* Brown S; Stockley, Myers, Pinault, White, Chilvers, Duguid, Izzet, Andrews, McGleish, Vine.
*Aldershot T:* Bull; Challinor, Sterling, Rees, Warburton (Taylor), Chewins, Miller, Shields, Sills, D'Sane, Charles.

**Gravesend & N (1) 1** *(Perkins 42)*
**Notts Co (0) 2** *(Fenton 69, Platt 90)* 2998
*Gravesend & N:* Wilkerson (O'Reilly); Lee, Gibbs■, Strouts, Moore, Shearer, Drury, McKimm, Perkins, Pinnock (Abbey), Walshe (Gradley).
*Notts Co:* Mildenhall; Jenkins, Nicholson, Bolland (Murray), Fenton, Richardson, Baldry, Caskey, Platt, Heffernan, Baraclough.

**Hornchurch (0) 0**
**Tranmere R (1) 1** *(Jones 26)* 3500
*Hornchurch:* Gay; Gooding, West, Martin, Kerrigan (Allen), Adedeji, Locke (Opara), Keeling, John, McGowan, Graham.
*Tranmere R:* Achterberg; Connelly, Tremarco, Linwood, Allen, Loran, Harrison, Mellon, Jones, Dadi (Hay), Beresford (Taylor).

**Macclesfield T (1) 1** *(Tipton 22 (pen))*
**Cambridge U (1) 1** *(Turner 23)* 2182
*Macclesfield T:* Wilson; Adams, Abbey■, Widdrington, Welch, Munroe, Little (Hitchen), Priest, Tipton, Carruthers, Whitaker.
*Cambridge U:* Marshall; Goodhind, Murray, Tann, Angus, Duncan, Nacca (Dutton), Guttridge, Taylor, Turner, Tudor.

**Northampton T (1) 4** *(Smith 36 (pen), Low 64, Richards 77, 90)*
**Weston-Super-Mare (0) 1** *(Clark 80)* 3948
*Northampton T:* Harper; Lyttle, Trollope, Lincoln, Willmott, Sampson (Chambers), Low (Richards), Asamoah, Walker, Smith, Hargreaves (Reeves).
*Weston-Super-Mare:* Jones; Jackson (Sorbara), McKeever■, Clark, Jarman, Benton (Howell), Skinner (Davis), Rose, McGregor, French, Slater.

**Oldham Ath (0) 2** *(Eyre 61, Johnson 90)*
**Blackpool (3) 5** *(Taylor 2, 20, 57, Southern 25, Richardson 73)* 6143
*Oldham Ath:* Pogliacomi; Clegg, Holden (Griffin), Boshell, Beharall (Hall D), Haining, Murray (Eyres), Sheridan J, Eyre, Johnson, Cooksey.
*Blackpool:* Jones L; Richardson, Evans, Southern, Flynn, Davis, Wellens, Bullock (Clarke), Murphy, Taylor (Sheron), Burns (McMahon).

**Peterborough U (1) 3** *(Clarke A 22, Thomson 47, Newton 65)*
**Grimsby T (1) 2** *(Jevons 24, Cas 84)* 4836
*Peterborough U:* Tyler; Gill, Jelleyman, Arber, Rea, Woodhouse, Newton, Thomson, Clarke A (Logan), McKenzie, Farrell.
*Grimsby T:* Davison; McDermott, Barnard (Young), Crowe, Edwards, Crane, Campbell, Hamilton, Jevons, Onuora (Mansaram), Anderson (Cas).

**Rochdale (0) 0**
**Luton T (1) 2** *(Robinson 20 (pen), Mansell 77)* 2807
*Rochdale:* Edwards; Evans, Simpkins, Beech (Patterson), Burgess, Grand, McCourt, Jones, Connor (McEvilly), Bishop (Townson), Doughty.
*Luton T:* Beresford; Hillier, Davis, Robinson, Boyce, Coyne, Mansell, Brkovic, Forbes, Howard, Holmes.

**Scunthorpe U (1) 2** *(Torpey 33, 71)*
**Sheffield W (0) 2** *(N'Dumbu-Nsungu 84, Holt 90)* 7418
*Scunthorpe U:* Evans; Barwick, Sharp, Butler, Jackson, Byrne, Sparrow, Kell, MacLean (Featherstone), Torpey, Beagrie.
*Sheffield W:* Pressman; Geary, Barry-Murphy, Haslam, Lee, Bromby, Mustoe, Proudlock (Wilson), Owusu (N'Dumbu-Nsungu), Holt, Reddy (Wood).

**Southend U (1) 3** *(Bramble 39, Gower 64, Corbett 89)*
**Lincoln C (0) 0** 4258
*Southend U:* Flahavan; McSweeney, Wilson, Maher, Cort, Hunt, Kightly (Constantine), Smith, Bramble (Husbands), Corbett (Broughton), Gower.
*Lincoln C:* Marriott; Bloomer (Bailey), Mayo, Weaver (May), Morgan, Futcher, Butcher, McNamara, Fletcher, Yeo, Gain.

**Swansea C (1) 2** *(Nugent 23, Trundle 51)*
**Stevenage B (0) 1** *(Elding 49)* 6125
*Swansea C:* Freestone; Duffy, Howard, Britton, O'Leary, Iriekpen, Durkan, Robinson, Nugent, Trundle, Johnrose.
*Stevenage B:* Perez; Warner, Holloway (Cook), Bunce (Carroll), Laker, Gould, Wormull, Watson, Maamria, Elding, Costello (Baptiste).

**Telford U (1) 3** *(Moore 26, 58, 80 (pen))*
**Brentford (0) 0** 2996
*Telford U:* MacKenzie; Clarke, Blackwood, Wilkinson, Whitehead, Challis, Hulbert, Simpson (Murphy), Mills (Grant), Moore (Naylor), Ricketts.
*Brentford:* Smith P; Dobson, Somner, Sonko■, Kitamirike, Smith J (Evans), Rougier (Hughes), O'Connor, May (Peters), Tabb, Hunt.

**Woking (0) 0**
**Kidderminster H (1) 3** *(Bennett 6, 64, Burton 74)* 3484
*Woking:* Bevan; Townsend (Cockerill), MacDonald, Canham, Boardman (Smith), Sharp, Nade, Selley, Foyewa, Sharpling, Ferguson (Haule).
*Kidderminster H:* Brock; Smith, Stamps, Burton (Coleman), Hinton, Hatswell, Gadsby, Bennett, Williams J (Shilton), White (Henriksen), Williams D.

**Yeovil T (3) 5** *(Pluck 9, Williams 18 (pen), 27, Crittenden 74, Edwards 78)*
**Barnet (1) 1** *(Beadle 10)* 5973
*Yeovil T:* Weale; Williams, Crittenden, Lockwood, Rodrigues, Pluck, Skiverton, Terry, Jackson (Edwards), Gall (Stansfield), Johnson (Gosling).
*Barnet:* Gore; Hendon, King, Lopez, Plummer, Maddix (Rooney), Strevens, Gamble (Hatch), Grazioli, Beadle (Williams), Yakubu.

Sunday, 7 December 2003

**Burton Alb (0) 0**
**Hartlepool U (0) 1** *(Porter 70)* 3132
*Burton Alb:* Duke; Henshaw, Webster, Stride, Wassall, Chettle, Dudley, Howard, Anderson (Ducros), Colkin (Talbot), Kirkwood.
*Hartlepool U:* Provett; Barron, Robson, Nelson, Westwood, Tinkler, Byrne (Robinson P), Humphreys, Williams E, Porter (Wilkinson), Strachan.

**Port Vale (0) 0**
**Scarborough (0) 1** *(Sestanovich 80)* 4651
*Port Vale:* Brain; Cummins, Reid, Collins, Burns (Birchall), Pilkington, Boyd (Bridge-Wilkinson), Littlejohn, McPhee, Paynter, Lipa (Brisco).
*Scarborough:* Walker; Lyth, Hotte, Kerr, Redmile, Cryan, Kelly, Sestanovich, Quayle (Rose), Marcelle, Gill.

## SECOND ROUND REPLAYS

Monday, 15 December 2003

**Accrington S (0) 0**
**Bournemouth (0) 0** 2585
*Accrington S:* Speare (Kennedy); Cavanagh, Halford, Williams, Howarth, Cook, Proctor, Gouck (Flitcroft), James, Mullin (Armstrong), Prendergast.
*Bournemouth:* Moss; Purches (Buxton), Cummings, Broadhurst, Fletcher C, Browning, Elliott (Hayter), Stock, Feeney, Fletcher S, O'Connor.
*aet; Accrington S won 5-3 on penalties.*

Tuesday, 16 December 2003

**Barnsley (2) 2** *(Kay 24, Monk 43)*
**Bristol C (0) 1** *(Roberts 65)* 5434
*Barnsley:* Ilic; O'Callaghan, Austin, Burns, Monk, Ireland, Kay, Hayward, Betsy, Walters (Neil), Carson (Lumsdon).
*Bristol C:* Phillips; Carey, Woodman, Clist (Roberts), Coles, Hill, Wilkshire, Tinnion, Peacock, Miller (Lita), Brown A (Bell).

**Cambridge U (0) 2** *(Turner 66, Tann 119)*
**Macclesfield T (1) 2** *(Miles 26, Tipton 101)* 2545
*Cambridge U:* Marshall; Goodhind, Murray, Duncan, Angus (Dutton), Tann, Nacca (Bridges), Guttridge, Taylor, Turner, Tudor (Venus).
*Macclesfield T:* Wilson; Abbey, Adams, Widdrington, Welch, Munroe■, Little (Haddrell), Priest (Brackenridge), Miles, Tipton (Carruthers), Whitaker.
*aet; Macclesfield T won 4-2 on penalties.*

**Mansfield T (1) 3** *(Lawrence 14, 72 (pen), 90 (pen))*
**Wycombe W (0) 2** *(McSporran 56, 59)* 5512
*Mansfield T:* Pilkington; Hassell, Vaughan (Dimech), Curtis, Artell, Day, Lawrence, Williamson, Mendes, Disley (Christie), Corden.
*Wycombe W:* Williams; Rogers, Vinnicombe, Simpemba, Thomson, Johnson, Roberts, Simpson, Dixon (Ryan), Faulconbridge, McSporran.

Wednesday, 17 December 2003

**Sheffield W (0) 0**
**Scunthorpe U (0) 0** 11,722
*Sheffield W:* Pressman; Geary, Barry-Murphy, Haslam, Lee, Bromby, Mustoe, N'Dumbu-Nsungu, Owusu (Smith D), Proudlock (Wilson), Holt (Beswetherick).
*Scunthorpe U:* Evans; Graves (Stanton), Sharp, Barwick, Butler, Byrne, Sparrow, Kell, MacLean, Torpey (Hayes), Beagrie.
*aet; Scunthorpe U won 3-1 on penalties.*

## THIRD ROUND

Saturday, 3 January 2004

**Accrington S (0) 0**
**Colchester U (0) 0** 4368
*Accrington S:* Speare; Howarth, Hollis, Cook, Williams, Halford (Armstrong), Proctor (Calcutt), Gouck (Flitcroft), James, Mullin, Prendergast.
*Colchester U:* Brown S; Stockley, Johnson, Pinault, Fitzgerald, Chilvers, Duguid, Izzet, Fagan, McGleish, Vine (Keith).

**Barnsley (0) 0**
**Scunthorpe U (0) 0** 10,839
*Barnsley:* Ilic; O'Callaghan, Austin, Burns, Monk, Ireland, Kay (Jack), Neil, Betsy, Walters (Rankin), Carson.
*Scunthorpe U:* Evans; Stanton, Sharp (Featherstone), Barwick, Butler, Byrne, Sparrow, Kell (Kilford), MacLean, Torpey, Beagrie (Hayes).

**Birmingham C (2) 4** *(Morrison 23, Clemence 36, Forssell 78, Hughes 84)*
**Blackburn R (0) 0** 18,688
*Birmingham C:* Maik Taylor; Kenna, Lazaridis (Carter), Cunningham, Upson (Hughes), Clemence, Johnson, Savage, Forssell, Morrison, Dunn (Kirovski).
*Blackburn R:* Friedel; Babbel, Gresko, Todd, Short (Taylor), Tugay, Neill, Flitcroft, Cole, Gallagher (Yorke), Mahon (Baggio).

**Bradford C (0) 1** *(Gray 83 (pen))*
**Luton T (1) 2** *(Forbes 20, 48)* 8222
*Bradford C:* Combe; Atherton, Heckingbottom, Kearney (Muirhead), Wetherall (Gavin), Bower, Evans, Windass, Armstrong, Gray (Branch), Farrelly.
*Luton T:* Beresford; Foley, Davis, Spring (Holmes), Boyce, Coyne, Mansell, Robinson, Forbes, Howard, Brkovic.

**Cardiff C (0) 0**
**Sheffield U (0) 1** *(Allison 74)* 10,525
*Cardiff C:* Margetson; Weston (Croft), Prior, Whalley (Campbell), Gabbidon, Vidmar, Langley, Kavanagh, Earnshaw (Lee), Thorne, Boland.
*Sheffield U:* Kenny; Jagielka, Kozluk, McCall, Morgan, Page, Sturridge (Peschisolido), Montgomery, Lester, Ward (Allison), Tonge.

**Coventry C (0) 2** *(McSheffrey 59, Joachim 61)*
**Peterborough U (0) 1** *(Clarke A 79)* 11,400
*Coventry C:* Ward; Whing, Warnock, Staunton, Konjic, Davenport, McSheffrey (Pitt), Safri, Adebola, Joachim, Doyle.
*Peterborough U:* Tyler; Kanu (Newton), Legg, Arber, Rea, Burton■, Woodhouse, Thomson, Logan (Willock), Williams, Farrell (Clarke A).

**Crewe Alex (0) 0**
**Telford U (1) 1** *(Mills 2)* 7085
*Crewe Alex:* Ince; Wright, Tonkin, Jones B, Foster, Higdon, Rix (Jeffs), Lunt, Ashton, Jones S, Varney (Robinson).
*Telford U:* MacKenzie; Clarke, Challis, Hulbert, Whitehead, Howarth, Murphy (Grant), Simpson, Mills, Moore (Naylor), Ricketts.

**Everton (2) 3** *(Kilbane 15, Ferguson 38 (pen), 70 (pen))*
**Norwich C (1) 1** *(Brennan 27)* 29,955
*Everton:* Martyn; Hibbert, Naysmith, Stubbs, Unsworth, Carsley, McFadden (Jeffers), Gravesen (Yobo), Ferguson (Campbell), Rooney, Kilbane.
*Norwich C:* Green; Edworthy, Drury, Fleming, Mackay, Holt, Brennan (Henderson), Francis (Mulryne), Huckerby, Roberts (Jarvis), McVeigh.

**Gillingham (3) 3** *(Johnson T 17, Sidibe 19, Smith 34)*
**Charlton Ath (1) 2** *(Cox 1 (og), Cole 90)* 10,894
*Gillingham:* Bossu; Nosworthy, Hills, Hope, Cox, Smith, Spiller, Johnson T (Henderson), Sidibe, Shaw, Southall.
*Charlton Ath:* Kiely; Kishishev (Euell), Hreidarsson, Holland, Perry (Di Canio), Fortune, Stuart, Jensen, Cole, Johansson, Konchesky.

**Ipswich T (0) 3** *(Naylor 54, Miller 69, Kuqi 89)*
**Derby Co (0) 0** 16,159
*Ipswich T:* Davis; Wilnis, Richards, Bart-Williams (Magilton), McGreal, Naylor, Reuser, Miller, Counago (Bowditch), Bent D (Kuqi), Wright.
*Derby Co:* Grant; Mills, Zavagno, Huddlestone, Mawene, Johnson (Holmes), Bolder, Taylor, Tudgay, Manel, Morris.

**Kidderminster H (0) 1** *(Williams J 77)*
**Wolverhampton W (0) 1** *(Rae 89)* 6005
*Kidderminster H:* Brock; Smith, Stamps, Christiansen, Hinton, Hatswell, Parrish, Bennett, Henriksen (Williams J), Ward, Williams D (Gadsby).
*Wolverhampton W:* Oakes; Irwin, Naylor, Cameron, Clyde, Craddock, Newton, Rae, Iversen, Miller (Ganea), Kennedy (Silas).

**Manchester C (1) 2** *(Anelka 27 (pen), 69)*
**Leicester C (1) 2** *(Dickov 4, Bent 66)* 30,617
*Manchester C:* Seaman; Jihai, Dunne, Sommeil, Distin, Bosvelt (Barton), Wright-Phillips (Sinclair), Reyna, Anelka, Fowler, McManaman (Sibierski).
*Leicester C:* Walker; Impey, Davidson, McKinlay, Heath, Scimeca (Stewart), Hignett, Izzet, Dickov (Ferdinand), Bent (Brooker), Scowcroft.

**Mansfield T (0) 0**
**Burnley (1) 2** *(Moore I 30, 73)* 8290
*Mansfield T:* Pilkington; Hassell, Clarke■, Curtis (Artell), Day, Dimech■, Lawrence, Williamson, Christie (Corden), Mendes, Disley (Buxton).
*Burnley:* Jensen; Roche, McEveley (Camara), Chaplow■, May, McGregor, Weller, Grant, Moore I, Blake, Chadwick (Moore A).

**Middlesbrough (1) 2** *(Richardson 25 (og), Zenden 64)*
**Notts Co (0) 0** 15,061
*Middlesbrough:* Jones; Mills, Queudrue, Southgate, Ehiogu (Riggott), Boateng, Downing, Nemeth, Ricketts (Morrison), Job (Maccarone), Zenden.
*Notts Co:* Mildenhall; Fenton, Nicholson, Riley, Barras■, Richardson, Baldry, Caskey, Platt (Harrad), Stallard, Baraclough (Brough).

**Millwall (2) 2** *(Braniff 33, Cahill 45)*

**Walsall (1) 1** *(Leitao 12)* 6977

*Millwall:* Warner; Muscat, Livermore, Cahill (Elliott), Lawrence, Ward, Sweeney (Fofana), Wise, Harris, Braniff, Roberts.
*Walsall:* Walker■; Bazeley, Aranalde (Vincent), Osborn, Roper, Ritchie, Wrack, Emblen, Leitao■, Birch (Hawley), Samways (Lawrence).

**Northampton T (0) 1** *(Smith 63)*

**Rotherham U (0) 1** *(Barker R 55)* 5741

*Northampton T:* Harper; Lyttle (Harsley), Carruthers, Sampson, Westwood, Reid, Trollope, Asamoah, Walker (Richards), Smith, Hargreaves.
*Rotherham U:* Pollitt; Barker S, Hurst, Talbot, Swailes, Branston, Sedgwick, Daws, Barker R, Byfield (Hoskins), Warne.

**Nottingham F (0) 1** *(King 54 (pen))*

**WBA (0) 0** 11,843

*Nottingham F:* Ward; Louis-Jean, Robertson, Gunnarsson, Morgan, Walker, Williams, Thompson, Taylor, King, Reid.
*WBA:* Hoult; Haas, Robinson, Moore, Gaardsoe, Clement, O'Connor, Sakiri (Dyer), Hulse, Horsfield (Dobie), Koumas.

**Portsmouth (1) 2** *(Schemmel 36, Yakubu 90)*

**Blackpool (1) 1** *(Taylor 43)* 13,479

*Portsmouth:* Wapenaar; Zivkovic, Taylor, Schemmel, Stefanovic, De Zeeuw, Hughes, Smertin, Yakubu (Robinson), Sheringham, Burton.
*Blackpool:* Jones L; Grayson, Evans■, Hilton, Flynn, Davis, Wellens (Clarke), Bullock, Murphy, Taylor (Johnson), Coid.

**Preston NE (3) 3** *(O'Neil 9, Fuller 32, 45)*

**Reading (3) 3** *(Goater 7, Jackson 13 (og), Davis 37 (og))* 9428

*Preston NE:* Gould; Alexander, Davis, O'Neil, Lucketti, Jackson, Keane, McKenna, Healy, Fuller (Abbott), Lewis.
*Reading:* Hahnemann; Murty, Shorey (Salako), Brown, Williams, Newman, Murray, Sidwell, Goater, Savage (Morgan), Harper.

**Southampton (0) 0**

**Newcastle U (2) 3** *(Dyer 24, 67, Robert 39)* 28,456

*Southampton:* Niemi; Dodd, Higginbotham, Telfer, Lundekvam, Svensson M, Prutton, Pahars (Ormerod), Beattie, Phillips, Svensson A.
*Newcastle U:* Given; Hughes, Bernard, Speed, Woodgate, Bramble, Solano (Ambrose), Jenas, Shearer, Dyer (Lua-Lua), Robert (Viana).

**Southend U (1) 1** *(Smith 9)*

**Scarborough (0) 1** *(Kerr 74)* 6902

*Southend U:* Flahavan; Jupp, Stuart, Maher, Cort, Hunt, Gower, Smith, Bramble (Broughton), Constantine, Jenkins (Kightly).
*Scarborough:* Walker; Lyth, Baker, Kerr, Cryan, Hotte, Kelly, Gill (Whitman), Quayle, Marcelle (Williams), Sestanovich.

**Sunderland (0) 1** *(Arca 53)*

**Hartlepool U (0) 0** 40,816

*Sunderland:* Poom; Wright, Arca, Bjorklund (Williams), Babb, McCartney, Oster (Butler), Whitley, Proctor, Stewart, Clark.
*Hartlepool U:* Provett; Barron, Robson, Nelson, Westwood, Tinkler (Clarke), Shuker (Istead), Humphreys, Williams E, Robinson P (Porter), Strachan.

**Swansea C (1) 2** *(Trundle 44, 70)*

**Macclesfield T (0) 1** *(Tipton 65)* 8112

*Swansea C:* Freestone; Duffy, Howard, Britton, O'Leary, Iriekpen, Maylett, Robinson (Coates), Thomas (Nugent), Trundle, Johnrose.
*Macclesfield T:* Wilson; Adams, Carr, Priest, Haddrell, Macauley■, Little, Brackenridge, Tipton, Carruthers (Miles), Whitaker.

**Tottenham H (2) 3** *(Kanoute 15, 20, 48)*

**Crystal Palace (0) 0** 32,340

*Tottenham H:* Keller; Carr, Taricco, Gardner, Doherty, King (Davies), Poyet■, Dalmat, Keane, Kanoute, Jackson (Zamora).
*Crystal Palace:* Berthelin; Butterfield■, Borrowdale (Granville), Symons (Smith), Popovic, Watson, Routledge, Gray, Johnson (Freedman), Shipperley, Hughes.

**Tranmere R (0) 1** *(Haworth 51)*

**Bolton W (0) 1** *(Nolan 78)* 10,587

*Tranmere R:* Achterberg; Taylor, Roberts, Linwood, Allen, Sharps (Navarro), Hume (Dadi), Mellon, Haworth, Jones, Beresford.
*Bolton W:* Poole; Hunt (Frandsen), Smith (Vaz Te), Barness, Emerson, Comyn-Platt, Giannakopoulos, Ba (Nolan), Pedersen, Facey, Livesey.

**Watford (2) 2** *(Helguson 5, Mahon 34)*

**Chelsea (2) 2** *(Gudjohnsen 33 (pen), Lampard 41)* 21,121

*Watford:* Pidgeley; Ardley, Smith, Vernazza, Dyche, Gayle, Devlin, Hyde, Helguson, Cook (Webber), Mahon.
*Chelsea:* Sullivan; Johnson, Babayaro, Makelele, Gallas, Desailly, Gronkjaer, Lampard, Gudjohnsen, Mutu, Geremi.

**Wigan Ath (0) 1** *(Quinn 90 (og))*

**West Ham U (0) 2** *(Mullins 80, Connolly 85)* 11,793

*Wigan Ath:* Filan; Eaden, Baines (Jackson), Mitchell, Breckin, De Vos, Teale, Bullard, Ellington, Roberts, McCulloch.
*West Ham U:* James; Stockdale, Quinn, Mullins, Repka (Dailly), Pearce, Carrick, Horlock (Hutchison), Harewood (Mellor), Connolly, Etherington.

**Wimbledon (0) 1** *(Nowland 73)*

**Stoke C (1) 1** *(Eustace 12)* 3609

*Wimbledon:* Banks; Darlington, Lewington, McAnuff, Gier, Leigertwood, Nowland, Small, Agyemang, Mackie (Gray), Reo-Coker.
*Stoke C:* Cutler; Halls, Hall, Thomas, Eustace, Russell, Johnson (Hoekstra), Akinbiyi (Greenacre), Asaba, Noel-Williams, Clarke.

Sunday, 4 January 2004

**Aston Villa (1) 1** *(Barry 19)*

**Manchester U (0) 2** *(Scholes 64, 68)* 40,371

*Aston Villa:* Sorensen; De la Cruz, Samuel, McCann, Johnsen, Mellberg, Hendrie (Hitzlsperger), Barry, Angel, Vassell (Moore S), Whittingham.
*Manchester U:* Howard; Neville G, O'Shea (Keane), Brown, Butt, Silvestre, Kleberson (Fletcher), Scholes, Forlan (Van Nistelrooy), Giggs, Fortune.

**Fulham (1) 2** *(Saha 13, 90)*

**Cheltenham T (1) 1** *(McCann 5)* 10,303

*Fulham:* Van der Sar; Djetou, Green, Knight, Goma (Melville), Davis, Legwinski, Inamoto (Hayles), Saha, Malbranque, Petta.
*Cheltenham T:* Higgs; Wilson, Victory, Forsyth, Brough, Duff M, Devaney, Finnigan, Taylor, Spencer (Odejayi), McCann.

**Leeds U (1) 1** *(Viduka 8)*

**Arsenal (2) 4** *(Henry 26, Edu 33, Pires 87, Toure 90)* 31,207

*Leeds U:* Robinson; Richardson, Harte, Matteo, Kilgallon, Duberry, Bakke (Sakho), Batty, Viduka, Smith, Milner (Lennon).
*Arsenal:* Lehmann; Lauren, Cole, Vieira, Campbell, Keown, Ljungberg (Parlour), Silva, Kanu (Pires), Henry, Edu (Toure).

**Yeovil T (0) 0**

**Liverpool (0) 2** *(Heskey 70, Murphy 77 (pen))* 9348

*Yeovil T:* Weale; Williams, Crittenden, Lockwood, Pluck (Jackson), Rodrigues, Skiverton, Way, Terry (Lindegaard) (Gosling), Gall, Johnson.
*Liverpool:* Dudek; Biscan, Riise, Hamann, Henchoz, Hyypia, Diouf (Le Tallec), Murphy, Sinama-Pongolle (Heskey), Smicer (Cheyrou), Kewell.

## THIRD ROUND REPLAYS

Tuesday, 13 January 2004

**Bolton W (0) 1** *(Shakes 90)*

**Tranmere R (0) 2** *(Dadi 82, Hume 91)* 8759

*Bolton W:* Poole; Barness, Smith, Frandsen, Livesey, Comyn-Platt, Giannakopoulos (Shakes), Vaz Te, Pedersen, Jardel (Nolan), Facey (Taylor).
*Tranmere R:* Achterberg; Taylor, Roberts, Harrison, Allen, Sharps, Jones, Mellon, Dadi, Hume (Navarro), Beresford (Hay).
*aet.*

**Colchester U (1) 2** *(Keith 11, 84)*

**Accrington S (0) 1** *(Mullin 89)* 5611

*Colchester U:* Brown S; Stockley, Halford, Pinault, Fitzgerald, Chilvers, Fagan (White), Izzet, Andrews (Vine), McGleish, Keith.
*Accrington S:* Kennedy; Cavanagh, Halford■, Cook, Howarth (Smith), Williams, Proctor, Flitcroft (Calcutt), James, Mullin, Prendergast.

**Reading (0) 1** *(Goater 84)*

**Preston NE (1) 2** *(Cresswell 28, Koumantarakis 47)* 9314

*Reading:* Hahnemann; Murty, Shorey, Ingimarsson, Williams, Newman (Sidwell), Murray, Hughes (Salako), Goater, Morgan, Harper (Watson).
*Preston NE:* Gould; Alexander, Keane, O'Neil, Edwards, Mears, McKenna, Etuhu, Cresswell, Koumantarakis (Abbott), Healy.

**Rotherham U (1) 1** *(Hurst 19)*

**Northampton T (1) 2** *(Walker 36, Smith 54)* 9405

*Rotherham U:* Pollitt; Barker S, Hurst, Talbot, Swailes, Minto, Sedgwick (Monkhouse), Mullin, Barker R (Butler), Byfield, Warne (Garner).
*Northampton T:* Harper; Lyttle, Carruthers, Sampson, Willmott, Reid, Trollope, Asamoah (Richards), Walker, Smith, Hargreaves.

**Scunthorpe U (1) 2** *(Torpey 14, McCombe 74)*

**Barnsley (0) 0** 6293

*Scunthorpe U:* Evans; Graves, Ridley (Featherstone), Barwick, Stanton, Byrne, Sparrow, Kilford, MacLean (Kell), Torpey, Hayes (McCombe).
*Barnsley:* Ilic; Austin, Crooks, Handyside (O'Callaghan), Monk, Ireland, Kay, Hayward (Lumsdon), Betsy, Rankin, Burns (Carson).

**Stoke C (0) 0**

**Wimbledon (1) 1** *(Nowland 32)* 6463

*Stoke C:* Cutler; Halls, Clarke, Thomas, Eustace, Russell, Neal (Commons), Svard (Johnson), Asaba, Greenacre (Iwelumo), Hoekstra.
*Wimbledon:* Banks; Darlington, Lewington, Tapp (Chorley), Gier, Leigertwood, McAnuff, Small (Gordon), Gray, Holdsworth (Mackie), Nowland.

**Wolverhampton W (1) 2** *(Miller 36, 65)*

**Kidderminster H (0) 0** 25,808

*Wolverhampton W:* Oakes; Luzhny, Andrews, Butler, Clyde, Craddock, Newton, Gudjonsson, Ganea (Iversen), Miller, Kennedy (Silas).
*Kidderminster H:* Brock; Smith, Stamps, Bennett, Hinton, Hatswell, Parrish (Rickards), Ward, Henriksen, Christiansen (Williams J), Williams D.

Wednesday, 14 January 2004

**Chelsea (2) 4** *(Mutu 7, 76, Hasselbaink 34, Gudjohnsen 84)*

**Watford (0) 0** 38,763

*Chelsea:* Cudicini; Melchiot, Babayaro, Makelele, Terry, Gallas (Huth), Gronkjaer, Lampard, Hasselbaink (Gudjohnsen), Mutu (Duff), Cole J.
*Watford:* Pidgeley; Ardley, Smith, Cox, Gayle, Hand (Doyley), Devlin, Hyde, Dyer (Webber), Mahon, Cook (Fitzgerald).

**Leicester C (0) 1** *(Ferdinand 73)*

**Manchester C (1) 3** *(Sibierski 12, Anelka 89, Macken 90)* 18,916

*Leicester C:* Walker; Curtis, Davidson, McKinlay, Heath, Sinclair, Scowcroft, Bent, Dickov, Ferdinand (Elliott), Stewart.
*Manchester C:* Ellegaard; Dunne, Tarnat, Sommeil, Distin, Barton, Sibierski, Bosvelt, Anelka, Macken, Sinclair.

**Scarborough (0) 1** *(Quayle 83)*

**Southend U (0) 0** 4859

*Scarborough:* Walker; Lyth, Baker, Kerr, Cryan, Hotte, Kelly, Whitman, Quayle, Marcelle, Sestanovich.
*Southend U:* Flahavan; Jupp, Stuart, Maher, Cort, Hunt, Gower (Clark), Smith, Bramble (Corbett), Constantine, Jenkins (Kightly).

## FOURTH ROUND

Saturday, 24 January 2004

**Arsenal (2) 4** *(Bergkamp 19, Ljungberg 28, 68, Bentley 90)*

**Middlesbrough (1) 1** *(Job 23)* 37,256

*Arsenal:* Lehmann; Lauren, Cole, Vieira (Clichy), Campbell, Toure, Parlour, Edu, Ljungberg, Bergkamp (Bentley), Pires.
*Middlesbrough:* Schwarzer; Mills, Queudrue, Riggott, Parnaby, Boateng■, Downing (Nemeth), Mendieta, Ricketts (Maccarone), Job (Juninho), Zenden.

**Birmingham C (1) 1** *(Hughes 4)*

**Wimbledon (0) 0** 22,159

*Birmingham C:* Maik Taylor; Tebily, Kenna, Cunningham, Purse, Hughes, Johnson, Savage, Morrison, John (Clapham), Dunn (Forssell).
*Wimbledon:* Banks; Darlington, Lewington, Chorley, Gier, Leigertwood, McAnuff, Small, Holdsworth (Gray), Mackie, Harding (Hawkins).

**Burnley (2) 3** *(Moore I 30, Blake 33, 64)*

**Gillingham (0) 1** *(Henderson 71)* 9735

*Burnley:* Jensen; Roche, Camara, Chaplow, May, McGregor, Little, Grant, Moore I, Blake, Moore A (Branch).
*Gillingham:* Bossu; Nosworthy, Hills, Hope, Ashby, Smith, Hessenthaler, Pouton (James), Henderson, Johnson T (Jarvis), Spiller (Johnson L).

**Coventry C (1) 1** *(Joachim 33)*

**Colchester U (1) 1** *(Adebola 30 (og))* 15,341

*Coventry C:* Ward; Whing, Gordon, Deloumeaux, Konjic, Davenport, Doyle, McSheffrey, Adebola (Gudjonsson), Morrell (Warnock), Joachim.
*Colchester U:* McKinney; Stockley, Duguid, Pinault, White, Chilvers, Fagan, Izzet, Andrews (Vine), McGleish, Keith.

**Ipswich T (0) 1** *(Reuser 90)*

**Sunderland (1) 2** *(Smith 45, Arca 68)* 21,406

*Ipswich T:* Davis; Wilnis, Richards (Reuser), Miller, Naylor, McGreal, Magilton, Wright, Counago, Kuqi, Westlake.
*Sunderland:* Poom; Williams (Ramsden), McCartney, Thirlwell, Babb, Bjorklund, McAteer (Thornton), Whitley, Kyle, Smith (Oster), Arca.

**Liverpool (1) 2** *(Cheyrou 2, 61)*

**Newcastle U (1) 1** *(Robert 4)* 41,365

*Liverpool:* Dudek; Finnan, Carragher, Hamann, Henchoz, Hyypia, Heskey (Le Tallec), Gerrard, Cheyrou, Owen, Kewell.
*Newcastle U:* Given; Hughes, Bernard, Speed, Woodgate, O'Brien, Solano (Ameobi), Jenas, Shearer, Dyer, Robert.

**Luton T (0) 0**

**Tranmere R (0) 1** *(Mellon 81)* 8767

*Luton T:* Beresford; Foley, Davis, Holmes, Boyce, Coyne, Leary, Nicholls (Crowe), Showunmi, Mansell (Keane), Brkovic.
*Tranmere R:* Achterberg; Taylor, Roberts, Sharps, Allen, Jones, Harrison, Mellon, Dadi (Hay), Hume, Beresford.

**Portsmouth (1) 2** *(Taylor 35, 66)*

**Scunthorpe U (0) 1** *(Parton 89)* 17,508

*Portsmouth:* Hislop; Primus, Taylor, Harper (Robinson), Pasanen, Stefanovic, Hughes, Smertin (Schemmel), Berger (Faye), Sheringham, Berkovic.
*Scunthorpe U:* Evans; Graves (Ridley), Sharp, Barwick, Stanton, Byrne, Sparrow, Kilford, Hayes (Parton), Torpey, Beagrie.

**Scarborough (0) 0**

**Chelsea (1) 1** *(Terry 10)* 5379

*Scarborough:* Walker; Lyth, Baker (Capper), Kerr, Cryan, Hotte, Kelly, Marcelle, Quayle, Whitman (Senior), Sestanovich.
*Chelsea:* Cudicini; Melchiot, Bridge, Nicolas (Oliveira), Terry, Gallas, Cole J, Lampard, Hasselbaink, Gudjohnsen, Gronkjaer (Petit).

**Swansea C (0) 2** *(Robinson 80, Trundle 82)*

**Preston NE (0) 1** *(Etuhu 58)* 10,201

*Swansea C:* Freestone; Jones S (Hylton), Howard, Britton, O'Leary, Iriekpen, Maylett, Martinez, Connolly (Thomas), Trundle, Robinson (Coates).
*Preston NE:* Gould; Alexander, Broomes, O'Neil, Davis, Etuhu, McKenna, Healy, Koumantarakis (Abbott), Fuller, Lewis.

Sunday, 25 January 2004

**Everton (0) 1** *(Jeffers 90)*

**Fulham (0) 1** *(Davis 49)* 27,862

*Everton:* Martyn; Hibbert, Pistone (Jeffers), Stubbs, Unsworth (Naysmith), Gravesen, Nyarko, Rooney, Ferguson, Radzinski, Kilbane.
*Fulham:* Van der Sar; Djetou, Bocanegra, Knight, Goma, Davis, Volz, Clark, Hayles (Sava), Boa Morte, Malbranque.

**Manchester C (1) 1** *(Anelka 11)*

**Tottenham H (0) 1** *(Doherty 57)* 28,840

*Manchester C:* Ellegaard; Jihai, Tarnat, Dunne, Distin, Bosvelt, Sibierski (Wright-Phillips), Reyna, Anelka, Fowler (Macken), Sinclair.
*Tottenham H:* Keller; Carr, Taricco (Jackson), Gardner, Doherty, King, Anderton (Dalmat), Brown, Keane, Postiga, Davies.

**Northampton T (0) 0**

**Manchester U (1) 3** *(Silvestre 34, Hargreaves 47 (og), Forlan 68)* 7356

*Northampton T:* Harper; Lyttle, Carruthers (Chambers), Sampson, Willmott, Reid, Lincoln (Harsley), Asamoah, Reeves (Richards), Smith, Hargreaves.
*Manchester U:* Carroll; O'Shea, Fortune (Pugh), Brown, Butt, Silvestre (Bardsley), Bellion, Fletcher, Forlan, Scholes (Richardson), Ronaldo.

**Nottingham F (0) 0**

**Sheffield U (1) 3** *(Lester 33 (pen), Morgan 79, Allison 90)* 17,306

*Nottingham F:* Ward; Louis-Jean, Robertson, Sonner, Doig, Walker, Williams, Bopp (Westcarr), Taylor, King, Reid.
*Sheffield U:* Kenny; Kozluk, Wright, McCall (Rankine), Morgan, Page, Montgomery, Allison, Lester (Whitlow), Peschisolido (Forte), Tonge.

**Wolverhampton W (1) 1** *(Ganea 23)*

**West Ham U (3) 3** *(Deane 4, Harewood 21, Connolly 32)* 24,413

*Wolverhampton W:* Oakes; Luzhny (Craddock), Naylor, Ince, Clyde, Butler, Silas (Gudjonsson), Cameron, Ganea, Miller (Clarke), Kennedy.
*West Ham U:* Bywater; Ferdinand (Quinn), Harley, Mullins, Dailly, Horlock, Carrick, Connolly, Harewood, Deane, Etherington.

Wednesday, 11 February 2004

**Telford U (0) 0**

**Millwall (1) 2** *(Ifill 37, Wise 83)* 5589

*Telford U:* MacKenzie; Hulbert, Challis, Howarth, Whitehead, Murphy, Ricketts, Simpson, Moore (Rowe), Naylor (Grant), Blackwood (Clarke).
*Millwall:* Gueret; Muscat, Ryan, Cahill, Lawrence, Ward, Ifill, Wise, Harris (Braniff), Dichio, Livermore.

## FOURTH ROUND REPLAYS

Tuesday, 3 February 2004

**Colchester U (2) 3** *(Vine 12, 43, 57)*

**Coventry C (1) 1** *(Joachim 25)* 5530

*Colchester U:* Brown S; Halford, Keith, Pinault, White, Chilvers, Duguid, Izzet, Fagan, McGleish (Andrews), Vine (Bowry).
*Coventry C:* Ward; Shaw, Staunton, Deloumeaux, Konjic (McSheffrey), Davenport■, Doyle, Gudjonsson, Morrell (Adebola), Joachim, Warnock (Gordon).

Wednesday, 4 February 2004

**Fulham (0) 2** *(Inamoto 57, Malbranque 102)*

**Everton (0) 1** *(Jeffers 90)* 11,551

*Fulham:* Van der Sar; Volz, Bocanegra, Knight, Goma, Davis, Djetou, Inamoto (Petta), Hayles (Sava), Boa Morte, Malbranque.
*Everton:* Martyn; Hibbert, Naysmith, Unsworth, Pistone, Carsley, Nyarko (Watson), Gravesen, Rooney, Radzinski (Jeffers), Kilbane.
*aet.*

**Tottenham H (3) 3** *(King 2, Keane 19, Ziege 42)*

**Manchester C (0) 4** *(Distin 48, Bosvelt 61, Wright-Phillips 80, Macken 90)* 30,400

*Tottenham H:* Keller; Carr, Ziege (Jackson), Gardner, Richards, King, Brown, Dalmat, Keane, Postiga (Poyet), Davies.
*Manchester C:* Arason; Jihai, Tarnat, Dunne, Distin, Barton■, Wright-Phillips, Bosvelt (Sibierski), Anelka (Macken), Fowler, Sinclair (McManaman).

## FIFTH ROUND

Saturday, 14 February 2004

**Fulham (0) 0**

**West Ham U (0) 0** 14,705

*Fulham:* Van der Sar; Volz, Bocanegra, Knight, Goma, Davis, Legwinski, Malbranque, McBride, Hayles, Boa Morte (Petta).
*West Ham U:* Bywater; Ferdinand, Horlock, Mullins, Repka, Dailly, Carrick, Connolly (Lomas), Harewood, Deane (Mellor), Etherington.

**Manchester U (1) 4** *(Scholes 34, Van Nistelrooy 71, 80, Ronaldo 74)*

**Manchester City (0) 2** *(Tarnat 78, Fowler 86)* 67,228

*Manchester U:* Howard; Neville G■, Fortune, O'Shea, Keane, Silvestre, Ronaldo, Neville P (Brown), Van Nistelrooy, Scholes, Giggs (Butt).
*Manchester City:* Arason; Wright-Phillips, Tarnat, Dunne, Distin, Van Buyten, Reyna, Barton, Fowler, McManaman, Sibierski.

**Millwall (0) 1** *(Dichio 70)*

**Burnley (0) 0** 10,420

*Millwall:* Gueret; Muscat, Ryan (Sweeney), Cahill, Lawrence, Ward, Ifill, Wise, Harris (Braniff), Dichio, Livermore.
*Burnley:* Jensen; Roche (Chadwick), Camara, Chaplow, May, McGregor (Moore A), Little, Grant, Moore I, Blake (Weller■), Wood.

**Sunderland (1) 1** *(Kyle 39)*

**Birmingham C (1) 1** *(Forssell 28)* 24,966

*Sunderland:* Poom; Wright, McCartney, McAteer, Breen, Bjorklund, Oster, Whitley, Kyle, Stewart, Arca.
*Birmingham C:* Maik Taylor; Upson, Kenna, Cunningham, Purse, Hughes (Carter), Johnson, Savage (Cisse■), Forssell, Morrison (Dugarry), Lazaridis.

**Tranmere R (1) 2** *(Taylor 24 (pen), Hume 59)*

**Swansea C (1) 1** *(Robinson 16)* 12,215

*Tranmere R:* Achterberg; Connelly, Roberts, Taylor, Allen, Jones, Harrison, Jennings (Linwood), Dadi (Hay), Hume, Navarro (Nicholson).
*Swansea C:* Freestone; Byrne (O'Leary), Howard (Thomas), Britton, Tate■, Iriekpen, Maylett, Martinez, Robinson, Trundle, Coates (Nugent).

Sunday, 15 February 2004

**Arsenal (0) 2** *(Reyes 56, 61)*

**Chelsea (1) 1** *(Mutu 40)* 38,136

*Arsenal:* Lehmann; Lauren, Cole, Vieira, Campbell, Toure, Parlour (Edu), Silva, Reyes (Clichy), Bergkamp, Pires.
*Chelsea:* Cudicini (Sullivan); Melchiot, Bridge, Makelele, Terry, Gallas, Parker, Lampard, Hasselbaink, Mutu (Gudjohnsen), Gronkjaer (Cole J).

**Liverpool (1) 1** *(Owen 2)*

**Portsmouth (0) 1** *(Taylor 77)* 34,669

*Liverpool:* Dudek; Finnan, Carragher, Hamann, Henchoz, Hyypia, Kewell (Le Tallec), Gerrard, Heskey, Owen, Cheyrou (Sinama-Pongolle).
*Portsmouth:* Hislop; Primus, Stefanovic, Faye, Pasanen, De Zeeuw, Smertin, Berkovic (Taylor), Yakubu, Mornar (Olszar), Quashie.

**Sheffield U (0) 1** *(Peschisolido 61)*

**Colchester U (0) 0** 17,074

*Sheffield U:* Kenny; Jagielka, Wright, McCall, Whitlow, Page, Ndlovu (Parkinson), Montgomery, Allison, Peschisolido, Bousatta (Rankine).
*Colchester U:* Brown S; Stockley, Tierney (McGleish), Pinault, White, Chilvers, Duguid, Izzet, Vine, Andrews, Keith.

## FIFTH ROUND REPLAYS

Sunday, 22 February 2004

**Portsmouth (0) 1** *(Hughes 72)*

**Liverpool (0) 0** 19,529

*Portsmouth:* Hislop; Primus, Stefanovic (Hughes), Smertin, Pasanen, De Zeeuw, Harper, Quashie, Yakubu, Berkovic, Taylor.
*Liverpool:* Kirkland; Finnan, Carragher, Hamann, Henchoz, Hyypia, Gerrard, Le Tallec (Murphy), Heskey (Baros), Owen, Cheyrou (Sinama-Pongolle).

Tuesday, 24 February 2004

**West Ham U (0) 0**

**Fulham (0) 3** *(McBride 76, Hayles 79, Boa Morte 90)* 27,934

*West Ham U:* Bywater; Ferdinand, Quinn, Horlock (Lee), Mullins, Dailly (Mellor), Carrick, Connolly, Harewood, Deane (Lomas), Etherington.
*Fulham:* Van der Sar; Volz, Bocanegra, Djetou (Knight), Goma, Davis (Pembridge), Legwinski, Malbranque, McBride, Boa Morte, Petta (Hayles).

Wednesday, 25 February 2004

**Birmingham C (0) 0**

**Sunderland (0) 2** *(Smith 99, 115)* 25,645

*Birmingham C:* Maik Taylor; Tebily (John), Kenna, Cunningham, Purse, Hughes, Johnson, Savage, Forssell, Morrison, Dunn (Clemence) (Carter).
*Sunderland:* Poom; Wright, McCartney, Thirlwell, Breen, Babb, Oster (Thornton), Whitley, Kyle, Stewart (Smith), Arca.
*aet.*

## SIXTH ROUND

Saturday, 6 March 2004

**Manchester U (1) 2** *(Van Nistelrooy 25, 62)*

**Fulham (1) 1** *(Malbranque 23 (pen))* 67,614

*Manchester U:* Howard; Neville P, O'Shea, Keane (Djemba-Djemba), Butt, Brown, Ronaldo (Solskjaer), Fletcher, Van Nistelrooy, Scholes, Giggs.
*Fulham:* Van der Sar; Volz, Green, Knight, Goma, Davis, Legwinski (Pembridge), Malbranque, McBride (Hayles), Clark (Petta), Boa Morte.

**Portsmouth (0) 1** *(Sheringham 90)*

**Arsenal (3) 5** *(Henry 25, 50, Ljungberg 43, 57, Toure 45)* 20,137

*Portsmouth:* Hislop; Primus, Taylor, Faye, Pasanen, De Zeeuw, Smertin, Berkovic (Stone), Yakubu, Mornar (Sheringham), Quashie (Hughes).
*Arsenal:* Lehmann; Lauren, Cole, Vieira (Clichy), Campbell, Toure, Silva, Edu, Reyes, Henry (Kanu), Ljungberg (Bentley).

Sunday, 7 March 2004

**Millwall (0) 0**

**Tranmere R (0) 0** 16,404

*Millwall:* Marshall; Muscat, Ryan (Sweeney), Cahill, Lawrence, Ward, Livermore, Wise, Harris (Braniff), Dichio, Ifill.
*Tranmere R:* Achterberg; Connelly, Roberts, Harrison, Goodison, Jones, Taylor, Mellon, Dadi, Hume, Beresford (Nicholson).

**Sunderland (1) 1** *(Smith 15)*

**Sheffield U (0) 0** 37,115

*Sunderland:* Poom; Wright, McCartney, McAteer, Breen, Babb, Oster (Stewart), Whitley, Kyle, Smith (Thornton), Arca (Thirlwell).
*Sheffield U:* Kenny; Jagielka, Kozluk, McCall (Wright), Morgan, Page, Ndlovu, Montgomery, Parkinson (Peschisolido), Ward (Allison), Tonge.

## SIXTH ROUND REPLAY

Tuesday, 16 March 2004

**Tranmere R (1) 1** *(Jones 41)*

**Millwall (2) 2** *(Cahill 11, Harris 16)* 15,510

*Tranmere R:* Achterberg; Connelly, Roberts, Taylor, Allen, Goodison, Harrison, Mellon, Hume, Jones, Beresford (Dadi).
*Millwall:* Marshall; Muscat, Ryan, Cahill, Lawrence, Ward, Ifill (Elliott), Livermore, Harris, Dichio (Sutton), Roberts.

**SEMI-FINAL (AT VILLA PARK)**

Saturday, 3 April 2004

**Arsenal (0) 0**

**Manchester U (1) 1** *(Scholes 32)* 39,939

*Arsenal:* Lehmann; Lauren, Clichy, Vieira, Campbell, Toure, Ljungberg, Edu (Kanu), Aliadiere (Reyes), Bergkamp, Pires (Henry).

*Manchester U:* Carroll; Neville G, O'Shea, Brown, Keane, Silvestre, Ronaldo (Bellion), Fletcher, Solskjaer (Neville P), Giggs, Scholes.

**SEMI-FINAL (AT OLD TRAFFORD)**

Sunday, 4 April 2004

**Sunderland (0) 0**

**Millwall (1) 1** *(Cahill 26)* 56,112

*Sunderland:* Poom; Wright (Thornton), McCartney, McAteer■, Breen, Babb (Piper), Oster, Thirlwell, Kyle (Stewart), Smith, Arca.

*Millwall:* Marshall; Muscat (Roberts), Ryan (Elliott), Cahill, Lawrence, Ward, Ifill (Sweeney), Wise, Harris, Dichio, Livermore.

**THE FA CUP FINAL**

Saturday, 22 May 2004

(at Millennium Stadium, Cardiff, attendance 72,350)

**Manchester U (1) 3** *(Ronaldo 42, Van Nistelrooy 64 (pen), 80)* **Millwall (0) 0**

*Manchester U:* Howard (Carroll); Neville G, O'Shea, Brown, Keane, Silvestre, Ronaldo (Solskjaer), Fletcher (Butt), Van Nistelrooy, Scholes, Giggs.

*Millwall:* Marshall; Elliott, Ryan (Cogan), Cahill, Lawrence, Ward, Ifill, Wise (Weston), Harris (McCammon), Livermore, Sweeney.

*Referee:* J. Winter (Stockton).

With half-time approaching, Manchester United's Cristiano Ronaldo heads past Millwall's goalkeeper Andy Marshall to break the Millwall resistance and put United 1-0 ahead in the FA Cup Final. (Colorsport)

# NATIONWIDE CONFERENCE 2003–04

Just as the Football League benefited from the institution of play-offs, so the Conference has followed and last season saw interest and attendances rise to a higher level than previously. Moreover the formation of a Second Division split into north and south sections as part of the restructuring of the non-league game will surely lead to even greater stability.

Celebrating the 25th anniversary of the original competition, then named the Alliance Premier League, attendances rose to a record 880,220, representing an average of 1905 per game.

In 2002–03 both semi-finals went to penalties. Away goals counting double would not have helped solve the problem. It would have made the difference in 2003–04, with Hereford United not Aldershot Town reaching the final. The final was also decided on a penalty shoot-out with Shrewsbury Town returning to the Football League after one season's absence. They had the highest average crowd at 4007 followed by Hereford's 3704.

Though Hereford were also aggrieved that finishing 21 points ahead of Aldershot and only a point behind automatically promoted Chester City, gave them nothing in the end, everyone knew the rules when the competition began.

In fact Aldershot, the only part-time team among the contenders, exceeded their most optimistic aspirations in getting so close to a return to the Football League 12 years after the old club was wound up. They were never out of the top five all season. In the summer they decided to go full-time.

Apart from a rally by Exeter City to force themselves back into the leading frame following earlier season promise, the four previously mentioned teams plus Barnet had settled down to jockey for positions among themselves, though Chester seemingly had matters in their own hands until Hereford's amazing 11 game winning streak challenged them at the death.

The foundation of Chester's achievement came from an unbeaten run of 18 matches from late August taking them into the first week in December. The sequence was ended by Stevenage Borough, who otherwise had a disappointing time having been expected to be among the serious challengers.

Morecambe dropped out of the running in late February though made a gallant revival towards the end. Woking, too, were fifth after half a dozen games. Of the other two newcomers, Accrington Stanley were invariably hovering in the pack below the top five, but Tamworth found the going tougher, though they did manage to avoid the relegation zone.

Halifax Town fell like a stone with ten consecutive defeats from February, while Northwich went 15 games without a win to leave them well adrift at the foot of the table. Leigh struggling for support averaged only 566, one fewer than the spectators at Dover for Margate matches.

Problems off the pitch affected Exeter, Margate and Telford. City were threatened on two fronts, firstly the possibility of points deduction because of going into administration, secondly over the registration of a player after an embargo on new signings. In both instances they were cleared.

Margate, sharing Dover Athletic's ground, decided their priority was a return to their own venue and plumped for a place in the new Second Division while Telford ended the season with manager and players axed because of their dire financial position followed then by liquidation; a warning of the financial pitfalls for all clubs.

Thus for the first time in the 25 year history of the competition, no club was relegated with further reprieves for Leigh and Northwich one of the founders. Because the Unibond League winners and runners-up were unqualified for a place in the Conference, there had already been a reprieve for Farnborough Town third from bottom.

From 2004–05 the competition will be known as Conference National.

## NATIONWIDE CONFERENCE PLAY-OFFS 2003–04

### SEMI-FINALS FIRST LEG

Thursday, 29 April 2004

**Aldershot T (1) 1** *(D'Sane 45 (pen))*
**Hereford U (1) 1** *(Brown 7)* 6379

*Aldershot T:* Bull; Downer (McLean 80), Sterling, Antwi (Chewins 76), Warburton, Giles, Gosling, Challinor, Sills, D'Sane (Nutter 90), Charles.
*Hereford U:* Baker; Green, Travis, James, Tretton, Smith, Pitman, Brown, Carey-Bertram (Beesley 68), Rose, Purdie (Betts 90).

**Barnet (1) 2** *(Strevens 13 (pen), Clist 90)*
**Shrewsbury T (1) 1** *(Rodgers 43 (pen))* 4171

*Barnet:* Gore; Hendon, King, Lopez (Clist 65), Plummer, Maddix, Strevens, Gamble, Grazioli, Hatch, Yakubu.
*Shrewsbury T:* Howie; Moss, Challis (Lawrence 76), O'Connor, Tinson (Sedgemore 46), Ridler, Lowe, Tolley, Rodgers (Quinn 85), Darby, Aiston.

### SEMI-FINAL SECOND LEG

Monday, 3 May 2004

**Hereford U (0) 0**
**Aldershot T (0) 0** 7044

*Hereford U:* Baker; Green, Travis (Betts 84), Smith, Tretton■, James, Pitman, Rose, Guinan (Beesley 73), Brown, Williams (Cozic 109).
*Aldershot T:* Bull; Downer (Chewins 60), Charles (D'Sane 70), Giles, Warburton, Sterling, Gosling, Antwi, Sills, McLean (Nutter 84), Challinor.
*aet; Aldershot T won 4-2 on penalties: D'Sane (hit bar), Brown (saved), Gosling (scored), Beesley (saved), Giles (scored), James (scored), Sills (scored), Smith (scored), Antwi (scored).*

**Shrewsbury T (1) 1** *(Rodgers 44 (pen))*
**Barnet (0) 0** 7012

*Shrewsbury T:* Howie; Moss, Challis, O'Connor (Edwards 46), Tinson, Ridler, Lowe, Tolley, Rodgers, Darby (Cramb 105), Aiston (Sedgemore 113).
*Barnet:* Gore; Hendon, King, Lopez (Clist 55), Plummer, Maddix (Redmile 59), Strevens, Gamble, Grazioli, Hatch, Yakubu.
*aet; Shrewsbury T won 5-3 on penalties: Sedgemore (scored), Strevens (scored), Tolley (scored), Grazioli (scored), Rodgers (scored), Yakubu (scored), Cramb (scored), Clist (saved), Moss (scored).*

### CONFERENCE FINAL (AT BRITANNIA STADIUM)

Sunday, 16 May 2004

**Shrewsbury T (1) 1** *(Darby 43)*
**Aldershot T (1) 1** *(McLean 35)* 19,216

*Shrewsbury T:* Howie; Sedgemore, Challis, O'Connor (Street), Tinson (Lawrence), Ridler, Lowe, Tolley, Rodgers, Darby (Cramb), Aiston.
*Aldershot T:* Bull; Downer (Hooper), Sterling, Antwi, Warburton, Giles, Gosling, Challinor, McLean (Sills), D'Sane (Charles), Miller.
*aet; Shrewsbury T won 3-0 on penalties: Rodgers (missed), Sills (saved), Tolley (scored), Giles (saved), Sedgemore (scored), Gosling (saved), Challis (scored).*
*Referee:* K. Stroud (Bournemouth).

## NATIONWIDE CONFERENCE 2003–04 FINAL LEAGUE TABLE

| | | | *Home* | | | | | *Away* | | | | | *Total* | | | | | | |
|---|---|---|---|---|---|---|---|---|---|---|---|---|---|---|---|---|---|---|---|
| | | *P* | *W* | *D* | *L* | *F* | *A* | *W* | *D* | *L* | *F* | *A* | *W* | *D* | *L* | *F* | *A* | *GD* | *Pts* |
| 1 | Chester C | 42 | 16 | 4 | 1 | 45 | 18 | 11 | 7 | 3 | 40 | 16 | 27 | 11 | 4 | 85 | 34 | 51 | 92 |
| 2 | Hereford U | 42 | 14 | 3 | 4 | 42 | 20 | 14 | 4 | 3 | 61 | 24 | 28 | 7 | 7 | 103 | 44 | 59 | 91 |
| 3 | Shrewsbury T | 42 | 13 | 6 | 2 | 38 | 14 | 7 | 8 | 6 | 29 | 28 | 20 | 14 | 8 | 67 | 42 | 25 | 74 |
| 4 | Barnet | 42 | 11 | 6 | 4 | 30 | 17 | 8 | 8 | 5 | 30 | 29 | 19 | 14 | 9 | 60 | 46 | 14 | 71 |
| 5 | Aldershot T | 42 | 12 | 6 | 3 | 40 | 24 | 8 | 4 | 9 | 40 | 43 | 20 | 10 | 12 | 80 | 67 | 13 | 70 |
| 6 | Exeter C | 42 | 10 | 7 | 4 | 33 | 24 | 9 | 5 | 7 | 38 | 33 | 19 | 12 | 11 | 71 | 57 | 14 | 69 |
| 7 | Morecambe | 42 | 14 | 4 | 3 | 43 | 25 | 6 | 3 | 12 | 23 | 41 | 20 | 7 | 15 | 66 | 66 | 0 | 67 |
| 8 | Stevenage B | 42 | 10 | 5 | 6 | 29 | 22 | 8 | 4 | 9 | 29 | 30 | 18 | 9 | 15 | 58 | 52 | 6 | 63 |
| 9 | Woking | 42 | 10 | 9 | 2 | 40 | 23 | 5 | 7 | 9 | 25 | 29 | 15 | 16 | 11 | 65 | 52 | 13 | 61 |
| 10 | Accrington S | 42 | 13 | 3 | 5 | 46 | 31 | 2 | 10 | 9 | 22 | 30 | 15 | 13 | 14 | 68 | 61 | 7 | 58 |
| 11 | Gravesend & N | 42 | 7 | 6 | 8 | 34 | 35 | 7 | 9 | 5 | 35 | 31 | 14 | 15 | 13 | 69 | 66 | 3 | 57 |
| 12 | Telford U | 42 | 10 | 3 | 8 | 28 | 28 | 5 | 7 | 9 | 21 | 23 | 15 | 10 | 17 | 49 | 51 | –2 | 55 |
| 13 | Dagenham & R | 42 | 8 | 3 | 10 | 30 | 34 | 7 | 6 | 8 | 29 | 30 | 15 | 9 | 18 | 59 | 64 | –5 | 54 |
| 14 | Burton Alb* | 42 | 7 | 4 | 10 | 30 | 29 | 8 | 3 | 10 | 27 | 30 | 15 | 7 | 20 | 57 | 59 | –2 | 51 |
| 15 | Scarborough | 42 | 8 | 9 | 4 | 32 | 25 | 4 | 6 | 11 | 19 | 29 | 12 | 15 | 15 | 51 | 54 | –3 | 51 |
| 16 | Margate | 42 | 8 | 2 | 11 | 30 | 32 | 6 | 7 | 8 | 26 | 32 | 14 | 9 | 19 | 56 | 64 | –8 | 51 |
| 17 | Tamworth | 42 | 9 | 6 | 6 | 32 | 30 | 4 | 4 | 13 | 17 | 38 | 13 | 10 | 19 | 49 | 68 | –19 | 49 |
| 18 | Forest Green R | 42 | 6 | 8 | 7 | 32 | 36 | 6 | 4 | 11 | 26 | 44 | 12 | 12 | 18 | 58 | 80 | –22 | 48 |
| 19 | Halifax T | 42 | 9 | 4 | 8 | 28 | 26 | 3 | 4 | 14 | 15 | 39 | 12 | 8 | 22 | 43 | 65 | –22 | 44 |
| 20 | Farnborough T | 42 | 7 | 6 | 8 | 31 | 34 | 3 | 3 | 15 | 22 | 40 | 10 | 9 | 23 | 53 | 74 | –21 | 39 |
| 21 | Leigh RMI | 42 | 4 | 6 | 11 | 26 | 44 | 3 | 2 | 16 | 20 | 53 | 7 | 8 | 27 | 46 | 97 | –51 | 29 |
| 22 | Northwich Vic | 42 | 2 | 8 | 11 | 15 | 38 | 2 | 3 | 16 | 15 | 42 | 4 | 11 | 27 | 30 | 80 | –50 | 23 |

**Burton Alb deducted 1pt for breach of rules.*

## NATIONWIDE CONFERENCE LEADING GOALSCORERS 2003–04

| | *League* | *P-offs* | *FA Cup* | *LDV* | *Trophy* | *Total* |
|---|---|---|---|---|---|---|
| Daryl Clare *(Chester C)* | 29 | 0 | 1 | 0 | 0 | 30 |
| Steve Guinan *(Hereford U)* | 25 | 0 | 3 | 1 | 0 | 29 |
| David McNiven *(Leigh RMI)* | 25 | 0 | 0 | 0 | 1 | 26 |
| Giuliano Grazioli *(Barnet)* | 24 | 0 | 2 | 0 | 0 | 26 |
| Roscoe D'Sane *(Aldershot T)* | 21 | 1 | 2 | 0 | 3 | 27 |
| Sean Devine *(Exeter C)* | 20 | 0 | 2 | 0 | 3 | 25 |
| Paul Mullin *(Accrington S)* | 20 | 0 | 3 | 0 | 1 | 24 |
| Darryn Stamp *(Chester C)* | 20 | 0 | 0 | 0 | 0 | 20 |
| Tim Sills *(Aldershot T)* | 18 | 0 | 1 | 0 | 2 | 21 |
| Anthony Elding *(Stevenage B)* | 17 | 0 | 2 | 0 | 0 | 19 |
| Lutel James *(Accrington S)* | 17 | 0 | 1 | 0 | 0 | 18 |
| Danny Carlton *(Morecambe)* | 17 | 0 | 0 | 0 | 0 | 17 |
| Mark Cooper *(Tamworth)* | 15 | 0 | 0 | 0 | 0 | 15 |
| David Brown *(Hereford U)* | 14 | 1 | 0 | 2 | 0 | 17 |
| Mark Quayle *(Scarborough)* | 14 | 0 | 1 | 0 | 0 | 15 |

## ATTENDANCES BY CLUB 2003–04

| | *Aggregate 2003–04* | *Average 2003–04* | *Highest Attendance 2003–04* |
|---|---|---|---|
| Shrewsbury Town | 84,150 | 4,007 | 6,738 v Telford United |
| Hereford United | 77,784 | 3,704 | 7,240 v Chester City |
| Exeter City | 76,957 | 3,665 | 8,256 v Accrington Stanley |
| Aldershot Town | 69,164 | 3,294 | 4,637 v Woking |
| Chester City | 64,362 | 3,065 | 5,987 v Scarborough |
| Woking | 48,746 | 2,321 | 4,158 v Aldershot Town |
| Telford United | 43,634 | 2,078 | 4,337 v Shrewsbury Town |
| Stevenage Borough | 42,044 | 2,002 | 3,019 v Barnet |
| Barnet | 38,436 | 1,830 | 2,988 v Leigh RMI |
| Accrington Stanley | 37,731 | 1,797 | 3,143 v Shrewsbury Town |
| Morecambe | 37,393 | 1,781 | 3,084 v Accrington Stanley |
| Burton Albion | 35,326 | 1,682 | 3,203 v Shrewsbury Town |
| Halifax Town | 31,617 | 1,506 | 2,160 v Morecambe |
| Dagenham & Redbridge | 30,302 | 1,443 | 1,948 v Stevenage Borough |
| Scarborough | 28,028 | 1,335 | 2,503 v Woking |
| Tamworth | 28,036 | 1,335 | 2,535 v Burton Albion |
| Gravesend & Northfleet | 24,746 | 1,178 | 1,725 v Margate |
| Farnborough Town | 19,847 | 945 | 3,233 v Aldershot Town |
| Forest Green Rovers | 18,949 | 902 | 1,576 v Hereford United |
| Northwich Victoria | 17,875 | 851 | 3,268 v Shrewsbury Town |
| Margate | 11,905 | 567 | 1,030 v Gravesend & Northfleet |
| Leigh RMI | 11,881 | 566 | 2,002 v Chester City |

## CHESTER CITY ROLL CALL 2003–04

| Player | Position | Height | Weight | Birthdate | Birthplace | Source |
|---|---|---|---|---|---|---|
| Mark Beesley | F | 5 11 | 11 00 | 10.11.1981 | Burscough | Preston NE |
| Phil Bolland | D | 6 4 | 13 12 | 26.08.1976 | Liverpool | Oxford U |
| Jon Brady | M | 5 8 | 11 01 | 14.01.1975 | Newcastle (Aus) | Woking |
| Steve Brodie | M | 5 7 | 10 06 | 14.01.1973 | Sunderland | Swansea C |
| Wayne Brown | G | 6 0 | 11 12 | 14.01.1977 | Southampton | Weston S Mare |
| Paul Carden | M | | | 29.03.1979 | Liverpool | Doncaster R |
| Shaun Carey | M | 5 9 | 11 01 | 13.05.1976 | Kettering | Rushden & D |
| Daryl Clare | F | 5 9 | 12 05 | 01.08.1978 | Jersey | Boston U |
| Danny Collins | D | 6 0 | 12 00 | 06.08.1980 | Chester | Buckley T |
| Ben Davies | M | 5 6 | 10 07 | 27.05.1981 | Birmingham | Kidderminster H |
| Ian Foster | F | 5 7 | 11 00 | 11.11.1976 | Liverpool | Kidderminster H |
| Scott Guyett | D | 6 2 | 12 09 | 20.01.1976 | Ascot | Oxford U |
| Andy Harris | M | 5 11 | 12 05 | 26.02.1977 | Springs (S Africa) | Leyton Orient |
| Jamie Heard | M | | | 11.08.1983 | Sheffield | Hull C |
| Chris Lane | D | | | 25.05.1979 | Liverpool | Leigh RMI |
| Ian McCaldon | G | 6 5 | 16 00 | 14.09.1974 | Liverpool | Oxford U |
| Kevin McIntyre | D | | | 23.12.1977 | Liverpool | Doncaster R |
| Kevin Rapley | F | 5 10 | 12 02 | 21.09.1977 | Reading | Colchester U |
| Carl Ruffer | D | | | 20.12.1974 | Chester | Runcorn |
| Alex Smith | M | 5 9 | 10 06 | 15.02.1976 | Liverpool | Reading |
| Darryn Stamp | F | 6 2 | 12 00 | 21.09.1978 | Beverley | Northampton T |
| Michael Twiss | M | 5 11 | 13 03 | 26.12.1977 | Salford | Leigh RMI |
| Andy Woods | M | | | 15.01.1976 | Colchester | Northwich Vic |

## SHREWSBURY TOWN ROLL CALL 2003-04

| Player | Position | Height | Weight | Birthdate | Birthplace | Source |
|---|---|---|---|---|---|---|
| Sam Aiston | M | 6 1 | 12 10 | 21.11.1976 | Newcastle | Sunderland |
| Jody Banim | F | | | 01.04.1978 | Manchester | Radcliffe Borough |
| Trevor Challis | D | 5 8 | 11 05 | 23.10.1975 | Paddington | Telford U |
| Colin Cramb | F | 5 11 | 12 04 | 23.06.1974 | Lanark | Bury |
| Duane Darby | F | 5 11 | 12 06 | 17.10.1973 | Birmingham | Rushden & D |
| Leon Drysdale | D | 5 10 | 11 11 | 03.02.1981 | Birmingham | Trainee |
| Ian Dunbavin | G | 6 2 | 13 00 | 27.05.1980 | Liverpool | Liverpool |
| Dave Edwards | M | 5 11 | 11 05 | 03.02.1986 | Shrewsbury | Trainee |
| Ian Fitzpatrick | M | 5 9 | 10 05 | 22.09.1980 | Manchester | Halifax T |
| Joe Hart | G | 6 3 | 13 03 | 19.04.1987 | Shrewsbury | Trainee |
| Scott Howie | G | 6 2 | 13 07 | 04.01.1972 | Glasgow | Bristol R |
| Ryan Lowe | M | 5 11 | 11 03 | 18.09.1978 | Liverpool | Burscough |
| Darren Moss | D | 5 10 | 11 00 | 24.05.1981 | Wrexham | Chester C |
| Martin O'Connor | M | 5 9 | 11 08 | 10.12.1967 | Walsall | Walsall |
| Dave Ridler | D | 6 1 | 12 02 | 12.03.1976 | Liverpool | Scarborough |
| Luke Rodgers | F | 5 7 | 11 00 | 01.01.1982 | Birmingham | Trainee |
| Jake Sedgemore | D | | | 10.10.1978 | Wolverhampton | Northwich Vic |
| Ross Stephens | M | 5 10 | 10 09 | 28.05.1985 | Landiloes | Trainee |
| Kevin Street | M | 5 10 | 10 08 | 25.11.1977 | Crewe | Bristol R |
| Darren Tinson | D | 6 0 | 12 12 | 15.11.1969 | Connah's Quay | Macclesfield T |
| Jamie Tolley | M | 6 0 | 11 03 | 12.05.1983 | Ludlow | Trainee |

# ACCRINGTON STANLEY Conference

*Ground:* The Crown Ground, Livingstone Road, Accrington, Lancashire.
*Tel:* 01254 397 869.
*Year Formed:* 1968 (formerly 1893).
*Record Gate:* 2,270 (1992 v Gateshead FA Cup First Round) (in Football League 17,634).
*Nickname:* Stanley.
*Manager:* John Coleman.
*Secretary:* Philip Terry.
*Colours:* Red shirts, white shorts, red stockings.

## ACCRINGTON STANLEY 2003–04 LEAGUE RECORD

| *Match No.* | *Date* | *Venue* | *Opponents* | *Result* | | *H/T Score* | *Lg. Pos.* | *Goalscorers* | *Attendance* |
|---|---|---|---|---|---|---|---|---|---|
| 1 | Aug 10 | A | Aldershot T | L | 1-2 | 1-2 | — | Proctor [26] | 3471 |
| 2 | 13 | H | Leigh RMI | W | 4-1 | 2-0 | — | James 2 [42, 45], Mullin [46], Prendergast [71] | 2003 |
| 3 | 16 | H | Shrewsbury T | L | 0-1 | 0-0 | 15 | | 3143 |
| 4 | 23 | A | Forest Green R | L | 1-2 | 0-2 | 18 | Jenkins (og) [58] | 711 |
| 5 | 25 | H | Scarborough | W | 1-0 | 0-0 | 14 | Mullin [77] | 2017 |
| 6 | 30 | A | Tamworth | D | 1-1 | 1-0 | 13 | Cavanagh [45] | 1215 |
| 7 | Sept 6 | A | Barnet | D | 0-0 | 0-0 | 13 | | 1621 |
| 8 | 13 | H | Margate | W | 3-2 | 1-2 | 10 | James 2 [17, 55], Durnin [63] | 1718 |
| 9 | 20 | A | Dagenham & R | W | 1-0 | 0-0 | 9 | Mullin [68] | 1542 |
| 10 | 23 | H | Burton Alb | W | 3-1 | 1-1 | — | Mullin [30], Hollis [67], James (pen) [90] | 1911 |
| 11 | 27 | H | Woking | D | 3-3 | 2-2 | 8 | James 3 (1 pen) [1, 17 (p), 90] | 2115 |
| 12 | Oct 4 | A | Northwich Vic | D | 3-3 | 3-3 | 7 | Prendergast [7], Mullin [13], Gouck [24] | 865 |
| 13 | 7 | A | Halifax T | D | 1-1 | 1-1 | — | Gouck [29] | 2116 |
| 14 | 11 | H | Farnborough T | W | 3-1 | 2-1 | 6 | Mullin [4], Cavanagh [14], James (pen) [65] | 1806 |
| 15 | 18 | H | Exeter C | L | 1-2 | 0-1 | 7 | Mullin [71] | 2342 |
| 16 | Nov 1 | A | Gravesend & N | D | 0-0 | 0-0 | 7 | | 1274 |
| 17 | 11 | H | Hereford U | W | 2-0 | 1-0 | — | James [40], Mullin [79] | 1824 |
| 18 | 15 | A | Stevenage Bor | L | 1-2 | 1-2 | 8 | Mullin [32] | 2121 |
| 19 | 22 | H | Telford U | L | 1-5 | 0-4 | 9 | Mullin [73] | 1448 |
| 20 | 25 | A | Chester C | D | 3-3 | 1-3 | — | Cook [21], James [63], Prendergast [81] | 2432 |
| 21 | 29 | H | Barnet | W | 2-0 | 0-0 | 8 | Mullin 2 [48, 61] | 1120 |
| 22 | Dec 13 | H | Aldershot T | W | 4-2 | 3-2 | 8 | Mullin 2 [2, 5], Gouck [41], Howarth [73] | 1407 |
| 23 | 20 | A | Leigh RMI | W | 2-1 | 2-0 | 8 | Gouck [14], Howarth [45] | 612 |
| 24 | 26 | H | Morecambe | W | 1-0 | 1-0 | 7 | James [33] | 2954 |
| 25 | Jan 1 | A | Morecambe | L | 0-1 | 0-0 | 7 | | 3084 |
| 26 | 17 | A | Shrewsbury T | D | 0-0 | 0-0 | 9 | | 3777 |
| 27 | 20 | H | Tamworth | W | 3-0 | 2-0 | — | James [5], Mullin 2 [12, 90] | 1301 |
| 28 | 24 | A | Burton Alb | D | 1-1 | 0-0 | 7 | McEvilly [82] | 1614 |
| 29 | Feb 7 | H | Dagenham & R | L | 2-3 | 1-1 | 8 | Prendergast [42], James [53] | 1601 |
| 30 | 14 | A | Woking | D | 2-2 | 1-0 | 8 | James [15], Mullin [57] | 2312 |
| 31 | 21 | H | Northwich Vic | D | 2-2 | 0-1 | 10 | James (pen) [60], Prendergast [64] | 1422 |
| 32 | 28 | A | Farnborough T | D | 1-1 | 0-1 | 9 | McEvilly [48] | 571 |
| 33 | Mar 6 | H | Halifax T | W | 2-1 | 1-0 | 8 | Flitcroft [43], Calcutt [52] | 1717 |
| 34 | 13 | A | Hereford U | L | 0-1 | 0-0 | 9 | | 3230 |
| 35 | 16 | A | Margate | L | 1-3 | 0-1 | — | Kempson [76] | 345 |
| 36 | 20 | H | Stevenage Bor | W | 2-1 | 0-1 | 7 | James [66], Mullin [69] | 1124 |
| 37 | Apr 3 | H | Chester C | L | 0-2 | 0-1 | 8 | | 2561 |
| 38 | 8 | A | Telford U | L | 0-1 | 0-0 | — | | 2031 |
| 39 | 10 | H | Forest Green R | W | 4-1 | 2-0 | 8 | Brannan [40], Mullin 2 [44, 61], Durnin [73] | 1058 |
| 40 | 12 | A | Scarborough | L | 1-2 | 1-0 | 10 | Gouck [26] | 1523 |
| 41 | 17 | H | Gravesend & N | D | 3-3 | 1-3 | 10 | Prendergast [7], Durnin 2 [66, 67] | 1139 |
| 42 | 24 | A | Exeter C | L | 2-3 | 1-1 | 10 | Proctor [45], Flitcroft [62] | 8256 |

**Final League Position: 10**

### GOALSCORERS

*League (68):* Mullin 20, James 17 (4 pens), Prendergast 6, Gouck 5, Durnin 4, Cavanagh 2, Flitcroft 2, Howarth 2, McEvilly 2, Proctor 2, Brannan 1, Calcutt 1, Cook 1, Hollis 1, Kempson 1, own goal 1.
*FA Cup (4):* Mullin 3, James 1.
*Trophy (2):* Howarth 1, Mullin 1.

| Speare 10 + 1 | Cavanagh 35 + 1 | Hollis 27 + 2 | Cook 28 + 6 | Williams 33 | Smith 18 + 4 | Proctor 36 + 3 | Armstrong 4 + 9 | James 40 + 1 | Mullin 41 | Prendergast 36 + 2 | Halford 24 + 2 | Calcutt 6 + 14 | Kennedy 32 + 1 | Gouck 20 + 6 | Durnin 4 + 12 | Waine — + 1 | Flitcroft 13 + 11 | Welch 1 + 1 | Madden — + 2 | Jackson — + 2 | Howarth 15 + 2 | Brannan 19 + 1 | McEvilly 3 + 3 | Kempson 9 + 2 | Fitzgerald 7 | Hindle 1 | Match No. |
|---|---|---|---|---|---|---|---|---|---|---|---|---|---|---|---|---|---|---|---|---|---|---|---|---|---|---|---|
| 1■ | 2 | 3 | 4 | 5 | 6[1] | 7 | 8[2] | 9 | 10 | 11[3] | 12 | 13 | 14 | | | | | | | | | | | | | | 1 |
| | 2 | 3 | 4[1] | 5 | 6 | 7 | 8[2] | 9[3] | 10 | 12 | | 11 | 1 | 13 | 14 | | | | | | | | | | | | 2 |
| | 2 | 3 | 4[1] | 5 | 6 | 7 | 8[2] | 9[3] | 10 | 11 | | 12 | 1 | 13 | 14 | | | | | | | | | | | | 3 |
| | 2 | 3 | 4[1] | 5 | 13 | 7 | | 9 | 10 | 11 | 6[2] | 8 | 1 | 12 | | | | | | | | | | | | | 4 |
| | 2 | 3 | 4■ | 5 | 6 | 7 | | 9[2] | 10 | 11 | | 8[1] | 1 | 12 | | 13 | | | | | | | | | | | 5 |
| | 2 | 3 | 4[1] | 5 | 6 | 12 | | 9 | 10 | 11 | | 7■ | 1 | 8 | | | | | | | | | | | | | 6 |
| | 2 | 3 | 4 | 5 | 6 | 12 | 13 | 9 | 10 | 11 | | | 1 | 8[2] | | | 7[1] | | | | | | | | | | 7 |
| | 2 | 3 | | 5 | 6 | 7 | 12 | 9 | 10 | 11 | | | 1 | 4[1] | 13 | | | 8[2] | | | | | | | | | 8 |
| | 2 | 3 | | 5 | | 7■ | 13 | 9 | 10 | 11[3] | 4[1] | 14 | 1 | 6[2] | 12 | | 8 | | | | | | | | | | 9 |
| | 2 | 3 | | 5 | 12 | 7 | 13 | 9 | 10 | 11 | 4[1] | | 1 | 6[2] | 8[3] | | 14 | | | | | | | | | | 10 |
| | 2 | 3 | 14 | 5[2] | 6[1] | 7 | 13 | 9 | 10 | 11 | 12 | | 1 | 4 | 8[3] | | | | | | | | | | | | 11 |
| | 2 | 3 | 4 | 5 | 6 | | | 9 | 10 | 11 | | | 1 | 8 | | | 7 | | | | | | | | | | 12 |
| | 2 | 3 | 4 | 5 | 12 | 7 | 13 | 9 | 10 | 11 | 6[1] | | 1 | 8[2] | | | | | | | | | | | | | 13 |
| | 2 | 3 | 4 | 5 | | 7 | | 9 | 10 | 11[2] | 6 | | 1 | 8[1] | | | | 12 | 13 | | | | | | | | 14 |
| | 2■ | 3 | 4 | 5 | | 7 | | 9 | 10 | 11 | 6 | | 1 | 8[1] | | | | | | 12 | | | | | | | 15 |
| | | 2 | 4[3] | 5 | 12 | 7 | 13 | 9 | | 11 | 3■ | 8[2] | 1 | | 10 | | 14 | | | | 6[1] | | | | | | 16 |
| | 2 | 3 | 4 | 5 | 6 | 7 | 12 | 9 | 10 | 11 | | | 1 | 8[1] | | | | | | | | | | | | | 17 |
| | 2 | 3 | 4 | 5 | 6 | 7 | | 9 | 10 | 11[2] | | 14 | 1 | 8[1] | 12 | | | | | 13[3] | | | | | | | 18 |
| | 2 | 3 | 6[1] | 5 | 4 | 7 | | 9 | 10 | | | 13 | 1 | 12 | 11[3] | | 8[2] | | 14 | | | | | | | | 19 |
| | 2 | | 4[1] | 5 | 6 | 7 | | 9 | 10 | 11 | 3 | 12 | 1 | | | | | | | | | 8 | | | | | 20 |
| 1 | | | | | 6 | 7 | 8 | 9 | 10 | 11 | 5 | | | 4 | | | | | | | 2 | 3 | | | | | 21 |
| 1 | 2■ | | 6[1] | 4 | | 7 | | 9 | 10 | 11[2] | | | | 8 | 13 | | 12 | | | | 5 | 3 | | | | | 22 |
| 1 | 2 | | 6 | 4 | | | 12 | 9 | 10 | | 3 | | | 8[1] | | | 7 | | | | 5 | 11 | | | | | 23 |
| 1 | 2 | | 4[1] | 6 | | 7 | | 9 | 10 | 11 | 3 | | | | | | 12 | | | | 5 | 8 | | | | | 24 |
| 1 | | 3 | 12 | 5 | | 7 | | 9 | 10 | 11 | 6 | | | 8[1] | | | | | | | 2 | 4 | | | | | 25 |
| | 2 | 12 | 4[2] | 5 | | 7 | | 9 | 10 | 11 | 3 | | 1 | | | | 13 | | | | 6 | 8[1] | | | | | 26 |
| 15 | 2■ | 12 | | 4 | | 7 | | 9[1] | 10 | 11 | 3 | | 1[G] | | | | 6 | | | | 5 | | 8 | | | | 27 |
| | 2 | | | 4 | 3 | 7[2] | | 9[3] | 10 | 11 | | 14 | 1 | | 12 | | 6 | | | | 5[1] | 13 | 8 | | | | 28 |
| | | 3 | | 4■ | | 7 | | 9 | 10 | 11 | | | 1 | | | | 12 | | | | 5 | 6 | 8[1] | 2 | | | 29 |
| | | 3 | 6[3] | 4 | | 7 | | 9 | 10 | 11 | | | 1 | 8[2] | 13 | | 14 | | | | | 2[1] | 12 | 5 | | | 30 |
| | | 3[2] | 6[1] | | | | | 9 | 10 | 11 | 4 | 12 | 1 | 8 | | | 7 | | | | 2 | | 13 | 5 | | | 31 |
| | 2 | | 4[2] | | | 7 | | 9 | 10 | 11 | 3 | | 1 | 8[1] | | | 13 | | | | 6 | | 12 | 5 | | | 32 |
| | 2 | | 12 | | | 13 | | 9 | 10 | 11 | 6 | 7[1] | 1 | | | | 8 | | | | | 4[2] | | 5 | 3 | | 33 |
| | 2 | | 12 | | | 7 | | 9 | 10 | 11[2] | 6■ | 14 | 1 | | | | 8[3] | | | | 13 | 4[1] | | 5 | 3 | | 34 |
| | 2 | | 13 | | | 7 | | 9 | 10 | 12 | 6 | 14 | 1 | | | | 11[3] | | | | 4[1] | 8[2] | | 5 | 3 | | 35 |
| | 2 | | 4[1] | 5 | | 7 | | 9 | 10 | 11 | 6 | | 1 | | | | 12 | | | | | 8 | | | 3 | | 36 |
| | 2 | 3[1] | 4[2] | 6■ | | 7 | | 9 | 10 | | | 12 | 1 | | 14 | | 13 | | | | | 8 | | 5 | 11[3] | | 37 |
| 1 | 2 | 3 | 4[1] | 8 | 6 | 7 | | 14 | 10 | 11 | | 13 | | | | | 12 | | | | 5[2] | 9[3] | | | | | 38 |
| 1 | 2 | 3 | 12 | 5 | | 7[2] | | 9[3] | 10 | 11 | 6 | 13 | | | 14 | | 8[1] | | | | | 4 | | | | | 39 |
| 1 | 12 | | | | 6[2] | 7 | | 9 | 10 | 11 | 3 | 13 | | 8[3] | | | | | | | 5[1] | 4 | | 14 | 2 | | 40 |
| 1 | 2 | 3 | 4 | | | 7[1] | | | 10 | 11 | 6 | | | 12 | 13 | | | | | | | 8 | | 5 | | 9[2] | 41 |
| | 2 | | 4 | | 5[1] | 7 | | 9 | 10 | | 3 | | 1 | | 14 | | 8[3] | | | | 13 | 11 | | 12 | 6[2] | | 42 |

**FA Cup**

| | | | |
|---|---|---|---|
| Fourth Qual | Leigh RMI | (h) | 2-0 |
| First Round | Huddersfield T | (h) | 1-0 |
| Second Round | Bournemouth | (a) | 1-1 |
| | | (h) | 0-0 |
| Third Round | Colchester U | (h) | 0-0 |
| | | (a) | 1-2 |

# ALDERSHOT TOWN Conference

*Ground:* Recreation Ground, High Street, Aldershot, Hampshire GU11 1TW.
*Tel:* (01252) 320 211.
*Year Formed:* 1992 (formerly 1926).
*Record Gate:* 7,500 (2000 v Brighton & Hove Albion FA Cup First Round) (in Football League 19,138).
*Nickname:* Shots.
*Manager:* Terry Brown.
*Secretary:* Andy Morgan.
*Colours:* Red shirts with blue trim, red shorts, red stockings with blue trim.

## ALDERSHOT TOWN 2003–04 LEAGUE RECORD

| Match No. | Date | Venue | Opponents | Result | | H/T Score | Lg. Pos. | Goalscorers | Attendance |
|---|---|---|---|---|---|---|---|---|---|
| 1 | Aug 10 | H | Accrington S | W | 2-1 | 2-1 | — | Sills [16], D'Sane [45] | 3471 |
| 2 | 12 | A | Margate | W | 2-1 | 0-0 | — | Sills [52], D'Sane [67] | 1005 |
| 3 | 16 | A | Telford U | W | 5-2 | 1-1 | 2 | McLean 2 [45, 84], Challinor [60], Sills [63], Manuella [79] | 2206 |
| 4 | 23 | H | Woking | W | 2-1 | 2-0 | 1 | Challinor [44], D'Sane [45] | 4637 |
| 5 | 25 | A | Hereford U | L | 3-4 | 2-2 | 2 | James (og) [5], Sills [9], McLean [67] | 4985 |
| 6 | 30 | H | Northwich Vic | W | 4-3 | 3-0 | 2 | Challinor 2 [14, 26], D'Sane [32], Sills [76] | 2801 |
| 7 | Sept 6 | A | Morecambe | L | 0-2 | 0-1 | 3 | | 1948 |
| 8 | 13 | H | Shrewsbury T | D | 1-1 | 1-1 | 4 | Charles L [18] | 3329 |
| 9 | 20 | A | Barnet | L | 1-2 | 0-1 | 5 | Sills [89] | 2208 |
| 10 | 23 | H | Farnborough T | W | 2-0 | 0-0 | — | McLean [83], Challinor [90] | 4166 |
| 11 | 27 | H | Burton Alb | W | 3-1 | 1-0 | 4 | Chewins [37], Charles L [53], McLean [76] | 2687 |
| 12 | Oct 4 | A | Leigh RMI | D | 2-2 | 1-1 | 4 | Challinor [10], Sills [68] | 545 |
| 13 | 7 | A | Gravesend & N | W | 3-1 | 2-1 | — | Sills 2 [16, 42], Warburton [63] | 1477 |
| 14 | 11 | H | Halifax T | W | 3-1 | 2-0 | 3 | D'Sane 2 (2 pens) [34, 87], Charles L [45] | 2882 |
| 15 | 18 | A | Tamworth | D | 3-3 | 0-2 | 3 | Ayres (og) [48], D'Sane (pen) [87], Taylor [90] | 1538 |
| 16 | Nov 1 | H | Forest Green R | W | 3-0 | 1-0 | 3 | Warburton [18], Miller [48], Charles L [67] | 2398 |
| 17 | 11 | H | Exeter C | W | 2-1 | 1-0 | — | Sills [37], Flack (og) [54] | 4112 |
| 18 | 15 | A | Scarborough | L | 0-1 | 0-0 | 3 | | 1624 |
| 19 | 22 | H | Chester C | D | 1-1 | 0-0 | 4 | Challinor [61] | 3610 |
| 20 | 29 | H | Morecambe | D | 2-2 | 1-0 | 5 | Charles L [37], D'Sane [65] | 2584 |
| 21 | Dec 13 | A | Accrington S | L | 2-4 | 2-3 | 5 | D'Sane 2 (1 pen) [7, 32 (p)] | 1407 |
| 22 | 16 | A | Stevenage Bor | W | 1-0 | 0-0 | — | Thomas [47] | 1794 |
| 23 | 20 | H | Margate | L | 0-2 | 0-1 | 4 | | 2529 |
| 24 | 26 | A | Dagenham & R | W | 3-2 | 2-1 | 3 | Miller 2 [20, 23], Mumford [79] | 1625 |
| 25 | Jan 1 | H | Dagenham & R | W | 2-1 | 1-0 | 3 | Sills [21], McLean [63] | 4168 |
| 26 | 3 | A | Northwich Vic | D | 1-1 | 1-1 | 3 | Sills [4] | 752 |
| 27 | 17 | H | Telford U | W | 3-1 | 0-1 | 3 | Sills [50], D'Sane 2 (1 pen) [67, 78 (p)] | 2831 |
| 28 | 24 | A | Farnborough T | L | 0-4 | 0-1 | 4 | | 3233 |
| 29 | Feb 6 | H | Barnet | D | 1-1 | 0-1 | — | Challinor [80] | 4217 |
| 30 | 21 | H | Leigh RMI | W | 2-0 | 1-0 | 4 | D'Sane 2 [2, 84] | 2412 |
| 31 | 24 | A | Halifax T | W | 2-1 | 1-1 | — | Sills 2 [22, 86] | 843 |
| 32 | Mar 6 | H | Gravesend & N | D | 2-2 | 1-0 | 4 | Challinor [31], D'Sane (pen) [81] | 2736 |
| 33 | 13 | A | Exeter C | L | 1-2 | 0-0 | 5 | Sills [81] | 3982 |
| 34 | 16 | A | Burton Alb | W | 4-1 | 1-0 | — | D'Sane 2 [20, 47], Challinor [50], Sills [81] | 1295 |
| 35 | 20 | H | Scarborough | L | 1-2 | 1-0 | 3 | D'Sane (pen) [34] | 2442 |
| 36 | 23 | A | Shrewsbury T | W | 2-1 | 1-0 | — | Challinor [6], D'Sane [62] | 3371 |
| 37 | 30 | H | Stevenage Bor | W | 2-0 | 1-0 | — | D'Sane [30], Gosling [90] | 2540 |
| 38 | Apr 6 | A | Chester C | L | 2-4 | 1-2 | — | Miller [37], Charles L [76] | 3432 |
| 39 | 10 | A | Woking | D | 2-2 | 2-1 | 3 | Challinor [8], Miller [12] | 4158 |
| 40 | 12 | H | Hereford U | L | 1-2 | 0-1 | 3 | Sills [47] | 4400 |
| 41 | 17 | A | Forest Green R | L | 1-3 | 1-0 | 4 | D'Sane (pen) [25] | 1330 |
| 42 | 24 | H | Tamworth | D | 1-1 | 0-0 | 5 | Charles L [62] | 4212 |

**Final League Position: 5**

### GOALSCORERS

*League (80):* D'Sane 21 (8 pens), Sills 18, Challinor 12, Charles L 7, McLean 6, Miller 5, Warburton 2, Chewins 1, Gosling 1, Manuella 1, Mumford 1, Taylor 1, Thomas 1, own goals 3.
*FA Cup (5):* D'Sane 2 (1 pen), McLean 1, Sills 1, Warburton 1.
*Trophy (12):* D'Sane 3 (1 pen), McLean 2, Miller 2, Sills 2, Charles L 1, Nutter 1, Warburton 1.
*Play-Offs (2):* D'Sane 1 (pen), McLean 1.

| Bull 24 | Hooper 29 | Sterling 33 + 5 | Roddis 9 + 1 | Warburton 40 | Rodwell 11 + 2 | D'Sane 39 + 1 | Challinor 36 | Sills 39 | McLean 24 + 13 | Tanfield 1 + 5 | Gedling 1 + 6 | Harper — + 12 | Nutter 10 + 11 | Manuella 8 | Chewins 26 + 9 | Barnard 18 + 3 | Charles L 20 + 10 | Hammond 7 | Rees 7 | Shields 12 + 1 | Taylor — + 3 | Miller 23 + 1 | Thomas 5 | Mumford 4 | Westell — + 1 | Antwi 13 | Johnson 1 + 5 | Smith 2 + 1 | Lovett 1 | Downer 8 | Giles 4 + 1 | Gosling 7 + 1 | Match No. |
|---|---|---|---|---|---|---|---|---|---|---|---|---|---|---|---|---|---|---|---|---|---|---|---|---|---|---|---|---|---|---|---|---|---|
| 1 | 2 | 3 | 4 | 5 | 6 | 7 | 8 | 9[1] | 10[2] | 11[3] | 12 | 13 | 14 | | | | | | | | | | | | | | | | | | | | 1 |
| 1 | 2 | 3 | 4 | 5 | 6■ | 7[1] | 8 | 9 | 10[2] | | | 13 | 12 | 11 | | | | | | | | | | | | | | | | | | | 2 |
| 1 | 2 | 3 | 4 | 5 | 6[1] | 7[2] | 8 | 9[3] | 10 | | 13 | 14 | | 11 | 12 | | | | | | | | | | | | | | | | | | 3 |
| 1 | 2 | 3 | 4■ | 5 | 6[3] | 7[1] | 8 | 9[2] | 10 | | 12 | 13 | | 11 | 14 | | | | | | | | | | | | | | | | | | 4 |
| 1[G] | | 6 | 2 | 5 | | 7■ | 8 | 9 | 10 | | | | 12 | 11[1] | 3 | 15 | 4 | | | | | | | | | | | | | | | | 5 |
| | 2 | 6 | 4[2] | 5 | | 7[1] | 8 | 9 | 10[3] | 12 | 13 | | | 11 | 3 | 1 | 14 | | | | | | | | | | | | | | | | 6 |
| 1 | 2 | 3[1] | | 5 | 6 | 7 | 8 | 9 | 10 | | 4[2] | | | 11 | 12 | | 13 | | | | | | | | | | | | | | | | 7 |
| 1 | 2 | 12 | | 5 | 6[1] | | 8 | 9 | 10 | 13 | | | | 11 | 3 | | 7[2] | 4 | | | | | | | | | | | | | | | 8 |
| 1[G] | 2 | 6[1] | | 5 | 12 | 7 | 8 | 9 | 10 | 13 | | | | 11[2] | 3 | 15 | | 4 | | | | | | | | | | | | | | | 9 |
| | 2 | | 7 | 5 | 6 | 11[1] | 8 | 9 | 10 | 12 | | | | | 3 | 1 | | 4 | | | | | | | | | | | | | | | 10 |
| | 2 | | 7 | 5 | 6 | 11[1] | 8 | 9 | 10 | | | | | | 3 | 1 | 12 | 4 | | | | | | | | | | | | | | | 11 |
| | 2 | 13 | 4[1] | 5 | 6 | 7[3] | 8[2] | 9 | 10 | 14 | | | 3 | | | 1 | 12 | 11 | | | | | | | | | | | | | | | 12 |
| | 2 | 3 | | 5 | 6 | 7 | | 9[1] | 10 | | | | 11 | | 4 | 1 | 12 | 8 | | | | | | | | | | | | | | | 13 |
| | 2 | 3 | | 5 | 12 | 10 | | 9 | | | 13 | | 11[2] | | 6 | 1 | 7[1] | 8 | 4 | | | | | | | | | | | | | | 14 |
| | | 3 | | 5 | 4[1] | 7 | | 9 | 10[2] | | | | 12 | | 6 | 1 | 11 | | 2 | 8 | 13 | | | | | | | | | | | | 15 |
| | 2 | 3 | 13[3] | 5 | | 7[1] | | 9 | 10[2] | | | | | | 14 | 1 | 11 | | 4 | 6 | 12 | 8 | | | | | | | | | | | 16 |
| | 2 | 13 | | 5 | | 10 | 8[2] | 9[1] | 12 | | | | | | 3 | 1 | 11 | | 4 | 6 | | 7 | | | | | | | | | | | 17 |
| | 2■ | 13 | | 5 | | 10[1] | 8[3] | 9 | 12 | | | | 14 | | 3 | 1 | 11[2] | | 4 | 6 | | 7 | | | | | | | | | | | 18 |
| 1 | 2 | | | 5 | | 12 | 8 | 9 | 10[1] | | | | | | 3 | | 11 | | 4 | 6 | | 7 | | | | | | | | | | | 19 |
| 1 | | 3 | | 5 | | 10 | 2 | | 9 | | | | 11 | | 6 | | 7 | | 4 | | | 8 | | | | | | | | | | | 20 |
| 1 | 2 | 5 | | | | 10[2] | 8 | 9 | 12 | | | 14 | | | 3 | | 11[1] | | | 4■ | 13 | 7 | 6[3] | | | | | | | | | | 21 |
| 1 | 2 | 6 | | 5 | | 10 | 8 | 9[2] | 13 | | | | | | 3 | | 11[1] | | | 7 | | 12 | 4 | | | | | | | | | | 22 |
| 1 | 2 | 3 | | 5 | | 10 | 8■ | 9 | 12 | | | 14 | 13 | | 6[2] | | 11[3] | | | | | 7 | 4[1] | | | | | | | | | | 23 |
| 1 | 2 | 3 | | 5 | | 10 | 8[3] | | 9[2] | | | 13 | 12 | | 6[1] | | | | | | | 11 | 4 | 7 | 14 | | | | | | | | 24 |
| 1 | | 6 | | 5 | | 10[1] | 8 | 9[2] | 11 | | | 13 | 12 | | 3 | | | | | | | 7 | 2 | 4 | | | | | | | | | 25 |
| 1 | | 6 | | 5 | | 10[1] | | 9[2] | 11 | | | | 3 | | 12 | | 13 | | | 8 | | 7 | | 4■ | | 2 | | | | | | | 26 |
| | 2 | 6 | | 5 | | 10 | | 9 | | | | | 12 | | 3 | 1 | 11 | | | 8 | | 7 | | | | 4[1] | | | | | | | 27 |
| | 2 | 6[1] | | 5 | | 10 | 4 | 9[3] | 12 | | | 14 | 13 | | 3[2] | 1 | 11 | | | 8 | | 7 | | | | | | | | | | | 28 |
| 1[G] | 2 | 3 | | 5 | | | 8 | 9 | 10 | | | | | | 12[2] | 15 | 11 | | | | | 7 | | 6[1] | | 4 | 13 | | | | | | 29 |
| | 2 | 6[3] | | 5 | | 7 | 4 | 9 | 10[2] | | 12 | | 3 | | | 1 | 11[1] | | | | | 8 | | | | | 13 | 14 | | | | | 30 |
| | 2 | | | | | 10 | 8 | 9 | 12 | | | | 3 | | | 1 | | | | 7[1] | | 11 | | | | 4 | 6 | | 5 | | | | 31 |
| | 2■ | 6[1] | | 5 | | 10 | 7 | 9[2] | | | | 13 | | | 3 | 1 | | | | 12 | | 11 | | | | 8 | | | | 4 | | | 32 |
| | 2[1] | 6 | | 5[3] | | 10 | 11 | 9 | | | | 14 | 12 | | 3[2] | 1 | 13 | | | 8■ | | | | | | 7 | | | | 4 | | | 33 |
| 1 | | 6 | | 5 | | 10[2] | 8 | 9[3] | 13 | | | 14 | 3[1] | | 12 | | 11 | | | | | 7 | | | | 4 | | | | 2 | | | 34 |
| 1 | | 6 | | 5[3] | | 10 | 8 | 9 | 12 | | | | | | 3 | | 11[2] | | | | | 7 | | | | 4[1] | | | | 2 | 14 | 13 | 35 |
| 1 | | 3 | | 5 | | 10 | 8 | | 9[1] | | | | | | | | 12 | | | | | 11 | | | | 4 | | | | 2 | 6■ | 7 | 36 |
| 1 | | 13 | | 5 | | 10 | 8 | 9[1] | 12 | | | | 3 | | | | | | | | | 11[2] | | | | 4 | | | | 2 | 6 | 7 | 37 |
| 1 | 2■ | 3 | | 5 | | 10 | 11[2] | 9 | | | | | | | 12 | | 13 | | | | | 8 | | | | 6 | | | | 4[1] | | 7 | 38 |
| 1 | | 6 | | 5 | | 10[2] | 8 | 9 | 13 | | | | | | 3 | | 11[1] | | | | | 7 | | | | | 12 | 2 | | | | 4 | 39 |
| 1 | | 6 | | 5 | | 10 | 4 | 9 | 12 | | | | 11[2] | | 3 | | 7[1] | | | | | 8 | | | | | 13 | | | | | 2 | 40 |
| | | 3 | | 5 | | 10 | 8 | 9 | 11 | | | | | | 12 | 1 | | | | | | | | | | 2 | | | | 4[1] | 6 | 7 | 41 |
| | | 6 | | 5 | | 10 | 11 | 9[1] | 12 | | | | | | 3[3] | 1 | 13 | | | | | | | | | 8 | 14 | 2[2] | | | 4 | 7 | 42 |

**FA Cup**

| | | | |
|---|---|---|---|
| Fourth Qual | Forest Green R | (a) | 3-1 |
| First Round | Grays Ath | (a) | 2-1 |
| Second Round | Colchester U | (a) | 0-1 |

**Play-Offs**

| | | | |
|---|---|---|---|
| Semi-Finals | Hereford U | (h) | 1-1 |
| | | (a) | 0-0 |
| Final | Shrewsbury T | | 1-1 |

# BARNET — Conference

*Ground:* Underhill Stadium, Barnet Lane, Barnet, Hertfordshire EN5 2BE.
*Tel:* (0208) 441 6932.
*Year Formed:* 1888.
*Record Gate:* 11,026 (1952 v Wycombe Wanderers FA Amateur Cup Fourth Round).
*Nickname:* The Bees.
*Manager:* Paul Fairclough.
*Secretary:* Andrew Adie.
*Colours:* Amber shirts with black trim, amber shorts, amber stockings.

## BARNET 2003–04 LEAGUE RECORD

| Match No. | Date | Venue | Opponents | Result | | H/T Score | Lg. Pos. | Goalscorers | Attendance |
|---|---|---|---|---|---|---|---|---|---|
| 1 | Aug 9 | H | Telford U | W | 2-0 | 0-0 | — | Strevens $^{49}$, Eustace (og) $^{78}$ | 1319 |
| 2 | 12 | A | Farnborough T | D | 1-1 | 1-1 | — | Grazioli $^{35}$ | 1063 |
| 3 | 16 | A | Dagenham & R | L | 2-5 | 0-2 | 11 | Grazioli 2 (1 pen) $^{70, 89 (p)}$ | 1735 |
| 4 | 23 | H | Hereford U | D | 1-1 | 0-0 | 13 | Hendon $^{84}$ | 1475 |
| 5 | 25 | A | Burton Alb | W | 3-2 | 1-0 | 8 | Grazioli 2 $^{36, 70}$, Henshaw (og) $^{59}$ | 1675 |
| 6 | 30 | H | Halifax T | W | 4-1 | 2-1 | 6 | Grazioli 3 $^{9, 51, 69}$, Plummer $^{45}$ | 1341 |
| 7 | Sept 6 | H | Accrington S | D | 0-0 | 0-0 | 5 | | 1621 |
| 8 | 13 | A | Stevenage Bor | W | 2-1 | 0-1 | 5 | Beadle $^{58}$, Grazioli $^{66}$ | 3019 |
| 9 | 20 | H | Aldershot T | W | 2-1 | 1-0 | 4 | Strevens $^{3}$, Grazioli $^{59}$ | 2208 |
| 10 | 23 | A | Margate | W | 1-0 | 0-0 | — | Grazioli $^{67}$ | 780 |
| 11 | 27 | A | Shrewsbury T | W | 1-0 | 0-0 | 3 | Grazioli $^{67}$ | 4063 |
| 12 | Oct 4 | H | Morecambe | W | 2-1 | 2-0 | 3 | Strevens $^{2}$, Hendon $^{26}$ | 1776 |
| 13 | 7 | H | Exeter C | L | 2-3 | 0-1 | — | Plummer $^{89}$, Grazioli (pen) $^{90}$ | 2037 |
| 14 | 11 | A | Tamworth | L | 0-2 | 0-1 | 4 | | 1304 |
| 15 | 18 | A | Leigh RMI | W | 4-1 | 0-0 | 4 | Grazioli 3 $^{49, 62, 64}$, Hogg $^{84}$ | 348 |
| 16 | Nov 1 | H | Northwich Vic | W | 1-0 | 1-0 | 4 | Grazioli $^{5}$ | 1852 |
| 17 | 11 | H | Gravesend & N | W | 1-0 | 0-0 | — | Plummer $^{90}$ | 1542 |
| 18 | 15 | A | Chester C | L | 0-1 | 0-1 | 4 | | 2638 |
| 19 | 22 | H | Forest Green R | W | 5-0 | 2-0 | 2 | Taggart $^{2}$, Beadle 2 $^{41, 53}$, Strevens $^{80}$, Hendon (pen) $^{90}$ | 1378 |
| 20 | 25 | A | Scarborough | D | 2-2 | 1-1 | — | Yakubu $^{33}$, Hendon (pen) $^{60}$ | 1208 |
| 21 | 29 | A | Accrington S | L | 0-2 | 0-0 | 3 | | 1120 |
| 22 | Dec 13 | A | Telford U | W | 2-1 | 1-1 | 3 | Pitcher $^{45}$, Grazioli $^{50}$ | 1562 |
| 23 | 20 | H | Farnborough T | L | 0-2 | 0-1 | 3 | | 1547 |
| 24 | 26 | A | Woking | D | 2-2 | 1-1 | 4 | Strevens 2 $^{24, 58}$ | 2856 |
| 25 | Jan 1 | H | Woking | D | 0-0 | 0-0 | 5 | | 2304 |
| 26 | 3 | A | Halifax T | W | 2-1 | 0-1 | 4 | Grazioli $^{54}$, Strevens $^{64}$ | 1517 |
| 27 | 17 | H | Dagenham & R | L | 2-4 | 1-2 | 4 | Grazioli 2 $^{25, 84}$ | 2006 |
| 28 | 24 | H | Margate | W | 3-1 | 2-0 | 3 | Grazioli 2 $^{30, 41}$, Hendon (pen) $^{58}$ | 1591 |
| 29 | Feb 6 | A | Aldershot T | D | 1-1 | 1-0 | — | Redmile $^{27}$ | 4217 |
| 30 | 21 | A | Morecambe | W | 3-1 | 3-0 | 3 | Gamble $^{3}$, Strevens $^{12}$, Clist $^{37}$ | 2014 |
| 31 | 28 | H | Tamworth | W | 1-0 | 0-0 | 3 | Hatch $^{53}$ | 1899 |
| 32 | Mar 6 | A | Exeter C | D | 1-1 | 0-1 | 3 | Hatch $^{65}$ | 3531 |
| 33 | 9 | H | Stevenage Bor | D | 0-0 | 0-0 | — | | 2066 |
| 34 | 13 | A | Gravesend & N | D | 1-1 | 0-1 | 4 | Pearson $^{64}$ | 1516 |
| 35 | 20 | H | Chester C | D | 0-0 | 0-0 | 4 | | 2455 |
| 36 | 27 | A | Forest Green R | D | 1-1 | 1-1 | 5 | Strevens $^{25}$ | 1013 |
| 37 | 30 | H | Shrewsbury T | L | 0-1 | 0-1 | — | | 1966 |
| 38 | Apr 3 | H | Scarborough | D | 0-0 | 0-0 | 6 | | 1560 |
| 39 | 10 | A | Hereford U | L | 0-2 | 0-1 | 6 | | 4447 |
| 40 | 12 | H | Burton Alb | W | 2-1 | 0-1 | 5 | Hatch $^{47}$, Hendon (pen) $^{88}$ | 1505 |
| 41 | 17 | A | Northwich Vic | D | 1-1 | 0-1 | 5 | Hatch $^{81}$ | 728 |
| 42 | 24 | H | Leigh RMI | W | 2-1 | 1-1 | 4 | Yakubu $^{16}$, Grazioli $^{58}$ | 2988 |

**Final League Position: 4**

### GOALSCORERS

*League (60):* Grazioli 24 (2 pens), Strevens 9, Hendon 6 (4 pens), Hatch 4, Beadle 3, Plummer 3, Yakubu 2, Clist 1, Gamble 1, Hogg 1, Pearson 1, Pitcher 1, Redmile 1, Taggart 1, own goals 2.
*FA Cup (8):* Beadle 2, Gamble 2, Grazioli 2, Hatch 2.
*LDV Vans Trophy (3):* Hatch 1, Henry 1 (pen), Lopez 1.
*Trophy (3):* Pitcher 2, Roach 1.
*Play-Offs (2):* Clist 1, Strevens 1 (pen).

| Naisbitt 7 | Rooney 23 + 6 | King 33 + 2 | Hendon 37 + 1 | Plummer 34 | Maddix 32 | Lopez 15 + 10 | Gamble 40 | Grazioli 38 | Strevens 35 + 4 | Taggart 8 + 14 | Pluck — + 1 | Williams 19 + 15 | Hogg 11 + 5 | Sylla — + 4 | Yakubu 32 + 7 | Saunders — + 1 | Henry — + 3 | Forde 7 | Beadle 10 + 3 | Millard 1 | Solomon — + 1 | Hatch 17 + 6 | Gore 19 | Roach — + 1 | Pitcher 5 | Silk 1 | McNamee 2 + 3 | Campion — + 1 | Scully 1 | Bankole 8 | Clist 13 + 2 | Redmile 12 | Pearson 2 + 8 | *Match No.* |
|---|---|---|---|---|---|---|---|---|---|---|---|---|---|---|---|---|---|---|---|---|---|---|---|---|---|---|---|---|---|---|---|---|---|---|
| 1 | $2^{1}$ | $3^{2}$ | 4 | 5 | 6 | $7^{3}$ | 8 | 9 | 10 | 11 | 12 | 13 | 14 | | | | | | | | | | | | | | | | | | | | | 1 |
| 1 | 2 | | 4 | 5 | 6 | $7^{1}$ | 8 | 9 | 10 | 3 | | $11^{2}$ | 12 | 13 | | | | | | | | | | | | | | | | | | | | 2 |
| 1 | $2^{1}$ | 3 | 4 | $5^{2}$ | 6 | 14 | 8 | 9 | 10 | 11 | | 12 | $7^{3}$ | | 13 | | | | | | | | | | | | | | | | | | | 3 |
| 1 | 2 | 3 | 4 | 5 | 6 | $7^{2}$ | 8 | 9 | $10^{1}$ | $11^{3}$ | | 12 | 13 | 14 | | | | | | | | | | | | | | | | | | | | 4 |
| 1 | 12 | 3 | 4 | 5 | 6 | | 8 | 9 | 10 | | | 2 | $7^{2}$ | | $11^{1}$ | 13 | | | | | | | | | | | | | | | | | | 5 |
| 1 | 12 | 3 | 4 | 5 | $6^{1}$ | | 8 | $9^{2}$ | 10 | | | 2 | 7 | 13 | $11^{3}$ | | 14 | | | | | | | | | | | | | | | | | 6 |
| 1 | | 3 | 4 | 5 | 6 | 12 | 8 | 9 | 10 | 13 | | 2 | $7^{1}$ | | $11^{2}$ | | | | | | | | | | | | | | | | | | | 7 |
| | 12 | | $4^{1}$ | 5 | 6 | | 8 | 9 | 13 | $11^{2}$ | | 2 | 7 | | 3 | | | 1 | 10 | | | | | | | | | | | | | | | 8 |
| | 2 | | | 5 | 6 | | 8 | 9 | 10 | 12 | | 7 | 4 | | 3 | | | 1 | $11^{1}$ | | | | | | | | | | | | | | | 9 |
| | 2 | | | 5 | 6 | 12 | 8 | 9 | 10 | | | 7 | $4^{1}$ | | 3 | | | 1 | 11 | | | | | | | | | | | | | | | 10 |
| | $2^{1}$ | 13 | 12 | 5 | 6 | 4 | 8 | 9 | 10 | | | $7^{2}$ | | | 3 | | | 1 | 11 | | | | | | | | | | | | | | | 11 |
| | | $3^{1}$ | 4 | 5 | 6 | 7 | 8 | | 10 | 12 | | $2^{2}$ | | 13 | 11 | | | 1 | 9 | | | | | | | | | | | | | | | 12 |
| | | $3^{1}$ | 4 | 5 | 6 | 13 | $8^{2}$ | 9 | 10 | 14 | | 12 | 2▮ | | 11 | | | 1 | $7^{3}$ | | | | | | | | | | | | | | | 13 |
| | | 12 | 4 | 5 | 6 | 2 | $8^{2}$ | 9 | $10^{3}$ | $11^{1}$ | | 14 | 13 | | 3 | | | 1 | 7 | | | | | | | | | | | | | | | 14 |
| | 2 | 3 | 4 | 5 | 6 | | 8 | $9^{2}$ | | 14 | | | 7 | | $11^{3}$ | | | | 12 | 1 | 13 | $10^{1}$ | | | | | | | | | | | | 15 |
| | $2^{3}$ | 3 | 4 | 5 | 6 | 7 | 8 | 9 | 12 | | | 14 | | | $11^{1}$ | | | | 13 | | | $10^{2}$ | 1 | | | | | | | | | | | 16 |
| | | 3 | 4 | 5 | 6▮ | | 8 | 9 | 12 | | | $2^{2}$ | 7 | | 11 | | | | 13 | | | $10^{1}$ | 1 | | | | | | | | | | | 17 |
| | | 3 | 2 | 5 | 6 | | 4 | 9 | 7 | | | 13 | | | 11 | | | | $8^{1}$ | | | $10^{2}$ | 1 | 12 | | | | | | | | | | 18 |
| | 2 | 3 | 4 | 5 | $6^{1}$ | | $8^{2}$ | | 10 | 11 | | 7 | 13 | | 12 | | 14 | | $9^{3}$ | | | | 1 | | | | | | | | | | | 19 |
| | 2 | 3 | 4 | 5 | 6 | | 8 | 9 | 13 | | | $7^{2}$ | | | 11 | | | | $10^{1}$ | | | 12 | 1 | | | | | | | | | | | 20 |
| | 2 | 3 | 4 | 5 | | 12 | 8 | 9 | 7 | 14 | | 13 | $6^{1}$ | | $11^{3}$ | | | | | | | $10^{2}$ | 1 | | | | | | | | | | | 21 |
| | 7 | $3^{1}$ | 2 | 5 | 6 | | 8 | 9 | $10^{2}$ | 13 | | | | | 12 | | | | | | | 11 | 1 | | 4 | | | | | | | | | 22 |
| | 2 | | | 5 | | | 8 | | | 14 | | $9^{3}$ | | | 3 | | 13 | | | | | 10 | 1 | | 4 | 6 | $7^{1}$ | 12 | $11^{2}$ | | | | | 23 |
| | 7 | $3^{2}$ | 2 | 5 | 6 | | 8 | 9 | 10 | | | | | | $11^{1}$ | | | | | | | 12 | 1 | | 4 | | 13 | | | | | | | 24 |
| | 7 | | 2 | 5 | | 12 | 8 | 9 | 10 | | | 13 | | | 3 | | | | | | | $11^{2}$ | 1 | | $4^{1}$ | | 6 | | | | | | | 25 |
| | 13 | 2 | 5 | | 6 | 4 | 8 | $9^{2}$ | 10 | $11^{1}$ | | 7 | | | 3 | | | | | | | | 1 | | | | 12 | | | | | | | 26 |
| | | 3 | 2 | 5▮ | 6 | 7 | | 9 | 10 | | | 13 | | | $11^{1}$ | | | | | | | $8^{2}$ | 1 | | 4 | | 12 | | | | | | | 27 |
| | | 3 | 2 | 5 | $6^{1}$ | 13 | 8 | $9^{3}$ | $10^{2}$ | 14 | | 12 | | | 11 | | | | | | | 7 | | | | | | | | 1 | 4 | | | 28 |
| | | 3 | 2 | | 6 | | 8 | 9 | 10 | | | | | | 7 | | | | | | | 11 | | | | | | | | 1 | 4 | 5 | | 29 |
| | 2 | 3 | 5 | | | 11 | 8 | $9^{1}$ | 10 | 12 | | 7 | | | 6 | | | | | | | | | | | | | | | 1 | 4 | | | 30 |
| | 2 | $3^{1}$ | 4 | 5 | | 13 | 8 | 9 | 10 | | | $12^{2}$ | | | $11^{3}$ | | | | | | | 14 | | | | | | | | 1 | 7 | 6 | | 31 |
| | $2^{1}$ | | 4 | 5 | | 13 | 8 | $9^{3}$ | $10^{2}$ | | | 12 | | | 3 | | | | | | | 11 | | | | | | | | 1 | 7 | 6 | 14 | 32 |
| | | 3 | 2▮ | | 6 | $7^{2}$ | 8 | 9 | 10 | | | 12 | | | 13 | | | | | | | $11^{1}$ | | | | | | | | 1 | $4^{3}$ | 5 | 14 | 33 |
| | | 3 | 2 | | 6 | 12 | 8 | | 10 | | | $7^{1}$ | | | $11^{2}$ | | | | | | | 9 | | | | | | | | 1 | 4 | 5 | 13 | 34 |
| | | 3 | 2 | | 6 | | 8 | 9 | 7 | | | 12 | | | $11^{1}$ | | | | | | | 10 | | | | | | | | 1 | 4 | 5 | | 35 |
| | 2 | 3 | | | 6 | | $8^{2}$ | 9 | 11 | 13 | | $7^{1}$ | | | 12 | | | | | | | 14 | 1 | | | | | | | | 4 | 5 | $10^{3}$ | 36 |
| | 12 | 3 | 2 | | 6 | | | 9 | 8 | 14 | | $7^{1}$ | | | 11 | | | | | | | $13^{3}$ | 1 | | | | | | | | 4 | 5 | $10^{2}$ | 37 |
| | | 3 | 2 | 6 | | | 8 | 9 | 10 | | | 7 | | | $11^{1}$ | | | | | | | | 1 | | | | | | | | 4 | 5 | 12 | 38 |
| | $7^{1}$ | 3 | 2 | 6 | | $11^{2}$ | 8 | 9 | $10^{3}$ | 14 | | | | | 12 | | | | | | | | 1 | | | | | | | | 4 | 5 | 13 | 39 |
| | 7 | 3 | 2 | 6 | | 11 | 8 | $9^{3}$ | $10^{2}$ | | | | | | 13 | | | | | | | 12 | 1 | | | | | | | | $4^{1}$ | 5 | 14 | 40 |
| | 7 | 3 | 2 | 6 | | 4 | 8 | $9^{3}$ | | $12^{2}$ | | | | | $11^{1}$ | | | | | | | 10 | 1 | | | | | | | | 13 | 5 | 14 | 41 |
| | 12 | 3 | 2 | 5 | 6 | 4 | 8 | $9^{3}$ | $7^{2}$ | | | | | | $11^{1}$ | | | | | | | 10 | 1 | | | | | | | | 13 | | 14 | 42 |

**LDV Vans Trophy**
First Round | Brentford | (h) | 3-3

**FA Cup**
Fourth Qual | Bracknell T | (a) | 3-0
First Round | Stalybridge C | (h) | 2-2
| | (a) | 2-0
Second Round | Yeovil T | (a) | 1-5

**Play-Offs**
Semi-Finals | Shrewsbury T | (h) | 2-1
| | (a) | 0-1

# BURTON ALBION — Conference

*Ground:* Eton Park, Princess Way, Burton-on-Trent DE14 2RU.
*Tel:* (01283) 565938.
*Year Formed:* 1950.
*Record Gate:* 5,860 (1964 v Weymouth Southern League Cup Final).
*Nickname:* Brewers.
*Manager:* Nigel Clough.
*Secretary:* Tony Kirkland.
*Colours:* All yellow with black trim.

## BURTON ALBION 2003–04 LEAGUE RECORD

| Match No. | Date | Venue | Opponents | Result | | H/T Score | Lg. Pos. | Goalscorers | Attendance |
|---|---|---|---|---|---|---|---|---|---|
| 1 | Aug 9 | A | Gravesend & N | W | 2-1 | 0-1 | — | Howard $^{64}$, Wright $^{90}$ | 1137 |
| 2 | 12 | H | Shrewsbury T | L | 0-1 | 0-0 | — | | 3203 |
| 3 | 16 | H | Stevenage Bor | D | 1-1 | 0-0 | 10 | Anderson $^{49}$ | 1572 |
| 4 | 23 | A | Scarborough | W | 2-1 | 2-1 | 6 | Moore $^{8}$, Anderson $^{21}$ | 1445 |
| 5 | 25 | H | Barnet | L | 2-3 | 0-1 | 11 | Talbot $^{84}$, Chettle $^{87}$ | 1675 |
| 6 | 30 | A | Morecambe | L | 1-2 | 0-0 | 14 | Williams $^{51}$ | 1789 |
| 7 | Sept 6 | H | Woking | W | 2-0 | 1-0 | 12 | Anderson $^{41}$, Moore $^{66}$ | 1482 |
| 8 | 13 | A | Telford U | D | 2-2 | 1-1 | 11 | Kirkwood 2 $^{7, 86}$ | 2035 |
| 9 | 19 | H | Hereford U | W | 4-1 | 2-0 | — | Talbot 3 $^{19, 56, 79}$, Howard $^{43}$ | 2502 |
| 10 | 23 | A | Accrington S | L | 1-3 | 1-1 | — | Halford (og) $^{43}$ | 1911 |
| 11 | 27 | A | Aldershot T | L | 1-3 | 0-1 | 11 | Webster (pen) $^{71}$ | 2687 |
| 12 | Oct 3 | H | Exeter C | L | 3-4 | 1-2 | — | Webster 2 (2 pens) $^{16, 88}$, Moore $^{72}$ | 1985 |
| 13 | 8 | H | Chester C | D | 1-1 | 0-0 | — | Webster (pen) $^{90}$ | 1411 |
| 14 | 11 | A | Forest Green R | D | 1-1 | 0-1 | 14 | Twigg $^{78}$ | 867 |
| 15 | 18 | A | Dagenham & R | W | 2-0 | 1-0 | 11 | Beckwith (og) $^{21}$, Sinton $^{50}$ | 1483 |
| 16 | Nov 1 | H | Farnborough T | W | 1-0 | 1-0 | 10 | Stride $^{10}$ | 1601 |
| 17 | 14 | H | Halifax T | D | 2-2 | 1-0 | — | Ducros $^{12}$, Webster (pen) $^{82}$ | 1541 |
| 18 | 22 | A | Margate | W | 2-1 | 0-0 | 13 | Webster $^{64}$, Anderson $^{84}$ | 564 |
| 19 | 25 | H | Leigh RMI | W | 3-2 | 2-1 | — | Anderson $^{39}$, Howard $^{45}$, Corbett $^{90}$ | 1327 |
| 20 | 29 | A | Woking | L | 0-1 | 0-0 | 13 | | 1947 |
| 21 | Dec 2 | A | Northwich Vic | W | 2-1 | 1-0 | — | Talbot $^{36}$, Williams $^{71}$ | 686 |
| 22 | 13 | H | Gravesend & N | W | 3-0 | 0-0 | 9 | Colkin $^{46}$, Talbot $^{59}$, Stride $^{70}$ | 1403 |
| 23 | 26 | H | Tamworth | L | 0-1 | 0-0 | 12 | | 3164 |
| 24 | Jan 1 | A | Tamworth | D | 1-1 | 0-1 | 13 | Stride $^{86}$ | 2535 |
| 25 | 3 | H | Morecambe | L | 0-1 | 0-0 | 14 | | 1478 |
| 26 | 17 | A | Stevenage Bor | L | 0-1 | 0-0 | 14 | | 2003 |
| 27 | 24 | H | Accrington S | D | 1-1 | 0-0 | 13 | Webster $^{47}$ | 1614 |
| 28 | Feb 7 | A | Hereford U | W | 2-1 | 1-1 | 12 | White $^{27}$, Talbot $^{56}$ | 3417 |
| 29 | 21 | A | Exeter C | L | 0-2 | 0-1 | 12 | | 2885 |
| 30 | 24 | A | Shrewsbury T | L | 0-1 | 0-1 | — | | 3115 |
| 31 | 28 | H | Forest Green R | L | 2-3 | 0-2 | 12 | Talbot $^{69}$, Howard $^{76}$ | 1442 |
| 32 | Mar 6 | A | Chester C | L | 1-3 | 1-2 | 14 | Talbot $^{7}$ | 3318 |
| 33 | 9 | H | Telford U | W | 2-1 | 1-1 | — | Wright $^{42}$, Talbot $^{73}$ | 1244 |
| 34 | 13 | H | Northwich Vic | L | 0-1 | 0-1 | 13 | | 1416 |
| 35 | 16 | H | Aldershot T | L | 1-4 | 0-1 | — | Stride $^{55}$ | 1295 |
| 36 | 27 | H | Margate | L | 0-1 | 0-1 | 17 | | 1240 |
| 37 | 30 | A | Halifax T | W | 4-1 | 2-0 | — | Kirkwood $^{5}$, Ducros $^{33}$, Gill $^{84}$, Anderson $^{86}$ | 1128 |
| 38 | Apr 3 | A | Leigh RMI | W | 1-0 | 1-0 | 12 | Anderson $^{12}$ | 339 |
| 39 | 10 | H | Scarborough | W | 2-0 | 1-0 | 13 | Kirkwood $^{43}$, Dudley $^{62}$ | 1370 |
| 40 | 12 | A | Barnet | L | 1-2 | 1-0 | 13 | Talbot $^{30}$ | 1505 |
| 41 | 17 | A | Farnborough T | L | 1-2 | 0-1 | 13 | Henshaw $^{76}$ | 812 |
| 42 | 24 | H | Dagenham & R | L | 0-1 | 0-0 | 14 | | 1361 |

**Final League Position: 14**

### GOALSCORERS

*League (57):* Talbot 11, Anderson 7, Webster 7 (5 pens), Howard 4, Kirkwood 4, Stride 4, Moore 3, Ducros 2, Williams 2, Wright 2, Chettle 1, Colkin 1, Corbett 1, Dudley 1, Gill 1, Henshaw 1, Sinton 1, Twigg 1, White 1, own goals 2.
*FA Cup (8):* Anderson 3, Talbot 2, Webster 2, own goal 1.
*Trophy (6):* Webster 3, Anderson 1, Howard 1, Stride 1.

| Duke 42 | Henshaw 29 + 2 | Colkin 12 + 2 | Stride 28 + 2 | Wright 15 + 4 | Chettle 22 + 2 | Howard 30 + 6 | Ducros 20 + 6 | Anderson 26 + 11 | Moore 8 + 3 | Kirkwood 19 + 6 | Webster 31 + 3 | Talbot 28 + 9 | Williams 13 + 5 | Sugden 2 + 2 | Sinton 2 + 3 | Wassall 27 + 3 | Clough 15 + 12 | Dudley 23 + 4 | Crosby — + 2 | Twigg 3 + 1 | Gummer — + 1 | Willis 6 | Corbett 10 + 15 | Hoyle 12 + 4 | Murray 2 | McMahon 12 + 3 | Baptiste 3 | White 3 | Shilton 15 | Gill 4 + 1 | *Match No.* |
|---|---|---|---|---|---|---|---|---|---|---|---|---|---|---|---|---|---|---|---|---|---|---|---|---|---|---|---|---|---|---|---|
| 1 | 2 | 3¹ | 4 | 5 | 6 | 7 | 8 | 9² | 10 | 11 | 12 | 13 | | | | | | | | | | | | | | | | | | | 1 |
| 1 | 2 | 3¹ | 4 | 5² | 6 | 7 | 14 | 12 | 10 | | | 9 | 13 | 8 | 11³ | | | | | | | | | | | | | | | | 2 |
| 1 | 2 | | 4 | | 6 | 7¹ | | 9 | 12 | 11 | 3 | 10² | 8 | 13 | | 5 | | | | | | | | | | | | | | | 3 |
| 1 | 2 | | 4 | | 6¹ | 7 | | 9 | 10 | 11 | 5 | 13³ | 8 | 14 | | 3² | 12 | | | | | | | | | | | | | | 4 |
| 1 | 2 | | 4¹ | | 6 | 12 | | 13 | 10■ | | 3 | 11 | 7 | 8² | 9³ | 5 | | 14 | | | | | | | | | | | | | 5 |
| 1 | 2 | 13 | 4 | 5 | 6 | 7 | | 9 | 14 | | 3 | 10³ | 8² | | 12 | | | 11¹ | | | | | | | | | | | | | 6 |
| 1 | 2 | 12 | 4² | 5 | 6 | 7 | | 9³ | 10 | 13 | 3¹ | | 8 | | 14 | | | 11 | | | | | | | | | | | | | 7 |
| 1 | 2 | 3 | | 5¹ | 6 | 7² | 13 | 9 | | 11 | | 10 | | | | 12 | 4 | 8 | | | | | | | | | | | | | 8 |
| 1 | 2 | | | 5 | | 7 | 12 | 9 | | 11 | 3 | 10¹ | | | | 4² | 8 | 6 | 13 | | | | | | | | | | | | 9 |
| 1 | 2 | | | 5¹ | 6 | 7 | 13 | 9² | | 11 | 3 | 10 | 12 | | | | 8 | 4 | | | | | | | | | | | | | 10 |
| 1 | 2 | | | | 6 | 7² | 8 | 12 | 10³ | | 3 | 14 | 4 | | | 5 | 13 | 11¹ | | 9 | | | | | | | | | | | 11 |
| 1 | 2 | | | | 6 | 7 | 8 | 9² | 12 | | 3 | 10¹ | 11 | | | 5 | 4 | | | 13 | | | | | | | | | | | 12 |
| 1 | 2 | | 4 | | 6 | 7¹ | | | 10 | 13 | 3 | 9² | 8 | | | 5 | 12 | | | 11 | | | | | | | | | | | 13 |
| 1 | 2 | | 4² | | 6 | 7¹ | 12 | | 10 | 11 | 3 | | 8■ | | | 5 | 13 | | | 9³ | 14 | | | | | | | | | | 14 |
| 1 | 2 | 4 | | | 6 | 13 | 8 | 9³ | | 11 | 3 | 14 | 7¹ | | 12 | 5 | 10² | | | | | | | | | | | | | | 15 |
| 1 | 2 | 6² | 4 | | | 13 | 8 | 9 | | 12 | 3 | 10³ | 14 | | | 5¹ | 7 | | | | | 11 | | | | | | | | | 16 |
| 1 | | | 4 | | | 7 | 8 | 9 | | 6 | 3 | 10¹ | 2 | | | | 5 | | | | | 11 | 12 | | | | | | | | 17 |
| 1 | 2 | 5¹ | 4 | | | | | 9 | | 11³ | 3 | | 14 | | | 6² | | | 12 | | | 7 | 8 | 13 | 10 | | | | | | 18 |
| 1 | 2 | | 12 | | | 11 | | 9³ | | 13 | 3 | 10 | | | | 5 | 8² | 7¹ | | | | 6 | 14 | | 4 | | | | | | 19 |
| 1 | 2 | 6² | 4 | | | 10 | | 14 | | 11 | 3 | 13 | | | | 5¹ | | 7³ | | | | 8 | 9 | 12 | | | | | | | 20 |
| 1 | 2 | 6 | 4 | | | | | 14 | | 13 | 3 | 10³ | 7 | | | | 12 | | | | | 5 | 9 | 8¹ | | 11² | | | | | 21 |
| 1 | 2 | 5 | 4 | | 6¹ | 7² | | 14 | | 11 | 3 | 9³ | | | | 12 | 13 | 8 | | | | | 10 | | | | | | | | 22 |
| 1 | 2 | 3 | 4 | | 6 | 11² | 13 | 9 | | | | 12 | | | | 5 | 8 | 7¹ | | | | | 10 | | | | | | | | 23 |
| 1 | 2 | 3 | 4 | | 6 | 7³ | 8 | 9 | | 11 | 14 | 12 | | | | 5¹ | | 10² | | | | | 13 | | | | | | | | 24 |
| 1 | 2 | 11² | 4 | | | | 8 | 13 | | 7 | 3 | 9³ | 6¹ | | | 5 | 14 | 12 | | | | | 10 | | | | | | | | 25 |
| 1 | 2 | | 6 | | | 4 | 8¹ | 10 | | | 3 | 9³ | 12² | | | 5 | 14 | 7 | | | | | 13 | | | 11 | | | | | 26 |
| 1 | 2 | | 6 | | | 4 | | 9 | | | 3 | 10¹ | | | | 5 | 8 | 7 | | | | | 12 | | | 11 | | | | | 27 |
| 1 | | | 8 | 6 | | | | 14 | | | 3 | 9³ | | | | 5 | 12 | 13 | | | | | 7 | | | 4¹ | 2 | 10 | 11² | | 28 |
| 1 | | | | | 6¹ | 7 | 8² | 9 | | | 3 | 14 | | | | 5 | | 12 | | | | | 13 | | | 4 | 2 | 10³ | 11 | | 29 |
| 1 | | | | | | 2 | 8 | 12 | | | 3 | 9² | | | | 5 | 4 | 7 | | | | | 13 | 6 | | | | 10¹ | 11 | | 30 |
| 1 | | | | 12 | | 4 | 8 | 9³ | | | 3 | 14 | | | | 5 | | 7 | | | | | 10 | 6² | | 13 | 2¹ | | 11 | | 31 |
| 1 | 13 | | | 2¹ | | 6 | 8² | 9³ | | | 3 | 10 | | | | 5 | | 7 | | | | | 14 | 12 | | 4 | | | 11 | | 32 |
| 1 | | | | 6 | | 2¹ | 8 | 9² | | | 3 | 10 | | | | 5 | | 7 | | | | | 13 | 12 | | 4 | | | 11 | | 33 |
| 1 | | | | 6 | | | 8 | 14 | | | 3 | 10³ | | | | 5 | 12 | 7² | | | | | 13 | 2 | | 4¹ | | | 11 | 9 | 34 |
| 1 | | | 12 | 6² | 13 | 7 | 8 | 9³ | | | 3¹ | | | | | 5 | 4 | | | | | | 14 | 2 | | | | | 11 | 10 | 35 |
| 1 | | | 7 | 6³ | | 11¹ | 8 | 13 | | | 12 | 9 | | | | 5 | | | | | | | 14 | 2 | | 4 | | | 3 | 10² | 36 |
| 1 | | | 11 | 12 | 6 | | 8 | 9 | | 5¹ | | 10³ | | | | | 4² | 7 | | | | | | 2 | | 13 | | | 3 | 14 | 37 |
| 1 | | | 11 | 13 | 6 | 8¹ | | 9³ | | 5² | | | | | | | 12 | 7 | | | | | 14 | 2 | | 4 | | | 3 | 10 | 38 |
| 1 | 13 | | 4 | 12 | 6¹ | 5 | | 9³ | | 11 | | 10² | | | | | | 7 | | | | | 14 | 2 | | 8 | | | 3 | | 39 |
| 1 | 2 | | 4 | 5 | | 13 | 8 | | | 14 | | 10² | | | | 12 | 9¹ | | | | | | 7 | 3 | | 6³ | | | 11 | | 40 |
| 1 | 2 | | 4 | 5¹ | 14 | 13 | 8² | | | 6³ | | 9 | | | | | 12 | 7 | | | | | 10 | 3 | | | | | 11 | | 41 |
| 1 | 2 | | 8² | | 6 | 14 | | | | 10³ | 3 | 9 | | | | | 4 | 7¹ | | | | | 12 | 5 | | 13 | | | 11 | | 42 |

**FA Cup**

| | | | |
|---|---|---|---|
| Fourth Qual | Buxton | (h) | 6-0 |
| First Round | Torquay U | (a) | 2-1 |
| Second Round | Hartlepool U | (h) | 0-1 |

# CHESTER CITY — FL Championship 2

*Ground:* Deva Stadium, Bumpers Lane, Chester CH1 4LT.
*Tel:* (01244) 371 809.
*Year Formed:* 1884.
*Record Gate:* 5,538 (1994 v Preston North End Football League Division 3) (formerly at Sealand Road, 20,500 1952 v Chelsea FA Cup First Round).
*Nickname:* The Blues.
*Manager:* Mark Wright.
*Secretary:* Michael Beech.
*Colours:* Blue and white striped shirts, blue shorts, white stockings.

## CHESTER CITY 2003–04 LEAGUE RECORD

| Match No. | Date | Venue | Opponents | Result | | H/T Score | Lg. Pos. | Goalscorers | Attendance |
|---|---|---|---|---|---|---|---|---|---|
| 1 | Aug 9 | A | Stevenage Bor | D | 0-0 | 0-0 | — | | 2502 |
| 2 | 12 | H | Tamworth | W | 1-0 | 0-0 | — | Ruffer [49] | 2267 |
| 3 | 16 | H | Forest Green R | W | 1-0 | 0-0 | 5 | Davies [90] | 1881 |
| 4 | 23 | A | Exeter C | L | 1-2 | 1-1 | 7 | Foster (pen) [20] | 3030 |
| 5 | 26 | H | Shrewsbury T | W | 2-1 | 1-0 | — | Stamp [23], Bolland [89] | 4665 |
| 6 | 30 | A | Gravesend & N | W | 4-0 | 2-0 | 3 | Stamp [33], Bolland [38], Twiss 2 [89, 90] | 939 |
| 7 | Sept 6 | A | Margate | W | 2-1 | 1-1 | 2 | Stamp [43], Brady [70] | 634 |
| 8 | 13 | H | Halifax T | W | 2-0 | 1-0 | 2 | Hatswell [19], Stamp [51] | 2628 |
| 9 | 20 | A | Farnborough T | W | 2-1 | 1-0 | 2 | Stamp 2 [35, 60] | 748 |
| 10 | 23 | H | Northwich Vic | W | 4-0 | 1-0 | — | Collins [42], Carden [60], Foster [66], Rapley [90] | 2817 |
| 11 | 27 | H | Telford U | D | 0-0 | 0-0 | 2 | | 2688 |
| 12 | Oct 4 | A | Dagenham & R | D | 0-0 | 0-0 | 2 | | 1497 |
| 13 | 8 | A | Burton Alb | D | 1-1 | 0-0 | — | Stamp [75] | 1411 |
| 14 | 11 | H | Woking | W | 2-1 | 1-0 | 2 | Davies [17], Twiss [57] | 2085 |
| 15 | 18 | H | Hereford U | D | 0-0 | 0-0 | 2 | | 4481 |
| 16 | Nov 1 | A | Scarborough | D | 2-2 | 2-0 | 2 | Stamp [34], Clare (pen) [39] | 1441 |
| 17 | 11 | A | Morecambe | W | 1-0 | 0-0 | — | Clare [76] | 1959 |
| 18 | 15 | H | Barnet | W | 1-0 | 1-0 | 1 | Smith [45] | 2638 |
| 19 | 22 | A | Aldershot T | D | 1-1 | 0-0 | 1 | Stamp [49] | 3610 |
| 20 | 25 | H | Accrington S | D | 3-3 | 3-1 | — | Davies [19], Clare 2 [39, 44] | 2432 |
| 21 | 29 | H | Margate | W | 3-0 | 0-0 | 1 | Davies [68], Clare [82], Stamp [90] | 1971 |
| 22 | Dec 6 | A | Halifax T | W | 3-0 | 1-0 | 1 | Davies [33], Collins [59], Clare [65] | 1928 |
| 23 | 13 | H | Stevenage Bor | L | 1-2 | 0-1 | 1 | Twiss [90] | 2145 |
| 24 | 20 | A | Tamworth | W | 5-1 | 2-0 | 1 | Ruffer [20], Clare 3 [37, 48, 83], Smith [71] | 1520 |
| 25 | 26 | H | Leigh RMI | W | 5-0 | 3-0 | 1 | Clare [10], Stamp 3 [18, 25, 73], Rapley [87] | 3044 |
| 26 | Jan 1 | A | Leigh RMI | W | 6-2 | 2-0 | 1 | Clare 3 [33, 88, 89], Stamp 2 [43, 47], Smith [90] | 2002 |
| 27 | 3 | H | Gravesend & N | D | 2-2 | 2-0 | 1 | Clare 2 (1 pen) [23, 29 (p)] | 2670 |
| 28 | 17 | A | Forest Green R | L | 1-2 | 1-0 | 1 | Clare [45] | 1164 |
| 29 | 24 | A | Northwich Vic | W | 4-0 | 2-0 | 1 | McIntyre [34], Stamp 2 [42, 52], Clare [49] | 2141 |
| 30 | Feb 7 | H | Farnborough T | W | 3-2 | 2-0 | 1 | Stamp [1], Clare 2 [27, 88] | 2665 |
| 31 | 21 | H | Dagenham & R | W | 2-1 | 1-0 | 1 | Clare (pen) [18], Stamp [90] | 2990 |
| 32 | 28 | A | Woking | W | 2-1 | 0-1 | 1 | Collins [78], Twiss [86] | 2554 |
| 33 | Mar 6 | H | Burton Alb | W | 3-1 | 2-1 | 1 | Clare 2 [33, 71], Guyett [36] | 3318 |
| 34 | 13 | H | Morecambe | W | 2-1 | 0-0 | 1 | Smith [46], Clare [80] | 3512 |
| 35 | 20 | A | Barnet | D | 0-0 | 0-0 | 1 | | 2455 |
| 36 | 30 | A | Telford U | W | 2-0 | 0-0 | — | Clare 2 (1 pen) [76 (p), 90] | 3503 |
| 37 | Apr 3 | A | Accrington S | W | 2-0 | 1-0 | 1 | Guyett [13], Clare (pen) [90] | 2561 |
| 38 | 6 | H | Aldershot T | W | 4-2 | 2-1 | — | Bolland 2 [2, 58], Clare 2 (1 pen) [10, 67 (p)] | 3432 |
| 39 | 10 | H | Exeter C | W | 3-2 | 0-0 | 1 | Twiss 2 [63, 87], Clare [70] | 4046 |
| 40 | 13 | A | Shrewsbury T | D | 0-0 | 0-0 | — | | 5827 |
| 41 | 17 | H | Scarborough | W | 1-0 | 1-0 | 1 | Stamp [19] | 5987 |
| 42 | 24 | A | Hereford U | L | 1-2 | 0-1 | 1 | James (og) [47] | 7240 |

**Final League Position: 1**

### GOALSCORERS

*League (85):* Clare 29 (6 pens), Stamp 20, Twiss 7, Davies 5, Bolland 4, Smith 4, Collins 3, Foster 2 (1 pen), Guyett 2, Rapley 2, Ruffer 2, Brady 1, Carden 1, Hatswell 1, McIntyre 1, own goal 1.
*FA Cup (1):* Clare 1.
*Trophy (1):* Bolland 1.

| Brown 16 + 1 | Collins 41 | McIntyre 40 | Harris 10 + 4 | Hatswell 8 | Ruffer 23 + 1 | Carden 33 + 2 | Davies 26 + 9 | Rapley 9 + 17 | Gill 3 + 1 | Heard 24 + 1 | Foster 10 + 10 | Beesley — + 3 | Brodie — + 2 | Carey 21 + 1 | Twiss 10 + 20 | McCaldon 13 | Bolland 30 + 5 | Brady 15 | Stamp 35 + 3 | Clare 27 + 3 | Guyett 24 + 3 | Smith 20 | Regan 4 | Turner 12 | Williams 5 | Lane 1 + 3 | Woods 1 + 1 | Elam 1 + 3 | *Match No.* |
|---|---|---|---|---|---|---|---|---|---|---|---|---|---|---|---|---|---|---|---|---|---|---|---|---|---|---|---|---|---|
| 1 | 2 | 3 | 4 | 5 | 6 | 7 | 8 | $9^{1}$ | $10^{2}$ | 11 | 12 | 13 | | | | | | | | | | | | | | | | | 1 |
| 1 | 2 | 3 | $4^{1}$ | 5 | 6 | 7 | 8 | $9^{2}$ | $10^{3}$ | 11 | 12 | 13 | 14 | | | | | | | | | | | | | | | | 2 |
| 1 | 2 | 3 | | 5 | 6 | 7 | 8 | $9^{1}$ | $10^{2}$ | 11 | 12 | | 13 | $4^{3}$ | 14 | | | | | | | | | | | | | | 3 |
| | 2 | 3 | | 5 | $6^{1}$ | 7 | 8 | | | | $4^{2}$ | 13 | | | 12 | 1 | 9 | 11 | 10 | | | | | | | | | | 4 |
| 1 | 2 | 3 | | 5 | | 7 | 8 | | 12 | 11 | $6^{1}$ | | | | 13 | | 4 | $10^{2}$ | 9 | | | | | | | | | | 5 |
| 1 | 2 | 3 | 12 | 5 | 13 | $7^{2}$ | 8 | | | $11^{3}$ | 10 | | | | 14 | | 4 | 6 | $9^{1}$ | | | | | | | | | | 6 |
| 1 | 2 | 3 | $4^{1}$ | 5 | | 7 | 8 | 13 | | | $10^{2}$ | | | | 12 | | 6 | 11 | 9 | | | | | | | | | | 7 |
| 1 | 2 | 3 | 4 | 5 | | 7 | 8 | 12 | | | $10^{1}$ | | | | | | 6 | 11 | 9 | | | | | | | | | | 8 |
| 1 | 2 | 3 | 4 | | 6 | 7 | 8 | 12 | | | $10^{1}$ | | | | | | 5 | 11 | 9 | | | | | | | | | | 9 |
| | 2 | 3 | 4 | | 6 | 7 | 8 | 12 | | | $10^{2}$ | | | | 13 | 1 | 5 | $11^{1}$ | 9 | | | | | | | | | | 10 |
| 1 | 2 | 3 | 4 | | 6 | 7 | 8 | 13 | | | $10^{3}$ | | | | 12 | | 5 | $11^{1}$ | $9^{2}$ | 14 | | | | | | | | | 11 |
| 1 | 2 | 3 | | | 6 | 7 | 8 | 12 | | | $10^{2}$ | | | | $4^{1}$ | | 5 | 11 | 9 | 13 | | | | | | | | | 12 |
| | 2 | 3 | | | 6 | 7 | 8 | $11^{1}$ | | 4 | $10^{2}$ | | | | 13 | 1 | 5 | | 9 | 12 | | | | | | | | | 13 |
| | 2 | 3 | | | $6^{1}$ | 7 | 8 | 13 | | 11 | 14 | | | | 4 | 1 | 5 | | $9^{3}$ | $10^{2}$ | 12 | | | | | | | | 14 |
| | 2 | 3 | | | 6 | 7 | 8 | 12 | | 4■ | 13 | | | | $11^{1}$ | 1 | 5 | | 9 | $10^{2}$ | | | | | | | | | 15 |
| | 2 | 3 | | | 6 | 7■ | 8 | | | | | | | 4 | 13 | 1 | 5 | 11 | $9^{1}$ | $10^{2}$ | 12 | | | | | | | | 16 |
| 15 | 2 | 3 | | | 6 | 7 | 8 | | | | 12 | | | | | $1^{6}$ | 5 | 11 | 10 | $9^{1}$ | 13 | $4^{2}$ | | | | | | | 17 |
| 1 | 2 | 3 | 13 | | 6 | | 8 | | | | | | | 7 | 12 | | | 11 | 10 | $9^{2}$ | 5 | $4^{1}$ | | | | | | | 18 |
| 1 | 2 | 3 | | | $6^{1}$ | 13 | 8 | | | 12 | 14 | | | 7 | | | | $11^{3}$ | 10 | 9 | 5 | $4^{2}$ | | | | | | | 19 |
| 1 | 2 | 3 | 4 | | | | 8 | 13 | | | 12 | | | 7 | | | | 11 | $10^{2}$ | $9^{1}$ | 5 | 6 | | | | | | | 20 |
| 1 | 2 | 3 | | | 6 | | 8 | $9^{3}$ | | | 13 | | | 7 | | | 12 | $11^{2}$ | 14 | 10 | $5^{1}$ | 4 | | | | | | | 21 |
| 1 | 2 | 3 | | | 6 | 12 | 8 | 10 | | $11^{2}$ | | | | 4 | | | 13 | | | 9 | 5 | $7^{1}$ | | | | | | | 22 |
| 1 | 2 | 3 | | | 6 | | 8 | $9^{2}$ | | | | | | 7 | 12 | | 4 | | 13 | 10 | $5^{1}$ | 11 | | | | | | | 23 |
| | 2 | $3^{2}$ | 12 | | 6 | 7 | | 14 | | | | | | 8 | | 1 | 13 | | 10 | $9^{3}$ | 5 | $11^{1}$ | 4 | | | | | | 24 |
| | 2 | 3 | | | 6 | 7 | 12 | 13 | | | | | | 8 | 14 | 1 | | | $10^{3}$ | $9^{2}$ | 5 | $4^{1}$ | 11 | | | | | | 25 |
| | 2 | $3^{2}$ | | | 6 | 7 | | | | | | | | 8 | 13 | 1 | 12 | | 10 | 9 | $5^{1}$ | 4 | 11 | | | | | | 26 |
| | 2 | | | | 6 | 7 | 13 | 14 | | | | | | $8^{2}$ | 11 | 1 | 12 | | $10^{3}$ | 9 | 5 | $4^{1}$ | 3 | | | | | | 27 |
| | 2 | 3 | 4 | | 6 | 8 | | 13 | | 11 | | | | | 12 | 1 | 5 | | $10^{2}$ | 9 | | $7^{1}$ | | | | | | | 28 |
| | 2 | 3 | | | | 7 | 12 | 14 | | 11 | | | | $6^{1}$ | 13 | 1 | 4 | | $10^{3}$ | $9^{2}$ | 5 | 8 | | | | | | | 29 |
| | 2 | 3 | | | | | 8 | | | 11 | | | | 7 | 12 | | 4 | | 10 | 9 | 5 | $6^{1}$ | | 1 | | | | | 30 |
| | 2 | 3 | | | | | 12 | | | 11 | | | | $7^{1}$ | 13 | | 4 | | 10 | 9 | 5 | $6^{2}$ | | 1 | 8 | | | | 31 |
| | 2 | 3 | | | | 8 | | | | 11 | | | | | 12 | | 4 | | 10 | 9 | 5 | $6^{1}$ | | 1 | 7 | | | | 32 |
| | 2 | 3 | | | | 8 | | | | 11 | | | | 12 | | | 4 | | 10 | 9 | 5 | 6 | | 1 | $7^{1}$ | | | | 33 |
| | 2 | 3 | | | | 7 | 12 | | | 11 | | | | | | | 4 | | 10 | 9 | 5 | 6 | | 1 | $8^{1}$ | | | | 34 |
| | 2 | 3 | | | | 8 | | 12 | | $11^{3}$ | | | | | 13 | | 4 | | 9 | $10^{1}$ | 5 | $6^{2}$ | | 1 | 7 | 14 | | | 35 |
| | 2 | 3 | | | | 8 | 13 | | | 11 | | | | 7 | 12 | | 4 | | $10^{2}$ | 9 | 5 | $6^{1}$ | | | | | 1 | | 36 |
| | 2 | 3 | | | | 8 | | | | 11 | | | | 7 | 6 | | 4 | | $10^{1}$ | 9 | 5 | | | 1 | | 12 | | | 37 |
| | 2 | 3■ | | | | 8 | 13 | | | $11^{3}$ | | | | $7^{1}$ | 6 | | 4 | | $10^{2}$ | 9 | 5 | | | 1 | | 12 | | 14 | 38 |
| | 2 | 3 | | | | 8 | 12 | 13 | | 11 | | | | $7^{1}$ | 6 | | 4 | | $10^{2}$ | $9^{3}$ | 5 | | | 1 | | | | 14 | 39 |
| | 2 | 3 | | | | 8 | 12 | 9 | | 11 | | | | $7^{1}$ | 6 | | 4 | | 10 | | 5 | | | 1 | | | | | 40 |
| | $2^{3}$ | 3 | 12 | | | 8 | 7 | 13 | | 11 | | | | | $6^{1}$ | | 4 | | 10 | $9^{2}$ | 5 | | | 1 | | | | 14 | 41 |
| | | | 2 | | | | 8 | $9^{2}$ | | 11 | 12 | | | $7^{1}$ | 6 | | 4 | | 13 | | 5 | | | $1^{6}$ | | 3 | 15 | 10 | 42 |

**LDV Vans Trophy**

| | | | |
|---|---|---|---|
| First Round | Doncaster R | (h) | 0-1 |

**FA Cup**

| | | | |
|---|---|---|---|
| Fourth Qual | Blyth S | (a) | 1-0 |
| First Round | Gravesend & N | (h) | 0-1 |

# DAGENHAM & REDBRIDGE Conference

*Ground:* Victoria Road, Dagenham, Essex RM10 7XL.
*Tel:* (0208) 592 7194.
*Year Formed:* 1992.
*Record Gate:* 5,500 (1992 v Leyton Orient FA Cup First Round).
*Nickname:* Daggers.
*Manager:* John Still.
*Secretary:* Derek Almond.
*Colours:* Red shirts, white shorts, red stockings.

## DAGENHAM & REDBRIDGE 2003–04 LEAGUE RECORD

| Match No. | Date | Venue | Opponents | Result | | H/T Score | Lg. Pos. | Goalscorers | Attendance |
|---|---|---|---|---|---|---|---|---|---|
| 1 | Aug 9 | A | Leigh RMI | L | 1-2 | 1-1 | — | Bruce [41] | 419 |
| 2 | 12 | H | Stevenage Bor | L | 1-2 | 0-1 | — | Vickers [73] | 1948 |
| 3 | 16 | H | Barnet | W | 5-2 | 2-0 | 14 | Bentley 2 [30, 34], Stein 3 [58, 61, 90] | 1735 |
| 4 | 23 | A | Morecambe | L | 2-3 | 1-2 | 17 | Stein 2 [45, 54] | 1477 |
| 5 | 25 | H | Forest Green R | W | 5-2 | 3-1 | 13 | Bentley 2 [2, 32], Shipp 2 [28, 81], Meechan [90] | 1540 |
| 6 | 30 | A | Shrewsbury T | L | 1-2 | 0-2 | 15 | Bentley [69] | 3468 |
| 7 | Sept 6 | H | Telford U | D | 1-1 | 0-1 | 16 | Piper C (pen) [51] | 1503 |
| 8 | 13 | A | Northwich Vic | W | 1-0 | 0-0 | 14 | Cole [48] | 575 |
| 9 | 20 | H | Accrington S | L | 0-1 | 0-0 | 14 | | 1542 |
| 10 | 22 | A | Exeter C | D | 1-1 | 1-1 | — | Cole [36] | 3344 |
| 11 | 27 | A | Tamworth | L | 0-2 | 0-0 | 14 | | 1147 |
| 12 | Oct 4 | H | Chester C | D | 0-0 | 0-0 | 14 | | 1497 |
| 13 | 7 | H | Margate | W | 4-0 | 1-0 | — | Bruce [25], Shipp [62], Meechan [69], Braithwaite [88] | 1540 |
| 14 | 13 | A | Hereford U | D | 1-1 | 0-0 | — | Beckwith [65] | 4325 |
| 15 | 18 | H | Burton Alb | L | 0-2 | 0-1 | 16 | | 1483 |
| 16 | Nov 1 | A | Halifax T | L | 0-3 | 0-3 | 17 | | 1379 |
| 17 | 11 | H | Farnborough T | W | 1-0 | 1-0 | — | Watts [41] | 1269 |
| 18 | 15 | A | Woking | D | 0-0 | 0-0 | 15 | | 2256 |
| 19 | 22 | H | Scarborough | W | 1-0 | 1-0 | 15 | Bentley [28] | 1107 |
| 20 | 25 | A | Gravesend & N | W | 2-1 | 0-1 | — | Piper C [53], Watts [89] | 1274 |
| 21 | 29 | A | Telford U | L | 0-1 | 0-1 | 14 | | 1321 |
| 22 | Dec 6 | H | Northwich Vic | W | 2-0 | 0-0 | 14 | Mustafa [53], Goodwin [67] | 1163 |
| 23 | 13 | H | Leigh RMI | L | 1-2 | 0-1 | 14 | Cole [83] | 1037 |
| 24 | 20 | A | Stevenage Bor | W | 2-0 | 1-0 | 14 | Moore [45], Cole [51] | 1749 |
| 25 | 26 | H | Aldershot T | L | 2-3 | 1-2 | 14 | Moore [35], Watts [90] | 1625 |
| 26 | Jan 1 | A | Aldershot T | L | 1-2 | 0-1 | 14 | Moore [71] | 4168 |
| 27 | 3 | H | Shrewsbury T | W | 5-0 | 3-0 | 13 | Moore 2 [29, 70], Piper C (pen) [33], Pacquette [38], Goodwin [73] | 1571 |
| 28 | 17 | A | Barnet | W | 4-2 | 2-1 | 11 | Plummer (og) [20], Cole [28], Janney [58], Hill [90] | 2006 |
| 29 | 24 | H | Exeter C | L | 0-2 | 0-0 | 11 | | 1909 |
| 30 | Feb 7 | A | Accrington S | W | 3-2 | 1-1 | 11 | Piper C [13], Moore [89], Jackson K [90] | 1601 |
| 31 | 21 | A | Chester C | L | 1-2 | 0-1 | 11 | Braithwaite [71] | 2990 |
| 32 | 27 | H | Hereford U | L | 0-9 | 0-3 | — | | 1617 |
| 33 | Mar 6 | A | Margate | D | 3-3 | 1-3 | 11 | Jackson J [12], Moore [82], Shipp [86] | 508 |
| 34 | 9 | H | Tamworth | D | 0-0 | 0-0 | — | | 984 |
| 35 | 13 | A | Farnborough T | D | 2-2 | 2-0 | 12 | Braithwaite [11], Moore [24] | 787 |
| 36 | 20 | H | Woking | W | 1-0 | 0-0 | 11 | Shipp [76] | 1345 |
| 37 | 27 | A | Scarborough | D | 0-0 | 0-0 | 11 | | 1302 |
| 38 | Apr 3 | H | Gravesend & N | L | 0-4 | 0-0 | 13 | | 1421 |
| 39 | 10 | H | Morecambe | L | 1-3 | 0-2 | 15 | Moore [73] | 1122 |
| 40 | 12 | A | Forest Green R | W | 3-1 | 2-0 | 14 | Janney [5], Braithwaite [9], Moore [90] | 762 |
| 41 | 17 | H | Halifax T | L | 0-1 | 0-1 | 14 | | 1344 |
| 42 | 24 | A | Burton Alb | W | 1-0 | 0-0 | 13 | Braithwaite [56] | 1361 |

**Final League Position: 13**

### GOALSCORERS

*League (59):* Moore 10, Bentley 6, Braithwaite 5, Cole 5, Shipp 5, Stein 5, Piper C 4 (2 pens), Watts 3, Bruce 2, Goodwin 2, Janney 2, Meechan 2, Beckwith 1, Hill 1, Jackson J 1, Jackson K 1, Mustafa 1, Pacquette 1, Vickers 1, own goal 1.
*FA Cup (1):* Shipp 1.
*LDV Vans Trophy (5):* Bentley 2, Scully 2, Braithwaite 1.
*Trophy (3):* Jackson K 2, Braithwaite 1.

| Pullen 9 | Mustafa 35 + 1 | Cole 29 | Terry 2 | Vickers 30 + 1 | Jackson J 17 + 2 | Janney 22 + 15 | Shipp 29 + 6 | Braithwaite 20 + 14 | Stein 6 | Bruce 30 + 6 | Matthews 15 + 1 | Meechan 6 + 10 | Bentley 23 + 2 | Smith 5 | Roberts 26 | Piper C 29 + 5 | Piper L 6 + 8 | Goodwin 15 + 5 | Hill 16 + 8 | Scully 13 | Kimble 19 + 3 | Beckwith 4 | McGowan — + 3 | Watts 7 + 7 | Gill 5 | Whitman 3 + 1 | Moore 19 + 1 | Naisbitt 7 | Pacquette 3 | Eaton — + 2 | Perfect 1 + 5 | Hoyle 1 | Rees 1 | Jackson K 4 | Venus 5 | *Match No.* |
|---|---|---|---|---|---|---|---|---|---|---|---|---|---|---|---|---|---|---|---|---|---|---|---|---|---|---|---|---|---|---|---|---|---|---|---|---|
| 1 | 2 | $3^{1}$ | 4 | 5 | 6 | $7^{2}$ | 8 | 9 | 10 | $11^{3}$ | 12 | 13 | 14 | | | | | | | | | | | | | | | | | | | | | | | 1 |
| 1 | $2^{1}$ | | 4 | 5 | $6^{2}$ | 12 | $8^{3}$ | 9 | 10 | 13 | 3 | 14 | 7 | 11 | | | | | | | | | | | | | | | | | | | | | | 2 |
| | 2 | | | 3 | | $7^{2}$ | 12 | $9^{3}$ | 10 | 11 | 4 | 14 | 8 | 5 | 1 | $6^{1}$ | 13 | | | | | | | | | | | | | | | | | | | 3 |
| | 2 | | | 3▮ | | $7^{1}$ | 8 | $9^{2}$ | $10^{3}$ | 11 | 6 | 14 | 4 | 5 | 1 | | 13 | 12 | | | | | | | | | | | | | | | | | | 4 |
| | | | | | 6 | 12 | 7 | $9^{3}$ | $10^{2}$ | 11 | 3 | 13 | 8 | 5 | 1 | | $4^{1}$ | 2 | 14 | | | | | | | | | | | | | | | | | 5 |
| | 3 | | | 13 | $6^{2}$ | 7 | | 9 | | 11 | 4 | 12 | 8 | 5 | 1 | | 14 | $2^{3}$ | $10^{1}$ | | | | | | | | | | | | | | | | | 6 |
| | 12 | 3 | | | | 13 | | 9 | | | 4 | 10 | 8 | | 1 | 6 | 14 | $5^{1}$ | $7^{3}$ | $11^{2}$ | 2 | | | | | | | | | | | | | | | 7 |
| | 2 | 5 | | | | 12 | | 14 | 10 | 13 | 4 | $9^{3}$ | 8 | | 1 | 7 | | | $6^{1}$ | $11^{2}$ | 3 | | | | | | | | | | | | | | | 8 |
| 1 | 2 | 4▮ | | | | | 12 | $9^{2}$ | | 13 | 5 | $8^{1}$ | 7 | | | 6 | 14 | | $10^{3}$ | 11 | 3 | | | | | | | | | | | | | | | 9 |
| 1 | $2^{2}$ | 4 | | | | 12 | $7^{3}$ | 13 | | 10 | 5 | | 8 | | | 6 | $9^{1}$ | | 14 | 11 | 3▮ | | | | | | | | | | | | | | | 10 |
| 1 | | 3 | | 5 | | 13 | 9 | | | 11 | 4 | 12 | $8^{1}$ | | | 6 | $10^{2}$ | | 7 | 2 | | | | | | | | | | | | | | | | 11 |
| 1 | | | | 5 | | 7 | 9 | | | 11 | | 10 | 8 | | | 2 | 6 | | | | 3 | 4 | | | | | | | | | | | | | | 12 |
| 1▮ | $3^{1}$ | | | 6 | | | 9 | 14 | | 11 | | 10 | 8 | | | 2 | $4^{3}$ | | 12 | $7^{2}$ | | 5 | 13 | | | | | | | | | | | | | 13 |
| 1 | 3 | | | 6 | | | 9 | 12 | | $11^{2}$ | | $10^{1}$ | 8 | | | 2 | $4^{3}$ | | 14 | 7 | 13 | 5 | | | | | | | | | | | | | | 14 |
| 1 | 2 | | | 5 | | $7^{1}$ | $9^{3}$ | 10 | | | | 14 | 8 | | | 6 | 12 | | | $11^{2}$ | 3 | 4 | | 13 | | | | | | | | | | | | 15 |
| | 2 | 3 | | 5 | | 13 | | 9 | | 11 | 6 | 12 | 8 | | 1 | | | | 4 | $7^{1}$ | | | | $10^{2}$ | | | | | | | | | | | | 16 |
| | 2 | 5 | | 6 | | 12 | 14 | 13 | | | | | 8 | | 1 | $7^{1}$ | | | $4^{3}$ | | 3 | | | 11 | 9 | $10^{2}$ | | | | | | | | | | 17 |
| | 2 | 5 | | 6 | | 13 | 11 | 14 | | | | | 8▮ | | 1 | | | 12 | $4^{1}$ | $7^{2}$ | 3 | | | | 9 | $10^{3}$ | | | | | | | | | | 18 |
| | | 5 | | 6 | | 2 | 11 | | | | | 13 | 8 | | 1 | 12 | | 4 | | $7^{1}$ | 3 | | | 14 | $9^{2}$ | $10^{3}$ | | | | | | | | | | 19 |
| | 3 | $5^{1}$ | | | | 12 | 7 | | | 11 | 6 | | 8 | | 1 | 4 | | 2 | | | | | | 9 | $10^{2}$ | | 13 | | | | | | | | | 20 |
| | 3 | | | 6 | | 12 | 8 | 14 | | 11 | 5 | | | | 1 | 4 | | $2^{1}$ | | $7^{2}$ | | | | 9 | $10^{3}$ | 13 | | | | | | | | | | 21 |
| | 3 | | | 5 | | 12 | 8 | $9^{3}$ | | 11 | 4 | | 13 | | 1 | $6^{2}$ | | $2^{1}$ | | 7 | 14 | | | 10 | | | | | | | | | | | | 22 |
| | 7 | 4 | | 3 | | 12 | 11 | | | 10 | 5 | | 8 | | | $6^{2}$ | | $2^{1}$ | 13 | | | | | 9 | | | | 1 | | | | | | | | 23 |
| | 2 | 4 | | 3 | | 12 | 7 | $9^{2}$ | | 11 | | | 8 | | | 6 | | $5^{1}$ | 14 | | | | | 13 | | | $10^{3}$ | 1 | | | | | | | | 24 |
| | 2 | 4 | | 5▮ | 3 | | 7 | 10 | | $11^{1}$ | | | 8 | | | $6^{2}$ | | | 13 | | | | | 12 | | | 9 | 1 | | | | | | | | 25 |
| | 2 | 5 | | 3 | 13 | 12 | $4^{2}$ | | | $11^{1}$ | | | 8 | | | 6 | | | | | | | | 7 | | | 9 | 1 | $10^{3}$ | 14 | | | | | | 26 |
| | 7 | 4 | | $5^{1}$ | 3 | | | | | 11 | | | | | | $6^{2}$ | | 2 | 8 | | | | 13 | 14 | | | 9 | 1 | $10^{3}$ | | 12 | | | | | 27 |
| | 2 | 4 | | | 3 | $7^{1}$ | 13 | 14 | | 11 | | | | | | $6^{2}$ | | | 8 | | | | | 12 | | | 9 | 1 | $10^{3}$ | | | 5 | | | | 28 |
| | 2 | 4 | | | 3 | $7^{1}$ | 13 | 12 | | 11 | | | | | | 6 | | | $8^{2}$ | | | | | 14 | | | $9^{3}$ | 1 | | | | | 5 | 10 | | 29 |
| | 2 | 4 | | $5^{1}$ | 3 | 7 | | 12 | | 11 | | | | | 1 | 6 | | | 8 | | | | | | | | 9 | | | | | | | 10 | | 30 |
| | 2 | 4 | | 5 | $3^{2}$ | 7 | 8 | 13 | | 11 | | | | | 1 | 12 | | | $6^{1}$ | | 14 | | | | | | $9^{3}$ | | | | | | | 10 | | 31 |
| | 2 | 4 | | 5 | 3 | $7^{1}$ | 8▮ | | | 11 | | | | | 1 | 12 | 13 | | $6^{2}$ | | | | | | | | 9 | | | | | | | 10 | | 32 |
| | $2^{1}$ | 4 | | 5 | $11^{3}$ | 7 | 8 | 10 | | 14 | | | | | 1 | 12 | 13 | | $6^{2}$ | | 3 | | | | | | 9 | | | | | | | | | 33 |
| | 2 | 4 | | 5 | $11^{1}$ | 7 | 8 | 10 | | 12 | | | | | 1 | 6 | | | | | 3 | | | | | | 9 | | | | | | | | | 34 |
| | 2 | 4 | | | 11 | $7^{1}$ | | 10 | | $8^{3}$ | | | | | 1 | 6 | | 12 | | | 3 | | | | | | $9^{2}$ | | | 13 | 14 | | | | 5 | 35 |
| | 2 | 4 | | | 11 | 7 | 14 | $10^{3}$ | | 8 | | | | | 1 | $6^{1}$ | | 13 | 12 | | 3 | | | | | | $9^{2}$ | | | | | | | | 5 | 36 |
| | 2 | 4 | | | 11 | $7^{1}$ | 8 | 13 | | 10 | | | | | 1 | 6 | | 12 | | | 3 | | | | | | $9^{2}$ | | | | | | | | 5 | 37 |
| | | | | 4 | 11 | 7 | 8 | 12 | | $10^{2}$ | | | | | 1 | 6▮ | | 2 | | | 3 | | | | | | $9^{1}$ | | | | 13 | | | | 5 | 38 |
| | 2 | | | 4 | | 7 | 10 | 12 | | $11^{2}$ | | | | | 1 | 14 | | 8 | $6^{3}$ | | 3 | | | | | | 9 | | | | 13 | | | | $5^{1}$ | 39 |
| | 11 | 4 | | 5 | | 7 | 8 | 10 | | | | | | | 1 | 6 | | 2 | | | 3 | | | | | | 9 | | | | | | | | | 40 |
| | $2^{3}$ | 5 | | 6 | 13 | 7 | 8 | $10^{1}$ | | 12 | | | | | 1 | | | 4 | | | 3 | | 14 | | | | $9^{2}$ | | | | 11 | | | | | 41 |
| | | 4 | | 5 | | 7 | 8 | $10^{1}$ | | 11 | | | | | 1 | 6 | | 2 | | | 3 | | | | | | 9 | | | | 12 | | | | | 42 |

**LDV Vans Trophy**

| | | | |
|---|---|---|---|
| First Round | Leyton Orient | (h) | 4-1 |
| Second Round | QPR | (a) | 1-2 |

**FA Cup**

| | | | |
|---|---|---|---|
| Fourth Qual | Thurrock | (a) | 1-2 |

# EXETER CITY

## Conference

*Ground:* St James Park, Exeter EX4 6PX.
*Tel:* (01392) 411 243.
*Year Formed:* 1904.
*Record Gate:* 20,984 v Sunderland, FA Cup 6th rd (replay), 4 March 1931.
*Nickname:* The Grecians.
*Manager:* Eamonn Dolan.
*Secretary:* Sally Cooke.
*Colours:* Red and white shirts, white shorts, white stockings.

### EXETER CITY 2003–04 LEAGUE RECORD

| Match No. | Date | Venue | Opponents | Result | | H/T Score | Lg. Pos. | Goalscorers | Attendance |
|---|---|---|---|---|---|---|---|---|---|
| 1 | Aug 9 | H | Halifax T | D | 1-1 | 1-0 | — | Flack [25] | 3723 |
| 2 | 12 | A | Telford U | L | 0-2 | 0-0 | — | | 2830 |
| 3 | 16 | A | Margate | W | 1-0 | 0-0 | 12 | McConnell (pen) [59] | 890 |
| 4 | 23 | H | Chester C | W | 2-1 | 1-1 | 8 | Coppinger [29], Moor [61] | 3030 |
| 5 | 25 | A | Woking | L | 0-1 | 0-1 | 12 | | 2556 |
| 6 | 30 | H | Farnborough T | D | 1-1 | 0-0 | 10 | Flack [61] | 2672 |
| 7 | Sept 6 | H | Stevenage Bor | W | 1-0 | 0-0 | 10 | Lee [82] | 3012 |
| 8 | 13 | A | Forest Green R | W | 5-2 | 1-1 | 8 | Lee 2 [16, 82], Gaia [48], Devine 2 [84, 85] | 1342 |
| 9 | 20 | A | Gravesend & N | L | 2-3 | 0-0 | 11 | Moor [71], Gaia [90] | 1155 |
| 10 | 22 | H | Dagenham & R | D | 1-1 | 1-1 | — | Devine (pen) [14] | 3344 |
| 11 | 27 | H | Scarborough | D | 0-0 | 0-0 | 10 | | 2776 |
| 12 | Oct 3 | A | Burton Alb | W | 4-3 | 2-1 | — | Devine 3 [3, 12, 82], Coppinger [71] | 1985 |
| 13 | 7 | A | Barnet | W | 3-2 | 1-0 | — | Gaia [42], Todd [72], Cronin [88] | 2037 |
| 14 | 11 | H | Northwich Vic | W | 2-0 | 0-0 | 5 | Devine 2 [73, 82] | 3090 |
| 15 | 18 | A | Accrington S | W | 2-1 | 1-0 | 5 | Devine [20], Sheldon [61] | 2342 |
| 16 | Nov 1 | H | Tamworth | W | 3-2 | 1-1 | 5 | Sheldon 2 [5, 63], Cronin [54] | 2979 |
| 17 | 11 | A | Aldershot T | L | 1-2 | 0-1 | — | Devine [85] | 4112 |
| 18 | 15 | H | Morecambe | W | 4-0 | 3-0 | — | Jeannin [4], Devine 2 [12, 16], Sheldon [54] | 2900 |
| 19 | 22 | A | Leigh RMI | D | 1-1 | 0-1 | 6 | Coppinger [58] | 630 |
| 20 | 25 | H | Shrewsbury T | W | 3-2 | 2-0 | — | Coppinger [29], McConnell [45], Devine (pen) [77] | 3470 |
| 21 | 29 | A | Stevenage Bor | D | 2-2 | 1-0 | 4 | Cronin [13], Gaia [62] | 2007 |
| 22 | Dec 6 | H | Forest Green R | D | 2-2 | 1-1 | 3 | Cronin [22], Sheldon [51] | 3637 |
| 23 | 13 | A | Halifax T | L | 0-2 | 0-0 | 4 | | 1267 |
| 24 | 20 | H | Telford U | L | 0-3 | 0-1 | 6 | | 3114 |
| 25 | 26 | A | Hereford U | D | 1-1 | 0-0 | 6 | Flack [73] | 4010 |
| 26 | Jan 1 | H | Hereford U | L | 0-1 | 0-1 | 6 | | 4943 |
| 27 | 3 | A | Farnborough T | W | 2-1 | 0-1 | 6 | Devine [52], Cronin [77] | 1354 |
| 28 | 17 | H | Margate | D | 1-1 | 1-0 | 6 | Devine [32] | 3439 |
| 29 | 24 | A | Dagenham & R | W | 2-0 | 0-0 | 6 | Canham [73], Coppinger (pen) [79] | 1909 |
| 30 | Feb 7 | H | Gravesend & N | L | 0-1 | 0-0 | 6 | | 3303 |
| 31 | 21 | H | Burton Alb | W | 2-0 | 1-0 | 6 | Sheldon [42], Flack [50] | 2885 |
| 32 | Mar 6 | H | Barnet | D | 1-1 | 1-0 | 7 | Devine [22] | 3531 |
| 33 | 13 | H | Aldershot T | W | 2-1 | 0-0 | 6 | Devine [63], Jeannin [83] | 3982 |
| 34 | 16 | A | Northwich Vic | D | 1-1 | 0-0 | — | Foran (og) [60] | 547 |
| 35 | 20 | A | Morecambe | W | 3-0 | 1-0 | 6 | Coppinger (pen) [45], Canham [48], Afful [54] | 1877 |
| 36 | 23 | A | Scarborough | W | 3-2 | 2-2 | — | Sheldon [13], Coppinger [40], Canham [54] | 1200 |
| 37 | 27 | H | Leigh RMI | W | 3-2 | 0-1 | 4 | Moxey [75], Devine 2 [88, 90] | 3635 |
| 38 | Apr 3 | A | Shrewsbury T | D | 2-2 | 0-0 | 4 | Moxey [85], Flack [89] | 4185 |
| 39 | 10 | A | Chester C | L | 2-3 | 0-0 | 5 | Devine [59], Canham [90] | 4046 |
| 40 | 12 | H | Woking | L | 1-2 | 1-0 | 6 | Sheldon [4] | 5236 |
| 41 | 17 | A | Tamworth | L | 1-2 | 0-1 | 6 | Afful [90] | 1803 |
| 42 | 24 | H | Accrington S | W | 3-2 | 1-1 | 6 | Coppinger [11], Canham [53], Flack [83] | 8256 |

**Final League Position: 6**

### GOALSCORERS

*League (71):* Devine 20 (2 pens), Coppinger 8 (2 pens), Sheldon 8, Flack 6, Canham 5, Cronin 5, Gaia 4, Lee 3, Afful 2, Jeannin 2, McConnell 2 (1 pen), Moor 2, Moxey 2, Todd 1, own goal 1.
*FA Cup (3):* Devine 2, Lee 1.
*Trophy (10):* Devine 3, Flack 3, Sheldon 3, Coppinger 1.

| Bittner 37 | McConnell 13 + 7 | Jeannin 39 | Cronin 40 | Hiley 42 | Todd 38 + 1 | Coppinger 36 + 3 | Ampadu 29 + 10 | Flack 24 + 13 | Moor 7 + 5 | Sheldon 30 + 4 | Afful 17 + 13 | Canham 10 + 11 | Thomas 5 + 6 | Gaia 39 | Cheeseman — + 2 | Lee 18 + 3 | Devine 24 + 9 | Reed — + 1 | Rice 5 + 2 | Moxey 9 + 8 | Taylor — + 7 | *Match No.* |
|---|---|---|---|---|---|---|---|---|---|---|---|---|---|---|---|---|---|---|---|---|---|---|
| 1 | 2 | 3 | 4 | 5 | 6 | 7 | $8^{1}$ | 9 | $10^{2}$ | $11^{3}$ | 12 | 13 | 14 | | | | | | | | | 1 |
| 1 | | 3 | 4 | $5^{1}$ | 6 | 7 | 13 | 9 | 10 | $11^{3}$ | 14 | 12 | $8^{2}$ | 2 | | | | | | | | 2 |
| 1 | 12 | 3 | 4 | $5^{1}$ | 6 | 7 | 8 | 9 | $10^{2}$ | | 13 | | 11 | 2 | | | | | | | | 3 |
| 1 | | 3 | 4 | 2 | 5 | $7^{1}$ | $8^{2}$ | 9 | $10^{3}$ | | 13 | 12 | 11 | 6 | 14 | | | | | | | 4 |
| 1 | 12 | 3 | 4 | $2^{1}$ | 6 | 7 | 8 | 9 | $10^{2}$ | | 13 | | $11^{3}$ | 5 | 14 | | | | | | | 5 |
| 1 | | 3■ | 4 | 2 | 6 | 7 | 8 | 9 | $10^{1}$ | | 12 | 13 | $11^{2}$ | 5 | | | | | | | | 6 |
| 1 | 12 | 3 | 4 | 2 | 6 | 7 | $8^{2}$ | $9^{3}$ | | | $11^{1}$ | 10 | | 5 | | 13 | 14 | | | | | 7 |
| 1 | $2^{1}$ | | 4■ | 3 | 6 | | 8 | 9 | | 13 | $7^{2}$ | $10^{3}$ | | 5 | | 11 | 14 | 12 | | | | 8 |
| 1 | 2 | | 4 | 3 | 6 | $7^{1}$ | $8^{2}$ | 9 | 12 | 13 | | $10^{3}$ | | 5 | | 11 | 14 | | | | | 9 |
| 1 | | 3 | 4 | 2 | 6 | 7 | 12 | $9^{3}$ | 13 | | $8^{1}$ | 14 | | 5 | | $11^{2}$ | 10 | | | | | 10 |
| 1 | | 3 | | 2 | 6 | 7 | 8 | 9 | | 12 | 4 | | | $5^{1}$ | | 11 | 10 | | | | | 11 |
| 1 | | 3 | 4 | 2 | 6 | 7 | 12 | 9 | | | $8^{1}$ | 13 | | 5 | | $11^{2}$ | 10 | | | | | 12 |
| | | 3 | 4 | 2 | 6 | 7 | $8^{1}$ | 9 | | | | 12 | | 5 | | 11 | 10■ | | 1 | | | 13 |
| | 13 | 3 | 4 | 2 | 6 | $7^{1}$ | $8^{2}$ | 9 | | 12 | | 14 | | 5 | | 11 | $10^{3}$ | | 1 | | | 14 |
| | 7 | 3 | 4 | 2 | $6^{1}$ | | | 9 | | 8 | | | | 5 | | 11 | 10 | | 1 | 12 | | 15 |
| | $7^{2}$ | 3 | 4 | 2 | 6 | 12 | 13 | 9 | | $11^{1}$ | | | | 5 | | 8 | 10 | | 1 | | | 16 |
| | 7 | 3 | 4 | $2^{2}$ | 6 | 12 | $8^{3}$ | 9 | 13 | $11^{1}$ | | | | 5 | | | 10 | | 1 | | 14 | 17 |
| 1 | $7^{2}$ | 3 | 4 | 2 | 6 | $9^{3}$ | 12 | | 13 | $8^{1}$ | | | | 5 | | 11 | 10 | | | | 14 | 18 |
| 1 | $7^{2}$ | 3 | 4 | 2 | 6 | 9 | 12 | 13 | | $8^{1}$ | | | | 5 | | 11 | 10 | | | | | 19 |
| 1 | $7^{3}$ | 3 | 4 | 2 | 6 | 9 | 12 | 13 | | $8^{1}$ | | | | 5 | | 11 | $10^{2}$ | | | | 14 | 20 |
| 1 | $7^{2}$ | 3 | 4 | 2 | 6 | 9 | 13 | 12 | | $8^{1}$ | | | | 5 | | 11 | 10 | | | | | 21 |
| 1 | $7^{2}$ | 3 | 4 | $2^{1}$ | 6 | 9 | | 12 | | 8 | 13 | | | 5 | | 11 | 10 | | | | | 22 |
| 1 | $7^{2}$ | 3 | | $2^{1}$ | 6 | 9 | $8^{3}$ | 12 | | 11 | 13 | | | 5 | | 4 | 10 | | | | 14 | 23 |
| 1 | $7^{3}$ | 3 | 4 | 2 | $6^{2}$ | 9 | 13 | 14 | | 11 | 12 | | | | | 8 | 10 | | | $5^{1}$ | | 24 |
| 1■ | | 3 | $4^{1}$ | 2 | | 7 | 12 | 9 | $10^{G}$ | 8 | | | | 5 | | 11 | | | 15 | 6 | | 25 |
| 1■ | | 3 | 4 | 2 | 6 | $7^{G}$ | | 9 | | 8 | 12 | | | $5^{1}$ | | 11 | 10 | | 15 | | | 26 |
| 1 | | 3 | 4 | $2^{1}$ | 6 | 7 | $8^{2}$ | 9 | | 11 | | | | 5 | | 12 | 10 | | | | 13 | 27 |
| 1 | | 3 | 4 | 2 | 6 | $9^{3}$ | 8 | | | 11 | $7^{1}$ | 13 | | 5 | | | $10^{2}$ | | | 12 | 14 | 28 |
| 1 | | 3 | 4 | 2 | | 9 | 8 | | 12 | 11 | $10^{1}$ | 6 | | 5 | | | | | | 7 | | 29 |
| 1 | | 3 | 4 | $2^{1}$ | 6 | 7 | $8^{2}$ | $9^{3}$ | | 11 | 14 | | 13 | 5 | | | 10 | | | 12 | | 30 |
| 1 | | 3 | 4 | 2 | 6 | 13 | 8 | 9 | | $11^{1}$ | $10^{3}$ | | 12 | 5 | | | 14 | | | $7^{2}$ | | 31 |
| 1 | | $3^{2}$ | 4 | 2 | 6 | 9 | $8^{1}$ | | | 11 | 7 | | | 5 | | 12 | 10 | | | 13 | | 32 |
| 1 | 12 | 3 | 4 | 2 | $6^{1}$ | 7 | 8 | 13 | | 11 | $9^{2}$ | | | 5 | | | $10^{3}$ | | | 14 | | 33 |
| 1 | 12 | 3 | 4 | $2^{1}$ | 6 | 7 | 8 | 13 | | 11 | 9 | | | 5 | | | $10^{2}$ | | | | | 34 |
| 1 | 12 | | 4 | 2 | 6 | 7 | $8^{2}$ | | | 11 | $9^{3}$ | 10 | 14 | $5^{1}$ | | | | | | 3 | 13 | 35 |
| 1 | | 5 | 4 | 2 | 6 | 7 | 8 | 12 | | $11^{3}$ | $9^{2}$ | $10^{1}$ | 14 | | | | 13 | | | 3 | | 36 |
| 1 | | 3 | 4 | 2 | | 7 | 8 | 12 | | 11 | $9^{2}$ | $10^{1}$ | | 5 | | | 13 | | | 6 | | 37 |
| 1 | | 3 | 4 | 2 | 6 | $7^{2}$ | 8 | 12 | | 11 | 9 | $10^{3}$ | | $5^{1}$ | | | 14 | | | 13 | | 38 |
| 1 | | 3 | 4 | 2 | 6 | 7 | $8^{2}$ | $9^{3}$ | | 11 | 13 | 14 | | $5^{1}$ | | | 10 | | | 12 | | 39 |
| 1 | | $3^{1}$ | 4 | 2 | 6 | 7■ | 8 | 13 | | 11 | $9^{3}$ | $10^{2}$ | | 5 | | | 14 | | | 12 | | 40 |
| 1 | | $3^{1}$ | 4 | 2 | 6 | | 8 | $9^{3}$ | | 11 | 13 | 14 | 12 | 5 | | | 10 | | | $7^{2}$ | | 41 |
| 1 | | $3^{1}$ | 4 | 2 | $12^{2}$ | 7 | 8 | 13 | | 11 | $9^{3}$ | 10 | | 5 | | | 14 | | | 6 | | 42 |

**LDV Vans Trophy**
First Round Hereford U (a) 0-2

**FA Cup**
Fourth Qual Gravesend & N (h) 0-0
(a) 3-3

# FARNBOROUGH TOWN Conference

*Ground:* Cherrywood Road, Farnborough, Hampshire GU14 8UD.
*Tel:* (01252) 541 469.
*Year Formed:* 1967.
*Record Gate:* 3,581 (1995 v Brentford FA Cup First Round).
*Nickname:* The Boro.
*Manager:* Dean Austin.
*Secretary:* Vince Williams.
*Colours:* All red and white.

## FARNBOROUGH TOWN 2003–04 LEAGUE RECORD

| Match No. | Date | Venue | Opponents | Result | | H/T Score | Lg. Pos. | Goalscorers | Attendance |
|---|---|---|---|---|---|---|---|---|---|
| 1 | Aug 9 | A | Scarborough | L | 1-2 | 0-1 | — | Charlery 83 | 1415 |
| 2 | 12 | H | Barnet | D | 1-1 | 1-1 | — | Weatherstone 40 | 1063 |
| 3 | 16 | H | Leigh RMI | D | 1-1 | 0-0 | 18 | Weatherstone 62 | 594 |
| 4 | 23 | A | Shrewsbury T | L | 0-3 | 0-1 | 20 | | 3403 |
| 5 | 25 | H | Gravesend & N | L | 1-2 | 0-1 | 21 | Belgrave 85 | 839 |
| 6 | 30 | A | Exeter C | D | 1-1 | 0-0 | 21 | Griffiths (pen) 88 | 2672 |
| 7 | Sept 6 | H | Hereford U | L | 0-5 | 0-3 | 22 | | 1334 |
| 8 | 13 | A | Woking | L | 2-3 | 0-0 | 22 | Charlery 76, Hodgson 89 | 2791 |
| 9 | 20 | H | Chester C | L | 1-2 | 0-1 | 22 | Fashanu 47 | 748 |
| 10 | 23 | A | Aldershot T | L | 0-2 | 0-0 | — | | 4166 |
| 11 | 27 | A | Morecambe | L | 2-3 | 2-1 | 22 | Chaaban 2 5, 32 | 1636 |
| 12 | Oct 4 | H | Tamworth | D | 3-3 | 1-0 | 22 | Fashanu (pen) 21, Hodgson 2 53, 69 | 770 |
| 13 | 7 | H | Forest Green R | L | 1-3 | 1-2 | — | Fashanu 12 | 525 |
| 14 | 11 | A | Accrington S | L | 1-3 | 1-2 | 22 | Beall 18 | 1806 |
| 15 | 18 | H | Telford U | W | 2-1 | 1-1 | 22 | MacKenzie (og) 31, Hayes 80 | 579 |
| 16 | Nov 1 | A | Burton Alb | L | 0-1 | 0-1 | 22 | | 1601 |
| 17 | 11 | A | Dagenham & R | L | 0-1 | 0-1 | — | | 1269 |
| 18 | 15 | H | Northwich Vic | W | 2-0 | 1-0 | 21 | Manuella 44, Burton 76 | 626 |
| 19 | 22 | A | Halifax T | L | 0-2 | 0-1 | 21 | | 1250 |
| 20 | 29 | A | Hereford U | L | 0-2 | 0-0 | 22 | | 2630 |
| 21 | Dec 6 | H | Margate | D | 1-1 | 0-1 | 21 | Burton 90 | 595 |
| 22 | 9 | H | Woking | W | 1-0 | 0-0 | — | Semple 58 | 1005 |
| 23 | 13 | H | Scarborough | L | 1-2 | 1-1 | 21 | Chaaban 37 | 620 |
| 24 | 20 | A | Barnet | W | 2-0 | 1-0 | 21 | Burton 42, Semple 87 | 1547 |
| 25 | 26 | H | Stevenage Bor | W | 2-0 | 1-0 | 20 | Hodgson 43, Chaaban 90 | 1403 |
| 26 | Jan 1 | A | Stevenage Bor | L | 2-3 | 2-2 | 20 | Hodgson (pen) 15, Harkness 24 | 2285 |
| 27 | 3 | H | Exeter C | L | 1-2 | 1-0 | 20 | Forington 29 | 1354 |
| 28 | 17 | A | Leigh RMI | W | 2-0 | 1-0 | 20 | Charlery 10, Forington 78 | 295 |
| 29 | 24 | H | Aldershot T | W | 4-0 | 1-0 | 19 | Charles 43, Burton 47, Doudou 54, Iffufo 73 | 3233 |
| 30 | Feb 7 | A | Chester C | L | 2-3 | 0-2 | 20 | Burton 52, Hodgson 68 | 2665 |
| 31 | 14 | H | Morecambe | L | 2-4 | 2-3 | 20 | Hodgson 36, Perkins (og) 43 | 704 |
| 32 | 21 | A | Tamworth | L | 1-2 | 0-1 | 20 | Hodgson 65 | 1084 |
| 33 | 28 | H | Accrington S | D | 1-1 | 1-0 | 20 | Harkness 40 | 571 |
| 34 | Mar 6 | A | Forest Green R | D | 1-1 | 0-1 | 20 | Harkness 88 | 781 |
| 35 | 13 | H | Dagenham & R | D | 2-2 | 0-2 | 20 | Fashanu 76, Roberts (og) 90 | 787 |
| 36 | 20 | A | Northwich Vic | D | 1-1 | 1-1 | 20 | Hodgson (pen) 17 | 510 |
| 37 | 27 | H | Halifax T | W | 1-0 | 0-0 | 20 | Burton 85 | 644 |
| 38 | Apr 3 | A | Margate | L | 0-3 | 0-1 | 20 | | 386 |
| 39 | 10 | H | Shrewsbury T | L | 1-3 | 0-0 | 20 | Hayes 90 | 1041 |
| 40 | 12 | A | Gravesend & N | L | 0-2 | 0-1 | 20 | | 1284 |
| 41 | 17 | H | Burton Alb | W | 2-1 | 1-0 | 20 | Burton 39, Mulhern 65 | 812 |
| 42 | 24 | A | Telford U | W | 4-2 | 3-1 | 20 | Burton 23, Fashanu 28, Forington (pen) 33, Harkness 80 | 3323 |

**Final League Position: 20**

### GOALSCORERS

*League (53):* Hodgson 9 (2 pens), Burton 8, Fashanu 5 (1 pen), Chaaban 4, Harkness 4, Charlery 3, Forington 3 (1 pen), Hayes 2, Semple 2, Weatherstone 2, Beall 1, Belgrave 1, Charles 1, Doudou 1, Griffiths 1 (pen), Iffufo 1, Manuella 1, Mulhern 1, own goals 3.
*FA Cup (2):* Clarke 1, Hayes 1.

| Osborn 39 | Neil 5 / Allen-Page 3+1 | Opinel 35 | Hutchings 20 | Weatherstone 19+2 / Christou 1+2 | Burton 30 | Hodgson 32+1 | Beall 31+3 | Charlery 12+11 | Belgrave 12+12 | Martin 3+2 | Lovett 3+6 / Oli 4 | Harkness 15+13 | Hayes 27+7 | Pardesi —+1 / Howell 2+2 | Reece 1+1 | Thompson 16+5 | Griffiths 5 | Green 1+1 / Theo 3+2 | Chaaban 18+5 | Pattison 8+10 | Sappleton 7 | Stanley —+1 / Mulhern 6 | Fashanu 7+6 | Clarke 6+3 / Donovan 7 | Packham 2 | Ifura 5+1 / Ashwood 1 | Moussali 1+1 | Manuella 9+5 | Charles 16 | Forington 21+4 | Semple 9 | Lavin 1 / Pitcher 3 | Iffufo 2+8 | Sombili Jalo 1 / Deacons 2+1 | Mendonca —+1 | Toms 4 / Peters 2+1 | Doudou 5+3 | *Match No.* |
|---|---|---|---|---|---|---|---|---|---|---|---|---|---|---|---|---|---|---|---|---|---|---|---|---|---|---|---|---|---|---|---|---|---|---|---|---|---|---|
| 1 | 2 | 3 | 4 | 5 | 6■ | 7 | 8[1] | 9 | 10[2] | 11[3] | 12 | 13 | 14 | | | | | | | | | | | | | | | | | | | | | | | | | 1 |
| 1 | 2 | 3 | 4 | 5 | 6 | 7 | 12 | 9[2] | 10 | | 13 | 11[3] | 8[1] | 14 | | | | | | | | | | | | | | | | | | | | | | | | 2 |
| 1 | 2[1] | 3 | 4 | 5 | 6[2] | 7[3] | 8 | | 10 | | 11 | 14 | | | 12 | 13 | 9 | | | | | | | | | | | | | | | | | | | | | 3 |
| 1 | 2 | 3 | 4[1] | 5 | | 7 | | | 10 | | 13 | 14 | 9 | | 6[3] | 12 | 8 | 11[2] | | | | | | | | | | | | | | | | | | | | 4 |
| 1 | 2[1] | 3 | 4[2] | 5 | 6 | 7 | | | 12 | | 13 | 11 | | | | 8 | 9 | | 10[3] | 14 | | | | | | | | | | | | | | | | | | 5 |
| 1 | | 3 | 4 | 5 | | 7 | 8 | | 12 | | 2[3] | 13 | 6[2] | | | 14 | 10 | | 9[1] | | 11 | | | | | | | | | | | | | | | | | 6 |
| 1 | | 3 | 4 | 5 | 6 | 7 | 8 | | 10[2] | | | 2[1] | | | | | 9[3] | | | | 11■ | 12 | 13 | 14 | | | | | | | | | | | | | | 7 |
| 1 | | 3 | 4[2] | 5 | 6 | 12 | 8 | 13 | | | 2 | 7 | 11 | | | | | | | 9[1] | | | 14 | 10[3] | | | | | | | | | | | | | | 8 |
| | | 3 | 4 | 5■ | 6 | 7 | 8 | 9[2] | 13 | | | | | | | 12 | | | 2[1] | | | | 14 | 10[3] | 1 | 11 | | | | | | | | | | | | 9 |
| | | 3 | 4[1] | 5 | 6 | 7■ | 8 | | 12 | | 13 | | | | | | | | 10[2] | | 2 | | 9 | 11 | 1 | | | | | | | | | | | | | 10 |
| 1 | | 3[1] | 4 | 5 | 6 | 7[2] | 8 | | | | | 14 | 12 | | | | | | 9 | | 2 | | 13 | 10[3] | | 11 | | | | | | | | | | | | 11 |
| 1 | | 3 | 4 | | | 7 | | 14 | 10[1] | | 12 | 13 | 6 | | | | | | 9[2] | 11■ | 2 | | 8[3] | | | 5 | | | | | | | | | | | | 12 |
| 1 | | 3 | 4 | 5 | | | | 13 | | | | 12 | 7 | | | | | | 9 | 11[2] | 2■ | | 10[3] | 14 | | 6 | 8[1] | | | | | | | | | | | 13 |
| 1 | | 3 | | 5[1] | | 7 | 8 | 6■ | 10 | | | | 14 | | | | | 13 | 9 | | 2 | | | | | 4 | 12[2] | 11[3] | | | | | | | | | | 14 |
| 1 | | 3 | | 12 | 6 | 7 | 8 | 9 | 10 | | | | 4 | | | 2[1] | | | 11[3] | | | | | 14 | | 13 | | | 5[2] | | | | | | | | | 15 |
| 1 | | 3 | 4 | | 6 | 7 | 8 | 9 | 12 | | | 13 | 2[2] | | | 10[1] | | | | | | | | 11 | | | | | 5 | | | | | | | | | 16 |
| 1 | | 3 | 4 | | | 7 | 8 | 12 | | | | 13 | 14 | | | 2 | | | 11[2] | | | | | 9[1] | | | | 6[3] | 5 | 10 | | | | | | | | 17 |
| 1 | | 3 | | | 6 | 7 | 8[2] | 9 | | | | 14 | 13 | | | 2 | | | 12 | 4[1] | | | | | | | | 11 | 5 | 10[3] | | | | | | | | 18 |
| 1 | | 3 | 4 | | 6 | 7 | 8 | 9 | 12 | | | 13 | 2 | | | 5 | | | | | | | | | | | | | | 10[2] | 11[1] | | | | | | | 19 |
| 1 | | 3 | | | 6 | 7[2] | 8 | 14 | 13 | | | 9 | 12 | | | 2 | | | | | | | | | | | | 4[1] | 5 | 10[3] | 11 | | | | | | | 20 |
| 1 | | | | 12 | 6 | | 8 | 9[3] | 14 | | | 10 | 11[2] | | | 2[1] | | | 13 | | | | | | | | | 7 | 5 | | 4 | 3 | | | | | | 21 |
| 1 | | 3 | | 5 | 6 | 11[2] | 8 | | 10 | | | | 12 | | | 2 | | | 9[3] | | | | | | | | | 7[1] | | 14 | 4 | | 13 | | | | | 22 |
| 1 | | 3 | | 5 | 6 | | 8[1] | | 10[3] | | | | 11[2] | | | 2 | | | 9 | 12 | | | | | | | | 4■ | | 14 | 7 | | 13 | | | | | 23 |
| 1 | | 3 | 4[2] | 2 | 6[1] | 11 | | | 9[3] | | | | 8 | | | 12 | | | 10 | | | | | | | | | 13 | 5 | 14 | 7 | | | | | | | 24 |
| 1 | | | 4 | 5 | | 7 | | | 10[3] | | | 14 | 3 | | | 2 | | | 9 | 13 | | | | | | | | 12 | 6 | 11[1] | 8[2] | | | | | | | 25 |
| 1 | | 3 | 4 | 5 | | 7[2] | 14 | 12 | | | | 9 | 11 | | | 2■ | | | 8[1] | 13 | | | | | | | | | 6 | 10[3] | | | | | | | | 26 |
| 1 | | 3 | 4 | 5 | | 7 | 12 | | | | | 11 | 8[2] | | | 2 | | | | 14 | | | | | | | | | 6 | 10[3] | | | | 9[1] | 13 | | | 27 |
| 1 | | 3 | | | | 7 | 8 | 5 | | | | | 2 | | | | | | 14 | | | | | | | | | 13 | 6 | 10 | 4[1] | | 12 | | | 11[2] | 9[3] | 28 |
| 1 | | 2 | | | 6[1] | 11 | 8 | 12 | | | | | 3 | | | | | | 14 | | | | | | | | | | 5 | 10[3] | 7 | | 13 | | | 4[2] | 9 | 29 |
| 1 | | 3 | | 13 | 6 | 7 | | | | 5[2] | | | 4 | | | 2[1] | | | 8 | | | | | | | | | 12 | | 10 | | | 14 | | | 11[3] | 9 | 30 |
| 1 | | 3 | | | 6 | 7 | 8 | | | 12 | 11 | | | | | 2 | | | 13 | | | | | | | | | | 5[2] | 10[3] | | | 14 | | | 4[1] | 9 | 31 |
| 1 | | 3 | | | 6 | 7 | 4 | 14 | | 5 | 8 | 13 | 11 | | | 2[1] | | | | | | | | | | | | 12 | | 10[2] | | | | | | | 9[3] | 32 |
| 1 | | 2 | | | 6 | 7[2] | 4 | 13 | | 14 | 9 | 11[1] | 3 | | | | | | | | | | | | | | | 8 | 5 | 10[3] | | | 12 | | | | | 33 |
| 1 | | | | | 6 | 7 | | 14 | | | 9[3] | 4 | 3 | | | | | 2 | 11 | 12 | | | | | | | | 8[1] | 5 | 10[2] | | | | | | | 13 | 34 |
| 1 | | | | | 6 | 7 | 8 | 12 | | | | 4[2] | 3 | | | | | 2 | 9[3] | 11 | | | 13 | | | | | | 5 | 10[1] | | | | | | | 14 | 35 |
| 1 | | 2■ | | | 6[1] | 7 | 8 | | | | | | 3 | | | | | 12 | | 13 | | 11 | 9[3] | 5 | | | | | | 10 | | 4[2] | | | | | 14 | 36 |
| 1 | | 2 | | 13 | 6 | | 8 | | | | | | 3 | | | | | | | 12 | | 7[1] | | 5 | | | | | | 10 | | 11 | | 4 | | 9[2] | | 37 |
| 1 | 12 | | | 9[3] | 6 | | 4 | | | | | | 3 | 11 | | | | | | 8 | | | | 5 | | | | | | 10 | | 7[2] | 13 | 2[1] | | 14 | | 38 |
| 1 | | | | | | | 4 | 6 | 12 | | | 7[1] | 3 | 14 | | | | 2 | | 8 | | 11 | 13 | 5 | | | | | | 10[2] | | | | | | 9[3] | | 39 |
| 1 | 2 | | | | | | 4 | 6 | 14 | | | 3 | | 13 | | | | 12 | | 8[2] | | 11[1] | 9 | 5■ | | | | | | 10[3] | | | 7 | | | | | 40 |
| 1 | 2 | 3 | | | 6 | | 4[1] | | 13 | | | 8 | | 7 | | | | | | 12 | | 11 | 9[3] | 5 | | | | | | 14 | | | 10[2] | | | | | 41 |
| | 2 | 3 | | | 6 | | 4 | | 14 | | | 8 | 7 | | | | | | | 13 | | 11[1] | 9[3] | 5 | | 1 | | | | 10[2] | | | | 12 | | | | 42 |

**FA Cup**

| | | | |
|---|---|---|---|
| Fourth Qual | Thame U | (a) | 2-1 |
| First Round | Weston-Super-Mare | (h) | 0-1 |

# FOREST GREEN ROVERS Conference

*Ground:* The Lawn, Nympsfield Road, Forest Green, Nailsworth GL6 0ET.
*Tel:* (01453) 834 860.
*Year Formed:* 1890.
*Record Gate:* 3,002 (1999 v St Albans City FA Umbro Trophy).
*Nickname:* Rovers.
*Manager:* Tim Harris.
*Secretary:* David Honeybill.
*Colours:* Black and white striped shirts, black shorts, red stockings.

## FOREST GREEN ROVERS 2003–04 LEAGUE RECORD

| Match No. | Date | Venue | Opponents | Result | H/T Score | Lg. Pos. | Goalscorers | Attendance |
|---|---|---|---|---|---|---|---|---|
| 1 | Aug 9 | H | Northwich Vic | D 0-0 | 0-0 | — | | 628 |
| 2 | 12 | A | Hereford U | L 1-5 | 1-2 | — | Grayson [41] | 3195 |
| 3 | 16 | A | Chester C | L 0-1 | 0-0 | 20 | | 1881 |
| 4 | 23 | H | Accrington S | W 2-1 | 2-0 | 16 | Cowe [12], Owers [40] | 711 |
| 5 | 25 | A | Dagenham & R | L 2-5 | 1-3 | 19 | Cowe 2 [45, 75] | 1540 |
| 6 | 30 | H | Margate | L 1-2 | 1-1 | 20 | Cowe [34] | 569 |
| 7 | Sept 6 | A | Leigh RMI | W 2-1 | 1-1 | 17 | Grayson 2 [38, 52] | 415 |
| 8 | 13 | H | Exeter C | L 2-5 | 1-1 | 17 | Rogers 2 [21, 89] | 1342 |
| 9 | 20 | A | Scarborough | D 2-2 | 1-1 | 19 | Grayson 2 (1 pen) [14, 70 (p)] | 1208 |
| 10 | 23 | H | Woking | D 2-2 | 1-1 | — | Rogers [21], Brodie [55] | 712 |
| 11 | 27 | H | Halifax T | L 1-2 | 1-0 | 20 | Rogers [25] | 722 |
| 12 | Oct 4 | A | Gravesend & N | D 1-1 | 0-0 | 20 | Brodie [90] | 1190 |
| 13 | 7 | A | Farnborough T | W 3-1 | 2-1 | — | Hutchings (og) [34], Brodie [45], Kennedy [70] | 525 |
| 14 | 11 | H | Burton Alb | D 1-1 | 1-0 | 18 | Grayson [45] | 867 |
| 15 | 18 | H | Stevenage Bor | W 3-1 | 1-1 | 15 | Foster [21], Moralee 2 [50, 84] | 676 |
| 16 | Nov 1 | A | Aldershot T | L 0-3 | 0-1 | 16 | | 2398 |
| 17 | 11 | A | Shrewsbury T | L 0-2 | 0-0 | — | | 3263 |
| 18 | 15 | H | Tamworth | W 2-1 | 1-0 | 16 | Rogers [13], Cant [73] | 782 |
| 19 | 22 | A | Barnet | L 0-5 | 0-2 | 16 | | 1378 |
| 20 | 25 | H | Morecambe | L 1-2 | 0-1 | — | Grayson [82] | 605 |
| 21 | 29 | H | Leigh RMI | D 2-2 | 0-0 | 16 | Meechan [68], Sykes [84] | 554 |
| 22 | Dec 6 | A | Exeter C | D 2-2 | 1-1 | 16 | Phillips 2 [7, 83] | 3637 |
| 23 | 13 | A | Northwich Vic | W 4-0 | 1-0 | 16 | Bowen 3 [31, 83, 85], Meechan [68] | 474 |
| 24 | 19 | H | Hereford U | L 1-7 | 0-4 | — | Searle [85] | 1576 |
| 25 | Jan 1 | H | Telford U | D 0-0 | 0-0 | 17 | | 1071 |
| 26 | 4 | A | Margate | L 0-2 | 0-0 | — | | 255 |
| 27 | 17 | H | Chester C | W 2-1 | 0-1 | 17 | Cowe [71], Rogers [75] | 1164 |
| 28 | 24 | A | Woking | D 1-1 | 0-0 | 17 | Foster [90] | 1815 |
| 29 | Feb 7 | H | Scarborough | W 4-0 | 2-0 | 17 | Rogers 2 [15, 53], Grayson 2 [39, 51] | 848 |
| 30 | 21 | H | Gravesend & N | L 1-2 | 1-0 | 18 | Meechan [9] | 752 |
| 31 | 28 | A | Burton Alb | W 3-2 | 2-0 | 17 | Moore [4], Foster [12], Rogers [90] | 1442 |
| 32 | Mar 6 | H | Farnborough T | D 1-1 | 1-0 | 17 | Ingram (pen) [28] | 781 |
| 33 | 9 | A | Halifax T | W 1-0 | 1-0 | — | Meechan [5] | 883 |
| 34 | 13 | H | Shrewsbury T | D 1-1 | 0-0 | 15 | Ingram [90] | 1484 |
| 35 | 20 | A | Tamworth | L 0-1 | 0-1 | 16 | | 1112 |
| 36 | 23 | A | Telford U | W 2-0 | 1-0 | — | Meechan [38], Sykes [48] | 1354 |
| 37 | 27 | H | Barnet | D 1-1 | 1-1 | 13 | Searle (pen) [29] | 1013 |
| 38 | Apr 3 | A | Morecambe | L 0-4 | 0-2 | 16 | | 1259 |
| 39 | 10 | A | Accrington S | L 1-4 | 0-2 | 17 | Searle (pen) [81] | 1058 |
| 40 | 12 | H | Dagenham & R | L 1-3 | 0-2 | 18 | Meechan [59] | 762 |
| 41 | 17 | H | Aldershot T | W 3-1 | 0-1 | 18 | Langan [50], Searle (pen) [73], Cowe [83] | 1330 |
| 42 | 24 | A | Stevenage Bor | L 1-2 | 0-1 | 18 | Sykes [47] | 1747 |

**Final League Position: 18**

### GOALSCORERS

*League (58):* Grayson 9 (1 pen), Rogers 9, Cowe 6, Meechan 6, Searle 4 (3 pens), Bowen 3, Brodie 3, Foster 3, Sykes 3, Ingram 2 (1 pen), Moralee 2, Phillips 2, Cant 1, Kennedy 1, Langan 1, Moore 1, Owers 1, own goal 1.
*FA Cup (1):* Cowe 1.
*Trophy (7):* Grayson 4, Foster 1, Ingram 1 (pen), Rogers 1.

| Perrin 42 | Jenkins 10 + 1 | Sykes 16 + 8 | Jones S 11 | Richardso n33 | Ingram 32 | Stoker 24 | Owers 14 | Grayson 24 + 1 | Gilroy 2 + 3 | Foster 42 | Cowe 21 + 13 | Rogers 27 + 12 | Cook — + 1 | Russell 3 + 1 | Cant 4 + 7 | Morgan 7 | Jones J 3 + 2 | Adams — + 4 | Langan 11 + 5 | Brodie 7 | Moralee 6 + 4 | Kennedy 11 + 2 | Jones L — + 9 | Searle 31 | Phillips 19 + 2 | Meechan 22 | Jones D 10 | Bowen 2 | McAuley 6 + 7 | Moore 4 + 2 | Simpson 2 + 1 | Aubrey 2 + 6 | Jordan 5 | Fitzpatrick 4 + 1 | Green 5 | *Match No.* |
|---|---|---|---|---|---|---|---|---|---|---|---|---|---|---|---|---|---|---|---|---|---|---|---|---|---|---|---|---|---|---|---|---|---|---|---|---|
| 1 | 2 | 3 | $4^1$ | 5 | 6 | $7^2$ | 8 | 9 | $10^3$ | 11 | 12 | 13 | 14 | | | | | | | | | | | | | | | | | | | | | | | 1 |
| 1 | 2 | $3^1$ | 4 | 5 | 6 | | $8^2$ | 9 | $10^3$ | 11 | 12 | 13 | | 7 | 14 | | | | | | | | | | | | | | | | | | | | | 2 |
| 1 | 2 | | 4 | 5 | 6 | | 8 | 9 | | 11 | | 12 | | 3 | | 7 | $10^1$ | | | | | | | | | | | | | | | | | | | 3 |
| 1 | 2 | | 4 | 5 | 6 | | 8 | 9 | 12 | $11^3$ | $3^2$ | 14 | | 13 | | 7 | $10^1$ | | | | | | | | | | | | | | | | | | | 4 |
| 1 | 2 | | $4^3$ | 5 | 6 | | 8 | 9 | 12 | 7 | $10^1$ | 13 | | $3^2$ | | 11 | 14 | | | | | | | | | | | | | | | | | | | 5 |
| 1 | $2^1$ | 12 | 4 | 5 | | | 8 | 9 | 13 | $11^3$ | 7 | 3 | | | | 6 | $10^2$ | 14 | | | | | | | | | | | | | | | | | | 6 |
| 1 | 2 | | 4 | 5 | 6 | | 8 | 9 | | 11 | 7 | $3^1$ | | | | | | | 12 | 10 | | | | | | | | | | | | | | | | 7 |
| 1 | 2 | | 4 | 5 | 6 | | $8^1$ | 9 | | $11^2$ | 7 | 3 | | | | | 12 | | 13 | 10 | | | | | | | | | | | | | | | | 8 |
| 1 | 2 | | 4 | 5 | 6 | | | 9 | | 7 | | $8^1$ | | | | 3 | | | 11 | 10 | 12 | | | | | | | | | | | | | | | 9 |
| 1 | 2 | | 4 | | 6 | | 8 | 9 | | 11 | | 7 | | | | 3 | | | 5 | 10 | | | | | | | | | | | | | | | | 10 |
| 1 | 13 | | 4 | | 6 | $7^2$ | 8 | 9 | | 10 | | $5^1$ | | | | 3■ | | | 2 | 11 | 12 | | | | | | | | | | | | | | | 11 |
| 1 | | | | | 2 | 7 | 8 | 9 | | 11 | | 10 | | | | | | $13^3$ | $4^2$ | 5 | 14 | $3^1$ | 12 | 6 | | | | | | | | | | | | 12 |
| 1 | | | | 5 | 6 | 7 | 8 | 9 | | 11 | | 12 | | | | | | | | $10^2$ | 13 | 4 | | 3 | $2^1$ | | | | | | | | | | | 13 |
| 1 | | | | 5 | 6 | 7 | $8^2$ | 9 | | 11 | | 13 | | | 12 | | | | | | 10 | 4 | | 3 | $2^1$ | | | | | | | | | | | 14 |
| 1 | | | | 5 | $6^2$ | 7 | 8 | $9^3$ | | 11 | | 14 | | | | | | | 13 | | 10 | 4 | 12 | 3 | $2^1$ | | | | | | | | | | | 15 |
| 1 | | 12 | | 5 | 6 | 7 | | | | 11 | $8^1$ | $4^2$ | | | 14 | | | | $2^3$ | | 10 | 9 | 13 | 3 | | | | | | | | | | | | 16 |
| 1 | | | | $5^1$ | 6 | 7 | | 9 | | 4 | 14 | $8^2$ | | | 13 | | | | 2 | | $10^3$ | 12 | | 3 | 11 | | | | | | | | | | | 17 |
| 1 | | 12 | | | 6 | | | 9 | | 11 | 7 | 8 | | | 13 | | | | $5^1$ | | $10^2$ | 4 | | 3 | 2 | | | | | | | | | | | 18 |
| 1 | | 13 | | | 6 | 7 | | 9 | | $8^2$ | $5^1$ | 11 | | | 10 | | | | | | | 4 | 12 | 3 | 2 | | | | | | | | | | | 19 |
| 1 | | | | $4^2$ | | $7^3$ | | 9 | | 11 | 14 | 8 | | | 6 | | | 12 | | | | 13 | | 3 | $2^1$ | 10 | 5 | | | | | | | | | 20 |
| 1 | | 12■ | | | 6 | | | 9 | | 11 | $4^1$ | $8^2$ | | | | | | | | | | 7 | 13 | 3 | 2 | 10 | 5 | | | | | | | | | 21 |
| 1 | | $7^1$ | | | 4 | | | | | 6 | 13 | $11^2$ | | | 12 | | | | | | 10 | 9 | | 3 | 2 | 8 | 5 | | | | | | | | | 22 |
| 1 | | | | | 6 | | | | | 7 | 12 | | | | 9 | | | | $4^1$ | | | 8 | 13 | 3 | 2 | 10 | 5 | $11^2$ | | | | | | | | 23 |
| 1 | | 12 | | | 6 | | | | | 7 | $4^2$ | 14 | | | $9^3$ | | | | | | | $8^1$ | 13 | 3 | 2 | 10 | 5 | 11 | | | | | | | | 24 |
| 1 | | | | 5 | 6 | 7 | | 9 | | 11 | $4^1$ | 12 | | | | | | | | | | | | 3 | 8 | 10 | 2 | | | | | | | | | 25 |
| 1 | | | | 6 | 4 | 7 | | 9 | | 11 | $8^1$ | 12 | | | 13 | | | | | | | | | $3^2$ | 2 | 10 | 5 | | | | | | | | | 26 |
| 1 | | 12 | | 5 | 6 | 4 | | | | 11 | $9^2$ | 7 | | | | | | | | | | | | 3 | $8^1$ | 10 | 2 | | 13 | | | | | | | 27 |
| 1 | | | | 5 | $6^1$ | 2 | | | | 8 | 10 | 9 | | | | | | | 12 | | | | | 3 | $4^2$ | 11 | 7 | | 13 | | | | | | | 28 |
| 1 | | $2^2$ | | 5 | 6 | | | $9^3$ | | 11 | 14 | 7 | | | | | | | $8^1$ | | | | | 3 | 12 | 10 | 4 | | 13 | | | | | | | 29 |
| 1 | | 13 | | 5 | 6 | $7^1$ | | | | 11 | 4 | 9 | | | | | | | | | | | 12 | 3 | 2 | $10^3$ | | | $8^2$ | 14 | | | | | | 30 |
| 1 | | 4 | | 5 | 6 | 7 | | | | 11 | 12 | 8 | | | | | | | | | | | | 3 | 2 | 10 | | | | $9^1$ | | | | | | 31 |
| 1 | | $4^1$ | | 5 | 6 | 7 | | 13 | | 11 | 14 | 8 | | | | | | | | | | | | 3 | 12 | $10^3$ | | | | $9^2$ | 2 | | | | | 32 |
| 1 | | $7^1$ | | 5 | 6 | 4 | | 9 | | 11 | 12 | 8 | | | | | | | | | | | | 3 | 2 | $10^2$ | | | | 13 | | | | | | 33 |
| 1 | | $7^2$ | | 5 | 6 | 4 | | | | 11 | 12 | 8 | | | | | | | | | | | | 3 | | 10 | | | 13 | $9^3$ | $2^1$ | 14 | | | | 34 |
| 1 | | 4 | | 5 | | 7 | | | | 11 | 6 | 8 | | | | | | | | | | | | 3 | $2^1$ | 10 | | | 12 | $9^2$ | | 13 | | | | 35 |
| 1 | | 9 | | 5 | | 7 | | | | 11 | $2^1$ | 4 | | | | | | | | | | | | 3 | | 10 | | | 12 | | | 13 | 6 | $8^2$ | | 36 |
| 1 | | 4 | | 5 | | 7 | | | | 11 | $2^1$ | 8 | | | | | | 13 | | | | | | 3 | | $10^3$ | | | 12 | | | 14 | 6 | $9^2$ | | 37 |
| 1 | | $4^2$ | | 5 | | 7 | | | | 11 | 14 | | | | | | | | | | | | | 3 | | 10 | | | 8 | | 12 | 13 | $6^1$ | $9^3$ | 2 | 38 |
| 1 | | 4 | | 5 | | | | | | 11 | 7 | | | | | | | | 12 | | | | | 3 | | $10^2$ | | | 8 | | | 13 | 6 | $9^1$ | 2 | 39 |
| 1 | | $4^1$ | | 5 | | | | | | 11 | $9^2$ | 8 | | | | | | | | | | | 13 | 3 | | 10 | | | 7 | | | | 6 | 12 | 2 | 40 |
| 1 | | 4 | | 5 | | | | | | 11 | 12 | 8 | | | | | | | 6 | | | | | 3 | | $10^1$ | | | 7 | | | 9 | | | 2 | 41 |
| 1 | | 4 | | 5 | | $7^1$ | | | | 11 | 8 | 12 | | | | | | | 6 | | | | | 3 | | | | | 10 | | | 9 | | | 2 | 42 |

**LDV Vans Trophy**
First Round Brighton & HA (a) 0-2

**FA Cup**
Fourth Qual Aldershot T (h) 1-3

# GRAVESEND & NORTHFLEET Conference

*Ground:* Stonebridge Road, Northfleet, Kent DA11 9BA.
*Tel:* (01474) 533 796.
*Year Formed:* 1946.
*Record Gate:* 12,036 (1963 v Sunderland FA Cup Fourth Round).
*Nickname:* The Fleet.
*Manager:* Andy Ford.
*Secretary:* Roly Edwards.
*Colours:* Red shirts, white shorts, red stockings.

## GRAVESEND & NORTHFLEET 2003–04 LEAGUE RECORD

| *Match No.* | *Date* | *Venue* | *Opponents* | *Result* | | *H/T Score* | *Lg. Pos.* | *Goalscorers* | *Attendance* |
|---|---|---|---|---|---|---|---|---|---|
| 1 | Aug 9 | H | Burton Alb | L | 1-2 | 1-0 | — | Strouts [12] | 1137 |
| 2 | 12 | A | Woking | L | 2-3 | 0-2 | — | Pinnock [70], Abbey [74] | 2096 |
| 3 | 16 | A | Halifax T | L | 0-1 | 0-0 | 21 | | 1675 |
| 4 | 23 | H | Telford U | L | 1-2 | 0-0 | 22 | Gradley [90] | 834 |
| 5 | 25 | A | Farnborough T | W | 2-1 | 1-0 | 20 | McKimm [33], Pinnock [48] | 839 |
| 6 | 30 | H | Chester C | L | 0-4 | 0-2 | 22 | | 939 |
| 7 | Sept 6 | A | Scarborough | L | 0-2 | 0-0 | 21 | | 1249 |
| 8 | 13 | H | Leigh RMI | W | 3-1 | 1-0 | 18 | Owen [43], Haworth [58], Moore [79] | 723 |
| 9 | 20 | H | Exeter C | W | 3-2 | 0-0 | 17 | Pinnock 2 [51, 70], Haworth [68] | 1155 |
| 10 | 23 | A | Stevenage Bor | D | 2-2 | 0-1 | — | Drury [75], Lee [90] | 1732 |
| 11 | 27 | A | Hereford U | D | 3-3 | 2-2 | 17 | Haworth 2 [19, 47], Miller [33] | 3731 |
| 12 | Oct 4 | H | Forest Green R | D | 1-1 | 0-0 | 17 | Drury [70] | 1190 |
| 13 | 7 | H | Aldershot T | L | 1-3 | 1-2 | — | Haworth [44] | 1477 |
| 14 | 11 | A | Morecambe | D | 2-2 | 0-0 | 19 | Abbey [71], Gradley [78] | 1539 |
| 15 | 18 | A | Northwich Vic | D | 0-0 | 0-0 | 19 | | 542 |
| 16 | Nov 1 | H | Accrington S | D | 0-0 | 0-0 | 19 | | 1274 |
| 17 | 11 | A | Barnet | L | 0-1 | 0-0 | — | | 1542 |
| 18 | 15 | H | Shrewsbury T | L | 0-3 | 0-1 | 19 | | 1397 |
| 19 | 22 | A | Tamworth | W | 3-1 | 3-1 | 18 | Perkins 2 [16, 45], Drury [27] | 1128 |
| 20 | 25 | H | Dagenham & R | L | 1-2 | 1-0 | — | Drury [17] | 1274 |
| 21 | 29 | H | Scarborough | D | 1-1 | 1-0 | 17 | Perkins [13] | 747 |
| 22 | Dec 13 | A | Burton Alb | L | 0-3 | 0-0 | 18 | | 1403 |
| 23 | 20 | H | Woking | D | 2-2 | 1-1 | 18 | Abbey [6], Drury (pen) [90] | 975 |
| 24 | 28 | A | Margate | W | 3-1 | 1-1 | — | Moore [45], Haworth [52], Abbey [58] | 1030 |
| 25 | Jan 1 | H | Margate | W | 2-1 | 2-1 | 16 | Moore [10], Duku [35] | 1725 |
| 26 | 3 | A | Chester C | D | 2-2 | 0-2 | 16 | Moore 2 [68, 71] | 2670 |
| 27 | 17 | H | Halifax T | W | 1-0 | 1-0 | 16 | Evans [10] | 985 |
| 28 | 24 | H | Stevenage Bor | L | 2-3 | 1-1 | 16 | Drury (pen) [19], Moore [74] | 1230 |
| 29 | Feb 7 | A | Exeter C | W | 1-0 | 0-0 | 16 | Essandoh [46] | 3303 |
| 30 | 14 | H | Hereford U | L | 2-5 | 2-3 | 17 | Abbey 2 [4, 36] | 1230 |
| 31 | 21 | A | Forest Green R | W | 2-1 | 0-1 | 16 | Essandoh 2 [69, 75] | 752 |
| 32 | 28 | H | Morecambe | W | 6-0 | 2-0 | 13 | Perkins 2 [13, 56], Owen [45], Pinnock 2 [52, 58], Drury (pen) [55] | 1061 |
| 33 | Mar 6 | A | Aldershot T | D | 2-2 | 0-1 | 13 | Essandoh [76], Omoyinmi [77] | 2736 |
| 34 | 13 | H | Barnet | D | 1-1 | 1-0 | 14 | Moore [3] | 1516 |
| 35 | 27 | H | Tamworth | W | 2-0 | 1-0 | 14 | Omoyinmi [31], Drury [72] | 1157 |
| 36 | 30 | A | Leigh RMI | W | 2-1 | 0-0 | — | Pinnock [73], Essandoh [75] | 304 |
| 37 | Apr 3 | A | Dagenham & R | W | 4-0 | 0-0 | 11 | Essandoh [48], Pinnock [58], Walshe 2 [82, 86] | 1421 |
| 38 | 10 | A | Telford U | D | 1-1 | 0-0 | 12 | Sidibe [54] | 1746 |
| 39 | 12 | H | Farnborough T | W | 2-0 | 1-0 | 11 | Drury [38], Essandoh [78] | 1284 |
| 40 | 17 | A | Accrington S | D | 3-3 | 3-1 | 11 | Essandoh 2 [27, 42], Perkins [34] | 1139 |
| 41 | 20 | A | Shrewsbury T | D | 1-1 | 0-1 | — | Shearer [69] | 2869 |
| 42 | 24 | H | Northwich Vic | D | 2-2 | 1-1 | 11 | Essandoh [44], Pinnock [79] | 1436 |

**Final League Position: 11**

### GOALSCORERS

*League (69):* Essandoh 10, Drury 9 (3 pens), Pinnock 9, Moore 7, Abbey 6, Haworth 6, Perkins 6, Gradley 2, Omoyinmi 2, Owen 2, Walshe 2, Duku 1, Evans 1, Lee 1, McKimm 1, Miller 1, Shearer 1, Sidibe 1, Strouts 1.
*FA Cup (5):* Abbey 1, Haworth 1, Moore 1, Perkins 1, Skinner 1 (pen).
*Trophy (2):* Abbey 1, Haworth 1.

| O'Reilly 10 + 1 | Pennock 4 | McClements 12 + 1 | Perkins 30 + 7 | Trott 1 + 1 | Duku 17 + 2 | Strouts 4 + 7 | McKimm 36 + 2 | Abbey 11 + 12 | Huggins 2 | Skinner 26 | Pinnock 22 + 8 | Gradley 12 + 1 | Kwashi 1 + 1 | Lee 25 + 4 | Owen 30 + 3 | Shearer 26 + 3 | Goodwin — + 2 | Evans 1 + 6 | Haworth 21 + 1 | Walshe 17 + 6 | Wilkerson 27 + 1 | Moore 33 | Miller 4 | Drury 25 + 6 | Finn — + 1 | Daly — + 1 | Gibbs 2 | Oli 5 | Protheroe 10 | Gledhill 12 + 1 | Essandoh 14 | Sidibe 5 + 7 | Omoyinmi 4 + 3 | Battersby — + 1 | Surey 7 + 1 | Rouse 1 + 1 | Mitten 5 | *Match No.* |
|---|---|---|---|---|---|---|---|---|---|---|---|---|---|---|---|---|---|---|---|---|---|---|---|---|---|---|---|---|---|---|---|---|---|---|---|---|---|---|
| 1 | $2^{1}$ | 3 | 4 | 5 | 6 | 7 | 8 | $9^{2}$ | $10^{3}$ | 11 | 12 | 13 | 14 | | | | | | | | | | | | | | | | | | | | | | | | | 1 |
| 1 | 2 | 3 | $4^{1}$ | | 6 | 7 | 8 | 9 | $10^{2}$ | | 13 | | $11^{3}$ | 5 | 14 | 12 | | | | | | | | | | | | | | | | | | | | | | 2 |
| 1 | 2 | | $4^{1}$ | 13 | $6^{2}$ | 7 | 8 | | | 3 | 9 | | | 5 | $10^{3}$ | 11 | 12 | 14 | | | | | | | | | | | | | | | | | | | | 3 |
| 1 | $2^{1}$ | | 6 | | | 13 | 8 | | | $11^{3}$ | 10 | 7 | | $3^{2}$ | 4 | 5 | 12 | 14 | 9 | | | | | | | | | | | | | | | | | | | 4 |
| 1 | | 3 | 4 | | | | 8 | 12 | | 11 | $6^{1}$ | 9 | | 2 | 7 | 5 | | | 10 | | | | | | | | | | | | | | | | | | | 5 |
| 1 | | $3^{1}$ | 4 | | | | 8 | 12 | | 6 | 11 | 7 | | 2 | 10 | 5 | | | 9 | | | | | | | | | | | | | | | | | | | 6 |
| 1■ | | 14 | 13 | | $6^{1}$ | 12 | 7■ | | | 10■ | $11^{3}$ | 8 | | 2 | 3 | 4 | | | $5^{2}$ | 9 | | | | | | | | | | | | | | | | | | 7 |
| $1^{G}$ | | | 12 | | | | 8 | 13 | | 11 | 10 | 7 | | 2 | 6 | 5 | | | $9^{2}$ | $4^{1}$ | 15 | 3 | | | | | | | | | | | | | | | | 8 |
| | | 3 | | | | 12 | | | | | 10 | $8^{2}$ | | 2 | 6 | 4 | | | 9 | 11 | 1 | 5 | $7^{1}$ | 13 | | | | | | | | | | | | | | 9 |
| | | $3^{1}$ | | | | | | | | | 10 | 8 | | 2 | 7 | 4 | | | 9 | 11 | 1 | 5 | 6■ | 12 | | | | | | | | | | | | | | 10 |
| | | $3^{2}$ | 12 | | 14 | $2^{1}$ | | | | | $10^{3}$ | 8 | | | 7 | 4 | | | 9 | 11 | 1 | 5■ | 6 | 13 | | | | | | | | | | | | | | 11 |
| | | | 2 | | | 13 | 12 | | | 3 | 10 | 11 | | | 7 | 6 | | | 9 | | 1 | 5 | $8^{2}$ | $4^{1}$ | | | | | | | | | | | | | | 12 |
| | | | 2■ | | | | 8 | 12 | | $3^{1}$ | 10 | 7 | | | | 4 | | | 9 | 11 | 1 | 5 | | $6^{2}$ | 13 | | | | | | | | | | | | | 13 |
| | | | 2 | | 6 | 12 | 8 | 14 | | | $10^{3}$ | 7 | | 3 | 4 | $5^{1}$ | | | 9 | $11^{2}$ | 1 | | | 13 | | | | | | | | | | | | | | 14 |
| | | | 2 | | 6 | | 8 | 13 | | | $10^{2}$ | $7^{1}$ | | 3 | 4 | | | | 9 | 11 | 1 | 5 | | 12 | | | | | | | | | | | | | | 15 |
| | | | $2^{2}$ | | 6 | | 8 | 10 | | $4^{1}$ | | | | 3 | 7 | | | | 9 | 11 | 1 | 5 | | 13 | | 12 | | | | | | | | | | | | 16 |
| | | | 4 | | 6 | 12 | 8 | 13 | | $3^{1}$ | $10^{2}$ | | | 2 | 11 | | | | 9 | | 1 | 5 | | 7 | | | | | | | | | | | | | | 17 |
| | | | 4 | | 6 | | 8 | 10 | | | 12 | | | $2^{1}$ | $11^{2}$ | 14 | | | $9^{3}$ | 13 | 1 | 5 | | 7 | | | 3 | | | | | | | | | | | 18 |
| | | 3 | 2 | | 6 | | 9 | | | | | | | 4 | 8 | | | | | 11 | 1 | 5 | | 7 | | | | 10 | | | | | | | | | | 19 |
| | | 3 | 8 | | 6 | 12 | $7^{1}$ | | | | | | | 2 | 4 | | | 13 | | $11^{2}$ | 1 | 5 | | 9 | | | | 10 | | | | | | | | | | 20 |
| | | 3 | 4 | | | | 8 | | | | 13■ | | | 2 | 7 | 6 | | | $9^{2}$ | 12 | 1 | 5 | | $11^{1}$ | | | | 10 | | | | | | | | | | 21 |
| | | | 10 | | 13 | | 8 | 12 | | | | | | 2 | | 4 | | | 9 | 11 | 1 | $5^{2}$ | | $7^{1}$ | | | 3 | | 6 | | | | | | | | | 22 |
| | | | 4 | | 6 | | 8 | 9 | | | | | | 2 | | | | | | 11 | 1 | 5 | | 7 | | | | 10 | 3 | | | | | | | | | 23 |
| | | 3 | | | 6 | | 8 | 10 | | | | | | | 4 | | | 12 | 9 | $11^{1}$ | 1 | 5 | | 7 | | | | | 2 | | | | | | | | | 24 |
| | | 3 | 14 | | 6 | | 8 | 10 | | | | | | 12 | 4 | | | 13 | 9 | $11^{2}$ | 1 | 5 | | $7^{3}$ | | | | | $2^{1}$ | | | | | | | | | 25 |
| | | | $11^{1}$ | | 6 | | 8 | 13 | | | | | | 3 | 4 | | | | $9^{2}$ | 12 | 1 | 5 | | 7 | | | | 10 | 2 | | | | | | | | | 26 |
| 15 | | | 12 | | 6 | | 8 | | | 3 | | | | | 4 | 5 | | 10 | 9 | $11^{2}$ | $1^{G}$ | | | $7^{1}$ | | | | | 2 | 13 | | | | | | | | 27 |
| 1 | | | 14 | | 6■ | | 8 | $9^{2}$ | | 3 | | | | | 11 | 12 | | 13 | | | | 5 | | 7 | | | | | 4 | $2^{1}$ | $10^{3}$ | | | | | | | 28 |
| 1 | | | 8 | | | | | $9^{1}$ | | 3 | 12 | | | | 11 | 6 | | | | | | 5 | | 7 | | | | | 4 | 2 | 10 | | | | | | | 29 |
| | | | $8^{2}$ | | | | 13 | 9 | | 3 | | | | | 11 | 6 | | | 12 | | 1 | 5 | | 7 | | | | | 4 | $2^{1}$ | 10 | | | | | | | 30 |
| | | | 8 | | | | 11 | $9^{2}$ | | 3 | 13 | | | | $4^{1}$ | 6 | | | | | 1 | 5 | | 7 | | | | | 2 | | 10 | 12 | | | | | | 31 |
| | | | 8 | | | | 11 | | | 3 | $9^{2}$ | | | | 4 | 6 | | | | | 1 | 5 | | $7^{1}$ | | | | | | 2 | $10^{3}$ | 12 | 13 | 14 | | | | 32 |
| | | | 8 | | | | 4 | $12^{2}$ | | 3 | 11 | | | 13 | $7^{3}$ | 6 | | | | | 1 | 5 | | | | | | | | $2^{1}$ | 10 | 14 | 9 | | | | | 33 |
| | | | 8 | | | | 4 | 12 | | 3 | $10^{1}$ | | | | 11 | 6 | | | | | 1 | 5 | | $7^{2}$ | | | | | | 2 | | 13 | 9 | | | | | 34 |
| | | | 11 | | | | 8 | | | 3 | | | | | $4^{2}$ | 6 | | | | | 1 | $5^{1}$ | | 7 | | | | | | 2 | 10 | 13 | 9 | | 12 | | | 35 |
| | | | | | | | 8 | | | 3 | 13 | | | 12 | | $6^{1}$ | | | | 14 | 1 | 5 | | 7 | | | | | | 2 | $10^{3}$ | 11 | $9^{2}$ | | 4 | | | 36 |
| | | | $6^{1}$ | | | | 8 | | | $3^{3}$ | $9^{2}$ | | | 7 | 12 | | | | | 13 | 1 | 5 | | | | | | | | 2 | 10 | 11 | | | 4 | 14 | | 37 |
| | | | 11 | | | | 8 | | | 3 | 12 | | | 6 | | | | | | | | 5 | | 7 | | | | | | 2 | 10 | $9^{1}$ | | | 4 | | 1 | 38 |
| | | | 12 | | | | 8 | | | 3 | $9^{3}$ | | | 6 | | | | | | 11 | | 5 | | $7^{2}$ | | | | | | 2 | 10 | 13 | 14 | | $4^{1}$ | | 1 | 39 |
| | | | 11 | | | | 8 | | | 3 | $9^{2}$ | | | 12 | | 6 | | | | | | 5 | | | | | | | | $2^{1}$ | 10 | 7 | 13 | | 4 | | 1 | 40 |
| | | | $11^{1}$ | | | | 8 | | | 3 | 9 | | | 2 | | 6 | | | | | | 5 | | 7 | | | | | | | 10 | 12 | | | 4 | | 1 | 41 |
| | | | | | | | 8 | 12 | | | 9 | | | 2 | 13 | 6 | | | | 14 | | $5^{1}$ | | 7 | | | | | | | 10 | $11^{3}$ | | | $4^{2}$ | 3 | 1 | 42 |

**FA Cup**

| | | | |
|---|---|---|---|
| Fourth Qual | Exeter C | (a) | 0-0 |
| | | (h) | 3-3 |
| First Round | Chester C | (a) | 1-0 |
| Second Round | Notts Co | (h) | 1-2 |

# HALIFAX TOWN — Conference

*Ground:* The Shay Stadium, Shay Syke, Halifax, West Yorkshire HX1 2YS.
*Tel:* (01422) 341 222.
*Year Formed:* 1911.
*Record Gate:* 36,885 (1953 v Tottenham Hotspur FA Cup Fifth Round).
*Nickname:* The Shaymen.
*Manager:* Chris Wilder
*Secretary:* Jenna Helliwell.
*Colours:* All blue.

## HALIFAX TOWN 2003–04 LEAGUE RECORD

| Match No. | Date | Venue | Opponents | Result | | H/T Score | Lg. Pos. | Goalscorers | Attendance |
|---|---|---|---|---|---|---|---|---|---|
| 1 | Aug 9 | A | Exeter C | D | 1-1 | 0-1 | — | Killeen 85 | 3723 |
| 2 | 12 | H | Morecambe | W | 1-0 | 1-0 | — | Cameron 23 | 2160 |
| 3 | 16 | H | Gravesend & N | W | 1-0 | 0-0 | 3 | Mallon 84 | 1675 |
| 4 | 23 | A | Leigh RMI | D | 1-1 | 0-0 | 4 | Midgley 60 | 849 |
| 5 | 25 | H | Tamworth | L | 1-2 | 0-1 | 7 | Midgley 66 | 1849 |
| 6 | 30 | A | Barnet | L | 1-4 | 1-2 | 11 | Midgley 15 | 1341 |
| 7 | Sept 6 | H | Northwich Vic | W | 5-3 | 2-0 | 9 | Killeen 2 17, 75, Elam 32, Lee 50, Midgley (pen) 71 | 1440 |
| 8 | 13 | A | Chester C | L | 0-2 | 0-1 | 13 | | 2628 |
| 9 | 20 | H | Margate | L | 0-1 | 0-1 | 13 | | 1452 |
| 10 | 23 | A | Shrewsbury T | L | 0-2 | 0-0 | — | | 3807 |
| 11 | 27 | A | Forest Green R | W | 2-1 | 0-1 | 12 | Elam 54, Farrell 82 | 722 |
| 12 | Oct 4 | H | Stevenage Bor | W | 2-1 | 1-1 | 11 | Farrell 8, Lee 50 | 1437 |
| 13 | 7 | H | Accrington S | D | 1-1 | 1-1 | — | Lee 23 | 2116 |
| 14 | 11 | A | Aldershot T | L | 1-3 | 0-2 | 11 | Monington 76 | 2882 |
| 15 | 18 | A | Woking | D | 2-2 | 1-2 | 12 | Mallon 35, Bushell 58 | 1917 |
| 16 | Nov 1 | H | Dagenham & R | W | 3-0 | 3-0 | 11 | Quinn 4, Sandwith 16, McCombe 27 | 1379 |
| 17 | 11 | H | Telford U | D | 1-1 | 0-0 | — | Lee 52 | 1332 |
| 18 | 14 | A | Burton Alb | D | 2-2 | 0-1 | — | Killeen 60, Midgley (pen) 90 | 1541 |
| 19 | 22 | H | Farnborough T | W | 2-0 | 1-0 | 11 | Midgley 2 (2 pens) 45, 75 | 1250 |
| 20 | 25 | A | Hereford U | L | 1-7 | 1-2 | — | Killeen 2 | 1875 |
| 21 | 29 | A | Northwich Vic | W | 1-0 | 0-0 | 12 | Bushell 86 | 757 |
| 22 | Dec 6 | H | Chester C | L | 0-3 | 0-1 | 13 | | 1928 |
| 23 | 13 | H | Exeter C | W | 2-0 | 0-0 | 12 | Sagare 49, Midgley (pen) 83 | 1267 |
| 24 | 20 | A | Morecambe | L | 0-2 | 0-1 | 13 | | 1603 |
| 25 | 26 | H | Scarborough | W | 1-0 | 0-0 | 10 | Lee 74 | 2136 |
| 26 | Jan 3 | H | Barnet | L | 1-2 | 1-0 | 11 | Killeen 37 | 1517 |
| 27 | 17 | A | Gravesend & N | L | 0-1 | 0-1 | 12 | | 985 |
| 28 | 24 | H | Shrewsbury T | D | 0-0 | 0-0 | 12 | | 1830 |
| 29 | Feb 8 | A | Margate | L | 0-2 | 0-1 | 14 | | 391 |
| 30 | 21 | A | Stevenage Bor | L | 0-1 | 0-0 | 14 | | 1715 |
| 31 | 24 | H | Aldershot T | L | 1-2 | 1-1 | — | Mallon 14 | 843 |
| 32 | Mar 6 | A | Accrington S | L | 1-2 | 0-1 | 16 | Owen 85 | 1717 |
| 33 | 9 | H | Forest Green R | L | 0-1 | 0-1 | — | | 883 |
| 34 | 13 | A | Telford U | L | 1-2 | 0-0 | 17 | Killeen 74 | 1337 |
| 35 | 25 | A | Scarborough | L | 0-1 | 0-0 | — | | 1220 |
| 36 | 27 | A | Farnborough T | L | 0-1 | 0-0 | 19 | | 644 |
| 37 | 30 | H | Burton Alb | L | 1-4 | 0-2 | — | Little 90 | 1128 |
| 38 | Apr 3 | H | Hereford U | L | 1-2 | 1-0 | 19 | Midgley (pen) 19 | 1389 |
| 39 | 9 | H | Leigh RMI | W | 2-1 | 2-0 | — | Allan 25, Bushell 45 | 1415 |
| 40 | 12 | A | Tamworth | L | 0-2 | 0-1 | 19 | | 1095 |
| 41 | 17 | A | Dagenham & R | W | 1-0 | 1-0 | 19 | Midgley (pen) 45 | 1344 |
| 42 | 24 | H | Woking | D | 2-2 | 2-1 | 19 | Little (pen) 37, Midgley 42 | 1191 |

**Final League Position: 19**

### GOALSCORERS

*League (43):* Midgley 11 (7 pens), Killeen 7, Lee 5, Bushell 3, Mallon 3, Elam 2, Farrell 2, Little 2 (1 pen), Allan 1, Cameron 1, McCombe 1, Monington 1, Owen 1, Quinn 1, Sagare 1, Sandwith 1.
*LDV Vans Trophy (6):* Killeen 1, Mallon 1, Midgley 1 (pen), Owen 1, Quinn 1, Sandwith 1.
*Trophy (6):* Farrell 3 (1 pen), Killeen 1, Quinn 1, own goal 1.

| Davies 8 | Sandwith 31 | Hockenhull 27 + 4 | Bushell 37 + 1 | Garnett 11 / Stoneman — + 1 | Monington 26 + 2 | Mallon 29 + 8 | Cameron 6 + 3 | Killeen 29 + 3 | Cullen 7 | Elam 14 + 1 | Midgley 28 + 10 | Hudson 21 + 7 | Parke — + 5 | Price 5 / Lowe 2 | Quinn 21 + 4 | Lee 17 + 9 | Farrell 6 + 12 | McAuley 11 + 4 | Cartwright 32 | Sagare 11 + 14 | Tozer 2 + 1 | Dudgeon 9 + 1 / Hoyle — + 1 | Golden — + 1 | Senior — + 4 | Naylor — + 1 | McCombe 7 | Yates 12 | Owen 15 + 2 | Allan 9 + 5 | Colley 6 + 1 | Parry 2 | Donaldson 2 + 2 | Thornley 1 + 2 | May 2 + 1 | Carney 2 + 1 | Ingram 6 | Little 8 | *Match No.* |
|---|---|---|---|---|---|---|---|---|---|---|---|---|---|---|---|---|---|---|---|---|---|---|---|---|---|---|---|---|---|---|---|---|---|---|---|---|---|---|
| 1 | 2 | $3^1$ | 4 | 5 | 6 | $7^2$ | 8 | 9 | 10 | $11^3$ | 12 | 13 | 14 | | | | | | | | | | | | | | | | | | | | | | | | | 1 |
| 1 | 2 | | 4 | 5 | 6 | $7^1$ | $8^2$ | 9 | 10 | $11^3$ | 12 | 14 | 13 | 3 | | | | | | | | | | | | | | | | | | | | | | | | 2 |
| 1 | 2 | | | 5 | $6^1$ | 7 | $8^3$ | 9 | 10 | 11 | 13 | $4^2$ | | 3 | 12 | 14 | | | | | | | | | | | | | | | | | | | | | | 3 |
| 1 | 2 | | 12 | $5^2$ | | 7 | $8^3$ | 9 | | 11 | 6 | $10^1$ | 13 | 3 | 4 | 14 | | | | | | | | | | | | | | | | | | | | | | 4 |
| 1 | 2 | | 4 | 5 | | $7^2$ | | 9 | $10^1$ | 11 | 12 | | 14 | 3 | 6 | $8^3$ | 13 | | | | | | | | | | | | | | | | | | | | | 5 |
| 1 | 2 | | 4 | 5 | | 12 | $8^2$ | 9 | | $11^1$ | 10 | 7 | | $3^3$ | 6 | 13 | 14 | | | | | | | | | | | | | | | | | | | | | 6 |
| 1 | 2 | 3 | 4 | 5 | 6 | $7^1$ | 14 | 9 | | $11^2$ | 8 | | | | | $10^3$ | 12 | 13 | | | | | | | | | | | | | | | | | | | | 7 |
| 1 | 2 | $3^1$ | 4 | 5 | 6 | 14 | | 9 | $10^2$ | 11 | 7 | | 13 | | 12 | $8^3$ | | | | | | | | | | | | | | | | | | | | | | 8 |
| | 2 | 3 | 4 | 5 | | 12 | 14 | 9 | $10^2$ | $11^1$ | 8 | | | | 6 | $7^3$ | | | 1 | 13 | | | | | | | | | | | | | | | | | | 9 |
| | 2 | 3 | 4 | 5 | 6 | | $8^3$ | 9 | $10^2$ | 12 | 7 | | | | | 13 | | | 1 | 14 | $11^1$ | | | | | | | | | | | | | | | | | 10 |
| | 2 | 3 | 4 | 5 | 6 | 7 | | | | $11^2$ | 13 | 8 | | | | $9^3$ | 12 | | 1 | 14 | $10^1$ | | | | | | | | | | | | | | | | | 11 |
| | 2 | 3 | $4^2$ | | 6 | 7 | | | | $11^1$ | 13 | 8 | | | | 10 | $9^3$ | | 1 | 14 | 12 | 5 | | | | | | | | | | | | | | | | 12 |
| | 2 | 3 | 4 | | 6 | 7 | 13 | 12 | | $11^1$ | | 8 | | | | $10^2$ | 9 | | 1 | | | 5 | | | | | | | | | | | | | | | | 13 |
| | 2 | 3 | 4 | | 6 | 7 | | 9 | | $11^1$ | 13 | 8 | | | | | $10^2$ | | 1 | 12 | | 5 | | | | | | | | | | | | | | | | 14 |
| | 2 | 3 | 4 | | $6^1$ | 7 | | $9^3$ | | 11 | 14 | 8 | | | 5 | 13 | | | 1 | $10^2$ | | 12 | | | | | | | | | | | | | | | | 15 |
| | 2 | 3 | 4 | | | $7^1$ | | | | | 11 | 8 | | | 5 | $9^2$ | | | 1 | $10^3$ | | | 12 | 13 | 14 | 6 | | | | | | | | | | | | 16 |
| | 2 | 3 | 4 | | | 7 | | 9 | | | 11 | 8 | | | 6 | $10^1$ | | | 1 | 12 | | | | | | 5 | | | | | | | | | | | | 17 |
| | 2 | | 4 | | | 7 | | 9 | | | 11 | 8 | | | 6 | | | 12 | 1 | $10^1$ | | | | | | 5 | 3 | | | | | | | | | | | 18 |
| | 2 | 13 | 4 | | | $7^2$ | | 9 | | | $11^1$ | 8 | | | | $10^3$ | 14 | 12 | 1 | | | 6 | | | | 5 | 3 | | | | | | | | | | | 19 |
| | 2 | | 4 | | 12 | 7 | | $9^3$ | | | 11 | 8 | | | | $10^2$ | 13 | | 1 | 14 | | $5^1$ | | | | 6 | 3 | | | | | | | | | | | 20 |
| | 2 | 12 | 4 | | 5 | 7 | | 9 | | | $11^1$ | 8 | | | | | $10^2$ | | 1 | 13 | | | | | | 6 | 3 | | | | | | | | | | | 21 |
| | | | 4 | | 5 | 7 | | 13 | | | 11 | $8^1$ | | | | $10^3$ | | 2 | 1 | $9^2$ | | | | | | 6 | 3 | 12 | 14 | | | | | | | | | 22 |
| | 3 | | 4 | | | 7 | | | | | 13 | $8^2$ | | | | $9^3$ | 12 | $10^1$ | 1 | 14 | | 5 | | | | | 2 | 11 | | 6 | | | | | | | | 23 |
| | 3■ | | | | | 7 | | 12 | | | $11^1$ | 8 | | | | 14 | $10^3$ | | 1 | $9^2$ | | 5 | | | | | 2 | 4 | 13 | 6 | | | | | | | | 24 |
| | 3 | 14 | 4 | | | $9^3$ | | | | | 11 | 12 | | | | 13 | $10^2$ | | 1 | $8^1$ | | 5■ | | | | | 2■ | 7 | | 6 | | | | | | | | 25 |
| | | | | | 4 | 7 | | 9 | | | 11 | $8^1$ | | | | $10^2$ | 13 | 3 | 1 | 12 | | 5 | | | | | 2 | 6 | | | | | | | | | | 26 |
| | 2 | 3 | | | 4 | | | 9 | | | $7^1$ | $8^2$ | | | 13 | | 12 | $11^3$ | | 14 | | | | | | | | 6 | 10■ | 5 | 1 | | | | | | | 27 |
| | 2 | 3 | 8 | | 4 | 7 | | 9 | | | $11^1$ | 12 | | | | 13 | | | 1 | $10^2$ | | | | | | | | 6 | | 5 | | | | | | | | 28 |
| | 2 | 3 | 11 | | 4 | 7 | | | | | 12 | 8 | | | 13 | $9^2$ | | | 1 | $10^3$ | | | | | | | | $6^1$ | | 5 | | 14 | | | | | | 29 |
| | 2 | 3 | 7 | | 4 | 12 | | | | | $11^1$ | 13 | | | 5 | | | | 1 | $10^3$ | | | | | | | | $6^2$ | 8 | 14 | | 9 | | | | | | 30 |
| | 2 | 3 | 8 | | 4 | $7^3$ | | | | | 11 | 12 | | | 5 | | | 14 | 1■ | 13 | | | | | | | | $6^1$ | 9 | | | $10^2$ | | | | | | 31 |
| | 2 | 3 | 8 | | 4 | 7 | | | | | 11■ | | | | 5 | | | | 1 | $10^2$ | | | | 12 | | | | 6 | $9^1$ | | | 13 | | | | | | 32 |
| | 2 | 12 | 8 | | 4 | $7^3$ | | | | | 11 | | | | 5 | | | | | $10^1$ | | | | | | | $3^2$ | 6 | 13 | | 1 | | 14 | 9 | | | | 33 |
| | | 2 | 8 | | 4 | | | 9 | | | $11^2$ | | | | 5 | 13 | | 3 | 1 | 12 | | | | | | | | $6^3$ | | | | | 7 | $10^1$ | 14 | | | 34 |
| | | $2^1$ | 4 | | | $7^2$ | | 9 | | | | 8 | | | 5 | | | 3 | 1 | 13 | | | | | | | | | | | | | 14 | 12 | $11^3$ | 6 | 10 | 35 |
| | | 2 | 11 | | 4 | 12 | | $9^2$ | | | | | | | 5 | 10 | | 3 | 1 | | | | | | | | 8 | $6^1$ | 13 | | | | | | | | 7 | 36 |
| | | 2 | 8 | 13 | | $7^2$ | | 9 | | | | | | | 5 | $10^1$ | | 3 | 1 | | | | | | | | 4 | 6 | 12 | | | | | | | | 11 | 37 |
| | | $2^1$ | 8 | | | 13 | | 9 | | | 11 | 14 | | | 5 | | 12 | 3 | 1 | | | | | | | | | $6^2$ | $10^3$ | | | | | | | 4 | 7 | 38 |
| | | 2 | 4 | | 13 | | | 9 | | | 11 | | | | 5 | | 14 | 3 | 1 | | | | | | | | | 12 | $8^2$ | | | | | | $7^1$ | 6 | $10^3$ | 39 |
| | | 2 | 8 | | 4 | 12 | | $9^3$ | | | 11 | | | | 6 | | 13 | $3^1$ | 1 | | | | | 14 | | | | | $10^2$ | | | | | | | 5 | 7 | 40 |
| | | 2 | 8 | | 4 | | | 9 | | | 11 | | | 3 | 6 | | | | 1 | | | | | | | | | | 10 | | | | | | | 5 | 7 | 41 |
| | | 2 | 8 | | 4 | 14 | | $9^3$ | | | $11^2$ | | | 3 | 5 | | | | 1 | | | 13 | | 12 | | | | | 10 | | | | | | | $6^1$ | 7 | 42 |

**LDV Vans Trophy**

| | | | |
|---|---|---|---|
| First Round | York C | (h) | 2-1 |
| Second Round | Scarborough | (a) | 1-0 |
| Quarter-Final | Lincoln C | (h) | 1-0 |
| Semi-Final | Blackpool | (a) | 2-3 |

**FA Cup**

| | | | |
|---|---|---|---|
| Fourth Qual | Northwich Vic | (a) | 0-1 |

# HEREFORD UNITED

## Conference

*Ground:* Edgar Street, Hereford, Herefordshire HR4 9JU.
*Tel:* (01432) 276 666.
*Year Formed:* 1924.
*Record Gate:* 18,114 (1958 v Sheffield Wednesday FA Cup Third Round).
*Nickname:* The Bulls.
*Manager:* Graham Turner.
*Secretary:* Joan Fennessy.
*Colours:* White and black shirts, black shorts, white stockings.

### HEREFORD UNITED 2003–04 LEAGUE RECORD

| Match No. | Date | Venue | Opponents | Result | H/T Score | Lg. Pos. | Goalscorers | Attendance |
|---|---|---|---|---|---|---|---|---|
| 1 | Aug 9 | A | Tamworth | W 3-1 | 1-0 | — | Guinan [28], Smith 2 [65, 69] | 2250 |
| 2 | 12 | H | Forest Green R | W 5-1 | 2-1 | — | Guinan 2 [16, 69], Purdey 2 [45, 54], Carey-Bertram [77] | 3195 |
| 3 | 16 | H | Morecambe | W 3-0 | 2-0 | 1 | Smith 2 [18, 52], Guinan [28] | 2941 |
| 4 | 23 | A | Barnet | D 1-1 | 0-0 | 2 | James (pen) [78] | 1475 |
| 5 | 25 | H | Aldershot T | W 4-3 | 2-2 | 1 | Williams [29], Rose [45], James (pen) [52], Brown [90] | 4985 |
| 6 | 30 | A | Stevenage Bor | W 2-0 | 1-0 | 1 | Smith [27], Guinan [65] | 2705 |
| 7 | Sept 6 | A | Farnborough T | W 5-0 | 3-0 | 1 | Parry [4], Smith [17], Guinan [25], James (pen) [56], Brown [84] | 1334 |
| 8 | 13 | H | Scarborough | W 2-1 | 1-0 | 1 | Rose [29], Parry [78] | 4850 |
| 9 | 19 | A | Burton Alb | L 1-4 | 0-2 | — | Parry [74] | 2502 |
| 10 | 23 | H | Telford U | W 2-1 | 1-0 | — | Guinan [6], Green [90] | 4190 |
| 11 | 27 | H | Gravesend & N | D 3-3 | 2-2 | 1 | Guinan [35], Brown [45], Smith [50] | 3731 |
| 12 | Oct 4 | A | Woking | W 1-0 | 0-0 | 1 | Guinan [82] | 2906 |
| 13 | 7 | A | Northwich Vic | W 5-1 | 1-0 | — | Williams [4], Brown [49], Guinan 2 [76, 90], Parry [85] | 1008 |
| 14 | 13 | H | Dagenham & R | D 1-1 | 0-0 | — | Smith [54] | 4325 |
| 15 | 18 | A | Chester C | D 0-0 | 0-0 | 1 | | 4481 |
| 16 | Nov 1 | H | Leigh RMI | L 0-1 | 0-0 | 1 | | 3231 |
| 17 | 11 | A | Accrington S | L 0-2 | 0-1 | — | | 1824 |
| 18 | 15 | H | Margate | W 2-1 | 0-0 | 2 | Parry [56], Murphy (og) [78] | 2320 |
| 19 | 22 | A | Shrewsbury T | L 1-4 | 0-2 | 3 | Mkandawire [89] | 6585 |
| 20 | 25 | H | Halifax T | W 7-1 | 2-1 | — | Smith 2 [10, 33], Guinan 3 [52, 55, 71], Purdey [72], Brown [81] | 1875 |
| 21 | 29 | H | Farnborough T | W 2-0 | 0-0 | 2 | Smith [69], Pitman [89] | 2630 |
| 22 | Dec 13 | H | Tamworth | L 0-1 | 0-1 | 2 | | 2561 |
| 23 | 19 | A | Forest Green R | W 7-1 | 4-0 | — | Parry 3 [13, 25, 58], Smith 2 [35, 60], Purdey [38], Pitman [79] | 1576 |
| 24 | 26 | H | Exeter C | D 1-1 | 0-0 | 2 | Purdey [53] | 4010 |
| 25 | Jan 1 | A | Exeter C | W 1-0 | 1-0 | 2 | Williams [45] | 4943 |
| 26 | 3 | H | Stevenage Bor | W 1-0 | 0-0 | 2 | Parry [90] | 2875 |
| 27 | 17 | A | Morecambe | D 2-2 | 1-1 | 2 | U'ddin [29], Teesdale [78] | 2003 |
| 28 | Feb 3 | A | Scarborough | D 3-3 | 1-1 | — | Brown [7], U'ddin [54], Guinan [69] | 1459 |
| 29 | 7 | H | Burton Alb | L 1-2 | 1-1 | 2 | James (pen) [15] | 3417 |
| 30 | 14 | A | Gravesend & N | W 5-2 | 3-2 | 2 | James (pen) [6], Brown 2 [14, 68], Guinan 2 [22, 90] | 1230 |
| 31 | 21 | H | Woking | L 0-1 | 0-0 | 2 | | 2817 |
| 32 | 27 | A | Dagenham & R | W 9-0 | 3-0 | — | James (pen) [15], Brown 3 [38, 71, 89], Guinan 2 [45, 48], Williams 2 [76, 88], Beesley [85] | 1617 |
| 33 | Mar 2 | A | Telford U | W 3-0 | 1-0 | — | Tretton [45], Brown 2 [80, 90] | 2554 |
| 34 | 6 | H | Northwich Vic | W 1-0 | 0-0 | 2 | Guinan [84] | 3064 |
| 35 | 13 | H | Accrington S | W 1-0 | 0-0 | 2 | James (pen) [75] | 3230 |
| 36 | 20 | A | Margate | W 3-1 | 2-0 | 2 | Guinan [32], Willis [45], Purdey [86] | 604 |
| 37 | 27 | H | Shrewsbury T | W 2-1 | 1-1 | 1 | Purdey [3], Guinan [54] | 5850 |
| 38 | Apr 3 | A | Halifax T | W 2-1 | 0-1 | 2 | Guinan [75], Tretton [77] | 1389 |
| 39 | 10 | H | Barnet | W 2-0 | 1-0 | 2 | Willis [38], James (pen) [76] | 4447 |
| 40 | 12 | A | Aldershot T | W 2-1 | 1-0 | 2 | Purdey [4], Carey-Bertram [81] | 4400 |
| 41 | 17 | A | Leigh RMI | W 5-0 | 3-0 | 2 | James (pen) [6], Guinan 2 [28, 89], Travis [43], Carey-Bertram [84] | 836 |
| 42 | 24 | H | Chester C | W 2-1 | 1-0 | 2 | Brown [20], Beesley [70] | 7240 |

**Final League Position: 2**

### GOALSCORERS

*League (103):* Guinan 25, Brown 14, Smith 13, James 9 (9 pens), Parry 9, Purdey 8, Williams 5, Carey-Bertram 3, Beesley 2, Pitman 2, Rose 2, Tretton 2, U'ddin 2, Willis 2, Green 1, Mkandawire 1, Teesdale 1, Travis 1, own goal 1.
*FA Cup (6):* Guinan 3, Smith 1, Carey-Bertram 1, Smith 1.
*LDV Vans Trophy (3):* Brown 2, Guinan 1.
*Trophy (2):* Carey-Bertram 1, Purdey 1.
*Play-Offs (1):* Brown 1.

| Baker 42 | Green 38 | Rose 37 + 1 | Williams 31 + 6 | Tretton 22 | James 42 | Smith 35 | Parry 25 | Guinan 34 + 2 | Purdey 34 + 2 | Pitman 39 | Carey-Bertram 2 + 18 | Sawyers — + 1 | Brown 25 + 13 | Craven 5 + 6 | Teesdale 4 + 8 | Mkandawire 14 | King 1 + 1 | U'ddin 9 | Beesley 4 + 8 | Palmer 3 | Travis 5 | Willis 8 | Betts 3 + 2 | Cozic — + 2 | *Match No.* |
|---|---|---|---|---|---|---|---|---|---|---|---|---|---|---|---|---|---|---|---|---|---|---|---|---|---|
| 1 | 2 | 3 | 4 | 5 | 6 | 7 | 8 | $9^1$ | $10^2$ | 11 | 12 | 13 | | | | | | | | | | | | | 1 |
| 1 | 2 | 3 | 4 | 5 | 6 | 7 | 8 | $9^1$ | 10 | 11 | 12 | | | | | | | | | | | | | | 2 |
| 1 | 2 | 3 | 4 | 5 | 6 | 7 | 8 | $9^1$ | $10^2$ | 11 | 12 | | 13 | | | | | | | | | | | | 3 |
| 1 | 2 | 3 | 4 | 5 | 6 | 7 | 8 | $9^1$ | $10^2$ | 11 | $13^3$ | | 14 | 12 | | | | | | | | | | | 4 |
| 1 | 2 | 3 | 4 | 5 | 6 | 7 | 8 | $9^1$ | 10 | 11 | | | 12 | | | | | | | | | | | | 5 |
| 1 | 2 | 3 | 4 | 5 | 6 | 7 | 8 | 9 | $10^1$ | 11 | | | 12 | | | | | | | | | | | | 6 |
| 1 | 2 | 3 | $4^1$ | 5 | 6 | 7 | 8 | 9 | 10 | 11 | | | 12 | | | | | | | | | | | | 7 |
| 1 | 2 | 3 | 4 | 5 | 6 | 7 | 8 | 9 | $10^1$ | 11 | | | 12 | | | | | | | | | | | | 8 |
| 1 | 2 | 3 | 4 | $5^1$ | 6 | 7 | 8 | $9^2$ | $10^3$ | 11 | 13 | | 14 | | 12 | | | | | | | | | | 9 |
| 1 | 2 | 3 | 4 | | 6 | 7 | 8 | 9 | | 11 | 12 | | $10^1$ | | 5 | | | | | | | | | | 10 |
| 1 | 2 | 3 | 4 | | 6 | 7 | 8 | 9 | | 11 | 12 | | $10^1$ | | 5 | | | | | | | | | | 11 |
| 1 | 2 | 3 | 4 | | 6 | 7 | 8 | 9 | | 5 | 12 | | $10^1$ | | | 11 | | | | | | | | | 12 |
| 1 | 2 | 3 | 4 | | 6 | 7 | 8 | 9 | | 5 | 12 | | $10^1$ | | | 11 | | | | | | | | | 13 |
| 1 | 2 | 3 | 4 | | 6 | 7 | 8 | 9 | | 11 | 12 | | $10^1$ | | | 5 | | | | | | | | | 14 |
| 1 | 2 | 3 | 4 | | 6 | 7 | 8 | 9 | | 11 | 12 | | $10^1$ | | | 5 | | | | | | | | | 15 |
| 1 | 2 | 3 | 4 | | 6 | 7 | | 9 | 12 | 11■ | $10^2$ | | 13 | $8^1$ | | 5 | | | | | | | | | 16 |
| 1 | 2 | 3 | 4 | | 6 | | 8 | 9 | 10 | 11 | | | 12 | | | 5 | $7^1$ | | | | | | | | 17 |
| 1 | 2 | 3 | 4 | | 5 | 7 | 8 | 9 | 10 | | | | | 11 | | 6■ | | | | | | | | | 18 |
| 1 | 2 | | 4 | | 6 | $7^1$ | 8 | 9 | $10^2$ | 11 | 13 | | 12 | 3 | | 5 | | | | | | | | | 19 |
| 1 | 2 | 3 | $4^2$ | | 6 | 7 | $8^3$ | 9 | 10 | 11 | | | 13 | 14 | 12 | $5^1$ | | | | | | | | | 20 |
| 1 | 2 | 3 | 4 | | 6 | 7 | 8 | 9 | $10^1$ | 11 | | | 12 | | 5 | | | | | | | | | | 21 |
| 1 | 2■ | 3 | 4 | | 6 | 7 | 8 | | $10^1$ | 11 | 12 | | 9 | | | | | 5 | | | | | | | 22 |
| 1 | 2 | 3 | $4^2$ | | $6^1$ | $7^3$ | 8 | | 10 | 11 | | | 9 | 13 | 12 | | 14 | 5 | | | | | | | 23 |
| 1 | 2 | 3 | $4^1$ | | 6 | 7 | 8 | | 10 | 11 | | | 9 | | | | | 5 | 12 | | | | | | 24 |
| 1 | | 3 | $4^1$ | | 6 | 7 | $8^2$ | 12 | 10 | 11 | | | | 13 | 5 | | | 2 | 9 | | | | | | 25 |
| 1 | 2 | 3 | 4 | | 6 | 7 | 8 | | $10^2$ | | | | 12 | 11 | 13 | | | 5 | $9^1$ | | | | | | 26 |
| 1 | 2 | 3■ | $4^1$ | | 6 | | | | 10 | 11 | 13 | | $9^3$ | 12 | 14 | | | 5 | $8^2$ | 7 | | | | | 27 |
| 1 | 2 | | 4 | | 6 | 7 | | 12 | 13 | 11 | | | 9 | 3 | | | | 5 | $10^1$ | $8^2$ | | | | | 28 |
| 1 | $2^1$ | 3 | $4^2$ | | 6 | 7 | | 9 | 10 | 11 | | | 8 | | 12 | | | 5 | 13 | | | | | | 29 |
| 1 | | 3 | 4 | 5 | 6 | $7^1$ | | 9 | 10 | | | | 8 | | 12 | | | 2 | | 11 | | | | | 30 |
| 1 | | 2 | $4^3$ | $5^1$ | 6 | | | 9 | 10 | 11 | 14 | | 8 | | 13 | 3 | | | 12 | | $7^2$ | | | | 31 |
| 1 | 2 | 3 | 12 | 5 | 6 | | | $9^2$ | 10 | $11^3$ | | | 8 | 14 | | 4 | | | 13 | | | $7^1$ | | | 32 |
| 1 | | 3 | | 5 | 6 | | | 9 | 10 | 11 | | | 8 | | | 4 | | | | | 2 | 7 | | | 33 |
| 1 | 2 | 3 | | 5 | 6 | | | 9 | 10 | 11 | | | 8 | | | 4 | | | 12 | | | $7^1$ | | | 34 |
| 1 | 2 | 3 | | 5 | 6 | 7 | | 9 | 10 | 11 | 12 | | 8 | | | | | | | | | $4^1$ | | | 35 |
| 1 | 2 | 3 | 12 | 5 | 6 | | | 9 | 10 | 11 | | | 8 | | | 4 | | | | | | $7^1$ | | | 36 |
| 1 | 2 | 3 | 12 | 5 | 6 | 7 | | 9 | 10 | 11 | | | 8 | | | | | | | | | $4^1$ | | | 37 |
| 1 | 2 | 3 | 12 | 5 | 6 | $7^1$ | | 9 | 10 | 11 | | | 8 | | | | | | | | | $4^2$ | 13 | | 38 |
| 1 | 2 | | 13 | 5 | 6 | 7 | | 9 | $10^1$ | 11 | | | $8^2$ | | | | | | | | 3 | 4■ | 12 | | 39 |
| 1 | 2 | | | 5 | 6 | 7 | | 9 | $10^3$ | $11^2$ | 12 | | $8^1$ | | | | | | 13 | | 3 | | 4 | 14 | 40 |
| 1 | 2 | 14 | | 5 | 6 | 7 | | 9 | $10^2$ | $11^1$ | 13 | | $8^3$ | | | | | | 12 | | 3 | | 4 | | 41 |
| 1 | 2 | 3 | 12 | 5 | 6 | 7 | | | 10 | 11 | $9^2$ | | $8^3$ | | | | | | 14 | | | | $4^1$ | 13 | 42 |

**LDV Vans Trophy**

| | | | |
|---|---|---|---|
| First Round | Exeter C | (h) | 2-0 |
| Second Round | Northampton T | (h) | 1-1 |

**FA Cup**

| | | | |
|---|---|---|---|
| Fourth Qual | Harrow B | (a) | 6-1 |
| First Round | Peterborough U | (a) | 0-2 |

**Play-Offs**

| | | | |
|---|---|---|---|
| Semi-Finals | Aldershot T | (a) | 1-1 |
| | | (h) | 0-0 |

# LEIGH RMI

## Conference

*Ground:* Hilton Park, Kirkhall Lane, Leigh, Lancashire WN7 1RN.
*Tel:* (01942) 743 743.
*Year Formed:* 1896.
*Record Gate:* 7,125 (1999 v Fulham FA Cup Third Round) (at Horwich 8,500 1954 v Wigan Athletic).
*Nickname:* Railwaymen.
*Manager:* Phil Starbuck.
*Secretary:* Alan Robinson.
*Colours:* Red and white shirts, black shorts, white stockings.

### LEIGH RMI 2003–04 LEAGUE RECORD

| Match No. | Date | Venue | Opponents | Result | | H/T Score | Lg. Pos. | Goalscorers | Attendance |
|---|---|---|---|---|---|---|---|---|---|
| 1 | Aug 9 | H | Dagenham & R | W | 2-1 | 1-1 | — | McNiven 2 [18, 49] | 419 |
| 2 | 13 | A | Accrington S | L | 1-4 | 0-2 | — | McNiven [88] | 2003 |
| 3 | 16 | A | Farnborough T | D | 1-1 | 0-0 | 13 | McNiven [52] | 594 |
| 4 | 23 | H | Halifax T | D | 1-1 | 0-0 | 14 | McNiven [80] | 849 |
| 5 | 25 | A | Northwich Vic | W | 1-0 | 1-0 | 9 | Maden [39] | 582 |
| 6 | 30 | H | Woking | L | 0-1 | 0-0 | 12 | | 435 |
| 7 | Sept 6 | H | Forest Green R | L | 1-2 | 1-1 | 15 | Robinson [34] | 415 |
| 8 | 13 | A | Gravesend & N | L | 1-3 | 0-1 | 16 | McNiven [63] | 723 |
| 9 | 20 | H | Tamworth | D | 1-1 | 1-0 | 16 | Redmond [38] | 427 |
| 10 | 23 | A | Morecambe | L | 0-1 | 0-0 | — | | 1393 |
| 11 | 27 | A | Stevenage Bor | L | 0-4 | 0-1 | 19 | | 1734 |
| 12 | Oct 4 | H | Aldershot T | D | 2-2 | 1-1 | 19 | McNiven 2 [22, 53] | 545 |
| 13 | 11 | A | Margate | L | 0-2 | 0-1 | 20 | | 429 |
| 14 | 18 | H | Barnet | L | 1-4 | 0-0 | 20 | McNiven (pen) [89] | 348 |
| 15 | Nov 1 | A | Hereford U | W | 1-0 | 0-0 | 20 | Barrowclough [86] | 3231 |
| 16 | 11 | H | Scarborough | L | 1-4 | 1-1 | — | Maden [9] | 375 |
| 17 | 15 | A | Telford U | L | 0-5 | 0-2 | 20 | | 1377 |
| 18 | 18 | H | Shrewsbury T | D | 2-2 | 0-0 | — | McNiven 2 [67, 76] | 1219 |
| 19 | 22 | H | Exeter C | D | 1-1 | 1-0 | 20 | Maden [41] | 630 |
| 20 | 25 | A | Burton Alb | L | 2-3 | 1-2 | — | McNiven [17], Maden [84] | 1327 |
| 21 | 29 | A | Forest Green R | D | 2-2 | 0-0 | 20 | McNiven [63], Peyton [90] | 554 |
| 22 | Dec 13 | A | Dagenham & R | W | 2-1 | 1-0 | 20 | Shepherd [42], McNiven [84] | 1037 |
| 23 | 20 | H | Accrington S | L | 1-2 | 0-2 | 20 | McNiven [89] | 612 |
| 24 | 26 | A | Chester C | L | 0-5 | 0-3 | 21 | | 3044 |
| 25 | Jan 1 | H | Chester C | L | 2-6 | 0-2 | 21 | Daniel [73], Peyton [78] | 2002 |
| 26 | 3 | A | Woking | L | 0-2 | 0-2 | 21 | | 2105 |
| 27 | 17 | H | Farnborough T | L | 0-2 | 0-1 | 21 | | 295 |
| 28 | 24 | H | Morecambe | W | 3-1 | 1-0 | 21 | McNiven 3 (1 pen) [42, 48, 63 (p)] | 605 |
| 29 | Feb 7 | A | Tamworth | L | 3-4 | 2-1 | 21 | McNiven [18], Barrowclough [42], Roscoe [68] | 905 |
| 30 | 14 | H | Stevenage Bor | L | 1-3 | 0-1 | 21 | McNiven [60] | 270 |
| 31 | 21 | A | Aldershot T | L | 0-2 | 0-1 | 21 | | 2412 |
| 32 | 28 | H | Margate | W | 4-2 | 3-1 | 21 | Brodie 2 [8, 34], McNiven (pen) [30], Daniel [66] | 302 |
| 33 | Mar 8 | A | Shrewsbury T | L | 1-3 | 1-1 | — | Brodie [29] | 3307 |
| 34 | 13 | A | Scarborough | L | 1-4 | 0-0 | 21 | Brodie [64] | 1093 |
| 35 | 20 | H | Telford U | D | 1-1 | 0-1 | 21 | Lancaster [89] | 315 |
| 36 | 27 | A | Exeter C | L | 2-3 | 1-0 | 21 | McNiven [13], Durkin [89] | 3635 |
| 37 | 30 | H | Gravesend & N | L | 1-2 | 0-0 | — | McNiven [90] | 304 |
| 38 | Apr 3 | H | Burton Alb | L | 0-1 | 0-1 | 21 | | 339 |
| 39 | 9 | A | Halifax T | L | 1-2 | 0-2 | — | Daniel [74] | 1415 |
| 40 | 12 | H | Northwich Vic | W | 1-0 | 1-0 | 21 | McNiven [29] | 339 |
| 41 | 17 | H | Hereford U | L | 0-5 | 0-3 | 21 | | 836 |
| 42 | 24 | A | Barnet | L | 1-2 | 1-1 | 21 | McNiven (pen) [6] | 2988 |

**Final League Position: 21**

### GOALSCORERS

*League (46):* McNiven 25 (4 pens), Brodie 4, Maden 4, Daniel 3, Barrowclough 2, Peyton 2, Durkin 1, Lancaster 1, Redmond 1, Robinson 1, Roscoe 1, Shepherd 1.
*Trophy (1):* McNiven 1.

| Coburn 10 / Tench 1 + 2 | Harrison 26 + 2 | Hill 9 + 1 / Coyne 1 + 1 | Peyton 27 + 7 | Lancaster 32 + 1 | Durkin 37 | Monk 14 + 7 / Ellison 4 | Kielty 7 + 3 | McNiven 41 | Robinson 9 | Heald 3 | Courtney — + 5 / McGrath 2 + 1 | Hallows — + 7 | Pendlebury — + 1 | Shepherd 25 + 4 | Maden 23 + 4 | Redmond 22 + 4 | Milligan 1 | Hardy 1 / Smith 1 + 2 | Roscoe 30 + 3 | Forrest 6 / Brodie 5 | Downey — + 4 | Kelly 14 / Gunby 8 + 2 | Starbuck 5 + 3 | Tickle 2 + 2 / Holmes 11 + 1 | Barrowclough1 2 + 3 | Orr 1 + 6 / Salisbury 2 | Rezai 16 + 4 | Fitzpatrick 2 / Whitman 7 + 1 | Harris 1 + 2 | Ashmole — + 1 / Price 4 | Martin 16 | Whitehead — + 11 | Rickers 3 | Daniel 10 + 6 | McHale 5 + 2 | Alford 1 / Williams 3 | Lane 2 | Match No. |
|---|---|---|---|---|---|---|---|---|---|---|---|---|---|---|---|---|---|---|---|---|---|---|---|---|---|---|---|---|---|---|---|---|---|---|---|---|---|---|
| 1 | 2 | 3 | 4 | 5 | 6 | 7 | 8 | $9^{1}$ | $10^{2}$ | $11^{3}$ | 12 | 13 | 14 | | | | | | | | | | | | | | | | | | | | | | | | | 1 |
| 1 | $2^{1}$ | 3 | 4 | 5 | 6 | $7^{2}$ | 8 | 9 | 10 | $11^{3}$ | 14 | | | 13 | 12 | | | | | | | | | | | | | | | | | | | | | | | 2 |
| 1 | | 3 | 4 | 5 | 6 | 12 | 8 | $9^{2}$ | $10^{3}$ | $2^{1}$ | 14 | 13 | | 11 | 7 | | | | | | | | | | | | | | | | | | | | | | | 3 |
| 1 | | 3 | 4 | 5 | 6 | 7 | 8 | 9 | $10^{1}$ | | 13 | 12 | | 11 | | $2^{2}$ | | | | | | | | | | | | | | | | | | | | | | 4 |
| 1 | | 3 | 4 | 5 | 6 | 7 | 8 | $9^{1}$ | $10^{2}$ | | 12 | 13 | | | 11 | 2 | | | | | | | | | | | | | | | | | | | | | | 5 |
| 1 | | 3 | 4 | 5 | 6 | 7 | $8^{1}$ | 9 | $10^{2}$ | | | 13 | | 12 | 11 | 2 | | | | | | | | | | | | | | | | | | | | | | 6 |
| 1 | | 13 | 4 | 5 | 6 | 7 | | $9^{3}$ | 10 | | | 14 | | 2 | 12 | 3 | $8^{1}$ | $11^{2}$ | | | | | | | | | | | | | | | | | | | | 7 |
| 1 | | | 4 | 5■ | 6 | 12 | | $9^{3}$ | $10^{2}$ | | | 14 | | 2 | 3■ | 7 | | | $8^{1}$ | 11 | 13 | | | | | | | | | | | | | | | | | 8 |
| | | | 4 | 5 | 6 | 12 | | 9 | $10^{2}$ | | | | | 2■ | 14 | 3 | | | 7 | 8 | $13^{3}$ | 1 | $11^{1}$ | | | | | | | | | | | | | | | 9 |
| 1 | | 3 | 4 | 5 | 6 | 7 | | 9 | | | | | | | 2 | | | | 8 | 11 | | | 10 | | | | | | | | | | | | | | | 10 |
| 1 | 12 | 3 | 5 | | 6 | 10 | | 9 | | | | | | 2 | | 4 | | | $7^{1}$ | 8 | 13 | | $11^{2}$ | | | | | | | | | | | | | | | 11 |
| | $2^{1}$ | 3 | 4 | | 6 | 7 | | 9 | | | | | | | 8 | 12 | | | $5^{2}$ | 11 | | 1 | 10 | 13 | | | | | | | | | | | | | | 12 |
| | 2 | | $4^{1}$ | | 6 | 14 | | $9^{2}$ | | | | | | 5 | 3 | | | | 12 | 7 | 13 | 1 | $10^{3}$ | 8 | 11 | | | | | | | | | | | | | 13 |
| | 2 | | 12 | $5^{1}$ | 6 | 7 | | 9 | | | | | | 3 | 8 | 4 | | | 13 | | | 1 | | $11^{2}$ | 10 | | | | | | | | | | | | | 14 |
| | $2^{1}$ | | 4 | 5 | 6 | 7 | | 9 | | | | | | | 8 | 3 | | | 11 | | | 1 | 12 | | 10 | | | | | | | | | | | | | 15 |
| | 2 | | 4 | 5 | 3 | 7 | | 9 | | | | | | 12 | 8 | $6^{2}$ | | | 11 | | | 1 | | | $10^{1}$ | 13 | | | | | | | | | | | | 16 |
| | 2 | | 4 | 5 | 6 | $7^{1}$ | | 9 | | | | | | 3 | | | | | 11 | | | 1 | 12 | | | 10 | 8 | | | | | | | | | | | 17 |
| | 2 | | 4 | 5 | 6 | $7^{1}$ | | 9 | | | | | | 3 | 8 | | | | $11^{2}$ | | | 1 | | 13 | | 12 | 10 | | | | | | | | | | | 18 |
| | 3 | | $4^{2}$ | 5 | 6 | 13 | | 9 | | | | | | 2 | 7 | | | | 11 | | | 1 | | | $10^{1}$ | 12 | 8 | | | | | | | | | | | 19 |
| | 2 | | $4^{1}$ | 5 | 6 | 12 | | 9 | | | | | | 3 | 7 | | | | $10^{2}$ | | | 1 | | | 11 | 13 | 8 | | | | | | | | | | | 20 |
| | 2 | | 4 | 5 | 6 | 12 | 13 | 9 | | | | | | 3 | $7^{2}$ | 14 | | | $10^{1}$ | | | 1 | | | 11 | | $8^{3}$ | | | | | | | | | | | 21 |
| | $3^{1}$ | | 12 | 2 | 5 | | | 9 | | | | | | 7 | 8 | 6 | | | 11 | | | 1 | | | $10^{2}$ | 13 | | 4 | | | | | | | | | | 22 |
| | 3 | | 12 | 2 | $5^{1}$ | | 14 | 9 | | | | | | 7 | 8 | 6 | | | 11 | | | 1 | | | $10^{3}$ | | 13 | $4^{2}$ | | | | | | | | | | 23 |
| | | | $5^{2}$ | 2 | | | 7 | 9 | | | | | | 4 | 11 | $6^{1}$ | | | | | | 1 | | | 10 | 12 | 8 | | 3 | 13 | | | | | | | | 24 |
| | 2 | | 13 | 5 | | | | 9 | | | | | | 7 | $8^{2}$ | $6^{1}$ | | | 11 | | | | | | | | $4^{3}$ | | 14 | | 1 | 12 | 3 | 10 | | | | 25 |
| | $2^{1}$ | | 3 | 5 | | | 12 | 9 | | | | | | 4 | | $6^{2}$ | | | 11 | | | | | | $7^{3}$ | | | | 13 | | 1 | 14 | 8 | 10 | | | | 26 |
| | | | 4 | $5^{1}$ | | | | 9 | | | | | | 2 | | 6 | | | 11 | | | | | | 13 | | 8 | | | | 1 | 12 | 7 | | 3 | $10^{2}$ | | 27 |
| | $3^{1}$ | | 12 | 5 | 4 | | | 9 | | | | | | 2 | | 6 | | | 11 | | | | | | 13 | | $8^{2}$ | | | | 1 | 14 | | | $10^{3}$ | | 7 | 28 |
| | | | 11 | 5 | 6 | | | 9 | | | | | | $4^{1}$ | 7■ | | | 13 | 3 | | | | | | $10^{2}$ | | 8■ | | | | 1 | | | 12 | | | 2 | 29 |
| | 12 | | 7 | 5 | 4 | | | 9 | | | | | | $2^{1}$ | | 6 | | | 3 | 11 | | | | | | | 8 | | | | 1 | | | 13 | $10^{2}$ | | | 30 |
| | 2 | | $3^{2}$ | | 4 | | | | | | | | | 6 | | 5■ | | 13 | $10^{3}$ | 9 | | $7^{1}$ | | 12 | 14 | | | | | | 1 | | | 11 | 8 | | | 31 |
| | 2 | | | 12 | 5 | | | $9^{2}$ | | | | | | $4^{1}$ | | 6 | | | 7 | 11 | | 3 | | 8 | | | | | | | 1 | 14 | | $10^{3}$ | 13 | | | 32 |
| | 2 | | 7 | 5 | 6 | | | 9 | | | | | | | | | | | $11^{2}$ | 10 | | 3 | | 4 | | 1 | | | | | | 12 | | $8^{1}$ | 13 | | | 33 |
| | 2 | | | $5^{1}$ | 6 | | | 9 | | | | | | | 13 | 12 | | | 11 | 10 | | $3^{2}$ | | 4 | | 1 | 14 | | | | | | | $8^{3}$ | 7 | | | 34 |
| | 2 | | | 5 | 4 | | | 9 | | | | | | | $7^{1}$ | 6 | | | 11 | | | $8^{2}$ | | 3 | | | 13 | $10^{3}$ | | | 1 | 12 | | 14 | | | | 35 |
| | $2^{1}$ | | 12 | 5 | 6 | | | 9 | | | | | | | 7 | | | | 13 | | | $8^{3}$ | | 11 | | | | 10 | | $3^{2}$ | 1 | | | 14 | | 4 | | 36 |
| 14 | 2 | | 12 | | 4 | | | 9 | | | | | | | 7 | $6^{2}$ | | | | | | | | 11 | | | 8 | $10^{3}$ | | $3^{1}$ | 1 | | | 13 | | 5 | | 37 |
| $8^{3}$ | 2 | | | | 6 | | | 9 | | | | | | | $7^{2}$ | | | | 3 | | | 13 | | 11 | | | 14 | 10 | | | 1 | 12 | | $4^{1}$ | | 5 | | 38 |
| | $2^{1}$ | 5 | | | 6 | 4 | | 9 | | | $10^{3}$ | | | 13 | | | | | 3 | | | $7^{2}$ | | 11 | | | 8 | 12 | | | 1 | | | 14 | | | | 39 |
| | | | | | 6 | 5 | | 9 | | | $4^{3}$ | | | $2^{1}$ | | | | | 3 | | | 14 | 12 | 7 | | | 8 | 10 | | | 1 | 13 | | $11^{2}$ | | | | 40 |
| 13 | | | | | 6 | $5^{1}$ | | $9^{3}$ | | | | | | | | 12 | | | 3 | | | $4^{2}$ | | 7 | | | 8 | 10 | | 2 | 1 | 14 | | 11 | | | | 41 |
| | | 12■ | | 5 | | $6^{1}$ | | 9 | | | 13 | | | | | | | 2 | $3^{2}$ | | | | | 4 | | | 8 | 10 | | 7 | 1 | 14 | | $11^{3}$ | | | | 42 |

**FA Cup**
Fourth Qual Accrington S (a) 0-2

# MARGATE — Conference South

*Ground:* Hartsdown Park, Hartsdown Road, Margate, Kent CT9 5OZ.
*Tel:* (01843) 221 769.
*Year Formed:* 1896.
*Record Gate:* 14,500 (1973 v Tottenham Hotspur FA Cup Third Round).
*Nickname:* The Gate.
*Manager:* Chris Kinnear.
*Secretary:* Kenneth Tomlinson.
*Colours:* Royal blue shirts, royal blue shorts, white stockings.

## MARGATE 2003–04 LEAGUE RECORD

| Match No. | Date | Venue | Opponents | Result | | H/T Score | Lg. Pos. | Goalscorers | Attendance |
|---|---|---|---|---|---|---|---|---|---|
| 1 | Aug 9 | A | Shrewsbury T | D | 1-1 | 0-1 | — | Patmore [83] | 4015 |
| 2 | 12 | H | Aldershot T | L | 1-2 | 0-0 | — | McFlynn [85] | 1005 |
| 3 | 16 | H | Exeter C | L | 0-1 | 0-0 | 19 | | 890 |
| 4 | 23 | A | Tamworth | D | 1-1 | 1-0 | 19 | Robinson (og) [33] | 1056 |
| 5 | 25 | H | Stevenage Bor | L | 1-4 | 0-4 | 22 | Pullman [59] | 755 |
| 6 | 30 | A | Forest Green R | W | 2-1 | 1-1 | 19 | McFlynn [43], Stadhart [69] | 569 |
| 7 | Sept 6 | H | Chester C | L | 1-2 | 1-1 | 20 | Sodje [39] | 634 |
| 8 | 13 | A | Accrington S | L | 2-3 | 2-1 | 20 | Omoyinmi [27], Oates [31] | 1718 |
| 9 | 20 | A | Halifax T | W | 1-0 | 1-0 | 18 | Sodje [40] | 1452 |
| 10 | 23 | H | Barnet | L | 0-1 | 0-0 | — | | 780 |
| 11 | 27 | H | Northwich Vic | W | 3-1 | 1-0 | 16 | Baltazar [1], Omoyinmi [55], Annon [74] | 478 |
| 12 | Oct 4 | A | Telford U | D | 1-1 | 1-0 | 16 | Porter [25] | 1529 |
| 13 | 7 | A | Dagenham & R | L | 0-4 | 0-1 | — | | 1540 |
| 14 | 11 | H | Leigh RMI | W | 2-0 | 1-0 | 16 | Clarke [14], Saunders [68] | 429 |
| 15 | 18 | A | Scarborough | W | 1-0 | 0-0 | 13 | Omoyinmi [63] | 1263 |
| 16 | Nov 1 | A | Morecambe | D | 3-3 | 1-0 | 14 | Watson 3 [36, 66, 79] | 1499 |
| 17 | 11 | H | Woking | L | 1-2 | 1-1 | — | Sharpling (og) [22] | 550 |
| 18 | 15 | A | Hereford U | L | 1-2 | 0-0 | 17 | Porter [53] | 2320 |
| 19 | 22 | H | Burton Alb | L | 1-2 | 0-0 | 17 | Piper [78] | 564 |
| 20 | 29 | A | Chester C | L | 0-3 | 0-0 | 18 | | 1971 |
| 21 | Dec 6 | A | Farnborough T | D | 1-1 | 1-0 | 17 | Piper [25] | 595 |
| 22 | 14 | H | Shrewsbury T | L | 0-2 | 0-0 | — | | 635 |
| 23 | 20 | A | Aldershot T | W | 2-0 | 1-0 | 17 | Piper [45], Leberl [47] | 2529 |
| 24 | 28 | H | Gravesend & N | L | 1-3 | 1-1 | — | Watson [12] | 1030 |
| 25 | Jan 1 | A | Gravesend & N | L | 1-2 | 1-2 | 18 | Keister [30] | 1725 |
| 26 | 4 | H | Forest Green R | W | 2-0 | 0-0 | — | Saunders [48], Leberl [69] | 255 |
| 27 | 17 | A | Exeter C | D | 1-1 | 0-1 | 18 | Omoyinmi [90] | 3439 |
| 28 | 24 | A | Barnet | L | 1-3 | 0-2 | 18 | Omoyinmi [55] | 1591 |
| 29 | Feb 8 | H | Halifax T | W | 2-0 | 1-0 | 18 | Colley (og) [10], Sigere [62] | 391 |
| 30 | 14 | A | Northwich Vic | W | 3-0 | 1-0 | 16 | Watson [21], Sigere [70], Clarke [85] | 428 |
| 31 | 21 | H | Telford U | W | 1-0 | 1-0 | 15 | Baptiste [30] | 400 |
| 32 | 28 | A | Leigh RMI | L | 2-4 | 1-3 | 16 | Clarke [31], Watson [89] | 302 |
| 33 | Mar 6 | H | Dagenham & R | D | 3-3 | 3-1 | 15 | Baptiste [2], Clarke (pen) [7], Sigere [20] | 508 |
| 34 | 13 | A | Woking | D | 0-0 | 0-0 | 16 | | 2109 |
| 35 | 16 | H | Accrington S | W | 3-1 | 1-0 | — | Baptiste 2 [32, 47], Sigere [86] | 345 |
| 36 | 20 | H | Hereford U | L | 1-3 | 0-2 | 15 | Baptiste [89] | 604 |
| 37 | 27 | A | Burton Alb | W | 1-0 | 1-0 | 15 | Stadhart [19] | 1240 |
| 38 | Apr 3 | H | Farnborough T | W | 3-0 | 1-0 | 14 | Clarke [33], Stadhart [56], Saunders [90] | 386 |
| 39 | 10 | H | Tamworth | W | 3-2 | 2-0 | 14 | Price (og) [5], Stadhart [10], Porter [70] | 448 |
| 40 | 12 | A | Stevenage Bor | L | 1-2 | 1-0 | 15 | Porter [44] | 1548 |
| 41 | 18 | H | Morecambe | D | 1-1 | 0-1 | 15 | Saunders [56] | 414 |
| 42 | 24 | H | Scarborough | L | 0-2 | 0-1 | 16 | | 404 |

**Final League Position: 16**

### GOALSCORERS

*League (56):* Watson 6, Baptiste 5, Clarke 5 (1 pen), Omoyinmi 5, Porter 4, Saunders 4, Sigere 4, Stadhart 4, Piper 3, Leberl 2, McFlynn 2, Sodje 2, Annon 1, Baltazar 1, Keister 1, Oates 1, Patmore 1, Pullman 1, own goals 4.
*FA Cup (6):* Saunders 2, Clarke 1 (pen), Patmore 1, Porter 1, Watson 1.
*Trophy (6):* Clarke 2, Saunders 2, Keister 1, Sodje 1.

| Smith 42 | Oates 36 | Annon 38 + 3 | O'Connell 4 + 3 | Porter 35 + 3 | Leberl 39 | Keister 26 + 5 | Saunders 36 | Patmore 6 | Sigere 18 + 13 | McFlynn 10 + 2 | Clarke 27 + 8 | Beard 1 + 1 | Stadhart 19 + 16 | Sodje 28 + 1 | Pullman 2 + 9 | Abbott — + 6 | Zoricich 11 | Kwashi — + 3 | Omoyinmi 13 + 1 | Baltazar 1 + 1 | Edwards 27 + 5 | Hankin 3 | Watson 9 + 13 | Murphy 12 | Piper 7 + 1 | Mitten — + 1 | Baptiste 12 | Whitby — + 1 | Jjunju — + 2 | *Match No.* |
|---|---|---|---|---|---|---|---|---|---|---|---|---|---|---|---|---|---|---|---|---|---|---|---|---|---|---|---|---|---|---|
| 1 | 2 | 3 | $4^1$ | 5 | 6 | $7^2$ | 8 | 9 | 10 | $11^3$ | 12 | 13 | 14 | | | | | | | | | | | | | | | | | 1 |
| 1 | 2 | 3 | $4^1$ | 5■ | 6 | $7^2$ | 8 | 9 | 10 | 11 | 12 | | 13 | | | | | | | | | | | | | | | | | 2 |
| 1 | 2 | 3 | $4^1$ | 5 | 6 | $7^2$ | 8 | 9 | $10^3$ | 11 | 13 | | 14 | 12 | | | | | | | | | | | | | | | | 3 |
| 1 | 2 | 3 | 12 | 5 | 6 | 13 | 8 | 9 | | $11^2$ | $7^1$ | | $10^3$ | 4 | 14 | | | | | | | | | | | | | | | 4 |
| 1 | 2 | 3 | | $5^1$ | 6 | 12 | 8 | 9 | | 11 | 7 | | $10^2$ | 4 | 13 | | | | | | | | | | | | | | | 5 |
| 1 | 2 | 3 | 12 | | 6 | 4 | 8 | $9^2$ | | 11 | 5 | | $13^3$ | 7 | $10^1$ | 14 | | | | | | | | | | | | | | 6 |
| 1 | 2 | 3 | | | | 7 | 8 | | | | $6^1$ | 4 | 9 | 11 | $10^2$ | 12 | 5 | 13 | | | | | | | | | | | | 7 |
| 1 | 2 | 3 | | | 6 | 7 | 8■ | | | $11^1$ | | | $9^2$ | 4 | 13 | | 5 | 12 | 10 | | | | | | | | | | | 8 |
| 1 | 2 | 3 | | 5 | 6 | $7^1$ | 8 | | | | | | $10^2$ | 11 | | | 4 | | 9 | 12 | 13 | | | | | | | | | 9 |
| 1 | $2^1$ | $3^2$ | | 5 | 11 | $7^3$ | 8 | | | | 14 | | 10 | 4 | | | 6 | 13 | 9 | | 12 | | | | | | | | | 10 |
| 1 | 2 | 3 | | 5 | 7 | | | | | | 8 | | $10^1$ | 4 | 12 | | 6 | | 9 | $11^2$ | 13 | | | | | | | | | 11 |
| 1 | 2 | $3^1$ | | 5 | 8 | | | | | | 7 | | 13 | 6 | | | 4 | | 9 | | 12 | 11 | $10^2$ | | | | | | | 12 |
| 1 | 2 | $3^2$ | | 5 | 8 | | | | 14 | | 7 | | 13 | $6^1$ | | | 4 | | 9 | | 12 | 11■ | $10^3$ | | | | | | | 13 |
| 1 | 2 | 12 | | 5 | 8 | | 7 | | $9^3$ | | 11 | | $10^2$ | 3 | | | $4^1$ | | 14 | | | 6 | 13 | | | | | | | 14 |
| 1 | 2 | 3 | | 5 | 8 | | 11 | | $10^1$ | 12 | 7 | | | 6 | | | 4 | | 9 | | | | | | | | | | | 15 |
| 1 | | 3 | 12 | $5^1$ | 8 | | 7 | | $10^2$ | 11 | | | 14 | 2 | | | 4 | | 9 | | 6 | | $13^3$ | | | | | | | 16 |
| 1 | | 3 | | 5 | 8 | 12 | 7 | | $10^2$ | $11^1$ | | | | 2 | | | 4 | | 9 | | 6 | | 13 | | | | | | | 17 |
| 1 | | 3 | | 5 | | 8 | 7 | | | 11 | 12 | | $10^2$ | 2■ | 13 | | | | 9 | | 4 | | | $6^1$ | | | | | | 18 |
| 1 | | $3^1$ | | 5 | 8 | $9^2$ | 7 | | | | 13 | | 10 | 2 | 12 | | | | | | 6 | | | 4 | 11 | | | | | 19 |
| $1^G$ | | 3 | 4 | 5 | 8 | $9^1$ | | | $10^2$ | | 7 | | 13 | | | | | | | | 2 | | 12 | 6 | 11 | 15 | | | | 20 |
| 1 | $2^1$ | 12 | | 5 | 8 | | 11 | | 13 | 14 | | | $10^3$ | 3 | | | | | | | 6 | | $9^2$ | 4 | 7 | | | | | 21 |
| 1 | 2 | 12 | | $5^1$ | 6 | $9^3$ | 7 | | 14 | | | | 10■ | 3 | | 13 | | | | | 8 | | | 4 | $11^2$ | | | | | 22 |
| 1 | 2 | 3 | | 5 | 8 | $10^1$ | 7 | | 13 | | 12 | | | 4 | | | | | | | 6 | | $9^2$ | | 11 | | | | | 23 |
| 1 | 4 | $3^1$ | | 5 | 8 | $10^3$ | 7 | | 13 | | 14 | | 12 | 2■ | | | | | | | 6 | | $9^2$ | | 11 | | | | | 24 |
| 1 | 2 | 3 | | 5 | 8 | $10^1$ | 7 | | 12 | | 11 | | | 4 | 13 | | | | | | 6 | | $9^2$ | | | | | | | 25 |
| 1 | 2 | | | 5 | 6 | 10 | 8 | | 13 | | 7 | | | 3 | 12 | | | | | | 4 | | $9^2$ | | $11^1$ | | | | | 26 |
| 1 | 2 | $3^1$ | | 5 | 8 | $10^3$ | 7 | | 13 | | $11^2$ | | 12 | | | | | | 9 | | 6 | | 14 | 4 | | | | | | 27 |
| 1 | | 3 | | 5 | 8 | 11 | 7 | | 13 | | $2^1$ | | $10^2$ | | | | | | 9 | | 6 | | 12 | 4 | | | | | | 28 |
| 1 | 2 | 3 | | 14 | 6 | | 7 | | $10^2$ | | 8 | | 12 | 4 | | | | | | | 5 | | $9^1$ | $11^3$ | 13 | | | | | 29 |
| 1 | 2 | $3^1$ | | 12 | 8 | | 7 | | 10 | | 11 | | 14 | 4 | | | | | $9^2$ | | 5 | | $13^3$ | 6 | | | | | | 30 |
| 1 | 2 | 3 | | 12 | 8 | 13 | 7 | | $10^3$ | | $11^1$ | | 14 | 4■ | | | | | | | 5 | | | 6 | | | $9^2$ | | | 31 |
| 1 | 2 | $3^1$ | | 5 | 8 | 12 | 7 | | $10^2$ | | 11 | | | | | | | | | | 6 | | 13 | 4 | | | 9 | | | 32 |
| 1 | 2 | 3 | | 5 | 6 | 7■ | | | $10^2$ | | 11 | | 12 | | | | | | | | 4 | | $9^1$ | | | | 8 | 13 | | 33 |
| 1 | 2 | 3 | | 5 | 8 | 7 | | | $10^2$ | | 11 | | 12 | | | | | | | | 4 | | 13 | 6 | | | $9^1$ | | | 34 |
| 1 | 2 | 3 | | 5 | 6■ | 7 | 8 | | $10^1$ | | 11 | | 12 | | | | | | | | 4 | | 13 | | | | $9^2$ | | | 35 |
| 1 | 2 | 3 | | 5 | 8 | | 7 | | $10^1$ | | 11 | | | 4 | | | | | | | 6 | | | | | | 9 | | 12 | 36 |
| 1 | 2 | 3 | | 5 | 8 | | 7 | | $10^2$ | | | | $9^1$ | 4■ | | 12 | | | | | 6 | | $13^3$ | | | | 11 | | 14 | 37 |
| 1 | 2 | 3 | | 5 | | $7^1$ | 8 | | 13 | | 11 | | $10^2$ | 4 | | 12 | | | | | 6 | | | | | | 9 | | | 38 |
| 1 | 2 | 3 | | 5 | 6 | $7^1$ | 8 | | 13 | | 11 | | $10^2$ | | | 12 | | | | | 4 | | | | | | 9 | | | 39 |
| 1 | 2 | $3^1$ | | 5 | 6 | 7 | 8 | | 12 | | 11 | | $10^2$ | | | | | | | | 4 | | 13 | | | | 9 | | | 40 |
| 1 | 2 | 3 | | | 6 | 4 | 7 | | $8^1$ | | 11 | | 10 | | | | | | | | 5 | | 12 | | | | 9 | | | 41 |
| 1 | 2 | 3 | | 5 | 6 | $7^1$ | 8 | | 13 | | 11 | | $10^2$ | | 12 | | | | | | 4 | | | | | | 9 | | | 42 |

**FA Cup**

| | | | |
|---|---|---|---|
| Fourth Qual | Grays Ath | (a) | 3-3 |
| | | (h) | 3-3 |

# MORECAMBE Conference

*Ground:* Christie Park, Lancaster Road, Morecambe, Lancashire LA4 5TJ.
*Tel:* (01524) 411 797.
*Year Formed:* 1920.
*Record Gate:* 9,326 (1962 v Weymouth FA Cup Third Round).
*Nickname:* The Shrimps.
*Manager:* Jim Harvey.
*Secretary:* Neil Marsdin.
*Colours:* Red shirts, white shorts, black stockings.

## MORECAMBE 2003–04 LEAGUE RECORD

| *Match No.* | *Date* | | *Venue* | *Opponents* | *Result* | | *H/T Score* | *Lg. Pos.* | *Goalscorers* | *Attendance* |
|---|---|---|---|---|---|---|---|---|---|---|
| 1 | Aug | 9 | H | Woking | W | 2-1 | 1-1 | — | Rigoglioso [8], Bentley [83] | 1772 |
| 2 | | 12 | A | Halifax T | L | 0-1 | 0-1 | — | | 2160 |
| 3 | | 16 | A | Hereford U | L | 0-3 | 0-2 | 17 | | 2941 |
| 4 | | 23 | H | Dagenham & R | W | 3-2 | 2-1 | 11 | Carlton 2 [19, 44], Lane [90] | 1477 |
| 5 | | 25 | A | Telford U | L | 1-2 | 0-0 | 15 | Collins [50] | 2613 |
| 6 | | 30 | H | Burton Alb | W | 2-1 | 0-0 | 9 | Howell [56], Drummond [83] | 1789 |
| 7 | Sept | 6 | H | Aldershot T | W | 2-0 | 1-0 | 6 | Stringfellow [9], Drummond (pen) [78] | 1948 |
| 8 | | 13 | A | Tamworth | W | 3-2 | 1-1 | 6 | Drummond 2 [33, 59], Carlton [65] | 1247 |
| 9 | | 20 | A | Northwich Vic | D | 1-1 | 0-0 | 7 | Curtis [61] | 853 |
| 10 | | 23 | H | Leigh RMI | W | 1-0 | 0-0 | — | Rigoglioso (pen) [88] | 1393 |
| 11 | | 27 | H | Farnborough T | W | 3-2 | 1-2 | 5 | Rigoglioso (pen) [45], Curtis [55], Thompson [87] | 1636 |
| 12 | Oct | 4 | A | Barnet | L | 1-2 | 0-2 | 6 | Thompson [61] | 1776 |
| 13 | | 7 | A | Scarborough | L | 0-1 | 0-0 | — | | 1219 |
| 14 | | 11 | H | Gravesend & N | D | 2-2 | 0-0 | 7 | Bentley [59], Walmsley [83] | 1539 |
| 15 | | 18 | A | Shrewsbury T | L | 0-2 | 0-1 | 8 | | 3404 |
| 16 | Nov | 1 | H | Margate | D | 3-3 | 0-1 | 8 | Carlton 2 [67, 85], Rogan [89] | 1499 |
| 17 | | 11 | H | Chester C | L | 0-1 | 0-0 | — | | 1959 |
| 18 | | 15 | A | Exeter C | L | 0-4 | 0-3 | 12 | | 2900 |
| 19 | | 22 | H | Stevenage Bor | W | 2-1 | 1-1 | 12 | McFlynn [41], Thompson [50] | 1354 |
| 20 | | 25 | A | Forest Green R | W | 2-1 | 1-0 | — | Thompson [39], Carlton [77] | 605 |
| 21 | | 29 | A | Aldershot T | D | 2-2 | 0-1 | 9 | Carlton [71], Thompson [90] | 2584 |
| 22 | Dec | 6 | H | Tamworth | W | 4-0 | 2-0 | 7 | Bentley [27], Carlton [39], Howell [66], Sugden [90] | 1449 |
| 23 | | 13 | A | Woking | L | 1-4 | 0-2 | 10 | Rogan [81] | 1588 |
| 24 | | 20 | H | Halifax T | W | 2-0 | 1-0 | 9 | McFlynn [12], Rogan [85] | 1603 |
| 25 | | 26 | A | Accrington S | L | 0-1 | 0-1 | 9 | | 2954 |
| 26 | Jan | 1 | H | Accrington S | W | 1-0 | 0-0 | 8 | Halford (og) [89] | 3084 |
| 27 | | 3 | A | Burton Alb | W | 1-0 | 0-0 | 7 | Carlton [68] | 1478 |
| 28 | | 17 | H | Hereford U | D | 2-2 | 1-1 | 7 | Carlton [33], Sugden [90] | 2003 |
| 29 | | 24 | A | Leigh RMI | L | 1-3 | 0-1 | 9 | Sugden [90] | 605 |
| 30 | Feb | 7 | H | Northwich Vic | W | 3-0 | 3-0 | 7 | Carlton 2 (1 pen) [29, 42 (p)], Thompson [37] | 1597 |
| 31 | | 14 | A | Farnborough T | W | 4-2 | 3-2 | 5 | McFlynn [7], Carlton [19], Howell [34], Sugden [82] | 704 |
| 32 | | 21 | H | Barnet | L | 1-3 | 0-3 | 7 | Carlton [74] | 2014 |
| 33 | | 28 | A | Gravesend & N | L | 0-6 | 0-2 | 7 | | 1061 |
| 34 | Mar | 6 | H | Scarborough | W | 2-1 | 1-0 | 6 | Carlton [44], Murphy [90] | 1623 |
| 35 | | 13 | A | Chester C | L | 1-2 | 0-0 | 8 | Drummond [90] | 3512 |
| 36 | | 20 | H | Exeter C | L | 0-3 | 0-1 | 9 | | 1877 |
| 37 | | 27 | A | Stevenage Bor | W | 1-0 | 0-0 | 7 | Walmsley [50] | 1687 |
| 38 | Apr | 3 | H | Forest Green R | W | 4-0 | 2-0 | 7 | Curtis 3 [20, 79, 90], Sugden [35] | 1259 |
| 39 | | 10 | A | Dagenham & R | W | 3-1 | 2-0 | 7 | Curtis (pen) [31], Carlton [41], Sugden [85] | 1122 |
| 40 | | 12 | H | Telford U | W | 1-0 | 0-0 | 7 | Bentley [69] | 1642 |
| 41 | | 18 | A | Margate | D | 1-1 | 1-0 | 7 | Carlton [10] | 414 |
| 42 | | 24 | H | Shrewsbury T | D | 3-3 | 1-2 | 7 | Curtis 2 (1 pen) [11 (p), 81], Rogan [48] | 2876 |

**Final League Position: 7**

## GOALSCORERS

*League (66):* Carlton 17 (1 pen), Curtis 8 (2 pens), Sugden 6, Thompson 6, Drummond 5 (1 pen), Bentley 4, Rogan 4, Howell 3, McFlynn 3, Rigoglioso 3 (2 pens), Walmsley 2, Collins 1, Lane 1, Murphy 1, Stringfellow 1, own goal 1.
*FA Cup (2):* Collins 1, Sugden 1.
*LDV Vans Trophy (1):* own goal 1.

| Mawson 39 + 1 | Lane 15 + 1 | Perkins 39 | Drummond 31 | Swan 14 + 5 | Bentley 36 | Thompson 29 + 6 | Stringfellow 26 + 3 | Rigoglioso 13 | Curtis 18 + 5 | Howell 24 + 6 | Black — + 4 | Carlton 28 + 10 | McKearney 26 + 8 | Collins 10 + 2 | Hunter 8 + 7 | Murphy 22 + 5 | Sugden 13 + 20 | Walmsley 27 | Rogan 3 + 21 | Dodgson — + 3 | Garnett 12 | McFlynn 16 + 3 | Blackburn 4 + 1 | Dunbavin 3 | Osborne 6 + 2 | *Match No.* |
|---|---|---|---|---|---|---|---|---|---|---|---|---|---|---|---|---|---|---|---|---|---|---|---|---|---|---|
| 1 | 2 | 3 | 4 | 5 | 6 | 7[1] | 8 | 9 | 10[2] | 11 | 12 | 13 | | | | | | | | | | | | | | 1 |
| 1 | 2[1] | 3 | 4 | 5 | 6 | 7 | 8 | 9[2] | 10[3] | 11 | 13 | 14 | 12 | | | | | | | | | | | | | 2 |
| 1 | 2 | 3 | 4 | 5[1] | 6 | 7[2] | 8 | 9 | 13 | 10 | 14 | | 12 | 11[3] | | | | | | | | | | | | 3 |
| 1 | 2 | 3 | 4 | 5 | | 7[1] | 8 | 9 | 13 | 11[2] | | 10 | 6 | | 12 | | | | | | | | | | | 4 |
| 1 | 2 | 3 | 4 | 5 | 6 | 7[1] | 12 | 9■ | | 11[3] | | 10 | 14 | 8[2] | | 13 | | | | | | | | | | 5 |
| 1 | 2 | 3 | 4 | 5[1] | 6 | 7[2] | 8 | 9[3] | | 11 | 13 | 10 | 12 | 14 | | | | | | | | | | | | 6 |
| 1 | 2 | 3 | 4 | 5[1] | 6 | | 8[2] | 9 | 13 | | | 10[3] | 7 | 11 | | 12 | 14 | | | | | | | | | 7 |
| 1 | 2 | 3[1] | 4 | | 6 | 14 | 8 | | 10[2] | 12 | | 9[3] | 5 | 7 | | 11 | 13 | | | | | | | | | 8 |
| 1 | 2 | 3 | 4 | | 6 | 12 | 8 | | 10[2] | | | 9[1] | 5 | 7 | | 11 | 13 | | | | | | | | | 9 |
| 1 | 2 | 3 | 4 | | 6 | 7 | 13 | 9[1] | 10 | | | 14 | 12 | 8[2] | | 5 | 11[3] | | | | | | | | | 10 |
| 1 | | 3 | 4 | | 6 | 7 | 8[1] | 9 | 10 | 13 | | 12 | | | | 5 | 11[2] | 2 | | | | | | | | 11 |
| 1 | 2 | 3 | 4[1] | | 6 | 7 | | 9 | 10■ | 12[2] | | 8[3] | 11 | | | 5 | 14 | | 13 | | | | | | | 12 |
| 1 | 2 | 3 | | 5[1] | 6 | | | 9 | 10 | 7 | | 13 | 11 | | | 4 | 8[2] | | 12 | | | | | | | 13 |
| 1 | 12 | 3 | | 5 | 6 | 7[2] | | 9 | 10 | 11[3] | | 13 | 2[1] | 4 | | | | 8 | 14 | | | | | | | 14 |
| 1 | 2 | | | 5 | 6 | 7 | 8 | 9[1] | | 11[2] | | 12 | 3 | 4 | | | 10 | | | 13 | | | | | | 15 |
| 1 | 2 | 3 | | 5 | 6 | 7 | 8 | | 10[1] | | | 4 | | 11 | 13 | | 9[2] | | 12 | | | | | | | 16 |
| 1 | | 3 | | 5[1] | 6 | 7 | 8 | | 10[2] | | | 9[3] | | 11 | 12 | 14 | | 2 | 13 | | 4 | | | | | 17 |
| 1 | 2 | 3 | | 5[2] | 6 | 7 | 8 | | 10[3] | 14 | | | 12 | | 13 | | 9 | 4[1] | | | 11 | | | | | 18 |
| 1 | | 3 | | | 6 | 7 | 8 | | | 11 | | 9[2] | 2 | | | | 13 | 4 | 12 | | 5 | 10[1] | | | | 19 |
| 1 | | 3 | | 12 | 6 | 10 | 8 | | | 7 | | 9[3] | 2 | | | | 13 | 4 | 14 | | 5[1] | 11[2] | | | | 20 |
| 1 | | 3 | | 12 | 6 | 7 | 8 | | | 11 | | 9[3] | 2[2] | | | 5[1] | 13 | 4 | 14 | | | 10 | | | | 21 |
| 1 | | 3 | | | 6 | 7 | 8 | | | 11 | | 9[3] | 2[1] | 12 | | 5 | 13 | 4 | 14 | | | 10[2] | | | | 22 |
| 1 | | 3 | | 12 | 6[1] | 7 | 8 | | | 11 | | 9[2] | 2 | | | 5 | 14 | 4 | 13 | | | 10[3] | | | | 23 |
| 1 | | 3 | 4 | | | 7[1] | 8 | | | 11 | | 9[3] | 2 | | | 5 | 14 | 6 | 13 | 12 | | 10[2] | | | | 24 |
| 1 | | 3 | 4 | | | 7 | 8 | | | 11[1] | | 9[3] | 2 | | 12 | 5 | 13■ | 6 | 14 | | | 10[2] | | | | 25 |
| 1 | | 3[1] | 4 | | | 7 | 12 | | | 11 | | 14 | 2 | | | 5 | 9[3] | 8 | 13 | | 6 | 10[2] | | | | 26 |
| 1 | | | 4 | 12 | | 7 | 8 | | | 11 | | 9[2] | 2 | | | 5 | 14 | 3 | 10[3] | | 6[1] | 13 | | | | 27 |
| 1 | | 3 | 4 | | 6 | 7 | 8 | | | 11[1] | | 9[3] | | | | | 14 | 2 | 12 | 13 | 5 | 10[2] | | | | 28 |
| 1 | | 3 | 4 | | 6 | | 8 | | | 13 | | | 2[1] | | | 7[2] | 9 | 11 | 10 | | 5 | 12 | | | | 29 |
| 1 | | 3 | 4 | | 6 | 7 | 8 | | | 11[1] | | 9 | 2 | | 12 | | | 5 | 13 | | | 10[2] | | | | 30 |
| 1 | | 3 | 4 | | 6 | 7 | 8 | | | 11 | | 9[2] | 12 | | | 13 | 14 | 2 | | | 5[1] | 10[3] | | | | 31 |
| 1 | | 3 | 4 | | 6 | 7 | 8 | | 13 | 11[2] | | 9 | 2[1] | | | | 14 | 5 | | | | 10[3] | 12 | | | 32 |
| 1 | | 3 | 4 | 12 | 6[1] | 7[2] | | | | 11[3] | | 9 | 13 | | | | 14 | 2 | | | 5 | 10 | 8 | | | 33 |
| | | 3 | 4 | | 6 | | | | | 13■ | | 9[3] | 2[1] | | 10 | 7 | 12 | 5 | 11[2] | | | | 8 | 1 | 14 | 34 |
| | | 3 | 4 | | 6 | | | | 13 | 11[1] | | 9[3] | 2 | | 12 | 8 | 10[2] | 5 | 14 | | | | 7 | 1 | | 35 |
| 15 | | 3[2] | 8 | | 6■ | | | | | | | 9 | 2 | | 7 | 4 | 10 | | 12 | | 5[1] | | 11 | 1[G] | 13 | 36 |
| 1 | | 3 | 4 | | 6 | | | | 10 | | | 13 | 2 | | 11 | 12 | 9[2] | 5 | | | 8[1] | | | | 7 | 37 |
| 1 | | 3 | 4 | 5 | | 12 | | | 10 | | | 13 | 2[1] | | 11 | 6 | 9[3] | 7 | | | | 14 | | | 8[2] | 38 |
| 1 | | 3 | 4 | | 6 | 14 | | | 7 | | | 9[2] | | | 11[1] | 5 | 13 | 2 | 12 | | | 10[3] | | | 8 | 39 |
| 1 | | 3 | 4 | | 6 | 13 | | | 10 | | | 9[3] | | | 7 | 5 | 12 | 2 | 14 | | | 11[2] | | | 8[1] | 40 |
| 1 | | 3 | 4 | | 6 | 12 | | | 10 | | | 9[3] | | | 8[2] | 5 | 14 | 2 | 13 | | | 11[1] | | | 7 | 41 |
| 1 | | | 4 | | 6 | 7 | | | 10 | | | | 3 | | 8 | 5 | 9[1] | 2 | 12 | | | | | | 11 | 42 |

**LDV Vans Trophy**
First Round — Wrexham — (a) — 1-4

**FA Cup**
Fourth Qual — Shrewsbury T — (h) — 2-4

# NORTHWICH VICTORIA Conference

*Ground:* Witton Albion FC, Wincham Park, Chapel Street, Northwich, Cheshire.
*Tel:* (01606) 43008.
*Year Formed:* 1874.
*Record Gate:* 12,000 (1977 v Watford FA Cup Fourth Round).
*Nickname:* The Vics.
*Manager:* Steve Burr.
*Secretary:* Derek Nuttall.
*Colours:* Green shirts with white trim, white shorts, black stockings.

## NORTHWICH VICTORIA 2003–04 LEAGUE RECORD

| Match No. | Date | Venue | Opponents | Result | | H/T Score | Lg. Pos. | Goalscorers | Attendance |
|---|---|---|---|---|---|---|---|---|---|
| 1 | Aug 9 | A | Forest Green R | D | 0-0 | 0-0 | — | | 628 |
| 2 | 12 | H | Scarborough | D | 1-1 | 0-1 | — | Ward [89] | 854 |
| 3 | 16 | H | Tamworth | W | 1-0 | 1-0 | 8 | Devlin [10] | 712 |
| 4 | 23 | A | Stevenage Bor | L | 0-1 | 0-0 | 12 | | 1869 |
| 5 | 25 | H | Leigh RMI | L | 0-1 | 0-1 | 16 | | 582 |
| 6 | 30 | A | Aldershot T | L | 3-4 | 0-3 | 17 | Ward [80], Devlin [85], Garvey [87] | 2801 |
| 7 | Sept 6 | A | Halifax T | L | 3-5 | 0-2 | 19 | Thompson [64], Garvey [66], Ward [90] | 1440 |
| 8 | 13 | H | Dagenham & R | L | 0-1 | 0-0 | 19 | | 575 |
| 9 | 20 | H | Morecambe | D | 1-1 | 0-0 | 20 | Ross [86] | 853 |
| 10 | 23 | A | Chester C | L | 0-4 | 0-1 | — | | 2817 |
| 11 | 27 | A | Margate | L | 1-3 | 0-1 | 21 | Garvey [90] | 478 |
| 12 | Oct 4 | H | Accrington S | D | 3-3 | 3-3 | 21 | Allan 2 [8, 36], Ward [11] | 865 |
| 13 | 7 | H | Hereford U | L | 1-5 | 0-1 | — | Norris [78] | 1008 |
| 14 | 11 | A | Exeter C | L | 0-2 | 0-0 | 21 | | 3090 |
| 15 | 18 | H | Gravesend & N | D | 0-0 | 0-0 | 21 | | 542 |
| 16 | Nov 1 | A | Barnet | L | 0-1 | 0-1 | 21 | | 1852 |
| 17 | 15 | A | Farnborough T | L | 0-2 | 0-1 | 22 | | 626 |
| 18 | 22 | H | Woking | L | 1-4 | 0-2 | 22 | Wright [47] | 627 |
| 19 | 25 | A | Telford U | W | 1-0 | 1-0 | — | Foran [11] | 1560 |
| 20 | 29 | H | Halifax T | L | 0-1 | 0-0 | 21 | | 757 |
| 21 | Dec 2 | H | Burton Alb | L | 1-2 | 0-1 | — | Potts [56] | 686 |
| 22 | 6 | A | Dagenham & R | L | 0-2 | 0-0 | 22 | | 1163 |
| 23 | 13 | H | Forest Green R | L | 0-4 | 0-1 | 22 | | 474 |
| 24 | 20 | A | Scarborough | L | 0-1 | 0-1 | 22 | | 1265 |
| 25 | 26 | A | Shrewsbury T | L | 1-3 | 0-1 | 22 | Wright [77] | 5059 |
| 26 | Jan 1 | H | Shrewsbury T | L | 0-2 | 0-1 | 22 | | 3268 |
| 27 | 3 | H | Aldershot T | D | 1-1 | 1-1 | 22 | Thompson [29] | 752 |
| 28 | 17 | A | Tamworth | L | 1-2 | 1-1 | 22 | Robinson (og) [4] | 1158 |
| 29 | 24 | H | Chester C | L | 0-4 | 0-2 | 22 | | 2141 |
| 30 | Feb 7 | A | Morecambe | L | 0-3 | 0-3 | 22 | | 1597 |
| 31 | 14 | H | Margate | L | 0-3 | 0-1 | 22 | | 428 |
| 32 | 21 | A | Accrington S | D | 2-2 | 1-0 | 22 | Thompson [33], Garvey [77] | 1422 |
| 33 | Mar 6 | A | Hereford U | L | 0-1 | 0-0 | 22 | | 3064 |
| 34 | 13 | A | Burton Alb | W | 1-0 | 1-0 | 22 | Foran [45] | 1416 |
| 35 | 16 | H | Exeter C | D | 1-1 | 0-0 | — | Nicholas [80] | 547 |
| 36 | 20 | H | Farnborough T | D | 1-1 | 1-1 | 22 | Ward [44] | 510 |
| 37 | 27 | A | Woking | L | 0-3 | 0-1 | 22 | | 1857 |
| 38 | Apr 10 | H | Stevenage Bor | L | 1-2 | 1-1 | 22 | Devlin [13] | 487 |
| 39 | 12 | A | Leigh RMI | L | 0-1 | 0-1 | 22 | | 339 |
| 40 | 17 | H | Barnet | D | 1-1 | 1-0 | 22 | Garvey (pen) [42] | 728 |
| 41 | 21 | H | Telford U | W | 1-0 | 1-0 | — | Wright [32] | 479 |
| 42 | 24 | A | Gravesend & N | D | 2-2 | 1-1 | 22 | Wright [15], Ward [53] | 1436 |

**Final League Position: 22**

### GOALSCORERS

*League (30):* Ward 6, Garvey 5 (1 pen), Wright 4, Devlin 3, Thompson 3, Allan 2, Foran 2, Nicholas 1, Norris 1, Potts 1, Ross 1, own goal 1.
*FA Cup (2):* Thompson 2.

| Woods 23 | Royle 30 + 3 | Woodyatt 19 + 7 | Devlin 35 | Foran 36 + 3 | Brazier 34 + 2 | Garvey 30 + 5 | Blackburn 25 + 3 | Thompson 18 + 9 | Allan 15 + 1 | Owen 8 + 5 / Briscoe 1 + 5 | Brough 3 + 2 | Ward 15 + 10 | Came 13 + 2 | Charnock 21 + 6 | Butterworth 1 + 4 | Barnard 8 | Norris 10 + 17 | Black 2 + 4 / Tolley 5 | Ross 3 | Connett 10 | Ralph 9 | McGuire 9 + 3 | Murray 3 | McAuley — + 1 | Bennett — + 1 | Wright 20 + 2 | Hankin 1 | Young 6 + 3 | Brown 6 | Potts 10 + 1 | McCoy — + 2 | Teale 5 + 1 | Willis 4 | Nicholas 12 | Mitchell 3 | Sawtell 2 | Rioch 7 | *Match No.* |
|---|---|---|---|---|---|---|---|---|---|---|---|---|---|---|---|---|---|---|---|---|---|---|---|---|---|---|---|---|---|---|---|---|---|---|---|---|---|---|
| 1 | 2 | $3^{1}$ | 4 | 5 | 6 | 7 | 8 | 9 | $10^{2}$ | 11 | 12 | 13 | | | | | | | | | | | | | | | | | | | | | | | | | | 1 |
| 1 | 2 | $3^{1}$ | 4 | 5 | 6 | 7 | 8 | 9 | 10 | $11^{2}$ | 13 | 12 | | | | | | | | | | | | | | | | | | | | | | | | | | 2 |
| 1 | 2 | 3 | 4 | 5 | 6 | $7^{1}$ | 8 | 9 | 13 | 11 | | $10^{2}$ | 12 | | | | | | | | | | | | | | | | | | | | | | | | | 3 |
| 1 | 2 | | 4 | 5 | 6 | $7^{1}$ | 8 | 9 | 10 | $11^{2}$ | $3^{3}$ | 12 | | 14 | 13 | | | | | | | | | | | | | | | | | | | | | | | 4 |
| 1 | 2 | | 4 | 5 | $6^{3}$ | 7 | 8 | $9^{2}$ | 10 | | $3^{1}$ | 12 | 14 | 11 | 13 | | | | | | | | | | | | | | | | | | | | | | | 5 |
| 1 | 2 | 3 | 4 | 5 | 6 | 7 | $8^{2}$ | 13 | 10 | | $11^{1}$ | 14 | | 12 | $9^{3}$ | | | | | | | | | | | | | | | | | | | | | | | 6 |
| 1 | 2 | | 4 | 5 | 6 | $7^{1}$ | $8^{2}$ | 9 | 10 | 13 | | 14 | | | | 3 | 12 | $11^{3}$ | | | | | | | | | | | | | | | | | | | | 7 |
| 1 | 2 | | $4^{1}$ | 5 | 6 | 12 | 14 | 9 | $10^{3}$ | 11 | | $8^{2}$ | | | 13 | 3 | 7 | | | | | | | | | | | | | | | | | | | | | 8 |
| 1 | 2 | | 4 | 5 | 6 | 7 | 13 | $9^{3}$ | $10^{2}$ | $8^{1}$ | | 14 | | | | 3 | 12 | | 11 | | | | | | | | | | | | | | | | | | | 9 |
| 1 | 2 | | 4 | | 6 | 7 | $8^{1}$ | $9^{3}$ | $10^{2}$ | 13 | | 14 | | 5 | | 3 | 12 | | 11 | | | | | | | | | | | | | | | | | | | 10 |
| 1 | 2 | | 4 | 5 | 6 | 7 | 12 | 13 | $10^{3}$ | 14 | | | | 8 | | 3 | $11^{1}$ | | $9^{2}$ | | | | | | | | | | | | | | | | | | | 11 |
| | $2^{1}$ | 12 | 4 | 5 | 6 | 7 | 8 | 13 | 10 | 11 | | $9^{2}$ | | | | 3 | | | | 1 | | | | | | | | | | | | | | | | | | 12 |
| 1 | | 3 | $4^{2}$ | 5 | 6 | 7 | 8 | 14 | 10 | $11^{1}$ | | $9^{3}$ | | 2 | | | 12 | 13 | | | | | | | | | | | | | | | | | | | | 13 |
| 1 | 2■ | 3 | 4 | $5^{1}$ | 6 | 13 | 8 | $9^{3}$ | 10 | 14 | | | | 7 | | | $11^{2}$ | 12 | | | | | | | | | | | | | | | | | | | | 14 |
| | 2 | 3 | $4^{1}$ | | 6 | $7^{2}$ | 8 | 14 | $10^{3}$ | 12 | | 9 | | 5 | | 11 | | 13 | | | 1 | | | | | | | | | | | | | | | | | 15 |
| | | 3 | $11^{2}$ | 5 | | | $8^{3}$ | 9 | 10 | | | | | 4 | | 2 | 13 | $6^{1}$ | | | 1 | 12 | 7 | 14 | | | | | | | | | | | | | | 16 |
| | 2 | $3^{1}$ | | 5 | 6 | $7^{2}$ | 8 | 9 | | | | | | 4 | 12 | | | | | | 1 | | 11 | | 13 | 10 | | | | | | | | | | | | 17 |
| | | 12 | | 5 | 6 | $7^{2}$ | 8 | | | | | | | 4 | | | | 13 | | | 1 | 3 | 11 | | | 10 | $2^{1}$ | 9 | | | | | | | | | | 18 |
| | 2 | | 4 | 5 | 6 | | 8 | | | | | 12■ | | 7 | | | | | | | 1 | 3 | | | | 10 | | $9^{1}$ | 11 | | | | | | | | | 19 |
| | 2 | | 3 | 5 | 6 | | $8^{2}$ | | | | | | | 4 | | | 13 | | | | 1 | $7^{1}$ | | | | 9 | | 10 | 11 | 12 | | | | | | | | 20 |
| | 2 | | 4 | 5 | 6 | | $8^{1}$ | | | | | 13 | | 3 | | | 12 | | | | 1 | | | | | 9 | | 10 | $11^{2}$ | 7 | | | | | | | | 21 |
| | 2 | | 4 | 5 | 6 | 12 | | 14 | | | | | | 3 | | | 13 | | | | 1 | $7^{2}$ | | | | 9 | | $10^{3}$ | $11^{1}$ | 8 | | | | | | | | 22 |
| | $2^{1}$ | | 4 | 5 | 6 | 7 | 8 | 12 | | | | | | 3 | | | | | | | 1 | | | | | 9 | | 10 | | 11 | | | | | | | | 23 |
| 1 | | 13 | 4 | 5 | 6 | 7 | 8 | | | | | $10^{2}$ | | 3 | | | $2^{1}$ | | | | | | | | | 9 | | 12 | | 11 | | | | | | | | 24 |
| 1 | 12 | $3^{1}$ | 4 | 5 | 6 | 7 | 8 | | | | | | | 2 | | | 11 | | | | | | | | | 10 | | 13 | | $9^{2}$ | | | | | | | | 25 |
| 1 | $2^{1}$ | 12 | 4 | 5 | 6 | $7^{2}$ | | 9 | | | | | | 14 | | | 8 | | | | | | | | | 10 | | | 3 | $11^{3}$ | 13 | | | | | | | 26 |
| 1 | | 3 | | | 6 | 7 | | 9 | | | | | | | | | 8 | | | | | 2 | | | | 10 | | 12 | $4^{1}$ | 11 | | 5 | | | | | | 27 |
| 1 | | | $4^{3}$ | 12 | $6^{1}$ | | 8 | | | | | | | 2 | | | 14 | | | | | 3 | | | | 13 | | | | $11^{2}$ | | 5 | 7 | 9 | 10 | | | 28 |
| 1 | | | $4^{2}$ | 12 | | 14 | 8 | | | | | | | $2^{1}$ | | | 13 | | | | | 6 | | | | 7 | | | | $11^{3}$ | | 5 | 3 | 9 | 10 | | | 29 |
| 1 | $2^{1}$ | 13 | 4 | 12 | | | 8 | 14 | | | | | 3 | | | | | | | | | $6^{2}$ | | | | | | | | 11 | | 5 | 9 | 7 | $10^{3}$ | | | 30 |
| 1 | | 3 | $4^{1}$ | 6 | | | 11 | 9 | | | | | 2 | | | | 12 | | | | | | | | | 13 | | | | | | 5 | 7 | 10 | | $8^{2}$ | | 31 |
| 1 | | 3 | | 5 | | 7 | | 9 | | | | $10^{1}$ | 6 | | | | 8 | | | | | | | | | 4 | | | | | 12 | | | 11 | | 2 | | 32 |
| 1 | 2 | 12 | 4 | 5 | | 7 | | 9 | | | | $10^{2}$ | 6 | | | | 13 | | | | | | | | | 8 | | | | | | | | $11^{1}$ | | | 3 | 33 |
| | 2 | 14 | 7 | 5 | 12 | 4 | | $10^{3}$ | | | | $9^{2}$ | $6^{1}$ | | | | 13 | | | 1 | | | | | | 8 | | | | | | | | 11 | | | 3 | 34 |
| | 2 | $8^{2}$ | | 5 | 12 | 4 | | | | 13 | | 9 | 6 | | | | $7^{1}$ | | | 1 | | | | | | 10 | | | | | | | | 11 | | | 3 | 35 |
| | 2 | 7 | | 5 | 8 | 4 | | | | 12 | | 9 | 6 | | | | | | | 1 | | | | | | 10■ | | | | | | | | $11^{1}$ | | | 3 | 36 |
| | $2^{1}$ | | | 5 | 6 | 8 | | | | 12 | | 9 | 4 | 14 | | | 13 | $7^{2}$ | | 1 | | | | | | 10 | | | | | | | | $11^{3}$ | | | 3■ | 37 |
| | 2 | 8 | 7 | 5 | 3 | $11^{2}$ | | 14 | | 12 | | $9^{3}$ | 6 | $4^{1}$ | | | 13 | | | 1 | | | | | | | | | | | | | | 10 | | | | 38 |
| | $3^{1}$ | 11 | 8 | 5 | 6 | 14 | | | | $9^{2}$ | | | 2 | 12 | | | 7 | 4 | | 1 | | | | | | | | | | | | 13 | | $10^{3}$ | | | | 39 |
| | 3 | 11 | 9 | 5 | 6 | 7 | | | | $12^{2}$ | | | 4 | 8 | | | 13 | $10^{1}$ | | 1 | | 2 | | | | | | | | | | | | | | | | 40 |
| | 14 | 11 | 7 | 5 | $3^{1}$ | $8^{3}$ | | | | | | 9 | 6 | 13 | | | | $4^{2}$ | | 1 | | 12 | | | | 10 | | | | | | | | | | | 2 | 41 |
| | 14 | | 7 | 5 | $3^{1}$ | 11 | | | | | | 9 | 6 | 4 | | | 12 | $8^{3}$ | | 1 | | 13 | | | | 10 | | | | | | | | | | | $2^{2}$ | 42 |

**FA Cup**

| | | | |
|---|---|---|---|
| Fourth Qual | Halifax T | (h) | 1-0 |
| First Round | Kidderminster H | (a) | 1-2 |

# SCARBOROUGH Conference

*Ground:* McCain Stadium, Seamer Road, Scarborough, Yorkshire YO12 4HF.
*Tel:* (01723) 375 094.
*Year Formed:* 1879.
*Record Gate:* 11,130 (1987 v Luton Town FA Cup Third Round).
*Nickname:* The Boro.
*Manager:* Nick Henry.
*Secretary:* Kevin Philliskirk.
*Colours:* All red.

## SCARBOROUGH 2003–04 LEAGUE RECORD

| Match No. | Date | Venue | Opponents | Result | H/T Score | Lg. Pos. | Goalscorers | Attendance |
|---|---|---|---|---|---|---|---|---|
| 1 | Aug 9 | H | Farnborough T | W 2-1 | 1-0 | — | Rose [9], Gilroy (pen) [89] | 1415 |
| 2 | 12 | A | Northwich Vic | D 1-1 | 1-0 | — | Gill [41] | 854 |
| 3 | 16 | A | Woking | L 1-2 | 0-2 | 9 | Henry [59] | 1901 |
| 4 | 23 | H | Burton Alb | L 1-2 | 1-2 | 15 | Quayle [19] | 1445 |
| 5 | 25 | A | Accrington S | L 0-1 | 0-0 | 17 | | 2017 |
| 6 | 30 | H | Telford U | D 1-1 | 1-0 | 16 | Quayle [42] | 1113 |
| 7 | Sept 6 | H | Gravesend & N | W 2-0 | 0-0 | 14 | Quayle (pen) [63], Senior [78] | 1249 |
| 8 | 13 | A | Hereford U | L 1-2 | 0-1 | 15 | Quayle [88] | 4850 |
| 9 | 20 | H | Forest Green R | D 2-2 | 1-1 | 15 | Quayle 2 (1 pen) [22 (p), 83] | 1208 |
| 10 | 23 | A | Tamworth | D 0-0 | 0-0 | — | | 1004 |
| 11 | 27 | A | Exeter C | D 0-0 | 0-0 | 15 | | 2776 |
| 12 | Oct 4 | H | Shrewsbury T | D 1-1 | 0-1 | 15 | Quayle [75] | 1201 |
| 13 | 7 | H | Morecambe | W 1-0 | 0-0 | — | Price [69] | 1219 |
| 14 | 11 | A | Stevenage Bor | D 2-2 | 0-1 | 13 | Blackman [54], Senior [87] | 1776 |
| 15 | 18 | H | Margate | L 0-1 | 0-0 | 17 | | 1263 |
| 16 | Nov 1 | H | Chester C | D 2-2 | 0-2 | 15 | Quayle (pen) [48], Marcelle [64] | 1441 |
| 17 | 11 | A | Leigh RMI | W 4-1 | 1-1 | — | Rose [24], Quayle 2 (1 pen) [75, 79 (p)], Senior [84] | 375 |
| 18 | 15 | H | Aldershot T | W 1-0 | 0-0 | 13 | Redmile [70] | 1624 |
| 19 | 22 | A | Dagenham & R | L 0-1 | 0-1 | 14 | | 1107 |
| 20 | 25 | H | Barnet | D 2-2 | 1-1 | — | Redmile [26], Kelly [85] | 1208 |
| 21 | 29 | A | Gravesend & N | D 1-1 | 0-1 | 15 | Cryan [73] | 747 |
| 22 | Dec 13 | A | Farnborough T | W 2-1 | 1-1 | 15 | Sestanovic [30], Quayle [46] | 620 |
| 23 | 20 | H | Northwich Vic | W 1-0 | 1-0 | 15 | Sestanovic [22] | 1265 |
| 24 | 26 | A | Halifax T | L 0-1 | 0-0 | 15 | | 2136 |
| 25 | Jan 17 | H | Woking | D 2-2 | 0-0 | 15 | Williams [49], Quayle (pen) [89] | 2503 |
| 26 | Feb 3 | H | Hereford U | D 3-3 | 1-1 | — | Marcelle [32], Downey G [49], Redmile [53] | 1459 |
| 27 | 7 | A | Forest Green R | L 0-4 | 0-2 | 15 | | 848 |
| 28 | 21 | A | Shrewsbury T | L 1-4 | 1-0 | 17 | Senior [19] | 3333 |
| 29 | Mar 6 | A | Morecambe | L 1-2 | 0-1 | 18 | Quayle [89] | 1623 |
| 30 | 13 | H | Leigh RMI | W 4-1 | 0-0 | 18 | Hackworth [58], Nicholson [61], Harrison (og) [67], Rose [88] | 1093 |
| 31 | 16 | H | Tamworth | L 0-1 | 0-0 | — | | 1059 |
| 32 | 20 | A | Aldershot T | W 2-1 | 0-1 | 17 | Ketchanke [69], Senior [86] | 2442 |
| 33 | 23 | H | Exeter C | L 2-3 | 2-2 | — | Kelly (pen) [10], Hackworth [16] | 1200 |
| 34 | 25 | H | Halifax T | W 1-0 | 0-0 | — | Senior [74] | 1220 |
| 35 | 27 | H | Dagenham & R | D 0-0 | 0-0 | 16 | | 1302 |
| 36 | Apr 3 | A | Barnet | D 0-0 | 0-0 | 17 | | 1560 |
| 37 | 6 | H | Stevenage Bor | D 2-2 | 0-0 | — | Marcelle [63], Rose [68] | 1018 |
| 38 | 10 | A | Burton Alb | L 0-2 | 0-1 | 16 | | 1370 |
| 39 | 12 | H | Accrington S | W 2-1 | 0-1 | 16 | Hackworth [61], Gilroy [90] | 1523 |
| 40 | 14 | A | Telford U | L 1-2 | 1-2 | — | Marcelle [44] | 1654 |
| 41 | 17 | A | Chester C | L 0-1 | 0-1 | 16 | | 5987 |
| 42 | 24 | A | Margate | W 2-0 | 1-0 | 15 | Gilroy [44], Quayle [87] | 404 |

**Final League Position: 15**

### GOALSCORERS

*League (51):* Quayle 14 (5 pens), Senior 6, Marcelle 4, Rose 4, Gilroy 3 (1 pen), Hackworth 3, Redmile 3, Kelly 2 (1 pen), Sestanovic 2, Blackman 1, Cryan 1, Downey G 1, Gill 1, Henry 1, Ketchanke 1, Nicholson 1, Price 1, Williams 1, own goal 1.
*FA Cup (7):* Kerr 3, Lyth 1, Quayle 1, Rose 1, Sestanovic 1.
*LDV Vans Trophy (2):* Kelly 1, Senior 1.
*Trophy (1):* Senior 1.

| Sollitt 7 + 2 | Price 12 + 4 | Capper 18 + 2 | Kerr 36 + 1 | Redmile 22 / Brownrigg 2 + 1 | Hotte 37 + 1 | Gilroy 5 + 7 | Gill 28 + 7 | Rose 23 + 4 | Quayle 35 + 1 | Williams 6 + 6 | Senior 7 + 33 | Henry 8 | Sherlock 1 + 6 | Raw 7 + 4 | Donaldson 2 | Baker 18 + 1 | Burt 1 | Walker 35 | Downey G 14 + 1 | Nesovic — + 1 | Kelly 30 | Dudgeon — + 1 | Lyth 22 + 5 | Blackman 5 + 1 | Marcelle 26 + 3 | McSweeney — + 3 | Graydon — + 1 | Cryan 10 | Sestanovic 7 | Bachelor — + 1 | Whitman 4 + 2 | O'Neill 1 | Robinson 2 | Davidson 2 | Ketchanke 5 | Hackworth 11 | Nicholson 13 | *Match No.* |
|---|---|---|---|---|---|---|---|---|---|---|---|---|---|---|---|---|---|---|---|---|---|---|---|---|---|---|---|---|---|---|---|---|---|---|---|---|---|---|
| 1 | 2 | 3 | 4 | 5 | 6 | 7 | 8 | 9 | 10 | $11^{1}$ | 12 | | | | | | | | | | | | | | | | | | | | | | | | | | | 1 |
| 1 | 2 | 3 | 4■ | 5 | 6 | 7 | 8 | $9^{1}$ | $10^{2}$ | | 12 | 11 | 13 | | | | | | | | | | | | | | | | | | | | | | | | | 2 |
| 1 | 2 | 3 | 4 | 5 | 6 | 7 | 8 | | 10 | | $11^{1}$ | 9 | | 12 | | | | | | | | | | | | | | | | | | | | | | | | 3 |
| 1 | 2 | 3 | 4 | 5 | 6 | $7^{1}$ | 8 | 12 | 10 | $11^{2}$ | 13 | | 14 | | $9^{3}$ | | | | | | | | | | | | | | | | | | | | | | | 4 |
| 1 | 2 | 3 | 4 | 5 | 6 | | 8 | $9^{1}$ | 10 | | 11 | | 12 | 7 | | | | | | | | | | | | | | | | | | | | | | | | 5 |
| 1 | 2 | 3 | | 5 | 6 | | 8 | 9 | 10 | | 12 | | | 11 | | 4 | $7^{1}$ | | | | | | | | | | | | | | | | | | | | | 6 |
| | | | | 5 | 6 | | 8 | 9■ | 10 | | 12 | $7^{3}$ | 14 | $4^{2}$ | | 3 | | 1 | $2^{1}$ | 13 | 11 | | | | | | | | | | | | | | | | | 7 |
| | 2 | | | 5 | 6 | | 8 | | 10 | | 14 | $7^{2}$ | 13 | | $9^{3}$ | 3 | | 1 | $4^{1}$ | | 11 | 12 | | | | | | | | | | | | | | | | 8 |
| | 12 | 3 | 14 | 5 | 6 | | $8^{2}$ | | 10 | | 13 | $4^{3}$ | | | | 2 | | 1 | | | 7 | | $11^{1}$ | 9 | | | | | | | | | | | | | | 9 |
| | 12 | $3^{1}$ | 4 | | 6 | | 8 | | 10 | | 14 | $7^{2}$ | | 13 | | 5 | | 1 | | | 11 | | 2 | $9^{3}$ | | | | | | | | | | | | | | 10 |
| | 12 | | 4 | 5 | 6 | | 14 | | 10 | | 13 | $7^{2}$ | | 8 | | $3^{1}$ | | 1 | | | 11 | | 2 | $9^{3}$ | | | | | | | | | | | | | | 11 |
| | $11^{1}$ | 3 | 4 | 5 | 6 | | $8^{2}$ | | 10 | | 14 | | | | | | | 1 | | | 7 | | 2 | $9^{3}$ | 12 | 13 | | | | | | | | | | | | 12 |
| | $2^{2}$ | | 4 | 5 | 6 | | 13 | | 10 | | 12 | | | $8^{1}$ | | 3 | | 1 | | | 7 | | 11 | | 9 | | | | | | | | | | | | | 13 |
| | | 3 | 4 | 5 | 6 | | | | $10^{3}$ | | 12 | | | $8^{2}$ | | 2 | | 1 | | | 11 | | $7^{1}$ | 14 | 9 | 13 | | | | | | | | | | | | 14 |
| | 2 | $3^{2}$ | 4 | 5 | | | 12 | | | | 11 | | | | | $6^{1}$ | | 1 | | | 8 | | 7 | $9^{3}$ | 10 | 14 | 13 | | | | | | | | | | | 15 |
| | | 3 | 4 | 5 | | | | 9 | 10 | | 12 | | | | | 2 | | 1 | | | 7 | | | | $8^{1}$ | | | 6 | 11 | | | | | | | | | 16 |
| | | 3 | 4 | 5 | | | 14 | $10^{2}$ | $9^{1}$ | 12 | 13 | | | | | 2 | | 1 | | | 7 | | | | $11^{3}$ | | | 6 | 8 | | | | | | | | | 17 |
| | | $3^{1}$ | 4 | 5 | 12 | | 10 | | 9 | 14 | 13 | $7^{3}$ | | | | 2 | | 1 | | | | | | | 11 | | | 6 | $8^{2}$ | | | | | | | | | 18 |
| | | | 4 | 5 | 3 | | 8 | 10 | | $11^{2}$ | 13 | | | | | $2^{1}$ | | 1 | | | 7 | | 12 | | $9^{3}$ | | | 6 | | 14 | | | | | | | | 19 |
| | | | 4 | 5 | 3 | 13 | 8 | $10^{2}$ | | $11^{1}$ | 12 | | | | | | | 1 | | | 7 | | 2 | | 9 | | | 6 | | | | | | | | | | 20 |
| | 5 | | 4 | | 3 | 12 | $8^{1}$ | 10 | $9^{2}$ | 14 | 13 | | | | | | | 1 | | | 7 | | 2 | | $11^{3}$ | | | 6 | | | | | | | | | | 21 |
| | 12 | | $4^{2}$ | 5■ | 3 | | $11^{3}$ | | 9 | 13 | | | | | | 14 | | 1 | | | 7 | | 2 | | 10 | | | 6 | $8^{1}$ | | | | | | | | | 22 |
| | | | 4 | | 5 | | $11^{1}$ | | 9 | 12 | 13 | | | | | 3 | | 1 | | | 7 | | 2 | | $10^{2}$ | | | 6 | 8 | | | | | | | | | 23 |
| | | | $4^{2}$ | 5■ | 3 | | 8■ | | $9^{3}$ | 14 | 12 | | | | | | | 1 | | | 7 | | $2^{1}$ | | 10 | | | 6 | 11 | | 13 | | | | | | | 24 |
| | | 12 | | | 3 | | | | 9 | 4 | 13 | | | | | $5^{1}$ | | 1 | | | 7 | | 2■ | | $10^{2}$ | | | 6 | 11 | | 8 | | | | | | | 25 |
| 15 | | 2 | 4 | $5^{1}$ | 6 | | $8^{2}$ | 12 | | 11 | 13 | | | | | | | $1^{6}$ | 3 | | 7 | | | | 9 | | | | | | 10 | | | | | | | 26 |
| | | 3 | 4 | | | | | 12 | 9 | | 13 | | $8^{1}$ | | | | | 1 | 6 | | 7 | | 2 | | 11 | | | | | | $10^{2}$ | 5 | | | | | | 27 |
| | $2^{1}$ | | 4■ | | 6 | | 8 | | 9 | | 10 | | | | | | | 1 | 5 | | 7 | | 12 | | | | | | | | 11 | | 3 | | | | | 28 |
| | | | | | 5 | | | 6 | 9 | | 10 | | 12 | | | 2■ | | 1 | 3 | | 7 | | | | 8 | | | | | | 13 | | $11^{2}$ | $4^{1}$ | | | | 29 |
| | | | 4 | | 5 | | 12 | 8 | $9^{2}$ | | 13 | | | | | 3 | | 1 | | | $7^{1}$ | | 2 | | | | | | | | | | | | 6 | 10 | 11 | 30 |
| | | | 4 | | 6 | | 13 | 8 | $9^{3}$ | | 14 | | | | | $3^{2}$ | | 1 | | | 7■ | | $2^{1}$ | | 12 | | | | | | | | | | 5 | 10 | 11 | 31 |
| | | | 4 | 2 | 6 | | 8 | 11 | | | 12 | | | | | | | 1 | | | 7 | | | | 9 | | | | | | | | | | $5^{1}$ | 10 | 3 | 32 |
| | | | $4^{2}$ | $2^{1}$ | 6 | | 13 | 8 | 9 | | 14 | | | | | | | 1 | | | 7 | | 12 | | $11^{3}$ | | | | | | | | | | 5 | 10 | 3 | 33 |
| | | | 4 | 12 | 6 | | | 8 | 9 | | 14 | | | | | | | 1 | 13 | | 7 | | $2^{3}$ | | 11 | | | | | | | | | | $5^{1}$ | $10^{2}$ | 3 | 34 |
| | | $2^{1}$ | 4 | | 6 | | 8 | 12 | 9 | | 10 | | | | | | | 1 | 5 | | 7 | | 13 | | 11 | | | | | | | | | | | | $3^{2}$ | 35 |
| | | 13 | 4 | | 6 | 12 | 11 | 8 | 9 | | $7^{1}$ | | | | | | | 1 | 5 | | | | 2 | | $10^{2}$ | | | | | | | | | | | | 3 | 36 |
| | | | 4 | | 6 | | 11 | 7 | 9 | | 13 | | | 12 | | | | 1 | 5 | | | | 2 | | $8^{1}$ | | | | | | | | | | | $10^{2}$ | 3 | 37 |
| | | | 4 | | 6 | 12 | 11 | 7 | $9^{2}$ | | 13 | | | 14 | | | | 1 | 5 | | | | $2^{1}$ | | $8^{3}$ | | | | | | | | | | | 10 | 3 | 38 |
| | | 2 | 4 | | 6 | 12 | $7^{1}$ | 11 | $9^{2}$ | | 13 | | | | | | | 1 | 5 | | | | | | 8 | | | | | | | | | | | 10 | 3 | 39 |
| 1 | | | 4 | | 6 | 13 | | 11 | $9^{3}$ | | 14 | | | 7 | | | | | 5 | | | | 12 | | $8^{2}$ | | | | | | | | | $2^{1}$ | | 10 | 3 | 40 |
| | | | 4 | | 6 | 9 | $7^{2}$ | $8^{1}$ | | | 13 | | | | | | | 1 | 5 | | 11 | | 2 | | 12 | | | | | | | | | | | 10 | 3 | 41 |
| 15 | | | 4 | | 6 | 12 | 11 | $8^{1}$ | 13 | | | | | | | | | $1^{6}$ | 5 | | 7 | | 2 | | 9 | | | | | | | | | | | $10^{2}$ | 3 | 42 |

**LDV Vans Trophy**

| | | | |
|---|---|---|---|
| First Round | Port Vale | (h) | 2-1 |
| Second Round | Halifax T | (h) | 0-1 |

**FA Cup**

| | | | |
|---|---|---|---|
| Fourth Qual | Hinckley U | (h) | 3-1 |
| First Round | Doncaster R | (h) | 1-0 |
| Second Round | Port Vale | (a) | 1-0 |
| Third Round | Southend U | (a) | 1-1 |
| | | (h) | 1-0 |
| Fourth Round | Chelsea | (h) | 0-1 |

# SHREWSBURY TOWN FL Championship 2

*Ground:* Gay Meadow, Abbey Foregate, Shrewsbury SY2 6AB.
*Tel:* (01743) 360 111.
*Year Formed:* 1886.
*Record Gate:* 18,917 v Walsall, Division 3, 26 April 1961.
*Nickname:* 'Town', 'Blues' or 'Salop'. The name 'Salop' is a colloquialism for the county of Shropshire. Since Shrewsbury is the only club in Shropshire, cries of 'Come on Salop' are frequently used!
*Manager:* Jimmy Quinn.
*Secretary:* Judy Shone.
*Colours:* Blue and amber.

## SHREWSBURY TOWN 2003–04 LEAGUE RECORD

| *Match No.* | *Date* | *Venue* | *Opponents* | *Result* | | *H/T Score* | *Lg. Pos.* | *Goalscorers* | *Attendance* |
|---|---|---|---|---|---|---|---|---|---|
| 1 | Aug 9 | H | Margate | D | 1-1 | 1-0 | — | Watts [17] | 4015 |
| 2 | 12 | A | Burton Alb | W | 1-0 | 0-0 | — | Rodgers [73] | 3203 |
| 3 | 16 | A | Accrington S | W | 1-0 | 0-0 | 4 | Cramb [81] | 3143 |
| 4 | 23 | H | Farnborough T | W | 3-0 | 1-0 | 3 | Cramb [24], Jagielka [54], Lowe [85] | 3403 |
| 5 | 26 | A | Chester C | L | 1-2 | 0-1 | — | Tolley J [53] | 4665 |
| 6 | 30 | H | Dagenham & R | W | 2-1 | 2-0 | 4 | Tolley J [34], Cramb [41] | 3468 |
| 7 | Sept 7 | H | Tamworth | W | 3-1 | 0-0 | 4 | Rodgers 3 [64, 89, 90] | 3882 |
| 8 | 13 | A | Aldershot T | D | 1-1 | 1-1 | 3 | Cramb [24] | 3329 |
| 9 | 20 | A | Woking | D | 3-3 | 1-0 | 3 | Rodgers 3 (1 pen) [12, 48, 90 (p)] | 2539 |
| 10 | 23 | H | Halifax T | W | 2-0 | 0-0 | — | Cramb [80], Lowe [88] | 3807 |
| 11 | 27 | H | Barnet | L | 0-1 | 0-0 | 6 | | 4063 |
| 12 | Oct 4 | A | Scarborough | D | 1-1 | 1-0 | 5 | Quinn [43] | 1201 |
| 13 | 18 | H | Morecambe | W | 2-0 | 1-0 | 6 | Rodgers [11], Quinn [75] | 3404 |
| 14 | Nov 1 | A | Stevenage Bor | L | 0-2 | 0-1 | 6 | | 2172 |
| 15 | 11 | H | Forest Green R | W | 2-0 | 0-0 | — | Tolley J [47], Quinn [51] | 3263 |
| 16 | 15 | A | Gravesend & N | W | 3-0 | 1-0 | 6 | Lowe 2 [17, 64], Cramb [90] | 1397 |
| 17 | 18 | A | Leigh RMI | D | 2-2 | 0-0 | — | Cramb [46], Street [90] | 1219 |
| 18 | 22 | H | Hereford U | W | 4-1 | 2-0 | 5 | O'Connor [13], Cramb [37], Street [55], Darby [81] | 6585 |
| 19 | 25 | A | Exeter C | L | 2-3 | 0-2 | — | Rodgers [65], Cramb [90] | 3470 |
| 20 | 29 | A | Tamworth | D | 1-1 | 1-0 | 6 | Cramb (pen) [14] | 1761 |
| 21 | Dec 9 | H | Telford U | D | 0-0 | 0-0 | — | | 6738 |
| 22 | 14 | A | Margate | W | 2-0 | 0-0 | — | Lowe [83], Banim [90] | 635 |
| 23 | 26 | H | Northwich Vic | W | 3-1 | 1-0 | 5 | Cramb [39], Lowe [63], Tinson [71] | 5059 |
| 24 | Jan 1 | A | Northwich Vic | W | 2-0 | 1-0 | 4 | Ridler [45], Cramb [58] | 3268 |
| 25 | 3 | A | Dagenham & R | L | 0-5 | 0-3 | 5 | | 1571 |
| 26 | 17 | H | Accrington S | D | 0-0 | 0-0 | 5 | | 3777 |
| 27 | 24 | A | Halifax T | D | 0-0 | 0-0 | 5 | | 1830 |
| 28 | Feb 21 | H | Scarborough | W | 4-1 | 0-1 | 5 | Darby 2 [54, 89], Sedgemore [61], O'Connor [73] | 3333 |
| 29 | 24 | H | Burton Alb | W | 1-0 | 1-0 | — | Rodgers [17] | 3115 |
| 30 | Mar 2 | H | Woking | W | 1-0 | 0-0 | — | Rodgers [72] | 3029 |
| 31 | 8 | H | Leigh RMI | W | 3-1 | 1-1 | — | Darby [11], Lowe [70], Banim [90] | 3307 |
| 32 | 13 | A | Forest Green R | D | 1-1 | 0-0 | 3 | Rogers (og) [68] | 1484 |
| 33 | 23 | H | Aldershot T | L | 1-2 | 0-1 | — | Darby [79] | 3371 |
| 34 | 27 | A | Hereford U | L | 1-2 | 1-1 | 6 | Lawrence [4] | 5850 |
| 35 | 30 | A | Barnet | W | 1-0 | 1-0 | — | Darby [37] | 1966 |
| 36 | Apr 3 | H | Exeter C | D | 2-2 | 0-0 | 5 | Lawrence [49], Darby [71] | 4185 |
| 37 | 6 | A | Telford U | L | 0-1 | 0-0 | — | | 4337 |
| 38 | 10 | A | Farnborough T | W | 3-1 | 0-0 | 4 | Darby 2 [47, 51], Rodgers [76] | 1041 |
| 39 | 13 | H | Chester C | D | 0-0 | 0-0 | — | | 5827 |
| 40 | 17 | H | Stevenage Bor | W | 3-1 | 0-0 | 3 | Ridler [66], Lowe [69], Darby [90] | 3650 |
| 41 | 20 | H | Gravesend & N | D | 1-1 | 1-0 | — | Rodgers [42] | 2869 |
| 42 | 24 | A | Morecambe | D | 3-3 | 2-1 | 3 | Lowe [7], Sedgemore (pen) [23], Quinn [68] | 2876 |

**Final League Position: 3**

### GOALSCORERS

*League (67):* Rodgers 13 (1 pen), Cramb 12 (1 pen), Darby 10, Lowe 9, Quinn 4, Tolley J 3, Banim 2, Lawrence 2, O'Connor 2, Ridler 2, Sedgemore 2 (1 pen), Street 2, Jagielka 1, Tinson 1, Watts 1, own goal 1.
*FA Cup (5):* Lowe 2, Quinn 2, Aiston 1.
*LDV Vans Trophy (1):* Lowe 1.
*Trophy (6):* Cramb 2 (1 pen), Aiston 1, Lowe 1, Moss 1, Street 1.
*Play-Offs (3):* Rodgers 2 (2 pens), Darby 1.

| Dunbavin 3 | Moss 37 + 1 | Rioch 18 + 2 | Tolley J 26 + 2 | Tinson 38 + 1 | Ridler 39 | Jagielka 8 + 3 | O'Connor 35 + 1 | Rodgers 26 + 8 | Watts 4 + 4 | Fitzpatrick 3 + 4 | Aiston 30 + 2 | Murray 4 + 2 | Sedgemore 27 + 8 | Cramb 24 + 10 | Howie 37 + 1 | Lowe 20 + 14 | Drysdale 1 | Edwards 7 + 9 | Quinn 8 + 8 | Bell 1 + 2 | Street 20 + 8 | Stevens — + 1 | Darby 20 + 4 | Potter 4 + 1 | Banim 7 + 9 | Lawrence 6 + 1 | Challis 7 + 1 | Hart 2 | *Match No.* |
|---|---|---|---|---|---|---|---|---|---|---|---|---|---|---|---|---|---|---|---|---|---|---|---|---|---|---|---|---|---|
| 1 | 2 | 3 | 4 | 5 | 6 | 7 | 8 | 9 | 10 | $11^{1}$ | 12 | | | | | | | | | | | | | | | | | | 1 |
| 1 | 2■ | 3 | 4 | 5 | 6 | 7 | $8^{2}$ | 9 | $10^{3}$ | $11^{1}$ | | 13 | 12 | 14 | | | | | | | | | | | | | | | 2 |
| $1^{6}$ | 2 | $3^{1}$ | 4 | 5 | 6 | 7 | 8 | 9 | | $11^{2}$ | | | 12 | 10 | 15 | 13 | | | | | | | | | | | | | 3 |
| | 2 | | 4 | 5 | 6 | 7 | $8^{1}$ | $9^{2}$ | | | 11 | 12 | 3 | 10 | 1 | 13 | | | | | | | | | | | | | 4 |
| | | | 4 | 5 | 6 | $7^{3}$ | 8 | 9 | 12 | 14 | 11 | | $3^{2}$ | $10^{1}$ | 1 | 13 | 2 | | | | | | | | | | | | 5 |
| | 2 | $3^{2}$ | 4 | 5 | 6 | 7 | 8 | 9 | 12 | | $11^{1}$ | | 13 | $10^{3}$ | 1 | 14 | | | | | | | | | | | | | 6 |
| | 2 | 3 | $4^{1}$ | 5 | 6 | 7 | 8 | 9 | 13 | 14 | $11^{3}$ | | | $10^{2}$ | 1 | 12 | | | | | | | | | | | | | 7 |
| | | 3 | | 5 | 6 | $7^{2}$ | 8 | 9 | 12 | | $11^{1}$ | 4 | 2 | 10 | 1 | | | 13 | | | | | | | | | | | 8 |
| | 2 | 3 | | 5 | $6^{1}$ | 13 | 8 | 9 | $7^{3}$ | | 11 | $4^{2}$ | 12 | 10 | 1 | | | | 14 | | | | | | | | | | 9 |
| | 2 | 3 | | 5 | | | 8 | 9 | $7^{2}$ | 12 | $11^{1}$ | 4 | 6 | 10 | 1 | 13 | | | | | | | | | | | | | 10 |
| | $2^{1}$ | 3 | | 5 | | 13 | $8^{2}$ | 9 | | 14 | $11^{3}$ | 4 | 6 | 10 | 1 | 7 | | | 12 | | | | | | | | | | 11 |
| | 2 | 3 | 4 | 5 | 6 | 12 | | | | | 11 | | | $10^{1}$ | 1 | 7 | | | 9 | 8 | | | | | | | | | 12 |
| | 2 | 3 | 4 | | 6 | | $8^{1}$ | 9 | | | 11 | | 5 | | 1 | 13 | | | $10^{2}$ | 12 | 7 | | | | | | | | 13 |
| | 12 | 3 | $4^{3}$ | 5 | $6^{2}$ | | 8 | 9 | | | 11 | | $2^{1}$ | | 1 | 13 | | | 10 | 14 | 7 | | | | | | | | 14 |
| | 2 | 3 | 4 | | 6 | | 8 | $9^{2}$ | | | $11^{3}$ | | 5 | 13 | 1 | $7^{1}$ | | | 10 | | 12 | 14 | | | | | | | 15 |
| | 2 | 3 | 4 | 5 | 6 | | 8 | 14 | | | $11^{1}$ | | | 13 | 1 | $7^{2}$ | | | $10^{3}$ | | 12 | | 9 | | | | | | 16 |
| | 2 | $3^{3}$ | 4 | $5^{2}$ | 6 | | 8 | 12 | | | $11^{1}$ | | 13 | 10 | 1 | 7 | | | | | 14 | | 9 | | | | | | 17 |
| | 2 | | 4 | 5 | 6 | | $8^{1}$ | 12 | | | | | | 10 | 1 | 7 | | | | | 11 | | 9 | 3 | | | | | 18 |
| | 2 | | 4 | 5 | $6^{3}$ | | $8^{2}$ | 12 | | | | | 13 | 10 | 1 | $7^{1}$ | | | 14 | | 11 | | 9 | 3 | | | | | 19 |
| | 2 | 12 | | 5 | $6^{3}$ | | 8■ | | | | | | 4 | $10^{1}$ | 1 | 7 | | 13 | 14 | | 11 | | $9^{2}$ | 3 | | | | | 20 |
| | 2 | | 4 | 5 | 6 | | 8 | $9^{3}$ | | | $11^{1}$ | | | 10 | 1 | 14 | | | | | 3 | | $7^{2}$ | 12 | 13 | | | | 21 |
| | 2 | 14 | $4^{1}$ | 5 | 6 | | | $9^{2}$ | | | $11^{3}$ | | 7 | | 1 | 12 | | | 10 | | 8 | | | 3 | 13 | | | | 22 |
| | 2 | 3 | | 5 | 6 | | $4^{2}$ | | | | 11 | | 8 | 10 | 1 | 12 | | 13 | | | $7^{1}$ | | | | 9 | | | | 23 |
| | 2 | 3 | | 6 | 5 | | 4 | | | | 11 | | 8 | $10^{3}$ | 1 | $7^{1}$ | | | 14 | | 12 | | 13 | | $9^{2}$ | | | | 24 |
| | 2 | $3^{1}$ | | 5 | 6 | | 4 | | | | 11 | | 8 | $10^{2}$ | 1 | $7^{3}$ | | | 12 | | 14 | | 13 | | 9 | | | | 25 |
| | 2 | | | 5 | 6 | | 12 | | | | 11 | | 3 | $10^{1}$ | 1 | | | 4 | $8^{2}$ | | 7 | | 9 | | 13 | | | | 26 |
| | 2 | | 12 | 5 | 6 | | $4^{1}$ | 9 | | | 11 | | 3 | 13 | 1 | | | 8 | | | 7 | | $10^{2}$ | | | | | | 27 |
| | 2 | | $4^{1}$ | 5 | 6 | | $8^{2}$ | 9■ | | | $11^{3}$ | | 3 | 13 | 1 | 7 | | 12 | | | 14 | | 10 | | | | | | 28 |
| | 2 | | | 5 | 6 | | 4 | $9^{1}$ | | | 12 | | 3 | 10 | 1 | 7 | | $8^{2}$ | | | 13 | | $11^{3}$ | | 14 | | | | 29 |
| | 2 | | 4 | 5 | 6 | | $8^{2}$ | 9 | | | 11■ | | 3 | $10^{1}$ | 1 | $7^{3}$ | | 13 | | | | | 12 | | 14 | | | | 30 |
| | 2 | | $4^{2}$ | 5 | 6 | | 8 | | | | $11^{1}$ | | 3 | 10 | 1 | 7 | | 13 | | | 12 | | $9^{3}$ | | 14 | | | | 31 |
| | 2 | | $4^{2}$ | 5 | 6 | | 8 | 12 | | | | | 3 | $10^{3}$ | 1 | 7 | | 13 | | | $11^{1}$ | | 9 | | 14 | | | | 32 |
| | 2 | | | 5 | 6 | | $8^{1}$ | 9 | | | | | 7 | 12 | 1 | | | $3^{2}$ | 14 | | 11 | | 10 | | 4 | $13^{3}$ | | | 33 |
| | 2 | | | 5 | 6 | | | 9 | | | | | 8 | | 1 | $7^{1}$ | | | 13 | | 4 | | $10^{2}$ | | 12 | 11 | 3 | | 34 |
| | 2 | | | 5 | | | 4 | 13 | | | | | 6 | 12 | 1 | $7^{1}$ | | | | | 11 | | 9 | | $10^{2}$ | 8 | 3 | | 35 |
| | | | | 5 | 6 | | 4 | 13 | | | | | 2 | 12 | 1 | 7 | | | | | 11 | | $9^{1}$ | | $10^{2}$ | 8 | 3 | | 36 |
| | | | 13 | 5 | 6 | | $4^{2}$ | 14 | | | $11^{1}$ | | 2 | | 1 | 12 | | | | | 7 | | 9 | | $10^{3}$ | 8 | 3 | | 37 |
| | 2 | | 4 | 5 | 6 | | | $10^{3}$ | | | $11^{2}$ | | 12 | 14 | 1 | 13 | | $8^{1}$ | | | 7 | | 9 | | | | 3 | | 38 |
| | 2 | | 4 | 5 | 6 | | | 9 | | | 11 | | | | 1 | | | 8 | | | 7 | | 10 | | | | 3 | | 39 |
| | 2 | | $4^{1}$ | 5 | 6 | | | $9^{3}$ | | | 11 | | 12 | 14 | 1 | 13 | | $8^{2}$ | | | 7 | | 10 | | | | 3 | | 40 |
| | 2■ | | 8 | 12 | 6 | | $4^{1}$ | 9 | | | $11^{3}$ | | 5 | $10^{2}$ | | 7 | | 14 | | | | | 13 | | | 3 | | 1 | 41 |
| | 2 | | $8^{2}$ | | 6 | | $4^{3}$ | | | | 11 | | 5 | | | 9 | | 13 | 10 | | 7 | | | | 14 | $3^{1}$ | 12 | 1 | 42 |

**LDV Vans Trophy**
First Round Scunthorpe U (a) 1-2

**FA Cup**
Fourth Qual Morecambe (a) 4-2

**Play-Offs**
Semi-Finals Barnet (a) 1-2
(h) 1-0
Final Aldershot T 1-1

# STEVENAGE BOROUGH Conference

*Ground:* Broadhall Way Stadium, Broadhall Way, Stevenage, Hertfordshire SG2 8RH.
*Tel:* (01438) 223 223.
*Year Formed:* 1976.
*Record Gate:* 6,489 (1997 v Kidderminster Harriers Conference).
*Nickname:* The Boro.
*Manager:* Graham Westley.
*Secretary:* Roger Austin.
*Colours:* Red and white shirts, black shorts, white stockings.

## STEVENAGE BOROUGH 2003–04 LEAGUE RECORD

| Match No. | Date | Venue | Opponents | Result | | H/T Score | Lg. Pos. | Goalscorers | Attendance |
|---|---|---|---|---|---|---|---|---|---|
| 1 | Aug 9 | H | Chester C | D | 0-0 | 0-0 | — | | 2502 |
| 2 | 12 | A | Dagenham & R | W | 2-1 | 1-0 | — | Elding [15], Costello [62] | 1948 |
| 3 | 16 | A | Burton Alb | D | 1-1 | 0-0 | 7 | Elding [74] | 1572 |
| 4 | 23 | H | Northwich Vic | W | 1-0 | 0-0 | 5 | Elding [57] | 1869 |
| 5 | 25 | A | Margate | W | 4-1 | 4-0 | 3 | Holloway 2 [7, 37], Baptiste [18], Elding [23] | 755 |
| 6 | 30 | H | Hereford U | L | 0-2 | 0-1 | 7 | | 2705 |
| 7 | Sept 6 | A | Exeter C | L | 0-1 | 0-0 | 8 | | 3012 |
| 8 | 13 | H | Barnet | L | 1-2 | 1-0 | 12 | Baptiste [14] | 3019 |
| 9 | 20 | A | Telford U | W | 2-0 | 1-0 | 10 | Elding [16], Goodliffe [60] | 1703 |
| 10 | 23 | H | Gravesend & N | D | 2-2 | 1-0 | — | Baptiste [41], Elding [88] | 1732 |
| 11 | 27 | H | Leigh RMI | W | 4-0 | 1-0 | 7 | Elding 2 [27, 90], Battersby [56], Richards [80] | 1734 |
| 12 | Oct 4 | A | Halifax T | L | 1-2 | 1-1 | 9 | Battersby [21] | 1437 |
| 13 | 7 | A | Woking | D | 1-1 | 1-1 | — | Travis [36] | 2592 |
| 14 | 11 | H | Scarborough | D | 2-2 | 1-0 | 9 | Battersby (pen) [36], Gould [78] | 1776 |
| 15 | 18 | A | Forest Green R | L | 1-3 | 1-1 | 9 | Bunce [5] | 676 |
| 16 | Nov 1 | H | Shrewsbury T | W | 2-0 | 1-0 | 9 | Maamria [41], Wormull [61] | 2172 |
| 17 | 11 | A | Tamworth | W | 2-1 | 1-0 | — | Wormull [33], Holloway [85] | 1006 |
| 18 | 15 | H | Accrington S | W | 2-1 | 2-1 | 7 | Elding 2 [6, 45] | 2121 |
| 19 | 22 | A | Morecambe | L | 1-2 | 1-1 | 7 | Cook [14] | 1354 |
| 20 | 29 | H | Exeter C | D | 2-2 | 0-1 | 10 | Elding 2 [67, 78] | 2007 |
| 21 | Dec 13 | A | Chester C | W | 2-1 | 1-0 | 11 | Elding [37], Baptiste [75] | 2145 |
| 22 | 16 | H | Aldershot T | L | 0-1 | 0-0 | — | | 1794 |
| 23 | 20 | H | Dagenham & R | L | 0-2 | 0-1 | 12 | | 1749 |
| 24 | 26 | A | Farnborough T | L | 0-2 | 0-1 | 13 | | 1403 |
| 25 | Jan 1 | H | Farnborough T | W | 3-2 | 2-2 | 10 | Carroll [3], Maamria [12], Charles (og) [86] | 2285 |
| 26 | 3 | A | Hereford U | L | 0-1 | 0-0 | 10 | | 2875 |
| 27 | 17 | H | Burton Alb | W | 1-0 | 0-0 | 10 | Richards [51] | 2003 |
| 28 | 24 | A | Gravesend & N | W | 3-2 | 1-1 | 10 | Maamria 2 (2 pens) [37, 64], Rogers [84] | 1230 |
| 29 | Feb 7 | H | Telford U | L | 0-1 | 0-0 | 10 | | 1744 |
| 30 | 14 | A | Leigh RMI | W | 3-1 | 1-0 | 10 | Maamria [43], Elding [55], Richards [70] | 270 |
| 31 | 21 | H | Halifax T | W | 1-0 | 0-0 | 9 | Maamria [49] | 1715 |
| 32 | Mar 6 | H | Woking | D | 1-1 | 1-1 | 10 | Elding [36] | 2489 |
| 33 | 9 | A | Barnet | D | 0-0 | 0-0 | — | | 2066 |
| 34 | 13 | H | Tamworth | W | 3-1 | 0-0 | 7 | Elding [82], Maamria 2 (1 pen) [84, 90 (p)] | 1646 |
| 35 | 20 | A | Accrington S | L | 1-2 | 1-0 | 8 | Brennan [31] | 1124 |
| 36 | 27 | H | Morecambe | L | 0-1 | 0-0 | 10 | | 1687 |
| 37 | 30 | A | Aldershot T | L | 0-2 | 0-1 | — | | 2540 |
| 38 | Apr 6 | A | Scarborough | D | 2-2 | 0-0 | — | Brough [79], Brennan [84] | 1018 |
| 39 | 10 | A | Northwich Vic | W | 2-1 | 1-1 | 9 | Elding [24], Boyd [82] | 487 |
| 40 | 12 | H | Margate | W | 2-1 | 0-1 | 8 | Maamria [60], Richards [84] | 1548 |
| 41 | 17 | A | Shrewsbury T | L | 1-3 | 0-0 | 9 | Barnard [80] | 3650 |
| 42 | 24 | H | Forest Green R | W | 2-1 | 1-0 | 8 | Brough [10], Flack [84] | 1747 |

**Final League Position: 8**

### GOALSCORERS

*League (58):* Elding 17, Maamria 9 (3 pens), Baptiste 4, Richards 4, Battersby 3 (1 pen), Holloway 3, Brennan 2, Brough 2, Wormull 2, Barnard 1, Boyd 1, Bunce 1, Carroll 1, Cook 1, Costello 1, Flack 1, Goodliffe 1, Gould 1, Rogers 1, Travis 1, own goal 1.
*FA Cup (6):* Maamria 3, Elding 2, Watson 1.
*Trophy (3):* Brady 1, Maamria 1, Richards 1.

| Perez 27 | Travis 20 + 2 | Laker 35 | Carroll 15 + 5 | Flynn 22 | Goodliffe 9 | Battersby 10 + 4 | Cook 15 + 11 | Watson 26 + 1 | Elding 33 + 3 | Pitcher 4 + 1 | Baptiste 9 + 11 | Costello 8 + 4 | Abbey 6 | Langston 1 + 1 | Holloway 13 + 11 | Bunce 24 | Marcelle — + 3 | Warner 30 + 5 | Richards 9 + 16 | Maamria 25 | Wormull 20 + 1 | Gould 26 + 1 | Brennan 13 + 4 | Smith 12 + 2 | Brady 13 + 7 | Scott 2 + 4 | Rogers 4 | Camara — + 1 | Boyd 4 + 7 | Cracknell — + 1 | Brough 11 | Weatherstone 2 + 2 | Westhead 9 + 1 | Hodgson 3 + 3 | Barnard 2 + 2 | Williams — + 1 | Flack — + 1 | *Match No.* |
|---|---|---|---|---|---|---|---|---|---|---|---|---|---|---|---|---|---|---|---|---|---|---|---|---|---|---|---|---|---|---|---|---|---|---|---|---|---|---|
| 1 | 2 | 3 | 4 | 5 | 6 | 7 | 8 | 9 | $10^1$ | $11^2$ | 12 | 13 | | | | | | | | | | | | | | | | | | | | | | | | | | 1 |
| | 2 | 3 | $4^1$ | 5 | 6 | 7 | $8^2$ | 9 | $10^3$ | | 14 | 11 | 1 | 12 | 13 | | | | | | | | | | | | | | | | | | | | | | | 2 |
| | 2 | 3 | 4 | 5 | 6 | 7 | $8^1$ | $9^2$ | 10 | 14 | 13 | $11^3$ | 1 | | 12 | | | | | | | | | | | | | | | | | | | | | | | 3 |
| | 2 | 3 | 4 | 5 | | $7^1$ | 8 | | $10^2$ | $11^3$ | 12 | 6 | 1 | | 14 | 9 | 13 | | | | | | | | | | | | | | | | | | | | | 4 |
| | 2 | 3 | | 5 | | 12 | 8 | | $10^2$ | 11 | $9^1$ | $7^3$ | 1 | | 6 | 4 | 13 | 14 | | | | | | | | | | | | | | | | | | | | 5 |
| | 2 | 3 | 12 | 5 | | | $8^2$ | | 10 | 11 | 9 | $7^1$ | 1 | | 6 | $4^3$ | 13 | | 14 | | | | | | | | | | | | | | | | | | | 6 |
| | 2 | $3^1$ | 4 | 5 | 6 | | 8 | 9■ | $10^2$ | | 14 | 7 | 1 | | 12 | | | 13 | | $11^3$ | | | | | | | | | | | | | | | | | | 7 |
| 1 | 2 | 3 | $4^1$ | 5 | 6 | | 8 | 9 | $10^3$ | | 11 | $7^2$ | | | 13 | | | 12 | 14 | | | | | | | | | | | | | | | | | | | 8 |
| 1 | $2^1$ | 3 | 4 | 5 | 6 | | 14 | | 10 | | $9^3$ | | | | 8 | 7 | | 12 | | | $11^2$ | 13 | | | | | | | | | | | | | | | | 9 |
| 1 | 2 | 3 | $4^2$ | $5^1$ | 6 | | 12 | | 10 | | $9^3$ | 14 | | | 8 | 7 | | | 13 | | 11 | | | | | | | | | | | | | | | | | 10 |
| 1 | 2 | 3 | | 5 | $6^1$ | $9^3$ | 12 | | 10 | | | | | | 8 | 4 | | 13 | 14 | | $11^2$ | | 7 | | | | | | | | | | | | | | | 11 |
| 1 | 2 | 3 | | 5 | | 7 | 13 | | 10 | | 12 | | | $4^2$ | 9 | $6^1$ | | | 14 | | 8 | | $11^3$ | | | | | | | | | | | | | | | 12 |
| 1 | $2^1$ | 3 | | 5 | | $7^3$ | 13 | | 10 | | | 12 | | | 6■ | 4 | | 11 | 14 | | 8 | $9^2$ | | | | | | | | | | | | | | | | 13 |
| 1 | $2^1$ | 3 | | 5 | | 7 | 12 | | $10^2$ | | | | | | 8 | 4 | | 11 | 13 | | 9 | 6 | | | | | | | | | | | | | | | | 14 |
| 1 | 2 | 3 | | 5 | | $9^2$ | 8■ | 12 | 13 | | | 6 | | | 7 | 4 | | 11 | | $10^1$ | | | | | | | | | | | | | | | | | | 15 |
| 1 | 13 | 3 | 4 | 5 | $6^1$ | | | $11^3$ | 10 | | 14 | $12^2$ | | | | | | 2 | | 9 | 7 | 8 | | | | | | | | | | | | | | | | 16 |
| 1 | $7^1$ | 5 | | 3 | | 14 | | 8 | | | 10 | | | | 13 | 4 | | 2 | | 9 | $11^2$ | $6^3$ | 12 | | | | | | | | | | | | | | | 17 |
| 1 | $7^1$ | 5 | | 3 | | 13 | 11 | 8 | 10 | | | | | | 12 | 4 | | 2 | | $9^2$ | | 6 | | | | | | | | | | | | | | | | 18 |
| 1 | $7^2$ | 5 | 14 | 3 | | | $11^3$ | 8 | 10 | | 12 | | | | 13 | $4^1$ | | 2 | | 9 | | 6 | | | | | | | | | | | | | | | | 19 |
| 1 | | 5 | $8^2$ | $3^1$ | | | 12 | | 10 | | 13 | | | | 11 | 4 | | 2 | 14 | $9^3$ | 7 | 6 | | | | | | | | | | | | | | | | 20 |
| 1 | | 5 | | | | | 12 | 8 | $10^1$ | | 11 | | | | 3 | 4 | | 2 | | $9^2$ | 7 | 6 | | 13 | | | | | | | | | | | | | | 21 |
| 1 | | 5 | 13 | | | | 12 | 8 | 10 | | 11 | | | | $3^2$ | $4^1$ | | 2 | | 9 | $7^3$ | 6 | | | 14 | | | | | | | | | | | | | 22 |
| 1 | | 5 | | $3^1$ | | | 14 | 8 | 10 | | 12 | | | | 13 | 4 | | 2 | | 9 | $7^2$ | $6^3$ | | | 11 | | | | | | | | | | | | | 23 |
| 1 | | 5 | 6 | $3^1$ | | | 12 | 8 | 14 | | 10 | | | | 13 | | | 2 | | $9^3$ | $7^2$ | | | 4 | 11 | | | | | | | | | | | | | 24 |
| 1 | | | 4 | | | | 11 | 8 | $10^1$ | | | | | | | | | 2 | 12 | 9 | 7 | 6 | | 5 | 3 | | | | | | | | | | | | | 25 |
| 1 | | | | | | | 11 | 8 | | | 13 | | | | 10 | | | 2 | 12 | 9 | $7^1$ | 6 | | 5 | 3 | $4^2$ | | | | | | | | | | | | 26 |
| 1 | 13 | | | | | | $11^3$ | 8 | | | | | | | 12 | | | 2 | 10 | 9 | $7^2$ | 6 | | 4 | $3^1$ | 14 | 5 | | | | | | | | | | | 27 |
| 1 | $4^1$ | | $8^3$ | | | 14 | 11 | | | | | | | | | | | 2 | 10 | 9 | 7 | $6^2$ | | 5 | 12 | 13 | 3 | | | | | | | | | | | 28 |
| 1 | 2 | | | | | 9 | | 8 | 14 | | | | | | | | | 3 | 10 | | 7 | $6^3$ | 13 | $5^1$ | 12 | $11^2$ | 4 | | | | | | | | | | | 29 |
| 1 | | | | | | | | 8 | $10^3$ | | | | | | | 4 | | 7 | 13 | 9 | | $6^2$ | 11 | $5^1$ | 3 | 14 | 2 | 12 | | | | | | | | | | 30 |
| 1 | | 5 | | | | | | $8^1$ | $10^3$ | | | | | | | 4 | | 2 | 13 | 9 | $7^2$ | 6 | 3 | | 11 | 12 | | | 14 | | | | | | | | | 31 |
| 1 | | 5 | | | | | | 8 | 10 | | | | | | | 4 | | 2 | $3^1$ | $9^3$ | | 6 | 11 | | | | | | 14 | 12 | $7^2$ | 13 | | | | | | 32 |
| $1^6$ | | 5 | | | | | | 8 | 10 | | | | | | | 4 | | 2 | 11 | 9■ | | $6^2$ | $7^1$ | | 13 | | | | 12 | | 3 | | 15 | | | | | 33 |
| | | 5 | | | | | | 8 | 10 | | | | | | | 4 | | 2 | $11^2$ | 9 | | $6^3$ | $7^1$ | | 13 | | | | 12 | | 3 | 14 | 1 | | | | | 34 |
| | | 5 | 13 | | | | | 8 | 10 | | | | | | | $4^2$ | | 2 | 14 | 9 | | | $3^1$ | | 12 | | | | 11 | | 7 | $6^3$ | 1 | | | | | 35 |
| | | 5 | | | | | | $8^2$ | 10 | | | | | | | $4^1$ | | 2 | $9^3$ | | | 6 | 3 | | 12 | | | | 11 | | 7 | | 1 | 13 | 14 | | | 36 |
| | | 4 | 8 | | | | | | $10^3$ | | | | | | | | | 2 | 14 | | 12 | | $3^1$ | 13 | 11 | | | | | | $6^2$ | 5 | 1 | 7 | 9 | | | 37 |
| | | | $4^1$ | | | | | | 10 | | | | | | | | | 2 | 9 | | $7^2$ | 6 | 12 | 5 | 11 | | | | 13 | | 3 | | 1 | $8^3$ | | 14 | | 38 |
| | | 4 | | | | | | $8^1$ | 10 | | | | | | | | | 2 | 12 | 9 | | $6^2$ | 7 | 5 | 11 | | | | 13 | | 3 | | 1 | | | | | 39 |
| | | 4 | | | | | | | $10^2$ | | | | | | | | | 2 | 12 | 9 | | $6^1$ | 7 | 5 | 11 | | | | 8 | | 3 | | 1 | 13 | | | | 40 |
| | | 4 | 12 | | | | | | | | | | | | | | | 2 | 10 | $9^3$ | | 6 | $8^2$ | $5^1$ | 11 | | | | 7 | | 3 | | 1 | 13 | 14 | | | 41 |
| | | 4 | | | | | | $8^2$ | | | | | | | | | | 2 | | 9 | | $6^1$ | 13 | 5 | 11 | | | | 12 | | 3 | | 1 | $7^3$ | 10 | | 14 | 42 |

**LDV Vans Trophy**

| | | | |
|---|---|---|---|
| First Round | Luton T | (h) | 0-1 |

**FA Cup**

| | | | |
|---|---|---|---|
| Fourth Qual | Eastbourne B | (a) | 2-2 |
| | | (h) | 1-0 |
| First Round | Stockport Co | (h) | 2-1 |
| Second Round | Swansea C | (a) | 1-2 |

# TAMWORTH

## Conference

*Ground:* The Lamb Ground, Kettlebrook, Tamworth, Staffordshire B77 1AA.
*Tel:* (01827) 65798.
*Year Formed:* 1933.
*Record Gate:* 4,920 (1948 v Atherstone Town Birmingham Combination).
*Nickname:* Lambs.
*Manager:* Mark Cooper.
*Secretary:* Russell Moore.
*Colours:* Red shirts with white sleeves, black shorts, red stockings.

### TAMWORTH 2003–04 LEAGUE RECORD

| Match No. | Date | Venue | Opponents | Result | | H/T Score | Lg. Pos. | Goalscorers | Attendance |
|---|---|---|---|---|---|---|---|---|---|
| 1 | Aug 9 | H | Hereford U | L | 1-3 | 0-1 | — | Cooper [76] | 2250 |
| 2 | 12 | A | Chester C | L | 0-1 | 0-0 | — | | 2267 |
| 3 | 16 | A | Northwich Vic | L | 0-1 | 0-1 | 22 | | 712 |
| 4 | 23 | H | Margate | D | 1-1 | 0-1 | 21 | Setchell [52] | 1056 |
| 5 | 25 | A | Halifax T | W | 2-1 | 1-0 | 18 | Rickards [45], Robinson [50] | 1849 |
| 6 | 30 | H | Accrington S | D | 1-1 | 0-1 | 18 | Setchell (pen) [90] | 1215 |
| 7 | Sept 7 | A | Shrewsbury T | L | 1-3 | 0-0 | 18 | Rioch (og) [88] | 3882 |
| 8 | 13 | H | Morecambe | L | 2-3 | 1-1 | 21 | Powell [13], Cooper [70] | 1247 |
| 9 | 20 | A | Leigh RMI | D | 1-1 | 0-1 | 21 | Rickards (pen) [81] | 427 |
| 10 | 23 | H | Scarborough | D | 0-0 | 0-0 | — | | 1004 |
| 11 | 27 | H | Dagenham & R | W | 2-0 | 0-0 | 18 | Whitman 2 [51, 69] | 1147 |
| 12 | Oct 4 | A | Farnborough T | D | 3-3 | 0-1 | 18 | Cooper 2 [64, 87], Follett [72] | 770 |
| 13 | 7 | A | Telford U | L | 0-2 | 0-1 | — | | 1725 |
| 14 | 11 | H | Barnet | W | 2-0 | 1-0 | 17 | Cooper 2 [5, 64] | 1304 |
| 15 | 18 | H | Aldershot T | D | 3-3 | 2-0 | 18 | Whitman [3], Watson 2 [4, 74] | 1538 |
| 16 | Nov 1 | A | Exeter C | L | 2-3 | 1-1 | 18 | Follett [22], Cooper [79] | 2979 |
| 17 | 11 | H | Stevenage Bor | L | 1-2 | 0-1 | — | Cooper [57] | 1006 |
| 18 | 15 | A | Forest Green R | L | 1-2 | 0-1 | 18 | Blunt [53] | 782 |
| 19 | 22 | H | Gravesend & N | L | 1-3 | 1-3 | 19 | Rickards [44] | 1128 |
| 20 | 25 | A | Woking | L | 0-4 | 0-0 | — | | 1565 |
| 21 | 29 | H | Shrewsbury T | D | 1-1 | 0-1 | 19 | Cooper [77] | 1761 |
| 22 | Dec 6 | A | Morecambe | L | 0-4 | 0-2 | 19 | | 1449 |
| 23 | 13 | A | Hereford U | W | 1-0 | 1-0 | 19 | Dryden [15] | 2561 |
| 24 | 20 | H | Chester C | L | 1-5 | 0-2 | 19 | Sylla [73] | 1520 |
| 25 | 26 | A | Burton Alb | W | 1-0 | 0-0 | 18 | Sylla [50] | 3164 |
| 26 | Jan 1 | H | Burton Alb | D | 1-1 | 1-0 | 19 | Sylla [45] | 2535 |
| 27 | 17 | H | Northwich Vic | W | 2-1 | 1-1 | 19 | Follett [8], Robinson [67] | 1158 |
| 28 | 20 | A | Accrington S | L | 0-3 | 0-2 | — | | 1301 |
| 29 | Feb 7 | H | Leigh RMI | W | 4-3 | 1-2 | 18 | Brooks [26], Scully [62], Cooper (pen) [76], Barnes [86] | 905 |
| 30 | 21 | H | Farnborough T | W | 2-1 | 1-0 | 19 | Cooper [19], Dryden [61] | 1084 |
| 31 | 28 | A | Barnet | L | 0-1 | 0-0 | 19 | | 1899 |
| 32 | Mar 6 | H | Telford U | L | 0-1 | 0-1 | 19 | | 1115 |
| 33 | 9 | A | Dagenham & R | D | 0-0 | 0-0 | — | | 984 |
| 34 | 13 | A | Stevenage Bor | L | 1-3 | 0-0 | 19 | Cooper [68] | 1646 |
| 35 | 16 | A | Scarborough | W | 1-0 | 0-0 | — | Cooper [75] | 1059 |
| 36 | 20 | H | Forest Green R | W | 1-0 | 1-0 | 18 | Barnes [20] | 1112 |
| 37 | 27 | A | Gravesend & N | L | 0-2 | 0-1 | 18 | | 1157 |
| 38 | Apr 3 | H | Woking | W | 2-0 | 1-0 | 18 | Smith N [45], Cooper (pen) [52] | 1053 |
| 39 | 10 | A | Margate | L | 2-3 | 0-2 | 18 | Smith N [76], Robinson [86] | 448 |
| 40 | 12 | H | Halifax T | W | 2-0 | 1-0 | 17 | Cooper (pen) [39], Sylla [77] | 1095 |
| 41 | 17 | H | Exeter C | W | 2-1 | 1-0 | 17 | Barnes 2 [19, 50] | 1803 |
| 42 | 24 | A | Aldershot T | D | 1-1 | 0-0 | 17 | Ebdon [51] | 4212 |

**Final League Position: 17**

### GOALSCORERS

*League (49):* Cooper 15 (3 pens), Barnes 4, Sylla 4, Follett 3, Rickards 3 (1 pen), Robinson 3, Whitman 3, Dryden 2, Setchell 2 (1 pen), Smith N 2, Watson 2, Blunt 1, Brooks 1, Ebdon 1, Powell 1, Scully 1, own goal 1.
*FA Cup (5):* Fisher 2, Jordan 2, Setchell 1 (pen).
*Trophy (6):* Barnes 2, Blunt 1, Ebdon 1, Quailey 1, Warner 1.

| Whiteh ead 15 | Setchell 17 | Follett 27 + 5 | Cooper 35 + 3 | Robinson 24 + 1 | Taylor 5 + 1 / Henderson 3 | Warner 34 + 5 | Fisher 14 + 1 | Collins 4 + 2 / Smith N 6 + 5 | McGregor 4 + 3 | Trainer 5 + 1 / Fox — + 1 | Barnard 3 + 3 | Darby 13 + 13 | Rickards 13 + 6 | Jordan 17 + 2 | Turner 3 + 5 | Scott 4 / Smith A 3 + 1 | Powell 5 | Hannie — + 2 / Scully 1 | Whitman 5 + 2 | Watson 6 + 1 / Brooks 1 | Langmead 2 | Johnson 6 + 5 | Ayres 23 | Stanford 6 + 1 / Price 8 | One 4 | Blunt 26 + 1 | Sylla 12 + 13 | Lindley 6 | Goodwin 2 + 2 | Dryden 22 | Ebdon 13 + 1 | Wilson — + 1 / Noon 5 + 2 | Quailey 14 + 3 | Brush 10 | Barnes 17 + 1 | Rodwell 6 / Colkin 9 | Baptiste 4 | *Match No.* |
|---|---|---|---|---|---|---|---|---|---|---|---|---|---|---|---|---|---|---|---|---|---|---|---|---|---|---|---|---|---|---|---|---|---|---|---|---|---|---|
| 1 | 2 | 3 | 4 | $5^1$ | 6 | 7 | 8 | 9 | $10^2$ | $11^3$ | 12 | 13 | 14 | | | | | | | | | | | | | | | | | | | | | | | | | 1 |
| 1 | 2 | | 4 | | | 7 | 8 | 9 | 10■ | 11 | 3 | 12 | $5^1$ | 6 | | | | | | | | | | | | | | | | | | | | | | | | 2 |
| 1 | 2 | | 4 | 5 | | $7^1$ | 8 | | | $11^2$ | 6 | 12 | 9 | 3 | 13 | 10 | | | | | | | | | | | | | | | | | | | | | | 3 |
| 1 | 2 | | 4 | 5 | | 7 | 8 | $9^1$ | 12 | $10^2$ | 14 | | 13 | 3 | | 11 | $6^3$ | | | | | | | | | | | | | | | | | | | | | 4 |
| 1 | 2 | | 4 | 5 | | 7 | 8 | 12 | | | 13 | 10 | 9 | 3 | | $11^1$ | $6^2$ | | | | | | | | | | | | | | | | | | | | | 5 |
| 1 | 2■ | | $4^1$ | 5 | | 3 | 8 | 13 | | 12 | 6 | $7^2$ | 9 | | | 10 | 11 | | | | | | | | | | | | | | | | | | | | | 6 |
| 1 | 2 | 3 | 4 | 5■ | | 7 | 8 | 9 | | | | 12 | 10 | | | | $6^2$ | 13 | $11^1$ | | | | | | | | | | | | | | | | | | | 7 |
| 1 | | 3 | 4 | 5 | 6 | 7 | 8 | | | | | $9^2$ | 12 | | | | $2^1$ | | | 10 | 11 | 13 | | | | | | | | | | | | | | | | 8 |
| 1 | | 3 | | 5 | 6 | 7 | 8 | | | $11^1$ | | 10 | 12 | 13 | | | | | | | $9^2$ | | 2 | 4 | | | | | | | | | | | | | | 9 |
| 1 | | 3 | | | $6^1$ | 2 | 8 | | | | | 10 | 9 | 5 | | | | 13 | | 7 | | 12 | 11 | $4^2$ | | | | | | | | | | | | | | 10 |
| 1 | 2 | 3 | 12 | | | 7 | 8■ | | | | | $10^1$ | 9 | 5 | | | | | 13 | $11^2$ | | | 4 | 6 | | | | | | | | | | | | | | 11 |
| 1 | 2 | 5 | 12 | | | 7 | 8 | | | | | $9^3$ | 10■ | 4 | | | | | 14 | | | 13 | $6^2$ | $3^1$ | 11 | | | | | | | | | | | | | 12 |
| 1 | 2 | 3 | 4 | $5^1$ | | 12 | 8 | | | | | | 13 | 6 | | | | | 11 | | | | 7 | 14 | $9^2$ | $10^3$ | | | | | | | | | | | | 13 |
| 1 | | 3 | 4 | | 12 | 7 | | | | | | 14 | 8 | 2 | | | | | $9^3$ | 13 | | | $6^1$ | 5 | $11^2$ | 10 | | | | | | | | | | | | 14 |
| 1 | | 3 | 4 | | | 7 | 12 | | | | | | | 5 | | | | | $10^1$ | 6 | | | 2 | 8 | | 11 | 9 | | | | | | | | | | | 15 |
| | 2 | 3 | 13 | | 6 | | 8 | | | | | | 14 | 5 | | | | | $10^2$ | $7^1$ | | | | | $9^3$ | 4 | 12 | 1 | 11 | | | | | | | | | 16 |
| | 2 | 3 | 4 | | | | | | 10 | | | 12 | $9^3$ | 6 | | | | | | $8^2$ | | | | | | $7^1$ | 14 | 1 | 13 | 5 | 11 | | | | | | | 17 |
| | 2 | 3 | | | | 7 | | | $10^1$ | | | 12 | 9 | 6 | | | | | | | | | | | | 8 | $11^2$ | 1 | | 5 | 4 | 13 | | | | | | 18 |
| | 2 | 3 | 4 | | | $7^1$ | | | | | | | 8 | $9^2$ | | | | | | | | 12 | | | | 10 | 13 | 1 | | 5 | 6 | | 11 | | | | | 19 |
| | 2 | 3 | 4 | | | 13 | | | | | | 14 | | 12 | | | | | | | | 6 | | | | 11 | $10^3$ | | $8^2$ | $5^1$ | 7 | | 9 | 1 | | | | 20 |
| | 2 | 3 | 4 | | | 12 | | | | | | $9^2$ | | 6 | | | | | | | | 5 | 7 | | | 11 | 13 | | | | 8 | | $10^1$ | 1 | | | | 21 |
| | 2 | 3 | 4 | | | 13 | | | | | | | 9 | $8^3$ | | | | | | | | $5^2$ | 11■ | | | 7 | | | 12 | | $6^1$ | | 14 | 1 | 10 | | | 22 |
| | | 3 | 4 | | | 7■ | | | | | | 9 | | | | | | | | | | 2 | 6 | | | | | | | 5 | | | 10 | 1 | | 8 | 11 | 23 |
| | | 3 | $6^1$ | | | 12 | | $11^2$ | | | | 9 | | | | | | | | | | 2 | | | | 7 | 13 | | | 5 | | | 10 | 1 | | 4 | 8 | 24 |
| | | 3 | 8 | 13 | | 2 | | | | | | 12 | | | | | | | | | | | 4 | | | 11 | $10^2$ | | | 5 | | | $9^1$ | 1 | | 6 | 7 | 25 |
| | | 3 | 4 | 5 | | | | | | | | 12 | | | | | | | | | | | $2^1$ | | | 11 | $10^2$ | | | 6 | | | 9 | 1 | 13 | 7 | 8 | 26 |
| | | 3 | 6 | 2 | | 7 | | 13 | 12 | | | | | | | | | | | | | | | | | 11 | $10^2$ | | | 5 | | | $8^1$ | 1 | 9 | 4 | | 27 |
| | | 3 | 4 | 5 | | $7^1$ | | 8 | | 13 | | $12^2$ | | | | | | | | | | | | | | 11 | 14 | | | 6 | | | $10^3$ | 1 | 9 | 2 | | 28 |
| | | $3^1$ | 4 | 5 | | 2 | | 12 | | | | | | | | 8 | | 11 | | $10^2$ | | | | | | 7 | 13 | | | 6 | | | | 1 | 9 | | | 29 |
| | | 3 | 4 | 5 | | 7 | | | | | | | | | 12 | $2^1$ | | | | | | | | | | 8 | 13 | 1 | | 6 | 11 | | $9^2$ | | 10 | | | 30 |
| | | $3^1$ | 4 | 6 | | 2 | | 13 | 14 | | | | | | 7 | | | | | | | | | | | 11 | 12 | 1 | | 5 | $8^2$ | | $9^3$ | | 10 | | | 31 |
| | | 4 | 7 | | | 2 | | 13 | | | | 8 | | 5 | | | | | | | | | 3 | 1 | | $11^2$ | 14 | | | $6^1$ | | 12 | $9^3$ | | 10 | | | 32 |
| | | 12 | 4 | 5 | | 3 | | | | | | | | | | | | | | | | | 7 | 1 | | 11 | $10^2$ | | | 6 | | $8^1$ | 13 | | 9 | 2 | | 33 |
| | | 13 | 4 | 5 | 1 | 3 | | | | | | | | | 12 | | | | | | | | 7 | | | 11 | $10^3$ | | | $6^2$ | | $8^1$ | 14 | | 9 | 2 | | 34 |
| | | | 7 | 4 | 1 | 2 | | 12 | | | | | | | | | | | | | | | 6 | | | 11 | 13 | | | 5 | | $8^1$ | $9^2$ | | 10 | 3 | | 35 |
| | | | 7 | 4 | 1 | 2 | | | | | | | | | 13 | | | | | | | | 6 | | | 11 | 12 | | | 5 | | 8 | $9^1$ | | $10^2$ | 3 | | 36 |
| | | | 7 | 4 | | 2 | | | | | | 13 | | | 12 | | | | | | | | $6^1$ | 1 | | 11 | $9^3$ | | | 5 | 14 | $8^2$ | | | 10 | 3■ | | 37 |
| | | | $4^1$ | 3 | | 2 | | 7 | | | | 9 | | | 5 | | | | | | | | 6 | 1 | | | | | | | 8 | 12 | | | 10 | 11 | | 38 |
| | | 12 | 7 | 2 | | $4^2$ | | 11 | | | | 9 | | | $3^1$ | | | | | | | | 6 | 1 | | | 13 | | | 5 | 8 | | | | 10 | | | 39 |
| | | 12 | 7 | | | 2 | | 11 | | | | 14 | | | | | | | | | | $4^1$ | 6 | 1 | | 13 | 9 | | | 5 | $8^2$ | | | | 10 | $3^3$ | | 40 |
| | | | 7 | 4 | | 2 | | | | | | | | | | 12 | | | | | | | 6 | 1 | | 11 | 9 | | | $5^1$ | 8 | | | | 10 | 3 | | 41 |
| | | 12 | | 5 | | $2^1$ | | 7 | | | | | | | | $4^2$ | | | | | | 13 | 6 | 1 | | 11 | 9 | | | | 8 | | | | 10 | 3 | | 42 |

**FA Cup**

| | | | |
|---|---|---|---|
| Fourth Qual | Telford U | (a) | 3-3 |
| | | (h) | 2-3 |

# TELFORD UNITED (before liquidation)

*Ground:* New Bucks Head Stadium, The Bucks Way, Telford, Shropshire TF1 2NT.
*Tel:* (01952) 640 064.
*Year Formed:* 1876.
*Record Gate:* 13,000 (1935 v Shrewsbury Town Birmingham League).
*Nickname:* The Bucks.
*Manager:* Mick Jones.
*Secretary:* Mike Ferriday.
Colours; Red shirts, blue shorts, red stockings.

## TELFORD UNITED 2003–04 LEAGUE RECORD

| *Match No.* | *Date* | *Venue* | *Opponents* | *Result* | *H/T Score* | *Lg. Pos.* | *Goalscorers* | *Attendance* |
|---|---|---|---|---|---|---|---|---|
| 1 | Aug 9 | A | Barnet | L 0-2 | 0-0 | — | | 1319 |
| 2 | 12 | H | Exeter C | W 2-0 | 0-0 | — | Mills [47], Williams [57] | 2830 |
| 3 | 16 | H | Aldershot T | L 2-5 | 1-1 | 16 | Green [5], Grant [87] | 2206 |
| 4 | 23 | A | Gravesend & N | W 2-1 | 0-0 | 10 | Ricketts [51], Blackwood [55] | 834 |
| 5 | 25 | H | Morecambe | W 2-1 | 0-0 | 6 | Lavery [52], Ricketts [86] | 2613 |
| 6 | 30 | A | Scarborough | D 1-1 | 0-1 | 8 | Mills [81] | 1113 |
| 7 | Sept 6 | A | Dagenham & R | D 1-1 | 1-0 | 11 | Mills [36] | 1503 |
| 8 | 13 | H | Burton Alb | D 2-2 | 1-1 | 9 | Grant 2 [40, 54] | 2035 |
| 9 | 20 | H | Stevenage Bor | L 0-2 | 0-1 | 12 | | 1703 |
| 10 | 23 | A | Hereford U | L 1-2 | 0-1 | — | Mills [83] | 4190 |
| 11 | 27 | A | Chester C | D 0-0 | 0-0 | 13 | | 2688 |
| 12 | Oct 4 | H | Margate | D 1-1 | 0-1 | 13 | Mills [79] | 1529 |
| 13 | 7 | H | Tamworth | W 2-0 | 1-0 | — | Murphy [45], Naylor [65] | 1725 |
| 14 | 18 | A | Farnborough T | L 1-2 | 1-1 | 14 | Naylor [45] | 579 |
| 15 | Nov 1 | H | Woking | W 1-0 | 1-0 | 13 | Mills [14] | 1334 |
| 16 | 11 | A | Halifax T | D 1-1 | 0-0 | — | Murphy [85] | 1332 |
| 17 | 15 | H | Leigh RMI | W 5-0 | 2-0 | 9 | Naylor [10], Murphy 3 [22, 76, 90], Moore P [80] | 1377 |
| 18 | 22 | A | Accrington S | W 5-1 | 4-0 | 8 | Murphy 2 [4, 62], Blackwood [7], Naylor [27], Mills [29] | 1448 |
| 19 | 25 | H | Northwich Vic | L 0-1 | 0-1 | — | | 1560 |
| 20 | 29 | H | Dagenham & R | W 1-0 | 1-0 | 11 | Hulbert [36] | 1321 |
| 21 | Dec 9 | A | Shrewsbury T | D 0-0 | 0-0 | — | | 6738 |
| 22 | 13 | H | Barnet | L 1-2 | 1-1 | 13 | Mills [14] | 1562 |
| 23 | 20 | A | Exeter C | W 3-0 | 1-0 | 10 | Mills [3], Blackwood [63], Naylor [90] | 3114 |
| 24 | Jan 1 | A | Forest Green R | D 0-0 | 0-0 | 12 | | 1071 |
| 25 | 17 | A | Aldershot T | L 1-3 | 1-0 | 13 | Naylor [35] | 2831 |
| 26 | Feb 7 | A | Stevenage Bor | W 1-0 | 0-0 | 13 | Naylor [56] | 1744 |
| 27 | 21 | A | Margate | L 0-1 | 0-1 | 13 | | 400 |
| 28 | Mar 2 | H | Hereford U | L 0-3 | 0-1 | — | | 2554 |
| 29 | 6 | A | Tamworth | W 1-0 | 1-0 | 12 | Naylor [20] | 1115 |
| 30 | 9 | A | Burton Alb | L 1-2 | 1-1 | — | Naylor [31] | 1244 |
| 31 | 13 | H | Halifax T | W 2-1 | 0-0 | 11 | Naylor [48], Ricketts [69] | 1337 |
| 32 | 20 | A | Leigh RMI | D 1-1 | 1-0 | 12 | Naylor [38] | 315 |
| 33 | 23 | H | Forest Green R | L 0-2 | 0-1 | — | | 1354 |
| 34 | 30 | H | Chester C | L 0-2 | 0-0 | — | | 3503 |
| 35 | Apr 6 | H | Shrewsbury T | W 1-0 | 0-0 | — | Ricketts [62] | 4337 |
| 36 | 8 | H | Accrington S | W 1-0 | 0-0 | — | Green [65] | 2031 |
| 37 | 10 | H | Gravesend & N | D 1-1 | 0-0 | 11 | Whitehead [87] | 1746 |
| 38 | 12 | A | Morecambe | L 0-1 | 0-0 | 12 | | 1642 |
| 39 | 14 | H | Scarborough | W 2-1 | 2-1 | — | Grant 2 [35, 38] | 1654 |
| 40 | 17 | A | Woking | L 1-3 | 0-1 | 12 | Grant [88] | 2326 |
| 41 | 21 | A | Northwich Vic | L 0-1 | 0-1 | — | | 479 |
| 42 | 24 | H | Farnborough T | L 2-4 | 1-3 | 12 | Stanley [40], Green [84] | 3323 |

**Final League Position: 12**

### GOALSCORERS

*League (49):* Naylor 11, Mills 9, Murphy 7, Grant 6, Ricketts 4, Blackwood 3, Green 3, Hulbert 1, Lavery 1, Moore P 1, Stanley 1, Whitehead P 1, Williams 1.
*FA Cup (13):* Moore P 4 (1 pen), Murphy 3, Mills 2, Blackwood 1, Green 1 (pen), Lavery 1, Ricketts 1.
*LDV Vans Trophy (1):* Mills 1.
*Trophy (12):* Grant 4, Naylor 3, Blackwood 2, Clarke 1, Green 1, Ricketts 1.

| MacKenzie 39 | Clarke 29 + 5 | Challis 33 | Green 16 + 4 | Howarth 26 | Eustace 6 | Williams 8 + 5 | Simpson2 8 + 3 | Mills 26 | Grant 20 + 15 | Blackwood 25 + 11 | Rowe 2 + 6 | Ricketts 39 + 2 | Murphy 15 + 9 | Moore P 18 + 12 | Lavery 23 + 8 | Whitehead 36 + 1 | Naylor 16 + 5 | Wilkinson 8 | Hulbert 21 + 1 | Stanley 11 + 1 | Uddin 6 | Rushbury 8 + 2 | Taylor 3 | Daniels — + 1 | Moore C — + 1 | *Match No.* |
|---|---|---|---|---|---|---|---|---|---|---|---|---|---|---|---|---|---|---|---|---|---|---|---|---|---|---|
| 1 | 2 | 3 | 4 | 5 | 6 | $7^{1}$ | 8 | 9 | $10^{2}$ | $11^{3}$ | 12 | 13 | 14 | | | | | | | | | | | | | 1 |
| 1 | 2 | 3 | 4 | 5 | 6 | 7 | 8 | 9 | 10 | 11 | | | | | | | | | | | | | | | | 2 |
| 1 | 2 | 3 | $4^{1}$ | 5 | 6 | $7^{2}$ | 8 | 9 | 10 | $11^{3}$ | | 12 | | 13 | 14 | | | | | | | | | | | 3 |
| 1 | 2 | 3 | 4 | | 6 | $7^{1}$ | 8 | $9^{2}$ | | 11 | 13 | 10 | 12 | | | 5 | | | | | | | | | | 4 |
| 1 | 2 | $3^{1}$ | 4 | 5 | | | 8 | $9^{2}$ | 13 | $10^{3}$ | 14 | 11 | 12 | | 7 | 6 | | | | | | | | | | 5 |
| 1 | 2 | $3^{1}$ | $4^{2}$ | 5 | | 13 | 8 | 9 | 14 | $11^{3}$ | | 10 | 12 | | 7 | 6 | | | | | | | | | | 6 |
| 1 | 2 | 3 | 4 | 5■ | | 12 | 8 | 9 | $10^{2}$ | | | $7^{1}$ | 13 | | 11 | 6 | | | | | | | | | | 7 |
| 1 | 2 | $3^{1}$ | $4^{2}$ | | 6 | 13 | 8 | $9^{3}$ | 10■ | 14 | | 7 | 12 | | 11 | 5 | | | | | | | | | | 8 |
| 1 | 2 | 3 | | | | $7^{1}$ | 8 | 9 | 10 | 12 | | 4 | $11^{2}$ | 13 | 6 | 5 | | | | | | | | | | 9 |
| 1 | 2 | 3 | | 5 | 6 | | 8 | 9 | 10 | | | 11 | | | 7 | 4 | | | | | | | | | | 10 |
| 1 | 2 | 3 | 4 | 5 | | | 8 | 9 | | $12^{2}$ | | 7 | 13 | | 6■ | 11 | $10^{1}$ | | | | | | | | | 11 |
| 1 | $2^{1}$ | $3^{2}$ | 4 | 5 | | 13 | 8 | 9 | | 12 | 14 | 7 | 11 | | | 6 | $10^{3}$ | | | | | | | | | 12 |
| 1 | 2 | 3 | 4 | 5 | | | 8 | 9 | | | | $7^{1}$ | 11 | | 12 | 6 | 10 | | | | | | | | | 13 |
| 1 | | $3^{1}$ | 4 | | | 7 | 8 | 9 | 13 | 12 | | 6 | 2 | $10^{2}$ | | 5 | 11 | | | | | | | | | 14 |
| 1 | 2 | 3 | $4^{1}$ | | | | 8 | $9^{2}$ | 13 | 11 | | 7 | 6 | 14 | 12 | 5 | $10^{3}$ | | | | | | | | | 15 |
| 1 | 2 | 3 | | 5 | | | $8^{1}$ | 9 | 13 | 12 | | 7 | 11 | $10^{2}$ | 6 | 4 | | | | | | | | | | 16 |
| 1 | 2 | 3 | | | | | $8^{1}$ | $9^{2}$ | 14 | 12 | | 6 | 11 | 13 | 7 | 5 | $10^{3}$ | 4 | | | | | | | | 17 |
| 1 | | 3 | | | | | 8 | $9^{2}$ | 13 | 11 | | 6 | $7^{1}$ | 14 | 12 | 5 | $10^{3}$ | 2 | 4 | | | | | | | 18 |
| 1 | $2^{1}$ | 3 | | | | | $8^{2}$ | 9 | 14 | 11 | | 7 | | 12 | 13 | 5 | 10 | 6 | $4^{3}$ | | | | | | | 19 |
| 1 | 2 | 3 | | | | | $8^{1}$ | $9^{2}$ | 13 | 11 | | 7 | | 10 | 12 | 5 | | 6 | 4 | | | | | | | 20 |
| 1 | 2 | 3 | | | | | 8 | $9^{3}$ | 13 | 12 | | 7 | $6^{1}$ | $10^{2}$ | | 5 | 14 | 4■ | 11 | | | | | | | 21 |
| 1 | $2^{1}$ | 3 | | | | | 8 | $9^{3}$ | 13 | $11^{2}$ | | 7 | | 10 | 12 | 5 | 14 | 4 | 6 | | | | | | | 22 |
| 1 | 2 | 3 | | 5 | | | 8 | 9 | | 11 | | 7 | | $10^{1}$ | | | 12 | 4 | 6 | | | | | | | 23 |
| 1 | 2 | 3 | | 5 | | | 8 | $9^{2}$ | 13 | $11^{1}$ | | 7 | 12 | $10^{3}$ | | 4 | 14 | | 6 | | | | | | | 24 |
| 1 | $2^{1}$ | 3 | | 5 | | | $8^{2}$ | $9^{3}$ | 14 | 12 | | 7 | 6 | 13 | | | 10 | 4 | 11 | | | | | | | 25 |
| 1 | | $3^{1}$ | | 5 | | | 8 | | | 11 | | 7 | 6 | 9 | 12 | 2 | 10 | | 4 | | | | | | | 26 |
| 1 | $2^{1}$ | 3 | | 5 | | | $8^{2}$ | | $9^{3}$ | 12 | | 7 | 11 | 14 | | 6 | 10 | | 4 | 13 | | | | | | 27 |
| 1 | $3^{1}$ | 6 | | 5 | | | | | 9 | | | 11 | | 12 | 7 | 2 | 10 | | 8 | 4 | | | | | | 28 |
| 1 | 2 | 3 | | 5 | | | | | 10 | | | 11 | | | 7 | 4 | 9 | | 6 | 8 | | | | | | 29 |
| 1 | $2^{1}$ | 3 | | | | | | | $9^{2}$ | 12 | | 7 | | 13 | 11 | 5 | 10 | | 8 | 4 | 6 | | | | | 30 |
| 1 | | 3 | | | | 12 | $2^{1}$ | | 13 | 11 | | 7 | | $9^{2}$ | | 5 | 10 | | 8 | 4 | 6 | | | | | 31 |
| 1 | | 3 | | 5 | | 7 | | | | 11 | | $8^{1}$ | | 9 | 6 | 12 | 10 | | | 4 | 2 | | | | | 32 |
| 1 | 12 | 6 | 13 | | | $3^{1}$ | | | $10^{3}$ | | | 11 | | 9 | 8 | 5 | 14 | | | 4 | 2 | $7^{2}$ | | | | 33 |
| | 2■ | | 14 | 6 | | | | | 10 | 11 | 12 | $7^{2}$ | | $9^{3}$ | 8 | 5 | | | | 4 | $3^{1}$ | 13 | 1 | | | 34 |
| 1 | | | | 6 | | | | | 10 | 11 | | 7 | 12 | $9^{1}$ | 4 | 5 | | | $8^{2}$ | 2 | 3 | 13 | | | | 35 |
| 1 | 13 | | 14 | 6 | | | | | 10 | 11 | | 7 | $3^{2}$ | $9^{3}$ | 8 | 5 | | | 12 | $4^{1}$ | | 2 | | | | 36 |
| 1 | 12 | | $2^{1}$ | | | | | 9 | $10^{3}$ | 11 | 13 | 7 | $6^{2}$ | 14 | 8 | 5 | | | 4 | | | 3 | | | | 37 |
| 1 | 2 | | | | | | 12 | | 14 | $11^{1}$ | $10^{3}$ | 7 | 6 | $9^{2}$ | 8 | 5 | | | 4 | | | 3 | | 13 | | 38 |
| 1 | | | 2 | 6 | | | | | 10 | 11 | | 7 | | 9 | 8 | 5 | | | 4 | | | 3 | | | | 39 |
| 1 | | | | 6 | | | 12 | | 10 | 11 | $8^{1}$ | 7 | | 9 | 2 | 5 | | | 4 | | | 3 | | | | 40 |
| | 12 | | 9 | 6 | | | 14 | | 10 | $11^{1}$ | | 7 | | 13 | 8 | 5 | | | $4^{3}$ | $2^{2}$ | | 3 | 1 | | | 41 |
| | 12 | | 14 | 6 | | | | | $10^{2}$ | 11 | | $7^{1}$ | | $9^{3}$ | 8 | 5 | | | 4 | 2 | | 3 | 1 | | 13 | 42 |

**LDV Vans Trophy**

| | | | |
|---|---|---|---|
| First Round | Lincoln C | (a) | 1-3 |

**FA Cup**

| | | | |
|---|---|---|---|
| Fourth Qual | Tamworth | (h) | 3-3 |
| | | (a) | 3-2 |
| First Round | Crawley T | (h) | 3-2 |
| Second Round | Brentford | (h) | 3-0 |
| Third Round | Crewe Alex | (a) | 1-0 |
| Fourth Round | Millwall | (h) | 0-2 |

# WOKING — Conference

*Ground:* Kingfield Sports Ground, Kingfield, Woking, Surrey GU22 9AA.
*Tel:* (01483) 772 470.
*Year Formed:* 1889.
*Record Gate:* 6,084 (1997 v Coventry City, FA Cup Third Round).
*Nickname:* The Cards.
*Manager:* Glenn Cockerill.
*Secretary:* Phil Ledger.
*Colours:* Red and white shirts, black shorts, red stockings.

## WOKING 2003–04 LEAGUE RECORD

| Match No. | Date | Venue | Opponents | Result | | H/T Score | Lg. Pos. | Goalscorers | Attendance |
|---|---|---|---|---|---|---|---|---|---|
| 1 | Aug 9 | A | Morecambe | L | 1-2 | 1-1 | — | Louis [40] | 1772 |
| 2 | 12 | H | Gravesend & N | W | 3-2 | 2-0 | — | Louis 2 (1 pen) [33 (p), 34], Foyewa [72] | 2096 |
| 3 | 16 | H | Scarborough | W | 2-1 | 2-0 | 6 | Louis [35], Foyewa [38] | 1901 |
| 4 | 23 | A | Aldershot T | L | 1-2 | 0-2 | 9 | Canham [62] | 4637 |
| 5 | 25 | H | Exeter C | W | 1-0 | 1-0 | 5 | Louis [7] | 2556 |
| 6 | 30 | A | Leigh RMI | W | 1-0 | 0-0 | 5 | Ferguson [56] | 435 |
| 7 | Sept 6 | A | Burton Alb | L | 0-2 | 0-1 | 7 | | 1482 |
| 8 | 13 | H | Farnborough T | W | 3-2 | 0-0 | 7 | Foyewa [48], Canham [54], Ferguson [72] | 2791 |
| 9 | 20 | H | Shrewsbury T | D | 3-3 | 0-1 | 6 | Haule [73], Selley (pen) [82], Foyewa [89] | 2539 |
| 10 | 23 | A | Forest Green R | D | 2-2 | 1-1 | — | Selley (pen) [45], Boardman [87] | 712 |
| 11 | 27 | A | Accrington S | D | 3-3 | 2-2 | 9 | Foyewa [15], Ferguson [28], Nade [86] | 2115 |
| 12 | Oct 4 | H | Hereford U | L | 0-1 | 0-0 | 10 | | 2906 |
| 13 | 7 | H | Stevenage Bor | D | 1-1 | 1-1 | — | Selley [45] | 2592 |
| 14 | 11 | A | Chester C | L | 1-2 | 0-1 | 10 | Nade [75] | 2085 |
| 15 | 18 | H | Halifax T | D | 2-2 | 2-1 | 10 | Haule [37], Ferguson [39] | 1917 |
| 16 | Nov 1 | A | Telford U | L | 0-1 | 0-1 | 12 | | 1334 |
| 17 | 11 | A | Margate | W | 2-1 | 1-1 | — | Zoricich (og) [6], Sodje (og) [56] | 550 |
| 18 | 15 | H | Dagenham & R | D | 0-0 | 0-0 | 10 | | 2256 |
| 19 | 22 | A | Northwich Vic | W | 4-1 | 2-0 | 10 | Sharpling 2 [6, 80], Nade 2 [27, 74] | 627 |
| 20 | 25 | H | Tamworth | W | 4-0 | 0-0 | — | Sharpling 2 [55, 79], Ferguson [65], Selley [77] | 1565 |
| 21 | 29 | H | Burton Alb | W | 1-0 | 0-0 | 7 | Haule [90] | 1947 |
| 22 | Dec 9 | A | Farnborough T | L | 0-1 | 0-0 | — | | 1005 |
| 23 | 13 | H | Morecambe | W | 4-1 | 2-0 | 7 | Sharp [22], Sharpling [45], Harris [50], Nade [80] | 1588 |
| 24 | 20 | A | Gravesend & N | D | 2-2 | 1-1 | 7 | Harris [31], Ferguson [48] | 975 |
| 25 | 26 | H | Barnet | D | 2-2 | 1-1 | 8 | Smith [5], Selley [90] | 2856 |
| 26 | Jan 1 | A | Barnet | D | 0-0 | 0-0 | 9 | | 2304 |
| 27 | 3 | H | Leigh RMI | W | 2-0 | 2-0 | 8 | Sharp [16], Foyewa [22] | 2105 |
| 28 | 17 | A | Scarborough | D | 2-2 | 0-0 | 8 | Smith 2 (1 pen) [81, 90 (p)] | 2503 |
| 29 | 24 | H | Forest Green R | D | 1-1 | 0-0 | 8 | Haule [69] | 1815 |
| 30 | Feb 14 | H | Accrington S | D | 2-2 | 0-1 | 9 | Foyewa [68], Nade [90] | 2312 |
| 31 | 21 | A | Hereford U | W | 1-0 | 0-0 | 8 | Ferguson [69] | 2817 |
| 32 | 28 | H | Chester C | L | 1-2 | 1-0 | 8 | Ferguson [1] | 2554 |
| 33 | Mar 2 | A | Shrewsbury T | L | 0-1 | 0-0 | — | | 3029 |
| 34 | 6 | A | Stevenage Bor | D | 1-1 | 1-1 | 9 | Noble [17] | 2489 |
| 35 | 13 | H | Margate | D | 0-0 | 0-0 | 10 | | 2109 |
| 36 | 20 | A | Dagenham & R | L | 0-1 | 0-0 | 10 | | 1345 |
| 37 | 27 | H | Northwich Vic | W | 3-0 | 1-0 | 9 | Cornwall [20], Murray [68], Ferguson [90] | 1857 |
| 38 | Apr 3 | A | Tamworth | L | 0-2 | 0-1 | 9 | | 1053 |
| 39 | 10 | H | Aldershot T | D | 2-2 | 1-2 | 10 | Selley (pen) [40], Cornwall [90] | 4158 |
| 40 | 12 | A | Exeter C | W | 2-1 | 0-1 | 9 | Cornwall [57], Foyewa [81] | 5236 |
| 41 | 17 | H | Telford U | W | 3-1 | 1-0 | 8 | Johnson [27], Selley (pen) [60], Foyewa [90] | 2326 |
| 42 | 24 | A | Halifax T | D | 2-2 | 1-2 | 9 | Foyewa [2], Selley (pen) [82] | 1191 |

**Final League Position: 9**

### GOALSCORERS

*League (65):* Foyewa 10, Ferguson 9, Selley 8 (5 pens), Nade 6, Louis 5 (1 pen), Sharpling 5, Haule 4, Cornwall 3, Smith 3 (1 pen), Canham 2, Harris 2, Sharp 2, Boardman 1, Johnson 1, Murray 1, Noble 1, own goals 2.
*FA Cup (6):* Ferguson 2, Selley 2 (1 pen), Haule 1, Sharpling 1.

| Bayes 35 | Townsend 33 + 5 | Smith 30 + 4 | Canham 33 + 4 | Boardman 37 | Sharp 23 + 1 | Narada 8 | Selley 30 | Louis 8 | Ferguson 32 + 7 | Nade 34 + 3 | Foyewa 20 + 14 | Sharpling 11 + 11 | Ajoge 7 + 1 | Haule 5 + 19 | Cockerill 20 + 3 | Simpemba 5 | MacDonald 32 | Pitcher 3 | Johnson 9 + 8 | Bevan 4 | Campbell 3 + 1 | Harris 7 | McNab — + 1 | Murray 13 | Parsons — + 3 | Giles 6 | Noble 5 | Oliver 1 + 1 | Cornwall 5 + 2 | Basoo 3 | Harlisha — + 1 | Allum — + 1 | *Match No.* |
|---|---|---|---|---|---|---|---|---|---|---|---|---|---|---|---|---|---|---|---|---|---|---|---|---|---|---|---|---|---|---|---|---|---|
| 1 | 2 | 3 | 4 | 5■ | 6 | 7 | 8 | $9^{1}$ | $10^{2}$ | $11^{3}$ | 12 | 13 | 14 | | | | | | | | | | | | | | | | | | | | 1 |
| 1 | 2 | 12 | 4 | 5 | 6 | 7 | 8 | 9 | 13 | 11 | $3^{2}$ | $10^{1}$ | | | | | | | | | | | | | | | | | | | | | 2 |
| 1 | 2 | 12 | 4 | 5 | 6 | 7 | 8 | $9^{1}$ | $10^{2}$ | 11 | $3^{3}$ | 14 | | 13 | | | | | | | | | | | | | | | | | | | 3 |
| 1 | $2^{1}$ | 3 | 4 | | 6 | | 8 | 9 | $10^{2}$ | 11 | $7^{3}$ | 13 | 5 | 14 | 12 | | | | | | | | | | | | | | | | | | 4 |
| 1 | | 3 | 4 | 5 | | 7 | 8 | 9 | 10 | $11^{1}$ | 6 | 12 | 2 | | | | | | | | | | | | | | | | | | | | 5 |
| 1 | 2 | 3 | 4 | 5 | | 7 | 8 | $9^{2}$ | $10^{1}$ | 11 | 13 | 12 | 6 | | | | | | | | | | | | | | | | | | | | 6 |
| 1 | 2 | $3^{1}$ | $4^{2}$ | 5 | | 7 | 8 | 9 | 10 | $11^{3}$ | 12 | 14 | 6 | 13 | | | | | | | | | | | | | | | | | | | 7 |
| 1 | 13 | 3 | 4 | 5 | | 7 | 8 | 9 | $10^{2}$ | 11 | $6^{1}$ | 12 | 2 | | | | | | | | | | | | | | | | | | | | 8 |
| 1 | 13 | 12 | 4 | 5 | | $7^{2}$ | 8 | | 10 | 11 | 9 | $6^{3}$ | 3 | 14 | | $2^{1}$ | | | | | | | | | | | | | | | | | 9 |
| 1 | 2 | 3 | 4 | 5 | | | 8 | | $10^{2}$ | 11 | 13 | | 6 | 12 | | 7 | $9^{1}$ | | | | | | | | | | | | | | | | 10 |
| 1 | 2 | 3 | $4^{1}$ | 5 | | | 8 | | $10^{2}$ | 11 | 9■ | 13 | | 12 | | 6 | 7 | | | | | | | | | | | | | | | | 11 |
| 1 | 2 | $3^{1}$ | 14 | 5 | | | 8 | | 10 | $11^{2}$ | $9^{3}$ | 12 | | 13 | | 6 | 7 | 4 | | | | | | | | | | | | | | | 12 |
| 1 | 2 | $3^{1}$ | $4^{2}$ | 5 | | | 8 | | 10 | 11 | | 12 | | 13 | | 7 | 6 | 9 | | | | | | | | | | | | | | | 13 |
| 1 | 2 | $3^{2}$ | $4^{1}$ | 5 | 6 | | 8 | | 10 | 13 | | | | 9 | 12 | | 7 | 11 | | | | | | | | | | | | | | | 14 |
| 1 | 2 | | 4 | 5 | 6 | | 8 | | 10 | $11^{1}$ | | 7 | | 9 | 12 | | 3 | | | | | | | | | | | | | | | | 15 |
| 1 | 2 | | 4 | 5 | 6 | | 8 | | $10^{2}$ | 11 | 9 | 12 | | $7^{1}$ | | | 3 | | 13 | | | | | | | | | | | | | | 16 |
| 1 | 2 | $3^{1}$ | 4 | 5 | 6 | | 8 | | | 10 | 9 | $11^{2}$ | | 12 | | | 7 | | 13 | | | | | | | | | | | | | | 17 |
| | 2 | | 4 | 5 | 6 | | 8 | | 13 | 10 | 9 | $7^{1}$ | | 12 | | | 3 | | $11^{2}$ | 1 | | | | | | | | | | | | | 18 |
| | 2 | | 4 | 5 | 6 | | 8 | | 10 | 9 | | 11 | | 12 | $7^{1}$ | | 3 | | | 1 | | | | | | | | | | | | | 19 |
| | 2 | | 4 | 5 | 6 | | 8 | | 10 | 9 | | 7 | | | 11 | | 3 | | | 1 | | | | | | | | | | | | | 20 |
| | 2 | 12 | 4 | $5^{1}$ | 6 | | 8 | | $10^{2}$ | 9 | 13 | 7 | | 14 | $11^{3}$ | | 3 | | | 1 | | | | | | | | | | | | | 21 |
| 1 | 2 | 3 | 12 | | 6 | | 8 | | 10 | 13 | 14 | 7 | | $9^{3}$ | $11^{1}$ | | 4 | | | | $5^{2}$ | | | | | | | | | | | | 22 |
| 1 | 2 | 3 | | | 6 | | 8 | | 13 | 9 | | 11 | | | $7^{1}$ | | 4 | | 12 | | 5 | $10^{2}$ | | | | | | | | | | | 23 |
| 1 | 2 | 3 | | | 6 | | 8 | | 12 | 9 | 13 | $11^{1}$ | | | 7 | | 4 | | | | 5■ | $10^{2}$ | | | | | | | | | | | 24 |
| 1 | 2 | 3 | | 5 | 6 | | 8 | | 7 | 9 | 12 | | | | 11 | | 4 | | | | | $10^{1}$ | | | | | | | | | | | 25 |
| 1 | 2 | 7 | 4 | 5 | 6 | | | | 8 | 9 | 13 | | | 14 | $11^{2}$ | | $3^{1}$ | | | | 12 | $10^{3}$ | | | | | | | | | | | 26 |
| 1 | | 2 | $4^{1}$ | 5 | 6 | | | | | 7 | 9 | | | 14 | | | 3 | | 11 | | | $10^{3}$ | 12 | $8^{2}$ | 13 | | | | | | | | 27 |
| 1 | 2 | 3 | | 5 | 6 | | | | | 7 | 9 | | | 12 | | | 4 | | 11 | | | $10^{1}$ | | 8 | | | | | | | | | 28 |
| 1 | 2 | 7 | 13 | 5 | 6 | | | | $10^{1}$ | 9 | 12 | | | 8 | | | 3 | | $11^{2}$ | | | | | 4 | | | | | | | | | 29 |
| 1 | 2 | 6 | 13 | 5 | | | | | 8 | 7 | 9 | | | | 3 | | | | $12^{2}$ | | | $10^{1}$ | | 11 | | 4 | | | | | | | 30 |
| 1 | 2 | 6 | 8 | 5 | | | | | $10^{2}$ | 9 | 13 | | | 12 | $11^{1}$ | | 3 | | | | | | | 7 | | 4 | | | | | | | 31 |
| 1 | $2^{1}$ | 6 | 8 | 5 | | | | | 10 | | 9 | | | 12 | 11 | | 3 | | | | | | | 7 | | 4 | | | | | | | 32 |
| 1 | 2 | 6 | | 5 | 13 | | | | 10 | 7 | 9 | | | 12■ | $11^{2}$ | | 3 | | | | | | | 8 | | $4^{1}$ | | | | | | | 33 |
| 1 | 12 | 6 | 8 | 5 | | | | | 10 | $7^{1}$ | 14 | | | | $11^{2}$ | | 3 | | 13 | | | | | 2 | | 4 | $9^{3}$ | | | | | | 34 |
| 1 | 2 | 6 | $8^{1}$ | 5 | | | | | 10 | | | | | 12 | $11^{2}$ | | 3 | | 13 | | | | | 7 | | 4 | $9^{3}$ | 14 | | | | | 35 |
| 1 | | 2 | 4 | 5 | 6 | | | | 7 | | | | | | 11 | | 3 | | 12 | | | | | 8 | | | $9^{1}$ | | 10 | | | | 36 |
| | 14 | 2 | 8 | 5 | 6 | | | | 7 | | 12 | | | | 11 | | 3 | | $13^{3}$ | | | | | 4 | | | $9^{1}$ | | $10^{2}$ | 1 | | | 37 |
| 1 | 2 | 6 | 7 | 5 | | | $8^{1}$ | | 10 | | 13 | | | | | | 3 | | 11 | | | | | 4 | | | $9^{2}$ | | 12 | | | | 38 |
| 1 | 12 | $2^{1}$ | 4 | 5 | $6^{2}$ | | 8 | | $10^{3}$ | 13 | 9 | | | | 11 | | 3 | | 7 | | | | | | | | | | 14 | | | | 39 |
| | 2 | | 4 | 5 | | | 8 | | 12 | 7 | $9^{1}$ | | | | 11 | | 3 | | 6 | | | | | | | | | | $10^{2}$ | 1 | 13 | | 40 |
| | 2 | | $4^{1}$ | 5 | | | 8 | | 14 | 7 | $9^{2}$ | | | | 11 | | 3 | | 6 | | | | | | 12 | | | | $10^{3}$ | 1 | | 13 | 41 |
| 1 | | | $4^{2}$ | | | | 8 | | 12 | 7 | 9 | | | | 11 | | 3 | | $5^{1}$ | | | | | 6 | 13 | | | 2 | 10 | | | | 42 |

**FA Cup**

| | | | |
|---|---|---|---|
| Fourth Qual | East Thurrock U | (a) | 1-1 |
| | | (h) | 2-0 |
| First Round | Histon | (h) | 3-1 |
| Second Round | Kidderminster H | (h) | 0-3 |

# REVIEW OF THE SCOTTISH SEASON 2003–04

It has been quite an interesting season, with plenty to talk about.

On the international front there has not been a great deal to enthuse about. We duly finished as runner-up in our Euro group, and there was more than a flicker of hope when we defeated Holland in the first leg of the play-off at Hampden. We were soon put in our place in the return match. Yes, there are hopeful signs from time to time, particularly at Under-21 level; but we do not have enough home players in first teams, and most of those who stray to the south seem somehow to lose their national fervour and appetite for success.

The Scottish women's team had some good results, but have not managed to qualify for Euro 2005.

Celtic again carried our flag into Europe. The highlight of their campaign came when they held Barcelona at Nou Camp and thus won the tie. It was good to find how welcome the Celtic fans were in the city. A further Spanish contest proved too much, but Celtic had again shown themselves fit company for anyone.

At home, they dominated the Premier League. An astonishing run of twenty-five wins in succession saw them well ahead of any opposition, and they finished seventeen points ahead of Rangers, and thirty points ahead of third-placed Hearts. Rangers had a rather sad season.

There were times when some of their players on the field looked uninterested and certainly overpaid, and that is no way to compete. They will come again, but the fire must be kindled. Hearts had a good season; Dunfermline challenged in the top area; Dundee United, after a poor start, worked their way up to fifth; and Motherwell did well with a side which included a number of young Scots – a welcome improvement after last season's reprieve. In the lower half, there was not much between the teams, and although Aberdeen were well behind the others, they were still well clear of the luckless Partick Thistle. There are few teams in this league who are not in financial difficulties, and this does not help the players much,

The almost customary relegation row broke out at the end of the season, and it is still not finally sorted.

In the First Division there was a robust and fascinating end to the season. At the beginning of December, the top six teams were all within two points of each other. Gradually Clyde and Inverness drew ahead, but, by the start of April, the former had what appeared a commanding lead of six points with half a dozen games to go. Three draws saw them losing ground, and the crunch fixture came in the penultimate game, when Clyde lost to the northerners in front of a crowd of four and a half thousand. There were over six thousand at the Caledonian Stadium to see Inverness clinch the title the following week. Then the fun started.

Brechin never quite made the grade at the foot of the table, but they tried gallantly; Ayr United join them in relegation.

There was an amazing transformation in the Second Division. In mid-November, Morton and East Fife were at the top. However, a string of eight games saw the Fifers collect only two points, and another series of losses in the new year found them in eighth place. Late in the season Arbroath overtook them, so East Fife are relegated, with Stenhousemuir. In January Morton had a ten-point lead over Berwick, in second place. They looked certainties for promotion. Gradually, however, they surrendered points here and there; Airdrie came right to the top, but Morton still looked good for second place. However, they still squandered points, and Hamilton Accies gratefully accepted second place and promotion.

Stranraer return at once from the Third Division to the Second. Although they had some ups and downs, they were fairly consistent. And they scored plenty of goals – which always helps. Stranraer had the inestimable advantage of keeping most of their team together for the whole campaign – ten of their players played in thirty matches or more. It does show. Stirling Albion join them in the Second Division next year. Gretna did well, and Peterhead looked good at times, but made too many mistakes to put in a credible challenge.

The Scottish Cup was won by Celtic, who defeated Dunfermline in a good final. The Pars were ahead at half-time, but a couple of inevitable goals from Henrik Larssen, and a third from Petrov were sufficient to send the trophy to Parkhead. There had been a replay in the semi-finals, when Dunfermline were hard put to defeat Inverness after an initial draw.

In the early rounds there was much interest in the progress of non-Scottish League club Spartans. After a first round win in the Highlands, they won against Alloa in a high-scoring game after a replay, and then knocked out Arbroath; in the fourth round they took on Livingston on their home ground. Spartans held the Premier League club in the first half, but eventually the pressure was too great. Livingston then went on as far as the semi-finals – against Celtic.

The CIS League Cup was won by Livingston, their first trophy, and a ray of light in the middle of deep financial trouble. In the final they beat Hibernian, who had dismissed both Celtic and Rangers from the competition. Not many clubs can claim to have done that. A notable first round win was in Inverness, where Queen's Park accounted for the home side – a side which had been extremely successful in the other cups. Inverness in fact won the Bell's Challenge Cup, beating Airdrie in the final in Perth.

Now we are on the verge of another season. Some new faces both as managers and players; the same hopes for international success; and, come what may, a keenness amongst supporters as usual.

ALAN ELLIOTT

# ABERDEEN

## Premier League

*Year Formed:* 1903. *Ground & Address:* Pittodrie Stadium, Pittodrie St, Aberdeen AB24 5QH. *Telephone:* 01224 650400. *Fax:* 01224 644173.
*Ground Capacity:* all seated: 21,487. *Size of Pitch:* 110yd × 72yd.
*Chairman:* Stewart Milne. *Chief Executive:* Keith Wyness. *Secretary:* Duncan Fraser. *Operations Manager:* John Morgan.
*Manager:* Jim Calderwood. *Assistant Manager:* Jimmy Nichol. *U-21/U-19 Manager:* Neil Cooper. *Physios:* David Wylie, John Sharp.
*Managers since 1975:* Ally MacLeod, Billy McNeill, Alex Ferguson, Ian Porterfield, Alex Smith and Jocky Scott, Willie Miller, Roy Aitken, Alex Miller, Paul Hegarty, Ebbe Skovdahl, Steve Paterson. *Club Nicknames(s):* The Dons. *Previous Grounds:* None.
*Record Attendance:* 45,061 v Hearts, Scottish Cup 4th rd, 13 Mar 1954.
*Record Transfer Fee received:* £1.75 million for Eoin Jess to Coventry City (February 1996).
*Record Transfer Fee paid:* £1m+ for Paul Bernard from Oldham Athletic (September 1995).
*Record Victory:* 13-0 v Peterhead, Scottish Cup, 9 Feb 1923.
*Record Defeat:* 0-8 v Celtic, Division 1, 30 Jan 1965.
*Most Capped Players:* Alex McLeish, 77, Scotland.
*Most League Appearances:* 556: Willie Miller, 1973-90.
*Most League Goals in Season (Individual):* 38: Benny Yorston, Division I, 1929-30.
*Most Goals Overall (Individual):* 199: Joe Harper.

### ABERDEEN 2003–04 LEAGUE RECORD

| Match No. | Date | Venue | Opponents | Result | | H/T Score | Lg. Pos. | Goalscorers | Attendance |
|---|---|---|---|---|---|---|---|---|---|
| 1 | Aug 9 | A | Hearts | L | 0-2 | 0-1 | — | | 14260 |
| 2 | 16 | H | Rangers | L | 2-3 | 1-2 | — | Zdrilic [23], Deloumeaux [89] | 16,348 |
| 3 | 23 | H | Dunfermline Ath | L | 1-2 | 1-1 | 11 | Zdrilic [23] | 10,810 |
| 4 | 30 | A | Hibernian | D | 1-1 | 1-0 | 11 | Anderson [6] | 10,682 |
| 5 | Sept 13 | H | Partick Th | W | 2-1 | 1-0 | 9 | Booth [5], Anderson [76] | 10,597 |
| 6 | 20 | A | Dundee | L | 0-2 | 0-1 | 10 | | 7887 |
| 7 | 27 | H | Livingston | L | 0-3 | 0-1 | 11 | | 10,307 |
| 8 | Oct 4 | A | Kilmarnock | W | 3-1 | 2-0 | 10 | Zdrilic [2], Tosh [14], Booth [47] | 6023 |
| 9 | 18 | H | Dundee U | L | 0-1 | 0-1 | 11 | | 11,234 |
| 10 | 25 | A | Celtic | L | 0-4 | 0-3 | 11 | | 59,574 |
| 11 | Nov 1 | H | Motherwell | L | 0-3 | 0-1 | 11 | | 9895 |
| 12 | 9 | H | Hearts | L | 0-1 | 0-1 | 11 | | 9687 |
| 13 | 22 | A | Rangers | L | 0-3 | 0-0 | 11 | | 49,962 |
| 14 | 29 | A | Dunfermline Ath | D | 2-2 | 1-0 | 11 | Deloumeaux [24], Booth [60] | 5254 |
| 15 | Dec 7 | H | Hibernian | W | 3-1 | 1-0 | 11 | Hinds [26], Booth 2 [84, 90] | 7863 |
| 16 | 13 | A | Partick Th | W | 3-0 | 1-0 | 11 | Anderson 2 [42, 48], Clark [90] | 5189 |
| 17 | 20 | H | Dundee | D | 2-2 | 1-1 | 11 | Anderson [42], Hinds [58] | 10,354 |
| 18 | 27 | A | Livingston | D | 1-1 | 1-0 | 11 | Booth [22] | 6020 |
| 19 | Jan 3 | H | Kilmarnock | W | 3-1 | 2-0 | 10 | Diamond [6], Tosh [43], Hinds [58] | 11,699 |
| 20 | 17 | A | Dundee U | L | 2-3 | 0-1 | 11 | Booth (pen) [55], Archibald (og) [65] | 8888 |
| 21 | 24 | H | Celtic | L | 1-3 | 0-2 | 11 | Tosh [61] | 16,452 |
| 22 | Feb 11 | A | Hearts | L | 0-1 | 0-0 | — | | 11,236 |
| 23 | 14 | H | Rangers | D | 1-1 | 1-0 | 11 | Diamond [1] | 15,815 |
| 24 | 21 | H | Dunfermline Ath | W | 2-0 | 1-0 | 11 | McGuire [36], Booth [52] | 11,035 |
| 25 | 24 | A | Motherwell | L | 0-1 | 0-0 | — | | 5220 |
| 26 | 28 | A | Hibernian | W | 1-0 | 1-0 | 11 | Morrison [5] | 10,416 |
| 27 | Mar 9 | H | Partick Th | D | 0-0 | 0-0 | — | | 7395 |
| 28 | 13 | A | Dundee | D | 1-1 | 0-1 | 9 | Hinds [60] | 6839 |
| 29 | 21 | H | Livingston | L | 1-2 | 0-1 | 9 | Hinds [83] | 7477 |
| 30 | 27 | A | Kilmarnock | L | 1-3 | 1-2 | 11 | Prunty [23] | 7251 |
| 31 | Apr 3 | H | Dundee U | W | 3-0 | 3-0 | 10 | Hinds [20], McGuire [23], Sheerin [42] | 8449 |
| 32 | 18 | H | Motherwell | L | 0-2 | 0-1 | 11 | | 7246 |
| 33 | 21 | A | Celtic | W | 2-1 | 0-1 | — | Prunty [55], Zdrilic [90] | 57,385 |
| 34 | 24 | A | Livingston | L | 0-2 | 0-1 | 11 | | 3133 |
| 35 | May 1 | A | Partick Th | L | 0-2 | 0-1 | 11 | | 2839 |
| 36 | 8 | H | Hibernian | L | 0-1 | 0-0 | 11 | | 6781 |
| 37 | 12 | A | Kilmarnock | L | 0-4 | 0-2 | — | | 4967 |
| 38 | 15 | H | Dundee | L | 1-2 | 1-0 | 11 | Foster [6] | 7878 |

**Final League Position: 11**

**Honours**
*League Champions:* Division I 1954-55. Premier Division 1979-80, 1983-84, 1984-85; *Runners-up:* Division I 1910-11, 1936-37, 1955-56, 1970-71, 1971-72. Premier Division 1977-78, 1980-81, 1981-82, 1988-89, 1989-90, 1990-91, 1992-93, 1993-94.
*Scottish Cup Winners:* 1947, 1970, 1982, 1983, 1984, 1986, 1990; *Runners-up:* 1937, 1953, 1954, 1959, 1967, 1978, 1993, 2000.
*League Cup Winners:* 1955-56, 1976-77, 1985-86, 1989-90, (Coca Cola cup) 1995-96; *Runners-up:* 1946-47, 1978-79, 1979-80, 1987-88, 1988-89, 1992-93, 1999-2000.
*Drybrough Cup Winners:* 1971, 1980.

**European:** *European Cup:* 12 matches (1980-81, 1984-85, 1985-86); *Cup Winners' Cup:* 39 matches (1967-68, 1970-71, 1978-79, 1982-83 winners, 1983-84 semi-finals, 1986-87, 1990-91, 1993-94); *UEFA Cup:* 48 matches (*Fairs Cup:* 1968-69. *UEFA Cup:* 1971-72, 1972-73, 1973-74, 1977-78, 1979-80, 1981-82, 1987-88, 1988-89, 1989-90, 1991-92, 1994-95, 1996-97, 2000-01, 2002-03).

**Club colours:** Shirt, Shorts, Stockings: Red with white trim.

**Goalscorers:** *League* (39): Booth 8 (1 pen), Hinds 6, Anderson 5, Zdrilic 4, Tosh 3, Deloumeaux 2, Diamond 2, McGuire 2, Prunty 2, Clark 1, Foster 1, Morrison 1, Sheerin 1, own goal 1
*Scottish Cup* (6): Zdrilic 2, Booth 1, Clark 1, Heikkinen 1, Muirhead 1
*CIS Cup* (10): Tosh 3, Hinds 2, Zdrilic 2, Booth 1, Muirhead 1, Sheerin 1

| Preece D 36 | McGuire P 16 + 1 | McNaughton K 15 + 2 | Anderson R 25 | McQuilken J 7 | Hart M 10 + 1 | Tosh S 24 + 2 | Heikkinen M 38 | Sheerin P 27 + 6 | Hinds L 23 + 7 | Zdrilic D 23 + 8 | Mackie D 4 + 12 | Booth S 20 + 1 | Clark C 18 + 5 | Deloumeaux E 8 + 3 | Muirhead S 24 + 8 | Bird M — + 2 | Tiernan F 3 + 3 | Diamond A 17 + 2 | Foster R 12 + 6 | Rutkiewicz K 16 | Morrison S 26 + 1 | Prunty B 6 + 12 | Stewart J 3 + 5 | Souter K 1 + 2 | Buckley R 6 + 2 | Higgins C 4 | Esson R 2 | O'Leary R 2 | Lombardi M — + 1 | McCulloch M 1 + 2 | Considine A 1 | Donald D — + 1 | Tarditi S — + 1 | *Match No.* |
|---|---|---|---|---|---|---|---|---|---|---|---|---|---|---|---|---|---|---|---|---|---|---|---|---|---|---|---|---|---|---|---|---|---|---|
| 1 | 2 | $3^{3}$ | 4 | 5 | 6 | 7 | 8 | 9 | $10^{1}$ | $11^{2}$ | 12 | 13 | 14 | | | | | | | | | | | | | | | | | | | | | 1 |
| 1 | 2 | 12 | 4 | $5^{2}$ | 3 | 7 | $6^{3}$ | 9 | | 11 | $8^{1}$ | 10 | 13 | 14 | | | | | | | | | | | | | | | | | | | | 2 |
| 1 | 2 | 14 | 4 | 5 | 6 | $7^{3}$ | 8 | 9 | 12 | $11^{1}$ | | $10^{2}$ | | 3 | 13 | | | | | | | | | | | | | | | | | | | 3 |
| 1 | | 3 | 4 | 5 | 2 | 7 | $6^{2}$ | 9 | $10^{1}$ | | 11 | | | | 8 | 12 | 13 | | | | | | | | | | | | | | | | | 4 |
| 1 | | 3 | 4 | 5 | 2 | 7 | $6^{3}$ | $9^{1}$ | 13 | $11^{2}$ | 12 | 10 | | 14 | 8 | | | | | | | | | | | | | | | | | | | 5 |
| 1 | | 3 | 4 | 5 | 2 | $7^{1}$ | 6 | 12 | 13 | $11^{2}$ | $10^{3}$ | | | | 9 | 14 | 8 | | | | | | | | | | | | | | | | | 6 |
| 1 | | 3 | 4 | 5 | 2 | 7 | $6^{1}$ | 9 | $10^{2}$ | 11 | 13 | | | 12 | 8 | | | | | | | | | | | | | | | | | | | 7 |
| 1 | 2 | $3^{3}$ | $4^{1}$ | | | 7 | 6 | 9 | | 11 | 13 | $10^{2}$ | 14 | 5 | 8 | | | 12 | | | | | | | | | | | | | | | | 8 |
| 1 | 2 | $3^{1}$ | 4 | | | 7 | 6 | $9^{2}$ | 13 | $11^{3}$ | 14 | 10 | 12 | 5 | 8 | | | | | | | | | | | | | | | | | | | 9 |
| 1 | 2 | | 4 | | | 5 | 6 | 9 | 12 | | $11^{1}$ | $10^{2}$ | 8 | 3 | 7 | | | | 13 | | | | | | | | | | | | | | | 10 |
| 1 | 2 | 3 | 4 | | | 7 | $6^{2}$ | $9^{1}$ | | $11^{3}$ | 14 | 10 | 12 | 5 | 8 | | | 13 | | | | | | | | | | | | | | | | 11 |
| 1 | | $3^{1}$ | 4 | | | 7■ | 6 | 14 | | 11■ | 13 | $10^{3}$ | | $5^{2}$ | 9 | | | 2 | | 8 | 12 | | | | | | | | | | | | | 12 |
| 1 | | | 4 | | | | $6^{2}$ | | $11^{1}$ | | 12 | 10 | 8 | 3 | 9 | | 13 | 2■ | | 7 | 5 | | | | | | | | | | | | | 13 |
| 1 | | 3 | 4 | | | 7 | $6^{2}$ | 13 | 12 | $11^{1}$ | 14 | $10^{3}$ | 9 | 5 | | | | | | 8 | 2 | | | | | | | | | | | | | 14 |
| 1 | | | 4 | | | 7 | 6 | | $11^{1}$ | 12 | 14 | 10 | $9^{3}$ | | 13 | | | 3 | $8^{2}$ | 5 | 2 | | | | | | | | | | | | | 15 |
| 1 | | | 4 | | | | 6 | $8^{3}$ | $11^{2}$ | 13 | 14 | 10 | 9 | | 12 | | | 3 | $7^{1}$ | 5 | 2 | | | | | | | | | | | | | 16 |
| 1 | | | 4 | | | 7 | 6 | 12 | $11^{3}$ | 14 | 13 | 10 | 9 | | | | | $3^{1}$ | 8 | $5^{2}$ | 2 | | | | | | | | | | | | | 17 |
| 1 | 12 | | $4^{1}$ | | | 7 | 6 | | $11^{2}$ | 13 | | 10 | 9 | | $8^{3}$ | | 5 | | 14 | 3 | 2 | | | | | | | | | | | | | 18 |
| 1 | | | 4 | | | $7^{3}$ | 6 | 14 | 11 | 12 | | $10^{1}$ | 9 | | 13 | | | 3 | $8^{2}$ | 5 | 2 | | | | | | | | | | | | | 19 |
| 1 | | | 4 | | | 7 | 6 | | $11^{1}$ | 12 | | 10 | 9 | | 8 | | | 3 | | 5 | 2 | | | | | | | | | | | | | 20 |
| 1 | 2 | $5^{3}$ | | | | 7 | 6 | 12 | $11^{2}$ | 10 | | | 9 | | $8^{1}$ | | | 3 | 13 | | 4 | 14 | | | | | | | | | | | | 21 |
| 1 | | 5 | 4 | | | | $6^{2}$ | 8 | $11^{1}$ | 10 | | | 9 | | 7 | | | 2 | 13 | | 3 | 12 | | | | | | | | | | | | 22 |
| 1 | | $5^{2}$ | 4 | | | | 6 | 8 | 11 | 9 | | 10 | $7^{1}$ | | 13 | | | 2 | | | 3 | 12 | | | | | | | | | | | | 23 |
| 1 | $2^{2}$ | | 4 | | | 13 | 6 | 8 | 11 | $9^{3}$ | | $10^{1}$ | 7 | | | | | 5 | 14 | | 3 | 12 | | | | | | | | | | | | 24 |
| 1 | 2 | | 4 | | | 13 | 6 | $8^{2}$ | $11^{3}$ | 9 | | $10^{1}$ | 7 | | 12 | | | 5 | | | 3 | 14 | | | | | | | | | | | | 25 |
| 1 | 2 | | 4 | | | 7 | 6 | | $11^{1}$ | 14 | | $10^{3}$ | 9 | | 12 | | | 5 | $8^{2}$ | | 3 | 13 | | | | | | | | | | | | 26 |
| 1 | 2 | 5 | | | 4 | | 6 | 8 | 11 | $10^{2}$ | | | 9 | | $7^{1}$ | | | | | | 3 | 12 | 13 | | | | | | | | | | | 27 |
| 1 | $2^{2}$ | 5 | | | 13 | | 6 | 8 | 11 | $10^{1}$ | | | 9 | | $7^{3}$ | | | 4 | | | 3 | 12 | 14 | | | | | | | | | | | 28 |
| 1 | 2 | | | | 4 | | $6^{2}$ | 9 | 11 | 12 | | | | | 13 | | 7 | 5 | $8^{1}$ | | 3 | $10^{3}$ | | 14 | | | | | | | | | | 29 |
| 1 | 2 | | | | $4^{3}$ | $7^{1}$ | 6 | $9^{2}$ | 11 | | | | | | 8 | | 12 | 5 | | | 3 | 10 | 13 | | 14 | | | | | | | | | 30 |
| 1 | $2^{3}$ | | | | | $7^{2}$ | 6 | 9 | 11 | 10 | | | | | 8 | | | 4 | | $5^{1}$ | 3 | 14 | | 13 | 12 | | | | | | | | | 31 |
| 1 | | | | | | 7 | 6 | 9 | $11^{1}$ | $10^{2}$ | | | | | 8 | | | | 13 | 4 | 3 | 12 | | | 5 | 2 | | | | | | | | 32 |
| 1 | | | | | | $7^{1}$ | 6 | 11 | | 10 | | | | | 8 | | | | 9 | 4 | 3 | 12 | | | 5 | 2 | | | | | | | | 33 |
| 1 | | | | | | | 6 | 9 | | 10 | | | | | 8 | | | | 7 | 4 | 3 | $11^{1}$ | 12 | | 5 | 2 | | | | | | | | 34 |
| 1 | | | | | | | 6 | 9 | | 10 | | | | | 8 | | | | $7^{1}$ | 4 | 3 | 11 | 12 | | 5 | 2 | | | | | | | | 35 |
| | | | | | | | $6^{2}$ | 9 | | | | | | | 8 | | | | $7^{1}$ | 4 | 3 | 11 | 10 | | 5 | | 1 | 2 | 12 | 13 | | | | 36 |
| 1 | | | | | | | 6 | 9 | 13 | | | | | | 8 | | | | 7 | 4 | 3 | 11 | $10^{2}$ | | $5^{1}$ | | | 2 | | 12 | | | | 37 |
| | | | | | | | $6^{1}$ | 9 | $11^{3}$ | | | | $8^{2}$ | | | | | | 7 | | 3 | 14 | 10 | 5 | | | 1 | | | 4 | 2 | 12 | 13 | 38 |

# AIRDRIE UNITED

## First Division

*Year Formed:* 2002. *Ground & Address:* Shyberry Excelsior Stadium, Broomfield Park, Craigneuk Avenue, Airdrie ML6 8QZ.
*Ground Capacity:* all seated: 10,000. *Size of Pitch:* 112yd × 76yd.
*Chairman:* James Ballantyne. *Secretary:* Ann Marie Ballantyne.
*Manager:* Sandy Stewart.
*Record Attendance:* 5704 v Morton, Second Division, 15 May 2004.
*Record Victory:* 6-0 v Berwick R, Second Division, 3 Apr 2004.
*Record Defeat:* 1-6 v Morton, Second Division, 1 Nov 2003.
*Most League Appearances:* 71, M. McGeown, 2002-04.
*Most League Goals in Season (Individual):* 18, Jerome Vareille, 2002-03.
*Most Goals Overall (Individual):* 28, Jerome Vareille, 2002-04.

### AIRDRIE UNITED 2003–04 LEAGUE RECORD

| Match No. | Date | Venue | Opponents | Result | | H/T Score | Lg. Pos. | Goalscorers | Attendance |
|---|---|---|---|---|---|---|---|---|---|
| 1 | Aug 9 | A | Morton | L | 1-3 | 1-0 | — | McKeown [12] | 3806 |
| 2 | 16 | H | Alloa Ath | W | 1-0 | 0-0 | 7 | Vareille [90] | 1445 |
| 3 | 23 | A | Hamilton A | L | 1-2 | 0-1 | 8 | Vareille [68] | 2007 |
| 4 | 30 | H | Dumbarton | W | 2-0 | 2-0 | 5 | Dunn [5], Glancy [22] | 1468 |
| 5 | Sept 13 | A | East Fife | L | 1-3 | 1-1 | 7 | Glancy [35] | 885 |
| 6 | 20 | H | Arbroath | W | 2-1 | 0-1 | 4 | Dunn [48], Docherty [54] | 1385 |
| 7 | 27 | A | Berwick R | W | 1-0 | 1-0 | 3 | Gow [37] | 752 |
| 8 | Oct 4 | A | Forfar Ath | D | 1-1 | 0-0 | 4 | Gow [88] | 650 |
| 9 | 11 | A | Alloa Ath | W | 4-1 | 3-1 | 3 | Docherty [33], Roberts [36], Gow [44], Vareille [68] | 636 |
| 10 | 18 | H | Stenhousemuir | W | 2-0 | 1-0 | 3 | Vareille [24], McKeown [83] | 1406 |
| 11 | Nov 1 | H | Morton | L | 1-6 | 0-3 | 3 | McKeown [80] | 3159 |
| 12 | 8 | H | East Fife | D | 1-1 | 0-0 | 3 | Docherty [65] | 1418 |
| 13 | 16 | A | Dumbarton | L | 0-2 | 0-0 | 5 | | 1361 |
| 14 | Dec 2 | A | Arbroath | D | 1-1 | 0-0 | — | Ronald [50] | 405 |
| 15 | 6 | H | Berwick R | D | 1-1 | 1-0 | 5 | Coyle [39] | 1254 |
| 16 | 13 | H | Forfar Ath | D | 3-3 | 1-1 | 5 | Coyle [4], Gow 2 (1 pen) [55, 80 (p)] | 1072 |
| 17 | 27 | A | Stenhousemuir | W | 1-0 | 1-0 | 3 | Gow [1] | 1005 |
| 18 | Jan 24 | H | Arbroath | L | 0-1 | 0-0 | 6 | | 1267 |
| 19 | Feb 7 | A | East Fife | W | 1-0 | 1-0 | 5 | Dunn [43] | 793 |
| 20 | 14 | H | Dumbarton | D | 1-1 | 1-0 | 5 | Vareille [10] | 1378 |
| 21 | 21 | H | Stenhousemuir | W | 4-0 | 4-0 | 4 | Vareille 4 [29, 34, 36, 42] | 1324 |
| 22 | Mar 2 | H | Hamilton A | W | 3-0 | 1-0 | — | Coyle 3 [39, 48, 67] | 1634 |
| 23 | 6 | H | Alloa Ath | W | 2-1 | 2-1 | 2 | McLaren 2 [38, 45] | 1542 |
| 24 | 9 | A | Morton | D | 1-1 | 0-1 | — | Gow [62] | 3252 |
| 25 | 13 | A | Hamilton A | W | 1-0 | 1-0 | 2 | Coyle [17] | 2559 |
| 26 | 16 | A | Berwick R | D | 1-1 | 0-1 | — | McLaren [80] | 502 |
| 27 | 23 | A | Forfar Ath | W | 3-1 | 2-1 | — | McLaren 2 [15, 75], Christie [18] | 710 |
| 28 | 27 | A | Dumbarton | W | 2-1 | 1-1 | 2 | Glancy [9], McLaren [62] | 1543 |
| 29 | 31 | H | East Fife | W | 2-1 | 1-0 | — | Dunn [36], McLaren [55] | 1597 |
| 30 | Apr 3 | H | Berwick R | W | 6-0 | 5-0 | 1 | Gow 2 [4, 22], Coyle 3 [7, 18, 86], Docherty [24] | 1546 |
| 31 | 10 | A | Arbroath | W | 4-0 | 1-0 | 1 | McKeown [42], McLaren [49], Wilson S [72], Lovering [80] | 1074 |
| 32 | 17 | A | Stenhousemuir | W | 3-0 | 1-0 | 1 | Lovering [15], Coyle [51], Gow (pen) [58] | 1197 |
| 33 | 24 | H | Forfar Ath | D | 2-2 | 0-1 | 1 | McLaren [47], Coyle [74] | 1959 |
| 34 | May 1 | H | Hamilton A | D | 1-1 | 0-0 | 1 | Gow [58] | 2936 |
| 35 | 8 | A | Alloa Ath | W | 1-0 | 1-0 | 1 | Coyle [26] | 1635 |
| 36 | 15 | H | Morton | W | 2-0 | 0-0 | 1 | Gow [52], McLaren [88] | 5704 |

**Final League Position: 1**

**Honours**
*League Champions:* Second Division 2003-04.
*Bell's League Challenge Cup runners-up:* 2003-04.

**Club colours:** Shirt: White with red diamond. Shorts: White with two red horizontal stripes. Stockings: White with red hoops.

**Goalscorers:** *League* (64): Coyle 12, Gow 12 (2 pens), McLaren 10, Vareille 9, Docherty 4, Dunn 4, McKeown 4, Glancy 3, Lovering 2, Christie 1, Roberts 1, Ronald 1, Wilson S 1
*Scottish Cup* (5): Coyle 2, McKeown 1, Roberts 1, Stewart 1
*CIS Cup* (3): Glancy 1, Roberts 1, Ronald 1
*Challenge Cup* (8) : Dunn 2, McKeown 2, Gow 1, Roberts 1, Vareille 1, Wilson S 1

| McGeown M 36 | Wilson W 21 + 2 | Dunn D 25 + 3 | Stewart A 13 + 1 | McManus A 28 + 1 | McGowan N 32 | Vareille J 21 + 12 | Wilson M 25 + 8 | McKeown S 10 + 18 | Docherty S 27 | Roberts M 19 + 11 | Ronald P 7 + 6 | Gow A 26 + 6 | Black K 4 | Wilson S 16 + 3 | Glancy M 14 + 12 | Singbo F 3 + 3 | McLaren W 18 + 3 | Coyle O 23 | Christie K 10 + 3 | Lovering P 18 | McKenna S — + 1 | Match No. |
|---|---|---|---|---|---|---|---|---|---|---|---|---|---|---|---|---|---|---|---|---|---|---|
| 1 | 2 | 3 | 4 | 5 | 6 | $7^{2}$ | 8 | 9 | $10^{1}$ | 11 | 12 | 13 | | | | | | | | | | 1 |
| 1 | 2 | | 4 | | $6^{2}$ | 7 | 8 | | 10 | $9^{1}$ | 12 | 11 | 3 | 5 | 13 | | | | | | | 2 |
| 1 | | 12 | $4^{2}$ | 2 | 6 | 7 | 8 | | | 11 | $10^{1}$ | 9 | 3 | 5 | 13 | | | | | | | 3 |
| 1 | 2 | 10 | | | 6 | $7^{1}$ | 4 | | | 9 | $8^{2}$ | 12 | 3 | 5 | 11 | 13 | | | | | | 4 |
| 1 | 2 | 10 | 12 | 4 | $6^{1}$ | 7 | 8 | | | $9^{2}$ | | 13 | 3 | 5 | 11 | | | | | | | 5 |
| 1 | 3 | 10 | 4 | 5 | 6 | | 8 | | 2 | 9 | 13 | $7^{1}$ | | | $11^{2}$ | 12 | | | | | | 6 |
| 1 | 3 | | 4 | 5 | 6 | 12 | 8 | 14 | 2 | 9 | | $7^{3}$ | | 13 | $11^{2}$ | $10^{1}$ | | | | | | 7 |
| 1 | $3^{3}$ | 10 | 4 | 5 | 6 | 13 | $8^{1}$ | 14 | 2 | 9 | | 7 | | | $11^{2}$ | 12 | | | | | | 8 |
| 1 | 2 | | 4 | 5 | 3 | $7^{1}$ | $8^{3}$ | 12 | 10 | $9^{2}$ | 14 | 11 | | 6 | 13 | | | | | | | 9 |
| 1 | 2 | 14 | 4 | 5 | 3■ | $7^{1}$ | 8 | 13 | 10 | $9^{2}$ | | 11 | | $6^{3}$ | 12 | | | | | | | 10 |
| 1 | $2^{2}$ | 10 | | | 3 | 7 | 8 | 12 | 4 | $9^{1}$ | | 11 | | 5 | 13 | 6 | | | | | | 11 |
| 1 | 2 | 3 | 4 | | 6 | $7^{3}$ | $8^{2}$ | 9 | 10 | $11^{1}$ | 13 | | | 5 | 12 | | 14 | | | | | 12 |
| 1 | 2 | 6 | 4 | | 3 | $7^{2}$ | 8 | 9 | 10 | | 13 | | | 5 | $11^{1}$ | | 12 | | | | | 13 |
| 1 | $3^{2}$ | 10 | $4^{3}$ | 5 | | $7^{1}$ | 8 | 12 | 2 | 11 | 6 | 13 | | | 14 | | | 9 | | | | 14 |
| 1 | | 11 | | 5 | 3 | 13 | 8 | $7^{1}$ | $2^{2}$ | $10^{3}$ | 6 | 12 | | | 14 | 4 | | 9 | | | | 15 |
| 1 | | 6 | | 4 | 3 | 12 | 8 | 10 | 2 | 13 | $7^{2}$ | 11 | | $5^{1}$ | | | | 9 | | | | 16 |
| 1 | | 12 | 4 | 5 | 3 | 13 | $8^{1}$ | 7 | 2 | $10^{2}$ | 6 | 11 | | | | | | 9 | | | | 17 |
| 1 | | | 4 | 5 | 3 | 12 | 8 | $7^{3}$ | 2 | 10 | $6^{1}$ | $11^{2}$ | | | 14 | | 13 | 9 | | | | 18 |
| 1 | | 6 | | 5 | 4 | 7 | | | 8 | | | 10 | | | | | 11 | 9 | 2 | 3 | | 19 |
| 1 | | 6 | | 5 | 4 | 7 | 14 | | 8 | 13 | | $10^{1}$ | | | 12 | | $11^{3}$ | $9^{2}$ | 2 | 3 | | 20 |
| 1 | | 6 | | | 4 | 7 | 14 | 13 | $8^{3}$ | 12 | | $10^{1}$ | | 5 | | | 11 | $9^{2}$ | 2 | 3 | | 21 |
| 1 | | 6 | | | 4 | 7 | 12 | 14 | $8^{1}$ | 13 | | 10 | | 5 | | | $11^{3}$ | $9^{2}$ | 2 | 3 | | 22 |
| 1 | | 6 | | 12 | 4 | $7^{3}$ | | 14 | 8 | 13 | | $10^{2}$ | | $5^{1}$ | | | 11 | 9 | 2 | 3 | | 23 |
| 1 | 12 | 6 | | 5 | 4 | $7^{1}$ | 14 | | $8^{3}$ | 13 | | 10 | | | | | 11 | $9^{2}$ | 2 | 3 | | 24 |
| 1 | 2 | 6 | | 5 | 4 | $7^{2}$ | 14 | 12 | 8 | $10^{1}$ | | | | | 13 | | 11 | $9^{3}$ | | 3 | | 25 |
| 1 | $2^{3}$ | 6 | | 5 | 4 | $7^{1}$ | | 13 | 8 | $10^{2}$ | | | | | 12 | | 11 | 9 | 14 | 3 | | 26 |
| 1 | | 6 | | 5 | 4 | $7^{3}$ | 12 | 14 | $8^{1}$ | $10^{2}$ | | 13 | | | | | 11 | 9 | 2 | 3 | | 27 |
| 1 | 13 | 6 | | 5 | 4 | | 14 | 12 | 8 | | | $10^{1}$ | | | $7^{3}$ | | $11^{2}$ | 9 | 2 | 3 | | 28 |
| 1 | 2 | 6 | | 5 | 4 | | 13 | 12 | 8 | | | $10^{1}$ | | | $7^{2}$ | | 11 | 9 | | 3 | | 29 |
| 1 | 2 | | | $5^{2}$ | 4 | 14 | 6 | 12 | $8^{1}$ | | | 10 | | 13 | $7^{3}$ | | 11 | 9 | | 3 | | 30 |
| 1 | 2 | | | 4 | | 12 | 8 | $6^{2}$ | | 13 | | 10 | | 5 | 7 | | $11^{1}$ | $9^{3}$ | | 3 | 14 | 31 |
| 1 | 2 | | | 4 | | 12 | $8^{3}$ | 6 | | 13 | | $10^{2}$ | | 5 | 7 | | 11 | $9^{1}$ | 14 | 3 | | 32 |
| 1 | 2 | | | 4 | | 12 | 8 | $6^{2}$ | | | | 10 | | 5 | $7^{1}$ | | 11 | 9 | 13 | 3 | | 33 |
| 1 | | $6^{2}$ | | 5 | 4 | 12 | 8 | 13 | | 14 | | $10^{3}$ | | | $7^{1}$ | | 11 | 9 | 2 | 3 | | 34 |
| 1 | | $6^{3}$ | | 5 | 4 | 12 | 8 | 14 | | 13 | | 10 | | | $7^{1}$ | | $11^{2}$ | 9 | 2 | 3 | | 35 |
| 1 | 2 | 6 | | 5 | 4 | $7^{2}$ | 8 | 12 | | 14 | | $10^{1}$ | | 13 | | | $11^{3}$ | 9 | | 3 | | 36 |

# ALBION ROVERS — Third Division

*Year Formed:* 1882. *Ground & Address:* Cliftonhill Stadium, Main St, Coatbridge ML5 3RB. *Telephone/Fax:* 01236 606334.
*Ground capacity:* total: 2496, seated: 538. *Size of Pitch:* 110yd × 72yd.
*Chairman:* Andrew Dick, *Company Secretary:* David Shanks BSc. *General Manager:* John Reynolds.
*Manager:* Kevin McAllister. *Assistant Manager:* Scott Crabbe. *Youth Development:* Jimmy Lindsay. *Physio:* Derek Kelly.
*Managers since 1975:* G. Caldwell, S. Goodwin, H. Hood, J. Baker, D. Whiteford, M. Ferguson, W. Wilson, B. Rooney, A. Ritchie, T. Gemmell, D. Provan, M. Oliver, B. McLaren, T. Gemmell, T Spence, J. Crease, V. Moore, B. McLaren, J. McVeigh, P. Hetherston.
*Club Nickname(s):* The Wee Rovers. *Previous Grounds:* Cowheath Park, Meadow Park, Whifflet.
*Record Attendance:* 27,381 v Rangers, Scottish Cup 2nd rd, 8 Feb 1936.
*Record Transfer Fee received:* £40,000 from Motherwell for Bruce Cleland.
*Record Transfer Fee paid:* £7000 for Gerry McTeague to Stirling Albion, September 1989.
*Record Victory:* 12-0 v Airdriehill, Scottish Cup, 3 Sept 1887.
*Record Defeat:* 1-11 v Partick T, League Cup, 11 Aug 1993.
*Most Capped Player:* Jock White, 1 (2), Scotland.
*Most League Appearances:* 399, Murdy Walls, 1921-36.
*Most League Goals in Season (Individual):* 41: Jim Renwick, Division II, 1932-33.
*Most Goals Overall (Individual):* 105: Bunty Weir, 1928-31.

## ALBION ROVERS 2003–04 LEAGUE RECORD

| Match No. | Date | Venue | Opponents | Result | H/T Score | Lg. Pos. | Goalscorers | Attendance |
|---|---|---|---|---|---|---|---|---|
| 1 | Aug 9 | H | Stranraer | D 1-1 | 1-1 | — | McManus [25] | 323 |
| 2 | 16 | A | Cowdenbeath | W 4-1 | 3-0 | 3 | Yardley 2 [31, 32], Mercer [34], McManus [53] | 362 |
| 3 | 23 | H | Queen's Park | W 3-1 | 2-0 | 2 | Yardley [24], Farrell [36], Smith [68] | 627 |
| 4 | 30 | A | Gretna | L 1-3 | 0-2 | 3 | Diack [51] | 385 |
| 5 | Sept 6 | H | Elgin C | L 1-2 | 1-0 | 3 | McManus [33] | 394 |
| 6 | 13 | H | Montrose | L 0-1 | 0-0 | 5 | | 262 |
| 7 | 20 | A | Stirling A | L 1-2 | 1-1 | 7 | Yardley [17] | 685 |
| 8 | 27 | H | Peterhead | W 2-0 | 0-0 | 5 | Yardley [84], McManus [90] | 283 |
| 9 | Oct 4 | H | East Stirling | W 5-0 | 1-0 | 4 | McManus 2 [41, 58], Yardley [59], McCaul [61], McBride [76] | 256 |
| 10 | 18 | A | Elgin C | W 5-1 | 2-1 | 3 | McManus [2], Yardley [33], McAllister [51], Mercer [76], Stirling [90] | 681 |
| 11 | 25 | H | Cowdenbeath | L 1-2 | 0-0 | 3 | McBride [74] | 415 |
| 12 | Nov 1 | A | Stranraer | L 0-5 | 0-1 | 5 | | 447 |
| 13 | 8 | A | Montrose | L 0-1 | 0-0 | 6 | | 267 |
| 14 | 14 | H | Gretna | L 1-3 | 0-1 | 7 | Stirling (pen) [82] | 357 |
| 15 | Dec 2 | H | Stirling A | L 0-3 | 0-3 | — | | 392 |
| 16 | 6 | A | Peterhead | L 1-2 | 0-2 | 8 | McManus [59] | 485 |
| 17 | 13 | A | East Stirling | W 4-3 | 2-2 | 7 | Stirling [26], McLaren (og) [40], Mercer [46], Yardley [90] | 175 |
| 18 | Jan 3 | A | Queen's Park | D 1-1 | 0-0 | 7 | McManus [68] | 454 |
| 19 | 24 | A | Stirling A | L 0-3 | 0-1 | 8 | | 629 |
| 20 | Feb 7 | H | Montrose | W 3-0 | 1-0 | 7 | Mercer [17], McManus [84], Smith [90] | 192 |
| 21 | 14 | A | Gretna | L 0-3 | 0-3 | 7 | | 418 |
| 22 | 17 | H | Stranraer | L 1-4 | 0-2 | — | Bradford [73] | 428 |
| 23 | 21 | A | Elgin C | W 2-1 | 1-0 | 7 | McManus [9], Patrick [79] | 425 |
| 24 | Mar 6 | A | Cowdenbeath | D 1-1 | 1-0 | 8 | Stirling [30] | 248 |
| 25 | 9 | H | East Stirling | W 5-1 | 4-0 | — | Yardley [11], Bradford [20], McManus [21], Mercer 2 [29, 90] | 179 |
| 26 | 13 | H | Queen's Park | W 3-1 | 2-1 | 7 | McManus 2 [15, 88], Ferry (og) [41] | 491 |
| 27 | 16 | H | Peterhead | D 3-3 | 3-1 | — | Stirling [5], Mercer [22], Yardley [30] | 253 |
| 28 | 20 | A | Montrose | L 1-3 | 0-0 | 7 | McManus [79] | 339 |
| 29 | 27 | H | Gretna | L 1-2 | 1-2 | 7 | Stevens (og) [37] | 287 |
| 30 | Apr 3 | A | Peterhead | L 0-5 | 0-3 | 8 | | 440 |
| 31 | 10 | H | Stirling A | L 3-5 | 2-2 | 8 | Mercer 2 [16, 90], Yardley [45] | 615 |
| 32 | 17 | H | Elgin C | L 1-2 | 1-1 | 8 | McManus [13] | 212 |
| 33 | 24 | A | East Stirling | W 8-1 | 2-1 | 7 | Bradford 2 [38, 51], Stirling [43], McManus 2 [47, 66], Crabbe [49], McKenzie [76], Mercer [85] | 223 |
| 34 | May 1 | A | Queen's Park | W 1-0 | 0-0 | 7 | McKenzie [52] | 516 |
| 35 | 8 | H | Cowdenbeath | L 2-4 | 1-2 | 7 | Stirling (pen) [27], Sweeney [64] | 307 |
| 36 | 15 | A | Stranraer | L 0-4 | 0-3 | 8 | | 1321 |

**Final League Position: 8**

**Honours**
*League Champions:* Division II 1933-34, Second Division 1988-89; *Runners-up:* Division II 1913-14, 1937-38, 1947-48.
*Scottish Cup Runners-up:* 1920.

**Club colours:** Shirt: Scarlet and yellow. Shorts: Scarlet. Stockings: Yellow.

**Goalscorers:** *League* (66): McManus 18, Yardley 11, Mercer 10, Stirling 7 (2 pens), Bradford 4, McBride 2, McKenzie 2, Smith 2, Crabbe 1, Diack 1, Farrell 1, McAllister 1, McCaul 1 Patrick 1, Sweeney 1, own goals 3
*Scottish Cup* (2): Mercer 1, own goal 1
*CIS Cup* (2): McAllister 1, McManus 1
*Challenge Cup* (3): Diack 2, McManus 1

| Fahey C 9 | McCaul G 18 | Stirling J 31 + 2 | Smith J 27 + 2 | Cormack P 17 + 4 | McCaig J 21 + 2 | McAllister K 12 + 2 | Farrell D 16 + 1 | McManus P 33 + 1 | Diack I 5 + 8 | Mercer J 33 | Yardley M 26 + 1 | Paterson A 29 + 2 | McBride K 5 + 7 | Connolly C 5 + 3 | Skinner S — + 2 | Bennett N 26 + 1 | Sweeney S 21 | McKenzie M 3 + 11 | Molloy M 2 + 3 | Denham G 1 | Bradford J 14 + 6 | Kerr C 6 + 2 | Patrick R 12 + 1 | Low A 4 + 6 | Crabbe S 13 | Selkirk A — + 2 | Carr M 1 | Potter K 3 + 2 | Valentine J — + 1 | Silvestro C 3 | Kerr S — + 1 | *Match No.* |
|---|---|---|---|---|---|---|---|---|---|---|---|---|---|---|---|---|---|---|---|---|---|---|---|---|---|---|---|---|---|---|---|---|
| 1 | 2 | 3 | 4 | 5 | 6 | $7^1$ | 8 | 9 | 10 | 11 | 12 | | | | | | | | | | | | | | | | | | | | | 1 |
| 1 | 8 | 3 | 4 | | 6 | $7^2$ | 5 | $10^1$ | 12 | 11 | 9 | 2 | 13 | | | | | | | | | | | | | | | | | | | 2 |
| 1 | 8 | $3^3$ | 12 | 6 | 5 | $7^1$ | 4 | $10^2$ | 13 | 11■ | 9 | 2 | 14 | | | | | | | | | | | | | | | | | | | 3 |
| 1 | | 3■ | 4 | 5 | 6 | 12 | 8 | 10 | $7^2$ | | 9■ | 2 | $11^1$ | 13 | | | | | | | | | | | | | | | | | | 4 |
| 1 | 8 | $3^1$ | | 5 | 6 | $7^2$ | 4 | 10 | 13 | 11 | 9 | $2^3$ | 12 | | 14 | | | | | | | | | | | | | | | | | 5 |
| 1 | 8 | 3 | | 5 | $6^1$ | 7 | 4 | 10 | 9 | 11 | | 2 | | | 12 | | | | | | | | | | | | | | | | | 6 |
| 1 | 7 | 3 | 8■ | 6 | 5 | 13 | $4^2$ | 10 | 12 | 11 | $9^1$ | 2 | | | | | | | | | | | | | | | | | | | | 7 |
| | 8 | | | | 5 | $7^1$ | 6 | 10 | $3^2$ | 11 | 9 | $2^3$ | 12 | | | 1 | 4 | 13 | 14 | | | | | | | | | | | | | 8 |
| | $8^2$ | | | | 5 | 7 | 4 | 10 | $3^1$ | 11 | 9 | 2 | 12 | | | 1 | 6 | | 13 | | | | | | | | | | | | | 9 |
| | 8 | 3 | | 12 | $5^1$ | 7 | 6 | $10^2$ | 13 | 11 | 9 | 2 | | | | 1 | 4 | | | | | | | | | | | | | | | 10 |
| | $8^2$ | 3 | | | $5^1$ | 7 | 6 | 10 | 13 | 11 | 9 | 2 | 12 | | | 1 | 4 | | | | | | | | | | | | | | | 11 |
| | 8 | | 2 | 5■ | 13 | $7^2$ | $6^3$ | 10 | 12 | 11 | $9^1$ | 14 | 3 | | | 1 | 4 | | | | | | | | | | | | | | | 12 |
| | 8 | 3 | 13 | | 5 | 7 | $6^1$ | 10 | 12 | 11 | | $2^3$ | 9 | | | 1 | $4^2$ | | 14 | | | | | | | | | | | | | 13 |
| | 8 | 3 | 4 | 13 | 5■ | 7 | | 10 | | 11 | | $2^1$ | 6 | | | 1 | | 12 | $9^2$ | | | | | | | | | | | | | 14 |
| | 8 | 13 | 4 | 3 | | | | 10 | | 11 | 9 | $2^1$ | $6^2$ | 12 | | 1 | 5 | 14 | $7^3$ | | | | | | | | | | | | | 15 |
| | $7^1$ | 6 | 8 | 3 | | | | 10 | | 11 | 9 | | | 2 | | 1 | 4 | | | 5 | 12 | | | | | | | | | | | 16 |
| | $7^3$ | 6 | 8 | $3^2$ | 5 | | | 10 | | 11 | 9 | 12 | 13 | $2^1$ | | 1 | 4 | | | | 14 | | | | | | | | | | | 17 |
| | $7^2$ | 6 | 4 | 5 | | | | 10 | | 11 | 9 | | | $2^1$ | | 1 | | 13 | | | 12 | 3 | 8 | | | | | | | | | 18 |
| | | 3 | 6 | | 5 | | | 12 | | 11 | 9 | | | $2^2$ | | 1 | 4 | 7 | | | $10^1$ | | 8 | 13 | | | | | | | | 19 |
| | $6^1$ | 13 | 5 | | | | | $10^3$ | | 11 | 9 | | | 2 | | 1 | 4 | 12 | | | 14 | 3 | 8 | $7^2$ | | | | | | | | 20 |
| | | 6 | 5 | | | | | 10 | | 11 | | $2^2$ | | 13 | | 1 | 4 | 12 | | | | 3 | 8 | $7^1$ | 9 | | | | | | | 21 |
| | | 6 | 5 | | | | | 10 | | 11 | | 2 | | | | 1 | 4 | $7^2$ | | | 13 | $3^1$ | 8 | 12 | 9 | | | | | | | 22 |
| | | 6 | 5 | | | | | $10^1$ | | 11 | | 2 | | | | 1 | 4 | | | | 12 | 3 | 8 | 7 | 9 | | | | | | | 23 |
| | | 6 | 5 | | 12 | | | 10 | | | | 2 | | | | 1 | 4 | | | | 11 | 3 | $8^1$ | 7 | 9 | | | | | | | 24 |
| | | 3 | | 5 | 4 | | $6^1$ | $10^3$ | | 11 | 9 | 2 | | | | 1 | | | | | $7^2$ | 12 | | 13 | 8 | 14 | | | | | | 25 |
| | | 3 | 5 | 6 | | | | 10 | | 11 | $9^2$ | 2 | | | | 1 | 4 | | | | $7^1$ | 12 | | 13 | 8 | | | | | | | 26 |
| | | 3 | 5 | | 6 | | | 10 | | 11 | $9^1$ | 2 | | | | 1 | 4■ | | | | 7 | | | 12 | 8 | | | | | | | 27 |
| | | 3 | 5 | 6 | 4 | | | 10 | | 11 | 9 | 2 | | | | 1 | | 12 | | | $7^1$ | | | | $8^2$ | 13 | | | | | | 28 |
| | | 3 | 5 | | 4 | | | 10 | | 11 | 9 | 2 | | | | 1 | 6 | | | | 7 | | | | 8 | | | | | | | 29 |
| | | 3 | $5^1$ | 12 | $4^2$ | | 6 | 10 | | 11 | 9 | 2 | | | | | | | | | $7^3$ | | 8 | 14 | | | 1 | 13 | | | | 30 |
| 1 | | 3 | 6 | 5 | $4^1$ | | | 10 | | 11 | 9 | 2 | | | | | | | | | 7 | | 8 | | | | | 12 | | | | 31 |
| $1^1$ | | 3 | 6 | 5 | | | | 10 | | 11 | 9 | 2 | | | | 12 | | 13 | | | $7^2$ | | 8 | | | | | 4 | | | | 32 |
| | | $3^1$ | 6 | | | | 12 | $10^2$ | | 11 | 9 | 2 | | | | 1 | 5 | 13 | | | 7 | | | | $8^3$ | | | 4 | 14 | | | 33 |
| | | 3 | 4 | | | | | $10^1$ | | 11 | $9^2$ | 2 | | | | 1 | 5 | 12 | | | 7 | | 13 | | 8 | | | | | 6 | | 34 |
| | | 3 | 4 | 12 | | | | | | 11 | | 2 | | | | 1 | 5 | $9^1$ | | | 7 | | 10 | | 8 | | | | | 6 | | 35 |
| | | 3 | 5 | 11 | | | $6^2$ | | | | | 2 | | | | 1 | | 12 | | | 9 | | $7^1$ | | 10 | | | 4 | | 8 | 13 | 36 |

# ALLOA ATHLETIC — Second Division

*Year Formed:* 1878. *Ground & Address:* Recreation Park, Clackmannan Rd, Alloa FK10 1RY. *Telephone:* 01259 722695.
*Ground Capacity:* total: 3100, seated: 400. *Size of Pitch:* 110yd × 75yd.
*Chairman:* David Murray. *Secretary:* Ewen G. Cameron.
*Manager:* Tom Hendrie. *Assistant Manager:* Graeme Armstrong. *Physio:* Jim Law.
*Managers since 1975:* H. Wilson, A. Totten, W. Garner, J. Thomson, D. Sullivan, G. Abel, B. Little, H. McCann, W. Lamont, P. McAuley, T. Hendrie, T. Christie. *Club Nickname(s):* The Wasps. *Previous Grounds:* None.
*Record Attendance:* 13,000 v Dunfermline Athletic, Scottish Cup 3rd rd replay, 26 Feb 1939.
*Record Transfer Fee received:* £100,000 for Martin Cameron to Bristol Rovers.
*Record Transfer Fee paid:* £26,000 for Ross Hamilton from Stenhousemuir.
*Record Victory:* 9-2 v Forfar Ath, Division II, 18 Mar 1933.
*Record Defeat:* 0-10 v Dundee, Division II, 8 Mar 1947 v Third Lanark, League Cup, 8 Aug 1953.
*Most Capped Player:* Jock Hepburn, 1, Scotland.
*Most League Goals in Season (Individual):* 49: 'Wee' Willie Crilley, Division II, 1921-22.

## ALLOA ATHLETIC 2003–04 LEAGUE RECORD

| Match No. | Date | Venue | Opponents | Result | | H/T Score | Lg. Pos. | Goalscorers | Attendance |
|---|---|---|---|---|---|---|---|---|---|
| 1 | Aug 9 | H | Dumbarton | L | 1-2 | 1-1 | — | Smith D (og) [4] | 446 |
| 2 | 16 | A | Airdrie U | L | 0-1 | 0-0 | 8 | | 1445 |
| 3 | 23 | H | Stenhousemuir | D | 2-2 | 0-0 | 9 | Hamilton [53], Little [82] | 447 |
| 4 | 30 | A | Berwick R | L | 2-3 | 1-1 | 10 | Callaghan 2 [16, 89] | 405 |
| 5 | Sept 13 | H | Arbroath | D | 2-2 | 1-0 | 10 | Nicolson [10], Hamilton [62] | 358 |
| 6 | 20 | A | East Fife | W | 1-0 | 1-0 | 9 | Walker R [44] | 595 |
| 7 | 27 | H | Forfar Ath | D | 1-1 | 1-0 | 9 | Callaghan (pen) [32] | 378 |
| 8 | Oct 4 | A | Hamilton A | W | 4-3 | 3-0 | 7 | Little 3 [32, 41, 70], Janczyk [39] | 1016 |
| 9 | 11 | H | Airdrie U | L | 1-4 | 1-3 | 8 | Janczyk [45] | 636 |
| 10 | 18 | H | Morton | L | 0-1 | 0-0 | 8 | | 1118 |
| 11 | Nov 1 | A | Dumbarton | L | 0-1 | 0-1 | 9 | | 742 |
| 12 | 8 | A | Arbroath | L | 1-3 | 0-2 | 10 | Little [89] | 448 |
| 13 | 16 | H | Berwick R | L | 2-3 | 1-1 | 10 | Little 2 [15, 65] | 391 |
| 14 | Dec 2 | H | East Fife | W | 2-0 | 2-0 | — | Nicolson [18], Hamilton [41] | 405 |
| 15 | 6 | A | Forfar Ath | D | 1-1 | 0-0 | 10 | Ferguson [65] | 502 |
| 16 | 13 | H | Hamilton A | L | 1-3 | 0-0 | 10 | Ferguson [69] | 504 |
| 17 | Jan 10 | A | Stenhousemuir | W | 3-1 | 0-1 | 9 | Nicolson [60], Callaghan (pen) [62], Hamilton [69] | 402 |
| 18 | 17 | H | Dumbarton | W | 3-0 | 1-0 | 9 | Hamilton [8], Daly [83], Callaghan [90] | 423 |
| 19 | 24 | A | East Fife | W | 1-0 | 0-0 | 9 | Ferguson [87] | 647 |
| 20 | 31 | H | Forfar Ath | W | 4-0 | 2-0 | 7 | Hamilton 3 [38, 44, 64], Walker R [89] | 321 |
| 21 | Feb 7 | H | Arbroath | W | 4-0 | 1-0 | 6 | Little [38], McGowan [64], Hamilton [75], Stevenson [85] | 442 |
| 22 | 14 | A | Berwick R | L | 1-3 | 0-0 | 7 | McGowan [70] | 445 |
| 23 | 21 | H | Morton | D | 3-3 | 2-1 | 7 | Callaghan [6], Walker R [17], Little [88] | 1145 |
| 24 | Mar 6 | A | Airdrie U | L | 1-2 | 1-2 | 7 | Daly [21] | 1542 |
| 25 | 13 | H | Stenhousemuir | W | 1-0 | 0-0 | 7 | Hamilton [84] | 444 |
| 26 | 16 | A | Hamilton A | W | 1-0 | 0-0 | — | McGowan [63] | 831 |
| 27 | 20 | A | Arbroath | L | 1-2 | 1-2 | 7 | Stevenson [8] | 449 |
| 28 | 27 | H | Berwick R | W | 4-2 | 2-2 | 6 | Bolochowescyj [12], McGowan [28], Little [67], Hamilton [75] | 365 |
| 29 | 30 | A | Morton | D | 2-2 | 1-2 | — | Hamilton [9], Walker R [79] | 2436 |
| 30 | Apr 10 | H | East Fife | D | 1-1 | 1-0 | 7 | Hamilton [15] | 567 |
| 31 | 13 | A | Forfar Ath | L | 0-2 | 0-2 | — | | 411 |
| 32 | 17 | A | Morton | L | 1-2 | 0-1 | 7 | Little [60] | 2618 |
| 33 | 24 | H | Hamilton A | D | 1-1 | 1-0 | 7 | Walker R [29] | 579 |
| 34 | May 1 | A | Stenhousemuir | W | 1-0 | 0-0 | 7 | Clark [65] | 480 |
| 35 | 8 | H | Airdrie U | L | 0-1 | 0-1 | 7 | | 1635 |
| 36 | 15 | A | Dumbarton | L | 1-3 | 1-0 | 7 | McGowan [39] | 1494 |

**Final League Position: 7**

**Honours**
*League Champions:* Division II 1921-22; Third Division 1997-98. *Runners-up:* Division II 1938-39. Second Division 1976-77, 1981-82, 1984-85, 1988-89, 1999-2000, 2001-02.
*Bell's League Challenge Winners:* 1999-2000. *Runners-up:* 2001-02.

**Club colours:** Shirt: Gold with black trim. Shorts: Black with gold stripe. Stockings: Gold, black hoop on top.

**Goalscorers:** *League* (55): Hamilton 13, Little 11, Callaghan 6 (2 pens), McGowan 5, Walker R 5, Ferguson 3, Nicolson 3, Daly 2, Janczyk 2, Stevenson 2, Bolochowescyj 1, Clark 1, own goal 1
*Scottish Cup* (6): Ferguson 2, Hamilton 1, McGowan 1, Walker R 1, Walker S 1
*CIS Cup* (0):
*Challenge Cup* (1): Callaghan (pen)

| McGlynn G 32 | Nicolson I 35 | Seaton A 20 | Valentine C 33 | McGowan J 34 | Ferguson A 33 + 1 | Walker R 35 | Hamilton R 35 | Crabbe S 1 + 9 | Callaghan S 35 | Little I 33 + 1 | Kelbie K — + 8 | McLaughlin P 8 + 4 | Evans G 1 + 5 | Janczyk N 10 + 2 | Watson M — + 4 | Walker S 11 | Evans J 4 + 2 | Bolochowescyj M 20 | Daly M 8 + 9 | Stevenson J 2 + 11 | Clark D 6 + 1 | *Match No.* |
|---|---|---|---|---|---|---|---|---|---|---|---|---|---|---|---|---|---|---|---|---|---|---|
| 1 | 2 | 3 | $4^{2}$ | 5 | 6 | $7^{3}$ | 8 | $9^{1}$ | 10 | 11 | 12 | 13 | 14 | | | | | | | | | 1 |
| 1 | 2 | 3 | | 5 | 6 | 7 | 8 | | 10 | 11 | 12 | 4 | $9^{1}$ | | | | | | | | | 2 |
| 1 | 2 | 3 | 4 | 5 | 6 | 7 | $9^{2}$ | 12 | 10 | $11^{3}$ | 13 | | | $8^{1}$ | 14 | | | | | | | 3 |
| 1 | 2 | 3 | 4 | | $6^{1}$ | 7 | $9^{2}$ | 12 | 10 | 11 | 13 | 5 | | 8 | | | | | | | | 4 |
| 1 | 2 | $3^{1}$ | 4 | 5 | 6 | 7 | 9 | | 10 | 11 | 12 | | | 8 | | | | | | | | 5 |
| 1 | 3 | | 2 | 5 | 6 | 7 | 9 | $12^{2}$ | 10 | 11 | | | | $8^{1}$ | | 4 | 13 | | | | | 6 |
| | 2 | 3 | 4 | 5 | $8^{2}$ | 7 | $9^{3}$ | 12 | 10 | $11^{1}$ | 14 | 13 | | | | 6 | 1 | | | | | 7 |
| | 2 | 3 | 4 | 5 | | 7 | $9^{1}$ | 12 | 10 | 11 | | | | 8 | | 6 | 1 | | | | | 8 |
| 1 | 2 | 3 | 4 | 5 | | 7 | $9^{1}$ | 12 | 10 | 11 | | | | 8 | | 6 | | | | | | 9 |
| 1 | 2 | | 4 | 5 | $3^{2}$ | $7^{3}$ | 9 | 12 | 10 | 11 | 13 | | | $8^{1}$ | 14 | 6 | | | | | | 10 |
| 1 | 2 | | 4 | 5 | $3^{1}$ | 7 | 9 | | 10 | 11 | | | | 8 | 12 | 6 | | | | | | 11 |
| 1 | 2 | 3 | 4 | 5 | 7 | | $9^{1}$ | | 10 | 11 | 12 | | | 8 | | 6 | | | | | | 12 |
| 1 | 2 | 3 | 4 | $5^{1}$ | 12 | 7 | 9 | | 10 | 11 | | | 13 | $8^{2}$ | | 6 | | | | | | 13 |
| 1 | 2 | 3 | 4 | 5 | 8 | $7^{2}$ | $9^{1}$ | 12 | 10 | $11^{3}$ | | | 13 | 14 | | 6 | | | | | | 14 |
| 1 | 2 | 3 | 4 | 5 | 8 | 7 | 9 | | 10 | 11 | | | | | | 6 | | | | | | 15 |
| 1 | 2 | $3^{1}$ | | 5 | 8 | 7 | 9 | 13 | 10 | $11^{2}$ | | 4 | | 12 | | 6 | | | | | | 16 |
| 1 | 2 | 3 | 4 | 6 | 8 | 7 | 9 | | 11 | | | 10 | | | | | | 5 | | | | 17 |
| $1^{G}$ | 3 | | 4 | 6 | 2 | 7 | 9 | | 11 | | | 10 | | | | | 15 | 5 | 8 | | | 18 |
| | 2 | 3 | 4 | 6 | 8 | 7 | $9^{2}$ | | 11 | 12 | | $10^{1}$ | | | | | 1 | 5 | 13 | | | 19 |
| 1 | 2 | 3 | 4 | 6 | $8^{1}$ | 7 | 9 | | 11 | 10 | | | | | | | | 5 | 12 | | | 20 |
| 1 | 2 | 3 | 4 | 6 | 8 | $7^{2}$ | 9 | | $11^{1}$ | 10 | | | | | | | | 5 | 13 | 12 | | 21 |
| 1 | 2 | $3^{2}$ | 4 | 6 | 8 | $7^{1}$ | 9 | | 11 | $10^{3}$ | | | 14 | | | | | 5 | 13 | 12 | | 22 |
| 1 | $2^{1}$ | | 3 | 6 | 8 | 7 | 9 | | 11 | 10 | | | | | | | | 5 | 4 | 12 | | 23 |
| 1 | 2 | | 4 | 6 | 3 | $7^{2}$ | 9 | | | 10 | | 13 | 12 | | 14 | | | 5 | $8^{3}$ | $11^{1}$ | | 24 |
| 1 | $2^{2}$ | 3 | 4 | 6 | 8 | $7^{1}$ | 9 | | 11 | $10^{3}$ | | 14 | | | | | | 5 | 13 | 12 | | 25 |
| 1 | 2 | 3 | 4 | 6 | 8 | $7^{1}$ | 9 | | 11 | 10 | | | | | | | | 5 | | 12 | | 26 |
| 1 | 2 | | 4 | | 3 | 7 | | | 11 | 10 | | 6 | | | | | | 5 | 8 | 9 | | 27 |
| 1 | 2 | | 4 | 6 | 3 | 7 | 9 | | 11 | 10 | | | | | | | | 5 | 8 | | | 28 |
| 1 | 2 | | 4 | 6 | 3 | 7 | 9 | | 11 | 10 | | | | | | | | 5 | 8 | | | 29 |
| 1 | 2 | | 4 | 6 | 3 | 7 | 9 | | 11 | $10^{1}$ | | | | | | | | 5 | $8^{2}$ | 12 | 13 | 30 |
| 1 | | | 4 | 6 | 2 | 7 | 9 | | 11 | 10 | | | | | | | | 5 | $8^{1}$ | 12 | 3 | 31 |
| 1 | 2 | | 4 | 6 | 8 | 7 | 9 | | 11 | $10^{1}$ | | | | | | | | 5 | | 12 | 3 | 32 |
| | 2 | | 4 | 6 | $8^{1}$ | 7 | 9 | | 11 | $10^{2}$ | | | | | | | 1 | 5 | 13 | 12 | 3 | 33 |
| 1 | 2 | | 4 | 6 | 8 | 7 | $9^{1}$ | | 11 | 10 | | | | | | | | 5 | 12 | | 3 | 34 |
| 1 | 2 | | 4 | 6 | $8^{1}$ | 7 | $9^{2}$ | | 11 | 10 | | | | | | | | 5 | 12 | 13 | 3 | 35 |
| 1 | 2 | | | 6 | $8^{1}$ | $7^{2}$ | 9 | | 11 | 10 | | 4 | | | | | | 5 | 12 | 13 | 3 | 36 |

# ARBROATH — Second Division

*Year Formed:* 1878. *Ground & Address:* Gayfield Park, Arbroath DD11 1QB. *Telephone and Fax:* 01241 431125.
*Ground Capacity:* 4020, seated: 715. *Size of Pitch:* 115yd × 71yd.
*President:* John D. Christison. *Secretary:* Dr Gary Callon. *Administrator:* Mike Cargill. *Commercial Manager:* M. Fairweather.
*Manager:* Steve Kirk. *Assistant Manager:* Jake Ferrier. *Physio:* John Cooper.
*Managers since 1975:* A. Henderson, I. J. Stewart, G. Fleming, J. Bone, J. Young, W. Borthwick, M. Lawson, D. McGrain MBE, J. Scott, J. Brogan, T. Campbell, G. Mackie, D. Baikie, J. Brownlie.
*Club Nickname(s):* The Red Lichties. *Previous Grounds:* None.
*Record Attendance:* 13,510 v Rangers, Scottish Cup 3rd rd, 23 Feb 1952.
*Record Transfer Fee received:* £120,000 for Paul Tosh to Dundee (Aug 1993).
*Record Transfer Fee paid:* £20,000 for Douglas Robb from Montrose (1981).
*Record Victory:* 36-0 v Bon Accord, Scottish Cup 1st rd, 12 Sept 1885.
*Record Defeat:* 1-9 v Celtic, League Cup 3rd rd, 25 Aug 1993.
*Most Capped Player:* Ned Doig, 2 (5), Scotland.
*Most League Appearances:* 445: Tom Cargill, 1966-81.
*Most League Goals in Season (Individual):* 45: Dave Easson, Division II, 1958-59.
*Most Goals Overall (Individual):* 120: Jimmy Jack, 1966-71.

## ARBROATH 2003–04 LEAGUE RECORD

| Match No. | Date | Venue | Opponents | Result | | H/T Score | Lg. Pos. | Goalscorers | Attendance |
|---|---|---|---|---|---|---|---|---|---|
| 1 | Aug 9 | H | Berwick R | W | 1-0 | 1-0 | — | Dow [20] | 565 |
| 2 | 16 | A | Dumbarton | D | 1-1 | 0-0 | 4 | Cargill [84] | 1070 |
| 3 | 23 | H | Forfar Ath | D | 0-0 | 0-0 | 4 | | 856 |
| 4 | 30 | H | Hamilton A | D | 2-2 | 1-1 | 3 | Cusick (pen) [36], McGlashan [63] | 650 |
| 5 | Sept 13 | A | Alloa Ath | D | 2-2 | 0-1 | 3 | Graham J [53], Henslee [81] | 358 |
| 6 | 20 | A | Airdrie U | L | 1-2 | 1-0 | 6 | Cargill [19] | 1385 |
| 7 | 27 | H | Morton | L | 0-4 | 0-3 | 7 | | 1116 |
| 8 | Oct 4 | A | Stenhousemuir | L | 0-1 | 0-1 | 9 | | 344 |
| 9 | 18 | H | East Fife | L | 0-1 | 0-1 | 9 | | 705 |
| 10 | 25 | H | Dumbarton | W | 2-1 | 1-0 | 7 | Cargill [45], McGlashan [70] | 506 |
| 11 | Nov 1 | A | Berwick R | L | 0-3 | 0-1 | 8 | | 383 |
| 12 | 8 | H | Alloa Ath | W | 3-1 | 2-0 | 7 | Dow [5], Cargill [9], McGlashan [63] | 448 |
| 13 | 22 | A | Hamilton A | L | 0-2 | 0-0 | 8 | | 1286 |
| 14 | Dec 2 | H | Airdrie U | D | 1-1 | 0-0 | — | Diack [56] | 405 |
| 15 | 6 | A | Morton | L | 4-6 | 2-2 | 8 | Cargill 2 [30, 72], McGlashan [45], Durno [80] | 2707 |
| 16 | 13 | H | Stenhousemuir | W | 2-1 | 1-0 | 8 | McGlashan [29], Diack [52] | 402 |
| 17 | 27 | A | East Fife | W | 1-0 | 1-0 | 7 | Diack [24] | 811 |
| 18 | Jan 17 | H | Berwick R | L | 1-2 | 1-0 | 8 | Cusick [16] | 411 |
| 19 | 24 | A | Airdrie U | W | 1-0 | 0-0 | 8 | McMullen [68] | 1267 |
| 20 | 31 | H | Morton | D | 2-2 | 1-1 | 9 | McLean [5], Cusick (pen) [88] | 805 |
| 21 | Feb 7 | A | Alloa Ath | L | 0-4 | 0-1 | 9 | | 442 |
| 22 | 14 | H | Hamilton A | L | 0-2 | 0-1 | 9 | | 502 |
| 23 | 21 | H | East Fife | D | 0-0 | 0-0 | 9 | | 596 |
| 24 | Mar 6 | A | Dumbarton | L | 0-1 | 0-1 | 9 | | 828 |
| 25 | 13 | H | Forfar Ath | L | 0-1 | 0-1 | 9 | | 702 |
| 26 | 16 | A | Forfar Ath | D | 2-2 | 1-1 | — | McGlashan [38], Diack [75] | 682 |
| 27 | 20 | H | Alloa Ath | W | 2-1 | 2-1 | 9 | McGlashan [22], Diack [45] | 449 |
| 28 | 27 | A | Hamilton A | D | 2-2 | 1-1 | 9 | Diack [27], McGlashan [78] | 1041 |
| 29 | 30 | A | Stenhousemuir | W | 3-0 | 1-0 | — | Cargill [22], Cusick (pen) [69], McLean [86] | 307 |
| 30 | Apr 3 | A | Morton | L | 0-1 | 0-1 | 9 | | 2493 |
| 31 | 10 | H | Airdrie U | L | 0-4 | 0-1 | 9 | | 1074 |
| 32 | 17 | A | East Fife | W | 2-1 | 1-1 | 8 | McLean 2 [6, 63] | 762 |
| 33 | 24 | H | Stenhousemuir | D | 1-1 | 0-1 | 8 | McLean [67] | 511 |
| 34 | May 1 | A | Forfar Ath | W | 2-1 | 1-1 | 8 | McGlashan [17], Diack (pen) [52] | 707 |
| 35 | 8 | H | Dumbarton | L | 0-3 | 0-2 | 8 | | 553 |
| 36 | 15 | A | Berwick R | W | 3-1 | 0-1 | 8 | Cusick [50], McLean [56], McGlashan [62] | 506 |

**Final League Position: 8**

**Honours**
*League Champions Runners-up:* Division II 1934-35, 1958-59, 1967-68, 1971-72; Second Division 2000-01; Third Division 1997-98.
*Scottish Cup: Quarter-finals:* 1993.

**Club colours:** Shirt: Maroon with white trim. Shorts: White. Stockings: Maroon.

**Goalscorers:** *League* (41): McGlashan 10, Cargill 7, Diack 7 (1 pen), McLean 6, Cusick 5 (3 pens), Dow 2, Durno 1, Graham J 1, Henslee 1, McMullen 1
*Scottish Cup* (3): McGlashan 3
*CIS Cup* (4): McGlashan 2, Cusick 1, Graham J 1
*Challenge Cup* (3): McGlashan 2, Graham J 1

| Peat M 33 | McMullen K 32 + 2 | King D 33 | Rennie S 32 | Denham C 3 | Cusick J 24 | Cargill A 25 | Dow A 18 | Graham J 14 + 1 | McGlashan J 34 | Kerrigan S 3 + 3 | Henslee C 20 + 11 | Swankie G 16 + 14 | Mitchell A 2 | Browne P 17 + 4 | Farquharson P — + 12 | Herkes J 7 + 8 | McAulay J 8 + 10 | Newall C — + 3 | Durno J 3 + 8 | Graham E 2 + 3 | Kirk S — + 1 | Shaw G — + 1 | Diack I 21 + 1 | McCulloch M 21 | Watson C — + 1 | Miller G 15 + 1 | McLean D 12 + 4 | Collier J — + 1 | Woodcock T 1 + 1 | Match No. |
|---|---|---|---|---|---|---|---|---|---|---|---|---|---|---|---|---|---|---|---|---|---|---|---|---|---|---|---|---|---|---|
| 1 | $2^{3}$ | 3 | 4 | 5 | $6^{1}$ | 7 | 8 | 9 | 10 | $11^{2}$ | 12 | 13 | | 14 | | | | | | | | | | | | | | | | 1 |
| 1 | | 3 | 4 | 5 | 6 | 7 | $8^{3}$ | $9^{1}$ | $10^{2}$ | 11 | 13 | 12 | | 2 | 14 | | | | | | | | | | | | | | | 2 |
| 1 | 2 | 3 | 4 | | $6^{1}$ | 7 | 8 | 9 | 10 | | 13 | $11^{2}$ | | 5 | | 12 | | | | | | | | | | | | | | 3 |
| | 2 | $3^{2}$ | 4 | | $6^{3}$ | 7 | 8 | $9^{1}$ | 10 | 12 | 14 | | 1 | 5 | 13 | 11 | | | | | | | | | | | | | | 4 |
| 1 | 2 | 3 | 4 | | $6^{3}$ | | 8 | 9 | 10 | $11^{2}$ | 13 | 12 | | 5 | | $7^{1}$ | 14 | | | | | | | | | | | | | 5 |
| 1 | 2 | 3 | 4 | | $6^{2}$ | $7^{3}$ | 8 | 9 | 10 | | 14 | $11^{1}$ | | 5 | | 12 | | 13 | | | | | | | | | | | | 6 |
| 1 | 14 | | 4 | 6 | | $8^{1}$ | 3 | 9 | 10 | | $2^{3}$ | | | 5 | | 13 | $11^{2}$ | 12 | 7 | | | | | | | | | | | 7 |
| 1 | 2 | 3 | 4 | | | | 8 | 9■ | 10 | | 7 | | | 5 | 13 | $6^{1}$ | | | $11^{3}$ | $12^{2}$ | 14 | | | | | | | | | 8 |
| 1 | 2 | 3 | 4■ | | | 7 | 6 | | 10 | | 9 | | | 5 | | $11^{2}$ | 13 | 12 | $8^{1}$ | | | | | | | | | | | 9 |
| 1 | 2 | $3^{2}$ | | | | 7 | $6^{1}$ | 9 | 10 | 14 | 8 | | | 5 | | 11 | 13 | | | 4 | | $12^{3}$ | | | | | | | | 10 |
| 1 | 2 | 3 | 4 | | | 7 | $6^{3}$ | 9 | 10 | 13 | $8^{2}$ | 12 | | 5 | | $11^{1}$ | 14 | | | | | | | | | | | | | 11 |
| 1 | $2^{1}$ | 3 | 4 | | | 7 | 6 | 9 | 10 | | 8 | $11^{2}$ | | 5 | | 13 | 12 | | | | | | | | | | | | | 12 |
| 1 | 2 | 3 | 4 | | | 7 | $6^{1}$ | $9^{2}$ | 10 | | 8 | | | 5 | | 12 | | | 13 | | | | 11 | | | | | | | 13 |
| 1 | 2 | 3 | 4 | | $6^{2}$ | 7 | | | 10 | | 8 | $11^{1}$ | | 5 | | 12 | 13 | | | | | | 9 | | | | | | | 14 |
| 1 | 2 | 3 | 4 | | $6^{2}$ | 7 | | | 10 | | $8^{3}$ | 11 | | 5 | | 12 | 13 | | 14 | | | | $9^{1}$ | | | | | | | 15 |
| 1 | 2 | 3 | 4 | | | $7^{2}$ | 6 | | 10 | | 12 | 11 | | 5 | | 13 | | | | | | | $9^{1}$ | 8 | | | | | | 16 |
| | 2 | 3 | | | | 7 | | | 10 | | 4 | $11^{1}$ | 1 | 5■ | 13 | 6 | 12 | | | | | | $9^{2}$ | 8 | | | | | | 17 |
| 1 | 13 | 3 | 4 | | $5^{2}$ | 7 | 6 | | 10 | | | 11 | | | | | 2 | | | | | | $9^{1}$ | 8 | 12 | | | | | 18 |
| 1 | 7 | 3 | 4 | | 5 | | 6 | | $10^{1}$ | | | $11^{2}$ | | 12 | 13 | | 2 | | | 14 | | | $9^{3}$ | 8 | | | | | | 19 |
| 1 | $2^{1}$ | $3^{2}$ | 4 | | 5 | | $6^{3}$ | | | | 12 | 14 | | 13 | | | 10 | | | | | | 9 | 8 | | 7 | 11 | | | 20 |
| 1 | | 3 | 4 | | | | $6^{3}$ | | 10 | | 14 | 12 | | 5 | 13 | | $2^{1}$ | | | | | | $9^{2}$ | 8 | | 7 | 11 | | | 21 |
| 1 | 2 | 3 | $4^{2}$ | | | $7^{1}$ | | 14 | 10 | | | 12 | | 13 | | | 5 | | | | | | 9 | 6 | | 8 | $11^{3}$ | | | 22 |
| 1 | 2 | 3 | $4^{1}$ | | 5 | 7 | | 11 | 10 | | | 14 | | | | | 12 | | | | | | $9^{2}$ | 6 | | $8^{3}$ | 13 | | | 23 |
| 1 | 2 | 5 | 4 | | 8 | | | $9^{1}$ | | | 10 | 13 | | | 14 | | $6^{2}$ | | | | | | 12 | 3 | | $7^{3}$ | 11 | | | 24 |
| 1 | 2 | 5 | 4 | | 6 | | | | 10 | | $8^{1}$ | $11^{2}$ | | | | | | | 13 | | | | 9 | 3 | | 7 | 12 | | | 25 |
| 1 | 2 | 5 | 4 | | 6 | | | | 10 | | 8 | $11^{1}$ | | | 12 | | | | | | | | 9 | 3 | | 7 | | | | 26 |
| 1 | 2 | 5 | 4 | | 6 | | | | 10 | | 8 | $11^{1}$ | | | | | | | | | | | 9 | 3 | | 7 | 12 | | | 27 |
| 1 | 2 | 5 | 4 | | 6 | | | | 10 | | 8 | $11^{1}$ | | | | | | | 13 | | | | $9^{2}$ | 3 | | 7 | 12 | | | 28 |
| 1 | 2 | 5 | | | 6 | 8 | | | 10 | | 12 | $11^{1}$ | | | | | | | 13 | | | | 9 | 3 | | 7 | $4^{2}$ | | | 29 |
| 1 | $2^{3}$ | | 4 | | $6^{1}$ | 8 | | | 10 | | 5 | $11^{2}$ | | | 14 | | | | 13 | 12 | | | | 3 | | 7 | 9 | | | 30 |
| 1 | 2 | | 4 | | 6 | 8 | | | 10 | | $5^{1}$ | 12 | | | 14 | | | | | | | | 9 | 3 | | $7^{3}$ | $11^{2}$ | 13 | | 31 |
| 1 | 2 | 5 | 4 | | 6 | $7^{2}$ | | | 10 | | 11 | 12 | | | 14 | | | | | 3 | | | | $8^{1}$ | | 13 | $9^{3}$ | | | 32 |
| 1 | 2 | 5 | 4 | | $6^{1}$ | 7 | | | 10 | | 8 | 12 | | | | | | | | | | | $9^{2}$ | 3 | | | 11 | | 13 | 33 |
| | $2^{1}$ | 5 | 4 | | | 7 | | | 10 | | | $8^{2}$ | | | | | 12 | | 13 | | | | 9 | 3 | | 6 | 11 | | 1 | 34 |
| 1 | 2 | 5 | 4 | | $6^{1}$ | 7 | | | $10^{2}$ | | 13 | 12 | | | | | | | 14 | | | | 9 | 3 | | 8 | $11^{3}$ | | | 35 |
| 1 | 2 | 5 | | | 6 | | | | 10 | | $7^{1}$ | 12 | | | 13 | | 4 | | | | | | 9 | 3 | | 8 | $11^{2}$ | | | 36 |

# AYR UNITED

## Second Division

*Year Formed:* 1910. *Ground & Address:* Somerset Park, Tryfield Place, Ayr KA8 9NB. *Telephone:* 01292 263435.
*Ground Capacity:* 10,185, seated: 1549. *Size of Pitch:* 110yd × 72yd.
*Chairman:* David Capperauld. *Administrator:* Brian Caldwell. *Lottery Manager:* Andrew Downie.
*Manager:* Campbell Money. *Physio:* John Kerr.
*Managers since 1975:* Alex Stuart, Ally MacLeod, Willie McLean, George Caldwell, Ally MacLeod, George Burley, Simon Stainrod, Gordon Dalziel. *Club Nickname(s):* The Honest Men. *Previous Grounds:* None.
*Record Attendance:* 25,225 v Rangers, Division I, 13 Sept 1969.
*Record Transfer Fee received:* £300,000 for Steven Nicol to Liverpool (Oct 1981).
*Record Transfer Fee paid:* £90,000 for Mark Campbell from Stranraer (March 1999).
*Record Victory:* 11-1 v Dumbarton, League Cup, 13 Aug 1952.
*Record Defeat:* 0-9 in Division I v Rangers (1929); v Hearts (1931); B Division v Third Lanark (1954).
*Most Capped Player:* Jim Nisbet, 3, Scotland.
*Most League Appearances:* 459, John Murphy, 1963-78.
*Most League League and Cup Goals in Season (Individual):* 66, Jimmy Smith, 1927-28.
*Most League and Cup Goals Overall (Individual):* 213, Peter Price, 1955-61.

### AYR UNITED 2003–04 LEAGUE RECORD

| *Match No.* | *Date* | *Venue* | *Opponents* | *Result* | | *H/T Score* | *Lg. Pos.* | *Goalscorers* | *Atten-dance* |
|---|---|---|---|---|---|---|---|---|---|
| 1 | Aug 9 | A | Clyde | L | 0-3 | 0-0 | — | | 1067 |
| 2 | 16 | H | Falkirk | D | 1-1 | 0-1 | 9 | Kean 88 | 2519 |
| 3 | 23 | A | Raith R | D | 1-1 | 1-0 | 9 | Ferguson A 16 | 2337 |
| 4 | 30 | H | Queen of the S | L | 1-4 | 0-1 | 9 | Campbell 82 | 2143 |
| 5 | Sept 13 | A | Inverness CT | L | 0-1 | 0-1 | 9 | | 1476 |
| 6 | 20 | A | Ross Co | D | 2-2 | 2-2 | 9 | Whalen 20, Chaplain 35 | 2911 |
| 7 | 27 | H | Brechin C | W | 3-2 | 2-1 | 9 | Craig 2, Chaplain 15, Dunlop 89 | 1427 |
| 8 | Oct 4 | A | St Johnstone | D | 1-1 | 0-0 | 9 | Kean 88 | 1906 |
| 9 | 18 | H | St Mirren | L | 0-2 | 0-1 | 9 | | 2447 |
| 10 | 25 | A | Falkirk | W | 1-0 | 1-0 | 9 | Ferguson A 8 | 2609 |
| 11 | Nov 1 | H | Clyde | D | 2-2 | 0-1 | 9 | Chaplain 52, Kean 75 | 1653 |
| 12 | 8 | H | Inverness CT | L | 0-3 | 0-2 | 9 | | 1464 |
| 13 | 16 | A | Queen of the S | L | 0-1 | 0-0 | 9 | | 3555 |
| 14 | 22 | A | Brechin C | L | 1-3 | 0-2 | 9 | Dunlop 50 | 508 |
| 15 | 29 | H | Ross Co | L | 1-3 | 1-2 | 9 | Hardy 35 | 977 |
| 16 | Dec 6 | A | St Mirren | L | 2-3 | 0-1 | 9 | Kean 47, Ferguson A 85 | 2567 |
| 17 | 13 | H | St Johnstone | D | 1-1 | 0-0 | 9 | Ramsay 89 | 1203 |
| 18 | 20 | A | Clyde | L | 1-2 | 0-0 | 9 | Chaplain 75 | 1049 |
| 19 | 27 | H | Raith R | W | 1-0 | 1-0 | 9 | Ferguson A 23 | 1791 |
| 20 | Jan 3 | H | Queen of the S | D | 1-1 | 0-1 | 9 | Ferguson A 80 | 2303 |
| 21 | 17 | A | Inverness CT | L | 1-2 | 0-1 | 9 | Doyle 61 | 1443 |
| 22 | 24 | A | Ross Co | D | 1-1 | 0-1 | 9 | Kean 72 | 2732 |
| 23 | 31 | H | Brechin C | L | 1-2 | 1-2 | 9 | Brown 39 | 1512 |
| 24 | Feb 14 | A | St Johnstone | L | 0-3 | 0-2 | 10 | | 2067 |
| 25 | 21 | H | St Mirren | W | 2-0 | 1-0 | 8 | Ferguson A 8, Kean 67 | 2252 |
| 26 | Mar 6 | H | Falkirk | L | 2-3 | 1-0 | 9 | Kean 32, Hardy (pen) 80 | 2048 |
| 27 | 13 | A | Raith R | L | 1-2 | 1-1 | 10 | Hardy 13 | 2231 |
| 28 | 20 | H | Inverness CT | D | 1-1 | 1-1 | 10 | Hardy 1 | 1207 |
| 29 | 27 | A | Queen of the S | D | 0-0 | 0-0 | 9 | | 1831 |
| 30 | Apr 3 | A | Brechin C | W | 3-0 | 0-0 | 9 | Black 54, Smyth 58, Kean 61 | 519 |
| 31 | 10 | H | Ross Co | L | 1-2 | 0-2 | 9 | Brown 90 | 1535 |
| 32 | 17 | A | St Mirren | L | 1-4 | 0-0 | 9 | Kean 63 | 3211 |
| 33 | 24 | H | St Johnstone | D | 1-1 | 1-0 | 9 | Forsyth (og) 7 | 1119 |
| 34 | May 1 | H | Clyde | D | 1-1 | 0-1 | 9 | Campbell 72 | 1816 |
| 35 | 8 | A | Falkirk | D | 0-0 | 0-0 | 9 | | 2077 |
| 36 | 15 | H | Raith R | W | 1-0 | 1-0 | 9 | Ferguson A 40 | 1283 |

**Final League Position: 9**

**Honours**
*League Champions:* Division II 1911-12, 1912-13, 1927-28, 1936-37, 1958-59, 1965-66. Second Division 1987-88, 1996-97;
*Runners-up:* Division II 1910-11, 1955-56, 1968-69.
*Scottish Cup:* Semi-final 2002.
*League Cup:* (CIS) Runners-up: 2001-02.
*B&Q Cup Runners-up:* 1990-91, 1991-92.

**Club colours:** Shirt: White with black trim. Shorts: Black. Stockings: White with black.

**Goalscorers:** *League* (37): Kean 9, Ferguson A 7, Chaplain 4, Hardy 4 (1 pen), Brown 2, Campbell 2, Dunlop 2, Black 1, Craig 1, Doyle 1, Ramsay 1, Smyth 1, Whalen 1, own goal 1
*Scottish Cup* (1): Craig 1
*CIS Cup* (1): Smyth 1
*Challenge Cup* (1): Kean 1

| Roy L 35 | Smyth M 30 + 4 | Kerr C 5 + 4 | Latta J 1 + 2 | Campbell M 25 | Ramsay D 29 | Chaplain S 29 + 5 | Black A 17 + 2 | Kean S 36 | Whalen S 7 + 2 | McGrady S 11 + 9 | Conway C — + 8 | Lyle W 26 + 5 | McColl M 2 + 12 | Craig D 33 | Ferguson S 9 | Dunlop M 18 + 5 | Mullen B — + 5 | Ferguson A 16 + 15 | Hillcoat J 1 + 1 | Burgess R 4 + 4 | Hardy L 24 | Kinniburgh W 7 | Crawford S 1 | Brown G 12 + 3 | Doyle J 6 + 1 | Miller S 1 + 5 | Tait J 11 | Match No. |
|---|---|---|---|---|---|---|---|---|---|---|---|---|---|---|---|---|---|---|---|---|---|---|---|---|---|---|---|---|
| 1 | 2 | $3^{2}$ | 4 | 5 | 6 | 7 | $8^{1}$ | 9 | $10^{3}$ | 11 | 12 | 13 | 14 | | | | | | | | | | | | | | | 1 |
| 1 | 4 | 3 | | 5 | 8 | $11^{2}$ | | 9 | | 10 | | $2^{3}$ | | 6 | $7^{1}$ | 12 | 13 | 14 | | | | | | | | | | 2 |
| 1 | 4 | 3 | | 5 | 8 | 7 | | 9 | | $2^{1}$ | 14 | 12 | | 6 | | $11^{2}$ | 13 | $10^{3}$ | | | | | | | | | | 3 |
| 1 | 4 | 3 | | 5 | | 8 | | 9 | 14 | $2^{2}$ | | 13 | | 6 | 7 | $11^{1}$ | $12^{3}$ | 10 | | | | | | | | | | 4 |
| 1 | 7 | | | 5 | 4 | | | 10 | $9^{1}$ | 11 | 13 | $2^{2}$ | | 6 | 8 | 3 | | 12 | | | | | | | | | | 5 |
| 1 | 4 | 12 | | 5 | 11 | 7 | | 10 | 9 | $3^{1}$ | | 2 | | 6 | 8 | | | | | | | | | | | | | 6 |
| 1 | $4^{1}$ | | | 5 | 11 | 7 | | 10 | $9^{2}$ | 3 | | 2 | 13 | 6 | 8 | 12 | | | | | | | | | | | | 7 |
| 1 | 4 | 12 | | 5 | 11 | 7 | | 10 | | $3^{1}$ | | 2 | 13 | 6 | | 8■ | | $9^{2}$ | | | | | | | | | | 8 |
| | 4 | 12 | | 5 | 11 | 7 | | 10 | | $3^{1}$ | | 2 | 13 | 6 | 8 | | | $9^{2}$ | 1 | | | | | | | | | 9 |
| 1 | 4 | 12 | | 5 | 11 | 7 | | 9 | | | | 2 | 13 | 6 | 8 | $3^{1}$ | | $10^{2}$ | | | | | | | | | | 10 |
| 1 | 4 | | 13 | 5 | 11 | $7^{2}$ | | 9 | | | | 2 | 12 | 6 | 8 | 3 | | $10^{1}$ | | | | | | | | | | 11 |
| 1 | 5 | $3^{1}$ | 14 | | 4 | 7 | | 9 | 10 | 13 | | 2 | $11^{2}$ | 6 | $8^{3}$ | | | | | 12 | | | | | | | | 12 |
| $1^{1}$ | 4 | | | | 8 | $7^{2}$ | 13 | 9 | | | | 2 | | 6 | | 11 | | 10 | 12 | | 3 | 5 | | | | | | 13 |
| 1 | 4 | | | | $8^{3}$ | 7 | | 9 | 12 | | 13 | $2^{2}$ | | 6 | | 11 | | $10^{1}$ | | 14 | 3 | 5 | | | | | | 14 |
| 1 | 8 | | | $5^{3}$ | 2 | 7 | $11^{1}$ | 9 | $10^{2}$ | | | | | 6 | | 12 | | 13 | | 14 | 3 | 4 | | | | | | 15 |
| 1 | 2 | | | | 8 | $7^{2}$ | 4 | $9^{3}$ | $10^{1}$ | | 13 | | | 6 | | 3 | 14 | 12 | | 5 | 11 | | | | | | | 16 |
| 1 | 2 | | | | 8 | 7 | $4^{1}$ | 9 | | 13 | | | 12 | 6 | | 3 | | 10 | | | $11^{2}$ | 5 | | | | | | 17 |
| 1 | 2 | | | | 8 | 7 | $4^{1}$ | 9 | | 13 | | | 12 | 6 | | 3 | | $10^{2}$ | | | 11 | 5 | | | | | | 18 |
| 1 | 2 | | | | 8 | $4^{1}$ | | 9 | | $7^{3}$ | 14 | 12 | 13 | 6 | | 3 | | 10 | | | $11^{2}$ | 5 | | | | | | 19 |
| 1 | 2 | | | | 8 | 4 | | 9 | | $7^{1}$ | | 12 | 13 | 6 | | | | 10 | | | 11 | 5 | $3^{2}$ | | | | | 20 |
| 1 | 4 | | | 5 | 8 | 7 | | 10 | | 13 | | 2 | $11^{1}$ | 6 | | | | 14 | | | $3^{2}$ | | | $9^{3}$ | 12 | | | 21 |
| 1 | 4 | | | | 8 | $7^{1}$ | | 10 | | 12 | | 2 | | 6 | | | | 13 | | 5 | 3 | | | $9^{2}$ | $11^{3}$ | 14 | | 22 |
| 1 | | | | | | 7 | 13 | 10 | | 12 | | 2 | | 6 | | $3^{3}$ | | 14 | | $5^{2}$ | 11 | | | 9 | $4^{1}$ | 8 | | 23 |
| 1 | 2 | | | | $8^{2}$ | 4 | | 10 | | 14 | | 7 | | 6 | | 3 | | 12 | | $5^{3}$ | 11 | | | $9^{1}$ | | 13 | | 24 |
| 1 | 4 | | | 5 | 8 | 13 | 7 | 9 | | | | 2 | | 6 | | | | $10^{1}$ | | | $11^{2}$ | | | 12 | | | 3 | 25 |
| 1 | 4 | | | 5 | 8 | 13 | $7^{2}$ | 9 | | 14 | | $2^{3}$ | | 6 | | | | $10^{1}$ | | | 11 | | | 12 | | | 3 | 26 |
| 1 | $4^{3}$ | | | 5 | 8 | 12 | 7 | 9 | | | | 2 | | 6 | | | | $10^{2}$ | | | 11 | | | 13 | | 14 | $3^{1}$ | 27 |
| 1 | 12 | | | 5 | 8 | $4^{1}$ | 7 | 9 | | | | 2 | | 6 | | 13 | | 14 | | | 11 | | | $10^{2}$ | | | $3^{3}$ | 28 |
| 1 | 13 | | | 5 | $8^{2}$ | $4^{3}$ | 7 | $9^{1}$ | | | | 2 | | 6 | | | | 12 | | | 11 | | | 10 | | 14 | 3 | 29 |
| 1 | 12 | | | 5 | $8^{1}$ | 4 | 7 | $9^{2}$ | | | | 2 | | 6 | | | | 13 | | | 11 | | | 10 | | | 3 | 30 |
| 1 | $8^{3}$ | | | 5 | | $4^{2}$ | 7 | 9 | | | 14 | 2 | | 6 | | | 13 | 12 | | | 11 | | | 10 | | | $3^{1}$ | 31 |
| 1 | $8^{1}$ | | | 5 | | 4 | 7 | 9 | | | | 2 | | 6 | | 12 | | | | | 11 | | | 10 | | | 3 | 32 |
| 1 | 4 | | | 5 | | | 7 | 9 | | 14 | | | | $6^{1}$ | | 3 | | 13 | | | 11 | | | 10 | $8^{3}$ | 12 | $2^{2}$ | 33 |
| 1 | | | | 5 | | $4^{2}$ | 7 | 9 | | | | 2 | 13 | 6 | | $3^{3}$ | | 12 | | 14 | 11 | | | $10^{1}$ | 8 | | | 34 |
| 1 | $6^{1}$ | | | 5 | | 13 | 7 | 9 | | | | 2 | 14 | | | $8^{2}$ | | 12 | | | 11 | | | $10^{3}$ | 4 | | 3 | 35 |
| 1 | 13 | | | 5 | $8^{3}$ | 14 | 7 | 9 | | | 12 | 2 | | | | $6^{1}$ | | 10 | | | $11^{2}$ | | | | 4 | | 3 | 36 |

# BERWICK RANGERS Second Division

*Year Formed:* 1881. *Ground & Address:* Shielfield Park, Tweedmouth, Berwick-upon-Tweed TD15 2EF. *Telephone:* 01289 307424. *Fax:* 01289 309424. Club 24 hour hotline 09068 800697. *Ground Capacity:* 4131, seated: 1366. *Size of Pitch:* 110yd × 70yd.
*Chairman:* Robert L. Wilson. *Vice-chairman:* Moray McLaren. *Company Secretary:* Ross Hood. *Club Secretary:* Dennis McCleary. *Treasurer:* J. N. Simpson.
*Manager:* Paul Smith. *Assistant Manager:* Greg Shaw. *Coach:* Ian Smith. *Physios:* Ian Smith & Jamie Dougal. *Ground/Kit:* Ian Oliver.
*Managers since 1975:* H. Melrose, G. Haig, W. Galbraith, D. Smith, F. Connor, J. McSherry, E. Tait, J. Thomson, J. Jefferies, R. Callachan, J. Anderson, J. Crease, T. Hendrie, I. Ross, J. Thomson.
*Club Nickname(s):* The Borderers. *Previous Grounds:* Bull Stob Close, Pier Field, Meadow Field, Union Park, Old Shielfield.
*Record Attendance:* 13,365 v Rangers, Scottish Cup 1st rd, 28 Jan 1967.
*Record Victory:* 8-1 v Forfar Ath, Division II, 25 Dec 1965; v Vale of Leithen, Scottish Cup, Dec 1966.
*Record Defeat:* 1-9 v Hamilton A, First Division, 9 Aug 1980.
*Most League Appearances:* 435: Eric Tait, 1970-87.
*Most League Goals in Season (Individual):* 38: Ken Bowron, Division II, 1963-64.
*Most Goals Overall (Individual):* 115: Eric Tait, 1970-87.

## BERWICK RANGERS 2003–04 LEAGUE RECORD

| Match No. | Date | Venue | Opponents | Result | | H/T Score | Lg. Pos. | Goalscorers | Attendance |
|---|---|---|---|---|---|---|---|---|---|
| 1 | Aug 9 | A | Arbroath | L | 0-1 | 0-1 | — | | 565 |
| 2 | 16 | H | Hamilton A | W | 3-1 | 1-0 | 5 | McCutcheon 2 [19, 72], Hampshire [63] | 552 |
| 3 | 23 | A | East Fife | L | 1-3 | 1-0 | 6 | Cowan [26] | 692 |
| 4 | 30 | H | Alloa Ath | W | 3-2 | 1-1 | 4 | Hutchison [20], Forrest 2 [83, 85] | 405 |
| 5 | Sept 13 | A | Dumbarton | D | 1-1 | 0-1 | 4 | Hutchison [52] | 751 |
| 6 | 20 | A | Stenhousemuir | W | 3-0 | 1-0 | 3 | Hutchison 2 [43, 58], McCutcheon [55] | 393 |
| 7 | 27 | H | Airdrie U | L | 0-1 | 0-1 | 4 | | 752 |
| 8 | Oct 4 | A | Morton | W | 3-1 | 1-0 | 3 | Connelly [19], McCutcheon [70], Hutchison [78] | 2896 |
| 9 | 18 | H | Forfar Ath | L | 0-4 | 0-1 | 4 | | 423 |
| 10 | 25 | A | Hamilton A | D | 2-2 | 1-0 | 5 | Connelly [34], McCutcheon [64] | 1143 |
| 11 | Nov 1 | H | Arbroath | W | 3-0 | 1-0 | 5 | Hutchison 3 [13, 84, 89] | 383 |
| 12 | 8 | H | Dumbarton | L | 1-4 | 1-4 | 5 | McCutcheon [36] | 395 |
| 13 | 16 | A | Alloa Ath | W | 3-2 | 1-1 | 4 | Hutchison [8], Bennett (pen) [68], Hampshire [76] | 391 |
| 14 | 29 | H | Stenhousemuir | W | 2-1 | 2-0 | 2 | McNicoll [13], McCutcheon [42] | 330 |
| 15 | Dec 6 | A | Airdrie U | D | 1-1 | 0-1 | 2 | Hutchison [72] | 1254 |
| 16 | 13 | H | Morton | L | 2-3 | 0-2 | 4 | McCutcheon [49], Neil M [54] | 882 |
| 17 | 27 | A | Forfar Ath | W | 5-1 | 3-1 | 2 | Forrest 3 [16, 43, 50], Connelly [36], McCutcheon [63] | 603 |
| 18 | Jan 3 | H | East Fife | L | 0-2 | 0-1 | 2 | | 501 |
| 19 | 17 | A | Arbroath | W | 2-1 | 0-1 | 2 | McCutcheon 2 [62, 83] | 411 |
| 20 | 24 | A | Stenhousemuir | L | 1-3 | 0-2 | 2 | Cowan [64] | 337 |
| 21 | Feb 7 | A | Dumbarton | L | 1-4 | 1-2 | 3 | Cowan [19] | 722 |
| 22 | 14 | H | Alloa Ath | W | 3-1 | 0-0 | 3 | Hutchison 2 [51, 56], Forrest [63] | 445 |
| 23 | 21 | H | Forfar Ath | W | 3-1 | 1-1 | 2 | Hutchison [32], Forrest [51], Cowan [68] | 435 |
| 24 | Mar 6 | H | Hamilton A | L | 2-4 | 0-2 | 4 | Hutchison [59], Hampshire [86] | 468 |
| 25 | 13 | A | East Fife | D | 2-2 | 0-2 | 5 | Hilland [3], Hutchison [44] | 498 |
| 26 | 16 | H | Airdrie U | D | 1-1 | 1-0 | — | Hilland [20] | 502 |
| 27 | 23 | A | Morton | L | 1-2 | 0-1 | — | Hutchison [89] | 2300 |
| 28 | 27 | A | Alloa Ath | L | 2-4 | 2-2 | 7 | Hutchison 2 [27, 31] | 365 |
| 29 | 30 | H | Dumbarton | L | 1-2 | 0-1 | — | Bennett (pen) [67] | 354 |
| 30 | Apr 3 | A | Airdrie U | L | 0-6 | 0-5 | 7 | | 1546 |
| 31 | 10 | H | Stenhousemuir | W | 3-0 | 2-0 | 6 | McCutcheon [11], Forrest [31], Hampshire [46] | 392 |
| 32 | 17 | A | Forfar Ath | W | 2-0 | 1-0 | 6 | McCutcheon [3], Hutchison [75] | 465 |
| 33 | 24 | H | Morton | W | 2-0 | 2-0 | 6 | Hutchison [1], McCutcheon [25] | 1175 |
| 34 | May 1 | H | East Fife | D | 1-1 | 0-0 | 5 | Hutchison [85] | 490 |
| 35 | 8 | A | Hamilton A | L | 0-2 | 0-2 | 5 | | 1591 |
| 36 | 15 | H | Arbroath | L | 1-3 | 1-0 | 5- | Hutchison [13] | 506 |

**Final League Position: 5**

**Honours**
*League Champions:* Second Division 1978-79; *Runners-up:* Second Division 1993-94. Third Division 1999-2000.
*Scottish Cup: Quarter-finals:* 1953-54, 1979-80.
*League Cup: Semi-finals:* 1963-64.

**Club colours:** Shirt: Black with broad gold vertical stripes. Shorts: Black with white trim. Stockings: Gold with black and white trim.

**Goalscorers:** *League* (61): Hutchison 22, McCutcheon 14, Forrest 8, Cowan 4, Hampshire 4, Connelly 3, Bennett 2 (2 pens), Hilland 2, McNicoll 1, Neil M 1
*Scottish Cup* (4): Hutchison 3, own goal 1
*CIS Cup* (0):
*Challenge Cup* (1): McNicoll 1

| Inglis N 25 | Murie D 35 | Neill A 20 + 2 | Cowan M 24 + 1 | McNicoll G 32 | Hampshire P 32 + 3 | Connelly G 27 + 4 | Forrest G 18 | McAllister J 1 + 2 | Hutchison G 36 | Bennett J 30 + 4 | McCormick M — + 4 | Birrell J — + 1 | Waldie C 11 + 2 | Connell G 25 + 2 | McCutcheon G 33 + 1 | Godfrey R 11 + 1 | Smith D 7 + 12 | Blackley D — + 5 | Hilland P 9 + 4 | Robertson M — + 3 | Neil M 16 + 4 | Kerrigan S — + 6 | Gordon K 3 + 10 | Elliot B — + 5 | Noon D 1 | Bain C — + 1 | Macdonald S — + 1 | Bracks K — + 1 | *Match No.* |
|---|---|---|---|---|---|---|---|---|---|---|---|---|---|---|---|---|---|---|---|---|---|---|---|---|---|---|---|---|---|
| 1 | 2 | 3 | $4^{1}$ | 5 | 6 | 7 | 8 | $9^{2}$ | 10 | 11 | 12 | 13 | | | | | | | | | | | | | | | | | 1 |
| $1^{2}$ | 2 | 5 | 4 | | 11 | | 6 | | 9 | 3 | | | 7 | 8 | $10^{1}$ | 13 | 12 | | | | | | | | | | | | 2 |
| | | 5 | $4^{1}$ | 2 | 11 | 12 | 6 | 14 | 9 | 3 | | | $7^{3}$ | $8^{2}$ | 10 | 1 | | 13 | | | | | | | | | | | 3 |
| | 2 | $5^{2}$ | | 4 | 11 | $7^{1}$ | 6 | | 9 | 3 | | | | 8 | 10 | 1 | 12 | | 13 | | | | | | | | | | 4 |
| | 2 | | 4 | 5 | 11 | $7^{2}$ | | | 9 | 8 | | | 12 | 6 | 10 | 1 | | 13 | $3^{1}$ | | | | | | | | | | 5 |
| | 2 | | 4 | 5 | 11 | $7^{2}$ | | | $9^{3}$ | $3^{1}$ | | | 6 | 8 | 10 | 1 | | 14 | 12 | 13 | | | | | | | | | 6 |
| | $2^{1}$ | | 4 | 5 | 11 | 7 | | 12 | 9 | 3 | | | 6 | 8 | 10 | 1 | | | | | | | | | | | | | 7 |
| | 2 | | 4 | 5 | 11 | 7 | | | 9 | 3 | | | 6 | 8 | $10^{1}$ | 1 | | 12 | | | | | | | | | | | 8 |
| | $2^{2}$ | | 4 | 5 | 11 | $7^{3}$ | | | 9 | $3^{1}$ | | | 6■ | 8 | 10 | 1 | | 14 | 12 | 13 | | | | | | | | | 9 |
| | 2 | | 5 | 4 | 11 | 7 | | | 9 | 6 | | | | 8 | 10 | 1 | | | 3 | | | | | | | | | | 10 |
| | 2 | | 5 | 4 | 11 | $7^{1}$ | | | 9 | $6^{2}$ | | | 12 | 8 | $10^{3}$ | 1 | | | 3 | 14 | 13 | | | | | | | | 11 |
| | 2 | | 5 | 4 | 11 | 7 | | | 9 | 6 | | | 8 | | 10 | 1 | | | $3^{1}$ | | 12 | | | | | | | | 12 |
| 1 | 2 | 4 | 5 | | $11^{2}$ | 12 | | | 9 | 3 | | | 6 | 8 | $10^{1}$ | | | | 13 | | 7■ | | | | | | | | 13 |
| 1 | 2 | | 5 | 4 | 11 | 7 | | | 9 | 3 | | | 6 | 8 | 10 | | | | | | | | | | | | | | 14 |
| 1 | 2 | | 5 | 4 | 11 | | | | $9^{2}$ | 3 | 12 | | $7^{1}$ | 8 | $10^{3}$ | | 14 | | | | 6 | 13 | | | | | | | 15 |
| 1 | 2 | 13 | 5 | 4■ | 11 | | | | 9 | $3^{3}$ | 12 | | $7^{1}$ | $8^{2}$ | 10 | | 14 | | | | 6 | | | | | | | | 16 |
| 1 | 2 | 4 | 5 | | 11 | $7^{1}$ | $8^{3}$ | | $9^{2}$ | 3 | 12 | | | | 10 | | 14 | | | | 6 | 13 | | | | | | | 17 |
| 1 | 2 | 4 | 5 | | 11 | 7 | $8^{2}$ | | 9 | $3^{1}$ | | | | | 10 | | 12 | | | | 6 | 13 | | | | | | | 18 |
| 1 | 2 | 3 | 5 | 4 | $11^{1}$ | 7 | 8 | | $9^{2}$ | | | | | | 10 | | 12 | | | | 6 | 13 | | | | | | | 19 |
| 1 | $2^{3}$ | 3 | 5 | 4 | $11^{2}$ | 7 | 8 | | 9 | | | | | 12 | 10 | | 13 | | | | $6^{1}$ | 14 | | | | | | | 20 |
| 1 | 2 | | 5 | 4 | 11 | 7 | $6^{1}$ | | 9 | $3^{2}$ | | | | 8 | $10^{3}$ | | 12 | | | | | 13 | 14 | | | | | | 21 |
| 1 | 2 | | 5 | 4 | 12 | 7 | 8 | | $9^{3}$ | 3 | | | | 6 | $10^{2}$ | | $11^{1}$ | | | | 14 | | 13 | | | | | | 22 |
| 1 | 2 | | 5 | 4 | | 7 | 8 | | 9 | 3 | | | | 6 | 10 | | $11^{1}$ | | | | | | 12 | | | | | | 23 |
| 1 | 2 | 12 | 4 | $5^{1}$ | 13 | $7^{3}$ | 8 | | 9 | $3^{2}$ | | | | 6 | 10 | | 11 | | | | | | 14 | | | | | | 24 |
| 1 | $2^{1}$ | 5 | | 4 | 11 | 7 | $8^{3}$ | | 9 | 14 | | | | 6 | $10^{2}$ | | | | 3 | | 12 | | 13 | | | | | | 25 |
| 1 | 2 | 5 | | 4 | $11^{1}$ | 7 | | | 9 | 12 | | | | 6 | $10^{2}$ | | | | 3 | | 8 | | 13 | | | | | | 26 |
| 1 | 2 | 5 | | 4 | $11^{2}$ | $7^{3}$ | | | 9 | 12 | | | | 6 | 10 | | 13 | | $3^{1}$ | | 8 | | 14 | | | | | | 27 |
| 1 | 2 | 5 | | 4 | $11^{2}$ | $7^{3}$ | | | 9 | 12 | | | | 6 | 10 | | 13 | | $3^{1}$ | | 8 | | | 14 | | | | | 28 |
| 1 | 2 | 5 | | 4 | 13 | 12 | 7 | | 9 | 3 | | | | $6^{1}$ | $10^{3}$ | | $11^{2}$ | | | | 8 | | 14 | | | | | | 29 |
| 1 | 2 | 5 | | 4 | 11 | 7 | 6 | | $9^{2}$ | 3 | | | | $8^{1}$ | 12 | | | | 10 | | | | | 13 | | | | | 30 |
| 1 | 2 | 5 | | 4 | 11 | 7 | $8^{2}$ | | $9^{3}$ | 3 | | | | $6^{1}$ | 10 | | 12 | | | | | | 13 | 14 | | | | | 31 |
| 1 | 2 | 5 | | 4 | 11 | 7 | 8 | | 9 | 3 | | | | | 10 | | | | | | 6 | | | | | | | | 32 |
| 1 | 2 | 5 | | 4 | 11 | 7 | 8 | | $9^{2}$ | 3 | | | | | $10^{1}$ | | | | | | 6 | | 13 | 12 | | | | | 33 |
| 1 | 2 | 5 | | 4 | 11 | | | | 9 | 3 | | | | 12 | 10 | | 8 | | | | 6 | | $7^{1}$ | | | | | | 34 |
| 1 | 2 | 5 | 14 | 4 | 11 | 13 | | | 9 | 3 | | | | | $10^{1}$ | | $8^{3}$ | | | | $6^{2}$ | | 7 | 12 | | | | | 35 |
| | 2 | | 5 | $4^{1}$ | 11 | | | | 9 | $3^{3}$ | | | | | | 1 | 8 | | | | 6 | | 7 | | $10^{2}$ | 12 | 13 | 14 | 36 |

# BRECHIN CITY — Second Division

*Year Formed:* 1906. *Ground & Address:* Glebe Park, Trinity Rd, Brechin, Angus DD9 6BJ. *Telephone:* 01356 622856. *Fax (to Secretary):* 01356 625524.
*Ground Capacity:* total: 3060, seated: 1518. *Size of Pitch:* 110yd × 67yd.
*Chairman:* David Birse. *Vice-Chairman:* Hugh Campbell Adamson. *Secretary:* Ken Ferguson.
*Manager:* Dick Campbell. *Assistant Manager:* Ian Campbell. *Youth Coach:* Paul Martin. *Physio:* Tom Gilmartin.
*Managers since 1975:* C. Dunn, I. Stewart, D. Houston, I. Fleming, J. Ritchie, I. Redford, J. Young.
*Club Nickname(s):* The City. *Previous Grounds:* Nursery Park.
*Record Attendance:* 8122 v Aberdeen, Scottish Cup 3rd rd, 3 Feb 1973.
*Record Transfer Fee received:* £100,000 for Scott Thomson to Aberdeen (1991).
*Record Transfer Fee paid:* £16,000 for Sandy Ross from Berwick Rangers (1991).
*Record Victory:* 12-1 v Thornhill, Scottish Cup 1st rd, 28 Jan 1926.
*Record Defeat:* 0-10 v Airdrieonians, Albion R and Cowdenbeath, all in Division II, 1937-38.
*Most League Appearances:* 459: David Watt, 1975-89.
*Most League Goals in Season (Individual):* 26: W. McIntosh, Division II, 1959-60.
*Most Goals Overall (Individual):* 131: Ian Campbell.

## BRECHIN CITY 2003–04 LEAGUE RECORD

| Match No. | Date | Venue | Opponents | Result | | H/T Score | Lg. Pos. | Goalscorers | Attendance |
|---|---|---|---|---|---|---|---|---|---|
| 1 | Aug 9 | A | Ross Co | L | 0-4 | 0-2 | — | | 2662 |
| 2 | 16 | H | Raith R | L | 0-3 | 0-1 | 10 | | 1013 |
| 3 | 23 | A | Clyde | L | 1-2 | 1-1 | 10 | Jablonski 6 | 1063 |
| 4 | 30 | A | St Johnstone | L | 1-3 | 0-0 | 10 | Gibson 90 | 2219 |
| 5 | Sept 13 | H | St Mirren | D | 1-1 | 1-1 | 10 | Fotheringham (pen) 11 | 956 |
| 6 | 20 | H | Inverness CT | L | 0-2 | 0-0 | 10 | | 652 |
| 7 | 27 | A | Ayr U | L | 2-3 | 1-2 | 10 | King 40, Hampshire 60 | 1427 |
| 8 | Oct 4 | H | Queen of the S | L | 0-1 | 0-0 | 10 | | 621 |
| 9 | 18 | A | Falkirk | L | 0-3 | 0-2 | 10 | | 2442 |
| 10 | 25 | A | Raith R | L | 1-2 | 0-2 | 10 | Fotheringham (pen) 73 | 1685 |
| 11 | Nov 1 | H | Ross Co | W | 4-2 | 1-2 | 10 | White 2 39, 54, Smith 63, McLeish 83 | 564 |
| 12 | 8 | A | St Mirren | D | 0-0 | 0-0 | 10 | | 2801 |
| 13 | 16 | H | St Johnstone | L | 0-1 | 0-1 | 10 | | 1434 |
| 14 | 22 | H | Ayr U | W | 3-1 | 2-0 | 10 | Templeman 10, Hampshire 39, McLeish 57 | 508 |
| 15 | 29 | A | Inverness CT | L | 0-5 | 0-3 | 10 | | 1393 |
| 16 | Dec 6 | H | Falkirk | D | 2-2 | 2-0 | 10 | Mitchell 6, Millar M (pen) 18 | 1043 |
| 17 | 13 | A | Queen of the S | L | 0-1 | 0-0 | 10 | | 1736 |
| 18 | 20 | A | Ross Co | L | 1-2 | 0-1 | 10 | Templeman 67 | 2545 |
| 19 | 27 | H | Clyde | L | 1-3 | 0-0 | 10 | Hampshire 73 | 808 |
| 20 | Jan 3 | A | St Johnstone | D | 2-2 | 0-2 | 10 | Mitchell 46, Hampshire 69 | 2171 |
| 21 | 17 | H | St Mirren | W | 2-0 | 0-0 | 10 | McCulloch S 54, Smith 78 | 878 |
| 22 | 24 | H | Inverness CT | L | 2-4 | 1-2 | 10 | Duffy 2 14, 61 | 669 |
| 23 | 31 | A | Ayr U | W | 2-1 | 2-1 | 10 | Millar M (pen) 25, King 33 | 1512 |
| 24 | Feb 14 | H | Queen of the S | W | 2-1 | 0-0 | 9 | King 72, Beith 79 | 642 |
| 25 | 21 | A | Falkirk | L | 0-5 | 0-4 | 10 | | 2060 |
| 26 | Mar 10 | H | Raith R | D | 1-1 | 0-1 | — | Duffy 70 | 925 |
| 27 | 13 | A | Clyde | D | 0-0 | 0-0 | 9 | | 1037 |
| 28 | 20 | A | St Mirren | D | 3-3 | 1-2 | 9 | McCulloch S 27, Templeman 49, Winter 61 | 2221 |
| 29 | 27 | H | St Johnstone | L | 0-2 | 0-1 | 10 | | 822 |
| 30 | Apr 3 | H | Ayr U | L | 0-3 | 0-0 | 10 | | 519 |
| 31 | 13 | A | Inverness CT | L | 0-1 | 0-0 | — | | 1198 |
| 32 | 17 | H | Falkirk | L | 0-1 | 0-0 | 10 | | 768 |
| 33 | 24 | A | Queen of the S | D | 2-2 | 0-1 | 10 | Winter 68, Gibson 74 | 1352 |
| 34 | May 1 | H | Ross Co | W | 1-0 | 0-0 | 10 | Gibson 90 | 464 |
| 35 | 8 | A | Raith R | D | 1-1 | 1-0 | 10 | Gibson 4 | 2311 |
| 36 | 15 | H | Clyde | L | 2-5 | 0-3 | 10 | Templeman 2 (1 pen) 80 (p), 88 | 1268 |

**Final League Position: 10**

**Honours**
*League Champions:* C Division 1953-54. Second Division 1982-83, 1989-90. Third Division 2001-02. *Runners-up:* Second Division 1992-93, 2002-03. Third Division 1995-96.
*Bell's League Challenge:* Finalists 2002-03. Semi-finalists 2001-02.

**Club colours:** Shirt, Shorts, Stockings: Red with white trimmings.

**Goalscorers:** *League* (37): Templeman 5 (1 pen), Gibson 4, Hampshire 4, Duffy 3, King 3, Fotheringham 2 (2 pens), McCulloch S 2, McLeigh 2, Millar M 2 (2 pens), Mitchell 2, Smith 2, White 2, Winter 2, Beith 1, Jablonski 1
*Scottish Cup* (1): King 1
*CIS Cup* (5): Fotheringham 1, Gibson 1, Hampshire 1, Templeman 1, White 1
*Challenge Cup* (7): Fotheringham 2, Templeman 2, Johnston 1, King 1, White 1

| Budinauckas K 8+1 | Davidson I 3+1 | McCulloch S 22+8 | Deas P 32 | White D 27+1 | Fotheringham K 8+4 | Mitchell A 27+2 | Johnson G 25 | Templeman C 22+11 | Gibson G 11+16 | Black R 5+5 | Miller G 7+10 | Shields D —+2 | Stein J 2+4 | Clark D 3+3 | Jackson C 1 | King C 27+5 | Hay D 16+2 | McCulloch M 3+3 | Jablonski N 15+1 | Soutar D 12 | Hampshire S 27 | McLeish K 11+9 | Smith J 26+2 | Millar M 19+1 | Boylan C 1+12 | Beith G 2+2 | Walker S 1 | Duffy D 8 | Dowie A 15 | Winter C 10 | *Match No.* |
|---|---|---|---|---|---|---|---|---|---|---|---|---|---|---|---|---|---|---|---|---|---|---|---|---|---|---|---|---|---|---|---|
| 1 | 2 | 3 | 4[1] | 5 | 6 | 7■ | 8 | 9 | 10[2] | 11[3] | 12 | 13 | 14 | | | | | | | | | | | | | | | | | | 1 |
| 1[G] | 2 | 3 | | 4 | 6 | | | 9 | 12 | | 7 | 13 | 11[2] | 5■ | 8 | 10[1] | 15 | | | | | | | | | | | | | | 2 |
| | 14 | 6 | 4 | 5 | 12 | 3 | 7[1] | 9 | 10[2] | | 2 | | 13 | | | | 1 | 8[3] | 11 | | | | | | | | | | | | 3 |
| | 4[3] | 14 | 8 | 5 | 6 | 3 | | 9[2] | 13 | | 2 | | | | | 12 | | 11 | 10[1] | 1 | 7 | | | | | | | | | | 4 |
| | | 4 | 3 | 5 | 6[2] | 11 | | 12 | 9[1] | | 2 | | | | | 13 | | 14 | 8 | 1 | 10 | 7[3] | | | | | | | | | 5 |
| | | 4 | 3 | 5 | | 11 | 8[2] | 12 | 7[1] | | 14 | | | | | 10 | | 13 | 6[3] | 1 | 9 | | 2 | | | | | | | | 6 |
| | | 10 | 3 | 5 | | 11 | 8[3] | 12 | 13 | | 2 | | | | | 7[2] | | 14 | 6 | 1 | 9[1] | | 4 | | | | | | | | 7 |
| | | 10 | 3 | 5 | 13 | 11 | 8[2] | 12 | | | 2[1] | | | | | 7 | | | 6 | 1 | 9 | | 4 | | | | | | | | 8 |
| | | 3 | 4 | 5 | | 8 | | 9 | 14 | | 12 | | 11[1] | 13 | | 7 | | 6 | | 1 | 10[3] | | 2[2] | | | | | | | | 9 |
| | | 4 | 3 | 5 | 12 | 8 | | 10[3] | 14 | | 2[1] | | 13 | | | 7 | | | 11[2] | 1 | 9 | | 6 | | | | | | | | 10 |
| | | 14 | 3 | 5 | | 6 | 8[3] | 9 | 12 | | 13 | | | | | 7[2] | | | 2 | 1 | 10[1] | 11 | 4 | | | | | | | | 11 |
| | | 14 | 3 | 5 | | 6 | 8 | 9 | | | | | | | | 7[1] | 13 | | 2[3] | 1[2] | 10 | 11 | 4 | 12 | | | | | | | 12 |
| | | | 3 | 5 | 14 | 11 | 4[3] | 9[1] | 12 | | 13 | | | | | 7 | 1 | | 8[2] | | 10 | | 6 | 2 | | | | | | | 13 |
| | | 12 | 3 | 5 | | | 4 | 10 | 14 | | 13 | | | | | 7 | 1 | | 8[2] | | 9 | 11[3] | 6[1] | 2 | | | | | | | 14 |
| | | 6 | 3 | 5 | | | 4[3] | 10[1] | 12 | | 13 | | 14 | | | 7 | 1 | | 8[2] | | 9 | 11 | | 2 | | | | | | | 15 |
| | | 12 | 3[1] | 5 | | 11 | 4 | 13 | 10 | | | | | | | 7[3] | | | 14 | 1■ | 9[2] | 8 | 6 | 2 | | | | | | | 16 |
| | | 5 | 3 | 4 | 6 | 11 | | 12 | 9[1] | | 13 | | | 2[2] | | 7 | 1 | | 8[3] | | | 10 | | | 14 | | | | | | 17 |
| | | | 3 | 5■ | 6 | 11 | | 12 | 10[2] | | 14 | | | | | 7[1] | | | 8 | 1 | 9 | | 4 | 2[3] | 13 | | | | | | 18 |
| | | | 5 | | 6 | 9 | 8[2] | 11[3] | 10 | | | | | | | | | | 4[1] | 1 | 7 | 12 | 3 | 2 | 14 | 13 | | | | | 19 |
| | | 13 | 3 | | 6[2] | 7 | 11 | 9[1] | 12 | | | | | | | 14 | 1 | | | | 10 | 8[3] | 4 | 2 | | | 5 | | | | 20 |
| | | 3 | 6 | | | 8 | 4 | | 14 | 12 | 13 | | | | | 7[2] | 1 | | | | 9[3] | | 5 | 2 | | 11[1] | | 10 | | | 21 |
| | | 8[1] | 5 | | | 11 | 7[3] | 13 | | 3[2] | | | | | | 12 | 1 | | | | 9 | 14 | 4 | 2 | | | | 10 | 6 | | 22 |
| | | | 3 | 5 | | 11 | 8 | 13 | 12 | | | | | | | 7[1] | 1 | | | | 9 | | 4 | 2 | | | | 10[2] | 6 | | 23 |
| | | | 3 | 5 | | | 8 | 9[3] | | 11[2] | | | | 6[1] | | 7 | 1 | | | | | 12 | 2 | | 14 | 13 | | 10 | 4 | | 24 |
| | | 12 | 3 | 5 | | 8 | 6[3] | 14 | | 13 | | | | | | 7 | 1 | | | | 10 | | 2 | | | 11[2] | | 9[1] | 4 | | 25 |
| 1 | | 5 | 6 | 4[1] | | 3[3] | | | | | | | | 14 | | 7 | | | | | 9 | 11[2] | 12 | 8 | 13 | | | 10 | 2 | | 26 |
| | | 5 | 3 | | | 11 | 4 | | | | | | | | | 7[2] | 1 | | | | 9 | 13 | 12 | 2 | 14 | | | 10[3] | 6 | 8[1] | 27 |
| | | 5 | | | | 11 | 6[3] | 12 | | | | | | 14 | | 7 | 1 | | | | 9[2] | 13 | 2 | 3 | | | | 10[1] | 4 | 8 | 28 |
| | | 3[2] | | 12 | | 11 | 6 | 9 | 13 | | | | | | | 7[1] | 1 | | | | 10 | 14 | 5 | 2 | | | | | 4 | 8[3] | 29 |
| | | 6 | 3 | 5 | | | 8[2] | 10[1] | 12 | | | | | | | | 1 | | | | 9 | 13 | 2[3] | 7 | 14 | | | | 4 | 11 | 30 |
| 12 | | 6 | 3 | 5 | | | 8[3] | 7 | | | | | | | | 13 | 1[1] | | | | 9[2] | | 2 | 11 | 14 | | | | 4 | 10 | 31 |
| 1 | | 6[1] | 3 | | | 12 | | 9 | 13 | 14 | | | | | | 11 | | | | | | 8[2] | 5 | 2 | 7[3] | | | | 4 | 10 | 32 |
| 1 | | 6 | 3[1] | 5[2] | | 11 | | 9 | 13 | 12 | | | | | | 7[3] | | | | | | | 2 | 10 | 14 | | | | 4 | 8 | 33 |
| 1 | | 6 | 3 | | | 11[3] | | 9 | 10 | 14 | | | | | | 7[1] | | | | | | 13 | 5 | 2 | 12 | | | | 4 | 8[2] | 34 |
| 1 | | | 3 | 5 | | 14 | 10 | 9 | 11 | 6[1] | | | | | | 7[2] | | | | | | 12 | 2[3] | | 13 | | | | 4 | 8 | 35 |
| 1 | | 12 | | 5 | | | 6 | 9 | 10 | 3[2] | | | | | | 7[1] | | | | | 11 | 2 | | | 13 | | | | 4 | 8 | 36 |

# CELTIC — Premier League

*Year Formed:* 1888. *Ground & Address:* Celtic Park, Glasgow G40 3RE. *Telephone:* 0141 556 2611. *Fax:* 0141 551 8106.
*Ground Capacity:* all seated: 60,355. *Size of Pitch:* 105m × 68m.
*Chairman:* Brian Quinn. *Executive Director:* Peter Lawwell. *Secretary:* Robert Howat.
*Manager:* Martin O'Neill. *Assistant Manager:* John Robertson. *First Team Coach:* Steve Walford. *Youth Development Manager:* Tommy Burns. *Head Youth Coach:* Willie McStay. *Physio:* Brian Scott. *Assistant Physio:* Neil McLeod. *Kit Manager:* John Clark.
*Managers since 1975:* Jock Stein, Billy McNeill, David Hay, Billy McNeill, Liam Brady, Lou Macari, Tommy Burns, Wim Jansen, Dr Jozef Venglos, John Barnes (Head Coach). *Club Nickname(s):* The Bhoys. *Previous Grounds:* None.
*Record Attendance:* 92,000 v Rangers, Division I, 1 Jan 1938.
*Record Transfer Fee received:* £4,700,000 for Paolo Di Canio to Sheffield W (August 1997).
*Record Transfer Fee paid:* £6,000,000 for Chris Sutton from Chelsea (July 2000).
*Record Victory:* 11-0 Dundee, Division I, 26 Oct 1895.
*Record Defeat:* 0-8 v Motherwell, Division I, 30 Apr 1937.
*Most Capped Player:* Pat Bonner 80, Republic of Ireland.
*Most League Appearances:* 486: Billy McNeill, 1957-75.
*Most League Goals in Season (Individual):* 50: James McGrory, Division I, 1935-36.
*Most Goals Overall (Individual):* 397: James McGrory, 1922-39.

**Honours**
*League Champions:* (39 times) Division I 1892-93, 1893-94, 1895-96, 1897-98, 1904-05, 1905-06, 1906-07, 1907-08, 1908-09, 1909-10, 1913-14, 1914-15, 1915-16, 1916-17, 1918-19, 1921-22, 1925-26, 1935-36, 1937-38, 1953-54, 1965-66, 1966-67,

## CELTIC 2003–04 LEAGUE RECORD

| Match No. | Date | Venue | Opponents | Result | H/T Score | Lg. Pos. | Goalscorers | Attendance |
|---|---|---|---|---|---|---|---|---|
| 1 | Aug 9 | A | Dunfermline Ath | D 0-0 | 0-0 | — | | 10082 |
| 2 | 16 | H | Dundee U | W 5-0 | 3-0 | 2 | Maloney 11, Agathe 26, Thompson (pen) 44, McNamara 66, Larsson 83 | 57004 |
| 3 | 23 | A | Partick Th | W 2-1 | 2-1 | 2 | Lambert 8, Thompson (pen) 42 | 9045 |
| 4 | 30 | H | Livingston | W 5-1 | 2-0 | 2 | Larsson 3 24, 55, 76, Maloney 38, Thompson 90 | 57,062 |
| 5 | Sept 13 | A | Dundee | W 1-0 | 1-0 | 2 | Balde 7 | 10,647 |
| 6 | 20 | H | Motherwell | W 3-0 | 0-0 | 2 | Larsson 47, Sutton 64, Maloney 70 | 57,492 |
| 7 | 27 | A | Hibernian | W 2-1 | 1-1 | 2 | Thompson (pen) 39, Larsson 51 | 12,032 |
| 8 | Oct 4 | A | Rangers | W 1-0 | 0-0 | 1 | Hartson 46 | 49,825 |
| 9 | 18 | H | Hearts | W 5-0 | 4-0 | 1 | Miller 2 8, 50, Stamp (og) 12, Larsson 35, Varga 41 | 59,511 |
| 10 | 25 | H | Aberdeen | W 4-0 | 3-0 | 1 | Larsson 3 3, 28, 54, Sutton (pen) 44 | 59,574 |
| 11 | Nov 1 | A | Kilmarnock | W 5-0 | 1-0 | 1 | Sutton 3 (2 pens) 19 (p), 75, 89 (p), Hartson 69, Maloney 83 | 12,460 |
| 12 | 8 | H | Dunfermline Ath | W 5-0 | 1-0 | 1 | Hartson 2 23, 76, Wallace 81, Varga 84, Larsson 87 | 58,258 |
| 13 | 22 | A | Dundee U | W 5-1 | 1-0 | 1 | Larsson 2 51, 58, Sutton 3 (1 pen) 61, 56, 81 (p) | 10,802 |
| 14 | 29 | H | Partick Th | W 3-1 | 2-1 | 1 | Larsson 22, Sutton 2 38, 59 | 58,194 |
| 15 | Dec 6 | A | Livingston | W 2-0 | 0-0 | 1 | Sutton 47, Thompson 84 | 8065 |
| 16 | 13 | H | Dundee | W 3-2 | 1-1 | 1 | Larsson 14, Balde 69, Kennedy 86 | 57,539 |
| 17 | 21 | A | Motherwell | W 2-0 | 1-0 | 1 | Hartson 3, Thompson 71 | 10,513 |
| 18 | 27 | H | Hibernian | W 6-0 | 2-0 | 1 | Sutton 2 (1 pen) 3, 53 (p), Hartson 2 44, 59, Larsson 65, Petrov 76 | 59,542 |
| 19 | Jan 3 | H | Rangers | W 3-0 | 1-0 | 1 | Petrov 19, Varga 59, Thompson 83 | 59,042 |
| 20 | 18 | A | Hearts | W 1-0 | 1-0 | 1 | Petrov 27 | 13,753 |
| 21 | 24 | A | Aberdeen | W 3-1 | 2-0 | 1 | Petrov 29, Larsson 42, Pearson 57 | 16,452 |
| 22 | 31 | H | Kilmarnock | W 5-1 | 0-0 | 1 | Agathe 55, Hartson 2 64, 88, Larsson 75, Pearson 77 | 59,046 |
| 23 | Feb 11 | A | Dunfermline Ath | W 4-1 | 3-1 | — | Larsson 2 23, 43, Varga 25, Thompson 68 | 9718 |
| 24 | 14 | H | Dundee U | W 2-1 | 0-0 | 1 | Maloney 80, Sutton (pen) 82 | 58,671 |
| 25 | 22 | A | Partick Th | W 4-1 | 2-0 | 1 | Sutton 2 34, 51, Varga 2 38, 80 | 8131 |
| 26 | 29 | H | Livingston | W 5-1 | 2-1 | 1 | Pearson 12, Sutton 35, Thompson 2 48, 79, Larsson 55 | 57,949 |
| 27 | Mar 14 | H | Motherwell | D 1-1 | 0-1 | 1 | Larsson 69 | 57,580 |
| 28 | 17 | A | Dundee | W 2-1 | 1-0 | — | Petrov 38, Larsson 68 | 8593 |
| 29 | 21 | A | Hibernian | W 4-0 | 2-0 | 1 | Agathe 2 17, 80, Larsson 2 33, 48 | 9456 |
| 30 | 28 | A | Rangers | W 2-1 | 1-0 | 1 | Larsson 19, Thompson 52 | 49,909 |
| 31 | Apr 3 | H | Hearts | D 2-2 | 0-1 | 1 | Sutton 87, Agathe 89 | 59,295 |
| 32 | 18 | A | Kilmarnock | W 1-0 | 1-0 | 1 | Petrov 31 | 14,516 |
| 33 | 21 | H | Aberdeen | L 1-2 | 1-0 | — | Larsson 15 | 57,385 |
| 34 | 25 | A | Hearts | D 1-1 | 1-0 | 1 | McGeady 17 | 12,112 |
| 35 | May 2 | H | Dunfermline Ath | L 1-2 | 0-1 | 1 | Larsson 46 | 59,719 |
| 36 | 8 | H | Rangers | W 1-0 | 0-0 | 1 | Sutton 89 | 59,180 |
| 37 | 12 | A | Motherwell | D 1-1 | 0-0 | 1 | Beattie 78 | 7749 |
| 38 | 16 | H | Dundee U | W 2-1 | 0-0 | 1 | Larsson 2 80, 86 | 58,364 |

**Final League Position: 1**

1967-68, 1968-69, 1969-70, 1970-71, 1971-72, 1972-73, 1973-74. Premier Division 1976-77, 1978-79, 1980-81, 1981-82, 1985-86, 1987-88, 1997-98, 2000-01, 2001-02, 2003–04. *Runners-up:* 26 times.
*Scottish Cup Winners:* (32 times) 1892, 1899, 1900, 1904, 1907, 1908, 1911, 1912, 1914, 1923, 1925, 1927, 1931, 1933, 1937, 1951, 1954, 1965, 1967, 1969, 1971, 1972, 1974, 1975, 1977, 1980, 1985, 1988, 1989, 1995, 2001, 2004. *Runners-up:* 18 times.
*League Cup Winners:* (12 times) 1956-57, 1957-58, 1965-66, 1966-67, 1967-68, 1968-69, 1969-70, 1974-75, 1982-83, 1997-98, 1999-2000, 2000-01. *Runners-up:* 11 times.

**European:** *European Cup:* 100 matches (1966-67 winners, 1967-68, 1968-69, 1969-70 runners-up, 1970-71, 1971-72 semi-finals, 1972-73, 1973-74 semi-finals, 1974-75, 1977-78, 1979-80, 1981-82, 1982-83, 1986-87, 1988-89, 1998-99, 2001-02, 2002-03, 2003-04). *Cup Winners' Cup:* 39 matches (1963-64 semi-finals, 1965-66 semi-finals, 1975-76, 1980-81, 1984-85, 1985-86, 1989-90, 1995-96). *UEFA Cup:* 73 matches (*Fairs Cup:* 1962-63, 1964-65. *UEFA Cup:* 1976-77, 1983-84, 1987-88, 1991-92, 1992-93, 1993-94, 1996-97, 1997-98, 1998-99, 1999-2000, 2000-01, 2001-02, 2002-03 runners-up, 2003-04 quarter-finals.

**Club colours:** Shirt: Emerald green and white hoops. Shorts: White with emerald trim. Stockings: White.

**Goalscorers:** *League* (105): Larsson 30, Sutton 19 (6 pens), Thompson 11 (3 pens), Hartson 9, Petrov 6, Varga 6, Agathe 5, Maloney 5, Pearson 3, Balde 2, Miller 2, Beattie 1, Kennedy 1, Lambert 1, McGeady 1, McNamara 1, Wallace 1, own goal 1
*Scottish Cup* (12): Larsson 5, Petrov 3, Sutton 2, Hartson 1, Lambert 1
*CIS Cup* (3): Beattie 1, Smith 1, Varga 1

| Douglas R 15 + 1 | Mjällby J 10 + 3 | Valgaeren J 4 + 3 | Balde D 30 + 1 | Thompson A 26 | Petrov S 33 + 2 | Lennon N 35 | Lambert P 9 + 4 | Agathe D 26 + 1 | Larsson H 36 + 1 | Maloney S 7 + 10 | Smith J 4 + 7 | Miller L 13 + 12 | Hedman M 12 | Varga S 35 | McNamara J 26 + 1 | Sylla M 5 + 9 | Beattie C 2 + 8 | Hartson J 14 + 1 | Crainey S 1 + 1 | Sutton C 25 | Gray M 2 + 5 | Kennedy J 9 + 3 | Wallace R 4 + 4 | Pearson S 16 + 1 | Marshall D 11 | McManus S 5 | McGeady A 3 + 1 | *Match No.* |
|---|---|---|---|---|---|---|---|---|---|---|---|---|---|---|---|---|---|---|---|---|---|---|---|---|---|---|---|---|
| 1 | 2 | 3 | 4 | 5 | 6 | $7^2$ | $8^1$ | 9 | 10 | 11 | 12 | 13 | | | | | | | | | | | | | | | | 1 |
| | | $3^1$ | 4 | 8 | $6^3$ | | | $9^2$ | 10 | 11 | 14 | 7 | 1 | 2 | 5 | 12 | 13 | | | | | | | | | | | 2 |
| 1 | | $3^1$ | 4 | 9 | 6 | 7 | $8^2$ | | 10 | 11 | | 12 | | 2 | 5 | 13 | | | | | | | | | | | | 3 |
| | | | 4 | 8 | $6^1$ | 5 | | $9^2$ | 10 | 11 | | 7 | 1 | 2 | $3^3$ | 13 | | 12 | 14 | | | | | | | | | 4 |
| | | | 4 | 8 | $6^3$ | 7 | | 9■ | 10 | 14 | | 12 | 1 | 2 | 5 | 13 | | $11^2$ | $3^1$ | | | | | | | | | 5 |
| | | | 4 | 5 | $6^3$ | $7^2$ | | | 10 | 12 | | 14 | 1 | 2 | 3 | 8 | | $11^1$ | | 9 | 13 | | | | | | | 6 |
| | | | 4■ | 5 | 6 | 7 | | 8 | 10 | $11^1$ | | 12 | 1 | 2 | 3 | | | | | 9 | | | | | | | | 7 |
| | | | | $5^1$ | 6 | 7 | | 8 | 10 | | | 4 | 1 | 2 | 3 | | | 11 | | 9 | 12 | | | | | | | 8 |
| | | | 4 | $5^2$ | $6^1$ | 7 | | 8 | 10 | 12 | | 9 | 1 | $2^3$ | 3 | | | 11 | | | 13 | 14 | | | | | | 9 |
| | | 3 | 4 | $5^1$ | | $7^2$ | | $8^3$ | 10 | 13 | | 6 | 1 | 2 | | 14 | | 11 | | 9 | 12 | | | | | | | 10 |
| | | | 4 | | 6 | $7^3$ | | | 10 | 13 | | 8 | 1 | 2 | 3 | 12 | | $11^2$ | | 9 | $5^1$ | | 14 | | | | | 11 |
| 1 | 14 | | $4^2$ | | $6^3$ | 7 | | 5 | 10 | $8^1$ | | | | 2 | 3 | 13 | | 11 | | 9 | | | 12 | | | | | 12 |
| 13 | 3 | | 4 | 5 | 6 | 7 | | 8 | $10^3$ | 14 | | 9 | $1^2$ | $2^1$ | 12 | | | | | 11 | | | | | | | | 13 |
| | 3 | | | | 13 | 7 | | | 10 | | | 6 | 1 | 2 | | $4^1$ | | $11^2$ | | 9 | 12 | 5 | 8 | | | | | 14 |
| | 12 | | 4 | 8 | 6 | 7 | | | 10 | | | 9 | 1 | 2 | $3^1$ | | | | | 11 | 5 | | | | | | | 15 |
| 1 | $3^2$ | | 4 | 5 | 6 | 7 | | | 10 | $11^1$ | 12 | 8 | | 2 | | | | | | 9 | | 13 | | | | | | 16 |
| 1 | 3 | | 4 | 5 | 6 | 7 | | | $10^1$ | | 12 | 8 | | 2 | | | | 11 | | 9 | | | | | | | | 17 |
| 1 | $3^3$ | | $4^2$ | 8 | 6 | 7 | | | 10 | | | 12 | | $2^1$ | 5 | | 14 | 11 | | 9 | | | 13 | | | | | 18 |
| 1 | | | 4 | 5 | 6 | 7 | | 8 | 10 | | | 12 | | 2 | 3 | | | $11^1$ | | 9 | | | | | | | | 19 |
| 1 | | | 4 | | 6 | 7 | | 8 | 10 | | | | | 2 | 3 | | 12 | $11^1$ | | 9 | | | | 5 | | | | 20 |
| 1 | | | | | 6 | 7 | | 8 | 10 | | | | | 2 | 3 | | | 11 | | 9 | | 4 | | 5 | | | | 21 |
| 1 | | 14 | | | $6^2$ | 7 | 13 | 8 | $10^1$ | 12 | | | | $2^3$ | 3 | | | 11 | | 9 | | 4 | | 5 | | | | 22 |
| 1 | | 12 | | 5 | 6 | $7^3$ | 14 | 8 | 10 | 13 | | | | 2 | 3 | | | | | 11 | | $4^1$ | | $9^2$ | | | | 23 |
| 1 | | | 4 | 5 | $6^2$ | 7 | 13 | 8 | 10 | 12 | | | | 2 | 3 | | | | | 11 | | | | $9^1$ | | | | 24 |
| 1 | | | 4 | 8 | 6 | $7^3$ | 13 | | 10 | 12 | | | | 2 | 5 | 14 | | | | $11^2$ | | 3 | | $9^1$ | | | | 25 |
| 1 | | 14 | 4 | 5 | 6 | 7 | | 8 | $10^1$ | | | | | $2^3$ | | 12 | 13 | | | $11^2$ | | 3 | | 9 | | | | 26 |
| | | | 4 | | 6 | | 8 | 13 | 12 | | 7 | | | 2 | | 5 | $10^1$ | | | | | 3 | $11^2$ | 9 | 1 | | | 27 |
| | | | 4 | 8 | 6 | 7 | | 11 | $10^3$ | | 13 | | | $2^1$ | 3 | $5^2$ | 14 | | | | | 12 | | 9 | 1 | | | 28 |
| | 12 | | 4 | | 6 | $7^2$ | $8^3$ | 11 | $10^1$ | | 14 | | | | 2 | | 13 | | | | | 3 | | 9 | 1 | 5 | | 29 |
| | | | 4 | 5 | 6 | 7 | | 8 | 10 | | | 12 | | 2 | | | | | | 11 | | 3 | | $9^1$ | 1 | | | 30 |
| | | | 4 | 5 | 13 | | 8 | 7 | 10 | | | 12 | | 3 | 2 | | | | | 11 | | | | $9^1$ | 1 | $6^2$ | | 31 |
| 1 | 5 | | 4 | | 6 | 7 | 8 | $11^1$ | 10 | | | 12 | | 3 | 2 | | | | | | | | | 9 | | | | 32 |
| | | | 13 | | 6 | 7 | 8 | $9^1$ | 10 | | 12 | 14 | | 3 | $2^2$ | 4 | | | | | | | 11 | | 1 | $5^3$ | | 33 |
| | 2 | | 4 | | 6 | 7 | | 11 | 10 | | 5 | 9 | | 3 | | | 12 | | | | | | | | 1 | | $8^1$ | 34 |
| | 2 | | | 5 | | 7 | 8 | | 10 | | $4^2$ | 13 | | 3 | | | 14 | | | 11 | | | | 12 | 1 | $6^1$ | $9^3$ | 35 |
| | | | 4 | 5 | 6 | 7 | | 8 | 10 | | | | | 3 | 2 | | | | | 11 | | | | $9^1$ | 1 | | 12 | 36 |
| | 2 | | | | | 7 | 8 | | | | 5 | 6 | | | | | 11 | | | | | | 10 | 9 | 1 | 4 | 3 | 37 |
| | | | 4 | $5^1$ | 6 | 7 | | 8 | 10 | | | | | 3 | 2 | | | | | 11 | | | 12 | 9 | 1 | | | 38 |

# CLYDE

## First Division

*Year Formed:* 1877. *Ground & Address:* Broadwood Stadium, Cumbernauld, G68 9NE. *Telephone:* 01236 451511.
*Ground Capacity:* all seated: 8200. *Size of Pitch:* 112yd × 76yd.
*Chairman:* W. B. Carmichael. *Secretary:* John D. Taylor.
*Manager:* Billy Reid. *Assistant Manager:* Stuart Balmer. *First Team Coach:* Denis McDaid. *Physio:* Ian McKinlay.
*Managers since 1975:* S. Anderson, C. Brown, J. Clark, A. Smith, G. Speirs, A. Maitland, A. Kernaghan.
*Club Nickname(s):* The Bully Wee. *Previous Grounds:* Barrowfield Park 1877-97, Shawfield Stadium 1897-1994.
*Record Attendance:* 52,000 v Rangers, Division I, 21 Nov 1908.
*Record Transfer Fee received:* £175,000 for Scott Howie to Norwich City (Aug 1993).
*Record Transfer Fee paid:* £14,000 for Harry Hood from Sunderland (1966).
*Record Victory:* 11-1 v Cowdenbeath, Division II, 6 Oct 1951.
*Record Defeat:* 0-11 v Dumbarton, Scottish Cup 4th rd, 22 Nov, 1879; v Rangers, Scottish Cup 4th rd, 13 Nov 1880.
*Most Capped Player:* Tommy Ring, 12, Scotland.
*Most League Appearances:* 428: Brian Ahern.
*Most League Goals in Season (Individual):* 32: Bill Boyd, 1932-33.

### CLYDE 2003–04 LEAGUE RECORD

| Match No. | Date | Venue | Opponents | Result | H/T Score | Lg. Pos. | Goalscorers | Attendance |
|---|---|---|---|---|---|---|---|---|
| 1 | Aug 9 | H | Ayr U | W 3-0 | 0-0 | — | Keogh 2 [56, 70], McLaughlin [60] | 1067 |
| 2 | 16 | A | Inverness CT | D 0-0 | 0-0 | 3 | | 1839 |
| 3 | 23 | H | Brechin C | W 2-1 | 1-1 | 1 | Harty [32], Hagen [90] | 1063 |
| 4 | 30 | A | St Mirren | L 1-2 | 0-0 | 4 | Gilhaney [52] | 3010 |
| 5 | Sept 13 | H | St Johnstone | W 2-0 | 1-0 | 2 | Harty [42], McConalogue [61] | 1468 |
| 6 | 20 | H | Falkirk | L 1-2 | 1-1 | 5 | McConalogue [29] | 2758 |
| 7 | 27 | A | Queen of the S | L 1-4 | 1-2 | 7 | McConalogue [42] | 1952 |
| 8 | Oct 4 | H | Ross Co | D 2-2 | 1-2 | 6 | McConalogue [29], McCunnie (og) [90] | 1056 |
| 9 | 18 | A | Raith R | W 1-0 | 1-0 | 6 | Gibson [8] | 1765 |
| 10 | Nov 1 | A | Ayr U | D 2-2 | 1-0 | 6 | Keogh 2 [4, 53] | 1653 |
| 11 | 5 | H | Inverness CT | W 1-0 | 0-0 | — | McConalogue [60] | 734 |
| 12 | 8 | A | St Johnstone | L 0-3 | 0-2 | 6 | | 2474 |
| 13 | 14 | H | St Mirren | W 2-0 | 1-0 | 5 | Keogh [41], Gilhaney [90] | 1811 |
| 14 | 22 | H | Queen of the S | W 3-1 | 0-1 | 5 | Smith 2 [53, 60], Harty [56] | 1271 |
| 15 | 29 | A | Falkirk | W 2-0 | 0-0 | 3 | McLaughlin [51], Smith [61] | 2898 |
| 16 | Dec 6 | H | Raith R | D 0-0 | 0-0 | 3 | | 1375 |
| 17 | 13 | A | Ross Co | W 1-0 | 1-0 | 2 | Harty [45] | 2721 |
| 18 | 20 | H | Ayr U | W 2-1 | 0-0 | 1 | McLaughlin [49], Harty [61] | 1049 |
| 19 | 27 | A | Brechin C | W 3-1 | 0-0 | 1 | Smith [54], Gibson [59], Harty [66] | 808 |
| 20 | Jan 3 | A | St Mirren | W 3-2 | 2-1 | 1 | Harty [14], Smith [25], McLaughlin [58] | 3355 |
| 21 | 24 | H | Falkirk | W 4-2 | 2-0 | 1 | Marshall [57], Harty [59], McLaughlin [77], Keogh [90] | 3137 |
| 22 | Feb 14 | H | Ross Co | W 1-0 | 1-0 | 2 | Harty (pen) [43] | 1139 |
| 23 | 21 | A | Raith R | W 3-0 | 1-0 | 1 | Harty 2 [25, 70], Marshall [60] | 1871 |
| 24 | Mar 6 | H | St Johnstone | L 2-3 | 1-1 | 1 | Smith [29], Keogh [78] | 1518 |
| 25 | 10 | A | Queen of the S | W 2-1 | 1-0 | — | Fotheringham [7], Harty [46] | 2169 |
| 26 | 13 | H | Brechin C | D 0-0 | 0-0 | 1 | | 1037 |
| 27 | 16 | A | Inverness CT | L 1-3 | 1-2 | — | Fotheringham [36] | 2645 |
| 28 | 20 | A | St Johnstone | W 3-1 | 2-0 | 1 | McConalogue [10], Smith [35], Harty [69] | 3512 |
| 29 | 27 | H | St Mirren | D 2-2 | 1-0 | 1 | Harty (pen) [10], Ross [84] | 1786 |
| 30 | Apr 3 | H | Queen of the S | W 2-0 | 0-0 | 1 | McConalogue [46], Ross [73] | 1207 |
| 31 | 10 | A | Falkirk | D 1-1 | 0-0 | 1 | Smith [73] | 2536 |
| 32 | 17 | H | Raith R | W 4-1 | 1-1 | 1 | Gibson 2 [21, 75], McCluskey [73], Keogh [84] | 1533 |
| 33 | 24 | A | Ross Co | D 0-0 | 0-0 | 1 | | 3220 |
| 34 | May 1 | A | Ayr U | D 1-1 | 1-0 | 1 | Keogh [15] | 1816 |
| 35 | 8 | H | Inverness CT | L 1-2 | 0-0 | 2 | Harty (pen) [72] | 4722 |
| 36 | 15 | A | Brechin C | W 5-2 | 3-0 | 2 | Keogh 3 [2, 20, 79], Smith 2 [25, 57] | 1268 |

**Final League Position: 2**

**Honours**
*League Champions:* Division II 1904-05, 1951-52, 1956-57, 1961-62, 1972-73. Second Division 1977-78, 1981-82, 1992-93, 1999-2000.
*Runners-up:* Division II 1903-04, 1905-06, 1925-26, 1963-64. Second Division 2003-04.
*Scottish Cup Winners:* 1939, 1955, 1958; *Runners-up:* 1910, 1912, 1949.

**Club colours:** Shirt: White with red and black trim. Shorts: Black. Stockings: white.

**Goalscorers:** *League* (64): Harty 15 (3 pens), Keogh 12, Smith 10, McConalogue 7, McLaughlin 5, Gibson 4, Fotheringham 2, Gilhaney 2, Marshall 2, Ross 2, Hagen 1, McCluskey 1, own goal 1
*Scottish Cup* (3): Smith 2, Ross 1
*CIS Cup* (4): Gilhaney 2, Keogh 1, Millen 1
*Challenge Cup* (2): Fraser 1, McConalogue 1

| Morrison A 16 + 1 | Mensing S 30 + 1 | McLaughlin M 29 + 2 | Kernaghan A 22 | Fraser J 16 + 2 | Ross J 35 | Hagen D 22 + 9 | Millen A 14 + 3 | Keogh P 10 + 15 | Harty I 29 + 5 | McConalogue S 17 + 7 | Gilhaney M 6 + 27 | Potter J 11 + 1 | Smith A 24 + 9 | Halliwell B 20 | Doyle P 1 + 6 | Gibson J 26 + 1 | McGroarty C 12 | Marshall C 24 + 2 | McCluskey S 17 | Fotheringham K 9 + 4 | McCann H 6 | Match No. |
|---|---|---|---|---|---|---|---|---|---|---|---|---|---|---|---|---|---|---|---|---|---|---|
| 1 | 2 | 3 | $4^{2}$ | 5 | 6 | 7 | 8 | $9^{3}$ | $10^{1}$ | 11 | 12 | 13 | 14 | | | | | | | | | 1 |
| | 2 | 3 | | 5 | 6 | 7 | 8 | | 10 | $11^{1}$ | 9 | 4 | 12 | 1 | | | | | | | | 2 |
| | 2 | $3^{1}$ | | $5^{3}$ | 6 | 7 | 8 | | 10 | $11^{2}$ | 13 | 4 | 9 | 1 | 12 | 14 | | | | | | 3 |
| | | | | 5 | 6 | 7 | 8 | | 9 | | 10 | 3 | 12 | 1 | 2 | $4^{1}$ | 11 | | | | | 4 |
| | 3 | 12 | 4 | 5 | 6 | | 8 | | $9^{2}$ | $11^{1}$ | 10 | 2 | 13 | 1 | | | 7 | | | | | 5 |
| | 3 | 14 | 4 | 5 | 6 | 12 | 8 | | $9^{1}$ | $11^{3}$ | $10^{2}$ | 2 | 13 | 1 | | | 7 | | | | | 6 |
| | 3 | 10 | $4^{1}$ | $5^{3}$ | 6 | 12 | 8 | | $9^{2}$ | 11 | 13 | 2 | 14 | 1 | | | 7 | | | | | 7 |
| | 3 | | 4 | 12 | 6 | | 8 | $9^{2}$ | 13 | 11 | $10^{3}$ | 2 | 14 | 1 | | $5^{1}$ | 7 | | | | | 8 |
| | | 3 | 4 | $5^{2}$ | 6 | 14 | 8 | 9 | 12 | $11^{1}$ | 13 | 2 | | 1 | | 10 | $7^{3}$ | | | | | 9 |
| 1 | | 3 | 4 | 5 | | 7 | 8 | 9 | 12 | $10^{2}$ | 13 | 2 | | | | | $11^{1}$ | 6 | | | | 10 |
| 1 | 12 | 3 | 4 | 5 | 6 | $7^{1}$ | 8 | $9^{2}$ | | $11^{3}$ | 14 | 2 | 13 | | | | 10 | | | | | 11 |
| 1 | 3 | | 4 | 5■ | 6 | $7^{1}$ | 8 | 9 | | $11^{2}$ | 12 | 2 | 13 | | | | $10^{3}$ | 14 | | | | 12 |
| 1 | 2 | 3 | 4 | | 6 | 11 | $8^{1}$ | $9^{2}$ | 13 | $10^{3}$ | 14 | | | | | 5 | 7 | 12 | | | | 13 |
| 1 | 2 | 3 | 4 | | 6 | 7 | 13 | | $11^{1}$ | | 12 | | 9 | | | $5^{2}$ | 10 | 8 | | | | 14 |
| 1 | 3 | $5^{1}$ | 4 | 2 | 6 | 7 | 12 | | $11^{3}$ | 14 | 13 | | $9^{2}$ | | | 10 | | 8 | | | | 15 |
| 1 | 3 | 5 | 4 | 2 | 6 | 7 | 13 | | $11^{3}$ | 14 | 12 | | $9^{1}$ | | | 10 | | $8^{2}$ | | | | 16 |
| 1 | 2 | 5 | 4 | | 6 | 7 | | | 11 | | 12 | | 9 | | | 10 | 3 | $8^{1}$ | | | | 17 |
| 1 | 2 | 3 | 4 | | 6 | 7 | 5 | | 11 | | 12 | | 9 | | | 10 | | $8^{1}$ | | | | 18 |
| 1 | 3 | 5 | 4■ | 2 | 6 | 7 | | 14 | $11^{2}$ | 12 | 13 | | $9^{3}$ | | | 10 | | $8^{1}$ | | | | 19 |
| 1 | $3^{2}$ | 5 | | 2 | 6 | 7 | | 14 | 11 | | 13 | | $9^{3}$ | | 12 | $10^{1}$ | | 8 | 4 | | | 20 |
| 1 | 3 | 5 | | $2^{1}$ | $6^{3}$ | 7 | | 12 | 11 | | 13 | | $9^{2}$ | | 14 | 10 | | 8 | 4 | | | 21 |
| 1 | 3 | 5 | 4 | | 6 | 7 | | 13 | $11^{1}$ | | 12 | | $9^{2}$ | | | 10 | | 8 | 2 | | | 22 |
| 1 | 3 | $5^{2}$ | 4 | 14 | 6 | 7 | | 12 | 11 | | | | $9^{1}$ | | 13 | 10 | | $8^{3}$ | 2 | | | 23 |
| 1 | 3 | 5 | 4 | | 6 | 7 | | 12 | 11 | | 13 | | $9^{2}$ | | | 10 | | $8^{3}$ | $2^{1}$ | 14 | | 24 |
| | 3 | 5 | 4 | | 6 | 12 | | 13 | $11^{3}$ | | 14 | | $9^{2}$ | 1 | | $10^{1}$ | | 8 | 2 | 7 | | 25 |
| | 3 | 5 | 4 | | 6 | 13 | | 10 | 11 | 14 | 12 | | $9^{1}$ | 1 | | | | 8 | $2^{2}$ | $7^{3}$ | | 26 |
| | 2 | 5 | | | 6 | $7^{1}$ | | 14 | $11^{2}$ | 13 | 12 | | 9 | 1 | | 10 | | 8 | $4^{3}$ | 3 | | 27 |
| 12 | 2 | 5 | | | 6 | 13 | | 14 | 11 | $7^{2}$ | | | $9^{3}$ | $1^{1}$ | | 10 | | 8 | 4 | 3 | | 28 |
| | 2 | 5 | | | 6 | 7 | | 13 | 11 | 14 | | | $9^{3}$ | 1 | 12 | $10^{2}$ | | 8 | 4 | $3^{1}$ | | 29 |
| | 2 | | | | 6 | | | 13 | 11 | $7^{2}$ | 12 | | $9^{1}$ | 1 | | 10 | | 8 | 4 | 5 | 3 | 30 |
| | 2 | | | | 6 | 14 | | 12 | $11^{1}$ | $7^{2}$ | 13 | | $9^{3}$ | 1 | | 10 | | 8 | 4 | 5 | 3 | 31 |
| | 2 | 5 | | | 6 | 13 | | 14 | $11^{3}$ | $7^{1}$ | 12 | | 9 | 1 | | 10 | | 8 | 4 | $3^{2}$ | | 32 |
| | 2 | 5 | | | 6 | 14 | | 13 | 11 | | $7^{2}$ | | $9^{3}$ | 1 | | 10 | | 8 | $4^{1}$ | 12 | 3 | 33 |
| | 2 | 5 | | | 6 | | | $7^{1}$ | 11 | 14 | 13 | | $9^{2}$ | 1 | | 10 | | 8 | 4 | 12 | $3^{3}$ | 34 |
| | | 5 | $4^{3}$ | | 6 | $7^{1}$ | | 13 | 11 | | 12 | | $9^{2}$ | 1 | | 10 | | 8 | 2 | 14 | 3 | 35 |
| | | 5 | | | $6^{3}$ | | | 11 | 14 | $7^{1}$ | 12 | | 9 | 1 | 13 | 10 | | 8 | 2 | $4^{2}$ | 3 | 36 |

# COWDENBEATH Third Division

*Year Formed:* 1881. *Ground & Address:* Central Park, Cowdenbeath KY4 9EY. *Telephone:* 01383 610166. *Fax:* 01383 512132.
*Ground Capacity:* total: 5268, seated: 1622. *Size of Pitch:* 107yd × 66yd.
*Chairman:* Gordon McDougall. *Secretary:* Tom Ogilvie. *General Manager:* Joe McNamara.
*Manager:* Keith Wright. *Assistant Manager:* Mickey Weir. *Physio:* Neil Bryson.
*Managers since 1975:* D. McLindon, F. Connor, P. Wilson, A. Rolland, H. Wilson, W. McCulloch, J. Clark, J. Craig, R. Campbell, J. Blackley, J. Brownlie, A. Harrow, J. Reilly, P Dolan, T. Steven, S. Conn, C. Levein, G. Kirk. *Previous Grounds:* North End Park, Cowdenbeath.
*Record Attendance:* 25,586 v Rangers, League Cup quarter-final, 21 Sept 1949.
*Record Transfer Fee received:* £30,000 for Nicky Henderson to Falkirk (March 1994).
*Record Victory:* 12-0 v Johnstone, Scottish Cup 1st rd, 21 Jan 1928.
*Record Defeat:* 1-11 v Clyde, Division II, 6 Oct 1951.
*Most Capped Player:* Jim Paterson, 3, Scotland.
*Most League and Cup Appearances:* 491 Ray Allan 1972-75, 1979-89.
*Most League Goals in Season (Individual):* 54, Rab Walls, Division II, 1938-39.
*Most Goals Overall (Individual):* 127, Willie Devlin, 1922-26, 1929-30.

## COWDENBEATH 2003–04 LEAGUE RECORD

| Match No. | Date | Venue | Opponents | Result | | H/T Score | Lg. Pos. | Goalscorers | Attendance |
|---|---|---|---|---|---|---|---|---|---|
| 1 | Aug 9 | A | Stirling A | D | 0-0 | 0-0 | — | | 576 |
| 2 | 16 | H | Albion R | L | 1-4 | 0-3 | 10 | Buchanan [86] | 362 |
| 3 | 23 | A | Montrose | W | 3-1 | 1-1 | 5 | Morris [18], Brown [52], Winter [84] | 338 |
| 4 | 30 | A | East Stirling | D | 1-1 | 0-0 | 6 | Morris [83] | 296 |
| 5 | Sept 13 | H | Queen's Park | L | 0-1 | 0-0 | 9 | | 339 |
| 6 | 20 | H | Gretna | L | 0-1 | 0-0 | 9 | | 235 |
| 7 | 27 | A | Elgin C | W | 4-0 | 2-0 | 7 | Buchanan [12], Shields 2 [67, 86], Ritchie [83] | 665 |
| 8 | Oct 4 | H | Stranraer | L | 0-1 | 0-1 | 7 | | 232 |
| 9 | 18 | A | Peterhead | W | 1-0 | 0-0 | 6 | Gilfillan [70] | 542 |
| 10 | 25 | A | Albion R | W | 2-1 | 0-0 | 6 | Fusco [46], Stewart [49] | 415 |
| 11 | Nov 1 | H | Stirling A | W | 2-0 | 0-0 | 4 | Gilfillan [53], Buchanan [88] | 468 |
| 12 | 8 | A | Queen's Park | D | 0-0 | 0-0 | 4 | | 554 |
| 13 | 14 | H | East Stirling | W | 2-1 | 0-0 | 4 | Shields 2 [67, 84] | 330 |
| 14 | Dec 2 | A | Gretna | L | 0-1 | 0-1 | — | | 401 |
| 15 | 6 | H | Elgin C | W | 3-2 | 2-1 | 5 | Shields [10], Brown [39], Mauchlen [89] | 242 |
| 16 | 13 | A | Stranraer | L | 0-2 | 0-1 | 5 | | 395 |
| 17 | 27 | H | Peterhead | W | 2-0 | 1-0 | 5 | McInally [8], Brown [90] | 308 |
| 18 | Jan 3 | H | Montrose | D | 3-3 | 2-2 | 5 | Shields [22], Brown 2 [36, 90] | 282 |
| 19 | 17 | A | Stirling A | D | 1-1 | 1-0 | 5 | Shields [57] | 790 |
| 20 | 24 | H | Gretna | L | 1-2 | 1-1 | 5 | Skinner [41] | 290 |
| 21 | Feb 7 | H | Queen's Park | W | 5-1 | 2-1 | 5 | Shields 2 [27, 37], Skinner [52], Buchanan 2 [81, 85] | 275 |
| 22 | 14 | A | East Stirling | W | 1-0 | 0-0 | 5 | Ritchie [62] | 308 |
| 23 | 21 | A | Peterhead | D | 0-0 | 0-0 | 5 | | 619 |
| 24 | Mar 6 | H | Albion R | D | 1-1 | 0-1 | 5 | Buchanan [64] | 248 |
| 25 | 9 | H | Stranraer | L | 1-2 | 1-0 | — | Winter [37] | 210 |
| 26 | 13 | A | Montrose | D | 1-1 | 1-1 | 5 | Shields [32] | 349 |
| 27 | 16 | A | Elgin C | D | 0-0 | 0-0 | — | | 312 |
| 28 | 20 | A | Queen's Park | W | 2-1 | 0-1 | 5 | Gilfillan [53], Ritchie [84] | 508 |
| 29 | 27 | H | East Stirling | W | 2-0 | 1-0 | 5 | Buchanan [3], Gilfillan [64] | 289 |
| 30 | Apr 3 | H | Elgin C | W | 2-0 | 1-0 | 5 | Buchanan [16], Ritchie [86] | 218 |
| 31 | 10 | A | Gretna | W | 1-0 | 0-0 | 5 | Gilfillan [70] | 429 |
| 32 | 17 | H | Peterhead | L | 0-3 | 0-0 | 5 | | 238 |
| 33 | 24 | A | Stranraer | L | 0-1 | 0-0 | 5 | | 457 |
| 34 | May 1 | H | Montrose | D | 0-0 | 0-0 | 5 | | 229 |
| 35 | 8 | A | Albion R | W | 4-2 | 2-1 | 5 | Shields 2 [16, 21], Gilfillan [84], Smith (og) [87] | 307 |
| 36 | 15 | H | Stirling A | L | 0-5 | 0-2 | 5 | | 692 |

**Final League Position: 5**

**Honours**
*League Champions:* Division II 1913-14, 1914-15, 1938-39; *Runners-up:* Division II 1921-22, 1923-24, 1969-70. Second Division 1991-92. *Runners-up:* Third Division 2000-01.
*Scottish Cup: Quarter-finals:* 1931.
*League Cup: Semi-finals:* 1959-60, 1970-71.

**Club colours:** Shirt: Royal blue with white cuffs and collar. Shorts: White. Stockings: White.

**Goalscorers:** *League* (46): Shields 12, Buchanan 8, Gilfillan 6, Brown 5, Ritchie 4, Morris 2, Skinner 2, Winter 2, Fusco 1, McInally 1, Mauchlen 1, Stewart 1, own goal 1
*Scottish Cup* (10): Gordon 2, Mauchlen 2, Buchanan 1, Fusco 1, Gilfillan 1, Shields 1, Winter 1, own goal 1
*CIS Cup* (3): McInally 2, Morris 1
*Challenge Cup* (1): Brown 1

| Carlin A 33 | Shand C 30 + 1 | McInally D 29 + 5 | Campbell A 18 + 3 | McKeown J 32 + 1 | Mowat D 33 + 3 | Gilfillan B 32 + 1 | Morris I 5 | Brown G 12 + 2 | Gordon K 7 + 8 | Boyle S 2 | Matheson R 3 + 6 | Fallon J 3 + 4 | Moffat A 2 + 2 | Winter C 21 | Buchanan L 8 + 17 | Mauchlen I 14 + 10 | Shields D 30 + 1 | Ritchie I 29 + 1 | Fusco G 22 + 5 | Slaven J 1 + 2 | Stewart S 3 + 1 | McGuinness S 11 + 5 | Skinner S 8 + 1 | Orhue P — + 1 | McCallum R 1 + 12 | Kelly J 4 + 6 | Bristow S — + 1 | Fleming A 3 + 1 | Bathgate S — + 1 | *Match No.* |
|---|---|---|---|---|---|---|---|---|---|---|---|---|---|---|---|---|---|---|---|---|---|---|---|---|---|---|---|---|---|---|
| 1 | 2 | 3 | 4 | $5^3$ | 6 | $7^1$ | 8 | 9■ | 10 | $11^2$ | 12 | 13 | 14 | | | | | | | | | | | | | | | | | 1 |
| 1 | 2 | 3 | 4 | 12 | 5 | 14 | 11 | | 10 | | $7^3$ | $9^2$ | $6^1$ | 8 | 13 | | | | | | | | | | | | | | | 2 |
| 1 | $2^1$ | 3 | 12 | 5 | 6 | 4 | 10 | $9^3$ | 13 | 11 | | | | 8 | 14 | $7^2$ | | | | | | | | | | | | | | 3 |
| 1 | 2 | 3 | | 5 | $6^1$ | 4 | 11 | 9 | 10 | | 13 | | $7^2$ | 8 | | | 12 | | | | | | | | | | | | | 4 |
| 1 | $2^2$ | 3 | | 5 | $6^3$ | 4 | 11■ | 9 | 12 | | 14 | | | 8 | | $7^1$ | 10 | 13 | | | | | | | | | | | | 5 |
| 1 | 2■ | 3 | | 5 | $6^3$ | 4 | | 9 | 10 | | $7^1$ | | 13 | 8 | 14 | 12 | $11^2$ | | | | | | | | | | | | | 6 |
| 1 | 13 | 3 | | 5 | $2^2$ | 4 | | 9 | | | 12 | | | 8 | $11^3$ | | 10 | 6 | $7^1$ | 14 | | | | | | | | | | 7 |
| 1 | 2 | $3^2$ | | 5 | 7 | 4 | | 9 | 12 | | $11^1$ | | | 8 | | | 10 | 6 | | 13 | | | | | | | | | | 8 |
| 1 | 2 | $3^3$ | | 5 | 13 | 4 | | | | | 14 | $9^1$ | | 8 | $11^2$ | | 10 | 6 | 12 | 7 | | | | | | | | | | 9 |
| 1 | 2 | 3 | | 5 | 14 | 4 | | | 13 | | | $9^2$ | | 8 | $11^1$ | | 10 | 6 | 12 | | $7^3$ | | | | | | | | | 10 |
| 1 | | 3 | 2 | 5 | 11 | $4^1$ | | $9^3$ | | | | 12 | | 8 | 14 | 13 | | 6 | 10 | | $7^2$ | | | | | | | | | 11 |
| 1 | 2 | 3 | | 5 | 11 | 4 | | $9^1$ | | | | 12 | | 8 | | 14 | $10^3$ | 6 | $7^2$ | | 13 | | | | | | | | | 12 |
| 1 | $2^3$ | 3 | | 5 | 11 | $4^1$ | | | | | | 14 | | 8 | 12 | 13 | 9 | 6 | 10 | | $7^2$ | | | | | | | | | 13 |
| 1 | | $3^1$ | 13 | 5 | 2 | 4 | | $9^2$ | 12 | | | | | 8 | | 7 | 10 | 6 | 11 | | | | | | | | | | | 14 |
| 1 | | 3 | | 5 | 12 | 4 | | $9^3$ | $7^2$ | | | | | 8 | 14 | 2 | 10 | 6 | 13 | | | $11^1$ | | | | | | | | 15 |
| 1 | 2 | $3^2$ | | 5 | 11 | $4^1$ | | $9^3$ | 14 | | | | | 8 | | 7 | 10 | 6■ | 12 | | | 13 | | | | | | | | 16 |
| 1 | 2 | 3 | 12 | | 5 | 4■ | | 13 | $10^1$ | | 14 | | | $8^3$ | | 7 | $9^2$ | 6 | 11 | | | | | | | | | | | 17 |
| 1 | 2 | $3^2$ | | 5 | 11 | | | 12 | $10^1$ | | | | | 8 | 14 | $7^3$ | 9 | 6 | 4 | | | 13 | | | | | | | | 18 |
| 1 | 2 | 3 | | 5 | 4 | | | | 12 | | | | | | | $7^2$ | 9 | 6 | 8 | | | 11 | $10^1$ | 13 | | | | | | 19 |
| 1 | 2 | $3^3$ | 4 | 5 | 7 | | | | 13 | | | | | | | 12 | 9 | 6 | $8^1$ | | | 11 | $10^2$ | | 14 | | | | | 20 |
| 1 | | $3^1$ | | 5 | 2 | 4 | | | | | | | | | 14 | 12 | 9 | 6 | 8 | | | $11^2$ | $10^3$ | | 13 | 7 | | | | 21 |
| 1 | 2 | $11^2$ | | 5 | 3 | 4 | | | | | | | | 8 | 12 | $7^3$ | 9 | 6 | | | | 13 | $10^1$ | | 14 | | | | | 22 |
| 1 | | 12 | 2 | 5 | 3 | 4 | | | | | | | | 8 | 13 | 7 | 9 | 6 | $11^1$ | | | | $10^2$ | | | | | | | 23 |
| 1 | 2 | $3^3$ | 6 | 5 | 11 | 4 | | | | | | | | 8 | 13 | $7^1$ | 9 | | 12 | | | | $10^2$ | | 14 | | | | | 24 |
| 1 | 2 | | 3 | 5 | 11 | $4^3$ | | | | | | | | 8 | $10^1$ | 13 | 9 | 6 | $7^2$ | | | | | | 14 | | 12 | | | 25 |
| | 2 | $11^2$ | 3 | 5■ | 8 | 4 | | | | | | | | | | 7 | 9 | 6 | | | | 13 | $10^1$ | | 12 | | | 1 | | 26 |
| 1 | 2 | $11^3$ | 3 | | 5 | 4 | | | | | | | | | 14 | 13 | 9 | 6 | 8 | | | | $10^1$ | | 12 | $7^2$ | | | | 27 |
| 1 | 2 | $11^2$ | 3 | 5 | 10 | $4^3$ | | | | | | | | | 14 | 7 | | 6 | 8 | | | 13 | | | 12 | $9^1$ | | | | 28 |
| | 2 | 13 | 3 | | 5 | 4 | | | | | | | | | $10^1$ | | 9 | 6 | 8 | | | $11^2$ | 12 | | $7^3$ | | | 1 | 14 | 29 |
| | $2^1$ | 14 | 3 | 5 | 7 | 4 | | | | | | | | | 10 | | $9^2$ | 6 | 8 | | | $11^3$ | | | 13 | 12 | | 1 | | 30 |
| 1 | 2 | 14 | 3 | 5 | 7 | $4^2$ | | | | | | | | | $10^1$ | 13 | 9 | 6 | 8 | | | $11^3$ | | | | 12 | | | | 31 |
| 1 | 2 | | 3 | 5 | 7 | $4^1$ | | | | | | | | | $10^2$ | 12 | 9 | 6 | 8 | | | $11^3$ | | | 13 | 14 | | | | 32 |
| 1 | $2^3$ | $10^1$ | 3 | 5 | 7 | $4^2$ | | | | | | | | | 14 | | 9 | 6 | 8 | | | 11 | | | 12 | 13 | | | | 33 |
| 1 | 2 | 13 | 3 | 5 | 10 | $4^1$ | | | | | | | | | 12 | | 9 | 6 | 8 | | | $11^3$ | | | 14 | $7^2$ | | | | 34 |
| 1 | 2 | $11^1$ | 3 | 5 | $7^2$ | 4 | | | | | | | | | 13 | | 9 | 6 | 8 | | | 10 | | | | 12 | | | | 35 |
| $1^1$ | 2 | $11^2$ | 3 | 5 | $10^3$ | 4 | | | | | | | | | 13 | 7 | 9 | 6 | 8 | | | | | | | 14 | | 12 | | 36 |

# DUMBARTON — Second Division

*Year Formed:* 1872. *Ground:* Strathclyde Homes Stadium, Dumbarton G82 1JJ. *Telephone:* 01389 762569/767864. *Fax:* 01389 762629
*Ground Capacity:* total: 2050. *Size of Pitch:* 110yd × 75yd.
*Chairman:* Ian MacFarlane. *Club Secretary:* David Prophet. *Company Secretary:* John Benn.
*Manager:* Brian Fairley. *Assistant Manager:* Allan McGonigal. *Physio:* Linda McIllwraith.
*Managers since 1975:* A. Wright, D. Wilson, S. Fallon, W. Lamont, D. Wilson, D. Whiteford, A. Totten, M. Clougherty, R. Auld, J. George, W. Lamont, M. MacLeod, J. Fallon, I. Wallace, T. Carson, D. Winnie. *Club Nickname(s):* The Sons.
*Previous Grounds:* Broadmeadow, Ropework Lane, Townend Ground, Boghead Park.
*Record Attendance:* 18,000 v Raith Rovers, Scottish Cup, 2 Mar 1957.
*Record Transfer Fee received:* £125,000 for Graeme Sharp to Everton (March 1982).
*Record Transfer Fee paid:* £50,000 for Charlie Gibson from Stirling Albion (1989).
*Record Victory:* 13-1 v Kirkintilloch Central. 1st rd, 1 Sept 1888.
*Record Defeat:* 1-11 v Albion Rovers, Division II; 30 Jan, 1926: v Ayr United, League Cup, 13 Aug 1952.
*Most Capped Player:* James McAulay, 9, Scotland.
*Most League Appearances:* 297: Andy Jardine, 1957-67.
*Most Goals in Season (Individual):* 38: Kenny Wilson, Division II, 1971-72. *(League and Cup):* 46 Hughie Gallacher, 1955-56.
*Most Goals Overall (Individual):* 169: Hughie Gallacher, 1954-62 (including C Division 1954-55). *(League and Cup):* 202 Hughie Gallacher, 1954-62

## DUMBARTON 2003–04 LEAGUE RECORD

| Match No. | Date | Venue | Opponents | Result | H/T Score | Lg. Pos. | Goalscorers | Attendance |
|---|---|---|---|---|---|---|---|---|
| 1 | Aug 9 | A | Alloa Ath | W 2-1 | 1-1 | — | Bradley [8], Flannery [48] | 446 |
| 2 | 16 | H | Arbroath | D 1-1 | 0-0 | 3 | Flannery [55] | 1070 |
| 3 | 23 | A | Morton | D 2-2 | 0-1 | 3 | Flannery [58], Boyle [59] | 3410 |
| 4 | 30 | A | Airdrie U | L 0-2 | 0-2 | 6 | | 1468 |
| 5 | Sept 13 | H | Berwick R | D 1-1 | 1-0 | 6 | Dillon [17] | 751 |
| 6 | 20 | A | Forfar Ath | L 1-3 | 0-1 | 8 | Collins [66] | 449 |
| 7 | 27 | H | Stenhousemuir | L 0-1 | 0-0 | 10 | | 730 |
| 8 | Oct 4 | A | East Fife | L 0-1 | 0-0 | 10 | | 518 |
| 9 | 18 | H | Hamilton A | L 0-3 | 0-1 | 10 | | 890 |
| 10 | 25 | A | Arbroath | L 1-2 | 0-1 | 10 | McEwan [57] | 506 |
| 11 | Nov 1 | H | Alloa Ath | W 1-0 | 1-0 | 10 | McEwan [38] | 742 |
| 12 | 8 | A | Berwick R | W 4-1 | 4-1 | 9 | Bonar [5], English [18], Dillon 2 [21, 23] | 395 |
| 13 | 16 | H | Airdrie U | W 2-0 | 0-0 | 9 | Dillon 2 [65, 69] | 1361 |
| 14 | Dec 6 | A | Stenhousemuir | D 1-1 | 1-1 | 7 | Bradley [31] | 447 |
| 15 | 13 | H | East Fife | W 3-1 | 1-0 | 7 | Dillon [18], Bonar [47], Russell [75] | 683 |
| 16 | Jan 3 | H | Morton | W 1-0 | 1-0 | 7 | Russell [6] | 2011 |
| 17 | 10 | H | Forfar Ath | W 2-1 | 1-1 | 5 | Dillon [43], Rodgers [52] | 781 |
| 18 | 17 | A | Alloa Ath | L 0-3 | 0-1 | 6 | | 423 |
| 19 | 24 | A | Forfar Ath | L 0-1 | 0-1 | 7 | | 540 |
| 20 | Feb 7 | H | Berwick R | W 4-1 | 2-1 | 7 | McEwan [1], Herd [6], Brittain [70], Russell [84] | 722 |
| 21 | 14 | A | Airdrie U | D 1-1 | 0-1 | 6 | Rodgers [87] | 1378 |
| 22 | 21 | H | Hamilton A | W 2-0 | 1-0 | 6 | Bonar [44], Russell [85] | 1015 |
| 23 | Mar 6 | H | Arbroath | W 1-0 | 1-0 | 6 | Rodgers [21] | 828 |
| 24 | 9 | A | Hamilton A | L 0-2 | 0-1 | — | | 949 |
| 25 | 13 | A | Morton | L 2-3 | 0-1 | 6 | McEwan [49], Bonar [84] | 3028 |
| 26 | 16 | A | East Fife | W 3-1 | 1-1 | — | Russell [9], Herd [85], Boyle [86] | 439 |
| 27 | 23 | H | Stenhousemuir | W 4-0 | 3-0 | — | Russell 2 [1, 12], Boyle [16], Bonar [75] | 552 |
| 28 | 27 | H | Airdrie U | L 1-2 | 1-1 | 4 | Herd [29] | 1543 |
| 29 | 30 | A | Berwick R | W 2-1 | 1-0 | — | Russell [23], Boyle [74] | 354 |
| 30 | Apr 3 | A | Stenhousemuir | W 2-1 | 1-0 | 3 | Ronald [2], Dillon [71] | 387 |
| 31 | 10 | H | Forfar Ath | D 1-1 | 0-1 | 4 | Herd [53] | 1007 |
| 32 | 17 | A | Hamilton A | L 1-2 | 1-1 | 4 | Collins [7] | 1343 |
| 33 | 24 | H | East Fife | W 1-0 | 1-0 | 4 | Russell [44] | 841 |
| 34 | May 1 | H | Morton | W 3-0 | 1-0 | 4 | Ronald [45], Herd [58], Russell [85] | 1882 |
| 35 | 8 | A | Arbroath | W 3-0 | 2-0 | 4 | Ronald [26], Herd 2 [33, 61] | 553 |
| 36 | 15 | H | Alloa Ath | W 3-1 | 0-1 | 3 | Herd [67], Skjelbred [72], Rodgers [84] | 1494 |

**Final League Position: 3**

**Honours**
*League Champions:* Division I 1890-91 (shared with Rangers), 1891-92. Division II 1910-11, 1971-72. Second Division 1991-92; *Runners-up:* First Division 1983-84. Division II 1907-08. Third Division 2001-02.
*Scottish Cup Winners:* 1883; *Runners-up:* 1881, 1882, 1887, 1891, 1897.

**Club colours:** Shirt: Yellow with black facing. Shorts: Yellow with black stripe. Stockings: Yellow.

**Goalscorers:** *League* (56): Russell 10, Dillon 8, Herd 8, Bonar 5, Boyle 4, McEwan 4, Rodgers 4, Flannery 3, Ronald 3, Bradley 2, Collins 2, Brittain 1, English 1, Skjelbred 1
*Scottish Cup* (0):
*CIS Cup* (3): Bonar 1, Flannery 1, Obidile 1
*Challenge Cup* (0):

| Grindlay S 34 | McKinstry J 35 | Brittain C 32 | Okoli J 2 | Duffy N 8 + 1 | Smith D 4 + 1 | Bonar S 35 | Bradley M 18 + 6 | Flannery P 9 + 2 | Russell I 26 + 7 | Dillon J 31 + 5 | Boyle C 17 + 11 | Herd G 11 + 9 | English I 8 + 1 | Donald B 24 + 2 | McEwan C 19 + 4 | Collins N 29 + 1 | Obidile E 8 + 2 | Wight J — + 1 | Dobbins I 12 + 5 | Robertson K 2 | Renicks S 7 + 11 | Mallan S 3 + 2 | Rodgers A 7 + 4 | Ronald P 13 + 1 | Laidler S — + 6 | Skjelbred B 2 + 6 | *Match No.* |
|---|---|---|---|---|---|---|---|---|---|---|---|---|---|---|---|---|---|---|---|---|---|---|---|---|---|---|---|
| 1 | 2 | 3 | 4 | 5 | 6 | 7 | 8 | $9^{3}$ | $10^{2}$ | $11^{1}$ | 12 | 13 | 14 | | | | | | | | | | | | | | 1 |
| 1 | 2 | 3 | 4 | 5 | 12 | $7^{3}$ | 13 | 9 | | $11^{2}$ | 6 | | 10 | $8^{1}$ | 14 | | | | | | | | | | | | 2 |
| 1 | 2 | 3 | | 5 | | $7^{1}$ | 13 | 9 | | 11 | 6 | | 10 | $8^{2}$ | 12 | 4 | | | | | | | | | | | 3 |
| 1 | 2 | 3 | | 5 | | 7 | 13 | 9 | | $11^{3}$ | $6^{2}$ | | $10^{1}$ | 8 | 14 | 4 | 12 | | | | | | | | | | 4 |
| $1^{1}$ | 2 | 3 | | 5 | | 7 | 8 | 10 | 14 | $11^{3}$ | $6^{2}$ | | | 13 | | 4 | 9 | 12 | | | | | | | | | 5 |
| 1 | 2 | 3 | | 5 | | 7 | 14 | 9 | $10^{1}$ | 12 | $6^{3}$ | | | $8^{2}$ | | 13 | 11 | | 4 | | | | | | | | 6 |
| | 2 | 3 | | $5^{3}$ | | $8^{1}$ | 12 | 9 | $10^{2}$ | 14 | 11 | | | | | 4■ | 7 | | 6 | 1 | 13 | | | | | | 7 |
| | 4 | 3 | | | 6 | 7 | 8 | 12 | 10 | $11^{2}$ | 13 | | | | | | $9^{1}$ | | 5 | 1 | 2 | | | | | | 8 |
| 1 | 2 | 3 | | | $6^{2}$ | | 13 | $9^{1}$ | 12 | 11 | 8 | | 10 | | 14 | 4 | 7 | | $5^{3}$ | | | | | | | | 9 |
| 1 | 4 | | | | $6^{2}$ | 7 | | 12 | $10^{1}$ | 11 | | | 9 | 8 | 2 | 5 | 13 | | | | 3 | | | | | | 10 |
| 1 | 4 | 3 | | | | 7 | 8 | | 12 | 11 | 6 | | $10^{1}$ | | 2 | 5 | 9 | | | | | | | | | | 11 |
| 1 | 3 | | | 5■ | | 7 | 8 | | 12 | 11 | $6^{2}$ | | $10^{1}$ | | 2 | 4 | 9 | | 13 | | | | | | | | 12 |
| 1 | | | | | | 7 | 8 | 4 | 12 | 11 | $6^{2}$ | | $10^{1}$ | 13 | 2 | 5 | 9 | | | | 3 | | | | | | 13 |
| 1 | 4 | 3 | | | | 7 | 8 | | 10 | $11^{1}$ | 12 | | | 6 | 2 | 5 | | | | | | 9 | | | | | 14 |
| 1 | 4 | 3 | | | | 7 | 8 | | 10 | 11 | | | | 6 | 2 | 5 | | | 12 | | $9^{1}$ | | | | | | 15 |
| 1 | 4 | 3 | | | | 7 | 8 | | $10^{2}$ | $11^{1}$ | $12^{3}$ | | | 6 | 2 | 5 | | | | | 14 | 13 | 9 | | | | 16 |
| 1 | 4 | 3 | | | | $7^{2}$ | 8 | | 10 | $11^{3}$ | 14 | | | 6 | 2 | 5 | | | | | 13 | 12 | $9^{1}$ | | | | 17 |
| 1 | 4 | 3 | | | | $7^{2}$ | 8 | | $10^{1}$ | 11 | | 13 | | 6 | 2 | 5 | | | | | 12 | 9 | | | | | 18 |
| 1 | 4 | 3 | | 13 | | 7 | 8 | | 10 | $11^{3}$ | | 12 | | 6 | $2^{2}$ | 5 | | | | | 14 | $9^{1}$ | | | | | 19 |
| 1 | 4 | 3 | | | | 7 | $8^{2}$ | | 12 | 11 | 13 | $10^{1}$ | | 6 | 2 | 5 | | | | | | | | 9 | | | 20 |
| 1 | 4 | 3 | | | | $7^{3}$ | 8 | | 13 | $11^{1}$ | 12 | $9^{2}$ | | 6 | 2 | 5 | | | | | | | 14 | 10 | | | 21 |
| 1 | 4 | 3 | | | | 7 | 8 | | 11 | 12 | $6^{1}$ | 13 | | | 2 | 5 | | | | | | | $9^{2}$ | 10 | | | 22 |
| 1 | 4 | 3 | | | | 7 | 8 | | $10^{1}$ | 11 | | 12 | | | 2 | 5 | | | | | | | 9 | 6 | | | 23 |
| 1 | 4 | $3^{1}$ | | | | $7^{1}$ | 8 | | 10 | $11^{2}$ | | 12 | | 6 | 2 | 5 | | | 13 | | 14 | | 9 | | | | 24 |
| 1 | 4 | 3 | | | | 7 | $8^{1}$ | | 10 | $11^{2}$ | | 12 | | 6 | 2 | 5 | | | | | 13 | | $9^{3}$ | 14 | | | 25 |
| 1 | 4 | 3 | | | | 7 | | | 8 | 11 | 12 | 13 | | $6^{1}$ | $2^{3}$ | 5 | | | | | | | $10^{2}$ | 9 | 14 | | 26 |
| 1 | 4 | 3 | | | | 7 | | | 10 | 11 | 6 | $9^{2}$ | | | $2^{1}$ | $5^{3}$ | | | 14 | | 12 | | 13 | 8 | | | 27 |
| 1 | 4 | 3 | | | | 7 | | | 10 | $11^{2}$ | $6^{3}$ | 9 | | | $2^{1}$ | 5 | | | 12 | | | | | 8 | 13 | 14 | 28 |
| 1 | 2 | 3 | | | | $7^{1}$ | | | 10 | $11^{2}$ | 6 | 9 | | 8 | | 5 | | | 4 | | 13 | | | | | 12 | 29 |
| 1 | 2 | 3 | | | | 7 | | | 10 | 13 | $11^{2}$ | $9^{1}$ | | 6 | | 5 | | | 4 | | | | 12 | 8 | | | 30 |
| 1 | 2 | 3 | | | | $7^{1}$ | | | 10 | 11 | $6^{2}$ | $9^{3}$ | | 8 | | 5 | | | 4 | | 14 | | | | 13 | 12 | 31 |
| 1 | 2 | 3 | | | | 7 | | | 10 | 14 | $11^{3}$ | $9^{2}$ | | $6^{1}$ | | 5 | | | 4 | | 12 | | | 8 | | 13 | 32 |
| 1 | 2 | 3 | | | | 7 | | | $10^{2}$ | $11^{1}$ | 12 | 13 | | 6 | | 5 | | | 4 | | | | | 8 | 14 | $9^{3}$ | 33 |
| 1 | 4 | 3 | | | | $7^{3}$ | | | 10 | $11^{2}$ | 13 | $9^{1}$ | | 6 | | | | | 5 | | 2 | | | 8 | 14 | 12 | 34 |
| 1 | 4 | 3 | | | | 7 | | | 10 | 11 | 12 | $9^{2}$ | | $6^{3}$ | | | | | 5 | | 2 | | | $8^{1}$ | 14 | 13 | 35 |
| 1 | 4 | | | | | 2 | | | 10 | 11 | | $9^{1}$ | | 6 | | | | | 5 | | 3 | | 12 | 8 | | 7 | 36 |

# DUNDEE Premier League

*Year Formed:* 1893. *Ground & Address:* Dens Park Stadium, Sandeman St, Dundee DD3 7JY. *Telephone:* 01382 889966. *Fax:* 01382 832284.
*Ground Capacity:* all seated: 11,760. *Size of Pitch:* 101m × 66m.
*Chairman:* Jim Marr. *Chief Executive:* Peter Marr.
*Manager:* Jim Duffy. *Goalkeeping Coach:* Paul Mathers. *Under 21 Coach:* Ray Farningham. *Under 18 Coach:* Steve Campbell. *Youth Development Coach:* Kenny Cameron. *Community Coach:* Kevin Lee. *Physio:* Jim Law.
*Managers since 1975:* David White, Tommy Gemmell, Donald Mackay, Archie Knox, Jocky Scott, Dave Smith, Gordon Wallace, Iain Munro, Simon Stainrod, Jim Duffy, John McCormack, John Scott, Ivano Bonetti.
*Club Nickname(s):* The Dark Blues or The Dee. *Previous Grounds:* Carolina Port 1893-98.
*Record Attendance:* 43,024 v Rangers, Scottish Cup, 1953.
*Record Transfer Fee received:* £500,000 for Tommy Coyne to Celtic (March 1989).
*Record Transfer Fee paid:* £200,000 for Jim Leighton (Feb 1992).
*Record Victory:* 10-0 Division II v Alloa, 9 Mar 1947 and v Dunfermline Ath, 22 Mar 1947.
*Record Defeat:* 0-11 v Celtic, Division I, 26 Oct 1895.
*Most Capped Player:* Alex Hamilton, 24, Scotland. *Most League Appearances:* 341: Doug Cowie, 1945-61.
*Most League Goals in Season (Individual):* 52: Alan Gilzean, 1963-64.
*Most Goals Overall (Individual):* 113: Alan Gilzean.

## DUNDEE 2003–04 LEAGUE RECORD

| Match No. | Date | Venue | Opponents | Result | | H/T Score | Lg. Pos. | Goalscorers | Attendance |
|---|---|---|---|---|---|---|---|---|---|
| 1 | Aug 9 | A | Motherwell | W | 3-0 | 2-0 | — | Rae $^{23}$, Wilkie $^{43}$, Smith $^{84}$ | 6812 |
| 2 | 17 | H | Dunfermline Ath | L | 0-2 | 0-1 | 6 | | 7750 |
| 3 | 23 | H | Livingston | W | 2-1 | 1-1 | 5 | Novo 2 (1 pen) $^{16, 83 (p)}$ | 5815 |
| 4 | 31 | A | Kilmarnock | D | 1-1 | 0-0 | 5 | Novo $^{54}$ | 5935 |
| 5 | Sept 13 | H | Celtic | L | 0-1 | 0-1 | 4 | | 10,647 |
| 6 | 20 | H | Aberdeen | W | 2-0 | 1-0 | 4 | Cowan $^{27}$, Novo $^{81}$ | 7887 |
| 7 | 27 | A | Rangers | L | 1-3 | 0-0 | 5 | Novo $^{77}$ | 49,548 |
| 8 | Oct 4 | A | Hearts | D | 2-2 | 1-0 | 5 | Novo $^{16}$, Rae $^{63}$ | 11,348 |
| 9 | 18 | H | Partick Th | W | 1-0 | 0-0 | 3 | Novo $^{52}$ | 6497 |
| 10 | 26 | A | Dundee U | D | 1-1 | 1-0 | 4 | Novo $^{19}$ | 12,767 |
| 11 | Nov 1 | H | Hibernian | D | 1-1 | 1-0 | 4 | Novo $^{32}$ | 7392 |
| 12 | 8 | H | Motherwell | L | 0-1 | 0-0 | 5 | | 6374 |
| 13 | 22 | A | Dunfermline Ath | L | 0-2 | 0-0 | 7 | | 5458 |
| 14 | 29 | A | Livingston | D | 1-1 | 0-0 | 7 | Fotheringham $^{83}$ | 3878 |
| 15 | Dec 6 | H | Kilmarnock | L | 1-2 | 1-2 | 8 | Novo (pen) $^{31}$ | 6954 |
| 16 | 13 | A | Celtic | L | 2-3 | 1-1 | 9 | Fotheringham $^{19}$, Mair $^{89}$ | 57,539 |
| 17 | 20 | A | Aberdeen | D | 2-2 | 1-1 | 9 | Hutchinson $^{44}$, Novo $^{51}$ | 10,354 |
| 18 | 28 | H | Rangers | L | 0-2 | 0-2 | 10 | | 10,948 |
| 19 | Jan 6 | H | Hearts | L | 1-2 | 0-0 | — | McLean $^{79}$ | 6387 |
| 20 | 17 | A | Partick Th | W | 2-1 | 0-1 | 9 | Novo $^{85}$, Smith $^{87}$ | 4690 |
| 21 | 25 | H | Dundee U | W | 2-1 | 0-1 | 7 | Novo $^{47}$, Lovell $^{70}$ | 10,747 |
| 22 | 31 | A | Hibernian | D | 1-1 | 1-0 | 8 | Fotheringham $^{43}$ | 8023 |
| 23 | Feb 11 | A | Motherwell | L | 3-5 | 2-2 | — | Novo 2 $^{10, 57}$, Hernandez $^{27}$ | 4247 |
| 24 | 14 | H | Dunfermline Ath | L | 0-1 | 0-1 | 9 | | 5643 |
| 25 | 21 | H | Livingston | W | 1-0 | 0-0 | 7 | Milne $^{58}$ | 6108 |
| 26 | 28 | A | Kilmarnock | L | 2-4 | 1-2 | 8 | Novo $^{5}$, Milne $^{62}$ | 5454 |
| 27 | Mar 13 | H | Aberdeen | D | 1-1 | 1-0 | 7 | Fotheringham $^{8}$ | 6839 |
| 28 | 17 | H | Celtic | L | 1-2 | 0-1 | — | Kneissl $^{90}$ | 8593 |
| 29 | 20 | A | Rangers | L | 0-4 | 0-1 | 8 | | 49,364 |
| 30 | 27 | A | Hearts | L | 1-3 | 1-0 | 10 | Milne $^{7}$ | 10,491 |
| 31 | Apr 3 | H | Partick Th | W | 2-1 | 1-1 | 9 | Milne $^{2}$, Novo $^{89}$ | 5084 |
| 32 | 11 | A | Dundee U | D | 2-2 | 2-0 | 9 | Lovell $^{17}$, Milne $^{38}$ | 9571 |
| 33 | 17 | H | Hibernian | D | 2-2 | 1-1 | 9 | Lovell $^{37}$, Milne $^{88}$ | 5508 |
| 34 | 24 | A | Partick Th | W | 1-0 | 0-0 | 9 | Lovell $^{73}$ | 2727 |
| 35 | May 1 | A | Hibernian | L | 0-1 | 0-1 | 10 | | 6180 |
| 36 | 8 | H | Kilmarnock | W | 2-0 | 1-0 | 8 | Milne $^{6}$, Novo $^{79}$ | 4942 |
| 37 | 12 | H | Livingston | W | 2-0 | 1-0 | — | Novo 2 $^{4, 89}$ | 4954 |
| 38 | 15 | A | Aberdeen | W | 2-1 | 0-1 | 7 | Milne $^{72}$, Lovell $^{90}$ | 7878 |

**Final League Position: 7**

**Honours**
*League Champions:* Division I 1961-62. First Division 1978-79, 1991-92, 1997-98. Division II 1946-47; *Runners-up:* Division I 1902-03, 1906-07, 1908-09, 1948-49, 1980-81.
*Scottish Cup Winners:* 1910; *Runners-up:* 1925, 1952, 1964, 2003.
*League Cup Winners:* 1951-52, 1952-53, 1973-74; *Runners-up:* 1967-68, 1980-81. *(Coca-Cola Cup):* 1995-96.
*B&Q (Centenary) Cup Winners:* 1990-91; *Runners-up:* 1994-95.

**European:** *European Cup:* 8 matches (1962-63 semi-finals). *Cup Winners' Cup:* 2 matches: (1964-65).
*UEFA Cup:* 22 matches: (*Fairs Cup:* 1967-68 semi-finals. *UEFA Cup:* 1971-72, 1973-74, 1974-75, 2003-04).

**Club colours:** Shirt: Navy with white and red shoulder and sleeve flashes. Shorts: White with navy/red piping. Stockings: Navy, top with two white hoops.

**Goalscorers:** *League* (48): Novo 20 (2 pens), Milne 8, Lovell 5, Fotheringham 4, Rae 2, Smith 2, Cowan 1, Hernandez 1, Hutchinson 1, Kneissl 1, McLean 1, Mair 1, Willkie 1
*Scottish Cup* (2): Novo 1, Robb 1
*CIS Cup* (6): Ravanelli 3, Linn 1, Novo 1, Wilkie 1

| Speroni J 37 | Mackay D 34 + 1 | Hernandez J 27 + 2 | Mair L 36 | Wilkie L 21 | Smith B 27 + 2 | Nemsadze G 9 | Rae G 11 + 2 | Brady G 35 + 2 | Lovell S 15 + 6 | Novo I 34 + 1 | Carranza L — + 2 | Jablonski N 3 + 9 | Caballero F 9 + 4 | Sancho B 20 + 1 | Sara J 3 + 7 | Cowan T 4 + 1 | Hutchinson T 8 + 4 | Fotheringham M 19 + 5 | Ravanelli F 5 | Linn R 3 + 9 | Burley C 1 + 1 | Macdonald C 6 | Cameron D 6 + 5 | McCafferty J — + 1 | McLean D 3 + 1 | Robb S 9 + 6 | Milne S 15 + 5 | Barrett N 10 + 2 | Kneissl S 5 + 6 | Hegarty C 1 + 3 | Clark N — + 2 | McNally S 1 + 1 | Youngson A — + 1 | Soutar D 1 | *Match No.* |
|---|---|---|---|---|---|---|---|---|---|---|---|---|---|---|---|---|---|---|---|---|---|---|---|---|---|---|---|---|---|---|---|---|---|---|---|
| 1 | 2 | 3 | 4 | 5 | 6 | 7¹ | 8² | 9 | 10³ | 11 | 12 | 13 | 14 | | | | | | | | | | | | | | | | | | | | | | 1 |
| 1 | | 3 | 4 | 5 | 6 | 7 | 8 | 9 | 10 | 11² | 13 | | 12 | 2¹ | | | | | | | | | | | | | | | | | | | | | 2 |
| 1 | 2 | 3 | 4 | 5 | 6 | 7 | 13 | 8 | 10¹ | 11 | | | 9² | | 12 | | | | | | | | | | | | | | | | | | | | 3 |
| 1 | | | 3¹ | 5 | 6 | 7 | 8 | 9 | 14 | 11³ | | | 10² | 4 | 13 | 2 | 12 | | | | | | | | | | | | | | | | | | 4 |
| 1 | 2¹ | 3 | 4 | 5 | 6³ | 7 | 8 | 14 | 10² | 11 | | | 9 | | 12 | | | 13 | | | | | | | | | | | | | | | | | 5 |
| 1 | 2 | | 4 | 5 | 12 | 7 | 8 | 6¹ | 13 | 11 | | | 9 | | 10² | 3 | | | | | | | | | | | | | | | | | | | 6 |
| 1 | 2 | | 4 | 5 | 6 | 7 | 8 | | | 11² | | | 10 | 9¹ | 12 | 3 | 13 | | | | | | | | | | | | | | | | | | 7 |
| 1 | 2 | 12 | 4 | 5 | 6 | 7 | 8 | 9² | | 11 | | | 10 | | | 3¹ | 13 | | | | | | | | | | | | | | | | | | 8 |
| 1 | 2 | 3 | | 4 | 6 | 7 | 8³ | 5 | | 11 | | | 10² | | 12 | 14 | | | 9¹ | 13 | | | | | | | | | | | | | | | 9 |
| 1 | 2 | 3¹ | 4 | 5 | 6 | | 8² | 7 | | 11 | | | 10 | | 14 | | | 13 | 9³ | | 12 | | | | | | | | | | | | | | 10 |
| 1 | 2 | | 4 | 5 | 6 | | | 7 | | 11 | | | 13 | | 12 | | | | 9² | 10¹ | 8■ | 3 | | | | | | | | | | | | | 11 |
| 1 | 2 | | 4 | 5 | 6 | | | 3 | | 11 | | | 12 | | 10 | | | | 9 | 8¹ | | | 7 | | | | | | | | | | | | 12 |
| 1 | 2 | 3¹ | 4 | 5 | 6 | | | 7² | | 11 | | | 10 | | 8 | | | | 9 | 13 | | | 12 | | | | | | | | | | | | 13 |
| 1 | 2 | 3 | 4 | 5 | 6 | | 13 | 8 | 10² | 11 | | | | | | | 7¹ | 9 | | 12 | | | | | | | | | | | | | | | 14 |
| 1 | 14 | 3 | 4 | 5 | 6 | | 8¹ | 7 | | 11 | | | | | | | 2 | 9² | | | | | 13 | 12 | 10³ | | | | | | | | | | 15 |
| 1 | 2 | 3 | 4 | 5 | 6 | | 8² | 10 | | 11 | | | | 7¹ | | | 13 | 9 | | 12 | | | | | | | | | | | | | | | 16 |
| 1 | 2 | 3 | 4¹ | 5 | 6 | | | 10 | | 11 | | | | 7 | | | 8 | 9 | | 12 | | | | | | | | | | | | | | | 17 |
| 1 | 2 | 3 | 4 | 5 | 6 | | | 8 | | 11 | | | | 7¹ | | | | 9 | | 10 | | | | | 12 | | | | | | | | | | 18 |
| 1 | 2 | 3 | | 5 | 6 | | | 8 | | 11 | | 7¹ | | 4 | | | | 9 | | | | | | | 10² | 12 | 13 | | | | | | | | 19 |
| 1 | 2 | 3 | 4 | 5 | 6 | | | 8 | | 11 | | 13 | | | | | | 9 | | | | | | | 10¹ | 7² | 12 | | | | | | | | 20 |
| 1 | 2 | 3 | 4 | 5¹ | 6 | | | 8 | 13 | 11 | | | | 12 | | | | 9 | | | | | | | | 14 | 10³ | 7² | | | | | | | 21 |
| 1 | 2 | 3 | 4 | | 6 | | | 8 | 13 | 11³ | | 14 | | 5 | | | | 9 | | | | | | | | 12 | 10² | 7¹ | | | | | | | 22 |
| 1 | 2 | 3 | 4 | | 13 | | | 8 | 12 | 11 | | | | | | | 5 | 9 | | | | | | | | 14 | 10³ | 7² | 6¹ | | | | | | 23 |
| 1 | 2 | 3 | 4 | | 6 | | | 8 | 10 | 11 | | | | | | | 5³ | 12 | | | | | | | | 14 | 13 | 7¹ | 9² | | | | | | 24 |
| 1 | 2 | | 4 | | 6 | | | 8 | 10¹ | | | 14 | | | | | 3 | 9 | | | | 5 | | | | 7² | 11³ | 13 | 12 | | | | | | 25 |
| 1 | 2 | 13 | 4 | | 6¹ | | | 8³ | 9 | 11 | | 12 | | | | | 3 | 7 | | | | 5² | | | | | 10 | | 14 | | | | | | 26 |
| 1 | 2 | 3² | 4 | | | | | 8¹ | | 11 | | | | 5 | | | | 7 | | 12 | | | 13 | | | 9 | 10 | 6 | | | | | | | 27 |
| 1 | 2 | 3 | 4 | | | | | 8 | | 11 | | | | 5 | | | | 7 | | 12 | | | 14 | | | 9² | 10¹ | 6³ | 13 | | | | | | 28 |
| 1 | 2 | 3 | 4 | | | | | 13 | 12 | 11 | | | | 5 | | | 6 | 7 | | | | | | | | 9¹ | 14 | 8² | 10³ | | | | | | 29 |
| 1 | 2 | | 4 | | | | | 8 | 9¹ | 11² | | 13 | | 3 | | | | 7³ | | | | | 5 | | | 6 | 10 | | 12 | 14 | | | | | 30 |
| 1 | 2 | | 4 | | | | | 8 | 9² | 11 | | | | 3 | | | | 7 | | | | | 5 | | | 12 | 10¹ | 6 | 13 | | | | | | 31 |
| 1 | 2 | 3 | 4 | | | | | 8 | 11¹ | | | | | 5 | | | | 7 | | | | | | | | 9 | 10 | 6 | | | 12 | | | | 32 |
| 1 | 2 | 3 | 4 | | | | | 8 | 11 | 12 | | | | 5 | | | | 7 | | | | | | | | 6² | 10 | 13 | 9¹ | | | | | | 33 |
| 1 | 2 | 3 | 4 | | | | | 8 | 9 | 11 | | 13 | | 5 | | | | 12 | | | | | 7¹ | | | | 10³ | 6² | | | | 14 | | | 34 |
| 1 | 2 | 3 | 4 | | | | | 8 | | 11 | | 9² | | 5 | | | | | | | | 6³ | 7¹ | | | | 10 | | | 13 | 12 | | 14 | | 35 |
| 1 | 2 | 3¹ | 4 | | 6³ | | | 8 | | 11 | | 12 | | 5 | | | | 13 | | 14 | | 7 | 9² | | | | 10 | | | | | | | | 36 |
| 1 | | | 4 | | 6 | | | 8 | 9³ | 11 | | 7² | | 5 | | | | | | 12 | | 2 | | | | | 14 | | 10¹ | 13 | | 3 | | | 37 |
| | 2 | 3 | 4 | | 6 | | | 8³ | 11 | | | 14 | | 5 | | | | | | | | | 13 | | | 9¹ | 10 | | 12 | 7² | | | | 1 | 38 |

# DUNDEE UNITED Premier League

*Year Formed:* 1909 (1923). *Ground & Address:* Tannadice Park, Tannadice St, Dundee DD3 7JW. *Telephone:* 01382 833166. *Fax:* 01382 889398. *Ground Capacity:* total: 14,223 all seated: stands: east 2868, west 2096, south 2201, Fair Play 1601, George Fox 5151, executive boxes 292.
*Size of Pitch:* 110yd × 72yd.
*Chairman:* Eddie Thomson. *Secretary:* Spence Anderson. *General Manager:* Bill Campbell. *Community Development Officer:* Gordon Grady.
*Manager:* Ian McCall. *Assistant Team Manager:* Gordon Chisholm. *Coaches:* Tony Docherty, Graeme Liveston. *Physio:* Jeff Clarke. *Stadium Manager:* Ron West.
*Managers since 1975:* J. McLean, I. Golac, W. Kirkwood, T. McLean, P. Sturrock, A. Smith. *Club Nickname(s):* The Terrors.
*Previous Grounds:* None.
*Record Attendance:* 28,000 v Barcelona, Fairs Cup, 16 Nov 1966.
*Record Transfer Fee received:* £4,000,000 for Duncan Ferguson from Rangers (July 1993).
*Record Transfer Fee paid:* £750,000 for Steven Pressley from Coventry C (July 1995).
*Record Victory:* 14-0 v Nithsdale Wanderers, Scottish Cup 1st rd, 17 Jan 1931.
*Record Defeat:* 1-12 v Motherwell, Division II, 23 Jan 1954.
*Most Capped Player:* Maurice Malpas, 55, Scotland.
*Most League Appearances:* 612, Dave Narey, 1973-94.
*Most Appearances in European Matches:* 76, Dave Narey (record for Scottish player).
*Most League Goals in Season (Individual):* 41: John Coyle, Division II, 1955-56.
*Most Goals Overall (Individual):* 158: Peter McKay.

## DUNDEE UNITED 2003–04 LEAGUE RECORD

| Match No. | Date | Venue | Opponents | Result | | H/T Score | Lg. Pos. | Goalscorers | Attendance |
|---|---|---|---|---|---|---|---|---|---|
| 1 | Aug 9 | H | Hibernian | L | 1-2 | 0-0 | — | Samuel 46 | 9809 |
| 2 | 16 | A | Celtic | L | 0-5 | 0-3 | 12 | | 57004 |
| 3 | 23 | A | Hearts | L | 0-3 | 0-3 | 12 | | 11,395 |
| 4 | 31 | H | Rangers | L | 1-3 | 0-1 | 12 | Dodds 82 | 11,111 |
| 5 | Sept 13 | A | Livingston | D | 0-0 | 0-0 | 12 | | 4226 |
| 6 | 20 | A | Partick Th | W | 2-0 | 1-0 | 11 | Miller 2 40, 63 | 4711 |
| 7 | 27 | H | Kilmarnock | D | 1-1 | 0-0 | 10 | McLaren 73 | 6529 |
| 8 | Oct 4 | H | Motherwell | L | 0-2 | 0-1 | 11 | | 6194 |
| 9 | 18 | A | Aberdeen | W | 1-0 | 1-0 | 10 | McLaren 11 | 11,234 |
| 10 | 26 | H | Dundee | D | 1-1 | 0-1 | 10 | McIntyre 56 | 12,767 |
| 11 | Nov 1 | A | Dunfermline Ath | L | 0-2 | 0-0 | 10 | | 5078 |
| 12 | 8 | A | Hibernian | D | 2-2 | 1-1 | 10 | McLaren 27, Robson 83 | 8756 |
| 13 | 22 | H | Celtic | L | 1-5 | 0-1 | 10 | McIntyre 75 | 10,802 |
| 14 | 30 | H | Hearts | W | 2-1 | 2-0 | 10 | Archibald 11, McInnes 43 | 6343 |
| 15 | Dec 6 | A | Rangers | L | 1-2 | 0-2 | 10 | Dodds 55 | 49,307 |
| 16 | 13 | H | Livingston | W | 2-0 | 1-0 | 10 | Dodds 2 41, 81 | 5421 |
| 17 | 23 | H | Partick Th | D | 0-0 | 0-0 | — | | 6440 |
| 18 | 27 | A | Kilmarnock | W | 2-0 | 1-0 | 7 | Dodds 19, McIntyre (pen) 82 | 6062 |
| 19 | Jan 3 | A | Motherwell | L | 1-3 | 1-0 | 8 | Wilson 15 | 5549 |
| 20 | 17 | H | Aberdeen | W | 3-2 | 1-0 | 7 | Robson 20, Miller 85, Dodds (pen) 90 | 8888 |
| 21 | 25 | A | Dundee | L | 1-2 | 1-0 | 9 | Dodds 43 | 10,747 |
| 22 | 31 | H | Dunfermline Ath | W | 1-0 | 0-0 | 7 | McIntyre 57 | 5564 |
| 23 | Feb 10 | H | Hibernian | D | 0-0 | 0-0 | — | | 6389 |
| 24 | 14 | A | Celtic | L | 1-2 | 0-0 | 8 | Archibald 60 | 58,671 |
| 25 | 21 | A | Hearts | L | 1-3 | 0-1 | 9 | McIntyre 52 | 10,265 |
| 26 | 29 | H | Rangers | W | 2-0 | 2-0 | 6 | Kerr 30, McIntyre 33 | 10,497 |
| 27 | Mar 13 | A | Partick Th | D | 1-1 | 0-0 | 6 | Robson 68 | 3510 |
| 28 | 20 | H | Kilmarnock | W | 4-1 | 4-0 | 6 | McIntyre 3 10, 26, 33, Miller 21 | 5757 |
| 29 | 24 | A | Livingston | W | 3-2 | 1-1 | — | Scotland 13, Samuel 79, McIntyre 83 | 3082 |
| 30 | 27 | H | Motherwell | W | 1-0 | 0-0 | 5 | Scotland 65 | 7585 |
| 31 | Apr 3 | A | Aberdeen | L | 0-3 | 0-3 | 5 | | 8449 |
| 32 | 11 | H | Dundee | D | 2-2 | 0-2 | 5 | Dodds 2 55, 84 | 9571 |
| 33 | 17 | A | Dunfermline Ath | D | 1-1 | 0-1 | 6 | McCracken 64 | 4405 |
| 34 | 24 | H | Rangers | D | 3-3 | 1-3 | 6 | Dodds 1, Scotland 2 59, 90 | 8339 |
| 35 | May 1 | H | Hearts | L | 0-2 | 0-1 | 6 | | 6620 |
| 36 | 8 | A | Motherwell | W | 1-0 | 0-0 | 5 | Wilson 52 | 5722 |
| 37 | 11 | H | Dunfermline Ath | W | 3-2 | 3-1 | — | Miller 17, Innes 22, Samuel 29 | 5998 |
| 38 | 16 | A | Celtic | L | 1-2 | 0-0 | 5 | Wilson (pen) 87 | 58,364 |

**Final League Position: 5**

**Honours**
*League Champions:* Premier Division 1982-83. Division II 1924-25, 1928-29; *Runners-up:* Division II 1930-31, 1959-60. First Division Runners-up 1995-96.
*Scottish Cup Winners:* 1994; *Runners-up:* 1974, 1981, 1985, 1987, 1988, 1991.
*League Cup Winners:* 1979-80, 1980-81; *Runners-up:* 1981-82, 1984-85, 1997-98.
*Summer Cup Runners-up:* 1964-65. *Scottish War Cup Runners-up:* 1939-40.

**European:** *European Cup:* 8 matches (1983-84, semi-finals). *Cup Winners' Cup:* 10 matches (1974-75, 1988-89, 1994-95). *UEFA Cup:* 84 matches (*Fairs Cup:* 1966-67, 1969-70, 1970-71. *UEFA Cup:* 1975-76, 1977-78, 1978-79, 1979-80, 1980-81, 1981-82, 1982-83, 1984-85, 1985-86, 1986-87 runners-up, 1987-88, 1989-90, 1990-91, 1993-94, 1997-98).

**Club colours:** Shirts: Tangerine. Shorts: Tangerine. Stockings: Tangerine.

**Goalscorers:** *League* (47): Dodds 10 (1 pen), McIntyre 10 (1 pen), Miller 5, Scotland 4, McLaren 3, Robson 3, Samuel 3, Wilson 3 (1 pen), Archibald 2, Innes 1, Kerr 1, McCracken 1, McInnes 1
*Scottish Cup* (1): McInnes 1
*CIS Cup* (3): McIntyre 2, McLaren 1

| Gallacher P 33 | Archibald A 38 | Paterson S 2 + 1 | Griffin D 9 + 4 | McInnes D 34 + 1 | Kerr M 30 + 3 | Paterson J 10 + 6 | Miller C 22 + 4 | Samuel C 11 + 15 | Dodds W 23 + 10 | Robson B 25 + 3 | Duff S 10 + 8 | McIntyre J 27 + 3 | Bollan G 1 + 1 | McCracken D 32 | Easton C 10 + 12 | Wilson M 31 + 1 | Bullock A 5 | Innes C 29 | Scotland J 10 + 11 | McLaren A 26 + 1 | Coyle O — + 3 | Holmes G — + 3 | Conway A — + 1 | Match No. |
|---|---|---|---|---|---|---|---|---|---|---|---|---|---|---|---|---|---|---|---|---|---|---|---|---|
| 1 | 2 | 3 | 4 | 5 | 6 | $7^3$ | $8^1$ | 9 | $10^2$ | 11■ | 12 | 13 | 14 | | | | | | | | | | | 1 |
| 1 | 2 | $3^1$ | 4 | 9 | 6 | 7 | $8^2$ | 11 | $10^3$ | | | 13 | | 5 | 12 | 14 | | | | | | | | 2 |
| 1 | 2 | | $4^1$ | 7 | 6 | | 14 | 9 | $10^2$ | 11 | 12 | 13 | $3^3$ | 5 | | 8 | | | | | | | | 3 |
| | 2 | | 4 | 7 | $6^3$ | 14 | 8 | $9^1$ | 13 | $11^2$ | 5 | 10 | | | | | 1 | 3 | 12 | | | | | 4 |
| | 2 | | 4 | 7 | 12 | | 6 | $8^1$ | $10^2$ | 14 | 5 | 11 | | | | | 1 | 3 | 13 | $9^3$ | | | | 5 |
| | 2 | | 4 | 7 | 13 | $6^1$ | 8 | 12 | 14 | | 5 | 11 | | | | | 1 | 3 | $10^3$ | $9^2$ | | | | 6 |
| | 2 | | 4 | 7 | $6^2$ | | 8 | $12^3$ | 13 | | 5 | 11 | | | 14 | | 1 | 3 | $10^1$ | 9 | | | | 7 |
| | 2 | | 4 | 7 | 6 | | | | 12 | | 5 | 11 | | | $8^1$ | | 1 | 3 | $10^2$ | 9 | 13 | | | 8 |
| 1 | 2 | | 13 | 7 | | $6^1$ | | | $10^2$ | 12 | | 11 | | 4 | 8 | 5 | | 3 | | $9^3$ | 14 | | | 9 |
| 1 | 2 | | | 7 | | 6 | | | $10^1$ | | | 11 | | 4 | 8 | 5 | | 3 | | 9 | 12 | | | 10 |
| 1 | 2 | | | 7 | 14 | $6^2$ | | 12 | | 13 | 8 | 11 | | 4 | $9^3$ | 5 | | 3 | | $10^1$ | | | | 11 |
| 1 | 2 | | 12 | $7^1$ | | | | | 10 | 8 | 13 | 11 | | 4 | 6 | $5^2$ | | 3 | | 9 | | | | 12 |
| 1 | 2 | | | 7 | | | | 12 | 10 | $8^1$ | | 11 | | 4 | 6 | 5 | | 3 | | 9 | | | | 13 |
| 1 | 2 | | | 7 | 8 | $6^1$ | | 13 | 10 | | 12 | 11 | | 4 | | 5 | | 3 | | $9^2$ | | | | 14 |
| 1 | 2 | | | 7 | $6^2$ | | 13 | 14 | $10^3$ | 8 | | 11 | | 4 | 12 | $5^1$ | | 3 | | 9 | | | | 15 |
| 1 | 2 | | 13 | 7 | 6 | | 12 | | 10 | 8 | | 11 | | 4 | | 5 | | $3^2$ | | $9^1$ | | | | 16 |
| 1 | 2 | | 3 | 7 | 6 | 12 | $8^1$ | 13 | 10 | | | 11 | | 4 | | 5 | | | | $9^2$ | | | | 17 |
| 1 | 2 | | 14 | 7 | $5^3$ | $6^2$ | | | 10 | 8 | 13 | 11 | | 4 | | 3 | | | 12 | $9^1$ | | | | 18 |
| 1 | 2 | | | 7 | 8 | $6^3$ | | 13 | 10 | | 12 | $11^2$ | | 4 | | 5 | | $3^1$ | 9 | 14 | | | | 19 |
| 1 | 2 | | | 7 | 6 | | 12 | $8^1$ | 10 | 11 | 3 | | | 4 | | 5 | | | | 9 | | | | 20 |
| 1 | 2 | | | 7 | $5^2$ | 6 | 8 | 12 | $10^1$ | 11 | | | | 4 | 13 | 3 | | | | 9 | | | | 21 |
| 1 | 2 | | | 12 | 6 | | 8 | | 10 | 7 | | $11^2$ | | 4 | 13 | 5 | | 3 | | $9^1$ | | | | 22 |
| 1 | 2 | | | 7 | 6 | | 8 | | 10 | 9 | | 11 | | 4 | | 5 | | 3 | | | | | | 23 |
| 1 | 2 | | | 7 | $6^2$ | | 8 | 13 | 10■ | $9^1$ | 3 | $11^3$ | | 4 | 12 | 5 | | | 14 | | | | | 24 |
| 1 | 2 | | | 7 | $6^2$ | 12 | $8^3$ | 10 | | $9^1$ | 3 | 11 | | 4 | 13 | 5 | | | 14 | | | | | 25 |
| 1 | 2 | | | 7 | 6 | | 8 | | | 10 | | 11 | | 4 | | 5 | | 3 | | 9 | | | | 26 |
| 1 | 2 | | | 7 | $6^1$ | | 8 | | 12 | 10 | | 11 | | 4 | 13 | $5^3$ | | 3 | 14 | $9^2$ | | | | 27 |
| 1 | 2 | | | 7 | 6 | | $8^1$ | | 12 | $10^2$ | | $11^3$ | | 4 | 14 | 5 | | 3 | 13 | 9 | | | | 28 |
| 1 | 2 | | | 7 | 6 | | 8 | 12 | | | | 11 | | 4 | | 5 | | 3 | $10^1$ | 9 | | | | 29 |
| 1 | 2 | | | 7 | 6 | | $8^1$ | | 12 | $10^3$ | | 11 | | 4 | 14 | 5 | | 3 | 13 | $9^2$ | | | | 30 |
| 1 | 2 | | | 7 | $6^2$ | | 8 | 14 | 13 | 10 | | $11^3$ | | 4 | | 5 | | 3 | 12 | $9^1$ | | | | 31 |
| 1 | 2 | | | | 6 | 13 | | 14 | 10 | 8 | | $11^1$ | | 4 | 7 | $5^3$ | | 3 | 12 | $9^2$ | | | | 32 |
| 1 | $2^3$ | | | $7^1$ | | | | 13 | 10 | 8 | 14 | | | 4 | 6 | 5 | | 3 | 11 | $9^2$ | | 12 | | 33 |
| 1 | 2 | | | $7^1$ | 6 | | 8 | 13 | 10 | 11 | | | | 4 | | 5 | | 3 | 12 | $9^2$ | | | | 34 |
| 1 | 2 | | | | 6 | 12 | | $9^2$ | 10 | 11 | | | | $4^1$ | 7 | 5 | | 3 | 8 | | | 13 | | 35 |
| 1 | 2 | | | 7 | 6 | | $8^3$ | $11^2$ | 12 | | 9 | | | 4 | 14 | 5 | | 3 | $10^1$ | | | | 13 | 36 |
| 1 | 2 | | | $7^1$ | 6 | | 8 | $11^2$ | 13 | 9 | 14 | | | 4 | 12 | 5 | | 3 | $10^3$ | | | | | 37 |
| 1 | 2 | 13 | | | 6 | 12 | 8 | $11^1$ | | 9 | | | | 4 | $7^3$ | 5 | | 3 | $10^2$ | | | 14 | | 38 |

# DUNFERMLINE ATHLETIC Premier League

*Year Formed:* 1885. *Ground & Address:* East End Park, Halbeath Rd, Dunfermline KY12 7RB. *Telephone:* 01383 724295. *Fax:* 01383 723468. *Ticket office telephone:* 0870 300 1201. *e-mail:* pars@dunfermline-ath.com
*Ground Capacity:* all seated: 12,500. *Size of Pitch:* 115yd × 71yd.
*Chairman:* John Yorkston. *Director of Football/Club Secretary:* Jim Leishman. *Commercial Manager:* Karen McNeil.
*Manager:* David Hay. *Assistant Manager:* Billy Kirkwood. *Physio:* Paul Atkinson.
*Coach and Youth Development Officer:* John Ritchie. *U-21 Coach:* Sandy Clark.
*Managers since 1975:* G. Miller, H. Melrose, P. Stanton, T. Forsyth, J. Leishman, I. Munro, J. Scott, B. Paton, R. Campbell, J. Calderwood. *Club Nickname(s):* The Pars. *Previous Grounds:* None.
*Record Attendance:* 27,816 v Celtic, Division I, 30 Apr 1968.
*Record Transfer Fee received:* £650,000 for Jackie McNamara to Celtic (Oct 1995).
*Record Transfer Fee paid:* £540,000 for Istvan Kozma from Bordeaux (Sept 1989).
*Record Victory:* 11-2 v Stenhousemuir, Division II, 27 Sept 1930.
*Record Defeat:* 1-11 v Hibernian, Scottish Cup, 3rd rd replay, 26 Oct 1889.
*Most Capped Player:* Colin Miller 16(61), Canada.
*Most League Appearances:* 497: Norrie McCathie, 1981-96.
*Most League Goals in Season (Individual):* 53: Bobby Skinner, Division II, 1925-26.
*Most Goals Overall (Individual):* 154: Charles Dickson.

## DUNFERMLINE ATHLETIC 2003–04 LEAGUE RECORD

| Match No. | Date | Venue | Opponents | Result | | H/T Score | Lg. Pos. | Goalscorers | Attendance |
|---|---|---|---|---|---|---|---|---|---|
| 1 | Aug 9 | H | Celtic | D | 0-0 | 0-0 | — | | 10082 |
| 2 | 17 | A | Dundee | W | 2-0 | 1-0 | 5 | Wilkie (og) 44, Crawford 81 | 7750 |
| 3 | 23 | A | Aberdeen | W | 2-1 | 1-1 | 3 | Brewster 30, Nicholson 56 | 10,810 |
| 4 | 31 | A | Hearts | L | 0-1 | 0-0 | 4 | | 11,934 |
| 5 | Sept 13 | A | Rangers | L | 0-4 | 0-3 | 6 | | 49,072 |
| 6 | 20 | H | Hibernian | D | 0-0 | 0-0 | 5 | | 8715 |
| 7 | 27 | H | Partick Th | W | 2-1 | 0-0 | 4 | Crawford 2 56, 70 | 4684 |
| 8 | Oct 4 | A | Livingston | D | 0-0 | 0-0 | 4 | | 3993 |
| 9 | 18 | H | Kilmarnock | L | 2-3 | 1-1 | 7 | Crawford 2 27, 54 | 4495 |
| 10 | Nov 1 | H | Dundee U | W | 2-0 | 0-0 | 6 | Thomson SM 59, Mehmet 89 | 5078 |
| 11 | 8 | A | Celtic | L | 0-5 | 0-1 | 8 | | 58,258 |
| 12 | 22 | H | Dundee | W | 2-0 | 0-0 | 5 | Crawford 2 51, 63 | 5458 |
| 13 | 25 | A | Motherwell | D | 2-2 | 2-0 | — | Crawford 14, Brewster 39 | 4220 |
| 14 | 29 | H | Aberdeen | D | 2-2 | 0-1 | 5 | Young Derek 62, Bullen 75 | 5254 |
| 15 | Dec 6 | H | Hearts | W | 2-1 | 1-1 | 4 | Young Derek 20, Wilson S 61 | 6147 |
| 16 | 14 | H | Rangers | W | 2-0 | 1-0 | 4 | Crawford 4, Vanoli (og) 82 | 8592 |
| 17 | 21 | A | Hibernian | W | 2-1 | 2-0 | 4 | Brewster 2 1, 35 | 9085 |
| 18 | 27 | A | Partick Th | L | 1-4 | 0-1 | 4 | Brewster 58 | 4377 |
| 19 | Jan 3 | H | Livingston | D | 2-2 | 1-1 | 4 | Nicholson (pen) 35, Crawford 79 | 5154 |
| 20 | 17 | A | Kilmarnock | D | 1-1 | 0-1 | 4 | Crawford 63 | 5715 |
| 21 | 24 | H | Motherwell | W | 1-0 | 0-0 | 4 | Young Derek 72 | 5270 |
| 22 | 31 | A | Dundee U | L | 0-1 | 0-0 | 4 | | 5564 |
| 23 | Feb 11 | H | Celtic | L | 1-4 | 1-3 | — | Hunt 14 | 9718 |
| 24 | 14 | A | Dundee | W | 1-0 | 1-0 | 4 | Hunt 31 | 5643 |
| 25 | 21 | A | Aberdeen | L | 0-2 | 0-1 | 4 | | 11,035 |
| 26 | 28 | H | Hearts | D | 0-0 | 0-0 | 4 | | 8422 |
| 27 | Mar 20 | H | Partick Th | W | 1-0 | 1-0 | 4 | Young Darren 9 | 4351 |
| 28 | 23 | A | Rangers | L | 1-4 | 1-4 | — | Tod 21 | 47,487 |
| 29 | 27 | A | Livingston | D | 0-0 | 0-0 | 4 | | 3558 |
| 30 | Apr 3 | H | Kilmarnock | W | 2-1 | 1-1 | 4 | Nicholson 40, Crawford 70 | 3914 |
| 31 | 13 | H | Hibernian | D | 1-1 | 0-1 | — | Dempsey 77 | 5041 |
| 32 | 15 | A | Motherwell | L | 0-1 | 0-1 | — | | 3920 |
| 33 | 17 | H | Dundee U | D | 1-1 | 1-0 | 4 | Shields 44 | 4405 |
| 34 | 24 | H | Motherwell | W | 3-0 | 1-0 | 4 | Nicholson 34, Dempsey 51, Young Derek 73 | 4250 |
| 35 | May 2 | A | Celtic | W | 2-1 | 1-0 | 4 | Nicholson 29, Dempsey 58 | 59,719 |
| 36 | 8 | A | Hearts | L | 1-2 | 1-1 | 4 | Tod 11 | 10,846 |
| 37 | 11 | A | Dundee U | L | 2-3 | 1-3 | — | Bullen 33, Crawford 46 | 5998 |
| 38 | 16 | H | Rangers | L | 2-3 | 1-2 | 4 | Dempsey 2 27, 67 | 6719 |

**Final League Position: 4**

**Honours**
*League Champions:* First Division 1988-89, 1995-96. Division II 1925-26. Second Division 1985-86; *Runners-up:* First Division 1986-87, 1993-94, 1994-95, 1999-2000. Division II 1912-13, 1933-34, 1954-55, 1957-58, 1972-73. Second Division 1978-79.
*Scottish Cup Winners:* 1961, 1968; *Runners-up:* 1965, 2004.
*League Cup Runners-up:* 1949-50, 1991-92.

**European**: *Cup Winners' Cup:* 14 matches (1961-62, 1968-69 semi-finals). *UEFA Cup:* 28 matches (*Fairs Cup:* 1962-63, 1964-65, 1965-66, 1966-67, 1969-70).

**Club colours:** Shirt: Black and white vertical stripes. Shorts: White. Stockings: White.

**Goalscorers:** *League* (45): Crawford 13, Brewster 5, Dempsey 5, Nicholson 5 (1 pen), Young Derek 4, Bullen 2, Hunt 2, Tod 2, Mehmet 1, Shields 1, Thomson SM 1, Wilson S 1, Young Darren 1, own goals 2
*Scottish Cup* (14): Brewster 4, Nicholson 4, Crawford 2, Bullen 1, Byrne 1, Skerla 1, Young Darren 1
*CIS Cup* (4): Crawford 2, Brewster 1, Young Darren 1

| Stillie D 37 | McGroarty C 2 | Tod A 22 + 8 | Skerla A 35 | Wilson S 28 | Young Darren 32 | Nicholson B 36 | Mason G 32 | Young Derek 25 + 3 | Crawford S 33 + 1 | Brewster C 23 + 3 | Grondin D 9 + 5 | Bullen L 19 + 8 | Dair J — + 1 | Dempsey G 15 + 17 | Mehmet W 5 + 13 | Kilgannon S 4 + 7 | Labonte A 8 + 13 | Thomson S 15 + 1 | Byrne R 10 + 3 | McDermott A 5 + 1 | McGarty M — + 1 | Hunt N 5 + 8 | Shields G 15 + 2 | Ruitenbeek M 1 | Clark P 1 + 1 | Wilson C 1 | Greenhill G — + 1 | McGuire K — + 1 | *Match No.* |
|---|---|---|---|---|---|---|---|---|---|---|---|---|---|---|---|---|---|---|---|---|---|---|---|---|---|---|---|---|---|
| 1 | 2 | 3 | 4 | 5 | 6 | 7 | 8 | $9^{1}$ | 10 | 11 | 12 | | | | | | | | | | | | | | | | | | 1 |
| 1 | $2^{1}$ | 3 | 4 | 5 | | 7 | 8 | $9^{3}$ | 10 | $11^{2}$ | | 6 | 12 | 13 | 14 | | | | | | | | | | | | | | 2 |
| 1 | | 3 | 4 | 5 | $6^{2}$ | 7 | 8 | | 10 | $11^{1}$ | 2 | 9 | | 13 | 12 | | | | | | | | | | | | | | 3 |
| 1 | | 3 | 4 | 5 | $6^{2}$ | 7 | 8 | | 10 | $11^{1}$ | 2 | 9 | | 13 | | 12 | | | | | | | | | | | | | 4 |
| 1 | | $3^{3}$ | 4 | 5 | 6 | 7 | 8 | | 10 | | $2^{2}$ | 9 | | $11^{1}$ | 12 | 13 | 14 | | | | | | | | | | | | 5 |
| 1 | | 3 | 4 | $5^{2}$ | 6 | 7 | 8 | | 10 | 11 | $2^{1}$ | 9 | | 13 | | 12 | | | | | | | | | | | | | 6 |
| 1 | | $3^{1}$ | 4 | | 6 | 7 | 8 | | $10^{3}$ | 11 | 2 | 5 | | | 14 | $9^{2}$ | 13 | 12 | | | | | | | | | | | 7 |
| 1 | | | 4 | 5 | 6 | $7^{2}$ | 8 | | 10 | 11 | | 2 | | 12 | | $9^{1}$ | | 3 | 13 | | | | | | | | | | 8 |
| 1 | | | 4 | 5 | 6 | 7 | 8 | | 10 | 11 | $2^{1}$ | 12 | | | | 9 | | 3 | | | | | | | | | | | 9 |
| 1 | | | 4 | 5 | 6 | 7 | 8 | | 10 | $11^{1}$ | | | | $9^{2}$ | 13 | | 12 | 3 | | 2 | | | | | | | | | 10 |
| 1 | | | 4 | 5 | 6 | | $8^{1}$ | | 10 | 13 | | 9 | | 12 | $11^{3}$ | | 7 | 3 | | $2^{2}$ | 14 | | | | | | | | 11 |
| 1 | | | | 5 | 6 | 7 | 8 | 13 | 10 | $11^{2}$ | $2^{1}$ | 12 | | 9 | | | | 3 | | 4 | | | | | | | | | 12 |
| 1 | | 2 | | 5 | 6 | 7 | 8 | $9^{2}$ | 10 | $11^{1}$ | | | | 13 | 12 | | 14 | 3 | | $4^{3}$ | | | | | | | | | 13 |
| 1 | | $2^{2}$ | 4 | 5 | 6 | 7 | 8 | $9^{3}$ | 10 | 11 | | 12 | | 13 | | | | $3^{1}$ | | | | 14 | | | | | | | 14 |
| 1 | | 3 | 4 | 5 | 6 | 7 | 8 | $9^{3}$ | 10 | $11^{2}$ | $2^{1}$ | 12 | | | | | 14 | | | | | 13 | | | | | | | 15 |
| 1 | | 3 | 4 | 5 | 6 | 7 | 8 | $9^{1}$ | 10 | $11^{2}$ | | 2 | | 12 | | | | | | | | 13 | | | | | | | 16 |
| 1 | | 3 | 4 | 5 | 6 | 7 | 8 | $9^{1}$ | 10 | $11^{2}$ | | 2 | | | | | | | | 12 | | 13 | | | | | | | 17 |
| 1 | | 13 | 4 | 5 | 6 | 7 | 8 | $9^{2}$ | $10^{1}$ | $11^{3}$ | | 2 | | 12 | | | | 3 | | | | 14 | | | | | | | 18 |
| 1 | | 3 | 4 | | 6 | 7 | $8^{2}$ | 11 | 10 | | 13 | 2 | | 9 | | | | | | $5^{1}$ | | 12 | | | | | | | 19 |
| 1 | | 2 | 4 | 5 | $6^{1}$ | 7 | 8 | 12 | $10^{2}$ | 11 | | | | 13 | | | 9 | 3 | | | | | | | | | | | 20 |
| 1 | | 14 | 4 | 5 | 6 | $7^{1}$ | 8 | 9 | 10 | $11^{2}$ | | | | $2^{3}$ | | | 13 | 3 | | | | | 12 | | | | | | 21 |
| 1 | | 12 | 4 | 5 | 6 | $7^{3}$ | $8^{2}$ | 11 | 10 | | | | | 14 | | | $9^{1}$ | 3 | | | | 13 | 2 | | | | | | 22 |
| 1 | | 8 | 4 | 5 | 6 | 7 | | $9^{1}$ | 10 | | | | | 12 | 13 | | | $3^{2}$ | | | | 11 | 2 | | | | | | 23 |
| 1 | | 14 | 4 | 5 | 6 | 7 | | 13 | 10 | | | | | $9^{2}$ | | | 12 | 3 | $8^{1}$ | | | $11^{3}$ | 2 | | | | | | 24 |
| 1 | | | 4 | 5 | | $7^{3}$ | | 9 | 10 | | 13 | 12 | | $8^{1}$ | $11^{2}$ | | 14 | 3 | 6 | | | | 2 | | | | | | 25 |
| 1 | | 8 | 4 | 5 | 6 | 7 | | $10^{3}$ | | | | 12 | | 14 | 13 | | | 3 | $9^{2}$ | | | $11^{1}$ | 2 | | | | | | 26 |
| 1 | | 14 | 4 | 5 | 6 | 7 | | $9^{3}$ | 10 | 11 | | 12 | | $8^{1}$ | | | 13 | | $3^{2}$ | | | | 2 | | | | | | 27 |
| 1 | | $3^{1}$ | 4 | 5 | 6 | 7 | $9^{3}$ | 11 | 10 | 12 | | | | | 14 | | $8^{2}$ | | 13 | | | | 2 | | | | | | 28 |
| 1 | | 14 | 4 | $5^{3}$ | 6 | 7 | $8^{2}$ | 9 | 10 | 11 | | | | 12 | 13 | | | | $3^{1}$ | | | | 2 | | | | | | 29 |
| 1 | | 5 | 4 | | 6 | 7 | 8 | $9^{2}$ | 10 | $11^{3}$ | | 12 | | 13 | 14 | | | | $3^{1}$ | | | | 2 | | | | | | 30 |
| 1 | | 14 | 4 | $5^{1}$ | $6^{2}$ | 7 | | 9 | 10 | $11^{3}$ | | 3 | | 8 | 13 | | 12 | | | | | | 2 | | | | | | 31 |
| 1 | | $3^{3}$ | 4 | | | 7 | 8 | 10 | 14 | 13 | | $5^{1}$ | | 9 | $11^{2}$ | | 6 | | 12 | | | | 2 | | | | | | 32 |
| | | 3 | | | 6 | | 8 | | | | 4 | | | 13 | 11 | $7^{2}$ | 5 | | | | | | 2 | 1 | $9^{3}$ | $10^{1}$ | 12 | 14 | 33 |
| 1 | | | 4 | | 6 | 7 | 8 | $11^{3}$ | $10^{2}$ | | 14 | 5 | | 9 | 13 | | 12 | | $3^{1}$ | | | | 2 | | | | | | 34 |
| 1 | | | 4 | | 6 | 7 | 8 | $10^{2}$ | | | | 5 | | $9^{3}$ | $11^{1}$ | 14 | 13 | | 3 | | | 12 | 2 | | | | | | 35 |
| 1 | | 3 | $4^{1}$ | | | 7 | 8 | 10 | | | | 6 | | 9 | | 13 | 12 | | 5 | | | $11^{2}$ | 2 | | | | | | 36 |
| 1 | | $3^{3}$ | 4 | | | 7 | $8^{1}$ | 9 | 10 | | 13 | 2 | | 6 | | 14 | 5 | | | | | 11 | $12^{2}$ | | | | | | 37 |
| 1 | | 13 | 4 | | | 7 | 8 | $9^{1}$ | 10 | $11^{3}$ | | 2 | | 6 | | 12 | 5 | | $3^{2}$ | | | | | | 14 | | | | 38 |

# EAST FIFE

## Third Division

*Year Formed:* 1903. *Ground & Address:* Bayview Stadium, Harbour View, Methil, Fife KY8 3RW. *Telephone:* 01333 426323. *Fax:* 01333 426376.
*Ground Capacity:* all seated: 2000. *Size of Pitch:* 115yd × 75yd.
*Chairman and Secretary:* Derrick Brown.
*Manager:* James Moffat. *Assistant Manager:* Craig Robertson.
*Managers since 1975:* Frank Christie, Roy Barry, David Clarke, Gavin Murray, Alex Totten, Steve Archibald, James Bone, Steve Kirk, Rab Shannon, David Clarke. *Club Nickname(s):* The Fifers. *Previous Ground:* Bayview Park.
*Record Attendance:* 22,515 v Raith Rovers, Division I, 2 Jan 1950.
*Record Transfer Fee received:* £150,000 for Paul Hunter from Hull C (March 1990).
*Record Transfer Fee paid:* £70,000 for John Sludden from Kilmarnock (July 1991).
*Record Victory:* 13-2 v Edinburgh City, Division II, 11 Dec 1937.
*Record Defeat:* 0-9 v Hearts, Division I, 5 Oct 1957.
*Most Capped Player:* George Aitken, 5 (8), Scotland.
*Most League Appearances:* 517: David Clarke, 1968-86.
*Most League Goals in Season (Individual):* 41: Jock Wood, Division II; 1926-27 and Henry Morris, Division II, 1947-48.
*Most Goals Overall (Individual):* 225: Phil Weir (215 in League).

### EAST FIFE 2003–04 LEAGUE RECORD

| Match No. | Date | Venue | Opponents | Result | | H/T Score | Lg. Pos. | Goalscorers | Attendance |
|---|---|---|---|---|---|---|---|---|---|
| 1 | Aug 9 | H | Stenhousemuir | W | 3-2 | 2-0 | — | Deuchar 39, McDonald G 43, Fairbairn 89 | 568 |
| 2 | 16 | A | Forfar Ath | W | 1-0 | 0-0 | 2 | McDonald G 78 | 708 |
| 3 | 23 | H | Berwick R | W | 3-1 | 0-1 | 1 | Mitchell 49, Fairbairn 80, Deuchar 87 | 692 |
| 4 | 30 | A | Morton | L | 1-2 | 1-0 | 2 | Donaldson 35 | 3270 |
| 5 | Sept 13 | H | Airdrie U | W | 3-1 | 1-1 | 2 | McDonald G 3, Donaldson 56, Deuchar 77 | 885 |
| 6 | 20 | H | Alloa Ath | L | 0-1 | 0-1 | 2 | | 595 |
| 7 | 27 | A | Hamilton A | D | 2-2 | 0-1 | 2 | McDonald G 57, Donaldson 59 | 1123 |
| 8 | Oct 4 | H | Dumbarton | W | 1-0 | 0-0 | 2 | Lynes 81 | 518 |
| 9 | 18 | A | Arbroath | W | 1-0 | 1-0 | 2 | Nicholas 36 | 705 |
| 10 | 25 | H | Forfar Ath | L | 2-3 | 2-2 | 2 | McDonald G 5, Hall 28 | 671 |
| 11 | Nov 1 | A | Stenhousemuir | L | 0-3 | 0-3 | 2 | | 532 |
| 12 | 8 | A | Airdrie U | D | 1-1 | 0-0 | 2 | Deuchar 71 | 1418 |
| 13 | 16 | H | Morton | D | 0-0 | 0-0 | 3 | | 1757 |
| 14 | Dec 2 | A | Alloa Ath | L | 0-2 | 0-2 | — | | 405 |
| 15 | 6 | H | Hamilton A | L | 2-3 | 1-0 | 6 | Hall 44, Nicholas 63 | 584 |
| 16 | 13 | A | Dumbarton | L | 1-3 | 0-1 | 6 | McDonald G 67 | 683 |
| 17 | 27 | H | Arbroath | L | 0-1 | 0-1 | 6 | | 811 |
| 18 | Jan 3 | A | Berwick R | W | 2-0 | 1-0 | 6 | McMillan 18, McDonald G 82 | 501 |
| 19 | 17 | H | Stenhousemuir | W | 1-0 | 0-0 | 3 | Deuchar 58 | 536 |
| 20 | 24 | H | Alloa Ath | L | 0-1 | 0-0 | 5 | | 647 |
| 21 | 31 | A | Hamilton A | L | 0-1 | 0-1 | 5 | | 1429 |
| 22 | Feb 7 | H | Airdrie U | L | 0-1 | 0-1 | 8 | | 793 |
| 23 | 14 | A | Morton | D | 1-1 | 0-0 | 8 | Deuchar 48 | 2894 |
| 24 | 21 | A | Arbroath | D | 0-0 | 0-0 | 8 | | 596 |
| 25 | Mar 6 | A | Forfar Ath | L | 0-1 | 0-0 | 8 | | 600 |
| 26 | 13 | H | Berwick R | D | 2-2 | 2-0 | 8 | Deuchar 2 11, 30 | 498 |
| 27 | 16 | H | Dumbarton | L | 1-3 | 1-1 | — | Fairbairn 31 | 439 |
| 28 | 27 | H | Morton | W | 1-0 | 0-0 | 8 | Deuchar 51 | 1114 |
| 29 | 31 | A | Airdrie U | L | 1-2 | 0-1 | — | Stein 77 | 1597 |
| 30 | Apr 3 | H | Hamilton A | L | 2-3 | 0-0 | 8 | McMillan 52, Deuchar 70 | 489 |
| 31 | 10 | A | Alloa Ath | D | 1-1 | 0-1 | 8 | Mortimer 76 | 567 |
| 32 | 17 | H | Arbroath | L | 1-2 | 1-1 | 9 | McMullen (og) 38 | 762 |
| 33 | 24 | A | Dumbarton | L | 0-1 | 0-1 | 9 | | 841 |
| 34 | May 1 | A | Berwick R | D | 1-1 | 0-0 | 9 | Deuchar 86 | 490 |
| 35 | 8 | H | Forfar Ath | W | 2-0 | 0-0 | 9 | McDonald G 51, McMillan 53 | 448 |
| 36 | 15 | A | Stenhousemuir | W | 1-0 | 0-0 | 9 | McDonald G 83 | 826 |

**Final League Position: 9**

**Honours**
*League Champions:* Division II 1947-48; *Runners-up:* Division II 1929-30, 1970-71. Second Division 1983-84, 1995-96. Third Division 2002-03
*Scottish Cup Winners:* 1938; *Runners-up:* 1927, 1950.
*League Cup Winners:* 1947-48, 1949-50, 1953-54.

**Club colours:** Shirt: Gold and black. Shorts: White. Stockings: Black.

**Goalscorers:** *League* (38): Deuchar 11, McDonald G 9, Donaldson 3, Fairbairn 3, McMillan 3, Hall 2, Nicholas 2, Lynes 1, Mitchell 1, Mortimer 1, Stein 1, own goal 1
*Scottish Cup* (6): Deuchar 1, Hall 1, McDonald G 1, Nicholas 1, own goals 2.
*CIS Cup* (0):
*Challenge Cup* (0):

| O'Connor G 34 | Kelly P 24 + 1 | Miller C 6 | Mortimer P 9 + 7 | Hall M 27 | Byle L 2 | McMillan C 36 | McDonald G 31 + 3 | Deuchar K 31 + 5 | Stewart W 14 + 7 | Donaldson E 31 + 1 | Lynes C 3 + 3 | Russell G 9 + 1 | Fairbairn B 10 + 20 | Love G 1 + 2 | Mitchell J 14 + 10 | Gilbert G 11 + 11 | Lumsden C 21 + 2 | Blair B 15 + 7 | McDonald I 9 | Nicholas S 10 + 1 | Graham M 2 | Stein J 12 + 1 | Herkes J 8 + 7 | Mathie G 16 | Bain K 10 + 1 | Match No. |
|---|---|---|---|---|---|---|---|---|---|---|---|---|---|---|---|---|---|---|---|---|---|---|---|---|---|---|
| 1 | 2 | 3 | 4 | 5 | $6^1$ | 7 | $8^2$ | $9^3$ | 10 | 11 | 12 | 13 | 14 | | | | | | | | | | | | | 1 |
| 1 | 6 | 3 | $4^1$ | 5 | 8 | $7^3$ | 12 | 9 | $10^2$ | 11 | | 2 | 13 | 14 | | | | | | | | | | | | 2 |
| 1 | 6 | 3 | | 5 | | 2 | 8 | 9 | $10^2$ | 11 | | 4 | 13 | $7^1$ | 12 | | | | | | | | | | | 3 |
| 1 | 6 | 3 | | 5 | | 2 | 8 | $9^2$ | $10^1$ | 11 | | 4 | 12 | 14 | $7^3$ | 13 | | | | | | | | | | 4 |
| 1 | 6 | 3 | 14 | 5 | | $7^3$ | 8 | 9 | | $11^1$ | | 2 | $10^2$ | | 13 | 12 | 4 | | | | | | | | | 5 |
| 1 | 6 | 3 | | 5 | | 7 | $8^3$ | 9 | | $11^2$ | | 2 | $10^1$ | | 12 | 13 | 4 | 14 | | | | | | | | 6 |
| 1 | 6 | | | 5 | | 2 | 8 | 9 | $10^2$ | 11 | | | 12 | | $7^1$ | 13 | 4 | | 3 | | | | | | | 7 |
| 1 | 6 | | | 5 | | 2 | 8 | $9^3$ | | 11 | 14 | | $10^2$ | | 7 | 12 | 4 | | $3^1$ | 13 | | | | | | 8 |
| 1 | 8 | | 12 | 5 | | 2 | $10^1$ | 9 | | 3 | 13 | | | | 7 | 14 | 4 | | $6^2$ | $11^3$ | | | | | | 9 |
| 1 | | | | 5 | | 2 | 8 | 9 | 12 | 3 | 6 | | 14 | | $10^2$ | $11^3$ | 4 | 13 | | $7^1$ | | | | | | 10 |
| 1 | | | | 5 | | 2 | $8^2$ | 9 | 14 | 3 | 6 | | 12 | | $10^1$ | 11 | 4 | 13 | | $7^3$ | | | | | | 11 |
| 1 | 8 | | | 5 | | 2 | | 9 | $10^3$ | 3 | $11^1$ | | 13 | | 14 | 12 | 4 | 6 | | $7^2$ | | | | | | 12 |
| 1 | 8 | | $12^2$ | $5^1$ | | 2 | 13 | 9 | $7^3$ | 3 | | | 14 | | | 11 | 4 | 6 | | 10 | | | | | | 13 |
| 1 | 12 | | | 5 | | 2 | 8 | 9 | $7^1$ | 3 | | | $11^2$ | | 13 | | 4 | 6 | | 10 | | | | | | 14 |
| | | | 12 | 5 | | 2 | 8 | 9 | 14 | 3 | | | 13 | | $7^2$ | 11 | 4 | $6^1$ | | $10^3$ | 1 | | | | | 15 |
| | 2 | | $6^3$ | 5 | | 7 | 8 | 9 | 13 | 3 | | | 12 | | | $11^1$ | 4 | 14 | | $10^2$ | 1 | | | | | 16 |
| 1 | 6 | | $4^2$ | 5 | | $7^1$ | 8 | 9 | $11^3$ | 3 | | 2 | 14 | | | 12 | | 13 | | 10 | | | | | | 17 |
| 1 | 6 | | | 5 | | 11 | 4 | 9 | 13 | 3 | | | 12 | | $7^2$ | | 2 | 8 | | $10^1$ | | | | | | 18 |
| 1 | 8 | | | 5 | | 2 | $4^1$ | 13 | $10^2$ | 3 | | | 9 | | $7^3$ | | 12 | 6 | | | | 11 | 14 | | | 19 |
| 1 | $8^1$ | | | 5 | | 2 | 12 | 9 | | 3 | | 4 | $10^2$ | | 7 | 14 | | 6 | | | | $11^3$ | 13 | | | 20 |
| 1 | 6 | | | 3 | | 2 | 4 | 9 | | 11 | | | 14 | | $7^2$ | | | $8^1$ | | | | $10^3$ | 13 | 5 | 12 | 21 |
| 1 | 6 | | | 3 | | 2 | 4 | 9 | 12 | 11 | | | | | | | | 8 | | | | $10^1$ | 7 | 5 | | 22 |
| 1 | 8 | | | 3 | | 2 | 4 | 9 | $10^2$ | 11 | | | | | 13 | | | 12 | | | | | 7 | 5 | $6^1$ | 23 |
| 1 | 8 | | | 3 | | 2 | 4 | 9 | $10^2$ | 11 | | | | | | | | 12 | | | | 13 | 7 | 5 | $6^1$ | 24 |
| 1 | 8 | | | | | 2 | 4 | 9 | $10^1$ | 3 | | | 12 | | | | | | | | | 11 | 7 | 5 | 6 | 25 |
| 1 | 8 | | | | | 2 | 4 | 9 | | 3 | | | $10^2$ | | 13 | | 12 | | | | | 11 | 7 | $5^1$ | 6 | 26 |
| 1 | 8 | | | | | 2 | 4 | 9 | | 3 | | | $10^1$ | | 12 | | | | | | | 11 | 7 | 5 | 6 | 27 |
| 1 | | | 14 | | | 2 | 10 | $9^2$ | 13 | | | | $7^1$ | | | | 4 | $8^3$ | 3 | | | 11 | 12 | 5 | 6 | 28 |
| 1 | 8 | | 12 | | | 6 | $4^1$ | 9 | $7^2$ | | | | 14 | | $10^3$ | 13 | 2 | | 3 | | | 11 | | 5 | | 29 |
| 1 | | | | | | 2 | | 9 | | | | 6 | $7^1$ | | | 12 | 4 | 8 | 3 | | | 11 | | 5 | 10 | 30 |
| 1 | | | 12 | | | 7 | 4 | 9 | | 13 | | | 14 | | | $11^3$ | 2 | $6^1$ | $3^2$ | | | 10 | | 5 | 8 | 31 |
| 1 | | | 6 | | | 7 | 4 | 9 | | | | 2 | 13 | | | $10^1$ | | | $3^2$ | | | 11 | 12 | 5 | 8 | 32 |
| 1 | | | 4 | | | 7 | 6 | 12 | | 11 | | | | | 13 | $10^1$ | 2 | | 3 | | | | $9^2$ | 5 | 8 | 33 |
| 1 | | | 4 | 3 | | $7^1$ | 8 | 13 | | 11 | | | 14 | | 12 | $10^2$ | 2 | 6 | | | | | $9^3$ | 5 | | 34 |
| 1 | | | 4 | 3 | | 7 | 8 | 12 | | 11 | | | | | $9^2$ | $10^1$ | 2 | 6 | | | | | 13 | 5 | | 35 |
| 1 | | | 4 | 3 | | $7^1$ | 8 | 13 | | 11 | | | 14 | | $9^3$ | $10^2$ | 2 | 6 | | | | | 12 | 5 | | 36 |

# EAST STIRLINGSHIRE Third Division

*Year Formed:* 1880. *Ground & Address:* Firs Park, Firs St, Falkirk FK2 7AY. *Telephone:* 01324 623583. *Fax:* 01324 637 862.
*Ground Capacity:* total: 1880, seated: 200. *Size of Pitch:* 112yd × 72yd.
*Chairman:* A. Mackin. *Vice Chairman:* Douglas Morrison. *Chief Executive/Secretary:* Leslie G. Thomson.
*Head Coach:* Dennis Newall. *Assistant Coach:* Alex Cleland. *Physio:* Laura Gillogley.
*Managers since 1975:* I. Ure, D. McLinden, W. P. Lamont, A. Ferguson, W. Little, D. Whiteford, D. Lawson, J. D. Connell, A. Mackin, D. Sullivan, B. McCulley, B. Little, J. Brownlie, H. McCann, G. Fairley, B. Ross, D. Diver.
*Club Nickname(s):* The Shire. *Previous Grounds:* Burnhouse, Randyford Park, Merchiston Park, New Kilbowie Park.
*Record Attendance:* 12,000 v Partick T, Scottish Cup 3rd rd, 21 Feb 1921.
*Record Transfer Fee received:* £35,000 for Jim Docherty to Chelsea (1978).
*Record Transfer Fee paid:* £6,000 for Colin McKinnon from Falkirk (March 1991).
*Record Victory:* 11-2 v Vale of Bannock, Scottish Cup 2nd rd, 22 Sept 1888.
*Record Defeat:* 1-12 v Dundee United, Division II, 13 Apr 1936.
*Most Capped Player:* Humphrey Jones, 5 (14), Wales.
*Most League Appearances:* 415: Gordon Russell, 1983-2001.
*Most League Goals in Season (Individual):* 36: Malcolm Morrison, Division II, 1938-39.

## EAST STIRLINGSHIRE 2003–04 LEAGUE RECORD

| *Match No.* | *Date* | *Venue* | *Opponents* | *Result* | *H/T Score* | *Lg. Pos.* | *Goalscorers* | *Attendance* |
|---|---|---|---|---|---|---|---|---|
| 1 | Aug 9 | A | Elgin C | L 1-3 | 0-2 | — | Livingstone [53] | 604 |
| 2 | 16 | H | Montrose | D 1-1 | 0-0 | 8 | Kelly (pen) [61] | 182 |
| 3 | 23 | A | Stirling A | L 1-5 | 1-2 | 10 | Polwart [12] | 581 |
| 4 | 30 | H | Cowdenbeath | D 1-1 | 0-0 | 10 | Ormiston [64] | 296 |
| 5 | Sept 13 | A | Stranraer | L 0-4 | 0-1 | 10 | | 358 |
| 6 | 20 | A | Peterhead | L 0-2 | 0-0 | 10 | | 520 |
| 7 | 27 | H | Queen's Park | L 1-2 | 0-1 | 10 | Ure [89] | 281 |
| 8 | Oct 4 | A | Albion R | L 0-5 | 0-1 | 10 | | 256 |
| 9 | 18 | H | Gretna | L 0-1 | 0-0 | 10 | | 198 |
| 10 | 25 | A | Montrose | L 1-5 | 1-1 | 10 | Ure [11] | 246 |
| 11 | Nov 1 | H | Elgin C | W 3-1 | 1-0 | 10 | Ure 2 [9, 49], Kelly [90] | 239 |
| 12 | 8 | H | Stranraer | L 1-4 | 1-1 | 10 | Rodden [15] | 245 |
| 13 | 14 | A | Cowdenbeath | L 1-2 | 0-0 | 10 | Ritchie (og) [63] | 330 |
| 14 | 29 | H | Peterhead | L 1-3 | 0-2 | 10 | Kelly [70] | 178 |
| 15 | Dec 6 | A | Queen's Park | L 0-3 | 0-2 | 10 | | 439 |
| 16 | 13 | H | Albion R | L 3-4 | 2-2 | 10 | Ure [10], Leishman [12], Kelly (pen) [49] | 175 |
| 17 | 27 | A | Gretna | L 1-2 | 0-0 | 10 | Kelly [68] | 532 |
| 18 | Jan 10 | H | Stirling A | L 2-4 | 1-0 | 10 | Ure 2 [22, 50] | 495 |
| 19 | 17 | A | Elgin C | L 0-3 | 0-2 | 10 | | 432 |
| 20 | 24 | A | Peterhead | L 0-6 | 0-4 | 10 | | 553 |
| 21 | Feb 7 | A | Stranraer | L 1-7 | 0-2 | 10 | McAuley [67] | 405 |
| 22 | 14 | H | Cowdenbeath | L 0-1 | 0-0 | 10 | | 308 |
| 23 | 21 | H | Gretna | L 2-4 | 1-2 | 10 | Baldwin [15], Reid C [54] | 187 |
| 24 | Mar 2 | H | Queen's Park | L 2-4 | 1-2 | — | McAuley 2 [1, 61] | 235 |
| 25 | 6 | H | Montrose | L 1-4 | 1-3 | 10 | Kelly [9] | 195 |
| 26 | 9 | A | Albion R | L 1-5 | 0-4 | — | Ure [47] | 179 |
| 27 | 13 | A | Stirling A | L 0-6 | 0-2 | 10 | | 739 |
| 28 | 24 | H | Stranraer | L 1-2 | 1-2 | — | Millar [20] | 181 |
| 29 | 27 | A | Cowdenbeath | L 0-2 | 0-1 | 10 | | 289 |
| 30 | Apr 3 | A | Queen's Park | L 0-1 | 0-1 | 10 | | 404 |
| 31 | 10 | H | Peterhead | L 0-3 | 0-2 | 10 | | 243 |
| 32 | 17 | A | Gretna | L 1-5 | 0-3 | 10 | Millar [60] | 311 |
| 33 | 24 | H | Albion R | L 1-8 | 1-2 | 10 | Kelly [25] | 223 |
| 34 | May 1 | H | Stirling A | L 0-3 | 0-1 | 10 | | 779 |
| 35 | 8 | A | Montrose | L 0-1 | 0-0 | 10 | | 360 |
| 36 | 15 | H | Elgin C | W 2-1 | 1-1 | 10 | Ure [37], Dickson H (og) [48] | 363 |

**Final League Position: 10**

**Honours**
*League Champions:* Division II 1931-32; C Division 1947-48. *Runners-up:* Division II 1962-63. Second Division 1979-80. Division Three 1923-24.

**Club colours:** Shirt: Black with white. Shorts: Black with white. Stockings: Black with white hoops.

**Goalscorers:** *League* (30): Ure 9, Kelly 7 (2 pens), McAuley 3, Millar 2, Baldwin 1, Leishman 1, Livingstone 1, Ormiston 1, Polwart 1, Reid C 1, Rodden 1, own goals 2
*Scottish Cup* (0):
*CIS Cup* (1): Rodden
*Challenge Cup* (2): Baldwin 1, Kelly 1

| Connolly J 19 | Penman C 1 | Polwart D 14 + 4 | Livingstone S 29 + 3 | Maughan R 26 | McGhee G 35 + 1 | Boyle G 1 + 7 | Mackay J 12 + 3 | Kelly S 20 + 11 | Ormiston D 7 | Baldwin C 23 + 1 | Leishman J 14 + 6 | Rodden P 7 + 12 | McLaren G 30 + 2 | McCann K 5 | McCulloch G 1 + 2 | Reid C 9 + 2 | McAuley S 24 + 5 | Hare R 11 + 4 | Todd C 13 + 1 | Ure D 26 + 2 | Oates S 16 | Irvine S 1 + 2 | Mulholland B 13 + 3 | Ogilvie F — + 1 | Ford K 9 + 1 | Carnaghan G 1 | Reid M — + 1 | Newell C 15 | Lynch C 2 + 3 | Millar D 8 + 2 | Gilpin R 4 | Kane P — + 3 | Match No. |
|---|---|---|---|---|---|---|---|---|---|---|---|---|---|---|---|---|---|---|---|---|---|---|---|---|---|---|---|---|---|---|---|---|---|
| 1 | $2^{2}$ | 3 | 4 | 5 | 6 | $7^{1}$ | 8 | 9 | 10 | 11 | 12 | 13 | | | | | | | | | | | | | | | | | | | | | 1 |
| 1 | | 4 | 7 | 2 | 6 | 12 | $8^{1}$ | 9 | $10^{2}$ | 11 | | 13 | 3 | 5 | | | | | | | | | | | | | | | | | | | 2 |
| 1 | | 4 | 7 | 2 | 6 | | $8^{2}$ | 9 | $10^{3}$ | $11^{1}$ | 12 | 14 | 3 | 5■ | 13 | | | | | | | | | | | | | | | | | | 3 |
| 1 | | 4 | 7 | 2 | 6 | | | 10 | 9 | | $11^{1}$ | 12 | 3 | | | 5 | 8 | | | | | | | | | | | | | | | | 4 |
| 1 | | 11 | $7^{1}$ | 2 | 6 | | $4^{2}$ | | 9 | | $10^{3}$ | 12 | 3 | 5 | 14 | | 8 | 13 | | | | | | | | | | | | | | | 5 |
| 1 | | 4 | 7 | 2 | 6 | | | 10 | 9 | $11^{1}$ | | 12 | 3 | 5 | | | 8 | | | | | | | | | | | | | | | | 6 |
| 1■ | | $4^{2}$ | | | 6 | | | 9 | 7 | $11^{1}$ | | $10^{3}$ | 3 | 5 | 2 | | 8 | 14 | 12 | 13 | | | | | | | | | | | | | 7 |
| | | $4^{2}$ | | 2 | 6 | 14 | 12 | 7 | | 11 | | $9^{3}$ | 3 | | | 5 | $8^{1}$ | 13 | 1 | 10 | | | | | | | | | | | | | 8 |
| 1 | | $3^{1}$ | $7^{2}$ | | 6 | 13 | 8 | 10 | | 11 | | 12 | | | | 5 | 4 | 2 | | 9 | | | | | | | | | | | | | 9 |
| 1 | | $3^{1}$ | 7 | | 6 | 14 | 8■ | $10^{2}$ | | 11 | | 13 | 12 | | | 5 | 4 | $2^{3}$ | | 9 | | | | | | | | | | | | | 10 |
| 1 | | 12 | 7 | 2 | 6 | | | 13 | | $11^{1}$ | $8^{3}$ | $10^{2}$ | 3 | | | | 14 | 4 | | 9 | 5 | | | | | | | | | | | | 11 |
| 1 | | 11 | | 2 | 6 | 14 | | 12 | | | $8^{2}$ | $10^{3}$ | 3 | | | | 13 | 4 | | 9 | 5 | $7^{1}$ | | | | | | | | | | | 12 |
| 1 | | 12 | 7 | 2 | 6 | | | 13 | | 11 | $8^{3}$ | $10^{2}$ | $3^{1}$ | | | | 14 | 4 | | 9 | 5 | | | | | | | | | | | | 13 |
| 1 | | | $7^{2}$ | 2 | 3 | 14 | | 10 | | | $11^{3}$ | | 4 | | | 12 | 8 | 6 | | 9 | $5^{1}$ | 13 | | | | | | | | | | | 14 |
| 1 | | | 7 | 2 | 6 | 13 | 14 | 10 | | | $11^{1}$ | | 5 | | | | 8 | $4^{3}$ | | $9^{2}$ | 3 | 12 | | | | | | | | | | | 15 |
| 1 | | | 7 | 2 | 6 | | | $10^{2}$ | | 11 | $8^{1}$ | | 5 | | | | | 4 | | 9■ | 3 | | 12 | 13 | | | | | | | | | 16 |
| 1 | | | $7^{1}$ | 2 | 3 | | 4 | 9 | | 11 | 12 | | 6 | | | 5 | | | | | | | 8 | | 10 | | | | | | | | 17 |
| 1 | | | 7 | 2 | 3 | | 4 | | | 11 | | | 6■ | | | 5■ | | 12 | | 10 | | | 8■ | | $9^{1}$ | | | | | | | | 18 |
| 1 | | 3 | 7 | 2 | 6 | | 4 | 13 | | $11^{3}$ | $8^{1}$ | | | | | | 12 | | | 10 | | | | | $9^{2}$ | 5 | 14 | | | | | | 19 |
| 1 | | 3 | 12 | 2 | 6 | | 4 | 13 | | $11^{3}$ | 14 | | | | | | $8^{1}$ | | | 10 | $5^{2}$ | | 7 | | 9 | | | | | | | | 20 |
| | | $3^{2}$ | | 2 | 13 | | 8 | 12 | | | | | 6 | | | | 11 | 4 | 1 | 10 | | | 7 | | $9^{1}$ | | | 5 | | | | | 21 |
| | | 13 | 12 | 2 | 6 | | $8^{1}$ | | | $11^{2}$ | | 14 | 3 | | | | 4 | | 1 | 10 | | | 7■ | | $9^{3}$ | | | 5 | | | | | 22 |
| | | 12 | $7^{1}$ | | 6 | | | | | $11^{2}$ | | | 3 | | | 2 | 8 | 4 | 1 | 10 | | | | | 9 | | | 5 | 13 | | | | 23 |
| | | | 7 | | 6 | | | 13 | | 11 | | | 3 | | | 2 | 8 | $4^{1}$ | 1 | 10 | | | | | $9^{2}$ | | | 5 | | 12 | | | 24 |
| | | | 12 | $2^{2}$ | 6 | | | 9 | | 7 | | | 3 | | | 13 | 8 | | 1 | 10 | | | | | $11^{3}$ | | | 5 | 14 | $4^{1}$ | | | 25 |
| | | | 4 | 2 | 6 | | 12 | 11 | | | | | 3 | | | | | | 1 | 10 | | | $7^{1}$ | | 13 | | | 5 | $9^{2}$ | 8 | | | 26 |
| | | | 9 | 4 | 6 | | | 12 | | 13 | | | 3 | | | $2^{2}$ | 14 | | 1 | 10 | | | 7 | | | | | 5 | $11^{1}$ | $8^{3}$ | | | 27 |
| | | | 7 | 2 | 5 | | | 12 | | $11^{1}$ | | | 3 | | | | 10 | | | 9 | 4 | | | | | | | 6 | | 8 | 1 | | 28 |
| | | | 7 | 2 | 6 | | | 12 | | $11^{1}$ | | | 3 | | | | 10 | | 1 | 9 | 4 | | 13 | | | | | 5 | | $8^{2}$ | | | 29 |
| | | | $7^{3}$ | 2 | 6 | | | | | $11^{1}$ | 12 | | $3^{2}$ | | | | 10 | | 1 | 9 | 4 | | 13 | | | | | 5 | | 8 | | 14 | 30 |
| | | | 6 | 2 | 5 | | | 10 | | | $8^{2}$ | $9^{1}$ | 3 | | | | 7 | | 1 | 12 | 4 | | 11 | | | | | | 13 | | | | 31 |
| | | | $7^{3}$ | | 5 | | | 13 | | | 14 | $10^{2}$ | 3 | | | | 8 | | 1 | 9 | 4 | | $11^{1}$ | | | | | 2 | | 6 | | 12 | 32 |
| | | | 2 | | 6 | | | $10^{3}$ | | | 7 | 14 | 12 | | | | 8 | | 1 | $9^{2}$ | 4 | | $3^{1}$ | | | | | 5 | | 11 | | 13 | 33 |
| | | | 7 | | 5 | | | 9 | | 11 | $10^{1}$ | 12 | 3 | | | | 6 | | | | 4 | | $8^{2}$ | | | | | 2 | | 13 | 1 | | 34 |
| | | | 2 | | 6 | | | 10 | | | 7 | 12 | 3 | | | | 8 | | | $9^{1}$ | 4 | | 11 | | | | | 5 | | | 1 | | 35 |
| | | | 2 | | 6 | | | 10 | | | 7 | | 3 | | | | 8 | | | 9 | 4 | | 11 | | | | | 5 | | | 1 | | 36 |

# ELGIN CITY — Third Division

*Year Formed:* 1893. *Ground and Address:* Borough Briggs, Borough Briggs Road, Elgin IV30 1AP.
*Telephone:* 01343 551114. *Fax:* 01343 547921.
*Ground Capacity:* 3927, seated 478, standing 3449. *Size of pitch:* 111yd × 72yd.
*Chairman:* Denis J. Miller. *Secretary:* John A. Milton. *Commercial Manager:* Michael Teasdale.
*Manager:* David Robertson. *Coach:* Neil MacLennan. *Physio:* Maurice O'Donnell.
*Managers since 1975:* McHardy, Wilson, McHardy, Dickson, Shewan, Tedcastle, Grant, Cochran, Cumming, Cowie, Paterson, Winton, Black, Teasdale, Fleming, McHardy, Tatters, Caldwell.
*Previous names:* 1893-1900 Elgin City, 1900-03 Elgin City United, 1903- Elgin City.
*Club Nickname(s):* City or Black & Whites. *Previous Grounds:* Association Park 1893-95; Milnfield Park 1895-1909; Station Park 1909-19; Cooper Park 1919-21.
*Record Attendance:* 12,608 v Arbroath, Scottish Cup, 17 Feb 1968.
*Record Transfer Fee received:* £32,000 for Michael Teasdale to Dundee (Jan 1994).
*Record Transfer Fee paid:* £10,000 to Fraserburgh for Russell McBride (July 2001).
*Record Victory:* 18-1 v Brora Rangers, North of Scotland Cup, 6 Feb 1960.
*Record Defeat:* 1-14 v Hearts, Scottish Cup, 4 Feb 1939.
*Most League Appearances:* 97: Martin Pirie, 2000-03.
*Most League Goals in Season (Individual):* 12, Ian Gilzean, 2001-02.
*Most Goals Overall (Individual):* David Ross, 14, 2000-03.

## ELGIN CITY 2003–04 LEAGUE RECORD

| Match No. | Date | Venue | Opponents | Result | H/T Score | Lg. Pos. | Goalscorers | Attendance |
|---|---|---|---|---|---|---|---|---|
| 1 | Aug 9 | H | East Stirling | W 3-1 | 2-0 | — | Ogboke 2 32, 40, Allison 78 | 604 |
| 2 | 16 | A | Queen's Park | L 2-5 | 1-2 | 5 | McCormick 35, Bone 88 | 556 |
| 3 | 23 | H | Peterhead | L 2-3 | 1-2 | 6 | Bone 43, Martin 57 | 748 |
| 4 | 30 | A | Montrose | D 3-3 | 1-2 | 8 | Bone 38, Coulter 57, Steele 69 | 324 |
| 5 | Sept 6 | A | Albion R | W 2-1 | 0-1 | 4 | Martin 2 52, 83 | 394 |
| 6 | 13 | H | Gretna | D 3-3 | 2-2 | 4 | Ogboke 2 30, 36, Bone 84 | 529 |
| 7 | 20 | A | Stranraer | L 3-4 | 1-3 | 6 | Bone 42, Ogboke 83, Martin 88 | 370 |
| 8 | 27 | H | Cowdenbeath | L 0-4 | 0-2 | 8 | | 665 |
| 9 | Oct 4 | A | Stirling A | L 0-3 | 0-2 | 8 | | 648 |
| 10 | 18 | H | Albion R | L 1-5 | 1-2 | 8 | McMullan 23 | 681 |
| 11 | 25 | H | Queen's Park | D 2-2 | 1-0 | 9 | Martin 14, White 90 | 548 |
| 12 | Nov 1 | A | East Stirling | L 1-3 | 0-1 | 9 | White 56 | 239 |
| 13 | 8 | A | Gretna | D 2-2 | 1-2 | 9 | Ogboke 25, McMillan 70 | 451 |
| 14 | 15 | H | Montrose | L 2-3 | 1-1 | 9 | Martin 13, Bone 57 | 475 |
| 15 | 29 | H | Stranraer | L 1-3 | 1-2 | 9 | Tully 41 | 410 |
| 16 | Dec 6 | A | Cowdenbeath | L 2-3 | 1-2 | 9 | Martin 8, Tully 77 | 242 |
| 17 | 13 | H | Stirling A | L 0-2 | 0-1 | 9 | | 478 |
| 18 | Jan 3 | A | Peterhead | L 1-5 | 1-1 | 9 | Tully 35 | 714 |
| 19 | 17 | H | East Stirling | W 3-0 | 2-0 | 9 | Tully 14, Hind 2 27, 88 | 432 |
| 20 | 24 | A | Stranraer | L 0-6 | 0-1 | 9 | | 393 |
| 21 | Feb 7 | H | Gretna | D 1-1 | 0-1 | 9 | Tully 90 | 383 |
| 22 | 14 | A | Montrose | L 3-4 | 1-3 | 9 | Bone 3 38, 71, 84 | 312 |
| 23 | 21 | H | Albion R | L 1-2 | 0-1 | 9 | Bone 48 | 425 |
| 24 | Mar 6 | A | Queen's Park | L 0-4 | 0-1 | 9 | | 444 |
| 25 | 10 | A | Stirling A | L 1-6 | 0-3 | — | Bone 88 | 527 |
| 26 | 13 | H | Peterhead | W 1-0 | 0-0 | 9 | Bone 59 | 675 |
| 27 | 16 | H | Cowdenbeath | D 0-0 | 0-0 | — | | 312 |
| 28 | 20 | A | Gretna | L 1-2 | 1-2 | 9 | Steele 8 | 360 |
| 29 | 27 | H | Montrose | W 2-1 | 0-0 | 9 | McCormick 47, Bone 88 | 499 |
| 30 | Apr 3 | A | Cowdenbeath | L 0-2 | 0-1 | 9 | | 218 |
| 31 | 10 | H | Stranraer | D 0-0 | 0-0 | 9 | | 663 |
| 32 | 17 | A | Albion R | W 2-1 | 1-1 | 9 | McKenzie 45, Bone 87 | 212 |
| 33 | 24 | H | Stirling A | L 0-1 | 0-1 | 9 | | 542 |
| 34 | May 1 | A | Peterhead | L 1-3 | 1-0 | 9 | Bone 27 | 616 |
| 35 | 8 | H | Queen's Park | L 1-3 | 1-3 | 9 | Bremner 16 | 421 |
| 36 | 15 | A | East Stirling | L 1-2 | 1-1 | 9 | Martin 23 | 363 |

**Final League Position: 9**

**Honours**
*Scottish Cup: Quarter Finals* 1968.
*Highland League Champions:* winners 15 times.
*Scottish Qualifying Cup (North):* winners 7 times.
*North of Scotland Cup:* winners 17 times.
*Highland League Cup:* winners 5 times.
*Inverness Cup:* winners twice.

**Club colours:** Shirt: Black and white vertical stripes. Shorts: Black. Stockings: Red.

**Goalscorers:** *League* (48): Bone 15, Martin 8, Ogboke 6, Tully 5, Hind 2, McCormick 2, Steele 2, White 2, Allison 1, Bremner 1, Coulter 1, McKenzie 1, McMillan 1, McMullan 1
*Scottish Cup* (1): Campbell 1
*CIS Cup* (0):
*Challenge Cup* (0):

| Pirie M 28 | Hind D 28 + 3 | Gallagher J 3 + 2 | White J 13 + 3 | Coulter R 16 + 1 | Allison J 32 | Martin W 30 + 4 | McLean C 2 | McCormick S 14 + 2 | Steele K 9 + 13 | Murphy J 6 + 1 | Ogboke C 9 + 10 | McLean N 19 + 7 | Bone A 30 + 3 | McMullan R 18 + 10 | Campbell C 28 | McMillan A 19 + 2 | Teasdale M 1 | Hamilton P 3 | Dickson H 18 + 1 | Goram A 5 | Dempsie A 21 | Bremner F 4 + 2 | Tully C 17 | Donald M — + 4 | Addicoat W 4 | McKenzie J 14 | Vigurs I 1 + 2 | Reid P 2 + 4 | Dickson M 1 + 1 | Charlesworth M — + 1 | Read C — + 1 | Anderson R — + 1 | Ralph J 1 | Thomson R — + 1 | Wood G — + 1 | *Match No.* |
|---|---|---|---|---|---|---|---|---|---|---|---|---|---|---|---|---|---|---|---|---|---|---|---|---|---|---|---|---|---|---|---|---|---|---|---|---|
| 1 | 2 | 3 | 4 | 5 | 6 | 7 | $8^{1}$ | $9^{2}$ | 10 | 11 | 12 | 13 | | | | | | | | | | | | | | | | | | | | | | | | 1 |
| 1 | 2 | 3 | $4^{2}$ | 5 | 6 | 7 | | $8^{3}$ | $10^{1}$ | 11 | 12 | 13 | 9 | 14 | | | | | | | | | | | | | | | | | | | | | | 2 |
| 1 | 2 | | 4 | 5 | 6 | 7 | | | 10 | 11 | 8 | | $9^{1}$ | 12 | 3 | | | | | | | | | | | | | | | | | | | | | 3 |
| 1 | 2 | | 4 | 5 | 6 | 7 | | 12 | 10 | 11 | $8^{1}$ | | 9 | | 3 | | | | | | | | | | | | | | | | | | | | | 4 |
| 1 | 2 | 12 | 4 | 5 | | 7 | | $8^{2}$ | $10^{1}$ | 6 | 13 | | 9 | | 11 | 3 | | | | | | | | | | | | | | | | | | | | 5 |
| 1 | 2 | 12 | 4 | 5 | 6 | $7^{2}$ | | | $10^{1}$ | | 11 | | 9 | 13 | 8 | 3 | | | | | | | | | | | | | | | | | | | | 6 |
| 1 | 2 | | | 5 | 6 | 7 | | $11^{3}$ | $10^{2}$ | 12 | 13 | | 9 | 14 | 8 | 3 | $4^{1}$ | | | | | | | | | | | | | | | | | | | 7 |
| | 4 | | | 5 | 6 | 7 | | | 12 | $11^{1}$ | 10 | $2^{2}$ | 9 | 13 | 8 | 3 | | 1 | | | | | | | | | | | | | | | | | | 8 |
| | | 3 | | 5 | 6 | 7 | | | | | $10^{1}$ | 8 | 9 | 12 | 11 | 4 | | 1 | 2 | | | | | | | | | | | | | | | | | 9 |
| | 8 | | 4 | 5 | 6 | 7 | | | | | 12 | $10^{1}$ | 9 | 11 | 3 | | | | 2 | 1 | | | | | | | | | | | | | | | | 10 |
| | 8 | | 4 | | 6 | 7 | | | | | 12 | 10 | $9^{1}$ | 11 | 3 | 5 | | | 2 | 1 | | | | | | | | | | | | | | | | 11 |
| | 8 | | 4 | | 6 | 7 | | | 13 | | 12 | $10^{2}$ | $9^{1}$ | 11 | 3 | 5 | | | 2■ | 1 | | | | | | | | | | | | | | | | 12 |
| | 8 | | 4 | | $6^{3}$ | $7^{1}$ | | | 13 | | 9 | $10^{2}$ | 12 | 11 | 2 | 5 | | | | 1 | 3 | 14 | | | | | | | | | | | | | | 13 |
| | 8 | | 4 | | 6 | 7 | | | 14 | | $9^{2}$ | $10^{3}$ | 13 | 11 | 2 | 5 | | | 12 | 1 | $3^{1}$ | | | | | | | | | | | | | | | 14 |
| 1 | 12 | | 4 | | 6 | $7^{2}$ | | | 14 | | 13 | $10^{3}$ | 9 | 11 | 2 | | | | $8^{1}$ | | 3 | | 5 | | | | | | | | | | | | | 15 |
| 1 | | | 14 | $4^{3}$ | 6 | 7 | | | 13 | | $12^{2}$ | 10 | 9 | $11^{1}$ | 2 | 8 | | | | | 3■ | | 5 | | | | | | | | | | | | | 16 |
| 1 | 12 | | 3 | 4 | 6 | $7^{2}$ | | | | | 14 | 10 | $9^{3}$ | 11 | 2 | $8^{1}$ | | | | | | | 5 | 13 | | | | | | | | | | | | 17 |
| 1 | 12 | | | | 6 | 7 | $8^{1}$ | | 13 | | | 10 | 9 | $11^{2}$ | 2 | | | | 4 | | 3 | | 5 | | | | | | | | | | | | | 18 |
| 1 | 8 | | | | 6 | 7 | | 13 | 14 | | $9^{2}$ | $10^{3}$ | | 12 | 2 | | | | 4 | | 3 | | 5 | | $11^{1}$ | | | | | | | | | | | 19 |
| 1 | 8 | | | 13 | 6 | 7 | | | 14 | | $9^{1}$ | $10^{2}$ | | | 2 | | | | 4■ | | 3 | | 5 | 12 | $11^{3}$ | | | | | | | | | | | 20 |
| 1 | 8 | | | 2 | 6 | | | | 12 | | | $10^{1}$ | 9 | 7 | | | | | | | 3 | | 5 | 13 | $11^{2}$ | 4 | | | | | | | | | | 21 |
| 1 | 8 | | 14 | 2 | 6 | 12 | | | | | | 13 | 9 | $7^{2}$ | 10 | | | | | | 3 | | $5^{3}$ | | $11^{1}$ | 4 | | | | | | | | | | 22 |
| 1 | 8 | | | 2 | 6 | 11 | | | | | | | 9 | 7 | 10 | | | | | | 3 | | 5 | | | 4 | | | | | | | | | | 23 |
| 1 | $8^{2}$ | | | 2 | 6 | 11 | | | $10^{1}$ | | | 12 | 9 | 7■ | 3 | 13 | | | | | | | 5 | | | 4■ | | | | | | | | | | 24 |
| 1 | $8^{2}$ | | 12 | | 6 | 7 | | 10 | 13 | | | | 9 | | 11 | 4 | | | 2 | | 3 | | $5^{1}$ | | | | | | | | | | | | | 25 |
| 1 | 4 | | | | 2 | 13 | | $11^{2}$ | | | | 12 | 9 | 7 | 10 | $6^{1}$ | | | 5 | | 3 | | | | | 8 | | | | | | | | | | 26 |
| 1 | 4 | | | | 2 | 13 | | 11 | 12 | | | | 9 | $7^{2}$ | $10^{1}$ | 6 | | | 5 | | 3 | | | | | 8 | | | | | | | | | | 27 |
| 1 | 4 | | | | 2 | 7 | | 11 | 10 | | | 12 | 9 | | | $6^{1}$ | | | 5■ | | 3 | | | | | 8 | | | | | | | | | | 28 |
| | 4 | | | | 2 | 10 | | $11^{1}$ | | | | 3 | 9 | $7^{2}$ | | 8 | | 1 | | | | 12 | $5^{3}$ | 13 | | 6 | 14 | | | | | | | | | 29 |
| 1 | 4 | | | | 2 | 10 | | $11^{1}$ | 13 | | | 3 | 9 | $7^{2}$ | | 8 | | | | | 5 | | | | | 6 | | 12 | | | | | | | | 30 |
| 1 | 4 | | | | 2 | $7^{2}$ | | $11^{1}$ | | | | 14 | 9 | 13 | $10^{3}$ | | | | 5 | | 3 | | 8 | | | 6 | | 12 | | | | | | | | 31 |
| 1 | 4 | | | | 2 | $7^{1}$ | | $11^{2}$ | | | | | 9 | 12 | 10 | 14 | | | 5 | | 3 | | 8 | | | $6^{3}$ | | 13 | | | | | | | | 32 |
| 1 | $4^{1}$ | | | | 2 | 13 | | $11^{3}$ | | | | | 12 | 14 | 10 | | | | 5 | | 3 | 7 | 8 | | | 6 | | $9^{2}$ | | | | | | | | 33 |
| 1 | | | | | | 10■ | | | | | | 8 | 9 | 11 | 2 | | | | 5 | | 3 | $7^{1}$ | 4 | | | $6^{2}$ | 13 | 12 | | | | | | | | 34 |
| 1 | | | | | | | | $11^{2}$ | | | | 10 | 9 | | | 8 | | | 5 | | 3 | $7^{3}$ | $4^{1}$ | | | 6 | | | 2 | 12 | 13 | 14 | | | | 35 |
| 1 | | | | | | 10 | | | | | | $6^{2}$ | 9 | | | 8 | | | 5 | | 2 | $7^{1}$ | | | | | 3 | $11^{3}$ | 13 | | | | 4 | 12 | 14 | 36 |

# FALKIRK — First Division

*Year Formed:* 1876. *Ground & Address:* Ochilview Park, Gladstone Rd, Stenhousemuir FK5 5QL. *Telephone:* 01324 666808. *Fax:* 01324 664539.
*Ground Capacity:* total: 2374, seated: 626. *Size of Pitch:* 110yd × 72yd.
*Chairman:* Campbell Christie. *Secretary:* Alex Blackwood. *General Manager:* Crawford Baptie.
*Head Coach:* John Hughes. *Assistant Coach:* Brian Rice. *Director of Football:* Alex Totten. *Youth Co-ordinator:* Ian McIntyre.
*Managers since 1975:* J. Prentice, G. Miller, W. Little, J. Hagart, A. Totten, G. Abel, W. Lamont, D. Clarke, J. Duffy, W. Lamont, J. Jefferies, J. Lambie E. Bannon, A. Totten, I. McCall. *Club Nickname(s):* The Bairns. *Previous Grounds:* Randyford 1876-81; Blinkbonny Grounds 1881-83; Brockville Park 1883-2003.
*Record Attendance:* 23,100 v Celtic, Scottish Cup 3rd rd, 21 Feb 1953.
*Record Transfer Fee received:* £380,000 for John Hughes to Celtic (Aug 1995).
*Record Transfer Fee paid:* £225,000 to Chelsea for Kevin McAllister (Aug 1991).
*Record Victory:* 12-1 v Laurieston, Scottish Cup 2nd rd, 23 Sept 1893.
*Record Defeat:* 1-11 v Airdrieonians, Division I, 28 Apr 1951.
*Most Capped Player:* Alex Parker, 14 (15), Scotland.
*Most League Appearances:* (post-war): 353, George Watson, 1975-87.
*Most League Goals in Season (Individual):* 43: Evelyn Morrison, Division I, 1928-29.
*Most Goals Overall (Individual):* Dougie Moran, 86, 1957-61 and 1964-67.

## FALKIRK 2003–04 LEAGUE RECORD

| Match No. | Date | Venue | Opponents | Result | H/T Score | Lg. Pos. | Goalscorers | Atten-dance |
|---|---|---|---|---|---|---|---|---|
| 1 | Aug 9 | H | Inverness CT | W 2-1 | 1-1 | — | McMenamin 36, Lee 83 | 2619 |
| 2 | 16 | A | Ayr U | D 1-1 | 1-0 | 4 | Lee 18 | 2519 |
| 3 | 23 | H | Queen of the S | D 0-0 | 0-0 | 4 | | 2202 |
| 4 | 30 | A | Raith R | W 1-0 | 0-0 | 1 | O'Neil (pen) 68 | 4222 |
| 5 | Sept 13 | H | Ross Co | L 0-2 | 0-1 | 5 | | 2970 |
| 6 | 20 | A | Clyde | W 2-1 | 1-1 | 4 | Henry 2 3, 64 | 2758 |
| 7 | 27 | H | St Johnstone | L 0-3 | 0-2 | 5 | | 3887 |
| 8 | Oct 4 | A | St Mirren | D 0-0 | 0-0 | 4 | | 3105 |
| 9 | 18 | H | Brechin C | W 3-0 | 2-0 | 4 | Henry 2 8, 25, O'Neil 64 | 2442 |
| 10 | 25 | H | Ayr U | L 0-1 | 0-1 | 5 | | 2609 |
| 11 | Nov 1 | A | Inverness CT | W 2-1 | 0-0 | 4 | Lawrie 69, Lee 83 | 2223 |
| 12 | 8 | A | Ross Co | W 2-1 | 2-1 | 3 | Lawrie 6, Lee 17 | 3206 |
| 13 | 14 | H | Raith R | W 3-2 | 2-1 | 3 | Sharp 4, McMenamin 2 24, 60 | 3237 |
| 14 | 22 | A | St Johnstone | W 4-0 | 2-0 | 1 | Latapy 9, James 35, McMenamin 60, McAnespie 84 | 4185 |
| 15 | 29 | H | Clyde | L 0-2 | 0-0 | 4 | | 2898 |
| 16 | Dec 6 | A | Brechin C | D 2-2 | 0-2 | 4 | White (og) 69, Lee 82 | 1043 |
| 17 | 13 | H | St Mirren | D 0-0 | 0-0 | 4 | | 2581 |
| 18 | 27 | A | Queen of the S | L 0-2 | 0-0 | 6 | | 4075 |
| 19 | Jan 3 | A | Raith R | L 0-2 | 0-1 | 6 | | 2885 |
| 20 | 17 | H | Ross Co | W 2-0 | 1-0 | 5 | Latapy 25, Colquhoun 49 | 2482 |
| 21 | 24 | A | Clyde | L 2-4 | 0-2 | 6 | McAnespie 25, Colquhoun 44 | 3137 |
| 22 | Feb 14 | A | St Mirren | D 1-1 | 1-0 | 6 | Hughes 56 | 2934 |
| 23 | 21 | H | Brechin C | W 5-0 | 4-0 | 6 | Hughes 3, Latapy 2 10, 26, Scally 37, Lee 77 | 2060 |
| 24 | Mar 2 | H | Inverness CT | W 2-1 | 1-1 | — | Lee 9, McAnespie 76 | 2268 |
| 25 | 6 | A | Ayr U | W 3-2 | 0-1 | 3 | Lee 52, Scally 57, Nicholls 81 | 2048 |
| 26 | 9 | H | St Johnstone | L 0-1 | 0-0 | — | | 2799 |
| 27 | 13 | H | Queen of the S | L 0-2 | 0-2 | 5 | | 2098 |
| 28 | 20 | A | Ross Co | D 1-1 | 0-0 | 5 | McPherson 67 | 2931 |
| 29 | 27 | H | Raith R | W 1-0 | 1-0 | 4 | O'Neil 38 | 2386 |
| 30 | Apr 3 | A | St Johnstone | L 1-2 | 1-1 | 4 | Latapy 8 | 2535 |
| 31 | 10 | H | Clyde | D 1-1 | 0-0 | 5 | Latapy 78 | 2536 |
| 32 | 17 | A | Brechin C | W 1-0 | 0-0 | 4 | Latapy 68 | 768 |
| 33 | 24 | H | St Mirren | W 1-0 | 1-0 | 4 | O'Neil 24 | 2386 |
| 34 | May 1 | A | Inverness CT | D 0-0 | 0-0 | 4 | | 2631 |
| 35 | 8 | H | Ayr U | D 0-0 | 0-0 | 4 | | 2077 |
| 36 | 15 | A | Queen of the S | L 0-1 | 0-1 | 4 | | 2751 |

**Final League Position: 4**

**Honours**
*League Champions:* Division II 1935-36, 1969-70, 1974-75. First Division 1990-91, 1993-94, 2002-03. Second Division 1979-80; *Runners-up:* Division I 1907-08, 1909-10. First Division 1985-86, 1988-89. Division II 1904-05, 1951-52, 1960-61.
*Scottish Cup Winners:* 1913, 1957; *Runners-up:* 1997. *League Cup Runners-up:* 1947-48. *B&Q Cup Winners:* 1993-94. *League Challenge Cup Winners:* 1997-98.

**Club colours:** Shirt: Navy blue with white seams. Shorts: Navy. Stockings: Navy with two white hoops.

**Goalscorers:** *League* (43): Lee 8, Latapy 7, Henry 4, McMenamin 4, O'Neil 4 (1 pen), McAnespie 3, Colquhoun 2, Hughes 2, Lawrie 2, Scally 2, James 1, McPherson 1, Nicholls 1, Sharp 1, own goal 1
*Scottish Cup* (2): Lee 1, Xausa 1
*CIS Cup* (5): Nicholls 2, Latapy 1, McMenamin 1, Rodgers 1
*Challenge Cup* (0):

| Hill D 19 + 1 | Lawrie A 34 + 1 | McPherson C 35 | Mackenzie S 26 + 1 | Hughes J 27 | Sharp J 30 | Rahim B 19 + 7 | Nicholls D 13 + 9 | Lee J 27 + 2 | Latapy R 32 | McMenamin C 13 + 4 | McLaren A 1 + 1 | Scally N 12 + 8 | May E 2 + 2 | Rodgers A 2 + 4 | O'Neil J 30 | Xausa D 10 + 5 | McAnespie K 12 + 14 | Henry J 5 + 2 | James K 13 | Ferguson A 17 | McCluskey S 1 | Colquhoun D 7 + 8 | Christie K 2 | MacSween I 5 + 5 | McStay R 2 + 4 | Barr D — + 1 | Ramsay M — + 2 | Twaddle M — + 3 | Creaney P — + 1 | Manson S — + 1 | *Match No.* |
|---|---|---|---|---|---|---|---|---|---|---|---|---|---|---|---|---|---|---|---|---|---|---|---|---|---|---|---|---|---|---|---|
| 1 | 2 | 3 | $4^1$ | 5 | 6 | 7 | $8^2$ | 9 | 10 | 11 | 12 | 13 | | | | | | | | | | | | | | | | | | | 1 |
| 1 | 2 | 3 | | 5 | 6 | $7^1$ | 8 | 9 | 10 | $11^2$ | 4 | | 12 | 13 | | | | | | | | | | | | | | | | | 2 |
| 1 | 2 | 3 | | $5^1$ | 6 | 7 | 8 | $9^2$ | 10 | 11 | | 4 | 12 | 13 | | | | | | | | | | | | | | | | | 3 |
| 1 | 5 | 3 | | | 6 | $2^1$ | 8 | 9 | 10 | $11^3$ | | 12 | $4^2$ | 14 | 7 | 13 | | | | | | | | | | | | | | | 4 |
| 1 | 5 | | | | 6 | | 8 | 9 | 10 | | | 2 | $4^1$ | 12 | 7 | 11 | $3^2$ | 13 | | | | | | | | | | | | | 5 |
| 1 | 2 | 3 | 5 | | | 13 | $4^3$ | 12 | $10^2$ | 9 | | 14 | | $11^1$ | 7 | | | 8 | 6 | | | | | | | | | | | | 6 |
| 1 | 2 | 3 | 5 | | | 13 | $4^2$ | | 10 | $9^1$ | | | | 11 | 7 | 12 | | 8 | 6 | | | | | | | | | | | | 7 |
| | 2 | 3 | 5 | | | | 11 | | 10 | 12 | | | | | 7 | $9^1$ | | 8 | 6 | 1 | 4 | | | | | | | | | | 8 |
| | $2^3$ | 3 | 4 | 5 | | | $11^2$ | | $10^1$ | 12 | | 14 | | | 7 | 9 | 13 | 8 | 6 | 1 | | | | | | | | | | | 9 |
| | 2 | 3 | $4^1$ | 5 | | | $10^2$ | | | 11 | | 14 | | | $7^3$ | 9 | 13 | 8 | 6 | 1 | | 12 | | | | | | | | | 10 |
| | 2 | 3 | 4 | 5 | 7 | 13 | | 9 | $10^2$ | 12 | | | | | $8^3$ | $11^1$ | | 14 | 6 | 1 | | | | | | | | | | | 11 |
| | 2 | 3 | 4 | 5 | 7 | 12 | | 9 | $10^1$ | 11 | | | | | $8^2$ | | 13 | | 6 | 1 | | | | | | | | | | | 12 |
| | 2 | 3 | 4 | 5 | 7 | $6^3$ | | $9^2$ | $10^1$ | 11 | | 14 | | | 8 | | 12 | | | 1 | | 13 | | | | | | | | | 13 |
| | 2 | 3 | | $5^1$ | 7 | $4^3$ | | 9 | $10^2$ | 11 | | 14 | | | 8 | 13 | 12 | | 6 | 1 | | | | | | | | | | | 14 |
| | 2 | 3 | | | 7 | $4^3$ | 14 | 9 | $10^1$ | 11 | | $5^2$ | | | 8 | 12 | 13 | | 6 | 1 | | | | | | | | | | | 15 |
| | 2 | 3 | | | $7^1$ | 4 | 13 | 9 | | 11 | | | | | 8 | $10^2$ | 12 | | 6 | 1 | | | 5 | | | | | | | | 16 |
| | 2 | 3 | | | 4 | 7 | 12 | 9 | | 13 | | | | | 8 | $10^2$ | 11 | | $6^1$ | 1 | | | 5 | | | | | | | | 17 |
| | | 3 | 12 | 5■ | $4^1$ | 2 | | 9 | 10 | $11^2$ | | | | | 7 | | 8 | | 6 | 1 | | 13 | | | | | | | | | 18 |
| 12 | 5 | 3 | | | | $2^2$ | | 9 | 10 | | | $4^1$ | | | 7 | 8 | 11 | | 6 | 1 | | 13 | | | | | | | | | 19 |
| 1 | 2 | 3 | 4 | 5 | 6 | | | | $10^3$ | | | 13 | | | $7^2$ | $8^1$ | 11 | | | | | 9 | | 12 | 14 | | | | | | 20 |
| 1 | 2 | 3 | 4 | 5 | 6 | 12 | | 13 | 10 | | | | | | $7^2$ | 8 | $11^1$ | | | | | 9 | | | | | | | | | 21 |
| | 2 | 3 | 4 | 5 | 6 | 12 | 14 | 9 | 10 | | | | | | $7^3$ | 13 | $11^1$ | | | 1 | | $8^2$ | | | | | | | | | 22 |
| | $2^2$ | 3 | 4 | 5 | $6^1$ | 8 | 12 | $9^3$ | 10 | | | 11 | | | 7 | | 13 | | | 1 | | 14 | | | | | | | | | 23 |
| | 2 | 3 | 4 | 5 | 6 | $8^1$ | 13 | 9 | $10^3$ | | | 11 | | | $7^2$ | | 12 | | | 1 | | | | 14 | | | | | | | 24 |
| 1 | 2 | 3 | 4 | 5 | 6 | 13 | $8^2$ | 9 | $10^1$ | | | 11 | | | 7 | | 12 | | | | | | | | | | | | | | 25 |
| 1 | 2 | $3^2$ | $4^3$ | 5 | 6 | | $8^1$ | 9 | 10 | | | 11 | | | 7 | | 12 | | | | | 14 | | 13 | | | | | | | 26 |
| 1 | $2^3$ | 3 | 4 | 5 | 6 | | $8^1$ | 9 | 10 | | | 11 | | | | | 12 | | | | | $7^2$ | | 13 | | 14 | | | | | 27 |
| 1 | 2 | 3 | 4 | 5 | 6 | $8^1$ | | 9 | 10 | | | 11 | | | 7 | | 12 | | | | | | | | | | | | | | 28 |
| 1 | 12 | 3 | 4 | 5 | 6 | $2^1$ | | $9^2$ | 10 | | | 11 | | | 7 | | 8 | | | | | 13 | | | | | | | | | 29 |
| | 2 | 3 | $4^3$ | 5 | 6 | 8 | 12 | $9^2$ | 10 | | | | | | 7 | | $11^1$ | | | 1 | | 13 | | 14 | | | | | | | 30 |
| | 2 | 3 | 4 | 5 | 6 | $8^1$ | 12 | | 10 | | | | | | 7 | | | | | 1 | | 9 | | 11 | | | | | | | 31 |
| 1 | 2 | 3 | 4 | 5 | 6 | $8^2$ | 12 | | 10 | | | | | | 7 | | | | | | | $9^1$ | | $11^3$ | 13 | | 14 | | | | 32 |
| 1 | 2 | $3^3$ | 4 | 5 | 6 | $8^1$ | | 9 | 10 | | | | | | $7^2$ | | 12 | | | | | | | 11 | 13 | | | 14 | | | 33 |
| 1 | 2 | 3 | 4 | 5 | 6 | | | 9 | 10 | | | 7 | | | | | $8^1$ | | | | | | | $11^2$ | 13 | | | | 12 | | 34 |
| 1 | 2 | 3 | 4 | 5 | 6 | | | 9 | 10 | | | | | | | | 8 | | | | | | | $11^1$ | 7 | | | 12 | | | 35 |
| 1 | 2 | 3 | 4 | 5 | 6 | | | $9^3$ | | | | | | | 7 | | $11^2$ | | | | | $10^1$ | | | 8 | | 13 | 12 | | 14 | 36 |

# FORFAR ATHLETIC — Second Division

*Year Formed:* 1885. *Ground & Address:* Station Park, Carseview Road, Forfar. *Telephone:* 01307 463576/462259. *Fax:* 01307 466956.
*Ground Capacity:* total: 4640, seated: 739. *Size of Pitch:* 115yd × 69yd.
*Chairman and Secretary:* David McGregor.
*Manager:* Raymond Stewart. *Assistant Manager:* Ian Miller. *Coaches:* Peter Castle, Donald Ritchie. *Physio:* Brian McNeil.
*Managers since 1975:* Jerry Kerr, Archie Knox, Alex Rae, Doug Houston, Henry Hall, Bobby Glennie, Paul Hegarty, Tommy Campbell, Ian McPhee, Neil Cooper. *Club Nickname(s):* Loons. *Previous Grounds:* None.
*Record Attendance:* 10,780 v Rangers, Scottish Cup 2nd rd, 2 Feb 1970.
*Record Transfer Fee received:* £65,000 for David Bingham to Dunfermline Ath (September 1995).
*Record Transfer Fee paid:* £50,000 for Ian McPhee from Airdrieonians (1991).
*Record Victory:* 14-1 v Lindertis, Scottish Cup 1st rd, 1 Sept 1988.
*Record Defeat:* 2-12 v King's Park, Division II, 2 Jan 1930.
*Most League Appearances:* 484: Ian McPhee, 1978-88 and 1991-98.
*Most League Goals in Season (Individual):* 45: Dave Kilgour, Division II, 1929-30.
*Most Goals Overall (Individual):* 124, John Clark.

## FORFAR ATHLETIC 2003–04 LEAGUE RECORD

| Match No. | Date | Venue | Opponents | Result | H/T Score | Lg. Pos. | Goalscorers | Attendance |
|---|---|---|---|---|---|---|---|---|
| 1 | Aug 9 | A | Hamilton A | W 2-1 | 0-0 | — | Tosh [59], Shields [60] | 1271 |
| 2 | 16 | H | East Fife | L 0-1 | 0-0 | 6 | | 708 |
| 3 | 23 | A | Arbroath | D 0-0 | 0-0 | 5 | | 856 |
| 4 | 30 | A | Stenhousemuir | L 0-2 | 0-1 | 9 | | 383 |
| 5 | Sept 13 | H | Morton | L 2-3 | 2-2 | 9 | Davidson [4], Henderson [14] | 1006 |
| 6 | 20 | H | Dumbarton | W 3-1 | 1-0 | 7 | Tosh [4], Henderson [56], Shields [83] | 449 |
| 7 | 27 | A | Alloa Ath | D 1-1 | 0-1 | 6 | Tosh [85] | 378 |
| 8 | Oct 4 | H | Airdrie U | D 1-1 | 0-0 | 8 | Sellars [63] | 650 |
| 9 | 18 | A | Berwick R | W 4-0 | 1-0 | 5 | Tosh 2 [38, 52], Shields [77], Taylor [89] | 423 |
| 10 | 25 | A | East Fife | W 3-2 | 2-2 | 4 | Shields 2 [32, 42], Tosh [76] | 671 |
| 11 | Nov 1 | H | Hamilton A | W 4-3 | 0-2 | 3 | Taylor [47], Tosh 2 [66, 82], Rattray [90] | 558 |
| 12 | 8 | A | Morton | D 1-1 | 1-1 | 4 | Henderson [20] | 3327 |
| 13 | 16 | H | Stenhousemuir | W 2-0 | 1-0 | 2 | McCulloch G (og) [2], Tosh [46] | 478 |
| 14 | Dec 6 | H | Alloa Ath | D 1-1 | 0-0 | 3 | Davidson [90] | 502 |
| 15 | 13 | A | Airdrie U | D 3-3 | 1-1 | 3 | Sellars [36], Davidson [52], Tosh [59] | 1072 |
| 16 | 27 | H | Berwick R | L 1-5 | 1-3 | 5 | Tosh [8] | 603 |
| 17 | Jan 10 | A | Dumbarton | L 1-2 | 1-1 | 6 | Lunan [17] | 781 |
| 18 | 20 | A | Hamilton A | L 1-2 | 0-2 | — | Ferry M [71] | 1099 |
| 19 | 24 | H | Dumbarton | W 1-0 | 1-0 | 4 | Tosh [24] | 540 |
| 20 | 31 | A | Alloa Ath | L 0-4 | 0-2 | 4 | | 321 |
| 21 | Feb 7 | H | Morton | W 2-1 | 1-1 | 4 | Ferry M [13], Tosh [67] | 958 |
| 22 | 14 | A | Stenhousemuir | W 2-0 | 0-0 | 4 | Shields [75], Ferry M [77] | 335 |
| 23 | 21 | A | Berwick R | L 1-3 | 1-1 | 5 | Tosh [14] | 435 |
| 24 | Mar 6 | H | East Fife | W 1-0 | 0-0 | 5 | Tosh [68] | 600 |
| 25 | 13 | A | Arbroath | W 1-0 | 1-0 | 5 | Henderson [24] | 702 |
| 26 | 16 | H | Arbroath | D 2-2 | 1-1 | — | Tosh 2 [18, 78] | 682 |
| 27 | 23 | H | Airdrie U | L 1-3 | 1-2 | — | Ferry M [22] | 710 |
| 28 | 27 | H | Stenhousemuir | D 1-1 | 1-0 | 5 | Rattray [35] | 407 |
| 29 | Apr 6 | A | Morton | D 1-1 | 1-0 | — | McClune [32] | 2453 |
| 30 | 10 | A | Dumbarton | D 1-1 | 1-0 | 5 | Maher [23] | 1007 |
| 31 | 13 | H | Alloa Ath | W 2-0 | 2-0 | — | Shields 2 [10, 38] | 411 |
| 32 | 17 | H | Berwick R | L 0-2 | 0-1 | 5 | | 465 |
| 33 | 24 | A | Airdrie U | D 2-2 | 1-0 | 5 | Davidson [35], Shields [73] | 1959 |
| 34 | May 1 | H | Arbroath | L 1-2 | 1-1 | 6 | Tosh [25] | 707 |
| 35 | 8 | A | East Fife | L 0-2 | 0-0 | 6 | | 448 |
| 36 | 15 | H | Hamilton A | L 0-4 | 0-1 | 6 | | 1496 |

**Final League Position: 6**

**Honours**
*League Champions:* Second Division 1983-84. Third Division 1994-95; *Runners-up:* 1996-97. C Division 1948-49.
*Scottish Cup:* Semi-finals 1982; Quarter-finals 2002.
*League Cup:* Semi-finals 1977-78.

**Club colours:** Shirt: Navy with sky blue side panels. Shorts: Sky blue with navy side panels. Stockings: Sky blue with navy tops.

**Goalscorers:** *League* (49): Tosh 18, Shields 9, Davidson 4, Ferry M 4, Henderson 4, Rattray 2, Sellars 2, Taylor 2, Lunan 1, McClune 1, Maher 1, own goal 1
*Scottish Cup* (4): Tosh 3 (1 pen), Rattray 1
*CIS Cup* (4): Henderson 2, Tosh 2
*Challenge Cup* (8): Shields 4, Maher 2, Davidson 1, Tosh 1

| Ferrie N 4 + 2 | Rattray A 23 | Lowing D 16 + 5 | Horn R 28 | Stewart D 11 | McClune D 28 + 1 | Lunan P 29 + 2 | Sellars B 28 + 1 | Tosh P 31 + 1 | Davidson H 33 + 1 | Shields P 25 + 8 | Maher M 11 + 17 | Henderson D 25 + 1 | Florence S 8 + 6 | Brown M 32 | Taylor S 3 + 10 | Byers K 20 + 5 | Vella S 4 | Williams D 1 + 6 | Ogunmade D 2 + 3 | Forbes B — + 1 | Ferry M 11 + 7 | King M 11 + 5 | MacNicol S 12 | Bremner C — + 1 | *Match No.* |
|---|---|---|---|---|---|---|---|---|---|---|---|---|---|---|---|---|---|---|---|---|---|---|---|---|---|
| 1 | 2 | $3^{3}$ | 4 | 5 | $6^{1}$ | $7^{2}$ | 8 | 9 | 10 | 11 | 12 | 13 | 14 | | | | | | | | | | | | 1 |
| | 2■ | 3 | 4■ | 5 | 6 | $7^{1}$ | $8^{2}$ | | 10 | 11 | 12 | | | 1 | 9 | 13 | | | | | | | | | 2 |
| | | 3 | | 5 | 6 | 2 | | 9 | 10 | 11 | $7^{1}$ | | | 1 | 12 | 8 | 4 | | | | | | | | 3 |
| | | $3^{3}$ | | 5 | 6 | $2^{2}$ | | 9 | 10 | 11 | $7^{1}$ | 8 | 13 | 1 | 12 | | 4 | 14 | | | | | | | 4 |
| | | $3^{1}$ | | 5 | 6 | 2 | | 9 | 8 | $11^{3}$ | 14 | $10^{2}$ | 12 | 1 | | 13 | 4 | | 7 | | | | | | 5 |
| | 3 | 12 | | 5 | 4 | $2^{2}$ | 13 | $9^{3}$ | 8 | 11 | 14 | 10 | | 1 | | 6 | | | $7^{1}$ | | | | | | 6 |
| | 4 | 3 | | 5 | | $2^{2}$ | 7 | 9 | 8 | 11 | 13 | $10^{3}$ | | 1 | 14 | $6^{1}$ | | | 12 | | | | | | 7 |
| | 2 | 3 | 4 | 5 | | | 7 | $9^{2}$ | 8 | $11^{1}$ | | 10 | | 1 | 12 | 6 | | | 13 | | | | | | 8 |
| | 3 | | 4 | 5 | | 2 | 7 | $9^{3}$ | 8 | $11^{2}$ | 12 | $10^{1}$ | | 1 | 13 | 6 | | 14 | | | | | | | 9 |
| | 3 | | $4^{2}$ | 5 | | 2 | 7 | 9 | 8 | 11 | | $10^{1}$ | 13 | 1 | | 6 | | | 12 | | | | | | 10 |
| 13 | 3 | | | 5■ | 4 | $2^{1}$ | 7 | 9 | 8 | | 12 | 10 | | 1■ | $11^{2}$ | 6 | | | | | | | | | 11 |
| 1 | 3 | | 5 | | 4 | 2 | 7 | 9 | 8 | 12 | | 10 | | | $11^{1}$ | 6 | | | | | | | | | 12 |
| | 3 | | 5 | | 4 | 2 | 7 | 9 | 8 | $11^{1}$ | | 10 | | 1 | 12 | 6 | | | | | | | | | 13 |
| | | 12 | 5 | | 4 | 2 | 7 | 9 | 8 | $11^{2}$ | 3 | 10 | | 1 | | $6^{1}$ | | 13 | | | | | | | 14 |
| | 3 | 13 | 5 | | 4 | 2 | $7^{1}$ | 9 | 8 | $11^{3}$ | 12 | $10^{2}$ | | 1 | 14 | 6 | | | | | | | | | 15 |
| | 3 | 14 | 4 | | 10 | 2 | 7 | 9 | 8 | $11^{2}$ | 12 | | | 1 | 13 | $6^{3}$ | $5^{1}$ | | | | | | | | 16 |
| | $2^{1}$ | 3 | 4 | | 5 | 10 | 6 | 9 | 8 | $11^{2}$ | $7^{3}$ | | | 1 | 13 | 12 | | | | 14 | | | | | 17 |
| 13 | 3 | 12 | 5 | | 4 | 2 | 7 | 9 | 8 | 14 | | $10^{1}$ | | $1^{2}$ | | | | | | | 6 | $11^{3}$ | | | 18 |
| 1 | | 3 | 5 | | 4 | $2^{1}$ | | 9 | 8 | 14 | 12 | $10^{2}$ | 13 | | | 7 | | | | | 6 | $11^{3}$ | | | 19 |
| 1 | 2 | 3 | 5 | | 4 | 13 | | 9 | 8 | 12 | | $10^{2}$ | | | 14 | $7^{1}$ | | | | | 6 | $11^{3}$ | | | 20 |
| | $2^{1}$ | | 5 | | 4 | 3 | 7 | 9 | 8 | 13 | | 10 | | 1 | | 12 | | | | | 6 | $11^{2}$ | | | 21 |
| | 2 | | 5 | | | $3^{2}$ | 7 | 9 | 8 | 12 | 13 | 10 | | 1 | | 4 | | | | | 6 | $11^{1}$ | | | 22 |
| | 2 | | 5 | | | 3 | 7 | 9 | 8 | 13 | 12 | $10^{3}$ | | 1 | | $4^{1}$ | | 14 | | | 6 | $11^{2}$ | | | 23 |
| | | | 5 | | 3 | $2^{2}$ | 7 | 9 | 8 | 11 | 13 | 10 | 12 | 1 | | $4^{1}$ | | | | | 6 | | | | 24 |
| | | | 5 | | 4 | 2 | 7 | 9 | 8 | $11^{1}$ | | 10 | | 1 | | | | | | | 6 | 12 | 3 | | 25 |
| | 2 | | 5 | | 4 | | 7 | 9 | $8^{2}$ | | 13 | 10 | | 1 | | 6 | | | | | 12 | $11^{1}$ | 3 | | 26 |
| | 2 | | 5 | | 12 | $4^{1}$ | 7 | 9 | 8 | 14 | 13 | | | 1 | | $10^{2}$ | | | | | 6 | $11^{3}$ | 3 | | 27 |
| | 2 | | 5 | | | 12 | 7 | 9 | | | 8 | $10^{1}$ | 4 | 1 | | | | | | | 6 | 11 | 3 | | 28 |
| | 5 | | | | 6 | 4 | 7 | | | 9 | 11 | 10 | 3 | 1 | | | | 12 | | | | $8^{1}$ | 2 | | 29 |
| | $5^{2}$ | | | | 6 | 4 | 7 | | 12 | 9 | 11 | $10^{1}$ | 3 | 1 | | | | 14 | | | 13 | $8^{3}$ | 2 | | 30 |
| | | 10 | 5 | | 6 | 4 | 7 | | $8^{1}$ | 9 | 11 | | 3 | 1 | | | | | | | 12 | | 2 | | 31 |
| | | $10^{1}$ | 5 | | 6 | 4 | 7 | 12 | 8 | $9^{3}$ | 11 | | | 1 | | 13 | | | | | $3^{2}$ | 14 | 2 | | 32 |
| | | $6^{2}$ | 5 | | 11 | $4^{1}$ | 7 | 9 | 8 | 10 | 12 | | 3 | 1 | | | | | | | 13 | | 2 | | 33 |
| | | 5 | 4 | | 6 | | $7^{2}$ | 9 | $8^{1}$ | 10 | 11 | | 3 | 1 | | | | | | | 13 | 12 | 2 | | 34 |
| | | 11 | 4 | | $6^{3}$ | | | 9 | 8 | 10 | $7^{2}$ | | 5 | 1 | | | | $3^{1}$ | | | 12 | 13 | 2 | 14 | 35 |
| | | 5 | 4 | | 7 | | | 9 | $8^{1}$ | 11 | 13 | $10^{3}$ | 3 | 1 | | $6^{2}$ | | | | | 14 | 12 | 2 | | 36 |

# GRETNA Third Division

*Year Formed:* 1946. *Ground & Address:* Raydale Park, Dominion Rd, Gretna DG16 5AP. *Telephone:* 01461 337602. *Fax:* 01461 338047. *e-mail:* info@gretnafootballclub.co.uk.
*Ground Capacity:* 2200.
*Club Shop:* Alan Watson, 01387 251550.
*President:* Brian Fulton. *Chairman:* Ron MacGregor. *Secretary:* Helen MacGregor. *Managing Director:* Brookes Mileson. *General Manager:* Colin Carter.
*Manager:* Rowan Alexander. *Assistant Manager:* David Irons. *Coaches:* Danny Lennon, Leigh Manson. *Physios:* William Bentley & Gael Moffat.
*Record Attendance:* 2307 v Rochdale, FA Cup, 16 Nov 1991.
*Record Victory:* 20-0 v Silloth, 1962.
*Record Defeat:* 0-6 v Worksop Town, 1994-95 and 0-6 v Bradford (Park Avenue) 1999-2000.
*Most League Appearances:* 69, David Irons, 2002-04.
*Most League Goals in Season (Individual):* 17, M. Cameron, 2003-04.
*Most Goals Overall (Individual):* 17, M. Cameron, 2003-04.

## GRETNA 2003–04 LEAGUE RECORD

| *Match No.* | *Date* | *Venue* | *Opponents* | *Result* | | *H/T Score* | *Lg. Pos.* | *Goalscorers* | *Attendance* |
|---|---|---|---|---|---|---|---|---|---|
| 1 | Aug 9 | H | Queen's Park | D | 1-1 | 0-0 | — | Cameron [84] | 420 |
| 2 | 16 | A | Peterhead | L | 0-2 | 0-2 | 9 | | 464 |
| 3 | 23 | H | Stranraer | D | 1-1 | 0-0 | 8 | Birch [67] | 367 |
| 4 | 30 | H | Albion R | W | 3-1 | 2-0 | 4 | Cameron 3 (1 pen) [31, 35, 76 (p)] | 385 |
| 5 | Sept 13 | A | Elgin C | D | 3-3 | 2-2 | 7 | Cameron 2 [38, 41], McGuffie [65] | 529 |
| 6 | 20 | A | Cowdenbeath | W | 1-0 | 0-0 | 4 | Mowat (og) [70] | 235 |
| 7 | 27 | H | Stirling A | L | 0-1 | 0-0 | 6 | | 482 |
| 8 | Oct 4 | H | Montrose | D | 1-1 | 1-1 | 6 | Cameron [11] | 356 |
| 9 | 18 | A | East Stirling | W | 1-0 | 0-0 | 5 | Stevens [55] | 198 |
| 10 | 25 | H | Peterhead | W | 3-2 | 0-1 | 4 | Cameron 2 [46, 89], Skelton [74] | 425 |
| 11 | Nov 1 | A | Queen's Park | W | 1-0 | 0-0 | 3 | Cameron [80] | 522 |
| 12 | 8 | H | Elgin C | D | 2-2 | 2-1 | 3 | Cameron 2 (1 pen) [32 (p), 40] | 451 |
| 13 | 14 | A | Albion R | W | 3-1 | 1-0 | 3 | Stevens 2 [27, 66], Skelton [47] | 357 |
| 14 | Dec 2 | H | Cowdenbeath | W | 1-0 | 1-0 | — | Baldacchino [8] | 401 |
| 15 | 6 | A | Stirling A | W | 1-0 | 1-0 | 3 | Stevens [11] | 682 |
| 16 | 13 | A | Montrose | L | 0-2 | 0-2 | 4 | | 438 |
| 17 | 27 | H | East Stirling | W | 2-1 | 0-0 | 3 | Gordon [50], Stevens [77] | 532 |
| 18 | Jan 3 | A | Stranraer | W | 2-1 | 1-0 | 3 | Birch [31], Galloway [76] | 534 |
| 19 | 17 | H | Queen's Park | L | 0-1 | 0-0 | 3 | | 419 |
| 20 | 24 | A | Cowdenbeath | W | 2-1 | 1-1 | 3 | Stevens [38], Galloway [80] | 290 |
| 21 | Feb 7 | A | Elgin C | D | 1-1 | 1-0 | 3 | Baldacchino [18] | 383 |
| 22 | 14 | H | Albion R | W | 3-0 | 3-0 | 3 | Cameron [2], Stevens [29], Townsley [39] | 418 |
| 23 | 21 | A | East Stirling | W | 4-2 | 2-1 | 3 | Cameron 3 [2, 74, 76], Galloway [20] | 187 |
| 24 | 28 | H | Montrose | L | 1-2 | 1-0 | 3 | Cameron [6] | 635 |
| 25 | Mar 2 | H | Stirling A | W | 1-0 | 1-0 | — | Wake [32] | 758 |
| 26 | 6 | A | Peterhead | L | 1-2 | 1-0 | 3 | Townsley [27] | 556 |
| 27 | 13 | H | Stranraer | D | 0-0 | 0-0 | 3 | | 736 |
| 28 | 20 | H | Elgin C | W | 2-1 | 2-1 | 3 | Maddison [10], Irons [40] | 360 |
| 29 | 27 | A | Albion R | W | 2-1 | 2-1 | 3 | Baldacchino [7], Stevens [25] | 287 |
| 30 | Apr 3 | A | Stirling A | W | 1-0 | 1-0 | 3 | Townsley [26] | 678 |
| 31 | 10 | H | Cowdenbeath | L | 0-1 | 0-0 | 3 | | 429 |
| 32 | 17 | H | East Stirling | W | 5-1 | 3-0 | 3 | McGhee (og) [5], Stevens [38], Townsley 3 [40, 75, 90] | 311 |
| 33 | 24 | A | Montrose | W | 4-1 | 2-0 | 3 | Wake 2 [6, 48], Townsley 2 [40, 84] | 395 |
| 34 | May 1 | A | Stranraer | L | 2-3 | 1-1 | 3 | Townsley [17], Wake [85] | 697 |
| 35 | 8 | H | Peterhead | W | 3-2 | 3-0 | 3 | Birch [27], Baldacchino [31], Stevens [33] | 418 |
| 36 | 15 | A | Queen's Park | D | 1-1 | 0-1 | 3 | Wake [87] | 541 |

**Final League Position: 3**

**Club colours:** Shirt: White with black detail. Shorts: White. Stockings: White topped with black hoops.

**Goalscorers:** *League* (59): Cameron 17 (2 pens), Stevens 10, Townsley 9, Wake 5, Baldacchino 4, Birch 3, Galloway 3, Skelton 2, Gordon 1, Irons 1, McGuffie 1, Maddison 1, own goals 2
*Scottish Cup* (9): Sevens 3, Skelton 2, Baldacchino 1, Cohen 1, Gordon 1, Holdsworth 1
*CIS Cup* (1): McGuffie 1
*Challenge Cup* (0):

| Mathieson D 35 | Knox K 2 + 1 | Skelton G 30 + 1 | Prokas R 27 + 3 | O'Neill P 2 | Holdsworth D 27 | Skinner S 1 | Galloway M 34 + 1 | Cameron M 24 + 2 | Cohen G 14 + 12 | Allan J 2 + 4 | McGuffie R 19 + 7 | Gordon W 4 + 15 | Robb R 1 | Grainger D 1 | Irons D 32 + 1 | Cosgrove S — + 4 | Birch M 23 | Baldacchino R 33 | Hore J 1 | Eccles M 5 + 5 | Maddison L 29 | Stevens I 23 + 5 | Wake B 6 + 5 | Lennon D 3 + 4 | Townsley D 15 | May K 1 + 2 | Summersgill C 1 | Spence C 1 | Match No. |
|---|---|---|---|---|---|---|---|---|---|---|---|---|---|---|---|---|---|---|---|---|---|---|---|---|---|---|---|---|---|
| 1 | 2 | 3 | 4 | 5 | 6 | 7² | 8 | 9 | 10 | 11¹ | 12 | 13 | | | | | | | | | | | | | | | | | 1 |
| 1 | 7 | 11³ | 4 | 5² | 6 | | 8 | 9 | 10 | | | 12 | 2 | 3¹ | 13 | 14 | | | | | | | | | | | | | 2 |
| 1 | | 3 | | | 6 | | 8 | 9 | 10 | | 4 | | | | 5 | | 2 | 7 | 11¹ | 12 | | | | | | | | | 3 |
| 1 | | 13 | | | 6 | | 8 | 9 | 10 | | 4¹ | | | | 5 | 12 | 2 | 7 | | 11² | 3 | | | | | | | | 4 |
| 1 | | 3 | | | 6 | | 8³ | 9 | 7² | 12 | 4 | 13 | | | 5 | 14 | 2 | | | 11¹ | | 10■ | | | | | | | 5 |
| 1 | 13 | | | | 6 | | 8 | 9 | 10² | | 4 | 12 | | | 5 | | 2 | 7 | | 11¹ | 3 | | | | | | | | 6 |
| 1 | | | 13 | | 6 | | 8 | 9 | 14 | | 4² | 10 | | | 5 | | 2 | 7 | | 11¹ | 3³ | 12 | | | | | | | 7 |
| 1 | | 11 | 4 | | 6 | | 8 | 9 | | | | 10¹ | | | 5 | | 2 | 7 | | | 3 | 12 | | | | | | | 8 |
| 1 | | 11 | 4 | | 6 | | 8 | 9¹ | 12 | | | 13 | | | 5 | | 2 | 7 | | | 3 | 10² | | | | | | | 9 |
| 1 | | 11² | 4 | | 6 | | 8¹ | 9 | | | 12 | | | | 5 | | 2 | 7 | | 13 | 3 | 10 | | | | | | | 10 |
| 1 | | 11¹ | 4 | | 6 | | 8 | 9² | | 13 | | 12 | | | 5 | | 2 | 7 | | | 3 | 10 | | | | | | | 11 |
| 1 | | 11 | 4 | | 6 | | 8 | 9 | | | | 12 | | | 5 | | 2 | 7 | | | 3 | 10¹ | | | | | | | 12 |
| 1 | | 11 | 4 | | 6 | | 8 | 9¹ | | 12 | | | | | 5 | | 2 | 7 | | | 3 | 10 | | | | | | | 13 |
| 1 | | 11 | 4 | | 6 | | 8 | 9 | | | | | | | 5 | | 2 | 7 | | | 3 | 10 | | | | | | | 14 |
| 1 | | 11 | 4 | | 6 | | 8 | 9¹ | | 12 | 13 | | | | 5 | | 2 | 7² | | | 3 | 10 | | | | | | | 15 |
| 1 | | 11 | 4 | | 6 | | 8 | | 13 | 9² | 12 | | | | 5■ | | 2 | 7¹ | | | 3 | 10 | | | | | | | 16 |
| 1 | | 11 | 4 | | 6 | | 8 | | 10 | | 5 | 12 | | | | | 2 | 7 | | | 3¹ | 9 | | | | | | | 17 |
| 1 | | 3 | 4 | | 6 | | 8 | | 10¹ | | 14 | 11³ | | | 5 | 13 | 2 | 7² | | | | 9 | 12 | | | | | | 18 |
| 1 | | 11 | 4¹ | | 6 | | 8 | 13 | 10³ | | | 14 | | | 5 | | 2 | 7 | | | 3 | 9² | | 12 | | | | | 19 |
| 1 | | 11 | 4 | | 6 | | 8 | 12 | 10¹ | | 2 | | | | 5 | | | 7 | | | 3 | 9 | | | | | | | 20 |
| 1 | | 11 | 4 | | | | 8 | 9 | | | 2 | | | | 5 | | | 7 | | | 3 | 10 | | | 6 | | | | 21 |
| 1 | | | 13 | | 6 | | 8² | 9¹ | 12 | | 2 | | | | 5 | | | 7 | | | 3 | 10 | | 4 | 11 | | | | 22 |
| 1 | | | | | 6 | | 8 | 9 | 12 | | 2 | | | | 5 | | | 7 | | | 3 | 10¹ | | 4 | 11 | | | | 23 |
| 1 | | | | | 6 | | 8 | 9¹ | 12 | | 2 | 13 | | | 5 | | | 7 | | | 3 | 10 | | 4 | 11² | | | | 24 |
| 1 | | 11 | 4 | | 6■ | | 8 | 9² | 12 | | 2 | 13 | | | 5 | | | 7 | | | 3 | | 10¹ | | | | | | 25 |
| 1 | | 11 | 4 | | | | 8 | 9 | 13 | | 2² | | | | 5 | | | 7 | | | 3 | 12 | 10¹ | | 6 | | | | 26 |
| 1 | | 11 | 4 | | | | 8 | 9 | 12 | | 2 | | | | 5 | | | 7 | | | 3 | | 10¹ | | 6 | | | | 27 |
| 1 | | 11 | 4 | | | | 8 | 9² | 12 | | 2 | | | | 5 | | | 7 | | | 3 | 13 | 10¹ | | 6 | | | | 28 |
| 1 | | 11 | 4 | | 6 | | 8 | 9¹ | 10² | | | | | | 5 | | | 7 | | | 3³ | 12 | 13 | 14 | 2 | | | | 29 |
| 1 | | 11 | 4 | | | | 8 | | 10³ | | 12 | | | | 5 | | 2 | 7 | | | 3 | 9² | 13 | 14 | 6¹ | | | | 30 |
| 1 | | 11² | 4 | | | | 8 | | 10¹ | | 14 | 13 | | | 5 | | 2³ | 7 | | | 3 | 9 | 12■ | | 6 | | | | 31 |
| 1 | | 11¹ | 4 | | | | 8³ | | | | 10 | 13 | | | 5 | | 2 | 7² | | 12 | 3 | 9 | | 14 | 6 | | | | 32 |
| 1 | | 3 | 4 | | | | | | 14 | | 6 | 11¹ | | | 5 | | 2² | 7 | | 12 | | 9³ | 10 | | 8 | 13 | | | 33 |
| 1 | | 11³ | 4 | | | | 12 | | | | 8² | 14 | | | 5 | | 2 | 7¹ | | | 3 | 9 | 10 | | 6 | 13 | | | 34 |
| 1 | | 11¹ | 4 | | 6 | | 8 | | 13 | | | | | | 5 | | 2 | 7 | | 12 | 3 | 9² | | | 10 | | | | 35 |
| | | 3 | 14 | | 6 | | 8 | | 9¹ | | 2 | 13 | | | | | | 7 | | 11³ | | | 12 | | 10 | 5 | 1 | 4² | 36 |

# HAMILTON ACADEMICAL First Division

*Year Formed:* 1874. *Ground:* New Douglas Park, Cadzow Avenue, Hamilton ML3 0FT. *Telephone:* 01698 368650. *Fax:* 01698 285422. *Ground Capacity:* 5396. *Size of Pitch:* 115yd × 75yd.
*Chairman:* Ronnie MacDonald. *Chief Executive:* George W. Fairley. *Secretary:* Scott A. Struthers BA. *Commercial Director:* Arthur Lynch.
*Manager:* Allan Maitland. *Assistant Manager:* Denis McDaid. *First Team Coach:* Jimmy McQuade. *Coach:* James Ward. *Physio:* Michael Valentine.
*Managers since 1975:* J. Eric Smith, Dave McParland, John Blackley, Bertie Auld, John Lambie, Jim Dempsey, John Lambie, Billy McLaren, Iain Munro, Sandy Clark, Colin Miller, Ally Dawson, Chris Hillcoat. *Club Nickname(s):* The Accies. *Previous Grounds:* Bent Farm, South Avenue, South Haugh, Douglas Park, Cliftonhill Stadium, Firhill Stadium.
*Record Attendance:* 28,690 v Hearts, Scottish Cup 3rd rd, 3 Mar 1937.
*Record Transfer Fee received:* £380,000 for Paul Hartley to Millwall (July 1996).
*Record Transfer Fee paid:* £60,000 for Paul Martin from Kilmarnock (Oct 1988) and for John McQuade from Dumbarton (Aug 1993).
*Record Victory:* 11-1 v Chryston, Lanarkshire Cup, 28 Nov 1885.
*Record Defeat:* 1-11 v Hibernian, Division I, 6 Nov 1965.
*Most Capped Player:* Colin Miller, 29, Canada, 1988-94.

## HAMILTON ACADEMICAL 2003–04 LEAGUE RECORD

| Match No. | Date | Venue | Opponents | Result | | H/T Score | Lg. Pos. | Goalscorers | Atten-dance |
|---|---|---|---|---|---|---|---|---|---|
| 1 | Aug 9 | H | Forfar Ath | L | 1-2 | 0-0 | — | McPhee 53 | 1271 |
| 2 | 16 | A | Berwick R | L | 1-3 | 0-1 | 9 | Whiteford 52 | 552 |
| 3 | 23 | H | Airdrie U | W | 2-1 | 1-0 | 7 | Carrigan 33, Convery 50 | 2007 |
| 4 | 30 | A | Arbroath | D | 2-2 | 1-1 | 8 | Carrigan 32, Thomson 82 | 650 |
| 5 | Sept 13 | H | Stenhousemuir | W | 2-0 | 0-0 | 5 | Hodge 71, Aitken 73 | 934 |
| 6 | 20 | A | Morton | D | 1-1 | 1-0 | 5 | Convery 42 | 3225 |
| 7 | 27 | H | East Fife | D | 2-2 | 1-0 | 5 | Bailey 39, Waddell A 89 | 1123 |
| 8 | Oct 4 | H | Alloa Ath | L | 3-4 | 0-3 | 6 | Aitken 46, Carrigan 47, Corcoran 85 | 1016 |
| 9 | 18 | A | Dumbarton | W | 3-0 | 1-0 | 6 | Corcoran 25, Quitongo 51, Thomson 70 | 890 |
| 10 | 25 | H | Berwick R | D | 2-2 | 0-1 | 6 | Aitken 75, Carrigan 77 | 1143 |
| 11 | Nov 1 | A | Forfar Ath | L | 3-4 | 2-0 | 6 | Carrigan 33, Quitongo 36, Bailey (pen) 88 | 558 |
| 12 | 8 | A | Stenhousemuir | W | 3-0 | 0-0 | 6 | McPhee 3 (2 pens) 49 (p), 52, 90 (p) | 576 |
| 13 | 22 | H | Arbroath | W | 2-0 | 0-0 | 6 | Carrigan 2 46, 55 | 1286 |
| 14 | Dec 2 | H | Morton | L | 1-2 | 0-1 | — | Carrigan (pen) 65 | 1905 |
| 15 | 6 | A | East Fife | W | 3-2 | 0-1 | 4 | Aitken 47, McPhee 2 (1 pen) 56, 64 (p) | 584 |
| 16 | 13 | A | Alloa Ath | W | 3-1 | 0-0 | 2 | Quitongo 50, Convery 2 62, 87 | 504 |
| 17 | Jan 20 | H | Forfar Ath | W | 2-1 | 2-0 | — | Carrigan 40, McPhee 43 | 1099 |
| 18 | 24 | A | Morton | D | 2-2 | 2-2 | 3 | Lumsden 1, Carrigan (pen) 11 | 2942 |
| 19 | 31 | H | East Fife | W | 1-0 | 1-0 | 2 | Quitongo 19 | 1429 |
| 20 | Feb 10 | H | Stenhousemuir | L | 0-1 | 0-0 | — | | 1111 |
| 21 | 14 | A | Arbroath | W | 2-0 | 1-0 | 2 | Quitongo 2, Aitken 63 | 502 |
| 22 | 21 | A | Dumbarton | L | 0-2 | 0-1 | 3 | | 1015 |
| 23 | Mar 2 | A | Airdrie U | L | 0-3 | 0-1 | — | | 1634 |
| 24 | 6 | A | Berwick R | W | 4-2 | 2-0 | 3 | McPhee 3, Aitken 9, Lumsden 73, Gribben 81 | 468 |
| 25 | 9 | H | Dumbarton | W | 2-0 | 1-0 | — | McPhee 24, Gribben 53 | 949 |
| 26 | 13 | H | Airdrie U | L | 0-1 | 0-1 | 2 | | 2559 |
| 27 | 16 | H | Alloa Ath | L | 0-1 | 0-0 | — | | 831 |
| 28 | 27 | H | Arbroath | D | 2-2 | 1-1 | 3 | Carrigan 25, Walker R 79 | 1041 |
| 29 | Apr 3 | A | East Fife | W | 3-2 | 0-0 | 4 | Walker R 49, McPhee 2 66, 74 | 489 |
| 30 | 6 | A | Stenhousemuir | W | 2-0 | 0-0 | — | McPhee 2 78, 82 | 296 |
| 31 | 10 | H | Morton | W | 6-1 | 3-0 | 3 | Walker R 13, McPhee 2 37, 38, Aitken 52, Carrigan 55, Corcoran 63 | 2692 |
| 32 | 17 | H | Dumbarton | W | 2-1 | 1-1 | 3 | Thomson 34, Gemmell 90 | 1343 |
| 33 | 24 | A | Alloa Ath | D | 1-1 | 0-1 | 3 | McPhee 64 | 579 |
| 34 | May 1 | A | Airdrie U | D | 1-1 | 0-0 | 3 | McPhee 82 | 2936 |
| 35 | 8 | H | Berwick R | W | 2-0 | 2-0 | 2 | Whiteford 1, Aitken 14 | 1591 |
| 36 | 15 | A | Forfar Ath | W | 4-0 | 1-0 | 2 | Carrigan 2 (1 pen) 34, 66 (p), McPhee 2 48, 54 | 1496 |

**Final League Position: 2**

*Most League Appearances:* 452: Rikki Ferguson, 1974-88.
*Most League Goals in Season (Individual):* 35: David Wilson, Division I; 1936-37.
*Most Goals Overall (Individual):* 246: David Wilson, 1928-39.

**Honours**
*League Champions:* First Division 1985-86, 1987-88; Third Division 2000-01. *Runners-up:* Division II 1903-04, 1952-53, 1964-65; Second Division 1996-97, 2003-04.
*Scottish Cup Runners-up:* 1911, 1935. *League Cup:* Semi-finalists three times.
*B&Q Cup Winners:* 1991-92, 1992-93.

**Club colours:** Shirt: Red and white hoops. Shorts: White. Stockings: White.

**Goalscorers:** *League* (70): McPhee 19 (3 pens), Carrigan 14 (3 pens), Aitken 8, Quitongo 5, Convery 4, Corcoran 3, Thomson 3, Walker R 3, Bailey 2 (1 pen), Gribben 2, Lumsden 2, Whiteford 2, Gemmell 1, Hodge 1, Waddell A 1
*Scottish Cup* (4): McPhee 2, Corcoran 1, Quitongo 1
*CIS Cup* (5): McPhee 2, Aitken 1, Carrigan 1, Corcoran 1
*Challenge Cup* (2): Aitken 1, McPhee 1

| McEwan D 36 | Fitter J 5 | Forbes B 4 + 4 | Thomson S 36 | Lumsden T 33 + 1 | Maxwell D 2 | Carrigan B 30 + 1 | Aitken C 32 + 1 | Convery S 12 + 4 | McPhee B 31 | Corcoran M 22 + 13 | Whiteford A 12 + 5 | Waddell A — + 5 | Sherry J 22 + 4 | Arbuckle A 23 + 6 | Paterson N — + 3 | Hodge S 31 + 1 | Gribben D 4 + 19 | Bailey J 4 + 3 | Jellema R — + 1 | Quitongo J 14 + 4 | Donnelly C 1 + 8 | Anderson D — + 1 | Walker R 21 + 2 | Ferguson D 3 + 1 | Gemmell J — + 8 | Blackadder R 10 + 5 | Waddell R 8 + 1 | Match No. |
|---|---|---|---|---|---|---|---|---|---|---|---|---|---|---|---|---|---|---|---|---|---|---|---|---|---|---|---|---|
| 1 | 2 | $3^{2}$ | 4 | 5 | 6 | 7 | $8^{3}$ | $9^{1}$ | 10 | 11 | 12 | 13 | 14 | | | | | | | | | | | | | | | 1 |
| 1 | $2^{1}$ | | 4 | 5 | $6^{2}$ | 7 | 8 | $9^{3}$ | 10 | 11 | 3 | 14 | | 12 | 13 | | | | | | | | | | | | | 2 |
| 1 | | | 4 | 5 | | $7^{2}$ | 8 | 9 | 10 | $11^{1}$ | 2 | | 6 | 12 | | 3 | 13 | | | | | | | | | | | 3 |
| 1 | | | 4 | $5^{3}$ | | 7 | 8 | $9^{1}$ | 10 | $11^{2}$ | 2 | | 6 | 12 | 14 | 3 | 13 | | | | | | | | | | | 4 |
| 1 | | 14 | 4 | 5 | | $7^{2}$ | 8 | 12 | $10^{3}$ | $11^{1}$ | 2 | | 6 | | | 3 | 13 | 9 | | | | | | | | | | 5 |
| 1 | | 12 | 4 | 5 | | $7^{2}$ | $8^{1}$ | $11^{3}$ | 10 | 13 | 2 | | 6 | | | 3 | 14 | 9 | | | | | | | | | | 6 |
| 1 | | $11^{2}$ | 4 | 5 | | $7^{1}$ | $8^{3}$ | | 10 | 12 | 2 | 13 | 6 | | | 3 | 14 | 9 | | | | | | | | | | 7 |
| $1^{1}$ | | $11^{3}$ | 4 | 5 | | 7 | 8 | | | 9 | 2 | 13 | $6^{2}$ | 14 | | 3 | | 10 | 12 | | | | | | | | | 8 |
| 1 | 2 | | 4 | 5 | | $7^{2}$ | 8 | $9^{1}$ | | 11 | | 13 | | 6 | | 3 | | | | 10 | 12 | | | | | | | 9 |
| 1 | $2^{1}$ | 12 | 4 | 5 | | 7 | 8 | 9 | | $11^{2}$ | | | | 6 | | 3 | | 13 | | 10 | | | | | | | | 10 |
| 1 | $2^{2}$ | 13 | 4 | 5 | | 7■ | 8■ | | $10^{1}$ | $11^{3}$ | | | | 6 | | 3 | | 12 | | 9■ | | 14 | | | | | | 11 |
| 1 | | $11^{1}$ | 4 | 5 | | | | $7^{2}$ | 10 | 9 | | | | 8 | 13 | 3 | 12 | 14 | | | $6^{3}$ | | 2 | | | | | 12 |
| 1 | | | 4 | 5 | | $7^{1}$ | 8 | $9^{2}$ | 10 | 12 | | | | 6 | | 3 | 14 | | | $11^{3}$ | 13 | | 2 | | | | | 13 |
| 1 | | | 4 | 5 | | 7 | 8 | 12 | $10^{3}$ | 13 | | | 11 | $6^{2}$ | | 3 | 14 | | | $9^{1}$ | | | 2 | | | | | 14 |
| 1 | | | 4 | 5 | | $7^{1}$ | 8 | 12 | 10 | 13 | | | 11 | 6 | | 3 | | | | $9^{2}$ | | | 2 | | | | | 15 |
| 1 | | | 4 | 5 | | | 8 | 7 | 10 | 12 | 13 | | $11^{1}$ | 6 | | 3 | 14 | | | $9^{3}$ | | | $2^{2}$ | | | | | 16 |
| 1 | | | 4 | 5 | | $7^{2}$ | 8 | | 10 | | 2 | | 12 | 6 | | 3 | | | | $9^{3}$ | 13 | | | $11^{1}$ | 14 | | | 17 |
| 1 | | | 4 | $5^{1}$ | | 7 | 8 | 14 | $10^{2}$ | 12 | 2 | | 11 | 6 | | 3 | | | | $9^{3}$ | | | | | 13 | | | 18 |
| 1 | | | 4 | 5 | | $7^{1}$ | 8 | | 10 | 12 | 2 | | 11 | 6 | | $3^{3}$ | | | | $9^{2}$ | | | 14 | | 13 | | | 19 |
| 1 | | | 4 | 5 | | 7 | | $9^{1}$ | 10 | $11^{2}$ | | | 6 | | | 3 | | | | 13 | | | 2 | $8^{3}$ | 12 | 14 | | 20 |
| 1 | | | 4 | 5 | | 7 | 8 | | $10^{3}$ | 12 | | | $11^{2}$ | 6 | | 3 | 14 | | | $9^{1}$ | | | 2 | | | 13 | | 21 |
| 1 | | | 4 | 5 | | 7 | 8 | | 10 | 11 | | | $6^{1}$ | 12 | | 3 | 13 | | | | | | 2 | | | $9^{2}$ | | 22 |
| 1 | | | 4 | 5 | | | 8 | 7 | 10 | $11^{2}$ | $2^{3}$ | | | 6 | | 3 | 13 | | | | | | 14 | $9^{1}$ | | 12 | | 23 |
| 1 | | | $4^{3}$ | 5 | | 7 | $8^{1}$ | | 10 | 12 | 14 | | | 6 | | 3 | 9 | | | | 13 | | 2 | | | $11^{2}$ | | 24 |
| 1 | | | 4 | 5 | | $7^{1}$ | $8^{2}$ | | 10 | 12 | | | 14 | 6 | | 3 | $9^{3}$ | | | | 13 | | 2 | | | 11 | | 25 |
| 1 | | | 4 | 5 | | 7 | $8^{1}$ | | $10^{2}$ | 13 | | | 12 | 6 | | 3 | 9 | | | | | | 2 | | | 11 | | 26 |
| 1 | | | 4 | 5 | | 7 | 12 | | | 11 | 14 | | 8 | $6^{3}$ | | 3 | $9^{2}$ | | | | 13 | | $2^{3}$ | | | 10 | | 27 |
| 1 | | | 4 | 5 | | $7^{2}$ | | | | 10 | | | 8 | $6^{3}$ | | $3^{1}$ | | | | 13 | | | 2 | 14 | 12 | 9 | 11 | 28 |
| 1 | | | 4 | 5 | | $7^{2}$ | 8 | | $10^{3}$ | 12 | | | 6 | 13 | | 3 | 14 | | | | | | 2 | | | 9 | $11^{1}$ | 29 |
| 1 | | | 4 | 5 | | 13 | 9 | | $10^{3}$ | 11 | | | 8 | 6 | | $3^{1}$ | 14 | | | $7^{2}$ | | | 2 | | | | 12 | 30 |
| 1 | | | 4 | 5 | | $7^{3}$ | $8^{2}$ | | $10^{1}$ | 11 | | | 6 | 3 | | | 12 | | | 14 | | | 2 | | | 13 | 9 | 31 |
| 1 | | | 4 | 5 | | 7 | 8 | | $10^{2}$ | $11^{1}$ | | | 6 | 3 | | | 12 | | | | | | 2 | | 13 | | 9 | 32 |
| 1 | | | 4 | 5 | | 7 | $8^{3}$ | | 10 | $11^{2}$ | | | 6 | $3^{1}$ | | 14 | 13 | | | | | | 2 | | | 12 | 9 | 33 |
| 1 | | | 4 | | | | 8 | | 10 | $11^{2}$ | | | 6 | | | 5 | 12 | | | $7^{1}$ | 13 | | $2^{3}$ | | 14 | 9 | 3 | 34 |
| 1 | | | 4 | | | | 8 | | $10^{3}$ | 11 | $6^{1}$ | | | | | 5 | 13 | | | $7^{2}$ | 12 | | 2 | | 14 | 9 | 3 | 35 |
| 1 | | | 4 | 14 | | $7^{2}$ | 8 | | 10 | $11^{3}$ | 12 | | | $6^{1}$ | | 5 | | | | 13 | | | 2 | | | 9 | 3 | 36 |

# HEART OF MIDLOTHIAN Premier League

*Year Formed:* 1874. *Ground & Address:* Tynecastle Stadium, Gorgie Rd, Edinburgh EH11 2NL. *Telephone:* 0131 200 7200. *Fax:* 0131 200 7222. *Website:* www.heartsfc.co.uk
*Ground Capacity:* 18,000. *Size of Pitch:* 108yd × 73yd.
*Chairman:* George Foulkes MP. *Chief Executive:* Christopher Robinson. *Sales and Marketing Manager:* Kenny Wittmann.
*Manager:* Craig Levein. *Assistant Coach:* Peter Houston. *Coach:* John McGlynn. *Physio:* Alan Rae.
*Managers since 1975:* J. Hagart, W. Ormond, R. Moncur, T. Ford, A. MacDonald, A. MacDonald & W. Jardine, A. MacDonald, J. Jordan, S. Clark, T. McLean, J. Jefferies.
*Club Nickname(s):* Hearts, Jambo's. *Previous Grounds:* The Meadows 1874, Powderhall 1878, Old Tynecastle 1881, (Tynecastle Park, 1886).
*Record Attendance:* 53,396 v Rangers, Scottish Cup 3rd rd, 13 Feb 1932.
*Record Transfer Fee received:* £2,100,000 for Alan McLaren from Rangers (October 1994).
*Record of Transfer paid:* £750,000 for Derek Ferguson to Rangers (July 1990).
*Record Victory:* 21-0 v Anchor, EFA Cup, 30 Oct 1880.
*Record Defeat:* 1-8 v Vale of Leven, Scottish Cup, 1888.
*Most Capped Player:* Bobby Walker, 29, Scotland.
*Most League Appearances:* 515: Gary Mackay, 1980-97.
*Most League Goals in Season (Individual):* 44: Barney Battles.
*Most Goals Overall (Individual):* 214: John Robertson, 1983-98.

## HEART OF MIDLOTHIAN 2003–04 LEAGUE RECORD

| *Match No.* | *Date* | *Venue* | *Opponents* | *Result* | *H/T Score* | *Lg. Pos.* | *Goalscorers* | *Attendance* |
|---|---|---|---|---|---|---|---|---|
| 1 | Aug 9 | H | Aberdeen | W 2-0 | 1-0 | — | De Vries [16], Kirk [90] | 14260 |
| 2 | 17 | A | Hibernian | L 0-1 | 0-0 | 7 | | 14,803 |
| 3 | 23 | H | Dundee U | W 3-0 | 3-0 | 4 | Stamp [20], Wilson (og) [22], De Vries [65] | 11,395 |
| 4 | 31 | H | Dunfermline Ath | W 1-0 | 0-0 | 3 | Wyness [61] | 11,934 |
| 5 | Sept 13 | A | Kilmarnock | W 2-0 | 2-0 | 3 | De Vries 2 [13, 40] | 6925 |
| 6 | 21 | H | Rangers | L 0-4 | 0-1 | 3 | | 14,732 |
| 7 | 27 | A | Motherwell | D 1-1 | 1-1 | 3 | Hartley [44] | 5888 |
| 8 | Oct 4 | H | Dundee | D 2-2 | 0-1 | 3 | Weir [72], Pressley [80] | 11,348 |
| 9 | 18 | A | Celtic | L 0-5 | 0-4 | 4 | | 59,511 |
| 10 | 25 | A | Partick Th | W 4-1 | 3-0 | 3 | Kirk 2 [12, 29], De Vries [26], Simmons [73] | 4814 |
| 11 | Nov 1 | H | Livingston | W 3-1 | 0-0 | 3 | Kirk 2 [67, 85], Pressley (pen) [89] | 11,233 |
| 12 | 9 | A | Aberdeen | W 1-0 | 1-0 | 3 | McKenna [12] | 9687 |
| 13 | 23 | H | Hibernian | W 2-0 | 1-0 | 3 | Orman (og) [9], Smith (og) [67] | 16,632 |
| 14 | 30 | A | Dundee U | L 1-2 | 0-2 | 3 | Severin [46] | 6343 |
| 15 | Dec 6 | A | Dunfermline Ath | L 1-2 | 1-1 | 3 | Maybury [40] | 6147 |
| 16 | 13 | H | Kilmarnock | W 2-1 | 0-0 | 3 | Kirk [63], Stamp [78] | 10,154 |
| 17 | 21 | A | Rangers | L 1-2 | 1-1 | 3 | Kirk [10] | 49,592 |
| 18 | 27 | H | Motherwell | D 0-0 | 0-0 | 3 | | 10,046 |
| 19 | Jan 6 | A | Dundee | W 2-1 | 0-0 | — | De Vries [47], Maybury [82] | 6387 |
| 20 | 18 | H | Celtic | L 0-1 | 0-1 | 3 | | 13,753 |
| 21 | 24 | H | Partick Th | W 2-0 | 1-0 | 3 | Wyness 2 [42, 78] | 10,264 |
| 22 | Feb 11 | H | Aberdeen | W 1-0 | 0-0 | — | Pressley [80] | 11,236 |
| 23 | 15 | A | Hibernian | D 1-1 | 0-1 | 3 | Pressley [47] | 15,016 |
| 24 | 21 | H | Dundee U | W 3-1 | 1-0 | 3 | Hartley [16], Wilson (og) [65], McKenna [72] | 10,265 |
| 25 | 24 | A | Livingston | W 3-2 | 1-1 | — | De Vries [25], Kirk [47], McKenna [83] | 4630 |
| 26 | 28 | A | Dunfermline Ath | D 0-0 | 0-0 | 3 | | 8422 |
| 27 | Mar 7 | A | Kilmarnock | D 1-1 | 0-0 | 3 | Webster [59] | 5297 |
| 28 | 13 | H | Rangers | D 1-1 | 0-0 | 3 | Wyness [75] | 14,596 |
| 29 | 27 | H | Dundee | W 3-1 | 0-1 | 3 | Hartley [51], Pressley (pen) [58], Hamill [65] | 10,491 |
| 30 | Apr 3 | A | Celtic | D 2-2 | 1-0 | 3 | McKenna [20], De Vries [77] | 59,295 |
| 31 | 7 | A | Motherwell | D 1-1 | 1-0 | — | Wyness [23] | 5500 |
| 32 | 10 | A | Partick Th | L 0-1 | 0-0 | 3 | | 4043 |
| 33 | 17 | H | Livingston | D 1-1 | 1-0 | 3 | McKenna [18] | 10,352 |
| 34 | 25 | H | Celtic | D 1-1 | 0-1 | 3 | De Vries [73] | 12,112 |
| 35 | May 1 | A | Dundee U | W 2-0 | 1-0 | 3 | De Vries [4], Webster [71] | 6620 |
| 36 | 8 | H | Dunfermline Ath | W 2-1 | 1-1 | 3 | De Vries 2 [41, 80] | 10,846 |
| 37 | 12 | A | Rangers | W 1-0 | 0-0 | — | Hamill [50] | 47,467 |
| 38 | 16 | H | Motherwell | W 3-2 | 1-2 | 3 | Wyness 2 [5, 67], McKenna [74] | 11,619 |

**Final League Position: 3**

**Honours**
*League Champions:* Division I 1894-95, 1896-97, 1957-58, 1959-60. First Division 1979-80; *Runners-up:* Division I 1893-94, 1898-99, 1903-04, 1905-06, 1914-15, 1937-38, 1953-54, 1956-57, 1958-59, 1964-65. Premier Division 1985-86, 1987-88, 1991-92. First Division 1977-78, 1982-83.
*Scottish Cup Winners:* 1891, 1896, 1901, 1906, 1956, 1998; *Runners-up:* 1903, 1907, 1968, 1976, 1986, 1996.
*League Cup Winners:* 1954-55, 1958-59, 1959-60, 1962-63; *Runners-up:* 1961-62, 1996-97.

**European:** *European Cup:* 4 matches (1958-59, 1960-61). *Cup Winners' Cup:* 10 matches (1976-77, 1996-97, 1998-99). *UEFA Cup:* 41 matches (*Fairs Cup:* 1961-62, 1963-64, 1965-66. *UEFA Cup:* 1984-85, 1986-87, 1988-89, 1990-91, 1992-93, 1993-94, 2000-01, 2003-04).

**Club colours:** Shirt: Maroon. Shorts: White. Stockings: Maroon.

**Goalscorers:** *League* (56): De Vries 12, Kirk 8, Wyness 7, McKenna 6, Pressley 5 (2 pens), Hartley 3, Hamill 2, Maybury 2, Stamp 2, Webster 2, Severin 1, Simmons 1, Weir 1, own goals 4
*Scottish Cup* (2): Hamill 1, own goal 1
*CIS Cup* (2): De Vries 1, Kirk 1

| Moilanen T 9 | Maybury A 32 + 1 | McCann HA 6 | Pressley S 31 | Webster A 31 + 1 | Sloan R 9 + 4 | Severin S 24 + 2 | Stamp P 23 + 2 | Hartley P 29 + 1 | De Vries M 26 + 5 | Wyness D 19 + 9 | McKenna K 22 + 10 | Kirk A 14 + 10 | Macfarlane N 24 + 6 | Boyack S 3 + 5 | McMullan P 1 + 1 | Hamill J 12 + 6 | Neilson R 25 + 4 | Kisnorbo P 28 + 3 | Weir G 7 + 11 | Valois J 5 + 6 | Simmons S 1 + 6 | Gordon C 29 | Berra C 3 + 3 | Wales G — + 1 | Janczyk N 4 + 7 | Tierney G 1 | *Match No.* |
|---|---|---|---|---|---|---|---|---|---|---|---|---|---|---|---|---|---|---|---|---|---|---|---|---|---|---|---|
| 1 | 2 | 3 | 4 | 5 | 6 | 7 | 8[3] | 9 | 10[1] | 11[2] | 12 | 13 | 14 | | | | | | | | | | | | | | 1 |
| 1 | 2 | 3 | 4 | 5 | 6[1] | 7 | 8 | 9 | 10[2] | 11[3] | 13 | 14 | | 12 | | | | | | | | | | | | | 2 |
| 1 | 2 | | 4 | 5 | | 7 | 8 | | 10[3] | 11 | 14 | | 9 | 12 | 3[2] | 6[1] | 13 | | | | | | | | | | 3 |
| 1 | 2 | | 4 | 5 | | 7 | 8 | | 10 | 11[3] | | | 9 | 13 | | 3[2] | 6[1] | 12 | 14 | | | | | | | | 4 |
| 1 | 2 | | 4 | 5 | | 7 | 8 | | 10[2] | 11 | | 13 | 9 | 12 | | 6[1] | | 3 | | | | | | | | | 5 |
| 1 | 2 | | 4 | 5 | | 7 | 8 | | 10[3] | 11[2] | 14 | 12 | 9 | | | 6[1] | | 3 | | 13 | | | | | | | 6 |
| 1 | 2 | | 4 | 5 | | 7 | 8 | 9[1] | 10[2] | 11[3] | 13 | | 6 | | | 12 | | 3 | 14 | | | | | | | | 7 |
| 1 | 2 | | 4 | 5 | | 7 | 8 | 9[1] | 10 | 11[2] | | | 6[3] | | | | | 3 | 13 | 12 | 14 | | | | | | 8 |
| 1 | 2 | | 4 | 5[1] | | 7 | 8[2] | 13 | 10[3] | | 12 | | 9 | | | | | 3 | 11 | 6 | 14 | | | | | | 9 |
| | 14 | | 4 | | | 7 | | 9 | 10[2] | 13 | 2 | 11[3] | 8[1] | | | | 5 | 3 | | 6 | 12 | 1 | | | | | 10 |
| | | | 4 | | | 7 | 8 | 9[3] | 10 | 14 | 2 | 11 | | | 12 | | 5[1] | 3 | | 6[2] | 13 | 1 | | | | | 11 |
| | 2 | 3 | 4 | 5 | | 7 | 12 | 8[2] | 10 | 9[1] | 6[3] | 11 | 13 | | | | | | | 14 | | 1 | | | | | 12 |
| | 2 | | 4[1] | 12 | | | | 9 | 10 | 13 | 5 | 11[2] | 8 | | | 14 | 7 | 3 | | 6[3] | | 1 | | | | | 13 |
| | 2 | | | 4 | | 7 | | | 10 | 12 | 5 | 11 | 8[3] | | | | 6 | 3[2] | | 13 | 9[1] | 1 | 14 | | | | 14 |
| | 2 | 6 | | 5 | | 7 | | 10[2] | | | 4 | | 9[1] | | | | 8 | 3 | 11 | 12 | | 1 | | 13 | | | 15 |
| | 2 | 6[2] | 4[1] | 5 | | 7 | 8 | 9 | 10[3] | | 12 | 11 | 14 | | | | 13 | 3 | | | | 1 | | | | | 16 |
| | | 2 | | | 6[1] | 7 | 8[2] | 10 | 13 | | 4 | 11 | 9 | | | | 5 | 3 | 12 | | | 1 | | | | | 17 |
| | | | | 2 | 6 | 7[3] | 8 | 10[1] | 13 | | 4[2] | 11 | 9 | | | | 5 | 3 | | 12 | | 1 | 14 | | | | 18 |
| | 2 | | 4 | 5 | 12 | | 8[1] | 9 | 10 | 14 | | 11[3] | 7 | | | | 13 | 3 | | 6[2] | | 1 | | | | | 19 |
| | 2 | | 4 | 5 | 6[1] | 7 | 8 | 9[2] | 10 | 11 | 13 | | | | | | | 3 | 12 | | | 1 | | | | | 20 |
| | 2 | | 4 | 5 | 6 | | 8 | 9 | 10[1] | 11 | 12 | | | | | 14 | 7[2] | 3 | | | 13[3] | 1 | | | | | 21 |
| | 2[1] | | 4 | 5 | 6 | | 8 | 9 | 10 | 11[3] | | 13 | 14 | | | 7[2] | 12 | 3 | | | | 1 | | | | | 22 |
| | 2 | | 4 | 5 | | | | 9 | 10 | 11[1] | 6 | | 8 | | | | 7 | 3 | 12 | | | 1 | | | | | 23 |
| | 2 | | 4 | 5 | 12 | | 8[1] | 9 | 10 | 11[2] | 6 | 13 | | | | | 7 | 3[3] | | | | 1 | | | 14 | | 24 |
| | 2 | | 4 | 5 | 13 | | 12 | 9[1] | 10[3] | 14 | 6 | 11 | 8[2] | | | | 7 | 3 | | | | 1 | | | | | 25 |
| | 2 | | 4 | 5 | 9[2] | | 8 | | | 11[1] | 6 | 10 | 13 | | | | 7 | 3 | 12 | | | 1 | | | | | 26 |
| | 2 | | | 5 | 9[2] | | 8 | | | | 4 | 11[1] | 10 | | | 6 | 7 | | 13 | | | 1 | 3 | | 12 | | 27 |
| | 2 | | 4 | 5[1] | | | 8 | 10[2] | | 12 | 6 | 14 | | | | 9 | 7 | 3 | 11[3] | | | 1 | | | 13 | | 28 |
| | 2 | | 4 | | | | 8[2] | 10[3] | 13 | 11 | 5 | | 9[1] | | | 6 | 7 | 3 | 14 | | | 1 | | | 12 | | 29 |
| | 2 | | 4 | | | 7 | | 10 | 12 | | 6[1] | | 9 | | | | 8 | 3 | 11[2] | | | 1 | 13 | | 5 | | 30 |
| | 2 | | 4 | | | 12 | | 9[3] | 10 | 11 | | 13 | 7 | | | | 6 | 3 | 8[2] | | | 1 | 5[1] | | 14 | | 31 |
| | 2 | | 4 | 5 | | | | 9[1] | 10 | 11[2] | 3 | 13 | 8[3] | | | 12 | 6 | | | | 14 | 1 | | | 7[1] | | 32 |
| | 2 | | 4 | 5 | | 13 | | | | 12 | 6 | 11 | 10[3] | 9[1] | | 14 | 8 | 3 | | | | 1 | 7[2] | | | | 33 |
| | 2 | | 4 | 5 | | 7 | 8[1] | 10 | 13 | | 6 | 11[3] | | | | 12 | 9 | 3[2] | 14 | | | 1 | | | | | 34 |
| | 2 | | 4 | 5 | | 7[2] | | 9[3] | 10 | 14 | 3 | | 13 | | | 8 | 6 | | 11[1] | | | 1 | | | 12 | | 35 |
| | 2 | | 4 | 5 | | 7[2] | | 11 | 10 | | 3 | | | 14 | | 9[1] | 8 | 13 | 12 | | | 1 | | | 6[3] | | 36 |
| | | | | 4 | 13 | 7 | | 10 | | | 12 | | 9 | 8[2] | | 5 | 6 | 3 | 11[1] | | | 1 | | | 2 | | 37 |
| | | | | 4 | | 7 | | 10 | | 11 | 3 | 14 | 9[3] | 8[2] | | 5 | 6 | 12 | | | | 1 | | | 13 | 2[1] | 38 |

# HIBERNIAN **Premier League**

*Year Formed:* 1875. *Ground & Address:* Easter Road Stadium, Albion Rd, Edinburgh EH7 5QG. *Telephone:* 0131 661 2159. *Fax:* 0131 659 6488.
*Ground Capacity:* total: 17,500. *Size of Pitch:* 112yd × 74yd.
*Chairman:* Ken Lewandowski. *Managing Director:* Rod Petrie. *Commercial Director:* Steven Powell.
*Manager:* Tony Mowbray. *Assistant Manager:* Mark Venus.
*Physio:* Malcolm Colquhoun.
*Managers since 1975:* Eddie Turnbull, Willie Ormond, Bertie Auld, Pat Stanton, John Blackley, Alex Miller, Jim Duffy, Alex McLeish, Frank Sauzee. *Club Nickname(s):* Hibees. *Previous Grounds:* Meadows 1875-78, Powderhall 1878-79, Mayfield 1879-80, First Easter Road 1880-92, Second Easter Road 1892-.
*Record Attendance:* 65,860 v Hearts, Division I, 2 Jan 1950.
*Record Victory:* 22-1 v 42nd Highlanders, 3 Sept 1881.
*Record Defeat:* 0-10 v Rangers, 24 Dec 1898.
*Most Capped Player:* Lawrie Reilly, 38, Scotland.
*Most League Appearances:* 446: Arthur Duncan.
*Most League Goals in Season (Individual):* 42: Joe Baker.
*Most Goals Overall (Individual):* 364: Gordon Smith.

## HIBERNIAN 2003–04 LEAGUE RECORD

| *Match No.* | *Date* | *Venue* | *Opponents* | *Result* | | *H/T Score* | *Lg. Pos.* | *Goalscorers* | *Attendance* |
|---|---|---|---|---|---|---|---|---|---|
| 1 | Aug 9 | A | Dundee U | W | 2-1 | 0-0 | — | Riordan 74, McManus (pen) 88 | 9809 |
| 2 | 17 | H | Hearts | W | 1-0 | 0-0 | 4 | O'Connor 90 | 14,803 |
| 3 | 23 | A | Rangers | L | 2-5 | 2-2 | 6 | Murray 28, McManus 34 | 49,642 |
| 4 | 30 | H | Aberdeen | D | 1-1 | 0-1 | 6 | Brown S 72 | 10,682 |
| 5 | Sept 13 | H | Motherwell | L | 0-2 | 0-1 | 7 | | 8387 |
| 6 | 20 | A | Dunfermline Ath | D | 0-0 | 0-0 | 6 | | 8715 |
| 7 | 27 | H | Celtic | L | 1-2 | 1-1 | 7 | Doumbe 38 | 12,032 |
| 8 | Oct 4 | A | Partick Th | W | 1-0 | 0-0 | 7 | Brebner 88 | 4125 |
| 9 | 18 | H | Livingston | L | 0-2 | 0-1 | 8 | | 8562 |
| 10 | 25 | H | Kilmarnock | W | 3-1 | 2-0 | 5 | Murdock 12, Riordan 15, McManus 78 | 7191 |
| 11 | Nov 1 | A | Dundee | D | 1-1 | 0-1 | 7 | Riordan 82 | 7392 |
| 12 | 8 | H | Dundee U | D | 2-2 | 1-1 | 7 | Brown S 14, McCracken (og) 90 | 8756 |
| 13 | 23 | A | Hearts | L | 0-2 | 0-1 | 8 | | 16,632 |
| 14 | 30 | H | Rangers | L | 0-1 | 0-0 | 9 | | 11,116 |
| 15 | Dec 7 | A | Aberdeen | L | 1-3 | 0-1 | 9 | Dobbie 58 | 7863 |
| 16 | 13 | A | Motherwell | W | 1-0 | 0-0 | 7 | Riordan 89 | 4533 |
| 17 | 21 | H | Dunfermline Ath | L | 1-2 | 0-2 | 8 | Riordan 63 | 9085 |
| 18 | 27 | A | Celtic | L | 0-6 | 0-2 | 9 | | 59,542 |
| 19 | Jan 3 | H | Partick Th | W | 3-2 | 2-0 | 7 | O'Connor 9, Dobbie 35, Whittaker 85 | 8875 |
| 20 | 17 | A | Livingston | L | 0-1 | 0-1 | 8 | | 4948 |
| 21 | 24 | A | Kilmarnock | W | 2-0 | 0-0 | 6 | Brown S 48, O'Connor 50 | 5571 |
| 22 | 31 | H | Dundee | D | 1-1 | 0-1 | 6 | Riordan 70 | 8023 |
| 23 | Feb 10 | A | Dundee U | D | 0-0 | 0-0 | — | | 6389 |
| 24 | 15 | H | Hearts | D | 1-1 | 1-0 | 6 | Riordan 24 | 15,016 |
| 25 | 21 | A | Rangers | L | 0-3 | 0-1 | 8 | | 49,698 |
| 26 | 28 | H | Aberdeen | L | 0-1 | 0-1 | 9 | | 10,416 |
| 27 | Mar 21 | H | Celtic | L | 0-4 | 0-2 | 10 | | 9456 |
| 28 | 24 | H | Motherwell | D | 3-3 | 2-0 | — | Nicol 5, Reid 36, Riordan 60 | 5568 |
| 29 | 27 | A | Partick Th | D | 1-1 | 0-0 | 9 | Murdock 67 | 3155 |
| 30 | Apr 3 | H | Livingston | W | 3-1 | 1-0 | 8 | McManus 38, Riordan 2 53, 82 | 6223 |
| 31 | 10 | H | Kilmarnock | W | 3-0 | 2-0 | 7 | Caldwell 22, Thomson 44, Riordan 63 | 7287 |
| 32 | 13 | A | Dunfermline Ath | D | 1-1 | 1-0 | — | Riordan 3 | 5041 |
| 33 | 17 | A | Dundee | D | 2-2 | 1-1 | 7 | Riordan 2 44, 49 | 5508 |
| 34 | 24 | A | Kilmarnock | L | 0-2 | 0-1 | 8 | | 4886 |
| 35 | May 1 | H | Dundee | W | 1-0 | 1-0 | 7 | Riordan 41 | 6180 |
| 36 | 5 | H | Partick Th | L | 1-2 | 1-1 | — | Murdock 32 | 5380 |
| 37 | 8 | A | Aberdeen | W | 1-0 | 0-0 | 7 | O'Connor 90 | 6781 |
| 38 | 15 | A | Livingston | L | 1-4 | 0-1 | 8 | Doumbe 75 | 4409 |

**Final League Position: 8**

**Honours**
*League Champions:* Division I 1902-03, 1947-48, 1950-51, 1951-52. First Division 1980-81, 1998-99. Division II 1893-94, 1894-95, 1932-33; *Runners-up:* Division I 1896-97, 1946-47, 1949-50, 1952-53, 1973-74, 1974-75.
*Scottish Cup Winners:* 1887, 1902; *Runners-up:* 1896, 1914, 1923, 1924, 1947, 1958, 1972, 1979, 2001.
*League Cup Winners:* 1972-73, 1991-92; *Runners-up:* 1950-51, 1968-69, 1974-75, 1993-94, 2003-04.

**European:** *European Cup:* 6 matches (1955-56 semi-finals). *Cup Winners' Cup:* 6 matches (1972-73). *UEFA Cup:* 61 matches (*Fairs Cup:* 1960-61 semi-finals, 1961-62, 1962-63, 1965-66, 1967-68, 1968-69, 1970-71. *UEFA Cup:* 1973-74, 1974-75, 1975-76, 1976-77, 1978-79, 1989-90, 1992-93, 2001-02).

**Club colours:** Shirt: Green with white sleeves and collar. Shorts: White with green stripe. Stockings: White with green trim.

**Goalscorers:** *League* (41): Riordan 15, McManus 4 (1 pen), O'Connor 4, Brown S 3, Murdock 3, Dobbie 2, Doumbe 2, Brebner 1, Caldwell 1, Murray 1, Nicol 1, Reid 1, Thomson 1, Whittaker 1, own goal 1
*Scottish Cup* (0):
*CIS Cup* (14): Dobbie 4, Riordan 3, O'Connor 2, Brebner 1, Brown S 1, Murray 1, Thomson 1, own goal 1

| Andersson D 38 | Orman A 13 + 5 | Smith G 19 | Zambernardi Y 7 + 1 | Doumbe M 33 | Murray I 14 | Wiss J 13 | Brebner G 22 | Glass S 9 + 3 | Riordan D 27 + 7 | Brown S 34 + 2 | McManus T 18 + 14 | Dobbie S 7 + 20 | O'Connor G 27 + 6 | Whittaker S 15 + 13 | Murdock C 32 | Edge R 20 | Reid A 16 + 4 | Thomson K 23 | Nicol K 11 + 4 | McCluskey J — + 1 | Caldwell G 16 + 1 | Baillie J 2 | Kane J — + 1 | Fletcher S 1 + 4 | Shields J 1 | McDonald K — + 1 | Match No. |
|---|---|---|---|---|---|---|---|---|---|---|---|---|---|---|---|---|---|---|---|---|---|---|---|---|---|---|---|
| 1 | 2 | 3 | 4 | 5 | 6 | 7 | 8 | $9^{1}$ | 10 | $11^{2}$ | 12 | 13 | | | | | | | | | | | | | | | 1 |
| 1 | 2 | 3 | 4 | 5 | 6 | $7^{3}$ | 8■ | 14 | 9 | $11^{1}$ | $10^{2}$ | 13 | 12 | | | | | | | | | | | | | | 2 |
| 1 | 2 | 3 | 4 | 5 | 6 | | 7 | 13 | $9^{3}$ | 8 | $10^{2}$ | 12 | $11^{1}$ | 14 | | | | | | | | | | | | | 3 |
| 1 | | 3 | 4 | 5 | 6 | $7^{1}$ | 8 | 12 | 13 | 9 | $10^{2}$ | 14 | $11^{3}$ | | 2 | | | | | | | | | | | | 4 |
| 1 | | 3 | 4 | 5 | 6 | | 8 | 7 | $9^{2}$ | 11 | 13 | 14 | $10^{3}$ | 12 | $2^{1}$ | | | | | | | | | | | | 5 |
| 1 | 4 | | | 5 | 6 | 7 | 8 | 9 | 12 | $11^{2}$ | 13 | | $10^{1}$ | | 2 | 3 | | | | | | | | | | | 6 |
| 1 | 4 | | | 5 | 6 | $7^{2}$ | 8 | $9^{3}$ | 13 | 12 | 14 | $11^{1}$ | 10 | | 2 | 3 | | | | | | | | | | | 7 |
| 1 | 4 | | | 5 | 6 | 7 | 8 | | 12 | $9^{2}$ | 13 | $11^{1}$ | 10 | | 2 | 3 | | | | | | | | | | | 8 |
| 1 | 4 | | | 5 | 6 | 7 | 8 | $9^{3}$ | 12 | $11^{2}$ | 14 | 13 | $10^{1}$ | | 2 | 3 | | | | | | | | | | | 9 |
| 1 | 4 | | | 5 | 6 | | 8 | $7^{1}$ | $9^{3}$ | | $11^{2}$ | 14 | 10 | 13 | 2 | 3 | 12 | | | | | | | | | | 10 |
| 1 | $4^{3}$ | 3 | | 5 | 6 | | | 7 | 9 | 12 | $11^{1}$ | 13 | $10^{2}$ | 14 | 2 | | | 8 | | | | | | | | | 11 |
| 1 | $4^{2}$ | 3 | | 5 | 6 | | 8 | | 9 | $11^{3}$ | 14 | 12 | $10^{1}$ | 13 | 2 | | | 7 | | | | | | | | | 12 |
| 1 | $4^{1}$ | 3 | | 5 | 6 | | 8 | | $9^{3}$ | 11 | 14 | 13 | $10^{2}$ | 12 | 2 | | | 7 | | | | | | | | | 13 |
| 1 | 4 | 3 | | 5 | $6^{1}$ | | 8 | | 9 | 11 | | 12 | 10 | | 2 | | | $7^{2}$ | 13 | | | | | | | | 14 |
| 1 | 12 | 3 | | 5 | | | 8 | | 9 | 11 | 13 | $7^{2}$ | 10 | | 2 | $4^{1}$ | | 6 | | | | | | | | | 15 |
| 1 | | 3 | | 4 | | | 8 | 7 | 9 | 11 | | | 10 | 5 | 2 | | | 6 | | | | | | | | | 16 |
| 1 | | 3 | | 4 | | | 8 | | 9 | 11 | $7^{1}$ | 12 | 10 | 5 | 2 | | | 6 | | | | | | | | | 17 |
| 1 | | 3 | | 4 | | | 8 | | 9■ | 11 | $7^{2}$ | 12 | $10^{1}$ | 5 | 2 | | 13 | $6^{3}$ | 14 | | | | | | | | 18 |
| 1 | 13 | 3 | | 4 | | | 8 | 7 | | $11^{2}$ | | $9^{1}$ | 10 | 5 | 2 | | 12 | 6 | | | | | | | | | 19 |
| 1 | | 3 | | 4 | | $7^{3}$ | | | 9 | 11 | 13 | 14 | $10^{2}$ | 5 | 2 | | 12 | $6^{1}$ | 8 | | | | | | | | 20 |
| 1 | | 3 | | 4 | | 7 | | | $9^{3}$ | $11^{1}$ | 12 | 14 | 10 | 5 | 2 | | $8^{2}$ | | 6 | 13 | | | | | | | 21 |
| 1 | | $3^{1}$ | | 4 | | $7^{2}$ | | | 9 | 11 | | 14 | 10 | 5 | 2 | | $8^{3}$ | 6 | 13 | | 12 | | | | | | 22 |
| 1 | | | | 4 | | 7 | | | 9 | | | 11 | 10 | 8 | 2 | 3 | | 6 | | | 5 | | | | | | 23 |
| 1 | | | | 4 | | $7^{2}$ | | | $9^{3}$ | 11 | 12 | 14 | 10 | 13 | 2 | 3 | $8^{1}$ | 6 | | | 5 | | | | | | 24 |
| 1 | $2^{2}$ | | | 4 | | $7^{1}$ | | | 13 | 11 | 14 | 12 | $10^{3}$ | 8 | | 3 | 9 | 6 | | | 5 | | | | | | 25 |
| 1 | | 3 | | 4 | | | | | 9 | 11 | $8^{1}$ | 12 | 10 | | 2 | 6 | | 7 | | | 5 | | | | | | 26 |
| 1 | | 3 | 13 | | | | | | 12 | 11 | 10 | $9^{2}$ | | 6 | | 4 | $8^{1}$ | | 7 | | 5 | 2 | | | | | 27 |
| 1 | | | | 4 | | | | | 9 | 11 | 10 | | | 12 | 2 | 3 | 8 | $6^{1}$ | 7 | | 5 | | | | | | 28 |
| 1 | | | | 4 | | | | | 9 | $11^{2}$ | 10 | | 13 | 12 | 2 | 3 | 8 | 6 | $7^{1}$ | | 5 | | | | | | 29 |
| 1 | 13 | | | | | | | | 9 | $11^{2}$ | $10^{1}$ | | 12 | 7 | 2 | 3 | 8 | $6^{3}$ | | | 5 | 4 | 14 | | | | 30 |
| 1 | | | | 4 | | | | | 9 | 11 | | | $10^{2}$ | $7^{1}$ | 2 | 3 | 8 | 6 | 12 | | 5 | | | 13 | | | 31 |
| 1 | | | | 4 | | | | | $9^{1}$ | 11 | $10^{2}$ | | 12 | 13 | 2 | 3 | 8 | 6 | 7 | | 5 | | | | | | 32 |
| 1 | 12 | | | 4 | | | | | 9 | 11 | $10^{2}$ | | 13 | 6 | 2 | $3^{1}$ | 8 | | 7 | | 5 | | | | | | 33 |
| 1 | | | | | | | | | 9 | 11 | $10^{1}$ | | 12 | $7^{2}$ | 2 | 3 | 8 | 6 | 4 | | 5 | | | 13 | | | 34 |
| 1 | | | | | | | $8^{1}$ | | $9^{3}$ | 11 | $10^{2}$ | 13 | | 12 | 2 | 3 | 7 | 6 | 4 | | 5 | | | 14 | | | 35 |
| 1 | 12 | | | | | | 8 | | | 11 | 10 | $9^{3}$ | | 13 | 2 | $3^{2}$ | 7 | $6^{1}$ | 4 | | 5 | | | 14 | | | 36 |
| 1 | | | 3 | 4 | | | 8 | | | 11 | 12 | | 10 | $6^{1}$ | 2 | | 9 | | 7 | | 5 | | | | | | 37 |
| 1 | | | 3 | 4 | | | 6 | | | $11^{2}$ | 9 | | 10 | 13 | | | 7 | | | | 5 | | | 8 | $2^{1}$ | 12 | 38 |

# INVERNESS CALEDONIAN THISTLE

## Premier League

*Year Formed:* 1994. *Ground & Address:* Caledonian Stadium, East Longman, Inverness IV1 1FF. *Telephone:* 01463 222880. *Fax:* 01463 715816.
*Ground Capacity:* 6500, seated: 2200. *Size of Pitch:* 115yd × 75yd.
*Chairman:* Kenneth Mackie. *President:* John MacDonald. *Secretary:* Jim Falconer. *Commercial Manager:* Debbie Ross.
*Youth Administrator:* Charlie Christie. *Football and Community Development Manager:* Danny MacDonald.
*Manager:* John Robertson. *Assistant Manager:* Donald Park. *First Team Coach:* John Docherty. *Physio:* Emily Goodlad.
*Managers since 1995:* Steven Paterson.
*Record Attendance:* 6290 v Aberdeen, Scottish Cup, 20 February 2000.
*Record Victory:* 8-1, v Annan Ath, Scottish Cup 3rd rd, 24 January 1998.
*Record Defeat:* 1-5, v Morton, First Division, 12 November 1999 and v Airdrieonians, First Division, 15 April 2000.
*Most League Appearances:* 308, Charlie Christie, 1995-2003.
*Most League Goals in Season:* 27, Iain Stewart, 1996-97; Denis Wyness 2002-03.
*Most Goals Overall (Individual):* 82, Iain Stewart, 1995-2001.

### INVERNESS CALEDONIAN THISTLE 2003–04 LEAGUE RECORD

| Match No. | Date | Venue | Opponents | Result | | H/T Score | Lg. Pos. | Goalscorers | Attendance |
|---|---|---|---|---|---|---|---|---|---|
| 1 | Aug 9 | A | Falkirk | L | 1-2 | 1-1 | — | McCaffrey [13] | 2619 |
| 2 | 16 | H | Clyde | D | 0-0 | 0-0 | 8 | | 1839 |
| 3 | 23 | A | St Johnstone | W | 2-1 | 0-0 | 6 | Bingham [53], Hislop [74] | 3031 |
| 4 | 30 | A | Ross Co | D | 1-1 | 1-1 | 7 | Mann [22] | 5020 |
| 5 | Sept 13 | H | Ayr U | W | 1-0 | 1-0 | 4 | Ritchie [21] | 1476 |
| 6 | 20 | A | Brechin C | W | 2-0 | 0-0 | 3 | McBain [60], Ritchie [77] | 652 |
| 7 | 27 | H | St Mirren | W | 2-0 | 2-0 | 2 | Ritchie [21], McCaffrey [36] | 1896 |
| 8 | Oct 4 | H | Raith R | W | 2-1 | 1-0 | 1 | Tokely [36], McCaffrey [72] | 1707 |
| 9 | 18 | A | Queen of the S | L | 2-3 | 0-0 | 2 | Ritchie [54], Bingham [89] | 3547 |
| 10 | Nov 1 | H | Falkirk | L | 1-2 | 0-0 | 5 | Hughes (og) [80] | 2223 |
| 11 | 5 | A | Clyde | L | 0-1 | 0-0 | — | | 734 |
| 12 | 8 | A | Ayr U | W | 3-0 | 2-0 | 4 | Golabek [17], Hart [37], Hislop [61] | 1464 |
| 13 | 14 | H | Ross Co | D | 3-3 | 3-1 | 4 | Bingham [30], Hislop [31], Wilson [34] | 3523 |
| 14 | 22 | A | St Mirren | W | 4-0 | 2-0 | 3 | Bingham 2 [30, 65], McBain 2 [34, 57] | 2204 |
| 15 | 29 | H | Brechin C | W | 5-0 | 3-0 | 1 | Hislop [1], Tokely 2 [36, 76], Keogh [44], Wilson [85] | 1393 |
| 16 | Dec 6 | H | Queen of the S | W | 4-1 | 0-1 | 1 | Hislop 2 [49, 76], McCaffrey [55], Wilson [84] | 1745 |
| 17 | 13 | A | Raith R | W | 3-1 | 0-1 | 1 | Munro [68], Bingham [83], Ritchie [90] | 1432 |
| 18 | 27 | H | St Johnstone | W | 1-0 | 0-0 | 2 | Wilson (pen) [80] | 2949 |
| 19 | Jan 3 | A | Ross Co | L | 0-1 | 0-0 | 2 | | 6020 |
| 20 | 17 | H | Ayr U | W | 2-1 | 1-0 | 2 | Ritchie [22], Bingham [81] | 1443 |
| 21 | 24 | A | Brechin C | W | 4-2 | 2-1 | 2 | Thomson [10], Ritchie [41], Bingham [47], Duncan [83] | 669 |
| 22 | 31 | H | St Mirren | D | 1-1 | 0-1 | 1 | Bingham [88] | 1913 |
| 23 | Feb 14 | H | Raith R | W | 3-0 | 1-0 | 1 | Bingham [44], Keogh [81], Wilson [86] | 1879 |
| 24 | 21 | A | Queen of the S | L | 1-2 | 0-2 | 2 | Ritchie [77] | 2021 |
| 25 | Mar 2 | A | Falkirk | L | 1-2 | 1-1 | — | Ritchie [35] | 2268 |
| 26 | 13 | A | St Johnstone | L | 2-3 | 0-2 | 2 | Ritchie 2 [64, 73] | 2913 |
| 27 | 16 | H | Clyde | W | 3-1 | 2-1 | — | Ritchie [35], Bingham [41], Wilson (pen) [88] | 2645 |
| 28 | 20 | A | Ayr U | D | 1-1 | 1-1 | 2 | Wilson (pen) [42] | 1207 |
| 29 | 27 | H | Ross Co | W | 1-0 | 0-0 | 2 | Wilson [60] | 4019 |
| 30 | Apr 3 | A | St Mirren | D | 0-0 | 0-0 | 2 | | 2272 |
| 31 | 13 | H | Brechin C | W | 1-0 | 0-0 | — | Wilson (pen) [67] | 1198 |
| 32 | 17 | H | Queen of the S | W | 4-1 | 2-0 | 2 | Hislop 2 [39, 81], Bingham [40], Wilson [65] | 2126 |
| 33 | 24 | A | Raith R | W | 1-0 | 1-0 | 2 | Ritchie [2] | 1748 |
| 34 | May 1 | H | Falkirk | D | 0-0 | 0-0 | 2 | | 2631 |
| 35 | 8 | A | Clyde | W | 2-1 | 0-0 | 1 | Keogh [54], Hislop [79] | 4722 |
| 36 | 15 | H | St Johnstone | W | 3-1 | 1-1 | 1 | Bingham [30], Wilson [55], Ritchie [76] | 6092 |

**Final League Position: 1**

**Honours**
*Scottish Cup:* Semi-finals 2003; Quarter-finals 1996.
*League Champions:* First Division 2003-04. Third Division 1996-97; *Runners-up:* Second Division 1998-99.
*Bell's League Challenge Cup Winners:* 2003-04. *Runners-up:* 1999-2000.

**Club colours:** Shirts: Royal blue with red stripes. Shorts: Royal blue. Stockings: Royal blue.

**Goalscorers:** *League* (67): Ritchie 14, Bingham 13, Wilson 11 (4 pens), Hislop 9, McCaffrey 4, Keogh 3, McBain 3, Tokely 3, Duncan 1, Golabek 1, Hart 1, Mann 1, Munro 1, Thomson 1, own goal 1
*Scottish Cup* (10): Ritchie 5, Bingham 2, McBain 1, Thomson 1, Wilson 1
*CIS Cup* (1): Ritchie 1
*Challenge Cup* (14): Hislop 5, Ritchie 3, Bingham 2, Hart 2, Wilson 2

| Brown M 36 | Tokely R 34 | Golabek S 34 | Mann R 33 | McCaffrey S 34 | Duncan R 33 | Hart R 15 + 5 | Hislop S 18 + 8 | Ritchie P 23 + 11 | McBain R 32 | Bingham D 31 + 2 | Christie C 2 + 1 | Procter D 4 + 7 | Thomson D 7 + 14 | Low A — + 1 | Wilson B 26 + 3 | Keogh L 21 + 8 | MacMillan C — + 10 | Munro G 8 + 7 | Mackie D 5 + 1 | Macrae D — + 2 | McKinnon L — + 1 | *Match No.* |
|---|---|---|---|---|---|---|---|---|---|---|---|---|---|---|---|---|---|---|---|---|---|---|
| 1 | 2 | 3 | 4 | 5 | 6 | 7 | $8^{2}$ | $9^{1}$ | 10 | 11 | 12 | 13 | | | | | | | | | | 1 |
| 1 | 2 | 3 | 4 | 5 | 6 | 7 | 8 | 13 | 11 | $9^{1}$ | $10^{2}$ | | 12 | | | | | | | | | 2 |
| 1 | 2 | 3 | 4 | 5 | 6 | 7 | $8^{2}$ | 12 | 11 | 9 | $10^{1}$ | 13 | | | | | | | | | | 3 |
| 1 | 2 | 3 | 4 | 5 | 6 | 7 | 8 | 9 | 10 | $11^{1}$ | | | | 12 | | | | | | | | 4 |
| 1 | $2^{1}$ | 3 | 4 | 5 | 8 | 10 | 13 | $9^{2}$ | 6 | $11^{3}$ | | 12 | 14 | | 7 | | | | | | | 5 |
| 1 | | 3 | 4 | 5 | 6 | 10 | | 9 | 8 | $11^{1}$ | | 2 | 12 | | 7 | | | | | | | 6 |
| 1 | 2 | 3 | 4 | 5 | 6 | | 12 | $9^{1}$ | 8 | 11 | | 10 | | | 7 | | | | | | | 7 |
| 1 | 2 | 3 | 4 | 5 | 6 | | 12 | 9 | 8 | 11 | | $10^{1}$ | | | $7^{2}$ | 13 | | | | | | 8 |
| 1 | 2 | 3 | 4 | 5 | 6 | | $8^{1}$ | $9^{3}$ | 10 | 11 | | | 12 | | $7^{2}$ | 13 | 14 | | | | | 9 |
| 1 | 2 | 3 | $4^{2}$ | 5 | 6 | 10 | $9^{1}$ | 12 | 8 | 11 | | | | | 7 | 13 | | | | | | 10 |
| 1 | 2 | 3 | | 5 | 6 | $10^{2}$ | $9^{1}$ | | 8 | 11 | | | 14 | | $7^{3}$ | 13 | 12 | 4 | | | | 11 |
| 1 | 2 | 3 | | 5 | 6 | $10^{1}$ | $9^{2}$ | | 8 | 11 | | | 12 | | $7^{3}$ | 14 | 13 | 4 | | | | 12 |
| 1 | 2 | 3 | | 5 | 6 | 10 | $9^{1}$ | 12 | 8 | $11^{2}$ | | | | | 7 | 13 | | 4 | | | | 13 |
| 1 | 2 | 3 | 4 | $5^{1}$ | $6^{2}$ | | $9^{3}$ | 14 | 8 | 11 | | | 13 | | 7 | 10 | | 12 | | | | 14 |
| 1 | $2^{2}$ | 3 | 4 | 5 | 6 | | $9^{1}$ | 12 | 8 | $11^{3}$ | | | 13 | | 7 | 10 | 14 | | | | | 15 |
| 1 | 2 | 3 | 4 | 5 | 6 | | $9^{2}$ | 13 | 8 | $11^{1}$ | | | 14 | | $7^{3}$ | 10 | 12 | | | | | 16 |
| 1 | 2 | 3 | $4^{1}$ | 5 | 6 | | $9^{3}$ | 13 | 8 | 11 | | | | | 7 | $10^{2}$ | 14 | 12 | | | | 17 |
| 1 | 2 | 3 | 4 | 5 | 6 | | $9^{1}$ | 12 | 8 | 11 | | | | | 7 | 10 | | | | | | 18 |
| 1 | $2^{3}$ | 3 | 4 | 5 | 6 | | | $9^{2}$ | 8 | 11 | | | 12 | | 7 | $10^{1}$ | 13 | 14 | | | | 19 |
| 1 | 2 | 3 | 4 | 5 | 6 | | | 9 | | 11 | | | $8^{1}$ | | 12 | 10 | | 13 | $7^{2}$ | | | 20 |
| 1 | 2 | 3 | 4 | 5 | 6 | | 13 | $9^{2}$ | | 11 | | | 8 | | | $10^{1}$ | | | 7 | 12 | | 21 |
| 1 | $2^{2}$ | 3 | 4 | 5 | 6 | | $12^{3}$ | $9^{1}$ | 8 | 11 | | | 13 | | | 10 | | 14 | 7 | | | 22 |
| 1 | 2 | 3 | 4 | | $6^{3}$ | | | $9^{1}$ | 8 | $11^{2}$ | | | 7 | | 12 | 10 | | 5 | | 14 | 13 | 23 |
| 1 | $2^{1}$ | 3 | 4 | | 6 | | | 9 | 8 | | | | 11 | | 7 | 10 | 12 | 5 | | | | 24 |
| 1 | $2^{3}$ | 3 | 4 | 5 | $6^{2}$ | 13 | | 9 | 8 | $11^{1}$ | | | 12 | | 7 | 10 | 14 | | | | | 25 |
| 1 | $2^{2}$ | 3 | 4 | 5 | 6 | | | 9 | 8 | 12 | | 13 | $11^{1}$ | | 7 | 10 | | | | | | 26 |
| 1 | 2 | 3 | 4 | 5 | 6 | 14 | | $9^{1}$ | 8 | $11^{2}$ | | 13 | | | $7^{3}$ | 10 | | 12 | | | | 27 |
| 1 | 2 | $3^{3}$ | 4 | 5 | 6 | 12 | | 9 | | $11^{1}$ | | | 14 | | 7 | $10^{2}$ | 13 | 8 | | | | 28 |
| 1 | 2 | 3 | 4 | 5 | 6 | 12 | | 9 | 8 | | | | $11^{1}$ | | 7 | 10 | | | | | | 29 |
| 1 | 2 | | 4 | 5 | 6 | 12 | 8 | 9 | | | | | $11^{1}$ | | 7 | 10 | | 3 | | | | 30 |
| 1 | 2 | | 4 | 5 | 6 | $10^{3}$ | $9^{1}$ | 13 | 8 | 11 | | | | | 12 | 14 | | 3 | $7^{2}$ | | | 31 |
| 1 | 2 | 3 | 4 | 5 | 6 | $10^{1}$ | 9 | 14 | 8 | $11^{3}$ | | | | | $7^{2}$ | 12 | | | 13 | | | 32 |
| 1 | 2 | 3 | 4 | 5 | | 6 | $11^{1}$ | $9^{2}$ | 8 | 13 | | 12 | | | | 10 | | | 7 | | | 33 |
| 1 | $2^{2}$ | 3 | 4 | 5 | | 6 | 12 | $9^{1}$ | 8 | $11^{3}$ | | 14 | 13 | | 7 | 10 | | | | | | 34 |
| 1 | | 3 | 4 | 5 | 6 | | 12 | $9^{1}$ | 8 | 11 | | $2^{2}$ | | | 7 | 10 | | 13 | | | | 35 |
| 1 | 2 | 3 | 4 | 5 | | 6 | 12 | 9 | 8 | 11 | | | | | 7 | $10^{1}$ | | | | | | 36 |

# KILMARNOCK — Premier League

*Year Formed:* 1869. *Ground & Address:* Rugby Park, Kilmarnock KA1 2DP. *Telephone:* 01563 545300. *Fax:* 01563 522181. *Website:* www.kilmarnockfc.co.uk
*Ground Capacity:* all seated: 18,128. *Size of Pitch:* 114yd × 72yd.
*Chairman:* James T. Moffat. *Secretary:* Angela Burnett. *General Manager:* David MacKinnon.
*Manager:* Jim Jefferies. *Assistant Manager:* Billy Brown. *Physio:* A. MacQueen.
*Managers since 1975:* W. Fernie, D. Sneddon, J. Clunie, E. Morrison, J. Fleeting, T. Burns, A. Totten, B. Brown.
*Club Nickname(s):* Killie. *Previous Grounds:* Rugby Park (Dundonald Road); The Grange; Holm Quarry; Present ground since 1899.
*Record Attendance:* 35,995 v Rangers, Scottish Cup, 10 Mar 1962.
*Record Transfer Fee received:* £300,000 for Shaun McSkimming to Motherwell (1995).
*Record Transfer Fee paid:* £300,000 for Paul Wright from St Johnstone (1995).
*Record Victory:* 11-1 v Paisley Academical, Scottish Cup, 18 Jan 1930 (15-0 v Lanemark, Ayrshire Cup, 15 Nov 1890).
*Record Defeat:* 1-9 v Celtic, Division I, 13 Aug 1938.
*Most Capped Player:* Joe Nibloe, 11, Scotland.
*Most League Appearances:* 481: Alan Robertson, 1972-88.
*Most League Goals in Season (Individual):* 34: Harry 'Peerie' Cunningham 1927-28 and Andy Kerr 1960-61.
*Most Goals Overall (Individual):* 148: W. Culley, 1912-23.

## KILMARNOCK 2003–04 LEAGUE RECORD

| Match No. | Date | Venue | Opponents | Result | | H/T Score | Lg. Pos. | Goalscorers | Attendance |
|---|---|---|---|---|---|---|---|---|---|
| 1 | Aug 9 | A | Rangers | L | 0-4 | 0-3 | — | | 49108 |
| 2 | 16 | H | Partick Th | W | 2-1 | 0-1 | 8 | Hardie 46, Boyd 60 | 6778 |
| 3 | 23 | A | Motherwell | L | 1-2 | 0-0 | 9 | Dindeleux 76 | 5087 |
| 4 | 31 | H | Dundee | D | 1-1 | 0-0 | 8 | Boyd 78 | 5935 |
| 5 | Sept 13 | H | Hearts | L | 0-2 | 0-2 | 10 | | 6925 |
| 6 | 20 | A | Livingston | W | 2-1 | 2-1 | 8 | Hessey 15, Boyd 22 | 4846 |
| 7 | 27 | A | Dundee U | D | 1-1 | 0-0 | 9 | Boyd 71 | 6529 |
| 8 | Oct 4 | H | Aberdeen | L | 1-3 | 0-2 | 9 | Nish 67 | 6023 |
| 9 | 18 | A | Dunfermline Ath | W | 3-2 | 1-1 | 9 | McSwegan 2 24, 83, Shields 68 | 4495 |
| 10 | 25 | A | Hibernian | L | 1-3 | 0-2 | 9 | Nish 81 | 7191 |
| 11 | Nov 1 | H | Celtic | L | 0-5 | 0-1 | 9 | | 12,460 |
| 12 | 9 | H | Rangers | L | 2-3 | 1-1 | 9 | McDonald 38, Canero 49 | 12,204 |
| 13 | 22 | A | Partick Th | W | 4-2 | 1-1 | 9 | Nish 2 26, 89, McDonald 2 60, 65 | 4445 |
| 14 | 29 | H | Motherwell | W | 2-0 | 1-0 | 8 | Canero 13, Boyd 59 | 6320 |
| 15 | Dec 6 | A | Dundee | W | 2-1 | 2-1 | 6 | Nish 7, Boyd 36 | 6954 |
| 16 | 13 | A | Hearts | L | 1-2 | 0-0 | 6 | McSwegan 89 | 10,154 |
| 17 | 20 | H | Livingston | L | 0-3 | 0-1 | 7 | | 5035 |
| 18 | 27 | H | Dundee U | L | 0-2 | 0-1 | 8 | | 6062 |
| 19 | Jan 3 | A | Aberdeen | L | 1-3 | 0-2 | 9 | Nish 81 | 11,699 |
| 20 | 17 | H | Dunfermline Ath | D | 1-1 | 1-0 | 10 | McSwegan 28 | 5715 |
| 21 | 24 | H | Hibernian | L | 0-2 | 0-0 | 10 | | 5571 |
| 22 | 31 | A | Celtic | L | 1-5 | 0-0 | 10 | McSwegan 84 | 59,046 |
| 23 | Feb 11 | A | Rangers | L | 0-2 | 0-1 | — | | 46,900 |
| 24 | 14 | H | Partick Th | W | 2-1 | 0-0 | 10 | Lilley 55, Boyd 57 | 5818 |
| 25 | 21 | A | Motherwell | L | 0-1 | 0-1 | 10 | | 5163 |
| 26 | 28 | H | Dundee | W | 4-2 | 2-1 | 10 | Skora 31, Invincibile 2 33, 63, Boyd 53 | 5454 |
| 27 | Mar 7 | H | Hearts | D | 1-1 | 0-0 | — | Invincibile 86 | 5297 |
| 28 | 20 | A | Dundee U | L | 1-4 | 0-4 | 11 | Invincibile 61 | 5757 |
| 29 | 27 | H | Aberdeen | W | 3-1 | 2-1 | 8 | Dargo 1, Boyd 2 27, 75 | 7251 |
| 30 | Apr 3 | A | Dunfermline Ath | L | 1-2 | 1-1 | 11 | Invincibile 9 | 3914 |
| 31 | 7 | A | Livingston | D | 1-1 | 0-0 | — | Dargo 84 | 2677 |
| 32 | 10 | A | Hibernian | L | 0-3 | 0-2 | 10 | | 7287 |
| 33 | 18 | H | Celtic | L | 0-1 | 0-1 | 10 | | 14,516 |
| 34 | 24 | H | Hibernian | W | 2-0 | 1-0 | 10 | Boyd 2 22, 85 | 4886 |
| 35 | May 1 | H | Livingston | W | 4-2 | 0-2 | 9 | Nish 2 54, 79, Canning 74, McSwegan 87 | 5023 |
| 36 | 8 | A | Dundee | L | 0-2 | 0-1 | 10 | | 4942 |
| 37 | 12 | H | Aberdeen | W | 4-0 | 2-0 | — | Skora 23, Boyd 2 35, 59, Nish 60 | 4967 |
| 38 | 15 | A | Partick Th | D | 2-2 | 1-1 | 10 | Boyd 5, Dargo 68 | 4124 |

**Final League Position: 10**

**Honours**
*League Champions:* Division I 1964-65. Division II 1897-98, 1898-99; *Runners-up:* Division I 1959-60, 1960-61, 1962-63, 1963-64. First Division 1975-76, 1978-79, 1981-82, 1992-93. Division II 1953-54, 1973-74. Second Division 1989-90.
*Scottish Cup Winners:* 1920, 1929, 1997; *Runners-up:* 1898, 1932, 1938, 1957, 1960.
*League Cup Runners-up:* 1952-53, 1960-61, 1962-63, 2000-01.

**European:** *European Cup:* 4 matches (1965-66). *Cup Winners' Cup:* 4 matches (1997-98). *UEFA Cup:* 24 matches (*Fairs Cup:* 1964-65, 1966-67, 1969-70, 1970-71, *UEFA Cup:* 1998-99, 1999-2000, 2001-02).

**Club colours:** Shirt: Blue and white vertical stripes. Shorts: Blue. Stockings: Blue.

**Goalscorers:** *League* (51): Boyd 15, Nish 9, McSwegan 6, Invincibile 5, Dargo 3, McDonald 3, Canero 2, Skora 2, Canning 1, Dindeleux 1, Hardie 1, Hessey 1, Lilley 1, Shields 1
*Scottish Cup* (3): McDonald 1, McSwegan 1, Nish 1
*CIS Cup* (0):

| Meldrum C 16 + 1 | Shields G 19 | Dindeleux F 33 | Hessey S 7 | Innes C 1 | Hay G 30 | Locke G 18 + 2 | Fulton S 21 | Invincibile D 19 + 3 | Boyd K 31 + 5 | Di Giacomo P 4 + 3 | McSwegan G 13 + 18 | Nish C 15 + 15 | Fowler J 25 + 7 | Hardie M 8 + 8 | McLaughlin B 14 + 2 | McDonald G 15 + 8 | Mahood A 2 + 3 | Murray S 22 + 7 | Canero P 12 + 1 | Dubourdeau F 19 | Dillon S 2 | Dodds R 9 + 2 | Greer G 23 + 2 | Dargo C 3 + 9 | Samson C 1 | Skora E 16 + 1 | Lilley D 14 | Smith G 2 + 1 | Naismith S — + 1 | Canning M 4 + 1 | *Match No.* |
|---|---|---|---|---|---|---|---|---|---|---|---|---|---|---|---|---|---|---|---|---|---|---|---|---|---|---|---|---|---|---|---|
| 1 | 2 | 3 | 4 | 5■ | 6 | 7 | 8 | 9 | $10^{1}$ | $11^{2}$ | 12 | 13 | | | | | | | | | | | | | | | | | | | 1 |
| 1 | 2 | 3 | 4 | | 5 | $7^{2}$ | 8 | $9^{1}$ | 10 | 12 | $11^{3}$ | | 6 | 13 | 14 | | | | | | | | | | | | | | | | 2 |
| 1 | | 3 | | | 5 | | 8 | | 10 | $9^{2}$ | 11 | 13 | 2■ | $6^{1}$ | 4 | $7^{3}$ | 12 | 14 | | | | | | | | | | | | | 3 |
| 1 | 2 | 3 | | | 5 | | 8 | | 10 | $9^{1}$ | 13 | 12 | | | 4 | $11^{2}$ | 6 | 7 | | | | | | | | | | | | | 4 |
| 1 | 2 | 3 | | | $5^{3}$ | | 8 | | 10 | | $11^{1}$ | 13 | 7 | 12 | 4 | | $6^{2}$ | 14 | 9 | | | | | | | | | | | | 5 |
| | 2 | 3 | 5 | | | | 8 | | $10^{1}$ | 12 | | $7^{2}$ | 6 | 11 | 4■ | | 13 | | 9 | 1 | | | | | | | | | | | 6 |
| | 2 | 3 | 4 | | | $8^{1}$ | 7 | 13 | 10 | | | $6^{2}$ | 5 | 11 | | | 12 | | 9 | 1 | | | | | | | | | | | 7 |
| | $2^{1}$ | 3 | 4 | | | 8 | 7 | $9^{3}$ | 10 | | 14 | 12 | $5^{2}$ | 11 | | | | 13 | 6 | 1 | | | | | | | | | | | 8 |
| | 2 | | 4 | | | | 8 | $9^{1}$ | 10 | | 11 | | 6 | | 3 | 13 | | 12 | | 1 | 5 | $7^{2}$ | | | | | | | | | 9 |
| | 2 | 3 | | | | | 8 | 9 | $10^{2}$ | | 11 | 13 | $6^{3}$ | | | 12 | | 14 | | 1 | 5 | $7^{1}$ | 4 | | | | | | | | 10 |
| | 2 | 3 | 5 | | | | 8 | $9^{2}$ | | $11^{3}$ | 14 | 13 | $6^{1}$ | | 4 | 10 | | | 12 | 1 | | | 7 | | | | | | | | 11 |
| | 2 | 3 | | | 5 | | $8^{3}$ | | $10^{1}$ | | 12 | 6 | | 13 | 14 | 11 | | $7^{2}$ | 9 | 1 | | | 4 | | | | | | | | 12 |
| | 2 | 3 | | | $5^{2}$ | | 8 | | 12 | | $10^{1}$ | 6 | | 13 | | 11 | | $7^{3}$ | 9 | 1 | | | 4 | 14 | | | | | | | 13 |
| | 2 | 3 | | | 5 | | $8^{3}$ | | $10^{1}$ | | 13 | $6^{2}$ | 14 | 12 | | 11 | | 7 | 9 | 1 | | | 4 | | | | | | | | 14 |
| | 2 | 3 | | | 5 | | $8^{3}$ | | 10 | 13 | 12 | $6^{2}$ | 14 | 11 | | | | $7^{1}$ | 9 | 1 | | | 4 | | | | | | | | 15 |
| | 2 | 3 | | | 5 | | 8 | | 10 | | 13 | 6 | | 12 | | $11^{2}$ | | $7^{1}$ | 9 | 1 | | | 4 | | | | | | | | 16 |
| | 2 | 3 | | | $5^{1}$ | | 8 | | 10 | | 12 | 6 | | | | 11 | | 7 | 9 | 1 | | | 4 | | | | | | | | 17 |
| | 2 | 3 | | | $5^{3}$ | | 8 | | 13 | | 10 | $6^{2}$ | 12 | 14 | | 11 | | $7^{1}$ | 9 | 1 | | | 4 | | | | | | | | 18 |
| | $2^{1}$ | 3 | | | 5 | $8^{3}$ | 7 | | $10^{2}$ | | | 6 | 12 | 13 | | 11 | | 14 | 9 | | | | 4 | | 1 | | | | | | 19 |
| | 2 | 3 | | | | 8 | 7 | 13 | 12 | | 10 | $6^{1}$ | 5 | | | 11 | | | | 1 | | $9^{2}$ | 4 | | | | | | | | 20 |
| | | 3 | | | | 8 | $7^{2}$ | 14 | 13 | | 10 | $6^{3}$ | 5 | | $2^{1}$ | 11 | | | | 1 | | 9 | 4 | | | 12 | | | | | 21 |
| 13 | | | | | $5^{2}$ | 8 | | 7 | | | 10 | | 12 | 9 | 2 | 11 | | | | 1 | | | $4^{1}$ | | | 6 | 3 | | | | 22 |
| | | | | | $5^{2}$ | | | 7 | 10 | | 12 | $9^{1}$ | 6 | | 2 | 14 | | 13 | | 1 | | $11^{3}$ | 4 | | | 8 | 3 | | | | 23 |
| | | | | | 5 | 8 | | | 12 | | $10^{2}$ | | 14 | 9 | 2 | | | $7^{3}$ | | 1 | | $11^{1}$ | 4 | 13 | | 6 | 3 | | | | 24 |
| | | | | | 5 | 8 | | | 10 | | $11^{1}$ | 13 | 14 | 9 | 2 | | | $7^{2}$ | | 1 | | | 4 | 12 | | 6 | $3^{3}$ | | | | 25 |
| 1 | | 3 | | | 5 | 8 | | 11 | $10^{3}$ | | 13 | 14 | 6 | | 2 | 12 | | 7 | | | | | | | | $9^{2}$ | $4^{1}$ | | | | 26 |
| $1^{1}$ | | 3 | | | 5 | 8 | | 11 | $10^{3}$ | | | 14 | 6 | | $2^{2}$ | | | 7 | | | | | 13 | | | 9 | 4 | 12 | | | 27 |
| 1 | | 3 | | | $5^{2}$ | 8 | | 9 | 10 | | | | 6 | | $2^{1}$ | 11 | | | | | | | 12 | 13 | | 7 | 4 | | | | 28 |
| 1 | | 3 | | | 5 | $8^{1}$ | | | $10^{3}$ | | 13 | 14 | 6 | | | | | 7 | | | | 12 | 2 | $11^{2}$ | | 9 | 4 | | | | 29 |
| 1 | | 3 | | | $5^{1}$ | 8 | | 11 | 10 | | 13 | 14 | $6^{3}$ | | | | | $7^{2}$ | | | | | 2 | 12 | | 9 | 4 | | | | 30 |
| 1 | | 3 | | | 5 | 8 | | $11^{1}$ | 10 | | 13 | 14 | 6 | | | | | $7^{2}$ | | | | | 2 | 12 | | 9 | $4^{3}$ | | | | 31 |
| 1 | | 3 | | | 5 | 8 | | | 10 | | | 12 | 6 | | | 14 | | $7^{2}$ | | | | | 2 | $11^{3}$ | | 9 | $4^{1}$ | | 13 | | 32 |
| 1 | | 3 | | | 5 | 8 | | $11^{2}$ | 10 | | 13 | | 6 | | | | | $7^{1}$ | | | | | 2 | 12 | | 9 | 4 | | | | 33 |
| 1 | | 3 | | | 5 | | | 9 | 10 | | 12 | | 4 | | | 14 | | $7^{2}$ | | | | 6 | 2 | $11^{1}$ | | $8^{3}$ | | | | 13 | 34 |
| 1 | | 3 | | | 5 | | | 11 | $10^{1}$ | | 14 | 12 | 4 | | | 13 | | 7 | | | | 6 | $2^{2}$ | | | 8 | | | | $9^{3}$ | 35 |
| 1 | | 3 | | | 2 | 12 | | 9 | 10 | | $11^{2}$ | | 4 | | | 13 | | 7 | | | | $5^{1}$ | | | | 8 | | | | 6 | 36 |
| | | 3 | | | 5 | | | 11 | $10^{2}$ | | 13 | $9^{3}$ | 4 | | | | | 7 | | | | 12 | | 14 | | $8^{1}$ | 2 | 1 | | 6 | 37 |
| | | 3 | | | 5 | 12 | | 9 | 10 | | | $8^{2}$ | 4 | | | 11 | | 7 | | | | | | 13 | | | 2 | 1 | | $6^{1}$ | 38 |

# LIVINGSTON

## Premier League

*Year Formed:* 1974. *Ground:* West Lothian Courier Stadium, Alderton Road, Livingston EH54 7DN. *Telephone:* 01506 417000. *Fax:* 01506 418888. *Email:* info@livingstonfc.co.uk
*Ground Capacity:* 10,024 (all seated). *Size of Pitch:* 105yd × 72yd.
*Chairman:* Dr A. Kinder. *General Manager:* David Hay. *Secretary:* J. R. S. Renton.
*Team Manager:* Allan Preston. *Assistant Manager:* Alan Kernaghan. *Physios:* Michael McBride, Arthur Duncan.
*Managers since 1975:* Jim Leishman, John Bain, Alec Ness, Willie MacFarlane, Terry Christie, Michael Lawson.
*Club Nickname:* Livi Lions. *Previous Grounds:* None.
*Record Attendance:* 10,024 v Celtic, Premier League, 18 Aug 2001.
*Record Transfer Fee received:* £1,000,000 for D. Fernandez to Celtic (June 2002).
*Record Transfer Fee paid:* £60,000 for Barry Wilson from Inverness CT (May 2000).
*Record Victory:* 7-0 v Queen of the South, Scottish Cup, 29 Jan 2000.
*Record Defeat:* 0-8 v Hamilton A. Division II, 14 Dec 1974.
*Most Capped Player (under 18):* I. Little.
*Most League Appearances:* 446: Walter Boyd, 1979-89.
*Most League Goals in Season (Individual):* 21: John McGachie, 1986-87. *(Team):* 69; Second Division, 1986-87.
*Most Goals Overall (Individual):* 64: David Roseburgh, 1986-93.

### LIVINGSTON 2003–04 LEAGUE RECORD

| Match No. | Date | Venue | Opponents | Result | | H/T Score | Lg. Pos. | Goalscorers | Attendance |
|---|---|---|---|---|---|---|---|---|---|
| 1 | Aug 9 | A | Partick Th | D | 1-1 | 0-1 | — | Pasquinelli [77] | 4220 |
| 2 | 16 | H | Motherwell | W | 1-0 | 0-0 | 3 | Lilley [78] | 4497 |
| 3 | 23 | A | Dundee | L | 1-2 | 1-1 | 7 | O'Brien [37] | 5815 |
| 4 | 30 | A | Celtic | L | 1-5 | 0-2 | 8 | Lilley [84] | 57,062 |
| 5 | Sept 13 | H | Dundee U | D | 0-0 | 0-0 | 8 | | 4226 |
| 6 | 20 | H | Kilmarnock | L | 1-2 | 1-2 | 9 | Makel [18] | 4846 |
| 7 | 27 | A | Aberdeen | W | 3-0 | 1-0 | 6 | Quino [45], Rubio [63], Pasquinelli [68] | 10,307 |
| 8 | Oct 4 | H | Dunfermline Ath | D | 0-0 | 0-0 | 8 | | 3993 |
| 9 | 18 | A | Hibernian | W | 2-0 | 1-0 | 5 | Lilley 2 [36, 81] | 8562 |
| 10 | 25 | H | Rangers | D | 0-0 | 0-0 | 6 | | 7689 |
| 11 | Nov 1 | A | Hearts | L | 1-3 | 0-0 | 8 | Lilley [52] | 11,233 |
| 12 | 8 | H | Partick Th | W | 2-0 | 2-0 | 6 | Lilley (pen) [16], Makel [44] | 4397 |
| 13 | 22 | A | Motherwell | D | 1-1 | 1-1 | 6 | Lilley [38] | 6357 |
| 14 | 29 | H | Dundee | D | 1-1 | 0-0 | 6 | Lilley (pen) [72] | 3878 |
| 15 | Dec 6 | H | Celtic | L | 0-2 | 0-0 | 7 | | 8065 |
| 16 | 13 | A | Dundee U | L | 0-2 | 0-1 | 8 | | 5421 |
| 17 | 20 | A | Kilmarnock | W | 3-0 | 1-0 | 5 | Camacho [19], Pasquinelli [80], O'Brien [90] | 5035 |
| 18 | 27 | H | Aberdeen | D | 1-1 | 0-1 | 5 | O'Brien [88] | 6020 |
| 19 | Jan 3 | A | Dunfermline Ath | D | 2-2 | 1-1 | 6 | McNamee [14], Makel [62] | 5154 |
| 20 | 17 | H | Hibernian | W | 1-0 | 1-0 | 5 | Makel [25] | 4948 |
| 21 | 24 | A | Rangers | L | 0-1 | 0-1 | 5 | | 48,638 |
| 22 | Feb 11 | A | Partick Th | L | 2-5 | 0-2 | — | Makel [85], McMenamin [90] | 3011 |
| 23 | 14 | H | Motherwell | W | 3-1 | 3-0 | 5 | McAllister [2], Lilley [29], Fernandez [44] | 3624 |
| 24 | 21 | A | Dundee | L | 0-1 | 0-0 | 6 | | 6108 |
| 25 | 24 | H | Hearts | L | 2-3 | 1-1 | — | Makel [5], McMenamin [56] | 4630 |
| 26 | 29 | A | Celtic | L | 1-5 | 1-2 | 7 | Lilley [40] | 57,949 |
| 27 | Mar 21 | A | Aberdeen | W | 2-1 | 1-0 | 7 | McMenamin [13], McGovern [87] | 7477 |
| 28 | 24 | H | Dundee U | L | 2-3 | 1-1 | — | McNamee [38], McLaughlin [71] | 3082 |
| 29 | 27 | H | Dunfermline Ath | D | 0-0 | 0-0 | 7 | | 3558 |
| 30 | Apr 3 | A | Hibernian | L | 1-3 | 0-1 | 7 | Lilley [50] | 6223 |
| 31 | 7 | H | Kilmarnock | D | 1-1 | 0-0 | — | Fernandez [83] | 2677 |
| 32 | 14 | H | Rangers | D | 1-1 | 0-1 | — | McMenamin [79] | 6092 |
| 33 | 17 | A | Hearts | D | 1-1 | 0-1 | 8 | McMenamin [73] | 10,352 |
| 34 | 24 | H | Aberdeen | W | 2-0 | 1-0 | 7 | McNamee [23], McMenamin [62] | 3133 |
| 35 | May 1 | A | Kilmarnock | L | 2-4 | 2-0 | 8 | Makel [13], O'Brien [22] | 5023 |
| 36 | 9 | H | Partick Th | D | 2-2 | 1-1 | 9 | O'Brien [22], McMenamin [68] | 2706 |
| 37 | 12 | A | Dundee | L | 0-2 | 0-1 | — | | 4954 |
| 38 | 15 | H | Hibernian | W | 4-1 | 1-0 | 9 | Lovell [7], Lilley [64], Fernandez [78], Makel [89] | 4409 |

**Final League Position: 9**

**Honours**
*League Champions:* First Division: Champions: 2000-01. Second Division 1986-87, 1998-99. Third Division 1995-96; *Runners-up:* Second Division 1982-83. First Division 1987-88.
*Scottish Cup:* Semi-finals 2004.
*League Cup Winners:* 2003-04. Semi-finals 1984-85. *B&Q Cup:* Semi-finals 1992-93, 1993-94, 2001.
*Bell's League Challenge Runners-up:* 2000-01.

**European:** *UEFA Cup:* 4 matches (2002-03).

**Club colours:** Shirt: Gold and white stripes with black trim. Shorts: Black with gold and white trim. Stockings: Gold with black trim.

**Goalscorers:** *League* (48): Lilley 12 (2 pens), Makel 8, McMenamin 7, O'Brien 5, Fernandez 3, McNamee 3, Pasquinelli 3, Camacho 1, Lovell 1, McAllister 1, McGovern 1, McLaughlin 1, Rubio 1, Quino 1
*Scottish Cup* (8): Lilley 3, Fernandez 2, McMenamin 1, O'Brien 1, own goal 1
*CIS Cup* (10): :Lilley 3, Makel 3, McAllister 1, Pasquinelli 1, Quino 1, own goal 1

| McKenzie R 35 | McNamee D 30 | McAllister J 34 | Rubio O 36 + 1 | Andrews M 38 | Whitmore T 2 + 1 | Makel L 36 | Wilson B 4 | O'Brien B 28 + 5 | McGovern J 11 + 16 | Pasquinelli F 16 + 5 | Kerr B 11 + 2 | Xausa D — + 1 | Main A 3 | Lilley D 29 + 7 | McLaughlin S 8 + 9 | Toure-Maman C 1 | Camacho J — + 6 | Capin S 2 | Quino F 6 + 6 | Fernandez D 25 + 2 | Ipoua G — + 1 | Dorado E 29 | Lovell S 24 + 1 | Brittain R 4 + 8 | McMenamin C 6 + 9 | McPake J — + 1 | Snowdon W — + 2 | Match No. |
|---|---|---|---|---|---|---|---|---|---|---|---|---|---|---|---|---|---|---|---|---|---|---|---|---|---|---|---|---|
| 1 | 2 | 3 | 4 | 5 | 6[2] | 7 | 8[1] | 9 | 10 | 11 | 12 | 13 | | | | | | | | | | | | | | | | 1 |
| | 2 | 3 | 4 | 5 | 6[1] | 7 | 8 | 9 | 10[2] | 11 | 12 | | 1 | 13 | | | | | | | | | | | | | | 2 |
| | 2 | 3[2] | 4 | 5 | 14 | 7[3] | 8[1] | 9 | 10 | 11 | 6 | | 1 | 12 | 13 | | | | | | | | | | | | | 3 |
| | 2[3] | 3 | 4 | 5 | | 7 | 8[2] | | 10 | 11 | 6 | | 1 | 12 | 14 | 9[1] | 13 | | | | | | | | | | | 4 |
| 1 | | 2 | 4 | 5 | | 7 | | | 10[1] | 11 | 6 | | | 12 | | | | 3 | 8 | 9 | | | | | | | | 5 |
| 1 | | 2 | 4 | 5[1] | | 7 | | | 14 | 11 | 6 | | | 9 | 12 | | | 3[3] | 8[2] | 10 | 13 | | | | | | | 6 |
| 1 | 2[1] | 3 | 4[3] | 5 | | 7 | | 14 | | 11[2] | 9 | | | 13 | 12 | | | | 8 | 10 | | 6 | | | | | | 7 |
| 1 | | 2[1] | 4 | 5 | | 7 | | | 10 | 11 | 6 | | | 13 | 12 | | | | 8[2] | 9 | | 3 | | | | | | 8 |
| 1 | 2 | 3 | 4 | 5 | | 7 | | 12 | 13 | | 8 | | | 11[2] | | | | | | 10 | | 6 | 9[1] | | | | | 9 |
| 1 | 2[2] | 3 | 4 | 5 | | 7 | | 12 | 13 | | 8 | | | 11 | | | | | | 10 | | 6 | 9[1] | | | | | 10 |
| 1 | 2■ | | 4 | 5 | | 7 | | 8 | 13 | | 6 | | | 11 | | | 12 | | | 10[2] | | 3[1] | 9 | | | | | 11 |
| 1 | | | 4 | 5 | | 7 | | 6 | 10 | | 3 | | | 11 | | | 12 | | | 9[1] | | 2 | 8 | | | | | 12 |
| 1 | | | 4 | 5 | | 7 | | 6 | 10 | | 3[1] | | | 11 | | | | | 12 | 9 | | 2 | 8 | | | | | 13 |
| 1 | 2 | 3 | 4 | 5 | | 7 | | 8 | | 12 | | | | 11[2] | | | | | 13 | 10 | | 6 | 9[1] | | | | | 14 |
| 1 | 2 | 3 | 4 | 5 | | | | 8 | 12 | 10 | | | | 11 | | | 13 | | 7 | | | 6[2] | 9[1] | | | | | 15 |
| 1 | 2 | 3 | 4 | 5 | | 7[1] | | 12 | 13 | 10[2] | | | | 11 | | | | | 8 | | | 6 | 9 | | | | | 16 |
| 1 | 2 | 3 | 4 | 5 | | 7 | | 8 | | 10[2] | | | | 11 | | | 12 | | 13 | | | 6[1] | 9 | | | | | 17 |
| 1 | 2 | 3 | 4[1] | 5 | | 7 | | 8 | | 10 | | | | 11 | | | 12 | | 13 | | | 6 | 9[2] | | | | | 18 |
| 1 | 2 | 3 | 4[1] | 5 | | 7 | | 8[2] | | 10[3] | | | | 11 | | | | | 13 | 12 | | 6 | 9 | 14 | | | | 19 |
| 1 | 2 | 3 | 4 | 5 | | 7 | | 8 | | 13 | | | | 11[2] | | | | | 12 | 10 | | 6 | 9[1] | | | | | 20 |
| 1 | 2 | 3 | 4 | 5 | | 7 | | 8 | | 12 | | | | 11[2] | | | | | | 10 | | 6 | 9[1] | 13 | | | | 21 |
| 1 | 2 | 3 | 4[2] | 5 | | 7 | | 8 | 12 | 10[1] | | | | 11 | | | | | | 9 | | 6 | | | 13 | | | 22 |
| 1 | 2[2] | 3 | 4 | 5 | | 7 | | 8 | 13 | | | | | 11 | 12 | | | | | 10[3] | | 6[1] | 9 | | 14 | | | 23 |
| 1 | 2 | 3[1] | 4 | 5 | | 7 | | 8 | | 12 | | | | 11 | | | | | | 10[3] | | 6 | 9[2] | 13 | 14 | | | 24 |
| 1 | 2 | | 4 | 5 | | 7 | | 8 | | 12 | | | | 11 | | | | | | 10 | | 3 | 6 | | 9[1] | | | 25 |
| 1 | 2 | 3 | 4[1] | 5 | | 7[2] | | 8 | 13 | 10 | | | | 11 | | | | | | | | 6 | 9 | | 12 | | | 26 |
| 1 | 2 | 3[1] | 4 | 5 | | | | 12 | 10 | 11[2] | | | | 13 | 7 | | | | | 14 | | 6 | | 8 | 9[3] | | | 27 |
| 1 | 2 | 3 | 4 | 5 | | 7 | | 8 | 12 | | | | | 11[3] | 13 | | | | | 10 | | 6[1] | 9[2] | | 14 | | | 28 |
| 1 | 2[1] | 3 | 4 | 5 | | 7 | | 8 | 12 | | | | | 11[2] | 9 | | | | | 10 | | | | 6 | 13 | | | 29 |
| 1 | | 3 | 4 | 5 | | 7 | | 8 | | | | | | 11[2] | 6 | | | | | 10 | | | 9[1] | 2 | 12 | 13 | | 30 |
| 1 | 2 | 3 | 4[2] | 5 | | 7 | | 8 | 13 | | | | | 11[1] | 9[3] | | | | | 10 | | 6 | | 14 | 12 | | | 31 |
| 1 | 2 | 3 | 4[2] | 5 | | 7 | | 8 | 13 | | | | | 11[1] | 9[3] | | | | | 10 | | 6 | | 14 | 12 | | | 32 |
| 1 | 2 | 3 | | 5 | | 7 | | | 8[1] | | | | | | 6 | | | | | 10 | | 4 | 9 | 12 | 11[2] | | 13 | 33 |
| 1 | 2[2] | 3 | 4 | 5 | | 7 | | 8 | | | | | | 10[3] | 13 | | | | | | | 6[1] | 9 | 14 | 11 | | 12 | 34 |
| 1 | | 3[2] | 4[1] | 5 | | 7 | | 8 | 13 | | | | | 11 | 6 | | | | | 10 | | 2 | 9 | 12 | | | | 35 |
| 1 | | 3 | 13 | 4 | | 7 | | 8 | 12 | | | | | 11[3] | 6[1] | | | | | 10 | | 2 | 14 | 5[2] | 9 | | | 36 |
| 1 | 2 | 3 | 4[1] | 5 | | 7 | | 8 | 12 | | | | | 11 | | | | | | | | 6 | 9 | | 10 | | | 37 |
| 1 | 2[1] | 3 | 4 | 5 | | 7 | | 6 | 9 | | | | | 11 | 12 | | | | | 10 | | | 8 | | | | | 38 |

# MONTROSE

## Third Division

*Year Formed:* 1879. *Ground & Address:* Links Park, Wellington St, Montrose DD10 8QD. *Telephone:* 01674 673200.
*Ground Capacity:* total: 3292, seated: 1338. *Size of Pitch:* 113yd × 70yd.
*Chairman:* John F. Paton. *Secretary:* Malcolm J. Watters.
*Manager:* Henry Hall.
*Managers since 1975:* A. Stuart, K. Cameron, R. Livingstone, S. Murray, D. D'Arcy, I. Stewart, C. McLelland, D. Rougvie, J. Leishman, J Holt, A. Dornan, D. Smith, T. Campbell, K. Drinkell.
*Club Nickname(s):* The Gable Endies. *Previous Grounds:* None.
*Record Attendance:* 8983 v Dundee, Scottish Cup 3rd rd, 17 Mar 1973.
*Record Transfer Fee received:* £50,000 for Gary Murray to Hibernian (Dec 1980).
*Record Transfer Fee paid:* £17,500 for Jim Smith from Airdrieonians (Feb 1992).
*Record Victory:* 12-0 v Vale of Leithen, Scottish Cup 2nd rd, 4 Jan 1975.
*Record Defeat:* 0-13 v Aberdeen, 17 Mar 1951.
*Most Capped Player:* Alexander Keillor, 2 (6), Scotland.
*Most League Appearances:* 426: David Larter, 1987-98.
*Most League Goals in Season (Individual):* 28: Brian Third, Division II, 1972-73.

### MONTROSE 2003–04 LEAGUE RECORD

| Match No. | Date | Venue | Opponents | Result | | H/T Score | Lg. Pos. | Goalscorers | Attendance |
|---|---|---|---|---|---|---|---|---|---|
| 1 | Aug 9 | H | Peterhead | L | 0-1 | 0-1 | — | | 411 |
| 2 | 16 | A | East Stirling | D | 1-1 | 0-0 | 6 | Gibson [70] | 182 |
| 3 | 23 | H | Cowdenbeath | L | 1-3 | 1-1 | 9 | Michie [16] | 338 |
| 4 | 30 | H | Elgin C | D | 3-3 | 2-1 | 9 | Kerrigan [9], Gibson [17], Black [58] | 324 |
| 5 | Sept 13 | A | Albion R | W | 1-0 | 0-0 | 8 | Kerrigan [74] | 262 |
| 6 | 20 | A | Queen's Park | D | 1-1 | 1-1 | 8 | Michie [39] | 490 |
| 7 | 27 | H | Stranraer | L | 2-4 | 0-2 | 9 | Kerrigan [76], Gibson [81] | 273 |
| 8 | Oct 4 | A | Gretna | D | 1-1 | 1-1 | 9 | Simpson [45] | 356 |
| 9 | 11 | A | Stirling A | L | 0-3 | 0-2 | 9 | | 490 |
| 10 | 18 | H | Stirling A | L | 2-3 | 0-2 | 9 | Smart 2 [74, 77] | 338 |
| 11 | 25 | H | East Stirling | W | 5-1 | 1-1 | 8 | Michie [28], Black 2 [52, 83], Kerrigan [80], Smith E [89] | 246 |
| 12 | Nov 1 | A | Peterhead | D | 0-0 | 0-0 | 8 | | 540 |
| 13 | 8 | H | Albion R | W | 1-0 | 0-0 | 7 | Kerrigan [63] | 267 |
| 14 | 15 | A | Elgin C | W | 3-2 | 1-1 | 6 | Michie [19], Kerrigan [71], Farnan [78] | 475 |
| 15 | Dec 2 | H | Queen's Park | D | 0-0 | 0-0 | — | | 279 |
| 16 | 6 | A | Stranraer | L | 0-2 | 0-1 | 6 | | 409 |
| 17 | 13 | H | Gretna | W | 2-0 | 2-0 | 6 | Black [38], Michie [44] | 438 |
| 18 | Jan 3 | A | Cowdenbeath | D | 3-3 | 2-2 | 6 | Smith E [18], Kerrigan [30], Smart [79] | 282 |
| 19 | 17 | H | Peterhead | W | 2-1 | 1-0 | 6 | Michie [19], Smart [56] | 512 |
| 20 | 24 | A | Queen's Park | D | 1-1 | 0-0 | 6 | Kerrigan [87] | 443 |
| 21 | 31 | H | Stranraer | L | 1-4 | 1-3 | 6 | Gibson [35] | 349 |
| 22 | Feb 7 | A | Albion R | L | 0-3 | 0-1 | 6 | | 192 |
| 23 | 14 | H | Elgin C | W | 4-3 | 3-1 | 6 | Gibson [2], Michie 2 [9, 63], Sharp [19] | 312 |
| 24 | 21 | H | Stirling A | L | 1-4 | 1-3 | 6 | Webster [34] | 466 |
| 25 | 28 | A | Gretna | W | 2-1 | 0-1 | 6 | Smart 2 [51, 72] | 635 |
| 26 | Mar 6 | A | East Stirling | W | 4-1 | 3-1 | 6 | Wood [2], Michie 2 [23, 70], Smith E [37] | 195 |
| 27 | 13 | H | Cowdenbeath | D | 1-1 | 1-1 | 6 | Michie [34] | 349 |
| 28 | 20 | H | Albion R | W | 3-1 | 0-0 | 6 | Smith E [59], Michie 2 [75, 82] | 339 |
| 29 | 27 | A | Elgin C | L | 1-2 | 0-0 | 6 | McQuillan [80] | 499 |
| 30 | Apr 3 | A | Stranraer | L | 0-6 | 0-2 | 6 | | 378 |
| 31 | 10 | H | Queen's Park | D | 1-1 | 1-0 | 6 | Smart [3] | 388 |
| 32 | 17 | A | Stirling A | D | 1-1 | 1-1 | 6 | Michie [23] | 672 |
| 33 | 24 | H | Gretna | L | 1-4 | 0-2 | 6 | Wood [62] | 395 |
| 34 | May 1 | A | Cowdenbeath | D | 0-0 | 0-0 | 6 | | 229 |
| 35 | 8 | H | East Stirling | W | 1-0 | 0-0 | 6 | Smart [90] | 360 |
| 36 | 15 | A | Peterhead | W | 2-1 | 1-1 | 6 | Henderson [43], Webster [83] | 604 |

**Final League Position: 6**

**Honours**
*League Champions:* Second Division 1984-85; *Runners-up:* 1990-91. Third Division, *Runners-up:* 1994-95.
*Scottish Cup:* Quarter-finals 1973, 1976.
*League Cup:* Semi-finals 1975-76.
*B&Q Cup:* Semi-finals 1992-93.
*League Challenge Cup:* Semi-finals: 1996-97.

**Club colours:** Shirt: Royal blue. Shorts: Royal blue. Stockings: White.

**Goalscorers:** *League* (52): Muchie 14, Kerrigan 8, Smart 8, Gibson 5, Black 4, Smith E 4, Webster 2, Wood 2, Farnan 1, Henderson 1, McQuillan 1, Sharp 1, Simpson 1
*Scottish Cup* (5): Michie 2, Wood 2, Ferguson 1
*CIS Cup* (2): Kerrigan 1, Smart 1
*Challenge Cup* (0)

| Butter J 30 | Donachie B 31 + 1 | Ferguson S 36 | Conway F 6 | Simpson M 10 + 1 | Smith G 9 + 4 | Gibson K 19 + 4 | Farnan C 6 + 7 | Smart C 24 + 2 | Wood M 26 + 3 | Kerrigan S 32 | Henderson R 4 + 16 | Webster K 26 + 6 | Sharp G 13 + 16 | Thomson G 2 | Michie S 30 + 1 | Watt J 1 + 9 | McQuillan J 33 | Black R 10 + 1 | Brash K 3 | Hankinson M 6 + 1 | Spink D 5 + 5 | Smith E 28 | Hall E 1 + 9 | Coulston D 2 + 4 | Budd A 2 | Stephen N 1 + 2 | *Match No.* |
|---|---|---|---|---|---|---|---|---|---|---|---|---|---|---|---|---|---|---|---|---|---|---|---|---|---|---|---|
| 1 | 2 | 3 | 4 | 5 | 6 | 7 | $8^3$ | $9^1$ | $10^2$ | 11 | 12 | 13 | 14 | | | | | | | | | | | | | | 1 |
| 1 | 2 | 3 | 4 | 5 | | 7 | 8 | | $10^3$ | $11^2$ | | 13 | 12 | $6^1$ | 9 | 14 | | | | | | | | | | | 2 |
| 1 | 2 | 3 | 6 | 5 | | 4 | $8^2$ | | | 10 | 14 | 7 | 12 | $11^1$ | $9^3$ | 13 | | | | | | | | | | | 3 |
| 1 | 2 | 3 | 6 | 5 | | 8 | | 12 | 13 | 10 | | 7 | | | $9^2$ | | 4 | $11^1$ | | | | | | | | | 4 |
| 1 | 2 | 3 | 6 | 5 | | 12 | 13 | 8 | | 10 | | $7^1$ | | | $9^3$ | 14 | 4 | | $11^2$ | | | | | | | | 5 |
| | 2 | 3 | 6 | 5 | | | 13 | $7^1$ | | 10 | | | 12 | | $9^3$ | 14 | 4 | | 11 | 1 | $8^2$ | | | | | | 6 |
| | | 3 | | 5 | | 7 | | | | 10 | 12 | | | | 9 | 13 | 4 | 8 | $11^1$ | 1 | $6^2$ | 2 | | | | | 7 |
| 1 | | 3 | | 5 | | 4 | 8 | | | $10^2$ | 12 | $7^1$ | | | 9 | 13 | 6 | 11 | | | | 2 | | | | | 8 |
| $1^2$ | 2 | 3 | | $5^1$ | 12 | 8 | 6 | | | 10 | 14 | 7 | | | $9^3$ | | 4 | | | 13 | | 11 | | | | | 9 |
| | 12 | 3 | | | $5^1$ | 13 | | 8 | 10 | 11 | 14 | 7 | | | | $9^2$ | 4 | $6^3$ | | 1 | | 2 | | | | | 10 |
| | 2 | 3 | | | | 12 | | 8 | $9^2$ | 6 | | 7 | 13 | | $10^1$ | 14 | 5 | $11^3$ | | 1 | | 4 | | | | | 11 |
| 1 | 2 | 3 | | | | 4 | 14 | $10^1$ | $9^3$ | 8 | | $7^2$ | 13 | | 12 | | 5 | 11 | | | | 6 | | | | | 12 |
| 1 | 2 | 3 | | | | 8 | | | $10^2$ | 6 | | 7 | 12 | | $9^1$ | 13 | 5 | 11 | | | | 4 | | | | | 13 |
| 1 | 2 | 3 | | | | 8 | 12 | | $10^1$ | 6 | | 7 | 13 | | $9^3$ | 14 | 5 | $11^2$ | | | | 4 | | | | | 14 |
| 1 | 2 | 3 | | | | 8[illegible] | 14 | $7^3$ | 10 | 6 | | 12 | $11^2$ | | $9^1$ | | 5 | 13 | | | | 4 | | | | | 15 |
| 1 | 2 | $3^3$ | | 14 | | | $6^1$ | 8 | 10 | | | 7 | 12 | | $9^2$ | | 5 | 11 | | | | 4 | 13 | | | | 16 |
| 1 | 2 | 3 | | | | 8 | 14 | $10^3$ | 12 | $6^2$ | | 7 | 13 | | $9^1$ | | 5 | 11 | | | | 4 | | | | | 17 |
| 1 | 2 | 3 | | 4 | | | 12 | 8 | 10 | $6^1$ | $9^2$ | 13 | 11 | | | | 5 | | | | | 7 | | | | | 18 |
| 1 | 2 | 3 | | | | | | 8 | 10 | 6 | 12 | 7 | 11 | | $9^1$ | | 5 | | | | | 4 | | | | | 19 |
| 1 | 2 | 3 | | | | $8^1$ | | $11^3$ | $10^2$ | 6 | 13 | 7 | 12 | | 9 | | 5 | | | | 14 | 4 | | | | | 20 |
| 1 | 2 | 3 | | | 12 | 8 | | 13 | 10 | 6 | | $7^3$ | $11^1$ | | $9^2$ | | 5 | | | | | 4 | 14 | | | | 21 |
| 1 | 2 | 3 | | | | 8 | | 7 | $10^2$ | | 12 | | $11^3$ | | $9^1$ | | 5 | | | | 6 | 4 | 13 | 14 | | | 22 |
| 1 | 2 | 3 | | | 13 | 8 | | 6 | 10 | | 12 | $7^1$ | $11^2$ | | 9 | | 5 | | | | | 4 | | | | | 23 |
| 1 | 2 | 3 | | | 12 | 8 | | 6 | $10^2$ | | 14 | 7 | 11 | | $9^1$ | | 5 | | | | 13 | $4^3$ | | | | | 24 |
| 1 | $2^1$ | 3 | | | 6 | 10 | | 11 | 9 | 8 | | 7 | 12 | | | | 5 | | | | | 4 | | | | | 25 |
| 1 | 2 | 3 | | | 6 | 13 | | $11^2$ | 10 | $8^3$ | | 12 | $7^1$ | | 9 | | 5 | | | | | 4 | 14 | | | | 26 |
| 1 | 2 | 3 | | | | 8 | | | 12 | 6 | $10^1$ | | 7 | | 9 | | 5 | | | | | 4 | 13 | $11^2$ | | | 27 |
| 1 | 2 | 3 | | | 4 | | | 11 | 10 | 6 | | $7^1$ | 12 | | 9 | | 5 | | | | | 8 | | | | | 28 |
| 1 | 2 | 3 | | | | | | 8 | $10^3$ | 6 | 13 | 7 | $11^1$ | | $9^2$ | | 5 | | | | | 4 | 14 | 12 | | | 29 |
| 1 | 2 | 3 | | | 6 | | | 11 | 10 | $8^3$ | | $7^1$ | | | 9 | | 5 | | | | 14 | $4^2$ | 13 | 12 | | | 30 |
| 1 | | 3 | | | 2 | | | 8 | 10 | 6 | 13 | 7 | 12 | | $9^2$ | | 5 | | | | | | | $11^1$ | 4 | | 31 |
| 1 | 2 | 3 | | | 4 | | | 8 | | 6 | $10^1$ | $7^3$ | $11^2$ | | 9 | | 5 | | | | 14 | | 13 | 12 | | | 32 |
| 1 | 2 | 3 | | | $4^1$ | | | | 10 | 6 | 13 | $7^2$ | 12 | | 9 | | 5 | | | | $8^3$ | 11 | 14 | | | | 33 |
| | 2 | 3 | | | | | | | 10 | 6 | 13 | 12 | $7^2$ | | $9^1$ | | 5 | | | 1 | 8 | 11 | | | | 4 | 34 |
| | 2 | 3 | | | | | | 8 | 10 | 6 | 13 | 7 | $11^2$ | | 9 | | 5 | | | 1 | | $4^1$ | | | | 12 | 35 |
| 1 | | $3^2$ | | | | | | 8 | 10 | $6^1$ | 9 | 7 | 14 | | | | 5 | | | | 12 | 4 | $11^3$ | | 2 | 13 | 36 |

# MORTON

## Second Division

*Year Formed:* 1874. *Ground & Address:* Cappielow Park, Sinclair St, Greenock. *Telephone:* 01475 723571. *Fax:* 01475 781084.
*Ground Capacity:* total: 11,612, seated: 6062. *Size of Pitch:* 110yd × 71yd.
*Commercial Manager:* Chris Norris.
*Manager:* John McCormack. *Managers since 1975:* Joe Gilroy, Benny Rooney, Alex Miller, Tommy McLean, Willie McLean, Allan McGraw, Billy Stark, Ian McCall, Allan Evans, Peter Cormack, Dave McPherson.
*Club Nickname(s):* The Ton. *Previous Grounds:* Grant Street 1874, Garvel Park 1875, Cappielow Park 1879, Ladyburn Park 1882, (Cappielow Park 1883).
*Record Attendance:* 23,500 v Celtic, 29 April 1922.
*Record Transfer Fee received:* £350,000 for Neil Orr to West Ham U.
*Record Transfer Fee paid:* £150,000 for Allan Mahood from Nottingham Forest.
*Record Victory:* 11-0 v Carfin Shamrock, Scottish Cup 1st rd, 13 Nov 1886.
*Record Defeat:* 1-10 v Port Glasgow Ath, Division II, 5 May, 1894 and v St Bernards, Division II, 14 Oct 1933.
*Most Capped Player:* Jimmy Cowan, 25, Scotland.
*Most League Appearances:* 358: David Hayes, 1969-84.
*Most League Goals in Season (Individual):* 58: Allan McGraw, Division II, 1963-64.

### MORTON 2003–04 LEAGUE RECORD

| *Match No.* | *Date* | *Venue* | *Opponents* | *Result* | *H/T Score* | *Lg. Pos.* | *Goalscorers* | *Attendance* |
|---|---|---|---|---|---|---|---|---|
| 1 | Aug 9 | H | Airdrie U | W 3-1 | 0-1 | — | Maisano J [53], Weatherson [76], Williams [77] | 3806 |
| 2 | 16 | A | Stenhousemuir | W 2-0 | 0-0 | 1 | Williams (pen) [49], Weatherson [90] | 1343 |
| 3 | 23 | H | Dumbarton | D 2-2 | 1-0 | 2 | Williams [31], Weatherson [83] | 3410 |
| 4 | 30 | H | East Fife | W 2-1 | 0-1 | 1 | Weatherson [55], Bottiglieri [83] | 3270 |
| 5 | Sept 13 | A | Forfar Ath | W 3-2 | 2-2 | 1 | Weatherson [15], Maisano M [23], Walker [82] | 1006 |
| 6 | 20 | H | Hamilton A | D 1-1 | 0-1 | 1 | Williams [52] | 3225 |
| 7 | 27 | A | Arbroath | W 4-0 | 3-0 | 1 | Weatherson 2 [28, 41], Greacen [35], Bottiglieri [59] | 1116 |
| 8 | Oct 4 | H | Berwick R | L 1-3 | 0-1 | 1 | Walker [54] | 2896 |
| 9 | 18 | A | Alloa Ath | W 1-0 | 0-0 | 1 | Williams [58] | 1118 |
| 10 | 25 | H | Stenhousemuir | W 5-2 | 2-1 | 1 | Williams [9], Weatherson 2 [26, 84], Maisano M [73], Uotinen [89] | 2880 |
| 11 | Nov 1 | A | Airdrie U | W 6-1 | 3-0 | 1 | Greacen 2 [20, 54], Maisano J 2 [22, 76], Williams [30], Walker [62] | 3159 |
| 12 | 8 | H | Forfar Ath | D 1-1 | 1-1 | 1 | Greacen [17] | 3327 |
| 13 | 16 | A | East Fife | D 0-0 | 0-0 | 1 | | 1757 |
| 14 | Dec 2 | A | Hamilton A | W 2-1 | 1-0 | — | Williams 2 [29, 90] | 1905 |
| 15 | 6 | H | Arbroath | W 6-4 | 2-2 | 1 | Walker [27], Bannerman [43], Millar [53], Weatherson [66], Maisano M [75], Williams [89] | 2707 |
| 16 | 13 | A | Berwick R | W 3-2 | 2-0 | 1 | Maisano J 2 [34, 39], Walker [59] | 882 |
| 17 | Jan 3 | A | Dumbarton | L 0-1 | 0-1 | 1 | | 2011 |
| 18 | 24 | H | Hamilton A | D 2-2 | 2-2 | 1 | Williams 2 [9, 23] | 2942 |
| 19 | 31 | A | Arbroath | D 2-2 | 1-1 | 1 | Weatherson [40], Williams [84] | 805 |
| 20 | Feb 7 | A | Forfar Ath | L 1-2 | 1-1 | 1 | Williams [4] | 958 |
| 21 | 14 | H | East Fife | D 1-1 | 0-0 | 1 | Bannerman [90] | 2894 |
| 22 | 21 | A | Alloa Ath | D 3-3 | 1-2 | 1 | Collins [40], Henderson [49], Maisano J [72] | 1145 |
| 23 | Mar 6 | A | Stenhousemuir | W 1-0 | 0-0 | 1 | Millar [80] | 1217 |
| 24 | 9 | H | Airdrie U | D 1-1 | 1-0 | 1 | Maisano J [37] | 3252 |
| 25 | 13 | H | Dumbarton | W 3-2 | 1-0 | 1 | Greacen [44], Millar [70], Williams [86] | 3028 |
| 26 | 23 | H | Berwick R | W 2-1 | 1-0 | — | Greacen [44], Cannie [60] | 2300 |
| 27 | 27 | A | East Fife | L 0-1 | 0-0 | 1 | | 1114 |
| 28 | 30 | H | Alloa Ath | D 2-2 | 2-1 | — | Greacen [5], Cannie [26] | 2436 |
| 29 | Apr 3 | H | Arbroath | W 1-0 | 1-0 | 2 | Weatherson [32] | 2493 |
| 30 | 6 | H | Forfar Ath | D 1-1 | 0-1 | — | Weatherson [48] | 2453 |
| 31 | 10 | A | Hamilton A | L 1-6 | 0-3 | 2 | Bannerman [80] | 2692 |
| 32 | 17 | H | Alloa Ath | W 2-1 | 1-0 | 2 | Cannie [5], Walker [89] | 2618 |
| 33 | 24 | A | Berwick R | L 0-2 | 0-2 | 2 | | 1175 |
| 34 | May 1 | A | Dumbarton | L 0-3 | 0-1 | 2 | | 1882 |
| 35 | 8 | H | Stenhousemuir | L 1-4 | 1-3 | 3 | Weatherson [13] | 3456 |
| 36 | 15 | A | Airdrie U | L 0-2 | 0-0 | 4 | | 5704 |

**Final League Position: 4**

**Honours**
*League Champions:* First Division 1977-78, 1983-84, 1986-87. Division II 1949-50, 1963-64, 1966-67. Second Division 1994-95. Third Division 2002-03. *Runners-up:* Division 1 1916-17, Division II 1899-1900, 1928-29, 1936-37.
*Scottish Cup Winners:* 1922; *Runners-up:* 1948. *League Cup Runners-up:* 1963-64.
*B&Q Cup Runners-up:* 1992-93.

**European:** *UEFA Cup:* 2 matches (*Fairs Cup:* 1968-69).

**Club colours:** Shirt: Royal blue with 3½ inch white hoops. Shorts: White with royal blue panel down side. Stockings: Royal blue with white tops.

**Goalscorers:** *League* (66): Williams 15 (1 pen), Weatherson 14, Greacen 7, Maisano J 7, Walker 6, Bannerman 3, Cannie 3, Maisano M 3, Millar 3, Bottiglieri 2, Collins 1, Henderson 1, Uotinen 1
*Scottish Cup* (4): Williams 2, Millar 1, Weatherson 1
*CIS Cup* (3): Bannerman 1, Bottiglieri 1, Weatherson 1
*Challenge Cup* (5): Weatherson 3 (1 pen), Hawke 1, Maisano J 1

| Coyle C 36 | Collins D 28 | Bottiglieri E 32 + 2 | MacGregor D 25 + 1 | Greacen S 32 | Bannerman S 17 + 8 | Millar C 35 + 1 | Maisano J 29 | Williams A 26 + 9 | Weatherson P 31 | Walker P 31 + 2 | Maisano M 28 + 3 | Hawke W 1 + 11 | Uotinen J 5 + 15 | Henderson R 20 + 1 | Cannie P 11 + 10 | McAlister J 1 + 8 | Adam J 2 + 3 | McLeod C 5 + 1 | Gaughan P 1 + 2 | McGlinchy P — + 7 | *Match No.* |
|---|---|---|---|---|---|---|---|---|---|---|---|---|---|---|---|---|---|---|---|---|---|
| 1 | 2 | 3 | 4 | 5 | 6 | $7^{1}$ | 8 | $9^{2}$ | 10 | $11^{3}$ | 12 | 13 | 14 | | | | | | | | 1 |
| 1 | 2 | 3 | | 5 | | 7 | 8 | $9^{1}$ | 10 | 11 | 6 | 12 | | 4 | | | | | | | 2 |
| 1 | 2 | 3 | | 5 | 14 | 7 | $8^{1}$ | $9^{2}$ | 10 | 11 | 6 | 13 | 12 | $4^{3}$ | | | | | | | 3 |
| 1 | 2 | 3 | 4 | 5 | 9 | 7 | $8^{1}$ | 12 | 10 | $11^{2}$ | 6 | | 13 | | | | | | | | 4 |
| 1 | 2 | 3 | 4 | 5 | $9^{3}$ | 7 | $8^{1}$ | 12 | 10 | 11 | $6^{2}$ | 14 | 13 | | | | | | | | 5 |
| 1 | 2 | 3 | 4 | 5 | $9^{2}$ | 7 | $8^{1}$ | 12 | 10 | 11 | 6 | | 13 | | | | | | | | 6 |
| 1 | 2 | 3 | 4 | 5 | 12 | 7 | $8^{2}$ | 9 | 10 | $11^{3}$ | $6^{1}$ | 13 | 14 | | | | | | | | 7 |
| 1 | $2^{3}$ | 3 | 4 | 5 | 13 | 7 | 8 | $9^{1}$ | 10 | 11 | $6^{2}$ | 12 | 14 | | | | | | | | 8 |
| 1 | 2 | 3 | 4 | 5 | 13 | 7 | $8^{2}$ | $9^{1}$ | 10 | 11■ | 6 | | | | 12 | | | | | | 9 |
| 1 | 2 | 3 | 4 | 5 | 12 | 7 | $8^{2}$ | 9 | 10 | | 6 | | 13 | | $11^{1}$ | | | | | | 10 |
| 1 | $2^{3}$ | 3 | 4 | $5^{2}$ | 12 | 7 | 8 | 9 | 10 | 11 | $6^{1}$ | | 14 | 13 | | | | | | | 11 |
| 1 | | 3 | 4 | 5 | 8 | 7 | | 9 | $10^{1}$ | 11 | $6^{2}$ | | 12 | 2 | 13 | | | | | | 12 |
| 1 | | 3 | 4 | 5 | | 7 | 8 | 9 | 10 | 11 | 6 | | | 2 | | | | | | | 13 |
| 1 | | 3 | 4 | 5 | 12 | 7 | $8^{1}$ | 9 | $10^{2}$ | 11 | 6 | | | 2 | 13 | | | | | | 14 |
| 1 | | 3 | 4 | 5 | 2 | 7 | 8 | 9 | $10^{1}$ | 11 | 6 | | | | 12 | | | | | | 15 |
| 1 | | 3 | 4 | 5 | 2 | $7^{1}$ | 8 | 9 | 10 | 11 | 6 | | | | 12 | | | | | | 16 |
| 1 | 2 | 3 | 4 | | $7^{1}$ | 12 | $8^{3}$ | $9^{2}$ | 10 | 11 | 6 | | | 5 | | 13 | 14 | | | | 17 |
| 1 | 2 | 3 | 4 | | | 7 | $8^{1}$ | $9^{2}$ | $10^{3}$ | 11 | 6 | 14 | 12 | | 13 | | | 5 | | | 18 |
| 1 | | 3 | 4 | | | 7 | $8^{1}$ | 9 | 10 | 11 | 6 | | 12 | | | | | 5 | 2 | | 19 |
| 1 | 2 | 3 | 4 | | | 7 | $8^{3}$ | $9^{2}$ | 10 | 11 | 6 | 13 | | | | 14 | | $5^{1}$ | 12 | | 20 |
| 1 | 2 | 3 | | 4 | 6 | $7^{2}$ | 8 | $9^{1}$ | 10 | 11 | 14 | $12^{3}$ | | | | | | 5 | | 13 | 21 |
| 1 | 2 | 3 | 13 | 4 | 6 | 7 | $8^{2}$ | 9 | $10^{1}$ | | | | | 11 | | 12 | | 5 | | | 22 |
| 1 | 2 | 3 | 4 | 5 | | 7 | | 9 | | | | | $8^{3}$ | 6 | $10^{2}$ | $11^{1}$ | 13 | | 14 | 12 | 23 |
| 1 | 2 | 12 | $4^{1}$ | 5 | | 7 | 8 | 9 | | 11 | 6 | | | $3^{3}$ | $10^{2}$ | | | 14 | | 13 | 24 |
| 1 | 2 | 3 | | 5 | | 7 | $8^{1}$ | $9^{2}$ | | $11^{3}$ | 6 | | | 4 | 13 | 12 | 10 | | | 14 | 25 |
| 1 | 2 | 3 | | 5 | 13 | 7 | $8^{1}$ | 9 | | $11^{3}$ | 6 | | | 4 | 12 | | $10^{2}$ | | | 14 | 26 |
| 1 | 2 | $3^{1}$ | | 5 | 8 | 7 | | $9^{2}$ | | 11 | 6 | | | 4 | 10 | 13 | | | | 12 | 27 |
| 1 | 2 | 3 | | 5 | 8 | 7 | | 12 | $9^{1}$ | 11 | 6 | | | 4 | 10 | | | | | | 28 |
| 1 | 2 | 3 | | 5 | 8 | 7 | | 13 | $9^{2}$ | 11 | | 12 | 6 | 4 | $10^{1}$ | | | | | | 29 |
| 1 | | 3 | | 5 | 6 | 7 | | 12 | 9 | 11 | 2 | | 8 | 4 | $10^{1}$ | | | | | | 30 |
| 1 | 2 | 3 | | 5 | 6 | 7 | $8^{1}$ | 9 | $10^{3}$ | 12 | $11^{2}$ | | 13 | 4 | 14 | | | | | | 31 |
| 1 | 2 | 13 | 3 | 5 | 6 | 7 | $8^{3}$ | 12 | 10 | 11 | | | 14 | $4^{2}$ | $9^{1}$ | | | | | | 32 |
| 1 | 2 | 3 | 4 | 5 | | 7 | 8 | 12 | $10^{2}$ | $11^{3}$ | 6 | | 14 | | $9^{1}$ | 13 | | | | | 33 |
| 1 | 2 | | 4 | 5 | | 7 | 8 | | $10^{2}$ | $11^{3}$ | | | 6 | 3 | $9^{1}$ | 12 | 14 | | | 13 | 34 |
| 1 | | | $4^{1}$ | 5 | 2 | 7 | $8^{2}$ | 9 | 10 | 11 | 12 | 14 | $6^{3}$ | 3 | 13 | | | | | | 35 |
| 1 | 2 | 11 | 4 | 5 | | 7 | | 13 | $9^{2}$ | 12 | $6^{3}$ | 10 | | 3 | $8^{1}$ | 14 | | | | | 36 |

# MOTHERWELL Premier League

*Year Formed:* 1886. *Ground & Address:* Fir Park Stadium, Motherwell ML1 2QN. *Telephone:* 01698 333333. *Fax:* 01698 338001.
*Ground Capacity:* all seated: 13,742. *Size of Pitch:* 110yd × 75yd.
*Chairman:* Willian H. Dickie. *Secretary:* Stewart Robertson.
*First Team Coach:* Terry Butcher. *Coach:* Maurice Malpas. *Physios:* John Porteous, Peter Salila.
*Managers since 1975:* Ian St. John, Willie McLean, Rodger Hynd, Ally MacLeod, David Hay, Jock Wallace, Bobby Watson, Tommy McLean, Alex McLeish, Harri Kampman, Billy Davies, Eric Black.
*Club Nickname(s):* The Well. *Previous Grounds:* Roman Road, Dalziel Park.
*Record Attendance:* 35,632 v Rangers, Scottish Cup 4th rd replay, 12 Mar 1952.
*Record Transfer Fee received:* £1,750,000 for Phil O'Donnell to Celtic (September 1994).
*Record Transfer Fee paid:* £500,000 for John Spencer from Everton (Jan 1999).
*Record Victory:* 12-1 v Dundee U, Division II, 23 Jan 1954.
*Record Defeat:* 0-8 v Aberdeen, Premier Division, 26 Mar 1979.
*Most Capped Player:* Tommy Coyne, 13, Republic of Ireland.
*Most League Appearances:* 626: Bobby Ferrier, 1918-37.
*Most League Goals in Season (Individual):* 52: Willie McFadyen, Division I, 1931-32.
*Most Goals Overall (Individual):* 283: Hugh Ferguson, 1916-25.

## MOTHERWELL 2003–04 LEAGUE RECORD

| *Match No.* | *Date* | *Venue* | *Opponents* | *Result* | | *H/T Score* | *Lg. Pos.* | *Goalscorers* | *Attendance* |
|---|---|---|---|---|---|---|---|---|---|
| 1 | Aug 9 | H | Dundee | L | 0-3 | 0-2 | — | | 6812 |
| 2 | 16 | A | Livingston | L | 0-1 | 0-0 | 11 | | 4497 |
| 3 | 23 | H | Kilmarnock | W | 2-1 | 0-0 | 8 | McFadden (pen) [64], Pearson [90] | 5087 |
| 4 | 30 | H | Partick Th | D | 2-2 | 1-1 | 7 | McFadden 2 [8, 68] | 6193 |
| 5 | Sept 13 | A | Hibernian | W | 2-0 | 1-0 | 5 | Clarkson 2 [44, 74] | 8387 |
| 6 | 20 | A | Celtic | L | 0-3 | 0-0 | 7 | | 57,492 |
| 7 | 27 | H | Hearts | D | 1-1 | 1-1 | 8 | Adams [28] | 5888 |
| 8 | Oct 4 | A | Dundee U | W | 2-0 | 1-0 | 6 | Adams 2 (1 pen) [21 (p), 89] | 6194 |
| 9 | 19 | H | Rangers | D | 1-1 | 1-1 | 6 | Pearson [25] | 10,824 |
| 10 | Nov 1 | A | Aberdeen | W | 3-0 | 1-0 | 5 | Craig [7], Pearson [76], Lasley [90] | 9895 |
| 11 | 8 | A | Dundee | W | 1-0 | 0-0 | 4 | Craig [52] | 6374 |
| 12 | 22 | H | Livingston | D | 1-1 | 1-1 | 4 | Clarkson [27] | 6357 |
| 13 | 25 | H | Dunfermline Ath | D | 2-2 | 0-2 | — | Pearson [70], Corrigan [90] | 4220 |
| 14 | 29 | A | Kilmarnock | L | 0-2 | 0-1 | 4 | | 6320 |
| 15 | Dec 7 | A | Partick Th | L | 0-1 | 0-0 | 5 | | 4124 |
| 16 | 13 | H | Hibernian | L | 0-1 | 0-0 | 5 | | 4533 |
| 17 | 21 | H | Celtic | L | 0-2 | 0-1 | 6 | | 10,513 |
| 18 | 27 | A | Hearts | D | 0-0 | 0-0 | 6 | | 10,046 |
| 19 | Jan 3 | H | Dundee U | W | 3-1 | 0-1 | 5 | Clarkson 3 [59, 67, 89] | 5549 |
| 20 | 17 | A | Rangers | L | 0-1 | 0-0 | 6 | | 48,925 |
| 21 | 24 | A | Dunfermline Ath | L | 0-1 | 0-0 | 8 | | 5270 |
| 22 | Feb 11 | H | Dundee | W | 5-3 | 2-2 | — | Lasley [14], Dair 2 [17, 73], Clarkson [50], Burns [61] | 4247 |
| 23 | 14 | A | Livingston | L | 1-3 | 0-3 | 7 | Adams [89] | 3624 |
| 24 | 21 | H | Kilmarnock | W | 1-0 | 1-0 | 5 | Quinn [14] | 5163 |
| 25 | 24 | H | Aberdeen | W | 1-0 | 0-0 | — | Wright [84] | 5220 |
| 26 | 28 | H | Partick Th | W | 3-0 | 1-0 | 5 | Hammell [8], Clarkson [51], Adams [80] | 5814 |
| 27 | Mar 14 | A | Celtic | D | 1-1 | 1-0 | 5 | Fagan [61] | 57,580 |
| 28 | 24 | A | Hibernian | D | 3-3 | 0-2 | — | Lasley [46], Adams [58], McDonald S [79] | 5568 |
| 29 | 27 | A | Dundee U | L | 0-1 | 0-0 | 6 | | 7585 |
| 30 | Apr 4 | H | Rangers | L | 0-1 | 0-1 | 6 | | 8967 |
| 31 | 7 | H | Hearts | D | 1-1 | 0-1 | — | Clarkson [60] | 5500 |
| 32 | 15 | H | Dunfermline Ath | W | 1-0 | 1-0 | — | Adams [9] | 3920 |
| 33 | 18 | A | Aberdeen | W | 2-0 | 1-0 | 5 | Burns [13], Craig [90] | 7246 |
| 34 | 24 | A | Dunfermline Ath | L | 0-3 | 0-1 | 5 | | 4250 |
| 35 | May 1 | A | Rangers | L | 0-4 | 0-1 | 5 | | 47,579 |
| 36 | 8 | H | Dundee U | L | 0-1 | 0-0 | 6 | | 5722 |
| 37 | 12 | H | Celtic | D | 1-1 | 0-0 | — | Clarkson [63] | 7749 |
| 38 | 16 | A | Hearts | L | 2-3 | 2-1 | 6 | McDonald S [36], Clarkson [45] | 11,619 |

**Final League Position: 6**

**Honours**
*League Champions:* Division I 1931-32. First Division 1981-82, 1984-85. Division II 1953-54, 1968-69; *Runners-up:* Premier Division 1994-95. Division I 1926-27, 1929-30, 1932-33, 1933-34. Division II 1894-95, 1902-03. *Scottish Cup:* 1952, 1991; *Runners-up:* 1931, 1933, 1939, 1951.
*League Cup:* 1950-51. *Runners-up:* 1954-55. *Scottish Summer Cup:* 1944, 1965.

**Club colours:** Shirt: Amber with claret hoop and trimmings. Shorts: Amber. Stockings: Amber with claret trim.

**European:** *Cup Winners' Cup:* 2 matches (1991-92). *UEFA Cup:* 6 matches (1994-95, 1995-96).

**Goalscorers:** *League* (42): Clarkson 11, Adams 7 (1 pen), Pearson 4, Craig 3, Lasley 3, McFadden 3 (1 pen), Burns 2, Dair 2, McDonald S 2, Corrigan 1, Fagan 1, Hammell 1, Quinn 1, Wright 1
*Scottish Cup* (6): Burns 2, Clarkson 2, Adams 1, McDonald S 1
*CIS Cup* (3): Craig 1, Lasley 1, Pearson 1

| Marshall G 33 | Corrigan M 38 | Partridge D 15 | Hammell S 37 | Craigan S 36 | MacDonald K 1 + 3 | Pearson S 17 + 1 | Leitch S 20 | Craig S 16 + 8 | Burns A 29 + 4 | Clarkson D 32 + 6 | McFadden J 2 + 1 | Lasley K 33 | Wright K 2 + 12 | Quinn P 24 + 2 | Adams D 31 | Dair J 19 + 10 | Fagan S 9 + 4 | O'Donnell P 7 + 2 | McDonald S 10 + 5 | Bollan G 1 + 2 | Corr B 5 | Kinniburgh W — + 1 | Fitzpatrick M 1 + 1 | Cowan D — + 1 | *Match No.* |
|---|---|---|---|---|---|---|---|---|---|---|---|---|---|---|---|---|---|---|---|---|---|---|---|---|---|
| 1 | 2 | 3 | 4 | 5 | 6 | 7 | 8 | $9^1$ | 10 | 11 | 12 | | | | | | | | | | | | | | 1 |
| 1 | 2 | 3 | 4 | 5 | | 7 | 8 | 12 | 10 | 11 | | 6 | $9^1$ | | | | | | | | | | | | 2 |
| 1 | 2 | 3 | 4 | | | 7 | 8 | 13 | $10^2$ | 12 | $11^1$ | 6 | | 5 | 9 | | | | | | | | | | 3 |
| 1 | 2 | 3 | 4 | | | 7■ | 8 | | $10^1$ | 12 | 11 | 6 | | 5 | 9 | | | | | | | | | | 4 |
| 1 | 2 | 3 | 4 | 5 | | 7 | $8^1$ | 13 | $10^2$ | 11 | | 6 | | | 9 | 12 | | | | | | | | | 5 |
| 1 | 2 | 3 | 4 | 5 | | 7 | $8^1$ | 10 | | 11 | | 6 | 12 | | 9 | | | | | | | | | | 6 |
| 1 | 2 | 3 | 4 | 5 | | 7 | $8^1$ | 10 | | 11 | | 6 | | | 9 | | 12 | | | | | | | | 7 |
| 1 | 2 | 3 | 4 | 5 | | 7 | 8 | $10^1$ | | 11 | | 6 | | | 9 | 12 | | | | | | | | | 8 |
| 1 | 2 | 3 | 4 | 5 | | 7 | 8 | $10^1$ | | 11 | | 6 | | | 9 | 12 | | | | | | | | | 9 |
| 1 | 2 | 3 | 4 | 5 | | 7 | 8 | 10 | | $11^1$ | | 6 | | | 9 | 12 | | | | | | | | | 10 |
| 1 | 2 | 3 | 4 | 5 | | 7 | 8 | 10 | 12 | $11^1$ | | $6^2$ | 13 | | 9 | | | | | | | | | | 11 |
| 1 | 2 | 3 | 4 | 5 | | 7 | 8 | 10 | 12 | $11^1$ | | 6 | | | 9 | | | | | | | | | | 12 |
| 1 | 2 | 3 | 4 | 5 | | 7 | $8^1$ | $10^2$ | 13 | 11 | | 6 | | | 9 | 12 | | | | | | | | | 13 |
| 1 | 2 | 3 | $4^1$ | 5 | | $7^2$ | $8^3$ | 10 | 14 | 11 | | 6 | | 13 | 9 | 12 | | | | | | | | | 14 |
| 1 | 2 | $3^2$ | 4 | 5 | | 7 | $8^1$ | | 10 | 11 | | 6 | 13 | | 9 | 12 | | | | | | | | | 15 |
| 1 | 2 | | 4 | 5 | | 7 | 8 | | 10 | 11 | | $6^1$ | | 12 | 9 | 3 | | | | | | | | | 16 |
| 1 | 2 | | 4 | 5 | | 7 | $8^1$ | | 10 | 11 | | 6 | | 3 | 9 | 12 | | | | | | | | | 17 |
| 1 | 2 | | 4 | 5 | | 12 | $8^3$ | 13 | $10^1$ | $11^2$ | | 6 | | 3 | 9 | 7 | 14 | | | | | | | | 18 |
| 1 | 2 | | 4 | 5 | | | $8^1$ | | 10 | 11 | | 6 | | 3 | 9 | 7 | | 12 | | | | | | | 19 |
| 1 | 2 | | 4 | 5 | | | $8^2$ | | $10^1$ | 11 | | 6 | | 3 | 9 | 7 | | | 12 | 13 | | | | | 20 |
| | 2 | | 4 | 5 | | | | | 10 | 11 | | $6^1$ | | 3 | 9 | 7 | | 8 | 12 | | 1 | | | | 21 |
| 1 | 2 | | 4 | 5 | | | | | 10 | 11 | | $6^1$ | | 3 | 9 | 7 | | $8^2$ | 12 | 13 | | | | | 22 |
| 1 | 2 | | | 5 | | | | | 10 | 11 | | 6 | 13 | 3 | 9 | 7 | | $8^1$ | 12 | $4^2$ | | | | | 23 |
| 1 | 2 | | 4 | 5 | | | | | 10 | $11^2$ | | 6 | 13 | 3 | 9 | 7 | | 12 | $8^1$ | | | | | | 24 |
| 1 | 2 | | 4 | 5 | 12 | | | 13 | 10 | 11 | | 6 | 14 | 3 | | $7^1$ | $9^3$ | | $8^2$ | | | | | | 25 |
| 1 | 2 | | 4 | 5 | 13 | | | 12 | $10^3$ | 11 | | 6 | 14 | 3 | 9 | | $7^2$ | | $8^1$ | | | | | | 26 |
| 1 | 2 | | 4 | 5 | | | | | 10 | $11^1$ | | 6 | 12 | 3 | 9 | 13 | $7^2$ | | 8 | | | | | | 27 |
| 1 | 2 | | $4^1$ | 5 | | | | | 10 | $11^2$ | | 6 | | 3 | 9 | 12 | 7 | | 8 | | | 13 | | | 28 |
| 1 | 2 | | 4 | 5 | | | | 12 | 10 | $11^1$ | | 6 | | 3 | | 7 | 9 | | 8 | | | | | | 29 |
| 1 | 2 | | 4 | 5 | | | | 11 | 10 | 12 | | | | 3 | | 7 | 9 | 6 | $8^1$ | | | | | | 30 |
| 1 | 2 | | 4 | 5 | | | | 8 | 10 | $11^1$ | | | 12 | 3 | 9 | 7 | | 6 | | | | | | | 31 |
| 1 | 2 | | 4 | 5 | | | | $11^1$ | 10 | 12 | | $6^2$ | | 3 | 9 | 7 | 13 | 8 | | | | | | | 32 |
| | 2 | | 4 | 5 | | | | 11 | $10^1$ | 12 | | 6 | | 3 | 9 | 7 | | 8 | | | 1 | | | | 33 |
| | 2 | | 4 | 5 | | | | $11^2$ | 10 | 13 | | 6 | 8 | 3 | 9 | $7^1$ | 12 | | | | 1 | | | | 34 |
| 1 | 2 | | 4 | 5 | | | | $8^1$ | 10 | 11 | | | 12 | 3 | 9 | $7^2$ | 6 | | 13 | | | | | | 35 |
| 1 | 2 | | 4 | 5 | | | | 12 | $10^1$ | 11 | | | | 3 | 9 | 7 | 6 | | 8 | | | | | | 36 |
| | 2 | | 4 | 5 | 14 | | | | 10 | $11^3$ | | 6 | 13 | 3 | | 7 | $9^1$ | | $8^2$ | | 1 | | 12 | | 37 |
| | 2 | | 4 | 5 | | | | | $10^2$ | 11 | | 6 | 12 | 3 | | 7 | | | 8 | | 1 | | $9^1$ | 13 | 38 |

# PARTICK THISTLE — First Division

*Year Formed:* 1876. *Ground & Address:* Firhill Stadium, 80 Firhill Rd, Glasgow G20 7AL. *Telephone:* 0141 579 1971. *Fax:* 0141 945 1525.
*Ground Capacity:* total: 13,141, seated: 10,921. *Size of Pitch:* 110yd × 75yd.
*Chairman:* Thomas Hughes. *Chief Executive Secretary:* Alan C. Dick. *Commercial Manager:* Amanda Barrie.
*Joint Managers:* Gerry Britton & Derek Whyte. *First Team Coach:* John McLaughlan. *Physio:* George Hannah.
*Managers since 1975:* R. Auld, P. Cormack, B. Rooney, R. Auld, D. Johnstone, W. Lamont, S. Clark, J. Lambie, M. MacLeod, J. McVeigh, T. Bryce, J. Lambie, G. Collins. *Club Nickname(s):* The Jags. *Previous Grounds:* Jordanvale Park; Muirpark; Inchview; Meadowside Park.
*Record Attendance:* 49,838 v Rangers, Division I, 18 Feb 1922. *Ground Record:* 54,728, Scotland v Ireland, 25 Feb 1928.
*Record Transfer Fee received:* £200,000 for Mo Johnston to Watford.
*Record Transfer Fee paid:* £85,000 for Andy Murdoch from Celtic (Feb 1991).
*Record Victory:* 16-0 v Royal Albert, Scottish Cup 1st rd, 17 Jan 1931.
*Record Defeat:* 0-10 v Queen's Park, Scottish Cup, 3 Dec 1881.
*Most Capped Player:* Alan Rough, 51 (53), Scotland.
*Most League Appearances:* 410: Alan Rough, 1969-82.
*Most League Goals in Season (Individual):* 41: Alex Hair, Division I, 1926-27.

## PARTICK THISTLE 2003–04 LEAGUE RECORD

| Match No. | Date | Venue | Opponents | Result | | H/T Score | Lg. Pos. | Goalscorers | Attendance |
|---|---|---|---|---|---|---|---|---|---|
| 1 | Aug 9 | H | Livingston | D | 1-1 | 1-0 | — | Milne [31] | 4220 |
| 2 | 16 | A | Kilmarnock | L | 1-2 | 1-0 | 9 | Grady [38] | 6778 |
| 3 | 23 | H | Celtic | L | 1-2 | 1-2 | 10 | Grady [25] | 9045 |
| 4 | 30 | A | Motherwell | D | 2-2 | 1-1 | 10 | Britton [25], Taylor [81] | 6193 |
| 5 | Sept 13 | A | Aberdeen | L | 1-2 | 0-1 | 11 | Mitchell [51] | 10,597 |
| 6 | 20 | H | Dundee U | L | 0-2 | 0-1 | 12 | | 4711 |
| 7 | 27 | A | Dunfermline Ath | L | 1-2 | 0-0 | 12 | Grady [50] | 4684 |
| 8 | Oct 4 | H | Hibernian | L | 0-1 | 0-0 | 12 | | 4125 |
| 9 | 18 | A | Dundee | L | 0-1 | 0-0 | 12 | | 6497 |
| 10 | 25 | H | Hearts | L | 1-4 | 0-3 | 12 | Waddell [62] | 4814 |
| 11 | Nov 1 | A | Rangers | L | 1-3 | 0-2 | 12 | Grady [82] | 49,551 |
| 12 | 8 | A | Livingston | L | 0-2 | 0-2 | 12 | | 4397 |
| 13 | 22 | H | Kilmarnock | L | 2-4 | 1-1 | 12 | Mitchell [18], Grady [80] | 4445 |
| 14 | 29 | A | Celtic | L | 1-3 | 1-2 | 12 | Grady [11] | 58,194 |
| 15 | Dec 7 | H | Motherwell | W | 1-0 | 0-0 | 12 | McBride [59] | 4124 |
| 16 | 13 | H | Aberdeen | L | 0-3 | 0-1 | 12 | | 5189 |
| 17 | 23 | A | Dundee U | D | 0-0 | 0-0 | — | | 6440 |
| 18 | 27 | H | Dunfermline Ath | W | 4-1 | 1-0 | 12 | Thomson [38], Grady 2 (1 pen) [55 (p), 89], Ross A [88] | 4377 |
| 19 | Jan 3 | A | Hibernian | L | 2-3 | 0-2 | 12 | Grady [53], Madaschi [73] | 8875 |
| 20 | 17 | H | Dundee | L | 1-2 | 1-0 | 12 | Rowson [30] | 4690 |
| 21 | 24 | A | Hearts | L | 0-2 | 0-1 | 12 | | 10,264 |
| 22 | Feb 1 | H | Rangers | L | 0-1 | 0-0 | 12 | | 8220 |
| 23 | 11 | H | Livingston | W | 5-2 | 2-0 | — | Grady [10], Britton 2 [41, 73], McNamee (og) [68], Thomson [81] | 3011 |
| 24 | 14 | A | Kilmarnock | L | 1-2 | 0-0 | 12 | Bonnes [50] | 5818 |
| 25 | 22 | H | Celtic | L | 1-4 | 0-2 | 12 | Britton [54] | 8131 |
| 26 | 28 | A | Motherwell | L | 0-3 | 0-1 | 12 | | 5814 |
| 27 | Mar 9 | A | Aberdeen | D | 0-0 | 0-0 | — | | 7395 |
| 28 | 13 | H | Dundee U | D | 1-1 | 0-0 | 12 | Rowson [65] | 3510 |
| 29 | 20 | A | Dunfermline Ath | L | 0-1 | 0-1 | 12 | | 4351 |
| 30 | 27 | H | Hibernian | D | 1-1 | 0-0 | 12 | Thomson (pen) [69] | 3155 |
| 31 | Apr 3 | A | Dundee | L | 1-2 | 1-1 | 12 | Thomson [14] | 5084 |
| 32 | 10 | H | Hearts | W | 1-0 | 0-0 | 12 | Thomson [51] | 4043 |
| 33 | 17 | A | Rangers | L | 0-2 | 0-1 | 12 | | 49,279 |
| 34 | 24 | H | Dundee | L | 0-1 | 0-0 | 12 | | 2727 |
| 35 | May 1 | H | Aberdeen | W | 2-0 | 1-0 | 12 | Grady [9], Mitchell [79] | 2839 |
| 36 | 5 | A | Hibernian | W | 2-1 | 1-1 | — | Grady [37], Mitchell [60] | 5380 |
| 37 | 9 | A | Livingston | D | 2-2 | 1-1 | 12 | Madaschi [4], Grady [63] | 2706 |
| 38 | 15 | H | Kilmarnock | D | 2-2 | 1-1 | 12 | Grady 2 [17, 89] | 4124 |

**Final League Position: 12**

**Honours**
*League Champions:* First Division 1975-76, 2001-02. Division II 1896-97, 1899-1900, 1970-71; Second Division 2000-01; *Runners-up:* First Division 1991-92. Division II 1901-02.
*Scottish Cup Winners:* 1921; *Runners-up:* 1930; *Semi-finals:* 2002.
*League Cup Winners:* 1971-72; *Runners-up:* 1953-54, 1956-57, 1958-59.

**European:** *Fairs Cup:* 4 matches (1963-64). *UEFA Cup:* 2 matches (1972-73). *Intertoto Cup:* 4 matches 1995-96.

**Club colours:** Shirt: Red and yellow halves with black sleeves. Shorts: Black. Stockings: Black.

**Goalscorers:** *League* (39): Grady 15 (1 pen), Thomson 5 (1 pen), Britton 4, Mitchell 4, Madaschi 2, Rowson 2, Bonnes 1, McBride 1, Milne 1, Ross A 1, Taylor 1, Waddell A 1, own goal 1
*Scottish Cup* (8): Britton 2, Grady 2, Bonnes 1, McBride 1, Mitchell 1, Rowson 1
*CIS Cup* (2): Milne 1, Mitchell 1

| Mikkelsen J 5 | Lilley D 15 | Murray G 36 | Whyte D 15 | Bonnes S 11+9 | Taylor S 6+7 | Rowson D 35 | McBride J 19+2 | Milne K 25 | Grady J 32+1 | Thomson A 13+8 | Britton G 15+12 | Ross I 15+3 | Anis J 20+4 | Panther E —+8 | Forrest E 3+2 | Mitchell J 30+2 | Waddell R 3+4 | Ross A 11+8 | Gemmell J —+5 | Arthur K 22 | Fleming D 20+4 | Madaschi A 23+1 | Howie W 5+5 | Langfield J 10 | Gibson A 4+7 | Gibson W 16 | Cadete J 1+4 | English T —+2 | Chiarini D 5+1 | Strachan A 2+3 | Pinkowski S 1 | *Match No.* |
|---|---|---|---|---|---|---|---|---|---|---|---|---|---|---|---|---|---|---|---|---|---|---|---|---|---|---|---|---|---|---|---|---|
| 1 | 2 | 3 | 4 | $5^{2}$ | 6 | 7 | $8^{1}$ | 9 | 10 | 11 | 12 | 13 | | | | | | | | | | | | | | | | | | | | 1 |
| 1 | 2■ | 3 | 4 | $5^{1}$ | $6^{2}$ | 7 | 8 | 9 | 10 | $11^{3}$ | 14 | | 12 | 13 | | | | | | | | | | | | | | | | | | 2 |
| 1 | | 3 | 4 | 13 | | 7 | $8^{1}$ | | 10 | $11^{2}$ | 9 | 6 | 5 | | 2 | 12 | | | | | | | | | | | | | | | | 3 |
| 1 | 2 | 3■ | 4 | | 8 | $7^{2}$ | | | 10 | 12 | 9 | 6 | $5^{3}$ | | | 14 | $11^{1}$ | 13 | | | | | | | | | | | | | | 4 |
| 1 | 2 | | $4^{1}$ | | 11 | 7 | $6^{2}$ | $5^{3}$ | 10 | 13 | 9 | | 12 | | 3 | 8 | | | 14 | | | | | | | | | | | | | 5 |
| | 2 | 3 | | | 11 | 7 | | 5 | 10 | 12 | 9 | 6 | $4^{1}$ | | | 8 | | | | 1 | | | | | | | | | | | | 6 |
| | | 3 | 4 | $11^{1}$ | 13 | 7 | $8^{3}$ | 5 | 10 | | 12 | | | | 2 | 9 | | $6^{2}$ | | 1 | 14 | | | | | | | | | | | 7 |
| | | 3 | 4 | | 13 | 7 | | 5 | $10^{1}$ | 12 | 9 | | 2 | | | 11 | | 8 | | 1 | $6^{2}$ | | | | | | | | | | | 8 |
| | | 3 | 4 | | 13 | $7^{2}$ | | 5 | $10^{3}$ | | 9 | | 2 | | | 11 | 12 | 8 | 14 | 1 | $6^{1}$ | | | | | | | | | | | 9 |
| | 2 | 3 | 4 | $10^{3}$ | 9 | 7 | | $6^{2}$ | | $11^{1}$ | 12 | | | 13 | | 8 | 14 | | | 1 | | 5 | | | | | | | | | | 10 |
| | $2^{3}$ | 3 | 4 | | | 7 | $8^{2}$ | 5 | 10 | | | | 14 | | | 9 | 11 | 12 | 13 | 1 | $6^{1}$ | | | | | | | | | | | 11 |
| | 2 | 3 | 4 | | | 7 | $9^{2}$ | 5 | 10 | | 13 | | | | | 11 | | $8^{1}$ | | 1 | $6^{3}$ | 12 | 14 | | | | | | | | | 12 |
| | | 3 | 4 | | 12 | $7^{1}$ | | 6 | 10 | | 9 | | 2 | | | 11 | | | | 1 | 13 | 5 | $8^{2}$ | | | | | | | | | 13 |
| | | 3 | 4 | | 13 | | 9 | 6 | 10 | | | | $2^{3}$ | 12 | | 11 | | $8^{2}$ | 14 | 1 | 7 | $5^{1}$ | | | | | | | | | | 14 |
| | 2 | 3 | 4 | | 13 | | $9^{1}$ | 6 | 10 | | | | | | | $11^{2}$ | | 8 | | 1 | 7 | 5 | 12 | | | | | | | | | 15 |
| | 2 | 3 | $4^{1}$ | | 14 | | $9^{3}$ | 6 | 10 | | | | | 13 | | 11 | | $8^{2}$ | 12 | 1 | 7 | 5 | | | | | | | | | | 16 |
| | 2 | 3 | | 13 | | 7 | $9^{1}$ | 5 | 10 | $11^{2}$ | | | | 14 | | 8 | | 12 | | 1 | $6^{3}$ | 4 | | | | | | | | | | 17 |
| | 2 | 3 | | 13 | | 7 | | 5 | 10 | $11^{2}$ | | 14 | | 12 | | $9^{1}$ | | 8 | | 1 | $6^{3}$ | 4 | | | | | | | | | | 18 |
| | 2 | 3 | | 13 | | 7 | | $5^{3}$ | 10 | $11^{2}$ | | 12 | | 14 | | 9 | | $8^{1}$ | | 1 | 6 | 4 | | | | | | | | | | 19 |
| | $2^{3}$ | 3 | | 13 | | 7 | 12 | 5 | 10 | $11^{2}$ | | 8 | | | 14 | 9 | | | | | $6^{1}$ | 4 | | 1 | | | | | | | | 20 |
| | 2 | 3 | | | | 7 | $9^{2}$ | 5 | 10 | 13 | | $8^{3}$ | | | | 11■ | 14 | | | | $6^{1}$ | 4 | | 1 | 12 | | | | | | | 21 |
| | | 3 | | 12 | | 7 | $8^{3}$ | 5 | 10 | 13 | $9^{2}$ | 6 | 2 | | | | $11^{1}$ | 14 | | 1 | | 4 | | | | | | | | | | 22 |
| | | 3 | | 11 | | 7 | 8 | | 10 | 13 | $9^{2}$ | 6 | $2^{1}$ | | 14 | | | | | 1 | | 4 | | | 12 | $5^{3}$ | | | | | | 23 |
| | | 3 | | $11^{1}$ | | 7 | 8 | | $10^{2}$ | 12 | 9 | 5 | | | | | 13 | 6 | | 1 | | 4 | | | | 2 | | | | | | 24 |
| | | 3 | | 14 | | 7 | $8^{2}$ | 5 | 10 | | $9^{3}$ | 6 | | | | $11^{1}$ | | | | 1 | | 4 | | | 12 | 2 | 13 | | | | | 25 |
| | | 3 | | | | 7 | | $5^{2}$ | $10^{1}$ | | 9 | 6 | | | | 11 | | | | 1 | | 4 | | | 8 | 2 | 12 | 13 | | | | 26 |
| | | 3 | | 11 | | 7 | | | | | 9 | 6 | 5 | | | $8^{3}$ | | | | | | $4^{1}$ | | 1 | 13 | 2 | $10^{2}$ | 14 | 12 | | | 27 |
| | | 3 | | $11^{1}$ | | 7 | | 5 | | | $9^{3}$ | 6 | 4 | | | 10 | | | | | 13 | | | 1 | 12 | $2^{2}$ | 14 | | 8 | | | 28 |
| | | 3 | | 10 | | 7 | 13 | $5^{2}$ | | $11^{1}$ | | 6 | 4 | | | 9 | | | | | | | | 1 | 14 | $2^{3}$ | 12 | | 8 | | | 29 |
| | | 3 | | $10^{2}$ | | 7 | | $5^{1}$ | | 11 | 13 | 6 | 4 | | | 9 | | | | | 12 | | | 1 | | 2 | | | 8 | | | 30 |
| | | 3 | | $10^{1}$ | | 7 | | | 12 | $11^{3}$ | 14 | 6 | 4 | | | 9 | | | | | $5^{2}$ | | 13 | 1 | | 2 | | | 8 | | | 31 |
| | | 3 | | | | 7 | $8^{1}$ | | 10 | $11^{2}$ | 13 | | 4 | | | 9 | | | | | 6 | 5 | 12 | 1 | | 2 | | | | | | 32 |
| | | 3 | | 14 | | 7 | $8^{3}$ | | $10^{2}$ | 11 | 13 | | $4^{1}$ | | | 9 | | | | | 6 | 5 | 12 | 1 | | 2 | | | | | | 33 |
| | | | | 13 | | 7 | $9^{1}$ | | 10 | | $11^{2}$ | | $4^{3}$ | | | | | 12 | | | 3 | 5 | 6 | 1 | | 2 | | | 8 | 14 | | 34 |
| | | 3 | | | | 7 | | | 10 | | 14 | | $4^{2}$ | | | $11^{3}$ | | 13 | | 1 | 6 | 5 | 8 | | 12 | 2 | | | | $9^{1}$ | | 35 |
| | | 3 | | | | 7 | | | 10 | | | | $4^{2}$ | | | 11 | | 12 | | 1 | 6 | 5 | $8^{1}$ | | 9 | 2 | | | | 13 | | 36 |
| | | 3 | | | | 7 | | | 10 | | 14 | | $4^{1}$ | | | $11^{3}$ | | 13 | | 1 | 6 | 5 | 8 | | $9^{2}$ | 2 | | | | 12 | | 37 |
| | | 3 | | | | 7 | | | 10 | | 14 | | 13 | 12 | | 11 | | $8^{1}$ | | | 4 | 5 | | | $9^{3}$ | 2 | | | | $6^{2}$ | 1 | 38 |

# PETERHEAD — Third Division

*Year Formed:* 1891. *Ground and Address:* Balmoor Stadium, Lord Catto Park, Peterhead AB42 1EU.
*Telephone:* 01779 478256. *Fax:* 01779 490682.
*Ground Capacity:* 3250, seated 1000.
*Chairman:* Roger Taylor. *General Manager:* Dave Watson. *Secretary:* George Moore.
*Manager:* Iain Stewart. *Assistant Manager:* Alan Lyons. *Physio:* Jennifer Johnson.
*Managers since 1975:* C. Grant, D. Darcy, I. Taylor, J. Harper, D. Smith, J. Hamilton, G. Adams, J. Guyan, I. Wilson, D. Watson, R. Brown, D. Watson, I. Wilson. *Club Nickname(s):* Blue Toon. *Previous Ground:* Recreation Park.
*Record Attendance:* 6310 friendly v Celtic, 1948.
*Record Victory:* 17-0 v Fort William, 1998-99 (in Highland League).
*Record Defeat:* 0-13 v Aberdeen, Scottish Cup, 1923-24.
*Most League Appearances:* 130, Martin Johnston, 2000-04.
*Most League Goals in Season (Individual):* 21, Iain Stewart, 2002-03.
*Most Goals Overall (Individual):* 57, Iain Stewart, 2000-04.

## PETERHEAD 2003–04 LEAGUE RECORD

| Match No. | Date | Venue | Opponents | Result | | H/T Score | Lg. Pos. | Goalscorers | Attendance |
|---|---|---|---|---|---|---|---|---|---|
| 1 | Aug 9 | A | Montrose | W | 1-0 | 1-0 | — | Duncan [37] | 411 |
| 2 | 16 | H | Gretna | W | 2-0 | 2-0 | 1 | Stewart I [19], Raeside [43] | 464 |
| 3 | 23 | A | Elgin C | W | 3-2 | 2-1 | 1 | Tindal [42], Bavidge [44], Stewart I [68] | 748 |
| 4 | 30 | H | Stranraer | L | 1-2 | 0-0 | 2 | Roddie [50] | 813 |
| 5 | Sept 13 | A | Stirling A | L | 1-3 | 1-0 | 2 | Johnston [41] | 711 |
| 6 | 20 | H | East Stirling | W | 2-0 | 0-0 | 2 | Johnston [57], Beith [64] | 520 |
| 7 | 27 | A | Albion R | L | 0-2 | 0-0 | 3 | | 283 |
| 8 | Oct 4 | A | Queen's Park | W | 2-0 | 2-0 | 3 | Beith [11], Perry [44] | 395 |
| 9 | 18 | H | Cowdenbeath | L | 0-1 | 0-0 | 4 | | 542 |
| 10 | 25 | A | Gretna | L | 2-3 | 1-0 | 5 | Stewart I [20], Stewart G [84] | 425 |
| 11 | Nov 1 | H | Montrose | D | 0-0 | 0-0 | 6 | | 540 |
| 12 | 8 | H | Stirling A | D | 2-2 | 0-2 | 5 | Bavidge [58], Johnston [72] | 589 |
| 13 | 15 | A | Stranraer | W | 2-0 | 1-0 | 5 | Good [36], Bavidge [82] | 428 |
| 14 | 29 | A | East Stirling | W | 3-1 | 2-0 | 3 | Johnston 2 [5, 62], Smith [16] | 178 |
| 15 | Dec 6 | H | Albion R | W | 2-1 | 2-0 | 4 | Mackay 2 [11, 35] | 485 |
| 16 | 13 | H | Queen's Park | W | 4-1 | 2-0 | 3 | Johnston 2 (1 pen) [37 (p), 80], Bavidge [40], Raeside [85] | 535 |
| 17 | 27 | A | Cowdenbeath | L | 0-2 | 0-1 | 4 | | 308 |
| 18 | Jan 3 | H | Elgin C | W | 5-1 | 1-1 | 4 | Johnston 3 [4, 55, 65], Tindal [70], Bavidge [75] | 714 |
| 19 | 17 | A | Montrose | L | 1-2 | 0-1 | 4 | Bavidge [55] | 512 |
| 20 | 24 | H | East Stirling | W | 6-0 | 4-0 | 4 | Stewart I 2 [7, 15], Johnston 2 [10, 70], Bavidge [13], Raeside [75] | 553 |
| 21 | Feb 7 | A | Stirling A | W | 2-0 | 1-0 | 4 | Raeside [43], Stewart I [80] | 651 |
| 22 | 14 | H | Stranraer | W | 2-0 | 2-0 | 4 | Raeside [36], Bavidge [39] | 615 |
| 23 | 21 | H | Cowdenbeath | D | 0-0 | 0-0 | 4 | | 619 |
| 24 | 28 | A | Queen's Park | L | 0-1 | 0-1 | 4 | | 581 |
| 25 | Mar 6 | H | Gretna | W | 2-1 | 0-1 | 4 | Roddie [77], Buchan [79] | 556 |
| 26 | 13 | A | Elgin C | L | 0-1 | 0-0 | 4 | | 675 |
| 27 | 16 | A | Albion R | D | 3-3 | 1-3 | — | Roddie [44], Johnston [55], Bavidge [76] | 253 |
| 28 | 20 | H | Stirling A | D | 0-0 | 0-0 | 4 | | 588 |
| 29 | 27 | A | Stranraer | D | 1-1 | 0-1 | 4 | Robertson [50] | 434 |
| 30 | Apr 3 | H | Albion R | W | 5-0 | 3-0 | 4 | Bavidge 3 [25, 38, 48], Buchan [30], Robertson [71] | 440 |
| 31 | 10 | A | East Stirling | W | 3-0 | 2-0 | 4 | Bavidge 2 [34, 44], Robertson [76] | 243 |
| 32 | 17 | A | Cowdenbeath | W | 3-0 | 0-0 | 4 | Gibson [47], Johnston [49], Buchan [85] | 238 |
| 33 | 24 | H | Queen's Park | D | 1-1 | 0-1 | 4 | Johnston (pen) [59] | 631 |
| 34 | May 1 | H | Elgin C | W | 3-1 | 0-1 | 4 | Johnston 2 [52, 59], Bavidge [62] | 616 |
| 35 | 8 | A | Gretna | L | 2-3 | 0-3 | 4 | Raeside [47], Bavidge [48] | 418 |
| 36 | 15 | H | Montrose | L | 1-2 | 1-1 | 4 | Johnston [43] | 604 |

**Final League Position: 4**

**Honours**
*Scottish Cup:* Quarter Finals 2001.
*Highland League Champions:* winners 5 times.
*Scottish Qualifying Cup (North):* winners 6 times.
*North of Scotland Cup:* winners 5 times.
*Aberdeenshire Cup:* winners: 20 times.

**Club colours:** Shirt: Royal blue with white; Shorts: Royal blue; Stockings: Royal blue tops with white hoops.

**Goalscorers:** *League* (67): Johnston 18 (2 pens), Bavidge 16, Raeside 6, Stewart I 6, Buchan 3, Robertson 3, Roddie 3, Beith 2, Mackay 2, Tindal 2, Duncan 1, Gibson 1, Good 1, Perry 1, Smith 1, Stewart G 1
*Scottish Cup* (2): Bavidge 2
*CIS Cup* (4): Stewart I 3, Mackay 1
*Challenge Cup* (4): Grant 1, Raeside 1, Stewart D 1, Stewart I 1

| Mathers P 33 | McGuinness K 20 + 3 | McSkimming S 20 + 2 | Raeside R 30 + 1 | Perry M 33 | Bain K 11 + 2 | Tindal K 17 + 4 | Duncan R 20 + 8 | Grant R 3 + 4 | Bavidge M 33 + 1 | Roddie A 25 + 2 | Stewart I 17 + 4 | Mackay S 11 + 8 | Johnston M 28 + 5 | Beith G 9 + 3 | Stewart D 1 + 9 | Smith D 11 + 12 | Good I 22 + 1 | Stewart G 4 + 3 | Brash K 6 + 4 | Buchan M 15 | Robertson S 16 | Milne D 1 + 4 | Buchanan R 3 | Gibson K 6 | Shand R 1 | Match No. |
|---|---|---|---|---|---|---|---|---|---|---|---|---|---|---|---|---|---|---|---|---|---|---|---|---|---|---|
| 1 | $2^{3}$ | 3 | 4 | 5 | $6^{2}$ | 7 | 8 | $9^{1}$ | 10 | 11 | 12 | 13 | 14 | | | | | | | | | | | | | 1 |
| 1 | 2 | 3 | 4 | 5 | 6 | 7 | 12 | $9^{2}$ | | $11^{1}$ | 8 | | | 10 | 13 | | | | | | | | | | | 2 |
| 1 | 2 | 3 | 4 | 5 | 6 | 7 | | | 10 | 11 | 8 | | | 9 | | | | | | | | | | | | 3 |
| 1 | $2^{1}$ | 3 | 4 | 5 | 6 | 7 | | 12 | 10 | 11 | 8 | | 13 | $9^{2}$ | | | | | | | | | | | | 4 |
| 1 | | 3 | 4 | 5 | | $7^{2}$ | 6■ | 14 | 10 | $11^{1}$ | 8 | | 9 | 13 | | $2^{3}$ | 12 | | | | | | | | | 5 |
| 1 | | 3 | 4 | 5 | 6 | | | 13 | | $11^{1}$ | $8^{3}$ | 7 | $10^{2}$ | 9 | 14 | 2 | | 12 | | | | | | | | 6 |
| 1 | $2^{1}$ | 3 | 4 | 5 | 6 | | | $9^{2}$ | 13 | | 8 | 7 | 10 | 11 | | 12 | | | | | | | | | | 7 |
| 1 | 14 | 3 | 4 | 5 | $6^{3}$ | | | | 10 | | $8^{2}$ | 7 | 13 | 9 | | 2 | $11^{1}$ | 12 | | | | | | | | 8 |
| 1 | 12 | 3 | 4 | 5 | $6^{2}$ | | | 14 | 10 | 11 | 8 | $7^{3}$ | | 9 | | $2^{1}$ | | 13 | | | | | | | | 9 |
| 1 | 2 | 3 | 4 | 5 | | | 12 | | 10 | $11^{1}$ | 8 | | 13 | $9^{3}$ | 14 | $7^{2}$ | | 6 | | | | | | | | 10 |
| 1 | 2 | 3 | 4 | 5 | | | 11 | | 10 | 13 | $8^{1}$ | | 12 | $9^{2}$ | $7^{3}$ | 14 | | 6 | | | | | | | | 11 |
| 1 | $2^{2}$ | 3 | $4^{1}$ | 5 | | | 6 | | 10 | 12 | | $7^{3}$ | 9 | 14 | | 13 | 11 | 8 | | | | | | | | 12 |
| 1 | 2 | 3 | | 5 | 7 | | 6 | | 10 | $11^{1}$ | | 12 | 9 | | | | 4 | 8 | | | | | | | | 13 |
| 1 | 2 | | | 5 | 6 | 13 | $8^{1}$ | | $10^{3}$ | 11 | 14 | $4^{2}$ | 9 | 12 | | 7 | 3 | | | | | | | | | 14 |
| 1 | | 13 | 4 | 5 | $6^{1}$ | 12 | $8^{2}$ | | $10^{3}$ | 11 | 14 | 7 | 9 | | | 2 | 3 | | | | | | | | | 15 |
| 1 | 12 | 3 | 4 | 5 | | 7 | | | $10^{2}$ | 11 | 13 | 8 | 9 | | | 2 | $6^{1}$ | | | | | | | | | 16 |
| 1 | | 3 | | 5 | | $2^{1}$ | $7^{2}$ | | 10 | 11 | 8 | 4 | 9 | | | 12 | 6 | | 13 | | | | | | | 17 |
| 1 | 2 | | | 5 | 14 | 7 | 4 | | $10^{2}$ | 11 | 8 | $6^{1}$ | $9^{3}$ | | 13 | 12 | 3 | | | | | | | | | 18 |
| 1 | 2 | | 4 | 5■ | | $7^{1}$ | | | 10 | 11 | $8^{2}$ | 6 | 9 | | 12 | 13 | 3 | | | | | | | | | 19 |
| 1 | 2 | | 4 | | 14 | | 6 | | 9 | 11 | $8^{3}$ | 12 | 10 | | | 13 | 3 | | $7^{2}$ | $5^{1}$ | | | | | | 20 |
| 1 | 2 | | 4 | 5 | | | 6 | | 9 | 11 | $8^{1}$ | 12 | 10 | | | | 3 | | | | 7 | | | | | 21 |
| 1 | 2 | | 4 | 5 | | | 6 | | 9 | 11 | 8 | 12 | 10 | | | | 3 | | | | $7^{1}$ | | | | | 22 |
| 1 | | | 4 | 5 | | 12 | $6^{2}$ | | 9 | 11 | $8^{1}$ | | 10 | | | 13 | 3 | | | 2 | 7 | | | | | 23 |
| 1 | | | 4 | 5 | | | 6 | | 9 | 11 | | 12 | 10 | | | $8^{1}$ | 3 | | | 2 | 7 | | | | | 24 |
| 1 | 2 | | 4 | 5 | | | 6 | | $9^{2}$ | 11 | | | 10 | | | $3^{1}$ | | | 12 | 8 | 7 | 13 | | | | 25 |
| 1 | 2 | | 4 | 5 | | 12 | 6 | | 9 | | | | $10^{2}$ | | | | $3^{1}$ | | 11 | 8 | 7 | 13 | | | | 26 |
| | 2 | 12 | 4 | 5 | | $6^{2}$ | 14 | | 9 | $11^{3}$ | | 13 | 10 | | | | | | $3^{1}$ | 8 | 7 | | 1 | | | 27 |
| 1 | 2 | 3 | 4 | 5 | | $6^{1}$ | 13 | | $9^{2}$ | 11 | | 12 | 10 | | | | | | | 8 | 7 | | | | | 28 |
| 1 | 2 | 3 | 4 | 5 | | | 12 | | 9 | $11^{1}$ | | | 10 | | | | | | | 8 | 7 | | | 6 | | 29 |
| 1 | | 3 | | 5 | | 2 | 12 | | 9 | $11^{1}$ | | | 10 | | | 13 | 4 | | 14 | $8^{2}$ | $7^{3}$ | | | 6 | | 30 |
| 1 | | $3^{1}$ | 12 | 5 | | 2 | 13 | | 9 | | | | $10^{3}$ | | | | 4 | | $11^{2}$ | 8 | 7 | 14 | | 6 | | 31 |
| 1 | | | $4^{3}$ | 5 | | 2 | 12 | | 9 | | | | 10 | | 14 | 13 | 3 | | $11^{2}$ | 8 | 7 | | | $6^{1}$ | | 32 |
| 1 | | | 4 | 5 | | | 11 | | 9 | | | | 10 | | 12 | $2^{1}$ | 3 | | | 8 | 7 | | | 6 | | 33 |
| | | | 4 | 5 | | $2^{3}$ | 11 | | 9 | | | | 10 | | 13 | 14 | $3^{1}$ | | 12 | 8 | $7^{2}$ | | 1 | 6 | | 34 |
| 1 | | 3 | 5 | | | 2 | $6^{1}$ | | 9 | | | | 10 | | | | 4 | | 11 | 8 | 7 | 12 | | | | 35 |
| | | | 4 | | | 7 | 11 | | 9 | | | | 10 | | 12 | 13 | 5 | | | 8 | 3 | $6^{1}$ | 1 | | $2^{2}$ | 36 |

# QUEEN OF THE SOUTH — First Division

*Year Formed:* 1919. *Ground & Address:* Palmerston Park, Dumfries DG2 9BA. *Telephone and Fax:* 01387 254853.
*Ground Capacity:* total: 8352, seated: 3549. *Size of Pitch:* 112yd × 73yd.
*Chairman:* David Rae. *Vice-Chairman:* Thomas Harkness. *Secretary:* Richard Shaw MBE. *Commercial Manager:* Margaret Heuchan.
*Manager:* Ian Scott.
*Managers since 1975:* M. Jackson, W. Hunter, B. Little, G. Herd, H. Hood, A. Busby, R. Clark, M. Jackson, D. Wilson, W. McLaren, F. McGarvey, A. MacLeod, D. Frye, W. McLaren, M. Shanks, R. Alexander, J. Connolly. *Club Nickname(s):* The Doonhamers. *Previous Grounds:* None.
*Record Attendance:* 24,500 v Hearts, Scottish Cup 3rd rd, 23 Feb 1952.
*Record Transfer Fee received:* £250,000 for Andy Thomson to Southend U (1994).
*Record Transfer Fee paid:* £30,000 for Jim Butter from Alloa Athletic (1995).
*Record Victory:* 11-1 v Stranraer, Scottish Cup 1st rd, 16 Jan 1932.
*Record Defeat:* 2-10 v Dundee, Division I, 1 Dec 1962.
*Most Capped Player:* Billy Houliston, 3, Scotland.
*Most League Appearances:* 731: Allan Ball, 1963-82.
*Most League Goals in Season (Individual):* 37: Jimmy Gray, Division II, 1927-28.
*Most Goals in Season:* 41: Jimmy Rutherford, 1931-32.
*Most Goals Overall (Individual):* 250: Jim Patterson, 1949-63.

## QUEEN OF THE SOUTH 2003–04 LEAGUE RECORD

| Match No. | Date | Venue | Opponents | Result | | H/T Score | Lg. Pos. | Goalscorers | Attendance |
|---|---|---|---|---|---|---|---|---|---|
| 1 | Aug 9 | A | St Johnstone | L | 1-4 | 0-2 | — | Bowey [63] | 2939 |
| 2 | 16 | H | Ross Co | W | 1-0 | 1-0 | 6 | Lyle [11] | 1734 |
| 3 | 23 | A | Falkirk | D | 0-0 | 0-0 | 7 | | 2202 |
| 4 | 30 | A | Ayr U | W | 4-1 | 1-0 | 5 | Paton [16], O'Connor 2 [59, 84], Burke [76] | 2143 |
| 5 | Sept 13 | H | Raith R | L | 0-2 | 0-1 | 7 | | 2142 |
| 6 | 20 | A | St Mirren | W | 2-1 | 2-1 | 6 | O'Connor [36], Burke [45] | 2681 |
| 7 | 27 | H | Clyde | W | 4-1 | 2-1 | 3 | Paton [12], O'Connor [38], Burke 2 [64, 69] | 1952 |
| 8 | Oct 4 | A | Brechin C | W | 1-0 | 0-0 | 2 | O'Connor [54] | 621 |
| 9 | 18 | H | Inverness CT | W | 3-2 | 0-0 | 1 | Bagan [65], O'Connor 2 [68, 74] | 3547 |
| 10 | 25 | A | Ross Co | L | 0-1 | 0-0 | 1 | | 2962 |
| 11 | Nov 1 | H | St Johnstone | D | 1-1 | 1-0 | 1 | McColligan [9] | 3159 |
| 12 | 8 | A | Raith R | W | 1-0 | 0-0 | 1 | Burke [48] | 1944 |
| 13 | 16 | H | Ayr U | W | 1-0 | 0-0 | 1 | Burke [46] | 3555 |
| 14 | 22 | A | Clyde | L | 1-3 | 1-0 | 2 | Wood [45] | 1271 |
| 15 | Dec 3 | H | St Mirren | L | 1-2 | 0-1 | — | Burke [55] | 2473 |
| 16 | 6 | A | Inverness CT | L | 1-4 | 1-0 | 6 | Wood [5] | 1745 |
| 17 | 13 | H | Brechin C | W | 1-0 | 0-0 | 5 | Wood [85] | 1736 |
| 18 | 20 | A | St Johnstone | D | 2-2 | 1-1 | 4 | O'Connor [36], Reid [82] | 1999 |
| 19 | 27 | H | Falkirk | W | 2-0 | 0-0 | 3 | O'Connor [49], Wood [67] | 4075 |
| 20 | Jan 3 | A | Ayr U | D | 1-1 | 1-0 | 3 | Bowey [20] | 2303 |
| 21 | 17 | H | Raith R | D | 1-1 | 0-0 | 3 | O'Connor [50] | 2089 |
| 22 | 24 | A | St Mirren | L | 1-3 | 0-1 | 3 | Bagan [56] | 2540 |
| 23 | Feb 14 | A | Brechin C | L | 1-2 | 0-0 | 5 | Bowey [55] | 642 |
| 24 | 21 | H | Inverness CT | W | 2-1 | 2-0 | 4 | O'Connor [9], Bowey [29] | 2021 |
| 25 | Mar 6 | H | Ross Co | D | 1-1 | 1-0 | 6 | Bowey [7] | 2047 |
| 26 | 10 | H | Clyde | L | 1-2 | 0-1 | — | Burke [71] | 2169 |
| 27 | 13 | A | Falkirk | W | 2-0 | 2-0 | 6 | Burke 2 [10, 23] | 2098 |
| 28 | 23 | A | Raith R | L | 1-3 | 1-2 | — | O'Connor [12] | 1482 |
| 29 | 27 | H | Ayr U | D | 0-0 | 0-0 | 6 | | 1831 |
| 30 | Apr 3 | A | Clyde | L | 0-2 | 0-0 | 6 | | 1207 |
| 31 | 10 | H | St Mirren | W | 1-0 | 1-0 | 6 | Bowey [8] | 2211 |
| 32 | 17 | A | Inverness CT | L | 1-4 | 0-2 | 6 | Burke [78] | 2126 |
| 33 | 24 | H | Brechin C | D | 2-2 | 1-0 | 6 | Jaconelli [15], Burke [46] | 1352 |
| 34 | May 1 | H | St Johnstone | D | 1-1 | 0-0 | 6 | Jaconelli [74] | 1629 |
| 35 | 8 | A | Ross Co | W | 2-1 | 1-1 | 5 | Bowey [43], Burke [66] | 2842 |
| 36 | 15 | H | Falkirk | W | 1-0 | 1-0 | 5 | Jaconelli [18] | 2751 |

**Final League Position: 5**

**Honours**
*League Champions:* Division II 1950-51. Second Division 2001-02. *Runners-up:* Division II 1932-33, 1961-62, 1974-75. Second Division 1980-81, 1985-86.
*Scottish Cup:* semi-finalists 1949-50.
*League Cup:* semi-finalists 1950-51, 1960-61.
*B&Q Cup:* semi-finalists 1991-92. *League Challenge Cup:* winners 2002-03; runners-up 1997-98.

**Club colours:** Shirt: Royal blue with white sleeves. Shorts: White with blue piping. Stockings: Royal blue.

**Goalscorers:** *League* (46): Burke 13, O'Connor 12, Bowey 7, Wood 4, Jaconelli 3, Bagan 2, Paton 2, Lyle 1, McColligan 1, Reid 1
*Scottish Cup* (3): O'Connor 3
*CIS Cup* (6): Burke 3, Bagan 1, Burns 1, Wood 1
*Challenge Cup* (1): Lyle 1

| Dodds J 12 + 1 | Paton E 35 | McAlpine J 19 + 3 | Allan D 15 + 3 | Aitken A 24 + 7 | Bagan D 29 + 2 | O'Connor S 19 + 8 | Bowey S 33 | Wood G 16 + 5 | Lyle D 8 + 7 | Gibson W 14 + 2 | Burke A 27 + 7 | Reid B 33 | Thomson J 26 + 1 | Burns P 23 + 6 | Scott C 10 | Talbot P 3 + 1 | McColligan B 18 + 5 | Jaconelli E 11 + 6 | Robertson K 2 | McMullan P 3 + 9 | Payne S 4 + 6 | Samson C 12 | *Match No.* |
|---|---|---|---|---|---|---|---|---|---|---|---|---|---|---|---|---|---|---|---|---|---|---|---|
| 1 | 2 | 3 | 4 | 5 | 6 | 7 | 8 | $9^{1}$ | 10 | 11 | 12 | | | | | | | | | | | | 1 |
| 1 | 2 | $3^{2}$ | 4 | 13 | $7^{1}$ | 14 | 8 | 9 | $10^{3}$ | 11 | | 5 | 6 | 12 | | | | | | | | | 2 |
| 1 | $2^{1}$ | 3 | 4 | | 7 | 12 | 8 | 9 | 10 | 11 | | 5 | 6 | | | | | | | | | | 3 |
| 1 | $2^{2}$ | 3 | 4 | | $7^{3}$ | 13 | 8 | 9 | 10 | $11^{1}$ | 12 | 5 | 6 | 14 | | | | | | | | | 4 |
| 1 | $2^{3}$ | 3 | 4 | | 7 | 12 | 8 | 9 | $10^{2}$ | $11^{1}$ | 13 | 5 | 6 | 14 | | | | | | | | | 5 |
| | 2 | 3 | | 13 | 4 | 7 | 8 | | $10^{1}$ | | $9^{2}$ | 5 | 6 | 12 | 1 | 11 | | | | | | | 6 |
| | 2 | 3 | | 12 | 4 | 7 | 8 | 13 | | | $9^{2}$ | 5 | 6 | 10 | 1 | $11^{1}$ | | | | | | | 7 |
| | 2 | 3 | 14 | | 4 | 7 | 8 | 13 | | | $9^{2}$ | 5 | 6 | $10^{3}$ | 1 | $11^{1}$ | 12 | | | | | | 8 |
| | 2 | 11 | | 3 | 4 | $7^{1}$ | 8 | 12 | | | 9 | 5 | 6 | 10 | 1 | | | | | | | | 9 |
| | 2 | 11 | | $3^{2}$ | 4 | $7^{1}$ | 8 | | 12 | 13 | 9 | 5 | 6 | 10 | 1 | | | | | | | | 10 |
| | 2 | 3 | | 14 | 4 | $7^{1}$ | | 8 | $12^{2}$ | 13 | $9^{3}$ | 5 | 6 | 10 | 1 | | 11 | | | | | | 11 |
| | 2 | 3 | 12 | | 4 | | 8 | 7 | | | 9 | 5 | 6 | $10^{1}$ | 1 | | 11 | | | | | | 12 |
| | 2 | 3 | | 12 | 4 | | 8 | 7 | 13 | | $9^{2}$ | 5 | 6■ | $10^{1}$ | 1 | | 11 | | | | | | 13 |
| 12 | 2 | 3 | | 6 | 4 | | $8^{3}$ | $7^{2}$ | 14 | | 9 | 5 | | 10 | $1^{1}$ | | 11 | 13 | | | | | 14 |
| | 2 | $3^{2}$ | | 12 | 4 | | | $9^{3}$ | 14 | $11^{1}$ | 10 | 5 | 6 | 7 | | | 8 | 13■ | 1 | | | | 15 |
| | 2 | | | 3 | 4 | 13 | 8 | $7^{1}$ | 10 | | 9 | 5 | 6 | | | 12 | $11^{2}$ | | 1 | | | | 16 |
| 1 | 2 | | 14 | 3 | 4 | 7 | 8 | 12 | $10^{1}$ | | $9^{3}$ | 5 | 6 | $11^{2}$ | | | 13 | | | | | | 17 |
| 1 | 2 | | | 3 | 4 | $7^{1}$ | 8 | 10 | 12 | | 9 | 5 | 6 | | | | 11 | | | | | | 18 |
| 1 | 2 | | | 3 | | 7 | 8 | 10 | 12 | | $9^{1}$ | 5 | 6 | 4 | | | 11 | | | | | | 19 |
| 1 | 2 | | | 3 | $4^{1}$ | 7 | 8 | 10 | | | 9 | 5 | 6 | 12 | | | $11^{2}$ | | | 13 | | | 20 |
| 1 | 2 | 12 | | 3 | | 7 | 8 | | | | $9^{3}$ | $5^{1}$ | 6 | 4 | | | 11 | 14 | | $10^{2}$ | 13 | | 21 |
| 1 | 2 | 3 | | 5 | 4 | 7 | 8 | 6 | | | $9^{2}$ | | | $10^{3}$ | | | 12 | 13 | | $11^{1}$ | 14 | | 22 |
| 1 | 2 | | | 12 | 4 | $7^{3}$ | 8 | | | | 14 | 5 | 6 | $10^{1}$ | | | 11 | 9 | | $3^{2}$ | 13 | | 23 |
| | 2 | $11^{2}$ | 6 | 3 | 4 | $7^{1}$ | 8 | | | | 12 | 5 | | 10 | | | | 9 | | 13 | | 1 | 24 |
| | 2 | | 6 | 3 | 4 | | 8 | 12 | | $11^{2}$ | $9^{1}$ | 5 | | 7 | | | | 10 | | 13 | | 1 | 25 |
| | 2 | $11^{3}$ | 4 | 3 | | | 8 | $9^{1}$ | | | 12 | 5 | $6^{2}$ | 7 | | | | 10 | | 14 | 13 | 1 | 26 |
| | 2 | | 6 | 3 | 4 | 7 | 8 | | | | 9 | 5 | | $10^{1}$ | | | 13 | | | 12 | $11^{2}$ | 1 | 27 |
| | | 13 | 6 | 3 | $4^{3}$ | $7^{1}$ | 8 | | | | 9 | 5 | 2 | $10^{2}$ | | | | 12 | | 14 | 11 | 1 | 28 |
| | 2 | $11^{1}$ | 4 | 3 | 12 | 7 | 8 | | | | 9 | | 6 | $5^{3}$ | | | 13 | 14 | | | $10^{2}$ | 1 | 29 |
| | 2 | | 6 | 3 | 13 | $7^{1}$ | 8 | | | $11^{2}$ | 9 | 5 | | | | | 4 | 10 | | 12 | | 1 | 30 |
| | 2 | | 6 | 3 | $7^{1}$ | | 8 | | | 11 | 9 | 5 | | | | | 4 | $10^{2}$ | | 13 | 12 | 1 | 31 |
| | 2 | | 6 | 3 | | | 8 | | | $11^{2}$ | 12 | 5 | 13 | 10 | | | 4 | 9 | | | $7^{1}$ | 1 | 32 |
| | 2 | | 6 | 3 | | 13 | 8 | | | $11^{3}$ | 9 | 5 | | $7^{2}$ | | | 4 | $10^{1}$ | | 12 | 14 | 1 | 33 |
| | 2 | | | 3 | 7 | | 8 | | | 11 | 9 | 5 | 6 | | | | 4 | 10 | | | | 1 | 34 |
| | 2 | | | 3 | $7^{2}$ | 12 | 8 | | | 11 | 9 | 5 | 6 | 13 | 1 | | 4 | $10^{1}$ | | | | | 35 |
| | 2 | 13 | | 3 | $7^{2}$ | 12 | | | | 11 | 9 | 5 | 6 | 8 | | | 4 | $10^{1}$ | | | | 1 | 36 |

# QUEEN'S PARK — Third Division

*Year Formed:* 1867. *Ground & Address:* Hampden Park, Mount Florida, Glasgow G42 9BA. *Telephone:* 0141 632 1275. *Fax:* 0141 636 1612.
*Ground Capacity:* all seated: 52,000. *Size of Pitch:* 115yd × 75yd.
*President:* David Gordon. *Secretary:* Alistair Mackay. *Treasurer:* Garry Templeman..
*Coach:* Kenneth Brannigan. *Physio:* R. C. Findlay.
*Coaches since 1975:* D. McParland, J. Gilroy, E. Hunter, H. McCann, J. McCormack. *Club Nickname(s):* The Spiders.
*Previous Grounds:* 1st Hampden (Recreation Ground); (Titwood Park was used as an interim measure between 1st & 2nd Hampdens); 2nd Hampden (Cathkin); 3rd Hampden.
*Record Attendance:* 95,772 v Rangers, Scottish Cup, 18 Jan 1930.
*Record for Ground:* 149,547 Scotland v England, 1937.
*Record Transfer Fee received:* Not applicable due to amateur status.
*Record Transfer Fee paid:* Not applicable due to amateur status.
*Record Victory:* 16-0 v St. Peters, Scottish Cup 1st rd, 29 Aug 1885.
*Record Defeat:* 0-9 v Motherwell, Division I, 26 Apr 1930.
*Most Capped Player:* Walter Arnott, 14, Scotland.
*Most League Appearances:* 532: Ross Caven.
*Most League Goals in Season (Individual):* 30: William Martin, Division I, 1937-38.
*Most Goals Overall (Individual):* 163: J. B. McAlpine.

## QUEEN'S PARK 2003–04 LEAGUE RECORD

| *Match No.* | *Date* | *Venue* | *Opponents* | *Result* | *H/T Score* | *Lg. Pos.* | *Goalscorers* | *Atten-dance* |
|---|---|---|---|---|---|---|---|---|
| 1 | Aug 9 | A | Gretna | D 1-1 | 0-0 | — | Carroll [90] | 420 |
| 2 | 16 | H | Elgin C | W 5-2 | 2-1 | 2 | Reilly 3 (3 pens) [3, 48, 64], Whelan 2 [39, 84] | 556 |
| 3 | 23 | A | Albion R | L 1-3 | 0-2 | 4 | Canning [88] | 627 |
| 4 | 30 | H | Stirling A | L 0-2 | 0-2 | 7 | | 638 |
| 5 | Sept 13 | A | Cowdenbeath | W 1-0 | 0-0 | 6 | Canning [48] | 339 |
| 6 | 20 | H | Montrose | D 1-1 | 1-1 | 5 | McAuley [30] | 490 |
| 7 | 27 | A | East Stirling | W 2-1 | 1-0 | 4 | McAuley 2 [12, 54] | 281 |
| 8 | Oct 4 | H | Peterhead | L 0-2 | 0-2 | 5 | | 395 |
| 9 | 18 | A | Stranraer | L 0-1 | 0-0 | 7 | | 464 |
| 10 | 25 | A | Elgin C | D 2-2 | 0-1 | 7 | Gallagher [82], McAuley [87] | 548 |
| 11 | Nov 1 | H | Gretna | L 0-1 | 0-0 | 7 | | 522 |
| 12 | 8 | H | Cowdenbeath | D 0-0 | 0-0 | 8 | | 554 |
| 13 | 15 | A | Stirling A | L 0-1 | 0-0 | 8 | | 590 |
| 14 | Dec 2 | A | Montrose | D 0-0 | 0-0 | — | | 279 |
| 15 | 6 | H | East Stirling | W 3-0 | 2-0 | 7 | Graham [7], McAuley 2 [32, 54] | 439 |
| 16 | 13 | A | Peterhead | L 1-4 | 0-2 | 8 | Graham [63] | 535 |
| 17 | Jan 3 | H | Albion R | D 1-1 | 0-0 | 8 | Gallagher [59] | 454 |
| 18 | 10 | H | Stranraer | L 0-4 | 0-3 | 8 | | 473 |
| 19 | 17 | A | Gretna | W 1-0 | 0-0 | 7 | Reilly [88] | 419 |
| 20 | 24 | H | Montrose | D 1-1 | 0-0 | 7 | Reilly [64] | 443 |
| 21 | Feb 7 | A | Cowdenbeath | L 1-5 | 1-2 | 8 | Whelan [2] | 275 |
| 22 | 14 | H | Stirling A | L 1-4 | 1-2 | 8 | Stewart [31] | 742 |
| 23 | 21 | A | Stranraer | L 1-3 | 0-0 | 8 | Carcary [65] | 435 |
| 24 | 28 | H | Peterhead | W 1-0 | 1-0 | 8 | Smith (og) [3] | 581 |
| 25 | Mar 2 | A | East Stirling | W 4-2 | 2-1 | — | McCallum [4], Graham [28], Carcary [64], Reilly [80] | 235 |
| 26 | 6 | H | Elgin C | W 4-0 | 1-0 | 7 | Canning [7], Harvey [81], Carcary 2 [87, 90] | 444 |
| 27 | 13 | A | Albion R | L 1-3 | 1-2 | 8 | Carroll [8] | 491 |
| 28 | 20 | H | Cowdenbeath | L 1-2 | 1-0 | 8 | Carroll [4] | 508 |
| 29 | 27 | A | Stirling A | D 0-0 | 0-0 | 8 | | 797 |
| 30 | Apr 3 | H | East Stirling | W 1-0 | 1-0 | 7 | Dunning [34] | 404 |
| 31 | 10 | A | Montrose | D 1-1 | 0-1 | 7 | Carcary [87] | 388 |
| 32 | 17 | H | Stranraer | L 0-2 | 0-2 | 7 | | 564 |
| 33 | 24 | A | Peterhead | D 1-1 | 1-0 | 8 | Reilly [14] | 631 |
| 34 | May 1 | H | Albion R | L 0-1 | 0-0 | 8 | | 516 |
| 35 | 8 | A | Elgin C | W 3-1 | 3-1 | 8 | Whelan 2 [23, 36], Canning [45] | 421 |
| 36 | 15 | H | Gretna | D 1-1 | 1-0 | 7 | McCallum [35] | 541 |

**Final League Position: 7**

**Honours**
*League Champions:* Division II 1922-23. B Division 1955-56. Second Division 1980-81. Third Division 1999-2000.
*Scottish Cup Winners:* 1874, 1875, 1876, 1880, 1881, 1882, 1884, 1886, 1890, 1893; *Runners-up:* 1892, 1900.
*League Cup:* —.
*FA Cup runners-up:* 1884, 1885.

**Club colours:** Shirt: White and black hoops. Shorts: White. Stockings: Black with white tops.

**Goalscorers:** *League* (41): Reilly 7 (3 pens), McAuley 6, Carcary 5, Whelan 5, Canning 4, Carroll 3, Graham 3, Gallagher 2, McCallum 2, Dunning 1, Harvey 1, Stewart 1, own goal 1
*Scottish Cup* (1): McAuley 1
*CIS Cup* (3): Clark 1, Graham 1, Reilly 1
*Challenge Cup* (2): Clark 1, Graham 1

| Scrimgour D 35 | Dunning A 12 + 2 | Clark R 27 + 2 | Sinclair R 20 + 1 | Agostini D 20 + 3 | Conlin R 1 + 1 | Reilly S 27 | Harvey P 19 + 6 | Graham A 20 + 1 | Whelan J 26 + 7 | Menelaws D 3 + 3 | Ferry D 24 + 2 | Moffat S 8 + 3 | Carroll F 17 + 7 | Fallon S 20 + 1 | Kettlewell S 15 + 12 | Carcary D 16 + 6 | Canning S 25 + 3 | McAuley S 13 + 4 | Thompson J 5 + 4 | Gallagher P 4 + 6 | McCallum D 18 + 1 | Crawford D 1 + 1 | Stewart D 13 + 2 | Bonnar M 7 + 6 | Weatherston D — + 5 | Quinn A — + 2 | Trouten A — + 1 | McCue B — + 1 | *Match No.* |
|---|---|---|---|---|---|---|---|---|---|---|---|---|---|---|---|---|---|---|---|---|---|---|---|---|---|---|---|---|---|
| 1 | 2 | 3 | $4^2$ | 5 | 6 | 7 | $8^1$ | 9 | 10 | $11^3$ | 12 | 13 | 14 | | | | | | | | | | | | | | | | 1 |
| 1 | $2^2$ | 7 | 4 | $5^1$ | | 8 | | 9 | 10 | $11^3$ | 3 | 12 | | 6 | 13 | 14 | | | | | | | | | | | | | 2 |
| 1 | $2^2$ | | 4 | | | 8■ | | 9■ | 10 | $11^3$ | 3 | 5 | | 6 | $7^1$ | 13 | 12 | 14 | | | | | | | | | | | 3 |
| 1 | 14 | 7 | 4 | | | | | | 10 | 12 | 2 | 5 | | 6 | | $11^3$ | $8^2$ | $9^1$ | 3 | 13 | | | | | | | | | 4 |
| 1 | | 7 | 5 | | | $8^1$ | 12 | 9 | 10 | | 2 | 3 | | 6 | | 13 | 4 | $11^2$ | | | | | | | | | | | 5 |
| 1 | | 7 | 5 | | | 4 | 12 | 9 | 10 | 13 | 2 | $3^3$ | | 6 | | | $8^1$ | $11^2$ | 14 | | | | | | | | | | 6 |
| 1 | | $7^3$ | 5 | | | 10 | 8 | 9 | 12 | 13 | | $4^1$ | | 6 | | | 2 | 11 | | 14 | $3^2$ | | | | | | | | 7 |
| 1 | | 7 | 5 | | | 8 | 4 | $9^1$ | 10 | | | | | 6 | | 12 | 2 | 11 | 13 | | $3^2$ | | | | | | | | 8 |
| 1 | | 8 | 4 | 5 | | | | 9 | 13 | | 2 | | 12 | 6 | 10■ | | $7^2$ | $11^1$ | | | 3 | | | | | | | | 9 |
| 1 | | 8 | 4 | 5 | | 7 | | 10 | $9^2$ | | 2 | | $11^1$ | 6 | | | | 12 | 3 | 13 | | | | | | | | | 10 |
| 1 | | 13 | 4 | 5 | | 8 | | 9 | $10^2$ | | 2 | | 14 | 6 | 12 | | | $11^3$ | 3 | $7^1$ | | | | | | | | | 11 |
| 1 | | 7 | $4^1$ | 5 | | | | 9 | $10^3$ | | 2 | 3 | | 6 | 8 | 13 | 14 | $11^2$ | 12 | | | | | | | | | | 12 |
| 1 | | 7 | | 5 | | | | $9^1$ | 10 | | 2 | 4 | 12 | 6 | 8 | | | 11 | 3 | | | | | | | | | | 13 |
| 1 | | | 4■ | 13 | | | 8 | 9 | 12 | | 14 | | 5 | 6 | $7^1$ | | $2^2$ | $11^3$ | 3 | 10 | | | | | | | | | 14 |
| 1 | | $7^1$ | | $5^3$ | | | 8 | 9 | 10 | | 2 | | $3^2$ | 6 | 12 | | 4 | 11 | 14 | 13 | | | | | | | | | 15 |
| 1■ | | | 3 | | 14 | $5^3$ | 8 | 9 | 4 | | 2 | | 10■ | | 7 | | $6^1$ | $11^2$ | | 13 | | 12 | | | | | | | 16 |
| | | 12 | | 5 | | 7 | 8 | $9^3$ | 14 | | 2 | $4^2$ | | 6 | | | 3 | $11^1$ | | 10 | 13 | 1 | | | | | | | 17 |
| 1 | | | | 5 | | 4 | 8 | $9^1$ | 14 | | 2 | 13 | | $6^2$ | $7^3$ | | 10 | 12 | | 11 | | | 3 | | | | | | 18 |
| 1 | | 4 | | 5 | | 8 | $11^1$ | | 10 | | 2 | | 9 | 6 | 12 | 7 | | | | | | | 3 | | | | | | 19 |
| 1 | | 4 | | 5 | | 8 | $7^1$ | | 10 | | 2 | | $9^2$ | 6 | 12 | 11 | | | | 13 | | | 3 | | | | | | 20 |
| 1 | | 4 | | $5^1$ | | 8 | $7^3$ | 13 | 10 | | 2 | | 9 | 6 | 12 | $11^2$ | | 14 | | | | | 3 | | | | | | 21 |
| 1 | | $4^2$ | 5 | | | 8 | 7■ | | 10 | | 2 | | $9^1$ | 14 | 13 | 11 | 12 | | | | $6^3$ | | 3 | | | | | | 22 |
| 1 | | 3 | 5 | | | 8 | | 9 | 12 | | 2 | | | 4 | | 11 | 7 | | | | $10^2$ | | $6^1$ | 13 | | | | | 23 |
| 1 | 4 | 6 | | 12 | | 8 | | $9^3$ | 10 | | 2 | | | | 13 | 11 | $7^2$ | | | | 3 | | $5^1$ | 14 | | | | | 24 |
| 1 | 4 | 6 | | 5 | | 8 | 14 | $9^1$ | 10 | | 2 | | 12 | | 13 | $11^3$ | $7^2$ | | | | 3 | | | | | | | | 25 |
| 1 | 4 | 6 | | 5 | | $8^2$ | $12^3$ | | $10^1$ | | 2 | | 9 | | 13 | 11 | 7 | | | | 3 | | | 14 | | | | | 26 |
| 1 | $4^2$ | $6^3$ | | $5^1$ | | 8 | | | 10■ | | 2 | | 9 | | 13 | 11 | 7 | | | | 3 | | 12 | 14 | | | | | 27 |
| 1 | $4^1$ | 6 | | | | 8 | 13 | | | | 2 | | 9 | | 12 | 11 | $10^2$ | | | | 3 | | 5 | 7 | | | | | 28 |
| 1 | $4^2$ | 6 | | | | 8 | 12 | | | | | | 9 | | 7 | $11^1$ | 10 | | | | 3 | | 5 | 2 | 13 | | | | 29 |
| 1 | 4 | 6 | | | | 8 | 11 | | | | | | $9^2$ | | 7 | 12 | 10 | | | | $3^1$ | | 5 | 2 | 13 | | | | 30 |
| 1 | $4^2$ | $6^1$ | 12 | | | 8 | $7^3$ | | 13 | | | | 14 | | 11 | 9 | 10 | | | | 3 | | 5 | 2 | | | | | 31 |
| 1 | $4^1$ | | 2 | 13 | | 8 | $7^3$ | | 10 | | | | 12 | | 6 | 9 | 11 | | | | 3 | | $5^2$ | 14 | | | | | 32 |
| 1 | | | 5 | 2 | | $8^1$ | 6 | | 10 | | | | $9^2$ | | 7 | | 11 | | | | 3 | | | 4 | 13 | 12 | | | 33 |
| 1 | 12 | 6 | $5^1$ | 2 | | | $8^2$ | | 10 | | | | 9 | | 7 | | 11 | | | | 3 | | | 4 | 13 | | | | 34 |
| 1 | | | | 5 | | | $7^3$ | | $10^1$ | | | | 9 | | 2 | $11^2$ | 8 | | | | 3 | | 4 | 6 | 13 | 12 | 14 | | 35 |
| $1^1$ | | 6 | $5^3$ | 4 | | | $7^2$ | | 10 | | | | 9 | | 2 | 11 | 8 | | | | 3 | | 14 | 13 | | | | 12 | 36 |

# RAITH ROVERS First Division

*Year Formed:* 1883. *Ground & Address:* Stark's Park, Pratt St, Kirkcaldy KY1 1SA. *Telephone:* 01592 263514. *Fax:* 01592 642833.
*Ground Capacity:* all seated: 10,104. *Size of Pitch:* 113yd × 70yd.
*Chairman:* Turnbull Hutton. *Office Manager:* Bob Mullen.
*Manager:* Claude Anelka. *Assistant Manager:* Francisco Ortez Rivas.
*Managers since 1975:* R. Paton, A. Matthew, W. McLean, G. Wallace, R. Wilson, F. Connor, J. Nicholl, J. Thomson, T. McLean, I. Munro, J. Nicholl, J. McVeigh, P. Hetherston, J. Scott, A. Calderon.
*Club Nickname:* Rovers. *Previous Grounds:* Robbie's Park.
*Record Attendance:* 31,306 v Hearts, Scottish Cup 2nd rd, 7 Feb 1953.
*Record Transfer Fee received:* £900,000 for S. McAnespie to Bolton Wanderers (Sept 1995).
*Record Transfer Fee paid:* £225,000 for Paul Harvey from Airdrieonians (1996).
*Record Victory:* 10-1 v Coldstream, Scottish Cup 2nd rd, 13 Feb 1954.
*Record Defeat:* 2-11 v Morton, Division II, 18 Mar 1936.
*Most Capped Player:* David Morris, 6, Scotland.
*Most League Appearances:* 430: Willie McNaught.
*Most League Goals in Season (Individual):* 38: Norman Haywood, Division II, 1937-38.
*Most Goals Overall (Individual):* 154: Gordon Dalziel (League), 1987-94.

## RAITH ROVERS 2003–04 LEAGUE RECORD

| Match No. | Date | Venue | Opponents | Result | | H/T Score | Lg. Pos. | Goalscorers | Attendance |
|---|---|---|---|---|---|---|---|---|---|
| 1 | Aug 9 | H | St Mirren | D | 1-1 | 1-0 | — | Brittain 28 | 3090 |
| 2 | 16 | A | Brechin C | W | 3-0 | 1-0 | 2 | Sutton 3 12, 72, 84 | 1013 |
| 3 | 23 | H | Ayr U | D | 1-1 | 0-1 | 3 | Dennis 70 | 2337 |
| 4 | 30 | H | Falkirk | L | 0-1 | 0-0 | 6 | | 4222 |
| 5 | Sept 13 | A | Queen of the S | W | 2-0 | 1-0 | 3 | Sutton 2 25, 78 | 2142 |
| 6 | 20 | A | St Johnstone | W | 1-0 | 1-0 | 2 | Calderon 28 | 2983 |
| 7 | 27 | H | Ross Co | L | 1-7 | 1-3 | 4 | Brown 11 | 2292 |
| 8 | Oct 4 | A | Inverness CT | L | 1-2 | 0-1 | 7 | Sutton 83 | 1707 |
| 9 | 18 | H | Clyde | L | 0-1 | 0-1 | 7 | | 1765 |
| 10 | 25 | H | Brechin C | W | 2-1 | 2-0 | 7 | Hawley 28, Sutton 36 | 1685 |
| 11 | Nov 1 | A | St Mirren | L | 1-2 | 1-1 | 7 | Rivas 43 | 3005 |
| 12 | 8 | H | Queen of the S | L | 0-1 | 0-0 | 8 | | 1944 |
| 13 | 14 | A | Falkirk | L | 2-3 | 1-2 | 8 | Sutton 35, Blackadder 80 | 3237 |
| 14 | 22 | A | Ross Co | L | 2-3 | 0-1 | 7 | Sutton 60, Calderon 78 | 2803 |
| 15 | 29 | H | St Johnstone | L | 1-4 | 0-1 | 8 | Hawley 62 | 1996 |
| 16 | Dec 6 | A | Clyde | D | 0-0 | 0-0 | 8 | | 1375 |
| 17 | 13 | H | Inverness CT | L | 1-3 | 1-0 | 8 | Sutton 45 | 1432 |
| 18 | 27 | A | Ayr U | L | 0-1 | 0-1 | 8 | | 1791 |
| 19 | Jan 3 | H | Falkirk | W | 2-0 | 1-0 | 8 | Sutton 8, Stanley 72 | 2885 |
| 20 | 17 | A | Queen of the S | D | 1-1 | 0-0 | 8 | Sutton 77 | 2089 |
| 21 | 24 | A | St Johnstone | L | 2-5 | 1-3 | 8 | Sutton 12, Patino 52 | 2576 |
| 22 | Feb 7 | H | Ross Co | D | 0-0 | 0-0 | 8 | | 1562 |
| 23 | 14 | A | Inverness CT | L | 0-3 | 0-1 | 8 | | 1879 |
| 24 | 21 | H | Clyde | L | 0-3 | 0-1 | — | | 1871 |
| 25 | Mar 6 | H | St Mirren | W | 2-0 | 1-0 | 8 | Ferrero 15, Pereira Gomez 71 | 1882 |
| 26 | 10 | A | Brechin C | D | 1-1 | 1-0 | — | Calderon 22 | 925 |
| 27 | 13 | H | Ayr U | W | 2-1 | 1-1 | 8 | Pereira Gomez 2 30, 67 | 2231 |
| 28 | 23 | H | Queen of the S | W | 3-1 | 2-1 | — | Pereira Gomez 1, Rivas 6, Thomson (og) 90 | 1482 |
| 29 | 27 | A | Falkirk | L | 0-1 | 0-1 | 8 | | 2386 |
| 30 | Apr 3 | A | Ross Co | D | 1-1 | 0-1 | 8 | Pereira Gomez 61 | 2414 |
| 31 | 10 | H | St Johnstone | D | 1-1 | 1-0 | 7 | Pereira Gomez 38 | 2676 |
| 32 | 17 | A | Clyde | L | 1-4 | 1-1 | 8 | Ferrero 2 | 1533 |
| 33 | 24 | H | Inverness CT | L | 0-1 | 0-1 | 8 | | 1748 |
| 34 | May 1 | A | St Mirren | D | 1-1 | 0-1 | 8 | Ferrero 63 | 2372 |
| 35 | 8 | H | Brechin C | D | 1-1 | 0-1 | 8 | O'Reilly 52 | 2311 |
| 36 | 15 | A | Ayr U | L | 0-1 | 0-1 | 8 | | 1283 |

**Final League Position: 8**

**Honours**
*League Champions:* First Division: 1992-93, 1994-95. Division II 1907-08, 1909-10 (shared), 1937-38, 1948-49; *Runners-up:* Division II 1908-09, 1926-27, 1966-67. Second Division 1975-76, 1977-78, 1986-87.
*Scottish Cup Runners-up:* 1913. *League Cup Winners: (Coca-Cola Cup):* 1994-95. *Runners-up:* 1948-49.

**European:** *UEFA Cup:* 6 matches (1995-96).

**Club colours:** Shirt: Navy blue with white sleeves. Shorts: White with navy and red trim. Stockings: Navy blue with white turnover.

**Goalscorers:** *League* (37): Sutton 13, Pereira Gomez 6, Calderon 3, Ferrero 3, Hawley 2, Rivas 2, Blackadder 1, Brittain 1, Brown 1, Dennis 1, O'Reilly 1, Patino 1, Stanley 1, own goal 1
*Scottish Cup* (1): Talio 1
*CIS Cup* (0):
*Challenge Cup* (10): Prest 3, Sutton 3, Calderon 1, Henry 1, Peers 1, Stanley 1

| Gonzalez R 17 + 1 | Patino C 20 | Calderon A 26 + 3 | Talio V 9 + 1 | Dennis S 23 | Brady D 24 + 5 | Stanley C 18 + 2 | Rivas F 33 | Sutton J 20 + 1 / Irons S — + 1 | Brittain R 9 + 4 | Prest M 8 + 3 / Raffell B — + 1 | Brown I 13 + 3 | Peers M 2 + 3 / Leiper C — + 1 | Blackadder R 8 + 9 | Martin J 1 + 4 | Henry J 2 + 1 | Stanic G 28 + 1 | Evans D 2 + 6 | Hawley K 4 + 7 | Robb S 8 + 3 | Jack M 6 | Langfield J 5 | Carranza L 2 + 1 | Boyle J 3 + 12 | Young L 9 + 5 | Pereira Gomez R 10 | Berthelot D 14 | Bornes J 13 | Neito J 11 + 1 | Ferrero S 12 | Glynn D 1 | Smart J 9 + 3 | Millar P 1 + 1 | Malcolm C 1 + 4 | Dow A 9 | Capin S 11 + 1 | Maxwell D 2 + 5 | O'Reilly C 2 + 2 | *Match No.* |
|---|---|---|---|---|---|---|---|---|---|---|---|---|---|---|---|---|---|---|---|---|---|---|---|---|---|---|---|---|---|---|---|---|---|---|---|---|---|---|
| 1 | 2 | $3^{2}$ | $4^{1}$ | 5 | 6 | 7 | 8 | 9 | $10^{3}$ | 11 | 12 | 13 | 14 | | | | | | | | | | | | | | | | | | | | | | | | | 1 |
| 1 | 2 | 3 | 14 | 5 | 4 | 6 | 8 | $9^{3}$ | 10 | $11^{2}$ | | $7^{1}$ | 12 | 13 | | | | | | | | | | | | | | | | | | | | | | | | 2 |
| 1 | 2 | 3 | | 5 | | 6 | 8 | $9^{3}$ | 4 | 11 | | $7^{2}$ | 13 | | $10^{1}$ | 12 | 14 | | | | | | | | | | | | | | | | | | | | | 3 |
| 1 | $2^{2}$ | 10 | | 5 | 12 | $7^{3}$ | 8 | 9 | 4 | 11 | | | 13 | | $6^{1}$ | 3 | 14 | | | | | | | | | | | | | | | | | | | | | 4 |
| 1 | 2 | | $3^{2}$ | | 4 | 6 | 8 | 9 | 7 | $11^{1}$ | 5 | | 10 | | 13 | | | 12 | | | | | | | | | | | | | | | | | | | | 5 |
| 1 | | 10 | | 5 | 4 | 6 | 8 | 9 | | | 2 | | 7 | | | 3 | | 12 | $11^{1}$ | | | | | | | | | | | | | | | | | | | 6 |
| 1 | | $10^{1}$ | | 5 | $4^{2}$ | 6 | 8 | 9 | 13 | 12 | $2^{3}$ | | 7 | | | 3 | | 14 | 11 | | | | | | | | | | | | | | | | | | | 7 |
| 1 | 2 | 10 | | | 4 | 6 | 8 | 9 | $7^{1}$ | | 5 | 13 | | | | 3 | | 12 | $11^{2}$ | | | | | | | | | | | | | | | | | | | 8 |
| 1 | 2 | 10 | $5^{2}$ | | $6^{3}$ | 7 | 8 | 9 | 4 | | | 13 | 14 | | | 3 | | 12 | $11^{1}$ | | | | | | | | | | | | | | | | | | | 9 |
| 1 | 2 | 10 | $4^{1}$ | | | 7 | 8 | 9 | 6 | | 5 | | 12 | | | 3 | | 11 | | | | | | | | | | | | | | | | | | | | 10 |
| 1 | 2 | $10^{2}$ | $4^{3}$ | | | 7 | 8 | $9^{1}$ | 6 | 12 | 5 | | 14 | | | 3 | | 11 | 13 | | | | | | | | | | | | | | | | | | | 11 |
| 1 | 2 | 10 | | | $6^{2}$ | 7 | 8 | 14 | 12 | $11^{3}$ | $5^{1}$ | | | | | 3 | | 9 | 13 | 4 | | | | | | | | | | | | | | | | | | 12 |
| 1 | 2 | $10^{1}$ | 5 | | $6^{2}$ | 12 | 8 | 9 | | 13 | | | 7 | | | 3 | 14 | | $11^{3}$ | 4 | | | | | | | | | | | | | | | | | | 13 |
| 1 | $2^{3}$ | 10 | | | $4^{2}$ | 6 | 8 | 9 | 13 | | 14 | | 7 | | | 3 | | 12 | $11^{1}$ | 5 | | | | | | | | | | | | | | | | | | 14 |
| | | $10^{3}$ | | 5 | | 6 | 8 | 9 | 13 | | 2 | | $7^{2}$ | | | 3 | | 11 | 14 | $4^{1}$ | 1 | 12 | | | | | | | | | | | | | | | | 15 |
| | 2 | | | 5 | | 7 | 8 | 9 | | 11 | 4 | | 12 | | | 3 | | | | 6 | 1 | $10^{1}$ | | | | | | | | | | | | | | | | 16 |
| | $2^{1}$ | 13 | | 5 | 6 | 14 | 8 | 9 | | 11 | 12 | | $7^{3}$ | | | $3^{2}$ | | | 10 | 4 | 1 | | | | | | | | | | | | | | | | | 17 |
| | 2 | 4 | | 5 | 12 | 6 | 8 | 9 | | | | | $7^{3}$ | 14 | | $3^{2}$ | | 13 | 11 | | 1 | $10^{1}$ | | | | | | | | | | | | | | | | 18 |
| | 2 | 3 | 4 | 5 | 6 | 7 | 8 | 9 | | | | | | 12 | | | $11^{1}$ | | | | 1 | | $10^{2}$ | 13 | | | | | | | | | | | | | | 19 |
| 1 | 2 | 3 | $7^{3}$ | | $4^{2}$ | 6 | 8 | 9 | | | 5 | | 14 | | | $11^{1}$ | 13 | | | | | | 12 | | 10 | | | | | | | | | | | | | 20 |
| 1 | 2 | 4 | 7 | | $6^{2}$ | | 8 | 9 | | | $5^{1}$ | | | | | 3 | 13 | | | | | | 12 | 11 | 10 | | | | | | | | | | | | | 21 |
| | $2^{1}$ | 6 | | 5 | 14 | | 8 | | | | | | | | | 3 | 13 | | | | | | 12 | $11^{3}$ | 10 | 1 | 4 | 7 | $9^{2}$ | | | | | | | | | 22 |
| | | 6 | | 5 | 12 | | | | | | | | | | | 3 | $11^{1}$ | | | | | | $10^{2}$ | $7^{3}$ | | 1 | 4 | 8 | 9 | | 2 | 13 | 14 | | | | | 23 |
| | | 10 | | | 6 | | 8 | | | | $5^{1}$ | | | | | 3 | | | | | | | | 14 | | 1 | 4 | $7^{2}$ | 9 | | 2 | | 13 | $11^{3}$ | 12 | | | 24 |
| | $2^{1}$ | | | 5 | 13 | | 8 | | | | | | | | | 6 | | | | | | | 14 | | $10^{3}$ | 1 | 4 | 7 | 9 | | 12 | | | $3^{2}$ | 11 | | | 25 |
| | | 4 | | 5 | 7 | | $8^{1}$ | | | | | | | | | 3 | | | | | | | 13 | 12 | $10^{3}$ | 1 | | | 9 | | 6 | | 14 | $11^{2}$ | 2 | | | 26 |
| | | 13 | | 5 | 6 | | | | | | | | | | | 11 | | | | | | | 12 | $7^{3}$ | 10 | 1 | 4 | 14 | 9 | | $2^{2}$ | | | $3^{1}$ | 8 | | | 27 |
| | | 3 | | 5 | 6 | | 8 | | | | | | | | | | | | | | | | 12 | $11^{1}$ | 10 | 1 | 4 | $7^{2}$ | 9 | | | | | | 2 | 13 | | 28 |
| | | 13 | | 5 | $6^{1}$ | | 8 | | | | | | | | | 3 | | | | | | | | $11^{2}$ | 10 | 1 | 4 | $7^{3}$ | 9 | | 12 | | | | 2 | 14 | | 29 |
| 13 | | 9 | | 5 | 6 | | 8 | | | | | | | $12^{3}$ | | 3 | | | | | | | 14 | $11^{1}$ | 10 | $1^{2}$ | 4 | 7 | | | | | | | 2 | | | 30 |
| | | 6 | | | | | 8 | | | | | | | | | 3 | | | | | | | | | 10 | 1 | 4 | 7 | 9 | | 5 | | | $11^{1}$ | 2 | 12 | | 31 |
| | | $11^{1}$ | | 5 | 6 | | 8 | | | | | | | | | 3 | | | | | | | 14 | | | 1 | 4 | $7^{2}$ | 9 | | 13 | | | $10^{3}$ | 2 | 12 | | 32 |
| | | | | 5 | 6 | | 8 | | | | | | | | | | | | | | | | 12 | 14 | | 1 | $4^{1}$ | $7^{2}$ | 9 | | $3^{3}$ | | | 11 | 2 | 10 | 13 | 33 |
| | | | | 5 | 6 | | $8^{2}$ | | | | | | | | | 3 | | | | | | | 14 | 12 | | 1 | 4 | $7^{3}$ | 9 | | 2 | | | $10^{1}$ | 11 | | 13 | 34 |
| | | | | 5 | $6^{3}$ | | 8 | | | | | | | | | 3 | | | | | | | 13 | 11 | | 1 | 4 | | | | 2 | | 14 | $9^{1}$ | 7 | 12 | $10^{2}$ | 35 |
| 1 | | | | | | | | 12 | | 13 | 4 | 14 | | $2^{1}$ | | | | | | | | | $3^{3}$ | 8 | | | | | | 10 | 5 | $7^{2}$ | 11 | | | 6 | 9 | 36 |

# RANGERS

## Premier League

*Year Formed:* 1873. *Ground & Address:* Ibrox Stadium, 150 Edmiston Drive, Glasgow G51 2XD.
*Telephone:* 0870 600 1972. *Fax:* 0870 600 1978. *Website:* www.rangers.co.uk
*Ground Capacity:* all seated: 50,444. *Size of Pitch:* 114.5m × 81.5m.
*Chairman:* John McClelland. *Hon. Chairman:* David Murray. *General Secretary/Director:* R. C. Ogilvie. *Director of Football Business:* Martin Bain.
*Manager:* Alex McLeish. *Assistant Manager:* Andy Watson. *First Team Coach:* Jan Wouters. *Physios:* David Henderson, Stuart Collie. *Reserve team coach:* John Brown.
*Managers since 1975:* Jock Wallace, John Greig, Jock Wallace, Graeme Souness, Walter Smith, Dick Advocaat.
*Club Nickname(s):* The Gers. *Previous Grounds:* Flesher's Haugh, Burnbank, Kinning Park, Old Ibrox.
*Record Attendance:* 118,567 v Celtic, Division I, 2 Jan 1939.
*Record Transfer Fee received:* £8,500,000 for G. Van Bronckhorst to Arsenal (2001).
*Record Transfer Fee paid:* £12 million for Tore Andre Flo from Chelsea (November 2000).
*Record Victory:* 14-2 v Blairgowrie, Scottish Cup 1st rd, 20 Jan, 1934. *Record Defeat:* 2-10 v Airdrieonians; 1886.
*Most Capped Player:* Ally McCoist, 60, Scotland. *Most League Appearances:* 496: John Greig, 1962-78.
*Most League Goals in Season (Individual):* 44: Sam English, Division I, 1931-32.
*Most Goals Overall (Individual):* 355: Ally McCoist; 1985-98.

**Honours**
*League Champions:* (50 times) Division I 1890-91 (shared), 1898-99, 1899-1900, 1900-01, 1901-02, 1910-11, 1911-12, 1912-13, 1917-18, 1919-20, 1920-21, 1922-23, 1923-24, 1924-25, 1926-27, 1927-28, 1928-29, 1929-30, 1930-31, 1932-33, 1933-34, 1934-35, 1936-37, 1938-39, 1946-47, 1948-49, 1949-50, 1952-53, 1955-56, 1956-57, 1958-59, 1960-61, 1962-63, 1963-64, 1974-75. Premier Division: 1975-76, 1977-78, 1986-87, 1988-89, 1989-90, 1990-91, 1991-92, 1992-93, 1993-94, 1994-95, 1995-96, 1996-97, 1998-99, 1999-2000, 2002-03; *Runners-up:* 25 times.

### RANGERS 2003–04 LEAGUE RECORD

| *Match No.* | *Date* | *Venue* | *Opponents* | *Result* | *H/T Score* | *Lg. Pos.* | *Goalscorers* | *Attendance* |
|---|---|---|---|---|---|---|---|---|
| 1 | Aug 9 | H | Kilmarnock | W 4-0 | 3-0 | — | Lovenkrands [14], Mols [38], Arteta 2 (1 pen) [43 (p), 72] | 49108 |
| 2 | 16 | A | Aberdeen | W 3-2 | 2-1 | — | de Boer R [37], Arteta [42], Mols [58] | 16,348 |
| 3 | 23 | H | Hibernian | W 5-2 | 2-2 | 1 | Mols 2 [33, 62], Murray (og) [43], Arteta [66], Burke [83] | 49,642 |
| 4 | 31 | A | Dundee U | W 3-1 | 1-0 | 1 | Capucho [13], Arveladze [80], Arteta [88] | 11,111 |
| 5 | Sept 13 | H | Dunfermline Ath | W 4-0 | 3-0 | 1 | Thompson [6], Mols [32], Arveladze [42], Capucho [65] | 49,072 |
| 6 | 21 | A | Hearts | W 4-0 | 1-0 | 1 | Arveladze 2 [44, 71], Lovenkrands [50], Ball [87] | 14,732 |
| 7 | 27 | H | Dundee | W 3-1 | 0-0 | 1 | Arveladze 2 [60, 88], Vanoli [85] | 49,548 |
| 8 | Oct 4 | H | Celtic | L 0-1 | 0-0 | 2 | | 49,825 |
| 9 | 19 | A | Motherwell | D 1-1 | 1-1 | 2 | Arveladze [14] | 10,824 |
| 10 | 25 | A | Livingston | D 0-0 | 0-0 | 2 | | 7689 |
| 11 | Nov 1 | H | Partick Th | W 3-1 | 2-0 | 2 | Arteta 2 (1 pen) [7, 75 (p)], Mols [69] | 49,551 |
| 12 | 9 | A | Kilmarnock | W 3-2 | 1-1 | 2 | Arveladze 2 [29, 63], Capucho [88] | 12,204 |
| 13 | 22 | H | Aberdeen | W 3-0 | 0-0 | 2 | Hughes [76], Lovenkrands 2 [88, 89] | 49,962 |
| 14 | 30 | A | Hibernian | W 1-0 | 0-0 | 2 | Hughes [90] | 11,116 |
| 15 | Dec 6 | H | Dundee U | W 2-1 | 2-0 | 2 | Capucho [16], Lovenkrands [19] | 49,307 |
| 16 | 14 | A | Dunfermline Ath | L 0-2 | 0-1 | 2 | | 8592 |
| 17 | 21 | H | Hearts | W 2-1 | 1-1 | 2 | Arveladze [20], Burke [52] | 49,592 |
| 18 | 28 | A | Dundee | W 2-0 | 2-0 | 2 | Capucho [6], Wilkie (og) [35] | 10,948 |
| 19 | Jan 3 | A | Celtic | L 0-3 | 0-1 | 2 | | 59,042 |
| 20 | 17 | H | Motherwell | W 1-0 | 0-0 | 2 | Arveladze [82] | 48,925 |
| 21 | 24 | H | Livingston | W 1-0 | 1-0 | 2 | Nerlinger [11] | 48,638 |
| 22 | Feb 1 | A | Partick Th | W 1-0 | 0-0 | 2 | Lovenkrands [75] | 8220 |
| 23 | 11 | H | Kilmarnock | W 2-0 | 1-0 | — | Moore [22], Namouchi [75] | 46,900 |
| 24 | 14 | A | Aberdeen | D 1-1 | 0-1 | 2 | de Boer F [87] | 15,815 |
| 25 | 21 | H | Hibernian | W 3-0 | 1-0 | 2 | Arveladze (pen) [9], Mols [65], Thompson (pen) [82] | 49,698 |
| 26 | 29 | A | Dundee U | L 0-2 | 0-2 | 2 | | 10,497 |
| 27 | Mar 13 | A | Hearts | D 1-1 | 0-0 | 2 | Moore (pen) [48] | 14,596 |
| 28 | 20 | H | Dundee | W 4-0 | 1-0 | 2 | Lovenkrands [41], de Boer F [47], Rae [80], Thompson [81] | 49,364 |
| 29 | 23 | H | Dunfermline Ath | W 4-1 | 4-1 | — | Hutton [2], Lovenkrands [11], de Boer R [26], Mols [28] | 47,487 |
| 30 | 28 | H | Celtic | L 1-2 | 0-1 | 2 | Thompson [82] | 49,909 |
| 31 | Apr 4 | A | Motherwell | W 1-0 | 1-0 | 2 | Hughes [43] | 8967 |
| 32 | 14 | A | Livingston | D 1-1 | 1-0 | — | Mols [24] | 6092 |
| 33 | 17 | H | Partick Th | W 2-0 | 1-0 | 2 | Thompson [39], Rae [49] | 49,279 |
| 34 | 24 | A | Dundee U | D 3-3 | 3-1 | 2 | Thompson 2 (1 pen) [5, 14 (p)], Namouchi [43] | 8339 |
| 35 | May 1 | H | Motherwell | W 4-0 | 1-0 | 2 | Arteta [44], Ross [46], Namouchi [50], Thompson [55] | 47,579 |
| 36 | 8 | A | Celtic | L 0-1 | 0-0 | 2 | | 59,180 |
| 37 | 12 | H | Hearts | L 0-1 | 0-0 | — | | 47,467 |
| 38 | 16 | A | Dunfermline Ath | W 3-2 | 2-1 | 2 | Ricksen [42], Burke [44], McCormack (pen) [53] | 6719 |

**Final League Position: 2**

*Scottish Cup Winners:* (31 times) 1894, 1897, 1898, 1903, 1928, 1930, 1932, 1934, 1935, 1936, 1948, 1949, 1950, 1953, 1960, 1962, 1963, 1964, 1966, 1973, 1976, 1978, 1979, 1981, 1992, 1993, 1996, 1999, 2000, 2002, 2003; *Runners-up:* 17 times.
*League Cup Winners:* (23 times) 1946-47, 1948-49, 1960-61, 1961-62, 1963-64, 1964-65, 1970-71, 1975-76, 1977-78, 1978-79, 1981-82, 1983-84, 1984-85, 1986-87, 1987-88, 1988-89, 1990-91, 1992-93, 1993-94, 1996-97, 1998-99, 2001-02, 2002-03; *Runners-up:* 6 times.

**European:** *European Cup:* 117 matches (1956-57, 1957-58, 1959-60 semi-finals, 1961-62, 1963-64, 1964-65, 1975-76, 1976-77, 1978-79, 1987-88, 1989-90, 1990-91, 1991-92, 1992-93 final pool, 1993-94, 1994-95, 1995-96; 1996-97, 1997-98, 1999-2000, 2000-01, 2003-04).
*Cup Winners' Cup:* 54 matches (1960-61 runners-up, 1962-63, 1966-67 runners-up, 1969-70, 1971-72 winners, 1973-74, 1977-78, 1979-80, 1981-82, 1983-84). *UEFA Cup:* 56 matches (*Fairs Cup:* 1967-68, 1968-69 semi-finals, 1970-71.
*UEFA Cup:* 1982-83, 1984-85, 1985-86, 1986-87, 1988-89, 1997-98, 1998-99, 1999-2000, 2000-01, 2002-03).

**Club colours:** Shirt: Royal blue; red chevrons at neck, white collar, red trim at cuffs. Shorts: White with royal blue side panels and red trim. Stockings: Black with red tops; or Royal blue with white tops.

**Goalscorers:** *League* (76): Arveladze 12 (1 pen). Mols 9, Arteta 8 (2 pens), Lovenkrands 8, Thompson 8 (2 pens). Capucho 5, Burke 3, Hughes 3, Namouchi 3, de Boer F 2, de Boer R 2, Moore 2 (1 pen), Rae 2, Ball 1, Hutton 1, McCormack 1 (1 pen), Nerlinger 1, Ricksen 1, Ross 1, Vanoli 1, own goals 2
*Scottish Cup* (4): Arveladze 2, de Boer R 1, Lovenkrands 1
*CIS Cup* (10): Nerlinger 3, Mols 2, Ostenstad 2, Burke 1, Capucho 1, Lovenkrands 1

| Klos S 34 | Ricksen F 29 + 1 | Moore C 16 + 1 | Khizanishvili Z 25 + 1 | Ball M 30 + 2 | Ross M 10 + 10 | Ferguson B 3 | Arteta M 23 | de Boer R 12 + 4 | Mols M 29 + 6 | Lovenkrands P 22 + 3 | Vanoli P 14 + 9 | Malcolm R 8 + 6 | Thompson S 9 + 7 | Berg H 20 | Nerlinger C 11 + 3 | Capucho N 18 + 4 | Arveladze S 17 + 2 | Burke C 11 + 9 | Emerson13 + 1 | Ostenstad E 2 + 9 | Hughes S 17 + 5 | Duffy D — + 1 | Rae G 9 + 1 | Namouchi H 4 + 3 | de Boer F 15 | Hutton A 11 | Fetai B — + 1 | Walker A — + 2 | Adams C 1 + 1 | McGregor A 4 | McCormack R 1 + 1 | McKenzie G — + 2 | Davidson R — + 1 | *Match No.* |
|---|---|---|---|---|---|---|---|---|---|---|---|---|---|---|---|---|---|---|---|---|---|---|---|---|---|---|---|---|---|---|---|---|---|---|
| 1 | $2^3$ | 3 | 4 | $5^1$ | 6 | 7 | $8^2$ | 9 | 10 | 11 | 12 | 13 | 14 | | | | | | | | | | | | | | | | | | | | | 1 |
| 1 | $2^3$ | | 4 | 5 | | 7 | 6 | $9^2$ | 10 | $11^1$ | 12 | 14 | 13 | 3 | 8 | | | | | | | | | | | | | | | | | | | 2 |
| 1 | 6 | | $4^3$ | 5 | | 7 | 8 | | 10 | | $2^1$ | 14 | | 3 | 12 | $9^2$ | 11 | 13 | | | | | | | | | | | | | | | | 3 |
| 1 | 2 | | 4 | | | | 7 | $9^1$ | 10 | | 3 | 5 | 12 | | 6 | $8^2$ | 11 | | 13 | | | | | | | | | | | | | | | 4 |
| 1 | 2 | | 4 | 5 | | | 7 | | 10 | 14 | 13 | | $9^1$ | $3^2$ | 6 | 12 | $11^3$ | | 8 | | | | | | | | | | | | | | | 5 |
| 1 | | | 4 | 5 | 2 | | 7 | | $10^1$ | 11 | | | | 3 | | 8 | 9 | | 6 | 12 | | | | | | | | | | | | | | 6 |
| 1 | | 12 | 4 | 5 | $2^3$ | | 7 | | 10 | $11^2$ | 13 | | | $3^1$ | | 8 | 9 | | 6 | | 14 | | | | | | | | | | | | | 7 |
| 1 | | $3^1$ | 4 | 5 | 12 | | 7 | | 10 | 11 | | | | 2 | | $8^2$ | 9 | | 6 | 13 | | | | | | | | | | | | | | 8 |
| 1 | $6^3$ | 3 | 4 | 5 | | | 7 | | 10 | $11^2$ | 12 | | | 2 | | 14 | 9 | | $8^1$ | 13 | | | | | | | | | | | | | | 9 |
| 1 | 6 | 3 | 4 | 5 | | | 7 | | | | 2 | | | | $8^2$ | 11 | | 13 | $9^1$ | 10 | 12 | | | | | | | | | | | | | 10 |
| 1 | $2^1$ | 3 | 12 | 5 | | | 7 | | 10 | 11 | | | | 4 | $6^3$ | 8 | 13 | | | $9^2$ | 14 | | | | | | | | | | | | | 11 |
| 1 | 2 | | | 5 | | | 7 | | $10^2$ | 11 | 3 | | | 4 | | 12 | 9 | | $8^1$ | 13 | 6 | | | | | | | | | | | | | 12 |
| 1 | 2 | | | 5 | | | $7^2$ | | 10 | 11 | 3 | | | 4 | | | 9 | 12 | $8^1$ | 13 | 6 | | | | | | | | | | | | | 13 |
| 1 | 2 | | 4 | 5 | 7 | | | | $10^2$ | 11 | | | | 3 | | $8^1$ | 9 | 12 | | 13 | 6 | | | | | | | | | | | | | 14 |
| 1 | 2 | | 4 | 5 | | | | | $10^2$ | 11 | 14 | 12 | | 3 | | 9 | | $8^3$ | $7^1$ | | 6 | 13 | | | | | | | | | | | | 15 |
| 1 | 6 | | | 5 | | | | | $10^2$ | 11 | 4 | 2 | | 3 | | $9^1$ | 12 | 8 | | 13 | 7 | | | | | | | | | | | | | 16 |
| 1 | 2 | | | 5 | 12 | | 7 | | $10^2$ | 11 | | 4 | | 3 | | | 9 | 8 | | 13 | $6^1$ | | | | | | | | | | | | | 17 |
| 1 | 2 | 3 | | 5 | | | 7 | | | $11^2$ | 13 | 6 | | 4 | 12 | 10 | $9^1$ | 8 | | | | | | | | | | | | | | | | 18 |
| 1 | 2 | 3 | | 5 | | | 7 | | 12 | 11 | | $6^2$ | | 4 | | 13 | 9 | 10 | | | | | $8^1$ | | | | | | | | | | | 19 |
| 1 | | 3 | 4 | | 14 | | $7^1$ | | 13 | 11 | 2 | $6^2$ | | 5 | 12 | 10 | 9 | | | | | | | $8^3$ | | | | | | | | | | 20 |
| 1 | 2 | 3 | 4 | 13 | 6 | | | 12 | $10^1$ | 11 | $5^2$ | | | | 7 | 8 | 9 | | | | | | | | | | | | | | | | | 21 |
| 1 | 6 | | $4^2$ | 5 | 13 | | | 12 | 10 | $11^3$ | | 14 | | 2 | 7 | $9^1$ | | | | | | | | 8 | 3 | | | | | | | | | 22 |
| 1 | 2 | 3 | | 5 | 6 | | | 9 | $10^1$ | | | | | | 7 | $11^2$ | | | 8 | 12 | | | | 13 | 4 | | | | | | | | | 23 |
| 1 | 2 | 3 | | $5^2$ | 6 | | | $9^3$ | 14 | | 13 | | | | $7^1$ | 11 | 10 | | 8 | | | | | 12 | 4 | | | | | | | | | 24 |
| 1 | 2 | | | | 5 | | $7^3$ | $9^1$ | 12 | | | | 13 | 3 | 6 | 11 | $10^2$ | | 8 | | 14 | | | | 4 | | | | | | | | | 25 |
| 1 | 2 | 3 | | 5 | 13 | | $7^2$ | 9 | 10 | | | | 12 | | $6^3$ | 11 | | | $8^1$ | | | | 14 | | 4 | | | | | | | | | 26 |
| 1 | 6 | 3 | | $5^2$ | 9 | | | $10^1$ | 12 | 11 | | | | 2 | | | | 13 | | | 7 | | 8 | | 4 | | | | | | | | | 27 |
| 1 | | $3^2$ | 2 | 5 | | | | $9^1$ | 12 | $11^3$ | | 13 | 10 | | | | | 14 | | | 7 | | 8 | | 4 | 6 | | | | | | | | 28 |
| 1 | | | 2 | 5 | | | | $9^1$ | $10^3$ | $11^2$ | | 3 | 12 | | | | | 13 | | | 7 | | 8 | | 4 | 6 | 14 | | | | | | | 29 |
| 1 | 14 | 3 | $2^1$ | 5 | | | | 9 | 10 | $11^2$ | | $4^3$ | 13 | | | | | 12 | | | 7 | | 8 | | | 6 | | | | | | | | 30 |
| 1 | | 3 | | 5 | 12 | | | | 10 | | 6 | | 11 | | | | | | | | 7 | | 8 | $9^2$ | 4 | $2^1$ | | 13 | | | | | | 31 |
| 1 | | | 3 | 5 | 14 | | | $9^2$ | 10 | | $6^1$ | | $11^3$ | | | | | 12 | | | 7 | | 8 | | 4 | 2 | | | 13 | | | | | 32 |
| | 2 | | 3 | 5 | | | $7^1$ | 12 | 10 | | | | $11^2$ | | | | | 9 | | | 13 | | $8^3$ | | 4 | 6 | | 14 | | 1 | | | | 33 |
| | 2 | | 3 | $5^3$ | 14 | | | | $10^1$ | | 13 | | 11 | | | | | 9 | | | 7 | | $8^2$ | 12 | 4 | 6 | | | | 1 | | | | 34 |
| 1 | 2 | | 3 | | 12 | | $8^2$ | | | | 6 | | 11 | | | | | 10 | | | 7 | | | $9^3$ | 4 | $5^1$ | | | | | 13 | 14 | | 35 |
| 1 | 2 | | 3 | 12 | | | 8 | | 10 | | 6 | | 11 | | | | | 9 | | | $7^1$ | | | | 4 | 5 | | | | | | | | 36 |
| | 2 | | 3 | | 13 | | 8 | 14 | $10^3$ | 12 | 6 | | 11 | | | | | 9 | | | $7^2$ | | | | $4^1$ | 5 | | | | 1 | | | | 37 |
| | 2 | | 3 | | $8^3$ | | | | $10^1$ | $12^2$ | 6 | | | | | | | 9 | | | 7 | | | | | 5 | | | 11 | 1 | $4^1$ | 14 | 13 | 38 |

# ROSS COUNTY First Division

*Year Formed:* 1929. *Ground & Address:* Victoria Park, Dingwall IV15 9QW. *Telephone:* 01349 860860. *Fax:* 01349 866277.
*Website:* www.rosscountyfootballclub.co.uk
*Ground Capacity:* 6700. *Size of Ground:* 105×68m.
*Chairman:* Roy McGregor. *Secretary:* Donnie MacBean.
*Manager:* Alex Smith. *Physio:* Douglas Sim.
*Managers since 1994:* Neale Cooper.
*Record Attendance:* 6600, benefit match v Celtic, 31 August 1970.
*Record Transfer Fee Received:* £200,000 for Neil Tarrant to Aston Villa (April 1999).
*Record Transfer Fee Paid:* £25,000 for Barry Wilson from Southampton (Oct. 1992).
*Record Victory:* 11-0 v St Cuthbert Wanderers, Scottish Cup, 11 Dec 1993.
*Record Defeat:* 1-10 v Inverness Thistle, Highland League.
*Most League Appearances:* 157: David Mackay, 1995-2001.
*Most League Goals in Season:* 22: D. Adams, 1996-97.
*Most League Goals (Overall):* 44: Steven Ferguson, 1996-2002.

## ROSS COUNTY 2003–04 LEAGUE RECORD

| *Match No.* | *Date* | *Venue* | *Opponents* | *Result* | *H/T Score* | *Lg. Pos.* | *Goalscorers* | *Attendance* |
|---|---|---|---|---|---|---|---|---|
| 1 | Aug 9 | H | Brechin C | W 4-0 | 2-0 | — | Mackay [18], Robertson [20], Hamilton (pen) [67], Tait [89] | 2662 |
| 2 | 16 | A | Queen of the S | L 0-1 | 0-1 | 5 | | 1734 |
| 3 | 23 | H | St Mirren | W 2-0 | 0-0 | 2 | Winters (pen) [68], Gemmill (og) [88] | 3053 |
| 4 | 30 | H | Inverness CT | D 1-1 | 1-1 | 2 | Hannah (pen) [2] | 5020 |
| 5 | Sept 13 | A | Falkirk | W 2-0 | 1-0 | 1 | Winters (pen) [11], Rankin [88] | 2970 |
| 6 | 20 | H | Ayr U | D 2-2 | 2-2 | 1 | Higgins 2 [3, 15] | 2911 |
| 7 | 27 | A | Raith R | W 7-1 | 3-1 | 1 | McGarry [7], Higgins [38], Winters 3 [45, 86, 88], Bayne [74], O'Donnell [79] | 2292 |
| 8 | Oct 4 | A | Clyde | D 2-2 | 2-1 | 3 | Rankin [22], O'Donnell [31] | 1056 |
| 9 | 18 | H | St Johnstone | L 0-3 | 0-3 | 3 | | 3195 |
| 10 | 25 | H | Queen of the S | W 1-0 | 0-0 | 2 | Webb [58] | 2962 |
| 11 | Nov 1 | A | Brechin C | L 2-4 | 2-1 | 2 | Bayne 2 [1, 44] | 564 |
| 12 | 8 | H | Falkirk | L 1-2 | 1-2 | 5 | Robertson [31] | 3206 |
| 13 | 14 | A | Inverness CT | D 3-3 | 1-3 | 6 | Winters [35], Bayne [70], McGarry [90] | 3523 |
| 14 | 22 | H | Raith R | W 3-2 | 1-0 | 6 | Winters 2 [44, 50], Gethins [59] | 2803 |
| 15 | 29 | A | Ayr U | W 3-1 | 2-1 | 6 | O'Donnell [25], Rankin 2 [47, 82] | 977 |
| 16 | Dec 6 | A | St Johnstone | D 1-1 | 0-1 | 5 | Hamilton [46] | 2478 |
| 17 | 13 | H | Clyde | L 0-1 | 0-1 | 6 | | 2721 |
| 18 | 20 | H | Brechin C | W 2-1 | 1-0 | 5 | McGarry [23], Higgins [52] | 2545 |
| 19 | 27 | A | St Mirren | D 1-1 | 0-1 | 4 | Rankin [90] | 3550 |
| 20 | Jan 3 | H | Inverness CT | W 1-0 | 0-0 | 4 | Gethins [83] | 6020 |
| 21 | 17 | A | Falkirk | L 0-2 | 0-1 | 4 | | 2482 |
| 22 | 24 | H | Ayr U | D 1-1 | 1-0 | 5 | Bayne [39] | 2732 |
| 23 | Feb 7 | A | Raith R | D 0-0 | 0-0 | 3 | | 1562 |
| 24 | 14 | A | Clyde | L 0-1 | 0-1 | 4 | | 1139 |
| 25 | 21 | H | St Johnstone | W 2-0 | 1-0 | 3 | Higgins [42], Winters [90] | 3050 |
| 26 | Mar 6 | A | Queen of the S | D 1-1 | 0-1 | 5 | McGarry [82] | 2047 |
| 27 | 13 | H | St Mirren | W 1-0 | 0-0 | 4 | Winters [77] | 2819 |
| 28 | 20 | H | Falkirk | D 1-1 | 0-0 | 4 | Bayne [72] | 2931 |
| 29 | 27 | A | Inverness CT | L 0-1 | 0-0 | 5 | | 4019 |
| 30 | Apr 3 | H | Raith R | D 1-1 | 1-0 | 5 | Hamilton [22] | 2414 |
| 31 | 10 | A | Ayr U | W 2-1 | 2-0 | 4 | McGarry [19], Hamilton [37] | 1535 |
| 32 | 17 | A | St Johnstone | D 1-1 | 1-1 | 5 | Dods (og) [39] | 2169 |
| 33 | 24 | H | Clyde | D 0-0 | 0-0 | 5 | | 3220 |
| 34 | May 1 | A | Brechin C | L 0-1 | 0-0 | 5 | | 464 |
| 35 | 8 | H | Queen of the S | L 1-2 | 1-1 | 6 | Hamilton [35] | 2842 |
| 36 | 15 | A | St Mirren | L 0-2 | 0-1 | 6 | | 2291 |

**Final League Position: 6**

**Honours**
*League Champions:* Third Division: 1998-99.

**Club colours:** Shirt: Navy blue with white side panels. Shorts: White with navy side panels. Stockings: Navy blue with two white hoops.

**Goalscorers:** *League* (49): Winters 10 (2 pens), Bayne 6, Hamilton 5 (1 pen), Higgins 5, McGarry 5, Rankin 5, O'Donnell 3, Gethins 2, Robertson 2, Hannah 1 (1 pen), Mackay 1, Tait 1, Webb 1, own goals 2
*Scottish Cup* (0):
*CIS Cup* (2): Cowie 1, Mackay 1
*Challenge Cup* (7): Winters 3, Hamilton 2, Rankin 1, own goal 1

| Stewart C 16 | McCunnie J 35 | Mackay S 20 + 1 | Tait J 8 + 1 | Malcolm S 23 + 1 | McCulloch M 33 + 3 | Rankin J 35 | Hannah D 32 | Higgins S 15 + 11 | Robertson H 18 + 2 | Winters D 21 + 11 | Hamilton J 12 + 10 | Gethins C 6 + 13 | Cowie D 8 + 15 | Webb S 12 + 2 | Bayne G 16 + 9 | McGarry S 19 + 9 | O'Donnell S 15 + 11 | Fridge L — + 1 | Smith G 20 | Canning M 14 + 1 | Lauchlan J 17 | Ogunmade D — + 4 | MacDonald N 1 | *Match No.* |
|---|---|---|---|---|---|---|---|---|---|---|---|---|---|---|---|---|---|---|---|---|---|---|---|---|
| 1 | 2 | 3 | 4 | 5 | 6 | 7 | 8 | 9³ | 10¹ | 11² | 12 | 13 | 14 | | | | | | | | | | | 1 |
| 1 | 2 | 3 | 4 | 5³ | 6 | 7 | 8 | 9¹ | 12 | 11 | 10² | 13 | | 14 | | | | | | | | | | 2 |
| 1 | 2 | 3 | 4 | 5 | 6 | 7 | 8 | 12 | | 11³ | 13 | 14 | 10¹ | | 9² | | | | | | | | | 3 |
| 1 | 2 | 3² | 4 | 5 | 6 | 7 | 8 | 9¹ | 10 | 11³ | 12 | 14 | 13 | | | | | | | | | | | 4 |
| 1 | 2 | 3 | 4¹ | 5 | 6 | 7 | 8 | 9³ | 10 | 11² | | | 12 | | 14 | 13 | | | | | | | | 5 |
| 1 | 2 | | 3 | 5 | 6 | 7 | 8² | 9³ | 10 | 11¹ | 14 | | 4 | | | 12 | 13 | | | | | | | 6 |
| 1 | 2 | 3 | | 5 | 4 | 7 | | 9³ | 12 | 11 | | | 13 | 6¹ | 14 | 10² | 8 | | | | | | | 7 |
| 1 | 2 | 3 | | 5 | 6 | 7 | | 9² | 4 | 11³ | 13 | | 12 | | 14 | 10¹ | 8 | | | | | | | 8 |
| 1 | 2 | 3 | 12 | 5 | 6 | 7 | 8 | 9² | | 11¹ | | 14 | | | 13 | 10³ | 4 | | | | | | | 9 |
| 1 | 2² | | 4 | 5 | 6 | 7 | 8 | | 10 | 11¹ | | 12 | 14 | 3³ | 9 | | 13 | | | | | | | 10 |
| 1 | 2 | | 4¹ | 5 | 6 | 7 | 8 | 13 | 10 | 11³ | | | 12 | 3 | 9² | 14 | | | | | | | | 11 |
| 1 | 2 | 3³ | | 5 | 6 | 7 | 8 | 9² | 10 | 14 | | 12 | 4 | | 11¹ | 13 | | | | | | | | 12 |
| 1 | 2 | 3¹ | | 5 | 6 | | 8 | 14 | 10 | 11² | | 12 | | 4 | 9 | 13 | 7³ | | | | | | | 13 |
| 1 | 2 | 14 | | 5 | 8 | 7³ | | 12 | 3 | 11 | | 10¹ | 13 | 6 | 9 | | 4² | | | | | | | 14 |
| 1 | 2 | | | | 6 | 7 | 8 | | 3 | 11¹ | 12 | 10³ | 13 | 5 | 9 | 14 | 4² | | | | | | | 15 |
| 1¹ | 2 | | | 5 | 6 | 7 | 8 | | 3 | 11² | 10 | 13 | | | 9 | | 4 | 12 | | | | | | 16 |
| | 2 | | | 5³ | 6 | 7 | 8 | | 3 | 12 | 10 | 11¹ | 14 | | 9² | 13 | 4 | | 1 | | | | | 17 |
| | 4¹ | | | 5 | 12 | 7 | 8 | 9² | 3 | | | | 11³ | 6 | 13 | 10 | 14 | | 1 | 2 | | | | 18 |
| | 2 | | | 5 | 13 | 7 | 8 | 9¹ | 3 | 14 | | | 11³ | 6 | 12 | 10 | | | 1 | 4² | | | | 19 |
| | 2 | | | | 4 | 7 | 8 | 9¹ | 3 | 11³ | | 13 | | 5 | 12 | 10² | 14 | | 1 | | 6 | | | 20 |
| | 2² | | | | 4 | 7 | 8 | | 3 | 11³ | 9 | 14 | 13 | 5 | | 12 | 10¹ | | 1 | | 6 | | | 21 |
| | 2 | | | 5 | 4 | 7 | 8 | | 3 | 11¹ | 13 | 12 | | | 9³ | 10² | 14 | | 1 | | 6 | | | 22 |
| | 2 | 3 | | 5 | 10 | 7 | 8 | | | 13 | 9³ | 11² | 14 | 4¹ | 12 | | | | 1 | | 6 | | | 23 |
| | 2 | 3³ | | 5 | 4 | 7 | 8 | 13 | | 11² | | | | | 9 | 14 | 10¹ | | 1 | 12 | 6 | | | 24 |
| | 2 | 3 | | | 4 | 7 | 8 | 9¹ | | 13 | | | | | 10 | 11² | 12 | | 1 | 5 | 6 | | | 25 |
| | 2 | 3² | | | 4 | 7 | 8 | 9¹ | | 12 | 14 | | | | 11³ | 10 | 13 | | 1 | 5 | 6 | | | 26 |
| | 2³ | 3 | | 13 | 4¹ | 7 | 8 | | | 14 | 9 | | | | 11² | 10 | 12 | | 1 | 5 | 6 | | | 27 |
| | 2 | 3 | | | 4 | 7 | 8 | 12 | | 11¹ | 13 | | | | 9³ | 10² | 14 | | 1 | 5 | 6 | | | 28 |
| | 2 | 3³ | | | 4 | 7 | 8 | 13 | | 11¹ | 12 | | | | 9 | 10² | 14 | | 1 | 5 | 6 | | | 29 |
| | 2 | 3 | | 4 | 13 | 7³ | 8 | | | | 9 | | | | 12 | 10¹ | 11² | | 1 | 5 | 6 | 14 | | 30 |
| | 2 | 3 | | | 4 | 7 | 8 | | | 12 | 9 | | 13 | | | 10¹ | 11² | | 1 | 5 | 6 | | | 31 |
| | 2 | | | | 4 | 7 | 8 | 14 | | 12 | 9 | | 13 | | | 10¹ | 11³ | | 1 | 5 | 6 | | 3² | 32 |
| | 2 | 3¹ | | | 4 | 7 | 8 | 14 | | 13 | 9³ | | 12 | | | 10 | 11² | | 1 | 5 | 6 | | | 33 |
| | 2³ | | | | 3 | 7² | 8 | 9¹ | | | | 12 | 4 | 14 | | 10 | 11 | | 1 | 5 | 6 | 13 | | 34 |
| | 2 | | | | 3 | 7² | 8 | 14 | | | 9³ | 11 | 4¹ | | | 10 | 12 | | 1 | 5 | 6 | 13 | | 35 |
| | | | | 4 | 2³ | 7 | | 13 | | 12 | 9 | 11¹ | 8 | 3 | | 10² | | | 1 | 5 | 6 | 14 | | 36 |

# ST JOHNSTONE — First Division

*Year Formed:* 1884. *Ground & Address:* McDiarmid Park, Crieff Road, Perth PH1 2SJ. *Telephone:* 01738 459090. *Fax:* 01738 625 771. *Clubcall:* 0898 121559. *Website:* www.stjohnstonefc.co.uk
*Ground Capacity:* all seated: 10,673. *Size of Pitch:* 115yd × 75yd.
*Chairman:* G.S. Brown. *Secretary and Managing Director:* Stewart Duff. *Sales Executive:* Susan Weir.
*Manager:* John Connolly. *Coach:* Jin Weir. *Physio:* Nick Summersgill. *Youth Co-ordinator:* Tommy Campbell.
*Managers since 1975:* J. Stewart, J. Storrie, A. Stuart, A. Rennie, I. Gibson, A. Totten, J. McClelland, P. Sturrock, S. Clark, B. Stark.
*Club Nickname(s):* Saints. *Previous Grounds:* Recreation Grounds, Muirton Park.
*Record Attendance:* (McDiarmid Park): 10,545 v Dundee, Premier Division, 23 May 1999.
*Record Transfer Fee received:* £1,750,000 for Calum Davidson to Blackburn R (March 1998).
*Record Transfer Fee paid:* £400,000 for Billy Dodds from Dundee (1994).
*Record Victory:* 9-0 v Albion R, League Cup, 9 Mar 1946.
*Record Defeat:* 1-10 v Third Lanark, Scottish Cup, 24 Jan 1903.
*Most Capped Player:* Nick Dasovic, 26, Canada.
*Most League Appearances:* 298: Drew Rutherford.
*Most League Goals in Season (Individual):* 36: Jimmy Benson, Division II, 1931-32.
*Most Goals Overall (Individual):* 140: John Brogan, 1977-83.

## ST JOHNSTONE 2003–04 LEAGUE RECORD

| Match No. | Date | Venue | Opponents | Result | H/T Score | Lg. Pos. | Goalscorers | Attendance |
|---|---|---|---|---|---|---|---|---|
| 1 | Aug 9 | H | Queen of the S | W 4-1 | 2-0 | — | Fotheringham [18], Parker 2 [23, 58], Malone [84] | 2939 |
| 2 | 16 | A | St Mirren | D 1-1 | 0-0 | 1 | Parker [61] | 3613 |
| 3 | 23 | H | Inverness CT | L 1-2 | 0-0 | 5 | Parker [66] | 3031 |
| 4 | 30 | H | Brechin C | W 3-1 | 0-0 | 3 | Paatelainen 2 [50, 72], Dods [78] | 2219 |
| 5 | Sept 13 | A | Clyde | L 0-2 | 0-1 | 6 | | 1468 |
| 6 | 20 | H | Raith R | L 0-1 | 0-1 | 7 | | 2983 |
| 7 | 27 | A | Falkirk | W 3-0 | 2-0 | 6 | MacDonald 2 [31, 44], Paatelainen [46] | 3887 |
| 8 | Oct 4 | H | Ayr U | D 1-1 | 0-0 | 5 | MacDonald [68] | 1906 |
| 9 | 18 | A | Ross Co | W 3-0 | 3-0 | 5 | Paatelainen 3 [8, 37, 41] | 3195 |
| 10 | 25 | H | St Mirren | W 1-0 | 1-0 | 3 | Robertson M [33] | 2677 |
| 11 | Nov 1 | A | Queen of the S | D 1-1 | 0-1 | 3 | McLaughlin [71] | 3159 |
| 12 | 8 | H | Clyde | W 3-0 | 2-0 | 2 | MacDonald [8], Donnelly 2 [43, 70] | 2474 |
| 13 | 16 | A | Brechin C | W 1-0 | 1-0 | 2 | MacDonald [42] | 1434 |
| 14 | 22 | H | Falkirk | L 0-4 | 0-2 | 4 | | 4185 |
| 15 | 29 | A | Raith R | W 4-1 | 1-0 | 2 | McLaughlin [42], Hay [61], Paatelainen [76], MacDonald [90] | 1996 |
| 16 | Dec 6 | H | Ross Co | D 1-1 | 1-0 | 2 | Paatelainen [15] | 2478 |
| 17 | 13 | A | Ayr U | D 1-1 | 0-0 | 3 | Bernard [64] | 1203 |
| 18 | 20 | H | Queen of the S | D 2-2 | 1-1 | 3 | Thomson (og) [32], Paatelainen [90] | 1999 |
| 19 | 27 | A | Inverness CT | L 0-1 | 0-0 | 5 | | 2949 |
| 20 | Jan 3 | H | Brechin C | D 2-2 | 2-0 | 5 | MacDonald [23], Paatelainen [28] | 2171 |
| 21 | 24 | H | Raith R | W 5-2 | 3-1 | 4 | Hay 2 [2, 62], McLaughlin [13], Taylor [23], MacDonald [81] | 2576 |
| 22 | Feb 14 | H | Ayr U | W 3-0 | 2-0 | 3 | Maxwell [8], McQuilken [42], Donnelly [61] | 2067 |
| 23 | 21 | A | Ross Co | L 0-2 | 0-1 | 5 | | 3050 |
| 24 | Mar 6 | A | Clyde | W 3-2 | 1-1 | 4 | Donnelly 2 [18, 65], Bernard [88] | 1518 |
| 25 | 9 | A | Falkirk | W 1-0 | 0-0 | — | Hay [87] | 2799 |
| 26 | 13 | H | Inverness CT | W 3-2 | 2-0 | 3 | Donnelly [14], Paatelainen [23], Parker [89] | 2913 |
| 27 | 16 | A | St Mirren | D 1-1 | 0-1 | — | Robertson J [61] | 2180 |
| 28 | 20 | H | Clyde | L 1-3 | 0-2 | 3 | Parker [90] | 3512 |
| 29 | 27 | A | Brechin C | W 2-0 | 1-0 | 3 | Hay [19], Baxter [60] | 822 |
| 30 | Apr 3 | H | Falkirk | W 2-1 | 1-1 | 3 | Hay 2 [44, 88] | 2535 |
| 31 | 10 | A | Raith R | D 1-1 | 0-1 | 3 | Donnelly (pen) [53] | 2676 |
| 32 | 17 | H | Ross Co | D 1-1 | 1-1 | 3 | Hay [3] | 2169 |
| 33 | 24 | A | Ayr U | D 1-1 | 0-1 | 3 | Hay [66] | 1119 |
| 34 | May 1 | A | Queen of the S | D 1-1 | 0-0 | 3 | Donnelly (pen) [62] | 1629 |
| 35 | 8 | H | St Mirren | L 1-3 | 0-1 | 3 | Parker [72] | 2363 |
| 36 | 15 | A | Inverness CT | L 1-3 | 1-1 | 3 | Parker [44] | 6092 |

**Final League Position: 3**

**Honours**
*League Champions:* First Division 1982-83, 1989-90, 1996-97. Division II 1923-24, 1959-60, 1962-63; *Runners-up:* Division II 1931-32. Second Division 1987-88.
*Scottish Cup:* Semi-finals 1934, 1968, 1989, 1991.
*League Cup Runners-up:* 1969, 1998.
*League Challenge Cup Runners-up:* 1996-97.

**European:** *UEFA Cup:* 10 matches (1971-72, 1999-2000).

**Club colours:** Shirt: Royal blue with white trim. Shorts: White. Stockings: Royal blue with white hoops.

**Goalscorers:** *League* (59): Paatelainen 11, Hay 9, Donnelly 8 (2 pens), MacDonald 8, Parker 8, McLaughlin 3, Bernard 2, Baxter 1, Dods 1, Fotheringham 1, McQuilken 1, Malone 1, Maxwell 1, Robertson J 1, Robertson M 1, Taylor 1, own goal 1
*Scottish Cup* (0):
*CIS Cup* (8): Dods 2, Donnelly 2, Paatelainen 2, MacDonald 1, McLaughlin 1
*Challenge Cup* (5): Parker 2, Donnelly 1, Forsyth 1, Paatelainen 1

| Cuthbert K 29 | Robertson J 27 | Forsyth R 18 + 4 | Donnelly S 35 + 1 | Dods D 24 + 2 | Maxwell I 33 | Parker K 13 + 18 | Reilly M 25 + 2 | Paatelainen M 28 + 5 | Fotheringham M 3 + 4 | Bernard P 24 + 1 | Baxter M 11 + 5 | Malone E 5 + 4 | Stevenson R 8 + 4 | Lovering P 4 + 1 | Ferry M 1 | Hay C 10 + 12 | McLaughlin B 23 + 7 | Robertson M 8 + 1 | MacDonald P 11 + 4 | Nelson C 7 | McQuilken J 15 | Vata R 15 | Weir J 9 | Taylor S 8 + 1 | Fraser S 2 | *Match No.* |
|---|---|---|---|---|---|---|---|---|---|---|---|---|---|---|---|---|---|---|---|---|---|---|---|---|---|---|
| 1 | 2 | 3 | $4^{3}$ | 5 | 6 | $7^{2}$ | 8 | 9 | $10^{1}$ | 11 | 12 | 13 | 14 | | | | | | | | | | | | | 1 |
| 1 | 2 | | 4 | 5 | 6 | 7 | $8^{1}$ | 9 | 12 | 10 | 13 | | $11^{2}$ | 3 | | | | | | | | | | | | 2 |
| 1 | 2 | | 4 | 5 | 6 | 7 | | 9 | | 10 | 13 | 11 | | $3^{2}$ | $8^{1}$ | 12 | | | | | | | | | | 3 |
| 1 | 2 | 12 | $10^{2}$ | 5 | $6^{1}$ | 7 | 8 | 9 | | $4^{3}$ | 3 | 11 | | | | | 13 | 14 | | | | | | | | 4 |
| 1 | 2 | | 10 | 5 | 6 | 7 | 8 | 9 | | $4^{2}$ | $3^{1}$ | 13 | | | | | 12 | 11 | | | | | | | | 5 |
| 1 | 2 | | $10^{1}$ | 5 | 6 | 7 | 8 | 9 | | $4^{2}$ | 13 | 3 | | | | | 12 | 11 | | | | | | | | 6 |
| 1 | 2 | 3 | 10 | 5 | 6 | 13 | 8 | 9 | | 4 | | 12 | | | | | $11^{1}$ | | $7^{2}$ | | | | | | | 7 |
| 1 | 2 | 3 | 10 | 5 | 6 | 12 | 8 | 9 | | | | $11^{1}$ | | | | | | 4 | 7 | | | | | | | 8 |
| 1 | 2 | 3 | 10 | 5 | 6 | 12 | $8^{2}$ | $9^{3}$ | | 4 | | | | | | 14 | 13 | 11 | $7^{1}$ | | | | | | | 9 |
| 1 | 2 | 3 | 10 | 5 | 6 | 12 | 8 | 9 | | 4 | | | | | | | 13 | $11^{2}$ | $7^{1}$ | | | | | | | 10 |
| 1 | 2 | 3 | 10 | 5 | 6 | $7^{1}$ | | 9 | | 4 | | | | | | | 11 | 8 | 12 | | | | | | | 11 |
| 1 | 2 | 3 | $10^{3}$ | 5 | 6 | 12 | | $9^{2}$ | 14 | 4 | | | | | | 13 | 11 | 8 | $7^{1}$ | | | | | | | 12 |
| 1 | 2 | 3 | 10 | 5 | 6 | | | 9 | 4 | | | | | | | | 11 | 8 | 7 | | | | | | | 13 |
| 1 | 2 | 3 | 10 | 5 | 6 | | | 9 | | 4 | 8 | | | | | | 11 | | 7 | | | | | | | 14 |
| 1 | 2 | 3 | 10 | | 6 | | | 9 | | 4 | 8 | | 5 | | | $7^{1}$ | 11 | | 12 | | | | | | | 15 |
| 1 | 2 | 3 | $10^{2}$ | 5 | 6 | 13 | | 9 | | 4 | | | 8 | | | $7^{1}$ | 11 | | 12 | | | | | | | 16 |
| 1 | 2 | 3 | 10 | 5 | 6 | | | 9 | | 4 | | | 8 | | | 12 | 11 | | $7^{1}$ | | | | | | | 17 |
| | 2 | $3^{2}$ | $10^{1}$ | 5 | 6 | 12 | | 9 | 14 | 4 | | | $8^{3}$ | 13 | | | 11 | | 7 | 1 | | | | | | 18 |
| | 2 | | 10 | 5 | 6 | 14 | 13 | $9^{3}$ | | 4 | | | $8^{2}$ | 3 | | 12 | 11 | | $7^{1}$ | 1 | | | | | | 19 |
| | 2 | | $4^{2}$ | 5 | 6 | 7 | 8 | 9 | 13 | | | | | 3 | | 12 | 11 | | $10^{1}$ | 1 | | | | | | 20 |
| | 2 | | 13 | | 6 | | 8 | $9^{1}$ | | | | | | | | $7^{2}$ | 11 | | 12 | 1 | 3 | 4 | 5 | 10 | | 21 |
| | $2^{2}$ | 12 | 9 | | $6^{1}$ | 14 | 8 | | | | | | 13 | | | $7^{3}$ | 11 | | | 1 | 3 | 4 | 5 | 10 | | 22 |
| | | | 9 | 12 | 6 | 14 | 8 | 13 | | 10 | $2^{2}$ | | | | | $7^{3}$ | 11 | | | 1 | 3 | 4 | $5^{1}$ | | | 23 |
| 1 | 2 | | 7 | | 6 | 13 | 8 | $9^{1}$ | | 10 | | | | | | 12 | $11^{2}$ | | | | 3 | 4 | 5 | | | 24 |
| 1 | 2 | | 7 | | 6 | 13 | 8 | $9^{2}$ | | 10 | | | | | | 12 | $11^{1}$ | | | | 3 | 4 | 5 | | | 25 |
| 1 | 2 | | 7 | | 6 | 10 | 8 | $9^{1}$ | | | | | 13 | | | 12 | $11^{2}$ | | | | 3 | 4 | 5 | | | 26 |
| 1 | 2 | | 7 | | 6 | $10^{2}$ | 8 | $9^{1}$ | | 12 | | | | | | 13 | 11 | | | | 3 | 4 | 5 | | | 27 |
| 1 | $2^{2}$ | 14 | 7 | | $6^{3}$ | 13 | 8 | $9^{1}$ | | 10 | | | | | | 12 | 11 | | | | 3 | 4 | 5 | | | 28 |
| 1 | | | 7 | 5 | 6 | 13 | 8 | 9 | | | 2 | | | | | $11^{2}$ | 12 | | | | 3 | 4 | | $10^{1}$ | | 29 |
| 1 | | 14 | 7 | 5 | 6 | 12 | 8 | 13 | | | 2 | | | | | $9^{2}$ | $11^{3}$ | | | | 3 | 4 | | $10^{1}$ | | 30 |
| 1 | | | 7 | 5 | 6 | 13 | 8 | $9^{2}$ | | | 2 | | | | | 11 | 12 | | | | 3 | 4 | | $10^{1}$ | | 31 |
| 1 | | 3 | 7 | $5^{1}$ | 6 | 13 | 8 | 14 | | 4 | 12 | | | | | 9 | $11^{2}$ | | | | | 2 | | $10^{3}$ | | 32 |
| 1 | | 6 | 7 | 5 | | 13 | 8 | 12 | | 10 | $2^{2}$ | | | | | 9 | | | | | 3 | 4 | | $11^{1}$ | | 33 |
| 1 | | 3 | 10 | | | 9 | 8 | | | 7 | 2 | | 12 | | | | | | | | 4 | 5 | | $11^{1}$ | 6 | 34 |
| 1 | | 3 | $10^{2}$ | 12 | 6 | 9 | $8^{3}$ | 13 | | | | 2 | 4 | | | | 11 | | | | 7 | $5^{1}$ | | 14 | | 35 |
| | | $4^{2}$ | 10 | | | 9 | 13 | | 8 | | 2 | 12 | $7^{3}$ | | | 14 | $11^{1}$ | | | 1 | 3 | | 5 | | 6 | 36 |

# ST MIRREN

## First Division

*Year Formed:* 1877. *Ground & Address:* St Mirren Park, Love St, Paisley PA3 2EJ. *Telephone:* 0141 889 2558/0141 840 1337. *Fax:* 0141 848 6444.
*Ground Capacity:* 10,866 (all seated). *Size of Pitch:* 112yd × 73yd.
*Chairman:* Stewart Gilmour. *Vice-Chairman:* George Campbell. *Secretary:* Allan Marshall.
*Manager:* Gus MacPherson. *Youth Development Officer:* Arthur Bell.
*Managers since 1975:* Alex Ferguson, Jim Clunie, Rikki MacFarlane, Alex Miller, Alex Smith, Tony Fitzpatrick, David Hay, Jimmy Bone, Tony Fitzpatrick, Tom Hendrie, John Coughlin. *Club Nickname(s):* The Buddies. *Previous Grounds:* Short Roods 1877-79, Thistle Park Greenhill 1879-83, Westmarch 1883-94.
*Record Attendance:* 47,438 v Celtic, League Cup, 20 Aug 1949.
*Record Transfer Fee received:* £850,000 for Ian Ferguson to Rangers (1988).
*Record Transfer Fee paid:* £400,000 for Thomas Stickroth from Bayer Uerdingen (1990).
*Record Victory:* 15-0 v Glasgow University, Scottish Cup 1st rd, 30 Jan 1960.
*Record Defeat:* 0-9 v Rangers, Division I, 4 Dec 1897.
*Most Capped Player:* Godmundor Torfason, 29, Iceland.
*Most League Appearances:* 351: Tony Fitzpatrick, 1973-88.
*Most League Goals in Season (Individual):* 45: Dunky Walker, Division I, 1921-22.
*Most Goals Overall (Individual):* 221: David McCrae, 1923-34.

### ST MIRREN 2003–04 LEAGUE RECORD

| *Match No.* | *Date* | *Venue* | *Opponents* | *Result* | | *H/T Score* | *Lg. Pos.* | *Goalscorers* | *Attendance* |
|---|---|---|---|---|---|---|---|---|---|
| 1 | Aug 9 | A | Raith R | D | 1-1 | 0-1 | — | Gillies (pen) [51] | 3090 |
| 2 | 16 | H | St Johnstone | D | 1-1 | 0-0 | 7 | O'Neil [63] | 3613 |
| 3 | 23 | A | Ross Co | L | 0-2 | 0-0 | 8 | | 3053 |
| 4 | 30 | H | Clyde | W | 2-1 | 0-0 | 8 | Russell 2 [65, 85] | 3010 |
| 5 | Sept 13 | A | Brechin C | D | 1-1 | 1-1 | 8 | Gillies [13] | 956 |
| 6 | 20 | H | Queen of the S | L | 1-2 | 1-2 | 8 | Gillies [45] | 2681 |
| 7 | 27 | A | Inverness CT | L | 0-2 | 0-2 | 8 | | 1896 |
| 8 | Oct 4 | H | Falkirk | D | 0-0 | 0-0 | 8 | | 3105 |
| 9 | 18 | A | Ayr U | W | 2-0 | 1-0 | 8 | Broadfoot 2 [11, 67] | 2447 |
| 10 | 25 | A | St Johnstone | L | 0-1 | 0-1 | 8 | | 2677 |
| 11 | Nov 1 | H | Raith R | W | 2-1 | 1-1 | 8 | O'Neil [7], Gillies [80] | 3005 |
| 12 | 8 | H | Brechin C | D | 0-0 | 0-0 | 7 | | 2801 |
| 13 | 14 | A | Clyde | L | 0-2 | 0-1 | 7 | | 1811 |
| 14 | 22 | H | Inverness CT | L | 0-4 | 0-2 | 8 | | 2204 |
| 15 | Dec 3 | A | Queen of the S | W | 2-1 | 1-0 | — | Gillies [12], Russell [54] | 2473 |
| 16 | 6 | H | Ayr U | W | 3-2 | 1-0 | 7 | Lappin [14], Gillies 2 [75, 90] | 2567 |
| 17 | 13 | A | Falkirk | D | 0-0 | 0-0 | 7 | | 2581 |
| 18 | 27 | H | Ross Co | D | 1-1 | 1-0 | 7 | Gillies [23] | 3550 |
| 19 | Jan 3 | H | Clyde | L | 2-3 | 1-2 | 7 | Dunn [16], Millen [52] | 3355 |
| 20 | 17 | A | Brechin C | L | 0-2 | 0-0 | 7 | | 878 |
| 21 | 24 | H | Queen of the S | W | 3-1 | 1-0 | 7 | O'Neil 2 [29, 50], McGinty [48] | 2540 |
| 22 | 31 | A | Inverness CT | D | 1-1 | 1-0 | 7 | Lappin [17] | 1913 |
| 23 | Feb 14 | H | Falkirk | D | 1-1 | 0-1 | 7 | Murray [28] | 2934 |
| 24 | 21 | A | Ayr U | L | 0-2 | 0-1 | 7 | | 2252 |
| 25 | Mar 6 | A | Raith R | L | 0-2 | 0-1 | 7 | | 1882 |
| 26 | 13 | A | Ross Co | L | 0-1 | 0-0 | 7 | | 2819 |
| 27 | 16 | H | St Johnstone | D | 1-1 | 1-0 | — | Murray [42] | 2180 |
| 28 | 20 | H | Brechin C | D | 3-3 | 2-1 | 7 | Dunn [8], Millar M (og) [13], Crilly [55] | 2221 |
| 29 | 27 | A | Clyde | D | 2-2 | 0-1 | 7 | Lappin [61], Russell [67] | 1786 |
| 30 | Apr 3 | H | Inverness CT | D | 0-0 | 0-0 | 7 | | 2272 |
| 31 | 10 | A | Queen of the S | L | 0-1 | 0-1 | 8 | | 2211 |
| 32 | 17 | H | Ayr U | W | 4-1 | 0-0 | 7 | Van Zanten 2 [70, 84], McGinty [77], Lappin [87] | 3211 |
| 33 | 24 | A | Falkirk | L | 0-1 | 0-1 | 7 | | 2386 |
| 34 | May 1 | H | Raith R | D | 1-1 | 1-0 | 7 | Broadfoot [26] | 2372 |
| 35 | 8 | A | St Johnstone | W | 3-1 | 1-0 | 7 | McGinty 3 (2 pens) [10 (p), 62, 76 (p)] | 2363 |
| 36 | 15 | H | Ross Co | W | 2-0 | 1-0 | 7 | McGowne [45], McGinty [80] | 2291 |

**Final League Position: 7**

**Honours**
*League Champions:* First Division 1976-77, 1999-2000. Division II 1967-68; *Runners-up:* 1935-36.
*Scottish Cup Winners:* 1926, 1959, 1987. *Runners-up:* 1908, 1934, 1962.
*League Cup Runners-up:* 1955-56.
*B&Q Cup Runners-up:* 1993-94. *Victory Cup:* 1919-20. *Summer Cup:* 1943-44. *Anglo-Scottish Cup:* 1979-80.

**European:** *Cup Winners' Cup:* 4 matches (1987-88). *UEFA Cup:* 10 matches (1980-81, 1983-84, 1985-86).

**Club colours:** Shirt: Black and white vertical stripes. Shorts: White with black trim. Stockings: White with 2 black hoops. Change colours: Predominantly red.

**Goalscorers:** *League* (39):Gillies 8 (1 pen), McGinty 6 (2 pens), Lappin 4, O'Neil 4, Russell 4, Broadfoot 3, Dunn 2, Murray 2, Van Zanten 2, Crilly 1, McGowne 1, Millen 1, own goal 1
*Scottish Cup* (2): Lavety 1, McKenna 1
*CIS Cup* (0):
*Challenge Cup* (7): O'Neil 3, Crilly 1, Gillies 1 (1 pen), McGinty 1, Russell 1

| Hinchcliffe C 28 | MacPherson A 9 | Ellis L 21 + 2 | McGowne K 29 + 1 | Broadfoot K 28 + 3 | Crilly M 18 + 7 | Gillies R 33 + 3 | O'Neil J 23 + 6 | McGinty B 23 + 5 | Dunn R 11 + 16 | Lappin S 23 + 1 | Russell A 17 + 9 | Van Zanten D 32 + 3 | Gemmill S — + 3 | Twaddle K 1 + 2 | Dempsie M 20 + 3 | Lavety B 4 + 9 | Muir A — + 3 | Walker S 1 | Annand E 6 + 3 | Murray H 27 + 3 | McKnight P — + 4 | McKenna D 1 + 8 | Millen A 19 | Woods S 8 | McGroarty C 12 + 1 | Molloy C 1 + 1 | McCay R 1 | *Match No.* |
|---|---|---|---|---|---|---|---|---|---|---|---|---|---|---|---|---|---|---|---|---|---|---|---|---|---|---|---|---|
| 1 | 2[2] | 3 | 4 | 5■ | 6 | 7 | 8 | 9[1] | 10[3] | 11 | 12 | 13 | 14 | | | | | | | | | | | | | | | 1 |
| 1 | 2 | 3 | 5 | 4 | 6 | 7 | 8 | | 10 | 11 | 9[1] | 12 | | | | | | | | | | | | | | | | 2 |
| 1 | 5 | 3 | 4 | 8 | 6 | 7 | 10 | | 11[2] | | 9[1] | 2 | 13 | 12 | | | | | | | | | | | | | | 3 |
| 1 | 5 | 3 | | 4 | 6[1] | 7 | 8 | 10[2] | 11[3] | | 9 | 2 | | | 12 | 13 | 14 | | | | | | | | | | | 4 |
| 1 | | 3 | 5 | 4 | 11 | 7 | 8 | | 2[2] | | 9 | | | | | 10[1] | | 6 | 12 | 13 | | | | | | | | 5 |
| 1 | | 3 | 5 | 4 | 11■ | 7 | 8[1] | | 12 | | 9 | 2[2] | | 13 | | 10[3] | | | 14 | 6 | | | | | | | | 6 |
| 1 | 4 | 3 | 5 | 8 | | 7 | | | | | 9 | 2 | | 11[1] | | 12 | 13 | | 10[3] | 6[2] | 14 | | | | | | | 7 |
| 1 | 4[2] | 3 | 5 | 8 | 11 | 7 | | 10[3] | | | 12 | 2 | | | 13 | 14 | | | 9[1] | 6 | | | | | | | | 8 |
| 1 | 4 | 3 | 5 | 8 | 11[2] | 7 | 13 | 10[1] | 14 | | | 2 | | | | | | | 9[3] | 6 | 12 | | | | | | | 9 |
| 1 | 4 | 3 | 5 | | 11 | 7 | 8[2] | 10 | 13 | | 9 | 2[3] | | | | 14 | | | | 6[1] | 12 | | | | | | | 10 |
| 1 | 4[1] | 3[2] | 5 | 6 | 11 | 7 | 8 | 10 | 14 | | 9[3] | 2 | | | 12 | 13 | | | | | | | | | | | | 11 |
| 1 | | 3 | 5 | 6 | 11 | 7[3] | 8 | 10[2] | 12 | | 9[1] | 2 | | | 4 | 13 | | | | | 14 | | | | | | | 12 |
| 1 | | 3 | 5 | 6 | 11 | 7 | 8[1] | 10[3] | 13 | | 9 | 2[2] | | | 4 | 14 | | | | 12 | | | | | | | | 13 |
| 1 | | 3 | 5 | 6[2] | 14 | 13 | 8■ | 12 | 7[1] | 11[3] | 9 | 2 | | | 4 | | | | | 10 | | | | | | | | 14 |
| 1 | | 3 | 5 | 6 | | 7 | | 9[2] | 12 | 11 | 10[1] | 2 | | | 4 | | | | | 8 | | 13 | | | | | | 15 |
| 1 | | 3 | 5 | 6 | | 7 | | 9[2] | 12 | 11 | 10[3] | 2 | | | 4[1] | 13 | | | | 8 | | 14 | | | | | | 16 |
| 1 | | 3 | | 5 | | 8 | | 9 | 7 | 11 | | 2 | | | 4 | 10[1] | | | | 6 | | 12 | | | | | | 17 |
| 1 | | 3[1] | 5 | | 14 | 7 | 12 | 9[3] | 10[2] | 11 | 13 | 2 | | | 6 | | | | | 8 | | | 4 | | | | | 18 |
| | | 3[1] | 5 | 14 | 13 | 7 | 12 | 9 | 10[2] | 11 | | 2 | | | 6 | | | | | 8[3] | | | 4 | 1 | | | | 19 |
| | | | 5 | 13 | 12 | 7 | 10[1] | | | 11 | | 2[3] | | | 6 | 9 | | | | 8 | | 14 | 4[2] | 1 | 3 | | | 20 |
| | | | 5[1] | 12 | | 7 | 10 | 9[2] | 13 | 11 | | 2 | | | 6 | | | | | 8 | | | 4 | 1 | 3 | | | 21 |
| | | | | 5 | 13 | 7[2] | 10 | 9[1] | 12 | 11 | | 2 | | | 6 | | | | | 8 | | | 4 | 1 | 3 | | | 22 |
| | | | | 5 | | 7 | 10[1] | 9[2] | 12 | 11 | 13 | 2 | | | 6 | | | | | 8 | | | 4 | 1 | 3 | | | 23 |
| | | | | 5 | 13 | 7[2] | 10[1] | 9[3] | 14 | 11 | 12 | 2 | | | 6 | | | | | 8 | | | 4 | 1 | 3 | | | 24 |
| | | | 5 | | | 7[3] | 13 | 10 | 12 | 11 | 9[1] | 2[2] | | | 6 | | | | | 8 | | 14 | 4 | 1 | 3 | | | 25 |
| | | | 5[3] | 8 | | 12 | 10 | 9[2] | 13 | 11 | 14 | 2[1] | | | 6 | | | | | 7 | | | 4 | 1 | 3 | | | 26 |
| 1 | | | | 5 | 12 | 7 | 10[2] | 9 | | 11[1] | 13 | 2 | | | 6 | | | | | 8 | | | 4 | | 3 | | | 27 |
| 1 | | | 12 | 5 | 11 | 7 | 10[2] | | 9[3] | | | 2 | 14 | | 6[1] | | | | | 8 | | 13 | 4 | | 3 | | | 28 |
| 1 | | | 5 | 6 | 10[2] | 7 | 9[1] | 13 | | 11 | 12 | 2 | | | | | | | | 8 | | | 4 | | 3 | | | 29 |
| 1 | | | 5 | 6 | 10[1] | 7 | | 12 | 13 | 11[3] | 9[2] | 2 | | | | | | | 14 | 8 | | | 4 | | 3 | | | 30 |
| 1 | | 12 | 5 | 6[1] | 7 | 14 | 10 | | 9[2] | 11[3] | 13 | 2 | | | | | | | | 8 | | | 4 | | 3 | | | 31 |
| 1 | | | 5 | 3 | | 7[3] | 14 | 12 | | 11 | 10[2] | 2 | | | 6 | 13 | | | 9[1] | 8 | | | 4 | | | | | 32 |
| 1 | | | 5 | 3 | | 7 | 14 | 12 | 13 | 11 | 10[1] | 2 | | | 6 | | | | 9[2] | 8[3] | | | 4 | | | | | 33 |
| 1 | | 14 | 5 | 3 | | 7 | | 10[1] | | 11[3] | | 2 | | | 6 | | | | 9[2] | 8 | | 12 | 4 | | 13 | | | 34 |
| 1 | | 3 | 5 | | 6 | 7 | 10[3] | 9[2] | | 11 | | 2 | | | | | 14 | | | 8[1] | | 13 | 4 | | | 12 | | 35 |
| 1 | | 3 | 5 | | 6 | 7 | 10 | 9 | | 13 | | 14 | | | | | | | | 12 | | 8[1] | 4 | | | 2[3] | 11[2] | 36 |

# STENHOUSEMUIR — Third Division

*Year Formed:* 1884. *Ground & Address:* Ochilview Park, Gladstone Rd, Stenhousemuir FK5 5QL. *Telephone:* 01324 562992. *Fax:* 01324 562980.
*Ground Capacity:* total: 2374, seated: 626. *Size of Pitch:* 110yd × 72yd.
*Chairman:* Mike Laing. *Secretary:* David O. Reid. *Commercial Manager:* Jock Rolland.
*Joint Managers:* Des McKeown & Tony Smith. *Assistant Manager:* Andy Smith. *Physio:* Alain Davidson.
*Managers since 1975:* H. Glasgow, J. Black, A. Rose, W. Henderson, A. Rennie, J. Meakin, D. Lawson, T. Christie, G. Armstrong, B. Fairley, J. McVeigh.
*Club Nickname(s):* The Warriors. *Previous Grounds:* Tryst Ground 1884-86, Goschen Park 1886-90.
*Record Attendance:* 12,500 v East Fife, Scottish Cup 4th rd, 11 Mar 1950.
*Record Transfer Fee received:* £70,000 for Euan Donaldson to St Johnstone (May 1995).
*Record Transfer Fee paid:* £20,000 to Livingston for Ian Little (June 1995).
*Record Victory:* 9-2 v Dundee U, Division II, 19 Apr 1937.
*Record Defeat:* 2-11 v Dunfermline Ath. Division II, 27 Sept 1930.
*Most League Appearances:* 360: Archie Rose.
*Most League Goals in Season (Individual):* 32: Robert Taylor, Division II, 1925-26.

## STENHOUSEMUIR 2003–04 LEAGUE RECORD

| Match No. | Date | Venue | Opponents | Result | | H/T Score | Lg. Pos. | Goalscorers | Attendance |
|---|---|---|---|---|---|---|---|---|---|
| 1 | Aug 9 | A | East Fife | L | 2-3 | 0-2 | — | McKenzie [66], Crawford [78] | 568 |
| 2 | 16 | H | Morton | L | 0-2 | 0-0 | 10 | | 1343 |
| 3 | 23 | A | Alloa Ath | D | 2-2 | 0-0 | 10 | Valentine (og) [47], Carr [64] | 447 |
| 4 | 30 | H | Forfar Ath | W | 2-0 | 1-0 | 7 | Mallan [11], Donnelly [46] | 383 |
| 5 | Sept 13 | A | Hamilton A | L | 0-2 | 0-0 | 8 | | 934 |
| 6 | 20 | H | Berwick R | L | 0-3 | 0-1 | 10 | | 393 |
| 7 | 27 | A | Dumbarton | W | 1-0 | 0-0 | 8 | Harty [89] | 730 |
| 8 | Oct 4 | H | Arbroath | W | 1-0 | 1-0 | 5 | Herkes (og) [19] | 344 |
| 9 | 18 | A | Airdrie U | L | 0-2 | 0-1 | 7 | | 1406 |
| 10 | 25 | A | Morton | L | 2-5 | 1-2 | 10 | McKenzie [31], Brown [64] | 2880 |
| 11 | Nov 1 | H | East Fife | W | 3-0 | 3-0 | 7 | Booth [13], Brown [22], McKenzie [38] | 532 |
| 12 | 8 | H | Hamilton A | L | 0-3 | 0-0 | 8 | | 576 |
| 13 | 16 | A | Forfar Ath | L | 0-2 | 0-1 | 8 | | 478 |
| 14 | 29 | A | Berwick R | L | 1-2 | 0-2 | 9 | McQuilter [83] | 330 |
| 15 | Dec 6 | H | Dumbarton | D | 1-1 | 1-1 | 9 | Brown [10] | 447 |
| 16 | 13 | A | Arbroath | L | 1-2 | 0-1 | 9 | Murphy S [53] | 402 |
| 17 | 27 | H | Airdrie U | L | 0-1 | 0-1 | 9 | | 1005 |
| 18 | Jan 10 | H | Alloa Ath | L | 1-3 | 1-0 | 10 | Murphy S [44] | 402 |
| 19 | 17 | A | East Fife | L | 0-1 | 0-0 | 10 | | 536 |
| 20 | 24 | H | Berwick R | W | 3-1 | 2-0 | 10 | Murphy S 2 [18, 90], Brown [31] | 337 |
| 21 | Feb 10 | A | Hamilton A | W | 1-0 | 0-0 | — | Knox J [88] | 1111 |
| 22 | 14 | H | Forfar Ath | L | 0-2 | 0-0 | 10 | | 335 |
| 23 | 21 | A | Airdrie U | L | 0-4 | 0-4 | 10 | | 1324 |
| 24 | Mar 6 | H | Morton | L | 0-1 | 0-0 | 10 | | 1217 |
| 25 | 13 | A | Alloa Ath | L | 0-1 | 0-0 | 10 | | 444 |
| 26 | 23 | A | Dumbarton | L | 0-4 | 0-3 | — | | 552 |
| 27 | 27 | A | Forfar Ath | D | 1-1 | 0-1 | 10 | Carr [86] | 407 |
| 28 | 30 | H | Arbroath | L | 0-3 | 0-1 | — | | 307 |
| 29 | Apr 3 | H | Dumbarton | L | 1-2 | 0-1 | 10 | Brown [87] | 387 |
| 30 | 6 | H | Hamilton A | L | 0-2 | 0-0 | — | | 296 |
| 31 | 10 | A | Berwick R | L | 0-3 | 0-2 | 10 | | 392 |
| 32 | 17 | H | Airdrie U | L | 0-3 | 0-1 | 10 | | 1197 |
| 33 | 24 | A | Arbroath | D | 1-1 | 1-0 | 10 | Booth (pen) [45] | 511 |
| 34 | May 1 | H | Alloa Ath | L | 0-1 | 0-0 | 10 | | 480 |
| 35 | 8 | A | Morton | W | 4-1 | 3-1 | 10 | Harty [5], Lauchlan [28], Savage 2 [39, 80] | 3456 |
| 36 | 15 | H | East Fife | L | 0-1 | 0-0 | 10 | | 826 |

**Final League Position: 10**

**Honours**
*League Champions:* Third Division runners-up: 1998-99. *Scottish Cup:* Semi-finals 1902-03. Quarter-finals 1948-49, 1949-50, 1994-95. *League Cup:* Quarter-finals 1947-48, 1960-61, 1975-76. *League Challenge Cup:* Winners 1995-96.

**Club colours:** Shirt: Maroon. Shorts: White. Stockings: Maroon.

**Goalscorers:** *League* (28): Brown 5, Murphy S 4, McKenzie 3, Booth 2 (1 pen), Carr 2, Harty 2, Savage 2, Crawford 1, Donnelly 1, Knox J 1, Lauchlan 1, McQuilter 1, Mallan 1, own goals 2
*Scottish Cup* (1): Brown 1
*CIS Cup* (1): Harty 1
*Challenge Cup* (0):

| McCulloch W 34 | Hamilton S 24 + 3 | McKenna G 17 + 5 | Tully C 6 + 1 | Gaughan K 15 | Easton S — + 1 | Booth M 23 + 6 | McCulloch G 13 + 3 | McKenzie J 16 | Brown A 27 + 5 | McDowell M 2 | Lauchlan M 21 + 7 | Crawford B 1 + 3 | Johnstone D 1 + 2 | Smith A 21 + 3 | McGowan M 9 + 1 | McCloy B 4 + 2 | Donnelly K 3 + 1 | Carr D 18 + 7 | Harty M 19 + 13 | Mallan S 5 + 1 | Bonar P 7 + 5 | McQuilter R 8 | Cairney C 2 + 2 | Hardie A 2 | Murphy S 10 + 3 | Flannery P 6 + 4 | Scott C — + 1 | Waldie C 11 + 1 | Miller C 6 + 1 | Murphy P 18 | Knox K 17 | Knox J 3 + 3 | Cosgrove S 11 + 5 | Kerrigan S 5 | Craig J 3 + 2 | Morrison D 5 + 2 | Savage J 3 | Sinclair T — + 1 | *Match No.* |
|---|---|---|---|---|---|---|---|---|---|---|---|---|---|---|---|---|---|---|---|---|---|---|---|---|---|---|---|---|---|---|---|---|---|---|---|---|---|---|---|
| 1 | $2^{1}$ | $3^{2}$ | 4 | 5 | | 6 | 7 | 8 | 9 | 10 | 11 | 12 | 13 | | | | | | | | | | | | | | | | | | | | | | | | | | 1 |
| 1 | 2 | 12 | | 5 | | $6^{1}$ | 4 | 8 | 14 | 7 | 11 | $9^{3}$ | 10 | $3^{2}$ | 13 | | | | | | | | | | | | | | | | | | | | | | | | 2 |
| 1 | 5 | 14 | 4 | 3 | | | 2 | 7 | $9^{2}$ | | $11^{1}$ | | | | | $6^{3}$ | 8 | 10 | 12 | 13 | | | | | | | | | | | | | | | | | | | 3 |
| 1 | 6 | | 4 | 3 | | | 2 | 5 | 12 | | 7 | | | | | 13 | 8 | $10^{1}$ | 11 | $9^{2}$ | | | | | | | | | | | | | | | | | | | 4 |
| 1 | 5 | 3 | 4 | 2 | | 13 | | 8 | 12 | | $7^{2}$ | | | | | $6^{1}$ | | $10^{3}$ | 11 | 9 | 14 | | | | | | | | | | | | | | | | | | 5 |
| 1 | $4^{2}$ | 3 | | 2 | | 6 | | 5 | $9^{1}$ | | 7 | | 12 | | | 13 | $8^{3}$ | | 14 | 10 | 11 | | | | | | | | | | | | | | | | | | 6 |
| 1 | | 14 | 12 | 4 | | $6^{1}$ | | 8 | | | 11 | | | 3 | $7^{3}$ | 2 | | 10 | 13 | $9^{2}$ | | 5 | | | | | | | | | | | | | | | | | 7 |
| 1 | 12 | 13 | | 4 | | 6 | | 8 | | | 11 | 14 | | $3^{1}$ | $7^{2}$ | 2 | | 10 | $9^{3}$ | | | 5 | | | | | | | | | | | | | | | | | 8 |
| 1 | 2 | | 4 | 5 | | $6^{3}$ | 14 | 8 | $10^{1}$ | | 7 | 13 | | 3 | | | | | 12 | $9^{2}$ | 11 | | | | | | | | | | | | | | | | | | 9 |
| 1 | | 2 | 6 | 4 | | 13 | 14 | $8^{3}$ | 12 | | | | | 3 | 7 | | | $10^{2}$ | | | 11 | 5 | $9^{1}$ | | | | | | | | | | | | | | | | 10 |
| 1 | $4^{1}$ | $3^{2}$ | | 2 | | 6 | | 5 | 9 | | 8 | | | 11 | 7 | | 14 | $10^{3}$ | 13 | | 12 | | | | | | | | | | | | | | | | | | 11 |
| 1 | 4 | 2 | | | | 6 | | 5 | 9 | | 8 | | | 3 | $7^{2}$ | | | $10^{1}$ | 12 | | 11 | | 13 | | | | | | | | | | | | | | | | 12 |
| | 4 | 3 | | | | 6 | 2 | 5 | 9 | | $10^{1}$ | | | 11 | $7^{2}$ | | | 13 | 8 | | 12 | | | 1 | | | | | | | | | | | | | | | 13 |
| | 14 | $2^{3}$ | | 3 | | $6^{1}$ | 12 | 5 | 9 | | 13 | | | 11 | | | | | 7 | | | 4 | | 1 | 8 | $10^{2}$ | | | | | | | | | | | | | 14 |
| 1 | | | | 2 | | 14 | $3^{2}$ | $5^{3}$ | 9 | | 8 | | | 6 | 7 | | | 12 | | | 11 | 4 | | | 13 | $10^{1}$ | | | | | | | | | | | | | 15 |
| 1 | $2^{1}$ | 3 | | 4 | | 6 | | | 9 | | $11^{3}$ | | | | $7^{2}$ | | | | 13 | | 12 | 5 | | | 8 | 10 | 14 | | | | | | | | | | | | 16 |
| 1 | 7 | 3 | | 4 | | $6^{2}$ | 2 | 8 | 9 | | 12 | | | | | | | | 11 | | | 5 | | | 13 | $10^{1}$ | | | | | | | | | | | | | 17 |
| 1 | | 2 | | | | | 4 | | $9^{3}$ | | 7 | | | 3 | | | | $10^{1}$ | 12 | | $11^{2}$ | 5 | | | 6 | 14 | | 8 | 13 | | | | | | | | | | 18 |
| 1 | 13 | 4 | | | | | | | $9^{1}$ | | 14 | | | 3 | 7 | | | 12 | 10 | | | | | | $6^{3}$ | | | 8 | $11^{2}$ | 2 | 5 | | | | | | | | 19 |
| 1 | 4 | 3 | | | | $8^{1}$ | 2 | | 9 | | | | | 12 | | | | | $11^{2}$ | | | | | | 10 | 13 | | 7 | | 6 | 5 | | | | | | | | 20 |
| 1 | 2 | $3^{2}$ | | | | $8^{1}$ | 6 | | 9 | | 14 | | | 13 | | | | | $11^{3}$ | | | | | | 10 | | | | | 4 | 5 | 7 | 12 | | | | | | 21 |
| 1 | 6 | 3 | | | | $8^{1}$ | $7^{3}$ | | 9 | | 12 | | | | | | | 13 | $11^{2}$ | | | | | | 10 | | | | | 4 | 5 | 2 | 14 | | | | | | 22 |
| 1 | 2 | 3 | | | | 6 | | | $9^{3}$ | | 12 | | | 13 | | | | | 14 | | | | | | $8^{2}$ | 11 | | | | 4 | 5 | $7^{1}$ | 10 | | | | | | 23 |
| 1 | $2^{1}$ | | | | | 13 | | | 9 | | 7 | | | $6^{2}$ | | | | $10^{3}$ | 11 | | | | | | | 14 | | | 3 | 5 | 4 | 12 | 8 | | | | | | 24 |
| 1 | $2^{1}$ | | | | | 13 | | | 9 | | 7 | | | $6^{2}$ | | | | $10^{3}$ | 11 | | | | | | | 14 | | | 3 | 5 | 4 | 12 | 8 | | | | | | 25 |
| 1 | | 13 | | | | 6 | | | 9 | | $7^{3}$ | | | 11 | | | | | 12 | | | | | | 14 | $10^{1}$ | | 2 | 3 | $5^{2}$ | 4 | | 8 | | | | | | 26 |
| 1 | | | | | | 11 | | | 10 | | | | | 6 | | | | 13 | 12 | | $3^{1}$ | | | | 8 | | | 2 | | 5 | 4 | | 7 | $9^{2}$ | | | | | 27 |
| 1 | | | | | | 6 | | | $10^{1}$ | | 13 | | | 3 | | | | 12 | 11 | | | | | | 8 | | | 2 | | 5 | $4^{2}$ | | 7 | 9 | | | | | 28 |
| 1 | | 3 | | | | | $8^{1}$ | | 14 | | | | | | | | | 11 | 12 | | | | $7^{2}$ | | | | | 2 | | 5 | 4 | 13 | 6 | $10^{3}$ | 9 | | | | 29 |
| 1 | 2 | | | | | 12 | $8^{2}$ | | 10 | | | | | | | | | 11 | 13 | | | | | | | | | 7 | 3 | 5 | 4 | | $6^{3}$ | | $9^{1}$ | 14 | | | 30 |
| 1 | 2 | | | | | $8^{2}$ | | | $9^{3}$ | | | | | | | | | 10 | 11 | | 12 | | | | | | | 7 | $3^{1}$ | 5 | 4 | | 6 | | 13 | 14 | | | 31 |
| 1 | 2 | | | | | 6 | | | 9 | | | | | | | | | $10^{2}$ | 3 | | | | 13 | | | | | 7 | | 5 | 4 | | 12 | | $8^{1}$ | 11 | | | 32 |
| 1 | 2 | | | | | 6 | | | 9 | | | | | $3^{1}$ | | | | 7 | 11 | | | | | | | | | | | 5 | 4 | | 12 | 10 | | 8 | | | 33 |
| 1 | 2 | | | | | | | | | | 10 | | | 3 | | | | 13 | $11^{2}$ | | | | | | | | | $7^{1}$ | | 5 | 4 | | 12 | 9 | | 6 | 8 | | 34 |
| 1 | 2 | | | | | | | | | | 7 | | | 11 | | | | $9^{1}$ | 3 | | | | | | | | | 12 | | 5 | 4 | | 8 | | | 6 | $10^{2}$ | 13 | 35 |
| 1 | | | | | 13 | $2^{2}$ | | | 9 | | 7 | | | 5 | | | | $11^{1}$ | 3 | | | | | | | | | | | 4 | | | 8 | | 12 | 6 | 10 | | 36 |

# STIRLING ALBION Second Division

*Year Formed:* 1945. *Ground & Address:* Forthbank Stadium, Springkerse Industrial Estate, Stirling FK7 7UJ. *Telephone:* 01786 450399. *Fax:* 01786 448592.
*Ground Capacity:* 3808, seated: 2508. *Size of Pitch:* 110yd × 74yd.
*Chairman:* Peter McKenzie. *Secretary:* Mrs Marlyn Hallam.
*Player/Coach:* Allan Moore. *Physio:* Michael McLaughlan.
*Managers since 1975:* A. Smith, G. Peebles, J. Fleeting, J. Brogan, K. Drinkell, J. Philliben. *Club Nickname(s):* The Binos.
*Previous Grounds:* Annfield 1945-92.
*Record Attendance:* 26,400 (at Annfield) v Celtic, Scottish Cup 4th rd, 14 Mar 1959; 3808 v Aberdeen, Scottish Cup 4th rd, 15 February 1996 (Forthbank).
*Record Transfer Fee received:* £70,000 for John Philliben to Doncaster R (Mar 1984).
*Record Transfer Fee paid:* £25,000 for Craig Taggart from Falkirk (Aug 1994).
*Record Victory:* 20-0 v Selkirk, Scottish Cup 1st rd, 8 Dec 1984.
*Record Defeat:* 0-9 v Dundee U, Division I, 30 Dec 1967.
*Most League Appearances:* 504: Matt McPhee, 1967-81.
*Most League Goals in Season (Individual):* 27: Joe Hughes, Division II, 1969-70.
*Most Goals Overall (Individual):* 129: Billy Steele, 1971-83.

## STIRLING ALBION 2003–04 LEAGUE RECORD

| *Match No.* | *Date* | *Venue* | *Opponents* | *Result* | | *H/T Score* | *Lg. Pos.* | *Goalscorers* | *Attendance* |
|---|---|---|---|---|---|---|---|---|---|
| 1 | Aug 9 | H | Cowdenbeath | D | 0-0 | 0-0 | — | | 576 |
| 2 | 16 | A | Stranraer | W | 1-0 | 1-0 | 4 | Davidson [19] | 436 |
| 3 | 23 | H | East Stirling | W | 5-1 | 2-1 | 3 | Davidson 2 [38, 45], Devine [54], Hay [85], McLean [88] | 581 |
| 4 | 30 | A | Queen's Park | W | 2-0 | 2-0 | 1 | McLean [23], O'Brien [29] | 638 |
| 5 | Sept 13 | H | Peterhead | W | 3-1 | 0-1 | 1 | McKinnon [66], McLean 2 [73, 83] | 711 |
| 6 | 20 | H | Albion R | W | 2-1 | 1-1 | 1 | McLean [23], McKinnon [77] | 685 |
| 7 | 27 | A | Gretna | W | 1-0 | 0-0 | 1 | McKinnon [80] | 482 |
| 8 | Oct 4 | H | Elgin C | W | 3-0 | 2-0 | 1 | McLean [34], O'Brien [38], Devine [80] | 648 |
| 9 | 11 | H | Montrose | W | 3-0 | 2-0 | 1 | Davidson [15], McKinnon [18], Elliot [62] | 490 |
| 10 | 18 | A | Montrose | W | 3-2 | 2-0 | 1 | Gibson [14], McKinnon 2 [27, 84] | 338 |
| 11 | 25 | H | Stranraer | W | 1-0 | 1-0 | 1 | McKinnon [16] | 924 |
| 12 | Nov 1 | A | Cowdenbeath | L | 0-2 | 0-0 | 1 | | 468 |
| 13 | 8 | A | Peterhead | D | 2-2 | 2-0 | 1 | Davidson 2 [28, 45] | 589 |
| 14 | 15 | H | Queen's Park | W | 1-0 | 0-0 | 1 | Ferguson [88] | 590 |
| 15 | Dec 2 | A | Albion R | W | 3-0 | 3-0 | — | Davidson [8], McLean [22], O'Brien [32] | 392 |
| 16 | 6 | H | Gretna | L | 0-1 | 0-1 | 1 | | 682 |
| 17 | 13 | A | Elgin C | W | 2-0 | 1-0 | 1 | Campbell (og) [21], McLean [48] | 478 |
| 18 | Jan 10 | A | East Stirling | W | 4-2 | 0-1 | 1 | Wilson [77], Kelly [88], McLean [89], Livingstone (og) [90] | 495 |
| 19 | 17 | H | Cowdenbeath | D | 1-1 | 0-1 | 1 | Lyle [63] | 790 |
| 20 | 24 | H | Albion R | W | 3-0 | 1-0 | 1 | O'Brien [35], McLean [51], Lyle [75] | 629 |
| 21 | Feb 7 | H | Peterhead | L | 0-2 | 0-1 | 1 | | 651 |
| 22 | 14 | A | Queen's Park | W | 4-1 | 2-1 | 1 | O'Brien [1], McKinnon [7], McLean [48], Lyle [89] | 742 |
| 23 | 21 | A | Montrose | W | 4-1 | 3-1 | 1 | Davidson [7], O'Brien [31], Lyle [45], Rowe [58] | 466 |
| 24 | Mar 2 | A | Gretna | L | 0-1 | 0-1 | — | | 758 |
| 25 | 6 | A | Stranraer | D | 1-1 | 0-0 | 1 | McKinnon [80] | 685 |
| 26 | 10 | H | Elgin C | W | 6-1 | 3-0 | — | McLean 3 [9, 12, 47], Rowe [47], Martin (og) [70], Lyle [79] | 527 |
| 27 | 13 | H | East Stirling | W | 6-0 | 2-0 | 1 | Lyle 3 [21, 50, 73], O'Brien 2 [35, 46], Rowe [79] | 739 |
| 28 | 20 | A | Peterhead | D | 0-0 | 0-0 | 1 | | 588 |
| 29 | 27 | H | Queen's Park | D | 0-0 | 0-0 | 1 | | 797 |
| 30 | Apr 3 | H | Gretna | L | 0-1 | 0-1 | 2 | | 678 |
| 31 | 10 | A | Albion R | W | 5-3 | 2-2 | 2 | Lyle 2 [5, 41], Devine [51], McLean [63], McKinnon [70] | 615 |
| 32 | 17 | H | Montrose | D | 1-1 | 1-1 | 2 | Davidson [44] | 672 |
| 33 | 24 | A | Elgin C | W | 1-0 | 1-0 | 2 | McKinnon [3] | 542 |
| 34 | May 1 | A | East Stirling | W | 3-0 | 1-0 | 2 | O'Brien [16], McLean 2 [72, 83] | 779 |
| 35 | 8 | H | Stranraer | D | 2-2 | 0-0 | 2 | Ferguson 2 [80, 85] | 2190 |
| 36 | 15 | A | Cowdenbeath | W | 5-0 | 2-0 | 2 | O'Brien [37], McLean 4 (1 pen) [44 (p), 64, 70, 82] | 692 |

**Final League Position: 2**

**Honours**
*League Champions:* Division II 1952-53, 1957-58, 1960-61, 1964-65. Second Division 1976-77, 1990-91, 1995-96; *Runners-up:* Division II 1948-49, 1950-51. Third Division 2003-04.

**Club colours:** Shirt: Red and white halves. Shorts: Red with white piping. Stockings: Red with 2 white hoops at top.

**Goalscorers:** *League* (78): McLean 21 (1 pen), McKinnon 11, Lyle 10, O'Brien 10, Davidson 9, Devine 3, Ferguson 3, Rowe 3, Elliot 1, Gibson 1, Hay 1, Kelly 1, Wilson 1, own goals 3
*Scottish Cup* (4): Kelly 2, O'Brien 1, Rowe 1
*CIS Cup* (0):
*Challenge Cup* (3): Elliot 2, McLean 1

| Hogarth M 35 | Nugent P 22 + 1 | Anderson D 25 + 3 | McNally M 22 | Rowe G 36 | Hay P 24 + 7 | Ferguson C 4 + 15 | McLean S 30 + 1 | Elliot B 3 + 16 | Devine S 19 + 7 | O'Brien D 32 + 3 | Davidson R 21 + 11 | Wilson D 11 + 8 | Smith A 30 + 2 | Gibson A 15 + 1 | Morrison S 1 | McKinnon C 26 + 2 | Scotland C 13 | Kelly G 7 + 12 | Lyle D 19 | Beveridge R 1 + 3 | *Match No.* |
|---|---|---|---|---|---|---|---|---|---|---|---|---|---|---|---|---|---|---|---|---|---|
| 1 | 2 | 3 | 4 | 5 | $6^{3}$ | $7^{1}$ | 8 | 9 | $10^{2}$ | 11 | 12 | 13 | 14 | | | | | | | | 1 |
| 1 | 2 | 3 | 4 | 5 | 6 | $7^{2}$ | 9 | | $11^{1}$ | 12 | 10 | | 8 | 13 | | | | | | | 2 |
| 1 | 2 | 3 | 4 | 5 | 13 | $6^{1}$ | 9 | 12 | 8 | 11 | 10 | | | $7^{2}$ | | | | | | | 3 |
| | 2 | 3 | 4 | 5 | 6 | 12 | 9 | 13 | 8 | 11 | $10^{2}$ | | | $7^{1}$ | 1 | | | | | | 4 |
| 1 | 2 | 3 | 4 | 5 | 13 | | 9 | 12 | $8^{3}$ | | $11^{1}$ | 14 | $6^{2}$ | 7 | | 10 | | | | | 5 |
| 1 | 2 | 3 | 4 | 5 | | | 9 | 13 | $11^{1}$ | 12 | $10^{2}$ | | 6 | 7 | | 8 | | | | | 6 |
| 1 | 2 | 3 | 4 | 5 | 13 | | $9^{1}$ | 12 | | $11^{2}$ | 10 | | 6 | 7 | | 8 | | | | | 7 |
| 1 | 2 | 3 | 4 | 5 | 14 | | $9^{1}$ | 12 | 13 | $11^{2}$ | 10 | | $6^{3}$ | 7 | | 8 | | | | | 8 |
| 1 | $2^{2}$ | 3 | 4 | 5 | 13 | 12 | 9 | 14 | | 11 | $10^{3}$ | | 6 | 7 | | $8^{1}$ | | | | | 9 |
| 1 | | 3 | 4 | 5 | 2 | | 9 | 12 | 13 | $11^{2}$ | $10^{1}$ | | 6 | 7 | | 8 | | | | | 10 |
| 1 | | 3 | 4 | 5 | 2 | | 9 | 13 | $11^{1}$ | 12 | $10^{2}$ | | 6 | 7 | | 8 | | | | | 11 |
| 1 | | 3 | 4 | 5 | $2^{1}$ | 12 | 9 | $10^{2}$ | | 11 | 13 | 14 | 6 | $7^{3}$ | | 8 | | | | | 12 |
| 1 | | 3 | 4 | 5 | 2 | 12 | 9 | 13 | | 11 | $10^{2}$ | | $6^{1}$ | 7 | | 8 | | | | | 13 |
| 1 | | | 4 | 5 | 3 | 12 | 9 | 13 | | $11^{3}$ | $10^{2}$ | 14 | 6 | 7 | | $8^{1}$ | 2 | | | | 14 |
| 1 | | 3 | 4 | 5 | 2 | 13 | 9 | | | 11 | 10 | 12 | $6^{2}$ | $7^{1}$ | | | | 8 | | | 15 |
| 1 | 12 | $3^{3}$ | 4 | 5 | 2 | | 9 | 14 | | 11 | 10 | 13 | 6 | $7^{2}$ | | | | $8^{1}$ | | | 16 |
| 1 | 2 | 3 | 4 | 5 | 12 | 13 | 9 | | | 11 | $10^{2}$ | | 6 | 7 | | | | $8^{1}$ | | | 17 |
| 1 | 2 | $3^{1}$ | 4 | 5 | | 12 | 9 | $10^{2}$ | | 11 | | 13 | 6 | | | | | 8 | 7 | | 18 |
| 1 | 2 | $3^{1}$ | 4 | 5 | 14 | | 9 | 13 | | $11^{2}$ | | 7 | $6^{3}$ | | | 12 | | 8 | 10 | | 19 |
| 1 | 2 | 3 | 4 | 5 | | | $9^{3}$ | 14 | 12 | 11 | 13 | 7 | | | | $6^{1}$ | | 8 | $10^{2}$ | | 20 |
| 1 | 2 | $3^{1}$ | 4 | 5 | | | 9 | | 12 | $11^{3}$ | 14 | 7 | 13 | | | 6 | | $8^{2}$ | 10 | | 21 |
| 1 | 4 | $3^{2}$ | | 5 | 2 | | $9^{3}$ | | 13 | 11 | | 7 | $6^{1}$ | | | 8 | | 12 | 10 | 14 | 22 |
| 1 | 4 | 3 | | 5 | 2 | 14 | | | 13 | 11 | 9 | $7^{1}$ | $6^{2}$ | | | $8^{3}$ | | 12 | 10 | | 23 |
| 1 | 2■ | 3■ | $4^{1}$ | 5 | 7 | | 13 | | 14 | 11 | $9^{2}$ | | $6^{3}$ | | | 8 | | 12 | 10 | | 24 |
| 1 | | | | 5 | 2 | | 9 | | 3 | 11 | 10 | | $6^{1}$ | | | 8 | 4 | 12 | 7 | | 25 |
| 1 | 2 | 12 | | 5 | 7 | 14 | $9^{2}$ | | 3 | $11^{1}$ | 13 | | 6 | | | $8^{3}$ | 4 | | 10 | | 26 |
| 1 | 2 | | | 5 | 7 | 12 | | 13 | 3 | 11 | $10^{2}$ | | $6^{3}$ | | | $8^{1}$ | 4 | 14 | 9 | | 27 |
| 1 | 2 | | | 5 | 7 | | $9^{1}$ | 12 | 3 | 11 | | | 6 | | | $8^{2}$ | 4 | 13 | 10 | | 28 |
| 1 | 2 | 12 | | 5 | 7■ | | 9■ | | $3^{1}$ | 11 | 14 | | $6^{2}$ | | | 8 | 4 | 13 | $10^{3}$ | | 29 |
| 1 | $2^{3}$ | | | 5 | | 8 | | | 3 | 11 | 10 | 7 | $6^{1}$ | | | 13 | 4 | 12 | $9^{2}$ | 14 | 30 |
| 1 | | 3 | | 5 | 2 | 12 | 9 | | 6 | $11^{1}$ | 14 | $7^{2}$ | | | | 8 | 4 | 13 | $10^{3}$ | | 31 |
| 1 | | $3^{2}$ | | 5 | 6 | 14 | | | 7 | 11 | $10^{1}$ | 13 | 2 | | | $8^{3}$ | 4 | | 9 | 12 | 32 |
| 1 | | | | 5 | 2 | | | | 3 | 11 | 12 | 7 | 6 | | | 8 | 4 | | 9 | $10^{1}$ | 33 |
| 1 | | 13 | | 5 | 2 | | 9 | | $3^{2}$ | 11 | 14 | 7 | $6^{1}$ | | | 8 | 4 | 12 | $10^{3}$ | | 34 |
| 1 | | | | 5 | 2 | 12 | 9 | | $3^{3}$ | 11 | 14 | 7 | $6^{2}$ | | | $8^{1}$ | 4 | 13 | 10 | | 35 |
| 1 | | | | 5 | 2 | 12 | 9 | | $3^{3}$ | 11 | 14 | 7 | $6^{2}$ | | | $8^{1}$ | 4 | 13 | 10 | | 36 |

# STRANRAER — Second Division

*Year Formed:* 1870. *Ground & Address:* Stair Park, London Rd, Stranraer DG9 8BS. *Telephone:* 01776 703271.
*Ground Capacity:* 5600. *Size of Pitch:* 110yd × 70yd.
*Chairman:* R. J. Clanachan. *Secretary:* Graham Rodgers. *Commercial Manager:* T. L. Sutherland.
*Manager:* Neil Watt. *Assistant Manager:* Stuart Millar. *Physio:* Walter Cannon.
*Managers since 1975:* J. Hughes, N. Hood, G. Hamilton, D. Sneddon, J. Clark, R. Clark, A. McAnespie, C. Money, W. McLaren. *Club Nickname(s):* The Blues. *Previous Grounds:* None.
*Record Attendance:* 6500 v Rangers, Scottish Cup 1st rd, 24 Jan 1948.
*Record Transfer Fee received:* £90,000 for Mark Campbell to Ayr Utd, 1999.
*Record Transfer Fee paid:* £15,000 for Colin Harkness from Kilmarnock (Aug 1989).
*Record Victory:* 7-0 v Brechin C, Division II, 6 Feb 1965.
*Record Defeat:* 1-11 v Queen of the South, Scottish Cup 1st rd, 16 Jan 1932.
*Most League Appearances:* 301, Keith Knox, 1986-90; 1999-2001.
*Most League Goals in Season (Individual):* 59, Tommy Sloan.

## STRANRAER 2003–04 LEAGUE RECORD

| *Match No.* | *Date* | *Venue* | *Opponents* | *Result* | *H/T Score* | *Lg. Pos.* | *Goalscorers* | *Attendance* |
|---|---|---|---|---|---|---|---|---|
| 1 | Aug 9 | A | Albion R | D 1-1 | 1-1 | — | Kerr [21] | 323 |
| 2 | 16 | H | Stirling A | L 0-1 | 0-1 | 6 | | 436 |
| 3 | 23 | A | Gretna | D 1-1 | 0-0 | 7 | Grant [73] | 367 |
| 4 | 30 | A | Peterhead | W 2-1 | 0-0 | 5 | Grant [67], Graham [75] | 813 |
| 5 | Sept 13 | H | East Stirling | W 4-0 | 1-0 | 3 | Finlayson 2 [19, 52], Moore 2 [67, 85] | 358 |
| 6 | 20 | H | Elgin C | W 4-3 | 3-1 | 3 | Moore [26], Sharp [31], Swift [45], Jenkins [54] | 370 |
| 7 | 27 | A | Montrose | W 4-2 | 2-0 | 2 | Moore 4 [5, 17, 52, 90] | 273 |
| 8 | Oct 4 | A | Cowdenbeath | W 1-0 | 1-0 | 2 | Moore [8] | 232 |
| 9 | 18 | H | Queen's Park | W 1-0 | 0-0 | 2 | Graham [68] | 464 |
| 10 | 25 | A | Stirling A | L 0-1 | 0-1 | 2 | | 924 |
| 11 | Nov 1 | H | Albion R | W 5-0 | 1-0 | 2 | Swift 2 [25, 55], Henderson [66], Moore [69], Graham [89] | 447 |
| 12 | 8 | A | East Stirling | W 4-1 | 1-1 | 2 | Jenkins 2 [26, 84], Moore [53], Graham [76] | 245 |
| 13 | 15 | H | Peterhead | L 0-2 | 0-1 | 2 | | 428 |
| 14 | 29 | A | Elgin C | W 3-1 | 2-1 | 2 | Graham [21], Moore [35], Swift [58] | 410 |
| 15 | Dec 6 | H | Montrose | W 2-0 | 1-0 | 2 | Finlayson [28], Crawford [77] | 409 |
| 16 | 13 | H | Cowdenbeath | W 2-0 | 1-0 | 2 | Ritchie (og) [39], Swift [52] | 395 |
| 17 | Jan 3 | H | Gretna | L 1-2 | 0-1 | 2 | Moore [52] | 534 |
| 18 | 10 | A | Queen's Park | W 4-0 | 3-0 | 2 | Henderson [26], Aitken [27], Jenkins [43], Moore [68] | 473 |
| 19 | 24 | H | Elgin C | W 6-0 | 1-0 | 2 | Finlayson 2 [39, 62], Moore 4 [49, 56, 65, 81] | 393 |
| 20 | 31 | A | Montrose | W 4-1 | 3-1 | 2 | Wright [17], Graham 2 [19, 43], Jenkins [81] | 349 |
| 21 | Feb 7 | H | East Stirling | W 7-1 | 2-0 | 2 | Moore [6], Graham 4 [28, 50, 72, 89], Finlayson 2 [69, 86] | 405 |
| 22 | 14 | A | Peterhead | L 0-2 | 0-2 | 2 | | 615 |
| 23 | 17 | A | Albion R | W 4-1 | 2-0 | — | Collins [17], Henderson [24], Graham [74], Sharp [90] | 428 |
| 24 | 21 | H | Queen's Park | W 3-1 | 0-0 | 2 | Sharp [52], Finlayson 2 [59, 81] | 435 |
| 25 | Mar 6 | H | Stirling A | D 1-1 | 0-0 | 2 | Moore [60] | 685 |
| 26 | 9 | A | Cowdenbeath | W 2-1 | 0-1 | — | Crawford [76], Wingate [79] | 210 |
| 27 | 13 | A | Gretna | D 0-0 | 0-0 | 2 | | 736 |
| 28 | 24 | A | East Stirling | W 2-1 | 2-1 | — | Moore [9], Henderson [30] | 181 |
| 29 | 27 | H | Peterhead | D 1-1 | 1-0 | 2 | Graham [34] | 434 |
| 30 | Apr 3 | H | Montrose | W 6-0 | 2-0 | 1 | Graham [5], Henderson [35], Swift 2 [58, 85], Moore [66], Crawford [88] | 378 |
| 31 | 10 | A | Elgin C | D 0-0 | 0-0 | 1 | | 663 |
| 32 | 17 | A | Queen's Park | W 2-0 | 2-0 | 1 | Moore [2], Graham [33] | 564 |
| 33 | 24 | H | Cowdenbeath | W 1-0 | 0-0 | 1 | Jenkins [81] | 457 |
| 34 | May 1 | H | Gretna | W 3-2 | 1-1 | 1 | Turnbull [28], Graham 2 [48, 64] | 697 |
| 35 | 8 | A | Stirling A | D 2-2 | 0-0 | 1 | Wright [63], Moore [75] | 2190 |
| 36 | 15 | H | Albion R | W 4-0 | 3-0 | 1 | Finlayson [9], Moore [28], Graham 2 [44, 67] | 1321 |

**Final League Position: 1**

**Honours**
*League Champions:* Second Division 1993-94, 1997-98. Third Division 2003-04.
*Qualifying Cup Winners:* 1937.
*Scottish Cup:* Quarter-finals 2003
*League Challenge Cup Winners:* 1996-97.

**Club colours:** Shirt: Blue with white side panels. Shorts: Blue with white side panels. Stockings: Blue with two white hoops.

**Goalscorers:** *League* (87): Moore 24, Graham 19, Finlayson 10, Swift 7, Jenkins 6, Henderson 5, Crawford 3, Sharp 3, Grant 2, Wright 2, Aitken 1, Collins 1, Kerr 1, Turnbull 1, Wingate 1, own goal 1
*Scottish Cup* (2): Jenkins 1, Moore 1
*CIS Cup* (0):
*Challenge Cup* (2): Moore 2

| McCondichie A 36 | Swift S 36 | Wright F 34 | Wingate D 36 | Henderson M 35 | Jenkins A 35 + 1 | Finlayson K 32 + 1 | McAllister T 3 + 7 | Moore M 30 + 1 | Kerr P 2 + 6 | Sharp L 35 | Aitken S 31 + 2 | Turnbull D 1 + 13 | Guy G 1 + 1 | Essler A 1 | Grant A 2 + 9 | Cruickshank C 1 + 5 | McPhee G 1 + 2 | Marshall S 1 + 6 | Graham D 30 + 2 | Crawford B 2 + 9 | Collins L 11 + 1 | Gaughan K — + 1 | *Match No.* |
|---|---|---|---|---|---|---|---|---|---|---|---|---|---|---|---|---|---|---|---|---|---|---|---|
| 1 | 2 | 3 | 4 | 5 | 6 | 7 | $8^{1}$ | 9 | $10^{2}$ | 11 | 12 | 13 | | | | | | | | | | | 1 |
| 1 | 2 | | 4 | 5 | 6 | 7 | $8^{3}$ | 9 | $10^{1}$ | | 14 | | 3 | $11^{2}$ | 12 | 13 | | | | | | | 2 |
| 1 | 2 | | 4 | | 6 | 7 | | $9^{1}$ | 12 | 11 | 8 | | | | 10 | 3 | $5^{2}$ | 13 | | | | | 3 |
| 1 | 2 | 3 | 4 | 5 | 6 | 7 | | $9^{2}$ | | 11 | $8^{1}$ | | | | 10 | | 12 | | 13 | | | | 4 |
| 1 | 2 | 3 | 4 | 5 | 6 | 7 | | $9^{2}$ | | 11 | 8 | 13 | | | 12 | | | | $10^{1}$ | | | | 5 |
| 1 | 2 | 3 | 4 | $5^{3}$ | 6 | 7 | | $9^{1}$ | | 11 | 8 | 13 | | | 12 | 14 | | | $10^{2}$ | | | | 6 |
| 1 | 2 | 3 | 4 | 5 | $6^{2}$ | 7 | | 9 | | 11 | 8 | | | | 12 | | | 13 | $10^{1}$ | | | | 7 |
| 1 | 2 | 3 | 4 | 5 | $6^{2}$ | $7^{3}$ | | $9^{1}$ | 12 | 11 | 8 | | | | | 14 | | 13 | 10 | | | | 8 |
| 1 | 2 | 3 | 4 | 5 | 6 | 7 | | $9^{1}$ | 12 | 11 | 8 | | | | | | | | 10 | | | | 9 |
| 1 | 2 | 3 | 4 | 5 | $6^{2}$ | 7 | | 9 | 14 | 11 | $8^{1}$ | | | | 13 | | | 12 | $10^{3}$ | | | | 10 |
| 1 | 2 | 3 | 4 | 5 | 6 | 7 | | $9^{1}$ | 12 | 11 | 8 | | | | | | | | 10 | | | | 11 |
| 1 | 2 | 3 | 4 | 5 | 6 | 7 | | $9^{3}$ | | 11 | $8^{1}$ | 14 | | | 13 | | | 12 | $10^{2}$ | | | | 12 |
| 1 | 2 | 3 | 4 | 5 | $6^{3}$ | 7 | 14 | 9 | 12 | $11^{1}$ | | | | | 13 | | | 8 | $10^{2}$ | | | | 13 |
| 1 | 2 | 3 | 4 | 5 | $6^{1}$ | 7 | | 9 | | 11 | 8 | | | | | | | 12 | $10^{2}$ | 13 | | | 14 |
| 1 | 2 | 3 | 4 | 5 | 6 | 7 | | 9 | | 11 | 8 | | | | | | | | $10^{1}$ | 12 | | | 15 |
| 1 | 2 | 3 | 4 | 5 | $6^{1}$ | 7 | | | | 11 | 8 | 13 | | | 14 | | 12 | | $10^{3}$ | $9^{2}$ | | | 16 |
| 1 | 2 | 3 | 4 | 5 | 12 | 7 | | 9 | | $11^{2}$ | 8 | | | | 13 | | | | 10 | | $6^{1}$ | | 17 |
| 1 | 2 | 3 | 4 | 5 | 6 | 7 | | $9^{1}$ | | 11 | 8 | 12 | | | | 13 | | | | | $10^{2}$ | | 18 |
| 1 | 2 | 3 | 4 | 5 | $6^{3}$ | $7^{2}$ | 12 | 9 | | 11 | 8 | 14 | | | | | | | 13 | | $10^{1}$ | | 19 |
| 1 | 2 | 3 | 4 | 5 | 6 | 7 | | $9^{1}$ | | 11 | 8 | 12 | | | | | | | 10 | | | | 20 |
| 1 | 2 | 3 | 4 | 5 | 6 | 7 | | 9 | | 11 | 8 | | | | | | | | 10 | | | | 21 |
| 1 | 2 | 3 | 4 | 5 | 6 | 7 | | $9^{1}$ | | 11 | 8 | 12 | | | | | | | 10 | | | | 22 |
| 1 | 2 | 3 | 4 | 5 | 6 | $7^{1}$ | | | | 11 | 8 | 12 | | | | | | | 10 | | 9 | | 23 |
| 1 | 2 | 3 | 4 | 5 | 6 | 7 | 12 | | | 11 | 8 | | | | | | | | 10 | | $9^{1}$ | | 24 |
| 1 | 2 | 3 | 4 | 5 | 6 | 7 | | 12 | | 11 | 8 | | | | | | | | 10 | | $9^{1}$ | | 25 |
| 1 | 2 | 3 | 4 | 5 | $6^{1}$ | | | 9 | | 11 | 8 | | | | | | | | 10 | 12 | 7 | | 26 |
| 1 | $2^{1}$ | 3 | 4 | 5 | 6 | | 13 | 9 | | 11 | $8^{2}$ | | | | | 12 | | | 10 | | 7 | | 27 |
| 1 | 2 | 3 | 4 | 5 | 6 | 12 | | 9 | | 11 | 8 | | | | | | | | 10 | | $7^{1}$ | | 28 |
| 1 | 2 | 3 | 4 | 5 | 6 | 7 | | 9 | | 11 | 8 | | | | | | | | 10 | | | | 29 |
| 1 | 2 | 3 | 4 | 5 | $6^{1}$ | 7 | 13 | 9 | | 11 | $8^{2}$ | | | | | | | | $10^{3}$ | 14 | 12 | | 30 |
| 1 | 2 | 3 | 4 | 5 | 6 | $7^{1}$ | | 9 | | 11 | | | | | | | | | 10 | 12 | 8 | | 31 |
| 1 | $2^{2}$ | 3 | 4 | 5 | 6 | 7 | 14 | $9^{1}$ | | 11 | | | | | | | | | 10 | 12 | $8^{3}$ | 13 | 32 |
| 1 | 2 | 3 | 4 | 5 | 6 | | $7^{2}$ | | | 11 | 8 | 12 | 13 | | | | | | 10 | $9^{1}$ | | | 33 |
| 1 | 2 | 3 | 4 | 5 | 6 | 7 | | | | 11 | 8 | $9^{1}$ | | | | | | | 10 | 12 | | | 34 |
| 1 | 2 | 3 | 4 | 5 | 6 | 7 | | $9^{1}$ | | 11 | 8 | 12 | | | | | | | $10^{2}$ | 13 | | | 35 |
| 1 | 2 | 3 | 4 | 5 | 6 | 7 | 14 | $9^{1}$ | | 11 | $8^{3}$ | 12 | | | | | | | $10^{2}$ | 13 | | | 36 |

# SCOTTISH LEAGUE TABLES 2003–04

## PREMIER DIVISION

| | | Home | | | | | Away | | | | | Total | | | | | | |
|---|---|---|---|---|---|---|---|---|---|---|---|---|---|---|---|---|---|---|
| | P | W | D | L | F | A | W | D | L | F | A | W | D | L | F | A | GD | Pts |
| 1 Celtic | 38 | 15 | 2 | 2 | 62 | 15 | 16 | 3 | 0 | 43 | 10 | 31 | 5 | 2 | 105 | 25 | 80 | 98 |
| 2 Rangers | 38 | 16 | 0 | 3 | 48 | 11 | 9 | 6 | 4 | 28 | 22 | 25 | 6 | 7 | 76 | 33 | 43 | 81 |
| 3 Hearts | 38 | 12 | 5 | 2 | 32 | 17 | 7 | 6 | 6 | 24 | 23 | 19 | 11 | 8 | 56 | 40 | 16 | 68 |
| 4 Dunfermline Ath | 38 | 9 | 7 | 3 | 28 | 19 | 5 | 4 | 10 | 17 | 33 | 14 | 11 | 13 | 45 | 52 | –7 | 53 |
| 5 Dundee U | 38 | 8 | 6 | 5 | 28 | 27 | 5 | 4 | 10 | 19 | 33 | 13 | 10 | 15 | 47 | 60 | –13 | 49 |
| 6 Motherwell | 38 | 7 | 7 | 5 | 25 | 22 | 5 | 3 | 11 | 17 | 27 | 12 | 10 | 16 | 42 | 49 | –7 | 46 |
| 7 Dundee | 38 | 8 | 3 | 8 | 21 | 20 | 4 | 7 | 8 | 27 | 37 | 12 | 10 | 16 | 48 | 57 | –9 | 46 |
| 8 Hibernian | 38 | 6 | 5 | 8 | 25 | 28 | 5 | 6 | 8 | 16 | 32 | 11 | 11 | 16 | 41 | 60 | –19 | 44 |
| 9 Livingston | 38 | 6 | 9 | 4 | 24 | 18 | 4 | 4 | 11 | 24 | 39 | 10 | 13 | 15 | 48 | 57 | –9 | 43 |
| 10 Kilmarnock | 38 | 8 | 3 | 8 | 29 | 31 | 4 | 3 | 12 | 22 | 43 | 12 | 6 | 20 | 51 | 74 | –23 | 42 |
| 11 Aberdeen | 38 | 5 | 3 | 11 | 22 | 29 | 4 | 4 | 11 | 17 | 34 | 9 | 7 | 22 | 39 | 63 | –24 | 34 |
| 12 Partick T | 38 | 5 | 4 | 10 | 24 | 32 | 1 | 4 | 14 | 15 | 35 | 6 | 8 | 24 | 39 | 67 | –28 | 26 |

## FIRST DIVISION

| | | Home | | | | | Away | | | | | Total | | | | | | |
|---|---|---|---|---|---|---|---|---|---|---|---|---|---|---|---|---|---|---|
| | P | W | D | L | F | A | W | D | L | F | A | W | D | L | F | A | GD | Pts |
| 1 Inverness CT | 36 | 13 | 4 | 1 | 37 | 12 | 8 | 3 | 7 | 30 | 21 | 21 | 7 | 8 | 67 | 33 | 34 | 70 |
| 2 Clyde | 36 | 11 | 4 | 3 | 34 | 17 | 9 | 5 | 4 | 30 | 23 | 20 | 9 | 7 | 64 | 40 | 24 | 69 |
| 3 St Johnstone | 36 | 8 | 5 | 5 | 34 | 27 | 7 | 7 | 4 | 25 | 18 | 15 | 12 | 9 | 59 | 45 | 14 | 57 |
| 4 Falkirk | 36 | 8 | 4 | 6 | 20 | 16 | 7 | 6 | 5 | 23 | 21 | 15 | 10 | 11 | 43 | 37 | 6 | 55 |
| 5 Queen of the S | 36 | 9 | 6 | 3 | 24 | 16 | 6 | 3 | 9 | 22 | 32 | 15 | 9 | 12 | 46 | 48 | –2 | 54 |
| 6 Ross Co | 36 | 8 | 6 | 4 | 24 | 17 | 4 | 7 | 7 | 25 | 24 | 12 | 13 | 11 | 49 | 41 | 8 | 49 |
| 7 St Mirren | 36 | 6 | 9 | 3 | 27 | 23 | 3 | 5 | 10 | 12 | 23 | 9 | 14 | 13 | 39 | 46 | –7 | 41 |
| 8 Raith R | 36 | 5 | 5 | 8 | 18 | 28 | 3 | 5 | 10 | 19 | 29 | 8 | 10 | 18 | 37 | 57 | –20 | 34 |
| 9 Ayr U | 36 | 4 | 7 | 7 | 21 | 29 | 2 | 6 | 10 | 16 | 29 | 6 | 13 | 17 | 37 | 58 | –21 | 31 |
| 10 Brechin C | 36 | 5 | 3 | 10 | 21 | 33 | 1 | 6 | 11 | 16 | 40 | 6 | 9 | 21 | 37 | 73 | –36 | 27 |

## SECOND DIVISION

| | | Home | | | | | Away | | | | | Total | | | | | | |
|---|---|---|---|---|---|---|---|---|---|---|---|---|---|---|---|---|---|---|
| | P | W | D | L | F | A | W | D | L | F | A | W | D | L | F | A | GD | Pts |
| 1 Airdrie U | 36 | 10 | 6 | 2 | 36 | 19 | 10 | 4 | 4 | 28 | 17 | 20 | 10 | 6 | 64 | 36 | 28 | 70 |
| 2 Hamilton A | 36 | 9 | 3 | 6 | 32 | 21 | 9 | 5 | 4 | 38 | 26 | 18 | 8 | 10 | 70 | 47 | 23 | 62 |
| 3 Dumbarton | 36 | 12 | 3 | 3 | 31 | 13 | 6 | 3 | 9 | 25 | 28 | 18 | 6 | 12 | 56 | 41 | 15 | 60 |
| 4 Morton | 36 | 8 | 8 | 2 | 37 | 30 | 8 | 3 | 7 | 29 | 28 | 16 | 11 | 9 | 66 | 58 | 8 | 59 |
| 5 Berwick R | 36 | 8 | 2 | 8 | 31 | 31 | 6 | 4 | 8 | 30 | 36 | 14 | 6 | 16 | 61 | 67 | –6 | 48 |
| 6 Forfar Ath | 36 | 7 | 4 | 7 | 25 | 30 | 5 | 7 | 6 | 24 | 27 | 12 | 11 | 13 | 49 | 57 | –8 | 47 |
| 7 Alloa Ath | 36 | 6 | 6 | 6 | 33 | 26 | 6 | 2 | 10 | 22 | 29 | 12 | 8 | 16 | 55 | 55 | 0 | 44 |
| 8 Arbroath | 36 | 5 | 6 | 7 | 17 | 27 | 6 | 4 | 8 | 24 | 30 | 11 | 10 | 15 | 41 | 57 | –16 | 43 |
| 9 East Fife | 36 | 7 | 2 | 9 | 24 | 24 | 4 | 6 | 8 | 14 | 21 | 11 | 8 | 17 | 38 | 45 | –7 | 41 |
| 10 Stenhousemuir | 36 | 4 | 1 | 13 | 12 | 29 | 3 | 3 | 12 | 16 | 36 | 7 | 4 | 25 | 28 | 65 | –37 | 25 |

## THIRD DIVISION

| | | Home | | | | | Away | | | | | Total | | | | | | |
|---|---|---|---|---|---|---|---|---|---|---|---|---|---|---|---|---|---|---|
| | P | W | D | L | F | A | W | D | L | F | A | W | D | L | F | A | GD | Pts |
| 1 Stranraer | 36 | 13 | 2 | 3 | 51 | 14 | 11 | 5 | 2 | 36 | 16 | 24 | 7 | 5 | 87 | 30 | 57 | 79 |
| 2 Stirling Alb | 36 | 10 | 5 | 3 | 37 | 12 | 13 | 3 | 2 | 41 | 15 | 23 | 8 | 5 | 78 | 27 | 51 | 77 |
| 3 Gretna | 36 | 9 | 5 | 4 | 29 | 18 | 11 | 3 | 4 | 30 | 21 | 20 | 8 | 8 | 59 | 39 | 20 | 68 |
| 4 Peterhead | 36 | 10 | 5 | 3 | 38 | 13 | 8 | 2 | 8 | 29 | 24 | 18 | 7 | 11 | 67 | 37 | 30 | 61 |
| 5 Cowdenbeath | 36 | 7 | 3 | 8 | 25 | 27 | 8 | 7 | 3 | 21 | 12 | 15 | 10 | 11 | 46 | 39 | 7 | 55 |
| 6 Montrose | 36 | 7 | 4 | 7 | 31 | 34 | 5 | 8 | 5 | 21 | 29 | 12 | 12 | 12 | 52 | 63 | –11 | 48 |
| 7 Queen's Park | 36 | 5 | 5 | 8 | 20 | 24 | 5 | 6 | 7 | 21 | 29 | 10 | 11 | 15 | 41 | 53 | –12 | 41 |
| 8 Albion R | 36 | 6 | 2 | 10 | 36 | 35 | 6 | 2 | 10 | 30 | 40 | 12 | 4 | 20 | 66 | 75 | –9 | 40 |
| 9 Elgin C | 36 | 4 | 5 | 9 | 23 | 34 | 2 | 2 | 14 | 25 | 59 | 6 | 7 | 23 | 48 | 93 | –45 | 25 |
| 10 East Stirlingshire | 36 | 2 | 2 | 14 | 22 | 51 | 0 | 0 | 18 | 8 | 67 | 2 | 2 | 32 | 30 | 118 | –88 | 8 |

# SCOTTISH LEAGUE ATTENDANCES 2003–04

**PREMIER LEAGUE**

| | *Average* | *Highest* | *Lowest* |
|---|---|---|---|
| Aberdeen | 10,385 | 16,452 | 6781 |
| Celtic | 58,442 | 59,719 | 57,004 |
| Dundee | 7109 | 10,948 | 4942 |
| Dundee U | 7928 | 12,767 | 5421 |
| Dunfermline Ath | 6092 | 10,082 | 3914 |
| Hearts | 11,961 | 16,632 | 10,046 |
| Hibernian | 9107 | 15,016 | 5380 |
| Kilmarnock | 6960 | 14,516 | 4886 |
| Livingston | 4551 | 8065 | 2677 |
| Motherwell | 6225 | 10,824 | 3920 |
| Partick Th | 4711 | 9045 | 2727 |
| Rangers | 48,992 | 49,962 | 46,900 |

**FIRST DIVISION**

| | | | |
|---|---|---|---|
| Ayr U | 1706 | 2519 | 977 |
| Brechin C | 809 | 1434 | 464 |
| Clyde | 1652 | 4722 | 734 |
| Falkirk | 2585 | 3887 | 2060 |
| Inverness CT | 2372 | 6092 | 1198 |
| Queen of the S | 2360 | 4075 | 1352 |
| Raith R | 2190 | 4222 | 1432 |
| Ross Co | 3173 | 6020 | 2414 |
| St Johnstone | 2622 | 4185 | 1906 |
| St Mirren | 2773 | 3613 | 2180 |

**SECOND DIVISION**

| | *Average* | *Highest* | *Lowest* |
|---|---|---|---|
| Airdrie U | 1861 | 5704 | 1072 |
| Alloa Ath | 589 | 1635 | 321 |
| Arbroath | 625 | 1116 | 402 |
| Berwick R | 522 | 1175 | 330 |
| Dumbarton | 1050 | 2011 | 552 |
| East Fife | 712 | 1757 | 439 |
| Forfar Ath | 663 | 1496 | 407 |
| Hamilton A | 1407 | 2692 | 831 |
| Morton | 2966 | 3806 | 2300 |
| Stenhousemuir | 600 | 1343 | 296 |

**THIRD DIVISION**

| | | | |
|---|---|---|---|
| Albion R | 349 | 627 | 179 |
| Cowdenbeath | 305 | 692 | 210 |
| East Stirlingshire | 278 | 779 | 175 |
| Elgin C | 527 | 748 | 312 |
| Gretna | 461 | 758 | 311 |
| Montrose | 355 | 512 | 246 |
| Peterhead | 579 | 813 | 440 |
| Queen's Park | 515 | 742 | 395 |
| Stirling A | 753 | 2190 | 490 |
| Stranraer | 503 | 1321 | 358 |

The Celtic players celebrate after winning the Scottish FA Cup Final 3-1 against Dunfermline Athletic at Hampden Park, completing the Scottish League and Cup double. (Actionimages)

# SCOTTISH LEAGUE HONOURS 1890 to 2004

*On goal average (ratio)/difference. †Held jointly after indecisive play-off. ‡Won on deciding match.
††Held jointly. ¶Two points deducted for fielding ineligible player.
Competition suspended 1940–45 during war; Regional Leagues operating. ‡‡Two points deducted for registration irregularities.

## PREMIER LEAGUE

| | First | Pts | Second | Pts | Third | Pts |
|---|---|---|---|---|---|---|
| | | | *Maximum points: 108* | | | |
| 1998–99 | Rangers | 77 | Celtic | 71 | St Johnstone | 57 |
| 1999–2000 | Rangers | 90 | Celtic | 69 | Hearts | 54 |
| | | | *Maximum points: 114* | | | |
| 2000–01 | Celtic | 97 | Rangers | 82 | Hibernian | 66 |
| 2001–02 | Celtic | 103 | Rangers | 85 | Livingston | 58 |
| 2002–03 | Rangers* | 97 | Celtic | 97 | Hearts | 63 |
| 2003–04 | Celtic | 98 | Rangers | 81 | Hearts | 68 |

## PREMIER DIVISION

| | First | Pts | Second | Pts | Third | Pts |
|---|---|---|---|---|---|---|
| | | | *Maximum points: 72* | | | |
| 1975–76 | Rangers | 54 | Celtic | 48 | Hibernian | 43 |
| 1976–77 | Celtic | 55 | Rangers | 46 | Aberdeen | 43 |
| 1977–78 | Rangers | 55 | Aberdeen | 53 | Dundee U | 40 |
| 1978–79 | Celtic | 48 | Rangers | 45 | Dundee U | 44 |
| 1979–80 | Aberdeen | 48 | Celtic | 47 | St Mirren | 42 |
| 1980–81 | Celtic | 56 | Aberdeen | 49 | Rangers* | 44 |
| 1981–82 | Celtic | 55 | Aberdeen | 53 | Rangers | 43 |
| 1982–83 | Dundee U | 56 | Celtic* | 55 | Aberdeen | 55 |
| 1983–84 | Aberdeen | 57 | Celtic | 50 | Dundee U | 47 |
| 1984–85 | Aberdeen | 59 | Celtic | 52 | Dundee U | 47 |
| 1985–86 | Celtic* | 50 | Hearts | 50 | Dundee U | 47 |
| | | | *Maximum points: 88* | | | |
| 1986–87 | Rangers | 69 | Celtic | 63 | Dundee U | 60 |
| 1987–88 | Celtic | 72 | Hearts | 62 | Rangers | 60 |
| | | | *Maximum points: 72* | | | |
| 1988–89 | Rangers | 56 | Aberdeen | 50 | Celtic | 46 |
| 1989–90 | Rangers | 51 | Aberdeen* | 44 | Hearts | 44 |
| 1990–91 | Rangers | 55 | Aberdeen | 53 | Celtic* | 41 |
| | | | *Maximum points: 88* | | | |
| 1991–92 | Rangers | 72 | Hearts | 63 | Celtic | 62 |
| 1992–93 | Rangers | 73 | Aberdeen | 64 | Celtic | 60 |
| 1993–94 | Rangers | 58 | Aberdeen | 55 | Motherwell | 54 |
| | | | *Maximum points: 108* | | | |
| 1994–95 | Rangers | 69 | Motherwell | 54 | Hibernian | 53 |
| 1995–96 | Rangers | 87 | Celtic | 83 | Aberdeen* | 55 |
| 1996–97 | Rangers | 80 | Celtic | 75 | Dundee U | 60 |
| 1997–98 | Celtic | 74 | Rangers | 72 | Hearts | 67 |

## FIRST DIVISION

| | First | Pts | Second | Pts | Third | Pts |
|---|---|---|---|---|---|---|
| | | | *Maximum points: 52* | | | |
| 1975–76 | Partick T | 41 | Kilmarnock | 35 | Montrose | 30 |
| | | | *Maximum points: 78* | | | |
| 1976–77 | St Mirren | 62 | Clydebank | 58 | Dundee | 51 |
| 1977–78 | Morton* | 58 | Hearts | 58 | Dundee | 57 |
| 1978–79 | Dundee | 55 | Kilmarnock* | 54 | Clydebank | 54 |
| 1979–80 | Hearts | 53 | Airdrieonians | 51 | Ayr U* | 44 |
| 1980–81 | Hibernian | 57 | Dundee | 52 | St Johnstone | 51 |
| 1981–82 | Motherwell | 61 | Kilmarnock | 51 | Hearts | 50 |
| 1982–83 | St Johnstone | 55 | Hearts | 54 | Clydebank | 50 |
| 1983–84 | Morton | 54 | Dumbarton | 51 | Partick T | 46 |
| 1984–85 | Motherwell | 50 | Clydebank | 48 | Falkirk | 45 |
| 1985–86 | Hamilton A | 56 | Falkirk | 45 | Kilmarnock | 44 |
| | | | *Maximum points: 88* | | | |
| 1986–87 | Morton | 57 | Dunfermline Ath | 56 | Dumbarton | 53 |
| 1987–88 | Hamilton A | 56 | Meadowbank T | 52 | Clydebank | 49 |
| | | | *Maximum points: 78* | | | |
| 1988–89 | Dunfermline Ath | 54 | Falkirk | 52 | Clydebank | 48 |
| 1989–90 | St Johnstone | 58 | Airdrieonians | 54 | Clydebank | 44 |
| 1990–91 | Falkirk | 54 | Airdrieonians | 53 | Dundee | 52 |
| | | | *Maximum points: 88* | | | |
| 1991–92 | Dundee | 58 | Partick T* | 57 | Hamilton A | 57 |
| 1992–93 | Raith R | 65 | Kilmarnock | 54 | Dunfermline Ath | 52 |
| 1993–94 | Falkirk | 66 | Dunfermline Ath | 65 | Airdrieonians | 54 |
| | | | *Maximum points: 108* | | | |
| 1994–95 | Raith R | 69 | Dunfermline Ath* | 68 | Dundee | 68 |
| 1995–96 | Dunfermline Ath | 71 | Dundee U* | 67 | Morton | 67 |
| 1996–97 | St Johnstone | 80 | Airdieonians | 60 | Dundee* | 58 |
| 1997–98 | Dundee | 70 | Falkirk | 65 | Raith R* | 60 |
| 1998–99 | Hibernian | 89 | Falkirk | 66 | Ayr U | 62 |
| 1999–2000 | St Mirren | 76 | Dunfermline Ath | 71 | Falkirk | 68 |
| 2000–01 | Livingston | 76 | Ayr U | 69 | Falkirk | 56 |
| 2001–02 | Partick T | 66 | Airdrieonians | 56 | Ayr U | 52 |
| 2002–03 | Falkirk | 81 | Clyde | 72 | St Johnstone | 67 |
| 2003–04 | Inverness CT | 70 | Clyde | 69 | St Johnstone | 57 |

## SECOND DIVISION

*Maximum points: 52*

| | First | Pts | Second | Pts | Third | Pts |
|---|---|---|---|---|---|---|
| 1975–76 | Clydebank* | 40 | Raith R | 40 | Alloa | 35 |
| | | | *Maximum points: 78* | | | |
| 1976–77 | Stirling A | 55 | Alloa | 51 | Dunfermline Ath | 50 |
| 1977–78 | Clyde* | 53 | Raith R | 53 | Dunfermline Ath | 48 |
| 1978–79 | Berwick R | 54 | Dunfermline Ath | 52 | Falkirk | 50 |
| 1979–80 | Falkirk | 50 | East Stirling | 49 | Forfar Ath | 46 |
| 1980–81 | Queen's Park | 50 | Queen of the S | 46 | Cowdenbeath | 45 |
| 1981–82 | Clyde | 59 | Alloa* | 50 | Arbroath | 50 |
| 1982–83 | Brechin C | 55 | Meadowbank T | 54 | Arbroath | 49 |
| 1983–84 | Forfar Ath | 63 | East Fife | 47 | Berwick R | 43 |
| 1984–85 | Montrose | 53 | Alloa | 50 | Dunfermline Ath | 49 |
| 1985–86 | Dunfermline Ath | 57 | Queen of the S | 55 | Meadowbank T | 49 |
| 1986–87 | Meadowbank T | 55 | Raith R* | 52 | Stirling A* | 52 |
| 1987–88 | Ayr U | 61 | St Johnstone | 59 | Queen's Park | 51 |
| 1988–89 | Albion R | 50 | Alloa | 45 | Brechin C | 43 |
| 1989–90 | Brechin C | 49 | Kilmarnock | 48 | Stirling A | 47 |
| 1990–91 | Stirling A | 54 | Montrose | 46 | Cowdenbeath | 45 |
| 1991–92 | Dumbarton | 52 | Cowdenbeath | 51 | Alloa | 50 |
| 1992–93 | Clyde | 54 | Brechin C* | 53 | Stranraer | 53 |
| 1993–94 | Stranraer | 56 | Berwick R | 48 | Stenhousemuir* | 47 |
| | | | *Maximum points: 108* | | | |
| 1994–95 | Morton | 64 | Dumbarton | 60 | Stirling A | 58 |
| 1995–96 | Stirling A | 81 | East Fife | 67 | Berwick R | 60 |
| 1996–97 | Ayr U | 77 | Hamilton A | 74 | Livingston | 64 |
| 1997–98 | Stranraer | 61 | Clydebank | 60 | Livingston | 59 |
| 1998–99 | Livingston | 77 | Inverness CT | 72 | Clyde | 53 |
| 1999–2000 | Clyde | 65 | Alloa Ath | 64 | Ross Co | 62 |
| 2000–01 | Partick T | 75 | Arbroath | 58 | Berwick R* | 54 |
| 2001–02 | Queen of the S | 67 | Alloa | 59 | Forfar Ath | 53 |
| 2002–03 | Raith R | 59 | Brechin C | 55 | Airdrie U | 54 |
| 2003–04 | Airdrie U | 70 | Hamilton A | 62 | Dumbarton | 60 |

## THIRD DIVISION

*Maximum points: 108*

| | | | | | | |
|---|---|---|---|---|---|---|
| 1994–95 | Forfar Ath | 80 | Montrose | 67 | Ross Co | 60 |
| 1995–96 | Livingston | 72 | Brechin C | 63 | Caledonian T | 57 |
| 1996–97 | Inverness CT | 76 | Forfar Ath* | 67 | Ross Co | 67 |
| 1997–98 | Alloa Ath | 76 | Arbroath | 68 | Ross Co* | 67 |
| 1998–99 | Ross Co | 77 | Stenhousemuir | 64 | Brechin C | 59 |
| 1999–2000 | Queen's Park | 69 | Berwick R | 66 | Forfar Ath | 61 |
| 2000–01 | Hamilton A* | 76 | Cowdenbeath | 76 | Brechin C | 72 |
| 2001–02 | Brechin C | 73 | Dumbarton | 61 | Albion R | 59 |
| 2002–03 | Morton | 72 | East Fife | 71 | Albion R | 70 |
| 2003–04 | Stranraer | 79 | Stirling A | 77 | Gretna | 68 |

## FIRST DIVISION to 1974–75

*Maximum points: a* 36; *b* 44; *c* 40; *d* 52; *e* 60; *f* 68; g 76; *h* 84.

| | | | | | | |
|---|---|---|---|---|---|---|
| 1890–91*a* | Dumbarton†† | 29 | Rangers†† | 29 | Celtic | 21 |
| 1891–92*b* | Dumbarton | 37 | Celtic | 35 | Hearts | 34 |
| 1892–93*a* | Celtic | 29 | Rangers | 28 | St Mirren | 20 |
| 1893–94*a* | Celtic | 29 | Hearts | 26 | St Bernard's | 23 |
| 1894–95*a* | Hearts | 31 | Celtic | 26 | Rangers | 22 |
| 1895–96*a* | Celtic | 30 | Rangers | 26 | Hibernian | 24 |
| 1896–97*a* | Hearts | 28 | Hibernian | 26 | Rangers | 25 |
| 1897–98*a* | Celtic | 33 | Rangers | 29 | Hibernian | 22 |
| 1898–99*a* | Rangers | 36 | Hearts | 26 | Celtic | 24 |
| 1899–1900*a* | Rangers | 32 | Celtic | 25 | Hibernian | 24 |
| 1900–01*c* | Rangers | 35 | Celtic | 29 | Hibernian | 25 |
| 1901–02*a* | Rangers | 28 | Celtic | 26 | Hearts | 22 |
| 1902–03*b* | Hibernian | 37 | Dundee | 31 | Rangers | 29 |
| 1903–04*d* | Third Lanark | 43 | Hearts | 39 | Celtic* | 38 |
| 1904–05*d* | Celtic‡ | 41 | Rangers | 41 | Third Lanark | 35 |
| 1905–06*e* | Celtic | 49 | Hearts | 43 | Airdrieonians | 38 |
| 1906–07*f* | Celtic | 55 | Dundee | 48 | Rangers | 45 |
| 1907–08*f* | Celtic | 55 | Falkirk | 51 | Rangers | 50 |
| 1908–09*f* | Celtic | 51 | Dundee | 50 | Clyde | 48 |
| 1909–10*f* | Celtic | 54 | Falkirk | 52 | Rangers | 46 |
| 1910–11*f* | Rangers | 52 | Aberdeen | 48 | Falkirk | 44 |
| 1911–12*f* | Rangers | 51 | Celtic | 45 | Clyde | 42 |
| 1912–13*f* | Rangers | 53 | Celtic | 49 | Hearts* | 41 |
| 1913–14*g* | Celtic | 65 | Rangers | 59 | Hearts* | 54 |
| 1914–15*g* | Celtic | 65 | Hearts | 61 | Rangers | 50 |
| 1915–16*g* | Celtic | 67 | Rangers | 56 | Morton | 51 |
| 1916–17*g* | Celtic | 64 | Morton | 54 | Rangers | 53 |
| 1917–18*f* | Rangers | 56 | Celtic | 55 | Kilmarnock* | 43 |
| 1918–19*f* | Celtic | 58 | Rangers | 57 | Morton | 47 |
| 1919–20*h* | Rangers | 71 | Celtic | 68 | Motherwell | 57 |
| 1920–21*h* | Rangers | 76 | Celtic | 66 | Hearts | 50 |

| | *First* | *Pts* | *Second* | *Pts* | *Third* | *Pts* |
|---|---|---|---|---|---|---|
| 1921–22*h* | Celtic | 67 | Rangers | 66 | Raith R | 51 |
| 1922–23*g* | Rangers | 55 | Airdrieonians | 50 | Celtic | 46 |
| 1923–24*g* | Rangers | 59 | Airdrieonians | 50 | Celtic | 46 |
| 1924–25*g* | Rangers | 60 | Airdrieonians | 57 | Hibernian | 52 |
| 1925–26*g* | Celtic | 58 | Airdrieonians* | 50 | Hearts | 50 |
| 1926–27*g* | Rangers | 56 | Motherwell | 51 | Celtic | 49 |
| 1927–28*g* | Rangers | 60 | Celtic* | 55 | Motherwell | 55 |
| 1928–29*g* | Rangers | 67 | Celtic | 51 | Motherwell | 50 |
| 1929–30*g* | Rangers | 60 | Motherwell | 55 | Aberdeen | 53 |
| 1930–31*g* | Rangers | 60 | Celtic | 58 | Motherwell | 56 |
| 1931–32*g* | Motherwell | 66 | Rangers | 61 | Celtic | 48 |
| 1932–33*g* | Rangers | 62 | Motherwell | 59 | Hearts | 50 |
| 1933–34*g* | Rangers | 66 | Motherwell | 62 | Celtic | 47 |
| 1934–35*g* | Rangers | 55 | Celtic | 52 | Hearts | 50 |
| 1935–36*g* | Celtic | 66 | Rangers* | 61 | Aberdeen | 61 |
| 1936–37*g* | Rangers | 61 | Aberdeen | 54 | Celtic | 52 |
| 1937–38*g* | Celtic | 61 | Hearts | 58 | Rangers | 49 |
| 1938–39*g* | Rangers | 59 | Celtic | 48 | Aberdeen | 46 |
| 1946–47*e* | Rangers | 46 | Hibernian | 44 | Aberdeen | 39 |
| 1947–48*e* | Hibernian | 48 | Rangers | 46 | Partick T | 36 |
| 1948–49*e* | Rangers | 46 | Dundee | 45 | Hibernian | 39 |
| 1949–50*e* | Rangers | 50 | Hibernian | 49 | Hearts | 43 |
| 1950–51*e* | Hibernian | 48 | Rangers* | 38 | Dundee | 38 |
| 1951–52*e* | Hibernian | 45 | Rangers | 41 | East Fife | 37 |
| 1952–53*e* | Rangers* | 43 | Hibernian | 43 | East Fife | 39 |
| 1953–54*e* | Celtic | 43 | Hearts | 38 | Partick T | 35 |
| 1954–55*e* | Aberdeen | 49 | Celtic | 46 | Rangers | 41 |
| 1955–56*f* | Rangers | 52 | Aberdeen | 46 | Hearts* | 45 |
| 1956–57*f* | Rangers | 55 | Hearts | 53 | Kilmarnock | 42 |
| 1957–58*f* | Hearts | 62 | Rangers | 49 | Celtic | 46 |
| 1958–59*f* | Rangers | 50 | Hearts | 48 | Motherwell | 44 |
| 1959–60*f* | Hearts | 54 | Kilmarnock | 50 | Rangers* | 42 |
| 1960–61*f* | Rangers | 51 | Kilmarnock | 50 | Third Lanark | 42 |
| 1961–62*f* | Dundee | 54 | Rangers | 51 | Celtic | 46 |
| 1962–63*f* | Rangers | 57 | Kilmarnock | 48 | Partick T | 46 |
| 1963–64*f* | Rangers | 55 | Kilmarnock | 49 | Celtic* | 47 |
| 1964–65*f* | Kilmarnock* | 50 | Hearts | 50 | Dunfermline Ath | 49 |
| 1965–66*f* | Celtic | 57 | Rangers | 55 | Kilmarnock | 45 |
| 1966–67*f* | Celtic | 58 | Rangers | 55 | Clyde | 46 |
| 1967–68*f* | Celtic | 63 | Rangers | 61 | Hibernian | 45 |
| 1968–69*f* | Celtic | 54 | Rangers | 49 | Dunfermline Ath | 45 |
| 1969–70*f* | Celtic | 57 | Rangers | 45 | Hibernian | 44 |
| 1970–71*f* | Celtic | 56 | Aberdeen | 54 | St Johnstone | 44 |
| 1971–72*f* | Celtic | 60 | Aberdeen | 50 | Rangers | 44 |
| 1972–73*f* | Celtic | 57 | Rangers | 56 | Hibernian | 45 |
| 1973–74*f* | Celtic | 53 | Hibernian | 49 | Rangers | 48 |
| 1974–75*f* | Rangers | 56 | Hibernian | 49 | Celtic | 45 |

## SECOND DIVISION to 1974–75

*Maximum points: a* 76; *b* 72; *c* 68; *d* 52; *e* 60; *f* 36; *g* 44.

| | | | | | | |
|---|---|---|---|---|---|---|
| 1893–94*f* | Hibernian | 29 | Cowlairs | 27 | Clyde | 24 |
| 1894–95*f* | Hibernian | 30 | Motherwell | 22 | Port Glasgow | 20 |
| 1895–96*f* | Abercorn | 27 | Leith Ath | 23 | Renton | 21 |
| 1896–97*f* | Partick T | 31 | Leith Ath | 27 | Kilmarnock* | 21 |
| 1897–98*f* | Kilmarnock | 29 | Port Glasgow | 25 | Morton | 22 |
| 1898–99*f* | Kilmarnock | 32 | Leith Ath | 27 | Port Glasgow | 25 |
| 1899–1900*f* | Partick T | 29 | Morton | 28 | Port Glasgow | 20 |
| 1900–01*f* | St Bernard's | 25 | Airdrieonians | 23 | Abercorn | 21 |
| 1901–02*g* | Port Glasgow | 32 | Partick T | 31 | Motherwell | 26 |
| 1902–03*g* | Airdrieonians | 35 | Motherwell | 28 | Ayr U* | 27 |
| 1903–04*g* | Hamilton A | 37 | Clyde | 29 | Ayr U | 28 |
| 1904–05*g* | Clyde | 32 | Falkirk | 28 | Hamilton A | 27 |
| 1905–06*g* | Leith Ath | 34 | Clyde | 31 | Albion R | 27 |
| 1906–07*g* | St Bernard's | 32 | Vale of Leven* | 27 | Arthurlie | 27 |
| 1907–08*g* | Raith R | 30 | Dumbarton*‡‡ | 27 | Ayr U | 27 |
| 1908–09*g* | Abercorn | 31 | Raith R* | 28 | Vale of Leven | 28 |
| 1909–10*g* | Leith Ath‡ | 33 | Raith R | 33 | St Bernard's | 27 |
| 1910–11*g* | Dumbarton | 31 | Ayr U | 27 | Albion R | 25 |
| 1911–12*g* | Ayr U | 35 | Abercorn | 30 | Dumbarton | 27 |
| 1912–13*d* | Ayr U | 34 | Dunfermline Ath | 33 | East Stirling | 32 |
| 1913–14*g* | Cowdenbeath | 31 | Albion R | 27 | Dunfermline Ath* | 26 |
| 1914–15*d* | Cowdenbeath* | 37 | St Bernard's* | 37 | Leith Ath | 37 |
| 1921–22*a* | Alloa | 60 | Cowdenbeath | 47 | Armadale | 45 |
| 1922–23*a* | Queen's Park | 57 | Clydebank¶ | 50 | St Johnstone¶ | 45 |
| 1923–24*a* | St Johnstone | 56 | Cowdenbeath | 55 | Bathgate | 44 |
| 1924–25*a* | Dundee U | 50 | Clydebank | 48 | Clyde | 47 |
| 1925–26*a* | Dunfermline Ath | 59 | Clyde | 53 | Ayr U | 52 |
| 1926–27*a* | Bo'ness | 56 | Raith R | 49 | Clydebank | 45 |
| 1927–28*a* | Ayr U | 54 | Third Lanark | 45 | King's Park | 44 |
| 1928–29*b* | Dundee U | 51 | Morton | 50 | Arbroath | 47 |
| 1929–30*a* | Leith Ath* | 57 | East Fife | 57 | Albion R | 54 |

| | *First* | *Pts* | *Second* | *Pts* | *Third* | *Pts* |
|---|---|---|---|---|---|---|
| 1930–31*a* | Third Lanark | 61 | Dundee U | 50 | Dunfermline Ath | 47 |
| 1931–32*a* | East Stirling* | 55 | St Johnstone | 55 | Raith R* | 46 |
| 1932–33*c* | Hibernian | 54 | Queen of the S | 49 | Dunfermline Ath | 47 |
| 1933–34*c* | Albion R | 45 | Dunfermline Ath* | 44 | Arbroath | 44 |
| 1934–35*c* | Third Lanark | 52 | Arbroath | 50 | St Bernard's | 47 |
| 1935–36*c* | Falkirk | 59 | St Mirren | 52 | Morton | 48 |
| 1936–37*c* | Ayr U | 54 | Morton | 51 | St Bernard's | 48 |
| 1937–38*c* | Raith R | 59 | Albion R | 48 | Airdrieonians | 47 |
| 1938–39*c* | Cowdenbeath | 60 | Alloa* | 48 | East Fife | 48 |
| 1946–47*d* | Dundee | 45 | Airdrieonians | 42 | East Fife | 31 |
| 1947–48*e* | East Fife | 53 | Albion R | 42 | Hamilton A | 40 |
| 1948–49*e* | Raith R* | 42 | Stirling A | 42 | Airdrieonians* | 41 |
| 1949–50*e* | Morton | 47 | Airdrieonians | 44 | Dunfermline Ath* | 36 |
| 1950–51*e* | Queen of the S* | 45 | Stirling A | 45 | Ayr U* | 36 |
| 1951–52*e* | Clyde | 44 | Falkirk | 43 | Ayr U | 39 |
| 1952–53*e* | Stirling A | 44 | Hamilton A | 43 | Queen's Park | 37 |
| 1953–54*e* | Motherwell | 45 | Kilmarnock | 42 | Third Lanark* | 36 |
| 1954–55*e* | Airdrieonians | 46 | Dunfermline Ath | 42 | Hamilton A | 39 |
| 1955–56*b* | Queen's Park | 54 | Ayr U | 51 | St Johnstone | 49 |
| 1956–57*b* | Clyde | 64 | Third Lanark | 51 | Cowdenbeath | 45 |
| 1957–58*b* | Stirling A | 55 | Dunfermline Ath | 53 | Arbroath | 47 |
| 1958–59*b* | Ayr U | 60 | Arbroath | 51 | Stenhousemuir | 46 |
| 1959–60*b* | St Johnstone | 53 | Dundee U | 50 | Queen of the S | 49 |
| 1960–61*b* | Stirling A | 55 | Falkirk | 54 | Stenhousemuir | 50 |
| 1961–62*b* | Clyde | 54 | Queen of the S | 53 | Morton | 44 |
| 1962–63*b* | St Johnstone | 55 | East Stirling | 49 | Morton | 48 |
| 1963–64*b* | Morton | 67 | Clyde | 53 | Arbroath | 46 |
| 1964–65*b* | Stirling A | 59 | Hamilton A | 50 | Queen of the S | 45 |
| 1965–66*b* | Ayr U | 53 | Airdrieonians | 50 | Queen of the S | 47 |
| 1966–67*a* | Morton | 69 | Raith R | 58 | Arbroath | 57 |
| 1967–68*b* | St Mirren | 62 | Arbroath | 53 | East Fife | 49 |
| 1968–69*b* | Motherwell | 64 | Ayr U | 53 | East Fife* | 48 |
| 1969–70*b* | Falkirk | 56 | Cowdenbeath | 55 | Queen of the S | 50 |
| 1970–71*b* | Partick T | 56 | East Fife | 51 | Arbroath | 46 |
| 1971–72*b* | Dumbarton* | 52 | Arbroath | 52 | Stirling A | 50 |
| 1972–73*b* | Clyde | 56 | Dumfermline Ath | 52 | Raith R* | 47 |
| 1973–74*b* | Airdrieonians | 60 | Kilmarnock | 58 | Hamilton A | 55 |
| 1974–75*a* | Falkirk | 54 | Queen of the S* | 53 | Montrose | 53 |

Elected to First Division: 1894 Clyde; 1895 Hibernian; 1896 Abercorn; 1897 Partick T; 1899 Kilmarnock; 1900 Morton and Partick T; 1902 Port Glasgow and Partick T; 1903 Airdrieonians and Motherwell; 1905 Falkirk and Aberdeen; 1906 Clyde and Hamilton A; 1910 Raith R; 1913 Ayr U and Dumbarton.

## RELEGATED FROM PREMIER LEAGUE

1998–99 Dunfermline Ath
1999–2000 *No relegation due to League reorganization*
2000–01 St Mirren
2001–02 St Johnstone
2002–03 *No relegated team*
2003–04 Partick T

## RELEGATED FROM PREMIER DIVISION

1974–75 *No relegation due to League reorganization*
1975–76 Dundee, St Johnstone
1976–77 Hearts, Kilmarnock
1977–78 Ayr U, Clydebank
1978–79 Hearts, Motherwell
1979–80 Dundee, Hibernian
1980–81 Kilmarnock, Hearts
1981–82 Partick T, Airdrieonians
1982–83 Morton, Kilmarnock
1983–84 St Johnstone, Motherwell
1984–85 Dumbarton, Morton
1985–86 *No relegation due to League reorganization*
1986–87 Clydebank, Hamilton A
1987–88 Falkirk, Dunfermline Ath, Morton
1988–89 Hamilton A
1989–90 Dundee
1990–91 *None*
1991–92 St Mirren, Dunfermline Ath
1992–93 Falkirk, Airdrieonians
1993–94 *See footnote*
1994–95 Dundee U
1995–96 Partick T, Falkirk
1996–97 Raith R
1997–98 Hibernian

## RELEGATED FROM DIVISION 1

1974–75 *No relegation due to League reorganization*
1975–76 Dunfermline Ath, Clyde
1976–77 Raith R, Falkirk
1977–78 Alloa Ath, East Fife
1978–79 Montrose, Queen of the S
1979–80 Arbroath, Clyde
1980–81 Stirling A, Berwick R
1981–82 East Stirling, Queen of the S
1982–83 Dunfermline Ath, Queen's Park
1983–84 Raith R, Alloa
1984–85 Meadowbank T, St Johnstone
1985–86 Ayr U, Alloa
1986–87 Brechin C, Montrose
1987–88 East Fife, Dumbarton
1988–89 Kilmarnock, Queen of the S
1989–90 Albion R, Alloa
1990–91 Clyde, Brechin C
1991–92 Montrose, Forfar Ath
1992–93 Meadowbank T, Cowdenbeath
1993–94 *See footnote*
1994–95 Ayr U, Stranraer
1995–96 Hamilton A, Dumbarton
1996–97 Clydebank, East Fife
1997–98 Partick T, Stirling A
1998–99 Hamilton A, Stranraer
1999–2000 Clydebank
2000–01 Morton, Alloa
2001–02 Raith R
2002–03 Alloa, Arbroath
2003–04 Ayr U, Brechin C

## RELEGATED FROM DIVISION 2

1994–95 Meadowbank T, Brechin C
1995–96 Forfar Ath, Montrose
1996–97 Dumbarton, Berwick R
1997–98 Stenhousemuir, Brechin C
1998–99 East Fife, Forfar Ath
1999–2000 Hamilton A**
2000–01 Queen's Park, Stirling A
2001–02 Morton
2002–03 Stranraer, Cowdenbeath
2003–04 East Fife, Stenhousemuir

## RELEGATED FROM DIVISION 1 (TO 1973–74)

1921–22 *Queen's Park, Dumbarton, Clydebank
1922–23 Albion R, Alloa Ath
1923–24 Clyde, Clydebank
1924–25 Third Lanark, Ayr U
1925–26 Raith R, Clydebank
1926–27 Morton, Dundee U
1927–28 Dunfermline Ath, Bo'ness
1928–29 Third Lanark, Raith R
1929–30 St Johnstone, Dundee U
1930–31 Hibernian, East Fife
1931–32 Dundee U, Leith Ath
1932–33 Morton, East Stirling
1933–34 Third Lanark, Cowdenbeath
1934–35 St Mirren, Falkirk
1935–36 Airdrieonians, Ayr U
1936–37 Dunfermline Ath, Albion R
1937–38 Dundee, Morton
1938–39 Queen's Park, Raith R
1946–47 Kilmarnock, Hamilton A
1947–48 Airdrieonians, Queen's Park
1948–49 Morton, Albion R
1949–50 Queen of the S, Stirling A
1950–51 Clyde, Falkirk
1951–52 Morton, Stirling A
1952–53 Motherwell, Third Lanark
1953–54 Airdrieonians, Hamilton A
1954–55 *No clubs relegated*
1955–56 Stirling A, Clyde
1956–57 Dunfermline Ath, Ayr U
1957–58 East Fife, Queen's Park
1958–59 Queen of the S, Falkirk
1959–60 Arbroath, Stirling A
1960–61 Ayr U, Clyde
1961–62 St Johnstone, Stirling A
1962–63 Clyde, Raith R
1963–64 Queen of the S, East Stirling
1964–65 Airdrieonians, Third Lanark
1965–66 Morton, Hamilton A
1966–67 St Mirren, Ayr U
1967–68 Motherwell, Stirling A
1968–69 Falkirk, Arbroath
1969–70 Raith R, Partick T
1970–71 St Mirren, Cowdenbeath
1971–72 Clyde, Dunfermline Ath
1972–73 Kilmarnock, Airdrieonians
1973–74 East Fife, Falkirk

*Season 1921–22 – only 1 club promoted, 3 clubs relegated. ***15pts deducted for failing to field a team.*

**Scottish League championship wins:** Rangers 50, Celtic 38, Aberdeen 4, Hearts 4, Hibernian 4, Dumbarton 2, Dundee 1, Dundee U 1, Kilmarnock 1, Motherwell 1, Third Lanark 1.

*At the end of the 1993–94 season four divisions were created assisted by the admission of two new clubs Ross County and Caledonian Thistle. Only one club was promoted from Division 1 and Division 2. The three relegated from the Premier joined with teams finishing second to seventh in Division 1 to form the new Division 1. Five relegated from Division 1 combined with those who finished second to sixth to form a new Division 2 and the bottom eight in Division 2 linked with the two newcomers to form a new Division 3. At the end of the 1997–98 season the nine clubs remaining in the Premier Division plus the promoted team from Division 1 formed a breakaway Premier League. At the end of the 1999–2000 season two teams were added to the Scottish League. There was no relegation from the Premier League but two promoted from the First Division and three from each of the Second and Third Divisions. One team was relegated from the First Division and one from the Second Division, leaving 12 teams in each division. In season 2002–03, Falkirk were not promoted to the Premier League due to the failure of their ground to meet League Standards. Inverness CT were promoted after a previous refusal in 2003–04 because of ground sharing.*

Celtic's Henrik Larsson heads home the opening goal ahead of Michael Ball of Rangers. (Empics)

# SCOTTISH LEAGUE CUP FINALS 1946–2004

| *Season* | *Winners* | *Runners-up* | *Score* |
|---|---|---|---|
| 1946–47 | Rangers | Aberdeen | 4-0 |
| 1947–48 | East Fife | Falkirk | 4-1 after 0-0 draw |
| 1948–49 | Rangers | Raith R | 2-0 |
| 1949–50 | East Fife | Dunfermline Ath | 3-0 |
| 1950–51 | Motherwell | Hibernian | 3-0 |
| 1951–52 | Dundee | Rangers | 3-2 |
| 1952–53 | Dundee | Kilmarnock | 2-0 |
| 1953–54 | East Fife | Partick T | 3-2 |
| 1954–55 | Hearts | Motherwell | 4-2 |
| 1955–56 | Aberdeen | St Mirren | 2-1 |
| 1956–57 | Celtic | Partick T | 3-0 after 0-0 draw |
| 1957–58 | Celtic | Rangers | 7-1 |
| 1958–59 | Hearts | Partick T | 5-1 |
| 1959–60 | Hearts | Third Lanark | 2-1 |
| 1960–61 | Rangers | Kilmarnock | 2-0 |
| 1961–62 | Rangers | Hearts | 3-1 after 1-1 draw |
| 1962–63 | Hearts | Kilmarnock | 1-0 |
| 1963–64 | Rangers | Morton | 5-0 |
| 1964–65 | Rangers | Celtic | 2-1 |
| 1965–66 | Celtic | Rangers | 2-1 |
| 1966–67 | Celtic | Rangers | 1-0 |
| 1967–68 | Celtic | Dundee | 5-3 |
| 1968–69 | Celtic | Hibernian | 6-2 |
| 1969–70 | Celtic | St Johnstone | 1-0 |
| 1970–71 | Rangers | Celtic | 1-0 |
| 1971–72 | Partick T | Celtic | 4-1 |
| 1972–73 | Hibernian | Celtic | 2-1 |
| 1973–74 | Dundee | Celtic | 1-0 |
| 1974–75 | Celtic | Hibernian | 6-3 |
| 1975–76 | Rangers | Celtic | 1-0 |
| 1976–77 | Aberdeen | Celtic | 2-1 |
| 1977–78 | Rangers | Celtic | 2-1 |
| 1978–79 | Rangers | Aberdeen | 2-1 |
| 1979–80 | Dundee U | Aberdeen | 3-0 after 0-0 draw |
| 1980–81 | Dundee U | Dundee | 3-0 |
| 1981–82 | Rangers | Dundee U | 2-1 |
| 1982–83 | Celtic | Rangers | 2-1 |
| 1983–84 | Rangers | Celtic | 3-2 |
| 1984–85 | Rangers | Dundee U | 1-0 |
| 1985–86 | Aberdeen | Hibernian | 3-0 |
| 1986–87 | Rangers | Celtic | 2-1 |
| 1987–88 | Rangers | Aberdeen | 3-3 |
| | | *(Rangers won 5-3 on penalties)* | |
| 1988–89 | Rangers | Aberdeen | 3-2 |
| 1989–90 | Aberdeen | Rangers | 2-1 |
| 1990–91 | Rangers | Celtic | 2-1 |
| 1991–92 | Hibernian | Dunfermline Ath | 2-0 |
| 1992–93 | Rangers | Aberdeen | 2-1 |
| 1993–94 | Rangers | Hibernian | 2-1 |
| 1994–95 | Raith R | Celtic | 2-2 |
| | | *(Raith R won 6-5 on penalties)* | |
| 1995–96 | Aberdeen | Dundee | 2-0 |
| 1996–97 | Rangers | Hearts | 4-3 |
| 1997–98 | Celtic | Dundee U | 3-0 |
| 1998–99 | Rangers | St Johnstone | 2-1 |
| 1999–2000 | Celtic | Aberdeen | 2-0 |
| 2000–01 | Celtic | Kilmarnock | 3-0 |
| 2001–02 | Rangers | Ayr U | 4-0 |
| 2002–03 | Rangers | Celtic | 2-1 |
| 2003–04 | Livingston | Hibernian | 2-0 |

## SCOTTISH LEAGUE CUP WINS

Rangers 23, Celtic 12, Aberdeen 5, Hearts 4, Dundee 3, East Fife 3, Dundee U 2, Hibernian 2, Livingston 1, Motherwell 1, Partick T 1, Raith R 1.

## APPEARANCES IN FINALS

Rangers 29, Celtic 25, Aberdeen 12, Hibernian 8, Dundee 6, Hearts 6, Dundee U 5, Kilmarnock 4, Partick T 4, East Fife 3, Dunfermline Ath 2, Motherwell 2, Raith R 2, St Johnstone 2, Ayr U 1, Falkirk 1, Livingston 1, Morton 1, St Mirren 1, Third Lanark 1.

# CIS SCOTTISH LEAGUE CUP 2003–04

■ *Denotes player sent off.*

## FIRST ROUND

Tuesday, 2 September 2003

**Arbroath (0) 1** *(Cusick 90)*
**Raith R (0) 0** 879
*Arbroath:* Peat; McMullen (MacAulay), King, Rennie, Browne, Cusick, Herkes (Henslee), Dow, Graham, McGlashan, Kerrigan (Swankie).
*Raith R:* Gonzalez; Talio, Stanic (Blackadder), Brown (Peers), Dennis, Brady, Brittain, Henry, Hawley, Calderon, Evans (Prest).

**Ayr U (0) 1** *(Smyth 75)*
**Dumbarton (1) 2** *(Flannery 37, Bonar 90)* 1048
*Ayr U:* Roy; Lyle, McGrady, Smyth■, Campbell (Mullen) (Conway), Craig, Ferguson S■, Ramsay, Kean (Ferguson A), Whalen, Chaplain.
*Dumbarton:* Grindlay; McKinstry, Brittain, Collins, Dobbins, Smith (Donald), McEwan, Bradley, Obidile, Flannery (Bonar), Boyle.

**Cowdenbeath (0) 3** *(McInally 65, 82, Morris 67)*
**Alloa Ath (0) 0** 288
*Cowdenbeath:* Carlin; Shand, McInally, Gilfillan, McKeown, Mowat, Mauchlen (Gordon), Winter, Brown, Shields (Matheson), Morris.
*Alloa Ath:* McGlynn; Nicolson, Seaton, Valentine, McLaughlin, Ferguson, Walker, Janczyk, Crabbe (Watson), Kelbie (Evans G), Little.

**East Fife (0) 0**
**Airdrie U (1) 2** *(Roberts 38, Ronald 88)* 766
*East Fife:* O'Connor; Russell, Miller (McDonald I), Lumsden, Hall, Kelly (Blair), Mitchell, McDonald G, Deuchar, Fairbairn, Donaldson (Gilbert).
*Airdrie U:* McGeown; Wilson W, Black, McManus, Wilson S, McGowan, Vareille (Ronald), Wilson M, Roberts (Gow), Dunn, Glancy.

**East Stirling (0) 1** *(Rodden 81)*
**Ross Co (0) 2** *(Cowie 67, Mackay 71)* 208
*East Stirling:* Connolly; Maughan, McLaren, Polwart, McCann, McGhee, Livingstone, McAuley (Rodden), Ormiston, Kelly (McCulloch), Baldwin (Boyle).
*Ross Co:* Stewart; McCunnie, Mackay, Tait (Cowie), Malcolm, McCulloch, Rankin, Hannah, Bayne, Hamilton (Winters), Robertson (McGarry).

**Elgin C (0) 0**
**Brechin C (1) 4** *(Fotheringham 33, White 55, Gibson 82, Templeman 85)* 486
*Elgin C:* Pirie; Hind, McMillan, White, Coulter, Allison, Martin, Ogboke (McCormick), Bone, Steele, Campbell.
*Brechin C:* Hay; Miller, McCulloch, Jablonski (McLeish), White, Fotheringham, King, Mitchell (Clark), Hampshire (Templeman), Gibson, Stein.

**Forfar Ath (0) 1** *(Henderson 85)*
**Berwick R (0) 0** 407
*Forfar Ath:* Brown; Lunan (Ogunmade), Lowing, Horn, Stewart, McClune, Byers, Henderson, Tosh, Davidson, Shields.
*Berwick R:* Godfrey; Murie, Hilland, Cowan, McNicoll, Connell, McAllister (Smith D), Bennett, Hutchison, McCutcheon, Hampshire.

**Gretna (1) 1** *(McGuffie 21)*
**Peterhead (0) 2** *(Stewart I 81, 89)* 386
*Gretna:* Mathieson; Birch, Maddison, McGuffie, Irons, Holdsworth, Baldacchino, Galloway, Cameron, Cohen (Cosgrove), Eccles (Skelton).
*Peterhead:* Mathers; Smith, McSkimming, Raeside, Perry, Bain (Johnston), Mackay (Grant), Stewart I, Beith (Duncan), Bavidge, Roddie.

**Hamilton A (2) 3** *(McPhee 26, 30, Aitken 90)*
**Albion R (0) 2** *(McManus 76, McAllister 78)* 824
*Hamilton A:* McEwan; Arbuckle (Fitter), Hodge, Thomson, Whiteford, Sherry, Carrigan, Aitken, Corcoran (Paterson), McPhee, Bailey.
*Albion R:* Fahey; Paterson, Farrell, Smith, Cormack, McCaig, McAllister, McCaul, Diack, McManus, Skinner (McBride).

**Inverness CT (1) 1** *(Ritchie 26)*
**Queen's Park (1) 2** *(Reilly 29, Graham 60)* 968
*Inverness CT:* Brown; Tokely (Proctor), Golabek, Mann, McCaffrey, Duncan, Wilson, Hislop (Thomson), Ritchie, Hart, McBain.
*Queen's Park:* Scrimgour; Sinclair, Ferry, Whelan, Moffat, Fallon, Clark (Gallagher), Reilly, Graham, Canning, McAuley (Carcary).

**Montrose (0) 2** *(Smart 46, Kerrigan 53)*
**Stirling Albion (0) 0** 252
*Montrose:* Butter; Donachie, Ferguson, McQuillan, Simpson, Conway, Webster, Wood (Michie), Smart, Kerrigan, Black (Farnan).
*Stirling Albion:* Hogarth; Nugent, Anderson, McNally, Rowe, Ferguson (McKinnon), Gibson, Devine, McLean, Elliot, O'Brien (Davidson).

**St Mirren (0) 0**
**St Johnstone (0) 2** *(Dods 98, Paatelainen 102)* 2590
*St Mirren:* Hinchcliffe; Van Zanten, Ellis, Broadfoot, MacPherson, Dunn (Twaddle), Gillies, O'Neil, Russell, Lavety (Gemmill), McGinty (Muir).
*St Johnstone:* Cuthbert; Robertson J, Baxter, Bernard, Dods, Maxwell, Parker, Reilly (Robertson M), Paatelainen, Donnelly, Malone.
*aet.*

**Stenhousemuir (1) 1** *(Harty 25)*
**Queen of the S (1) 2** *(Wood 4, Bagan 85)* 415
*Stenhousemuir:* McCulloch W; McCulloch G, Gaughan, Hamilton, McCloy (Johnstone), McKenzie, Lauchlan (McKenna), Donnelly, Mallan, Carr (Brown), Harty.
*Queen of the S:* Dodds; Bagan, McAlpine, Allan, Reid, Thomson, O'Connor, Bowie, Wood (Gibson), Lyle, Burke (Burn).

Wednesday, 3 September 2003

**Morton (1) 2** *(Bottiglieri 37, Bannerman 83)*
**Stranraer (0) 0** 2758
*Morton:* Coyle; Collins, Bottiglieri, MacGregor, Greacan, Maisano M, Millar, Maisano J (Uotinen), Bannerman, Weatherson, Walker (Williams).
*Stranraer:* McCondichie; Swift, Wright, Wingate, Henderson, Jenkins, Finlayson, Aitken (McPhee), Moore (Kerr), Grant (Graham), Sharp.

## SECOND ROUND

Tuesday, 23 September 2003

**Aberdeen (2) 3** *(Zdrilic 15, 45, Hinds 49)*
**Dumbarton (0) 1** *(Grindlay 46)* 3944
*Aberdeen:* Preece; Diamond, McQuilken (Muirhead), Anderson, McNaughton, Heikkinen (Deloumeaux), Tosh, Hart, Sheerin, Zdrilic, Hinds (Bird).
*Dumbarton:* Grindlay; McKinstry, Brittain, Collins, Duffy, Dobbins, Bonar, Donald (Flannery), Obidile, Bradley (Russell), Boyle (Dillon).

**Arbroath (0) 3** *(McGlashan 77, 79, Graham 115)*
**Falkirk (1) 4** *(McMenamin 36, Rodgers 83, Nicholls 108, 119)* 923
*Arbroath:* Peat; McMullen (Newall), Dow, Rennie, Browne, Henslee, Swankie (Durno), Cargill, Graham, McGlashan, Herkes (McAulay).
*Falkirk:* Hill; Lawrie, McPherson, Nicholls, MacKenzie, James (Sharp), O'Neil, Henry, McMenamin, Latapy (Rahim), Rodgers.
*aet.*

**Brechin C (1) 1** *(Hampshire 18)*
**Kilmarnock (0) 0** 813
*Brechin C:* Soutar; Smith, Deas, White, McCulloch S, Jablonski, Miller (Clark), Johnson, Hampshire (Gibson), King (Templeman), Mitchell.
*Kilmarnock:* Dubourdeaux; Shields, Dindeleux, McLaughlin (Murray), Hessey, Fowler (Di Giacomo), Nish (McSwegan), Fulton, Canero, Boyd, Hardie.

**Clyde (0) 2** *(Millen 55, Gilhaney 70)*
**Airdrie U (0) 1** *(Glancy 53)* 1401
*Clyde:* Halliwell; Potter, Mensing, Kernaghan, Fraser, Ross, Hagen, Millen, Harty, McLaughlin, McConalogue (Gilhaney).
*Airdrie U:* McGeown; Docherty, Wilson W (Vareille), Stewart (Singbo), McManus, McGowan, Gow, Wilson M, Roberts, Dunn■, Glancy.

**Dundee U (2) 3** *(McLaren 10, McIntyre 36, 84)*
**Morton (0) 1** *(Weatherson 74)* 5638
*Dundee U:* Bullock; Archibald, Innes, Griffin, Paterson J (Kerr), Duff, McInnes, Miller, McLaren (Samuel), Scotland (Dodds), McIntyre.
*Morton:* Coyle; Collins, Bottiglieri, Macgregor, Greacen, Maisano M, Miller (Hawke), Maisano J, Williams (Uotinen), Weatherson, Walker (Bannerman).

**Forfar Ath (1) 3** *(Henderson 30, Tosh 51, 54)*
**Motherwell (1) 3** *(Craig 31, Lasley 52, Pearson 60)* 1110
*Forfar Ath:* Brown; Lunan (Williams), Rattray, McClune (Lowing), Stewart, Byers, Sellars, Davidson, Tosh, Henderson (Maher), Shields.
*Motherwell:* Marshall; Corrigan, Partridge, Hammell, Craigan, Lasley (Dair), Pearson, Leitch, Adams, Craig (Wright), Clarkson.
*aet; Forfar Ath won 4-2 on penalties.*

**Hibernian (4) 9** *(Dobbie 1, 29, 31, O'Connor 18, 85, Murray 66, Kerrigan (og) 70, Riordan 78, Brown S 86)*
**Montrose (0) 0** 5032
*Hibernian:* Andersson; Murdock, Edge, Orman (Whittaker), Doumbe, Murray, Glass, Brebner, McManus (Brown S), O'Connor, Dobbie (Riordan).
*Montrose:* Hankinson; Donachie, Ferguson, McQuillan, Simpson, Smith G (Sharp), Gibson (Brash), Farnan, Michie, Kerrigan, Black.

**Queen's Park (0) 1** *(Clark 89)*
**Livingston (2) 3** *(Makel 11, 79, Quino 40)* 1011
*Queen's Park:* Scrimgour; Clark, Reilly, Moffat, Sinclair, Fallon, Canning, Harvey (Gallagher), Graham, Whelan (McCallum), McAuley.
*Livingston:* McKenzie; McAllister, McNamee, Rubio, Dorado, Kerr, Makel, Quino (McGovern), O'Brien, Fernandez (Lilley), Pasquinelli (Ipoua).

**Ross Co (0) 0**
**Queen of the S (2) 3** *(Burke 6, 38, Burns 51)* 959
*Ross Co:* Stewart; McCunnie, Mackay, Tait (O'Donnell), Malcolm, McCulloch, Rankin, Cowie, Higgins (Hamilton), Robertson, McGarry (Bayne).
*Queen of the S:* Scott; Paton, McAlpine, Bagan (McColligan), Reid, Thomson, O'Connor, Bowey, Burke (Wood), Burns, Talbot (Aitken).

**St Johnstone (0) 3** *(Donnelly 59, McLaughlin 90, Paatelainen 107)*
**Hamilton A (0) 2** *(Carrigan 73, Corcoran 77)* 1471
*St Johnstone:* Cuthbert; Robertson J, Forsyth, Bernard, Dods, Maxwell, Parker (Paatelainen), Reilly, Robertson M, Donnelly (MacDonald), McLaughlin (Malone).
*Hamilton A:* McEwan; Whiteford, Hodge, Thomson, Lumsden (Corcoran), Sherry (Paterson), Carrigan, Aitken, Bailey (Forbes), McPhee, Convery.
*aet.*

Wednesday, 24 September 2003

**Dunfermline Ath (0) 2** *(Crawford 55, Brewster 65)*
**Cowdenbeath (0) 0** 3582
*Dunfermline Ath:* Stillie; Bullen, Tod, Skerla, Dempsey (Byrne), Darren Young, Nicholson, Mason, Kilgannon, Crawford, Brewster (Mehmet).
*Cowdenbeath:* Carlin; Mowat, McInally, Gilfillan, McKeown, Ritchie, Shields (Fusco), Winter, Brown, Gordon, Buchanan (Mauchlen).

**Peterhead (1) 2** *(Mackay 30, Stewart I 116)*
**Partick T (1) 2** *(Mitchell 3, Milne 108)* 1352
*Peterhead:* Mathers; McGuiness (Smith), McSkimming, Raeside, Perry, Bain (Stewart G), Mackay, Stewart I, Grant, Johnston, Beith.
*Partick T:* Arthur; Lilley (Bonnes), Murray, Whyte, Milne, Taylor, Rowson, Mitchell, Waddell (Forrest), Grady (Britton), Thomson.
*aet; Partick T won 4-3 on penalties.*

## THIRD ROUND

Tuesday, 28 October 2003

**Aberdeen (4) 5** *(Tosh 10, Booth 12, Muirhead 36, Sheerin 39, Hinds 84)*
**Brechin C (0) 0** 3631
*Aberdeen:* Preece; McGuire (Rutkiewicz), Deloumeaux, Anderson, Muirhead, Heikkenen (Tiernan), Tosh, Clark (Hinds), Sheerin, Booth, Mackie.
*Brechin C:* Soutar; Smith (Miller), McCulloch S (McCulloch M), White, Deas, Fotheringham, King, Mitchell, Hampshire, Jablonski, Stein (Templeman).

**Hibernian (2) 2** *(Riordan 11, 23)*
**Queen of the S (0) 1** *(Burke 89)* 7613
*Hibernian:* Andersson; Murdock■, Edge (Reid), Orman, Doumbe, Murray, Glass, Brebner (Whittaker), Riordan, O'Connor, Glass.
*Queen of the S:* Scott; Paton, Aitken, Bagan, Reid, Thomson, O'Connor, Bowey, Burke, Burns, McAlpine (Wood).

**Rangers (2) 6** *(Nerlinger 15, 53, 69, Lovenkrands 23, Capucho 49, Ostenstad 74)*
**Forfar Ath (0) 0** 26,330
*Rangers:* McGregor; Ross (Duffy), Moore, Khizanishvili, Vanoli (Ricksen), Emerson, Hughes, Nerlinger, Capucho, Ostenstad, Lovenkrands (Burke).
*Forfar Ath:* Brown; Lunan (Maher), Rattray, Horn (McClune), Stewart (Lowing), Byers, Sellars, Davidson, Tosh, Henderson, Shields.

**St Johnstone (1) 3** *(Donnelly 8, Dods 68, MacDonald 72)*
**Dunfermline Ath (0) 2** *(Crawford 80, Darren Young 83)* 2680
*St Johnstone:* Cuthbert; Robertson J, Forsyth, Bernard, Dods, Maxwell, MacDonald (Hay), Robertson M, Parker, Donnelly, McLaughlin (Malone).
*Dunfermline Ath:* Stillie; Bullen (Dempsey), Thomson SM, Grondin (Mehmet), Wilson, Darren Young, Nicholson, Mason, Kilgannon (Labonte), Crawford, Brewster.

Wednesday, 29 October 2003

**Clyde (1) 2** *(Keogh 2, Gilhaney 78)*
**Dundee (1) 5** *(Novo 4, Wilkie 66, Ravanelli 71, 74, 76)* 1701
*Clyde:* Halliwell; Mensing, McLaughlin, Kernaghan, Fraser, Ross (Marshall), Hagen, Millen, Keogh, Gibson (Gilhaney), McConalogue (Harty).
*Dundee:* Speroni; Mackay, Macdonald, Mair, Willkie, Smith, Burley (Fotheringham), Brady, Sara, Caballero (Ravanelli), Novo (Linn).

**Dundee U (0) 0**
**Livingston (1) 1** *(Gallacher (og) 19)* 2899
*Dundee U:* Gallacher; Archibald, Innes, McCracken, Wilson (Samuel), Paterson J (Robson), Kerr, Easton, McLaren, Dodds (Coyle), McIntyre.
*Livingston:* McKenzie; McNamee, McAllister (O'Brien), Rubio, Andrews, Dorado, Makel (Quinn), Kerr, Lovell, Fernandez, Lilley.

**Hearts (0) 2** *(De Vries 53, Kirk 85)*
**Falkirk (0) 1** *(Latapy 58)* 8687
*Hearts:* Gordon; McKenna, Kisnorbo, Pressley, Neilson, Valois, Severin, Simmons (Wyness), Hartley, De Vries, Kirk.
*Falkirk:* Ferguson; Lawrie, McPherson, MacKenzie, Hughes, James, Sharp, Nicholls (McAnespie), Xausa, Latapy (Rahim), McMenamin (Colquhoun).

**Partick T (0) 0**
**Celtic (1) 2** *(Beattie 30, Smith 76)* 5700
*Partick T:* Arthur; Anis, Murray, Whyte, Lilley, Milne, Ross A, Fleming (Taylor), McBride (Howie), Grady (Gemmell), Mitchell.
*Celtic:* Marshall; Mjällby, Kennedy, McNamara (Laursen), Sylla, Crainey, Gray, Lambert (Guppy), Smith, Maloney, Beattie.

## QUARTER-FINALS

Tuesday, 2 December 2003

**Aberdeen (1) 2** *(Tosh 33, 59)*
**Livingston (1) 3** *(Lilley 15, Pasqinelli 47, Makel 96)* 6090
*Aberdeen:* Preece; Diamond, Deloumeaux, Anderson, McNaughton (Clark), Heikkinen (Sheerin), Tosh, Rutkiewicz, Muirhead (Mackie), Booth, Zdrilic.
*Livingston:* McKenzie; McNamee (McGovern), McAllister (Queno), Rubio, Andrews, Dorado, Makel, O'Brien, Lovell, Fernandez (Pasquinelli), Lilley.
*aet.*

Wednesday, 3 December 2003

**Dundee (0) 1** *(Linn 107)*
**Hearts (0) 0** 7130
*Dundee:* Speroni; Mackay, Hernandez, Mair, Wilkie, Smith, Fotheringham, Rae (Sancho), Brady, Lovell (Linn), Novo.
*Hearts:* Gordon; Maybury, Kisnorbo, Webster, Neilson, Macfarlane, Stamp (Valois), Wyness (Severin), Hartley, De Vries (McKenna), Kirk.
*aet.*

**Rangers (1) 3** *(Burke16, Ostenstad 59, Mols 90)*
**St Johnstone (0) 0** 28,395
*Rangers:* McGregor; Ricksen, Malcolm, Khizanishvili, Vanoli, Hughes, Emerson, Burke (Ross), Ostenstad (Capucho), Mols, Lovenkrands.
*St Johnstone:* Cuthbert; Robertson J, Forsyth, Bernard, Dods, Maxwell, Parker (Paatelainen), Robertson M (Stevenson), MacDonald, Donnelly, McLaughlin (Malone).

Saturday, 20 December 2003

**Hibernian (0) 2** *(Brebner 62, Thomson 81)*
**Celtic (0) 1** *(Varga 56)* 9246
*Hibernian:* Andersson; Baillie, Smith, Whittaker, Doumbe, Thomson, Brebner, McManus (Dobbie), Riordan, O'Connor, Brown S.
*Celtic:* Douglas; Kennedy, Varga, Balde, Crainey, Thompson, Miller, Lambert (Beattie), Sutton (Maloney), Larsson, Wallace.

## SEMI-FINALS (at Easter Road)

Tuesday, 3 February 2004

**Dundee (0) 0**
**Livingston (0) 1** *(Lilley 89)* 7231
*Dundee:* Speroni; Mackay, Hernandez, Mair, Sancho, Smith, Fotheringham, Barrett, Brady, Lovell (Milne), Novo.
*Livingston:* McKenzie; McNamee, McAllister, Rubio (Pasquinelli), Andrews, Dorado, Makel, O'Brien, Lovell, Fernandez, Lilley.

Thursday, 5 February 2004

**Hibernian (0) 1** *(Dobbie 77)*
**Rangers (1) 1** *(Mols 39)* 27,954
*Hibernian:* Andersson; Murdock, Edge (Dobbie), Caldwell, Doumbe, Thomson, Wiss (Whittaker), Reid (McManus), Riordan, O'Connor, Brown S.
*Rangers:* Klos; Ricksen, Moore, de Boer F, Ball, Ross (Vanoli), Arteta (Khizanishvili), Nerlinger, de Boer R (Ostenstad), Mols, Arveladze.
*aet; Hibernian won 4-3 on penalties.*

## FINAL

Sunday, 14 March 2004

(at Hampden Park)

**Livingston (0) 2** *(Lilley 49, McAllister 52)*
**Hibernian (0) 0** 45,443
*Livingston:* McKenzie; McNamee (McLaughlin), McAllister, Rubio, Andrews, Dorado, Makel, O'Brien (McGovern), Lovell, Fernandez (Pasquinelli), Lilley.
*Hibernian:* Andersson; Murdock, Smith (McManus), Edge, Doumbe, Caldwell, Thomson, Reid (Dobbie), Riordan, O'Connor, Brown S.
*Referee:* Willie Young.

Jamie McAllister of Livingston scores the second goal against Hibernian in the 2-0 CIS Scottish League Cup Final win at Hampden Park. (Actionimages)

# BELL'S LEAGUE CHALLENGE 2003–04

■ *Denotes player sent off.*

## FIRST ROUND

Saturday, 2 August 2003

**Airdrie U (0) 2** *(McKeown 55, 61)*
**Montrose (0) 0** 1151
*Airdrie U:* McGeown; Wilson W, Dunn (Glancy), Stewart, McManus, McGowan, Vareille, Wilson M, McKeown, Docherty (Gow), Roberts (Ronald).
*Montrose:* Butter; Donachie, Ferguson, Farnan, Simpson, Smith G, Webster (Sharp), Gibson, Smart (Henderson), Wood, Thomson.

**Albion R (0) 1** *(Diack 82)*
**East Fife (0) 0** 250
*Albion R:* Fahey; Paterson (Diack), Stirling, Smith, Cormack, McCaig, McAllister (Connolly), Farrell, McManus (Robertson), McCaul, Mercer.
*East Fife:* O'Connor; Kelly, Miller, Mortimer, Hall, McDonald, McMillan, Byle, Deuchar, Stewart (Fairbairn), Donaldson (Mitchell).

**Alloa Ath (0) 1** *(Callaghan 69 (pen))*
**Clyde (1) 2** *(McConalogue 44, Fraser 90)* 633
*Alloa Ath:* McGlynn; Ferguson, McLaughlin (Elliot), Valentine, McGowan, Hamilton, Walker, Kelbie (Evans G), Crabbe, Callaghan, Little.
*Clyde:* Halliwell■; Mensing, McLaughlin, Potter, Fraser, Ross, Hagen, Millen, Keogh, Harty (Gilhaney), McConalogue (Clark).

**Ayr U (0) 1** *(Kean 48)*
**Stirling Albion (1) 2** *(Elliot 14, 108)* 1115
*Ayr U:* Roy; Smyth, Kerr, Latta, Campbell, Burgess (Lyle), Chaplain, Black, Kean, Whalen, McColl (Conway).
*Stirling Albion:* Hogarth; Nugent, Anderson, McNally, Rowe, Hay, Ferguson (McKinnon), Devine, McLean (Beveridge), Elliot, O'Brien (Wilson).
*aet.*

**Brechin C (0) 1** *(King 75)*
**Falkirk (0) 0** 938
*Brechin C:* Budinauckas; Davidson, Black (McCulloch S), White, Deas, Fotheringham, King (Stein), Johnson, Templeman, Shields (Gibson), Mitchell.
*Falkirk:* Hill; Lawrie, McPherson, MacKenzie, Hughes, Sharp, Henry, Christie (McSween), Lee, McMenamin (Rodgers), Scally.

**Cowdenbeath (1) 1** *(Brown 14)*
**Ross Co (1) 2** *(Campbell (og) 22, Rankin 80)* 325
*Cowdenbeath:* Carlin; Shand, McInally, Campbell, McKeown, Mowat (Matheson), Morris (Buchanan), Winter, Brown, Gordon, Fallon (Gilfillan).
*Ross Co:* Stewart (Fridge); McCunnie, Mackay, Tait (O'Donnell), Malcolm, McCulloch, Rankin, Hannah, Higgins (Bayne), Robertson, Winter.

**East Stirling (0) 2** *(Kelly 58, Baldwin 83)*
**Raith R (1) 5** *(Sutton 24, 69, Peers 49, Prest 65, Stanley 88)* 556
*East Stirling:* Todd C; Maughan, Reid, McGhee, McLaren, Livingstone, Mackay, Polwart (Penman), Baldwin, Kelly, Ormiston.
*Raith R:* Gonzalez; Paquito, Dennis, Patino, Calderon, Brittain (Blackadder), Brady, Stanley, Peers, Sutton (Martin), Prest (Brown).

**Forfar Ath (0) 4** *(Shields 63, Tosh 66, Davidson 67, Maher 90)*
**Elgin C (0) 0** 444
*Forfar Ath:* Ferry; Rattray, Lowing, Horn, Stewart, McClune (Maher), Lunan, Sellars, Tosh (Williams), Davidson, Shields (Taylor).
*Elgin C:* Pirie; Hind, Gallagher, White, Coulter, Allison, Martin, McLean C (McLean N), Bone (McCormick), Steele, Murphy (McMullan).

**Gretna (0) 0**
**Inverness CT (1) 5** *(Bingham 22, Hislop 49, Ritchie 50, Hart 60, 62)* 628
*Gretna:* Mathieson; Cleeland (Gordon), Skelton, Robb, Neill, Holdsworth, Henney, Galloway, Cameron, Cohen, Allen (Skinner).
*Inverness CT:* Brown; Tokely (Proctor), Golabek, Mann, McCaffrey, Duncan, Hart, Hislop (Christie), Ritchie (Thomson), McBain, Bingham.

**Hamilton A (1) 2** *(Aitken 38, McPhee 77)*
**St Johnstone (0) 3** *(Paatelainen 59, Parker 64, Donnelly 102)* 1097
*Hamilton A:* McEwan; Sutter (Whiteford), Forbes (Maxwell), Thomson, Lumsden, Sherry (Ferguson), Carrigan, Aitken, Convery, McPhee, Corcoran.
*St Johnstone:* Cuthbert; Robertson, Forsyth■, Stevenson (Baxter), Dodds, Maxwell, Parker, Reilly, Paatelainen, Fotheringham, McLaughlin (Donnelly).
*aet.*

**Morton (3) 4** *(Weatherson 4 (pen), 31, 90, Hawke 12)*
**Arbroath (1) 3** *(McGlashan 8, 89, Graham 66)* 2241
*Morton:* Coyle; Collins, MacGregor, Henderson, Bottiglieri, Bannerman (McDonald), Millar, Maisano J (Uotinen), Hawke (Cannie), Weatherson, Walker.
*Arbroath:* Peat; McAulay (McMullan), Dow, Denholm, King, Cargill, Herkes, Henslee (Cusick), McGlashan, Graham, Swankie (Kerrigan).

**St Mirren (0) 3** *(Crilly 63, McGinty 88 (pen), O'Neil 95)*
**Queen's Park (2) 2** *(Clark 14, Graham 19)* 1868
*St Mirren:* Hinchcliffe; Van Zanten (O'Neil), Ellis, McGowne, MacPherson, Broadfoot, Gillies (McHarg), Crilly, McGinty, McKnight (Dunn), Lappin.
*Queen's Park:* Scrimgour; Dunning (Canning), McCallum (Ferry), Sinclair, Agostini, Fallon, Clark, Kettlewell, Graham, Reilly, Menelaws (McAuley).
*aet.*

**Stenhousemuir (0) 0**
**Peterhead (0) 3** *(Raeside 74, Grant 76, Stewart I 85)* 256
*Stenhousemuir:* McCulloch W; Hamilton, Smith■, McCulloch G, Gaughan, Booth, McGowan (Harty), McKenzie, Brown (Johnstone), McDowell, Laughlan.
*Peterhead:* Mathers; McGuiness (Johnston), McSkimming, Raeside, Perry, Bain, Tindal, Bavidge, Grant (Stewart I), Duncan (Stewart G), Roddie.

**Stranraer (1) 2** *(Moore 28, 68)*
**Queen of the S (0) 1** *(Lyle 80)* 828
*Stranraer:* McCondichie; Swift, Wright, Wingate, Henderson, Jenkins, Finlayson, McAllister, Moore (Grant), Kerr (Turnbull), Sharp.
*Queen of the S:* Dodds; Paton, Hodge, Bagan, Aitken, Thomson, O'Connor, Bowey, Burke (Gibson), Lyle, McAlpine.

## SECOND ROUND

Tuesday, 12 August 2003

**Brechin C (2) 3** *(Templeman 5, Johnston 42, Fotheringham 88 (pen))*
**Stirling Albion (0) 1** *(McLean 62)* 468
*Brechin C:* Budinauckas; Millar M, McCulloch S■, Johnston, White, Fotheringham, King (Davidson), McCulloch M, Templeman, Clark (Mitchell), Stein (Gibson).
*Stirling Albion:* Hogarth; Nugent, Anderson, Scotland (O'Brien), Rowe, Hay (Wilson), Ferguson, McLean (Davidson), Elliot, Devine, Smith.

**Clyde (0) 0**
**St Johnstone (0) 1** *(Parker 67)* 1521
*Clyde:* Halliwell; Mensing, McLaughlin, Potter, Fraser, Ross, Hagen, Millen, Keogh (Gilhaney), Harty, McConalogue (Baird).
*St Johnstone:* Cuthbert; Robertson J (Baxter), Lovering (Stevenson), Donnelly, Dods, Maxwell, Parker, Reilly, Paatelainen, Bernard, Malone.

**Forfar Ath (1) 4** *(Shields 40, 66, 97, Maher 96)*
**Albion R (1) 2** *(McManus 45, Diack 51)* 423
*Forfar Ath:* Brown; Rattray, Florence (Lowing), Horn, Stewart, McClune, Byers (Maher), Sellars, Taylor (Williams), Davidson, Shields.
*Albion R:* Fahey; Paterson, Stirling, McCaul, Cormack (Selkirk), McCaig, McBride (Connelly■), Diack (McAllister), Yardley, McManus, Mercer.
*aet.*

**Morton (0) 1** *(Maisano J 46)*
**Airdrie U (0) 2** *(Vareille 60, Roberts 70)* 3317
*Morton:* Coyle; Collins, Bottiglieri (Henderson), MacGregor■, Greacen, Maisano M, Bannerman (Millar), Maisano J (Hawke), Williams, Weatherson, Walker.
*Airdrie U:* McGeown; Docherty, Black (Wilson S), Stewart, McManus■, McGowan, Vareille (Glancy), Wilson M, McKeown (Ronald), Gow, Roberts.

**Peterhead (0) 1** *(Stewart D 86)*
**Inverness CT (1) 2** *(Hislop 14, 82)* 886
*Peterhead:* Mathers; Tindal, Good, Duncan (Johnston), Perry, Bayne, Mackay, Stewart I, Grant (Stewart G), Bavidge (Stewart D), Roddie.
*Inverness CT:* Brown; Tokely, Golabek, Mann, McCaffrey, Duncan, Hart, Hislop, Bingham (Ritchie), Christie (Thomson), McBain.

**Raith R (0) 2** *(Calderon 62, Sutton 80)*
**Stranraer (0) 0** 1396
*Raith R:* Gonzalez; Patino, Talio (Calderon■), Brady, Brown, Stanley, Peers (Blackadder), Ortiz Rivas, Sutton, Brittain, Prest (McCann).
*Stranraer:* McCondichie; Swift, Wright (Guy) (Turnbull), Wingate, Henderson, Jenkins, Finlayson, McAllister (Aitken), Moore, Kerr, Sharp.

**Ross Co (1) 5** *(Winters 30, 82, 85, Hamilton 71, 75)*
**Dumbarton (0) 0** 861
*Ross Co:* Stewart; McCunnie (Campbell), Mackay, O'Donnell (Tait), Malcolm, Webb, Cowie, Hannah, Hamilton, Gethins (Higgins), Winters.
*Dumbarton:* Grindlay; McKinstry, Brittain, Collins, Duffy, Smith, Bonar, Bradley, Flannery, Russell (Herd) (English), Dillon (Boyle).

**St Mirren (1) 2** *(Gillies 32 (pen), O'Neil 75)*
**Berwick R (0) 1** *(McNicoll 85)* 1747
*St Mirren:* Hinchcliffe; MacPherson, Ellis, Van Zanten, McWilliam, Crilly, Gillies, O'Neil, McGinty (Gemmill), Russell (Dunn), Lappin.
*Berwick R:* Inglis; Murie, Neill A, Bennett, McNicoll, Forrest, Connelly (McAllister), Connell, Hampshire, McCormick (Blackley), Hutchison (Noon).

## QUARTER-FINALS

Tuesday, 26 August 2003

**Forfar Ath (0) 0**
**Airdrie U (0) 2** *(Wilson S 54, Dunn 74)* 752
*Forfar Ath:* Brown; Rattray, Lowing (Taylor), Vella, Stewart, McClune, Lunan (Maher), Byres■, Tosh, Davidson, Shields.
*Airdrie U:* McGeown; McManus (Wilson W), Black, Stewart, Wilson S, McGowan, Vareille (Ronald), Wilson M, Roberts, Dunn, Glancy (Gow).

**Inverness CT (0) 1** *(Hislop 49)*
**Ross Co (0) 0** 2631
*Inverness CT:* Brown; Tokely, Golabek, Mann, McCaffrey, Duncan, Hart, Hislop (Proctor), Ritchie, McBain, Bingham (Thomson).
*Ross Co:* Stewart; McCunnie, Mackay, Tait, Malcolm, McCulloch, Rankin, Hannah, Higgins (Bayne), Hamilton (Gethins), Winters (O'Donnell).

**Raith R (2) 3** *(Prest 27, 62, Henry 33)*
**St Mirren (1) 2** *(Russell 40, O'Neil 74)* 1948
*Raith R:* Gonzalez; Patino, Stanic, Brittain, Brown, Henry, Stanley, Rivas, Sutton, Blackadder, Prest (Boyle).
*St Mirren:* Hinchcliffe; Van Zanten (McGinty), Ellis, McGowne (Dempsie), Broadfoot, Crilly, Gillies, Dunn, Russell, O'Neil, Twaddle (Gemmill).

**St Johnstone (0) 1** *(Forsyth 89)*
**Brechin C (2) 2** *(Templeman 3, Fotheringham 34)* 1919
*St Johnstone:* Cuthbert; Robertson, Forsyth, Donnelly, Dods (Baxter), Maxwell, Parker, Fotheringham (Hay), Paatelainen, Bernard, Malone.
*Brechin C:* Hay; Davidson, Mitchell, White, Deas, Fotheringham, Millar, Jablonski, Gibson (Shields), Templeman (Jackson), McCulloch M (King).

## SEMI-FINALS

Tuesday, 16 September 2003

**Raith R (0) 0**
**Inverness CT (3) 4** *(Wilson 28, 81, Ritchie 30, 43)* 2110
*Raith R:* Gonzalez; Patino, Stanic, Brady (Calderon), Dennis, Brittain (Hawley), Stanley, Ortiz Rivas, Sutton, Blackadder (Robb), Prest.
*Inverness CT:* Brown; Proctor, Golabek, Mann (Munro), McCaffrey, Duncan, Wilson, McBain, Ritchie (Hislop), Hart, Bingham (Thomson).

Wednesday, 17 September 2003

**Brechin C (1) 1** *(White 15)*
**Airdrie U (1) 2** *(Dunn 35, Gow 112)* 803
*Brechin C:* Soutar; Millar, Deas, McCulloch, White, Fotheringham (Gibson), Mitchell (Stein), Jablonski (King), Templeman, Hampshire, Johnston.
*Airdrie U:* McGeown; Wilson W, Black (Singbo), McManus, Wilson S (Docherty), McGowan, Vareille■, Wilson M, Roberts, Dunn, Glancy (Gow).
*aet.*

## FINAL (at McDiarmid Park)

Sunday, 26 October 2003

**Inverness CT (0) 2** *(Bingham 78, Hislop 89)*
**Airdrie U (0) 0** 5428
*Inverness CT:* Brown; Tokely, Golabek, Mann, McCaffrey, Duncan, Wilson, Hart (Keogh), Ritchie (Hislop), McBain, Bingham (Thomson).
*Airdrie U:* McGeown; Docherty (Singbo), Wilson W, Stewart, McManus, Wilson S (Ronald), Vareille (McKeown S), Wilson M, Roberts, Dunn, Gow.
*Referee:* Willie Young.

# LEAGUE CHALLENGE FINALS 1991–2004

| *Year* | *Winners* | *Runners-up* | *Score* |
|---|---|---|---|
| 1991 | Dundee | Ayr U | 3-2 |
| 1992 | Hamilton A | Ayr U | 1-0 |
| 1993 | Hamilton A | Morton | 3-2 |
| 1994 | St Mirren | Falkirk | 9-3 |
| 1995 | Airdrieonians | Dundee | 3-2 |
| 1996 | Stenhousemuir | Dundee U | 0-0 |
| | *(Stenhousemuir won 5-4 on penalties)* | | |
| 1997 | Stranraer | St Johnstone | 1-0 |
| 1998 | Falkirk 1 Qeeen of the South 0 | | |
| 1999 | no competition | | |
| 2000 | Alloa | Inverness CT | 4-4 |
| | *(Alloa won 5-4 on penalties)* | | |
| 2001 | Airdrieonians | Livingston | 2-2 |
| | *(Airdrieonians won 3-2 on penalties)* | | |
| 2002 | Airdrieonians | Alloa | 2-1 |
| 2003 | Queen of the S | Brechin C | 2-0 |
| 2004 | Inverness CT | Airdrie U | 2-0 |

# SCOTTISH CUP FINALS 1874–2004

| *Year* | *Winners* | *Runners-up* | *Score* |
|---|---|---|---|
| 1874 | Queen's Park | Clydesdale | 2-0 |
| 1875 | Queen's Park | Renton | 3-0 |
| 1876 | Queen's Park | Third Lanark | 2-0 after 1-1 draw |
| 1877 | Vale of Leven | Rangers | 3-2 after 0-0 and 1-1 draws |
| 1878 | Vale of Leven | Third Lanark | 1-0 |
| 1879 | Vale of Leven* | Rangers | |
| 1880 | Queen's Park | Thornlibank | 3-0 |
| 1881 | Queen's Park† | Dumbarton | 3-1 |
| 1882 | Queen's Park | Dumbarton | 4-1 after 2-2 draw |
| 1883 | Dumbarton | Vale of Leven | 2-1 after 2-2 draw |
| 1884 | Queen's Park‡ | Vale of Leven | |
| 1885 | Renton | Vale of Leven | 3-1 after 0-0 draw |
| 1886 | Queen's Park | Renton | 3-1 |
| 1887 | Hibernian | Dumbarton | 2-1 |
| 1888 | Renton | Cambuslang | 6-1 |
| 1889 | Third Lanark§ | Celtic | 2-1 |
| 1890 | Queen's Park | Vale of Leven | 2-1 after 1-1 draw |
| 1891 | Hearts | Dumbarton | 1-0 |
| 1892 | Celtic¶ | Queen's Park | 5-1 |
| 1893 | Queen's Park | Celtic | 2-1 |
| 1894 | Rangers | Celtic | 3-1 |
| 1895 | St Bernard's | Renton | 2-1 |
| 1896 | Hearts | Hibernian | 3-1 |
| 1897 | Rangers | Dumbarton | 5-1 |
| 1898 | Rangers | Kilmarnock | 2-0 |
| 1899 | Celtic | Rangers | 2-0 |
| 1900 | Celtic | Queen's Park | 4-3 |
| 1901 | Hearts | Celtic | 4-3 |
| 1902 | Hibernian | Celtic | 1-0 |
| 1903 | Rangers | Hearts | 2-0 after 1-1 and 0-0 draws |
| 1904 | Celtic | Rangers | 3-2 |
| 1905 | Third Lanark | Rangers | 3-1 after 0-0 draw |
| 1906 | Hearts | Third Lanark | 1-0 |
| 1907 | Celtic | Hearts | 3-0 |
| 1908 | Celtic | St Mirren | 5-1 |
| 1909 | •• | | |
| 1910 | Dundee | Clyde | 2-1 after 2-2 and 0-0 draws |
| 1911 | Celtic | Hamilton A | 2-0 after 0-0 draw |
| 1912 | Celtic | Clyde | 2-0 |
| 1913 | Falkirk | Raith R | 2-0 |
| 1914 | Celtic | Hibernian | 4-1 after 0-0 draw |
| 1920 | Kilmarnock | Albion R | 3-2 |
| 1921 | Partick T | Rangers | 1-0 |
| 1922 | Morton | Rangers | 1-0 |
| 1923 | Celtic | Hibernian | 1-0 |
| 1924 | Airdrieonians | Hibernian | 2-0 |
| 1925 | Celtic | Dundee | 2-1 |
| 1926 | St Mirren | Celtic | 2-0 |
| 1927 | Celtic | East Fife | 3-1 |
| 1928 | Rangers | Celtic | 4-0 |
| 1929 | Kilmarnock | Rangers | 2-0 |
| 1930 | Rangers | Partick T | 2-1 after 0-0 draw |
| 1931 | Celtic | Motherwell | 4-2 after 2-2 draw |
| 1932 | Rangers | Kilmarnock | 3-0 after 1-1 draw |
| 1933 | Celtic | Motherwell | 1-0 |
| 1934 | Rangers | St Mirren | 5-0 |
| 1935 | Rangers | Hamilton A | 2-1 |
| 1936 | Rangers | Third Lanark | 1-0 |
| 1937 | Celtic | Aberdeen | 2-1 |
| 1938 | East Fife | Kilmarnock | 4-2 after 1-1 draw |
| 1939 | Clyde | Motherwell | 4-0 |
| 1947 | Aberdeen | Hibernian | 2-1 |
| 1948 | Rangers | Morton | 1-0 after 1-1 draw |
| 1949 | Rangers | Clyde | 4-1 |
| 1950 | Rangers | East Fife | 3-0 |
| 1951 | Celtic | Motherwell | 1-0 |
| 1952 | Motherwell | Dundee | 4-0 |
| 1953 | Rangers | Aberdeen | 1-0 after 1-1 draw |
| 1954 | Celtic | Aberdeen | 2-1 |
| 1955 | Clyde | Celtic | 1-0 after 1-1 draw |
| 1956 | Hearts | Celtic | 3-1 |
| 1957 | Falkirk | Kilmarnock | 2-1 after 1-1 draw |
| 1958 | Clyde | Hibernian | 1-0 |
| 1959 | St Mirren | Aberdeen | 3-1 |
| 1960 | Rangers | Kilmarnock | 2-0 |
| 1961 | Dunfermline Ath | Celtic | 2-0 after 0-0 draw |
| 1962 | Rangers | St Mirren | 2-0 |
| 1963 | Rangers | Celtic | 3-0 after 1-1 draw |
| 1964 | Rangers | Dundee | 3-1 |
| 1965 | Celtic | Dunfermline Ath | 3-2 |
| 1966 | Rangers | Celtic | 1-0 after 0-0 draw |
| 1967 | Celtic | Aberdeen | 2-0 |
| 1968 | Dunfermline Ath | Hearts | 3-1 |
| 1969 | Celtic | Rangers | 4-0 |
| 1970 | Aberdeen | Celtic | 3-1 |

| *Year* | *Winners* | *Runners-up* | *Score* |
|---|---|---|---|
| 1971 | Celtic | Rangers | 2-1 after 1-1 draw |
| 1972 | Celtic | Hibernian | 6-1 |
| 1973 | Rangers | Celtic | 3-2 |
| 1974 | Celtic | Dundee U | 3-0 |
| 1975 | Celtic | Airdrieonians | 3-1 |
| 1976 | Rangers | Hearts | 3-1 |
| 1977 | Celtic | Rangers | 1-0 |
| 1978 | Rangers | Aberdeen | 2-1 |
| 1979 | Rangers | Hibernian | 3-2 after 0-0 and 0-0 draws |
| 1980 | Celtic | Rangers | 1-0 |
| 1981 | Rangers | Dundee U | 4-1 after 0-0 draw |
| 1982 | Aberdeen | Rangers | 4-1 (aet) |
| 1983 | Aberdeen | Rangers | 1-0 (aet) |
| 1984 | Aberdeen | Celtic | 2-1 (aet) |
| 1985 | Celtic | Dundee U | 2-1 |
| 1986 | Aberdeen | Hearts | 3-0 |
| 1987 | St Mirren | Dundee U | 1-0 (aet) |
| 1988 | Celtic | Dundee U | 2-1 |
| 1989 | Celtic | Rangers | 1-0 |
| 1990 | Aberdeen | Celtic | 0-0 (aet) |
| | | *(Aberdeen won 9-8 on penalties)* | |
| 1991 | Motherwell | Dundee U | 4-3 (aet) |
| 1992 | Rangers | Airdrieonians | 2-1 |
| 1993 | Rangers | Aberdeen | 2-1 |
| 1994 | Dundee U | Rangers | 1-0 |
| 1995 | Celtic | Airdrieonians | 1-0 |
| 1996 | Rangers | Hearts | 5-1 |
| 1997 | Kilmarnock | Falkirk | 1-0 |
| 1998 | Hearts | Rangers | 2-1 |
| 1999 | Rangers | Celtic | 1-0 |
| 2000 | Rangers | Aberdeen | 4-0 |
| 2001 | Celtic | Hibernian | 3-0 |
| 2002 | Rangers | Celtic | 3-2 |
| 2003 | Rangers | Dundee | 1-0 |
| 2004 | Celtic | Dunfermline Ath | 3-1 |

*Vale of Leven awarded cup, Rangers failing to appear for replay after 1-1 draw.
†After Dumbarton protested the first game, which Queen's Park won 2-1.
‡Queen's Park awarded cup, Vale of Leven failing to appear.
§Replay by order of Scottish FA because of playing conditions in first match, won 3-0 by Third Lanark.
¶After mutually protested game which Celtic won 1-0.
••Owing to riot, the cup was withheld after two drawn games – between Celtic and Rangers 2-2 and 1-1.

## SCOTTISH CUP WINS

Celtic 32, Rangers 31, Queen's Park 10, Aberdeen 7, Hearts 6, Clyde 3, Kilmarnock 3, St Mirren 3, Vale of Leven 3, Dunfermline Ath 2, Falkirk 2, Hibernian 2, Motherwell 2, Renton 2, Third Lanark 2, Airdrieonians 1, Dumbarton 1, Dundee 1, Dundee U 1, East Fife 1, Morton 1, Partick T 1, St Bernard's 1.

## APPEARANCES IN FINAL

Celtic 51, Rangers 48, Aberdeen 15, Queen's Park 12, Hearts 12, Hibernian 11, Kilmarnock 8, Vale of Leven 7, Clyde 6, Dumbarton 6, Dundee U 7, Motherwell 6, St Mirren 6, Third Lanark 6, Dundee 5, Renton 5, Airdrieonians 4, Dunfermline Ath 4, East Fife 3, Falkirk 3, Hamilton A 2, Morton 2, Partick T 2, Albion R 1, Cambuslang 1, Clydesdale 1, Raith R 1, St Bernard's 1, Thornlibank 1.

# TENNENT'S SCOTTISH CUP 2003–04

▪ *Denotes player sent off.*

## FIRST ROUND

Saturday, 22 November 2003

**Clachnacuddin (0) 0**
**Stranraer (2) 2** *(Moore 43, Jenkins 45)* 408
*Clachnacuddin:* Rae; Mackay, MacLeod, MacDonald, Matheson, Morrison (Campbell), Lewis (Mitchell), MacCuish, Polworth (McCraw), Ross, Michael Sanderson.
*Stranraer:* McCondichie; Swift, Wright, Wingate, Henderson, Jenkins, Finlayson (Marshall), Aitken, Moore, Graham, Sharp.

**Cowdenbeath (4) 5** *(Gilfillan 3, Seeley J (og) 4, Mauchlen 22, Fusco 41, Shields 57)*
**Edinburgh C (0) 0** 293
*Cowdenbeath:* Carlin; Shand (Gordon), McInally, Gilfillan (Buchanan), McKeown, Ritchie, Mauchlen, Winter, Shields, Fusco (Fallon), Mowat.
*Edinburgh C:* Mackintosh; Ferry, Moriarty, Seeley J, Foster, Macnamara, Godden, Donachie (Burgess), Nye (Gordon), McColl, Seeley C (Whyte).

**Elgin C (1) 1** *(Campbell 44)*
**Peterhead (2) 2** *(Bavidge 14, 42)* 726
*Elgin C:* Goram (Pirie); Campbell, Dempsie, White, Tully, Allison (Ogboke), Martin, Dickson, Bone, McLean N, McMullan.
*Peterhead:* Mathers; Mackay, McSkimming (Stewart D), Bain, Perry, Good, Stewart G (Smith), Duncan (Stewart I), Johnston, Bavidge, Roddie.

**Forfar Ath (0) 1** *(Rattray 48)*
**East Fife (0) 1** *(Hall 87)* 651
*Forfar Ath:* Brown; Lunan, Rattray, McClune, Horn, Byers, Sellars, Davidson, Tosh (Williams), Henderson (Maher), Shields.
*East Fife:* O'Connor; McMillan (Fairbairn), Donaldson, Lumsden, Hall, Blair, Stewart (Mitchell), McDonald, Deuchar, Nicholas, Gilbert.

**Gretna (1) 4** *(Stevens 6, Skelton 73, Holdsworth 81, Gordon 86)*
**Dumbarton (0) 0** 652
*Gretna:* Matheson; Birch, Maddison, Prokas, Irons, Holdsworth, Baldacchino (Gordon), Galloway (Cosgrove), Cameron (Allan), Stevens, Skelton.
*Dumbarton:* Grindlay (White); McEwan, Brittain, McKinstry, Collins, Boyle, Bonar, Bradley, Obidile, English (Russell), Dillon (Dobbins).

**Montrose (0) 1** *(Wood 50)*
**Albion R (1) 1** *(Mercer 25)* 367
*Montrose:* Butter; Donachie, Ferguson, Smith E, McQuillan, Kerrigan, Webster, Gibson (Smart), Michie, Wood (Farnan), Black (Sharp).
*Albion R:* Bennett; Paterson, Stirling (Valentine), Smith, McCaig, McBride, McAllister, McCaul, Yardley, McManus, Mercer.

**Spartans (3) 6** *(McLeod 38, 65, Johnston J 40, Manson 42, Hobbins 69, 88)*
**Buckie T (1) 1** *(More 28)* 358
*Spartans:* Brown; Rae, Fairlie, Johnson P (Vintner), Burns, Thomson (Tough), McLeod (Crawford), Johnston J, Hobbins, Manson, Henretty.
*Buckie T:* Main; Shewan, Lamberton, Slater, Small (Smith), Munro, Catto (Davidson), Taylor, Milne, More (Coutts), Macdonald.

**Stirling Albion (0) 3** *(Rowe 51, O'Brien 61, Kelly 73)*
**Queen's Park (1) 1** *(McAuley 4)* 617
*Stirling Albion:* Hogarth; Hay, Anderson, McNally, Rowe, Smith (Scotland), Wilson, Ferguson (Kelly), McLean (Beveridge), Elliot, O'Brien.
*Queen's Park:* Scrimgour; Clark, Thomson, Fallon, Agostini, Moffar (Ferry), Reilly, Whelan, Kettlewell, Graham (Carcary), McAuley (Carroll).

## FIRST ROUND REPLAYS

Saturday, 29 November 2003

**Albion R (1) 1** *(McQuillan (og) 42)*
**Montrose (0) 3** *(Michie 60, 74, Ferguson 63)* 230
*Albion R:* Bennett; Paterson (Connolly), Cormack, Smith, McCaig (McKenzie), Sweeney, Malloy (Valentine), McBride, Yardley, McManus, Mercer.
*Montrose:* Butter; Donachie, Ferguson, Smith E, McQuillan, Kerrigan (Farnan), Webster, Gibson (Smart), Michie, Wood (Sharp), Black.

**East Fife (1) 3** *(Horn (og) 32, McClune (og) 61, Deuchar 113)*
**Forfar Ath (0) 3** *(Tosh 62 (pen), 89, 93)* 561
*East Fife:* O'Connor; McMillan, Donaldson, Lumsden, Hall, Blair, Stewart (Mitchell), McDonald, Deuchar, Nicholas (Fairbairn), Gilbert.
*Forfar Ath:* Brown; Lowing (Maher), Rattray, McClune, Horn, Byers, Sellars, Davidson, Tosh, Henderson, Shields.
*(aet; East Fife won 4-1 on penalties)*

## SECOND ROUND

Saturday, 20 December 2003

**Alloa Ath (3) 3** *(Ferguson 17, Hamilton 22, Walker R 28)*
**Spartans (2) 3** *(Thomson 25, Johnston P 38, Manson 69)* 477
*Alloa Ath:* McGlynn; Nicolson, Little, McLaughlin, McGowan, Walker S, Walker R, Ferguson, Hamilton, Callaghan, Evans G (Kelbie).
*Spartans:* Brown; Rae, Fowlie, Johnson P, Burns, Thomson, McLeod, Johnston J (Crawford), Hobbins, Manson, Henretty (Tough).

**Berwick R (3) 4** *(Redford (og) 7, Hutchison 16, 25, 67)*
**Huntly (1) 2** *(Farmer 10, Stainer 76)* 255
*Berwick R:* Inglis; Murie, Neill A, McNicoll (Hilland), Cowan, Neil M, Waldie, Connell (McCormick), Hutchison (Kerrigan), McCutcheon, Hampshire.
*Huntly:* Thompson; Redford, Scott, Stephen, Henderson (Green), McGowan, Craig (Stainer), Guild, O'Driscoll, Gray, Farmer (De Barros).

**East Stirling (0) 0**
**Cowdenbeath (1) 5** *(Winter 35, Gordon 46, 55, Mauchlen 73, Buchanan 88)* 244
*East Stirling:* Connolly; Maughan, McGhee, Hare, Reid, McLaren (Boyle), Livingstone (Irvine), Leishman (Mackay), Ure, Kelly, Baldwin.
*Cowdenbeath:* Carlin; Shand, Mowat, Gilfillan, McKeown, Fusco, Mauchlen (Matheson), Winter, Shields, Gordon (Buchanan), McGuiness (McInally).

**Gretna (1) 5** *(Stevens 36, 54, Cohen 70, Skelton 77, Baldacchino 87)*
**Stenhousemuir (0) 1** *(Brown 55)* 426
*Gretna:* Mathieson; Birch, Maddison, Prokas (Cosgrove), Irons, Holdsworth, Baldacchino, Galloway, Stevens, Cohen, Skelton (Gordon).
*Stenhousemuir:* McCulloch; Gaughan, McKenna, McQuilter, McKenzie, Murphy, Harty, Hamilton (Lauchlan), Brown, Flannery (Carr), Bonar.

**Inverurie Locos (0) 1** *(Ross 86)*
**Airdrie U (3) 5** *(Coyle 2, 84, McKeown 24, Stewart 27, Roberts 64)* 1523
*Inverurie Locos:* Thain; Fraser, Buchan, Wilson, Young, Park, Singer (Mackay), Walker (Copland), Coull (Low), Ross, McWilliam.
*Airdrie U:* McGeown; Docherty, Black, Stewart (Wilson W), McManus, Ronald (McLaren), McKeown, Wilson M, Coyle, Roberts (Glancy), Gow.

**Peterhead (0) 0**
**East Fife (1) 2** *(McDonald 39, Nicholas 86)* 654
*Peterhead:* Mathers; Smith (Stewart I), McSkimming, Raeside, Perry, Good, Tindal (Duncan), Mackay, Johnston, Bavidge, Roddie.

*East Fife:* O'Connor; Kelly, Donaldson, Russell, Hall, Mortimer, McMillan, McDonald, Deuchar (Gilbert), Nicholas (Mitchell), Stewart (Blair).

**Stirling Albion (1) 1** *(Kelly 33)*
**Arbroath (1) 2** *(McGlashan 13, 85)* 647
*Stirling Albion:* Hogarth; Hay, Anderson, McNally, Rowe, Smith, Wilson (Devine), Kelly, McLean (Elliot), Davidson (Cumming), O'Brien.
*Arbroath:* Peat; McMullen (McAulay), King, Rennie, Browne, Dow (Henslee), Cargill, McCulloch, Diack, McGlashan, Swankie (Herkes).

Saturday, 27 December 2003

**Montrose (0) 1** *(Wood 83)*
**Threave R (0) 0** 520
*Montrose:* Butter; Donachie, Ferguson, Smith E, McQuillan, Kerrigan, Webster (Shanks), Gibson, Smart, Wood (Farnan), Black (Henderson).
*Threave R:* Gall; McMinn, Wilson, McGinley P, Whiteford, Haney, Sloan, Neilson, Budrys, Nicol, Baker (Adams).

**Morton (2) 4** *(Weatherson 15, Williams 45, 57, Miller 54)*
**Vale of Leithen (0) 0** 3231
*Morton:* Coyle; Collins, Bottiglieri, MacGregor, Greacen (Bannerman), Maisano M (Hawke), Millar, Maisano J, Williams, Weatherson (Adam), Walker.
*Vale of Leithen:* Lumsden; Weir (Baxter), Lothian C, Lothian G, Pilon, Hume, Kayser, Lockhart (Shanks), Hastie (Edge), Morrell, Palicza.

**Stranraer (0) 0**
**Hamilton A (0) 1** *(Quitongo 75)* 820
*Stranraer:* McCondichie; Swift, Wright, Wingate, Henderson, Jenkins (McAllister), Finlayson (Crawford), Aitken, Moore, Graham, Sharp (Grant).
*Hamilton A:* McEwan; Walker (Whiteford), Hodge, Thomson, Lumsden, Arbuckle, Carrigan, Aitken, Quitongo, McPhee (Gribben), Corcoran (Donnelly).

## SECOND ROUND REPLAY

Saturday, 27 December 2003

**Spartans (1) 5** *(Valentine (og) 10, Manson 70, McLeod 73, Hughes 100, Crawford 107)*
**Alloa Ath (2) 3** *(McGowan 19, Walker S 32, Ferguson 89)* 590
*Spartans:* Brown; Rae, Fowlie, Johnson P, Burns, Thomson, McLeod (Hughes), Johnston J (Crawford), Hobbins, Manson (Vinter), Henretty.
*Alloa Ath:* McGlynn; Nicolson, Seaton (Evans G), McGowan, Walker S, Valentine, Walker R, Ferguson, Hamilton, Little, Callaghan.
*aet.*

## THIRD ROUND

Saturday, 10 January 2004

**Aberdeen (0) 0**
**Dundee (0) 0** 11,012
*Aberdeen:* Preece; Diamond, Morrison, Anderson, Rutkiewicz, Heikkinen (Sheerin), Tosh, Foster (Muirhead), Clark, Booth, Hinds (Zdrilic).
*Dundee:* Speroni; Mackay, Hernandez, Mair, Wilkie, Smith, Fotheringham, Robb, Brady, Novo (Jablonski), McLean (Sancho).

**Arbroath (1) 1** *(McGlashan 10)*
**Spartans (2) 4** *(McLeod 21, Manson 43, 66, Johnson P 67)* 1017
*Arbroath:* Peat; McMullen, King, Rennie, Browne (Farquharson), McCulloch, Cargill, Henslee (Herkes), Diack, McGlashan, Swankie (Dow).
*Spartans:* Brown; Rae, Fowlie, Johnson P, Burns, Thomson (Hoy), McLeod (Vinter), Hughes, Hobbins, Manson (Crawford), Henretty.

**Ayr U (1) 1** *(Craig 28)*
**Falkirk (1) 2** *(Lee 20, Xausa 75)* 2632
*Ayr U:* Roy; Smyth, Dunlop (McGrady), Chaplain, Campbell, Craig, McColl, Ramsay, Kean, Ferguson, Hardy.
*Falkirk:* Hill; Lawrie, McPherson, Mackenzie, Sharp, James, O'Neil (Scally), Xausa, Lee (Colquhoun), Latapy, McAnespie.

**Celtic (0) 2** *(Hartson 74, Lambert 78)*
**Ross Co (0) 0** 29,615
*Celtic:* Douglas; McNamara, Sutton, Balde, Lennon, Agathe (Pearson), Wallace (Beattie), Lambert, Maloney (Petrov), Larsson, Hartson.
*Ross Co:* Smith; McCunnie, Robertson, McCulloch, Webb, Lauchlan, Rankin, Hannah, Bayne (Cowie), O'Donnell (Higgins), Winters (Gethins).

**Clyde (0) 3** *(Smith 57, 64, Ross 89)*
**Gretna (0) 0** 1060
*Clyde:* Morrison (Halliwell); Mensing, McCluskey, Kernaghan, McLaughlin, Ross, Fraser, Marshall, Smith, Gibson, Harty (McConalogue).
*Gretna:* Mathieson; Birch, Skelton, Prokas (Cosgrove), Irons, Holdsworth, Baldacchino, Galloway (Lennon), Stevens, Cohen, Gordon (Cameron).

**Dunfermline Ath (2) 3** *(Crawford 16, 36, Brewster 49)*
**Dundee U (1) 1** *(McInnes 38)* 6140
*Dunfermline Ath:* Stillie; Wilson, Thomson SM, Skerla, Dempsey (Tod), Darren Young, Nicholson, Mason, Derek Young (Bullen), Crawford (Hunt), Brewster.
*Dundee U:* Gallacher; Archibald, McCracken (Paterson J), Wilson, Duff, Easton, McInnes, Miller (Holmes), McLaren, Dodds, Samuel (Scotland).

**East Fife (0) 0**
**Queen of the S (0) 1** *(O'Connor 75)* 1063
*East Fife:* O'Connor; McMillan, Donaldson, McDonald, Hall, Kelly, Mitchell (Stewart), Blair, Deuchar (Fairbairn), Nicholas, Gilbert (Stein).
*Queen of the S:* Dodds; Paton, Aitken, Bagan (Burns), Reid, Thomson, O'Connor, Bowey, Burke, Wood (McMullen), McColligan.

**Hamilton A (1) 2** *(McPhee 25, 46)*
**Cowdenbeath (0) 0** 1096
*Hamilton A:* McEwan; Whiteford, Hodge, Thomson, Lumsden, Arbuckle, Carrigan (Gribben), Aitken, Quitongo, McPhee (Corcoran), Ferguson (Sherry).
*Cowdenbeath:* Carlin; Mowat, McInally, Gilfillan (McGuiness), McKeown (Campbell), Ritchie, Mauchlen, Winter, Shields, Buchanan (Shand), Fusco.

**Hearts (1) 2** *(Cowan (og) 27, Hamill 65)*
**Berwick R (0) 0** 8516
*Hearts:* Gordon; Maybury, Pressley (Neilson), Kisnorbo, Webster, Sloan, Severin, Macfarlane (Hamill), Hartley, De Vries, Kirk (Wyness).
*Berwick R:* Inglis; Murie, Hampshire (Bennett), McNicoll, Cowan, Neill A (Hilland), Connolly (Connell), Neil M, Hutchison, McCutcheon, Forrest.

**Hibernian (0) 0**
**Rangers (1) 2** *(Arveladze 35, Lovenkrands 49)* 11,392
*Hibernian:* Andersson; Murdock, Smith, Doumbe, Whittaker, Thomson, Brown, Brebner (Nicol), Riordan, O'Connor, Dobbie.
*Rangers:* Klos; Ricksen, Berg, Khizanishvili, Vanoli, Malcolm, Arteta, Capucho (Mols), Burke (Namouchi), Arveladze, Lovenkrands.

**Inverness CT (3) 5** *(Ritchie 8, 9, 68, Bingham 23, McBain 56)*
**Brechin C (0) 1** *(King 51)* 1412
*Inverness CT:* Brown; Tokely, Golabek, Mann, McCaffrey, Duncan, Mackie, McBain (Thomson), Ritchie (Macmillan), Keogh, Bingham (MacRae).
*Brechin C:* Hay; Millar M, Deas, Johnson, White, Smith, King, McLeish (McCulloch S), Templeman (Miller G), Gibson (Boylan), Mitchell.

**Livingston (1) 1** *(Fernandez 16)*
**Montrose (0) 0** 2657
*Livingston:* McKenzie; McNamee, McAllister, Dorado, Andrews, O'Brien, Makel, Lovell, Lilley, Fernandez, Pasquinelli (McGovern).
*Montrose:* Butter; Donachie, Ferguson, Smith E, McQuillan, Kerrigan, Webster (Henderson), Gibson (Smith G), Smart, Wood, Sharp (Hall).

**Morton (0) 0**
**Partick T (1) 3** *(Rowson 35, Grady 52, 89)* 6613
*Morton:* Coyle; Collins, Bottiglieri, MacGregor, Gaughan (Cannie), Maisano M (Bannerman), Millar, Maisano J, Williams (Uotinen), Weatherson, Walker.

*Partick T:* Arthur (Pinkowski); Lilley (Forrest), Murray, Madaschi, Milne, Ross I, Rowson, Mitchell, McBride, Grady, Thomson (Bonnes).

**Raith R (0) 1** *(Talio 54)*
**Kilmarnock (3) 3** *(McSwegan 27, McDonald 31, Nish 34)* 3610
*Raith R:* Gonzalez; Patino, Stanic, Talio (Martin), Calderon, Brady, Stanley, Rivas, Sutton, Boyle (Prest), Evans (Gomez).
*Kilmarnock:* Dubourdeau; Shields, Dindeleux, Greer, Hay, Fowler, Fulton, Locke, Nish (Boyd), McSwegan (Invincibile), McDonald.

**St Johnstone (0) 0**
**Motherwell (2) 3** *(Clarkson 23, 32, McDonald S 89)* 4092
*St Johnstone:* Nelson; Baxter, McQuilken, Bernard, Robertson J, Maxwell, MacDonald, Reilly, Paatelainen (Parker), Donnelly (Hay), McLaughlin (Taylor).
*Motherwell:* Marshall; Corrigan, Craigan, Hammell, Dair, Lasley (Fagan), Quinn, Leitch, Adams (O'Donnell), Burns, Clarkson (McDonald S).

**St Mirren (0) 2** *(Lavety 83, McKenna 90)*
**Airdrie U (0) 0** 3049
*St Mirren:* Woods; Broadfoot, Lappin, Millen, McGowne, Dempsie, Gillies (Crilly), O'Neil, Dunn (Lavety), McGinty (McKenna), Murray.
*Airdrie U:* McGeown; Docherty, McGowan, Stewart, McManus, Ronald, McKeown (Dunn), Wilson M (Christie), Coyle, Roberts (Vareille), Gow.

## THIRD ROUND REPLAY

Wednesday, 21 January 2004

**Dundee (1) 2** *(Robb 9, Novo 89)*
**Aberdeen (1) 3** *(Clark 4, Heikkinen 77, Zdrilic 88)* 5857
*Dundee:* Speroni; Mackay, Hernandez, Mair, Wilkie, Smith, Jablonski (Milne), Robb, Brady, Novo, Linn (Lovell).
*Aberdeen:* Preece; Diamond, Morrison, Anderson, McNaughton (Muirhead), Heikkinen (Sheerin), Tosh, Clark, Prunty (Zdrilic), Booth, Hinds.

## FOURTH ROUND

Saturday, 7 February 2004

**Clyde (1) 1** *(McLaughlin 29)*
**Dunfermline Ath (2) 2** *(Hunt 4, Nicholson 22)* 3893
*Clyde:* Morrison; Mensing, Fotheringham, McCluskey, McLaughlin, Ross, Hagen, Marshall, Smith, Gibson, Harty.
*Dunfermline Ath:* Stillie; Tod, Thomson SM, Skerla, Wilson, Darren Young, Nicholson, Byrne, Hunt, Crawford, Derek Young.
*Match abandoned after 57 minutes – heavy snow.*

**Falkirk (0) 0**
**Aberdeen (0) 2** *(Zdrilic 60, Booth 64)* 4747
*Falkirk:* Ferguson; Lawrie, McPherson, MacKenzie, Hughes, Sharp, O'Neil, Xausa (Lee), Colquhoun, Latapy, McAnespie (Nicholls).
*Aberdeen:* Preece; Diamond, Morrison, Anderson, McNaughton (McGuire), Heikkinen, Tosh, Clark, Zdrilic (Muirhead), Booth (Prunty), Hinds.

**Hearts (0) 0**
**Celtic (2) 3** *(Petrov 3, 33, Larsson 90)* 14,712
*Hearts:* Gordon; Maybury, Pressley, Kisnorbo (Kirk), Webster, Stamp, Sloan (Neilson), Macfarlane (McKenna), Hartley, De Vries, Wyness.
*Celtic:* Douglas; McNamara, Varga, Kennedy, Thompson, Petrov, Lennon, Pearson, Agathe, Larsson, Sutton.

**Motherwell (3) 3** *(Adams 2, Burns 17, 44)*
**Queen of the S (0) 2** *(O'Connor 64, 69)* 8101
*Motherwell:* Marshall; Corrigan, Craigan, Hammell, Dair, Lasley (Bollan), Quinn, O'Donnell, Adams, Burns (McDonald S), Clarkson.
*Queen of the S:* Dodds; Paton, McAlpine (McMullen), Bagan, Reid, Aitken, O'Connor, Bowey, Wood (Jaconelli), Payne (McColligan), Burns.

**Partick T (1) 5** *(Mitchell 39, Britton 53, 61, McBride 80, Bonnes 83)*
**Hamilton A (0) 1** *(Corcoran 89)* 4004
*Partick T:* Arthur; Gibson W, Ross I (Fleming), Madaschi, Milne, Murray, Rowson, Mitchell (Anis), McBride, Grady, Britton (Bonnes).
*Hamilton A:* McEwan; Whiteford, Hodge, Thomson, Lumsden, Arbuckle, Carrigan, Aitken, Quitongo (Blackadder), McPhee (Convery), Sherry (Corcoran).

**St Mirren (0) 0**
**Inverness CT (0) 1** *(Thomson 78)* 3859
*St Mirren:* Woods; Van Zanten (Dunn), McGroarty, Millen, Broadfoot, Dempsie, Gillies, Murray (Lavety), McGinty, O'Neil, Lappin.
*Inverness CT:* Brown; Tokely, Golabek, Mann, Munro, Duncan (Christie), Thomson, McBain, Ritchie, Keogh, Bingham.

Sunday, 8 February 2004

**Kilmarnock (0) 0**
**Rangers (0) 2** *(de Boer R 62, Arveladze 67)* 11,072
*Kilmarnock:* Dubourdeau; McLaughlin, Greer, Hay, Fowler, Skora, Invincibile (Murray), Locke (Dodds), Hardie, McSwegan, McDonald (Boyd).
*Rangers:* Klos; Ricksen, Moore, Berg, Ball, Ross, Arteta (Ostenstad), Nerlinger (Vanoli), de Boer R, Arveladze, Capucho (Namouchi).

**Spartans (0) 0**
**Livingston (0) 4** *(Lilley 52, 60, 70, Fernandez 58)* 3000
*Spartans:* Brown; Rae, Fowlie, Johnson P (Vinter), Burns, Thomson (Johnston J), McLeod, Hughes (Bennett), Hobbins, Manson, Henretty.
*Livingston:* McKenzie; McNamee, McAllister (McLaughlin), Dorado, Andrews, O'Brien, Makel, Lovell (Brittain), Lilley, Fernandez, Pasquinelli (McMenamin).

Tuesday, 24 February 2004

**Clyde (0) 0**
**Dunfermline Ath (3) 3** *(Nicholson 18, 37, Bullen 40)* 2441
*Clyde:* Halliwell; Mensing, Fotheringham (Doyle), Kernaghan, McCluskey, Ross, Hagen, Marshall, Keogh, Fraser (Smith), Harty (Gilhaney).
*Dunfermline Ath:* Stillie; Tod, Thomson SM (Mason), Skerla (Grondin), Wilson (Kilgannon), Bullen, Nicholson, Byrne, Dempsey, Labonte, Mehmet.

## QUARTER-FINALS

Saturday, 6 March 2004

**Aberdeen (0) 1** *(Muirhead 56)*
**Livingston (0) 1** *(Anderson (og) 50)* 11,593
*Aberdeen:* Preece; McGuire, Morrison, Anderson, Diamond (Hart), Heikkinen, Tosh (Muirhead), Foster, Clark, Prunty (Zdrilic), Hinds.
*Livingston:* McKenzie; McNamee, McAllister, Rubio, Andrews, Dorado, Makel, O'Brien, Lovell, Fernandez, Lilley.

**Motherwell (0) 0**
**Inverness CT (1) 1** *(Wilson 9)* 7934
*Motherwell:* Marshall; Corrigan, Quinn, Hammell, Craigan, Lasley, Fagan (O'Donnell), McDonald S, Adams, Burns, Clarkson (Wright).
*Inverness CT:* Brown; Tokely, Golabek, Mann, McCaffrey, Duncan, Wilson, McBain, Ritchie (Proctor), Keogh, Thomson (Munro).

**Partick T (0) 0**
**Dunfermline Ath (2) 3** *(Byrne 10, Nicholson 36, Brewster 68)* 5335
*Partick T:* Arthur; Gibson W, Murray, Madaschi, Milne (Fleming), Ross I, Rowson, Chiarini (Cadete), Britton, Bonnes (Gibson A), Mitchell.
*Dunfermline Ath:* Stillie; Bullen, Tod, Skerla, Wilson, Darren Young, Nicholson, Mason (Dempsey), Byrne, Crawford (Derek Young), Brewster (Hunt).

Sunday, 7 March 2004

**Celtic (0) 1** *(Larsson 55)*
**Rangers (0) 0** 58,665
*Celtic:* Douglas; Varga, Valgaeren (Kennedy), Balde, Thompson, Petrov, Lennon, McNamara, Pearson (Beattie) (Sylla), Larsson, Agathe.
*Rangers:* Klos; Ricksen, Moore, de Boer F, Berg, Ball, Hughes (Thompson), Rae, Arteta (de Boer R), Arveladze, Lovenkrands.

## QUARTER-FINAL REPLAY

Thursday, 18 March 2004

**Livingston (1) 1** *(O'Brien 26)*
**Aberdeen (0) 0** 4487
*Livingston:* McKenzie; McNamee, McAllister, Rubio, Andrews, Dorado, Makel, O'Brien, Lovell (McLaughlin), Fernandez, Lilley.
*Aberdeen:* Preece; McGuire, Morrison, Hart, Diamond, Heikkinen, Muirhead (Foster), Sheerin, Clark (Tiernan), Zdrilic (Prunty), Hinds.

## SEMI-FINALS (at Hampden Park)

Saturday, 10 April 2004

**Inverness CT (1) 1** *(Ritchie 45)*
**Dunfermline Ath (0) 1** *(Brewster 67)* 13,255
*Inverness CT:* Brown; Tokely, Golabek, Mann, McCaffrey, Duncan, Wilson (Thomson), McBain, Ritchie (Hislop), Keogh, Bingham (Proctor).
*Dunfermline Ath:* Stillie; Bullen, Tod, Skerla, Mason (Grondin), Darren Young, Nicholson, Byrne (Dempsey), Derek Young, Crawford, Brewster.

Sunday, 11 April 2004

**Livingston (0) 1** *(McMenamin 78)*
**Celtic (1) 3** *(Sutton 36, 64, Larsson 49)* 26,152
*Livingston:* McKenzie; McNamee, Dorado, Rubio (Brittain), Andrews, McLaughlin, Makel, O'Brien, Lovell (McGovern), Lilley, Pasquinelli (McMenamin).
*Celtic:* Marshall; Varga, Valgaeren, Balde, Thompson (Miller), Petrov, Lennon, Agathe, Pearson, Larsson (Mjällby), Sutton (Beattie).

## SEMI-FINAL REPLAY (at Pittodrie)

Tuesday, 20 April 2004

**Inverness CT (1) 2** *(Ritchie 8, Bingham 89)*
**Dunfermline Ath (1) 3** *(Darren Young 25, Brewster 64, Nicholson 79)* 5728
*Inverness CT:* Brown; Tokely (Proctor), Golabek, Mann, McCaffrey, Duncan (Thomson), Hislop, McBain, Ritchie (Mackie), Keogh, Bingham.
*Dunfermline Ath:* Stillie; Bullen, Mason (Labonte), Skerla, Wilson, Darren Young, Nicholson, Dempsey (Byrne), Derek Young, Crawford, Brewster.

## FINAL (at Hampden Park)

Saturday, 22 May 2004

**Celtic (0) 3** *(Larsson 58, 71, Petrov 83)*
**Dunfermline Ath (1) 1** *(Skerla 40)* 50,846
*Celtic:* Marshall; McNamara, Varga, Balde, Thompson, Petrov, Lennon, Agathe, Pearson (Wallace), Larsson, Sutton.
*Dunfermline Ath:* Stillie; Labonte, Mason (Grondin), Skerla, Byrne (Tod), Darren Young, Nicholson, Dempsey (Bullen), Derek Young, Crawford, Brewster.
*Referee:* Stuart Dougal.

Dunfermline Athletic's Andre Skerla celebrates the opening goal of the Tennent's Scottish Cup Final. Celtic hit back after half-time with goals from Larsson (2) and Petrov to lift the cup with a 3-1 triumph. (Empics)

# WELSH FOOTBALL 2003–04

'And the pain goes on' . . . – the headline in the *Western Mail* newspaper said it all.

The day after the night before was the moment it really sank in: Wales would not be going to the finals of a major tournament for the first time in 46 years. A qualifying campaign that began with a bang had ended with a whimper when the Welsh blew their chance of reaching Euro 2004 by losing 1-0 to Russia at the Millennium Stadium in Cardiff.

But that hugely disappointing night in November, when Wales failed to finally throw off the mantle of the 'nearly men' of international football, turned out to be not quite the end of their bid to reach Portugal. A failed drugs test by one of the Russian players meant the battle moved from the pitch to the appeal court before ultimately being unsuccessful.

After four successive wins, Wales could only manage a solitary draw in the second half of their campaign. Political unrest in Belgrade meant that the game against Serbia and Montenegro in early April had to be postponed until August by which time the lost momentum resulted in a 1-0 defeat. A 4-0 thrashing in Italy followed and their last two home matches produced a 1-1 draw with Finland and a 3-2 win for Serbia and Montenegro. It all came down to a two-legged play-off final against Russia and a choice of tactics.

Spot-on in Moscow where he employed his usual five-man midfield to secure a typically battling 0-0 draw, manager Mark Hughes failed to seize the moment by declining to change tack in the return leg in Cardiff. Instead of seizing the initiative and going for goals, he opted for the same rigid defensive formation. John Hartson was left to labour all alone up front while the First Division's top scorer, Cardiff City's Robert Earnshaw, inexplicably kicked his heels on the bench.

Poor marking at a free-kick gave the Russians the lead midway through the first half and from then on, Wales were chasing the game. True, Ryan Giggs hit a post just before the interval but even when Earnshaw was introduced after about an hour, he was played out of position wide on the right and never threatened to score his fourth goal in his fifth Welsh appearance at the Millennium Stadium. The result showed that tactical flexibility is just as important as the defensive stability on which the turnaround in Welsh fortunes under Hughes has been based. It perfectly illustrated the SAS motto 'who dares wins'. In such a significant one-off match, Wales should have been more adventurous but the inherent caution of Hughes and his coaching team meant they didn't dare – and they missed out again.

But criticism of the team's tactics was largely eclipsed by immediate post-match uncertainty over the manager's future and then by the revelation in January that Yegor Titov had tested positive for the banned drug, bromantan, after the first game in Moscow. Although he had been an unused substitute in Russia, the Spartak Moscow midfielder played for an hour of the second leg. Wales immediately cried foul!, lodged a protest to Uefa and insisted they should be awarded a 3-0 win and take Russia's place in Portugal. The Welsh FA were right to appeal – despite the estimated £200,000 cost and slim chance of success – and the case went all the way to the Court of Arbitration in Sport before eventually being dismissed in May.

Back on the pitch, Wales bounced back through a resounding 4-0 defeat of Scotland – with Earnshaw scoring a hat-trick – and a 2-1 win in Hungary. They then drew 0-0 in Norway and beat Canada 1-0 at the Racecourse in Wrexham with Cardiff's Paul Parry rounding off a fairytale season by scoring his first international goal. The former Hereford United winger is one of a crop of emerging youngsters and Wales can approach their 2006 World Cup qualifying campaign – including games against England and Northern Ireland – with cautious optimism.

For the country's three Nationwide League clubs, the season proved to be anti-climactic. Cardiff lacked the consistency to reach the play-offs but did well to finish halfway up the Division One table, Wrexham, beset by growing financial problems, made an encouraging return to Division Two while Swansea began their campaign in sensational style but were distracted by a wonderful FA Cup run and ended up three places and 15 points outside the top seven. Their slump in form cost director of football Brian Flynn his job and another former Welsh international, Kenny Jackett, took his place.

Newport County were the most successful of the three English pyramid clubs. After not winning one of their first 10 games, Peter Nicholas' side recovered well to finish seventh in the Dr Martens League Premier Division and secure a place in Conference Two (South) as part of the newly formed second tier of English non-League football. Merthyr missed out on automatic promotion to the new division by a single point and then lost to Redditch in a sudden-death play-off while Colwyn Bay failed to reach the new Northern Premier League after finishing 16th in Division One of the Unibond League.

Pride of place in domestic Welsh football must go to Rhyl who, under their manager John Hulse, completed a memorable hat-trick by winning the Premier League title for the first time and then lifting the Welsh and League Cups. They narrowly failed to complete a clean sweep by losing to Wrexham in the FAW Premier Cup Final. The demise of the former league champions, Barry Town, was equally spectacular. After nearly a decade of unparalleled success, the League of Wales' first fully professional side were relegated as a result of a series of financial problems involving their relationship with the local council. Their 2-1 home win over Macedonia's FK Vardar in the Champions League was the only bright spot in an otherwise depressing set of European games but it failed to prevent an 4-2 aggregate defeat. TNS Llansantffraid and Cwmbran Town lost heavily to Manchester City and Israel's Maccabi Haifa respectively in the UEFA Cup while Bangor City went out to Gloria Bistrita of Romania in the Intertoto Cup.

Rhyl, TNS, Haverfordwest and Aberystywyth will fly the Welsh flag in the 2004–05 season and although crowds are on the increase – average Premier League attendances have reached 300 for the first time since its formation in 1992 – there's still much room for improvement in results in Europe.

Wales may not have qualified for the European Championships but at least Mark Hughes had something to smile about at the end of the season. Glorious failure has its compensations because the Welsh manager was rewarded by having his MBE upgraded to an OBE in the Queen's Birthday Honours List. The irony of the announcement being made on the day that Euro 2004 kicked off wasn't lost on the man who, having rejuvenated Welsh football over the last five years, dedicated the honour to his family, players, staff and the loyal Welsh supporters. But, despite his obvious pride in receiving his latest award, I'm sure that Hughes would have swapped it for a place in the finals in Portugal in the summer.

GRAHAME LLOYD

## JT HUGHES/MITSUBISHI WELSH PREMIER LEAGUE 2003–04

| | Aberystwyth Town | Afan Lido | Bangor City | Barry Town | Caernarfon Town | Caersws | Carmarthen Town | Connah's Quay Nomads | Cwmbran Town | Haverfordwest County | Newi Cefn Druids | Newtown | Porthmadog | Port Talbot Town | Rhyl | TNS | Welshpool Town |
|---|---|---|---|---|---|---|---|---|---|---|---|---|---|---|---|---|---|
| Aberystwyth Town | — | 1-2 | 1-2 | 3-1 | 2-1 | 2-0 | 5-1 | 2-1 | 1-0 | 1-1 | 1-0 | 2-1 | 1-0 | 1-1 | 2-2 | 0-3 | 5-0 |
| Afan Lido | 0-1 | — | 0-0 | 1-1 | 0-0 | 0-0 | 3-3 | 2-0 | 0-4 | 0-0 | 3-1 | 0-1 | 1-0 | 1-2 | 1-2 | 2-3 | 1-0 |
| Bangor City | 2-3 | 3-0 | — | 2-1 | 1-1 | 1-1 | 2-2 | 2-1 | 7-2 | 3-3 | 0-3 | 2-1 | 4-1 | 4-1 | 2-3 | 0-1 | 5-0 |
| Barry Town | 1-2 | 0-1 | 0-3 | — | 0-5 | 1-3 | 0-0 | 0-2 | 0-2 | 0-2 | 0-1 | 3-2 | 2-3 | 3-1 | 0-3 | 2-3 | 5-4 |
| Caernarfon Town | 3-2 | 2-2 | 4-5 | 8-0 | — | 2-4 | 1-1 | 5-5 | 1-0 | 0-1 | 3-2 | 0-3 | 2-0 | 2-0 | 1-1 | 2-2 | 4-1 |
| Caersws | 0-0 | 2-2 | 1-4 | 1-0 | 2-2 | — | 3-0 | 0-1 | 4-1 | 0-0 | 3-1 | 4-0 | 3-2 | 1-0 | 3-3 | 0-2 | 3-0 |
| Carmarthen Town | 1-2 | 2-1 | 1-4 | 0-0 | 1-4 | 1-7 | — | 2-2 | 0-2 | 0-1 | 2-0 | 0-1 | 1-0 | 1-2 | 0-0 | 1-4 | 0-2 |
| Connah's Quay Nomads | 0-4 | 4-0 | 3-2 | 4-1 | 3-0 | 3-5 | 1-1 | — | 3-2 | 0-1 | 0-1 | 2-3 | 1-3 | 1-3 | 0-2 | 1-1 | 1-1 |
| Cwmbran Town | 2-1 | 4-1 | 1-2 | 2-1 | 0-1 | 2-2 | 3-1 | 3-3 | — | 0-1 | 0-2 | 1-2 | 1-0 | 3-0 | 1-1 | 0-1 | 2-1 |
| Haverfordwest County | 3-1 | 0-0 | 1-0 | 2-2 | 1-1 | 3-0 | 1-0 | 1-2 | 2-1 | — | 1-0 | 1-0 | 1-0 | 1-1 | 2-1 | 1-2 | 1-1 |
| Newi Cefn Druids | 1-3 | 5-3 | 1-5 | 2-1 | 1-3 | 2-2 | 2-2 | 1-2 | 0-2 | 1-0 | — | 2-1 | 3-0 | 0-1 | 0-2 | 0-2 | 4-2 |
| Newtown | 1-1 | 2-0 | 2-5 | 3-0 | 2-0 | 0-0 | 1-1 | 2-1 | 1-3 | 1-1 | 2-3 | — | 1-0 | 1-0 | 0-2 | 2-5 | 1-0 |
| Porthmadog | 2-1 | 2-0 | 0-1 | 2-2 | 3-2 | 2-3 | 3-1 | 1-1 | 0-2 | 0-2 | 3-1 | 3-2 | — | 1-2 | 0-2 | 1-1 | 3-0 |
| Port Talbot Town | 1-3 | 0-2 | 0-0 | 2-2 | 4-1 | 0-2 | 3-1 | 1-1 | 2-3 | 2-0 | 3-2 | 2-0 | 3-2 | — | 1-2 | 1-4 | 0-1 |
| Rhyl | 5-3 | 3-0 | 2-0 | 4-0 | 7-1 | 2-1 | 4-0 | 1-1 | 1-0 | 1-1 | 2-0 | 1-1 | 6-1 | 2-1 | — | 1-0 | 3-0 |
| TNS | 1-0 | 5-0 | 2-1 | 3-0 | 4-1 | 1-3 | 4-0 | 3-2 | 2-1 | 2-0 | 2-1 | 2-1 | 4-0 | 4-0 | 2-3 | — | 1-1 |
| Welshpool Town | 0-2 | 0-2 | 3-1 | 1-1 | 3-3 | 1-0 | 1-1 | 1-4 | 0-1 | 2-4 | 3-1 | 3-2 | 0-1 | 2-2 | 1-2 | 0-5 | — |

## JT HUGHES/MITSUBISHI WELSH PREMIER LEAGUE

| | | | Home | | | | | Away | | | | | Total | | | | | | |
|---|---|---|---|---|---|---|---|---|---|---|---|---|---|---|---|---|---|---|---|
| | | *P* | *W* | *D* | *L* | *F* | *A* | *W* | *D* | *L* | *F* | *A* | *W* | *D* | *L* | *F* | *A* | *GD* | *Pts* |
| 1 | Rhyl | 32 | 13 | 3 | 0 | 45 | 10 | 10 | 5 | 1 | 31 | 16 | 23 | 8 | 1 | 76 | 26 | 50 | 77 |
| 2 | TNS | 32 | 13 | 1 | 2 | 40 | 14 | 11 | 3 | 2 | 37 | 14 | 24 | 4 | 4 | 77 | 28 | 49 | 76 |
| 3 | Haverfordwest County | 32 | 10 | 5 | 1 | 22 | 10 | 7 | 6 | 3 | 18 | 13 | 17 | 11 | 4 | 40 | 23 | 17 | 62 |
| 4 | Aberystwyth Town | 32 | 10 | 3 | 3 | 30 | 16 | 8 | 2 | 6 | 29 | 23 | 18 | 5 | 9 | 59 | 39 | 20 | 59 |
| 5 | Caersws | 32 | 8 | 5 | 3 | 30 | 18 | 7 | 5 | 4 | 33 | 23 | 15 | 10 | 7 | 63 | 41 | 22 | 55 |
| 6 | Bangor City | 32 | 7 | 4 | 5 | 37 | 25 | 9 | 2 | 5 | 35 | 22 | 16 | 6 | 10 | 72 | 47 | 25 | 54 |
| 7 | Cwmbran Town | 32 | 7 | 3 | 6 | 22 | 20 | 8 | 0 | 8 | 26 | 24 | 15 | 3 | 14 | 48 | 44 | 4 | 48 |
| 8 | Connah's Quay Nomads | 32 | 6 | 3 | 7 | 29 | 28 | 5 | 6 | 5 | 29 | 27 | 11 | 9 | 12 | 58 | 55 | 3 | 42 |
| 9 | Caernarfon Town | 32 | 6 | 5 | 5 | 38 | 31 | 5 | 4 | 7 | 27 | 34 | 11 | 9 | 12 | 65 | 65 | 0 | 42 |
| 10 | Newtown | 32 | 7 | 4 | 5 | 22 | 22 | 5 | 1 | 10 | 21 | 28 | 12 | 5 | 15 | 43 | 50 | –7 | 41 |
| 11 | Port Talbot Town | 32 | 6 | 3 | 7 | 25 | 26 | 5 | 3 | 8 | 16 | 25 | 11 | 6 | 15 | 41 | 51 | –10 | 39 |
| 12 | Porthmadog | 32 | 7 | 3 | 6 | 26 | 23 | 4 | 0 | 12 | 15 | 31 | 11 | 3 | 18 | 41 | 54 | –13 | 36 |
| 13 | Newi Cefn Druids | 32 | 6 | 2 | 8 | 25 | 31 | 5 | 0 | 11 | 19 | 28 | 11 | 2 | 19 | 44 | 59 | –15 | 35 |
| 14 | Afan Lido | 32 | 4 | 5 | 7 | 15 | 19 | 4 | 3 | 9 | 16 | 35 | 8 | 8 | 16 | 31 | 54 | –23 | 32 |
| 15 | Welshpool Town | 32 | 4 | 4 | 8 | 21 | 32 | 2 | 3 | 11 | 14 | 39 | 6 | 7 | 19 | 35 | 71 | –36 | 25 |
| 16 | Carmarthen Town | 32 | 3 | 3 | 10 | 13 | 32 | 0 | 8 | 8 | 15 | 37 | 3 | 11 | 18 | 28 | 69 | –41 | 20 |
| 17 | Barry Town | 32 | 3 | 1 | 12 | 17 | 37 | 0 | 6 | 10 | 13 | 40 | 3 | 7 | 22 | 30 | 77 | –47 | 16 |

## WELSH CUP 2003–04

**FIRST ROUND**

Aberaman Athletic v Fields Park Pontllanfraith 2-4
AFC Llwydcoed v Penrhiwceiber Rangers 3-2
Ammanford AFC v Cardiff Corinthians 1-2
Blaenrhondda v Tredegar Town 3-1
Bodedem v Prestatyn Town 2-1
Brickfield Rangers v Conwy United 1-0
Bridgend Town v Garden Village 6-5
Bryntirion Athletic v Treharris Athletic 3-4
Caldicot Town v Merthyr Saints 1-3
Cemaes Bay v Holyhead Hotspurs 2-3
Chirk AAA v Penrhyncoch 2-3
Flint Town United v Brynteg Villa 5-0
Gresford Athletic v Corwen 5-2
Guilsfield United v Caerau Ely 1-0
Holywell Town v Glantraeth 1-4
Llanfairpwll v Rhos Aelwyd 2-1
Llanidloes Town v Newcastle Emlyn 1-2
Llanwern v Ely Rangers 2-3
Mold Alexandra v Bala Town 2-0
Morriston Town v Dinas Powys 4-3
Newport YMCA v Treowen Stars 0-1
Pontyclun v Grange Harlequins 0-2
Pontypridd Town v Caerleon 1-2
Porthcawl Town v Cwmaman United 1-2
Porth Tywyn Suburbs v Troedyrhiw 3-2
Presteigne St Andrews v Llanrhaeadr 1-0
Taffs Well v Skewen Athletic 0-4

**SECOND ROUND**

Aberystwyth Town v Lex XI 12-2
Barry Town v Risca & Gelli United 1-2
Bangor City v Glantraeth 6-7 *(aet & pens)*
Bodedem v Penrhyncoch 5-1
Brickfield Rangers v Buckley Town 0-2
Briton Ferry Athletic v Blaenrhondda 3-1
Caerleon v Skewen Athletic 4-3 *(aet & pens)*
Caernarfon Town v Llandudno 5-0
Cardiff Corinthians v AFC Llwydcoed 0-3 *(aet)*
Cwmbran Town v Merthyr Saints 5-1
Ely Rangers v Port Talbot Town 0-2
Flint Town United v Ruthin Town 2-1
Grange Harlequins v Ton Pentre 0-1 *(aet)*
Guilsfield United v Connah's Quay Nomads 1-8
Gwynfi United v Bridgend Town 1-4
Halkyn United v Llangefni Town 1-3
Haverfordwest County v Afan Lido 0-2
Holyhead Hotspurs v Gresford Athletic 3-0
Llanelli v Morriston Town 5-0
Maesteg Park Athletic v Goytre United 0-1
Mold Alexandra v Welshpool Town 1-4
Neath v Cwmaman United 4-3 *(aet & pens)*
Newcastle Emlyn v Pontardawe Town 0-1
Newi Cefn Druids v Porthmadog 3-0
Newtown v Amlwch Town 3-0
Porth Tywyn Suburbs v Garw Athletic 1-0
Presteigne St Andrews v Llanfairpwll 1-4
Rhyl v Airbus UK 2-0
Total Network Solutions v Caersws 2-0
Treharris Athletic v Bettws 3-1 *(aet & pens)*
Treowen Stars v Fields Park Pontllanfraith 3-1
UWIC Inter Cardiff v Carmarthen Town 2-1

**THIRD ROUND**

Bodedem v Connah's Quay Nomads 1-2
Bridgend Town v Treowen Stars 3-2
Buckley Town v Newi Cefn Druids 0-7
Caerleon v Porth Tywyn Suburbs 0-1 *(aet)*
Caernarfon Town v Holyhead Hotspurs 3-2
Flint Town United v Glantraeth 0-3
Llanelli v Cwmbran Town 0-1
Llanfairpwll v Rhyl 1-4
Pontardawe Town v Afan Lido 0-2
Port Talbot Town v Aberystwyth Town 2-1 *(aet)*
Risca & Gelli United v AFC Llwydcoed 0-1
Ton Pentre v Neath 4-1
Total Network Solutions v Llangefni Town 5-1
Treharris Athletic v Goytre United 0-2
UWIC Inter Cardiff v Briton Ferry Athletic 2-0
Welshpool Town v Newtown 3-1

**FOURTH ROUND**

Caernarfon Town v Cwmbran Town 1-2
Connah's Quay Nomads v Total Network Solutions 0-1
AFC Llwydcoed v Rhyl 0-2
Newi Cefn Druids v Goytre United 3-0
Porth Tywyn Suburbs v Afan Lido
*(Porth Tywyn Suburbs withdrew; tie awarded to Afan Lido).*
Ton Pentre v Port Talbot Town 0-1
UWIC Inter Cardiff v Bridgend Town 2-0
Welshpool Town v Glantraeth 3-2
*(Welshpool Town fielded an ineligible player; tie awarded to Glantraeth).*

**FIFTH ROUND**

Afan Lido v Rhyl 1-2
Cwmbran Town v UWIC Inter Cardiff 2-1 *(aet)*
Newi Cefn Druids v Port Talbot Town 0-1
Total Network Solutions v Glantraeth 4-1

**SEMI-FINALS**

Cwmbran Town v Rhyl 2-4
Total Network Solutions v Port Talbot Town 1-0

## WELSH CUP FINAL

(at Newtown FC)

9 May 2004

**Rhyl (0) 1 Total Network Solutions (0) 0**

*(aet)*

*Rhyl:* Smith; Limbert, Graves (Adamson 82), Atherton, Edwards, Brewerton, Powell M, Walters (McGinn 32), Moran, Powell G (Jackson 107), Wilson.
*Scorer:* Taylor 91 (og).

*Total Network Solutions:* Acton; Naylor (Bridgewater 19) (Perry 85), Davies (Aggrey 108), Taylor, Evans, Holmes, Hogan, Wood, Toner, Wilde, Ruscoe.

*Referee:* J. Collins.

*Attendance:* 1300

## FAW PREMIER CUP

| *Group A* | *P* | *W* | *D* | *L* | *F* | *A* | *GD* | *Pts* |
|---|---|---|---|---|---|---|---|---|
| TNS | 6 | 3 | 2 | 1 | 19 | 8 | 11 | 11 |
| Caersws | 6 | 3 | 0 | 3 | 11 | 24 | –13 | 9 |
| Bangor City | 6 | 2 | 2 | 2 | 24 | 17 | 7 | 8 |
| Aberystwyth Town | 6 | 1 | 2 | 3 | 11 | 16 | –5 | 5 |

| *Group B* | *P* | *W* | *D* | *L* | *F* | *A* | *GD* | *Pts* |
|---|---|---|---|---|---|---|---|---|
| Rhyl | 6 | 4 | 1 | 1 | 9 | 6 | 3 | 13 |
| Newport County | 6 | 3 | 2 | 1 | 12 | 5 | 7 | 11 |
| Connah's Quay Nomads | 6 | 1 | 3 | 2 | 7 | 9 | –2 | 6 |
| Afan Lido | 6 | 0 | 2 | 4 | 5 | 13 | –8 | 2 |

**QUARTER-FINALS**

| | |
|---|---|
| Newport County v Cardiff City | 0-1 |
| TNS v Wrexham | 0-2 |
| Rhyl v Barry Town | 8-0 |
| Caersws v Swansea City | 2-4 |

**SEMI-FINALS**

| | |
|---|---|
| Wrexham v Cardiff City | 2-2 |
| *( Wrexham won 7-6 on penalties).* | |
| Rhyl v Swansea City | 2-0 |

**FINAL**

| | |
|---|---|
| Wrexham v Rhyl | 4-1 |

## THE MOTAQUOTE INSURANCE WELSH LEAGUE

**DIVISION ONE**

| | *P* | *W* | *D* | *L* | *F* | *A* | *GD* | *Pts* |
|---|---|---|---|---|---|---|---|---|
| Llanelli | 34 | 26 | 4 | 4 | 74 | 28 | +46 | 82 |
| Goytre United | 34 | 22 | 9 | 3 | 73 | 24 | +49 | 75 |
| Grange Harlequins | 34 | 22 | 8 | 4 | 74 | 26 | +48 | 74 |
| UWIC | 34 | 21 | 6 | 7 | 72 | 33 | +39 | 69 |
| Ton Pentre | 34 | 20 | 6 | 8 | 96 | 38 | +58 | 66 |
| Dinas Powys | 34 | 14 | 11 | 9 | 58 | 41 | +17 | 53 |
| Maesteg Park | 34 | 14 | 11 | 9 | 39 | 36 | +3 | 53 |
| Neath | 34 | 15 | 5 | 14 | 65 | 56 | +9 | 50 |
| Briton Ferry | 34 | 11 | 11 | 12 | 53 | 45 | +8 | 44 |
| Bridgend Town | 34 | 12 | 7 | 15 | 50 | 60 | –10 | 43 |
| Garw | 34 | 11 | 5 | 18 | 46 | 66 | –20 | 38 |
| Caerleon | 34 | 10 | 7 | 17 | 56 | 62 | –6 | 37 |
| Bettws | 34 | 9 | 5 | 20 | 39 | 66 | –27 | 32 |
| Ely Rangers | 34 | 8 | 7 | 19 | 42 | 64 | –22 | 31 |
| Gwynfi United | 34 | 8 | 7 | 19 | 37 | 77 | –40 | 31 |
| Cardiff Corries | 34 | 7 | 6 | 21 | 39 | 65 | –26 | 27 |
| Pontardawe | 34 | 7 | 6 | 21 | 37 | 103 | –66 | 27 |
| Llanwern | 34 | 6 | 5 | 23 | 36 | 96 | –60 | 23 |

## HUWS GRAY – FITLOCK CYMRU ALLIANCE LEAGUE

| | *P* | *W* | *D* | *L* | *F* | *A* | *GD* | *Pts* |
|---|---|---|---|---|---|---|---|---|
| Airbus UK | 32 | 27 | 4 | 1 | 88 | 31 | +57 | 85 |
| Buckley Town | 32 | 20 | 6 | 6 | 74 | 33 | +41 | 66 |
| Ruthin Town | 32 | 19 | 7 | 6 | 78 | 48 | +30 | 64 |
| Glantraeth | 32 | 18 | 8 | 6 | 74 | 44 | +30 | 62 |
| Llangefni Town | 32 | 15 | 7 | 10 | 71 | 54 | +17 | 52 |
| Guilsfield | 32 | 15 | 7 | 10 | 68 | 56 | +12 | 52 |
| Llandudno | 32 | 15 | 6 | 11 | 63 | 50 | +13 | 51 |
| Halkyn United | 32 | 15 | 5 | 12 | 64 | 57 | +7 | 50 |
| Llanfairpwll | 32 | 12 | 7 | 13 | 51 | 52 | -1 | 43 |
| Flint Town United | 32 | 10 | 9 | 13 | 61 | 62 | -1 | 39 |
| Holyhead Hotspur | 32 | 10 | 8 | 14 | 51 | 67 | -16 | 38 |
| Lex XI | 32 | 9 | 8 | 15 | 77 | 85 | -8 | 35 |
| Gresford Athletic | 32 | 10 | 4 | 18 | 48 | 64 | -16 | 34 |
| Holywell Town | 32 | 8 | 8 | 16 | 38 | 61 | -23 | 32 |
| Mold Alexandra | 32 | 6 | 6 | 20 | 43 | 84 | -41 | 24 |
| Cemaes Bay | 32 | 5 | 7 | 20 | 37 | 70 | -33 | 22 |
| Amlwch Town | 32 | 2 | 5 | 25 | 34 | 102 | -68 | 11 |

## PREVIOUS WELSH LEAGUE WINNERS

| | | | | | |
|---|---|---|---|---|---|
| 1993 | Cwmbran Town | 1997 | Barry Town | 2001 | Barry Town |
| 1994 | Bangor City | 1998 | Barry Town | 2002 | Barry Town |
| 1995 | Bangor City | 1999 | Barry Town | 2003 | Barry Town |
| 1996 | Barry Town | 2000 | TNS | 2004 | Wrexham |

## PREVIOUS WELSH CUP WINNERS

| | | | | | |
|---|---|---|---|---|---|
| 1878 | Wrexham Town | 1921 | Wrexham | 1966 | Swansea Town |
| 1879 | White Star Newtown | 1922 | Cardiff City | 1967 | Cardiff City |
| 1880 | Druids | 1923 | Cardiff City | 1968 | Cardiff City |
| 1881 | Druids | 1924 | Wrexham | 1969 | Cardiff City |
| 1882 | Druids | 1925 | Wrexham | 1970 | Cardiff City |
| 1883 | Wrexham | 1926 | Ebbw Vale | 1971 | Cardiff City |
| 1884 | Oswestry United | 1927 | Cardiff City | 1972 | Wrexham |
| 1885 | Druids | 1928 | Cardiff City | 1973 | Cardiff City |
| 1886 | Druids | 1929 | Connah's Quay | 1974 | Cardiff City |
| 1887 | Chirk | 1930 | Cardiff City | 1975 | Wrexham |
| 1888 | Chirk | 1931 | Wrexham | 1976 | Cardiff City |
| 1889 | Bangor | 1932 | Swansea Town | 1977 | Shrewsbury Town |
| 1890 | Druids | 1933 | Chester | 1978 | Wrexham |
| 1891 | Shrewsbury Town | 1934 | Bristol City | 1979 | Shrewsbury Town |
| 1892 | Chirk | 1935 | Tranmere Rovers | 1980 | Newport County |
| 1893 | Wrexham | 1936 | Crewe Alexandra | 1981 | Swansea City |
| 1894 | Chirk | 1937 | Crewe Alexandra | 1982 | Swansea City |
| 1895 | Newtown | 1938 | Shrewsbury Town | 1983 | Swansea City |
| 1896 | Bangor | 1939 | South Liverpool | 1984 | Shrewsbury Town |
| 1897 | Wrexham | 1940 | Wellington Town | 1985 | Shrewsbury Town |
| 1898 | Druids | 1947 | Chester | 1986 | Wrexham |
| 1899 | Druids | 1948 | Lovell's Athletic | 1987 | Merthyr Tydfil |
| 1900 | Aberystwyth | 1949 | Merthyr Tydfil | 1988 | Cardiff City |
| 1901 | Oswestry United | 1950 | Swansea Town | 1989 | Swansea City |
| 1902 | Wellington Town | 1951 | Merthyr Tydfil | 1990 | Hereford United |
| 1903 | Wrexham | 1952 | Rhyl | 1991 | Swansea City |
| 1904 | Druids | 1953 | Rhyl | 1992 | Cardiff City |
| 1905 | Wrexham | 1954 | Flint Town United | 1993 | Cardiff City |
| 1906 | Wellington Town | 1955 | Barry Town | 1994 | Barry Town |
| 1907 | Oswestry United | 1956 | Cardiff City | 1995 | Wrexham |
| 1908 | Chester | 1957 | Wrexham | 1996 | TNS |
| 1909 | Wrexham | 1958 | Wrexham | 1997 | Barry Town |
| 1910 | Wrexham | 1959 | Cardiff City | 1998 | Bangor City |
| 1911 | Wrexham | 1960 | Wrexham | 1999 | Inter Cable-Tel |
| 1912 | Cardiff City | 1961 | Swansea Town | 2000 | Bangor City |
| 1913 | Swansea Town | 1962 | Bangor City | 2001 | Barry Town |
| 1914 | Wrexham | 1963 | Borough United | 2002 | Barry Town |
| 1915 | Wrexham | 1964 | Cardiff City | 2003 | Barry Town |
| 1920 | Cardiff City | 1965 | Cardiff City | 2004 | Rhyl |

# NORTHERN IRISH FOOTBALL 2003–04

Northern Ireland football underwent a dramatic change in season 2003–04 – not specifically on the playing pitch, but in the corridors of power.

The system of a Council with a series of sub-committees which has operated comparatively successfully for more than a century was abandoned and a 17-member Executive Board, given total authority, was set up to run the affairs, including what is, in effect, an amalgamation of the Irish Football Association and the Irish Football League under one roof. In other words, the Council, which will meet, perhaps, four times a year, will be an irrelevancy.

The changes follow two years' discussion on the report from a Government Task Force on the future of football, which culminated in £8m grant aid over three years for development of the game at all levels. With it went stipulations, and until they were met the cash could not be released. The new set-up, however, is to be examined after two years but, frankly, most people assume the concept has been written in stone. 'Let's give it a chance', says Irish FA president Jim Boyce.

And there was depression and drama with the international team. It went 1,298 minutes and 15 matches without scoring a goal until David Healy, the Preston striker, ended the drought against Norway and went on to establish a new all-time Irish scoring record of 14 – one more than that which had existed for years and was held by Colin Clarke, the ex-Portsmouth centre-forward, and the late Billy Gillespie, Sheffield United icon of the 1920's.

Sammy McIlroy resigned as manager 24 hours after the final European Championship qualifier against Greece in Athens to join Stockport County. Jimmy Nicholl, Dunfermline's assistant coach, appeared a certainty to succeed him, but the job went to Lawrie Sanchez, Wimbledon's FA Cup Final hero, who played three times for Northern Ireland under Billy Bingham.

Sanchez brought a new dimension to management, got the team on a winning streak – five matches undefeated – lifted morale and, at last, the public found themselves with a feel-good factor. Confidence had been restored as the World Cup qualifiers against England, Wales, Poland, Austria and Azerbaijan loomed.

Domestically it was a season pockmarked with problems for clubs attempting to make ends meet. Ards, for instance, remain without a stadium after selling Castlereagh Park four years ago to meet pressing debts, but they expect work to be started soon on their new site given by the Borough Council.

Ironically, Glenavon, whose Mourneview Park stadium ranks among the finest in Ireland, were relegated from the Premiership for the first time in their history and they also opted against having a reserve side in the coming season, but plan continuing with the youth development policy. Adding salt to the wound, Loughgall, near neighbours, were promoted.

Linfield regained the Irish Premier Division title, Glentoran won the Nationwide Irish Cup, while the Irish FA announced that Germany would provide the opposition for the 125th anniversary game in June 2005 – the actual celebrations are in November – and the European Under-19 Championships will be staged in Northern Ireland that year to coincide with the anniversary.

A new era commences for Northern Ireland, but, frankly, what the future holds remains to be seen. The time has arrived when legislators must take a firm grip, make hard decisions to handle their own affairs without outside influence. Progress can be made, but it will take all-round unanimity.

DR MALCOLM BRODIE

**DAILY MIRROR IRISH LEAGUE PREMIER DIVISION**

| | *P* | *W* | *D* | *L* | *F* | *A* | *GD* | *Pts* |
|---|---|---|---|---|---|---|---|---|
| Linfield | 30 | 22 | 7 | 1 | 67 | 16 | +51 | 73 |
| Portadown | 30 | 22 | 4 | 4 | 71 | 22 | +49 | 70 |
| Lisburn Distillery | 30 | 16 | 7 | 7 | 45 | 30 | +15 | 55 |
| Coleraine | 30 | 14 | 9 | 7 | 48 | 36 | +12 | 51 |
| Glentoran | 30 | 15 | 5 | 10 | 48 | 27 | +21 | 50 |
| Ballymena United | 30 | 13 | 8 | 9 | 41 | 35 | +6 | 47 |
| Limavady United | 30 | 12 | 5 | 13 | 41 | 43 | −2 | 41 |
| Ards | 30 | 9 | 11 | 10 | 36 | 46 | −10 | 38 |
| Crusaders | 30 | 10 | 6 | 14 | 33 | 38 | −5 | 36 |
| Dungannon Swifts | 30 | 10 | 6 | 14 | 36 | 46 | −12 | 36 |
| Institute | 30 | 9 | 7 | 14 | 38 | 53 | −15 | 34 |
| Newry Town | 30 | 8 | 9 | 13 | 35 | 53 | −18 | 33 |
| Omagh town | 30 | 9 | 4 | 17 | 37 | 58 | −21 | 31 |
| Larne | 30 | 7 | 8 | 15 | 42 | 51 | −9 | 29 |
| Cliftonville | 30 | 6 | 8 | 16 | 27 | 45 | −18 | 26 |
| Glenavon* | 30 | 4 | 4 | 22 | 24 | 67 | −43 | 16 |

**Relegated.*

**PROMOTION/RELEGATION PLAY-OFF**

**First Leg**
Armagh City 0, Cliftonville 3 *(at Holm Park, Armagh)*

**Second Leg**
Cliftonville 1, Armagh City 1 *(at Solitude, Belfast)*

*Leading goalscorers:* 34 Ferguson (Linfield); 27 Hamilton (Portadown); 23 Arkins (Portadown); 21 Fitzgerald (Ards); 20 Smith A (Glentoran); 19 Parkhouse (Institute); 18 Kennedy (Ards), Hamill (Coleraine); 14 Morgan (Linfield), Halliday (Glentoran); 13 Crawford (Omagh Town), Armstrong (Coleraine), Delaney (Larne), Willis (Crusaders); 12 Picking (Linfield), Brown (Limavady United), Crawford (Cliftonville), Sweeney (Limavady United); 11 Tolan (Coleraine), Armour (Glentoran), Kearney (Ballymena United), Candlish (Larne).

**DAILY MIRROR FIRST DIVISION**

| | *P* | *W* | *D* | *L* | *F* | *A* | *GD* | *Pts* |
|---|---|---|---|---|---|---|---|---|
| Loughgall | 22 | 14 | 6 | 2 | 37 | 20 | +17 | 48 |
| Armagh City | 22 | 13 | 4 | 5 | 30 | 15 | +15 | 43 |
| Ballyclare Comrades | 22 | 13 | 4 | 5 | 34 | 21 | +13 | 43 |
| Bangor | 22 | 11 | 6 | 5 | 35 | 20 | +15 | 39 |
| HW Welders | 22 | 9 | 6 | 7 | 29 | 24 | +5 | 33 |
| Ballymoney United | 22 | 7 | 8 | 7 | 22 | 26 | −4 | 29 |
| Carrick Rangers | 22 | 6 | 7 | 9 | 30 | 35 | −5 | 25 |
| Donegal Celtic | 22 | 5 | 8 | 9 | 29 | 27 | +2 | 23 |
| Ballinamallard United | 22 | 5 | 6 | 11 | 20 | 31 | −11 | 21 |
| Moyola Park | 22 | 4 | 6 | 12 | 34 | 41 | −7 | 18 |
| Lurgan Celtic* | 22 | 3 | 9 | 10 | 24 | 44 | −20 | 18 |
| Brantwood* | 22 | 4 | 6 | 12 | 18 | 38 | −20 | 18 |

**INTERMEDIATE SECOND DIVISION**

| | *P* | *W* | *D* | *L* | *F* | *A* | *GD* | *Pts* |
|---|---|---|---|---|---|---|---|---|
| Coagh United | 22 | 16 | 2 | 4 | 60 | 28 | +32 | 50 |
| Dundela | 22 | 14 | 4 | 4 | 49 | 23 | +26 | 46 |
| Dergview | 22 | 13 | 4 | 5 | 45 | 26 | +19 | 43 |
| Tobermore United | 22 | 12 | 6 | 4 | 42 | 27 | +15 | 42 |
| Wakehurst | 22 | 11 | 4 | 7 | 39 | 26 | +13 | 37 |
| PSNI | 22 | 12 | 1 | 9 | 49 | 47 | +2 | 37 |
| Banbridge Town | 22 | 8 | 2 | 12 | 42 | 49 | −7 | 26 |
| Portstewart | 22 | 6 | 7 | 9 | 25 | 26 | −1 | 25 |
| Chimney Corner | 22 | 6 | 6 | 10 | 28 | 35 | −7 | 24 |
| Queens University | 22 | 6 | 4 | 12 | 36 | 43 | −7 | 22 |
| Annagh United | 22 | 4 | 4 | 14 | 25 | 51 | −26 | 16 |
| Crewe United | 22 | 0 | 4 | 18 | 10 | 69 | −59 | 4 |

**IFL RESERVE LEAGUE**

| | *P* | *W* | *D* | *L* | *F* | *A* | *GD* | *Pts* |
|---|---|---|---|---|---|---|---|---|
| Linfield Swifts | 26 | 17 | 5 | 4 | 82 | 35 | +47 | 56 |
| Glentoran II | 26 | 16 | 4 | 6 | 58 | 35 | +23 | 52 |
| Institute II | 25 | 14 | 7 | 4 | 51 | 36 | +15 | 49 |
| Dungannon Swifts Res | 26 | 14 | 5 | 7 | 73 | 53 | +20 | 47 |
| Crusaders Res | 26 | 14 | 5 | 7 | 51 | 21 | +30 | 47 |
| Portadown Res | 26 | 14 | 1 | 11 | 55 | 46 | +9 | 43 |
| Cliftonville Olympic | 24 | 11 | 2 | 11 | 45 | 43 | +2 | 35 |
| Lisburn Distillery II | 26 | 11 | 2 | 13 | 47 | 49 | −2 | 35 |
| Omagh Town Res | 26 | 9 | 5 | 12 | 43 | 52 | −9 | 32 |
| Glenavon Res | 26 | 9 | 4 | 13 | 36 | 49 | −13 | 31 |
| Limavady United Res | 24 | 7 | 4 | 13 | 41 | 48 | −7 | 25 |
| Ards II | 26 | 7 | 2 | 17 | 31 | 87 | −56 | 23 |
| Ballymena United Res | 25 | 6 | 2 | 17 | 39 | 68 | −29 | 20 |
| Coleraine Res | 24 | 3 | 4 | 17 | 33 | 63 | −30 | 13 |

**IFL YOUTH LEAGUE**

| | *P* | *W* | *D* | *L* | *F* | *A* | *GD* | *Pts* |
|---|---|---|---|---|---|---|---|---|
| Glenavon III | 28 | 22 | 4 | 2 | 85 | 22 | +63 | 70 |
| Donegal Celtic Youth | 28 | 21 | 2 | 5 | 90 | 33 | +57 | 65 |
| Glentoran Colts | 28 | 20 | 4 | 4 | 62 | 30 | +32 | 64 |
| Crusaders Colts | 27 | 15 | 5 | 7 | 63 | 38 | +25 | 50 |
| Linfield Rangers | 24 | 13 | 7 | 4 | 43 | 23 | +20 | 46 |
| Ballyclare Comrades Colts | 24 | 11 | 1 | 12 | 40 | 46 | −6 | 34 |
| Limavady United III | 26 | 9 | 4 | 13 | 51 | 38 | +13 | 31 |
| Ards Colts | 25 | 8 | 3 | 14 | 49 | 77 | −28 | 27 |
| Ballinamallard United Youth | 21 | 8 | 2 | 11 | 32 | 39 | −7 | 26 |
| Cliftonville Strollers | 25 | 7 | 3 | 15 | 44 | 57 | −13 | 24 |
| Lisburn Distillery III | 24 | 6 | 4 | 14 | 42 | 71 | −29 | 22 |
| Ballymena United III | 25 | 5 | 6 | 14 | 36 | 56 | −20 | 21 |
| Coleraine Colts | 25 | 5 | 2 | 18 | 27 | 74 | −47 | 17 |
| Institute Academy | 20 | 3 | 5 | 12 | 19 | 56 | −37 | 14 |
| Newry Town Wanderers | 18 | 3 | 4 | 11 | 18 | 41 | −23 | 13 |

## ULSTER CUP WINNERS

1949 Linfield
1950 Larne
1951 Glentoran
1952
1953 Glentoran
1954 Crusaders
1955 Glenavon
1956 Linfield
1957 Linfield
1958 Distillery
1959 Glenavon
1960 Linfield
1961 Ballymena U
1962 Linfield
1963 Crusaders
1964 Linfield
1965 Coleraine
1966 Glentoran
1967 Linfield
1968 Coleraine
1969 Coleraine
1970 Linfield
1971 Linfield
1972 Coleraine
1973 Ards
1974 Linfield
1975 Coleraine
1976 Glentoran
1977 Linfield
1978 Linfield
1979 Linfield
1980 Ballymena U
1981 Glentoran
1982 Glentoran
1983 Glentoran
1984 Linfield
1985 Coleraine
1986 Coleraine
1987 Larne
1988 Glentoran
1989 Glentoran
1990 Portadown
1991 Bangor
1992 Linfield
1993 Crusaders
1994 Bangor
1995 Portadown
1996 Portadown
1997 Coleraine
1998 Ballyclare Comrades
1999 Distillery
2000 *No competition*
2001 *No competition*
2002 *No competition*
2003 Dungannon Swifts *(Confined to First Division clubs)*
2004 *No competition*

## IRISH LEAGUE CHAMPIONSHIP WINNERS

| | |
|---|---|
| 1891 | Linfield |
| 1892 | Linfield |
| 1893 | Linfield |
| 1894 | Glentoran |
| 1895 | Linfield |
| 1896 | Distillery |
| 1897 | Glentoran |
| 1898 | Linfield |
| 1899 | Distillery |
| 1900 | Belfast Celtic |
| 1901 | Distillery |
| 1902 | Linfield |
| 1903 | Distillery |
| 1904 | Linfield |
| 1905 | Glentoran |
| 1906 | Cliftonville |
| | Distillery |
| 1907 | Linfield |
| 1908 | Linfield |
| 1909 | Linfield |
| 1910 | Cliftonville |
| 1911 | Linfield |
| 1912 | Glentoran |
| 1913 | Glentoran |
| 1914 | Linfield |
| 1915 | Belfast Celtic |
| 1920 | Belfast Celtic |
| 1921 | Glentoran |
| 1922 | Linfield |
| 1923 | Linfield |
| 1924 | Queen's Island |
| 1925 | Glentoran |
| 1926 | Belfast Celtic |
| 1927 | Belfast Celtic |
| 1928 | Belfast Celtic |
| 1929 | Belfast Celtic |
| 1930 | Linfield |
| 1931 | Glentoran |
| 1932 | Linfield |
| 1933 | Belfast Celtic |
| 1934 | Linfield |
| 1935 | Linfield |
| 1936 | Belfast Celtic |
| 1937 | Belfast Celtic |
| 1938 | Belfast Celtic |
| 1939 | Belfast Celtic |
| 1940 | Belfast Celtic |
| 1948 | Belfast Celtic |
| 1949 | Linfield |
| 1950 | Linfield |
| 1951 | Glentoran |
| 1952 | Glenavon |
| 1953 | Glentoran |
| 1954 | Linfield |
| 1955 | Linfield |
| 1956 | Linfield |
| 1957 | Glentoran |
| 1958 | Ards |
| 1959 | Linfield |
| 1960 | Glenavon |
| 1961 | Linfield |
| 1962 | Linfield |
| 1963 | Distillery |
| 1964 | Glentoran |
| 1965 | Derry City |
| 1966 | Linfield |
| 1967 | Glentoran |
| 1968 | Glentoran |
| 1969 | Linfield |
| 1970 | Glentoran |
| 1971 | Linfield |
| 1972 | Glentoran |
| 1973 | Crusaders |
| 1974 | Coleraine |
| 1975 | Linfield |
| 1976 | Crusaders |
| 1977 | Glentoran |
| 1978 | Linfield |
| 1979 | Linfield |
| 1980 | Linfield |
| 1981 | Glentoran |
| 1982 | Linfield |
| 1983 | Linfield |
| 1984 | Linfield |
| 1985 | Linfield |
| 1986 | Linfield |
| 1987 | Linfield |
| 1988 | Glentoran |
| 1989 | Linfield |
| 1990 | Portadown |
| 1991 | Portadown |
| 1992 | Glentoran |
| 1993 | Linfield |
| 1994 | Linfield |
| 1995 | Crusaders |
| 1996 | Portadown |
| 1997 | Crusaders |
| 1998 | Cliftonville |
| 1999 | Glentoran |
| 2000 | Linfield |
| 2001 | Linfield |
| 2002 | Portadown |
| 2003 | Glentoran |
| 2004 | Linfield |

## FIRST DIVISION

| | |
|---|---|
| 1996 | Coleraine |
| 1997 | Ballymena United |
| 1998 | Newry Town |
| 1999 | Distillery |
| 2000 | Omagh Town |
| 2001 | Ards |
| 2002 | Lisburn Distillery |
| 2003 | Dungannon Swifts |
| 2004 | Loughgall |

## NATIONWIDE IRISH CUP 2003–04

### FIFTH ROUND

| | |
|---|---|
| Crusaders v Brantwood | 0-1 |
| Coleraine v HW Welders | 1-1, 4-1 |
| Loughgall v Killyleagh | 3-1 |
| Linfield v Carrick Rangers | 0-0, 4-1 |
| Larne v Institute | 2-0 |
| Newry Town v Ballymoney United | 2-2, 3-1 |
| Ballyclare Comrades v Donegal Celtic | 3-0 |
| Limavady United v Armagh City | 4-1 |
| Ards v Donard Hospital | 10-0 |
| Dungannon Swifts v Ballymure OB | 4-1 |
| Portadown v Glenavon | 0-1 |
| Omagh Town v Albert Foundry | 5-3 |
| Tobermore United v Nortel | 3-1 |
| Cliftonville v Lisburn Distillery | 5-1 |
| Glentoran v Ballymena United | 4-2 |
| Lurgan Celtic v Bangor | 1-3 |

### SIXTH ROUND

| | |
|---|---|
| Bangor v Linfield | 0-0, 0-7 |
| Loughgall v Glentoran | 0-0. 0-2 |
| Ballyclare Comrades v Ards | 0-2 |
| Newry Town v Larne | 2-1 |
| Omagh Town v Brantwood | 2-1 |
| Dungannon Swifts v Glenavon | 1-1, 0-1 |
| Tobermore United v Limavady United | 0-4 |
| Cliftonville v Coleraine | 0-1 |

### QUARTER-FINALS

| | |
|---|---|
| Linfield v Glentoran | 0-1 |
| Limavady United v Glenavon | 2-0 |
| Newry Town v Coleraine | 1-1, 1-3 |
| Ards v Omagh Town | 1-2 |

### SEMI-FINALS

| | |
|---|---|
| Coleraine v Limavady United *(at The Showground, Ballymena)* | 3-1 |
| Glentoran v Omagh Town *(at Mourneview Park, Lurgan)* | 4-1 |

## NATIONWIDE IRISH CUP FINAL 2003–04

(at Windsor Park)

**Glentoran 1 Coleraine 0**

*Glentoran:* Morris; Nixon, Glendinning, Melaugh, Leeman, Smyth G, McCann (Kilmartin), Lockhart, Smith A, Halliday (Armour), Keegan (McCallion).
*Scorer:* Halliday.

*Coleraine:* O'Hare; Clanaghan, Flynn, Gaston, McAuley (Johnson), Beatty, Curran (Armstrong), Hamill, Tolan, Haveron, Gorman.
*Referee:* D. Malcolm (Bangor).

*Attendance:* 8300.

*Man of the Match:* Michael Halliday (Glentoran).

*Player of the Tournament:* Michael Halliday.

## IRISH CUP FINALS (from 1946–47)

| | |
|---|---|
| 1946–47 | Belfast Celtic 1, Glentoran 0 |
| 1947–48 | Linfield 3, Coleraine 0 |
| 1948–49 | Derry City 3, Glentoran 1 |
| 1949–50 | Linfield 2, Distillery 1 |
| 1950–51 | Glentoran 3, Ballymena U 1 |
| 1951–52 | Ards 1, Glentoran 0 |
| 1952–53 | Linfield 5, Coleraine 0 |
| 1953–54 | Derry City 1, Glentoran 0 |
| 1954–55 | Dundela 3, Glenavon 0 |
| 1955–56 | Distillery 1, Glentoran 0 |
| 1956–57 | Glenavon 2, Derry City 0 |
| 1957–58 | Ballymena U 2, Linfield 0 |
| 1958–59 | Glenavon 2, Ballymena U 0 |
| 1959–60 | Linfield 5, Ards 1 |
| 1960–61 | Glenavon 5, Linfield 1 |
| 1961–62 | Linfield 4, Portadown 0 |
| 1962–63 | Linfield 2, Distillery 1 |
| 1963–64 | Derry City 2, Glentoran 0 |
| 1964–65 | Coleraine 2, Glenavon 1 |
| 1965–66 | Glentoran 2, Linfield 0 |
| 1966–67 | Crusaders 3, Glentoran 1 |
| 1967–68 | Crusaders 2, Linfield 0 |
| 1968–69 | Ards 4, Distillery 2 |
| 1969–70 | Linfield 2, Ballymena U 1 |
| 1970–71 | Distillery 3, Derry City |
| 1971–72 | Coleraine 2, Portadown 1 |
| 1972–73 | Glentoran 3, Linfield 2 |
| 1973–74 | Ards 2, Ballymena U 1 |
| 1974–75 | Coleraine 1:0:1, Linfield 1:0:0 |
| 1975–76 | Carrick Rangers 2, Linfield 1 |
| 1976–77 | Coleraine 4, Linfield 1 |
| 1977–78 | Linfield 3, Ballymena U 1 |
| 1978–79 | Cliftonville 3, Portadown 2 |
| 1979–80 | Linfield 2, Crusaders 0 |
| 1980–81 | Ballymena U 1, Glenavon 0 |
| 1981–82 | Linfield 2, Coleraine 1 |
| 1982–83 | Glentoran 1:2, Linfield 1:1 |
| 1983–84 | Ballymena U 4, Carrick Rangers 1 |
| 1984–85 | Glentoran 1:1, Linfield 1:0 |
| 1985–86 | Glentoran 2, Coleraine 1 |
| 1986–87 | Glentoran 1, Larne 0 |
| 1987–88 | Glentoran 1, Glenavon 0 |
| 1988–89 | Ballymena U 1, Larne 0 |
| 1989–90 | Glentoran 3, Portadown 0 |
| 1990–91 | Portadown 2, Glenavon 1 |
| 1991–92 | Glenavon 2, Linfield 1 |
| 1992–93 | Bangor 1:1:1, Ards 1:1:0 |
| 1993–94 | Linfield 2, Bangor 0 |
| 1994–95 | Linfield 3, Carrick Rangers 1 |
| 1995–96 | Glentoran 1, Glenavon 0 |
| 1996–97 | Glenavon 1, Cliftonville 0 |
| 1997–98 | Glentoran 1, Glenavon 0 |
| 1998–99 | *Portadown awarded trophy after Cliftonville were eliminated for using an ineligible player in semi-final.* |
| 1999–2000 | Glentoran 1, Portadown 0 |
| 2000–01 | Glentoran 1, Linfield 0 |
| 2001–02 | Linfield 2, Portadown 1 |
| 2002–03 | Coleraine 1 Glentoran 0 |
| 2003–04 | Glentoran 1 Coleraine 0 |

## COUNTY ANTRIM SHIELD

**FIRST ROUND**

| | |
|---|---|
| Glentoran v Donegal Celtic | 6-1 |
| Linfield v Islandmagee | 4-2 |
| Crusaders v Bangor | 3-0 |
| Ballymena United v Dunmurry YM | 3-1 |
| Larne v Larne Tech OB | 4-0 |
| Ards v Carrick Rangers | 4-1 |
| Lisburn Distillery v Ballyclare Comrades | 0-1 |
| Cliftonville v Holywood FC | 6-0 |

**SECOND ROUND**

| | |
|---|---|
| Glentoran v Cliftonville | 3-0 |
| Ballyclare Comrades v Ards | 0-1 |
| Linfield v Larne | 3-0 |
| Cruaders v Ballymena United | 0-1 |

**SEMI-FINALS**

Ards v Ballymena United 1-0
*(at Seaview, Belfast)*
Glentoran v Linfield 0-1
*(at The Oval)*
*(Armed, masked robbers snatched £20,000 gate receipts at this semi-final. County Antrim FA compensated clubs from their own funds).*

### COUNTY ANTRIM SHIELD FINAL

(at The Oval)

**Linfield 2 Ards 0**

*Linfield:* Mannus; Wall, McShane, Irons (McCann), Murphy W, Gault, Morgan (Larmour), Picking (O'Kane), Ferguson, King, Bailie.
*Scorers:* Hunter (og), Larmour.

*Ards:* Fox; Watson (Murphy D), Scannell, McCombe (Rainey), Gollogly, Campbell, Quinn, Feeney, Hunter M (Lowry), Fitzgerald, Kennedy.

*Referee:* D. Malcolm (Bangor).

## CIS INSURANCE IRISH LEAGUE CUP

**FINAL SECTION TABLES**

| **Section A** | *P* | *W* | *D* | *L* | *F* | *A* | *Pts* |
|---|---|---|---|---|---|---|---|
| Glentoran | 6 | 6 | 0 | 0 | 18 | 1 | 18 |
| Cliftonville | 6 | 2 | 0 | 4 | 5 | 6 | 6 |
| Omagh Town | 6 | 2 | 0 | 4 | 5 | 8 | 6 |
| Dungannon Swifts | 6 | 2 | 0 | 4 | 2 | 15 | 6 |

| **Section B** | *P* | *W* | *D* | *L* | *F* | *A* | *Pts* |
|---|---|---|---|---|---|---|---|
| Portadown | 6 | 4 | 2 | 0 | 13 | 5 | 14 |
| Institute | 6 | 3 | 1 | 2 | 11 | 9 | 10 |
| Glenavon | 6 | 2 | 1 | 3 | 7 | 8 | 7 |
| Ballymena United | 6 | 1 | 0 | 5 | 6 | 15 | 3 |

| **Section C** | *P* | *W* | *D* | *L* | *F* | *A* | *Pts* |
|---|---|---|---|---|---|---|---|
| Coleraine | 6 | 4 | 1 | 1 | 16 | 7 | 13 |
| Crusaders | 6 | 3 | 2 | 1 | 8 | 4 | 11 |
| Ards | 6 | 3 | 1 | 2 | 8 | 8 | 10 |
| Limavady United | 6 | 0 | 0 | 6 | 3 | 16 | 0 |

| **Section D** | *P* | *W* | *D* | *L* | *F* | *A* | *Pts* |
|---|---|---|---|---|---|---|---|
| Linfield | 6 | 6 | 0 | 0 | 17 | 4 | 18 |
| Larne | 6 | 4 | 0 | 2 | 9 | 7 | 12 |
| Lisburn Distillery | 6 | 1 | 0 | 5 | 6 | 12 | 3 |
| Newry Town | 6 | 1 | 0 | 5 | 5 | 14 | 3 |

**QUARTER-FINALS**

| | |
|---|---|
| Linfield v Crusaders | 0-1 |
| Portadown v Cliftonville | 0-3 |
| Coleraine v Larne | 2-4 |
| Glentoran v Institute | 6-1 |

**SEMI-FINALS**

Cliftonville v Crusaders 1-1
*Cliftonville won 4-1 on penalties.*
Glentoran v Larne *(match postponed to investigate non-registration of Gary Smyth (Glentoran) with the Irish FA. Glentoran were eliminated and Larne automatically entered in the Final).*

### CIS INSURANCE IRISH LEAGUE CUP FINAL

(at Windsor Park)

**Cliftonville 1 Larne 1**

*aet; Cliftonville won 5-4 on penalties.*

*Cliftonville:* Straney; Fleming, Brannigan (McMullan C), Small, Mulvenna, Quigley, McMullan G (Vernon), Crawford, Patton, Hagan, Donnelly.
*Scorer:* Mulvenna.

*Larne:* McDonald; Clifford, Maxwell, Murphy, McDonagh, Dickson, O'Connor (McKinstry), Ogden (Cowie), Delaney, Parker (Walsh), McCloskey.
*Scorer:* Delaney.

*Referee:* F. Hiles (Coleraine).

*Attendance:* 3000.

## WHERE THE TROPHIES WENT

| **Daily Mirror Irish Premier League** | *Winners* | *Runners-up* |
|---|---|---|
| Premier Division | Linfield | Portadown |
| First Division | Loughgall | Armagh City |
| Irish Reserve League | Linfield Swifts | Glentoran II |
| Irish League Youth Cup | Glenavon III | Glentoran Colts |
| Nationwide Irish Cup | Glentoran | Coleraine |
| CIS Insurance Irish League Cup | Cliftonville | Larne |
| County Antrim Shield | Linfield | Ards |
| Steel and Sons Cup | Donegal Celtic | Killyleagh YM |
| County Antrim Junior Shield | Ardoyne WMC | Crumlin United II |
| Belfast Telegraph Intermediate Cup | Linfield Swifts | Larne Tech OB |
| Irish Junior Cup | Irvinestown Wanderers | West Belfast |
| Rushmere Shopping Mid Ulster Cup | Loughgall | Newry Town |
| Village Windows NW Senior Cup | Coleraine | Limavady United |
| Harry Cavan Youth Cup | Linfield Rangers | Coleraine Colts |
| George Wilson Memorial Cup | Dungannon Swifts | Linfield Swifts |
| Daily Mirror Trophy Final | Carrick Rangers | Moyola Park |

# CHAMPIONS LEAGUE REVIEW 2003–04

Nothing seems to satisfy the purists. If the favourites fail to reach the final, the competition is deemed second rate. Should they succeed, the standard of play is disappointing. Yet when one simply analyses the Champions League 2003–04, there is far more in it to praise than decry the ultimate outcome.

For FC Porto and their charismatic coach Jose Mourinho, success merely set light to the fuse which threatened to launch him into the stratosphere of the English Premier League if he so desired. Variously described in the informative *Champions* magazine as the essence of the thinking girl's crumpet and boasting confidence just a little short of arrogance, at 41 he reached the high peak of his career when his Portuguese pulling-power propelled his team to a comprehensive 3-0 win over Monaco in the Gelsenkirchen final. He had won the UEFA Cup the previous season of course.

In truth they did not make the best of starts to their group matches, held to a draw away to Partizan, then well beaten 3-1 at home by Real Madrid, in hindsight the Spaniards' best performance of the season and arguably one of their last such. After that they managed single goal successes in the next three and learned a lesson from the Real reverse by drawing in Spain. In the first knock-out round Manchester United were beaten 2-1 and held 1-1 at Old Trafford, but only with a last gasp equaliser. Lyon proved slightly less of a problem in the quarter-final, until Porto were on the back foot again in the semis.

At home in the first leg facing Deportivo La Coruna, they were unable to break the visitors' defence down and prospects for the return leg seemed distinctly dire, given the Spaniards' display against AC Milan. But Mourinho had other ideas and after they took the lead with a penalty on the hour, the subsequent dismissal of La Coruna's Nouredine Naybet eased the likelihood of a Spanish revival.

In contrast to the cloaked closeness of the majority of Porto's matches, Monaco were swashbuckling adventurers, capable of high scoring – witness their incredible 8-3 win over La Coruna, but just as likely to struggle for a breakthrough on other occasions. However in the quarter-finals they virtually ended Real Madrid's season at home and abroad.

Trailing 4-2 from the Spanish leg, Monaco went further behind just after half an hour in the second game, levelled before the break, then carried on to win 3-1 and clinch the tie on away goals. In the semi-final they took full advantage of Claudio Ranieri's apparent senior moment when he made ill-judged substitutions at half-time and allowed a 1-1 scoreline to be transformed into 3-1 defeat against ten opponents. Then at Stamford Bridge it finished 2-2 after the Blues discarded a two-goal lead.

English clubs' hopes had rested heavily on the new millionaires from west London, especially as Chelsea had pulled off the seemingly impossible by disposing of Arsenal in the quarter-finals, ending the Blues' dismal overall record against the Gunners in recent years.

This after Arsenal had turned in one of their finest European performances in devastating Internazionale 5-1 in Milan in their penultimate group match, when even qualification was being threatened for them.

Chelsea had had to scramble through from the third qualifying round along with Newcastle United, who found themselves highly embarrassed by Partizan after taking a 1-0 lead from Serbia; they were pegged back at St James Park and then defeated by the English curse – penalty kicks.

The quarter-finals also saw the demise of AC Milan, who in company with Real Madrid were favoured by those in the know. But La Coruna pulled off a sensational victory after crashing 4-1 in Italy in the first leg. Three first half goals wiped out Milan's advantage and the Spaniards underlined their triumph with a fourth.

Arsenal's Kolo Toure can only look on as Frank Lampard draws Chelsea level in the European Champions League quarter final second leg tie at Highbury. (ASP)

# EUROPEAN CUP

## EUROPEAN CUP FINALS 1956–1992

| Year | Winners | Runners-up | Venue | Attendance | Referee |
|---|---|---|---|---|---|
| 1956 | Real Madrid 4 | Reims 3 | Paris | 38,000 | Ellis (E) |
| 1957 | Real Madrid 2 | Fiorentina 0 | Madrid | 124,000 | Horn (Ho) |
| 1958 | Real Madrid 3 | AC Milan 2 *(aet)* | Brussels | 67,000 | Alsteen (Bel) |
| 1959 | Real Madrid 2 | Reims 0 | Stuttgart | 80,000 | Dutsch (WG) |
| 1960 | Real Madrid 7 | Eintracht Frankfurt 3 | Glasgow | 135,000 | Mowat (S) |
| 1961 | Benfica 3 | Barcelona 2 | Berne | 28,000 | Dienst (Sw) |
| 1962 | Benfica 5 | Real Madrid 3 | Amsterdam | 65,000 | Horn (Ho) |
| 1963 | AC Milan 2 | Benfica 1 | Wembley | 45,000 | Holland (E) |
| 1964 | Internazionale 3 | Real Madrid 1 | Vienna | 74,000 | Stoll (A) |
| 1965 | Internazionale 1 | Benfica 0 | Milan | 80,000 | Dienst (Sw) |
| 1966 | Real Madrid 2 | Partizan Belgrade 1 | Brussels | 55,000 | Kreitlein (WG) |
| 1967 | Celtic 2 | Internazionale 1 | Lisbon | 56,000 | Tschenscher (WG) |
| 1968 | Manchester U 4 | Benfica 1 *(aet)* | Wembley | 100,000 | Lo Bello (I) |
| 1969 | AC Milan 4 | Ajax 1 | Madrid | 50,000 | Ortiz (Sp) |
| 1970 | Feyenoord 2 | Celtic 1 *(aet)* | Milan | 50,000 | Lo Bello (I) |
| 1971 | Ajax 2 | Panathinaikos 0 | Wembley | 90,000 | Taylor (E) |
| 1972 | Ajax 2 | Internazionale 0 | Rotterdam | 67,000 | Helies (F) |
| 1973 | Ajax 1 | Juventus 0 | Belgrade | 93,500 | Guglovic (Y) |
| 1974 | Bayern Munich 1 | Atletico Madrid 1 | Brussels | 49,000 | Loraux (Bel) |
| *Replay* | Bayern Munich 4 | Atletico Madrid 0 | Brussels | 23,000 | Delcourt (Bel) |
| 1975 | Bayern Munich 2 | Leeds U 0 | Paris | 50,000 | Kitabdjian (F) |
| 1976 | Bayern Munich 1 | St Etienne 0 | Glasgow | 54,864 | Palotai (H) |
| 1977 | Liverpool 3 | Moenchengladbach 1 | Rome | 57,000 | Wurtz (F) |
| 1978 | Liverpool 1 | FC Brugge 0 | Wembley | 92,000 | Corver (Ho) |
| 1979 | Nottingham F 1 | Malmo 0 | Munich | 57,500 | Linemayr (A) |
| 1980 | Nottingham F 1 | Hamburg 0 | Madrid | 50,000 | Garrido (P) |
| 1981 | Liverpool 1 | Real Madrid 0 | Paris | 48,360 | Palotai (H) |
| 1982 | Aston Villa 1 | Bayern Munich 0 | Rotterdam | 46,000 | Konrath (F) |
| 1983 | Hamburg 1 | Juventus 0 | Athens | 80,000 | Rainea (R) |
| 1984 | Liverpool 1 | Roma 1 | Rome | 69,693 | Fredriksson (Se) |
| | *(aet; Liverpool won 4-2 on penalties)* | | | | |
| 1985 | Juventus 1 | Liverpool 0 | Brussels | 58,000 | Daina (Sw) |
| 1986 | Steaua Bucharest 0 | Barcelona 0 | Seville | 70,000 | Vautrot (F) |
| | *(aet; Steaua won 2-0 on penalties)* | | | | |
| 1987 | Porto 2 | Bayern Munich 1 | Vienna | 59,000 | Ponnet (Bel) |
| 1988 | PSV Eindhoven 0 | Benfica 0 | Stuttgart | 70,000 | Agnolin (I) |
| | *(aet; PSV won 6-5 on penalties)* | | | | |
| 1989 | AC Milan 4 | Steaua Bucharest 0 | Barcelona | 97,000 | Tritschler (WG) |
| 1990 | AC Milan 1 | Benfica 0 | Vienna | 57,500 | Kohl (A) |
| 1991 | Red Star Belgrade 0 | Marseille 0 | Bari | 56,000 | Lanese (I) |
| | *(aet; Red Star won 5-3 on penalties)* | | | | |
| 1992 | Barcelona 1 | Sampdoria 0 *(aet)* | Wembley | 70,827 | Schmidhuber (G) |

## UEFA CHAMPIONS LEAGUE FINALS 1993–2004

| | | | | | |
|---|---|---|---|---|---|
| 1993 | Marseille* 1 | AC Milan 0 | Munich | 64,400 | Rothlisberger (Sw) |
| 1994 | AC Milan 4 | Barcelona 0 | Athens | 70,000 | Don (E) |
| 1995 | Ajax 1 | AC Milan 0 | Vienna | 49,730 | Craciunescu (Ro) |
| 1996 | Juventus 1 | Ajax 1 | Rome | 67,000 | Vega (Sp) |
| | *(aet; Juventus won 4-2 on penalties)* | | | | |
| 1997 | Borussia Dortmund 3 | Juventus 1 | Munich | 59,000 | Puhl (H) |
| 1998 | Real Madrid 1 | Juventus 0 | Amsterdam | 47,500 | Krug (G) |
| 1999 | Manchester U 2 | Bayern Munich 1 | Barcelona | 90,000 | Collina (I) |
| 2000 | Real Madrid 3 | Valencia 0 | Paris | 78,759 | Braschi (I) |
| 2001 | Bayern Munich 1 | Valencia 1 | Milan | 71,500 | Jol (Ho) |
| | *(aet; Bayern Munich won 5-4 on penalties)* | | | | |
| 2002 | Real Madrid 2 | Leverkusen 1 | Glasgow | 52,000 | Meier (Sw) |
| 2003 | AC Milan 0 | Juventus 0 | Manchester | 63,215 | Merk (G) |
| | *(aet; AC Milan won 3-2 on penalties)* | | | | |
| 2004 | Porto 3 | Monaco 0 | Gelsenkirchen | 52,000 | Nielsen (Den) |

**Subsequently stripped of title.*

# UEFA CHAMPIONS LEAGUE 2003–04

■ *Denotes player sent off.*

## FIRST QUALIFYING ROUND FIRST LEG

Wednesday, 16 July 2003

**BATE Borisov (1) 1** *(Lashankov 25)*
**Bohemians (0) 0** 5000
*BATE Borisov:* Zhevnov; Likhtarovich, Baga, Mardas, Stripeikis (Chumachenko 46), Lashankov, Shkabara (Rubnenka 78), Tarasenka, Shmihera, Biahanski (Kobets 68), Molosh.
*Bohemians:* Gregg; Lynch, Webb, Hunt, Heary, Hawkins, Ryan (Harkin 78), Caffrey, Doyle (Keegan 80), Crowe, Rutherford.

**Dynamo Tbilisi (2) 3** *(Melkadze 6, Anchabadze 45, Daraselia 50 (pen))*
**SK Tirana (0) 0** 4500
*Dynamo Tbilisi:* Zoidze (Gvaramadze 81); Shashiashvili, Daraselia (Da Rocha 86), Gogoberishvili, Burduli, Anchabadze, Akhalaia, Kvirkvelia, Melkadze (Kandelaki 66), Amisulashvili, Khizaneishvili.
*SK Tirana:* Egbo; Sina, Dabulla, Dede, Bulku E (Hajdari 46), Mukaj, Fortuzi, Halili (Patushi 46), Lici (Merkoci 72), Xhafa, Pinari.

**Glentoran (0) 0**
**HJK Helsinki (0) 0** 2523
*Glentoran:* Morris; Nixon, Glendinning, Walker (Armour 27), Leeman, Smyth, Keegan, Young (O'Neill 73), Smith, Lockhart, McCann TM (McCann T 73).
*HJK Helsinki:* Vilnrotter; Peltola, Turpeinen, Jensen, Aalto, Eremenko Sr (Fekete 69), Kallio, Heinola, Makela (Eremenko Jr 60), Hakanpaa, Kottila.

**Grevenmacher (0) 0**
**Leotar (0) 0** 500
*Grevenmacher:* Joubert; Kordian, Albrecht, El Aouad, Thimmesch (Huss 50), Rodrigues Da Cruz, Groune (Buschmann 65), Birtz, Henrot, Martin, Toppmoller.
*Leotar:* Stojkovic; Jucinic, Simic, Milosevic, Milenkovic, Saraba, Popovic, Kerkez (Stojonovic 66) (Jankovic 90), Mulina, Krunic, Delibasic (Jovanovic 73).

**HB Torshavn (0) 0**
**Kaunas (0) 1** *(Opic 75)* 600
*HB Torshavn:* Johannesen; Christiansen, Lag, Dogaru (Joensen 87), Nolsoe, Jacobsen R, From K (Akselsen 76), Flotum, Dam, Eliasen, Danielsen.
*Kaunas:* Padimanskas; Gvildys, Kancelskis, Pastva (Puotkalis 80), Bezykornovas (Belicka 84), Regelskis, Gedgaudas■, Sirmelis, Zelmikas, Karalius (Opic 71), Barevicius.

**Omonia (0) 0**
**Irtysh (0) 0** 15,531
*Omonia:* Michopoulos; Theodotou (Stjepanovic 84), Ioakim, Nicolaou M (Mihajlovic 78), Korolovszky, Haber■, Georgiou (Alonaftis 76), Nicolaou C, Rauffmann, Kaiafas, Kozlej.
*Irtysh:* Novikov; Timofeev, Schastka, Davletov, Kumisbeckov, Zakharov, Nurdaletov, Irismetov, Kucheryavykh, Agayev (Dostayev 85), Tieshev (Ivanov 46) (Juska 80).

**Pyunik (0) 1** *(Pachajian 61)*
**KR Reykjavik (0) 0** 15,000
*Pyunik:* Bete; Art Mkrchyan, Zeciu, Bilibio, Nazarian (Balep Ba 84), Partsikian, Lombe, Ag Mkrchyan (Manucharian 79), Peralta, Pachajian (Hovhannisian 89), Cisterna.
*KR Reykjavik:* Finnbogason; Eyjolfsson (Johannsson 58), Gislason (Bergsteinsson 61), Magnusson, Danielsson (Davidsson 82), Einarsson, Sigurgeirsson, Skaftason, Sigurdsson, Elisabetarson, Gunnarsson.

**Serif (0) 1** *(Tudor 88)*
**Flora Tallinn (0) 0** 6133
*Serif:* Hutan; Testimitanu, Priganiuc, Tarkhnishvili, Ivanov, Tudor, Boret, Dadu (Nesteruk 75), Bandi (Barisev 31), Gumenik (Farias 62), Lacusta.
*Flora Tallinn:* Kaalma; Allas, Stepanov, Jaager, Saviauk, Reinumae, Rooba M, Kristal, Viikmae, Zahovaiko, Lindpere (Klavan 90).

**Sliema Wanderers (0) 2** *(Bogdanovic 62, Doncic 68 (pen))*
**Skonto Riga (0) 0** 473
*Sliema Wanderers:* Akanji; Laferla, Said, Chetcuti, Turner, Giglio, Brincat, Mamo, Anonam, Doncic, Bogdanovic (Veselji 90).
*Skonto Riga:* Piedels; Isakovs, Zemlinskis, Buitkus, Verpakovskis (Kalnins 87), Blanks (Korgalidze 70), Lobanovs, Semyonovs, Dedura, Nguimbat, Morozs.

**Vardar (1) 3** *(Dos Santos 38, 70, Ristovski 49)*
**Barry Town (0) 0** 3000
*Vardar:* Zekir; Veselinovski, Dosevski, Anyanviu, Grozdanovski (Tasevski 78), Petkov (Da Costa 65), Zaharievski, Ristovski, Georgievski, Brankovic, Dos Santos (Nacevski 81).
*Barry Town:* Ovendale; Jarman, Lloyd (Cotterrell 67), Jenkins, Morgan, Phillips, Molloy (Kennedy 75), French, Moralee, Ramasut, Akinfenwa (Ocquaye 63).

## FIRST QUALIFYING ROUND SECOND LEG

Wednesday, 23 July 2003

**Barry Town (1) 2** *(Jarman 1, Moralee 63)*
**Vardar (0) 1** *(Da Costa 60)* 1126
*Barry Town:* Ovendale; Jarman, Kennedy, Morgan, Phillips, French, Moralee, Ramasut (Jenkins 85), Akinfenwa, Cotterrell (Molloy 76), Ocquaye (Moss 76).
*Vardar:* Zekir; Veselinovski, Dosevski, Anyanviu, Trajcev, Petkov (Da Costa 46), Zaharievski, Ristovski, Georgievski (Bozinovski 83), Brankovic, Dos Santos (Milevski 90).

**Bohemians (2) 3** *(Caffrey 38, Ryan 45, Crowe 58)*
**BATE Borisov (0) 0** 5300
*Bohemians:* Kelly; Lynch, Webb, Hunt, Heary, Hawkins, Ryan (Harkin 73), Caffrey, Doyle, Crowe (Pereplyotkin 90), Rutherford (Morrison 89).
*BATE Borisov:* Zhevnov; Baga, Mardas, Chumachenko (Shchahrykovich 78), Stripeikis, Lashankov, Shkabara (Rubnenka 69), Tarasenka, Shmihera (Kobets 61), Klimovich, Likhtarovich.

**Flora Tallinn (0) 1** *(Viikmae 88)*
**Serif (0) 1** *(Nesteruk 80)* 800
*Flora Tallinn:* Kaalma; Allas (Rahn 80), Stepanov, Jaager, Saviauk (Klavan 66), Reinumae, Viikmae, Kristal, Hamre (Saharov 74), Lindpere, Zahovaiko.
*Serif:* Hutan; Testimitanu, Priganiuc, Tarkhnishvili, Ivanov (Necsulescu 85), Tudor (Farias 84), Boret, Dadu (Nesteruk 72), Odiah, Barisev, Lacusta.

**HJK Helsinki (0) 1** *(Makela 72)*
**Glentoran (0) 0** 4270
*HJK Helsinki:* Vilnrotter; Turpeinen■, Nylund, Jensen, Aalto, Eremenko Jr (Peltola 19), Kallio (Sund 66), Heinola, Makela (Savolianen 89), Hakanpaa, Kottila.
*Glentoran:* Morris; Nixon, Glendinning, Leeman, Young (Kilmartin 85), Smyth, McCann T, O'Neill, Smith, Lockhart (McCann TM 85), Keegan (Armour 76).

**Irtysh (1) 1** *(Agayev 21)*

**Omonia (0) 2** *(Rauffmann 61, Georgiou 90)* 12,000

*Irtysh:* Novikov; Timofeev, Schastka, Davletov, Kucheryavykh, Zakharov (Kumisbeckov 46), Nurdaletov, Irismetov, Zheylitbayev, Agayev (Skorikh 73), Usmanov (Tieshev 70).
*Omonia:* Michopoulos; Theodotou, Ioakim, Korolovszky, Nicolaou C, Georgiou, Kozlej (Panayiotou 85), Nicolaou M (Charalambous 90), Rauffmann, Mihajlovic (Stjepanovic 46), Kaiafas.

**KR Reykjavik (0) 1** *(Arnar Gunnlaugsson 82 (pen))*

**Pyunik (0) 1** *(Ag Mkrchyan 73)* 2069

*KR Reykjavik:* Finnbogason; Gislason (Eyjolfsson 82), Magnusson (Olafsson 68), Danielsson (Bjarki Gunnlaugsson 46), Davidsson, Einarsson, Johannsson, Sigurdsson, Elisabetarson, Arnar Gunnlaugsson, Gunnarsson.
*Pyunik:* Bete; Zeciu, Bilibio, Ag Mkrchyan, Peralta (Manucharian 62), Cisterna, Balep Ba (Minasian 84), Pachajian (Nazarian 89), Art Mkrchyan, Partsikian, Lombe.

**Kaunas (3) 4** *(Beniusis 5, 77, Kancelskis 36, Opic 40)*

**HB Torshavn (1) 1** *(Jacobsen R 9)* 3500

*Kaunas:* Padimanskas; Gvildys, Kancelskis, Bezykornovas (Pastva 53), Opic, Regelskis, Papeckys, Sirmelis (Velicka 77), Zelmikas, Beniusis (Karalius 80), Barevicius.
*HB Torshavn:* Johannesen; Christiansen, Lag (Joensen 58), Dogaru, Nolsoe, Jacobsen R■, Flotum, Dam, Akselsen (From K 68), Eliasen, Danielsen (Jorgensen 79).

**Leotar (1) 2** *(Kerkez 23, 83)*

**Grevenmacher (0) 0** 3105

*Leotar:* Stojkovic, Saraba, Milosevic, Mulina, Delibasic (Simic 46), Krunic, Kerkez, Milenkovic■, Popovic, Jucinic (Corlija 76), Stojonovic (Jovanovic 76).
*Grevenmacher:* Joubert; Kandu M, Kordian, Albrecht, Huss (Toppmoller 46), Rodrigues Da Cruz, Birtz, Henrot, Martin, Thimmesch (Morocutti 65), El Aouad.

**SK Tirana (1) 3** *(Lici 11, Fortuzi 64, Halili 77)*

**Dynamo Tbilisi (0) 0** 2100

*SK Tirana:* Egbo; Sina (Merkoci 84), Dede, Bulku E (Bulku S 64), Mukaj, Fortuzi, Hajdari, Lici, Xhafa (Halili 64), Patushi, Pinari.
*Dynamo Tbilisi:* Zoidze; Shashiashvili, Daraselia (Da Rocha 64), Gogoberishvili, Burduli, Anchabadze (Kandelaki 22), Akhalaia, Kvirkvelia, Melkadze (Samkharadze 58), Amisulashvili, Khizaneishvili.
*aet; SK Tirana won 4-2 on penalties.*

**Skonto Riga (1) 3** *(Buitkus 14, Verpakovskis 64, Dedura 70)*

**Sliema Wanderers (0) 1** *(Brincat 90)* 3250

*Skonto Riga:* Piedels; Morozs■, Zemlinskis, Nguimbat, Lobanovs (Korgalidze 90), Dedura, Buitkus, Verpakovskis, Blanks (Ksanavicius 46), Semyonovs, Kalnins (Lagiewka 77).
*Sliema Wanderers:* Akanji (Farrugia 38); Mamo (Veselji 74), Said, Turner, Doncic, Bogdanovic, Chetcuti, Anonam, Giglio, Pace (Laferla 55), Brincat.

---

## SECOND QUALIFYING ROUND FIRST LEG

Wednesday, 30 July 2003

**Bohemians (0) 0**

**Rosenborg (1) 1** *(Karadas 35)* 7930

*Bohemians:* Kelly; Lynch, Webb, Hunt, Heary, Hawkins, Ryan (Harkin 83), Caffrey, Doyle (Keegan 60), Crowe, Rutherford (Pereplyotkin 70).
*Rosenborg:* Johnsen E; Hoftun, Winsnes (Strand 83), Basma, Berg, Johnsen F, Riseth, George (Solli 70), Karadas, Stensaas, Brattbakk.

**CSKA Moscow (0) 1** *(Samodin 89)*

**Vardar (0) 2** *(Grozdanovski 54, Dos Santos 64)* 12,000

*CSKA Moscow:* Akinfeev; Semberas, Yanovski, Gusev, Gogniyev (Kirichenko 34), Laizans (Kusov 58), Jarosik, Popov (Samodin 77), Evsikov, Rahimic, Shershun.
*Vardar:* Zekir; Veselinovski, Dosevski, Anyanviu, Grozdanovski (Milevski 86), Trajcev, Zaharievski, Ristovski, Georgievski (Bozinovski 77), Brankovic, Dos Santos (Da Costa 79).

**FC Copenhagen (3) 4** *(Zuma 24, 28 (pen), Larsen R 65, Jonsson 45)*

**Sliema Wanderers (0) 1** *(Doncic 50)* 14,197

*FC Copenhagen:* Raboczki; Rooba U, Svensson, Albrechtsen, Mykland (Lonstrup 77), Nielsen, Larsen R, Zuma (Zivkovic 88), Jonsson (Moller 73), Tobiasen, Norregaard.
*Sliema Wanderers:* Akanji; Said, Turner (Grima 74), Chetcuti, Giglio, Mamo, Brincat, Anonam, Doncic (Sammut 90), Bogdanovic (Veselji 56), Laferla.

**Kaunas (0) 0**

**Celtic (2) 4** *(Larsson 12, Sutton 28, Maloney 54, Miller 86)* 4000

*Kaunas:* Padimanskas; Gvildys, Kancelskis, Petrenka, Regelskis, Papeckys (Opic 66), Gedgaudas, Sirmelis (Pastva 75), Zelmikas, Beniusis (Karalius 80), Barevicius.
*Celtic:* Douglas; Agathe, Thompson (Smith 70), Mjallby, Varga, Valgaeren, Lambert, Lennon (Maloney 46), Sutton (Miller 72), Larsson, Petrov.

**Leotar (1) 1** *(Delibasic 42 (pen))*

**Slavia Prague (1) 2** *(Da Silva 16, Dostalek 49)* 4256

*Leotar:* Stojkovic; Saraba (Corlija 77), Gerinic, Milosevic, Mulina, Delibasic, Krunic (Jankovic 80), Kerkez, Popovic, Vucinic (Jovanovic 61), Stojonovic.
*Slavia Prague:* Cerny; Dosek L, Kuka, Dostalek (Zacalias 90), Skacel, Gedeon, Petrous, Hrdlicka, Pitak, Bejbl (Muller 46), Da Silva (Dosek T 74).

**MTK Budapest (2) 3** *(Da Silva 37, 42, Rednic 90)*

**HJK Helsinki (0) 1** *(Kottila 53)* 1213

*MTK Budapest:* Vegh; Pusztai (Halmai 61), Juhasz, Komlosi, Jezdimirovic, Fuzi, Zavadszky, Pisont (Czvitkovics 61), Da Silva, Torghelle, Szabo (Rednic 78).
*HJK Helsinki:* Vilnrotter; Peltola, Nylund, Jensen, Aalto, Zeneli (Makela 64), Sund (Fekete 79), Kallio, Heinola, Hakanpaa, Kottila.

**Maribor (1) 1** *(Pekic 36)*

**Dynamo Zagreb (1) 1** *(Kranjcar 33)* 6443

*Maribor:* Kuzma; Golob (Mostarlic 60), Ceh, Teinovic, Franci, Karic, Pekic, Filekovic, Pitamic, Balajic, Vuksanovic.
*Dynamo Zagreb:* Jozic; Sedloski, Mijatovic, Agic, Mujcin, Mikic (Cesar 46), Kranjcar, Mitu (Zahora 88), Tomic, Bartolovic (Da Silva 44), Drpic.

**Partizan Belgrade (0) 1** *(Ilic 59)*

**Djurgaarden (0) 1** *(Makondele 72)* 23,400

*Partizan Belgrade:* Radakovic; Cirkovic, Djordjevic, West, Malbasa, Duljaj, Nadj, Cakar (Drulovic 82), Ilic, Iliev, Stojanoski (Brnovic 63).
*Djurgaarden:* Isaksson; Stenman (Bergtoft 85), Kuivasto, Arneng, Den Ouden (Wowoah 57), Johansson A, Karlsson, Kallstrom, Rasck, Corr Nyang (Sjolund 68), Makondele.

**Pyunik (0) 0**

**CSKA Sofia (1) 2** *(Yanchev 20, Mukassi 48)* 14,000

*Pyunik:* Bete; Art Mkrchyan (Nazarian 78), Zeciu, Bilibio, Lombe, Partsikian, Cisterna, Ag Mkrchyan, Minasian (Manucharian 70), Pachajian, Peralta (Diawara 53).
*CSKA Sofia:* Petrov; Georgiev■, Gueye, Joao Carlos, Tomovski, Stefanov, Yanchev, Haxhi, Gargorov (Yanev 89), Joao Paulo Brito (Yordanov 63), Mukassi (Todorov 71).

**Rapid Bucharest (0) 0**

**Anderlecht (0) 0** 12,000

*Rapid Bucharest:* Dossey; Soava, Badoi, Ziyati, Ilyes (Makinwa 79), Perja, Bratu (Nita 89), Niculae (Lutu 58), Godfroid, Iencsi, Maftei.
*Anderlecht:* Zitka; Deschacht, Lovre, Jestrovic (Mornar 75), Baseggio, Doll, Hasi, Seol, Dindane, Kompany, Tihinen.

**SK Tirana (1) 1** *(Xhafa 5)*

**Graz (3) 5** *(Bazina 14, Aufhauser 32, Naumoski 41, 82, Standfest 56)* 7200

*SK Tirana:* Egbo; Sina, Dabulla (Bulku S 46), Dede, Mukaj, Fortuzi (Merkoci 72), Hajdari, Lici, Xhafa, Patushi, Pinari (Halili 57).
*Graz:* Schranz; Tokic, Ehmann, Ramusch (Potscher 70), Standfest, Naumoski, Milinkovic, Pogatetz, Dollinger (Amerhauser 75), Aufhauser (Kulovits 58), Bazina.

**Serif (0) 0**

**Shakhtjor Donetsk (0) 0** 10,224

*Serif:* Hutan; Testimitanu, Priganiuc, Tarkhnishvili, Ivanov, Tudor (Nesteruk 71), Boret, Farias (Dadu 60), Blanco, Odiah, Barisev.
*Shakhtjor Donetsk:* Pletikosa; Tymoschuk, Popov, Vukic (Pukanych 82), Vorobei (Srna 75), Lewandowski, Hay, Bielik (Brandao 61), Zakarlyuka, Pazin, Rat.

**Wisla (3) 5** *(Zurawski 12, 49, Frankowski 19, Baszczynski 45, Dubicki 70)*

**Omonia (0) 2** *(Rauffmann 76 (pen), 86)* 6500

*Wisla:* Piekutowski; Baszczynski, Nawotczynski, Jop, Stolarczyk, Pater, Strak, Szymkowiak, Brasilia, Frankowski (Dubicki 64), Zurawski (Gorawski 71).
*Omonia:* Michopoulos; Theodotou (Charalambous 71), Ioakim, Panayiotou (Nicolaou M 81), Korolovszky, Georgiou, Stjepanovic (Alonaftis 46), Nicolaou C, Rauffmann, Kaiafas, Kozlej.

**Zilina (0) 1** *(Bazik 86)*

**Maccabi Tel Aviv (0) 0** 5988

*Zilina:* Trabalik; Konecny, Durica, Strba, Labant, Zabavnik, Barcik, Stas (Drahno 66), Sninsky, Fabus (Gottwald 68), Putik (Bazik 76).
*Maccabi Tel Aviv:* Shtrauber; Brumer, Abu-Siam, Banin (Crispis 66), Nimni, Pantsil, Prohorenkovs, Bruno Reis, Biton (Cohen L 79), Ben Haim, Cohen T.

## SECOND QUALIFYING ROUND SECOND LEG

Wednesday, 6 August 2003

**Anderlecht (0) 3** *(Jestrovic 50, Zetteberg 52, Seol 75)*

**Rapid Bucharest (2) 2** *(Ilyes 42, Bratu 45)* 22,432

*Anderlecht:* Zitka; Deschacht, Jestrovic (Hendrikx 86), Baseggio, Doll, Hasi (Wilhelmsson 46), Seol, Zetteberg, Dindane, Kompany, Tihinen.
*Rapid Bucharest:* Dolha; Soava, Badoi, Ziyati (Lutu 77), Ilyes (Makinwa 88), Perja, Bratu (Nita 70), Niculae, Godfroid, Iencsi, Maftei.

**CSKA Sofia (0) 1** *(Da Silva 90 (pen))*

**Pyunik (0) 0** 6500

*CSKA Sofia:* Petrov; Todorov, Gueye, Joao Carlos (Varbanov 80), Haxhi, Yanchev, Stefanov, Lima, Joao Paulo Brito (Yanev 65), Gargorov, Mukasi (Yordanov 71).
*Pyunik:* Bete; Aleksanyian, Zeciu, Bilibio, Partsikian, Cisterna, Lombe (Balep Ba 89), Ag Mkrchyan, Pachajian, Diawara (Manucharian 82), Petrosian (Hovhannisian 86).

**Celtic (1) 1** *(Gvildys 21 (og))*

**Kaunas (0) 0** 40,104

*Celtic:* Douglas; Sylla (Lennon 57), Balde, Mjallby, Smith, Valgaeren, Lambert, Maloney (Beattie 57), Sutton, Miller, Thompson (Wallace 80).
*Kaunas:* Padimanskas; Gvildys, Kancelskis, Petrenko, Beniusis (Karalius 35), Opic (Sanajevas 87), Regelskis, Papeckys (Puotkalis 77), Gedgaudas, Barevicius, Zelmikas.

**Djurgaarden (1) 2** *(Johansson A 10, Wowoah 77)*

**Partizan Belgrade (0) 2** *(Ilic 61, Malbasa 66 (pen))* 28,287

*Djurgaarden:* Isaksson; Stenman, Kuivasto, Arneng (Bapupa-Ngabu 27), Den Ouden (Wowoah 70), Johansson A, Karlsson, Stefanidis (Blomqvist 68), Kallstrom, Rasck, Makondele.
*Partizan Belgrade:* Kralj; Djordjevic, Cirkovic, Malbasa, West, Nadj, Duljaj, Cakar (Drulovic 46), Ilic, Stojanoski (Bajic 76), Iliev (Radoncic 90).

**Dynamo Zagreb (0) 2** *(Mijatovic 59, Drpic 63)*

**Maribor (1) 1** *(Balajic 10)* 8790

*Dynamo Zagreb:* Jozic; Sedloski, Mijatovic, Agic, Mujcin, Mikic, Kranjcar (Cesar 87), Mitu■, Tomic (Strok 56), Da Silva (Zahora 90), Drpic.
*Maribor:* Kuzma; Golob, Ceh (Komljenovic 83), Teinovic, Rakovic, Karic, Pekic, Filekovic (Brezic 64), Pitamic, Balajic, Vuksanovic (Franci 73).

**Graz (1) 2** *(Sick 16, Kollmann 75)*

**SK Tirana (0) 1** *(Agolli 90)* 5090

*Graz:* Schranz; Potscher, Tokic, Ramusch, Milinkovic (Bazina 57), Goossens, Kulovits, Pogatetz (Standfest 75), Dollinger (Amerhauser 66), Sick, Kollmann.
*SK Tirana:* Egbo; Sina, Dabulla, Dede, Bulku S (Prenga 87), Mukaj, Halili, Agolli, Xhafa (Fortuzi 42), Patushi (Lici 59), Pinari.

**HJK Helsinki (0) 1** *(Makela 63)*

**MTK Budapest (0) 0** 2650

*HJK Helsinki:* Vilnrotter; Peltola (Aalto 64), Nylund, Jensen, Zeneli (Fekete 62), Sund, Kallio (Poulsen 81), Heinola, Makela, Hakanpaa, Kottila.
*MTK Budapest:* Vegh; Pusztai, Juhasz, Komlosi, Fuzi, Zavadszky, Jezdimirovic, Halmai, Torghelle (Pisont 70), Da Silva (Zabos 90), Szabo (Rednic 73).

**Maccabi Tel Aviv (1) 1** *(Pantsil 25)*

**Zilina (1) 1** *(Sninsky 16)* 491

*Maccabi Tel Aviv:* Strauber; Strul, Abu-Siam, Ben Haim, Pantsil, Banin, Nimni, Prohorenkovs (Biton 61), Cohen L (Mussa 75), Oved, Bruno Reis (Goldberg 61).
*Zilina:* Trabalik; Konecny, Durica, Strba, Labant, Zabavnik, Barcik, Bazik, Stas (Drahno 78), Sninsky, Cervenec (Putik 32) (Klago 90).

**Omonia (1) 2** *(Rauffmann 16, Charalambous 51)*

**Wisla (1) 2** *(Zurawski 6, 72)* 12,500

*Omonia:* Michopoulos; Theodotou (Alonaftis 37), Ioakim, Georgiou, Korolovszky, Haber (Stjepanovic 64), Charalambous, Nicolaou C, Rauffmann, Kaiafas (Mihajlovic 79), Kozlej.
*Wisla:* Piekutowski; Baszczynski, Jop, Nawotczynski, Stolarczyk■, Gorawski (Kuzera 51), Strak, Szymkowiak, Brasilia (Brozek 84), Dubicki, Zurawski.

**Rosenborg (1) 4** *(Karadas 43, Brattbakk 51, Strand 68, Johnsen F 76)*

**Bohemians (0) 0** 15,911

*Rosenborg:* Johnsen E; Hoftun, Winsnes (Enerly 80), Basma, Strand (Solli 69), Berg, Johnsen F, Riseth, Karadas (George 85), Stensaas, Brattbakk.
*Bohemians:* Kelly; Lynch, Webb, Hunt, Heary, Hawkins, Ryan (Morrison 65), Caffrey, Doyle, Crowe (Keegan 76), Rutherford (Harkin 56).

**Shakhtjor Donetsk (0) 2** *(Vukic 60, Brandao 89)*

**Serif (0) 0** 31,600

*Shakhtjor Donetsk:* Pletikosa; Tymoschuk, Popov, Bakharev (Srna 56), Vukic (Pukanych 89), Vorobei, Lewandowski, Hay, Bielik (Brandao 70), Pazin, Rat.
*Serif:* Hutan; Testimitanu, Priganiuc, Tarkhnishvili■, Ivanov, Tudor (Farias 24), Boret, Dadu (Nesteruk 70), Blanco, Odiah, Barisev (Comlionoc 81).

**Slavia Prague (1) 2** *(Kuka 42, Skacel 73)*
**Leotar (0) 0** 6154
*Slavia Prague:* Cerny; Dosek L (Muller 46), Kuka, Dostalek, Skacel, Gedeon, Petrous, Hrdlicka, Zacalias, Da Silva (Fort 77), Dosek T (Pitak 61).
*Leotar:* Stojkovic; Jerinic, Simic (Miljanovic 90), Milosevic, Mulina, Delibasic (Jovanovic 52), Krunic, Kerkez, Corlija, Popovic, Stojonovic.

**Sliema Wanderers (0) 0**
**FC Copenhagen (3) 6** *(Jonsson 17, 41, Norregaard 36, Chetcuti 46 (og), Zuma 49, Larsen R 68)* 735
*Sliema Wanderers:* Akanji; Mamo, Said (Lombardi 55) (Grima 68), Turner, Doncic, Bogdanovic, Veselji (Pace 46), Chetcuti, Anonam, Brincat, Laferla.
*FC Copenhagen:* Raboczki; Rooba U, Svensson, Albrechtsen, Mykland, Nielsen (Lonstrup 68), Larsen R, Zuma (Pettersson 68), Jonsson (Moller 46), Tobiasen, Norregaard.

**Vardar (0) 1** *(Dos Santos 64)*
**CSKA Moscow (1) 1** *(Gogniyev 30)* 12,000
*Vardar:* Zekir; Veselinovski, Dosevski, Anyanviu, Grozdanovski (Da Costa 55), Trajcev, Zaharievski, Ristovski (Braga de Jesus 74), Georgievski, Brankovic, Dos Santos (Petkov 71).
*CSKA Moscow:* Mandrikin; Berezutski A, Yanovski (Kirichenko 46) (Samodin 79), Gusev, Gogniyev, Jarosik, Popov, Evsikov, Berezutski V, Rahimic, Shershun (Laizans 62).

## THIRD QUALIFYING ROUND FIRST LEG

### Tuesday, 12 August 2003

**Celta Vigo (1) 3** *(Mostovoi 17, Jesuli 49, Edu 55)*
**Slavia Prague (0) 0** 13,500
*Celta Vigo:* Cavallero; Velasco, Silvinho, Caceres, Giovanella, Milosevic (Catanha 64), Mostovoi, Contreras, Jose Ignacio, Edu (Angel Lopez 68), Jesuli (Jandro 82).
*Slavia Prague:* Cerny; Dosek L (Latka 87), Kuka, Dostalek, Skacel, Gedeon, Petrous, Hrdlicka (Lukes 65), Pitak, Zacalias, Da Silva (Dosek T 57).

**Dynamo Kiev (2) 3** *(Fedorov 32, Leko 39, Gusev 82)*
**Dynamo Zagreb (1) 1** *(Kranjcar 42)* 8200
*Dynamo Kiev:* Shovkovskyi; Khatskevich (Dmitrulin 60), Fedorov, Mori Nunes (Gusev 68), Belkevich, Gusin, Diogo Rincon (Cernat 76), Nesmachni, Gavrancic, Leko, Shatskikh.
*Dynamo Zagreb:* Jozic; Sedloski, Mijatovic, Agic, Mujcin (Krznar 87), Mikic, Kranjcar, Tomic, Bartolovic (Strok 60), Da Silva (Zahora 74), Drpic.

**Graz (0) 1** *(Pogatetz 56)*
**Ajax (0) 1** *(Sneijder 79)* 12,382
*Graz:* Schranz; Potscher, Tokic, Ehmann, Ramusch, Naumoski (Goossens 73), Milinkovic (Kulovits 60), Pogatetz, Dollinger (Amerhauser 69), Aufhauser, Kollmann.
*Ajax:* Stekelenburg; Trabelsi, Escude, Pienaar (Sikora 69), Van der Vaart, Maxwell, Wamberto, Sneijder (Van Damme 86), Sonck (Ibrahimovic 64), Yakubu, Grygera.

### Wednesday, 13 August 2003

**Anderlecht (2) 3** *(Jestrovic 13, Lovre 38, Dindane 59)*
**Wisla (0) 1** *(Zurawski 77 (pen))* 17,630
*Anderlecht:* Zitka; Deschacht, Lovre (Zetteberg 86), Jestrovic (Wilhelmsson 39), Baseggio, Doll, Hasi, Seol, Dindane, Kompany, Tihinen.
*Wisla:* Piekutowski; Baszczynski, Jop, Nawotczynski, Paszulewicz, Pater (Dubicki 46), Strak, Szymkowiak, Brasilia, Frankowski (Ouadja 46), Zurawski.

**FC Brugge (2) 2** *(Ceh 33, Verheyen 44)*
**Borussia Dortmund (0) 1** *(Amoroso 53)* 19,364
*FC Brugge:* Verlinden; De Cock, Simons, Rozehnal, Van der Heyden, Clement, Verheyen, Ceh, Martens (Saertens 73), Mendoza (Smolders 86), Stoica (Gvodzenovic 86).
*Borussia Dortmund:* Weidenfeller; Worns, Kehl, Conceicao, Reuter, Koller, Rosicky (Ricken 86), Dede, Amoroso (Ewerthon 71), Madouni, Bergdolmo (Addo 46).

**FK Austria (0) 0**
**Marseille (1) 1** *(Sytchev 4)* 28,300
*FK Austria:* Mandl; Rudi, Afolabi, Dospel, Wagner, Vastic, Janocko (Kitzbichler 59), Verlaat, Ratajczyk (Scharner 50), Dundee, Gilewicz (Rushfeldt 76).
*Marseille:* Runje; Van Buyten, Hemdani, Mido (Drogba 67), Fernandao (N'Diaye 67), Meite, Vachousek, Johansen, Sytchev (Olembe 82), Beye, Celestini.

**Galatasaray (3) 3** *(Hasan Sas 3, Hakan Sukur 6, Arif 37)*
**CSKA Sofia (0) 0** 66,300
*Galatasaray:* Mondragon; Bulent K, Joao Batista, Frank de Boer, Umit K (Arif 30), Hakan Sukur (Erdogan 90), Hasan Sas, Volkan (Ayhan 73), Cesar Prates, Hakan Unsal, Ergun.
*CSKA Sofia:* Petrov; Todorov (Lima 57), Gueye, Varbanov, Tomovski, Haxhi, Stefanov, Yanchev, Gargorov, Dimitrov (De Souza Cardoso 79), Mukassi (Yordanov■ 46).

**Grasshoppers (0) 1** *(Nunez 83)*
**AEK Athens (0) 0** 12,400
*Grasshoppers:* Borer; Gamboa, Tararache, Eduardo (Magro 84), Petric, Castillo, Spycher, Chatruc, Lichtsteiner, Nunez, Mitreski A.
*AEK Athens:* Hiotis; Borbokis, Kostenoglou (Georgatos 66), Zagorakis, Maladenis (Moras 87), Tsartas, Georgeas, Kasapis, Katsouranis, Ivic (Okkas 66), Kapsis.

**Lazio (1) 3** *(Corradi 16, Fiore 54, Mihajlovic 80)*
**Benfica (0) 1** *(Simao Sabrosa 65)* 57,926
*Lazio:* Peruzzi; Albertini (Sergio Conceicao 74), Zauri, Lopez C (Giannichedda 87), Corradi, Stankovic, Mihajlovic, Fiore, Favalli (Liverani 74), Oddo, Stam.
*Benfica:* Moreira; Argel, Roland, Petit, Zahovic (Roger 55), Geovanni (Feher M 85), Aguiar (Andersson 55), Simao Sabrosa, Miguel, Sokota, Ricardo Rocha.

**MTK Budapest (0) 0**
**Celtic (2) 4** *(Larsson 17, Agathe 36, Petrov 70, Sutton 90)* 4773
*MTK Budapest:* Vegh; Molnar (Pisont 72), Juhasz, Pusztai, Fuzi, Zavadszky, Halmai, Jezdimirovic (Torghelle 24), Da Silva, Illes, Rednic (Szabo 64).
*Celtic:* Douglas; Agathe (Sylla 78), Balde (Crainey 81), Thompson, Varga, Valgaeren, Lennon, Lambert, Sutton, Larsson, Petrov (Miller 78).

**Partizan Belgrade (0) 0**
**Newcastle United (1) 1** *(Solano 39)* 27,300
*Partizan Belgrade:* Kralj; Cirkovic, Malbasa, Djordjevic, West, Bajic, Duljaj (Drulovic 46), Ilic, Delibasic (Stojanoski 60), Iliev, Nadj.
*Newcastle United:* Given; Griffin, Bernard, Solano (Jenas 83), O'Brien, Woodgate, Dyer, Speed, Shearer, Bellamy, Robert (Ameobi 65).

**Rangers (1) 1** *(Lovenkrands 8)*
**FC Copenhagen (0) 1** *(Jonsson 50)* 47,401
*Rangers:* Klos; Ricksen, Moore, Ferguson B, Mols, Ronald de Boer (Thompson 69), Arteta, Khizanishvili, Ball, Ross (Capucho 59), Lovenkrands.
*FC Copenhagen:* Raboczki; Rooba U, Svensson, Albrechtsen, Mykland, Nielsen, Larsen R, Zuma, Jonsson (Moller 75), Tobiasen, Norregaard.

**Rosenborg (0) 0**
**La Coruna (0) 0** 21,166
*Rosenborg:* Johnsen E; Hoftun, Basma, Strand, Berg, Enerly (George 46), Johnsen F, Riseth, Karadas (Solli 72), Stensaas, Brattbakk.
*La Coruna:* Molina; Jorge Andrade, Naybet, Sergio, Mauro Silva, Victor (Scaloni 75), Amavisca, Valeron, Hector, Romero (Capdevila 79), Diego Tristan (Pandiani 65).

**Shakhtjor Donetsk (0) 1** *(Vukic 56 (pen))*
**Lokomotiv Moscow (0) 0** 31,700
*Shakhtjor Donetsk:* Pletikosa; Tymoschuk, Popov, Bakharev (Srna 80), Vukic, Vorobei, Lewandowski, Hay, Bielik (Aghahowa 60), Pazin, Rat.
*Lokomotiv Moscow:* Ovchinnikov; Nizhegorodov, Lekgetho, Ignashevich, Maminov, Loskov (Buznikin 67) (Wanger 74), Pachinine■, Parks, Sennikov, Khokhlov, Ashvetia (Izmailov 41).

**Vardar (0) 2** *(Da Costa 61, Georgievski 74)*
**Sparta Prague (2) 3** *(Poborsky 37, 89, Gluscevic I 41)* 14,000
*Vardar:* Zekir; Veselinovski, Anyanviu, Brankovic, Ristovski, Nacevski (Petkov 61), Grozdanovski (Tasevski 67), Georgievski, Zaharievski, Da Costa (Braga de Jesus 61), Dos Santos.
*Sparta Prague:* Blazek; Poborsky, Jezek (Michalik 69), Sionko (Jun 62), Kovac, Hubschmann, Johana, Poledica■, Petras, Nemec, Gluscevic I (Flachbart 74).

**Zilina (0) 0**
**Chelsea (1) 2** *(Gudjohnsen 42, Drahno 75 (og))* 6211
*Zilina:* Trabalik; Konecny, Stas (Drahno 66), Strba, Zabavnik, Labant, Barcik, Sninsky, Bazik, Varadin (Fabus 83), Durica (Putik 66).
*Chelsea:* Cudicini; Johnson, Bridge, Lampard, Terry, Desailly, Veron, Geremi, Forssell (Gronkjaer 58), Gudjohnsen, Duff (Cole J 70).

## THIRD QUALIFYING ROUND SECOND LEG

Tuesday, 26 August 2003

**Chelsea (1) 3** *(Johnson 32, Huth 67, Hasselbaink 78)*
**Zilina (0) 0** 23,408
*Chelsea:* Cudicini; Johnson, Babayaro, Lampard (Petit 46), Terry, Desailly (Huth 64), Gronkjaer (Stanic 69), Geremi, Hasselbaink, Gudjohnsen, Cole J.
*Zilina:* Rzeszoto; Koneckny, Stas, Sninsky, Zabavnik, Labant, Kosmel (Strba 90), Bazik, Varadin (Fabus 72), Barcik, Durica (Putik 83).

**La Coruna (1) 1** *(Luque 16)*
**Rosenborg (0) 0** 22,153
*La Coruna:* Molina; Hector, Jorge Andrade, Naybet, Romero, Mauro Silva, Sergio, Victor (Scaloni 81), Valeron, Diego Tristan (Pandiani 46), Luque (Fran 74).
*Rosenborg:* Johnsen E; Hoftun, Winsnes (Solli 75), Basma, Strand, Berg, Johnson F, Riseth, Karadas (Storflor 65), Stensaas (Knutsen 86), Brattbakk.

**Sparta Prague (1) 2** *(Poborsky 33, Sionko 85)*
**Vardar (1) 2** *(Georgievski 31, Anyanviu 66)* 12,345
*Sparta Prague:* Blazek; Poborsky, Jezek (Michalik 58), Kovac, Hubschman, Johana, Petras, Nemec, Jun (Kinci 90), Zboncak, Gluscevic I (Sionko 69).
*Vardar:* Jovcev; Veselinovski, Anyanviu, Grozdanovski (Petkov 63), Zaharievski, Ristovski, Georgievski, Brankovic, Da Costa, Dos Santos (Miserdovski 81), Braga de Jesus.

**Wisla (0) 0**
**Anderlecht (0) 1** *(Dindane 85)* 8200
*Wisla:* Piekutowski; Baszczynski, Jop, Stolarczyk (Dubicki 65), Paszulewicz (Nawotczynski 71), Gorawski, Szymkowiak (Pater 76), Brasilia, Strak, Zurawski, Frankowski.
*Anderlecht:* Zitka; Deschacht, Lovre (Wilhelmsson 72), Baseggio, Doll, Hasi, Seol, Zetteberg (Hendrikx 87), Dindane (Mornar 87), Kompany, Tihinen.

Wednesday, 27 August 2003

**AEK Athens (3) 3** *(Katsouranis 20, Lymberopoulos N 25, Castillo 39 (og))*
**Grasshoppers (0) 1** *(Nunez 68)* 11,500
*AEK Athens:* Hiotis; Borbokis, Zagorakis, Okkas, Tsartas (Maladenis 53), Georgeas, Abonsah, Katsouranis, Georgatos (Nalitzis 61), Kapsis, Lymberopoulos N (Kostenoglou 80).
*Grasshoppers:* Borer; Gamboa■, Magro (Chatruc 55), Tararache, Eduardo (Empefe 46), Petric, Castillo■, Spycher, Lichtsteiner (Gane 79), Nunez, Mitreski A.

**Ajax (1) 2** *(Ibrahimovic 15, Galasek 103 (pen))*
**Graz (1) 1** *(Kollmann 40)* 48,470
*Ajax:* Lobont; Pasanen, Escude, Galasek, Pienaar (Sonck 94), Ibrahimovic, Van der Vaart, Sikora (Wamberto 68), Van Damme (Sneijder 56), Maxwell, Grygera.
*Graz:* Schranz; Potscher■, Tokic, Ehmann■, Ramusch (Standfest 74), Naumoski (Bazina 100), Milinkovic, Pogatetz, Dollinger, Aufhauser, Kollmann.

**Benfica (0) 0**
**Lazio (1) 1** *(Cesar 28)* 16,974
*Benfica:* Moreira; Argel, Petit, Zahovic (Roger 33), Geovanni, Simao Sabrosa, Miguel, Feher M, Tiago (Andersson 69), Helder, Ricardo Rocha (Cristiano 73).
*Lazio:* Peruzzi; Albertini, Lopez C (Giannichedda 78), Cesar, Corradi, Stankovic, Mihajlovic, Fiore (Sergio Conceicao 84), Favalli, Oddo, Stam (Fernando Couto 57).

**Borussia Dortmund (1) 2** *(Amoroso 3, Ewerthon 86)*
**FC Brugge (1) 1** *(Mendoza 26)* 62,000
*Borussia Dortmund:* Weidenfeller; Worns, Kehl, Reuter (Fernandez 86), Koller, Rosicky, Dede, Addo, Amoroso, Madouni (Ewerthon 75), Bergdolmo.
*FC Brugge:* Butina; De Cock, Simons, Rozehnal■, Van der Heyden, Clement, Verheyen (Maertens 114), Englebert, Martens (Saertens 82), Mendoza, Stoica (Ceh 46).
*aet; FC Brugge won 4-2 on penalties.*

**CSKA Sofia (0) 0**
**Galatasaray (1) 3** *(Cesar Prates 28, Sabri 53, Arif 86)* 34,067
*CSKA Sofia:* Petrov; Todorov, Gueye (Varbanov 75), Joao Carlos, Charras (Joao Paulo Brito 55), Yanchev, Haxhi, Dimitrov, De Souza Cardoso, Lima (Mukasi 61), Gargorov.
*Galatasaray:* Mondragon; Bulent K, Frank de Boer, Joao Batista, Hakan Sukur, Hasan Sas (Arif 74), Cesar Prates, Tamas (Berkant 68), Sabri, Hakan Unsal (Orhan 79), Ergun.

**Celtic (1) 1** *(Sutton 14)*
**MTK Budapest (0) 0** 43,008
*Celtic:* Hedman; Balde (Kennedy 46), Thompson, Agathe, Varga, Crainey, Lambert, Miller, Sutton, Larsson (Hartson 59), Petrov (Petta 46).
*MTK Budapest:* Vegh; Molnar, Komlosi, Juhasz, Halmai, Jezdimirovic, Zavadszky, Pisont (Czvitkovics 46), Torghelle (Da Silva 80), Illes (Szabo 70), Fuzi.

**Dynamo Zagreb (0) 0**
**Dynamo Kiev (0) 2** *(Shatskikh 47, Diogo Rincon 70)* 22,000
*Dynamo Zagreb:* Jozic; Sedloski, Mijatovic, Agic, Mujcin, Mikic, Kranjcar, Tomic (Poldrugac 57), Bartolovic (Strok 72), Da Silva (Zahora 82), Drpic.
*Dynamo Kiev:* Shovkovskyi; Fedorov, Dmitrulin, Belkevich, Diogo Rincon (Khatskevich 72), Ghioane, Gusev, Nesmachni, Gavrancic (Onischenko 83), Leko (Sablic 87), Shatskikh.

**FC Copenhagen (0) 1** *(Santos 83)*
**Rangers (0) 2** *(Arteta 52 (pen), Arveladze 86)* 35,519
*FC Copenhagen:* Raboczki; Tobiasen (Moller 75), Rooba U, Mykland (Pettersson 67), Svensson, Albrechtsen, Norregaard, Nielsen, Zuma, Jonsson (Santos 67), Larsen R.
*Rangers:* Klos; Ricksen, Ball, Ferguson B, Berg (Malcolm 65), Khizanishvili, Arteta, Nerlinger, Arveladze, Mols (Thompson 65), Ronald de Boer (Vanoli 73).

**Lokomotiv Moscow (2) 3** *(Ashvetia 28, 45, Ignashevich 85 (pen))*
**Shakhtjor Donetsk (0) 1** *(Lewandowski 71)* 30,000
*Lokomotiv Moscow:* Ovchinnikov; Nizhegorodov, Lekgetho, Ignashevich, Izmailov, Maminov, Loskov, Buznikin (Leandro 66), Evseyev, Khokhlov, Ashvetia (Pimenov 85).
*Shakhtjor Donetsk:* Pletikosa; Tymoschuk, Popov, Bakharev, Vukic (Srna 76), Vorobei, Lewandowski, Hay, Pazin (Bielik 88), Brandao (Aghahowa 69), Rat.

**Marseille (0) 0**
**FK Austria (0) 0** 41,253
*Marseille:* Runje; Van Buyten, Hemdani, Fernandao (Vachousek 58), Drogba, Meite, Johansen (Perez 86), Ecker (N'Diaye 74), Sytchev, Beye, Celestini.
*FK Austria:* Mandl; Troyansky (Blanchard 71), Afolabi, Dospel, Flogel (Gilewicz 71), Vastic, Janocko (Dundee 81), Verlaat, Ratajczyk, Scharner, Rushfeldt.

**Newcastle United (0) 0**
**Partizan Belgrade (0) 1** *(Iliev 50)* 37,293
*Newcastle United:* Given; Hughes, Bernard, Solano (Lua-Lua 106), O'Brien, Woodgate, Dyer, Speed (Jenas 90), Shearer, Ameobi, Viana (Robert 86).
*Partizan Belgrade:* Kralj; Cirkovic, Malbasa, Djordjevic, Stojanoski, West, Duljaj, Ilic, Delibasic (Cakar 117), Iliev, Nadj.
*aet; Partizan Belgrade won 4-3 on penalties.*

**Slavia Prague (2) 2** *(Skacel 18, Hrdlicka 30)*
**Celta Vigo (0) 0** 8091
*Slavia Prague:* Kozacik; Dosek L, Dosek T, Kuka (Da Silva 60), Dostalek, Skacel, Petrous, Hrdlicka (Latka 72), Pitak (Fort 82), Bejbl, Zacalias.
*Celta Vigo:* Cavallero; Velasco, Silvinho, Caceres, Giovanella (Gustavo Lopez 59) (Contreras 85), Milosevic (Catanha 89), Mostovoi■, Jose Ignacio, Angel Lopez, Edu, Sergio Fernandez.

## GROUP STAGE

### GROUP A

Wednesday, 17 September 2003

**Bayern Munich (0) 2** *(Makaay 73, 86)*
**Celtic (0) 1** *(Thompson 56)* 48,500
*Bayern Munich:* Kahn; Sagnol, Lizarazu (Santa Cruz 73), Salihamidzic (Rau 73), Kovac, Linke, Hargreaves, Ballack, Pizarro, Makaay, Ze Roberto.
*Celtic:* Hedman; Agathe, Thompson, Varga, Balde, McNamara, Lennon, Sutton, Hartson (Miller 66), Larsson, Petrov.

**Lyon (1) 1** *(Juninho 26 (pen))*
**Anderlecht (0) 0** 37,002
*Lyon:* Coupet; Deflandre, Edmilson, Muller, Reveillere, Essien, Dhorasoo, Diarra, Juninho (Carriere 70), Govou (Malouda 72), Elber (Luyindula 88).
*Anderlecht:* Zitka; Zewlakow, De Boeck, Tihinen, Deschacht, Wilhelmsson, Hasi (Mornar 64), Zetteberg, Baseggio, Seol, Dindane.

Tuesday, 30 September 2003

**Anderlecht (0) 1** *(Mornar 53)*
**Bayern Munich (0) 1** *(Santa Cruz 74)* 21,788
*Anderlecht:* Zitka; Zewlakow, Kompany, Tihinen, Deschacht, Hendrikx (Kolar 82), Hasi, Baseggio, Seol, Mornar (Zetteberg 87), Aruna.
*Bayern Munich:* Kahn; Kuffour (Salihamidzic 74), Kovac, Linke, Lizarazu, Hargreaves (Schweinsteiger 63), Demichelis, Ballack, Pizarro■, Makaay, Ze Roberto (Santa Cruz 63).

**Celtic (0) 2** *(Miller 70, Sutton 78)*
**Lyon (0) 0** 58,027
*Celtic:* Hedman; Agathe, Thompson, Varga, Balde, McNamara, Lennon, Sutton, Hartson (Miller 63), Larsson, Petrov.
*Lyon:* Coupet; Deflandre, Edmilson, Muller, Reveillere, Govou (Malouda 78), Diarra, Dhorasoo (Luyindula 78), Juninho, Carriere (Essien 62), Elber.

Tuesday, 21 October 2003

**Anderlecht (0) 1** *(Dindane 72)*
**Celtic (0) 0** 27,000
*Anderlecht:* Zitka; Zewlakow, De Boeck■, Kompany, Deschacht, Wilhelmsson (Hendrikx 88), Baseggio, Hasi, Kolar (Tihinen 90), Dindane, Mornar.
*Celtic:* Hedman; Agathe, Thompson, Varga, Balde, McNamara (Valgaeren 46), Lennon (Miller 80), Sutton, Hartson, Larsson, Petrov.

**Lyon (0) 1** *(Luyindula 88)*
**Bayern Munich (1) 1** *(Makaay 25)* 37,659
*Lyon:* Coupet; Deflandre (Malouda 46), Edmilson, Muller, Reveillere, Govou (Luyindula 68), Diarra, Dhorasoo (Carriere 71), Essien, Juninho, Elber.
*Bayern Munich:* Kahn; Kuffour, Kovac, Linke, Lizarazu, Deisler, Demichelis (Jeremies 46), Ballack, Ze Roberto (Salihamidzic 90), Santa Cruz, Makaay.

Wednesday, 5 November 2003

**Bayern Munich (1) 1** *(Makaay 15)*
**Lyon (1) 2** *(Juninho 6, Elber 53)* 58,000
*Bayern Munich:* Kahn; Sagnol (Scholl 73), Kuffour, Kovac, Lizarazu, Salihamidzic, Demichelis (Jeremies 72), Ballack, Ze Roberto, Pizarro (Santa Cruz 67), Makaay.
*Lyon:* Coupet; Reveillere, Muller, Edmilson, Berthou, Essien (Govou 77), Diarra, Juninho (Carriere 90), Malouda, Elber (Cacapa 79), Luyindula.

**Celtic (3) 3** *(Larsson 12, Miller 17, Sutton 29)*
**Anderlecht (0) 1** *(Dindane 77)* 59,057
*Celtic:* Hedman; Agathe, McNamara, Varga, Balde, Miller (Gray 75), Lennon, Sutton, Hartson (Maloney 83) (Sylla 90), Larsson, Petrov.
*Anderlecht:* Zitka; Zewlakow, Tihinen, Kompany, Deschacht, Wilhelmsson, Baseggio, Hendrikx (Kolar 62), Hasi, Mornar, Dindane.

Tuesday, 25 November 2003

**Anderlecht (0) 1** *(Tihinen 70)*
**Lyon (0) 0** 20,779
*Anderlecht:* Zitka; Tihinen, Kompany, Deschacht, Zewlakow (Hendrikx 68), Hasi, Baseggio, Kolar (Iachtchouk 89), Zetteberg (Vanderhaeghe 84), Wilhelmsson, Mornar.
*Lyon:* Puydebois; Reveillere, Edmilson, Muller, Berthod (Cacapa 81), Govou, Diarra (Carriere 74), Luyindula, Juninho, Malouda, Elber.

**Celtic (0) 0**
**Bayern Munich (0) 0** 59,506
*Celtic:* Hedman; Agathe (Miller 62), Thompson, Varga, Balde, McNamara, Lennon, Sutton, Hartson (Sylla 86), Larsson, Petrov.
*Bayern Munich:* Kahn; Sagnol, Kuffour, Kovac, Lizarazu, Salihamidzic, Jeremies, Ballack, Hargreaves, Makaay, Santa Cruz (Pizarro 72).

Wednesday, 10 December 2003

**Bayern Munich (1) 1** *(Makaay 42 (pen))*

**Anderlecht (0) 0** 52,000

*Bayern Munich:* Kahn; Kuffour, Linke, Pizarro, Lizarazu, Salihamidzic (Schweinsteiger 79), Ballack, Ze Roberto (Sagnol 67), Santa Cruz, Makaay, Hargreaves.
*Anderlecht:* Zitka; Tihinen, Kompany, Deschacht, Zewlakow (Wilhelmsson 64), Baseggio, Hendrikx (Kolar 86), Hasi (Iachtchouk 79), Mornar, Zetteberg, Dindane.

**Lyon (1) 3** *(Elber 6, Juninho 52, 86 (pen))*

**Celtic (1) 2** *(Hartson 24, Sutton 75)* 40,125

*Lyon:* Coupet; Reveillere, Edmilson, Cacapa, Diarra, Berthod (Carriere 76), Govou, Luyindula, Juninho (Muller 89), Malouda, Elber (Dhorasoo 87).
*Celtic:* Hedman; Mjallby, Gray (Wallace 67), Miller, Balde, Varga, Lennon, Sutton (Kennedy 80), Hartson (Sylla 67), Larsson, Petrov.

| Group A Final Table | P | W | D | L | F | A | Pts |
|---|---|---|---|---|---|---|---|
| Lyon | 6 | 3 | 1 | 2 | 7 | 7 | 10 |
| Bayern Munich | 6 | 2 | 3 | 1 | 6 | 5 | 9 |
| Celtic | 6 | 2 | 1 | 3 | 8 | 7 | 7 |
| Anderlecht | 6 | 2 | 1 | 3 | 4 | 6 | 7 |

## GROUP B

Wednesday, 17 September 2003

**Arsenal (0) 0**

**Internazionale (3) 3** *(Julio Cruz 22, Van der Meyde 24, Martins 41)* 34,393

*Arsenal:* Lehmann; Lauren, Cole, Vieira, Campbell, Toure, Ljungberg, Silva (Kanu 66), Wiltord (Parlour 79), Henry, Pires (Bergkamp 65).
*Internazionale:* Toldo; Zanetti J, Cordoba, Zanetti C, Cannavaro, Materazzi, Van der Meyde (Helveg 71), Emre (Lamouchi 66), Julio Cruz (Kallon 85), Martins, Kily Gonzalez.

**Dynamo Kiev (0) 2** *(Diogo Rincon 63, 90)*

**Lokomotiv Moscow (0) 0** 79,500

*Dynamo Kiev:* Shovkovskyi; Dmitrulin (Khatskevich 46), Gavrancic, Fedorov, Nesmachni, Gusev (Diogo Rincon 62), Ghioane (Cernat 79), Leko, Belkevich, Peev, Shatskikh.
*Lokomotiv Moscow:* Ovchinnikov; Sennikov, Ignashevich, Nizhegorodov, Lekgetho, Pachinine, Maminov, Izmailov (Leandro 67), Loskov, Khokhlov, Ashvetia (Pimenov 88).

Tuesday, 30 September 2003

**Internazionale (1) 2** *(Adani 23, Vieri 90)*

**Dynamo Kiev (1) 1** *(Fedorov 34)* 24,325

*Internazionale:* Toldo; Zanetti J, Adani, Cannavaro, Cordoba, Van der Meyde (Helveg 61), Zanetti C, Emre, Julio Cruz (Kallon 77), Martins (Vieri 58), Kily Gonzalez.
*Dynamo Kiev:* Shovkovskyi; Dmitrulin (Khatskevich 68), Fedorov, Sablic, Nesmachni, Ghioane, Peev, Diogo Rincon, Leko, Belkevich, Shatskikh (Melaschenko 85).

**Lokomotiv Moscow (0) 0**

**Arsenal (0) 0** 27,000

*Lokomotiv Moscow:* Ovchinnikov; Sennikov, Ignashevich, Pashinine, Evseyev (Nizhegorodov 73), Maminov, Khokhlov, Gurenko, Loskov, Izmailov, Ashvetia (Pimenov 65).
*Arsenal:* Lehmann; Lauren, Cole, Silva, Toure, Keown, Parlour, Edu, Wiltord, Henry, Pires.

Tuesday, 21 October 2003

**Dynamo Kiev (1) 2** *(Shatskikh 27, Belkevich 64)*

**Arsenal (0) 1** *(Henry 80)* 60,000

*Dynamo Kiev:* Shovkovskyi; Dmitrulin (Sablic 34), Fedorov, Gavrancic, Nesmachni, Peev, Leko, Ghioane (Khatskevich 78), Belkevich, Shatskikh, Gusev (Rincon 62).
*Arsenal:* Lehmann; Lauren, Cole, Silva, Campbell, Toure, Parlour (Ljungberg 72), Edu (Vieira 60), Wiltord (Kanu 72), Henry, Pires.

**Lokomotiv Moscow (1) 3** *(Loskov 2, Ashvetia 50, Khokhlov 57)*

**Internazionale (0) 0** 20,000

*Lokomotiv Moscow:* Ovchinnikov; Evseyev (Gurenko 75), Ignashevich, Sennikov, Lekgetho, Maminov, Khokhlov, Buznikin (Pachinine 46), Loskov, Izmailov, Ashvetia.
*Internazionale:* Toldo; Cordoba, Cannavaro, Materazzi (Emre 61), Brechet (Coco 72), Zanetti J, Almeyda, Zanetti C, Recoba, Vieri, Julio Cruz (Martins 61).

Wednesday, 5 November 2003

**Arsenal (0) 1** *(Cole 88)*

**Dynamo Kiev (0) 0** 34,419

*Arsenal:* Lehman; Lauren, Cole, Silva, Campbell, Toure, Ljungberg (Wiltord 69), Parlour (Kanu 76), Henry, Bergkamp (Edu 90), Pires.
*Dynamo Kiev:* Shovkovskyi; Peev, Gavrancic, Fedorov, Nesmachni, Onichenko (Sablic 22), Gusev (Rincon 60), Leko, Belkevich, Ghioane, Shatskikh (Nanni 71).

**Internazionale (1) 1** *(Recoba 14)*

**Lokomotiv Moscow (0) 1** *(Loskov 54)* 22,822

*Internazionale:* Toldo; Adani, Materazzi, Cannavaro, Helveg, Almeyda, Zanetti C (Lamouchi 68), Zanetti J, Recoba (Julio Cruz 76), Vieri, Kily Gonzalez (Karagounis 90).
*Lokomotiv Moscow:* Ovchinnikov; Evseyev, Pachinin, Sennikov, Lekgetho, Maminov, Ignashevich, Khokhlov, Loskov, Izmailov (Nizhegorodov 90), Ashvetia (Buznikin 76).

Tuesday, 25 November 2003

**Internazionale (1) 1** *(Vieri 32)*

**Arsenal (1) 5** *(Henry 25, 85, Ljungberg 49, Edu 87, Pires 89)* 44,884

*Internazionale:* Toldo; Cordoba, Materazzi, Cannavaro (Pasquale 59), Zanetti J, Zanetti C, Lamouchi (Almeyda 57), Brechet, Martins, Vieri, Van der Meyde (Julio Cruz 69).
*Arsenal:* Lehmann; Toure, Cole, Edu, Campbell, Cygan, Ljungberg, Parlour, Kanu (Silva 73), Henry (Aliadiere 88), Pires.

**Lokomotiv Moscow (2) 3** *(Buznikin 28, Ignashevich 45 (pen), Parks 89)*

**Dynamo Kiev (1) 2** *(Belkevich 37, Shatskikh 65)* 25,000

*Lokomotiv Moscow:* Ovchinnikov; Evseyev, Pachinin, Sennikov, Ignashevich, Lekgetho, Maminov, Khokhlov, Buznikin (Parks 83) (Nizhegorodov 90), Loskov, Ashvetia.
*Dynamo Kiev:* Shovkovskyi; Sablic, Gavrancic, Nesmachni, Gusev, Dmishenko (Peev 66), Ghioane (Khatskevich 57), Dmitrulin, Belkevich, Shatskikh, Rincon.

Wednesday, 10 December 2003

**Arsenal (1) 2** *(Pires 12, Ljungberg 67)*

**Lokomotiv Moscow (0) 0** 35,343

*Arsenal:* Lehmann; Toure, Cole, Vieira, Campbell, Cygan, Ljungberg, Silva, Henry, Bergkamp (Kanu 75), Pires.
*Lokomotiv Moscow:* Ovchinnikov; Evseyev, Sennikov, Pachinine, Lekgetho■, Ignashevich, Buznikin (Gurenko 46), Maminov, Khokhlov, Loskov, Ashvetia (Parks 46).

**Dynamo Kiev (0) 1** *(Rincon 85)*

**Internazionale (0) 1** *(Adani 68)* 81,500

*Dynamo Kiev:* Shovkovskyi; Nesmachni, Gavrancic, Sablic, Leko, Peev (Milevski 84), Rincon, Ghioane (Gusev 74), Dmitrulin (Cernat 78), Belkevich, Shatskikh.
*Internazionale:* Toldo; Cordoba, Cannavaro, Emre (Recoba 88), Adani, Pasquale, Zanetti J, Van der Meyde (Martins 49), Julio Cruz (Lamouchi 82), Almeyda, Vieri.

| Group B Final Table | P | W | D | L | F | A | Pts |
|---|---|---|---|---|---|---|---|
| Arsenal | 6 | 3 | 1 | 2 | 9 | 6 | 10 |
| Lokomotiv Moscow | 6 | 2 | 2 | 2 | 7 | 7 | 8 |
| Internazionale | 6 | 2 | 2 | 2 | 8 | 11 | 8 |
| Dynamo Kiev | 6 | 2 | 1 | 3 | 8 | 8 | 7 |

## GROUP C

Wednesday, 17 September 2003

**AEK Athens (0) 1** *(Tsartas 86)*
**La Coruna (1) 1** *(Pandiani 12)* 16,600
*AEK Athens:* Hiotis; Kreek (Nalitzis 80), Borbokis, Georgeas, Kostenoglou, Zagorakis, Katsouranis, Kapsis (Moras 20), Tsartas, Lymberopoulos N (Ivic 65), Okkas.
*La Coruna:* Molina; Hector, Naybet, Jorge Andrade, Romero, Mauro Silva, Sergio (Duscher 65), Victor, Luque (Diego Tristan 70), Valeron, Pandiani (Scaloni 77).

**PSV Eindhoven (0) 1** *(Bouma 65)*
**Monaco (1) 2** *(Morientes 31, Cisse 56)* 25,000
*PSV Eindhoven:* Waterreus; Colin, Ooijer, Bouma, Lee, Rommedahl, Van Bommel, Van der Schaaf (Vennegoor of Hesselink 46), Robbati (De Jong 83), Park, Kezman.
*Monaco:* Roma; Givet, Squillaci, Rodriguez, Evra, Cisse (Plasil 73), Bernardi, Zikos, Rothen (Prso 89), Giuly (Adebayor 86), Morientes.

Tuesday, 30 September 2003

**La Coruna (1) 2** *(Sergio 19, Pandiani 51 (pen))*
**PSV Eindhoven (0) 0** 24,300
*La Coruna:* Molina; Manuel Pablo, Naybet, Jorge Andrade, Capdevila, Mauro Silva, Sergio, Victor, Valeron (Munitis 80), Luque (Fran 46), Pandiani (Diego Tristan 58).
*PSV Eindhoven:* Waterreus; Ooijer, Bouma, Hofland, Lee, Van Bommel, Van der Schaaf (Robbati 54), Vogel (Vennegoor of Hesselink 76), Park, Rommedahl, Kezman.

**Monaco (2) 4** *(Giuly 23, Morientes 27, 56, Prso 86)*
**AEK Athens (0) 0** 12,000
*Monaco:* Roma; Givet, Squillaci, Rodriguez, Evra, Giuly, Zikos, Bernardi, Rothen (Plasil 85), Morientes (Prso 76), Adebayor (Cisse 69).
*AEK Athens:* Hiotis; Georgeas, Moras (Tsartas 62), Abonsah, Kreek (Kostenoglou 75), Okkas, Katsouranis, Zagorakis (Kasapis 75), Maladenis, Georgatos, Lymberopoulos N.

Tuesday, 21 October 2003

**AEK Athens (0) 0**
**PSV Eindhoven (1) 1** *(Lucius 37)* 11,500
*AEK Athens:* Michaildis; Georgeas, Abonsah■, Kapsis, Kasapis (Borbokis 78), Katsouranis, Zagorakis, Rusev (Lakis 81), Tsartas, Okkas, Lymberopoulos N (Ivic 61).
*PSV Eindhoven:* Waterreus; Ooijer, Hofland (Colin 63), Bouma, Lee, Lucius, Vogel, Rommedahl, De Jong, Robben, Kezman.

**La Coruna (0) 1** *(Diego Tristan 83)*
**Monaco (0) 0** 27,000
*La Coruna:* Molina; Manuel Pablo, Naybet, Jorge Andrade, Romero, Duscher, Sergio, Victor (Scaloni 80), Luque (Fran 57), Valeron (Pandiani 65), Diego Tristan.
*Monaco:* Roma; Givet, Squillaci, Evra, Rodriguez, Plasil (Prso 87), Rothen, Bernardi, Cisse, Giuly, Morientes (Adebayor 79).

Wednesday, 5 November 2003

**Monaco (5) 8** *(Rothen 2, Giuly 11, Prso 26, 30, 45, 49, Plasil 47, Cisse 67)*
**La Coruna (2) 3** *(Diego Tristan 39, 52, Scaloni 45)* 16,000
*Monaco:* Roma; Givet, Squilliaci, Rodriguez, Evra (Ibarra 83), Giuly, Cisse, Bernardi, Rothen, Plasil (Zikos 67), Prso (Adebayor 75).
*La Coruna:* Molina (Munua 46); Manuel Pablo (Munitis 46), Naybet, Jorge Andrade, Rothen, Mauro Silva, Sergio (Pandiani 60), Scaloni, Valeron, Amavisca, Diego Tristan.

**PSV Eindhoven (0) 2** *(Bouma 51, Robben 63)*
**AEK Athens (0) 0** 28,000
*PSV Eindhoven:* Waterreus; Colin, Hofland, Bouma, Lee, Ooijer, Park, Lucius, Robben, De Jong, Kezman.
*AEK Athens:* Michaildis; Georgeas, Kostenoglou, Moras, Kasapis, Lakis (Konstantinidis 68), Zagorakis, Katsouranis, Rusev (Tsartas 32), Okkas (Ivic 78), Lymberopoulos N.

Tuesday, 25 November 2003

**La Coruna (1) 3** *(Hector 22, Valeron 51, Luque 71)*
**AEK Athens (0) 0** 35,000
*La Coruna:* Molina; Hector, Cesar (Romero 72), Jorge Andrade, Capdevila, Sergio, Duscher, Valeron (Luque 59), Victor (Scaloni 69), Fran, Pandiani.
*AEK Athens:* Michaildis; Borbokis, Abonsah, Kapsis, Kasapis (Kostenoglou 44), Lakis (Petkov 73), Katsouranis, Zagorakis, Tsartas, Okkas (Konstantinidis 77), Nalitzis.

**Monaco (1) 1** *(Morientes 33)*
**PSV Eindhoven (0) 1** *(Vennegoor of Hesselink 84)* 17,000
*Monaco:* Roma; Givet, Squillaci, Rodriguez, Evra (Ibarra 75), Giuly■, Zikos■, Bernardi, Rothen, Morientes (Adebayor 81), Prso (Cisse 59).
*PSV Eindhoven:* Waterreus; Bogelund (Colin 72), Faber, Bouma, Lee (De Jong 78), Park, Lucius■, Vogel, Robben, Vonlanten (Vennegoor of Hesselink 64), Kezman.

Wednesday, 10 December 2003

**AEK Athens (0) 0**
**Monaco (0) 0** 4000
*AEK Athens:* Michaildis; Borbokis, Kapsis, Kreek, Moras, Katsouranis, Lakis (Nalitis 56), Lymberopoulos N (Maladenis 67), Zagorakis, Okkas (Konstantinidis 83), Tsartas.
*Monaco:* Sylva; Givet, Rodriguez, Squillaci, Evra, Ibarra (Carole 73), Plasil, Bernardi, Morientes, Cisse, Adebayor (Camara 62).

**PSV Eindhoven (1) 3** *(De Jong 14, 90, Robben 48)*
**La Coruna (0) 2** *(Luque 59, Pandiani 83)* 32,000
*PSV Eindhoven:* Waterreus; Ooijer, Bouma, Lee, Vogel, De Jong, Bogelund, Park (Rommedahl 46), Robben, Vennegoor of Hesselink, Kezman.
*La Coruna:* Molina; Jorge Andrade, Hector, Sergio (Luque 57), Scaloni (Cesar 84), Capdevila, Naybet, Fran, Valeron, Duscher, Diego Tristan (Pandiani 63).

| Group C Final Table | P | W | D | L | F | A | Pts |
|---|---|---|---|---|---|---|---|
| Monaco | 6 | 3 | 2 | 1 | 15 | 6 | 11 |
| La Coruna | 6 | 3 | 1 | 2 | 12 | 12 | 10 |
| PSV Eindhoven | 6 | 3 | 1 | 2 | 8 | 7 | 10 |
| AEK Athens | 6 | 0 | 2 | 4 | 1 | 11 | 2 |

## GROUP D

Wednesday, 17 September 2003

**Juventus (1) 2** *(Del Piero 5, 73)*
**Galatasaray (1) 1** *(Hakan Sukur 17)* 14,420
*Juventus:* Buffon; Thuram, Ferrara, Montero, Zambrotta, Tacchinardi (Davids 46), Appiah, Camoranesi (Tudor 63), Nedved, Del Piero, Trezeguet (Di Vaio 78).
*Galatasaray:* Mondragon; Cesar Prates, Frank De Boer, Bulent K, Hakan Unsal (Tamas 62), Fabio Pinto (Arif 80), Sabri, Joao Batista, Ergun, Hasan Sas (Cihan 64), Hakan Sukur.

**Real Sociedad (0) 1** *(Kovacevic 79 (pen))*
**Olympiakos (0) 0** 29,000
*Real Sociedad:* Westerveld; Lopez Rekarte, Jauregi, Schurrer, Aranzabal, Karpin, Xabi Alonso, Aranburu, Barkero (Lee 61), De Paula (Nihat 61), Kovacevic.
*Olympiakos:* Katergiannakis; Mavrogenidis (Pantos 74), Kostoulas, Karembeu, Anatolakis, Georgiadis, Stoltidis, Kafes (Gonias 51), Venetidis, Giovanni (Choutos 64), Djordjevic.

Tuesday, 30 September 2003

**Galatasaray (0) 1** *(Hakan Sukur 61)*

**Real Sociedad (1) 2** *(Kovacevic 3, Xabi Alonso 71)* 55,000

*Galatasaray:* Mondragon; Tamas (Arif 46), Bulent K, Frank de Boer, Ergun, Ayhan, Cihan (Baljic 84), Cesar Prates (Joao Batista 40), Sabri, Hasan Sas■, Hakan Sukur.
*Real Sociedad:* Westerveld; Potillon, Kvarme, Jauregi, Aranzabal, Karpin, Xabi Alonso, Aranburu, Gabilondo (Lee 67), Nihat (Alkiza 65), Kovacevic (De Paula 78).

**Olympiakos (1) 1** *(Stoltidis 11)*

**Juventus (1) 2** *(Nedved 21, 79)* 16,000

*Olympiakos:* Katergiannakis; Pantos, Kostoulas, Antzas, Venetidis, Mavrogenidis (Gonias 65), Karembeu, Stoltidis, Djordjevic, Castillo (Tatsis 75), Giovanni (Georgiadis 66).
*Juventus:* Buffon; Thuram, Legrottaglie, Montero, Zambrotta, Appiah, Tacchinardi, Davids, Nedved (Birindelli 89), Trezeguet, Di Vaio (Miccoli 56).

Tuesday, 21 October 2003

**Galatasaray (1) 1** *(Cihan 9)*

**Olympiakis (0) 0** 50,000

*Galatasaray:* Mondragon; Cesar Prates (Hakan Unsal 69), Frank de Boer, Bulent K, Ergun, Sabri (Suat 90), Ayhan, Joao Batista, Cihan, Arif (Petre 76), Hakan Sukur.
*Olympiakis:* Bucek; Pantos, Antzas, Anatolakis, Venetidis, Mavrogenidis (Tatsis 85), Karembeu, Stoltidis (Kafes 62), Djordjevic, Castillo (Georgiadis 77), Giovanni.

**Juventus (3) 4** *(Trezeguet 3, 63, Di Vaio 7, 45)*

**Real Sociedad (0) 2** *(Tudor 67 (og), Di Pedro 80)* 17,246

*Juventus:* Buffon; Thuram, Tudor (Montero 75), Iuliano, Zambrotta, Camoranesi (Davids 66), Tacchinardi, Appiah, Nedved, Di Vaio (Birindelli 84), Trezeguet.
*Real Sociedad:* Westerveld; Potillon, Jauregi, Schurrer, Aranzabal, Lee (Di Pedro 66), Karpin, Xabi Alonso (Aranburu 81), Alkiza, Kovacevic (Nihat 73), Gabilondo.

Wednesday, 5 November 2003

**Olympiakos (2) 3** *(Mavrogenidis 6, Castillo 34, Giovanni 90)*

**Galatasaray (0) 0** 14,000

*Olympiakos:* Katergiannakis; Georgiadis (Niniadis 89), Antzas, Anatolakis, Venetidis, Mavrogenidis (Kostoulas 80), Karembeu, Stoltidis, Djordjevic■, Castillo (Kafes 65), Giovanni.
*Galatasaray:* Mondragon; Cesar Prates (Sabri 81), Frank de Boer, Bulent K, Orhan, Cihan (Baljic 40), Petre, Ayhan■, Ergun (Lukunku 68), Hasan Sas, Hakan Sukur.

**Real Sociedad (0) 0**

**Juventus (0) 0** 27,000

*Real Sociedad:* Westerveld; Lopez Rekarte, Jauregi, Schurrer, Aranzabal, Xabi Alonso, Alkiza, Karpin, Nihat, Di Pedro (Lee 75), Kovacevic.
*Juventus:* Buffon; Birindelli, Ferrara, Iuliano, Pessotto (Appiah 69), Conte (Tacchinardi 82), Tudor, Davids, Nedved, Di Viao (Zalayeta 78), Miccoli.

Tuesday, 25 November 2003

**Olympiakos (0) 2** *(Stoltidis 58, Castillo 71)*

**Real Sociedad (1) 2** *(Gabilondo 31, Schurrer 73)* 14,000

*Olympiakos:* Katergiannakis; Pantos, Anatolakis, Antzas (Kates 46), Venetidis (Tatsis 86), Mavrogenidis (Niniadis 53), Karembeu, Stoltidis, Georgiadis, Castillo, Giovanni.
*Real Sociedad:* Westerveld; Lopez Rekarte, Jauregi, Schurrer, Aranzabal, Karpin (Aranburu 80), Xabi Alonso (Boris 89), Alkiza, Gabilondo, Nihat (Lee 74), Kovacevic■.

Tuesday, 2 December 2003

**Galatasaray (0) 2** *(Hakan Sukur 47, 90)*

**Juventus (0) 0** 45,000

*Galatasaray:* Mondragon; Tomas, Frank de Boer (Bulent K 84), Orhan, Cesar Prates (Hasan Sas 44), Sabri, Petre, Ergun, Hakan Unsal, Hakan Sukur (Cihan 90), Berkant.
*Juventus:* Chimenti; Tudor, Ferrara, Iuliano (Appiah 74), Pessotto, Zalayeta, Conte (Camoranesi 86), Davids, Maresca, Miccoli, Di Vaio.
*In Dortmund.*

Wednesday, 10 December 2003

**Juventus (4) 7** *(Trezeguet 14, 25, Miccoli 19, Maresca 28, Di Vaio 62, Del Piero 67, Zalayeta 79)*

**Olympiakos (0) 0** 12,578

*Juventus:* Chimenti; Tudor, Montero, Pessotto, Birindelli, Iuliano (Zambrotta 84), Miccoli (Del Piero 66), Maresca, Conte, Trezeguet (Di Vaio 58), Zalayeta.
*Olympiakos:* Eleftheropoulos; Venetidis, Djordjevic, Kafes (Gonias 61), Pantos, Mavrogenidis, Karembeu, Castillo, Giovanni (Niniadis 77), Kostoulas, Anatolakis (Georgiadis 68).

**Real Sociedad (0) 1** *(De Paulo 51)*

**Galatasaray (1) 1** *(Hakan Sukur 26)* 22,276

*Real Sociedad:* Alberto; De Paula (Aranburu 72), Kvarme, Aranzabal, Xabi Alonso, Schurrer, Karpin, Lopez Rekarte, Nihat (Jauregi 90), Gabilondo, Alkiza (Boris 87).
*Galatasaray:* Mondragon; Bulent K, Frank de Boer (Umit A 86), Berkant, Petre, Tomas, Sabri, Hakan Unsal (Cihan 76), Ergun, Hasan Sas (Arif 66), Hakan Sukur.

| **Group D Final Table** | *P* | *W* | *D* | *L* | *F* | *A* | *Pts* |
|---|---|---|---|---|---|---|---|
| Juventus | 6 | 4 | 1 | 1 | 15 | 6 | 13 |
| Real Sociedad | 6 | 2 | 3 | 1 | 8 | 8 | 9 |
| Galatasaray | 6 | 2 | 1 | 3 | 6 | 8 | 7 |
| Olympiakos | 6 | 1 | 1 | 4 | 6 | 13 | 4 |

## GROUP E

Tuesday, 16 September 2003

**Manchester United (4) 5** *(Silvestre 13, Fortune 15, Solskjaer 33, Butt 40, Djemba Djemba 83)*

**Panathinaikos (0) 0** 66,520

*Manchester United:* Howard; Neville G, O'Shea (Fletcher 57), Ferdinand, Neville P, Silvestre, Solskjaer (Bellion 46), Butt (Djemba Djemba 57), Van Nistelrooy, Giggs, Fortune.
*Panathinaikos:* Nikopolidis (Chalkias 46); Seitaridis, Fyssas, Goumas (Epalle 46), Kyrgiakos, Henriksen, Papadopoulos (Olisadebe 62), Maric, Constadinou, Zutautas, Sanmartean.

**Rangers (0) 2** *(Nerlinger 74, Lovenkrands 79)*

**Stuttgart (1) 1** *(Kuranyi 45)* 47,957

*Rangers:* Klos; Ricksen (Ross 33), Ball, Arteta, Berg, Khizanishvili, Emerson (Capucho 63), Nerlinger, Arveladze, Mols, Vanoli (Lovenkrands 46).
*Stuttgart:* Hildebrand; Hinkel, Gerber (Szabics 80), Hleb, Bordon, Fernando Meira, Tiffert, Soldo, Cacau (Amantidis 46), Kuranyi, Heldt (Meissener 70).

Wednesday, 1 October 2003

**Panathinaikos (0) 1** *(Konstantinidis 87)*

**Rangers (1) 1** *(Emerson 35)* 13,718

*Panathinaikos:* Chalkias; Seitaridis, Morris, Kyrgiakos (Goumas■ 46), Fyssas, Michaelsen, Epalle (Konstantinidis 78), Zutautas, Maric, Constadinou, Vlaovic (Papadopoulos 64).
*Rangers:* Klos; Khizanishvili, Ball, Arteta, Moore, Berg, Capucho, Emerson, Arveladze (Nerlinger 84), Mols, Lovenkrands (Vanoli 76).

**Stuttgart (0) 2** *(Szabics 50, Kuranyi 52)*

**Manchester United (0) 1** *(Van Nistelrooy 67 (pen))* 50,348

*Stuttgart:* Hildebrand; Hinkel, Fernando Meira, Bordon, Lahm (Gerber 71), Vranjes (Tiffert 73), Soldo, Hleb (Meissener 87), Heldt, Kuranyi, Szabics.

*Manchester United:* Howard; Neville G, O'Shea (Fortune 65), Ferdinand (Forlan 82), Keane, Silvestre, Scholes, Neville P, Van Nistelrooy, Giggs, Ronaldo (Fletcher 90).

Wednesday, 22 October 2003

**Rangers (0) 0**

**Manchester United (1) 1** *(Neville P 5)* 48,730

*Rangers:* Klos; Khizanishvili (Ross 86), Ball, Ricksen, Berg, Moore, Lovenkrands, Arteta, Mols, Arveladze, Vanoli (Nerlinger 67).
*Manchester United:* Howard; Neville G, O'Shea, Ferdinand, Keane, Silvestre, Neville P (Butt 85), Scholes, Van Nistelrooy, Giggs, Fortune (Djemba Djemba 90).

**Stuttgart (2) 2** *(Szabics 13, Soldo 25)*

**Panathinaikos (0) 0** 50,346

*Stuttgart:* Hildebrand; Hinkel, Fernando Meira, Bordon, Lahm, Vranjes (Meissener 77), Soldo, Hleb, Heldt (Tiffert 62), Szabics (Amanatidis 84), Kuranyi.
*Panathinaikos:* Nikopolidis; Morris, Henriksen, Seitaridis, Michaelsen, Basinas, Zutautas, Fyssas, Maric, Munch (Konstantinidis 69), Papadopoulos (Constadinou 46).

Tuesday, 4 November 2003

**Manchester United (2) 3** *(Forlan 6, Van Nistelrooy 44, 60)*

**Rangers (0) 0** 66,707

*Manchester United:* Howard; Neville G, Fortune, Ferdinand, Keane, Silvestre, Ronaldo, Neville P, Van Nistelrooy (Fletcher 77), Forlan (Bellion 67), Giggs (Kleberson 67).
*Rangers:* Klos; Khizanshvili, Ball, Arteta, Berg, Moore (Ross 67), Lovenkrands, Hughes, Mols (Capucho 57), Arveladze, Vanoli (Burke 83).

**Panathinaikos (0) 1** *(Constadinou 60)*

**Stuttgart (0) 3** *(Fyssas 65 (og), Kuranyi 75, Hinkel 77)* 6015

*Panathinaikos:* Nikopolidis; Goumas, Henriksen, Fyssas, Seitaridis, Michaelsen (Sanmartean 72), Basinas, Zutautas, Maric (Konstantinidis 79), Constadinou, Papadopoulos.
*Stuttgart:* Hildebrand; Hinkel, Fernando Meira, Wenzel, Lahm, Soldo, Tiffert, Vranjes (Hleb 46), Amanatidis (Heldt 46), Kuranyi, Szabics (Meissener 79).

Wednesday, 26 November 2003

**Panathinaikos (0) 0**

**Manchester United (0) 1** *(Forlan 85)* 6890

*Panathinaikos:* Nikopolidis; Seitaridis, Henriksen, Goumas, Munch, Sanmartean (Epalle 46), Basinas, Zutautas, Maric, Papadopoulos (Sapanis 62), Constadinou (Vlaovic 75).
*Manchester United:* Howard; O'Shea, Fortune, Ferdinand, Butt, Silvestre, Ronaldo, Fletcher (Bellion 75), Forlan, Kleberson, Giggs.

**Stuttgart (1) 1** *(Wenzel 45)*

**Rangers (0) 0** 50,348

*Stuttgart:* Hildebrand; Hinkel, Fernando Meira, Wenzel, Lahm, Soldo, Hleb (Centurion 73), Heldt (Tiffert 50), Meissner, Kuranyi, Szabics (Branco 89).
*Rangers:* Klos; Ross (Ostenstad 70), Ball, Capucho, Berg, Khizanishvili, Ricksen, Vanoli (Mols 55), Arveladze, Lovenkrands (Burke 79), Hughes.

Tuesday, 9 December 2003

**Manchester United (1) 2** *(Van Nistelrooy 45, Giggs 58)*

**Stuttgart (0) 0** 67,141

*Manchester United:* Carroll; Neville G, O'Shea, Ferdinand, Neville P, Silvestre, Fletcher, Scholes (Djemba Djemba 79), Van Nistelrooy (Forlan 71), Giggs (Bellion 71), Fortune.
*Stuttgart:* Hildebrand; Hinkel, Fernando Meira, Wenzel, Lahm, Vranjes (Tiffert 46), Soldo, Hleb (Centurion 76), Heldt, Kuranyi, Szabics (Cacau 46).

**Rangers (1) 1** *(Mols 28)*

**Panathinaikos (1) 3** *(Zutautas 32, Basinas 62, Constadinou 80)* 48,588

*Rangers:* Klos; Ross (Duffy 83), Ball, Burke (Ostenstad 69), Berg, Khizanishvili (Vanoli 69), Ricksen, Hughes, Mols, Capucho, Lovenkrands.
*Panathinaikos:* Nikopolidis; Seitaridis, Morris, Munch, Henriksen, Goumas, Sanmartean (Epalle 46), Basinas, Zutautas, Sapanis (Vlaovic 78), Constadinou.

| **Group E Final Table** | *P* | *W* | *D* | *L* | *F* | *A* | *Pts* |
|---|---|---|---|---|---|---|---|
| Manchester United | 6 | 5 | 0 | 1 | 13 | 2 | 15 |
| Stuttgart | 6 | 4 | 0 | 2 | 9 | 6 | 12 |
| Panathinaikos | 6 | 1 | 1 | 4 | 5 | 13 | 4 |
| Rangers | 6 | 1 | 1 | 4 | 4 | 10 | 4 |

## GROUP F

Tuesday, 16 September 2003

**Partizan Belgrade (0) 1** *(Delibasic 54)*

**Porto (1) 1** *(Costinha 21)* 33,000

*Partizan Belgrade:* Radakovic; Cirkovic (Savic 46), Djordjevic, West, Rzasa, Duljaj, Nadj, Stojanoski (Drulovic 46), Ilic, Delibasic, Iliev (Brnovic 84).
*Porto:* Vitor Baia; Paulo Ferreira, Jorge Costa, Ricardo Carvalho, Nuno Valente, Pedro Mendes, Costinha, Deco (Ricardo Fernandes 80), Maniche (Bosingwa 79), Derlei, McCarthy (Jankauskas 70).

**Real Madrid (2) 4** *(Roberto Carlos 29, Ronaldo 34, 56, Figo 61 (pen))*

**Marseille (1) 2** *(Drogba 25, Van Buyten 83)* 73,000

*Real Madrid:* Casillas; Michel Salgado, Roberto Carlos, Cambiasso (Guti 73), Raul Bravo, Pavon, Beckham, Figo, Raul, Ronaldo (Portillo 86), Zidane (Solari 86).
*Marseille:* Runje; Beye, Van Buyten, Hemdani (Vachousek 62), Ecker, Meite, Marlet (Johansen 38), Celestini, Meriem, Drogba (N'Diaye 86), Mido.

Wednesday, 1 October 2003

**Marseille (0) 3** *(Drogba 62, 68, 85)*

**Partizan Belgrade (0) 0** 53,000

*Marseille:* Runje; Perez, Van Buyten, Meite, Ecker, Marlet (Fernandao 61), Vachousek, Meriem (Hemdani 73), Celestini, Mido (Sytchev 76), Drogba.
*Partizan Belgrade:* Radakovic; Cirkovic (Savic 85), Djordjevic, Stojanoski, West, Malbasa, Duljaj, Nadj, Delibasic■, Ilic (Drulovic 81), Iliev (Brnovic 81).

**Porto (1) 1** *(Costinha 7)*

**Real Madrid (2) 3** *(Helguera 27, Solari 37, Zidane 67)* 37,506

*Porto:* Vitor Baia; Paulo Ferreira, Pedro Emanuel (Jankauskas 70), Ricardo Carvalho, Nuno Valente, Maniche, Costinha, Pedro Mendes (McCarthy 46), Ricardo Fernandes (Bosingwa 46), Deco, Derlei.
*Real Madrid:* Casillas; Michel Salgado, Roberto Carlos, Helguera, Raul Bravo, Pavon, Figo, Guti, Ronaldo (Raul 83), Zidane, Solari (Cambiasso 90).

Wednesday, 22 October 2003

**Marseille (1) 2** *(Drogba 24, Marlet 84)*

**Porto (2) 3** *(Maniche 31, Derlei 35, Alenichev 81)* 57,000

*Marseille:* Runje; Perez (Sychev 66), Van Buyten, Meite, Ecker, Meriem, Celestini, Hemdani, Marlet, Drogba, Mido (Vachousek 67).
*Porto:* Vitor Baia; Paulo Ferreira, Jorge Costa, Ricardo Carvalho, Nuno Valente, Maniche, Costinha, Deco, Marco Ferreira (Alenichev 73), Derlei (Jankauskas 88), Cesar Peixoto (Bosingwa 65).

**Real Madrid (1) 1** *(Raul 38)*

**Partizan Belgrade (0) 0** 58,000

*Real Madrid:* Casillas; Michel Salgado, Pavon (Guti 46), Raul Bravo, Roberto Carlos, Helguera, Figo, Beckham, Zidane (Solari 79), Raul, Ronaldo (Portillo 79).
*Partizan Belgrade:* Pantic; Savic, Malbasa, Djordjevic (Brnovic 90), Ognjanovic, Duljaj, Nadj (Cakar 90), Rzasa (Stojanoski 46), Ilic, Iliev, Drulovic.

Tuesday, 4 November 2003

**Partizan Belgrade (0) 0**

**Real Madrid (0) 0** 32,000

*Partizan Belgrade:* Pantic; Savic, Bajic, West, Djordjevic, Duljaj, Malbasa (Rzasa 19), Nadj (Drulovic 67), Ilic, Delibasic (Stojanoski 46), Iliev.
*Real Madrid:* Casillas; Michel Salgado, Pavon, Raul Bravo, Roberto Carlos (Guti 12), Figo, Helguera, Beckham, Zidane, Ronaldo, Raul.

**Porto (1) 1** *(Alenichev 21)*

**Marseille (0) 0** 40,000

*Porto:* Vitor Baia; Paulo Ferreira, Jorge Costa, Ricardo Carvalho, Nuno Valente (Ricardo Costa 60), Alenichev, Costinha, Maniche, Bosingwa (Pedro Mendes 83), McCarthy (Marco Ferreira 63), Derlei.
*Marseille:* Runje; Meite, Van Buyten, Christanval, Ecker, Perez (Mido 51), Hemdani, Meriem, Vachousek (Johansen 80), Marlet (Sychev 80), Drogba.

Wednesday, 26 November 2003

**Marseille (0) 1** *(Mido 63)*

**Real Madrid (1) 2** *(Beckham 35, Ronaldo 73)* 53,000

*Marseille:* Runje; Meite, Van Buyten, Christanval, Ecker, Meriem, Hemdani, Celestini, Vachousek (Sychev 72), Drogba, Mido (Fernandao 82).
*Real Madrid:* Casillas; Michel Salgado, Helguera, Raul Bravo, Roberto Carlos (Solari 82), Figo, Beckham, Cambiasso, Zidane (Guti 87), Raul, Ronaldo (Ruben 90).

**Porto (1) 2** *(McCarthy 25, 50)*

**Partizan Belgrade (0) 1** *(Delibasic 90)* 22,177

*Porto:* Vitor Baia; Paulo Ferreira, Jorge Costa, Ricardo Carvalho, Mario Silva, Bosingwa (Pedro Mendes 46), Costinha, Deco, Maniche, McCarthy (Hugo Almeida 67), Derlei (Jankausas 80).
*Partizan Belgrade:* Pantic; Djordjevic, Stojanoski (Drulovic 78), Savic, Cirkovic (Radovic 38), Duljaj, Ivic, Malbasa, Ilic (Cakar 58), Iliev, Delibasic.

Tuesday, 9 December 2003

**Partizan Belgrade (0) 1** *(Delibasic 80)*

**Marseille (0) 1** *(Mido 61)* 28,000

*Partizan Belgrade:* Pantic; Savic, Cirkovic, Duljaj, Ognjanovic, Malbasa, Rzasa (Drulovic 66), Iliev (Radoncic 88), Ivic, Ilic (Cakar 88), Delibasic.
*Marseille:* Gavanon; Van Buyten, Christanval (Beye 16), Hemdani, N'Diaye, Mido, Drogba, Meite, Vachousek, Johansen, Ecker.

**Real Madrid (1) 1** *(Solari 9)*

**Porto (1) 1** *(Derlei 34 (pen))* 48,715

*Real Madrid:* Cesar Sanchez; Michel Salgado, Roberto Carlos, Raul Bravo, Pavon, Borja (Jordi 89), Cambiasso, Solari, Zidane, Ronaldo (Portillo 46), Figo (Minambres 46).
*Porto:* Vitor Baia; Pedro Emanuel, Ricardo Carvalho, Ricardo Costa, Costinha, Jankausas (Hugo Almeida 74), Deco, Derlei, Alenichev (Bosingwa 81), Paulo Ferreira, Pedro Mendes.

| **Group F Final Table** | *P* | *W* | *D* | *L* | *F* | *A* | *Pts* |
|---|---|---|---|---|---|---|---|
| Real Madrid | 6 | 4 | 2 | 0 | 11 | 5 | 14 |
| Porto | 6 | 3 | 2 | 1 | 9 | 8 | 11 |
| Marseille | 6 | 1 | 1 | 4 | 9 | 11 | 4 |
| Partizan Belgrade | 6 | 0 | 3 | 3 | 3 | 8 | 3 |

GROUP G

Tuesday, 16 September 2003

**Besiktas (0) 0**

**Lazio (1) 2** *(Stam 37, Fiore 78)* 23,000

*Besiktas:* Cordoba; Zago, Ronaldo, Ahmet Y, Kaan Dobra, Tayfur, Giunti (Sinan 72), Ibrahim, Tumer (Hassan 56), Pancu, Ilhan (Sergen 56).
*Lazio:* Peruzzi; Oddo, Stam, Fernando Couto, Favalli, Sergio Conceicao (Giannichedda 60), Albertini, Stankovic, Fiore, Corradi (Liverani 83), Lopez C (Muzzi 69).

**Sparta Prague (0) 0**

**Chelsea (0) 1** *(Gallas 85)* 16,597

*Sparta Prague:* Blazek; Petras (Sionko 46), Labant (Jezek 37), Nemec, Johana, Hubschmann, Poborsky, Kovac, Glusevic I, Jun, Michalik (Zboncak 57).
*Chelsea:* Cudicini; Johnson, Bridge, Makelele, Gallas, Desailly, Geremi, Petit (Lampard 46), Crespo (Hasselbaink 72), Mutu (Duff 47), Veron.

Wednesday, 1 October 2003

**Chelsea (0) 0**

**Besiktas (2) 2** *(Sergen 25, 29)* 32,957

*Chelsea:* Cudicini; Terry, Babayaro (Bridge 23), Makelele, Gallas, Desailly, Veron, Lampard, Crespo (Hasselbaink 46), Mutu (Duff 46), Geremi.
*Besiktas:* Cordoba; Emre, Ronaldo, Zago, Okan (Kaan Dobra 60), Tayfur, Giunti (Yasin 67), Ibrahim, Pancu, Sergen (Hassan 82), Ilhan■.

**Lazio (0) 2** *(Inzaghi 46, 60 (pen))*

**Sparta Prague (2) 2** *(Sionko 27, Poborsky 38)* 25,405

*Lazio:* Peruzzi; Oddo, Stam, Mihajlovic, Favalli, Sergio Conceicao (Muzzi 61), Albertini (Liverani 46), Stankovic, Fiore, Corradi, Inzaghi (Dabo 82).
*Sparta Prague:* Blazek; Flachbart, Hubschmann, Johana, Labant, Sionko (Michalik 87), Kovac, Pergl, Poborsky, Zelenka (Krmas 90), Kinci (Gluscevic I 82).

Wednesday, 22 October 2003

**Chelsea (0) 2** *(Lampard 57, Mutu 65)*

**Lazio (1) 1** *(Inzaghi 39)* 40,405

*Chelsea:* Cudicini; Johnson, Bridge, Makelele, Terry, Gallas, Veron (Gronkjaer 64), Lampard, Gudjohnsen, Mutu (Cole 87), Duff (Geremi 78).
*Lazio:* Peruzzi; Oddo, Stam, Mihajlovic, Favalli, Sergio Conceicao, Albertini, Stankovic (Liverani 84), Zauri (Fiore 74), Corradi, Inzaghi (Muzzi 68).

**Sparta Prague (0) 2** *(Zelenka 58, Poborsky 84)*

**Besiktas (0) 1** *(Pancu 60 (pen))* 14,512

*Sparta Prague:* Blazek; Pergl, Hubschmann, Johana, Labant, Kovac, Nemec, Sionko (Jun 88), Zelenka (Michalik 90), Poborsky, Kinci (Gluscevic I 86).
*Besiktas:* Cordoba; Emre, Ronaldo, Zago, Tayfur, Giunti, Kaan Dobra, Pancu, Ibrahim, Sergen (Hassan 81), Ahmet D (Sinan 85).

Tuesday, 4 November 2003

**Besiktas (0) 1** *(Ronaldo 82)*

**Sparta Prague (0) 0** 18,000

*Besiktas:* Cordoba; Zago, Ronaldo, Ahmet Y, Giunti, Kaan (Hassan 62), Tayfur, Pancu, Ibrahim (Tumer 72), Ilhan, Sergen (Ahmet D 90).
*Sparta Prague:* Blazek; Pergl, Hubschman, Johana, Labant, Kovac, Krmas (Gluscevic I 84), Sionko (Jun 60), Zelenka, Poborsky, Kinci (Michalik 77).

**Lazio (0) 0**

**Chelsea (1) 4** *(Crespo 15, Gudjohnsen 70, Duff 75, Lampard 80)* 48,485

*Lazio:* Sereni; Zauri, Fernando Couto, Mihajlovic■, Favalli, Fiore (Negro 59), Albertini (Muzzi 71), Liverani, Stankovic, Corradi, Inzaghi (Claudio Lopez 71).
*Chelsea:* Cudicini; Johnson■, Bridge, Makelele, Terry, Gallas, Veron (Cole 75), Lampard, Crespo (Gudjohnsen 67), Mutu (Gronkjaer 57), Duff.

Wednesday, 26 November 2003

**Chelsea (0) 0**

**Sparta Prague (0) 0** 40,152

*Chelsea:* Cudicini; Melchiot, Bridge, Makelele, Terry, Gallas, Cole (Geremi 72), Lampard, Crespo (Gudjohnsen 73), Mutu, Duff.
*Sparta Prague:* Blazek; Pergl, Homola, Hubschman, Labant, Poborsky, Kovac, Krmas, Michalik (Gluscevic I 71), Zelenka (Flachbart 86), Sionko (Jezek 90).

**Lazio (0) 1** *(Muzzi 56)*

**Besiktas (1) 1** *(Pancu 45 (pen))* 49,000

*Lazio:* Peruzzi; Oddo, Stam, Negro, Favalli (Zauri 53), Albertini, Giannichedda (Fiore 46), Sergio Conceicao (Muzzi 46), Stankovic, Corradi, Inzaghi.

*Besiktas:* Cordoba; Emre, Ronaldo, Zago, Okan, Tayfur, Giunti (Ahmet Y 90), Ibrahim, Pancu, Sergen (Tumer 80), Ilhan.

Tuesday, 9 December 2003

**Besiktas (0) 0**

**Chelsea (0) 2** *(Hasselbaink 77, Bridge 85)* 52,000

*Besiktas:* Cordoba; Emre, Ronaldo, Zago, Kaan (Okan 71), Tayfur, Yasin (Hassan 81), Pancu, Sergen (Tumer 75), Ibrahim, Ilhan.
*Chelsea:* Cudicini; Johnson, Babayaro (Bridge 83), Gallas, Terry, Desailly, Lampard, Makelele, Hasselbaink, Geremi, Gronkjaer (Duff 72).
*In Gelsenkirchen.*

**Sparta Prague (0) 1** *(Kinci 90)*

**Lazio (0) 0** 17,850

*Sparta Prague:* Blazek; Labant, Pergl, Johana, Hubschmann, Kovac, Gluscevic I (Jezek 85), Poborsky, Michalik (Kinci 73), Sionko (Jun 89), Zelenka.
*Lazio:* Peruzzi; Negro, Fernando Couto, Stam, Albertini, Stankovic, Gattuso (Liverani 53), Muzzi (Inzaghi 73), Favalli (Sergio Conceicao 89), Corradi, Fiore.

| **Group G Final Table** | *P* | *W* | *D* | *L* | *F* | *A* | *Pts* |
|---|---|---|---|---|---|---|---|
| Chelsea | 6 | 4 | 1 | 1 | 9 | 3 | 13 |
| Sparta Prague | 6 | 2 | 2 | 2 | 5 | 5 | 8 |
| Besiktas | 6 | 2 | 1 | 3 | 5 | 7 | 7 |
| Lazio | 6 | 1 | 2 | 3 | 6 | 10 | 5 |

## GROUP H

Tuesday, 16 September 2003

**AC Milan (0) 1** *(Inzaghi 68)*

**Ajax (0) 0** 48,000

*AC Milan:* Dida; Cafu, Nesta, Maldini, Costacurta (Laursen 33), Gattuso■, Pirlo, Kaka, Seedorf (Serginho 54), Shevchenko, Inzaghi (Ambrosini 73).
*Ajax:* Lobont; Yakubu, Pasanen, Escude (Soetaers 70), Trabelsi, Pienaar (Sikora 80), Galasek, Maxwell, Van der Vaart, Sonck (Sneijder 55), Ibrahimovic.

**FC Brugge (0) 1** *(Juanfran 84 (og))*

**Celta Vigo (0) 1** *(Juanfran 50)* 25,000

*FC Brugge:* Butina; De Cock, Clement, Maertens (Gvodzenovic 70), Van der Heyden, Verheyen, Stoica (Englebert 31), Simons, Ceh (Saertens 79), Martens■, Mendoza■.
*Celta Vigo:* Pinto; Angel (Velasco 79), Sergio Fernandez, Berizzo, Contreras, Juanfran, Vagner, Jose Ignacio, Jesuli (Silvinho 83), Lopez (Jandro 65), Milosevic.

Wednesday, 1 October 2003

**Ajax (1) 2** *(Sonck 11, 53)*

**FC Brugge (0) 0** 49,371

*Ajax:* Lobont; Trabelsi, Pasanen, Escude, Maxwell, Pienaar (De Jong 60), Galasek, Van der Vaart (Van Damme 77), Sonck, Soetaers (Sneijder 46), Ibrahimovic.
*FC Brugge:* Butina; De Cock, Clement, Rozehnal, Van der Heyden, Cornelis, Simons, Englebert (Ceh 54), Gvodzenovic (Simic 79), Verheyen, Saertens.

**Celta Vigo (0) 0**

**AC Milan (0) 0** 30,000

*Celta Vigo:* Pinto; Velasco, Contreras (Sergio Fernandez 46), Caceres, Juanfran, Angel Lopez, Vagner, Giovanella, Gustavo Lopez (Milosevic 58), Jesuli (Jandro 84), Mostovoi.
*AC Milan:* Dida; Cafu, Nesta, Maldini, Costacurta, Kaka (Rivaldo 63), Pirlo, Ambrosini, Rui Costa, Serginho (Inzaghi 62), Shevchenko (Brocchi 73).

Wednesday, 22 October 2003

**AC Milan (0) 0**

**FC Brugge (1) 1** *(Mendoza 33)* 43,823

*AC Milan:* Dida; Cafu, Nesta, Maldini, Pancaro, Brocchi, Pirlo, Seedorf (Serginho 62), Kaka (Rui Costa 62), Shevchenko (Tomasson 75), Inzaghi.

*FC Brugge:* Verlinden; Maertens, Simons, Rozehnal, De Cock, Clement, Ceh (Stoica 90), Gvodzenovic, Van der Heyden, Martens (Verheyen 79), Mendoza (Saertens 79).

**Ajax (0) 1** *(Ibrahimovic 53)*

**Celta Vigo (0) 0** 48,514

*Ajax:* Lobont; Trabelsi (De Jong 64), Pasanen, Van Damme, Maxwell, Pienaar, Galasek, Sneijder, Van der Vaart (Mitea 39), Sonck (Yakubu 79), Ibrahimovic.
*Celta Vigo:* Pinto; Velasco, Caceres (Angel 85), Berizzo, Silvinho, Luccin, Giovanella (Catanha 81), Jesuli, Mostovoi, Juanfran, Milosevic.

Tuesday, 4 November 2003

**Celta Vigo (2) 3** *(Luccin 25 (pen), Milosevic 39, Vagner 63)*

**Ajax (0) 2** *(Sonck 53, Van der Vaart 82)* 21,572

*Celta Vigo:* Pinto; Angel, Caceres, Sergio, Silvinho, Luccin, Vagner (Contreras 85), Jesuli (Lopez 83), Mostovoi (Oubina 90), Juanfran, Milosevic.
*Ajax:* Lobont; Grygera■, Yakubu (Heitinga 65), Escude, Maxwell, De Jong, Galasek (Wamberto 75), Van der Vaart, Mitea, Sonck, Ibrahimovic (Litmanen 70).

**FC Brugge (0) 0**

**AC Milan (0) 1** *(Kaka 86)* 40,000

*FC Brugge:* Verlinden; De Cock, Maertens, Simons, Rozehnal, Van der Heyden, Verheyen, Clement (Saertens 77), Ceh (Stoica 62), Gvodzenovic, Mendoza.
*AC Milan:* Dida; Cafu, Nesta■, Maldini (Costacurta 35), Pancaro, Gattuso, Pirlo, Seedorf, Kaka (Ambrosini 87), Shevchenko, Tomasson (Simic 42).

Wednesday, 26 November 2003

**Ajax (0) 0**

**AC Milan (0) 1** *(Shevchenko 52)* 50,210

*Ajax:* Lobont; De Jong, Yakubu, Heitinga, Escude, Maxwell, Galasek, Obodai (Wamberto 54), Mitea (Sikora 77), Sneijder, Ibrahimovic (Litmanen 40).
*AC Milan:* Dida; Cafu, Laursen (Pancaro 46), Maldini, Costacurta, Gattuso, Pirlo, Kaka (Rui Costa 77), Seedorf, Shevchenko, Inzaghi (Ambrosini 72).

**Celta Vigo (0) 1** *(Mostovoi 74)*

**FC Brugge (0) 1** *(Lange 90)* 17,000

*Celta Vigo:* Cavalero (Pinto 62); Angel, Sergio, Perizzo, Silvinho (Gustavo Lopez 46), Jose Ignacio, Luccin, Jesuli, Mostovoi (Jandro 78), Juanfran, Milosevic.
*FC Brugge:* Verlinden; De Cock, Simons, Rozehnal, Gvodzenovic (Lange 81), Englebert, Clement, Ceh (Roelandts 85), Martens, Verheyen, Saertens.

Tuesday, 9 December 2003

**AC Milan (1) 1** *(Kaka 40)*

**Celta Vigo (1) 2** *(Jesuli 42, Jose Ignacio 71)* 36,207

*AC Milan:* Abbiati; Costacurta (Abate 68), Simic, Borriello, Redondo, Kaladze, Seedorf (Rui Costa 46), Kaka (Tomasson 46), Laursen, Serginho, Brocchi.
*Celta Vigo:* Cavallero; Silvinho, Caceres, Berizzo, Angel, Milosevic (Catanha 84), Gustavo Lopez (Contreras 89), Juanfran, Jose Ignacio (Giovanella 80), Jesuli, Luccin.

**FC Brugge (1) 2** *(Lange 27, Saertens 84)*

**Ajax (1) 1** *(Sonck 42 (pen))* 28,041

*FC Brugge:* Verlinden; De Cock, Simons, Rozehnal (Smolders 79), Van der Heyden, Clement, Verheyen, Englebert, Ceh, Martens (Cornelis 89), Lange (Saertens 66).
*Ajax:* Lobont; Grygera (Van Damme 85), Mitea (Soetaers 75), Sneijder, Sonck, Van der Vaart, Escude, Ibrahimovic (Litmanen 72), Heitinga, Maxwell, De Jong.

| **Group H Final Table** | *P* | *W* | *D* | *L* | *F* | *A* | *Pts* |
|---|---|---|---|---|---|---|---|
| AC Milan | 6 | 3 | 1 | 2 | 4 | 3 | 10 |
| Celta Vigo | 6 | 2 | 3 | 1 | 7 | 6 | 9 |
| FC Brugge | 6 | 2 | 2 | 2 | 5 | 6 | 8 |
| Ajax | 6 | 2 | 0 | 4 | 6 | 7 | 6 |

# KNOCK-OUT STAGE

## KNOCK-OUT ROUND FIRST LEG

Tuesday, 24 February 2004

**Bayern Munich (0) 1** *(Makaay 75)*

**Real Madrid (0) 1** *(Roberto Carlos 83)* 59,000

*Bayern Munich:* Kahn; Sagnol, Lizarazu (Salihamidzic 46), Kuffour, Kovac, Demichelis (Jeremies 90), Makaay, Ze Roberto, Ballack, Pizarro (Santa Cruz 76), Hargreaves.
*Real Madrid:* Casillas; Michel Salgado, Roberto Carlos, Helguera, Raul Bravo, Zidane, Beckham, Ronaldo (Solari 90), Raul, Guti, Figo.

**Celta Vigo (1) 2** *(Edu 27, Jose Ignacio 64)*

**Arsenal (1) 3** *(Edu 18, 58, Pires 80)* 21,000

*Celta Vigo:* Cavallero; Velasco, Silvinho, Luccin, Sergio, Berizzo, Angel (Vagner 64), Jose Ignacio, Edu (Pinilia 75), Milosevic, Mostovoi.
*Arsenal:* Lehmann; Lauren, Clichy (Cygan 90), Vieira, Campbell, Toure, Ljungberg (Bentley 90), Edu, Reyes (Kanu 78), Henry, Pires.

**Lokomotiv Moscow (1) 2** *(Izmailov 32, Maminov 59)*

**Monaco (0) 1** *(Morientes 69)* 28,000

*Lokomotiv Moscow:* Ovchinnikov; Izmailov (Parks 79), Maminov, Loskov, Pachinine, Evseyev, Sennikov, Khokhlov (Nizhegorodov 83), Asatiani, Ashvetia (Obiorah 46), Gurenko.
*Monaco:* Roma; Evra, Ibarra, Bernardi, Prso (Adebayor 64), Morientes, Cisse, Zikos, Rothen, Rodriguez, Givet.

**Sparta Prague (0) 0**

**AC Milan (0) 0** 20,640

*Sparta Prague:* Blazek; Labant, Pergl, Zelenka, Poborsky, Michalik, Kovac, Hubschmann, Johana, Stajner (Gluscevic V 85), Gluscevic I (Baranek 73).
*AC Milan:* Dida; Cafu, Maldini, Costacurta, Pirlo, Pancaro, Kaka, Gattuso, Inzaghi (Serginho 85), Shevchenko, Seedorf.

Wednesday, 25 February 2004

**La Coruna (1) 1** *(Luque 37)*

**Juventus (0) 0** 28,000

*La Coruna:* Molina; Romero, Naybet, Mauro Silva, Sergio, Diego Tristan (Pandiani 69), Scaloni, Jorge Andrade, Victor (Manuel Pablo 85), Luque (Fran 81), Valeron.
*Juventus:* Buffon; Tacchinardi, Montero (Birindelli 56), Pessotto (Conte 63), Zambrotta, Appiah, Thuram, Legrottaglie, Trezeguet (Miccoli 46), Del Piero, Nedved.

**Porto (1) 2** *(McCarthy 29, 78)*

**Manchester United (1) 1** *(Fortune 14)* 49,977

*Porto:* Vitor Baia; Paulo Ferreira, Nuno Valente, Jorge Costa, Ricardo Carvalho, Pedro Mendes, Maniche, Alenichev (Jankauskas 63), Carlos Alberto (Ricardo Fernandes 75), McCarthy (Bruno Moraes 83), Deco.
*Manchester United:* Howard; Neville P (O'Shea 70), Fortune, Neville G, Keane■, Brown, Scholes, Butt, Van Nistelrooy, Saha (Ronaldo 76), Giggs.

**Real Sociedad (0) 0**

**Lyon (1) 1** *(Schurrer 18 (og))* 29,000

*Real Sociedad:* Westerveld; Kvarme, Aranzabal, Xabi Alonso (Aranburu 74), Schurrer, Karpin, Kovacevic, Lopez Rekarte, Nihat (De Paula 80), Gabilondo (Lee 64), Alkiza.
*Lyon:* Coupet; Deflandre, Edmilson, Essien, Diarra, Juninho, Malouda, Govou (Dhorasoo 80), Luyindula, Muller, Sartre (Berthod 66).

**Stuttgart (0) 0**

**Chelsea (1) 1** *(Fernando Meira 12 (og))* 50,000

*Stuttgart:* Hildebrand; Hinkel, Lahm, Heldt (Cacau 66), Fernando Meira, Bordon, Meissner (Tiffert 46), Soldo, Kuranyi, Szabics, Hleb.
*Chelsea:* Cudicini; Johnson, Bridge, Makelele, Terry, Gallas, Geremi, Lampard, Gudjohnsen (Hasselbaink 76), Crespo (Cole 88), Gronkjaer (Duff 66).

## KNOCK-OUT ROUND SECOND LEG

Tuesday, 9 March 2004

**Chelsea (0) 0**

**Stuttgart (0) 0** 36,657

*Chelsea:* Cudicini; Johnson (Desailly 30), Bridge, Makelele, Terry, Gallas, Gronkjaer, Lambert, Crespo, Duff (Mutu 82), Parker (Geremi 61).
*Stuttgart:* Hildebrand; Hinkel (Gomez 81), Lahm, Soldo, Zivkovic, Bordon, Fernando Meira, Meissner (Tiffert 63), Kuranyi, Cacau (Szabics 40), Hleb.

**Juventus (0) 0**

**La Coruna (1) 1** *(Pandiani 12)* 24,680

*Juventus:* Buffon; Ferrara, Tacchinardi, Montero, Appiah, Thuram, Legrottaglie (Pessotto 46), Camoranesi (Chiumento 70), Di Vaio, Del Piero (Miccoli 8), Nedved.
*La Coruna:* Molina; Naybet, Mauro Silva, Jorge Andrade, Capdevila, Victor, Valeron (Duscher 77), Sergio, Pandiani (Diego Tristan 82), Scaloni, Luque (Fran 62).

**Lyon (0) 1** *(Juninho 77)*

**Real Sociedad (0) 0** 38,914

*Lyon:* Coupet (Vercoutre 16); Deflandre, Edmilson, Essien, Diarra, Juninho, Malouda, Govou, Luyindula (Elber 83), Muller, Dhorasoo (Berthod 87).
*Real Sociedad:* Alberto; Xabi Alonso, Schurrer (De Paula 85), Jauregi, Karpin, Kovacevic, Aranburu (Nihat 60), Lopez Rekarte, Gabilondo (De Pedro 60), Alkiza, Potillon.

**Manchester United (1) 1** *(Scholes 32)*

**Porto (0) 1** *(Costinha 90)* 67,029

*Manchester United:* Howard; Neville P, O'Shea, Neville G, Butt, Brown, Djemba-Djemba (Saha 46), Fletcher (Ronaldo 75) (Solskjaer 83), Van Nistelrooy, Scholes, Giggs.
*Porto:* Vitor Baia; Paulo Ferreira, Nuno Valente, Deco, Jorge Costa (Pedro Emanuel 37), Ricardo Carvalho, Alenichev (Ricardo Fernandes 81), Costinha, Carlos Alberto (Jankauskas 61), McCarthy, Maniche.

Wednesday, 10 March 2004

**AC Milan (1) 4** *(Inzaghi 45, Shevchenko 66, 79, Gattuso 85)*

**Sparta Prague (0) 1** *(Jun 59)* 50,000

*AC Milan:* Dida; Cafu (Costacurta 88), Maldini, Nesta, Ambrosini, Pirlo, Gattuso, Pancaro, Inzaghi (Tomasson 76), Shevchenko (Rui Costa 86), Kaka.
*Sparta Prague:* Blazek; Sivok, Labant, Pergl, Johana, Kovac, Zelenka (Jun 57), Poborsky, Hubschmann, Michalik (Gluscevic V 71), Stajner (Poledica 88).

**Arsenal (2) 2** *(Henry 14, 34)*

**Celta Vigo (0) 0** 35,402

*Arsenal:* Lehmann; Lauren, Cole, Vieira, Campbell, Toure, Ljungberg, Edu (Silva 70), Henry, Bergkamp (Kanu 77), Pires (Reyes 70).
*Celta Vigo:* Cavallero; Velasco, Silvinho (Contreras■ 22), Oubina, Caceres, Sergio, Jose Ignacio, Luccin (Jesuli 29), Mostovoi, Pinilia, Gustavo Lopez (Vagner 71).

**Monaco (0) 1** *(Prso 60)*

**Lokomotiv Moscow (0) 0** 16,500

*Monaco:* Roma; Zikos, Evra, Ibarra, Adebayor (Cisse 77), Rodriguez, Bernardi, Givet, Prso (Plasil 90), Morientes, Rothen.
*Lokomotiv Moscow:* Ovchinnikov; Nizhegorodov, Obiorah, Sennikov (Gurenko 65), Evseyev, Izmailov, Maminov, Ashvetia (Parks 67), Loskov■, Pachinine, Asatiani.

**Real Madrid (1) 1** *(Zidane 32)*

**Bayern Munich (0) 0** 78,000

*Real Madrid:* Casillas; Michel Salgado, Raul Bravo, Mejia, Helguera, Guti (Borja 90), Figo, Beckham, Raul, Zidane, Solari (Cambiasso 90).
*Bayern Munich:* Kahn; Sagnol (Salihamidzic 67), Lizarazu, Kuffour, Kovac, Demichelis, Pizarro (Santa Cruz 68), Ballack, Ze Roberto, Makaay, Hargreaves (Schweinsteiger 46).

## QUARTER-FINALS FIRST LEG

Tuesday, 23 March 2004

**AC Milan (1) 4** *(Kaka 45, 49, Shevchenko 46, Pirlo 53)*

**La Coruna (1) 1** *(Pandiani 11)* 60,335

*AC Milan:* Dida; Cafu, Maldini, Gattuso, Costacurta, Pirlo, Pancaro (Serginho 73), Kaka, Inzaghi (Ambrosini 79), Shevchenko (Tomasson 84), Seedorf.
*La Coruna:* Molina; Jorge Andrade, Capdevila, Naybet, Duscher (Fran 66), Mauro Silva, Pandiani, Sergio (Manuel Pablo 81), Scaloni, Valeron, Luque (Diego Tristan 83).

**Porto (1) 2** *(Deco 44, Ricardo Carvalho 71)*

**Lyon (0) 0** 46,910

*Porto:* Vitor Baia; Paulo Ferreira, Pedro Emanuel, Ricardo Carvalho, Maniche, Costinha (Bosingwa 78), Deco, Nuno Valente, Alenichev (Ricardo Fernandes 82), McCarthy, Carlos Alberto (Jankauskas 58).
*Lyon:* Coupet; Deflandre (Reveillere 73), Edmilson, Essien, Malouda, Govou, Diarra, Juninho (Dhorasoo 46), Elber, Muller, Luyindula.

Wednesday, 24 March 2004

**Chelsea (0) 1** *(Gudjohnsen 53)*

**Arsenal (0) 1** *(Pires 59)* 40,778

*Chelsea:* Ambrosio; Gallas, Bridge, Makelele, Terry, Desailly■, Parker (Cole 72), Lampard, Gudjohnsen (Melchiot 86), Mutu (Crespo 72), Duff.
*Arsenal:* Lehmann; Lauren, Cole, Vieira, Campbell, Toure, Ljungberg (Reyes 78), Edu, Henry, Bergkamp (Silva 72), Pires.

**Real Madrid (0) 4** *(Helguera 51, Zidane 69, Figo 76, Ronaldo 81)*

**Monaco (1) 2** *(Squillaci 43, Morientes 83)* 70,000

*Real Madrid:* Casillas; Michel Salgado, Raul Bravo, Guti (Borja 77), Helguera, Mejia, Beckham, Figo, Ronaldo (Solari 82), Raul, Zidane.
*Monaco:* Roma; Givet, Evra (El-Fakiri 89), Zikos, Squillaci, Rodriguez, Cisse (Plasil 66), Bernardi, Morientes, Giuly, Rothen.

## QUARTER-FINALS SECOND LEG

Tuesday, 6 April 2004

**Arsenal (1) 1** *(Reyes 45)*

**Chelsea (0) 2** *(Lampard 51, Bridge 87)* 35,486

*Arsenal:* Lehmann; Lauren, Cole, Vieira, Campbell, Toure, Ljungberg, Edu, Reyes, Henry (Bergkamp 81), Pires.
*Chelsea:* Ambrosio; Melchiot, Bridge, Makelele, Terry, Gallas, Parker (Gronkjaer 46), Lampard, Hasselbaink (Crespo 83), Gujohnsen, Duff (Cole 83).

**Monaco (1) 3** *(Giuly 45, 66, Morientes 48)*

**Real Madrid (1) 1** *(Raul 35)* 18,000

*Monaco:* Roma; Givet, Evra, Plasil, Ibarra, Rodriguez, Rothen, Cisse, Morientes (Adebayor 84), Prso (Nonda 61), Giuly (El-Fakiri 81).
*Real Madrid:* Casillas; Michel Salgado (Raul Bravo 84), Roberto Carlos, Guti (Portillo 87), Helguera, Mejia, Borja (Solari 71), Figo, Ronaldo, Raul, Zidane.

Wednesday, 7 April 2004

**La Coruna (3) 4** *(Pandiani 5, Valeron 35, Luque 44, Fran 76)*

**AC Milan (0) 0** 29,000

*La Coruna:* Molina; Manuel Pablo, Romero, Naybet, Jorge Andrade, Mauro Silva, Pandiani, Sergio (Duscher 87), Valeron (Djalminha 90), Victor, Luque (Fran 66).
*AC Milan:* Dida; Cafu, Maldini, Nesta, Pirlo (Serginho 59), Pancaro (Rui Costa 77), Shevchenko, Gattuso, Kaka, Tomasson (Inzaghi 67), Seedorf.

**Lyon (1) 2** *(Luyindula 14, Elber 90)*

**Porto (1) 2** *(Maniche 6, 47)* 40,000

*Lyon:* Coupet; Berthod, Edmilson■, Essien (Reveillere 60), Muller, Dhorasoo (Deflandre 76), Diarra, Juninho (Bergougnoux 60), Elber, Luyindula, Malouda.
*Porto:* Vitor Baia; Jorge Costa, Carlos Alberto (Pedro Emanuel 47), Ricardo Carvalho, Paulo Ferreira, Costinha, Alenichev, Nuno Valente, McCarthy (Jankauskas 57), Deco (Pedro Mendes 76), Maniche.

## SEMI-FINALS FIRST LEG

Tuesday, 20 April 2004

**Monaco (1) 3** *(Prso 17, Morientes 78, Nonda 83)*

**Chelsea (1) 1** *(Crespo 22)* 15,000

*Monaco:* Roma; Ibarra, Evra, Zikos■, Givet, Rodriguez, Bernardi, Giuly (Nonda 83), Morientes, Prso (Cisse 57), Rothen (Plasil 88).
*Chelsea:* Ambrosio; Melchiot (Hasselbaink 62), Bridge, Makelele, Terry, Desailly, Parker (Huth 69), Lampard, Crespo, Gudjohnsen, Gronkjaer (Veron 46).

Wednesday, 21 April 2004

**Porto (0) 0**

**La Coruna (0) 0** 50,818

*Porto:* Vitor Baia; Jorge Costa, Carlos Alberto, Ricardo Carvalho, Paulo Ferreira, Costinha (Pedro Mendes 46), Alenichev (Jankausas 46), Nuno Valente, McCarthy (Ferreira 70), Deco, Maniche.
*La Coruna:* Molina; Manuel Pablo, Romero, Naybet, Andrade■, Mauro Silva, Pandiani, Sergio (Duscher 79), Valeron, Victor (Cesar 88), Luque (Fran 45).

## SEMI-FINALS SECOND LEG

Tuesday, 4 May 2004

**La Coruna (0) 0**

**Porto (0) 1** *(Derlei 60 (pen))* 34,600

*La Coruna:* Molina; Manuel Pablo, Romero, Duscher, Cesar, Naybet■, Victor (Scaloni 55), Sergio (Diego Tristan 67), Luque, Pandiani, Valeron.
*Porto:* Vitor Baia; Paulo Ferreira, Nuno Valente, Pedro Mendes, Jorge Costa, Ricardo Carvalho, Costinha, Maniche, Derlei (McCarthy 90), Carlos Alberto (Pedro Emanuel 68), Deco.

Wednesday, 5 May 2004

**Chelsea (2) 2** *(Gronkjaer 22, Lampard 44)*

**Monaco (1) 2** *(Ibarra 45, Morientes 60)* 37,132

*Chelsea:* Cudicini; Melchiot (Johnson 64), Bridge, Lampard, Terry, Gallas, Gronkjaer, Geremi (Parker 69), Hasselbaink (Crespo 69), Gudjohnsen, Cole.
*Monaco:* Roma; Givet, Evra, Bernardi, Squillaci (Plasil 46), Rodriguez, Ibarra, Cisse, Morientes (Nonda 81), Giuly (Prso 67), Rothen.

### UEFA CHAMPIONS LEAGUE FINAL 2004

**Porto (1) 3** *(Carlos Alberto 39, Deco 71, Alenichev 75)* **Monaco (0) 0**

Wednesday, 26 May 2004

(at Arena AufSchalke, Gelsenkirchen, Germany, 52,000)

*Porto:* Vitor Baia; Paulo Ferreira, Nuno Valente, Costinha, Jorge Costa, Ricardo Carvalho, Pedro Mendes, Deco (Pedro Emanuel 85), Carlos Alberto (Alenichev 60), Derlei (McCarthy 78), Maniche.

*Monaco:* Roma; Ibarra, Evra, Zikos, Givet (Squillaci 73), Rodriguez, Cisse (Nonda 64), Bernardi, Giuly (Prso 23), Morientes, Rothen.

*Referee:* K.M. Nielsen (Denmark)

The Porto players celebrate with the European Champions League trophy after their 3-0 victory over Monaco. (ASP)

# UEFA CHAMPIONS LEAGUE 2004–05

(Early results)

| | 1st Leg | | 2nd Leg |
|---|---|---|---|
| Pobeda | 1-3 | Pyunik | 21/07 |
| Şliema | 0-2 | Kaunas | 21/07 |
| Široki Brijeg | 2-1 | Neftchi | 21/07 |
| Gomel | 0-2 | Tirana | 21/07 |
| Linfield | 0-1 | HJK | 21/07 |
| Sheriff | 2-0 | Jeunesse Esch | 21/07 |
| WIT | 5-0 | HB | 21/07 |
| KR | 2-2 | Shelbourne | 21/07 |
| Skonto | 4-0 | Rhyl | 21/07 |
| Flora | 2-4 | Gorica | 21/07 |

# EUROPEAN CUP-WINNERS' CUP FINALS 1961–99

| Year | Winners | Runners-up | Venue | Attendance | Referee |
|---|---|---|---|---|---|
| 1961 | Fiorentina 2 | Rangers 0 *(1st Leg)* | Glasgow | 80,000 | Steiner (A) |
| | Fiorentina 2 | Rangers 1 *(2nd Leg)* | Florence | 50,000 | Hernadi (H) |
| 1962 | Atletico Madrid 1 | Fiorentina 1 | Glasgow | 27,389 | Wharton (S) |
| *Replay* | Atletico Madrid 3 | Fiorentina 0 | Stuttgart | 38,000 | Tschenscher (WG) |
| 1963 | Tottenham Hotspur 5 | Atletico Madrid 1 | Rotterdam | 49,000 | Van Leuwen (Ho) |
| 1964 | Sporting Lisbon 3 | MTK Budapest 3 *(aet)* | Brussels | 3000 | Van Nuffel (Bel) |
| *Replay* | Sporting Lisbon 1 | MTK Budapest 0 | Antwerp | 19,000 | Versyp (Bel) |
| 1965 | West Ham U 2 | Munich 1860 0 | Wembley | 100,000 | Szolt (H) |
| 1966 | Borussia Dortmund 2 | Liverpool 1 *(aet)* | Glasgow | 41,657 | Schwinte (F) |
| 1967 | Bayern Munich 1 | Rangers 0 *(aet)* | Nuremberg | 69,480 | Lo Bello (I) |
| 1968 | AC Milan 2 | Hamburg 0 | Rotterdam | 53,000 | Ortiz (Sp) |
| 1969 | Slovan Bratislava 3 | Barcelona 2 | Basle | 19,000 | Van Ravens (Ho) |
| 1970 | Manchester C 2 | Gornik Zabrze 1 | Vienna | 8,000 | Schiller (A) |
| 1971 | Chelsea 1 | Real Madrid 1 *(aet)* | Athens | 42,000 | Scheurer (Sw) |
| *Replay* | Chelsea 2 | Real Madrid 1 *(aet)* | Athens | 35,000 | Bucheli (Sw) |
| 1972 | Rangers 3 | Moscow Dynamo 2 | Barcelona | 24,000 | Ortiz (Sp) |
| 1973 | AC Milan 1 | Leeds U 0 | Salonika | 45,000 | Mihas (Gr) |
| 1974 | Magdeburg 2 | AC Milan 0 | Rotterdam | 4000 | Van Gemert (Ho) |
| 1975 | Dynamo Kiev 3 | Ferencvaros 0 | Basle | 13,000 | Davidson (S) |
| 1976 | Anderlecht 4 | West Ham U 2 | Brussels | 58,000 | Wurtz (F) |
| 1977 | Hamburg 2 | Anderlecht 0 | Amsterdam | 65,000 | Partridge (E) |
| 1978 | Anderlecht 4 | Austria/WAC 0 | Paris | 48,679 | Adlinger (WG) |
| 1979 | Barcelona 4 | Fortuna Dusseldorf 3 *(aet)* | Basle | 58,000 | Palotai (H) |
| 1980 | Valencia 0 | Arsenal 0 | Brussels | 36,000 | Christov (Cz) |
| | *(aet; Valencia won 5-4 on penalties)* | | | | |
| 1981 | Dynamo Tbilisi 2 | Carl Zeiss Jena 1 | Dusseldorf | 9000 | Lattanzi (I) |
| 1982 | Barcelona 2 | Standard Liege 1 | Barcelona | 100,000 | Eschweiler (WG) |
| 1983 | Aberdeen 2 | Real Madrid 1 *(aet)* | Gothenburg | 17,804 | Menegali (I) |
| 1984 | Juventus 2 | Porto 1 | Basle | 60,000 | Prokop (EG) |
| 1985 | Everton 3 | Rapid Vienna 1 | Rotterdam | 50,000 | Casarin (I) |
| 1986 | Dynamo Kiev 3 | Atletico Madrid 0 | Lyon | 39,300 | Wohrer (A) |
| 1987 | Ajax 1 | Lokomotiv Leipzig 0 | Athens | 35,000 | Agnolin (I) |
| 1988 | Mechelen 1 | Ajax 0 | Strasbourg | 39,446 | Pauly (WG) |
| 1989 | Barcelona 2 | Sampdoria 0 | Berne | 45,000 | Courtney (E) |
| 1990 | Sampdoria 2 | Anderlecht 0 | Gothenburg | 20,103 | Galler (Sw) |
| 1991 | Manchester U 2 | Barcelona 1 | Rotterdam | 42,000 | Karlsson (Se) |
| 1992 | Werder Bremen 2 | Monaco 0 | Lisbon | 16,000 | D'Elia (I) |
| 1993 | Parma 3 | Antwerp 1 | Wembley | 37,393 | Assenmacher (G) |
| 1994 | Arsenal 1 | Parma 0 | Copenhagen | 33,765 | Krondl (Czr) |
| 1995 | Zaragoza 2 | Arsenal 1 | Paris | 42,424 | Ceccarini (I) |
| 1996 | Paris St Germain 1 | Rapid Vienna 0 | Brussels | 37,500 | Pairetto (I) |
| 1997 | Barcelona 1 | Paris St Germain 0 | Rotterdam | 45,000 | Merk (G) |
| 1998 | Chelsea 1 | Stuttgart 0 | Stockholm | 30,216 | Braschi (I) |
| 1999 | Lazio 2 | Mallorca 1 | Villa Park | 33,021 | Benko (A) |

# INTER-CITIES FAIRS CUP FINALS 1958–71

*(Winners in italics)*

| Year | First Leg | Attendance | Second Leg | Attendance |
|---|---|---|---|---|
| 1958 | London 2 Barcelona 2 | 45,466 | *Barcelona* 6 London 0 | 62,000 |
| 1960 | Birmingham C 0 Barcelona 0 | 40,500 | *Barcelona* 4 Birmingham C 1 | 70,000 |
| 1961 | Birmingham C 2 Roma 2 | 21,005 | *Roma* 2 Birmingham C 0 | 60,000 |
| 1962 | Valencia 6 Barcelona 2 | 65,000 | Barcelona 1 *Valencia* 1 | 60,000 |
| 1963 | Dynamo Zagreb 1 Valencia 2 | 40,000 | *Valencia* 2 Dynamo Zagreb 0 | 55,000 |
| 1964 | *Zaragoza* 2 Valencia 1 | 50,000 | (in Barcelona) | |
| 1965 | *Ferencvaros* 1 Juventus 0 | 25,000 | (in Turin) | |
| 1966 | Barcelona 0 Zaragoza 1 | 70,000 | Zaragoza 2 *Barcelona* 4 | 70,000 |
| 1967 | Dynamo Zagreb 2 Leeds U 0 | 40,000 | Leeds U 0 *Dynamo Zagreb* 0 | 35,604 |
| 1968 | Leeds U 1 Ferencvaros 0 | 25,368 | Ferencvaros 0 *Leeds U* 0 | 70,000 |
| 1969 | Newcastle U 3 Ujpest Dozsa 0 | 60,000 | Ujpest Dozsa 2 *Newcastle U* 3 | 37,000 |
| 1970 | Anderlecht 3 Arsenal 1 | 37,000 | *Arsenal* 3 Anderlecht 0 | 51,612 |
| 1971 | Juventus 0 Leeds U 0 *(abandoned 51 minutes)* | 42,000 | | |
| | Juventus 2 Leeds U 2 | 42,000 | *Leeds U* 1* Juventus 1 | 42,483 |

# UEFA CUP FINALS 1972–97

*(Winners in italics)*

| Year | First Leg | Attendance | Second Leg | Attendance |
|---|---|---|---|---|
| 1972 | Wolverhampton W 1 Tottenham H 2 | 45,000 | *Tottenham H* 1 Wolverhampton W 1 | 48,000 |
| 1973 | Liverpool 0 Moenchengladbach 0 *(abandoned 27 minutes)* | 44,967 | | |
| | Liverpool 3 Moenchengladbach 0 | 41,169 | Moenchengladbach 2 *Liverpool* 0 | 35,000 |
| 1974 | Tottenham H 2 Feyenoord 2 | 46,281 | *Feyenoord* 2 Tottenham H 0 | 68,000 |
| 1975 | Moenchengladbach 0 Twente 0 | 45,000 | Twente 1 *Moenchengladbach* 5 | 24,500 |
| 1976 | Liverpool 3 FC Brugge 2 | 56,000 | FC Brugge 1 *Liverpool* 1 | 32,000 |
| 1977 | Juventus 1 Athletic Bilbao 0 | 75,000 | Athletic Bilbao 2 *Juventus* 1* | 43,000 |
| 1978 | Bastia 0 PSV Eindhoven 0 | 15,000 | *PSV Eindhoven* 3 Bastia 0 | 27,000 |
| 1979 | Red Star Belgrade 1 Moenchengladbach 1 | 87,500 | *Moenchengladbach* 1 Red Star Belgrade 0 | 45,000 |
| 1980 | Moenchengladbach 3 Eintracht Frankfurt 2 | 25,000 | *Eintracht Frankfurt* 1* Moenchengladbach 0 | 60,000 |
| 1981 | Ipswich T 3 AZ 67 Alkmaar 0 | 27,532 | AZ 67 Alkmaar 4 *Ipswich T* 2 | 28,500 |
| 1982 | Gothenburg 1 Hamburg 0 | 42,548 | Hamburg 0 *Gothenburg* 3 | 60,000 |
| 1983 | Anderlecht 1 Benfica 0 | 45,000 | Benfica 1 *Anderlecht* 1 | 80,000 |
| 1984 | Anderlecht 1 Tottenham H 1 | 40,000 | *Tottenham H* 1[1] Anderlecht 1 | 46,258 |
| 1985 | Videoton 0 Real Madrid 3 | 30,000 | *Real Madrid* 0 Videoton 1 | 98,300 |
| 1986 | Real Madrid 5 Cologne 1 | 80,000 | Cologne 2 *Real Madrid* 0 | 15,000 |
| 1987 | Gothenburg 1 Dundee U 0 | 50,023 | Dundee U 1 *Gothenburg* 1 | 20,911 |
| 1988 | Espanol 3 Bayer Leverkusen 0 | 42,000 | *Bayer Leverkusen* 3[2] Espanol 0 | 22,000 |
| 1989 | Napoli 2 Stuttgart 1 | 83,000 | Stuttgart 3 *Napoli* 3 | 67,000 |
| 1990 | Juventus 3 Fiorentina 1 | 45,000 | Fiorentina 0 *Juventus* 0 | 32,000 |
| 1991 | Internazionale 2 Roma 0 | 68,887 | Roma 1 *Internazionale* 0 | 70,901 |
| 1992 | Torino 2 Ajax 2 | 65,377 | *Ajax* 0* Torino 0 | 40,000 |
| 1993 | Borussia Dortmund 1 Juventus 3 | 37,000 | *Juventus* 3 Borussia Dortmund 0 | 62,781 |
| 1994 | Salzburg 0 Internazionale 1 | 47,500 | *Internazionale* 1 Salzburg 0 | 80,326 |
| 1995 | Parma 1 Juventus 0 | 23,000 | Juventus 1 *Parma* 1 | 80,750 |
| 1996 | Bayern Munich 2 Bordeaux 0 | 62,000 | Bordeaux 1 *Bayern Munich* 3 | 36,000 |
| 1997 | Schalke 1 Internazionale 0 | 56,824 | Internazionale 1 *Schalke* 0[3] | 81,670 |

**won on away goals* [1]*aet; Tottenham H won 4-3 on penalties* [2]*aet; Bayer Leverkusen won 3-2 on penalties*
[3]*aet; Schalke won 4-1 on penalties*

# UEFA CUP FINALS 1998–2004

| Year | Winners | Runners-up | Venue | Attendance | Referee |
|---|---|---|---|---|---|
| 1998 | Internazionale 3 | Lazio 0 | Paris | 42,938 | Nieto (Sp) |
| 1999 | Parma 3 | Marseille 0 | Moscow | 61,000 | Dallas (S) |
| 2000 | Galatasaray 0 *(aet; Galatasaray won 4-1 on penalties).* | Arsenal 0 | Copenhagen | 38,919 | Nieto (Sp) |
| 2001 | Liverpool 5 *(aet; Liverpool won on sudden death).* | Alaves 4 | Dortmund | 65,000 | Veissiere (F) |
| 2002 | Feyenoord 3 | Borussia Dortmund 2 | Rotterdam | 45,000 | Pereira (P) |
| 2003 | Porto 3 *(aet).* | Celtic 2 | Seville | 52,972 | Michel (Slv) |
| 2004 | Valencia 2 | Marseille 0 | Gothenburg | 40,000 | Collina (I) |

# UEFA CUP 2003–04

■ *Denotes player sent off.*

### QUALIFYING ROUND, FIRST LEG

AIK Stockholm (0) 1 *(Quansah 89)*, Fylkir (0) 0 7556
Atyrau (0) 1 *(Agabayev 88)*, Levski (4) 4 *(Chilikov 9, Gonzo 13, 33, Temile 20)* 9000
Birkirkara (0) 0, Ferencvaros (1) 5 *(Rosa 31, 90, Jovic 55, 60, Gera 73)* 3000
Brondby (2) 3 *(Jakobsson 3, Wieghorst 19, Bagger 89)*, Dynamo Minsk (0) 0 9376
Cement (0) 0, Katowice (0) 0 5000
Dinamo Bucharest (2) 5 *(Danciulescu 18, 88, Petre 31, 73, Barcauan 60)*, Metalurgs (1) 2 *(Dobrecovs 45 (pen), Safranko 59)* 7500
Dinamo Tirana (0) 0, Lokeren (3) 4 *(De Beule 19, 54, Baldvinsson 40, Van Hoeylandt 45)* 2000
Ekranas (1) 1 *(Luksys 17)*, Debrecen (0) 1 *(Bajzat 74)* 4000
Esbjerg (3) 5 *(Lovenkrands 14, 23, Thorup 41, 76, Hansen 63)*, Santa Coloma (0) 0 1605
Etzella (1) 1 *(Mischo 21)*, Kamen (1) 2 *(Zekic 29, 50)* 1000
Groclin (1) 2 *(Rasiak 37, 53)*, Atlantas (0) 0 4000
Haka (2) 2 *(Popovich 14, Ristila 42)*, Hajduk Split (1) 1 *(Krpan 2)* 2500
Hapoel Tel Aviv (1) 1 *(Rozen 45)*, Banants (0) 1 *(Amiryan 73)* 500
*(in Rotterdam).*
Karnten (1) 2 *(Schellander 28, Kabat 77 (pen))*, Grindavik (0) 1 *(Floventsson 84)* 2300
Lens (0) 3 *(Moreira 69, Utaka 82, Diop 85)*, Torpedo Kutaisi (0) 0 26,443
Levadia (0) 1 *(Rotskov 55)*, Varteks (1) 3 *(Mumlek 33, 65, Rezic 71)* 2000
Liteks (0) 0, Zimbru Chisinau (0) 0 3000
Molde (2) 2 *(Hoset 35 (pen), Ljung 37)*, KI (0) 0 868
MyPa (2) 3 *(Okkonen 2 (pen), 71, Luiz Antonio 23)*, Young Boys (1) 2 *(Fonseca 19, Magnin 57)* 1515
Neman (0) 1 *(Dolya 70)*, Steaua (0) 1 *(Oprita 90)* 2000
Nordsjaelland (2) 4 *(Sorensen 12, 45, 48, Rasmussen 56)*, Shirak (0) 0 2363
NSI (0) 1 *(Hansen 87)*, Lyn (2) 3 *(Sundgot 22, Gudmundsson J 38, Sigurdsson H 80)* 800
Odense (1) 1 *(Miti 25)*, VMK (0) 1 *(Kurjanov 61)* 4221
Petrzalka (1) 1 *(Durica 14)*, Dudelange (0) 0 5000
Matador Puchov (1) 3 *(Breska 48, 90, Pernis 79)*, Sioni (0) 0 2500
Publikum (4) 7 *(Kriznik 6, Brulc 11, 21, Maletic 35, Cadikovski 47, 60, Robnik 82)*, Belasica (0) 2 *(Baldovaliev 49, 85)* 3961
Red Star Belgrade (3) 5 *(Zigic 8, 20, 49, Vidic 45 (pen), Boskovic 46)*, Otaci (0) 0 25,000
Sarajevo (0) 1 *(Kovacevic 83 (og))*, Sartid (1) 1 *(Mirosavljevic 5)* 25,000
Torpedo Moscow (2) 5 *(Volkov 22, Shirko 30, 56, Osipov 49, Zyryanov 87)*, Domagnano (0) 0 4000
Vaduz (0) 0, Dnepr (0) 1 *(Rykun 88)* 750
Valletta (0) 0 *Agius*■, Neuchatel Xamax (2) 2 *(Griffiths 18, Mangane 35)* 1500
Ventspils (0) 1 *(Butriks 61)*, Plock (1) 1 *(Gesior 43)* 2000
Viktoria Zizkov (0) 3 *(Dirnbach 54, Chihuri 60, Mikolanda 90)*, Zhenis (0) 0 3500
Zeljeznicar (0) 1 *(Gredic 71)*, Anorthosis (0) 0 8000

Thursday, 14 August 2003

**Apoel (1) 2** *(Kowalczyk 22, Okkarides 55)*
**Derry City (1) 1** *(Beckett 44)* 9000
*Apoel:* Morfis; Charalambous (Elia 22), Amanatidis, Okkarides, Kowalczyk, Malekkos (Music 80), Satsias, Daskalakis, Charalambides, Papandreon (Vakouftsis 70), Michael.
*Derry City:* Bennett; McCallion, Hargan, Hutton, McLaughlin, Doherty, Martyn, Beckett (Moran 90), Coyle (McGlynn 71), McChrystal, Holt (Deery 46).

**Coleraine (2) 2** *(Gaston 10, Hamill 45)*
**Uniao Leiria (1) 1** *(Joao Manuel 43)* 1700
*Coleraine:* O'Hare; Clamachan, Flynn, Gaston, McAuley, Beatty, Hamill, Tolan, McAllister, Gorman, McCoosh.
*Uniao Leiria:* Da Silva Arruda; Bilro, Atz (Maciel■ 53), Sousa Gomes, Pereira Barros, Douala (Alhandra 75), Joao Manuel, Paulo Duarte, Dos Santos (Sergio Gameiro 85), Joao Paulo, Da Silva.

**Cwmbran Town (0) 0**
**Maccabi Haifa (2) 3** *(Tal 9, Zandberg 29, Lopez 90)* 1052
*Cwmbran Town:* Ellacott; Carter, Smothers, Jones, Warton, David, Summer (McCormick 89), Moore, Mainwaring, Wallace (Green 74), Edwards (Hurlin 77).
*Maccabi Haifa:* Davidovich; Harazi, Benado, Keise, Lopez, Tal (Zano 68), Rosso, Britez, Ejiofor, Zandberg (Levy 76), Katan (Valid 59).

**Malmo (2) 4** *(Mattison 23, Yngvesson 29, 57, Skoog 77)*
**Portadown (0) 0** 5941
*Malmo:* Asper; Persson, Maistorovic, Olsson (Chanko 76), Mattisson (Jonsson 82), Elanga, Skoog, Hoiland, Ijeh, Yngvesson, Johansson (Concha 67).
*Portadown:* Wells; Feeney (Boyle 76), O'Hara (Craig 82), McGibbon, Convery, Clarke, Fitzgerald (Neill 76), Hamilton, Arkins, McCann P, McCann M.

**Manchester City (1) 5** *(Sinclair 14, Wright-Phillips 51, Jihai 60, Sommeil 74, Anelka 87)*
**TNS (0) 0** 34,103
*Manchester City:* Seaman; Jihai, Tarnat (Tiatto 79), Sommeil, Distin, Bosvelt (Barton 64), Wright-Phillips, Berkovic, Anelka, Fowler (Wanchope 71), Sinclair.
*TNS:* Doherty; Naylor, King, Leah, Taylor, Aggrey, Bridgewater (Wood 79), Brabin, Ward (Toner 54), Davies, Ruscoe.

**Olimpija (0) 1** *(Jusufbegovic 72)*
**Shelbourne (0) 0** 2000
*Olimpija:* Mavric; Lazic, Budicin, Handanagic (Mirtic 18), Barun, Jusufbegovic, Rudonja, Zlogar, Aljancic (Kreftl 87), Kmetec (Puc 60), Kosic.
*Shelbourne:* Williams; Heary, Crawley, Doherty, Byrne S (Houlihan 11), Cahill, Baker R (Baker D 80), Crawford, Byrne J (McCarthy 78), Morgan, Rogers.

**Vllaznia (0) 0**
**Dundee (1) 2** *(Lovell 44, Novo 50)* 10,000
*Vllaznia:* Grima (Mustafa 58); Teli, Zmijani, Salihi, Belisha, Cungu (Martini 69), Devolli, Asllani (Luka 52), Ishka, Mancaku, Sinani.
*Dundee:* Speroni; MacKay, Hernandez, Wilkie, Mair, Nemsadze (Sancho 90), Novo (Carranza 89), Rae, Lovell (Sara 83), Smith, Brady.

### QUALIFYING ROUND, SECOND LEG

Anorthosis (1) 1 *(Joldic 20 (og))*, Zeljeznicar (2) 3 *(Gredic 8, Jahic 25, 72)* 6500
Atlantas (0) 1 *(Tarvydas 90)*, Groclin (2) 4 *(Rasiak 30, Krizanac 34, Niedzielan 47, 65)* 1500
Banants (0) 1 *(Amiryan 67)*, Hapoel Tel Aviv (1) 2 *(Solchaga 13, Edri 53)* 2500
Belasica (0) 0, Publikum (2) 5 *(Budimir 30, Kriznik 37, Cadikovski 64, Kvas 72, Plastovski 75)* 1000
Debrecen (1) 2 *(Bajzat 41, 97)*, Ekranas (0) 1 *(Kavaliauskas 60)* 4500
Dnepr (0) 1 *(Rykun 75)*, Vaduz (0) 0 8500
Domagnano (0) 0, Torpedo Moscow (1) 4 *(Leonchenko 44 (pen), Samusevas 54, Volkov 56, Oper 74)* 500
Dudelange (0) 0, Petrzalka (0) 1 *(Durica 87)* 1200
Dynamo Minsk (0) 0, Brondby (1) 2 *(Retov 25, Jonson 81)* 5000
Ferencvaros (0) 1 *(Dragoner 90)*, Birkirkara (0) 0 10,000
Fylkir (0) 0, AIK Stockholm (0) 0 1200

Grindavik (0) 1 *(Jonsson 74)*, Karnten (0) 1 *(Hota 90)* 1500
Hajduk Split (1) 1 *(Racunica 9)*, Haka (0) 0 15,000
Kamen (1) 7 *(Bajsic 33 (pen), Popovic 49, 60, Lisnic 63, Kovac 68, Kopunovic 82, 87)*, Etzella (0) 0 3500
Katowice (0) 1 *(Kowalczyk 57)*, Cement (1) 1 *(Bajramovski 24)* 7500
KI (0) 0, Molde (2) 4 *(Hestad 28, Gustafson 35, Hulsker 75, Ljung 89)* 250
Levski (1) 2 *(Angelov 27 (pen), Telkiyski 69)*, Atyrau (0) 0 8000
Lokeren (1) 3 *(Baldvinsson 29, Fofana 56, 77)*, Dinamo Tirana (1) 1 *(Xhihani 11)* 4500
Lyn (3) 6 *(Hadzimehmedovic 11, 31, 42, 49, 50, 58)*, NSI (0) 0 532
Metalurgs (1) 1 *(Grebis 45)*, Dinamo Bucharest (1) 1 *(Zicu 24)* 20,000
Neuchatel Xamax (1) 2 *(Griffiths 45, Portillo 90)*, Valletta (0) 0 7500
Otaci (1) 2 *(Bursuc 27, 65)*, Red Star Belgrade (2) 3 *(Bogavac 2, Krivokapic 10, Perovic 87)* 5000
Plock (2) 2 *(Jelen 12, 41)*, Ventspils (0) 2 *(Rimkus 51, Zangareyev 68)* 2500
Santa Coloma (1) 1 *(Walker 38)*, Esbjerg (3) 4 *(Lovenkrands 9, Thorup 10, Hansen 31, Hogh 62)* 500
Sartid (1) 3 *(Pantelic 30 (pen), Zecevic 65, Mudrinic 89)*, Sarajevo (0) 0 15,000
Shirak (0) 0, Nordsjaelland (1) 2 *(Rasmussen 43, 89)* 3000
Sioni (0) 0, Matador Puchov (3) 3 *(Nemec 17, 34, Gegic 45)* 2500
Steaua (0) 0, Neman (0) 0 25,000
Torpedo Kutaisi (0) 0, Lens (2) 2 *(Bakari 35, 41)* 5600
Varteks (1) 3 *(Karic 34, Kristic 58, Safaric 71)*, Levadia (0) 2 *(Leitan 72, 87)* 5000
VMK (0) 0, Odense (0) 3 *(Berg 68, Miti 80, 84)* 3500
Young Boys (1) 2 *(Sermeter 24, 77)*, MyPa (0) 2 *(Luiz Antonio 71, Taipale 86)* 7300
Zhenis (0) 1 *(Kozulin 89)*, Viktoria Zizkov (2) 3 *(Oravec 14, Pikl 27, Chihuri 79)* 9500
Zimbru Chisinau (0) 2 *(Balasa 67, Cebotari 81 (pen))*, Liteks (0) 0 6000

Thursday, 28 August 2003

**Derry City (0) 0**
**Apoel (1) 3** *(Malekkos 36, Charalambides 80, Papandreon 90)* 2200

*Derry City:* Gough; McCallion, Hargan, Hutton, McLaughlin, Doherty, Deery, Martyn (McGlynn 83), Beckett, Coyle, Holt (Friars 83).
*Apoel:* Morfis; Amanatidis■, Okkarides, Malekos, Votava (Petkofski 60), Satzias, Daskalakis, Elia (Petrou 77), Charalambides, Michael, Kowalczyk (Papandreon 43).

**Dundee (2) 4** *(Novo 2, 89, Sara 40, Rae 50)*
**Vllaznia (0) 0** 8254

*Dundee:* Speroni; MacKay, Wilkie, Mair, Hernandez (Hutchinson 68), Nemsadze (Boylan 73), Smith, Carranza (Sara 40), Rae, Novo, Lovell.
*Vllaznia:* Grima; Zmijani, Luka, Teli, Osja, Salihi, Asllani (Hoti 69), Belisha, Sinani, Martini (Kraja 72), Cungu.

**Maccabi Haifa (2) 3** *(Katan 36, Rosso 45, Zandberg 61)*
**Cwmbran Town (0) 0** 200
*(Played in Izmir).*

*Maccabi Haifa:* Davidovich; Harazi, Benado, Valid (Zandberg 58), Keise, Lopez, Tal (Azaria 65), Rosso, Britez, Zano, Katan (Barda 67).
*Cwmbran Town:* Ellacott; Carter, Smothers, Jones, Green (Mohamed 69), David, Summer, Moore, Mainwaring (Davies 73), Wallace, Edwards (Hurlin 63).

**Portadown (0) 0**
**Malmo (0) 2** *(Ijeh 60, 62)* 1000

*Portadown:* Wells; Feeney, O'Hara, McGibbon (Craig 46), Convery, Fitzgerald, Boyle, Hamilton, Arkins, McCann P, Neill (Clarke 76).
*Malmo:* Asper; Concha, Maistorovic, Nuorela, Bergstrom, Johansson, Persson (Jonsson 5) (Nilsson 82), Chanko, Yngvesson (Elanga 46), Rosenberg, Ijeh.

**Shelbourne (1) 2** *(Cahill 14, Byrne J 90)*
**Olimpija (2) 3** *(Jusufbegovic 9, Zlogar 45, Kmetec 56)* 3500

*Shelbourne:* Williams; Heary (McCarthy 80), Crawley (Geoghegan 56), Byrne S, Cahill, Baker R, Crawford, Houlihan, Byrne J, Doherty, Rogers.
*Olimpija:* Mavric; Aljancic, Barun, Handanagic, Lazic, Budicin (Mirtic 24), Kosic (Pokorn 74), Zlogar, Rudonja, Jusufbegovic, Kmetec (Ilic 81).

**TNS (0) 0**
**Manchester City (1) 2** *(Negouai 43, Huckerby 81)* 10,123
*(At Millennium Stadium).*

*TNS:* Williams; Naylor, King, Leah, Taylor, Aggrey, Ruscoe, Brabin, Ward (Bridgewater 69), Wood (Wilde 62), Davies (Beck 81).
*Manchester City:* Weaver; Flood, Tiatto, Dunne, Wiekens, Bischoff, Bosvelt (Whelan 73), Negouai, Huckerby, Macken (Wright-Phillips 58), Berkovic (Barton 80).

**Uniao Leiria (0) 5** *(Ludemar 58, 79, Edson 73, 76, Caico 90)*
**Coleraine (0) 0** 7500

*Uniao Leiria:* Helton; Bilro, Paulo Gomes (Alhandra 39), Ludemar, Douala (Gabrel 78), Joao Manuel, Paulo Duarte, Caico, Fredy (Sergio Gameiro 60), Joao Paulo, Edson.
*Coleraine:* O'Hare; Clanachan■, Flynn (Armstrong 78), Gaston, McAuley, Beatty■, Hamill (Johnston 85), Tolan (McHugh 78), McAllister, Gorman, Haveron.

**FIRST ROUND, FIRST LEG**
AIK Stockholm (0) 0, Valencia (0) 1 *(Ricardo Oliveira 65)* 25,433
Apoel (0) 1 *(Papandreou 46)*, Mallorca (1) 2 *(Gonzalez 22, Bruggink 56)* 7000
Auxerre (1) 1 *(Kalou 7)*, Neuchatel Xamax (0) 0 12,000
Bordeaux (2) 2 *(Riera 7, Darchville 36)*, Petrzalka (1) 1 *(Krejci 16)* 11,461
Brondby (0) 1 *(Jonson 64)*, Viktoria Zizkov (0) 0 8939
Cement (0) 0, Lens (0) 1 *(Diop 90)* 5000
CSKA Sofia (1) 1 *(Dimitrov 17)*, Torpedo Moscow (0) 1 *(Semshov 78)* 12,000
Dinamo Bucharest (0) 2 *(Niculescu 86, Zicu 88) Semeghin*■, Shakhtjor Donetsk (0) 0 *Srna*■ 13,000
Dynamo Zagreb (1) 3 *(Da Silva 38, Agic 48, Sedloski 56) Drpic*■, MTK Budapest (1) 1 *(Torghelle 3)* 6000
Feyenoord (0) 2 *(Kuijt 64, Buffel 77)*, Karnten (0) 1 *(Maric 57)* 25,000
Ferencvaros (1) 1 *(Kriston 37)*, FC Copenhagen (1) 1 *(Jonsson 1)* 7500
FK Austria (1) 1 *(Janocko 39)*, Borussia Dortmund (1) 2 *(Addo 38, Ricken 67)* 30,500
Gaziantep (0) 1 *(Hasan Ozer 87)*, Hapoel Tel Aviv (0) 0 8000
Grasshoppers (1) 1 *(Eduardo 40)*, Hajduk Split (0) 1 *(Neretljak 56) Andric*■ 8100
Hamburg (0) 2 *(Hoogma 50 (pen), Romeo 81)*, Dnepr (1) 1 *(Venglinski 11)* 26,831
Hapoel Ramat Gan (0) 0, Levski (0) 1 *(Kolev 80)* 100
*(Played in Streda).*
Hertha Berlin (0) 0, Groclin (0) 0 23,142
Kaiserslautern (0) 1 *(Klose 57)*, Teplice (1) 2 *(Rezek 6, Bencik 64)* 18,511
Kamen (0) 0, Schalke (0) 0 10,000
La Louviere (1) 1 *(Odemwingie 15)*, Benfica (0) 1 *(Sabrosa 53)* 14,200
Maccabi Haifa (1) 2 *(Badir 8, Katan 84)*, Publikum (0) 1 *(Kvas 90)* 250
*(Played in Izmir).*
Malatya (0) 0, Basle (1) 2 *(Yakin M 16, 76)* 8000
Metalurgs (1) 1 *(Shyshchenko 44)*, Parma (0) 1 *(Adriano 67)* 14,000
MyPa (0) 0 *Korhonen*■, Sochaux (1) 1 *(Diawara 45)* 2275
Odense (1) 2 *(Miti 17, Borre 90)*, Red Star Belgrade (1) 2 *(Zigic 22, 64)* 7795

Panionios (2) 2 *(Smiljanic 30, Majewski 33),* Nordsjaelland (0) 1 *(Ziberi 67)* 2500
PAOK Salonika (0) 0, Lyn (1) 1 *(Sigurdsson 39)* 10,000
Matador Puchov (0) 1 *(Jambor 90),* Barcelona (0) 1 *(Kluivert 49)* 18,500
Roma (2) 4 *(Dellas 12, De Rossi 20, Carew 54, Delvecchio 90),* Vardar (0) 0 17,082
Salzburg (0) 0, Udinese (1) 1 *(Fava 36)* 10,000
Sartid (0) 1 *(Kocic 90) Paunovic*■, Slavia Prague (2) 2 *(Dosek 43, Bejbl 45 (pen))* 7000
Spartak Moscow (2) 2 *(Pavlenko 14, Kalinichenko 33),* Esbjerg (0) 0 6500
Sporting Lisbon (1) 2 *(Lourenco 15, Liedson 85),* Malmo (0) 0 25,552
Uniao Leiria (0) 1 *(Caico 56),* Molde (0) 0 2000
Utrecht (1) 2 *(Van de Haar 44, Tanghe 85),* Zilina (0) 0 10,000
Varteks (1) 1 *(Kastel 45) Kristic*■, Debrecen (1) 3 *(Sandor 23, Kiss 57, Dombi 89)* 4000
Ventspils (0) 1 *(Rimkus 81 (pen)),* Rosenborg (3) 4 *(Johnsen F 23, Stensaas 32, Storflor 40, Brattbakk 68)* 1100
Villarreal (0) 0, Trabzonspor (0) 0 17,000
Valerenga (0) 0, Graz (0) 0 2594
Wisla (1) 2 *(Frankowski 29, 56),* NEC Nijmegen (0) 1 *(Wielaert 65 (pen))* 6000
Zimbru Chisinau (0) 1 *(Balasa 57),* Aris Salonika (1) 1 *(Mallous 25)* 5000

Wednesday, 24 September 2004

**Dundee (0) 1** *(Novo 64)*
**Perugia (0) 2** *(Di Loreto 50, Fusani 84)* 9911
*Dundee:* Speroni; MacKay, Hernandez, Smith, Mair (Cowan 87), Wilkie, Sara, Rae, Lovell, Nemsadze (Brady 60), Novo.
*Perugia:* Kalac; Ze Maria, Tedesco, Grosso (Berrettoni 70) Margiotta, Souleymane, Vryzas (Do Prado 87), Alioui, Fusani, Di Loreto, Gatti.

**Genclerbirligi (2) 3** *(Skoko 42, Youla 43, 60)*
**Blackburn Rovers (0) 1** *(Emerton 57)* 18,000
*Genclerbirligi:* Gokhan (Botonjic 46); El Saka, Umit B, Mercimek, Tandogan (M'Bayo 79), Serkan, Deniz, Skoko, Daems, Youla, Ozkan (Bulent A 87).
*Blackburn Rovers:* Friedel; Neill, Gresko, Babbel, Amoruso, Tugay, Emerton, Baggio (Reid 68), Jansen (Cole 46), Yorke (Grabbi 68), Thompson.

**Hearts (1) 2** *(De Vries 28, Webster 60)*
**Zeljeznicar (0) 0** 15,830
*Hearts:* Moilanen; Maybury, Kisnorbo, Pressley, Webster, Sverin, Macfarlane, Hartley (Hamill 81), De Vries, Wyness (Weir 47), Boyack (Valois 23).
*Zeljeznicar:* Hasagic; Kajtaz, Alihodzic, Karic, Gredic (Avdija 86), Muharemovic, Spahic, Jahic, Vuksanovic (Biscevic 72), Obad (Admir 69), Agic.

**Manchester City (1) 3** *(Siberski 8, Fowler 77, Anelka 80 (pen))*
**Lokeren (2) 2** *(Zoundi 14, Kristinsson 40)* 29,067
*Manchester City:* Seaman; Jihai, Tiatto (Dunne 69), Sommeil, Distin, Bosvelt (Wright-Phillips 65), Siberski, Reyna, Anelka, Fowler, McManaman.
*Lokeren:* Dabanovic; Conte, Muzinga, Zanzan, Van Hoey, Doba, Zoundi, Vidarsson, Gretarsson, De Beule, Kristinsson.

**Newcastle United (2) 5** *(Bellamy 31, 37, Bramble 59, Shearer 77, Ambrose 89)*
**NAC Breda (0) 0** 36,007
*Newcastle United:* Given; Hughes, Bernard (Viana 84), Speed, Bramble, O'Brien, Dyer (Ambrose 79), Jenas, Shearer, Bellamy (Ameobi 84), Robert.
*NAC Breda:* Babos; Fehir, Penders, Schenning, Gudelj, Diba (Boussaboun 73), Slot (Koning 62), Peto, Engelaar, Seedorf, Elmander.

**Southampton (0) 1** *(Phillips 52)*
**Steaua (1) 1** *(Raducanu 20)* 30,557
*Southampton:* Jones; Dodd (Delap 84), Le Saux, Oakley, Lundekvam, Svensson M, Fernandes (Telfer 85), Svensson A, Beattie, Phillips, Marsden (McCann 67).
*Steaua:* Hamutovski; Dumitru, Radoi, Rachita, Mutica, Stoica, Aliuta (Paraschiv 84), Falemi, Bostina, Raducanu (Nicolescu 87), Oprita (Ogararu 75).

**Olimpija (0) 1** *(Zlogar 66)*
**Liverpool (0) 1** *(Owen 78)* 10,000
*Olimpija:* Mavric; Aljancic (Pokorn 36), Lazic (Grabic 46), Handanagic (Mirtic 28), Budicin, Zlogar, Ilic, Barun, Jusufbegovic, Rudonja, Puc.
*Liverpool:* Dudek; Diao (Finnan 69), Riise, Le Tallec (Welsh 86), Biscan, Hyypia, Murphy (Gerrard 14), Smicer, Heskey, Owen, Kewell.

FIRST ROUND, SECOND LEG

Aris Salonika (1) 2 *(Koltsidas 44, Lazanas 86),* Zimbru Chisinau (1) 1 *(Shishelov 18)* 3000
Barcelona (3) 8 *(Ronaldinho 6, 19, 57, Motta 41, Luis Enrique 63, 75, Saviola 71, 89),* Matador Puchov (0) 0 29,000
Basle (0) 1 *(Streller 90),* Malatya (0) 2 *(Kocak 64, 85)* 26,600
Benfica (0) 1 *(Feher 58),* La Louviere (0) 0 20,000
Borussia Dortmund (1) 1 *(Ricken 17),* FK Austria (0) 0 50,500
Debrecen (2) 3 *(Kiss 44, Eger 45, Habi 90),* Varteks (1) 2 *(Safaric 26, Vuckovic 57)* 8000
Dnepr (1) 3 *(Mikhalenko 5, Rykun 68, Venglinski 78),* Hamburg (0) 0 25,700
Esbjerg (0) 1 *(Jorgensen 88),* Spartak Moscow (1) 1 *(Pavlyuchenko 43)* 6448
FC Copenhagen (0) 1 *(Nielsen 90 (pen)),* Ferencvaros (0) 1 *(Lipcsei 83)* 16,600
*(aet; FC Copenhagen won 4-3 on penalties.)*
Graz (1) 1 *(Ramusch 32),* Valerenga (0) 1 *(Berre 58)* 9000
Groclin (0) 1 *(Rasiak 83),* Hertha Berlin (0) 0 4450
Hajduk Split (0) 0, Grasshoppers (0) 0 30,000
Hapoel Tel Aviv (0) 0, Gaziantep (0) 0 2500
*(Played in Rotterdam).*
Karnten (0) 0, Feyenoord (1) 1 *(Buffel 15)* 7000
Lens (2) 5 *(Condon 14, Moreira 45, Utaka 53 (pen), Coulibaly 58, Bakiri 90),* Cement (0) 0 22,671
Levski (1) 4 *(Chilikov 23, Ivanov 76, Simonovic 79, Demba-Nyren 90),* Hapoel Ramat Gan (0) 0 2510
Lyn (0) 0, PAOK Salonika (0) 3 *(Giasemi 52, Koutsis 55, Vokolos 62)* 2068
MTK (0) 0, Dynamo Zagreb (0) 0 4000
Mallorca (1) 4 *(Eto'o 30, 61, 71, Correa 89),* Apoel Nicosia (1) 2 *(Okkarides 9, Amanatidis 90)* 7000
Malmo (0) 0, Sporting Lisbon (0) 1 *(Liedson 48)* 6360
Molde (1) 3 *(Hoseth 34 (pen), 74 (pen), Hestad 51),* Uniao Leiria (1) 1 *(Maciel 56)* 1787
Neuchatel Xamax (0) 0, Auxerre (0) 1 *(Lachuer 53)* 5585
NEC Nijmegen (1) 1 *(Zonneveld 33),* Wisla (1) 2 *(Frankowski 45, 68)* 4500
Nordsjaelland (0) 0, Panionios (0) 1 *(Raguel 90)* 4528
Parma (1) 3 *(Gilardino 43, 46, Marchionni 72),* Metalurg (0) 0 8308
Petrzalka(0) 1 *(Krejci 90),* Bordeaux (0) 1 *(Darcheville 86)* 3300
Publikum (1) 2 *(Koren 43, 60),* Maccabi Haifa (0) 2 *(Tal 61, Rosso 81)* 2000
Red Star Belgrade (3) 4 *(Zigic 4, 86, Vidic 12, Djordjic 26),* Odense (2) 3 *(Stokholm 10, 77, Hojer 39)* 35,000
Rosenborg (3) 6 *(Karadas 17, Brattbakk 29, 90, Hoftun 45, Solli 57, Zavoronkovs 89 (og)),* Ventspils (0) 0 17,000
Schalke (0) 1 *(Hanke 77),* Kamen (0) 0 52,600
Shakhtjor Donetsk (2) 2 *(Aghahowa 18, 45), Dinamo Bucharest (1) 3 (Niculescu 28, Marica 76, Danciulescu 86)* 30,000
Slavia Prague (2) 2 *(Dostalek 5, Adauto 30),* Sartid (0) 1 *(Mirosavljevic 47)* 4243
Sochaux (0) 2 *(Monsoreau 58, Dos Santos 80),* MyPa (0) 0 8885
Teplice (0) 1 *(Bencik 70),* Kaiserslautern (0) 0 14,300

Torpedo Moscow (1) 1 *(Oper 11)*, CSKA Sofia (0) 1 *(Dimitrov 90)* 8500
*(aet; Torpedo Moscow won 3-2 on penalties.)*
Trabzonspor (0) 2 *(Karadeniz 73, Tekke 82)*, Villarreal (0) 3 *(Anderson 61, Jose Mari 66, 90)*, 21,000
Udinese (1) 1 *(Bertotto 15)*, Salzburg (0) 2 *(Hassler 65, Kahraman 79)* 15,000
Valencia (0) 1 *(Mista 70)*, AIK Stockholm (0) 0 20,000
Vardar (1) 1 *(Zaharievski 41)*, Roma (0) 1 *(Mancini 63)* 15,000
Viktoria Zizkov (0) 0, Brondby (0) 1 *(Daugaard 87)* 3162
Zilina (0) 0, Utrecht (1) 4 *(Van de Haar 29, 65, Lamey 80, Tanghe 83)* 6673

Wednesday, 15 October 2003

**Blackburn Rovers (0) 1** *(Jansen 65)*

**Genclerbirligi (0) 1** *(Ozkan 66)* 14,573

*Blackburn Rovers:* Friedel; Reid, Gresko (Yorke 62), Todd (Taylor 77), Amoruso, Tugay, Emerton, Flitcroft, Grabbi (Baggio 60), Jansen, Thompson.
*Genclerbirligi:* Botonjic; Mercimek, Umit B, El Saka, Tandogan, Skoko (Bulent K 90), Deniz, Serkan, Daems, Ozkan (Ozbey 75), Youla (Cihan 82).

**Liverpool (2) 3** *(Le Tallec 30, Heskey 37, Kewell 47)*

**Olimpija (0) 0** 42,880

*Liverpool:* Dudek; Finnan, Riise, Le Tallec (Sinama-Pongolle 61), Biscan, Hyypia, Gerrard (Diao 76), Diouf, Heskey, Kewell, Smicer (Henchoz 67).
*Olimpija:* Mavric; Ilic, Grabic, Mirtic, Pokorn (Kmetec 46), Kosic (Aljancic 39), Zlogar, Barun, Budicin, Rudonja (Puc 61), Jusufbegovic.

**Lokeren (0) 0**

**Manchester City (0) 1** *(Anelka 19 (pen))* 10,000

*Lokeren:* Van der Jeugt; Conte (Vanhoeylandt 76), Doba, Katana, Muzinga, Coulibali, Vidarsson, Gretarsson, De Beule, Kristinsson, Fofana (Baldvinsson 66).
*Manchester City:* Seaman; Jihai, Tarnat, Sommeil, Distin, Bosvelt, Wright-Phillips, McManaman, Anelka, Wanchope (Reyna 78), Sinclair (Barton 89).

**NAC Breda (0) 0**

**Newcastle United (0) 1** *(Robert 86)* 15,564

*NAC Breda:* Babos (Coutinho 37); Collen, Penders, Koning (Barakat 69), Gudelj, Seedorf, Stam, Slot, Engelaar, Boussaboun (Vos 69), Elmander.
*Newcastle United:* Harper; Griffin, Bernard, Solano (Ambrose 78), Bramble (Caldwell S 78), O'Brien, Dyer (Lua-Lua 84), Jenas, Ameobi, Viana, Robert.

**Perugia (0) 1** *(Margiotta 71)*

**Dundee (0) 0** 8685

*Perugia:* Kalac; Souleymane, Ignoffo, Di Loreto, Obodo, Loumpoutis, Ze Maria, Tedesco, Bothroyd (Do Prado 73), Fusani, Vryzas (Margiotta 64).
*Dundee:* Speroni; MacKay (Carranza 76), Wilkie, Mair, Hernandez, Nemsadze, Rae, Smith, Novo, Sara, Caballero (McLean 83).

**Steaua (0) 1** *(Raducanu 82)*

**Southampton (0) 0** 29,000

*Steaua:* Hamutovski; Radoi, Rachita, Mutica, Dumitru, Paraschiv, Aliuta (Falemi 57), Bostina, Stoica, Oprita (Dinita 70), Raducanu (Ogararu 89).
*Southampton:* Niemi; Dodd, Higginbotham, Delap, Lundekvam, Svensson M, Telfer, Svensson A, Beattie (Tessem 86), Phillips, Fernandes.

**Zeljeznicar (0) 0**

**Hearts (0) 0** 20,000

*Zeljeznicar:* Hasagic; Biscevic, Kajtaz, Mulalic, Alihodzic, Karic, Gredic (Joldic 77), Muharemovic, Jahic, Vuksanovic (Avdija 71), Obad (Dzeko 63).
*Hearts:* Moilanen; Maybury, Pressley, Webster, Severin, Stamp (Hartley 84), De Vries (McKenna 88), Valois, Macfarlane, Kisnorbo, Weir (Wyness 76).

## SECOND ROUND, FIRST LEG

Benfica (1) 3 *(Nuno Gomes 18, 54, Geovanni 51)*, Molde (0) 1 *(Hestad 76)* 35,385
Borussia Dortmund (0) 2 *(Senesie 67, Ewerthon 76)*, Sochaux (2) 2 *(Dos Santos 12, Frau 27)* 40,500
Dynamo Zagreb (0) 0, Dnepr (1) 2 *(Venglinski 8, Maxymyuk 84)* 12,000
FC Copenhagen (1) 1 *(Albrechtsen 31)*, Mallorca (1) 2 *(Albrechtsen 27 (og), Nagore 73)* 20,487
Feyenoord (0) 0, Teplice (1) 2 *(Dolezal 3, Rezek 57)* 27,000
Gaziantep (1) 3 *(Ayhan 43, Bouazzi 60, Lazarov 65)*, Lens (0) 0 12,000
Genclerbirligi (0) 1 *(Cihan 56)*, Sporting Lisbon (0) 1 *(Liedson 50)* 20,000
PAOK Salonika (1) 1 *(Karadimos 11)*, Debrecen (1) 1 *(Bajzat 25)* 10,000
Panionios (0) 0, Barcelona (1) 3 *(Luis Garcia 42, Kluivert 46, Xavi 90)* 10,000
Perugia (0) 2 *(Margiotta 46, 89)*, Aris Salonika (0) 0 10,000
Roma (0) 1 *(Cassano 90)*, Hajduk Split (0) 0 20,000
Rosenborg (0) 0, Red Star Belgrade (0) 0 12,600
Salzburg (0) 0, Parma (0) 4 *(Filippini 60, Gilardino 65, Nakata 84, Rosina 86)* 6000
Schalke (0) 2 *(Hanke 60, 72)*, Brondby (1) 1 *(Jakobsson 34)* 50,000
Slavia Prague (1) 2 *(Kuka 23, Fort 90)*, Levski (0) 2 *(Ivanov 77, Muller 89 (og))* 4200
Spartak Moscow (1) 4 *(Pjanovic 21, 62, Kalinicenko 58, Pavlenko 73)*, Dinamo Bucharest (0) 0 8500
Utrecht (0) 0, Auxerre (0) 0 20,000
Valencia (0) 0, Maccabi Haifa (0) 0 35,000
Valerenga (0) 0, Wisla (0) 0 3716
Villarreal (0) 2 *(Riquelme 51, 68)*, Torpedo Moscow (0) 0 10,000

Thursday, 6 November 2003

**Basle (2) 2** *(Cantaluppi 11, Chipperfield 15)*

**Newcastle United (2) 3** *(Robert 14, Bramble 37, Ameobi 75)* 30,000

*Basle:* Zuberbuhler; Atouba, Yakin M, Zwyssig, Degen P, Huggel, Cantaluppi, Chipperfield, Yakin H (Rossi 60), Streller, Gimenez (Barberis 81).
*Newcastle United:* Given; Hughes, Bernard, Speed, Bramble, O'Brien, Solano (Ambrose 86), Jenas, Shearer, Ameobi, Robert (Viana 90).

**Bordeaux (0) 0**

**Hearts (0) 1** *(De Vries 78)* 15,536

*Bordeaux:* Rame; Alicarte, Bruno Basto, Jemmali, Jurietti (Deivid 80), Pochettino, Eduardo Costa, Paulo Costa (Riera 66), Feindouno, Chamack, Darcheville.
*Hearts:* Gordon; McKenna, Pressley, Webster, Neilson (McCann 72), Maybury, Stamp (Severin 79), Wyness, Valois (Hartley 68), Kisnorbo, De Vries.

**Manchester City (1) 1** *(Anelka 6)*

**Groclin (0) 1** *(Mila 65)* 32,506

*Manchester City:* Seaman; Jihai, Tarnat, Dunne, Distin, Barton, Wright-Phillips, Reyna (Bosvelt 25), McManaman (Tiatto 64), Anelka, Fowler (Wanchope 69).
*Groclin:* Liberda; Mynar, Koziol, Pawlak, Krizanac, Zajac (Kaczmarczyk 89), Wieszczycki, Mila, Sedlacek, Rasiak, Niedzielan (Piechniak 71).

**Steaua (0) 1** *(Raducanu 69)*

**Liverpool (1) 1** *(Traore 23)* 25,000

*Steaua:* Hamutovski; Radoi, Rachita, Mutica, Dumitru, Ngassam Nana, Aliuta (Neaga 72), Bostina (Pitu 60), Stoica, Oprita (Nesu 86), Raducanu.
*Liverpool:* Dudek; Finnan, Traore, Gerrard, Biscan, Hyypia, Diouf (Le Tallec 56), Murphy, Heskey, Kewell, Riise.

## SECOND ROUND, SECOND LEG

Aris Salonika (0) 1 *(Papadopoulos 90)*, Perugia (1) 1 *(Margiotta 28)* 20,000

Auxerre (2) 4 *(Cisse 22, 48, Kapo 30, Kalou 58)*, Utrecht (0) 0 16,000
Barcelona (2) 2 *(Saviola 33, Luis Garcia 44)*, Panionios (0) 0 25,321
Brondby (1) 2 *(Jakobsson 16 (pen), Jonson 70)*, Schalke (0) 1 *(Agali 55)* 25,817
*(aet; Brondby won 3-1 on penalties.)*
Debrecen (0) 0, PAOK Salonika (0) 0 8000
Dynamo Bucharest (1) 3 *(Danciulescu 29, 79 (pen), Iordache 59)*, Spartak Moscow (0) 1 *(Parfyonov 84 (pen))* 7000
Dnepr (0) 1 *(Venglinski 65)*, Dynamo Zagreb (0) 1 *(Sedloski 62)* 15,000
Hajduk Split (1) 1 *(Bule 33)*, Roma (0) 1 *(Cassano 85)* 35,000
Lens (0) 1 *(Fanni 73)*, Gaziantep (1) 3 *(Bolukbasi 40, Namli 56, Lazarov 85 (pen)* 37,372
Levski (0) 0, Slavia Prague (0) 0 30,000
Maccabi Haifa (0) 0, Valencia (2) 4 *(Mista 11, Baraja 24, Albelda 89, Angulo 90)* 2333
*(Played in Rotterdam).*
Mallorca (0) 1 *(Campano 68)*, FC Copenhagen (0) 1 *(Albrechtsen 87)* 9000
Molde (0) 0, Benfica (2) 2 *(Tiago 29, 43)* 4181
Parma (3) 5 *(Carbone 1, 7, Filippini 43, Sorrentino 47, 86)*, Salzburg (0) 0 6000
Red Star Belgrade (0) 0, Rosenborg (0) 1 *(Brattbakk 51)* 55,000
Sochaux (1) 4 *(Frau 6 (pen), Dos Santos 64, Oruma 76, Mathieu 89)*, Borussia Dortmund (0) 0 18,384
Sporting Lisbon (0) 0, Genclerbirligi (2) 3 *(Mario Sergio 44 (og), Tandogan 45, Cihan 49)* 27,949
Teplice (1) 1 *(Horvath 40 (pen))*, Feyenoord (1) 1 *(Snoyl 37)* 17,054
Torpedo Moscow (0) 1 *(Semshov 74)*, Villarreal (0) 0 4000
Wisla (0) 0, Valerenga (0) 0 10,000
*(aet; Valerenga won 4-3 on penalties.)*

Thursday, 27 November 2003

**Groclin (0) 0**

**Manchester City (0) 0** 5500

*Groclin:* Liberda; Mynar, Pawlak, Ivica, Sedlacek, Zajac (Gorszkow 88), Koziol, Wieszczycki, Mila, Rasiak, Niedzielan (Piechniak 81).
*Manchester City:* Seaman; Jihai, Dunne, Sommeil, Distin, Barton, Wright-Phillips (Reyna 79), McManaman, Anelka (Macken 75), Fowler (Wanchope 75), Sinclair.

**Hearts (0) 0**

**Bordeaux (1) 2** *(Riera 8, Fendouno 66)* 17,587

*Hearts:* Gordon; Nielson, McKenna, Maybury, Webster, Hartley (Severin 29), Macfarlane (Simmons 46), Stamp, Kisnorbo, Valois (Kirk 73), De Vries.
*Bordeaux:* Rame; Caneira, Planus, Pochettino, Alicarte, Jurietti, Eduardo Costa, Feindouno, Riera (Paulo Costa 46), Chamack (Sahnoun 90), Darcheville (Celades 82).

**Liverpool (0) 1** *(Kewell 49)*

**Steaua (0) 0** 42,837

*Liverpool:* Kirkland; Diao, Traore, Hamann, Biscan, Hyypia, Diouf (Smicer 70), Gerrard, Sinama-Pongolle (Heskey 70), Owen (Murphy 89), Kewell.
*Steaua:* Hamutovski; Radoi, Rachita, Mutica, Dumitru, Falemi (Dinita 80), Aliuta (Paraschiv 15), Stoica, Bostina, Oprita (Pitu 80), Raducanu.

**Newcastle United (1) 1** *(Smiljanic 14 (og))*

**Basle (0) 0** 40,385

*Newcastle United:* Given; Hughes, Bernard, Speed, Bramble, O'Brien, Dyer (Solano 78), Jenas, Shearer, Ameobi, Robert (Ambrose 78).
*Basle:* Zuberbuhler; Degen P, Quennoz, Zwyssig (Smiljanic 4), Antouba, Barberis (Degen D 53), Cantaluppi, Chipperfield, Yakin H, Streller, Rossi (Tum 62).

## THIRD ROUND, FIRST LEG

Auxerre (0) 0, *Kapo*■, Panathinaikos (0) 0 19,000
Benfica (0) 1 *(Zahovic 59)*, Rosenborg (0) 0 40,000
Brondby (0) 0, Barcelona (0) 1 *(Ronaldinho 63)* 26,031
FC Brugge (1) 1 *(Lange 40)*, Debrecen (0) 0 21,400
Galatasaray (1) 2 *(Murat 26, Cesar Prates 52)*, Villarreal (2) 2 *(Anderson 7, Riquelme 22) Ballesteros*■ 55,000
Gaziantep (1) 1 *(Yusuf 19)*, Roma (0) 0 18,000
Groclin (0) 0, Bordeaux (0) 1 *(Chamakh 90) Costa*■ 5000
Marseille (0) 1 *(Drogba 54 (pen))*, Dnepr (0) 0 15,500
Parma (0) 0, Genclerbirligi (0) 1 *(Skoko 60)* 3598
Perugia (0) 0, PSV Eindhoven (0) 0 7000
Sochaux (0) 2 *(Frau 59, 81)*, Internazionale (1) 2 *(Vieri 8, Recoba 61)* 19,551
Spartak Moscow (0) 0, Mallorca (0) 3 *(Eto'o 67, Rodriguez 81, Jesus Perera 85)* 15,000
Valencia (2) 3 *(Sissoko 25, Canobbio 43, Navarro 90)*, Besiktas (2) 2 *(Pancu 17, 39)* 15,000

Thursday, 26 February 2004

**Celtic (2) 3** *(Larsson 3, 90, Sutton 12)*

**Teplice (0) 0** 48,947

*Celtic:* Douglas; Agathe, Thompson, Varga, Balde, McNamara (Valgaeren 86), Lambert, Pearson (Sylla 72), Sutton, Larsson, Petrov.
*Teplice:* Postulka; Leitner, Hunal, Verbir, Ryska, Dolezal, Tesarik, Rada, Masek, Kowalik (Rilke 46), Skala.

**Liverpool (0) 2** *(Gerrard 67, Kewell 70)*

**Levski (0) 0** 39,149

*Liverpool:* Kirkland; Finnan, Carragher, Hamann, Henchoz, Hyypia, Murphy, Gerrard, Baros (Cheyrou 90), Owen, Kewell (Diouf 85).
*Levski:* Ivankov; Borimirov (Stankov 77), Wagner, Topuzakov, Stoyanov, Markov, Temile (Telkiyaki 71), Bukarev, Ivanov G, Golovskoy, Vidolov (Chilikov 71).

**Valerenga (0) 1** *(Normann 54)*

**Newcastle United (1) 1** *(Bellamy 39)* 17,039

*Valerenga:* Bolthof; Brocken, Normann (Ovrebo 82), Hagen, Rekdal, Hovi (Edvardsen 25) (Krogstad 88), Berre, Gashi, Dos Santos, Hanssen, Fredheim.
*Newcastle United:* Given; Hughes, Bernard, Speed, O'Brien, Bramble, Ambrose (Dyer 51), Jenas, Ameobi (Bridges 74), Bellamy, Viana (Robert 74).

## THIRD ROUND, SECOND LEG

Barcelona (2) 2 *(Luis Garcia 31, Cocu 42)*, Brondby (0) 1 *(Nielsen 86)* 46,589
Besiktas (0) 0 *Zago*■, Valencia (1) 2 *(Angulo 12, Sanchez 56)* 30,000
Bordeaux (2) 4 *(Planus 41, Chamakh 42, Krizanac 64 (og), Riera 74 (pen)) Afanou*■, Groclin (0) 1 *(Wieszczycki 90)* 9197
Debrecen (0) 0, FC Brugge (0) 0 7000
Dnepr (0) 0, Marseille (0) 0 25,000
Genclerbirligi (1) 3 *(Daems 36 (pen), Ferrari 81 (og), Tandogan 90)*, Parma (0) 0 *Frey*■ 25,000
Internazionale (0) 0 *Vieri*■, Sochaux (0) 0 15,900
Mallorca (0) 0, Spartak Moscow (1) 1 *(Samedov 43)* 3000
Panathinaikos (0) 0, Auxerre (0) 1 *(Kalou 71)* 24,000
PSV Eindhoven (2) 3 *(Hofland 22, Kezman 44, 48)*, Perugia (0) 1 *(Ze Maria 88)* 31,500
Roma (2) 2 *(Emerson 22, Cassano 42)*, Gaziantep (0) 0 24,000
Rosenborg (2) 2 *(Berg 8, Karadas 16)*, Benfica (1) 1 *(Nuno Gomes 21)* 18,328
Villarreal (0) 3 *(Anderson 48, Roger 52, Riquelme 90)*, Galatasaray (0) 0 11,000

Wednesday, 3 March 2004

**Levski (2) 2** *(Ivanov G 27, Simonovic 40)*

**Liverpool (3) 4** *(Gerrard 7, Owen 11, Hamann 44, Hyypia 67)* 40,281

*Levski:* Ivankov; Topuzakov, Markov, Bukarev (Golovskoy 62), Stoyanov (Borimirov 62), Temile, Simonovic, Chilikov, Ivanov G, Vidolov, Angelov (Kolev 71).
*Liverpool:* Kirkland; Finnan (Biscan 58), Carragher, Hamann, Henchoz, Hyypia, Murphy, Gerrard, Cheyrou (Baros 69), Owen, Kewell (Le Tallec 80).

**Newcastle United (1) 3** *(Shearer 19, Ameobi 47, 89)*

**Valerenga (1) 1** *(Hagen 25)* 38,531

*Newcastle United:* Given; Hughes, O'Brien, Speed, Woodgate, Bramble, Bridges (Brittan 76), Jenas, Shearer, Bellamy (Ameobi 46), Robert.
*Valerenga:* Bolthof; Brocken, Hanssen (Waehler 65), Jailand, Hovi, Rekdal (Normann 70), Hagen, Berre, Dos Santos, Gashi, Holm.

**Teplice (1) 1** *(Masek 35)*

**Celtic (0) 0** 10,000

*Teplice:* Postulka; Leitner (Styvar 90), Hunal, Verbir (Mares 88), Rada, Dolezal, Tesarik, Kuchar, Masek, Rilke (Ryska 75), Skala.
*Celtic:* Douglas; Kennedy, McNamara (Valgaeren 84), Agathe, Balde, Varga, Lambert, Petrov, Sutton (Pearson 72), Larsson, Thompson.

## FOURTH ROUND, FIRST LEG

Auxerre (1) 1 *(Tainio 36),* PSV Eindhoven (0) 1 *(Lucius 68)* 13,000
Benfica (0) 0, Internazionale (0) 0 64,569
Bordeaux (0) 3 *(Celades 59, 71, Riera 87),* FC Brugge (0) 1 *(Verheyen 58)* 14,498
Genclerbirligi (1) 1 *(Daems 12 (pen)),* Valencia (0) 0 20,000
Villarreal (2) 2 *(Anderson 30, Jose Mari 35),* Roma (0) 0 17,000

Thursday, 11 March 2004

**Celtic (0) 1** *(Thompson 59)*

**Barcelona (0) 0** 59,539

*Celtic:* Douglas■; Agathe, McNamara, Beattie (Marshall 46), Balde, Varga, Lennon, Petrov, Larsson, Pearson, Thompson (Sylla 83).
*Barcelona:* Victor Valdes; Reiziger (Lopez 64), Gabri, Cocu, Oleguer, Puyol, Xavi, Motta■, Saviola■, Ronaldinho (Overmars 88), Luis Garcia (Quaresma 72).

**Liverpool (0) 1** *(Baros 55)*

**Marseille (0) 1** *(Drogba 78)* 41,270

*Liverpool:* Kirkland; Finnan (Biscan 89), Carragher, Hamann, Henchoz, Hyypia, Murphy (Heskey 82), Gerrard, Baros, Owen, Kewell.
*Marseille:* Barthez; Perez (Ferreira 62), Dos Santos, Beye, Hemdani, Meite, Flamini, N'Diaye, Marlet, Drogba, Batiles (Meriem 67).

**Newcastle United (0) 4** *(Bellamy 67, Shearer 71, Robert 74, Bramble 84)*

**Mallorca (0) 1** *(Correa 57)* 38,012

*Newcastle United:* Given; Hughes, Bernard, Speed, O'Brien, Bramble, Dyer (Ambrose 86), Jenas, Shearer, Bellamy, Robert.
*Mallorca:* Leo Franco; Cortes, Moya■, Arbizu, Lussenhoff, Nino, Campano, Colsa (Martin 64), Correa (George 64), Eto'o, Nene.

## FOURTH ROUND, SECOND LEG

FC Brugge (0) 0, Bordeaux (0) 1 *(Chamack 84)* 23,717
Internazionale (1) 4 *(Martins 45, 70, Recoba 60, Vieri 64),* Benfica (1) 3 *(Nuno Gomes 36, 67, Tiago 77)* 27,638
PSV Eindhoven (2) 3 *(Kezman 4, 27, Van Bommel 73),* Auxerre (0) 0 30,000
Roma (1) 2 *(Emerson 10, Cassano 51) Zebina*■, Villarreal (0) 1 *(Anderson 66)* 29,088
Valencia (0) 2 *(Mista 64, Vicente 94),* Genclerbirligi (0) 0 29,000
*(Valencia won on sudden death).*

Thursday, 25 March 2004

**Barcelona (0) 0**

**Celtic (0) 0** 80,000

*Barcelona:* Victor Valdes; Reiziger (Overmars 83), Gabri, Xavi, Oleguer, Puyol (Marquez 33), Gerard, Cocu, Luis Enrique (Sergio Garcia 64), Ronaldinho, Luis Garcia.
*Celtic:* Marshall; Agathe, McNamara (Miller 51), Pearson, Varga, Kennedy, Petrov, Lennon, Sutton (Sylla 83), Larsson, Thompson.

**Mallorca (0) 0**

**Newcastle United (0) 3** *(Shearer 46, 89, Bellamy 78)* 12,000

*Mallorca:* Miki; George, Gonzalez (Nino 46), Ramis (Eto'o 53), Lussenhoff, Poli, Marcos (Campano 38), Arbizu, Perera, Bruggink, Nene.
*Newcastle United:* Given; O'Brien (Taylor 80), Bernard, Speed (Bellamy 77), Woodgate, Bramble, Ambrose, Jenas, Shearer, Ameobi, Robert (Viana 66).

**Marseille (1) 2** *(Drogba 38 (pen), Meite 58)*

**Liverpool (1) 1** *(Heskey 15)* 55,000

*Marseille:* Barthez; Ferreira, Dos Santos, Beye, Hemdani, Meite, Flamini, N'Diaye, Marlet (Meriem 79), Drogba, Batiles (Mido 72).
*Liverpool:* Dudek; Carragher, Riise, Hamann, Biscan■, Hyypia, Gerrard, Murphy (Cheyrou 69), Heskey, Owen (Baros 62), Kewell (Sinama-Pongolle 82).

## QUARTER-FINALS, FIRST LEG

Bordeaux (1) 1 *(Riera 18), Mavuba*■, Valencia (0) 2 *(Baraja 75, Rufete 87)* 29,000
Marseille (0) 1 *(Drogba 47),* Internazionale (0) 0 58,000

Thursday, 8 April 2004

**Celtic (0) 1** *(Larsson 64)*

**Villarreal (1) 1** *(Josico 9)* 58,493

*Celtic:* Marshall; Agathe, McNamara, Pearson (Miller 78), Varga, Balde, Petrov, Lennon, Sutton, Larsson, Thompson.
*Villarreal:* Reina; Venta, Arruabarrena, Battaglia, Coloccini, Ballesteros, Jose Mari, Josico (Marti 78), Roman, Anderson, Garcia.

**PSV Eindhoven (1) 1** *(Kezman 15)*

**Newcastle United (1) 1** *(Jenas 45)* 35,000

*PSV Eindhoven:* Waterreus; Bogelund, Lee, Van der Schaaf (Vogel 66), Colin, Bouma, Park, Van Bommel, Kezman, Vennegoor of Hesselink, De Jong (Rommedahl 67).
*Newcastle United:* Given; Hughes, Bernard, Speed, Woodgate, Bramble, Ambrose, Jenas, Shearer (Ameobi 90), Bellamy, Robert.

## QUARTER-FINALS, SECOND LEG

Internazionale (0) 0, Marseille (0) 1 *(Meriem 73)* 36,044
Valencia (0) 2 *(Pellegrino 51, Rufete 60),* Bordeaux (0) 1 *(Costa 71)* 40,000

Wednesday, 14 April 2004

**Newcastle United (1) 2** *(Shearer 9, Speed 66)*

**PSV Eindhoven (0) 1** *(Kezman 52 (pen)* 50,083

*Newcastle United:* Given; Hughes, Bernard, Speed, Woodgate, Bramble (O'Brien 77), Ambrose (Ameobi 81), Jenas, Shearer, Bellamy, Robert (Viana 90).
*PSV Eindhoven:* Waterreus; Bogelund, Lee, Vogel (Von Lanten 76), Colin, Bouma, Rommedahl (Vennegoor of Hesselink 46), Van Bommel, Kezman, De Jong, Park.

**Villarreal (1) 2** *(Anderson 6, Roger 68)*

**Celtic (0) 0** 23,000

*Villarreal:* Reina; Belletti, Arruabarrena, Battaglia, Coloccini, Ballesteros, Jose Mari (Venta 84), Riquelme, Anderson, Roger, Josico.
*Celtic:* Marshall; Agathe, Valgaeren, McNamara, Varga, Balde, Miller (Smith 70), Lennon, Petrov, Larsson, Pearson (Wallace 70).

**SEMI-FINALS, FIRST LEG**
Villarreal (0) 0, Valencia (0) 0 23,000

Thursday, 22 April 2004

**Newcastle United (0) 0**
**Marseille (0) 0** 52,004

*Newcastle United:* Given; Hughes, Bernard, Speed, Woodgate, O'Brien, Ambrose, Viana, Shearer, Ameobi (Bridges 77), Robert.
*Marseille:* Barthez; Ferreira, Dos Santos, Meite, Beye, Hemdani, Batiles (Celestini 90), Flamini, Drogba, N'Diaye, Meriem.

**SEMI-FINALS, SECOND LEG**
Valencia (1) 1 *(Mista 16 (pen))*, Villarreal (0) 0 52,000

Thursday, 6 May 2004

**Marseille (1) 2** *(Drogba 18, 82)*
**Newcastle United (0) 0** 57,500

*Marseille:* Barthez; Ferreira, Dos Santos, Meite, Beye, Hemdani, Flamini, N'Diaye, Marlet (Batiles 81), Drogba (Vachousek 90), Meriem.
*Newcastle United:* Given; Hughes, Bernard, Speed, O'Brien, Bramble, Ambrose, Viana (Bowyer 65), Shearer, Ameobi, Robert.

**UEFA CUP FINAL 2004**

Wednesday, 19 May 2004

(in Gothenburg, 40,000)

**Valencia (1) 2** *(Vicente 45 (pen), Mista 47)* **Marseille (0) 0**

*Valencia:* Canizares; Curro Torres, Carboni, Baraja, Ayala, Marchena (Pellegrino 86), Rufete (Aimar 64), Albelda, Angulo (Sissoko 83), Mista, Vicente.

*Marseille:* Barthez■; Ferreira, Dos Santos, Beye, Hemdani, Meite, Flamini (Batiles 71), Meriem (Gavanon 45), Marlet, Drogba, N'Diaye (Celestini 84).

*Referee:* P. Collina (Italy).

Valencia's Mista fires in their second goal in the 2-0 UEFA Cup final win against Marseille in Gothenburg. (Empics)

# UEFA CHAMPIONS LEAGUE 2004–05

## NEW SYSTEM

The 2004–05 season will see the start of UEFA's club licensing system. In order for a club to be admitted to any of the UEFA club competitions, minimum standards in areas including sporting matters, infrastructure, personnel and administration, legal matters and financial matters must be fulfilled.

## UEFA CHAMPIONS LEAGUE

| *IOC* | *Stage* | *Club* |
|---|---|---|
| – | Grp | FC Porto – holders |
| ESP | Grp | Valencia CF |
| ESP | Grp | FC Barcelona |
| ESP | Q3 | RC Deportivo La Coruña |
| ESP | Q3 | Real Madrid CF |
| ITA | Grp | AC Milan |
| ITA | Grp | AS Roma |
| ITA | Q3 | Juventus FC |
| ITA | Q3 | FC Internazionale |
| ENG | Grp | Arsenal FC |
| ENG | Grp | Chelsea FC |
| ENG | Q3 | Manchester United FC |
| ENG | Q3 | Liverpool FC |
| GER | Grp | SV Werder Bremen |
| GER | Grp | FC Bayern München |
| GER | Q3 | Bayer 04 Leverkusen |
| FRA | Grp | Olympique Lyonnais |
| FRA | Grp | Paris Saint-Germain FC |
| FRA | Q3 | AS Monaco FC |
| GRE | Grp | Panathinaikos FC |
| GRE | Grp | Olympiacos CFP |
| GRE | Q3 | FC PAOK |
| POR | Q3 | SL Benfica |
| HOL | Grp | AFC Ajax |
| HOL | Q3 | PSV Eindhoven |
| SCO | Grp | Celtic FC |
| SCO | Q3 | Rangers FC |
| TUR | Grp | Fenerbahçe SK |
| TUR | Q2 | Trabzonspor |
| BEL | Q3 | RSC Anderlecht |
| BEL | Q2 | Club Brugge KV |
| CZE | Q3 | FC Baník Ostrava |
| CZE | Q2 | AC Sparta Praha |
| SUI | Q3 | FC Basel 1893 |
| SUI | Q2 | BSC Young Boys |
| UKR | Q3 | FC Dynamo Kyiv |
| UKR | Q2 | FC Shakhtar Donetsk |
| ISR | Q3 | Maccabi Haifa FC |
| ISR | Q2 | Maccabi Tel-Aviv FC |
| AUT | Q3 | Grazer AK |
| POL | Q2 | Wisla Kraków |
| RUS | Q2 | PFC CSKA Moskva |
| SMN | Q2 | FK Crvena Zvezda |
| NOR | Q2 | Rosenborg BK |
| BUL | Q2 | PFC Lokomotiv Plovdiv |
| CRO | Q2 | HNK Hajduk Split |
| SWE | Q2 | Djurgårdens IF |
| DEN | Q2 | FC København |
| SVK | Q2 | MŠK Žilina |
| ROM | Q2 | FC Dinamo Bucuresti |
| HUN | Q2 | Ferencvárosi TC |
| CYP | Q2 | APOEL FC |
| SLO | Q1 | NK Gorica |
| FIN | Q1 | HJK Helsinki |
| LAT | Q1 | FC Skonto |
| MOL | Q1 | FC Sheriff |
| GEO | Q1 | FC WIT Georgia |
| BHZ | Q1 | NK Široki Brijeg |
| LIT | Q1 | FBK Kaunas |
| ISL | Q1 | KR Reykjavík |
| MKD | Q1 | FK Pobeda |
| BLS | Q1 | FC Gomel |
| IRL | Q1 | Shelbourne FC |
| MLT | Q1 | Sliema Wanderers FC |
| ARM | Q1 | FC Pyunik |
| WAL | Q1 | Rhyl FC |
| ALB | Q1 | KF Tirana |
| EST | Q1 | FC Flora |
| NIR | Q1 | Linfield FC |
| LUX | Q1 | AS Jeunesse Esch |
| FAR | Q1 | HB Tórshavn |
| AZE | Q1 | FK Neftchi |

# UEFA CUP 2004–05

From the 2004–05 season, the UEFA Cup will adopt a new format that will include a group stage alongside the traditional two-legged format, with the final continuing as a single match.

## ALTERED FORMAT

Two qualifying rounds and the first round proper will open the competition, at which point 40 clubs will advance to the group stage. This part of the competition comprises eight groups of five teams with two matches at home and two matches away for each team in each group. The winners, runners-up and third-placed team advance to the knock-out phase, at which point they are joined by the eight clubs which finish in third place in each of the groups in the UEFA Champions League group phase. From this point, the 32 clubs embark on a knock-out competition, playing two matches against each other on a home and away basis. The club scoring the greater aggregate of goals qualifies for the next round. In the event of both teams scoring the same number of goals, the team which scores more goals away qualifies. The final is decided by a single match.

## BRITISH PARTICIPATING CLUBS

Middlesbrough, Millwall, Newcastle U (England); Dunfermline Ath, Hearts (Scotland); Bohemians, Longford T (Republic of Ireland); Haverfordwest, TNS (Wales); Glentoran, Portadown (Northern Ireland).

## FIRST QUALIFYING ROUND

| | | *1st Leg* | *2nd Leg* |
|---|---|---|---|
| MIKA | Kispest | 0-1 | 29/07 |
| Lev. Tallinn | Bohemians | 15/07 | 27/07 |
| Haverfordwest | Hafnarfjördur | 15/07 | 29/07 |
| Öster | TNS | 15/07 | 29/07 |
| Portadown | Žalgiris | 15/07 | 29/07 |
| B68 | Ventspils | 15/07 | 29/07 |
| Ekranas | Dudelange | 15/07 | 29/07 |
| Vaduz | Longford | 15/07 | 29/07 |
| B36 | Metalurgs | 15/07 | 29/07 |
| ÍA | TVMK | 15/07 | 29/07 |
| Glentoran | Allianssi | 15/07 | 29/07 |
| Haka | Etzella | 15/07 | 29/07 |
| Santa Coloma | Modrica | 15/07 | 29/07 |
| Sileks | Maribor | 15/07 | 29/07 |
| Marsaxlokk | Primorje | 15/07 | 29/07 |
| Pennarossa | Željeznicar | 15/07 | 29/07 |
| Otelul | Dinamo Tirana | 15/07 | 29/07 |
| Omonia | Sloga | 15/07 | 29/07 |
| Partizani | Birkirkara | 15/07 | 29/07 |
| Illichivets | Banants | 15/07 | 29/07 |
| Tbilisi | Shamkir | 15/07 | 29/07 |
| BATE | Dinamo Tbilisi | 15/07 | 29/07 |
| Shirak | Tiraspol | 15/07 | 29/07 |
| Nistru | Shakhtyor | 15/07 | 29/07 |
| Banská Bystrica | Karabakh | 15/07 | 29/07 |

# SUMMARY OF APPEARANCES

## EUROPEAN CUP AND CHAMPIONS LEAGUE (1955–2004)

**ENGLISH CLUBS**
15 Manchester U
14 Liverpool
8 Arsenal
4 Leeds U
3 Newcastle U, Nottingham F
2 Chelsea, Derby Co, Wolverhampton W, Everton, Aston Villa
1 Burnley, Tottenham H, Ipswich T, Manchester C, Blackburn R

**SCOTTISH CLUBS**
23 Rangers
19 Celtic
3 Aberdeen
2 Hearts
1 Dundee, Dundee U, Kilmarnock, Hibernian

**WELSH CLUBS**
6 Barry T
1 Cwmbran T, TNS

**NORTHERN IRELAND CLUBS**
20 Linfield
10 Glentoran
3 Crusaders, Portadown
1 Glenavon, Ards, Distillery, Derry C, Coleraine, Cliftonville

**EIRE CLUBS**
7 Shamrock R, Dundalk
6 Waterford
4 Shelbourne, Bohemians
3 Drumcondra, St Patrick's Ath,
2 Sligo R, Limerick, Athlone T, Derry C*
1 Cork Hibs, Cork Celtic, Cork City

**Winners: Celtic 1966–67; Manchester U 1967–68, 1998–99; Liverpool 1976–77, 1977–78, 1980–81, 1983–84; Nottingham F 1978–79, 1979–80; Aston Villa 1981–82**

**Finalists: Celtic 1969–70; Leeds U 1974–75; Liverpool 1984–85**

## EUROPEAN CUP-WINNERS' CUP (1960–99)

**ENGLISH CLUBS**
6 Tottenham H
5 Manchester U, Liverpool, Chelsea
4 West Ham U
3 Arsenal, Everton
2 Manchester C
1 Wolverhampton W, Leicester C, WBA, Leeds U, Sunderland, Southampton, Ipswich T, Newcastle U

**SCOTTISH CLUBS**
10 Rangers
8 Aberdeen, Celtic
3 Hearts
2 Dunfermline Ath, Dundee U
1 Dundee, Hibernian, St Mirren, Motherwell, Airdrieonians, Kilmarnock

**WELSH CLUBS**
14 Cardiff C
8 Wrexham
7 Swansea C
3 Bangor C
1 Borough U, Newport Co, Merthyr Tydfil, Barry T, Llansantfraid, Cwmbran T

**NORTHERN IRELAND CLUBS**
9 Glentoran
5 Glenavon
4 Ballymena U, Coleraine
3 Crusaders, Linfield
2 Ards, Bangor
1 Derry C, Distillery, Portadown, Carrick Rangers, Cliftonville

**EIRE CLUBS**
6 Shamrock R
4 Shelbourne
3 Limerick, Waterford, Dundalk, Bohemians
2 Cork Hibs, Galway U, Derry C*, Cork City
1 Cork Celtic, St Patrick's Ath, Finn Harps, Home Farm, University College Dublin, Bray W, Sligo R

**Winners: Tottenham H 1962–63; West Ham U 1964–65; Manchester C 1969–70; Chelsea 1970–71, 1997–98; Rangers 1971–72; Aberdeen 1982–83; Everton 1984–85; Manchester U 1990–91; Arsenal 1993–94**

**Finalists: Rangers 1960–61, 1966–67; Liverpool 1965–66; Leeds U 1972–73; West Ham U 1975–76; Arsenal 1979–80, 1994–95**

## EUROPEAN FAIRS CUP & UEFA CUP (1955–2004)

**ENGLISH CLUBS**
13 Leeds U
12 Liverpool
10 Aston Villa, Ipswich T
9 Arsenal
8 Newcastle U
7 Manchester U
6 Everton, Southampton, Tottenham H, Chelsea
5 Nottingham F, Manchester C
4 Birmingham C, Wolverhampton W, WBA, Blackburn R
3 Sheffield W
2 Stoke C, Derby Co, QPR, Leicester C
1 Burnley, Coventry C, Norwich C, London Rep XI, Watford, West Ham U, Fulham

**SCOTTISH CLUBS**
18 Dundee U
15 Hibernian, Aberdeen, Celtic
13 Rangers
11 Hearts
7 Kilmarnock
5 Dunfermline Ath, Dundee
3 St Mirren
2 Partick T, Motherwell, St Johnstone
1 Morton, Raith R, Livingston

**WELSH CLUBS**
4 Bangor C
3 Inter Cardiff (formerly Inter Cable-Tel), Cwmbran T, TNS
2 Newtown, Barry T
1 Afan Lido

**NORTHERN IRELAND CLUBS**
14 Glentoran
8 Coleraine, Linfield
5 Portadown, Glenavon
3 Crusaders
1 Ards, Ballymena U, Bangor

**EIRE CLUBS**
11 Bohemians
6 Dundalk, Shelbourne
5 Shamrock R
4 Cork City
3 Finn Harps, St Patrick's Ath, Derry C*
2 Drumcondra
1 Cork Hibs, Athlone T, Limerick, Drogheda U, Galway U, Bray Wanderers, Longford T

**Winners: Leeds U 1967–68, 1970–71; Newcastle U 1968–69; Arsenal 1969–70; Tottenham H 1971–72, 1983–84; Liverpool 1972–73, 1975–76, 2000–01; Ipswich T 1980–81**

**Finalists: London 1955–58, Birmingham C 1958–60, 1960–61; Leeds U 1966–67; Wolverhampton W 1971–72; Tottenham H 1973–74; Dundee U 1986–87**

** Now play in League of Ireland*

# INTERTOTO CUP 2003

## FIRST ROUND

| *Home Team First Leg* | *Away Team First Leg* | *1st Leg Score* | *2nd Leg Score* | *Aggregate Score* |
|---|---|---|---|---|
| Partizani* | M. Netanya | 2-0 | 1-3 | 3-3 |
| Brno* | Kotayk | 1-0 | 2-3 | 3-3 |
| Györ* | Achnas | 1-1 | 2-2 | 3-3 |
| Bangor | Gloria | 0-1 | 2-5 | 2-6 |
| Dubnica | Olympiakos | 3-0 | 4-1 | 7-1 |
| Dacia | GI | 4-1 | 1-0 | 5-1 |
| Sloboda | KA | 1-1 | 1-1 | 2-2 |
| *aet: Sloboda won 3-2 on penalties.* | | | | |
| Shakhtyor | Omagh | 1-0 | 7-1 | 8-1 |
| OFK | Trans | 6-1 | 5-3 | 11-4 |
| Dinaburg | Wil | 1-0 | 0-2 | 1-2 |
| Odra | Shamrock Rovers | 1-2 | 0-1 | 1-3 |
| Spartak | Pobeda | 1-5 | 1-2 | 2-7 |
| Allianssi | Hibernians | 1-0 | 1-1 | 2-1 |
| Pasching* | WIT | 1-0 | 1-2 | 2-2 |
| Koper | Zagreb | 1-0 | 2-2 | 3-2 |
| Zalgiris | Örgryte | 1-1 | 0-3 | 1-4 |
| Encamp | Lierse | 0-3 | 1-4 | 1-7 |
| Videoton | Marek | 2-2 | 2-3 | 4-5 |
| Polonia | Tobol | 0-3 | 1-2 | 1-5 |
| Tampere* | Ceahlaul | 1-0 | 1-2 | 2-2 |
| Sutjeska | US Luxembourg | 3-0 | 1-1 | 4-1 |

## SECOND ROUND

| | | | | |
|---|---|---|---|---|
| Örgryte | Nice* | 3-2 | 1-2 | 4-4 |
| Thun | Brno | 2-3 | 1-1 | 3-4 |
| Brescia | Gloria | 2-1 | 1-1 | 3-2 |
| Marek | Wolfsburg | 1-1 | 0-2 | 1-3 |
| Shakhtyor | Cibalia | 1-1 | 2-4 | 3-5 |
| Willem II | Wil | 2-1 | 1-3 | 3-4 |
| Pobeda | Pasching | 1-1 | 1-2 | 2-3 |
| Sloboda | Lierse | 1-0 | 1-5 | 2-5 |
| Dacia | Partizani | 2-0 | 3-0 | 5-0 |
| Koper* | Dubnica | 1-0 | 2-3 | 3-3 |
| Sint-Truiden | Tobol | 0-2 | 0-1 | 0-3 |
| Synot | OFK | 1-0 | 3-3 | 4-3 |
| Racing* | Györ | 1-0 | 1-2 | 2-2 |
| Liberec | Shamrock Rovers | 2-0 | 2-0 | 4-0 |
| Akratitos | Allianssi | 0-1 | 0-0 | 0-1 |
| Tampere | Sutjeska | 0-0 | 1-0 | 1-0 |

* *Won on away goals rule.*

## THIRD ROUND

| | | | | |
|---|---|---|---|---|
| Tobol | Pasching | 0-1 | 0-3 | 0-4 |
| Perugia | Allianssi | 2-0 | 2-0 | 4-0 |
| Egaleo | Koper | 2-3 | 2-2 | 4-5 |
| Nantes | Wil | 2-1 | 3-2 | 5-3 |
| Nice | Werder Bremen | 0-0 | 0-1 | 0-1 |
| Villarreal | Brescia | 2-0 | 1-1 | 3-1 |
| Guingamp | Brno | 2-1 | 2-4 | 4-5 |
| Dacia | Schalke | 0-1 | 1-2 | 1-3 |
| Racing | Liberec | 0-1 | 1-2 | 1-3 |
| Synot | Wolfsburg | 0-1 | 0-2 | 0-3 |
| Tampere | Cibalia | 0-2 | 1-0 | 1-2 |
| Heerenveen | Lierse | 4-1 | 1-0 | 5-1 |

## SEMI-FINAL

| *Home Team First Leg* | *Away Team First Leg* | *1st Leg Score* | *2nd Leg Score* | *Aggregate Score* |
|---|---|---|---|---|
| Nantes | Perugia | 0-1 | 0-0 | 0-1 |
| Pasching | Werder Bremen | 4-0 | 1-1 | 5-1 |
| Brno | Villarreal | 1-1 | 0-2 | 1-3 |
| Schalke | Liberec | 2-1 | 0-0 | 2-1 |
| Heerenveen | Koper | 2-0 | 0-1 | 2-1 |
| Cibalia | Wolfsburg | 1-4 | 0-4 | 1-8 |

## FINALS

| *Home Team First Leg* | *Away Team First Leg* | *1st Leg Score* | *2nd Leg Score* | *Aggregate Score* |
|---|---|---|---|---|
| Pasching | Schalke | 0-2 | 0-0 | 0-2 |
| Heerenveen | Villarreal | 1-2 | 0-0 | 1-2 |
| Perugia | Wolfsburg | 1-0 | 2-0 | 3-0 |

*Schalke, Villarreal and Perugia qualified for the UEFA Cup.*

## INTERTOTO CUP – PREVIOUS WINNERS

| *Year* | *Winners* | *Runners-up* | *Score* |
| --- | --- | --- | --- |
| 1995 | Karlsruhe | Bursa | 3-3 |
| | *Karlsruhe won 6-5 on penalties.* | | |
| | Strasbourg | Metz | 2-0 |
| | Bordeaux | Heerenveen | 2-0 |
| | Tirol | Leverkusen | 2-2 |
| | *Tirol won 5-3 on penalties.* | | |
| 1996 | Silkeborg | Segesta | 2-1, 0-1 |
| | Guingamp | Volgograd | 1-2, 1-0 |
| | Karlsruhe | Standard Liege | 0-1, 3-1 |
| 1997 | Bastia | Halmstad | 1-0, 1-1 |
| | Auxerre | Duisburg | 0-0, 2-0 |
| | Lyon | Montpellier | 1-0, 3-2 |
| 1998 | Valencia | Salzburg | 2-0, 2-1 |
| | Werder Bremen | Vojvodina | 1-0, 1-1 |
| | Bologna | Ruch | 1-0, 2-0 |
| 1999 | Montpellier | Hamburg | 1-1, 1-1 |
| | *Montpellier won 3-0 on penalties.* | | |
| | West Ham U | Metz | 0-1, 3-1 |
| | Juventus | Rennes | 2-0, 2-2 |
| 2000 | Stuttgart | Auxerre | 2-0, 1-1 |
| | Udinese | Sigma | 2-2, 4-2 |
| | Celta Vigo | Zenit | 2-1, 2-2 |
| 2001 | Aston Villa | Basle | 1-1, 4-1 |
| | Troyes | Newcastle U | 0-0, 4-4 |
| | Paris St Germain | Brescia | 0-0, 1-1 |
| 2002 | Malaga | Villareal | 1-0, 1-1 |
| | Fulmam | Bologna | 3-1, 2-2 |
| | Stuttgart | Lille | 2-0, 0-1 |
| 2003 | Shalke | Pasching | 0-0 2-0 |
| | Villarreal | Heerenveen | 0-0, 2-1 |
| | Perugia | Wolfsburg | 1-0, 2-0 |

# INTERTOTO CUP 2004

### FIRST ROUND

| | *Agg.* | | *1st Leg* | *2nd Leg* |
| --- | --- | --- | --- | --- |
| Hibernians | 2-4 | Slaven | 2-1 | 0-3 |
| Aberystwyth | 0-4 | Dinaburg | 0-0 | 0-4 |
| EfB | 7-1 | NSÍ | 3-1 | 4-0 |
| Achnas | 2-10 | Vardar | 1-5 | 1-5 |
| Sopron | 2-3 | Teplice | 1-0 | 1-3 |
| Spartak Trnava | 4-4 | Debrecen | 3-0 | 1-4 |
| *Spartak Trnava won on away goals.* | | | | |
| Publikum | 2-2 | Sloboda | 2-1 | 0-1 |
| *Sloboda won on away goals.* | | | | |
| Cork | 4-1 | Malmö | 3-1 | 1-0 |
| Vetra | 4-0 | Trans | 3-0 | 1-0 |
| OB | 7-0 | Ballymena | 0-0 | 7-0 |
| Vllaznia | 4-2 | H. Beer-Sheva | 1-2 | 3-0* |
| **H. Beer-Sheva forfeited match.* | | | | |
| Sant Julià | 0-11 | Sartid | 0-8 | 0-3 |
| Bregenz | 1-5 | Khazar | 0-3* | 1-2 |
| **Bregenz Sheva forfeited match.* | | | | |
| AA Gent | 3-1 | Fylkir | 2-1 | 1-0 |
| Odra | 1-2 | Dinamo Minsk | 1-0 | 0-2 |
| Teuta | 0-4 | Dubnica | 0-0 | 0-4 |
| MyPa | 3-4 | Zlín | 1-1 | 2-3 |
| Marek | 2-0 | Dila | 0-0 | 2-0 |
| Spartak Moskva | 2-1 | Atlantas | 2-0 | 0-1 |
| Thun | 2-0 | Gloria | 2-0 | 0-0 |
| Grevenmacher | 1-1 | Tampere | 1-1 | 0-0 |
| *Tampere won on away goals.* | | | | |

### SECOND ROUND

| | *Agg.* | | *1st Leg* | *2nd Leg* |
| --- | --- | --- | --- | --- |
| OB | 0-5 | Villarreal | 0-3 | 0-2 |
| Teplice | 1-4 | Shinnik | 1-2 | 0-2 |
| Dubnica | 1-7 | Liberec | 1-2 | 0-5 |
| Westerlo | 0-3 | Zlín | 0-0 | 0-3 |
| Hibernian | 1-2 | Vetra | 1-1 | 0-1 |
| Spartak Moskva | 5-1 | Kamen Ingrad | 4-1 | 1-0 |
| Spartak Trnava | 3-1 | Sloboda | 2-1 | 1-0 |
| Vardar | 1-1 | AA Gent | 1-0 | 0-1 |
| *Vardar won 4-3 on penalties.* | | | | |
| Slaven | 2-1 | Vllaznia | 2-0 | 0-1 |
| NEC | 0-1 | Cork | 0-0 | 0-1 |
| EfB | 2-1 | Nice | 1-0 | 1-1 |
| Wolfsburg | 3-7 | Thun | 2-3 | 1-4 |
| OFK | 5-1 | Dinaburg | 3-1 | 2-0 |
| Genk | 2-1 | Marek | 2-1 | 0-0 |
| Tampere | 3-1 | Khazar | 3-0 | 0-1 |
| Dinamo Minsk | 4-3 | Sartid | 1-2 | 3-1 |
| *Dinamo Minsk won on Silver Goal.* | | | | |

### THIRD ROUND

Genk v Dortmund
Thun v Hamburg
Shinnik v Leiria
Schalke v Vardar
Liberec v Roda
Lille v Dinamo Minsk
Slaven v Spartak Trnava
Zlín v Atlético
Villarreal v Spartak Moskva
Vetra v EfB
Nantes v Cork
Tampere v OFK

# WORLD CLUB CHAMPIONSHIP

Played annually up to 1974 and intermittently since then between the winners of the European Cup and the winners of the South American Champions Cup — known as the Copa Libertadores. In 1980 the winners were decided by one match arranged in Tokyo in February 1981 and the venue has been the same since. AC Milan replaced Marseille who had been stripped of their European Cup title in 1993.

1960 Real Madrid beat Penarol 0-0, 5-1
1961 Penarol beat Benfica 0-1, 5-0, 2-1
1962 Santos beat Benfica 3-2, 5-2
1963 Santos beat AC Milan 2-4, 4-2, 1-0
1964 Inter-Milan beat Independiente 0-1, 2-0, 1-0
1965 Inter-Milan beat Independiente 3-0, 0-0
1966 Penarol beat Real Madrid 2-0, 2-0
1967 Racing Club beat Celtic 0-1, 2-1, 1-0
1968 Estudiantes beat Manchester United 1-0, 1-1
1969 AC Milan beat Estudiantes 3-0, 1-2
1970 Feyenoord beat Estudiantes 2-2, 1-0
1971 Nacional beat Panathinaikos* 1-1, 2-1
1972 Ajax beat Independiente 1-1, 3-0
1973 Independiente beat Juventus* 1-0
1974 Atlético Madrid* beat Independiente 0-1, 2-0
1975 Independiente and Bayern Munich could not agree dates; no matches.
1976 Bayern Munich beat Cruzeiro 2-0, 0-0
1977 Boca Juniors beat Borussia Moenchengladbach* 2-2, 3-0
1978 Not contested
1979 Olimpia beat Malmö* 1-0, 2-1
1980 Nacional beat Nottingham Forest 1-0
1981 Flamengo beat Liverpool 3-0
1982 Penarol beat Aston Villa 2-0
1983 Gremio Porto Alegre beat SV Hamburg 2-1
1984 Independiente beat Liverpool 1-0
1985 Juventus beat Argentinos Juniors 4-2 on penalties after a 2-2 draw
1986 River Plate beat Steaua Bucharest 1-0
1987 FC Porto beat Penarol 2-1 after extra time
1988 Nacional (Uru) beat PSV Eindhoven 7-6 on penalties after 1-1 draw
1989 AC Milan beat Atletico Nacional (Col) 1-0 after extra time
1990 AC Milan beat Olimpia 3-0
1991 Red Star Belgrade beat Colo Colo 3-0
1992 Sao Paulo beat Barcelona 2-1
1993 Sao Paulo beat AC Milan 3-2
1994 Velez Sarsfield beat AC Milan 2-0
1995 Ajax beat Gremio Porto Alegre 4-3 on penalties after 0-0 draw
1996 Juventus beat River Plate 1-0
1997 Borussia Dortmund beat Cruzeiro 2-0
1998 Real Madrid beat Vasco da Gama 2-1
1999 Manchester U beat Palmeiras 1-0
2000 Boca Juniors beat Real Madrid 2-1
2001 Bayern Munich beat Boca Juniors 1-0 after extra time
2002 Real Madrid beat Olimpia 2-0

*European Cup runners-up; winners declined to take part.

**2003**

14 December 2003, in Yokohama

**Boca Juniors (1) 1 AC Milan (1) 1** 68,000

*aet; Boca Juniors won 3-1 on penalties*: Schiavi, Donnet and Cascini scored for Boca Juniors; Rui Costa for AC Milan. Battaglia missed for Boca Juniors, Pirlo, Seedorf and Costacurta missed for AC Milan.

*Boca Juniors:* Abbondanzieri; Perea, Schiavi, Burdisso, Rodriguez, Donnet, Battaglia, Cascini, Cagna, Iarley, Schelotto (Tevez 73).

*Scorer:* Donnet 29.

*AC Milan:* Dida; Cafu, Pancaro, Pirlo, Costacurta, Maldini, Gattuso (Ambrosini 102), Kaka (Rui Costa 78), Shevchenko, Tomasson (Inzaghi 60), Seedorf.

*Scorer:* Tomasson 24.

*Referee:* M. Ivanov (Russia).

# EUROPEAN SUPER CUP

Played annually between the winners of the European Champions' Cup and the European Cup-Winners' Cup (UEFA Cup from 2000). AC Milan replaced Marseille in 1993–94.

1972 Ajax beat Rangers 3-1, 3-2
1973 Ajax beat AC Milan 0-1, 6-0
1974 Not contested
1975 Dynamo Kiev beat Bayern Munich 1-0, 2-0
1976 Anderlecht beat Bayern Munich 4-1, 1-2
1977 Liverpool beat Hamburg 1-1, 6-0
1978 Anderlecht beat Liverpool 3-1, 1-2
1979 Nottingham F beat Barcelona 1-0, 1-1
1980 Valencia beat Nottingham F 1-0, 1-2
1981 Not contested
1982 Aston Villa beat Barcelona 0-1, 3-0
1983 Aberdeen beat Hamburg 0-0, 2-0
1984 Juventus beat Liverpool 2-0
1985 Juventus v Everton not contested due to UEFA ban on English clubs
1986 Steaua Bucharest beat Dynamo Kiev 1-0
1987 FC Porto beat Ajax 1-0, 1-0
1988 KV Mechelen beat PSV Eindhoven 3-0, 0-1
1989 AC Milan beat Barcelona 1-1, 1-0
1990 AC Milan beat Sampdoria 1-1, 2-0
1991 Manchester U beat Red Star Belgrade 1-0
1992 Barcelona beat Werder Bremen 1-1, 2-1
1993 Parma beat AC Milan 0-1, 2-0
1994 AC Milan beat Arsenal 0-0, 2-0
1995 Ajax beat Zaragoza 1-1, 4-0
1996 Juventus beat Paris St Germain 6-1, 3-1
1997 Barcelona beat Borussia Dortmund 2-0, 1-1
1998 Chelsea beat Real Madrid 1-0
1999 Lazio beat Manchester U 1-0
2000 Galatasaray beat Real Madrid 2-1
2001 Liverpool beat Bayern Munich 3-2
2002 Real Madrid beat Feyenoord 3-1

**2003–04**

29 August 2003, Monaco

**AC Milan (1) 1** *(Shevchenko 10)* **Porto (0) 0** 18,500

*AC Milan:* Dida; Simic, Nesta, Maldini, Pancaro, Gattuso, Pirlo, Rui Costa (Cafu 86), Seedorf (Ambrosini 70), Shevchenko (Rivaldo 76), Inzaghi.

*Porto:* Vitor Baia; Paulo Ferreira, Jorge Costa, Ricardo Carvalho, Ricardo Costa, Alenichev (Ricardo Fernandes 76), Deco, Costinha (Bosingwa 67), Maniche, McCarthy (Jankauskas 60), Derlei.

*Referee:* P. Barber (England).

# INTERNATIONAL DIRECTORY

The latest available information has been given regarding numbers of clubs and players registered with FIFA, the world governing body. Where known, official colours are listed. With European countries, League tables show a number of signs. * indicates relegated teams, + play-offs, *+ relegated after play-offs, ++ promoted.

There are 197 member associations and one provisional member, Palestine. The four home countries, England, Scotland, Northern Ireland and Wales, are dealt with elsewhere in the Yearbook; but basic details appear in this directory.

## EUROPE

The Football Association of Albania, Rruga Labinoti, Pallati Perballe Shkolles 'Gjuhet e Huaja'.
*Founded:* 1930; *Number of Clubs:* 49; *Number of Players:* 5,192; *National Colours:* Red shirts, black shorts, red stockings.
*Telephone:* 00-355-43/46 601; *Fax:* 00-355-43/46 609.

**International matches 2003**
Vietnam (h) 5-0, Russia (h) 3-1, Eire (h) 0-0, Bulgaria (a) 0-2, Eire (a) 1-2, Switzerland (a) 2-3, Macedonia (a) 1-3, Georgia (a) 0-3, Georgia (h) 3-1, Portugal (a) 3-5, Estonia (h) 2-0.

**League Championship wins (1930–37; 1945–2004)**
SK Tirana 21 (including 17 Nentori 8); Dinamo Tirana 16; Partizani Tirana 15; Vllaznia 9; Flamurtari 1; Elbasan 2 (including Labinoti 1); Skenderbeu 1; Teuta 1.

**Cup wins (1948–2004)**
Partizani Tirana 15; Dinamo Tirana 13; SK Tirana 10 (including 17 Nentori 6); Vllaznia 5; Teuta 3; Elbasan 3 (including Labintoti 1); Flamurtari 2; Apolonia 1.

**Final League Table 2003–04**

| | *P* | *W* | *D* | *L* | *F* | *A* | *Pts* |
|---|---|---|---|---|---|---|---|
| SK Tirana | 36 | 24 | 8 | 4 | 90 | 36 | 80 |
| Dinamo | 36 | 21 | 8 | 7 | 68 | 39 | 71 |
| Vllaznia | 36 | 21 | 5 | 10 | 77 | 51 | 68 |
| Partizani | 36 | 20 | 7 | 9 | 65 | 39 | 67 |
| Teuta | 36 | 14 | 10 | 12 | 57 | 49 | 52 |
| Lushnja | 36 | 11 | 9 | 16 | 35 | 52 | 42 |
| Shkumbini | 36 | 12 | 5 | 19 | 44 | 61 | 41 |
| Elbasan | 36 | 10 | 10 | 16 | 47 | 55 | 40 |
| Besa* | 36 | 8 | 5 | 23 | 36 | 81 | 29 |
| Flamurtari* | 36 | 3 | 5 | 28 | 24 | 80 | 14 |

*Top scorer:* Sinani (Vllaznia) 36.
*Cup Final:* Partizani 1, Dinamo 0.

### ANDORRA

Federacio Andorrana de Futbol, Avinguda Carlemany 67, 3er Pis, Apartado postal 65, Escaldes-Engordany, Principat D'Andorra.
*Founded:* 1994; *Number of Clubs:* 12; *Number of Players:* 300; *National Colours:* Yellow shirts, red shorts, blue stockings.
*Telephone:* 00376/805 830; *Fax:* 00376/862 006.

**International matches 2003**
Croatia (a) 0-2, Estonia (h) 0-2, Estonia (a) 0-2, Belgium (a) 0-3, Gabon (h) 0-2, Croatia (h) 0-3, Bulgaria (h) 0-3.

**League Championship wins (1996–2004)**
Principat 3; Santa Coloma 2; Dicoansa 1; Constelacio 1; St Julia 1; Encamp 1.

**Cup wins (1996–2004)**
Principat 4; Santa Coloma 3; Constelacio 1; Lusitanos 1.

**Qualifying League Table 2003–04**

| | *P* | *W* | *D* | *L* | *F* | *A* | *Pts* |
|---|---|---|---|---|---|---|---|
| Santa Coloma | 14 | 11 | 1 | 2 | 34 | 13 | 34 |
| St Julia | 14 | 10 | 2 | 2 | 47 | 13 | 32 |
| Rangers | 14 | 8 | 3 | 3 | 30 | 11 | 27 |
| Encamp | 14 | 7 | 3 | 4 | 27 | 11 | 24 |
| Principat | 14 | 6 | 2 | 6 | 29 | 31 | 20 |
| Lusitanos | 14 | 3 | 3 | 8 | 11 | 21 | 12 |
| Inter | 14 | 2 | 1 | 11 | 13 | 34 | 7 |
| Engordany | 14 | 1 | 1 | 12 | 10 | 67 | 4 |

**Championship Play-Offs**

| | *P* | *W* | *D* | *L* | *F* | *A* | *Pts* |
|---|---|---|---|---|---|---|---|
| Santa Coloma | 20 | 14 | 3 | 3 | 44 | 21 | 45 |
| St Julia | 20 | 13 | 4 | 3 | 57 | 18 | 43 |
| Rangers | 20 | 10 | 4 | 6 | 34 | 17 | 34 |
| Encamp | 20 | 8 | 4 | 8 | 31 | 20 | 28 |

**Relegation Play-Offs**

| | P | W | D | L | F | A | Pts |
|---|---|---|---|---|---|---|---|
| Principat | 20 | 9 | 4 | 7 | 52 | 41 | 31 |
| Lusitanos | 20 | 5 | 6 | 9 | 24 | 29 | 21 |
| Inter | 20 | 3 | 3 | 14 | 20 | 43 | 12 |
| Engordany* | 20 | 3 | 2 | 15 | 20 | 93 | 11 |

*Cup Final:* Santa Coloma 1, St Julia 0.

### ARMENIA

Football Federation of Armenia, Saryan 38, Yerevan, 375 010, Armenia.
*Founded:* 1992; *Number of Clubs:* 32; *Number of Players:* 15,000; *National Colours:* Red shirts, blue shorts, orange stockings.
*Telephone:* 00374-1/535 084; *Fax:* 00374-1/539517.

**International matches 2003**
Israel (a) 0-2, N Ireland (h) 1-0, Spain (a) 0-3, Ukraine (a) 3-4, Greece (h) 0-1, N Ireland (a) 1-0, Spain (h) 0-4.

**League Championship wins (1992–2003)**
Pyunik 5; Shirak Gyumri 4*; Ararat Yerevan 2*; Homenmen 1; FC Yerevan 1; Tsement 1; Araks 1.
*Includes one unofficial title.

**Cup wins (1992–2004)**
Ararat Erevan 5; Pyunik 3; Tsement 2; Mika 2; Banants 1.

**Final League Table 2003**

| | *P* | *W* | *D* | *L* | *F* | *A* | *Pts* |
|---|---|---|---|---|---|---|---|
| Pyunik | 28 | 23 | 5 | 0 | 87 | 11 | 74 |
| Banants | 28 | 21 | 3 | 4 | 89 | 15 | 66 |
| Shirak | 28 | 17 | 2 | 9 | 63 | 34 | 53 |
| Mika | 28 | 15 | 6 | 7 | 49 | 29 | 51 |
| Kotaik | 28 | 8 | 7 | 13 | 29 | 56 | 31 |
| Dinamo | 28 | 5 | 4 | 19 | 18 | 69 | 19 |
| Lernagorts | 28 | 3 | 6 | 19 | 20 | 72 | 15 |
| Araks* | 28 | 2 | 3 | 23 | 17 | 86 | 9 |

*Ararat Yerevan excluded; Lernayin withdrew.*
*Top scorer:* Hakobian (Banants) 45.
*Cup Final:* Pyunik 0, Banants 0.
*Pyunik won 6-5 on penalties.*

### AUSTRIA

Oesterreichischer Fussball-Bund, Ernst-Happel Stadion - Sektor A/F, Postfach 340, Meierestrasse 7, Wien 1021.
*Founded:* 1904; *Number of Clubs:* 2,081; *Number of Players:* 253,576; *National Colours:* White shirts, black shorts, white stockings.
*Telephone:* 0043-1/727 180; *Fax:* 0043-1/ 728 1632.

**International matches 2003**
Greece (h) 2-2, Czech Republic (a) 0-4, Scotland (a) 2-0, Moldova (a) 0-1, Belarus (h) 5-0, Costa Rica (h) 2-0, Holland (a) 1-3, Czech Republic (h) 2-3.

**League Championship wins (1912–2004)**
Rapid Vienna 30; FK Austria 23; Tirol-Svarowski-Innsbruck 10; Admira-Energie-Wacker 9; First Vienna 6; Wiener Sportklub 3; Austria Salzburg 3; Sturm Graz 2; FAC 1; Hakoah 1; Linz ASK 1; WAF 1; Voest Linz 1; Graz 1.

**Cup wins (1919–2003)**
FK Austria 26; Rapid Vienna 14; TS Innsbruck (formerly Wacker Innsbruck) 7; Admira-Energie-Wacker (formerly Sportklub Admira & Admira-Energie) 5; Graz 4; First Vienna 3; Sturm Graz 3; Linz ASK 1; Wacker Vienna 1; WAF 1; Wiener Sportklub 1; Stockerau 1; Ried 1; Karnten 1.

**Final League Table 2003–04**

| | *P* | *W* | *D* | *L* | *F* | *A* | *Pts* |
|---|---|---|---|---|---|---|---|
| Graz | 36 | 21 | 9 | 6 | 62 | 32 | 72 |
| FK Austria | 36 | 21 | 8 | 7 | 63 | 31 | 71 |
| Pasching | 36 | 17 | 12 | 7 | 59 | 41 | 63 |
| Rapid | 36 | 16 | 9 | 11 | 50 | 47 | 57 |
| Bregenz | 36 | 11 | 12 | 13 | 47 | 58 | 45 |
| Admira Modling | 36 | 11 | 9 | 16 | 42 | 49 | 42 |
| Salzburg | 36 | 11 | 5 | 20 | 44 | 48 | 38 |
| Mattersburg | 36 | 9 | 10 | 17 | 39 | 61 | 37 |
| Sturm Graz | 36 | 8 | 11 | 17 | 39 | 52 | 35 |
| Karnten* | 36 | 7 | 11 | 18 | 36 | 62 | 32 |

*Top scorer:* Kollmann (Graz) 27.
*Cup Final:* Graz 3, FK Austria 3.
*Graz won 5-4 on penalties.*
*Admira combined with Modling*

## AZERBAIJAN

Association of Football Federations of Azerbaijan, 42 Gussi Gadjiev Street, Baku 370 009.
*Founded:* 1992; *Number of Clubs:* 1,500;. *Number of Players:* 95,000; *National Colours:* White shirts, blue shorts, white stockings.
*Telephone:* 00994-12/944 916; *Fax:* 00994-12/ 989 393.

**International matches 2003**
Serbia (a) 2-2, Wales (a) 0-4, Serbia (h) 2-1, Finland (h) 1-2, Italy (a) 0-4.

**League Championship wins (1992–2004)**
Kopaz 3; Shamkir 3; Neftchi 3; Karabakh 2; Turan 1.
*Includes one unofficial title for Shamkir in 2002.*

**Cup wins (1992–2004)**
Kopaz 4; Neftchi 4; Karabakh 1; Inshatchi 1; Shafa 1.

**Final League Table 2003–04**

| | *P* | *W* | *D* | *L* | *F* | *A* | *Pts* |
|---|---|---|---|---|---|---|---|
| Neftchi | 26 | 22 | 3 | 1 | 66 | 15 | 69 |
| Shamkir | 26 | 20 | 4 | 2 | 67 | 11 | 64 |
| Karabakh | 26 | 19 | 3 | 4 | 63 | 17 | 60 |
| Xazar Uni | 26 | 15 | 6 | 5 | 43 | 16 | 51 |
| Dinamo Baku | 26 | 12 | 5 | 9 | 45 | 32 | 41 |
| Safa | 26 | 12 | 3 | 11 | 40 | 23 | 39 |
| Bakili | 26 | 10 | 4 | 12 | 40 | 46 | 34 |
| MOIK | 26 | 7 | 8 | 11 | 25 | 32 | 29 |
| Adliyya | 26 | 7 | 8 | 11 | 27 | 40 | 29 |
| Shahdagh | 26 | 7 | 6 | 13 | 29 | 41 | 27 |
| Kopaz | 26 | 6 | 5 | 15 | 22 | 45 | 23 |
| Xazar | 26 | 7 | 1 | 18 | 32 | 78 | 22 |
| Turan | 26 | 4 | 4 | 18 | 15 | 59 | 16 |
| Lokomotiv | 26 | 4 | 0 | 22 | 17 | 76 | 12 |

*Lokomotiv removed after 15 matches; remaining games awarded 0-3 against them.*
*Umid removed from competition; record annulled.*
*Top scorer:* Musayev (Karabach) 20.
*Cup Final:* Neftchi 1, Shamkir 0.

## BELARUS

Belarus Football Federation, Kirova Street 8/2, Minsk 220 600, Belarus.
*Founded:* 1992; *Number of Clubs:* 455; *Number of Players:* 120,000; *National Colours:* Red shirts, green shorts, red stockings.
*Telephone:* 00375-17/227 2920; *Fax:* 00375-17/227 2920.

**International matches 2003**
Moldova (h) 2-1, Uzbekistan (h) 2-2, Uzbekistan (a) 2-1, Holland (h) 0-2, Austria (a) 0-5, Iran (h) 2-1, Czech Republic (h) 1-3, Moldova (a) 1-2.

**League Championship wins (1992–2003)**
Dynamo Minsk 6; Slavia Mozyr (formerly MPKC Mozyr) 2; BATE Borisov 2; Dnepr Mogilev 1; Belshina 1; Gomel 1.

**Cup wins (1992–2004)**
Belshina 3; Dynamo Minsk 3; Slavia Mozyr (formerly MPKC Mozyr) 2; Neman 1; Dynamo 93 Minsk 1; Lokomotiv 96 1; Gomel 1; Shakhter 1.

**Final League Table 2003**

| | *P* | *W* | *D* | *L* | *F* | *A* | *Pts* |
|---|---|---|---|---|---|---|---|
| Gomel | 30 | 23 | 5 | 2 | 56 | 12 | 74 |
| BATE Borisov | 30 | 20 | 6 | 4 | 70 | 21 | 66 |
| Dynamo Minsk | 30 | 20 | 4 | 6 | 62 | 24 | 64 |
| Torpedo Minsk | 30 | 19 | 7 | 4 | 54 | 20 | 64 |
| Shakhter | 30 | 19 | 7 | 4 | 60 | 23 | 64 |
| Torpedo Zhodino | 30 | 13 | 10 | 7 | 44 | 25 | 49 |
| Neman | 30 | 10 | 9 | 11 | 24 | 35 | 39 |
| Naftan | 30 | 10 | 5 | 15 | 39 | 49 | 35 |
| Dnepr | 30 | 8 | 10 | 12 | 38 | 46 | 34 |
| Belshina | 30 | 8 | 8 | 14 | 44 | 50 | 32 |
| Dynamo Brest | 30 | 5 | 12 | 13 | 21 | 49 | 27 |
| Zvezda | 30 | 7 | 4 | 19 | 23 | 64 | 25 |
| Daryda | 30 | 7 | 4 | 19 | 22 | 45 | 25 |
| Slavia | 30 | 6 | 7 | 17 | 29 | 64 | 25 |
| Lakamatyu* | 30 | 5 | 9 | 16 | 16 | 42 | 24 |
| Molodechno* | 30 | 3 | 7 | 20 | 19 | 52 | 16 |

*Top scorers:* Bliznyuk (Gomel), Karnilenka (Dynamo Minsk) 18.
*Cup Final:* Shakhter 1, Gomel 0.

## BELGIUM

Union Royale Belge Des Societes De Football Association, 145 Avenue Houba de Strooper, B-1020 Bruxelles.
*Founded:* 1895; *Number of Clubs:* 2,120; *Number of Players:* 390,468; *National Colours:* All red.
*Telephone:* 0032-2/477 1211; *Fax:* 0032-2/ 478 2391.

**International matches 2003**
Algeria (a) 3-1, Croatia (a) 0-4, Poland (h) 3-1, Bulgaria (a) 2-2, Andorra (h) 3-0, Holland (h) 1-1, Croatia (h) 2-1, Estonia (h) 2-0.

**League Championship wins (1896–2004)**
Anderlecht 27; FC Brugge 12; Union St Gilloise 11; Standard Liege 8; Beerschot 7; RC Brussels 6; FC Liege 5; Daring Brussels 5; Antwerp 4; Mechelen 4; Lierse SK 4; SV Brugge 3; Beveren 2; Genk 2; RWD Molenbeek 1.

**Cup wins (1954–2004)**
FC Brugge 9; Anderlecht 8; Standard Liege 5; Beerschot 2; Waterschei 2; Beveren 2; Gent 2; Antwerp 2; Lierse SK 2; Genk 2; Racing Doornik 1; Waregem 1; SV Brugge 1; Mechelen 1; FC Liege 1; Ekeren 1; Westerlo 1; La Louviere 1.

**Final League Table 2003–04**

| | *P* | *W* | *D* | *L* | *F* | *A* | *Pts* |
|---|---|---|---|---|---|---|---|
| Anderlecht | 34 | 25 | 6 | 3 | 77 | 27 | 81 |
| FC Brugge | 34 | 22 | 6 | 6 | 77 | 31 | 72 |
| Standard Liege | 34 | 18 | 11 | 5 | 68 | 31 | 65 |
| Genk | 34 | 17 | 8 | 9 | 58 | 40 | 59 |
| Mouscron | 34 | 15 | 14 | 5 | 64 | 42 | 59 |
| Westerlo | 34 | 14 | 10 | 10 | 51 | 45 | 52 |
| Beerschot | 34 | 11 | 11 | 12 | 34 | 40 | 44 |
| La Louviere | 34 | 10 | 14 | 10 | 45 | 46 | 44 |
| Gent | 34 | 8 | 16 | 10 | 33 | 34 | 40 |
| Lokeren | 34 | 10 | 9 | 15 | 45 | 54 | 39 |
| Lierse | 34 | 8 | 15 | 11 | 33 | 40 | 39 |
| Beveren | 34 | 11 | 5 | 18 | 45 | 58 | 38 |
| St Truiden | 34 | 9 | 11 | 14 | 36 | 50 | 38 |
| CS Brugge | 34 | 7 | 14 | 13 | 28 | 52 | 35 |
| Charleroi | 34 | 8 | 9 | 17 | 35 | 47 | 33 |
| Mons | 34 | 7 | 12 | 15 | 29 | 52 | 33 |
| Heusden* | 34 | 7 | 7 | 20 | 36 | 68 | 28 |
| Antwerp* | 34 | 7 | 6 | 21 | 30 | 67 | 27 |

*Top scorer:* Pieroni (Mouscron) 28.
*Cup Final:* FC Brugge 4, Beveren 2.

## BOSNIA HERZEGOVINA

Football Federation of Bosnia & Herzegovina, Ferhadija 30, Sarajevo 71000.
*Founded:* 1992; *National Colours:* White shirts, blue shorts, white stockings.
*Telephone:* 00387-33/276 660; *Fax:* 00387-33/444 332.

**International matches 2003**
Wales (a) 2-2, Luxembourg (h) 2-0, Denmark (a) 2-0, Romania (a) 0-2, Norway (h) 1-0, Luxembourg (a) 1-0, Denmark (h) 1-1.

**League Championship wins (1996–2004)**
Zeljeznicar 3; Brotnjo 1; Leotar 1; Siroki 1.

**Cup wins (1996–2004)**
Zeljeznicar 3; Sarajevo 2; Bosna 1; Celik 1; Modrica 1.

**Final League Table 2003–04**

| | *P* | *W* | *D* | *L* | *F* | *A* | *Pts* |
|---|---|---|---|---|---|---|---|
| Siroki | 30 | 19 | 4 | 7 | 58 | 32 | 61 |
| Zeljeznicar | 30 | 18 | 5 | 7 | 67 | 35 | 59 |
| Sarajevo | 30 | 17 | 5 | 8 | 58 | 25 | 56 |
| Leotar | 30 | 17 | 5 | 8 | 46 | 23 | 56 |
| Sloboda | 30 | 11 | 9 | 10 | 38 | 36 | 42 |
| Modrica | 30 | 11 | 7 | 12 | 43 | 43 | 40 |
| Borac | 30 | 11 | 6 | 13 | 40 | 42 | 39 |
| Orasje | 30 | 12 | 3 | 15 | 40 | 51 | 39 |
| Rudar | 30 | 11 | 6 | 13 | 31 | 43 | 39 |
| Posusje | 30 | 11 | 6 | 13 | 35 | 48 | 39 |
| Zrinjski | 30 | 11 | 5 | 14 | 40 | 47 | 38 |
| Celik | 30 | 9 | 10 | 11 | 42 | 43 | 37 |
| Zepce | 30 | 10 | 7 | 13 | 26 | 38 | 37 |
| Travnik | 30 | 10 | 7 | 13 | 30 | 43 | 37 |
| Glasinac* | 30 | 9 | 6 | 15 | 34 | 49 | 33 |
| Brotnjo* | 30 | 4 | 7 | 19 | 29 | 59 | 19 |

*Top scorer:* Skoro (Sarajevo) 20.
*Cup Final:* Modrica 1, Borac 1.
*Modrica won 4-2 on penalties.*

## BULGARIA

Bulgarian Football Union, Karnigradska Street 19, BG-1000 Sofia.
*Founded:* 1923; *Number of Clubs:* 376; *Number of Players:* 48,240; *National Colours:* White shirts, green shorts, white stockings.
*Telephone:* 00359-2/987 7490; *Fax:* 00359-2/986 2538.

**International matches 2003**
Serbia (a) 2-1, Estonia (a) 0-0, Albania (h) 2-0, Belgium (h) 2-2, Lithuania (h) 3-0, Estonia (h) 2-0, Andorra (a) 3-0, Croatia (a) 0-1, South Korea (a) 1-0.

**League Championship wins (1925–2004)**
CSKA Sofia 29; Levski Sofia 22; Slavia Sofia 7; Vladislav Varna 3; Lokomotiv Sofia 3; Liteks 2; Trakia Plovdiv 2; AC 23 Sofia 1; Botev Plovdiv 1; SC Sofia 1; Sokol Varna 1; Spartak Plovdiv 1; Tichka Varna 1; JSZ Sofia 1; Beroe Stara Zagora 1; Etur 1; Lokomotiv Plovdiv 1.

**Cup wins (1946–2004)**
Levski Sofia 22; CSKA Sofia 16; Slavia Sofia 7; Lokomotiv Sofia 4; Liteks 2; Botev Plovdiv 1; Spartak Plovdiv 1; Spartak Sofia 1; Marek Stanke 1; Trakia Plovdiv 1; Spartak Varna 1; Sliven 1.

**Qualifying League Table 2003-04**

| | *P* | *W* | *D* | *L* | *F* | *A* | *Pts* |
|---|---|---|---|---|---|---|---|
| Lokomotiv Plovdiv | 30 | 24 | 3 | 3 | 74 | 24 | 75 |
| Levski Sofia | 30 | 22 | 6 | 2 | 59 | 16 | 72 |
| CSKA Sofia | 30 | 20 | 5 | 5 | 65 | 28 | 65 |
| Liteks | 30 | 18 | 10 | 2 | 43 | 20 | 64 |
| Slavia Sofia | 30 | 18 | 3 | 9 | 57 | 30 | 57 |
| Cherno Varna | 30 | 10 | 8 | 12 | 45 | 53 | 38 |
| Marek | 30 | 12 | 2 | 16 | 33 | 50 | 38 |
| Naftex | 30 | 9 | 8 | 13 | 49 | 38 | 35 |
| Lokomotiv Sofia | 30 | 8 | 9 | 13 | 37 | 48 | 33 |
| Rodopa | 30 | 10 | 3 | 17 | 28 | 47 | 33 |
| Belasitsa | 30 | 8 | 7 | 15 | 34 | 52 | 31 |
| Vidima | 30 | 6 | 12 | 12 | 32 | 48 | 30 |
| Spartak Varna | 30 | 8 | 6 | 16 | 35 | 46 | 30 |
| Botev Plovdiv* | 30 | 7 | 6 | 17 | 33 | 60 | 27 |
| Makedonska* | 30 | 8 | 2 | 20 | 32 | 58 | 26 |
| Chernomorets* | 30 | 4 | 6 | 20 | 30 | 68 | 18 |

*Top scorer:* Kamburov (Lokomotiv Plovdiv) 25.
*Cup Final:* Liteks 2, CSKA Sofia 2.
*Litets won 4-3 on penalties.*

## CROATIA

Croatian Football Federation, Rusanova 13, Zagreb, 10 3000, Croatia.
*Founded:* 1912; *Number of Clubs:* 1,221; *Number of Players:* 78,127; *National Colours:* Red & white shirts, white shorts, blue stockings.
*Telephone:* 00385-1/236 1555; *Fax:* 00385-1/244 1501.

**International matches 2003**
Macedonia (h) 2-2, Poland (h) 0-0, Belgium (h) 4-0, Andorra (h) 2-0, Sweden (a) 2-1, Estonia (a) 1-0, England (a) 1-3, Andorra (a) 3-0, Belgium (a) 1-2, Bulgaria (h) 1-0, Slovenia (h) 1-1, Slovenia (a) 1-0.

**League Championship wins (1941–44; 1992–2004)**
Dynamo Zagreb (formerly Croatia Zagreb) 7; Hajduk Split 5; Gradanski 3; Concordia 1; Zagreb 1.

**Cup wins (1993–2004)**
Dynamo Zagreb (formerly Croatia Zagreb) 7; Hajduk Split 4; Osijek 1.

**Qualifying Table 2003–04**

| | *P* | *W* | *D* | *L* | *F* | *A* | *Pts* |
|---|---|---|---|---|---|---|---|
| Hajduk Split | 22 | 18 | 1 | 3 | 46 | 18 | 55 |
| Dynamo Zagreb | 22 | 15 | 5 | 2 | 47 | 16 | 50 |
| Rijeka | 22 | 8 | 7 | 7 | 26 | 25 | 31 |
| Osijek | 22 | 8 | 5 | 9 | 36 | 40 | 29 |
| Varteks | 22 | 7 | 8 | 7 | 21 | 25 | 29 |
| Zadar | 22 | 7 | 7 | 8 | 37 | 44 | 28 |
| Kamen | 22 | 8 | 4 | 10 | 32 | 27 | 28 |
| Inker | 22 | 6 | 9 | 7 | 22 | 23 | 27 |
| Slaven | 22 | 6 | 8 | 8 | 22 | 27 | 26 |
| Cibalia | 22 | 5 | 5 | 12 | 25 | 35 | 20 |
| Zagreb | 22 | 3 | 10 | 9 | 21 | 32 | 19 |
| Marsonia | 22 | 4 | 5 | 13 | 25 | 48 | 17 |

**Championship Play-Off Table 2003-04**

| | *P* | *W* | *D* | *L* | *F* | *A* | *Pts* |
|---|---|---|---|---|---|---|---|
| Hajduk Split | 32 | 25 | 3 | 4 | 63 | 24 | 78 |
| Dynamo Zagreb | 32 | 23 | 7 | 2 | 77 | 25 | 76 |
| Rijeka | 32 | 11 | 9 | 12 | 36 | 41 | 42 |
| Osijek | 32 | 11 | 6 | 15 | 50 | 57 | 39 |
| Varteks | 32 | 9 | 11 | 12 | 33 | 42 | 38 |
| Zadar | 32 | 7 | 11 | 14 | 46 | 71 | 32 |

**Relegation Table 2003-04**

| | *P* | *W* | *D* | *L* | *F* | *A* | *Pts* |
|---|---|---|---|---|---|---|---|
| Kamen | 32 | 13 | 7 | 12 | 45 | 36 | 46 |
| Inker | 32 | 11 | 9 | 12 | 40 | 38 | 42 |
| Slaven | 32 | 10 | 10 | 12 | 37 | 39 | 40 |
| Zagreb | 32 | 8 | 12 | 12 | 33 | 41 | 36 |
| Cibalia+ | 32 | 8 | 7 | 17 | 39 | 53 | 31 |
| Marsonia* | 32 | 5 | 10 | 17 | 32 | 64 | 25 |

*Top scorer:* Spehar (Osijek) 17.
*Cup Final:* Varteks 1, 0, Dynamo Zagreb 1, 0.

## CYPRUS

Cyprus Football Association, 1 Stasinos Str., Engomi, P.O. Box 25071, Nicosia 2404.
*Founded:* 1934; *Number of Clubs:* 85; *Number of Players:* 6,000; *National Colours:* Blue shirts, white shorts, blue stockings.
*Telephone:* 00357-22/590 960; *Fax:* 00357-22/590 544.

**International matches 2003**
Greece (h) 1-2, Russia (h) 0-1, Slovakia (h) 1-3, Israel (h) 1-1, Slovenia (a) 1-4, Israel (a) 0-2, Malta (a) 2-1, France (a) 0-5, Slovenia (h) 2-2.

**League Championship wins (1935–2004)**
Omonia 19; Apoel 18; Anorthosis 11; AEL 5; EPA 3; Olympiakos 3; Apollon 2; Pezoporikos 2; Chetin Kayal 1; Trast 1.

**Cup wins (1935–2004)**
Apoel 17; Omonia 11; Anorthosis 7; AEL 6; EPA 5; Apollon 5; Trast 3; Chetin Kayal 2; Olympiakos 1; Pezoporikos 1; Salamina 1; AEK 1.

**Final League Table 2003–04**

| | P | W | D | L | F | A | Pts |
|---|---|---|---|---|---|---|---|
| Apoel | 26 | 20 | 5 | 1 | 56 | 20 | 65 |
| Omonia | 26 | 20 | 2 | 4 | 68 | 29 | 62 |
| Apollon | 26 | 16 | 1 | 9 | 50 | 23 | 49 |
| AEL | 26 | 14 | 7 | 5 | 52 | 26 | 49 |
| Anorthosis | 26 | 15 | 3 | 8 | 57 | 35 | 48 |
| Ethnikos Achnas | 26 | 11 | 5 | 10 | 51 | 37 | 38 |
| AEP | 26 | 12 | 2 | 12 | 41 | 36 | 38 |
| ENP | 26 | 10 | 6 | 10 | 40 | 36 | 36 |
| AEK | 26 | 9 | 5 | 12 | 50 | 52 | 32 |
| Olympiakos | 26 | 8 | 7 | 11 | 45 | 44 | 31 |
| Digenis | 26 | 7 | 7 | 12 | 27 | 38 | 28 |
| Anagennisis* | 26 | 4 | 6 | 16 | 17 | 44 | 18 |
| Onisilos* | 26 | 3 | 4 | 19 | 22 | 63 | 13 |
| Doxa* | 26 | 1 | 4 | 21 | 18 | 111 | 7 |

*Top scorers:* Sosin (Apollon), Koslej (Omonia) 21.
*Cup Final:* AEK 2, AEL 1.

## CZECH REPUBLIC

Football Association of Czech Republic, Diskarska 100, Prague 6 16017 - Strahov, Czech Republic.
*Founded:* 1901; *Number of Clubs:* 3,836; *Number of Players:* 319,500; *National Colours:* Red shirts, white shorts, blue stockings.
*Telephone:* 00420-2/3302 9111; *Fax:* 00420-2/3335 3107.

**International matches 2003**
France (a) 2-0, Holland (a) 1-1, Austria (h) 4-0, Turkey (h) 4-0, Moldova (h) 5-0, Belarus (a) 3-1, Holland (h) 3-1, Austria (a) 3-2, Canada (h) 5-1.

**League Championship wins (1926–93)**
Sparta Prague 19; Slavia Prague 12; Dukla Prague (prev. UDA) 11; Slovan Bratislava 7; Spartak Trnava 5; Banik Ostrava 3; Inter-Bratislava 1; Spartak Hradec Kralove 1; Viktoria Zizkov 1; Zbrojovka Brno 1; Bohemians 1; Vitkovice 1.

**Cup wins (1961–93)**
Dukla Prague 8; Sparta Prague 8; Slovan Bratislava 5; Spartak Trnava 4; Banik Ostrava 3; Lokomotiv Kosice 3; TJ Gottwaldov 1; Dunajska Streda 1.
*From 1993–94, there were two separate countries; the Czech Republic and Slovakia.*

**League Championship wins (1994–2004)**
Sparta Prague 8; Slavia Prague 1; Slovan Liberec 1; Banik Ostrava 1.

**Cup wins (1994–2004)**
Slavia Prague 4; Viktoria Zizkov 2; Sparta Prague 2; Spartak Hradec Kralove 1; Jablonec 1; Slovan Liberec 1; Teplice 1.

**Final League Table 2003–04**

| | P | W | D | L | F | A | Pts |
|---|---|---|---|---|---|---|---|
| Banik Ostrava | 30 | 18 | 9 | 3 | 60 | 25 | 63 |
| Sparta Prague | 30 | 16 | 10 | 4 | 48 | 24 | 58 |
| Sigma Olomouc | 30 | 16 | 7 | 7 | 43 | 24 | 55 |
| Slavia Prague | 30 | 15 | 7 | 8 | 43 | 24 | 52 |
| Synot | 30 | 14 | 6 | 10 | 43 | 37 | 48 |
| Slovan Liberec | 30 | 12 | 10 | 8 | 38 | 27 | 46 |
| Zlin | 30 | 12 | 5 | 13 | 31 | 39 | 41 |
| Ceske | 30 | 11 | 7 | 12 | 38 | 38 | 40 |
| Teplice | 30 | 9 | 12 | 9 | 32 | 32 | 39 |
| Jablonec | 30 | 8 | 14 | 8 | 27 | 32 | 38 |
| Marila Pribram | 30 | 10 | 7 | 13 | 33 | 37 | 37 |
| Opava | 30 | 8 | 7 | 15 | 34 | 55 | 31 |
| Chmel Blsany | 30 | 8 | 6 | 16 | 34 | 54 | 30 |
| Brno | 30 | 7 | 9 | 14 | 33 | 43 | 30 |
| Viktoria Zizkov* | 30 | 6 | 9 | 15 | 18 | 34 | 27 |
| Plzen* | 30 | 4 | 7 | 19 | 23 | 53 | 19 |

*Top scorer:* Heinz (Banik Ostrava) 19.
*Cup Final:* Sparta Prague 2, Banik Ostrava 1.

## DENMARK

Danish Football Association, Idraettens Hus, Brondby Stadion 20, DK-2605, Brondby.
*Founded:* 1889; *Number of Clubs:* 1,555; *Number of Players:* 268,517; *National Colours:* Red shirts, white shorts, red stockings.
*Telephone:* 0045-43/262 222; *Fax:* 0045-43/262 245.

**International matches 2003**
Egypt (a) 4-1, Romania (a) 5-2, Bosnia (h) 0-2, Ukraine (h) 1-0, Norway (h) 1-0, Luxembourg (a) 2-0, Finland (h) 1-1, Romania (h) 2-2, Bosnia (a) 1-1, England (a) 3-2.

**League Championship wins (1913–2004)**
KB Copenhagen 15; B 93 Copenhagen 10; AB (Akademisk) 9; Brondby 9; B 1903 Copenhagen 7; Frem 6; Esbjerg BK 5; Vejle BK 5; AGF Aarhus 5; FC Copenhagen 4; Hvidovre 3; Odense BK 3; AaB Aalborg 2; B 1909 Odense 2; Koge BK 2; Lyngby 2; Silkeborg 1; Herfolge 1.

**Cup wins (1955–2004)**
Aarhus GF 9; Vejle BK 6; OB Odense 4; Brondby 4; Randers Freja 3; Lyngby 3; FC Copenhagen 3; B1909 Odense 2; Aalborg BK 2; Esbjerg BK 2; Frem 2; B 1903 Copenhagen 2; B 93 Copenhagen 1; KB Copenhagen 1; Vanlose 1; Hvidovre 1; B1913 Odense 1, AB Copenhagen 1, Viborg 1; Silkeborg 1.

**Final League Table 2003–04**

| | P | W | D | L | F | A | Pts |
|---|---|---|---|---|---|---|---|
| FC Copenhagen | 33 | 20 | 8 | 5 | 56 | 27 | 68 |
| Brondby | 33 | 20 | 7 | 6 | 55 | 29 | 67 |
| Esbjerg | 33 | 18 | 8 | 7 | 71 | 44 | 62 |
| Odense | 33 | 16 | 9 | 8 | 66 | 46 | 57 |
| Aalborg | 33 | 16 | 9 | 8 | 55 | 41 | 57 |
| Midtjylland | 33 | 14 | 6 | 13 | 65 | 51 | 48 |
| Viborg | 33 | 11 | 9 | 13 | 47 | 44 | 42 |
| Aarhus | 33 | 11 | 3 | 19 | 45 | 67 | 36 |
| Nordsjaelland | 33 | 7 | 11 | 15 | 35 | 59 | 32 |
| Herfolge | 33 | 8 | 7 | 18 | 34 | 57 | 31 |
| Frem* | 33 | 8 | 3 | 22 | 40 | 65 | 27 |
| AB Copenhagen* | 33 | 8 | 2 | 23 | 31 | 70 | 17 |

*Nordsjaelland formerly Farum; AB Copenhagen deducted 9 points for player registration discrepancy.*
*Top scorers:* Bechmann (Esbjerg), Miti (Odense), Hojer (Odense), Zidan (Midtjylland) 19.
*Cup Final:* FC Copenhagen 1, Aalborg 0.

## ENGLAND

The Football Association, 25 Soho Square, London W1D 4FA.
*Founded:* 1863; *Number of Clubs:* 42,000; *Number of Players:* 2,250,000; *National Colours:* White shirts with navy blue collar, navy shorts, white stockings.
*Telephone:* 020 7745 4545, 020 7402 7151; *Fax:* 020 7745 4546; *Website:* www.the-fa.org

## ESTONIA

Estonian Football Association, Rapia 8/10, Tallinn 11312.
*Founded:* 1921; *Number of Clubs:* 40; *Number of Players:* 12,000; *National Colours:* Blue shirts, black shorts, white stockings.
*Telephone:* 00372-6/512 720; *Fax:* 00372-6/512 729.

**International matches 2003**
Ecuador (a) 0-1, Ecuador (a) 1-2, China (a) 0-1, Canada (h) 2-1, Bulgaria (h) 0-0, Andorra (a) 2-0, Andorra (h) 2-0, Croatia (h) 0-1, Lithuania (h) 1-5, Latvia (h) 0-0, Poland (h) 1-2, Bulgaria (a) 0-2, Belgium (a) 0-2, Albania (a) 0-2, Hungary (a) 1-0, Saudi Arabia (a) 1-1, Oman (a) 1-3.

**League Championship wins (1922–40; 1992–2003)**
Flora Tallinn 7; Sport 8; Estonia 5; Norma Tallinn 2; Tallinn JK 2; Kalev 2; Levadia 2; LFLS 1; Olimpia 1; Lantana 1.

**Cup wins (1992–2003)**
Levadia (merged with Sadam) 4; Levadia Tallinn 2; VMV Tallinn 1; Nikol Tallinn 1; Norma Tallinn 1; Lantana 1; Flora Tallinn 1; Trans 1.

**Final League Table 2003**

| | P | W | D | L | F | A | Pts |
|---|---|---|---|---|---|---|---|
| Flora | 28 | 24 | 4 | 0 | 105 | 21 | 76 |
| VMK | 28 | 20 | 5 | 3 | 82 | 26 | 65 |
| Levadia | 28 | 15 | 4 | 9 | 54 | 30 | 49 |
| Trans | 28 | 14 | 5 | 9 | 58 | 43 | 47 |
| Tulevik | 28 | 8 | 6 | 14 | 44 | 56 | 30 |
| Levadia Tallinn | 28 | 8 | 4 | 16 | 44 | 63 | 28 |
| Valga+ | 28 | 3 | 8 | 17 | 25 | 63 | 17 |
| Kuressaare* | 28 | 1 | 2 | 25 | 11 | 121 | 5 |

*Top scorer:* Hamre (Flora) 39.
*Cup Final:* Levadia Tallinn 3, VMK 0.

## FAEROE ISLANDS

Fotboltssamband Foroya, The Faeroes' Football Assn., Gundalur, P.O. Box 3028, FR-110, Torshavn.
*Founded:* 1979; *Number of Clubs:* 16; *Number of Players:* 1,014; *National Colours:* White shirts, blue shorts, white stockings.
*Telephone:* 00298/316 707; *Fax:* 00298/319 079.

**International matches 2003**
Kazakhstan (h) 3-2, Kazakhstan (h) 2-1, Iceland (a) 1-2, Germany (h) 0-2, Iceland (h) 1-2, Scotland (a) 1-3, Lithuania (h) 1-3.

**League Championship wins (1942–2003)**
HB Torshavn 17; KI Klaksvik 16; TB Tvoroyri 7; GI Gotu 7; B36 Torshavn 7; B68 Toftir 3; SI Sorvag 1; IF Fuglafjordur 1; B71 Sandur 1; VB 1.

**Cup wins (1955–2003)**
HB Torshavn 25; KI Klaksvik 5; GI Gotu 5; TB Tvoroyri 4; B36 Torshavn 3; NSI Runavik 2; VB Vagur 1; B71 Sandur 1.

**Final League Table 2003**

| | *P* | *W* | *D* | *L* | *F* | *A* | *Pts* |
|---|---|---|---|---|---|---|---|
| HB | 18 | 12 | 5 | 1 | 41 | 17 | 41 |
| B36 | 18 | 12 | 1 | 5 | 38 | 20 | 37 |
| B68 | 18 | 10 | 5 | 3 | 26 | 15 | 35 |
| NSI | 18 | 9 | 5 | 4 | 33 | 18 | 32 |
| KI | 18 | 7 | 3 | 8 | 29 | 30 | 24 |
| EB/Streymur | 18 | 6 | 6 | 6 | 33 | 36 | 24 |
| GI | 18 | 5 | 5 | 8 | 26 | 33 | 20 |
| VB | 18 | 4 | 4 | 10 | 16 | 30 | 16 |
| Skala+ | 18 | 4 | 0 | 14 | 16 | 39 | 12 |
| Vagar* | 18 | 3 | 2 | 13 | 25 | 45 | 11 |

*Top scorer:* Elttor (KI) 13.
*Cup Final:* B36 3, GI 1.

## FINLAND

Suomen Palloliitto Finlands Bollfoerbund, Urheilukatu 5, P.O. Box 191, Helsinki 00251.
*Founded:* 1907; *Number of Clubs:* 1,135; *Number of Players:* 66,100; *National Colours:* White shirts, blue shorts, white stockings.
*Telephone:* 00358-9/7421 51; *Fax:* 00358-9/7421 4200.

**International matches 2003**
Barbados (a) 0-0, Trinidad & Tobago (a) 2-1, N Ireland (a) 1-0, Serbia (h) 3-0, Italy (a) 0-2, Iceland (h) 3-0, Norway (a) 0-2, Italy (h) 0-2, Denmark (a) 1-1, Azerbaijan (a) 2-1, Wales (a) 1-1, Canada (h) 3-2, Honduras (a) 2-1, Costa Rica (a) 1-2.

**League Championship wins (1949–2003)**
HJK Helsinki 12; Valkeakosken Haka 8; Turun Palloseura 5; Kuopion Palloseura 5; Kuusysi 4; Lahden Reipas 3; IF Kamraterna 3; Ilves-Kissat 2; Jazz Pori 2; Kotkan TP 2; OPS Oulu 2; Torun Pyrkiva 1; IF Kronohagens 1; Helsinki PS 1; Kokkolan PV 1; Vasa 1; TPV Tampere 1; Tampere U 1.

**Cup wins (1955–2003)**
Valkeakosken Haka 11; HJK Helsinki 8; Lahden Reipas 7; Kotkan TP 4; Mikkeli 2; Kuusysi 2; Kuopion Palloseura 2; Ilves Tampere 2; TPS Turku 2; ; MyPa 2; IFK Abo 1; Drott 1; Helsinki PS 1; Pallo-Peikot 1; Rovaniemi PS 1; Jokerit 1 (formerly PK-35); Atlantis 1.

**Final League Table 2003**

| | *P* | *W* | *D* | *L* | *F* | *A* | *Pts* |
|---|---|---|---|---|---|---|---|
| HJK Helsinki | 26 | 17 | 6 | 3 | 51 | 15 | 57 |
| Haka | 26 | 16 | 5 | 5 | 54 | 16 | 53 |
| Tampere U | 26 | 14 | 5 | 7 | 39 | 21 | 47 |
| MyPa | 26 | 13 | 4 | 9 | 46 | 29 | 43 |
| Lahti | 26 | 11 | 8 | 7 | 40 | 31 | 41 |
| Allianssi | 26 | 10 | 6 | 10 | 43 | 44 | 36 |
| Inter | 26 | 10 | 5 | 11 | 43 | 41 | 35 |
| Jaro | 26 | 9 | 8 | 9 | 36 | 38 | 35 |
| TPS Turku | 26 | 8 | 8 | 10 | 30 | 35 | 32 |
| Jokerit | 26 | 7 | 7 | 12 | 29 | 37 | 28 |
| Hameenlinna | 26 | 7 | 7 | 12 | 25 | 48 | 28 |
| Jazz Pori | 26 | 7 | 7 | 12 | 31 | 55 | 28 |
| Kotka+ | 26 | 6 | 4 | 16 | 28 | 53 | 22 |
| KuPS* | 26 | 4 | 6 | 16 | 25 | 57 | 18 |

*Top scorer:* Puhakainen (MyPa) 14.
*Cup Final:* HJK Helsinki 2, Allianssi 1.

## FRANCE

Federation Francaise De Football, 60 Bis Avenue d'Iena, Paris 75116.
*Founded:* 1919; *Number of Clubs:* 21,629; *Number of Players:* 1,692,205; *National Colours:* Blue shirts, white shorts, red stockings.
*Telephone:* 0033-1/ 4431 7300; *Fax:* 0033-1/4720 8296.

**International matches 2003**
Czech Republic (h) 0-2, Malta (h) 6-0, Israel (a) 2-1, Egypt (h) 5-0, Colombia (n) 1-0, Japan (n) 2-1, New Zealand (n) 5-0, Turkey (n) 3-2, Cameroon (n) 1-0, Switzerland (a) 2-0, Cyprus (h) 5-0, Slovenia (a) 2-0, Israel (h) 3-0, Germany (a) 3-0.

**League Championship wins (1933–2004)**
Saint Etienne 10; Olympique Marseille 8; Nantes 8; AS Monaco 7; Stade de Reims 6; Girondins Bordeaux 5; OGC Nice 4; Lille OSC 3; Lyon 3; Paris St Germain 2; FC Sete 2; Sochaux 2; Racing Club Paris 1; Roubaix-Tourcoing 1; Strasbourg 1; Auxerre 1; Lens 1.

**Cup wins (1918–2004)**
Olympique Marseille 10; Saint Etienne 6; AS Monaco 6; Lille OSC 5; Racing Club Paris 5; Red Star 5; Paris St Germain 5; Olympique Lyon 3; Girondins Bordeaux 3; OGC Nice 3; Nantes 3; Racing Club Strasbourg 3; Auxerre 3; CAS Genereaux 2; Nancy 2; Sedan 2; FC Sete 2; Stade de Reims 2; SO Montpellier 2; Stade Rennes 2; AS Cannes 1; Club Français 1; Excelsior Roubaix 1; Le Havre 1; Olympique de Pantin 1; CA Paris 1; Sochaux 1; Toulouse 1; Bastia 1; Metz 1; Lorient 1.

**Final League Table 2003–04**

| | *P* | *W* | *D* | *L* | *F* | *A* | *Pts* |
|---|---|---|---|---|---|---|---|
| Lyon | 38 | 24 | 7 | 7 | 64 | 26 | 79 |
| Paris St Germain | 38 | 22 | 10 | 6 | 50 | 28 | 76 |
| Monaco | 38 | 21 | 12 | 5 | 59 | 30 | 75 |
| Auxerre | 38 | 19 | 8 | 11 | 60 | 34 | 65 |
| Sochaux | 38 | 18 | 9 | 11 | 54 | 42 | 63 |
| Nantes | 38 | 17 | 9 | 12 | 47 | 35 | 60 |
| Marseille | 38 | 17 | 6 | 15 | 51 | 45 | 57 |
| Lens | 38 | 15 | 8 | 15 | 34 | 48 | 53 |
| Rennes | 38 | 14 | 10 | 14 | 56 | 44 | 52 |
| Lille | 38 | 14 | 9 | 15 | 41 | 41 | 51 |
| Nice | 38 | 11 | 17 | 10 | 42 | 39 | 50 |
| Bordeaux | 38 | 13 | 11 | 14 | 40 | 43 | 50 |
| Strasbourg | 38 | 10 | 13 | 15 | 43 | 50 | 43 |
| Metz | 38 | 11 | 9 | 18 | 34 | 42 | 42 |
| Ajaccio | 38 | 10 | 10 | 18 | 33 | 55 | 40 |
| Toulouse | 38 | 9 | 12 | 17 | 31 | 44 | 39 |
| Bastia | 38 | 9 | 12 | 17 | 33 | 49 | 39 |
| Guingamp* | 38 | 10 | 8 | 20 | 36 | 58 | 38 |
| Le Mans* | 38 | 9 | 11 | 18 | 35 | 57 | 38 |
| Montpellier* | 38 | 8 | 7 | 23 | 41 | 74 | 31 |

*Top scorer:* Cisse (Auxerre) 17.
*Cup Final:* Paris St Germain 1, Chateauroux 0.

## GEORGIA

Georgian Football Federation, 76a Tchavtchavadze Avenue, Tbilisi 380062.
*Founded:* 1990; *Number of Clubs:* 4050. *Number of Players:* 115,000; *National Colours:* All white.
*Telephone:* 00995-32/912 610; *Fax:* 00995-32/001 128.

**International matches 2003**
Moldova (h) 2-2, Eire (h) 1-2, Switzerland (h) 0-0, Russia (h) 1-0, Eire (a) 0-2, Albania (h) 3-0, Albania (a) 1-3, Russia (a) 1-3.

**League Championship wins (1990–2004)**
Dynamo Tbilisi 11; Torpedo Kutaisi 3; WIT 1.

**Cup wins (1990–2004)**
Dynamo Tbilisi 8; Torpedo Kutaisi 2; Lokomotivi 2; Dynamo Batumi 1; Guria 1.

**Qualifying League Table 2003–04**

| | P | W | D | L | F | A | Pts |
|---|---|---|---|---|---|---|---|
| Dynamo Tbilisi | 22 | 15 | 5 | 2 | 49 | 8 | 50 |
| WIT | 22 | 12 | 6 | 4 | 38 | 15 | 42 |
| Sioni | 22 | 11 | 7 | 4 | 31 | 18 | 40 |
| Tbilisi | 22 | 10 | 5 | 7 | 41 | 26 | 35 |
| Lokomotivi | 22 | 10 | 4 | 8 | 32 | 24 | 34 |
| Dila Gori | 22 | 10 | 4 | 8 | 28 | 20 | 34 |
| Torpedo Kutaisi | 22 | 10 | 4 | 8 | 27 | 26 | 34 |
| Dynamo Batumi | 22 | 10 | 2 | 10 | 26 | 28 | 32 |
| Kolkheti | 22 | 7 | 3 | 12 | 18 | 35 | 24 |
| Mtskheta | 22 | 6 | 2 | 14 | 25 | 55 | 20 |
| Spartak Lazika | 22 | 4 | 4 | 14 | 14 | 47 | 16 |
| Mertskhali | 22 | 2 | 4 | 16 | 18 | 45 | 10 |

*Merani changed name to Tbilisi.*
*Top scorer:* Akhalaia (Dynamo Tbilisi) 8.

**Championship Table 2003–04**

| | P | W | D | L | F | A | Pts |
|---|---|---|---|---|---|---|---|
| Sioni | 10 | 6 | 3 | 1 | 14 | 5 | 41 |
| WIT | 10 | 6 | 2 | 2 | 10 | 3 | 41 |
| Dynamo Tbilisi | 10 | 4 | 3 | 3 | 15 | 10 | 40 |
| Tbilisi | 10 | 3 | 5 | 2 | 12 | 8 | 32 |
| Lokomotivi | 10 | 1 | 5 | 4 | 6 | 11 | 25 |
| Dila Gori | 10 | 0 | 2 | 8 | 2 | 22 | 19 |

**Championship Play-Off**
WIT 2, Sioni 0.

**Relegation Table 2003–04**

| | P | W | D | L | F | A | Pts |
|---|---|---|---|---|---|---|---|
| Torpedo Kutaisi | 10 | 5 | 2 | 3 | 19 | 12 | 34 |
| Kolkheti | 10 | 6 | 3 | 1 | 14 | 6 | 33 |
| Mtskheta+ | 10 | 6 | 3 | 1 | 14 | 5 | 31 |
| Dynamo Batumi+ | 10 | 3 | 0 | 7 | 6 | 14 | 25 |
| Spartaki* | 10 | 5 | 1 | 4 | 18 | 11 | 24 |
| Mertskhali* | 10 | 0 | 1 | 9 | 4 | 27 | 6 |

*Spartak Lazika renamed Spartaki.*
*Top scorer:* Davitashvili (Torpedo Kutaisi) 20.
*Cup Final:* Dynamo Tbilisi 2, Torpedo Kutaisi 1.

## GERMANY

Deutscher Fussball-Bund, Otto-Fleck-Schneise 6, Postfach 710265, Frankfurt Am Main 60492.
*Founded:* 1900; *Number of Clubs:* 26,760; *Number of Players:* 5,260,320; *National Colours:* White shirts, black shorts, white stockings.
*Telephone:* 0049-69/678 80; *Fax:* 0049-69/678 8266.

**International matches 2003**
Spain (a) 1-3, Lithuania (h) 1-1, Serbia (h) 1-0, Canada (h) 4-1, Scotland (a) 1-1, Faeroes (a) 2-0, Italy (h) 0-1, Iceland (a) 0-0, Scotland (h) 2-1, Iceland (h) 3-0, France (h) 0-3.

**League Championship wins (1903–2004)**
Bayern Munich 18; IFC Nuremberg 9; Schalke 04 7; Borussia Dortmund 6; SV Hamburg 6; Borussia Moenchengladbach 5; VfB Stuttgart 4; IFC Kaiserslautern 4; Werder Bremen 4; VfB Leipzig 3; SpVgg Furth 3; IFC Cologne 3; Viktoria Berlin 2; Hertha Berlin 2; Hannover 96 2; Dresden SC 2; Munich 1860 1; Union Berlin 1; FC Freiburg 1; Phoenix Karlsruhe 1; Karlsruher FV 1; Holstein Kiel 1; Fortuna Dusseldorf 1; Rapid Vienna 1; VfR Mannheim 1; Rot-Weiss Essen 1; Eintracht Frankfurt 1; Eintracht Brunswick 1.

**Cup wins (1935–2004)**
Bayern Munich 11; Werder Bremen 5; IFC Cologne 4; Eintracht Frankfurt 4; Schalke 04 4; IFC Nuremberg 3; SV Hamburg 3; Moenchengladbach 3; VfB Stuttgart 3; Dresden SC 2; Fortuna Dusseldorf 2; Karlsruhe SC 2; Munich 1860 2; Borussia Dortmund 2; Kaiserslautern 2; First Vienna 1; VfB Leipzig 1; Kickers Offenbach 1; Rapid Vienna 1; Rot-Weiss Essen 1; SW Essen 1; Bayer Uerdingen 1; Hannover 96 1; Leverkusen 1.

**Final League Table 2003–04**

| | P | W | D | L | F | A | Pts |
|---|---|---|---|---|---|---|---|
| Werder Bremen | 34 | 22 | 8 | 4 | 79 | 38 | 74 |
| Bayern Munich | 34 | 20 | 8 | 6 | 70 | 39 | 68 |
| Leverkusen | 34 | 19 | 8 | 7 | 73 | 39 | 65 |
| Stuttgart | 34 | 18 | 10 | 6 | 52 | 24 | 64 |
| Bochum | 34 | 15 | 11 | 8 | 57 | 39 | 56 |
| Borussia Dortmund | 34 | 16 | 7 | 11 | 59 | 48 | 55 |
| Schalke | 34 | 13 | 11 | 10 | 49 | 42 | 50 |
| Hamburg | 34 | 14 | 7 | 13 | 47 | 60 | 49 |
| Hansa Rostock | 34 | 12 | 8 | 14 | 55 | 54 | 44 |
| Wolfsburg | 34 | 13 | 3 | 18 | 56 | 61 | 42 |
| Moenchengladbach | 34 | 10 | 9 | 15 | 40 | 49 | 39 |
| Hertha | 34 | 9 | 12 | 13 | 42 | 59 | 39 |
| Freiburg | 34 | 10 | 8 | 16 | 42 | 67 | 38 |
| Hannover | 34 | 9 | 10 | 15 | 49 | 63 | 37 |
| Kaiserslautern (-3) | 34 | 11 | 6 | 17 | 39 | 62 | 36 |
| Eintracht Frankfurt* | 34 | 9 | 5 | 20 | 36 | 53 | 32 |
| Munich 1860* | 34 | 8 | 8 | 18 | 32 | 55 | 32 |
| Cologne* | 34 | 6 | 5 | 23 | 32 | 57 | 23 |

*Top scorer:* Ailton (Werder Bremen) 28.
*Cup Final:* Werder Bremen 3, Alemannia 2.

## GREECE

Hellenic Football Federation, Singrou Avenue 137, Nea Smirni, 17121 Athens.
*Founded:* 1926; *Number of Clubs:* 4,050; *Number of Players:* 180,000; *National Colours:* Blue shirts, white shorts, blue stockings.
*Telephone:* 0030-210/930 6000; *Fax:* 0030-210/935 9666.

**International matches 2003**
Cyprus (a) 2-1, Norway (h) 1-0, Austria (a) 2-2, N Ireland (a) 2-0, Slovakia (a) 2-2, Spain (a) 1-0, Ukraine (h) 1-0, Sweden (a) 2-1, Armenia (a) 1-0, N Ireland (h) 1-0, Portugal (a) 1-1.

**League Championship wins (1928–2004)**
Olympiakos 32; Panathinaikos 19; AEK Athens 11; Aris Salonika 3; PAOK Salonika 2; Larissa 1.

**Cup wins (1932–2004)**
Olympiakos 21; Panathinaikos 17; AEK Athens 13; PAOK Salonika 4; Panionios 2; Aris Salonika 1; Ethnikos 1; Iraklis 1; Kastoria 1; Larissa 1; OFI Crete 1.

**Final League Table 2003–04**

| | P | W | D | L | F | A | Pts |
|---|---|---|---|---|---|---|---|
| Panathinaikos | 30 | 24 | 5 | 1 | 62 | 18 | 77 |
| Olympiakos | 30 | 24 | 3 | 3 | 70 | 19 | 75 |
| PAOK Salonika | 30 | 18 | 6 | 6 | 47 | 27 | 60 |
| AEK Athens | 30 | 16 | 7 | 7 | 57 | 32 | 55 |
| Aigaleo | 30 | 15 | 7 | 8 | 37 | 26 | 52 |
| Panionios | 30 | 12 | 11 | 7 | 40 | 29 | 47 |
| Halkidona | 30 | 13 | 6 | 11 | 40 | 39 | 45 |
| Iraklis | 30 | 12 | 6 | 12 | 40 | 39 | 42 |
| Ionikos | 30 | 9 | 6 | 15 | 33 | 43 | 33 |
| Xanthi | 30 | 8 | 6 | 16 | 28 | 42 | 30 |
| OFFI Crete | 30 | 7 | 8 | 15 | 27 | 44 | 29 |
| Kalithea | 30 | 5 | 12 | 13 | 37 | 42 | 27 |
| Aris Salonika | 30 | 7 | 6 | 17 | 24 | 46 | 27 |
| Akratitos+ | 30 | 5 | 8 | 17 | 31 | 69 | 23 |
| Paniliakos* | 30 | 4 | 9 | 17 | 28 | 56 | 21 |
| Proodeftiki* | 30 | 4 | 8 | 18 | 26 | 56 | 20 |

*Top scorer:* Giovanni (Olympiakos) 21.
*Cup Final:* Panathinaikos 3, Olympiakos 1.

## HOLLAND

Koninklijke Nederlandsche Voetbalbond, Woudenbergseweg 56–58, Postbus 515, NL-3700 AM, Zeist.
*Founded:* 1889; *Number of Clubs:* 3,097; *Number of Players:* 962,397; *National Colours:* Orange shirts, black shorts, orange stockings.
*Telephone:* 0031-343/499 201; *Fax:* 0031-343/499 189.

**International matches 2003**
Argentina (h) 1-0, Czech Republic (h) 1-1, Moldova (a) 2-1, Portugal (h) 1-1, Belarus (a) 2-0, Belgium (a) 1-1, Austria (h) 3-1, Czech Republic (a) 1-3, Moldova (h) 5-0, Scotland (a) 0-1, Scotland (h) 6-0.

**League Championship wins (1898–2004)**
Ajax Amsterdam 29; PSV Eindhoven 17; Feyenoord 14; HVV The Hague 8; Sparta Rotterdam 6; Go Ahead Deventer 4; HBS The Hague 3; Willem II Tilburg 3; RAP 2; Heracles 2; ADO The Hague 2; Quick The Hague 1; BVV Den Bosch 2; NAC Breda 1; Eindhoven 1; Enschede 1; Volewijckers Amsterdam 1; Limburgia 1; Rapid JC Heerlen 3; DOS Utrecht 1; DWS Amsterdam 1; Haarlem 1; Be Quick Groningen 1; AZ 67 Alkmaar 1.

**Cup wins (1899–2004)**
Ajax Amsterdam 15; Feyenoord 10; PSV Eindhoven 7; Quick The Hague 4; AZ 67 Alkmaar 3; Rotterdam 3; Utrecht 3; DFC 2; Fortuna Geleen 2; Haarlem 2; HBS The Hague 2; RCH Haarlem 2; Roda 2; VOC 2; Wageningen 2; Willem II Tilburg 2; FC Den Haag 2; Twente Enschede 2; Concordia Rotterdam 1; CVV 1; Eindhoven 1; HVV The Hague 1; Longa 1; Quick Nijmegen 1; RAP 1; Roermond 1; Schoten 1; Velocitas Breda 1; Velocitas Groningen 1; VSV 1; VUC 1; VVV Groningen 1; ZFC 1; NAC Breda 1.

**Final League Table 2003–04**

| | *P* | *W* | *D* | *L* | *F* | *A* | *Pts* |
|---|---|---|---|---|---|---|---|
| Ajax | 34 | 25 | 5 | 4 | 79 | 31 | 80 |
| PSV Eindhoven | 34 | 23 | 5 | 6 | 92 | 30 | 74 |
| Feyenoord | 34 | 20 | 8 | 6 | 71 | 38 | 68 |
| Heerenveen | 34 | 17 | 7 | 10 | 45 | 35 | 58 |
| AZ | 34 | 17 | 6 | 11 | 65 | 42 | 57 |
| Roda JC | 34 | 14 | 11 | 9 | 60 | 41 | 53 |
| Willem II | 34 | 13 | 10 | 11 | 47 | 54 | 49 |
| Twente | 34 | 15 | 3 | 16 | 56 | 53 | 48 |
| NAC Breda | 34 | 12 | 10 | 12 | 58 | 55 | 46 |
| Utrecht | 34 | 13 | 7 | 14 | 42 | 52 | 46 |
| RKC Waalwijk | 34 | 10 | 10 | 14 | 47 | 55 | 40 |
| Roosendaal | 34 | 10 | 10 | 14 | 34 | 47 | 40 |
| Groningen | 34 | 9 | 10 | 15 | 38 | 53 | 37 |
| NEC Nijmegen | 34 | 10 | 4 | 20 | 44 | 62 | 34 |
| ADO The Hague | 34 | 9 | 7 | 18 | 36 | 61 | 34 |
| Vitesse+ | 34 | 4 | 16 | 14 | 39 | 56 | 28 |
| Volendam+ | 34 | 7 | 6 | 21 | 31 | 79 | 27 |
| Zwolle* | 34 | 5 | 11 | 18 | 27 | 67 | 26 |

*Top scorer:* Kezman (PSV Eindhoven) 31.
*Cup Final:* Utrecht 1, Twente 0.

## HUNGARY

Hungarian Football Federation, Robert Karoly krt 61-65, Robert Haz Budapest 1134.
*Founded:* 1901; *Number of Clubs:* 1944; *Number of Players:* 95,986; *National Colours:* Red shirts, white shorts, green stockings.
*Telephone:* 0036-1/412 3340; *Fax:* 0036-1/452 0360.

**International matches 2003**
Poland (a) 0-0, Sweden (h) 1-2, Luxembourg (h) 5-1, Latvia (h) 3-1, San Marino (a) 5-0, Slovenia (a) 1-2, Latvia (a) 1-3, Poland (h) 1-2, Estonia (h) 0-1.

**League Championship wins (1901–2004)**
Ferencvaros 28; MTK-VM Budapest 21; Ujpest Dozsa 20; Kispest Honved 13; Vasas Budapest 6; Csepel 4; Raba Gyor 3; BTC 2; Nagyvarad 1; Vac 1; Dunaferr 1; Zalaegerszeg 1.

**Cup wins (1910–2004)**
Ferencvaros 19; MTK-VM Budapest 12; Ujpest Dozsa 9; Raba Gyor 4; Kispest Honved 5; Vasas Budapest 4; Diósgyör 2; Debrecen 2; Bocskai 1; III Ker 1; Kispesti AC 1; Soroksar 1; Szolnoki MAV 1; Siofok Banyasz 1; Bekescsaba 1; Pecsi 1.
*Cup not regularly held until 1964.*

**Qualifying League Table 2003–04**

| | *P* | *W* | *D* | *L* | *F* | *A* | *Pts* |
|---|---|---|---|---|---|---|---|
| Ferencvaros | 22 | 12 | 8 | 2 | 29 | 15 | 44 |
| Balaton | 22 | 12 | 5 | 5 | 24 | 11 | 41 |
| Debrecen | 22 | 11 | 6 | 5 | 34 | 17 | 39 |
| MTK | 22 | 10 | 8 | 4 | 35 | 21 | 38 |
| Ujpest | 22 | 9 | 8 | 5 | 32 | 22 | 35 |
| Matav | 22 | 8 | 7 | 7 | 35 | 28 | 31 |
| Pecsi | 22 | 6 | 9 | 7 | 19 | 21 | 27 |
| Videoton | 22 | 5 | 8 | 9 | 27 | 37 | 23 |
| Zalaegerszeg | 22 | 5 | 5 | 12 | 24 | 35 | 20 |
| Gyor | 22 | 5 | 5 | 12 | 23 | 38 | 20 |
| Bekescsaba | 22 | 4 | 7 | 11 | 23 | 34 | 19 |
| Haladas | 22 | 3 | 8 | 11 | 12 | 38 | 17 |

*Ferencvaros deducted six points for pitch invasion previous season; Balaton formerly Siofok.*

**Final Championship Table 2003–04**

| | *P* | *W* | *D* | *L* | *F* | *A* | *Pts* |
|---|---|---|---|---|---|---|---|
| Ferencvaros | 32 | 16 | 9 | 7 | 44 | 30 | 57 |
| Ujpest | 32 | 15 | 11 | 6 | 48 | 29 | 56 |
| Debrecen | 32 | 16 | 8 | 8 | 51 | 32 | 56 |
| Balaton | 32 | 14 | 8 | 10 | 34 | 24 | 50 |
| Matav | 32 | 13 | 9 | 10 | 53 | 42 | 48 |
| MTK | 32 | 11 | 11 | 10 | 42 | 40 | 44 |

**Promotion/Relegation Table 2003–04**

| | *P* | *W* | *D* | *L* | *F* | *A* | *Pts* |
|---|---|---|---|---|---|---|---|
| Videoton | 32 | 10 | 10 | 12 | 55 | 51 | 40 |
| Pecsi | 32 | 9 | 13 | 10 | 36 | 37 | 40 |
| Zalaegerszeg | 32 | 11 | 6 | 15 | 45 | 47 | 39 |
| Gyor | 32 | 10 | 6 | 16 | 36 | 54 | 36 |
| Bekescsaba+ | 32 | 8 | 8 | 16 | 36 | 50 | 32 |
| Haladas+ | 32 | 4 | 11 | 17 | 19 | 63 | 23 |

*Top scorer:* Toth (Matav) 17.
*Cup Final:* Ferencvaros 3, Kispest Honved 1.

## ICELAND

Knattspyrnusamband Island, Laugardal, 104 Reykjavik.
*Founded:* 1929; *Number of Clubs:* 73; *Number of Players:* 23,673; *National Colours;* All blue.
*Telephone:* 00354/510 2900; *Fax:* 00354/568 9793.

**International matches 2003**
Scotland (a) 1-2, Finland (a) 0-3, Faeroes (h) 2-1, Lithuania (a) 3-0, Faeroes (a) 2-1, Germany (h) 0-0, Germany (a) 0-3, Mexico (a) 0-0.

**League Championship wins (1912–2003)**
KR 24; Valur 19; Fram 18; IA Akranes 18; Vikingur 5; IBV Vestmann 4; IBK Keflavik 3; KA Akureyri 1.

**Cup wins (1960–2003)**
KR 10; Valur 8; Fram 7; IA Akranes 8; IBV Vestmann 4; IBK Keflavik 2; Fylkir 2; IBA Akureyri 1; Vikingur 1.

**Final League Table 2003**

| | *P* | *W* | *D* | *L* | *F* | *A* | *Pts* |
|---|---|---|---|---|---|---|---|
| KR | 18 | 10 | 3 | 5 | 28 | 27 | 33 |
| FH | 18 | 9 | 3 | 6 | 36 | 24 | 30 |
| IA | 18 | 8 | 6 | 4 | 27 | 21 | 30 |
| Fylkir | 18 | 9 | 2 | 7 | 29 | 24 | 29 |
| IBV | 18 | 7 | 3 | 8 | 25 | 25 | 24 |
| Grindavik | 18 | 7 | 2 | 9 | 24 | 31 | 23 |
| Fram | 18 | 7 | 2 | 9 | 22 | 30 | 23 |
| KA | 18 | 6 | 4 | 8 | 29 | 27 | 22 |
| Throttur* | 18 | 7 | 1 | 10 | 27 | 29 | 22 |
| Valur* | 18 | 6 | 2 | 10 | 24 | 33 | 20 |

*Top scorers:* Thorvaldsson (IBV), Hermansen (Throttur), Takefusa (Throttur) 10.
*Cup Final:* IA 1, FH 0.

## REPUBLIC OF IRELAND

The Football Association of Ireland (Cumann Peile Na H-Eireann), 80 Merrion Square, South Dublin 2.
*Founded:* 1921; *Number of Clubs:* 3,190; *Number of Players:* 124,615; *National Colours:* Green shirts, white shorts, green and white stockings.
*Telephone:* 00353-1/676 6864; *Fax:* 00353-1/661 0931.

**League Championship wins (1922–2003)**
Shamrock Rovers 15; Shelbourne 11; Dundalk 9; Bohemians 9; St Patrick's Athletic 8; Waterford 6; Cork United 5; Drumcondra 5; St James's Gate 2; Cork Athletic 2; Sligo Rovers 2; Limerick 2; Athlone Town 2; Derry City 2; Dolphin 1; Cork Hibernians 1; Cork Celtic 1; Cork City 1.

**Cup wins (1922–2003)**
Shamrock Rovers 24; Dundalk 9; Shelbourne 6; Bohemians 6; Drumcondra 5; Derry City 3; Cork Athletic 2; Cork United 2; St James's Gate 2; St Patrick's Athletic 2; Cork Hibernians 2; Limerick 2; Waterford 2; Athlone Town 2; Sligo 2; Bray Wanderers 2; Alton United 1; Cork 1; Fordsons 1; Transport 1; Finn Harps 1; Home Farm 1; UCD 1; Galway United 1; Cork City 1; Longford Town 1.

**Final League Table 2003**

| | *P* | *W* | *D* | *L* | *F* | *A* | *Pts* |
|---|---|---|---|---|---|---|---|
| Shelbourne | 36 | 19 | 12 | 5 | 52 | 28 | 69 |
| Bohemians | 36 | 18 | 10 | 8 | 58 | 37 | 64 |
| Cork City | 36 | 13 | 14 | 9 | 43 | 33 | 53 |
| Longford Town | 36 | 12 | 12 | 12 | 46 | 44 | 48 |
| St Patrick's Athletic | 36 | 10 | 16 | 10 | 48 | 48 | 46 |
| Waterford United | 36 | 11 | 12 | 13 | 44 | 58 | 45 |
| Shamrock Rovers | 36 | 10 | 14 | 12 | 45 | 46 | 44 |
| Drogheda United | 36 | 9 | 10 | 17 | 38 | 50 | 37 |
| Derry City+ | 36 | 7 | 15 | 14 | 33 | 51 | 36 |
| UCD* | 36 | 7 | 13 | 16 | 27 | 39 | 34 |

*Top scorer:* Byrne J (Shelbourne) 21.
*Cup Final:* Longford Town 2, St Patrick's Athletic 0.

## ISRAEL

Israel Football Association, Ramat-Gan Stadium, 299 Aba Hilell Street, Ramat-Gan 52134.
*Founded:* 1948; *Number of Clubs:* 544; *Number of Players:* 30,449; *National Colours:* Blue shirts, white shorts, blue stockings.
*Telephone:* 00972-3/617 1503; *Fax:* 00972-3/ 570 2044.

**International matches 2003**
Armenia (h) 2-0, Moldova (h) 0-0, Cyprus (a) 1-1, France (h) 1-2, Cyprus (h) 2-0, Slovenia (h) 0-0, Russia (a) 2-1, Slovenia (a) 1-3, Malta (h) 2-2, France (a) 0-3.

**League Championship wins (1932–2004)**
Maccabi Tel Aviv 19; Hapoel Tel Aviv 13; Maccabi Haifa 8; Hapoel Petach Tikva 6; Maccabi Netanya 5; Beitar Jerusalem 4; Hakoah Ramat Gan 2; Hapoel Beersheba 2; Bnei Yehouda 1; British Police 1; Hapoel Kfar Sava 1; Hapoel Ramat Gan 1; Hapoel Haifa 1.

**Cup wins (1928–2004)**
Maccabi Tel Aviv 21; Hapoel Tel Aviv 11; Beitar Jerusalem 5; Maccabi Haifa 5; Hapoel Haifa 3; Hapoel Kfar Sava 3; Beitar Tel Aviv 2; Bnei Yehouda 2; Hakoah Ramat Gan 2; Hapoel Petah Tikva 2; Maccabi Petach Tikva 2; British Police 1; Hapoel Jerusalem 1; Hapoel Lod 1; Maccabi Netanya 1; Hapoel Beersheba 1; Hapoel Ramat Gan 1; Hapoel Bnei Sakhnin 1.

**Final League Table 2003–04**

| | *P* | *W* | *D* | *L* | *F* | *A* | *Pts* |
|---|---|---|---|---|---|---|---|
| Maccabi Haifa | 33 | 19 | 6 | 8 | 54 | 25 | 63 |
| Maccabi Tel Aviv | 33 | 16 | 9 | 8 | 35 | 22 | 57 |
| Maccabi Petach Tikva | 33 | 16 | 8 | 9 | 49 | 35 | 56 |
| Hapoel Beersheba | 33 | 16 | 7 | 10 | 48 | 36 | 55 |
| Hapoel Tel Aviv | 33 | 13 | 10 | 10 | 48 | 37 | 49 |
| Bnei Yehouda | 33 | 12 | 9 | 12 | 34 | 42 | 45 |
| Ashdod | 33 | 11 | 9 | 13 | 47 | 49 | 42 |
| Hapoel Petah Tikva | 33 | 11 | 9 | 13 | 46 | 52 | 42 |
| Beitar Jerusalem | 33 | 10 | 9 | 14 | 32 | 42 | 39 |
| Hapoel Bnei Sakhnin | 33 | 8 | 11 | 14 | 31 | 38 | 35 |
| Maccabi Netanya* | 33 | 8 | 7 | 18 | 28 | 52 | 31 |
| Maccabi Nazareth* (-3) | 33 | 8 | 6 | 19 | 40 | 62 | 27 |

*Top scorers:* Haim (Hapoel Beersheba), Holtzman (Ashdod) 16.
*Cup Final:* Hapoel Bnei Sakhnin 4, Hapoel Haifa 1.

## ITALY

Federazione Italiana Giuoco Calcio, Via Gregorio Allegri 14, Roma 00198.
*Founded:* 1898; *Number of Clubs:* 20,961; *Number of Players:* 1,420,160; *National Colours:* Blue shirts, white shorts, blue stockings.
*Telephone:* 0039-06/84 911; *Fax:* 0039-06/84 912 526.

**International matches 2003**
Portugal (h) 1-0, Finland (h) 2-0, Switzerland (a) 2-1, N Ireland (h) 2-0, Finland (a) 2-0, Germany (a) 1-0, Wales (h) 4-0, Serbia (a) 1-1, Azerbaijan (h) 4-0, Poland (a) 1-3, Romania (h) 1-0.

**League Championship wins (1898–2004)**
Juventus 27; AC Milan 17; Inter-Milan 13; Genoa 9; Torino 8; Pro Vercelli 7; Bologna 7; AS Roma 3; Fiorentina 2; Lazio 2; Napoli 2; Casale 1; Novese 1; Cagliari 1; Verona 1; Sampdoria 1.

**Cup wins (1922–2004)**
Juventus 9; AS Roma 8; Fiorentina 6; AC Milan 5; Torino 4; Sampdoria 4; Lazio 4; Inter-Milan 3; Napoli 3; Parma 3; Bologna 2; Atalanta 1; Genoa 1; Vado 1; Venezia 1; Vicenza 1.

**Final League Table 2003–04**

| | *P* | *W* | *D* | *L* | *F* | *A* | *Pts* |
|---|---|---|---|---|---|---|---|
| AC Milan | 34 | 25 | 7 | 2 | 65 | 24 | 82 |
| Roma | 34 | 21 | 8 | 5 | 68 | 19 | 71 |
| Juventus | 34 | 21 | 6 | 7 | 67 | 42 | 69 |
| Internazionale | 34 | 17 | 8 | 9 | 59 | 37 | 59 |
| Parma | 34 | 16 | 10 | 8 | 57 | 46 | 58 |
| Lazio | 34 | 16 | 8 | 10 | 52 | 38 | 56 |
| Udinese | 34 | 13 | 11 | 10 | 44 | 40 | 50 |
| Sampdoria | 34 | 11 | 13 | 10 | 40 | 42 | 46 |
| Chievo | 34 | 11 | 11 | 12 | 36 | 37 | 44 |
| Lecce | 34 | 11 | 8 | 15 | 43 | 56 | 41 |
| Brescia | 34 | 9 | 13 | 12 | 52 | 57 | 40 |
| Bologna | 34 | 10 | 9 | 15 | 45 | 53 | 39 |
| Siena | 34 | 8 | 10 | 16 | 41 | 54 | 34 |
| Reggina | 34 | 6 | 16 | 12 | 29 | 45 | 34 |
| Perugia+ | 34 | 6 | 14 | 14 | 44 | 56 | 32 |
| Modena* | 34 | 6 | 12 | 16 | 27 | 46 | 30 |
| Empoli* | 34 | 7 | 9 | 18 | 26 | 54 | 30 |
| Ancona* | 34 | 2 | 7 | 25 | 21 | 70 | 13 |

*Serie A extended to twenty clubs with three relegated, five promoted and one play-off.*
*Top scorer:* Shevchenko (AC Milan) 24.
*Cup Final:* Lazio 2, 2, Juventus 0, 2.

## KAZAKHSTAN

The Football Union of Kazakhstan, Satpayev Street, 29/3 Almaty 480 072, Kazakhstan.
*Founded:* 1914; *Number of Clubs:* 5,793; *Number of Players:* 260,000; *National Colours:* Blue shirts, blue shorts, yellow stockings.
*Telephone:* 007-3272/920 444; *Fax:* 007-3272/921 885.

**International matches 2003**
Malta (a) 2-2, Faeroes (a) 2-3, Faeroes (a) 1-2, Poland (a) 0-3, Portugal (a) 0-1.

**League Championship wins (1992-2003)**
Irtysh 5; Yelimai 3; Zhenis 2; Kairat 1; Taraz 1.

**Cup wins (1992–2003)**
Kairat 5; Zhenis 2; Dostyk 1; Vostok 1; Yelimai 1; Irtysh 1; Kaisar 1.

**Final League Table 2003**

| | *P* | *W* | *D* | *L* | *F* | *A* | *Pts* |
|---|---|---|---|---|---|---|---|
| Irtysh | 32 | 25 | 3 | 4 | 59 | 20 | 78 |
| Tobol | 32 | 24 | 4 | 4 | 55 | 19 | 76 |
| Jenis | 32 | 20 | 4 | 8 | 65 | 33 | 64 |
| Atyrau | 32 | 16 | 5 | 11 | 48 | 42 | 53 |
| Aqtobe | 32 | 13 | 12 | 7 | 40 | 29 | 51 |
| Ordabasy | 32 | 15 | 4 | 13 | 33 | 29 | 49 |
| Kairat | 32 | 14 | 7 | 11 | 51 | 42 | 49 |
| Jetisu | 32 | 14 | 6 | 12 | 46 | 38 | 48 |
| Yelimai | 32 | 12 | 7 | 13 | 35 | 35 | 43 |
| Shakhter | 32 | 10 | 12 | 10 | 37 | 29 | 42 |
| Yesil Bogatyr | 32 | 10 | 6 | 16 | 42 | 53 | 36 |
| Taraz | 32 | 10 | 4 | 18 | 35 | 45 | 34 |
| Kaysar | 32 | 9 | 7 | 16 | 26 | 42 | 34 |
| Vostok+ | 32 | 8 | 8 | 16 | 34 | 46 | 32 |
| Yekibastuzets+ | 32 | 8 | 4 | 20 | 30 | 56 | 28 |
| Batys* | 32 | 8 | 2 | 22 | 25 | 74 | 26 |
| Yesil* | 32 | 4 | 9 | 19 | 13 | 42 | 15 |

*Yesil six points deducted for administration discrepancies; they withdrew for financial reasons and remaining matches awarded 0-3 against them.*
*Ordabasy formerly Dostyk.*
*Top scorer:* Finonchenko (Shakhter) 18.
*Cup Final:* Kairat 3, Tobol 1.

## LATVIA

Latvian Football Federation, Augsiela 1, LV-1009, Riga.
*Founded:* 1921; *Number of Clubs:* 50; *Number of Players:* 12,000; *National Colours:* Carmine red shirts, white shorts, carmine red stockings.
*Telephone:* 00371/729 2988; *Fax:* 00371/ 731 5604.

**International matches 2003**
Lithuania (h) 2-1, Ukraine (a) 0-1, San Marino (h) 3-0, Hungary (a) 1-3, Lithuania (h) 2-1, Estonia (a) 0-0, Uzbekistan (h) 0-3, Poland (h) 0-2, Hungary (h) 3-1, Sweden (a) 1-0, Turkey (h) 1-0, Turkey (a) 2-2.

**League Championship wins (1922–2003)**
Skonto Riga 13; ASK Riga 9; RFK Riga 8; Olympia Liepaya 7; Sarkanais Metalurgs Liepaya 7; VEF Riga 6; Energija Riga 4; Elektrons Riga 3; Torpedo Riga 3; Daugava Liepaya 2; ODO Riga 2; Khimikis Daugavpils 2; RAF Yelgava 2; Keisermezhs Riga 2; Dinamo Riga 1; Zhmilyeva Team 1; Darba Rezervi 1; REZ Riga 1; Start Brotseni 1; Venta Ventspils 1; Yurnieks Riga 1; Alfa Riga 1; Gauya Valmiera 1.

**Cup wins (1937–2003)**
Elektrons Riga 7; Skonto Riga 7; Sarkanais Metalurgs Liepaya 5; ODO Riga 3; VEF Riga 3; ASK Riga 3; Tseltnieks Riga 3; RAF Yelgava 3; RFK Riga 2; Daugava Liepaya 2; Start Brotseni 2; Selmash Liepaya 2; Yurnieks Riga 2; Khimikis Daugavpils 2; Rigas Vilki 1; Dinamo Liepaya 1; Dinamo Riga 1; REZ Riga 1; Voulkan Kouldiga 1; Baltija Liepaya 1; Venta Ventspils 1; Pilot Riga 1; Lielupe Yurmala 1; Energija Riga 1; Torpedo Riga 1; Daugava SKIF Riga 1; Tseltnieks Daugavpils 1; Olympia Riga 1; FK Riga 1; FK Ventspils 1.

**Final League Table 2003**

| | *P* | *W* | *D* | *L* | *F* | *A* | *Pts* |
|---|---|---|---|---|---|---|---|
| Skonto Riga | 28 | 23 | 4 | 1 | 91 | 9 | 73 |
| Metalurgs Liepaya | 28 | 22 | 2 | 4 | 100 | 29 | 68 |
| FK Ventspils | 28 | 19 | 4 | 5 | 89 | 19 | 61 |
| Dinaburg Daugavpils | 28 | 13 | 5 | 10 | 43 | 36 | 44 |
| FK Riga | 28 | 8 | 5 | 15 | 34 | 63 | 29 |
| Gauja Valmiera | 28 | 6 | 5 | 17 | 27 | 70 | 23 |
| Auda Riga | 28 | 4 | 1 | 23 | 21 | 88 | 13 |
| RKB Arma Riga* | 28 | 2 | 4 | 22 | 23 | 115 | 10 |

*Top scorer:* Dobrecovs (Metalurgs Liepaya) 36.
*Cup Final:* FK Ventspils 4, Skonto Riga 0.

## LIECHTENSTEIN

Liechtensteiner Fussball-Verband, Malbuner Huus Altenbach 11, Postfach 165, 9490 Vaduz.
*Founded:* 1934; *Number of Clubs:* 7; *Number of Players:* 1,247; *National Colours:* Blue shirts, red shorts, blue stockings.
*Telephone:* 00423/237 4747; *Fax:* 00423/237 4748.

**International matches 2003**
England (h) 0-2, Slovakia (a) 0-4, Saudi Arabia (h) 1-0, Macedonia (a) 1-3, San Marino (h) 2-2, Turkey (h) 0-3, England (a) 0-2, Slovakia (h) 0-2.
Liechtenstein has no national league. Teams compete in Swiss regional leagues.

**Cup wins (1946–2004)**
Vaduz 33; Balzers 11; Triesen 8; Eschen/Mauren 4; Schaan 3.
*Cup Final:* Vaduz 5, Balzers 0.

## LITHUANIA

Lithuanian Football Federation, Seimyniskiu str. 15, 2005 Vilnius.
*Founded:* 1922; *Number of Clubs:* 152; *Number of Players:* 16,600; *National Colours:* Yellow shirts, green shorts, yellow stockings.
*Telephone:* 00370/5263 8741; *Fax:* 00370/5263 8740.

**International matches 2003**
Latvia (a) 1-2, Germany (a) 1-1, Scotland (h) 1-0, Romania (h) 0-1, Iceland (h) 0-3, Estonia (a) 5-1, Latvia (a) 1-2, Bulgaria (a) 0-3, Faeroes (a) 3-1, Scotland (a) 0-1, Poland (h) 1-3.

**League Championship wins (1922–2003)**
Kovas Kaunas 6; KSS Klaipeda 6; FBK Kaunas 5; LFLS Kaunas 4; Zalgiris Vilnius 4; LGSF Kaunas 2; Kareda 2; MSK Kaunas 1; Ekranas Panevezys 1; Romar Mazeikiai 1; Inkaras Grifas 1.

**Cup wins (1992–2003)**
Zalgiris Vilnius 4; Kareda 2; Ekranas 2; Atlantas 2; Inkaras 1; Kaunas 1.

**Final League Table 2003**

| | *P* | *W* | *D* | *L* | *F* | *A* | *Pts* |
|---|---|---|---|---|---|---|---|
| FBK Kaunas | 28 | 21 | 5 | 2 | 64 | 20 | 68 |
| Ekranas | 28 | 18 | 8 | 2 | 50 | 19 | 62 |
| Vetra | 28 | 13 | 8 | 7 | 42 | 22 | 47 |
| Zalgiris | 28 | 9 | 7 | 12 | 37 | 37 | 34 |
| Atlantas | 28 | 9 | 6 | 13 | 27 | 30 | 33 |
| Suduva | 28 | 8 | 8 | 12 | 39 | 45 | 32 |
| Sviesa | 28 | 7 | 5 | 16 | 25 | 38 | 26 |
| Sakalas* | 28 | 1 | 5 | 22 | 13 | 86 | 8 |

*Inkaras withdrew.*
*Top scorer:* Beniusis (FBK Kaunas) 16 (including 6 for Atlantas).
*Cup Final:* Zalgiris 3, Ekranas 1.

## LUXEMBOURG

Federation Luxembourgeoise De Football (F.L.F.), 68 Rue De Gasperich, Luxembourg 1617.
*Founded:* 1908; *Number of Clubs:* 126; *Number of Players:* 21,684; *National Colours:* All red.
*Telephone:* 00352/488 665 1; *Fax:* 00352/488 665 82.

**International matches 2003**
Bosnia (a) 0-2, Norway (h) 0-2, Hungary (a) 1-5, Denmark (h) 0-2, Malta (h) 1-1, Romania (a) 0-4, Bosnia (h) 0-1, Norway (a) 0-1, Moldova (h) 1-2.

**League Championship wins (1910–2004)**
Jeunesse Esch 27; Spora Luxembourg 11; Stade Dudelange 10; Avenir Beggen 7; Red Boys Differdange 6; US Hollerich-Bonnevoie 5; Fola Esch 5; US Luxembourg 5; Aris Bonnevoie 3; Progres Niedercorn 3; F91 Dudelange 3; Grevenmacher 1.

**Cup wins (1922–2004)**
Red Boys Differdange 16; Jeunesse Esch 12; US Luxembourg 10; Spora Luxembourg 8; Avenir Beggen 7; Stade Dudelange 4; Progres Niedercorn 4; Fola Esch 3; Grevenmacher 3; Alliance Dudelange 2; US Rumelange 2; Aris Bonnevoie 1; US Dudelange 1; Jeunesse Hautcharage 1; National Schiffige 1; Racing Luxembourg 1; SC Tetange 1; Hesperange 1; Etzella 1; F91 Dudelange 1.

**Qualifying Table 2003–04**

| | *P* | *W* | *D* | *L* | *F* | *A* | *Pts* |
|---|---|---|---|---|---|---|---|
| Jeunesse Esch | 22 | 19 | 1 | 2 | 56 | 13 | 58 |
| F91 Dudelange | 22 | 14 | 4 | 4 | 52 | 19 | 46 |
| Etzella | 22 | 12 | 8 | 2 | 56 | 29 | 44 |
| Grevenmacher | 22 | 11 | 3 | 8 | 47 | 33 | 36 |
| Spora | 22 | 12 | 0 | 10 | 49 | 48 | 36 |
| Union Luxembourg | 22 | 9 | 5 | 8 | 31 | 21 | 32 |
| Hesperange | 22 | 8 | 1 | 13 | 28 | 41 | 25 |
| Victoria Rosport | 22 | 7 | 3 | 12 | 32 | 38 | 24 |
| Avenir Beggen | 22 | 5 | 5 | 12 | 20 | 46 | 20 |
| Rumelange | 22 | 4 | 6 | 12 | 28 | 55 | 18 |
| Mondercange | 22 | 5 | 3 | 14 | 24 | 52 | 18 |
| FC Wiltz 71 | 22 | 5 | 3 | 14 | 20 | 48 | 18 |

**Championship Table 2003–04**

| | *P* | *W* | *D* | *L* | *F* | *A* | *Pts* |
|---|---|---|---|---|---|---|---|
| Jeunesse Esch | 28 | 22 | 2 | 4 | 70 | 23 | 68 |
| F91 Dudelange | 28 | 18 | 5 | 5 | 62 | 26 | 59 |
| Etzella | 28 | 13 | 9 | 6 | 63 | 41 | 48 |
| Grevenmacher | 28 | 13 | 4 | 11 | 56 | 44 | 43 |

**Promotion/Relegation Table 2003–04**

| **Group A** | *P* | *W* | *D* | *L* | *F* | *A* | *Pts* |
|---|---|---|---|---|---|---|---|
| Spora | 28 | 14 | 2 | 12 | 56 | 57 | 44 |
| Hesperange | 28 | 10 | 2 | 16 | 34 | 47 | 32 |
| Avenir Beggen | 28 | 7 | 7 | 14 | 28 | 54 | 28 |
| Mondercange* | 28 | 7 | 6 | 15 | 32 | 58 | 27 |

| **Group B** | *P* | *W* | *D* | *L* | *F* | *A* | *Pts* |
|---|---|---|---|---|---|---|---|
| Union Luxembourg | 28 | 11 | 6 | 11 | 44 | 31 | 39 |
| Victoria Rosport | 28 | 9 | 4 | 15 | 38 | 50 | 31 |
| FC Wiltz 71 | 28 | 7 | 7 | 14 | 31 | 54 | 28 |
| Rumelange* | 28 | 6 | 8 | 14 | 37 | 66 | 26 |

*Top scorer:* Gomes (Spora) 24.
*Cup Final:* F91 Dudelange 3, Etzella 1.

## MACEDONIA

Football Association of Macedonia, VIII-ma Udarna Brigada 31-A, Skopje 1000.
*Founded:* 1948; *Number of Clubs:* 598; *Number of Players:* 15,165; *National Colours:* All red.
*Telephone:* 00389-2/3129 291; *Fax:* 00389-2/3165 448.

**International matches 2003**
Croatia (a) 2-2, Poland (a) 0-3, Slovakia (h) 0-2, Portugal (a) 0-1, Liechtenstein (h) 3-1, Turkey (a) 2-3, Albania (h) 3-1, England (h) 1-2, Slovakia (a) 1-1, Ukraine (a) 0-0.

**League Championship wins (1993–2004)**
Vardar 5; Sileks 3; Sloga 3; Pobeda 1.

**Cup wins (1993–2004)**
Vardar 4; Sloga 2; Sileks 1; Pellister 1; Pobeda 1; Cement 1.

**Final League Table 2003–04**

| | P | W | D | L | F | A | Pts |
|---|---|---|---|---|---|---|---|
| Pobeda | 33 | 22 | 5 | 6 | 78 | 42 | 71 |
| Sileks | 33 | 20 | 6 | 7 | 67 | 32 | 66 |
| Vardar | 33 | 17 | 9 | 7 | 66 | 39 | 60 |
| Rabotnicki | 33 | 16 | 10 | 7 | 58 | 40 | 58 |
| Sloga | 33 | 17 | 6 | 10 | 69 | 36 | 57 |
| Madzari | 33 | 14 | 8 | 11 | 44 | 30 | 50 |
| Cement | 33 | 11 | 12 | 10 | 48 | 41 | 45 |
| Baskimi | 33 | 14 | 1 | 18 | 44 | 54 | 43 |
| Napredok | 33 | 12 | 5 | 16 | 51 | 52 | 41 |
| Belasica | 33 | 10 | 6 | 17 | 37 | 55 | 36 |
| Tikves* | 33 | 5 | 4 | 24 | 25 | 62 | 19 |
| Bregalnica* (-3) | 33 | 2 | 4 | 27 | 20 | 124 | 7 |

*Cup Final:* Sloga 1, Napredok 0.

## MALTA

Malta Football Association, 280 St Paul Street, Valletta VLT07.
*Founded:* 1900; *Number of Clubs:* 252; *Number of Players:* 5,544; *National Colours:* Red shirts, white shorts, red stockings.
*Telephone:* 00356-21/232 581; *Fax:* 00356-21/245 136.

**International matches 2003**
Kazakhstan (h) 2-2, France (a) 0-6, Slovenia (h) 1-3, Cyprus (h) 1-2, Luxembourg (a) 1-1, Israel (a) 2-2, Poland (h) 0-4.

**League Championship wins (1910–2004)**
Floriana 25; Sliema Wanderers 25; Valletta 18; Hibernians 9; Hamrun Spartans 7; Rabat Ajax 2; St George's 1; KOMR 1; Birkirkara 1.

**Cup wins (1935–2004)**
Sliema Wanderers 19; Floriana 18; Valletta 10; Hamrun Spartans 6; Hibernians 6; Birkirkara 2; Gzira United 1; Melita 1; Zurrieq 1; Rabat Ajax 1.

**Qualifying League Table 2003–04**

| | P | W | D | L | F | A | Pts |
|---|---|---|---|---|---|---|---|
| Sliema Wanderers | 18 | 13 | 2 | 3 | 37 | 15 | 41 |
| Birkirkara | 18 | 11 | 2 | 5 | 41 | 18 | 35 |
| Hibernians | 18 | 10 | 4 | 4 | 31 | 25 | 34 |
| Marsaxlokk | 18 | 9 | 4 | 5 | 30 | 22 | 31 |
| Floriana | 18 | 7 | 6 | 5 | 33 | 26 | 27 |
| Pieta Hotspurs | 18 | 7 | 6 | 5 | 28 | 25 | 27 |
| Valletta | 18 | 6 | 5 | 7 | 27 | 29 | 23 |
| Balzan Youths | 18 | 5 | 3 | 10 | 22 | 37 | 18 |
| Msida St Joseph | 18 | 2 | 4 | 12 | 18 | 35 | 10 |
| Hamrun Spartans | 18 | 0 | 4 | 14 | 11 | 46 | 4 |

**Championship Table 2003–04**

| | P | W | D | L | F | A | Pts |
|---|---|---|---|---|---|---|---|
| Sliema Wanderers | 28 | 20 | 3 | 5 | 61 | 27 | 43 |
| Birkirkara | 28 | 17 | 5 | 6 | 59 | 30 | 39 |
| Hibernians | 28 | 16 | 4 | 8 | 47 | 38 | 35 |
| Marsaxlokk | 28 | 12 | 6 | 10 | 46 | 39 | 27 |
| Pieta Hotspurs | 28 | 9 | 9 | 10 | 40 | 40 | 23 |
| Floriana | 28 | 8 | 7 | 13 | 41 | 51 | 18 |

**Promotion/Relegation Table 2003–04**

| | P | W | D | L | F | A | Pts |
|---|---|---|---|---|---|---|---|
| Valletta | 24 | 11 | 5 | 8 | 41 | 33 | 27 |
| Msida St Joseph | 24 | 6 | 5 | 13 | 32 | 42 | 18 |
| Balzan Youths* | 24 | 7 | 3 | 14 | 28 | 51 | 15 |
| Hamrun Spartans* | 24 | 0 | 5 | 19 | 16 | 60 | 3 |

*Top scorer:* Doncic (Sliema Wanderers) 19.
*Cup Final:* Sliema Wanderers 2, Marsaxlokk 0.

## MOLDOVA

Football Association of Moldova, 39 Tricolorului Str, 2012, Chisinau.
*Founded:* 1990; *Number of Clubs:* 143; *Number of Players:* 75,000; *National Colours:* Red shirts, blue shorts, red stockings.
*Telephone:* 00373-22/210 413; *Fax:* 00373-22/210 432.

**International matches 2003**
Georgia (a) 2-2, Israel (a) 0-0, Belarus (a) 1-2, Holland (h) 1-2, Austria (h) 1-0, Czech Republic (a) 0-5, Turkey (a) 0-2, Belarus (h) 2-1, Holland (a) 0-5, Luxembourg (a) 2-1.

**League Championship wins (1992–2004)**
Zimbru Chisinau 8; Serif 3; Constructorul 1.

**Cup wins (1992–2004)**
Tiligul 4; Zimbru Chisinau 4; Serif 3; Combat 1; Constructorul 1.

**Final League Table 2003–04**

| | P | W | D | L | F | A | Pts |
|---|---|---|---|---|---|---|---|
| Serif | 26 | 19 | 5 | 2 | 46 | 14 | 62 |
| Otaci | 26 | 16 | 6 | 4 | 46 | 23 | 54 |
| Zimbru Chisinau | 26 | 12 | 7 | 7 | 35 | 21 | 43 |
| Tiraspol | 26 | 11 | 8 | 7 | 29 | 20 | 41 |
| Dacia | 26 | 8 | 8 | 10 | 23 | 27 | 32 |
| Tiligul | 26 | 5 | 13 | 8 | 20 | 23 | 28 |
| Unisport+ | 26 | 6 | 5 | 15 | 27 | 47 | 23 |
| Agro* | 26 | 0 | 2 | 24 | 12 | 63 | 2 |

*Top scorer:* Shishelov (Zimbru Chisinau) 14.
*Cup Final:* Zimbru Chisinau 2, Serif 1.

## NORTHERN IRELAND

Irish Football Association Ltd, 20 Windsor Avenue, Belfast BT9 6EE.
*Founded:* 1880; *Number of Clubs:* 1,555; *Number of Players:* 24,558; *National Colours:* Green shirts, white shorts, green stockings.
*Telephone:* 0044-28/9066 9458; *Fax:* 0044-28/9066 7620.

## NORWAY

Norges Fotballforbund, Ullevaal Stadion, Sognsveien 75J, Serviceboks 1, Oslo 0855.
*Founded:* 1902; *Number of Clubs:* 1,810; *Number of Players:* 300,000; *National Colours:* Red shirts, white shorts, blue stockings.
*Telephone:* 0047/2102 9300; *Fax:* 0047/2102 9301.

**International matches 2003**
UAE (a) 1-1, Oman (a) 2-1, Greece (a) 0-1, Luxembourg (a) 2-0, Eire (a) 0-1, Denmark (a) 0-1, Finland (h) 2-0, Romania (h) 1-1, Scotland (h) 0-0, Bosnia (a) 0-1, Portugal (h) 0-1, Luxemborg (h) 1-0, Spain (a) 1-2, Spain (h) 0-3.

**League Championship wins (1938–2003)**
Rosenborg Trondheim 17; Fredrikstad 9; Viking Stavanger 8; Lillestroem 6; Valerengen 4; Larvik Turn 3; Brann Bergen 2; Lyn Oslo 2; IK Start 2; Friedig 1; Skeid Oslo 1; Strömsgodset Drammen 1; Moss 1.

**Cup wins (1902–2003)**
Odds Bk Skien 11; Fredrikstad 10; Lyn Oslo 8; Skeid Oslo 8; Rosenborg Trondheim 8; Sarpsborg FK 6; Brann Bergen 5; Viking Stavanger 5; Orn F Horten 4; Lillestroem 4; Strömsgodset Drammen 4; Frigg 3; Mjondalens F 3; Valerenga 3; Bodo-Glimt 2; Mercantile 2; Tromso 2; Grane Nordstrand 1; Kvik Halden 1; Sparta 1; Gjovik 1; Moss 1; Byrne 1; Molde 1; Stabaek 1; Odd Grenland 1.
*(Known as the Norwegian Championship for HM The King's Trophy).*

**Final League Table 2003**

| | P | W | D | L | F | A | Pts |
|---|---|---|---|---|---|---|---|
| Rosenborg | 26 | 19 | 4 | 3 | 68 | 28 | 61 |
| Bodo-Glimt | 26 | 14 | 5 | 7 | 45 | 30 | 47 |
| Stabaek | 26 | 11 | 9 | 6 | 51 | 35 | 42 |
| Odd | 26 | 11 | 5 | 10 | 46 | 43 | 38 |
| Viking | 26 | 9 | 10 | 7 | 46 | 34 | 37 |
| Brann | 26 | 10 | 7 | 9 | 45 | 47 | 37 |
| Lillestrom | 26 | 10 | 7 | 9 | 33 | 35 | 37 |
| Sogndal | 26 | 9 | 8 | 9 | 43 | 46 | 35 |
| Molde | 26 | 9 | 4 | 13 | 32 | 41 | 31 |
| Lyn | 26 | 8 | 6 | 12 | 34 | 45 | 30 |
| Tromso | 26 | 8 | 5 | 13 | 30 | 52 | 29 |
| Valerenga+ | 26 | 6 | 10 | 10 | 30 | 33 | 28 |
| Aalesund* | 26 | 7 | 7 | 12 | 30 | 43 | 28 |
| Bryne* | 26 | 7 | 1 | 18 | 35 | 56 | 22 |

*Top scorer:* Brattbakk (Rosenborg) 17.
*Cup Final:* Rosenborg 3, Bodo-Glimt 1.

## POLAND

Polish Football Association, Polski Zwiazek Pilki Noznej, Miodowa 1, Warsaw 00-080.

*Founded:* 1919; *Number of Clubs:* 5,881; *Number of Players:* 317,442; *National Colours:* White shirts, red shorts, white stockings.
*Telephone:* 0048-22/827 0914; *Fax:* 0048-22/827 0704.

**International matches 2003**
Croatia (a) 0-0, Macedonia (h) 3-0, Hungary (h) 0-0, San Marino (h) 5-0, Belgium (a) 1-3, Kazakhstan (h) 3-0, Sweden (a) 0-3, Estonia (a) 2-1, Latvia (a) 2-0, Sweden (h) 0-2, Hungary (a) 2-1, Italy (h) 3-1, Serbia (h) 4-3, Malta (a) 4-0, Lithuania (a) 3-1.

**League Championship wins (1921–2004)**
Gornik Zabrze 14; Ruch Chorzow 13; Wisla Krakow 10; Legia Warsaw 7; Widzew Lodz 6; Lech Poznan 5; Pogon Lwow 4; Cracovia 3; Warta Poznan 2; Polonia Bytom 2; Stal Mielec 2; LKS Lodz 2; Polonia Warsaw 2; Garbarnia Krakow 1; Slask Wroclaw 1; Szombierki Bytom 1; Zaglebie Lubin 1.

**Cup wins (1951–2004)**
Legia Warsaw 12; Gornik Zabrze 6; Zaglebie Sosnowiec 4; Lech Poznan 4; GKS Katowice 3; Ruch Chorzow 3; Amica Wronki 3; Wisla Krakow 3; Slask Wroclaw 2; Polonia Warsaw 2; Gwardia Warsaw 1; LKS Lodz 1; Stal Rzeszow 1; Arka Gdynia 1; Lechia Gdansk 1; Widzew Lodz 1; Miedz Legnica 1.

**Final League Table 2003–04**

| | *P* | *W* | *D* | *L* | *F* | *A* | *Pts* |
|---|---|---|---|---|---|---|---|
| Wisla | 26 | 21 | 2 | 3 | 73 | 30 | 65 |
| Legia | 26 | 18 | 6 | 2 | 56 | 19 | 60 |
| Amica | 26 | 14 | 6 | 6 | 47 | 25 | 48 |
| Groclin | 26 | 13 | 7 | 6 | 59 | 31 | 46 |
| Wisla Plock | 26 | 10 | 8 | 8 | 41 | 39 | 38 |
| Lech | 26 | 10 | 7 | 9 | 43 | 34 | 37 |
| Gornik Zabrze | 26 | 8 | 9 | 9 | 26 | 33 | 33 |
| Leczna | 26 | 10 | 3 | 13 | 22 | 38 | 33 |
| Odra | 26 | 8 | 4 | 14 | 27 | 40 | 28 |
| Katowice | 26 | 6 | 8 | 12 | 20 | 42 | 26 |
| Polonia | 26 | 6 | 7 | 13 | 25 | 40 | 25 |
| Polkowice+ | 26 | 6 | 5 | 15 | 17 | 37 | 23 |
| Lukullus* | 26 | 5 | 7 | 14 | 21 | 42 | 22 |
| Widzew* | 26 | 4 | 7 | 15 | 25 | 52 | 19 |

*Top scorer:* Zurawski (Wisla) 20.
*Cup Final:* Lech 2, 0, Legia 0, 1.

## PORTUGAL

Federacao Portuguesa De Futebol, Praca De Alegria N.25, Apartado 21.100, P-1127, Lisboa 1250-004.
*Founded:* 1914; *Number of Clubs:* 204; *Number of Players:* 79,235; *National Colours:* Red shirts, green shorts, red stockings.
*Telephone:* 00351-21/325 2700; *Fax:* 00351-21/325 2780.

**International matches 2003**
Italy (a) 0-1, Brazil (h) 2-1, Macedonia (h) 1-0, Holland (a) 1-1, Paraguay (h) 0-0, Bolivia (h) 4-0, Kazakhstan (h) 1-0, Spain (h) 0-3, Norway (a) 1-0, Albania (h) 5-3, Greece (h) 1-1, Kuwait (h) 8-0.

**League Championship wins (1935–2004)**
Benfica 30; FC Porto 20; Sporting Lisbon 18; Belenenses 1; Boavista 1.

**Cup wins (1939–2004)**
Benfica 24; Sporting Lisbon 13; FC Porto 12; Boavista 5; Belenenses 3; Vitoria Setubal 2; Academica Coimbra 1; Leixoes Porto 1; Sporting Braga 1; Amadora 1; Beira Mar 1.

**Final League Table 2003–04**

| | *P* | *W* | *D* | *L* | *F* | *A* | *Pts* |
|---|---|---|---|---|---|---|---|
| Porto | 34 | 25 | 7 | 2 | 63 | 19 | 82 |
| Benfica | 34 | 22 | 8 | 4 | 62 | 28 | 74 |
| Sporting Lisbon | 34 | 23 | 4 | 7 | 60 | 33 | 73 |
| Nacional | 34 | 17 | 5 | 12 | 56 | 35 | 56 |
| Braga | 34 | 15 | 9 | 10 | 36 | 38 | 54 |
| Maritimo | 34 | 12 | 12 | 10 | 35 | 33 | 48 |
| Rio Ave | 34 | 12 | 12 | 10 | 42 | 37 | 48 |
| Boavista | 34 | 12 | 11 | 11 | 32 | 31 | 47 |
| Moreirense | 34 | 12 | 10 | 12 | 33 | 33 | 46 |
| Uniao Leiria | 34 | 11 | 12 | 11 | 43 | 45 | 45 |
| Beira Mar | 34 | 11 | 8 | 15 | 36 | 45 | 41 |
| Gil Vicente | 34 | 10 | 10 | 14 | 43 | 40 | 40 |
| Academica | 34 | 11 | 5 | 18 | 40 | 42 | 38 |
| Guimaraes | 34 | 9 | 10 | 15 | 31 | 40 | 37 |
| Belenenses | 34 | 8 | 11 | 15 | 35 | 54 | 35 |
| Alverca* | 34 | 10 | 5 | 19 | 33 | 49 | 35 |
| Pacos* | 34 | 8 | 4 | 22 | 27 | 53 | 28 |
| Amadora* | 34 | 4 | 5 | 25 | 22 | 74 | 17 |

*Top scorer:* McCarthy (Porto) 20.
*Cup Final:* Benfica 2, Porto 1.

## ROMANIA

Federatia Romana De Fotbal, House of Football, Str. Serg. Serbanica Vasile 12, Bucharest 73412.
*Founded:* 1909; *Number of Clubs:* 414; *Number of Players:* 22,920; *National Colours:* All yellow.
*Telephone:* 0040-21/325 0678; *Fax:* 0040-21/325 0679.

**International matches 2003**
Slovakia (h) 2-1, Russia (a) 2-4, Denmark (h) 2-5, Lithuania (a) 1-0, Bosnia (h) 2-0, Norway (a) 1-1, Ukraine (a) 2-0, Luxembourg (h) 4-0, Denmark (a) 2-2, Japan (h) 1-1, Italy (a) 0-1.

**League Championship wins (1910–2004)**
Steaua Bucharest 21; Dinamo Bucharest 17; Venus Bucharest 8; Chinezul Timisoara 6; UT Arad 6; Ripensia Temesvar 4; Uni Craiova 4; Petrolul Ploesti 3; Rapid Bucharest 3; Olimpia Bucharest 2; Colentina Bucharest 2; Arges Pitesti 2; ICO Oradea 2; Soc RA Bucharest 1; Prahova Ploesti 1; Coltea Brasov 1; Juventus Bucharest 1; Metalochimia Resita 1; Ploesti United 1; Unirea Tricolor 1.

**Cup wins (1934–2004)**
Steaua Bucharest 20; Rapid Bucharest 11; Dinamo Bucharest 11; Uni Craiova 6; UT Arad 2; Ripensia Temesvar 2; Politehnica Timisoara 2; Petrolul Ploesti 2; ICO Oradeo 1; Metalochimia Resita 1; Stinta Cluj 1; CFR Turnu Severin 1; Chimia Ramnicu Vilcea 1; Jiul Petroseni 1; Progresul Bucharest 1; Progresul Oradea 1; Gloria Bistrita 1.

**Final League Table 2003–04**

| | *P* | *W* | *D* | *L* | *F* | *A* | *Pts* |
|---|---|---|---|---|---|---|---|
| Dinamo | 30 | 22 | 4 | 4 | 71 | 30 | 70 |
| Steaua | 30 | 18 | 10 | 2 | 60 | 20 | 64 |
| Rapid | 30 | 16 | 7 | 7 | 51 | 32 | 55 |
| Uni Craiova | 30 | 11 | 11 | 8 | 38 | 34 | 44 |
| Otelul | 30 | 10 | 13 | 7 | 30 | 26 | 43 |
| Apulum | 30 | 11 | 8 | 11 | 32 | 47 | 41 |
| National | 30 | 11 | 6 | 13 | 36 | 39 | 39 |
| Timisoara | 30 | 9 | 12 | 9 | 30 | 40 | 39 |
| Farul | 30 | 9 | 10 | 11 | 39 | 42 | 37 |
| Arges | 30 | 9 | 9 | 12 | 31 | 35 | 36 |
| Brasov | 30 | 10 | 6 | 14 | 40 | 42 | 36 |
| Gloria | 30 | 9 | 8 | 13 | 36 | 48 | 35 |
| Bacau | 30 | 7 | 10 | 13 | 29 | 43 | 31 |
| Ceahlaul* | 30 | 7 | 9 | 14 | 34 | 50 | 30 |
| Petrolul* | 30 | 6 | 9 | 15 | 38 | 55 | 27 |
| Oradea* | 30 | 6 | 6 | 18 | 38 | 50 | 23 |

*Top scorer:* Danciulescu (Dinamo) 21.
*Cup Final:* Dinamo 2, Otelul 0.

## RUSSIA

Football Union of Russia; Luzhnetskaya Naberezyhnaja 8, Moscow 119 992.
*Founded:* 1912; *Number of Clubs:* 43,700; *Number of Players:* 785,000; *National Colours:* All white.
*Telephone:* 007-095/201 1637; *Fax:* 007-502/220 2037.

**International matches 2003**
Cyprus (a) 1-0, Romania (h) 4-2, Albania (a) 1-3, Georgia (a) 0-1, Switzerland (a) 2-2, Israel (h) 1-2, Eire (a) 1-1, Switzerland (h) 4-1, Georgia (h) 3-1, Wales (h) 0-0, Wales (a) 1-0.

**League Championship wins (1945–2003)**
Spartak Moscow 20; Dynamo Kiev 13; Dynamo Moscow 11; CSKA Moscow 8; Torpedo Moscow 3; Dynamo Tbilisi 2; Dnepr Dnepropetrovsk 2; Saria Voroshilovgrad 1; Ararat Erevan 1; Dynamo Minsk 1; Zenit Leningrad 1; Spartak Vladikavkaz 1; Lokomotiv Moscow 1.

**Cup wins (1936–2004)**
Spartak Moscow 13; Dynamo Kiev 10; Torpedo Moscow 7; Dynamo Moscow 7; Lokomotiv Moscow 6; CSKA

Moscow 6; Shakhtjor Donetsk 4; Dynamo Tbilisi 2; Ararat Erevan 2; Zenit Leningrad 2; Karpaty Lvov 1; SKA Rostov 1; Metallist Kharkov 1; Dnepr 1; Terek 1.

**Final League Table 2003**

| | P | W | D | L | F | A | Pts |
|---|---|---|---|---|---|---|---|
| CSKA Moscow | 30 | 17 | 8 | 5 | 56 | 32 | 59 |
| Zenit | 30 | 16 | 8 | 6 | 48 | 32 | 56 |
| Rubin | 30 | 15 | 8 | 7 | 44 | 29 | 53 |
| Lokomotiv Moscow | 30 | 15 | 7 | 8 | 54 | 33 | 52 |
| Shinnik | 30 | 12 | 11 | 7 | 43 | 34 | 47 |
| Dynamo Moscow | 30 | 12 | 10 | 8 | 42 | 29 | 46 |
| Saturn | 30 | 12 | 9 | 9 | 40 | 37 | 45 |
| Torpedo Moscow | 30 | 11 | 10 | 9 | 42 | 38 | 43 |
| Krylia Sovekov | 30 | 11 | 9 | 10 | 38 | 33 | 42 |
| Spartak Moscow | 30 | 10 | 6 | 14 | 38 | 48 | 36 |
| Rostov | 30 | 8 | 10 | 12 | 30 | 42 | 34 |
| Volgograd | 30 | 9 | 5 | 16 | 33 | 44 | 32 |
| Spartak Alania | 30 | 9 | 4 | 17 | 23 | 43 | 31 |
| Torpedo Metallurg | 30 | 8 | 5 | 17 | 25 | 39 | 29 |
| Uralan* | 30 | 6 | 10 | 14 | 23 | 47 | 28 |
| Chernomorets* | 30 | 6 | 6 | 18 | 30 | 49 | 24 |

*Spartak Alania formerly Vladikavkaz.*
*Torpedo Metallurg formerly Torpedo ZIL.*
*Top scorer:* Loskov (Lokomotiv Moscow) 14.
*Cup Final:* Terek 1, Krylia Sovekov 0.

## SAN MARINO

Federazione Sammarinese Giuoco Calcio, Viale Campo dei Giudei, 14; Rep. San Marino 47890.
*Founded:* 1931; *Number of Clubs:* 17; *Number of Players:* 1,033; *National Colours:* All light blue.
*Telephone:* 00378-054/999 0515; *Fax:* 00378-054/999 2348.

**International matches 2003**
Poland (a) 0-5, Latvia (a) 0-3, Sweden (h) 0-6, Hungary (h) 0-5, Liechtenstein (a) 2-2, Sweden (a) 0-5.

**League Championship wins (1986–2004)**
Tre Fiori 4; Faetano 3; Folgore 3; Domagnano 3; Fiorita 2; Montevito 1; Libertas 1; Cosmos 1; Pennarossa 1.

**Cup wins (1986–2004)**
Domagnano 7; Libertas 3; Faetano 3; Cosmos 2; Fiorita 1; Tre Penne 1; Murata 1; Pennarossa 1.

**Qualifying League Table 2003–04**

| Group A | P | W | D | L | F | A | Pts |
|---|---|---|---|---|---|---|---|
| Pennarossa | 21 | 14 | 4 | 3 | 41 | 20 | 46 |
| Juvenes/Dogana | 21 | 13 | 5 | 3 | 49 | 18 | 44 |
| Cailungo | 21 | 13 | 1 | 7 | 43 | 22 | 40 |
| Libertas | 21 | 9 | 6 | 6 | 29 | 20 | 33 |
| Tre Penne | 21 | 7 | 2 | 12 | 22 | 35 | 23 |
| San Giovanni | 21 | 5 | 7 | 9 | 23 | 37 | 22 |
| La Fiorita | 21 | 5 | 6 | 10 | 24 | 33 | 21 |
| Folgore/Falciano | 21 | 1 | 4 | 16 | 15 | 58 | 7 |

| Group B | P | W | D | L | F | A | Pts |
|---|---|---|---|---|---|---|---|
| Domagnano | 20 | 12 | 5 | 3 | 39 | 23 | 41 |
| Murata | 20 | 12 | 5 | 3 | 32 | 14 | 41 |
| Virtus | 20 | 11 | 5 | 4 | 48 | 24 | 38 |
| Tre Fiore | 20 | 10 | 5 | 5 | 35 | 20 | 35 |
| Faetano | 20 | 5 | 6 | 9 | 23 | 28 | 21 |
| Cosmos | 20 | 3 | 2 | 15 | 15 | 48 | 11 |
| Montevito | 20 | 1 | 3 | 16 | 16 | 54 | 6 |

*Play-Offs:* Murata 2, Cailungo 1; Juvenes/Dogana 1, Virtus 3; Pennarossa 5, Murata 3; Domagnano 2, Virtus 1; Cailungo 4, Virtus 2; Juvenes/Dogana 1, Murata 3; Pennarossa 1, Domagnano 4; Cailungo 3, Murata 1; Pennarossa 3, Cailungo 0.
*Final:* Domagnano 2, Pennarossa 2.
*Pennarossa won 4-2 on penalties.*
*Top scorer:* Vannucci (Virtus) 15.
*Cup Final:* Pennarossa 3, Domagnano 0.

## SCOTLAND

The Scottish Football Association Ltd, Hampden Park, Glasgow G42 9AY.
*Founded:* 1873; *Number of Clubs:* 6,148; *Number of Players:* 135,474; *National Colours:* Dark blue shirts, white shorts, dark blue stockings.
*Telephone:* 0044-141/616 6000; *Fax:* 0044-141/616 6001.

## SERBIA-MONTENEGRO

Football Association of Serbia and Montenegro, Terazije 35, P.O. Box 263, 11000 Beograd.
*Founded:* 1919; *Number of Clubs:* 6,532; *Number of Players:* 229,024; *National Colours:* Blue shirts, white shorts, red stockings.
*Telephone:* 00381-11/ 323 4253; *Fax:* 00381-11/323 3433.

**International matches 2003**
Azerbaijan (h) 2-2, Bulgaria (h) 1-2, Germany (a) 0-1, England (a) 1-2, Finland (a) 0-3, Azerbaijan (a) 1-2, Wales (h) 1-0, Italy (h) 1-1, Wales (a) 3-2, Poland (a) 3-4.

**League Championship wins (1923–2004)**
Red Star Belgrade 23; Partizan Belgrade 18; Hajduk Split 9; Gradjanski Zagreb 5; BSK Belgrade 5; Dynamo Zagreb 4; Jugoslavija Belgrade 2; Concordia Zagreb 2; FC Sarajevo 2; Vojvodina Novi Sad 2; HASK Zagreb 1; Zeljeznicar 1; Obilic 1.

**Cup wins (1947–2004)**
Red Star Belgrade 20; Hajduk Split 9; Partizan Belgrade 9; Dynamo Zagreb 8; BSK Belgrade 2; OFK Belgrade 2; Rijeka 2; Velez Mostar 2; Vardar Skopje 1; Borac Banjaluka 1; Sartid 1.

**Final League Table 2003–04**

| | P | W | D | L | F | A | Pts |
|---|---|---|---|---|---|---|---|
| Red Star Belgrade | 30 | 23 | 5 | 2 | 59 | 13 | 74 |
| Partizan Belgrade | 30 | 19 | 6 | 5 | 48 | 20 | 63 |
| Zeleznik | 30 | 17 | 7 | 6 | 48 | 20 | 58 |
| OFK Belgrade | 30 | 14 | 9 | 7 | 36 | 31 | 51 |
| Sartid | 30 | 14 | 7 | 9 | 43 | 36 | 49 |
| Obilic | 30 | 14 | 4 | 12 | 42 | 29 | 46 |
| Zemun | 30 | 11 | 8 | 11 | 27 | 29 | 41 |
| Niksic | 30 | 12 | 4 | 14 | 38 | 36 | 40 |
| Vojvodina | 30 | 10 | 10 | 10 | 33 | 33 | 40 |
| Hajduk Kula | 30 | 11 | 5 | 14 | 28 | 29 | 38 |
| Golubovci | 30 | 10 | 6 | 14 | 38 | 41 | 36 |
| Borac | 30 | 8 | 11 | 11 | 30 | 41 | 35 |
| Buducnost* | 30 | 10 | 4 | 16 | 30 | 49 | 34 |
| Napredak* | 30 | 7 | 4 | 19 | 28 | 46 | 25 |
| Radnicki* | 30 | 4 | 12 | 14 | 18 | 47 | 24 |
| Kom* | 30 | 4 | 2 | 24 | 21 | 67 | 14 |

*Top scorer:* Digic (Red Star Belgrade) 19.
*Cup Final:* Red Star Belgrade 1, Buducnost 0.

## SLOVAKIA

Slovak Football Association, Junacka 6, 83280 Bratislava, Slovakia.
*Founded:* 1993; *Number of Clubs:* 2,140; *Number of Players:* 141,000; *National Colours:* All blue and white.
*Telephone:* 00421-2/4924 9151; *Fax:* 00421-2/4924 9595.

**International matches 2003**
Romania (a) 1-2, Cyprus (a) 3-1, Macedonia (a) 2-0, Liechtenstein (h) 4-0, Greece (h) 2-2, Turkey (h) 0-1, England (a) 1-2, Colombia (a) 0-0, Macedonia (h) 1-1, Liechtenstein (a) 2-0, Costa Rica (a) 0-0.

**League Championship wins (1939–44; 1994–2004)**
Slovan Bratislava 8; Zilina 3; Kosice 2; Inter 2; Bystrica 1; OAP Bratislava 1.

**Cup wins (1994–2004)**
Inter 3; Slovan Bratislava 2; Tatran Presov 1; Humenne 1; Spartak Trnava 1; Koba 1; Matador 1; Petrzalka 1.

**Final League Table 2003–04**

| | P | W | D | L | F | A | Pts |
|---|---|---|---|---|---|---|---|
| Zilina | 36 | 17 | 13 | 6 | 62 | 35 | 64 |
| Bystrica | 36 | 17 | 13 | 6 | 58 | 36 | 64 |
| Ruzomberok | 36 | 15 | 10 | 11 | 53 | 47 | 55 |
| Spartak Trnava | 36 | 15 | 8 | 13 | 46 | 46 | 53 |
| Trencin | 36 | 13 | 9 | 14 | 37 | 43 | 48 |
| Dubnica | 36 | 12 | 10 | 14 | 41 | 42 | 46 |
| Inter | 36 | 12 | 9 | 15 | 38 | 44 | 45 |
| Petrzalka | 36 | 10 | 14 | 12 | 43 | 44 | 44 |
| Matador | 36 | 10 | 9 | 17 | 34 | 54 | 39 |
| Slovan Bratislava* | 36 | 6 | 11 | 19 | 37 | 58 | 29 |

*Top scorer:* Stevko (Ruzomberok) 17.
*Cup Final:* Petrzalka 2, Steel Trans 0.

## SLOVENIA

Football Association of Slovenia, Nogometna zveza Slovenije, Cerinova 4, P.P. 3986, 1001 Ljubljana, Slovenia.
*Founded:* 1920; *Number of Clubs:* 375; *Number of Players:* 20,117; *National Colours:* White shirts with green sleeves, white shorts, white stockings.
*Telephone:* 00386-1/530 0400; *Fax:* 00386-1/530 0410.

**International matches 2003**
Switzerland (h) 1-5, Cyprus (h) 4-1, Malta (a) 3-1, Israel (a) 0-0, Hungary (h) 2-1, Israel (h) 3-1, France (h) 0-2, Cyprus (a) 2-2, Croatia (a) 1-1, Croatia (h) 0-1.

**League Championship wins (1992–2004)**
Maribor 7; SCT Olimpija 4; Gorica 2.

**Cup wins (1992–2004)**
Maribor 5; SCT Olimpija 4; Gorica 2; Mura 1; Rudar 1.

**Qualifying League Table 2003–04**

| | *P* | *W* | *D* | *L* | *F* | *A* | *Pts* |
|---|---|---|---|---|---|---|---|
| Gorica | 22 | 12 | 6 | 4 | 46 | 21 | 42 |
| Olimpija | 22 | 12 | 5 | 5 | 42 | 27 | 41 |
| Maribor | 22 | 12 | 5 | 5 | 29 | 23 | 41 |
| Primorje | 22 | 10 | 8 | 4 | 49 | 25 | 38 |
| Koper | 22 | 10 | 7 | 5 | 28 | 17 | 37 |
| Mura | 22 | 10 | 4 | 8 | 41 | 41 | 34 |
| Publikum | 22 | 8 | 4 | 10 | 43 | 36 | 28 |
| Esotech | 22 | 6 | 8 | 8 | 27 | 35 | 26 |
| Domzale | 22 | 7 | 3 | 12 | 26 | 42 | 24 |
| Ljubljana | 22 | 5 | 4 | 13 | 22 | 44 | 19 |
| Dravograd | 22 | 5 | 4 | 13 | 24 | 47 | 19 |
| Drava | 22 | 3 | 6 | 13 | 23 | 42 | 15 |

**Championship Play-Off**

| | *P* | *W* | *D* | *L* | *F* | *A* | *Pts* |
|---|---|---|---|---|---|---|---|
| Gorica | 32 | 15 | 11 | 6 | 55 | 29 | 56 |
| Olimpija | 32 | 16 | 7 | 9 | 55 | 39 | 55 |
| Maribor | 32 | 15 | 9 | 8 | 41 | 34 | 54 |
| Koper | 32 | 13 | 11 | 8 | 41 | 31 | 50 |
| Mura | 32 | 14 | 7 | 11 | 53 | 54 | 49 |
| Primorjè | 32 | 12 | 12 | 8 | 59 | 36 | 48 |

**Relegation Play-Off**

| | *P* | *W* | *D* | *L* | *F* | *A* | *Pts* |
|---|---|---|---|---|---|---|---|
| Domzale | 32 | 11 | 8 | 13 | 47 | 53 | 41 |
| Esotech | 32 | 10 | 10 | 12 | 43 | 48 | 40 |
| Publikum | 32 | 11 | 6 | 15 | 61 | 52 | 39 |
| Ljubljana (-3) | 32 | 12 | 6 | 14 | 38 | 53 | 39 |
| Drava+ | 32 | 7 | 7 | 18 | 34 | 60 | 28 |
| Dravograd* (-1) | 32 | 7 | 4 | 21 | 35 | 73 | 24 |

*Top scorer:* Zezelj (Primorje) 19.
*Cup Final:* Maribor 4, 3, Dravograd 0, 4.

## SPAIN

Real Federacion Espanola De Futbol, Ramon y Cajal, s/n, Apartado Postale 385, Madrid 28230.
*Founded:* 1913; *Number of Clubs:* 10,240; *Number of Players:* 408,135; *National Colours:* Red shirts, blue shorts, blue stockings with red, blue and yellow border.
*Telephone:* 0034-91/495 9800; *Fax:* 0034-91/495 9801.

**International matches 2003**
Germany (h) 3-1, Ukraine (a) 2-2, Armenia (h) 3-0, Ecuador (h) 4-0, Greece (h) 0-1, N Ireland (a) 0-0, Portugal (a) 3-0, Ukraine (h) 2-1, Armenia (a) 4-0, Norway (h) 2-1, Norway (a) 3-0.

**League Championship wins (1929–36; 1940–2004)**
Real Madrid 29; Barcelona 16; Atletico Madrid 9; Athletic Bilbao 8; Valencia 6; Real Sociedad 2; Real Betis 1; Seville 1; La Coruna 1.

**Cup wins (1902–2004)**
Barcelona 24; Athletic Bilbao 23; Real Madrid 17; Atletico Madrid 9; Valencia 6; Real Zaragoza 6; Real Union de Irun 3; Seville 3; Espanyol 3; La Coruna 2; Arenas 1; Ciclista Sebastian 1; Racing de Irun 1; Vizcaya Bilbao 1; Real Betis 1; Real Sociedad 1; Mallorca 1.

**Final League Table 2003–04**

| | *P* | *W* | *D* | *L* | *F* | *A* | *Pts* |
|---|---|---|---|---|---|---|---|
| Valencia | 38 | 23 | 8 | 7 | 71 | 27 | 77 |
| Barcelona | 38 | 21 | 9 | 8 | 63 | 39 | 72 |
| La Coruna | 38 | 21 | 8 | 9 | 60 | 34 | 71 |
| Real Madrid | 38 | 21 | 7 | 10 | 72 | 54 | 70 |
| Athletic Bilbao | 38 | 15 | 11 | 12 | 53 | 49 | 56 |
| Sevilla | 38 | 15 | 10 | 13 | 56 | 45 | 55 |
| Atletico Madrid | 38 | 15 | 10 | 13 | 51 | 53 | 55 |
| Villarreal | 38 | 15 | 9 | 14 | 47 | 49 | 54 |
| Betis | 38 | 13 | 13 | 12 | 46 | 43 | 52 |
| Malaga | 38 | 15 | 6 | 17 | 50 | 55 | 51 |
| Mallorca | 38 | 15 | 6 | 17 | 54 | 66 | 51 |
| Zaragoza | 38 | 13 | 9 | 16 | 46 | 55 | 48 |
| Osasuna | 38 | 11 | 15 | 12 | 38 | 37 | 48 |
| Albacete | 38 | 13 | 8 | 17 | 40 | 48 | 47 |
| Real Sociedad | 38 | 11 | 13 | 14 | 49 | 53 | 46 |
| Espanyol | 38 | 13 | 4 | 21 | 48 | 64 | 43 |
| Santander (-1) | 38 | 11 | 10 | 17 | 48 | 63 | 42 |
| Valladolid* | 38 | 10 | 11 | 17 | 46 | 56 | 41 |
| Celta* | 38 | 9 | 12 | 17 | 48 | 68 | 39 |
| Murcia* | 38 | 5 | 11 | 22 | 29 | 57 | 26 |

*Top scorer:* Ronaldo (Real Madrid) 24.
*Cup Final:* Zaragoza 3, Real Madrid 2.

## SWEDEN

Svenska Fotbollfoerbundet, Box 1216, S-17123 Solna.
*Founded:* 1904; *Number of Clubs:* 3,250; *Number of Players:* 485,000; *National Colours:* Yellow shirts, blue shorts, yellow stockings.
*Telephone:* 0046-8/735 0900; *Fax:* 0046-8/735 0901.

**International matches 2003**
Tunisia (a) 0-1, Qatar (h) 3-2, South Korea (h) 1-1, Thailand (a) 4-1, North Korea (h) 4-0, Hungary (a) 2-1, Croatia (h) 1-2, San Marino (a) 6-0, Poland (h) 3-0, Greece (h) 1-2, San Marino (h) 5-0, Poland (a) 2-0, Latvia (h) 0-1, Egypt (a) 0-1.

**League Championship wins (1896–2003)**
IFK Gothenburg 18; Oergryte IS Gothenburg 14; Malmo FF 14; IFK Norrköping 11; AIK Stockholm 10; Djurgaarden 10; GAIS Gothenburg 6; IF Helsingborg 6; Boras IF Elfsborg 4; Oster Vaxjo 4; Halmstad 4; Atvidaberg 2; IFK Ekilstune 1; IF Gavic Brynas 1; IF Gothenburg 1; Fassbergs 1; Norrköping IK Sleipner 1; Hammarby 1.

**Cup wins (1941–2003)**
Malmo FF 13; AIK Stockholm 8; IFK Norrköping 6; IFK Gothenburg 4; Atvidaberg 2; Kalmar 2; Helsingborg 2; Djurgaarden 2; GAIS Gothenburg 1; IF Raa 1; Landskrona 1; Oster Vaxjo 1; Degerfors 1; Halmstad 1; Orgryte 1; Elfsborg 1.

**Final League Table 2003**

| | *P* | *W* | *D* | *L* | *F* | *A* | *Pts* |
|---|---|---|---|---|---|---|---|
| Djurgaarden | 26 | 19 | 1 | 6 | 62 | 26 | 58 |
| Hammarby | 26 | 15 | 6 | 5 | 50 | 30 | 51 |
| Malmo | 26 | 14 | 6 | 6 | 50 | 23 | 48 |
| Orgryte | 26 | 14 | 3 | 9 | 42 | 40 | 45 |
| AIK | 26 | 11 | 6 | 9 | 39 | 34 | 39 |
| Helsingborg | 26 | 11 | 5 | 10 | 35 | 36 | 38 |
| IFK Gothenburg | 26 | 10 | 7 | 9 | 37 | 28 | 37 |
| Orebro | 26 | 10 | 7 | 9 | 29 | 33 | 37 |
| Halmstad | 26 | 11 | 3 | 12 | 41 | 37 | 36 |
| Elfsborg | 26 | 9 | 7 | 10 | 29 | 34 | 34 |
| Landskrona | 26 | 8 | 8 | 10 | 26 | 39 | 32 |
| Sundsvall+ | 26 | 3 | 10 | 13 | 25 | 43 | 19 |
| Osters* | 26 | 3 | 8 | 15 | 31 | 56 | 17 |
| Enkopings* | 26 | 3 | 5 | 18 | 22 | 59 | 14 |

*Top scorer:* Skoog (Malmo) 22.
*Cup Final:* Elfsborg 2, Assyriska 0.

## SWITZERLAND

Schweizerisher Fussballverband, Postfach 3000, Berne 15.
*Founded:* 1895; *Number of Clubs:* 1,473; *Number of Players:* 185,286; *National Colours:* Red shirts, white shorts, red stockings.
*Telephone:* 0041-31/950 8111; *Fax:* 0041-31/950 8181.

**International matches 2003**
Slovenia (a) 5-1, Georgia (a) 0-0, Italy (h) 1-2, Russia (h) 2-2, Albania (h) 3-2, France (h) 0-2, Russia (a) 1-4, Eire (h) 2-0.

**League Championship wins (1898–2004)**
Grasshoppers 26; Servette 17; Young Boys Berne 11; FC Basle 10; FC Zurich 9; Lausanne 7; La Chaux-de-Fonds 3; FC Lugano 3; Winterthur 3; FX Aarau 3; Neuchatel Xamax 3; Sion 2; St Gallen 2; FC Anglo-American 1; FC Brühl 1; Cantonal-Neuchatel 1; Biel 1; Bellinzona 1; FC Etoile La Chaux-de-Fonds 1; Lucerne 1.

**Cup wins (1926–2004)**
Grasshoppers 18; FC Sion 9; Lausanne 9; Servette 7; FC Basle 7; La Chaux-de-Fonds 6; Young Boys Berne 6; FC Zurich 6; Lucerne 2; FC Lugano 2; FC Granges 1; St Gallen 1; Urania Geneva 1; Young Fellows Zurich 1; Aarau 1; Wil 1.

**Final League Table 2003–04**

| | *P* | *W* | *D* | *L* | *F* | *A* | *Pts* |
|---|---|---|---|---|---|---|---|
| Basle | 36 | 26 | 7 | 3 | 86 | 32 | 85 |
| Young Boys | 36 | 22 | 6 | 8 | 75 | 48 | 72 |
| Servette | 36 | 15 | 7 | 14 | 61 | 62 | 52 |
| Zurich | 36 | 14 | 8 | 14 | 58 | 52 | 50 |
| St Gallen | 36 | 14 | 8 | 14 | 54 | 57 | 50 |
| Thun | 36 | 13 | 10 | 13 | 51 | 57 | 49 |
| Grasshoppers | 36 | 12 | 5 | 19 | 42 | 74 | 41 |
| Aarau | 36 | 9 | 11 | 16 | 57 | 69 | 38 |
| Neuchatel Xamax+ | 36 | 10 | 6 | 20 | 46 | 63 | 36 |
| Wil* | 36 | 7 | 8 | 21 | 37 | 73 | 29 |

*Top scorer:* Chapuisat (Young Boys) 23.
*Cup Final:* Wil 3, Grasshoppers 2.

### TURKEY

Turkiye Futbol Federasyonu, Konaklar Mah. Ihlamurlu Sok. 9, 4 Levent, Istanbul 80620.
*Founded:* 1923; *Number of Clubs:* 230; *Number of Players:* 64,521; *National Colours:* All white.
*Telephone:* 0090-212/282 7020; *Fax:* 0090-212/282 7015.

**International matches 2003**
Ukraine (h) 0-0, England (a) 0-2, Czech Republic (a) 0-4, Slovakia (a) 1-0, Macedonia (h) 3-2, USA (n) 2-1, Cameroon (n) 0-1, Brazil (n) 2-2, France (n) 2-3, Colombia (n) 2-1, Moldova (h) 2-0, Liechtenstein (a) 3-0, Eire (a) 2-2, England (h) 0-0, Latvia (a) 0-1, Latvia (h) 2-2.

**League Championship wins (1960–2004)**
Galatasaray 15; Fenerbahce 15; Besiktas 11; Trabzonspor 6.

**Cup wins (1963–2004)**
Galatasaray 13; Trabzonspor 7; Besiktas 6; Fenerbahce 4; Goztepe Izmir 2; Altay Izmir 2; Ankaragucu 2; Genclerbirligi 2; Kocaeli 2; Eskisehirspor 1; Bursapor 1; Sakaryaspor 1.

**Final League Table 2003–04**

| | *P* | *W* | *D* | *L* | *F* | *A* | *Pts* |
|---|---|---|---|---|---|---|---|
| Fenerbahce | 34 | 23 | 7 | 4 | 82 | 41 | 76 |
| Trabzonspor | 34 | 22 | 6 | 6 | 60 | 38 | 72 |
| Besiktas | 34 | 18 | 8 | 8 | 65 | 45 | 62 |
| Gaziantep | 34 | 18 | 3 | 13 | 52 | 51 | 57 |
| Denizli | 34 | 17 | 4 | 13 | 52 | 43 | 55 |
| Galatasaray | 34 | 15 | 9 | 10 | 56 | 47 | 54 |
| Samsun | 34 | 13 | 7 | 14 | 46 | 47 | 46 |
| Malatya | 34 | 11 | 12 | 11 | 51 | 40 | 45 |
| Ankaragucu | 34 | 13 | 6 | 15 | 48 | 53 | 45 |
| Genclerbirligi | 34 | 12 | 8 | 14 | 56 | 52 | 44 |
| Konya | 34 | 10 | 14 | 10 | 53 | 54 | 44 |
| Diyarbakir | 34 | 12 | 7 | 15 | 44 | 54 | 43 |
| Akcaabat | 34 | 11 | 9 | 14 | 45 | 53 | 42 |
| Rize | 34 | 13 | 3 | 18 | 37 | 53 | 42 |
| Istanbul | 34 | 11 | 8 | 15 | 46 | 45 | 41 |
| Bursa* | 34 | 10 | 10 | 14 | 40 | 40 | 40 |
| Adana* | 34 | 6 | 4 | 24 | 38 | 73 | 22 |
| Elazig* | 34 | 5 | 7 | 22 | 37 | 79 | 22 |

*Top scorer:* Van Hooijdonk (Fenerbahce), Zafer (Konya) 24.
*Cup Final:* Trabzonspor 4, Genclerbirligi 0.

### UKRAINE

Football Federation of Ukraine, Laboratorna Str. 1, P.O. Box 293, Kiev 03150.
*Founded:* 1991; *Number of Clubs:* 1500; *Number of Players:* 759,500; *National Colours:* All yellow and blue.
*Telephone:* 00380-44/252 8498; *Fax:* 00380-44/252 8513.

**International matches 2003**
Turkey (a) 0-0, Spain (h) 2-2, Latvia (h) 1-0, Denmark (a) 0-1, Armenia (h) 4-3, Greece (a) 0-1, Romania (h) 0-2, N Ireland (h) 0-0, Spain (a) 1-2, Macedonia (h) 0-0.

**League Championship wins (1992–2004)**
Dynamo Kiev 10; Tavriya Simferopol 1; Shakhtjor Donetsk 1.

**Cup wins (1992–2004)**
Dynamo Kiev 6; Shakhtjor Donetsk 5; Chernomorets 2.

**Final League Table 2003–04**

| | *P* | *W* | *D* | *L* | *F* | *A* | *Pts* |
|---|---|---|---|---|---|---|---|
| Dynamo Kiev | 30 | 23 | 4 | 7 | 68 | 20 | 73 |
| Shakhtjor Donestsk | 30 | 22 | 4 | 4 | 62 | 19 | 70 |
| Dnepr | 30 | 16 | 9 | 5 | 44 | 23 | 56 |
| Metalurg Donetsk | 30 | 14 | 10 | 6 | 51 | 34 | 52 |
| Chernomorets | 30 | 11 | 12 | 7 | 38 | 33 | 45 |
| Borysfen | 30 | 11 | 8 | 11 | 25 | 29 | 41 |
| Obolon | 30 | 11 | 8 | 11 | 34 | 35 | 41 |
| Mariupol | 30 | 10 | 10 | 10 | 34 | 36 | 40 |
| Arsenal | 30 | 10 | 7 | 13 | 38 | 44 | 37 |
| Krivbas | 30 | 10 | 6 | 14 | 26 | 41 | 36 |
| Tavriya | 30 | 7 | 11 | 12 | 22 | 28 | 32 |
| Metalurg Zapor | 30 | 8 | 8 | 14 | 26 | 40 | 32 |
| Volyn | 30 | 7 | 8 | 15 | 25 | 44 | 29 |
| Vorskla | 30 | 6 | 9 | 15 | 26 | 49 | 27 |
| Karpaty* | 30 | 6 | 8 | 16 | 22 | 39 | 26 |
| Zirka* (-3) | 30 | 3 | 8 | 19 | 16 | 43 | 14 |

Metalurg Zapor relegated in 2003 but reinstated when Olexandriya became defunct.
*Top scorer:* Demetradze (Metalurg Donetsk) 17.
*Cup Final:* Shakhtjor Donetsk 2, Dnepr 0.

### WALES

The Football Association of Wales Limited, Plymouth Chambers, 3 Westgate Street, Cardiff, CF10 1DP.
*Founded:* 1876; *Number of Clubs:* 2,326; *Number of Players:* 53,926; *National Colours:* All red.
*Telephone:* 0044-29/2037 2325; *Fax:* 0044-29/2034 3961.

## SOUTH AMERICA

### ARGENTINA

Asociacion Del Futbol Argentina, Viamonte 1366/76, 1053 Buenos Aires.
*Founded:* 1893; *Number of Clubs:* 3,035; *Number of Players:* 306,365; *National Colours:* Light blue and white vertical striped shirts, dark blue shorts, white stockings.
*Telephone:* 0054-11/4372 7900; *Fax:* 0054-11/4375 4410.
*International matches 2003*
Honduras (a) 3-1, Mexico (a) 1-0, USA (a) 1-0, Holland (a) 0-1, Libya (a) 3-1, Japan (a) 4-1, South Korea (a) 1-0, Uruguay (h) 2-2, Uruguay (h) 3-2, Chile (h) 2-2, Venezuela (a) 3-0, Bolivia (h) 3-0, Colombia (a) 1-1.

### BOLIVIA

Federacion Boliviana De Futbol, Av. Libertador Bolivar No. 1168, Casilla de Correo 484, Cochabamba, Bolivia.
*Founded:* 1925; *Number of Clubs:* 305; *Number of Players:* 15,290; *National Colours:* Green shirts, white shorts, green stockings.
*Telephone:* 00591-4/424 4982; *Fax:* 00591-4/428 2132.
*International matches 2003*
Mexico (a) 0-2, Portugal (a) 0-4, Panama (h) 3-0, Uruguay (a) 0-5, Colombia (h) 4-0, Honduras (h) 1-0, Argentina (a) 0-3, Venezuela (a) 1-2.

### BRAZIL

Confederacao Brasileira De Futebol, Rua Victor Civita 66, Bloco 1-Edificio 5-5 Andar, Barra da Tijuca, Rio De Janeiro 22775-040.
*Founded:* 1914; *Number of Clubs:* 12,987; *Number of Players:* 551,358; *National Colours:* Yellow shirts with green collar and cuffs, blue shorts, white stockings with green and yellow border.
*Telephone:* 0055-21/3870 3610; *Fax:* 0055-21/3870 3612.

*International matches 2003*
China (a) 0-0, Portugal (a) 1-2, Mexico (a) 0-0, Algeria (a) 3-0, Cameroon (n) 0-1, USA (n) 1-0, Turkey (n) 2-2, Mexico (n) 0-1, Honduras (n) 2-1, Colombia (n) 2-0, USA (n) 2-1, Mexico (n) 0-1, Colombia (a) 2-1, Ecuador (h) 1-0, Peru (a) 1-1, Uruguay (h) 3-3, Jamaica (h) 1-0.

### CHILE

Federacion De Futbol De Chile, Avda. Quillin No. 5635, Casilla postal 3733, Correo Central, Santiago de Chile.
*Founded:* 1895; *Number of Clubs:* 4,598; *Number of Players:* 609,724; *National Colours:* Red shirts with blue collar and cuffs, blue shorts, white stockings.
*Telephone:* 0056-2/284 9000; *Fax:* 0056-2/284 3510.
*International matches 2003*
Peru (h) 2-0, Peru (a) 0-3, Costa Rica (h) 1-0, Costa Rica (a) 0-1, Honduras (a) 2-1, China (a) 0-0, Argentina (a) 2-2, Peru (h) 2-1, Uruguay (a) 1-2, Paraguay (h) 0-1.

### COLOMBIA

Federacion Colombiana De Futbol, Avenida 32, No. 16–22 piso 4o. Apartado Aereo 17602, Santafe de Bogota.
*Founded:* 1924; *Number of Clubs:* 3,685; *Number of Players:* 188,050; *National Colours:* Yellow shirts, blue shorts, red stockings.
*Telephone:* 0057-1/288 9740; *Fax:* 0057-1/288 9559.
*International matches 2003*
Mexico (a) 0-0, South Korea (a) 0-0, Honduras (h) 0-0, Ecuador (h) 0-0, France (n) 0-1, New Zealand (n) 3-1, Japan (n) 1-0, Cameroon (n) 0-1, Turkey (n) 1-2, Jamaica (n) 1-0, Guatemala (n) 1-1, Brazil (n) 0-2, Slovakia (h) 0-0, Brazil (h) 1-2, Bolivia (a) 0-4, Venezuela (h) 0-1, Argentina (h) 1-1.

### ECUADOR

Federacion Ecuatoriana del Futbol, km 4 1/2 via a la Costa (Avda. del Bombero), PO Box 09-01-7447 Guayaquil.
*Founded:* 1925; *Number of Clubs:* 170; *Number of Players:* 15,700; *National Colours:* Yellow shirts, blue shorts, red stockings.
*Telephone:* 00593-4/235 2372; *Fax:* 00593-4/235 2116.
*International matches 2003*
Estonia (h) 1-0, Estonia (h) 2-1, Spain (a) 0-4, Colombia (a) 0-0, Peru (h) 2-2, Guatemala (h) 2-0, Venezuela (h) 2-0, Brazil (a) 0-1, Paraguay (a) 1-2, Peru (h) 0-0.

### PARAGUAY

Asociacion Paraguaya de Futbol, Estadio De Los Defensores del Chaco, Calles Mayor Martinez 1393, Asuncion.
*Founded:* 1906; *Number of Clubs:* 1,500; *Number of Players:* 140,000; *National Colours:* Red and white shirts, blue shorts, blue stockings.
*Telephone:* 00595-21/480 120; *Fax:* 00595-21/480 124.
*International matches 2003*
Mexico (a) 1-1, Costa Rica (a) 1-2, Honduras (a) 1-1, Peru (a) 1-0, Portugal (a) 0-0, Japan (a) 0-0, El Salvador (h) 1-0, USA (a) 0-2, Jamaica (a) 0-2, Panama (a) 2-1, Peru (a) 1-4, Uruguay (h) 4-1, Ecuador (h) 2-1, Chile (a) 1-0.

### PERU

Federacion Peruana De Futbol, Av. Aviacion 2085, San Luis, Lima 30.
*Founded:* 1922; *Number of Clubs:* 10,000; *Number of Players:* 325,650; *National Colours:* White shirts with red stripe, white shorts with red lines, white stockings with red line.
*Telephone:* 0051-1/225 8236; *Fax:* 0051-1/225 8240.
*International matches 2003*
Haiti (h) 5-1, Chile (a) 0-2, Chile (h) 3-0, Paraguay (h) 0-1, Ecuador (a) 2-2, Venezuela (h) 1-0, Guatemala (h) 2-1, Uruguay (h) 3-4, Uruguay (a) 0-1, Mexico (a) 3-1, Guatemala (h) 0-0, Paraguay (h) 4-1, Chile (a) 0-2, Brazil (h) 1-1, Ecuador (a) 0-0.

### URUGUAY

Asociacion Uruguaya De Futbol, Guayabo 1531, 11200 Montevideo.
*Founded:* 1900; *Number of Clubs:* 1,091; *Number of Players:* 134,310; *National Colours:* Sky blue shirts with white collar/cuffs, black shorts and stockings with sky blue borders.
*Telephone:* 0059-82/400 4814; *Fax:* 0059-82/409 0550.
*International matches 2003*
Iran (a) 1-1, Japan (a) 2-2, South Korea (a) 2-0, Argentina (a) 2-2, Peru (a) 4-3, Peru (h) 1-0, Argentina (a) 2-3, Bolivia (h) 5-0, Paraguay (a) 1-4, Chile (h) 2-1, Brazil (a) 3-3, Mexico (a) 2-0.

### VENEZUELA

Federacion Venezolana De Futbol, Avda. Santos Erminy Ira, Calle las Delicias Torre Mega II, P.H. Sabana Grande, Caracas 1050.
*Founded:* 1926; *Number of Clubs:* 1,753; *Number of Players:* 63,175; *National Colours:* Burgundy shirts, white shorts and stockings.
*Telephone:* 0058-212/762 4472; *Fax:* 0058-212/762 0596.
*International matches 2003*
USA (a) 0-2, Jamaica (h) 2-0, Trinidad & Tobago (h) 3-0, Honduras (h) 2-1, Peru (a) 0-1, Trinidad & Tobago (a) 2-2, Nigeria (a) 0-1, Haiti (h) 3-2, Ecuador (a) 0-2, Argentina (h) 0-3, Colombia (a) 1-0, Bolivia (h) 2-1.

## ASIA

### AFGHANISTAN

Afghanistan Football Federation, PO Box 5099, Kabul.
*Founded:* 1933; *Number of Clubs*: 30; *Number of Players*: 3,300; *National Colours*: All white with red lines.
*Telephone:* 0093-20/210 2417; *Fax:* 0093-20/210 2417

### BAHRAIN

Bahrain Football Association, P.O. Box 5464, Manama.
*Founded:* 1957; *Number of Clubs:* 25; *Number of Players:* 2,030; *National Colours:* All red.
*Telephone:* 00973/689 569; *Fax:* 00973/781 188.

### BANGLADESH

Bangladesh Football Federation, Bangabandhu National Stadium-1, Dhaka 1000.
*Founded:* 1972; *Number of Clubs:* 1,265; *Number of Players:* 30,385; *National Colours:* Orange shirts, white shorts, green stockings.
*Telephone:* 00880-2/955 6072; *Fax:* 00880-2/956 3419.

### BHUTAN

Bhutan Football Federation, P.O. Box 365, Thimphu.
*National Colours:* All yellow and red.
*Telephone:* 00975-2/322 350; *Fax:* 00975-2/321 131.

### BRUNEI DARUSSALAM

The Football Association of Brunei Darussalam, P.O. Box 2010, 1920 Bandar Seri Begawan BS 8674.
*Founded:* 1959; *Number of Clubs:* 22; *Number of Players:* 830; *National Colours:* Yellow shirts, black shorts, black and white stockings.
*Telephone:* 00673-2/382 761; *Fax:* 00673-2/382 760.

### CAMBODIA

Cambodian Football Federation, Chaeng Maeng Village, Rd. Kab Srov, Sangkat Samrong Krom, Khan Dangkor, Phnom-Penh .
*Founded:* 1933; *Number of Clubs:* 30; *Number of Players:* 650; *National Colours:* All blue.
*Telephone:* 00855-23/364 889; *Fax:* 00855-23/220 780.

### CHINA PR

Football Association of The People's Republic of China, 9 Tiyuguan Road, Beijing 100763.
*Founded:* 1924; *Number of Clubs:* 1,045; *Number of Players:* 2,250,000; *National Colours:* All white.
*Telephone:* 0086-10/6711 7019; *Fax:* 0086-10/6714 2533.

### CHINA TAIPEI

Chinese Taipei Football Association, 2F No. Yu Men St., Taipei, Taiwan 104.
*Founded:* 1936; *Number of Players:* 17,000; *National Colours:* Blue shirts and shorts, white stockings.
*Telephone:* 00886-2/2596 1185; *Fax:* 00886-2/2595 1594.

### GUAM

Guam Football Association, P.O.Box 5093, Agana, Guam 96932.
*Founded:* 1975; *National Colours:* Blue shirts, white shorts, blue stockings.
*Telephone:* 001-671/477 5423; *Fax:* 001-671/477 5424.

### HONG KONG

The Hong Kong Football Association Ltd, 55 Fat Kwong Street, Homantin, Kowloon, Hong Kong.
*Founded:* 1914; *Number of Clubs:* 69; *Number of Players:* 3,274; *National Colours:* All red.
*Telephone:* 00852/2712 9122; *Fax:* 00852/2760 4303.

### INDIA

All India Football Federation, Nehru Stadium (West Stand), Fatorda Margao-Goa 403 602.
*Founded:* 1937; *Number of Clubs:* 2,000; *Number of Players:* 56,000; *National Colours:* Sky blue shirts, navy blue shorts, sky and navy blue stockings.
*Telephone:* 0091-832/2742 603; *Fax:* 0091-832/2741 172.

### INDONESIA

Football Association of Indonesia, Gelora Bung Karno, Pintu X-XI, Jakarta 10270.
*Founded:* 1930; *Number of Clubs:* 2,880; *Number of Players:* 97,000; *National Colours:* Red shirts, white shorts, red stockings.
*Telephone:* 0062-21/570 4762; *Fax:* 0062-21/573 4386.

### IRAN

IR Iran Football Federation, No. 16-4th deadend, Pakistan Street, PO Box 15316-6967 Shahid Beheshti Avenue, Tehran 15316.
*Founded:* 1920; *Number of Clubs:* 6,326; *Number of Players:* 306,000; *National Colours:* All white.
*Telephone:* 0098-21/873 2754; *Fax:* 0098-21/873 0305.

### IRAQ

Iraqi Football Association, Olympic Committee Building, Palestine Street, PO Box 484, Baghdad.
*Founded:* 1948; *Number of Clubs:* 155; *Number of Players:* 4,400; *National Colours:* All black.
*Telephone:* 00964-1/772 9990; *Fax:* 00964-1/885 4321.

### JAPAN

Japan Football Association, JFA House, 3-10-15, Hongo, Bunkyo-ku, Tokyo 113-0033.
*Founded:* 1921; *Number of Clubs:* 13,047; *Number of Players:* 358,989; *National Colours:* Blue shirts, white shorts, blue stockings.
*Telephone:* 0081-3/3830 2004; *Fax:* 0081-3/3830 2005.

### JORDAN

Jordan Football Association, P.O. Box 962024 Al Hussein Sports City, 11196 Amman.
*Founded:* 1949; *Number of Clubs:* 98; *Number of Players:* 4,305; *National Colours:* All white and red.
*Telephone:* 00962-6/565 7662; *Fax:* 00962-6/565 7660.

### KOREA, NORTH

Football Association of The Democratic People's Rep. of Korea, Kumsong-dong, Kwangbok Street, Mangyongdae Distr, PO Box 56, Pyongyang FNJ-PRK.
*Founded:* 1945; *Number of Clubs:* 90; *Number of Players:* 3,420; *National Colours:* All white.
*Telephone:* 00850-2/18 222; *Fax:* 00850-2/381 4403.

### KOREA, SOUTH

Korea Football Association, 1-131 Sinmunno, 2-ga, Jongno-Gu, Seoul 110-062.
*Founded:* 1928; *Number of Clubs:* 476; *Number of Players:* 2,047; *National Colours:* Red shirts, blue shorts, red stockings.
*Telephone:* 0082-2/733 6764; *Fax:* 0082-2/735 2755.

### KUWAIT

Kuwait Football Association, P.O. Box 2029, Udiliya, Block 4 Al-Ittihad Street, Safat 13021.
*Founded:* 1952; *Number of Clubs:* 14 (senior); *Number of Players:* 1,526; *National Colours:* All blue.
*Telephone:* 00965/255 5851; *Fax:* 00965/254 9955.

### KYRGYZSTAN

Football Federation of Kyrgyz Republic, PO Box 1484, Kurenkeeva Street 195, Bishkek 720040, Kyrgyzstan.
*Founded:* 1992; *Number of Players:* 20,000; *National Colours:* Red shirts, white shorts, red stockings.
*Telephone:* 00996-312/670 573; *Fax:* 00996-312/670 573.

### LAOS

Federation Lao de Football, National Stadium, Kounboulo Street, PO Box 3777, Vientiane 856-21, Laos.
*Founded:* 1951; *Number of Clubs:* 76; *Number of Players:* 2,060; *National Colours:* All red.
*Telephone:* 00856-21/251 593; *Fax:* 00856-21/213 460.

### LEBANON

Federation Libanaise De Football-Association, P.O. Box 4732, Verdun Street, Bristol, Radwan Centre Building, Beirut.
*Founded:* 1933; *Number of Clubs:* 105; *Number of Players:* 8,125; *National Colours:* Red shirts, white shorts, red stockings.
*Telephone:* 00961-1/745 745; *Fax:* 00961-1/349 529.

### MACAO

Associacao De Futebol De Macau (AFM), Ave. da Amizade 405, Seng Vo Kok, 13 Andar "A", Macau.
*Founded:* 1939; *Number of Clubs:* 52; *Number of Players:* 800; *National Colours:* All green.
*Telephone:* 00853/781 883; *Fax:* 00853/782 383.

### MALAYSIA

Football Association of Malaysia, 3rd Floor, Wisma Fam, Jalan, SSA/9, Kelana Jaya Selangor Darul Ehsan 47301.
*Founded:* 1933; *Number of Clubs:* 450; *Number of Players:* 11,250; *National Colours:* All yellow and black.
*Telephone:* 0060-3/7876 3766; *Fax:* 0060-3/7875 7984.

### MALDIVES REPUBLIC

Football Association of Maldives, National Stadium G. Banafsaa Magu 20-04, Male.
*Founded:* 1982; *Number of Clubs: Number of Players: National Colours:* Red shirts, Green shorts, white stockings.
*Telephone:* 00960/317 006; *Fax:* 00960/317 005.

### MONGOLIA

Mongolia Football Federation, PO Box 259 Ulaan-Baatar 210646.
*National Colours:* White shirts, red shorts, white stockings.
*Telephone:* 00976-11/312 145; *Fax:* 00976-11/312 145.

### MYANMAR

Myanmar Football Federation, Youth Training Centre, Thingankyun Township, Yangon.
*Founded:* 1947; *Number of Clubs:* 600; *Number of Players:* 21,000; *National Colours:* Red shirts, white shorts, red stockings.
*Telephone:* 00951/577 366; *Fax:* 00951/570 000.

### NEPAL

All-Nepal Football Association, AMFA House, Ward No. 4, Bishalnagar, PO Box 12582, Kathmandu.
*Founded:* 1951; *Number of Clubs:* 85; *Number of Players:* 2,550; *National Colours:* All red.
*Telephone:* 00977-1/5539 059; *Fax:* 00977-1/442 4314.

### OMAN

Oman Football Association, P.O. Box 3462, Ruwi Postal Code 112.
*Founded:* 1978; *Number of Clubs:* 47; *Number of Players:* 2,340; *National Colours:* All white.
*Telephone:* 00968/787 635; *Fax:* 00968/787 632.

### PAKISTAN

Pakistan Football Federation, 6 National Hockey Stadium, Feroze Pure Road, Lahore, Pakistan.
*Founded:* 1948; *Number of Clubs:* 882; *Number of Players:* 21,000; *National Colours:* All green and white.
*Telephone:* 0092-42/923 0821; *Fax:* 0092-42/923 0823.

### PALESTINE

Palestinian Football Federation, Al-Yarmouk, Gaza.
*National Colours:* White shirts, black shorts, white stockings.
*Telephone:* 00972-8/283 4339; *Fax:* 00972-8/282 5208.

### PHILIPPINES

Philippine Football Federation, Room 405, Building V, Philsports Complex, Meralco Avenue, Pasig City, Metro Manila.
*Founded:* 1907; *Number of Clubs:* 650; *Number of Players:* 45,000; *National Colours:* All blue.
*Telephone:* 0063-2/687 1594; *Fax:* 0063-2/687 1598.

### QATAR

Qatar Football Association, 7th Floor, QNOC Building, Cornich, P.O. Box 5333, Doha.
*Founded:* 1960; *Number of Clubs:* 8 (senior); *Number of Players:* 1,380; *National Colours:* All white.
*Telephone:* 00974/494 4411; *Fax:* 00974/494 4414.

### SAUDI ARABIA

Saudi Arabian Football Federation, Al Mather Quarter (Olympic Complex), Prince Faisal Bin Fahad Street, P.O. Box 5844, Riyadh 11432.
*Founded:* 1959; *Number of Clubs:* 120; *Number of Players:* 9,600; *National Colours:* White shirts, green shorts, white stockings.
*Telephone:* 00966-1/482 2240; *Fax:* 00966-1/482 1215.

### SINGAPORE

Football Association of Singapore, Jalan Besar Stadium, 100 Tyrwhitt Road, Singapore 207542.
*Founded:* 1892; *Number of Clubs:* 250; *Number of Players:* 8,000; *National Colours:* All red.
*Telephone:* 0065/6348 3477; *Fax:* 0065/6293 3728.

### SRI LANKA

Football Federation of Sri Lanka, 100/9, Independence Avenue, Colombo 07.
*Founded:* 1939; *Number of Clubs:* 600; *Number of Players:* 18,825; *National Colours:* All white.
*Telephone:* 0094-11/268 6120; *Fax:* 0094-11/2682 471.

### SYRIA

Syrian Football Federation, PO Box 421, Maysaloon Street, Damascus.
*Founded:* 1936; *Number of Clubs:* 102; *Number of Players:* 30,600; *National Colours:* All red.
*Telephone:* 00963-11/333 5866; *Fax:* 00963-11/333 1511.

### TAJIKISTAN

Tajikistan Football Federation, 22 Shotemur Ave., Dushanbe 734 025.
*Founded:* 1991; *Number of Clubs:* 1,804; *Number of Players:* 71,400; *National Colours:* All white.
*Telephone:* 00992-372/210 265; *Fax:* 00992-372/510 157.

### THAILAND

The Football Association of Thailand, Gate 3, Rama I Road, Patumwan, Bangkok 10330.
*Founded:* 1916; *Number of Clubs:* 168; *Number of Players:* 15,000; *National Colours:* All red.
*Telephone:* 0066-2/216 4691; *Fax:* 0066-2/215 4494.

### TURKMENISTAN

Football Association of Turkmenistan, 32 Belinskiy Street, Stadium Kopetdag, Ashgabat 744 001.
*Founded:* 1992; *Number of Players:* 75,000; *National Colours:* Green shirts, white shorts, green stockings.
*Telephone:* 00993-12/362 392; *Fax:* 00993-12/362 355.

### UNITED ARAB EMIRATES

United Arab Emirates Football Association, P.O. Box 916, Abu Dhabi.
*Founded:* 1971; *Number of Clubs:* 23 (senior); *Number of Players:* 1,787; *National Colours:* All white.
*Telephone:* 00971-2/444 5600; *Fax:* 00971-2/444 8558.

### UZBEKISTAN

Uzbekistan Football Federation, Massiv Almazar Furkat Street 15/1, 700003 Tashkent, Uzbekistan.
*Founded:* 1946; *Number of Clubs:* 15,000; *Number of Players:* 217,000; *National Colours:* All white.
*Telephone:* 00998-71/144 1684; *Fax:* 00998-71/144 1683.

### VIETNAM

Vietnam Football Federation, 18 Ly van Phuc, Dong Da District, Hanoi 844.
*Founded:* 1962; *Number of Clubs:* 55 (senior); *Number of Players:* 16,000; *National Colours:* All red.
*Telephone:* 0084-4/845 2480; *Fax:* 0084-4/823 3119.

### YEMEN

Yemen Football Association, Quarter of Sport - Al Jeraf, Behind the Stadium of Ali Mushsen, Al Moreissy in the Sport, Al-Thawra City.
*Founded:* 1962; *Number of Clubs:* 26; *Number of Players:* 1750; *National Colours:* All green.
*Telephone:* 00967-1/310 927. *Fax:* 00967-1/310 921.

## CONCACAF

### ANGUILLA

Anguilla Football Association, P.O. Box 1318, The Valley, Anguilla, BWI.
*National Colours:* Turquoise, white, orange and blue shirts and shorts, turquoise and orange stockings.
*Telephone:* 001-264/497 7323; *Fax:* 001-264/497 7324.

### ANTIGUA & BARBUDA

The Antigua/Barbuda Football Association, Newgate Street, P.O. Box 773, St John's.
*Founded:* 1928; *Number of Clubs:* 60; *Number of Players:* 1,008; *National Colours:* Red, black, yellow and blue shirts, black shorts and stockings.
*Telephone:* 001-268/727 8869; *Fax:* 001-268/562 1681.

### ARUBA

Arubaanse Voetbal Bond, Ferguson Street, Z/N P.O. Box 376, Oranjestad, Aruba.
*Founded:* 1932; *Number of Clubs:* 50; *Number of Players:* 1,000; *National Colours:* Yellow shirts, blue shorts, yellow and blue stockings.
*Telephone:* 00297/829 550; *Fax:* 00297/829 550.

## BAHAMAS

Bahamas Football Association, Plaza on the Way, West Bay Street, P.O. Box N 8434, Nassau, NP.
*Founded:* 1967; *Number of Clubs:* 14; *Number of Players:* 700; *National Colours:* Yellow shirts, black shorts, yellow stockings.
*Telephone:* 001-242/322 5897; *Fax:* 001-242/322 5898.

## BARBADOS

Barbados Football Association, Hildor No. 4, 10th Avenue, P.O. Box 1362, Belleville-St. Michael, Barbados.
*Founded:* 1910; *Number of Clubs:* 92; *Number of Players:* 1,100; *National Colours:* Royal blue and gold shirts, gold shorts, white, gold and blue stockings.
*Telephone::* 001-246/228 1707; *Fax:* 001-246/228 6484.

## BELIZE

Belize National Football Association, 26 Hummingbird Highway, Belmopan, P.O. Box 1742, Belize City.
*Founded:* 1980; *National Colours:* Red, white and black shirts, black shorts, red and black stockings.
*Telephone:* 00501-822/3410; *Fax:* 00501-822/3377.

## BERMUDA

The Bermuda Football Association, 48 Cedar Avenue, Hamilton HM12.
*Founded:* 1928; *Number of Clubs:* 30; *Number of Players:* 1,947; *National Colours:* All blue.
*Telephone:* 001-441/295 2199; *Fax:* 001-441/295 0773.

## BRITISH VIRGIN ISLANDS

British Virgin Islands Football Association, P.O. Box 29, Road Town, Tortola, BVI.
*National Colours:* Gold and green shirts, green shorts, and stockings.
*Telephone:* 001-284/494 5655; *Fax:* 001-284/494 8968.

## US VIRGIN ISLANDS

USVI Soccer Federation Inc., 54, Castle Coakley, PO Box 2346, Kingshill, St Croix 00851.
*National Colours:* Royal blue and gold shirts, royal blue shorts and stockings.
*Telephone:* 001-340/711 9676; *Fax:* 00-340/711 9707.

## CANADA

The Canadian Soccer Association, Place Soccer Canada, 237 Metcalfe Street, Ottawa, ONT K2P 1R2.
*Founded:* 1912; *Number of Clubs:* 1,600; *Number of Players:* 224,290; *National Colours:* All red.
*Telephone:* 001-613/237 7678; *Fax:* 001-613/237 1516.

## CAYMAN ISLANDS

Cayman Islands Football Association, PO Box 178 GT, Truman Bodden Sports Complex, Olympic Way Off Walkers Rd, George Town, Grand Cayman, Cayman Islands WI.
*Founded:* 1966; *Number of Clubs:* 25; *Number of Players:* 875; *National Colours:* Red and white shirts, blue and white shorts, white and red stockings.
*Telephone:* 001-345/949 5775. *Fax:* 001-345/945 7673.

## COSTA RICA

Federacion Costarricense De Futbol, Costado Norte Estatua Leon Cortes, San Jose 670-1000.
*Founded:* 1921; *Number of Clubs:* 431; *Number of Players:* 12,429; *National Colours:* Red shirts, blue shorts, white stockings.
*Telephone:* 00506/222 1544; *Fax:* 00506/255 2674.

## CUBA

Asociacion de Futbol de Cuba, Calle 13 No. 661, Esq. C. Vedado, ZP 4, La Habana.
*Founded:* 1924; *Number of Clubs:* 70; *Number of Players:* 12,900; *National Colours:* All red, white and blue.
*Telephone:* 0053-7/545 024; *Fax:* 0053-7/335 310.

## DOMINICA

Dominica Football Association, 33 Great Marlborough Street, Roseau.
*Founded:* 1970; *Number of Clubs:* 30; *Number of Players:* 500; *National Colours:* Emerald green shirts, black shorts, green stockings.
*Telephone:* 001-767/448 7577; *Fax:* 001-767/448 7587.

## DOMINICAN REPUBLIC

Federacion Dominicana De Futbol, Centro Olimpico Juan Pablo Duarte, Ensanche Miraflores, Apartado De Correos No. 1953, Santo Domingo.
*Founded:* 1953; *Number of Clubs:* 128; *Number of Players:* 10,706; *National Colours:* Navy blue shirts, white shorts, red stockings.
*Telephone:* 001-809/542 6923; *Fax:* 001-809/547 5363.

## EL SALVADOR

Federacion Salvadorena De Futbol, Primera Calle Poniente No. 2025, San Salvador CA1029.
*Founded:* 1935; *Number of Clubs:* 944; *Number of Players:* 21,294; *National Colours:* All blue.
*Telephone:* 00503/263 7525; *Fax:* 00503/260 3129.

## GRENADA

Grenada Football Association, P.O. Box 326, National Stadium, Queens Park, St George's, Grenada, W.I.
*Founded:* 1924; *Number of Clubs:* 15; *Number of Players:* 200; *National Colours:* Green and yellow striped shirts, red shorts, yellow stockings.
*Telephone:* 001-473/440 9903; *Fax:* 001-473/440 9973.

## GUATEMALA

Federacion Nacional de Futbol de Guatemala, 2a Calle 15-57, Zona 15, Boulevard Vista Hermosa, Guatemala City 01009.
*Founded:* 1946; *Number of Clubs:* 1,611; *Number of Players:* 43,516; *National Colours:* Blue shirts, white shorts, blue stockings.
*Telephone:* 00502/279 1746; *Fax:* 00502/379 8345.

## GUYANA

Guyana Football Federation, 159 Rupununi Street, Bel Air Park, P.O. Box 10727, Georgetown.
*Founded:* 1902; *Number of Clubs:* 103; *Number of Players:* 1,665; *National Colours:* Green shirts and shorts, yellow stockings.
*Telephone:* 00592-2/278 758; *Fax:* 00592-2/262 641.

## HAITI

Federation Haitienne De Football, 128 Avenue Christiophe, P.O. Box 2258, Port-Au-Prince.
*Founded:* 1904; *Number of Clubs:* 40; *Number of Players:* 4,000; *National Colours:* Blue shirts, red shorts, blue stockings.
*Telephone:* 00509/244 0115; *Fax:* 00509/244 0117.

## HONDURAS

Federacion Nacional Autonoma De Futbol De Honduras, Colonia Florencia Norte, Ave Roble, Edificio Plaza America, Ave. Roble 1 y 2 Nivel, Tegucigalpa, D.C.
*Founded:* 1951; *Number of Clubs:* 1,050; *Number of Players:* 15,300; *National Colours:* All white.
*Telephone:* 00504/232 0572; *Fax:* 00504/239 8826.

## JAMAICA

Jamaica Football Federation Ltd, 20 St Lucia Crescent, Kingston 5.
*Founded:* 1910; *Number of Clubs:* 266; *Number of Players:* 45,200; *National Colours:* Gold shirts, black shorts, gold stockings.
*Telephone:* 001-876/929 8036; *Fax:* 001-876/929 0483.

### MEXICO

Federacion Mexicana De Futbol Asociacion, A.C., Colima No. 373, Colonia Roma Mexico DF 06700.
*Founded:* 1927; *Number of Clubs:* 77 (senior); *Number of Players:* 1,402,270; *National Colours:* Green shirts with white collar, white shorts, red stockings.
*Telephone:* 0052-55/5241 0190; *Fax:* 0052-55/5241 0191.

### MONSERRAT

Monserrat Football Association Inc., P.O. Box 505, Woodlands, Monserrat.
*National Colours:* Green shirts with black and white stripes, green shorts with white stripes, green stockings with black and white stripes.
*Telephone:* 001-664/491 8744; *Fax:* 001-664/491 8801.

### NETHERLANDS ANTILLES

Nederlands Antiliaanse Voetbal Unie, Bonamweg 49, Curacao, NA.
*Founded:* 1921; *Number of Clubs:* 85; *Number of Players:* 4,500; *National Colours:* White shirts with red and blue stripes, red shorts with blue and white stripes, white stockings with red stripes.
*Telephone:* 00599-9736 5040; *Fax:* 00599/9736 5047.

### NICARAGUA

Federacion Nicaraguense De Futbol, Hospital Pautista 1, Cuadra avajo, 1 cuada al Sur y 1/2, Cuadra Abajo, Managua 976.
*Founded:* 1931; *Number of Clubs:* 31; *Number of Players:* 160 (senior); *National Colours:* Blue shirts, white shorts, blue stockings.
*Telephone:* 00505/222 7035; *Fax:* 00505/222 7885.

### PANAMA

Federacion Panamena De Futbol, Estadio Rommel Fernandez, Puerta 24, Ave. Jose Aeustin Araneo, Apartado Postal 8-391, Zona 8, Panama.
*Founded:* 1937; *Number of Clubs:* 65; *Number of Players:* 4,225; *National Colours:* All red.
*Telephone:* 00507/233 3896; *Fax:* 00507/233 0582.

### PUERTO RICO

Federacion Puertorriquena De Futbol, P.O. Box 193590 San Juan 00919.
*Founded:* 1940; *Number of Clubs:* 175; *Number of Players:* 4,200; *National Colours:* Red, blue and white shirts and shorts, red and blue stockings.
*Telephone:* 001-787/759 7544; *Fax:* 001-787/759 7544.

### SAINT KITTS & NEVIS

St Kitts & Nevis Football Association, P.O. Box 465, Warner Park, Basseterre, St Kitts, W.I.
*Founded:* 1932; *Number of Clubs:* 36; *Number of Players:* 600; *National Colours:* Green and yellow shirts, red shorts, yellow stockings.
*Telephone:* 001-869/466 8502; *Fax:* 001-869/465 9033.

### SAINT LUCIA

St Lucia National Football Association, PO Box 255, Sans Souci, Castries, St Lucia.
*Founded:* 1979; *Number of Clubs:* 100; *Number of Players:* 4,000; *National Colours:* White shirts and shorts with yellow, blue and black stripes, white, blue and yellow stockings.
*Telephone:* 001-758/453 0687; *Fax:* 001-758/456 0510.

### SAINT VINCENT & THE GRENADINES

St Vincent & The Grenadines Football Federation, Sharpe Street, PO Box 1278, Saint George.
*Founded:* 1979; *Number of Clubs:* 500; *Number of Players:* 5,000; *National Colours:* Green shirts with yellow border, blue shorts, yellow stockings.
*Telephone:* 001-784/456 1092; *Fax:* 001-784/457 2193.

### SURINAM

Surinaamse Voetbal Bond, Letitia Vriesde Laan 7, P.O. Box 1223, Paramaribo.
*Founded:* 1920; *Number of Clubs:* 168; *Number of Players:* 4,430; *National Colours:* White, green and red shirts, green and white shirts and stockings.
*Telephone:* 00597/473 112; *Fax:* 00597/479 718.

### TRINIDAD & TOBAGO

Trinidad & Tobago Football Federation, 24–26 Dundonald Street, PO Box 400, Port of Spain.
*Founded:* 1908; *Number of Clubs:* 124; *Number of Players:* 5,050; *National Colours:* Red shirts, black shorts, white stockings.
*Telephone:* 001-868/623 7312; *Fax:* 001-868/623 8109.

### TURKS & CAICOS

Turks & Caicos Islands Football Association, P.O. Box 626, Tropicana Plaza, Leeward Highway, Providenciales.
*National Colours:* All white.
*Telephone:* 001-649/941 5532; *Fax:* 001-649/941 5554.

### USA

US Soccer Federation, US Soccer House, 1801–1811 S. Prairie Avenue, Chicago, Illinois 60616.
*Founded:* 1913; *Number of Clubs:* 7,000; *Number of Players:* 1,411,500; *National Colours:* White shirts, blue shorts, white stockings.
*Telephone:* 001-312/808 1300; *Fax:* 001-312/808 1301.

## OCEANIA

### AMERICAN SAMOA

American Samoa Football Association, P.O. Box 282, Pago Pago AS 96799.
*National Colours:* Navy blue shirts, white shorts, red stockings.
*Telephone:* 00684/699 7380; *Fax:* 00684/699 7381.

### AUSTRALIA

Soccer Australia Ltd, Level 3, East Stand, Stadium Australia, Edwin Flack Avenue, Homebush, NSW 2127.
*Founded:* 1961; *Number of Clubs:* 6,816; *Number of Players:* 433,957; *National Colours:* All green with gold trim.
*Telephone:* 0061-2/9739 5555; *Fax:* 0061-2/9739 5590.

### COOK ISLANDS

Cook Islands Football Association, Victoria Road, Tupapa, P.O. Box 29, Avarua, Rarotonga, Cook Islands.
*Founded:* 1971; *Number of Clubs:* 9; *National Colours:* Green shirts with white sleeves, green shorts, white stockings.
*Telephone:* 00682/28 980; *Fax:* 00682/28 981.

### FIJI

Fiji Football Association, PO Box 2514, Government Buildings, Suva.
*Founded:* 1938; *Number of Clubs;* 140: *Number of Players:* 21,300; *National Colours:* White shirts, blue shorts and stockings.
*Telephone:* 00679/330 0453; *Fax:* 00679/330 4642.

### NEW ZEALAND

New Zealand Soccer Inc., PO Box 301 043, Albany, Auckland, New Zealand.
*Founded:* 1891; *Number of Clubs:* 312; *Number of Players:* 52,969; *National Colours:* All white.
*Telephone:* 0064-9/414 0175; *Fax:* 0064-9/414 0176.

### PAPUA NEW GUINEA

Papua New Guinea Football Association, PO Box 957, Room II Level I, Haus Tisa, Lae.
*Founded:* 1962; *Number of Clubs:* 350; *Number of Players:* 8,250; *National Colours:* Red and yellow shirts, black shorts, yellow stockings.
*Telephone:* 00675/479 1998; *Fax:* 00675/479 1999.

### SAMOA

The Samoa Football Soccer Federation, P.O. Box 960, Apia.
*Founded:* 1968; *National Colours:* Blue, white and red shirts, blue and white shorts, red and blue stockings.
*Telephone:* 00685/26 504; *Fax:* 00685/20 341.

### SOLOMON ISLANDS

Solomon Islands Football Federation, PO Box 854, Honiara, Solomon Islands.
*Founded:* 1978; *Number of Players:* 4,000; *National Colours:* Gold and blue shirts, blue and white shorts, white and blue stockings.
*Telephone:* 00677/26 496; *Fax:* 00677/26 497.

### TAHITI

Federation Tahitienne de Football, Rue Coppenrath Stade de Fautana, PO Box 50858 Pirae 98716.
*Founded:* 1989; *National Colours:* Red shirts, white shorts, red stockings.
*Telephone:* 00689/540 954; *Fax:* 00689/419 629.

### TONGA

Tonga Football Association, Tungi Arcade, Taufa'Ahau Road, P.O. Box 852, Nuku'Alofa, Tonga.
*Founded:* 1965; *Number of Clubs:* 23; *Number of Players:* 350; *National Colours:* Red shirts, white shorts, red stockings.
*Telephone:* 00676/24 442; *Fax:* 00676/23 340.

### VANUATU

Vanuatu Football Federation, P.O. Box 266, Port Vila, Vanuatu.
*Founded:* 1934; *National Colours:* Gold and black shirts, black shorts, gold and black stockings.
*Telephone:* 00678/25 236; *Fax:* 00678/25 236.

## AFRICA

### ALGERIA

Federation Algerienne De Foot-ball, Chemin Ahmed Ouaked, Boite Postale No. 39, Dely-Ibrahim-Alger.
*Founded:* 1962; *Number of Clubs:* 780; *Number of Players:* 58,567; *National Colours:* Green shirts, white shorts, green stockings.
*Telephone:* 00213-21/372 929; *Fax:* 00213-21/367 266.

### ANGOLA

Federation Angolaise De Football, Compl. da Cidadela Desportiva, B.P. 3449, Luanda.
*Founded:* 1979; *Number of Clubs:* 276; *Number of Players:* 4,269; *National Colours:* Red shirts, black shorts, red stockings.
*Telephone:* 00244-2/264 948; *Fax:* 00244-2/260 566.

### BENIN

Federation Beninoise De Football, Stade Rene Pleven d'Akpakpa, B.P. 965, Cotonou 01.
*Founded:* 1962; *Number of Clubs:* 117; *Number of Players:* 6,700; *National Colours:* Green shirts, Yellow shorts, red stockings.
*Telephone:* 00229/330 537; *Fax:* 00229/330 537

### BOTSWANA

Botswana Football Association, P.O. Box 1396, Gabarone.
*Founded:* 1970; *National Colours:* Blue, white and black striped shirts, blue, white and black shorts and stockings.
*Telephone:* 00267/390 0279; *Fax:* 00267/ 390 0280.

### BURKINA FASO

Federation Burkinabe De Foot-Ball, 01 B.P. 57, Ouagadougou 01.
*Founded:* 1960; *Number of Clubs:* 57; *Number of Players:* 4,672; *National Colours:* All green, red and white.
*Telephone:* 00226/318 815; *Fax:* 00226/318 843.

### BURUNDI

Federation De Football Du Burundi, Bulding Nyogozi, Boulevard de l'Uprona, B.P. 3426, Bujumbura.
*Founded:* 1948; *Number of Clubs:* 132; *Number of Players:* 3,930; *National Colours:* Red and white shirts, white and red shorts, green stockings.
*Telephone :* 00257/921 105; *Fax:* 00257/242 892.

### CAMEROON

Federation Camerounaise De Football, B.P. 1116, Yaounde.
*Founded:* 1959; *Number of Clubs:* 200; *Number of Players:* 9,328; *National Colours:* Green shirts, red shorts, yellow stockings.
*Telephone:* 00237/221 0012; *Fax:* 00237/221 6662.

### CAPE VERDE ISLANDS

Federacao Cabo-Verdiana De Futebol, Praia Cabo Verde, FCF CX, P.O. Box 234, Praia.
*Founded:* 1982; *National Colours:* Blue and white shirts and shorts, blue and red stockings.
*Telephone :* 00238/611 362; *Fax:* 00238/611 362.

### CENTRAL AFRICAN REPUBLIC

Federation Centrafricaine De Football, Immeuble Soca Constructa, B.P. 344, Bangui.
*Founded:* 1937; *Number of Clubs:* 256; *Number of Players:* 7,200; *National Colours:* Blue and white shirts, white shorts, blue stockings.
*Telephone:* 00236/619 545; *Fax:* 00236/615 660.

### CHAD

Federation Tchadienne de Football, B.P. 886, N'Djamena.
*Founded:* 1962; *National Colours:* Blue shirts, yellow shorts, red stockings.
*Telephone:* 00235/515 982; *Fax:* 00235/525 538.

### CONGO

Federation Congolaise De Football, 80 Rue Eugene-Etienne, Centre Ville, PO Box 11, Brazzaville.
*Founded:* 1962; *Number of Clubs:* 250; *Number of Players:* 5,940; *National Colours:* Green shirts, yellow shorts, red stockings.
*Telephone:* 00242/811 563; *Fax:* 00242/812 524.

### CONGO DR

Federation Congolaise De Football-Association, Av. de l'Enseignemt 210, C/Kasa-Vubu, Kinshasa 1.
*Founded:* 1919; *Number of Clubs:* 3,800; *Number of Players:* 64,627; *National Colours:* Blue and yellow shirts, yellow and blue shorts, white and blue stockings.
*Telephone:* 00243/993 9635; *Fax:* 00243/139 8426.

### DJIBOUTI

Federation Djiboutienne de Football, Stade el Haoj Hassan Gouled, B.P. 2694, Djibouti.
*Founded:* 1977; *Number of Players:* 2,000; *National Colours:* Green shirts, white shorts, blue stockings.
*Telephone:* 00253/341 964; *Fax:* 00253/341 963.

### EGYPT

Egyptian Football Association, 5 Gabalaya Street, Guezira, El Borg Post Office, Cairo.
*Founded:* 1921; *Number of Clubs:* 247; *Number of Players:* 19,735; *National Colours:* Red shirts, white shorts, black stockings.
*Telephone:* 0020-2/735 1793; *Fax:* 0020-2/736 7817.

### ERITREA

The Eritrean National Football Federation, Sematat Avenue 29–31, P.O. Box 3665, Asmara.
*National Colours:* Blue shirts, red shorts, green stockings.
*Telephone:* 00291-1/120 335; *Fax:* 00291-1/126 821.

### ETHIOPIA

Ethiopia Football Federation, Addis Ababa Stadium, P.O. Box 1080, Addis Ababa.
*Founded:* 1943; *Number of Clubs:* 767; *Number of Players:* 20,594; *National Colours:* Green shirts, yellow shorts, red stockings.
*Telephone:* 00251-1/514 453; *Fax:* 00251-1/515 899.

### GABON

Federation Gabonaise De Football, B.P. 181, Libreville.
*Founded:* 1962; *Number of Clubs:* 320; *Number of Players:* 10,000; *National Colours:* Green, yellow and blue shirts, blue and yellow shorts, white stockings with tri-colour trims.
*Telephone:* 00241/730 460; *Fax:* 00241/730 460.

### GAMBIA

Gambia Football Association, Independence Stadium, Bakau, P.O. Box 523, Banjul.
*Founded:* 1952; *Number of Clubs:* 30; *Number of Players:* 860; *National Colours:* All red, blue and white.
*Telephone:* 00220/494 509; *Fax:* 00220/494 509.

### GHANA

Ghana Football Association, National Sports Council, P.O. Box 1272, Accra.
*Founded:* 1957; *Number of Clubs:* 347; *Number of Players:* 11,275; *National Colours:* All yellow.
*Telephone:* 00233-21/671 501; *Fax:* 00233-21/668 590.

### GUINEA

Federation Guineenne De Football, P.O. Box 3645, Conakry.
*Founded:* 1959; *Number of Clubs:* 351; *Number of Players:* 10,000; *National Colours:* Red shirts, yellow shorts, green stockings.
*Telephone:* 00224/455 878; *Fax:* 00224/455 879.

### GUINEA-BISSAU

Federacao De Football Da Guinea-Bissau, Alto Bandim (Nova Sede), PO Box 375 Bissau 1035.
*Founded:* 1974; *National Colours:* Red, green and yellow shirts, green and yellow shorts, red, green and yellow stockings.
*Telephone:* 00245/201 918; *Fax:* 00245/211 414.

### GUINEA, EQUATORIAL

Federacion Ecuatoguineana De Futbol, c/P Patricio Lumumba (Estadio La Paz), Malabo 1071.
*Founded:* 1986; *National Colours:* All red.
*Telephone:* 00240-9/74 049; *Fax:* 00240-9/2257.

### IVORY COAST

Federation Ivoirienne De Football, 01 PO Box 1202, Abidjan 01.
*Founded:* 1960; *Number of Clubs:* 84 (senior); *Number of Players:* 3,655; *National Colours:* Orange shirts, black shorts, green stockings.
*Telephone:* 00225/2124 0027; *Fax:* 00225/2125 9352.

### KENYA

Kenya Football Federation, Nyayo National Stadium, P.O. Box 40234, Nairobi.
*Founded:* 1960; *Number of Clubs:* 351; *Number of Players:* 8,880; *National Colours:* All red.
*Telephone:* 00254-2/608 422; *Fax:* 00254-2/249 855.

### LESOTHO

Lesotho Football Association, P.O. Box 1879, Maseru-100, Lesotho.
*Founded:* 1932; *Number of Clubs:* 88; *Number of Players:* 2,076; *National Colours:* Blue shirts, green shorts, white stockings.
*Telephone:* 00266/2231 1879; *Fax:* 00266/2231 0586.

### LIBERIA

Liberia Football Association, Broad and Center Streets, PO Box 10-1066, Monrovia 1000.
*Founded:* 1936; *National Colours:* Blue shirts, white shorts, red stockings.
*Telephone:* 00231/226 385; *Fax:* 00231/226 092.

### LIBYA

Libyan Football Federation, Asayadi Street, Near Janat Al-Areet, P.O. Box 5137, Tripoli.
*Founded:* 1963; *Number of Clubs:* 89; *Number of Players:* 2,941; *National Colours:* Green and black shirts, black shorts and stockings.
*Telephone:* 00218-21/334 3600; *Fax:* 00218-21/444 1274.

### MADAGASCAR

Federation Malagasy de Football, Immeuble Preservatrice Vie-Lot IBF-9B, Rue Rabearivelo-Antsahavola, PO Box 4409, Antananarivo 101.
*Founded:* 1961; *Number of Clubs:* 775; *Number of Players:* 23,536; *National Colours:* Red and green shirts, white and green shorts, green and white stockings.
*Telephone:* 00261-20/226 8374; *Fax:* 00261-20/226 8373.

### MALAWI

Football Association of Malawi, Mpira House, Old Chileka Road, P.O. Box 865, Blantyre.
*Founded:* 1966; *Number of Clubs:* 465; *Number of Players:* 12,500; *National Colours:* Red shirts, white shorts, red and black stockings.
*Telephone:* 00265-1/623 197; *Fax:* 00265-1/623 204.

### MALI

Federation Malienne De Football, Avenue du Mali, Hamdallaye ACI 2000, PO Box 1020, Bamako 12582.
*Founded:* 1960; *Number of Clubs:* 128; *Number of Players:* 5,480; *National Colours:* Green shirts, yellow shorts, red stockings.
*Telephone:* 00223/223 8844; *Fax:* 00223/222 4254.

### MAURITANIA

Federation De Foot-Ball De La Rep. Islamique. De Mauritanie, B.P. 566, Nouakchott.
*Founded:* 1961; *Number of Clubs:* 59; *Number of Players:* 1,930; *National Colours:* Green and yellow shirts, yellow shorts, green stockings.
*Telephone:* 00222-5/241 860; *Fax:* 00222-5/241 861.

### MAURITIUS

Mauritius Football Association, Chancery House, 2nd Floor Nos. 303–305, 14 Lislet Geoffroy Street, Port Louis.
*Founded:* 1952; *Number of Clubs:* 397; *Number of Players:* 29,375; *National Colours:* All red.
*Telephone:* 00230/212 1418; *Fax:* 00230/208 4100.

### MOROCCO

Federation Royale Marocaine De Football, 51 Bis Av. Ibn Sina, PO Box 51, Agdal, Rabat 10 000.
*Founded:* 1955; *Number of Clubs:* 350; *Number of Players:* 19,768; *National Colours:* All green white and red.
*Telephone:* 00212-37/672 706; *Fax:* 00212-37/671 070.

### MOZAMBIQUE

Federacao Mocambicana De Futebol, Av. Samora Machel 11-2, Caixa Postal 1467, Maputo.
*Founded:* 1978; *Number of Clubs:* 144; *National Colours:* Red shirts, black shorts, red and black stockings.
*Telephone:* 00258-1/300 366; *Fax:* 00258-1/300 367.

## NAMIBIA

Namibia Football Association, Abraham Mashego Street 8521, Katurua Council of Churches in Namibia, P.O. Box 1345, Windhoek 9000, Namibia.
*Founded:* 1990; *Number of Clubs:* 244; *Number of Players:* 7320; *National Colours:* All red.
Telephone: 00264-61/265 691; Fax: 00264-61/265 693.

## NIGER

Federation Nigerienne De Football, Rue de la Tapoa, PO Box 10299, Niamey.
*Founded:* 1967; *Number of Clubs:* 64; *Number of Players:* 1,525; *National Colours:* Orange shirts, white shorts, green stockings.
*Telephone:* 00227/725 127; *Fax:* 00227/725 127.

## NIGERIA

Nigeria Football Association, Plot 2033, Olusegun, Obasanjo Way, Zone 7, Wuse Abuja, PO Box 5101 Garki, Abuja, Nigeria.
*Founded:* 1945; *Number of Clubs:* 326; *Number of Players:* 80,190; *National Colours:* All green and white.
*Telephone:* 00234-9/523 7326; *Fax:* 00234-9/523 7327.

## RWANDA

Federation Rwandaise De Football Amateur, B.P. 2000, Kigali.
*Founded:* 1972; *Number of Clubs:* 167; *National Colours:* Red, green and yellow shirts, green shorts, red stockings.
*Telephone:* 00250/571 596; *Fax:* 00250/571 597.

## SENEGAL

Federation Senegalaise De Football, Stade Leopold Sedar Senghor, Route De L'Aeroport De Yoff, B.P. 130 21, Dakar.
*Founded:* 1960; *Number of Clubs:* 75 (senior); *Number of Players:* 3,977; *National Colours:* All white and green.
*Telephone:* 00221/827 2935; *Fax:* 00221/827 3524.

## SEYCHELLES

Seychelles Football Federation, P.O. Box 843, People's Stadium, Victoria-Mahe, Seychelles.
*Founded:* 1979; *National Colours:* Red and green shirts and shorts, red stockings.
*Telephone:* 00248/324 632; *Fax:* 00248/225 468.

## ST THOMAS AND PRINCIPE

Federation Santomense De Futebol, Rua Ex-Joao de Deus No. QXXIII-426/26, PO Box 440, Sao Tome.
*Founded:* 1975; *National Colours:* Green and red shirts, yellow shorts, green stockings.
*Telephone:* 00239-2/22 4231; *Fax:* 00239-2/21 333.

## SIERRA LEONE

Sierra Leone Football Association, 21 Battery Street, Kingtorn, P.O. Box 672, National Stadium, Brookfields, Freetown.
*Founded:* 1967; *Number of Clubs:* 104; *Number of Players:* 8,120; *National Colours:* Green and blue shirts, green, blue and white shorts and stockings.
*Telephone:* 00232-22/241 872; *Fax:* 00232-22/227 771.

## SOMALIA

Somali Football Federation, PO Box 222, Mogadishu BN 03040.
*Founded:* 1951; *Number of Clubs:* 46 (senior); *Number of Players:* 1,150; *National Colours:* Sky blue and white shirts and shorts, white and sky blue stockings.
*Telephone:* 00252-1/229 843; *Fax:* 00252-1/215 513.

## SOUTH AFRICA

South African Football Association, First National Bank Stadium, PO Box 910, Johannesburg 2000, South Africa.
*Founded:* 1991; *Number of Teams:* 51,944; *Number of Players:* 1,039,880; *National Colours:* White shirts with yellow striped sleeves, white shorts with yellow stripes, white stockings.
*Telephone:* 0027-11/494 3522; *Fax:* 0027-11/494 3013.

## SUDAN

Sudan Football Association, Bladia Street, Khartoum.
*Founded:* 1936; *Number of Clubs:* 750; *Number of Players:* 42,200; *National Colours:* Red shirts, white shorts, black stockings.
*Telephone:* 00249-11/773 495; *Fax:* 00249-11/776 633.

## SWAZILAND

National Football Association of Swaziland, Sigwaca House, Plot 582, Sheffield Road, PO Box 641, Mbabane H100.
*Founded:* 1968; *Number of Clubs:* 136; *National Colours:* Blue shirts, gold shorts, red stockings.
*Telephone:* 00268/404 6852; *Fax:* 00268/404 6206.

## TANZANIA

Football Association of Tanzania, Uhuru/Shaurimoyo Road, Karume Memorial Stadium, P.O. Box 1574, Ilala/Dar Es Salaam.
*Founded:* 1930; *Number of Clubs:* 51; *National Colours:* Green, yellow and blue shirts, black shorts, green stockings with horizontal stripe.
*Telephone:* 00255-22/286 1815; *Fax:* 00255-22/286 1815.

## TOGO

Federation Togolaise De Football, C.P. 5, Lome.
*Founded:* 1960; *Number of Clubs:* 144; *Number of Players:* 4,346; *National Colours:* White shirts, green shorts, red stockings with yellow and green stripes.
*Telephone:* 00228/221 2698; *Fax:* 00228/222 1413.

## TUNISIA

Federation Tunisienne De Football, Maison des Federations Sportives, Cite Olympique, Tunis 1003.
*Founded:* 1956; *Number of Clubs:* 215; *Number of Players:* 18,300; *National Colours:* Red shirts, white shorts, red stockings.
*Telephone:* 00216-71/233 303; *Fax:* 00216-71/767 929.

## UGANDA

Federation of Uganda Football Associations, Plot No. 879, Kyadondo Block 8, Mengo Wakaliga Road, P.O. Box 22518, Kampala.
*Founded:* 1924; *Number of Clubs:* 400; *Number of Players:* 1,518; *National Colours:* All yellow, red and white.
*Telephone:* 00256-41/272 702; *Fax:* 00256-41/272 702.

## ZAMBIA

Football Association of Zambia, Football House, Alick Nkhata Road, P.O. Box 34751, Lusaka.
*Founded:* 1929; *Number of Clubs:* 20 (senior); *Number of Players:* 4,100; *National Colours:* White and green shirts, green and white shorts, white and green stockings.
*Telephone:* 00260-1/250 946; *Fax:* 00260-1/250 946.

## ZIMBABWE

Zimbabwe Football Association, P.O. Box CY 114, Causeway, Harare.
*Founded:* 1965; *National Colours:* All green and gold.
*Telephone:* 00263-4/721 026; *Fax:* 00263-4/721 045.

# THE WORLD CUP 2006

## QUALIFYING FIXTURES

### SOUTH AMERICA

*Top four qualify for finals; fifth placed team enters play-off against Oceania winners for a place in finals.*

04/05.09.04 Brazil v Bolivia
04/05.09.04 Chile v Colombia
04/05.09.04 Paraguay v Venezuela
04/05.09.04 Peru v Argentina
04/05.09.04 Uruguay v Ecuador
09/10.10.04 Argentina v Uruguay
09/10.10.04 Bolivia v Peru
09/10.10.04 Colombia v Paraguay
09/10.10.04 Ecuador v Chile
09/10.10.04 Venezuela v Brazil
12/13.10.04 Bolivia v Uruguay
12/13.10.04 Brazil v Colombia
12/13.10.04 Chile v Argentina
12/13.10.04 Paraguay v Peru
12/13.10.04 Venezuela v Ecuador
16/17.11.04 Argentina v Venezuela
16/17.11.04 Colombia v Bolivia
16/17.11.04 Ecuador v Brazil
16/17.11.04 Peru v Chile
16/17.11.04 Uruguay v Paraguay
26/27.03.05 Bolivia v Argentina
26/27.03.05 Brazil v Peru
26/27.03.05 Chile v Uruguay
26/27.03.05 Ecuador v Paraguay
26/27.03.05 Venezuela v Colombia
29/30.03.05 Argentina v Colombia
29/30.03.05 Bolivia v Venezuela
29/30.03.05 Paraguay v Chile
29/30.03.05 Peru v Ecuador
29/30.03.05 Uruguay v Brazil
04/05.06.05 Brazil v Paraguay
04/05.06.05 Chile v Bolivia
04/05.06.05 Colombia v Peru
04/05.06.05 Ecuador v Argentina
04/05.06.05 Venezuela v Uruguay
07/08.06.05 Argentina v Brazil
07/08.06.05 Chile v Venezuela
07/08.06.05 Colombia v Ecuador
07/08.06.05 Paraguay v Bolivia
07/08.06.05 Peru v Uruguay
03/04.09.05 Bolivia v Ecuador
03/04.09.05 Brazil v Chile
03/04.09.05 Paraguay v Argentina
03/04.09.05 Uruguay v Colombia
03/04.09.05 Venezuela v Peru
08/09.10.05 Argentina v Peru
08/09.10.05 Bolivia v Brazil
08/09.10.05 Colombia v Chile
08/09.10.05 Ecuador v Uruguay
08/09.10.05 Venezuela v Paraguay
11/12.10.05 Brazil v Venezuela
11/12.10.05 Chile v Ecuador
11/12.10.05 Paraguay v Colombia
11/12.10.05 Peru v Bolivia
11/12.10.05 Uruguay v Argentina

### EUROPE

*Group winners and two best runners-up qualify for finals. Remaining six runners-up paired in two leg play-off matches, the winners of which also qualify for finals. Group runners-up ranked according to results against teams finishing in order in their respective groups.*

**GROUP 1**

18.08.04 Macedonia v Armenia
18.08.04 Romania v Finland
04.09.04 Finland v Andorra
04.09.04 Romania v Macedonia
08.09.04 Andorra v Romania
08.09.04 Armenia v Finland
08.09.04 Holland v Czech Republic
09.10.04 Czech Republic v Romania
09.10.04 Finland v Armenia
09.10.04 Macedonia v Holland
13.10.04 Andorra v Macedonia
13.10.04 Armenia v Czech Republic
13.10.04 Holland v Finland
17.11.04 Andorra v Holland
17.11.04 Armenia v Romania
17.11.04 Macedonia v Czech Republic
09.02.05 Macedonia v Andorra
26.03.05 Armenia v Andorra
26.03.05 Czech Republic v Finland
26.03.05 Romania v Holland
30.03.05 Andorra v Czech Republic
30.03.05 Holland v Armenia
30.03.05 Macedonia v Romania
04.06.05 Armenia v Macedonia
04.06.05 Czech Republic v Andorra
04.06.05 Holland v Romania
08.06.05 Czech Republic v Macedonia
08.06.05 Finland v Holland
08.06.05 Romania v Armenia
17.08.05 Macedonia v Finland
17.08.05 Romania v Andorra
03.09.05 Andorra v Finland
03.09.05 Armenia v Holland
03.09.05 Romania v Czech Republic
07.09.05 Czech Republic v Armenia
07.09.05 Finland v Macedonia
07.09.05 Holland v Andorra
08.10.05 Czech Republic v Holland
08.10.05 Finland v Romania
12.10.05 Andorra v Armenia
12.10.05 Finland v Czech Republic
12.10.05 Holland v Macedonia

**GROUP 2**

04.09.04 Albania v Greece
04.09.04 Denmark v Ukraine
04.09.04 Turkey v Georgia
08.09.04 Georgia v Albania
08.09.04 Greece v Turkey
08.09.04 Kazakhstan v Ukraine
09.10.04 Albania v Denmark
09.10.04 Turkey v Kazakhstan
09.10.04 Ukraine v Greece
13.10.04 Denmark v Turkey
13.10.04 Kazakhstan v Albania
13.10.04 Ukraine v Georgia
17.11.04 Georgia v Denmark
17.11.04 Greece v Kazakhstan
17.11.04 Turkey v Ukraine
09.02.05 Albania v Ukraine
09.02.05 Greece v Denmark
09.02.05 Kazakhstan v Georgia
26.03.05 Denmark v Kazakhstan
26.03.05 Georgia v Greece
26.03.05 Turkey v Albania
30.03.05 Georgia v Turkey
30.03.05 Greece v Albania
30.03.05 Ukraine v Denmark
04.06.05 Albania v Georgia
04.06.05 Turkey v Greece
04.06.05 Ukraine v Kazakhstan
08.06.05 Denmark v Albania
08.06.05 Greece v Ukraine
08.06.05 Kazakhstan v Turkey

| | |
|---|---|
| 03.09.05 | Albania v Kazakhstan |
| 03.09.05 | Georgia v Ukraine |
| 03.09.05 | Turkey v Denmark |
| 07.09.05 | Denmark v Georgia |
| 07.09.05 | Kazakhstan v Greece |
| 07.09.05 | Ukraine v Turkey |
| 08.10.05 | Denmark v Greece |
| 08.10.05 | Georgia v Kazakhstan |
| 08.10.05 | Ukraine v Albania |
| 12.10.05 | Albania v Turkey |
| 12.10.05 | Greece v Georgia |
| 12.10.05 | Kazakhstan v Denmark |

**GROUP 3**

| | |
|---|---|
| 18.08.04 | Liechtenstein v Estonia |
| 18.08.04 | Slovakia v Luxembourg |
| 04.09.04 | Estonia v Luxembourg |
| 04.09.04 | Latvia v Portugal |
| 04.09.04 | Russia v Slovakia |
| 08.09.04 | Luxembourg v Latvia |
| 08.09.04 | Portugal v Estonia |
| 08.09.04 | Slovakia v Liechtenstein |
| 09.10.04 | Liechtenstein v Portugal |
| 09.10.04 | Luxembourg v Russia |
| 09.10.04 | Slovakia v Latvia |
| 13.10.04 | Latvia v Estonia |
| 13.10.04 | Luxembourg v Liechtenstein |
| 13.10.04 | Portugal v Russia |
| 17.11.04 | Liechtenstein v Latvia |
| 17.11.04 | Luxembourg v Portugal |
| 17.11.04 | Russia v Estonia |
| 26.03.05 | Estonia v Slovakia |
| 26.03.05 | Liechtenstein v Russia |
| 30.03.05 | Estonia v Russia |
| 30.03.05 | Latvia v Luxembourg |
| 30.03.05 | Slovakia v Portugal |
| 04.06.05 | Estonia v Liechtenstein |
| 04.06.05 | Portugal v Slovakia |
| 04.06.05 | Russia v Latvia |
| 08.06.05 | Estonia v Portugal |
| 08.06.05 | Latvia v Liechtenstein |
| 08.06.05 | Luxembourg v Slovakia |
| 17.08.05 | Latvia v Russia |
| 17.08.05 | Liechtenstein v Slovakia |
| 03.09.05 | Estonia v Latvia |
| 03.09.05 | Portugal v Luxembourg |
| 03.09.05 | Russia v Liechtenstein |
| 07.09.05 | Latvia v Slovakia |
| 07.09.05 | Liechtenstein v Luxembourg |
| 07.09.05 | Russia v Portugal |
| 08.10.05 | Portugal v Liechtenstein |
| 08.10.05 | Russia v Luxembourg |
| 08.10.05 | Slovakia v Estonia |
| 12.10.05 | Luxembourg v Estonia |
| 12.10.05 | Portugal v Latvia |
| 12.10.05 | Slovakia v Russia |

**GROUP 4**

| | |
|---|---|
| 04.09.04 | France v Israel |
| 04.09.04 | Republic of Ireland v Cyprus |
| 04.09.04 | Switzerland v Faeroes |
| 08.09.04 | Faeroes v France |
| 08.09.04 | Israel v Cyprus |
| 08.09.04 | Switzerland v Republic of Ireland |
| 09.10.04 | Cyprus v Faeroes |
| 09.10.04 | France v Republic of Ireland |
| 09.10.04 | Israel v Switzerland |
| 13.10.04 | Cyprus v France |
| 13.10.04 | Republic of Ireland v Faeroes |
| 17.11.04 | Cyprus v Israel |
| 26.03.05 | Israel v Republic of Ireland |
| 26.03.05 | France v Switzerland |
| 30.03.05 | Israel v France |
| 30.03.05 | Switzerland v Cyprus |
| 04.06.05 | Faeroes v Switzerland |
| 04.06.05 | Republic of Ireland v Israel |
| 08.06.05 | Faeroes v Republic of Ireland |
| 17.08.05 | Faeroes v Cyprus |
| 03.09.05 | France v Faeroes |
| 03.09.05 | Switzerland v Israel |
| 07.09.05 | Cyprus v Switzerland |
| 07.09.05 | Faeroes v Israel |
| 07.09.05 | Republic of Ireland v France |
| 08.10.05 | Cyprus v Republic of Ireland |
| 08.10.05 | Switzerland v France |
| 08.10.05 | Israel v Faeroes |
| 12.10.05 | France v Cyprus |
| 12.10.05 | Republic of Ireland v Switzerland |

**GROUP 5**

| | |
|---|---|
| 04.09.04 | Italy v Norway |
| 04.09.04 | Slovenia v Moldova |
| 08.09.04 | Moldova v Italy |
| 08.09.04 | Norway v Belarus |
| 08.09.04 | Scotland v Slovenia |
| 09.10.04 | Belarus v Moldova |
| 09.10.04 | Scotland v Norway |
| 09.10.04 | Slovenia v Italy |
| 13.10.04 | Italy v Belarus |
| 13.10.04 | Moldova v Scotland |
| 13.10.04 | Norway v Slovenia |
| 28.03.05 | Italy v Scotland |
| 30.03.05 | Moldova v Norway |
| 30.03.05 | Slovenia v Belarus |
| 04.06.05 | Belarus v Slovenia |
| 04.06.05 | Norway v Italy |
| 04.06.05 | Scotland v Moldova |
| 08.06.05 | Belarus v Scotland |
| 03.09.05 | Moldova v Belarus |
| 03.09.05 | Scotland v Italy |
| 03.09.05 | Slovenia v Norway |
| 07.09.05 | Belarus v Italy |
| 07.09.05 | Moldova v Slovenia |
| 07.09.05 | Norway v Scotland |
| 08.10.05 | Italy v Slovenia |
| 08.10.05 | Norway v Moldova |
| 08.10.05 | Scotland v Belarus |
| 12.10.05 | Belarus v Norway |
| 12.10.05 | Italy v Moldova |
| 12.10.05 | Slovenia v Scotland |

**GROUP 6**

| | |
|---|---|
| 04.09.04 | Austria v England |
| 04.09.04 | Azerbaijan v Wales |
| 04.09.04 | Northern Ireland v Poland |
| 08.09.04 | Austria v Azerbaijan |
| 08.09.04 | Poland v England |
| 08.09.04 | Wales v Northern Ireland |
| 09.10.04 | Austria v Poland |
| 09.10.04 | Azerbaijan v Northern Ireland |
| 09.10.04 | England v Wales |
| 13.10.04 | Azerbaijan v England |
| 13.10.04 | Northern Ireland v Austria |
| 13.10.04 | Wales v Poland |
| 26.03.05 | England v Northern Ireland |
| 26.03.05 | Poland v Azerbaijan |
| 26.03.05 | Wales v Austria |
| 30.03.05 | Austria v Wales |
| 30.03.05 | England v Azerbaijan |
| 30.03.05 | Poland v Northern Ireland |
| 04.06.05 | Azerbaijan v Poland |
| 03.09.05 | Northern Ireland v Azerbaijan |
| 03.09.05 | Poland v Austria |
| 03.09.05 | Wales v England |
| 07.09.05 | Azerbaijan v Austria |
| 07.09.05 | Northern Ireland v England |
| 07.09.05 | Poland v Wales |
| 08.10.05 | England v Austria |
| 08.10.05 | Northern Ireland v Wales |
| 12.10.05 | Austria v Northern Ireland |
| 12.10.05 | England v Poland |
| 12.10.05 | Wales v Azerbaijan |

**GROUP 7**

| | |
|---|---|
| 04.09.04 | Belgium v Lithuania |
| 04.09.04 | San Marino v Serbia-Montenegro |
| 08.09.04 | Bosnia v Spain |
| 08.09.04 | Lithuania v San Marino |
| 09.10.04 | Bosnia v Serbia-Montenegro |
| 09.10.04 | Spain v Belgium |
| 13.10.04 | Lithuania v Spain |
| 13.10.04 | Serbia-Montenegro v San Marino |
| 17.11.04 | Belgium v Serbia-Montenegro |
| 17.11.04 | San Marino v Lithuania |
| 09.02.05 | Spain v San Marino |
| 26.03.05 | Belgium v Bosnia |
| 30.03.05 | Bosnia v Lithuania |

| | |
|---|---|
| 30.03.05 | San Marino v Belgium |
| 30.03.05 | Serbia-Montenegro v Spain |
| 04.06.05 | San Marino v Bosnia |
| 04.06.05 | Serbia-Montenegro v Belgium |
| 04.06.05 | Spain v Lithuania |
| 08.06.05 | Spain v Bosnia |
| 03.09.05 | Bosnia v Belgium |
| 03.09.05 | Serbia-Montenegro v Lithuania |
| 07.09.05 | Belgium v San Marino |
| 07.09.05 | Lithuania v Bosnia |
| 07.09.05 | Spain v Serbia-Montenegro |
| 08.10.05 | Belgium v Spain |
| 08.10.05 | Bosnia v San Marino |
| 08.10.05 | Lithuania v Serbia-Montenegro |
| 12.10.05 | Lithuania v Belgium |
| 12.10.05 | San Marino v Spain |
| 12.10.05 | Serbia-Montenegro v Bosnia |

**GROUP 8**

| | |
|---|---|
| 04.09.04 | Croatia v Hungary |
| 04.09.04 | Iceland v Bulgaria |
| 04.09.04 | Malta v Sweden |
| 08.09.04 | Hungary v Iceland |
| 08.09.04 | Sweden v Croatia |
| 09.10.04 | Croatia v Bulgaria |
| 09.10.04 | Malta v Iceland |
| 09.10.04 | Sweden v Hungary |
| 13.10.04 | Bulgaria v Malta |
| 13.10.04 | Iceland v Sweden |
| 17.11.04 | Malta v Hungary |
| 26.03.05 | Bulgaria v Sweden |
| 26.03.05 | Croatia v Iceland |
| 30.03.05 | Croatia v Malta |
| 30.03.05 | Hungary v Bulgaria |
| 04.06.05 | Bulgaria v Croatia |
| 04.06.05 | Iceland v Hungary |
| 04.06.05 | Sweden v Malta |
| 08.06.05 | Iceland v Malta |
| 03.09.05 | Hungary v Malta |
| 03.09.05 | Iceland v Croatia |
| 03.09.05 | Sweden v Bulgaria |
| 07.09.05 | Bulgaria v Iceland |
| 07.09.05 | Hungary v Sweden |
| 07.09.05 | Malta v Croatia |
| 08.10.05 | Bulgaria v Hungary |
| 08.10.05 | Croatia v Sweden |
| 12.10.05 | Hungary v Croatia |
| 12.10.05 | Malta v Bulgaria |
| 12.10.05 | Sweden v Iceland |

# THE WORLD CUP 1930–2002

| Year | Winners | Runners-up | Venue | Attendance | Referee |
|---|---|---|---|---|---|
| 1930 | Uruguay 4 | Argentina 2 | Montevideo | 90,000 | Langenus (B) |
| 1934 | Italy 2 *(after extra time)* | Czechoslovakia 1 | Rome | 50,000 | Eklind (Se) |
| 1938 | Italy 4 | Hungary 2 | Paris | 45,000 | Capdeville (F) |
| 1950 | Uruguay 2 | Brazil 1 | Rio de Janeiro | 199,854 | Reader (E) |
| 1954 | West Germany 3 | Hungary 2 | Berne | 60,000 | Ling (E) |
| 1958 | Brazil 5 | Sweden 2 | Stockholm | 49,737 | Guigue (F) |
| 1962 | Brazil 3 | Czechoslovakia 1 | Santiago | 68,679 | Latychev (USSR) |
| 1966 | England 4 *(after extra time)* | West Germany 2 | Wembley | 93,802 | Dienst (Sw) |
| 1970 | Brazil 4 | Italy 1 | Mexico City | 107,412 | Glockner (EG) |
| 1974 | West Germany 2 | Holland 1 | Munich | 77,833 | Taylor (E) |
| 1978 | Argentina 3 *(after extra time)* | Holland 1 | Buenos Aires | 77,000 | Gonella (I) |
| 1982 | Italy 3 | West Germany 1 | Madrid | 90,080 | Coelho (Br) |
| 1986 | Argentina 3 | West Germany 2 | Mexico City | 114,580 | Filho (Br) |
| 1990 | West Germany 1 | Argentina 0 | Rome | 73,603 | Mendez (Mex) |
| 1994 | Brazil 0 *(Brazil won 3-2 on penalties aet)* | Italy 0 | Los Angeles | 94,194 | Puhl (H) |
| 1998 | France 3 | Brazil 0 | St-Denis | 75,000 | Belqola (Mor) |
| 2002 | Brazil 2 | Germany 0 | Yokohama | 69,029 | Collina (I) |

## GOALSCORING AND ATTENDANCES IN WORLD CUP FINAL ROUNDS

| *Venue* | *Matches* | *Goals (av)* | *Attendance (av)* |
|---|---|---|---|
| 1930, Uruguay | 18 | 70 (3.9) | 434,500 (24,138) |
| 1934, Italy | 17 | 70 (4.1) | 395,000 (23,235) |
| 1938, France | 18 | 84 (4.6) | 483,000 (26,833) |
| 1950, Brazil | 22 | 88 (4.0) | 1,337,000 (60,772) |
| 1954, Switzerland | 26 | 140 (5.4) | 943,000 (36,270) |
| 1958, Sweden | 35 | 126 (3.6) | 868,000 (24,800) |
| 1962, Chile | 32 | 89 (2.8) | 776,000 (24,250) |
| 1966, England | 32 | 89 (2.8) | 1,614,677 (50,458) |
| 1970, Mexico | 32 | 95 (2.9) | 1,673,975 (52,311) |
| 1974, West Germany | 38 | 97 (2.5) | 1,774,022 (46,684) |
| 1978, Argentina | 38 | 102 (2.7) | 1,610,215 (42,374) |
| 1982, Spain | 52 | 146 (2.8) | 2,064,364 (38,816) |
| 1986, Mexico | 52 | 132 (2.5) | 2,441,731 (46,956) |
| 1990, Italy | 52 | 115 (2.2) | 2,515,168 (48,368) |
| 1994, USA | 52 | 141 (2.7) | 3,567,415 (68,604) |
| 1998, France | 64 | 171 (2.6) | 2,775,400 (43,366) |
| 2002, Japan/S. Korea | 64 | 161 (2.5) | 2,705,566 (42,274) |

## LEADING GOALSCORERS

| *Year* | *Player* | *Goals* |
|---|---|---|
| 1930 | Guillermo Stabile (Argentina) | 8 |
| 1934 | Angelo Schiavio (Italy), Oldrich Nejedly (Czechoslovakia), Edmund Conen (Germany) | 4 |
| 1938 | Leonidas da Silva (Brazil) | 8 |
| 1950 | Ademir (Brazil) | 9 |
| 1954 | Sandor Kocsis (Hungary) | 11 |
| 1958 | Just Fontaine (France) | 13 |
| 1962 | Valentin Ivanov (USSR), Leonel Sanchez (Chile), Garrincha, Vava (both Brazil), Florian Albert (Hungary), Drazen Jerkovic (Yugoslavia) | 4 |
| 1966 | Eusebio (Portugal) | 9 |
| 1970 | Gerd Muller (West Germany) | 10 |
| 1974 | Grzegorz Lato (Poland) | 7 |
| 1978 | Mario Kempes (Argentina) | 6 |
| 1982 | Paolo Rossi (Italy) | 6 |
| 1986 | Gary Lineker (England) | 6 |
| 1990 | Salvatore Schillaci (Italy) | 6 |
| 1994 | Oleg Salenko (Russia) Hristo Stoichkov (Bulgaria) | 6 |
| 1998 | Davor Suker (Croatia) | 6 |
| 2002 | Ronaldo (Brazil) | 8 |

# THE WORLD CUP 2006

## QUALIFYING RESULTS – SOUTH AMERICA

Buenos Aires, 6 September 2003, 35,372

**Argentina (2) 2** *(Kily Gonzalez 32, Aimar 36)*

**Chile (0) 2** *(Mirosevic 60, Navia 77)*

*Argentina:* Cavallero; Vivas, Ayala, Samuel■, Zanetti, Veron (Almeyda 65), Kily Gonzalez, Aimar, D'Alessandro, Delgado, Crespo (Saviola 71).
*Chile:* Tapia N; Alvarez■, Contreras, Olarra, Perez, Martel, Marcos Gonzalez, Melendez (Mirosevic 38), Mark Gonzalez (Acuna 57), Tapia H (Pinilla 57), Navia■.
*Referee:* Aquino (Paraguay).

Quito, 6 September 2003, 30,000

**Ecuador (1) 2** *(Espinoza G 6, Tenorio C 67)*

**Venezuela (0) 0**

*Ecuador:* Cevallos; De la Cruz, Espinoza G, Hurtado I, Reasco, Ayovi, Obregon, Mendez, Chala, Aguinaga (Tenorio O 43), Tenorio C.
*Venezuela:* Angelucci; Vallenilla, Rey, Alvarado, Rojas, Mea Vitali, Jimenez, Arango, Paez (Noriega 60), Urdaneta (Gonzalez 60), Moran (Casseres 67).
*Referee:* Selman (Chile).

Lima, 6 September 2003, 43,000

**Peru (2) 4** *(Solano 34, Mendoza 42, Jorge Soto 83, Farfan 90)*

**Paraguay (1) 1** *(Gamarra 24)*

*Peru:* Delgado; Jorge Soto, Rebosio, Galliquio, Hidalgo, Jayo, Zegarra, Solano (Jose Soto 89), Palacios (Ciurlizza 76), Mendoza (Farfan 70), Pizarro.
*Paraguay:* Tavarelli; Arce, Gamarra, Da Silva, Caceres, Toledo (Alvarenga 60), Enciso, Paredes, Bonet (Cuevas 81), Santa Cruz, Cardozo.
*Referee:* Baldassi (Argentina).

Barranquilla, 7 September 2003, 55,000

**Colombia (1) 1** *(Angel 38)*

**Brazil (1) 2** *(Ronaldo 25, Kaka 60)*

*Colombia:* Cordoba O; Martinez, Cordoba I, Yepes, Bedoya (Perea 35), Caballero, Restrepo (Becerra 63), Grisales, Patino (Molina 75), Hernandez, Angel.
*Brazil:* Dida; Cafu, Lucio, Roque Junior, Roberto Carlos, Emerson (Renato 59), Gilberto Silva, Ze Roberto, Alex (Kaka 59), Ronaldo, Rivaldo (Diego 87).
*Referee:* Elizondo (Argentina).

Montevideo, 7 September 2003, 42,000

**Uruguay (2) 5** *(Forlan 17, Chevanton 38, 60, Abeijon 82, Bueno 87)*

**Bolivia (0) 0**

*Uruguay:* Munua; Gonzalez, Lopez, Lago, Sosa (Abeijon 69), Liguera (Oliveira 77), Nunez, Recoba, Bueno, Chevanton, Forlan (Sanchez 76).
*Bolivia:* Fernandez L; Hoyos, Sanchez, Pena, Gatti Ribeiro (Baldivieso 46), Rojas, Cristaldo, Ricardi■, Morejon (Botero 46), Castillo, Mendez.
*Referee:* Hidalgo (Peru).

Santiago, 9 September 2003, 55,000

**Chile (1) 2** *(Pinilla 35, Norambuena 70)*

**Peru (0) 1** *(Mendoza 57)*

*Chile:* Tapia N; Rojas, Contreras, Olarra, Martel (Mark Gonzalez 46), Acuna, Marcos Gonzalez (Pizarro 46), Mirosevic, Perez, Tapia H (Norambuena 67), Pinilla.
*Peru:* Delgado; Jorge Soto, Galliquio, Rebosio, Hidalgo, Jayo, Zegarra, Solano (Jose Soto 81), Palacios (Farfan 75), Mendoza, Pizarro.
*Referee:* Aquino (Paraguay).

Caracas, 9 September 2003, 25,000

**Venezuela (0) 0**

**Argentina (3) 3** *(Aimar 7, Crespo 25, Delgado 32)*

*Venezuela:* Angelucci; Gonzalez (Vallenilla 46), Rey, Alvaravo, Rojas, Vera, Jimenez, Arango (Moreno 61), Paez, Moran (Urdaneta 46), Noriega.
*Argentina:* Cavallero; Vivas, Ayala, Piacente, Zanetti, Veron, Kily Gonzalez, Aimar (Heinze 63), D'Alessandro (Luis Gonzalez 85), Delgado (Almeyda 81), Crespo.
*Referee:* Vazquez (Uruguay).

La Paz, 10 September 2003, 30,000

**Bolivia (2) 4** *(Baldivieso 12, Botero 28, 49, 58)*

**Colombia (0) 0**

*Bolivia:* Fernandez L (Fernandez JC 46); Paz Garcia, Pena, Sanchez, Gatti Ribeiro, Rojas (Garcia R 74), Cristaldo, Baldivieso, Mendez, Botero, Suarez (Justinano 62).
*Colombia:* Cordoba O; Martinez, Cordoba I■, Yepes, Cortes, Viafara, Vargas (Restrepo 46), Patino (Molina 46), Hernandez (Castillo 46), Angel, Aristizabal.
*Referee:* Oliveira (Brazil).

Manaus, 10 September 2003, 35,000

**Brazil (1) 1** *(Ronaldinho 13)*

**Ecuador (0) 0**

*Brazil:* Dida; Cafu, Lucio, Roque Junior, Roberto Carlos, Emerson (Renato 62), Gilberto Silva, Ze Roberto, Ronaldinho (Kaka 68), Ronaldo, Rivaldo (Alex 90).
*Ecuador:* Cevallos; De la Cruz, Hurtado I, Espinoza G, Reasco, Obregon, Tenorio E, Ayovi, Mendez, Chala, Tenorio C (Tenorio O 83).
*Referee:* Solozano (Venezuela).

Asuncion, 10 September 2003, 20,000

**Paraguay (1) 4** *(Cardozo 27, 58, 73, Paredes 54)*

**Uruguay (1) 1** *(Chevanton 24)*

*Paraguay:* Villar; Arce, Gamarra, Da Silva, Caceres, Bonet, Enciso (Ortiz 90), Paredes, Santa Cruz, Cardozo, Campos (Gavilan 81).
*Uruguay:* Munua; Gonzalez, Sorondo, Aguiai, Regueiro (Nunez 78), Abeijon, Oliveira, Giacomazzi (Liguera 46), Chevanton, Bueno (Recoba 61), Forlan.
*Referee:* Ruiz (Colombia).

Buenos Aires, 15 November 2003, 30,042

**Argentina (0) 3** *(D'Alessandro 56, Crespo 61, Aimar 63)*

**Bolivia (0) 0**

*Argentina:* Cavallero; Quiroga, Ayala, Samuel, Zanetti, Almeyda (Cambiasso 89), Kily Gonzalez, Aimar, D'Alessandro (Sorin 84), Crespo (Saviola 80), Delgado.
*Bolivia:* Fernandez L; Raldes, Sanchez, Paz Garcia, Ricaldi, Gatti Ribeiro, Justiniano, Reyes, Suarez (Etcheverry 69), Mercado (Castillo 64), Botero (Mendez 64).
*Referee:* Hidalgo (Peru).

Barranquilla, 15 November 2003, 20,000

**Colombia (0) 0**

**Venezuela (1) 1** *(Arango 8)*

*Colombia:* Mondragon; Vallejo, Perez, Yepes, Viveros, Lozano, Bolano (Arriaga 54), Hernandez (Patino 46), Grisales, Becerra, Angel.
*Venezuela:* Angelucci; Vallenilla, Hernandez, Rey, Cichero, Jimenez, Mea Vitali (Vielna 6), Paez (Gonzalez 57), Urdaneta (Rojas 57), Arango, Noriega.
*Referee:* Chandia (Chile).

Asuncion, 15 November 2003, 30,000

**Paraguay (1) 2** *(Santa Cruz 30, Cardozo 70)*

**Ecuador (0) 1** *(Mendez 59)*

*Paraguay:* Villar; Arce, Caceres, Gamarra, Caniza, Bonet (Gavilan 72), Ortiz, Paredes, Campos (Cuevas 61), Santa Cruz, Cardozo (Alvarenga 87).
*Ecuador:* Cevallos; De la Cruz, Hurtado I, Espinoza G, Corozo, Mendez, Tenorio E (Fernandez 63), Ambrossi (Salas 77), Gomez, Chala, Ordonez.
*Referee:* Paniagua (Bolivia).

Montevideo, 15 November 2003, 60,000

**Uruguay (1) 2** *(Chevanton 31, Romero 48)*

**Chile (1) 1** *(Melendez 20)*

*Uruguay:* Munua; Gonzalez, Lopez, Lago, Munoz (Romero 46), Sosa, Nunez, Liguera (Recoba 70), Chevanton, Bueno, Forlan (Hornos 46).
*Chile:* Tapia N; Rojas, Olarra, Ramirez, Perez, Martel (Ormazabal 53), Nunoz, Melendez, Mark Gonzalez (Mirosevic 53), Navia (Norambuena 75), Pinilla.
*Referee:* Martin (Argentina).

Santiago, 16 November 2003, 63,000

**Chile (0) 0**

**Paraguay (1) 1** *(Paredes 30)*

*Chile:* Tapia N; Contreras, Ramirez, Olarra, Alvarez (Ormazabal 46), Marcos Gonzalez (Melendez 46), Perez, Mirosevic, Pizarro, Pinilla, Navia (Norambuena 62).
*Paraguay:* Villar; Arce, Caceres, Gamarra, Caniza, Bonet (Gavilan 79), Ortiz, Paredes (Da Silva 88), Enciso, Santa Cruz, Cardozo (Alvarenga 87).
*Referee:* Mendez (Uruguay).

Lima, 16 November 2003, 70,000

**Peru (0) 1** *(Solano 58)*

**Brazil (1) 1** *(Rivaldo 20 (pen))*

*Peru:* Ibanez; Jorge Soto, Galliquio, Rebosio, Hidalgo (Salas 52), Jayo, Ciurlizza, Solano, Palacios (Garcia 74), Mendoza, Pizarro.
*Brazil:* Dida; Cafu, Lucio, Roque Junior, Junior, Gilberto Silva, Ze Roberto, Emerson (Renato 61), Kaka (Alex 74), Rivaldo (Luis Fabiano 84), Ronaldo.
*Referee:* Ruiz (Colombia).

Maracaibo, 18 November 2003, 25,000

**Venezuela (0) 2** *(Rey 89, Arango 90)*

**Bolivia (0) 1** *(Botero 60)*

*Venezuela:* Angelucci; Vallenilla, Cichero, Rey, Hernandez (Rojas 61), Jimenez, Arango, Urdaneta, Paez, Moran (Rondon 59), Noriega (Moreno 52).
*Bolivia:* Fernandez L; Raldes (Sandy 79), Sanchez, Paz Garcia, Reyes, Alvarez, Gatti Ribeiro, Justiniano, Suarez (Mendez 69), Mercado (Vaca 66), Botero.
*Referee:* Reinoso (Ecuador).

Barranquilla, 19 November 2003, 30,000

**Colombia (0) 1** *(Angel 47)*

**Argentina (1) 1** *(Crespo 26)*

*Colombia:* Cordoba O; Martinez, Cordoba I, Yepes, Viveros, Grisales, Viafara, Lozano (Bolano 20), Patino (Arriaga 46), Montoya (Becerra 71), Angel.
*Argentina:* Cavallero; Quiroga, Ayala, Samuel, Zanetti, Almeyda, Piacente, Kily Gonzalez, Aimar (D'Alessandro 70), Delgado (Veron 46), Crespo (Saviola 71).
*Referee:* Simon (Brazil).

Quito, 19 November 2003, 43,000

**Ecuador (0) 0**

**Peru (0) 0**

*Ecuador:* Cevallos; De la Cruz, Hurtado I, Reasco, Espinoza G, Ayovi, Obregon (Fernandez 66), Chala (Aguinaga 79), Mendez, Tenorio C, Ordonez (Salas 46).
*Peru:* Ibanez; Jorge Soto, Rebosio, Galliquio, Salas, Jayo, Ciurlizza, Garcia, Palacios (Moran 53), Mendoza (Farfan 46), Pizarro.
*Referee:* Gonzalez (Paraguay).

Curitiba, 19 November 2003, 30,000

**Brazil (2) 3** *(Kaka 19, Ronaldo 29, 87)*

**Uruguay (0) 3** *(Forlan 57, 76, Gilberto Silva 79 (og))*

*Brazil:* Dida; Cafu, Lucio, Roque Junior, Junior, Renato (Juninho Pernambucano 79), Gilberto Silva, Ze Roberto, Kaka (Alex 72), Rivaldo (Luis Fabiano 80), Ronaldo.
*Uruguay:* Munua; Romero (Recoba 46), Bizera, Lopez, Lago, Sosa, Abeijon (Nunez 36), Liguera, Hornos (Chevanton 55), Zalayeta, Forlan.
*Referee:* Elizondo (Argentina).

Buenos Aires, 30 March 2004, 55,000

**Argentina (0) 1** *(Crespo 60)*

**Ecuador (0) 0**

*Argentina:* Cavallero; Ayala, Sorin, Rodriguez, Luis Gonzalez, Heinze, Gonzalez M (Tevez 46), D'Alessandro, Aimar (Riquelme 55), Delgado (Burdisso 66), Crespo.
*Ecuador:* Cevallos; Hurtado I, De la Cruz, Obregon, Tenorio C (Salas 73), Ayovi, Chala (Delgado 63), Espinoza G, Reasco, Mendez, Tenorio E (Kaviedes 67).
*Referee:* Vazquez (Uruguay).

La Paz, 30 March 2004, 42,000

**Bolivia (0) 0**

**Chile (1) 2** *(Villarroel 38, Mark Gonzalez 60)*

*Bolivia:* Fernandez L; Sanchez, Pena, Pizarro, Suarez (Gatti Ribeiro 46), Angulo, Reyes (Vaca 61), Pachi, Da Rosa, Castillo, Botero (Mendez 46).
*Chile:* Tapia N; Rojas, Vargas, Olarra, Perez, Villarroel (Maldonado 55), Melendez, Mark Gonzalez, Martel (Valenzuela 74), Salas, Galaz (Pinilla 55).
*Referee:* Martin (Argentina).

Asuncion, 31 March 2004, 40,000

**Paraguay (0) 0**

**Brazil (0) 0**

*Paraguay:* Tavarelli; Arce, Caceres (Da Silva 73), Gamarra, Bonet (Ortiz 30), Paredes, Toledo (Campos 56), Enciso, Caniza, Cardozo, Santa Cruz.
*Brazil:* Dida; Cafu, Lucio, Roque Junior, Roberto Carlos, Renato (Juninho Pernambucano 67), Gilberto Silva, Ze Roberto, Kaka, Ronaldinho, Ronaldo.
*Referee:* Ruiz (Colombia).

Lima, 31 March 2004, 29,325

**Peru (0) 0**

**Colombia (2) 2** *(Grisales 30, Oviedo 42)*

*Peru:* Ibanez; Rebosio, Jorge Soto, Hidalgo (Farfan 46), Jayo, Palacios (Silva 58), Quinteros (Salas 46), Ciurlizza, Galliquio, Pizarro, Mendoza.
*Colombia:* Calero; Cordoba I, Yepes, Vargas, Oviedo, Murillo (Viveros 72), Perea, Ramirez (Viafara 90), Grisales (Patino 78), Bedoya, Angel.
*Referee:* Rezende (Brazil).

Montevideo, 31 March 2004, 40,000

**Uruguay (0) 0**

**Venezuela (1) 3** *(Urdaneta 18, Hector Gonzalez 65, Arango 80)*

*Uruguay:* Munua; Lopez■, Sorondo, Rodriguez, Liguera, Sosa, Nunez, Recoba, Chevanton (Correa 59), Hornos (Pandiani 46), Forlan (Bueno 72).
*Venezuela:* Angelucci; Vallenilla, Rey, Cichero, Hernandez, Jimenez, Vera, Paez (Rojas 61), Arango (Andre Gonzalez 83), Urdaneta (Hector Gonzalez 61), Rondon.
*Referee:* Ortube (Bolivia).

La Paz, 1 June 2004, 20,000

**Bolivia (1) 2** *(Cristaldo 9, Suarez 72)*

**Paraguay (1) 1** *(Cardozo 33)*

*Bolivia:* Fernandez L; Jauregui, Raldes, Pena■, Gatti Ribeiro (Solis 90), Cristaldo, Sanchez, Alvarez (Suarez 60), Baldivieso, Gutierrez (Angulo 86), Botero.
*Paraguay:* Villa; Espinola, Lugo (Cabanas 82), Gamarra, Da Silva, Edgar Gonzalez, Ortiz, Duarte (De Los Santos 74), Enciso, Cardozo, Santa Cruz (Ramirez 63).
*Referee:* Resende de Freitas (Brazil).

Montevideo, 1 June 2004, 30,000

**Uruguay (0) 1** *(Forlan 73)*

**Peru (2) 3** *(Solano 12, Pizarro 19, Farfan 62)*

*Uruguay:* Munua; De Souza, Sorondo■, Lembo, Guigou (Romero 46), Sosa, Garcia, Pacheco (Forlan 46), Nunez, Chevanton, Pandiani (Dario Silva 72).
*Peru:* Ibanez; Galliquio, Acasiete, Rebosio (Garcia 80), Vilchez, Zegarra, Solano, Jayo, Palacios (Jose Soto 59), Pizarro (Mendoza 46), Farfan.
*Referee:* Selma (Chile).

San Cristobal, 1 June 2004, 30,000

**Venezuela (0) 0**

**Chile (0) 1** *(Pinilla 84)*

*Venezuela:* Angelucci; Vallenilla (Hector Gonzalez 65), Cichero, Rey, Hernandez, Jimenez, Vielma (Andre Gonzalez 75), Urdaneta (Margiotta 46), Paez, Arango, Rondon.
*Chile:* Tapia N; Rojas, Vargas, Olarra, Perez, Maldonado, Melendez, Mark Gonzalez (Mirosevic 59), Pizarro (Valenzuela 79), Galaz (Pinilla 46), Navia.
*Referee:* Torres (Paraguay).

Belo Horizonte, 2 June 2004, 48,000

**Brazil (1) 3** *(Ronaldo 16 (pen), 67 (pen), 90 (pen))*

**Argentina (0) 1** *(Sorin 80)*

*Brazil:* Dida; Cafu, Juan, Roque Junior, Roberto Carlos, Edmilson, Juninho Pernambucano (Julio Baptista 75), Ze Roberto, Kaka (Alex 75), Luis Fabiano, Ronaldo.
*Argentina:* Cavallero; Quiroga, Samuel, Heinze, Zanetti, Mascherano, Luis Gonzalez (Aimar 61), Sorin, Delgado (Rosales 36) (Saviola 61), Crespo, Kily Gonzalez.
*Referee:* Ruiz (Colombia).

Quito, 2 June 2004, 40,000

**Ecuador (1) 2** *(Delgado 3, Salas 66)*

**Colombia (0) 1** *(Oviedo 56)*

*Ecuador:* Espinoza J; De la Cruz, Hurtado I, Espinoza G, Ambrossi, Ayovi (Lastra 87), Tenorio E, Mendez (Aguinaga 65), Chala, Figueroa (Salas 50), Delgado.
*Colombia:* Calero; Perea, Yepes, Cordoba I, Bedoya (Ferreira 78), Vargas, Ramirez, Viafara (Viveros 46), Oviedo, Valentierra (Murillo■ 70), Rey.
*Referee:* Baldassi (Argentina).

Quito, 5 June 2004, 40,000

**Ecuador (3) 3** *(Solis 29 (og), Delgado 33, De la Cruz 40)*

**Bolivia (0) 2** *(Gutierrez 58, Castillo 75)*

*Ecuador:* Espinoza J; De la Cruz, Hurtado I, Espinoza G, Reasco, Tenorio E, Obregon (Aguinaga 70), Ambrossi (Ayovi 80), Chala (Mendez 66), Delgado, Salas.
*Bolivia:* Fernandez L; Solis (Gatti Ribeiro 46), Sanchez, Raldes, Jauregui, Alvarez, Angulo (Galindo 46), Suarez (Castillo 67), Baldivieso, Botero, Gutierrez.
*Referee:* Brand (Venezuela).

Buenos Aires, 6 June 2004, 30,000

**Argentina (0) 0**

**Paraguay (0) 0**

*Argentina:* Abbondanzieri; Ayala, Samuel, Heinze, Luis Gonzalez (Rosales 69), Mascherano, Sorin, Tevez, Saviola, Crespo, Kily Gonzalez.
*Paraguay:* Villar; Caniza, Caceres, Gamarra, Da Silva, Gavilan (Sarabia 90), Ortiz■, Toledo (Edgar Gonzalez 64), Enciso, Santa Cruz, Cardozo (Ramirez 84).
*Referee:* Simon (Brazil).

Santiago, 6 June 2004, 65,000

**Chile (0) 1** *(Navia 89 (pen))*

**Brazil (1) 1** *(Luis Fabiano 16)*

*Chile:* Tapia N; Rojas (Alvarez 46), Fuentes, Olarra, Perez, Helo (Galaz 46), Melendez, Maldonado, Mark Gonzalez (Mirosevic 56), Pizarro, Navia.
*Brazil:* Dida; Cafu, Roberto Carlos, Juninho Pernambucano, Juan, Roque Junior, Edmilson, Kaka (Julio Baptista 72), Ronaldo, Luis Fabiano, Edu.
*Referee:* Elizondo (Argentina).

Barranquilla, 6 June 2004, 20,000

**Colombia (3) 5** *(Pacheco 18, 32, Moreno 20, Restrepo 81, Herrera 86)*

**Uruguay (0) 0**

*Colombia:* Calero; Palacios, Perea, Yepes, Bedoya, Ramirez, Restrepo, Oviedo (Vargas 74), Pacheco (Ferreira 84), Moreno (Arriaga 74), Herrera.
*Uruguay:* Munua; Gonzalez, Lembo, De Souza (Lago 64), Romero (De Los Santos 46), Romero, Garcia, Delgado, Canobbio (Forlan 46), Recoba, Chevanton.
*Referee:* Carlos (Paraguay).

Lima, 6 June 2004, 45,000

**Peru (0) 0**

**Venezuela (0) 0**

*Peru:* Ibanez; Jorge Soto, Rebosio, Acasiete, Hidalgo (Vilchez 67), Jayo, Zegarra, Solano, Palacios (Orejuela 67), Farfan, Mendoza (Silva 79).
*Venezuela:* Angelucci; Vallenilla, Cichero, Rey, Hernandez, Mea Vitali, Jimenez, Urdaneta (Margiotta 79), Paez (Hector Gonzalez 66), Arango, Rondon (Moran 61).
*Referee:* Larrionda (Uruguay).

# EUROPEAN FOOTBALL CHAMPIONSHIP
## (formerly EUROPEAN NATIONS' CUP)

| *Year* | *Winners* | | *Runners-up* | | *Venue* | *Attendance* |
|---|---|---|---|---|---|---|
| 1960 | USSR | 2 | Yugoslavia | 1 | Paris | 17,966 |
| 1964 | Spain | 2 | USSR | 1 | Madrid | 120,000 |
| 1968 | Italy<br>After 1-1 draw | 2 | Yugoslavia | 0 | Rome | 60,000<br>75,000 |
| 1972 | West Germany | 3 | USSR | 0 | Brussels | 43,437 |
| 1976 | Czechoslovakia<br>*(Czechoslovakia won on penalties)* | 2 | West Germany | 2 | Belgrade | 45,000 |
| 1980 | West Germany | 2 | Belgium | 1 | Rome | 47,864 |
| 1984 | France | 2 | Spain | 0 | Paris | 48,000 |
| 1988 | Holland | 2 | USSR | 0 | Munich | 72,308 |
| 1992 | Denmark | 2 | Germany | 0 | Gothenburg | 37,800 |
| 1996 | Germany<br>*(Germany won on sudden death)* | 2 | Czech Republic | 1 | Wembley | 73,611 |
| 2000 | France<br>*(France won on sudden death)* | 2 | Italy | 1 | Rotterdam | 50,000 |
| 2004 | Greece | 1 | Portugal | 0 | Lisbon | 62,865 |

# BRITISH & IRISH INTERNATIONAL MANAGERS

**England**
Walter Winterbottom 1946–1962 (after period as coach); Alf Ramsey 1963–1974; Joe Mercer (caretaker) 1974; Don Revie 1974–1977; Ron Greenwood 1977–1982; Bobby Robson 1982–1990; Graham Taylor 1990–1993; Terry Venables (coach) 1994–1996; Glenn Hoddle 1996–1999; Kevin Keegan 1999–2000; Sven-Goran Eriksson from January 2001.

**Northern Ireland**
Peter Doherty 1951–1952; Bertie Peacock 1962–1967; Billy Bingham 1967–1971; Terry Neill 1971–1975; Dave Clements (player-manager) 1975–1976; Danny Blanchflower 1976–1979; Billy Bingham 1980–1994; Bryan Hamilton 1994–1998; Lawrie McMenemy 1998–1999; Sammy McIlroy 2000–03; Lawrie Sanchez from January 2004.

**Scotland (since 1967)**
Bobby Brown 1967–1971; Tommy Docherty 1971–1972; Willie Ormond 1973–1977; Ally MacLeod 1977–1978; Jock Stein 1978–1985; Alex Ferguson (caretaker) 1985–1986 Andy Roxburgh (coach) 1986–1993; Craig Brown 1993–2001; Berti Vogts from March 2002.

**Wales (since 1974)**
Mike Smith 1974–1979; Mike England 1980–1988; David Williams (caretaker) 1988; Terry Yorath 1988–1993; John Toshack 1994 for one match; Mike Smith 1994–1995; Bobby Gould 1995–1999; Mark Hughes from November 1999.

**Republic of Ireland**
Liam Tuohy 1971–1972; Johnny Giles 1973–1980 (after period as player-manager); Eoin Hand 1980–1985; Jack Charlton 1986–1996; Mick McCarthy 1996–2002; Brian Kerr from January 2003.

# EURO 2004

## QUALIFYING RESULTS

▪ *Denotes player sent off.*
*NB: Places for teams level on points determined by results between them.*

### GROUP 1

Nicosia, 7 September 2002, 11,898

**Cyprus (1) 1** *(Okkas 14)*

**France (1) 2** *(Cisse 39, Wiltord 52)*

*Cyprus:* Panayiotou N; Theodotou, Daskalakis (Michael 68), Ioakim, Konnafis, Spyrou, Kaiafas, Satsias, Nicolaou N (Agathocleous 74), Rauffmann (Yiasoumi 62), Okkas.
*France:* Coupet; Thuram, Christanval, Desailly, Silvestre, Wiltord (Kapo 79), Makelele, Zidane, Vieira, Marlet (Govou 70), Cisse.
*Referee:* Fandel (Germany).

Ljubljana, 7 September 2002, 15,000

**Slovenia (1) 3** *(Debono 37 (og), Siljak 59, Cimerotic 90)*

**Malta (0) 0**

*Slovenia:* Simeunovic; Vugdalic, Bulajic, Knavs, Karic, Sukalo (Gajser 74), Acimovic (Radosavljevic 86), Zahovic, Pavlin, Siljak, Cimerotic.
*Malta:* Muscat; Said, Dimech, Carabott, Debono, Chetcuti, Agius, Giglio▪, Mallia (Bogdanovic 71), Nwoko, Michael Mifsud (Mifsud A 88).
*Referee:* Borovilos (Greece).

Stade de France, 12 October 2002, 77,619

**France (2) 5** *(Vieira 10, Marlet 35, 64, Wiltord 79, Govou 86)*

**Slovenia (0) 0**

*France:* Barthez; Thuram (Sagnol 84), Silvestre, Vieira, Gallas, Desailly, Wiltord (Cheyrou 87), Makelele, Marlet (Govou 80), Zidane, Henry.
*Slovenia:* Simeunovic; Gajser▪, Karic (Filekovic 88), Sukalo, Vugdalic, Cipot, Zahovic, Radosavljevic (Zlogar 68), Siljak, Pavlin, Cimerotic (Ceh N 46).
*Referee:* Nielsen (Denmark).

Valletta, 12 October 2002, 4000

**Malta (0) 0**

**Israel (0) 2** *(Balili 57, Revivo 77)*

*Malta:* Muscat; Said, Dimech, Chetcuti, Carabott, Debono, Agius (Mallia 84), Turner, Brincat (Mifsud A 76), Nwoko (Bogdanovic 64), Michael Mifsud.
*Israel:* Auat; Zano, Domb, Banin, Badir, Benado, Keissi, Balili (Benayoun 71), Revivo, Tal (Antebi 82), Berkovic.
*Referee:* Shebek (Ukraine).

Valletta, 16 October 2002, 12,000

**Malta (0) 0**

**France (2) 4** *(Henry 25, 35, Wiltord 59, Carriere 84)*

*Malta:* Muscat; Carabott, Chetcuti, Debono (Miguel Mifsud 87), Said, Dimech, Agius, Michael Mifsud, Giglio, Nwoko (Bogdanovic 46), Brincat (Mallia 69).
*France:* Barthez; Thuram, Silvestre, Vieira (Dacourt 70), Gallas (Mexes 84), Desailly, Wiltord, Makelele, Marlet, Zidane, Henry (Carriere 78).
*Referee:* Tudor (Romania).

Nicosia, 20 November 2002, 5000

**Cyprus (0) 2** *(Rauffmann 50, Okkas 74)*

**Malta (0) 1** *(Michael Mifsud 90)*

*Cyprus:* Panayiotou N; Konnafis, Ioakim, Spyrou, Okkarides, Theodotou, Satsias (Michael), Kaiafas, Okkas, Rauffmann (Yiasoumi 71), Constantinou M (Nicolaou N 66).
*Malta:* Muscat; Said, Mamo (Miguel Mifsud 74), Giglio (Theuma 80), Chetcuti, Carabott, Agius, Dimech, Michael Mifsud, Bogdanovic, Mifsud A (Mallia 61).
*Referee:* Guenov (Bulgaria).

Limassol, 29 March 2003, 5000

**Cyprus (0) 1** *(Rauffmann 61)*

**Israel (1) 1** *(Afek 2)*

*Cyprus:* Panayiotou N; Okkarides, Ioakim (Nicolaou N 46) (Daskalakis 77), Konnafis, Spyrou, Theodotou, Engomitis (Rauffmann 60), Kaiafas, Tomic, Constantinou M, Okkas.
*Israel:* Auat; Benado, Ben-Haim, Keissi, Harazi A, Banin, Badir (Abuksis 85), Tal, Afek (Benayoun 73), Zandberg (Nimny 66), Revivo.
*Referee:* McCurry (Scotland).

Lens, 29 March 2003, 40,775

**France (2) 6** *(Wiltord 36, Henry 38, 54, Zidane 57 (pen), 81, Trezeguet 70)*

**Malta (0) 0**

*France:* Barthez; Thuram (Sagnol 65), Lizarazu, Pedretti, Gallas, Silvestre, Wiltord (Govou 75), Makelele, Trezeguet, Zidane, Henry (Rothen 80).
*Malta:* Muscat; Carabott, Ciantar, Said, Vella, Mamo (Chetcuti 71), Bogdanovic (Turner 62), Dimech, Mallia, Michael Mifsud, Nwoko.
*Referee:* Bozinovski (Macedonia).

Palermo, 2 April 2003, 5000

**Israel (1) 1** *(Afek 2)*

**France (2) 2** *(Trezeguet 23, Zidane 45)*

*Israel:* Auat; Benado, Ben-Haim, Keissi, Harazi A, Abuksis, Banin (Benayoun 74), Tal (Badir 56), Afek, Turgeman (Zandberg 46), Revivo.
*France:* Barthez; Thuram, Lizarazu, Vieira, Gallas, Silvestre, Wiltord (Govou 66), Makelele, Trezeguet (Cisse 74), Zidane, Henry.
*Referee:* Barber (England).

Ljubljana, 2 April 2003, 5000

**Slovenia (4) 4** *(Siljak 5, 14, Zahovic 39 (pen), Ceh A 43)*

**Cyprus (1) 1** *(Constantinou M 10)*

*Slovenia:* Simeunovic; Cipot, Karic, Vugdalic, Bulajic, Zahovic, Ceh A, Pavlin, Sukalo, Koren (Zlogar 85), Siljak (Rakovic 90).
*Cyprus:* Panayiotou N; Konnafis (Ioakim 46), Daskalakis, Spyrou (Constantinou G 75), Theodotou, Kaiafas, Okkarides, Rauffmann (Charalambides 46), Tomic, Okkas, Constantinou M.
*Referee:* Gomes (Portugal).

Palermo, 30 April 2003, 1000

**Israel (0) 2** *(Badir 88, Holtzman 90)*

**Cyprus (0) 0**

*Israel:* Elimelech; Zano, Afek, Benado, Ben-Haim, Banin (Badir 85), Keissi, Abuksis, Revivo, Turgeman (Benayoun 52), Zandberg (Holtzman 67).
*Cyprus:* Panayiotou N; Konnafis, Germanou, Nicolaou N, Tomic (Kaiafas 62), Engomitis (Chrisostomos 80), Theodotou, Nicolaou C (Yiasoumi 89), Okkarides, Okkas, Constantinou M.
*Referee:* Benes (Czech Republic).

Valletta, 30 April 2003, 2500

**Malta (0) 1** *(Michael Mifsud 90)*

**Slovenia (2) 3** *(Zahovic 15, Siljak 36, 57)*

*Malta:* Muscat; Ciantar, Vella, Carabott, Said, Turner, Dimech, Giglio (Camenzuli 69), Mallia, Michael Mifsud, Nwoko (Bogdanovic 63).
*Slovenia:* Simeunovic; Cipot, Vugdalic, Karic, Oslaj (Snofl 61), Sukalo, Ceh N, Zahovic, Pavlin, Siljak (Rakovic 90), Gajser (Koren 78).
*Referee:* Hanacsek (Hungary).

Antalya, 7 June 2003, 2500

**Israel (0) 0**

**Slovenia (0) 0**

*Israel:* Elimelech; Benado, Banin, Keissi, Afek (Zandberg 71), Nimny, Tal (Bachar 76), Abuksis (Holtzman 86), Revivo, Zano, Benayoun.
*Slovenia:* Simeunovic; Cipot, Vugdalic, Knavs, Gajser (Koren 71), Sukalo, Pavlin, Karic, Zahovic, Acimovic (Snofl 86), Siljak.
*Referee:* Busacca (Switzerland).

Ta'Qali, 7 June 2003, 3000

**Malta (0) 1** *(Dimech 72)*

**Cyprus (1) 2** *(Constantinou M 23 (pen), 52)*

*Malta:* Darmanin■; Camenzuli, Said (Bogdanovic 86), Carabott, Vella, Giglio, Dimech, Mallia (Agius 66), Turner, Michael Mifsud, Nwoko (Muscat 23).
*Cyprus:* Panayiotou N; Konnafis, Charalambides (Garpozis 90), Daskalakis (Foukaris 65), Christodoulou, Satsias, Okkarides, Michael, Ilia, Okkas (Yiasoumi 78), Constantinou M.
*Referee:* Brugger (Austria).

Saint-Denis, 6 September 2003, 55,000

**France (3) 5** *(Trezeguet 7, 82, Wiltord 20, 41, Henry 59)*

**Cyprus (0) 0**

*France:* Barthez; Thuram (Sagnol 65), Lizarazu, Makelele, Desailly, Silvestre, Wiltord, Vieira (Dacourt 71), Trezeguet, Henry (Marlet 78), Pires.
*Cyprus:* Panayiotou N; Okkarides, Georghiou N, Theodotou, Konnafis (Ioakim 46), Engomitis (Michael C 58), Nicolaou N, Kaiafas, Satsias, Okkas, Constantinou M (Yiasoumi 67).
*Referee:* Irvine (Northern Ireland).

Ljubljana, 6 September 2003, 8000

**Slovenia (2) 3** *(Siljak 35, Knavs 37, Ceh N 78)*

**Israel (0) 1** *(Revivo 69)*

*Slovenia:* Simeunovic; Cipot, Karic, Snofl, Knavs, Sukalo, Ceh N (Rudonja 89), Zahovic, Kapic (Seslar 84), Acimovic, Siljak (Cimerotic 64).
*Israel:* Elimelech; Harazi, Ben-Haim■, Benado, Keissi (Balili 46), Abuksis (Badir 77), Tal, Berkovic, Benayoun, Revivo, Nimny■.
*Referee:* Fandel (Germany).

Antalya, 10 September 2003, 300

**Israel (1) 2** *(Revivo 16, Abuksis 78)*

**Malta (0) 2** *(Michael Mifsud 51 (pen), Carabott 52)*

*Israel:* Elimelech; Harazi, Benado, Gershon, Zandberg (Benayoun 62), Revivo, Abuksis, Berkovic (Afek 43), Tal, Balili, Badir.
*Malta:* Muscat; Barbara, Chetcuti, Carabott, Said, Camenzuli, Turner, Giglio (Theuma 79), Michael Mifsud, Bogdanovic (Galea 69), Nwoko (Mifsud A 88).
*Referee:* Blareau (Bulgaria).

Ljubljana, 10 September 2003, 8000

**Slovenia (0) 0**

**France (1) 2** *(Trezeguet 10, Dacourt 71)*

*Slovenia:* Simeunovic; Vugdalic (Snofl 83), Knavs, Cipot, Karic, Acimovic, Sukalo (Kapic 55), Pavlin, Ceh N, Zahovic (Cimerotic 65), Siljak.
*France:* Barthez; Thuram, Lizarazu, Makelele■, Desailly, Silvestre, Wiltord (Sagnol 76), Vieira, Trezeguet (Dacourt 69), Henry, Zidane (Pires 79).
*Referee:* Messina (Italy).

Limassol, 11 October 2003, 2346

**Cyprus (0) 2** *(Georgiou S 74, Yiasoumi 84)*

**Slovenia (2) 2** *(Siljak 12, 42)*

*Cyprus:* Panayiotou N; Georgiou S, Georgiou N (Lambrou 80), Antoniou, Nicolaou N, Ilia, Constantinou M (Charalambous 46), Yiasoumi, Okkarides, Iakovou, Engomitis (Eleftheriou 42).
*Slovenia:* Simeunovic; Cipot (Bulajic 26), Vugdalic, Knavs, Sukalo, Ceh N, Siljak, Pavlin, Rudonja (Koren 85), Kapic, Acimovic.
*Referee:* Ovrebo (Norway).

Saint-Denis, 11 October 2003, 57,009

**France (3) 3** *(Henry 9, Trezeguet 25, Boumsong 43)*

**Israel (0) 0**

*France:* Barthez; Reveillere, Thuram, Boumsong, Lizarazu, Dacourt, Pedretti, Pires (Giuly 85), Zidane, Henry (Cisse 77), Trezeguet (Marlet 85).
*Israel:* Davidovich; Harazi, Benado, Gershon, Keissi, Zeituni (Balili 89), Tal, Badir (Udi 76), Benayoun, Zandberg (Abuksis 46), Revivo.
*Referee:* Bolognino (Italy).

| **Group 1 Final Table** | *P* | *W* | *D* | *L* | *F* | *A* | *Pts* |
|---|---|---|---|---|---|---|---|
| France | 8 | 8 | 0 | 0 | 29 | 2 | 24 |
| Slovenia | 8 | 4 | 2 | 2 | 15 | 12 | 14 |
| Israel | 8 | 2 | 3 | 3 | 9 | 11 | 9 |
| Cyprus | 8 | 2 | 2 | 4 | 9 | 18 | 8 |
| Malta | 8 | 0 | 1 | 7 | 5 | 24 | 1 |

## GROUP 2

Sarajevo, 7 September 2002, 4500

**Bosnia (0) 0**

**Romania (3) 3** *(Chivu 8, Munteanu D 10, Ganea 28)*

*Bosnia:* Piplica; Beslija (Brkic 41), Music, Hibic, Rizvic, Hota, Ikanovic (Huric 37), Bajramovic (Akrapovic 46), Salihamidzic, Muratovic, Mulina.
*Romania:* Stelea (Vintila 33); Contra, Radoi, Popescu, Chivu, Codrea (Ghioane 84), Munteanu D, Munteanu V, Mutu, Ganea, Niculae (Cernat 66).
*Referee:* Cardoso (Portugal).

Oslo, 7 September 2002, 25,114

**Norway (0) 2** *(Riise 55, Carew 90)*

**Denmark (1) 2** *(Tomasson 23, 72)*

*Norway:* Grodas; Basma, Berg, Johnsen R, Bergdolmo, Leonhardsen (Strand 77), Andersen T (Carew 77), Bakke (Larsen S 88), Riise, Iversen, Solskjaer.
*Denmark:* Sorensen; Helveg, Laursen, Lustu, Jensen N, Rommedahl (Michaelsen 59), Poulsen, Gravesen, Gronkjaer (Jensen C 70), Tomasson (Nielsen P 90), Sand.
*Referee:* Dallas (Scotland).

Copenhagen, 12 October 2002, 40,259

**Denmark (0) 2** *(Tomasson 51 (pen), Sand 71)*

**Luxembourg (0) 0**

*Denmark:* Jensen S; Bogelund, Jensen N, Gravesen, Henriksen, Poulsen, Rommedahl (Gronkjaer 67), Jensen C (Lovenkrands 67), Tomasson, Sand, Jorgensen (Roll 75).
*Luxembourg:* Besic; Ferron, Deville F, Reiter, Hoffmann, Strasser, Remy, Holtz (Di Domenico 72), Leweck, Braun G (Huss 79), Cardoni.
*Referee:* Bede (Hungary).

Bucharest, 12 October 2002, 21,000

**Romania (0) 0**

**Norway (0) 1** *(Iversen 84)*

*Romania:* Vintila; Contra, Rat, Radoi, Popescu, Chivu, Codrea, Munteanu D (Pancu 85), Ganea (Niculae 64), Moldovan (Ilie 64), Mutu.
*Norway:* Myhre; Bergdolmo, Basma, Bakke, Lundekvam, Berg, Iversen, Andersen T, Carew (Leonhardsen 80), Solskjaer (Rushfeldt 89), Riise.
*Referee:* Ivanov (Russia).

Luxembourg, 16 October 2002, 2056

**Luxembourg (0) 0**

**Romania (4) 7** *(Moldovan 2, 5, Radoi 24, Contra 45, 47, 86, Ghioane 80)*

*Luxembourg:* Besic; Ferron, Deville F, Leweck, Hoffmann, Strasser, Holtz (Rohmann 76), Reiter, Remy, Braun G (Huss 71), Cardoni (Schneider 60).
*Romania:* Vintila; Contra, Rat, Munteanu D, Radoi, Popescu, Codrea (Ghioane 36), Moldovan (Cernat 69), Ilie, Ganea (Pancu 46), Miu.
*Referee:* Lajuks (Latvia).

Oslo, 16 October 2002, 24,169

**Norway (2) 2** *(Lundekvam 7, Riise 27)*

**Bosnia (0) 0**

*Norway:* Olsen; Basma, Bergdolmo, Andersen T (Larsen S 90), Berg, Lundekvam, Leonhardsen (Carew 65), Bakke, Solskjaer (Rushfeldt 89), Iversen, Riise.
*Bosnia:* Tolja; Bosnjak (Mujcin 65), Papac, Bajramovic, Hibic, Konjic, Salihamidzic (Miskovic 85), Grujic, Baljic, Sabic (Huric 57), Music.
*Referee:* Benes (Czech Republic).

Zenica, 29 March 2003, 12,000

**Bosnia (0) 2** *(Bolic 54, Barbarez 77)*

**Luxembourg (0) 0**

*Bosnia:* Hasagic; Biscevic (Berberovic 68), Konjic, Alihodzic, Bajramovic, Bolic (Turkovic 82), Beslija (Hrgovic 80), Baljic, Grujic, Music, Barbarez.
*Luxembourg:* Besic; Peters, Hoffmann, Strasser, Federspiel, Schauls, Remy, Molitor, Christophe (Huss 86), Braun G (Schneider 88), Leweck (Di Domenico 79).
*Referee:* Hyytia (Finland).

Bucharest, 29 March 2003, 50,000

**Romania (1) 2** *(Mutu 5, Munteanu D 47)*

**Denmark (1) 5** *(Rommedahl 9, 90, Gravesen 53, Tomasson 71, Contra 73 (og))*

*Romania:* Lobont; Radoi, Popescu, Filipescu, Chivu, Contra, Codrea (Reghecampf 60), Munteanu D, Pancu (Bratu 68), Ganea, Mutu.
*Denmark:* Sorensen; Rytter (Michaelsen 34), Henriksen, Laursen, Jensen N, Rommedahl, Poulsen (Weighorst 68), Gravesen, Lovenkrands (Jorgensen 56), Tomasson, Sand.
*Referee:* Gonzalez (Spain).

Copenhagen, 2 April 2003, 30,845

**Denmark (0) 0**

**Bosnia (2) 2** *(Barbarez 23, Baljic 29)*

*Denmark:* Sorensen; Michaelsen, Henriksen, Albrechtsen, Jensen N (Frandsen 81), Rommedahl, Jensen C (Wieghorst 60), Gravesen, Jorgensen, Tomasson (Berg S 85), Sand.
*Bosnia:* Hasagic; Berberovic, Music, Konjic, Bajramovic, Hibic, Beslija (Mulina 84), Hrgovic (Grujic 67), Biscevic, Baljic (Blatnjak 77), Barbarez.
*Referee:* Stredak (Slovakia).

Luxembourg, 2 April 2003, 3000

**Luxembourg (0) 0**

**Norway (0) 2** *(Rushfeldt 60, Solskjaer 74)*

*Luxembourg:* Besic; Peters, Federspiel, Hoffmann, Strasser, Remy, Schauls, Molitor, Braun G (Schneider 75), Leweck (Lassine 89), Christophe (Huss 83).
*Norway:* Olsen; Bergdolmo, Johnsen, Berg, Basma, Rudi (Tessem 46), Andersen T, Bakke (Larsen S 86), Riise, Flo T (Rushfeldt 46), Solskjaer.
*Referee:* Dobrinov (Bulgaria).

Copenhagen, 7 June 2003, 41,824

**Denmark (1) 1** *(Gronkjaer 6)*

**Norway (0) 0**

*Denmark:* Sorensen; Helveg, Laursen, Henriksen, Jensen N, Wieghorst, Gravesen, Gronkjaer (Rommedahl 70), Jensen C (Larsen 62), Jorgensen (Nielsen P 83), Sand.
*Norway:* Olsen; Basma, Johnsen R, Lundekvam, Bakke, Iversen, Andersen T (Bergdolmo 46), Leonhardsen (Flo T 62), Riise, Carew, Solskjaer (Flo H 89).
*Referee:* Poll (England).

Craiova, 7 June 2003, 37,000

**Romania (0) 2** *(Mutu 46, Ganea 88)*

**Bosnia (0) 0**

*Romania:* Lobont; Contra, Iencsi, Chivu, Rat, Radoi, Codrea (Bundea 66), Pancu, Ganea, Mutu (Miu 86), Ilie (Soava 73).
*Bosnia:* Hasagic; Berberovic (Blatnjak 73), Music, Konjic, Bajramovic, Hibic, Bolic, Beslija (Bartolovic 47), Grujic, Barbarez, Hrgovic.
*Referee:* Bossen (Holland).

Luxembourg, 11 June 2003, 6869

**Luxembourg (0) 0**

**Denmark (1) 2** *(Jensen C 22, Gravesen 50)*

*Luxembourg:* Besic; Federspiel, Schauls, Strasser, Remy, Reiter, Molitor, Leweck, Braun G (Christophe 70), Posing, Braun M.
*Denmark:* Sorensen; Bogelund (Larsen 52), Laursen, Henriksen, Jensen N, Wieghorst, Gravesen, Gronkjaer (Rommedahl 63), Jensen C, Jorgensen, Sand (Skoubo 74).
*Referee:* Baskakov (Russia).

Oslo, 11 June 2003, 24,890

**Norway (0) 1** *(Solskjaer 78 (pen))*

**Romania (0) 1** *(Ganea 64)*

*Norway:* Olsen; Bergdolmo, Berg (Lundekvam 86), Johnsen R, Basma, Solskjaer, Bakke, Andersen T, Johnsen F (Flo T 70), Riise, Carew (Iversen 81).
*Romania:* Lobont; Contra, Iencsi, Chivu, Rat, Radoi, Soava, Pancu (Bratu 86), Ganea, Mutu, Ilie (Stoica 46).
*Referee:* Michel (Slovakia).

Zenica, 6 September 2003, 18,000

**Bosnia (0) 1** *(Bajramovic 86)*

**Norway (0) 0**

*Bosnia:* Hasagic; Spahic, Konjic, Hibic, Papac, Salihamidzic (Beslija 66), Bajramovic, Grujic, Barbarez (Biscevic 87), Music (Hrgovic 70), Bolic.
*Norway:* Johnsen E; Basma, Berg H, Johnsen R, Bergdolmo, Solskjaer (Iversen 85), Andresen, Hangeland, Strand R (Solli 87), Riise, Carew (Flo T 77).
*Referee:* Bre (France).

Ploiesti, 6 September 2003, 4500

**Romania (3) 4** *(Mutu 39, Pancu 42, Ganea 44, Bratu 77)*

**Luxembourg (0) 0**

*Romania:* Lobont; Stoican, Rat, Iencsi, Chivu (Soava 46), Radoi, Dumitru, Munteanu D, Ganea, Mutu (Bratu 46), Pancu (Stoica A 76).
*Luxembourg:* Besic; Peters, Federspiel, Hoffmann, Strasser, Remy, Schauls, Reiter, Leweck, Cardoni (Mannon 84), Braun G (Huss 84).
*Referee:* Yefet (Israel).

Copenhagen, 10 September 2003, 42,049

**Denmark (1) 2** *(Tomasson 35 (pen), Laursen 90)*

**Romania (0) 2** *(Mutu 61, Pancu 72)*

*Denmark:* Sorensen; Wieghorst (Poulsen 64), Henriksen, Laursen, Jensen N, Helveg, Gravesen, Gronkjaer (Rommedahl 80), Tomasson (Jensen C 55), Martin Jorgensen, Sand.
*Romania:* Lobont; Stoican, Iencsi, Chivu, Rat, Dumitru (Cernat 70), Radoi, Pancu, Munteanu D, Ganea (Bratu 77), Mutu (Soava 90).
*Referee:* Meier (Switzerland).

Luxembourg, 10 September 2003, 3500

**Luxembourg (0) 0**

**Bosnia (1) 1** *(Barbarez 36)*

*Luxembourg:* Besic; Peters, Federspiel (Engeldinger 55), Hoffmann, Strasser, Remy, Schauls, Reiter, Leweck, Braun G (Mannon 22), Huss.
*Bosnia:* Hasagic; Spahic, Turkovic, Konjic, Bajramovic, Hibic, Bolic (Beslija 62), Huric (Biscevic 62), Barbarez, Salihamidzic, Hrgovic (Papac 78).
*Referee:* Kapitanis (Cyprus).

Sarajevo, 11 October 2003, 35,500

**Bosnia (1) 1** *(Bolic 39)*

**Denmark (1) 1** *(Martin Jorgensen 12)*

*Bosnia:* Hasagic; Spahic (Baljic 46), Music, Konjic (Hrgovic 79), Hibic, Bajramovic, Grujic (Biscevic 85), Barbarez, Salihamidzic, Beslija, Bolic.

*Denmark:* Sorensen; Wieghorst, Henriksen, Laursen, Helveg, Jensen N (Nielsen P 90), Gravesen▪, Gronkjaer (Larsen 85), Poulsen, Tomasson, Martin Jorgensen (Rommedahl 55).
*Referee:* Barber (England).

Oslo, 11 October 2003, 22,255

**Norway (1) 1** *(Flo T 18)*

**Luxembourg (0) 0**

*Norway:* Johnsen E; Basma, Lundekvam, Berg H, Riise, Strand R, Andresen, Winsnes (Andersen 80), Flo H (Johnsen F 69), Flo T (Rushfeldt 85), Brattbakk.
*Luxembourg:* Besic; Peters, Hoffmann, Schauls, Federspiel, Mannon (Di Domenico 71), Remy, Strasser, Leweck, Braun G, Huss.
*Referee:* Szabo (Hungary).

| **Group 2 Final Table** | *P* | *W* | *D* | *L* | *F* | *A* | *Pts* |
|---|---|---|---|---|---|---|---|
| Denmark | 8 | 4 | 3 | 1 | 15 | 9 | 15 |
| Norway | 8 | 4 | 2 | 2 | 9 | 5 | 14 |
| Romania | 8 | 4 | 2 | 2 | 21 | 9 | 14 |
| Bosnia | 8 | 4 | 1 | 3 | 7 | 8 | 13 |
| Luxembourg | 8 | 0 | 0 | 8 | 0 | 21 | 0 |

## GROUP 3

Vienna, 7 September 2002, 18,300

**Austria (2) 2** *(Herzog 4 (pen), 30 (pen))*

**Moldova (0) 0**

*Austria:* Manninger; Dospel, Baur, Martin Hiden, Panis, Schopp (Wimmer 58), Aufhauser, Herzog, Flogel, Vastic (Wagner 81), Wallner (Krankl 68).
*Moldova:* Hmaruc; Covalenco, Rebeja, Olexic, Sosnovschi, Priganiuc (Boret 68), Boicenco (Cebotari 46), Berco (Catinsus 46), Rogaciov, Ivanov, Clescenco.
*Referee:* Dougal (Scotland).

Eindhoven, 7 September 2002, 34,000

**Holland (2) 3** *(Davids 35, Kluivert 37, Hasselbaink 73)*

**Belarus (0) 0**

*Holland:* Van der Sar; Ricksen, Stam, Frank de Boer, Zenden, Van der Meyde, Van Bommel, Cocu, Davids (Van der Vaart 70) (Reiziger 83), Kluivert, Van Nistelrooy (Hasselbaink 70).
*Belarus:* Shantalosov (Khomutovski 88); Kulchi, Lukhvich, Ostrovski, Shtanyuk, Gurenko, Khatskevich (Kovba 82), Hleb, Omelyunchuk (Shuneiko 76), Romashchenko▪, Kutuzov.
*Referee:* Barber (England).

Minsk, 12 October 2002, 23,000

**Belarus (0) 0**

**Austria (0) 2** *(Schopp 57, Akagunduz 89)*

*Belarus:* Tumilovich; Hleb, Gurenko, Lukhvich▪, Ostrovski, Shtanyuk, Kulchi, Yaskovich (Omelyanchuk 51), Shuneiko (Vasilyuk 64), Khatskevich, Kutuzov (Ryndyuk 83).
*Austria:* Manninger; Schopp, Cerny, Martin Hiden, Baur, Dospel, Kovacevic (Aufhauser 90), Flogel, Kahraman (Herzog 82), Wallner (Akagunduz 75), Wagner.
*Referee:* Poulat (France).

Chisinau, 12 October 2002, 3000

**Moldova (0) 0**

**Czech Republic (0) 2** *(Jankulovski 70 (pen), Rosicky 80)*

*Moldova:* Hmaruc; Catinsus, Cebotari, Sosnovschi▪, Olexic, Covalenco, Rebeja, Pusca, Covalciuc (Budanov 70), Clescenco (Patula 46), Boret (Ivanov 65).
*Czech Republic:* Cech; Grygera, Jankulovski, Galasek (Jarosik 55), Bolf, Ujfalusi, Poborsky, Rosicky (Lokvenc 84), Vachousek (Dostalek 88), Koller, Stajner.
*Referee:* Irvine (Northern Ireland).

Vienna, 16 October 2002, 46,300

**Austria (0) 0**

**Holland (3) 3** *(Seedorf 16, Cocu 20, Makaay 30)*

*Austria:* Manninger; Schopp, Weissenberger (Akagunduz 76), Martin Hiden▪, Baur, Dospel, Flogel, Herzog (Aufhauser 46), Wallner (Scharner 80), Wagner, Cerny.
*Holland:* Van der Sar; Ricksen, Zenden (Bouma 69), Van Bommel (Ronald de Boer 77), Frank de Boer, Stam, Seedorf, Cocu, Makaay (Hasselbaink 80), Kluivert, Davids.
*Referee:* Collina (Italy).

Teplice, 16 October 2002, 12,850

**Czech Republic (2) 2** *(Poborsky 7, Baros 23)*

**Belarus (0) 0**

*Czech Republic:* Cech; Jiranek (Grygera 86), Bolf, Ujfalusi, Poborsky, Galasek, Rosicky (Jarosik 90), Koller (Vachousek 56), Baros, Jankulovski, Nedved.
*Belarus:* Tumilovich; Yaskovich (Lavrik 26), Khrapkovski, Shuneiko (Omelyunchuk 46), Shantyuk, Romashchenko, Gurenko, Kulchi, Hleb (Ryndyuk 69), Khatskevich, Kutuzov.
*Referee:* Fleischer (Germany).

Minsk, 29 March 2003, 8000

**Belarus (1) 2** *(Kutuzov 43, Gurenko 58)*

**Moldova (1) 1** *(Cebotari 14)*

*Belarus:* Tumilovich; Omelyunchuk, Kulchi, Ostrovski, Lavrik, Gurenko, Hleb (Romashchenko 80), Belkevich, Shuneiko, Khatskevich, Kutuzov (Kovba 87).
*Moldova:* Hmaruc; Olexic, Catinsus, Priganiuc, Covalenco, Testimitanu, Rebeja, Rogaciov (Popovich 25) (Berco 62), Covalciuc, Cebotari (Golban 79), Clescenco.
*Referee:* Verbist (Belgium).

Rotterdam, 29 March 2003, 45,000

**Holland (1) 1** *(Van Nistelrooy 45)*

**Czech Republic (0) 1** *(Koller 68)*

*Holland:* Waterreus; Ricksen, Stam, Frank de Boer, Van Bronckhorst (Van der Vaart 39), Seedorf, Van Bommel, Davids, Zenden, Kluivert, Van Nistelrooy (Makaay 81).
*Czech Republic:* Cech; Grygera, Bolf, Ujfalusi, Jankulovski, Poborsky, Galasek, Rosicky, Nedved, Smicer (Jiranek 79), Koller (Lokvenc 88).
*Referee:* Nielsen (Denmark).

Prague, 2 April 2003, 17,150

**Czech Republic (2) 4** *(Nedved 19, Koller 32, 62, Jankulovski 57 (pen))*

**Austria (0) 0**

*Czech Republic:* Cech; Grygera, Bolf, Ujfalusi, Jankulovski, Poborsky, Galasek, Smicer (Rosicky 63), Nedved (Vachousek 74), Baros, Koller (Lokvenc 79).
*Austria:* Mandl; Schamer, Stranzl, Hieblinger, Pogatetz, Schopp, Aufhauser, Flogel (Wagner 46), Weissenberger, Herzog (Kovacevic▪ 53), Haas (Dospel 64).
*Referee:* Lopez (Spain).

Tiraspol, 2 April 2003, 13,000

**Moldova (1) 1** *(Boret 16)*

**Holland (1) 2** *(Van Nistelrooy 37, Van Bommel 84)*

*Moldova:* Hmaruc; Covalenco, Olexic, Testimitanu, Catinsus, Priganiuc, Covalciuc (Berco 79), Ivanov, Boret, Cebotari (Pogreban 88), Clescenco (Golban 63).
*Holland:* Waterreus; Reiziger, Stam (Ricksen 63), Frank de Boer, Van Bommel, Davids, Seedorf (Ronald de Boer 65), Van der Vaart (Van Hooijdonk 74), Van Nistelrooy, Kluivert, Zenden.
*Referee:* Sars (France).

Minsk, 7 June 2003, 8000

**Belarus (0) 0**

**Holland (0) 2** *(Overmars 62, Kluivert 68)*

*Belarus:* Tumilovich; Ostrovski, Lukhvich, Shtanyuk (Omelyunchuk 90), Shuneiko (Kovba 75), Belkevich, Romashchenko (Hleb 52), Gurenko, Kulchi, Kutuzov, Lavrik.
*Holland:* Van der Sar; Reiziger (Bosvelt 46), Frank de Boer, Stam, Van Bronckhorst (Overmars 60), Seedorf, Van Bommel, Cocu, Zenden, Kluivert, Van Nistelrooy (Van der Vaart 75).
*Referee:* Ovrevo (Norway).

Tiraspol, 7 June 2003, 10,000

**Moldova (0) 1** *(Frunza 60)*

**Austria (0) 0**

*Moldova:* Hmaruc; Testimitanu, Priganiuc, Catinsus, Olexic, Ivanov, Frunza (Valuta 84), Covalciuc, Cebotari (Patula 77), Boret (Andriuta 67), Rogaciov.
*Austria:* Mandl; Schamer (Eder 79), Dospel (Cerny 56), Stranzl, Ehmann, Aufhauser, Schopp, Flogel, Wagner (Wallner 69), Haas, Kirchler.
*Referee:* Da Silva (Portugal).

Innsbruck, 11 June 2003, 8100

**Austria (1) 5** *(Aufhauser 33, Haas 47, Kirchler 52, Wallner 62, Cerny 69)*

**Belarus (0) 0**

*Austria:* Mandl (Payer 85); Schamer, Dospel, Stranzl (Hieblinger 46), Ehmann, Aufhauser, Cerny, Flogel, Wagner, Haas (Wallner 60), Kirchler.
*Belarus:* Tumilovich; Kulchi, Ostrovski, Lukhvich, Shtanyuk (Khraphovsky 66), Gurenko, Omelyunchuk, Lavrik, Belkevich (Kovba 55), Romashchenko, Kutuzov (Vasilyuk 46).
*Referee:* Frojdfeldt (Sweden).

Olomouc, 11 June 2003, 12,097

**Czech Republic (1) 5** *(Smicer 41, Koller 72 (pen), Stajner 81, Lokvenc 88, 90)*

**Moldova (0) 0**

*Czech Republic:* Cech; Grygera, Bolf, Ujfalusi, Jankulovski, Poborsky (Stajner 65), Galasek, Smicer (Baros 59), Rosicky, Nedved, Koller (Lokvenc 79).
*Moldova:* Hmaruc; Testimitanu, Priganiuc■, Catinsus, Olexic, Covalenco, Ivanov, Covalciuc (Pogreban 83), Cebotari (Frunza 76), Boret, Rogaciov (Patula 76).
*Referee:* Jakobsson (Iceland).

Minsk, 6 September 2003, 11,000

**Belarus (1) 1** *(Bulyga 14)*

**Czech Republic (1) 3** *(Nedved 37, Baros 54, Smicer 85)*

*Belarus:* Tumilovich; Kulchi, Ostrovski, Lukhvich, Shtanyuk, Rovneiko (Khrapkovsky 90), Kutuzov (Hleb 56), Romashchenko, Geraschenko, Gurenko (Volodenkov 82), Bulyga.
*Czech Republic:* Cech; Grygera, Ujfalusi, Bolf, Jankulovski, Poborsky, Tyce (Smicer 35), Rosicky (Vachousek 83), Nedved, Koller, Baros (Hubschman 66).
*Referee:* McCurry (Scotland).

Rotterdam, 6 September 2003, 47,000

**Holland (1) 3** *(Van der Vaart 30, Kluivert 60, Cocu 64)*

**Austria (1) 1** *(Pogatetz 34)*

*Holland:* Van der Sar; Reiziger, Frank de Boer, Stam, Van der Meyde (Robben 72), Cocu, Van Bommel, Davids (Van Hooijdonk 46), Zenden (Overmars 46), Kluivert, Van der Vaart.
*Austria:* Mandl; Dospel, Ehmann, Martin Hiden, Pogatetz, Schopp, Aufhauser, Flogel, Ivanschitz (Dollinger 84), Glieder (Kirchler 66), Kollmann (Haas 66).
*Referee:* Poulat (France).

Prague, 10 September 2003, 18,356

**Czech Republic (2) 3** *(Koller 15 (pen), Poborsky 38, Baros 90)*

**Holland (0) 1** *(Van der Vaart 62)*

*Czech Republic:* Cech; Grygera (Hubschman 25), Ujfalusi, Galasek, Bolf, Smicer (Vachousek 81), Poborsky, Jiranek, Rosicky (Baros 60), Nedved, Koller.
*Holland:* Van der Sar; Reiziger, Stam, Frank de Boer (Ooijer 46), Cocu, Van Bommel, Overmars (Bosvelt 20), Davids■, Van Nistelrooy (Van Hooijdonk 71), Kluivert, Van der Vaart.
*Referee:* Batista (Portugal).

Tiraspol, 10 September 2003, 7000

**Moldova (1) 2** *(Dadu 23, Covalciuc 88)*

**Belarus (0) 1** *(Vasilyuk 89 (pen))*

*Moldova:* Hmaruc; Covalenco (Savinov 74), Olexic, Barisev, Catinsus, Valuta (Boret 69), Covalciuc, Ivanov, Rogaciov, Cebotari, Dadu (Clescenco 68).
*Belarus:* Tumilovich; Kulchi, Ostrovski, Lukhvich, Shtanyuk (Omelyunchuk 40), Gurenko, Rovneiko, Geraschenko, Bulyga, Romashchenko (Vasilyuk 66), Kutuzov (Volodenkov 52).
*Referee:* Delevic (Serbia).

Vienna, 11 October 2003, 32,350

**Austria (0) 2** *(Haas 51, Ivanschitz 77)*

**Czech Republic (1) 3** *(Jankulovski 27, Vachousek 79, Koller 90)*

*Austria:* Mandl; Standfest, Stranzl, Martin Hiden, Pogatetz, Aufhauser, Schopp■, Flogel (Dospel 68), Glieder (Wagner 68), Ivanschitz, Haas (Linz 76).
*Czech Republic:* Cech; Petrous, Galasek, Boli, Jankulovski (Vorisek 83), Heinz (Koller 68), Stajner, Nedved, Lokvenc, Vachousek, Jiranek (Tyce 41).
*Referee:* Kasnaferis (Greece).

Eindhoven, 11 October 2003, 30,995

**Holland (1) 5** *(Kluivert 43, Sneider 51, Van Hooijdonk 74 (pen), Van der Vaart 80, Robben 89)*

**Moldova (0) 0**

*Holland:* Van der Sar; Reiziger (Makaay 33), Stam, Ooijer, Van Bronckhorst, Van der Meyde, Cocu, Sneider, Overmars (Robben 65), Kluivert (Van Hooijdonk 71), Van der Vaart.
*Moldova:* Hmaruc; Covalenco (Testimitanu 63), Savinov, Valuta, Catinsus, Covalciuc, Priganiuc, Ivanov (Miterev 82), Cebotari, Barisev, Dadu (Golban 74).
*Referee:* Siric (Croatia).

| **Group 3 Final Table** | *P* | *W* | *D* | *L* | *F* | *A* | *Pts* |
|---|---|---|---|---|---|---|---|
| Czech Republic | 8 | 7 | 1 | 0 | 23 | 5 | 22 |
| Holland | 8 | 6 | 1 | 1 | 20 | 6 | 19 |
| Austria | 8 | 3 | 0 | 5 | 12 | 14 | 9 |
| Moldova | 8 | 2 | 0 | 6 | 5 | 19 | 6 |
| Belarus | 8 | 1 | 0 | 7 | 4 | 20 | 3 |

## GROUP 4

Riga, 7 September 2002, 9000

**Latvia (0) 0**

**Sweden (0) 0**

*Latvia:* Kolinko; Stepanovs IN, Astafjevs, Zemlinsky, Laizans, Blagonadezhdin, Isakov, Bleidelis, Rubins, Pahars (Stolcers 80), Verpakovsky.
*Sweden:* Hedman; Mellberg, Jakobsson, Michael Svensson, Antonelius, Linderoth, Alexandersson, Farnerud (Jonson 56), Magnus Svensson (Johansson 76), Ibrahimovic (Kallstrom 65), Allback.
*Referee:* De Bleeckere (Belgium).

Serravalle, 7 September 2002, 2000

**San Marino (0) 0**

**Poland (0) 2** *(Kaczorowski 75, Kukielka 88)*

*San Marino:* Gasperoni F; Gennari, Vannucci (Selva R 83), Matteoni, Albani, Bacciocchi, Mauro Marani, Michele Marani, Moretti L (Zonzini 70), Selva A, Ugolini (De Luigi 78).
*Poland:* Kowalewski; Glowacki, Klos, Bak J, Kaczorowski, Kukielka, Kaluzny (Marcin Zewlakow 60), Kosowski, Wichniarek (Dawidowski 46), Zurawski, Olisadebe (Lewandowski M 80).
*Referee:* McKeon (Republic of Ireland).

Warsaw, 12 October 2002, 12,000

**Poland (0) 0**

**Latvia (1) 1** *(Laizans 30)*

*Poland:* Dudek; Hajto, Michal Zewlakow (Surma 46), Kukielka, Zielinski, Ratajczak, Dawidowski, Lewandowski M, Wichniarek (Marcin Zewlakow 46), Zurawski, Kosowski (Mieciel 63).

*Latvia:* Kolinko; Blagonadezhdin, Laizans, Rubins, Stepanovs IN, Zemlinsky, Isakov, Astafjevs, Verpakovsky (Stolcers 89), Pahars (Prohorenkovs 58), Bleidelis.
*Referee:* Busacca (Switzerland).

Stockholm, 12 October 2002, 35,084

**Sweden (0) 1** *(Ibrahimovic 76)*

**Hungary (1) 1** *(Kenesei 5)*

*Sweden:* Isaksson; Mellberg, Antonelius (Jonson 67), Linderoth, Jakobsson, Michael Svensson, Alexandersson (Kallstrom 59), Ljungberg, Andersson A, Ibrahimovic (Allback 76), Anders Svensson.
*Hungary:* Kiraly; Feher C, Low, Urban, Dragoner, Gyepes, Lipcsei, Lisztes, Tokoli (Feher M 59), Kenesei (Gera 70), Dardai.
*Referee:* Stark (Germany).

Budapest, 16 October 2002, 8000

**Hungary (0) 3** *(Gera 49, 60, 85)*

**San Marino (0) 0**

*Hungary:* Kiraly; Feher C, Low, Urban, Dragoner, Gyepes, Lipcsei, Lisztes (Miriuta 84), Tokoli, Kenesei (Gera 46), Dardai (Feher M 78).
*San Marino:* Gasperoni F; Gennari, Gobbi, Bacciocchi, Valentini C (Zonzini 81), Albani, Moretti L (Selva R 55), Michele Marani, Muccioli (Montagna 73), Selva A, Vannucci.
*Referee:* Orrason (Iceland).

Serravalle, 20 November 2002, 600

**San Marino (0) 0**

**Latvia (0) 1** *(Valentini C 89 (og))*

*San Marino:* Gasperoni F; Valentini C, Matteoni, Gobbi, Gennari (Albani 86), Bacciocchi, Muccioli, Michele Marani (Zonzini 53), Selva A, Vannucci, Montagna (De Luigi 59).
*Latvia:* Kolinko; Stepanovs IN, Kolesnichenko (Prohorenkovs 57), Blagonadezhdin, Astafjevs, Zemlinsky, Isakov, Bleidelis (Stolcers 46), Rubins, Pahars, Verpakovsky (Mikholap 63).
*Referee:* Khudiev (Azerbaijan).

Chorzow, 29 March 2003, 48,000

**Poland (0) 0**

**Hungary (0) 0**

*Poland:* Dudek; Bak J, Hajto, Stolarczyk, Szymkowiak, Kaluzny, Swierczewski, Kosowski, Zajac (Dawidowski 71), Kuzba, Olisadebe.
*Hungary:* Kiraly; Feher C, Urban, Dragoner, Juhar, Lipcsei, Dardai, Lisztes, Low, Tokoli (Boor 85), Kenesei (Sebok 69).
*Referee:* De Santis (Italy).

Budapest, 2 April 2003, 30,000

**Hungary (0) 1** *(Lisztes 65)*

**Sweden (1) 2** *(Allback 34, 66)*

*Hungary:* Kiraly; Feher C, Juhar, Urban (Bodnar 61), Dragoner, Lipcsei (Boor 80), Dardai, Lisztes, Low, Tokoli (Sebok 68), Kenesei.
*Sweden:* Isaksson; Lucic, Michael Svensson, Edman, Mellberg, Andersson A, Anders Svensson (Kallstrom 61), Mjallby, Ljungberg, Larsson, Allback (Jonson 90).
*Referee:* Bastista (Portugal).

Ostrowiec, 2 April 2003, 8500

**Poland (2) 5** *(Szymkowiak 4, Kosowski 27, Kuzba 55, 90, Karwan 82)*

**San Marino (0) 0**

*Poland:* Dudek; Bak J (Wasilewski 63), Zielinski, Sznaucner, Zajac (Karwan 46), Szymkowiak, Burkhardt, Kosowski, Zurawski, Kuzba, Olisadebe (Krzynowek 39).
*San Marino:* Gasperoni F; Albani, Bacciocchi, Matteoni, Michele Marani, Zonzini (Gasperoni B 67), Moretti L, Muccioli, Selva A (Ugolini 89), Vannucci, Montagna (De Luigi 74).
*Referee:* Loizou (Cyprus).

Riga, 30 April 2003, 7500

**Latvia (2) 3** *(Prohorenkovs 9, Bleidelis 20, 74)*

**San Marino (0) 0**

*Latvia:* Kolinko; Zirnis, Stepanovs IN, Zemlinsky, Laizans, Isakov, Prohorenkovs, Rubins, Bleidelis (Dobretsov 83), Verpakovsky (Rimkus 60), Mikholap (Stolcers 78).
*San Marino:* Gasperoni F; Valentini F, Gennari, Albani, Bacciocchi, Matteoni (Moretti 77), Muccioli (Gasperoni B 90), Michele Marani, Selva A, Vannucci, Montagna (De Luigi 64).
*Referee:* Byrne (Republic of Ireland).

Budapest, 7 June 2003, 3000

**Hungary (0) 3** *(Szabics 51, 58, Gera 87)*

**Latvia (1) 1** *(Verpakovsky 38)*

*Hungary:* Vegh; Urban, Dragoner (Gera 40), Juhar■, Feher C, Lisztes (Boor 77), Dardai, Lipcsei, Low, Kenesei (Lendvai 64), Szabics.
*Latvia:* Kolinko; Blagonadezhdin, Stepanovs IN, Zemlinsky, Isakov, Rubins, Astafjevs (Semyonov 85), Laizans, Bleidelis (Stolcers 79), Verpakovsky, Lobanov (Mikholap 71).
*Referee:* Merk (Germany).

Serravalle, 7 June 2003, 2184

**San Marino (0) 0**

**Sweden (1) 6** *(Jonson 16, 59, 70, Allback 52, 85, Ljungberg 53)*

*San Marino:* Gasperoni F; Valentini C (Zonzini 66), Albani, Matteoni, Gennari, Moretti L (Selva R 86), Bacciocchi, Selva A, Gasperoni B, Montagna, Vannucci (De Luigi 77).
*Sweden:* Isaksson; Lucic, Mellberg, Jakobsson, Edman, Mjallby (Nilsson 73), Andersson A, Kallstrom (Anders Svensson 57), Ljungberg (Johansson 73), Allback, Jonson.
*Referee:* Delevic (Serbia).

Serravalle, 11 June 2003, 1000

**San Marino (0) 0**

**Hungary (2) 5** *(Boor 5, Lisztes 20, 82, Kenesei 62, Szabics 77)*

*San Marino:* Gasperoni F; Valentini C, Albani, Matteoni, Mauro Marani, Bacciocchi, Gasperoni B, Zonzini, De Luigi (Montagna 74), Selva R, Vannucci (Gennari 65).
*Hungary:* Vegh; Bodog, Dragoner, Szekeres (Fuzi 56), Boor, Lipcsei (Lendvai 74), Dardai (Zavadszky 80), Lisztes, Low, Kenesei, Szabics.
*Referee:* Clark (Scotland).

Stockholm, 11 June 2003, 35,220

**Sweden (2) 3** *(Anders Svensson 16, 71, Allback 43)*

**Poland (0) 0**

*Sweden:* Isaksson; Lucic (Michael Svensson 87), Mellberg, Jakobsson, Edman, Ljungberg, Mjallby, Nilsson, Anders Svensson, Allback, Jonson (Magnus Svensson 72).
*Poland:* Dudek; Baszczynski (Klos 46), Bak J, Hajto, Stolarczyk, Szymkowiak (Burkhardt 76), Dawidowski, Zdebel, Kosowski (Zajac 64), Krzynowek, Wichniarek.
*Referee:* Veissiere (France).

Riga, 6 September 2003, 9000

**Latvia (0) 0**

**Poland (2) 2** *(Szymkowiak 36, Klos 38)*

*Latvia:* Kolinko; Isakov, Zemlinsky, Stepanovs IN, Blagonadezhdin, Bleidelis, Lobanov, Laizans■, Rubins (Semyonov 77), Prohorenkovs (Rimkus 80), Verpakovsky (Stolcers 82).
*Poland:* Dudek; Klos, Bak J, Hajto, Ratajczyk, Lewandowski M (Kosowski 68), Sobolewski, Szymkowiak (Zdebel 89), Krzynowek, Zurawski, Kryszalowicz (Saganowski 46).
*Referee:* Vassaras (Greece).

Gothenburg, 6 September 2003, 31,098

**Sweden (1) 5** *(Jonson M 33, Jakobsson 49, Ibrahimovic 56, 83 (pen), Kallstrom 68 (pen))*

**San Marino (0) 0**

*Sweden:* Isaksson; Lucic, Mellberg, Michael Svensson, Edman, Jakobsson (Linderoth 65), Nilsson M, Anders Svensson (Johansson A 65), Kallstrom, Ibrahimovic, Jonson M (Skoog 73).
*San Marino:* Gasperoni F; Albani, Matteoni, Bacciocchi, Valentini C, Vannucci, Moretti L, Michele Marani, Gennari (Nanni 26), Gasperoni A (Zonzini 9) (Selva A 85), Montagna.
*Referee:* Messner (Austria).

Riga, 10 September 2003, 7500

**Latvia (2) 3** *(Verpakovsky 38, 51, Bleidelis 42)*

**Hungary (0) 1** *(Lisztes 53)*

*Latvia:* Kolinko; Stepanovs IN, Astafjevs, Zemlinsky, Lobanov, Blagonadezhdin, Zirnis, Bleidelis, Verpakovsky (Kolesnichenko 89), Rubins, Rimkus (Semyonov 75).
*Hungary:* Kiraly; Feher C, Dragoner, Lovv (Boor 46), Juhar, Lipcsei, Szabics, Dardai, Feher M (Kenesei 46), Lisztes, Gera (Kovacs 86).
*Referee:* Larsen (Denmark).

Chorzow, 10 September 2003, 20,000

**Poland (0) 0**

**Sweden (2) 2** *(Nilsson M 2, Mellberg 36)*

*Poland:* Dudek; Klos, Sobolewski, Michal Zewlakow, Szymkowiak, Bak J, Hajto■, Krzynowek, Lewandowski M (Kosowski 68), Saganowski (Rasiak 64), Zurawski (Kryszalowicz 73).
*Sweden:* Isaksson; Lucic, Mellberg, Michael Svensson, Edman, Jakobsson, Nilsson M, Anders Svensson, Ljungberg, Allback (Ibrahimovic 87), Jonson M (Anders Andersson 84).
*Referee:* Riley (England).

Budapest, 11 October 2003, 15,500

**Hungary (0) 1** *(Szabics 49)*

**Poland (1) 2** *(Niedzielan 10, 62)*

*Hungary:* Kiraly; Bodog, Dragoner, Juhar, Boor, Lipcsei (Gera 46), Dardai, Fuzi, Lisztes, Feher M (Kenesei 65), Szabics.
*Poland:* Dudek; Klos, Bak J, Rzasa, Michal Zewlakow, Sobolewski, Szymkowiak (Lewandowski M 85), Mila (Kosowski 53), Krzynowek, Rasiak, Niedzielan (Saganowski 87).
*Referee:* Gonzalez (Spain).

Stockholm, 11 October 2003, 32,095

**Sweden (0) 0**

**Latvia (1) 1** *(Verpakovsky 23)*

*Sweden:* Isaksson; Lucic (Dorsin 46), Mellberg, Michael Svensson, Andersson C (Johansson A 81), Jakobsson, Nilsson M, Anders Svensson, Kallstrom (Ibrahimovic 64), Allback, Jonson M.
*Latvia:* Kolinko; Stepanovs IN, Astafjevs, Zemlinsky, Lobanov, Blagonadezhdin, Zirnis■, Bleidelis, Verpakovsky (Stolcers 87), Rubins (Pucinsks 81), Rimkus (Isakov 75).
*Referee:* De Santis (Italy).

| **Group 4 Final Table** | *P* | *W* | *D* | *L* | *F* | *A* | *Pts* |
|---|---|---|---|---|---|---|---|
| Sweden | 8 | 5 | 2 | 1 | 19 | 3 | 17 |
| Latvia | 8 | 5 | 1 | 2 | 10 | 6 | 16 |
| Poland | 8 | 4 | 1 | 3 | 11 | 7 | 13 |
| Hungary | 8 | 3 | 2 | 3 | 15 | 9 | 11 |
| San Marino | 8 | 0 | 0 | 8 | 0 | 30 | 0 |

## GROUP 5

Toftir, 7 September 2002, 4000

**Faeroes (2) 2** *(Petersen J 7, 13)*

**Scotland (0) 2** *(Lambert 62, Ferguson B 83)*

*Faeroes:* Knudsen; Johannesen O, Hansen JK, Thorsteinsson, Jacobsen JR, Elltor (Lakjuni 89), Benjaminsen, Johnsson, Jacobsen C (Jacobsen R 76), Borg, Petersen J (Flotum 80).
*Scotland:* Douglas; Ross (Alexander 75), Crainey, Ferguson B, Weir, Dailly, Lambert, Dobie (Thompson S 83), Dickov (Crawford 46), Kyle, Johnston.
*Referee:* Granat (Poland).

Kaunas, 7 September 2002, 8500

**Lithuania (0) 0**

**Germany (1) 2** *(Ballack 25, Stankevicius 58 (og))*

*Lithuania:* Stauce; Skarbalius, Stankevicius, Gleveckas, Dedura, Semberas, Zutautas, Razanauskas (Morinas 71), Mikalajunas, Poskus, Jankauskas (Fomenka 77).
*Germany:* Kahn; Linke, Ramelow, Metzelder, Frings, Schneider (Jeremies 85), Hamann, Ballack, Bohme, Jancker (Neuville 68), Klose.
*Referee:* Poll (England).

Reykjavik, 12 October 2002, 6611

**Iceland (0) 0**

**Scotland (1) 2** *(Dailly 7, Naysmith 63)*

*Iceland:* Arason; Thorsteinsson, Vidarsson (Baldvinsson 66), Ingimarsson, Sigurdsson L, Hreidarsson, Gudnason (Gudjonsson B 77), Kristinsson R, Gudjohnsen E, Sigurdsson H (Helguson 46), Gunnarsson.
*Scotland:* Douglas; Ross, Naysmith (Anderson R 90), Dailly, Pressley, Wilkie, Lambert, Ferguson B, Crawford, Thompson S (Severin 89), McNamara (Davidson 34).
*Referee:* Sars (France).

Kaunas, 12 October 2002, 4000

**Lithuania (2) 2** *(Razanauskas 23 (pen), Poskus 37)*

**Faeroes (0) 0**

*Lithuania:* Stauce; Zutautas (Barasa 75), Cesnauskis D (Slavickas 77) (Stankevicius 84), Skarbalius, Poskus, Gleveckas, Razanauskas, Skerla, Fomenka, Dziaukstas, Mikalajunas.
*Faeroes:* Mikkelsen; Johannesen O, Jacobsen C (Flotum 60), Johnsson J (Jacobsen R 68), Petersen J, Thorsteinsson (Joensen J 73), Jacobsen JR, Hansen O, Benjaminsen, Hansen JK, Borg.
*Referee:* Delevic (Yugoslavia).

Hanover, 16 October 2002, 36,000

**Germany (1) 2** *(Ballack 2 (pen), Klose 59)*

**Faeroes (1) 1** *(Friedrich 45 (og))*

*Germany:* Kahn; Schneider (Kehl 87), Frings, Friedrich, Ramelow (Freier 46), Worns, Jeremies, Hamann, Jancker (Neuville 69), Klose, Ballack.
*Faeroes:* Mikkelsen; Thorsteinsson, Hansen JK, Benjaminsen, Johannesen O, Jacobsen JR, Borg (Elltor 71), Johnsson, Petersen J (Petersen H 87), Flotum (Jacobsen C 78), Hansen O.
*Referee:* Koren (Israel).

Reykjavik, 16 October 2002, 5000

**Iceland (0) 3** *(Helguson 50, Gudjohnsen E 60, 73)*

**Lithuania (0) 0**

*Iceland:* Arason; Thorsteinsson (Gudjonsson B 37), Vidarsson, Ingimarsson, Gunnarsson, Hreidarsson, Gudnason, Stigsson (Einarsson 65), Helguson, Gudjohnsen E, Gudjonsson J (Sigurdsson H 75).
*Lithuania:* Stauce; Dziaukstas, Gleveckas, Skerla, Stankevicius, Cesnauskis D■, Razanauskas, Mikalajunas, Barasa, Fomenka, Poskus.
*Referee:* Gilewski (Poland).

Nuremberg, 29 March 2003, 40,754

**Germany (1) 1** *(Ramelow 8)*

**Lithuania (0) 1** *(Razanauskas 73)*

*Germany:* Kahn; Friedrich, Worns, Rau (Freier 83), Frings, Ramelow, Hamann, Bohme (Rehmer 46), Schneider, Klose, Bobic (Kuranyi 72).
*Lithuania:* Stauce; Semberas, Zvirgdauskas, Dedura, Barasa, Morinas, Petrenko (Dziaukstas 87), Pukelevicius (Maciulevicius 46), Mikalajunas, Razanauskas, Jankauskas (Fomenka 90).
*Referee:* Torres (Spain).

Glasgow, 29 March 2003, 37,938

**Scotland (1) 2** *(Miller 12, Wilkie 70)*

**Iceland (0) 1** *(Gudjohnsen E 48)*

*Scotland:* Douglas; Wilkie, Alexander, Ferguson, Pressley, Dailly, Lambert, Hutchison (Devlin 66), Crawford, Miller (McNamara 82), Naysmith.
*Iceland:* Arason; Thorsteinsson, Sigurdsson L, Bergsson, Gunnarsson (Gudjonsson T 74), Kristinsson R, Gudjonsson J, Ingimarsson, Vidarsson (Sigurdsson I 83), Gudjohnsen E (Gudmundsson T 89), Gretarsson.
*Referee:* Temmink (Holland).

Kaunas, 2 April 2003, 8000

**Lithuania (0) 1** *(Razanauskas 74 (pen))*

**Scotland (0) 0**

*Lithuania:* Stauce; Semberas, Zvirgzdauskas, Dedura, Barasa, Morinas, Petrenko (Maciulevicius 71), Razanauskas, Gleveckas, Mikalajunas (Buitkus 89), Jankauskas (Fomenka 63).
*Scotland:* Gallacher; Alexander, Naysmith, Wilkie, Pressley, Dailly, McNamara (Gray 81), Lambert, Crawford (Devlin 57), Miller, Hutchison (Cameron 78).
*Referee:* Stuchlik (Austria).

Reykjavik, 7 June 2003, 6038

**Iceland (0) 2** *(Sigurdsson H 49, Gudmundsson T 89)*

**Faeroes (0) 1** *(Jacobsen JR 62)*

*Iceland:* Arason; Sigurdsson I (Gudmundsson T 75), Bergsson, Hreidarsson, Vidarsson, Kristinsson R, Sigurdsson L, Gudjonsson J, Sigurdsson H (Gretarsson 75), Gudjohnsen E, Gudjonsson T.
*Faeroes:* Mikkelsen; Jacobsen C, Joensen J, Jacobsen JR, Olsen, Borg, Jacobsen R, Petersen H (Johnsson 61), Benjaminsen, Petersen J, Flotum (Elltor 64).
*Referee:* Liba (Czech Republic).

Glasgow, 7 June 2003, 48,047

**Scotland (0) 1** *(Miller 69)*

**Germany (1) 1** *(Bobic 23)*

*Scotland:* Douglas; Ross (McNamara 75), Naysmith, Dailly, Pressley, Webster, Devlin (Rae 60), Cameron, Crawford, Miller (Thompson 90), Lambert.
*Germany:* Kahn; Frings, Rau (Freier 57), Friedrich, Ramelow, Worns, Jeremies, Ballack, Bobic, Klose (Neuville 74), Schneider (Kehl 86).
*Referee:* Messina (Italy).

Torshavn, 11 June 2003, 6130

**Faeroes (0) 0**

**Germany (0) 2** *(Klose 89, Bobic 90)*

*Faeroes:* Mikkelsen; Johannesen O, Joensen J, Thorsteinsson, Jacobsen JR, Jacobsen R, Benjaminsen, Johnsson, Borg (Elltor 61), Petersen J, Jacobsen C (Petersen JI 77).
*Germany:* Kahn (Rost 46); Friedrich, Freier, Rau (Hartmann 72), Ramelow, Worns, Jeremies (Klose 65), Kehl, Bobic, Neuville, Schneider.
*Referee:* Wegereef (Holland).

Kaunas, 11 June 2003, 8000

**Lithuania (0) 0**

**Iceland (0) 3** *(Gudjonsson T 60, Gudjohnsen E 72, Hreidarsson 90)*

*Lithuania:* Stauce; Semberas■, Dedura, Barasa (Maciulevicius 72), Petrenko, Zvirgzdauskas, Zutautas (Karcemarskas 70), Morinas, Razanauskas, Jankauskas (Danilevicius 79), Skarbalius.
*Iceland:* Arason; Sigurdsson L, Bergsson, Hreidarsson, Vidarsson, Gunnarsson, Kristinsson R, Gudjonsson J (Gretarsson 89), Sigurdsson H (Gudmundsson T 82), Gudjohnsen E, Gudjonsson T.
*Referee:* Corpodea (Romania).

Torshavn, 20 August 2003, 3416

**Faeroes (0) 1** *(Jacobsen R 65)*

**Iceland (1) 2** *(Gudjohnsen E 5, Marteinsson 70)*

*Faeroes:* Mikkelsen; Thorsteinsson (Joensen J 78), Jacobsen JR, Johannesen, Olsen, Jacobsen C, Johnsson J, Petersen JI, Jacobsen R, Petersen J (Petersen H 78), Flotum (Elltor 56).
*Iceland:* Arason; Marteinsson, Bjarnason, Hreidarsson, Gudjonsson T, Gudjonsson J, Gunnarsson B (Gretarsson 71), Kristinsson R (Helguson 77), Vidarsson, Gudjohnsen E, Sigurdsson H (Sigurdsson I 84).
*Referee:* Gonzalez (Spain).

Reykjavik, 6 September 2003, 7035

**Iceland (0) 0**

**Germany (0) 0**

*Iceland:* Arason; Sigurdsson L, Bjarnason, Hreidarsson, Gudjonsson T, Gudjonsson J, Marteinsson (Gretarsson 75), Kristinsson R, Sigurdsson I (Vidarsson 83), Gudjohnsen E, Helguson (Sigurdsson H 78).
*Germany:* Kahn; Friedrich, Worns, Baumann, Schneider (Deisler 76), Ramelow, Ballack, Kehl, Rahn (Hartmann 60), Klose, Neuville (Kuranyi 46).
*Referee:* Barber (England).

Glasgow, 6 September 2003, 40,909

**Scotland (2) 3** *(McCann 7, Dickov 45, McFadden 74)*

**Faeroes (0) 1** *(Johnsson J 35)*

*Scotland:* Douglas; McNamara, Naysmith, Ferguson B, Webster, Wilkie, Devlin (McFadden 59), Cameron, Dickov (Rae 68), Crawford (Thompson S 75), McCann.
*Faeroes:* Mikkelsen; Petersen JI, Thorsteinsson, Jacobsen JR, Johannesen, Petersen H (Akselsen 66), Benjaminsen, Johnsson J (Danielsen 85), Borg (Holst 85), Jacobsen R, Petersen J.
*Referee:* Ceferen (Slovenia).

Toftir, 10 September 2003, 2175

**Faeroes (1) 1** *(Olsen 43)*

**Lithuania (1) 3** *(Morinas 23, 57, Vencevicius 88)*

*Faeroes:* Knudsen; Hansen HF, Olsen, Thorsteinsson (Jacobsen R 50), Jacobsen JR, Petersen JI, Benjaminsen, Johnsson J (Danielsen 85), Borg (Akselsen 70), Petersen J, Jacobsen C.
*Lithuania:* Kurskis; Dziaukstas, Dedura, Barasa, Cesnauskis E, Zvirgzdauskas, Morinas (Kucys 78), Cesnauskis D, Jankauskas, Poderis (Tamosauskas 46), Vencevicius (Guscinas 90).
*Referee:* Trivkovic (Croatia).

Dortmund, 10 September 2003, 67,000

**Germany (1) 2** *(Bobic 25, Ballack 50 (pen))*

**Scotland (0) 1** *(McCann 60)*

*Germany:* Kahn; Friedrich, Baumann, Worns, Schneider (Kehl 81), Rehmer, Ramelow, Rau, Ballack, Bobic (Klose 76), Kuranyi.
*Scotland:* Douglas; McNamara, Naysmith, Ferguson B, Pressley, Dailly, McFadden (Rae 53), Lambert (Ross■ 46), Thompson S, Cameron, McCann.
*Referee:* Frisk (Sweden).

Hamburg, 11 October 2003, 50,780

**Germany (1) 3** *(Ballack 9, Bobic 59, Kuranyi 79)*

**Iceland (0) 0**

*Germany:* Kahn; Friedrich, Ramelow, Worns, Hinkel, Baumann, Rahn, Schneider, Ballack, Bobic (Klose 70), Kuranyi (Neuville 85).
*Iceland:* Arason; Bjarnason, Vidarsson, Hreidarsson, Sigurdsson I (Dadason 65), Gretarsson (Gunnarsson V 80), Kristinsson R, Ingimarsson, Gudjonsson T, Gudjohnsen E, Sigurdsson H (Gunnarsson B 80).
*Referee:* Ivanov (Russia).

Glasgow, 11 October 2003, 50,343

**Scotland (0) 1** *(Fletcher 70)*

**Lithuania (0) 0**

*Scotland:* Douglas; McNamara, Naysmith, Cameron (Fletcher 65), Pressley, Dailly, Rae, Ferguson, Crawford, Miller (Hutchison 65), McFadden (Alexander 90).
*Lithuania:* Stauce; Dziaukstas, Zvirgzdauskas (Cesnauskis D 46), Dedura, Regelskis (Beniusis 85), Barasa, Razanauskas, Vencevicius (Maciulevicius 79), Baravicius, Jankauskas, Poskus.
*Referee:* Colombo (France).

| **Group 5 Final Table** | *P* | *W* | *D* | *L* | *F* | *A* | *Pts* |
|---|---|---|---|---|---|---|---|
| Germany | 8 | 5 | 3 | 0 | 13 | 4 | 18 |
| Scotland | 8 | 4 | 2 | 2 | 12 | 8 | 14 |
| Iceland | 8 | 4 | 1 | 3 | 11 | 9 | 13 |
| Lithuania | 8 | 3 | 1 | 4 | 7 | 11 | 10 |
| Faeroes | 8 | 0 | 1 | 7 | 7 | 16 | 1 |

## GROUP 6

Erevan, 7 September 2002, 9000

**Armenia (0) 2** *(Art Petrossian 73, Sarkissian 90)*

**Ukraine (2) 2** *(Serebrennikov 2, Zubov 33)*

*Armenia:* Berezovski; Artur Mkrtchian (Sarkissian 60), Hovsepian, Vardanian, Minasian (Voskanian 46), Khachatrian R, Art Petrossian, Bilibio, Dokhoyan, Art Karamian, Arm Karamian (Movsisian 71).
*Ukraine:* Reva; Luzhny, Tymoshchuk, Yezersky■, Nesmachni, Kormiltsev, Serebrennikov, Gusin (Maksimioek 65) (Popov 90), Moroz, Zubov (Spivak 69), Vorobei.
*Referee:* Vuorela (Finland).

Athens, 7 September 2002, 17,000

**Greece (0) 0**

**Spain (1) 2** *(Raul 8, Valeron 76)*

*Greece:* Nikopolidis; Patsatzoglou, Dabizas, Dellas, Fyssas (Vryzas 72), Konstantinidis (Karagounis 40), Zagorakis (Basinas 46), Tsartas, Giannakopoulos, Charisteas, Nikolaidis.
*Spain:* Casillas; Michel Salgado, Marchena, Garcia Calvo, Raul Bravo, Joaquin (Mendieta 59), Xavi (Baraja 59), Valeron (Cesar 87), Helguera, Vicente, Raul.
*Referee:* Merk (Germany).

Albacete, 12 October 2002, 16,000

**Spain (1) 3** *(Baraja 19, 88, Guti 59)*

**Northern Ireland (0) 0**

*Spain:* Casillas; Michel Salgado, Raul Bravo, Xavi, Puyol, Helguera, Joaquin (Mendieta 79), Baraja, Raul (Morientes 63), Guti (Capi 83), Vicente.
*Northern Ireland:* Taylor; Hughes A, McCartney, Murdock, Taggart (McCann 70), Lomas, Johnson D, Mulryne, Gillespie, McVeigh (Healy 65), Horlock (Hughes M 65).
*Referee:* Dobrinov (Bulgaria).

Kiev, 12 October 2002, 55,000

**Ukraine (0) 2** *(Vorobei 51, Voronin 90)*

**Greece (0) 0**

*Ukraine:* Reva; Tymoshchuk, Luzhny, Starostiak, Moroz (Radchenko 25), Gusin, Kormiltsev (Rebrov 71), Zubov, Kalinitchenko, Vorobei, Serebrennikov (Voronin 24).
*Greece:* Nikopolidis; Seitaridis, Lakis (Giannakopoulos 66), Dabizas, Dellas, Venetidis, Zagorakis (Basinas 69), Karagounis, Tsartas, Nikolaidis (Vryzas 66), Charisteas.
*Referee:* Temmink (Holland).

Athens, 16 October 2002, 5500

**Greece (1) 2** *(Nikolaidis 2, 59)*

**Armenia (0) 0**

*Greece:* Nikopolidis; Seitaridis, Georgiadis (Giannakopoulos 46), Dellas, Dabizas, Venetidis (Vryzas 60), Basinas, Kafes, Charisteas, Nikolaidis, Tsartas (Zagorakis 46).
*Armenia:* Berezovski; Sarkissian (Melikian 82), Vardanian, Khachatrian R (Minasian 46), Bilibio, Hovsepian, Art Petrossian, Art Karamian, Arm Karamian (Mkhitarian 66), Voskanian, Dokhoyan.
*Referee:* Ceferin (Slovenia).

Belfast, 16 October 2002, 9288

**Northern Ireland (0) 0**

**Ukraine (0) 0**

*Northern Ireland:* Taylor; Lomas, Horlock, Mulryne (McCann 80), Hughes A, McCartney, Gillespie, Johnson D (Murdock 84), McVeigh (Kirk 65), Healy, Hughes M.
*Ukraine:* Reva; Starostiak, Luzhny, Tymoshchuk, Kormiltsev (Lysytski 89), Gusin, Zubov, Kalynychenko (Rebrov 54), Voronin, Radchenko, Vorobei (Melashchenko 76).
*Referee:* Bolognino (Italy).

Erevan, 29 March 2003, 9000

**Armenia (0) 1** *(Art Petrossian 87)*

**Northern Ireland (0) 0**

*Armenia:* Berezovski; Melikian, Dokhoyan, Hovsepian, Vardanian, Bilibio, Art Petrossian (Mkhitarian 89), Voskanian, Sarkissian (Artur Mkrtchian 89), Art Karamian (Agvan Mkrtchian 89), Arm Karamian.
*Northern Ireland:* Taylor; Hughes A, McCann, Lomas, Williams, Craigan, Gillespie, Johnson D, Healy, Quinn (Elliott 70), McVeigh.
*Referee:* Beck (Liechtenstein).

Kiev, 29 March 2003, 82,000

**Ukraine (1) 2** *(Voronin 11, Gorchkov 90)*

**Spain (0) 2** *(Raul 83, Etxeberria 87)*

*Ukraine:* Shovkovskyi; Nesmachni, Dmitrulin, Fedorov, Tymoshchuk, Kormiltsev (Kalynychenko 62), Gusin, Gorchkov, Voronin, Vorobei, Shevchenko (Serebrennikov 67).
*Spain:* Casillas; Michel Salgado, Aranzabal, Albelda (Xavi 65), Marchena, Cesar, Etxeberria, Baraja, Guti (Valeron 65), Raul, Vicente (Diego Tristan 77).
*Referee:* Riley (England).

Belfast, 2 April 2003, 7196

**Northern Ireland (0) 0**

**Greece (1) 2** *(Charisteas 2, 55)*

*Northern Ireland:* Taylor; Hughes A, McCartney, Lomas, Williams, Craigan, Gillespie■, Johnson D, Healy (Kirk 68), Quinn■, McCann (McVeigh 68).
*Greece:* Nikopolidis; Giannakopoulos, Venetidis (Fyssas 70), Dabizas, Kyrgiakos, Konstantinidis, Zagorakis, Tsartas (Kafes 75), Charisteas, Nikolaidis (Vryzas 41), Karagounis.
*Referee:* Gilewski (Poland).

Amilivia, 2 April 2003, 13,500

**Spain (0) 3** *(Diego Tristan 63, Helguera 69, Joaquin 90)*

**Armenia (0) 0**

*Spain:* Casillas; Michel Salgado, Bravo, Albelda, Helguera, Marchena, Etxeberria (Joaquin 46), Xavi (Vicente 54), Valeron (Baraja 63), Raul, Diego Tristan.
*Armenia:* Berezovski; Dokhoyan, Vardanian, Melikian, Hovsepian, Art Petrossian (Mkhitarian 81) (Minasian 84), Khachatrian R, Voskanian, Sarkissian, Art Karamian (Bilibio 89), Arm Karamian.
*Referee:* Yefet (Israel).

Zaragoza, 7 June 2003, 32,000

**Spain (0) 0**

**Greece (1) 1** *(Giannakopoulos 42)*

*Spain:* Casillas; Michel Salgado, Raul Bravo, Marchena (Sergio 76), Puyol, Helguera, Etxeberria (Joaquin 57), Valeron, Raul, Morientes, Vicente (De Pedro 57).
*Greece:* Nikopolidis; Seitaridis, Dellas, Dabizas, Kapsis, Venetidis■, Zagorakis, Tsartas (Karagounis 36), Giannakopoulos, Vryzas, Charisteas (Lakis 34).
*Referee:* Sars (France).

Lvov, 7 June 2003, 30,000

**Ukraine (1) 4** *(Gorchkov 28, Shevchenko 65 (pen), 70, Fedorov 90)*

**Armenia (1) 3** *(Sarkissian 13 (pen), 50, Art Petrossian 72 (pen))*

*Ukraine:* Shutkov; Luzhny, Fedorov, Nesmachni, Zakarlyuka (Radchenko 63), Popov (Kalynychenko 65), Gorchkov, Voronin, Rebrov (Venhlynsky 80), Shevchenko, Vorobei.
*Armenia:* Berezovski; Partsikian, Dokhoyan, Vardanian, Hovsepian, Art Petrossian (Bilibio 75), Khachatrian B, Voskanian, Sarkissian, Art Karamian (Arutiunian 83), Arm Karamian.
*Referee:* Albrecht (Germany).

Athens, 11 June 2003, 15,000

**Greece (0) 1** *(Charisteas 86)*

**Ukraine (0) 0**

*Greece:* Nikopolidis; Seitaridis, Dabizas, Dellas, Fyssas, Kapsis, Zagorakis (Tsartas 72), Lakis (Houtos 65), Karagounis, Vryzas (Charisteas 46), Giannakopoulos.
*Ukraine:* Shovkovskyi; Nesmachni, Fedorov, Golovko, Tymoshchuk, Gusin, Shevchuk, Zakarlyuka, Voronin, Shevchenko, Rebrov (Vorobei 61).
*Referee:* De Bleeckere (Belgium).

Belfast, 11 June 2003, 11,365

**Northern Ireland (0) 0**

**Spain (0) 0**

*Northern Ireland:* Taylor; Baird, Kennedy, Griffin, Hughes A, McCartney, Healy, Johnson, Smith (Williams 90), Jones (McVeigh 73), Doherty (Toner 80).
*Spain:* Casillas; Puyol, Juanfran, Sergio (Joaquin 66), Marchena, Helguera, Etxeberria (De Pedro 78), Baraja, Valeron, Raul, Vicente (Morientes 66).
*Referee:* Larsen (Denmark).

Erevan, 6 September 2003, 6500

**Armenia (0) 0**

**Greece (1) 1** *(Vryzas 34)*

*Armenia:* Berezovski; Melikian, Bilibio, Zeciu, Vardanian, Khachatrian R, Art Petrossian, Voskanian, Sarkissian, Art Karamian, Arm Karamian (Movsesian 65).
*Greece:* Nikopolidis; Seitaridis, Fyssas, Antzas, Dellas, Basinas, Kapsis, Vryzas, Karagounis (Zagorakis 89), Giannakopoulos (Nikolaidis 87), Charisteas.
*Referee:* Temmink (Holland).

Donetsk, 6 September 2003, 24,000

**Ukraine (0) 0**

**Northern Ireland (0) 0**

*Ukraine:* Shovkovskyi; Luzhny, Fedorov, Tymoshchuk, Nesmachni, Horshkov, Gusin (Gusev 16), Zubov, Rebrov (Melaschenko 72), Voronin, Vorobei.
*Northern Ireland:* Taylor; Baird, Kennedy, Griffin, Hughes A, McCartney, Gillespie, Doherty (Mulryne 67), Johnson D, Healy (Smith 62), Hughes M (Jones 81).
*Referee:* Stark (Germany).

Belfast, 10 September 2003, 8616

**Northern Ireland (0) 0**

**Armenia (1) 1** *(Arm Karamian 29)*

*Northern Ireland:* Taylor; Baird, McCann, Griffin, Hughes A, McCartney, Gillespie (Jones 29), Doherty (Mulryne 29), Johnson D, Healy (McVeigh 78), Smith.
*Armenia:* Berezovski; Melikian, Bilibio, Hovsepian, Zeciu, Khachatrian R, Art Petrossian (Arm Karamian 12), Voskanian, Sarkissian, Art Karamian (Partsikian 87), Movsesian (Hakobian A 75).
*Referee:* Stredak (Slovakia).

Elche, 10 September 2003, 38,000

**Spain (0) 2** *(Raul 59, 71)*

**Ukraine (0) 1** *(Shevchenko 84)*

*Spain:* Casillas; Michel Salgado, Juanito, Marchena, Puyol, Etxeberria, Alonso, Baraja (Xavi 85), Vicente (Valeron 64), Raul, Fernando Torres (Reyes 64).
*Ukraine:* Shovkovskyi; Luzhny, Fedorov, Tymoshchuk, Nesmachni, Dmitrulin (Zubov 65), Popov (Serebrennikov 18), Horshkov, Voronin (Gusev 52), Shevchenko, Vorobei.
*Referee:* Hauge (Norway).

Erevan, 11 October 2003, 15,000

**Armenia (0) 0**

**Spain (1) 4** *(Valeron 7, Raul 76, Reyes 87, 90)*

*Armenia:* Berezovski; Melikian, Dokhoyan K, Hovsepian, Vardanian, Khachatrian R, Secu (Bilibio 88), Voskanian (Movsesian 78), Sarkissian, Art Karamian, Arm Karamian (Petrossian G 87).
*Spain:* Casillas; Michel Salgado, Helguera, Marchena, Puyol, Baraja (Xabi Alonso 66), Albelda, Etxeberria, Valeron, Vicente (Reyes 62), Raul (Luque 78).
*Referee:* Meier (Switzerland).

Athens, 11 October 2003, 15,500

**Greece (0) 1** *(Tsartas 69 (pen))*

**Northern Ireland (0) 0**

*Greece:* Nikopolidis; Dabizas (Venetidis 46), Dellas, Antzas, Seitaridis, Basinas (Zagorakis 90), Tsartas, Vryzas, Fyssas, Charisteas (Nikolaidis 46), Giannakopoulos.
*Northern Ireland:* Taylor; Baird, Kennedy, Griffin (Jones 88), Hughes A, McCartney■, Gillespie (Smith 63), Whitley Jeff, Healy, Elliott (Murdock 70), Hughes M.
*Referee:* Batista (Portugal).

| **Group 6 Final Table** | *P* | *W* | *D* | *L* | *F* | *A* | *Pts* |
|---|---|---|---|---|---|---|---|
| Greece | 8 | 6 | 0 | 2 | 8 | 4 | 18 |
| Spain | 8 | 5 | 2 | 1 | 16 | 4 | 17 |
| Ukraine | 8 | 2 | 4 | 2 | 11 | 10 | 10 |
| Armenia | 8 | 2 | 1 | 5 | 7 | 16 | 7 |
| Northern Ireland | 8 | 0 | 3 | 5 | 0 | 8 | 3 |

## GROUP 7

Vaduz, 7 September 2002, 1200

**Liechtenstein (0) 1** *(Michael Stocklasa 90)*

**Macedonia (1) 1** *(Hristov 7)*

*Liechtenstein:* Jehle; Ritter, Gigon (Burgmeier 83), Hasler D, Michael Stocklasa, Martin Stocklasa, Telser (D'Elia 83), Frick M, Gerster, Beck T, Beck M (Buchel 46).
*Macedonia:* Milosevski; Braga (Grncarov 85), Sedloski, Nikolovski, Petrov, Mitreski I, Sumolikoski, Sakiri, Pandev (Stoikov 70), Hristov (Popov 58), Mitreski A.
*Referee:* Goduljan (Ukraine).

Istanbul, 7 September 2002, 20,000

**Turkey (2) 3** *(Serhat 14, Arif 45, 65)*

**Slovakia (0) 0**

*Turkey:* Rustu; Fatih, Bulent K, Alpay, Hakan Unsal, Okan (Nihat 63), Tugay, Emre B (Cihan 78), Basturk, Serhat (Umit D 87), Arif.
*Slovakia:* Bucek; Karhan, Spilar, Dzurik, Labant (Michalik 61), Kisel, Cisovski, Kozlej (Reiter 55), Gresko (Hlinka 72), Janocko, Vittek.
*Referee:* Nieto (Spain).

Skopje, 12 October 2002, 12,000

**Macedonia (1) 1** *(Grozdanovski 2)*

**Turkey (1) 2** *(Okan 29, Nihat 54)*

*Macedonia:* Milosevski; Mitreski I, Vasovski, Sedloski, Stojanovski, Mitreski A, Trajanov (Nacevski 68), Sumolikoski (Petrov 46), Sakiri, Hristov (Popov 46), Grozdanovski.
*Turkey:* Rustu; Fatih, Okan (Umit D 79), Bulent K, Alpay, Tugay (Serhat 46), Emre B, Basturk, Arif (Hasan Sas 46), Nihat, Ergun.
*Referee:* Fisker (Denmark).

Bratislava, 12 October 2002, 30,000

**Slovakia (1) 1** *(Nemeth S 24)*

**England (0) 2** *(Beckham 65, Owen 82)*

*Slovakia:* Konig; Pinte (Kozlej 88), Leitner, Zeman, Dzurik, Hlinka, Karhan, Janocko (Mintal 88), Nemeth S, Petras, Vittek (Reiter 80).
*England:* Seaman; Neville G, Ashley Cole, Southgate, Woodgate, Butt, Beckham, Gerrard (Dyer 77), Heskey (Smith 90), Owen (Hargreaves 86), Scholes.
*Referee:* Messina (Italy).

Southampton, 16 October 2002, 32,095

**England (2) 2** *(Beckham 14, Gerrard 36)*

**Macedonia (2) 2** *(Sakiri 11, Trajanov 25)*

*England:* Seaman; Neville G, Ashley Cole, Gerrard (Butt 56), Campbell, Woodgate, Beckham, Scholes, Smith■, Owen, Bridge (Vassell 58).
*Macedonia:* Milosevski; Popov, Petrov, Sumolikoski, Sedloski, Vasovski, Grozdanovski, Mitreski A, Sakiri, Trajanov (Stojanovski 90), Toleski (Pandev 62).
*Referee:* Ibanez (Spain).

Istanbul, 16 October 2002, 15,000

**Turkey (3) 5** *(Okan 7, Umit D 14, Ilhan 23, Serhat 81, 90)*

**Liechtenstein (0) 0**

*Turkey:* Rustu; Umit D, Ergun, Bulent K (Fatih 46), Alpay, Tugay, Okan (Hakan Unsal 60), Emre B, Ilhan (Serhat 79), Arif, Nihat.
*Liechtenstein:* Jehle; Telser, Michael Stocklasa, Nigg (Burgmeier 72), Hasler D, D'Elia, Martin Stocklasa (Beck M 79), Buchel (Ospelt 85), Beck T, Frick M, Gerster.
*Referee:* Baskakov (Russia).

Vaduz, 29 March 2003, 3548

**Liechtenstein (0) 0**

**England (1) 2** *(Owen 28, Beckham 53)*

*Liechtenstein:* Jehle; Telser, Hasler D, Michael Stocklasa, D'Elia, Beck T, Martin Stocklasa, Buchel (Beck M 86), Zech (Burgmeier 62), Frick M (Nigg 82), Gerster.
*England:* James; Neville G, Bridge, Gerrard (Butt 66), Ferdinand, Southgate, Beckham (Murphy 70), Scholes, Heskey (Rooney 80), Owen, Dyer.
*Referee:* Kasnaferis (Greece).

Skopje, 29 March 2003, 8000

**Macedonia (0) 0**

**Slovakia (1) 2** *(Petras 28, Reiter 90)*

*Macedonia:* Milosevski; Braga, Lazarevski (Stoikov 81), Sedloski, Mitreski I, Sumolikovski (Naumoski 52), Jancevski, Krstev M, Sakiri, Krstev S (Grozdanovski 61), Pandev.
*Slovakia:* Konig; Petras, Klimpl, Hlinka, Leitner, Karhan (Hanek 90), Demo (Labant 81), Michalik, Janocko, Nemeth S (Reiter 75), Vittek.
*Referee:* Duhamel (France).

Sunderland, 2 April 2003, 47,667

**England (0) 2** *(Vassell 76, Beckham 90 (pen))*

**Turkey (0) 0**

*England:* James; Neville G, Bridge, Butt, Campbell, Ferdinand, Beckham, Scholes, Rooney (Dyer 89), Owen (Vassell 58), Gerrard.
*Turkey:* Rustu; Fatih (Hakan Sukur 79), Ergun, Alpay, Bulent K, Tugay, Okan (Umit D 59), Emre B, Basturk (Hasan Sas 70), Nihat, Ilhan.
*Referee:* Meier (Switzerland).

Trnava, 2 April 2003

**Slovakia (1) 4** *(Reiter 18, Nemeth S 51, 64, Janocko 90)*

**Liechtenstein (0) 0**

*Slovakia:* Konig; Petras, Klimpl, Hlinka, Leitner, Karhan (Hanek 90), Demo (Labant 68), Michalik (Mintal 81), Janocko, Kozlej (Nemeth S 46), Reiter.
*Liechtenstein:* Jehle; Telser, Hasler D, Michael Stocklasa, D'Elia, Beck T, Martin Stocklasa, Buchel (Gigon 71), Burgmeier, Frick M (Nigg 60), Gerster (Ospelt 85).
*Match played behind closed doors.*
*Referee:* Ceferen (Slovenia).

Skopje, 7 June 2003, 6000

**Macedonia (1) 3** *(Sedloski 39 (pen), Krstev M 52, Stoikov 82)*

**Liechtenstein (1) 1** *(Beck T 20)*

*Macedonia:* Milosevski; Sumolikoski, Sedloski, Vasovski, Lazarevski, Trajanov (Jancevski 60), Mitreski A, Sakiri (Bajevski 55), Stoikov, Naumoski (Dimitrovski 46), Krstev M.
*Liechtenstein:* Jehle; Ospelt, Hasler D, Gigon, Maierhofer (Wolfinger 89), D'Elia, Gerster, Frick M, Telser, Beck M (Vogt 89), Beck T (Rohrer 79).
*Referee:* Jara (Czech Republic).

Bratislava, 7 June 2003, 15,000

**Slovakia (0) 0**

**Turkey (1) 1** *(Nihat 12)*

*Slovakia:* Konig; Zeman, Hlinka (Vittek 46), Klimpl, Labant, Karhan (Mintal 71), Janocko, Petras, Demo, Michalik (Kisel 77), Nemeth S.
*Turkey:* Rustu; Fatih, Alpay, Bulent K, Ergun, Okan (Tayfun 58), Basturk (Volkan 80), Tugay, Emre B (Ibrahim 90), Nihat, Hakan Sukur.
*Referee:* Hauge (Norway).

Middlesbrough, 11 June 2003, 35,000

**England (0) 2** *(Owen 62 (pen), 73)*

**Slovakia (1) 1** *(Janocko 31)*

*England:* James; Mills (Hargreaves 43), Ashley Cole, Neville P, Southgate, Upson, Gerrard, Scholes, Rooney (Vassell 58), Owen, Lampard.
*Slovakia:* Konig; Hanek, Labant (Debnar 38), Zabavnik, Zeman, Petras, Demo (Mintal 55), Janocko, Nemeth S (Reiter 75), Vittek, Michalik.
*Referee:* Stark (Germany).

Istanbul, 11 June 2003, 22,000

**Turkey (1) 3** *(Nihat 27, Gokdeniz 48, Hakan Sukur 59)*

**Macedonia (2) 2** *(Grozdanovski 23, Sakiri 29)*

*Turkey:* Rustu; Fatih, Alpay (Yildirin 72), Bulent K, Ergun, Emre B (Gokdeniz 43), Tayfun (Okan 46), Tugay, Ibrahim, Hakan Sukur (Volkan 78), Nihat.
*Macedonia:* Milosevski; Sumolikoski, Sedloski, Vasovski, Lazarevski, Bozinovski (Poleski 76), Mitreski A, Sakiri, Stoikov, Grozdanovski (Nuhiji 56), Jancevski.
*Referee:* Rosetti (Italy).

Vaduz, 6 September 2003, 3548

**Liechtenstein (0) 0**

**Turkey (2) 3** *(Tumer 14, Okan 41, Hakan Sukur 50)*

*Liechtenstein:* Jehle; Telser, Michael Stocklasa (Maierhofer 80), Hasler D, Ritter, Martin Stocklasa, Beck T (Beck R 59), Gerster, D'Elia, Frick M, Burgmeier (Buchel 59).
*Turkey:* Rustu; Umit D, Bulent K (Deniz 64), Alpay, Ibrahim, Tumer (Hasan Sas 64), Tugay, Okan (Gokdeniz 75), Ergun, Hakan Sukur, Tuncay.
*Referee:* Van Egmond (Holland).

Skopje, 6 September 2003, 20,500

**Macedonia (1) 1** *(Hristov 28)*

**England (0) 2** *(Rooney 53, Beckham 63 (pen))*

*Macedonia:* Milosevski; Stojanovski, Mitreski I, Stavrevski, Grozdanovski (Braga 56), Trajanov, Pandev (Gjuzelov 48), Sumolikoski, Sakiri, Naumoski, Hristov (Dimitrovski 88).
*England:* James; Neville G, Ashley Cole, Lampard (Heskey 46), Terry, Campbell, Beckham, Butt, Rooney (Neville P 74), Owen (Dyer 86), Hargreaves.
*Referee:* De Bleeckere (Belgium).

Old Trafford, 10 September 2003, 64,931

**England (0) 2** *(Owen 46, Rooney 52)*

**Liechtenstein (0) 0**

*England:* James; Neville G, Bridge, Gerrard (Hargreaves 58), Terry, Upson, Beckham (Neville P 58), Rooney (Cole J 69), Beattie, Owen, Lampard.
*Liechtenstein:* Jehle; Telser, Michael Stocklasa (Maierhofer 46), Hasler D, Ritter, Martin Stocklasa, Burgmeier, Gerster, Beck R (Beck T 57), D'Elia (Buchel 73), Frick M.
*Referee:* Fisker (Denmark).

Zilina, 10 September 2003, 2286

**Slovakia (1) 1** *(Nemeth S 25)*

**Macedonia (0) 1** *(Dimitrovski 62)*

*Slovakia:* Konig; Petras, Labant V, Klimpl, Zabavnik, Labant B, Durica (Kisel 71), Oravec, Janocko (Sninsky 89), Mintal (Urban 71), Nemeth S.
*Macedonia:* Milosevski; Stojanovski, Mitreski I, Stavrevski, Sedloski, Jancevski, Pandev (Kapinkovski 73), Trajanov, Grozdanovski (Georgievski 90), Sakiri, Naumoski (Dimitrovski 33).
*Referee:* Sundell (Sweden).

Vaduz, 11 October 2003, 1500

**Liechtenstein (0) 0**

**Slovakia (1) 2** *(Vittek 40, 56)*

*Liechtenstein:* Heeb; Telser, Maierhofer, Hasler D, Michael Stocklasa, Ritter, Beck T (Beck R 46), Beck M (Rohrer 46), D'Elia (Buchel 76), Frick M, Burgmeier.
*Slovakia:* Konig; Klimpl, Leitner, Labant B, Varga, Zabavnik, Kisel (Urban 46), Michalik (Babnic 84), Janocko, Nemeth S (Oravec 76), Vittek.
*Referee:* Hyylia (Finland).

Istanbul, 11 October 2003, 42,000

**Turkey (0) 0**

**England (0) 0**

*Turkey:* Rustu; Fatih, Alpay, Bulent K, Ibrahim, Okan (Ilhan 67), Tugay, Emre B (Ergun 79), Sergen (Tuncay 61), Nihat, Hakan Sukur.
*England:* James; Neville G, Ashley Cole, Gerrard, Campbell, Terry, Beckham, Butt, Rooney (Dyer 73), Heskey (Vassell 68), Scholes (Lampard 90).
*Referee:* Collina (Italy).

| Group 7 Final Table | P | W | D | L | F | A | Pts |
|---|---|---|---|---|---|---|---|
| England | 8 | 6 | 2 | 0 | 14 | 5 | 20 |
| Turkey | 8 | 6 | 1 | 1 | 17 | 5 | 19 |
| Slovakia | 8 | 3 | 1 | 4 | 11 | 9 | 10 |
| Macedonia | 8 | 1 | 3 | 4 | 11 | 14 | 6 |
| Liechtenstein | 8 | 0 | 1 | 7 | 2 | 22 | 1 |

## GROUP 8

Brussels, 7 September 2002, 20,000

**Belgium (0) 0**

**Bulgaria (1) 2** *(Jankovic 17, Stilian Petrov 63)*

*Belgium:* De Vlieger; Vreven, Van Buyten, Simons, Van der Heyden (Peeters B 64), Englebert (Mpenza M 53), Vanderhaeghe, Baseggio, Goor, Mpenza E (Thijs 70), Sonck.
*Bulgaria:* Zdravkov; Kishishev, Kirilov, Petov I, Petrov M, Peev (Petkov G 83), Stilian Petrov, Balakov, Petov M (Zagorcic 90), Pazin, Jankovic (Chilikov 77).
*Referee:* Hauge (Norway).

Osijek, 7 September 2002, 12,000

**Croatia (0) 0**

**Estonia (0) 0**

*Croatia:* Pletikosa; Zivkovic, Babic, Simic D, Tokic, Vugrinec, Tapalovic, Saric (Tomas 79), Maric T (Petric 60), Olic, Maric S (Rapajic 46).
*Estonia:* Poom; Allas, Stepanovs, Piroja, Saviauk, Rooba M, Reim, Kristal, Lindpere (Rooba U 59), Zelinski, Oper.
*Referee:* Marin (Spain).

Andorra, 12 October 2002, 700

**Andorra (0) 0**

**Belgium (0) 1** *(Sonck 61)*

*Andorra:* Koldo; Ayala, Txema (Escura 66), Jonas, Lima A, Fernandez (Silva 6), Emiliano, Jimenez (Lucendo 75), Juli Sanchez, Ruiz, Sonejee.
*Belgium:* De Vlieger; De Cock, Dheedene, Buffel, Valgaeren, Simons, Vanderhaeghe, Baseggio (Thijs 81), Sonck (Soeters 90), Van Houdt, Goor.
*Referee:* Nalbandian (Armenia).

Sofia, 12 October 2002, 43,000

**Bulgaria (2) 2** *(Stilian Petrov 22, Berbatov 37)*

**Croatia (0) 0**

*Bulgaria:* Zdravkov; Kishishev, Petov I, Stilian Petrov, Pazin, Kirilov, Peev (Ivanov G 90), Jankovic, Berbatov (Chilikov 39), Petrov M (Petrov G 66), Balakov.
*Croatia:* Pletikosa; Simic D (Olic 18), Zivkovic, Tomas, Kovac R, Tudor, Vugrinec, Leko, Rapajic (Maric M 46), Boksic (Maric S 69), Stanic.
*Referee:* Frisk (Sweden).

Sofia, 16 October 2002, 38,000

**Bulgaria (1) 2** *(Chilikov 37, Balakov 59)*

**Andorra (0) 1** *(Lima A 81)*

*Bulgaria:* Zdravkov; Kishishev, Jankovic (Gonzo 77), Peev, Pazin, Kirilov, Stilian Petrov, Balakov (Svetoslav Petrov 62), Petrov M (Manchev 75), Chilikov, Petkov I.
*Andorra:* Koldo; Ayala, Jonas, Lima A■, Fernandez, Escura, Emiliano (Silva 64), Lima I, Jimenez (Marc 80), Sonejee, Ruiz.
*Referee:* Richards (Wales).

Tallinn, 16 October 2002, 4000

**Estonia (0) 0**

**Belgium (1) 1** *(Sonck 2)*

*Estonia:* Poom; Allas, Rooba U, Anniste (Haavistu 46), Stepanovs, Piiroja, Reim, Kristal (Lindpere 83), Oper, Zelinski, Terehhov (Viikmae 60).
*Belgium:* De Vlieger; De Cock, Dheedene, Vanderhaeghe, Valgaeren, Simons, Buffel (Van Hout 89), Baseggio, Sonck, Van Houdt, Goor.
*Referee:* Riley (England).

Zagreb, 29 March 2003, 22,000

**Croatia (1) 4** *(Srna 9, Prso 53, Maric T 68, Leko 76)*

**Belgium (0) 0**

*Croatia:* Pletikosa; Simic D, Simunic, Kovac R, Zivkovic, Rapajic, Tudor (Kovac N 77), Srna, Rosso (Leko 46), Prso (Stanic 70), Maric T.
*Belgium:* Vandendriessche; De Cock (Deflandre 57), Valgaeren (Van Damme 67), Van Buyten, Van der Heyden, Buffel, Simons, Englebert (Baseggio 55), Goor, Sonck, Mpenza E.
*Referee:* Fandel (Germany).

Varazdin, 2 April 2003, 10,000

**Croatia (2) 2** *(Rapajic 11 (pen), 44)*

**Andorra (0) 0**

*Croatia:* Pletikosa; Simic D, Simunic (Kovac N 46), Kovac R, Zivkovic, Rapajic (Babic 65), Tudor, Srna, Leko, Prso, Maric T (Stanic 46).
*Andorra:* Koldo; Ayala, Txema, Jonas, Fernandez, Sonejee, Emiliano (Motwani 89), Marc, Pol Perez (Lucendo 79), Jimenez (Escura 55), Juli Sanchez.
*Referee:* Salomir (Romania).

Tallinn, 2 April 2003, 3200

**Estonia (0) 0**

**Bulgaria (0) 0**

*Estonia:* Poom; Allas, Lemsalu, Jaager, Rooba U, Leetma, Kristal, Oper, Haavistu (Reinumae 63), Terehov, Zelinski (Viikmae 63).
*Bulgaria:* Zdravkov; Kishishev, Pazin, Petkov I, Kirilov, Stilian Petrov, Peev, Balakov, Petrov M (Petkov M 70), Berbatov, Jankovic (Todorov 46).
*Referee:* Plautz (Austria).

La Vella, 30 April 2003, 500

**Andorra (0) 0**

**Estonia (1) 2** *(Zelinski 26, 74)*

*Andorra:* Koldo; Ayala (Silva 90), Txema, Escura, Fernandez, Emiliano, Marc (Alvarez 80), Sonejee, Juli Sanchez,Ruiz, Jimenez (Lucendo 71).
*Estonia:* Poom; Allas, Stepanovs, Lemsalu, Rooba U, Reim, Haavistu (Reinumae 69), Kristal, Terehhov (Lindpere 55), Viikmae (Rooba M 89), Zelinski.
*Referee:* Aydin (Turkey).

Sofia, 7 June 2003, 42,000

**Bulgaria (0) 2** *(Berbatov 53, Todorov 71 (pen))*

**Belgium (1) 2** *(Stilian Petrov 31 (og), Clement 57)*

*Bulgaria:* Zdravkov; Stankov, Kirilov, Stoyanov, Petkov I, Borimirov, Stilian Petrov, Hristov (Manchev 72), Petrov M, Dimitrov (Alexandrov 81), Berbatov (Todorov 54).
*Belgium:* De Vlieger; Deflandre, Simons, Van Buyten, Dheedene, Mpenza M, Baseggio, Clement, Goor, Buffel, Sonck (Mpenza E 73).
*Referee:* Collina (Italy).

Tallinn, 7 June 2003, 2700

**Estonia (2) 2** *(Allas 22, Viikmae 31)*

**Andorra (0) 0**

*Estonia:* Poom; Allas, Stepanovs, Piroja, Rooba U (Saviauk 49), Leetma, Kristal, Zahovalko, Haavistu (Rooba M 70), Viikmae, Lindpere (Reinumae 88).
*Andorra:* Koldo; Escura, Txema, Juli, Lima A, Lima I, Emiliano (Silva 83), Jimenez (Marc 53), Sonejee, Ruiz, Juli Sanchez.
*Referee:* Juhos (Hungary).

Ghent, 11 June 2003, 12,000

**Belgium (2) 3** *(Goor 20, 65, Sonck 44)*

**Andorra (0) 0**

*Belgium:* De Vlieger; De Cock, Simons, Van Buyten, Dheedene (Van der Heyden 79), Clement, Baseggio, Goor (Soetars 83), Mpenza M, Sonck, Buffel (Martens 73).
*Andorra:* Koldo; Ayala, Txema, Jonas, Sonejee (Lucendo 81), Lima A, Lima I, Emiliano (Alvarez 70), Juli Sanchez (Escura 58), Fernandez, Marc.
*Referee:* Shmolik (Belarus).

Tallinn, 11 June 2003, 6000

**Estonia (0) 0**

**Croatia (0) 1** *(Kovac N 77)*

*Estonia:* Poom; Allas (Zahovalko 82), Stepanovs, Piiroja, Rooba U, Leetma, Kristal, Oper, Rooba M (Reinumae 71), Lindpere (Lemsalu 83), Zelinski.
*Croatia:* Pletikosa; Simunic, Tomas, Zivkovic, Simic D (Maric T 61), Babic (Leko 73), Rapajic (Rosso 79), Kovac N, Srna, Olic, Prso.
*Referee:* Hamer (Luxembourg).

La Vella, 6 September 2003, 800

**Andorra (0) 0**

**Croatia (2) 3** *(Kovac N 4, Simunic 16, Rosso 71)*

*Andorra:* Koldo; Ramirez, Txema, Jonas (Garcia 68), Lima A, Fernandez, Ayala, Juli Sanchez, Sonejee, Emiliano (Silva 49), Ruiz.
*Croatia:* Pletikosa; Simic D, Simunic, Tomas, Kovac R, Leko (Tudor 46), Rapajic, Rosso, Mornar, Kovac N (Vranjes 32), Olic (Prso 57).
*Referee:* Liba (Czech Republic).

Sofia, 6 September 2003, 25,128

**Bulgaria (1) 2** *(Petrov M 16, Berbatov 67)*

**Estonia (0) 0**

*Bulgaria:* Ivankov; Borimirov, Kirilov, Stoyanov (Zhelev 88), Petkov I, Stilian Petrov, Hristov, Dimitrov (Peev 71), Jankovic (Krastev 63), Petrov M, Berbatov.
*Estonia:* Poom; Allas, Stepanovs, Jaager, Rooba U, Leetma, Rooba M (Reinumae 60), Kristal, Viikmae, Oper■, Lindpere (Klavan 74).
*Referee:* Wack (Germany).

La Vella, 10 September 2003, 1000

**Andorra (0) 0**

**Bulgaria (2) 3** *(Berbatov 10, 23, Hristov 58)*

*Andorra:* Koldo; Ramirez, Txema, Jonas (Juli Sanchez 60), Lima A, Ayala (Escura 80), Sonejee, Jimenez, Fernandez, Marc, Ruiz (Lucendo 90).
*Bulgaria:* Ivankov; Borimirov, Kirilov, Pazin, Petkov I, Stilian Petrov, Peev (Manchev 63), Hristov, Jankovic (Dimitrov 59), Petrov M, Berbatov.
*Referee:* Mikulski (Poland).

Brussels, 10 September 2003, 35,000

**Belgium (2) 2** *(Sonck 34, 42)*

**Croatia (1) 1** *(Simic D 35)*

*Belgium:* De Vlieger; Deflandre, Simons, Van Buyten, Van Damme, Baseggio, Goor, Clement, Walasiak, Buffel (Martens 88), Sonck (Soetars 90).
*Croatia:* Pletikosa; Simic D, Simunic■, Tomas, Kovac R, Zivkovic, Rapajic (Maric 78), Rosso (Srna 65), Mornar, Kovac N, Olic (Prso 46).
*Referee:* Poll (England).

Liege, 11 October 2003, 26,000

**Belgium (1) 2** *(Reinumae 45 (og), Buffel 61)*

**Estonia (0) 0**

*Belgium:* De Vlieger; Deflandre, Van Buyten, Simons, Van Damme (Deschacht 56), Mpenza M, Baseggio, Clement, Goor, Sonck (Mpenza E 80), Buffel (Roussel 87).
*Estonia:* Poom; Jaager, Lemsalu, Piroja, Rooba U, Reinumae, Haavistu (Zahhoraiko 78), Reim, Rooba M, Klavan (Terehhov 64), Viikmae.
*Referee:* Busacca (Switzerland).

Zagreb, 11 October 2003, 37,000

**Croatia (0) 1** *(Olic 48)*

**Bulgaria (0) 0**

*Croatia:* Pleitkosa; Simic D, Vranjes, Kovac R, Tudor, Zivkovic, Rapajic (Babic 54), Srna (Olic 46), Prso, Leko, Mornar (Rosso 76).
*Bulgaria:* Zdravkov; Krastev, Kirilov, Petkov I, Pazin, Borimirov, Dimitrov (Manchev 62), Peev (Jankovic 72), Hristov, Stilian Petrov, Berbatov.
*Referee:* Veissiere (France).

| **Group 8 Final Table** | *P* | *W* | *D* | *L* | *F* | *A* | *Pts* |
|---|---|---|---|---|---|---|---|
| Bulgaria | 8 | 5 | 2 | 1 | 13 | 4 | 17 |
| Croatia | 8 | 5 | 1 | 2 | 12 | 4 | 16 |
| Belgium | 8 | 5 | 1 | 2 | 11 | 9 | 16 |
| Estonia | 8 | 2 | 2 | 4 | 4 | 6 | 8 |
| Andorra | 8 | 0 | 0 | 8 | 1 | 18 | 0 |

## GROUP 9

Baku, 7 September 2002, 37,000

**Azerbaijan (0) 0**

**Italy (1) 2** *(Akhmedov 32 (og), Del Piero 63)*

*Azerbaijan:* Kramarenko; Kuliyev K, Kerimov A, Akhmedov, Kuliyev E, Imamaliev, Kurbanov M (Musayev 68), Aliyev, Kurbanov K (Ismailov 90), Sadykhov, Agayev (Nabiev 88).
*Italy:* Buffon; Panucci, Nesta, Cannavaro, Coco, Gattuso, Di Biagio (Ambrosini 57), Del Piero, Tommasi, Inzaghi (Pirlo 78), Vieri (Montella 57).
*Referee:* Vassaras (Greece).

Helsinki, 7 September 2002, 35,833

**Finland (0) 0**

**Wales (1) 2** *(Hartson 30, Davies 72)*

*Finland:* Niemi; Nylund (Johansson 69), Saarinen (Kopteff 78), Hyypia, Tihinen, Nurmela (Kottila 86), Riihilahti, Tainio, Kolkka, Litmanen, Kuqi.
*Wales:* Jones; Delaney, Gabbidon, Savage, Melville, Pembridge, Speed, Johnson (Bellamy 76), Hartson, Davies, Giggs.
*Referee:* Plautz (Austria).

Helsinki, 12 October 2002, 11,853

**Finland (1) 3** *(Akhmedov 14 (og), Tihinen 59, Hyypia 71)*

**Azerbaijan (0) 0**

*Finland:* Niemi; Pasanen, Saarinen, Riihilahti, Tihinen, Hyypia (Kuivasto 79), Nurmela, Tainio (Wiss 74), Sumiala (Kuqi 85), Litmanen, Kolkka.
*Azerbaijan:* Gasanzade; Kerimov A, Akhmedov, Agayev, Kuliyev K, Kuliyev E, Mamedov R (Mamedov F 90), Kurbanov M (Sadykhov 65), Kurbanov G, Aliyev, Imamaliev (Vasilyev 83).
*Referee:* Hamer (Luxembourg).

Naples, 12 October 2002, 42,661

**Italy (1) 1** *(Del Piero 39)*

**Yugoslavia (1) 1** *(Mijatovic 28)*

*Italy:* Buffon; Panucci, Zauri (Oddo 32), Pirlo (Ambrosini 34), Nesta, Cannavaro, Tommasi, Doni (Montella 46), Inzaghi, Del Piero, Gattuso.
*Yugoslavia:* Jevric; Lazetic, Dragutinovic, Vidic, Mihajlovic, Krstajic, Trobok, Mirkovic (Duljaj 8), Kovacevic D (Milosevic 69), Mijatovic (Kezman 66), Stankovic D.
*Referee:* Gonzalez (Spain).

Cardiff, 16 October 2002, 70,000

**Wales (1) 2** *(Davies 12, Bellamy 71)*

**Italy (1) 1** *(Del Piero 32)*

*Wales:* Jones P; Delaney, Speed, Pembridge, Melville, Gabbidon, Davies, Savage, Hartson, Bellamy (Blake 90), Giggs.
*Italy:* Buffon; Panucci, Zauri, Pirlo, Nesta, Cannavaro, Tommasi, Di Biagio (Gattuso 65) (Marazzina 85), Del Piero, Montella (Maccarone 70), Ambrosini.
*Referee:* Veissiere (France).

Belgrade, 16 October 2002, 35,000

**Yugoslavia (0) 2** *(Kovacevic D 56, Mihajlovic 84 (pen))*

**Finland (0) 0**

*Yugoslavia:* Jevric; Njegus (Krstajic 46), Dragutinovic, Stankovic D, Vidic, Mihajlovic, Lazetic, Duljaj, Kovacevic D (Milosevic 71), Kezman (Brnovic N 62), Mijatovic.
*Finland:* Niemi; Saarinen, Kuivasto, Pasanen (Reini■ 63), Hyypia, Riihilahti, Nurmela, Tainio (Kuqi 82), Litmanen, Kolkka, Sumiala (Johansson 57).
*Referee:* Van Hulten (Holland).

Baku, 20 November 2002, 8000

**Azerbaijan (0) 0**

**Wales (1) 2** *(Speed 9, Hartson 68)*

*Azerbaijan:* Gasanzade; Kerimov A (Mamedov F 46), Niftaliev, Sadykhov, Yadullayev, Akhmedov (Asadov 76), Kurbanov M (Ismailov 64), Imamaliev, Kurbanov A, Vasilyev, Aliyev.
*Wales:* Jones P; Delaney (Weston 71), Barnard, Robinson C (Trollope 90), Melville, Page, Davies, Speed, Earnshaw (Roberts N 89), Hartson, Giggs.
*Referee:* Huyghe (Belgium).

Podgorica, 13 February 2003, 8000

**Yugoslavia (1) 2** *(Mijatovic 33 (pen), Lazetic 52)*

**Azerbaijan (0) 2** *(Kurbanov G 58, 77)*

*Yugoslavia:* Jevric; Djordjevic, Dudic, Bunjevcevic, Vukic, Lazetic (Markovic 74), Boskovic, Stankovic D, Mijatovic (Ljuboja 70), Kezman (Duljaj 59), Milosevic.
*Azerbaijan:* Gasanzade; Kuliyev K, Sadykhov, Kuliyev E, Akhmedov, Kurbanov M (Mamedov F 90), Mamedov R, Imamaliev, Aliyev (Mamedov K 87), Kurbanov G, Ismailov (Musayev 55).
*Referee:* Granat (Poland).

Palermo, 29 March 2003, 34,074

**Italy (2) 2** *(Vieri 6, 22)*

**Finland (0) 0**

*Italy:* Buffon; Panucci, Zambrotta, Zanetti C, Cannavaro, Nesta, Perrotta, Camoranesi, Totti (Miccoli 86), Delvecchio (Birindelli 69), Vieri (Corradi 82).
*Finland:* Niemi; Pasanen, Tihinen, Hyypia, Saarinen, Riihilahti (Johansson 36), Ilola, Nurmela (Kopteff 75), Tainio, Kolkka (Kuqi 89), Forssell.
*Referee:* Ivanov (Russia).

Cardiff, 29 March 2003, 72,500

**Wales (3) 4** *(Bellamy 1, Speed 40, Hartson 44, Giggs 52)*

**Azerbaijan (0) 0**

*Wales:* Jones; Davies, Speed (Trollope 46), Pembridge, Melville, Page, Oster, Savage (Robinson C 19), Hartson, Bellamy (Edwards 71), Giggs.
*Azerbaijan:* Gasanzade; Akhmedov, Kuliyev K, Aliyev (Tagizade 76), Kuliyev E (Yadullayev 46), Hajiyev (Mamedov F 46), Kurbanov M, Mamedov R, Kurbanov G, Imamaliev, Musayev.
*Referee:* Leuba (Switzerland).

Helsinki, 7 June 2003, 17,343

**Finland (2) 3** *(Hyypia 20, Kolkka 45, Forssell 57)*

**Serbia-Montenegro (0) 0**

*Finland:* Jaaskelainen; Pasanen, Hyypia, Tihinen, Saarinen, Valakari, Nurmela (Riihilahti 88), Vayrynen, Litmanen, Forssell (Kuqi 81), Kolkka (Kopteff 67).
*Serbia-Montenegro:* Jevric; Mirkovic (Kovacevic M 81), Vidic, Mihajlovic■, Dmitrovic, Duljaj, Markovic, Krstajic, Mijatovic (Vukic 46), Kovacevic D, Milosevic (Jestrovic 46).
*Referee:* Colombo (France).

Baku, 11 June 2003, 3500

**Azerbaijan (0) 2** *(Kurbanov G 88 (pen), Aliyev 90)*

**Serbia-Montenegro (1) 1** *(Boskovic 27)*

*Azerbaijan:* Kramarenko; Agayev (Tagizade 84), Akhmedov, Kuliyev E, Kerimov, Kuliyev K, Kurbanov M, Sadykhov, Aliyev, Kurbanov G (Yadullayev 90), Musayev (Ismailov 59).
*Serbia-Montenegro:* Jevric (Zilic 46); Mirkovic, Njegus, Djordjevic N, Malbasa, Duljaj (Milosevic 88), Vukic, Krstajic, Boskovic, Kovacevic D, Mijatovic (Kovacevic N 68).
*Referee:* Fisker (Denmark).

Helsinki, 11 June 2003, 36,850

**Finland (0) 0**

**Italy (1) 2** *(Totti 32, Del Piero 73)*

*Finland:* Jaaskelainen; Pasanen, Hyypia, Tihinen, Saarinen, Valakari (Riihilahti 82), Nurmela (Kopteff 69), Vayrynen, Litmanen, Forssell, Kolkka (Johansson 79).
*Italy:* Buffon; Panucci, Zambrotta, Perrotta, Nesta, Cannavaro (Legrottaglie 90), Zanetti C, Fiore (Oddo 83), Totti, Del Piero, Corradi (Delvecchio 85).
*Referee:* Siric (Croatia).

Belgrade, 20 August 2003, 25,000

**Serbia-Montenegro (0) 1** *(Mladenovic 73)*

**Wales (0) 0**

*Serbia-Montenegro:* Jevric; Gavrancic, Krstajic, Stefanovic, Cirkovic, Mladenovic, Dragutinovic, Stankovic D (Djordjevic P 81), Vukic (Ilic 68), Kovacevic D, Kezman (Milosevic 71).
*Wales:* Jones P; Delaney, Speed, Pembridge, Page, Gabbidon, Davies, Savage, Blake (Earnshaw), Bellamy, Giggs.
*Referee:* Frisk (Sweden).

Baku, 6 September 2003, 450

**Azerbaijan (0) 1** *(Ismailov 89)*

**Finland (0) 2** *(Tainio 52, Nurmela 76)*

*Azerbaijan:* Kramarenko; Agayev (Musayev 11), Akhmedov■, Kuliyev E, Kuliyev K, Kurbanov M, Yadullayev, Sadykhov, Ismailov, Aliyev, Vasilyev.
*Finland:* Niemi; Saarinen, Hyypia, Pasanen, Vayrynen (Riihilahti 69), Nurmela, Tainio (Valakari 86), Kolkka, Reini, Forssell, Johansson (Kopteff 46).
*Referee:* Hrinak (Slovakia).

Milan, 6 September 2003, 68,000

**Italy (0) 4** *(Inzaghi 59, 63, 70, Del Piero 76 (pen))*

**Wales (0) 0**

*Italy:* Buffon; Panucci (Oddo 58), Nesta, Cannavaro, Zambrotta, Camoranesi, Perrotta (Fiore 86), Zanetti C, Del Piero, Inzaghi (Gattuso 74), Vieri.
*Wales:* Jones P; Delaney, Speed, Pembridge (Johnson 79), Page, Savage, Koumas (Earnshaw 71), Davies, Hartson (Blake 82), Bellamy, Giggs.
*Referee:* Merk (Germany).

Belgrade, 10 September 2003, 35,000

**Serbia-Montenegro (0) 1** *(Ilic 82)*

**Italy (1) 1** *(Inzaghi 22)*

*Serbia-Montenegro:* Jevric; Gavrancic, Krstajic, Stefanovic, Cirkovic, Mladenovic, Dragutinovic (Boskovic 70), Ilic, Djordjevic P, Kezman (Ljuboja 60), Milosevic.
*Italy:* Buffon; Panucci, Nesta, Cannavaro, Zambrotta, Tacchinardi, Perrotta, Camoranesi (Gattuso 51), Del Piero, Inzaghi (Fiore 64), Vieri (Corradi 79).
*Referee:* Hamer (Luxembourg).

Cardiff, 10 September 2003, 72,500

**Wales (1) 1** *(Davies 3)*

**Finland (0) 1** *(Forssell 79)*

*Wales:* Jones P; Weston (Johnson 72), Speed, Pembridge, Page, Melville, Davies, Koumas■, Hartson (Blake 81), Earnshaw, Giggs.
*Finland:* Niemi; Pasanen (Kopteff 81), Hyypia, Tihinen, Saarinen (Reini 46), Nurmela, Riihilahti, Tainio, Vayrynen (Kuqi 57), Kolkka, Forssell.
*Referee:* Ibanez (Spain).

Reggio Calabria, 11 October 2003, 30,000

**Italy (2) 4** *(Vieri 16, Inzaghi 24, 88, Di Vaio 65)*

**Azerbaijan (0) 0**

*Italy:* Buffon; Oddo, Nesta (Ferrari 77), Cannavaro, Zambrotta, Camoranesi (Gattuso 87), Zanetti, Perrotta, Totti, Inzaghi, Vieri (Di Vaio 55).
*Azerbaijan:* Kramarenko (Gasanzade 56); Agayev, Kerimov, Imamaliev, Kuliyev E, Kuliyev K, Kurbanov M (Mamedov R 84), Tagizade (Vasilyev 74), Yadullayev, Sadykhov, Aliyev.
*Referee:* Dougal (Scotland).

Cardiff, 11 October 2003, 72,514

**Wales (1) 2** *(Hartson 24 (pen), Earnshaw 90)*

**Serbia-Montenegro (1) 3** *(Vukic 4, Milosevic 82, Ljuboja 87)*

*Wales:* Jones P; Weston (Edwards 73), Barnard, Speed, Gabbidon, Delaney, Robinson C (Oster 88), Bellamy, Earnshaw, Hartson (Blake 86), Giggs.
*Serbia-Montenegro:* Jevric; Gavrancic, Bunjevcevic, Djordjevic N, Cirkovic (Brnovic 74), Vukic, Mladenovic, Boskovic, Sarac, Kezman (Milosevic 60), Kovacevic D (Ljuboja 75).
*Referee:* Stuchlik (Austria).

| **Group 9 Final Table** | *P* | *W* | *D* | *L* | *F* | *A* | *Pts* |
|---|---|---|---|---|---|---|---|
| Italy | 8 | 5 | 2 | 1 | 17 | 4 | 17 |
| Wales | 8 | 4 | 1 | 3 | 13 | 10 | 13 |
| Serbia-Montenegro | 8 | 3 | 3 | 2 | 11 | 11 | 12 |
| Finland | 8 | 3 | 1 | 4 | 9 | 10 | 9 |
| Azerbaijan | 8 | 1 | 1 | 6 | 5 | 20 | 4 |

**Serbia-Montenegro: changed name from Yugoslavia in February 2003.*

## GROUP 10

Moscow, 7 September 2002, 23,000

**Russia (2) 4** *(Kariaka 20, Bestchastnykh 24, Kerzhakov 71, Babb 88 (og))*

**Republic of Ireland (0) 2** *(Doherty 69, Morrison 76)*

*Russia:* Ovchinnikov; Loskov, Yanovsky, Ignachevitch, Onopko, Nizhegorodov, Kariaka, Aldonin, Bestchastnykh (Kerzhakov 46), Semak (Khokhlov 75), Gusev (Solomatin 28).
*Republic of Ireland:* Given; Finnan, Harte, Cunningham, Breen, Kinsella, McAteer (Doherty 65), Holland, Robbie Keane, Duff (Morrison 18), Kilbane (Babb 85).
*Referee:* Colombo (France).

Basle, 7 September 2002, 20,500

**Switzerland (1) 4** *(Frei 37, Yakin H 63, Muller P 74, Chapuisat 82)*

**Georgia (0) 1** *(Arveladze A 62)*

*Switzerland:* Stiel; Haas, Henchoz, Yakin M, Magnin (Berner 83), Cabanas, Vogel (Celestini 68), Muller P, Frei, Chapuisat, Yakin H (Wicky 74).
*Georgia:* Gvaramadze; Kobiashvili, Shekiladze, Kaladze, Sajaia (Rekhviashvili 46) (Kavelashvili 84), Nemsadze, Tskitishvili, Jamarauli, Demetradze, Arveladze A, Kinkladze (Burduli 46).
*Referee:* Krinak (Slovakia).

Tirana, 12 October 2002, 15,000

**Albania (0) 1** *(Murati 79)*

**Switzerland (1) 1** *(Yakin M 38)*

*Albania:* Strakosha; Fakaj, Duro (Sina 88), Murati, Cipi, Xhumba, Hasi, Lala, Vata F, Tare (Myrtaj 71), Haxhi (Bushi 60).
*Switzerland:* Stiel; Haas, Magnin, Cabanas (Cantaluppi 81), Yakin M, Muller P, Vogel, Yakin H (Celestini 63), Frei (Thurre 84), Chapuisat, Wicky.
*Referee:* Erdemir (Turkey).

Dublin, 16 October 2002, 40,000

**Republic of Ireland (0) 1** *(Magnin 78 (og))*

**Switzerland (1) 2** *(Yakin H 45, Celestini 87)*

*Republic of Ireland:* Given; Kelly G, Harte (Doherty 86), Holland, Breen, Cunningham, Healy, Kinsella, Robbie Keane, Duff (Butler 82), Kilbane (Morrison 61).
*Switzerland:* Stiel; Haas, Magnin, Vogel, Yakin M, Muller, Cabanas, Yakin H (Celestini 84), Frei (Thurre 70), Chapuisat, Wicky (Cantaluppi 84).
*Referee:* Pedersen (Norway).

Moscow, 16 October 2002, 15,000

**Russia (2) 4** *(Kerzhakov 3, Semak 42, 55, Onopko 52)*

**Albania (1) 1** *(Duro 13)*

*Russia:* Ovchinnikov; Nizhegorodov, Ignachevitch, Smertin, Semak, Yanovsky, Onopko, Gusev (Yevseyev 81), Solomatin, Loskov (Aldonin 46), Kerzhakov (Popov 64).
*Albania:* Strakosha; Cipi, Xhumba, Fakaj, Murati, Hasi, Lala, Duro, Vata F (Sina 60), Tare (Myrtaj 69), Haxhi (Bushi 56).
*Referee:* Sundell (Sweden).

Tirana, 29 March 2003, 16,000

**Albania (1) 3** *(Rraklli 20, Lala 80, Tare 83)*

**Russia (0) 1** *(Kariaka 77)*

*Albania:* Strakosha; Beqiri, Cipi, Aliaj, Duro, Lala, Hasi, Murati (Bellai 68), Skela (Dede 84), Rraklli (Myrtaj 71), Tare.
*Russia:* Ovchinnikov; Nizhegorodov, Ignachevitch, Berezutski, Gusev (Bestchastnykh 56), Aldonin, Smertin (Yanovsky 73), Tochilin (Kariaka 46), Loskov, Semak, Kerzhakov.
*Referee:* Alaerts (Belgium).

Tbilisi, 29 March 2003, 15,000

**Georgia (0) 1** *(Kobiashvili 61)*

**Republic of Ireland (1) 2** *(Duff 18, Doherty 84)*

*Georgia:* Lomaia; Khizanishvili, Shashiashvili, Amisulashvili, Nemsadze, Tskitishvili, Jamarauli, Kinkladze (Didava 70), Kobiashvili, Ketsbaia (Demetradze 46), Iashvili.
*Republic of Ireland:* Given; Carr, O'Shea, Kinsella, Breen, Cunningham, Carsley, Holland, Doherty, Kilbane, Duff.
*Referee:* Vassaras (Greece).

Tirana, 2 April 2003, 17,000

**Albania (0) 0**

**Republic of Ireland (0) 0**

*Albania:* Strakosha; Duro, Murati (Bellai 67), Beqiri, Cipi, Aliaj, Lala, Hasi, Skela (Bushi 86), Rraklli (Myrtaj 69), Tare.
*Republic of Ireland:* Given; Carr, O'Shea, Holland, Green, Cunningham, Carsley, Kinsella, Keane (Doherty 57), Duff, Kilbane.
*Referee:* Farina (Italy).

Tbilisi, 2 April 2003, 10,000

**Georgia (0) 0**

**Switzerland (0) 0**

*Georgia:* Lomaia; Khizanishvili, Kemoklidze, Khizaneishvili, Kvirkvelia, Tskitishvili, Nemsadze (Didava 46), Rekhviashvili, Kobiashvili, Demetradze (Ashvetia 72), Iashvili (Arveladze S 46).
*Switzerland:* Zuberbuhler; Haas, Berner, Vogel, Yakin M, Meyer, Cabanas (Cantaluppi 68), Yakin H (Thurre 0), Frei (Celestini 59), Chapuisat, Wicky.
*Referee:* Trivkovic (Croatia).

Tbilisi, 30 April 2003, 11,000

**Georgia (1) 1** *(Asatiani 11)*

**Russia (0) 0**

*Georgia:* Lomaia; Khizanishvili, Khizaneishvili, Kaladze, Tskitishvili, Nemsadze, Kvirkvelia, Burduli (Shashiashvili 0), Ashvetia (Alexidze 84), Asatiani (Didava 75), Demetradze.
*Russia:* Mandrykin; Nizhegorodov, Ignachevitch (Evsikov 4), Onopko, Aldonin (Sychev 79), Alenichev, Smertin, Titov, Kariaka, Semak, Izmailov (Kerzhakov 46).
*Referee:* Wack (Germany).

Dublin, 7 June 2003, 33,000

**Republic of Ireland (1) 2** *(Keane 6, Aliaj 90)*

**Albania (1) 1** *(Skela 9)*

*Republic of Ireland:* Given; Carr, O'Shea, Kinsella (Carsley 55), Cunningham, Breen, Kilbane (Reid 76), Holland, Robbie Keane, Connolly (Doherty 65), Duff.
*Albania:* Strakosha (Beqaj 77); Beqiri, Cipi, Aliaj, Duro, Lala, Hasi, Skela, Murati (Bellai 57), Rraklli (Myrtaj 86), Tare.
*Referee:* Mikulski (Poland).

Basle, 7 June 2003, 30,500

**Switzerland (2) 2** *(Frei 14, 16)*

**Russia (1) 2** *(Ignachevitch 24, 68 (pen))*

*Switzerland:* Stiel; Haas, Yakin M, Muller P (Henchoz 2), Magnin (Berner 61), Cabanas, Celestini, Wicky (Vogel 71), Yakin H, Frei, Chapuisat.
*Russia:* Ovchinnikov; Berezutski, Ignachevitch, Kovtun, Gusev, Smertin, Yanovski, Aldonin, Karyaka (Bystrov 2), Popov (Sychev 46), Semak (Evsikov 82).
*Referee:* Ibanez (Spain).

Dublin, 11 June 2003, 36,000

**Republic of Ireland (1) 2** *(Doherty 43, Robbie Keane 59)*

**Georgia (0) 0**

*Republic of Ireland:* Given; Carr, O'Shea, Carsley, Cunningham, Breen, Healy (Kinsella 86), Holland, Robbie Keane, Doherty (Lee 88), Kilbane.
*Georgia:* Lomaia; Khizanishvili, Khizaneishvili, Kaladze, Rekhviashvili, Burduli, Didava (Aleksidze 76), Asatiani, Amisulashvili, Demetradze (Daraselia 62), Arveladze S.
*Referee:* Gonzalez (Spain).

Geneva, 11 June 2003, 26,000

**Switzerland (2) 3** *(Haas 10, Frei 32, Cabanas 72)*

**Albania (1) 2** *(Lala 23, Skela 86 (pen))*

*Switzerland:* Stiel; Haas, Henchoz (Zwyssig 75), Yakin M, Berner, Cabanas, Vogel, Wicky (Spycher 64), Yakin H, Frei (Celestini 83), Chapuisat.
*Albania:* Strakosha; Beqiri, Cipi (Cana 46), Aliaj, Duro (Dragusha 74), Hasi, Lala, Skela, Bellai, Bushai (Rraklli 2), Tare.
*Referee:* Bennett (England).

Tbilisi, 6 September 2003, 18,000

**Georgia (3) 3** *(Arveladze S 9, 44, Ashvetia 18)*

**Albania (0) 0**

*Georgia:* Lomaia; Khizanishvili, Kemoklidze, Burduli (Rekhviashvili 70), Kvirkvelia, Kobiashvili, Nemsadze, Iashvili, Ashvetia, Jamarauli (Asatiani 58), Arveladze S (Demetradze 60).
*Albania:* Strakosha; Cipi, Dede (Jupi 10), Cana, Hasi, Murati, Bushai (Tare 61), Aliaj, Skela, Bellai (Duro 46), Dragusha.
*Referee:* Voliquartz (Denmark).

Dublin, 6 September 2003, 36,000

**Republic of Ireland (1) 1** *(Duff 35)*

**Russia (1) 1** *(Ignachevitch 42)*

*Republic of Ireland:* Given; Carr, O'Shea (Harte 26), Cunningham, Breen, Carsley (Reid 46), Kilbane, Holland, Morrison (Doherty 73), Healy, Duff.
*Russia:* Ovchinnikov; Evseev, Ignachevitch, Onopko, Sennikov, Gusev, Smertin, Mostovoi, Yesipov (Kerzhakov 33), Alenichev (Aldonin 39), Bulykin.
*Referee:* Michel (Slovakia).

Tirana, 10 September 2003, 10,500

**Albania (0) 3** *(Hasi 52, Tare 54, Bushi 80)*

**Georgia (0) 1** *(Arveladze S 63)*

*Albania:* Strakosha; Beqiri, Cipi, Cana (Myrtaj 85), Hasi, Murati (Haxhi 18), Shkembi, Rraklli (Bushi 58), Aliaj, Tare, Duro.
*Georgia:* Lomaia; Khizanishvili, Kemoklidze (Rekhviashvili 40), Didava (Kinkladze 54), Kvirkvelia, Kobiashvili, Nemsadze, Ashvetia, Iashvili (Demetradze 54), Jamarauli, Arveladze S.
*Referee:* Salomir (Romania).

Moscow, 10 September 2003, 29,000

**Russia (2) 4** *(Bulykin 20, 33, 59, Mostovoi 72)*

**Switzerland (1) 1** *(Karyaka 12 (og))*

*Russia:* Ovchinnikov; Radimov, Solomatin (Sennikov 46), Karyaka, Ignachevitch, Onopko, Gusev (Izmailov 58), Smertin, Kerzhakov (Sychev 77), Mostovoi, Bulykin.
*Switzerland:* Zuberbuhler; Meyer, Berner (Wicky 71), Henchoz, Yakin M, Vogel, Cabanas■, Muller P (Huggel 64), Frei (Rama 79), Celestini, Chapuisat.
*Referee:* Collina (Italy).

Moscow, 11 October 2003, 30,000

**Russia (2) 3** *(Bulykin 29, Titov 45, Sychev 73)*

**Georgia (1) 1** *(Iashvili 5)*

*Russia:* Ovchinnikov; Evseev, Sennikov, Titov, Karayaka (Izmailov 46), Ignachevitch, Onopko, Gusev (Aldonin 63), Bulykin, Mostovoi, Kerzhakov (Sychev 56).
*Georgia:* Lomaia; Khizanishvili, Kemoklidze, Kobiashvili, Kvirkvelia, Tskitishvili (Asatiani 54), Nemsadze, Ashvetia (Daraselia 58), Iashvili, Jamarauli (Burduli 46), Demetradze.
*Referee:* Plautz (Austria).

Basle, 11 October 2003, 31,006

**Switzerland (1) 2** *(Yakin H 6, Frei 60)*

**Republic of Ireland (0) 0**

*Switzerland:* Stiel; Haas, Yakin M, Muller P, Spycher, Huggel, Vogel, Yakin H (Celestini 55), Wicky, Frei (Henchoz 90), Chapuisat (Streller 68).
*Republic of Ireland:* Given; Carr, Harte, Holland (Kinsella 74), Breen, O'Shea, Duff, Healy, Robbie Keane, Connolly (Morrison 56), Kilbane (Finnan 74).
*Referee:* Frisk (Sweden).

| **Group 10 Final Table** | *P* | *W* | *D* | *L* | *F* | *A* | *Pts* |
|---|---|---|---|---|---|---|---|
| Switzerland | 8 | 4 | 3 | 1 | 15 | 11 | 15 |
| Russia | 8 | 4 | 2 | 2 | 19 | 12 | 14 |
| Republic of Ireland | 8 | 3 | 2 | 3 | 10 | 11 | 11 |
| Albania | 8 | 2 | 2 | 4 | 11 | 15 | 8 |
| Georgia | 8 | 2 | 1 | 5 | 8 | 14 | 7 |

**PLAY-OFFS FIRST LEG**

Zagreb, 15 November 2003, 35,000

**Croatia (1) 1** *(Prso 5)*

**Slovenia (1) 1** *(Siljak 22)*

*Croatia:* Pleitkosa; Simic D, Neretjak, Tomas, Tudor, Zivkovic (Srna 59), Mornar, Leko (Rosso 46), Kovac N, Prso, Olic (Rapajic 46).
*Slovenia:* Dabanovic; Cipot, Karic, Vugdalic, Knavs, Sukalo, Ceh N (Bulajic 86), Zahovic, Pavlin, Acimovic (Kapic 76), Siljak (Cesar 89).
*Referee:* Merk (Germany).

Riga, 15 November 2003, 8000

**Latvia (1) 1** *(Verpakovsky 29)*

**Turkey (0) 0**

*Latvia:* Kolinko; Isakov, Lobanov, Stepanovs IN, Astafjevs, Korabiovs, Laizans, Bleidelis, Rubins (Pucinsks 83), Rimkus (Stolcers 86), Verpakovsky (Kolesnichenko 89).
*Turkey:* Rustu; Fatih, Bulent K, Ibrahim, Emre A■, Tugay, Ergun, Emre B (Tumer 88), Okan (Gokdeniz 84), Nihat (Deniz 77), Ilhan.
*Referee:* Veissiere (France).

Moscow, 15 November 2003, 29,000

**Russia (0) 0**

**Wales (0) 0**

*Russia:* Ovchinnikov; Evseev, Ignachevitch, Onopko, Sennikov, Smertin (Gusev 59), Mostovoi, Alenichev, Loskov, Sychev (Izmailov 46), Bulykin.
*Wales:* Jones P; Delaney, Barnard, Speed, Gabbidon, Melville, Johnson, Savage, Hartson (Blake 83), Koumas, Giggs.
*Referee:* Batista (Portugal).

Glasgow, 15 November 2003, 50,670

**Scotland (1) 1** *(McFadden 22)*

**Holland (0) 0**

*Scotland:* Douglas; McNamara, Naysmith, Dailly, Pressley, Wilkie, Fletcher, Ferguson, Dickov (Miller 66), McFadden (Hutchison 90), McCann (Pearson 71).
*Holland:* Van der Sar; Ooijer, Stam, Frank de Boer, Van Bronckhorst (Seedorf 46), Van der Meyde, Cocu, Davids (Van der Vaart 60), Overmars, Kluivert (Makaay 77), Van Nistelrooy.
*Referee:* Hauge (Norway).

Valencia, 15 November 2003, 53,000

**Spain (1) 2** *(Raul 20, Berg H 85 (og))*

**Norway (1) 1** *(Iversen 14)*

*Spain:* Casillas; Michel Salgado, Helguera, Marchena, Puyol, Etxeberria (Joaquin 77), Albelda, Baraja, Reyes (Vicente 77), Raul, Fernando Torres (Valeron 68).
*Norway:* Johnsen E; Basma, Berg H, Lundekvam, Riise, Strand R (Brattbakk 25), Iversen (Johnsen F 77), Andresen (Berg R 87), Andersen, Solli, Flo T.
*Referee:* Poll (England).

**PLAY-OFFS SECOND LEG**

Amsterdam, 19 November 2003, 51,000

**Holland (3) 6** *(Sneider 14, Ooijer 32, Van Nistelrooy 37, 51, 67, Frank de Boer 65)*

**Scotland (0) 0**

*Holland:* Van der Sar; Reiziger, Ooijer (Frank de Boe 46), Cocu, Bouma (Seedorf 68), Van der Meyde, Sneider Davids, Overmars, Van der Vaart, Van Nistelroo (Kluivert 77).
*Scotland:* Douglas; McNamara, Naysmith (Ross 46) Ferguson, Pressley, Wilkie, Fletcher, Rae, Dicko (Crawford 46), McFadden, McCann (Miller 62).
*Referee:* Michel (Slovakia).

Oslo, 19 November 2003, 25,106

**Norway (0) 0**

**Spain (1) 3** *(Raul 34, Vicente 49, Etxeberria 55)*

*Norway:* Johnsen E (Olsen 61); Basma, Lundekvam Johnsen R, Stensaas, Iversen, Andresen (Johnsen F 73) Andersen (Flo H 46), Solli, Riise, Flo T.
*Spain:* Casillas; Michel Salgado, Helguera, Cesar, Puyol Xabi Alonso, Albelda (Baraja 84), Etxeberria (Joaqui 77), Valeron (Guti 73), Vicente, Raul.
*Referee:* Collina (Italy).

Ljubljana, 19 November 2003, 9000

**Slovenia (0) 0**

**Croatia (0) 1** *(Prso 61)*

*Slovenia:* Dabanovic; Cipot (Bulajic 90), Karic, Vugdalic Knavs, Sukalo (Rakovic 69), Ceh N, Zahovic, Pavlir Rudonja (Kapic 46), Acimovic.
*Croatia:* Pletikosa; Srna, Simunic (Babic 53), Kovac R Tudor■, Zivkovic, Rapajic (Tomas 69), Rosso, Prs (Leko 76), Kovac N, Sokota.
*Referee:* Meier (Switzerland).

Istanbul, 19 November 2003, 25,000

**Turkey (1) 2** *(Ilhan 21, Hakan Sukur 64)*

**Latvia (0) 2** *(Laizans 66, Verpakovsky 77)*

*Turkey:* Omer; Umit D (Hasan Sas 78), Bulent K Ibrahim, Deniz, Emre B, Tumer (Gokdeniz 60), Tuga (Tuncay 80), Nihat, Hakan Sukur, Ilhan.
*Latvia:* Kolinko; Stepanovs IN, Astafjevs, Zemlinsky Laizans, Zirnis, Isakov, Bleidelis, Verpakovsky, Rubins Rimkus (Stolcers 79).
*Referee:* Frisk (Sweden).

Cardiff, 19 November 2003, 73,062

**Wales (0) 0**

**Russia (1) 1** *(Evseev 23)*

*Wales:* Jones P; Delaney, Barnard, Speed, Gabbidor Melville, Koumas (Blake 74), Johnson (Earnshaw 58) Hartson, Savage, Giggs.
*Russia:* Malafeev; Evseev, Ignachevitch, Onopkc Sennikov, Smertin, Gusev, Titov (Radimov 59) Alenichev, Izmailov, Bulykin.
*Referee:* Gonzalez (Spain).

# EURO 2004

Who would have expected Greece to win Euro 2004? Certainly not the majority of people living outside the country who were not of Greek origin. With the most modest of international records they not only finished as triumphant winners but in the process beat the host nation Portugal, then the holders France and capped it all by defeating the Portuguese again in the final itself.

Before the tournament started you might have thought that Greece would beat Russia at least in the group matches and that would be all they could have realistically hoped for over the initial stages. But perversely Greece lost 2-1 to Russia!

But back to the beginning and that 2-1 win over Portugal which set the pattern not only for Greece's subsequent performances, but also other upsets which accounted for other fancied teams.

Indeed Portugal only snatched a goal in the dying moments during that defeat. On the same day Portugal's Iberian neighbours Spain were managing to beat Russia 1-0 without too much conviction.

Group B opened with Switzerland and Croatia playing it cautiously and goalless. Later England seemed likely to be on the way to turning favourites France over with a 1-0 lead which could have been two had David Beckham not missed from the penalty spot.

Then a free-kick and a penalty for a Zinedine Zidane double and England were beaten in injury time. Group C saw another scoreless affair with Denmark and Italy sharing it. At last there were goals as Sweden trounced Bulgaria 5-0.

The final group saw surprise finalists Latvia shake the Czech Republic by going ahead only to lose 2-1 late on. Then the Dutch and the Germans played out a 1-1 draw. For the second matches Greece caused another round of raised eyebrows by drawing with Spain, but Portugal looked better in beating Russia 2-0. Group B saw England 3-0 winners over the Swiss with Wayne Rooney getting two goals.

Croatia then held France while in Group C Bulgaria suffered their second defeat 2-0 to Denmark. Italy again failed to win drawing 1-1 with Sweden. But close to another shock came when Latvia were unlucky not to beat Germany in Group D.

Then came the outstanding game of the entire finals in which the Czechs edged out Holland 3-2; a match of fine attacking football. This was the end of the second stage of games, then came the crunch with the last of them.

The Iberian clash of Portugal and Spain meant that the losers would have to pack their bags. Portugal won 1-0 and the Spanish under-achievers lived up to their reputation. Meanwhile Greece were losing 2-1 to Russia of course.

Rooney was again a double scoring hero as England beat Croatia 4-2 and France succeeded in a 3-1 victory over Switzerland. But despite beating Bulgaria 2-1, Italy were out as the Danes and Sweden drew 2-2.

A brace from Ruud Van Nistelrooy including a penalty saw the Dutch beat Latvia 3-0, but it was curtains for the Germans as the Czechs edged them 2-1.

The quarter-finals produced drama as Portugal needed penalties to dispose of England and France lost to the rampant Greeks. A shoot-out had to settle Sweden's match with Holland who went through. Milan Baros hit two goals as the Czechs beat Denmark 3-0.

Semi-finals found the Dutch wanting against Portugal and they only reduced the arrears at 2-1 with an own goal. Then Greece accounted for the Czechs with a silver goal from a corner to set up another meeting with the hosts Portugal.

Having adhered to their strategy of soaking up pressure, man marking and launching counter-attacks at specific moments during the match, the Greeks had the edge in tactics over Portugal who gradually became more and more frustrated. And again it was from a corner that they scored the only goal of the game, though it was poorly defended for all that.

With France, Italy, Spain and finally the hosts losing out not to mention the disappointment of England losing in their traditional method of exit from the penalty spot, this was surely the tournament of the underdog. Few could decry the Greeks for their prize, only the manner of winning based on a defensive system designed to totally frustrate the opposition upsetting the purists.

# EURO 2004

## FINAL COMPETITION

### GROUP A

Estadio Dragao, Oporto, 12 June 2004, 52,000

**Portugal (0) 1** *(Ronaldo 90)*

**Greece (1) 2** *(Karagounis 7, Basinas 51 (pen))*

*Portugal:* Ricardo; Paulo Ferreira, Rui Jorge, Rui Costa, Jorge Andrade, Fernando Couto, Figo, Costinha (Nuno Gomes 66), Simao Sabrosa (Ronaldo 46), Pauleta, Maniche.
*Greece:* Nikopolidis; Seitaridis, Fyssas, Karagounis (Katsouranis 46), Dellas, Kapsis, Zagorakis, Basinas, Charisteas (Lakis 74), Vryzas, Giannakopoulos (Nikolaidis 68).
*Referee:* Collina (Italy).

Faro-Loule, 12 June 2004, 30,000

**Spain (0) 1** *(Valeron 60)*

**Russia (0) 0**

*Spain:* Casillas; Puyol, Raul Bravo, Baraja (Xabi Alonso 58), Helguera, Marchena, Albelda, Etxeberria, Raul (Torres 77), Morientes (Valeron 58), Vicente.
*Russia:* Ovchinnikov; Evseyev, Sennikov, Gusev (Radinov 46), Sharonov■, Smertin, Aldonin (Sychev 67), Mostovoi, Bulykin, Izmailov (Kirlia 73), Alenichev.
*Referee:* Meier (Switzerland).

Estadio Do Bessa Sec. XXI, Oporto, 16 June 2004, 25,444

**Greece (0) 1** *(Charisteas 66)*

**Spain (1) 1** *(Morientes 28)*

*Greece:* Nikopolidis; Seitaridis, Fyssas (Venetidis 85), Karagounis (Tsartas 52), Dellas, Kapsis, Giannakopoulos (Nikolaidis 49), Zagorakis, Charisteas, Vryzas, Katsouranis.
*Spain:* Casillas; Puyol, Raul Bravo, Baraja, Helguera, Marchena, Etxeberria (Joaquin 46), Albelda, Raul (Torres 80), Morientes (Valeron 65), Vicente.
*Referee:* Michel (Slovakia).

Estadio Da Luz, Lisbon, 16 June 2004, 58,000

**Russia (0) 0**

**Portugal (1) 2** *(Maniche 7, Rui Costa 89)*

*Russia:* Ovchinnikov■; Evseyev, Sennikov, Aldonin, Smertin, Bugayev, Alenichev, Loskov, Izmailov (Bystrov 72), Kerzkhov, Kariaka (Bulykin 80).
*Portugal:* Ricardo; Miguel, Nuno Valente, Costinha, Jorge Andrade, Ricardo Carvalho, Simao Sabrosa (Rui Costa 63), Maniche, Deco, Pauleta, Figo (Ronaldo 78).
*Referee:* Hauge (Norway).

Faro-Loule, 20 June 2004, 25,000

**Russia (2) 2** *(Kirichenko 2, Bulykin 17)*

**Greece (1) 1** *(Vryzas 43)*

*Russia:* Malafeyev; Anyukov, Evseyev, Gusev, Sharanov (Sennikov 56), Bugayev, Alenichev, Radimov, Bulykin (Sychev 46), Kariaka, Kirichenko.
*Greece:* Nikopolidis; Seitaridis, Venetidis (Fyssas 89), Katsouranis, Dellas, Kapsis, Basinas (Tsartas 42), Zagorakis, Papadopoulos (Nikolaidis 69), Charisteas, Vryzas.
*Referee:* Veissiere (France).

Estadio Jose Alvalade XXI, Lisbon, 20 June 2004, 47,491

**Spain (0) 0**

**Portugal (0) 1** *(Nuno Gomes 57)*

*Spain:* Casillas; Puyol, Raul Bravo, Xabi Alonso, Helguera, Juanito (Morientes 80), Joaquin (Luque 72), Albelda (Baraja 66), Raul, Torres, Vicente.
*Portugal:* Ricardo; Miguel, Nuno Valente, Costinha, Jorge Andrade, Ricardo Carvalho, Figo (Petit 78), Maniche, Pauleta (Nuno Gomes 46), Deco, Ronaldo (Fernando Couto 84).
*Referee:* Frisk (Sweden).

### GROUP A FINAL TABLE

| | P | W | L | D | F | A | GD | Pts |
|---|---|---|---|---|---|---|---|---|
| Portugal | 3 | 2 | 1 | 0 | 4 | 2 | 2 | 6 |
| Greece | 3 | 1 | 1 | 1 | 4 | 4 | 0 | 4 |
| Spain | 3 | 1 | 1 | 1 | 2 | 2 | 0 | 4 |
| Russia | 3 | 1 | 2 | 0 | 2 | 4 | −2 | 3 |

### GROUP B

Leiria, 13 June 2004, 25,000

**Switzerland (0) 0**

**Croatia (0) 0**

*Switzerland:* Stiel; Haas, Spycher, Vogel■, Yakin M, Muller P, Huggel, Wicky (Henchoz 83), Chapuisat (Celestini 55), Frei, Yakin H (Gygax 85).
*Croatia:* Butina; Simic D (Srna 61), Zivkovic, Bjelica (Rosso 73), Kovac R, Simunic, Mornar, Kovac N, Sokota, Prso, Olic (Rapaic 46).
*Referee:* Batista (Portugal).

Estadio Da Luz, Lisbon, 13 June 2004, 62,487

**France (0) 2** *(Zidane 89, 90 (pen))*

**England (1) 1** *(Lampard 38)*

*France:* Barthez; Gallas, Lizarazu, Makelele, Thuram, Silvestre (Sagnol 79), Vieira, Zidane, Trezeguet, Henry, Pires (Wiltord 76).
*England:* James; Neville G, Cole A, Gerrard, Campbell, King, Beckham, Lampard, Rooney (Heskey 76), Owen (Vassell 69), Scholes (Hargreaves 76).
*Referee:* Merk (Germany).

Coimbra, 17 June 2004, 30,616

**England (1) 3** *(Rooney 23, 75, Gerrard 82)*

**Switzerland (0) 0**

*England:* James; Neville G, Cole A, Gerrard, Campbell, Terry, Beckham, Lampard, Rooney (Dyer 83), Owen (Vassell 72), Scholes (Hargreaves 70).
*Switzerland:* Stiel; Haas■, Spycher, Celestini (Cabanas 53), Yakin M, Muller P, Huggel, Wicky, Chapuisat (Gygaz 46), Frei, Yakin H (Vonlanthen 83).
*Referee:* Ivanov (Russia).

Leiria, 17 June 2004, 30,000

**Croatia (0) 2** *(Rapaic 48, Prso 52)*

**France (1) 2** *(Tudor 22 (og), Trezeguet 64)*

*Croatia:* Butina; Simic D, Simunic, Rosso, Kovac R, Tudor, Bjelica (Leko 68), Kovac N, Sokota (Olic 73), Prso, Rapaic (Mornar 87).
*France:* Barthez; Gallas (Sagnol 81), Silvestre, Vieira, Thuram, Desailly, Wiltord (Pires 70), Dacourt (Pedretti 78), Trezeguet, Henry, Zidane.
*Referee:* Nielsen (Denmark).

Estadio Da Luz, Lisbon, 21 June 2004, 63,000

**Croatia (1) 2** *(Kovac N 5, Tudor 73)*

**England (2) 4** *(Scholes 40, Rooney 45, 68, Lampard 79)*

*Croatia:* Butina; Simic D (Srna 67), Simunic, Rosso, Kovac R (Mornar 46), Tudor, Kovac N, Zivkovic, Prso, Rapaic (Olic 55), Sokota.
*England:* James; Neville G, Cole A, Lampard (Neville P 84), Campbell, Terry, Beckham, Gerrard, Rooney (Vassell 71), Owen, Scholes (King 70).
*Referee:* Collina (Italy).

Coimbra, 21 June 2004, 30,000

**Switzerland (1) 1** *(Vonlanthen 26)*

**France (1) 3** *(Zidane 20, Henry 76, 84)*

*Switzerland:* Stiel; Henchoz (Magnin 85), Spycher, Vogel, Yakin M, Muller P, Cabanas, Gygax (Rama 85), Wicky, Yakin H (Huggel 60), Vonlanthen.
*France:* Barthez; Sagnol (Gallas 46), Lizarazu, Makelele, Thuram, Silvestre, Vieira, Zidane, Trezeguet (Saha 75), Henry, Pires.
*Referee:* Michel (Slovakia).

**GROUP B FINAL TABLE**

| | P | W | L | D | F | A | GD | Pts |
|---|---|---|---|---|---|---|---|---|
| France | 3 | 2 | 0 | 1 | 7 | 4 | 3 | 7 |
| England | 3 | 2 | 1 | 0 | 8 | 4 | 4 | 6 |
| Croatia | 3 | 0 | 1 | 2 | 4 | 6 | –2 | 2 |
| Switzerland | 3 | 0 | 2 | 1 | 1 | 6 | –5 | 1 |

**GROUP C**

Guimaraes, 14 June 2004, 29,595

**Denmark (0) 0**

**Italy (0) 0**

*Denmark:* Sorensen; Helveg, Jensen N, Jensen D, Laursen, Henriksen, Poulsen (Priske 76), Jorgensen (Perez 72), Rommedahl, Sand (Jensen C 69), Tomasson.
*Italy:* Buffon; Panucci, Zambrotta, Perrotta, Nesta, Cannavaro, Zanetti C (Gattuso 57), Camoranesi (Fiore 68), Del Piero (Cassano 64), Vieri, Totti.
*Referee:* Gonzalez (Spain).

Estadio Jose Alvalade XXI, Lisbon, 14 June 2004, 52,000

**Sweden (1) 5** *(Ljungberg 32, Larsson 57, 58, Ibrahimovic 78 (pen), Allback 90)*

**Bulgaria (0) 0**

*Sweden:* Isaksson; Lucic (Wilhelmsson 41), Edman, Linderoth, Mellberg, Jakobsson, Nilsson, Svensson A (Kallstrom 77), Ibrahimovic (Allback 81), Larsson, Ljungberg.
*Bulgaria:* Zdravkov; Ivanov, Petkov I, Hristov, Pazin, Kirilov, Peev, Petrov S, Berbatov (Manchev 76), Jankovic (Dimitrov 62), Petrov M (Lazarov 84).
*Referee:* Riley (England).

Braga, 18 June 2004, 24,131

**Bulgaria (0) 0**

**Denmark (1) 2** *(Tomasson 44, Gronkjaer 90)*

*Bulgaria:* Zdravkov; Ivanov (Lazarov 51), Petkov I (Zagorcic 40), Hristov, Kirilov, Stoianov, Peev, Petrov S■, Berbatov, Yankovich (Petkov M 81), Petrov M.
*Denmark:* Sorensen; Helveg, Jensen N, Gravesen, Laursen, Henriksen, Tomasson, Jensen D, Rommedahl (Gronkjaer 23), Sand, Jorgensen (Jensen C 72).
*Referee:* Batista (Portugal).

Estadio Dragao, Oporto, 18 June 2004, 44,926

**Italy (0) 1** *(Cassano 37)*

**Sweden (0) 1** *(Ibrahimovic 85)*

*Italy:* Buffon; Panucci, Zambrotta, Pirlo, Nesta, Cannavaro, Gattuso (Favalli 76), Perrotta, Del Piero (Camoranesi 82), Vieri, Cassano (Fiore 70).
*Sweden:* Isaksson; Nilsson, Edman (Allback 76), Linderoth, Mellberg, Jakobsson, Wilhelmsson (Jonson 65), Svensson A (Kallstrom 55), Ibrahimovic, Larsson, Ljungberg.
*Referee:* Meier (Switzerland).

Estadio Do Bessa Sec. XXI, Oporto, 22 June 2004, 29,000

**Denmark (1) 2** *(Tomasson 28, 66)*

**Sweden (0) 2** *(Larsson 47 (pen), Jonson 89)*

*Denmark:* Sorensen; Helveg, Jensen N (Bogelund 46), Gravesen, Laursen, Henriksen, Tomasson, Jensen D (Poulsen 66), Sand, Jorgensen (Rommedahl 57), Gronkjaer.
*Sweden:* Isaksson; Nilsson, Edman, Jonson, Mellberg, Jakobsson, Andersson A (Allback 82), Kallstrom (Wilhelmsson 72), Ibrahimovic, Larsson, Ljungberg.
*Referee:* Merk (Germany).

Guimaraes, 22 June 2004, 16,002

**Italy (0) 2** *(Perrotta 48, Cassano 90)*

**Bulgaria (1) 1** *(Petrov M 45)*

*Italy:* Buffon; Panucci, Zambrotta, Pirlo, Nesta, Materazzi (Di Vaio 83), Fiore, Perrotta (Oddo 68), Del Piero, Corradi (Vieri 54), Cassano.
*Bulgaria:* Zdravkov; Borimirov, Stoianov, Yankovich (Bozhinov 46), Zagorcic, Pazin (Kotev 64), Petov M, Lazarov, Berbatov, Petrov M, Hristov (Dimitrov 79).
*Referee:* Ivanov (Russia).

**GROUP C FINAL TABLE**

| | P | W | L | D | F | A | GD | Pts |
|---|---|---|---|---|---|---|---|---|
| Sweden | 3 | 1 | 0 | 2 | 8 | 3 | 5 | 5 |
| Denmark | 3 | 1 | 0 | 2 | 4 | 2 | 2 | 5 |
| Italy | 3 | 1 | 0 | 2 | 3 | 2 | 1 | 5 |
| Bulgaria | 3 | 0 | 3 | 0 | 1 | 9 | –8 | 0 |

**GROUP D**

Aveiro, 15 June 2004, 25,000

**Czech Republic (0) 2** *(Baros 73, Heinz 85)*

**Latvia (1) 1** *(Verpakovsky 45)*

*Czech Republic:* Cech; Grygera (Heinz 56), Jankulovski, Galasek (Smicer 64), Bolf, Ujfalusi, Poborsky, Rosicky, Baros (Jiranek 87), Koller, Nedved.
*Latvia:* Kolinko; Isakov, Blagonadezdin, Lobanov (Rimkus 90), Zemlinsky, Stepanovs IN, Astafjevs, Bleidelis, Verpakovsky (Pahars 82), Prohorenkovs (Laizans 71), Rubins.
*Referee:* Veissiere (France).

Estadio Dragao, Oporto, 15 June 2004, 46,000

**Germany (1) 1** *(Frings 30)*

**Holland (0) 1** *(Van Nistelrooy 81)*

*Germany:* Kahn; Friedrich, Lahm, Hamann, Worns, Nowotny, Baumann, Schneider (Schweinsteiger 68), Kuranyi (Bobic 85), Frings (Ernst 79), Ballack.
*Holland:* Van der Sar; Heitinga (Van Hooijdonk 74), Van Bronckhorst, Cocu, Stam, Bouma, Davids (Sneijder 46), Van der Vaart, Van Nistelrooy, Van der Meyde, Zenden (Overmars 46).
*Referee:* Frisk (Sweden).

Estadio Do Bessa Sec. XXI, Oporto, 19 June 2004, 30,000

**Latvia (0) 0**

**Germany (0) 0**

*Latvia:* Kolinko; Izakov, Blagonadezdin, Lobanov (Laizans 70), Stepanovs IN, Zemlinsky, Bleidelis, Astafjevs, Verpakovsky (Zirnis 90), Prohorenkovs (Pahars 67), Rubins.
*Germany:* Kahn; Friedrich, Lahm, Hamann, Worns, Baumann, Schneider (Schweinsteiger 46), Ballack, Kuranyi (Brdaric 78), Bobic (Klose 67), Frings.
*Referee:* Riley (England).

Aveiro, 19 June 2004, 29,935

**Holland (2) 2** *(Bouma 4, Van Nistelrooy 19)*

**Czech Republic (1) 3** *(Koller 23, Baros 71, Smicer 88)*

*Holland:* Van der Sar; Heitinga■, Van Bronckhorst, Cocu, Stam, Bouma, Seedorf (Van der Vaart 85), Davids, Van Nistelrooy, Van der Meyde (Reiziger 79), Robben (Bosvelt 60).
*Czech Republic:* Cech; Grygera (Smicer 25), Galasek (Heinz 62), Poborsky, Ujfalusi, Jiranek, Rosicky, Jankulovski, Koller (Rozehnal 75), Baros, Nedved.
*Referee:* Gonzalez (Spain).

Estadio Jose Alvalade XXI, Lisbon, 23 June 2004, 46,849

**Germany (1) 1** *(Ballack 21)*

**Czech Republic (1) 2** *(Heinz 30, Baros 77)*

*Germany:* Kahn; Frings (Podolski 46), Schweinsteiger (Jeremies 86), Friedrich, Nowotny, Worns, Lahm, Hamann (Klose 79), Kuranyi, Ballack, Schneider.
*Czech Republic:* Blazek; Jiranek, Mares, Plasil, Bolf, Rozehnal, Tyce, Galasek (Hubschman 46), Heinz, Lokvenc (Baros 59), Vachousek.
*Referee:* Hauge (Norway).

Braga, 23 June 2004, 30,000

**Holland (2) 3** *(Van Nistelrooy 27 (pen), 35, Makaay 84)*

**Latvia (0) 0**

*Holland:* Van der Sar; Reiziger, Van Bronckhorst, Van der Meyde (Overmars 63), Frank De Boer, Stam, Seedorf, Cocu, Van Nistelrooy (Makaay 71), Davids (Sneijder 72), Robben.
*Latvia:* Kolinko; Isakov, Blagonadezdin, Lobanov, Zemlinsky, Stepanovs IN, Bleidelis (Stolcers 83), Rubins, Verpakovsky (Pahars 62), Prohorenkovs (Laizans 74), Astafjevs.
*Referee:* Nielsen (Denmark).

## GROUP D FINAL TABLE

| | P | W | L | D | F | A | GD | Pts |
|---|---|---|---|---|---|---|---|---|
| Czech Republic | 3 | 3 | 0 | 0 | 7 | 4 | 3 | 9 |
| Netherlands | 3 | 1 | 1 | 1 | 6 | 4 | 2 | 4 |
| Germany | 3 | 0 | 1 | 2 | 2 | 3 | –1 | 2 |
| Latvia | 3 | 0 | 2 | 1 | 1 | 5 | –4 | 1 |

## QUARTER-FINALS

Estadio Da Luz, Lisbon, 24 June 2004, 62,564

**Portugal (0) 2** *(Postiga 83, Rui Costa 110)*

**England (1) 2** *(Owen 3, Lampard 115)*

*Portugal:* Ricardo; Miguel (Rui Costa 77), Nuno Valente, Maniche, Ricardo Carvalho, Jorge Andrade, Costinha (Simao Sabrosa 62), Deco, Figo (Postiga 74), Nuno Gomes, Ronaldo.
*England:* James; Neville G, Cole A, Gerrard (Hargreaves 81), Terry, Campbell, Beckham, Lampard, Rooney (Vassell 27), Owen, Scholes (Neville P 56).
*aet; Portugal won 6-5 on penalties: Beckham missed, Deco scored, Owen scored, Simao Sabrosa scored, Lampard scored, Rui Costa missed, Terry scored, Ronaldo scored, Hargreaves scored, Maniche scored, Cole scored, Postiga scored, Vassell saved, Ricardo scored.*
*Referee:* Meier (Switzerland).

Estadio Jose Alvalade XXI, Lisbon, 25 June 2004, 45,390

**France (0) 0**

**Greece (0) 1** *(Charisteas 65)*

*France:* Barthez; Gallas, Lizarazu, Makelele, Thuram, Silvestre, Dacourt (Wiltord 70), Zidane, Trezeguet (Saha 70), Henry, Pires (Rothen 70).
*Greece:* Nikopolidis; Seitaridis, Fyssas, Basinas (Tsartas 85), Kapsis, Dellas, Zagorakis, Karagounis, Charisteas, Nikolaidis (Lakis 60), Katsouranis.
*Referee:* Frisk (Sweden).

Faro-Loule, 26 June 2004, 30,000

**Sweden (0) 0**

**Holland (0) 0**

*Sweden:* Isaksson; Ostlund, Nilsson, Linderoth, Mellberg, Jakobsson, Jonson (Wilhelmsson 65), Svensson A (Kallstrom 81), Ibrahimovic, Larsson, Ljungberg.
*Holland:* Van der Sar; Reiziger, Van Bronckhorst, Cocu, Frank De Boer (Bouma 36), Stam, Seedorf, Van der Meyde (Makaay 87), Van Nistelrooy, Davids (Heitinga 62), Robben.
*aet; Holland won 5-4 on penalties: Kalstrom scored, Van Nistelrooy scored, Larsson scored, Heitinga scored, Ibrahimovic missed, Reiziger scored, Ljungberg scored, Cocu hit post, Wilhelmsson scored, Makaay scored, Mellberg saved, Robben scored.*
*Referee:* Michel (Slovakia).

Estadio Dragao, Oporto, 27 June 2004, 41,092

**Czech Republic (0) 3** *(Koller 49, Baros 63, 65)*

**Denmark (0) 0**

*Czech Republic:* Cech; Jiranek (Grygera 39), Jankulovski, Galasek, Ujfalusi, Bolf, Poborsky, Rosicky, Koller, Baros (Heinz 71), Nedved.
*Denmark:* Sorensen; Helveg, Bogelund, Gravesen, Laursen, Henriksen, Poulsen, Jensen C (Madsen 71), Tomasson, Jorgensen (Lovenkrands 85), Gronkjaer (Rommedahl 77).
*Referee:* Ivanov (Russia).

## SEMI-FINALS

Estadio Jose Alvalade XXI, Lisbon, 30 June 2004, 46,679

**Portugal (1) 2** *(Ronaldo 26, Maniche 58)*

**Holland (0) 1** *(Jorge Andrade 63 (og))*

*Portugal:* Ricardo; Miguel, Nuno Valente, Maniche (Fernando Couto 87), Ricardo Carvalho, Jorge Andrade, Costinha, Figo, Pauleta (Nuno Gomes 74), Deco, Ronaldo (Petit 67).
*Holland:* Van der Sar; Reiziger, Van Bronckhorst, Cocu, Bouma (Van der Vaart 55), Stam, Seedorf, Davids, Van Nistelrooy, Robben (Van Hooijdonk 81), Overmars (Makaay 46).
*Referee:* Frisk (Sweden).

Estadio Dragao, Oporto, 1 July 2004, 45,000

**Greece (0) 1** *(Dellas 105)*

**Czech Republic (0) 0**

*Greece:* Nikopolidis; Seitaridis, Fyssas, Basinas (Giannakopoulos 72), Kapsis, Dellas, Zakorakis, Karagounis, Charisteas, Vryzas (Tsartas 90), Katsouranis.
*Czech Republic:* Cech; Grygera, Jankulovski, Galasek, Ujfalusi, Bolf, Poborsky, Rosicky, Koller, Baros, Nedved (Smicer 40).
*aet; Greece won on slow death.*
*Referee:* Collina (Italy).

## FINAL

Estadio Da Luz, Lisbon, 4 July 2004, 62,865

**Greece (0) 1** *(Charisteas 57)*

**Portugal (0) 0**

*Greece:* Nikopolidis; Seitaridis, Fyssas, Basinas, Kapsis, Dellas, Katsouranis, Zagorakis, Charisteas, Vryzas (Papadopoulos 81), Giannakopoulos (Venetidis 76).
*Portugal:* Ricardo; Miguel (Paulo Ferreira 43), Nuno Valente, Costinha (Rui Costa 58), Jorge Andrade, Ricardo Carvalho, Figo, Maniche, Pauleta (Nuno Gomes 74), Deco, Ronaldo.
*Referee:* Merk (Germany).

## EURO 2004 – STATISTICS

Official attendance figures for Euro 2004 showed a marked increase over the previous competition staged four years ago in Holland and Belgium. The aggregate figure for the finals in Portugal was 1,165,192 for an average of 37,587. This compared with 1,126,443 in 2000.

The crowd for the final between Greece and Portugal was given as 62,865 while England's enthralling match with Portugal produced 62,564. England's opening clash with France which was no less dramatic was watched by 62,487.

However for Euro 96 when the finals were held in England the average attendance had been 41,167 and the figure in West Germany as it was still known in 1988 had the highest average at 56,656.

UEFA also produced a squad of 23 for the tournament highlighting the outstanding players in their opinion. Greece the champions were rewarded with five names: Nikopolidis, Dellas, Seitaridis, Charisteas and Zagorakis who was voted the player of the tournament.

England and the beaten finalists Portugal had four each: Campbell, Cole, Lampard and Rooney for England, Figo, Ronaldo, Ricardo Carvalho and Maniche for Portugal. The Czech Republic had three nominated: Cech, Nedved and Baros, Sweden two in Mellberg and Larsson. The remaining names came singly from one country: Ballack (Germany), Van Nistelrooy (Holland), Zidane (France), Zambrotta (Italy) and Tomasson (Denmark).

Greek delight as Charisteas nods home the winner in their 1-0 victory over host nation Portugal to become European Champions. (Colorsport)

# BRITISH AND IRISH INTERNATIONAL RESULTS 1872–2004

*Note:* In the results that follow, WC=World Cup, EC=European Championship, UI=Umbro International Trophy. TF = Tournoi de France. For Ireland, read Northern Ireland from 1921. *After extra time.

## ENGLAND v SCOTLAND

*Played: 110; England won 45, Scotland won 41, Drawn 24. Goals: England 192, Scotland 169.*

| | | | *E* | *S* |
|---|---|---|---|---|
| 1872 | 30 Nov | Glasgow | 0 | 0 |
| 1873 | 8 Mar | Kennington Oval | 4 | 2 |
| 1874 | 7 Mar | Glasgow | 1 | 2 |
| 1875 | 6 Mar | Kennington Oval | 2 | 2 |
| 1876 | 4 Mar | Glasgow | 0 | 3 |
| 1877 | 3 Mar | Kennington Oval | 1 | 3 |
| 1878 | 2 Mar | Glasgow | 2 | 7 |
| 1879 | 5 Apr | Kennington Oval | 5 | 4 |
| 1880 | 13 Mar | Glasgow | 4 | 5 |
| 1881 | 12 Mar | Kennington Oval | 1 | 6 |
| 1882 | 11 Mar | Glasgow | 1 | 5 |
| 1883 | 10 Mar | Sheffield | 2 | 3 |
| 1884 | 15 Mar | Glasgow | 0 | 1 |
| 1885 | 21 Mar | Kennington Oval | 1 | 1 |
| 1886 | 31 Mar | Glasgow | 1 | 1 |
| 1887 | 19 Mar | Blackburn | 2 | 3 |
| 1888 | 17 Mar | Glasgow | 5 | 0 |
| 1889 | 13 Apr | Kennington Oval | 2 | 3 |
| 1890 | 5 Apr | Glasgow | 1 | 1 |
| 1891 | 6 Apr | Blackburn | 2 | 1 |
| 1892 | 2 Apr | Glasgow | 4 | 1 |
| 1893 | 1 Apr | Richmond | 5 | 2 |
| 1894 | 7 Apr | Glasgow | 2 | 2 |
| 1895 | 6 Apr | Everton | 3 | 0 |
| 1896 | 4 Apr | Glasgow | 1 | 2 |
| 1897 | 3 Apr | Crystal Palace | 1 | 2 |
| 1898 | 2 Apr | Glasgow | 3 | 1 |
| 1899 | 8 Apr | Birmingham | 2 | 1 |
| 1900 | 7 Apr | Glasgow | 1 | 4 |
| 1901 | 30 Mar | Crystal Palace | 2 | 2 |
| 1902 | 3 Mar | Birmingham | 2 | 2 |
| 1903 | 4 Apr | Sheffield | 1 | 2 |
| 1904 | 9 Apr | Glasgow | 1 | 0 |
| 1905 | 1 Apr | Crystal Palace | 1 | 0 |
| 1906 | 7 Apr | Glasgow | 1 | 2 |
| 1907 | 6 Apr | Newcastle | 1 | 1 |
| 1908 | 4 Apr | Glasgow | 1 | 1 |
| 1909 | 3 Apr | Crystal Palace | 2 | 0 |
| 1910 | 2 Apr | Glasgow | 0 | 2 |
| 1911 | 1 Apr | Everton | 1 | 1 |
| 1912 | 23 Mar | Glasgow | 1 | 1 |
| 1913 | 5 Apr | Chelsea | 1 | 0 |
| 1914 | 14 Apr | Glasgow | 1 | 3 |
| 1920 | 10 Apr | Sheffield | 5 | 4 |
| 1921 | 9 Apr | Glasgow | 0 | 3 |
| 1922 | 8 Apr | Aston Villa | 0 | 1 |
| 1923 | 14 Apr | Glasgow | 2 | 2 |
| 1924 | 12 Apr | Wembley | 1 | 1 |
| 1925 | 4 Apr | Glasgow | 0 | 2 |
| 1926 | 17 Apr | Manchester | 0 | 1 |
| 1927 | 2 Apr | Glasgow | 2 | 1 |
| 1928 | 31 Mar | Wembley | 1 | 5 |
| 1929 | 13 Apr | Glasgow | 0 | 1 |
| 1930 | 5 Apr | Wembley | 5 | 2 |
| 1931 | 28 Mar | Glasgow | 0 | 2 |
| 1932 | 9 Apr | Wembley | 3 | 0 |
| 1933 | 1 Apr | Glasgow | 1 | 2 |
| 1934 | 14 Apr | Wembley | 3 | 0 |
| 1935 | 6 Apr | Glasgow | 0 | 2 |
| 1936 | 4 Apr | Wembley | 1 | 1 |
| 1937 | 17 Apr | Glasgow | 1 | 3 |
| 1938 | 9 Apr | Wembley | 0 | 1 |
| 1939 | 15 Apr | Glasgow | 2 | 1 |
| 1947 | 12 Apr | Wembley | 1 | 1 |
| 1948 | 10 Apr | Glasgow | 2 | 0 |
| 1949 | 9 Apr | Wembley | 1 | 3 |
| WC1950 | 15 Apr | Glasgow | 1 | 0 |
| 1951 | 14 Apr | Wembley | 2 | 3 |
| 1952 | 5 Apr | Glasgow | 2 | 1 |
| 1953 | 18 Apr | Wembley | 2 | 2 |
| WC1954 | 3 Apr | Glasgow | 4 | 2 |
| 1955 | 2 Apr | Wembley | 7 | 2 |
| 1956 | 14 Apr | Glasgow | 1 | 1 |
| 1957 | 6 Apr | Wembley | 2 | 1 |
| 1958 | 19 Apr | Glasgow | 4 | 0 |
| 1959 | 11 Apr | Wembley | 1 | 0 |
| 1960 | 9 Apr | Glasgow | 1 | 1 |
| 1961 | 15 Apr | Wembley | 9 | 3 |
| 1962 | 14 Apr | Glasgow | 0 | 2 |
| 1963 | 6 Apr | Wembley | 1 | 2 |
| 1964 | 11 Apr | Glasgow | 0 | 1 |
| 1965 | 10 Apr | Wembley | 2 | 2 |
| 1966 | 2 Apr | Glasgow | 4 | 3 |
| EC1967 | 15 Apr | Wembley | 2 | 3 |
| EC1968 | 24 Jan | Glasgow | 1 | 1 |
| 1969 | 10 May | Wembley | 4 | 1 |
| 1970 | 25 Apr | Glasgow | 0 | 0 |
| 1971 | 22 May | Wembley | 3 | 1 |
| 1972 | 27 May | Glasgow | 1 | 0 |
| 1973 | 14 Feb | Glasgow | 5 | 0 |
| 1973 | 19 May | Wembley | 1 | 0 |
| 1974 | 18 May | Glasgow | 0 | 2 |
| 1975 | 24 May | Wembley | 5 | 1 |
| 1976 | 15 May | Glasgow | 1 | 2 |
| 1977 | 4 June | Wembley | 1 | 2 |
| 1978 | 20 May | Glasgow | 1 | 0 |
| 1979 | 26 May | Wembley | 3 | 1 |
| 1980 | 24 May | Glasgow | 2 | 0 |
| 1981 | 23 May | Wembley | 0 | 1 |
| 1982 | 29 May | Glasgow | 1 | 0 |
| 1983 | 1 June | Wembley | 2 | 0 |
| 1984 | 26 May | Glasgow | 1 | 1 |
| 1985 | 25 May | Glasgow | 0 | 1 |
| 1986 | 23 Apr | Wembley | 2 | 1 |
| 1987 | 23 May | Glasgow | 0 | 0 |
| 1988 | 21 May | Wembley | 1 | 0 |
| 1989 | 27 May | Glasgow | 2 | 0 |
| EC1996 | 15 June | Wembley | 2 | 0 |
| EC1999 | 13 Nov | Glasgow | 2 | 0 |
| EC1999 | 17 Nov | Wembley | 0 | 1 |

## ENGLAND v WALES

*Played: 97; England won 62, Wales won 14, Drawn 21. Goals: England 239, Wales 90.*

| | | | *E* | *W* |
|---|---|---|---|---|
| 1879 | 18 Jan | Kennington Oval | 2 | 1 |
| 1880 | 15 Mar | Wrexham | 3 | 2 |
| 1881 | 26 Feb | Blackburn | 0 | 1 |
| 1882 | 13 Mar | Wrexham | 3 | 5 |
| 1883 | 3 Feb | Kennington Oval | 5 | 0 |
| 1884 | 17 Mar | Wrexham | 4 | 0 |

| | | | E | W |
|---|---|---|---|---|
| 1885 | 14 Mar | Blackburn | 1 | 1 |
| 1886 | 29 Mar | Wrexham | 3 | 1 |
| 1887 | 26 Feb | Kennington Oval | 4 | 0 |
| 1888 | 4 Feb | Crewe | 5 | 1 |
| 1889 | 23 Feb | Stoke | 4 | 1 |
| 1890 | 15 Mar | Wrexham | 3 | 1 |
| 1891 | 7 May | Sunderland | 4 | 1 |
| 1892 | 5 Mar | Wrexham | 2 | 0 |
| 1893 | 13 Mar | Stoke | 6 | 0 |
| 1894 | 12 Mar | Wrexham | 5 | 1 |
| 1895 | 18 Mar | Queen's Club, Kensington | 1 | 1 |
| 1896 | 16 Mar | Cardiff | 9 | 1 |
| 1897 | 29 Mar | Sheffield | 4 | 0 |
| 1898 | 28 Mar | Wrexham | 3 | 0 |
| 1899 | 20 Mar | Bristol | 4 | 0 |
| 1900 | 26 Mar | Cardiff | 1 | 1 |
| 1901 | 18 Mar | Newcastle | 6 | 0 |
| 1902 | 3 Mar | Wrexham | 0 | 0 |
| 1903 | 2 Mar | Portsmouth | 2 | 1 |
| 1904 | 29 Feb | Wrexham | 2 | 2 |
| 1905 | 27 Mar | Liverpool | 3 | 1 |
| 1906 | 19 Mar | Cardiff | 1 | 0 |
| 1907 | 18 Mar | Fulham | 1 | 1 |
| 1908 | 16 Mar | Wrexham | 7 | 1 |
| 1909 | 15 Mar | Nottingham | 2 | 0 |
| 1910 | 14 Mar | Cardiff | 1 | 0 |
| 1911 | 13 Mar | Millwall | 3 | 0 |
| 1912 | 11 Mar | Wrexham | 2 | 0 |
| 1913 | 17 Mar | Bristol | 4 | 3 |
| 1914 | 16 Mar | Cardiff | 2 | 0 |
| 1920 | 15 Mar | Highbury | 1 | 2 |
| 1921 | 14 Mar | Cardiff | 0 | 0 |
| 1922 | 13 Mar | Liverpool | 1 | 0 |
| 1923 | 5 Mar | Cardiff | 2 | 2 |
| 1924 | 3 Mar | Blackburn | 1 | 2 |
| 1925 | 28 Feb | Swansea | 2 | 1 |
| 1926 | 1 Mar | Crystal Palace | 1 | 3 |
| 1927 | 12 Feb | Wrexham | 3 | 3 |
| 1927 | 28 Nov | Burnley | 1 | 2 |
| 1928 | 17 Nov | Swansea | 3 | 2 |
| 1929 | 20 Nov | Chelsea | 6 | 0 |
| 1930 | 22 Nov | Wrexham | 4 | 0 |
| 1931 | 18 Nov | Liverpool | 3 | 1 |
| 1932 | 16 Nov | Wrexham | 0 | 0 |
| 1933 | 15 Nov | Newcastle | 1 | 2 |
| 1934 | 29 Sept | Cardiff | 4 | 0 |
| 1936 | 5 Feb | Wolverhampton | 1 | 2 |
| 1936 | 17 Oct | Cardiff | 1 | 2 |
| 1937 | 17 Nov | Middlesbrough | 2 | 1 |
| 1938 | 22 Oct | Cardiff | 2 | 4 |
| 1946 | 13 Nov | Manchester | 3 | 0 |
| 1947 | 18 Oct | Cardiff | 3 | 0 |
| 1948 | 10 Nov | Aston Villa | 1 | 0 |
| WC1949 | 15 Oct | Cardiff | 4 | 1 |
| 1950 | 15 Nov | Sunderland | 4 | 2 |
| 1951 | 20 Oct | Cardiff | 1 | 1 |
| 1952 | 12 Nov | Wembley | 5 | 2 |
| WC1953 | 10 Oct | Cardiff | 4 | 1 |
| 1954 | 10 Nov | Wembley | 3 | 2 |
| 1955 | 27 Oct | Cardiff | 1 | 2 |
| 1956 | 14 Nov | Wembley | 3 | 1 |
| 1957 | 19 Oct | Cardiff | 4 | 0 |
| 1958 | 26 Nov | Aston Villa | 2 | 2 |
| 1959 | 17 Oct | Cardiff | 1 | 1 |
| 1960 | 23 Nov | Wembley | 5 | 1 |
| 1961 | 14 Oct | Cardiff | 1 | 1 |
| 1962 | 21 Oct | Wembley | 4 | 0 |
| 1963 | 12 Oct | Cardiff | 4 | 0 |
| 1964 | 18 Nov | Wembley | 2 | 1 |
| 1965 | 2 Oct | Cardiff | 0 | 0 |
| EC1966 | 16 Nov | Wembley | 5 | 1 |
| EC1967 | 21 Oct | Cardiff | 3 | 0 |
| 1969 | 7 May | Wembley | 2 | 1 |
| 1970 | 18 Apr | Cardiff | 1 | 1 |
| 1971 | 19 May | Wembley | 0 | 0 |
| 1972 | 20 May | Cardiff | 3 | 0 |
| WC1972 | 15 Nov | Cardiff | 1 | 0 |
| WC1973 | 24 Jan | Wembley | 1 | 1 |
| 1973 | 15 May | Wembley | 3 | 0 |
| 1974 | 11 May | Cardiff | 2 | 0 |
| 1975 | 21 May | Wembley | 2 | 2 |
| 1976 | 24 Mar | Wrexham | 2 | 1 |
| 1976 | 8 May | Cardiff | 1 | 0 |
| 1977 | 31 May | Wembley | 0 | 1 |
| 1978 | 3 May | Cardiff | 3 | 1 |
| 1979 | 23 May | Wembley | 0 | 0 |
| 1980 | 17 May | Wrexham | 1 | 4 |
| 1981 | 20 May | Wembley | 0 | 0 |
| 1982 | 27 Apr | Cardiff | 1 | 0 |
| 1983 | 23 Feb | Wembley | 2 | 1 |
| 1984 | 2 May | Wrexham | 0 | 1 |

## ENGLAND v IRELAND

*Played: 96; England won 74, Ireland won 6, Drawn 16. Goals: England 319, Ireland 80.*

| | | | E | I |
|---|---|---|---|---|
| 1882 | 18 Feb | Belfast | 13 | 0 |
| 1883 | 24 Feb | Liverpool | 7 | 0 |
| 1884 | 23 Feb | Belfast | 8 | 1 |
| 1885 | 28 Feb | Manchester | 4 | 0 |
| 1886 | 13 Mar | Belfast | 6 | 1 |
| 1887 | 5 Feb | Sheffield | 7 | 0 |
| 1888 | 31 Mar | Belfast | 5 | 1 |
| 1889 | 2 Mar | Everton | 6 | 1 |
| 1890 | 15 Mar | Belfast | 9 | 1 |
| 1891 | 7 Mar | Wolverhampton | 6 | 1 |
| 1892 | 5 Mar | Belfast | 2 | 0 |
| 1893 | 25 Feb | Birmingham | 6 | 1 |
| 1894 | 3 Mar | Belfast | 2 | 2 |
| 1895 | 9 Mar | Derby | 9 | 0 |
| 1896 | 7 Mar | Belfast | 2 | 0 |
| 1897 | 20 Feb | Nottingham | 6 | 0 |
| 1898 | 5 Mar | Belfast | 3 | 2 |
| 1899 | 18 Feb | Sunderland | 13 | 2 |
| 1900 | 17 Mar | Dublin | 2 | 0 |
| 1901 | 9 Mar | Southampton | 3 | 0 |
| 1902 | 22 Mar | Belfast | 1 | 0 |
| 1903 | 14 Feb | Wolverhampton | 4 | 0 |
| 1904 | 12 Mar | Belfast | 3 | 1 |
| 1905 | 25 Feb | Middlesbrough | 1 | 1 |
| 1906 | 17 Feb | Belfast | 5 | 0 |
| 1907 | 16 Feb | Everton | 1 | 0 |
| 1908 | 15 Feb | Belfast | 3 | 1 |
| 1909 | 13 Feb | Bradford | 4 | 0 |
| 1910 | 12 Feb | Belfast | 1 | 1 |
| 1911 | 11 Feb | Derby | 2 | 1 |
| 1912 | 10 Feb | Dublin | 6 | 1 |
| 1913 | 15 Feb | Belfast | 1 | 2 |
| 1914 | 14 Feb | Middlesbrough | 0 | 3 |
| 1919 | 25 Oct | Belfast | 1 | 1 |
| 1920 | 23 Oct | Sunderland | 2 | 0 |
| 1921 | 22 Oct | Belfast | 1 | 1 |
| 1922 | 21 Oct | West Bromwich | 2 | 0 |
| 1923 | 20 Oct | Belfast | 1 | 2 |
| 1924 | 22 Oct | Everton | 3 | 1 |
| 1925 | 24 Oct | Belfast | 0 | 0 |
| 1926 | 20 Oct | Liverpool | 3 | 3 |
| 1927 | 22 Oct | Belfast | 0 | 2 |

| | | | E | I |
|---|---|---|---|---|
| 1928 | 22 Oct | Everton | 2 | 1 |
| 1929 | 19 Oct | Belfast | 3 | 0 |
| 1930 | 20 Oct | Sheffield | 5 | 1 |
| 1931 | 17 Oct | Belfast | 6 | 2 |
| 1932 | 17 Oct | Blackpool | 1 | 0 |
| 1933 | 14 Oct | Belfast | 3 | 0 |
| 1935 | 6 Feb | Everton | 2 | 1 |
| 1935 | 19 Oct | Belfast | 3 | 1 |
| 1936 | 18 Nov | Stoke | 3 | 1 |
| 1937 | 23 Oct | Belfast | 5 | 1 |
| 1938 | 16 Nov | Manchester | 7 | 0 |
| 1946 | 28 Sept | Belfast | 7 | 2 |
| 1947 | 5 Nov | Everton | 2 | 2 |
| 1948 | 9 Oct | Belfast | 6 | 2 |
| WC1949 | 16 Nov | Manchester | 9 | 2 |
| 1950 | 7 Oct | Belfast | 4 | 1 |
| 1951 | 14 Nov | Aston Villa | 2 | 0 |
| 1952 | 4 Oct | Belfast | 2 | 2 |
| WC1953 | 11 Nov | Everton | 3 | 1 |
| 1954 | 2 Oct | Belfast | 2 | 0 |
| 1955 | 2 Nov | Wembley | 3 | 0 |
| 1956 | 10 Oct | Belfast | 1 | 1 |
| 1957 | 6 Nov | Wembley | 2 | 3 |
| 1958 | 4 Oct | Belfast | 3 | 3 |
| 1959 | 18 Nov | Wembley | 2 | 1 |
| 1960 | 8 Oct | Belfast | 5 | 2 |
| 1961 | 22 Nov | Wembley | 1 | 1 |
| 1962 | 20 Oct | Belfast | 3 | 1 |
| 1963 | 20 Nov | Wembley | 8 | 3 |
| 1964 | 3 Oct | Belfast | 4 | 3 |
| 1965 | 10 Nov | Wembley | 2 | 1 |
| EC1966 | 20 Oct | Belfast | 2 | 0 |
| EC1967 | 22 Nov | Wembley | 2 | 0 |
| 1969 | 3 May | Belfast | 3 | 1 |
| 1970 | 21 Apr | Wembley | 3 | 1 |
| 1971 | 15 May | Belfast | 1 | 0 |
| 1972 | 23 May | Wembley | 0 | 1 |
| 1973 | 12 May | Everton | 2 | 1 |
| 1974 | 15 May | Wembley | 1 | 0 |
| 1975 | 17 May | Belfast | 0 | 0 |
| 1976 | 11 May | Wembley | 4 | 0 |
| 1977 | 28 May | Belfast | 2 | 1 |
| 1978 | 16 May | Wembley | 1 | 0 |
| EC1979 | 7 Feb | Wembley | 4 | 0 |
| 1979 | 19 May | Belfast | 2 | 0 |
| EC1979 | 17 Oct | Belfast | 5 | 1 |
| 1980 | 20 May | Wembley | 1 | 1 |
| 1982 | 23 Feb | Wembley | 4 | 0 |
| 1983 | 28 May | Belfast | 0 | 0 |
| 1984 | 24 Apr | Wembley | 1 | 0 |
| WC1985 | 27 Feb | Belfast | 1 | 0 |
| WC1985 | 13 Nov | Wembley | 0 | 0 |
| EC1986 | 15 Oct | Wembley | 3 | 0 |
| EC1987 | 1 Apr | Belfast | 2 | 0 |

## SCOTLAND v WALES

*Played: 103; Scotland won 60, Wales won 20, Drawn 23. Goals: Scotland 238, Wales 116.*

| | | | S | W |
|---|---|---|---|---|
| 1876 | 25 Mar | Glasgow | 4 | 0 |
| 1877 | 5 Mar | Wrexham | 2 | 0 |
| 1878 | 23 Mar | Glasgow | 9 | 0 |
| 1879 | 7 Apr | Wrexham | 3 | 0 |
| 1880 | 3 Apr | Glasgow | 5 | 1 |
| 1881 | 14 Mar | Wrexham | 5 | 1 |
| 1882 | 25 Mar | Glasgow | 5 | 0 |
| 1883 | 12 Mar | Wrexham | 3 | 0 |
| 1884 | 29 Mar | Glasgow | 4 | 1 |
| 1885 | 23 Mar | Wrexham | 8 | 1 |
| 1886 | 10 Apr | Glasgow | 4 | 1 |
| 1887 | 21 Mar | Wrexham | 2 | 0 |
| 1888 | 10 Mar | Edinburgh | 5 | 1 |
| 1889 | 15 Apr | Wrexham | 0 | 0 |
| 1890 | 22 Mar | Paisley | 5 | 0 |
| 1891 | 21 Mar | Wrexham | 4 | 3 |
| 1892 | 26 Mar | Edinburgh | 6 | 1 |
| 1893 | 18 Mar | Wrexham | 8 | 0 |
| 1894 | 24 Mar | Kilmarnock | 5 | 2 |
| 1895 | 23 Mar | Wrexham | 2 | 2 |
| 1896 | 21 Mar | Dundee | 4 | 0 |
| 1897 | 20 Mar | Wrexham | 2 | 2 |
| 1898 | 19 Mar | Motherwell | 5 | 2 |
| 1899 | 18 Mar | Wrexham | 6 | 0 |
| 1900 | 3 Feb | Aberdeen | 5 | 2 |
| 1901 | 2 Mar | Wrexham | 1 | 1 |
| 1902 | 15 Mar | Greenock | 5 | 1 |
| 1903 | 9 Mar | Cardiff | 1 | 0 |
| 1904 | 12 Mar | Dundee | 1 | 1 |
| 1905 | 6 Mar | Wrexham | 1 | 3 |
| 1906 | 3 Mar | Edinburgh | 0 | 2 |
| 1907 | 4 Mar | Wrexham | 0 | 1 |
| 1908 | 7 Mar | Dundee | 2 | 1 |
| 1909 | 1 Mar | Wrexham | 2 | 3 |
| 1910 | 5 Mar | Kilmarnock | 1 | 0 |
| 1911 | 6 Mar | Cardiff | 2 | 2 |
| 1912 | 2 Mar | Tynecastle | 1 | 0 |
| 1913 | 3 Mar | Wrexham | 0 | 0 |
| 1914 | 28 Feb | Glasgow | 0 | 0 |
| 1920 | 26 Feb | Cardiff | 1 | 1 |
| 1921 | 12 Feb | Aberdeen | 2 | 1 |
| 1922 | 4 Feb | Wrexham | 1 | 2 |
| 1923 | 17 Mar | Paisley | 2 | 0 |
| 1924 | 16 Feb | Cardiff | 0 | 2 |
| 1925 | 14 Feb | Tynecastle | 3 | 1 |
| 1925 | 31 Oct | Cardiff | 3 | 0 |
| 1926 | 30 Oct | Glasgow | 3 | 0 |
| 1927 | 29 Oct | Wrexham | 2 | 2 |
| 1928 | 27 Oct | Glasgow | 4 | 2 |
| 1929 | 26 Oct | Cardiff | 4 | 2 |
| 1930 | 25 Oct | Glasgow | 1 | 1 |
| 1931 | 31 Oct | Wrexham | 3 | 2 |
| 1932 | 26 Oct | Edinburgh | 2 | 5 |
| 1933 | 4 Oct | Cardiff | 2 | 3 |
| 1934 | 21 Nov | Aberdeen | 3 | 2 |
| 1935 | 5 Oct | Cardiff | 1 | 1 |
| 1936 | 2 Dec | Dundee | 1 | 2 |
| 1937 | 30 Oct | Cardiff | 1 | 2 |
| 1938 | 9 Nov | Edinburgh | 3 | 2 |
| 1946 | 19 Oct | Wrexham | 1 | 3 |
| 1947 | 12 Nov | Glasgow | 1 | 2 |
| WC1948 | 23 Oct | Cardiff | 3 | 1 |
| 1949 | 9 Nov | Glasgow | 2 | 0 |
| 1950 | 21 Oct | Cardiff | 3 | 1 |
| 1951 | 14 Nov | Glasgow | 0 | 1 |
| WC1952 | 18 Oct | Cardiff | 2 | 1 |
| 1953 | 4 Nov | Glasgow | 3 | 3 |
| 1954 | 16 Oct | Cardiff | 1 | 0 |
| 1955 | 9 Nov | Glasgow | 2 | 0 |
| 1956 | 20 Oct | Cardiff | 2 | 2 |
| 1957 | 13 Nov | Glasgow | 1 | 1 |
| 1958 | 18 Oct | Cardiff | 3 | 0 |
| 1959 | 4 Nov | Glasgow | 1 | 1 |
| 1960 | 20 Oct | Cardiff | 0 | 2 |
| 1961 | 8 Nov | Glasgow | 2 | 0 |
| 1962 | 20 Oct | Cardiff | 3 | 2 |
| 1963 | 20 Nov | Glasgow | 2 | 1 |
| 1964 | 3 Oct | Cardiff | 2 | 3 |
| EC1965 | 24 Nov | Glasgow | 4 | 1 |
| EC1966 | 22 Oct | Cardiff | 1 | 1 |

| | | | S | W |
|---|---|---|---|---|
| 1967 | 22 Nov | Glasgow | 3 | 2 |
| 1969 | 3 May | Wrexham | 5 | 3 |
| 1970 | 22 Apr | Glasgow | 0 | 0 |
| 1971 | 15 May | Cardiff | 0 | 0 |
| 1972 | 24 May | Glasgow | 1 | 0 |
| 1973 | 12 May | Wrexham | 2 | 0 |
| 1974 | 14 May | Glasgow | 2 | 0 |
| 1975 | 17 May | Cardiff | 2 | 2 |
| 1976 | 6 May | Glasgow | 3 | 1 |
| wc1976 | 17 Nov | Glasgow | 1 | 0 |
| 1977 | 28 May | Wrexham | 0 | 0 |
| wc1977 | 12 Oct | Liverpool | 2 | 0 |
| 1978 | 17 May | Glasgow | 1 | 1 |
| 1979 | 19 May | Cardiff | 0 | 3 |
| 1980 | 21 May | Glasgow | 1 | 0 |
| 1981 | 16 May | Swansea | 0 | 2 |
| 1982 | 24 May | Glasgow | 1 | 0 |
| 1983 | 28 May | Cardiff | 2 | 0 |
| 1984 | 28 Feb | Glasgow | 2 | 1 |
| wc1985 | 27 Mar | Glasgow | 0 | 1 |
| wc1985 | 10 Sept | Cardiff | 1 | 1 |
| 1997 | 27 May | Kilmarnock | 0 | 1 |
| 2004 | 18 Feb | Cardiff | 0 | 4 |

## SCOTLAND v IRELAND

*Played: 93; Scotland won 62, Ireland won 15, Drawn 16. Goals: Scotland 257, Ireland 81.*

| | | | S | I |
|---|---|---|---|---|
| 1884 | 26 Jan | Belfast | 5 | 0 |
| 1885 | 14 Mar | Glasgow | 8 | 2 |
| 1886 | 20 Mar | Belfast | 7 | 2 |
| 1887 | 19 Feb | Glasgow | 4 | 1 |
| 1888 | 24 Mar | Belfast | 10 | 2 |
| 1889 | 9 Mar | Glasgow | 7 | 0 |
| 1890 | 29 Mar | Belfast | 4 | 1 |
| 1891 | 28 Mar | Glasgow | 2 | 1 |
| 1892 | 19 Mar | Belfast | 3 | 2 |
| 1893 | 25 Mar | Glasgow | 6 | 1 |
| 1894 | 31 Mar | Belfast | 2 | 1 |
| 1895 | 30 Mar | Glasgow | 3 | 1 |
| 1896 | 28 Mar | Belfast | 3 | 3 |
| 1897 | 27 Mar | Glasgow | 5 | 1 |
| 1898 | 26 Mar | Belfast | 3 | 0 |
| 1899 | 25 Mar | Glasgow | 9 | 1 |
| 1900 | 3 Mar | Belfast | 3 | 0 |
| 1901 | 23 Feb | Glasgow | 11 | 0 |
| 1902 | 1 Mar | Belfast | 5 | 1 |
| 1902 | 9 Aug | Belfast | 3 | 0 |
| 1903 | 21 Mar | Glasgow | 0 | 2 |
| 1904 | 26 Mar | Dublin | 1 | 1 |
| 1905 | 18 Mar | Glasgow | 4 | 0 |
| 1906 | 17 Mar | Dublin | 1 | 0 |
| 1907 | 16 Mar | Glasgow | 3 | 0 |
| 1908 | 14 Mar | Dublin | 5 | 0 |
| 1909 | 15 Mar | Glasgow | 5 | 0 |
| 1910 | 19 Mar | Belfast | 0 | 1 |
| 1911 | 18 Mar | Glasgow | 2 | 0 |
| 1912 | 16 Mar | Belfast | 4 | 1 |
| 1913 | 15 Mar | Dublin | 2 | 1 |
| 1914 | 14 Mar | Belfast | 1 | 1 |
| 1920 | 13 Mar | Glasgow | 3 | 0 |
| 1921 | 26 Feb | Belfast | 2 | 0 |
| 1922 | 4 Mar | Glasgow | 2 | 1 |
| 1923 | 3 Mar | Belfast | 1 | 0 |
| 1924 | 1 Mar | Glasgow | 2 | 0 |
| 1925 | 28 Feb | Belfast | 3 | 0 |
| 1926 | 27 Feb | Glasgow | 4 | 0 |
| 1927 | 26 Feb | Belfast | 2 | 0 |
| 1928 | 25 Feb | Glasgow | 0 | 1 |
| 1929 | 23 Feb | Belfast | 7 | 3 |
| 1930 | 22 Feb | Glasgow | 3 | 1 |
| 1931 | 21 Feb | Belfast | 0 | 0 |
| 1931 | 19 Sept | Glasgow | 3 | 1 |
| 1932 | 12 Sept | Belfast | 4 | 0 |
| 1933 | 16 Sept | Glasgow | 1 | 2 |
| 1934 | 20 Oct | Belfast | 1 | 2 |
| 1935 | 13 Nov | Edinburgh | 2 | 1 |
| 1936 | 31 Oct | Belfast | 3 | 1 |
| 1937 | 10 Nov | Aberdeen | 1 | 1 |
| 1938 | 8 Oct | Belfast | 2 | 0 |
| 1946 | 27 Nov | Glasgow | 0 | 0 |
| 1947 | 4 Oct | Belfast | 0 | 2 |
| 1948 | 17 Nov | Glasgow | 3 | 2 |
| 1949 | 1 Oct | Belfast | 8 | 2 |
| 1950 | 1 Nov | Glasgow | 6 | 1 |
| 1951 | 6 Oct | Belfast | 3 | 0 |
| 1952 | 5 Nov | Glasgow | 1 | 1 |
| 1953 | 3 Oct | Belfast | 3 | 1 |
| 1954 | 3 Nov | Glasgow | 2 | 2 |
| 1955 | 8 Oct | Belfast | 1 | 2 |
| 1956 | 7 Nov | Glasgow | 1 | 0 |
| 1957 | 5 Oct | Belfast | 1 | 1 |
| 1958 | 5 Nov | Glasgow | 2 | 2 |
| 1959 | 3 Oct | Belfast | 4 | 0 |
| 1960 | 9 Nov | Glasgow | 5 | 2 |
| 1961 | 7 Oct | Belfast | 6 | 1 |
| 1962 | 7 Nov | Glasgow | 5 | 1 |
| 1963 | 12 Oct | Belfast | 1 | 2 |
| 1964 | 25 Nov | Glasgow | 3 | 2 |
| 1965 | 2 Oct | Belfast | 2 | 3 |
| 1966 | 16 Nov | Glasgow | 2 | 1 |
| 1967 | 21 Oct | Belfast | 0 | 1 |
| 1969 | 6 May | Glasgow | 1 | 1 |
| 1970 | 18 Apr | Belfast | 1 | 0 |
| 1971 | 18 May | Glasgow | 0 | 1 |
| 1972 | 20 May | Glasgow | 2 | 0 |
| 1973 | 16 May | Glasgow | 1 | 2 |
| 1974 | 11 May | Glasgow | 0 | 1 |
| 1975 | 20 May | Glasgow | 3 | 0 |
| 1976 | 8 May | Glasgow | 3 | 0 |
| 1977 | 1 June | Glasgow | 3 | 0 |
| 1978 | 13 May | Glasgow | 1 | 1 |
| 1979 | 22 May | Glasgow | 1 | 0 |
| 1980 | 17 May | Belfast | 0 | 1 |
| wc1981 | 25 Mar | Glasgow | 1 | 1 |
| 1981 | 19 May | Glasgow | 2 | 0 |
| wc1981 | 14 Oct | Belfast | 0 | 0 |
| 1982 | 28 Apr | Belfast | 1 | 1 |
| 1983 | 24 May | Glasgow | 0 | 0 |
| 1983 | 13 Dec | Belfast | 0 | 2 |
| 1992 | 19 Feb | Glasgow | 1 | 0 |

## WALES v IRELAND

*Played: 90; Wales won 42, Ireland won 27, Drawn 21. Goals: Wales 182, Ireland 127.*

| | | | W | I |
|---|---|---|---|---|
| 1882 | 25 Feb | Wrexham | 7 | 1 |
| 1883 | 17 Mar | Belfast | 1 | 1 |
| 1884 | 9 Feb | Wrexham | 6 | 0 |
| 1885 | 11 Apr | Belfast | 8 | 2 |
| 1886 | 27 Feb | Wrexham | 5 | 0 |
| 1887 | 12 Mar | Belfast | 1 | 4 |
| 1888 | 3 Mar | Wrexham | 11 | 0 |
| 1889 | 27 Apr | Belfast | 3 | 1 |

| | | | W | I |
|---|---|---|---|---|
| 1890 | 8 Feb | Shrewsbury | 5 | 2 |
| 1891 | 7 Feb | Belfast | 2 | 7 |
| 1892 | 27 Feb | Bangor | 1 | 1 |
| 1893 | 8 Apr | Belfast | 3 | 4 |
| 1894 | 24 Feb | Swansea | 4 | 1 |
| 1895 | 16 Mar | Belfast | 2 | 2 |
| 1896 | 29 Feb | Wrexham | 6 | 1 |
| 1897 | 6 Mar | Belfast | 3 | 4 |
| 1898 | 19 Feb | Llandudno | 0 | 1 |
| 1899 | 4 Mar | Belfast | 0 | 1 |
| 1900 | 24 Feb | Llandudno | 2 | 0 |
| 1901 | 23 Mar | Belfast | 1 | 0 |
| 1902 | 22 Mar | Cardiff | 0 | 3 |
| 1903 | 28 Mar | Belfast | 0 | 2 |
| 1904 | 21 Mar | Bangor | 0 | 1 |
| 1905 | 18 Apr | Belfast | 2 | 2 |
| 1906 | 2 Apr | Wrexham | 4 | 4 |
| 1907 | 23 Feb | Belfast | 3 | 2 |
| 1908 | 11 Apr | Aberdare | 0 | 1 |
| 1909 | 20 Mar | Belfast | 3 | 2 |
| 1910 | 11 Apr | Wrexham | 4 | 1 |
| 1911 | 28 Jan | Belfast | 2 | 1 |
| 1912 | 13 Apr | Cardiff | 2 | 3 |
| 1913 | 18 Jan | Belfast | 1 | 0 |
| 1914 | 19 Jan | Wrexham | 1 | 2 |
| 1920 | 14 Feb | Belfast | 2 | 2 |
| 1921 | 9 Apr | Swansea | 2 | 1 |
| 1922 | 4 Apr | Belfast | 1 | 1 |
| 1923 | 14 Apr | Wrexham | 0 | 3 |
| 1924 | 15 Mar | Belfast | 1 | 0 |
| 1925 | 18 Apr | Wrexham | 0 | 0 |
| 1926 | 13 Feb | Belfast | 0 | 3 |
| 1927 | 9 Apr | Cardiff | 2 | 2 |
| 1928 | 4 Feb | Belfast | 2 | 1 |
| 1929 | 2 Feb | Wrexham | 2 | 2 |
| 1930 | 1 Feb | Belfast | 0 | 7 |
| 1931 | 22 Apr | Wrexham | 3 | 2 |
| 1931 | 5 Dec | Belfast | 0 | 4 |
| 1932 | 7 Dec | Wrexham | 4 | 1 |
| 1933 | 4 Nov | Belfast | 1 | 1 |
| 1935 | 27 Mar | Wrexham | 3 | 1 |

| | | | W | I |
|---|---|---|---|---|
| 1936 | 11 Mar | Belfast | 2 | 3 |
| 1937 | 17 Mar | Wrexham | 4 | 1 |
| 1938 | 16 Mar | Belfast | 0 | 1 |
| 1939 | 15 Mar | Wrexham | 3 | 1 |
| 1947 | 16 Apr | Belfast | 1 | 2 |
| 1948 | 10 Mar | Wrexham | 2 | 0 |
| 1949 | 9 Mar | Belfast | 2 | 0 |
| WC1950 | 8 Mar | Wrexham | 0 | 0 |
| 1951 | 7 Mar | Belfast | 2 | 1 |
| 1952 | 19 Mar | Swansea | 3 | 0 |
| 1953 | 15 Apr | Belfast | 3 | 2 |
| WC1954 | 31 Mar | Wrexham | 1 | 2 |
| 1955 | 20 Apr | Belfast | 3 | 2 |
| 1956 | 11 Apr | Cardiff | 1 | 1 |
| 1957 | 10 Apr | Belfast | 0 | 0 |
| 1958 | 16 Apr | Cardiff | 1 | 1 |
| 1959 | 22 Apr | Belfast | 1 | 4 |
| 1960 | 6 Apr | Wrexham | 3 | 2 |
| 1961 | 12 Apr | Belfast | 5 | 1 |
| 1962 | 11 Apr | Cardiff | 4 | 0 |
| 1963 | 3 Apr | Belfast | 4 | 1 |
| 1964 | 15 Apr | Cardiff | 2 | 3 |
| 1965 | 31 Mar | Belfast | 5 | 0 |
| 1966 | 30 Mar | Cardiff | 1 | 4 |
| EC1967 | 12 Apr | Belfast | 0 | 0 |
| EC1968 | 28 Feb | Wrexham | 2 | 0 |
| 1969 | 10 May | Belfast | 0 | 0 |
| 1970 | 25 Apr | Swansea | 1 | 0 |
| 1971 | 22 May | Belfast | 0 | 1 |
| 1972 | 27 May | Wrexham | 0 | 0 |
| 1973 | 19 May | Everton | 0 | 1 |
| 1974 | 18 May | Wrexham | 1 | 0 |
| 1975 | 23 May | Belfast | 0 | 1 |
| 1976 | 14 May | Swansea | 1 | 0 |
| 1977 | 3 June | Belfast | 1 | 1 |
| 1978 | 19 May | Wrexham | 1 | 0 |
| 1979 | 25 May | Belfast | 1 | 1 |
| 1980 | 23 May | Cardiff | 0 | 1 |
| 1982 | 27 May | Wrexham | 3 | 0 |
| 1983 | 31 May | Belfast | 1 | 0 |
| 1984 | 22 May | Swansea | 1 | 1 |

## OTHER BRITISH INTERNATIONAL RESULTS 1908–2002

## ENGLAND

| | | v ALBANIA | E | A |
|---|---|---|---|---|
| wc1989 | 8 Mar | Tirana | 2 | 0 |
| wc1989 | 26 Apr | Wembley | 5 | 0 |
| wc2001 | 28 Mar | Tirana | 3 | 1 |
| wc2001 | 5 Sept | Newcastle | 2 | 0 |

| | | v ARGENTINA | E | A |
|---|---|---|---|---|
| 1951 | 9 May | Wembley | 2 | 1 |
| 1953 | 17 May | Buenos Aires | 0 | 0 |
| *(abandoned after 21 mins)* | | | | |
| wc1962 | 2 June | Rancagua | 3 | 1 |
| 1964 | 6 June | Rio de Janeiro | 0 | 1 |
| wc1966 | 23 July | Wembley | 1 | 0 |
| 1974 | 22 May | Wembley | 2 | 2 |
| 1977 | 12 June | Buenos Aires | 1 | 1 |
| 1980 | 13 May | Wembley | 3 | 1 |
| wc1986 | 22 June | Mexico City | 1 | 2 |
| 1991 | 25 May | Wembley | 2 | 2 |
| wc1998 | 30 June | St Etienne | 2 | 2 |
| 2000 | 23 Feb | Wembley | 0 | 0 |
| wc2002 | 7 June | Sapporo | 1 | 0 |

| | | v AUSTRALIA | E | A |
|---|---|---|---|---|
| 1980 | 31 May | Sydney | 2 | 1 |
| 1983 | 11 June | Sydney | 0 | 0 |
| 1983 | 15 June | Brisbane | 1 | 0 |
| 1983 | 18 June | Melbourne | 1 | 1 |
| 1991 | 1 June | Sydney | 1 | 0 |
| 2003 | 12 Feb | West Ham | 1 | 3 |

| | | v AUSTRIA | E | A |
|---|---|---|---|---|
| 1908 | 6 June | Vienna | 6 | 1 |
| 1908 | 8 June | Vienna | 11 | 1 |
| 1909 | 1 June | Vienna | 8 | 1 |
| 1930 | 14 May | Vienna | 0 | 0 |
| 1932 | 7 Dec | Chelsea | 4 | 3 |
| 1936 | 6 May | Vienna | 1 | 2 |
| 1951 | 28 Nov | Wembley | 2 | 2 |
| 1952 | 25 May | Vienna | 3 | 2 |
| wc1958 | 15 June | Boras | 2 | 2 |
| 1961 | 27 May | Vienna | 1 | 3 |
| 1962 | 4 Apr | Wembley | 3 | 1 |
| 1965 | 20 Oct | Wembley | 2 | 3 |
| 1967 | 27 May | Vienna | 1 | 0 |
| 1973 | 26 Sept | Wembley | 7 | 0 |
| 1979 | 13 June | Vienna | 3 | 4 |

| | | v BELGIUM | E | B |
|---|---|---|---|---|
| 1921 | 21 May | Brussels | 2 | 0 |
| 1923 | 19 Mar | Highbury | 6 | 1 |
| 1923 | 1 Nov | Antwerp | 2 | 2 |
| 1924 | 8 Dec | West Bromwich | 4 | 0 |
| 1926 | 24 May | Antwerp | 5 | 3 |
| 1927 | 11 May | Brussels | 9 | 1 |
| 1928 | 19 May | Antwerp | 3 | 1 |
| 1929 | 11 May | Brussels | 5 | 1 |
| 1931 | 16 May | Brussels | 4 | 1 |
| 1936 | 9 May | Brussels | 2 | 3 |
| 1947 | 21 Sept | Brussels | 5 | 2 |

| | | | E | B |
|---|---|---|---|---|
| 1950 | 18 May | Brussels | 4 | 1 |
| 1952 | 26 Nov | Wembley | 5 | 0 |
| WC1954 | 17 June | Basle | 4 | 4* |
| 1964 | 21 Oct | Wembley | 2 | 2 |
| 1970 | 25 Feb | Brussels | 3 | 1 |
| EC1980 | 12 June | Turin | 1 | 1 |
| WC1990 | 27 June | Bologna | 1 | 0* |
| 1998 | 29 May | Casablanca | 0 | 0 |
| 1999 | 10 Oct | Sunderland | 2 | 1 |

| | | v BOHEMIA | E | B |
|---|---|---|---|---|
| 1908 | 13 June | Prague | 4 | 0 |

| | | v BRAZIL | E | B |
|---|---|---|---|---|
| 1956 | 9 May | Wembley | 4 | 2 |
| WC1958 | 11 June | Gothenburg | 0 | 0 |
| 1959 | 13 May | Rio de Janeiro | 0 | 2 |
| WC1962 | 10 June | Vina del Mar | 1 | 3 |
| 1963 | 8 May | Wembley | 1 | 1 |
| 1964 | 30 May | Rio de Janeiro | 1 | 5 |
| 1969 | 12 June | Rio de Janeiro | 1 | 2 |
| WC1970 | 7 June | Guadalajara | 0 | 1 |
| 1976 | 23 May | Los Angeles | 0 | 1 |
| 1977 | 8 June | Rio de Janeiro | 0 | 0 |
| 1978 | 19 Apr | Wembley | 1 | 1 |
| 1981 | 12 May | Wembley | 0 | 1 |
| 1984 | 10 June | Rio de Janeiro | 2 | 0 |
| 1987 | 19 May | Wembley | 1 | 1 |
| 1990 | 28 Mar | Wembley | 1 | 0 |
| 1992 | 17 May | Wembley | 1 | 1 |
| 1993 | 13 June | Washington | 1 | 1 |
| UI1995 | 11 June | Wembley | 1 | 3 |
| TF1997 | 10 June | Paris | 0 | 1 |
| 2000 | 27 May | Wembley | 1 | 1 |
| WC2002 | 21 June | Shizuoka | 1 | 2 |

| | | v BULGARIA | E | B |
|---|---|---|---|---|
| WC1962 | 7 June | Rancagua | 0 | 0 |
| 1968 | 11 Dec | Wembley | 1 | 1 |
| 1974 | 1 June | Sofia | 1 | 0 |
| EC1979 | 6 June | Sofia | 3 | 0 |
| EC1979 | 22 Nov | Wembley | 2 | 0 |
| 1996 | 27 Mar | Wembley | 1 | 0 |
| EC1998 | 10 Oct | Wembley | 0 | 0 |
| EC1999 | 9 June | Sofia | 1 | 1 |

| | | v CAMEROON | E | C |
|---|---|---|---|---|
| WC1990 | 1 July | Naples | 3 | 2* |
| 1991 | 6 Feb | Wembley | 2 | 0 |
| 1997 | 15 Nov | Wembley | 2 | 0 |
| 2002 | 26 May | Kobe | 2 | 2 |

| | | v CANADA | E | C |
|---|---|---|---|---|
| 1986 | 24 May | Burnaby | 1 | 0 |

| | | v CHILE | E | C |
|---|---|---|---|---|
| WC1950 | 25 June | Rio de Janeiro | 2 | 0 |
| 1953 | 24 May | Santiago | 2 | 1 |
| 1984 | 17 June | Santiago | 0 | 0 |
| 1989 | 23 May | Wembley | 0 | 0 |
| 1998 | 11 Feb | Wembley | 0 | 2 |

| | | v CHINA | E | C |
|---|---|---|---|---|
| 1996 | 23 May | Beijing | 3 | 0 |

| | | v CIS | E | C |
|---|---|---|---|---|
| 1992 | 29 Apr | Moscow | 2 | 2 |

| | | v COLOMBIA | E | C |
|---|---|---|---|---|
| 1970 | 20 May | Bogota | 4 | 0 |
| 1988 | 24 May | Wembley | 1 | 1 |
| 1995 | 6 Sept | Wembley | 0 | 0 |
| WC1998 | 26 June | Lens | 2 | 0 |

| | | v CROATIA | E | C |
|---|---|---|---|---|
| 1996 | 24 Apr | Wembley | 0 | 0 |
| 2003 | 20 Aug | Ipswich | 3 | 1 |
| EC2004 | 21 June | Lisbon | 4 | 2 |

| | | v CYPRUS | E | C |
|---|---|---|---|---|
| EC1975 | 16 Apr | Wembley | 5 | 0 |
| EC1975 | 11 May | Limassol | 1 | 0 |

| | | v CZECHOSLOVAKIA | E | C |
|---|---|---|---|---|
| 1934 | 16 May | Prague | 1 | 2 |
| 1937 | 1 Dec | Tottenham | 5 | 4 |
| 1963 | 29 May | Bratislava | 4 | 2 |
| 1966 | 2 Nov | Wembley | 0 | 0 |
| WC1970 | 11 June | Guadalajara | 1 | 0 |
| 1973 | 27 May | Prague | 1 | 1 |
| EC1974 | 30 Oct | Wembley | 3 | 0 |
| EC1975 | 30 Oct | Bratislava | 1 | 2 |
| 1978 | 29 Nov | Wembley | 1 | 0 |
| WC1982 | 20 June | Bilbao | 2 | 0 |
| 1990 | 25 Apr | Wembley | 4 | 2 |
| 1992 | 25 Mar | Prague | 2 | 2 |

| | | v CZECH REPUBLIC | E | C |
|---|---|---|---|---|
| 1998 | 18 Nov | Wembley | 2 | 0 |

| | | v DENMARK | E | D |
|---|---|---|---|---|
| 1948 | 26 Sept | Copenhagen | 0 | 0 |
| 1955 | 2 Oct | Copenhagen | 5 | 1 |
| WC1956 | 5 Dec | Wolverhampton | 5 | 2 |
| WC1957 | 15 May | Copenhagen | 4 | 1 |
| 1966 | 3 July | Copenhagen | 2 | 0 |
| EC1978 | 20 Sept | Copenhagen | 4 | 3 |
| EC1979 | 12 Sept | Wembley | 1 | 0 |
| EC1982 | 22 Sept | Copenhagen | 2 | 2 |
| EC1983 | 21 Sept | Wembley | 0 | 1 |
| 1988 | 14 Sept | Wembley | 1 | 0 |
| 1989 | 7 June | Copenhagen | 1 | 1 |
| 1990 | 15 May | Wembley | 1 | 0 |
| EC1992 | 11 June | Malmo | 0 | 0 |
| 1994 | 9 Mar | Wembley | 1 | 0 |
| WC2002 | 15 June | Niigata | 3 | 0 |
| 2004 | 16 Nov | Old Trafford | 2 | 3 |

| | | v ECUADOR | E | Ec |
|---|---|---|---|---|
| 1970 | 24 May | Quito | 2 | 0 |

| | | v EGYPT | E | Eg |
|---|---|---|---|---|
| 1986 | 29 Jan | Cairo | 4 | 0 |
| WC1990 | 21 June | Cagliari | 1 | 0 |

| | | v FIFA | E | FIFA |
|---|---|---|---|---|
| 1938 | 26 Oct | Highbury | 3 | 0 |
| 1953 | 21 Oct | Wembley | 4 | 4 |
| 1963 | 23 Oct | Wembley | 2 | 1 |

| | | v FINLAND | E | F |
|---|---|---|---|---|
| 1937 | 20 May | Helsinki | 8 | 0 |
| 1956 | 20 May | Helsinki | 5 | 1 |
| 1966 | 26 June | Helsinki | 3 | 0 |
| WC1976 | 13 June | Helsinki | 4 | 1 |
| WC1976 | 13 Oct | Wembley | 2 | 1 |
| 1982 | 3 June | Helsinki | 4 | 1 |
| WC1984 | 17 Oct | Wembley | 5 | 0 |
| WC1985 | 22 May | Helsinki | 1 | 1 |
| 1992 | 3 June | Helsinki | 2 | 1 |
| WC2000 | 11 Oct | Helsinki | 0 | 0 |
| WC2001 | 24 Mar | Liverpool | 2 | 1 |

| | | v FRANCE | E | F |
|---|---|---|---|---|
| 1923 | 10 May | Paris | 4 | 1 |
| 1924 | 17 May | Paris | 3 | 1 |
| 1925 | 21 May | Paris | 3 | 2 |
| 1927 | 26 May | Paris | 6 | 0 |
| 1928 | 17 May | Paris | 5 | 1 |
| 1929 | 9 May | Paris | 4 | 1 |
| 1931 | 14 May | Paris | 2 | 5 |
| 1933 | 6 Dec | Tottenham | 4 | 1 |
| 1938 | 26 May | Paris | 4 | 2 |
| 1947 | 3 May | Highbury | 3 | 0 |
| 1949 | 22 May | Paris | 3 | 1 |

| | | | E | F |
|---|---|---|---|---|
| 1951 | 3 Oct | Highbury | 2 | 2 |
| 1955 | 15 May | Paris | 0 | 1 |
| 1957 | 27 Nov | Wembley | 4 | 0 |
| EC1962 | 3 Oct | Sheffield | 1 | 1 |
| EC1963 | 27 Feb | Paris | 2 | 5 |
| WC1966 | 20 July | Wembley | 2 | 0 |
| 1969 | 12 Mar | Wembley | 5 | 0 |
| WC1982 | 16 June | Bilbao | 3 | 1 |
| 1984 | 29 Feb | Paris | 0 | 2 |
| 1992 | 19 Feb | Wembley | 2 | 0 |
| EC1992 | 14 June | Malmo | 0 | 0 |
| TF1997 | 7 June | Montpellier | 1 | 0 |
| 1999 | 10 Feb | Wembley | 0 | 2 |
| 2000 | 2 Sept | Paris | 1 | 1 |
| EC2004 | 13 June | Lisbon | 1 | 2 |

| | | **v GEORGIA** | E | G |
|---|---|---|---|---|
| WC1996 | 9 Nov | Tbilisi | 2 | 0 |
| WC1997 | 30 Apr | Wembley | 2 | 0 |

| | | **v GERMANY** | E | G |
|---|---|---|---|---|
| 1930 | 10 May | Berlin | 3 | 3 |
| 1935 | 4 Dec | Tottenham | 3 | 0 |
| 1938 | 14 May | Berlin | 6 | 3 |
| 1991 | 11 Sept | Wembley | 0 | 1 |
| 1993 | 19 June | Detroit | 1 | 2 |
| EC1996 | 26 June | Wembley | 1 | 1* |
| EC2000 | 17 June | Charleroi | 1 | 0 |
| WC2000 | 7 Oct | Wembley | 0 | 1 |
| WC2001 | 1 Sept | Munich | 5 | 1 |

| | | **v EAST GERMANY** | E | EG |
|---|---|---|---|---|
| 1963 | 2 June | Leipzig | 2 | 1 |
| 1970 | 25 Nov | Wembley | 3 | 1 |
| 1974 | 29 May | Leipzig | 1 | 1 |
| 1984 | 12 Sept | Wembley | 1 | 0 |

| | | **v WEST GERMANY** | E | WG |
|---|---|---|---|---|
| 1954 | 1 Dec | Wembley | 3 | 1 |
| 1956 | 26 May | Berlin | 3 | 1 |
| 1965 | 12 May | Nuremberg | 1 | 0 |
| 1966 | 23 Feb | Wembley | 1 | 0 |
| WC1966 | 30 July | Wembley | 4 | 2* |
| 1968 | 1 June | Hanover | 0 | 1 |
| WC1970 | 14 June | Leon | 2 | 3* |
| EC1972 | 29 Apr | Wembley | 1 | 3 |
| EC1972 | 13 May | Berlin | 0 | 0 |
| 1975 | 12 Mar | Wembley | 2 | 0 |
| 1978 | 22 Feb | Munich | 1 | 2 |
| WC1982 | 29 June | Madrid | 0 | 0 |
| 1982 | 13 Oct | Wembley | 1 | 2 |
| 1985 | 12 June | Mexico City | 3 | 0 |
| 1987 | 9 Sept | Dusseldorf | 1 | 3 |
| WC1990 | 4 July | Turin | 1 | 1* |

| | | **v GREECE** | E | G |
|---|---|---|---|---|
| EC1971 | 21 Apr | Wembley | 3 | 0 |
| EC1971 | 1 Dec | Piraeus | 2 | 0 |
| EC1982 | 17 Nov | Salonika | 3 | 0 |
| EC1983 | 30 Mar | Wembley | 0 | 0 |
| 1989 | 8 Feb | Athens | 2 | 1 |
| 1994 | 17 May | Wembley | 5 | 0 |
| WC2001 | 6 June | Athens | 2 | 0 |
| WC2001 | 6 Oct | Old Trafford | 2 | 2 |

| | | **v HOLLAND** | E | H |
|---|---|---|---|---|
| 1935 | 18 May | Amsterdam | 1 | 0 |
| 1946 | 27 Nov | Huddersfield | 8 | 2 |
| 1964 | 9 Dec | Amsterdam | 1 | 1 |
| 1969 | 5 Nov | Amsterdam | 1 | 0 |
| 1970 | 14 Jun | Wembley | 0 | 0 |
| 1977 | 9 Feb | Wembley | 0 | 2 |
| 1982 | 25 May | Wembley | 2 | 0 |
| 1988 | 23 Mar | Wembley | 2 | 2 |
| EC1988 | 15 June | Dusseldorf | 1 | 3 |
| WC1990 | 16 June | Cagliari | 0 | 0 |

| | | | E | H |
|---|---|---|---|---|
| WC1993 | 28 Apr | Wembley | 2 | 2 |
| WC1993 | 13 Oct | Rotterdam | 0 | 2 |
| EC1996 | 18 June | Wembley | 4 | 1 |
| 2001 | 15 Aug | Tottenham | 0 | 2 |
| 2002 | 13 Feb | Amsterdam | 1 | 1 |

| | | **v HUNGARY** | E | H |
|---|---|---|---|---|
| 1908 | 10 June | Budapest | 7 | 0 |
| 1909 | 29 May | Budapest | 4 | 2 |
| 1909 | 31 May | Budapest | 8 | 2 |
| 1934 | 10 May | Budapest | 1 | 2 |
| 1936 | 2 Dec | Highbury | 6 | 2 |
| 1953 | 25 Nov | Wembley | 3 | 6 |
| 1954 | 23 May | Budapest | 1 | 7 |
| 1960 | 22 May | Budapest | 0 | 2 |
| WC1962 | 31 May | Rancagua | 1 | 2 |
| 1965 | 5 May | Wembley | 1 | 0 |
| 1978 | 24 May | Wembley | 4 | 1 |
| WC1981 | 6 June | Budapest | 3 | 1 |
| WC1982 | 18 Nov | Wembley | 1 | 0 |
| EC1983 | 27 Apr | Wembley | 2 | 0 |
| EC1983 | 12 Oct | Budapest | 3 | 0 |
| 1988 | 27 Apr | Budapest | 0 | 0 |
| 1990 | 12 Sept | Wembley | 1 | 0 |
| 1992 | 12 May | Budapest | 1 | 0 |
| 1996 | 18 May | Wembley | 3 | 0 |
| 1999 | 28 Apr | Budapest | 1 | 1 |

| | | **v ICELAND** | E | I |
|---|---|---|---|---|
| 1982 | 2 June | Reykjavik | 1 | 1 |
| 2004 | 5 June | City of Manchester | 6 | 1 |

| | | **v REPUBLIC OF IRELAND** | E | RI |
|---|---|---|---|---|
| 1946 | 30 Sept | Dublin | 1 | 0 |
| 1949 | 21 Sept | Everton | 0 | 2 |
| WC1957 | 8 May | Wembley | 5 | 1 |
| WC1957 | 19 May | Dublin | 1 | 1 |
| 1964 | 24 May | Dublin | 3 | 1 |
| 1976 | 8 Sept | Wembley | 1 | 1 |
| EC1978 | 25 Oct | Dublin | 1 | 1 |
| EC1980 | 6 Feb | Wembley | 2 | 0 |
| 1985 | 26 Mar | Wembley | 2 | 1 |
| EC1988 | 12 June | Stuttgart | 0 | 1 |
| WC1990 | 11 June | Cagliari | 1 | 1 |
| EC1990 | 14 Nov | Dublin | 1 | 1 |
| EC1991 | 27 Mar | Wembley | 1 | 1 |
| 1995 | 15 Feb | Dublin | 0 | 1 |

*(abandoned after 27 mins)*

| | | **v ISRAEL** | E | I |
|---|---|---|---|---|
| 1986 | 26 Feb | Ramat Gan | 2 | 1 |
| 1988 | 17 Feb | Tel Aviv | 0 | 0 |

| | | **v ITALY** | E | I |
|---|---|---|---|---|
| 1933 | 13 May | Rome | 1 | 1 |
| 1934 | 14 Nov | Highbury | 3 | 2 |
| 1939 | 13 May | Milan | 2 | 2 |
| 1948 | 16 May | Turin | 4 | 0 |
| 1949 | 30 Nov | Tottenham | 2 | 0 |
| 1952 | 18 May | Florence | 1 | 1 |
| 1959 | 6 May | Wembley | 2 | 2 |
| 1961 | 24 May | Rome | 3 | 2 |
| 1973 | 14 June | Turin | 0 | 2 |
| 1973 | 14 Nov | Wembley | 0 | 1 |
| 1976 | 28 May | New York | 3 | 2 |
| WC1976 | 17 Nov | Rome | 0 | 2 |
| WC1977 | 16 Nov | Wembley | 2 | 0 |
| EC1980 | 15 June | Turin | 0 | 1 |
| 1985 | 6 June | Mexico City | 1 | 2 |
| 1989 | 15 Nov | Wembley | 0 | 0 |
| WC1990 | 7 July | Bari | 1 | 2 |
| WC1997 | 12 Feb | Wembley | 0 | 1 |
| TF1997 | 4 June | Nantes | 2 | 0 |
| WC1997 | 11 Oct | Rome | 0 | 0 |
| 2000 | 15 Nov | Turin | 0 | 1 |
| 2002 | 27 Mar | Leeds | 1 | 2 |

| | | **v JAPAN** | E | J |
|---|---|---|---|---|
| UI1995 | 3 June | Wembley | 2 | 1 |
| 2004 | 1 June | City of Manchester | 1 | 1 |

| | | v KUWAIT | E | K |
|---|---|---|---|---|
| WC1982 | 25 June | Bilbao | 1 | 0 |

| | | v LIECHTENSTEIN | E | L |
|---|---|---|---|---|
| EC2003 | 29 Mar | Vaduz | 2 | 0 |
| EC2003 | 10 Sept | Old Trafford | 2 | 0 |

| | | v LUXEMBOURG | E | L |
|---|---|---|---|---|
| 1927 | 21 May | Esch-sur-Alzette | 5 | 2 |
| WC1960 | 19 Oct | Luxembourg | 9 | 0 |
| WC1961 | 28 Sept | Highbury | 4 | 1 |
| WC1977 | 30 Mar | Wembley | 5 | 0 |
| WC1977 | 12 Oct | Luxembourg | 2 | 0 |
| EC1982 | 15 Dec | Wembley | 9 | 0 |
| EC1983 | 16 Nov | Luxembourg | 4 | 0 |
| EC1998 | 14 Oct | Luxembourg | 3 | 0 |
| EC1999 | 4 Sept | Wembley | 6 | 0 |

| | | v MACEDONIA | E | M |
|---|---|---|---|---|
| EC2002 | 16 Oct | Southampton | 2 | 2 |
| EC2003 | 6 Sept | Skopje | 2 | 1 |

| | | v MALAYSIA | E | M |
|---|---|---|---|---|
| 1991 | 12 June | Kuala Lumpur | 4 | 2 |

| | | v MALTA | E | M |
|---|---|---|---|---|
| EC1971 | 3 Feb | Valletta | 1 | 0 |
| EC1971 | 12 May | Wembley | 5 | 0 |
| 2000 | 3 June | Valletta | 2 | 1 |

| | | v MEXICO | E | M |
|---|---|---|---|---|
| 1959 | 24 May | Mexico City | 1 | 2 |
| 1961 | 10 May | Wembley | 8 | 0 |
| WC1966 | 16 July | Wembley | 2 | 0 |
| 1969 | 1 June | Mexico City | 0 | 0 |
| 1985 | 9 June | Mexico City | 0 | 1 |
| 1986 | 17 May | Los Angeles | 3 | 0 |
| 1997 | 29 Mar | Wembley | 2 | 0 |
| 2001 | 25 May | Derby | 4 | 0 |

| | | v MOLDOVA | E | M |
|---|---|---|---|---|
| WC1996 | 1 Sept | Chisinau | 3 | 0 |
| WC1997 | 10 Sept | Wembley | 4 | 0 |

| | | v MOROCCO | E | M |
|---|---|---|---|---|
| WC1986 | 6 June | Monterrey | 0 | 0 |
| 1998 | 27 May | Casablanca | 1 | 0 |

| | | v NEW ZEALAND | E | NZ |
|---|---|---|---|---|
| 1991 | 3 June | Auckland | 1 | 0 |
| 1991 | 8 June | Wellington | 2 | 0 |

| | | v NIGERIA | E | N |
|---|---|---|---|---|
| 1994 | 16 Nov | Wembley | 1 | 0 |
| WC2002 | 12 June | Osaka | 0 | 0 |

| | | v NORWAY | E | N |
|---|---|---|---|---|
| 1937 | 14 May | Oslo | 6 | 0 |
| 1938 | 9 Nov | Newcastle | 4 | 0 |
| 1949 | 18 May | Oslo | 4 | 1 |
| 1966 | 29 June | Oslo | 6 | 1 |
| WC1980 | 10 Sept | Wembley | 4 | 0 |
| WC1981 | 9 Sept | Oslo | 1 | 2 |
| WC1992 | 14 Oct | Wembley | 1 | 1 |
| WC1993 | 2 June | Oslo | 0 | 2 |
| 1994 | 22 May | Wembley | 0 | 0 |
| 1995 | 11 Oct | Oslo | 0 | 0 |

| | | v PARAGUAY | E | P |
|---|---|---|---|---|
| WC1986 | 18 June | Mexico City | 3 | 0 |
| 2002 | 17 Apr | Liverpool | 4 | 0 |

| | | v PERU | E | P |
|---|---|---|---|---|
| 1959 | 17 May | Lima | 1 | 4 |
| 1962 | 20 May | Lima | 4 | 0 |

| | | v POLAND | E | P |
|---|---|---|---|---|
| 1966 | 5 Jan | Everton | 1 | 1 |
| 1966 | 5 July | Chorzow | 1 | 0 |
| WC1973 | 6 June | Chorzow | 0 | 2 |
| WC1973 | 17 Oct | Wembley | 1 | 1 |
| WC1986 | 11 June | Monterrey | 3 | 0 |
| WC1989 | 3 June | Wembley | 3 | 0 |
| WC1989 | 11 Oct | Katowice | 0 | 0 |
| EC1990 | 17 Oct | Wembley | 2 | 0 |
| EC1991 | 13 Nov | Poznan | 1 | 1 |
| WC1993 | 29 May | Katowice | 1 | 1 |
| WC1993 | 8 Sept | Wembley | 3 | 0 |
| WC1996 | 9 Oct | Wembley | 2 | 1 |
| WC1997 | 31 May | Katowice | 2 | 0 |
| EC1999 | 27 Mar | Wembley | 3 | 1 |
| EC1999 | 8 Sept | Warsaw | 0 | 0 |

| | | v PORTUGAL | E | P |
|---|---|---|---|---|
| 1947 | 25 May | Lisbon | 10 | 0 |
| 1950 | 14 May | Lisbon | 5 | 3 |
| 1951 | 19 May | Everton | 5 | 2 |
| 1955 | 22 May | Oporto | 1 | 3 |
| 1958 | 7 May | Wembley | 2 | 1 |
| WC1961 | 21 May | Lisbon | 1 | 1 |
| WC1961 | 25 Oct | Wembley | 2 | 0 |
| 1964 | 17 May | Lisbon | 4 | 3 |
| 1964 | 4 June | São Paulo | 1 | 1 |
| WC1966 | 26 July | Wembley | 2 | 1 |
| 1969 | 10 Dec | Wembley | 1 | 0 |
| 1974 | 3 Apr | Lisbon | 0 | 0 |
| EC1974 | 20 Nov | Wembley | 0 | 0 |
| EC1975 | 19 Nov | Lisbon | 1 | 1 |
| WC1986 | 3 June | Monterrey | 0 | 1 |
| 1995 | 12 Dec | Wembley | 1 | 1 |
| 1998 | 22 Apr | Wembley | 3 | 0 |
| EC2000 | 12 June | Eindhoven | 2 | 3 |
| 2002 | 7 Sept | Villa Park | 1 | 1 |
| 2004 | 18 Feb | Faro | 1 | 1 |
| EC2004 | 24 June | Lisbon | 2 | 2* |

| | | v ROMANIA | E | R |
|---|---|---|---|---|
| 1939 | 24 May | Bucharest | 2 | 0 |
| 1968 | 6 Nov | Bucharest | 0 | 0 |
| 1969 | 15 Jan | Wembley | 1 | 1 |
| WC1970 | 2 June | Guadalajara | 1 | 0 |
| WC1980 | 15 Oct | Bucharest | 1 | 2 |
| WC1981 | 29 April | Wembley | 0 | 0 |
| WC1985 | 1 May | Bucharest | 0 | 0 |
| WC1985 | 11 Sept | Wembley | 1 | 1 |
| 1994 | 12 Oct | Wembley | 1 | 1 |
| WC1998 | 22 June | Toulouse | 1 | 2 |
| EC2000 | 20 June | Charleroi | 2 | 3 |

| | | v SAN MARINO | E | SM |
|---|---|---|---|---|
| WC1992 | 17 Feb | Wembley | 6 | 0 |
| WC1993 | 17 Nov | Bologna | 7 | 1 |

| | | v SAUDI ARABIA | E | SA |
|---|---|---|---|---|
| 1988 | 16 Nov | Riyadh | 1 | 1 |
| 1998 | 23 May | Wembley | 0 | 0 |

| | | v SERBIA-MONTENEGRO | E | S-M |
|---|---|---|---|---|
| 2003 | 3 June | Leicester | 2 | 1 |

| | | v SLOVAKIA | E | S |
|---|---|---|---|---|
| EC2002 | 12 Oct | Bratislava | 2 | 1 |
| EC2003 | 11 June | Middlesbrough | 2 | 1 |

| | | v SOUTH AFRICA | E | SA |
|---|---|---|---|---|
| 1997 | 24 May | Old Trafford | 2 | 1 |
| 2003 | 22 May | Durban | 2 | 1 |

| | | v SOUTH KOREA | E | SK |
|---|---|---|---|---|
| 2002 | 21 May | Seoguipo | 1 | 1 |

| | | v SPAIN | E | S |
|---|---|---|---|---|
| 1929 | 15 May | Madrid | 3 | 4 |
| 1931 | 9 Dec | Highbury | 7 | 1 |
| WC1950 | 2 July | Rio de Janeiro | 0 | 1 |
| 1955 | 18 May | Madrid | 1 | 1 |
| 1955 | 30 Nov | Wembley | 4 | 1 |
| 1960 | 15 May | Madrid | 0 | 3 |
| 1960 | 26 Oct | Wembley | 4 | 2 |
| 1965 | 8 Dec | Madrid | 2 | 0 |
| 1967 | 24 May | Wembley | 2 | 0 |
| EC1968 | 3 Apr | Wembley | 1 | 0 |
| EC1968 | 8 May | Madrid | 2 | 1 |
| 1980 | 26 Mar | Barcelona | 2 | 0 |
| EC1980 | 18 June | Naples | 2 | 1 |
| 1981 | 25 Mar | Wembley | 1 | 2 |
| WC1982 | 5 July | Madrid | 0 | 0 |

| | | | E | S |
|---|---|---|---|---|
| 1987 | 18 Feb | Madrid | 4 | 2 |
| 1992 | 9 Sept | Santander | 0 | 1 |
| EC 1996 | 22 June | Wembley | 0 | 0 |
| 2001 | 28 Feb | Villa Park | 3 | 0 |

| | | v SWEDEN | E | S |
|---|---|---|---|---|
| 1923 | 21 May | Stockholm | 4 | 2 |
| 1923 | 24 May | Stockholm | 3 | 1 |
| 1937 | 17 May | Stockholm | 4 | 0 |
| 1947 | 19 Nov | Highbury | 4 | 2 |
| 1949 | 13 May | Stockholm | 1 | 3 |
| 1956 | 16 May | Stockholm | 0 | 0 |
| 1959 | 28 Oct | Wembley | 2 | 3 |
| 1965 | 16 May | Gothenburg | 2 | 1 |
| 1968 | 22 May | Wembley | 3 | 1 |
| 1979 | 10 June | Stockholm | 0 | 0 |
| 1986 | 10 Sept | Stockholm | 0 | 1 |
| WC1988 | 19 Oct | Wembley | 0 | 0 |
| WC1989 | 6 Sept | Stockholm | 0 | 0 |
| EC1992 | 17 June | Stockholm | 1 | 2 |
| UI1995 | 8 June | Leeds | 3 | 3 |
| EC1998 | 5 Sept | Stockholm | 1 | 2 |
| EC1999 | 5 June | Wembley | 0 | 0 |
| 2001 | 10 Nov | Old Trafford | 1 | 1 |
| WC2002 | 2 June | Saitama | 1 | 1 |
| 2004 | 31 Mar | Gothenburg | 0 | 1 |

| | | v SWITZERLAND | E | S |
|---|---|---|---|---|
| 1933 | 20 May | Berne | 4 | 0 |
| 1938 | 21 May | Zurich | 1 | 2 |
| 1947 | 18 May | Zurich | 0 | 1 |
| 1948 | 2 Dec | Highbury | 6 | 0 |
| 1952 | 28 May | Zurich | 3 | 0 |
| WC1954 | 20 June | Berne | 2 | 0 |
| 1962 | 9 May | Wembley | 3 | 1 |
| 1963 | 5 June | Basle | 8 | 1 |
| EC1971 | 13 Oct | Basle | 3 | 2 |
| EC1971 | 10 Nov | Wembley | 1 | 1 |
| 1975 | 3 Sept | Basle | 2 | 1 |
| 1977 | 7 Sept | Wembley | 0 | 0 |
| WC1980 | 19 Nov | Wembley | 2 | 1 |
| WC1981 | 30 May | Basle | 1 | 2 |
| 1988 | 28 May | Lausanne | 1 | 0 |
| 1995 | 15 Nov | Wembley | 3 | 1 |
| EC1996 | 8 June | Wembley | 1 | 1 |
| 1998 | 25 Mar | Berne | 1 | 1 |
| EC2004 | 17 June | Coimbra | 3 | 0 |

| | | v TUNISIA | E | T |
|---|---|---|---|---|
| 1990 | 2 June | Tunis | 1 | 1 |
| WC1998 | 15 June | Marseilles | 2 | 0 |

| | | v TURKEY | E | T |
|---|---|---|---|---|
| WC1984 | 14 Nov | Istanbul | 8 | 0 |
| WC1985 | 16 Oct | Wembley | 5 | 0 |
| EC1987 | 29 Apr | Izmir | 0 | 0 |
| EC1987 | 14 Oct | Wembley | 8 | 0 |
| EC1991 | 1 May | Izmir | 1 | 0 |
| EC1991 | 16 Oct | Wembley | 1 | 0 |
| WC1992 | 18 Nov | Wembley | 4 | 0 |
| WC1993 | 31 Mar | Izmir | 2 | 0 |
| EC2003 | 2 Apr | Sunderland | 2 | 0 |
| EC2003 | 11 Oct | Istanbul | 0 | 0 |

| | | v UKRAINE | E | U |
|---|---|---|---|---|
| 2000 | 31 May | Wembley | 2 | 0 |

| | | v URUGUAY | E | U |
|---|---|---|---|---|
| 1953 | 31 May | Montevideo | 1 | 2 |
| WC1954 | 26 June | Basle | 2 | 4 |
| 1964 | 6 May | Wembley | 2 | 1 |
| WC1966 | 11 July | Wembley | 0 | 0 |
| 1969 | 8 June | Montevideo | 2 | 1 |
| 1977 | 15 June | Montevideo | 0 | 0 |
| 1984 | 13 June | Montevideo | 0 | 2 |
| 1990 | 22 May | Wembley | 1 | 2 |
| 1995 | 29 Mar | Wembley | 0 | 0 |

| | | v USA | E | USA |
|---|---|---|---|---|
| WC1950 | 29 June | Belo Horizonte | 0 | 1 |
| 1953 | 8 June | New York | 6 | 3 |
| 1959 | 28 May | Los Angeles | 8 | 1 |
| 1964 | 27 May | New York | 10 | 0 |
| 1985 | 16 June | Los Angeles | 5 | 0 |
| 1993 | 9 June | Foxboro | 0 | 2 |
| 1994 | 7 Sept | Wembley | 2 | 0 |

| | | v USSR | E | USSR |
|---|---|---|---|---|
| 1958 | 18 May | Moscow | 1 | 1 |
| WC1958 | 8 June | Gothenburg | 2 | 2 |
| WC1958 | 17 June | Gothenburg | 0 | 1 |
| 1958 | 22 Oct | Wembley | 5 | 0 |
| 1967 | 6 Dec | Wembley | 2 | 2 |
| EC1968 | 8 June | Rome | 2 | 0 |
| 1973 | 10 June | Moscow | 2 | 1 |
| 1984 | 2 June | Wembley | 0 | 2 |
| 1986 | 26 Mar | Tbilisi | 1 | 0 |
| EC1988 | 18 June | Frankfurt | 1 | 3 |
| 1991 | 21 May | Wembley | 3 | 1 |

| | | v YUGOSLAVIA | E | Y |
|---|---|---|---|---|
| 1939 | 18 May | Belgrade | 1 | 2 |
| 1950 | 22 Nov | Highbury | 2 | 2 |
| 1954 | 16 May | Belgrade | 0 | 1 |
| 1956 | 28 Nov | Wembley | 3 | 0 |
| 1958 | 11 May | Belgrade | 0 | 5 |
| 1960 | 11 May | Wembley | 3 | 3 |
| 1965 | 9 May | Belgrade | 1 | 1 |
| 1966 | 4 May | Wembley | 2 | 0 |
| EC1968 | 5 June | Florence | 0 | 1 |
| 1972 | 11 Oct | Wembley | 1 | 1 |
| 1974 | 5 June | Belgrade | 2 | 2 |
| EC1986 | 12 Nov | Wembley | 2 | 0 |
| EC1987 | 11 Nov | Belgrade | 4 | 1 |
| 1989 | 13 Dec | Wembley | 2 | 1 |

## SCOTLAND

| | | v ARGENTINA | S | A |
|---|---|---|---|---|
| 1977 | 18 June | Buenos Aires | 1 | 1 |
| 1979 | 2 June | Glasgow | 1 | 3 |
| 1990 | 28 Mar | Glasgow | 1 | 0 |

| | | v AUSTRALIA | S | A |
|---|---|---|---|---|
| WC1985 | 20 Nov | Glasgow | 2 | 0 |
| WC1985 | 4 Dec | Melbourne | 0 | 0 |
| 1996 | 27 Mar | Glasgow | 1 | 0 |
| 2000 | 15 Nov | Glasgow | 0 | 2 |

| | | v AUSTRIA | S | A |
|---|---|---|---|---|
| 1931 | 16 May | Vienna | 0 | 5 |
| 1933 | 29 Nov | Glasgow | 2 | 2 |
| 1937 | 9 May | Vienna | 1 | 1 |
| 1950 | 13 Dec | Glasgow | 0 | 1 |
| 1951 | 27 May | Vienna | 0 | 4 |
| WC1954 | 16 June | Zurich | 0 | 1 |
| 1955 | 19 May | Vienna | 4 | 1 |
| 1956 | 2 May | Glasgow | 1 | 1 |
| 1960 | 29 May | Vienna | 1 | 4 |
| 1963 | 8 May | Glasgow | 4 | 1 |
| (*abandoned after 79 mins*) | | | | |
| WC1968 | 6 Nov | Glasgow | 2 | 1 |
| WC1969 | 5 Nov | Vienna | 0 | 2 |
| EC1978 | 20 Sept | Vienna | 2 | 3 |
| EC1979 | 17 Oct | Glasgow | 1 | 1 |
| 1994 | 20 Apr | Vienna | 2 | 1 |
| WC1996 | 31 Aug | Vienna | 0 | 0 |
| WC1997 | 2 Apr | Celtic Park | 2 | 0 |
| 2003 | 30 Apr | Glasgow | 0 | 2 |

| | | v BELARUS | S | B |
|---|---|---|---|---|
| WC1997 | 8 June | Minsk | 1 | 0 |
| WC1997 | 7 Sept | Aberdeen | 4 | 1 |

| | | v BELGIUM | S | B |
|---|---|---|---|---|
| 1947 | 18 May | Brussels | 1 | 2 |
| 1948 | 28 Apr | Glasgow | 2 | 0 |

| | | | *S* | *B* |
|---|---|---|---|---|
| 1951 | 20 May | Brussels | 5 | 0 |
| EC1971 | 3 Feb | Liège | 0 | 3 |
| EC1971 | 10 Nov | Aberdeen | 1 | 0 |
| 1974 | 2 June | Brussels | 1 | 2 |
| EC1979 | 21 Nov | Brussels | 0 | 2 |
| EC1979 | 19 Dec | Glasgow | 1 | 3 |
| EC1982 | 15 Dec | Brussels | 2 | 3 |
| EC1983 | 12 Oct | Glasgow | 1 | 1 |
| EC1987 | 1 Apr | Brussels | 1 | 4 |
| EC1987 | 14 Oct | Glasgow | 2 | 0 |
| wc2001 | 24 Mar | Glasgow | 2 | 2 |
| wc2001 | 5 Sept | Brussels | 0 | 2 |

| | | **v BOSNIA** | *S* | *B* |
|---|---|---|---|---|
| EC1999 | 4 Sept | Sarajevo | 2 | 1 |
| EC1999 | 5 Oct | Glasgow | 1 | 0 |

| | | **v BRAZIL** | *S* | *B* |
|---|---|---|---|---|
| 1966 | 25 June | Glasgow | 1 | 1 |
| 1972 | 5 July | Rio de Janeiro | 0 | 1 |
| 1973 | 30 June | Glasgow | 0 | 1 |
| wc1974 | 18 June | Frankfurt | 0 | 0 |
| 1977 | 23 June | Rio de Janeiro | 0 | 2 |
| wc1982 | 18 June | Seville | 1 | 4 |
| 1987 | 26 May | Glasgow | 0 | 2 |
| wc1990 | 20 June | Turin | 0 | 1 |
| wc1998 | 10 June | Saint-Denis | 1 | 2 |

| | | **v BULGARIA** | *S* | *B* |
|---|---|---|---|---|
| 1978 | 22 Feb | Glasgow | 2 | 1 |
| EC1986 | 10 Sept | Glasgow | 0 | 0 |
| EC1987 | 11 Nov | Sofia | 1 | 0 |
| EC1990 | 14 Nov | Sofia | 1 | 1 |
| EC1991 | 27 Mar | Glasgow | 1 | 1 |

| | | **v CANADA** | *S* | *C* |
|---|---|---|---|---|
| 1983 | 12 June | Vancouver | 2 | 0 |
| 1983 | 16 June | Edmonton | 3 | 0 |
| 1983 | 20 June | Toronto | 2 | 0 |
| 1992 | 21 May | Toronto | 3 | 1 |
| 2002 | 15 Oct | Easter Road | 3 | 1 |

| | | **v CHILE** | *S* | *C* |
|---|---|---|---|---|
| 1977 | 15 June | Santiago | 4 | 2 |
| 1989 | 30 May | Glasgow | 2 | 0 |

| | | **v CIS** | *S* | *C* |
|---|---|---|---|---|
| EC1992 | 18 June | Norrkoping | 3 | 0 |

| | | **v COLOMBIA** | *S* | *C* |
|---|---|---|---|---|
| 1988 | 17 May | Glasgow | 0 | 0 |
| 1996 | 30 May | Miami | 0 | 1 |
| 1998 | 23 May | New York | 2 | 2 |

| | | **v COSTA RICA** | *S* | *CR* |
|---|---|---|---|---|
| wc1990 | 11 June | Genoa | 0 | 1 |

| | | **v CROATIA** | *S* | *C* |
|---|---|---|---|---|
| wc2000 | 11 Oct | Zagreb | 1 | 1 |
| wc2001 | 1 Sept | Glasgow | 0 | 0 |

| | | **v CYPRUS** | *S* | *C* |
|---|---|---|---|---|
| wc1968 | 17 Dec | Nicosia | 5 | 0 |
| wc1969 | 11 May | Glasgow | 8 | 0 |
| wc1989 | 8 Feb | Limassol | 3 | 2 |
| wc1989 | 26 Apr | Glasgow | 2 | 1 |

| | | **v CZECHOSLOVAKIA** | *S* | *C* |
|---|---|---|---|---|
| 1937 | 22 May | Prague | 3 | 1 |
| 1937 | 8 Dec | Glasgow | 5 | 0 |
| wc1961 | 14 May | Bratislava | 0 | 4 |
| wc1961 | 26 Sept | Glasgow | 3 | 2 |
| wc1961 | 29 Nov | Brussels | 2 | 4* |
| 1972 | 2 July | Porto Alegre | 0 | 0 |
| wc1973 | 26 Sept | Glasgow | 2 | 1 |
| wc1973 | 17 Oct | Prague | 0 | 1 |
| wc1976 | 13 Oct | Prague | 0 | 2 |
| wc1977 | 21 Sept | Glasgow | 3 | 1 |

| | | **v CZECH REPUBLIC** | *S* | *C* |
|---|---|---|---|---|
| EC1999 | 31 Mar | Glasgow | 1 | 2 |
| EC1999 | 9 June | Prague | 2 | 3 |

| | | **v DENMARK** | *S* | *D* |
|---|---|---|---|---|
| 1951 | 12 May | Glasgow | 3 | 1 |
| 1952 | 25 May | Copenhagen | 2 | 1 |
| 1968 | 16 Oct | Copenhagen | 1 | 0 |
| EC1970 | 11 Nov | Glasgow | 1 | 0 |
| EC1971 | 9 June | Copenhagen | 0 | 1 |
| wc1972 | 18 Oct | Copenhagen | 4 | 1 |
| wc1972 | 15 Nov | Glasgow | 2 | 0 |
| EC1975 | 3 Sept | Copenhagen | 1 | 0 |
| EC1975 | 29 Oct | Glasgow | 3 | 1 |
| wc1986 | 4 June | Nezahualcayotl | 0 | 1 |
| 1996 | 24 Apr | Copenhagen | 0 | 2 |
| 1998 | 25 Mar | Glasgow | 0 | 1 |
| 2002 | 21 Aug | Glasgow | 0 | 1 |
| 2004 | 28 Apr | Copenhagen | 0 | 1 |

| | | **v ECUADOR** | *S* | *E* |
|---|---|---|---|---|
| 1995 | 24 May | Toyama | 2 | 1 |

| | | **v EGYPT** | *S* | *E* |
|---|---|---|---|---|
| 1990 | 16 May | Aberdeen | 1 | 3 |

| | | **v ESTONIA** | *S* | *E* |
|---|---|---|---|---|
| wc1993 | 19 May | Tallinn | 3 | 0 |
| wc1993 | 2 June | Aberdeen | 3 | 1 |
| wc1997 | 11 Feb | Monaco | 0 | 0 |
| wc1997 | 29 Mar | Kilmarnock | 2 | 0 |
| EC1998 | 10 Oct | Edinburgh | 3 | 2 |
| EC1999 | 8 Sept | Tallinn | 0 | 0 |
| 2004 | 27 May | Tallinn | 1 | 0 |

| | | **v FAEROES** | *S* | *F* |
|---|---|---|---|---|
| EC1994 | 12 Oct | Glasgow | 5 | 1 |
| EC1995 | 7 June | Toftir | 2 | 0 |
| EC1998 | 14 Oct | Aberdeen | 2 | 1 |
| EC1999 | 5 June | Toftir | 1 | 1 |
| EC2002 | 7 Sept | Toftir | 2 | 2 |
| EC2003 | 6 Sept | Glasgow | 3 | 1 |

| | | **v FINLAND** | *S* | *F* |
|---|---|---|---|---|
| 1954 | 25 May | Helsinki | 2 | 1 |
| wc1964 | 21 Oct | Glasgow | 3 | 1 |
| wc1965 | 27 May | Helsinki | 2 | 1 |
| 1976 | 8 Sept | Glasgow | 6 | 0 |
| 1992 | 25 Mar | Glasgow | 1 | 1 |
| EC1994 | 7 Sept | Helsinki | 2 | 0 |
| EC1995 | 6 Sept | Glasgow | 1 | 0 |
| 1998 | 22 Apr | Edinburgh | 1 | 1 |

| | | **v FRANCE** | *S* | *F* |
|---|---|---|---|---|
| 1930 | 18 May | Paris | 2 | 0 |
| 1932 | 8 May | Paris | 3 | 1 |
| 1948 | 23 May | Paris | 0 | 3 |
| 1949 | 27 Apr | Glasgow | 2 | 0 |
| 1950 | 27 May | Paris | 1 | 0 |
| 1951 | 16 May | Glasgow | 1 | 0 |
| wc1958 | 15 June | Orebro | 1 | 2 |
| 1984 | 1 June | Marseilles | 0 | 2 |
| wc1989 | 8 Mar | Glasgow | 2 | 0 |
| wc1989 | 11 Oct | Paris | 0 | 3 |
| 1997 | 12 Nov | St Etienne | 1 | 2 |
| 2000 | 29 Mar | Glasgow | 0 | 2 |
| 2002 | 27 Mar | Paris | 0 | 5 |

| | | **v GERMANY** | *S* | *G* |
|---|---|---|---|---|
| 1929 | 1 June | Berlin | 1 | 1 |
| 1936 | 14 Oct | Glasgow | 2 | 0 |
| EC1992 | 15 June | Norrkoping | 0 | 2 |
| 1993 | 24 Mar | Glasgow | 0 | 1 |
| 1998 | 28 Apr | Bremen | 1 | 0 |
| EC2003 | 7 June | Glasgow | 1 | 1 |
| EC2003 | 10 Sept | Dortmund | 1 | 2 |

| | | **v EAST GERMANY** | *S* | *EG* |
|---|---|---|---|---|
| 1974 | 30 Oct | Glasgow | 3 | 0 |
| 1977 | 7 Sept | East Berlin | 0 | 1 |
| EC1982 | 13 Oct | Glasgow | 2 | 0 |
| EC1983 | 16 Nov | Halle | 1 | 2 |
| 1985 | 16 Oct | Glasgow | 0 | 0 |
| 1990 | 25 Apr | Glasgow | 0 | 1 |

| | | **v WEST GERMANY** | *S* | *WG* |
|---|---|---|---|---|
| 1957 | 22 May | Stuttgart | 3 | 1 |
| 1959 | 6 May | Glasgow | 3 | 2 |
| 1964 | 12 May | Hanover | 2 | 2 |
| wc1969 | 16 Apr | Glasgow | 1 | 1 |
| wc1969 | 22 Oct | Hamburg | 2 | 3 |

| | | | *S* | *WG* |
|---|---|---|---|---|
| 1973 | 14 Nov | Glasgow | 1 | 1 |
| 1974 | 27 Mar | Frankfurt | 1 | 2 |
| WC1986 | 8 June | Queretaro | 1 | 2 |

| | | **v GREECE** | *S* | *G* |
|---|---|---|---|---|
| EC1994 | 18 Dec | Athens | 0 | 1 |
| EC1995 | 16 Aug | Glasgow | 1 | 0 |

| | | **v HOLLAND** | *S* | *H* |
|---|---|---|---|---|
| 1929 | 4 June | Amsterdam | 2 | 0 |
| 1938 | 21 May | Amsterdam | 3 | 1 |
| 1959 | 27 May | Amsterdam | 2 | 1 |
| 1966 | 11 May | Glasgow | 0 | 3 |
| 1968 | 30 May | Amsterdam | 0 | 0 |
| 1971 | 1 Dec | Rotterdam | 1 | 2 |
| WC1978 | 11 June | Mendoza | 3 | 2 |
| 1982 | 23 Mar | Glasgow | 2 | 1 |
| 1986 | 29 Apr | Eindhoven | 0 | 0 |
| EC1992 | 12 June | Gothenburg | 0 | 1 |
| 1994 | 23 Mar | Glasgow | 0 | 1 |
| 1994 | 27 May | Utrecht | 1 | 3 |
| EC1996 | 10 June | Birmingham | 0 | 0 |
| 2000 | 26 Apr | Arnhem | 0 | 0 |
| EC2003 | 15 Nov | Glasgow | 1 | 0 |
| EC2003 | 19 Nov | Amsterdam | 0 | 6 |

| | | **v HONG KONG XI** | *S* | *HK* |
|---|---|---|---|---|
| †2002 | 23 May | Hong Kong | 4 | 0 |

†*match not recognised by FIFA*

| | | **v HUNGARY** | *S* | *H* |
|---|---|---|---|---|
| 1938 | 7 Dec | Glasgow | 3 | 1 |
| 1954 | 8 Dec | Glasgow | 2 | 4 |
| 1955 | 29 May | Budapest | 1 | 3 |
| 1958 | 7 May | Glasgow | 1 | 1 |
| 1960 | 5 June | Budapest | 3 | 3 |
| 1980 | 31 May | Budapest | 1 | 3 |
| 1987 | 9 Sept | Glasgow | 2 | 0 |

| | | **v ICELAND** | *S* | *I* |
|---|---|---|---|---|
| WC1984 | 17 Oct | Glasgow | 3 | 0 |
| WC1985 | 28 May | Reykjavik | 1 | 0 |
| EC2002 | 12 Oct | Reykjavik | 2 | 0 |
| EC2003 | 29 Mar | Glasgow | 2 | 1 |

| | | **v IRAN** | *S* | *I* |
|---|---|---|---|---|
| WC1978 | 7 June | Cordoba | 1 | 1 |

| | | **v REPUBLIC OF IRELAND** | *S* | *RI* |
|---|---|---|---|---|
| WC1961 | 3 May | Glasgow | 4 | 1 |
| WC1961 | 7 May | Dublin | 3 | 0 |
| 1963 | 9 June | Dublin | 0 | 1 |
| 1969 | 21 Sept | Dublin | 1 | 1 |
| EC1986 | 15 Oct | Dublin | 0 | 0 |
| EC1987 | 18 Feb | Glasgow | 0 | 1 |
| 2000 | 30 May | Dublin | 2 | 1 |
| 2003 | 12 Feb | Glasgow | 0 | 2 |

| | | **v ISRAEL** | *S* | *I* |
|---|---|---|---|---|
| WC1981 | 25 Feb | Tel Aviv | 1 | 0 |
| WC1981 | 28 Apr | Glasgow | 3 | 1 |
| 1986 | 28 Jan | Tel Aviv | 1 | 0 |

| | | **v ITALY** | *S* | *I* |
|---|---|---|---|---|
| 1931 | 20 May | Rome | 0 | 3 |
| WC1965 | 9 Nov | Glasgow | 1 | 0 |
| WC1965 | 7 Dec | Naples | 0 | 3 |
| 1988 | 22 Dec | Perugia | 0 | 2 |
| WC1992 | 18 Nov | Glasgow | 0 | 0 |
| WC1993 | 13 Oct | Rome | 1 | 3 |

| | | **v JAPAN** | *S* | *J* |
|---|---|---|---|---|
| 1995 | 21 May | Hiroshima | 0 | 0 |

| | | **v LATVIA** | *S* | *L* |
|---|---|---|---|---|
| WC1996 | 5 Oct | Riga | 2 | 0 |
| WC1997 | 11 Oct | Glasgow | 2 | 0 |
| WC2000 | 2 Sept | Riga | 1 | 0 |
| WC2001 | 6 Oct | Glasgow | 2 | 1 |

| | | **v LITHUANIA** | *S* | *L* |
|---|---|---|---|---|
| EC1998 | 5 Sept | Vilnius | 0 | 0 |
| EC1999 | 9 Oct | Glasgow | 3 | 0 |
| EC2003 | 2 Apr | Kaunas | 0 | 1 |
| EC2003 | 11 Oct | Glasgow | 1 | 0 |

| | | **v LUXEMBOURG** | *S* | *L* |
|---|---|---|---|---|
| 1947 | 24 May | Luxembourg | 6 | 0 |
| EC1986 | 12 Nov | Glasgow | 3 | 0 |
| EC1987 | 2 Dec | Esch | 0 | 0 |

| | | **v MALTA** | *S* | *M* |
|---|---|---|---|---|
| 1988 | 22 Mar | Valletta | 1 | 1 |
| 1990 | 28 May | Valletta | 2 | 1 |
| WC1993 | 17 Feb | Glasgow | 3 | 0 |
| WC1993 | 17 Nov | Valletta | 2 | 0 |
| 1997 | 1 June | Valletta | 3 | 2 |

| | | **v MOROCCO** | *S* | *M* |
|---|---|---|---|---|
| WC1998 | 23 June | St Etienne | 0 | 3 |

| | | **v NEW ZEALAND** | *S* | *NZ* |
|---|---|---|---|---|
| WC1982 | 15 June | Malaga | 5 | 2 |
| 2003 | 27 May | Tynecastle | 1 | 1 |

| | | **v NIGERIA** | *S* | *N* |
|---|---|---|---|---|
| 2002 | 17 Apr | Aberdeen | 1 | 2 |

| | | **v NORWAY** | *S* | *N* |
|---|---|---|---|---|
| 1929 | 28 May | Oslo | 7 | 3 |
| 1954 | 5 May | Glasgow | 1 | 0 |
| 1954 | 19 May | Oslo | 1 | 1 |
| 1963 | 4 June | Bergen | 3 | 4 |
| 1963 | 7 Nov | Glasgow | 6 | 1 |
| 1974 | 6 June | Oslo | 2 | 1 |
| EC1978 | 25 Oct | Glasgow | 3 | 2 |
| EC1979 | 7 June | Oslo | 4 | 0 |
| WC1988 | 14 Sept | Oslo | 2 | 1 |
| WC1989 | 15 Nov | Glasgow | 1 | 1 |
| 1992 | 3 June | Oslo | 0 | 0 |
| WC1998 | 16 June | Bordeaux | 1 | 1 |
| 2003 | 20 Aug | Oslo | 0 | 0 |

| | | **v PARAGUAY** | *S* | *P* |
|---|---|---|---|---|
| WC1958 | 11 June | Norrkoping | 2 | 3 |

| | | **v PERU** | *S* | *P* |
|---|---|---|---|---|
| 1972 | 26 Apr | Glasgow | 2 | 0 |
| WC1978 | 3 June | Cordoba | 1 | 3 |
| 1979 | 12 Sept | Glasgow | 1 | 1 |

| | | **v POLAND** | *S* | *P* |
|---|---|---|---|---|
| 1958 | 1 June | Warsaw | 2 | 1 |
| 1960 | 4 June | Glasgow | 2 | 3 |
| WC1965 | 23 May | Chorzow | 1 | 1 |
| WC1965 | 13 Oct | Glasgow | 1 | 2 |
| 1980 | 28 May | Poznan | 0 | 1 |
| 1990 | 19 May | Glasgow | 1 | 1 |
| 2001 | 25 Apr | Bydgoszcz | 1 | 1 |

| | | **v PORTUGAL** | *S* | *P* |
|---|---|---|---|---|
| 1950 | 21 May | Lisbon | 2 | 2 |
| 1955 | 4 May | Glasgow | 3 | 0 |
| 1959 | 3 June | Lisbon | 0 | 1 |
| 1966 | 18 June | Glasgow | 0 | 1 |
| EC1971 | 21 Apr | Lisbon | 0 | 2 |
| EC1971 | 13 Oct | Glasgow | 2 | 1 |
| 1975 | 13 May | Glasgow | 1 | 0 |
| EC1978 | 29 Nov | Lisbon | 0 | 1 |
| EC1980 | 26 Mar | Glasgow | 4 | 1 |
| WC1980 | 15 Oct | Glasgow | 0 | 0 |
| WC1981 | 18 Nov | Lisbon | 1 | 2 |
| WC1992 | 14 Oct | Glasgow | 0 | 0 |
| WC1993 | 28 Apr | Lisbon | 0 | 5 |
| 2002 | 20 Nov | Braga | 0 | 2 |

| | | **v ROMANIA** | *S* | *R* |
|---|---|---|---|---|
| EC1975 | 1 June | Bucharest | 1 | 1 |
| EC1975 | 17 Dec | Glasgow | 1 | 1 |
| 1986 | 26 Mar | Glasgow | 3 | 0 |
| EC1990 | 12 Sept | Glasgow | 2 | 1 |
| EC1991 | 16 Oct | Bucharest | 0 | 1 |
| 2004 | 31 Mar | Glasgow | 1 | 2 |

| | | **v RUSSIA** | *S* | *R* |
|---|---|---|---|---|
| EC1994 | 16 Nov | Glasgow | 1 | 1 |
| EC1995 | 29 Mar | Moscow | 0 | 0 |

| | | **v SAN MARINO** | *S* | *SM* |
|---|---|---|---|---|
| EC1991 | 1 May | Serravalle | 2 | 0 |
| EC1991 | 13 Nov | Glasgow | 4 | 0 |
| EC1995 | 26 Apr | Serravalle | 2 | 0 |
| EC1995 | 15 Nov | Glasgow | 5 | 0 |
| WC2000 | 7 Oct | Serravalle | 2 | 0 |
| WC2001 | 28 Mar | Glasgow | 4 | 0 |

| | | **v SAUDI ARABIA** | *S* | *SA* |
|---|---|---|---|---|
| 1988 | 17 Feb | Riyadh | 2 | 2 |

| | | **v SOUTH AFRICA** | *S* | *SA* |
|---|---|---|---|---|
| 2002 | 20 May | Hong Kong | 0 | 2 |

| | | **v SOUTH KOREA** | *S* | *SK* |
|---|---|---|---|---|
| 2002 | 16 May | Busan | 1 | 4 |

| | | **v SPAIN** | *S* | *Sp* |
|---|---|---|---|---|
| WC1957 | 8 May | Glasgow | 4 | 2 |
| WC1957 | 26 May | Madrid | 1 | 4 |
| 1963 | 13 June | Madrid | 6 | 2 |
| 1965 | 8 May | Glasgow | 0 | 0 |
| EC1974 | 20 Nov | Glasgow | 1 | 2 |
| EC1975 | 5 Feb | Valencia | 1 | 1 |
| 1982 | 24 Feb | Valencia | 0 | 3 |
| WC1984 | 14 Nov | Glasgow | 3 | 1 |
| WC1985 | 27 Feb | Seville | 0 | 1 |
| 1988 | 27 Apr | Madrid | 0 | 0 |

| | | **v SWEDEN** | *S* | *Sw* |
|---|---|---|---|---|
| 1952 | 30 May | Stockholm | 1 | 3 |
| 1953 | 6 May | Glasgow | 1 | 2 |
| 1975 | 16 Apr | Gothenburg | 1 | 1 |
| 1977 | 27 Apr | Glasgow | 3 | 1 |
| WC1980 | 10 Sept | Stockholm | 1 | 0 |
| WC1981 | 9 Sept | Glasgow | 2 | 0 |
| WC1990 | 16 June | Genoa | 2 | 1 |
| 1995 | 11 Oct | Stockholm | 0 | 2 |
| WC1996 | 10 Nov | Glasgow | 1 | 0 |
| WC1997 | 30 Apr | Gothenburg | 1 | 2 |

| | | **v SWITZERLAND** | *S* | *Sw* |
|---|---|---|---|---|
| 1931 | 24 May | Geneva | 3 | 2 |
| 1948 | 17 May | Berne | 1 | 2 |
| 1950 | 26 Apr | Glasgow | 3 | 1 |
| WC1957 | 19 May | Basle | 2 | 1 |
| WC1957 | 6 Nov | Glasgow | 3 | 2 |
| 1973 | 22 June | Berne | 0 | 1 |
| 1976 | 7 Apr | Glasgow | 1 | 0 |
| EC1982 | 17 Nov | Berne | 0 | 2 |

| | | | *S* | *Sw* |
|---|---|---|---|---|
| EC1983 | 30 May | Glasgow | 2 | 2 |
| EC1990 | 17 Oct | Glasgow | 2 | 1 |
| EC1991 | 11 Sept | Berne | 2 | 2 |
| WC1992 | 9 Sept | Berne | 1 | 3 |
| WC1993 | 8 Sept | Aberdeen | 1 | 1 |
| EC1996 | 18 June | Birmingham | 1 | 0 |

| | | **v TRINIDAD & TOBAGO** | *S* | *T* |
|---|---|---|---|---|
| 2004 | 30 May | Edinburgh | 4 | 1 |

| | | **v TURKEY** | *S* | *T* |
|---|---|---|---|---|
| 1960 | 8 June | Ankara | 2 | 4 |

| | | **v URUGUAY** | *S* | *U* |
|---|---|---|---|---|
| WC1954 | 19 June | Basle | 0 | 7 |
| 1962 | 2 May | Glasgow | 2 | 3 |
| 1983 | 21 Sept | Glasgow | 2 | 0 |
| WC1986 | 13 June | Nezahualcoyotl | 0 | 0 |

| | | **v USA** | *S* | *USA* |
|---|---|---|---|---|
| 1952 | 30 Apr | Glasgow | 6 | 0 |
| 1992 | 17 May | Denver | 1 | 0 |
| 1996 | 26 May | New Britain | 1 | 2 |
| 1998 | 30 May | Washington | 0 | 0 |

| | | **v USSR** | *S* | *USSR* |
|---|---|---|---|---|
| 1967 | 10 May | Glasgow | 0 | 2 |
| 1971 | 14 June | Moscow | 0 | 1 |
| WC1982 | 22 June | Malaga | 2 | 2 |
| 1991 | 6 Feb | Glasgow | 0 | 1 |

| | | **v YUGOSLAVIA** | *S* | *Y* |
|---|---|---|---|---|
| 1955 | 15 May | Belgrade | 2 | 2 |
| 1956 | 21 Nov | Glasgow | 2 | 0 |
| WC1958 | 8 June | Vasteras | 1 | 1 |
| 1972 | 29 June | Belo Horizonte | 2 | 2 |
| WC1974 | 22 June | Frankfurt | 1 | 1 |
| 1984 | 12 Sept | Glasgow | 6 | 1 |
| WC1988 | 19 Oct | Glasgow | 1 | 1 |
| WC1989 | 6 Sept | Zagreb | 1 | 3 |

| | | **v ZAIRE** | *S* | *Z* |
|---|---|---|---|---|
| WC1974 | 14 June | Dortmund | 2 | 0 |

## WALES

| | | **v ALBANIA** | *W* | *A* |
|---|---|---|---|---|
| EC1994 | 7 Sept | Cardiff | 2 | 0 |
| EC1995 | 15 Nov | Tirana | 1 | 1 |

| | | **v ARGENTINA** | *W* | *A* |
|---|---|---|---|---|
| 1992 | 3 June | Tokyo | 0 | 1 |
| 2002 | 13 Feb | Cardiff | 1 | 1 |

| | | **v ARMENIA** | *W* | *A* |
|---|---|---|---|---|
| WC2001 | 24 Mar | Erevan | 2 | 2 |
| WC2001 | 1 Sept | Cardiff | 0 | 0 |

| | | **v AUSTRIA** | *W* | *A* |
|---|---|---|---|---|
| 1954 | 9 May | Vienna | 0 | 2 |
| EC1955 | 23 Nov | Wrexham | 1 | 2 |
| EC1974 | 4 Sept | Vienna | 1 | 2 |
| 1975 | 19 Nov | Wrexham | 1 | 0 |
| 1992 | 29 Apr | Vienna | 1 | 1 |

| | | **v AZERBAIJAN** | *W* | *A* |
|---|---|---|---|---|
| EC2002 | 20 Nov | Baku | 2 | 0 |
| EC2003 | 29 Mar | Cardiff | 4 | 0 |

| | | **v BELARUS** | *W* | *B* |
|---|---|---|---|---|
| EC1998 | 14 Oct | Cardiff | 3 | 2 |
| EC1999 | 4 Sept | Minsk | 2 | 2 |
| WC2000 | 2 Sept | Minsk | 1 | 2 |
| WC2001 | 6 Oct | Cardiff | 1 | 0 |

| | | **v BELGIUM** | *W* | *B* |
|---|---|---|---|---|
| 1949 | 22 May | Liège | 1 | 3 |
| 1949 | 23 Nov | Cardiff | 5 | 1 |
| EC1990 | 17 Oct | Cardiff | 3 | 1 |
| EC1991 | 27 Mar | Brussels | 1 | 1 |
| WC1992 | 18 Nov | Brussels | 0 | 2 |
| WC1993 | 31 Mar | Cardiff | 2 | 0 |
| WC1997 | 29 Mar | Cardiff | 1 | 2 |
| WC1997 | 11 Oct | Brussels | 2 | 3 |

| | | **v BOSNIA** | *W* | *B* |
|---|---|---|---|---|
| 2003 | 12 Feb | Cardiff | 2 | 2 |

| | | **v BRAZIL** | *W* | *B* |
|---|---|---|---|---|
| WC1958 | 19 June | Gothenburg | 0 | 1 |
| 1962 | 12 May | Rio de Janeiro | 1 | 3 |
| 1962 | 16 May | São Paulo | 1 | 3 |
| 1966 | 14 May | Rio de Janeiro | 1 | 3 |
| 1966 | 18 May | Belo Horizonte | 0 | 1 |
| 1983 | 12 June | Cardiff | 1 | 1 |
| 1991 | 11 Sept | Cardiff | 1 | 0 |
| 1997 | 12 Nov | Brasilia | 0 | 3 |
| 2000 | 23 May | Cardiff | 0 | 3 |

| | | **v BULGARIA** | *W* | *B* |
|---|---|---|---|---|
| EC1983 | 27 Apr | Wrexham | 1 | 0 |
| EC1983 | 16 Nov | Sofia | 0 | 1 |
| EC1994 | 14 Dec | Cardiff | 0 | 3 |
| EC1995 | 29 Mar | Sofia | 1 | 3 |

| | | **v CANADA** | *W* | *C* |
|---|---|---|---|---|
| 1986 | 10 May | Toronto | 0 | 2 |
| 1986 | 20 May | Vancouver | 3 | 0 |
| 2004 | 30 May | Wrexham | 1 | 0 |

| | | **v CHILE** | *W* | *C* |
|---|---|---|---|---|
| 1966 | 22 May | Santiago | 0 | 2 |

| | | **v COSTA RICA** | *W* | *CR* |
|---|---|---|---|---|
| 1990 | 20 May | Cardiff | 1 | 0 |

| | | **v CROATIA** | *W* | *C* |
|---|---|---|---|---|
| 2002 | 21 Aug | Varazdin | 1 | 1 |

| | | **v CYPRUS** | *W* | *C* |
|---|---|---|---|---|
| WC1992 | 14 Oct | Limassol | 1 | 0 |
| WC1993 | 13 Oct | Cardiff | 2 | 0 |

| | | v CZECHOSLOVAKIA | W | C |
|---|---|---|---|---|
| WC1957 | 1 May | Cardiff | 1 | 0 |
| WC1957 | 26 May | Prague | 0 | 2 |
| EC1971 | 21 Apr | Swansea | 1 | 3 |
| EC1971 | 27 Oct | Prague | 0 | 1 |
| WC1977 | 30 Mar | Wrexham | 3 | 0 |
| WC1977 | 16 Nov | Prague | 0 | 1 |
| WC1980 | 19 Nov | Cardiff | 1 | 0 |
| WC1981 | 9 Sept | Prague | 0 | 2 |
| EC1987 | 29 Apr | Wrexham | 1 | 1 |
| EC1987 | 11 Nov | Prague | 0 | 2 |
| WC1993 | 28 Apr | Ostrava† | 1 | 1 |
| WC1993 | 8 Sept | Cardiff† | 2 | 2 |

*†Czechoslovakia played as RCS (Republic of Czechs and Slovaks).*

| | | v CZECH REPUBLIC | W | CR |
|---|---|---|---|---|
| 2002 | 27 Mar | Cardiff | 0 | 0 |

| | | v DENMARK | W | D |
|---|---|---|---|---|
| WC1964 | 21 Oct | Copenhagen | 0 | 1 |
| WC1965 | 1 Dec | Wrexham | 4 | 2 |
| EC1987 | 9 Sept | Cardiff | 1 | 0 |
| EC1987 | 14 Oct | Copenhagen | 0 | 1 |
| 1990 | 11 Sept | Copenhagen | 0 | 1 |
| EC1998 | 10 Oct | Copenhagen | 2 | 1 |
| EC1999 | 9 June | Liverpool | 0 | 2 |

| | | v ESTONIA | W | E |
|---|---|---|---|---|
| 1994 | 23 May | Tallinn | 2 | 1 |

| | | v FINLAND | W | F |
|---|---|---|---|---|
| EC1971 | 26 May | Helsinki | 1 | 0 |
| EC1971 | 13 Oct | Swansea | 3 | 0 |
| EC1987 | 10 Sept | Helsinki | 1 | 1 |
| EC1987 | 1 Apr | Wrexham | 4 | 0 |
| WC1988 | 19 Oct | Swansea | 2 | 2 |
| WC1989 | 6 Sept | Helsinki | 0 | 1 |
| 2000 | 29 Mar | Cardiff | 1 | 2 |
| EC2002 | 7 Sept | Helsinki | 2 | 0 |
| EC2003 | 10 Sept | Cardiff | 1 | 1 |

| | | v FAEROES | W | F |
|---|---|---|---|---|
| WC1992 | 9 Sept | Cardiff | 6 | 0 |
| WC1993 | 6 June | Toftir | 3 | 0 |

| | | v FRANCE | W | F |
|---|---|---|---|---|
| 1933 | 25 May | Paris | 1 | 1 |
| 1939 | 20 May | Paris | 1 | 2 |
| 1953 | 14 May | Paris | 1 | 6 |
| 1982 | 2 June | Toulouse | 1 | 0 |

| | | v GEORGIA | W | G |
|---|---|---|---|---|
| EC1994 | 16 Nov | Tbilisi | 0 | 5 |
| EC1995 | 7 June | Cardiff | 0 | 1 |

| | | v GERMANY | W | G |
|---|---|---|---|---|
| EC1995 | 26 Apr | Dusseldorf | 1 | 1 |
| EC1995 | 11 Oct | Cardiff | 1 | 2 |
| 2002 | 14 May | Cardiff | 1 | 0 |

| | | v EAST GERMANY | W | EG |
|---|---|---|---|---|
| WC1957 | 19 May | Leipzig | 1 | 2 |
| WC1957 | 25 Sept | Cardiff | 4 | 1 |
| WC1969 | 16 Apr | Dresden | 1 | 2 |
| WC1969 | 22 Oct | Cardiff | 1 | 3 |

| | | v WEST GERMANY | W | WG |
|---|---|---|---|---|
| 1968 | 8 May | Cardiff | 1 | 1 |
| 1969 | 26 Mar | Frankfurt | 1 | 1 |
| 1976 | 6 Oct | Cardiff | 0 | 2 |
| 1977 | 14 Dec | Dortmund | 1 | 1 |
| EC1979 | 2 May | Wrexham | 0 | 2 |
| EC1979 | 17 Oct | Cologne | 1 | 5 |
| WC1989 | 31 May | Cardiff | 0 | 0 |
| WC1989 | 15 Nov | Cologne | 1 | 2 |
| EC1991 | 5 June | Cardiff | 1 | 0 |
| EC1991 | 16 Oct | Nuremberg | 1 | 4 |

| | | v GREECE | W | G |
|---|---|---|---|---|
| WC1964 | 9 Dec | Athens | 0 | 2 |
| WC1965 | 17 Mar | Cardiff | 4 | 1 |

| | | v HOLLAND | W | H |
|---|---|---|---|---|
| WC1988 | 14 Sept | Amsterdam | 0 | 1 |
| WC1989 | 11 Oct | Wrexham | 1 | 2 |
| 1992 | 30 May | Utrecht | 0 | 4 |
| WC1996 | 5 Oct | Cardiff | 1 | 3 |
| WC1996 | 9 Nov | Eindhoven | 1 | 7 |

| | | v HUNGARY | W | H |
|---|---|---|---|---|
| WC1958 | 8 June | Sanviken | 1 | 1 |
| WC1958 | 17 June | Stockholm | 2 | 1 |
| 1961 | 28 May | Budapest | 2 | 3 |
| EC1962 | 7 Nov | Budapest | 1 | 3 |
| EC1963 | 20 Mar | Cardiff | 1 | 1 |
| EC1974 | 30 Oct | Cardiff | 2 | 0 |
| EC1975 | 16 Apr | Budapest | 2 | 1 |
| 1985 | 16 Oct | Cardiff | 0 | 3 |
| 2004 | 31 Mar | Budapest | 2 | 1 |

| | | v ICELAND | W | I |
|---|---|---|---|---|
| WC1980 | 2 June | Reykjavik | 4 | 0 |
| WC1981 | 14 Oct | Swansea | 2 | 2 |
| WC1984 | 12 Sept | Reykjavik | 0 | 1 |
| WC1984 | 14 Nov | Cardiff | 2 | 1 |
| 1991 | 1 May | Cardiff | 1 | 0 |

| | | v IRAN | W | I |
|---|---|---|---|---|
| 1978 | 18 Apr | Teheran | 1 | 0 |

| | | v REPUBLIC OF IRELAND | W | RI |
|---|---|---|---|---|
| 1960 | 28 Sept | Dublin | 3 | 2 |
| 1979 | 11 Sept | Swansea | 2 | 1 |
| 1981 | 24 Feb | Dublin | 3 | 1 |
| 1986 | 26 Mar | Dublin | 1 | 0 |
| 1990 | 28 Mar | Dublin | 0 | 1 |
| 1991 | 6 Feb | Wrexham | 0 | 3 |
| 1992 | 19 Feb | Dublin | 1 | 0 |
| 1993 | 17 Feb | Dublin | 1 | 2 |
| 1997 | 11 Feb | Cardiff | 0 | 0 |

| | | v ISRAEL | W | I |
|---|---|---|---|---|
| WC1958 | 15 Jan | Tel Aviv | 2 | 0 |
| WC1958 | 5 Feb | Cardiff | 2 | 0 |
| 1984 | 10 June | Tel Aviv | 0 | 0 |
| 1989 | 8 Feb | Tel Aviv | 3 | 3 |

| | | v ITALY | W | I |
|---|---|---|---|---|
| 1965 | 1 May | Florence | 1 | 4 |
| WC1968 | 23 Oct | Cardiff | 0 | 1 |
| WC1969 | 4 Nov | Rome | 1 | 4 |
| 1988 | 4 June | Brescia | 1 | 0 |
| 1996 | 24 Jan | Terni | 0 | 3 |
| EC1998 | 5 Sept | Liverpool | 0 | 2 |
| EC1999 | 5 June | Bologna | 0 | 4 |
| EC2002 | 16 Oct | Cardiff | 2 | 1 |
| EC2003 | 6 Sept | Milan | 0 | 4 |

| | | v JAMAICA | W | J |
|---|---|---|---|---|
| 1998 | 25 Mar | Cardiff | 0 | 0 |

| | | v JAPAN | W | J |
|---|---|---|---|---|
| 1992 | 7 June | Matsuyama | 1 | 0 |

| | | v KUWAIT | W | K |
|---|---|---|---|---|
| 1977 | 6 Sept | Wrexham | 0 | 0 |
| 1977 | 20 Sept | Kuwait | 0 | 0 |

| | | v LUXEMBOURG | W | L |
|---|---|---|---|---|
| EC1974 | 20 Nov | Swansea | 5 | 0 |
| EC1975 | 1 May | Luxembourg | 3 | 1 |
| EC1990 | 14 Nov | Luxembourg | 1 | 0 |
| EC1991 | 13 Nov | Cardiff | 1 | 0 |

| | | v MALTA | W | M |
|---|---|---|---|---|
| EC1978 | 25 Oct | Wrexham | 7 | 0 |
| EC1979 | 2 June | Valletta | 2 | 0 |
| 1988 | 1 June | Valletta | 3 | 2 |
| 1998 | 3 June | Valletta | 3 | 0 |

| | | v MEXICO | W | M |
|---|---|---|---|---|
| WC1958 | 11 June | Stockholm | 1 | 1 |
| 1962 | 22 May | Mexico City | 1 | 2 |

| | | v MOLDOVA | W | M |
|---|---|---|---|---|
| EC1994 | 12 Oct | Kishinev | 2 | 3 |
| EC1995 | 6 Sept | Cardiff | 1 | 0 |

| | | **v NORWAY** | *W* | *N* |
|---|---|---|---|---|
| EC1982 | 22 Sept | Swansea | 1 | 0 |
| EC1983 | 21 Sept | Oslo | 0 | 0 |
| 1984 | 6 June | Trondheim | 0 | 1 |
| 1985 | 26 Feb | Wrexham | 1 | 1 |
| 1985 | 5 June | Bergen | 2 | 4 |
| 1994 | 9 Mar | Cardiff | 1 | 3 |
| WC2000 | 7 Oct | Cardiff | 1 | 1 |
| WC2001 | 5 Sept | Oslo | 2 | 3 |
| 2004 | 27 May | Oslo | 0 | 0 |

| | | **v POLAND** | *W* | *P* |
|---|---|---|---|---|
| WC1973 | 28 Mar | Cardiff | 2 | 0 |
| WC1973 | 26 Sept | Katowice | 0 | 3 |
| 1991 | 29 May | Radom | 0 | 0 |
| WC2000 | 11 Oct | Warsaw | 0 | 0 |
| WC2001 | 2 June | Cardiff | 1 | 2 |

| | | **v PORTUGAL** | *W* | *P* |
|---|---|---|---|---|
| 1949 | 15 May | Lisbon | 2 | 3 |
| 1951 | 12 May | Cardiff | 2 | 1 |
| 2000 | 2 June | Chaves | 0 | 3 |

| | | **v QATAR** | *W* | *Q* |
|---|---|---|---|---|
| 2000 | 23 Feb | Doha | 1 | 0 |

| | | **v ROMANIA** | *W* | *R* |
|---|---|---|---|---|
| EC1970 | 11 Nov | Cardiff | 0 | 0 |
| EC1971 | 24 Nov | Bucharest | 0 | 2 |
| 1983 | 12 Oct | Wrexham | 5 | 0 |
| WC1992 | 20 May | Bucharest | 1 | 5 |
| WC1993 | 17 Nov | Cardiff | 1 | 2 |

| | | **v RUSSIA** | *W* | *R* |
|---|---|---|---|---|
| EC2003 | 15 Nov | Moscow | 0 | 0 |
| EC2003 | 19 Nov | Cardiff | 0 | 1 |

| | | **v SAN MARINO** | *W* | *SM* |
|---|---|---|---|---|
| WC1996 | 2 June | Serravalle | 5 | 0 |
| WC1996 | 31 Aug | Cardiff | 6 | 0 |

| | | **v SAUDI ARABIA** | *W* | *SA* |
|---|---|---|---|---|
| 1986 | 25 Feb | Dahran | 2 | 1 |

| | | **v SERBIA-MONTENEGRO** | *W* | *SM* |
|---|---|---|---|---|
| EC2003 | 20 Aug | Belgrade | 0 | 1 |
| EC2003 | 11 Oct | Cardiff | 2 | 3 |

| | | **v SPAIN** | *W* | *S* |
|---|---|---|---|---|
| WC1961 | 19 Apr | Cardiff | 1 | 2 |
| WC1961 | 18 May | Madrid | 1 | 1 |
| 1982 | 24 Mar | Valencia | 1 | 1 |
| WC1984 | 17 Oct | Seville | 0 | 3 |
| WC1985 | 30 Apr | Wrexham | 3 | 0 |

| | | **v SWEDEN** | *W* | *S* |
|---|---|---|---|---|
| WC1958 | 15 June | Stockholm | 0 | 0 |
| 1988 | 27 Apr | Stockholm | 1 | 4 |
| 1989 | 26 Apr | Wrexham | 0 | 2 |
| 1990 | 25 Apr | Stockholm | 2 | 4 |
| 1994 | 20 Apr | Wrexham | 0 | 2 |

| | | **v SWITZERLAND** | *W* | *S* |
|---|---|---|---|---|
| 1949 | 26 May | Berne | 0 | 4 |
| 1951 | 16 May | Wrexham | 3 | 2 |
| 1996 | 24 Apr | Lugano | 0 | 2 |
| EC1999 | 31 Mar | Zurich | 0 | 2 |
| EC1999 | 9 Oct | Wrexham | 0 | 2 |

| | | **v TUNISIA** | *W* | *T* |
|---|---|---|---|---|
| 1998 | 6 June | Tunis | 0 | 4 |

| | | **v TURKEY** | *W* | *T* |
|---|---|---|---|---|
| EC1978 | 29 Nov | Wrexham | 1 | 0 |
| EC1979 | 21 Nov | Izmir | 0 | 1 |
| WC1980 | 15 Oct | Cardiff | 4 | 0 |
| WC1981 | 25 Mar | Ankara | 1 | 0 |
| WC1996 | 14 Dec | Cardiff | 0 | 0 |
| WC1997 | 20 Aug | Istanbul | 4 | 6 |

| | | **v REST OF UNITED KINGDOM** | *W* | *UK* |
|---|---|---|---|---|
| 1951 | 5 Dec | Cardiff | 3 | 2 |
| 1969 | 28 July | Cardiff | 0 | 1 |

| | | **v UKRAINE** | *W* | *U* |
|---|---|---|---|---|
| WC2001 | 28 Mar | Cardiff | 1 | 1 |
| WC2001 | 6 June | Kiev | 1 | 1 |

| | | **v USA** | *W* | *USA* |
|---|---|---|---|---|
| 2003 | 27 May | San Jose | 0 | 2 |

| | | **v URUGUAY** | *W* | *U* |
|---|---|---|---|---|
| 1986 | 21 Apr | Wrexham | 0 | 0 |

| | | **v USSR** | *W* | *USSR* |
|---|---|---|---|---|
| WC1965 | 30 May | Moscow | 1 | 2 |
| WC1965 | 27 Oct | Cardiff | 2 | 1 |
| WC1981 | 30 May | Wrexham | 0 | 0 |
| WC1981 | 18 Nov | Tbilisi | 0 | 3 |
| 1987 | 18 Feb | Swansea | 0 | 0 |

| | | **v YUGOSLAVIA** | *W* | *Y* |
|---|---|---|---|---|
| 1953 | 21 May | Belgrade | 2 | 5 |
| 1954 | 22 Nov | Cardiff | 1 | 3 |
| EC1976 | 24 Apr | Zagreb | 0 | 2 |
| EC1976 | 22 May | Cardiff | 1 | 1 |
| EC1982 | 15 Dec | Titograd | 4 | 4 |
| EC1983 | 14 Dec | Cardiff | 1 | 1 |
| 1988 | 23 Mar | Swansea | 1 | 2 |

## NORTHERN IRELAND

| | | **v ALBANIA** | *NI* | *A* |
|---|---|---|---|---|
| WC1965 | 7 May | Belfast | 4 | 1 |
| WC1965 | 24 Nov | Tirana | 1 | 1 |
| EC1982 | 15 Dec | Tirana | 0 | 0 |
| EC1983 | 27 Apr | Belfast | 1 | 0 |
| WC1992 | 9 Sept | Belfast | 3 | 0 |
| WC1993 | 17 Feb | Tirana | 2 | 1 |
| WC1996 | 14 Dec | Belfast | 2 | 0 |
| WC1997 | 10 Sept | Zurich | 0 | 1 |

| | | **v ALGERIA** | *NI* | *A* |
|---|---|---|---|---|
| WC1986 | 3 June | Guadalajara | 1 | 1 |

| | | **v ARGENTINA** | *NI* | *A* |
|---|---|---|---|---|
| WC1958 | 11 June | Halmstad | 1 | 3 |

| | | **v ARMENIA** | *NI* | *A* |
|---|---|---|---|---|
| WC1996 | 5 Oct | Belfast | 1 | 1 |
| WC1997 | 30 Apr | Erevan | 0 | 0 |
| EC2003 | 29 Mar | Erevan | 0 | 1 |
| EC2003 | 10 Sept | Belfast | 0 | 1 |

| | | **v AUSTRALIA** | *NI* | *A* |
|---|---|---|---|---|
| 1980 | 11 June | Sydney | 2 | 1 |
| 1980 | 15 June | Melbourne | 1 | 1 |
| 1980 | 18 June | Adelaide | 2 | 1 |

| | | **v AUSTRIA** | *NI* | *A* |
|---|---|---|---|---|
| WC1982 | 1 July | Madrid | 2 | 2 |
| EC1982 | 13 Oct | Vienna | 0 | 2 |
| EC1983 | 21 Sept | Belfast | 3 | 1 |
| EC1990 | 14 Nov | Vienna | 0 | 0 |
| EC1991 | 16 Oct | Belfast | 2 | 1 |
| EC1994 | 12 Oct | Vienna | 2 | 1 |
| EC1995 | 15 Nov | Belfast | 5 | 3 |

| | | **v BARBADOS** | *NI* | *B* |
|---|---|---|---|---|
| 2004 | 30 May | Waterford | 1 | 1 |

| | | **v BELGIUM** | *NI* | *B* |
|---|---|---|---|---|
| WC1976 | 10 Nov | Liège | 0 | 2 |
| WC1977 | 16 Nov | Belfast | 3 | 0 |
| 1997 | 11 Feb | Belfast | 3 | 0 |

| | | **v BRAZIL** | *NI* | *B* |
|---|---|---|---|---|
| WC1986 | 12 June | Guadalajara | 0 | 3 |

| | | **v BULGARIA** | *NI* | *B* |
|---|---|---|---|---|
| WC1972 | 18 Oct | Sofia | 0 | 3 |
| WC1973 | 26 Sept | Sheffield | 0 | 0 |
| EC1978 | 29 Nov | Sofia | 2 | 0 |
| EC1979 | 2 May | Belfast | 2 | 0 |
| WC2001 | 28 Mar | Sofia | 3 | 4 |
| WC2001 | 2 June | Belfast | 0 | 1 |

| | | **v CANADA** | *NI* | *C* |
|---|---|---|---|---|
| 1995 | 22 May | Edmonton | 0 | 2 |
| 1999 | 27 Apr | Belfast | 1 | 1 |

| | | **v CHILE** | *NI* | *C* |
|---|---|---|---|---|
| 1989 | 26 May | Belfast | 0 | 1 |
| 1995 | 25 May | Edmonton | 1 | 2 |

| | | **v COLOMBIA** | *NI* | *C* |
|---|---|---|---|---|
| 1994 | 4 June | Boston | 0 | 2 |

| | | **v CYPRUS** | *NI* | *C* |
|---|---|---|---|---|
| EC1971 | 3 Feb | Nicosia | 3 | 0 |
| EC1971 | 21 Apr | Belfast | 5 | 0 |
| WC1973 | 14 Feb | Nicosia | 0 | 1 |
| WC1973 | 8 May | London | 3 | 0 |
| 2002 | 21 Aug | Belfast | 0 | 0 |

| | | **v CZECHOSLOVAKIA** | *NI* | *C* |
|---|---|---|---|---|
| WC1958 | 8 June | Halmstad | 1 | 0 |
| WC1958 | 17 June | Malmo | 2 | 1* |

**After extra time*

| | | **v CZECH REPUBLIC** | *NI* | *C* |
|---|---|---|---|---|
| WC2001 | 24 Mar | Belfast | 0 | 1 |
| WC2001 | 6 June | Teplice | 1 | 3 |

| | | **v DENMARK** | *NI* | *D* |
|---|---|---|---|---|
| EC1978 | 25 Oct | Belfast | 2 | 1 |
| EC1979 | 6 June | Copenhagen | 0 | 4 |
| 1986 | 26 Mar | Belfast | 1 | 1 |
| EC1990 | 17 Oct | Belfast | 1 | 1 |
| EC1991 | 13 Nov | Odense | 1 | 2 |
| WC1992 | 18 Nov | Belfast | 0 | 1 |
| WC1993 | 13 Oct | Copenhagen | 0 | 1 |
| WC2000 | 7 Oct | Belfast | 1 | 1 |
| WC2001 | 1 Sept | Copenhagen | 1 | 1 |

| | | **v ESTONIA** | *NI* | *E* |
|---|---|---|---|---|
| 2004 | 31 Mar | Tallinn | 1 | 0 |

| | | **v FAEROES** | *NI* | *F* |
|---|---|---|---|---|
| EC1991 | 1 May | Belfast | 1 | 1 |
| EC1991 | 11 Sept | Landskrona | 5 | 0 |

| | | **v FINLAND** | *NI* | *F* |
|---|---|---|---|---|
| WC1984 | 27 May | Pori | 0 | 1 |
| WC1984 | 14 Nov | Belfast | 2 | 1 |
| EC1998 | 10 Oct | Belfast | 1 | 0 |
| EC1998 | 9 Oct | Helsinki | 1 | 4 |
| 2003 | 12 Feb | Belfast | 0 | 1 |

| | | **v FRANCE** | *NI* | *F* |
|---|---|---|---|---|
| 1928 | 21 Feb | Paris | 0 | 4 |
| 1951 | 12 May | Belfast | 2 | 2 |
| 1952 | 11 Nov | Paris | 1 | 3 |
| WC1958 | 19 June | Norrkoping | 0 | 4 |
| 1982 | 24 Mar | Paris | 0 | 4 |
| WC1982 | 4 July | Madrid | 1 | 4 |
| 1986 | 26 Feb | Paris | 0 | 0 |
| 1988 | 27 Apr | Belfast | 0 | 0 |
| 1999 | 18 Aug | Belfast | 0 | 1 |

| | | **v GERMANY** | *NI* | *G* |
|---|---|---|---|---|
| 1992 | 2 June | Bremen | 1 | 1 |
| 1996 | 29 May | Belfast | 1 | 1 |
| WC1996 | 9 Nov | Nuremberg | 1 | 1 |
| WC1997 | 20 Aug | Belfast | 1 | 3 |
| EC1999 | 27 Mar | Belfast | 0 | 3 |
| EC1999 | 8 Sept | Dortmund | 0 | 4 |

| | | **v WEST GERMANY** | *NI* | *WG* |
|---|---|---|---|---|
| WC1958 | 15 June | Malmo | 2 | 2 |
| WC1960 | 26 Oct | Belfast | 3 | 4 |
| WC1961 | 10 May | Hamburg | 1 | 2 |
| 1966 | 7 May | Belfast | 0 | 2 |
| 1977 | 27 Apr | Cologne | 0 | 5 |
| EC1982 | 17 Nov | Belfast | 1 | 0 |
| EC1983 | 16 Nov | Hamburg | 1 | 0 |

| | | **v GREECE** | *NI* | *G* |
|---|---|---|---|---|
| WC1961 | 3 May | Athens | 1 | 2 |
| WC1961 | 17 Oct | Belfast | 2 | 0 |
| 1988 | 17 Feb | Athens | 2 | 3 |
| EC2003 | 2 Apr | Belfast | 0 | 2 |
| EC2003 | 11 Oct | Athens | 0 | 1 |

| | | **v HOLLAND** | *NI* | *H* |
|---|---|---|---|---|
| 1962 | 9 May | Rotterdam | 0 | 4 |
| WC1965 | 17 Mar | Belfast | 2 | 1 |
| WC1965 | 7 Apr | Rotterdam | 0 | 0 |
| WC1976 | 13 Oct | Rotterdam | 2 | 2 |
| WC1977 | 12 Oct | Belfast | 0 | 1 |

| | | **v HONDURAS** | *NI* | *H* |
|---|---|---|---|---|
| WC1982 | 21 June | Zaragoza | 1 | 1 |

| | | **v HUNGARY** | *NI* | *H* |
|---|---|---|---|---|
| WC1988 | 19 Oct | Budapest | 0 | 1 |
| WC1989 | 6 Sept | Belfast | 1 | 2 |
| 2000 | 26 Apr | Belfast | 0 | 1 |

| | | **v ICELAND** | *NI* | *I* |
|---|---|---|---|---|
| WC1977 | 11 June | Reykjavik | 0 | 1 |
| WC1977 | 21 Sept | Belfast | 2 | 0 |
| WC2000 | 11 Oct | Reykjavik | 0 | 1 |
| WC2001 | 5 Sept | Belfast | 3 | 0 |

| | | **v REPUBLIC OF IRELAND** | *NI* | *RI* |
|---|---|---|---|---|
| EC1978 | 20 Sept | Dublin | 0 | 0 |
| EC1979 | 21 Nov | Belfast | 1 | 0 |
| WC1988 | 14 Sept | Belfast | 0 | 0 |
| WC1989 | 11 Oct | Dublin | 0 | 3 |
| WC1993 | 31 Mar | Dublin | 0 | 3 |
| WC1993 | 17 Nov | Belfast | 1 | 1 |
| EC1994 | 16 Nov | Belfast | 0 | 4 |
| EC1995 | 29 Mar | Dublin | 1 | 1 |
| 1999 | 29 May | Dublin | 1 | 0 |

| | | **v ISRAEL** | *NI* | *I* |
|---|---|---|---|---|
| 1968 | 10 Sept | Jaffa | 3 | 2 |
| 1976 | 3 Mar | Tel Aviv | 1 | 1 |
| WC1980 | 26 Mar | Tel Aviv | 0 | 0 |
| WC1981 | 18 Nov | Belfast | 1 | 0 |
| 1984 | 16 Oct | Belfast | 3 | 0 |
| 1987 | 18 Feb | Tel Aviv | 1 | 1 |

| | | **v ITALY** | *NI* | *I* |
|---|---|---|---|---|
| WC1957 | 25 Apr | Rome | 0 | 1 |
| 1957 | 4 Dec | Belfast | 2 | 2 |
| WC1958 | 15 Jan | Belfast | 2 | 1 |
| 1961 | 25 Apr | Bologna | 2 | 3 |
| 1997 | 22 Jan | Palermo | 0 | 2 |
| 2003 | 3 June | Campobasso | 0 | 2 |

| | | **v LATVIA** | *NI* | *L* |
|---|---|---|---|---|
| WC1993 | 2 June | Riga | 2 | 1 |
| WC1993 | 8 Sept | Belfast | 2 | 0 |
| EC1995 | 26 Apr | Riga | 1 | 0 |
| EC1995 | 7 June | Belfast | 1 | 2 |

| | | **v LIECHTENSTEIN** | *NI* | *L* |
|---|---|---|---|---|
| EC1994 | 20 Apr | Belfast | 4 | 1 |
| EC1995 | 11 Oct | Eschen | 4 | 0 |
| 2002 | 27 Mar | Vaduz | 0 | 0 |

| | | **v LITHUANIA** | *NI* | *L* |
|---|---|---|---|---|
| WC1992 | 28 Apr | Belfast | 2 | 2 |
| WC1993 | 25 May | Vilnius | 1 | 0 |

| | | **v LUXEMBOURG** | *NI* | *L* |
|---|---|---|---|---|
| 2000 | 23 Feb | Luxembourg | 3 | 1 |

| | | **v MALTA** | *NI* | *M* |
|---|---|---|---|---|
| WC1988 | 21 May | Belfast | 3 | 0 |
| WC1989 | 26 Apr | Valletta | 2 | 0 |
| 2000 | 28 Mar | Valletta | 3 | 0 |
| WC2000 | 2 Sept | Belfast | 1 | 0 |
| WC2001 | 6 Oct | Valletta | 1 | 0 |

| | | **v MEXICO** | *NI* | *M* |
|---|---|---|---|---|
| 1966 | 22 June | Belfast | 4 | 1 |
| 1994 | 11 June | Miami | 0 | 3 |

| | | **v MOLDOVA** | *NI* | *M* |
|---|---|---|---|---|
| EC1998 | 18 Nov | Belfast | 2 | 2 |
| EC1999 | 31 Mar | Chisinau | 0 | 0 |

| | | **v MOROCCO** | *NI* | *M* |
|---|---|---|---|---|
| 1986 | 23 Apr | Belfast | 2 | 1 |

| | | **v NORWAY** | *NI* | *N* |
|---|---|---|---|---|
| 1922 | 25 May | Bergen | 1 | 2 |
| EC1974 | 4 Sept | Oslo | 1 | 2 |
| EC1975 | 29 Oct | Belfast | 3 | 0 |
| 1990 | 27 Mar | Belfast | 2 | 3 |
| 1996 | 27 Mar | Belfast | 0 | 2 |
| 2001 | 28 Feb | Belfast | 0 | 4 |
| 2004 | 18 Feb | Belfast | 1 | 4 |

| | | **v POLAND** | *NI* | *P* |
|---|---|---|---|---|
| EC1962 | 10 Oct | Katowice | 2 | 0 |
| EC1962 | 28 Nov | Belfast | 2 | 0 |
| 1988 | 23 Mar | Belfast | 1 | 1 |
| 1991 | 5 Feb | Belfast | 3 | 1 |
| 2002 | 13 Feb | Limassol | 1 | 4 |

| | | **v PORTUGAL** | *NI* | *P* |
|---|---|---|---|---|
| WC1957 | 16 Jan | Lisbon | 1 | 1 |
| WC1957 | 1 May | Belfast | 3 | 0 |
| WC1973 | 28 Mar | Coventry | 1 | 1 |
| WC1973 | 14 Nov | Lisbon | 1 | 1 |
| WC1980 | 19 Nov | Lisbon | 0 | 1 |
| WC1981 | 29 Apr | Belfast | 1 | 0 |
| EC1994 | 7 Sept | Belfast | 1 | 2 |
| EC1995 | 3 Sept | Lisbon | 1 | 1 |
| WC1997 | 29 Mar | Belfast | 0 | 0 |
| WC1997 | 11 Oct | Lisbon | 0 | 1 |

| | | **v ROMANIA** | *NI* | *R* |
|---|---|---|---|---|
| WC1984 | 12 Sept | Belfast | 3 | 2 |
| WC1985 | 16 Oct | Bucharest | 1 | 0 |
| 1994 | 23 Mar | Belfast | 2 | 0 |

| | | **v ST KITTS & NEVIS** | *NI* | *SK* |
|---|---|---|---|---|
| 2004 | 2 June | Basseterre | 2 | 0 |

| | | **v SERBIA-MONTENEGRO** | *NI* | *SM* |
|---|---|---|---|---|
| 2004 | 28 Apr | Belfast | 1 | 1 |

| | | **v SLOVAKIA** | *NI* | *S* |
|---|---|---|---|---|
| 1998 | 25 Mar | Belfast | 1 | 0 |

| | | **v SOUTH AFRICA** | *NI* | *SA* |
|---|---|---|---|---|
| 1924 | 24 Sept | Belfast | 1 | 2 |

| | | **v SPAIN** | *NI* | *S* |
|---|---|---|---|---|
| 1958 | 15 Oct | Madrid | 2 | 6 |
| 1963 | 30 May | Bilbao | 1 | 1 |
| 1963 | 30 Oct | Belfast | 0 | 1 |
| EC1970 | 11 Nov | Seville | 0 | 3 |
| EC1972 | 16 Feb | Hull | 1 | 1 |
| WC1982 | 25 June | Valencia | 1 | 0 |
| 1985 | 27 Mar | Palma | 0 | 0 |
| WC1986 | 7 June | Guadalajara | 1 | 2 |
| WC1988 | 21 Dec | Seville | 0 | 4 |
| WC1989 | 8 Feb | Belfast | 0 | 2 |
| WC1992 | 14 Oct | Belfast | 0 | 0 |
| WC1993 | 28 Apr | Seville | 1 | 3 |
| 1998 | 2 June | Santander | 1 | 4 |
| 2002 | 17 Apr | Belfast | 0 | 5 |
| EC2002 | 12 Oct | Albacete | 0 | 3 |
| EC2003 | 11 June | Belfast | 0 | 0 |

| | | **v SWEDEN** | *NI* | *S* |
|---|---|---|---|---|
| EC1974 | 30 Oct | Solna | 2 | 0 |
| EC1975 | 3 Sept | Belfast | 1 | 2 |
| WC1980 | 15 Oct | Belfast | 3 | 0 |
| WC1981 | 3 June | Solna | 0 | 1 |
| 1996 | 24 Apr | Belfast | 1 | 2 |

| | | **v SWITZERLAND** | *NI* | *S* |
|---|---|---|---|---|
| WC1964 | 14 Oct | Belfast | 1 | 0 |
| WC1964 | 14 Nov | Lausanne | 1 | 2 |
| 1998 | 22 Apr | Belfast | 1 | 0 |

| | | **v THAILAND** | *NI* | *T* |
|---|---|---|---|---|
| 1997 | 21 May | Bangkok | 0 | 0 |

| | | **v TRINIDAD & TOBAGO** | *NI* | *TT* |
|---|---|---|---|---|
| 2004 | 6 June | Bacolet | 3 | 0 |

| | | **v TURKEY** | *NI* | *T* |
|---|---|---|---|---|
| WC1968 | 23 Oct | Belfast | 4 | 1 |
| WC1968 | 11 Dec | Istanbul | 3 | 0 |
| EC1983 | 30 Mar | Belfast | 2 | 1 |
| EC1983 | 12 Oct | Ankara | 0 | 1 |
| WC1985 | 1 May | Belfast | 2 | 0 |
| WC1985 | 11 Sept | Izmir | 0 | 0 |
| EC1986 | 12 Nov | Izmir | 0 | 0 |
| EC1987 | 11 Nov | Belfast | 1 | 0 |
| EC1998 | 5 Sept | Istanbul | 0 | 3 |
| EC1999 | 4 Sept | Belfast | 0 | 3 |

| | | **v UKRAINE** | *NI* | *U* |
|---|---|---|---|---|
| WC1996 | 31 Aug | Belfast | 0 | 1 |
| WC1997 | 2 Apr | Kiev | 1 | 2 |
| EC2002 | 16 Oct | Belfast | 0 | 0 |
| EC2003 | 6 Sept | Donetsk | 0 | 0 |

| | | **v URUGUAY** | *NI* | *U* |
|---|---|---|---|---|
| 1964 | 29 Apr | Belfast | 3 | 0 |
| 1990 | 18 May | Belfast | 1 | 0 |

| | | **v USSR** | *NI* | *USSR* |
|---|---|---|---|---|
| WC1969 | 19 Sept | Belfast | 0 | 0 |
| WC1969 | 22 Oct | Moscow | 0 | 2 |
| EC1971 | 22 Sept | Moscow | 0 | 1 |
| EC1971 | 13 Oct | Belfast | 1 | 1 |

| | | **v YUGOSLAVIA** | *NI* | *Y* |
|---|---|---|---|---|
| EC1975 | 16 Mar | Belfast | 1 | 0 |
| EC1975 | 19 Nov | Belgrade | 0 | 1 |
| WC1982 | 17 June | Zaragoza | 0 | 0 |
| EC1987 | 29 Apr | Belfast | 1 | 2 |
| EC1987 | 14 Oct | Sarajevo | 0 | 3 |
| EC1990 | 12 Sept | Belfast | 0 | 2 |
| EC1991 | 27 Mar | Belgrade | 1 | 4 |
| 2000 | 16 Aug | Belfast | 1 | 2 |

## REPUBLIC OF IRELAND

| | | **v ALBANIA** | *RI* | *A* |
|---|---|---|---|---|
| WC1992 | 26 May | Dublin | 2 | 0 |
| WC1993 | 26 May | Tirana | 2 | 1 |
| EC2003 | 2 Apr | Tirana | 0 | 0 |
| EC2003 | 7 June | Dublin | 2 | 1 |

| | | **v ALGERIA** | *RI* | *A* |
|---|---|---|---|---|
| 1982 | 28 Apr | Algiers | 0 | 2 |

| | | **v ANDORRA** | *RI* | *A* |
|---|---|---|---|---|
| WC2001 | 28 Mar | Barcelona | 3 | 0 |
| WC2001 | 25 Apr | Dublin | 3 | 1 |

| | | **v ARGENTINA** | *RI* | *A* |
|---|---|---|---|---|
| 1951 | 13 May | Dublin | 0 | 1 |
| †1979 | 29 May | Dublin | 0 | 0 |
| 1980 | 16 May | Dublin | 0 | 1 |
| 1998 | 22 Apr | Dublin | 0 | 2 |

†*Not considered a full international.*

| | | **v AUSTRALIA** | *RI* | *A* |
|---|---|---|---|---|
| 2003 | 19 Aug | Dublin | 2 | 1 |

| | | **v AUSTRIA** | *RI* | *A* |
|---|---|---|---|---|
| 1952 | 7 May | Vienna | 0 | 6 |
| 1953 | 25 Mar | Dublin | 4 | 0 |
| 1958 | 14 Mar | Vienna | 1 | 3 |
| 1962 | 8 Apr | Dublin | 2 | 3 |
| EC1963 | 25 Sept | Vienna | 0 | 0 |
| EC1963 | 13 Oct | Dublin | 3 | 2 |
| 1966 | 22 May | Vienna | 0 | 1 |
| 1968 | 10 Nov | Dublin | 2 | 2 |
| EC1971 | 30 May | Dublin | 1 | 4 |
| EC1971 | 10 Oct | Linz | 0 | 6 |
| EC1995 | 11 June | Dublin | 1 | 3 |
| EC1995 | 6 Sept | Vienna | 1 | 3 |

| | | **v BELGIUM** | *RI* | *B* |
|---|---|---|---|---|
| 1928 | 12 Feb | Liège | 4 | 2 |
| 1929 | 30 Apr | Dublin | 4 | 0 |
| 1930 | 11 May | Brussels | 3 | 1 |
| WC1934 | 25 Feb | Dublin | 4 | 4 |
| 1949 | 24 Apr | Dublin | 0 | 2 |
| 1950 | 10 May | Brussels | 1 | 5 |
| 1965 | 24 Mar | Dublin | 0 | 2 |
| 1966 | 25 May | Liège | 3 | 2 |
| WC1980 | 15 Oct | Dublin | 1 | 1 |
| WC1981 | 25 Mar | Brussels | 0 | 1 |
| EC1986 | 10 Sept | Brussels | 2 | 2 |
| EC1987 | 29 Apr | Dublin | 0 | 0 |
| WC1997 | 29 Oct | Dublin | 1 | 1 |
| WC1997 | 16 Nov | Brussels | 1 | 2 |

| | | **v BOLIVIA** | *RI* | *B* |
|---|---|---|---|---|
| 1994 | 24 May | Dublin | 1 | 0 |
| 1996 | 15 June | New Jersey | 3 | 0 |

| | | **v BRAZIL** | *RI* | *B* |
|---|---|---|---|---|
| 1974 | 5 May | Rio de Janeiro | 1 | 2 |
| 1982 | 27 May | Uberlandia | 0 | 7 |
| 1987 | 23 May | Dublin | 1 | 0 |
| 2004 | 18 Feb | Dublin | 0 | 0 |

| | | **v BULGARIA** | *RI* | *B* |
|---|---|---|---|---|
| WC1977 | 1 June | Sofia | 1 | 2 |
| WC1977 | 12 Oct | Dublin | 0 | 0 |
| EC1979 | 19 May | Sofia | 0 | 1 |
| EC1979 | 17 Oct | Dublin | 3 | 0 |
| WC1987 | 1 Apr | Sofia | 1 | 2 |
| WC1987 | 14 Oct | Dublin | 2 | 0 |

| | | **v CAMEROON** | *RI* | *C* |
|---|---|---|---|---|
| WC2002 | 1 June | Niigata | 1 | 1 |

| | | **v CANADA** | *RI* | *C* |
|---|---|---|---|---|
| 2003 | 18 Nov | Dublin | 3 | 0 |

| | | **v CHILE** | *RI* | *C* |
|---|---|---|---|---|
| 1960 | 30 Mar | Dublin | 2 | 0 |
| 1972 | 21 June | Recife | 1 | 2 |
| 1974 | 12 May | Santiago | 2 | 1 |
| 1982 | 22 May | Santiago | 0 | 1 |
| 1991 | 22 May | Dublin | 1 | 1 |

| | | **v CHINA** | *RI* | *C* |
|---|---|---|---|---|
| 1984 | 3 June | Sapporo | 1 | 0 |

| | | **v CROATIA** | *RI* | *C* |
|---|---|---|---|---|
| 1996 | 2 June | Dublin | 2 | 2 |
| EC1998 | 5 Sept | Dublin | 2 | 0 |
| EC1999 | 4 Sept | Zagreb | 0 | 1 |
| 2001 | 15 Aug | Dublin | 2 | 2 |

| | | **v CYPRUS** | *RI* | *C* |
|---|---|---|---|---|
| WC1980 | 26 Mar | Nicosia | 3 | 2 |
| WC1980 | 19 Nov | Dublin | 6 | 0 |
| WC2001 | 24 Mar | Nicosia | 4 | 0 |
| WC2001 | 6 Oct | Dublin | 4 | 0 |

| | | **v CZECHOSLOVAKIA** | *RI* | *C* |
|---|---|---|---|---|
| 1938 | 18 May | Prague | 2 | 2 |
| EC1959 | 5 Apr | Dublin | 2 | 0 |
| EC1959 | 10 May | Bratislava | 0 | 4 |
| WC1961 | 8 Oct | Dublin | 1 | 3 |
| WC1961 | 29 Oct | Prague | 1 | 7 |
| EC1967 | 21 May | Dublin | 0 | 2 |
| EC1967 | 22 Nov | Prague | 2 | 1 |
| WC1969 | 4 May | Dublin | 1 | 2 |
| WC1969 | 7 Oct | Prague | 0 | 3 |
| 1979 | 26 Sept | Prague | 1 | 4 |
| 1981 | 29 Apr | Dublin | 3 | 1 |
| 1986 | 27 May | Reykjavik | 1 | 0 |

| | | **v CZECH REPUBLIC** | *RI* | *C* |
|---|---|---|---|---|
| 1994 | 5 June | Dublin | 1 | 3 |
| 1996 | 24 Apr | Prague | 0 | 2 |
| 1998 | 25 Mar | Olomouc | 1 | 2 |
| 2000 | 23 Feb | Dublin | 3 | 2 |
| 2004 | 31 Mar | Dublin | 2 | 1 |

| | | **v DENMARK** | *RI* | *D* |
|---|---|---|---|---|
| WC1956 | 3 Oct | Dublin | 2 | 1 |
| WC1957 | 2 Oct | Copenhagen | 2 | 0 |
| WC1968 | 4 Dec | Dublin | 1 | 1 |
| (*abandoned after 51 mins*) | | | | |
| WC1969 | 27 May | Copenhagen | 0 | 2 |
| WC1969 | 15 Oct | Dublin | 1 | 1 |
| EC1978 | 24 May | Copenhagen | 3 | 3 |
| EC1979 | 2 May | Dublin | 2 | 0 |
| WC1984 | 14 Nov | Copenhagen | 0 | 3 |
| WC1985 | 13 Nov | Dublin | 1 | 4 |
| WC1992 | 14 Oct | Copenhagen | 0 | 0 |
| WC1993 | 28 Apr | Dublin | 1 | 1 |
| 2002 | 27 Mar | Dublin | 3 | 0 |

| | | **v ECUADOR** | *RI* | *E* |
|---|---|---|---|---|
| 1972 | 19 June | Natal | 3 | 2 |

| | | **v EGYPT** | *RI* | *E* |
|---|---|---|---|---|
| WC1990 | 17 June | Palermo | 0 | 0 |

| | | **v ENGLAND** | *RI* | *E* |
|---|---|---|---|---|
| 1946 | 30 Sept | Dublin | 0 | 1 |
| 1949 | 21 Sept | Everton | 2 | 0 |
| WC1957 | 8 May | Wembley | 1 | 5 |
| WC1957 | 19 May | Dublin | 1 | 1 |
| 1964 | 24 May | Dublin | 1 | 3 |
| 1976 | 8 Sept | Wembley | 1 | 1 |
| EC1978 | 25 Oct | Dublin | 1 | 1 |
| EC1980 | 6 Feb | Wembley | 0 | 2 |
| 1985 | 26 Mar | Wembley | 1 | 2 |
| EC1988 | 12 June | Stuttgart | 1 | 0 |
| WC1990 | 11 June | Cagliari | 1 | 1 |
| EC1990 | 14 Nov | Dublin | 1 | 1 |
| EC1991 | 27 Mar | Wembley | 1 | 1 |
| 1995 | 15 Feb | Dublin | 1 | 0 |
| (*abandoned after 27 mins*) | | | | |

| | | **v ESTONIA** | *RI* | *E* |
|---|---|---|---|---|
| WC2000 | 11 Oct | Dublin | 2 | 0 |
| WC2001 | 6 June | Tallinn | 2 | 0 |

| | | **v FINLAND** | *RI* | *F* |
|---|---|---|---|---|
| WC1949 | 8 Sept | Dublin | 3 | 0 |
| WC1949 | 9 Oct | Helsinki | 1 | 1 |
| 1990 | 16 May | Dublin | 1 | 1 |
| 2000 | 15 Nov | Dublin | 3 | 0 |
| 2002 | 21 Aug | Helsinki | 3 | 0 |

| | | **v FRANCE** | *RI* | *F* |
|---|---|---|---|---|
| 1937 | 23 May | Paris | 2 | 0 |
| 1952 | 16 Nov | Dublin | 1 | 1 |
| WC1953 | 4 Oct | Dublin | 3 | 5 |
| WC1953 | 25 Nov | Paris | 0 | 1 |
| WC1972 | 15 Nov | Dublin | 2 | 1 |
| WC1973 | 19 May | Paris | 1 | 1 |
| WC1976 | 17 Nov | Paris | 0 | 2 |
| WC1977 | 30 Mar | Dublin | 1 | 0 |
| WC1980 | 28 Oct | Paris | 0 | 2 |
| WC1981 | 14 Oct | Dublin | 3 | 2 |
| 1989 | 7 Feb | Dublin | 0 | 0 |

| | | **v GEORGIA** | *RI* | *G* |
|---|---|---|---|---|
| EC2003 | 29 Mar | Tbilisi | 2 | 1 |
| EC2003 | 11 June | Dublin | 2 | 0 |

| | | **v GERMANY** | *RI* | *G* |
|---|---|---|---|---|
| 1935 | 8 May | Dortmund | 1 | 3 |
| 1936 | 17 Oct | Dublin | 5 | 2 |
| 1939 | 23 May | Bremen | 1 | 1 |
| 1994 | 29 May | Hanover | 2 | 0 |
| WC2002 | 5 June | Ibaraki | 1 | 1 |

| | | **v WEST GERMANY** | *RI* | *WG* |
|---|---|---|---|---|
| 1951 | 17 Oct | Dublin | 3 | 2 |
| 1952 | 4 May | Cologne | 0 | 3 |
| 1955 | 28 May | Hamburg | 1 | 2 |
| 1956 | 25 Nov | Dublin | 3 | 0 |
| 1960 | 11 May | Dusseldorf | 1 | 0 |
| 1966 | 4 May | Dublin | 0 | 4 |
| 1970 | 9 May | Berlin | 1 | 2 |
| 1975 | 1 Mar | Dublin | 1 | 0† |
| 1979 | 22 May | Dublin | 1 | 3 |
| 1981 | 21 May | Bremen | 0 | 3† |
| 1989 | 6 Sept | Dublin | 1 | 1 |

†*v West Germany 'B'*

| | | **v GREECE** | *RI* | *G* |
|---|---|---|---|---|
| 2000 | 26 Apr | Dublin | 0 | 1 |
| 2002 | 20 Nov | Athens | 0 | 0 |

| | | **v HOLLAND** | *RI* | *N* |
|---|---|---|---|---|
| 1932 | 8 May | Amsterdam | 2 | 0 |
| 1934 | 8 Apr | Amsterdam | 2 | 5 |
| 1935 | 8 Dec | Dublin | 3 | 5 |
| 1955 | 1 May | Dublin | 1 | 0 |
| 1956 | 10 May | Rotterdam | 4 | 1 |
| WC1980 | 10 Sept | Dublin | 2 | 1 |
| WC1981 | 9 Sept | Rotterdam | 2 | 2 |
| EC1982 | 22 Sept | Rotterdam | 1 | 2 |
| EC1983 | 12 Oct | Dublin | 2 | 3 |
| EC1988 | 18 June | Gelsenkirchen | 0 | 1 |
| WC1990 | 21 June | Palermo | 1 | 1 |
| 1994 | 20 Apr | Tilburg | 1 | 0 |
| WC1994 | 4 July | Orlando | 0 | 2 |
| EC1995 | 13 Dec | Liverpool | 0 | 2 |
| 1996 | 4 June | Rotterdam | 1 | 3 |
| WC2000 | 2 Sept | Amsterdam | 2 | 2 |
| WC2001 | 1 Sept | Dublin | 1 | 0 |
| 2004 | 5 June | Amsterdam | 1 | 0 |

| | | **v HUNGARY** | *RI* | *H* |
|---|---|---|---|---|
| 1934 | 15 Dec | Dublin | 2 | 4 |
| 1936 | 3 May | Budapest | 3 | 3 |
| 1936 | 6 Dec | Dublin | 2 | 3 |
| 1939 | 19 Mar | Cork | 2 | 2 |
| 1939 | 18 May | Budapest | 2 | 2 |
| WC1969 | 8 June | Dublin | 1 | 2 |
| WC1969 | 5 Nov | Budapest | 0 | 4 |
| WC1989 | 8 Mar | Budapest | 0 | 0 |
| WC1989 | 4 June | Dublin | 2 | 0 |
| 1991 | 11 Sept | Gyor | 2 | 1 |

| | | **v ICELAND** | *RI* | *I* |
|---|---|---|---|---|
| EC1962 | 12 Aug | Dublin | 4 | 2 |
| EC1962 | 2 Sept | Reykjavik | 1 | 1 |
| EC1982 | 13 Oct | Dublin | 2 | 0 |
| EC1983 | 21 Sept | Reykjavik | 3 | 0 |
| 1986 | 25 May | Reykjavik | 2 | 1 |
| WC1996 | 10 Nov | Dublin | 0 | 0 |
| WC1997 | 6 Sept | Reykjavik | 4 | 2 |

| | | **v IRAN** | *RI* | *I* |
|---|---|---|---|---|
| 1972 | 18 June | Recife | 2 | 1 |
| WC2001 | 10 Nov | Dublin | 2 | 0 |
| WC2001 | 15 Nov | Tehran | 0 | 1 |

| | | **v N. IRELAND** | *RI* | *NI* |
|---|---|---|---|---|
| EC1978 | 20 Sept | Dublin | 0 | 0 |
| EC1979 | 21 Nov | Belfast | 0 | 1 |
| WC1988 | 14 Sept | Belfast | 0 | 0 |
| WC1989 | 11 Oct | Dublin | 3 | 0 |
| WC1993 | 31 Mar | Dublin | 3 | 0 |
| WC1993 | 17 Nov | Belfast | 1 | 1 |
| EC1994 | 16 Nov | Belfast | 4 | 0 |
| EC1995 | 29 Mar | Dublin | 1 | 1 |
| 1999 | 29 May | Dublin | 0 | 1 |

| | | **v ISRAEL** | *RI* | *I* |
|---|---|---|---|---|
| 1984 | 4 Apr | Tel Aviv | 0 | 3 |
| 1985 | 27 May | Tel Aviv | 0 | 0 |
| 1987 | 10 Nov | Dublin | 5 | 0 |

| | | **v ITALY** | *RI* | *I* |
|---|---|---|---|---|
| 1926 | 21 Mar | Turin | 0 | 3 |
| 1927 | 23 Apr | Dublin | 1 | 2 |
| EC1970 | 8 Dec | Rome | 0 | 3 |
| EC1971 | 10 May | Dublin | 1 | 2 |
| 1985 | 5 Feb | Dublin | 1 | 2 |
| WC1990 | 30 June | Rome | 0 | 1 |
| 1992 | 4 June | Foxboro | 0 | 2 |
| WC1994 | 18 June | New York | 1 | 0 |

| | | **v JAMAICA** | *RI* | *J* |
|---|---|---|---|---|
| 2004 | 2 June | Charlton | 1 | 0 |

| | | **v LATVIA** | *RI* | *L* |
|---|---|---|---|---|
| WC1992 | 9 Sept | Dublin | 4 | 0 |
| WC1993 | 2 June | Riga | 2 | 1 |
| EC1994 | 7 Sept | Riga | 3 | 0 |
| EC1995 | 11 Oct | Dublin | 2 | 1 |

| | | **v LIECHTENSTEIN** | *RI* | *L* |
|---|---|---|---|---|
| EC1994 | 12 Oct | Dublin | 4 | 0 |
| EC1995 | 3 June | Eschen | 0 | 0 |
| WC1996 | 31 Aug | Eschen | 5 | 0 |
| WC1997 | 21 May | Dublin | 5 | 0 |

| | | **v LITHUANIA** | *RI* | *L* |
|---|---|---|---|---|
| WC1993 | 16 June | Vilnius | 1 | 0 |
| WC1993 | 8 Sept | Dublin | 2 | 0 |
| WC1997 | 20 Aug | Dublin | 0 | 0 |
| WC1997 | 10 Sept | Vilnius | 2 | 1 |

| | | **v LUXEMBOURG** | *RI* | *L* |
|---|---|---|---|---|
| 1936 | 9 May | Luxembourg | 5 | 1 |
| WC1953 | 28 Oct | Dublin | 4 | 0 |
| WC1954 | 7 Mar | Luxembourg | 1 | 0 |
| EC1987 | 28 May | Luxembourg | 2 | 0 |
| EC1987 | 9 Sept | Dublin | 2 | 1 |

| | | **v MACEDONIA** | *RI* | *M* |
|---|---|---|---|---|
| WC1996 | 9 Oct | Dublin | 3 | 0 |
| WC1997 | 2 Apr | Skopje | 2 | 3 |
| EC1999 | 9 June | Dublin | 1 | 0 |
| EC1999 | 9 Oct | Skopje | 1 | 1 |

| | | **v MALTA** | *RI* | *M* |
|---|---|---|---|---|
| EC1983 | 30 Mar | Valletta | 1 | 0 |
| EC1983 | 16 Nov | Dublin | 8 | 0 |
| WC1989 | 28 May | Dublin | 2 | 0 |
| WC1989 | 15 Nov | Valletta | 2 | 0 |
| 1990 | 2 June | Valletta | 3 | 0 |
| EC1998 | 14 Oct | Dublin | 5 | 0 |
| EC1999 | 8 Sept | Valletta | 3 | 2 |

| | | **v MEXICO** | *RI* | *M* |
|---|---|---|---|---|
| 1984 | 8 Aug | Dublin | 0 | 0 |
| WC1994 | 24 June | Orlando | 1 | 2 |
| 1996 | 13 June | New Jersey | 2 | 2 |
| 1998 | 23 May | Dublin | 0 | 0 |
| 2000 | 4 June | Chicago | 2 | 2 |

| | | **v MOROCCO** | *RI* | *M* |
|---|---|---|---|---|
| 1990 | 12 Sept | Dublin | 1 | 0 |

| | | **v NIGERIA** | *RI* | *N* |
|---|---|---|---|---|
| 2002 | 16 May | Dublin | 1 | 2 |
| 2004 | 29 May | Charlton | 0 | 3 |

| | | **v NORWAY** | *RI* | *N* |
|---|---|---|---|---|
| WC1937 | 10 Oct | Oslo | 2 | 3 |
| WC1937 | 7 Nov | Dublin | 3 | 3 |
| 1950 | 26 Nov | Dublin | 2 | 2 |
| 1951 | 30 May | Oslo | 3 | 2 |
| 1954 | 8 Nov | Dublin | 2 | 1 |
| 1955 | 25 May | Oslo | 3 | 1 |
| 1960 | 6 Nov | Dublin | 3 | 1 |
| 1964 | 13 May | Oslo | 4 | 1 |
| 1973 | 6 June | Oslo | 1 | 1 |
| 1976 | 24 Mar | Dublin | 3 | 0 |
| 1978 | 21 May | Oslo | 0 | 0 |
| WC1984 | 17 Oct | Oslo | 0 | 1 |
| WC1985 | 1 May | Dublin | 0 | 0 |
| 1988 | 1 June | Oslo | 0 | 0 |
| WC1994 | 28 June | New York | 0 | 0 |
| 2003 | 30 Apr | Dublin | 1 | 0 |

| | | **v PARAGUAY** | *RI* | *P* |
|---|---|---|---|---|
| 1999 | 10 Feb | Dublin | 2 | 0 |

| | | **v POLAND** | *RI* | *P* |
|---|---|---|---|---|
| 1938 | 22 May | Warsaw | 0 | 6 |
| 1938 | 13 Nov | Dublin | 3 | 2 |
| 1958 | 11 May | Katowice | 2 | 2 |
| 1958 | 5 Oct | Dublin | 2 | 2 |
| 1964 | 10 May | Kracow | 1 | 3 |
| 1964 | 25 Oct | Dublin | 3 | 2 |
| 1968 | 15 May | Dublin | 2 | 2 |
| 1968 | 30 Oct | Katowice | 0 | 1 |
| 1970 | 6 May | Dublin | 1 | 2 |
| 1970 | 23 Sept | Dublin | 0 | 2 |
| 1973 | 16 May | Wroclaw | 0 | 2 |
| 1973 | 21 Oct | Dublin | 1 | 0 |
| 1976 | 26 May | Poznan | 2 | 0 |
| 1977 | 24 Apr | Dublin | 0 | 0 |
| 1978 | 12 Apr | Lodz | 0 | 3 |
| 1981 | 23 May | Bydgoszcz | 0 | 3 |
| 1984 | 23 May | Dublin | 0 | 0 |
| 1986 | 12 Nov | Warsaw | 0 | 1 |
| 1988 | 22 May | Dublin | 3 | 1 |
| EC1991 | 1 May | Dublin | 0 | 0 |
| EC1991 | 16 Oct | Poznan | 3 | 3 |
| 2004 | 28 Apr | Bydgoszcz | 0 | 0 |

| | | **v PORTUGAL** | *RI* | *P* |
|---|---|---|---|---|
| 1946 | 16 June | Lisbon | 1 | 3 |
| 1947 | 4 May | Dublin | 0 | 2 |
| 1948 | 23 May | Lisbon | 0 | 2 |
| 1949 | 22 May | Dublin | 1 | 0 |
| 1972 | 25 June | Recife | 1 | 2 |
| 1992 | 7 June | Boston | 2 | 0 |
| EC1995 | 26 Apr | Dublin | 1 | 0 |
| EC1995 | 15 Nov | Lisbon | 0 | 3 |
| 1996 | 29 May | Dublin | 0 | 1 |
| WC2000 | 7 Oct | Lisbon | 1 | 1 |
| WC2001 | 2 June | Dublin | 1 | 1 |

**v ROMANIA**

| | | | RI | R |
|---|---|---|---|---|
| 1988 | 23 Mar | Dublin | 2 | 0 |
| WC1990 | 25 June | Genoa | 0 | 0* |
| WC1997 | 30 Apr | Bucharest | 0 | 1 |
| WC1997 | 11 Oct | Dublin | 1 | 1 |
| 2004 | 27 May | Dublin | 1 | 0 |

**v RUSSIA**

| | | | RI | R |
|---|---|---|---|---|
| 1994 | 23 Mar | Dublin | 0 | 0 |
| 1996 | 27 Mar | Dublin | 0 | 2 |
| 2002 | 13 Feb | Dublin | 2 | 0 |
| EC2002 | 7 Sept | Moscow | 2 | 4 |
| EC2003 | 6 Sept | Dublin | 1 | 1 |

**v SAUDI ARABIA**

| | | | RI | SA |
|---|---|---|---|---|
| WC2002 | 11 June | Yokohama | 3 | 0 |

**v SCOTLAND**

| | | | RI | S |
|---|---|---|---|---|
| WC1961 | 3 May | Glasgow | 1 | 4 |
| WC1961 | 7 May | Dublin | 0 | 3 |
| 1963 | 9 June | Dublin | 1 | 0 |
| 1969 | 21 Sept | Dublin | 1 | 1 |
| EC1986 | 15 Oct | Dublin | 0 | 0 |
| EC1987 | 18 Feb | Glasgow | 1 | 0 |
| 2000 | 30 May | Dublin | 1 | 2 |
| 2003 | 12 Feb | Glasgow | 2 | 0 |

**v SOUTH AFRICA**

| | | | RI | SA |
|---|---|---|---|---|
| 2000 | 11 June | New Jersey | 2 | 1 |

**v SPAIN**

| | | | RI | S |
|---|---|---|---|---|
| 1931 | 26 Apr | Barcelona | 1 | 1 |
| 1931 | 13 Dec | Dublin | 0 | 5 |
| 1946 | 23 June | Madrid | 1 | 0 |
| 1947 | 2 Mar | Dublin | 3 | 2 |
| 1948 | 30 May | Barcelona | 1 | 2 |
| 1949 | 12 June | Dublin | 1 | 4 |
| 1952 | 1 June | Madrid | 0 | 6 |
| 1955 | 27 Nov | Dublin | 2 | 2 |
| EC1964 | 11 Mar | Seville | 1 | 5 |
| EC1964 | 8 Apr | Dublin | 0 | 2 |
| WC1965 | 5 May | Dublin | 1 | 0 |
| WC1965 | 27 Oct | Seville | 1 | 4 |
| WC1965 | 10 Nov | Paris | 0 | 1 |
| EC1966 | 23 Oct | Dublin | 0 | 0 |
| EC1966 | 7 Dec | Valencia | 0 | 2 |
| 1977 | 9 Feb | Dublin | 0 | 1 |
| EC1982 | 17 Nov | Dublin | 3 | 3 |
| EC1983 | 27 Apr | Zaragoza | 0 | 2 |
| 1985 | 26 May | Cork | 0 | 0 |
| WC1988 | 16 Nov | Seville | 0 | 2 |
| WC1989 | 26 Apr | Dublin | 1 | 0 |
| WC1992 | 18 Nov | Seville | 0 | 0 |
| WC1993 | 13 Oct | Dublin | 1 | 3 |
| WC2002 | 16 June | Suwon | 1 | 1 |

**v SWEDEN**

| | | | RI | S |
|---|---|---|---|---|
| WC1949 | 2 June | Stockholm | 1 | 3 |
| WC1949 | 13 Nov | Dublin | 1 | 3 |
| 1959 | 1 Nov | Dublin | 3 | 2 |
| 1960 | 18 May | Malmo | 1 | 4 |
| EC1970 | 14 Oct | Dublin | 1 | 1 |
| EC1970 | 28 Oct | Malmo | 0 | 1 |
| 1999 | 28 Apr | Dublin | 2 | 0 |

**v SWITZERLAND**

| | | | RI | S |
|---|---|---|---|---|
| 1935 | 5 May | Basle | 0 | 1 |
| 1936 | 17 Mar | Dublin | 1 | 0 |
| 1937 | 17 May | Berne | 1 | 0 |
| 1938 | 18 Sept | Dublin | 4 | 0 |
| 1948 | 5 Dec | Dublin | 0 | 1 |
| EC1975 | 11 May | Dublin | 2 | 1 |
| EC1975 | 21 May | Berne | 0 | 1 |
| 1980 | 30 Apr | Dublin | 2 | 0 |
| WC1985 | 2 June | Dublin | 3 | 0 |
| WC1985 | 11 Sept | Berne | 0 | 0 |
| 1992 | 25 Mar | Dublin | 2 | 1 |
| EC2002 | 16 Oct | Dublin | 1 | 2 |
| EC2003 | 11 Oct | Basle | 0 | 2 |

**v TRINIDAD & TOBAGO**

| | | | RI | TT |
|---|---|---|---|---|
| 1982 | 30 May | Port of Spain | 1 | 2 |

**v TUNISIA**

| | | | RI | T |
|---|---|---|---|---|
| 1988 | 19 Oct | Dublin | 4 | 0 |

**v TURKEY**

| | | | RI | T |
|---|---|---|---|---|
| EC1966 | 16 Nov | Dublin | 2 | 1 |
| EC1967 | 22 Feb | Ankara | 1 | 2 |
| EC1974 | 20 Nov | Izmir | 1 | 1 |
| EC1975 | 29 Oct | Dublin | 4 | 0 |
| 1976 | 13 Oct | Ankara | 3 | 3 |
| 1978 | 5 Apr | Dublin | 4 | 2 |
| 1990 | 26 May | Izmir | 0 | 0 |
| EC1990 | 17 Oct | Dublin | 5 | 0 |
| EC1991 | 13 Nov | Istanbul | 3 | 1 |
| EC2000 | 13 Nov | Dublin | 1 | 1 |
| EC2000 | 17 Nov | Bursa | 0 | 0 |
| 2003 | 9 Sept | Dublin | 2 | 2 |

**v URUGUAY**

| | | | RI | U |
|---|---|---|---|---|
| 1974 | 8 May | Montevideo | 0 | 2 |
| 1986 | 23 Apr | Dublin | 1 | 1 |

**v USA**

| | | | RI | USA |
|---|---|---|---|---|
| 1979 | 29 Oct | Dublin | 3 | 2 |
| 1991 | 1 June | Boston | 1 | 1 |
| 1992 | 29 Apr | Dublin | 4 | 1 |
| 1992 | 30 May | Washington | 1 | 3 |
| 1996 | 9 June | Boston | 1 | 2 |
| 2000 | 6 June | Boston | 1 | 1 |
| 2002 | 17 Apr | Dublin | 2 | 1 |

**v USSR**

| | | | RI | USSR |
|---|---|---|---|---|
| WC1972 | 18 Oct | Dublin | 1 | 2 |
| WC1973 | 13 May | Moscow | 0 | 1 |
| EC1974 | 30 Oct | Dublin | 3 | 0 |
| EC1975 | 18 May | Kiev | 1 | 2 |
| WC1984 | 12 Sept | Dublin | 1 | 0 |
| WC1985 | 16 Oct | Moscow | 0 | 2 |
| EC1988 | 15 June | Hanover | 1 | 1 |
| 1990 | 25 Apr | Dublin | 1 | 0 |

**v WALES**

| | | | RI | W |
|---|---|---|---|---|
| 1960 | 28 Sept | Dublin | 2 | 3 |
| 1979 | 11 Sept | Swansea | 1 | 2 |
| 1981 | 24 Feb | Dublin | 1 | 3 |
| 1986 | 26 Mar | Dublin | 0 | 1 |
| 1990 | 28 Mar | Dublin | 1 | 0 |
| 1991 | 6 Feb | Wrexham | 3 | 0 |
| 1992 | 19 Feb | Dublin | 0 | 1 |
| 1993 | 17 Feb | Dublin | 2 | 1 |
| 1997 | 11 Feb | Cardiff | 0 | 0 |

**v YUGOSLAVIA**

| | | | RI | Y |
|---|---|---|---|---|
| 1955 | 19 Sept | Dublin | 1 | 4 |
| 1988 | 27 Apr | Dublin | 2 | 0 |
| EC1998 | 18 Nov | Belgrade | 0 | 1 |
| EC1999 | 1 Sept | Dublin | 2 | 1 |

# OTHER BRITISH AND IRISH INTERNATIONAL MATCHES 2003–04

## FRIENDLIES

Ipswich, 20 August 2003, 28,700

**England (1) 3** *(Beckham 10 (pen), Owen 51, Lampard 80)*

**Croatia (0) 1** *(Mornar 78)*

*England:* James (Robinson 46); Neville P (Mills 82), Cole A (Bridge 60), Butt (Lampard 27), Terry, Ferdinand (Upson 60), Beckham (Sinclair 60), Gerrard (Murphy 82), Heskey (Beattie 77), Owen (Dyer 60), Scholes (Cole J 60).
*Croatia:* Pletikosa (Butina 70); Simic (Babic 46), Zivkovic (Seric 73), Tomas, Kovac R, Simunic, Leko (Rosso 60), Maric (Mornar 46), Olic, Kovac N (Agic 73), Rapaic (Srna 46).
*Referee:* Bo Larsen (Denmark).

Old Trafford, 16 November 2003, 64,159

**England (2) 2** *(Rooney 5, Cole J 9)*

**Denmark (2) 3** *(Jorgensen 8, 30 (pen), Tomasson 82)*

*England:* James (Robinson 46); Neville G (Johnson 16), Cole A (Bridge 46), Butt (Neville P 46), Terry, Upson, Beckham (Jenas 66), Lampard, Heskey (Beattie 46), Rooney (Parker 66), Cole J (Murphy 76).
*Denmark:* Sorensen; Helveg (Priske 46), Jensen N, Gravesen, Nielsen (Gaardsoe 71), Henriksen, Wieghorst (Jensen D 29), Jorgensen (Madsen 84), Rommedahl (Perez 19), Sand (Tomasson 46), Gronkjaer (Lovenkrands 61).
*Referee:* Hrinak (Slovakia).

Faro-Loule, 18 February 2004, 27,000

**Portugal (0) 1** *(Pauleta 70)*

**England (0) 1** *(King 47)*

*Portugal:* Ricardo; Paulo Ferreira, Rui Jorge (Valente 46), Petit (Viana 83), Jorge Andrade (Ricardo Carvalho 75), Fernando Couto (Beto 83), Costinha (Deco 46), Figo (Boa Morte 66), Simao Sabrosa (Ronaldo 46), Pauleta (Almeida 78), Rui Costa
*England:* James; Neville P (Mills 46), Cole A (Bridge 18) (Carragher 86), Butt (Jenas 86), Southgate, King, Beckham (Hargreaves 86), Scholes (Dyer 46), Lampard (Cole J 46), Rooney (Heskey 71), Owen (Smith 71).
*Referee:* Kassai (Hungary).

Gothenburg, 31 March 2004, 40,464

**Sweden (0) 1** *(Ibrahimovic 54)*

**England (0) 0**

*Sweden:* Isaksson (Kihistedt 46); Lucic, Edman, Andersson A (Kallstrom 46), Mellberg, Mjallby (Linderoth 46), Nilsson, Svensson A (Jonson 46), Ibrahimovic (Ostlund 90), Elmander (Hansson 46), Wilhelmsson.
*England:* James; Neville P, Carragher, Butt (Parker 78), Terry (Gardner 46), Woodgate (Southgate 46), Hargreaves (Jenas 60), Gerrard (Cole J 60), Rooney (Smith 60), Vassell (Defoe 12), Thompson (Heskey 60).
*Referee:* Ovrebo (Norway).

City of Manchester, 1 June 2004, 38,581

**England (1) 1** *(Owen 22)*

**Japan (0) 1** *(Ono 53)*

*England:* James; Neville G (Neville P 86), Cole A, Gerrard (Hargreaves 82), Terry (King 88), Campbell, Beckham (Cole J 82), Lampard (Butt 82), Rooney (Heskey 77), Owen (Vassell 77), Scholes (Dyer 77).
*Japan:* Narazaki; Kaji, Santos, Tauboi, Miyamoto, Nakazawa, Inamoto (Fukunishi 90), Nakamura, Tamada (Suzuki 60), Kubo (Yanagisawa 60), Ono.
*Referee:* Rosetti (Italy).

City of Manchester, 5 June 2004, 43,500

**England (3) 6** *(Lampard 25, Rooney 27, 38, Vassell 57, 77, Bridge 68)*

**Iceland (1) 1** *(Helguson 42)*

*England:* Robinson (Walker 61); Neville G (Neville P 46), Cole A (Bridge 46), Gerrard (Hargreaves 46), Carragher (Defoe 83), Campbell (King 46), Beckham (Dyer 46), Lampard (Butt 46), Rooney (Vassell 46), Owen (Heskey 46), Scholes (Cole J 46).
*Iceland:* Arason; Gudjonsson T (Gudmundsson J 77), Sigurdsson I (Jonsson 77), Ingimarsson, Marteinsson (Sigurdsson K 46), Hreidarsson, Gudjonsson J (Helgason 86), Gretarsson, Helguson (Gudmundsson T 84), Sigurdsson H (Gudjonsson B 68), Gudjohnsen.
*Referee:* Wegereef (Holland).

Oslo, 20 August 2003, 12,858

**Norway (0) 0**

**Scotland (0) 0**

*Norway:* Johnsen E; Basma (Aas 70), Bergdolmo (Iversen S 68), Hangeland (Andersen T 46), Berg (Johnsen R 46), Lundekvam, Andresen, Johnsen F (Solli 46), Solskjaer, Carew (Flo H 81), Riise.
*Scotland:* Douglas; Ross (Fletcher 60), Dailly, Ferguson B, Webster, Pressley, Cameron (Rae 84), Lambert, Crawford (Devlin 80), Hutchison, Naysmith.
*Referee:* Vuorela (Finland).

Hampden Park, 31 March 2004, 20,433

**Scotland (0) 1** *(McFadden 57)*

**Romania (1) 2** *(Chivu 37, Pancu 51)*

*Scotland:* Gallacher; Alexander, McCann, Kennedy (Crainey 18), Pressley, Dailly, Caldwell G, Rae, Miller (McFadden 51), Thompson S (Crawford 63), Cameron.
*Romania:* Stelea (Lobont 46); Stoican, Rat, Petre O, Iensci, Chivu, Petre F (Mitea 46), Pancu (Danciulescu 89), Cernat (Soava 63), Ganea (Cristea 81), Mutu.
*Referee:* Hyyria (Finland).

Copenhagen, 28 April 2004, 22,885

**Denmark (0) 1** *(Sand 60)*

**Scotland (0) 0**

*Denmark:* Sorensen; Helveg, Jensen N (Perez 46), Jensen C (Sennels 46), Laursen, Henriksen (Kroldrup 66), Jensen D, Wieghorst (Retov 80), Jorgensen (Rommedahl 66), Tomasson (Sand 46), Gronkjaer (Rasmussen 88).
*Scotland:* Gallacher; Caldwell G, Crainey, Holt (Canero 16), Pressley, Mackay, Cameron (McCann 46), Fletcher, Kyle, McFadden, Dailly.
*Referee:* Ingvarsson (Sweden).

Tallinn, 27 May 2004, 4000

**Estonia (0) 0**

**Scotland (0) 1** *(McFadden 76)*

*Estonia:* Kaalma; Allas, Stepanov, Jaager, Klavan, Rahn, Terehov (Reinumae 85), Reim, Viikmae, Oper, Lindpere (Kink 75).
*Scotland:* Gallacher; McNamee, Hughes, Caldwell G, Mackay, Pressley (Webster 46), Fletcher, Holt, Miller (Crawford 79), McFadden (Kerr 89), Quashie.
*Referee:* Poulsen (Denmark).

Easter Road, 30 May 2004, 16,187

**Scotland (4) 4** *(Fletcher 6, Holt 14, Caldwell G 23, Quashie 34)*

**Trinidad & Tobago (0) 1** *(John 55)*

*Scotland:* Gordon; McNamara, McAllister, Caldwell G (Caldwell S 80), Pressley, Mackay (McNamee 85), Quashie (Hughes 72), Fletcher, Crawford (Miller 67),

McFadden (Webster 85), Holt.
*Trinidad & Tobago:* Ince; Edwards (Theobald 90), Mason, Sancho, Cox, Andrews, Eve (Jermot 82), Dwarika (Nixon 74), John, Glen (Boucard 28), Jones (Rojas 46).
*Referee:* Vink (Holland).

Cardiff, 18 February 2004, 47,124

**Wales (2) 4** *(Earnshaw 1, 35, 58, Taylor 78)*

**Scotland (0) 0**

*Wales:* Crossley (Ward 46); Edwards, Gabbidon, Speed (Robinson C 72), Melville (Symons 67), Page, Oster, Savage (Fletcher 72), Earnshaw, Giggs (Taylor 46), Davies (Parry 33).
*Scotland:* Douglas; McNamara, Naysmith (Murty 46), Caldwell S, Ritchie, Dailly, Fletcher (Webster 86), Cameron (Gallagher 68), Pearson (McFadden 46), Miller, Dickov.
*Referee:* Ross (Northern Ireland).

Budapest, 31 March 2004, 15,000

**Hungary (1) 1** *(Kenesei 17 (pen))*

**Wales (1) 2** *(Koumas 20, Earnshaw 81)*

*Hungary:* Babos; Bodnar, Low (Bodor 89), Peto, Stark, Komiosi (Dveri 89), Molnar, Lisztes (Toth 52), Kenesei (Szabics 46), Torghelle (Sebok J 69), Gera.
*Wales:* Jones P (Coyne 46); Gabbidon, Thatcher (Edwards 54), Robinson C (Fletcher 89), Melville, Page, Koumas, Savage, Earnshaw, Taylor, Vaughan (Roberts G 64).
*Referee:* Meyer (Germany).

Oslo, 27 May 2004, 14,137

**Norway (0) 0**

**Wales (0) 0**

*Norway:* Myhre; Basma, Riise, Helstad (Flo T 61), Johnsen R (Andersen 88), Berg (Lundekvam 17), Andresen, Hoset, Solskjaer (Solli 61), Saeternes (Lange 46), Pedersen (Bergdolmo 46).
*Wales:* Coyne; Delaney, Thatcher, Robinson C (Edwards 75), Collins, Gabbidon, Oster (Barnard 90), Fletcher, Earnshaw (Roberts N 71), Bellamy (Llewellyn 80), Parry (Roberts G 71).
*Referee:* Hansson (Sweden).

Wrexham, 30 May 2004, 10,805

**Wales (1) 1** *(Parry 21)*

**Canada (0) 0**

*Wales:* Coyne (Margetson 46); Delaney, Thatcher, Robinson C (Edwards 79), Collins, Gabbidon, Oster, Fletcher, Bellamy, Giggs (Llewellyn 89), Parry (Earnshaw 67).
*Canada:* Onstad; Imhof, Jazic, De Guzman, Watson, De Vos, Hulme (Occean 79), Hutchinson (Peschisolido 46), Radzinski (McKenna 72), De Rosario (Klukowski 83), Brennan (Bircham 46).
*Referee:* McKeon (Republic of Ireland).

Windsor Park, 18 February 2004, 11,288

**Northern Ireland (0) 1** *(Healy 56)*

**Norway (3) 4** *(Pedersen 17, 35, Iversen 43, Gillespie 57 (og))*

*Northern Ireland:* Taylor; Baird, Kennedy (Jones 77), Hughes A, McCartney, Griffin (Williams 46), Gillespie (McVeigh 73), Johnson, Healy, Smith, Hughes M.
*Norway:* Myhre (Holtan 70); Andresen, El Fakiri, Hangeland, Helstad (Hoiland 89), Hoseth, Iversen, Johnsen F, Riise (Hanstveit 70), Rushfeldt (Flo H 46), Pedersen (Odegaard 80).
*Referee:* Thomson (Scotland).

Tallinn, 31 March 2004, 2000

**Estonia (0) 0**

**Northern Ireland (1) 1** *(Healy 45)*

*Estonia:* Kaalma; Jaager, Stepanov, Piiroja (Rahn 81), Klavan, Reim, Smirnov (Reinumae 85), Kristal, Zelinski (Teever 64), Rooba M (Lindpere 73), Kink (Terehhov 71).
*Northern Ireland:* Taylor; Baird, Capaldi, Craigan, Williams, Sonner (Duff M 78), Mulryne (McCann 68), Jeff Whitley, Healy, Smith, Jones.
*Referee:* Petteri (Finland).

Windsor Park, 28 April 2004, 9690

**Northern Ireland (1) 1** *(Quinn 17)*

**Serbia-Montenegro (1) 1** *(Paunovic 7)*

*Northern Ireland:* Taylor (Carroll 46); Baird, Capaldi, Craigan, Williams, Doherty (Hughes M 78), Gillespie (Jones 46), Jeff Whitley (Sonner 78), Healy (Hamilton 46), Quinn (Smith 78), Mulryne (McVeigh 46).
*Serbia-Montenegro:* Kovacevic; Cirkovic (Markoski 83), Dudic, Gavrancic, Dragutinovic (Milivoje Vitakic 46), Nadj, Trobok (Vladimir Ivic 46), Vukic, Kezman, Petokvic, Paunovic (Kolakovic 69).
*Referee:* Richards (Wales).

Waterford, 30 May 2004, 1500

**Barbados (1) 1** *(Skinner 40)*

**Northern Ireland (0) 1** *(Healy 71)*

*Barbados:* Chase; Braithwaite, Burrowes, James, Parris, Forde (Goodridge 46), Grosvenor, Hall, Lovell (Hawkesworth), Lucas (Burgess), Skinner (Riley 65).
*Northern Ireland:* Taylor; Baird (Jones 67), Capaldi (Elliott 67), Craigan, Williams■, Johnson, Gillespie (Murdock 46), Sonner (McVeigh 67), Healy (Hamilton 80), Quinn, Mulryne (Smith 46).
*Referee:* Brizan (Trinidad & Tobago).

Basseterre, 2 June 2004, 1800

**St Kitts & Nevis (0) 0**

**Northern Ireland (0) 2** *(Healy 81, Jones 86)*

*St Kitts & Nevis:* Byron (Benjamin 85); Lewis, Eddy (Lawrence 87), Leader, Saddler K (Sargeant 75), Isaac, Huggins (Saddler A 75), Burton (Riley 54), Gomez, Lake (Francis 59), Gumbs.
*Northern Ireland:* Taylor; Baird, Capaldi, Craigan, Murdock, Jeff Whitley (Johnson 65), McVeigh (Mulryne 65), Sonner (Jones 52), Hamilton (Healy 65), Smith, Elliott (Gillespie 65).
*Referee:* Matthews (St Kitts & Nevis).

Bacolet, 6 June 2004, 5100

**Trinidad & Tobago (0) 0**

**Northern Ireland (2) 3** *(Healy 4, 65, Elliott 41)*

*Trinidad & Tobago:* Ince; Sancho (Thomas 46), Cox, Andrews, Rougier (Roberts 76), Eve, Jemmott (Theobald 83), Boucard (Fitzwilliams 68), Edwards, Mason (Yorke 46), John.
*Northern Ireland:* Taylor (Mannus 82); Baird, Capaldi, Craigan (Murdock 46), Williams, Jeff Whitley, Johnson (Gillespie 72), Mulryne (Sonner 72), Healy (McVeigh 66), Quinn (Smith 61), Elliott (Jones 46).
*Referee:* Callender (Barbados).

Dublin, 19 August 2003, 37,200

**Republic of Ireland (0) 2** *(O'Shea 74, Morrison 81)*

**Australia (0) 1** *(Viduka 49)*

*Republic of Ireland:* Colgan; Carr (Harte 57), O'Shea, Holland (Healy 19), Breen (O'Brien 46), Cunningham (Dunne 84), Finnan (Kilbane 66), Kinsella, Doherty (Morrison 57), Robbie Keane (Connolly 46), Duff (Quinn 80).
*Australia:* Schwarzer; Neill, Lazaridis, Okon (Grelia 66), Foxe, Popovic, Emerton, Bresciano, Viduka (Aloisi 78), Chipperfield, Tiatto (Vidmar 69).
*Referee:* Vidlak (Czech Republic).

Dublin, 9 September 2003, 27,000

**Republic of Ireland (1) 2** *(Connolly 35, Dunne 90)*

**Turkey (0) 2** *(Hakan Sukur 51, Okan Y 86)*

*Republic of Ireland:* Colgan (Murphy 72); Finnan, Harte (Carr 90), Healy (McPhail 86), Breen (Morrison 86), O'Brien (Dunne 72), Kinsella, Connolly, Doherty, Kilbane, Duff (Reid S 46).
*Turkey:* Rustu (Omer 61) (Zafer 86); Fatih, Ergun, Tugay (Ahmet 72), Bulent K (Umit D 86), Tayfun (Deniz 46), Alpay (Okan B 46), Emre (Gokdeniz 61), Hakan Sukur (Tumer 86), Tuncay (Okan Y 72), Hasan Sas (Ibrahim 46).
*Referee:* Wegereef (Holland).

Dublin, 18 November 2003, 23,253

**Republic of Ireland (0) 3** *(Duff 23, Robbie Keane 60, 84)*

**Canada (0) 0**

*Republic of Ireland:* Given (Colgan 82); Carr (Harte 46), O'Shea (Thompson 87), Kavanagh (Holland 11), Dunne, Cunningham, Reid S (Delap 61), Reid A (McPhail 73), Doherty (Morrison 46), Robbie Keane, Duff (Kilbane 87).
*Canada:* Hirschfeld; Stalteri, Jazic, Bircham (Nash 79), De Vos (Rogers 82), McKenna, Bent, Imhof, Radzinski, Peschisolido (Bernier 75), Hastings (Fenwick 87).
*Referee:* Whitby (Wales).

Dublin, 18 February 2004, 44,000

**Republic of Ireland (0) 0**

**Brazil (0) 0**

*Republic of Ireland:* Given; Carr, O'Shea, Holland, O'Brien, Cunningham, Kilbane, Kavanagh, Robbie Keane, Morrison, Reid A (McAteer 64).
*Brazil:* Dida; Cafu, Roberto Carlos, Silva (Edmilson 14), Roque Junior, Lucio, Kleberson (Julio Baptista 46), Kaka, Ronaldo, Ronaldinho, Ze Roberto.
*Referee:* Frisk (Sweden).

Dublin, 31 March 2004, 42,000

**Republic of Ireland (0) 2** *(Harte 52, Robbie Keane 90)*

**Czech Republic (0) 1** *(Baros 81)*

*Republic of Ireland:* Given (Kenny 82); Maybury, Harte, Holland, Doherty (Miller 70), Cunningham, Reid A (Delap 66), Kilbane, Robbie Keane, Morrison (Lee 76), Duff (Kinsella 76).
*Czech Republic:* Cech (Vaniak 46); Giranek (Plasil 69), Jankulovski, Galasek, Bolf (Rozehnal 58), Ujfalusi, Sionko (Stajner 46), Tyce, Baros (Vorisek 84), Koller (Lokvenc 46), Nedved (Heinz 46).
*Referee:* Fisker (Denmark).

Bydgoszcz, 28 April 2004, 18,000

**Poland (0) 0**

**Republic of Ireland (0) 0**

*Poland:* Dudek (Boruc 58); Zewlakow (Kaczorowski 83), Rzasa, Szymkowiak (Radomski 85), Klos (Bosacki 80), Glowacki (Hajto 46), Lewandowski, Zurawski, Olisadebe (Niedzielan 46), Krzynowek (Kosowski 46), Mila (Smolarek 65).
*Republic of Ireland:* Given (Colgan 70); O'Shea, Harte (Maybury 63), Miller, Doherty (O'Brien 80), Cunningham, Reid S, Kinsella, Reid A (Douglas 80), Morrison (Byrne 89), Lee (Barrett 63).
*Referee:* Shebek (Ukraine).

Dublin, 27 May 2004, 42,356

**Republic of Ireland (0) 1** *(Holland 85)*

**Romania (0) 0**

*Republic of Ireland:* Given; Finnan, Maybury, Roy Keane, O'Brien, Cunningham, Miller, Holland, Robbie Keane, Morrison, Reid A (Rowlands 78).
*Romania:* Lobont (Stelea 46); Dumitru, Dancia (Petre M 78), Plesan (Alluta 61), Icensi (Barcuan 90), Ghianes, Radoi (Constianin 84), Soava (Petre O 90), Danciulescu (Neaga 61), Ganea (Niculae 88), Dica (Alexa 78).
*Referee:* Jara (Czech Republic).

Charlton, 29 May 2004, 7438

**Republic of Ireland (0) 0**

**Nigeria (1) 3** *(Ogbeche 36, 69, Martins 49)*

*Republic of Ireland:* Colgan; Finnan, Maybury (Clarke 46), Holland (Douglas 67), Doherty, Cunningham, Miller (Rowlands 46), Kinsella, Robbie Keane (Barrett 84), Lee, McPhail.
*Nigeria:* Rotimi; Abbey (Adamu 90), Lawal, Olofinjana (Obiefule 86), Olajengbesi, Enakhire, Utaka, Obodo, Martins (Showunmi 84), Ogbeche (Baita 72), Ekwueme.
*Referee:* D'Urso (England).

Charlton, 2 June 2004, 6155

**Republic of Ireland (1) 1** *(Barrett 26)*

**Jamaica (0) 0**

*Republic of Ireland:* Kenny; Maybury, O'Shea (Clarke 46), Quinn (Holland 83), Doherty, O'Brien, Barrett, Kinsella, Morrison, Lee (McGeady 83), Reid A (Rowlands 77).
*Jamaica:* Ricketts; Neil, Reid, Chin-Sue (Langley 66), Stewart, Goodison, Davis, Hyde, Lisbie (Johnson 83), King (Dobson 85), Burton (Bernard 83).
*Referee:* Styles (England).

Amsterdam, 5 June 2004, 43,000

**Holland (0) 0**

**Republic of Ireland (1) 1** *(Robbie Keane 45)*

*Holland:* Van der Sar; Reiziger (Heitinga 46), Van Bronckhorst, Cocu, Stam, Bouma (Van Hooijdonk 84), Sneijder (Seedorf 46) (Bosvelt 63), Van der Vaart, Davids (Robben 63), Van Nistelrooy (Makaay 66), Kluivert (Van der Meyde 46).
*Republic of Ireland:* Given; Finnan, Maybury (Doyle 88), Holland, Cunningham, O'Brien, Barrett, Quinn, Robbie Keane, Morrison (Lee 83), Reid A.
*Referee:* Dean (England).

# INTERNATIONAL APPEARANCES 1872–2004

This is a list of full international appearances by Englishmen, Irishmen, Scotsmen and Welshmen in matches against the Home Countries and against foreign nations. It does not include unofficial matches against Commonwealth and Empire countries. The year indicated refers to the season; ie 2004 is the 2003–04 season.
Explanatory code for matches played by all five countries: A represents Austria; Alb, Albania; Alg, Algeria; An, Angola; And, Andorra; Arg, Argentina; Arm, Armenia; Aus, Australia; Az, Azerbaijan; B, Bohemia; Bar, Barbados; Bel, Belgium; Bl, Belarus; Bol, Bolivia; Bos, Bosnia; Br, Brazil; Bul, Bulgaria; C,CIS; Ca, Canada; Cam, Cameroon; Ch, Chile; Chn, China; Co, Colombia; Cr, Costa Rica; Cro, Croatia; Cy, Cyprus; Cz, Czechoslovakia; CzR, Czech Republic; D, Denmark; E, England; Ec, Ecuador; Ei, Republic of Ireland; EG, East Germany; Eg, Egypt; Es, Estonia; F, France; Fa, Faeroes; Fi, Finland; G, Germany; Ge, Georgia; Gh, Ghana; Gr, Greece; H, Hungary; Hk, Hong Kong; Ho, Holland; Hon, Honduras; I, Italy; Ic, Iceland; Ir, Iran; Is, Israel; J, Japan; Jam, Jamaica; K, Kuwait; L, Luxembourg; La, Latvia; Li, Lithuania; Lie, Liechtenstein; M, Mexico; Ma, Malta; Mac, Macedonia; Mal, Malaysia; Mol, Moldova; Mor, Morocco; N, Norway; Ng, Nigeria; Ni, Northern Ireland; Nz, New Zealand; P, Portugal; Para, Paraguay; Pe, Peru; Pol, Poland; R, Romania; RCS, Republic of Czechs and Slovaks; R of E, Rest of Europe; R of UK, Rest of United Kingdom; R of W, Rest of World; Ru, Russia; S.Af, South Africa; S.Ar, Saudi Arabia; S, Scotland; Se, Sweden; Ser, Serbia-Montenegro; Sk, South Korea; Slovakia; Slv, Slovenia; Sm, San Marino; Sp, Spain; Stk, St Kitts & Nevis; Slo Sw, Switzerland; T, Turkey; Th, Thailand; Tr, Trinidad & Tobago; Tun, Tunisia; U, Uruguay; Uk, Ukraine; US, United States of America; USSR, Soviet Union; W, Wales; WG, West Germany; Y, Yugoslavia; Z, Zaire.
*As at July 2004.*

## ENGLAND

Abbott, W. (Everton), 1902 v W (1)
A'Court, A. (Liverpool), 1958 v Ni, Br, A, USSR; 1959 v W (5)
Adams, T. A. (Arsenal), 1987 v Sp, T, Br; 1988 v WG, T, Y, Ho, H, S, Co, Sw, Ei, Ho, USSR; 1989 v D, Se, S.Ar.; 1991 v Ei (2); 1993 v N, T, Sm, T, Ho, Pol, N; 1994 v Pol, Ho, D, Gr, N; 1995 v US, R, Ei, U; 1996 v Co, N, Sw, P, Chn, Sw, S, Ho, Sp, G; 1997 v Ge (2); 1998 v I, Ch, P, S.Ar, Tun, R, Co, Arg; 1999 v Se, F; 2000 v L, Pol, Bel, S (2), Uk, P; 2001 v F, G (66)
Adcock, H. (Leicester C), 1929 v F, Bel, Sp; 1930 v Ni, W (5)
Alcock, C. W. (Wanderers), 1875 v S (1)
Alderson, J. T. (C Palace), 1923 v F (1)
Aldridge, A. (WBA), 1888 v Ni; (with Walsall Town Swifts), 1889 v Ni (2)
Allen, A. (Stoke C) 1960 v Se, W, Ni (3)
Allen, A. (Aston Villa), 1888 v Ni (1)
Allen, C. (QPR), 1984 v Br (sub), U, Ch; (with Tottenham H), 1987 v T; 1988 v Is (5)
Allen, H. (Wolverhampton W), 1888 v S, W, Ni; 1889 v S; 1890 v S (5)
Allen, J. P. (Portsmouth), 1934 v Ni, W (2)
Allen, R. (WBA), 1952 v Sw; 1954 v Y, S; 1955 v WG, W (5)
Alsford, W. J. (Tottenham H), 1935 v S (1)
Amos, A. (Old Carthusians), 1885 v S; 1886 v W (2)
Anderson, R. D. (Old Etonians), 1879 v W (1)
Anderson, S. (Sunderland), 1962 v A, S (2)
Anderson, V. (Nottingham F), 1979 v Cz, Se; 1980 v Bul, Sp; 1981 v N, R, W, S; 1982 v Ni, Ic; 1984 v Ni; (with Arsenal), 1985 v T, Ni, Ei, R, Fi, S, M, US; 1986 v USSR, M; 1987 v Se, Ni (2), Y, Sp, T; (with Manchester U), 1988 v WG, H, Co (30)
Anderton, D. R. (Tottenham H), 1994 v D, Gr, N; 1995 v US, Ei, U, J, Se, Br; 1996 v H, Chn, Sw, S, Ho, Sp, G; 1998 v S.Ar, Mor, Tun, R, Co, Arg; 1999 v Se, Bul, L, CzR, F; 2001 v F, I (sub); 2002 v Se (sub) (30)
Angus, J. (Burnley), 1961 v A (1)
Armfield, J. C. (Blackpool), 1959 v Br, Pe, M, US; 1960 v Y, Sp, H, S; 1961 v L, P, Sp, M, I, A, W, Ni, S; 1962 v A, Sw, Pe, W, Ni, S, L, P, H, Arg, Bul, Br; 1963 v F (2), Br, EG, Sw, Ni, W, S; 1964 v R of W, W, Ni, S; 1966 v Y, Fi (43)
Armitage, G. H. (Charlton Ath), 1926 v Ni (1)
Armstrong, D. (Middlesbrough), 1980 v Aus; (with Southampton), 1983 v WG; 1984 v W (3)
Armstrong, K. (Chelsea), 1955 v S (1)
Arnold, J. (Fulham), 1933 v S (1)
Arthur, J. W. H. (Blackburn R), 1885 v S, W, Ni; 1886 v S, W; 1887 v W, Ni (7)
Ashcroft, J. (Woolwich Arsenal), 1906 v Ni, W, S (3)
Ashmore, G. S. (WBA), 1926 v Bel (1)
Ashton, C. T. (Corinthians), 1926 v Ni (1)
Ashurst, W. (Notts Co), 1923 v Se (2); 1925 v S, W, Bel (5)
Astall, G. (Birmingham C), 1956 v Fi, WG (2)
Astle, J. (WBA), 1969 v W; 1970 v S, P, Br (sub), Cz (5)
Aston, J. (Manchester U), 1949 v S, W, D, Sw, Se, N, F; 1950 v S, W, Ni, Ei, I, P, Bel, Ch, US; 1951 v Ni (17)
Athersmith, W. C. (Aston Villa), 1892 v Ni, 1897 v S, W, Ni; 1898 v S, W, Ni; 1899 v S, W, Ni; 1900 v S, W (12)
Atyeo, P. J. W. (Bristol C), 1956 v Br, Se, Sp; 1957 v D, Ei (2) (6)
Austin, S. W. (Manchester C), 1926 v Ni (1)
Bach, P. (Sunderland), 1899 v Ni (1)
Bache, J. W. (Aston Villa), 1903 v W; 1904 v W, Ni; 1905 v S; 1907 v Ni; 1910 v Ni; 1911 v S (7)
Baddeley, T. (Wolverhampton W), 1903 v S, Ni; 1904 v S, W, Ni (5)
Bagshaw, J. J. (Derby Co), 1920 v Ni (1)
Bailey, G. R. (Manchester U), 1985 v Ei, M (2)
Bailey, H. P. (Leicester Fosse), 1908 v W, A (2), H, B (5)
Bailey, M. A. (Charlton Ath), 1964 v US; 1965 v W (2)
Bailey, N. C. (Clapham Rovers), 1878 v S; 1879 v S, W; 1880 v S; 1881 v S; 1882 v S, W; 1883 v S, W; 1884 v S, W, Ni; 1885 v S, W, Ni; 1886 v S, W; 1887 v S, W (19)
Baily, E. F. (Tottenham H), 1950 v Sp; 1951 v Y, Ni, W; 1952 v A (2), Sw, W; 1953 v Ni (9)
Bain, J. (Oxford University), 1887 v S (1)
Baker, A. (Arsenal), 1928 v W (1)
Baker, B. H. (Everton), 1921 v Bel; (with Chelsea), 1926 v Ni (2)
Baker, J. H. (Hibernian), 1960 v Y, Sp, H, Ni, S; (with Arsenal) 1966 v Sp, Pol, Ni (8)
Ball, A. J. (Blackpool), 1965 v Y, WG, Se; 1966 v S, Sp, Fi, D, U, Arg, P, WG (2), Pol (2); (with Everton), 1967 v W, S, Ni, A, Cz, Sp; 1968 v W, S, USSR, Sp (2), Y, WG; 1969 v Ni, W, S, R (2), M, Br, U; 1970 v P, Co, Ec, R, Br, Cz (sub), WG, W, S, Bel; 1971 v Ma, EG, Gr, Ma (sub), Ni, S; 1972 v Sw, Gr; (with Arsenal) WG (2), S; 1973 v W (3), Y, S (2), Cz, Ni, Pol; 1974 v P (sub); 1975 v WG, Cy (2), Ni, W, S (72)
Ball, J. (Bury), 1928 v Ni (1)
Ball, M. J. (Everton), 2001 v Sp (sub) (1)
Balmer, W. (Everton), 1905 v Ni (1)
Bamber, J. (Liverpool), 1921 v W (1)
Bambridge, A. L. (Swifts), 1881 v W; 1883 v W; 1884 v Ni (3)
Bambridge, E. C. (Swifts), 1879 v S; 1880 v S; 1881 v S; 1882 v S, W, Ni; 1883 v W; 1884 v S, W, Ni; 1885 v S, W, Ni; 1886 v S, W; 1887 v S, W, Ni (18)
Bambridge, E. H. (Swifts), 1876 v S (1)
Banks, G. (Leicester C), 1963 v S, Br, Cz, EG; 1964 v W, Ni, S, R of W, U, P (2), US, Arg; 1965 v Ni, S, H, Y, WG, Se; 1966 v Ni, S, Sp, Pol (2), WG (2), Y, Fi, U, M, F, Arg, P; 1967 v Ni, W, S, Cz; (with Stoke C), 1968 v W, Ni, S, USSR (2), Sp, WG, Y; 1969 v Ni, S, R (2), F, U, Br; 1970 v W, Ni, S, Ho, Bel, Co, Ec, R, Br, Cz; 1971 v Gr, Ma (2), Ni, S; 1972 v Sw, Gr, WG (2), W, S (73)
Banks, H. E. (Millwall), 1901 v Ni (1)
Banks, T. (Bolton W), 1958 v USSR (3), Br, A; 1959 v Ni (6)
Bannister, W. (Burnley), 1901 v W; (with Bolton W), 1902 v Ni (2)
Barclay, R. (Sheffield U), 1932 v S; 1933 v Ni; 1936 v S (3)
Bardsley, D. J. (QPR), 1993 v Sp (sub), Pol (2)
Barham, M. (Norwich C), 1983 v Aus (2) (2)
Barkas, S. (Manchester C), 1936 v Bel; 1937 v S; 1938 v W, Ni, Cz (5)
Barker, J. (Derby Co), 1935 v I, Ho, S, W, Ni; 1936 v G, A, S, W, Ni; 1937 v W (11)
Barker, R. (Herts Rangers), 1872 v S (1)
Barker, R. R. (Casuals), 1895 v W (1)
Barlow, R. J. (WBA), 1955 v Ni (1)
Barmby, N. J. (Tottenham H), 1995 v U (sub), Se (sub); (with Middlesbrough), 1996 v Co, N, P, Chn, Sw (sub), Ho (sub), Sp (sub); 1997 v Mol; (with Everton), 2000 v Br (sub), Uk

(sub), Ma, G (sub), R (sub); (with Liverpool), 2001 v F, G, I, Sp; 2002 v Ho (sub), G, Alb, Gr (23)
Barnes, J. (Watford), 1983 v Ni (sub), Aus (sub), Aus (2); 1984 v D, L (sub), F (sub), S, USSR, Br, U, Ch; 1985 v EG, Fi, T, Ni, R, Fi, S, I (sub), M, WG (sub), US (sub); 1986 v R (sub), Is (sub), M (sub), Ca (sub), Arg (sub); 1987 v Se, T (sub), Br; (with Liverpool), 1988 v WG, T, Y, Is, Ho, S, Co, Sw, Ei, Ho, USSR; 1989 v Se, Gr, Alb, Pol, D; 1990 v Se, I, Br, D, U, Tun, Ei, Ho, Eg, Bel, Cam; 1991 v H, Pol, Cam, Ei, T, USSR, Arg; 1992 v Cz, Fi; 1993 v Sm, T, Ho, Pol, US, G; 1995 v US, R, Ng, U, Se; 1996 v Co (sub) (79)
Barnes, P. S. (Manchester C), 1978 v I, WG, Br, W, S, H; 1979 v D, Ei, Cz, Ni (2), S, Bul, A; (with WBA), 1980 v D, W; 1981 v Sp (sub), Br, W, Sw (sub); (with Leeds U), 1982 v N (sub), Ho (sub) (22)
Barnet, H. H. (Royal Engineers), 1882 v Ni (1)
Barrass, M. W. (Bolton W), 1952 v W, Ni; 1953 v S (3)
Barrett, A. F. (Fulham), 1930 v Ni (1)
Barrett, E. D. (Oldham Ath), 1991 v Nz; (with Aston Villa), 1993 v Br, G (3)
Barrett, J. W. (West Ham U), 1929 v Ni (1)
Barry, G. (Aston Villa), 2000 v Uk (sub), Ma (sub); 2001 v F, G (sub), Fi, I ; 2003 v S.Af (sub), Ser (sub) (8)
Barry, L. (Leicester C), 1928 v F, Bel; 1929 v F, Bel, Sp (5)
Barson, F. (Aston Villa), 1920 v W (1)
Barton, J. (Blackburn R), 1890 v Ni (1)
Barton, P. H. (Birmingham), 1921 v Bel; 1922 v Ni; 1923 v F; 1924 v Bel, S, W; 1925 v Ni (7)
Barton, W. D. (Wimbledon), 1995 v Ei; (with Newcastle U), Se, Br (sub) (3)
Bassett, W. I. (WBA), 1888 v Ni, 1889 v S, W; 1890 v S, W; 1891 v S, Ni; 1892 v S; 1893 v S, W; 1894 v S; 1895 v S, Ni; 1896 v S, W, Ni (16)
Bastard, S. R. (Upton Park), 1880 v S (1)
Bastin, C. S. (Arsenal), 1932 v W; 1933 v I, Sw; 1934 v S, Ni, W, H, Cz; 1935 v S, Ni, I; 1936 v S, W, G, A; 1937 v W, Ni; 1938 v S, G, Sw, F (21)
Batty, D. (Leeds U), 1991 v USSR (sub), Arg, Aus, Nz, Mal; 1992 v G, T, H (sub), F, Se; 1993 v N, Sm, US, Br; (with Blackburn R), 1994 v D (sub); 1995 v J, Br; (with Newcastle U), 1997 v Mol (sub), Ge, I, M, Ge, S.Af (sub), Pol (sub), F; 1998 v Mol, I, Ch, Sw (sub), P, S.Ar, Tun, R, Co (sub), Arg (sub); 1999 v Bul (sub), L; (with Leeds U), H, Se, Bul; 2000 v L, Pol (42)
Baugh, R. (Stafford Road), 1886 v Ni; (with Wolverhampton W) 1890 v Ni (2)
Bayliss, A. E. J. M. (WBA), 1891 v Ni (1)
Baynham, R. L. (Luton T), 1956 v Ni, D, Sp (3)
Beardsley, P. A. (Newcastle U), 1986 v Eg (sub), Is, USSR, M, Ca (sub), P (sub), Pol, Para, Arg; 1987 v Ni (2), Y, Sp, Br, S; (with Liverpool), 1988 v WG, T, Y, Is, Ho, H, S, Co, Sw, Ei, Ho; 1989 v D, Se, S.Ar, Gr (sub), Alb (sub+1), Pol, D; 1990 v Se, Pol, I, Br, U (sub), Tun (sub), Ei, Eg (sub), Cam (sub), WG, I; 1991 v Pol (sub), Ei (2), USSR (sub); (with Newcastle U), 1994 v D, Gr, N; 1995 v Ng, Ei, U, J, Se; 1996 v P (sub), Chn (sub) (59)
Beasant, D. J. (Chelsea), 1990 v I (sub), Y (sub) (2)
Beasley, A. (Huddersfield T), 1939 v S (1)
Beats, W. E. (Wolverhampton W), 1901 v W; 1902 v S (2)
Beattie, J. S. (Southampton), 2003 v Aus, Ser (sub); 2004 v Cro (sub), Lie, D (sub) (5)
Beattie, T. K. (Ipswich T), 1975 v Cy (2), S; 1976 v Sw, P; 1977 v Fi, I (sub), Ho; 1978 v L (sub) (9)
Beckham, D. R. J. (Manchester U), 1997 v Mol, Pol, Ge, I, Ge, S.Af (sub), Pol, I, F; 1998 v Mol, I, Cam, P, S.Ar, Bel (sub), R (sub), Co, Arg; 1999 v L, CzR, F, Pol, Se; 2000 v L, Pol, S(2), Arg, Br, Uk, Ma, P, G, R; 2001 v F, G, I, Sp, Fi, Alb, M, Gr; 2002 v Ho, G, Alb, Gr, Se, Ho, I, Se, Arg, Ng, D, Br; 2003 v Slo, Mac, Aus, Lie, T, S.Af; (with Real Madrid), 2004 v Cro, Mac, Lie, T, D, P, J, Ic, F, Sw, Cro, P (72)
Becton, F. (Preston NE), 1895 v Ni; (with Liverpool), 1897 v W (2)
Bedford, H. (Blackpool), 1923 v Se; 1925 v Ni (2)
Bell, C. (Manchester C), 1968 v Se, WG; 1969 v W, Bul, F, U, Br; 1970 v Ni (sub), Ho (2), P, Br (sub), Cz, WG (sub); 1972 v Gr, WG (2), W, Ni, S; 1973 v W (3), Y, S (2), Ni, Cz, Pol; 1974 v A, Pol, I, W, Ni, S, Arg, EG, Bul, Y; 1975 v Cz, P, WG, Cy (2), Ni, S; 1976 v Sw, Cz (48)
Bennett, W. (Sheffield U), 1901 v S, W (2)
Benson, R. W. (Sheffield U), 1913 v Ni (1)
Bentley, R. T. F. (Chelsea), 1949 v Se; 1950 v S, P, Bel, Ch, USA; 1953 v W, Bel; 1955 v W, WG, Sp, P (12)
Beresford, J. (Aston Villa), 1934 v Cz (1)
Berry, A. (Oxford University), 1909 v Ni (1)
Berry, J. J. (Manchester U), 1953 v Arg, Ch, U; 1956 v Se (4)
Bestall, J. G. (Grimsby T), 1935 v Ni (1)
Betmead, H. A. (Grimsby T), 1937 v Fi (1)
Betts, M. P. (Old Harrovians), 1877 v S (1)
Betts, W. (Sheffield W), 1889 v W (1)
Beverley, J. (Blackburn R), 1884 v S, W, Ni (3)
Birkett, R. H. (Clapham Rovers), 1879 v S (1)
Birkett, R. J. E. (Middlesbrough), 1936 v Ni (1)
Birley, F. H. (Oxford University), 1874 v S; (with Wanderers), 1875 v S (2)
Birtles, G. (Nottingham F), 1980 v Arg (sub), I; 1981 v R (3)
Bishop, S. M. (Leicester C), 1927 v S, Bel, L, F (4)
Blackburn, F. (Blackburn R), 1901 v S; 1902 v Ni; 1904 v S (3)
Blackburn, G. F. (Aston Villa), 1924 v F (1)
Blenkinsop, E. (Sheffield W), 1928 v F, Bel; 1929 v S, W, Ni, F, Bel, Sp; 1930 v S, W, Ni, G, A; 1931 v S, W, Ni, F, Bel; 1932 v S, W, Ni, Sp; 1933 v S, W, Ni, A (26)
Bliss, H. (Tottenham H), 1921 v S (1)
Blissett, L. (Watford), 1983 v WG (sub), L, W, Gr (sub), H, Ni, S (sub), Aus (1+1 sub); (with AC Milan), 1984 v D (sub), H, W (sub), S, USSR (14)
Blockley, J. P. (Arsenal), 1973 v Y (1)
Bloomer, S. (Derby Co), 1895 v S, Ni; 1896 v W, Ni; 1897 v S, W, Ni; 1898 v S; 1899 v S, W, Ni; 1900 v S; 1901 v S, W; 1902 v S, W, Ni; 1904 v S; 1905 v S, W, Ni; (with Middlesbrough), 1907 v S, W (23)
Blunstone, F. (Chelsea), 1955 v W, S, F, P; 1957 v Y (5)
Bond, R. (Preston NE), 1905 v Ni, W; 1906 v S, W, Ni; (with Bradford C), 1910 v S, W, Ni (8)
Bonetti, P. P. (Chelsea), 1966 v D; 1967 v Sp, A; 1968 v Sp; 1970 v Ho, P, WG (7)
Bonsor, A. G. (Wanderers), 1873 v S; 1875 v S (2)
Booth, F. (Manchester C), 1905 v Ni (1)
Booth, T. (Blackburn R), 1898 v W; (with Everton), 1903 v S (2)
Bould, S. A. (Arsenal), 1994 v Gr, N (2)
Bowden, E. R. (Arsenal), 1935 v W, I; 1936 v W, Ni, A; 1937 v H (6)
Bower, A. G. (Corinthians), 1924 v Ni, Bel; 1925 v W, Bel; 1927 v W (5)
Bowers, J. W. (Derby Co), 1934 v S, Ni, W (3)
Bowles, S. (QPR), 1974 v P, W, Ni; 1977 v I, Ho (5)
Bowser, S. (WBA), 1920 v Ni (1)
Bowyer, L. D. (Leeds U), 2003 v P (1)
Boyer, P. J. (Norwich C), 1976 v W (1)
Boyes, W. (WBA), 1935 v Ho; (with Everton), 1939 v W, R of E (3)
Boyle, T. W. (Burnley), 1913 v Ni (1)
Brabrook, P. (Chelsea), 1958 v USSR; 1959 v Ni; 1960 v Sp (3)
Bracewell, P. W. (Everton), 1985 v WG (sub), US; 1986 v Ni (3)
Bradford, G. R. W. (Bristol R), 1956 v D (1)
Bradford, J. (Birmingham), 1924 v Ni; 1925 v Bel; 1928 v S; 1929 v Ni, W, F, Sp; 1930 v S, Ni, G, A; 1931 v W (12)
Bradley, W. (Manchester U), 1959 v I, US, M (sub) (3)
Bradshaw, F. (Sheffield W), 1908 v A (1)
Bradshaw, T. H. (Liverpool), 1897 v Ni (1)
Bradshaw, W. (Blackburn R), 1910 v W, Ni; 1912 v Ni; 1913 v W (4)
Brann, G. (Swifts), 1886 v S, W; 1891 v W (3)
Brawn, W. F. (Aston Villa), 1904 v W, Ni (2)
Bray, J. (Manchester C), 1935 v W; 1936 v S, W, Ni, G; 1937 v S (6)
Brayshaw, E. (Sheffield W), 1887 v Ni (1)
Bridge W. M. (Southampton), 2002 v Ho, I, Para, Sk (sub), Cam, Arg (sub), Ng (sub); 2003 v P (sub), Mac, Lie, T, Ser (sub); (with Chelsea), 2004 v Cro (sub), Lie, D (sub), P (sub), Ic (sub) (17)
Bridges, B. J. (Chelsea), 1965 v S, H, Y; 1966 v A (4)
Bridgett, A. (Sunderland), 1905 v S; 1908 v S, A (2), H, B; 1909 v Ni, W, H (2), A (11)
Brindle, T. (Darwen), 1880 v S, W (2)
Brittleton, J. T. (Sheffield W), 1912 v S, W, Ni; 1913 v S; 1914 v W (5)
Britton, C. S. (Everton), 1935 v S, W, Ni, I; 1937 v S, Ni, H, N, Se (9)
Broadbent, P. F. (Wolverhampton W), 1958 v USSR; 1959 v S, W, Ni, I, Br; 1960 v S (7)
Broadis, I. A. (Manchester C), 1952 v S, A, I; 1953 v S, Arg, Ch, U, US; (with Newcastle U), 1954 v S, H, Y, Bel, Sw, U (14)
Brockbank, J. (Cambridge University), 1872 v S (1)
Brodie, J. B. (Wolverhampton W), 1889 v S, Ni; 1891 v Ni (3)
Bromilow, T. G. (Liverpool), 1921 v W; 1922 v S, W; 1923 v Bel; 1926 v Ni (5)
Bromley-Davenport, W. E. (Oxford University), 1884 v S, W (2)

Brook, E. F. (Manchester C), 1930 v Ni; 1933 v Sw: 1934 v S, W, Ni, F, H, Cz; 1935 v S, W, Ni, I; 1936 v S, W, Ni; 1937 v H; 1938 v W, Ni (18)
Brooking, T. D. (West Ham U), 1974 v P, Arg, EG, Bul, Y; 1975 v Cz (sub), P; 1976 v P, W, Br, I, Fi; 1977 v Ei, Fi, I, Ho, Ni, W; 1978 v I, WG, W, S (sub), H; 1979 v D, Ei, Ni, W (sub), S, Bul, Se (sub), A; 1980 v D, Ni, Arg (sub), W, Ni, S, Bel, Sp; 1981 v Sw, Sp, R, H; 1982 v H, S, Fi, Sp (sub) (47)
Brooks, J. (Tottenham H), 1957 v W, Y, D (3)
Broome, F. H. (Aston Villa), 1938 v G, Sw, F; 1939 v N, I, R, Y (7)
Brown, A. (Aston Villa), 1882 v S, W, Ni (3)
Brown, A. S. (Sheffield U), 1904 v W; 1906 v Ni (2)
Brown, A. (WBA), 1971 v W (1)
Brown, G. (Huddersfield T), 1927 v S, W, Ni, Bel, L, F; 1928 v W; 1929 v S; (with Aston Villa), 1933 v W (9)
Brown, J. (Blackburn R), 1881 v W; 1882 v Ni; 1885 v S, W, Ni (5)
Brown, J. H. (Sheffield W), 1927 v S, W, Bel, L, F; 1930 v Ni (6)
Brown, K. (West Ham U), 1960 v Ni (1)
Brown, W. (West Ham U), 1924 v Bel (1)
Brown, W. M. (Manchester U), 1999 v H; 2001 v Fi (sub), Alb (sub); 2002 v Ho, Sk (sub), Cam; 2003 v Aus (sub) (7)
Bruton, J. (Burnley), 1928 v F, Bel; 1929 v S (3)
Bryant, W. I. (Clapton), 1925 v F (1)
Buchan, C. M. (Sunderland), 1913 v Ni; 1920 v W; 1921 v W, Bel; 1923 v F; 1924 v S (6)
Buchanan, W. S. (Clapham R), 1876 v S (1)
Buckley, F. C. (Derby Co), 1914 v Ni (1)
Bull, S. G. (Wolverhampton W), 1989 v S (sub), D (sub); 1990 v Y, Cz, D (sub), U (sub), Tun (sub), Ei (sub), Ho (sub), Eg, Bel (sub); 1991 v H, Pol (13)
Bullock, F. E. (Huddersfield T), 1921 v Ni (1)
Bullock, N. (Bury), 1923 v Bel; 1926 v W; 1927 v Ni (3)
Burgess, H. (Manchester C), 1904 v S, W, Ni; 1906 v S (4)
Burgess, H. (Sheffield W), 1931 v S, Ni, F, Bel (4)
Burnup, C. J. (Cambridge University), 1896 v S (1)
Burrows, H. (Sheffield W), 1934 v H, Cz; 1935 v Ho (3)
Burton, F. E. (Nottingham F), 1889 v Ni (1)
Bury, L. (Cambridge University), 1877 v S; (with Old Etonians), 1879 v W (2)
Butcher, T. (Ipswich T), 1980 v Aus; 1981 v Sp; 1982 v W, S, F, Cz, WG, Sp; 1983 v D, WG, L, W, Gr, H, Ni, S, Aus (3); 1984 v D, H, L, F, Ni; 1985 v EG, Fi, T, Ni, Ei, R, Fi, S, I, WG, US; 1986 v Is, USSR, S, M, Ca, P, Mor, Pol, Para, Arg; (with Rangers), 1987 v Se, Ni (2), Y, Sp, Br, S; 1988 v T, Y; 1989 v D, Se, Gr, Alb (2), Ch, S, Pol, D; 1990 v Se, Pol, I, Y, Br, Cz, D, U, Tun, Ei, Ho, Bel, Cam, WG (77)
Butler, J. D. (Arsenal), 1925 v Bel (1)
Butler, W. (Bolton W), 1924 v S (1)
Butt, N. (Manchester U), 1997 v M (sub), S.Af (sub); 1998 v Mol (sub), I (sub), Ch, Bel, CzR; 1999 v H; 2001 v I, Sp, Fi (sub), Alb, M (sub), Gr (sub); 2002 v Se, Ho (sub), I, Para, Arg, Ng, D, Br; 2003 v P, Slo, Mac (sub), Lie (sub), T; 2004 v Cro, Mac, T, D, P, Se, J (sub), Ic (sub) (35)
Byrne, G. (Liverpool), 1963 v S; 1966 v N (2)
Byrne, J. J. (C Palace), 1962 v Ni; (with West Ham U), 1963 v Sw; 1964 v S, U, P (2), Ei, Br, Arg; 1965 v W, S (11)
Byrne, R. W. (Manchester U), 1954 v S, H, Y, Bel, Sw, U; 1955 v S, W, Ni, WG, F, Sp, P; 1956 v S, W, Ni, Br, Se, Fi, WG, D, Sp; 1957 v S, W, Ni, Y, D (2), Ei (2); 1958 v W, Ni, F (33)

Callaghan, I. R. (Liverpool), 1966 v Fi, F; 1978 v Sw, L (4)
Calvey, J. (Nottingham F), 1902 v Ni (1)
Campbell, A. F. (Blackburn R), 1929 v W, Ni; (with Huddersfield T), 1931 v W, S, Ni; 1932 v W, Ni, Sp (8)
Campbell, S. (Tottenham H), 1996 v H (sub), S (sub); 1997 v Ge, I, Ge, S.Af (sub), Pol, F, Br; 1998 v Mol, I, Cam, Ch, P, Mor, Bel, Tun, R, Co, Arg; 1999 v Se, Bul, L, CzR, Pol, Se, Bul; 2000 v S (2), Arg, Br, Uk, Ma, P, G, R; 2001 v F, Sp, Fi, Alb; (with Arsenal), 2002 v G, Alb, Ho, I, Sk, Cam, Se, Arg, Ng, D, Br; 2003 v Mac, Aus, T; 2004 v Mac, T, J, Ic, F, Sw, Cro, P (62)
Camsell, G. H. (Middlesbrough), 1929 v F, Bel; 1930 v Ni, W; 1934 v F; 1936 v S, G, A, Bel (9)
Capes, A. J. (Stoke C), 1903 v S (1)
Carr, J. (Middlesbrough), 1920 v Ni; 1923 v W (2)
Carr, J. (Newcastle U), 1905 v Ni; 1907 v Ni (2)
Carr, W. H. (Owlerton, Sheffield), 1875 v S (1)
Carragher, J. L. (Liverpool), 1999 v H (sub); 2001 v I (sub), M (sub); 2002 v Ho, G (sub), Alb (sub), Se, Para (sub); 2003 v Ser (sub); 2004 v P (sub), Se, Ic (12)
Carrick, M. (West Ham U), 2001 v M (sub); 2002 v Ho (sub) (2)
Carter, H. S. (Sunderland), 1934 v S, H; 1936 v G; 1937 v S, Ni, H; (with Derby Co), 1947 v S, W, Ni, Ei, Ho, F, Sw (13)
Carter, J. H. (WBA), 1926 v Bel; 1929 v Bel, Sp (3)
Catlin, A. E. (Sheffield W), 1937 v W, Ni, H, N, Se (5)
Chadwick, A. (Southampton), 1900 v S, W (2)
Chadwick, E. (Everton), 1891 v S, W; 1892 v S; 1893 v S; 1894 v S; 1896 v Ni; 1897 v S (7)
Chamberlain, M (Stoke C), 1983 v L (sub); 1984 v D (sub), S, USSR, Br, U, Ch; 1985 v Fi (sub) (8)
Chambers, H. (Liverpool), 1921 v S, W, Bel; 1923 v S, W, Ni, Bel; 1924 v Ni (8)
Channon, M. R. (Southampton), 1973 v Y, S (2), Ni, W, Cz, USSR, I; 1974 v A, Pol, I, P, W, Ni, S, Arg, EG, Bul, Y; 1975 v Cz, P, WG, Cy (2), Ni (sub), W, S; 1976 v Sw, Cz, P, W, Ni, S, Br, I, Fi; 1977 v Fi, I, L, Ni, W, S, Br (sub), Arg, U; (with Manchester C), 1978 v Sw (46)
Charles, G. A. (Nottingham F), 1991 v Nz, Mal (2)
Charlton, J. (Leeds U), 1965 v S, H, Y, WG, Se; 1966 v W, Ni, S, A, Sp, Pol (2), WG (2), Y, Fi, D, U, M, F, Arg, P; 1967 v W, S, Ni, Cz; 1968 v W, Sp; 1969 v W, R, F; 1970 v Ho (2), P, Cz (35)
Charlton, R. (Manchester U), 1958 v S, P, Y; 1959 v S, W, Ni, USSR, I, Br, Pe, M, US; 1960 v W, S, Se, Y, Sp, H; 1961 v Ni, W, S, L, P, Sp, M, I, A; 1962 v W, Ni, S, A, Sw, Pe, L, P, H, Arg, Bul, Br; 1963 v S, F, Br, Cz, EG, Sw; 1964 v S, W, Ni, R of W, U, P, Ei, Br, Arg, US (sub); 1965 v Ni, S, Ho; 1966 v W, Ni, S, A, Sp, WG (2), Y, Fi, N, Pol, U, M, F, Arg, P; 1967 v Ni, W, S, Cz; 1968 v W, Ni, S, USSR (2), Sp (2), Se, Y; 1969 v S, W, Ni, R (2), Bul, M, Br; 1970 v W, Ni, Ho (2), P, Co, Ec, Cz, R, Br, WG (106)
Charnley, R. O. (Blackpool), 1963 v F (1)
Charsley, C. C. (Small Heath), 1893 v Ni (1)
Chedgzoy, S. (Everton), 1920 v W; 1921 v W, S, Ni; 1922 v Ni; 1923 v S; 1924 v W; 1925 v Ni (8)
Chenery, C. J. (C Palace), 1872 v S; 1873 v S; 1874 v S (3)
Cherry, T. J. (Leeds U), 1976 v W, S (sub), Br, Fi; 1977 v Ei, I, L, Ni, S (sub), Br, Arg, U; 1978 v Sw, L, I, Br, W; 1979 v Cz, W, Se; 1980 v Ei, Arg (sub), W, Ni, S, Aus, Sp (sub) (27)
Chilton, A. (Manchester U), 1951 v Ni; 1952 v F (2)
Chippendale, H. (Blackburn R), 1894 v Ni (1)
Chivers, M. (Tottenham H), 1971 v Ma (2), Gr, Ni, S; 1972 v Sw (1+1 sub), Gr, WG (2), Ni (sub), S; 1973 v W (3), S (2), Ni, Cz, Pol, USSR, I; 1974 v A, Pol (24)
Christian, E. (Old Etonians), 1879 v S (1)
Clamp, E. (Wolverhampton W), 1958 v USSR (2), Br, A (4)
Clapton, D. R. (Arsenal), 1959 v W (1)
Clare, T. (Stoke C), 1889 v Ni; 1892 v Ni; 1893 v W; 1894 v S (4)
Clarke, A. J. (Leeds U), 1970 v Cz; 1971 v EG, Ma, Ni, W (sub), S (sub); 1973 v S (2), W, Cz, Pol, USSR, I; 1974 v A, Pol, I; 1975 v P; 1976 v Cz, P (sub) (19)
Clarke, H. A. (Tottenham H), 1954 v S (1)
Clay, T. (Tottenham H), 1920 v W; 1922 v W, S, Ni (4)
Clayton, R. (Blackburn R), 1956 v Ni, Br, Se, Fi, WG, Sp; 1957 v S, W, Ni, Y, D (2), Ei (2); 1958 v S, W, Ni, F, P, Y, USSR; 1959 v S, W, Ni, USSR, I, Br, Pe, M, US; 1960 v W, Ni, S, Se, Y (35)
Clegg, J. C. (Sheffield W), 1872 v S (1)
Clegg, W. E. (Sheffield W), 1873 v S; (with Sheffield Albion), 1879 v W (2)
Clemence, R. N. (Liverpool), 1973 v W (2); 1974 v EG, Bul, Y; 1975 v Cz, P, WG, Cy, Ni, W, S; 1976 v Sw, Cz, P, W (2), Ni, S, Br, Fi; 1977 v Ei, Fi, I, Ho, L, S, Br, Arg, U; 1978 v Sw, L, I, WG, Ni, S; 1979 v D, Ei, Ni (2), S, Bul, A (sub); 1980 v D, Bul, Ei, Arg, W, S, Bel, Sp; 1981 v R, Sp, Br, Sw, H; (with Tottenham H), 1982 v N, Ni, Fi; 1983 v L; 1984 v L (61)
Clement, D. T. (QPR), 1976 v W (sub+1), I; 1977 v I, Ho (5)
Clough, B. H. (Middlesbrough), 1960 v W, Se (2)
Clough, N. H. (Nottingham F), 1989 v Ch; 1991 v Arg (sub), Aus, Mal; 1992 v F, Cz, C; 1993 v Sp, T (sub), Pol (sub), N (sub), US, Br, G (14)
Coates, R. (Burnley), 1970 v Ni; 1971 v Gr (sub); (with Tottenham H), Ma, W (4)
Cobbold, W. N. (Cambridge University), 1883 v S, Ni; 1885 v S, Ni; 1886 v S, W; (with Old Carthusians), 1887 v S, W, Ni (9)
Cock, J. G. (Huddersfield T), 1920 v Ni; (with Chelsea), v S (2)
Cockburn, H. (Manchester U), 1947 v W, Ni, Ei; 1948 v S, I; 1949 v S, Ni, D, Sw, Se; 1951 v Arg, P; 1952 v F (13)
Cohen, G. R. (Fulham), 1964 v U, P, Ei, US, Br; 1965 v W, S, Ni, Bel, H, Ho, Y, WG, Se; 1966 v W, S, Ni, A, Sp, Pol (2), WG (2), N, D, U, M, F, Arg, P; 1967 v W, S, Ni, Cz, Sp; 1968 v W, Ni (37)
Cole, A. (Manchester U), 1995 v U (sub); 1997 v I (sub); 1999 v F (sub), Pol, Se; 2000 v S (sub), Arg (sub); 2001 v F, G, Fi, Sp, Fi, Alb; 2002 v Ho, Gr (sub) (15)

Cole, A. (Arsenal), 2001 v Alb, M, Gr; 2002 v Ho, G, Alb, Gr, Sk, Se, Arg, Ng, D, Br; 2003 v P, Slo, Mac, Aus, Ser, Slo; 2004 v Cro, Mac, T, D, P, J, Ic, F, Sw, Cro, P (30)
Cole, J. J. (West Ham U), 2001 v M (sub); 2002 v Ho (sub), I (sub), Para (sub), Sk (sub), Cam, Se (sub); 2003 v P (sub), S.Af (sub), Ser (sub); (with Chelsea), 2004 v Cro (sub), Lie (sub), D, P (sub), Se (sub), J (sub), Ic (sub) (17)
Colclough, H. (C Palace), 1914 v W (1)
Coleman, E. H. (Dulwich Hamlet), 1921 v W (1)
Coleman, J. (Woolwich Arsenal), 1907 v Ni (1)
Collymore, S. V. (Nottingham F), 1995 v J, Br (sub); (with Aston Villa), 1998 v Mol (sub) (3)
Common, A. (Sheffield U), 1904 v W, Ni; (with Middlesbrough), 1906 v W (3)
Compton, L. H. (Arsenal), 1951 v W, Y (2)
Conlin, J. (Bradford C), 1906 v S (1)
Connelly, J. M. (Burnley), 1960 v W, N, S, Se; 1962 v W, A, Sw, P; 1963 v W, F; (with Manchester U), 1965 v H, Y, Se; 1966 v W, Ni, S, A, N, D, U (20)
Cook, T. E. R. (Brighton), 1925 v W (1)
Cooper, C. T. (Nottingham F), 1995 v Se, Br (2)
Cooper, N. C. (Cambridge University), 1893 v Ni (1)
Cooper, T. (Derby Co), 1928 v Ni; 1929 v W, Ni, S, F, Bel, Sp; 1931 v F; 1932 v W, Sp; 1933 v S; 1934 v S, H, Cz; 1935 v W (15)
Cooper, T. (Leeds U), 1969 v W, S, F, M; 1970 v Ho, Bel, Co, Ec, R, Cz, Br, WG; 1971 v EG, Ma, Ni, W, S; 1972 v Sw (2); 1975 v P (20)
Coppell, S. J. (Manchester U), 1978 v I, WG, Br, W, Ni, S, H; 1979 v D, Ei, Cz, Ni (2), W (sub), S, Bul, A; 1980 v D, Ni, Ei (sub), Sp, Arg, W, S, Bel, I; 1981 v R (sub), Sw, R, Br, W, S, Sw, H; 1982 v H, S, Fi, F, Cz, K, WG; 1983 v L, Gr (42)
Copping, W. (Leeds U), 1933 v I, Sw; 1934 v S, Ni, W, F; (with Arsenal), 1935 v Ni, I; 1936 v A, Bel; 1937 v N, Se, Fi; 1938 v S, W, Ni, Cz; 1939 v W, R of E; (with Leeds U), R (20)
Corbett, B. O. (Corinthians), 1901 v W (1)
Corbett, R. (Old Malvernians), 1903 v W (1)
Corbett, W. S. (Birmingham), 1908 v A, H, B (3)
Corrigan, J. T. (Manchester C), 1978 v I (sub), Br; 1979 v W; 1980 v Ni, Aus; 1981 v W, S; 1982 v W, Ic (9)
Cottee, A. R. (West Ham U), 1987 v Se (sub), Ni (sub); 1988 v H (sub); (with Everton) 1989 v D (sub), Se (sub), Ch (sub), S (7)
Cotterill, G. H. (Cambridge University), 1891 v Ni; (with Old Brightonians), 1892 v W; 1893 v S, Ni (4)
Cottle, J. R. (Bristol C), 1909 v Ni (1)
Cowan, S. (Manchester C), 1926 v Bel; 1930 v A; 1931 v Bel (3)
Cowans, G. (Aston Villa), 1983 v W, H, Ni, S, Aus (3); (with Bari), 1986 v Eg, USSR; (with Aston Villa), 1991 v Ei (10)
Cowell, A. (Blackburn R), 1910 v Ni (1)
Cox, J. (Liverpool), 1901 v Ni; 1902 v S; 1903 v S (3)
Cox, J. D. (Derby Co), 1892 v Ni (1)
Crabtree, J. W. (Burnley), 1894 v Ni; 1895 v Ni, S; (with Aston Villa), 1896 v W, S, Ni; 1899 v S, W, Ni; 1900 v S, W, Ni; 1901 v W; 1902 v W (14)
Crawford, J. F. (Chelsea), 1931 v S (1)
Crawford, R. (Ipswich T), 1962 v Ni, A (2)
Crawshaw, T. H. (Sheffield W), 1895 v Ni; 1896 v S, W, Ni; 1897 v S, W, Ni; 1901 v Ni; 1904 v W, Ni (10)
Crayston, W. J. (Arsenal), 1936 v S, W, G, A, Bel; 1938 v W, Ni, Cz (8)
Creek, F. N. S. (Corinthians), 1923 v F (1)
Cresswell, W. (South Shields), 1921 v W; (with Sunderland), 1923 v F; 1924 v Bel; 1925 v Ni; 1926 v W; 1927 v Ni; (with Everton), 1930 v Ni (7)
Crompton, R. (Blackburn R), 1902 v S, W, Ni; 1903 v S, W; 1904 v S, W, Ni; 1906 v S, W, Ni; 1907 v S, W, Ni; 1908 v S, W, Ni, A (2), H, B; 1909 v S, W, Ni, H (2), A; 1910 v S, W; 1911 v S, W, Ni; 1912 v S, W, Ni; 1913 v S, W, Ni; 1914 v S, W, Ni (41)
Crooks, S. D. (Derby Co), 1930 v S, G, A; 1931 v S, W, Ni, F, Bel; 1932 v S, W, Ni, Sp; 1933 v Ni, W, A; 1934 v S, Ni, W, F, H, Cz; 1935 v Ni; 1936 v S, W; 1937 v W, H (26)
Crowe, C. (Wolverhampton W), 1963 v F (1)
Cuggy, F. (Sunderland), 1913 v Ni; 1914 v Ni (2)
Cullis, S. (Wolverhampton W), 1938 v S, W, Ni, F, Cz; 1939 v S, Ni, R of E, N, I, R, Y (12)
Cunliffe, A. (Blackburn R), 1933 v Ni, W (2)
Cunliffe, D. (Portsmouth), 1900 v Ni (1)
Cunliffe, J. N. (Everton), 1936 v Bel (1)
Cunningham, L. (WBA), 1979 v W, Se, A (sub); (with Real Madrid), 1980 v Ei, Sp (sub); 1981 v R (sub) (6)
Curle, K. (Manchester C), 1992 v C (sub), H, D (3)
Currey, E. S. (Oxford University), 1890 v S, W (2)
Currie, A. W. (Sheffield U), 1972 v Ni; 1973 v USSR, I; 1974 v A, Pol, I; 1976 v Sw; (with Leeds U), 1978 v Br, W (sub), Ni, S, H (sub); 1979 v Cz, Ni (2), W, Se (17)
Cursham, A. W. (Notts Co), 1876 v S; 1877 v S; 1878 v S; 1879 v W; 1883 v S, W (6)
Cursham, H. A. (Notts Co), 1880 v W; 1882 v S, W, Ni; 1883 v S, W, Ni; 1884 v Ni (8)

Daft, H. B. (Notts Co), 1889 v Ni; 1890 v S, W; 1891 v Ni; 1892 v Ni (5)
Daley, A. M. (Aston Villa), 1992 v Pol (sub), C, H, Br, Fi (sub), D (sub), Se (7)
Danks, T. (Nottingham F), 1885 v S (1)
Davenport, P. (Nottingham F), 1985 v Ei (sub) (1)
Davenport, J. K. (Bolton W), 1885 v W; 1890 v Ni (2)
Davis, G. (Derby Co), 1904 v W, Ni (2)
Davis, H. (Sheffield W), 1903 v S, W, Ni (3)
Davison, J. E. (Sheffield W), 1922 v W (1)
Dawson, J. (Burnley), 1922 v S, Ni (2)
Day, S. H. (Old Malvernians), 1906 v Ni, W, S (3)
Dean, W. R. (Everton), 1927 v S, W, F, Bel, L; 1928 v S, W, Ni, F, Bel; 1929 v S, W, Ni; 1931 v S; 1932 v Sp; 1933 v Ni (16)
Deane, B. C. (Sheffield U), 1991 v Nz (sub + 1); 1993 v Sp (sub) (3)
Deeley, N. V. (Wolverhampton W), 1959 v Br, Pe (2)
Defoe, J. C. (Tottenham H), 2004 v Se (sub), Ic (sub) (2)
Devey, J. H. G. (Aston Villa), 1892 v Ni; 1894 v Ni (2)
Devonshire, A. (West Ham U), 1980 v Aus (sub), Ni; 1982 v Ho, Ic; 1983 v WG, W, Gr; 1984 v L (8)
Dewhurst, F. (Preston NE), 1886 v W, Ni; 1887 v S, W, Ni; 1888 v S, W, Ni; 1889 v W (9)
Dewhurst, G. P. (Liverpool Ramblers), 1895 v W (1)
Dickinson, J. W. (Portsmouth), 1949 v N, F; 1950 v S, W, Ei, P, Bel, Ch, US, Sp; 1951 v Ni, W, Y; 1952 v W, Ni, S, A (2), I, Sw; 1953 v W, Ni, S, Bel, Arg, Ch, U, US; 1954 v W, Ni, S, R of E, H (2), Y, Bel, Sw, U; 1955 v Sp, P; 1956 v W, Ni, S, D, Sp; 1957 v W, Y, D (48)
Dimmock, J. H. (Tottenham H), 1921 v S; 1926 v W, Bel (3)
Ditchburn, E. G. (Tottenham H), 1949 v Sw, Se; 1953 v US; 1957 v W, Y, D (6)
Dix, R. W. (Derby Co), 1939 v N (1)
Dixon, J. A. (Notts Co), 1885 v W (1)
Dixon, K. M. (Chelsea), 1985 v M (sub), WG, US; 1986 v Ni, Is, M (sub), Pol (sub); 1987 v Se (8)
Dixon, L. M. (Arsenal), 1990 v Cz; 1991 v H, Pol, Ei (2), Cam, T, Arg; 1992 v G, T, Pol, Cz (sub); 1993 v Sp, N, T, Sm, T, Ho, N, US; 1994 v Sm; 1999 v F (22)
Dobson, A. T. C. (Notts Co), 1882 v Ni; 1884 v S, W, Ni (4)
Dobson, C. F. (Notts Co), 1886 v Ni (1)
Dobson, J. M. (Burnley), 1974 v P, EG, Bul, Y; (with Everton), 1975 v Cz (5)
Doggart, A. G. (Corinthians), 1924 v Bel (1)
Dorigo, A. R. (Chelsea), 1990 v Y (sub), Cz (sub), D (sub), I; 1991 v H (sub), USSR; (with Leeds U), 1992 v G, Cz (sub), H, Br; 1993 v Sm, Pol, US, Br; 1994 v H (15)
Dorrell, A. R. (Aston Villa), 1925 v W, Bel, F; 1926 v Ni (4)
Douglas, B. (Blackburn R), 1958 v S, W, Ni, F, P, Y, USSR (2), Br, A; 1959 v S, USSR; 1960 v Y, H; 1961 v Ni, W, S, L, P, Sp, M, I, A; 1962 v W, Ni, S, Pe, L, P, H, Arg, Bul, Br; 1963 v S, Br, Sw (36)
Downs, R. W. (Everton), 1921 v Ni (1)
Doyle, M. (Manchester C), 1976 v W, S (sub), Br, I; 1977 v Ho (5)
Drake, E. J. (Arsenal), 1935 v Ni, I; 1936 v W; 1937 v H; 1938 v F (5)
Dublin, D. (Coventry C), 1998 v Ch, Mor, Bel (sub); (with Aston Villa), 1999 v CzR (4)
Ducat, A. (Woolwich Arsenal), 1910 v S, W, Ni; (with Aston Villa), 1920 v S, W; 1921 v Ni (6)
Dunn, A. T. B. (Cambridge University), 1883 v Ni; 1884 v Ni; (with Old Etonians), 1892 v S, W (4)
Dunn, D. J. I. (Blackburn R), 2003 v P (sub) (1)
Duxbury, M. (Manchester U), 1984 v L, F, W, S, USSR, Br, U, Ch; 1985 v EG, Fi (10)
Dyer, K. C. (Newcastle U), 2000 v L, Pol (sub), Bel, Arg, Uk (sub); 2001 v F (sub), G (sub), I; 2002 v Para, Se (sub), D (sub), Br (sub); 2003 v Slo (sub), Aus, Lie, T (sub); 2004 v Cro (sub), Mac (sub), T (sub), P (sub), J (sub), Ic (sub), Sw (sub) (23)

Earle, S. G. J. (Clapton), 1924 v F; (with West Ham U), 1928 v Ni (2)
Eastham, G. (Arsenal), 1963 v Br, Cz, EG; 1964 v W, Ni, S, R of W, U, P, Ei, US, Br, Arg; 1965 v H, WG, Se; 1966 v Sp, Pol, D (19)

Eastham, G. R. (Bolton W), 1935 v Ho (1)
Eckersley, W. (Blackburn R), 1950 v Sp; 1951 v S, Y, Arg, P; 1952 v A (2), Sw; 1953 v Ni, Arg, Ch, U, US; 1954 v W, Ni, R of E, H (17)
Edwards, D. (Manchester U), 1955 v S, F, Sp, P; 1956 v S, Br, Se, Fi, WG; 1957 v S, Ni, Ei (2), D (2); 1958 v W, Ni, F (18)
Edwards, J. H. (Shropshire Wanderers), 1874 v S (1)
Edwards, W. (Leeds U), 1926 v S, W; 1927 v W, Ni, S, F, Bel, L; 1928 v S, F, Bel; 1929 v S, W, Ni; 1930 v W, Ni (16)
Ehiogu, U. (Aston Villa), 1996 v Chn (sub); (with Middlesbrough), 2001 v Sp (sub); 2002 v Ho (sub), I (sub) (4)
Ellerington, W. (Southampton), 1949 v N, F (2)
Elliott, G. W. (Middlesbrough), 1913 v Ni; 1914 v Ni; 1920 v W (3)
Elliott, W. H. (Burnley), 1952 v I, A; 1953 v Ni, W, Bel (5)
Evans, R. E. (Sheffield U), 1911 v S, W, Ni; 1912 v W (4)
Ewer, F. H. (Casuals), 1924 v F; 1925 v Bel (2)

Fairclough, P. (Old Foresters), 1878 v S (1)
Fairhurst, D. (Newcastle U), 1934 v F (1)
Fantham, J. (Sheffield W), 1962 v L (1)
Fashanu, J. (Wimbledon), 1989 v Ch, S (2)
Felton, W. (Sheffield W), 1925 v F (1)
Fenton, M. (Middlesbrough), 1938 v S (1)
Fenwick, T. (QPR), 1984 v W (sub), S, USSR, Br, U, Ch; 1985 v Fi, S, M, US; 1986 v R, T, Ni, Eg, M, P, Mor, Pol, Arg; (with Tottenham H), 1988 v Is (sub) (20)
Ferdinand, L. (QPR), 1993 v Sm, Ho, N, US; 1994 v Pol, Sm; 1995 v US (sub); (with Newcastle U), 1996 v P, Bul, H; 1997 v Pol, Ge, I (sub); (with Tottenham H), 1998 v Mol, S.Ar (sub), Mor (sub), Bel (17)
Ferdinand, R. G. (West Ham U), 1998 v Cam (sub), Sw, Bel (sub); 1999 v L, CzR, F (sub), H, Se (sub); 2000 v Arg (sub); 2001 v I; (with Leeds U), Sp, Fi, Alb, M, Gr; 2002 v G, Alb, Gr, Se, Ho, Sk, Cam, Se, Arg, Ng, D, Br; (with Manchester U), 2003 v P, Aus, Lie, T, S.Af ; 2004 v Cro (33)
Field, E. (Clapham Rovers), 1876 v S; 1881 v S (2)
Finney, T. (Preston NE), 1947 v W, Ni, Ei, Ho, F, P; 1948 v S, W, Ni, Bel, Se, I; 1949 v S, W, Ni, Se, N, F; 1950 v S, W, Ni, Ei, I, P, Bel, Ch, US, Sp; 1951 v W, S, Arg, P; 1952 v W, Ni, S, F, I, Sw, A; 1953 v W, Ni, S, Bel, Arg, Ch, U, US; 1954 v W, S, Bel, Sw, U, H, Y; 1955 v WG; 1956 v S, W, Ni, D, Sp; 1957 v S, W, Y, D (2), Ei (2); 1958 v W, S, F, P, Y, USSR (2); 1959 v Ni, USSR (76)
Fleming, H. J. (Swindon T), 1909 v S, H (2); 1910 v W, Ni; 1911 v W, Ni; 1912 v Ni; 1913 v S, W; 1914 v S (11)
Fletcher, A. (Wolverhampton W), 1889 v W; 1890 v W (2)
Flowers, R. (Wolverhampton W), 1955 v F; 1959 v S, W, I, Br, Pe, US, M (sub); 1960 v W, Ni, S, Se, Y, Sp, H; 1961 v Ni, W, S, L, P, Sp, M, I, A; 1962 v W, Ni, S, A, Sw, Pe, L, P, H, Arg, Bul, Br; 1963 v Ni, W, S, F (2), Sw; 1964 v Ei, US, P; 1965 v W, Ho, WG; 1966 v N (49)
Flowers, T. D. (Southampton), 1993 v Br; (with Blackburn R), 1994 v Gr; 1995 v Ng, U, J, Se, Br; 1996 v Chn; 1997 v I; 1998 v Sw, Mor (11)
Forman, Frank (Nottingham F), 1898 v S, Ni; 1899 v S, W, Ni; 1901 v S; 1902 v S, Ni; 1903 v W (9)
Forman, F. R. (Nottingham F), 1899 v S, W, Ni (3)
Forrest, J. H. (Blackburn R), 1884 v W; 1885 v S, W, Ni; 1886 v S, W; 1887 v S, W, Ni; 1889 v S; 1890 v Ni (11)
Fort, J. (Millwall), 1921 v Bel (1)
Foster, R. E. (Oxford University), 1900 v W; (with Corinthians), 1901 v W, Ni, S; 1902 v W (5)
Foster, S. (Brighton & HA), 1982 v Ni, Ho, K (3)
Foulke, W. J. (Sheffield U), 1897 v W (1)
Foulkes, W. A. (Manchester U), 1955 v Ni (1)
Fowler, R. B. (Liverpool), 1996 v Bul (sub), Cro, Chn (sub), Ho (sub), Sp (sub); 1997 v M; 1998 v Cam; 1999 v CzR (sub), Bul; 2000 v L, Pol, Br (sub), Uk, Ma (sub); 2001 v I (sub), Fi (sub), M, Gr; 2002 v Ho, Alb (sub), Gr, Se (sub); (with Leeds U), I (sub), Para (sub), Cam (sub), D (sub) (26)
Fox, F. S. (Millwall), 1925 v F (1)
Francis, G. C. J. (QPR), 1975 v Cz, P, W, S; 1976 v Sw, Cz, P, W, Ni, S, Br, Fi (12)
Francis, T. (Birmingham C), 1977 v Ho, L, S, Br; 1978 v Sw, L, I (sub), WG (sub), Br, W, S, H; (with Nottingham F), 1979 v Bul (sub), Se, A (sub); 1980 v Ni, Bul, Sp; 1981 v Sp, R, S (sub), Sw; (with Manchester C), 1982 v N, Ni, W, S (sub), Fi (sub), F, Cz, K, WG, Sp; (with Sampdoria), 1983 v D, Gr, H, Ni, S, Aus (3); 1984 v D, Ni, USSR; 1985 v EG (sub), T (sub), Ni (sub), R, Fi, S, I, M; 1986 v S (52)
Franklin, C. F. (Stoke C), 1947 v S, W, Ni, Ei, Ho, F, Sw, P; 1948 v S, W, Ni, Bel, Se, I; 1949 v S, W, Ni, D, Sw, N, F, Se; 1950 v W, S, Ni, Ei, I (27)
Freeman, B. C. (Everton), 1909 v S, W; (with Burnley), 1912 v S, W, Ni (5)
Froggatt, J. (Portsmouth), 1950 v Ni, I; 1951 v S; 1952 v S, A (2), I, Sw; 1953 v Ni, W, S, Bel, US (13)
Froggatt, R. (Sheffield W), 1953 v W, S, Bel, US (4)
Fry, C. B. (Corinthians), 1901 v Ni (1)
Furness, W. I. (Leeds U), 1933 v I (1)

Galley, T. (Wolverhampton W), 1937 v N, Se (2)
Gardner, A. (Tottenham H), 2004 v Se (sub) (1)
Gardner, T. (Aston Villa), 1934 v Cz; 1935 v Ho (2)
Garfield, B. (WBA), 1898 v Ni (1)
Garratty, W. (Aston Villa), 1903 v W (1)
Garrett, T. (Blackpool), 1952 v S, I; 1954 v W (3)
Gascoigne, P. J. (Tottenham H), 1989 v D (sub), S.Ar (sub), Alb (sub), Ch, S (sub); 1990 v Se (sub), Br (sub), Cz, D, U, Tun, Ei, Ho, Eg, Bel, Cam, WG; 1991 v H, Pol, Cam; (with Lazio), 1993 v N, T, Sm, T, Ho, Pol, N; 1994 v Pol, D; 1995 v J (sub), Se (sub), Br (sub); (with Rangers), 1996 v Co, Sw, P, Bul, Cro, Chn, Sw, S, Ho, Sp, G; 1997 v Mol, Pol, Ge, S.Af, Pol, I (sub), F, Br; 1998 v Mol, I, Cam; (with Middlesbrough), S.Ar (sub), Mor, Bel (57)
Gates, E. (Ipswich T), 1981 v N, R (2)
Gay, L. H. (Cambridge University), 1893 v S; (with Old Brightonians), 1894 v S, W (3)
Geary, F. (Everton), 1890 v Ni; 1891 v S (2)
Geaves, R. L. (Clapham Rovers), 1875 v S (1)
Gee, C. W. (Everton), 1932 v W, Sp; 1937 v Ni (3)
Geldard, A. (Everton), 1933 v I, Sw; 1935 v S; 1938 v Ni (4)
George, C. (Derby Co), 1977 v Ei (1)
George, W. (Aston Villa), 1902 v S, W, Ni (3)
Gerrard, S. G. (Liverpool), 2000 v Uk, G (sub); 2001 v Fi, M, Gr; 2002 v G, Alb, Gr, Ho, Para; 2003 v P, Slo, Mac, Lie, T, S.Af, Ser, Slo; 2004 v Cro, Lie, T, Se, J, Ic, F, Sw, Cro, P (28)
Gibbins, W. V. T. (Clapton), 1924 v F; 1925 v F (2)
Gidman, J. (Aston Villa), 1977 v L (1)
Gillard, I. T. (QPR), 1975 v WG, W; 1976 v Cz (3)
Gilliat, W. E. (Old Carthusians), 1893 v Ni (1)
Goddard, P. (West Ham U), 1982 v Ic (sub) (1)
Goodall, F. R. (Huddersfield T), 1926 v S; 1927 v S, F, Bel, L; 1928 v S, W, F, Bel; 1930 v S, G, A; 1931 v S, W, Ni, Bel; 1932 v Ni; 1933 v W, Ni, A, I, Sw; 1934 v W, Ni, F (25)
Goodall, J. (Preston NE), 1888 v S, W; 1889 v S, W; (with Derby Co), 1891 v S, W; 1892 v S; 1893 v W; 1894 v S; 1895 v S, Ni; 1896 v S, W; 1898 v W (14)
Goodhart, H. C. (Old Etonians), 1883 v S, W, Ni (3)
Goodwyn, A. G. (Royal Engineers), 1873 v S (1)
Goodyer, A. C. (Nottingham F), 1879 v S (1)
Gosling, R. C. (Old Etonians), 1892 v W; 1893 v S; 1894 v W; 1895 v W, S (5)
Gosnell, A. A. (Newcastle U), 1906 v Ni (1)
Gough, H. C. (Sheffield U), 1921 v S (1)
Goulden, L. A. (West Ham U), 1937 v Se, N; 1938 v W, Ni, Cz, G, Sw, F; 1939 v S, W, R of E, I, R, Y (14)
Graham, L. (Millwall), 1925 v S, W (2)
Graham, T. (Nottingham F), 1931 v F; 1932 v Ni (2)
Grainger, C. (Sheffield U), 1956 v Br, Se, Fi, WG; 1957 v W, Ni; (with Sunderland), 1957 v S (7)
Gray, A. A. (C Palace), 1992 v Pol (1)
Gray, M. (Sunderland), 1999 v H (sub), Se (sub), Bul (3)
Greaves, J. (Chelsea), 1959 v Pe, M, US; 1960 v W, Se, Y, Sp; 1961 v Ni, W, S, L, P, Sp, I, A; (with Tottenham H), 1962 v S, Sw, Pe, H, Arg, Bul, Br; 1963 v Ni, W, S, F (2), Br, Cz, Sw; 1964 v W, Ni, R of W, P (2), Ei, Br, U, Arg; 1965 v Ni, S, Bel, Ho, H, Y; 1966 v W, A, Y, N, D, Pol, U, M, F; 1967 v S, Sp, A (57)
Green, F. T. (Wanderers), 1876 v S (1)
Green, G. H. (Sheffield U), 1925 v F; 1926 v S, Bel, W; 1927 v W, Ni; 1928 v F, Bel (8)
Greenhalgh, E. H. (Notts Co), 1872 v S; 1873 v S (2)
Greenhoff, B. (Manchester U), 1976 v W, Ni; 1977 v Ei, Fi, I, Ho, Ni, W, S, Br, Arg, U; 1978 v Br, W, Ni, S (sub), H (sub); (with Leeds U), 1980 v Aus (sub) (18)
Greenwood, D. H. (Blackburn R), 1882 v S, Ni (2)
Gregory, J. (QPR), 1983 v Aus (3); 1984 v D, H, W (6)
Grimsdell, A. (Tottenham H), 1920 v S, W; 1921 v S, Ni; 1923 v W, Ni (6)
Grosvenor, A. T. (Birmingham), 1934 v Ni, W, F (3)
Gunn, W. (Notts Co), 1884 v S, W (2)
Guppy, S. (Leicester C), 2000 v Bel (1)
Gurney, R. (Sunderland), 1935 v S (1)

Hacking, J. (Oldham Ath), 1929 v S, W, Ni (3)
Hadley, N. (WBA), 1903 v Ni (1)
Hagan, J. (Sheffield U), 1949 v D (1)

Haines, J. T. W. (WBA), 1949 v Sw (1)
Hall, A. E. (Aston Villa), 1910 v Ni (1)
Hall, G. W. (Tottenham H), 1934 v F; 1938 v S, W, Ni, Cz; 1939 v S, Ni, R of E, I, Y (10)
Hall, J. (Birmingham C), 1956 v S, W, Ni, Br, Se, Fi, WG, D, Sp; 1957 v S, W, Ni, Y, D (2), Ei (2) (17)
Halse, H. J. (Manchester U), 1909 v A (1)
Hammond, H. E. D. (Oxford University), 1889 v S (1)
Hampson, J. (Blackpool), 1931 v Ni, W; 1933 v A (3)
Hampton, H. (Aston Villa), 1913 v S, W; 1914 v S, W (4)
Hancocks, J. (Wolverhampton W), 1949 v Sw; 1950 v W; 1951 v Y (3)
Hapgood, E. (Arsenal), 1933 v I, Sw; 1934 v S, Ni, W, H, Cz; 1935 v S, Ni, W, I, Ho; 1936 v S, Ni, W, G, A, Bel; 1937 v Fi; 1938 v S, G, Sw, F; 1939 v S, W, Ni, R of E, N, I, Y (30)
Hardinge, H. T. W. (Sheffield U), 1910 v S (1)
Hardman, H. P. (Everton), 1905 v W; 1907 v S, Ni; 1908 v W (4)
Hardwick, G. F. M. (Middlesbrough), 1947 v S, W, Ni, Ei, Ho, F, Sw, P; 1948 v S, W, Ni, Bel, Se (13)
Hardy, H. (Stockport Co), 1925 v Bel (1)
Hardy, S. (Liverpool), 1907 v S, W, Ni; 1908 v S; 1909 v S, W, Ni, H (2), A; 1910 v S, W, Ni; 1912 v Ni; (with Aston Villa), 1913 v S; 1914 v Ni, W, S; 1920 v S, W, Ni (21)
Harford, M. G. (Luton T), 1988 v Is (sub); 1989 v D (2)
Hargreaves, F. W. (Blackburn R), 1880 v W; 1881 v W; 1882 v Ni (3)
Hargreaves, J. (Blackburn R), 1881 v S, W (2)
Hargreaves, O. (Bayern Munich) 2002 v Ho, G (sub), I (sub), Para (sub), Sk, Cam, Se, Arg; 2003 v P (sub), Slo (sub), Aus (sub), Ser (sub), Slo (sub); 2004 v Mac, Lie (sub), P (sub), Se, J (sub), Ic (sub), F (sub), Sw (sub), P (sub) (22)
Harper, E. C. (Blackburn R), 1926 v S (1)
Harris, G. (Burnley), 1966 v Pol (1)
Harris, P. P. (Portsmouth), 1950 v Ei; 1954 v H (2)
Harris, S. S. (Cambridge University), 1904 v S; (with Old Westminsters), 1905 v Ni, W; 1906 v S, W, Ni (6)
Harrison, A. H. (Old Westminsters), 1893 v S, Ni (2)
Harrison, G. (Everton), 1921 v Bel; 1922 v Ni (2)
Harrow, J. H. (Chelsea), 1923 v Ni, Se (2)
Hart, E. (Leeds U), 1929 v W; 1930 v W, Ni; 1933 v S, A; 1934 v S, H, Cz (8)
Hartley, F. (Oxford C), 1923 v F (1)
Harvey, A. (Wednesbury Strollers), 1881 v W (1)
Harvey, J. C. (Everton), 1971 v Ma (1)
Hassall, H. W. (Huddersfield T), 1951 v S, Arg, P; 1952 v F; (with Bolton W), 1954 v Ni (5)
Hateley, M. (Portsmouth), 1984 v USSR (sub), Br, U, Ch; (with AC Milan), 1985 v EG (sub), Fi, Ni, Ei, Fi, S, I, M; 1986 v R, T, Eg, S, M, Ca, P, Mor, Para (sub); 1987 v T (sub), Br (sub), S; (with Monaco), 1988 v WG (sub), Ho (sub), H (sub), Co (sub), Ei (sub), Ho (sub), USSR (sub); (with Rangers), 1992 v Cz (32)
Hawkes, R. M. (Luton T), 1907 v Ni; 1908 v A (2), H, B (5)
Haworth, G. (Accrington), 1887 v Ni, W, S; 1888 v S; 1890 v S (5)
Hawtrey, J. P. (Old Etonians), 1881 v S, W (2)
Haygarth, E. B. (Swifts), 1875 v S (1)
Haynes, J. N. (Fulham), 1955 v Ni; 1956 v S, Ni, Br, Se, Fi, WG, Sp; 1957 v W, Y, D, Ei (2); 1958 v W, Ni, S, F, P, Y, USSR (3), Br, A; 1959 v S, Ni, USSR, I, Br, Pe, M, US; 1960 v Ni, Y, Sp, H; 1961 v Ni, W, S, L, P, Sp, M, I, A; 1962 v W, Ni, S, A, Sw, Pe, P, H, Arg, Bul, Br (56)
Healless, H. (Blackburn R), 1925 v Ni; 1928 v S (2)
Hector, K. J. (Derby Co), 1974 v Pol (sub), I (sub) (2)
Hedley, G. A. (Sheffield U), 1901 v Ni (1)
Hegan, K. E. (Corinthians), 1923 v Bel, F; 1924 v Ni, Bel (4)
Hellawell, M. S. (Birmingham C), 1963 v Ni, F (2)
Hendrie, L. A. (Aston Villa), 1999 v CzR (sub) (1)
Henfrey, A. G. (Cambridge University), 1891 v Ni; (with Corinthians), 1892 v W; 1895 v W; 1896 v S, W (5)
Henry, R. P. (Tottenham H), 1963 v F (1)
Heron, F. (Wanderers), 1876 v S (1)
Heron, G. H. H. (Uxbridge), 1873 v S; 1874 v S; (with Wanderers), 1875 v S; 1876 v S; 1878 v S (5)
Heskey, E. W. (Leicester C), 1999 v H (sub), Bul (sub); 2000 v Bel (sub), S (sub), Arg; (with Liverpool), Uk (sub), Ma (sub), P (sub), R (sub); 2001 v Fi, I, Sp (sub), Fi (sub), Alb (sub), M, Gr; 2002 v G, Alb, Gr, Se, Ho, I, Sk, Cam, Se, Arg, Ng, D, Br; 2003 v P, Slo, Lie, S.Af, Ser; 2004 v Cro, Mac (sub), T, D, P (sub), Se (sub); (with Birmingham C), J (sub), Ic (sub), F (sub) (43)
Hibbert, W. (Bury), 1910 v S (1)
Hibbs, H. E. (Birmingham), 1930 v S, W, A, G; 1931 v S, W, Ni; 1932 v W, Ni, Sp; 1933 v S, W, Ni, A, I, Sw; 1934 v Ni, W, F; 1935 v S, W, Ni, Ho; 1936 v G, W (25)
Hill, F. (Bolton W), 1963 v Ni, W (2)
Hill, G. A. (Manchester U), 1976 v I; 1977 v Ei (sub), Fi (sub), L; 1978 v Sw (sub), L (6)
Hill, J. H. (Burnley), 1925 v W; 1926 v S; 1927 v S, Ni, Bel, F; 1928 v Ni, W; (with Newcastle U), 1929 v F, Bel, Sp (11)
Hill, R. (Luton T), 1983 v D (sub), WG; 1986 v Eg (sub) (3)
Hill, R. H. (Millwall), 1926 v Bel (1)
Hillman, J. (Burnley), 1899 v Ni (1)
Hills, A. F. (Old Harrovians), 1879 v S (1)
Hilsdon, G. R. (Chelsea), 1907 v Ni; 1908 v S, W, Ni, A, H, B; 1909 v Ni (8)
Hinchcliffe, A. G. (Everton), 1997 v Mol, Pol, Ge; 1998 v Cam; (with Sheffield W), Sw, S.Ar; 1999 v Bul (7)
Hine, E. W. (Leicester C), 1929 v W, Ni; 1930 v W, Ni; 1932 v W, Ni (6)
Hinton, A. T. (Wolverhampton W), 1963 v F; (with Nottingham F), 1965 v W, Bel (3)
Hirst, D. E. (Sheffield W), 1991 v Aus, Nz (sub); 1992 v F (3)
Hitchens, G. A. (Aston Villa), 1961 v M, I, A; (with Inter-Milan), 1962 v Sw, Pe, H, Br (7)
Hobbis, H. H. F. (Charlton Ath), 1936 v A, Bel (2)
Hoddle, G. (Tottenham H), 1980 v Bul, W, Aus, Sp; 1981 v Sp, W, S; 1982 v N, Ni, W, Ic, Cz (sub), K; 1983 v L (sub), Ni, S; 1984 v H, L, F; 1985 v Ei (sub), S, I (sub), M, WG, US; 1986 v R, T, Ni, Is, USSR, S, M, Ca, P, Mor, Pol, Para, Arg; 1987 v Se, Ni, Y, Sp, T, S; (with Monaco), 1988 v WG, T (sub), Y (sub), Ho (sub), H (sub), Co (sub), Ei (sub), Ho, USSR (53)
Hodge, S. B. (Aston Villa), 1986 v USSR (sub), S, Ca, P (sub), Mor (sub), Pol, Para, Arg; 1987 v Se, Ni, Y; (with Tottenham H), Sp. Ni, T, S; (with Nottingham F), 1989 v D; 1990 v I (sub), Y (sub), Cz, D, U, Tun; 1991 v Cam (sub), T (sub) (24)
Hodgetts, D. (Aston Villa), 1888 v S, W, Ni; 1892 v S, Ni; 1894 v Ni (6)
Hodgkinson, A. (Sheffield U), 1957 v S, Ei (2), D; 1961 v W (5)
Hodgson, G. (Liverpool), 1931 v S, Ni, W (3)
Hodkinson, J. (Blackburn R), 1913 v W, S; 1920 v Ni (3)
Hogg, W. (Sunderland), 1902 v S, W, Ni (3)
Holdcroft, G. H. (Preston NE), 1937 v W, Ni (2)
Holden, A. D. (Bolton W), 1959 v S, I, Br, Pe, M (5)
Holden, G. H. (Wednesbury OA), 1881 v S; 1884 v S, W, Ni (4)
Holden-White, C. (Corinthians), 1888 v W, S (2)
Holford, T. (Stoke), 1903 v Ni (1)
Holley, G. H. (Sunderland), 1909 v S, W, H (2), A; 1910 v W; 1912 v S, W, Ni; 1913 v S (10)
Holliday, E. (Middlesbrough), 1960 v W, Ni, Se (3)
Hollins, J. W. (Chelsea), 1967 v Sp (1)
Holmes, R. (Preston NE), 1888 v Ni; 1891 v S; 1892 v S; 1893 v S, W; 1894 v Ni; 1895 v Ni (7)
Holt, J. (Everton), 1890 v W; 1891 v S, W; 1892 v S, Ni; 1893 v S; 1894 v S, Ni; 1895 v S; (with Reading), 1900 v Ni (10)
Hopkinson, E. (Bolton W), 1958 v W, Ni, S, F, P, Y; 1959 v S, I, Br, Pe, M, US; 1960 v W, Se (14)
Hossack, A. H. (Corinthians), 1892 v W; 1894 v W (2)
Houghton, W. E. (Aston Villa), 1931 v Ni, W, F, Bel; 1932 v S, Ni; 1933 v A (7)
Houlker, A. E. (Blackburn R), 1902 v S; (with Portsmouth), 1903 v S, W; (with Southampton), 1906 v W, Ni (5)
Howarth, R. H. (Preston NE), 1887 v Ni; 1888 v S, W; 1891 v S; (with Everton), 1894 v Ni (5)
Howe, D. (WBA), 1958 v S, W, Ni, F, P, Y, USSR (3), Br, A; 1959 v S, W, Ni, USSR, I, Br, Pe, M, US; 1960 v W, Ni, Se (23)
Howe, J. R. (Derby Co), 1948 v I; 1949 v S, Ni (3)
Howell, L. S. (Wanderers), 1873 v S (1)
Howell, R. (Sheffield U), 1895 v Ni; (with Liverpool) 1899 v S (2)
Howey, S. N. (Newcastle U), 1995 v Ng; 1996 v Co, P, Bul (4)
Hudson, A. A. (Stoke C), 1975 v WG, Cy (2)
Hudson, J. (Sheffield), 1883 v Ni (1)
Hudspeth, F. C. (Newcastle U), 1926 v Ni (1)
Hufton, A. E. (West Ham U), 1924 v Bel; 1928 v S, Ni; 1929 v F, Bel, Sp (6)
Hughes, E. W. (Liverpool), 1970 v W, Ni, S, Ho, P, Bel; 1971 v EG, Ma (2), Gr, W; 1972 v Sw, Gr, WG (2), W, Ni, S; 1973 v W (3), S (2), Pol, USSR, I; 1974 v A, Pol, I, W, Ni, S, Arg, EG, Bul, Y; 1975 v Cz, P, Cy (sub), Ni; 1977 v I, L, W, S, Br, Arg, U; 1978 v Sw, L, I, WG, Ni, S, H; 1979 v D, Ei, Ni, W, Se; (with Wolverhampton W), 1980 v Sp (sub), Ni, S (sub) (62)
Hughes, L. (Liverpool), 1950 v Ch, US, Sp (3)
Hulme, J. H. A. (Arsenal), 1927 v S, Bel, F; 1928 v S, Ni, W; 1929 v Ni, W; 1933 v S (9)
Humphreys, P. (Notts Co), 1903 v S (1)

Hunt, G. S. (Tottenham H), 1933 v I, Sw, S (3)
Hunt, Rev K. R. G. (Leyton), 1911 v S, W (2)
Hunt, R. (Liverpool), 1962 v A; 1963 v EG; 1964 v S, US, P; 1965 v W; 1966 v S, Sp, Pol (2), WG (2), Fi, N, U, M, F, Arg, P; 1967 v Ni, W, Cz, Sp, A; 1968 v W, Ni, USSR (2), Sp (2), Se, Y; 1969 v R (2) (34)
Hunt, S. (WBA), 1984 v S (sub), USSR (sub) (2)
Hunter, J. (Sheffield Heeley), 1878 v S; 1880 v S, W; 1881 v S, W; 1882 v S, W (7)
Hunter, N. (Leeds U), 1966 v WG, Y, Fi, Sp (sub); 1967 v A; 1968 v Sp, Se, Y, WG, USSR; 1969 v R, W; 1970 v Ho, WG (sub); 1971 v Ma; 1972 v WG (2), W, Ni, S; 1973 v W (2) USSR (sub); 1974 v A, Pol, Ni (sub), S; 1975 v Cz (28)
Hurst, G. C. (West Ham U), 1966 v S, WG (2), Y, Fi, D, Arg, P; 1967 v Ni, W, S, Cz, Sp, A; 1968 v W, Ni, S, Se (sub), WG, USSR (2); 1969 v Ni, S, R (2), Bul, F, M, U, Br; 1970 v W, Ni, S, Ho (1+1 sub), Bel, Co, Ec, R, Br, WG; 1971 v EG, Gr, W, S; 1972 v Sw (2), Gr, WG (49)

Ince, P. E. C. (Manchester U), 1993 v Sp, N, T (2), Ho, Pol, US, Br, G; 1994 v Pol, Ho, Sm, D, N; 1995 v R, Ei; (with Internazionale), 1996 v Bul, Cro, H, Sw, S, Ho, G; 1997 v Mol, Pol, Ge, I, M, Ge, Pol, I, F (sub), Br; (with Liverpool), 1998 v I, Cam, Ch (sub), Sw, P, Mor, Tun, R, Co, Arg; 1999 v Se, F; (with Middlesbrough), 2000 v Bel, S (2), Br, Ma (sub), P, G, R (53)
Iremonger, J. (Nottingham F), 1901 v S; 1902 v Ni (2)

Jack, D. N. B. (Bolton W), 1924 v S, W; 1928 v F, Bel; (with Arsenal), 1930 v S, G, A; 1933 v W, A (9)
Jackson, E. (Oxford University), 1891 v W (1)
James. D. B. (Liverpool), 1997 v M; (with Aston Villa), 2001 v I, Sp, M (sub); (with West Ham U), 2002 v Ho (sub + sub), I (sub), Sk (sub), Cam (sub); 2003 v P, Aus, Lie, T, S.Af, Ser, Slo; 2004 v Cro, Mac, Lie, T, D; (with Manchester C), P, Se, J, F, Sw, Cro, P (28)
Jarrett, B. G. (Cambridge University), 1876 v S; 1877 v S; 1878 v S (3)
Jefferis, F. (Everton), 1912 v S, W (2)
Jeffers, F. (Arsenal), 2003 v Aus (sub) (1)
Jenas, J. A. (Newcastle U), 2003 v Aus (sub), S.Af (sub), Ser (sub); 2004 v D (sub), P (sub), Se (sub) (6)
Jezzard, B. A. G. (Fulham), 1954 v H; 1956 v Ni (2)
Johnson, D. E. (Ipswich T), 1975 v W, S; 1976 v Sw; (with Liverpool), 1980 v Ei, Arg, Ni, S, Bel (8)
Johnson, E. (Saltley College), 1880 v W; (with Stoke C), 1884 v Ni (2)
Johnson, G. M. C. (Chelsea), 2004 v D (sub) (1)
Johnson, J. A. (Stoke C), 1937 v N, Se, Fi, S, Ni (5)
Johnson, S. A. M. (Derby Co), 2001 v I (sub) (1)
Johnson, T. C. F. (Manchester C), 1926 v Bel; 1930 v W; (with Everton), 1932 v S, Sp; 1933 v Ni (5)
Johnson, W. H. (Sheffield U), 1900 v S, W, Ni; 1903 v S, W, Ni (6)
Johnston, H. (Blackpool), 1947 v S, Ho; 1951 v S; 1953 v Arg, Ch, U, US; 1954 v W, Ni, H (10)
Jones, A. (Walsall Swifts), 1882 v S, W; (with Great Lever), 1883 v S (3)
Jones, H. (Blackburn R), 1927 v S, Bel, L, F; 1928 v S, Ni (6)
Jones, H. (Nottingham F), 1923 v F (1)
Jones, M. D. (Sheffield U), 1965 v WG, Se; (with Leeds U), 1970 v Ho (3)
Jones, R. (Liverpool), 1992 v F; 1994 v Pol, Gr, N; 1995 v US, R, Ng, U (8)
Jones, W. (Bristol C), 1901 v Ni (1)
Jones, W. H. (Liverpool), 1950 v P, Bel (2)
Joy, B. (Casuals), 1936 v Bel (1)

Kail, E. I. L. (Dulwich Hamlet), 1929 v F, Bel, Sp (3)
Kay, A. H. (Everton), 1963 v Sw (1)
Kean, F. W. (Sheffield W), 1923 v S, Bel; 1924 v W; 1925 v Ni; 1926 v Ni, Bel; 1927 v L; (with Bolton W), 1929 v F, Sp (9)
Keegan, J. K. (Liverpool), 1973 v W (2); 1974 v W, Ni, Arg, EG, Bul, Y; 1975 v Cz, WG, Cy (2), Ni, S; 1976 v Sw, Cz, P, W (2), Ni, S, Br, Fi; 1977 v Ei, Fi, I, Ho, L; (with SV Hamburg), W, Br, Arg, U; 1978 v Sw, I, WG, Br, H; 1979 v D, Ei, Cz, Ni, W, S, Bul, Se, A; 1980 v D, Ni, Ei, Sp (2), Arg, Bel, I; (with Southampton), 1981 v Sp, Sw, H; 1982 v N, H, Ni, S, Fi, Sp (sub) (63)
Keen, E. R. L. (Derby Co), 1933 v A; 1937 v W, Ni, H (4)
Kelly, R. (Burnley), 1920 v S; 1921 v S, W, Ni; 1922 v S, W; 1923 v S; 1924 v Ni; 1925 v W, Ni, S; (with Sunderland), 1926 v W; (with Huddersfield T), 1927 v L; 1928 v S (14)
Kennedy, A. (Liverpool), 1984 v Ni, W (2)
Kennedy, R. (Liverpool), 1976 v W (2), Ni, S; 1977 v L, W, S, Br (sub), Arg (sub); 1978 v Sw, L; 1980 v Bul, Sp, Arg, W, Bel (sub), I (17)
Kenyon-Slaney, W. S. (Wanderers), 1873 v S (1)
Keown, M. R. (Everton), 1992 v F, Cz, C, H, Br, Fi, D, Fe, Se; (with Arsenal), 1993 v Ho, G (sub); 1997 v M, S.Af, I, Br; 1998 v Sw, Mor, Bel; 1999 v CzR, F, Pol, H, Se; 2000 v L, Pol, Bel, S, Arg, Br, Ma, P (sub), G, R; 2001 v F, G, Fi, M, Gr; 2002 v Ho, Gr, Para, Sk (sub), Cam (sub) (43)
Kevan, D. T. (WBA), 1957 v S; 1958 v W, Ni, S, P. Y, USSR (3), Br, A; 1959 v M, US; 1961 v M (14)
Kidd, B. (Manchester U), 1970 v Ni, Ec (sub) (2)
King, L. B. (Tottenham H), 2002 v I (sub); 2003 v Aus (sub); 2004 v P, J (sub), Ic (sub), F, Cro (sub) (7)
King, R. S. (Oxford University), 1882 v Ni (1)
Kingsford, R. K. (Wanderers), 1874 v S (1)
Kingsley, M. (Newcastle U), 1901 v W (1)
Kinsey, G. (Wolverhampton W), 1892 v W; 1893 v S; (with Derby Co), 1896 v W, Ni (4)
Kirchen, A. J. (Arsenal), 1937 v N, Se, Fi (3)
Kirton, W. J. (Aston Villa), 1922 v Ni (1)
Knight, A. E. (Portsmouth), 1920 v Ni (1)
Knowles, C. (Tottenham H), 1968 v USSR, Sp, Se, WG (4)
Konchesky, P. M. (Charlton Ath), 2003 v Aus (sub) (1)

Labone, B. L. (Everton), 1963 v Ni, W, F; 1967 v Sp, A; 1968 v S, Sp, Se, Y, USSR, WG; 1969 v Ni, S, R, Bul, M, U, Br; 1970 v S, W, Bel, Co, Ec, R, Br, WG (26)
Lampard, F. J. (West Ham U), 2000 v Bel; 2001 v Sp (sub); (with Chelsea), 2002 v Ho (sub), Se (sub), Ho (sub), I, Para (sub); 2003 v Aus, S.Af (sub), Ser, Slo; 2004 v Cro (sub), Mac, Lie, T (sub), D, P, J, Ic, F, Sw, Cro, P (23)
Lampard, F. R. G. (West Ham U), 1973 v Y; 1980 v Aus (2)
Langley, E. J. (Fulham), 1958 v S, P, Y (3)
Langton, R. (Blackburn R), 1947 v W, Ni, Ei, Ho, F, Sw; 1948 v Se; (with Preston NE), 1949 v D, Se; (with Bolton W), 1950 v S; 1951 v Ni (11)
Latchford, R. D. (Everton), 1978 v I, Br, W; 1979 v D, Ei, Cz (sub), Ni (2), W, S, Bul, A (12)
Latheron, E. G. (Blackburn R), 1913 v W; 1914 v Ni (2)
Lawler, C. (Liverpool), 1971 v Ma, W, S; 1972 v Sw (4)
Lawton, T. (Everton), 1939 v S, W, Ni, R of E, N, I, R, Y; (with Chelsea), 1947 v S, W, Ni, Ei, Ho, F, Sw, P; 1948 v W, Ni, Bel; (with Notts Co), 1948 v S, Se, I; 1949 v D (23)
Leach, T. (Sheffield W), 1931 v W, Ni (2)
Leake, A. (Aston Villa), 1904 v S, Ni; 1905 v S, W, Ni (5)
Lee, E. A. (Southampton), 1904 v W (1)
Lee, F. H. (Manchester C), 1969 v Ni, W, S, Bul, F, M, U; 1970 v W, Ho (2), P, Bel, Co, Ec, R, Br, WG; 1971 v EG, Gr, Ma, Ni, W, S; 1972 v Sw (2), Gr, WG (27)
Lee, J. (Derby Co), 1951 v Ni (1)
Lee, R. M. (Newcastle U), 1995 v R, Ng; 1996 v Co (sub), N, Sw, Bul (sub), H; 1997 v M, Ge, S.Af, Pol, F (sub), Br (sub); 1998 v Cam (sub), Ch, Sw, Bel, Co (sub); 1999 v Se (sub), Bul, L (sub) (21)
Lee, S. (Liverpool), 1983 v Gr, L, W, Gr, H, S, Aus; 1984 v D, H, L, F, Ni, W, Ch (sub) (14)
Leighton, J. E. (Nottingham F), 1886 v Ni (1)
Le Saux, G. P. (Blackburn R), 1994 v D, Gr, N; 1995 v US, R, Ng, Ei, U, Se, Br; 1996 v Co, P (sub); 1997 v I, M, Ge, S.Af, Pol, I, F, Br; (with Chelsea), 1998 v I, Ch (sub), P, Mor, Bel, Tun, R, Co, Arg; 1999 v Se, Bul (sub), CzR, F, Pol, Se; 2001 v G (36)
Le Tissier, M. P. (Southampton), 1994 v D (sub), Gr (sub), N (sub); 1995 v R, Ng (sub), Ei; 1997 v Mol (sub), I (8)
Lilley, H. E. (Sheffield U), 1892 v W (1)
Linacre, H. J. (Nottingham F), 1905 v W, S (2)
Lindley, T. (Cambridge University), 1886 v S, W, Ni; 1887 v S, W, Ni; 1888 v S, W, Ni; (with Nottingham F), 1889 v S; 1890 v S, W; 1891 v Ni (13)
Lindsay, A. (Liverpool), 1974 v Arg, EG, Bul, Y (4)
Lindsay, W. (Wanderers), 1877 v S (1)
Lineker, G. (Leicester C), 1984 v S (sub); 1985 v Ei, R (sub), S (sub), I (sub), WG, US; (with Everton), 1986 v R, T, Ni, Eg, USSR, Ca, P, Mor, Pol, Para, Arg; (with Barcelona), 1987 v Ni (2), Y, Sp, T, Br; 1988 v WG, T, Y, Ho, H, S, Co, Sw, Ei, Ho, USSR; 1989 v Se, S.Ar, Gr, Alb (2), Pol, D; (with Tottenham H), 1990 v Se, Pol, I, Y, Br, Cz, D, U, Tun, Ei, Ho, Eg, Bel, Cam, WG, I; 1991 v H, Pol, Ei (2), Cam, T, Arg, Aus, Nz, Mal; 1992 v G, T, Pol, F (sub), Cz (sub), C, H, Br, Fi, D, F, Se (80)
Lintott, E. H. (QPR), 1908 v S, W, Ni; (with Bradford C), 1909 v S, Ni, H (2) (7)
Lipsham, H. B. (Sheffield U), 1902 v W (1)
Little, B. (Aston Villa), 1975 v W (sub) (1)

Lloyd, L. V. (Liverpool), 1971 v W; 1972 v Sw, Ni; (with Nottingham F), 1980 v W (4)
Lockett, A. (Stoke C), 1903 v Ni (1)
Lodge, L. V. (Cambridge University), 1894 v W; 1895 v S, W; (with Corinthians), 1896 v S, Ni (5)
Lofthouse, J. M. (Blackburn R), 1885 v S, W, Ni; 1887 v S, W; (with Accrington), 1889 v Ni; (with Blackburn R), 1890 v Ni (7)
Lofthouse, N. (Bolton W), 1951 v Y; 1952 v W, Ni, S, A (2), I, Sw; 1953 v W, Ni, S, Bel, Arg, Ch, U, US; 1954 v W, Ni, R of E, Bel, U; 1955 v Ni, S, F, Sp, P; 1956 v W, S, Sp, D, Fi (sub); 1959 v W, USSR (33)
Longworth, E. (Liverpool), 1920 v S; 1921 v Bel; 1923 v S, W, Bel (5)
Lowder, A. (Wolverhampton W), 1889 v W (1)
Lowe, E. (Aston Villa), 1947 v F, Sw, P (3)
Lucas, T. (Liverpool), 1922 v Ni; 1924 v F; 1926 v Bel (3)
Luntley, E. (Nottingham F), 1880 v S, W (2)
Lyttelton, Hon. A. (Cambridge University), 1877 v S (1)
Lyttelton, Hon. E. (Cambridge University), 1878 v S (1)

McCall, J. (Preston NE), 1913 v S, W; 1914 v S; 1920 v S; 1921 v Ni (5)
McCann, G. P. (Sunderland), 2001 v Sp (sub) (1)
McDermott, T. (Liverpool), 1978 v Sw, L; 1979 v Ni, W, Se; 1980 v D, Ni (sub), Ei, Ni, S, Bel (sub), Sp; 1981 v N, R, Sw, R (sub), Br, Sw (sub), H; 1982 v N, H, W (sub), Ho, S (sub), Ic (25)
McDonald, C. A. (Burnley), 1958 v USSR (3), Br, A; 1959 v W, Ni, USSR (8)
McFarland, R. L. (Derby Co), 1971 v Gr, Ma (2), Ni, S; 1972 v Sw, Gr, WG, W, S; 1973 v W (3), Ni, S, Cz, Pol, USSR, I; 1974 v A, Pol, I, W, Ni; 1976 v Cz, S; 1977 v Ei, I (28)
McGarry, W. H. (Huddersfield T), 1954 v Sw, U; 1956 v W, D (4)
McGuinness, W. (Manchester U), 1959 v Ni, M (2)
McInroy, A. (Sunderland), 1927 v Ni (1)
McMahon, S. (Liverpool), 1988 v Is, H, Co, USSR; 1989 v D (sub); 1990 v Se, Pol, I, Y (sub), Br, Cz (sub), D, Ei (sub), Eg, Bel, I; 1991 v Ei (17)
McManaman, S. (Liverpool), 1995 v Ng (sub), U (sub), J (sub); 1996 v Co, N, Sw, P (sub), Bul, Cro, Chn, Sw, S, Ho, Sp, G; 1997 v Pol, I, M; 1998 v Cam, Sw, Mor, Co (sub); 1999 v Pol, H; (with Real Madrid), 2000 v L, Pol, Uk, Ma (sub), P; 2001 v F (sub), Fi (sub+1), Alb, Gr (sub); 2002 v G (sub), Alb (sub), Gr (sub) (37)
McNab, R. (Arsenal), 1969 v Ni, Bul, R (1+1 sub) (4)
McNeal, R. (WBA), 1914 v S, W (2)
McNeil, M. (Middlesbrough), 1961 v W, Ni, S, L, P, Sp, M, I; 1962 v L (9)
Mabbutt, G. (Tottenham H), 1983 v WG, Gr, L, W, Gr, H, Ni, S (sub); 1984 v H; 1987 v Y, Ni, T; 1988 v WG; 1992 v T, Pol, Cz (16)
Macaulay, R. H. (Cambridge University), 1881 v S (1)
Macdonald, M. (Newcastle U), 1972 v W, Ni, S (sub); 1973 v USSR (sub); 1974 v P, S (sub), Y (sub); 1975 v WG, Cy (2), Ni; 1976 v Sw (sub), Cz, P (14)
Macrae, S. (Notts Co), 1883 v S, W, Ni; 1884 v S, Ni (5)
Maddison, F. B. (Oxford University), 1872 v S (1)
Madeley, P. E. (Leeds U), 1971 v Ni; 1972 v Sw (2), Gr, WG (2), W, S; 1973 v S, Cz, Pol, USSR, I; 1974 v A, Pol, I; 1975 v Cz, P, Cy; 1976 v Cz, P, Fi; 1977 v Ei, Ho (24)
Magee, T. P. (WBA), 1923 v W, Se; 1925 v S, Bel, F (5)
Makepeace, H. (Everton), 1906 v S; 1910 v S; 1912 v S, W (4)
Male, C. G. (Arsenal), 1935 v S, Ni, I, Ho; 1936 v S, W, Ni, G, A, Bel; 1937 v S, Ni, H, N, Se, Fi; 1939 v I, R, Y (19)
Mannion, W. J. (Middlesbrough), 1947 v S, W, Ni, Ei, Ho, F, Sw, P; 1948 v W, Ni, Bel, Se, I; 1949 v N, F; 1950 v S, Ei, P, Bel, Ch, US; 1951 v Ni, W, S, Y; 1952 v F (26)
Mariner, P. (Ipswich T), 1977 v L (sub), Ni; 1978 v L, W (sub), S; 1980 v W, Ni (sub), S, Aus, I (sub), Sp (sub); 1981 v N, Sw, Sp, Sw, H; 1982 v N, H, Ho, S, Fi, F, Cz, K, WG, Sp; 1983 v D, WG, Gr, W; 1984 v D, H, L; (with Arsenal), 1985 v EG, R (35)
Marsden, J. T. (Darwen), 1891 v Ni (1)
Marsden, W. (Sheffield W), 1930 v W, S, G (3)
Marsh, R. W. (QPR), 1972 v Sw (sub); (with Manchester C), WG (sub+1), W, Ni, S; 1973 v W (2), Y (9)
Marshall, T. (Darwen), 1880 v W; 1881 v W (2)
Martin, A. (West Ham U), 1981 v Br, S (sub); 1982 v H, Fi; 1983 v Gr, L, W, Gr, H; 1984 v H, L, W; 1985 v Ni; 1986 v Is, Ca, Para; 1987 v Se (17)
Martin, H. (Sunderland), 1914 v Ni (1)
Martyn, A. N. (C Palace), 1992 v C (sub), H; 1993 v G; (with Leeds U), 1997 v S.Af; 1998 v Cam, Ch, Bel; 1999 v CzR, F (sub); 2000 v L, Pol, Bel (sub), Uk, R; 2001 v Sp (sub), M; 2002 v Ho, Gr, Se, Ho, I, Sk, Cam (23)
Marwood, B. (Arsenal), 1989 v S.Ar (sub) (1)
Maskrey, H. M. (Derby Co), 1908 v Ni (1)
Mason, C. (Wolverhampton W), 1887 v Ni; 1888 v W; 1890 v Ni (3)
Matthews, R. D. (Coventry C), 1956 v S, Br, Se, WG; 1957 v Ni (5)
Matthews, S. (Stoke C), 1935 v W, I; 1936 v G; 1937 v S; 1938 v S, W, Cz, G, Sw, F; 1939 v S, W, Ni, R of E, N, I, Y; 1947 v S; (with Blackpool), 1947 v Sw, P; 1948 v S, W, Ni, Bel, I; 1949 v S, W, Ni, D, Sw; 1950 v Sp; 1951 v Ni, S; 1954 v Ni, R of E, H, Bel, U; 1955 v Ni, W, S, F, WG, Sp, P; 1956 v W, Br; 1957 v S, W, Ni, Y, D (2), Ei (54)
Matthews, V. (Sheffield U), 1928 v F, Bel (2)
Maynard, W. J. (1st Surrey Rifles), 1872 v S; 1876 v S (2)
Meadows, J. (Manchester C), 1955 v S (1)
Medley, L. D. (Tottenham H), 1951 v Y, W; 1952 v F, A, W, Ni (6)
Meehan, T. (Chelsea), 1924 v Ni (1)
Melia, J. (Liverpool), 1963 v S, Sw (2)
Mercer, D. W. (Sheffield U), 1923 v Ni, Bel (2)
Mercer, J. (Everton), 1939 v S, Ni, I, R, Y (5)
Merrick, G. H. (Birmingham C), 1952 v Ni, S, A (2), I, Sw; 1953 v Ni, W, S, Bel, Arg, Ch, U; 1954 v W, Ni, S, R of E, H (2), Y, Bel, Sw, U (23)
Merson, P. C. (Arsenal), 1992 v G (sub), Cz, H, Br (sub), Fi (sub), D, Se (sub); 1993 v Sp (sub), N (sub), Ho (sub), Br (sub), G; 1994 v Ho, Gr; 1997 v I (sub); (with Middlesbrough), 1998 v Sw, P (sub), Bel, Arg (sub); 1999 v Se (sub); (with Aston Villa), CzR (21)
Metcalfe, V. (Huddersfield T), 1951 v Arg, P (2)
Mew, J. W. (Manchester U), 1921 v Ni (1)
Middleditch, B. (Corinthians), 1897 v Ni (1)
Milburn, J. E. T. (Newcastle U), 1949 v S, W, Ni, Sw; 1950 v W, P, Bel, Sp; 1951 v W, Arg, P; 1952 v F; 1956 v D (13)
Miller, B. G. (Burnley), 1961 v A (1)
Miller, H. S. (Charlton Ath), 1923 v Se (1)
Mills, D. J. (Leeds U), 2001 v M (sub); 2002 v Ho (sub), Se (sub), I, Para (sub), Sk, Cam (sub), Se, Arg, Ng, D, Br; 2003 v P, Aus (sub), S.Af, Ser, Slo; 2004 v Cro (sub), P (sub) (19)
Mills, G. R. (Chelsea), 1938 v W, Ni, Cz (3)
Mills, M. D. (Ipswich T), 1973 v Y; 1976 v W (2), Ni, S, Br, I (sub), Fi; 1977 v Fi (sub), I, Ni, W, S; 1978 v WG, Br, W, Ni, S, H; 1979 v D, Ei, Ni (2), S, Bul, A; 1980 v D, Ni, Sp (2); 1981 v Sw (2), H; 1982 v N, H, S, Fi, F, Cz, K, WG, Sp (42)
Milne, G. (Liverpool), 1963 v Br, Cz, EG; 1964 v W, Ni, S, R of W, U, P, Ei, Br, Arg; 1965 v Ni, Bel (14)
Milton, C. A. (Arsenal), 1952 v A (1)
Milward, A. (Everton), 1891 v S, W; 1897 v S, W (4)
Mitchell, C. (Upton Park), 1880 v W; 1881 v S; 1883 v S, W; 1885 v W (5)
Mitchell, J. F. (Manchester C), 1925 v Ni (1)
Moffat, H. (Oldham Ath), 1913 v W (1)
Molyneux, G. (Southampton), 1902 v S; 1903 v S, W, Ni (4)
Moon, W. R. (Old Westminsters), 1888 v S, W; 1889 v S, W; 1890 v S, W; 1891 v S (7)
Moore, H. T. (Notts Co), 1883 v Ni; 1885 v W (2)
Moore, J. (Derby Co), 1923 v Se (1)
Moore, R. F. (West Ham U), 1962 v Pe, H, Arg, Bul, Br; 1963 v W, Ni, S, F (2), Br, Cz, EG, Sw; 1964 v W, Ni, S, R of W, U, P (2), Ei, Br, Arg; 1965 v Ni, S, Bel, H, Y, WG, Se; 1966 v W, Ni, S, A, Sp, Pol (2), WG (2), N, D, U, M, F, Arg, P; 1967 v W, Ni, S, Cz, Sp, A; 1968 v W, Ni, S, USSR (2), Sp (2), Se, Y, WG; 1969 v Ni, W, S, R, Bul, F, M, U, Br; 1970 v W, Ni, S, Ho, P, Bel, Co, Ec, R, Br, Cz, WG; 1971 v EG, Gr, Ma, Ni, S; 1972 v Sw (2), Gr, WG (2), W, S; 1973 v W (3), Y, S (2), Ni, Cz, Pol, USSR, I; 1974 v I (108)
Moore, W. G. B. (West Ham U), 1923 v Se (1)
Mordue, J. (Sunderland), 1912 v Ni; 1913 v Ni (2)
Morice, C. J. (Barnes), 1872 v S (1)
Morley, A. (Aston Villa), 1982 v H (sub), Ni, W, Ic; 1983 v D, Gr (6)
Morley, H. (Notts Co), 1910 v Ni (1)
Morren, T. (Sheffield U), 1898 v Ni (1)
Morris, F. (WBA), 1920 v S; 1921 v Ni (2)
Morris, J. (Derby Co), 1949 v N, F; 1950 v Ei (3)
Morris, W. W. (Wolverhampton W), 1939 v S, Ni, R (3)
Morse, H. (Notts Co), 1879 v S (1)
Mort, T. (Aston Villa), 1924 v W, F; 1926 v S (3)
Morten, A. (C Palace), 1873 v S (1)
Mortensen, S. H. (Blackpool), 1947 v P; 1948 v W, S, Ni, Bel, Se, I; 1949 v S, W, Ni, Se, N; 1950 v S, W, Ni, I, P, Bel, Ch, US, Sp; 1951 v S, Arg; 1954 v R of E, H (25)
Morton, J. R. (West Ham U), 1938 v Cz (1)

Mosforth, W. (Sheffield W), 1877 v S; (with Sheffield Albion), 1878 v S; 1879 v S, W; 1880 v S, W; (with Sheffield W), 1881 v W; 1882 v S, W (9)
Moss, F. (Arsenal), 1934 v S, H, Cz; 1935 v I (4)
Moss, F. (Aston Villa), 1922 v S, Ni; 1923 v Ni; 1924 v S, Bel (5)
Mosscrop, E. (Burnley), 1914 v S, W (2)
Mozley, B. (Derby Co), 1950 v W, Ni, Ei (3)
Mullen, J. (Wolverhampton W), 1947 v S; 1949 v N, F; 1950 v Bel (sub), Ch, US; 1954 v W, Ni, S, R of E, Y, Sw (12)
Mullery, A. P. (Tottenham H), 1965 v Ho; 1967 v Sp, A; 1968 v W, Ni, S, USSR, Sp (2), Se, Y; 1969 v Ni, S, R, Bul, F, M, U, Br; 1970 v W, Ni, S (sub), Ho (sub), Bel, P, Co, Ec, R, Cz, WG, Br; 1971 v Ma, EG, Gr; 1972 v Sw (35)
Murphy, D. B. (Liverpool), 2002 v Se (sub), I (sub), Para (sub), Sk; 2003 v P (sub), Aus (sub), Lie (sub); 2004 v Cro (sub), D (sub) (9)

Neal, P. G. (Liverpool), 1976 v W, I; 1977 v W, S, Br, Arg, U; 1978 v Sw, I, WG, Ni, S, H; 1979 v D, Ei, Ni (2), S, Bul, A; 1980 v D, Ni, Sp, Arg, W, Bel, I; 1981 v R, Sw, Sp, Br, H; 1982 v N, H, W, Ho, Ic, F (sub), K; 1983 v D, Gr, L, W, Gr, H, Ni, S, Aus (2); 1984 v D (50)
Needham, E. (Sheffield U), 1894 v S; 1895 v S; 1897 v S, W, Ni; 1898 v S, W; 1899 v S, W, Ni; 1900 v S, Ni; 1901 v S, W, Ni; 1902 v W (16)
Neville, G. A. (Manchester U), 1995 v J, Br; 1996 v Co, N, Sw, P, Bul, Cro, H, Chn, Sw, S, Ho, Sp; 1997 v Mol, Pol, I, Ge, Pol, I (sub), F, Br (sub); 1998 v Mol, Ch, P, S.Ar, Bel, R, Co, Arg; 1999 v Bul, Pol; 2000 v L (sub), Pol, Br, Ma, P, G, R; 2001 v G, I, Sp (sub), Fi, Alb; 2002 v Ho, G, Alb, Gr, Se, Ho, I (sub), Para; 2003 v Slo, Mac, Aus, Lie, T; 2004 v Mac, Lie, T, D, J, Ic, F, Sw, Cro, P (67)
Neville, P. J. (Manchester U), 1996 v Chn; 1997 v S.Af, Pol (sub), I, F, Br; 1998 v Mol, Cam, Ch, P (sub), S.Ar (sub), Bel; 1999 v L, Pol (sub), H, Se, Bul; 2000 v L (sub), Pol (sub), Bel (sub), S (2), Arg (sub), Br, Uk, Ma, P, G, R; 2001 v Fi, Sp, M, Gr; 2002 v Se (sub), Ho (sub), I (sub), Para (sub); 2003 v S.Af, Ser, Slo; 2004 v Cro, Mac (sub), Lie (sub), D (sub), P, Se, J (sub), Ic (sub), Cro (sub), P (sub) (50)
Newton, K. R. (Blackburn R), 1966 v S, WG; 1967 v Sp, A; 1968 v W, S, Sp, Se, Y, WG; 1969 v Ni, W, S, R, Bul, M, U, Br, F; (with Everton), 1970 v Ni, S, Ho, Co, Ec, R, Cz, WG (27)
Nicholls, J. (WBA), 1954 v S, Y (2)
Nicholson, W. E. (Tottenham H), 1951 v P (1)
Nish, D. J. (Derby Co), 1973 v Ni; 1974 v P, W, Ni, S (5)
Norman, M. (Tottenham H), 1962 v Pe, H, Arg, Bul, Br; 1963 v S, F, Br, Cz, EG; 1964 v W, Ni, S, R of W, U, P (2), US, Br, Arg; 1965 v Ni, Bel, Ho (23)
Nuttall, H. (Bolton W), 1928 v W, Ni; 1929 v S (3)

Oakley, W. J. (Oxford University), 1895 v W; 1896 v S, W, Ni; (with Corinthians), 1897 v S, W, Ni; 1898 v S, W, Ni; 1900 v S, W, Ni; 1901 v S, W, Ni (16)
O'Dowd, J. P. (Chelsea), 1932 v S; 1933 v Ni, Sw (3)
O'Grady, M. (Huddersfield T), 1963 v Ni; (with Leeds U), 1969 v F (2)
Ogilvie, R. A. M. M. (Clapham R), 1874 v S (1)
Oliver, L. F. (Fulham), 1929 v Bel (1)
Olney, B. A. (Aston Villa), 1928 v F, Bel (2)
Osborne, F. R. (Fulham), 1923 v Ni, F; (with Tottenham H), 1925 v Bel; 1926 v Bel (4)
Osborne, R. (Leicester C), 1928 v W (1)
Osgood, P. L. (Chelsea), 1970 v Bel, R (sub), Cz (sub); 1974 v I (4)
Osman, R. (Ipswich T), 1980 v Aus; 1981 v Sp, R, Sw; 1982 v N, Ic; 1983 v D, Aus (3); 1984 v D (11)
Ottaway, C. J. (Oxford University), 1872 v S; 1874 v S (2)
Owen, J. R. B. (Sheffield), 1874 v S (1)
Owen, M. J. (Liverpool), 1998 v Ch, Sw, P (sub), Mor (sub), Bel (sub), Tun (sub), R (sub), Co, Arg; 1999 v Se, Bul, L, F; 2000 v L (sub), Pol (sub), Bel (sub), S (2), Br, P, G, R; 2001 v F (sub), G, Sp, Fi, Alb, M, Gr; 2002 v Ho (sub), G, Alb, I, Para, Sk, Cam, Se, Arg, Ng, D, Br; 2003 v P, Slo, Mac, Aus, Lie, T, S.Af, Ser, Slo; 2004 v Cro, Mac, Lie, P, J, Ic, F, Sw, Cro, P (60)
Owen, S. W. (Luton T), 1954 v H, Y, Bel (3)

Page, L. A. (Burnley), 1927 v S, W, Bel, L, F; 1928 v W, Ni (7)
Paine, T. L. (Southampton), 1963 v Cz, EG; 1964 v W, Ni, S, R of W, U, US, P; 1965 v Ni, H, Y, WG, Se; 1966 v W, A, Y, N, M (19)
Pallister, G. A. (Middlesbrough), 1988 v H; 1989 v S.Ar; (with Manchester U), 1991 v Cam (sub), T; 1992 v G; 1993 v N, US, Br, G; 1994 v Pol, Ho, Sm, D; 1995 v US, R, Ei, U, Se; 1996 v N, Sw; 1997 v Mol, Pol (sub) (22)
Palmer, C. L. (Sheffield W), 1992 v C, H, Br, Fi (sub), D, F, Se; 1993 v Sp (sub), N (sub), T, Sm, T, Ho, Pol, N, US, Br (sub); 1994 v Ho (18)
Pantling, H. H. (Sheffield U), 1924 v Ni (1)
Paravacini, P. J. de (Cambridge University), 1883 v S, W, Ni (3)
Parker, P. A. (QPR), 1989 v Alb (sub), Ch, D; 1990 v Y, U, Ho, Eg, Bel, Cam, WG, I; 1991 v H, Pol, USSR, Aus, Nz; (with Manchester U), 1992 v G; 1994 v Ho, D (19)
Parker, S. M. (Charlton Ath), 2004 v D (sub); (with Chelsea), v Se (sub) (2)
Parker, T. R. (Southampton), 1925 v F (1)
Parkes, P. B. (QPR), 1974 v P (1)
Parkinson, J. (Liverpool), 1910 v S, W (2)
Parlour, R. (Arsenal), 1999 v Pol (sub), Se (sub), Bul (sub); 2000 v L, S (sub), Arg (sub), Br (sub); 2001 v G (sub), Fi, I (10)
Parr, P. C. (Oxford University), 1882 v W (1)
Parry, E. H. (Old Carthusians), 1879 v W; 1882 v W, S (3)
Parry, R. A. (Bolton W), 1960 v Ni, S (2)
Patchitt, B. C. A. (Corinthians), 1923 v Se (2) (2)
Pawson, F. W. (Cambridge University), 1883 v Ni; (with Swifts), 1885 v Ni (2)
Payne, J. (Luton T), 1937 v Fi (1)
Peacock, A. (Middlesbrough), 1962 v Arg, Bul; 1963 v Ni, W; (with Leeds U), 1966 v W, Ni (6)
Peacock, J. (Middlesbrough), 1929 v F, Bel, Sp (3)
Pearce, S. (Nottingham F), 1987 v Br, S; 1988 v WG (sub), Is, H; 1989 v D, Se, S.Ar, Gr, Alb (2), Ch, S, Pol, D; 1990 v Se, Pol, I, Y, Br, Cz, D, U, Tun, Ei, Ho, Eg, Bel, Cam, WG; 1991 v H, Pol, Ei (2), Cam, T, Arg, Aus, Nz (2), Mal; 1992 v T, Pol, F, Cz, Br (sub), Fi, D, F, Se; 1993 v Sp, N, T; 1994 v Pol, Sm, Gr (sub); 1995 v R (sub), J, Br; 1996 v N, Sw, P, Bul, Cro, H, Sw, S, Ho, Sp, G; 1997 v Mol, Pol, I, M, S.Af, I; (with West Ham U), 2000 v L, Pol (78)
Pearson, H. F. (WBA), 1932 v S (1)
Pearson, J. H. (Crewe Alex), 1892 v Ni (1)
Pearson, J. S. (Manchester U), 1976 v W, Ni, S, Br, Fi; 1977 v Ei, Ho (sub), W, S, Br, Arg, U; 1978 v I (sub), WG, Ni (15)
Pearson, S. C. (Manchester U), 1948 v S; 1949 v S, Ni; 1950 v Ni, I; 1951 v P; 1952 v S, I (8)
Pease, W. H. (Middlesbrough), 1927 v W (1)
Pegg, D. (Manchester U), 1957 v Ei (1)
Pejic, M. (Stoke C), 1974 v P, W, Ni, S (4)
Pelly, F. R. (Old Foresters), 1893 v Ni; 1894 v S, W (3)
Pennington, J. (WBA), 1907 v S, W; 1908 v S, W, Ni, A; 1909 v S, W, H (2), A; 1910 v S, W; 1911 v S, W, Ni; 1912 v S, W, Ni; 1913 v S, W; 1914 v S, Ni; 1920 v S, W (25)
Pentland, F. B. (Middlesbrough), 1909 v S, W, H (2), A (5)
Perry, C. (WBA), 1890 v Ni; 1891 v Ni; 1893 v W (3)
Perry, T. (WBA), 1898 v W (1)
Perry, W. (Blackpool), 1956 v Ni, S, Sp (3)
Perryman, S. (Tottenham H), 1982 v Ic (sub) (1)
Peters, M. (West Ham U), 1966 v Y, Fi, Pol, M, F, Arg, P, WG; 1967 v Ni, W, S, Cz; 1968 v W, Ni, S, USSR (2), Sp (2), Se, Y; 1969 v Ni, S, R, Bul, F, M, U, Br; 1970 v Ho (2), P (sub), Bel; (with Tottenham H), W, Ni, S, Co, Ec, R, Br, Cz, WG; 1971 v EG, Gr, Ma (2), Ni, W, S; 1972 v Sw, Gr, WG (1+1 sub), Ni (sub); 1973 v S (2), Ni, W, Cz, Pol, USSR, I; 1974 v A, Pol, I, P, S (67)
Phelan, M. C. (Manchester U), 1990 v I (sub) (1)
Phillips, K. (Sunderland), 1999 v H; 2000 v Bel, Arg (sub), Br (sub), Ma; 2001 v I (sub); 2002 v Se, Ho (sub) (8)
Phillips, L. H. (Portsmouth), 1952 v Ni; 1955 v W, WG (3)
Pickering, F. (Everton), 1964 v US; 1965 v Ni, Bel (3)
Pickering, J. (Sheffield U), 1933 v S (1)
Pickering, N. (Sunderland), 1983 v Aus (1)
Pike, T. M. (Cambridge University), 1886 v Ni (1)
Pilkington, B. (Burnley), 1955 v Ni (1)
Plant, J. (Bury), 1900 v S (1)
Platt, D. (Aston Villa), 1990 v I (sub), Y (sub), Br, D (sub), Tun (sub), Ho (sub), Eg (sub), Bel (sub), Cam, WG, I; 1991 v H, Pol, Ei (2), T, USSR, Arg, Aus, Nz (2), Mal; (with Bari), 1992 v G, T, Pol, Cz, C, Br, Fi, D, F, Se; (with Juventus), 1993 v Sp, N, T, Sm, T, Ho, Pol, N, Br (sub), G; (with Sampdoria), 1994 v Pol, Ho, Sm, D, Gr, N; 1995 v US, Ng, Ei, U, J, Se, Br; (with Arsenal), 1996 v Bul (sub), Cro, H, Sw (sub), Ho (sub), Sp, G (62)
Plum, S. L. (Charlton Ath), 1923 v F (1)
Pointer, R. (Burnley), 1962 v W, L, P (3)
Porteous, T. S. (Sunderland), 1891 v W (1)
Powell, C. G. (Charlton Ath), 2001 v Sp, Fi, M (sub); 2002 v Ho (sub+sub) (5)
Priest, A. E. (Sheffield U), 1900 v Ni (1)

Prinsep, J. F. M. (Clapham Rovers), 1879 v S (1)
Puddefoot, S. C. (Blackburn R), 1926 v S, Ni (2)
Pye, J. (Wolverhampton W), 1950 v Ei (1)
Pym, R. H. (Bolton W), 1925 v S, W; 1926 v W (3)

Quantrill, A. (Derby Co), 1920 v S, W; 1921 v W, Ni (4)
Quixall, A. (Sheffield W), 1954 v W, Ni, R of E; 1955 v Sp, P (sub) (5)

Radford, J. (Arsenal), 1969 v R; 1972 v Sw (sub) (2)
Raikes, G. B. (Oxford University), 1895 v W; 1896 v W, Ni, S (4)
Ramsey, A. E. (Southampton), 1949 v Sw; (with Tottenham H), 1950 v S, I, P, Bel, Ch, US, Sp; 1951 v S, Ni, W, Y, Arg, P; 1952 v S, W, Ni, F, A (2), I, Sw; 1953 v Ni, W, S, Bel, Arg, Ch, U, US; 1954 v R of E, H (32)
Rawlings, A. (Preston NE), 1921 v Bel (1)
Rawlings, W. E. (Southampton), 1922 v S, W (2)
Rawlinson, J. F. P. (Cambridge University), 1882 v Ni (1)
Rawson, H. E. (Royal Engineers), 1875 v S (1)
Rawson, W. S. (Oxford University), 1875 v S; 1877 v S (2)
Read, A. (Tufnell Park), 1921 v Bel (1)
Reader, J. (WBA), 1894 v Ni (1)
Reaney, P. (Leeds U), 1969 v Bul (sub); 1970 v P; 1971 v Ma (3)
Redknapp, J. F. (Liverpool), 1996 v Co, N, Sw, Chn, S (sub); 1997 v M (sub), Ge (sub), S.Af; 1999 v Se, Bul, F, Pol (sub), H (sub), Bul; 2000 v Bel, S (2) (17)
Reeves, K. (Norwich C), 1980 v Bul; (with Manchester C), Ni (2)
Regis, C. (WBA), 1982 v Ni (sub), W (sub), Ic; 1983 v WG; (with Coventry C), 1988 v T (sub) (5)
Reid, P. (Everton), 1985 v M (sub), WG, US (sub); 1986 v R, S (sub), Ca (sub), Pol, Para, Arg; 1987 v Br; 1988 v WG, Y (sub), Sw (sub) (13)
Revie, D. G. (Manchester C), 1955 v Ni, S, F; 1956 v W, D; 1957 v Ni (6)
Reynolds, J. (WBA), 1892 v S; 1893 v S, W; (with Aston Villa), 1894 v S, Ni; 1895 v S; 1897 v S, W (8)
Richards, C. H. (Nottingham F), 1898 v Ni (1)
Richards, G. H. (Derby Co), 1909 v A (1)
Richards, J. P. (Wolverhampton W), 1973 v Ni (1)
Richardson, J. R. (Newcastle U), 1933 v I, Sw (2)
Richardson, K. (Aston Villa), 1994 v Gr (1)
Richardson, W. G. (WBA), 1935 v Ho (1)
Rickaby, S. (WBA), 1954 v Ni (1)
Ricketts, M. B. (Bolton W), 2002 v Ho (1)
Rigby, A. (Blackburn R), 1927 v S, Bel, L, F; 1928 v W (5)
Rimmer, E. J. (Sheffield W), 1930 v S, G, A; 1932 v Sp (4)
Rimmer, J. J. (Arsenal), 1976 v I (1)
Ripley, S. E. (Blackburn R), 1994 v Sm; 1998 v Mol (sub) (2)
Rix, G. (Arsenal), 1981 v N, R, Sw (sub), Br, W, S; 1982 v Ho (sub), Fi (sub), F, Cz, K, WG, Sp; 1983 v D, WG (sub), Gr (sub); 1984 v Ni (17)
Robb, G. (Tottenham H), 1954 v H (1)
Roberts, C. (Manchester U), 1905 v Ni, W, S (3)
Roberts, F. (Manchester C), 1925 v S, W, Bel, F (4)
Roberts, G. (Tottenham H), 1983 v Ni, S; 1984 v F, Ni, S, USSR (6)
Roberts, H. (Arsenal), 1931 v S (1)
Roberts, H. (Millwall), 1931 v Bel (1)
Roberts, R. (WBA), 1887 v S; 1888 v Ni; 1890 v Ni (3)
Roberts, W. T. (Preston NE), 1924 v W, Bel (2)
Robinson, J. (Sheffield W), 1937 v Fi; 1938 v G, Sw; 1939 v W (4)
Robinson, J. W. (Derby Co), 1897 v S, Ni; (with New Brighton Tower), 1898 v S, W, Ni; (with Southampton), 1899 v W, S; 1900 v S, W, Ni; 1901 v Ni (11)
Robinson, P. W. (Leeds U), 2003 v Aus (sub), S.Af (sub); 2004 v Cro (sub), D (sub); (with Tottenham H), Ic (5)
Robson, B. (WBA), 1980 v Ei, Aus; 1981 v N, R, Sw, Sp, R, Br, W, S, Sw, H; 1982 v N; (with Manchester U), H, Ni, W, Ho, S, Fi, F, Cz, WG, Sp; 1983 v D, Gr, L, S; 1984 v H, L, F, Ni, S, USSR, Br, U, Ch; 1985 v EG, Fi, T, Ei, R, Fi, S, M, I, WG, US; 1986 v R, T, Is, M, P, Mor; 1987 v Ni (2), Sp, T, Br, S; 1988 v T, Y, Ho, H, S, Co, Sw, Ei, Ho, USSR; 1989 v S, Se, S.Ar, Gr, Alb (2), Ch, S, Pol, D; 1990 v Pol, I, Y, Cz, U, Tun, Ei, Ho; 1991 v Cam, Ei; 1992 v T (90)
Robson, R. (WBA), 1958 v F, USSR (2), Br, A; 1960 v Sp, H; 1961 v Ni, W, S, L, P, Sp, M, I; 1962 v W, Ni, Sw, L, P (20)
Rocastle, D. (Arsenal), 1989 v D, S.Ar, Gr, Alb (2), Pol (sub), D; 1990 v Se (sub), Pol, Y, D (sub); 1992 v Pol, Cz, Br (sub) (14)
Rooney, W. (Everton), 2003 v Aus (sub), Lie (sub), T, Ser (sub), Slo; 2004 v Mac, Lie, T, D, P, Se, J, Ic, F, Sw, Cro, P (17)
Rose, W. C. (Wolverhampton W), 1884 v S, W, Ni; (with Preston NE), 1886 v Ni; (with Wolverhampton W), 1891 v Ni (5)
Rostron, T. (Darwen), 1881 v S, W (2)
Rowe, A. (Tottenham H), 1934 v F (1)
Rowley, J. F. (Manchester U), 1949 v Sw, Se, F; 1950 v Ni, I; 1952 v S (6)
Rowley, W. (Stoke C), 1889 v Ni; 1892 v Ni (2)
Royle, J. (Everton), 1971 v Ma; 1973 v Y; (with Manchester C), 1976 v Ni (sub), I; 1977 v Fi, L (6)
Ruddlesdin, H. (Sheffield W), 1904 v W, Ni; 1905 v S (3)
Ruddock, N. (Liverpool), 1995 v Ng (1)
Ruffell, J. W. (West Ham U), 1926 v S; 1927 v Ni; 1929 v S, W, Ni; 1930 v W (6)
Russell, B. B. (Royal Engineers), 1883 v W (1)
Rutherford, J. (Newcastle U), 1904 v S; 1907 v S, Ni, W; 1908 v S, Ni, W, A (2), H, B (11)

Sadler, D. (Manchester U), 1968 v Ni, USSR; 1970 v Ec (sub); 1971 v EG (4)
Sagar, C. (Bury), 1900 v Ni; 1902 v W (2)
Sagar, E. (Everton), 1936 v S, Ni, A, Bel (4)
Salako, J. A. (C Palace), 1991 v Aus (sub), Nz (sub + 1), Mal; 1992 v G (5)
Sandford, E. A. (WBA), 1933 v W (1)
Sandilands, R. R. (Old Westminsters), 1892 v W; 1893 v Ni; 1894 v W; 1895 v W; 1896 v W (5)
Sands, J. (Nottingham F), 1880 v W (1)
Sansom, K. (C Palace), 1979 v W; 1980 v Bul, Ei, Arg, W (sub), Ni, S, Bel, I; (with Arsenal), 1981 v N, R, Sw, Sp, R, Br, W, S, Sw; 1982 v Ni, W, Ho, S, Fi, F, Cz, WG, Sp; 1983 v D, WG, Gr, L, Gr, H, Ni, S; 1984 v D, H, L, F, S, USSR, Br, U, Ch; 1985 v EG, Fi, T, Ni, Ei, R, Fi, S, I, M, WG, US; 1986 v R, T, Ni, Eg, Is, USSR, S, M, Ca, P, Mor, Pol, Para, Arg; 1987 v Se, Ni (2), Y, Sp, T; 1988 v WG, T, Y, Ho, S, Co, Sw, Ei, Ho, USSR (86)
Saunders, F. E. (Swifts), 1888 v W (1)
Savage, A. H. (C Palace), 1876 v S (1)
Sayer, J. (Stoke C), 1887 v Ni (1)
Scales, J. R. (Liverpool), 1995 v J, Se (sub), Br (3)
Scattergood, E. (Derby Co), 1913 v W (1)
Schofield, J. (Stoke C), 1892 v W; 1893 v W; 1895 v Ni (3)
Scholes, P. (Manchester U), 1997 v S.Af (sub), I, Br; 1998 v Mol, Cam, P, S.Ar, Tun, R, Co, Arg; 1999 v Se, Bul, L, F (sub), Pol, Se; 2000 v Pol, S (2), Arg, Br, Uk, Ma, P, G, R; 2001 v F, G, Fi, Sp, Fi, Alb, M, Gr; 2002 v Ho, G, Alb, Gr, Se, Ho, Para, Sk, Cam, Se, Arg, Ng, D, Br; 2003 v Slo, Mac, Aus, Lie, T, S.Af, Ser, Slo; 2004 v Cro, T, P, J, Ic, F, Sw, Cro, P (66)
Scott, L. (Arsenal), 1947 v S, W, Ni, Ei, Ho, F, Sw, P; 1948 v S, W, Ni, Bel, Se, I; 1949 v W, Ni, D (17)
Scott, W. R. (Brentford), 1937 v W (1)
Seaman, D. A. (QPR), 1989 v S.Ar, D (sub); 1990 v Cz (sub); (with Arsenal), 1991 v Cam, Ei, T, Arg; 1992 v Cz, H (sub); 1994 v Pol, Ho, Sm, D, N; 1995 v US, R, Ei; 1996 v Co, N, Sw, P, Bul, Cro, H, Sw, S, Ho, Sp, G; 1997 v Mol, Pol, Ge (2), Pol, F, Br; 1998 v Mol, I, P, S.Ar, Tun, R, Co, Arg; 1999 v Se, Bul, L, F, Pol, H, Se, Bul; 2000 v Bel, S (2), Arg, Br, P, G; 2001 v F, G, Fi (2), Alb, Gr; 2002 v G, Alb, Para, Se, Arg, Ng, D, Br; 2003 v Slo, Mac (75)
Seddon, J. (Bolton W), 1923 v F, Se (2); 1924 v Bel; 1927 v W; 1929 v S (6)
Seed, J. M. (Tottenham H), 1921 v Bel: 1923 v W, Ni, Bel; 1925 v S (5)
Settle, J. (Bury), 1899 v S, W, Ni; (with Everton), 1902 v S, Ni; 1903 v Ni (6)
Sewell, J. (Sheffield W), 1952 v Ni, A, Sw; 1953 v Ni; 1954 v H (2) (6)
Sewell, W. R. (Blackburn R), 1924 v W (1)
Shackleton, L. F. (Sunderland), 1949 v W, D; 1950 v W; 1955 v W, WG (5)
Sharp, J. (Everton), 1903 v Ni; 1905 v S (2)
Sharpe, L. S. (Manchester U), 1991 v Ei (sub); 1993 v T (sub), N, US, Br, G; 1994 v Pol, Ho (8)
Shaw, G. E. (WBA), 1932 v S (1)
Shaw, G. L. (Sheffield U), 1959 v S, W, USSR, I; 1963 v W (5)
Shea, D. (Blackburn R), 1914 v W, Ni (2)
Shearer, A. (Southampton), 1992 v F, C, F; (with Blackburn R), 1993 v Sp, N, T; 1994 v Ho, D, Gr, N; 1995 v US, R, Ng, Ei, J, Se, Br; 1996 v Co, N, Sw, P, H (sub), Chn, Sw, S, Ho, Sp, G; (with Newcastle U), 1997 v Mol, Pol, I, Ge, Pol, F, Br; 1998 v Ch (sub), Sw, P, S.Ar, Tun, R, Co, Arg; 1999 v Se, Bul, L, F, Pol, H, Se, Bul; 2000 v L, Pol, Bel, S (2), Arg, Br, Uk, Ma, P, G, R (63)
Shellito, K. J. (Chelsea), 1963 v Cz (1)

Shelton A. (Notts Co), 1889 v Ni; 1890 v S, W; 1891 v S, W; 1892 v S (6)
Shelton, C. (Notts Rangers), 1888 v Ni (1)
Shepherd, A. (Bolton W), 1906 v S; (with Newcastle U), 1911 v Ni (2)
Sheringham, E. P. (Tottenham H), 1993 v Pol, N; 1995 v US, R (sub), Ng (sub), U, J (sub), Se, Br; 1996 v Co (sub), N (sub), Sw, Bul, Cro, H, Sw, S, Ho, Sp, G; 1997 v Ge, M, Ge, S.Af, Pol, I, F (sub), Br; (with Manchester U), 1998 v I, Ch, Sw (sub), P, S.Ar, Tun, R; 1999 v Se (sub), Bul (sub), Bul; 2001 v Fi, Alb (sub), M (sub); (with Tottenham H), 2002 v Gr (sub), Se (sub), I (sub), Para (sub), Sk (sub), Cam (sub), Arg (sub), Ng (sub), D (sub), Br (sub) (51)
Sherwood, T. A. (Tottenham H), 1999 v Pol, H, Se (3)
Shilton, P. L. (Leicester C), 1971 v EG, W; 1972 v Sw, Ni; 1973 v Y, S (2), Ni, W, Cz, Pol, USSR, I; 1974 v A, Pol, I, W, Ni, S, Arg; (with Stoke C), 1975 v Cy; 1977 v Ni, W; (with Nottingham F), 1978 v W, H; 1979 v Cz, Se, A; 1980 v Ni, Sp, I; 1981 v N, Sw, R; 1982 v H, Ho, S, F, Cz, K, WG, Sp; (with Southampton), 1983 v D, WG, Gr, W, Gr, H, Ni, S, Aus (3); 1984 v D, H, F, Ni, W, S, USSR, Br, U, Ch; 1985 v EG, Fi, T, Ni, R, Fi, S, I, WG; 1986 v R, T, Ni, Eg, Is, USSR, S, M, Ca, P, Mor, Pol, Para, Arg; 1987 v Se, Ni (2), Sp, Br; (with Derby Co), 1988 v WG, T, Y, Ho, S, Co, Sw, Ei, Ho; 1989 v D, Se, Gr, Alb (2), Ch, S, Pol, D; 1990 v Se, Pol, I, Y, Br, Cz, D, U, Tun, Ei, Ho, Eg, Bel, Cam, WG, I (125)
Shimwell, E. (Blackpool), 1949 v Se (1)
Shutt, G. (Stoke C), 1886 v Ni (1)
Silcock, J. (Manchester U), 1921 v S, W; 1923 v Se (3)
Sillett, R. P. (Chelsea), 1955 v F, Sp, P (3)
Simms, E. (Luton T), 1922 v Ni (1)
Simpson, J. (Blackburn R), 1911 v S, W, Ni; 1912 v S, W, Ni; 1913 v S; 1914 v W (8)
Sinclair, T. (West Ham U), 2002 v Se, I, Para (sub), Sk (sub), Cam (sub), Arg (sub), Ng, D, Br; 2003 v P (sub), S.Af; (with Manchester C), 2004 v Cro (sub) (12)
Sinton, A. (QPR), 1992 v Pol, C, H (sub), Br, F, Se; 1993 v Sp, T, Br, G; (with Sheffield W), 1994 v Ho (sub), Sm (12)
Slater, W. J. (Wolverhampton W), 1955 v W, WG; 1958 v S, P, Y, USSR (3), Br, A; 1959 v USSR; 1960 v S (12)
Smalley, T. (Wolverhampton W), 1937 v W (1)
Smart, T. (Aston Villa), 1921 v S; 1924 v S, W; 1926 v Ni; 1930 v W (5)
Smith, A. (Nottingham F), 1891 v S, W; 1893 v Ni (3)
Smith, A. (Leeds U), 2001 v M (sub), Gr (sub); 2002 v Ho (sub); 2003 v P, Slo (sub), Mac; 2004 v P (sub), Se (sub) (8)
Smith, A. K. (Oxford University), 1872 v S (1)
Smith, A. M. (Arsenal), 1989 v S.Ar (sub), Gr, Alb (sub), Pol (sub); 1991 v T, USSR, Arg; 1992 v G, T, Pol (sub), H (sub), D, Se (sub) (13)
Smith, B. (Tottenham H), 1921 v S; 1922 v W (2)
Smith, C. E. (C Palace), 1876 v S (1)
Smith, G. O. (Oxford University), 1893 v Ni; 1894 v W, S; 1895 v W; 1896 v Ni, W, S; (with Old Carthusians), 1897 v Ni, W, S; 1898 v Ni, W, S; (with Corinthians), 1899 v Ni, W, S; 1899 v Ni, W, S; 1901 v S (20)
Smith, H. (Reading), 1905 v W, S; 1906 v W, Ni (4)
Smith, J. (WBA), 1920 v Ni; 1923 v Ni (2)
Smith, Joe (Bolton W), 1913 v Ni; 1914 v S, W; 1920 v W, Ni (5)
Smith, J. C. R. (Millwall), 1939 v Ni, N (2)
Smith, J. W. (Portsmouth), 1932 v Ni, W, Sp (3)
Smith, Leslie (Brentford), 1939 v R (1)
Smith, Lionel (Arsenal), 1951 v W; 1952 v W, Ni; 1953 v W, S, Bel (6)
Smith, R. A. (Tottenham H), 1961 v Ni, W, S, L, P, Sp; 1962 v S; 1963 v S, F, Br, Cz, EG; 1964 v W, Ni, R of W (15)
Smith, S. (Aston Villa), 1895 v S (1)
Smith, S. C. (Leicester C), 1936 v Ni (1)
Smith, T. (Birmingham C), 1960 v W, Se (2)
Smith, T. (Liverpool), 1971 v W (1)
Smith, W. H. (Huddersfield T), 1922 v W, S; 1928 v S (3)
Sorby, T. H. (Thursday Wanderers, Sheffield), 1879 v W (1)
Southgate, G. (Aston Villa), 1996 v P (sub), Bul, H (sub), Chn, Sw, S, Ho, Sp, G; 1997 v Mol, Pol, Ge, M, Ge (sub), S.Af, Pol, I, F, Br; 1998 v Mol, I, Cam, Sw, S.Ar, Mor, Tun, Arg (sub); 1999 v Se, Bul, L, Bul; 2000 v Bel, S, Arg, Uk, Ma (sub), R (sub); 2001 v F (sub), G, Fi, I, M (sub); (with Middlesbrough), 2002 v Ho (sub), Se, Ho (sub), I, Para, Sk (sub), Cam (sub); 2003 v P, Slo, Lie, S.Af, Ser, Slo; 2004 v P, Se (sub) (57)
Southworth, J. (Blackburn R), 1889 v W; 1891 v W; 1892 v S (3)
Sparks, F. J. (Herts Rangers), 1879 v S; (with Clapham Rovers), 1880 v S, W (3)
Spence, J. W. (Manchester U), 1926 v Bel; 1927 v Ni (2)
Spence, R. (Chelsea), 1936 v A, Bel (2)
Spencer, C. W. (Newcastle U), 1924 v S; 1925 v W (2)
Spencer, H. (Aston Villa), 1897 v S, W; 1900 v W; 1903 v Ni; 1905 v W, S (6)
Spiksley, F. (Sheffield W), 1893 v S, W; 1894 v S, Ni; 1896 v Ni; 1898 v S, W (7)
Spilsbury, B. W. (Cambridge University), 1885 v Ni; 1886 v Ni, S (3)
Spink, N. (Aston Villa), 1983 v Aus (sub) (1)
Spouncer, W. A. (Nottingham F), 1900 v W (1)
Springett, R. D. G. (Sheffield W), 1960 v Ni, S, Y, Sp, H; 1961 v Ni, S, L, P, Sp, M, I, A; 1962 v W, Ni, S, A, Sw, Pe, L, P, H, Arg, Bul, Br; 1963 v Ni, W, F (2), Sw; 1966 v W, A, N (33)
Sproston, B. (Leeds U), 1937 v W; 1938 v S, W, Ni, Cz, G, Sw, F; (with Tottenham H), 1939 v W, R of E; (with Manchester C), N (11)
Squire, R. T. (Cambridge University), 1886 v S, W, Ni (3)
Stanbrough, M. H. (Old Carthusians), 1895 v W (1)
Staniforth, R. (Huddersfield T), 1954 v S, H, Y, Bel, Sw, U; 1955 v W, WG (8)
Starling, R. W. (Sheffield W), 1933 v S; (with Aston Villa), 1937 v S (2)
Statham, D. (WBA), 1983 v W, Aus (2) (3)
Steele, F. C. (Stoke C), 1937 v S, W, Ni, N, Se, Fi (6)
Stein, B. (Luton T), 1984 v F (1)
Stephenson, C. (Huddersfield T), 1924 v W (1)
Stephenson, G. T. (Derby Co), 1928 v F, Bel; (with Sheffield W), 1931 v F (3)
Stephenson, J. E. (Leeds U), 1938 v S; 1939 v Ni (2)
Stepney, A. C. (Manchester U), 1968 v Se (1)
Sterland, M. (Sheffield W), 1989 v S.Ar (1)
Steven, T. M. (Everton), 1985 v Ni, Ei, R, Fi, I, US (sub); 1986 v T (sub), Eg, USSR (sub), M (sub), Pol, Para, Arg; 1987 v Se, Y (sub), Sp (sub); 1988 v T, Y, Ho, H, S, Sw, Ho, USSR; 1989 v S; (with Rangers), 1990 v Cz, Cam (sub), WG (sub), I; 1991 v Cam; (with Marseille), 1992 v G, C, Br, Fi, D, F (36)
Stevens, G. A. (Tottenham H), 1985 v Fi (sub), T (sub), Ni; 1986 v S (sub), M (sub), Mor (sub), Para (sub) (7)
Stevens, M. G. (Everton), 1985 v I, WG; 1986 v R, T, Ni, Eg, Is, S, Ca, P, Mor, Pol, Para, Arg; 1987 v Br, S; 1988 v T, Y, Is, Ho, H (sub), S, Sw, Ei, Ho, USSR; (with Rangers), 1989 v D, Se, Gr, Alb (2), S, Pol; 1990 v Se, Pol, I, Br, D, Tun, Ei, I; 1991 v USSR; 1992 v C, H, Br, Fi (46)
Stewart, J. (Sheffield W), 1907 v S, W; (with Newcastle U), 1911 v S (3)
Stewart, P. A. (Tottenham H), 1992 v G (sub), Cz (sub), C (sub) (3)
Stiles, N. P. (Manchester U), 1965 v S, H, Y, Se; 1966 v W, Ni, S, A, Sp, Pol (2), WG (2), N, D, U, M, F, Arg, P; 1967 v Ni, W, S, Cz; 1968 v USSR; 1969 v R; 1970 v Ni, S (28)
Stoker, J. (Birmingham), 1933 v W; 1934 v S, H (3)
Stone, S. B. (Nottingham F), 1996 v N (sub), Sw (sub), P, Bul, Cro, Chn (sub), Sw (sub), S (sub), Sp (sub) (9)
Storer, H. (Derby Co), 1924 v F; 1928 v Ni (2)
Storey, P. E. (Arsenal), 1971 v Gr, Ni, S; 1972 v Sw, WG, W, Ni, S; 1973 v W (3), Y, S (2), Ni, Cz, Pol, USSR, I (19)
Storey-Moore, I. (Nottingham F), 1970 v Ho (1)
Strange, A. H. (Sheffield W), 1930 v S, A, G; 1931 v S, W, Ni, F, Bel; 1932 v S, W, Ni, Sp; 1933 v S, Ni, A, I, Sw; 1934 v Ni, W, F (20)
Stratford, A. H. (Wanderers), 1874 v S (1)
Streten, B. (Luton T), 1950 v Ni (1)
Sturgess, A. (Sheffield U), 1911 v Ni; 1914 v S (2)
Summerbee, M. G. (Manchester C), 1968 v S, Sp, WG; 1972 v Sw, WG (sub), W, Ni; 1973 v USSR (sub) (8)
Sunderland, A. (Arsenal), 1980 v Aus (1)
Sutcliffe, J. W. (Bolton W), 1893 v W; 1895 v S, Ni; 1901 v S; (with Millwall), 1903 v W (5)
Sutton, C. R. (Blackburn R), 1998 v Cam (sub) (1)
Swan, P. (Sheffield W), 1960 v Y, Sp, H; 1961 v Ni, W, S, L, P, Sp, M, I, A; 1962 v W, Ni, S, A, Sw, L, P (19)
Swepstone, H. A. (Pilgrims), 1880 v S; 1882 v S, W; 1883 v S, W, Ni (6)
Swift, F. V. (Manchester C), 1947 v S, W, Ni, Ei, Ho, F, Sw, P; 1948 v S, W, Ni, Bel, Se, I; 1949 v S, W, Ni, D, N (19)

Tait, G. (Birmingham Excelsior), 1881 v W (1)
Talbot, B. (Ipswich T), 1977 v Ni (sub), S, Br, Arg, U; (with Arsenal), 1980 v Aus (6)
Tambling, R. V. (Chelsea), 1963 v W, F; 1966 v Y (3)
Tate, J. T. (Aston Villa), 1931 v F, Bel; 1933 v W (3)
Taylor, E. (Blackpool), 1954 v H (1)
Taylor, E. H. (Huddersfield T), 1923 v S, W, Ni, Bel; 1924 v S, Ni, F; 1926 v S (8)

Taylor, J. G. (Fulham), 1951 v Arg, P (2)
Taylor, P. H. (Liverpool), 1948 v W, Ni, Se (3)
Taylor, P. J. (C Palace), 1976 v W (sub+1), Ni, S (4)
Taylor, T. (Manchester U), 1953 v Arg, Ch, U; 1954 v Bel, Sw; 1956 v S, Br, Se, Fi, WG; 1957 v Ni, Y (sub), D (2), Ei (2); 1958 v W, Ni, F (19)
Temple, D. W. (Everton), 1965 v WG (1)
Terry, J. G. (Chelsea), 2003 v Ser (sub); 2004 v Cro, Mac, Lie, T, D, Se, J, Sw, Cro, P (11)
Thickett, H. (Sheffield U), 1899 v S, W (2)
Thomas, D. (Coventry C), 1983 v Aus (1+1 sub) (2)
Thomas, D. (QPR), 1975 v Cz (sub), P, Cy (sub+1), W, S (sub); 1976 v Cz (sub), P (sub) (8)
Thomas, G. R. (C Palace), 1991 v T, USSR, Arg, Aus, Nz (2), Mal; 1992 v Pol, F (9)
Thomas, M. L. (Arsenal), 1989 v S.Ar; 1990 v Y (2)
Thompson, A. (Celtic), 2004 v Se (1)
Thompson, P. (Liverpool), 1964 v P (2), Ei, US, Br, Arg; 1965 v Ni, W, S, Bel, Ho; 1966 v Ni; 1968 v Ni, WG; 1970 v S, Ho (sub) (16)
Thompson, P. B. (Liverpool), 1976 v W (2), Ni, S, Br, I, Fi; 1977 v Fi; 1979 v Ei (sub), Cz, Ni, S, Bul, Se (sub), A; 1980 v D, Ni, Bul, Ei, Sp (2), Arg, W, S, Bel, I; 1981 v N, R, H; 1982 v N, H, W, Ho, S, Fi, F, Cz, K, WG, Sp; 1983 v WG, Gr (42)
Thompson T. (Aston Villa), 1952 v W; (with Preston NE), 1957 v S (2)
Thomson, R. A. (Wolverhampton W), 1964 v Ni, US, P, Arg; 1965 v Bel, Ho, Ni, W (8)
Thornewell, G. (Derby Co), 1923 v Se (2); 1924 v F; 1925 v F (4)
Thornley, I. (Manchester C), 1907 v W (1)
Tilson, S. F. (Manchester C), 1934 v H, Cz; 1935 v W; 1936 v Ni (4)
Titmuss, F. (Southampton), 1922 v W; 1923 v W (2)
Todd, C. (Derby Co), 1972 v Ni; 1974 v P, W, Ni, S, Arg, EG, Bul, Y; 1975 v P (sub), WG, Cy (2), Ni, W, S; 1976 v Sw, Cz, P, Ni, S, Br, Fi; 1977 v Ei, Fi, Ho (sub), Ni (27)
Toone, G. (Notts Co), 1892 v S, W (2)
Topham, A. G. (Casuals), 1894 v W (1)
Topham, R. (Wolverhampton W), 1893 v Ni; (with Casuals) 1894 v W (2)
Towers, M. A. (Sunderland), 1976 v W, Ni (sub), I (3)
Townley, W. J. (Blackburn R), 1889 v W; 1890 v Ni (2)
Townrow, J. E. (Clapton Orient), 1925 v S; 1926 v W (2)
Tremelling, D. R. (Birmingham), 1928 v W (1)
Tresadern, J. (West Ham U), 1923 v S, Se (2)
Tueart, D. (Manchester C), 1975 v Cy (sub), Ni; 1977 v Fi, Ni, W (sub), S (sub) (6)
Tunstall, F. E. (Sheffield U), 1923 v S; 1924 v S, W, Ni, F; 1925 v Ni, S (7)
Turnbull, R. J. (Bradford), 1920 v Ni (1)
Turner, A. (Southampton), 1900 v Ni; 1901 v Ni (2)
Turner, H. (Huddersfield T), 1931 v F, Bel (2)
Turner, J. A. (Bolton W), 1893 v W; (with Stoke C) 1895 v Ni; (with Derby Co) 1898 v Ni (3)
Tweedy, G. J. (Grimsby T), 1937 v H (1)

Ufton, D. G. (Charlton Ath), 1954 v R of E (1)
Underwood A. (Stoke C), 1891 v Ni; 1892 v Ni (2)
Unsworth, D. G. (Everton), 1995 v J (1)
Upson, M. J. (Birmingham C), 2003 v S.Af (sub), Ser, Slo; 2004 v Cro (sub), Lie, D (6)
Urwin, T. (Middlesbrough), 1923 v Se (2); 1924 v Bel; (with Newcastle U), 1926 v W (4)
Utley, G. (Barnsley), 1913 v Ni (1)

Vassell, D. (Aston Villa), 2002 v Ho, I (sub), Para, Sk, Cam, Se, Ng (sub), Br (sub); 2003 v Mac (sub), Aus (sub), T (sub), S.Af (sub), Ser (sub), Slo (sub); 2004 v T (sub), Se, J (sub), Ic (sub), F (sub), Sw (sub), Cro (sub), P (sub) (22)
Vaughton, O. H. (Aston Villa), 1882 v S, W, Ni; 1884 v S, W (5)
Veitch, C. C. M. (Newcastle U), 1906 v S, W, Ni; 1907 v S, W; 1909 v W (6)
Veitch, J. G. (Old Westminsters), 1894 v W (1)
Venables, T. F. (Chelsea), 1965 v Ho, Bel (2)
Venison, B. (Newcastle U), 1995 v US, U (2)
Vidal, R. W. S. (Oxford University), 1873 v S (1)
Viljoen, C. (Ipswich T), 1975 v Ni, W (2)
Viollet, D. S. (Manchester U), 1960 v H; 1962 v L (2)
Von Donop (Royal Engineers), 1873 v S; 1875 v S (2)

Wace, H. (Wanderers), 1878 v S; 1879 v S, W (3)
Waddle, C. R. (Newcastle U), 1985 v Ei, R (sub), Fi (sub), S (sub), I, M (sub), WG, US; (with Tottenham H), 1986 v R, T, Ni, Is, USSR, S, M, Ca, P, Mor, Pol (sub), Arg (sub); 1987 v Se (sub), Ni (2), Y, Sp, T, Br, S; 1988 v WG, Is, H, S (sub), Co, Sw (sub), Ei, Ho (sub); 1989 v Se, S.Ar, Alb (2), Ch, S, Pol, D (sub); (with Marseille), 1990 v Se, Pol, I, Y, Br, D, U, Tun, Ei, Ho, Eg, Bel, Cam, WG, I (sub); 1991 v H (sub), Pol (sub); 1992 v T (62)
Wadsworth, S. J. (Huddersfield T), 1922 v S; 1923 v S, Bel; 1924 v S, Ni; 1925 v S, Ni; 1926 v W; 1927 v Ni (9)
Wainscoat, W. R. (Leeds U), 1929 v S (1)
Waiters, A. K. (Blackpool), 1964 v Ei, Br; 1965 v W, Bel, Ho (5)
Walden, F. I. (Tottenham H), 1914 v S; 1922 v W (2)
Walker, D. S. (Nottingham F), 1989 v D (sub), Se (sub), Gr, Alb (2), Ch, S, Pol, D; 1990 v Se, Pol, I, Y, Br, Cz, D, U, Tun, Ei, Ho, Eg, Bel, Cam, WG, I; 1991 v H, Pol, Ei (2), Cam, T, Arg, Aus, Nz (2), Mal; 1992 v T, Pol, F, Cz, C, H, Br, Fi, D, F, Se; (with Sampdoria), 1993 v Sp, N, T, Sm, T, Ho, Pol, N, US (sub), Br, G; (with Sheffield W), 1994 v Sm (59)
Walker, I. M. (Tottenham H), 1996 v H (sub), Chn (sub); 1997 v I; (with Leicester C), 2004 v Ic (sub) (4)
Walker, W. H. (Aston Villa), 1921 v Ni; 1922 v Ni, W, S; 1923 v Se (2); 1924 v S; 1925 v Ni, W, S, Bel, F; 1926 v Ni, W, S; 1927 v Ni, W; 1933 v A (18)
Wall, G. (Manchester U), 1907 v W; 1908 v Ni; 1909 v S; 1910 v W, S; 1912 v S; 1913 v Ni (7)
Wallace, C. W. (Aston Villa), 1913 v W; 1914 v Ni; 1920 v S (3)
Wallace, D. L. (Southampton), 1986 v Eg (1)
Walsh, P. (Luton T), 1983 v Aus (2 + 1 sub); 1984 v F, W (5)
Walters, A. M. (Cambridge University), 1885 v S, N; 1886 v S; 1887 v S, W; (with Old Carthusians), 1889 v S, W; 1890 v S, W (9)
Walters, K. M. (Rangers), 1991 v Nz (1)
Walters, P. M. (Oxford University), 1885 v S, Ni; (with Old Carthusians), 1886 v S, W, Ni; 1887 v S, W; 1888 v S, Ni; 1889 v S, W; 1890 v S, W (13)
Walton, N. (Blackburn R), 1890 v Ni (1)
Ward, J. T. (Blackburn Olympic), 1885 v W (1)
Ward, P. (Brighton & HA), 1980 v Aus (sub) (1)
Ward, T. V. (Derby Co), 1948 v Bel; 1949 v W (2)
Waring, T. (Aston Villa), 1931 v F, Bel; 1932 v S, W, Ni (5)
Warner, C. (Upton Park), 1878 v S (1)
Warren, B. (Derby Co), 1906 v S, W, Ni; 1907 v S, W, Ni; 1908 v S, W, Ni, A (2), H, B; (with Chelsea), 1909 v S, Ni, W, H (2), A; 1911 v S, Ni, W (22)
Waterfield, G. S. (Burnley), 1927 v W (1)
Watson, D. (Norwich C), 1984 v Br, U, Ch; 1985 v M, US (sub); 1986 v S; (with Everton), 1987 v Ni; 1988 v Is, Ho, S, Sw (sub), USSR (12)
Watson, D. V. (Sunderland), 1974 v P, S (sub), Arg, EG, Bul, Y; 1975 v Cz, P, WG, Cy (2), Ni, W, S; (with Manchester C), 1976 v Sw, Cz (sub), P; 1977 v Ho, L, Ni, W, S, Br, Arg, U; 1978 v Sw, L, I, WG, Br, W, Ni, S, H; 1979 v D, Ei, Cz, Ni (2), W, S, Bul, Se, A; (with Werder Bremen), 1980 v D; (with Southampton), Ni, Bul, Ei, Sp (2), Arg, Ni, S, Bel, I; 1981 v N, R, Sw, R, W, S, Sw, H; (with Stoke C), 1982 v Ni, Ic (65)
Watson, V. M. (West Ham U), 1923 v W, S; 1930 v S, G, A (5)
Watson, W. (Burnley), 1913 v S; 1914 v Ni; 1920 v Ni (3)
Watson, W. (Sunderland), 1950 v Ni, I; 1951 v W, Y (4)
Weaver, S. (Newcastle U), 1932 v S, 1933 v S, Ni (3)
Webb, G. W. (West Ham U), 1911 v S, W (2)
Webb, N. J. (Nottingham F), 1988 v WG (sub), T, Y, Is, Ho, S, Sw, Ei, USSR (sub); 1989 v D, Se, Gr, Alb (2), Ch, S, Pol, D; (with Manchester U), 1990 v Se, I (sub); 1992 v F, H, Br (sub), Fi, D (sub), Se (26)
Webster, M. (Middlesbrough), 1930 v S, A, G (3)
Wedlock, W. J. (Bristol C), 1907 v S, Ni, W; 1908 v S, Ni, W, A (2), H, B; 1909 v S, W, Ni, H (2), A; 1910 v S, W, Ni; 1911 v S, W, Ni; 1912 v S, W, Ni; 1914 v W (26)
Weir, D. (Bolton W), 1889 v S, Ni (2)
Welch, R. de C. (Wanderers), 1872 v S; (with Harrow Chequers), 1874 v S (2)
Weller, K. (Leicester C), 1974 v W, Ni, S, Arg (4)
Welsh, D. (Charlton Ath), 1938 v G, Sw; 1939 v R (3)
West, G. (Everton), 1969 v W, Bul, M (3)
Westwood, R. W. (Bolton W), 1935 v S, W, Ho; 1936 v Ni, G; 1937 v W (6)
Whateley, O. (Aston Villa), 1883 v S, Ni (2)
Wheeler, J. E. (Bolton W), 1955 v Ni (1)
Wheldon, G. F. (Aston Villa), 1897 v Ni; 1898 v S, W, Ni (4)
White, D. (Manchester C), 1993 v Sp (1)
White, T. A. (Everton), 1933 v I (1)
Whitehead, J. (Accrington), 1893 v W; (with Blackburn R), 1894 v Ni (2)
Whitfeld, H. (Old Etonians), 1879 v W (1)

Whitham, M. (Sheffield U), 1892 v Ni (1)
Whitworth, S. (Leicester C), 1975 v WG, Cy, Ni, W, S; 1976 v Sw, P (7)
Whymark, T. J. (Ipswich T), 1978 v L (sub) (1)
Widdowson, S. W. (Nottingham F), 1880 v S (1)
Wignall, F. (Nottingham F), 1965 v W, Ho (2)
Wilcox, J. M. (Blackburn R), 1996 v H; 1999 v F (sub); (with Leeds U), 2000 v Arg (3)
Wilkes, A. (Aston Villa), 1901 v S, W; 1902 v S, W, Ni (5)
Wilkins, R. G. (Chelsea), 1976 v I; 1977 v Ei, Fi, Ni, Br, Arg, U; 1978 v Sw (sub), L, I, WG, W, Ni, S, H; 1979 v D, Ei, Cz, Ni, W, S, Bul, Se (sub), A; (with Manchester U), 1980 v D, Ni, Bul, Sp (2), Arg, W (sub), Ni, S, Bel, I; 1981 v Sp (sub), R, Br, W, S, Sw, H (sub); 1982 v Ni, W, Ho, S, Fi, F, Cz, K, WG, Sp; 1983 v D, WG; 1984 v D, Ni, W, S, USSR, Br, U, Ch; (with AC Milan), 1985 v EG, Fi, T, Ni, Ei, R, Fi, S, I, M; 1986 v T, Ni, Is, Eg, USSR, S, M, Ca, P, Mor; 1987 v Se, Y (sub) (84)
Wilkinson, B. (Sheffield U), 1904 v S (1)
Wilkinson, L. R. (Oxford University), 1891 v W (1)
Williams, B. F. (Wolverhampton W), 1949 v F; 1950 v S, W, Ei, I, P, Bel, Ch, US, Sp; 1951 v Ni, W, S, Y, Arg, P; 1952 v W, F; 1955 v S, WG, F, Sp, P; 1956 v W (24)
Williams, O. (Clapton Orient), 1923 v W, Ni (2)
Williams, S. (Southampton), 1983 v Aus (1+1 sub); 1984 v F; 1985 v EG, Fi, T (6)
Williams, W. (WBA), 1897 v Ni; 1898 v W, Ni, S; 1899 v W, Ni (6)
Williamson, E. C. (Arsenal), 1923 v Se (2) (2)
Williamson, R. G. (Middlesbrough), 1905 v Ni; 1911 v Ni, S, W; 1912 v S, W; 1913 v Ni (7)
Willingham, C. K. (Huddersfield T), 1937 v Fi; 1938 v S, G, Sw, F; 1939 v S, W, Ni, R of E, N, I, Y (12)
Willis, A. (Tottenham H), 1952 v F (1)
Wilshaw, D. J. (Wolverhampton W), 1954 v W, Sw, U; 1955 v S, F, Sp, P; 1956 v W, Ni, Fi, WG; 1957 v Ni (12)
Wilson, C. P. (Hendon), 1884 v S, W (2)
Wilson, C. W. (Oxford University), 1879 v W; 1881 v S (2)
Wilson, G. (Sheffield W), 1921 v S, W, Bel; 1922 v S, Ni; 1923 v S, W, Ni, Bel; 1924 v W, Ni, F (12)
Wilson, G. P. (Corinthians), 1900 v S, W (2)
Wilson, R. (Huddersfield T), 1960 v S, Y, Sp, H; 1962 v W, Ni, S, A, Sw, Pe, P, H, Arg, Bul, Br; 1963 v Ni, F, Br, Cz, EG, Sw; 1964 v W, S, R of W, U, P (2), Ei, Br, Arg; (with Everton), 1965 v S, H, Y, WG, Se; 1966 v WG (sub), W, Ni, A, Sp, Pol (2), Y, Fi, D, U, M, F, Arg, P, WG; 1967 v Ni, W, S, Cz, A; 1968 v Ni, S, USSR (2), Sp (2), Y (63)
Wilson, T. (Huddersfield T), 1928 v S (1)
Winckworth, W. N. (Old Westminsters), 1892 v W; 1893 v Ni (2)
Windridge, J. E. (Chelsea), 1908 v S, W, Ni, A (2), H, B; 1909 v Ni (8)
Wingfield-Stratford, C. V. (Royal Engineers), 1877 v S (1)
Winterburn, N. (Arsenal), 1990 v I (sub); 1993 v G (sub) (2)
Wise, D. F. (Chelsea), 1991 v T, USSR, Aus (sub), Nz (2); 1994 v N; 1995 v R (sub), Ng; 1996 v Co, N, P, H (sub); 2000 v Bel (sub), Arg, Br, Ma, P (sub), G, R; 2001 v F, Fi (21)
Withe, P. (Aston Villa), 1981 v Br, W, S; 1982 v N (sub), W, Ic; 1983 v H, Ni, S; 1984 v H (sub); 1985 v T (11)
Wollaston, C. H. R. (Wanderers), 1874 v S; 1875 v S; 1877 v S; 1880 v S (4)
Wolstenholme, S. (Everton), 1904 v S; (with Blackburn R), 1905 v W, Ni (3)
Wood, H. (Wolverhampton W), 1890 v S, W; 1896 v S (3)
Wood, R. E. (Manchester U), 1955 v Ni, W; 1956 v Fi (3)
Woodcock, A. S. (Nottingham F), 1978 v Ni; 1979 v Ei (sub), Cz, Bul (sub), Se; 1980 v Ni; (with Cologne), Bul, Ei, Sp (2), Arg, Bel, I; 1981 v N, R, Sw, R, W (sub), S; 1982 v Ni (sub), Ho, Fi (sub), WG (sub), Sp; (with Arsenal), 1983 v WG (sub), Gr, L, Gr; 1984 v L, F (sub), Ni, W, S, Br, U (sub); 1985 v EG, Fi, T, Ni; 1986 v R (sub), T (sub), Is (sub) (42)
Woodgate, J. S. (Leeds U), 1999 v Bul; 2003 v P (sub), Slo, Mac; (with Newcastle U), 2004 v Se (5)
Woodger, G. (Oldham Ath), 1911 v Ni (1)
Woodhall, G. (WBA), 1888 v S, W (2)
Woodley, V. R. (Chelsea), 1937 v S, N, Se, Fi; 1938 v S, W, Ni, Cz, G, Sw, F; 1939 v S, W, Ni, R of E, N, I, R, Y (19)
Woods, C. C. E. (Norwich C), 1985 v US; 1986 v Eg (sub), Is (sub), Ca (sub); (with Rangers), 1987 v Y, Sp (sub), Ni (sub), T, S; 1988 v Is, H, Sw (sub), USSR; 1989 v D (sub); 1990 v Br (sub), D (sub); 1991 v H, Pol, Ei, USSR, Aus, Nz (2), Mal; (with Sheffield W), 1992 v G, T, Pol, F, C, Br, Fi, D, F, Se; 1993 v Sp, N, T, Sm, T, Ho, Pol, N, US (43)
Woodward, V. J. (Tottenham H), 1903 v S, W, Ni; 1904 v S, Ni; 1905 v S, W, Ni; 1907 v S; 1908 v S, W, Ni, A (2), H, B; 1909 v W, Ni, H (2), A; (with Chelsea), 1910 v Ni; 1911 v W (23)
Woosnam, M. (Manchester C), 1922 v W (1)
Worrall, F. (Portsmouth), 1935 v Ho; 1937 v Ni (2)
Worthington, F. S. (Leicester C), 1974 v Ni (sub), S, Arg, EG, Bul, Y; 1975 v Cz, P (sub) (8)
Wreford-Brown, C. (Oxford University), 1889 v Ni; (with Old Carthusians), 1894 v W; 1895 v W; 1898 v S (4)
Wright, E, G. D. (Cambridge University), 1906 v W (1)
Wright, I. E. (C Palace), 1991 v Cam, Ei (sub), USSR, Nz; (with Arsenal), 1992 v H (sub); 1993 v N, T (2), Pol (sub), N (sub), US (sub), Br, G (sub); 1994 v Pol, Ho (sub), Sm, Gr (sub), N (sub); 1995 v US (sub), R; 1997 v Ge (sub), I (sub), M (sub), S.Af, I, F, Br (sub); 1998 v Mol, I, S.Ar (sub), Mor; (with West Ham U), 1999 v L (sub), CzR (33)
Wright, J. D. (Newcastle U), 1939 v N (1)
Wright, M. (Southampton), 1984 v W; 1985 v EG, Fi, T, Ei, R, I, WG; 1986 v R, T, Ni, Eg, USSR; 1987 v Y, Ni, S; (with Derby Co), 1988 v Is, Ho (sub), Co, Sw, Ei, Ho; 1990 v Cz (sub), Tun (sub), Ho, Eg, Bel, Cam, WG, I; 1991 v H, Pol, Ei (2), Cam, USSR, Arg, Aus, Nz, Mal; (with Liverpool), 1992 v F, Fi; 1993 v Sp; 1996 v Cro, H (45)
Wright, R. I. (Ipswich T), 2000 v Ma; (with Arsenal), 2002 v Ho (sub) (2)
Wright, T. J. (Everton), 1968 v USSR; 1969 v R (2), M (sub), U, Br; 1970 v W, Ho, Bel, R (sub), Br (11)
Wright, W. A. (Wolverhampton W), 1947 v S, W, Ni, Ei, Ho, F, Sw, P; 1948 v S, W, Ni, Bel, Se, I; 1949 v S, W, Ni, D, Sw, Se, N, F; 1950 v S, W, Ni, Ei, I, P, Bel, Ch, US, Sp; 1951 v Ni, S, Arg; 1952 v W, Ni, S, F, A (2), I, Sw; 1953 v Ni, W, S, Bel, Arg, Ch, U, US; 1954 v W, Ni, S, R of E, H (2), Y, Bel, Sw, U; 1955 v W, Ni, S, WG, F, Sp, P; 1956 v Ni, W, S, Br, Se, Fi, WG, D, Sp; 1957 v S, W, Ni, Y, D (2), Ei (2); 1958 v W, Ni, S, P, Y, USSR (3), Br, A, F; 1959 v W, Ni, S, USSR, I, Br, Pe, M, US (105)
Wylie, J. G. (Wanderers), 1878 v S (1)

Yates, J. (Burnley), 1889 v Ni (1)
York, R. E. (Aston Villa), 1922 v S; 1926 v S (2)
Young, A. (Huddersfield T), 1933 v W; 1937 v S, H, N, Se; 1938 v G, Sw, F; 1939 v W (9)
Young, G. M. (Sheffield W), 1965 v W (1)
R. E. Evans also played for Wales against E, Ni, S; J. Reynolds also played for Ireland against E, W, S.

## NORTHERN IRELAND

Addis, D. J. (Cliftonville), 1922 v N (1)
Aherne, T. (Belfast C), 1947 v E; 1948 v S; 1949 v W; (with Luton T), 1950 v W (4)
Alexander, T. E. (Cliftonville), 1895 v S (1)
Allan, C. (Cliftonville), 1936 v E (1)
Allen, J. (Limavady), 1887 v E (1)
Anderson, J. (Distillery), 1925 v S.Af (1)
Anderson, T. (Manchester U), 1973 v Cy, E, S, W; 1974 v Bul, P; (with Swindon T), 1975 v S (sub); 1976 v Is; 1977 v Ho, Bel, WG, E, S, W, Ic; 1978 v Ic, Ho, Bel; (with Peterborough U), S, E, W; 1979 v D (sub) (22)
Anderson, W. (Linfield), 1898 v W, E, S; (with Cliftonville), 1899 v S (4)
Andrews, W. (Glentoran), 1908 v S; (with Grimsby T), 1913 v E, S (3)
Armstrong, G. J. (Tottenham H), 1977 v WG, E, W (sub), Ic (sub); 1978 v Bel, S, E, W; 1979 v Ei, D, Bul, E, Bul, E, S, W, D; 1980 v E, Ei, Is, S, E, W, Aus (3); 1981 v Se; (with Watford), P, S, P, S, Se; 1982 v S, Is, E, F, W, Y, Hon, Sp, A, F; 1983 v A, T, Alb, S, E, W; (with Real Mallorca), 1984 v A, WG, E, W, Fi; 1985 v R, Fi, E, Sp; (with WBA), 1986 v T, R (sub), E (sub), F (sub); (with Chesterfield), D (sub), Br (sub) (63)

Baird, C. P. (Southampton), 2003 v I, Sp; 2004 v Uk, Arm, Gr, N, Es, Ser, Bar, Stk, Tr (11)
Baird, G. (Distillery), 1896 v S, E, W (3)
Baird, H. C. (Huddersfield T), 1939 v E (1)
Balfe, J. (Shelbourne), 1909 v E; 1910 v W (2)
Bambrick, J. (Linfield), 1929 v W, S, E; 1930 v W, S, E; 1932 v W; (with Chelsea), 1935 v W; 1936 v E, S; 1938 v W (11)

Banks, S. J. (Cliftonville), 1937 v W (1)
Barr, H. H. (Linfield), 1962 v E; (with Coventry C), 1963 v E, Pol (3)
Barron, J. H. (Cliftonville), 1894 v E, W, S; 1895 v S; 1896 v S; 1897 v E, W (7)
Barry, J. (Cliftonville), 1888 v W, S; 1889 v E (3)
Barry, J. (Bohemians), 1900 v S (1)
Baxter, R. A. (Distillery), 1887 v S (1)
Baxter, S. N. (Cliftonville), 1887 v W (1)
Bennett, L. V. (Dublin University), 1889 v W (1)
Best, G. (Manchester U), 1964 v W, U; 1965 v E, Ho (2), S, Sw (2), Alb; 1966 v S, E, Alb; 1967 v E; 1968 v S; 1969 v E, S, W, T; 1970 v S, E, W, USSR; 1971 v Cy (2), Sp, E, S, W; 1972 v USSR, Sp; 1973 v Bul; 1974 v P; (with Fulham), 1977 v Ho, Bel, WG; 1978 v Ic, Ho (37)
Bingham, W. L. (Sunderland), 1951 v F; 1952 v E, S, W; 1953 v E, S, F, W; 1954 v E, S, W; 1955 v E, S, W; 1956 v E, S, W; 1957 v E, S, W, P (2), I; 1958 v S, E, W, I (2), Arg, Cz (2), WG, F; (with Luton T), 1959 v E, S, W, Sp; 1960 v S, E, W; (with Everton), 1961 v E, S, WG (2), Gr, I; 1962 v E, Gr; 1963 v E, S, Pol (2), Sp; (with Port Vale), 1964 v S, E, Sp (56)
Black, K. T. (Luton T), 1988 v Fr (sub), Ma (sub); 1989 v Ei, H, Sp (2), Ch (sub); 1990 v H, N, U; 1991 v Y (2), D, A, Pol, Fa; (with Nottingham F), 1992 v Fa, A, D, S, Li, G; 1993 v Sp, D (sub), Alb, Ei (sub), Sp; 1994 v D (sub), Ei (sub), R (sub) (30)
Black, T. (Glentoran), 1901 v E (1)
Blair, H. (Portadown), 1928 v F; 1931 v S; 1932 v S; (with Swansea), 1934 v S (4)
Blair, J. (Cliftonville), 1907 v W, E, S; 1908 v E, S (5)
Blair, R. V. (Oldham Ath), 1975 v Se (sub), S (sub), W; 1976 v Se, Is (5)
Blanchflower, J. (Manchester U), 1954 v W; 1955 v E, S; 1956 v S, W; 1957 v S, E, P; 1958 v S, E, I (2) (12)
Blanchflower, R. D. (Barnsley), 1950 v S, W; 1951 v E, S; (with Aston Villa), F; 1952 v W; 1953 v E, S, W, F; 1954 v E, S, W; 1955 v E, S (with Tottenham H), W; 1956 v E, S, W; 1957 v E, S, W, I, P (2); 1958 v E, S, W, I (2), Cz (2), Arg, F, WG; 1959 v E, S, W, Sp; 1960 v E, S, W; 1961 v E, S, W, WG (2); 1962 v E, S, W, Gr, Ho; 1963 v E, S, Pol (2) (56)
Bookman, L. J. O. (Bradford C), 1914 v W; (with Luton T), 1921 v S, W; 1922 v E (4)
Bothwell, A. W. (Ards), 1926 v S, E, W; 1927 v E, W (5)
Bowler, G. C. (Hull C), 1950 v E, S, W (3)
Boyle, P. (Sheffield U), 1901 v E; 1902 v E; 1903 v S, W; 1904 v E (5)
Braithwaite, R. M. (Linfield), 1962 v W; 1963 v P, Sp; (with Middlesbrough), 1964 v W, U; 1965 v E, S, Sw (2), Ho (10)
Breen, T. (Belfast C), 1935 v E, W; 1937 v E, S; (with Manchester U), 1937 v W; 1938 v E, S; 1939 v W, S (9)
Brennan, B. (Bohemians), 1912 v W (1)
Brennan, R. A. (Luton T), 1949 v W; (with Birmingham C), 1950 v E, S, W; (with Fulham), 1951 v E (5)
Briggs, W. R. (Manchester U), 1962 v W; (with Swansea T), 1965 v Ho (2)
Brisby, D. (Distillery), 1891 v S (1)
Brolly, T. H. (Millwall), 1937 v W; 1938 v W; 1939 v E, W (4)
Brookes, E. A. (Shelbourne), 1920 v S (1)
Brotherston, N. (Blackburn R), 1980 v S, E, W, Aus (3); 1981 v Se, P; 1982 v S, Is, E, F, S, W, Hon (sub), A (sub); 1983 v A (sub), WG, Alb, T, Alb, S (sub), E (sub), W; 1984 v T; 1985 v Is (sub), T (27)
Brown, J. (Glenavon), 1921 v W; (with Tranmere R), 1924 v E, W (3)
Brown, J. (Wolverhampton W), 1935 v E, W; 1936 v E; (with Coventry C), 1937 v E, W; 1938 v S, W; (with Birmingham C), 1939 v E, S, W (10)
Brown, N. M. (Limavady), 1887 v E (1)
Brown, W. G. (Glenavon), 1926 v W (1)
Browne, F. (Cliftonville), 1887 v E, S, W; 1888 v E, S (5)
Browne, R. J. (Leeds U), 1936 v E, W; 1938 v E, W; 1939 v E, S (6)
Bruce, A. (Belfast C), 1925 v S.Af (1)
Bruce, W. (Glentoran), 1961 v S; 1967 v W (2)
Buckle, H. R. (Cliftonville), 1903 v S; (with Sunderland), 1904 v E; (with Bristol R), 1908 v W (3)
Buckle, J. (Cliftonville), 1882 v E (1)
Burnett, J. (Distillery), 1894 v E, W, S; (with Glentoran), 1895 v E, W (5)
Burnison, J. (Distillery), 1901 v E, W (2)
Burnison, S. (Distillery), 1908 v E; 1910 v E, S; (with Bradford), 1911 v E, S, W; (with Distillery), 1912 v E; 1913 v W (8)
Burns, J. (Glenavon), 1923 v E (1)
Burns, W. (Glentoran), 1925 v S.Af (1)
Butler, M. P. (Blackpool), 1939 v W (1)

Campbell, A. C. (Crusaders), 1963 v W; 1965 v Sw (2)
Campbell, D. A. (Nottingham F), 1986 v Mor (sub), Br; 1987 v E (2), T, Y; (with Charlton Ath), 1988 v Y, T (sub), Gr (sub), Pol (sub) (10)
Campbell, James (Cliftonville), 1897 v E, S, W; 1898 v E, S, W; 1899 v E; 1900 v E, S; 1901 v S, W; 1902 v S; 1903 v E; 1904 v S (14)
Campbell, John (Cliftonville), 1896 v W (1)
Campbell, J. P. (Fulham), 1951 v E, S (2)
Campbell, R. M. (Bradford C), 1982 v S, W (sub) (2)
Campbell, W. G. (Dundee), 1968 v S, E; 1969 v T; 1970 v S, W, USSR (6)
Capaldi, A. C. (Plymouth Arg), 2004 v Es, Ser, Bar, Stk, Tr (5)
Carey, J. J. (Manchester U), 1947 v E, S, W; 1948 v E; 1949 v E, S, W (7)
Carroll, E. (Glenavon), 1925 v S (1)
Carroll, R. E. (Wigan Ath), 1997 v Th (sub); 1999 v Ei (sub); 2000 v L, Ma; 2001 v Ma, D, Ic, CzR, Bul; (with Manchester U), 2002 v Lie (sub), Sp (sub); 2003 v Fi (sub), I (sub); 2004 v Ser (sub) (14)
Casey, T. (Newcastle U), 1955 v W; 1956 v W; 1957 v E, S, W, I, P (2); 1958 v WG, F; (with Portsmouth), 1959 v E, Sp (12)
Caskey, W. (Derby Co), 1979 v Bul, E, Bul, E, S (sub), D (sub); 1980 v E (sub); (with Tulsa R), 1982 v F (sub) (8)
Cassidy, T. (Newcastle U), 1971 v E (sub); 1972 v USSR (sub); 1974 v Bul (sub), S, E, W; 1975 v N; 1976 v S, E, W; 1977 v WG (sub); 1980 v E, Ei (sub), Is, S, E, W, Aus (3); (with Burnley), 1981 v Se, P; 1982 v Is, Sp (sub) (24)
Caughey, M. (Linfield), 1986 v F (sub), D (sub) (2)
Chambers, R. J. (Distillery), 1921 v W; (with Bury), 1928 v E, S, W; 1929 v E, S, W; 1930 v S, W; (with Nottingham F), 1932 v E, S, W (12)
Chatton, H. A. (Partick T), 1925 v E, S; 1926 v E (3)
Christian, J. (Linfield), 1889 v S (1)
Clarke, C. J. (Bournemouth), 1986 v F, D, Mor, Alg (sub), Sp, Br; (with Southampton), 1987 v E, T, Y; 1988 v Y, T, Gr, Pol, F, Ma; 1989 v Ei, H, Sp (1+1 sub); (with QPR), Ma, Ch; 1990 v H, Ei, N; (with Portsmouth), 1991 v Y (sub), D, A, Pol, Y (sub), Fa; 1992 v Fa, D, S, G; 1993 v Alb, Sp, D (38)
Clarke, R. (Belfast C), 1901 v E, S (2)
Cleary, J. (Glentoran), 1982 v S, W; 1983 v W (sub); 1984 v T (sub); 1985 v Is (5)
Clements, D. (Coventry C), 1965 v W, Ho; 1966 v M; 1967 v S, W; 1968 v S, E; 1969 v T (2), S, W; 1970 v S, E, W, USSR (2); 1971 v Sp, E, S, W, Cy; (with Sheffield W), 1972 v USSR (2), Sp, E, S, W; 1973 v Bul, Cy (2), P, E, S, W; (with Everton), 1974 v Bul, P, S, E, W; 1975 v N, Y, E, S, W; 1976 v Se, Y; (with New York Cosmos), E, W (48)
Clugston, J. (Cliftonville), 1888 v W; 1889 v W, S, E; 1890 v E, S; 1891 v E, W; 1892 v E, S, W; 1893 v E, S, W (14)
Cochrane, D. (Leeds U), 1939 v E, W; 1947 v E, S, W; 1948 v E, S, W; 1949 v S, W; 1950 v S, E (12)
Cockrane, G. (Cliftonville), 1903 v S (1)
Cochrane, G. T. (Coleraine), 1976 v N (sub); (with Burnley), 1978 v S (sub), E (sub), W (sub); 1979 v Ei (sub); (with Middlesbrough), D, Bul, E, Bul, E; 1980 v Is, E (sub), W (sub), Aus (1+2 sub); 1981 v Se (sub), P (sub), S, P, S, Se; 1982 v E (sub), F; (with Gillingham), 1984 v S, Fi (sub) (26)
Cochrane, M. (Distillery), 1898 v S, W, E; 1899 v E; 1900 v E, S, W; (with Leicester Fosse), 1901 v S (8)
Collins, F. (Celtic), 1922 v S (1)
Collins, R. (Cliftonville), 1922 v N (1)
Condy, J. (Distillery), 1882 v W; 1886 v E, S (3)
Connell, T. E. (Coleraine), 1978 v W (sub) (1)
Connor, J. (Glentoran), 1901 v S, E; (with Belfast C), 1905 v E, S, W; 1907 v E, S; 1908 v E, S; 1909 v W; 1911 v S, E, W (13)
Connor, M. J. (Brentford), 1903 v S, W; (with Fulham), 1904 v E (3)
Cook, W. (Celtic), 1933 v E, W, S; (with Everton), 1935 v E; 1936 v S, W; 1937 v E, S, W; 1938 v E, S, W; 1939 v E, S, W (15)
Cooke, S. (Belfast YMCA), 1889 v E; (with Cliftonville), 1890 v E, S (3)
Coote, A. (Norwich C), 1999 v Ca, Ei (sub); 2000 v Fi (sub), L (sub), Ma (sub), H (sub) (6)
Coulter, J. (Belfast C), 1934 v E, S, W; (with Everton), 1935 v E, S, W; 1937 v S, W; (with Grimsby T), 1938 v S, W; (with Chelmsford C), 1939 v S (11)
Cowan, J. (Newcastle U), 1970 v E (sub) (1)
Cowan, T. S. (Queen's Island), 1925 v W (1)
Coyle, F. (Coleraine), 1956 v E, S; 1957 v P; (with Nottingham F), 1958 v Arg (4)
Coyle, L. (Derry C), 1989 v Ch (sub) (1)

Coyle, R. I. (Sheffield W), 1973 v P, Cy (sub), W (sub); 1974 v Bul (sub), P (sub) (5)
Craig, A. B. (Rangers), 1908 v E, S, W; 1909 v S; (with Morton), 1912 v S, W; 1914 v E, S, W (9)
Craig, D. J. (Newcastle U), 1967 v W; 1968 v W; 1969 v T (2), E, S, W; 1970 v E, S, W, USSR; 1971 v Cy (2), Sp, S (sub); 1972 v USSR, S (sub); 1973 v Cy (2), E, S, W; 1974 v Bul, P; 1975 v N (25)
Craigan, S. J. (Partick T), 2003 v Fi (sub), Arm, Gr; (with Motherwell), 2004 v Es, Ser, Bar, Stk, Tr (8)
Crawford, A. (Distillery), 1889 v E, W; (with Cliftonville), 1891 v E, S, W; 1893 v E, W (7)
Croft, T. (Queen's Island), 1922 v N; 1924 v E; 1925 v S.Af (3)
Crone, R. (Distillery), 1889 v S; 1890 v E, S, W (4)
Crone, W. (Distillery), 1882 v W; 1884 v E, S, W; 1886 v E, S, W; 1887 v E; 1888 v E, W; 1889 v S; 1890 v W (12)
Crooks, W. J. (Manchester U), 1922 v W (1)
Crossan, E. (Blackburn R), 1950 v S; 1951 v E; 1955 v W (3)
Crossan, J. A. (Sparta-Rotterdam), 1960 v E; (with Sunderland), 1963 v W, P, Sp; 1964 v E, S, W, U, Sp; 1965 v E, S, Sw (2); (with Manchester C), W, Ho (2), Alb; 1966 v S, E, Alb, WG; 1967 v E, S; (with Middlesbrough), 1968 v S (24)
Crothers, C. (Distillery), 1907 v W (1)
Cumming, L. (Huddersfield T), 1929 v W, S; (with Oldham Ath), 1930 v E (3)
Cunningham, W. (Ulster), 1892 v S, E, W; 1893 v E (4)
Cunningham, W. E. (St Mirren), 1951 v W; 1953 v E; 1954 v S; 1955 v S; (with Leicester C), 1956 v E, S, W; 1957 v E, S, W, I, P (2); 1958 v S, W, I, Cz (2), Arg, WG, F; 1959 v E, S, W; 1960 v E, S, W; (with Dunfermline Ath), 1961 v W; 1962 v W, Ho (30)
Curran, S. (Belfast C), 1926 v S, W; 1928 v F, S (4)
Curran, J. J. (Glenavon), 1922 v W, N; (with Pontypridd), 1923 v E, S; (with Glenavon), 1924 v E (5)
Cush, W. W. (Glenavon), 1951 v E, S; 1954 v S, E; 1957 v W, I, P (2); (with Leeds U), 1958 v I (2), W, Cz (2), Arg, WG, F; 1959 v E, S, W, Sp; 1960 v E, S, W; (with Portadown), 1961 v WG, Gr; 1962 v Gr (26)

Dalrymple, J. (Distillery), 1922 v N (1)
Dalton, W. (YMCA), 1888 v S; (with Linfield), 1890 v S, W; 1891 v S, W; 1892 v E, S, W; 1894 v E, S, W (11)
D'Arcy, S. D. (Chelsea), 1952 v W; 1953 v E; (with Brentford), 1953 v S, W, F (5)
Darling, J. (Linfield), 1897 v E, S; 1900 v S; 1902 v E, S, W; 1903 v E, S (2), W; 1905 v E, S, W; 1906 v E, S, W; 1908 v W; 1909 v E; 1910 v E, S, W; 1912 v S (22)
Davey, H. H. (Reading), 1926 v E; 1927 v E, S; 1928 v E; (with Portsmouth), 1928 v W (5)
Davis, T. L. (Oldham Ath), 1937 v E (1)
Davison, A. J. (Bolton W), 1996 v Se; (with Bradford C), 1997 v Th; (with Grimsby T), 1998 v G (3)
Davison, J. R. (Cliftonville), 1882 v E, W; 1883 v E, W; 1884 v E, W, S; 1885 v E (8)
Dennison, R. (Wolverhampton W), 1988 v F, Ma; 1989 v H, Sp Ch (sub); 1990 v Ei, U; 1991 v Y (2), A. Pol, Fa (sub); 1992 v Fa, A, D (sub); 1993 v Sp (sub); 1994 v Co (sub); 1997 v I (sub) (18)
Devine, A. O. (Limavady), 1886 v E, W; 1887 v W; 1888 v W (4)
Devine, J. (Glentoran), 1990 v U (sub) (1)
Dickson, D. (Coleraine), 1970 v S (sub), W; 1973 v Cy, P (4)
Dickson, T. A. (Linfield), 1957 v S (1)
Dickson, W. (Chelsea), 1951 v W, F; 1952 v E, S, W; 1953 v E, S, W, F; (with Arsenal), 1954 v E, W; 1955 v E (12)
Diffin, W. J. (Belfast C), 1931 v W (1)
Dill, A. H. (Knock), 1882 v E, W; (with Down Ath), 1883 v W; (with Cliftonville), 1884 v E, S, W; 1885 v E, S, W (9)
Doherty, I. (Belfast C), 1901 v E (1)
Doherty, J. (Portadown), 1928 v F (1)
Doherty, J. (Cliftonville), 1933 v E, W (2)
Doherty, L. (Linfield), 1985 v Is; 1988 v T (sub) (2)
Doherty, M. (Derry C), 1938 v S (1)
Doherty, P. D. (Blackpool), 1935 v E, W; 1936 v E, S; (with Manchester C), 1937 v E, W; 1938 v E, S; 1939 v E, W; (with Derby Co), 1947 v E; (with Huddersfield T), 1947 v W; 1948 v E, W; 1949 v S; (with Doncaster R), 1951 v S (16)
Doherty, T. E. (Bristol C), 2003 v I, Sp; 2004 v Uk, Arm, Ser (5)
Donaghey, B. (Belfast C), 1903 v S (1)
Donaghy, M. M. (Luton T), 1980 v S, E, W; 1981 v Se, P, S (sub); 1982 v S, Is, E, F, S, W, Y, Hon, Sp, F; 1983 v A, WG, Alb, T, Alb, S, E, W; 1984 v A, T, WG, S, E, W, Fi; 1985 v R, Fi, E, Sp, T; 1986 v T, R, E, F, D, Mor, Alg, Sp, Br; 1987 v E (2), T, Is, Y; 1988 v Y, T, Gr, Pol, F, Ma; 1989 v Ei, H; (with Manchester U), Sp (2), Ma, Ch; 1990 v Ei, N; 1991 v Y (2), D, A, Pol, Fa; 1992 v Fa, A, D, S, Li, G; (with Chelsea), 1993 v Alb, Sp, D, Alb, Ei, Sp, Li, La; 1994 v La, D, Ei, R, Lie, Co, M (91)
Donnelly, L. (Distillery), 1913 v W (1)
Doran, J. F. (Brighton), 1921 v E; 1922 v E, W (3)
Dougan, A. D. (Portsmouth), 1958 v Cz; (with Blackburn R), 1960 v S; 1961 v E, W, I, Gr; (with Aston Villa), 1963 v S, Pol (2); (with Leicester C), 1966 v S, E, Alb, W, WG, M; 1967 v E, S; (with Wolverhampton W), W; 1968 v S, W; 1969 v Is, T (2), E, S, W; 1970 v USSR (2), S, E; 1971 v Sp, Cy (2), E, S, W; 1972 v USSR (2), S, E, W; 1973 v Bul, Cy (43)
Douglas, J. P. (Belfast C), 1947 v E (1)
Dowd, H. O. (Glenavon), 1974 v W; (with Sheffield W), 1975 v N (sub), Se (3)
Dowie, I. (Luton T), 1990 v N (sub), U; 1991 v Y, D, A (sub), (with West Ham U), Y, Fa; (with Southampton) 1992 v Fa, A, D (sub), S (sub), Li; 1993 v Alb (2), Ei, Sp (sub), Li, La; 1994 v La, D, Ei (sub), R (sub), Lie, Co, M (sub); 1995 v A, Ei; (with C Palace) Ei, La, Ca, Ch, La; 1996 v P; (with West Ham U), A, N, G; 1997 v Uk, Arm, G, Alb, P, Uk, Arm, Th; 1998 v Alb, P; (with QPR), Slo, Sw, Sp; 1999 v T, Fi, Mol, G, Mol, Ca, Ei; 2000 v F, T, G (59)
Duff, M. J. (Cheltenham T), 2002 v Pol (sub); 2003 v Cy (sub); 2004 v Es (sub) (3)
Duggan, H. A. (Leeds U), 1930 v E; 1931 v E, W; 1933 v E; 1934 v E; 1935 v S, W; 1936 v S (8)
Dunlop, G. (Linfield), 1985 v Is; 1987 v E, Y; 1990 v Ei (4)
Dunne, J. (Sheffield U), 1928 v W; 1931 v W, E; 1932 v E, S; 1933 v E, W (7)

Eames, W. L. E. (Dublin U), 1885 v E, S, W (3)
Eglington, T. J. (Everton), 1947 v S, W; 1948 v E, S, W; 1949 v E (6)
Elder, A. R. (Burnley), 1960 v W; 1961 v S, E, W, WG (2), Gr; 1962 v E, S, Gr; 1963 v E, S, W, Pol (2), Sp; 1964 v W, U; 1965 v E, S, W, Sw (2), Ho (2), Alb; 1966 v E, S, W, M, Alb; 1967 v E, S, W; (with Stoke C), 1968 v E, W; 1969 v E (sub), S, W; 1970 v USSR (40)
Elleman, A. R. (Cliftonville), 1889 v W; 1890 v E (2)
Elliott, S. (Motherwell), 2001 v Ma, D, Ic, N (sub), CzR, Bul (2), CzR; 2002 v D (sub), Ma, Pol (sub), Lie (sub), Sp; (with Hull C), 2003 v Fi (sub), Arm (sub), I (sub); 2004 v Gr, Bar (sub), Stk, Tr (20)
Elwood, J. H. (Bradford), 1929 v W; 1930 v E (2)
Emerson, W. (Glentoran), 1920 v E, S, W; 1921 v E; 1922 v E, S; (with Burnley), 1922 v W; 1923 v E, S, W; 1924 v E (11)
English, S. (Rangers), 1933 v W, S (2)
Enright, J. (Leeds C), 1912 v S (1)

Falloon, E. (Aberdeen), 1931 v S; 1933 v S (2)
Farquharson, T. G. (Cardiff C), 1923 v S, W; 1924 v E, S, W; 1925 v E, S (7)
Farrell, P. (Distillery), 1901 v S, W (2)
Farrell, P. (Hibernian), 1938 v W (1)
Farrell, P. D. (Everton), 1947 v S, W; 1948 v E, S, W; 1949 v E, W (7)
Feeney, J. M. (Linfield), 1947 v S; (with Swansea T), 1950 v E (2)
Feeney, W. (Glentoran), 1976 v Is (1)
Feeney, W. J. (Bournemouth), 2002 v Lie, Sp; 2003 v Cy (sub) (3)
Ferguson, G. (Linfield), 1999 v Ca (sub); 2001 v N, CzR (sub), Bul (sub), CzR (sub) (5)
Ferguson, W. (Linfield), 1966 v M; 1967 v E (2)
Ferris, J. (Belfast C), 1920 v E, W; (with Chelsea), 1921 v S, E; (with Belfast C), 1928 v F, S (6)
Ferris, R. O. (Birmingham C), 1950 v S; 1951 v F; 1952 v S (3)
Fettis, A. W. (Hull C), 1992 v D, Li; 1993 v D; 1994 v M; 1995 v P, Ei, La, Ca, Ch, La; 1996 v P, Lie, A; (with Nottingham F), v N, G; 1997 v Uk, Arm (2); (with Blackburn R), 1998 v P, Slo, Sw, Sp; 1999 v T, Fi, Mol (25)
Finney, T. (Sunderland), 1975 v N, E (sub), S, W; 1976 v N, Y, S; (with Cambridge U), 1980 v E, Is, S, E, W, Aus (2) (14)
Fitzpatrick, J. C. (Bohemians), 1896 v E, S (2)
Flack, H. (Burnley), 1929 v S (1)
Fleming, J. G. (Nottingham F), 1987 v E (2), Is, Y; 1988 v T, Gr, Pol; 1989 v Ma, Ch; (with Manchester C), 1990 v H, Ei; (with Barnsley), 1991 v Y; 1992 v Li (sub), G; 1993 v Alb, Sp, D, Alb, Sp, Li, La; 1994 v La, D, Ei, R, Lie, Co, M; 1995 v P, A, Ei (31)
Forbes, G. (Limavady), 1888 v W; (with Distillery), 1891 v E, S (3)
Forde, J. T. (Ards), 1959 v Sp; 1961 v E, S, WG (4)
Foreman, T. A. (Cliftonville), 1899 v S (1)

'orsyth, J. (YMCA), 1888 v E, S (2)
ox, W. T. (Ulster), 1887 v E, S (2)
rame, T. (Linfield), 1925 v S.Af (1)
ulton, R. P. (Larne), 1928 v F; (Belfast C), 1930 v W; 1931 v E, S, W; 1932 v W, E; 1933 v E, S; 1934 v E, W, S; 1935 v E, W, S; 1936 v S, W; 1937 v E, S, W; 1938 v W (21)

iaffikin, G. (Linfield Ath), 1890 v S, W; 1891 v S, W; 1892 v E, S, W; 1893 v E, S, W; 1894 v E, S, W; 1895 v E, W (15)
ialbraith, W. (Distillery), 1890 v W (1)
iallagher, P. (Celtic), 1920 v E, S; 1922 v S; 1923 v S, W; 1924 v S, W; 1925 v S, W, E; (with Falkirk), 1927 v S (11)
iallogly, C. (Huddersfield T), 1951 v E, S (2)
iara, A. (Preston NE), 1902 v E, S, W (3)
iardiner, A. (Cliftonville), 1930 v S, W; 1931 v S; 1932 v E, S (5)
iarrett, J. (Distillery), 1925 v W (1)
iaston, R. (Oxford U), 1969 v Is (sub) (1)
iaukrodger, G. (Linfield), 1895 v W (1)
iaussen, A. D. (Moyola Park), 1884 v E, S; (with Magherafelt), 1888 v E, W; 1889 v E, W (6)
ieary, J. (Glentoran), 1931 v S; 1932 v S (2)
iibb, J. T. (Wellington Park) 1884 v S, W; 1885 v S, E, W; 1886 v S; 1887 v S, E, W; (with Cliftonville), 1889 v S (10)
iibb, T. J. (Cliftonville), 1936 v W (1)
iibson W. K. (Cliftonville), 1894 v S, W, E; 1895 v S; 1897 v W; 1898 v S, W, E; 1901 v S, W, E; 1902 v S, W; 1903 v S (14)
iillespie, K. R. (Manchester U), 1995 v P, A, Ei; (with Newcastle U), Ei, La, Ca, Ch (sub), La (sub); 1996 v P, A, N, G; 1997 v Uk, Arm, Bel, P, Uk; 1998 v G, Alb, Slo, Sw; 1999 v T, Fi, Mol; (with Blackburn R), G, Mol; 2000 v F (sub), T (sub), G (sub), L, Ma, H; 2001 v Y (sub), CzR, Bul (2); 2002 v D, Ic, Pol, Lie, Sp; 2003 v Cy, Sp, Uk, Fi, Arm, Gr; (with Leicester C), 2004 v Uk, Arm, Gr, N, Ser, Bar, Stk (sub), Tr (sub) (55)
iillespie, S. (Hertford), 1886 v E, S, W; 1887 v E, S, W (6)
iillespie, W. (Sheffield U), 1913 v E, S; 1914 v E, W; 1920 v S, W; 1921 v E; 1922 v E, S, W; 1923 v E, S, W; 1924 v E, S, W; 1925 v E, S; 1926 v S, W; 1927 v E, W; 1928 v E; 1929 v E; 1931 v E (25)
iillespie, W. (West Down), 1889 v W (1)
ioodall, A. L. (Derby Co), 1899 v S, W; 1900 v E, W; 1901 v E; 1902 v S; 1903 v E, W; (with Glossop), 1904 v E, W (10)
ioodbody, M. F. (Dublin University), 1889 v E; 1891 v W (2)
iordon, H. (Linfield), 1895 v E; 1896 v E, S (3)
iordon R. W. (Linfield), 1891 v S; 1892 v W, E, S; 1893 v E, S, W (7)
iordon, T. (Linfield), 1894 v W; 1895 v E (2)
iorman, W. C. (Brentford), 1947 v E, S, W; 1948 v W (4)
iough, J. (Queen's Island), 1925 v S.Af (1)
iowdy, J. (Glentoran), 1920 v E; (with Queen's Island), 1924 v W; (with Falkirk), 1926 v E, S; 1927 v E, S (6)
iowdy, W. A. (Hull C), 1932 v S; (with Sheffield W), 1933 v S; (with Linfield), 1935 v E, S, W; (with Hibernian), 1936 v W (6)
iraham, W. G. L. (Doncaster R), 1951 v W, F; 1952 v E, S, W; 1953 v S, F; 1954 v E, W; 1955 v S, W; 1956 v E, S; 1959 v E (14)
iray, P. (Luton T), 1993 v D (sub), Alb, Ei, Sp; (with Sunderland), 1994 v La, D, Ei, R, Lie (sub); 1995 v P, A, Ei, Ca, Ch (sub); 1996 v P (sub), Lie, A; (with Nancy), 1997 v Uk, Arm, G (sub); (with Luton T), 1999 v Mol (sub); (with Burnley), 2001 v Ma (sub), D (sub), Ic (sub); (with Oxford U), N (sub), CzR (sub) (26)
ireer, W. (QPR), 1909 v E, S, W (3)
iregg, H. (Doncaster R), 1954 v W; 1957 v E, S, W, I, P (2); 1958 v E, I; (with Manchester U), 1958 v Cz, Arg, WG, F, W; 1959 v E, W; 1960 v S, E, W; 1961 v E, S; 1962 v S, Gr; 1964 v S, E (25)
iriffin, D. J. (St Johnstone), 1996 v G; 1997 v Uk, I, Bel (sub), Th; 1998 v G (sub), Alb; 1999 v Mol, Ei (sub); 2000 v L, Ma, H; (with Dundee U), 2001 v Y (sub), N (sub), CzR, Bul (2), CzR; 2002 v D, Ic, Ma, Pol; 2003 v Cy, I, Sp; 2004 v Uk, Arm, Gr; (with Stockport Co), N (29)

Iall, G. (Distillery), 1897 v E (1)
Ialligan, W. (Derby Co), 1911 v W; (with Wolverhampton W), 1912 v E (2)
Iamill, M. (Manchester U), 1912 v E; 1914 v E, S; (with Belfast C), 1920 v E, S, W; (with Manchester C), 1921 v S (7)
Iamill, R. (Glentoran), 1999 v Ca (sub) (1)
Iamilton, B. (Linfield), 1969 v T; 1971 v Cy (2), E, S, W; (with Ipswich T), 1972 v USSR (1+1 sub), Sp; 1973 v Bul, Cy (2), P, E, S, W; 1974 v Bul, S, E, W; 1975 v N, Se, Y, E; 1976 v Se, N, Y; (with Everton), Is, S, E, W; 1977 v Ho, Bel, WG, E, S, W, Ic; (with Millwall), 1978 v S, E, W; 1979 v Ei (sub); (with Swindon T), Bul (2), E, S, W, D; 1980 v Aus (2 sub) (50)
Hamilton, G. (Portadown), 2003 v I (sub); 2004 v Ser (sub), Bar (sub), Stk (4)
Hamilton, J. (Knock), 1882 v E, W (2)
Hamilton, R. (Rangers), 1928 v S; 1929 v E; 1930 v S, E; 1932 v S (5)
Hamilton, W. D. (Dublin Association), 1885 v W (1)
Hamilton, W. J. (Distillery), 1908 v W (1)
Hamilton, W. J. (Dublin Association), 1885 v W (1)
Hamilton, W. R. (QPR), 1978 v S (sub); (with Burnley), 1980 v S, E, W, Aus (2); 1981 v Se, P, S, P, S, Se; 1982 v S, Is, E, W, Y, Hon, Sp, A, F; 1983 v A, WG, Alb (2), S, E, W; 1984 v A, T, WG, S, E, W, Fi; (with Oxford U), 1985 v R, Sp; 1986 v Mor (sub), Alg, Sp (sub), Br (sub) (41)
Hampton, H. (Bradford C), 1911 v E, S, W; 1912 v E, W; 1913 v E, S, W; 1914 v E (9)
Hanna, J. (Nottingham F), 1912 v S, W (2)
Hanna, J. D. (Royal Artillery, Portsmouth), 1899 v W (1)
Hannon, D. J. (Bohemians), 1908 v E, S; 1911 v E, S; 1912 v W; 1913 v E (6)
Harkin, J. T. (Southport), 1968 v W; 1969 v T; (with Shrewsbury T), W (sub); 1970 v USSR; 1971 v Sp (5)
Harland, A. I. (Linfield), 1922 v N; 1923 v E (2)
Harris, J. (Cliftonville), 1921 v W; (with Glenavon), 1925 v S.Af (2)
Harris, V. (Shelbourne), 1906 v E; 1907 v E, W; 1908 v E, W, S; (with Everton), 1909 v E, W, S; 1910 v E, S, W; 1911 v E, S, W; 1912 v E; 1913 v E, S; 1914 v S, W (20)
Harvey, M. (Sunderland), 1961 v I; 1962 v Ho; 1963 v W, Sp; 1964 v S, E, W, U, Sp; 1965 v E, S, W, Sw (2), Ho (2), Alb; 1966 v S, E, W, M, Alb, WG; 1967 v E, S; 1968 v E, W; 1969 v Is, T (2), E; 1970 v USSR; 1971 v Cy, W (sub) (34)
Hastings, J. (Knock), 1882 v E, W; (with Ulster), 1883 v W; 1884 v E, S; 1886 v E, S (7)
Hatton, S. (Linfield), 1963 v S, Pol (2)
Hayes, W. E. (Huddersfield T), 1938 v E, S; 1939 v E, S (4)
Healy, D. J. (Manchester U), 2000 v L, Ma, H; 2001 v Y, Ma, D, Ic; (with Preston NE), N, CzR, Bul (2), CzR; 2002 v D, Ic, Ma, Pol, Lie, Sp; 2003 v Cy, Sp (sub), Uk, Fi, Arm, Gr, I, Sp; 2004 v Uk, Arm, Gr, N, Es, Ser, Bar, Stk (sub), Tr (35)
Healy, P. J. (Coleraine), 1982 v S, W, Hon (sub); (with Glentoran), 1983 v A (sub) (4)
Hegan, D. (WBA), 1970 v USSR; (with Wolverhampton W), 1972 v USSR, E, S, W; 1973 v Bul, Cy (7)
Henderson, J. (Ulster), 1885 v E, S, W (3)
Hewison, G. (Moyola Park), 1885 v E, S (2)
Hill, C. F. (Sheffield U), 1990 v N, U; 1991 v Pol, Y; 1992 v A, D; (with Leicester C), 1995 v Ei, La; 1996 v P, Lie, A, N, Se, G; 1997 v Uk, Arm, G, Alb, P, Uk, Arm, Th; (with Trelleborg), 1998 v G, Alb, P; (with Northampton T), Slo; 1999 v T (27)
Hill, M. J. (Norwich C), 1959 v W; 1960 v W; 1961 v WG; 1962 v S; (with Everton), 1964 v S, E, Sp (7)
Hinton, E. (Fulham), 1947 v S, W; 1948 v S, E, W; (with Millwall), 1951 v W, F (7)
Holmes, S. P. (Wrexham), 2002 v Lie (sub) (1)
Hopkins, J. (Brighton), 1926 v E (1)
Horlock, K. (Swindon T), 1995 v La, Ca; 1997 v G, Alb, I; (with Manchester C), v Bel, Uk, Arm, Th; 1998 v G, Alb, P; 1999 v T, Fi, G, Mol, Ca; 2000 v F, T, G, Ma (sub); 2001 v Y, Ma, D, Ic; 2002 v D, Ic, Ma, Sp; 2003 v Cy, Sp, Uk (32)
Houston, J. (Linfield), 1912 v S, W; 1913 v W; (with Everton), 1913 v E, S; 1914 v S (6)
Houston, W. (Linfield), 1933 v W (1)
Houston, W. J. (Moyola Park), 1885 v E, S (2)
Hughes, A. W. (Newcastle U), 1998 v Slo, Sw, Sp (sub); 1999 v T, Fi, Mol (sub), Ca, Ei; 2000 v F, T, L, H; 2001 v Y, Ma, D, Ic, N, CzR, Bul, CzR; 2002 v D, Ic, Pol, Sp; 2003 v Sp, Uk, Fi, Arm, Gr, I, Sp; 2004 v Uk, Arm, Gr, N (35)
Hughes, M. E. (Manchester C), 1992 v D, S, Li, G; (with Strasbourg), 1993 v Alb, Sp, D, Ei, Sp, Li, La; 1994 v La, D, Ei, R, Lie, Co, M; 1995 v P, A, Ei (2) La, Ca, Ch, La; 1996 v P, Lie, A, N, G; (with West Ham U), 1997 v Uk, Arm, G, Alb, I, Uk; 1998 v G; (with Wimbledon), P, Slo, Sw, Sp; 1999 v T, Fi, Mol, G, Mol; 2000 v F, T, G, Fi, L (sub), Ma, H; 2001 v CzR, Bul (2), CzR; 2002 v D, Ic, Ma, Pol, Lie (sub); 2003 v Sp (sub), Uk; (with C Palace), 2004 v Uk, Gr, N, Ser (sub) (69)
Hughes, P. A. (Bury), 1987 v E, T, Is (3)
Hughes, W. (Bolton W), 1951 v W (1)
Humphries, W. M. (Ards), 1962 v W; (with Coventry C), 1962 v Ho; 1963 v E, S, W, Pol, Sp; 1964 v S, E, Sp; 1965 v S, Ho; (with Swansea T), 1965 v W, Alb (14)

Hunter, A. (Distillery), 1905 v W; 1906 v W, E, S; (with Belfast C), 1908 v W; 1909 v W, E, S (8)
Hunter, A. (Blackburn R), 1970 v USSR; 1971 v Cy (2), E, S, W; (with Ipswich T), 1972 v USSR (2), Sp, E, S, W; 1973 v Bul, Cy (2), P, E, S, W; 1974 v Bul, S, E, W; 1975 v N, Se, Y, E, S, W; 1976 v Se, N, Y, Is, S, E, W; 1977 v Ho, Bel, WG, E, S, W, Ic; 1978 v Ic, Ho, Bel; 1979 v Ei, D, S, W, D; 1980 v E, Ei (53)
Hunter, B. V. (Wrexham), 1995 v La; 1996 v P, Lie, A, Se, G; (with Reading), 1997 v Arm, G, Alb, I, Bel; 1999 v Ca, Ei; 2000 v F, T (15)
Hunter, R. J. (Cliftonville), 1884 v E, S, W (3)
Hunter, V. (Coleraine), 1962 v E; 1964 v Sp (2)

Irvine, R. J. (Linfield), 1962 v Ho; 1963 v E, S, W, Pol (2), Sp; (with Stoke C), 1965 v W (8)
Irvine, R. W. (Everton), 1922 v S; 1923 v E, W; 1924 v E, S; 1925 v E; 1926 v E; 1927 v E, W; 1928 v E, S; (with Portsmouth), 1929 v E; 1930 v S; (with Connah's Quay), 1931 v E; (with Derry C), 1932 v W (15)
Irvine, W. J. (Burnley), 1963 v W, Sp; 1965 v S, W, Sw, Ho (2), Alb; 1966 v S, E, W, M, Alb; 1967 v E, S; 1968 v E, W; (with Preston NE), 1969 v Is, T, E; (with Brighton & HA), 1972 v E, S, W (23)
Irving, S. J. (Dundee), 1923 v S, W; 1924 v S, E, W; 1925 v S, E, W; 1926 v S, W; (with Cardiff C), 1927 v S, E, W; 1928 v S, E, W; (with Chelsea), 1929 v E; 1931 v W (18)

Jackson, T. A. (Everton), 1969 v Is, E, S, W; 1970 v USSR (1+1 sub); (with Nottingham F), 1971 v Sp; 1972 v E, S, W; 1973 v Cy, E, S, W; 1974 v Bul, P, S (sub), E (sub), W (sub); 1975 v N (sub), Se, Y, E, S, W; (with Manchester U); 1976 v Se, N, Y; 1977 v Ho, Bel, WG, E, S, W, Ic (35)
Jamison, J. (Glentoran), 1976 v N (1)
Jenkins, I. (Chester C), 1997 v Arm, Th; 1998 v Slo; (with Dundee U), Sw, Sp; 2000 v Fi (6)
Jennings, P. A. (Watford), 1964 v W, U; (with Tottenham H), 1965 v E, S, Sw (2), Ho, Alb; 1966 v S, E, W, Alb, WG; 1967 v E, S; 1968 v S, E, W; 1969 v Is, T (2), E, S, W; 1970 v S, E, USSR (2); 1971 v Cy (2), E, S, W; 1972 v USSR, Sp, S, E, W; 1973 v Bul, Cy, P, E, S, W; 1974 v P, S, E, W; 1975 v N, Se, Y, E, S, W; 1976 v Se, N, Y, Is, S, E, W; 1977 v Ho, Bel, WG, E, S, W, Ic; (with Arsenal), 1978 v Ic, Ho, Bel; 1979 v Ei, D, Bul, E, Bul, E, S, W, D; 1980 v E, Ei, Is; 1981 v S, P, S, Se; 1982 v S, Is, E, W, Y, Hon, Sp, F; 1983 v Alb, S, E, W; 1984 v A, T, WG, S, W, Fi; 1985 v R, Fi, E, Sp, T; (with Tottenham H), 1986 v T, R, E, F, D; (with Everton), Mor; (with Tottenham H), Alg, Sp, Br (119)
Johnson, D. M. (Blackburn R), 1999 v Ei (sub); 2000 v Fi (sub), L, Ma (sub), H (sub); 2001 v Y, Ma, Ic, N (sub), Bul (sub+1), CzR; 2002 v Ma, Pol; (with Birmingham C), Lie, Sp; 2003 v Cy, Sp, Uk, Fi, Arm, Gr, I, Sp; 2004 v Uk, Arm, N, Bar, Stk (sub), Tr (30)
Johnston, H. (Portadown), 1927 v W (1)
Johnston, R. S. (Distillery), 1882 v W; 1884 v E; 1886 v E, S (4)
Johnston, R. S. (Distillery), 1905 v W (1)
Johnston, S. (Linfield), 1890 v W; 1893 v S, W; 1894 v E (4)
Johnston, W. (Oldpark), 1885 v S, W (2)
Johnston, W. C. (Glenavon), 1962 v W; (with Oldham Ath), 1966 v M (sub) (2)
Jones, J. (Linfield), 1930 v S, W; 1931 v S, W, E; 1932 v S, E; 1933 v S, E, W; 1934 v S, E, W; 1935 v S, E, W; 1936 v E, S; (with Hibernian), 1936 v W; 1937 v E, W, S; (with Glenavon), 1938 v E (23)
Jones, J. (Glenavon), 1956 v W; 1957 v E, W (3)
Jones, S. (Distillery), 1934 v E; (with Blackpool), 1934 v W (2)
Jones, S. G. (Crewe Alex), 2003 v I (sub), Sp; 2004 v Uk (sub), Arm (sub), Gr (sub), N (sub), Es, Ser (sub), Bar (sub), Stk (sub), Tr (sub) (11)
Jordan, T. (Linfield), 1895 v E, W (2)

Kavanagh, P. J. (Celtic), 1930 v E (1)
Keane, T. R. (Swansea T), 1949 v S (1)
Kearns, A. (Distillery), 1900 v E, S, W; 1902 v E, S, W (6)
Kee, P. V. (Oxford U), 1990 v N; 1991 v Y (2), D, A, Pol, Fa; (with Ards), 1995 v A, Ei (9)
Keith, R. M. (Newcastle U), 1958 v E, W, Cz (2), Arg, I, WG, F; 1959 v E, S, W, Sp; 1960 v S, E; 1961 v S, E, W, I, WG (2), Gr; 1962 v W, Ho (23)
Kelly, H. R. (Fulham), 1950 v E, W; (with Southampton), 1951 v E, S (4)
Kelly, J. (Glentoran), 1896 v E (1)
Kelly, J. (Derry C), 1932 v E, W; 1933 v E, W, S; 1934 v W; 1936 v E, S, W; 1937 v S, E (11)
Kelly, P. J. (Manchester C), 1921 v E (1)
Kelly, P. M. (Barnsley), 1950 v S (1)

Kennedy, A. L. (Arsenal), 1923 v W; 1925 v E (2)
Kennedy, P. H. (Watford), 1999 v Mol, G (sub); 2000 v F, T G, Fi; 2001 v N, Bul (sub), CzR (sub); (with Wigan Ath) 2002 v D, Ic, Ma, Pol; 2003 v Cy, Fi, I, Sp; 2004 v Uk, Gr, N (20)
Kernaghan, N. (Belfast C), 1936 v W; 1937 v S; 1938 v E (3)
Kirk, A. (Hearts), 2000 v H; 2001 v N (sub); 2003 v Uk (sub), Fi (sub), Gr (sub) (5)
Kirkwood, H. (Cliftonville), 1904 v W (1)
Kirwan, J. (Tottenham H), 1900 v W; 1902 v E, W; 1903 v E, S W; 1904 v E, S, W; 1905 v E, S, W; (with Chelsea), 1906 v E S, W; 1907 v W; (with Clyde), 1909 v S (17)

Lacey, W. (Everton), 1909 v E, S, W; 1910 v E, S, W; 1911 v E S, W; 1912 v E; (with Liverpool), 1913 v W; 1914 v E, S, W 1920 v E, S, W; 1921 v E, S, W; 1922 v E, S; (with New Brighton), 1925 v E (23)
Lawther, R. (Glentoran), 1888 v E, S (2)
Lawther, W. I. (Sunderland), 1960 v W; 1961 v I; (with Blackburn R), 1962 v S, Ho (4)
Leatham, J. (Belfast C), 1939 v W (1)
Ledwidge, J. J. (Shelbourne), 1906 v S, W (2)
Lemon, J. (Glentoran), 1886 v W; (with Belfast YMCA), 188 v S; 1889 v W (3)
Lennon, N. F. (Crewe Alex), 1994 v M (sub); 1995 v Ch; 199 v P, Lie, A; (with Leicester C), v N; 1997 v Uk, Arm, G Alb, Bel, P, Uk, Arm, Th; 1998 v G, Alb, P, Slo, Sw, Sp 1999 v T, Fi, Mol, G, Mol, Ei; 2000 v F, T, G, Fi, Ma, H 2001 v D, Ic; (with Celtic), N, CzR, Bul (2); 2002 v Pol (sub (40)
Leslie, W. (YMCA), 1887 v E (1)
Lewis, J. (Glentoran), 1899 v S, E, W; (with Distillery), 1900 S (4)
Lockhart, H. (Russell School), 1884 v W (1)
Lockhart, N. H. (Linfield), 1947 v E; (with Coventry C), 195 v W; 1951 v W; 1952 v W; (with Aston Villa), 1954 v S, E 1955 v W; 1956 v W (8)
Lomas, S. M. (Manchester C), 1994 v R, Lie, Co (sub), M 1995 v P, A; 1996 v P, Lie, A, N, Se, G; 1997 v Uk, Arm, G Alb, I, Bel; (with West Ham U), P, Uk, Arm, Th; 1998 Alb, P, Slo, Sw; 1999 v Mol, G, Mol, Ca; 2000 v F, T, G, L Ma; 2001 v Ma, D, Ic; 2002 v Pol, Lie; 2003 v Sp, Uk, F Arm, Gr (45)
Loyal, J. (Clarence), 1891 v S (1)
Lutton, R. J. (Wolverhampton W), 1970 v S, E; (with Wes Ham U), 1973 v Cy (sub), S (sub), W (sub); 1974 v P (6)
Lynas, R. (Cliftonville), 1925 v S.Af (1)
Lyner, D. R. (Glentoran), 1920 v E, W; 1922 v S, W; (with Manchester U), 1923 v E; (with Kilmarnock), 1923 v W (6)
Lytle, J. (Glentoran), 1898 W (1)

McAdams, W. J. (Manchester C), 1954 v W; 1955 v S; 1957 E; 1958 v S, I; (with Bolton W), 1961 v E, S, W, I, WG (2) Gr; 1962 v E, Gr; (with Leeds U), Ho (15)
McAlery, J. M. (Cliftonville), 1882 v E, W (2)
McAlinden, J. (Belfast C), 1938 v S; 1939 v S; (with Portsmouth), 1947 v E; (with Southend U), 1949 v E (4)
McAllen, J. (Linfield), 1898 v E; 1899 v E, S, W; 1900 v E, S W; 1901 v W; 1902 v S (9)
McAlpine, S. (Cliftonville), 1901 v S (1)
McArthur, A. (Distillery), 1886 v W (1)
McAuley, J. L. (Huddersfield T), 1911 v E, W; 1912 v E, S 1913 v E, S (6)
McAuley, P. (Belfast C), 1900 v S (1)
McBride, S. D. (Glenavon), 1991 v D (sub), Pol (sub); 1992 Fa (sub), D (4)
McCabe, J. J. (Leeds U), 1949 v S, W; 1950 v E; 1951 v W 1953 v W; 1954 v S (6)
McCabe, W. (Ulster), 1891 v E (1)
McCambridge, J. (Ballymena), 1930 v S, W; (with Cardiff C) 1931 v W; 1932 v E (4)
McCandless, J. (Bradford), 1912 v W; 1913 v W; 1920 v W, S 1921 v E (5)
McCandless, W. (Linfield), 1920 v E, W; 1921 v E; (with Rangers), 1921 v W; 1922 v S; 1924 v W, S; 1925 v S; 1929 W (9)
McCann, G. S. (West Ham U), 2002 v Ma (sub), Pol (sub) Lie; 2003 v Sp (sub), Uk (sub); (with Cheltenham T), Arm Gr; 2004 v Arm, Es (sub) (9)
McCann, P. (Belfast C), 1910 v E, S, W; 1911 v E; (with Glentoran), 1911 v S; 1912 v E; 1913 v W (7)
McCarthy, J. D. (Port Vale), 1996 v Se; 1997 v I, Arm, Th (with Birmingham C), 1998 v P (sub), Slo (sub), Sp; 1999 Fi (sub), Mol (sub), G (sub), Ca, Ei; 2000 v F, T, G, Fi; 200 v N, Bul (sub) (18)

McCartney, A. (Ulster), 1903 v S, W; (with Linfield), 1904 v S, W; (with Everton), 1905 v E, S; (with Belfast C), 1907 v E, S, W; 1908 v E, S, W; (with Glentoran), 1909 v E, S, W (15)
McCartney, G. (Sunderland), 2002 v Ic, Ma, Pol (sub), Lie, Sp; 2003 v Cy, Sp, Uk, Fi, Gr, I, Sp; 2004 v Uk, Arm, Gr, N (16)
McCashin, J. W. (Cliftonville), 1896 v W; 1898 v S, W; 1899 v S; 1903 v S (5)
McCavana, W. T. (Coleraine), 1955 v S; 1956 v E, S (3)
McCaw, D. (Malone), 1882 v E (1)
McCaw, J. H. (Linfield), 1927 v W; 1928 v F; 1930 v S; 1931 v E, S, W (6)
McClatchey, J. (Distillery), 1886 v E, S, W (3)
McClatchey, T. (Distillery), 1895 v S (1)
McCleary, J. W. (Cliftonville), 1955 v W (1)
McCleery, W. (Cliftonville), 1922 v N; (Linfield), 1930 v E, W; 1931 v E, S, W; 1932 v S, W; 1933 v E, W (10)
McClelland, J. (Mansfield T), 1980 v S (sub), Aus (3); 1981 v Se, S; (with Rangers), S, Se (sub); 1982 v S, W, Y, Hon, Sp, A, F; 1983 v A, WG, Alb, T, Alb, S, E, W; 1984 v A, T, WG, S, E, W, Fi; 1985 v R, Is; (with Watford), Fi, E, Sp, T; 1986 v T, F (sub); 1987 v E (2), T, Is, Y; 1988 v T, Gr, F, Ma; 1989 v Ei, H, Sp (2), Ma; (with Leeds U), 1990 v N (53)
McClelland, J. T. (Arsenal), 1961 v W, I, WG (2), Gr; (with Fulham), 1966 v M (6)
McCluggage, A. (Cliftonville), 1922 v N; (Bradford), 1924 v E; (with Burnley), 1927 v S, W; 1928 v S, E, W; 1929 v S, E, W; 1930 v W; 1931 v E, W (13)
McClure, G. (Cliftonville), 1907 v S, W; 1908 v E; (with Distillery), 1909 v E (4)
McConnell, E. (Cliftonville), 1904 v S, W; (with Glentoran), 1905 v S; (with Sunderland), 1906 v E; 1907 v E; 1908 v S, W; (with Sheffield W), 1909 v S, W; 1910 v S, W, E (12)
McConnell, P. (Doncaster R), 1928 v W; (with Southport), 1932 v E (2)
McConnell, W. G. (Bohemians), 1912 v W; 1913 v E, S; 1914 v E, S, W (6)
McConnell, W. H. (Reading), 1925 v W; 1926 v E, W; 1927 v E, S, W; 1928 v E, W (8)
McCourt, F. J. (Manchester C), 1952 v E, W; 1953 v E, S, W, F (6)
McCourt, P. J. (Rochdale), 2002 v Sp (sub) (1)
McCoy, R. K. (Coleraine), 1987 v Y (sub) (1)
McCoy, S. (Distillery), 1896 v W (1)
McCracken, E. (Barking), 1928 v F (1)
McCracken, R. (C Palace), 1921 v E; 1922 v E, S, W (4)
McCracken, R. (Linfield), 1922 v N (1)
McCracken, W. R. (Distillery), 1902 v E, W; 1903 v S, E; 1904 v E, S, W; (with Newcastle U), 1905 v E, S, W; 1907 v E; 1920 v E; 1922 v E, S, W; (with Hull C), 1923 v S (16)
McCreery, D. (Manchester U), 1976 v S (sub), E, W; 1977 v Ho, Bel, WG, E, S, W, Ic; 1978 v Ic, Ho, Bel, S, E, W; 1979 v Ei, D, Bul, E, Bul, W, D; (with QPR), 1980 v E, Ei, S (sub), E (sub), W (sub), Aus (1+1 sub); 1981 v Se (sub), P (sub); (with Tulsa R), S, P, Se; 1982 v S, Is, E (sub), F, Y, Hon, Sp, A, F; (with Newcastle U), 1983 v A; 1984 v T (sub); 1985 v R, Sp (sub); 1986 v T (sub), R, E, F, D, Alg, Sp, Br; 1987 v T, E, Y; 1988 v Y; 1989 v Sp, Ma, Ch; (with Hearts), 1990 v H, Ei, N, U (sub) (67)
McCrory, S. (Southend U), 1958 v E (1)
McCullough, K. (Belfast C), 1935 v W; 1936 v E; (with Manchester C), 1936 v S; 1937 v E, S (5)
McCullough, W. J. (Arsenal), 1961 v I; 1963 v Sp; 1964 v S, E, W, U, Sp; 1965 v E, Sw; (with Millwall), 1967 v E (10)
McCurdy, C. (Linfield), 1980 v Aus (sub) (1)
McDonald, A. (QPR), 1986 v R, E, F, D, Mor, Alg, Sp, Br; 1987 v E (2), T, Is, Y; 1988 v Y, T, Pol, F, Ma; 1989 v Ei, H, Sp, Ch; 1990 v H, Ei, U; 1991 v Y, D, A, Fa; 1992 v Fa, S, Li, G; 1993 v Alb, Sp, D, Alb, Ei, Sp, Li, La; 1994 v D, Ei; 1995 v P, A, Ei, La, Ca, Ch, La; 1996 v A (sub), N (52)
McDonald, R. (Rangers), 1930 v S; 1932 v E (2)
McDonnell, J. (Bohemians), 1911 v E, S; 1912 v W; 1913 v W (4)
McElhinney, G. M. A. (Bolton W), 1984 v WG, S, E, W, Fi; 1985 v R (6)
McEvilly, L. R. (Rochdale), 2002 v Sp (sub) (1)
McFaul, W. S. (Linfield), 1967 v E (sub); (with Newcastle U), 1970 v W; 1971 v Sp; 1972 v USSR; 1973 v Cy; 1974 v Bul (6)
McGarry, J. K. (Cliftonville), 1951 v W, F, S (3)
McGaughey, M. (Linfield), 1985 v Is (sub) (1)
McGibbon, P. C. G. (Manchester U), 1995 v Ca (sub), Ch, La; 1996 v Lie (sub); 1997 v Th; (with Wigan Ath), 1998 v Alb; 2000 v L (sub) (7)
McGrath, R. C. (Tottenham H), 1974 v S, E, W; 1975 v N; 1976 v Is (sub); 1977; (with Manchester U), Ho, Bel, WG, E, S, W, Ic; 1978 v Ic, Ho, Bel, S, E, W; 1979 v Bul (sub), E (2 sub) (21)
McGregor, S. (Glentoran), 1921 v S (1)
McGrillen, J. (Clyde), 1924 v S; (with Belfast C), 1927 v S (2)
McGuire, E. (Distillery), 1907 v S (1)
McGuire, J. (Linfield), 1928 v F (1)
McIlroy, H. (Cliftonville), 1906 v E (1)
McIlroy, J. (Burnley), 1952 v E, S, W; 1953 v E, S, W; 1954 v E, S, W; 1955 v E, S, W; 1956 v E, S, W; 1957 v E, S, W, I, P (2); 1958 v E, S, W, I (2), Cz (2), Arg, WG, F; 1959 v E, S, W, Sp; 1960 v E, S, W; 1961 v E, W, WG (2), Gr; 1962 v E, S, Gr, Ho; 1963 v E, S, Pol (2); (with Stoke C), 1963 v W; 1966 v S, E, Alb (55)
McIlroy, S. B. (Manchester U), 1972 v Sp, S (sub); 1974 v S, E, W; 1975 v N, Se, Y, E, S, W; 1976 v Se, N, Y, S, E, W; 1977 v Ho, Bel, E, S, W, Ic; 1978 v Ic, Ho, Bel, S, E, W; 1979 v Ei, D, Bul, E, Bul, E, S, W, D; 1980 v E, Ei, Is, S, E, W; 1981 v Se, P, S, P, S, Se; 1982 v S, Is; (with Stoke C), E, F, S, W, Y, Hon, Sp, A, F; 1983 v A, WG, Alb, T, Alb, S, E, W; 1984 v A, T, S, E, W, Fi; 1985 v Fi, E, T; (with Manchester C), 1986 v T, R, E, F, D, Mor, Alg, Sp, Br; 1987 v E (sub) (88)
McIlvenny, P. (Distillery), 1924 v W (1)
McIlvenny, R. (Distillery), 1890 v E; (with Ulster), 1891 v E (2)
McKeag, W. (Glentoran), 1968 v S, W (2)
McKeague, T. (Glentoran), 1925 v S.Af (1)
McKee, F. W. (Cliftonville), 1906 v S, W; (with Belfast C), 1914 v E, S, W (5)
McKelvey, H. (Glentoran), 1901 v W; 1903 v S (2)
McKenna, J. (Huddersfield), 1950 v E, S, W; 1951 v E, S, F; 1952 v E (7)
McKenzie, H. (Distillery), 1922 v N; 1923 v S (2)
McKenzie, R. (Airdrie), 1967 v W (1)
McKeown, N. (Linfield), 1892 v E, S, W; 1893 v S, W; 1894 v S, W (7)
McKie, H. (Cliftonville), 1895 v E, S, W (3)
McKinney, D. (Hull C), 1921 v S; (with Bradford C), 1924 v S (2)
McKinney, V. J. (Falkirk), 1966 v WG (1)
McKnight, A. D. (Celtic), 1988 v Y, T, Gr, Pol, F, Ma; (with West Ham U), 1989 v Ei, H, Sp (2) (10)
McKnight, J. (Preston NE), 1912 v S; (with Glentoran), 1913 v S (2)
McLaughlin, J. C. (Shrewsbury T), 1962 v E, S, W, Gr; 1963 v W; (with Swansea T), 1964 v W, U; 1965 v E, W, Sw (2); 1966 v W (12)
McLean, T. (Limavady), 1885 v S (1)
McMahon, G. J. (Tottenham H), 1995 v Ca (sub), Ch, La; 1996 v Lie, N (sub), Se, G; (with Stoke C), 1997 v Arm (sub), Alb (sub), Bel, P (sub), Uk (sub), Arm (sub), Th (sub); 1998 v G (sub), Alb (sub), P (sub) (17)
McMahon, J. (Bohemians), 1934 v S (1)
McMaster, G. (Glentoran), 1897 v E, S, W (3)
McMichael, A. (Newcastle U), 1950 v E, S; 1951 v E, S, F; 1952 v E, S, W; 1953 v E, S, W, F; 1954 v E, S, W; 1955 v E, W; 1956 v W; 1957 v E, S, W, I, P (2); 1958 v E, S, W, I (2), Cz (2), Arg, WG, F; 1959 v S, W, Sp; 1960 v E, S, W (40)
McMillan, G. (Distillery), 1903 v E; 1905 v W (2)
McMillan, S. T. (Manchester U), 1963 v E, S (2)
McMillen, W. S. (Manchester U), 1934 v E; 1935 v S; 1937 v S; (with Chesterfield), 1938 v S, W; 1939 v E, S (7)
McMordie, A. S. (Middlesbrough), 1969 v Is, T (2), E, S, W; 1970 v E, S, W, USSR; 1971 v Cy (2), E, S, W; 1972 v USSR, Sp, E, S, W; 1973 v Bul (21)
McMorran, E. J. (Belfast C), 1947 v E; (with Barnsley), 1951 v E, S, W; 1952 v E, S, W; 1953 v E, S, F; (with Doncaster R), 1953 v W; 1954 v E; 1956 v W; 1957 v I, P (15)
McMullan, D. (Liverpool), 1926 v E, W; 1927 v S (3)
McNally, B. A. (Shrewsbury T), 1986 v Mor; 1987 v T (sub); 1988 v Y, Gr, Ma (sub) (5)
McNinch, J. (Ballymena), 1931 v S; 1932 v S, W (3)
McParland, P. J. (Aston Villa), 1954 v W; 1955 v E, S; 1956 v E, S; 1957 v E, S, W, P; 1958 v E, S, W, I (2), Cz (2), Arg, WG, F; 1959 v E, S, W, Sp; 1960 v E, S, W; 1961 v E, S, W, I, WG (2), Gr; (with Wolverhampton W), 1962 v Ho (34)
McShane, J. (Cliftonville), 1899 v S; 1900 v E, S, W (4)
McVeigh, P. (Tottenham H), 1999 v Ca (sub); (with Norwich C), 2002 v Ic (sub), Pol (sub); 2003 v Sp, Uk, Fi, Arm, Gr (sub), I, Sp (sub); 2004 v Arm (sub), N (sub), Ser (sub), Bar (sub), Stk, Tr (sub) (16)
McVicker, J. (Linfield), 1888 v E; (with Glentoran), 1889 v S (2)
McWha, W. B. R. (Knock), 1882 v E, W; (with Cliftonville), 1883 v E, W; 1884 v E; 1885 v E, W (7)
Mackie, J. (Arsenal), 1923 v W; (with Portsmouth), 1935 v S, W (3)

Madden, O. (Norwich C), 1938 v E (1)
Magee, G. (Wellington Park), 1885 v E, S, W (3)
Magill, E. J. (Arsenal), 1962 v E, S, Gr; 1963 v E, S, W, Pol (2), Sp; 1964 v E, S, W, U, Sp; 1965 v E, S, Sw (2), Ho, Alb; 1966 v S; (with Brighton & HA), E, Alb, W, WG, M (26)
Magilton, J. (Oxford U), 1991 v Pol, Y, Fa; 1992 v Fa, A, D, S, Li, G; 1993 v Alb, D, Alb, Ei, Li, La; 1994 v La, D, Ei; (with Southampton), R, Lie, Co, M; 1995 v P, A, Ei (2), Ca, Ch, La; 1996 v P, N, G; 1997 v Uk (sub), Arm (sub), Bel, P; 1998 v G; (with Sheffield W), P, Sp; (with Ipswich T), 2000 v L; 2001 v Y, Ma, D, Ic, N, CzR, Bul; 2002 v D, Ic, Ma, Pol, Lie (52)
Maginnis, H. (Linfield), 1900 v E, S, W; 1903 v S, W; 1904 v E, S, W (8)
Mahood, J. (Belfast C), 1926 v S; 1928 v E, S, W; 1929 v E, S, W; 1930 v W; (with Ballymena), 1934 v S (9)
Mannus, A. (Linfield), 2004 v Tr (sub) (1)
Manderson, R. (Rangers), 1920 v W, S; 1925 v S, E; 1926 v S (5)
Mansfield, J. (Dublin Freebooters), 1901 v E (1)
Martin, C. (Cliftonville), 1882 v E, W; 1883 v E (3)
Martin, C. (Bo'ness), 1925 v S (1)
Martin, C. J. (Glentoran), 1947 v S; (with Leeds U), 1948 v E, S, W; (with Aston Villa), 1949 v E; 1950 v W (6)
Martin, D. K. (Belfast C), 1934 v E, S, W; 1935 v S; (with Wolverhampton W), 1935 v E; 1936 v W; (with Nottingham F), 1937 v S; 1938 v E, S; 1939 v S (10)
Mathieson, A. (Luton T), 1921 v W; 1922 v E (2)
Maxwell, J. (Linfield), 1902 v W; 1903 v W, E; (with Glentoran), 1905 v W, S; (with Belfast C), 1906 v W; 1907 v S (7)
Meek, H. L. (Glentoran), 1925 v W (1)
Mehaffy, J. A. C. (Queen's Island), 1922 v W (1)
Meldon, P. A. (Dublin Freebooters), 1899 v S, W (2)
Mercer, H. V. A. (Linfield), 1908 v E (1)
Mercer, J. T. (Distillery), 1898 v E, S, W; 1899 v E; (with Linfield), 1902 v E, W; (with Distillery), 1903 v S (2), W; (with Derby Co), 1904 v E, W; 1905 v S (12)
Millar, W. (Barrow), 1932 v W; 1933 v S (2)
Miller, J. (Middlesbrough), 1929 v W, S; 1930 v E (3)
Milligan, D. (Chesterfield), 1939 v W (1)
Milne, R. G. (Linfield), 1894 v E, S, W; 1895 v E, W; 1896 v E, S, W; 1897 v E, S; 1898 v E, S, W; 1899 v E, W; 1901 v W; 1902 v E, S, W; 1903 v E, S (2); 1904 v E, S, W; 1906 v E, S, W (28)
Mitchell, E. J. (Cliftonville), 1933 v S; (with Glentoran), 1934 v W (2)
Mitchell, W. (Distillery), 1932 v E, W; 1933 v E, W; (with Chelsea), 1934 v W, S; 1935 v S, E; 1936 v S, E; 1937 v E, S, W; 1938 v E, S (15)
Molyneux, T. B. (Ligoniel), 1883 v E, W; (with Cliftonville), 1884 v E, W, S; 1885 v E, W; 1886 v E, W, S; 1888 v S (11)
Montgomery, F. J. (Coleraine), 1955 v E (1)
Moore, C. (Glentoran), 1949 v W (1)
Moore, P. (Aberdeen), 1933 v E (1)
Moore, R. (Linfield Ath), 1891 v E, S, W (3)
Moore, R. L. (Ulster), 1887 v S, W (2)
Moore, W. (Falkirk), 1923 v S (1)
Moorhead, F. W. (Dublin University), 1885 v E (1)
Moorhead, G. (Linfield), 1923 v S; 1928 v F, S; 1929 v S (4)
Moran, J. (Leeds C), 1912 v S (1)
Moreland, V. (Derby Co), 1979 v Bul (2 sub), E, S; 1980 v E, Ei (6)
Morgan, G. F. (Linfield), 1922 v N; 1923 v E; (with Nottingham F), 1924 v S; 1927 v E; 1928 v E, S, W; 1929 v E (8)
Morgan, S. (Port Vale), 1972 v Sp; 1973 v Bul (sub), P, Cy, E, S, W; (with Aston Villa), 1974 v Bul, P, S, E; 1975 v Se; 1976 v Se (sub), N, Y; (with Brighton & HA), S, W (sub); (with Sparta Rotterdam), 1979 v D (18)
Morrison, R. (Linfield Ath), 1891 v E, W (2)
Morrison, T. (Glentoran), 1895 v E, S, W; (with Burnley), 1899 v W; 1900 v W; 1902 v E, S (7)
Morrogh, D. (Bohemians), 1896 v S (1)
Morrow, S. J. (Arsenal), 1990 v U (sub); 1991 v A (sub), Pol, Y; 1992 v Fa, S (sub), G (sub); 1993 v Sp (sub), Alb, Ei; 1994 v R, Co, M (sub); 1995 v P, Ei (2), La; 1996 v P, Se; 1997 v Uk, G, Alb, I, Bel; (with QPR), P, Uk, Arm; 1998 v G, P, Slo, Sw, Sp; 1999 v T, Fi, Mol, G, Mol; 2000 v G, Fi (39)
Morrow, W. J. (Moyola Park), 1883 v E, W; 1884 v S (3)
Muir, R. (Oldpark), 1885 v S, W (2)
Mulholland, S. (Celtic), 1906 v S, E (2)
Mullan, G. (Glentoran), 1983 v S, E, W, Alb (sub) (4)
Mulligan, J. (Manchester C), 1921 v S (1)
Mulryne, P. P. (Manchester U), 1997 v Bel (sub), Arm (sub), Th; 1998 v Alb (sub), Sp (sub); 1999 v T, Fi; (with Norwich C), Ca; 2001 v Y, D (sub), Bul (sub), CzR; 2002 v D, Ic, Pol Lie; 2003 v Sp, Uk; 2004 v Uk (sub), Arm (sub), Es, Ser Bar, Stk (sub), Tr (25)
Murdock, C. J, (Preston NE), 2000 v L (sub), Ma, H (sub) 2001 v Y, Ma, D, Ic, N, CzR, Bul (2), CzR; 2002 v D, Ma 2003 v Cy, Sp, Uk (sub); (with Hibernian), 2004 v Gr (sub) Bar (sub), Stk, Tr (sub) (21)
Murphy, J. (Bradford C), 1910 v E, S, W (3)
Murphy, N. (QPR), 1905 v E, S, W (3)
Murray, J. M. (Motherwell), 1910 v E, S; (with Sheffield W) 1910 v W (3)

Napier, R. J. (Bolton W), 1966 v WG (1)
Neill, W. J. T. (Arsenal), 1961 v I, Gr, WG; 1962 v E, S, W, Gr 1963 v E, W, Pol, Sp; 1964 v S, E, W, U, Sp; 1965 v E, S, W Sw, Ho (2), Alb; 1966 v S, E, W, Alb, WG, M; 1967 v S, W 1968 v S, E; 1969 v E, S, W, Is, T (2); 1970 v S, E, W, USSR (2); (with Hull C), 1971 v Cy, Sp; 1972 v USSR (2), Sp, S, E W; 1973 v Bul, Cy (2), P, E, S, W (59)
Nelis, P. (Nottingham F), 1923 v E (1)
Nelson, S. (Arsenal), 1970 v W, E (sub); 1971 v Cy, Sp, E, S W; 1972 v USSR (2), Sp, E, S, W; 1973 v Bul, Cy, P; 1974 v S, E; 1975 v Se, Y; 1976 v Se, N, Is, E; 1977 v Bel (sub), WG W, Ic; 1978 v Ic, Ho, Bel; 1979 v Ei, D, Bul, E, Bul, E, S, W D; 1980 v E, Ei, Is; 1981 v S, P, S, Se; (with Brighton & HA), 1982 v E, S, Sp (sub), A (51)
Nicholl, C. J. (Aston Villa), 1975 v Se, Y, E, S, W; 1976 v Se N, Y, S, E, W; 1977 v W; (with Southampton), 1978 v Be (sub), S, E, W; 1979 v Ei, Bul, E, Bul, E, W; 1980 v Ei, Is, S E, W, Aus (3); 1981 v Se, P, S, P, S, Se; 1982 v S, Is, E, F, W Y, Hon, Sp, A, F; 1983 v S (sub), E, W; (with Grimsby T) 1984 v A, T (51)
Nicholl, H. (Belfast C), 1902 v E, W; 1905 v E (3)
Nicholl, J. M. (Manchester U), 1976 v Is, W (sub); 1977 v Ho Bel, E, S, W, Ic; 1978 v Ic, Ho, Bel, S, E, W; 1979 v Ei, D Bul, E, Bul, E, S, W, D; 1980 v E, Ei, Is, S, E, W, Aus (3) 1981 v Se, P, S, P, S, Se; 1982 v S, Is, E; (with Toronto B), F W, Y, Hon, Sp, A, F; (with Sunderland), 1983 v A, WG Alb, T, Alb; (with Toronto B), S, E, W; 1984 v T; (with Rangers), WG, S, E; (with Toronto B), Fi; 1985 v R; (with WBA), Fi, E, Sp, T; 1986 v T, R, E, F, Alg, Sp, Br (73)
Nicholson, J. J. (Manchester U), 1961 v S, W; 1962 v E, W, Gr Ho; 1963 v E, S, Pol (2); (with Huddersfield T), 1965 v W Ho (2), Alb; 1966 v S, E, W, Alb, M; 1967 v S, W; 1968 v S E, W; 1969 v S, E, W, T (2); 1970 v S, E, W, USSR (2); 197[illegible] v Cy (2), E, S, W; 1972 v USSR (2) (41)
Nixon, R. (Linfield), 1914 v S (1)
Nolan, I. R. (Sheffield W), 1997 v Arm, G, Alb, P, Uk; 1998 v G, P; 2000 v G, Fi, L, Ma, H; (with Bradford C), 2001 v Y Ma, Bul (2), CzR; (with Wigan Ath), 2002 v Sp (18)
Nolan-Whelan, J. V. (Dublin Freebooters), 1901 v E, W; 190[illegible] v S, W; 1903 v S (5)

O'Boyle, G. (Dunfermline Ath), 1994 v Co (sub), M; (with S[illegible] Johnstone), 1995 v P (sub), La (sub), Ca (sub), Ch (sub) 1996 v Se (sub), G (sub); 1997 v I (sub), Bel (sub); 1998 [illegible] Slo (sub), Sw (sub); 1999 v Fi (sub) (13)
O'Brien, M. T. (QPR), 1921 v S; (with Leicester C), 1922 v S W; 1924 v S, W; (with Hull C), 1925 v S, E, W; 1926 v W (with Derby Co), 1927 v W (10)
O'Connell, P. (Sheffield W), 1912 v E, S; (with Hull C), 1914 v E, S, W (5)
O'Doherty, A. (Coleraine), 1970 v E, W (sub) (2)
O'Driscoll, J. F. (Swansea T), 1949 v E, S, W (3)
O'Hagan, C. (Tottenham H), 1905 v S, W; 1906 v S, W, E (with Aberdeen), 1907 v E, S, W; 1908 v S, W; 1909 v E (11)
O'Hagan, W. (St Mirren), 1920 v E, W (2)
O'Hehir, J. C. (Bohemians), 1910 v W (1)
O'Kane, W. J. (Nottingham F), 1970 v E, W, S (sub); 1971 [illegible] Sp, E, S, W; 1972 v USSR (2); 1973 v P, Cy; 1974 v Bul, P, S E, W; 1975 v N, Se, E, S (20)
O'Mahoney, M. T. (Bristol R), 1939 v S (1)
O'Neill, C. (Motherwell), 1989 v Ch (sub); 1990 v Ei (sub) 1991 v D (3)
O'Neill, J. (Sunderland), 1962 v W (1)
O'Neill, J. P. (Leicester C), 1980 v Is, S, E, W, Aus (3); 1981 [illegible] P, S, P, S, Se; 1982 v S, Is, E, F, S, F (sub); 1983 v A, WG Alb, T, Alb, S; 1984 v S (sub); 1985 v Is, Fi, E, Sp, T; 1986 [illegible] T, R, E, F, D, Mor, Alg, Sp, Br (39)
O'Neill, M. A. M. (Newcastle U), 1988 v Gr, Pol, F, Ma; 198[illegible] v Ei, H, Sp (sub), Sp (sub), Ma (sub), Ch; (with Dundee U) 1990 v H (sub), Ei; 1991 v Pol; 1992 v Fa (sub), S (sub), [illegible] (sub); 1993 v Alb (sub + 1), Ei, Sp, Li, La; (with Hibernian) 1994 v Lie (sub); 1995 v A (sub), Ei; 1996 v Lie, A, N, Se (with Coventry C), 1997 v Uk (sub), Arm (sub) (31)

'Neill, M. H. M. (Distillery), 1972 v USSR (sub), (with Nottingham F), Sp (sub), W (sub); 1973 v P, Cy, E, S, W; 1974 v Bul, P, E (sub), W; 1975 v Se, Y, E, S; 1976 v Y (sub); 1977 v E (sub), S; 1978 v Ic, Ho, S, E, W; 1979 v Ei, D, Bul, E, Bul, D; 1980 v Ei, Is, Aus (3); 1981 v Se, P; (with Norwich C), P, S, Se; (with Manchester C), 1982 v S; (with Norwich C), E, F, S, Y, Hon, Sp, A, F; 1983 v A, WG, Alb, T, Alb, S, E; (with Notts Co), 1984 v A, T, WG, E, W, Fi; 1985 v R, Fi (64)
'Reilly, H. (Dublin Freebooters), 1901 v S, W; 1904 v S (3)

arke, J. (Linfield), 1964 v S; (with Hibernian), 1964 v E, Sp; (with Sunderland), 1965 v Sw, S, W, Ho (2), Alb; 1966 v WG; 1967 v E, S; 1968 v S, E (14)
atterson, D. J. (C Palace), 1994 v Co (sub), M (sub); 1995 v Ei (sub+1), La, Ca, Ch (sub), La (sub); (with Luton T), 1996 v N (sub), Se; 1998 v Sw, Sp; (with Dundee U), 1999 v Fi, Mol, G, Mol, Ei (17)
eacock, R. (Celtic), 1952 v S; 1953 v F; 1954 v W; 1955 v E, S; 1956 v E, S; 1957 v W, I, P; 1958 v S, E, W, I (2), Arg, Cz (2), WG; 1959 v E, S, W; 1960 v S, E; 1961 v E, S, I, WG (2), Gr; (with Coleraine), 1962 v S (31)
eden, J. (Distillery), 1887 v S, W; 1888 v W, E; 1889 v S, E; 1890 v W, S; 1891 v W, E; 1892 v W, E; 1893 v E, S, W; 1896 v W, E, S; 1897 v W, S; 1898 v W, E, S; 1899 v W (24)
enney, S. (Brighton & HA), 1985 v Is; 1986 v T, R, E, F, D, Mor, Alg, Sp; 1987 v E, T, Is; 1988 v Pol, F, Ma; 1989 v Ei, Sp (17)
ercy, J. C. (Belfast YMCA), 1889 v W (1)
latt, J. A. (Middlesbrough), 1976 v Is (sub); 1978 v S, E, W; 1980 v S, E, W, Aus (3); 1981 v Se, P; 1982 v F, S, W (sub), A; 1983 v A, WG, Alb, T; (with Ballymena U), 1984 v E, W (sub); (with Coleraine), 1986 v Mor (sub) (23)
ollock, W. (Belfast C), 1928 v F (1)
onsonby, J. (Distillery), 1895 v S, W; 1896 v E, S, W; 1897 v E, S, W; 1899 v E (9)
otts, R. M. C. (Cliftonville), 1883 v E, W (2)
riestley, T. J. M. (Coleraine), 1933 v S; (with Chelsea), 1934 v E (2)
yper, Jas. (Cliftonville), 1897 v S, W; 1898 v S, E, W; 1899 v S; 1900 v E (7)
yper, John (Cliftonville), 1897 v E, S, W; 1899 v E, W; 1900 v E, W, S; 1902 v S (9)
yper, M. (Linfield), 1932 v W (1)

uinn, J. M. (Blackburn R), 1985 v Is, Fi, E, Sp, T; 1986 v T, R, E, F, D (sub), Mor (sub); 1987 v E (sub), T; (with Swindon T), 1988 v Y (sub), T, Gr, Pol, F (sub), Ma; (with Leicester C), 1989 v Ei, H (sub), Sp (sub+1); (with Bradford C), Ma, Ch; 1990 v H; (with West Ham U), N; 1991 v Y (sub); (with Bournemouth), 1992 v Li; (with Reading), 1993 v Sp, D, Alb (sub), Ei (sub), La (sub); 1994 v La, D (sub), Ei, R, Lie, Co, M; 1995 v P, A (sub), La (sub); 1996 v Lie, A (sub) (46)
uinn, S. J. (Blackpool), 1996 v Se (sub); 1997 v Alb (sub), I, Bel, P, Uk (sub), Arm, Th (sub); 1998 v G, Alb; (with WBA), Slo, Sw; 1999 v T (sub), Fi (sub), Ei; 2000 v F (sub), T (sub), G (sub), Fi, L, Ma; 2001 v Y (sub), Bul (sub), CzR (sub); 2002 v Ma (sub); (with Willem II), 2003 v Cy, Fi, Arm, Gr; 2004 v Ser, Bar, Tr (32)

afferty, P. (Linfield), 1980 v E (sub) (1)
amsey, P. C. (Leicester C), 1984 v A, WG, S; 1985 v Is, E, Sp, T; 1986 v T, Mor; 1987 v Is, E, Y (sub); 1988 v Y; 1989 v Sp (14)
ankine, J. (Alexander), 1883 v E, W (2)
attray, D. (Avoniel), 1882 v E; 1883 v E, W (3)
ea, R. (Glentoran), 1901 v E (1)
edmond, R. (Cliftonville), 1884 v W (1)
eid, G. H. (Cardiff C), 1923 v S (1)
eid, J. (Ulster), 1883 v E; 1884 v W; 1887 v S; 1889 v W; 1890 v S, W (6)
eid, S. E. (Derby Co), 1934 v E, W; 1936 v E (3)
eid, W. (Hearts), 1931 v E (1)
eilly, M. M. (Portsmouth), 1900 v E; 1902 v E (2)
enneville, W. T. J. (Leyton), 1910 v S, E, W; (with Aston Villa), 1911 v W (4)
eynolds, J. (Distillery), 1890 v E, W; (with Ulster), 1891 v E, S, W (5)
eynolds, R. (Bohemians), 1905 v W (1)
ice, P. J. (Arsenal), 1969 v Is; 1970 v USSR; 1971 v E, S, W; 1972 v USSR, Sp, E, S, W; 1973 v Bul, Cy, E, S, W; 1974 v Bul, P, S, E, W; 1975 v N, Y, E, S, W; 1976 v Se, N, Y, Is, S, E, W; 1977 v Ho, Bel, WG, E, S, Ic; 1978 v Ic, Ho, Bel; 1979 v Ei, D, E (2), S, W, D; 1980 v E (49)
oberts, F. C. (Glentoran), 1931 v S (1)

Robinson, P. (Distillery), 1920 v S; (with Blackburn R), 1921 v W (2)
Robinson, S. (Bournemouth), 1997 v Th (sub); 1999 v Mol, Ei; 2000 v L (sub), H (sub) (5)
Rogan, A. (Celtic), 1988 v Y (sub), Gr, Pol (sub); 1989 v Ei (sub), H, Sp (2), Ma (sub), Ch; 1990 v H, N (sub), U; 1991 v Y (2), D, A; (with Sunderland), 1992 v Li (sub); (with Millwall), 1997 v G (sub) (18)
Rollo, D. (Linfield), 1912 v W; 1913 v W; 1914 v W, E; (with Blackburn R), 1920 v S, W; 1921 v E, S, W; 1922 v E; 1923 v E; 1924 v S, W; 1925 v W; 1926 v E; 1927 v E (16)
Roper, E. O. (Dublin University), 1886 v W (1)
Rosbotham, A. (Cliftonville), 1887 v E, S, W; 1888 v E, S, W; 1889 v E (7)
Ross, W. E. (Newcastle U), 1969 v Is (1)
Rowland, K. (West Ham U), 1994 v La (sub); 1995 v Ca, Ch, La; 1996 v P (sub), Lie (sub), N (sub), Se, G (sub); 1997 v Uk, Arm, I (sub); 1998 v Alb; (with QPR), 1999 v T, Fi, Mol, G, Ca, Ei (19)
Rowley, R. W. M. (Southampton), 1929 v S, W; 1930 v W, E; (with Tottenham H), 1931 v W; 1932 v S (6)
Rushe, F. (Distillery),1925 v S.Af (1)
Russell, A. (Linfield), 1947 v E (1)
Russell, S. R. (Bradford C), 1930 v E, S; (with Derry C), 1932 v E (3)
Ryan, R. A. (WBA), 1950 v W (1)

Sanchez, L. P. (Wimbledon), 1987 v T (sub); 1989 v Sp, Ma (3)
Scott, E. (Liverpool), 1920 v S; 1921 v E, S, W; 1922 v E; 1925 v W; 1926 v E, S, W; 1927 v E, S, W; 1928 v E, S, W; 1929 v E, S, W; 1930 v E; 1931 v E; 1932 v W; 1933 v E, S, W; 1934 v E, S, W; (with Belfast C), 1935 v S; 1936 v E, S, W (31)
Scott, J. (Grimsby), 1958 v Cz, F (2)
Scott, J. E. (Cliftonville), 1901 v S (1)
Scott, L. J. (Dublin University), 1895 v S, W (2)
Scott, P. W. (Everton), 1975 v W; 1976 v Y; (with York C), Is, S, E (sub), W; 1978 v S, E, W; (with Aldershot), 1979 v S (sub) (10)
Scott, T. (Cliftonville), 1894 v E, S; 1895 v S, W; 1896 v S, E, W; 1897 v E, W; 1898 v E, S, W; 1900 v W (13)
Scott, W. (Linfield), 1903 v E, S, W; 1904 v E, S, W; (with Everton), 1905 v E, S; 1907 v E, S; 1908 v E, S, W; 1909 v E, S, W; 1910 v E, S; 1911 v E, S, W; 1912 v E; (with Leeds City), 1913 v E, S, W (25)
Scraggs, M. J. (Glentoran), 1921 v W; 1922 v E (2)
Seymour, H. C. (Bohemians), 1914 v W (1)
Seymour, J. (Cliftonville), 1907 v W; 1909 v W (2)
Shanks, T. (Woolwich Arsenal), 1903 v S; 1904 v W; (with Brentford), 1905 v E (3)
Sharkey, P. G. (Ipswich T), 1976 v S (1)
Sheehan, Dr G. (Bohemians), 1899 v S; 1900 v E, W (3)
Sheridan, J. (Everton), 1903 v W, E, S; 1904 v E, S; (with Stoke C), 1905 v E (6)
Sherrard, J. (Limavady), 1885 v S; 1887 v W; 1888 v W (3)
Sherrard, W. C. (Cliftonville), 1895 v E, W, S (3)
Sherry, J. J. (Bohemians), 1906 v E; 1907 v W (2)
Shields, R. J. (Southampton), 1957 v S (1)
Silo, M. (Belfast YMCA), 1888 v E (1)
Simpson, W. J. (Rangers), 1951 v W, F; 1954 v E, S; 1955 v E; 1957 v I, P; 1958 v S, E, W, I; 1959 v S (12)
Sinclair, J. (Knock), 1882 v E, W (2)
Slemin, J. C. (Bohemians), 1909 v W (1)
Sloan, A. S. (London Caledonians), 1925 v W (1)
Sloan, D. (Oxford U), 1969 v Is; 1971 v Sp (2)
Sloan, H. A. de B. (Bohemians), 1903 v E; 1904 v S; 1905 v E; 1906 v W; 1907 v E, W; 1908 v W; 1909 v S (8)
Sloan, J. W. (Arsenal), 1947 v W (1)
Sloan, T. (Manchester U), 1979 v S, W (sub), D (sub) (3)
Sloan, T. (Cardiff C), 1926 v S, W, E; 1927 v W, S; 1928 v E, W; 1929 v E; (with Linfield), 1930 v W, S; 1931 v S (11)
Small, J. M. (Clarence), 1887 v E; (with Cliftonville), 1893 v E, S, W (4)
Smith, A. W. (Glentoran), 2003 v I, Sp; 2004 v Uk (sub), Arm, Gr (sub), N, Es, Ser (sub), Bar (sub), Stk, Tr (sub) (11)
Smith, E. E. (Cardiff C), 1921 v S; 1923 v W, E; 1924 v E (4)
Smith, J. E. (Distillery), 1901 v S, W (2)
Smyth, R. H. (Dublin University), 1886 v W (1)
Smyth, S. (Wolverhampton W), 1948 v E, S, W; 1949 v S, W; 1950 v E, S, W; (with Stoke C), 1952 v E (9)
Smyth, W. (Distillery), 1949 v E, S; 1954 v S, E (4)
Snape, A. (Airdrie), 1920 v E (1)
Sonner, D. J. (Ipswich T), 1998 v Alb (sub); (with Sheffield W), 1999 v G (sub), Ca (sub); 2000 v L (sub), Ma (sub), H; (with Birmingham C), 2001 v N (sub); (with Nottingham F), 2004 v Es, Ser (sub), Bar, Stk, Tr (sub) (12)

Spence, D. W. (Bury), 1975 v Y, E, S, W; 1976 v Se, Is, E, W, S (sub); (with Blackpool), 1977 v Ho (sub), WG (sub), E (sub), S (sub), W (sub), Ic (sub); 1979 v Ei, D (sub), E (sub), Bul (sub), E (sub), S, W, D; 1980 v Ei; (with Southend U), Is (sub), Aus (sub); 1981 v S (sub), Se (sub); 1982 v F (sub) (29)
Spencer, S. (Distillery), 1890 v E, S; 1892 v E, S, W; 1893 v E (6)
Spiller, E. A. (Cliftonville), 1883 v E, W; 1884 v E, W, S (5)
Stanfield, O. M. (Distillery), 1887 v E, S, W; 1888 v E, S, W; 1889 v E, S, W; 1890 v E, S; 1891 v E, S, W; 1892 v E, S, W; 1893 v E, W; 1894 v E, S, W; 1895 v E, S; 1896 v E, S, W; 1897 v E, S, W (30)
Steele, A. (Charlton Ath), 1926 v W, S; (with Fulham), 1929 v W, S (4)
Stevenson, A. E. (Rangers), 1934 v E, S, W; (with Everton), 1935 v E, S; 1936 v S, W; 1937 v E, W; 1938 v E, W; 1939 v E, S, W; 1947 v S, W; 1948 v S (17)
Stewart, A. (Glentoran), 1967 v W; 1968 v S, E; (with Derby Co), 1968 v W; 1969 v Is, T (1+1 sub) (7)
Stewart, D. C. (Hull C), 1978 v Bel (1)
Stewart, I. (QPR), 1982 v F (sub); 1983 v A, WG, Alb, T, Alb, S, E, W; 1984 v A, T, WG, S, E, W, Fi; 1985 v R, Fi, Is, E, Sp, T; (with Newcastle U), 1986 v R, E, D, Mor, Alg (sub), Sp (sub), Br; 1987 v E, Is (sub) (31)
Stewart, R. K. (St Columb's Court), 1890 v E, S, W; (with Cliftonville), 1892 v E, S, W; 1893 v E, W; 1894 v E, S, W (11)
Stewart, T. C. (Linfield), 1961 v W (1)
Swan, S. (Linfield), 1899 v S (1)

Taggart, G. P. (Barnsley), 1990 v N, U; 1991 v Y, D, A, Pol, Fa; 1992 v Fa, A, D, S, Li, G; 1993 v Alb, Sp, D, Alb, Ei, Sp, Li, La; 1994 v La, D, Ei, R, Lie, Co, M; 1995 v P (sub), A, Ei (2), Ca, Ch, La; (with Bolton W), 1997 v G, Alb, I, Bel, P, Uk, Arm; 1998 v G, P, Sp; (with Leicester C), 2000 v H; 2001 v Ma, D, Ic, N; 2003 v Sp (51)
Taggart, J. (Walsall), 1899 v W (1)
Taylor, M. S. (Fulham), 1999 v G, Mol, Ca, Ei; 2000 v F, T, G, Fi, L (sub), Ma (sub), H; 2001 v Y, N, Bul, CzR; 2002 v D, Ic, Ma, Pol, Lie, Sp; 2003 v Cy, Sp, Uk, Fi, Arm, Gr, I, Sp; 2004 v Uk, Arm, Gr, N; (with Birmingham C), Es, Ser, Bar, Stk, Tr (38)
Thompson, F. W. (Cliftonville), 1910 v E, S, W; (with Linfield), 1911 v W; (with Bradford C), 1911 v E; 1912 v E, W; 1913 v E, S, W; (with Clyde), 1914 v E, S (12)
Thompson, J. (Distillery), 1897 v S (1)
Thompson, R. (Queen's Island), 1928 v F (1)
Thompson, W. (Belfast Ath), 1889 v S (1)
Thunder, P. J. (Bohemians), 1911 v W (1)
Todd, S. J. (Burnley), 1966 v M (sub); 1967 v E; 1968 v W; 1969 v E, S, W; 1970 v S, USSR; (with Sheffield W), 1971 v Cy (2), Sp (sub) (11)
Toner, C. (Leyton Orient), 2003 v I (sub), Sp (sub) (2)
Toner, J. (Arsenal), 1922 v W; 1923 v W; 1924 v W, E; 1925 v E, S; (with St Johnstone), 1927 v E, S (8)
Torrans, R. (Linfield), 1893 v S (1)
Torrans, S. (Linfield), 1889 v S; 1890 v S, W; 1891 v S, W; 1892 v E, S, W; 1893 v E, S; 1894 v E, S, W; 1895 v E; 1896 v E, S, W; 1897 v E, S, W; 1898 v E, S; 1899 v E, W; 1901 v S, W (26)
Trainor, D. (Crusaders), 1967 v W (1)
Tully, C. P. (Celtic), 1949 v E; 1950 v E; 1952 v S; 1953 v E, S, W, F; 1954 v S; 1956 v E; 1959 v Sp (10)
Turner, A. (Cliftonville), 1896 v W (1)
Turner, E. (Cliftonville), 1896 v E (1)
Turner, W. (Cliftonville), 1886 v E, S; 1888 v S (3)
Twoomey, J. F. (Leeds U), 1938 v W; 1939 v E (2)

Uprichard, W. N. M. C. (Swindon T), 1952 v E, S, W; 1953 v E, S; (with Portsmouth), 1953 v W, F; 1955 v E, S, W; 1956 v E, S, W; 1958 v S, I, Cz; 1959 v S, Sp (18)

Vernon, J. (Belfast C), 1947 v E, S; (with WBA), 1947 v W; 1948 v E, S, W; 1949 v E, S, W; 1950 v E, S; 1951 v E, S, W, F; 1952 v S, E (17)

Waddell, T. M. R. (Cliftonville), 1906 v S (1)
Walker, J. (Doncaster R), 1955 v W (1)
Walker, T. (Bury), 1911 v S (1)
Walsh, D. J. (WBA), 1947 v S, W; 1948 v E, S, W; 1949 v E, S W; 1950 v W (9)
Walsh, W. (Manchester C), 1948 v E, S, W; 1949 v E, S (5)
Waring, J. (Cliftonville), 1899 v E (1)
Warren, P. (Shelbourne), 1913 v E, S (2)
Watson, J. (Ulster), 1883 v E, W; 1886 v E, S, W; 1887 v S, W 1889 v E, W (9)
Watson, P. (Distillery), 1971 v Cy (sub) (1)
Watson, T. (Cardiff C), 1926 v S (1)
Wattie, J. (Distillery), 1899 v E (1)
Webb, C. G. (Brighton), 1909 v S, W; 1911 v S (3)
Weir, E. (Clyde), 1939 v W (1)
Welsh, E. (Carlisle U), 1966 v W, WG, M; 1967 v W (4)
Whiteside, N. (Manchester U), 1982 v Y, Hon, Sp, A, F; 1983 WG, Alb, T; 1984 v A, T, WG, S, E, W, Fi; 1985 v R, Fi, Is E, Sp, T; 1986 v R, E, F, D, Mor, Alg, Sp, Br; 1987 v E (2 Is, Y; 1988 v T, Pol, F; (with Everton), 1990 v H, Ei (38)
Whiteside, T. (Distillery), 1891 v E (1)
Whitfield, E. R. (Dublin University), 1886 v W (1)
Whitley, Jeff (Manchester C), 1997 v Bel (sub), Th (sub); 199 v Sp (sub); 2000 v Fi; 2001 v Y, D, N; (with Sunderland 2004 v Gr, Es, Ser, Stk, Tr (12)
Whitley, Jim (Manchester C), 1998 v Sp; 1999 v T (sub); 2000 Fi (sub) (3)
Williams, J. R. (Ulster), 1886 v E, S (2)
Williams, M. S. (Chesterfield), 1999 v G, Mol, Ca, Ei; (wit Watford), 2000 v F, T, G, Fi, L, Ma, H (sub); (wit Wimbledon), 2001 v Y, Ic (sub), N (sub), CzR, Bul, CzR 2002 v Lie, Sp; 2003 v Cy, Fi; (with Stoke C), Arm, Gr, (sub), Sp (sub); (with Wimbledon), 2004 v N (sub), Es, Se Bar, Tr (30)
Williams, P. A. (WBA), 1991 v Fa (sub) (1)
Williamson, J. (Cliftonville), 1890 v E; 1892 v S; 1893 v S (3)
Willighan, T. (Burnley), 1933 v W; 1934 v S (2)
Willis, G. (Linfield), 1906 v S, W; 1907 v S; 1912 v S (4)
Wilson, D. J. (Brighton & HA), 1987 v T, Is, E (sub); (wit Luton T), 1988 v Y, T, Gr, Pol, F, Ma; 1989 v Ei, H, Sp, Ma Ch; 1990 v H, Ei, N, U; (with Sheffield W), 1991 v Y, D, A Fa; 1992 v A (sub), S (24)
Wilson, H. (Linfield), 1925 v W, S.Af (2)
Wilson, K. J. (Ipswich T), 1987 v Is, E, Y; (with Chelsea), 198 v Y, T, Gr (sub), Pol (sub), F (sub); 1989 v H (sub), Sp (2 Ma, Ch; 1990 v Ei (sub), N, U; 1991 v Y (2), A, Pol, Fa; 199 v Fa, A, D, S; (with Notts Co), Li, G; 1993 v Alb, Sp, D, S Li, La; 1994 v La, D, Ei, R, Lie, Co, M; (with Walsall), 199 v Ei (sub), La (42)
Wilson, M. (Distillery), 1884 v E, S, W (3)
Wilson, R. (Cliftonville), 1888 v S (1)
Wilson, S. J. (Glenavon), 1962 v S; 1964 v S; (with Falkirk 1964 v E, W, U, Sp; 1965 v E, Sw; (with Dundee), 1966 v W WG; 1967 v S; 1968 v E (12)
Wilton, J. M. (St Columb's Court), 1888 v E, W; 1889 v S, E (with Cliftonville), 1890 v E; (with St Columb's Court), 189 v W, S (7)
Wood, T. J. (Walsall), 1996 v Lie (sub) (1)
Worthington, N. (Sheffield W), 1984 v W, Fi (sub); 1985 v I Sp (sub); 1986 v T, R (sub), E (sub), D, Alg, Sp; 1987 v E (2), T, Is, Y; 1988 v Y, T, Gr, Pol, F, Ma; 1989 v Ei, H, Sp Ma; 1990 v H, Ei, U; 1991 v Y, D, A, Fa; 1992 v A, D, S, L G; 1993 v Alb, Sp, D, Ei, Sp, Li, La; 1994 v La, D, Ei, Li Co, M; (with Leeds U), 1995 v P, A, Ei (2), La, Ca (sub Ch, La; 1996 v P, Lie, A, N, Se, G; (with Stoke C), 1997 v Bel (sub) (66)
Wright, J. (Cliftonville), 1906 v E, S, W; 1907 v E, S, W (6)
Wright, T. J. (Newcastle U), 1989 v Ma, Ch; 1990 v H, U; 199 v Fa, A, S, G; 1993 v Alb, Sp, Alb, Ei, Sp, Li, La; 1994 v La (with Nottingham F), D, Ei, R, Lie, Co, M (sub); 1997 v C Alb, I, Bel; (with Manchester C), P, Uk; 1998 v Alb; 1999 Ca (sub); 2000 v F (sub) (31)

Young, S. (Linfield), 1907 v E, S; 1908 v E, S; (with Airdrie 1909 v E; 1912 v S; (with Linfield), 1914 v E, S, W (9)

## SCOTLAND

Adams, J. (Hearts), 1889 v Ni; 1892 v W; 1893 v Ni (3)
Agnew, W. B. (Kilmarnock), 1907 v Ni; 1908 v W, Ni (3)
Aird, J. (Burnley), 1954 v N (2), A, U (4)
Aitken, A. (Newcastle U), 1901 v E; 1902 v E; 1903 v E, W; 1904 v E; 1905 v E, W; 1906 v E; (with Middlesbrough), 1907 v E, W; 1908 v E; (with Leicester Fosse), 1910 v E; 1911 v E, Ni (14)
Aitken, G. G. (East Fife), 1949 v E, F; 1950 v W, Ni, Sw; (with Sunderland), 1953 v W, Ni; 1954 v E (8)
Aitken, R. (Dumbarton), 1886 v E; 1888 v Ni (2)
Aitken, R. (Celtic), 1980 v Pe (sub), Bel, W (sub), E, Pol; 1983 v Bel, Ca (1+1 sub); 1984 v Bel (sub), Ni, W (sub); 1985 v E, Ic; 1986 v W, EG, Aus (2), Is, R, E, D, WG, U; 1987 v Bul, Ei (2), L, Bel, E, Br; 1988 v H, Bel, Bul, L, S.Ar, Ma, Sp, Co, E; 1989 v N, Y, I, Cy, F, Cy, E, Ch; 1990 v Y, F, N; (with Newcastle U), Arg (sub), Pol, Ma, Cr, Se, Br; (with St Mirren), 1992 v R (sub) (57)
Aitkenhead, W. A. C. (Blackburn R), 1912 v Ni (1)
Albiston, A. (Manchester U), 1982 v Ni; 1984 v U, Bel, EG, W, E; 1985 v Y, Ic, Sp (2), W; 1986 v EG, Ho, U (14)
Alexander, D. (East Stirlingshire), 1894 v W, Ni (2)
Alexander, G. (Preston NE), 2002 v Ng (sub), Sk, S.Af (sub), Hk (sub); 2003 v D (sub), Fa (sub), Ca, P, Ei, Ic, Li, Nz (sub); 2004 v Li (sub), R (14)
Allan, D. S. (Queen's Park), 1885 v E, W; 1886 v W (3)
Allan, G. (Liverpool), 1897 v E (1)
Allan, H. (Hearts), 1902 v W (1)
Allan, J. (Queen's Park), 1887 v E, W (2)
Allan, T. (Dundee), 1974 v WG, N (2)
Ancell, R. F. D. (Newcastle U), 1937 v W, Ni (2)
Anderson, A. (Hearts), 1933 v E; 1934 v A, E, W, Ni; 1935 v E, W, Ni; 1936 v E, W, Ni; 1937 v G, E, W, Ni, A; 1938 v E, W, Ni, Cz, Ho; 1939 v W, H (23)
Anderson, F. (Clydesdale), 1874 v E (1)
Anderson, G. (Kilmarnock), 1901 v Ni (1)
Anderson, H. A. (Raith R), 1914 v W (1)
Anderson, J. (Leicester C), 1954 v Fi (1)
Anderson, K. (Queen's Park), 1896 v Ni; 1898 v E, Ni (3)
Anderson, R. (Aberdeen), 2003 v Ic (sub), Ca, P, Ei (4)
Anderson, W. (Queen's Park), 1882 v E; 1883 v E, W; 1884 v E; 1885 v E, W (6)
Andrews, P. (Eastern), 1875 v E (1)
Archibald, A. (Rangers), 1921 v W; 1922 v W, E; 1923 v Ni; 1924 v E, W; 1931 v E; 1932 v E (8)
Archibald, S. (Aberdeen), 1980 v P (sub); (with Tottenham H), Ni, Pol, H; 1981 v Se (sub), Is, Ni, Is, Ni, E; 1982 v Ni, P, Sp (sub), Ho, Nz (sub), Br, USSR; 1983 v EG, Sw (sub), Bel; 1984 v EG, E, F; (with Barcelona), 1985 v Sp, E, Ic (sub); 1986 v WG (27)
Armstrong, M. W. (Aberdeen), 1936 v W, Ni; 1937 v G (3)
Arnott, W. (Queen's Park), 1883 v W; 1884 v E, Ni; 1885 v E, W; 1886 v E; 1887 v E, W; 1888 v E; 1889 v E; 1890 v E; 1891 v E; 1892 v E; 1893 v E (14)
Auld, J. R. (Third Lanark), 1887 v E, W; 1889 v W (3)
Auld, R. (Celtic), 1959 v H, P; 1960 v W (3)

Baird, A. (Queen's Park), 1892 v Ni; 1894 v W (2)
Baird, D. (Hearts), 1890 v Ni; 1891 v E; 1892 v W (3)
Baird, H. (Airdrieonians), 1956 v A (1)
Baird, J. C. (Vale of Leven), 1876 v E; 1878 v W; 1880 v E (3)
Baird, S. (Rangers), 1957 v Y, Sp (2), Sw, WG; 1958 v F, Ni (7)
Baird, W. U. (St Bernard), 1897 v Ni (1)
Bannon, E. (Dundee U), 1980 v Bel; 1983 v Ni, W, E, Ca; 1984 v EG; 1986 v Is, R, E, D (sub), WG (11)
Barbour, A. (Renton), 1885 v Ni (1)
Barker, J. B. (Rangers), 1893 v W; 1894 v W (2)
Barrett, F. (Dundee), 1894 v Ni; 1895 v W (2)
Battles, B. (Celtic), 1901 v E, W, Ni (3)
Battles, B. jun. (Hearts), 1931 v W (1)
Bauld, W. (Hearts), 1950 v E, Sw, P (3)
Baxter, J. C. (Rangers), 1961 v Ni, Ei (2), Cz; 1962 v Ni, W, E, Cz (2), U; 1963 v W, Ni, E, A, N, Ei, Sp; 1964 v W, E, N, WG; 1965 v W, Ni, Fi; (with Sunderland), 1966 v P, Br, Ni, W, E, I; 1967 v W, E, USSR; 1968 v W (34)
Baxter, R. D. (Middlesbrough), 1939 v E, W, H (3)
Beattie, A. (Preston NE), 1937 v E, A, Cz; 1938 v E; 1939 v W, Ni, H (7)
Beattie, R. (Preston NE), 1939 v W (1)
Begbie, I. (Hearts), 1890 v Ni; 1891 v E; 1892 v W; 1894 v E (4)
Bell, A. (Manchester U), 1912 v Ni (1)
Bell, J. (Dumbarton), 1890 v Ni; 1892 v E; (with Everton), 1896 v E; 1897 v E; 1898 v E; (with Celtic), 1899 v E, W, Ni; 1900 v E, W (10)
Bell, M. (Hearts), 1901 v W (1)
Bell, W. J. (Leeds U), 1966 v P, Br (2)
Bennett, A. (Celtic), 1904 v W; 1907 v Ni; 1908 v W; (with Rangers), 1909 v W, Ni, E; 1910 v E, W; 1911 v E, W; 1913 v Ni (11)
Bennie, R. (Airdrieonians), 1925 v W, Ni; 1926 v Ni (3)
Bernard, P. R. J. (Oldham Ath), 1995 v J (sub), Ec (2)
Berry, D. (Queen's Park), 1894 v W; 1899 v W, Ni (3)
Berry, W. H. (Queen's Park), 1888 v E; 1889 v E; 1890 v E; 1891 v E (4)
Bett, J. (Rangers), 1982 v Ho; 1983 v Bel; (with Lokeren), 1984 v Bel, W, E, F; 1985 v Y, Ic, Sp (2), W, E, Ic; (with Aberdeen), 1986 v W, Is, Ho; 1987 v Bel; 1988 v H (sub); 1989 v Y; 1990 v F (sub), N, Arg, Eg, Ma, Cr (25)
Beveridge, W. W. (Glasgow University), 1879 v E, W; 1880 v W (3)
Black, A. (Hearts), 1938 v Cz, Ho; 1939 v H (3)
Black, D. (Hurlford), 1889 v Ni (1)
Black, E. (Metz), 1988 v H (sub), L (sub) (2)
Black, I. H. (Southampton), 1948 v E (1)
Blackburn, J. E. (Royal Engineers), 1873 v E (1)
Blacklaw, A. S. (Burnley), 1963 v N, Sp; 1966 v I (3)
Blackley, J. (Hibernian), 1974 v Cz, E, Bel, Z; 1976 v Sw; 1977 v W, Se (7)
Blair, D. (Clyde), 1929 v W, Ni; 1931 v E, A, I; 1932 v W, Ni; (with Aston Villa), 1933 v W (8)
Blair, J. (Sheffield W), 1920 v E, Ni; (with Cardiff C), 1921 v E; 1922 v E; 1923 v E, W, Ni; 1924 v W (8)
Blair, J. (Motherwell), 1934 v W (1)
Blair, J. A. (Blackpool), 1947 v W (1)
Blair, W. (Third Lanark), 1896 v W (1)
Blessington, J. (Celtic), 1894 v E, Ni; 1896 v E, Ni (4)
Blyth, J. A. (Coventry C), 1978 v Bul, W (2)
Bone, J. (Norwich C), 1972 v Y (sub); 1973 v D (2)
Booth, S. (Aberdeen), 1993 v G (sub), Es (2 subs); 1994 v Sw, Ma (sub); 1995 v Fa, Ru; 1996 v Fi, Sm, Aus (sub), US, Ho, Sw (sub); (with Borussia Dortmund), 1998 v D, Fi, Co (sub), Mor (sub); (with Twente), 2001 v Pol; 2002 v Cro, Bel (sub), La (sub) (21)
Bowie, J. (Rangers), 1920 v E, Ni (2)
Bowie, W. (Linthouse), 1891 v Ni (1)
Bowman, D. (Dundee U), 1992 v Fi, US (sub); 1993 v G, Es; 1994 v Sw, I (6)
Bowman, G. A. (Montrose), 1892 v Ni (1)
Boyd, J. M. (Newcastle U), 1934 v Ni (1)
Boyd, R. (Mossend Swifts), 1889 v Ni; 1891 v W (2)
Boyd, T. (Motherwell), 1991 v R (sub), Sw, Bul, USSR; (with Chelsea), 1992 v Sw, R; (with Celtic), Fi, Ca, N, C; 1993 v Sw, P, I, Ma, G, Es (2); 1994 v I, Ma (sub), Ho (sub), A; 1995 v Fi, Fa, Ru, Gr, Ru, Sm; 1996 v Gr, Fi, Se, Sm, Aus, D, US, Co, Ho, E, Sw; 1997 v A, La, Se, Es (2), A, Se, W, Ma, Bl; 1998 v Bl, La, F, D, Fi (sub), Co, US, Br, N, Mor; 1999 v Li, Es, Fa, CzR, G, Fa, CzR; 2001 v La, Cro, Aus, Bel, Sm (sub), Pol; 2002 v Bel (72)
Boyd, W. G. (Clyde), 1931 v I, Sw (2)
Brackenbridge, T. (Hearts), 1888 v Ni (1)
Bradshaw, T. (Bury), 1928 v E (1)
Brand, R. (Rangers), 1961 v Ni, Cz, Ei (2); 1962 v Ni, W, Cz, U (8)
Branden, T. (Blackburn R), 1896 v E (1)
Brazil, A. (Ipswich T), 1980 v Pol (sub), H; 1982 v Sp, Ho (sub), Ni, W, E, Nz, USSR (sub); 1983 v EG, Sw; (with Tottenham H), W, E (sub) (13)
Bremner, D. (Hibernian), 1976 v Sw (sub) (1)
Bremner, W. J. (Leeds U), 1965 v Sp; 1966 v E, Pol, P, Br, I (2); 1967 v W, Ni, E; 1968 v W, E; 1969 v W, E, Ni, D, A, WG, Cy (2); 1970 v Ei, WG, A; 1971 v W, E; 1972 v P, Bel, Ho, Ni, W, E, Y, Cz, Br; 1973 v D (2), E (2), Ni (sub), Sw, Br; 1974 v Cz, WG, Ni, W, E, Bel, N, Z, Br, Y; 1975 v Sp (2); 1976 v D (54)
Brennan, F. (Newcastle U), 1947 v W, Ni; 1953 v W, Ni, E; 1954 v Ni, E (7)
Breslin, B. (Hibernian), 1897 v W (1)
Brewster, G. (Everton), 1921 v E (1)
Brogan, J. (Celtic), 1971 v W, Ni, P, E (4)
Brown, A. (St Mirren), 1890 v W; 1891 v W (2)
Brown, A. (Middlesbrough), 1904 v E (1)
Brown, A. D. (East Fife), 1950 v Sw, P, F; (with Blackpool), 1952 v USA, D, Se; 1953 v W; 1954 v W, E, N (2), Fi, A, U (14)

Brown, G. C. P. (Rangers), 1931 v W; 1932 v E, W, Ni; 1933 v E; 1934 v A; 1935 v E, W; 1936 v E, W; 1937 v G, E, W, Ni, Cz; 1938 v E, W, Cz, Ho (19)
Brown, H. (Partick T), 1947 v W, Bel, L (3)
Brown, J. (Cambuslang), 1890 v W (1)
Brown, J. B. (Clyde), 1939 v W (1)
Brown, J. G. (Sheffield U), 1975 v R (1)
Brown, R. (Dumbarton), 1884 v W, Ni (2)
Brown, R. (Rangers), 1947 v Ni; 1949 v Ni; 1952 v E (3)
Brown, R. jun. (Dumbarton), 1885 v W (1)
Brown, W. D. F. (Dundee), 1958 v F; 1959 v E, W, Ni; (with Tottenham H), 1960 v W, Ni, Pol, A, H, T; 1962 v Ni, W, E, Cz; 1963 v W, Ni, E, A; 1964 v Ni, W, N; 1965 v E, Fi, Pol, Sp; 1966 v Ni, Pol, I (28)
Browning, J. (Celtic), 1914 v W (1)
Brownlie, J. (Third Lanark), 1909 v E, Ni; 1910 v E, W, Ni; 1911 v W, Ni; 1912 v W, Ni, E; 1913 v W, Ni, E; 1914 v W, Ni, E (16)
Brownlie, J. (Hibernian), 1971 v USSR; 1972 v Pe, Ni, E; 1973 v D (2); 1976 v R (7)
Bruce, D. (Vale of Leven), 1890 v W (1)
Bruce, R. F. (Middlesbrough), 1934 v A (1)
Buchan, M. M. (Aberdeen), 1972 v P (sub), Bel; (with Manchester U), W, Y, Cz, Br; 1973 v D (2), E; 1974 v WG, Ni, W, N, Br, Y; 1975 v EG, Sp, P; 1976 v D, R; 1977 v Fi, Cz, Ch, Arg, Br; 1978 v EG, W (sub), Ni, Pe, Ir, Ho; 1979 v A, N, P (34)
Buchanan, J. (Cambuslang), 1889 v Ni (1)
Buchanan, J. (Rangers), 1929 v E; 1930 v E (2)
Buchanan, P. S. (Chelsea), 1938 v Cz (1)
Buchanan, R. (Abercorn), 1891 v W (1)
Buckley, P. (Aberdeen), 1954 v N; 1955 v W, Ni (3)
Buick, A. (Hearts), 1902 v W, Ni (2)
Burchill, M. J. (Celtic), 2000 v Bos (sub), Li, E (sub + sub), F (sub), Ho (sub) (6)
Burley, C. W. (Chelsea), 1995 v J, Ec, Fa; 1996 v Gr, Se, Aus, D, US, Co (sub), Ho (sub), E (sub), Sw; 1997 v A, La, Se, Es, A, Se, Ma, Bl; (with Celtic), 1998 v Bl, La, F, Co, US (sub), Br, N, Mor; 1999 v Fa, CzR; 2000 v Bos, Es, Bos, Li, E (2); (with Derby Co), Ho, Ei; 2001 v Cro, Aus, Bel, Sm; 2002 v Cro, Bel, La; 2003 v A (46)
Burley, G. (Ipswich T), 1979 v W, Ni, E, Arg, N; 1980 v P, Ni, E (sub), Pol; 1982 v W (sub), E (11)
Burns, F. (Manchester U), 1970 v A (1)
Burns, K. (Birmingham C), 1974 v WG; 1975 v EG (sub), Sp (2); 1977 v Cz (sub), W, Se, W (sub); (with Nottingham F), 1978 v Ni (sub), W, E, Pe, Ir; 1979 v N; 1980 v Pe, A, Bel; 1981 v Is, Ni, W (20)
Burns, T. (Celtic), 1981 v Ni; 1982 v Ho (sub), W; 1983 v Bel (sub), Ni, Ca (1 + 1 sub); 1988 v E (sub) (8)
Busby, M. W. (Manchester C), 1934 v W (1)

Cairns, T. (Rangers), 1920 v W; 1922 v E; 1923 v E, W; 1924 v Ni; 1925 v W, E, Ni (8)
Calderhead, D. (Q of S Wanderers), 1889 v Ni (1)
Calderwood, C. (Tottenham H), 1995 v Ru, Sm, J, Ec, Fa; 1996 v Gr, Fi, Se, Sm, US, Co, Ho, E, Sw; 1997 v A, La, Se, Es (2), A, Se; 1998 v Bl, La, F, D, Fi, Co, US, Br, N; 1999 v Li, Es; (with Aston Villa), Fa, CzR; 2000 v Bos (1 + sub) (36)
Calderwood, R. (Cartvale), 1885 v Ni, E, W (3)
Caldow, E. (Rangers), 1957 v Sp (2), Sw, WG, E; 1958 v Ni, W, Sw, Par, H, Pol, Y, F; 1959 v E, W, Ni, WG, Ho, P; 1960 v E, W, Ni, A, H, T; 1961 v E, W, Ni, Ei (2), Cz; 1962 v Ni, W, E, Cz (2), U; 1963 v W, Ni, E (40)
Caldwell, G. (Newcastle U), 2002 v F, Ng (sub), Sk, S.Af; (with Hibernian), 2004 v R, D, Es, Tr (8)
Caldwell, S. (Newcastle U), 2001 v Pol (sub); 2003 v Ei; 2004 v W, Tr (sub) (4)
Callaghan, P. (Hibernian), 1900 v Ni (1)
Callaghan, W. (Dunfermline Ath), 1970 v Ei (sub), W (2)
Cameron, C. (Hearts), 1999 v G (sub), Fa (sub); 2000 v Li (sub), F, Ei (sub); 2001 v La (sub), Sm, Cro, Aus, Sm, Pol; (with Wolverhampton W), 2002 v Cro (sub), Bel (sub), La, F; 2003 v Ei (sub), Li (sub), A (sub), G; 2004 v N, Fa, G, Li, W, R, D (26)
Cameron, J. (Rangers), 1886 v Ni (1)
Cameron, J. (Queen's Park), 1896 v Ni (1)
Cameron, J. (St Mirren), 1904 v Ni; (with Chelsea), 1909 v E (2)
Campbell, C. (Queen's Park), 1874 v E; 1876 v W; 1877 v E, W; 1878 v E; 1879 v E; 1880 v E; 1881 v E; 1882 v E, W; 1884 v E; 1885 v E; 1886 v E (13)
Campbell, H. (Renton), 1889 v W (1)
Campbell, Jas (Sheffield W), 1913 v W (1)
Campbell, J. (South Western), 1880 v W (1)
Campbell, J. (Kilmarnock), 1891 v Ni; 1892 v W (2)
Campbell, John (Celtic), 1893 v E, Ni; 1898 v E, Ni; 1900 v E, Ni; 1901 v E, W, Ni; 1902 v W, Ni; 1903 v W (12)
Campbell, John (Rangers), 1899 v E, W, Ni; 1901 v Ni (4)
Campbell, K. (Liverpool), 1920 v E, W, Ni; (with Partick T), 1921 v W, Ni; 1922 v W, Ni, E (8)
Campbell, P. (Rangers), 1878 v W; 1879 v W (2)
Campbell, P. (Morton), 1898 v W (1)
Campbell, R. (Falkirk), 1947 v Bel, L; (with Chelsea), 1950 v Sw, P, F (5)
Campbell, W. (Morton), 1947 v Ni; 1948 v E, Bel, Sw, F (5)
Canero, P. (Leicester C), 2004 v D (sub) (1)
Carabine, J. (Third Lanark), 1938 v Ho; 1939 v E, Ni (3)
Carr, W. M. (Coventry C), 1970 v Ni, W, E; 1971 v D; 1972 v Pe; 1973 v D (sub) (6)
Cassidy, J. (Celtic), 1921 v W, Ni; 1923 v Ni; 1924 v W (4)
Chalmers, S. (Celtic), 1965 v W, Fi; 1966 v P (sub), Br; 1967 v Ni (5)
Chalmers, W. (Rangers), 1885 v Ni (1)
Chalmers, W. S. (Queen's Park), 1929 v Ni (1)
Chambers, T. (Hearts), 1894 v W (1)
Chaplin, G. D. (Dundee), 1908 v W (1)
Cheyne, A. G. (Aberdeen), 1929 v E, N, G, Ho; 1930 v F (5)
Christie, A. J. (Queen's Park), 1898 v W; 1899 v E, Ni (3)
Christie, R. M. (Queen's Park), 1884 v E (1)
Clark, J. (Celtic), 1966 v Br; 1967 v W, Ni, USSR (4)
Clark, R. B. (Aberdeen), 1968 v W, Ho; 1970 v Ni; 1971 v W, Ni, E, D, P, USSR; 1972 v Bel, Ni, W, E, Cz, Br; 1973 v D, E (17)
Clarke, S. (Chelsea), 1988 v H, Bel, Bul, S.Ar, Ma; 1994 v Ho (6)
Cleland, J. (Royal Albert), 1891 v Ni (1)
Clements, R. (Leith Ath), 1891 v Ni (1)
Clunas, W. L. (Sunderland), 1924 v E; 1926 v W (2)
Collier, W. (Raith R), 1922 v W (1)
Collins, J. (Hibernian), 1988 v S.Ar; 1990 v EG, Pol (sub), Ma (sub); (with Celtic), 1991 v Sw (sub), Bul (sub); 1992 v Ni (sub), Fi; 1993 v P, Ma, G, P, Es (2); 1994 v Sw, Ho (sub), A, Ho; 1995 v Fi, Fa, Ru, Gr, Ru, Sm, Fa; 1996 v Gr, Fi, Se, Sm, Aus, D, US (sub), Co, Ho, E, Sw; (with Monaco), 1997 v A, La, Se, Es, A, Se, Ma; 1998 v Bl, La, F, Fi, Co, US, Br, N, Mor; (with Everton), 1999 v Li; 2000 v Bos, Es, Bos, E (2) (58)
Collins, R. Y. (Celtic), 1951 v W, Ni, A; 1955 v Y, A, H; 1956 v Ni, W; 1957 v E, W, Sp (2), Sw, WG; 1958 v Ni, W, Sw, H, Pol, Y, F, Par; (with Everton), 1959 v E, W, Ni, WG, Ho, P; (with Leeds U), 1965 v E, Pol, Sp (31)
Collins, T. (Hearts), 1909 v W (1)
Colman, D. (Aberdeen), 1911 v E, W, Ni; 1913 v Ni (4)
Colquhoun, E. P. (Sheffield U), 1972 v P, Ho, Pe, Y, Cz, Br; 1973 v D (2), E (9)
Colquhoun, J. (Hearts), 1988 v S.Ar (sub), Ma (sub) (2)
Combe, J. R. (Hibernian), 1948 v E, Bel, Sw (3)
Conn, A. (Hearts), 1956 v A (1)
Conn, A. (Tottenham H), 1975 v Ni (sub), E (2)
Connachan, E. D. (Dunfermline Ath), 1962 v Cz, U (2)
Connelly, G. (Celtic), 1974 v Cz, WG (2)
Connolly, J. (Everton), 1973 v Sw (1)
Connor, J. (Airdrieonians), 1886 v Ni (1)
Connor, J. (Sunderland), 1930 v F; 1932 v Ni; 1934 v E; 1935 v Ni (4)
Connor, R. (Dundee), 1986 v Ho; (with Aberdeen), 1988 v S.Ar (sub); 1989 v E; 1991 v R (4)
Cook, W. L. (Bolton W), 1934 v E; 1935 v W, Ni (3)
Cooke, C. (Dundee), 1966 v W, I; (with Chelsea), P, Br; 1968 v E, Ho; 1969 v W, Ni, A, WG (sub), Cy (2); 1970 v A; 1971 v Bel; 1975 v Sp, P (16)
Cooper, D. (Rangers), 1980 v Pe, A (sub); 1984 v W, E; 1985 v Y, Ic, Sp (2), W; 1986 v W (sub), EG, Aus (2), Ho, WG (sub), U (sub); 1987 v Bul, L, Ei, Br; (with Motherwell), 1990 v N, Eg (22)
Cormack, P. B. (Hibernian), 1966 v Br; 1969 v D (sub); 1970 v Ei, WG; (with Nottingham F), 1971 v D (sub), W, P, E; 1972 v Ho (sub) (9)
Cowan, J. (Aston Villa), 1896 v E; 1897 v E; 1898 v E (3)
Cowan, J. (Morton), 1948 v Bel, Sw; F; 1949 v E, W, F; 1950 v E, W, Ni, Sw, P, F; 1951 v E, W, Ni, A (2), D, F, Bel; 1952 v Ni, W, USA, D, Se (25)
Cowan, W. D. (Newcastle U), 1924 v E (1)
Cowie, D. (Dundee), 1953 v E, Se; 1954 v Ni, W, Fi, N, A, U; 1955 v W, Ni, A, H; 1956 v W, A; 1957 v Ni, W; 1958 v H, Pol, Y, Par (20)
Cox, C. J. (Hearts), 1948 v F (1)
Cox, S. (Rangers), 1949 v E, F; 1950 v E, F, W, Ni, Sw, P; 1951 v E, D, F, Bel, A; 1952 v Ni, W, USA, D, Se; 1953 v W, Ni, E; 1954 v W, Ni, E (24)

Craig, A. (Motherwell), 1929 v N, Ho; 1932 v E (3)
Craig, J. (Celtic), 1977 v Se (sub) (1)
Craig, J. P. (Celtic), 1968 v W (1)
Craig, T. (Rangers), 1927 v Ni; 1928 v Ni; 1929 v N, G, Ho; 1930 v Ni, E, W (8)
Craig, T. B. (Newcastle U), 1976 v Sw (1)
Crainey, S. (Celtic), 2002 v F, Ng; 2003 v D (sub), Fa; (with Southampton), 2004 v R (sub), D (6)
Crapnell, J. (Airdrieonians), 1929 v E, N, G; 1930 v F; 1931 v Ni, Sw; 1932 v E, F; 1933 v Ni (9)
Crawford, D. (St Mirren), 1894 v W, Ni; 1900 v W (3)
Crawford, J. (Queen's Park), 1932 v F, Ni; 1933 v E, W, Ni (5)
Crawford, S. (Raith R), 1995 v Ec (sub); (with Dunfermline Ath), 2001 v Pol (sub); 2002 v F; 2003 v Fa (sub), Ic, Ca, P, Ei, Ic, Li, A (sub), Nz, G; 2004 v N, Fa, Li, Ho (sub), R (sub), Es (sub), Tr (20)
Crerand, P. T. (Celtic), 1961 v Ei (2), Cz; 1962 v Ni, W, E, Cz (2), U; 1963 v W, Ni; (with Manchester U), 1964 v Ni; 1965 v E, Pol, Fi; 1966 v Pol (16)
Cringan, W. (Celtic), 1920 v W; 1922 v E, Ni; 1923 v W, E (5)
Crosbie, J. A. (Ayr U), 1920 v W; (with Birmingham), 1922 v E (2)
Croal, J. A. (Falkirk), 1913 v Ni; 1914 v E, W (3)
Cropley, A. J. (Hibernian), 1972 v P, Bel (2)
Cross, J. H. (Third Lanark), 1903 v Ni (1)
Cruickshank, J. (Hearts), 1964 v WG; 1970 v W, E; 1971 v D, Bel; 1976 v R (6)
Crum, J. (Celtic), 1936 v E; 1939 v Ni (2)
Cullen, M. J. (Luton T), 1956 v A (1)
Cumming, D. S. (Middlesbrough), 1938 v E (1)
Cumming, J. (Hearts), 1955 v E, H, P, Y; 1960 v E, Pol, A, H, T (9)
Cummings, G. (Partick T), 1935 v E; 1936 v W, Ni; (with Aston Villa), E; 1937 v G; 1938 v W, Ni, Cz; 1939 v E (9)
Cummings, W. (Chelsea), 2002 v Hk (sub) (1)
Cunningham, A. N. (Rangers), 1920 v Ni; 1921 v W, E; 1922 v Ni; 1923 v E, W; 1924 v E, Ni; 1926 v E, Ni; 1927 v E, W (12)
Cunningham, W. C. (Preston NE), 1954 v N (2), U, Fi, A; 1955 v W, E, H (8)
Curran, H. P. (Wolverhampton W), 1970 v A; 1971 v Ni, E, D, USSR (sub) (5)

Dailly, C. (Derby Co), 1997 v W, Ma, Bl; 1998 v Bl, La, F, D, Fi, Co, US, Br, N, Mor; (with Blackburn R), 1999 v Li; 2000 v Bos (sub), Es, Bos, Li, E (2), F, Ho, Ei; 2001 v La, Sm, Aus; (with West Ham U), Pol; 2002 v Cro, Bel, La, F, Ng, Sk, S.Af, Hk; 2003 v D, Fa, Ic, Ca, P, Ei, Ic, Li, A, Nz, G; 2004 v N, G, Li, Ho, W, R, D (53)
Dalglish, K. (Celtic), 1972 v Bel (sub), Ho; 1973 v D (1+1 sub), E (2), W, Ni, Sw, Br; 1974 v Cz (2), WG (2), Ni, W, E, Bel, N (sub), Z, Br, Y; 1975 v EG, Sp (sub+1), Se, P, W, Ni, E, R; 1976 v D (2), R, Sw, Ni, E; 1977 v Fi, Cz, W (2), Se, Ni, E, Ch, Arg, Br; (with Liverpool), 1978 v EG, Cz, W, Bul, Ni (sub), W, E, Pe, Ir, Ho; 1979 v A, N, P, W, Ni, E, Arg, N; 1980 v Pe, A, Bel (2), P, Ni, W, E, Pol, H; 1981 v Se, P, Is; 1982 v Se, Ni, P (sub), Sp, Ho, Ni, W, E, Nz, Br (sub); 1983 v Bel, Sw; 1984 v U, Bel, EG; 1985 v Y, Ic, Sp, W; 1986 v EG, Aus, R; 1987 v Bul (sub), L (102)
Davidson, C. I. (Blackburn R), 1999 v Li (sub), Es, Fa, CzR, G, Fa, CzR; 2000 v Es, Bos, Li, E, F; (with Leicester C), 2001 v La, Pol; 2002 v La; 2003 v Ic (sub), Ca (sub) (17)
Davidson, D. (Queen's Park), 1878 v W; 1879 v W; 1880 v W; 1881 v E, W (5)
Davidson, J. A. (Partick T), 1954 v N (2), A, U; 1955 v W, Ni, E, H (8)
Davidson, S. (Middlesbrough), 1921 v E (1)
Dawson, A. (Rangers), 1980 v Pol (sub), H; 1983 v Ni, Ca (2) (5)
Dawson, J. (Rangers), 1935 v Ni; 1936 v E; 1937 v G, E, W, Ni, A, Cz; 1938 v W, Ho, Ni; 1939 v E, Ni, H (14)
Deans, J. (Celtic), 1975 v EG, Sp (2)
Delaney, J. (Celtic), 1936 v W, Ni; 1937 v G, E, A, Cz; 1938 v Ni; 1939 v W, Ni; (with Manchester U), 1947 v E; 1948 v E, W, Ni (13)
Devlin, P. J. (Birmingham C), 2003 v Ca, P (sub), Ei (sub), Ic (sub), Li (sub), A, Nz, G; 2004 v N (sub), Fa (10)
Dewar, G. (Dumbarton), 1888 v Ni; 1889 v E (2)
Dewar, N. (Third Lanark), 1932 v E, F; 1933 v W (3)
Dick, J. (West Ham U), 1959 v E (1)
Dickie, M. (Rangers), 1897 v Ni; 1899 v Ni; 1900 v W (3)
Dickov, P. (Manchester C), 2001 v Sm (sub), Cro (sub), Aus (sub); (with Leicester C), 2003 v Fa; 2004 v Fa, Ho (2), W (8)
Dickson, W. (Dumbarton), 1888 v Ni (1)
Dickson, W. (Kilmarnock), 1970 v Ni, W, E; 1971 v D, USSR (5)
Divers, J. (Celtic), 1895 v W (1)
Divers, J. (Celtic), 1939 v Ni (1)
Divine, A. (Falkirk), 1910 v W (1)
Dobie, R. S. (WBA), 2002 v Sk, S.Af, Hk (sub); 2003 v D (sub), Fa, P (6)
Docherty, T. H, (Preston NE), 1952 v W; 1953 v E, Se; 1954 v N (2), A, U; 1955 v W, E, H (2), A; 1957 v E, Y, Sp (2), Sw, WG; 1958 v Ni, W, E, Sw; (with Arsenal), 1959 v W, E, Ni (25)
Dodds, D. (Dundee U), 1984 v U (sub), Ni (2)
Dodds, J. (Celtic), 1914 v E, W, Ni (3)
Dodds, W. (Aberdeen), 1997 v La (sub), W, Bl (sub); 1998 v Bl (sub); (with Dundee U), 1999 v Es (sub), Fa, G, Fa, CzR; 2000 v Bos, Es, Bos, Li (sub), E (2); (with Rangers), F, Ho, Ei; 2001 v La, Sm, Aus, Bel, Sm, Pol; 2002 v Cro (sub), Bel (26)
Doig, J. E. (Arbroath), 1887 v Ni; 1889 v Ni; (with Sunderland), 1896 v E; 1899 v E; 1903 v E (5)
Donachie, W. (Manchester C), 1972 v Pe, Ni, E, Y, Cz, Br; 1973 v D, E, W, Ni; 1974 v Ni; 1976 v R, Ni, W, E; 1977 v Fi, Cz, W (2), Se, Ni, E, Ch, Arg, Br; 1978 v EG, W, Bul, W, E, Ir, Ho; 1979 v A, N, P (sub) (35)
Donaldson, A. (Bolton W), 1914 v E, Ni, W; 1920 v E, Ni; 1922 v Ni (6)
Donnachie, J. (Oldham Ath), 1913 v E; 1914 v E, Ni (3)
Donnelly, S. (Celtic), 1997 v W (sub), Ma (sub); 1998 v La (sub), F (sub), D (sub), Fi (sub), Co (sub), US (sub); 1999 v Es (sub), Fa (10)
Dougall, C. (Birmingham C), 1947 v W (1)
Dougall, J. (Preston NE), 1939 v E (1)
Dougan, R. (Hearts), 1950 v Sw (1)
Douglas, A. (Chelsea), 1911 v Ni (1)
Douglas, J. (Renfrew), 1880 v W (1)
Douglas, R. (Celtic), 2002 v Ng, S.Af, Hk; 2003 v D, Fa, Ic, P, Ic, Nz, G; 2004 v N, Fa, G, Li, Ho (2), W (17)
Dowds, P. (Celtic), 1892 v Ni (1)
Downie, R. (Third Lanark), 1892 v W (1)
Doyle, D. (Celtic), 1892 v E; 1893 v W; 1894 v E; 1895 v E, Ni; 1897 v E; 1898 v E, Ni (8)
Doyle, J. (Ayr U), 1976 v R (1)
Drummond, J. (Falkirk), 1892 v Ni; (with Rangers), 1894 v Ni; 1895 v Ni, E; 1896 v E, Ni; 1897 v Ni; 1898 v E; 1900 v E; 1901 v E; 1902 v E, W, Ni; 1903 v Ni (14)
Dunbar, M. (Cartvale), 1886 v Ni (1)
Duncan, A. (Hibernian), 1975 v P (sub), W, Ni, E, R; 1976 v D (sub) (6)
Duncan, D. (Derby Co), 1933 v E, W; 1934 v A, W; 1935 v E, W; 1936 v E, W, Ni; 1937 v G, E, W, Ni; 1938 v W (14)
Duncan, D. M. (East Fife), 1948 v Bel, Sw, F (3)
Duncan, J. (Alexandra Ath), 1878 v W; 1882 v W (2)
Duncan, J. (Leicester C), 1926 v W (1)
Duncanson, J. (Rangers), 1947 v Ni (1)
Dunlop, J. (St Mirren), 1890 v W (1)
Dunlop, W. (Liverpool), 1906 v E (1)
Dunn, J. (Hibernian), 1925 v W, Ni; 1927 v Ni; 1928 v Ni, E; (with Everton), 1929 v W (6)
Durie, G. S. (Chelsea), 1988 v Bul (sub); 1989 v I (sub), Cy; 1990 v Y, EG, Eg, Se; 1991 v Sw (sub), Bul (2), USSR (sub), Sm; (with Tottenham H), 1992 v Sw, R, Sm, Ni (sub), Fi, Ca, N (sub), Ho, G; 1993 v Sw, I; 1994 v Sw, I; (with Rangers), Ho (2); 1996 v US, Ho, E, Sw; 1997 v A (sub), Se (sub), Ma (sub), Bl; 1998 v Bl, La, F, Fi (sub), Co, Br, N, Mor (43)
Durrant, I. (Rangers), 1988 v H, Bel, Ma, Sp; 1989 v N (sub); 1993 v Sw (sub), P (sub), I, P (sub); 1994 v I (sub), Ma; (with Kilmarnock), 1999 v Es, Fa (sub), G, Fa, CzR; 2000 v Bos (sub), Es, Ho (sub), Ei (sub) (20)
Dykes, J. (Hearts), 1938 v Ho; 1939 v Ni (2)

Easson, J. F. (Portsmouth), 1931 v A, Sw; 1934 v W (3)
Elliott, M. S. (Leicester C), 1998 v F (sub), D, Fi; 1999 v Li, Fa, CzR, Fa; 2000 v Ho, Ei; 2001 v La, Sm, Cro, Aus (sub), Bel, Sm; 2002 v Cro, Bel, La (18)
Ellis, J. (Mossend Swifts), 1892 v Ni (1)
Evans, A. (Aston Villa), 1982 v Ho, Ni, E, Nz (4)
Evans, R. (Celtic), 1949 v E, W, Ni, F; 1950 v W, Ni, Sw, P; 1951 v E, A; 1952 v Ni; 1953 v Se; 1954 v Ni, W, E, N, Fi; 1955 v Ni, P, Y, A, H; 1956 v E, Ni, W, A; 1957 v WG, Sp; 1958 v Ni, W, E, Sw, H, Pol, Y, Par, F; 1959 v E, WG, Ho, P; 1960 v E, Ni, W, Pol; (with Chelsea), 1960 v A, H, T (48)
Ewart, J. (Bradford C), 1921 v E (1)
Ewing, T. (Partick T), 1958 v W, E (2)

Farm, G. N. (Blackpool), 1953 v W, Ni, E, Se; 1954 v Ni, W, E; 1959 v WG, Ho, P (10)

Ferguson, B. (Rangers), 1999 v Li; 2000 v Bos, Es (sub), E (2), F, Ei; 2001 v La, Aus, Bel; 2003 v D, Fa, Ic, Ei, Ic; 2004 v N (with Blackburn R), Fa, G, Li, Ho (2) (21)
Ferguson, D. (Rangers), 1988 v Ma, Co (sub) (2)
Ferguson, D. (Dundee U), 1992 v US (sub), Ca, Ho (sub); 1993 v G; (with Everton) 1995 v Gr; 1997 v A, Es (7)
Ferguson, I. (Rangers), 1989 v I, Cy (sub), F; 1993 v Ma (sub), Es; 1994 v Ma, A (sub), Ho (sub); 1997 v Es (sub) (9)
Ferguson, J. (Vale of Leven), 1874 v E; 1876 v E, W; 1877 v E, W; 1878 v W (6)
Ferguson, R. (Kilmarnock), 1966 v W, E, Ho, P, Br; 1967 v W, Ni (7)
Fernie, W. (Celtic), 1954 v Fi, A, U; 1955 v W, Ni; 1957 v E, Ni, W, Y; 1958 v W, Sw, Par (12)
Findlay, R. (Kilmarnock), 1898 v W (1)
Fitchie, T. T. (Woolwich Arsenal), 1905 v W; 1906 v W, Ni; (with Queen's Park), 1907 v W (4)
Flavell, R. (Airdrieonians), 1947 v Bel, L (2)
Fleck, R. (Norwich C), 1990 v Arg, Se, Br (sub); 1991 v USSR (4)
Fleming, C. (East Fife), 1954 v Ni (1)
Fleming, J. W. (Rangers), 1929 v G, Ho; 1930 v E (3)
Fleming, R. (Morton), 1886 v Ni (1)
Fletcher, D. B. (Manchester U), 2004 v N (sub), Li (sub), Ho (2), W, D, Es, Tr (8)
Forbes, A. R. (Sheffield U), 1947 v Bel, L, E; 1948 v W, Ni; (with Arsenal), 1950 v E, P, F; 1951 v W, Ni, A; 1952 v W, D, Se (14)
Forbes, J. (Vale of Leven), 1884 v E, W, Ni; 1887 v W, E (5)
Ford, D. (Hearts), 1974 v Cz (sub), WG (sub), W (3)
Forrest, J. (Rangers), 1966 v W, I; (with Aberdeen), 1971 v Bel (sub), D, USSR (5)
Forrest, J. (Motherwell), 1958 v E (1)
Forsyth, A. (Partick T), 1972 v Y, Cz, Br; 1973 v D; (with Manchester U), E; 1975 v Sp, Ni (sub), R, EG; 1976 v D (10)
Forsyth, C. (Kilmarnock), 1964 v E; 1965 v W, Ni, Fi (4)
Forsyth, T. (Motherwell), 1971 v D; (with Rangers), 1974 v Cz; 1976 v Sw, Ni, W, E; 1977 v Fi, Se, W, Ni, E, Ch, Arg, Br; 1978 v Cz, W, Ni, W (sub), E, Pe, Ir (sub), Ho (22)
Foyers, R. (St Bernards), 1893 v W; 1894 v W (2)
Fraser, D. M. (WBA), 1968 v Ho; 1969 v Cy (2)
Fraser, J. (Moffat), 1891 v Ni (1)
Fraser, M. J. E. (Queen's Park), 1880 v W; 1882 v W, E; 1883 v W, E (5)
Fraser, J. (Dundee), 1907 v Ni (1)
Fraser, W. (Sunderland), 1955 v W, Ni (2)
Freedman, D. A. (C Palace), 2002 v La, F (2)
Fulton, W. (Abercorn), 1884 v Ni (1)
Fyfe, J. H. (Third Lanark), 1895 v W (1)

Gabriel, J. (Everton), 1961 v W; 1964 v N (sub) (2)
Gallacher, H. K. (Airdrieonians), 1924 v Ni; 1925 v E, W, Ni; 1926 v W; (with Newcastle U), 1926 v E, Ni; 1927 v E, W, Ni; 1928 v E, W; 1929 v E, W, Ni; 1930 v W, Ni, F; (with Chelsea), 1934 v E; (with Derby Co), 1935 v E (20)
Gallacher, K. W. (Dundee U), 1988 v Co, E (sub); 1989 v N, I; (with Coventry C), 1991 v Sm; 1992 v R (sub), Sm (sub), Ni (sub), N (sub), Ho (sub), G (sub), C; 1993 v Sw (sub), P; (with Blackburn R), P, Es (2); 1994 v I, Ma; 1996 v Aus (sub), D, Co (sub), Ho; 1997 v Se (sub), Es (2), A, Se, W, Ma, Bl; 1998 v Bl, La, F, Fi (sub), US, Br, N, Mor; 1999 v Li, Es, Fa, CzR; 2000 v Bos (sub); (with Newcastle U), Bos, Li (sub), E, F, Ei (sub); 2001 v Sm, Cro, Bel (sub), Sm (sub) (53)
Gallacher, P. (Sunderland), 1935 v Ni (1)
Gallacher, P. (Dundee U), 2002 v Hk (sub); 2003 v Ca, Ei (sub), Li, A; 2004 v R, D, Es (8)
Gallagher, P. (Blackburn R), 2004 v W (sub) (1)
Galloway, M. (Celtic), 1992 v R (1)
Galt, J. H. (Rangers), 1908 v W, Ni (2)
Gardiner, I. (Motherwell), 1958 v W (1)
Gardner, D. R. (Third Lanark), 1897 v W (1)
Gardner, R. (Queen's Park), 1872 v E; 1873 v E; (with Clydesdale), 1874 v E; 1875 v E; 1878 v E (5)
Gemmell, T. (St Mirren), 1955 v P, Y (2)
Gemmell, T. (Celtic), 1966 v E; 1967 v W, Ni, E, USSR; 1968 v Ni, E; 1969 v W, Ni, E, D, A, WG, Cy; 1970 v E, Ei, WG; 1971 v Bel (18)
Gemmill, A. (Derby Co), 1971 v Bel; 1972 v P, Ho, Pe, Ni, W, E; 1976 v D, R, Ni, W, E; 1977 v Fi, Cz, W (2), Ni (sub), E (sub), Ch (sub), Arg, Br; 1978 v EG (sub); (with Nottingham F), Bul, Ni, W, E (sub), Pe (sub), Ir, Ho; 1979 v A, N, P, N; (with Birmingham C), 1980 v A, P, Ni, W, E, H; 1981 v Se, P, Is, Ni (43)
Gemmill, S. (Nottingham F), 1995 v J, Ec, Fa (sub); 1996 v Sm D (sub), US; 1997 v Es, Se (sub), W, Ma (sub), Bl (sub) 1998 v D, Fi; (with Everton), 1999 v G, Fa (sub); 2001 v Sm (sub), Pol (sub); 2002 v Cro (sub), F (sub), Ng, Sk, S.Af Hk; 2003 v Ca, Ei (sub), A (sub) (26)
Gibb, W. (Clydesdale), 1873 v E (1)
Gibson, D. W. (Leicester C), 1963 v A, N, Ei, Sp; 1964 v Ni 1965 v W, Fi (7)
Gibson, J. D. (Partick T), 1926 v E; 1927 v E, W, Ni; (with Aston Villa), 1928 v E, W; 1930 v W, Ni (8)
Gibson, N. (Rangers), 1895 v E, Ni; 1896 v E, Ni; 1897 v E, Ni 1898 v E; 1899 v E, W, Ni; 1900 v E, Ni; 1901 v W; (with Partick T), 1905 v Ni (14)
Gilchrist, J. E. (Celtic), 1922 v E (1)
Gilhooley, M. (Hull C), 1922 v W (1)
Gillespie, G. (Rangers), 1880 v W; 1881 v E, W; 1882 v E (with Queen's Park), 1886 v W; 1890 v W; 1891 v Ni (7)
Gillespie, G. T. (Liverpool), 1988 v Bel, Bul, Sp; 1989 v N, F Ch; 1990 v Y, EG, Eg, Pol, Ma, Br (sub); 1991 v Bul (13)
Gillespie, Jas (Third Lanark), 1898 v W (1)
Gillespie, John (Queen's Park), 1896 v W (1)
Gillespie, R. (Queen's Park), 1927 v W; 1931 v W; 1932 v F 1933 v E (4)
Gillick, T. (Everton), 1937 v A, Cz; 1939 v W, Ni, H (5)
Gilmour, J. (Dundee), 1931 v W (1)
Gilzean, A. J. (Dundee), 1964 v W, E, N, WG; 1965 v Ni, (with Tottenham H), Sp; 1966 v Ni, W, Pol, I; 1968 v W; 1969 v W E, WG, Cy (2), A (sub); 1970 v Ni, E (sub), WG, A; 1971 v P (22)
Glass, S. (Newcastle U), 1999 v Fa (sub) (1)
Glavin, R. (Celtic), 1977 v Se (1)
Glen, A. (Aberdeen), 1956 v E, Ni (2)
Glen, R. (Renton), 1895 v W; 1896 v W; (with Hibernian) 1900 v Ni (3)
Goram, A. L. (Oldham Ath), 1986 v EG (sub), R, Ho; 1987 v Br; (with Hibernian), 1989 v Y, I; 1990 v EG, Pol, Ma; 1991 v R, Sw, Bul (2), USSR, Sm; (with Rangers), 1992 v Sw, R Sm, Fi, N, Ho, G, C; 1993 v Sw, P, I, Ma, P; 1994 v Ho; 1995 v Fi, Fa, Ru, Gr; 1996 v Se (sub), D (sub), Co, Ho, E, Sw 1997 v A, La, Es; 1998 v D (sub) (43)
Gordon, C. S. (Hearts), 2004 v Tr (1)
Gordon, J. E. (Rangers), 1912 v E, Ni; 1913 v E, Ni, W; 1914 v E, Ni; 1920 v W, E, Ni (10)
Gossland, J. (Rangers), 1884 v Ni (1)
Goudle, J. (Abercorn), 1884 v Ni (1)
Gough, C. R. (Dundee U), 1983 v Sw, Ni, W, E, Ca (3); 1984 v U, Bel, EG, Ni, W, E, F; 1985 v Sp, E, Ic; 1986 v W, EG Aus, Is, R, E, D, WG, U; (with Tottenham H), 1987 v Bul L, Ei (2), Bel, E, Br; 1988 v H; (with Rangers), S.Ar, Sp, Co E; 1989 v Y, I, Cy, F, Cy; 1990 v F, Arg, EG, Eg, Pol, Ma Cr; 1991 v USSR, Bul; 1992 v Sm, Ni, Ca, N, Ho, G, C; 1993 v Sw, P (61)
Gould, J. (Celtic), 2000 v Li; 2001 v Aus (2)
Gourlay, J. (Cambuslang), 1886 v Ni; 1888 v W (2)
Govan, J. (Hibernian), 1948 v E, W, Bel, Sw, F; 1949 v Ni (6)
Gow, D. R. (Rangers), 1888 v E (1)
Gow, J. J. (Queen's Park), 1885 v E (1)
Gow, J. R. (Rangers), 1888 v Ni (1)
Graham, A. (Leeds U), 1978 v EG (sub); 1979 v A (sub), N W, Ni, E, Arg, N; 1980 v A; 1981 v W (10)
Graham, G. (Arsenal), 1972 v P, Ho, Ni, Y, Cz, Br; 1973 v D (2); (with Manchester U), E, W, Ni, Br (sub) (12)
Graham, J. (Annbank), 1884 v Ni (1)
Graham, J. A. (Arsenal), 1921 v Ni (1)
Grant, J. (Hibernian), 1959 v W, Ni (2)
Grant, P. (Celtic), 1989 v E (sub), Ch (2)
Gray, A. (Hibernian), 1903 v Ni (1)
Gray, A. D. (Bradford C), 2003 v Li (sub), Nz (sub) (2)
Gray, A. M. (Aston Villa), 1976 v R, Sw; 1977 v Fi, Cz; 1979 v A, N; (with Wolverhampton W), 1980 v P, E (sub); 1981 v Se, P, Is (sub), Ni; 1982 v Se (sub), Ni (sub); 1983 v Ni, W, E, Ca (1+1 sub); (with Everton), 1985 v Ic (20)
Gray, D. (Rangers), 1929 v W, Ni, G, Ho; 1930 v W, E, Ni; 1931 v W; 1933 v W, Ni (10)
Gray, E. (Leeds U), 1969 v E, Cy; 1970 v WG, A; 1971 v W, Ni; 1972 v Bel, Ho; 1976 v W, E; 1977 v Fi, W (12)
Gray, F. T. (Leeds U), 1976 v Sw; 1979 v N, P, W, Ni, E, Arg (sub); (with Nottingham F), 1980 v Bel (sub); 1981 v Se, P, Is, Ni, Is, W; (with Leeds U), Ni, E; 1982 v Se, Ni, P, Sp, Ho W, Nz, Br, USSR; 1983 v EG, Sw, Bel, Sw, W, E, Ca (32)
Gray, W. (Pollokshields Ath), 1886 v E (1)
Green, A. (Blackpool), 1971 v Bel (sub), P (sub), Ni, E; (with Newcastle U), 1972 v W, E (sub) (6)
Greig, J. (Rangers), 1964 v E, WG; 1965 v W, Ni, E, Fi (2), Sp Pol; 1966 v Ni, W, E, Pol, I (2), P, Ho, Br; 1967 v W, Ni, E 1968 v Ni, W, E, Ho; 1969 v W, Ni, E, D, A, WG, Cy (2)

1970 v W, E, Ei, WG, A; 1971 v D, Bel, W (sub), Ni, E; 1976 v D (44)
Groves, W. (Hibernian), 1888 v W; (with Celtic), 1889 v Ni; 1890 v E (3)
Guilliland, W. (Queen's Park), 1891 v W; 1892 v Ni; 1894 v E; 1895 v E (4)
Gunn, B. (Norwich C), 1990 v Eg; 1993 v Es (2); 1994 v Sw, I, Ho (sub) (6)

Haddock, H. (Clyde), 1955 v E, H (2), P, Y; 1958 v E (6)
Haddow, D. (Rangers), 1894 v E (1)
Haffey, F. (Celtic), 1960 v E; 1961 v E (2)
Hamilton, A. (Queen's Park), 1885 v E, W; 1886 v E; 1888 v E (4)
Hamilton, A. W. (Dundee), 1962 v Cz, U, W, E; 1963 v W, Ni, E, A, N, Ei; 1964 v Ni, W, E, N, WG; 1965 v Ni, W, E, Fi (2), Pol, Sp; 1966 v Pol, Ni (24)
Hamilton, G. (Aberdeen), 1947 v Ni; 1951 v Bel, A; 1954 v N (2) (5)
Hamilton, G. (Port Glasgow Ath), 1906 v Ni (1)
Hamilton, J. (Queen's Park), 1892 v W; 1893 v E, Ni (3)
Hamilton, J. (St Mirren), 1924 v Ni (1)
Hamilton, R. C. (Rangers), 1899 v E, W, Ni; 1900 v W; 1901 v E, Ni; 1902 v W, Ni; 1903 v E; 1904 v Ni; (with Dundee), 1911 v W (11)
Hamilton, T. (Hurlford), 1891 v Ni (1)
Hamilton, T. (Rangers), 1932 v E (1)
Hamilton, W. M. (Hibernian), 1965 v Fi (1)
Hannah, A. B. (Renton), 1888 v W (1)
Hannah, J. (Third Lanark), 1889 v W (1)
Hansen, A. D. (Liverpool), 1979 v W, Arg; 1980 v Bel, P; 1981 v Se, P, Is; 1982 v Se, Ni, P, Sp, Ni (sub), W, E, Nz, Br, USSR; 1983 v EG, Sw, Bel, Sw; 1985 v W (sub); 1986 v R (sub); 1987 v Ei (2), L (26)
Hansen, J. (Partick T), 1972 v Bel (sub), Y (sub) (2)
Harkness, J. D. (Queen's Park), 1927 v E, Ni; 1928 v E; (with Hearts), 1929 v W, E, Ni; 1930 v E, W; 1932 v W, F; 1934 v Ni, W (12)
Harper, J. M. (Aberdeen), 1973 v D (1+1 sub); (with Hibernian), 1976 v D; (with Aberdeen), 1978 v Ir (sub) (4)
Harper, W. (Hibernian), 1923 v E, Ni, W; 1924 v E, Ni, W; 1925 v E, Ni, W; (with Arsenal), 1926 v E, Ni (11)
Harris, J. (Partick T), 1921 v W, Ni (2)
Harris, N. (Newcastle U), 1924 v E (1)
Harrower, W. (Queen's Park), 1882 v E; 1884 v Ni; 1886 v W (3)
Hartford, R. A. (WBA), 1972 v Pe, W (sub), E, Y, Cz, Br; (with Manchester C), 1976 v D, R, Ni (sub); 1977 v Cz (sub), W (sub), Se, W, Ni, E, Ch, Arg, Br; 1978 v EG, Cz, W, Bul, W, E, Pe, Ir, Ho; 1979 v A, N, P, W, Ni, E, Arg, N; (with Everton), 1980 v Pe, Bel; 1981 v Ni (sub), Is, W, Ni, E; 1982 v Se; (with Manchester C), Ni, P, Sp, Ni, W, E, Br (50)
Harvey, D. (Leeds U), 1973 v D; 1974 v Cz, WG, Ni, W, E, Bel, Z, Br, Y; 1975 v EG, Sp (2); 1976 v D (2); 1977 v Fi (sub) (16)
Hastings, A. C. (Sunderland), 1936 v Ni; 1938 v Ni (2)
Haughney, M. (Celtic), 1954 v E (1)
Hay, D. (Celtic), 1970 v Ni, W, E; 1971 v D, Bel, W, P, Ni; 1972 v P, Bel, Ho; 1973 v W, Ni, E, Sw, Br; 1974 v Cz (2), WG, Ni, W, E, Bel, N, Z, Br, Y (27)
Hay, J. (Celtic), 1905 v Ni; 1909 v Ni; 1910 v W, Ni, E; 1911 v Ni, E; (with Newcastle U), 1912 v E, W; 1914 v E, Ni (11)
Hegarty, P. (Dundee U), 1979 v W, Ni, E, Arg, N (sub); 1980 v W, E; 1983 v Ni (8)
Heggie, C. (Rangers), 1886 v Ni (1)
Henderson, G. H. (Rangers), 1904 v Ni (1)
Henderson, J. G. (Portsmouth), 1953 v Se; 1954 v Ni, E, N; 1956 v W; (with Arsenal), 1959 v W, Ni (7)
Henderson, W. (Rangers), 1963 v W, Ni, E, A, N, Ei, Sp; 1964 v W, Ni, E, N, WG; 1965 v Fi, Pol, E, Sp; 1966 v Ni, W, Pol, I, Ho; 1967 v W, Ni; 1968 v Ho; 1969 v Ni, E, Cy; 1970 v Ei; 1971 v P (29)
Hendry, E. C. J. (Blackburn R), 1993 v Es (2); 1994 v Ma, Ho, A, Ho; 1995 v Fi, Fa, Gr, Ru, Sm; 1996 v Fi, Se, Sm, Aus, D, US, Co, Ho, E, Sw; 1997 v A, Se, Es (2), A, Se; 1998 v La, D, Fi, Co, US, Br, N, Mor; (with Rangers), 1999 v Li, Es, Fa, G; 2000 v Bos, Es, Bos, E (2); (with Coventry C), F; 2001 v La, Sm, Cro, Aus (sub); (with Bolton W), Bel, Sm (51)
Hepburn, J. (Alloa Ath), 1891 v W (1)
Hepburn, R. (Ayr U), 1932 v Ni (1)
Herd, A. C. (Hearts), 1935 v Ni (1)
Herd, D. G. (Arsenal), 1959 v E, W, Ni; 1961 v Ei, Cz (5)
Herd, G. (Clyde), 1958 v E; 1960 v H, T; 1961 v W, Ni (5)
Herriot, J. (Birmingham C), 1969 v Ni, E, D, Cy (2), W (sub); 1970 v Ei (sub), WG (8)
Hewie, J. D. (Charlton Ath), 1956 v E, A; 1957 v E, Ni, W, Y, Sp (2), Sw, WG; 1958 v H, Pol, Y, F; 1959 v Ho, P; 1960 v Ni, W, Pol (19)
Higgins, A. (Kilmarnock), 1885 v Ni (1)
Higgins, A. (Newcastle U), 1910 v E, Ni; 1911 v E, Ni (4)
Highet, T. C. (Queen's Park), 1875 v E; 1876 v E, W; 1878 v E (4)
Hill, D. (Rangers), 1881 v E, W; 1882 v W (3)
Hill, D. A. (Third Lanark), 1906 v Ni (1)
Hill, F. R. (Aberdeen), 1930 v F; 1931 v W, Ni (3)
Hill, J. (Hearts), 1891 v E; 1892 v W (2)
Hogg, G (Hearts), 1896 v E, Ni (2)
Hogg, J. (Ayr U), 1922 v Ni (1)
Hogg, R. M. (Celtic), 1937 v Cz (1)
Holm, A. H. (Queen's Park), 1882 v W; 1883 v E, W (3)
Holt, D. D. (Hearts), 1963 v A, N, Ei, Sp; 1964 v WG (sub) (5)
Holt, G. J. (Kilmarnock), 2001 v La (sub), Cro (sub); (with Norwich C), 2002 v F (sub); 2004 v D, Es, Tr (6)
Holton, J. A. (Manchester U), 1973 v W, Ni, E, Sw, Br; 1974 v Cz, WG, Ni, W, E, N, Z, Br, Y; 1975 v EG (15)
Hope, R. (WBA), 1968 v Ho; 1969 v D (2)
Hopkin, D. (C Palace), 1997 v Ma, Bl; (with Leeds U), 1998 v Bl (sub), F (sub); 1999 v CzR; 2000 v Bos (2) (7)
Houliston, W. (Queen of the South), 1949 v E, Ni, F (3)
Houston, S. M. (Manchester U), 1976 v D (1)
Howden, W. (Partick T), 1905 v Ni (1)
Howe, R. (Hamilton A), 1929 v N, Ho (2)
Howie, H. (Hibernian), 1949 v W (1)
Howie, J. (Newcastle U), 1905 v E; 1906 v E; 1908 v E (3)
Howieson, J. (St Mirren), 1927 v Ni (1)
Hughes, J. (Celtic), 1965 v Pol, Sp; 1966 v Ni, I (2); 1968 v E; 1969 v A; 1970 v Ei (8)
Hughes, R. D. (Portsmouth), 2004 v Es, Tr (sub) (2)
Hughes, W. (Sunderland), 1975 v Se (sub) (1)
Humphries, W. (Motherwell), 1952 v Se (1)
Hunter, A. (Kilmarnock), 1972 v Pe, Y; (with Celtic), 1973 v E; 1974 v Cz (4)
Hunter, J. (Dundee), 1909 v W (1)
Hunter, J. (Third Lanark), 1874 v E; (with Eastern), 1875 v E; (with Third Lanark), 1876 v E; 1877 v W (4)
Hunter, R. (St Mirren), 1890 v Ni (1)
Hunter, W. (Motherwell), 1960 v H, T; 1961 v W (3)
Husband, J. (Partick T), 1947 v W (1)
Hutchison, D. (Everton), 1999 v CzR (sub), G; 2000 v Bos, Es, Li, E (2), F, Ho, Ei; (with Sunderland), 2001 v La, Sm, Cro, Aus, Bel, Sm; (with West Ham U), 2002 v Cro, Bel, La; 2003 v Ei, Ic, Li, A; 2004 v N, Li (sub), Ho (sub) (26)
Hutchison, T. (Coventry C), 1974 v Cz (2), WG (2), Ni, W, Bel (sub), N, Z (sub), Y (sub); 1975 v EG, Sp (2), P, E (sub), R (sub); 1976 v D (17)
Hutton, J. (Aberdeen), 1923 v E, W, Ni; 1924 v Ni; 1926 v W, E, Ni; (with Blackburn R), 1927 v Ni; 1928 v W, Ni (10)
Hutton, J. (St Bernards), 1887 v Ni (1)
Hyslop, T. (Stoke C), 1896 v E; (with Rangers), 1897 v E (2)

Imlach, J. J. S. (Nottingham F), 1958 v H, Pol, Y, F (4)
Imrie, W. N. (St Johnstone), 1929 v N, G (2)
Inglis, J. (Rangers), 1883 v E, W (2)
Inglis, J. (Kilmarnock Ath), 1884 v Ni (1)
Irons, J. H. (Queen's Park), 1900 v W (1)
Irvine, B. (Aberdeen), 1991 v R; 1993 v G, Es (2); 1994 v Sw, I, Ma, A, Ho (9)

Jackson, A. (Cambuslang), 1886 v W; 1888 v Ni (2)
Jackson, A. (Aberdeen), 1925 v E, W, Ni; (with Huddersfield T), 1926 v E, W, Ni; 1927 v W, Ni; 1928 v E, W; 1929 v E, W, Ni; 1930 v E, W, Ni, F (17)
Jackson, C. (Rangers), 1975 v Se, P (sub), W; 1976 v D, R, Ni, W, E (8)
Jackson, D. (Hibernian), 1995 v Ru, Sm, J, Ec, Fa; 1996 v Gr, Fi (sub), Se (sub), Sm (sub), Aus (sub), D (sub), US; 1997 v La, Se, Es, A, Se, W, Ma, Bl; (with Celtic), 1998 v D, Fi, Co, US, Br, N; 1999 v Li, Es (sub) (28)
Jackson, J. (Partick T), 1931 v A, I, Sw; 1933 v E; (with Chelsea), 1934 v E; 1935 v E; 1936 v W, Ni (8)
Jackson, T. A. (St Mirren), 1904 v W, E, Ni; 1905 v W; 1907 v W, Ni (6)
James, A. W. (Preston NE), 1926 v W; 1928 v E; 1929 v E, Ni; (with Arsenal), 1930 v E, W, Ni; 1933 v W (8)
Jardine, A. (Rangers), 1971 v D (sub); 1972 v P, Bel, Ho; 1973 v E, Sw, Br; 1974 v Cz (2), WG (2), Ni, W, E, Bel, N, Z, Br, Y; 1975 v EG, Sp (2), Se, P, W, Ni, E; 1977 v Se (sub), Ch (sub), Br (sub); 1978 v Cz, W, Ni, Ir; 1980 v Pe, A, Bel (2) (38)
Jarvie, A. (Airdrieonians), 1971 v P (sub), Ni (sub), E (sub) (3)

Jenkinson, T. (Hearts), 1887 v Ni (1)
Jess, E. (Aberdeen), 1993 v I (sub), Ma; 1994 v Sw (sub), I, Ho (sub), A, Ho (sub); 1995 v Fi (sub); 1996 v Se (sub), Sm; (with Coventry C), US, Co (sub), E (sub); (with Aberdeen), 1998 v D (sub); 1999 v CzR, G (sub), Fa (sub), CzR (sub) (18)
Johnston, A. (Sunderland), 1999 v Es, Fa, CzR (sub), G, Fa, CzR; 2000 v Es, F (sub), Ei (sub); (with Rangers), 2001 v Sm (sub), Cro, Sm; (with Middlesbrough), 2002 v Ng (sub), Sk, S.Af, Hk; 2003 v D (sub), Fa (18)
Johnston, L. H. (Clyde), 1948 v Bel, Sw (2)
Johnston, M. (Watford), 1984 v W (sub), E (sub), F; 1985 v Y; (with Celtic), Ic, Sp (2), W; 1986 v EG; 1987 v Bul, Ei (2), L; (with Nantes), 1988 v H, Bel, L, S.Ar, Sp, Co, E; 1989 v N, Y, I, Cy, F, Cy, E, Ch (sub); (with Rangers), 1990 v F, N, EG, Pol, Ma, Cr, Se, Br; 1992 v Sw, Sm (sub) (38)
Johnston, R. (Sunderland), 1938 v Cz (1)
Johnston, W. (Rangers), 1966 v W, E, Pol, Ho; 1968 v W, E; 1969 v Ni (sub); 1970 v Ni; 1971 v D; (with WBA), 1977 v Se, W (sub), Ni, E, Ch, Arg, Br; 1978 v EG, Cz, W (2), E, Pe (22)
Johnstone, D. (Rangers), 1973 v W, Ni, E, Sw, Br; 1975 v EG (sub), Se (sub); 1976 v Sw, Ni (sub), E (sub); 1978 v Bul (sub), Ni, W; 1980 v Bel (14)
Johnstone, J. (Abercorn), 1888 v W (1)
Johnstone, J. (Celtic), 1965 v W, Fi; 1966 v E; 1967 v W, USSR; 1968 v W; 1969 v A, WG; 1970 v E, WG; 1971 v D, E; 1972 v P, Bel, Ho, Ni, E (sub); 1974 v W, E, Bel, N; 1975 v EG, Sp (23)
Johnstone, Jas (Kilmarnock), 1894 v W (1)
Johnstone, J. A. (Hearts), 1930 v W; 1933 v W, Ni (3)
Johnstone, R. (Hibernian), 1951 v E, D, F; 1952 v Ni, E; 1953 v E, Se; 1954 v W, E, N, Fi; 1955 v Ni, H; (with Manchester C), 1955 v E; 1956 v E, Ni, W (17)
Johnstone, W. (Third Lanark), 1887 v Ni; 1889 v W; 1890 v E (3)
Jordan, J. (Leeds U), 1973 v E (sub), Sw (sub), Br; 1974 v Cz (sub+1), WG (sub), Ni (sub), W, E, Bel, N, Z, Br, Y; 1975 v EG, Sp (2); 1976 v Ni, W, E; 1977 v Cz, W, Ni, E; 1978 v EG, Cz, W; (with Manchester U), Bul, Ni, E, Pe, Ir, Ho; 1979 v A, P, W (sub), Ni, E, N; 1980 v Bel, Ni (sub), W, E, Pol; 1981 v Is, W, E; (with AC Milan), 1982 v Se, Ho, W, E, USSR (52)

Kay, J. L. (Queen's Park), 1880 v E; 1882 v E, W; 1883 v E, W; 1884 v W (6)
Keillor, A. (Montrose), 1891 v W; 1892 v Ni; (with Dundee), 1894 v Ni; 1895 v W; 1896 v W; 1897 v W (6)
Keir, L. (Dumbarton), 1885 v W; 1886 v Ni; 1887 v E, W; 1888 v E (5)
Kelly, H. T. (Blackpool), 1952 v USA (1)
Kelly, J. (Renton), 1888 v E; (with Celtic), 1889 v E; 1890 v E; 1892 v E; 1893 v E, Ni; 1894 v W; 1896 v Ni (8)
Kelly, J. C. (Barnsley), 1949 v W, Ni (2)
Kelso, R. (Renton), 1885 v W, Ni; 1886 v W; 1887 v E, W; 1888 v E, Ni; (with Dundee), 1898 v Ni (8)
Kelso, T. (Dundee), 1914 v W (1)
Kennaway, J. (Celtic), 1934 v A (1)
Kennedy, A. (Eastern), 1875 v E; 1876 v E, W; (with Third Lanark), 1878 v E; 1882 v W; 1884 v W (6)
Kennedy, J. (Hibernian), 1897 v W (1)
Kennedy, J. (Celtic), 1964 v W, E, WG; 1965 v W, Ni, Fi (6)
Kennedy, J. (Celtic), 2004 v R (1)
Kennedy, S. (Aberdeen), 1978 v Bul, W, E, Pe, Ho; 1979 v A, P; 1982 v P (sub) (8)
Kennedy, S. (Partick T), 1905 v W (1)
Kennedy, S. (Rangers), 1975 v Se, P, W, Ni, E (5)
Ker, G. (Queen's Park), 1880 v E; 1881 v E, W; 1882 v W, E (5)
Ker, W. (Granville), 1872 v E; (with Queen's Park), 1873 v E (2)
Kerr, A. (Partick T), 1955 v A, H (2)
Kerr, B. (Newcastle U), 2003 v Nz (sub); 2004 v Es (sub) (2)
Kerr, P. (Hibernian), 1924 v Ni (1)
Key, G. (Hearts), 1902 v Ni (1)
Key, W. (Queen's Park), 1907 v Ni (1)
King, A. (Hearts), 1896 v E, W; (with Celtic), 1897 v Ni; 1898 v Ni; 1899 v Ni, W (6)
King, J. (Hamilton A), 1933 v Ni; 1934 v Ni (2)
King, W. S. (Queen's Park), 1929 v W (1)
Kinloch, J. D. (Partick T), 1922 v Ni (1)
Kinnaird, A. F. (Wanderers), 1873 v E (1)
Kinnear, D. (Rangers), 1938 v Cz (1)
Kyle, K. (Sunderland), 2002 v Sk (sub), S.Af, Hk; 2003 v D, Fa, Ca (sub), P (sub), Nz ; 2004 v D (9)

Lambert, P. (Motherwell), 1995 v J, Ec (sub); (with Borussia Dortmund), 1997 v La (sub), Se (sub), A, Se, Bl; 1998 v Bl, La; (with Celtic), Fi (sub), Co, US, Br, N, Mor; 1999 v Li, CzR, G, Fa, CzR; 2000 v Bos, Li, Ho, Ei; 2001 v Bel, Sm; 2002 v Cro, Bel, F, Ng; 2003 v D, Fa, Ic, P, Ei, Ic, Li, G; 2004 v N, G (40)
Lambie, J. A. (Queen's Park), 1886 v Ni; 1887 v Ni; 1888 v E (3)
Lambie, W. A. (Queen's Park), 1892 v Ni; 1893 v W; 1894 v E; 1895 v E, Ni; 1896 v E, Ni; 1897 v E, Ni (9)
Lamont, D. (Pilgrims), 1885 v Ni (1)
Lang, A. (Dumbarton), 1880 v W (1)
Lang, J. J. (Clydesdale), 1876 v W; (with Third Lanark), 1878 v W (2)
Latta, A. (Dumbarton), 1888 v W; 1889 v E (2)
Law, D. (Huddersfield T), 1959 v W, Ni, Ho, P; 1960 v Ni, W; (with Manchester C), 1960 v E, Pol, A; 1961 v E, Ni; (with Torino), 1962 v Cz (2), E; (with Manchester U), 1963 v W, Ni, E, A, N, Ei, Sp; 1964 v W, E, N, WG; 1965 v W, Ni, E, Fi (2), Pol, Sp; 1966 v Ni, E, Pol; 1967 v W, E, USSR; 1968 v Ni; 1969 v Ni, A, WG; 1972 v Pe, Ni, W, E, Y, Cz, Br; (with Manchester C), 1974 v Cz (2), WG (2), Ni, Z (55)
Law, G. (Rangers), 1910 v E, Ni, W (3)
Law, T. (Chelsea), 1928 v E; 1930 v E (2)
Lawrence, J. (Newcastle U), 1911 v E (1)
Lawrence, T. (Liverpool), 1963 v Ei; 1969 v W, WG (3)
Lawson, D. (St Mirren), 1923 v E (1)
Leckie, R. (Queen's Park), 1872 v E (1)
Leggat, G. (Aberdeen), 1956 v E; 1957 v W; 1958 v Ni, H, Pol, Y, Par; (with Fulham), 1959 v E, W, Ni, WG, Ho; 1960 v E, Ni, W, Pol, A, H (18)
Leighton, J. (Aberdeen), 1983 v EG, Sw, Bel, Sw, W, E, Ca (2); 1984 v U, Bel, Ni, W, E, F; 1985 v Y, Ic, Sp (2), W, E, Ic; 1986 v W, EG, Aus (2), Is, D, WG, U; 1987 v Bul, Ei (2), L, Bel, E; 1988 v H, Bel, Bul, L, S.Ar, Ma, Sp; (with Manchester U), Co, E; 1989 v N, Cy, F, Cy, E, Ch; 1990 v Y, F, N, Arg, Ma (sub, Cr, Se, Br; (with Hibernian), 1994 v Ma, A, Ho; 1995 v Gr (sub), Ru, Sm, J, Ec, Fa; 1996 v Gr, Fi, Se, Sm, Aus, D, US; 1997 v Se, Es, A, Se, W (sub), Ma, Bl; (with Aberdeen), 1998 v Bl, La, D, Fi, US, Br, N, Mor; 1999 v Li, Es (91)
Lennie, W. (Aberdeen), 1908 v W, Ni (2)
Lennox, R. (Celtic), 1967 v Ni, E, USSR; 1968 v W, L; 1969 v D, A, WG, Cy (sub); 1970 v W (sub) (10)
Leslie, L. G. (Airdrieonians), 1961 v W, Ni, Ei (2), Cz (5)
Levein, C. (Hearts), 1990 v Arg, EG, Eg (sub), Pol, Ma (sub), Se; 1992 v R, Sm; 1993 v P, G, P; 1994 v Sw, Ho; 1995 v Fi, Fa, Ru (16)
Liddell, W. (Liverpool), 1947 v W, Ni; 1948 v E, W, Ni; 1950 v E, W, P, F; 1951 v W, Ni, E, A; 1952 v W, Ni, E, USA, D, Se; 1953 v W, Ni, E; 1954 v W; 1955 v P, Y, A, H; 1956 v Ni (28)
Liddle, D. (East Fife), 1931 v A, I, Sw (3)
Lindsay, D. (St Mirren), 1903 v Ni (1)
Lindsay, J. (Dumbarton), 1880 v W; 1881 v W, E; 1884 v W, E; 1885 v W, E; 1886 v E (8)
Lindsay, J. (Renton), 1888 v E; 1893 v E, Ni (3)
Linwood, A. B. (Clyde), 1950 v W (1)
Little, R. J. (Rangers), 1953 v Se (1)
Livingstone, G. T. (Manchester C), 1906 v E; (with Rangers), 1907 v W (2)
Lochhead, A. (Third Lanark), 1889 v W (1)
Logan, J. (Ayr U), 1891 v W (1)
Logan, T. (Falkirk), 1913 v Ni (1)
Logie, J. T. (Arsenal), 1953 v Ni (1)
Loney, W. (Celtic), 1910 v W, Ni (2)
Long, H. (Clyde), 1947 v Ni (1)
Longair, W. (Dundee), 1894 v Ni (1)
Lorimer, P. (Leeds U), 1970 v A (sub); 1971 v W, Ni; 1972 v Ni (sub), W, E; 1973 v D (2), E (2); 1974 v WG (sub), E, Bel, N, Z, Br, Y; 1975 v Sp (sub); 1976 v D (2), R (sub) (21)
Love, A. (Aberdeen), 1931 v A, I, Sw (3)
Low, A. (Falkirk), 1934 v Ni (1)
Low, T. P. (Rangers), 1897 v Ni (1)
Low, W. L. (Newcastle U), 1911 v E, W; 1912 v Ni; 1920 v E, Ni (5)
Lowe, J. (St Bernards), 1887 v Ni (1)
Lowe, J. (Cambuslang), 1891 v Ni (1)
Lundie, J. (Hibernian), 1886 v W (1)
Lyall, J. (Sheffield W), 1905 v E (1)

McAdam, J. (Third Lanark), 1880 v W (1)
McAllister, B. (Wimbledon), 1997 v W, Ma, Bl (sub) (3)
McAllister, G. (Leicester C), 1990 v EG, Pol, Ma (sub); (with Leeds U), 1991 v R, Sw, Bul, USSR (sub), Sm; 1992 v Sw (sub), Sm, Ni, Fi (sub), US, Ca, N, Ho, G, C; 1993 v Sw, P, I,

Ma; 1994 v Sw, I, Ma, Ho, A, Ho; 1995 v Fi, Ru, Gr, Ru, Sm; 1996 v Gr, Fi, Se, Sm, Aus, D, US (sub), Co, Ho, E, Sw; (with Coventry C), 1997 v A, La, Es (2), A, Se, W, Ma, Bl; 1998 v Bl, La, F; 1999 v CzR (57)
McAllister, J. R. (Livingston), 2004 v Tr (1)
McArthur, D. (Celtic), 1895 v E, Ni; 1899 v W (3)
McAtee, A. (Celtic), 1913 v W (1)
McAulay, J. (Arthurlie), 1884 v Ni (1)
McAulay, J. D. (Dumbarton), 1882 v W; 1883 v E, W; 1884 v E; 1885 v E, W; 1886 v E; 1887 v E, W (9)
McAuley, R. (Rangers), 1932 v Ni, W (2)
McAvennie, F. (West Ham U), 1986 v Aus (2), D (sub), WG (sub); (with Celtic), 1988 v S.Ar (5)
McBain, E. (St Mirren), 1894 v W (1)
McBain, N. (Manchester U), 1922 v E; (with Everton), 1923 v Ni; 1924 v W (3)
McBride, J. (Celtic), 1967 v W, Ni (2)
McBride, P. (Preston NE), 1904 v E; 1906 v E; 1907 v E, W; 1908 v E; 1909 v W (6)
McCall, J. (Renton), 1886 v W; 1887 v E, W; 1888 v E; 1890 v E (5)
McCall, S. M. (Everton), 1990 v Arg, EG, Eg (sub), Pol, Ma, Cr, Se, Br; 1991 v Sw, USSR, Sm; (with Rangers), 1992 v Sw, R, Sm, US, Ca, N, Ho, G, C; 1993 v Sw, P (2); 1994 v I, Ho, A (sub), Ho; 1995 v Fi (sub), Ru, Gr; 1996 v Gr, D, US (sub), Co, Ho, E, Sw; 1997 v A, La; 1998 v D (sub) (40)
McCalliog, J. (Sheffield W), 1967 v E, USSR; 1968 v Ni; 1969 v D; (with Wolverhampton W), 1971 v P (5)
McCallum, N. (Renton), 1888 v Ni (1)
McCann, N. (Hearts), 1999 v Li (sub); (with Rangers), CzR; 2000 v Bos, Es (sub), E, F (sub), Ho, Ei; 2001 v La, Sm, Aus (sub); 2002 v Cro, La, F, Ng; 2003 v Ei; (with Southampton), 2004 v Fa, G, Ho (2), R, D (sub) (22)
McCann, R. J. (Motherwell), 1959 v WG; 1960 v E, Ni, W; 1961 v E (5)
McCartney, W. (Hibernian), 1902 v Ni (1)
McClair, B. (Celtic), 1987 v L, Ei, E, Br (sub); (with Manchester U), 1988 v Bul, Ma (sub), Sp (sub); 1989 v N, Y, I (sub), Cy, F (sub); 1990 v N (sub), Arg (sub); 1991 v Bul (2), Sm; 1992 v Sw (sub), R, Ni, US, Ca (sub), N, Ho, G, C; 1993 v Sw, P (sub), Es (2) (30)
McClory, A. (Motherwell), 1927 v W; 1928 v Ni; 1935 v W (3)
McCloy, P. (Ayr U), 1924 v E; 1925 v E (2)
McCloy, P. (Rangers), 1973 v W, Ni, Sw, Br (4)
McCoist, A. (Rangers), 1986 v Ho; 1987 v L (sub), Ei (sub), Bel, E, Br; 1988 v H, Bel, Ma, Sp, Co, E; 1989 v Y (sub), F, Cy, E; 1990 v Y, F, N, EG (sub), Eg, Pol, Ma (sub), Cr (sub), Se (sub), Br; 1991 v R, Sw, Bul (2), USSR; 1992 v Sw, Sm, Ni, Fi (sub), US, Ca, N, Ho, G, C; 1993 v Sw, P, I, Ma, P; 1996 v Gr (sub), Fi (sub), Sm (sub), Aus, D (sub), Co, E (sub), Sw; 1997 v A, Se (sub), Es (sub), A (sub); 1998 v Bl (sub); (with Kilmarnock), 1999 v Li, Es (61)
McColl, A. (Renton), 1888 v Ni (1)
McColl, I. M. (Rangers), 1950 v E, F; 1951 v W, Ni, Bel; 1957 v E, Ni, W, Y, Sp, Sw, WG; 1958 v Ni, E (14)
McColl, R. S. (Queen's Park), 1896 v W, Ni; 1897 v Ni; 1898 v Ni; 1899 v Ni, E, W; 1900 v E, W; 1901 v E, W; (with Newcastle U), 1902 v E; (with Queen's Park), 1908 v Ni (13)
McColl, W. (Renton), 1895 v W (1)
McCombie, A. (Sunderland), 1903 v E, W; (with Newcastle U), 1905 v E, W (4)
McCorkindale, J. (Partick T), 1891 v W (1)
McCormick, R. (Abercorn), 1886 v W (1)
McCrae, D. (St Mirren), 1929 v N, G (2)
McCredie, A. (Rangers), 1893 v W; 1894 v E (2)
McCreadie, E. G. (Chelsea), 1965 v E, Sp, Fi, Pol; 1966 v P, Ni, W, Pol, I; 1967 v E, USSR; 1968 v Ni, W, E, Ho; 1969 v W, Ni, E, D, A, WG, Cy (2) (23)
McCulloch, D. (Hearts), 1935 v W; (with Brentford), 1936 v E; 1937 v W, Ni; 1938 v Cz; (with Derby Co), 1939 v H, W (7)
MacDonald, A. (Rangers), 1976 v Sw (1)
McDonald, J. (Edinburgh University), 1886 v E (1)
McDonald, J. (Sunderland), 1956 v W, Ni (2)
MacDougall, E. J. (Norwich C) 1975 v Se, P, W, Ni, E; 1976 v D, R (sub) (7)
McDougall, J. (Vale of Leven), 1877 v E, W; 1878 v E; 1879 v E, W (5)
McDougall, J. (Airdrieonians), 1926 v Ni (1)
McDougall, J. (Liverpool), 1931 v I, A (2)
McFadden, J. (Motherwell), 2002 v S.Af (sub); 2003 v Ca (sub), A, Nz; (with Everton), 2004 v Fa (sub), G, Li, Ho (2), W (sub), R (sub), D, Es, Tr (14)
McFadyen, W. (Motherwell), 1934 v A, W (2)
Macfarlane, A. (Dundee), 1904 v W; 1906 v W; 1908 v W; 1909 v Ni; 1911 v W (5)
Macfarlane, W. (Hearts), 1947 v L (1)
McFarlane, R. (Greenock Morton), 1896 v W (1)
McGarr, E. (Aberdeen), 1970 v Ei, A (2)
McGarvey, F. P. (Liverpool), 1979 v Ni (sub), Arg; (with Celtic), 1984 v U, Bel (sub), EG (sub), Ni, W (7)
McGeoch, A. (Dumbreck), 1876 v E, W; 1877 v E, W (4)
McGhee, J. (Hibernian), 1886 v W (1)
McGhee, M. (Aberdeen), 1983 v Ca (1+1 sub); 1984 v Ni (sub), E (4)
McGinlay, J. (Bolton W), 1994 v A, Ho; 1995 v Fa, Ru, Gr, Ru, Sm, Fa; 1996 v Se; 1997 v Se, Es (1 + sub), A (sub) (13)
McGonagle, W. (Celtic), 1933 v E; 1934 v A, E, Ni; 1935 v Ni, W (6)
McGrain, D. (Celtic), 1973 v W, Ni, E, Sw, Br; 1974 v Cz (2), WG, W (sub), E, Bel, N, Z, Br, Y; 1975 v Sp, Se, P, W, Ni, E, R; 1976 v D (2), Sw, Ni, W, E; 1977 v Fi, Cz, W (2), Se, Ni, E, Ch, Arg, Br; 1978 v EG, Cz; 1980 v Bel, P, Ni, W, E, Pol, H; 1981 v Se, P, Is, Ni, Is, W (sub), Ni, E; 1982 v Se, Sp, Ho, Ni, E, Nz, USSR (sub) (62)
McGregor, J. C. (Vale of Leven), 1877 v E, W; 1878 v E; 1880 v E (4)
McGrory, J. (Celtic), 1928 v Ni; 1931 v E; 1932 v Ni, W; 1933 v E, Ni; 1934 v Ni (7)
McGrory, J. E. (Kilmarnock), 1965 v Ni, Fi; 1966 v P (3)
McGuire, W. (Beith), 1881 v E, W (2)
McGurk, F. (Birmingham), 1934 v W (1)
McHardy, H. (Rangers), 1885 v Ni (1)
McInally, A. (Aston Villa), 1989 v Cy (sub), Ch; (with Bayern Munich), 1990 v Y (sub), F (sub), Arg, Pol (sub), Ma, Cr (8)
McInally, J. (Dundee U), 1987 v Bel, Br; 1988 v Ma (sub); 1991 v Bul (2); 1992 v US (sub), N (sub), C (sub); 1993 v G, P (10)
McInally, T. B. (Celtic), 1926 v Ni; 1927 v W (2)
McInnes, D. (WBA), 2003 v D (sub), P (sub) (2)
McInnes, T. (Cowlairs), 1889 v Ni (1)
McIntosh, W. (Third Lanark), 1905 v Ni (1)
McIntyre, A. (Vale of Leven), 1878 v E; 1882 v E (2)
McIntyre, H. (Rangers), 1880 v W (1)
McIntyre, J. (Rangers), 1884 v W (1)
MacKay, D. (Celtic), 1959 v E, WG, Ho, P; 1960 v E, Pol, A, H, T; 1961 v W, Ni; 1962 v Ni, Cz, U (sub) (14)
Mackay, D. C. (Hearts), 1957 v Sp; 1958 v F; 1959 v W, Ni; (with Tottenham H), 1959 v WG, E; 1960 v W, Ni, A, Pol, H, T; 1961 v W, Ni, E; 1963 v E, A, N; 1964 v Ni, W, N; 1966 v Ni (22)
Mackay, G. (Hearts), 1988 v Bul (sub), L (sub), S.Ar (sub), Ma (4)
Mackay, M. (Norwich C), 2004 v D, Es, Tr (3)
McKay, J. (Blackburn R), 1924 v W (1)
McKay, R. (Newcastle U), 1928 v W (1)
McKean, R. (Rangers), 1976 v Sw (sub) (1)
McKenzie, D. (Brentford), 1938 v Ni (1)
Mackenzie, J. A. (Partick T), 1954 v W, E, N, Fi, A, U; 1955 v E, H; 1956 v A (9)
McKeown, M. (Celtic), 1889 v Ni; 1890 v E (2)
McKie, J. (East Stirling), 1898 v W (1)
McKillop, T. R. (Rangers), 1938 v Ho (1)
McKimmie, S. (Aberdeen), 1989 v E, Ch; 1990 v Arg, Eg, Cr (sub), Br; 1991 v R, Sw, Bul, Sm; 1992 v Sw, R, Ni, Fi, US, Ca (sub), N (sub), Ho, G, C; 1993 v P, Es (sub); 1994 v Sw, I, Ho, A, Ho; 1995 v Fi, Fa, Ru, Gr, Ru, Fa; 1996 v Gr, Fi, Se, D, Co, Ho, E (40)
McKinlay, D. (Liverpool), 1922 v W, Ni (2)
McKinlay, T. (Celtic), 1996 v Gr, Fi, D, Co, E, Sw; 1997 v A, La, Se, Es (sub + 1), A, Se, W, Ma, Bl; 1998 v Bl, La (sub), F (sub), US, Br (sub), Mor (sub) (22)
McKinlay, W. (Dundee U), 1994 v Ma, Ho (sub), A, Ho; 1995 v Fa (sub), Ru, Gr, Ru (sub), Sm (sub), J, Ec, Fa; 1996 v Fi (sub), Se (sub); (with Blackburn R), Sm (sub), Aus, D (sub), Ho (sub); 1997 v Se, Es (sub); 1998 v La (sub), F, D, Fi, Co (sub), US, Br (sub); 1999 v Es, Fa (29)
McKinnon, A. (Queen's Park), 1874 v E (1)
McKinnon, R. (Rangers), 1966 v W, E, I (2), Ho, Br; 1967 v W, Ni, E; 1968 v Ni, W, E, Ho; 1969 v D, A, WG, Cy; 1970 v Ni, W, E, Ei, WG, A; 1971 v D, Bel, P, USSR, D (28)
McKinnon, R. (Motherwell), 1994 v Ma; 1995 v J, Fa (3)
MacKinnon, W. (Dumbarton), 1883 v E, W; 1884 v E, W (4)
MacKinnon, W. W. (Queen's Park), 1872 v E; 1873 v E; 1874 v E; 1875 v E; 1876 v E, W; 1877 v E; 1878 v E; 1879 v E (9)
McLaren, A. (St Johnstone), 1929 v N, G, Ho; 1933 v W, Ni (5)
McLaren, A. (Preston NE), 1947 v E, Bel, L; 1948 v W (4)
McLaren, A. (Hearts), 1992 v US, Ca, N; 1993 v I, Ma, G, Es (sub + 1); 1994 v I, Ma, Ho, A; 1995 v Fi, Fa; (with Rangers), Ru, Gr, Ru, Sm, J, Ec, Fa; 1996 v Fi, Se, Sm (24)
McLaren, A. (Kilmarnock), 2001 v Pol (sub) (1)

McLaren, J. (Hibernian), 1888 v W; (with Celtic), 1889 v E; 1890 v E (3)
McLean, A. (Celtic), 1926 v W, Ni; 1927 v W, E (4)
McLean, D. (St Bernards), 1896 v W; 1897 v Ni (2)
McLean, D. (Sheffield W), 1912 v E (1)
McLean, G. (Dundee), 1968 v Ho (1)
McLean, T. (Kilmarnock), 1969 v D, Cy, W; 1970 v Ni, W; 1971 v D (6)
McLeish, A. (Aberdeen), 1980 v P, Ni, W, E, Pol, H; 1981 v Se, Is, Ni, Is, Ni, E; 1982 v Se, Sp, Ni, Br (sub); 1983 v Bel, Sw (sub), W, E, Ca (3); 1984 v U, Bel, EG, Ni, W, E, F; 1985 v Y, Ic, Sp (2), W, E, Ic; 1986 v W, EG, Aus (2), E, Ho, D; 1987 v Bel, E, Br; 1988 v Bel, Bul, L, S.Ar (sub), Ma, Sp, Co, E; 1989 v N, Y, I, Cy, F, Cy, E, Ch; 1990 v Y, F, N, Arg, EG, Eg, Cr, Se, Br; 1991 v R, Sw, USSR, Bul; 1993 v Ma (77)
McLeod, D. (Celtic), 1905 v Ni; 1906 v E, W, Ni (4)
McLeod, J. (Dumbarton), 1888 v Ni; 1889 v W; 1890 v Ni; 1892 v E; 1893 v W (5)
MacLeod, J. M. (Hibernian), 1961 v E, Ei (2), Cz (4)
MacLeod, M. (Celtic), 1985 v E (sub); 1987 v Ei, L, E, Br; (with Borussia Dortmund), 1988 v Co, E; 1989 v I, Ch; 1990 v Y, F, N (sub), Arg, EG, Pol, Se Br; (with Hibernian), 1991 v R, Sw, USSR (sub) (20)
McLeod, W. (Cowlairs), 1886 v Ni (1)
McLintock, A. (Vale of Leven), 1875 v E; 1876 v E; 1880 v E (3)
McLintock, F. (Leicester C), 1963 v N (sub), Ei, Sp; (with Arsenal), 1965 v Ni; 1967 v USSR; 1970 v Ni; 1971 v W, Ni, E (9)
McLuckie, J. S. (Manchester C), 1934 v W (1)
McMahon, A. (Celtic), 1892 v E; 1893 v E, Ni; 1894 v E; 1901 v Ni; 1902 v W (6)
McMenemy, J. (Celtic), 1905 v Ni; 1909 v Ni; 1910 v E, W; 1911 v Ni, W, E; 1912 v W; 1914 v W, Ni, E; 1920 v Ni (12)
McMenemy, J. (Motherwell), 1934 v W (1)
McMillan, I. L. (Airdrieonians), 1952 v E, USA, D; 1955 v E; 1956 v E; (with Rangers), 1961 v Cz (6)
McMillan, J. (St Bernards), 1897 v W (1)
McMillan, T. (Dumbarton), 1887 v Ni (1)
McMullan, J. (Partick T), 1920 v W; 1921 v W, Ni, E; 1924 v E, Ni; 1925 v E; 1926 v W; (with Manchester C), 1926 v E; 1927 v E, W; 1928 v E, W; 1929 v W, E, Ni (16)
McNab, A. (Morton), 1921 v E, Ni (2)
McNab, A. (Sunderland), 1937 v A; (with WBA), 1939 v E (2)
McNab, C. D. (Dundee), 1931 v E, W, A, I, Sw; 1932 v E (6)
McNab, J. S. (Liverpool), 1923 v W (1)
McNair, A. (Celtic), 1906 v W; 1907 v Ni; 1908 v E, W; 1909 v E; 1910 v W; 1912 v E, W, Ni; 1913 v E; 1914 v E, Ni; 1920 v E, W, Ni (15)
McNamara, J. (Celtic), 1997 v La (sub), Se, Es, W (sub); 1998 v D, Co, US (sub), N (sub), Mor; 2000 v Ho; 2001 v Sm; 2002 v Bel (sub), F (sub); 2003 v Ic (1+sub), Li, Nz, G (sub); 2004 v Fa, G, Li, Ho (2), W, Tr (25)
McNamee, D. (Livingston), 2004 v Es, Tr (sub) (2)
McNaught, W. (Raith R), 1951 v A, W, Ni; 1952 v E; 1955 v Ni (5)
McNaughton, K. (Aberdeen), 2002 v Ng; 2003 v D (2)
McNiel, H. (Queen's Park), 1874 v E; 1875 v E; 1876 v E, W; 1877 v W; 1878 v E; 1879 v E, W; 1881 v E, W (10)
McNiel, M. (Rangers), 1876 v W; 1880 v E (2)
McNeill, W. (Celtic), 1961 v E, Ei (2), Cz; 1962 v Ni, E, Cz, U; 1963 v Ei, Sp; 1964 v W, E, WG; 1965 v E, Fi, Pol, Sp; 1966 v Ni, Pol; 1967 v USSR; 1968 v E; 1969 v Cy, W, E, Cy (sub); 1970 v WG; 1972 v Ni, W, E (29)
McPhail, J. (Celtic), 1950 v W; 1951 v W, Ni, A; 1954 v Ni (5)
McPhail, R. (Airdrieonians), 1927 v E; (with Rangers), 1929 v W; 1931 v E, Ni; 1932 v W, Ni, F; 1933 v E, Ni; 1934 v A, Ni; 1935 v E; 1937 v G, E, Cz; 1938 v W, Ni (17)
McPherson, D. (Kilmarnock), 1892 v Ni (1)
McPherson, D. (Hearts), 1989 v Cy, E; 1990 v N, Ma, Cr, Se, Br; 1991 v Sw, Bul (2), USSR (sub), Sm; 1992 v Sw, R, Sm, Ni, Fi, US, Ca, N, Ho, G, C; (with Rangers), 1993 v Sw, I, Ma, P (27)
McPherson, J. (Clydesdale), 1875 v E (1)
McPherson, J. (Vale of Leven), 1879 v E, W; 1880 v E; 1881 v W; 1883 v E, W; 1884 v E; 1885 v Ni (8)
McPherson, J. (Kilmarnock), 1888 v W; (with Cowlairs), 1889 v E; 1890 v Ni, E; (with Rangers), 1892 v W; 1894 v E; 1895 v E, Ni; 1897 v Ni (9)
McPherson, J. (Hearts), 1891 v E (1)
McPherson, R. (Arthurlie), 1882 v E (1)
McQueen, G. (Leeds U), 1974 v Bel; 1975 v Sp (2), P, W, Ni, E, R; 1976 v D; 1977 v Cz, W (2), Ni, E; 1978 v EG, Cz, W; (with Manchester U), Bul, Ni, W; 1979 v A, N, P, Ni, E, N; 1980 v Pe, A, Bel; 1981 v W (30)
McQueen, M. (Leith Ath), 1890 v W; 1891 v W (2)
McRorie, D. M. (Morton), 1931 v W (1)
McSpadyen, A. (Partick T), 1939 v E, H (2)
McStay, P. (Celtic), 1984 v U, Bel, EG, Ni, W, E (sub); 1985 v Y, Ic, Sp (2), W; 1986 v EG (sub), Aus, Is, U; 1987 v Bul, Ei (1+1 sub), L (sub), Bel, E, Br; 1988 v H, Bel, Bul, L, S.Ar, Sp, Co, E; 1989 v N, Y, I, Cy, F, Cy, E, Ch; 1990 v Y, F, N, Arg, EG (sub), Eg, Pol (sub), Ma, Cr, Se (sub), Br; 1991 v R, USSR, Bul; 1992 v Sm, Fi, US, Ca, N, Ho, G, C; 1993 v Sw, P, I, Ma, P, Es (2); 1994 v I (sub), Ho; 1995 v Fi, Fa, Ru; 1996 v Aus; 1997 v Es (2), A (sub) (76)
McStay, W. (Celtic), 1921 v W, Ni; 1925 v E, Ni, W; 1926 v E, Ni, W; 1927 v E, Ni, W; 1928 v W, Ni (13)
McSwegan, G. (Hearts), 2000 v Bos (sub), Li (2)
McTavish, J. (Falkirk), 1910 v Ni (1)
McWattie, G. C. (Queen's Park), 1901 v W, Ni (2)
McWilliam, P. (Newcastle U), 1905 v E; 1906 v E; 1907 v E, W; 1909 v E, W; 1910 v E; 1911 v W (8)
Macari, L. (Celtic), 1972 v W (sub), E, Y, Cz, Br; 1973 v D; (with Manchester U), E (2), W (sub), Ni (sub); 1975 v Se, P (sub), W, E (sub), R; 1977 v Ni (sub), E (sub), Ch, Arg; 1978 v EG, W, Bul, Pe (sub), Ir (24)
Macauley, A. R. (Brentford), 1947 v E; (with Arsenal), 1948 v E, W, Ni, Bel, Sw, F (7)
Madden, J. (Celtic), 1893 v W; 1895 v W (2)
Main, F. R. (Rangers), 1938 v W (1)
Main, J. (Hibernian), 1909 v Ni (1)
Maley, W. (Celtic), 1893 v E, Ni (2)
Malpas, M. (Dundee U), 1984 v F; 1985 v E, Ic; 1986 v W, Aus (2), Is, R, E, Ho, D, WG; 1987 v Bul, Ei, Bel; 1988 v Bel, Bul, L, S.Ar, Ma; 1989 v N, Y, I, Cy, F, Cy, E, Ch; 1990 v Y, F, N, Eg, Pol, Ma, Cr, Se, Br; 1991 v R, Bul (2), USSR, Sm; 1992 v Sw, R, Sm, Ni, Fi, US, Ca (sub), N, Ho, G; 1993 v Sw, P, I (55)
Marshall, G. (Celtic), 1992 v US (1)
Marshall, H. (Celtic), 1899 v W; 1900 v Ni (2)
Marshall, J. (Third Lanark), 1885 v Ni; 1886 v W; 1887 v E, W (4)
Marshall, J. (Middlesbrough), 1921 v E, W, Ni; 1922 v E, W, Ni; (with Llanelly), 1924 v W (7)
Marshall, J. (Rangers), 1932 v E; 1933 v E; 1934 v E (3)
Marshall, R. W. (Rangers), 1892 v Ni; 1894 v Ni (2)
Martin, B. (Motherwell), 1995 v J, Ec (2)
Martin, F. (Aberdeen), 1954 v N (2), A, U; 1955 v E, H (6)
Martin, N. (Hibernian), 1965 v Fi, Pol; (with Sunderland), 1966 v I (3)
Martis, J. (Motherwell), 1961 v W (1)
Mason, J. (Third Lanark), 1949 v E, W, Ni; 1950 v Ni; 1951 v Ni, Bel, A (7)
Massie, A. (Hearts), 1932 v Ni, W, F; 1933 v Ni; 1934 v E, Ni; 1935 v E, Ni, W; 1936 v W, Ni; (with Aston Villa), 1936 v E; 1937 v G, E, W, Ni, A; 1938 v W (18)
Masson, D. S. (QPR), 1976 v Ni, W, E; 1977 v Fi, Cz, W, Ni, E, Ch, Arg, Br; 1978 v EG, Cz, W; (with Derby Co), Ni, E, Pe (17)
Mathers, D. (Partick T), 1954 v Fi (1)
Matteo, D. (Leeds U), 2001 v Aus, Bel, Sm; 2002 v Cro, Bel, F (6)
Maxwell, W. S. (Stoke C), 1898 v E (1)
May, J. (Rangers), 1906 v W, Ni; 1908 v E, Ni; 1909 v W (5)
Meechan, P. (Celtic), 1896 v Ni (1)
Meiklejohn, D. D. (Rangers), 1922 v W; 1924 v W; 1925 v W, Ni, E; 1928 v W, Ni; 1929 v E, Ni; 1930 v E, Ni; 1931 v E; 1932 v W, Ni; 1934 v A (15)
Menzies, A. (Hearts), 1906 v E (1)
Mercer, R. (Hearts), 1912 v W; 1913 v Ni (2)
Middleton, R. (Cowdenbeath), 1930 v Ni (1)
Millar, A. (Hearts), 1939 v W (1)
Millar, J. (Rangers), 1897 v E; 1898 v E, W (3)
Millar, J. (Rangers), 1963 v A, Ei (2)
Miller, C. (Dundee U), 2001 v Pol (1)
Miller, J. (St Mirren), 1931 v E, I, Sw; 1932 v F; 1934 v E (5)
Miller, K. (Rangers), 2001 v Pol (sub); (with Wolverhampton W), 2003 v Ic, Li, A (sub), G; 2004 v Li, Ho (sub + sub), W, R, Es, Tr (sub) (12)
Miller, P. (Dumbarton), 1882 v E; 1883 v E, W (3)
Miller, T. (Liverpool), 1920 v E; (with Manchester U), 1921 v E, Ni (3)
Miller, W. (Third Lanark), 1876 v E (1)
Miller, W. (Celtic), 1947 v E, W, Bel, L; 1948 v W, Ni (6)
Miller, W. (Aberdeen), 1975 v R; 1978 v Bul; 1980 v Bel, W, E, Pol, H; 1981 v Se, P, Is (sub), Ni, W, Ni, E; 1982 v Ni, P, Ho, Br, USSR; 1983 v EG, Sw (2), W, E, Ca (3); 1984 v U, Bel, EG, W, E, F; 1985 v Y, Ic, Sp (2), W, E, Ic; 1986 v W, EG, Aus (2), Is, R, E, Ho, D, WG, U; 1987 v Bul, E, Br; 1988 v H, L, S.Ar, Ma, Sp, Co, E; 1989 v N, Y; 1990 v Y, N (65)

Mills, W. (Aberdeen), 1936 v W, Ni; 1937 v W (3)
Milne, J. V. (Middlesbrough), 1938 v E; 1939 v E (2)
Mitchell, D. (Rangers), 1890 v Ni; 1892 v E; 1893 v E, Ni; 1894 v E (5)
Mitchell, J. (Kilmarnock), 1908 v Ni; 1910 v Ni, W (3)
Mitchell, R. C. (Newcastle U), 1951 v D, F (2)
Mochan, N. (Celtic), 1954 v N, A, U (3)
Moir, W. (Bolton W), 1950 v E (1)
Moncur, R. (Newcastle U), 1968 v Ho; 1970 v Ni, W, E, Ei; 1971 v D, Bel, W, P, Ni, E, D; 1972 v Pe, Ni, W, E (16)
Morgan, H. (St Mirren), 1898 v W; (with Liverpool), 1899 v E (2)
Morgan, W. (Burnley), 1968 v Ni; (with Manchester U), 1972 v Pe, Y, Cz, Br; 1973 v D (2), E (2), W, Ni, Sw, Br; 1974 v Cz (2), WG (2), Ni, Bel (sub), Br, Y (21)
Morris, D. (Raith R), 1923 v Ni; 1924 v E, Ni; 1925 v E, W, Ni (6)
Morris, H. (East Fife), 1950 v Ni (1)
Morrison, T. (St Mirren), 1927 v E (1)
Morton, A. L. (Queen's Park), 1920 v W, Ni; (with Rangers), 1921 v E; 1922 v E, W; 1923 v E, W, Ni; 1924 v E, W, Ni; 1925 v E, W, Ni; 1927 v E, Ni; 1928 v E, W, Ni; 1929 v E, W, Ni; 1930 v E, W, Ni; 1931 v E, W, Ni; 1932 v E, W, F (31)
Morton, H. A. (Kilmarnock), 1929 v G, Ho (2)
Mudie, J. K. (Blackpool), 1957 v W, Ni, E, Y, Sw, Sp (2), WG; 1958 v Ni, E, W, Sw, H, Pol, Y, Par, F (17)
Muir, W. (Dundee), 1907 v Ni (1)
Muirhead, T. A. (Rangers), 1922 v Ni; 1923 v E; 1924 v W; 1927 v Ni; 1928 v Ni; 1929 v W, Ni; 1930 v W (8)
Mulhall, G. (Aberdeen), 1960 v Ni; (with Sunderland), 1963 v Ni; 1964 v Ni (3)
Munro, A. D. (Hearts), 1937 v W, Ni; (with Blackpool), 1938 v Ho (3)
Munro, F. M. (Wolverhampton W), 1971 v Ni (sub), E (sub), D, USSR; 1975 v Se, W (sub), Ni, E, R (9)
Munro, I. (St Mirren), 1979 v Arg, N; 1980 v Pe, A, Bel, W, E (7)
Munro, N. (Abercorn), 1888 v W; 1889 v E (2)
Murdoch, J. (Motherwell), 1931 v Ni (1)
Murdoch, R. (Celtic), 1966 v W, E, I (2); 1967 v Ni; 1968 v Ni; 1969 v W, Ni, E, WG, Cy; 1970 v A (12)
Murphy, F. (Celtic), 1938 v Ho (1)
Murray, I. (Hibernian), 2003 v Ca (sub) (1)
Murray, J. (Renton), 1895 v W (1)
Murray, J. (Hearts), 1958 v E, H, Pol, Y, F (5)
Murray, J. W. (Vale of Leven), 1890 v W (1)
Murray, P. (Hibernian), 1896 v Ni; 1897 v W (2)
Murray, S. (Aberdeen), 1972 v Bel (1)
Murty, G. S. (Reading), 2004 v W (sub) (1)
Mutch, G. (Preston NE), 1938 v E (1)

Napier, C. E. (Celtic), 1932 v E; 1935 v E, W; (with Derby Co), 1937 v Ni, A (5)
Narey, D. (Dundee U), 1977 v Se (sub); 1979 v P, Ni (sub), Arg; 1980 v P, Ni, Pol, H; 1981 v W, E (sub); 1982 v Ho, W, E, Nz (sub), Br, USSR; 1983 v EG, Sw, Bel, Ni, W, E, Ca (3); 1986 v Is, R, Ho, WG, U; 1987 v Bul, E, Bel; 1989 v I, Cy (35)
Naysmith, G. A. (Hearts), 2000 v Ei; 2001 v La (sub), Sm, Cro; (with Everton), 2002 v Cro, Bel; 2003 v D, Ic, P, Ei, Ic, Li, A, Nz, G; 2004 v N, Fa, G, Li, Ho (2), W (22)
Neil, R. G. (Hibernian), 1896 v W; (with Rangers), 1900 v W (2)
Neill, R. W. (Queen's Park), 1876 v W; 1877 v E, W; 1878 v W; 1880 v E (5)
Nellies, P. (Hearts), 1913 v Ni; 1914 v W (2)
Nelson, J. (Cardiff C), 1925 v W, Ni; 1928 v E; 1930 v F (4)
Nevin, P. K. F. (Chelsea), 1986 v R (sub), E (sub); 1987 v L, Ei, Bel (sub); 1988 v L; (with Everton), 1989 v Cy, E; 1991 v R (sub), Bul (sub), Sm (sub); 1992 v US, G (sub), C (sub); (with Tranmere R), 1993 v Ma, P (sub), Es; 1994 v Sw, Ma, Ho, A (sub), Ho; 1995 v Fa, Ru (sub), Sm; 1996 v Se (sub), Sm, Aus (sub) (28)
Niblo, T. D. (Aston Villa), 1904 v E (1)
Nibloe, J. (Kilmarnock), 1929 v E, N, Ho; 1930 v W; 1931 v E, Ni, A, I, Sw; 1932 v E, F (11)
Nicholas, C. (Celtic), 1983 v Sw, Ni, E, Ca (3); (with Arsenal), 1984 v Bel, F (sub); 1985 v Y (sub), Ic (sub), Sp (sub), W (sub); 1986 v Is, R (sub), E, D, U (sub); 1987 v Bul, E (sub); (with Aberdeen), 1989 v Cy (sub) (20)
Nicholson, B. (Dunfermline Ath), 2001 v Pol; 2002 v La (2)
Nicol, S. (Liverpool), 1985 v Y, Ic, Sp, W; 1986 v W, EG, Aus, E, D, WG, U; 1988 v H, Bul, S.Ar, Sp, Co, E; 1989 v N, Y, Cy, F; 1990 v Y, F; 1991 v Sw, USSR, Sm; 1992 v Sw (27)
Nisbet, J. (Ayr U), 1929 v N, G, Ho (3)
Niven, J. B. (Moffatt), 1885 v Ni (1)

O'Connor, G. (Hibernian), 2002 v Ng (sub), Sk, Hk (sub) (3)
O'Donnell, F. (Preston NE), 1937 v E, A, Cz; 1938 v W; (with Blackpool), E, Ho (6)
O'Donnell, P. (Motherwell), 1994 v Sw (sub) (1)
Ogilvie, D. H. (Motherwell), 1934 v A (1)
O'Hare, J. (Derby Co), 1970 v W, Ni, E; 1971 v D, Bel, W, Ni; 1972 v P, Bel, Ho (sub), Pe, Ni, W (13)
O'Neil, B. (Celtic), 1996 v Aus; (with Wolfsburg), 1999 v G (sub); 2000 v Li, Ho (sub), Ei; (with Derby Co), 2001 v Aus (6)
O'Neil, J. (Hibernian), 2001 v Pol (1)
Ormond, W. E. (Hibernian), 1954 v E, N, Fi, A, U; 1959 v E (6)
O'Rourke, F. (Airdrieonians), 1907 v Ni (1)
Orr, J. (Kilmarnock), 1892 v W (1)
Orr, R. (Newcastle U), 1902 v E; 1904 v E (2)
Orr, T. (Morton), 1952 v Ni, W (2)
Orr, W. (Celtic), 1900 v Ni; 1903 v Ni; 1904 v W (3)
Orrock, R. (Falkirk), 1913 v W (1)
Oswald, J. (Third Lanark), 1889 v E; (with St Bernards), 1895 v E; (with Rangers), 1897 v W (3)

Parker, A. H. (Falkirk), 1955 v P, Y, A; 1956 v E, Ni, W, A; 1957 v Ni, W, Y; 1958 v Ni, W, E, Sw; (with Everton), Par (15)
Parlane, D. (Rangers), 1973 v W, Sw, Br; 1975 v Sp (sub), Se, P, W, Ni, E, R; 1976 v D (sub); 1977 v W (12)
Parlane, R. (Vale of Leven), 1878 v W; 1879 v E, W (3)
Paterson, G. D. (Celtic), 1939 v Ni (1)
Paterson, J. (Leicester C), 1920 v E (1)
Paterson, J. (Cowdenbeath), 1931 v A, I, Sw (3)
Paton, A. (Motherwell), 1952 v D, Se (2)
Paton, D. (St Bernards), 1896 v W (1)
Paton, M. (Dumbarton), 1883 v E; 1884 v W; 1885 v W, E; 1886 v E (5)
Paton, R. (Vale of Leven), 1879 v E, W (2)
Patrick, J. (St Mirren), 1897 v E, W (2)
Paul, H. McD. (Queen's Park), 1909 v E, W, Ni (3)
Paul, W. (Partick T), 1888 v W; 1889 v W; 1890 v W (3)
Paul, W. (Dykebar), 1891 v Ni (1)
Pearson, S. P. (Motherwell), 2004 v Ho (sub); (with Celtic), W (2)
Pearson, T. (Newcastle U), 1947 v E, Bel (2)
Penman, A. (Dundee), 1966 v Ho (1)
Pettigrew, W. (Motherwell), 1976 v Sw, Ni, W; 1977 v W (sub), Se (5)
Phillips, J. (Queen's Park), 1877 v E, W; 1878 v W (3)
Plenderleith, J. B. (Manchester C), 1961 v Ni (1)
Porteous, W. (Hearts), 1903 v Ni (1)
Pressley, S. J. (Hearts), 2000 v F (sub), Ei (sub); 2003 v Ic, Ca, P, Ic, Li, A, Nz, G; 2004 v N, G, Li, Ho (2), R, D, Es, Tr (19)
Pringle, C. (St Mirren), 1921 v W (1)
Provan, D. (Rangers), 1964 v Ni, N; 1966 v I (2), Ho (5)
Provan, D. (Celtic), 1980 v Bel (2 sub), P (sub), Ni (sub); 1981 v Is, W, E; 1982 v Se, P, Ni (10)
Pursell, P. (Queen's Park), 1914 v W (1)

Quashie, N. F. (Portsmouth), 2004 v Es, Tr (2)
Quinn, J. (Celtic), 1905 v Ni; 1906 v Ni, W; 1908 v Ni, E; 1909 v E; 1910 v E, Ni, W; 1912 v E, W (11)
Quinn, P. (Motherwell), 1961 v E, Ei (2); 1962 v U (4)

Rae, G. (Dundee), 2001 v Pol; 2002 v La (sub); 2003 v G (sub); 2004 v N (sub), Fa (sub), G (sub), Li, Ho; (with Rangers), R (9)
Rae, J. (Third Lanark), 1889 v W; 1890 v Ni (2)
Raeside, J. S. (Third Lanark), 1906 v W (1)
Raisbeck, A. G. (Liverpool), 1900 v E; 1901 v E; 1902 v E; 1903 v E, W; 1904 v E; 1906 v E; 1907 v E (8)
Rankin, G. (Vale of Leven), 1890 v Ni; 1891 v E (2)
Rankin, R. (St Mirren), 1929 v N, G, Ho (3)
Redpath, W. (Motherwell), 1949 v W, Ni; 1951 v E, D, F, Bel, A; 1952 v Ni, E (9)
Reid, J. G. (Airdrieonians), 1914 v W; 1920 v W; 1924 v Ni (3)
Reid, R. (Brentford), 1938 v E, Ni (2)
Reid, W. (Rangers), 1911 v E, W, Ni; 1912 v Ni; 1913 v E, W, Ni; 1914 v E, Ni (9)
Reilly, L. (Hibernian), 1949 v E, W, F; 1950 v W, Ni, Sw, F; 1951 v W, E, D, F, Bel, A; 1952 v Ni, W, E, USA, D, Se; 1953 v Ni, W, E, Se; 1954 v W; 1955 v H (2), P, Y, A, E; 1956 v E, W, Ni, A; 1957 v E, Ni, W, Y (38)
Rennie, H. G. (Hearts), 1900 v E, Ni; (with Hibernian), 1901 v E; 1902 v E, Ni, W; 1903 v Ni, W; 1904 v Ni; 1905 v W; 1906 v Ni; 1908 v Ni, W (13)
Renny-Tailyour, H. W. (Royal Engineers), 1873 v E (1)
Rhind, A. (Queen's Park), 1872 v E (1)

Richmond, A. (Queen's Park), 1906 v W (1)
Richmond, J. T. (Clydesdale), 1877 v E; (with Queen's Park), 1878 v E; 1882 v W (3)
Ring, T. (Clyde), 1953 v Se; 1955 v W, Ni, E, H; 1957 v E, Sp (2), Sw, WG; 1958 v Ni, Sw (12)
Rioch, B. D. (Derby Co), 1975 v P, W, Ni, E, R; 1976 v D (2), R, Ni, W, E; 1977 v Fi, Cz, W; (with Everton), W, Ni, E, Ch, Br; 1978 v Cz; (with Derby Co), Ni, E, Pe, Ho (24)
Ritchie, A. (East Stirlingshire), 1891 v W (1)
Ritchie, H. (Hibernian), 1923 v W; 1928 v Ni (2)
Ritchie, J. (Queen's Park), 1897 v W (1)
Ritchie, P. S. (Hearts), 1999 v G (sub), CzR; 2000 v Li, E; (with Bolton W), F, Ho; (with Walsall), 2004 v W (7)
Ritchie, W. (Rangers), 1962 v U (sub) (1)
Robb, D. T. (Aberdeen), 1971 v W, E, P, D (sub), USSR (5)
Robb, W. (Rangers), 1926 v W; (with Hibernian), 1928 v W (2)
Robertson, A. (Clyde), 1955 v P, A, H; 1958 v Sw, Par (5)
Robertson, D. (Rangers), 1992 v Ni; 1994 v Sw, Ho (3)
Robertson, G. (Motherwell), 1910 v W; (with Sheffield W), 1912 v W; 1913 v E, Ni (4)
Robertson, G. (Kilmarnock), 1938 v Cz (1)
Robertson, H. (Dundee), 1962 v Cz (1)
Robertson, J. (Dundee), 1931 v A, I (2)
Robertson, J. (Hearts), 1991 v R, Sw, Bul (sub), Sm (sub); 1992 v Sm, Ni (sub), Fi; 1993 v I (sub), Ma (sub), G, Es; 1995 v J (sub), Ec, Fa (sub); 1996 v Gr (sub), Se (16)
Robertson, J. N. (Nottingham F), 1978 v Ni, W (sub), Ir; 1979 v P, N; 1980 v Pe, A, Bel (2), P; 1981 v Se, P, Is, Ni, Is, Ni, E; 1982 v Se, Ni (2), E (sub), Nz, Br, USSR; 1983 v EG, Sw; (with Derby Co), 1984 v U, Bel (28)
Robertson, J. G. (Tottenham H), 1965 v W (1)
Robertson, J. T. (Everton), 1898 v E; (with Southampton), 1899 v E; (with Rangers), 1900 v E, W; 1901 v W, Ni, E; 1902 v W, Ni, E; 1903 v E, W; 1904 v E, W, Ni; 1905 v W (16)
Robertson, P. (Dundee), 1903 v Ni (1)
Robertson, T. (Queen's Park), 1889 v Ni; 1890 v E; 1891 v W; 1892 v Ni (4)
Robertson, T. (Hearts), 1898 v Ni (1)
Robertson, W. (Dumbarton), 1887 v E, W (2)
Robinson, R. (Dundee), 1974 v WG (sub); 1975 v Se, Ni, R (sub) (4)
Ross, M. (Rangers), 2002 v Sk, S.Af, Hk; 2003 v D, Fa, Ic, Ca, P, Nz, G; 2004 v N, G (sub), Ho (sub) (13)
Rough, A. (Partick T), 1976 v Sw, Ni, W, E; 1977 v Fi, Cz, W (2), Se, Ni, E, Ch, Arg, Br; 1978 v Cz, W, Ni, E, Pe, Ir, Ho; 1979 v A, P, W, Arg, N; 1980 v Pe, A, Bel (2), P, W, E, Pol, H; 1981 v Se, P, Is, Ni, Is, W, E; 1982 v Se, Ni, Sp, Ho, W, E, Nz, Br, USSR; (with Hibernian), 1986 v W (sub), E (53)
Rougvie, D. (Aberdeen), 1984 v Ni (1)
Rowan, A. (Caledonian), 1880 v E; (with Queen's Park), 1882 v W (2)
Russell, D. (Hearts), 1895 v E, Ni; (with Celtic), 1897 v W; 1898 v Ni; 1901 v W, Ni (6)
Russell, J. (Cambuslang), 1890 v Ni (1)
Russell, W. F. (Airdrieonians), 1924 v W; 1925 v E (2)
Rutherford, E. (Rangers), 1948 v F (1)

St John, I. (Motherwell), 1959 v WG; 1960 v E, Ni, W, Pol, A; 1961 v E; (with Liverpool), 1962 v Ni, W, E, Cz (2), U; 1963 v W, Ni, E, N, Ei (sub), Sp; 1964 v Ni; 1965 v E (21)
Sawers, W. (Dundee), 1895 v W (1)
Scarff, P. (Celtic), 1931 v Ni (1)
Schaedler, E. (Hibernian), 1974 v WG (1)
Scott, A. S. (Rangers), 1957 v Ni, Y, WG; 1958 v W, Sw; 1959 v P; 1962 v Ni, W, E, Cz, U; (with Everton), 1964 v W, N; 1965 v Fi; 1966 v P, Br (16)
Scott, J. (Hibernian), 1966 v Ho (1)
Scott, J. (Dundee), 1971 v D (sub), USSR (2)
Scott, M. (Airdrieonians), 1898 v W (1)
Scott, R. (Airdrieonians), 1894 v Ni (1)
Scoular, J. (Portsmouth), 1951 v D, F, A; 1952 v E, USA, D, Se; 1953 v W, Ni (9)
Sellar, W. (Battlefield), 1885 v E; 1886 v E; 1887 v E, W; 1888 v E; (with Queen's Park), 1891 v E; 1892 v E; 1893 v E, Ni (9)
Semple, W. (Cambuslang), 1886 v W (1)
Severin, S. (Hearts), 2002 v La (sub), Sk (sub), S.Af (sub), Hk; 2003 v D (sub), Ic (sub), Ca (sub), P (sub) (8)
Shankly, W. (Preston NE), 1938 v E; 1939 v E, W, Ni, H (5)
Sharp, G. M. (Everton), 1985 v Ic; 1986 v W, Aus (2 sub), Is, R, U; 1987 v Ei; 1988 v Bel (sub), Bul, L, Ma (12)
Sharp, J. (Dundee), 1904 v W; (with Woolwich Arsenal), 1907 v W, E; 1908 v E; (with Fulham), 1909 v W (5)
Shaw, D. (Hibernian), 1947 v W, Ni; 1948 v E, Bel, Sw, F; 1949 v W, Ni (8)
Shaw, F. W. (Pollokshields Ath), 1884 v E, W (2)
Shaw, J. (Rangers), 1947 v E, Bel, L; 1948 v Ni (4)
Shearer, D. (Aberdeen), 1994 v A (sub), Ho (sub); 1995 v Fi, Ru (sub), Sm, Fa; 1996 v Gr (7)
Shearer, R. (Rangers), 1961 v E, Ei (2), Cz (4)
Sillars, D. C. (Queen's Park), 1891 v Ni; 1892 v E; 1893 v W; 1894 v E; 1895 v W (5)
Simpson, J. (Third Lanark), 1895 v E, W, Ni (3)
Simpson, J. (Rangers), 1935 v E, W, Ni; 1936 v E, W, Ni; 1937 v G, E, W, Ni, A, Cz; 1938 v W, Ni (14)
Simpson, N. (Aberdeen), 1983 v Ni; 1984 v U (sub), F (sub); 1987 v E; 1988 v E (5)
Simpson, R. C. (Celtic), 1967 v E, USSR; 1968 v Ni, E; 1969 v A (5)
Sinclair, G. L. (Hearts), 1910 v Ni; 1912 v W, Ni (3)
Sinclair, J. W. E. (Leicester C), 1966 v P (1)
Skene, L. H. (Queen's Park), 1904 v W (1)
Sloan, T. (Third Lanark), 1904 v W (1)
Smellie, R. (Queen's Park), 1887 v Ni; 1888 v W; 1889 v E; 1891 v E; 1893 v E, Ni (6)
Smith, A. (Rangers), 1898 v E; 1900 v E, Ni, W; 1901 v E, Ni, W; 1902 v E, Ni, W; 1903 v E, Ni, W; 1904 v Ni; 1905 v W; 1906 v E, Ni; 1907 v W; 1911 v E, Ni (20)
Smith, D. (Aberdeen), 1966 v Ho; (with Rangers), 1968 v Ho (2)
Smith, G. (Hibernian), 1947 v E, Ni; 1948 v W, Bel, Sw, F; 1952 v E, USA; 1955 v P, Y, A, H; 1956 v E, Ni, W; 1957 v Sp (2), Sw (18)
Smith, H. G. (Hearts), 1988 v S.Ar (sub); 1992 v Ni, Ca (3)
Smith, J. (Ayr U), 1924 v E (1)
Smith, J. (Rangers), 1935 v Ni; 1938 v Ni (2)
Smith, J. (Aberdeen), 1968 v Ho (sub); (with Newcastle U), 1974 v WG, Ni (sub), W (sub) (4)
Smith, J. (Celtic), 2003 v Ei (sub), A (sub) (2)
Smith, J. E. (Celtic), 1959 v H, P (2)
Smith, Jas (Queen's Park), 1872 v E (1)
Smith, John (Mauchline), 1877 v E, W; 1879 v E, W; (with Edinburgh University), 1880 v E; (with Queen's Park), 1881 v W, E; 1883 v E, W; 1884 v E (10)
Smith, N. (Rangers), 1897 v E; 1898 v W; 1899 v E, W, Ni; 1900 v E, W, Ni; 1901 v Ni, W; 1902 v E, Ni (12)
Smith, R. (Queen's Park), 1872 v E; 1873 v E (2)
Smith, T. M. (Kilmarnock), 1934 v E; (with Preston NE), 1938 v E (2)
Somers, P. (Celtic), 1905 v E, Ni; 1907 v Ni; 1909 v W (4)
Somers, W. S. (Third Lanark), 1879 v E, W; (with Queen's Park), 1880 v W (3)
Somerville, G. (Queen's Park), 1886 v E (1)
Souness, G. J. (Middlesbrough), 1975 v EG, Sp, Se; (with Liverpool), 1978 v Bul, W, E (sub), Ho; 1979 v A, N, W, Ni, E; 1980 v Pe, A, Bel, P, Ni; 1981 v P, Is (2); 1982 v Ni, P, Sp, W, E, Nz, Br, USSR; 1983 v EG, Sw, Bel, Sw, W, E, Ca (2 + 1 sub); 1984 v U, Ni, W; (with Sampdoria), 1985 v Y, Ic, Sp (2), W, E, Ic; 1986 v EG, Aus (2), R, E, D, WG (54)
Speedie, D. R. (Chelsea), 1985 v E; 1986 v W, EG (sub), Aus, E; (with Coventry C), 1989 v Y (sub), I (sub), Cy (1+1 sub), Ch (10)
Speedie, F. (Rangers), 1903 v E, W, Ni (3)
Speirs, J. H. (Rangers), 1908 v W (1)
Spencer, J. (Chelsea), 1995 v Ru (sub), Gr (sub), Sm (sub), J; 1996 v Fi, Aus, D, US (sub), Co, Ho (sub), E, Sw (sub); 1997 v La; (with QPR), W (sub) (14)
Stanton, P. (Hibernian), 1966 v Ho; 1969 v Ni; 1970 v Ei, A; 1971 v D, Bel, P, USSR, D; 1972 v P, Bel, Ho, W; 1973 v W, Ni; 1974 v WG (16)
Stark, J. (Rangers), 1909 v E, Ni (2)
Steel, W. (Morton), 1947 v E, Bel, L; (with Derby Co), 1948 v F, E, W, Ni; 1949 v E, W, Ni, F; 1950 v E, W, Ni, Sw, P, F; (with Dundee), 1951 v W, Ni, E, A (2), D, F, Bel; 1952 v W; 1953 v W, E, Ni, Se (30)
Steele, D. M. (Huddersfield), 1923 v E, W, Ni (3)
Stein, C. (Rangers), 1969 v W, Ni, D, E, Cy (2); 1970 v A (sub), Ni (sub), W, E, Ei, WG; 1971 v D, USSR, Bel, D; 1972 v Cz (sub); (with Coventry C), 1973 v E (2 sub), W (sub), Ni (21)
Stephen, J. F. (Bradford), 1947 v W; 1948 v W (2)
Stevenson, G. (Motherwell), 1928 v W, Ni; 1930 v Ni, E, F; 1931 v E, W; 1932 v W, Ni; 1933 v Ni; 1934 v E; 1935 v Ni (12)
Stewart, A. (Queen's Park), 1888 v Ni; 1889 v W (2)
Stewart, A. (Third Lanark), 1894 v W (1)
Stewart, D. (Dumbarton), 1888 v Ni (1)
Stewart, D. (Queen's Park), 1893 v W; 1894 v Ni; 1897 v Ni (3)
Stewart, D. S. (Leeds U), 1978 v EG (1)

Stewart, G. (Hibernian), 1906 v W, E; (with Manchester C), 1907 v E, W (4)
Stewart, J. (Kilmarnock), 1977 v Ch (sub); (with Middlesbrough), 1979 v N (2)
Stewart, M. J. (Manchester U), 2002 v Ng (sub), Sk, S.Af (sub) (3)
Stewart, R. (West Ham U), 1981 v W, Ni, E; 1982 v Ni, P, W; 1984 v F; 1987 v Ei (2), L (10)
Stewart, W. E. (Queen's Park), 1898 v Ni; 1900 v Ni (2)
Stockdale, R. K. (Middlesbrough), 2002 v Ng, Sk (sub), S.Af, Hk; 2003 v D (5)
Storrier, D. (Celtic), 1899 v E, W, Ni (3)
Strachan, G. (Aberdeen), 1980 v Ni, W, E, Pol, H (sub); 1981 v Se, P; 1982 v Ni, P, Sp, Ho (sub), Nz, Br, USSR; 1983 v EG, Sw, Bel, Sw, Ni (sub), W, E, Ca (2 + 1 sub); 1984 v EG, Ni, E, F; (with Manchester U), 1985 v Sp (sub), E, Ic; 1986 v W, Aus, R, D, WG, U; 1987 v Bul, Ei (2); 1988 v H; 1989 v F (sub); (with Leeds U), 1990 v F; 1991 v USSR, Bul, Sm; 1992 v Sw, R, Ni, Fi (50)
Sturrock, P. (Dundee U), 1981 v W (sub), Ni, E (sub); 1982 v P, Ni (sub), W (sub), E (sub); 1983 v EG (sub), Sw, Bel (sub), Ca (3); 1984 v W; 1985 v Y (sub); 1986 v Is (sub), Ho, D, U; 1987 v Bel (20)
Sullivan, N. (Wimbledon), 1997 v W; 1998 v F, Co; 1999 v Fa, CzR, G, Fa, CzR; 2000 v Bos, Es, Bos, E (2), F, Ho, Ei; (with Tottenham H), 2001 v La, Sm, Cro, Bel, Sm, Pol; 2002 v Cro, Bel, La, F, Sk; 2003 v Ei (28)
Summers, W. (St Mirren), 1926 v E (1)
Symon, J. S. (Rangers), 1939 v H (1)

Tait, T. S. (Sunderland), 1911 v W (1)
Taylor, J. (Queen's Park), 1872 v E; 1873 v E; 1874 v E; 1875 v E; 1876 v E, W (6)
Taylor, J. D. (Dumbarton), 1892 v W; 1893 v W; 1894 v Ni; (with St Mirren), 1895 v Ni (4)
Taylor, W. (Hearts), 1892 v E (1)
Telfer, P. N. (Coventry C), 2000 v F (1)
Telfer, W. (Motherwell), 1933 v Ni; 1934 v Ni (2)
Telfer, W. D. (St Mirren), 1954 v W (1)
Templeton, R. (Aston Villa), 1902 v E; (with Newcastle U), 1903 v E, W; 1904 v E; (with Woolwich Arsenal), 1905 v W; (with Kilmarnock), 1908 v Ni; 1910 v E, Ni; 1912 v E, Ni; 1913 v W (11)
Thompson, S. (Dundee U), 2002 v F (sub), Ng, Hk; 2003 v D, Fa (sub), Ic, Ca; (with Rangers), Ei (sub), A, G (sub); 2004 v Fa (sub), G, R (13)
Thomson, A. (Arthurlie), 1886 v Ni (1)
Thomson, A. (Third Lanark), 1889 v W (1)
Thomson, A. (Airdrieonians), 1909 v Ni (1)
Thomson, A. (Celtic), 1926 v E; 1932 v F; 1933 v W (3)
Thomson, C. (Hearts), 1904 v Ni; 1905 v E, Ni, W; 1906 v W, Ni; 1907 v E, W, Ni; 1908 v E, W, Ni; (with Sunderland), 1909 v W; 1910 v E; 1911 v Ni; 1912 v E, W; 1913 v E, W; 1914 v E, Ni (21)
Thomson, C. (Sunderland), 1937 v Cz (1)
Thomson, D. (Dundee), 1920 v W (1)
Thomson, J. (Celtic), 1930 v F; 1931 v E, W, Ni (4)
Thomson, J. J. (Queen's Park), 1872 v E; 1873 v E; 1874 v E (3)
Thomson, J. R. (Everton), 1933 v W (1)
Thomson, R. (Celtic), 1932 v W (1)
Thomson, R. W. (Falkirk), 1927 v E (1)
Thomson, S. (Rangers), 1884 v W, Ni (2)
Thomson, W. (Dumbarton), 1892 v W; 1893 v W; 1898 v Ni, W (4)
Thomson, W. (Dundee), 1896 v W (1)
Thomson, W. (St Mirren), 1980 v Ni; 1981 v Ni (sub+1) 1982 v P; 1983 v Ni, Ca; 1984 v EG (7)
Thornton, W. (Rangers), 1947 v W, Ni; 1948 v E, Ni; 1949 v F; 1952 v D, Se (7)
Toner, W. (Kilmarnock), 1959 v W, Ni (2)
Townsley, T. (Falkirk), 1926 v W (1)
Troup, A. (Dundee), 1920 v E; 1921 v W, Ni; 1922 v Ni; (with Everton), 1926 v E (5)
Turnbull, E. (Hibernian), 1948 v Bel, Sw; 1951 v A; 1958 v H, Pol, Y, Par, F (8)
Turner, T. (Arthurlie), 1884 v W (1)
Turner, W. (Pollokshields Ath), 1885 v Ni; 1886 v Ni (2)

Ure, J. F. (Dundee), 1962 v W, Cz; 1963 v W, Ni, E, A, N, Sp; (with Arsenal), 1964 v Ni, N; 1968 v Ni (11)
Urquhart, D. (Hibernian), 1934 v W (1)

Vallance, T. (Rangers), 1877 v E, W; 1878 v E; 1879 v E, W; 1881 v E, W (7)
Venters, A. (Cowdenbeath), 1934 v Ni; (with Rangers), 1936 v E; 1939 v E (3)

Waddell, T. S. (Queen's Park), 1891 v Ni; 1892 v E; 1893 v E, Ni; 1895 v E, Ni (6)
Waddell, W. (Rangers), 1947 v W; 1949 v E, W, Ni, F; 1950 v E, Ni; 1951 v E, D, F, Bel, A; 1952 v Ni, W; 1954 v Ni; 1955 v W, Ni (17)
Wales, H. M. (Motherwell), 1933 v W (1)
Walker, A. (Celtic), 1988 v Co (sub); 1995 v Fi, Fa (sub) (3)
Walker, F. (Third Lanark), 1922 v W (1)
Walker, G. (St Mirren), 1930 v F; 1931 v Ni, A, Sw (4)
Walker, J. (Hearts), 1895 v Ni; 1897 v W; 1898 v Ni; (with Rangers), 1904 v W, Ni (5)
Walker, J. (Swindon T), 1911 v E, W, Ni; 1912 v E, W, Ni; 1913 v E, W, Ni (9)
Walker, J. N. (Hearts), 1993 v G; (with Partick T), 1996 v US (sub) (2)
Walker, R. (Hearts), 1900 v E, Ni; 1901 v E, W; 1902 v E, W, Ni; 1903 v E, W, Ni; 1904 v E, W, Ni; 1905 v E, W, Ni; 1906 v Ni; 1907 v E, Ni; 1908 v E, W, Ni; 1909 v E, W; 1912 v E, W, Ni; 1913 v E, W (29)
Walker, T. (Hearts), 1935 v E, W; 1936 v E, W, Ni; 1937 v G, E, W, Ni, A, Cz; 1938 v E, W, Ni, Cz, Ho; 1939 v E, W, Ni, H (20)
Walker, W. (Clyde), 1909 v Ni; 1910 v Ni (2)
Wallace, I. A. (Coventry C), 1978 v Bul (sub); 1979 v P (sub), W (3)
Wallace, W. S. B. (Hearts), 1965 v Ni; 1966 v E, Ho; (with Celtic), 1967 v E, USSR (sub); 1968 v Ni; 1969 v E (sub) (7)
Wardhaugh, J. (Hearts), 1955 v H; 1957 v Ni (2)
Wark, J. (Ipswich T), 1979 v W, Ni, E, Arg, N (sub); 1980 v Pe, A, Bel (2); 1981 v Is, Ni; 1982 v Se, Sp, Ho, Ni, Nz, Br, USSR; 1983 v EG, Sw (2), Ni, E (sub); 1984 v U, Bel, EG; (with Liverpool), E, F; 1985 v Y (29)
Watson, A. (Queen's Park), 1881 v E, W; 1882 v E (3)
Watson, J. (Sunderland), 1903 v E, W; 1904 v E; 1905 v E; (with Middlesbrough), 1909 v E, Ni (6)
Watson, J. (Motherwell), 1948 v Ni; (with Huddersfield T), 1954 v Ni (2)
Watson, J. A. K. (Rangers), 1878 v W (1)
Watson, P. R. (Blackpool), 1934 v A (1)
Watson, R. (Motherwell), 1971 v USSR (1)
Watson, W. (Falkirk), 1898 v W (1)
Watt, F. (Kilbirnie), 1889 v W, Ni; 1890 v W; 1891 v E (4)
Watt, W. W. (Queen's Park), 1887 v Ni (1)
Waugh, W. (Hearts), 1938 v Cz (1)
Webster, A. (Hearts), 2003 v A, Nz, G; 2004 v N, Fa, W (sub), Es (sub), Tr (sub) (8)
Weir, A. (Motherwell), 1959 v WG; 1960 v E, P, A, H, T (6)
Weir, D. G. (Hearts), 1997 v W, Ma (sub); 1998 v F, D (sub), Fi (sub), N (sub), Mor; 1999 v Es, Fa; (with Everton), CzR, G, Fa, CzR; 2000 v Bos, Es, Bos, Li, E (2), Ho; 2001 v La, Sm (sub), Cro, Aus, Bel, Sm, Pol (sub); 2002 v Cro, Bel, La, F, Ng, Sk, S.Af, Hk; 2003 v D, Fa (37)
Weir, J. (Third Lanark), 1887 v Ni (1)
Weir, J. B. (Queen's Park), 1872 v E; 1874 v E; 1875 v E; 1878 v W (4)
Weir, P. (St Mirren), 1980 v Ni, W, Pol (sub), H; (with Aberdeen), 1983 v Sw; 1984 v Ni (6)
White, John (Albion R), 1922 v W; (with Hearts), 1923 v Ni (2)
White, J. A. (Falkirk), 1959 v WG, Ho, P; 1960 v Ni; (with Tottenham H), 1960 v W, Pol, A, T; 1961 v W; 1962 v Ni, W, E, Cz (2); 1963 v W, Ni, E; 1964 v Ni, W, E, N, WG (22)
White, W. (Bolton W), 1907 v E; 1908 v E (2)
Whitelaw, A. (Vale of Leven), 1887 v Ni; 1890 v W (2)
Whyte, D. (Celtic), 1988 v Bel (sub), L; 1989 v Ch (sub); 1992 v US (sub); (with Middlesbrough), 1993 v P, I; 1995 v J (sub), Ec; 1996 v US; 1997 v La; (with Aberdeen), 1998 v Fi; 1999 v G (sub) (12)
Wilkie, L. (Dundee), 2002 v S.Af (sub), Hk; 2003 v Ic, Ca, P, Ic, Li, A; 2004 v Fa, Ho (2) (11)
Williams, G. (Nottingham F), 2002 v Ng, Sk (sub), S.Af, Hk (sub); 2003 v P (sub) (5)
Wilson, A. (Sheffield W), 1907 v E; 1908 v E; 1912 v E; 1913 v E, W; 1914 v Ni (6)
Wilson, A. (Portsmouth), 1954 v Fi (1)
Wilson, A. N. (Dunfermline), 1920 v E, W, Ni; 1921 v E, W, Ni; (with Middlesbrough), 1922 v E, W, Ni; 1923 v E, W, Ni (12)
Wilson, D. (Queen's Park), 1900 v W (1)
Wilson, D. (Oldham Ath), 1913 v E (1)
Wilson, D. (Rangers), 1961 v E, W, Ni, Ei (2), Cz; 1962 v Ni, W, E, Cz, U; 1963 v W, E, A, N, Ei, Sp; 1964 v E, WG; 1965 v Ni, E, Fi (22)

Wilson, G. W. (Hearts), 1904 v W; 1905 v E, Ni; 1906 v W; (with Everton), 1907 v E; (with Newcastle U), 1909 v E (6)
Wilson, Hugh, (Newmilns), 1890 v W; (with Sunderland), 1897 v E; (with Third Lanark), 1902 v W; 1904 v Ni (4)
Wilson, I. A. (Leicester C), 1987 v E, Br; (with Everton), 1988 v Bel, Bul, L (5)
Wilson, J. (Vale of Leven), 1888 v W; 1889 v E; 1890 v E; 1891 v E (4)
Wilson, P. (Celtic), 1926 v Ni; 1930 v F; 1931 v Ni; 1933 v E (4)
Wilson, P. (Celtic), 1975 v Sp (sub) (1)
Wilson, R. P. (Arsenal), 1972 v P, Ho (2)
Winters, R. (Aberdeen), 1999 v G (sub) (1)
Wiseman, W. (Queen's Park), 1927 v W; 1930 v Ni (2)
Wood, G. (Everton), 1979 v Ni, E, Arg (sub); (with Arsenal), 1982 v Ni (4)
Woodburn, W. A. (Rangers), 1947 v E, Bel, L; 1948 v W, Ni; 1949 v E, F; 1950 v E, W, Ni, P, F; 1951 v E, W, Ni, A (2), D, F, Bel; 1952 v E, W, Ni, USA (24)
Wotherspoon, D. N. (Queen's Park), 1872 v E; 1873 v E (2)
Wright, K. (Hibernian), 1992 v Ni (1)
Wright, S. (Aberdeen), 1993 v G, Es (2)
Wright, T. (Sunderland), 1953 v W, Ni, E (3)
Wylie, T. G. (Rangers), 1890 v Ni (1)

Yeats, R. (Liverpool), 1965 v W; 1966 v I (2)
Yorston, B. C. (Aberdeen), 1931 v Ni (1)
Yorston, H. (Aberdeen), 1955 v W (1)
Young, A. (Everton), 1905 v E; 1907 v W (2)
Young, A. (Hearts), 1960 v E, A (sub), H, T; 1961 v W, Ni; (with Everton), Ei; 1966 v P (8)
Young, G. L. (Rangers), 1947 v E, Ni, Bel, L; 1948 v E, Ni, Bel, Sw, F; 1949 v E, W, Ni, F; 1950 v E, W, Ni, Sw, P, F; 1951 v E, W, Ni, A (2), D, F, Bel; 1952 v E, W, Ni, USA, D, Se; 1953 v W, E, Ni, Se; 1954 v Ni, W; 1955 v W, Ni, P, Y; 1956 v Ni, W, E, A; 1957 v E, Ni, W, Y, Sp, Sw (53)
Young, J. (Celtic), 1906 v Ni (1)
Younger, T. (Hibernian), 1955 v P, Y, A, H; 1956 v E, Ni, W, A; (with Liverpool), 1957 v E, Ni, W, Y, Sp (2), Sw, WG; 1958 v Ni, W, E, Sw, H, Pol, Y, Par (24)

## WALES

Adams, H. (Berwyn R), 1882 v Ni, E; (with Druids), 1883 v Ni, E (4)
Aizlewood, M. (Charlton Ath), 1986 v S.Ar, Ca (2); 1987 v Fi; (with Leeds U), USSR, Fi (sub); 1988 v D (sub), Se, Ma, I; 1989 v Ho, Se (sub), WG; (with Bradford C), 1990 v Fi, WG, Ei, Cr; (with Bristol C), 1991 v D, Bel (2), L, Ei, Ic, Pol, WG; 1992 v Br, L, Ei, A, R, Ho, Arg, J; 1993 v Ei, Bel, Fa; 1994 v RCS, Cy; (with Cardiff C), 1995v Bul (39)
Allchurch, I. J. (Swansea T), 1951 v E, Ni, P, Sw; 1952 v E, S, Ni, R of UK; 1953 v S, E, Ni, F, Y; 1954 v S, E, Ni, A; 1955 v S, E, Ni, Y; 1956 v E, S, Ni, A; 1957 v E, S; 1958 v Ni, Is (2), H (2), M, Sw, Br; (with Newcastle U), 1959 v E, S, Ni; 1960 v E, S; 1961 v Ni, H, Sp (2); 1962 v E, S, Br (2), M; (with Cardiff C), 1963 v S, E, Ni, H (2); 1964 v E; 1965 v S, E, Ni, Gr, I, USSR; (with Swansea T), 1966 v USSR, E, S, D, Br (2), Ch (68)
Allchurch, L. (Swansea T), 1955 v Ni; 1956 v A; 1958 v S, Ni, EG, Is; 1959 v S; (with Sheffield U), 1962 v S, Ni, Br; 1964 v E (11)
Allen, B. W. (Coventry C), 1951 v S, E (2)
Allen, M. (Watford), 1986 v S.Ar (sub), Ca (1 + 1 sub); (with Norwich C), 1989 v Is (sub); 1990 v Ho, WG; (with Millwall), Ei, Se, Cr (sub); 1991 v L (sub), Ei (sub); 1992 v A; 1993 v Ei (sub); (with Newcastle U), 1994 v R (sub) (14)
Arridge, S. (Bootle), 1892 v S, Ni; (with Everton), 1894 v Ni; 1895 v Ni; 1896 v E; (with New Brighton Tower), 1898 v E, Ni; 1899 v E (8)
Astley, D. J. (Charlton Ath), 1931 v Ni; (with Aston Villa), 1932 v E; 1933 v E, S, Ni; 1934 v E, S; 1935 v S; 1936 v E, Ni; (with Derby Co), 1939 v E, S; (with Blackpool), F (13)
Atherton, R. W. (Hibernian), 1899 v E, Ni; 1903 v E, S, Ni; (with Middlesbrough), 1904 v E, S, Ni; 1905 v Ni (9)

Bailiff, W. E. (Llanelly), 1913 v E, S, Ni; 1920 v Ni (4)
Baker, C. W. (Cardiff C), 1958 v M; 1960 v S, Ni; 1961 v S, E, Ei; 1962 v S (7)
Baker, W. G. (Cardiff C), 1948 v Ni (1)
Bamford, T. (Wrexham), 1931 v E, S, Ni; 1932 v Ni; 1933 v F (5)
Barnard, D. S. (Barnsley), 1998 v Jam; 1999 v I, D, Bl, I, D; 2000 v Bl, Sw, Q, Fi, Br (sub), P; 2001 v Uk, Pol, Uk; 2002 v Arm (sub); (with Grimsby T), 2003 v Cro, Az; 2004 v Ser, Ru (2), N (sub) (22)
Barnes, W. (Arsenal), 1948 v E, S, Ni; 1949 v E, S, Ni; 1950 v E, S, Ni, Bel; 1951 v E, S, Ni, P; 1952 v E, S, Ni, R of UK; 1954 v E, S; 1955 v S, Y (22)
Bartley, T. (Glossop NE), 1898 v E (1)
Bastock, A. M. (Shrewsbury), 1892 v Ni (1)
Beadles, G. H. (Cardiff C), 1925 v E, S (2)
Bell, W. S. (Shrewsbury Engineers), 1881 v E, S; (with Crewe Alex), 1886 v E, S, Ni (5)
Bellamy, C. D. (Norwich C), 1998 v Jam (sub), Ma, Tun; 1999 v D (sub), Sw (sub), I, D (sub); 2000 v Br (sub), P; (with Coventry C), 2001 v Bl, Arm, Uk; (with Newcastle U), 2002 v Arm, N, Bl, Arg; 2003 v Fi (sub), I, Bos, Az; 2004 v Ser, I, Ser, N, Ca (25)
Bennion, S. R. (Manchester U), 1926 v S; 1927 v S; 1928 v S, E, Ni; 1929 v S, E, Ni; 1930 v S; 1932 v Ni (10)
Berry, G. F. (Wolverhampton W), 1979 v WG; 1980 v Ei, WG (sub), T; (with Stoke C), 1983 v E (sub) (5)
Blackmore, C. G. (Manchester U), 1985 v N (sub); 1986 v S (sub), H (sub), S.Ar, Ei, U; 1987 v Fi (2), USSR, Cz; 1988 v D (2), Cz, Y, Se, Ma, I; 1989 v Ho, Fi, Is, WG; 1990 v F; Ho, WG, Cr; 1991 v Bel, L; 1992 v Ei (sub), A, R (sub), Ho, Arg, J; 1993 v Fa, Cy, Bel, RCS; 1994 v Se (sub); (with Middlesbrough), 1997 v Bel (39)
Blake, N. A. (Sheffield U), 1994 v N, Se (sub); 1995 v Alb, Mol; 1996 v G (with Bolton W), I (sub); 1998 v T; 1999 v I, D, Bl; (with Blackburn R) Sw; 2000 v Bl, Sw, Q, Fi; 2001 v Bl (sub), N, Pol (2), Uk; 2002 v N (sub); (with Wolverhampton W), CzR; 2003 v I (sub); 2004 v Ser, I (sub), Fi (sub), Ser (sub), Ru (sub + sub) (29)
Blew, H. (Wrexham), 1899 v E, S, Ni; 1902 v S, Ni; 1903 v E, S; 1904 v E, S, Ni; 1905 v S, Ni; 1906 v E, S, Ni; 1907 v S; 1908 v E, S, Ni; 1909 v E, S; 1910 v E (22)
Boden, T. (Wrexham), 1880 v E (1)
Bodin, P. J. (Swindon T), 1990 v Cr; 1991 v D, Bel, L, Ei; (with C Palace), Bel, Ic, Pol, WG; 1992 v Br, G, L (sub); (with Swindon T), Ei (sub), Ho, Arg; 1993 v Ei, Bel, RCS, Fa; 1994 v R, Se, Es (sub); 1995 v Alb (23)
Boulter, L. M. (Brentford), 1939 v Ni (1)
Bowdler, H. E. (Shrewsbury), 1893 v S (1)
Bowdler, J. C. H. (Shrewsbury), 1890 v Ni; (with Wolverhampton W), 1891 v S; 1892 v Ni; (with Shrewsbury), 1894 v E (4)
Bowen, D. L. (Arsenal), 1955 v S, Y; 1957 v Ni, Cz, EG; 1958 v E, S, Ni, EG, Is (2), H (2), M, Se, Br; 1959 v E, S, Ni (19)
Bowen, E. (Druids), 1880 v S; 1883 v S (2)
Bowen, J. P. (Swansea C), 1994 v Es; (with Birmingham C), 1997 v Ho (2)
Bowen, M. R. (Tottenham H), 1986 v Ca (2 sub); (with Norwich C), 1988 v Y (sub); 1989 v Fi (sub), Is, Se, WG (sub); 1990 v Fi (sub), Ho, WG, Se; 1992 v Br (sub), G, L, Ei, A, R, Ho (sub), J; 1993 v Fa, Cy, Bel (1 + sub), RCS (sub); 1994 v RCS, Se; 1995 v Mol, Ge, Bul (2), G, Ge; 1996 v Mol, G, Alb, Sw, Sm; (with West Ham U), 1997 v Sm, Ho (2), Ei (sub) (41)
Bowsher, S. J. (Burnley), 1929 v Ni (1)
Boyle, T. (C Palace), 1981 v Ei, S (sub) (2)
Britten, T. J. (Parkgrove), 1878 v S; (with Presteigne), 1880 v S (2)
Brookes, S. J. (Llandudno), 1900 v E, Ni (2)
Brown, A. I. (Aberdare Ath), 1926 v Ni (1)
Browning, M. T. (Bristol R), 1996 v I (sub), Sm; 1997 v Sm, Ho (with Huddersfield T), S (sub) (5)
Bryan, T. (Oswestry), 1886 v E, Ni (2)
Buckland, T. (Bangor), 1899 v E (1)
Burgess, W. A. R. (Tottenham H), 1947 v E, S, Ni; 1948 v E, S; 1949 v E, S, Ni, P, Bel, Sw; 1950 v E, S, Ni, Bel; 1951 v S, Ni, P, Sw; 1952 v E, S, Ni, R of UK; 1953 v S, E, Ni, F, Y; 1954 v S, E, Ni, A (32)
Burke, T. (Wrexham), 1883 v E; 1884 v S; 1885 v E, S, Ni; (with Newton Heath), 1887 v E, S; 1888 v S (8)
Burnett, T. B. (Ruabon), 1877 v S (1)
Burton, A. D. (Norwich C), 1963 v Ni, H; (with Newcastle U), 1964 v E; 1969 v S, E, Ni, I, EG; 1972 v Cz (9)
Butler, J. (Chirk), 1893 v E, S, Ni (3)
Butler, W. T. (Druids), 1900 v S, Ni (2)

Cartwright, L. (Coventry C), 1974 v E (sub), S, Ni; 1976 v S (sub); 1977 v WG (sub); (with Wrexham), 1978 v Ir (sub); 1979 v Ma (7)
Carty, T. See McCarthy (Wrexham).
Challen, J. B. (Corinthians), 1887 v E, S; 1888 v E; (with Wellingborough GS), 1890 v E (4)
Chapman, T. (Newtown), 1894 v E, S, Ni; 1895 v S, Ni; (with Manchester C), 1896 v E; 1897 v E (7)
Charles, J. M. (Swansea C), 1981 v Cz, T (sub), S (sub), USSR (sub); 1982 v Ic; 1983 v N (sub), Y (sub), Bul (sub), S, Ni, Br; 1984 v Bul (sub); (with QPR), Y (sub), S; (with Oxford U), 1985 v Ic (sub), Sp, Ic; 1986 v Ei; 1987 v Fi (19)
Charles, M. (Swansea T), 1955 v Ni; 1956 v E, S, A; 1957 v E, Ni, Cz (2), EG; 1958 v E, S, EG, Is (2), H (2), M, Se, Br; 1959 v E, S; (with Arsenal), 1961 v Ni, H, Sp (2); 1962 v E, S; (with Cardiff C), 1962 v Br, Ni; 1963 v S, H (31)
Charles, W. J. (Leeds U), 1950 v Ni; 1951 v Sw; 1953 v Ni, F, Y; 1954 v E, S, Ni, A; 1955 v S, E, Ni, Y; 1956 v E, S, A, Ni; 1957 v E, S, Ni, Cz (2), EG; (with Juventus), 1958 v Is (2), H (2) M, Se; 1960 v S; 1962 v E, Br (2), M; (with Leeds U), 1963 v S; (with Cardiff C), 1964 v S; 1965 v S, USSR (38)
Clarke, R. J. (Manchester C), 1949 v E; 1950 v S, Ni, Bel; 1951 v E, S, Ni, P, Sw; 1952 v S, E, Ni, R of UK; 1953 v S, E; 1954 v E, S, Ni; 1955 v Y, S, E; 1956 v Ni (22)
Coleman, C. (C Palace), 1992 v A (sub); 1993 v Ei (sub); 1994 v N, Es; 1995 v Alb, Mol, Ge, Bul (2), G; 1996 v Mol; (with Blackburn R), I, Sw, Sm; 1997 v Sm; 1998 v Br; (with Fulham), Jam, Ma, Tun; 1999 v I, D, Bl, Sw, D; 2000 v Bl, Sw, Q, Fi; 2001 v Bl, N, Pol; 2002 v G (sub) (32)
Collier, D. J. (Grimsby T), 1921 v S (1)
Collins, J. M. (Cardiff C), 2004 v N, Ca (2)
Collins, W. S. (Llanelly), 1931 v S (1)
Conde, C. (Chirk), 1884 v E, S, Ni (3)
Cook, F. C. (Newport Co), 1925 v E, S; (with Portsmouth), 1928 v E, S; 1930 v E, S, Ni; 1932 v E (8)
Cornforth, J. M. (Swansea C), 1995 v Bul (sub), Ge (2)
Coyne, D. (Tranmere R), 1996 v Sw; (with Grimsby T), 2002 v CzR (sub); (with Leicester C), 2004 v H (sub), N, Ca (5)
Crompton, W. (Wrexham), 1931 v E, S, Ni (3)
Cross, E. A. (Wrexham), 1876 v S; 1877 v S (2)
Crosse, K. (Druids), 1879 v S; 1881 v E, S (3)
Crossley, M. G. (Nottingham F), 1997 v Ei; 1999 v Sw (sub); 2000 v Fi; (with Middlesbrough), 2002 v Arg (sub), G; 2003 v Bos (sub); (with Fulham), 2004 v S (7)
Crowe, V. H. (Aston Villa), 1959 v E, Ni; 1960 v E, Ni; 1961 v S, E, Ni, Ei, H, Sp (2); 1962 v E, S, Br, M; 1963 v H (16)
Cumner, R. H. (Arsenal), 1939 v E, S, Ni (3)
Curtis, A. (Swansea C), 1976 v E, Y (sub), S, Ni, Y (sub), E; 1977 v WG, S (sub), Ni (sub); 1978 v WG, E, S; 1979 v WG, S; (with Leeds U), E, Ni, Ma; 1980 v Ei, WG, T; (with Swansea C), 1982 v Cz, Ic, USSR, Sp, E, S, Ni; 1983 v N; 1984 v R (sub); (with Southampton), S; 1985 v Sp, N (1 + 1 sub); 1986 v H; (with Cardiff C), 1987 v USSR (35)
Curtis, E. R. (Cardiff C), 1928 v S; (with Birmingham), 1932 v S; 1934 v Ni (3)

Daniel, R. W. (Arsenal), 1951 v E, Ni, P; 1952 v E, S, Ni, R of UK; 1953 v S, E, Ni, F, Y; (with Sunderland), 1954 v E, S, Ni; 1955 v E, Ni; 1957 v S, E, Ni, Cz (21)
Darvell, S. (Oxford University), 1897 v S, Ni (2)
Davies, A. (Manchester U), 1983 v Ni, Br; 1984 v E, Ni; 1985 v Ic (2), N; (with Newcastle U), 1986 v H; (with Swansea C), 1988 v Ma, I; 1989 v Ho; (with Bradford C), 1990 v Fi, Ei (13)
Davies, A. (Wrexham), 1876 v S; 1877 v S (2)
Davies, A. (Druids), 1904 v S; (with Middlesbrough), 1905 v S (2)
Davies, A. O. (Barmouth), 1885 v Ni; 1886 v E, S; (with Swifts), 1887 v E, S; 1888 v E, Ni; (with Wrexham), 1889 v S; (with Crewe Alex), 1890 v E (9)
Davies, A. T. (Shrewsbury), 1891 v Ni (1)
Davies, C. (Charlton Ath), 1972 v R (sub) (1)
Davies, D. (Bolton W), 1904 v S, Ni; 1908 v E (sub) (3)
Davies, D. C. (Brecon), 1899 v Ni; (with Hereford); 1900 v Ni (2)
Davies, D. W. (Treharris), 1912 v Ni; (with Oldham Ath), 1913 v Ni (2)
Davies, E. Lloyd (Stoke C), 1904 v E; 1907 v E, S, Ni; (with Northampton T), 1908 v S; 1909 v Ni; 1910 v Ni; 1911 v E, S; 1912 v E, S; 1913 v E, S; 1914 v Ni, E, S (16)
Davies, E. R. (Newcastle U), 1953 v S, E; 1954 v E, S; 1958 v E, EG (6)
Davies, G. (Fulham), 1980 v T, Ic; 1982 v Sp (sub), F (sub); 1983 v E, Bul, S, Ni, Br; 1984 v R (sub), S (sub), E, Ni; 1985 v Ic; (with Manchester C), 1986 v S.Ar, Ei (16)
Davies, Rev. H. (Wrexham), 1928 v Ni (1)
Davies, Idwal (Liverpool Marine), 1923 v S (1)
Davies, J. E. (Oswestry), 1885 v E (1)
Davies, Jas (Wrexham), 1878 v S (1)
Davies, John (Wrexham), 1879 v S (1)
Davies, Jos (Newton Heath), 1888 v E, S, Ni; 1889 v S; 1890 v E; (with Wolverhampton W), 1892 v E; 1893 v E (7)
Davies, Jos (Everton), 1889 v S, Ni; (with Chirk), 1891 v Ni; (with Ardwick), v E, S; (with Sheffield U), 1895 v E, S, Ni; (with Manchester C), 1896 v E; (with Millwall), 1897 v E; (with Reading), 1900 v E (11)
Davies, J. P. (Druids), 1883 v E, Ni (2)
Davies, Ll. (Wrexham), 1907 v Ni; 1910 v Ni, S, E; (with Everton), 1911 v S, Ni; (with Wrexham), 1912 v Ni, S, E; 1913 v Ni, S, E; 1914 v Ni (13)
Davies, L. S. (Cardiff C), 1922 v E, S, Ni; 1923 v E, S, Ni; 1924 v E, S, Ni; 1925 v S, Ni; 1926 v E, Ni; 1927 v E, Ni; 1928 v S, Ni, E; 1929 v S, Ni, E; 1930 v E, S (23)
Davies, O. (Wrexham), 1890 v S (1)
Davies, R. (Wrexham), 1883 v Ni; 1884 v Ni; 1885 v Ni (3)
Davies, R. (Druids), 1885 v E (1)
Davies, R. O. (Wrexham), 1892 v Ni, E (2)
Davies, R. T. (Norwich C), 1964 v Ni; 1965 v E; 1966 v Br (2), Ch; (with Southampton), 1967 v S, E, Ni; 1968 v S, Ni, WG; 1969 v S, E, Ni, I, WG, R of UK; 1970 v E, S, Ni; 1971 v Cz, S, E, Ni; 1972 v R, E, S, N; (with Portsmouth), 1974 v E (29)
Davies, R. W. (Bolton W), 1964 v E; 1965 v E, S, Ni, D, Gr, USSR; 1966 v E, S, Ni, USSR, D, Br (2), Ch (sub); 1967 v S; (with Newcastle U), E; 1968 v S, Ni, WG; 1969 v S, E, Ni, I; 1970 v EG; 1971 v R, Cz; (with Manchester C), 1972 v E, S, Ni; (with Manchester U), 1973 v E, S (sub), Ni; (with Blackpool), 1974 v Pol (34)
Davies, S. (Tottenham H), 2001 v Uk (sub+1); 2002 v Arm, N, Bl, Arg, CzR, G; 2003 v Cro, Fi, I, Az, Bos, Az, US; 2004 v Ser, I, Fi, S (19)
Davies, S. I. (Manchester U), 1996 v Sw (sub) (1)
Davies, Stanley (Preston NE), 1920 v E, S, Ni; (with Everton), 1921 v E, S, Ni; (with WBA), 1922 v E, S, Ni; 1923 v S; 1925 v S, Ni; 1926 v S, E, Ni; 1927 v S; 1928 v S; (with Rotherham U), 1930 v Ni (18)
Davies, T. (Oswestry), 1886 v E (1)
Davies, T. (Druids), 1903 v E, Ni, S; 1904 v S (4)
Davies, W. (Wrexham), 1884 v Ni (1)
Davies, W. (Swansea T), 1924 v E, S, Ni; (with Cardiff C), 1925 v E, S, Ni; 1926 v E, S, Ni; 1927 v S; 1928 v Ni; (with Notts Co), 1929 v E, S, Ni; 1930 v E, S, Ni (17)
Davies, William (Wrexham), 1903 v Ni; 1905 v Ni; (with Blackburn R), 1908 v E, S; 1909 v E, S, Ni; 1911 v E, S, Ni; 1912 v Ni (11)
Davies, W. C. (C Palace), 1908 v S; (with WBA), 1909 v E; 1910 v S; (with C Palace), 1914 v E (4)
Davies, W. D. (Everton), 1975 v H, L, S, E, Ni; 1976 v Y (2), E, Ni; 1977 v WG, S (2), Cz, E, Ni; 1978 v K; (with Wrexham), S, Cz, WG, Ir, E, S, Ni; 1979 v Ma, T, WG, S, E, Ni, Ma; 1980 v Ei, WG, T, E, S, Ni, Ic; 1981 v T, Cz, Ei, T, S, E, USSR; (with Swansea C), 1982 v Cz, Ic, USSR, Sp, E, S, F; 1983 v Y (52)
Davies, W. H. (Oswestry), 1876 v S; 1877 v S; 1879 v E; 1880 v E (4)
Davies, W. O. (Millwall Ath), 1913 v E, S, Ni; 1914 v S, Ni (5)
Davis, G. (Wrexham), 1978 v Ir, E (sub), Ni (3)
Day, A. (Tottenham H), 1934 v Ni (1)
Deacy, N. (PSV Eindhoven), 1977 v Cz, S, E, Ni; 1978 v K (sub), S (sub), Cz (sub), WG, Ir, S (sub), Ni; (with Beringen), 1979 v T (12)
Dearson, D. J. (Birmingham), 1939 v S, Ni, F (3)
Delaney, M. A. (Aston Villa), 2000 v Sw, Q, Br, P; 2001 v N, Pol, Arm, Uk (2); 2002 v Arm, N, Bl, Arg, CzR, G; 2003 v Cro, Fi, I, Az; 2004 v Ser, I, Ser, Ru (2), N, Ca (26)
Derrett, S. C. (Cardiff C), 1969 v S, WG; 1970 v I; 1971 v Fi (4)
Dewey, F. T. (Cardiff Corinthians), 1931 v E, S (2)
Dibble, A. (Luton T), 1986 v Ca (1+1 sub); (with Manchester C), 1989 v Is (3)
Doughty, J. (Druids), 1886 v S; (with Newton Heath), 1887 v S, Ni; 1888 v E, S, Ni; 1889 v S; 1890 v E (8)
Doughty, R. (Newton Heath and Druids), 1888 v S, Ni (2)
Durban, A. (Derby Co), 1966 v Br (sub); 1967 v Ni; 1968 v E, S, Ni, WG; 1969 v EG, S, E, Ni, WG; 1970 v E, S, Ni, EG, I; 1971 v R, S, E, Ni, Cz, Fi; 1972 v Fi, Cz, E, S, Ni (27)
Dwyer, P. (Cardiff C), 1978 v Ir, E, S, Ni; 1979 v T, S, E, Ni, Ma (sub); 1980 v WG (10)

Earnshaw, R. (Cardiff C), 2002 v G; 2003 v Cro, Az, Bos; 2004 v Ser (sub), I (sub), Fi, Ser, Ru (sub), S, H, N, Ca (sub) (13)
Edwards, C. (Wrexham), 1878 v S (1)
Edwards, C. N. H. (Swansea C), 1996 v Sw (sub) (1)

Edwards, G. (Birmingham C), 1947 v E, S, Ni; 1948 v E, S, Ni; (with Cardiff C), 1949 v Ni, P, Bel, Sw; 1950 v E, S (12)
Edwards, H. (Wrexham Civil Service), 1878 v S; 1880 v E, S; 1882 v E, S; 1883 v S; 1884 v Ni; 1887 v Ni (8)
Edwards, J. H. (Wanderers), 1876 v S (1)
Edwards, J. H. (Oswestry), 1895 v Ni; 1897 v E, Ni (3)
Edwards, J. H. (Aberystwyth), 1898 v Ni (1)
Edwards, L. T. (Charlton Ath), 1957 v Ni, EG (2)
Edwards, R. I. (Chester), 1978 v K (sub); 1979 v Ma, WG; (with Wrexham), 1980 v T (sub) (4)
Edwards, R. O. (Aston Villa), 2003 v Az (sub); 2004 v Ser (sub), S, H (sub), N (sub), Ca (sub) (6)
Edwards, R. W. (Bristol C), 1998 v T (sub), Bel, Ma (sub), Tun (sub) (4)
Edwards, T. (Linfield), 1932 v S (1)
Egan, W. (Chirk), 1892 v S (1)
Ellis, B. (Motherwell), 1932 v E; 1933 v E, S; 1934 v S; 1936 v E; 1937 v S (6)
Ellis, E. (Nunhead), 1931 v S; (with Oswestry), E; 1932 v Ni (3)
Emanuel, W. J. (Bristol C), 1973 v E (sub), Ni (sub) (2)
England, H. M. (Blackburn R), 1962 v Ni, Br, M; 1963 v Ni, H; 1964 v E, S, Ni; 1965 v E, D, Gr (2), USSR, Ni, I; 1966 v E, S, Ni, USSR, D; (with Tottenham H), 1967 v S, E; 1968 v E, Ni, WG; 1969 v EG; 1970 v R of UK, EG, E, S, Ni, I; 1971 v R; 1972 v Fi, E, S, Ni; 1973 v E (3), S; 1974 v Pol; 1975 v H, L (44)
Evans, B. C. (Swansea C), 1972 v Fi, Cz; 1973 v E (2), Pol, S; (with Hereford U), 1974 v Pol (7)
Evans, D. G. (Reading), 1926 v Ni; 1927 v Ni, E; (with Huddersfield T), 1929 v S (4)
Evans, H. P. (Cardiff C), 1922 v E, S, Ni; 1924 v E, S, Ni (6)
Evans, I. (C Palace), 1976 v A, E, Y (2), E, Ni; 1977 v WG, S (2), Cz, E, Ni; 1978 v K (13)
Evans, J. (Oswestry), 1893 v Ni; 1894 v E, Ni (3)
Evans, J. (Cardiff C), 1912 v Ni; 1913 v Ni; 1914 v S; 1920 v S, Ni; 1922 v Ni; 1923 v E, Ni (8)
Evans, J. H. (Southend U), 1922 v E, S, Ni; 1923 v S (4)
Evans, Len (Aberdare Ath), 1927 v Ni; (with Cardiff C), 1931 v E, S; (with Birmingham), 1934 v Ni (4)
Evans, M. (Oswestry), 1884 v E (1)
Evans, P. S. (Brentford), 2002 v CzR (sub); (with Bradford C), Cro (sub) (2)
Evans, R. (Clapton), 1902 v Ni (1)
Evans, R. E. (Wrexham), 1906 v E, S; (with Aston Villa), Ni; 1907 v E; 1908 v E, S; (with Sheffield U), 1909 v S; 1910 v E, S, Ni (10)
Evans, R. O. (Wrexham), 1902 v Ni; 1903 v E, S, Ni; (with Blackburn R), 1908 v Ni; (with Coventry C), 1911 v E, Ni; 1912 v E, S, Ni (10)
Evans, R. S. (Swansea T), 1964 v Ni (1)
Evans, T. J. (Clapton Orient), 1927 v S; 1928 v E, S; (with Newcastle U), Ni (4)
Evans, W. (Tottenham H), 1933 v Ni; 1934 v E, S; 1935 v E; 1936 v E, Ni (6)
Evans, W. A. W. (Oxford University), 1876 v S; 1877 v S (2)
Evans, W. G. (Bootle), 1890 v E; 1891 v E; (with Aston Villa), 1892 v E (3)
Evelyn, E. C. (Crusaders), 1887 v E (1)
Eyton-Jones, J. A. (Wrexham), 1883 v Ni; 1884 v Ni, E, S (4)

Farmer, G. (Oswestry), 1885 v E, S (2)
Felgate, D. (Lincoln C), 1984 v R (sub) (1)
Finnigan, R. J. (Wrexham), 1930 v Ni (1)
Fletcher, C. N. (Bournemouth), 2004 v S (sub), H (sub), N, Ca (4)
Flynn, B. (Burnley), 1975 v L (2 sub), H (sub), S, E, Ni; 1976 v A, E, Y (2), E, Ni; 1977 v WG (sub), S (2), Cz, E, Ni; 1978 v K (2), S; (with Leeds U), Cz, WG, Ir (sub), E, S, Ni; 1979 v Ma, T, S, E, Ni, Ma; 1980 v Ei, WG, E, S, Ni, Ic; 1981 v T, Cz, Ei, T, S, E, USSR; 1982 v Cz, USSR, E, S, Ni, F; 1983 v N; (with Burnley), Y, E, Bul, S, Ni, Br; 1984 v N, R, Bul, Y, S, N, Is (66)
Ford, T. (Swansea T), 1947 v S; (with Aston Villa), 1947 v Ni; 1948 v S, Ni; 1949 v E, S, Ni, P, Bel, Sw; 1950 v E, S, Ni, Bel; 1951 v S; (with Sunderland), 1951 v E, Ni, P, Sw; 1952 v E, S, Ni, R of UK; 1953 v S, E, Ni, F, Y; (with Cardiff C), 1954 v A; 1955 v S, E, Ni, Y; 1956 v S, Ni, E, A; 1957 v S (38)
Foulkes, H. E. (WBA), 1932 v Ni (1)
Foulkes, W. I. (Newcastle U), 1952 v E, S, Ni, R of UK; 1953 v E, S, F, Y; 1954 v E, S, Ni (11)
Foulkes, W. T. (Oswestry), 1884 v Ni; 1885 v S (2)
Fowler, J. (Swansea T), 1925 v E; 1926 v E, Ni; 1927 v S; 1928 v S; 1929 v E (6)
Freestone, R. (Swansea C), 2000 v Br (1)

Gabbidon, D. L. (Cardiff C), 2002 v CzR; 2003 v Cro, Fi, I; 2004 v Ser (2), Ru (2), S, H, N, Ca (12)
Garner, J. (Aberystwyth), 1896 v S (1)
Giggs, R. J. (Manchester U), 1992 v G (sub), L (sub), R (sub); 1993 v Fa (sub), Bel (sub + 1), RCS, Fa; 1994 v RCS, Cy, R; 1995 v Alb, Bul; 1996 v G, Alb, Sm; 1997 v Sm, T, Bel; 1998 v T, Bel; 1999 v I (2), D; 2000 v Bl, Fi; 2001 v Bl, N, Pol, Uk, Pol, Uk; 2002 v Arm, N, Arg, G; 2003 v Fi, I, Az (2); 2004 v Ser, I, Fi, Ser, Ru (2), S, Ca (48)
Giles, D. (Swansea C), 1980 v E, S, Ni, Ic; 1981 v T, Cz, T (sub), E (sub), USSR (sub); (with C Palace), 1982 v Sp (sub); 1983 v Ni (sub), Br (12)
Gillam, S. G. (Wrexham), 1889 v S (sub), Ni; (with Shrewsbury), 1890 v E, Ni; (with Clapton), 1894 v S (5)
Glascodine, G. (Wrexham), 1879 v E (1)
Glover, E. M. (Grimsby T), 1932 v S; 1934 v Ni; 1936 v S; 1937 v E, S, Ni; 1939 v Ni (7)
Godding, G. (Wrexham), 1923 v S, Ni (2)
Godfrey, B. C. (Preston NE), 1964 v Ni; 1965 v D, I (3)
Goodwin, U. (Ruthin), 1881 v E (1)
Goss, J. (Norwich C), 1991 v Ic, Pol (sub); 1992 v A; 1994 v Cy (sub), R (sub), Se; 1995 v Alb; 1996 v Sw (sub), Sm (sub) (9)
Gough, R. T. (Oswestry White Star), 1883 v S (1)
Gray, A. (Oldham Ath), 1924 v E, S, Ni; 1925 v E, S, Ni; 1926 v E, S; 1927 v S; (with Manchester C), 1928 v E, S; 1929 v E, S, Ni; (with Manchester Central), 1930 v S; (with Tranmere R), 1932 v E, S, Ni; (with Chester), 1937 v E, S, Ni; 1938 v E, S, Ni (24)
Green, A. W. (Aston Villa), 1901 v Ni; (with Notts Co), 1903 v E; 1904 v S, Ni; 1906 v Ni, E; (with Nottingham F), 1907 v E; 1908 v S (8)
Green, C. R. (Birmingham C), 1965 v USSR, I; 1966 v E, S, USSR, Br (2); 1967 v E; 1968 v E, S, Ni, WG; 1969 v S, I, Ni (sub) (15)
Green, G. H. (Charlton Ath), 1938 v Ni; 1939 v E, Ni, F (4)
Green, R. M. (Wolverhampton W), 1998 v Ma, Tun (2)
Grey, Dr W. (Druids), 1876 v S; 1878 v S (2)
Griffiths, A. T. (Wrexham), 1971 v Cz (sub); 1975 v A, H (2), L (2), E, Ni; 1976 v A, E, S, E (sub), Ni, Y (2); 1977 v WG, S (17)
Griffiths, F. J. (Blackpool), 1900 v E, S (2)
Griffiths, G. (Chirk), 1887 v Ni (1)
Griffiths, J. H. (Swansea T), 1953 v Ni (1)
Griffiths, L. (Wrexham), 1902 v S (1)
Griffiths, M. W. (Leicester C), 1947 v Ni; 1949 v P, Bel; 1950 v E, S, Bel; 1951 v E, Ni, P, Sw; 1954 v A (11)
Griffiths, P. (Chirk), 1884 v E, Ni; 1888 v E; 1890 v S, Ni; 1891 v Ni (6)
Griffiths, P. H. (Everton), 1932 v S (1)
Griffiths, T. P. (Everton), 1927 v E, Ni; 1929 v E; 1930 v E; 1931 v Ni; 1932 v Ni, S, E; (with Bolton W), 1933 v E, S, Ni; (with Middlesbrough), F; 1934 v E, S; 1935 v E, Ni; 1936 v S; (with Aston Villa), Ni; 1937 v E, S, Ni (21)

Hall, G. D. (Chelsea), 1988 v Y (sub), Ma, I; 1989 v Ho, Fi, Is; 1990 v Ei; 1991 v Ei; 1992 v A (sub) (9)
Hallam, J. (Oswestry), 1889 v E (1)
Hanford, H. (Swansea T), 1934 v Ni; 1935 v S; 1936 v E; (with Sheffield W), 1936 v Ni; 1938 v E, S; 1939 v F (7)
Harrington, A. C. (Cardiff C), 1956 v Ni; 1957 v E, S; 1958 v S, Ni, Is (2); 1961 v S, E; 1962 v E, S (11)
Harris, C. S. (Leeds U), 1976 v E, S; 1978 v WG, Ir, E, S, Ni; 1979 v Ma, T, WG, E (sub), Ma; 1980 v Ni (sub), Ic (sub); 1981 v T, Cz (sub), Ei, T, S, E, USSR; 1982 v Cz, Ic, E (sub) (24)
Harris, W. C. (Middlesbrough), 1954 v A; 1957 v EG, Cz; 1958 v E, S, EG (6)
Harrison, W. C. (Wrexham), 1899 v E; 1900 v E, S, Ni; 1901 v Ni (5)
Hartson, J. (Arsenal), 1995 v Bul, G (sub), Ge (sub); 1996 v Mol (sub), Sw; 1997 v Ho, T (sub), Ei; (with West Ham U), Bel (sub), S; 1998 v Bel, Jam, Ma, Tun; (with Wimbledon), 1999 v Sw (sub), I (sub), D; 2000 v Sw (sub); 2001 v N, Pol; (with Coventry C), Arm, Uk, Pol, Uk; (with Celtic), 2002 v N, Bl, Arg, CzR, G; 2003 v Cro, Fi, I, Az, Bos, Az; 2004 v I, Fi, Ser, Ru (2) (40)
Haworth, S. O. (Cardiff C), 1997 v S (sub); (with Coventry C), 1998 v Br, Jam (sub), Ma (sub), Tun (sub) (5)
Hayes, A. (Wrexham), 1890 v Ni; 1894 v Ni (2)
Hennessey, W. T. (Birmingham C), 1962 v Ni, Br (2); 1963 v S, E, H (2); 1964 v E, S; 1965 v S, E, D, Gr, USSR; 1966 v E, USSR; (with Nottingham F), 1966 v S, Ni, D, Br (2), Ch; 1967 v S, E; 1968 v E, S, Ni; 1969 v WG, EG, R of UK; 1970 v EG; (with Derby Co), E, S, Ni; 1972 v Fi, Cz, E, S; 1973 v E (39)
Hersee, A. M. (Bangor), 1886 v S, Ni (2)

Hersee, R. (Llandudno), 1886 v Ni (1)
Hewitt, R. (Cardiff C), 1958 v Ni, Is, Se, H, Br (5)
Hewitt, T. J. (Wrexham), 1911 v E, S, Ni; (with Chelsea), 1913 v E, S, Ni; (with South Liverpool), 1914 v E, S (8)
Heywood, D. (Druids), 1879 v E (1)
Hibbott, H. (Newtown Excelsior), 1880 v E, S; (with Newtown), 1885 v S (3)
Higham, G. G. (Oswestry), 1878 v S; 1879 v E (2)
Hill, M. R. (Ipswich T), 1972 v Cz, R (2)
Hockey, T. (Sheffield U), 1972 v Fi, R; 1973 v E (2); (with Norwich C), Pol, S, E, Ni; (with Aston Villa), 1974 v Pol (9)
Hoddinott, T. F. (Watford), 1921 v E, S (2)
Hodges, G. (Wimbledon), 1984 v N (sub), Is (sub); 1987 v USSR, Fi, Cz; (with Newcastle U), 1988 v D; (with Watford), D (sub), Cz (sub), Se, Ma (sub), I (sub); 1990 v Se, Cr; (with Sheffield U), 1992 v Br (sub), Ei (sub), A; 1996 v G (sub), I (18)
Hodgkinson, A. V. (Southampton), 1908 v Ni (1)
Holden, A. (Chester C), 1984 v Is (sub) (1)
Hole, B. G. (Cardiff C), 1963 v Ni; 1964 v Ni; 1965 v S, E, Ni, D, Gr (2), USSR, I; 1966 v E, S, Ni, USSR, D, Br (2), Ch; (with Blackburn R), 1967 v S, E, Ni; 1968 v E, S, Ni, WG; (with Aston Villa), 1969 v I, WG, EG; 1970 v I; (with Swansea C), 1971 v R (30)
Hole, W. J. (Swansea T), 1921 v Ni; 1922 v E; 1923 v E, Ni; 1928 v E, S, Ni; 1929 v E, S (9)
Hollins, D. M. (Newcastle U), 1962 v Br (sub), M; 1963 v Ni, H; 1964 v E; 1965 v Ni, Gr, I; 1966 v S, D, Br (11)
Hopkins, I. J. (Brentford), 1935 v S, Ni; 1936 v E, Ni; 1937 v E, S, Ni; 1938 v E, Ni; 1939 v E, S, Ni (12)
Hopkins, J. (Fulham), 1983 v Ni, Br; 1984 v N, R, Bul, Y, S, E, Ni, N, Is; 1985 v Ic (1 + 1 sub), N; (with C Palace), 1990 v Ho, Cr (16)
Hopkins, M. (Tottenham H), 1956 v Ni; 1957 v Ni, S, E, Cz (2), EG; 1958 v E, S, Ni, EG, Is (2), H (2), M, Se, Br; 1959 v E, S, Ni; 1960 v E, S; 1961 v Ni, H, Sp (2); 1962 v Ni, Br (2), M; 1963 v S, Ni, H (34)
Horne, B. (Portsmouth), 1988 v D (sub), Y, Se (sub), Ma, I; 1989 v Ho, Fi, Is; (with Southampton), Se, WG; 1990 v WG (sub), Ei, Se, Cr; 1991 v D, Bel (2), L, Ei, Ic, Pol, WG; 1992 v Br, G, L, Ei, A, R, Ho, Arg, J; (with Everton), 1993 v Fa, Cy, Bel, Ei, Bel, RCS, Fa; 1994 v RCS, Cy, R, N, Se, Es; 1995 v Mol, Ge, Bul, G, Ge; 1996 v Mol, G, I, Sw, Sm; (with Birmingham C), 1997 v Sm, Ho, T, Ei, Bel (59)
Howell, E. G. (Builth), 1888 v Ni; 1890 v E; 1891 v E (3)
Howells, R. G. (Cardiff C), 1954 v E, S (2)
Hugh, A. R. (Newport Co), 1930 v Ni (1)
Hughes, A. (Rhos), 1894 v E, S (2)
Hughes, A. (Chirk), 1907 v Ni (1)
Hughes, C. M. (Luton T), 1992 v Ho (sub); 1994 v N (sub), Se (sub), Es; 1996 v Alb; 1997 v Ei (sub); (with Wimbledon), 1998 v T, Bel (8)
Hughes, E. (Everton), 1899 v S, Ni; (with Tottenham H), 1901 v E, S; 1902 v Ni; 1904 v E, Ni, S; 1905 v E, Ni, S; 1906 v E, Ni; 1907 v E (14)
Hughes, E. (Wrexham), 1906 v S; (with Nottingham F), 1906 v Ni; 1908 v S, E; 1910 v Ni, E, S; 1911 v Ni, E, S; (with Wrexham), 1912 v Ni, E, S; (with Manchester C), 1913 v E, S; 1914 v N (16)
Hughes, F. W. (Northwich Victoria), 1882 v E, Ni; 1883 v E, Ni, S; 1884 v S (6)
Hughes, I. (Luton T), 1951 v E, Ni, P, Sw (4)
Hughes, J. (Cambridge University), 1877 v S; (with Aberystwyth), 1879 v S (2)
Hughes, J. (Liverpool), 1905 v E, S, Ni (3)
Hughes, J. I. (Blackburn R), 1935 v Ni (1)
Hughes, L. M. (Manchester U), 1984 v E, Ni; 1985 v Ic, Sp, Ic, N, S, Sp, N; 1986 v S, H, U; (with Barcelona), 1987 v USSR, Cz; 1988 v D (2), Cz, Se, Ma, I; (with Manchester U), 1989 v Ho, Fi, Is, Se, WG; 1990 v Fi, WG, Cr; 1991 v D, Bel (2), L, Ic, Pol, WG; 1992 v Br, G, L, Ei, R, Ho, Arg, J; 1993 v Fa, Cy, Bel, Ei, Bel, RCS, Fa; 1994 v RCS, Cy, N; 1995 v Ge, Bul, G, Ge; (with Chelsea), 1996 v Mol, I, Sm; 1997 v Sm, Ho, T, Ei, Bel; 1998 v T; (with Southampton), 1999 v I, D, Bl, Sw, I, D (72)
Hughes, P. W. (Bangor), 1887 v Ni; 1889 v Ni, E (3)
Hughes, W. (Bootle), 1891 v E; 1892 v S, Ni (3)
Hughes, W. A. (Blackburn R), 1949 v E, Ni, P, Bel, Sw (5)
Hughes, W. M. (Birmingham), 1938 v E, Ni, S; 1939 v E, Ni, S, F; 1947 v E, S, Ni (10)
Humphreys, J. V. (Everton), 1947 v Ni (1)
Humphreys, R. (Druids), 1888 v Ni (1)
Hunter, A. H. (FA of Wales Secretary), 1887 v Ni (1)

Jackett, K. (Watford), 1983 v N, Y, E, Bul, S; 1984 v N, R, Y, S, Ni, N, Is; 1985 v Ic, Sp, Ic, N, S, Sp, N; 1986 v S, H, S.Ar, Ei, Ca (2); 1987 v Fi (2); 1988 v D, Cz, Y, Se (31)
Jackson, W. (St Helens Rec), 1899 v Ni (1)
James, E. (Chirk), 1893 v E, Ni; 1894 v E, S, Ni; 1898 v S, E; 1899 v Ni (8)
James, E. G. (Blackpool), 1966 v Br (2), Ch; 1967 v Ni; 1968 v S; 1971 v Cz, S, E, Ni (9)
James, L. (Burnley), 1972 v Cz, R, S (sub); 1973 v E (3), Pol, S, Ni; 1974 v Pol, E, S, Ni; 1975 v A, H (2), L (2), S, E, Ni; 1976 v A; (with Derby Co), S, E, Y (2), Ni; 1977 v WG, S (2), Cz, E, Ni; 1978 v K (2); (with QPR), WG; (with Burnley), 1979 v T; (with Swansea C), 1980 v E, S, Ni, Ic; 1981 v T, Ei, T, S, E; 1982 v Cz, Ic, USSR, E (sub), S, Ni, F; (with Sunderland), 1983 v E (sub) (54)
James, R. M. (Swansea C), 1979 v Ma, WG (sub), S, E, Ni, Ma; 1980 v WG; 1982 v Cz (sub), Ic, Sp, E, S, Ni, F; 1983 v N, Y, E, Bul; (with Stoke C), 1984 v N, R, Bul, Y, S, E, Ni, N, Is; 1985 v Ic, Sp, Ic; (with QPR), N, S, Sp, N; 1986 v S, S.Ar, Ei, U, Ca (2); 1987 v Fi (2), USSR, Cz; (with Leicester C), 1988 v D (2); (with Swansea C), Y (47)
James, W. (West Ham U), 1931 v Ni; 1932 v Ni (2)
Jarrett, R. H. (Ruthin), 1889 v Ni; 1890 v S (2)
Jarvis, A. L. (Hull C), 1967 v S, E, Ni (3)
Jenkins, E. (Lovell's Ath), 1925 v E (1)
Jenkins, J. (Brighton), 1924 v Ni, E, S; 1925 v S, Ni; 1926 v E, S; 1927 v S (8)
Jenkins, R. W. (Rhyl), 1902 v Ni (1)
Jenkins, S. R. (Swansea C), 1996 v G; (with Huddersfield T), Alb, I; 1997 v Ho (sub), T, S; 1998 v T, Bel, Br, Jam; 1999 v I (sub), D; 2001 v Pol (sub), Uk (sub); 2002 v Arm, N (16)
Jenkyns, C. A. L. (Small Heath), 1892 v E, S, Ni; 1895 v E; (with Woolwich Arsenal), 1896 v S; (with Newton Heath), 1897 v Ni; (with Walsall), 1898 v S, E (8)
Jennings, W. (Bolton W), 1914 v E, S; 1920 v S; 1923 v Ni, E; 1924 v E, S, Ni; 1927 v S, Ni; 1929 v S (11)
John, R. F. (Arsenal), 1923 v S, Ni; 1925 v Ni; 1926 v E; 1927 v E; 1928 v E, Ni; 1930 v E, S; 1932 v E; 1933 v F, Ni; 1935 v Ni; 1936 v S; 1937 v E (15)
John, W. R. (Walsall), 1931 v Ni; (with Stoke C), 1933 v E, S, Ni, F; 1934 v E, S; (with Preston NE), 1935 v E, S; (with Sheffield U), 1936 v E, S, Ni; (with Swansea T), 1939 v E, S (14)
Johnson, A. J. (Nottingham F), 1999 v I, D, Bl, Sw; 2000 v Fi (sub), Br (sub), P (sub); (with WBA), 2003 v Cro, Fi, US; 2004 v I (sub), Fi (sub), Ru (2) (14)
Johnson, M. G. (Swansea T), 1964 v Ni (1)
Jones, A. (Port Vale), 1987 v Fi, Cz (sub); 1988 v D, (with Charlton Ath), D (sub), Cz (sub); 1990 v Hol (sub) (6)
Jones, A. F. (Oxford University), 1877 v S (1)
Jones, A. T. (Nottingham F), 1905 v E; (with Notts Co), 1906 v E (2)
Jones, Bryn (Wolverhampton W), 1935 v Ni; 1936 v E, S, Ni; 1937 v E, S, Ni; 1938 v E, S, Ni; (with Arsenal), 1939 v E, S, Ni; 1947 v S, Ni; 1948 v E; 1949 v S (17)
Jones, B. S. (Swansea T), 1963 v S, E, Ni, H (2); 1964 v S, Ni; (with Plymouth Arg), 1965 v D; (with Cardiff C), 1969 v S, E, Ni, I (sub), WG, EG, R of UK (15)
Jones, Charlie (Nottingham F), 1926 v E; 1927 v S, Ni; 1928 v E; (with Arsenal), 1930 v E, S; 1932 v E; 1933 v F (8)
Jones, Cliff (Swansea T), 1954 v A; 1956 v E, Ni, S, A; 1957 v E, S, Ni, Cz (2), EG; 1958 v EG, E, S, Is (2); (with Tottenham H), 1958 v Ni, H (2), M, Se, Br; 1959 v Ni; 1960 v E, S, Ni; 1961 v S, E, Ni, Sp, H, Ei; 1962 v E, Ni, S, Br (2), M; 1963 v S, Ni, H; 1964 v E, S, Ni; 1965 v E, S, Ni, D, Gr (2), USSR, I; 1967 v S, E; 1968 v E, S, WG; (with Fulham), 1969 v I, R of UK (59)
Jones, C. W. (Birmingham), 1935 v Ni; 1939 v F (2)
Jones, D. (Chirk), 1888 v S, Ni; (with Bolton W), 1889 v E, S, Ni; 1890 v E; 1891 v S; 1892 v Ni; 1893 v E; 1894 v E; 1895 v E; 1898 v S; (with Manchester C), 1900 v E, Ni (14)
Jones, D. E. (Norwich C), 1976 v S, E (sub); 1978 v S, Cz, WG, Ir, E; 1980 v E (8)
Jones, D. O. (Leicester C), 1934 v E, Ni; 1935 v E, S; 1936 v E, Ni; 1937 v Ni (7)
Jones, Evan (Chelsea), 1910 v S, Ni; (with Oldham Ath), 1911 v E, S; 1912 v E, S; (with Bolton W), 1914 v Ni (7)
Jones, F. R. (Bangor), 1885 v E, Ni; 1886 v S (3)
Jones, F. W. (Small Heath), 1893 v S (1)
Jones, G. P. (Wrexham), 1907 v S, Ni (2)
Jones, H. (Aberaman), 1902 v Ni (1)
Jones, Humphrey (Bangor), 1885 v E, Ni, S; 1886 v E, Ni, S; (with Queen's Park), 1887 v E; (with East Stirlingshire), 1889 v E, Ni; 1890 v E, S, Ni; (with Queen's Park), 1891 v E, S (14)

Jones, Ivor (Swansea T), 1920 v S, Ni; 1921 v Ni, E; 1922 v S, Ni; (with WBA), 1923 v E, Ni; 1924 v S; 1926 v Ni (10)
Jones, Jeffrey (Llandrindod Wells), 1908 v Ni; 1909 v Ni; 1910 v S (3)
Jones, J. (Druids), 1876 v S (1)
Jones, J. (Berwyn Rangers), 1883 v S, Ni; 1884 v S (3)
Jones, J. (Wrexham), 1925 v Ni (1)
Jones, J. L. (Sheffield U), 1895 v E, S, Ni; 1896 v Ni, S, E; 1897 v Ni, S, E; (with Tottenham H), 1898 v Ni, E, S; 1899 v S, Ni; 1900 v S; 1902 v E, S, Ni; 1904 v E, S, Ni (21)
Jones, J. Love (Stoke C), 1906 v S; (with Middlesbrough), 1910 v Ni (2)
Jones, J. O. (Bangor), 1901 v S, Ni (2)
Jones, J. P. (Liverpool), 1976 v A, E, S; 1977 v WG, S (2), Cz, E, Ni; 1978 v K (2), S, Cz, WG, Ir, E, S, Ni; (with Wrexham), 1979 v Ma, T, WG, S, E, Ni, Ma; 1980 v Ei, WG, T, E, S, Ni, Ic; 1981 v T, Ei, T, S, E, USSR; 1982 v Cz, Ic, USSR, Sp, E, S, Ni, F; 1983 v N; (with Chelsea), Y, E, Bul, S, Ni, Br; 1984 v N, R, Bul, Y, S, E, Ni, N, Is; 1985 v Ic, N, S, N; (with Huddersfield T), 1986 v S, H, Ei, U, Ca (2) (72)
Jones, J. T. (Stoke C), 1912 v E, S, Ni; 1913 v E, Ni; 1914 v S, Ni; 1920 v E, S, Ni; (with C Palace), 1921 v E, S; 1922 v E, S, Ni (15)
Jones, K. (Aston Villa), 1950 v S (1)
Jones, Leslie J. (Cardiff C), 1933 v F; (with Coventry C), 1935 v Ni; 1936 v S; 1937 v E, S, Ni; (with Arsenal), 1938 v E, S, Ni; 1939 v E, S (11)
Jones, M. G. (Leeds U), 2000 v Sw (sub), Q, Br, P; 2001 v Pol (sub); (with Leicester C), Arm (sub), Uk, Pol (sub); 2002 v Arm (sub), N (sub), Bl; 2003 v Bos (sub), US (13)
Jones, P. L. (Liverpool), 1997 v S (sub); (with Tranmere R), 1998 v T (sub) (2)
Jones, P. S. (Stockport Co), 1997 v S (sub); (with Southampton), 1998 v T (sub), Br, Jam, Ma; 1999 v I, D, Bl, Sw, I, D; 2000 v Bl, Sw, Q; 2001 v Bl, N, Pol, Arm, Uk, Pol, Uk; 2002 v Arm, N, Bl, Arg; 2003 v Cro, Fi, I, Az (2), US; 2004 v Ser, I, Fi, Ser, Ru (2); (with Wolverhampton W), H (38)
Jones, P. W. (Bristol R), 1971 v Fi (1)
Jones, R. (Bangor), 1887 v S; 1889 v E; (with Crewe Alex), 1890 v E (3)
Jones, R. (Leicester Fosse), 1898 v S (1)
Jones, R. (Druids), 1899 v S (1)
Jones, R. (Bangor), 1900 v S, Ni (2)
Jones, R. (Millwall), 1906 v S, Ni (2)
Jones, R. A. (Druids), 1884 v E, Ni, S; 1885 v S (4)
Jones, R. A. (Sheffield W), 1994 v Es (1)
Jones, R. S. (Everton), 1894 v Ni (1)
Jones, S. (Wrexham), 1887 v Ni; (with Chester), 1890 v S (2)
Jones, S. (Wrexham), 1893 v S, Ni; (with Burton Swifts), 1895 v S; 1896 v E, Ni; (with Druids), 1899 v E (6)
Jones, T. (Manchester U), 1926 v Ni; 1927 v E, Ni; 1930 v Ni (4)
Jones, T. D. (Aberdare), 1908 v Ni (1)
Jones, T. G. (Everton), 1938 v Ni; 1939 v E, S, Ni; 1947 v E, S; 1948 v E, S, Ni; 1949 v E, Ni, P, Bel, Sw; 1950 v E, S, Bel (17)
Jones, T. J. (Sheffield W), 1932 v Ni; 1933 v F (2)
Jones, V. P. (Wimbledon), 1995 v Bul (2), G, Ge; 1996 v Sw; 1997 v Ho, T, Ei, Bel (9)
Jones, W. E. A. (Swansea T), 1947 v E, S; (with Tottenham H), 1949 v E, S (4)
Jones, W. J. (Aberdare), 1901 v E, S; (with West Ham U), 1902 v E, S (4)
Jones, W. Lot (Manchester C), 1905 v E, Ni; 1906 v E, S, Ni; 1907 v E, S, Ni; 1908 v S; 1909 v E, S, Ni; 1910 v E; 1911 v E; 1913 v E, S; 1914 v S, Ni; (with Southend U), 1920 v E, Ni (20)
Jones, W. P. (Druids), 1889 v E, Ni; (with Wynstay), 1890 v S, Ni (4)
Jones, W. R. (Aberystwyth), 1897 v S (1)

Keenor, F. C. (Cardiff C), 1920 v E, Ni; 1921 v E, Ni, S; 1922 v Ni; 1923 v E, Ni, S; 1924 v E, Ni, S; 1925 v E, Ni, S; 1926 v S; 1927 v E, Ni, S; 1928 v E, Ni, S; 1929 v E, Ni, S; 1930 v E, Ni, S; 1931 v E, Ni, S; (with Crewe Alex), 1933 v S (32)
Kelly, F. C. (Wrexham), 1899 v S, Ni; (with Druids), 1902 v Ni (3)
Kelsey, A. J. (Arsenal), 1954 v Ni, A; 1955 v S, Ni, Y; 1956 v E, Ni, S, A; 1957 v E, Ni, S, Cz (2), EG; 1958 v E, S, Ni, Is (2), H (2), M, Se, Br; 1959 v E, S; 1960 v E, Ni, S; 1961 v E, Ni, S, H, Sp (2); 1962 v E, S, Ni, Br (2) (41)
Kenrick, S. L. (Druids), 1876 v S; 1877 v S; (with Oswestry), 1879 v E, S; (with Shropshire Wanderers), 1881 v E (5)
Ketley, C. F. (Druids), 1882 v Ni (1)
King, J. (Swansea T), 1955 v E (1)
Kinsey, N. (Norwich C), 1951 v Ni, P, Sw; 1952 v E; (with Birmingham C), 1954 v Ni; 1956 v E, S (7)
Knill, A. R. (Swansea C), 1989 v Ho (1)
Koumas, J. (Tranmere R), 2001 v Uk (sub); 2002 v CzR; (with WBA), 2003 v Bos (sub), US; 2004 v I, Fi, Ru (2), H (9)
Krzywicki, R. L. (WBA), 1970 v EG, I; (with Huddersfield T), Ni, E, S; 1971 v R, Fi; 1972 v Cz (sub) (8)

Lambert, R. (Liverpool), 1947 v S; 1948 v E; 1949 v P, Bel, Sw (5)
Latham, G. (Liverpool), 1905 v E, S; 1906 v S; 1907 v E, S, Ni; 1908 v E; 1909 v Ni; (with Southport Central), 1910 v E; (with Cardiff C), 1913 v Ni (10)
Law, B. J. (QPR), 1990 v Se (1)
Lawrence, E. (Clapton Orient), 1930 v Ni; (with Notts Co), 1932 v S (2)
Lawrence, S. (Swansea T), 1932 v Ni; 1933 v F; 1934 v S, E, Ni; 1935 v E, S; 1936 v S (8)
Lea, A. (Wrexham), 1889 v E; 1891 v S, Ni; 1893 v Ni (4)
Lea, C. (Ipswich T), 1965 v Ni, I (2)
Leary, P. (Bangor), 1889 v Ni (1)
Leek, K. (Leicester C), 1961 v S, E, Ni, H, Sp (2); (with Newcastle U), 1962 v S; (with Birmingham C), v Br (sub), M; 1963 v E; 1965 v S, Gr; (with Northampton T), 1965 v Gr (13)
Legg, A. (Birmingham C), 1996 v Sw, Sm (sub); 1997 v Ho (sub), Ei; (with Cardiff C), 1999 v D (sub); 2001 v Arm (6)
Lever, A. R. (Leicester C), 1953 v S (1)
Lewis, B. (Chester), 1891 v Ni; (with Wrexham), 1892 v S, E, Ni; (with Middlesbrough), 1893 v S, E; (with Wrexham), 1894 v S, E, Ni; 1895 v S (10)
Lewis, D. (Arsenal), 1927 v E; 1928 v Ni; 1930 v E (3)
Lewis, D. (Swansea C), 1983 v Br (sub) (1)
Lewis, D. J. (Swansea T), 1933 v E, S (2)
Lewis, D. M. (Bangor), 1890 v Ni, S (2)
Lewis, J. (Bristol R), 1906 v E (1)
Lewis, J. (Cardiff C), 1926 v S (1)
Lewis, T. (Wrexham), 1881 v E, S (2)
Lewis, W. (Bangor), 1885 v E; 1886 v E, S; 1887 v E, S; 1888 v E; 1889 v E, Ni, S; (with Crewe Alex), 1890 v E; 1891 v E, S; 1892 v E, S, Ni; 1894 v E, S, Ni; (with Chester), 1895 v S, Ni, E; 1896 v E, S, Ni; (with Manchester C), 1897 v E, S; (with Chester), 1898 v Ni (27)
Lewis, W. L. (Swansea T), 1927 v E, Ni; 1928 v E, Ni; 1929 v S; (with Huddersfield T), 1930 v E (6)
Llewellyn, C. M. (Norwich C), 1998 v Ma (sub), Tun (sub); (with Wrexham), 2004 v N (sub), Ca (sub) (4)
Lloyd, B. W. (Wrexham), 1976 v A, E, S (3)
Lloyd, J. W. (Wrexham), 1879 v S; (with Newtown), 1885 v S (2)
Lloyd, R. A. (Ruthin), 1891 v Ni; 1895 v S (2)
Lockley, A. (Chirk), 1898 v Ni (1)
Lovell, S. (C Palace), 1982 v USSR (sub); (with Millwall), 1985 v N; 1986 v S (sub), H (sub), Ca (1+1 sub) (6)
Lowrie, G. (Coventry C), 1948 v E, S, Ni; (with Newcastle U), 1949 v P (4)
Lowndes, S. (Newport Co), 1983 v S (sub), Br (sub); (with Millwall), 1985 v N (sub); 1986 v S.Ar (sub), Ei, U, Ca (2); (with Barnsley), 1987 v Fi (sub); 1988 v Se (sub) (10)
Lucas, P. M. (Leyton Orient), 1962 v Ni, M; 1963 v S, E (4)
Lucas, W. H. (Swansea T), 1949 v S, Ni, P, Bel, Sw; 1950 v E; 1951 v E (7)
Lumberg, A. (Wrexham), 1929 v Ni; 1930 v E, S; (with Wolverhampton W), 1932 v S (4)

McCarthy, T. P. (Wrexham), 1899 v Ni (1)
McMillan, R. (Shrewsbury Engineers), 1881 v E, S (2)
Maguire, G. T. (Portsmouth), 1990 v Fi (sub), Ho, WG, Ei, Se; 1992 v Br (sub), G (7)
Mahoney, J. F. (Stoke C), 1968 v E; 1969 v EG; 1971 v Cz; 1973 v E (3), Pol, S, Ni; 1974 v Pol, E, S, Ni; 1975 v A, H (2), L (2), S, E, Ni; 1976 v A, Y (2), E, Ni; 1977 v WG, Cz, S, E, Ni; (with Middlesbrough), 1978 v K (2), S, Cz, Ir, E (sub), S, Ni; 1979 v WG, S, E, Ni, Ma; (with Swansea C), 1980 v Ei, WG, T (sub); 1982 v Ic, USSR; 1983 v Y, E (51)
Mardon, P. J. (WBA), 1996 v G (sub) (1)
Margetson, M. W. (Cardiff C), 2004 v Ca (sub) (1)
Marriott, A. (Wrexham), 1996 v Sw (sub); 1997 v S; 1998 v Bel, Br (sub), Tun (5)
Martin, T. J. (Newport Co), 1930 v Ni (1)
Marustik, C. (Swansea C), 1982 v Sp, E, S, Ni, F; 1983 v N (6)
Mates, J. (Chirk), 1891 v Ni; 1897 v E, S (3)
Mathews, R. W. (Liverpool), 1921 v Ni; (with Bristol C), 1923 v E; (with Bradford), 1926 v Ni (3)
Matthews, W. (Chester), 1905 v Ni; 1908 v E (2)

Matthias, J. S. (Brymbo), 1896 v S, Ni; (with Shrewsbury), 1897 v E, S; (with Wolverhampton W), 1899 v S (5)
Matthias, T. J. (Wrexham), 1914 v S, E; 1920 v Ni, S, E; 1921 v S, E, Ni; 1922 v S, E, Ni; 1923 v S (12)
Mays, A. W. (Wrexham), 1929 v Ni (1)
Medwin, T. C. (Swansea T), 1953 v Ni, F, Y; (with Tottenham H), 1957 v E, S, Ni, Cz (2), EG; 1958 v E, S, Ni, Is (2), H (2), M, Br; 1959 v E, S, Ni; 1960 v E, S, Ni; 1961 v S, Ei, E, Sp; 1963 v E, H (30)
Melville, A. K. (Swansea C), 1990 v WG, Ei, Se, Cr (sub); (with Oxford U), 1991 v Ic, Pol, WG; 1992 v Br, G, L, R, Ho, J (sub); 1993 v RCS, Fa (sub); (with Sunderland), 1994 v RCS (sub), R, N, Se, Es; 1995 v Alb, Mol (sub), Ge, Bul; 1996 v G, Alb, Sm; 1997 v Sm, Ho (2), T; 1998 v T; (with Fulham), 1999 v I, D; 2000 v Bl, Q, Fi, Br, P; 2001 v Bl, N, Pol, Arm, Uk, Pol, Uk; 2002 v Arm, Bl, Arg, CzR, G; 2003 v Cro, Fi, I, Az, Bos, Az, US; 2004 v Fi, Ru (2); (with West Ham U), S, H (63)
Meredith, S. (Chirk), 1900 v S; 1901 v S, E, Ni; (with Stoke C), 1902 v E; 1903 v Ni; 1904 v E; (with Leyton), 1907 v E (8)
Meredith, W. H. (Manchester C), 1895 v E, Ni; 1896 v E, Ni; 1897 v E, Ni, S; 1898 v E, Ni; 1899 v E; 1900 v E, Ni; 1901 v E, Ni; 1902 v E, S; 1903 v E, S, Ni; 1904 v E; 1905 v E, S; (with Manchester U), 1907 v E, S, Ni; 1908 v E, Ni; 1909 v E, S, Ni; 1910 v E, S, Ni; 1911 v E, S, Ni; 1912 v E, S, Ni; 1913 v E, S, Ni; 1914 v E, S, Ni; 1920 v E, S, Ni (48)
Mielczarek, R. (Rotherham U), 1971 v Fi (1)
Millership, H. (Rotherham Co), 1920 v E, S, Ni; 1921 v E, S, Ni (6)
Millington, A. H. (WBA), 1963 v S, E, H; (with C Palace), 1965 v E, USSR; (with Peterborough U), 1966 v Ch, Br; 1967 v E, Ni; 1968 v Ni, WG; 1969 v I, EG; (with Swansea T), 1970 v E, S, Ni; 1971 v Cz, Fi; 1972 v Fi (sub), Cz, R (21)
Mills, T. J. (Clapton Orient), 1934 v E, Ni; (with Leicester C), 1935 v E, S (4)
Mills-Roberts, R. H. (St Thomas' Hospital), 1885 v E, S, Ni; 1886 v E; 1887 v E; (with Preston NE), 1888 v E, Ni; (with Llanberis), 1892 v E (8)
Moore, G. (Cardiff C), 1960 v E, S, Ni; 1961 v Ei, Sp; (with Chelsea), 1962 v Br; 1963 v Ni, H; (with Manchester U), 1964 v S, Ni; (with Northampton T), 1966 v Ni, Ch; (with Charlton Ath), 1969 v S, E, Ni, R of UK; 1970 v E, S, Ni, I; 1971 v R (21)
Morgan, J. R. (Cambridge University), 1877 v S; (with Swansea T), 1879 v S; (with Derby School Staff), 1880 v E, S; 1881 v E, S; 1882 v E, S, Ni; (with Swansea T), 1883 v E (10)
Morgan, J. T. (Wrexham), 1905 v Ni (1)
Morgan-Owen, H. (Oxford University), 1902 v S; 1906 v E, Ni; (with Welshpool), 1907 v S (5)
Morgan-Owen, M. M. (Oxford University), 1897 v S, Ni; 1898 v E, S; 1899 v S; 1900 v E; (with Corinthians), 1901 v S, E; 1903 v S; 1906 v S, E, Ni; 1907 v E (13)
Morley, E. J. (Swansea T), 1925 v E; (with Clapton Orient), 1929 v E, S, Ni (4)
Morris, A. G. (Aberystwyth), 1896 v E, Ni, S; (with Swindon T), 1897 v E; 1898 v S; (with Nottingham F), 1899 v E, S; 1903 v E, S; 1905 v E, S; 1907 v E, S; 1908 v E; 1910 v E, S, Ni; 1911 v E, S, Ni; 1912 v E (21)
Morris, C. (Chirk), 1900 v E, S, Ni; (with Derby Co), 1901 v E, S, Ni; 1902 v E; 1903 v E, S, Ni; 1904 v Ni; 1905 v E, S, Ni; 1906 v S; 1907 v S; 1908 v E, S; 1909 v E, S, Ni; 1910 v E, S, Ni; (with Huddersfield T), 1911 v E, S, Ni (27)
Morris, E. (Chirk), 1893 v E, S, Ni (3)
Morris, H. (Sheffield U), 1894 v S; (with Manchester C), 1896 v E; (with Grimsby T), 1897 v E (3)
Morris, J. (Oswestry), 1887 v S (1)
Morris, J. (Chirk), 1898 v Ni (1)
Morris, R. (Chirk), 1900 v E, Ni; 1901 v Ni; 1902 v S; (with Shrewsbury T), 1903 v E, Ni (6)
Morris, R. (Druids), 1902 v E, S; (with Newtown), Ni; (with Liverpool), 1903 v S, Ni; 1904 v E, S, Ni; (with Leeds C), 1906 v S; (with Grimsby T), 1907 v Ni; (with Plymouth Arg), 1908 v Ni (11)
Morris, S. (Birmingham), 1937 v E, S; 1938 v E, S; 1939 v F (5)
Morris, W. (Burnley), 1947 v Ni; 1949 v E; 1952 v S, Ni, R of UK (5)
Moulsdale, J. R. B. (Corinthians), 1925 v Ni (1)
Murphy, J. P. (WBA), 1933 v F, E, Ni; 1934 v E, S; 1935 v E, S, Ni; 1936 v E, S, Ni; 1937 v S, Ni; 1938 v E, S (15)

Nardiello, D. (Coventry C), 1978 v Cz, WG (sub) (2)
Neal, J. E. (Colwyn Bay), 1931 v E, S (2)
Neilson, A. B. (Newcastle U), 1992 v Ei; 1994 v Se, Es; 1995 v Ge; (with Southampton), 1997 v Ho (5)
Newnes, J. (Nelson), 1926 v Ni (1)
Newton, L. F. (Cardiff Corinthians), 1912 v Ni (1)
Nicholas, D. S. (Stoke C), 1923 v S; (with Swansea T), 1927 v E, Ni (3)
Nicholas, P. (C Palace), 1979 v S (sub), Ni (sub), Ma; 1980 v Ei, WG, T, E, S, Ni, Ic; 1981 v T, Cz, E; (with Arsenal), T, S, E, USSR; 1982 v Cz, Ic, USSR, Sp, E, S, Ni, F; 1983 v Y, Bul, S, Ni; 1984 v N, Bul, N, Is; (with C Palace), 1985 v Sp; (with Luton T), N, S, Sp, N; 1986 v S, H, S.Ar, Ei, U, Ca (2); 1987 v Fi (2) USSR, Cz; (with Aberdeen), 1988 v D (2), Cz, Y, Se; (with Chelsea), 1989 v Ho, Fi, Is, Se, WG; 1990 v Fi, Ho, WG, Ei, Se, Cr; 1991 v D (sub), Bel, L, Ei; (with Watford), Bel, Pol, WG; 1992 v L (73)
Nicholls, J. (Newport Co), 1924 v E, Ni; (with Cardiff C), 1925 v E, S (4)
Niedzwiecki, E. A. (Chelsea), 1985 v N (sub); 1988 v D (2)
Nock, W. (Newtown), 1897 v Ni (1)
Nogan, L. M. (Watford), 1992 v A (sub); (with Reading), 1996 v Mol (2)
Norman, A. J. (Hull C), 1986 v Ei (sub), U, Ca; 1988 v Ma, I (5)
Nurse, M. T. G. (Swansea T), 1960 v E, Ni; 1961 v S, E, H, Ni, Ei, Sp (2); (with Middlesbrough), 1963 v E, H; 1964 v S (12)

O'Callaghan, E. (Tottenham H), 1929 v Ni; 1930 v S; 1932 v S, E; 1933 v Ni, S, E; 1934 v Ni, S, E; 1935 v E (11)
Oliver, A. (Blackburn R), 1905 v E; (with Bangor), S (2)
Oster, J. M. (Everton), 1998 v Bel (sub), Br, Jam; (with Sunderland), 2000 v Sw; 2003 v Bos (sub), Az, US; 2004 v Ser (sub), S, N, Ca (11)
O'Sullivan, P. A. (Brighton), 1973 v S (sub); 1976 v S; 1979 v Ma (sub) (3)
Owen, D. (Oswestry), 1879 v E (1)
Owen, E. (Ruthin Grammar School), 1884 v E, Ni, S (3)
Owen, G. (Chirk), 1888 v S; (with Newton Heath), 1889 v S, Ni; 1893 v Ni (4)
Owen, J. (Newton Heath), 1892 v E (1)
Owen, Trevor (Crewe Alex), 1899 v E, S (2)
Owen, T. (Oswestry), 1879 v E (1)
Owen, W. (Chirk), 1884 v E; 1885 v Ni; 1887 v E; 1888 v E; 1889 v E, Ni, S; 1890 v S, Ni; 1891 v E, S, Ni; 1892 v E, S; 1893 v S, Ni (16)
Owen, W. P. (Ruthin), 1880 v E, S; 1881 v E, S; 1882 v E, S, Ni; 1883 v E, S; 1884 v E, S, Ni (12)
Owens, J. (Wrexham), 1902 v S (1)

Page, M. E. (Birmingham C), 1971 v Fi; 1972 v S, Ni; 1973 v E (1+1 sub), Ni; 1974 v S, Ni; 1975 v H, L, S, E, Ni; 1976 v E, Y (2), E, Ni; 1977 v WG, S; 1978 v K (sub+1), WG, Ir, E, S; 1979 v Ma, WG (28)
Page, R. J. (Watford), 1997 v T, Bel, S; 1998 v T, Bel (sub), Br, I; 2000 v Bl, Sw, Q, Fi, Br, P; 2001 v Bl, N, Pol, Arm, Uk, Pol, Uk; (with Sheffield U ), 2002 v N, Bl (sub), Arg, CzR, G; 2003 v Az, Bos, Az ; 2004 v Ser, I, Fi, S, H (33)
Palmer, D. (Swansea T), 1957 v Cz; 1958 v E, EG (3)
Parris, J. E. (Bradford), 1932 v Ni (1)
Parry, B. J. (Swansea T), 1951 v S (1)
Parry, C. (Everton), 1891 v E, S; 1893 v E; 1894 v E; 1895 v E, S; (with Newtown), 1896 v E, S, Ni; 1897 v Ni; 1898 v E, S, Ni (13)
Parry, E. (Liverpool), 1922 v S; 1923 v E, Ni; 1925 v Ni; 1926 v Ni (5)
Parry, M. (Liverpool), 1901 v E, S, Ni; 1902 v E, S, Ni; 1903 v E, S; 1904 v E, Ni; 1906 v E; 1908 v E, S, Ni; 1909 v E, S (16)
Parry, P. I. (Cardiff C), 2004 v S (sub), N, Ca (3)
Parry, T. D. (Oswestry), 1900 v E, S, Ni; 1901 v E, S, Ni; 1902 v E (7)
Parry, W. (Newtown), 1895 v Ni (1)
Pascoe, C. (Swansea C), 1984 v N, Is; (with Sunderland), 1989 v Fi, Is, WG (sub); 1990 v Ho (sub), WG (sub); 1991 v Ei, Ic (sub); 1992 v Br (10)
Paul, R. (Swansea T), 1949 v E, S, Ni, P, Sw; 1950 v E, S, Ni, Bel; (with Manchester C), 1951 v S, E, Ni, P, Sw; 1952 v E, S, Ni, R of UK; 1953 v S, E, Ni, F, Y; 1954 v E, S, Ni; 1955 v S, E, Y; 1956 v E, Ni, S, A (33)
Peake, E. (Aberystwyth), 1908 v Ni; (with Liverpool), 1909 v Ni, S, E; 1910 v S, Ni; 1911 v Ni; 1912 v E; 1913 v E, Ni; 1914 v Ni (11)
Peers, E. J. (Wolverhampton W), 1914 v Ni, S, E; 1920 v E, S; 1921 v S, Ni, E; (with Port Vale), 1922 v E, S, Ni; 1923 v E (12)
Pembridge, M. A. (Luton T), 1992 v Br, Ei, R; (with Derby Co), Ho, J (sub); 1993 v Bel (sub), Ei; 1994 v N (sub); 1995 v Alb (sub), Mol, Ge (sub); (with Sheffield W), 1996 v Mol, G, Alb, Sw, Sm; 1997 v Sm, Ho (2), T, Ei, Bel, S; 1998 v Bel, Br, Jam, Ma, Tun; (with Benfica), 1999 v D (sub), Bl, Sw, I (sub), D (sub); (with Everton), 2000 v Bl, Q, Fi; 2001 v Arm, Pol, Uk; 2002 v Bl, Arg, G; 2003 v Cro, Fi, I, Bos, Az, US; 2004 v Ser; (with Fulham), I, Fi (51)

Perry, E. (Doncaster R), 1938 v E, S, Ni (3)
Perry, J. (Cardiff C), 1994 v N (1)
Phennah, E. (Civil Service), 1878 v S (1)
Phillips, C. (Wolverhampton W), 1931 v Ni; 1932 v E; 1933 v S; 1934 v E, S, Ni; 1935 v E, S, Ni; 1936 v S; (with Aston Villa), 1936 v E, Ni; 1938 v S (13)
Phillips, D. (Plymouth Arg), 1984 v E, Ni, N; (with Manchester C), 1985 v Sp, Ic, S, Sp, N; 1986 v S, H, S.Ar, Ei, U; (with Coventry C), 1987 v Fi, Cz; 1988 v D (2), Cz, Y, Se; 1989 v Se, WG; (with Norwich C), 1990 v Fi, Ho, WG, Ei, Se; 1991 v D, Bel, Ic, Pol, WG; 1992 v L, Ei, A, R, Ho (sub), Arg, J; 1993 v Fa, Cy, Bel, Ei, Bel, RCS, Fa; (with Nottingham F), 1994 v RCS, Cy, R, N, Se, Es; 1995 v Alb, Mol, Ge, Bul (2), G, Ge; 1996 v Mol (sub), Alb, I (62)
Phillips, L. (Cardiff C), 1971 v Cz, S, E, Ni; 1972 v Cz, R, S, Ni; 1973 v E; 1974 v Pol (sub), Ni; 1975 v A; (with Aston Villa), H (2), L (2), S, E, Ni; 1976 v A, E, Y (2), E, Ni; 1977 v WG, S (2), Cz, E; 1978 v K (2), S, Cz, WG, E, S; 1979 v Ma; (with Swansea C), T, WG, S, E, Ni, Ma; 1980 v Ei, WG, T, S (sub), Ni, Ic; 1981 v T, Cz, T, S, E, USSR; (with Charlton Ath), 1982 v Cz, USSR (58)
Phillips, T. J. S. (Chelsea), 1973 v E; 1974 v E; 1975 v H (sub); 1978 v K (4)
Phoenix, H. (Wrexham), 1882 v S (1)
Pipe, D. R. (Coventry C), 2003 v US (sub) (1)
Poland, G. (Wrexham), 1939 v Ni, F (2)
Pontin, K. (Cardiff C), 1980 v E (sub), S (2)
Powell, A. (Leeds U), 1947 v E, S; 1948 v E, S, Ni; (with Everton), 1949 v E; 1950 v Bel; (with Birmingham C), 1951 v S (8)
Powell, D. (Wrexham), 1968 v WG; (with Sheffield U), 1969 v S, E, Ni, I, WG; 1970 v E, S, Ni, EG; 1971 v R (11)
Powell, I. V. (QPR), 1947 v E; 1948 v E, S, Ni; (with Aston Villa), 1949 v Bel; 1950 v S, Bel; 1951 v S (8)
Powell, J. (Druids), 1878 v S; 1880 v E, S; 1882 v E, S, Ni; 1883 v E, S, Ni; (with Bolton W), 1884 v E; (with Newton Heath), 1887 v E, S; 1888 v E, S, Ni (15)
Powell, Seth (WBA), 1885 v S; 1886 v E, Ni; 1891 v E, S; 1892 v E, S (7)
Price, H. (Aston Villa), 1907 v S; (with Burton U), 1908 v Ni; (with Wrexham), 1909 v S, E, Ni (5)
Price, J. (Wrexham), 1877 v S; 1878 v S; 1879 v E; 1880 v E, S; 1881 v E, S; (with Druids), 1882 v S, E, Ni; 1883 v S, Ni (12)
Price, P. (Luton T), 1980 v E, S, Ni, Ic; 1981 v T, Cz, Ei, T, S, E, USSR; (with Tottenham H), 1982 v USSR, Sp, F; 1983 v N, Y, E, Bul, S, Ni; 1984 v N, R, Bul, Y, S (sub) (25)
Pring, K. D. (Rotherham U), 1966 v Ch, D; 1967 v Ni (3)
Pritchard, H. K. (Bristol C), 1985 v N (sub) (1)
Pryce-Jones, A. W. (Newtown), 1895 v E (1)
Pryce-Jones, W. E. (Cambridge University), 1887 v S; 1888 v S, E, Ni; 1890 v Ni (5)
Pugh, A. (Rhostyllen), 1889 v S (sub) (1)
Pugh, D. H. (Wrexham), 1896 v S, Ni; 1897 v S, Ni; (with Lincoln C), 1900 v S; 1901 v S, E (7)
Pugsley, J. (Charlton Ath), 1930 v Ni (1)
Pullen, W. J. (Plymouth Arg), 1926 v E (1)

Rankmore, F. E. J. (Peterborough), 1966 v Ch (sub) (1)
Ratcliffe, K. (Everton), 1981 v Cz, Ei, T, S, E, USSR; 1982 v Cz, Ic, USSR, Sp, E; 1983 v Y, E, Bul, S, Ni, Br; 1984 v N, R, Bul, Y, S, E, Ni, N, Is; 1985 v Ic, Sp, Ic, N, S, Sp; 1986 v S, H, S.Ar, U; 1987 v Fi (2), USSR, Cz; 1988 v D (2), Cz; 1989 v Fi, Is, Se, WG; 1990 v Fi; 1991 v D, Bel (2), L, Ei, Ic, Pol, WG; 1992 v Br, G; (with Cardiff C), 1993 v Bel (59)
Rea, J. C. (Aberystwyth), 1894 v Ni, S, E; 1895 v S; 1896 v S, Ni; 1897 v S, Ni; 1898 v Ni (9)
Ready, K. (QPR), 1997 v Ei; 1998 v Bel, Br, Ma, Tun (5)
Reece, G. I. (Sheffield U), 1966 v E, S, Ni, USSR; 1967 v S; 1969 v R of UK (sub); 1970 v I (sub); 1971 v S, E, Ni, Fi; 1972 v Fi, R, E (sub), S, Ni; (with Cardiff C), 1973 v E (sub), Ni; 1974 v Pol (sub), E, S, Ni; 1975 v A, H (2), L (2), S, Ni (29)
Reed, W. G. (Ipswich T), 1955 v S, Y (2)
Rees, A. (Birmingham C), 1984 v N (sub) (1)
Rees, J. M. (Luton T), 1992 v A (sub) (1)
Rees, R. R. (Coventry C), 1965 v S, E, Ni, D, Gr (2), I, R; 1966 v E, S, Ni, R, D, Br (2), Ch; 1967 v E, Ni; 1968 v E, S, Ni; (with WBA), WG; 1969 v I; (with Nottingham F), 1969 v WG, EG, S (sub), R of UK; 1970 v E, S, Ni, EG, I; 1971 v Cz, R, E (sub), Ni (sub), Fi; 1972 v Cz (sub), R (39)
Rees, W. (Cardiff C), 1949 v Ni, Bel, Sw; (with Tottenham H), 1950 v Ni (4)
Richards, A. (Barnsley), 1932 v S (1)
Richards, D. (Wolverhampton W), 1931 v Ni; 1933 v E, S, Ni; 1934 v E, S, Ni; 1935 v E, S, Ni; 1936 v S; (with Brentford), 1936 v E, Ni; 1937 v S, E; (with Birmingham), Ni; 1938 v E, S, Ni; 1939 v E, S (21)
Richards, G. (Druids), 1899 v E, S, Ni; (with Oswestry), 1903 v Ni; (with Shrewsbury), 1904 v S; 1905 v Ni (6)
Richards, R. W. (Wolverhampton W), 1920 v E, S; 1921 v Ni; 1922 v E, S; (with West Ham U), 1924 v E, S, Ni; (with Mold), 1926 v S (9)
Richards, S. V. (Cardiff C), 1947 v E (1)
Richards, W. E. (Fulham), 1933 v Ni (1)
Roach, J. (Oswestry), 1885 v Ni (1)
Robbins, W. W. (Cardiff C), 1931 v E, S; 1932 v Ni, E, S; (with WBA), 1933 v F, E, S, Ni; 1934 v S; 1936 v S (11)
Roberts, A. M. (QPR), 1993 v Ei (sub); 1997 v Sm (sub) (2)
Roberts, D. F. (Oxford U), 1973 v Pol, E (sub), Ni; 1974 v E, S; 1975 v A; (with Hull C), L, Ni; 1976 v S, Ni, Y; 1977 v E (sub), Ni; 1978 v K (1+1 sub), S, Ni (17)
Roberts, G. W. (Tranmere R), 2000 v Fi (sub), Br, P; 2001 v Bl; 2004 v H (sub), N (sub) (6)
Roberts, I. W. (Watford), 1990 v Ho; (with Huddersfield T), 1992 v A, Arg, J; (with Leicester C), 1994 v Se; 1995 v Alb (sub), Mol; (with Norwich C), 2000 v Fi (sub), Br, P; 2001 v Bl, N (sub), Arm (sub); 2002 v Arm, Bl (sub) (15)
Roberts, Jas (Wrexham), 1913 v S, Ni (2)
Roberts, J. (Corwen), 1879 v S; 1880 v E, S; 1882 v E, S, Ni; (with Berwyn R), 1883 v E (7)
Roberts, J. (Ruthin), 1881 v S; 1882 v S (2)
Roberts, J. (Bradford C), 1906 v Ni; 1907 v Ni (2)
Roberts, J. G. (Arsenal), 1971 v S, E, Ni, Fi; 1972 v Fi, E, Ni; (with Birmingham C), 1973 v E (2), Pol, S, Ni; 1974 v Pol, E, S, Ni; 1975 v A, H, S, E; 1976 v E, S (22)
Roberts, J. H. (Bolton), 1949 v Bel (1)
Roberts, N. W. (Wrexham), 2000 v Sw (sub); (with Wigan Ath), 2003 v Az (sub), US (sub) (3)
Roberts, P. S. (Portsmouth), 1974 v E; 1975 v A, H, L (4)
Roberts, R. (Druids), 1884 v S; (with Bolton W), 1887 v S; 1888 v S, E; 1889 v S, E; 1890 v S; 1892 v Ni; (with Preston NE), S (9)
Roberts, R. (Wrexham), 1886 v Ni; 1887 v Ni; 1891 v Ni (3)
Roberts, R. (Rhos), 1891 v Ni; (with Crewe Alex), 1893 v E (2)
Roberts, R. L. (Chester), 1890 v Ni (1)
Roberts, W. (Llangollen), 1879 v E, S; 1880 v E, S; (with Berwyn R), 1881 v S; 1883 v S (6)
Roberts, W. (Wrexham), 1886 v E, S, Ni; 1887 v Ni (4)
Roberts, W. H. (Ruthin), 1882 v E, S; 1883 v E, S, Ni; (with Rhyl), 1884 v S (6)
Robinson, C. P. (Wolverhampton W), 2000 v Bl (sub), P (sub); 2001 v Arm (sub), Uk; 2002 v Arm, N, Bl (sub), Arg (sub); (with Portsmouth), 2003 v Cro, Az (1+sub), US (sub); 2004 v Ser, S, H, N, Ca (17)
Robinson, J. R. C. (Charlton Ath), 1996 v Alb (sub), Sw, Sm; 1997 v Sm, Ho (1 + sub), Ei, S; 1998 v Bel, Br; 1999 v I, D (sub), Bl, Sw, I, D; 2000 v Bl, Sw, Q, Fi, Br, P; 2001 v Bl, N, Pol, Arm; 2002 v N (sub), Bl, Arg (sub), CzR (30)
Rodrigues, P. J. (Cardiff C), 1965 v Ni, Gr (2); 1966 v USSR, E, S, D; (with Leicester C), Ni, Br (2), Ch; 1967 v S; 1968 v E, S, Ni; 1969 v E, Ni, EG, R of UK; 1970 v E, S, Ni, EG; (with Sheffield W), 1971 v R, E, S, Cz, Ni; 1972 v Fi, Cz, R, E, Ni (sub); 1973 v E (3), Pol, S, Ni; 1974 v Pol (40)
Rogers, J. P. (Wrexham), 1896 v E, S, Ni (3)
Rogers, W. (Wrexham), 1931 v E, S (2)
Roose, L. R. (Aberystwyth), 1900 v Ni; (with London Welsh), 1901 v E, S, Ni; (with Stoke C), 1902 v E, S; 1904 v E; (with Everton), 1905 v S, E; (with Stoke C), 1906 v E, S, Ni; 1907 v E, S, Ni; (with Sunderland), 1908 v E, S; 1909 v E, S, Ni; 1910 v E, S, Ni; 1911 v S (24)
Rouse, R. V. (C Palace), 1959 v Ni (1)
Rowlands, A. C. (Tranmere R), 1914 v E (1)
Rowley, T. (Tranmere R), 1959 v Ni (1)
Rush, I. (Liverpool), 1980 v S (sub), Ni; 1981 v E (sub); 1982 v Ic (sub), USSR, E, S, Ni, F; 1983 v N, Y, E, Bul; 1984 v N, R, Bul, Y, S, E, Ni; 1985 v Ic, N, S, Sp; 1986 v S, S.Ar, Ei, U; 1987 v Fi (2), USSR, Cz; (with Juventus), 1988 v D, Cz, Y, Se, Ma, I; (with Liverpool), 1989 v Ho, Fi, Se, WG; 1990 v Fi, Ei; 1991 v D, Bel (2), L, Ei, Pol, WG; 1992 v G, L, R; 1993 v Fa, Cy, Bel (2), RCS, Fa; 1994 v RCS, Cy, R, N, Se, Es; 1995 v Alb, Ge, Bul, G, Ge; 1996 v Mol, I (73)
Russell, M. R. (Merthyr T), 1912 v S, Ni; 1914 v E; (with Plymouth Arg), 1920 v E, S, Ni; 1921 v E, S, Ni; 1922 v E, Ni; 1923 v E, S, Ni; 1924 v E, S, Ni; 1925 v E, S; 1926 v E, S; 1928 v S; 1929 v E (23)

Sabine, H. W. (Oswestry), 1887 v Ni (1)
Saunders, D. (Brighton & HA), 1986 v Ei (sub), Ca (2); 1987 v Fi, USSR (sub); (with Oxford U), 1988 v Y, Se, Ma, I (sub); 1989 v Ho (sub), Fi; (with Derby Co), Is, Se, WG; 1990 v Fi,

Ho, WG, Se, Cr; 1991 v D, Bel (2), L, Ei, Ic, Pol, WG; (with Liverpool), 1992 v Br, G, Ei, R, Ho, Arg, J; 1993 v Fa; (with Aston Villa), Cy, Bel (2), RCS, Fa; 1994 v RCS, Cy, R, N (sub); 1995 v Ge, Bul (2), G, Ge; (with Galatasaray), 1996 v G, Alb, Sm; (with Nottingham F), 1997 v Sm, Ho (2), T, Bel, S; 1998 v T, Bel, Br; (with Sheffield U), Ma, Tun; 1999 v I (sub), D, Bl; (with Benfica) Sw, I, D; (with Bradford C), 2000 v Bl, Sw, Fi (sub), Br; 2001 v Arm, Uk (sub) (75)
Savage, R. W. (Crewe Alex), 1996 v Alb (sub), Sw (sub), Sm (sub); 1997 v Ei (sub), S; (with Leicester C), 1998 v T, Bel, Jam, Tun; 1999 v I (sub), D, Bl, Sw; 2000 v Sw, Fi, Br; 2001 v Bl, N, Pol (2); 2002 v Arm, N, Arg, CzR, G; (with Birmingham C), 2003 v Fi, I, Bos, Az; 2004 v Ser, I, Ru (2), S, H (35)
Savin, G. (Oswestry), 1878 v S (1)
Sayer, P. (Cardiff C), 1977 v Cz, S, E, Ni; 1978 v K (2), S (7)
Scrine, F. H. (Swansea T), 1950 v E, Ni (2)
Sear, C. R. (Manchester C), 1963 v E (1)
Shaw, E. G. (Oswestry), 1882 v Ni; 1884 v S, Ni (3)
Sherwood, A. T. (Cardiff C), 1947 v E, Ni; 1948 v S, Ni; 1949 v E, S, Ni, P, Sw; 1950 v E, S, Ni, Bel; 1951 v E, S, Ni, P, Sw; 1952 v E, S, Ni, R of UK; 1953 v S, E, Ni, F, Y; 1954 v E, S, Ni, A; 1955 v S, E, Y, Ni; 1956 v E, S, Ni, A; (with Newport Co), 1957 v E, S (41)
Shone, W. W. (Oswestry), 1879 v E (1)
Shortt, W. W. (Plymouth Arg), 1947 v Ni; 1950 v Ni, Bel; 1952 v E, S, Ni, R of UK; 1953 v S, E, Ni, F, Y (12)
Showers, D. (Cardiff C), 1975 v E (sub), Ni (2)
Sidlow, C. (Liverpool), 1947 v E, S; 1948 v E, S, Ni; 1949 v S; 1950 v E (7)
Sisson, H. (Wrexham Olympic), 1885 v Ni; 1886 v S, Ni (3)
Slatter, N. (Bristol R), 1983 v S; 1984 v N (sub), Is; 1985 v Ic, Sp, Ic, N, S, Sp, N; (with Oxford U), 1986 v H (sub), S.Ar, Ca (2); 1987 v Fi (sub), Cz; 1988 v D (2), Cz, Ma, I; 1989 v Is (sub) (22)
Smallman, D. P. (Wrexham), 1974 v E (sub), S (sub), Ni; (with Everton), 1975 v H (sub), E, Ni (sub); 1976 v A (7)
Southall, N. (Everton), 1982 v Ni; 1983 v N, E, Bul, S, Ni, Br; 1984 v N, R, Bul, Y, S, E, Ni, N, Is; 1985 v Ic, Sp, Ic, N, S, Sp, N; 1986 v S, H, S.Ar, Ei; 1987 v USSR, Fi, Cz; 1988 v D, Cz, Y, Se; 1989 v Ho, Fi, Se, WG; 1990 v Fi, Ho, WG, Ei, Se, Cr; 1991 v D, Bel (2), L, Ei, Ic, Pol, WG; 1992 v Br, G, L, Ei, A, R, Ho, Arg, J; 1993 v Fa, Cy, Bel, Ei, Bel, RCS, Fa; 1994 v RCS, Cy, R, N, Se, Es; 1995 v Alb, Mol, Ge, Bul (2), G, Ge; 1996 v Mol, G, Alb, I, Sm; 1997 v Sm, Ho (2), T, Bel; 1998 v T (92)
Speed, G. A. (Leeds U), 1990 v Cr (sub); 1991 v D, L (sub), Ei (sub), Ic, WG (sub); 1992 v Br, G (sub), L, Ei, R, Ho,Arg,J; 1993 v Fa, Cy, Bel, Ei, Bel, Fa (sub); 1994 v RCS (sub), Cy, R, N, Se; 1995 v Alb, Mol, Ge, Bul (2), G; 1996 v Mol, G, I, Sw (sub); (with Everton), 1997 v Sm (sub), Ho (2), T, Ei, Bel, S; 1998 v T, Br; (with Newcastle U), Jam, Ma, Tun; 1999 v I, D, Sw, I, D; 2000 v Bl, Sw, Q, Fi, Br, P; 2001 v Bl, N, Pol, Arm, Uk, Pol, Uk; 2002 v Bl, Arg, G; 2003 v Fi, I, Az, Bos, Az; 2004 v Ser, I, Fi, Ser, Ru (2), S (80)
Sprake, G. (Leeds U), 1964 v S, Ni; 1965 v S, D, Gr; 1966 v E, Ni, USSR; 1967 v S; 1968 v E, S; 1969 v S, E, Ni, WG, R of UK; 1970 v EG, I; 1971 v R, S, E, Ni; 1972 v Fi, E, S, Ni; 1973 v E (2), Pol, S, Ni; 1974 v Pol; (with Birmingham C), S, Ni; 1975 v A, H, L (37)
Stansfield, F. (Cardiff C), 1949 v S (1)
Stevenson, B. (Leeds U), 1978 v Ni; 1979 v Ma, T, S, E, Ni, Ma; 1980 v WG, T, Ic (sub); 1982 v Cz; (with Birmingham C), Sp, S, Ni, F (15)
Stevenson, N. (Swansea C), 1982 v E, S, Ni; 1983 v N (4)
Stitfall, R. F. (Cardiff C), 1953 v E; 1957 v Cz (2)
Sullivan, D. (Cardiff C), 1953 v Ni, F, Y; 1954 v Ni; 1955 v E, Ni; 1957 v E, S; 1958 v Ni, H (2), Se, Br; 1959 v S, Ni; 1960 v E, S (17)
Symons, C. J. (Portsmouth), 1992 v Ei, Ho, Arg, J; 1993 v Fa, Cy, Bel, Ei, RCS, Fa; 1994 v RCS, Cy, R; 1995 v Mol, Ge (sub), Bul, G, Ge; (with Manchester C), 1996 v Mol, G, I, Sw; 1997 v Ho (2), Ei, Bel, S; (with Fulham), 1999 v I, D, Bl, Sw; 2000 v Q (sub); 2001 v Pol; 2002 v Arm, N, Bl; (with C Palace), 2004 v S (sub) (37)

Tapscott, D. R. (Arsenal), 1954 v A; 1955 v S, E, Ni, Y; 1956 v E, Ni, S, A; 1957 v Ni, Cz, EG; (with Cardiff C), 1959 v E, Ni (14)
Taylor, G. K. (C Palace), 1996 v Alb, I (sub); (with Sheffield U), Sw; 1997 v Sm (sub), Ho (sub), Ei (sub); 1998 v Bel (sub), Jam; (with Burnley), 2002 v CzR (sub); 2003 v Cro (sub), Bos (sub), US; (with Nottingham F), 2004 v S (sub), H (14)
Taylor, J. (Wrexham), 1898 v E (1)
Taylor, O. D. S. (Newtown), 1893 v S, Ni; 1894 v S, Ni (4)
Thatcher, B. D. (Leicester C), 2004 v H, N, Ca (3)
Thomas, C. (Druids), 1899 v Ni; 1900 v S (2)
Thomas, D. A. (Swansea T), 1957 v Cz; 1958 v EG (2)
Thomas, D. S. (Fulham), 1948 v E, S, Ni; 1949 v S (4)
Thomas, E. (Cardiff Corinthians), 1925 v E (1)
Thomas, G. (Wrexham), 1885 v E, S (2)
Thomas, H. (Manchester U), 1927 v E (1)
Thomas, M. (Wrexham), 1977 v WG, S (1+1 sub), Ni (sub); 1978 v K (sub), S, Cz, Ir, E, Ni (sub); 1979 v Ma; (with Manchester U), T, WG, Ma (sub); 1980 v Ei, WG (sub), T, E, S, Ni; 1981 v Cz, S, E, USSR; (with Everton), 1982 v Cz; (with Brighton & HA), USSR (sub), Sp, E, S (sub), Ni (sub); 1983 (with Stoke C), v N, Y, E, Bul, S, Ni, Br; 1984 v R, Bul, Y; (with Chelsea), S, E; 1985 v Ic, Sp, Ic, S, Sp, N; 1986 v S; (with WBA), H, S.Ar (sub) (51)
Thomas, M. R. (Newcastle U), 1987 v Fi (1)
Thomas, R. J. (Swindon T), 1967 v Ni; 1968 v WG; 1969 v E, Ni, I, WG, R of UK; 1970 v E, S, Ni, EG, I; 1971 v S, E, Ni, R, Cz; 1972 v Fi, Cz, R, E, S, Ni; 1973 v E (3), Pol, S, Ni; 1974 v Pol; (with Derby Co), E, S, Ni; 1975 v H (2), L (2), S, E, Ni; 1976 v A, Y, E; 1977 v Cz, S, E, Ni; 1978 v K, S; (with Cardiff C), Cz (50)
Thomas, T. (Bangor), 1898 v S, Ni (2)
Thomas, W. R. (Newport Co), 1931 v E, S (2)
Thomson, D. (Druids), 1876 v S (1)
Thomson, G. F. (Druids), 1876 v S; 1877 v S (2)
Toshack, J. B. (Cardiff C), 1969 v S, E, Ni, WG, EG, R of UK; 1970 v EG, I; (with Liverpool), 1971 v S, E, Ni, Fi; 1972 v Fi, E; 1973 v E (3), Pol, S; 1975 v A, H (2), L (2), S, E; 1976 v Y (2), E; 1977 v S; 1978 v K (2), S, Cz; (with Swansea C), 1979 v WG (sub), S, E, Ni, Ma; 1980 v WG (40)
Townsend, W. (Newtown), 1887 v Ni; 1893 v Ni (2)
Trainer, H. (Wrexham), 1895 v E, S, Ni (3)
Trainer, J. (Bolton W), 1887 v S; (with Preston NE), 1888 v S; 1889 v E; 1890 v S; 1891 v S; 1892 v Ni, S; 1893 v E; 1894 v Ni, E; 1895 v Ni, E; 1896 v S; 1897 v Ni, S, E; 1898 v S, E; 1899 v Ni, S (20)
Trollope, P. J. (Derby Co), 1997 v S; 1998 v Br (sub); (with Fulham), Jam (sub), Ma, Tun; (with Coventry C), 2002 v CzR (sub); (with Northampton T), 2003 v Cro (sub), Az (sub+sub) (9)
Turner, H. G. (Charlton Ath), 1937 v E, S, Ni; 1938 v E, S, Ni; 1939 v Ni, F (8)
Turner, J. (Wrexham), 1892 v E (1)
Turner, R. E. (Wrexham), 1891 v E, Ni (2)
Turner, W. H. (Wrexham), 1887 v E, Ni; 1890 v S; 1891 v E, S (5)

Van Den Hauwe, P. W. R. (Everton), 1985 v Sp; 1986 v S, H; 1987 v USSR, Fi, Cz; 1988 v D (2), Cz, Y, I; 1989 v Fi, Se (13)
Vaughan, D. O. (Crewe Alex), 2003 v US; 2004 v H (2)
Vaughan, Jas (Druids), 1893 v E, S, Ni; 1899 v E (4)
Vaughan, John (Oswestry), 1879 v S; 1880 v S; 1881 v E, S; 1882 v E, S, Ni; 1883 v E, S, Ni; (with Bolton W), 1884 v E (11)
Vaughan, J. O. (Rhyl), 1885 v Ni; 1886 v Ni, E, S (4)
Vaughan, N. (Newport Co), 1983 v Y (sub), Br; 1984 v N; (with Cardiff C), R, Bul, Y, Ni (sub), N, Is; 1985 v Sp (sub) (10)
Vaughan, T. (Rhyl), 1885 v E (1)
Vearncombe, G. (Cardiff C), 1958 v EG; 1961 v Ei (2)
Vernon, T. R. (Blackburn R), 1957 v Ni, Cz (2), EG; 1958 v E, S, EG, Se; 1959 v S; (with Everton), 1960 v Ni; 1961 v S, E, Ei; 1962 v Ni, Br (2), M; 1963 v S, E, H; 1964 v E, S; (with Stoke C), 1965 v Ni, Gr, I; 1966 v E, S, Ni, USSR, D; 1967 v Ni; 1968 v E (32)
Villars, A. K. (Cardiff C), 1974 v E, S, Ni (sub) (3)
Vizard, E. T. (Bolton W), 1911 v E, S, Ni; 1912 v E, S; 1913 v S; 1914 v E, Ni; 1920 v E; 1921 v E, S, Ni; 1922 v E, S; 1923 v E, Ni; 1924 v E, S, Ni; 1926 v E, S; 1927 v S (22)

Walley, J. T. (Watford), 1971 v Cz (1)
Walsh, I. (C Palace), 1980 v Ei, T, E, S, Ic; 1981 v T, Cz, Ei, T, S, E, USSR; 1982 v Cz (sub), Ic; (with Swansea C), Sp, S (sub), Ni (sub), F (18)
Ward, D. (Bristol R), 1959 v E; (with Cardiff C), 1962 v E (2)
Ward, D. (Notts Co), 2000 v P; (with Nottingham F), 2002 v CzR; 2003 v Bos, US (sub); 2004 v S (sub) (5)
Warner, J. (Swansea T), 1937 v E; (with Manchester U), 1939 v F (2)
Warren, F. W. (Cardiff C), 1929 v Ni; (with Middlesbrough), 1931 v Ni; 1933 v F, E; (with Hearts), 1937 v Ni; 1938 v Ni (6)
Watkins, A. E. (Leicester Fosse), 1898 v E, S; (with Aston Villa), 1900 v E, S; (with Millwall), 1904 v Ni (5)

Watkins, W. M. (Stoke C), 1902 v E; 1903 v E, S; (with Aston Villa); 1904 v E, S, Ni; (with Sunderland), 1905 v E, S, Ni; (with Stoke C), 1908 v Ni (10)
Webster, C. (Manchester U), 1957 v Cz; 1958 v H, M, Br (4)
Weston, R. D. (Arsenal), 2000 v P (sub); (with Cardiff C), 2003 v Cro (sub), Az (sub), Bos; 2004 v Fi, Ser (6)
Whatley, W. J. (Tottenham H), 1939 v E, S (2)
White, P. F. (London Welsh), 1896 v Ni (1)
Wilcock, A. R. (Oswestry), 1890 v Ni (1)
Wilding, J. (Wrexham Olympians), 1885 v E, S, Ni; 1886 v E, Ni; (with Bootle), 1887 v E; 1888 v S, Ni; (with Wrexham), 1892 v S (9)
Williams, A. (Reading), 1994 v Es; 1995 v Alb, Mol, G (sub), Ge; 1996 v Mol, I; (with Wolverhampton W), 1998 v Br (sub), Jam; 1999 v I, D, I; (with Reading), 2003 v US (13)
Williams, A. L. (Wrexham), 1931 v E (1)
Williams, A. P. (Southampton), 1998 v Br (sub), Ma (2)
Williams, B. (Bristol C), 1930 v Ni (1)
Williams, B. D. (Swansea T), 1928 v Ni, E; 1930 v E, S; (with Everton), 1931 v Ni; 1932 v E; 1933 v E, S, Ni; 1935 v Ni (10)
Williams, D. G. (Derby Co), 1988 v Cz, Y, Se, Ma, I; 1989 v Ho, Is, Se, WG; 1990 v Fi, Ho; (with Ipswich T), 1993 v Ei; 1996 v G (sub) (13)
Williams, D. M. (Norwich C), 1986 v S.Ar (sub), U, Ca (2); 1987 v Fi (5)
Williams, D. R. (Merthyr T), 1921 v E, S; (with Sheffield W), 1923 v S; 1926 v S; 1927 v E, Ni; (with Manchester U), 1929 v E, S (8)
Williams, E. (Crewe Alex), 1893 v E, S (2)
Williams, E. (Druids), 1901 v E, Ni, S; 1902 v E, Ni (5)
Williams, G. (Chirk), 1893 v S; 1894 v S; 1895 v E, S, Ni; 1898 v Ni (6)
Williams, G. E. (WBA), 1960 v Ni; 1961 v S, E, Ei; 1963 v Ni, H; 1964 v E, S, Ni; 1965 v S, E, Ni, D, Gr (2), USSR, I; 1966 v Ni, Br (2), Ch; 1967 v S, E, Ni; 1968 v Ni; 1969 v I (26)
Williams, G. G. (Swansea T), 1961 v Ni, H, Sp (2); 1962 v E (5)
Williams, G. J. J. (Cardiff C), 1951 v Sw (1)
Williams, G. O. (Wrexham), 1907 v Ni (1)
Williams, H. J. (Swansea), 1965 v Gr (2); 1972 v R (3)
Williams, H. T. (Newport Co), 1949 v Ni, Sw; (with Leeds U), 1950 v Ni; 1951 v S (4)
Williams, J. H. (Oswestry), 1884 v E (1)
Williams, J. J. (Wrexham), 1939 v F (1)
Williams, J. T. (Middlesbrough), 1925 v Ni (1)
Williams, J. W. (C Palace), 1912 v S, Ni (2)
Williams, R. (Newcastle U), 1935 v S, E (2)
Williams, R. P. (Caernarvon), 1886 v S (1)
Williams, S. G. (WBA), 1954 v A; 1955 v E, Ni; 1956 v E, S, A; 1958 v E, S, Ni, Is (2), H (2), M, Se, Br; 1959 v E, S, Ni; 1960 v E, S, Ni; 1961 v Ni, Ei, H, Sp (2); 1962 v E, S, Ni, Br (2), M; (with Southampton), 1963 v S, E, H (2); 1964 v E, S; 1965 v S, E, D; 1966 v D (43)
Williams, W. (Druids), 1876 v S; 1878 v S; (with Oswestry), 1879 v E, S; (with Druids), 1880 v E; 1881 v E, S; 1882 v E, S, Ni; 1883 v Ni (11)
Williams, W. (Northampton T), 1925 v S (1)
Witcomb, D. F. (WBA), 1947 v E, S; (with Sheffield W), 1947 v Ni (3)
Woosnam, A. P. (Leyton Orient), 1959 v S; (with West Ham U), E; 1960 v E, S, Ni; 1961 v S, E, Ni, Ei, Sp, H; 1962 v E, S, Ni, Br; (with Aston Villa), 1963 v Ni, H (17)
Woosnam, G. (Newton White Star), 1879 v S (1)
Worthington, T. (Newtown), 1894 v S (1)
Wynn, G. A. (Wrexham), 1909 v E, S, Ni; (with Manchester C), 1910 v E; 1911 v Ni; 1912 v E, S; 1913 v E, S; 1914 v E, S (11)
Wynn, W. (Chirk), 1903 v Ni (1)

Yorath, T. C. (Leeds U), 1970 v I; 1971 v S, E, Ni; 1972 v Cz, E, S, Ni; 1973 v E, Pol, S; 1974 v Pol, E, S, Ni; 1975 v A, H (2), L (2), S; 1976 v A, E, S, Y (2), E, Ni; (with Coventry C), 1977 v WG, S (2), Cz, E, Ni; 1978 v K (2), S, Cz, WG, Ir, E, S, Ni; 1979 v T, WG, S, E, Ni; (with Tottenham H), 1980 v Ei, T, E, S, Ni, Ic; 1981 v T, Cz; (with Vancouver W), Ei, T, USSR (59)
Young, E. (Wimbledon), 1990 v Cr; (with C Palace), 1991 v D, Bel (2), L, Ei; 1992 v G, L, Ei, A; 1993 v Fa, Cy, Bel, Ei, Bel, Fa; 1994 v RCS, Cy, R, N; (with Wolverhampton W), 1996 v Alb (21)

## REPUBLIC OF IRELAND

Aherne, T. (Belfast C), 1946 v P, Sp; (with Luton T), 1950 v Fi, E, Fi, Se, Bel; 1951 v N, Arg, N; 1952 v WG (2), A, Sp; 1953 v F; 1954 v F (16)
Aldridge, J. W. (Oxford U), 1986 v W, U, Ic, Cz; 1987 v Bel, S, Pol; (with Liverpool), S, Bul, Bel, Br, L; 1988 v Bul, Pol, N, E, USSR, Ho; 1989 v Ni, Tun, Sp, F (sub), H, Ma (sub), H; 1990 v WG; (with Real Sociedad), Ni, Ma, Fi (sub), T. E, Eg, Ho, R, I; 1991 v T, E (2), Pol; (with Tranmere R), 1992 v H (sub), T, W (sub), Sw (sub), US (sub), Alb, I, P (sub); 1993 v La, D, Sp, D, Alb, La, Li; 1994 v Li, Ni, CzR, I (sub), M (sub), N; 1995 v La, Ni, P, Lie; 1996 v La, P, Ho, Ru; 1997 v Mac (sub) (69)
Ambrose, P. (Shamrock R), 1955 v N, Ho; 1964 v Pol, N, E (5)
Anderson, J. (Preston NE), 1980 v Cz (sub), US (sub); 1982 v Ch, Br, Tr; (with Newcastle U), 1984 v Chn; 1986 v W, Ic, Cz; 1987 v Bul, Bel, Br, L; 1988 v R (sub), Y (sub); 1989 v Tun (16)
Andrews, P. (Bohemians), 1936 v Ho (1)
Arrigan, T. (Waterford), 1938 v N (1)

Babb, P. A. (Coventry C), 1994 v Ru, Ho, Bol, G, CzR (sub), I, M, N, Ho; (with Liverpool), 1995 v La, Lie, Ni (2), P, Lie, A; 1996 v La, P, Ho, CzR; 1997 v Ic; 1998 v Li (sub), R, Arg (sub), M; 1999 v Cro, Para (sub), Se (sub), Ni; 2000 v CzR (sub), S, M (sub), US, S.Af; (with Sunderland), 2003 v Ru (sub) (35)
Bailham, E. (Shamrock R), 1964 v E (1)
Barber, E. (Shelbourne), 1966 v Sp; (with Birmingham C), 1966 v Bel (2)
Barrett, G. (Arsenal), 2003 v Fi (sub); (with Coventry C), 2004 v Pol (sub), Ng (sub), Jam, Ho (5)
Barry, P. (Fordsons), 1928 v Bel; 1929 v Bel (2)
Beglin, J. (Liverpool), 1984 v Chn; 1985 v M, D, I, Is, E, N, Sw; 1986 v Sw, USSR, D, W; 1987 v Bel (sub), S, Pol (15)
Bermingham, J. (Bohemians), 1929 v Bel (1)
Bermingham, P. (St James' Gate), 1935 v H (1)
Braddish, S. (Dundalk), 1978 v T (sub), Pol (2)
Bonner, P. (Celtic), 1981 v Pol; 1982 v Alg; 1984 v Ma, Is, Chn; 1985 v I, Is, E, N; 1986 v U, Ic; 1987 v Bel (2), S (2), Pol, Bul, Br, L; 1988 v Bul, R, Y, N, E, USSR, Ho; 1989 v Sp, F, H, Sp, Ma, H; 1990 v WG, Ni, Ma, W, Fi, T, E, Eg, Ho, R, I; 1991 v Mor, T, E (2), W, Pol, US; 1992 v H, Pol, T, W, Sw, Alb, I; 1993 v La, D, Sp, W, Ni, D, Alb, La, Li; 1994 v Li, Sp, Ni, Ru, Ho, Bol, CzR, I, M, N, Ho; 1995 v Lie; 1996 v M, Bol (sub) (80)
Bradshaw, P. (St James' Gate), 1939 v Sw, Pol, H (2), G (5)
Brady, F. (Fordsons), 1926 v I; 1927 v I (2)
Brady, T. R. (QPR), 1964 v A (2), Sp (2), Pol, N (6)
Brady, W. L. (Arsenal), 1975 v USSR, T, Sw, USSR, Sw, WG; 1976 v T, N, Pol; 1977 v E, T, F (2), Sp, Bul; 1978 v Bul, N; 1979 v Ni, E, D, Bul, WG; 1980 v W, Bul, E, Cy; (with Juventus), 1981 v Ho, Bel, F, Cy, Bel; 1982 v Ho, F, Ch, Br, Tr; (with Sampdoria), 1983 v Ho, Sp, Ic, Ma; 1984 v Ic, Ho, Ma, Pol, Is; (with Internazionale), 1985 v USSR, N, D, I, E, N, Sp, Sw; 1986 v Sw, USSR, D, W; (with Ascoli), 1987 v Bel, S (2), Pol; (with West Ham U), Bul, Bel, Br, L; 1988 v L, Bul; 1989 v F, H (sub), H (sub); 1990 v WG, Fi (72)
Branagan, K. G. (Bolton W), 1997 v W (1)
Breen, G. (Birmingham C), 1996 v P (sub), Cro, Ho, US, M, Bol (sub); 1997 v Lie, Mac, Ic; (with Coventry C), v Mac; 1998 v Li (sub), R, CzR, Arg, M; 1999 v Ma, Y, Para, Se, Mac; 2000 v Y, Cro, Ma, Mac, T (2), Gr, S, M, US, S.Af; 2001 v Ho, P, Es, Fi, Cy, And (2); 2002 v Cy, Ir (2), Ru (sub), US, Cam, G, S.Ar, Sp; (with West Ham U), 2003 v Fi, Ru, Sw, S, Ge, Alb, N, Alb, Ge; (with Sunderland), 2004 v Aus, Ru, T, Sw (60)
Breen, T. (Manchester U), 1937 v Sw, F; (with Shamrock R), 1947 v E, Sp, P (5)
Brennan, F. (Drumcondra), 1965 v Bel (1)
Brennan, S. A. (Manchester U), 1965 v Sp; 1966 v Sp, A, Bel; 1967 v Sp, T, Sp; 1969 v Cz, D, H; 1970 v S, Cz, D, H, Pol (sub), WG; (with Waterford), 1971 v Pol, Se, I (19)
Brown, J. (Coventry C), 1937 v Sw, F (2)
Browne, W. (Bohemians), 1964 v A, Sp, E (3)
Buckley, L. (Shamrock R), 1984 v Pol (sub); (with Waregem), 1985 v M (2)
Burke, F. (Cork Ath), 1952 v WG (1)
Burke, J. (Shamrock R), 1929 v Bel (1)

Burke, J. (Cork), 1934 v Bel (1)
Butler, P. J. (Sunderland), 2000 v CzR (1)
Butler, T. (Sunderland), 2003 v Fi, Sw (sub) (2)
Byrne, A. B. (Southampton), 1970 v D, Pol, WG; 1971 v Pol, Se (2), I (2), A; 1973 v F, USSR (sub), F, N; 1974 v Pol (14)
Byrne, D. (Shelbourne), 1929 v Bel; (with Shamrock R), 1932 v Sp; (with Coleraine), 1934 v Bel (3)
Byrne, J. (Bray Unknowns), 1928 v Bel (1)
Byrne, J. (QPR), 1985 v I, Is (sub), E (sub), Sp (sub); 1987 v S (sub), Bel (sub), Br, L (sub); 1988 v L, Bul (sub), Is, R, Y (sub), Pol (sub); (with Le Havre), 1990 v WG (sub), W, Fi, T (sub), Ma; (with Brighton & HA), 1991 v W; (with Sunderland), 1992 v T, W; (with Millwall), 1993 v W (23)
Byrne, J. (Shelbourne), 2004 v Pol (sub) (1)
Byrne, P. (Dolphin), 1931 v Sp; 1932 v Ho; (with Drumcondra), 1934 v Ho (3)
Byrne, P. (Shamrock R), 1984 v Pol, Chn; 1985 v M; 1986 v D (sub), W (sub), U (sub), Ic (sub), Cz (8)
Byrne, S. (Bohemians), 1931 v Sp (1)

Campbell, A. (Santander), 1985 v I (sub), Is, Sp (3)
Campbell, N. (St Patrick's Ath), 1971 v A (sub); (with Fortuna Cologne), 1972 v Ir, Ec, Ch, P; 1973 v USSR, F (sub); 1975 v WG; 1976 v N; 1977 v Sp, Bul (sub) (11)
Cannon, H. (Bohemians), 1926 v I; 1928 v Bel (2)
Cantwell, N. (West Ham U), 1954 v L; 1956 v Sp, Ho; 1957 v D, WG, E (2); 1958 v D, Pol, A; 1959 v Pol, Cz (2); 1960 v Se, Ch, Se; 1961 v N; (with Manchester U), S (2); 1962 v Cz (2), A; 1963 v Ic (2), S; 1964 v A, Sp, E; 1965 v Pol, Sp; 1966 v Sp (2), A, Bel; 1967 v Sp, T (36)
Carey, B. P. (Manchester U), 1992 v US (sub); 1993 v W; (with Leicester C), 1994 v Ru (3)
Carey, J. J. (Manchester U), 1938 v N, Cz, Pol; 1939 v Sw, Pol, H (2), G; 1946 v P, Sp; 1947 v E, Sp, P; 1948 v P, Sp; 1949 v Sw, Bel, P, Se, Sp; 1950 v Fi, E, Fi, Se; 1951 v N, Arg, N; 1953 v F, A (29)
Carolan, J. (Manchester U), 1960 v Se, Ch (2)
Carr, S. (Tottenham H), 1999 v Se, Ni, Mac; 2000 v Y (sub), Cro, Ma, T (2), S, M, US, S.Af; 2001 v Ho, P, Es, And (sub), P, Es; 2003 v S, Ge, Alb, N, Alb, Ge; 2004 v Aus, Ru, T (sub), Sw, Ca, Br (30)
Carroll, B. (Shelbourne), 1949 v Bel; 1950 v Fi (2)
Carroll, T. R. (Ipswich T), 1968 v Pol; 1969 v Pol, A, D; 1970 v Cz, Pol, WG; 1971 v Se; (with Birmingham C), 1972 v Ir, Ec, Ch, P; 1973 v USSR (2), Pol, F, N (17)
Carsley, L. K. (Derby Co), 1998 v R, Bel (1 + sub), CzR, Arg, M; 1999 v Cro (sub), Ma (sub), Para (sub); (with Blackburn R) Ni, Mac; 2000 v Y (sub), Cro, Ma, T; 2001 v Fi (sub); (with Coventry C), 2002 v Cro, Cy (sub), Ru (sub); (with Everton), S.Ar (sub); 2003 v Fi, Gr, S (sub), Ge, Alb, N (sub), Alb (sub), Ge; 2004 v Ru (29)
Cascarino, A. G. (Gillingham), 1986 v Sw, USSR, D; (with Millwall), 1988 v Pol, N (sub), USSR (sub), Ho (sub); 1989 v Ni, Tun, Sp, F, H, Sp, Ma, H; 1990 v WG (sub), Ni, Ma; (with Aston Villa), W, Fi, T, E, Eg, Ho (sub), R (sub), I (sub); 1991 v Mor (sub),T(sub), E (2 sub), Pol (sub), Ch (sub), US; (with Celtic), 1992 v Pol, T; (with Chelsea), W, Sw, US (sub); 1993 v W, Ni (sub), D (sub), Alb (sub), La (sub); 1994 v Li (sub), Sp (sub), Ni (sub), Ru, Bol (sub), G, CzR, Ho (sub); (with Marseille), 1995 v La (sub), Ni (sub), P (sub), Lie (sub), A (sub); 1996 v A (sub), P (sub), Ho, Ru (sub), P, Cro (sub), Ho; 1997 v Lie (sub), Mac, Ic; (with Nancy), v W, Mac, R (sub), Lie (sub); 1998 v Li (sub), Ic (sub), Li, R, Bel (2); 1999 v Cro (sub), Ma (sub), Y (sub), Para (sub), Se (sub), Ni (sub), Mac (sub); 2000 v Y (sub), Cro, Mac (sub), T (1 + sub) (88)
Chandler, J. (Leeds U), 1980 v Cz (sub), US (2)
Chatton, H. A. (Shelbourne), 1931 v Sp; (with Dumbarton), 1932 v Sp; (with Cork), 1934 v Ho (3)
Clarke, C. R. (Stoke C), 2004 v Ng (sub), Jam (sub) (2)
Clarke, J. (Drogheda U), 1978 v Pol (sub) (1)
Clarke, K. (Drumcondra), 1948 v P, Sp (2)
Clarke, M. (Shamrock R), 1950 v Bel (1)
Clinton, T. J. (Everton), 1951 v N; 1954 v F, L (3)
Coad, P. (Shamrock R), 1947 v E, Sp, P; 1948 v P, Sp; 1949 v Sw, Bel, P, Se; 1951 v N (sub); 1952 v Sp (11)
Coffey, T. (Drumcondra), 1950 v Fi (1)
Colfer, M. D. (Shelbourne), 1950 v Bel; 1951 v N (2)
Colgan, N. (Hibernian), 2002 v D (sub); 2003 v S (sub), N (sub); 2004 v Aus, T, Ca (sub), Pol (sub), Ng (8)
Collins, F. (Jacobs), 1927 v I (1)
Conmy, O. M. (Peterborough U), 1965 v Bel; 1967 v Cz; 1968 v Cz, Pol; 1970 v Cz (5)
Connolly, D. J. (Watford), 1996 v P, Ho, US, M; 1997 v R, Lie; (with Feyenoord), 1998 v Li, Ic, Li, Bel (1 + sub), CzR, M; (with Wolverhampton W), 1999 v Y, Para (sub), Se, Ni (sub), Mac (sub); (with Excelsior), 2000 v T (1 + sub), CzR (sub), Gr; 2001 v Ho (sub), Fi (sub), Cy, And; (with Feyenoord), And; (with Wimbledon), 2002 v Cro (sub), Cy, Ir, D (sub), US (sub), Ng (sub), Sp (sub); 2003 v S (sub), N, Alb; (with West Ham U), 2004 v Aus (sub), T, Sw (40)
Connolly, H. (Cork), 1937 v G (1)
Connolly, J. (Fordsons), 1926 v I (1)
Conroy, G. A. (Stoke C), 1970 v Cz, D, H, Pol, WG; 1971 v Pol, Se (2), I; 1973 v USSR, F, USSR, N; 1974 v Pol, Br, U, Ch; 1975 v T, Sw, USSR, Sw, WG (sub); 1976 v T (sub), Pol; 1977 v E, T, Pol (27)
Conway, J. P. (Fulham), 1967 v Sp, T, Sp; 1968 v Cz; 1969 v A (sub), H; 1970 v S, Cz, D, H, Pol, WG; 1971 v I, A; 1974 v U, Ch; 1975 v WG (sub); 1976 v N, Pol; (with Manchester C), 1977 v Pol (20)
Corr, P. J. (Everton), 1949 v P, Sp; 1950 v E, Se (4)
Courtney, E. (Cork U), 1946 v P (1)
Coyle, O. C. (Bolton W), 1994 v Ho (sub) (1)
Coyne, T. (Celtic), 1992 v Sw, US, Alb (sub), US (sub), I (sub), P (sub); 1993 v W (sub), La (sub); (with Tranmere R), Ni; (with Motherwell), 1994 v Ru (sub), Ho, Bol, G (sub), CzR (sub), I, M, Ho; 1995 v Lie, Ni (sub), A; 1996 v Ru (sub); 1998 v Bel (sub) (22)
Crowe, G. (Bohemians), 2003 v Gr, N (sub) (2)
Cummins, G. P. (Luton T), 1954 v L (2); 1955 v N (2), WG; 1956 v Y, Sp; 1958 v D, Pol, A; 1959 v Pol, Cz (2); 1960 v Se, Ch, WG, Se; 1961 v S (2) (19)
Cuneen, T. (Limerick), 1951 v N (1)
Cunningham, K. (Wimbledon), 1996 v CzR, P, Cro, Ho (sub), US, Bol; 1997 v Ic (sub), W, R, Lie; 1998 v Li, Ic, Li, Bel (2), CzR; 1999 v Cro, Ma, Y, Para, Se, Ni, Mac; 2000 v Y, Cro, Ma, Mac, T (2), CzR, Gr; 2001 v Cy, And; 2002 v Ir (sub), Ru, D, US (sub), Ng, G (sub), Sp (sub); (with Birmingham C), 2003 v Fi, Ru, Sw, Gr, Ge, Alb (2), Ge; 2004 v Aus, Ru, Ca, Br, CzR, Pol, R, Ng, Ho (57)
Curtis, D. P. (Shelbourne), 1957 v D, WG; (with Bristol C), 1957 v E (2); 1958 v D, Pol, A; (with Ipswich T), 1959 v Pol; 1960 v Se, Ch, WG, Se; 1961 v N, S; 1962 v A; 1963 v Ic; (with Exeter C), 1964 v A (17)
Cusack, S. (Limerick), 1953 v F (1)

Daish, L. S. (Cambridge U), 1992 v W, Sw (sub); (with Coventry C), 1996 v CzR (sub), Cro, M (5)
Daly, G. A. (Manchester U), 1973 v Pol (sub), N; 1974 v Br (sub), U (sub); 1975 v Sw (sub), WG; 1977 v E, T, F; (with Derby Co), F, Bul; 1978 v Bul, T, D; 1979 v Ni, E, D, Bul; 1980 v Ni, E, Cy, Sw, Arg; (with Coventry C), 1981 v WG 'B', Ho, Bel, Cy, W, Bel, Cz, Pol (sub); 1982 v Alg, Ch, Br, Tr; 1983 v Ho, Sp (sub); 1984 v Is (sub), Ma; (with Birmingham C), 1985 v M (sub), N, Sp, Sw; 1986 v Sw; (with Shrewsbury T), U, Ic (sub), Cz (sub); 1987 v S (sub) (48)
Daly, J. (Shamrock R), 1932 v Ho; 1935 v Sw (2)
Daly, M. (Wolverhampton W), 1978 v T, Pol (2)
Daly, P. (Shamrock R), 1950 v Fi (sub) (1)
Davis, T. L. (Oldham Ath), 1937 v G, H; (with Tranmere R), 1938 v Cz, Pol (4)
Deacy, E. (Aston Villa), 1982 v Alg (sub), Ch, Br, Tr (4)
Delap, R. J. (Derby Co), 1998 v CzR (sub), Arg (sub), M (sub); 2000 v T (2), Gr (sub); (with Southampton), 2002 v US; 2003 v Fi (sub), Gr (sub); 2004 v Ca (sub), CzR (sub) (11)
De Mange, K. J. P. P. (Liverpool), 1987 v Br (sub); (with Hull C), 1989 v Tun (sub) (2)
Dempsey, J. T. (Fulham), 1967 v Sp, Cz; 1968 v Cz, Pol; 1969 v Pol, A, D; (with Chelsea), 1969 v Cz, D; 1970 v H, WG; 1971 v Pol, Se (2), I; 1972 v Ir, Ec, Ch, P (19)
Dennehy, J. (Cork Hibernians), 1972 v Ec (sub), Ch; (with Nottingham F), 1973 v USSR (sub), Pol, F, N; 1974 v Pol (sub); 1975 v T (sub), WG (sub); (with Walsall), 1976 v Pol (sub); 1977 v Pol (sub) (11)
Desmond, P. (Middlesbrough), 1950 v Fi, E, Fi, Se (4)
Devine, J. (Arsenal), 1980 v Cz, Ni; 1981 v WG 'B', Cz; 1982 v Ho, Alg; 1983 v Sp, Ma; (with Norwich C), 1984 v Ic, Ho, Is; 1985 v USSR, N (13)
Doherty, G. M. T. (Luton T), 2000 v Gr (sub); (with Tottenham H), US, S.Af (sub); 2001 v Cy (sub), And (sub+1), P (sub), Es (sub); 2002 v US (sub); 2003 v Fi (sub), Ru (sub), Sw (sub), Gr, S, Ge, Alb (sub+sub), Ge; 2004 v Aus, Ru (sub), T, Ca, CzR, Pol, Ng, Jam (26)
Donnelly, J. (Dundalk), 1935 v H, Sw, G; 1936 v Ho, Sw, H, L; 1937 v G, H; 1938 v N (10)
Donnelly, T. (Drumcondra), 1938 v N; (Shamrock R), 1939 v Sw (2)
Donovan, D. C. (Everton), 1955 v N, Ho, N, WG; 1957 v E (5)
Donovan, T. (Aston Villa), 1980 v Cz; 1981 v WG 'B'(sub) (2)
Douglas, J. (Blackburn R), 2004 v Pol (sub), Ng (sub) (2)

Dowdall, C. (Fordsons), 1928 v Bel; (with Barnsley), 1929 v Bel; (with Cork), 1931 v Sp (3)
Doyle, C. (Shelbourne), 1959 v Cz (1)
Doyle, D. (Shamrock R), 1926 v I (1)
Doyle, L. (Dolphin), 1932 v Sp (1)
Doyle, M. P. (Coventry C), 2004 v Ho (sub) (1)
Duff, D. A. (Blackburn R), 1998 v CzR, M; 1999 v Cro, Ma, Y, Para, Se (sub), Ni, Mac; 2000 v Cro, Ma (sub), T (sub + sub), S (sub); 2001 v P (sub), Es (sub), Cy (sub), And, P (sub), Es; 2002 v Cro, Ho, Ru, D, US, Ng, Cam, G, S.Ar, Sp; 2003 v Fi, Ru, Sw, Ge, Alb, N, Alb; (with Chelsea), 2004 v Aus, Ru, T, Sw, Ca, CzR (43)
Duffy, B. (Shamrock R), 1950 v Bel (1)
Duggan, H. A. (Leeds U), 1927 v I; 1930 v Bel; 1936 v H, L; (with Newport Co), 1938 v N (5)
Dunne, A. P. (Manchester U), 1962 v A; 1963 v Ic, S; 1964 v A, Sp, Pol, N, E; 1965 v Pol, Sp; 1966 v Sp (2), A, Bel; 1967 v Sp, T, Sp; 1969 v Pol, D, H; 1970 v H; 1971 v Se, I, A; (with Bolton W), 1974 v Br (sub), U, Ch; 1975 v T, Sw, USSR, Sw, WG; 1976 v T (33)
Dunne, J. (Sheffield U), 1930 v Bel; (with Arsenal), 1936 v Sw, H, L; (with Southampton), 1937 v Sw, F; (with Shamrock R), 1938 v N (2), Cz, Pol; 1939 v Sw, Pol, H (2), G (15)
Dunne, J. C. (Fulham), 1971 v A (1)
Dunne, L. (Manchester C), 1935 v Sw, G (2)
Dunne, P. A. J. (Manchester U), 1965 v Sp; 1966 v Sp (2), WG; 1967 v T (5)
Dunne, R. P. (Everton), 2000 v Gr, S (sub), M; 2001 v Ho, P, Es; (with Manchester C), Fi, And, P, Es; 2002 v Cro, Ho, Ru (sub), D (sub); 2003 v Gr, S (sub), N; 2004 v Aus (sub), T (sub), Ca (20)
Dunne, S. (Luton T), 1953 v F, A; 1954 v F, L; 1956 v Sp, Ho; 1957 v D, WG, E; 1958 v D, Pol, A; 1959 v Pol; 1960 v WG, Se (15)
Dunne, T. (St Patrick's Ath), 1956 v Ho; 1957 v D, WG (3)
Dunning, P. (Shelbourne), 1971 v Se, I (2)
Dunphy, E. M. (York C), 1966 v Sp; (with Millwall), 1966 v WG; 1967 v T, Sp, T, Cz; 1968 v Cz, Pol; 1969 v Pol, A, D (2), H; 1970 v D, H, Pol, WG (sub); 1971 v Pol, Se (2), I (2), A (23)
Dwyer, N. M. (West Ham U), 1960 v Se, Ch, WG, Se; (with Swansea T), 1961 v W, N, S (2); 1962 v Cz (2); 1964 v Pol (sub), N, E; 1965 v Pol (14)

Eccles, P. (Shamrock R), 1986 v U (sub) (1)
Egan, R. (Dundalk), 1929 v Bel (1)
Eglington, T. J. (Shamrock R), 1946 v P, Sp; (with Everton), 1947 v E, Sp, P; 1948 v P; 1949 v Sw, P, Se; 1951 v N, Arg; 1952 v WG (2), A, Sp; 1953 v F, A; 1954 v F, L, F; 1955 v N, Ho, WG; 1956 v Sp (24)
Ellis, P. (Bohemians), 1935 v Sw, G; 1936 v Ho, Sw, L; 1937 v G, H (7)
Evans, M. J. (Southampton), 1998 v R (sub) (1)

Fagan, E. (Shamrock R), 1973 v N (sub) (1)
Fagan, F. (Manchester C), 1955 v N; 1960 v Se; (with Derby Co), 1960 v Ch, WG, Se; 1961 v W, N, S (8)
Fagan, J. (Shamrock R), 1926 v I (1)
Fairclough, M. (Dundalk), 1982 v Ch (sub), Tr (sub) (2)
Fallon, S. (Celtic), 1951 v N; 1952 v WG (2), A, Sp; 1953 v F; 1955 v N, WG (8)
Fallon, W. J. (Notts Co), 1935 v H; 1936 v H; 1937 v H, Sw, F; 1939 v Sw, Pol; (with Sheffield W), 1939 v H, G (9)
Farquharson, T. G. (Cardiff C), 1929 v Bel; 1930 v Bel; 1931 v Sp; 1932 v Sp (4)
Farrell, P. (Hibernian), 1937 v Sw, F (2)
Farrell, P. D. (Shamrock R), 1946 v P, Sp; (with Everton), 1947 v Sp, P; 1948 v P, Sp; 1949 v Sw, P (sub), Sp; 1950 v E, Fi, Se; 1951 v Arg, N; 1952 v WG (2), A, Sp; 1953 v F, A; 1954 v F (2); 1955 v N, Ho, WG; 1956 v Y, Sp; 1957 v E (28)
Farrelly, G. (Aston Villa), 1996 v P, US, Bol; (with Everton), 1998 v CzR, M; (with Bolton W), 2000 v US (6)
Feenan, J. J. (Sunderland), 1937 v Sw, F (2)
Finnan, S. (Fulham), 2000 v Gr, S; 2001 v P (sub), Es (sub), Fi, And (sub+sub); 2002 v Cro (sub), Ho (sub), Cy, Ir (2), Ru, US, Ng, Cam (sub), G, S.Ar, Sp; 2003 v Ru, Gr, N (sub); (with Liverpool), 2004 v Aus, T, Sw (sub), R, Ng, Ho (28)
Finucane, A. (Limerick), 1967 v T, Cz; 1969 v Cz, D, H; 1970 v S, Cz; 1971 v Se, I (1+sub); 1972 v A (11)
Fitzgerald, F. J. (Waterford), 1955 v Ho; 1956 v Ho (2)
Fitzgerald, P. J. (Leeds U), 1961 v W, N, S; (with Chester), 1962 v Cz (2) (5)
Fitzpatrick, K. (Limerick), 1970 v Cz (1)
Fitzsimons, A. G. (Middlesbrough), 1950 v Fi, Bel; 1952 v WG (2), A, Sp; 1953 v F, A; 1954 v F, L, F; 1955 v Ho, N, WG; 1956 v Y, Sp, Ho; 1957 v D, WG, E (2); 1958 v D, Pol, A; 1959 v Pol; (with Lincoln C), 1959 v Cz (26)
Fleming, C. (Middlesbrough), 1996 v CzR (sub), P, Cro (sub), Ho (sub), US (sub), M, Bol; 1997 v Lie (sub); 1998 v R (sub), M (10)
Flood, J. J. (Shamrock R), 1926 v I; 1929 v Bel; 1930 v Bel; 1931 v Sp; 1932 v Sp (5)
Fogarty, A. (Sunderland), 1960 v WG, Se; 1961 v S; 1962 v Cz (2); 1963 v Ic (2), S (sub); 1964 v A (2); (with Hartlepools U), Sp (11)
Foley, D. J. (Watford), 2000 v S (sub), M (sub), US, S.Af; 2001 v Es (sub), Fi (6)
Foley, J. (Cork), 1934 v Bel, Ho; (with Celtic), 1935 v H, Sw, G; 1937 v G, H (7)
Foley, M. (Shelbourne), 1926 v I (1)
Foley, T. C. (Northampton T), 1964 v Sp, Pol, N; 1965 v Pol, Bel; 1966 v Sp (2), WG; 1967 v Cz (9)
Foy, T. (Shamrock R), 1938 v N; 1939 v H (2)
Fullam, J. (Preston NE), 1961 v N; (with Shamrock R), 1964 v Sp, Pol, N; 1966 v A, Bel; 1968 v Pol; 1969 v Pol, A, D; 1970 v Cz (sub) (11)
Fullam, R. (Shamrock R), 1926 v I; 1927 v I (2)

Gallagher, C. (Celtic), 1967 v T, Cz (2)
Gallagher, M. (Hibernian), 1954 v L (1)
Gallagher, P. (Falkirk), 1932 v Sp (1)
Galvin, A. (Tottenham H), 1983 v Ho, Ma; 1984 v Ho (sub), Is (sub); 1985 v M, USSR, N, D, I, N, Sp; 1986 v U, Ic, Cz; 1987 v Bel (2), S, Bul, L; (with Sheffield W), 1988 v L, Bul, R, Pol, N, E, USSR, Ho; 1989 v Sp; (with Swindon T), 1990 v WG (29)
Gannon, E. (Notts Co), 1949 v Sw; (with Sheffield W), 1949 v Bel, P, Se, Sp; 1950 v Fi; 1951 v N; 1952 v WG, A; 1954 v L, F; 1955 v N; (with Shelbourne), 1955 v N, WG (14)
Gannon, M. (Shelbourne), 1972 v A (1)
Gaskins, P. (Shamrock R), 1934 v Bel, Ho; 1935 v H, Sw, G; (with St James' Gate), 1938 v Cz, Pol (7)
Gavin, J. T. (Norwich C), 1950 v Fi (2); 1953 v F; 1954 v L; (with Tottenham H), 1955 v Ho, WG; (with Norwich C), 1957 v D (7)
Geoghegan, M. (St James' Gate), 1937 v G; 1938 v N (2)
Gibbons, A. (St Patrick's Ath), 1952 v WG; 1954 v L; 1956 v Y, Sp (4)
Gilbert, R. (Shamrock R), 1966 v WG (1)
Giles, C. (Doncaster R), 1951 v N (1)
Giles, M. J. (Manchester U), 1960 v Se, Ch; 1961 v W, N, S (2); 1962 v Cz (2), A; 1963 v Ic, S; (with Leeds U), 1964 v A (2), Sp (2), Pol, N, E; 1965 v Sp; 1966 v Sp (2), A, Bel; 1967 v Sp, T (2); 1969 v A, D, Cz; 1970 v S, Pol, WG; 1971 v I; 1973 v F, USSR; 1974 v Br, U, Ch; 1975 v USSR, T, Sw, USSR, Sw; (with WBA), 1976 v T; 1977 v E, T, F (2), Pol, Bul; (with Shamrock R), 1978 v Bul, T, Pol, N, D; 1979 v Ni, D, Bul, WG (59)
Given, S. J. J. (Blackburn R), 1996 v Ru, CzR, P, Cro, Ho, US, Bol; 1997 v Lie (2); (with Newcastle U), 1998 v Li, Ic, Li, Bel (2), CzR, Arg, M; 1999 v Cro, Ma, Y, Para, Se, Ni; 2000 v Gr, S.Af; 2001 v Fi, Cy, And (2), P, Es; 2002 v Cro, Ho, Cy, Ir (2), Ru, US, Ng, Cam, G, S.Ar, Sp; 2003 v Fi (sub), Ru, Sw, Gr, Ge, Alb, N, Alb, Ge; 2004 v Ru, Sw, Ca, Br, CzR, Pol, R, Ho (60)
Givens, D. J. (Manchester U), 1969 v D, H; 1970 v S, Cz, D, H; (with Luton T), 1970 v Pol, WG; 1971 v Se, I (2), A; 1972 v Ir, Ec, P; (with QPR), 1973 v F, USSR, Pol, F, N; 1974 v Pol, Br, U, Ch; 1975 v USSR, T, Sw, USSR, Sw, WG; 1976 v T, N, Pol; 1977 v E, T, F (2), Sp, Bul; 1978 v Bul, N, D; (with Birmingham C), 1979 v Ni (sub), E, D, Bul, WG; 1980 v US (sub), Ni (sub), Sw, Arg; 1981 v Ho, Bel, Cy (sub), W; (with Neuchatel X), 1982 v F (sub) (56)
Glen, W. (Shamrock R), 1927 v I; 1929 v Bel; 1930 v Bel; 1932 v Sp; 1936 v Ho, Sw, H, L (8)
Glynn, D. (Drumcondra), 1952 v WG; 1955 v N (2)
Godwin, T. F. (Shamrock R), 1949 v P, Se, Sp; 1950 v Fi, E; (with Leicester C), 1950 v Fi, Se, Bel; 1951 v N; (with Bournemouth), 1956 v Ho; 1957 v E; 1958 v D, Pol (13)
Golding, J. (Shamrock R), 1928 v Bel; 1930 v Bel (2)
Goodman, J. (Wimbledon), 1997 v W, Mac, R (sub), Lie (sub) (4)
Goodwin, J. (Stockport Co), 2003 v Fi (sub) (1)
Gorman, W. C. (Bury), 1936 v Sw, H, L; 1937 v G, H; 1938 v N, Cz, Pol; 1939 v Sw, Pol; (with Brentford), H; 1947 v E, P (13)
Grace, J. (Drumcondra), 1926 v I (1)
Grealish, A. (Orient), 1976 v N, Pol; 1978 v N, D; 1979 v Ni, E, WG; (with Luton T), 1980 v W, Cz, Bul, US, Ni, E, Cy, Sw, Arg; 1981 v WG 'B', Ho, Bel, F, Cy, W, Bel, Pol; (with Brighton & HA), 1982 v Ho, Alg, Ch, Br, Tr; 1983 v Ho, Sp,

Ic, Sp; 1984 v Ic, Ho; (with WBA), Pol, Chn; 1985 v M, USSR, N, D, Sp (sub), Sw; 1986 v USSR, D (45)
Gregg, E. (Bohemians), 1978 v Pol, D (sub); 1979 v E (sub), D, Bul, WG; 1980 v W, Cz (8)
Griffith, R. (Walsall), 1935 v H (1)
Grimes, A. A. (Manchester U), 1978 v T, Pol, N (sub); 1980 v Bul, US, Ni, E, Cy; 1981 v WG 'B' (sub), Cz, Pol; 1982 v Alg; 1983 v Sp (2); (with Coventry C), 1984 v Pol, Is; (with Luton T), 1988 v L, R (18)

Hale, A. (Aston Villa), 1962 v A; (with Doncaster R), 1963 v Ic; 1964 v Sp (2); (with Waterford), 1967 v Sp; 1968 v Pol (sub); 1969 v Pol, A, D; 1970 v S, Cz; 1971 v Pol (sub); 1972 v A (sub); 1974 v Pol (sub) (14)
Hamilton, T. (Shamrock R), 1959 v Cz (2) (2)
Hand, E. K. (Portsmouth), 1969 v Cz (sub); 1970 v Pol, WG; 1971 v Pol, A; 1973 v USSR, F, USSR, Pol, F; 1974 v Pol, Br, U, Ch; 1975 v T, Sw, USSR, Sw, WG; 1976 v T (20)
Harrington, W. (Cork), 1936 v Ho, Sw, H, L; 1938 v Pol (sub) (5)
Harte, I. P. (Leeds U), 1996 v Cro (sub), Ho, M, Bol; 1997 v Lie, Mac, Ic (sub), W, Mac (sub), R, Lie; 1998 v Li, Ic, Li, Bel (2), Arg, M; 1999 v Para; 2000 v Cro (sub), Ma (sub), CzR; 2001 v Ho, P, Es, Fi, Cy, And (2), P, Es; 2002 v Cro, Ho, Cy, Ir (2), Ru, D, US, Ng, Cam, G, S.Ar, Sp; 2003 v Fi, Ru, Sw, S, N; 2004 v Aus (sub), Ru (sub), T, Sw, Ca (sub), CzR, Pol (56)
Hartnett, J. B. (Middlesbrough), 1949 v Sp; 1954 v L (2)
Haverty, J. (Arsenal), 1956 v Ho; 1957 v D, WG, E (2); 1958 v D, Pol, A; 1959 v Pol; 1960 v Se, Ch; 1961 v W, N, S (2); (with Blackburn R), 1962 v Cz (2); (with Millwall), 1963 v S; 1964 v A, Sp, Pol, N, E; (with Celtic), 1965 v Pol; (with Bristol R), 1965 v Sp; (with Shelbourne), 1966 v Sp (2), WG, A, Bel; 1967 v T, Sp (32)
Hayes, A. W. P. (Southampton), 1979 v D (1)
Hayes, W. E. (Huddersfield T), 1947 v E, P (2)
Hayes, W. J. (Limerick), 1949 v Bel (1)
Healey, R. (Cardiff C), 1977 v Pol; 1980 v E (sub) (2)
Healy, C. (Celtic), 2002 v Ru, D (sub), US; 2003 v Fi (sub), Sw, Gr, S (sub), N (sub), Ge; (with Sunderland), 2004 v Aus (sub), Ru, T, Sw (13)
Heighway, S. D. (Liverpool), 1971 v Pol, Se (2), I, A; 1973 v USSR; 1975 v USSR, T, USSR, WG; 1976 v T, N; 1977 v E, F (2), Sp, Bul; 1978 v Bul, N, D; 1979 v Ni, Bul; 1980 v Bul, US, Ni, E, Cy, Arg; 1981 v Bel, F, Cy, W, Bel; (with Minnesota K), 1982 v Ho (34)
Henderson, B. (Drumcondra), 1948 v P, Sp (2)
Hennessy, J. (Shelbourne), 1965 v Pol, Bel, Sp; 1966 v WG; (with St Patrick's Ath), 1969 v A (5)
Herrick, J. (Cork Hibernians), 1972 v A, Ch (sub); (with Shamrock R), 1973 v F (sub) (3)
Higgins, J. (Birmingham C), 1951 v Arg (1)
Holland, M. R. (Ipswich T), 2000 v Mac (sub), M, US, S.Af; 2001 v P (sub), Fi, Cy (sub), And (2), P (sub), Es; 2002 v Ho, Cy, Ir (2), Ru (sub), D, US (sub), Ng, Cam, G, S.Ar, Sp; 2003 v Fi (sub), Ru, Sw, Gr, S, Ge, Alb, N, Alb, Ge; (with Charlton Ath), 2004 v Aus, Ru, Sw, Ca (sub), Br, CzR, R, Ng, Jam (sub), Ho (43)
Holmes, J. (Coventry C), 1971 v A (sub); 1973 v F, USSR, Pol, F, N; 1974 v Pol, Br; 1975 v USSR, Sw; 1976 v T, N, Pol; 1977 v E, T, F, Sp; (with Tottenham H), F, Pol, Bul; 1978 v Bul, T, Pol, N, D; 1979 v Ni, E, D, Bul; (with Vancouver W), 1981 v W (30)
Horlacher, A. F. (Bohemians), 1930 v Bel; 1932 v Sp, Ho; 1934 v Ho (sub); 1935 v H;1936 v Ho, Sw (7)
Houghton, R. J. (Oxford U), 1986 v W, U, Ic, Cz; 1987 v Bel (2), S (2), Pol, L; 1988 v L, Bul; (with Liverpool), Is, Y, N, E, USSR, Ho; 1989 v Ni, Tun, Sp, F, H, Sp, Ma, H; 1990 v Ni, Ma, Fi, E, Eg, Ho, R, I; 1991 v Mor, T, E (2), Pol, Ch, US; 1992 v H, Alb, US, I, P; (with Aston Villa), 1993 v D, Sp, Ni, D, Alb, La, Li; 1994 v Li, Sp, Ni, Bol, G (sub), I, M, N, Ho; (with C Palace), 1995 v P, A; 1996 v A, CzR; 1997 v Lie, R, Lie; (with Reading), 1998 v Li, R, Bel (1 + sub) (73)
Howlett, G. (Brighton & HA), 1984 v Chn (sub) (1)
Hoy, M. (Dundalk), 1938 v N; 1939 v Sw, Pol, H (2), G (6)
Hughton, C. (Tottenham H), 1980 v US, E, Sw, Arg; 1981 v Ho, Bel, F, Cy, W, Bel, Pol; 1982 v F; 1983 v Ho, Sp, Ma, Sp; 1984 v Ic, Ho, Ma; 1985 v M (sub), USSR, N, I, Is, E, Sp; 1986 v Sw, USSR, U, Ic; 1987 v Bel, Bul; 1988 v Is, Y, Pol, N, E, USSR, Ho; 1989 v Ni, F, H, Sp, Ma, H; 1990 v W (sub), USSR (sub), Fi, T (sub), Ma; 1991 v T; (with West Ham U), Ch; 1992 v T (53)
Hurley, C. J. (Millwall), 1957 v E; (with Sunderland), 1958 v D, Pol, A; 1959 v Cz (2); 1960 v Se, Ch, WG, Se; 1961 v W, N, S (2); 1962 v Cz (2), A; 1963 v Ic (2), S; 1964 v A (2), Sp (2), Pol, N; 1965 v Sp; 1966 v WG, A, Bel; 1967 v T, Sp, T, Cz; 1968 v Cz, Pol; 1969 v Pol, D, Cz, (with Bolton W), H (40)
Hutchinson, F. (Drumcondra), 1935 v Sw, G (2)

Irwin, D. J. (Manchester U), 1991 v Mor, T, W, E, Pol, US; 1992 v H, Pol, W, US, Alb, US (sub), I; 1993 v La, D, Sp, Ni, D, Alb, La, Li; 1994 v Li, Sp, Ni, Bol, G, I, M; 1995 v La, Lie, Ni, E, Ni, P, Lie, A; 1996 v A, P, Ho, CzR; 1997 v Lie, Mac, Ic, Mac, R; 1998 v Li, Bel, Arg (sub); 1999 v Cro, Y, Para, Mac; 2000 v Y, Mac, T (2) (56)

Jordan, D. (Wolverhampton W), 1937 v Sw, F (2)
Jordan, W. (Bohemians), 1934 v Ho; 1938 v N (2)

Kavanagh, G. A. (Stoke C), 1998 v CzR (sub); 1999 v Se (sub), Ni (sub); (with Cardiff C), 2004 v Ca, Br (5)
Kavanagh, P. J. (Celtic), 1931 v Sp; 1932 v Sp (2)
Keane, R. D. (Wolverhampton W), 1998 v CzR (sub), Arg, M; 1999 v Cro, Ma, Para, Se (sub), Ni, Mac; (with Coventry C), 2000 v Y, Ma, Mac, T, CzR, Gr, S, M, S.Af (sub); (with Internazionale), 2001 v Ho, P, Es, Fi, Cy, And, P; (with Leeds U), 2002 v Cro, Ho, Ir (2), Ru, D, US, Ng, Cam, G, S.Ar, Sp; 2003 v Fi; (with Tottenham H), Ru, Sw, Alb, N, Alb, Ge; 2004 v Aus, Sw, Ca, Br, CzR, R, Ng, Ho (52)
Keane, R. M. (Nottingham F), 1991 v Ch; 1992 v H, Pol, W, Sw, Alb, US; 1993 v La, D, Sp, W, Ni, D, Alb, La, Li; (with Manchester U), 1994 v Li, Sp, Ni, Bol, G, CzR (sub), I, M, N, Ho; 1995 v Ni (2); 1996 v A, Ru; 1997 v Ic, W, Mac, R, Lie; 1998 v Li, Ic, Li; 1999 v Cro, Ma, Y, Para; 2000 v Y, T (2), CzR; 2001 v Ho, P, Es, Cy, And, P; 2002 v Cro, Ho, Cy, Ir, Ru, Ng; 2004 v R (59)
Keane, T. R. (Swansea T), 1949 v Sw, P, Se, Sp (4)
Kearin, M. (Shamrock R), 1972 v A (1)
Kearns, F. T. (West Ham U), 1954 v L (1)
Kearns, M. (Oxford U), 1971 v Pol (sub); (with Walsall), 1974 v Pol (sub), U, Ch; 1976 v N, Pol; 1977 v E, T, F (2), Sp, Bul; 1978 v N, D; 1979 v Ni, E; (with Wolverhampton W), 1980 v US, Ni (18)
Kelly, A. T. (Sheffield U), 1993 v W (sub); 1994 v Ru (sub), G; 1995 v La, Ni, E, Ni, P, Lie, A; 1996 v A, La, P, Ho; 1997 v Mac, Ic, Mac, R; 1998 v R, Arg (sub); 1999 v Para (sub), Mac; (with Blackburn R), 2000 v Y, Cro, Ma, Mac, T, CzR, S, US; 2001 v Ho, P, Es; 2002 v Cro (sub) (34)
Kelly, D. T. (Walsall), 1988 v Is, R, Y; (with West Ham U), 1989 v Tun (sub); (with Leicester C), 1990 v USSR, Ma; 1991 v Mor, W (sub), Ch, US; 1992 v H; (with Newcastle U), I (sub), P; 1993 v Sp (sub), Ni; (with Wolverhampton W), 1994 v Ru, N (sub); 1995 v E, Ni; (with Sunderland), 1996 v La (sub); 1997 v Ic, W (sub), Mac (sub); (with Tranmere R), 1998 v Li (sub), R (sub), Bel (sub) (26)
Kelly, G. (Leeds U), 1994 v Ru, Ho, Bol (sub), G (sub), CzR, N, Ho; 1995 v La, Lie, Ni (2), P, Lie, A; 1996 v A, La, P, Ho; 1997 v W (sub), R, Lie; 1998 v Ic, Li, Bel (2), CzR, Arg, M; 2000 v Cro, Mac, CzR; 2001 v Ho (sub), Fi, Cy, And (2), P, Es; 2002 v Cro, Ho, Ir (sub+sub), Ru (sub), D, US (sub), Ng (sub), Cam, G, S.Ar, Sp; 2003 v Fi, Sw (52)
Kelly, J. (Derry C), 1932 v Ho; 1934 v Bel; 1936 v Sw, L (4)
Kelly, J. A. (Drumcondra), 1957 v WG, E; (with Preston NE), 1962 v A; 1963 v Ic (2), S; 1964 v A (2), Sp (2), Pol; 1965 v Bel; 1966 v A, Bel; 1967 v Sp (2), T, Cz; 1968 v Pol, Cz; 1969 v Pol, A, D, Cz, D, H; 1970 v S, D, H, Pol, WG; 1971 v Pol, Se (2), I (2), A; 1972 v Ir, Ec, Ch, P; 1973 v USSR, F, USSR, Pol, F, N (47)
Kelly, J. P. V. (Wolverhampton W), 1961 v W, N, S; 1962 v Cz (2) (5)
Kelly, M. J. (Portsmouth), 1988 v Y, Pol (sub); 1989 v Tun; 1991 v Mor (4)
Kelly, N. (Nottingham F), 1954 v L (1)
Kendrick, J. (Everton), 1927 v I; (with Dolphin) 1934 v Bel, Ho; 1936 v Ho (4)
Kenna, J. J. (Blackburn R), 1995 v P (sub), Lie (sub), A (sub); 1996 v La, P, Ho, Ru (sub), CzR, P, Cro, Ho, US; 1997 v Lie, Mac, Ic, R (sub), Lie; 1998 v Li, Ic, R, Bel (1 + sub), CzR, Arg; 1999 v Cro (sub), Ma; 2000 v T (sub) (27)
Kennedy, M. F. (Portsmouth), 1986 v Ic, Cz (sub) (2)
Kennedy, M. J. (Liverpool), 1996 v A, La (sub), P, Ru, CzR, Cro, Ho (sub), US (sub), M, Bol (sub); 1997 v R, Lie; 1998 v Li, Ic (sub), R, Bel (2), (with Wimbledon), M (sub); 1999 v Ma (sub), Se, Ni, Mac; (with Manchester C), 2000 v Y, Ma, Mac, CzR, S, M, US (sub), S.Af (sub); 2001 v And; (with Wolverhampton W), 2002 v Cro, Cy, Ru (sub) (34)
Kennedy, W. (St James' Gate), 1932 v Ho; 1934 v Bel, Ho (3)
Kenny, P. (Sheffield U), 2004 v CzR (sub), Jam (2)
Keogh, J. (Shamrock R), 1966 v WG (sub) (1)
Keogh, S. (Shamrock R), 1959 v Pol (1)

Kernaghan, A. N. (Middlesbrough), 1993 v La, D (2), Alb, La, Li; 1994 v Li; (with Manchester C), Sp, Ni, Bol (sub), CzR; 1995 v Lie, E; 1996 v A, P (sub), Ho (sub), Ru, P, Cro (sub), Ho, US, Bol (22)
Kiely, D. L. (Charlton Ath), 2000 v T (sub + 1), Gr (sub), M; 2002 v Ru (sub), D; 2003 v Fi, S (8)
Kiernan, F. W. (Shamrock R), 1951 v Arg, N; (with Southampton), 1952 v WG (2), A (5)
Kilbane, K. D. (WBA), 1998 v Ic, CzR (sub), Arg; 1999 v Se (sub), Mac (sub); 2000 v Y, Cro (sub), Ma, T (2); (with Sunderland), CzR, Gr, S, M (sub), US, S.Af (sub); 2001 v Ho, P, Es, Fi, Cy, And (2), P, Es; 2002 v Cro (sub), Ho, Cy, Ir (2), Ru, US, Ng, Cam, G, S.Ar, Sp; 2003 v Fi (sub), Ru, Sw, S, Ge, Alb, N, Alb, Ge; 2004 v Aus (sub); (with Everton), Ru, T, Sw, Ca (sub), Br, CzR (53)
Kinnear, J. P. (Tottenham H), 1967 v T; 1968 v Cz, Pol; 1969 v A; 1970 v Cz, D, H, Pol; 1971 v Se (sub), I; 1972 v Ir, Ec, Ch, P; 1973 v USSR, F; 1974 v Pol, Br, U, Ch; 1975 v USSR, T, Sw, USSR, WG; (with Brighton & HA), 1976 v T (sub) (26)
Kinsella, J. (Shelbourne), 1928 v Bel (1)
Kinsella, M. A. (Charlton Ath), 1998 v CzR, Arg; 1999 v Cro, Ma, Y, Para, Se, Ni, Mac; 2000 v Y, Cro, Ma, Mac, T, CzR, Gr; 2001 v Ho, P, Es, Fi, Cy, And, P, Es; 2002 v Ir, D, US, Ng (sub), Cam, G, S.Ar, Sp; 2003 v Fi; (with Aston Villa), Ru, Sw, S, Ge, Alb, N, Alb, Ge (sub); 2004 v Aus, T, Sw (sub); (with WBA), CzR (sub), Pol, Ng, Jam (48)
Kinsella, O. (Shamrock R), 1932 v Ho; 1938 v N (2)
Kirkland, A. (Shamrock R), 1927 v I (1)

Lacey, W. (Shelbourne), 1927 v I; 1928 v Bel; 1930 v Bel (3)
Langan, D. (Derby Co), 1978 v T, N; 1980 v Sw, Arg; (with Birmingham C), 1981 v WG 'B', Ho, Bel, F, Cy, W, Bel, Cz, Pol; 1982 v Ho, F; (with Oxford U), 1985 v N, Sp, Sw; 1986 v W, U; 1987 v Bel, S, Pol, Br (sub), L (sub); 1988 v L (26)
Lawler, J. F. (Fulham), 1953 v A; 1954 v L, F; 1955 v N, H, N, WG; 1956 v Y (8)
Lawlor, J. C. (Drumcondra), 1949 v Bel; (with Doncaster R), 1951 v N, Arg (3)
Lawlor, M. (Shamrock R), 1971 v Pol, Se (2), I (sub); 1973 v Pol (5)
Lawrenson, M. (Preston NE), 1977 v Pol; (with Brighton), 1978 v Bul, Pol, N (sub); 1979 v Ni, E; 1980 v E, Cy, Sw; 1981 v Ho, Bel, F, Cy, Pol; (with Liverpool), 1982 v Ho, F; 1983 v Ho, Sp, Ic, Ma, Sp; 1984 v Ic, Ho, Ma, Is; 1985 v USSR, N, D, I, E, N; 1986 v Sw, USSR, D; 1987 v Bel, S; 1988 v Bul, Is (38)
Lee, A. D. (Rotherham U), 2003 v N (sub), Ge (sub); (with Cardiff C), 2004 v CzR (sub), Pol, Ng, Jam, Ho (sub) (7)
Leech, M. (Shamrock R), 1969 v Cz, D, H; 1972 v A, Ir, Ec, P; 1973 v USSR (sub) (8)
Lennon, C. (St James' Gate), 1935 v H, Sw, G (3)
Lennox, G. (Dolphin), 1931 v Sp; 1932 v Sp (2)
Lowry, D. (St Patrick's Ath), 1962 v A (sub) (1)
Lunn, R. (Dundalk), 1939 v Sw, Pol (2)
Lynch, J. (Cork Bohemians), 1934 v Bel (1)

McAlinden, J. (Portsmouth), 1946 v P, Sp (2)
McAteer, J. W. (Bolton W), 1994 v Ru, Ho (sub), Bol (sub), G, CzR (sub), I (sub), M (sub), N, Ho (sub); 1995 v La, Lie, Ni (2 sub), Lie; (with Liverpool), 1996 v La, P, Ho (sub), Ru; 1997 v Mac, Ic, W, Mac; 1998 v Ic (sub), Li, R; 1999 v Cro, Ma, Y; (with Blackburn R), Para, Se; 2000 v CzR (sub), S, M, US (sub), S.Af; 2001 v Ho, P, Es, Fi (sub), Cy; 2002 v Cro (sub), Ho; (with Sunderland), Ir (2), Ru (sub), D, Ng, Cam, S.Ar (sub); 2003 v Fi, Ru; 2004 v Br (sub) (52)
McCann, J. (Shamrock R), 1957 v WG (1)
McCarthy, J. (Bohemians), 1926 v I; 1928 v Bel; 1930 v Bel (3)
McCarthy, M. (Shamrock R), 1932 v Ho (1)
McCarthy, M. (Manchester C), 1984 v Pol, Chn; 1985 v M, D, I, Is, E, Sp, Sw; 1986 v Sw, USSR, W (sub), U, Ic, Cz; 1987 v S (2), Pol, Bul, Bel (with Celtic), Br, L; 1988 v Bul, Is, R, Y, N, E, USSR, Ho; 1989 v Ni, Tun, Sp, F, H, Sp; (with Lyon), 1990 v WG, Ni (with Millwall), W, USSR, Fi, T, E, Eg, Ho, R, I; 1991 v Mor, T, E, US; 1992 v H, T, Alb (sub), US, I, P (57)
McConville, T. (Dundalk), 1972 v A; (with Waterford), 1973 v USSR, F, USSR, Pol, F (6)
McDonagh, Jacko (Shamrock R), 1984 v Pol (sub), Ma (sub); 1985 v M (sub) (3)
McDonagh, J. (Everton), 1981 v WG 'B', W, Bel, Cz; (with Bolton W), 1982 v Ho, F, Ch, Br; 1983 v Ho, Sp, Ic, Ma, Sp; (with Notts Co), 1984 v Ic, Ho, Pol; 1985 v M, USSR, N, D, Sp, Sw; 1986 v Sw, USSR; (with Wichita Wings) D (25)
McEvoy, M. A. (Blackburn R), 1961 v S (2); 1963 v S; 1964 v A, Sp (2), Pol, N, E; 1965 v Pol, Bel, Sp; 1966 v Sp (2); 1967 v Sp, T, Cz (17)
McGeady, A. (Celtic), 2004 v Jam (sub) (1)
McGee, P. (QPR), 1978 v T, N (sub), D (sub); 1979 v Ni, E, D (sub), Bul (sub); 1980 v Cz, Bul; (with Preston NE), US, Ni, Cy, Sw, Arg; 1981 v Bel (sub) (15)
McGoldrick, E. J. (C Palace), 1992 v Sw, US, I, P (sub); 1993 v D, W, Ni (sub), D; (with Arsenal), 1994 v Ni, Ru, Ho, CzR; 1995 v La (sub), Lie, E (15)
McGowan, D. (West Ham U), 1949 v P, Se, Sp (3)
McGowan, J. (Cork U), 1947 v Sp (1)
McGrath, M. (Blackburn R), 1958 v A; 1959 v Pol, Cz (2); 1960 v Se, WG, Se; 1961 v W; 1962 v Cz (2); 1963 v S; 1964 v A (2), E; 1965 v Pol, Bel, Sp; 1966 v Sp; (with Bradford), 1966 v WG, A, Bel; 1967 v T (22)
McGrath, P. (Manchester U), 1985 v I (sub), Is, E, N (sub), Sw (sub); 1986 v Sw (sub), D, W, Ic, Cz; 1987 v Bel (2), S (2), Pol, Bul, Br, L; 1988 v L, Bul, Y, Pol, N, E, Ho; 1989 v Ni, F, H, Sp, Ma, H; (with Aston Villa), 1990 v WG, Ma, USSR, Fi, T, E, Eg, Ho, R, I; 1991 v E (2), W, Pol, Ch (sub), US; 1992 v Pol, T, Sw, US, Alb, US, I, P; 1993 v La, Sp, Ni, D, La, Li; 1994 v Sp, Ni, G, CzR, I, M, N, Ho; 1995 v La, Ni, E, Ni, P, Lie, A; 1996 v A, La, P, Ho, Ru, CzR; (with Derby Co), 1997 v W (83)
McGuire, W. (Bohemians), 1936 v Ho (1)
McKenzie, G. (Southend U), 1938 v N (2), Cz, Pol; 1939 v Sw, Pol, H (2), G (9)
Mackey, G. (Shamrock R), 1957 v D, WG, E (3)
McLoughlin, A. F. (Swindon T), 1990 v Ma, E (sub), Eg (sub); 1991 v Mor (sub), E (sub); (with Southampton), W, Ch (sub); 1992 v H (sub), W (sub); (with Portsmouth), US (1 + sub), I (sub), P; 1993 v W; 1994 v Ni (sub), Ru, Ho (sub); 1995 v Lie (sub); 1996 v P, Cro, Ho, US, M, Bol (sub); 1997 v Lie, Mac, Ic, W, Mac; 1998 v Li (sub), Ic, Li, R, Bel, CzR (sub); 1999 v Y, Para (sub), Se, Ni (sub); 2000 v Cro, Ma (sub), Mac (42)
McLoughlin, F. (Fordsons), 1930 v Bel; (with Cork), 1932 v Sp (2)
McMillan, W. (Belfast Celtic), 1946 v P, Sp (2)
McNally, J. B. (Luton T), 1959 v Cz; 1961 v S; 1963 v Ic (3)
McPhail, S. (Leeds U), 2000 v S, US, S.Af; 2002 v Cro (sub), Cy (sub); 2003 v Fi (sub), Gr; 2004 v T (sub), Ca (sub), Ng (10)
Macken, A. (Derby Co), 1977 v Sp (1)
Madden, O. (Cork), 1936 v H (1)
Maguire, J. (Shamrock R), 1929 v Bel (1)
Mahon, A. J. (Tranmere R), 2000 v Gr (sub), S.Af (2)
Malone, G. (Shelbourne), 1949 v Bel (1)
Mancini, T. J. (QPR), 1974 v Pol, Br, U, Ch; (with Arsenal), 1975 v USSR (5)
Martin, C. (Bo'ness), 1927 v I (1)
Martin, C. J. (Glentoran), 1946 v P (sub), Sp; 1947 v E; (with Leeds U), 1947 v Sp; 1948 v P, Sp; (with Aston Villa), 1949 v Sw, Bel, P, Se, Sp; 1950 v Fi, E, Fi, Se, Bel; 1951 v Arg; 1952 v WG, A, Sp; 1954 v F (2), L; 1955 v N, Ho, N, WG; 1956 v Y, Sp, Ho (30)
Martin, M. P. (Bohemians), 1972 v A, Ir, Ec, Ch, P; 1973 v USSR; (with Manchester U), 1973 v USSR, Pol, F, N; 1974 v Pol, Br, U, Ch; 1975 v USSR, T, Sw, USSR, Sw, WG; (with WBA), 1976 v T, N, Pol; 1977 v E, T, F (2), Sp, Pol, Bul; (with Newcastle U), 1979 v D, Bul, WG; 1980 v W, Cz, Bul, US, Ni; 1981 v WG 'B', F, Bel, Cz; 1982 v Ho, F, Alg, Ch, Br, Tr; 1983 v Ho, Sp, Ma, Sp (52)
Maybury, A. (Leeds U), 1998 v CzR; 1999 v Ni; (with Hearts), 2004 v CzR, Pol (sub), R, Ng, Jam, Ho (8)
Meagan, M. K. (Everton), 1961 v S; 1962 v A; 1963 v Ic; 1964 v Sp; (with Huddersfield T), 1965 v Bel; 1966 v Sp (2), A, Bel; 1967 v Sp, T, Sp, T, Cz; 1968 v Cz, Pol; (with Drogheda), 1970 v S (17)
Meehan, P. (Drumcondra), 1934 v Ho (1)
Miller, L. W. P. (Celtic), 2004 v CzR (sub), Pol, R, Ng, (4)
Milligan, M. J. (Oldham Ath), 1992 v US (sub) (1)
Monahan, P. (Sligo R), 1935 v Sw, G (2)
Mooney, J. (Shamrock R), 1965 v Pol, Bel (2)
Moore, A. (Middlesbrough), 1996 v CzR, Cro (sub), Ho, M, Bol; 1997 v Lie (sub), Mac (sub), Ic (sub) (8)
Moore, P. (Shamrock R), 1931 v Sp; 1932 v Ho; (with Aberdeen), 1934 v Bel, Ho; 1935 v H, G; (with Shamrock R), 1936 v Ho; 1937 v G, H (9)
Moran, K. (Manchester U), 1980 v Sw, Arg; 1981 v WG 'B', Bel, F, Cy, W (sub), Bel, Cz, Pol; 1982 v F, Alg; 1983 v Ic; 1984 v Ic, Ho, Ma, Is; 1985 v M; 1986 v D, Ic, Cz; 1987 v Bel (2), S (2), Pol, Bul, Br, L; 1988 v L, Bul, Is, R, Y, Pol, N, E, USSR, Ho; (with Sporting Gijon), 1989 v Ni, Sp, H, Sp, Ma, H; 1990 v Ni, Ma; (with Blackburn R), W, USSR (sub), Ma, E, Eg, Ho, R, I; 1991 v T (sub), W, E, Pol, Ch, US; 1992 v Pol, US; 1993 v D, Sp, Ni, Alb; 1994 v Li, Sp, Ho, Bol (71)

Moroney, T. (West Ham U), 1948 v Sp; 1949 v P, Se, Sp; 1950 v Fi, E, Fi, Bel; 1951 v N (2); 1952 v WG; (with Evergreen U), 1954 v F (12)
Morris, C. B. (Celtic), 1988 v Is, R, Y, Pol, N, E, USSR, Ho; 1989 v Ni, Tun, Sp, F, H (1+sub); 1990 v WG, Ni, Ma (sub), W, USSR, Fi (sub), T, E, Eg, Ho, R, I; 1991 v E; 1992 v H (sub), Pol, W, Sw, US (2), P; (with Middlesbrough), 1993 v W (35)
Morrison, C. H. (C Palace), 2002 v Cro (sub), Cy (sub), Ir (sub), Ru (sub), D, US (sub), Ng (sub); (with Birmingham C), 2003 v Ru (sub), Sw (sub), S; 2004 v Aus (sub), Ru, T (sub), Sw (sub), Ca (sub), Br, CzR, Pol, R, Jam, Ho (21)
Moulson, C. (Lincoln C), 1936 v H, L; (with Notts Co), 1937 v H, Sw, F (5)
Moulson, G. B. (Lincoln C), 1948 v P, Sp; 1949 v Sw (3)
Mucklan, C. (Drogheda U), 1978 v Pol (1)
Muldoon, T. (Aston Villa), 1927 v I (1)
Mulligan, P. M. (Shamrock R), 1969 v Cz, D, H; 1970 v S, Cz, D; (with Chelsea), 1970 v H, Pol, WG; 1971 v Pol, Se, I; 1972 v A, Ir, Ec, Ch, P; (with C Palace), 1973 v F, USSR, Pol, F, N; 1974 v Pol, Br, U, Ch; 1975 v USSR, T, Sw, USSR, Sw; (with WBA), 1976 v T, Pol; 1977 v E, T, F (2), Pol, Bul; 1978 v Bul, N, D; 1979 v E, D, Bul (sub), WG; (with Shamrock R), 1980 v W, Cz, Bul, US (sub) (50)
Munroe, L. (Shamrock R), 1954 v L (1)
Murphy, A. (Clyde), 1956 v Y (1)
Murphy, B. (Bohemians), 1986 v U (1)
Murphy, J. (C Palace), 1980 v W, US, Cy (3)
Murphy, J. (WBA), 2004 v T (sub) (1)
Murray, T. (Dundalk), 1950 v Bel (1)

Newman, W. (Shelbourne), 1969 v D (1)
Nolan, R. (Shamrock R), 1957 v D, WG, E; 1958 v Pol; 1960 v Ch, WG, Se; 1962 v Cz (2); 1963 v Ic (10)

O'Brien, A. J. (Newcastle U), 2001 v Es (sub); 2002 v Cro (sub), Ho (sub), Ru, US; 2003 v S (sub); 2004 v Aus (sub), T, Br, Pol (sub), R, Jam, Ho (13)
O'Brien, F. (Philadelphia F), 1980 v Cz, E, Cy (sub) (3)
O'Brien, L. (Shamrock R), 1986 v U; (with Manchester U), 1987 v Br; 1988 v Is (sub), R (sub), Y (sub), Pol (sub); 1989 v Tun; (with Newcastle U), Sp (sub); 1992 v Sw (sub); 1993 v W; (with Tranmere R), 1994 v Ru; 1996 v Cro, Ho, US, Bol; 1997 v Mac (sub) (16)
O'Brien, M. T. (Derby Co), 1927 v I; (with Walsall), 1929 v Bel; (with Norwich C), 1930 v Bel; (with Watford), 1932 v Ho (4)
O'Brien, R. (Notts Co), 1976 v N, Pol; 1977 v Sp, Pol; 1980 v Arg (sub) (5)
O'Byrne, L. B. (Shamrock R), 1949 v Bel (1)
O'Callaghan, B. R. (Stoke C), 1979 v WG (sub); 1980 v W, US; 1981 v W; 1982 v Br, Tr (6)
O'Callaghan, K. (Ipswich T), 1981 v WG 'B', Cz, Pol; 1982 v Alg, Ch, Br, Tr (sub); 1983 v Sp, Ic (sub), Ma (sub), Sp (sub); 1984 v Ic, Ho, Ma; 1985 v M (sub), N (sub), D (sub), (with Portsmouth) E (sub); 1986 v Sw (sub), USSR (sub); 1987 v Br (21)
O'Connell, A. (Dundalk), 1967 v Sp; (with Bohemians), 1971 v Pol (sub) (2)
O'Connor, T. (Shamrock R), 1950 v Fi, E, Fi, Se (4)
O'Connor, T. (Fulham), 1968 v Cz; (with Dundalk), 1972 v A, Ir (sub), Ec (sub), Ch; (with Bohemians), 1973 v F (sub), Pol (sub) (7)
O'Driscoll, J. F. (Swansea T), 1949 v Sw, Bel, Se (3)
O'Driscoll, S. (Fulham), 1982 v Ch, Br, Tr (sub) (3)
O'Farrell, F. (West Ham U), 1952 v A; 1953 v A; 1954 v F; 1955 v Ho, N; 1956 v Y, Ho; (with Preston NE), 1958 v D; 1959 v Cz (9)
O'Flanagan, K. P. (Bohemians), 1938 v N, Cz, Pol; 1939 v Pol, H (2), G; (with Arsenal), 1947 v E, Sp, P (10)
O'Flanagan, M. (Bohemians), 1947 v E (1)
O'Hanlon, K. G. (Rotherham U), 1988 v Is (1)
O'Kane, P. (Bohemians), 1935 v H, Sw, G (3)
O'Keefe, E. (Everton), 1981 v W; (with Port Vale), 1984 v Chn; 1985 v M, USSR (sub), E (5)
O'Keefe, T. (Cork), 1934 v Bel; (with Waterford), 1938 v Cz, Pol (3)
O'Leary, D. (Arsenal), 1977 v E, F (2), Sp, Bul; 1978 v Bul, N, D; 1979 v E, Bul, WG; 1980 v W, Bul, Ni, E, Cy; 1981 v WG 'B',Ho, Cz, Pol; 1982 v Ho, F; 1983 v Ho, Ic, Sp; 1984 v Pol, Is, Chn; 1985 v USSR, N, D, Is, E (sub), N, Sp, Sw; 1986 v Sw, USSR, D, W; 1989 v Sp, Ma, H; 1990 v WG, Ni (sub), Ma, W (sub), USSR, Fi, T, Ma, R (sub); 1991 v Mor, T, E (2), Pol, Ch; 1992 v H, Pol, T, W, Sw, US, Alb, I, P; 1993 v W (68)

O'Leary, P. (Shamrock R), 1980 v Bul, US, Ni, E (sub), Cz, Arg; 1981 v Ho (7)
O'Mahoney, M. T. (Bristol R), 1938 v Cz, Pol; 1939 v Sw, Pol, H, G (6)
O'Neill, F. S. (Shamrock R), 1962 v Cz (2); 1965 v Pol, Bel, Sp; 1966 v Sp (2), WG, A; 1967 v Sp, T, Sp, T; 1969 v Pol, A, D, Cz, D (sub), H (sub); 1972 v A (20)
O'Neill, J. (Everton), 1952 v Sp; 1953 v F, A; 1954 v F, L, F; 1955 v N, Ho, N, WG; 1956 v Y, Sp; 1957 v D; 1958 v A; 1959 v Pol, Cz (2) (17)
O'Neill, J. (Preston NE), 1961 v W (1)
O'Neill, K. P. (Norwich C), 1996 v P (sub), Cro, Ho (sub), US (sub), M, Bol; 1997 v Lie, Mac (1 + sub); 1999 v Cro, Y (sub); (with Middlesbrough), Ni (sub); 2000 v Mac (sub) (13)
O'Neill, W. (Dundalk), 1936 v Ho, Sw, H, L; 1937 v G, H, Sw, F; 1938 v N; 1939 v H, G (11)
O'Regan, K. (Brighton & HA), 1984 v Ma, Pol; 1985 v M, Sp (sub) (4)
O'Reilly, J. (Brideville), 1932 v Ho; (with Aberdeen), 1934 v Bel, Ho; (with Brideville), 1936 v Ho; Sw, H, L; (with St James' Gate), 1937 v G, H, Sw, F; 1938 v N (2), Cz, Pol; 1939 v Sw, Pol, H (2), G (20)
O'Reilly, J. (Cork U), 1946 v P, Sp (2)
O'Shea, J. F. (Manchester U), 2002 v Cro (sub); 2003 v Gr, S, Ge, Alb (2), Ge; 2004 v Aus, Ru, Sw, Ca, Br, Pol, Jam (14)

Peyton, G. (Fulham), 1977 v Sp (sub); 1978 v Bul, T, Pol; 1979 v D, Bul, WG; 1980 v W, Cz, Bul, E, Cy, Sw, Arg; 1981 v Ho, Bel, F, Cy; 1982 v Tr; 1985 v M (sub); 1986 v W, Cz; (with Bournemouth), 1988 v L, Pol; 1989 v Ni, Tun; 1990 v USSR, Ma; 1991 v Ch; (with Everton) 1992 v US (2), I (sub), P (33)
Peyton, N. (Shamrock R), 1957 v WG; (with Leeds U), 1960 v WG, Se (sub); 1961 v W; 1963 v Ic, S (6)
Phelan, T. (Wimbledon), 1992 v H, Pol (sub), T, W, Sw, US, I (sub), P; (with Manchester C), 1993 v La (sub), D, Sp, Ni, Alb, La, Li; 1994 v Li, Sp, Ni, Ho, Bol, G, CzR, I, M, Ho; 1995 v E; 1996 v La; (with Chelsea), Ho, Ru, P, Cro, Ho, US, M (sub), Bol; (with Everton), 1997 v W, Mac; 1998 v R; (with Fulham), 2000 v S (sub), M, US, S.Af (42)

Quinn, A. (Sheffield W), 2003 v N (sub); 2004 v Aus (sub), Jam, Ho (4)
Quinn, B. S. (Coventry C), 2000 v Gr, M, US (sub), S.Af (sub) (4)
Quinn, N. J. (Arsenal), 1986 v Ic (sub), Cz; 1987 v Bul (sub), Br (sub); 1988 v L (sub), Bul (sub), Is, R (sub), Pol (sub), E (sub); 1989 v Tun (sub), Sp (sub), H (sub); (with Manchester C), 1990 v USSR, Ma, Eg (sub), Ho, R, I; 1991 v Mor, T, E(2) W, Pol; 1992 v H, W (sub), US, Alb, US, I (sub), P; 1993 v La, D, Sp, Ni, D, Alb, La, Li; 1994 v Li, Sp, Ni; 1995 v La, Lie, Ni, E, Ni, P, Lie, A; 1996 v A, La, P, Ru, CzR, P (sub), Cro, Ho (sub), US; (with Sunderland), 1997 v Lie; 1998 v Li, Arg; 1999 v Ma, Y, Para, Se, Ni, Mac; 2000 v Y, Cro (sub), Ma, Mac, T, CzR, S, M, US (sub), S.Af; 2001 v Ho, P, Es, P, Es; 2002 v Ho (sub), Cy, Ir, Ru (sub), G (sub), S.Ar (sub), Sp (sub) (91)

Reid, A. M. (Nottingham F), 2004 v Ca, Br, CzR, Pol, R, Jam, Ho (7)
Reid, C. (Brideville), 1931 v Sp (1)
Reid, S. J. (Millwall), 2002 v Cro, Ru, D (sub), US (sub), Ng (sub), Cam (sub), G (sub); 2003 v S, Alb (sub); (with Blackburn R), 2004 v Ru (sub), T (sub), Ca, Pol (13)
Richardson, D. J. (Shamrock R), 1972 v A (sub); (with Gillingham), 1973 v N (sub); 1980 v Cz (3)
Rigby, A. (St James' Gate), 1935 v H, Sw, G (3)
Ringstead, A. (Sheffield U), 1951 v Arg, N; 1952 v WG (2), A, Sp; 1953 v A; 1954 v F; 1955 v N; 1956 v Y, Sp, Ho; 1957 v E (2); 1958 v D, Pol, A; 1959 v Pol, Cz (2) (20)
Robinson, J. (Bohemians), 1928 v Bel; (with Dolphin), 1931 v Sp (2)
Robinson, M. (Brighton & HA), 1981 v WG 'B', F, Cy, Bel, Pol; 1982 v Ho, F, Alg, Ch; 1983 v Ho, Sp, Ic, Ma; (with Liverpool), 1984 v Ic, Ho, Is; 1985 v USSR, N; (with QPR), N, Sp, Sw; 1986 v D (sub), W, Cz (24)
Roche, P. J. (Shelbourne), 1972 v A; (with Manchester U), 1975 v USSR, T, Sw, USSR, Sw, WG; 1976 v T (8)
Rogers, E. (Blackburn R), 1968 v Cz, Pol; 1969 v Pol, A, D, Cz, D, H; 1970 v S, D, H; 1971 v I (2), A; (with Charlton Ath), 1972 v Ir, Ec, Ch, P; 1973 v USSR (19)
Rowlands, M. C. (QPR), 2004 v R (sub), Ng (sub), Jam (sub) (3)

Ryan, G. (Derby Co), 1978 v T; (with Brighton & HA), 1979 v E, WG; 1980 v W, Cy (sub), Sw, Arg (sub); 1981 v WG 'B' (sub), F (sub), Pol (sub); 1982 v Br (sub), Ho (sub), Alg (sub), Ch (sub), Tr; 1984 v Pol, Chn; 1985 v M (18)
Ryan, R. A. (WBA), 1950 v Se, Bel; 1951 v N, Arg, N; 1952 v WG (2), A, Sp; 1953 v F, A; 1954 v F, L, F; 1955 v N; (with Derby Co), 1956 v Sp (16)

Sadlier, R. T. (Millwall), 2002 v Ru (sub) (1)
Savage, D. P. T. (Millwall), 1996 v P (sub), Cro (sub), US (sub), M, Bol (5)
Saward, P. (Millwall), 1954 v L; (with Aston Villa), 1957 v E (2); 1958 v D, Pol, A; 1959 v Pol, Cz; 1960 v Se, Ch, WG, Se; 1961 v W, N; (with Huddersfield T), 1961 v S; 1962 v A; 1963 v Ic (2) (18)
Scannell, T. (Southend U), 1954 v L (1)
Scully, P. J. (Arsenal), 1989 v Tun (sub) (1)
Sheedy, K. (Everton), 1984 v Ho (sub), Ma; 1985 v D, I, Is, Sw; 1986 v Sw, D; 1987 v S, Pol; 1988 v Is, R, Pol, E (sub), USSR; 1989 v Ni, Tun, H, Sp, Ma, H; 1990 v Ni, Ma, W (sub), USSR, Fi (sub), T, E, Eg, Ho, R, I; 1991 v W, E, Pol, Ch, US; 1992 v H, Pol, T, W; (with Newcastle U), Sw (sub), Alb; 1993 v La, W (sub) (45)
Sheridan, J. J. (Leeds U), 1988 v R, Y, Pol, N (sub); 1989 v Sp; (with Sheffield W), 1990 v W, T (sub), Ma, I (sub); 1991 v Mor (sub), T, Ch, US (sub); 1992 v H; 1993 v La; 1994 v Sp (sub), Ho, Bol, G, CzR, I, M, N, Ho; 1995 v La, Lie, Ni, E, Ni, P, Lie, A; 1996 v A, Ho (34)
Slaven, B. (Middlesbrough), 1990 v W, Fi, T (sub), Ma; 1991 v W, Pol (sub); 1993 v W (7)
Sloan, J. W. (Arsenal), 1946 v P, Sp (2)
Smyth, M. (Shamrock R), 1969 v Pol (sub) (1)
Squires, J. (Shelbourne), 1934 v Ho (1)
Stapleton, F. (Arsenal), 1977 v T, F, Sp, Bul; 1978 v Bul, N, D; 1979 v Ni, E (sub), D, WG; 1980 v W, Bul, Ni, E, Cy; 1981 v WG 'B', Ho, Bel, F, Cy, Bel, Cz, Pol; (with Manchester U), 1982 v Ho, F, Alg; 1983 v Ho, Sp, Ic, Ma, Sp; 1984 v Ic, Ho, Ma, Pol, Is, Chn; 1985 v N, D, I, Is, E, N, Sw; 1986 v Sw, USSR, D, U, Ic, Cz (sub); 1987 v Bel (2), S (2), Pol, Bul, L; (with Ajax), 1988 v L, Bul, R, Y, N, E, USSR, Ho; (with Le Havre), 1989 v F, Sp, Ma; (with Blackburn R), 1990 v WG, Ma (sub) (71)
Staunton, S. (Liverpool), 1989 v Tun, Sp (2), Ma, H; 1990 v WG, Ni, Ma, W, USSR, Fi, T, Ma, E, Eg, Ho, R, I; 1991 v Mor, T, E (2), W, Pol, Ch, US; (with Aston Villa), 1992 v Pol, T, Sw, US, Alb, US, I, P; 1993 v La, Sp, Ni, D, Alb, La, Li; 1994 v Li, Sp, Ho, Bol, G, CzR, I, M, N, Ho; 1995 v La, Lie, Ni, E, Ni, P, Lie, A; 1996 v La, P, Ru; 1997 v Lie, Mac (2), W, R, Lie; 1998 v Li, Ic, Li, Bel (2), Arg; (with Liverpool), 1999 v Cro, Ma, Y, Se; 2000 v Y, Cro, Ma, Mac, CzR (sub), Gr; 2001 v Ho (sub), Fi (sub); (with Aston Villa), And (sub), P, Es; 2002 v Cro, Ho, Cy, Ir (2), Ru (sub), D, US (sub), Ng, Cam, G, S.Ar, Sp (102)
Stevenson, A. E. (Dolphin), 1932 v Ho; (with Everton), 1947 v E, Sp, P; 1948 v P, Sp; 1949 v Sw (7)
Strahan, F. (Shelbourne), 1964 v Pol, N, E; 1965 v Pol; 1966 v WG (5)
Sullivan, J. (Fordsons), 1928 v Bel (1)
Swan, M. M. G. (Drumcondra), 1960 v Se (sub) (1)
Synnott, N. (Shamrock R), 1978 v T, Pol; 1979 v Ni (3)

Taylor, T. (Waterford), 1959 v Pol (sub) (1)
Thomas, P. (Waterford), 1974 v Pol, Br (2)
Thompson, J. (Nottingham F), 2004 v Ca (sub) (1)
Townsend, A. D. (Norwich C), 1989 v F, Sp (sub), Ma (sub), H; 1990 v WG (sub), Ni, Ma, W, USSR, Fi (sub), T, Ma (sub), E, Eg, Ho, R, I; (with Chelsea), 1991 v Mor, T, E (2), W, Pol, Ch, US; 1992 v Pol, W, US, Alb, US, I; 1993 v La, D, Sp, Ni, D, Alb, La, Li; (with Aston Villa), 1994 v Li, Ni, Ho, Bol, G, CzR, I, M, N, Ho; 1995 v La, Ni, E, Ni, P; 1996 v A, La, Ho, Ru, CzR, P; 1997 v Lie, Mac (2), Ic, R, Lie; 1998 v Li; (with Middlesbrough), Ic, Bel (2) (70)
Traynor, T. J. (Southampton), 1954 v L; 1962 v A; 1963 v Ic (2), S; 1964 v A (2), Sp (8)
Treacy, R. C. P. (WBA), 1966 v WG; 1967 v Sp, Cz; 1968 v Cz; (with Charlton Ath), 1968 v Pol; 1969 v Pol, Cz, D; 1970 v S, D, H (sub), Pol (sub), WG (sub); 1971 v Pol, Se (sub+1), I, A; (with Swindon T), 1972 v Ir, Ec, Ch, P; 1973 v USSR, F, USSR, Pol, F, N; 1974 v Pol; (with Preston NE), Br; 1975 v USSR, Sw (2), WG; 1976 v T, N (sub), Pol (sub); (with WBA), 1977 v F, Pol; (with Shamrock R), 1978 v T, Pol; 1980 v Cz (sub) (42)
Tuohy, L. (Shamrock R), 1956 v Y; 1959 v Cz (2); (with Newcastle U), 1962 v A; 1963 v Ic (2); (with Shamrock R), 1964 v A; 1965 v Bel (8)
Turner, C. J. (Southend U), 1936 v Sw; 1937 v G, H, Sw, F; 1938 v N (2); (with West Ham U), Cz, Pol; 1939 v H (10)
Turner, P. (Celtic), 1963 v S; 1964 v Sp (2)

Vernon, J. (Belfast C), 1946 v P, Sp (2)

Waddock, G. (QPR), 1980 v Sw, Arg; 1981 v W, Pol (sub); 1982 v Alg; 1983 v Ic, Ma, Sp, Ho (sub); 1984 v Ma (sub), Ic, Ho, Is; 1985 v I, Is, E, N, Sp; 1986 v USSR; (with Millwall), 1990 v USSR, T (21)
Walsh, D. J. (Linfield), 1946 v P, Sp; (with WBA), 1947 v Sp, P; 1948 v P, Sp; 1949 v Sw, P, Se, Sp; 1950 v E, Fi, Se; 1951 v N; (with Aston Villa), Arg, N; 1952 v Sp; 1953 v A; 1954 v F (2) (20)
Walsh, J. (Limerick), 1982 v Tr (1)
Walsh, M. (Blackpool), 1976 v N, Pol; 1977 v F (sub), Pol; (with Everton), 1979 v Ni (sub); (with QPR), D (sub), Bul, WG (sub); (with Porto), 1981 v Bel (sub), Cz; 1982 v Alg (sub); 1983 v Sp, Ho (sub), Sp (sub); 1984 v Ic (sub), Ma, Pol, Chn; 1985 v USSR, N (sub), D (21)
Walsh, M. (Everton), 1982 v Ch, Br, Tr; 1983 v Ic (4)
Walsh, W. (Manchester C), 1947 v E, Sp, P; 1948 v P, Sp; 1949 v Bel; 1950 v E, Se, Bel (9)
Waters, J. (Grimsby T), 1977 v T; 1980 v Ni (sub) (2)
Watters, F. (Shelbourne), 1926 v I (1)
Weir, E. (Clyde), 1939 v H (2), G (3)
Whelan, R. (St Patrick's Ath), 1964 v A, E (sub) (2)
Whelan, R. (Liverpool), 1981 v Cz (sub); 1982 v Ho (sub), F; 1983 v Ic, Ma, Sp; 1984 v Is; 1985 v USSR, N, I (sub), Is, E, N (sub), Sw (sub); 1986 v USSR (sub), W; 1987 v Bel (sub), S, Bul, Bel, Br, L; 1988 v L, Bul, Pol, N, E, USSR, Ho; 1989 v Ni, F, H, Sp, Ma; 1990 v WG, Ni, Ma, W, Ho (sub); 1991 v Mor, E; 1992 v Sw; 1993 v La, W (sub), Li (sub); 1994 v Li (sub), Sp, Ru, Ho, G (sub), N (sub); (with Southend U), 1995 v Lie, A (53)
Whelan, W. (Manchester U), 1956 v Ho; 1957 v D, E (2) (4)
White, J. J. (Bohemians), 1928 v Bel (1)
Whittaker, R. (Chelsea), 1959 v Cz (1)
Williams, J. (Shamrock R), 1938 v N (1)

# BRITISH AND IRISH INTERNATIONAL GOALSCORERS SINCE 1872

Where two players with the same surname and initials have appeared for the same country, and one or both have scored, they have been distinguished by reference to the club which appears *first* against their name in the international appearances section.

**ENGLAND**

| | |
|---|---|
| A'Court, A. | 1 |
| Adams, T. A. | 5 |
| Adcock, H. | 1 |
| Alcock, C. W. | 1 |
| Allen, A. | 3 |
| Allen, R. | 2 |
| Amos, A. | 1 |
| Anderson, V. | 2 |
| Anderton, D. R. | 7 |
| Astall, G. | 1 |
| Athersmith, W. C. | 3 |
| Atyeo, P. J. W. | 5 |
| Bache, J. W. | 4 |
| Bailey, N. C. | 2 |
| Baily, E. F. | 5 |
| Baker, J. H. | 3 |
| Ball, A. J. | 8 |
| Bambridge, A. L. | 1 |
| Bambridge, E. C. | 11 |
| Barclay, R. | 2 |
| Barmby, N. J. | 4 |
| Barnes, J. | 11 |
| Barnes, P. S. | 4 |
| Barton, J. | 1 |
| Bassett, W. I. | 8 |
| Bastin, C. S. | 12 |
| Beardsley, P. A. | 9 |
| Beasley, A. | 1 |
| Beattie, T. K. | 1 |
| Beckham, D. R. J. | 13 |
| Becton, F. | 2 |
| Bedford, H. | 1 |
| Bell, C. | 9 |
| Bentley, R. T. F. | 9 |
| Bishop, S. M. | 1 |
| Blackburn, F. | 1 |
| Blissett, L. | 3 |
| Bloomer, S. | 28 |
| Bond, R. | 2 |
| Bonsor, A. G. | 1 |
| Bowden, E. R. | 1 |
| Bowers, J. W. | 2 |
| Bowles, S. | 1 |
| Bradford, G. R. W. | 1 |
| Bradford, J. | 7 |
| Bradley, W. | 2 |
| Bradshaw, F. | 3 |
| Brann, G. | 1 |
| Bridge, W. M. | 1 |
| Bridges, B. J. | 1 |
| Bridgett, A. | 3 |
| Brindle, T. | 1 |
| Britton, C. S. | 1 |
| Broadbent, P. F. | 2 |
| Broadis, I. A. | 8 |
| Brodie, J. B. | 1 |
| Bromley-Davenport, W. | 2 |
| Brook, E. F. | 10 |
| Brooking, T. D. | 5 |
| Brooks, J. | 2 |
| Broome, F. H. | 3 |
| Brown, A. | 4 |
| Brown, A. S. | 1 |
| Brown, G. | 5 |
| Brown, J. | 3 |
| Brown, W. | 1 |
| Buchan, C. M. | 4 |
| Bull, S. G. | 4 |
| Bullock, N. | 2 |
| Burgess, H. | 4 |
| Butcher, T. | 3 |
| Byrne, J. J. | 8 |
| Campbell, S. J. | 1 |
| Camsell, G. H. | 18 |
| Carter, H. S. | 7 |
| Carter, J. H. | 4 |
| Chadwick, E. | 3 |
| Chamberlain, M. | 1 |
| Chambers, H. | 5 |
| Channon, M. R. | 21 |
| Charlton, J. | 6 |
| Charlton, R. | 49 |
| Chenery, C. J. | 1 |
| Chivers, M. | 13 |
| Clarke, A. J. | 10 |
| Cobbold, W. N. | 6 |
| Cock, J. G. | 2 |
| Cole, A. | 1 |
| Cole, J. J. | 2 |
| Common, A. | 2 |
| Connelly, J. M. | 7 |
| Coppell, S. J. | 7 |
| Cotterill, G. H. | 2 |
| Cowans, G. | 2 |
| Crawford, R. | 1 |
| Crawshaw, T. H. | 1 |
| Crayston, W. J. | 1 |
| Creek, F. N. S. | 1 |
| Crooks, S. D. | 7 |
| Currey, E. S. | 2 |
| Currie, A. W. | 3 |
| Cursham, A. W. | 2 |
| Cursham, H. A. | 5 |
| Daft, H. B. | 3 |
| Davenport, J. K. | 2 |
| Davis, G. | 1 |
| Davis, H. | 1 |
| Day, S. H. | 2 |
| Dean, W. R. | 18 |
| Devey, J. H. G. | 1 |
| Dewhurst, F. | 11 |
| Dix, W. R. | 1 |
| Dixon, K. M. | 4 |
| Dixon, L. M. | 1 |
| Dorrell, A. R. | 1 |
| Douglas, B. | 11 |
| Drake, E. J. | 6 |
| Ducat, A. | 1 |
| Dunn, A. T. B. | 2 |
| Eastham, G. | 2 |
| Edwards, D. | 5 |
| Ehiogu, U. | 1 |
| Elliott, W. H. | 3 |
| Evans, R. E. | 1 |
| Ferdinand, L. | 5 |
| Ferdinand, R. G. | 1 |
| Finney, T. | 30 |
| Fleming, H. J. | 9 |
| Flowers, R. | 10 |
| Forman, Frank | 1 |
| Forman, Fred | 3 |
| Foster, R. E. | 3 |
| Fowler, R. B. | 7 |
| Francis, G. C. J. | 3 |
| Francis, T. | 12 |
| Freeman, B. C. | 3 |
| Froggatt, J. | 2 |
| Froggatt, R. | 2 |
| Galley, T. | 1 |
| Gascoigne, P. J. | 10 |
| Geary, F. | 3 |
| Gerrard, S. G. | 4 |
| Gibbins, W. V. T. | 3 |
| Gilliatt, W. E. | 3 |
| Goddard, P. | 1 |
| Goodall, J. | 12 |
| Goodyer, A. C. | 1 |
| Gosling, R. C. | 2 |
| Goulden, L. A. | 4 |
| Grainger, C. | 3 |
| Greaves, J. | 44 |
| Grovesnor, A. T. | 2 |
| Gunn, W. | 1 |
| Haines, J. T. W. | 2 |
| Hall, G. W. | 9 |
| Halse, H. J. | 2 |
| Hampson, J. | 5 |
| Hampton, H. | 2 |
| Hancocks, J. | 2 |
| Hardman, H. P. | 1 |
| Harris, S. S. | 2 |
| Hassall, H. W. | 4 |
| Hateley, M. | 9 |
| Haynes, J. N. | 18 |
| Hegan, K. E. | 4 |
| Henfrey, A. G. | 2 |
| Heskey, E. W. | 5 |
| Hilsdon, G. R. | 14 |
| Hine, E. W. | 4 |
| Hinton, A. T. | 1 |
| Hirst, D. E. | 1 |
| Hitchens, G. A. | 5 |
| Hobbis, H. H. F. | 1 |
| Hoddle, G. | 8 |
| Hodgetts, D. | 1 |
| Hodgson, G. | 1 |
| Holley, G. H. | 8 |
| Houghton, W. E. | 5 |
| Howell, R. | 1 |
| Hughes, E. W. | 1 |
| Hulme, J. H. A. | 4 |
| Hunt, G. S. | 1 |
| Hunt, R. | 18 |
| Hunter, N. | 2 |
| Hurst, G. C. | 24 |
| Ince, P. E. C. | 2 |
| Jack, D. N. B. | 3 |
| Jeffers, F. | 1 |
| Johnson, D. E. | 6 |
| Johnson, E. | 2 |
| Johnson, J. A. | 2 |
| Johnson, T. C. F. | 5 |
| Johnson, W. H. | 1 |
| Kail, E. I. L. | 2 |
| Kay, A. H. | 1 |
| Keegan, J. K. | 21 |
| Kelly, R. | 8 |
| Kennedy, R. | 3 |
| Kenyon-Slaney, W. S. | 2 |
| Keown, M. R. | 2 |
| Kevan, D. T. | 8 |
| Kidd, B. | 1 |
| King, L. B. | 1 |
| Kingsford, R. K. | 1 |
| Kirchen, A. J. | 2 |
| Kirton, W. J. | 1 |
| Lampard, F. J. | 5 |
| Langton, R. | 1 |
| Latchford, R. D. | 5 |
| Latherton, E. G. | 1 |
| Lawler, C. | 1 |
| Lawton, T. | 22 |
| Lee, F. | 10 |
| Lee, J. | 1 |
| Lee, R. M. | 2 |
| Lee, S. | 2 |
| Le Saux, G. P. | 1 |
| Lindley, T. | 14 |
| Lineker, G. | 48 |
| Lofthouse, J. M. | 3 |
| Lofthouse, N. | 30 |
| Hon. A. Lyttelton | 1 |
| Mabbutt, G. | 1 |
| Macdonald, M. | 6 |
| Mannion, W. J. | 11 |
| Mariner, P. | 13 |
| Marsh, R. W. | 1 |
| Matthews, S. | 11 |
| Matthews, V. | 1 |
| McCall, J. | 1 |
| McDermott, T. | 3 |
| McManaman, S. | 3 |
| Medley, L. D. | 1 |
| Melia, J. | 1 |
| Mercer, D. W. | 1 |
| Merson, P. C. | 3 |
| Milburn, J. E. T. | 10 |
| Miller, H. S. | 1 |
| Mills, G. R. | 3 |
| Milward, A. | 3 |
| Mitchell, C. | 5 |
| Moore, J. | 1 |
| Moore, R. F. | 2 |
| Moore, W. G. B. | 2 |
| Morren, T. | 1 |
| Morris, F. | 1 |
| Morris, J. | 3 |
| Mortensen, S. H. | 23 |
| Morton, J. R. | 1 |
| Mosforth, W. | 3 |
| Mullen, J. | 6 |
| Mullery, A. P. | 1 |
| Murphy, D. B | 1 |
| Neal, P. G. | 5 |
| Needham, E. | 3 |
| Nicholls, J. | 1 |
| Nicholson, W. E. | 1 |
| O'Grady, M. | 3 |
| Osborne, F. R. | 3 |
| Owen, M. J. | 26 |
| Own goals | 24 |
| Page, L. A. | 1 |
| Paine, T. L. | 7 |
| Palmer, C. L. | 1 |
| Parry, E. H. | 1 |
| Parry, R. A. | 1 |
| Pawson, F. W. | 1 |
| Payne, J. | 2 |

| | |
|---|---|
| Peacock, A. | 3 |
| Pearce, S. | 5 |
| Pearson, J. S. | 5 |
| Pearson, S. C. | 5 |
| Perry, W. | 2 |
| Peters, M. | 20 |
| Pickering, F. | 5 |
| Platt, D. | 27 |
| Pointer, R. | 2 |
| | |
| Quantrill, A. | 1 |
| | |
| Ramsay, A. E. | 3 |
| Revie, D. G. | 4 |
| Redknapp, J. F. | 1 |
| Reynolds, J. | 3 |
| Richardson, J. R. | 2 |
| Rigby, A. | 3 |
| Rimmer, E. J. | 2 |
| Roberts, F. | 2 |
| Roberts, H. | 1 |
| Roberts, W. T. | 2 |
| Robinson, J. | 3 |
| Robson, B. | 26 |
| Robson, R. | 4 |
| Rooney, W. | 9 |
| Rowley, J. F. | 6 |
| Royle, J. | 2 |
| Rutherford, J. | 3 |
| | |
| Sagar, C. | 1 |
| Sandilands, R. R. | 3 |
| Sansom, K. | 1 |
| Schofield, J. | 1 |
| Scholes, P. | 14 |
| Seed, J. M. | 1 |
| Settle, J. | 6 |
| Sewell, J. | 3 |
| Shackleton, L. F. | 1 |
| Sharp, J. | 1 |
| Shearer, A. | 30 |
| Shelton, A. | 1 |
| Shepherd, A. | 2 |
| Sheringham, E. P. | 11 |
| Simpson, J. | 1 |
| Smith, A. | 1 |
| Smith, A. M. | 2 |
| Smith, G. O. | 11 |
| Smith, Joe | 1 |
| Smith, J. R. | 2 |
| Smith, J. W. | 4 |
| Smith, R. | 13 |
| Smith, S. | 1 |
| Sorby, T. H. | 1 |
| Southgate, G. | 2 |
| Southworth, J. | 3 |
| Sparks, F. J. | 3 |
| Spence, J. W. | 1 |
| Spiksley, F. | 5 |
| Spilsbury, B. W. | 5 |
| Steele, F. C. | 8 |
| Stephenson, G. T. | 2 |
| Steven, T. M. | 4 |
| Stewart, J. | 2 |
| Stiles, N. P. | 1 |
| Storer, H. | 1 |
| Stone, S. B. | 2 |
| Summerbee, M. G. | 1 |
| | |
| Tambling, R. V. | 1 |
| Taylor, P. J. | 2 |
| Taylor, T. | 16 |
| Thompson, P. B. | 1 |
| Thornewell, G. | 1 |
| Tilson, S. F. | 6 |
| Townley, W. J. | 2 |
| Tueart, D. | 2 |
| | |
| Vassell, D. | 6 |
| Vaughton, O. H. | 6 |
| Veitch, J. G. | 3 |
| Violett, D. S. | 1 |
| | |
| Waddle, C. R. | 6 |
| Walker, W. H. | 9 |
| Wall, G. | 2 |
| Wallace, D. | 1 |
| Walsh, P. | 1 |
| Waring, T. | 4 |
| Warren, B. | 2 |
| Watson, D. V. | 4 |
| Watson, V. M. | 4 |
| Webb, G. W. | 1 |
| Webb, N. | 4 |
| Wedlock, W. J. | 2 |
| Weller, K. | 1 |
| Welsh, D. | 1 |
| Whateley, O. | 2 |
| Wheldon, G. F. | 6 |
| Whitfield, H. | 1 |
| Wignall, F. | 2 |
| Wilkes, A. | 1 |
| Wilkins, R. G. | 3 |
| Willingham, C. K. | 1 |
| Wilshaw, D. J. | 10 |
| Wilson, G. P. | 1 |
| Winckworth, W. N. | 1 |
| Windridge, J. E. | 7 |
| Wise, D. F. | 1 |
| Withe, P. | 1 |
| Wollaston, C. H. R. | 1 |
| Wood, H. | 1 |
| Woodcock, T. | 16 |
| Woodhall, G. | 1 |
| Woodward, V. J. | 29 |
| Worrall, F. | 2 |
| Worthington, F. S. | 2 |
| Wright, I. E. | 9 |
| Wright, M. | 1 |
| Wright, W. A. | 3 |
| Wylie, J. G. | 1 |
| | |
| Yates, J. | 3 |

**NORTHERN IRELAND**

| | |
|---|---|
| Anderson, T. | 4 |
| Armstrong, G. | 12 |
| | |
| Bambrick, J. | 12 |
| Barr, H. H. | 1 |
| Barron, H. | 3 |
| Best, G. | 9 |
| Bingham, W. L. | 10 |
| Black, K. | 1 |
| Blanchflower, D. | 2 |
| Blanchflower, J. | 1 |
| Brennan, B. | 1 |
| Brennan, R. A. | 1 |
| Brotherston, N. | 3 |
| Brown, J. | 1 |
| Browne, F. | 2 |
| | |
| Campbell, J. | 1 |
| Campbell, W. G. | 1 |
| Casey, T. | 2 |
| Caskey, W. | 1 |
| Cassidy, T. | 1 |
| Chambers, J. | 3 |
| Clarke, C. J. | 13 |
| Clements, D. | 2 |
| Cochrane, T. | 1 |
| Condy, J. | 1 |
| Connor, M. J. | 1 |
| Coulter, J. | 1 |
| Croft, T. | 1 |
| Crone, W. | 1 |
| Crossan, E. | 1 |
| Crossan, J. A. | 10 |
| Curran, S. | 2 |
| Cush, W. W. | 5 |
| | |
| Dalton, W. | 4 |
| D'Arcy, S. D. | 1 |
| Darling, J. | 1 |
| Davey, H. H. | 1 |
| Davis, T. L. | 1 |
| Dill, A. H. | 1 |
| Doherty, L. | 1 |
| Doherty, P. D. | 3 |
| Dougan, A. D. | 8 |
| Dowie, I. | 12 |
| Dunne, J. | 4 |
| | |
| Elder, A. R. | 1 |
| Elliott, S. | 2 |
| Emerson, W. | 1 |
| English, S. | 1 |
| | |
| Feeney, W | 1 |
| Ferguson, W. | 1 |
| Ferris, J. | 1 |
| Ferris, R. O. | 1 |
| Finney, T. | 2 |
| | |
| Gaffkin, J. | 4 |
| Gara, A. | 3 |
| Gaukrodger, G. | 1 |
| Gibb, J. T. | 2 |
| Gibb, T. J. | 1 |
| Gillespie, K. R. | 1 |
| Gillespie, W. | 13 |
| Goodall, A. L. | 2 |
| Griffin, D. J. | 1 |
| Gray, P. | 6 |
| | |
| Halligan, W. | 1 |
| Hamill, M. | 1 |
| Hamilton, B. | 4 |
| Hamilton, W. R. | 5 |
| Hannon, D. J. | 1 |
| Harkin, J. T. | 2 |
| Harvey, M. | 3 |
| Healy, D. J. | 14 |
| Hill, C. F. | 1 |
| Hughes, M. E. | 5 |
| Humphries, W. | 1 |
| Hunter, A. (*Distillery*) | 1 |
| Hunter, A. (*Blackburn R*) | 1 |
| Hunter, B. V. | 1 |
| | |
| Irvine, R. W. | 3 |
| Irvine, W. J. | 8 |
| | |
| Johnston, H. | 2 |
| Johnston, S. | 2 |
| Johnston, W. C. | 1 |
| Jones, S. | 1 |
| Jones, S. (*Crewe Alex*) | 1 |
| Jones, J. | 1 |
| | |
| Kelly, J. | 4 |
| Kernaghan, N. | 2 |
| Kirwan, J. | 2 |
| | |
| Lacey, W. | 3 |
| Lemon, J. | 2 |
| Lennon, N. F. | 2 |
| Lockhart, N. | 3 |
| Lomas, S. M. | 3 |
| | |
| Magilton, J. | 5 |
| Mahood, J. | 2 |
| Martin, D. K. | 3 |
| Maxwell, J. | 2 |
| McAdams, W. J. | 7 |
| McAllen, J. | 1 |
| Mcauley, J. L. | 1 |
| McCartney, G. | 1 |
| McCandless, J. | 3 |
| McCaw, J. H. | 1 |
| McClelland, J. | 1 |
| McCluggage, A. | 2 |
| McCracken, W. | 1 |
| McCrory, S. | 1 |
| McCurdy, C. | 1 |
| McDonald, A. | 3 |
| McGarry, J. K. | 1 |
| McGrath, R. C. | 4 |
| McIlroy, J. | 10 |
| McIlroy, S. B. | 5 |
| McKenzie, H | 1 |
| McKnight, J. | 2 |
| McLaughlin, J. C. | 6 |
| McMahon, G. J. | 2 |
| McMordie, A. S. | 3 |
| McMorran, E. J. | 4 |
| McParland, P. J. | 10 |
| McWha, W. B. R. | 1 |
| Meldon, J. | 1 |
| Mercer, J. T. | 1 |
| Millar, W. | 1 |
| Milligan, D. | 1 |
| Milne, R. G. | 2 |
| Molyneux, T. B. | 1 |
| Moreland, V. | 1 |
| Morgan, S. | 3 |
| Morrow, S. J. | 1 |
| Morrow, W. J. | 1 |
| Mulryne, P. P. | 3 |
| Murphy, N. | 1 |
| | |
| Neill, W. J. T. | 2 |
| Nelson, S. | 1 |
| Nicholl, C. J. | 3 |
| Nicholl, J. M. | 1 |
| Nicholson, J. J. | 6 |
| | |
| O'Boyle, G. | 1 |
| O'Hagan, C. | 2 |
| O'Kane, W. J. | 1 |
| O'Neill, J. | 2 |
| O'Neill, M. A. | 4 |
| O'Neill, M. H. | 8 |
| Own goals | 6 |
| | |
| Patterson, D. J. | 1 |
| Peacock, R. | 2 |
| Peden, J. | 7 |
| Penney, S. | 2 |
| Pyper, James | 2 |
| Pyper, John | 1 |
| | |
| Quinn, J. M. | 12 |
| Quinn, S. J. | 4 |
| | |
| Reynolds, J. | 1 |
| Rowland, K. | 1 |
| Rowley, R. W. M. | 2 |
| Rushe, F. | 1 |
| | |
| Sheridan, J. | 2 |
| Sherrard, J. | 1 |
| Sherrard, W. C. | 2 |
| Simpson, W. J. | 5 |
| Sloan, H. A. de B. | 4 |
| Smyth, S. | 5 |
| Spence, D. W. | 3 |
| Stanfield, O. M. | 11 |
| Stevenson, A. E. | 5 |
| Stewart, I. | 2 |
| | |
| Taggart, G. P. | 7 |
| Thompson, F. W. | 2 |
| Torrans, S. | 1 |
| Tully, C. P. | 3 |
| Turner, E. | 1 |
| | |
| Walker, J. | 1 |
| Walsh, D. J. | 5 |
| Welsh, E. | 1 |
| Whiteside, N. | 9 |
| Whiteside, T. | 1 |
| Whitley, Jeff | 1 |
| Williams, J. R. | 1 |
| Williams, M. S. | 1 |
| Williamson, J. | 1 |
| Wilson, D. J. | 1 |
| Wilson, K. J. | 6 |
| Wilson, S. J. | 7 |
| Wilton, J. M. | 2 |
| | |
| Young, S. | 1 |

*N.B. In 1914 Young goal should be credited to Gillespie W v Wales*

**SCOTLAND**

| | |
|---|---|
| Aitken, R. (*Celtic*) | 1 |
| Aitken, R. (*Dumbarton*) | 1 |
| Aitkenhead, W. A. C. | 2 |
| Alexander, D. | 1 |
| Allan, D. S. | 4 |
| Allan, J. | 2 |
| Anderson, F. | 1 |
| Anderson, W. | 4 |
| Andrews, P. | 1 |
| Archibald, A. | 1 |
| Archibald, S. | 4 |
| Baird, D. | 2 |
| Baird, J. C. | 2 |
| Baird, S. | 2 |
| Bannon, E. | 1 |
| Barbour, A. | 1 |
| Barker, J. B. | 4 |
| Battles, B. Jr | 1 |
| Bauld, W. | 2 |
| Baxter, J. C. | 3 |
| Bell, J. | 5 |
| Bennett, A. | 2 |
| Berry, D. | 1 |
| Bett, J. | 1 |
| Beveridge, W. W. | 1 |
| Black, A. | 3 |
| Black, D. | 1 |
| Bone, J. | 1 |
| Booth, S. | 6 |
| Boyd, R. | 2 |
| Boyd, T. | 1 |
| Boyd, W. G. | 1 |
| Brackenridge, T. | 1 |
| Brand, R. | 8 |
| Brazil, A. | 1 |
| Bremner, W. J. | 3 |
| Brown, A. D. | 6 |
| Buchanan, P. S. | 1 |
| Buchanan, R. | 1 |
| Buckley, P. | 1 |
| Buick, A. | 2 |
| Burley, C. W. | 3 |
| Burns, K. | 1 |
| Cairns, T. | 1 |
| Caldwell, G. | 1 |
| Calderwood, C. | 1 |
| Calderwood, R. | 2 |
| Caldow, E. | 4 |
| Cameron, C. | 2 |
| Campbell, C. | 1 |
| Campbell, John (*Celtic*) | 5 |
| Campbell, John (*Rangers*) | 4 |
| Campbell, P. | 2 |
| Campbell, R. | 1 |
| Cassidy, J. | 1 |
| Chalmers, S. | 3 |
| Chambers, T. | 1 |
| Cheyne, A. G. | 4 |
| Christie, A. J. | 1 |
| Clunas, W. L. | 1 |
| Collins, J. | 12 |
| Collins, R. Y. | 10 |
| Combe, J. R. | 1 |
| Conn, A. | 1 |
| Cooper, D. | 6 |
| Craig, J. | 1 |
| Craig, T. | 1 |
| Crawford, S. | 4 |
| Cunningham, A. N. | 5 |
| Curran, H. P. | 1 |
| Dailly, C. | 4 |
| Dalglish, K. | 30 |
| Davidson, D. | 1 |
| Davidson, J. A. | 1 |
| Delaney, J. | 3 |
| Devine, A. | 1 |
| Dewar, G. | 1 |
| Dewar, N. | 4 |
| Dickov, P. | 1 |
| Dickson, W. | 4 |
| Divers, J. | 1 |
| Dobie, R. S. | 1 |
| Docherty, T. H. | 1 |
| Dodds, D. | 1 |
| Dodds, W. | 7 |
| Donaldson, A. | 1 |
| Donnachie, J. | 1 |
| Dougall, J. | 1 |
| Drummond, J. | 2 |
| Dunbar, M. | 1 |
| Duncan, D. | 7 |
| Duncan, D. M. | 1 |
| Duncan, J. | 1 |
| Dunn, J. | 2 |
| Durie, G. S. | 7 |
| Easson, J. F. | 1 |
| Elliott, M. S. | 1 |
| Ellis, J. | 1 |
| Ferguson, B. | 2 |
| Ferguson, J. | 6 |
| Fernie, W. | 1 |
| Fitchie, T. T. | 1 |
| Flavell, R. | 2 |
| Fleming, C. | 2 |
| Fleming, J. W. | 3 |
| Fletcher, D. | 2 |
| Fraser, M. J. E. | 3 |
| Freedman, D. A. | 1 |
| Gallacher, H. K. | 23 |
| Gallacher, K. W. | 9 |
| Gallacher, P. | 1 |
| Galt, J. H. | 1 |
| Gemmell, T. (*St Mirren*) | 1 |
| Gemmell, T. (*Celtic*) | 1 |
| Gemmill, A. | 8 |
| Gemmill, S. | 1 |
| Gibb, W. | 1 |
| Gibson, D. W. | 3 |
| Gibson, J. D. | 1 |
| Gibson, N. | 1 |
| Gillespie, Jas. | 3 |
| Gillick, T. | 3 |
| Gilzean, A. J. | 12 |
| Gossland, J. | 2 |
| Goudie, J. | 1 |
| Gough, C. R. | 6 |
| Gourlay, J. | 1 |
| Graham, A. | 2 |
| Graham, G. | 3 |
| Gray, A. | 6 |
| Gray, E. | 3 |
| Gray, F. | 1 |
| Greig, J. | 3 |
| Groves, W. | 4 |
| Hamilton, G. | 4 |
| Hamilton, J. (*Queen's Park*) | 3 |
| Hamilton, R. C. | 14 |
| Harper, J. M. | 2 |
| Harrower, W. | 5 |
| Hartford, R. A. | 4 |
| Heggie, C. | 5 |
| Henderson, J. G. | 1 |
| Henderson, W. | 5 |
| Hendry, E. C. J. | 3 |
| Herd, D. G. | 3 |
| Herd, G. | 1 |
| Hewie, J. D. | 2 |
| Higgins, A. (*Newcastle U*) | 1 |
| Higgins, A. (*Kilmarnock*) | 4 |
| Highet, T. C. | 1 |
| Holt, G.J. | 1 |
| Holton, J. A. | 2 |
| Hopkin, D. | 2 |
| Houliston, W. | 2 |
| Howie, H. | 1 |
| Howie, J. | 2 |
| Hughes, J. | 1 |
| Hunter, W. | 1 |
| Hutchison, D. | 6 |
| Hutchison, T. | 1 |
| Hutton, J. | 1 |
| Hyslop, T. | 1 |
| Imrie, W. N. | 1 |
| Jackson, A. | 8 |
| Jackson, C. | 1 |
| Jackson, D. | 4 |
| James, A. W. | 4 |
| Jardine, A. | 1 |
| Jenkinson, T. | 1 |
| Jess, E. | 2 |
| Johnston, A. | 2 |
| Johnston, L. H. | 1 |
| Johnston, M. | 14 |
| Johnstone, D. | 2 |
| Johnstone, J. | 4 |
| Johnstone, Jas. | 1 |
| Johnstone, R. | 9 |
| Johnstone, W. | 1 |
| Jordan, J. | 11 |
| Kay, J. L. | 5 |
| Keillor, A. | 3 |
| Kelly, J. | 1 |
| Kelso, J. | 1 |
| Ker, G. | 10 |
| King, A. | 1 |
| King, J. | 1 |
| Kinnear, D. | 1 |
| Kyle, K. | 1 |
| Lambert, P. | 1 |
| Lambie, J. | 1 |
| Lambie, W. A. | 5 |
| Lang, J. J. | 1 |
| Law, D. | 30 |
| Leggat, G. | 8 |
| Lennie, W. | 1 |
| Lennox, R. | 3 |
| Liddell, W. | 6 |
| Lindsay, J. | 6 |
| Linwood, A. B. | 1 |
| Logan, J. | 1 |
| Lorimer, P. | 4 |
| Love, A. | 1 |
| Lowe, J. (*Cambuslang*) | 1 |
| Lowe, J. (*St Bernards*) | 1 |
| Macari, L. | 5 |
| MacDougall, E. J. | 3 |
| MacLeod, M. | 1 |
| Mackay, D. C. | 4 |
| Mackay, G. | 1 |
| MacKenzie, J. A. | 1 |
| MacKinnon, W. W. | 6 |
| Madden, J. | 5 |
| Marshall, H. | 1 |
| Marshall, J. | 1 |
| Mason, J. | 4 |
| Massie, A. | 1 |
| Masson, D. S. | 5 |
| McAdam, J. | 1 |
| McAllister, G. | 5 |
| McAulay, J. D. | 1 |
| McAvennie, F. | 1 |
| McCall, J. | 1 |
| McCall, S. M. | 1 |
| McCalliog, J. | 1 |
| McCallum, N. | 1 |
| McCann, N. | 3 |
| McClair, B. J. | 2 |
| McCoist, A. | 19 |
| McColl, R. S. | 13 |
| McCulloch, D. | 3 |
| McDougall, J. | 4 |
| McFarlane, A. | 1 |
| McFadden, J. | 4 |
| McFadyen, W. | 2 |
| McGhee, M. | 2 |
| McGinlay, J. | 4 |
| McGrory, J. | 6 |
| McGuire, W. | 1 |
| McInally, A. | 3 |
| McInnes, T. | 2 |
| McKie, J. | 2 |
| McKimmie, S. | 1 |
| McKinlay, W. | 4 |
| McKinnon, A. | 1 |
| McKinnon, R. | 1 |
| McLaren, A. | 4 |
| McLaren, J. | 1 |
| McLean, A. | 1 |
| McLean, T. | 1 |
| McLeish, A. | 1 |
| McLintock, F. | 1 |
| McMahon, A. | 6 |
| McMenemy, J. | 5 |
| McMillan, I. L. | 2 |
| McNeil, H. | 5 |
| McNeill, W. | 3 |
| McPhail, J. | 3 |
| McPhail, R. | 7 |
| McPherson, J. | 8 |
| McPherson, R. | 1 |
| McQueen, G. | 5 |
| McStay, P. | 9 |
| McSwegan, G. | 1 |
| Meiklejohn, D. D. | 3 |
| Millar, J. | 2 |
| Miller, K. | 2 |
| Miller, T. | 2 |
| Miller, W. | 1 |
| Mitchell, R. C. | 1 |
| Morgan, W. | 1 |
| Morris, D. | 1 |
| Morris, H. | 3 |
| Morton, A. L. | 5 |
| Mudie, J. K. | 9 |
| Mulhall, G. | 1 |
| Munro, A. D. | 1 |
| Munro, N. | 1 |
| Murdoch, R. | 5 |
| Murphy, F. | 1 |
| Murray, J. | 1 |
| Napier, C. E. | 3 |
| Narey, D. | 1 |
| Naysmith, G. A. | 1 |
| Neil, R. G. | 2 |
| Nevin, P. K. F. | 5 |
| Nicholas, C. | 5 |
| Nisbet, J. | 2 |
| O'Donnell, F. | 2 |
| O'Hare, J. | 5 |
| Ormond, W. E. | 1 |
| O'Rourke, F. | 1 |
| Orr, R. | 1 |
| Orr, T. | 1 |
| Oswald, J. | 1 |
| Own goals | 15 |
| Parlane, D. | 1 |
| Paul, H. McD. | 2 |
| Paul, W. | 6 |
| Pettigrew, W. | 2 |
| Provan, D. | 1 |
| Quashie, N. F. | 1 |
| Quinn, J. | 7 |
| Quinn, P. | 1 |
| Rankin, G. | 2 |
| Rankin, R. | 2 |
| Reid, W. | 4 |
| Reilly, L. | 22 |
| Renny-Tailyour, H. W. | 1 |
| Richmond, J. T. | 1 |
| Ring, T. | 2 |
| Rioch, B. D. | 6 |
| Ritchie, J. | 1 |
| Ritchie, P. S. | 1 |

| | |
|---|---|
| Robertson, A. | 2 |
| Robertson, J. | 2 |
| Robertson, J. N. | 9 |
| Robertson, J. T. | 2 |
| Robertson, T. | 1 |
| Robertson, W. | 1 |
| Russell, D. | 1 |
| Scott, A. S. | 5 |
| Sellar, W. | 4 |
| Sharp, G. | 1 |
| Shaw, F. W. | 1 |
| Shearer, D. | 2 |
| Simpson, J. | 1 |
| Smith, A. | 5 |
| Smith, G. | 4 |
| Smith, J. | 1 |
| Smith, John | 13 |
| Somerville, G. | 1 |
| Souness, G. J. | 4 |
| Speedie, F. | 2 |
| St John, I. | 9 |
| Steel, W. | 12 |
| Stein, C. | 10 |
| Stevenson, G. | 4 |
| Stewart, A. | 1 |
| Stewart, R. | 1 |
| Stewart, W. E. | 1 |
| Strachan, G. | 5 |
| Sturrock, P. | 3 |
| Taylor, J. D. | 1 |
| Templeton, R. | 1 |
| Thompson, S. | 2 |
| Thomson, A. | 1 |
| Thomson, C. | 4 |
| Thomson, R. | 1 |
| Thomson, W. | 1 |
| Thornton, W. | 1 |
| Waddell, T. S. | 1 |
| Waddell, W. | 6 |
| Walker, J. | 2 |
| Walker, R. | 7 |
| Walker, T. | 9 |
| Wallace, I. A. | 1 |
| Wark, J. | 7 |
| Watson, J. A. K. | 1 |
| Watt, F. | 2 |
| Watt, W. W. | 1 |
| Weir, A. | 1 |
| Weir, D. | 1 |
| Weir, J. B. | 2 |
| White, J. A. | 3 |
| Wilkie, L. | 1 |
| Wilson, A. | 2 |
| Wilson, A. N. | 13 |
| Wilson, D. (*Queen's Park*) | 2 |
| Wilson, D. (*Rangers*) | 9 |
| Wilson, H. | 1 |
| Wylie, T. G. | 1 |
| Young, A. | 5 |

**WALES**

| | |
|---|---|
| Allchurch, I. J. | 23 |
| Allen, M. | 3 |
| Astley, D. J. | 12 |
| Atherton, R. W. | 2 |
| Bamford, T. | 1 |
| Barnes, W. | 1 |
| Bellamy, C. D. | 6 |
| Blackmore, C. G. | 1 |
| Blake, N. A. | 4 |
| Bodin, P. J. | 3 |
| Boulter, L. M. | 1 |
| Bowdler, J. C. H. | 3 |
| Bowen, D. L. | 1 |
| Bowen, M. | 3 |
| Boyle, T. | 1 |
| Bryan, T. | 1 |
| Burgess, W. A. R. | 1 |
| Burke, T. | 1 |
| Butler, W. T. | 1 |
| Chapman, T. | 2 |
| Charles, J. | 1 |
| Charles, M. | 6 |
| Charles, W. J. | 15 |
| Clarke, R. J. | 5 |
| Coleman, C. | 4 |
| Collier, D. J. | 1 |
| Crosse, K. | 1 |
| Cumner, R. H. | 1 |
| Curtis, A. | 6 |
| Curtis, E. R. | 3 |
| Davies, D. W. | 1 |
| Davies, E. Lloyd | 1 |
| Davies, G. | 2 |
| Davies, L. S. | 6 |
| Davies, R. T. | 9 |
| Davies, R. W. | 6 |
| Davies, S. | 5 |
| Davies, Simon | 4 |
| Davies, W. | 6 |
| Davies, W. H. | 1 |
| Davies, William | 5 |
| Davis, W. O. | 1 |
| Deacy, N. | 4 |
| Doughty, J. | 6 |
| Doughty, R. | 2 |
| Durban, A. | 2 |
| Dwyer, P. | 2 |
| Earnshaw, R. | 7 |
| Edwards, G. | 2 |
| Edwards, R. I. | 4 |
| England, H. M. | 4 |
| Evans, I. | 1 |
| Evans, J. | 1 |
| Evans, R. E. | 2 |
| Evans, W. | 1 |
| Eyton-Jones, J. A. | 1 |
| Flynn, B. | 7 |
| Ford, T. | 23 |
| Foulkes, W. I. | 1 |
| Fowler, J. | 3 |
| Giles, D. | 2 |
| Giggs, R. J. | 8 |
| Glover, E. M. | 7 |
| Godfrey, B. C. | 2 |
| Green, A. W. | 3 |
| Griffiths, A. T. | 6 |
| Griffiths, M. W. | 2 |
| Griffiths, T. P. | 3 |
| Harris, C. S. | 1 |
| Hartson, J. | 11 |
| Hersee, R. | 1 |
| Hewitt, R. | 1 |
| Hockey, T. | 1 |
| Hodges, G. | 2 |
| Hole, W. J. | 1 |
| Hopkins, I. J. | 2 |
| Horne, B. | 2 |
| Howell, E. G. | 3 |
| Hughes, L. M. | 16 |
| James, E. | 2 |
| James, L. | 10 |
| James, R. | 7 |
| Jarrett, R. H. | 3 |
| Jenkyns, C. A. | 1 |
| Jones, A. | 1 |
| Jones, Bryn | 6 |
| Jones, B. S. | 2 |
| Jones, Cliff | 16 |
| Jones, C. W. | 1 |
| Jones, D. E. | 1 |
| Jones, Evan | 1 |
| Jones, H. | 1 |
| Jones, I. | 1 |
| Jones, J. L. | 1 |
| Jones, J. O. | 1 |
| Jones, J. P. | 1 |
| Jones, Leslie J. | 1 |
| Jones, R. A. | 2 |
| Jones, W. L. | 6 |
| Keenor, F. C. | 2 |
| Koumas, J. | 1 |
| Krzywicki, R. L. | 1 |
| Leek, K. | 5 |
| Lewis, B. | 4 |
| Lewis, D. M. | 2 |
| Lewis, W. | 8 |
| Lewis, W. L. | 3 |
| Lovell, S. | 1 |
| Lowrie, G. | 2 |
| Mahoney, J. F. | 1 |
| Mays, A. W. | 1 |
| Medwin, T. C. | 6 |
| Melville, A. K | 3 |
| Meredith, W. H. | 11 |
| Mills, T. J. | 1 |
| Moore, G. | 1 |
| Morgan, J. R. | 2 |
| Morgan-Owen, H. | 1 |
| Morgan-Owen, M. M. | 2 |
| Morris, A. G. | 9 |
| Morris, H. | 2 |
| Morris, R. | 1 |
| Morris, S. | 2 |
| Nicholas, P. | 2 |
| O'Callaghan, E. | 3 |
| O'Sullivan, P. A. | 1 |
| Owen, G. | 2 |
| Owen, W. | 4 |
| Owen, W. P. | 6 |
| Own goals | 13 |
| Palmer, D. | 3 |
| Parry, P. I. | 1 |
| Parry, T. D. | 3 |
| Paul, R. | 1 |
| Peake, E. | 1 |
| Pembridge, M. | 6 |
| Perry, E. | 1 |
| Phillips, C. | 5 |
| Phillips, D. | 2 |
| Powell, A. | 1 |
| Powell, D. | 1 |
| Price, J. | 4 |
| Price, P. | 1 |
| Pryce-Jones, W. E. | 3 |
| Pugh, D. H. | 2 |
| Reece, G. I. | 2 |
| Rees, R. R. | 3 |
| Richards, R. W. | 1 |
| Roach, J. | 2 |
| Robbins, W. W. | 4 |
| Roberts, J. (*Corwen*) | 1 |
| Roberts, Jas. | 1 |
| Roberts, P. S. | 1 |
| Roberts, R. (*Druids*) | 1 |
| Roberts, W. (*Llangollen*) | 2 |
| Roberts, W. (*Wrexham*) | 1 |
| Roberts, W. H. | 1 |
| Robinson, J. R. C. | 3 |
| Rush, I. | 28 |
| Russell, M. R. | 1 |
| Sabine, H. W. | 1 |
| Saunders, D. | 22 |
| Savage, R. W. | 2 |
| Shaw, E. G. | 2 |
| Sisson, H. | 4 |
| Slatter, N. | 2 |
| Smallman, D. P. | 1 |
| Speed, G. A. | 6 |
| Symons, C. J. | 2 |
| Tapscott, D. R. | 4 |
| Taylor, G. K. | 1 |
| Thomas, M. | 4 |
| Thomas, T. | 1 |
| Toshack, J. B. | 12 |
| Trainer, H. | 2 |
| Vaughan, John | 2 |
| Vernon, T. R. | 8 |
| Vizard, E. T. | 1 |
| Walsh, I. | 7 |
| Warren, F. W. | 3 |
| Watkins, W. M. | 4 |
| Wilding, J. | 4 |
| Williams, A. | 1 |
| Williams, D. R. | 2 |
| Williams, G. E. | 1 |
| Williams, G. G. | 1 |
| Williams, W. | 1 |
| Woosnam, A. P. | 3 |
| Wynn, G. A. | 1 |
| Yorath, T. C. | 2 |
| Young, E. | 1 |

**REPUBLIC OF IRELAND**

| | |
|---|---|
| Aldridge, J. | 19 |
| Ambrose, P. | 1 |
| Anderson, J. | 1 |
| Barrett, G. | 2 |
| Bermingham, P. | 1 |
| Bradshaw, P. | 4 |
| Brady, L. | 9 |
| Breen, G. | 6 |
| Brown, D. | 1 |
| Byrne, J. (*Bray*) | 1 |
| Byrne, J. (*QPR*) | 4 |
| Cantwell, J. | 14 |
| Carey, J. | 3 |
| Carroll, T. | 1 |
| Cascarino, A. | 19 |
| Coad, P. | 3 |
| Connolly, D. J. | 9 |
| Conroy, T. | 2 |
| Conway, J. | 3 |
| Coyne, T. | 6 |
| Cummings, G. | 5 |
| Curtis, D. | 8 |
| Daly, G. | 13 |
| Davis, T. | 4 |
| Dempsey, J. | 1 |
| Dennehy, M. | 2 |
| Doherty, G. M. T. | 4 |
| Donnelly, J. | 4 |
| Donnelly, T. | 1 |
| Duff, D. A. | 6 |
| Duffy, B. | 1 |
| Duggan, H. | 1 |
| Dunne, J. | 13 |
| Dunne, L. | 1 |
| Dunne, R. P. | 4 |
| Eglington, T. | 2 |
| Ellis, P. | 2 |
| Fagan, F. | 5 |
| Fallon, S. | 2 |
| Fallon, W. | 2 |
| Farrell, P. | 3 |
| Finnan, S. | 1 |
| Fitzgerald, P. | 2 |
| Fitzgerald, J. | 1 |

| | | | | | | | |
|---|---|---|---|---|---|---|---|
| Fitzsimmons, A. | 7 | Irwin, D. | 4 | Mancini, T. | 1 | Ringstead, A. | 7 |
| Flood, J. J. | 4 | | | Martin, C. | 6 | Robinson, M. | 4 |
| Fogarty, A. | 3 | Jordan, D. | 1 | Martin, M. | 4 | Rogers, E. | 5 |
| Foley, D. | 2 | | | Mooney, J. | 1 | Ryan, G. | 1 |
| Fullam, J. | 1 | Kavanagh, G. A. | 1 | Moore, P. | 7 | Ryan, R. | 3 |
| Fullam, R. | 1 | Keane, R. D. | 20 | Moran, K. | 6 | | |
| | | Keane, R. M. | 9 | Morrison, C. H. | 5 | Sheedy, K. | 9 |
| Galvin, A. | 1 | Kelly, D. | 9 | Moroney, T. | 1 | Sheridan, J. | 5 |
| Gavin, J. | 2 | Kelly, G. | 2 | Mulligan, P. | 1 | Slaven, B. | 1 |
| Geoghegan, M. | 2 | Kelly, J. | 2 | | | Sloan, W. | 1 |
| Giles, J. | 5 | Kennedy, M. | 3 | O'Callaghan, K. | 1 | Squires, J. | 1 |
| Givens, D. | 19 | Kernaghan, A. N. | 1 | O'Connor, T. | 2 | Stapleton, F. | 20 |
| Glynn, D. | 1 | Kilbane, K. D. | 4 | O'Farrell, F. | 2 | Staunton, S. | 7 |
| Grealish, T. | 8 | Kinsella, M. A. | 3 | O'Flanagan, K. | 3 | Strahan, J. | 1 |
| Grimes, A. A. | 1 | | | O'Keefe, E. | 1 | Sullivan, J. | 1 |
| | | Lacey, W. | 1 | O'Leary, D. A. | 1 | | |
| Hale, A. | 2 | Lawrenson, M. | 5 | O'Neill, F. | 1 | Townsend, A. D. | 7 |
| Hand, E. | 2 | Leech, M. | 2 | O'Neill, K. P. | 4 | Treacy, R. | 5 |
| Harte, I. P. | 9 | | | O'Reilly, J. (*Brideville*) | 2 | Touhy, L. | 4 |
| Haverty, J. | 3 | McAteer, J. W. | 3 | O'Reilly, J. (*Cork*) | 1 | | |
| Healy, C. | 1 | McCann, J. | 1 | O'Shea, J. F. | 1 | Waddock, G. | 3 |
| Holland, M. R. | 5 | McCarthy, M. | 2 | Own goals | 10 | Walsh, D. | 5 |
| Holmes, J. | 1 | McEvoy, A. | 6 | | | Walsh, M. | 3 |
| Horlacher, A. | 2 | McGee, P. | 4 | Quinn, N. | 21 | Waters, J. | 1 |
| Houghton, R. | 6 | McGrath, P. | 8 | | | White, J. J. | 2 |
| Hughton, C. | 1 | McLoughlin, A. F. | 2 | Reid, S. J. | 2 | Whelan, R. | 3 |
| Hurley, C. | 2 | McPhail, S. J. P. | 1 | | | | |

Frank Lampard equalises for England against Portugal in the Quarter-Final of EURO 2004 in Lisbon. Portugal progressed, winning 6-5 on penalties. (Colorsport)

# SOUTH AMERICA

## COPA LIBERTADORES 2004

| GROUP 1 | P | W | D | L | F | A | Pts |
|---|---|---|---|---|---|---|---|
| America (Mexico) | 6 | 4 | 1 | 1 | 11 | 5 | 13 |
| Sao Caetano | 6 | 2 | 2 | 2 | 10 | 8 | 8 |
| Penarol | 6 | 2 | 2 | 2 | 9 | 7 | 8 |
| The Strongest | 6 | 1 | 1 | 4 | 4 | 14 | 4 |
| **GROUP 2** | P | W | D | L | F | A | Pts |
| Once Caldas | 6 | 4 | 1 | 1 | 11 | 6 | 13 |
| Union Atletico | 6 | 2 | 2 | 2 | 10 | 9 | 8 |
| Velez Sarsfield | 6 | 2 | 1 | 3 | 7 | 9 | 7 |
| Fenix | 6 | 1 | 2 | 3 | 6 | 10 | 5 |
| **GROUP 3** | P | W | D | L | F | A | Pts |
| Cruzeiro | 6 | 4 | 1 | 1 | 15 | 6 | 13 |
| Santos Laguna | 6 | 3 | 3 | 0 | 10 | 6 | 12 |
| Caracas | 6 | 2 | 0 | 4 | 8 | 12 | 6 |
| Univ Concepcion | 6 | 0 | 2 | 4 | 7 | 16 | 2 |
| **GROUP 4** | P | W | D | L | F | A | Pts |
| Sao Paulo | 6 | 5 | 0 | 1 | 11 | 7 | 15 |
| LDU Quito | 6 | 4 | 0 | 2 | 13 | 3 | 12 |
| Alianza | 6 | 3 | 0 | 3 | 6 | 8 | 9 |
| Cobreloa | 6 | 0 | 0 | 6 | 3 | 15 | 0 |
| **GROUP 5** | P | W | D | L | F | A | Pts |
| Nacional (Uru) | 6 | 3 | 3 | 0 | 7 | 4 | 12 |
| Independiente | 6 | 2 | 2 | 2 | 9 | 7 | 8 |
| Cienciano | 6 | 2 | 1 | 3 | 10 | 12 | 7 |
| El Nacional | 6 | 1 | 2 | 3 | 6 | 9 | 5 |
| **GROUP 6** | P | W | D | L | F | A | Pts |
| River Plate | 6 | 3 | 2 | 1 | 10 | 6 | 11 |
| Tachira | 6 | 2 | 4 | 0 | 8 | 4 | 10 |
| Tolima | 6 | 1 | 2 | 3 | 6 | 9 | 5 |
| Libertad | 6 | 1 | 2 | 3 | 5 | 10 | 5 |
| **GROUP 7** | P | W | D | L | F | A | Pts |
| Santos | 6 | 5 | 1 | 0 | 6 | 6 | 16 |
| Barcelona | 6 | 2 | 2 | 2 | 9 | 6 | 8 |
| Guarani | 6 | 1 | 3 | 2 | 6 | 7 | 6 |
| Jorge Wilstermann | 6 | 0 | 2 | 4 | 5 | 17 | 2 |
| **GROUP 8** | P | W | D | L | F | A | Pts |
| Boca Juniors | 6 | 4 | 0 | 2 | 10 | 4 | 12 |
| Dep Cali | 6 | 3 | 0 | 3 | 9 | 9 | 9 |
| Bolivar | 6 | 3 | 0 | 3 | 7 | 9 | 9 |
| Colo Colo | 6 | 2 | 0 | 4 | 6 | 10 | 6 |
| **GROUP 9** | P | W | D | L | F | A | Pts |
| Sporting Cristal | 6 | 3 | 1 | 2 | 13 | 9 | 10 |
| Rosario Central | 6 | 3 | 1 | 2 | 8 | 8 | 10 |
| Coritiba | 6 | 2 | 2 | 2 | 7 | 8 | 8 |
| Olimpia | 6 | 1 | 2 | 3 | 7 | 10 | 5 |

### RUNNERS-UP PLAY-OFFS
Sao Caetano 2, Independiente 2
*Sao Caetano won 4-2 on penalties.*
Barcelona 6, Union Atletico 1

### SECOND ROUND FIRST LEG
Santos Laguna 0, River Plate 1
Sporting Cristal 2, Boca Juniors 3
Tachira 3, Nacional (Uru) 0
Sao Caetano 2, America (Mexico) 1
LDU Quito 4, Santos 2
Dep Cali 1, Cruzeiro 0
Rosario Central 1, Sao Paulo 0
Barcelona 0, Once Caldas 0

### SECOND ROUND SECOND LEG
River Plate 1, Santos Laguna 2
*River Plate won 4-2 on penalties.*
Boca Juniors 2, Sporting Cristal 1
Nacional (Uru) 2, Tachira 2
America (Mexico) 1, Sao Caetano 1
Santos 2, LDU Quito 0
*Santos won 5-3 on penalties.*
Cruzeiro 2, Dep Cali 1
*Dep Cali won 3-0 on penalties.*
Sao Paulo 2, Rosario Central 1
*Sao Paulo won 5-4 on penalties.*
Once Caldas 1, Barcelona 1
*Once Caldas won 4-2 on penalties.*

### QUARTER-FINALS FIRST LEG
Sao Paulo 3, Tachira 0
Santos 1, Once Caldas 1
Sao Caetano 0, Boca Juniors 0
River Plate 1, Dep Cali 0

### QUARTER-FINALS SECOND LEG
Tachira 1, Sao Paulo 4
Once Caldas 1, Santos 0
Boca Juniors 1, Sao Caetano 1
*Boca Juniors won 4-3 on penalties.*
Dep Cali 1, River Plate 3

### SEMI-FINALS FIRST LEG
Sao Paulo 0, Once Caldas 0
Boca Juniors 1, River Plate 0

### SEMI-FINALS SECOND LEG
Once Caldas 2, Sao Paulo 1
River Plate 2, Boca Juniors 1
*Boca Juniors won 5-4 on penalties.*

### FINAL FIRST LEG
Boca Juniors 0, Once Caldas 0

### FINAL SECOND LEG
Once Caldas 1, Boca Juniors 1
*Once Caldas won 2-0 on penalties.*

## COPA LIBERTADORES PAST WINNERS

1960 Penarol (Uruguay)
1961 Penarol
1962 Santos (Brazil)
1963 Santos
1964 Independiente (Argentina)
1965 Independiente
1966 Penarol
1967 Racing Club (Argentina)
1968 Estudiantes (Argentina)
1969 Estudiantes
1970 Estudiantes
1971 Nacional (Uruguay)
1972 Independiente
1973 Independiente
1974 Independiente
1975 Independiente
1976 Cruzeiro (Brazil)
1977 Boca Juniors (Argentina)
1978 Boca Juniors
1979 Olimpia (Paraguay)
1980 Nacional
1981 Flamengo (Brazil)
1982 Penarol
1983 Gremio Porto Alegre (Brazil)
1984 Independiente
1985 Argentinos Juniors (Argentina)
1986 River Plate (Argentina)
1987 Penarol
1988 Nacional (Uruguay)
1989 Nacional (Colombia)
1990 Olimpia
1991 Colo Colo (Chile)
1992 São Paulo (Brazil)
1993 São Paulo
1994 Velez Sarsfield (Argentina)
1995 Gremio Porto Alegre
1996 River Plate
1997 Cruzeiro
1998 Vasco da Gama
1999 Palmeiras
2000 Boca Juniors
2001 Boca Juniors
2002 Olimpia
2003 Boca Juniors
2004 Once Caldas

## COPA SUDAMERICANA

River Plate 3, 0, Cienciano 3, 1

## COPA AMERICA 2004

**GROUP A**
Colombia 1, Venezuela 0
Peru 2, Bolivia 2
Colombia 1, Bolivia 0
Peru 3, Venezuela 1
Venezuela 1, Bolivia 1
Peru 2, Colombia 2

| GROUP A | P | W | D | L | F | A | GD | Pts |
|---|---|---|---|---|---|---|---|---|
| Colombia | 3 | 2 | 1 | 0 | 4 | 2 | 2 | 7 |
| Peru | 3 | 1 | 2 | 0 | 7 | 5 | 2 | 5 |
| Bolivia | 3 | 0 | 2 | 1 | 3 | 4 | –1 | 2 |
| Venezuela | 3 | 0 | 1 | 2 | 2 | 5 | –3 | 1 |

**GROUP B**
Uruguay 2, Mexico 2
Argentina 6, Ecuador 1
Uruguay 2, Ecuador 1
Argentina 0, Mexico 1
Mexico 2, Ecuador 1
Argentina 4, Uruguay 2

| GROUP B | P | W | D | L | F | A | GD | Pts |
|---|---|---|---|---|---|---|---|---|
| Mexico | 3 | 2 | 1 | 1 | 5 | 3 | 2 | 7 |
| Argentina | 3 | 2 | 0 | 1 | 10 | 4 | 6 | 6 |
| Uruguay | 3 | 1 | 1 | 1 | 6 | 7 | –1 | 4 |
| Ecuador | 3 | 0 | 0 | 3 | 3 | 10 | –7 | 0 |

**GROUP C**
Paraguay 1, Costa Rica 0
Brazill 1, Chile 0
Brazil 4, Costa Rica 1
Paraguay 1, Chile 1
Costa Rica 2, Chile 1
Brazil 1, Paraguay 2

| GROUP C | P | W | D | L | F | A | GD | Pts |
|---|---|---|---|---|---|---|---|---|
| Paraguay | 3 | 2 | 1 | 0 | 4 | 2 | 2 | 7 |
| Brazil | 3 | 2 | 0 | 1 | 6 | 3 | 3 | 6 |
| Costa Rica | 3 | 1 | 0 | 2 | 3 | 6 | –3 | 3 |
| Chile | 3 | 0 | 1 | 2 | 2 | 4 | –2 | 1 |

**QUARTER-FINALS**
Peru v Argentina
Colombia v Costa Rica
Paraguay v Uruguay
Mexico v Brazil

## COPA AMERICA PAST WINNERS

1916 Uruguay
1917 Uruguay
1919 Brazil
1920 Uruguay
1921 Argentina
1922 Brazil
1923 Uruguay
1924 Uruguay
1925 Argentina
1926 Uruguay
1927 Argentina
1929 Argentina
1935 Uruguay
1937 Argentina
1939 Peru
1941 Argentina
1942 Uruguay
1945 Argentina
1946 Argentina
1947 Argentina
1949 Brazil
1953 Paraguay
1955 Argentina
1956 Uruguay
1957 Argentina
1959 Argentina
1959 Uruguay
1963 Bolivia
1967 Uruguay
1975 Peru
1979 Paraguay
1983 Uruguay
1987 Uruguay
1989 Brazil
1991 Argentina
1993 Argentina
1995 Uruguay
1997 Brazil
1999 Brazil
2001 Colombia

## GOLD CUP FINAL

Mexico 1, Brazil 0

# CONCACAF

## CONCACAF CUP OF THE CHAMPIONS 2004

**FINAL FIRST LEG**
Morelia (Mexico) 3, Toluca (Mexico) 3

**FINAL SECOND LEG**
Toluca (Mexico) 2, Morelia (Mexico) 1

## CONCACAF CHAMPIONS CUP 2004

**FINAL FIRST LEG**
Saprissa (Costa Rica) 1, Alajuelense (Costa Rica) 1

**FINAL SECOND LEG**
Alajuelense 4, Saprissa 0

# ASIA

## ARABIAN CHAMPIONS CUP

**FINAL**
Zamalek (Egypt) 2, Al Kuwait 1

# NORTH AMERICA

## MLS CUP 2004

**FINAL**
San Jose Earthquakes 4, Chicago Fire 2

# AFRICA

## AFRICAN NATIONS CUP 2004

### Final Tournament in Tunisia

**GROUP A**
Tunisia 2, Rwanda 1
DR Congo 1, Guinea 2
Rwanda 1, Guinea 1
Tunisia 3, DR Congo 0
Tunisia 1, Guinea 1
Rwanda 1, DR Congo 0

**GROUP B**
Senegal 0, Burkina Faso 0
Kenya 1, Mali 3
Senegal 3, Kenya 0
Burkina Faso 1, Mali 3
Senegal 1, Mali 1
Burkina Faso 0, Kenya 3

**GROUP C**
Zimbabwe 1, Egypt 2
Cameroon 1, Algeria 1
Cameroon 5, Zimbabwe 3
Algeria 2, Egypt 1
Cameroon 0, Egypt 0
Algeria 1, Zimbabwe 2

**GROUP D**
Nigeria 0, Morocco 1
South Africa 2, Benin 0
Nigeria 4, South Africa 0
Morocco 4, Benin 0
Morocco 1, South Africa 1
Nigeria 2, Benin 1

**QUARTER-FINALS**
Tunisia 1, Senegal 0
Mali 2, Guinea 1
Cameroon 1, Nigeria 2
Morocco 3, Algeria 1

**SEMI-FINALS**
Tunisia 1, Nigeria 1
*Tunisia won 5-3 on penalties.*
Mali 0, Morocco 4

**MATCH FOR THIRD PLACE**
Nigeria 2, Mali 1

**FINAL**
Tunisia 2, Morocco 1

## AFRICAN CHAMPIONS LEAGUE FINAL 2004

**FINAL FIRST LEG**
Enyimba (Nigeria) 2, Ismaili (Egypt) 0

**FINAL SECOND LEG**
Ismaili (Egypt) 1, Enyimba (Nigeria) 0

## AFRICAN CUP-WINNERS' CUP 2004

**FINAL FIRST LEG**
Julius Berger (Nigeria) 2, Etoile Sahel (Tunisia) 0

**FINAL SECOND LEG**
Etoile Sahel (Tunisia) 3, Julius Berger (Nigeria) 0

## CAF CUP 2004

**FINAL FIRST LEG**
Raja (Morocco) 2, Cotonsport (Cameroon) 0

**FINAL SECOND LEG**
Cotonsport (Cameroon) 0, Raja (Morocco) 0

## AFRICAN SUPER CUP 2004

**FINAL**
Enyimba (Nigeria) 1, Etoile Sahel (Tunisia) 0

## COSAFA CUP 2004

**FINAL**
Malawi 1, 0, Zimbabwe 2, 2

## CECAFA CUP 2004

**FINAL**
Uganda 2, Rwanda 0

# UEFA UNDER-21 CHAMPIONSHIP 2002–04

**GROUP 1**
Slovenia 1, Malta 0
Cyprus 0, France 1
Malta 0, Israel 1
France 1, Slovenia 0
Malta 0, France 3
Cyprus 2, Malta 0
Cyprus 2, Israel 0
France 2, Malta 0
Israel 0, France 3
Slovenia 2, Cyprus 0
Malta 0, Slovenia 0
Israel 0, Cyprus 3
Israel 0, Slovenia 0
Malta 0, Cyprus 1
Slovenia 1, Israel 2
France 2, Cyprus 0
Israel 3, Malta 0
Slovenia 0, France 0
France 2, Israel 0
Cyprus 4, Slovenia 0

**GROUP 2**
Norway 3, Denmark 0
Bosnia 2, Romania 1
Denmark 9, Luxembourg 0
Romania 0, Norway 1
Norway 0, Bosnia 0
Luxembourg 0, Romania 2
Bosnia 1, Luxembourg 0
Romania 0, Denmark 1
Denmark 3, Bosnia 0
Luxembourg 0, Norway 5
Romania 0, Bosnia 1
Denmark 2, Norway 0
Norway 2, Romania 1
Luxembourg 0, Denmark 6
Bosnia 1, Norway 3
Romania 2, Luxembourg 0
Denmark 0, Romania 0
Luxembourg 0, Bosnia 1
Norway 5, Luxembourg 0
Bosnia 0, Denmark 3

**GROUP 3**
Holland 0, Belarus 1
Austria 1, Moldova 0
Belarus 0, Austria 1
Moldova 0, Czech Republic 2
Austria 1, Holland 1
Czech Republic 3, Belarus 0
Holland 0, Czech Republic 3
Belarus 3, Moldova 1
Czech Republic 3, Austria 1
Moldova 2, Holland 2
Belarus 2, Holland 1
Moldova 0, Austria 1
Czech Republic 3, Moldova 0
Austria 0, Belarus 2
Belarus 1, Czech Republic 0
Holland 0, Austria 0
Czech Republic 1, Holland 2
Moldova 0, Belarus 2
Austria 0, Czech Republic 2
Holland 0, Moldova 0

**GROUP 4**
Latvia 0, Sweden 4
San Marino 1, Poland 5
Poland 3, Latvia 0
Sweden 1, Hungary 0
Hungary 4, San Marino 1
San Marino 0, Latvia 2
Poland 3, Hungary 2
Poland 7, San Marino 0
Hungary 5, Sweden 2
Latvia 4, San Marino 0
Hungary 3, Latvia 1
San Marino 1, Sweden 5
Sweden 1, Poland 1
San Marino 1, Hungary 2
Latvia 0, Poland 2
Sweden 0, San Marino 3
Poland 1, Sweden 1
Latvia 2, Hungary 0
Sweden 3, Latvia 2
Hungary 1, Poland 2

**GROUP 5**
Lithuania 1, Germany 4
Iceland 0, Scotland 2
Iceland 1, Lithuania 2
Scotland 1, Iceland 0
Germany 1, Lithuania 0
Lithuania 2, Scotland 1
Scotland 2, Germany 2
Lithuania 3, Iceland 0
Iceland 1, Germany 3
Germany 0, Scotland 1
Scotland 3, Lithuania 2
Germany 1, Iceland 0

**GROUP 6**
Armenia 1, Ukraine 1
Greece 1, Spain 0
Ukraine 1, Greece 1
Spain 1, Northern Ireland 0
Northern Ireland 1, Ukraine 1
Greece 2, Armenia 1
Armenia 2, Northern Ireland 0
Ukraine 0, Spain 0
Northern Ireland 2, Greece 6
Spain 5, Armenia 0
Ukraine 4, Armenia 0
Spain 2, Greece 0
Northern Ireland 1, Spain 4
Greece 0, Ukraine 0
Ukraine 1, Northern Ireland 0
Armenia 0, Greece 0
Northern Ireland 3, Armenia 1
Spain 2, Ukraine 0
Armenia 0, Spain 2
Greece 0, Northern Ireland 1

**GROUP 7**
Turkey 2, Slovakia 1
Portugal 1, Macedonia 0
Macedonia 0, Turkey 4
Slovakia 0, England 4
Turkey 4, Portugal 2
England 3, Macedonia 1
Portugal 4, England 2
Macedonia 0, Slovakia 2
Slovakia 0, Portugal 2
England 1, Turkey 1
Slovakia 0, Turkey 1
Macedonia 1, Portugal 4
Turkey 3, Macedonia 0
England 2, Slovakia 0
Macedonia 1, England 1
Portugal 1, Turkey 2
England 1, Portugal 2
Slovakia 5, Macedonia 1
Turkey 1, England 0
Portugal 4, Slovakia 1

**GROUP 8**
Croatia 3, Estonia 1
Belgium 3, Bulgaria 1
Bulgaria 1, Croatia 3
Estonia 0, Belgium 1
Croatia 1, Belgium 1
Estonia 1, Bulgaria 1
Bulgaria 2, Belgium 1
Estonia 0, Croatia 0
Bulgaria 1, Estonia 0
Belgium 0, Croatia 2
Croatia 0, Bulgaria 1
Belgium 4, Estonia 2

**GROUP 9**
Finland 2, Wales 1
Azerbaijan 0, Italy 3
Finland 3, Azerbaijan 0
Italy 4, Serbia-Montenegro 1
Serbia-Montenegro 3, Finland 3
Wales 1, Italy 2
Azerbaijan 0, Wales 1
Serbia-Montenegro 3, Azerbaijan 0
Wales 1, Azerbaijan 0
Italy 1, Finland 0
Finland 1, Serbia-Montenegro 2
Finland 1, Italy 2
Azerbaijan 0, Serbia-Montenegro 2
Serbia-Montenegro 3, Wales 0
Italy 8, Wales 1
Azerbaijan 0, Finland 1
Wales 0, Finland 0
Serbia-Montenegro 1, Italy 0
Wales 0, Serbia-Montenegro 1
Italy 6, Azerbaijan 0

**GROUP 10**
Russia 2, Republic of Ireland 0
Switzerland 2, Georgia 0
Albania 0, Switzerland 0
Georgia 0, Russia 3
Republic of Ireland 2, Switzerland 3
Russia 1, Albania 0
Georgia 1, Republic of Ireland 1
Albania 1, Russia 4
Albania 1, Republic of Ireland 0
Georgia 0, Switzerland 2
Switzerland 1, Russia 0
Republic of Ireland 0, Albania 3
Switzerland 2, Albania 1
Republic of Ireland 1, Georgia 1
Republic of Ireland 2, Russia 0
Georgia 3, Albania 1
Albania 3, Georgia 0
Russia 1, Switzerland 2
Switzerland 0, Republic of Ireland 2
Russia 3, Georgia 2

**PLAY-OFFS FIRST LEG**
Serbia-Montenegro 5, Norway 1
Germany 1, Turkey 0
Portugal 1, France 2
Denmark 1, Italy 1
Belarus 1, Poland 1
Sweden 2, Spain 0
Switzerland 1, Czech Republic 2
Croatia 2, Scotland 0

**PLAY-OFFS SECOND LEG**
Norway 3, Serbia-Montenegro 0
Turkey 1, Germany 1
France 1, Portugal 2
*Portugal won 4-1 on penalties.*
Italy 0, Denmark 0
Poland 0, Belarus 4
Spain 1, Sweden 1
Czech Republic 1, Switzerland 2
*Switzerland won 4-3 on penalties.*
Scotland 1, Croatia 0

## FINALS IN GERMANY

**GROUP A**
Serbia-Montenegro 3, Croatia 2
Italy 1, Belarus 2
Belarus 1, Croatia 1
Italy 2, Serbia-Montenegro 1
Italy 1, Croatia 0
Belarus 1, Serbia-Montenegro 2

**GROUP B**
Germany 2, Switzerland 1
Sweden 3, Portugal 1
Germany 1, Sweden 2
Switzerland 2, Portugal 2
Germany 1, Portugal 2
Switzerland 1, Sweden 3

**SEMI-FINALS**
Sweden 1, Serbia-Montenegro 1
*Serbia-Montenegro won 6-5 on penalties.*
Italy 3, Portugal 1

**MATCH FOR 3RD PLACE**
Sweden 2, Portugal 3

**FINAL**
Italy 3, Serbia-Montenegro 0
*Italy, Serbia-Montenegro and Portugal qualified for the Olympics.*

**PREVIOUS WINNERS**
1978 Yugoslavia
1980 USSR
1982 England
1984 England
1986 Spain
1988 France
1990 USSR
1992 Italy
1994 Italy
1996 Italy
1998 Spain
2000 Italy
2002 Czech Republic

# WORLD YOUTH CUP

(Finals in UAE)

| GROUP A | P | W | D | L | F | A | Pts |
|---|---|---|---|---|---|---|---|
| Burkina Faso | 3 | 2 | 1 | 0 | 2 | 0 | 7 |
| Slovakia | 3 | 2 | 0 | 1 | 5 | 2 | 6 |
| UAE | 3 | 1 | 1 | 1 | 3 | 5 | 4 |
| Panama | 3 | 0 | 0 | 3 | 1 | 4 | 0 |

| GROUP B | P | W | D | L | F | A | Pts |
|---|---|---|---|---|---|---|---|
| Argentina | 3 | 3 | 0 | 0 | 7 | 3 | 9 |
| Spain | 3 | 2 | 0 | 1 | 4 | 2 | 6 |
| Mali | 3 | 1 | 0 | 2 | 4 | 7 | 3 |
| Uzbekistan | 3 | 0 | 0 | 3 | 3 | 6 | 0 |

| GROUP C | P | W | D | L | F | A | Pts |
|---|---|---|---|---|---|---|---|
| Australia | 3 | 2 | 1 | 0 | 6 | 4 | 7 |
| Brazil | 3 | 1 | 1 | 1 | 5 | 4 | 4 |
| Canada | 3 | 1 | 0 | 2 | 2 | 4 | 3 |
| Czech Republic | 3 | 0 | 2 | 1 | 2 | 3 | 2 |

| GROUP D | P | W | D | L | F | A | Pts |
|---|---|---|---|---|---|---|---|
| Japan | 3 | 2 | 0 | 1 | 3 | 4 | 6 |
| Colombia | 3 | 1 | 2 | 0 | 4 | 1 | 5 |
| Egypt | 3 | 1 | 1 | 1 | 1 | 1 | 4 |
| England | 3 | 0 | 1 | 2 | 0 | 2 | 1 |

| GROUP E | P | W | D | L | F | A | Pts |
|---|---|---|---|---|---|---|---|
| Republic of Ireland | 3 | 2 | 1 | 0 | 6 | 3 | 7 |
| Ivory Coast | 3 | 1 | 2 | 0 | 4 | 3 | 5 |
| Saudi Arabia | 3 | 0 | 2 | 1 | 2 | 3 | 2 |
| Mexico | 3 | 0 | 1 | 2 | 2 | 5 | 1 |

| GROUP F | P | W | D | L | F | A | Pts |
|---|---|---|---|---|---|---|---|
| USA | 3 | 2 | 0 | 1 | 6 | 4 | 6 |
| Paraguay | 3 | 2 | 0 | 1 | 4 | 3 | 6 |
| South Korea | 3 | 1 | 0 | 2 | 2 | 3 | 3 |
| Germany | 3 | 1 | 0 | 2 | 3 | 5 | 3 |

**SECOND ROUND**
Japan 2, South Korea 1
Burkina Faso 0, Canada1
Argentina 2, Egypt 1
USA 2, Ivory Coast 0
Brazil 2, Slovakia 1
Australia 0, UAE 1
Paraguay 0, Spain 1
Republic of Ireland 2, Colombia 3

**QUARTER-FINALS**
Canada 1, Spain 2
USA 1, Argentina 2
Colombia 1, UAE 0
Japan 1, Brazil 5

**SEMI-FINALS**
Brazil 1, Argentina 0
Spain 1, Colombia 0

**MATCH FOR THIRD PLACE**
Colombia 2, Argentina 1

**FINAL**
Spain 0, Brazil 1

# UEFA UNDER-19 CHAMPIONSHIP

(Finals in Liechtenstein)

**GROUP A**
Liechtenstein 0, Portugal 5
Norway 0, Italy 1
Portugal 1, Italy 1
Liechtenstein 1, Norway 2
Portugal 2, Norway 2
Italy 5, Liechtenstein 1

**GROUP B**
England 1, Austria 2
France 3, Czech Republic 3
France 0, England 2
Czechoslovakia 1, Austria 4
Czech Republic 3, England 0
Austria 1, France 1

**SEMI-FINALS**
Austria 3, Portugal 6
Italy 1, Czechoslovakia 0

**FINAL**
Italy 2, Portugal 0

# UEFA UNDER-17 CHAMPIONSHIP

(Finals in France)

**GROUP A**
Spain 1, Turkey 0
France 3, Northern Ireland 0
Northern Ireland 2, Turkey 5
France 1, Spain 0
Turkey 1, France 2
Northern Ireland 1, Spain 4

**GROUP B**
Ukraine 0, England 2
Austria 0, Portugal 0
Ukraine 1, Austria 2
England 3, Portugal 1
Portugal 4, Ukraine 0
England 1, Austria 0

**SEMI-FINALS**
France 3, Portugal 1
England 1, Spain 2

**MATCH FOR 3rd PLACE**
Portugal 4, England 4
*Portugal won 3-2 on penalties.*

**FINAL**
France 2, Spain 1

# ENGLAND UNDER-21 RESULTS 1976–2004

*EC UEFA Competition for Under-21 Teams*

| Year | Date | | Venue | | |
|---|---|---|---|---|---|
| | | | **v ALBANIA** | Eng | Alb |
| EC1989 | Mar | 7 | Shkroda | 2 | 1 |
| EC1989 | April | 25 | Ipswich | 2 | 0 |
| EC2001 | Mar | 27 | Tirana | 1 | 0 |
| EC2001 | Sept | 4 | Middlesbrough | 5 | 0 |
| | | | **v ANGOLA** | Eng | Ang |
| 1995 | June | 10 | Toulon | 1 | 0 |
| 1996 | May | 28 | Toulon | 0 | 2 |
| | | | **v ARGENTINA** | Eng | Arg |
| 1998 | May | 18 | Toulon | 0 | 2 |
| 2000 | Feb | 22 | Fulham | 1 | 0 |
| | | | **v AUSTRIA** | Eng | Aus |
| 1994 | Oct | 11 | Kapfenberg | 3 | 1 |
| 1995 | Nov | 14 | Middlesbrough | 2 | 1 |
| | | | **v BELGIUM** | Eng | Bel |
| 1994 | June | 5 | Marseille | 2 | 1 |
| 1996 | May | 24 | Toulon | 1 | 0 |
| | | | **v BRAZIL** | Eng | B |
| 1993 | June | 11 | Toulon | 0 | 0 |
| 1995 | June | 6 | Toulon | 0 | 2 |
| 1996 | June | 1 | Toulon | 1 | 2 |
| | | | **v BULGARIA** | Eng | Bul |
| EC1979 | June | 5 | Pernik | 3 | 1 |
| EC1979 | Nov | 20 | Leicester | 5 | 0 |
| 1989 | June | 5 | Toulon | 2 | 3 |
| EC1998 | Oct | 9 | West Ham | 1 | 0 |
| EC1999 | June | 8 | Vratsa | 1 | 0 |
| | | | **v CROATIA** | Eng | Cro |
| 1996 | Apr | 23 | Sunderland | 0 | 1 |
| 2003 | Aug | 19 | West Ham | 0 | 3 |
| | | | **v CZECHOSLOVAKIA** | Eng | Cz |
| 1990 | May | 28 | Toulon | 2 | 1 |
| 1992 | May | 26 | Toulon | 1 | 2 |
| 1993 | June | 9 | Toulon | 1 | 1 |
| | | | **v CZECH REPUBLIC** | Eng | CzR |
| 1998 | Nov | 17 | Ipswich | 0 | 1 |
| | | | **v DENMARK** | Eng | Den |
| EC1978 | Sept | 19 | Hvidovre | 2 | 1 |
| EC1979 | Sept | 11 | Watford | 1 | 0 |
| EC1982 | Sept | 21 | Hvidovre | 4 | 1 |
| EC1983 | Sept | 20 | Norwich | 4 | 1 |
| EC1986 | Mar | 12 | Copenhagen | 1 | 0 |
| EC1986 | Mar | 26 | Manchester | 1 | 1 |
| 1988 | Sept | 13 | Watford | 0 | 0 |
| 1994 | Mar | 8 | Brentford | 1 | 0 |
| 1999 | Oct | 8 | Bradford | 4 | 1 |
| | | | **v EAST GERMANY** | Eng | EG |
| EC1980 | April | 16 | Sheffield | 1 | 2 |
| EC1980 | April | 23 | Jena | 0 | 1 |
| | | | **v FINLAND** | Eng | Fin |
| EC1977 | May | 26 | Helsinki | 1 | 0 |
| EC1977 | Oct | 12 | Hull | 8 | 1 |
| EC1984 | Oct | 16 | Southampton | 2 | 0 |
| EC1985 | May | 21 | Mikkeli | 1 | 3 |
| EC2000 | Oct | 10 | Valkeakoski | 2 | 2 |
| EC2001 | Mar | 23 | Barnsley | 4 | 0 |
| | | | **v FRANCE** | Eng | Fra |
| EC1984 | Feb | 28 | Sheffield | 6 | 1 |
| EC1984 | Mar | 28 | Rouen | 1 | 0 |
| 1987 | June | 11 | Toulon | 0 | 2 |
| EC1988 | April | 13 | Besancon | 2 | 4 |
| EC1988 | April | 27 | Highbury | 2 | 2 |
| 1988 | June | 12 | Toulon | 2 | 4 |
| 1990 | May | 23 | Toulon | 7 | 3 |
| 1991 | June | 3 | Toulon | 1 | 0 |
| 1992 | May | 28 | Toulon | 0 | 0 |
| 1993 | June | 15 | Toulon | 1 | 0 |
| 1994 | May | 31 | Aubagne | 0 | 3 |
| 1995 | June | 10 | Toulon | 0 | 2 |
| 1998 | May | 14 | Toulon | 1 | 1 |
| 1999 | Feb | 9 | Derby | 2 | 1 |
| | | | **v GEORGIA** | Eng | Geo |
| EC1996 | Nov | 8 | Batumi | 1 | 0 |
| EC1997 | April | 29 | Charlton | 0 | 0 |
| 2000 | Aug | 31 | Middlesbrough | 6 | 1 |
| | | | **v GERMANY** | Eng | Ger |
| 1991 | Sept | 10 | Scunthorpe | 2 | 1 |
| EC2000 | Oct | 6 | Derby | 1 | 1 |
| EC2001 | Aug | 31 | Frieburg | 2 | 1 |
| | | | **v GREECE** | Eng | Gre |
| EC1982 | Nov | 16 | Piraeus | 0 | 1 |
| EC1983 | Mar | 29 | Portsmouth | 2 | 1 |
| 1989 | Feb | 7 | Patras | 0 | 1 |
| EC1997 | Nov | 13 | Heraklion | 0 | 2 |
| EC1997 | Dec | 17 | Norwich | 4 | 2 |
| EC2001 | June | 5 | Athens | 1 | 3 |
| EC2001 | Oct | 5 | Ewood Park | 2 | 1 |
| | | | **v HOLLAND** | Eng | H |
| EC1993 | April | 27 | Portsmouth | 3 | 0 |
| EC1993 | Oct | 12 | Utrecht | 1 | 1 |
| 2001 | Aug | 14 | Reading | 4 | 0 |
| EC2001 | Nov | 9 | Utrecht | 2 | 2 |
| EC2001 | Nov | 13 | Derby | 1 | 0 |
| 2004 | Feb | 17 | Hull | 3 | 2 |
| | | | **v HUNGARY** | Eng | Hun |
| EC1981 | June | 5 | Keszthely | 2 | 1 |
| EC1981 | Nov | 17 | Nottingham | 2 | 0 |
| EC1983 | April | 26 | Newcastle | 1 | 0 |
| EC1983 | Oct | 11 | Nyiregyhaza | 2 | 0 |
| 1990 | Sept | 11 | Southampton | 3 | 1 |
| 1992 | May | 12 | Budapest | 2 | 2 |
| 1999 | April | 27 | Budapest | 2 | 2 |
| | | | **v ITALY** | Eng | Italy |
| EC1978 | Mar | 8 | Manchester | 2 | 1 |
| EC1978 | April | 5 | Rome | 0 | 0 |
| EC1984 | April | 18 | Manchester | 3 | 1 |
| EC1984 | May | 2 | Florence | 0 | 1 |
| EC1986 | April | 9 | Pisa | 0 | 2 |
| EC1986 | April | 23 | Swindon | 1 | 1 |
| EC1997 | Feb | 12 | Bristol | 1 | 0 |
| EC1997 | Oct | 10 | Rieti | 1 | 0 |
| EC2000 | May | 27 | Bratislava | 0 | 2 |
| 2000 | Nov | 14 | Monza* | 0 | 0 |
| 2002 | Mar | 26 | Valley Parade | 1 | 1 |
| EC2002 | May | 20 | Basle | 1 | 2 |
| 2003 | Feb | 11 | Pisa | 0 | 1 |
| *Abandoned 11 mins; fog.* | | | | | |
| | | | **v ISRAEL** | Eng | Isr |
| 1985 | Feb | 27 | Tel Aviv | 2 | 1 |
| | | | **v LATVIA** | Eng | Lat |
| 1995 | April | 25 | Riga | 1 | 0 |
| 1995 | June | 7 | Burnley | 4 | 0 |
| | | | **v LUXEMBOURG** | Eng | Lux |
| EC1998 | Oct | 13 | Greven Macher | 5 | 0 |
| EC1999 | Sept | 3 | Reading | 5 | 0 |
| | | | **v MACEDONIA** | Eng | M |
| EC2002 | Oct | 15 | Reading | 3 | 1 |
| EC2003 | Sept | 5 | Skopje | 1 | 1 |
| | | | **v MALAYSIA** | Eng | Mal |
| 1995 | June | 8 | Toulon | 2 | 0 |
| | | | **v MEXICO** | Eng | Mex |
| 1988 | June | 5 | Toulon | 2 | 1 |
| 1991 | May | 29 | Toulon | 6 | 0 |
| 1992 | May | 25 | Toulon | 1 | 1 |
| 2001 | May | 24 | Leicester | 3 | 0 |
| | | | **v MOLDOVA** | Eng | Mol |
| EC1996 | Aug | 31 | Chisinau | 2 | 0 |
| EC1997 | Sept | 9 | Wycombe | 1 | 0 |

| | | | v MOROCCO | Eng | Mor |
|---|---|---|---|---|---|
| 1987 | June | 7 | Toulon | 2 | 0 |
| 1988 | June | 9 | Toulon | 1 | 0 |

| | | | v NORWAY | Eng | Nor |
|---|---|---|---|---|---|
| EC1977 | June | 1 | Bergen | 2 | 1 |
| EC1977 | Sept | 6 | Brighton | 6 | 0 |
| 1980 | Sept | 9 | Southampton | 3 | 0 |
| 1981 | Sept | 8 | Drammen | 0 | 0 |
| EC1992 | Oct | 13 | Peterborough | 0 | 2 |
| EC1993 | June | 1 | Stavanger | 1 | 1 |
| 1995 | Oct | 10 | Stavanger | 2 | 2 |

| | | | v POLAND | Eng | Pol |
|---|---|---|---|---|---|
| EC1982 | Mar | 17 | Warsaw | 2 | 1 |
| EC1982 | April | 7 | West Ham | 2 | 2 |
| EC1989 | June | 2 | Plymouth | 2 | 1 |
| EC1989 | Oct | 10 | Jastrzebie | 3 | 1 |
| EC1990 | Oct | 16 | Tottenham | 0 | 1 |
| EC1991 | Nov | 12 | Pila | 1 | 2 |
| EC1993 | May | 28 | Zdroj | 4 | 1 |
| EC1993 | Sept | 7 | Millwall | 1 | 2 |
| EC1996 | Oct | 8 | Wolverhampton | 0 | 0 |
| EC1997 | May | 30 | Katowice | 1 | 1 |
| EC1999 | Mar | 26 | Southampton | 5 | 0 |
| EC1999 | Sept | 7 | Plock | 1 | 3 |

| | | | v PORTUGAL | Eng | Por |
|---|---|---|---|---|---|
| 1987 | June | 13 | Toulon | 0 | 0 |
| 1990 | May | 21 | Toulon | 0 | 1 |
| 1993 | June | 7 | Toulon | 2 | 0 |
| 1994 | June | 7 | Toulon | 2 | 0 |
| EC1994 | Sept | 6 | Leicester | 0 | 0 |
| 1995 | Sept | 2 | Lisbon | 0 | 2 |
| 1996 | May | 30 | Toulon | 1 | 3 |
| 2000 | Apr | 16 | Stoke | 0 | 1 |
| EC2002 | May | 22 | Zurich | 1 | 3 |
| EC2003 | Mar | 28 | Rio Major | 2 | 4 |
| EC2003 | Sept | 9 | Everton | 1 | 2 |

| | | | v REPUBLIC OF IRELAND | Eng | RoI |
|---|---|---|---|---|---|
| 1981 | Feb | 25 | Liverpool | 1 | 0 |
| 1985 | Mar | 25 | Portsmouth | 3 | 2 |
| 1989 | June | 9 | Toulon | 0 | 0 |
| EC1990 | Nov | 13 | Cork | 3 | 0 |
| EC1991 | Mar | 26 | Brentford | 3 | 0 |
| 1994 | Nov | 15 | Newcastle | 1 | 0 |
| 1995 | Mar | 27 | Dublin | 2 | 0 |

| | | | v ROMANIA | Eng | Rom |
|---|---|---|---|---|---|
| EC1980 | Oct | 14 | Ploesti | 0 | 4 |
| EC1981 | April | 28 | Swindon | 3 | 0 |
| EC1985 | April | 30 | Brasov | 0 | 0 |
| EC1985 | Sept | 10 | Ipswich | 3 | 0 |

| | | | v RUSSIA | Eng | Rus |
|---|---|---|---|---|---|
| 1994 | May | 30 | Bandol | 2 | 0 |

| | | | v SAN MARINO | Eng | SM |
|---|---|---|---|---|---|
| EC1993 | Feb | 16 | Luton | 6 | 0 |
| EC1993 | Nov | 17 | San Marino | 4 | 0 |

| | | | v SENEGAL | Eng | Sen |
|---|---|---|---|---|---|
| 1989 | June | 7 | Toulon | 6 | 1 |
| 1991 | May | 27 | Toulon | 2 | 1 |

| | | | v SERBIA-MONTENEGRO | Eng | S-M |
|---|---|---|---|---|---|
| 2003 | June | 2 | Hull | 3 | 2 |

| | | | v SCOTLAND | Eng | Sco |
|---|---|---|---|---|---|
| 1977 | April | 27 | Sheffield | 1 | 0 |
| EC1980 | Feb | 12 | Coventry | 2 | 1 |
| EC1980 | Mar | 4 | Aberdeen | 0 | 0 |
| EC1982 | April | 19 | Glasgow | 1 | 0 |
| EC1982 | April | 28 | Manchester | 1 | 1 |
| EC1988 | Feb | 16 | Aberdeen | 1 | 0 |
| EC1988 | Mar | 22 | Nottingham | 1 | 0 |
| 1993 | June | 13 | Toulon | 1 | 0 |

| | | | v SLOVAKIA | Eng | Slo |
|---|---|---|---|---|---|
| EC2002 | June | 1 | Bratislava | 0 | 2 |
| EC2002 | Oct | 11 | Trnava | 4 | 0 |
| EC2003 | June | 10 | Sunderland | 2 | 0 |

| | | | v SLOVENIA | Eng | Slo |
|---|---|---|---|---|---|
| 2000 | Feb | 12 | Nova Gorica | 1 | 0 |

| | | | v SOUTH AFRICA | Eng | SA |
|---|---|---|---|---|---|
| 1998 | May | 16 | Toulon | 3 | 1 |

| | | | v SPAIN | Eng | Spa |
|---|---|---|---|---|---|
| EC1984 | May | 17 | Seville | 1 | 0 |
| EC1984 | May | 24 | Sheffield | 2 | 0 |
| 1987 | Feb | 18 | Burgos | 2 | 1 |
| 1992 | Sept | 8 | Burgos | 1 | 0 |
| 2001 | Feb | 27 | Birmingham | 0 | 4 |

| | | | v SWEDEN | Eng | Swe |
|---|---|---|---|---|---|
| 1979 | June | 9 | Vasteras | 2 | 1 |
| 1986 | Sept | 9 | Ostersund | 1 | 1 |
| EC1988 | Oct | 18 | Coventry | 1 | 1 |
| EC1989 | Sept | 5 | Uppsala | 0 | 1 |
| EC1998 | Sept | 4 | Sundvall | 2 | 0 |
| EC1999 | June | 4 | Huddersfield | 3 | 0 |
| 2004 | Mar | 30 | Kristiansund | 2 | 2 |

| | | | v SWITZERLAND | Eng | Swit |
|---|---|---|---|---|---|
| EC1980 | Nov | 18 | Ipswich | 5 | 0 |
| EC1981 | May | 31 | Neuenburg | 0 | 0 |
| 1988 | May | 28 | Lausanne | 1 | 1 |
| 1996 | April | 1 | Swindon | 0 | 0 |
| 1998 | Mar | 24 | Brugglifeld | 0 | 2 |
| EC2002 | May | 17 | Zurich | 2 | 1 |

| | | | v USA | Eng | USA |
|---|---|---|---|---|---|
| 1989 | June | 11 | Toulon | 0 | 2 |
| 1994 | June | 2 | Toulon | 3 | 0 |

| | | | v TURKEY | Eng | Tur |
|---|---|---|---|---|---|
| EC1984 | Nov | 13 | Bursa | 0 | 0 |
| EC1985 | Oct | 15 | Bristol | 3 | 0 |
| EC1987 | April | 28 | Izmir | 0 | 0 |
| EC1987 | Oct | 13 | Sheffield | 1 | 1 |
| EC1991 | April | 30 | Izmir | 2 | 2 |
| 1991 | Oct | 15 | Reading | 2 | 0 |
| EC1992 | Nov | 17 | Orient | 0 | 1 |
| EC1993 | Mar | 30 | Izmir | 0 | 0 |
| EC2000 | May | 29 | Bratislava | 6 | 0 |
| EC2003 | April | 1 | Newcastle | 1 | 1 |
| EC2003 | Oct | 10 | Istanbul | 0 | 1 |

| | | | v USSR | Eng | USSR |
|---|---|---|---|---|---|
| 1987 | June | 9 | Toulon | 0 | 0 |
| 1988 | June | 7 | Toulon | 1 | 0 |
| 1990 | May | 25 | Toulon | 2 | 1 |
| 1991 | May | 31 | Toulon | 2 | 1 |

| | | | v WALES | Eng | Wales |
|---|---|---|---|---|---|
| 1976 | Dec | 15 | Wolverhampton | 0 | 0 |
| 1979 | Feb | 6 | Swansea | 1 | 0 |
| 1990 | Dec | 5 | Tranmere | 0 | 0 |

| | | | v WEST GERMANY | Eng | WG |
|---|---|---|---|---|---|
| EC1982 | Sept | 21 | Sheffield | 3 | 1 |
| EC1982 | Oct | 12 | Bremen | 2 | 3 |
| 1987 | Sept | 8 | Ludenscheid | 0 | 2 |

| | | | v YUGOSLAVIA | Eng | Yugo |
|---|---|---|---|---|---|
| EC1978 | April | 19 | Novi Sad | 1 | 2 |
| EC1978 | May | 2 | Manchester | 1 | 1 |
| EC1986 | Nov | 11 | Peterborough | 1 | 1 |
| EC1987 | Nov | 10 | Zemun | 5 | 1 |
| EC2000 | Mar | 29 | Barcelona | 3 | 0 |
| 2002 | Sept | 6 | Bolton | 1 | 1 |

# BRITISH AND IRISH UNDER-21 TEAMS 2003–04

■ *Denotes player sent off.*

## ENGLAND UNDER-21 TEAMS 2003–04

West Ham, 19 August 2003, 11,008

**England (0) 0**

**Croatia (1) 3** *(Ljubojevic 12, 52, Pranjic 90)*

*England:* Murray; Johnson, Konchesky, Prutton, Parnaby, Clarke (Jagielka 73), Pennant■, Jenas, Jeffers (Cole C 70), Defoe, Barry (Sidwell 46).

Skopje, 5 September 2003, 2700

**Macedonia (0) 1** *(Stojkov 60)*

**England (1) 1** *(Jagielka 35)*

*England:* Kirkland; Johnson, Konchesky, Barton, Clarke, Jagielka, Pennant (Wright-Phillips 62), Sidwell, Jeffers, Ameobi, Defoe (Tonge 71).

Everton, 9 September 2003, 23,744

**England (1) 1** *(Barton 37)*

**Portugal (1) 2** *(Quaresma 4, Postiga 78)*

*England:* Grant; Jagielka, Konchesky, Barton, Dawson, Clarke, Johnson, Prutton (Defoe 78), Jeffers, Ameobi, Barry.

Istanbul, 10 October 2003, 4000

**Turkey (1) 1** *(Sonkaya 2)*

**England (0) 0**

*England:* Grant; Johnson■, Taylor M, Prutton (Bent D 80), Davies, Jagielka, Wright-Phillips, Sidwell (Reo-Coker 61), Jenas, Ameobi, Defoe.

Hull, 17 February 2004, 25,280

**England (1) 3** *(Ashton 23, Bentley 72, Bent D 87)*

**Holland (0) 2** *(Tuyp 47, Huntelaar 74)*

*England:* Carson; Hunt (Hoyte 46), Ridgewell, Reo-Coker (Chaplow 84), Johnson, Taylor S, Bentley, Welsh, Ashton (Stead 69), Cole C (Bent D 84), Downing (Whittingham 69).

Kristiansund, 30 March 2004, 7330

**Sweden (0) 2** *(Nilsson P 58, Andersson J 70)*

**England (1) 2** *(Ashton 14, Chopra 90)*

*England:* Carson (Grant 69); Hoyte, Ridgewell, Reo-Coker (Jones 79), Dawson, Taylor S (Kilgallon 63), Bentley (Chopra 79), Tonge (Ambrose 63), Ashton (Stead 63), Cole C (Bent D 69), Downing (Milner 79).

## SCOTLAND UNDER-21 TEAMS 2003-04

Skien, 19 August 2003, 2000

**Norway (0) 3** *(Pedersen 54, 71, Hoff 87)*

**Scotland (1) 1** *(Lynch 21)*

*Scotland:* McGregor (Gordon 46); Caldwell G, Hammell, McCracken (Dowie 46), Crainey (Doig 46), Williams, Duff, Pearson (Noble 61), Kyle (Gallagher 46), Stewart (Hughes 58), Lynch (McManus 46) (Kennedy 90).

Ahlen, 9 September 2003, 4500

**Germany (0) 0**

**Scotland (0) 1** *(Maloney 62)*

*Scotland:* Soutar; Caldwell G, Pearson, McCracken, Crainey, Williams, Duff, Murray I, Kyle, Stewart (Fletcher 57), Lynch (Maloney 50).

Perth, 10 October 2003, 5289

**Scotland (0) 3** *(Hammell 79, Hughes 89, 90)*

**Lithuania (1) 2** *(Stankevicius 5, Kucys 71 (pen))*

*Scotland:* Soutar; Caldwell G, Hammell, Kennedy, McCracken, Williams (Hughes 61), Canero (McManus 70), Kerr, Lynch (Gallagher 75), Maloney, Stewart.

Varazdin, 13 November 2003, 4000

**Croatia (2) 2** *(Babic 7, Ljubojevic 11)*

**Scotland (0) 0**

*Scotland:* Gordon; Caldwell G, Hammell, McCracken, Kennedy, Kerr, Canero, Murray I, Kyle, Stewart (Hughes 84), McManus (Maloney 46).

Edinburgh, 18 November 2003, 11,992

**Scotland (1) 1** *(O'Connor 11)*

**Croatia (0) 0**

*Scotland:* Gordon; Duff, Hammell, Williams, Kennedy, Kerr, Canero (Montgomery 90), Murray I, Kyle (Lynch 36), Maloney (Hughes 68), O'Connor.

Livingston, 18 February 2004, 1544

**Scotland (1) 1** *(Maloney 31 (pen))*

**Hungary (0) 2** *(Csehi 86, Jovanczai 90)*

*Scotland:* Smith (Marshall 46); Lawson (Dempster 46), Lappin (Morrison 55), Kennedy, Dowie (Diamond 46), McCunnie, Foy (Wallace 65), Wilson (Sweeney 46), O'Connor (Beattie 46), Maloney (Reilly 83), Prunty.

Firhill, 30 March 2004, 1967

**Scotland (0) 0**

**Romania (1) 2** *(Piesan 5, Mihai-Florescu 89)*

*Scotland:* Samson; Lawson, Lappin, Hutton (Kinniburgh 56), Dowie, Fotheringham, Wilson (Burke 64), McCunnie, O'Connor (Boyd 73), Riordan (Foy 51), Beattie (Prunty 84).

Helsingor, 27 April 2004, 500

**Denmark (1) 2** *(Krohn-Delhi 45, 84)*

**Scotland (0) 2** *(Clarkson 73, Beattie 89)*

*Scotland:* Marshall (Smith 46); Wilson, Lappin (Morrison 46), Dowie, Quinn, Sweeney (Beattie 67), Hutton (Burke 72), Brown (Fotheringham 55), Boyd (Clarkson 46), Foy (Murray S 12), Gallagher.

Galway, 25 May 2004, 2200

**Republic of Ireland (3) 3** *(Fitzgerald 10, 35, McCarthy 20)*

**Scotland (1) 1** *(Beattie 15)*

*Republic of Ireland:* Henderson (Murphy B 46); Kelly, McCarthy, Fitzgerald, Capper, Foley K (Brennan 80), Whelan, Potter, Kearney (Foley 87), Murphy (Behan 87), Tabb (Zayed 70).
*Scotland:* Samson (Smith 46); Lawson (Murray S 71), Lappin, Dowie, Robertson, McCunnie, Wilson, Morrison (Sweeney 57), Boyd, Prunty, Beattie (Fotheringham 46).

## NORTHERN IRELAND UNDER-21 TEAMS 2003-04

Donetsk, 5 September 2003, 2500

**Ukraine (0) 1** *(Danylovskyi 59)*

**Northern Ireland (0) 0**

*Northern Ireland:* Blayney; Hughes, Capaldi, Buchanan, Webb, Melaugh (Davis 78), Clingan, McFlynn, McEvilly, Feeney, Davey (Clarke 79).

Coleraine, 9 September 2003, 250

**Northern Ireland (0) 3** *(Feeney 52, McFlynn 71, Davey 87)*

**Armenia (1) 1** *(Pachajyan 3)*

*Northern Ireland:* Blayney; Close, Capaldi, Buchanan, Webb, Melaugh (McFlynn 80), Hughes (Davis 55), Clingan, McEvilly, Feeney (Clarke 87), Davey.

Athens, 10 October 2003, 300

**Greece (0) 0**

**Northern Ireland (1) 1** *(Feeney 24)*

*Northern Ireland:* Blayney; Close, Capaldi, Buchanan, Webb, Clingan, Melaugh (Hughes 86), McFlynn, McEvilly (Braniff 73), Feeney, Davey.

## WALES UNDER-21 TEAMS 2003-04

Novi Sad, 19 August 2003, 8000

**Serbia-Montenegro (1) 3** *(Matic I 12, Lazovic 59, Milovanovic 75)*

**Wales (0) 0**

*Wales:* Brown; Moss, Price (Somner), Pejic, Rees, Tolley, Pipe (Powell), Fowler, Collins (Williams M), Williams G, Gall.

Pavia, 5 September 2003, 5000

**Italy (3) 8** *(Gilardino 18, 48, 67, Sculli 21, Borriello 36, 62, 90, Brighi 84)*

**Wales (1) 1** *(Vaughan 28)*

*Wales:* Brown; Pejic, Somner, Fowler, Rees, Collins (Powell), Pipe, Brough, Gall, Vaughan, Williams G (Williams M).

Merthyr, 9 September 2003, 1311

**Wales (0) 0**

**Finland (0) 0**

*Wales:* Brown; Powell, Price, Fowler, Pejic, Morgan, Pipe (Collins), Brough, Gall, Williams M, Stock.

Barry, 10 October 2003, 750

**Wales (0) 0**

**Serbia-Montenegro (1) 1** *(Matic I 30)*

*Wales:* Brown; Moss, Price, Collins, Day, Stock, Pipe, Jones, Gall (Crowell), Tolley (Morgan), Williams M (Williams G).

## REPUBLIC OF IRELAND UNDER-21 TEAMS 2003–04

Gdansk, 19 August 2003, 2500

**Poland (1) 1** *(Abbott 13)*

**Republic of Ireland (2) 5** *(Elliott 2, 82, 88, Hoolahan 28, O'Flynn 72)*

*Republic of Ireland:* Connor; Kelly, Kohlmann (Capper 76), Byrne, Cryan, Keegan, Gilroy (Cash 67), Elliott, O'Flynn (Zayed 76), O'Connor (Ward 80), Hoolahan.

Waterford, 5 September 2003, 4000

**Republic of Ireland (0) 2** *(Barrett 65, Rogochiy 81 (og))*

**Russia (0) 0**

*Republic of Ireland:* Connor; Kelly, Cryan (Byrne 81), Thompson, Kohlmann, Butler, Miller, O'Connor (Doyle M 76), Reid, O'Flynn (Elliott 88), Barrett.

Neuchatel, 10 October 2003, 2500

**Switzerland (0) 0**

**Republic of Ireland (0) 2** *(Walters 61, 74)*

*Republic of Ireland:* Connor; Kelly, Thompson, Fitzgerald, Kohlmann, Thornton, Keegan, O'Connor (Whelan 90), Hoolahan, Elliott, Walters (Deane 81).

Funchal, 23 February 2004, 4000

**Portugal (0) 0**

**Republic of Ireland (0) 0**

*Republic of Ireland:* Henderson; Kelly, Fitzgerald, Paisley (McStay 46), Kohlmann, Flood (Deane 46), Keegan, Whelan, Foley, Doyle (Murphy 76), Yeates (Bradley 78).

Funchal, 25 February 2004, 2500

**Italy (0) 0**

**Republic of Ireland (0) 1** *(Kearney 81)*

*Republic of Ireland:* Henderson; Kelly (Whelan 46), Cooney, Paisley, Kohlmann, Flood, Keegan (Cregg 46), Foley, Kearney, Murphy (Doyle 68), Bradley (Deane 68).

Funchal, 27 February 2004, 4000

**Madeira Selection (0) 0**

**Republic of Ireland (2) 4** *(Doyle 23, 31, Paisley 54, Flood 79)*

*Republic of Ireland:* Henderson (Doyle C 83); Kelly, Fitzgerald, Cooney, Paisley, Flood, Keegan, Whelan, Kearney (Deane 81), Doyle (Cogan 73), Yeates (Murphy 46).

Grudziadz, 27 April 2004, 3000

**Poland (1) 2** *(Pawel Brozek 21, Piotr Brozek 53)*

**Republic of Ireland (0) 2** *(Elliott 66, Fitzgerald 89)*

*Republic of Ireland:* Henderson; Kelly, Fitzgerald, McCarthy, Capper (Dillon 19), Potter (Ward 74), Whelan, Thornton, Flood, Elliott, Doyle (Mehmet 46).

# OTHER INTERMEDIATE INTERNATIONALS

## SCOTLAND B

Aberdeen, 21 October 2003, 1417

**Scotland (0) 0**

**Germany (0) 1** *(Daun 79)*

*Scotland:* Alexander; Stockdale, McAllister, Nicholson (McGovern 72), Anderson, Wilkie, McManus (Boyd 81), Kerr, O'Connor (Gallagher 46), Gray, Murray I.

Tannadice Park, 10 December 2003, 1450

**Scotland (1) 1** *(Caldwell S 29)*

**Turkey (0) 1** *(Ates 61)*

*Scotland:* Gordon (Shearer 46); Murty (Shields 46), McAllister, Caldwell S, Webster, Caldwell G, Murray S, Canero, McCulloch (McIndoe 71), Severin (McManus 63), Pearson.

## NORTHERN IRELAND UNDER-23

Lurgan, 27 April 2004

**Northern Ireland (0) 0**

**Serbia-Montenegro (0) 0**

*Northern Ireland:* Blayney (Mannus 46); Close, O'Hara, Webb, Buchanan, Clingan, Davis (Hughes 46), McFlynn, McEvilly, Braniff (Clarke 59), Davey (Brunt 46).

## WALES UNDER-20

Stoke, 14 November 2003

**Wales (0) 0**

**England (1) 2** *(Johnson 44, 51)*

*Wales:* Williams G (Brimble); Powell L (Spender), Powell R, Edwards D, Rewbury (Owen), Collins, Pipe, Parkins (Jones R), Birchall (Fish), Davies A, Fleetwood.

# BRITISH UNDER-21 APPEARANCES 1976–2004

## ENGLAND

Ablett, G. (Liverpool), 1988 v F (1)
Adams, A. (Arsenal). 1985 v Ei, Fi; 1986 v D; 1987 v Se, Y (5)
Adams, N. (Everton), 1987 v Se (1)
Allen, B. (QPR), 1992 v H, M, Cz, F; 1993 v N (sub), T, P, Cz (sub) (8)
Allen, C. A. (Oxford U), 1995 v Br (sub), F (sub) (2)
Allen, C. (QPR), 1980 v EG (sub); (with C Palace), 1981 v N, R (3)
Allen, M. (QPR), 1987 v Se (sub); 1988 v Y (sub) (2)
Allen, P. (West Ham U), 1985 v Ei, R; (with Tottenham H), 1986 v R (3)
Allen, R. W. (Tottenham H), 1998 v F (sub), S.Af, Arg (sub) (3)
Ambrose, D. P. F. (Ipswich T), 2003 v I (sub); (with Newcastle U), Ser (sub); 2004 v Se (sub) (3)
Ameobi, F. (Newcastle U), 2001 v Sp (sub), Fi (sub), Alb (sub), M, Gr (sub); 2002 v Ho (sub+1), Slv (sub), Sw (sub), I (sub), P (sub); 2003 v Y (sub), Slo, Mac, I, P, Ser, Slo; 2004 v Mac, P, T (19)
Anderson, V. A. (Nottingham F), 1978 v I (1)
Anderton, D. R. (Tottenham H), 1993 v Sp, Sm, Ho, Pol, N, P, Cz, Br, S, F; 1994 v Pol, Sm (12)
Andrews, I. (Leicester C), 1987 v Se (1)
Ardley, N. C. (Wimbledon), 1993 v Pol, N, P, Cz, Br, S, F, 1994 v Pol (sub), Ho, Sm (10)
Ashcroft, L. (Preston NE), 1992 v H (sub) (1)
Ashton, D. (Crewe Alex), 2004 v Ho, Se (2)
Atherton, P. (Coventry C), 1992 v T (1)
Atkinson, B. (Sunderland), 1991 v W (sub), Sen, M, USSR (sub), F; 1992 v Pol (sub) (6)
Awford, A. T. (Portsmouth), 1993 v Sp, N, T, P, Cz, Br, S, F; 1994 v Ho (9)

Bailey, G. R. (Manchester U), 1979 v W, Bul; 1980 v D, S (2), EG; 1982 v N; 1983 v D, Gr; 1984 v H, F (2), I, Sp (14)
Baker, G. E. (Southampton), 1981 v N, R (2)
Ball, M. J. (Everton), 1999 v Se, Bul, L, CzR, Pol; 2000 v L, D (sub) (7)
Barker, S. (Blackburn R), 1985 v Is (sub), Ei, R; 1986 v I (4)
Barmby, N. J. (Tottenham H), 1994 v D; 1995 v P, A (sub); (with Everton), 1998 v Sw (4)
Bannister, G. (Sheffield W), 1982 v Pol (1)
Barnes, J. (Watford), 1983 v D, Gr (2)
Barnes, P. S. (Manchester C), 1977 v W (sub), S, Fi, N; 1978 v N, Fi, I (2), Y (9)
Barrett, E. D. (Oldham Ath), 1990 v P, F, USSR, Cz (4)
Barry, G. (Aston Villa), 1999 v CzR, F, H; 2000 v Y; 2001 v Sp, Fi, Alb; 2002 v Ho, G, Alb, Gr, Ho (sub), Slv, I, P, Sw, I, P; 2003 v Y, Slo, Mac, I, P, T, Slo; 2004 v Cro, P (27)
Barton, J. (Manchester C), 2004 v Mac, P (2)
Bart-Williams, C. G. (Sheffield W), 1993 v Sp, N, T; 1994 v D, Ru, F, Bel, P; 1995 v P, A, Ei (2), La (2); ( with Nottingham F), 1996 v P (sub), A (16)
Batty, D. (Leeds U), 1988 v Sw (sub); 1989 v Gr (sub), Bul, Sen, Ei, US; 1990 v Pol (7)
Bazeley, D. S. (Watford), 1992 v H (sub) (1)
Beagrie, P. (Sheffield U), 1988 v WG, T (2)
Beardsmore, R. (Manchester U), 1989 v Gr, Alb (sub), Pol, Bul, USA (5)
Beattie, J. S. (Southampton), 1999 v CzR (sub), F (sub), Pol, H; 2000 v Pol (5)
Beckham, D. R. J. (Manchester U), 1995 v Br, Mal, An, F; 1996 v P, A (sub), Bel, An, P (9)
Bent, D. A. (Ipswich T), 2003 v I (sub), Ser (sub); 2004 v T (sub), Ho (sub), Se (sub) (5)
Bent, M. N. (C Palace), 1998 v S.Af (sub), Arg (2)
Bentley, D. M. (Arsenal), 2004 v Ho, Se (2)
Beeston, C (Stoke C), 1988 v USSR (1)
Benjamin, T. J. (Leicester C), 2001 v M (sub) (1)
Bertschin, K. E. (Birmingham C), 1977 v S; 1978 v Y (2) (3)
Birtles, G. (Nottingham F), 1980 v Bul, EG (sub) (2)
Blackwell, D. R. (Wimbledon), 1991 v W, T, Sen (sub), M, USSR, F (6)
Blake, M. A. (Aston Villa), 1990 v F (sub), Cz (sub); 1991 v H, Pol, Ei (2), W; 1992 v Pol (8)
Blissett, L. L. (Watford), 1979 v W, Bul (sub), Se; 1980 v D (4)
Booth, A. D. (Huddersfield T), 1995 v La (2 subs); 1996 v N (3)
Bothroyd, J. (Coventry C), 2001 v M (sub) (1)
Bowyer, L. D. (Charlton Ath), 1996 v N (sub), Bel, P, Br; (with Leeds U), 1997 v Mol, I, Sw, Ge; 1998 v Mol; 1999 v F, Pol; 2000 v D, Arg (13)
Bracewell, P. (Stoke C), 1983 v D, Gr (1 + 1 sub), H; 1984 v D, H, F (2), I (2), Sp (2); 1985 v T (13)
Bradbury, L. M. (Portsmouth), 1997 v Pol; (with Manchester C), 1998 v Mol (sub), I (sub) (3)
Bramble, T. M. (Ipswich T), 2001 v Ge, G, Fi, Alb (sub), M; 2002 v Ho (sub); (with Newcastle U), 2003 v Y, Slo, Mac, P (10)
Branch, P. M. (Everton), 1997 v Pol (sub) (1)
Bradshaw, P. W. (Wolverhampton W), 1977 v W, S; 1978 v Fi, Y (4)
Breacker, T. (Luton T), 1986 v I (2) (2)
Brennan, M. (Ipswich T), 1987 v Y, Sp, T, Mor, F (5)
Bridge, W. M. (Southampton), 1999 v H (sub); 2001 v Sp; 2002 v Ho, G, Alb, Gr, Ho (2) (8)
Bridges, M. (Sunderland), 1997 v Sw (sub); 1999 v F; (with Leeds U), 2000 v D (3)
Brightwell, I. (Manchester C), 1989 v D, Alb; 1990 v Se (sub), Pol (4)
Briscoe, L. S. (Sheffield W), 1996 v Cro, Bel (sub), An, Br; 1997 v Sw (sub) (5)
Brock, K. (Oxford U), 1984 v I, Sp (2); 1986 v I (4)
Broomes, M. C. (Blackburn R), 1997 v Sw, Ge (2)
Brown, M. R. (Manchester C), 1996 v Cro, Bel, An, P (4)
Brown, W. M. (Manchester U), 1999 v Se, Bul, L, CzR, Pol, Se, Bul; 2001 v G (8)
Bull, S. G. (Wolverhampton W), 1989 v Alb (2) Pol; 1990 v Se, Pol (5)
Bullock, M. J. (Barnsley), 1998 v Gr (sub) (1)
Burrows, D. (WBA), 1989 v Se (sub); (with Liverpool), Gr, Alb (2), Pol; 1990 v Se, Pol (7)
Butcher, T. I. (Ipswich T), 1979 v Se; 1980 v D, Bul, S (2), EG (2) (7)
Butt, N. (Manchester U), 1995 v Ei (2), La; 1996 v P, A; 1997 v Ge, Pol (7)
Butters, G. (Tottenham H), 1989 v Bul, Sen (sub), Ei (sub) (3)
Butterworth, I. (Coventry C), 1985 v T, R; (with Nottingham F), 1986 v R, T, D (2), I (2) (8)
Bywater, S. (West Ham U), 2001 v M (sub), Gr; 2002 v Ho (sub), I (sub); 2003 v P, Ser (sub) (6)

Cadamarteri, D. L. (Everton), 1999 v CzR (sub); 2000 v Y (sub); 2001 v M (sub) (3)
Caesar, G. (Arsenal), 1987 v Mor, USSR (sub), F (3)
Callaghan, N. (Watford), 1983 v D, Gr (sub), H (sub); 1984 v D, H, F (2), I, Sp (9)
Campbell, A. P. (Middlesbrough), 2000 v Y, T (sub), Slo (sub); 2001 v Ge (sub) (4)
Campbell, K. J. (Arsenal), 1991 v H, T (sub); 1992 v G, T (4)
Campbell, S. (Tottenham), 1994 v D, Ru, F, US, Bel, P; 1995 v P, A, Ei; 1996 v N, A (11)
Carbon, M. P. (Derby Co), 1996 v Cro (sub); 1997 v Ge, I, Sw (4)
Carr, C. (Fulham), 1985 v Ei (sub) (1)
Carr, F. (Nottingham F), 1987 v Se, Y, Sp (sub), Mor, USSR; 1988 v WG (sub), T, Y, F (9)
Carragher, J. L. (Liverpool), 1997 v I (sub), Sw, Ge, Pol; 1998 v Mol (sub), I, Gr, Sw (sub), F, S.Af, Arg; 1999 v Se, Bul, L, CzR, F, Pol, Se, Bul; 2000 v L, Pol, D, Arg, Y, I, T, Slo (27)
Carlisle, C. J. (QPR), 2001 v Ge (sub), G (sub), Fi (sub) (3)
Carrick, M. (West Ham U), 2001 v Ge, G, Fi, I, Gr; 2002 v Gr, Ho (2), P; 2003 v Y, Slo, Mac, I, P (14)
Carson, S. P. (Leeds U), 2004 v Ho, Se (2)
Casper, C. M. (Manchester U), 1995 v Mal (1)
Caton, T. (Manchester C), 1982 v N, H (sub), Pol (2), S; 1983 v WG (2), Gr; 1984 v D, H, F (2), I (2) (14)
Chadwick, L. H. (Manchester U), 2000 v L, D, Arg, I (sub), Slo (sub); 2001 v Ge (sub), I, Sp, Fi, Alb; 2002 v Ho, G, Alb (13)

Challis, T. M. (QPR), 1996 v An, P (2)
Chamberlain, M. (Stoke C), 1983 v Gr; 1984 v F (sub), I, Sp (4)
Chaplow, R. D. (Burnley), 2004 v Ho (sub) (1)
Chapman, L. (Stoke C), 1981 v Ei (1)
Charles, G. A. (Nottingham F), 1991 v H, W (sub), Ei; 1992 v T (4)
Chettle, S. (Nottingham F), 1988 v M, USSR, Mor, F; 1989 v D, Se, Gr, Alb (2), Bul; 1990 v Se, Pol (12)
Chopra, R, M. (Newcastle U), 2004 v Se (sub) (1)
Clark, L. R. (Newcastle U), 1992 v Cz, F; 1993 v Sp, N, T, Ho (sub), Pol (sub), Cz, Br, S; 1994 v Ho (11)
Clarke, P. M. (Everton), 2003 v Slo (sub), I, T, Ser, Slo; 2004 v Cro, Mac, P (8)
Christie, M. N. (Derby Co), 2001 v Fi (sub), Sp, Fi, Alb, M, Gr; 2002 v Ho (sub), Gr (sub), Ho, Slv, P (11)
Clegg, M. J. (Manchester U), 1998 v Fr (sub), S.Af (sub) (2)
Clemence, S. N. (Tottenham H), 1999 v Se (sub) (1)
Clough, N. (Nottingham F), 1986 v D (sub); 1987 v Se, Y, T, USSR, F (sub), P; 1988 v WG, T, Y, S (2), M, Mor, F (15)
Cole, A. A. (Arsenal), 1992 v H, Cz (sub), F (sub); (with Bristol C), 1993 v Sm; (with Newcastle U), Pol, N; 1994 v Pol, Ho (8)
Cole, A. (Arsenal), 2001 v Ge, G, Fi, I (4)
Cole, C. (Chelsea), 2003 v T (sub), Ser (sub), Slo (sub); 2004 v Cro (sub), Ho, Se (6)
Cole, J. J. (West Ham U), 2000 v Arg (sub); 2001 v Ge, Gr; 2002 v G; 2003 v Slo, Mac, P, T (8)
Coney, D. (Fulham), 1985 v T (sub); 1986 v R; 1988 v T, WG (4)
Connor, T. (Brighton & HA), 1987 v Y (1)
Cooke, R. (Tottenham H), 1986 v D (sub) (1)
Cooke, T. J. (Manchester U), 1996 v Cro, Bel, An (sub), P (4)
Cooper, C. (Middlesbrough), 1988 v F (2), M, USSR, Mor; 1989 v D, Se, Gr (8)
Corrigan, J. T. (Manchester C), 1978 v I (2), Y (3)
Cort, C. E. R. (Wimbledon), 1999 v L (sub), CzR, H (sub), Se, Bul; 2000 v L (sub), Pol, D (sub), Arg, I, T, Slo (12)
Cottee, A. (West Ham U), 1985 v Fi (sub), Is (sub), Ei, R, Fi; 1987 v Sp, P; 1988 v WG (8)
Couzens, A. J. (Leeds U), 1995 v Mal (sub), An, F (sub) (3)
Cowans, G. S. (Aston Villa), 1979 v W, Se; 1980 v Bul, EG; 1981 v R (5)
Cox, N. J. (Aston Villa), 1993 v T, Ho, Pol, N; 1994 v Pol, Sm (6)
Cranson, I. (Ipswich T), 1985 v Fi, Is, R; 1986 v R, I (5)
Cresswell, R. P. W. (York C), 1999 v F (sub); (with Sheffield W) H (sub), Se, Bul (4)
Croft, G. (Grimsby T), 1995 v Br, Mal, An, F (4)
Crooks, G. (Stoke C), 1980 v Bul, S (2), EG (sub) (4)
Crossley, M. G. (Nottingham F), 1990 v P, USSR, Cz (3)
Crouch, P. J. (Portsmouth), 2002 v I (sub), P (sub), Sw; (with Aston Villa), 2003 v Mac (sub), P (sub) (5)
Cundy, J. V. (Chelsea), 1991 v Ei (2); 1992 v Pol (3)
Cunningham, L. (WBA), 1977 v S, Fi, N (sub); 1978 v N, Fi, I (6)
Curbishley, L. C. (Birmingham C), 1981 v Sw (1)
Curtis, J. C. K. (Manchester U), 1998 v I (sub), Gr, Sw, F, S.Af, Arg; 1999 v Se (sub), Bul, L, CzR, F, Pol (sub), H, Se (sub), Bul; 2000 v Pol (16)

Daniel, P. W. (Hull C), 1977 v S, Fi, N; 1978 v Fi, I, Y (2) (7)
Davies, A. J. (Middlesbrough), 2004 v T (1)
Davies, K. C. (Southampton), 1998 v Gr (sub); (with Blackburn R), 1999 v CzR; (with Southampton), 2000 v Y (sub) (3)
Davis, K. G. (Luton T), 1995 v An; 1996 v Cro (sub), P (3)
Davis, P. (Arsenal), 1982 v Pol, S; 1983 v D, Gr (1 + 1 sub), H (sub); 1987 v T; 1988 v WG, T, Y, Fr (11)
Davis, S. (Fulham), 2001 v Fi, Alb, M, Gr; 2002 v Ho, G, Al, Ho (2), P, Sw (11)
Dawson, M. R. (Nottingham F), 2003 v Slo (sub), I, P, T; 2004 v P, Se (6)
Day, C. N. (Tottenham H), 1996 v Cro, Bel, Br; (with C Palace), 1997 v Mol, Ge, Sw (6)
D'Avray, M. (Ipswich T), 1984 v I, Sp (sub) (2)
Deehan, J. M. (Aston Villa), 1977 v N; 1978 v N, Fi, I; 1979 v Bul, Se (sub); 1980 v D (7)

Defoe, J. C. (West Ham U), 2001 v M, Gr; 2002 v H[o] (sub), G (sub), Alb, Gr, Ho (2), Slv, I, P (sub), Sw, I, F 2003 v Y, P, T, Ser, Slo; 2004 v Cro, Mac (sub), P (sub) T (23)
Dennis, M. E. (Birmingham C), 1980 v Bul; 1981 v N, [R] (3)
Dichio, D. S. E. (QPR), 1996 v N (sub) (1)
Dickens, A. (West Ham U), 1985 v Fi (sub) (1)
Dicks, J. (West Ham U), 1988 v Sw (sub), M, Mor, F (4)
Digby, F. (Swindon T), 1987 v Sp (sub), USSR, P; 1988 [v] T; 1990 v Pol (5)
Dillon, K. P. (Birmingham C), 1981 v R (1)
Dixon, K. (Chelsea), 1985 v Fi (1)
Dobson, A. (Coventry C), 1989 v Bul, Sen, Ei, US (4)
Dodd, J. R. (Southampton), 1991 v Pol, Ei, T, Sen, M, F 1992 v G, Pol (8)
Donowa, L. (Norwich C), 1985 v Is, R (sub), Fi (sub) (3)
Dorigo, A. (Aston Villa), 1987 v Se, Sp, T, Mor, USSR F, P; 1988 v WG, Y, S (2) (11)
Downing, S. (Middlesbrough), 2004 v Ho, Se (2)
Dozzell, J. (Ipswich T), 1987 v Se, Y (sub), Sp, USSR, F P; 1989 v Se, Gr (sub); 1990 v Se (sub) (9)
Draper, M. A. (Notts Co), 1991 v Ei (sub); 1992 v G, Po[l] (3)
Duberry, M. W. (Chelsea), 1997 v Mol, Pol, Ge; 1998 [v] Mol, Gr (5)
Dunn, D. J. I. (Blackburn R), 1999 v CzR (sub); 2000 v [Y] (sub), T, Slo; 2001 v Ge, G, Fi, I, Sp, M, Gr; 2002 v Ho Gr, Ho (2), Slv, P, Sw, I, P (20)
Duxbury, M. (Manchester U), 1981 v Sw (sub), Ei (sub) R (sub), Sw; 1982 v N; 1983 v WG (2) (7)
Dyer, B. A. (C Palace), 1994 v Ru, F, US, Bel, P; 1995 [v] P (sub); 1996 v Cro; 1997 v Mol, Ge; 1998 v Mol, G[r] (10)
Dyer, K. C. (Ipswich T), 1998 v Mol, I, Gr, Sw, S.Af, Arg 1999 v Se, Bul, CzR, Se; (with Newcastle U), 2000 v Y (11)
Dyson, P. I. (Coventry C), 1981 v N, R, Sw, Ei (4)

Eadie, D. M. (Norwich C), 1994 v F (sub), US; 1997 [v] Mol, Ge (2), I; 1998 v I (7)
Ebbrell, J. (Everton), 1989 v Sen, Ei, US (sub); 1990 v P F, USSR, Cz; 1991 v H, Pol, Ei, W, T; 1992 v G, T (14)
Edghill, R. A. (Manchester C), 1994 v D, Ru; 1995 v A[n] (3)
Ehiogu, U. (Aston Villa), 1992 v H, M, Cz, F; 1993 v Sp N, T, Sm, T, Ho, Pol, N; 1994 v Pol, Ho, Sm (15)
Elliott, P. (Luton T), 1985 v Fi; 1986 v T, D (3)
Elliott, R. J. (Newcastle U), 1996 v P, A (2)
Elliott, S. W. (Derby Co), 1998 v F, Arg (sub) (2)
Etherington, N, (Tottenham H), 2002 v Slv (sub), I; 200[3] v Y (sub) (3)
Euell, J. J. (Wimbledon), 1998 v F, Arg (sub); 1999 v Se (sub), Bul (se), Pol (sub), H (6)
Evans, R. (Chelsea), 2003 v Ser, Slo (2)

Fairclough, C. (Nottingham F), 1985 v T, Is, Ei; 1987 v Sp, T; (with Tottenham H), 1988 v Y, F (7)
Fairclough, D. (Liverpool), 1977 v W (1)
Fashanu, J. (Norwich C), 1980 v EG; 1981 v N (sub), R Sw, Ei (sub), H; (with Nottingham F), 1982 v N, H, Pol S; 1983 v WG (sub) (11)
Fear, P. (Wimbledon), 1994 v Ru, F, US (sub) (3)
Fenton, G. A. (Aston Villa), 1995 v Ei (1)
Fenwick, T. W. (C Palace), 1981 v N, R, Sw, Ei; (with QPR), R; 1982 v N, H, S (2); 1983 v WG (2) (11)
Ferdinand, R. G. (West Ham U), 1997 v Sw, Ge; 1998 v I Gr; 2000 v Y (5)
Fereday, W. (QPR), 1985 v T, Ei (sub). Fi; 1986 v T (sub), I (5)
Flitcroft, G. W. (Manchester C), 1993 v Sm, Hol, N, P, Cz, Br, S, F; 1994 v Pol, Ho (10)
Flowers, T. (Southampton), 1987 v Mor, F; 1988 v WG (sub) (3)
Ford, M. (Leeds U), 1996 v Cro; 1997 v Mol (2)
Forster, N. M. (Brentford), 1995 v Br, Mal, An, F (4)
Forsyth, M. (Derby Co), 1988 v Sw (1)
Foster, S. (Brighton & HA), 1980 v EG (sub) (1)
Fowler, R. B. (Liverpool), 1994 v Sm, Ru (sub), F, US; 1995 v P, A; 1996 v P, A (8)
Froggatt, S. J. (Aston Villa), 1993 v Sp, Sm (sub) (2)
Futcher, P. (Luton T), 1977 v W, S, Fi, N; (with Manchester C), 1978 v N, Fi, I (2), Y (2); 1979 v D (11)

Gabbiadini, M. (Sunderland), 1989 v Bul, USA (2)
Gale, A. (Fulham), 1982 v Pol (1)

Gallen, K. A. (QPR), 1995 v Ei, La (2); 1996 v Cro (4)
Gardner, A. (Tottenham H), 2002 v I (sub) (1)
Gascoigne, P. (Newcastle U), 1987 v Mo, USSR, P; 1988 v WG, Y, S (2), F (2), Sw, M, USSR (sub), Mor (13)
Gayle, H. (Birmingham C), 1984 v I, Sp (2) (3)
Gernon, T. (Ipswich T), 1983 v Gr (1)
Gerrard, P. W. (Oldham Ath), 1993 v T, Ho, Pol, N, P, Cz, Br, S, F; 1994 v D, Ru; 1995 v P, A, Ei (2), La (2); 1996 v P (18)
Gerrard, S. G. (Liverpool), 2000 v L, Pol, D, Y (4)
Gibbs, N. (Watford), 1987 v Mor, USSR, F, P; 1988 v T (5)
Gibson, C. (Aston Villa), 1982 v N (1)
Gilbert, W. A. (C Palace), 1979 v W, Bul; 1980 v Bul; 1981 v N, R, Sw, R, Sw, H; 1982 v N (sub), H (11)
Goddard, P. (West Ham U), 1981 v N, Sw, Ei (sub); 1982 v N (sub), Pol, S; 1983 v WG (2) (8)
Gordon, D. (Norwich C), 1987 v T (sub), Mor (sub), F, P (4)
Gordon, D. D. (C Palace), 1994 v Ru, F, US, Bel, P; 1995 v P, A, Ei (2), La (2); 1996 v P, N (13)
Grant, A. J. (Everton), 1996 v An (sub) (1)
Grant, L. A. (Derby Co), 2003 v I (sub); 2004 v P, T, Se (sub) (4)
Granville, D. P. (Chelsea), 1997 v Ge (sub), Pol; 1998 v Mol (3)
Gray, A. (Aston Villa), 1988 v S, F (2)
Greening, J. (Manchester U), 1999 v H, Se (sub), Bul; 2000 v Pol; 2001 v Ge, G, Fi, I, Sp (sub), Fi, Alb; (with Middlesbrough), 2002 v Ho, G, Alb, Gr, Ho (sub), I, P (18)
Griffin, A. (Newcastle U), 1999 v H; 2001 v I, Sp (3)
Guppy, S. A. (Leicester C), 1998 v Sw (1)

Haigh, P. (Hull C), 1977 v N (sub) (1)
Hall, M. T. J. (Coventry C), 1997 v Pol (2), I, Sw, Ge; 1998 v Mol, Gr (2) (8)
Hall, R. A. (Southampton), 1992 v H (sub), F; 1993 v Sm, T, Ho, Pol, P, Cz, Br, S, F (11)
Hamilton, D. V. (Newcastle U), 1997 v Pol (1)
Hardyman, P. (Portsmouth), 1985 v Ei; 1986 v D (2)
Hargreaves, O. (Bayern Munich), 2001 v Ge (sub), I, Sp (3)
Harley, J. (Chelsea), 2000 v Arg (sub), T (sub), Slo (3)
Hateley, M. (Coventry C), 1982 v Pol, S; 1983 v Gr (2), H; (with Portsmouth), 1984 v F (2), I, Sp (2) (10)
Hayes, M. (Arsenal), 1987 v Sp, T; 1988 v F (sub) (3)
Hazell, R. J. (Wolverhampton W), 1979 v D (1)
Heaney, N. A. (Arsenal), 1992 v H, M, Cz, F; 1993 v N, T (6)
Heath, A. (Stoke C), 1981 v R, Sw, H; 1982 v N, H; (with Everton), Pol, S; 1983 v WG (8)
Hendon, I. M. (Tottenham H), 1992 v H, M, Cz, F; 1993 v Sp, N, T (7)
Hendrie, L. A. (Aston Villa), 1996 v Cro (sub); 1998 v Sw (sub); 1999 v Se, Bul, L, F, Pol; 2000 v L, D, Arg, Y, I, Slo (sub) (13)
Hesford, I. (Blackpool), 1981 v Ei (sub), Pol (2), S (2); 1983 v WG (2) (7)
Heskey, E. W. I. (Leicester C), 1997 v I, Ge, Pol (2); 1998 v I, Gr (2), Sw, F, S.Af, Arg; 1999 v Se, Bul, L; 2000 v L; (with Liverpool), Y (16)
Hilaire, V. (C Palace), 1980 v Bul, S (1+1 sub), EG (2); 1981 v N, R, Sw (sub); 1982 v Pol (sub) (9)
Hill, D. R. L. (Tottenham H), 1995 v Br, Mal, An, F (4)
Hillier, D. (Arsenal), 1991 v T (1)
Hinchcliffe, A. (Manchester C), 1989 v D (1)
Hinshelwood, P. A. (C Palace), 1978 v N; 1980 v EG (2)
Hirst, D. (Sheffield W), 1988 v USSR, F; 1989 v D, Bul (sub), Sen, Ei, US (7)
Hislop, N. S. (Newcastle U), 1998 v Sw (1)
Hoddle, G. (Tottenham H), 1977 v W (sub); 1978 v Fi (sub), I (2), Y; 1979 v D, W, Bul; 1980 v S (2), EG (2) (12)
Hodge, S. (Nottingham F), 1983 v Gr (sub); 1984 v D, F, I, Sp (2); (with Aston Villa), 1986 v R, T (8)
Hodgson, D. J. (Middlesbrough), 1981 v N, R (sub), Sw, Ei; 1982 v Pol; 1983 v WG (6)
Holdsworth, D. (Watford), 1989 v Gr (sub) (1)
Holland, C. J. (Newcastle U), 1995 v La; 1996 v N (sub), A (sub), Cro, Bel, An, Br; 1997 v Mol, Pol, Sw (10)
Holland, P. (Mansfield T), 1995 v Br, Mal, An, F (4)
Holloway, D. (Sunderland), 1998 v Sw (sub) (1)
Horne, B. (Millwall), 1989 v Gr (sub), Pol, Bul, Ei, US (5)
Howe, E. J. F. (Bournemouth), 1998 v S.Af (sub), Arg (2)
Hoyte, J. R. (Arsenal), 2004 v Ho (sub), Se (2)
Hucker, P. (QPR), 1984 v I, Sp (2)
Huckerby, D. (Coventry C), 1997 v I (sub), Sw, Ge (sub), Pol (sub) (4)
Hughes, S. J. (Arsenal), 1997 v I, Sw, Ge, Pol; 1998 v Mol, I, Gr, Sw (sub) (8)
Humphreys, R. J. (Sheffield W), 1997 v Pol, Ge (sub), Sw (3)
Hunt, N. B. (Bolton W), 2004 v Ho (1)

Impey, A. R. (QPR), 1993 v T (1)
Ince, P. (West Ham U), 1989 v Alb; 1990 v Se (2)

Jackson, M. A. (Everton), 1992 v H, M, Cz, F; 1993 v Sm (sub), T, Ho, Pol, N; 1994 v Pol (10)
Jagielka, P. N. (Sheffield U), 2003 v Ser, Slo; 2004 v Cro (sub), Mac, P, T (6)
James, D. (Watford), 1991 v Ei (2), T, Sen, M, USSR, F; 1992 v G, T, Pol (10)
James, J. C. (Luton T), 1990 v F, USSR (2)
Jansen, M. B (C Palace), 1999 v Se, Bul, L; (with Blackburn R), F (sub), Pol; 2000 v I (sub) (6)
Jeffers, F. (Everton), 2000 v L, Arg, I, T, Slo; 2001 v Ge; (with Arsenal), 2002 v Ho, G (sub), Alb; 2003 v Y, Slo, Mac, T; 2004 v Cro, Mac, P (16)
Jemson, N. B. (Nottingham F), 1991 v W (1)
Jenas, J. A. (Newcastle U), 2002 v Slo, I, P (sub); 2003 v Y, Slo, Mac, T; 2004 v Cro, T (9)
Joachim, J. K. (Leicester C), 1994 v D (sub); 1995 v P, A, Ei, Br, Mal, An, F; 1996 v N (9)
Johnson, G. M. C. (West Ham U), 2003 v T (sub), Ser (sub); (with Chelsea), 2004 v Cro, Mac, P, T, Ho (7)
Johnson, S. A. M. (Crewe Alex), 1999 v L (sub), CzR (sub), F (sub), Pol; (with Derby Co), Se, Bul; 2000 v D, Arg (sub), Y, I, T; 2001 v Fi; 2002 v Ho (sub), Alb (sub); (with Leeds U), P (15)
Johnson, T. (Notts Co), 1991 v H (sub), Ei (sub); 1992 v G, T, Pol; (with Derby Co), M, Cz (sub) (7)
Johnston, C. P. (Middlesbrough), 1981 v N, Ei (2)
Jones, D. R. (Everton), 1977 v W (1)
Jones, C. H. (Tottenham H), 1978 v Y (sub) (1)
Jones, D. F. L. (Manchester U), 2004 v Se (sub) (1)
Jones, R. (Liverpool), 1993 v Sm, Ho (2)

Keegan, G. A. (Manchester C), 1977 v W (1)
Kenny, W. (Everton), 1993 v T (1)
Keown, M. (Aston Villa), 1987 v Sp, Mor, USSR, P; 1988 v T, S, F (2) (8)
Kerslake, D. (QPR), 1986 v T (1)
Kilcline, B. (Notts C), 1983 v D, Gr (2)
Kilgallon, M. (Leeds U), 2004 v Se (sub) (1)
King, A. E. (Everton), 1977 v W; 1978 v Y (2)
King, L. B. (Tottenham H), 2000 v L (sub), I, T, Slo; 2001 v I, Sp (sub), Fi; 2002 v G, Alb, Gr, Ho (2) (12)
Kirkland, C. E. (Coventry C), 2001 v M; (with Liverpool), 2002 v Gr, Ho (2), P (sub); 2003 v Y, Mac; 2004 v Mac (8)
Kitson, P. (Leicester C), 1991 v Sen (sub), M, F; 1992 v Pol; (with Derby Co), M, Cz, F (7)
Knight, A. (Portsmouth), 1983 v Gr, H (2)
Knight, I. (Sheffield W), 1987 v Se (sub), Y (2)
Knight, Z. (Fulham), 2002 v Slo (sub), I (2), P (4)
Konchesky, P. M. (Charlton Ath), 2002 v Slo, P, Sw, I, P; 2003 Y, Slo, Mac, P, T, Ser, Slo; 2004 v Cro, Mac, P (15)
Kozluk, R. (Derby Co), 1998 v F, Arg (sub) (2)

Lake, P. (Manchester C), 1989 v D, Alb (2), Pol; 1990 v Pol (5)
Lampard, F. J. (West Ham U), 1998 v Gr (2), Sw, F, S.Af, Arg; 1999 v Se, Bul, L, CzR, F, Pol, Se; 2000 v L, Arg, Y, I, T, Slo (19)
Langley, T. W. (Chelsea), 1978 v I (sub) (1)
Lee, D. J. (Chelsea), 1990 v F; 1991 v H, Pol, Ei (2), T, Sen, USSR, F; 1992 v Pol (10)
Lee, R. (Charlton Ath), 1986 v I (sub); 1987 v Se (sub) (2)
Lee, S. (Liverpool), 1981 v R, Sw, H; 1982 v S; 1983 v WG (2) (6)
Le Saux, G. (Chelsea), 1990 v P, F, USSR, Cz (4)
Lescott, J. P. (Wolverhampton W), 2003 v Y (sub), I (sub) (2)
Lowe, D. (Ipswich T), 1988 v F, Sw (sub) (2)

Lukic, J. (Leeds U), 1981 v N, R, Ei, R, Sw, H; 1982 v H (7)
Lund, G. (Grimsby T), 1985 v T; 1986 v R, T (3)

McCall, S. H. (Ipswich T), 1981 v Sw, H; 1982 v H, S; 1983 v WG (2) (6)
McDonald, N. (Newcastle U), 1987 v Se (sub), Sp, T; 1988 v WG, Y (sub) (5)
McEveley, J. (Blackburn R), 2003 v I (sub) (1)
McGrath, L. (Coventry C), 1986 v D (1)
MacKenzie, S. (WBA), 1982 v N, S (2) (3)
McLeary, A. (Millwall), 1988 v Sw (1)
McMahon, S. (Everton), 1981 v Ei; 1982 v Pol; 1983 v D, Gr (2); (with Aston Villa), 1984 v H (6)
McManaman, S. (Liverpool), 1991 v W, M (sub); 1993 v N, T, Sm, T; 1994 v Pol (7)
Mabbutt, G. (Bristol R), 1982 v Pol (2), S; (with Tottenham H), 1983 v D; 1984 v F; 1986 v D, I (7)
Makin, C. (Oldham Ath), 1994 v Ru (sub), F, US, Bel, P (5)
Marriott, A. (Nottingham F), 1992 v M (1)
Marsh, S. T. (Oxford U), 1998 v F (1)
Marshall, A. J. (Norwich C), 1995 v Mal, An; 1997 v Pol, I (4)
Marshall, L. K. (Norwich C), 1999 v F (sub) (1)
Martin, L. (Manchester U), 1989 v Gr (sub), Alb (sub) (2)
Martyn, N. (Bristol R), 1988 v S (sub), M, USSR, Mor, F; 1989 v D, Se, Gr, Alb (2); 1990 v Se (11)
Matteo, D. (Liverpool), 1994 v F (sub), Bel, P; 1998 v Sw (4)
Matthew, D. (Chelsea), 1990 v P, USSR (sub), Cz; 1991 v Ei, M, USSR, F; 1992 v G (sub), T (9)
May, A. (Manchester C), 1986 v I (sub) (1)
Merson, P. (Arsenal), 1989 v D, Gr, Pol (sub); 1990 v Pol (4)
Middleton, J. (Nottingham F), 1977 v Fi, N; (with Derby Co), 1978 v N (3)
Miller, A. (Arsenal), 1988 v Mor (sub); 1989 v Sen; 1991 v H, Pol (4)
Mills, D. J. (Charlton Ath), 1999 v Se, Bul (sub), L, Pol, H, Se; (with Leeds U), 2000 v L, Pol, D, Arg, Y (sub), I, T, Slo (14)
Mills, G. R. (Nottingham F), 1981 v R; 1982 v N (2)
Milner, J. P. (Leeds U), 2004 v Se (sub) (1)
Mimms, R. (Rotherham U), 1985 v Is (sub), Ei (sub); (with Everton), 1986 v I (3)
Minto, S. C. (Charlton Ath), 1991 v W; 1992 v H, M, Cz; 1993 v T; 1994 v Ho (6)
Moore, I. (Tranmere R), 1996 v Cro (sub), Bel (sub), An, P, Br; 1997 v Mol (sub); (with Nottingham F), Sw (sub) (7)
Moran, S. (Southampton), 1982 v N (sub); 1984 v F (2)
Morgan, S. (Leicester C), 1987 v Se, Y (2)
Morris, J. (Chelsea), 1997 v Pol (sub), Sw (sub), Ge (sub); 1999 v Bul (sub), L (sub), CzR; 2000 v Pol (7)
Mortimer, P. (Charlton Ath), 1989 v Sen, Ei (2)
Moses, A. P. (Barnsley), 1997 v Pol; 1998 v Gr (sub) (2)
Moses, R. M. (WBA), 1981 v N (sub), Sw, Ei, R, Sw, H; 1982 v N (sub); (with Manchester U), H (8)
Mountfield, D. (Everton), 1984 v Sp (1)
Muggleton, C. D. (Leicester C), 1990 v F (1)
Mullins, H. I. (C Palace), 1999 v Pol (sub), H, Bul (3)
Murphy, D. B. (Liverpool), 1998 v Mol, Gr (sub); 2000 v T, Slo (4)
Murray, P. (QPR), 1997 v I, Pol; 1998 v I, Gr (4)
Murray, M. W. (Wolverhampton W), 2003 v Slo, Mac (sub), I, T; 2004 v Cro (5)
Mutch, A. (Wolverhampton W), 1989 v Pol (1)
Myers. A. (Chelsea), 1995 v Br, Mal, An (sub), F (4)

Naylor, L. M. (Wolverhampton W), 2000 v Arg; 2001 v M, Gr (3)
Nethercott, S. (Tottenham), 1994 v D, Ru, F, US, Bel, P; 1995 v La (2) (8)
Neville, P. J. (Manchester U), 1995 v Br, Mal, An, F; 1996 v P, N (sub); 1997 v Ge (7)
Newell, M. (Luton T), 1986 v D (1 + 1 sub), I (1 + 1 sub) (4)
Newton, A. L. (West Ham U), 2001 v Ge (1)
Newton, E. J. I. (Chelsea), 1993 v T (sub); 1994 v Sm (2)
Newton, S. O. (Charlton Ath), 1997 v Mol, Pol, Ge (3)
Nicholls, A. (Plymouth Arg), 1994 v F (1)
Nolan, K. A. J. (Bolton W), 2003 v I (sub) (1)

Oakes, M. C. (Aston Villa), 1994 v D (sub), F (sub), US Bel, P; 1996 v A (6)
Oakes, S. J. (Luton T), 1993 v Br (sub) (1)
Oakley, M. (Southampton), 1997 v Ge; 1998 v F, S.A Arg (4)
O'Brien, A. J. (Bradford C), 1999 v F (1)
O'Connor, J. (Everton), 1996 v Cro, An, Br (3)
Oldfield, D. (Luton T), 1989 v Se (1)
Olney, I. A. (Aston Villa), 1990 v P, F, USSR, Cz; 1991 H, Pol, Ei (2), T; 1992 v Pol (sub) (10)
Ord, R. J. (Sunderland), 1991 v W, M, USSR (3)
Osman, R. C. (Ipswich T), 1979 v W (sub), Se; 1980 v D S (2), EG (2) (7)
Owen, G. A. (Manchester C), 1977 v S, Fi, N; 1978 v N Fi, I (2), Y; 1979 v D, W; (with WBA), Bul, Se (sub 1980 v D, S (2), EG; 1981 v Sw, R; 1982 v N (sub), H 1983 v WG (2) (22)
Owen, M. J. (Liverpool), 1998 v Gr (1)

Painter, I. (Stoke C), 1986 v I (1)
Palmer, C. (Sheffield W), 1989 v Bul, Sen, Ei, US (4)
Parker, G. (Hull C), 1986 v I (2); (with Nottingham F), F 1987 v Se, Y (sub), Sp (6)
Parker, P. (Fulham), 1985 v Fi, T, Is (sub), Ei, R, Fi; 198 v T, D (8)
Parker, S. M. (Charlton Ath), 2001 v Ge (sub), G, F (sub), Alb (sub); 2002 v Ho (sub), G (sub), Alb, Slo, (sub), Sw (sub), I (sub), P (sub) (12)
Parkes, P. B. F. (QPR), 1979 v D (1)
Parkin, S. (Stoke C), 1987 v Sp (sub); 1988 v WG (sub T, S (sub), F (5)
Parlour, R. (Arsenal), 1992 v H, M, Cz, F; 1993 v Sp, N T; 1994 v D, Ru, Bel, P; 1995 v A (12)
Parnaby, S. (Middlesbrough), 2003 v Y (sub), Ser, Slo 2004 v Cro (4)
Peach, D. S. (Southampton), 1977 v S, Fi, N; 1978 v N, (2) (6)
Peake, A. (Leicester C), 1982 v Pol (1)
Pearce, I. A. (Blackburn R), 1995 v Ei, La; 1996 v N (3)
Pearce, S. (Nottingham F), 1987 v Y (1)
Pennant, J. (Arsenal), 2001 v M (sub), Gr (sub); 2002 Ho (sub), Alb (sub), Gr, Ho (2), Slv, I (sub), P (sub Sw, I, P; 2003 v Y, P (sub), Ser, Slo; 2004 v Cro, Ma (19)
Pickering N. (Sunderland), 1983 v D (sub), Gr, H; 1984 F (sub + 1), I (2), Sp; 1985 v Is, R, Fi; 1986 v R, T; (wit Coventry C), D, I (15)
Platt, D. (Aston Villa), 1988 v M, Mor, F (3)
Plummer, C. S. (QPR), 1996 v Cro (sub), Bel, An, (sub), Br (5)
Pollock, J. (Middlesbrough), 1995 v Ei (sub); 1996 v N, A (3)
Porter, G. (Watford), 1987 v Sp (sub), T, Mor, USSR, F P (sub); 1988 v T (sub), Y, S (2), F, Sw (12)
Potter, G. S. (Southampton), 1997 v Mol (1)
Pressman, K. (Sheffield W), 1989 v D (sub) (1)
Proctor, M. (Middlesbrough), 1981 v Ei (sub), Sw; (wit Nottingham F) 1982 v N, Pol (4)
Prutton, D. T. (Nottingham F), 2001 v Ge (sub), G (sub Fi, Sp (sub), M, Gr (sub); 2002 v Ho (sub), G, Gr (sub Slv (sub), I, Sw (sub), I, P; 2003 v Y, Slo, Mac; (wit Southampton), I, P, T, Ser, Slo; 2004 v Cro, P, T (25)
Purse, D. J. (Birmingham C), 1998 v F. S.Af (2)

Quashie, N. F. (QPR), 1997 v Pol; 1998 v Mol, Gr, Sw (4
Quinn, W. R. (Sheffield U), 1998 v Mol (sub), I (2)

Ramage, C. D. (Derby Co), 1991 v Pol (sub), W; 1992 Fr (sub) (3)
Ranson, R. (Manchester C), 1980 v Bul, EG; 1981 v (sub), R, Sw (1 + 1 sub), H, Pol (2), S (10)
Redknapp, J. F. (Liverpool), 1993 v Sm, Pol, N, P, Cz, B S, F; 1994 v Pol, Ho (sub), D, Ru, F, US, Bel, P; 1995 P, A; 1998 v Sw (19)
Redmond, S. (Manchester C), 1988 v F (2), M, USSR Mor, F; 1989 v D, Se, Gr, Alb (2), Pol; 1990 v Se, Pc (14)
Reeves, K. P. (Norwich C), 1978 v I, Y (2); 1979 v N, W Bul, Sw; 1980 v D, S; (with Manchester C), EG (10)
Regis, C. (WBA), 1979 v D, Bul, Se; 1980 v S, EG; 1983 D (6)
Reid, N. S. (Manchester C), 1981 v H (sub); 1982 v H, Pc (2), S (2) (6)
Reid, P. (Bolton W), 1977 v S, Fi, N; 1978 v Fi, I, Y (6)
Reo-Coker, N. S. A. (Wimbledon), 2004 v T (sub); (wit West Ham U), Ho, Se (3)

Richards, D. I. (Wolverhampton W), 1995 v Br, Mal, An, F (4)
Richards, J. P. (Wolverhampton W), 1977 v Fi, N (2)
Rideout, P. (Aston Villa), 1985 v Fi, Is, Ei (sub), R; (with Bari), 1986 v D (5)
Ridgewell, L. M. (Aston Villa), 2004 v Ho, Se (2)
Riggott, C. M. (Derby Co), 2001 v Sp (sub), Fi (sub), Alb, M (sub); 2002 v Ho (sub), Slv, P, Sw (8)
Ripley, S. (Middlesbrough), 1988 v USSR, F (sub); 1989 v D (sub), Se, Gr, Alb (2); 1990 v Se (8)
Ritchie, A. (Brighton & HA), 1982 v Pol (1)
Rix, G. (Arsenal), 1978 v Fi (sub), Y; 1979 v D, Se; 1980 v D (sub), Bul, S (7)
Roberts, A. J. (Millwall), 1995 v Ei, La (2); (with C Palace), 1996 v N, A (5)
Roberts, B. J. (Middlesbrough), 1997 v Sw (sub) (1)
Robins, M. G. (Manchester U), 1990 v P, F, USSR, Cz; 1991 v H (sub), Pol (6)
Robinson, P. P. (Watford), 1999 v Se, Bul; 2000 v Pol (3)
Robinson, P. W. (Leeds U), 2000 v D; 2001 v Ge, G, Fi, Sp; 2002 v Slv, I, P, Sw, I, P (11)
Robson, B. (WBA), 1979 v W, Bul (sub), Se; 1980 v D, Bul, S (2) (7)
Robson, S. (Arsenal), 1984 v I; 1985 v Fi, Is, Fi; 1986 v R, I; (with West Ham U); 1988 v S, Sw (8)
Rocastle, D. (Arsenal), 1987 v Se, Y, Sp, T; 1988 v WG, T, Y, S (2), F (2 subs), M, USSR, Mor (14)
Roche, L. P. (Manchester U), 2001 v Fi (1)
Rodger, G. (Coventry C), 1987 v USSR, F, P; 1988 v WG (4)
Rogers, A. (Nottingham F), 1998 v F, S.Af, Arg (3)
Rosario, R. (Norwich C), 1987 v T (sub), Mor, F, P (sub) (4)
Rose, M. (Arsenal), 1997 v Ge (sub), I (2)
Rowell, G. (Sunderland), 1977 v Fi (1)
Ruddock, N. (Southampton), 1989 v Bul (sub), Sen, Ei, US (4)
Rufus, R. R. (Charlton Ath), 1996 v Cro, Bel, An, P, Br; 1997 v I (6)
Ryan, J. (Oldham Ath), 1983 v H (1)
Ryder, S.H. (Walsall), 1995 v Br, An, F (3)

Samuel, J. (Aston Villa), 2002 v I; 2003 v Y, Slo, Mac, I, P, T (7)
Samways, V. (Tottenham H), 1988 v Sw (sub), USSR, F; 1989 v D, Se (5)
Sansom, K. G. (C Palace), 1979 v D, W, Bul, Se; 1980 v S (2), EG (2) (8)
Scimeca, R. (Aston Villa), 1996 v P; 1997 v Mol, Pol, Ge, I; 1998 v Mol, I, Gr (2) (9)
Scowcroft, J. B. (Ipswich T), 1997 v Pol, Ge (2), I (sub); 1998 v Gr (sub) (5)
Seaman, D. (Birmingham C), 1985 v Fi, T, Is, Ei, R, Fi; 1986 v R, F, D, I (10)
Sedgley, S. (Coventry C), 1987 v USSR, F (sub), P; 1988 v F; 1989 v D (sub), Se, Gr, Alb (2), Pol; (with Tottenham H), 1990 v Se (11)
Sellars, S. (Blackburn R), 1988 v S (sub), F, Sw (3)
Selley, I. (Arsenal), 1994 v Ru (sub), F (sub), US (3)
Serrant, C. (Oldham Ath), 1998 v Gr (2) (2)
Sharpe, L. (Manchester U), 1989 v Gr; 1990 v P (sub), F, USSR, Cz; 1991 v H, Pol (sub), Ei (8)
Shaw, G. R. (Aston Villa), 1981 v Ei, Sw, H; 1982 v H, S; 1983 v WG (2) (7)
Shearer, A. (Southampton), 1991 v Ei (2), W, T, Sen, M, USSR, F; 1992 v G, T, Pol (11)
Shelton, G. (Sheffield W), 1985 v Fi (1)
Sheringham, T. (Millwall), 1988 v Sw (1)
Sheron, M. N. (Manchester C), 1992 v H, F; 1993 v N (sub), T (sub), Sm, Ho, Pol, N, P, Cz, Br, S, F; 1994 v Pol (sub), Ho, Sm (16)
Sherwood, T. A. (Norwich C), 1990 v P, F, USSR, Cz (4)
Shipperley, N. J. (Chelsea), 1994 v Sm (sub); (with Southampton) 1995 v Ei, La (2); 1996 v P, N, A (7)
Sidwell, S. J. (Reading), 2003 v Ser, Slo; 2004 v Cro (sub), Mac, T (5)
Simonsen, S. P. A. (Tranmere R), 1998 v F; (with Everton), l999 v CzR, F, Bul (4)
Simpson, P. (Manchester C), 1986 v D (sub); 1987 v Y, Mor, F, P (5)
Sims, S. (Leicester C), 1977 v W, S, Fi, N; 1978 v N, Fi, I (2), Y (2) (10)
Sinclair, T. (QPR), 1994 v Ho, Sm, D, Ru, F, US, Bel, P; 1995 v P, Ei (2), La; 1996 v P; (with West Ham U), 1998 v Sw (5)
Sinnott, L. (Watford), 1985 v Is (sub) (1)
Slade, S. A. (Tottenham H), 1996 v Bel, An, P, Br (4)
Slater, S. I. (West Ham U), 1990 v P, USSR (sub), Cz (sub) (3)
Small, B. (Aston Villa), 1993 v Sm, T, Ho, Pol, N, P, Cz, Br, S, F; 1994 v Pol, Sm (12)
Smith, A. (Leeds U), 2000 v D, Arg (sub); 2001 v G, Fi, Sp; 2002 v I, P, Sw, I, P (10)
Smith, D. (Coventry C), 1988 v M, USSR (sub), Mor; 1989 v D, Se, Alb (2), Pol; 1990 v Se, Pol (10)
Smith, M. (Sheffield W), 1981 v Ei, R, Sw, H; 1982 v Pol (sub) (5)
Smith, M. (Sunderland), 1995 v Ei (sub) (1)
Smith, T. W. (Watford), 2001 v Ge (sub) (1)
Snodin, I. (Doncaster R), 1985 v T, Is, R, Fi (4)
Statham, B. (Tottenham H), 1988 v Sw; 1989 v D (sub), Se (3)
Statham, D. J. (WBA), 1978 v Fi, 1979 v W, Bul, Se; 1980 v D; 1983 v D (6)
Stead, J. G. (Blackburn R), 2004 v Ho (sub), Se (sub) (2)
Stein, B. (Luton T), 1984 v D, H, I (3)
Sterland, M. (Sheffield W), 1984 v D, H, F (2), I, Sp (2) (7)
Steven, T. (Everton), 1985 v Fi, T (2)
Stevens, G. (Brighton & HA), 1983 v H; (with Tottenham H), 1984 v H, F (1+1 sub), I (sub), Sp (1+1 sub); 1986 v I (8)
Stewart, J. (Leicester C), 2003 v P (sub) (1)
Stewart, P. (Manchester C), 1988 v F (1)
Stockdale, R. K. (Middlesbrough), 2001 v Ge (sub) (1)
Stuart, G. C. (Chelsea), 1990 v P (sub), F, USSR, Cz; 1991 v T (sub) (5)
Stuart, J. C. (Charlton Ath), 1996 v Bel, An, P, Br (4)
Suckling, P. (Coventry C), 1986 v D; (with Manchester C), 1987 v Se (sub), Y, Sp, T; (with C Palace), 1988 v S (2), F (2), Sw (10)
Summerbee, N.J. (Swindon T), 1993 v P (sub), S (sub), F (3)
Sunderland, A. (Wolverhampton W), 1977 v W (1)
Sutton, C. R. (Norwich), 1993 v Sp (sub), T (sub + 1), Ho, P (sub), Cz, Br, S, F; 1994 v Pol, Ho, Sm, D (13)
Swindlehurst, D. (C Palace), 1977 v W (1)
Sutch, D. (Norwich C), 1992 v H, M, Cz; 1993 v T (4)

Talbot, B. (Ipswich T), 1977 v W (1)
Taylor, M. (Blackburn R), 2001 v M (sub) (1)
Taylor, M. S. (Portsmouth), 2003 v Slo (sub), I; 2004 v T (3)
Taylor, S. J. (Arsenal), 2002 v Ho, G, Alb (3)
Taylor, S. V. (Newcastle U), 2004 v Ho, Se (2)
Terry, J. G. (Chelsea), 2001 v Fi, Sp, Fi, Alb, M, Gr; 2002 v Ho (3) (9)
Thatcher, B. D. (Millwall), 1996 v Cro; (with Wimbledon), 1997 v Mol, Pol; 1998 v I (4)
Thelwell, A. A. (Tottenham H), 2001 v Sp (sub) (1)
Thirlwell, P. (Sunderland), 2001 v Ge (sub) (1)
Thomas, D. (Coventry C), 1981 v Ei; 1983 v WG (2), Gr, H; (with Tottenham H), I, Sp (7)
Thomas, M. (Luton T), 1986 v T, D, I (3)
Thomas, M. (Arsenal), 1988 v Y, S, F (2), M, USSR, Mor; 1989 v Gr, Alb (2), Pol; 1990 v Se (12)
Thomas, R. E. (Watford), 1990 v P (1)
Thompson, A. (Bolton W), 1995 v La; 1996 v P (2)
Thompson, D. A. (Liverpool), 1997 v Pol (sub), Ge; 2000 v L (sub), Pol (sub), D (sub), I, T (sub) (7)
Thompson, G. L. (Coventry C), 1981 v R, Sw, H; 1982 v N, H, S (6)
Thorn, A. (Wimbledon), 1988 v WG (sub). Y, S, F, Sw (5)
Thornley, B. L. (Manchester U), 1996 v Bel, P, Br (3)
Tiler, C. (Barnsley), 1990 v P, USSR, Cz; 1991 v H, Pol, Ei (2), T, Sen, USSR, F; (with Nottingham F), 1992 v G, T (13)
Tonge, M. W. E. (Sheffield U), 2004 v Mac, Se (2)

Unsworth, D. G. (Everton), 1995 v A, Ei (2), La; 1996 v N, A (6)
Upson, M. J. (Arsenal), 1999 v Se, Bul, L, F; 2000 v L, Pol, D; 2001 v I, Sp (sub), M (sub), Gr (11)

Vassell, D. (Aston Villa), 1999 v H (sub); 2000 v Pol (sub); 2001 v Ge, G, Fi, I, Fi, Alb; 2002 v Ho, G, Gr (11)
Venison, B. (Sunderland), 1983 v D, Gr; 1985 v Fi, T, Is, Fi; 1986 v R, T, D (2) (10)
Vernazza, P. A. P. (Arsenal), 2001 v G (sub); (with Watford), M (sub) (2)

Vinnicombe, C. (Rangers), 1991 v H (sub), Pol, Ei (2), T, Sen, M, USSR (sub), F; 1992 v G, T, Pol (12)

Waddle, C. (Newcastle U), 1985 v Fi (1)
Wallace, D. (Southampton), 1983 v Gr, H; 1984 v D, H, F (2), I, Sp (sub); 1985 v Fi, T, Is; 1986 v R, D, I (14)
Wallace, Ray (Southampton), 1989 v Bul, Sen (sub), Ei; 1990 v Se (4)
Wallace, Rod (Southampton), 1989 v Bul, Ei (sub), US; 1991 v H, Pol, Ei, T, Sen, M, USSR, F (11)
Walker, D. (Nottingham F), 1985 v Fi; 1987 v Se, T; 1988 v WG, T, S (2) (7)
Walker, I. M. (Tottenham H), 1991 v W; 1992 v H, Cz, F; 1993 v Sp, N, T, Sm; 1994 v Pol (9)
Walsh, G. (Manchester U), 1988 v WG, Y (2)
Walsh, P. M. (Luton T), 1983 v D (sub), Gr (2), H (4)
Walters, K. (Aston Villa), 1984 v D (sub), H (sub); 1985 v Is, Ei, R; 1986 v R, T, D, I (sub) (9)
Ward, P. D. (Brighton & HA), 1978 v N; 1980 v EG (2)
Warhurst, P. (Oldham Ath), 1991 v H, Pol, W, Sen, M (sub), USSR, F (sub); (with Sheffield W), 1992 v G (8)
Watson, D. (Norwich C), 1984 v D, F (2), I (2), Sp (2) (7)
Watson, D. N. (Barnsley), 1994 v Ho, Sm; 1995 v Br, F; 1996 v N (5)
Watson, G. (Sheffield W), 1991 v Sen, USSR (2)
Watson, S. C. (Newcastle U), 1993 v Sp (sub), N; 1994 v Sm (sub), D; 1995 v P, A, Ei (2), La (2); 1996 v N, A (12)
Weaver, N. J. (Manchester C), 2000 v L, Pol, Arg, I, T, Slo; 2001 v I, Fi, Alb; 2002 v Slv (sub) (10)
Webb, N. (Portsmouth), 1985 v Ei; (with Nottingham F), 1986 v D (2) (3)
Welsh, J. J. (Liverpool), 2004 v Ho (1)
Whelan, P. J. (Ipswich T), 1993 v Sp, T (sub), P (3)
Whelan, N. (Leeds U), 1995 v A (sub), Ei (2)
Whittingham, P. (Aston Villa), 2004 v Ho (sub) (1)
Wilson, M. A. (Manchester U), 2001 v Sp, Fi (sub), Alb, M (sub); (with Middlesbrough), 2002 v Ho (sub), Alb (sub) (6)
White, D. (Manchester C), 1988 v S (2), F, USSR; 1989 v Se; 1990 v Pol (6)
Whyte, C. (Arsenal), 1982 v S (1+1 sub); 1983 v D, Gr (4)
Wicks, S. (QPR), 1982 v S (1)
Wilkins, R. C. (Chelsea), 1977 v W (1)
Wilkinson, P. (Grimsby T), 1985 v Ei, R (sub); (with Everton), 1986 v R (sub), I (4)
Williams, D. (Sunderland), 1998 v Sw (sub); 1999 v F (2)
Williams, P. (Charlton Ath), 1989 v Bul, Sen, Ei, US (sub) (4)
Williams, P. D. (Derby Co), 1991 v Sen, M, USSR; 1992 v G, T, Pol (6)
Williams, S. C. (Southampton), 1977 v S, Fi, N; 1978 v N, I (1 + 1 sub), Y (2); 1979 v D, Bul, Se (sub); 1980 v D, EG (2) (14)
Winterburn, N. (Wimbledon), 1986 v I (1)
Wise, D. (Wimbledon), 1988 v Sw (1)
Woodcook, A. S. (Nottingham F), 1978 v Fi, I (2)
Woodgate, J. S. (Leeds U), 2000 v Arg (1)
Woodhouse, C. (Sheffield U), 1999 v H, Se, Bul; 2000 v Pol (sub) (4)
Woods, C. C. E. (Nottingham F), 1979 v W (sub), Se; (with QPR), 1980 v Bul, EG; 1981 v Sw; (with Norwich C), 1984 v D (6)
Wright, A. G. (Blackburn), 1993 v Sp, N (2)
Wright, M. (Southampton), 1983 v Gr, H; 1984 v D, H (4)
Wright, R. I. (Ipswich T), 1997 v Ge, Pol; 1998 v Mol, I, Gr (2), S.Af, Arg; 1999 v Se, Bul, L, Pol, H, Se; 2000 v Y (15)
Wright, S. J. (Liverpool), 2001 v Ge (sub), G, M (sub); 2002 v Ho (sub), G, Alb, Ho, Slv, I, P (10)
Wright, W. (Everton), 1979 v D, W, Bul; 1980 v D, S (2) (6)
Wright-Phillips, S. C. (Manchester C), 2002 v I; 2003 v Y (sub), Mac (sub), I; 2004 v Mac (sub), T (6)

Yates, D. (Notts Co), 1989 v D (sub), Bul, Sen, Ei, US (5)
Young, L. P. (Tottenham H), 1999 v H; 2000 v D (sub), Arg (sub), T, Slo; (with Charlton Ath), 2002 v Ho, Gr, Ho, P (sub), Sw, I, P (12)

Zamora, R. L. (Brighton & HA), 2002 v P (sub), I (sub), P (sub); 2003 v I, Ser, Slo (sub) (6)

## SCOTLAND

Aitken, R. (Celtic), 1977 v Cz, W, Sw; 1978 v Cz, W; 1979 v P, N (2); 1980 v Bel, E; 1984 v EG, Y (2); 1985 v WG, Ic, Sp (16)
Albiston, A. (Manchester U), 1977 v Cz, W, Sw; 1978 v Sw, Cz (5)
Alexander, N. (Stenhousemuir), 1997 v P; 1998 v Bl, Ei, I; (with Livingston), 1999 v Li, Es, Bel (2), CzR, G (10)
Anderson, I. (Dundee), 1997 v Co (sub), US, CzR, P; 1998 v Bl, La, Fi, D (sub), Ei (sub), Ni; 1999 v G (sub), Ei, Ni, CzR; (with Toulouse), 2000 v Bos (15)
Anderson, R. (Aberdeen), 1997 v Es, A, Se; 1998 v La (sub), Fi, Ei, I; 1999 v Es, Bel, G, Ei, Ni, CzR; 2000 v Bos, Es (15)
Anthony, M. (Celtic), 1997 v La (sub), Es (sub), Col (3)
Archdeacon, O. (Celtic), 1987 v WG (sub) (1)
Archibald, A. (Partick T), 1998 v Fi, Ei, Ni, I; 1999 v Li (5)
Archibald, S. (Aberdeen), 1980 v B, E (2), WG; (with Tottenham H), 1981 v D (5)

Bagen, D. (Kilmarnock), 1997 v Es, A (sub), Se (sub), Bl (4)
Bain, K. (Dundee), 1993 v P, I, Ma, P (4)
Baker, M. (St. Mirren), 1993 v F, M, E; 1994 v Ma, A; 1995 v Gr, M, F (sub), Sk (sub); 1996 v H (sub) (10)
Baltacha, S. S. (St Mirren), 2000 v Bos, Li (sub), F (sub) (3)
Bannon, E. J. P. (Hearts), 1979 v US; (with Chelsea), P, N (2); (with Dundee U), 1980 v Bel, WG, E (7)
Beattie, C. (Celtic), 2004 v H (sub), R, D (sub), Ei (4)
Beattie, J. (St Mirren), 1992 v D, US, P, Y (4)
Beaumont, D. (Dundee U), 1985 v Ic (1)
Bell, D. (Aberdeen), 1981 v D; 1984 v Y (2)
Bernard, P. R. J. (Oldham Ath), 1992 v R (sub), D, Se (sub), US; 1993 v Sw, P, I, Ma, P, F, Bul, M, E; 1994 v I, Ma (15)
Bett, J. (Rangers), 1981 v Se, D; 1982 v Se, D, I, E (2) (7)
Black, E. (Aberdeen), 1983 v EG, Sw (2), Bel; 1985 v Ic, Sp (2), Ic (8)
Blair, A. (Coventry C), 1980 v E; 1981 v Se; (with Aston Villa), 1982 v Se, D, I (5)
Bollan, G. (Dundee U), 1992 v D, G (sub), US, P, Y; 1993 v Sw, P, I, P, F, Bul, M, E; 1994 v Sw; 1995 v Gr; (with Rangers) v Ru, Sm (17)
Bonar, P. (Raith R), 1997 v A, La, Es (sub), Se (4)
Booth, S. (Aberdeen), 1991 v R (sub), Bul (sub + 1), Pol, F (sub); 1992 v Sw, R, D, Se, US, P, Y; 1993 v Ma, P (14)
Bowes, M. J. (Dunfermline Ath), 1992 v D (sub) (1)
Bowman, D. (Hearts), 1985 v WG (sub) (1)
Boyack, S. (Rangers), 1997 v Se (1)
Boyd, K. (Kilmarnock), 2003 v Bel (sub); 2004 v R (sub), D, Ei (4)
Boyd, T. (Motherwell), 1987 v WG, Ei (2), Bel; 1988 v Bel (5)
Brazil, A. (Hibernian), 1978 v W (1)
Brazil, A. (Ipswich T), 1979 v N; 1980 v Bel (2), E (2), WG; 1981 v Se; 1982 v Se (8)
Brebner, G. I. (Manchester U), 1997 v Col, CzR (sub), US (sub), P; 1998 v Bl, La, Fi, D; (with Reading), 1999 v Li, Es, Bel (2), CzR, G, Ei, Ni, CzR; (with Hibernian), 2000 v Bos (18)
Brough, J. (Hearts), 1981 v D (1)
Brown, A. H. (Hibernian), 2004 v D (1)
Browne, P. (Raith R), 1997 v A (1)
Buchan, J. (Aberdeen), 1997 v Se, Col, CzR, P; 1998 v Bl, La, Fi; 1999 v Li, Es, Bel, CzR, G, Ei (13)
Burchill, M. (Celtic), 1998 v Fi, D (sub); 1999 v Li, Es (sub), Bel (2), CzR, Ei, Ni, CzR; 2000 v Bos, Es; 2001 v La, Bel, Pol (15)
Burke, A. (Kilmarnock), 1997 v Es, A, Bl (sub); 1998 v Ei (sub) (4)
Burke, C. (Rangers), 2004 v R (sub), D (sub) (2)
Burley, G. E. (Ipswich T), 1977 v Cz, W, Sw; 1978 v Sw, Cz (5)
Burley, C. (Chelsea), 1992 v D; 1993 v Sw, P, I, P; 1994 v Sw, I (sub) (7)
Burns, H. (Rangers), 1985 v Sp, Ic (sub) (2)

ırns, T. (Celtic), 1977 v Cz, W, E; 1978 v Sw; 1982 v E (5)

aldwell, G. (Newcastle U), 2000 v F, Ni, W; 2002 v Cro, Bel, La; 2003 v Is (sub), Ic, Gh, Bel, Ei, Ic, Li, A, G; 2004 v N, G, Li, Cro (19)
ıldwell, S. (Newcastle U), 2001 v La, Cro, Bel; 2002 v Cro (4)
ampbell, S. (Dundee), 1989 v N (sub), Y, F (3)
ampbell, S. P. (Leicester C), 1998 v Fi (sub), D, Ei, Ni (sub), I; 1999 v Li, Es, Bel (2), CzR, G, Ei, Ni, CzR (sub); 2000 v Bos (sub) (15)
anero, P. (Kilmarnock), 2000 v F; 2001 v La (sub), Cro (sub), Bel, Pol; 2002 v La (sub); 2003 v D, Ni, Bel (sub), Ei, ic, Li, A, G; 2004 v Li, Cro (2) (17)
arey, L. A. (Bristol C), 1998 v D (1)
asey, J. (Celtic), 1978 v W (1)
hristie, M. (Dundee), 1992 v D, P (sub), Y (3)
lark, R. (Aberdeen), 1977 v Cz, W, Sw (3)
larke, S. (St Mirren), 1984 v Bel, EG, Y; 1985 v WG, Ic, Sp (2), Ic (8)
larkson, D. (Motherwell), 2004 v D (sub) (1)
leland, A. (Dundee U), 1990 v F, N (2); 1991 v R, Sw, Bul; 1992 v Sw, R, G, Se (2) (11)
ollins, J. (Hibernian), 1988 v Bel, E; 1989 v N, Y, F; 1990 v Y, F, N (8)
onnolly, P. (Dundee U), 1991 v R (sub), Sw, Bul (3)
onnor, R. (Ayr U), 1981 v Se; 1982 v Se (2)
ooper, D. (Clydebank), 1977 v Cz, W, Sw, E; (with Rangers), 1978 v Sw, Cz (6)
ooper, N. (Aberdeen), 1982 v D, E (2); 1983 v Bel, EG, Sw (2); 1984 v Bel, EG, Y; 1985 v Ic, Sp, Ic (13)
rabbe, S. (Hearts), 1990 v Y (sub), F (2)
raig, M. (Aberdeen), 1998 v Bl, La (2)
raig, T. (Newcastle U), 1977 v E (1)
rainey, S. D. (Celtic), 2000 v F (sub); 2003 v Bel, Ei (sub), A, G; 2004 v N, G (7)
rainie, D. (Celtic), 1983 v Sw (sub) (1)
rawford, S. (Raith R), 1994 v A, Eg, P, Bel; 1995 v Fi, Ru,Gr, Ru, Sm, M, F (sub), Sk (sub), Br (sub); 1996 v Gr, Fi (sub), H (1 + sub), Sp (sub), F (sub) (19)
reaney, G. (Celtic), 1991 v Sw, Bul (2), Pol, F; 1992 v Sw, R, G (2), Se (2) (11)
ummings, W. (Chelsea), 2000 v F, Ni; 2001 v La, Cro, Bel, Pol; 2002 v Cro, Bel (8)

ailly, C. (Dundee U), 1991 v R; 1992 v US, R; 1993 v Sw, P, I, Ic, P, F, Bul, M, E; 1994 v Sw, I, Ma, A, Eg, P, Bel; 1995 v Fi, Ru, Gr, Ru, Sm, M, F, Sk, Br; 1996 v Fi, Sm, H (2), Sp, F (34)
alglish, P. (Newcastle U), 1999 v Es, Bel, CzR; (with Norwich C), 2000 v Es (sub), Bos, Li (sub) (6)
argo, C. (Raith R), 1998 v Fi, Ei, Ni (sub), I; 1999 v Es, Bel (1+sub), CzR (sub), G, Ni (sub) (10)
avidson, C. (St Johnstone), 1997 v Se, Bl (2)
avidson, H. N. (Dundee U), 2000 v Es (sub), Li, F (3)
awson, A. (Rangers), 1979 v P, N (2); 1980 v B (2), E (2), WG (8)
eas, P. A. (St Johnstone), 1992 v D (sub); 1993 v Ma (2)
empster, J. (Rushden & D), 2004 v H (sub) (1)
ennis, S. (Raith R), 1992 v Sw (1)
iamond, A. (Aberdeen), 2004 v H (sub) (1)
ickov, P. (Arsenal), 1992 v Y; 1993 v F, M, E (4)
odds, D. (Dundee U), 1978 v W (1)
ods, D. (Hibernian), 1997 v La, Es, Se (2), Bl (5)
oig, C. R. (Nottingham F), 2000 v Ni, W; 2001 v La, Cro, Pol; 2003 v D, Is, Ni, Ic, Gh, Bel, Ei; 2004 v N (sub) (13)
onald, G. S. (Hibernian), 1992 v US (sub), P, Y (sub) (3)
onnelly, S. (Celtic), 1994 v Eg, P, Bel; 1995 v Fi, Gr (sub); 1996 v Gr (sub), Sm, H (2), Sp, F (11)
ow, A. (Dundee), 1993 v Ma (sub), Ic; (with Chelsea) 1994 v I (3)
owie, A. J. (Rangers), 2003 v D, Is; 2004 v N (sub), H, R, D. Ei (7)
uffy, J. (Dundee), 1987 v Ei (1)
uff, S. (Dundee U), 2003 v Is, Ni (sub), Ic, Gh, Bel, Ei (sub); 2004 v N, G, Cro (9)
urie, G. S. (Chelsea), 1987 v WG, Ei, Bel; 1988 v Bel (4)
urrant, I. (Rangers), 1987 v WG, Ei, Bel; 1988 v E (4)
oyle, J. (Partick Th), 1981 v D, I (sub) (2)

aston, C. (Dundee U), 1997 v Col, US, CzR, P; 1998 v Bl, Fi, D, Ei, Ni, I; 1999 v Li, Es, Bel (1+sub); 2000 v Li, F; 2001 v La (sub), Cro, Bel; 2002 v Cro, Bel (21)
Elliot, B. (Celtic), 1998 v Ni; 1999 v Li (sub) (2)
Esson, R. (Aberdeen), 2000 v Li, Ni; 2001 v La, Cro, Bel, Pol; 2002 v Bel (7)

Ferguson, B. (Rangers), 1997 v Col (sub), US, CzR, P; 1998 v Bl, La, Fi, D (sub), Ei, Ni, I; 1999 v Bel (12)
Ferguson, D. (Rangers), 1987 v WG, Ei, Bel; 1988 v E; 1990 v Y (5)
Ferguson, D. (Dundee U), 1992 v D, G, Se (2); 1993 v Sw, I, Ma (7)
Ferguson, D. (Manchester U), 1992 v US, P (sub), Y; 1993 v Sw, Ma (5)
Ferguson, I. (Dundee), 1983 v EG (sub), Sw (sub); 1984 v Bel (sub), EG (4)
Ferguson, I. (Clyde), 1987 v WG (sub), Ei; (with St Mirren), Ei, Bel; 1988 v Bel; (with Rangers), E (sub) (6)
Ferguson, R. (Hamilton A), 1977 v E (1)
Findlay, W. (Hibernian), 1991 v R, Pol, Bul (2), Pol (5)
Fitzpatrick, A. (St Mirren), 1977 v W (sub), Sw (sub), E; 1978 v Sw, Cz (5)
Flannigan, C. (Clydebank), 1993 v Ic (sub) (1)
Fleck, R. (Rangers), 1987 v WG (sub), Ei, Bel; (with Norwich C), 1988 v E (2); 1989 v Y (6)
Fletcher, D. B. (Manchester U), 2003 v Ic (sub); 2004 v G (sub) (2)
Fotheringham, M. M. (Dundee), 2004 v R, D (sub), Ei (sub) (3)
Fowler, J. (Kilmarnock), 2002 v Cro (sub), Bel, La (3)
Foy, R. A. (Liverpool), 2004 v H, R (sub), D (3)
Fraser, S. T. (Luton T), 2000 v Ni (sub), W; 2001 v La, Cro (4)
Freedman, D. A. (Barnet), 1995 v Ru (sub + 1), Sm, M, F, Sk, Br; (with C Palace) 1996 v Sm (sub) (8)
Fridge, L. (St Mirren), 1989 v F; 1990 v Y (2)
Fullarton, J. (St. Mirren), 1993 v F, Bul; 1994 v Ma, A, Eg, P, Bel; 1995 v M, F, Sk, Br; 1996 v Gr, Fi, H (sub + 1), Sp (sub), F (17)
Fulton, M. (St Mirren), 1980 v Bel, WG, E; 1981 v Se, D (sub) (5)
Fulton, S. (Celtic), 1991 v R, Sw, Bul, Pol, F; 1992 v G (2) (7)

Gallacher, K. (Dundee U), 1987 v WG, Ei (2), Bel (sub); 1988 v E (2); 1990 v Y (7)
Gallacher, P. (Dundee U), 1999 v Ei, Ni, CzR; 2000 v Bos, Es, Bos, F (7)
Gallagher, P. (Blackburn R), 2003 v G (sub); 2004 v N (sub), Li (sub), D (4)
Galloway, M. (Hearts), 1989 v F; (with Celtic), 1990 v N (2)
Gardiner, J. (Hibernian), 1993 v F (1)
Geddes, R. (Dundee), 1982 v Se, D, E (2); 1988 v E (5)
Gemmill, S. (Nottingham F), 1992 v Sw, R (sub), G (sub), Se (sub) (4)
Germaine, G. (WBA), 1997 v Se (1)
Gilles, R. (St Mirren), 1997 v A (1 + sub), La, Es (2), Se, Bl (7)
Gillespie, G. (Coventry C), 1979 v US; 1980 v E; 1981 v D; 1982 v Se, D, I (2), E (8)
Glass, S. (Aberdeen), 1995 v M, F, Sk, Br; 1996 v Gr, Fi, H, Sp; 1997 v A (2), Es (11)
Glover, L. (Nottingham F), 1988 v Bel (sub); 1989 v N; 1990 v Y (3)
Goram, A. (Oldham Ath), 1987 v Ei (1)
Gordon, C. (Hearts), 2003 v Is (sub), Gh; 2004 v N (sub), Cro (2) (5)
Gough, C. R. (Dundee U), 1983 v EG, Sw, Bel; 1984 v Y (2) (5)
Graham, D. (Rangers), 1998 v Bl (sub), La (sub), Fi (sub), D, Ei (sub), Ni, I; 1999 v Li (8)
Grant, P. (Celtic), 1985 v WG, Ic, Sp; 1987 v WG, Ei (2), Bel; 1988 v Bel, E (2) (10)
Gray S. (Celtic), 1995 v F, Sk, Br; 1996 v Gr, H, Sp, F (7)
Gray, S. (Aberdeen), 1987 v WG (1)
Gunn, B. (Aberdeen), 1984 v EG, Y (2); 1985 v WG, Ic, Sp (2), Ic; 1990 v F (9)

Hagen, D. (Rangers), 1992 v D (sub), US (sub), P, Y; 1993 v Sw (sub), P, Ic, P (8)
Hammell, S. (Motherwell), 2001 v Pol (sub); 2002 v La; 2003 v Is, Ni, Gh, Bel (sub), Ei; 2004 v N, Li, Cro (2) (11)

Hamilton, B. (St Mirren), 1989 v Y, F (sub); 1990 v F, N (4)
Hamilton, J. (Dundee) 1995 v Sm (sub), Br; 1996 v Fi (sub), Sm, H (sub), Sp (sub), F; 1997 v A, La, Es, Se; (with Hearts), Es, A, Se (14)
Handyside, P. (Grimsby T), 1993 v Ic (sub), Bul, M, E; 1995 v Ru; 1996 v Fi, Sm (7)
Hannah, D. (Dundee U), 1993 v F (sub), Bul, M; 1994 v A, Eg, P, Bel; 1995 v Fi, Ru (sub), Gr, Ru, M, F, Sk, Br; 1996 v Gr (16)
Harper, K. (Hibernian), 1995 v Ru (sub); 1996 v Fi; 1997 v A (2), La, Es, Se (7)
Hartford, R. A. (Manchester C), 1977 v Sw (1)
Hartley, P. (Millwall), 1997 v A (sub) (1)
Hegarty, P. (Dundee U), 1987 v WG, Bel; 1988 v E (2); 1990 v F, N (6)
Hendry, J. (Tottenham H), 1992 v D (sub) (1)
Hetherston, B. (St Mirren), 1997 v Es (sub) (1)
Hewitt, J. (Aberdeen), 1982 v I; 1983 v EG, Sw (2); 1984 v Bel, Y (sub) (6)
Hogg, G. (Manchester U), 1984 v Y; 1985 v WG, Ic, Sp (4)
Hood, G. (Ayr U), 1993 v F, E (sub); 1994 v A (3)
Horn, R. (Hearts), 1997 v US, CzR, P; 1998 v Bl, La, D (sub) (6)
Howie, S. (Cowdenbeath), 1993 v Ma, Ic, P; 1994 v Sw, I (5)
Hughes, R. D. (Bournemouth), 1999 v CzR, Ei, Ni, CzR; 2000 v Bos, Es; 2001 v La, Cro, Bel (9)
Hughes, S. (Rangers), 2002 v La; 2003 v D, Ic, Gh, Be, Ei (sub), Ic (sub), A; 2004 v N (sub), Li (sub), Cro (sub+sub) (12)
Hunter, G. (Hibernian), 1987 v Ei (sub); 1988 v Bel, E (3)
Hunter, P. (East Fife), 1989 v N (sub), F (sub); 1990 v F (sub) (3)
Hutton, A, (Rangers), 2004 v R, D (2)

James, K. F. (Falkirk), 1997 v Bl (1)
Jardine, I. (Kilmarnock), 1979 v US (1)
Jess, E. (Aberdeen), 1990 v F (sub), N (sub); 1991 v R, Sw, Bul (2), Pol, F; 1992 v Sw, R, G (2), Se (1 + 1 sub) (14)
Johnson, G. I. (Dundee U), 1992 v US, P, Y; 1993 v Sw, P, Ma (6)
Johnston, A. (Hearts), 1994 v Bel; 1995 v Ru, 1996 v Sp (3)
Johnston, F. (Falkirk), 1993 v Ic (1)
Johnston, M. (Partick Th), 1984 v EG (sub); (with Watford), Y (2) (3)
Jordan, A. J. (Bristol C), 2000 v Bos (sub), Li, F (3)
Jupp, D. A. (Fulham), 1995 v Fi, Ru (2), Sm, M, F, Sk, Br; 1997 v Se (9)

Kirkwood, D. (Hearts), 1990 v Y (1)
Kennedy, J. (Celtic), 2003 v Is (sub), Ni, Ic, Gh, Bel, Ei, Ic, Li, A, G; 2004 v N (sub), Li, Cro (2), H (15)
Kerr, B. (Newcastle U), 2003 v D, Is, Ni, Ic, Gh, Bel, Ei, Ic, Li, A, G; 2004 v Li, Cro (2) (14)
Kerr, M. (Kilmarnock), 2001 v Pol (sub) (1)
Kerr, S. (Celtic), 1993 v Bul, M, E; 1994 v Ma, A, Eg, P, Bel; 1995 v Fi, Gr (10)
Kinniburgh, W. D. (Motherwell), 2004 v R (sub) (1)
Kyle, K. (Sunderland), 2001 v La (sub), Cro (sub), Pol (sub); 2003 v Ic, Ei, Ic, Li, G; 2004 v N. G, Cro (2) (12)

Lambert, P. (St Mirren), 1991 v R, Sw, Bul (2), Pol, F; 1992 v Sw, R, G (2), Se (11)
Langfield, J. (Dundee), 2000 v W; 2002 v Cro (2)
Lappin, S. (St Mirren), 2004 v H, R, D, Ei (4)
Lauchlan, J. (Kilmarnock), 1998 v Ei, Ni, I; 1999 v CzR, G, Ni, CzR; 2000 v Bos, Es, Bos, Li (11)
Lavety, B. (St. Mirren), 1993 v Ic, Bul (sub), M (sub), E; 1994 v Ma, A (sub), Eg (sub), Bel (sub); 1995 v Fi (sub) (9)
Lavin, G. (Watford), 1993 v F, Bul, M; 1994 v Ma, Eg, P, Bel (7)
Lawson, P. (Celtic), 2004 v H, R, Ei (3)
Leighton, J. (Aberdeen), 1982 v I (1)
Levein, C. (Hearts), 1985 v Sp, Ic (2)
Liddell, A. M. (Barnsley), 1994 v Ma (sub); 1995 v Sm (sub), M (sub), F, Sk; 1996 v Gr, Fi, Sm, H (2), Sp, F (sub) (12)
Lindsey, J. (Motherwell), 1979 v US (1)
Locke, G. (Hearts), 1994 v Ma, A, Eg, P; 1995 v Fi; 1996 v Fi, H; 1997 v Es, A, Bl (10)
Love, G. (Hibernian), 1995 v Ru (1)

Lynch, S. (Celtic), 2003 v Is (sub), Ni (sub), Ic (sub), (
(sub), Bel; (with Preston NE), Ei (sub), Li (sub),
(sub), G; 2004 v N, G, Li, Cro (sub) (13)

McAllister, G. (Leicester C), 1990 v N (1)
McAlpine, H. (Dundee U), 1983 v EG, Sw (2), Bel; 19
v Bel (5)
McAnespie, K. (St Johnstone), 1998 v Fi (sub); 1999 v
(sub); 2000 v Ni, W (4)
McAuley, S. (St. Johnstone), 1993 v P (sub) (1)
McAvennie, F. (St Mirren), 1982 v I, E; 1985 v Is, Ei,
(5)
McBride, J. (Everton), 1981 v D (1)
McBride, J. P. (Celtic), 1998 v Ni (sub), I (sub) (2)
McCall, S. (Bradford C), 1988 v E; (with Everton), 199
F (2)
McCann, N. (Dundee), 1994 v A, Eg, P, Bel; 1995 v
Gr (sub), Sm; 1996 v Fi, Sm (9)
McClair, B. (Celtic), 1984 v Bel (sub), EG, Y (1 + 1 su
1985 v WG, Ic, Sp, Ic (8)
McCluskey, G. (Celtic), 1979 v US, P; 1980 v Bel (
1982 v D, I (6)
McCluskey, S. (St Johnstone), 1997 v Es (2), A, Se, C
US, CzR; 1998 v Bl, La, D, Ei (sub), Ni, I; 1999 v
(14)
McCoist, A. (Rangers), 1984 v Bel (1)
McConnell, I. (Clyde), 1997 v A (sub) (1)
McCracken, D. (Dundee U), 2002 v La; 2004 v N, G, I
Cro (5)
McCulloch, A. (Kilmarnock); 1981 v Se (1)
McCulloch, I. (Notts Co), 1982 v E (2)
McCulloch, L. (Motherwell), 1997 v La (sub), Es (1
sub), Se (sub + 1), A (sub), Col (sub); 1998 v Bl (su
Fi (sub), D, Ei, Ni; 1999 v CzR, G (14)
McCunnie, J. (Dundee U), 2001 v Pol; 2002 v Cro; 2003
D. Is, Ni; (with Ross Co), 2004 v H, R, Ei (8)
MacDonald, J. (Rangers), 1980 v WG (sub); 1981 v S
1982 v Se (sub), L, I (2), E (2 sub) (8)
McDonald, C. (Falkirk), 1995 v Fi (sub), Ru, M (sub),
(sub), Br (sub) (5)
McEwan, C. (Clyde), 1997 v Col, US (sub), CzR (sub),
(with Raith R), 1998 v Bl, La, Fi, D, Ei, Ni, I; 1999 v
Es (sub), Bel (2), CzR, G (sub) (17)
McEwan, D. (Livingston), 2003 v Ni (sub), Gh (sub) (2)
McFadden, J. (Motherwell), 2003 v D (sub), Is, Ni, G
Ei (sub), Ic, Li (7)
McFarlane, D. (Hamilton A), 1997 v Col, US (sub),
(sub) (3)
McGarry, S. (St Mirren), 1997 v US, CzR, P (sub) (3)
McGarvey, F. (St Mirren), 1977 v E; 1978 v Cz; (wi
Celtic), 1982 v D (3)
McGarvey, S. (Manchester U), 1982 v E (sub); 1983
Bel, Sw; 1984 v Bel (4)
McGhee, M. (Aberdeen), 1981 v D (1)
McGinnis, G. (Dundee U), 1985 v Sp (1)
McGregor, A. (Rangers), 2003 v D (sub), Is, Bel (sub),
(sub), A (sub); 2004 v N (6)
McGrillen, P. (Motherwell), 1994 v Sw (sub), I (2)
McGuire, D. (Aberdeen), 2002 v Bel, La (2)
McInally, J. (Dundee U), 1989 v F (1)
McKenzie, R. (Hearts), 1997 v Es, Bl (2)
McKimmie, S. (Aberdeen), 1985 v WG, Ic (2) (3)
McKinlay, T. (Dundee), 1984 v EG (sub); 1985 v WG,
Sp (2), Ic (6)
McKinlay, W. (Dundee U), 1989 v N, Y (sub), F; 1990
Y, F, N (6)
McKinnon, R. (Dundee U), 1991 v R, Pol (sub); 1992 v
(2), Se (2) (6)
McLaren, A, (Hearts), 1989 v F; 1990 v Y, N; 1991 v S
Bul, Po1, F; 1992 v R, G, Se (2) (11)
McLaren, A. (Dundee U), 1993 v I, Ma (sub); 1994 v S
I (sub) (4)
McLaughlin, B. (Celtic), 1995 v Ru, Sm, M, Sk (sub),
(sub); 1996 v Gr (sub), Sm (sub), H (8)
McLaughlin, J. (Morton), 1981 v D; 1982 v Se, D, I, E (
1983 v EG, Sw (2), Bel (10)
McLean, S. (Rangers), 2003 v D (sub), Ni (sub), C
(sub), Bel (sub) (4)
McLeish, A. (Aberdeen), 1978 v W; 1979 v US; 1980
Bel, E (2); 1987 v Ei (6)
MacLeod, A. (Hibernian), 1979 v P, N (2) (3)
McLeod, J. (Dundee U), 1989 v N; 1990 v F (2)
MacLeod, M. (Dumbarton), 1979 v US; (with Celtic),
(sub), N (2); 1980 v Bel (5)

McManus, T. (Hibernian), 2001 v Bel (sub), Pol (sub); 2002 v Cro, Bel, La; 2003 v D (sub), Ni (sub), Ic, Gh, A, G (sub); 2004 v N (sub), Li (sub), Cro (14)
McMillan, S. (Motherwell), 1997 v A (sub + sub), Se, Bl (4)
McNab, N. (Tottenham H), 1978 v W (1)
McNally, M. (Celtic), 1991 v Bul; 1993 v Ic (2)
McNamara, J. (Dunfermline Ath), 1994 v A, Bel; 1995 v Gr, Ru, Sm; 1996 v Gr, Fi; (with Celtic), Sm, H (2), Sp, F (12)
McNaughton, K. (Aberdeen), 2002 v La (sub) (1)
McNichol, J. (Brentford), 1979 v P, N (2); 1980 v Bel (2), WG, E (7)
McNiven, D. (Leeds U), 1977 v Cz, W (sub), Sw (sub) (3)
McNiven, S. A. (Oldham Ath), 1996 v Sm (sub) (1)
McParland, A. (Celtic), 2003 v Gh (sub) (1)
McPhee, S. (Port Vale), 2002 v La (sub) (1)
McPherson, D. (Rangers), 1984 v Bel; 1985 v Sp; (with Hearts), 1989 v N, Y (4)
McQuilken, J. (Celtic), 1993 v Bul, E (2)
McStay, P. (Celtic), 1983 v EG, Sw (2); 1984 v Y (2) (5)
McWhirter, N. (St Mirren), 1991 v Bul (sub) (1)
Main, A. (Dundee U), 1988 v E; 1989 v Y; 1990 v N (3)
Malcolm, R. (Rangers), 2001 v Pol (1)
Maloney, S. (Celtic), 2002 v Cro (sub), Bel (sub), La; 2003 v D, Is, Ni, Bel, Ei, Ic (sub), Li (sub), A; 2004 v G (sub), Li, Cro (1+sub), H (16)
Malpas, M. (Dundee U), 1983 v Bel, Sw (1+1 sub); 1984 v Bel, EG, Y (2); 1985 v Sp (8)
Marshall, D. J. (Celtic), 2004 v H (sub), D (2)
Marshall, S. R. (Arsenal), 1995 v Ru, Gr; 1996 v H, Sp, F (5)
Mason, G. R. (Manchester C), 1999 v Li (sub); (with Dunfermline Ath), 2002 v Bel (2)
Mathieson, D. (Queen of the South), 1997 v Col; 1998 v La; 1999 v G (sub) (3)
May, E. (Hibernian), 1989 v Y (sub), F (2)
Meldrum, C. (Kilmarnock), 1996 v F (sub); 1997 v A (2), La, Es, Se (6)
Melrose, J. (Partick Th), 1977 v Sw; 1979 v US, P, N (2); 1980 v Bel (sub), WG, E (8)
Miller, C. (Rangers), 1995 v Gr, Ru; 1996 v Gr, Sp, F; 1997 v A, La, Es (8)
Miller, J. (Aberdeen), 1987 v Ei (sub); 1988 v Bel; (with Celtic), E; 1989 v N, Y; 1990 v F, N (7)
Miller, K. (Hibernian), 2000 v F, Ni, W; (with Rangers), 2001 v Cro, Bel; 2002 v Cro, Bel (7)
Miller, W. (Aberdeen), 1978 v Sw, Cz (2)
Miller, W. (Hibernian), 1991 v R, Sw, Bul, Pol, F; 1992 v R, G (sub) (7)
Milne, K. (Hearts), 2000 v F (1)
Milne, R. (Dundee U), 1982 v Se (sub); 1984 v Bel, EG (3)
Money, I. C. (St Mirren), 1987 v Ei; 1988 v Bel; 1989 v N (3)
Montgomery, N. A. (Sheffield U), 2003 v A (sub); 2004 v Cro (sub) (2)
Morrison, S. A. (Aberdeen), 2004 v H (sub), D (sub), Ei (3)
Muir, L. (Hibernian), 1977 v Cz (sub) (1)
Murray, H. (St Mirren), 2000 v F (sub), Ni (sub), W (sub) (3)
Murray, I. (Hibernian), 2001 v Bel (sub), Pol; 2002 v Cro, Bel, La; 2003 v D, Ic, Gh, Bel, Ic, Li, G; 2004 v G, Cro (2) (15)
Murray, N. (Rangers), 1993 v P (sub), Ma, Ic, P; 1994 v Sw, I; 1995 v Fi, Ru, Gr, Sm; 1996 v Gr (sub), Fi, Sm, H (2), F (16)
Murray, R. (Bournemouth), 1993 v Ic (sub) (1)
Murray, S. (Kilmarnock), 2004 v D (sub), Ei (sub) (2)

Narey, D. (Dundee U), 1977 v Cz, Sw; 1978 v Sw, Cz (4)
Naysmith, G. (Hearts), 1997 v La, Es (1 + sub), Se, A, Col, US, CzR, P; 1998 v La, D; 1999 v Es, Bel (2), CzR, G, Ei, CzR; 2000 v Bos, Es, Bos, Li (22)
Neilson, R. (Hearts), 2000 v Ni (1)
Nevin, P. (Chelsea), 1985 v WG, Ic, Sp (2), Ic (5)
Nicholas, C. (Celtic), 1981 v Se; 1982 v Se; 1983 v EG, Sw, Bel; (with Arsenal), 1984 v Y (6)
Nicholson, B. (Rangers), 1999 v G, Ni, CzR (sub); 2000 v Bos (sub), Es, Bos, Li (7)
Nicol, S. (Ayr U), 1981 v Se; 1982 v Se, D; (with Liverpool), I (2), E (2); 1983 v EG, Sw (2), Bel; 1984 v Bel, EG, Y (14)
Nisbet, S. (Rangers), 1989 v N, Y, F; 1990 v Y, F (5)
Noble, D. J. (West Ham U), 2003 v A (sub); 2004 v N (sub) (2)
Notman, A. M. (Manchester U), 1999 v Li (sub), Es, Bel (sub+sub); 2000 v Li, F (sub), Ni, W; 2001 v La, Cro (10)

O'Brien, B. (Blackburn R), 1999 v Ei (sub), Ni (sub), CzR (sub); 2000 v Bos (sub); (with Livingston), 2003 v Is (sub), Gh (sub) (6)
O'Connor, G. (Hibernian), 2003 v D; 2004 v Cro, H, R (4)
O'Donnell, P. (Motherwell), 1992 v Sw (sub), R, D, G (2), Se (1 + 1 sub); 1993 v P (8)
O'Neil, B. (Celtic), 1992 v D, G, Se (2); 1993 v Sw, P, I (7)
O'Neil, J. (Dundee U), 1991 v Bul (sub) (1)
O'Neill, M. (Clyde), 1995 v Ru (sub), F, Sk, Br; 1997 v Se (sub), Bl (sub) (6)
Orr, N. (Morton), 1978 v W (sub); 1979 v US, P, N (2); 1980 v Bel, E (7)

Parker, K. (St Johnstone), 2001 v Pol (sub) (1)
Parlane, D. (Rangers), 1977 v W (1)
Paterson, C. (Hibernian), 1981 v Se; 1982 v I (2)
Paterson, J. (Dundee U), 1997 v Col, US, CzR; 1999 v Bel (sub+sub); 2000 v Es, Bos, Li; 2002 v Cro (sub) (9)
Payne, G. (Dundee U), 1978 v Sw, Cz, W (3)
Peacock, L. A. (Carlisle U), 1997 v Bl (1)
Pearson, S. (Motherwell), 2003 v Is, Ni, Bel (sub), Ei, A, G; 2004 v N, G (8)
Pressley, S. (Rangers), 1993 v Ic, F, Bul, M, E; 1994 v Sw, I, M, A, Eg, P, Bel; 1995 v Fi; (with Coventry C), Ru (2), Sm, M, F, Sk, Br; (with Dundee U), 1996 v Gr, Sm, H (2), Sp, F (26)
Provan, D. (Kilmarnock), 1977 v Cz (sub) (1)
Prunty, B. (Aberdeen), 2004 v H, R (sub), Ei (3)

Quinn, P. C. (Motherwell), 2004 v D (1)

Rae, A. (Millwall), 1991 v Bul (sub + 1), F (sub); 1992 v Sw, R, G (sub), Se (2) (8)
Rae, G. (Dundee), 1999 v Ei (sub), Ni, CzR; 2000 v Bos, Es, Bos (6)
Redford, I. (Rangers), 1981 v Se (sub); 1982 v Se, D, I (2), E (6)
Reid, B. (Rangers), 1991 v F; 1992 v D, US, P (4)
Reid, C. (Hibernian), 1993 v Sw, P, I (3)
Reid, M. (Celtic), 1982 v E; 1984 v Y (2)
Reid, R. (St Mirren), 1977 v W, Sw, E (3)
Reilly, A. (Wycombe W), 2004 v H (sub) (1)
Renicks, S. (Hamilton A), 1997 v Bl (1)
Rice, B. (Hibernian), 1985 v WG (1)
Richardson, L. (St Mirren), 1980 v WG, E (sub) (2)
Riordan, D. G. (Hibernian), 2004 v R (1)
Ritchie, A. (Morton), 1980 v Bel (1)
Ritchie, P. R. (Hearts), 1996 v H; 1997 v A (2), La, Es (2), Se (7)
Robertson, A. (Rangers) 1991 v F (1)
Robertson, C. (Rangers), 1977 v E (sub) (1)
Robertson, D. (Aberdeen), 1987 v Ei (sub); 1988 v E (2); 1989 v N, Y; 1990 v Y, N (7)
Robertson, G. A. (Nottingham F), 2004 v Ei (1)
Robertson, H. (Aberdeen), 1994 v Eg; 1995 v Fi (2)
Robertson, J. (Hearts), 1985 v WG, Ic (sub) (2)
Robertson, L. (Rangers), 1993 v F, M (sub), E (sub) (3)
Robertson, S. (St Johnstone), 1998 v Fi, Ni (2)
Roddie, A. (Aberdeen), 1992 v US, P; 1993 v Sw (sub), P, Ic (5)
Ross, T. W. (Arsenal), 1977 v W (1)
Rowson, D. (Aberdeen), 1997 v La, Es, Se (2), Bl (5)
Russell, R. (Rangers), 1978 v W; 1980 v Bel; 1984 v Y (3)

Salton, D. B. (Luton T), 1992 v D, US, P, Y; 1993 v Sw, I (6)
Samson, C. I. (Kilmarnock), 2004 v R, Ei (2)
Scott, P. (St Johnstone), 1994 v A (sub), Eg (sub), P, Bel (4)
Scrimgour, D. (St Mirren), 1997 v US, CzR; 1998 v D (3)
Seaton, A. (Falkirk), 1998 v Bl (sub) (1)
Severin, S. D. (Hearts), 2000 v Es, Bos, Li (sub), F, Ni, W; 2001 v La, Bel; 2002 v Cro, Bel (10)
Shannon, R. (Dundee), 1987 v WG, Ei (2), Bel; 1988 v Bel, E (2) (7)
Sharp, G. (Everton), 1982 v E (1)
Sharp, R. (Dunfermline Ath), 1990 v N (sub); 1991 v R, Sw, Bul (4)

Sheerin, P. (Southampton), 1996 v Sm (1)
Shields, G. (Rangers), 1997 v A, La (2)
Simmons, S. (Hearts), 2003 v Gh (sub) (1)
Simpson, N. (Aberdeen), 1982 v I (2), E; 1983 v EG, Sw (2), Bel; 1984 v Bel, EG, Y; 1985 v Sp (11)
Sinclair, G. (Dumbarton), 1977 v E (1)
Skilling, M. (Kilmarnock), 1993 v Ic (sub); 1994 v I (2)
Smith, B. M. (Celtic), 1992 v G (2), US, P, Y (5)
Smith, G. (Rangers), 1978 v W (1)
Smith, G> (Rangers), 2004 v H, D (sub), Ei (sub) (3)
Smith, H. G. (Hearts), 1987 v WG, Bel (2)
Sneddon, A. (Celtic), 1979 v US (1)
Soutar, D. (Dundee), 2003 v D, Ni, Ic, Bel, Ei, Ic, Li, A, G; 2004 v G, Li (11)
Speedie, D. (Chelsea), 1985 v Sp (1)
Spencer, J. (Rangers), 1991 v Sw (sub), F; 1992 v Sw (3)
Stanton, P. (Hibernian), 1977 v Cz (1)
Stark, W. (Aberdeen), 1985 v Ic (1)
Stephen, R. (Dundee), 1983 v Bel (sub) (1)
Stevens, G. (Motherwell), 1977 v E (1)
Stewart, C. (Kilmarnock), 2002 v La (1)
Stewart, J. (Kilmarnock), 1978 v Sw, Cz; (with Middlesbrough), 1979 v P (3)
Stewart, M. J. (Manchester U), 2000 v Ni; 2001 v La, Cro, Bel, Pol; 2002 v La; 2003 v D, Is, Ni, Ei (sub), Ic, Li, A; 2004 v N, G, Li, Cro (17)
Stewart, R. (Dundee U), 1979 v P, N (2); (with West Ham U), 1980 v Bel (2), E (2), WG; 1981 v D; 1982 v I (2), E (12)
Stillie, D. (Aberdeen), 1995 v Ru (2), Sm, M, F, Sk, Br; 1996 v Gr, Fi, Sm, H (2), Sp, F (14)
Strachan, G. D. (Aberdeen), 1980 v Bel (1)
Strachan, G. D. (Coventry C), 1998 v D, Ei; 1999 v Li, Es, Bel (2); 2000 v Li (7)
Sturrock, P. (Dundee U), 1977 v Cz, W, Sw, E; 1978 v Sw, Cz; 1982 v Se, I, E (9)
Sweeney, P. H. (Millwall), 2004 v H (sub), D, Ei (sub) (3)
Sweeney, S. (Clydebank), 1991 v R, Sw (sub), Bul (2), Pol; 1992 v Sw, R (7)

Tarrant, N. K. (Aston Villa), 1999 v Ni (sub); 2000 v Es (sub), Bos (sub), Li, Ni (sub) (5)
Teale, G. (Clydebank), 1997 v La (sub), Es, Bl; (with Ayr U), 1999 v CzR (sub), G (sub), Ei (sub) (6)
Telfer, P. (Luton T), 1993 v Ma, P; 1994 v Sw (3)
Thomas, K. (Hearts), 1993 v F (sub), Bul, M, E; 1994 v Sw, Ma; 1995 v Gr; 1997 v A (8)
Thompson, S. (Dundee U), 1997 v US, CzR, P; 1998 v Bl, La; 1999 v G (sub), Ei, Ni, CzR; 2000 v Bos, Es, Bos (12)
Thomson, W. (Partick Th), 1977 v E (sub); 1978 v W; (with St Mirren), 1979 v US, N (2); 1980 v Bel (2), E (2), WG (10)
Tolmie, J. (Morton), 1980 v Bel (sub) (1)
Tortolano, J. (Hibernian), 1987 v WG, Ei (2)
Tweed, S. (Hibernian), 1993 v Ic; 1994 v Sw, I (3)

Wales, G. (Hearts), 2000 v F (1)
Walker, A. (Celtic), 1988 v Bel (1)
Wallace, I. (Coventry C), 1978 v Sw (1)
Wallace, R. (Celtic), 2004 v H (sub) (1)
Walsh, C. (Nottingham F), 1984 v EG, Sw (2), Bel; 1984 v EG (5)
Wark, J. (Ipswich T), 1977 v Cz, W, Sw; 1978 v W; 1979 v P; 1980 v E (2), WG (8)
Watson, A. (Aberdeen), 1981 v Se, D; 1982 v D, I (sub) (4)
Watson, K. (Rangers), 1977 v E; 1978 v Sw (sub) (2)
Watt, M. (Aberdeen), 1991 v R, Sw, Bul (2), Pol, F; 1992 v Sw, R, G (2), Se (2) (12)
Webster, A. (Hearts), 2003 v Ic, Li (2)
Whiteford, A. (St Johnstone), 1997 v US (1)
Whyte, D. (Celtic), 1987 v Ei (2), Bel; 1988 v E (2); 1989 v N, Y; 1990 v Y, N (9)
Wilkie, L. (Dundee), 2000 v Bos, F, Ni, W; 2001 v La, Cro (6)
Will, J. A. (Arsenal), 1992 v D (sub), Y; 1993 v Ic (sub) (3)
Williams, G. (Nottingham F), 2002 v Bel (sub); 2003 v Ic, Ei, Ic, Li; 2004 v N, G, Li, Cro (9)
Wilson, M. (Dundee U), 2004 v H, R, D, Ei (4)
Wilson, S. (Rangers), 1999 v Es, Bel (2), G, Ei, CzR; 2000 v Bos (7)
Wilson, T. (St Mirren), 1983 v Sw (sub) (1)
Wilson, T. (Nottingham F), 1988 v E; 1989 v N, Y; 1990 v F (4)
Winnie, D. (St Mirren), 1988 v Bel (1)
Wright, P. (Aberdeen), 1989 v Y, F; (with QPR), 1990 v Y (sub) (3)
Wright, S. (Aberdeen), 1991 v Bul, Pol, F; 1992 v Sw, G (2), Se (2); 1993 v Sw, P, I, Ma; 1994 v I, Ma (14)
Wright, T. (Oldham Ath), 1987 v Bel (sub) (1)

Young, Darren (Aberdeen), 1997 v Es (sub), Se, Col, CzR (sub), P; 1998 v La (sub); 1999 v CzR (sub), G (sub) (8)
Young, Derek (Aberdeen), 2000 v W; 2001 v Cro (sub), Bel (sub), Pol; 2002 v Cro (5)

## WALES

Aizlewood, M. (Luton T), 1979 v E; 1981 v Ho (2)

Baddeley, L. M. (Cardiff C), 1996 v Mol (sub), G (sub) (2)
Balcombe, S. (Leeds U), 1982 v F (sub) (1)
Barnhouse, D. J. (Swansea), 1995 v Mol; 1996 v Mol, Sm (3)
Bater, P. T. (Bristol R), 1977 v E, S (2)
Bellamy, C. D. (Norwich C), 1996 v Sm (sub); 1997 v Sm, T, Bel; 1998 v T, Bel, I; 1999 v I (8)
Birchall, A. S. (Arsenal), 2003 v Fi, I, Az (3)
Bird, A. (Cardiff C), 1993 v Cy (sub); 1994 v Cy (sub); 1995 v Mol, Ge (sub), Bul; 1996 v G (sub) (6)
Blackmore, C. (Manchester U), 1984 v N, Bul, Y (3)
Blake, N. (Cardiff C), 1991 v Pol (sub); 1993 v Cy, Bel, RCS; 1994 v RCS (5)
Blaney, S. D. (West Ham U), 1997 v Sm, Ho, T (3)
Bodin, P. (Cardiff C), 1983 v Y (1)
Bowen, J. P. (Swansea C), 1993 v Cy, Bel (2); 1994 v RCS, R (sub) (5)
Bowen, M. (Tottenham H), 1983 v N; 1984 v Bul, Y (3)
Boyle, T. (C Palace), 1982 v F (1)
Brace, D. P. (Wrexham), 1995 v Ge, Bul (2); 1997 v Sm Ho; 1998 v T (6)
Brough, M. (Notts Co), 2003 v As (sub); 2004 v I, Fi (3)
Brown, J. R. (Gillingham), 2003 v Fi, I, Az; 2004 v Ser, I, Fi, Ser (7)
Byrne, M. T. (Bolton W), 2003 v Az (sub) (1)

Cegielski, W. (Wrexham), 1977 v E (sub), S (2)
Chapple, S. R. (Swansea C), 1992 v R; 1993 v Cy, Bel (2), RCS; 1994 v RCS; Bul (2) (8)
Charles, J. M. (Swansea C), 1979 v E; 1981 v Ho (2)
Clark, J. (Manchester U), 1978 v S; (with Derby Co), 1979 v E (2)
Coates, J. S. (Swansea C), 1996 v Mol, G; 1997 v Ho, T (sub); 1998 v T (sub) (5)
Coleman, C. (Swansea C), 1990 v Pol; 1991 v E, Pol (3)
Collins, J. M. (Cardiff C), 2003 v I (sub), Az (sub+1); 2004 v Ser, I, Fi (sub), Ser (7)
Coyne, D. (Tranmere R), 1992 v R; 1994 v Cy (sub), R; 1995 v Mol, Ge, Bul (2) (7)
Crowell, M. T. (Wrexham), 2004 v Ser (sub) (1)
Curtis, A. T. (Swansea C), 1977 v E (1)

Davies, A. (Manchester U), 1982 v F (2), Ho; 1983 v N, Y, Bul (6)
Davies, D. (Barry T), 1999 v D (sub) (1)
Davies, G. M. (Hereford U), 1993 v Bel, RCS; 1995 v Mol (sub), Ge, Bul (2); (with C Palace), 1996 v Mol (7)
Davies, I. C. (Norwich C), 1978 v S (sub) (1)
Davies, S. (Peterborough U), 1999 v D, Bl, Sw, I, D; (with Tottenham H), 2000 v S; 2001 v Bl, N, Pol, Arm (10)
Day, R. (Manchester C), 2000 v S (sub), Ni; 2001 v Uk, Pol, Uk; 2002 v Arm, N, Bl; 2003 v Fi, I, Az; (with Mansfield T), Az; 2004 v Ser (11)
Deacy, N. (PSV Eindhoven), 1977 v S (1)
De-Vulgt, L. S. (Swansea C), 2002 v Arm (sub), Bl (2)
Dibble, A. (Cardiff C), 1983 v Bul; 1984 v N, Bul (3)

Doyle, S. C. (Preston NE), 1979 v E (sub); (with Huddersfield T), 1984 v N (2)
Dwyer, P. J. (Cardiff C), 1979 v E (1)

Earnshaw, R. (Cardiff C), 1999 v P (sub), I, D; 2000 v S, Ni; 2001 v Bl (sub), N, Pol (2), Uk (10)
Ebdon, M. (Everton), 1990 v Pol; 1991 v E (2)
Edwards, C. N. H. (Swansea C), 1996 v G; 1997 v Sm, Ho (2), T, Bel; 1998 v T (7)
Edwards, R. I. (Chester), 1977 v S; 1978 v W (2)
Edwards, R. W. (Bristol C), 1991 v Pol; 1992 v R; 1993 v Cy, Bel (2), RCS; 1994 v RCS, Cy, R; 1995 v Ge, Bul; 1996 v Mol, G (13)
Evans, A. (Bristol R), 1977 v E (1)
Evans, K. (Leeds U), 1999 v I (sub), D; (with Cardiff C), 2001 v N (sub), Pol (sub) (4)
Evans, P. S. (Shrewsbury T), 1996 v G (1)
Evans, S. J. (C Palace), 2001 v Bl, Arm (2)
Evans, T. (Cardiff C), 1995 v Bul (sub); 1996 v Mol, G (3)

Folland, R. W. (Oxford U), 2000 v Ni (sub) (1)
Foster, M. G. (Tranmere R), 1993 v RCS (1)
Fowler, L. A. (Coventry C), 2003 v I; 2004 v Ser, I, Fi (4)
Freestone, R. (Chelsea), 1990 v Pol (1)

Gabbidon, D. L. (WBA), 1999 v D, P, Sw, I (sub), D; 2000 v Bl, Sw, S, Ni; (with Cardiff C), 2001 v N, Pol, Arm, Uk, Pol, Uk; 2002 v Arm, N (17)
Gale, D. (Swansea C), 1983 v Bul; 1984 v N (sub) (2)
Gall, K. A. (Bristol R), 2002 v N (sub), Bl (sub); 2003 v Fi (sub), Az; (with Yeovil T), 2004 v Ser, I, Fi, Ser (8)
Gibson, N. D. (Tranmere R), 1999 v D (sub), Bl (sub), P; 2000 v S (sub), Ni; (with Sheffield W), 2001 v Uk, Pol, Uk; 2002 v Arm, N, Bl (11)
Giggs, R. (Manchester U), 1991 v Pol (1)
Giles, D. C. (Cardiff C), 1977 v S; 1978 v S; (with Swansea C), 1981 v Ho; (with C Palace), 1983 v Y (4)
Giles, P. (Cardiff C), 1982 v F (2), Ho (3)
Graham, D. (Manchester U), 1991 v E (1)
Green, R. M. (Wolverhampton W), 1998 v I; 1999 v I, D, Bl, Sw, I, D; 2000 v Bl, S, Ni; 2001 v Bl, N, Pol, Arm, Uk, Pol (16)
Griffith, C. (Cardiff C), 1990 v Pol (1)
Griffiths, C. (Shrewsbury T), 1991 v Pol (sub) (1)

Hall, G. D. (Chelsea), 1990 v Pol (1)
Hartson, J. (Luton T), 1994 v Cy, R; 1995 v Mol, Ge, Bul; (with Arsenal), 1996 v G, Sm; 1997 v Sm, Ho (9)
Haworth, S. O. (Cardiff C), 1997 v Ho, T, Bel; (with Coventry C), 1998 v T, Bel; I; 1999 v I, D; (with Wigan Ath), Bl, Sw; 2000 v Bl, Sw (12)
Hillier, I. M. (Tottenham H), 2001 v Uk (sub), Pol (sub), Uk; (with Luton T), 2002 v Arm, N (5)
Hodges, G. (Wimbledon), 1983 v Y (sub), Bul (sub); 1984 v N, Bul, Y (5)
Holden, A. (Chester C), 1984 v Y (sub) (1)
Holloway, C. D. (Exeter C), 1999 v P, D (2)
Hopkins, J. (Fulham), 1982 v F (sub), Ho; 1983 v N, Y, Bul (5)
Hopkins, S. A. (Wrexham), 1999 v P (sub) (1)
Huggins, D. S. (Bristol C), 1996 v Sm (1)
Hughes, D. R. (Southampton), 1994 v R (1)
Hughes, R. D. (Aston Villa), 1996 v Sm; 1997 v Sm (sub), Ho (2), T, Bel; 1998 v T, Bel, I; 1999 v I, Sw, I; (with Shrewsbury T), 2000 v Sw (13)
Hughes, I. (Bury), 1992 v R; 1993 v Cy, Bel (sub), RCS; 1994 v Cy, R; 1995 v Mol, Ge, Bul; 1996 v Mol (sub), G (11)
Hughes, L. M. (Manchester U), 1983 v N, Y; 1984 v N, Bul, Y (5)
Hughes, W. (WBA), 1977 v E, S; 1978 v S (3)

Jackett, K. (Watford), 1981 v Ho; 1982 v F (2)
James, R. M. (Swansea C), 1977 v E, S; 1978 v S (3)
Jarman, L. (Cardiff C), 1996 v Sm; 1997 v Sm, Ho (2), Bel; 1998 v T, Bel; 1999 v I, P; 2000 v Bl (10)
Jeanne, L. C. (QPR), 1999 v P (sub), Sw, I; 2000 v Bl, Sw, S, Ni; 2001 v Bl (8)
Jelleyman, G. A. (Peterborough U), 1999 v D (sub) (1)
Jenkins, L. D. (Swansea C), 1998 v T (sub); 2000 v Bl, Sw, S, Ni; 2001 v N, Pol, Arm, Uk (9)
Jenkins, S. R. (Swansea C), 1993 v Cy (sub), Bel (2)
Jones, E. P. (Blackpool), 2000 v Ni (sub) (1)
Jones, F. (Wrexham), 1981 v Ho (1)
Jones, J. A. (Swansea C); 2001 v Pol, Uk; 2002 v N (sub) (3)
Jones, L. (Cardiff C), 1982 v F (2), Ho (3)
Jones, M. A. (Wrexham), 2004 v Ser (1)
Jones, M. G. (Leeds U), 1998 v Bel; 1999 v I, D, Bl, Sw, I; 2000 v Sw (7)
Jones, P. L. (Liverpool), 1992 v R; 1993 v Cy, Bel (2), RCS; 1994 v RCS (sub), Cy, R; 1995 v Mol, Ge; 1996 v Mol, G (12)
Jones, R. (Sheffield W), 1994 v R; 1995 v Bul (2) (3)
Jones, V. (Bristol R), 1979 v E; 1981 v Ho (2)

Kendall, L. M. (C Palace), 2001 v N, Pol (2)
Kendall, M. (Tottenham H), 1978 v S (1)
Kenworthy, J. R. (Tranmere R), 1994 v Cy; 1995 v Mol, Bul (3)
Knott, G. R. (Tottenham H), 1996 v Sm (1)

Law, B. J. (QPR), 1990 v Pol; 1991 v E (2)
Letheran, G. (Leeds U), 1977 v E, S (2)
Lewis, D. (Swansea C), 1982 v F (2), Ho; 1983 v N, Y, Bul; 1984 v N, Bu1, Y (9)
Lewis, J. (Cardiff C), 1983 v N (1)
Llewellyn, C. M. (Norwich C), 1998 v T (sub), Bel (sub), I; 1999 v I, D, Bl, I; 2000 v Bl, Sw, S; 2001 v N, Pol, Arm, Uk (14)
Loveridge, J. (Swansea C), 1982 v Ho; 1983 v N, Bul (3)
Low, J. D. (Bristol R), 1999 v P; (with Cardiff C), 2002 v Arm (sub), N (sub), Bl (1)
Lowndes, S. R. (Newport Co), 1979 v E; 1981 v Ho; (with Millwall), 1984 v Bul, Y (4)

McCarthy, A. J. (QPR), 1994 v RCS, Cy, R (3)
Maddy, P. (Cardiff C), 1982 v Ho; 1983 v N (sub) (2)
Margetson, M. W. (Manchester C), 1992 v R; 1993 v Cy, Bel (2), RCS; 1994 v RCS, Cy (7)
Martin, A. P. (C Palace), 1999 v D (1)
Marustik, C. (Swansea C), 1982 v F (2); 1983 v Y, Bul; 1984 v N, Bul, Y (7)
Maxwell, L. J. (Liverpool), 1999 v Sw (sub), I; 2000 v Sw (sub), S, Ni; 2001 v Bl, Pol, Arm, Uk, Pol, Uk; (with Cardiff C), 2002 v Arm, N, Bl (sub) (14)
Meaker, M. J. (QPR), 1994 v RCS (sub), R (sub) (2)
Melville, A. K. (Swansea C), 1990 v Pol; (with Oxford U), 1991 v E (2)
Micallef, C. (Cardiff C), 1982 v F, Ho; 1983 v N (3)
Morgan, A. M. (Tranmere R), 1995 v Mol, Bul; 1996 v Mol, G (4)
Morgan, C. (Wrexham), 2004 v Fi, Ser (sub) (2)
Moss, D. M. (Shrewsbury T), 2003 v Fi, I, Az (2); 2004 v Ser (2) (6)
Mountain, P. D. (Cardiff C), 1997 v Ho, T (2)
Mumford, A. O. (Swansea C), 2003 v Fi, I, Az (2) (4)

Nardiello, D. (Coventry C), 1978 v S (1)
Neilson, A. B. (Newcastle U), 1993 v Cy, Bel (2), RCS; 1994 v RCS, Cy, R (7)
Nicholas, P. (C Palace), 1978 v S; 1979 v E; (with Arsenal), 1982 v F (3)
Nogan, K. (Luton T), 1990 v Pol; 1991 v E (2)
Nogan, L. (Oxford U) 1991 v E (1)

Oster, J. M. (Grimsby T), 1997 v Sm (sub), Ho (sub), T, Bel; (with Everton), 1998 v T, Bel, I; 1999 v I, Sw (9)
Owen, G. (Wrexham), 1991 v E (sub), Pol; 1992 v R; 1993 v Cy, Bel (2); 1994 v Cy, R (8)

Page, R. J. (Watford), 1995 v Mol, Ge, Bul; 1996 v Mol (4)
Partridge, D. W. (West Ham U), 1997 v T (1)
Pascoe, C. (Swansea C), 1983 v Bul (sub); 1984 v N (sub), Bul, Y (4)
Pejic, S. M. (Wrexham), 2003 v Fi, I, Az; 2004 v Ser, I, Fi (6)
Pembridge, M. (Luton T), 1991 v Pol (1)
Perry, J. (Cardiff C), 1990 v Pol; 1991 v E, Pol (3)
Peters, M. (Manchester C), 1992 v R; (with Norwich C), 1993 v Cy, RCS (3)
Phillips, D. (Plymouth Arg), 1984 v N, Bul, Y (3)
Phillips, G. R. (Swansea C), 2001 v Uk (sub); 2002 v Arm (sub), Bl (3)
Phillips, L. (Swansea C), 1979 v E; (with Charlton Ath), 1983 v N (2)
Pipe, D. R. (Coventry C), 2003 v As (2); 2004 v Ser, I, Fi, Ser (6)
Pontin, K. (Cardiff C), 1978 v S (1)
Powell, L. (Southampton), 1991 v Pol (sub); 1992 v R (sub); 1993 v Bel (sub); 1994 v RCS (4)

Powell, L. (Leicester C), 2004 v Ser (sub), I (sub) Fi (3)
Price, J. J. (Swansea C), 1998 v I (sub); 1999 v I (sub), D, Bl, P; 2000 v Bl, Sw (7)
Price, M. D. (Everton), 2001 v Uk. Pol (sub), Uk; (with Hull C), 2002 v Arm, N, Bl; 2003 v Fi, I; (with Scarborough), Az (2); 2004 v Ser, Fi, Ser (13)
Price, P. (Luton T), 1981 v Ho (1)
Pugh, D. (Doncaster R), 1982 v F (2) (2)
Pugh, S. (Wrexham), 1993 v Bel (sub + sub) (2)

Ramasut, M. W. T. (Bristol R), 1997 v Ho, Bel; 1998 v T, I (4)
Ratcliffe, K. (Everton), 1981 v Ho; 1982 v F (2)
Ready, K. (QPR), 1992 v R; 1993 v Bel (2); 1994 v RCS, Cy (5)
Rees, A. (Birmingham C), 1984 v N (1)
Rees, J. (Luton T), 1990 v Pol; 1991 v E, Pol (3)
Rees, M. R. (Millwall), 2003 v Fi (sub), Az; 2004 v Ser, I (4)
Roberts, A. (QPR), 1991 v E, Pol (2)
Roberts, C. J. (Cardiff C), 1999 v D (sub) (1)
Roberts, G. (Hull C), 1983 v Bul (1)
Roberts, G. W. (Liverpool), 1997 v Ho, T, Bel; 1998 v T, I; 1999 v I, D, Bl, P; (with Panionios), D; (with Tranmere R), 2000 v Sw (11)
Roberts, J. G. (Wrexham), 1977 v E (1)
Roberts, N. W. (Wrexham), 1999 v I (sub), P; 2000 v Sw (sub) (3)
Roberts, P. (Porthmadog), 1997 v Ho (sub) (1)
Roberts, S. I. (Swansea C), 1999 v Sw, I (sub), D; 2000 v Bl (sub), Ni; 2001 v Bl (sub), N, Pol, Arm, Uk; 2002 v Arm, N, Bl (13)
Roberts, S. W. (Wrexham), 2000 v S; 2001 v Bl, N (sub) (3)
Robinson, C. P. (Wolverhampton W), 1996 v Sm; 1997 v Sm, Ho (2), T, Bel (6)
Robinson, J. (Brighton & HA), 1992 v R; (with Charlton Ath), 1993 v Bel; 1994 v RCS, Cy, R (5)
Rowlands, A. J. R. (Manchester C), 1996 v Sm; 1997 v Sm, Ho (1 + sub), T (sub) (5)
Rush, I. (Liverpool), 1981 v Ho; 1982 v F (2)

Savage, R. W. (Crewe Alex), 1995 v Bul; 1996 v Mol, G (3)
Sayer, P. A. (Cardiff C), 1977 v E, S (2)
Searle, D. (Cardiff C), 1991 v Pol (sub); 1992 v R; 1993 v Cy, Bel (2), RCS; 1994 v RCS (6)
Slatter, D. (Chelsea), 2000 v Sw (sub), S; 2001 v Bl, N (sub), Pol (sub), Uk (sub) (6)
Slatter, N. (Bristol R), 1983 v N, Y, Bul; 1984 v N, Bul, Y (6)
Somner, M. J. (Brentford), 2004 v Ser (sub), I (2)
Speed, G. A. (Leeds U), 1990 v Pol; 1991 v E, Pol (3)
Stevenson, N. (Swansea C), 1982 v F, Ho (2)
Stevenson, W. B. (Leeds U), 1977 v E, S; 1978 v S (3)
Stock, B. B. (Bournemouth), 2003 v Fi (sub), I (sub); 2004 v Fi, Ser (4)
Symons, K. (Portsmouth), 1991 v E, Pol (2)

Taylor, G. K. (Bristol R), 1995 v Ge, Bul (2); 1996 v Mo (4)
Thomas, D. J. (Watford), 1998 v T, Bel (2)
Thomas, J. A. (Blackburn R), 1996 v Sm; 1997 v Sm, H (2), T, Bel; 1998 v Bel; 1999 v D, Bl, P; 2000 v Bl (sub 2001 v Bl, N, Pol, Arm, Uk, Pol, Uk; 2002 v Arm, N, B (21)
Thomas, Martin R. (Bristol R), 1979 v E; 1981 v Ho (2)
Thomas, Mickey R. (Wrexham), 1977 v E; 1978 v S (2)
Thomas, S. (Wrexham), 2001 v Pol, Uk; 2002 v Arm, N Bl (5)
Thomas, D. G. (Leeds U), 1977 v E; 1979 v E; 1984 v (3)
Tibbott, L. (Ipswich T), 1977 v E, S (2)
Tipton, M. J. (Oldham Ath), 1998 v I (sub); 1999 v P, Sw (sub); 2000 v Ni; 2001 v Arm (sub), Uk (sub) (6)
Tolley, J. C. (Shrewsbury T), 2001 v Pol, Uk (sub); 2003 Fi, I, Az (2); 2004 v Ser (2) (8)
Twiddy, C. (Plymouth Arg), 1995 v Mol, Ge; 1996 v (sub) (3)

Vaughan, D. O. (Crewe Alex), 2003 v Fi, Az; 2004 v I (3)
Vaughan, N. (Newport Co), 1982 v F, Ho (2)
Valentine, R. D. (Everton), 2001 v Pol, Uk; 2002 v Arm N, Bl; (with Darlington), 2003 v Fi, I, Az (8)

Walsh, D. (Wrexham), 2000 v S, Ni; 2001 v Bl, Arm, Uk 2002 v Arm, N, Bl (8)
Walsh, I. P. (C Palace), 1979 v E; (with Swansea C), 198 v Bul (2)
Walton, M. (Norwich C.), 1991 v Pol (sub) (1)
Ward, D. (Notts Co), 1996 v Mol, G (2)
Weston, R. D. (Arsenal), 2001 v Bl, N, Pol; (with Cardif C), Arm (4)
Whitfield, P. M. (Wrexham), 2003 v Az (1)
Williams, A. P. (Southampton), 1998 v Bel, I; 1999 v I, D (sub), Bl, Sw, I; 2000 v Bl, Sw (9)
Williams, A. S. (Blackburn R), 1996 v Sm; 1997 v Sm Ho, Bel; 1998 v T, Bel, I; 1999 v I, D, Bl, P, Sw, I, D 2000 v Bl, Sw (16)
Williams, D. (Bristol R), 1983 v Y (1)
Williams, D. I. L. (Liverpool), 1998 v I; 1999 v D, Bl (with Wrexham) I, D; 2000 v Bl, S, Ni; 2001 v Bl (9)
Williams, E. (Caernarfon T), 1997 v Ho (sub), T (sub) (2)
Williams, G. (Bristol R), 1983 v Y, Bul (2)
Williams, G. A. (C Palace), 2003 v I (sub), Az; 2004 v Ser I, Ser (sub) (5)
Williams, M. (Manchester U), 2001 v Pol (sub), Uk (sub) 2002 v Bl (sub); 2003 v Fi, I, Az (sub); 2004 v Ser (sub) I (sub), Fi, Ser (10)
Williams, S. J. (Wrexham), 1995 v Mol, Ge, Bul (2) (4)
Wilmot, R. (Arsenal), 1982 v F (2), Ho; 1983 v N, Y; 1984 v Y (6)
Wright, A. A. (Oxford U), 1998 v Bel, I (sub); 1999 v D (sub) (3)

Young, S. (Cardiff C), 1996 v Sm; 1997 v Sm, Ho (2), Be (sub) (5)

## NORTHERN IRELAND

Bailie, N. (Linfield), l990 v Is; 1994 v R (sub) (2)
Baird, C. P. (Southampton), 2002 v G; 2003 v S, Sp, Uk, Fi, Gr (6)
Beatty, S. (Chelsea), 1990 v Is; (with Linfield), 1994 v R (2)
Black, J. (Tottenham H), 2003 v Uk (sub) (1)
Black, K. T. (Luton T), 1990 v Is (1)
Black, R. Z. (Morecambe), 2002 v G (1)
Blackledge, G. (Portadown), 1978 v Ei (1)
Blayney, A. (Southampton), 2003 v Fi (sub); 2004 v Uk, Arm, Gr (4)
Boyle, W. S. (Leeds U), 1998 v Sw (sub), S (sub); 2001 v CzR (sub), Bul (1+sub), CzR; 2002 v Ma (7)
Braniff, K. R. (Millwall), 2002 v G; 2003 v S (sub), Sp (sub), Fi, Arm (sub), Gr, Sp; 2004 v Gr (sub) (8)
Brotherston, N. (Blackburn R), 1978 v Ei (sub) (1)
Browne, G. (Manchester C), 2003 v S, Sp, Uk, Fi (sub), Sp (5)
Buchanan, W. B. (Bolton W), 2002 v G (sub); 2003 v Uk (sub); (with Lisburn Distillery), 2004 v Uk, Arm, Gr (5)
Burns, L. (Port Vale), 1998 v Sw, S, Ei; 1999 v T, Fi, Mol, G, Mol, Ei; 2000 v F, T, G, Fi (13)

Campbell, S. (Ballymena U), 2003 v Sp (sub) (1)
Capaldi, A. C. (Birmingham C), 2002 v D (sub), Ic, Ma, G; 2003 v S, Sp, Uk, Fi, Arm, Gr; (with Plymouth Arg), Sp; 2004 v Uk, Arm, Gr (14)
Carlisle, W. T. (C Palace), 2000 v Fi (sub); 2001 v Ma, Ic, Bul (1+sub), CzR; 2002 v D, Ic, Ma (9)
Carroll, R. E. (Wigan Ath), 1998 v S, Ei; 1999 v T, Fi, Mol, G, Mol, Ei; 2000 v T, G, Fi (11)
Carson, S. (Rangers), 2000 v Ma; (wirh Dundee U), 2002 v D (sub) (2)
Clarke, L. (Peterborough U), 2003 v Sp (sub); 2004 v Uk (sub), Arm (sub) (3)
Clarke, R. D. J. (Portadown), 1999 v Ei (sub), S; 2000 v F (sub), S, W (sub) (5)
Clingan, S. G. (Wolverhampton W), 2003 v Arm (sub); 2004 v Uk, Arm, Gr (4)
Close, B. (Middlesbrough), 2002 v Ic, Ma (sub), G; 2003 v S, Sp, Uk, Arm, Sp; 2004 v Arm, Gr (10)
Clyde, M. G. (Wolverhampton W), 2002 v G; 2003 v S, Sp, Uk, Fi (5)
Connell, T. E. (Coleraine), 1978 v Ei (sub) (1)
Coote, A. (Norwich C), 1998 v Sw (sub), S, Ei; 1999 v T, Fi,Mol, G, Mol, Ei; 2000 v F, T, G (12)

onvery, J. (Celtic), 2000 v S, W; 2001 v D, Ic (4)

avey, H. (UCD), 2004 v Uk, Arm, Gr (3)
avis, S. (Aston Villa), 2004 v Uk (sub), Arm (sub) (2)
evine, D. (Omagh T), 1994 v R (1)
evine, J. (Glentoran), 1990 v Is (1)
ickson, H. (Wigan Ath). 2002 v Ma (1)
olan, J. (Millwall), 2000 v Fi, Ma, S; 2001 v Ma, D, Ic (6)
onaghy, M. M. (Larne), 1978 v Ei (1)
owie, I. (Luton T), 1990 v Is (1)
uff, S. (Cheltenham T), 2003 v Sp (1)

lliott, S. (Glentoran), 1999 v Fi (sub), Ei, S (sub) (3)

eeney, L. (Linfield), 1998 v Ei (sub); 1999 v T, Fi, Mol; (with Rangers), G (sub), Ei, S; 2000 v Fi (8)
eeney, W. (Bournemouth), 2002 v D, Ic (sub); 2003 v Fi, Arm, Gr; 2004 v Uk, Arm, Gr (8)
erguson, M. (Glentoran), 2000 v T (sub), Ma (sub) (2)
itzgerald, D. (Rangers), 1998 v Sw, S; 1999 v T (sub), Fi (4)
riars, S. M. (Liverpool), 1998 v Sw, S, Ei; (with Ipswich T), 1999 v T, Fi, Mol, G, Mol; 2000 v F, T, G, Ma, S, W; 2001 v Ma, D, Ic, CzR, Bul (2), CzR (21)

illespie, K. R. (Manchester U), 1994 v R (1)
lendinning, M. (Bangor), 1994 v R (1)
raham, G. L. (C Palace), 1999 v S; 2000 v F, T, G, Fi (5)
raham, R. S. (QPR), 1999 v Fi (sub), Mol, Ei (sub); 2000 v F (sub), T (sub), G (sub), Fi (sub), Ma, S, W; 2001 v Ma, D, CzR (sub), Bul (sub), CzR (sub) (15)
ray, P. (Luton T), 1990 v Is (sub) (1)
riffin, D. J. (St Johnstone), 1998 v S (sub), Ei; 1999 v T, Fi, G, Mol, Ei, S; 2000 v F, T (10)

amilton, G. (Blackburn R), 2000 v Ma (sub), S, W (sub); 2001 v Ma, D, Ic, CzR, Bul (2), CzR; (wirh Portadown), 2002 v Ic, Ma (12)
amilton, W. R. (Linfield), 1978 v Ei (1)
arkin, M. P. (Wycombe W), Ma (sub), S (sub), W; 2001 v Ma (sub), D (sub), Ic, CzR, Bul (sub+1) (9)
arvey, J. (Arsenal), 1978 v Ei (1)
awe, S. (Blackburn R), 2001 v Cz (1+sub) (2)
ayes, T. (Luton T), 1978 v Ei (1)
ealy, D. J. (Manchester U), 1999 v Mol (sub), G (sub), Ei (sub), S; 2000 v F (sub), T, G, Fi (8)
erron, C. J. (QPR), 2003 v Arm, Gr (2)
olmes, S. (Manchester C), Ma, S, W; 2001 v Ma, D, Ic, CzR, Bul (2), CzR; (with Wrexham), 2002 v D, Ic, Ma (13)
ughes, M. A. (Tottenham H), 2003 v Sp (sub), Uk (sub), Fi, Arm, Gr, Sp; 2004 v Uk, Arm, Gr (sub) (9)
ughes, M. E. (Manchester C), 1990 v Is (sub)
unter, M. (Glentoran), 2002 v G (sub) (1)

ngham, M. (Sunderland), 2001 v CzR, Bul (2), CzR (4)

ohnson, D. M. (Blackburn R), 1998 v Sw, S, Ei; 1999 v T, Fi, G, Mol, Ei; 2000 v F, T, G (11)
ohnston, B. (Cliftonville), 1978 v Ei (1)

ee, P. V. (Oxford U), 1990 v Is (1)
elly, D. (Derry C), 2000 v Ma, W; 2001 v Ma, Ic (sub), CzR, Bul (2), CzR; 2002 v D, Ic, Ma (11)
elly, N. (Oldham Ath), 1990 v Is (sub) (1)
irk, A. (Hearts), 1999 v S; 2000 v Ma, S, W; 2001 v Ma, D, Ic (sub); 2002 v D, Ic (9)

ennon, N. F. (Manchester C), 1990 v Is; (with Crewe Alex), 1994 v R (2)
yttle, G. (Celtic), 1998 v Sw, S; (with Peterborough U), 1999 v T (sub), Mol (2), S; 2000 v G, Fi (8)

Magee, J. (Bangor), 1994 v R (sub) (1)
Magilton, J. (Liverpool), 1990 v Is (1)
Matthews, N. P. (Blackpool), 1990 v Is (1)
McAreavey, P. (Swindon T), 2000 v Ma, S; 2001 v Ma, D; 2002 v D, Ic (sub), Ma (sub) (7)
McBride, J. (Glentoran), 1994 v R (sub) (1)
McCallion, E. (Coleraine), 1998 v Sw (sub) (1)
McCann, G. S. (West Ham U), 2000 v S (sub), W; 2001 v D (sub), Ic, CzR, Bul (2), CzR; 2002 v D, Ic, Ma (11)
McCann, P. (Portadown), 2003 v Sp (1)
McCann, R. (Rangers), 2002 v G (sub); (with Linfield), 2003 v S (sub) (2)
McCartney, G. (Sunderland), 2001 v D, CzR, Bul (2); 2002 v D (5)
McCourt, P. J. (Rochdale), 2002 v G; 2003 v S (sub), Sp, Uk, Fi (sub), Arm (sub), Gr (sub) (6)
McCoy, R. K. (Coleraine), 1990 v Is (1)
McCreery, D. (Manchester U), 1978 v Ei (1)
McEvilly, L. (Rochdale), 2003 v S, Sp, Uk, Fi (sub), Arm, Gr (sub); 2004 v Uk, Arm, Gr (9)
McFlynn, T. M. (QPR), 2000 v Ma (sub), W (sub); 2001 v Ma (sub), CzR (sub), Bul (sub+sub), CzR; (with Woking), 2002 v D (sub), Ic (sub); (wirh Margate), G; 2003 v S (sub), Sp (sub), Fi (sub), Arm, Gr (sub), Sp (sub); 2004 v Uk, Arm (sub), Gr (19)
McGibbon, P. C. G. (Manchester U), 1994 v R (1)
McGlinchey, B. (Manchester C), 1998 v Sw, S, Ei; (with Port Vale), 1999 v T, Fi, Mol, G, Mol, Ei, S; (with Gillingham), 2000 v F, G, T, Fi (14)
McIlroy, T. (Linfield), 1994 v R (sub) (1)
McKnight, P. (Rangers), 1998 v Sw; 1999 v T (sub), Mol (sub) (3)
McMahon, G. J. (Tottenham H),1994 v R (sub) (1)
McVeigh, A. (Ayr U), 2002 v G (sub) (1)
McVeigh, P. F. (Tottenham H), 1998 v S (sub), Ei; 1999 v T, Mol, G, Mol, Ei; 2000 v F, T (sub), G (sub), Fi (11)
Melaugh, G. M. (Aston Villa), 2002 v G; 2003 v S, Sp, Uk, Fi, Arm, Gr, Sp; (with Glentoran), 2004 v Uk, Arm, Gr (11)
Millar, W. P. (Port Vale), 1990 v Is (1)
Miskelly, D. T. (Oldham Ath), 2000 v F, Ma, S, W; 2001 v Ma, D, Ic; 2002 v D, Ic, Ma (10)
Moreland, V. (Glentoran), 1978 v Ei (sub) (1)
Morgan, M, P. T. (Preston NE), 1999 v S (1)
Morris, E. J. (WBA), 2002 v G; (with Glentoran), 2003 v S, Sp, Uk, Fi, Arm, Gr, Sp (8)
Morrison, O. (Sheffield W), 2001 v Bul (sub); 2002 v Ma (sub); 2003 S, Fi; (with Sheffield U) Arm, Gr, Sp (7)
Morrow, A. (Northampton T), 2001 v D (sub) (1)
Mulryne, P. P. (Manchester U), Sw, S, Ei; (with Norwich C), 1999 v G, Mol (5)
Murray, W. (Linfield), 1978 v Ei (sub) (1)

Nicholl, J. M. (Manchester U), 1978 v Ei (1)
Nixon, C. (Glentoran), 2000 v Fi (sub) (1)

O'Hara, G. (Leeds U), 1994 v R (1)
O'Neill, M. A. M. (Hibernian), 1994 v R (1)
O'Neill, J. P. (Leicester C), 1978 v Ei (1)

Patterson, D. J. (C Palace), 1994 v R (1)

Quinn, S. J. (Blackpool), 1994 v R (1)

Robinson, S. (Tottenham H), 1994 v R (1)

Simms, G. (Hartlepool U), 2001 v Bul (2), CzR; 2002 v D, Ic, Ma, G; 2003 v S, Sp, Uk, Fi, Arm, Gr, Sp (14)
Skates, G. (Blackburn R), 2000 v Ma; 2001 v Ic (sub), CzR (2) (4)
Sloan, T. (Ballymena U), 1978 v Ei (1)

Taylor, M. S. (Fulham), 1998 v Sw (1)
Toner, C. (Tottenham H), 2000 v Ma (sub), S (sub), W; 2001 v D, Ic, CzR, Bul (2), CzR; 2002 v D, Ic, Ma; (with Leyton Orient), 2003 v S, Sp, Uk, Fi, Gr (17)

Waterman, D. G. (Portsmouth), 1998 v Sw, S, Ei; 1999 v T, Fi, Mol, G, Mol, Ei, S (sub); 2000 v F, T, G, Fi (14)
Webb, S. M. (Ross Co), 2004 v Uk, Arm, Gr (3)
Wells, D. P. (Barry T), 1999 v S (1)
Whitley, Jeff (Manchester C), 1998 v Sw, S, Ei; 1999 v T, Fi, Mol, G, Ei, S; 2000 v F, G, T, Ma, S, W; 2001 v Ma, Ic (17)

# ENGLAND NATIONAL GAME XI 2003–04

4 Nov

**England 2** *(Ricketts, Rodgers)*
**Belgium 2** 3166
*(at Darlington).*
*England:* Bittner (Exeter City); Cavanagh (Accrington Stanley), Jordan (Tamworth), Charles (Farnborough Town), Perkins (Morecambe), Hogg (Barnet), Ricketts (Telford United), McLean (Aldershot Town), Rodgers (Shrewsbury Town), D'Sane (Aldershot Town), Elding (Stevenage Borough).
*(Subs all used: Murphy (Telford United), Smith (Margate), Cowan (Canvey Island), Rickards (Tamworth)).*

11 Feb

**England 1** *(Sheldon)*
**Italy 4** 3703
*(at Shrewsbury).*
*England:* Bittner; Cavanagh, Boardman (Woking), Collins (Chester City), Perkins, Miller (Aldershot Town), Challinor (Aldershot Town), Murray (Woking), Sheldon (Exeter City), D'Sane, Rodgers.
*(Subs all used: McLean, Kennedy (Accrington Stanley), Charles, Purdie (Hereford United), Yakubu (Barnet)).*

27 May

**England 1** *(Hatch)*
**Iraq 5** 396
*(at Macclesfield).*
*England:* Baker; Perkins, Vickers (Dagenham & Redbridge), Sedgemore, Kennedy (Canvey Island), Thompson, Kerr, Southam, McNiven, Hatch, Sheldon.
*(Subs all used: Kennedy, Carlton (Morecambe), Cowan (Canvey Island), Proctor (Accrington Stanley), Baco (Hucknall Town)).*

9 June

**USA 0**
**England 0** 186
*(at Charleston).*
*England:* Baker; Sedgemore, Boardman, Tretton, Perkins, Southam, Kennedy, Sheldon, Crane (Altrinchm), Hatch, Guinan.
*(Subs all used: Kennedy, Thompson, Yakubu, McNiven, Boylan (Canvey Island)).*

# FOUR NATIONS TOURNAMENT

(in Scotland)

18 May

**Republic of Ireland 3**
**England 2** *(Guinan 2)* 390
*(at Banff).*
*England:* Baker (Hereford United); Cavanagh, Tretton (Hereford United), Redmile (Barnet), Perkins, Thompson (Morecambe), Ricketts, Kerr (Scarborough), Sheldon, Guinan (Hereford United), Hatch (Barnet).
*(Subs all used: Sedgemore (Shrewsbury Town), Foyewa (Woking), Southam (Dagenham & Redbridge), McDonnell (Worcester City), Boardman, McNiven (Leigh RMI)).*

20 May

**Wales 2**
**England 0** 240
*(at Keith).*
*England:* McDonnell; Redmile, Boardman, Tretton, Sedgemore, Southam, Kerr, Thompson, Guinan, Hatch, Sheldon.
*(Subs all used: Foyewa, Ricketts, McNiven, Baker).*

23 May

**Scotland 1**
**England 3** *(Guinan (pen), Southam, Hatch)* 2214
*(at Banff).*
*England:* Baker; Redmile, Perkins, Tretton, Sedgemore, Southam, Kerr, Ricketts, Guinan, Hatch, Sheldon.
*(Subs all used: Foyewa, McNiven, McDonnell, Thompson, Boardman).*

| | *P* | *W* | *D* | *L* | *F* | *A* | *Pts* |
|---|---|---|---|---|---|---|---|
| Wales | 3 | 2 | 1 | 0 | 6 | 1 | 7 |
| Scotland | 3 | 1 | 1 | 1 | 3 | 3 | 4 |
| England | 3 | 1 | 0 | 2 | 5 | 6 | 3 |
| Republic of Ireland | 3 | 1 | 0 | 2 | 4 | 8 | 3 |

# FA SCHOOLS & YOUTH GAMES 2003–04

** World Youth Cup; # (to come); + (to come); ++ (to come); * (to come).

## ENGLAND UNDER-20

Hoyte, Thomas, Bentley (Arsenal); Cooke (Aston Villa); Carter (Birmingham C); McEveley (Blackburn R); Pidgeley (Chelsea); Camp (Derby Co); Kilgallon, Milner (Leeds U); Wright (Leicester C); Welsh (Liverpool); Croft (Manchester C); Johnson, Fox (Manchester U); Taylor A (Middlesbrough); Taylor S, Chopra (Newcastle U); Carruthers (Northampton T); O'Neil (Portsmouth); Lonergan (Preston NE); Howard, Cranie (Southampton); Bowditch, Ifil (Tottenham H).

9 Oct
**England 2** *(Chopra 5, Bentley 47)*
**Czech Republic 0**
*(at Stevenage).*
*England:* Lonergan; Hoyte, McEveley, Carter, Taylor S, Kilgallon, Thomas, O'Neil, Chopra, Bentley, Milner.

14 Nov
**England 2** *(Johnson 44, 51)*
**Wales 0**
*(at Stoke).*
*England:* Lonergan (Camp 45); Hoyte (Cranie 45), Carruthers (Taylor A 71), Fox, Taylor S, McEveley, Johnson, O'Neil, Chopra, Carter, Milner.

29 Nov**
**England 0**
**Japan 1**
*(in Dubai).*
*England:* Lonergan; Carruthers (McEveley 46), Fox (Wright 65), Taylor S, Kilgallon, Thomas, O'Neil, Chopra, Carter, Welsh, Johnson (Croft 77).

2 Dec**
**Egypt 1**
**England 0**
*(in Dubai).*
*England:* Lonergan; Carruthers (McEveley 34), Taylor S, Kilgallon, Thomas (Johnson 76), O'Neil (Taylor A 53), Chopra, Carter, Ifil, Welsh, Wright.

5 Dec**
**Colombia 0**
**England 0**
*(in Dubai).*
*England:* Lonergan; Bowditch (Carter 69), Fox, Taylor S, Kilgallon, Chopra, Cranie, McEveley, Croft (Thomas 78), Welsh, Johnson (Wright 67).

## ENGLAND UNDER-19

Sadler, Kilkenny (Birmingham C); Chaplow (Burnley); Long, Sankofa (Charlton Ath); Tillen (Chelsea); Giddings (Coventry C); Wilson, Jones (Crewe Alex); Borrowdale, Routledge (Crystal Palace); Huddlestone, Holmes (Derby Co); Brown (Everton); Hogg, Bowditch (Ipswich T); Milner (Leeds U); Raven, Smyth (Liverpool); Croft, Proffitt (Manchester C); Turnbull (Middlesbrough); Samba (Millwall); Guy (Newcastle U); Jarvis, Henderson (Norwich C); Biggins, Gardner, Groves (Nottingham F); Young (Reading); Roma (Sheffield U); Blackstock (Southampton); Collins, Leadbitter (Sunderland); Ifil (Tottenham H); Martin (Wimbledon).

20 Sept#
**England 2** *(Long 68, Guy 70)*
**Liechtenstein 0**
*(in Moscow).*
*England:* Turnbull; Biggins, Sadler, Gardner, Raven (Hogg 65), Collins, Croft (Wilson 78), Brown (Guy 45), Proffitt, Long, Samba.

22 Sept#
**Andorra 0**
**England 4** *(Guy 5, 53, Croft 60, Brown 82)*
*(in Moscow).*
*England:* Sadler (Proffitt 72); Collins (Biggins 70), Brown, Samba (Croft 23), Tillen, Young, Roma, Groves, Guy, Wilson, Hogg.

24 Sept#
**Russia 0**
**England 1** *(Proffit 73)*
*(in Moscow).*
*England:* Turnbull; Biggins, Sadler (Proffit 28), Gardner, Collins, Croft, Brown, Long, Tillen, Guy, Hogg.

17 Feb
**Netherlands 0**
**England 2** *(Milner 11, Henderson 42)*
*(at Harderwijk).*
*England:* Turnbull (Young 45); Jones (Ifil 72), Borrowdale, Gardner, Raven, Collins (Sankofa 45), Routledge (Holmes 72), Groves (Kilkenny 45), Henderson, Long (Huddlestone 85), Milner (Bowditch 65).

30 Mar
**Germany 1**
**England 1** *(Holmes 43).*
*(at Celje).*
*England:* Turnbull (Martin 45); Ifil (Sankofa 78), Borrowdale (Biggins 88), Gardner, Raven, Collins, Henderson, Chaplow (Leadbitter 84), Jarvis (Smyth 45), Long (Brown 68), Holmes (Croft 46).

28 Apr#
**Slovenia 2**
**England 1** *(Brown 30)*
*(at Celje).*
*England:* Long (Leadbitter 77); Raven, Sankofa, Brown, Proffitt (Groves 70), Blackstock, Giddings, Gardner, Jarvis, Ifil, Turnbull.

30 Apr#
**England 3** *(Blackstock 3, Jarvis 27, Henderson 38)*
**Denmark 0**
*(at Kidricevo).*
*England:* Giddings; Biggins, Raven, Turnbull, Brown, Long (Groves 69), Blackstock (Proffitt 45), Gardner, Jarvis, Henderson (Wilson 76), Collins.

2 May#
**Ukraine 1**
**England 1** *(Collins 85)*
*(at Celje).*
*England:* Giddings; Wilson (Groves 45), Biggins (Ifil 77), Raven, Turnbull, Brown, Long, Gardner (Leadbitter 77), Jarvis, Henderson, Collins.

## ENGLAND UNDER-18

Howard (Arsenal); Nix (Aston Villa); Barker, Taylor A (Blackburn R); Giddings (Coventry C); Wilson, Hopkins (Everton); Dodds (Leicester C); Peltier (Liverpool), Heaton, Jones R (Manchester U); Bates, Morrison, Liddle, Taylor A, McMahon (Middlesbrough); Hoskins (Rotherham U); Forte (Sheffield U); Cranie, Blackstock, Mills (Southampton); O'Hara (Tottenham H); Carter (Wimbledon).

31 Mar
**England 1** *(Morrison 20)*
**Belgium 0**
*(at Northampton).*
*England:* Heaton (Howard 45); Peltier (McMahon 76); Gidings, Jones R (O'Hara 53), Bates (Mills 45), Cranie, Morrison, Liddle (Hopkins 70), Blackstock, Taylor A (Middlesbrough) (Wilson 83), Forte (Dodds 61).

29 Apr
**England 0**
**Sweden 2**
*(at York).*
*England:* Heaton; Peltier, Taylor A (Middlesbrough), Jones R, Bates, Cranie (Mills 7), Morrison, Liddle, Barker (Nix 24), O'Hara (Taylor A (Blackburn R: 12)), Carter (Hoskins 44).

## ENGLAND UNDER-17

Gilbert, Lewis S, Muamba, Murphy (Arsenal); Paul (Aston Villa); Jones Z, Woods (Blackburn R); Ashton, Walker, Weston (Charlton Ath); Brand, Grant, Mancienne, Simmonds, Smith, Watkins (Chelsea); Jones B, Roberts (Crewe Alex); Berry (Crystal Palace); Ainsworth, Doyle (Derby Co); Wright (Everton); James (Fulham); Krause (Ipswich T); Parker, Walton (Leeds U); Porter, Stearman (Leicester C); Guthrie, Holmes (Liverpool); Campbell (Manchester U); Knight, Reed, Wheater (Middlesbrough); Ashikodi (Millwall); Lewis J (Norwich C); Donnelly (QPR); Alnwick (Sunderland); Dawkins (Tottenham H); Cohen, Noble, Reid (West Ham U); Martin (Wimbledon); Davies (Wolverhampton W).

7 Jul
**England 1** *(Ashikodi 80)*
**USA 0**
*(at Notts County).*
*England:* Lewis J; Gilbert (Mancienne 57), Wheater, Dawkins (Reed 46), Ashikodi, Davies (James 73), Weston (Parker 60), Wright, Roberts (Lewis S 57), Simmonds, Jones B.

10 Jul
**England 0**
**Portugal 1**
*(at Notts County).*
*England:* Alnwick; Gilbert, Parker, Lewis S (Davies 55), Mancienne, James, Weston (Simmonds 57), Roberts, Watkins (Ashikodi 62), Reed, Jones B.

13 Jul
**England 0**
**Brazil 0**
*(at Notts County).*
*England:* Alnwick; Gilbert (Wheater 46), Parker (Wright 46), Mancienne, Dawkins (Weston 49), James, Ashikodi (Watkins 80), Davies (Reed 69), Roberts, Simmonds, Jones B.

29 Jul
**England 3** *(Donnelly 14, Campbell 28, Smith 77)*
**Iceland 0**
*(at Hamar).*
*England:* Knight; Walton, Krause (Ashton 77), Grant (Holmes 56), Campbell (Walker 68), Smith, Muamba (Guthrie 65), Berry, Porter (Woods 70), Stearman (Brand 61), Donnelly.

30 Jul
**Denmark 3**
**England 0**
*(at Hamar).*
*England:* Jones Z; Holmes, Ashton, Guthrie, Walker, Grant (Donnelly 55), Berry (Campbell 55), Porter (Krause 73), Brand, Woods (Smith J 66), Stearman (Walton 62).

1 Aug
**Norway 1**
**England 1** *(Smith J 41)*
*(at Hamar).*
*England:* Knight; Holmes, Ashton, Guthrie (Donnelly 57), Walton, Walker, Campbell (Berry 77), Smith J, Muamba, Brand, Woods (Porter 60).

3 Aug
**England 1** *(Guthrie 40)*
**Sweden 3**
*(at Briskeby).*
*England:* Jones Z; Ashton, Guthrie, Krause, Walker (Woods 64), Grant (Brand 41), Campbell (Berry 48), Smith J, Porter, Stearman (Walton 41), Donnelly (Muamba 79).

12 Nov
**England 1** *(Paul 10)*
**Switzerland 1**
*(at Bristol).*
*England:* Lewis J (Alnwick 40); Walton, Porter (Parker 40), Martin (Simmonds 52), Gilbert (Wheater 67), Walker, Noble, Cohen (Murphy 57), Paul (Ainsworth 67), Doyle (Roberts 40), Jones B.

21 Feb
**Portugal 0**
**England 0**
*(in Algarve).*
*England:* Lewis J; Reid (Davies), Doyle, James, Martin, Noble, Simmonds (Campbell), Mancienne, Walker (Paul), Wheater, Parker.

22 Feb
**France 1**
**England 1** *(Paul 50 (pen))*
*(in Algarve).*
*England:* Knight; Weston, Davies, Wheater, Doyle (Martin), Campbell, Mancienne, Stearman (Parker!), Ashton, Paul, Noble.

24 Feb
**Finland 0**
**England 3** *(Paul 22, Wheater 76, Walker 78)*
*(in Algarve).*
*England:* Lewis J (Knight); Mancienne (Doyle), James (Martin), Noble, Paul, Ashton, Reid (Campbell), Stearman, Walker, Wheater, Simmonds (Davies).

24 Mar+
**England 3** *(Noble 18 (pen), Paul 70, Campbell 80)*
**Armenia 0**
*(at Sheffield)*
*England:* Alnwick; Ashton, Doyle, Mancienne, Noble, Paul (James), Reid, Roberts, Simmonds (Davies), Stearman, Walker (Campbell).

26 Mar+
**England 1** *(Campbell 80)*
**Iceland 0**
*(at Doncaster).*
*England:* Lewis J; Stearman, Porter (Walker), Davies, Doyle, Campbell, Mancienne, Roberts, Parker (Ashton), Paul, Noble (James).

28 Mar+
**Norway 1**
**England 2** *(Reid 10, Campbell 67)*
*(at Sheffield).*
*England:* Alnwick; Reid, Doyle, James, Gilbert, Ashton, Simmonds, Mancienne, Campbell, Walker, Stearman.

4 May++
**England 2** *(Paul, Doyle)*
**Ukraine 0**
*(in Avoine).*
*England:* Alnwick; Stearman, Ashton, Noble, Wheater, Doyle, James, Roberts (Walton), Paul, Walker (Porter), Reid (Campbell).

6 May++
**England 3** *(Paul 2, Davies)*
**Portugal 1**
*(in Tours).*
*England:* Alnwick; Ashton, Noble, Roberts, Paul (Walton), James (Davies), Walker, Reid, Stearman, Doyle, Wheater.

9 May++
**England 1** *(Porter)*
**Austria 0**
*(in Blois).*
*England:* Alnwick; Ashton, Noble, Roberts, Paul (Porter), James, Walker (Campbell), Reid (Davies), Stearman, Doyle, Wheater.

12 May++
**England 1** *(Reid)*
**Spain 2**
*(in Tours).*
*England:* Alnwick; Jones B, Ashton, Roberts, Noble, Wheater, Paul, Campbell (Walker), Reid (Porter), Stearman, Davies (Doyle).

15 May++
**England 4** *(Walker 2, Reid, Davies)*
**Portugal 4**
*(in Chateauroux).*
*England:* Lewis; Jones B, Ashton, Roberts, Paul, Campbell, Walker, Reid, Stearman, Doyle, Wheater.

## ENGLAND UNDER-16

Baidoo (Arsenal); Bridges, MacDonald (Aston Villa); Jones Z, Woods, Garner (Blackburn R); Weston (Charlton Ath); Irving, Molyneux, Phelan, Morrison, Johnson (Everton); Omozusi (Fulham); Knights (Ipswich T); Gardner (Leeds U); Holmes, Barnett, Burns (Liverpool); Richards (Manchester C); Mullen (Manchester U); Hines, Cattermole (Middlesbrough); McGugan, Gamble (Nottingham F); Walcott (Southampton); Mills (Swindon T); Martin, Button, Peprah, Riley (Tottenham H); Ephraim, Tomkins (West Ham U).

17 Oct*
**England 4** *(Ephraim 3, Phelan 11, McGugan 64, Richards 69)*
**Northern Ireland 0**
*(at Rushden).*
*England:* Jones Z (Button 40); Irving (Peprah 56), Molyneux (Woods 56), McGugan (Richards 67), Hines, Holmes, Baidoo (Mullen 40), Phelan, Ephraim, Martin, Knights.

31 Oct*
**England 4** *(Burns 40, MacDonald 53, Mills 73, Cattermole 80)*
**Wales 2**
*(at Gillingham).*
*England:* Button (Gamble 40); Omozusi (Riley 50), Bridges, Cattermole, Mills, Hines, Barnett (Gardner 64), Morrison (MacDonald 40), Garner, Johnson, Burns (Weston 52).

28 Nov*
**Scotland 1**
**England 1** *(Weston 27)*
*(in Glasgow).*
*England:* Gamble (Jones Z 40); Riley, Richards, Peprah (Mills 40), Holmes, Mullen, MacDonald, Garner, Woods, Weston, Knights.

7 Apr
**England 0**
**Ivory Coast 1**
*(in Montaigu).*
*England:* Riley; Molyneux, Richards (McGugan 40), Phelan (Weston 25), Mullen (Walcott 11), Ephraim (Garner 18), Knights, MacDonald (Martin 11), Button, Holmes, Tomkins.

8 Apr
**England 3** *(Weston 48, Garner 64, Knights 66)*
**United States 1**
*(in Montaigu).*
*England:* Gamble; Riley, Molyneux (MacDonald 15), Bridges, Phelan, Walcott (Mullen 20), Garner (Ephraim 13), Martin, Weston (Knights 20), McGugan, Tomkins.

10 Apr
**England 2** *(44 (og), Knights 60)*
**Italy 3**
*(in Montaigu).*
*England:* Riley (Richards 26) (Cattermole 67); Bridges, Phelan (Ephraim 9), Walcott, Garner, MacDonald (Knights 26), Button, Martin, Weston (Mullen), Holmes, McGugan.

12 Apr
**France 2**
**England 1** *(Ephraim 44)*
*(in Montaigu).*
*England:* Gamble; Riley (Bridges 30), Molyneux, Phelan, Mullen (Weston 13), Walcott, Ephraim (MacDonald 9), Knights, Martin, Holmes, McGugan (Garner 27).

# WOMEN'S FOOTBALL 2003–04

The 2003-04 season proved to be the closest run Championship ever. It also showed that there is increasing competition in the women's game. Going into the last match of the season any one of three teams could have won the Premier Division title. The scenario was that Arsenal had to play Fulham at Highbury after their men's team had completed their undefeated season. If Arsenal won, the title was theirs; if Fulham won, it was their title and if the two teams drew, Charlton would be champions.

In the event the Gunners won by 3-1 and completed their 6th Championship. Not only that but they annexed the Women's FA Cup for the 6th time with a stunning 3-0 victory over Charlton Athletic at Loftus Road in May. A hat-trick from Julie Fleeting (who had recently left the American Pro League and had less than 24 hours before represented Scotland) helped lift the Trophy in front of a 12,244 crowd. It was the eighteenth trophy in as many years, master-minded by Arsenal's manager Vic Akers. Not bad for the club who for the first time had won nothing the season before, but will now be England's representative in the 2004–05 UEFA Women's Cup.

Charlton who finished second in the League to show their considerable progress won the Women's Premier League Cup, defeating Fulham, last year's triple champions, by 1-0 with a headed goal from Emma Cross in the thirty-fourth minute at Barnet's Underhill Stadium in March. It also underlined London's dominance as Charlton finished runners-up to Arsenal in the League with Fulham third. It was the fourth time Arsenal had completed the 'double'. Thus Arsenal and Charlton will contest the 2004–05 Women's Community Shield.

Tranmere Rovers, who finished bottom, and Aston Villa of the Premier Division will have to play their football next season in the Northern Division.

The Northern Division itself was won by Liverpool, who achieved 50 points from their 20 matches and are promoted to the Premier Division alongside Bristol City, who won the Southern Division with 58 points from their 24 games. Bristol's margin was one point over Southampton Saints, whereas Liverpool's differential was a whopping 13 over Sunderland. Bangor City and Chesterfield were relegated from the Northern Division and Barnet and Merthyr Tydfil went down from the Southern Division. Replacing the four relegated clubs will be Blackburn Rovers, Cardiff City, Coventry City and Crystal Palace, the latter emulating their men's team by winning promotion. The new League season kicks off on 19 August 2004.

On the international scene, England's women in friendly games defeated Australia 1-0; Iceland 1-0; Denmark 2-0 and Scotland 5-0. They drew 2-2 with Russia in Moscow but lost 4-0 to Germany in Germany and 3-0 to Nigeria at home.

One of the biggest boosts for the game in England comes in June 2005, when England hosts the UEFA Women's Championship for the first time. England qualify as hosts with 7 others also competing, of whom World Champions Germany and runners-up Sweden have already won through. Hope Powell, the Women's National Coach was able to pick 26 hopefuls for a summer training camp after the FA launched an England Women's Under-21 team which will help to bridge the gap between the Under-19s and senior levels.

Domestically things have continued to grow at a very impressive rate with a 20% increase year on year. The total number of women and girls playing affiliated League and Cup competitions for 2003–04 season grew to 101,173 with almost 7,500 clubs involved. It is expected that the hosting of the European Championships will encourage and also boost the numbers even more.

There are a number of Academies for coaching girls, many affiliated to Premier and Nationwide clubs and one of the most progressive is Arsenal. Here last season it was mentioned that the London Football Coaches' Association coach their under 14s and under 12s once per month bringing in top coaches for that purpose, including last season the former FA Assistant Technical Director Les Reed and Aston Villa goalkeeping coach Eric Steele. A one-off session for the girls was held by John Cartwright, former FA Youth Team Coach and also one time Technical Director of the National School. His company Premier Skills Coaching has already held courses for over 200 ladies in the last 12 months, mainly in the West Midlands area, including soccer mums, school teachers, girl footballers, as well as a special course set up for Hindu ladies.

More information concerning women's football can be obtained from the FA's Marketing and PR Manager Bev Ward on 0207 454 716 or 07970 237082. There is also a Women's Football Newsletter regularly available and a magazine devoted to the Women's Game, entitled 'Fairgame', which has just celebrated its first year of publication.

The Women's Football structure consists of Tessa Hayward – the Women's League co-ordinator and Secretary for the FA Women's Premier League; Penny Kift – the League's administrator; Helen Nicolaou, International Teams Development co-ordinator. Sally Cunnington, who deals with Youth teams; Mike Appelby – Leagues Manager for both women and men; and Bev Ward, the Media and Communications Officer.

KEN GOLDMAN

Winners of the numerous prestigious annual awards were:

**THE NATIONWIDE PLAYER OF THE YEAR**
Jayne Ludlow — Arsenal
*(The third time for the Wales Captain)*

**THE UMBRO YOUNG PLAYER OF THE YEAR**
Ann Marie Heatherston — Charlton Ath

**THE NATIONWIDE MANAGER OF THE YEAR**
Keith Boanas — Charlton Ath

**THE NATIONWIDE INTERNATIONAL PLAYER OF THE YEAR**
Rachel Unitt — Fulham

**THE FA FAIR PLAY AWARD**
Oldham Curzon — Northern Division

A Special Achievement Award was presented by the FA to Kath Tranter for 30 years work as player and administrator. Sky Sports shared the FA National Media Award.

## NATIONAL DIVISION

| | P | W | D | L | F | A | GD | Pts |
|---|---|---|---|---|---|---|---|---|
| Arsenal | 18 | 15 | 2 | 1 | 65 | 11 | 54 | 47 |
| Charlton Ath | 18 | 15 | 1 | 2 | 52 | 17 | 35 | 46 |
| Fulham | 18 | 14 | 2 | 2 | 60 | 20 | 40 | 44 |
| Leeds U | 18 | 8 | 4 | 6 | 32 | 28 | 4 | 28 |
| Doncaster Belles | 18 | 8 | 3 | 7 | 41 | 40 | 1 | 27 |
| Everton | 18 | 6 | 2 | 10 | 21 | 36 | –15 | 20 |
| Birmingham C | 18 | 4 | 5 | 9 | 17 | 31 | –14 | 17 |
| Bristol R | 18 | 3 | 3 | 12 | 27 | 37 | –10 | 12 |
| Aston Villa* | 18 | 1 | 4 | 13 | 18 | 63 | –45 | 7 |
| Tranmere R* | 18 | 1 | 4 | 13 | 13 | 63 | –50 | 7 |

## NORTHERN DIVISION

| | P | W | D | L | F | A | GD | Pts |
|---|---|---|---|---|---|---|---|---|
| Liverpool | 20 | 15 | 5 | 0 | 51 | 12 | 39 | 50 |
| Sunderland | 20 | 10 | 7 | 3 | 56 | 31 | 25 | 37 |
| Stockport Co | 20 | 10 | 4 | 6 | 41 | 22 | 19 | 34 |
| Oldham Curzon | 20 | 9 | 7 | 4 | 39 | 21 | 18 | 34 |
| Wolves Women | 20 | 6 | 9 | 5 | 27 | 22 | 5 | 27 |
| Middlesbrough | 20 | 7 | 5 | 8 | 25 | 28 | –3 | 26 |
| Manchester C | 20 | 7 | 3 | 10 | 35 | 45 | –10 | 24 |
| Lincoln C | 20 | 6 | 5 | 9 | 34 | 38 | –4 | 23 |
| Sheffield W | 20 | 6 | 4 | 10 | 30 | 45 | –15 | 22 |
| Chesterfield* | 20 | 5 | 6 | 9 | 23 | 50 | –27 | 21 |
| Bangor C* | 20 | 0 | 3 | 17 | 12 | 59 | –47 | 3 |

## SOUTHERN DIVISION

| | P | W | D | L | F | A | GD | Pts |
|---|---|---|---|---|---|---|---|---|
| Bristol C | 24 | 18 | 4 | 2 | 78 | 31 | 47 | 58 |
| Southampton Saints | 24 | 18 | 3 | 3 | 54 | 18 | 36 | 57 |
| AFC Wimbledon | 24 | 17 | 2 | 5 | 57 | 38 | 19 | 53 |
| Chelsea | 24 | 13 | 6 | 5 | 60 | 38 | 22 | 45 |
| Watford | 24 | 9 | 5 | 10 | 34 | 38 | –4 | 32 |
| Brighton | 24 | 8 | 7 | 9 | 43 | 44 | –1 | 31 |
| Langford | 24 | 9 | 4 | 11 | 37 | 42 | –5 | 31 |
| Millwall Lionesses | 24 | 8 | 6 | 10 | 35 | 38 | –3 | 30 |
| Ipswich T | 24 | 8 | 5 | 11 | 39 | 44 | –5 | 29 |
| Portsmouth | 24 | 9 | 1 | 14 | 43 | 48 | –5 | 28 |
| Enfield T | 24 | 4 | 4 | 16 | 17 | 54 | –37 | 16 |
| Merthyr Tydfil* | 24 | 3 | 6 | 15 | 27 | 61 | –34 | 15 |
| Barnet* | 24 | 2 | 7 | 15 | 31 | 61 | –30 | 11 |

## NATIONAL DIVISION LEAGUE – PREVIOUS WINNERS

| | | | | | |
|---|---|---|---|---|---|
| 1992–93 | Arsenal | 1996–97 | Arsenal | 2000–01 | Arsenal |
| 1993–94 | Doncaster Belles | 1997–98 | Everton | 2001–02 | Arsenal |
| 1994–95 | Arsenal | 1998–99 | Croydon | 2002–03 | Fulham |
| 1995–96 | Croydon | 1999–00 | Croydon | 2003–04 | Arsenal |

# THE FA WOMEN'S CUP 2003–04

## IN PARTNERSHIP WITH CARLSBERG

**FIRST QUALIFYING ROUND**

| | |
|---|---|
| Liverpool Feds v Darwen | 1-8 |
| Bolton Ambassadors v Corwen | 2-1 |
| Huddersfield Town v Crook Town | 3-2 |
| Bury Girls & Ladies v Stockport Celtic | 7-2 |
| Hull City v North Ferriby United | 3-4 |
| Blyth Spartans v York City | 2-1 |
| Wigan withdrew v Thorpe United w.o. | |
| Macclesfield Town v Bolton Wanderers | 0-3 |
| Kirklees v Chester-Le-Street Town | 0-13 |
| Ossett Albion v Wardley Eagles | 0-3 |
| Lumley Ladies v Gateshead Cleveland Hall | 10-3 |
| Morley Spurs v Killingworth YPC | 2-4 |
| Hopwood v Greyhound Gunners | 13-0 |
| Preston North End v Penrith Sapphires | 9-1 |
| Darlington RA v Blyth Town | 3-1 |
| Durham City v Windscale | 3-1 |
| Loughborough Dynamo v Walsall | 3-2 |
| Telford United v Stone Dominoes | 0-2 |
| TNS Ladies w.o. v Cambridge City withdrew. | |
| Leicester City v Kidderminster Harriers | 12-1 |
| Birstall United v Kettering Town | 2-1 |
| US Valerio Vixens v Barwell | 3-0 |
| Sporting Links (Caistor) v Eye United | 2-3 |
| Derby County v Cosford | 4-0 |
| Buxton v Atherstone United | 5-3 |
| South Normanton Athletic v Leafield Athletic | 0-5 |
| Cambridge United v Southam United | 7-1 |
| Northampton Town v Wollaston Victoria | 0-0 |
| *Wollaston Victoria won 4-3 on penalties.* | |

| | |
|---|---|
| Redbridge Raiders w.o. v Mansfield Road withdrew. | |
| Dagenham & Redbridge v Harlow Town | 17-0 |
| Aylesbury United v Redhill | 1-0 |
| Luton Borough v Tring Athletic | 1-4 |
| Brentwood Town v Whitehawk | 1-4 |
| Haywards Heath Town v Luton Town Belles | 1-4 |
| Thurrock & Tilbury v Tottenham Hotspur | 1-11 |
| Viking v MK Wanderers | 2-5 |
| London Women v Woking | 2-3 |
| Chelmsford City v Caversham | 5-6 |
| Wycombe Wanderers v Clapton Orient | 4-2 |
| Dynamo & North London v Hastings United | 3-3 |
| *Dynamo & North London won 5-4 on penalties.* | |
| London Colney v Haywood United | 3-1 |
| Brentford v Carterton Rangers | 3-2 |
| Billericay Town v Southwark Town United | 1-4 |
| Haringey Borough v Basildon United | 5-1 |
| Hitchin Town v Bushey Rangers | 2-2 |
| *Hitchin Town won 7-6 on penalties.* | |
| Lordswood v London Ladies | 1-4 |
| Crowborough Athletic v Maidstone Mavrix | 7-1 |
| Hendon v Leighton Linslade | 2-2 |
| *Leighton Linslade won 4-3 on penalties.* | |
| Lewes v Thatcham Town | 7-1 |
| Launceston v Team Bath | 0-5 |
| Bristol Manor Farm v Bath City | 1-2 |
| Madron v Alphington | 0-7 |
| Buckfastleigh Rangers v Cogan Corinthian | 6-1 |
| Plymouth Oak Villa v Ashdown Rovers | 7-3 |
| Swindon Spitfires w.o. v Caldicott Town removed. | |
| Penzance v Newquay | 3-1 |
| Keynsham Town v Marazion Blues | 12-0 |

**SECOND QUALIFYING ROUND**

| | |
|---|---|
| Bury Girls & Ladies v South Durham Royals | 7-4 |
| Chester-Le-Street Town v Lumley Ladies | 3-1 |
| Bolton Wanderers v Huddersfield Town | 7-1 |
| Hopwood v Wardley Eagles | 5-2 |
| Darwen v Darlington RA | 4-0 |
| Bradford City v Thorpe United | 4-1 |
| Blyth Spartans v North Ferriby United | 3-0 |
| Bolton Ambassadors v Preston North End | 2-3 |
| Durham City v Killingworth YPC | 2-3 |
| Wollaston Victoria v Cambridge United | 0-1 |
| Eye United v Leafield Athletic | 3-8 |
| Birstall United v Solihull Blades | 4-0 |
| Derby County v Loughborough Dynamo | 6-0 |
| TNS Ladies v US Valerio Vixens | 10-0 |
| Buxton v Leicester City | 0-7 |
| Peterborough United v Stone Dominoes | 3-1 |
| Edgware Town v Redbridge Raiders | 0-3 |
| Wycombe Wanderers v Luton Town Belles | 2-3 |
| Woking v Hitchin Town | 5-1 |
| Southwark Town United v Royston Town | 7-1 |
| Brentford v MK Wanderers | 10-1 |
| Haringey Borough v Tottenham Hotspur | 0-7 |
| Caversham v Woodbridge Town | 2-1 |
| Dynamo & North London v Crowborough Athletic | 0-1 |
| Leyton Orient v Tring Athletic | 6-0 |
| London Colney v London Ladies | 8-1 |
| Dagenham & Redbridge v Aylesbury United | 5-1 |
| Abbey Rangers v Whitstable Town | 4-0 |
| Whitehawk v Woodstock | 5-0 |
| Lewes v Leighton Linslade | 5-1 |
| Alphington v Gloucester City | 3-2 |
| Plymouth Oak Villa v Keynsham Town | 8-6 |
| Southampton v Bath City | 0-3 |
| Team Bath v Buckfastleigh Rangers | 1-0 |
| Penzance v Swindon Spitfires | 4-0 |

**FIRST ROUND**

| | |
|---|---|
| Crewe Vagrants v Chester-Le-Street Town | 3-2 |
| Manchester United v Newsham PH | 2-0 |
| Blackburn Rovers v Newcastle | 1-0 |
| Bolton Wanderers v East Durham | 1-5 |
| Blyth Spartans v Bury Girls & Ladies | 2-4 |
| Killingworth YPC v Hopwood | 1-2 |
| Bradford City v TNS Ladies | 1-3 |
| Scunthorpe United v Blackpool Wren Rovers | 1-2 |
| Chester City v Barnsley | 2-0 |
| Shrewsbury Town v Garswood Saints | 1-2 |
| Preston North End v Rotherham United | 5-4 |
| Darwen w.o. v Ilkeston Town withdrew | |
| Doncaster Parklands Rovers v Leeds City Vixens | 5-0 |
| Loughborough Students v Luton Town Belles | 2-0 |
| Derby County v Leafield Athletic | 3-5 |
| Nottingham Forest v Rushden & Diamonds | 3-2 |
| Leicester City v Bedford Town Belles | 2-1 |
| Lichfield Diamonds v Coventry City | 3-8 |
| Cambridge United v Peterborough United | 1-0 |
| Birstall United v Stafford Rangers | 3-0 |
| Crystal Palace v Southwark Town United | 1-0 |
| Reading v Stowmarket Sophtlogic | 3-3 |
| *Reading won 4-2 on penalties.* | |
| Brook House v Reading Royals | 2-3 |
| Brentford v Gillingham | 5-5 |
| *Gillingham won 8-7 on penalties.* | |
| Leyton Orient v Woking | 2-1 |
| Dagenham & Redbridge v Tottenham Hotspur | 2-3 |
| Crowborough Athletic v Abbey Rangers | 4-2 |
| Redbridge Raiders v Chesham United | 3-5 |
| Colchester United v Barking | 2-0 |
| Lewes v Norwich City | 1-0 |
| London Colney v West Ham United | 2-5 |
| Caversham v Whitehawk | 0-3 |
| Denham United v Queens Park Rangers | 2-4 |
| Forest Green Rovers v Rover Oxford | 7-3 |
| Bath City v Alphington | 3-5 |
| Newton Abbot v Plymouth Argyle | 4-0 |
| Team Bath v Cardiff City | 1-5 |
| Exeter City v Clevedon Town | 1-3 |
| Yeovil Town v Penzance | 0-1 |
| Plymouth Oak Villa v Swindon Town | 7-6 |

**SECOND ROUND**

| | |
|---|---|
| Darwen v Chester City | 3-2 |
| Bury Girls & Ladies v Blackburn Rovers | 0-7 |
| Garswood Saints v Manchester United | 1-4 |
| Hopwood v Crewe Vagrants | 0-5 |
| Blackpool Wren Rovers v Doncaster Parklands Rovers | 1-0 |
| East Durham v Preston North End | 4-2 |
| Nottingham Forest v TNS Ladies | 2-0 |
| Birstall United v Coventry City | 1-5 |
| Leafield Athletic v Leicester City | 0-2 |
| Cambridge United v Loughborough Students | 1-5 |
| Whitehawk v West Ham United | 1-1 |
| *West Ham United won 4-3 on penalties.* | |
| Gillingham v Lewes | 4-4 |
| *Gillingham won 4-2 on penalties.* | |
| Crystal Palace v Crowborough Athletic | 7-1 |
| Leyton Orient v Colchester United | 3-1 |
| Queens Park Rangers v Tottenham Hotspur | 5-4 |
| Newton Abbot v Reading | 2-2 |
| *(Abandoned 90 minutes; waterlogged pitch)* | 1-4 |
| Clevedon Town v Plymouth Oak Villa | 4-1 |
| Cardiff City v Chesham United | 5-1 |
| Penzance v Forest Green Rovers | 1-2 |
| Alphington v Reading Royals | 0-3 |

**THIRD ROUND**

| | |
|---|---|
| Stockport County v Blackburn Rovers | 2-1 |
| Leicester City v Sunderland AFC Ladies | 2-3 |
| Nottingham Forest v Crewe Vagrants | 3-1 |
| Loughborough Students v Blackpool Wren Rovers | 6-2 |
| Lincoln City v Manchester City | 3-1 |
| Chesterfield v Manchester United | 1-2 |
| East Durham v Oldham Curzon | 1-2 |
| Darwen v Sheffield Wednesday | 2-5 |
| Wolverhampton Wanderers v Liverpool | 2-1 |
| Middlesbrough v Bangor City | 2-0 |
| Queens Park Rangers v Merthyr Tydfil | 0-2 |
| Bristol City v Reading Royals | 0-3 |
| Portsmouth v Forest Green Rovers | 3-2 |
| Chelsea v Gillingham | 6-3 |
| Barnet v Cardiff City | 2-4 |
| Enfield Town v Crystal Palace | 0-0 |
| *Crystal Palace won 4-2 on penalties.* | |
| Watford v Brighton & Hove Albion | 1-2 |
| Coventry City v Southampton Saints | 2-3 |
| Reading v AFC Wimbledon | 0-3 |
| West Ham United v Langford | 1-1 |
| *Langford won 4-3 on penalties.* | |
| Clevedon Town v Millwall Lionesses | 1-3 |
| Leyton Orient v Ipswich Town | 4-2 |

**FOURTH ROUND**

| | |
|---|---|
| Reading Royals v Millwall Lionesses | 2-1 |
| Lincoln City v Leyton Orient | 1-3 |
| Doncaster Rovers Belles v Leeds United | 2-1 |
| Middlesbrough v Southampton Saints | 1-0 |
| Chelsea v Manchester United | 2-0 |

| | |
|---|---|
| Birmingham City v Loughborough Students | 1-0 |
| Wolverhampton Wanderers v AFC Wimbledon | 6-2 |
| Charlton Athletic v Portsmouth | 3-0 |
| Tranmere Rovers v Brighton & Hove Albion | 5-3 |
| Bristol Rovers v Aston Villa | 1-0 |
| Arsenal v Stockport County | 3-0 |
| Everton v Langford | 2-1 |
| Cardiff City v Merthyr Tydfil | 3-1 |
| Fulham v Sunderland AFC Ladies | 5-0 |
| Nottingham Forest v Oldham Curzon | 3-0 |
| Sheffield Wednesday v Crystal Palace | 1-0 |

**FIFTH ROUND**

| | |
|---|---|
| Chelsea v Nottingham Forest | 3-3 |
| *Nottingham Forest won 3-1 on penalties.* | |
| Doncaster Rovers Belles v Wolverhampton Wanderers | 4-0 |
| Charlton Athletic v Fulham | 2-1 |
| Reading Royals v Bristol Rovers | 1-9 |
| Tranmere Rovers v Sheffield Wednesday | 1-0 |
| Middlesbrough v Arsenal | 1-6 |
| Cardiff City v Everton | 2-1 |
| Leyton Orient v Birmingham City | 1-6 |

**SIXTH ROUND**

| | |
|---|---|
| Doncaster Rovers Belles v Charlton Athletic | 0-1 |
| Tranmere Rovers v Birmingham City | 2-3 |
| Nottingham Forest v Bristol Rovers | 0-3 |
| Arsenal v Cardiff City | 11-1 |

**SEMI-FINALS**

| | |
|---|---|
| Birmingham City v Charlton Athletic | 0-1 |
| Bristol Rovers v Arsenal | 0-2 |

**THE FA WOMEN'S CUP FINAL**

Monday, 3 May 2004
(at Loftus Road)

**Arsenal (2) 3** *(Fleeting 23, 25, 83)*
**Charlton Athletic (0) 0** 12,244

*Arsenal:* Byrne; Pealling, Wheatley, White, Asante, Champ, Ludlow, Maggs (Lorton 90), Sanderson (Potter 73), Fleeting (Scott 90), Grant.
*Charlton Athletic:* Cope; Murphy, Fletcher (Coss 70), Smith (Hunn 81), Stoney, Mills, Williams, Broadhurst, Barr, Walker, Heatherson (Aluko 70).
*Referee:* A. Rayner (Leicestershire & Rutland).

## THE FA WOMEN'S CUP – PREVIOUS WINNERS

| *Year* | *Winners* | *Runners-up* | *Score* |
|---|---|---|---|
| 1971 | Southampton | Stewarton & Thistle | 4-1 |
| 1972 | Southampton | Lee's Ladies | 3-2 |
| 1973 | Southampton | West Horn United | 2-0 |
| 1974 | Foxdens | Southampton | 2-1 |
| 1975 | Southampton | Warminster | 4-2 |
| 1976 | Southampton | QPR | 2-1 |
| 1977 | QPR | Southampton | 1-0 |
| 1978 | Southampton | QPR | 8-2 |
| 1979 | Southampton | Lowestoft | 1-0 |
| 1980 | St Helens | Preston North End | 1-0 |
| 1981 | Southampton | St Helens | 4-2 |
| 1982 | Lowestoft | Cleveland Spartans | 2-0 |
| 1983 | Doncaster Belles | St Helens | 3-2 |
| 1984 | Howbury Grange | Doncaster Belles | 4-2 |
| 1985 | Friends of Fulham | Doncaster Belles | 2-0 |
| 1986 | Norwich | Doncaster Belles | 4-3 |
| 1987 | Doncaster Belles | St Helens | 2-0 |
| 1988 | Doncaster Belles | Leasowe Pacific | 3-1 |
| 1989 | Leasowe Pacific | Friends of Fulham | 3-2 |
| 1990 | Doncaster Belles | Friends of Fulham | 1-0 |
| 1991 | Millwall Lionesses | Doncaster Belles | 1-0 |
| 1992 | Doncaster Belles | Red Star Southampton | 4-0 |
| 1993 | Arsenal | Doncaster Belles | 3-0 |
| 1994 | Doncaster Belles | Knowsley United | 1-0 |
| 1995 | Arsenal | Liverpool | 3-2 |
| 1996 | Croydon | Liverpool | 1-1 |
| | *Croydon won 4-2 on penalties.* | | |
| 1997 | Millwall Lionesses | Wembley | 1-0 |
| 1998 | Arsenal | Croydon | 3-2 |
| 1999 | Arsenal | Southampton Saints | 2-0 |
| 2000 | Croydon | Doncaster Belles | 2-1 |
| 2001 | Arsenal | Fulham | 1-0 |
| 2002 | Fulham | Doncaster Belles | 2-1 |
| 2003 | Fulham | Charlton Atheltic | 3-0 |
| 2004 | Arsenal | Charlton Athletic | 3-0 |

# THE FA NATIONWIDE PREMIER LEAGUE CUP 2003–04

**PRELIMINARY ROUND**

| | |
|---|---|
| Chesterfield v Middlesbrough | 2-3 |
| Portsmouth v Millwall Lionesses | 2-1 |

**FIRST ROUND**

| | |
|---|---|
| Arsenal v Ipswich Town | 4-0 |
| Aston Villa v AFC Wimbledon | 5-0 |
| Barnet v Bangor City | 2-4 |
| Birmingham City v Fulham | 0-4 |
| Brighton & Hove Albion v Charlton Athletic | 0-7 |
| Enfield Town v Lincoln City | 1-5 |
| Everton v Manchester City | 3-0 |
| Langford v Sheffield Wednesday | 1-0 |
| Leeds United v Bristol City | 3-1 |
| Liverpool v Bristol Rovers | 0-1 |
| Oldham Curzon v Merthyr Tydfil | 3-1 |
| Southampton Saints v Doncaster Rovers Belles | 1-3 |
| Sunderland v Stockport County | 3-0 |
| Watford v Tranmere Rovers | 1-7 |
| Wolves Women v Portsmouth | 2-1 |

*Bye:* Middlesbrough

**SECOND ROUND**

| | |
|---|---|
| Middlesbrough v Bristol Rovers | 1-5 |
| Charlton Athletic v Bangor City | 10-1 |
| Arsenal v Sunderland | 4-2 |
| Tranmere Rovers v Doncaster Rovers Belles | 1-5 |
| Fulham v Langford | 9-0 |
| Wolves Women v Lincoln City | 1-1 |
| *Wolves Women won 4-2 on penalties.* | |
| Leeds United v Everton | 7-0 |
| Aston Villa v Oldham Curzon | 2-1 |

**THIRD ROUND**

| | |
|---|---|
| Arsenal v Doncaster Rovers Belles | 4-0 |
| Bristol Rovers v Aston Villa | 4-1 |
| Wolves Women v Charlton Athletic | 0-4 |
| Leeds United v Fulham | 2-3 |

**SEMI-FINALS**

| | |
|---|---|
| Fulham v Bristol Rovers | 7-0 |
| Charlton Athletic v Arsenal | 2-1 |

**FINAL**

| | |
|---|---|
| Fulham v Charlton Athletic | 0-1 |

## THE WOMEN'S PREMIER LEAGUE CUP – PREVIOUS WINNERS

| *Year* | *Winners* | *Runners-up* | *Score* |
|---|---|---|---|
| 1993 | Arsenal | Knowsley | 3-0 |
| 1994 | Arsenal | Doncaster Belles | 4-0 |
| 1995 | Wimbledon | Villa Aztecs | 2-0 |
| 1996 | Wembley | Doncaster Belles | 2-2 |
| | *Wembley won 5-3 on penalties.* | | |
| 1997 | Millwall Lionesses | Everton | 2-1 |
| 1998 | Arsenal | Croydon | 3-2 |
| 1999 | Arsenal | Everton | 3-1 |
| 2000 | Arsenal | Leeds United | 5-1 |
| 2001 | Arsenal | Tranmere Rovers | 3-0 |
| 2002 | Fulham | Birmingham City | 7-1 |
| 2003 | Fulham | Arsenal | 1-1 |
| | *Fulham won 3-2 on penalties.* | | |
| 2004 | Charlton Athletic | Fulham | 1-0 |

## FIFA WOMEN'S WORLD CUP 2003
(in USA)

**GROUP A**
Nigeria 0, North Korea 3
USA 3, Sweden 1
Sweden 1, North Korea 0
USA 5, Nigeria 0
Sweden 3, Nigeria 0
North Korea 0, USA 3

**GROUP B**
Norway 2, France 0
Brazil 3, South Korea 0
Norway 1, Brazil 4
France 1, South Korea 0
South Korea 1, Norway 7
France 1, Brazil 1

**GROUP C**
Germany 4, Canada 1
Japan 6, Argentina 0
Germany 3, Japan 0
Canada 3, Argentina 0
Canada 3, Japan 1
Argentina 1, Germany 6

**GROUP D**
China 1, Ghana 0
Australia 1, Russia 2
Ghana 0, Russia 3
China 1, Australia 1
Ghana 2, Australia 1
China 1, Russia 0

**QUARTER-FINALS**
USA 1, Norway 0
Sweden 2, Brazil 1
Germany 7, Russia 1
China 0, Canada 1

**SEMI-FINALS**
USA 0, Germany 3
Sweden 2, Canada 1

**MATCH FOR THIRD PLACE**
USA 3, Canada 1

**FINAL**
Germany 1, Sweden 1
*Germany won 2-1 on sudden death.*

## FIFA WOMEN'S WORLD CUP PAST WINNERS

1991 USA 2, Norway 1 (in China)
1995 Norway 2, Germany 0 (in Sweden)
1999 USA 0, China 0 (in USA)
*USA won 5-4 on penalties.*
2003 Germany 1, Sweden 1
*Germany won 2-1 on sudden death.*

## UEFA WOMEN'S CUP 2002–03

**FINAL FIRST LEG**
Umea 4, Hjorring 1

**FINAL SECOND LEG**
Hjorring 0, Umea 3

## UEFA WOMEN'S CUP 2003–04
From Quarter-Finals onwards

**QUARTER-FINALS, FIRST LEG**
Brondby 9, Gomrukcu Baku 0
Frankfurt 3, Fulham 1
Energy 1, Umea 2
Malmo 2, Kolbotn 0

**QUARTER-FINALS, SECOND LEG**
Gomrukcu Baku 0, Brondby 3
Fulham 1, Frankfurt 4
Umea 2, Energy 1
Kolbotn 1, Malmo 0

**SEMI-FINALS, FIRST LEG**
Brondby 2, Umea 3
Malmo 0, Frankfurt 0

**SEMI-FINALS, SECOND LEG**
Umea 1, Brondby 0
Frankfurt 4, Malmo 1

**FINAL FIRST LEG**
Umea 3, Frankfurt 0

**FINAL SECOND LEG**
Frankfurt 0, Umea 5

## UEFA WOMEN'S CUP PAST WINNERS

2001–02 Frankfurt 2, Umea 0
2002–03 Umea 4, 3, Fortuna Hjorring 1, 0
2003–04 Frankfurt 0, Umea 5

## UEFA WOMEN'S CHAMPIONSHIP PAST WINNERS

1984 Sweden 1, 0, England 0, 1
*Sweden won 4-3 on penalties.*
1987 Norway 2, Sweden 1
1989 Germany 4, Norway 1
1991 Germany 3, Norway 1
1993 Norway 1, Italy 0
1995 Germany 3, Sweden 2
1997 Germany 2, Italy 0
2001 Germany 1, Sweden 0
2002 France 1, 1, England 0, 0

## UEFA WOMEN'S UNDER-19 CHAMPIONSHIP PAST WINNERS

1998 Denmark 2, 2, France 3, 0
1999 Sweden
2000 Germany 4, Spain 2
2001 Germany 3, Norway 2
2002 Germany 3, France 1
2003 France 2, Norway 0

## FIFA WOMEN'S UNDER-19'S CHAMPIONSHIP PAST WINNERS

2002 USA 1, Canada 0 (in Canada)

## WOMEN'S OLYMPICS PAST WINNERS

1996 USA 2, China 1 (in Atlanta)
2000 Norway 3, USA 2 (in Sydney)

## ENGLAND WOMEN'S INTERNATIONAL APPEARANCES 2003-04

*Appearances include those as substitute.*
Brown (Everton) 3; Champ (Arsenal) 5; Unitt (Fulham) 7; Chapman (Fulham) 7; Stoney (Charlton Athletic) 7; Phillip (Fulham) 7; Moore (Floya) 5; Exley (Doncaster RB) 4; Walker (Charlton Athletic) 3; Smith K (Philadelphia C) 7; Yankey (Fulham) 7; Handley (Doncaster RB) 6; McArthur (Fulham) 2; McDougall (Everton) 3; Barr (Charlton Athletic) 6; Smith S (Leeds United) 5; Cope (Charlton Athletic) 3; Williams (Charlton Athletic) 6; Yorston (Fulham) 2; Burke (Doncaster RB) 1; White (Arsenal) 4; Maggs (Arsenal) 2; Hall (Leeds United) 2; Pealling (Arsenal) 1; Asante (Arsenal) 1.

## WOMEN'S INTERNATIONAL RESULTS 2003–04

| *Date* | *Match* | *Result* | | *Venue* |
|---|---|---|---|---|
| **SENIOR TEAM** | | | | |
| 03/09/03 | England v Australia | 1-0 | Won | Burnley |
| 11/09/03 | Germany v England | 0-4 | Lost | Darmstadt |
| 21/10/03 | Russia v England | 2-2 | Draw | Moscow |
| 13/11/03 | England v Scotland | 5-0 | Won | Preston |
| 19/02/04 | England v Denmark | 2-0 | Won | Portsmouth |
| 22/04/04 | England v Nigeria | 0-3 | Lost | Reading |
| 14/05/04 | England v Iceland | 1-0 | Won | Peterborough |
| **UNDER-19 TEAM** | | | | |
| *European Championship Finals* | | | | |
| 25/07/03 | England v Sweden | 2-1 | Won | Markranstadt |
| 27/07/03 | England v Italy | 3-1 | Won | Markeleeberg |
| 29/07/03 | England v Germany | 0-6 | Lost | Torgau |
| 01/08/03 | England v France | 0-2 | Lost | Markranstadt |
| *European Championship Qualifying* | | | | |
| 23/09/03 | England v Scotland | 0-0 | Draw | Mogosoaia |
| 27/09/03 | England v Romania | 5-1 | Won | Mogosoaia |
| 26/03/04 | England v Belgium | 2-0 | Won | Calais |
| 28/03/04 | England v Holland | 2-2 | Draw | Calais |
| 30/03/04 | England v France | 0-3 | Lost | Calais |
| *Friendlies* | | | | |
| 19/03/04 | England v Republic of Ireland | 3-1 | Won | Gravesend |
| 20/05/04 | England v Sweden | 2-3 | Lost | Solihull |
| **UNDER-17 TEAM** | | | | |
| *International Friendly* | | | | |
| 30/10/03 | England v Belgium | 3-1 | Won | Yeading |
| *Castlebar Tournament* | | | | |
| 13/04/04 | England v N Ireland | 3-0 | Won | Castlebar |
| 15/04/04 | England v Scotland | 2-2* | Draw | Castlebar |
| 17/04/04 | England v USA Region 1 | 2-2** | Draw | Castlebar |

*England won Castlebar Tournament.*
** England won 3-1 on penalties.*
*** England won 6-5 on penalties.*

Arsenal ladies celebrate their 3-0 FA Cup final win over Charlton Athletic. Julie Fleeting helped herself to a hat-trick in the Loftus Road showpiece. (Colorsport)

# UNIBOND LEAGUE 2003–04

## PREMIER DIVISION

| | | | *Home* | | | | | *Away* | | | | | *Total* | | | | | | |
|---|---|---|---|---|---|---|---|---|---|---|---|---|---|---|---|---|---|---|---|
| | | *P* | *W* | *D* | *L* | *F* | *A* | *W* | *D* | *L* | *F* | *A* | *W* | *D* | *L* | *F* | *A* | *GD* | *Pts* |
| 1 | Hucknall Town | 44 | 15 | 5 | 2 | 38 | 14 | 14 | 3 | 5 | 45 | 24 | 29 | 8 | 7 | 83 | 38 | 45 | 95 |
| 2 | Droylsden | 44 | 15 | 4 | 3 | 51 | 29 | 11 | 4 | 7 | 45 | 35 | 26 | 8 | 10 | 96 | 64 | 32 | 86 |
| 3 | Barrow | 44 | 14 | 4 | 4 | 41 | 20 | 8 | 10 | 4 | 41 | 32 | 22 | 14 | 8 | 82 | 52 | 30 | 80 |
| 4 | Alfreton Town | 44 | 14 | 5 | 3 | 45 | 18 | 9 | 4 | 9 | 28 | 25 | 23 | 9 | 12 | 73 | 43 | 30 | 78 |
| 5 | Harrogate Town | 44 | 15 | 2 | 5 | 44 | 26 | 9 | 3 | 10 | 35 | 37 | 24 | 5 | 15 | 79 | 63 | 16 | 77 |
| 6 | Southport | 44 | 10 | 7 | 5 | 36 | 25 | 10 | 3 | 9 | 35 | 27 | 20 | 10 | 14 | 71 | 52 | 19 | 70 |
| 7 | Worksop Town | 44 | 10 | 6 | 6 | 34 | 22 | 9 | 7 | 6 | 35 | 28 | 19 | 13 | 12 | 69 | 50 | 19 | 70 |
| 8 | Lancaster City | 44 | 12 | 4 | 6 | 40 | 25 | 8 | 5 | 9 | 22 | 24 | 20 | 9 | 15 | 62 | 49 | 13 | 69 |
| 9 | Vauxhall Motors | 44 | 12 | 5 | 5 | 44 | 32 | 7 | 5 | 10 | 34 | 43 | 19 | 10 | 15 | 78 | 75 | 3 | 67 |
| 10 | Gainsborough Trinity | 44 | 12 | 5 | 5 | 46 | 25 | 5 | 8 | 9 | 24 | 27 | 17 | 13 | 14 | 70 | 52 | 18 | 64 |
| 11 | Stalybridge Celtic | 44 | 8 | 6 | 8 | 35 | 33 | 10 | 4 | 8 | 37 | 33 | 18 | 10 | 16 | 72 | 66 | 6 | 64 |
| 12 | Altrincham | 44 | 9 | 8 | 5 | 36 | 24 | 7 | 7 | 8 | 30 | 27 | 16 | 15 | 13 | 66 | 51 | 15 | 63 |
| 13 | Runcorn FC Halton | 44 | 5 | 9 | 8 | 32 | 32 | 11 | 4 | 7 | 35 | 31 | 16 | 13 | 15 | 67 | 63 | 4 | 61 |
| 14 | Ashton United | 44 | 7 | 5 | 10 | 34 | 44 | 10 | 3 | 9 | 25 | 35 | 17 | 8 | 19 | 59 | 79 | –20 | 59 |
| 15 | Whitby Town | 44 | 9 | 3 | 10 | 24 | 34 | 5 | 8 | 9 | 31 | 36 | 14 | 11 | 19 | 55 | 70 | –15 | 53 |
| 16 | Marine | 44 | 8 | 5 | 9 | 32 | 31 | 5 | 7 | 10 | 30 | 43 | 13 | 12 | 19 | 62 | 74 | –12 | 51 |
| 17 | Bradford Park Avenue | 44 | 2 | 9 | 11 | 23 | 32 | 10 | 5 | 7 | 25 | 30 | 12 | 14 | 18 | 48 | 62 | –14 | 50 |
| 18 | Spennymoor United | 44 | 8 | 2 | 12 | 30 | 51 | 6 | 4 | 12 | 25 | 42 | 14 | 6 | 24 | 55 | 93 | –38 | 48 |
| 19 | Burscough | 44 | 6 | 8 | 8 | 27 | 30 | 4 | 7 | 11 | 20 | 37 | 10 | 15 | 19 | 47 | 67 | –20 | 45 |
| 20 | Radcliffe Borough | 44 | 9 | 1 | 12 | 39 | 46 | 3 | 5 | 14 | 35 | 53 | 12 | 6 | 26 | 74 | 99 | –25 | 42 |
| 21 | Blyth Spartans | 44 | 5 | 7 | 10 | 30 | 40 | 5 | 3 | 14 | 24 | 34 | 10 | 10 | 24 | 54 | 74 | –20 | 40 |
| 22 | Frickley Athletic | 44 | 8 | 4 | 10 | 29 | 32 | 3 | 3 | 16 | 22 | 51 | 11 | 7 | 26 | 51 | 83 | –32 | 40 |
| 23 | Wakefield & Emley | 44 | 4 | 2 | 16 | 18 | 45 | 4 | 4 | 14 | 27 | 54 | 8 | 6 | 30 | 45 | 99 | –54 | 30 |

## DIVISION ONE

| | | | *Home* | | | | | *Away* | | | | | *Total* | | | | | | |
|---|---|---|---|---|---|---|---|---|---|---|---|---|---|---|---|---|---|---|---|
| | | *P* | *W* | *D* | *L* | *F* | *A* | *W* | *D* | *L* | *F* | *A* | *W* | *D* | *L* | *F* | *A* | *GD* | *Pts* |
| 1 | Hyde United | 42 | 14 | 4 | 3 | 42 | 14 | 10 | 4 | 7 | 37 | 35 | 24 | 8 | 10 | 79 | 49 | 30 | 80 |
| 2 | Matlock Town | 42 | 14 | 3 | 4 | 46 | 23 | 9 | 4 | 8 | 32 | 28 | 23 | 7 | 12 | 78 | 51 | 27 | 76 |
| 3 | Farsley Celtic | 42 | 11 | 7 | 3 | 44 | 25 | 9 | 7 | 5 | 34 | 31 | 20 | 14 | 8 | 78 | 56 | 22 | 74 |
| 4 | Lincoln United | 42 | 11 | 8 | 2 | 38 | 18 | 9 | 3 | 9 | 35 | 35 | 20 | 11 | 11 | 73 | 53 | 20 | 71 |
| 5 | Witton Albion | 42 | 8 | 7 | 6 | 35 | 27 | 9 | 5 | 7 | 26 | 29 | 17 | 12 | 13 | 61 | 56 | 5 | 63 |
| 6 | Gateshead | 42 | 12 | 1 | 8 | 37 | 36 | 9 | 3 | 9 | 28 | 32 | 21 | 4 | 17 | 65 | 68 | –3 | 63 |
| 7 | Workington | 42 | 9 | 5 | 7 | 38 | 25 | 8 | 6 | 7 | 32 | 33 | 17 | 11 | 14 | 70 | 58 | 12 | 62 |
| 8 | Leek Town | 42 | 8 | 6 | 7 | 29 | 24 | 8 | 7 | 6 | 27 | 23 | 16 | 13 | 13 | 56 | 47 | 9 | 61 |
| 9 | Guiseley | 42 | 9 | 6 | 6 | 35 | 23 | 7 | 6 | 8 | 31 | 31 | 16 | 12 | 14 | 66 | 54 | 12 | 60 |
| 10 | Bamber Bridge | 42 | 8 | 7 | 6 | 35 | 25 | 8 | 5 | 8 | 29 | 28 | 16 | 12 | 14 | 64 | 53 | 11 | 60 |
| 11 | Bridlington Town | 42 | 11 | 5 | 5 | 40 | 28 | 5 | 5 | 11 | 30 | 40 | 16 | 10 | 16 | 70 | 68 | 2 | 58 |
| 12 | Prescot Cables | 42 | 11 | 1 | 9 | 34 | 28 | 5 | 9 | 7 | 29 | 37 | 16 | 10 | 16 | 63 | 65 | –2 | 58 |
| 13 | Bishop Auckland | 42 | 8 | 6 | 7 | 36 | 33 | 6 | 7 | 8 | 25 | 31 | 14 | 13 | 15 | 61 | 64 | –3 | 55 |
| 14 | Ossett Town | 42 | 6 | 6 | 9 | 31 | 30 | 9 | 4 | 8 | 31 | 43 | 15 | 10 | 17 | 62 | 73 | –11 | 55 |
| 15 | Rossendale United | 42 | 7 | 9 | 5 | 32 | 25 | 6 | 3 | 12 | 21 | 37 | 13 | 12 | 17 | 53 | 62 | –9 | 51 |
| 16 | Colwyn Bay | 42 | 6 | 7 | 8 | 30 | 39 | 8 | 2 | 11 | 26 | 43 | 14 | 9 | 19 | 56 | 82 | –26 | 51 |
| 17 | North Ferriby United | 42 | 8 | 4 | 9 | 35 | 30 | 5 | 7 | 9 | 29 | 40 | 13 | 11 | 18 | 64 | 70 | –6 | 50 |
| 18 | Chorley | 42 | 10 | 4 | 7 | 37 | 28 | 3 | 6 | 12 | 17 | 42 | 13 | 10 | 19 | 54 | 70 | –16 | 49 |
| 19 | Stocksbridge PS | 42 | 9 | 4 | 8 | 36 | 32 | 3 | 8 | 10 | 21 | 37 | 12 | 12 | 18 | 57 | 69 | –12 | 48 |
| 20 | Belper Town | 42 | 7 | 8 | 6 | 21 | 19 | 2 | 7 | 12 | 23 | 39 | 9 | 15 | 18 | 44 | 58 | –14 | 42 |
| 21 | Kendal Town | 42 | 7 | 4 | 10 | 30 | 39 | 4 | 3 | 14 | 23 | 41 | 11 | 7 | 24 | 53 | 80 | –27 | 40 |
| 22 | Kidsgrove Athletic | 42 | 7 | 4 | 10 | 29 | 32 | 3 | 5 | 13 | 17 | 35 | 10 | 9 | 23 | 46 | 67 | –21 | 39 |

**4 points deducted for breach of rule.*

**LEADING GOALSCORERS (in order of League goals)**

**Premier Division**

| | *Lge* | *Cup* | *Total* |
|---|---|---|---|
| Fearns (Vauxhall Motors) | 35 | 2 | 37 |
| Hughes (Lancaster Cicy) | 22 | 9 | 31 |
| Cumiskey (Vauxhall Motors) | 22 | 8 | 30 |
| Ricketts (Hucknall Town) | 22 | 5 | 27 |
| Byrne (Droylsden) | 21 | 6 | 27 |
| Morris (Frickley Athletic) | 18 | 6 | 24 |
| Hayward (Stalybridge Celtic) | 20 | 3 | 23 |
| Bacon (Hucknall Town) | 19 | 4 | 23 |
| Banim (Rad B now Shrewsbury T) | 18 | 4 | 22 |
| Godber (Alfreton Town) | 18 | 4 | 22 |
| Rendell (Runcorn FC Halton) | 11 | 11 | 22 |

**Division One**

| | *Lge* | *Cup* | *Total* |
|---|---|---|---|
| Holland (Matlock Town) | 31 | 10 | 41 |
| Moseley (Witton Athletic) | 25 | 8 | 33 |
| Tolson (Hyde United) | 21 | 10 | 31 |
| Midwood (Farsley Celtic) | 18 | 9 | 27 |
| Irvine (Bishop Auckland) | 18 | 8 | 26 |
| Thompson (Gateshead) | 21 | 2 | 23 |
| Whittaker (Leek Town) | 17 | 6 | 23 |
| Wane (Bamber Bridge) | 18 | 3 | 21 |
| Bradshaw (North Ferriby United) | 15 | 6 | 21 |

**ATTENDANCES**

**Premier Division**

Highest Average Attendance: 1159 Barrow
Highest Attendances: 1750 Barrow v Lancaster City
1451 Barrow v Alfreton Town
1416 Barrow v Hucknall Town

**ATTENDANCES**

**Division One**

Highest Average Attendance: 350 Matlock Town
Highest Attendances: 792 Matlock Town v Belper Town
652 Belper Town v Matlock Town
618 Hyde U v North Ferriby U

## UNIBOND LEAGUE – PREMIER DIVISION RESULTS 2003–04

| | Alfreton Town | Altrincham | Ashton United | Barrow | Blyth Spartans | Bradford Park Avenue | Burscough | Droylsden | Frickley Athletic | Gainsborough Trinity | Harrogate Town | Hucknall Town | Lancaster City | Marine | Radcliffe Borough | Runcorn FC Halton | Southport | Spennymoor United | Stalybridge Celtic | Vauxhall Motors | Wakefield & Emley | Whitby Town | Worksop Town |
|---|---|---|---|---|---|---|---|---|---|---|---|---|---|---|---|---|---|---|---|---|---|---|---|
| Alfreton Town | — | 0-0 | 5-0 | 1-1 | 2-1 | 1-1 | 1-0 | 4-2 | 1-2 | 3-1 | 2-0 | 2-1 | 3-0 | 4-0 | 0-0 | 0-2 | 0-2 | 1-1 | 3-1 | 5-1 | 2-1 | 3-0 | 2-1 |
| Altrincham | 0-1 | — | 1-2 | 1-1 | 1-2 | 1-0 | 3-0 | 1-0 | 1-1 | 2-2 | 0-0 | 2-3 | 0-0 | 3-3 | 4-1 | 1-0 | 1-0 | 1-1 | 3-3 | 3-1 | 1-2 | 4-0 | 2-1 |
| Ashton United | 1-1 | 0-2 | — | 1-2 | 2-0 | 0-2 | 0-0 | 1-1 | 3-2 | 1-1 | 3-4 | 1-6 | 2-1 | 4-3 | 3-3 | 4-2 | 2-1 | 1-2 | 2-1 | 0-1 | 2-3 | 1-3 | 0-3 |
| Barrow | 1-2 | 2-1 | 3-0 | — | 3-0 | 4-0 | 3-3 | 2-1 | 3-1 | 3-0 | 1-2 | 1-0 | 4-3 | 1-1 | 2-0 | 1-0 | 1-1 | 2-0 | 0-2 | 0-1 | 3-2 | 0-0 | 1-0 |
| Blyth Spartans | 1-0 | 2-2 | 2-0 | 0-2 | — | 0-0 | 0-1 | 1-5 | 1-3 | 1-1 | 3-4 | 1-2 | 0-0 | 5-0 | 1-0 | 3-3 | 1-4 | 0-2 | 0-1 | 3-6 | 1-0 | 1-1 | 3-3 |
| Bradford Park Avenue | 0-1 | 1-1 | 2-1 | 2-2 | 1-1 | — | 0-2 | 0-2 | 0-0 | 0-0 | 2-3 | 1-2 | 0-2 | 1-1 | 1-1 | 1-1 | 0-1 | 0-0 | 2-3 | 6-2 | 1-2 | 2-3 | 0-1 |
| Burscough | 4-1 | 3-1 | 1-2 | 1-1 | 1-2 | 1-1 | — | 1-3 | 3-1 | 0-0 | 1-0 | 0-1 | 0-1 | 0-0 | 3-6 | 1-3 | 0-3 | 2-1 | 0-0 | 3-1 | 1-1 | 1-1 | 0-0 |
| Droylsden | 2-1 | 1-4 | 1-2 | 1-1 | 3-3 | 3-0 | 2-0 | — | 4-0 | 2-1 | 3-1 | 3-1 | 0-0 | 4-2 | 5-4 | 1-2 | 3-2 | 2-0 | 2-0 | 2-1 | 3-1 | 2-1 | 2-2 |
| Frickley Athletic | 0-3 | 1-1 | 1-2 | 4-2 | 2-1 | 0-1 | 2-0 | 0-3 | — | 0-0 | 0-0 | 0-1 | 0-2 | 4-3 | 3-0 | 1-2 | 1-2 | 3-2 | 1-2 | 0-2 | 2-1 | 3-1 | 1-1 |
| Gainsborough Trinity | 2-4 | 2-3 | 3-0 | 0-0 | 2-0 | 3-3 | 4-1 | 1-2 | 3-0 | — | 2-0 | 2-1 | 3-2 | 2-0 | 6-2 | 0-1 | 1-2 | 3-1 | 0-0 | 0-0 | 3-0 | 2-2 | 2-1 |
| Harrogate Town | 1-0 | 1-0 | 2-1 | 2-1 | 2-1 | 0-1 | 2-1 | 4-4 | 2-1 | 0-2 | — | 1-2 | 0-1 | 4-1 | 3-0 | 1-1 | 3-1 | 3-1 | 4-3 | 3-2 | 5-0 | 1-0 | 0-2 |
| Hucknall Town | 3-3 | 2-1 | 2-0 | 3-1 | 1-0 | 0-0 | 1-0 | 1-1 | 3-0 | 2-0 | 1-0 | — | 3-0 | 1-1 | 1-1 | 1-0 | 4-0 | 2-1 | 1-3 | 2-0 | 0-1 | 1-0 | 3-1 |
| Lancaster City | 0-1 | 1-0 | 1-1 | 0-3 | 1-1 | 1-3 | 4-0 | 2-1 | 1-1 | 0-1 | 1-4 | 3-1 | — | 3-1 | 4-2 | 0-1 | 1-0 | 6-0 | 2-1 | 0-0 | 3-0 | 4-3 | 2-0 |
| Marine | 0-1 | 0-1 | 0-2 | 1-2 | 1-0 | 2-0 | 4-0 | 1-2 | 2-1 | 3-1 | 2-2 | 1-1 | 1-1 | — | 3-2 | 1-3 | 1-1 | 1-3 | 0-2 | 3-2 | 3-0 | 2-2 | 0-2 |
| Radcliffe Borough | 1-0 | 1-3 | 1-2 | 2-3 | 2-3 | 2-0 | 1-2 | 4-2 | 4-2 | 2-1 | 3-1 | 1-6 | 0-2 | 3-1 | — | 1-2 | 1-3 | 1-1 | 3-2 | 1-2 | 4-1 | 0-5 | 1-2 |
| Runcorn FC Halton | 2-2 | 0-3 | 1-2 | 0-0 | 1-0 | 1-2 | 0-0 | 2-2 | 2-0 | 2-2 | 4-1 | 1-2 | 0-1 | 0-2 | 2-2 | — | 1-1 | 1-2 | 3-0 | 1-1 | 5-3 | 1-1 | 2-3 |
| Southport | 1-0 | 2-2 | 0-0 | 1-1 | 1-0 | 0-1 | 2-1 | 4-1 | 3-1 | 2-0 | 3-2 | 1-1 | 3-0 | 0-0 | 2-1 | 0-3 | — | 2-3 | 2-3 | 1-1 | 1-1 | 3-0 | 2-3 |
| Spennymoor United | 1-0 | 2-1 | 3-2 | 2-4 | 0-5 | 2-4 | 0-2 | 0-1 | 3-2 | 0-6 | 1-5 | 1-3 | 0-1 | 0-2 | 3-1 | 2-1 | 0-2 | — | 1-3 | 2-1 | 4-4 | 2-0 | 1-1 |
| Stalybridge Celtic | 3-0 | 1-0 | 1-1 | 2-2 | 2-0 | 2-0 | 1-1 | 2-1 | 5-0 | 2-0 | 1-2 | 1-2 | 0-3 | 1-1 | 0-2 | 2-2 | 2-1 | 0-2 | — | 3-4 | 3-3 | 1-3 | 0-3 |
| Vauxhall Motors | 2-0 | 1-1 | 1-2 | 1-1 | 2-1 | 6-2 | 3-2 | 2-4 | 2-1 | 0-2 | 3-0 | 1-3 | 2-1 | 1-0 | 0-5 | 6-0 | 3-2 | 4-2 | 1-1 | — | 1-0 | 1-1 | 1-1 |
| Wakefield & Emley | 0-3 | 2-0 | 1-2 | 2-5 | 1-2 | 0-1 | 2-2 | 0-2 | 0-2 | 0-2 | 0-2 | 0-3 | 1-0 | 0-4 | 2-1 | 3-5 | 0-1 | 2-0 | 1-3 | 0-1 | — | 0-3 | 1-1 |
| Whitby Town | 0-4 | 2-3 | 0-1 | 3-2 | 2-1 | 0-1 | 1-1 | 1-2 | 2-1 | 2-1 | 0-2 | 0-0 | 2-1 | 1-2 | 1-0 | 1-0 | 0-5 | 1-0 | 0-2 | 1-1 | 2-1 | — | 2-3 |
| Worksop Town | 0-0 | 0-0 | 3-0 | 2-4 | 1-0 | 1-2 | 1-1 | 1-3 | 3-0 | 0-0 | 1-0 | 0-3 | 0-0 | 1-2 | 4-1 | 0-1 | 1-0 | 4-0 | 2-1 | 4-3 | 4-0 | 1-1 | — |

## UNIBOND LEAGUE – DIVISION ONE RESULTS 2003–04

| | Bamber Bridge | Belper Town | Bishop Auckland | Bridlington Town | Chorley | Colwyn Bay | Farsley Celtic | Gateshead | Guiseley | Hyde United | Kendal Town | Kidsgrove Athletic | Leek Town | Lincoln United | Matlock Town | North Ferriby United | Ossett Town | Prescot Cables | Rossendale United | Stocksbridge PS | Witton Albion | Workington |
|---|---|---|---|---|---|---|---|---|---|---|---|---|---|---|---|---|---|---|---|---|---|---|
| Bamber Bridge | — | 2-1 | 1-3 | 2-0 | 0-0 | 1-1 | 1-2 | 0-2 | 1-2 | 2-3 | 5-1 | 3-0 | 0-0 | 1-0 | 4-4 | 1-1 | 0-0 | 2-2 | 2-1 | 4-0 | 1-2 | 2-0 |
| Belper Town | 2-1 | — | 1-1 | 0-2 | 2-0 | 2-0 | 1-1 | 1-1 | 1-0 | 0-1 | 3-0 | 1-1 | 0-2 | 0-1 | 0-2 | 0-3 | 3-0 | 2-2 | 0-0 | 1-0 | 0-0 | 1-1 |
| Bishop Auckland | 0-1 | 2-4 | — | 3-2 | 1-1 | 4-1 | 4-2 | 2-1 | 1-0 | 2-3 | 2-0 | 2-0 | 2-3 | 1-1 | 0-1 | 0-4 | 2-0 | 1-1 | 3-3 | 2-2 | 1-2 | 1-1 |
| Bridlington Town | 1-0 | 1-3 | 2-0 | — | 2-0 | 4-1 | 3-1 | 1-0 | 2-1 | 3-1 | 5-1 | 2-1 | 3-2 | 0-1 | 1-1 | 2-2 | 2-4 | 1-1 | 0-1 | 2-2 | 1-1 | 2-4 |
| Chorley | 0-1 | 1-1 | 2-1 | 1-1 | — | 3-2 | 1-2 | 4-1 | 1-2 | 1-0 | 2-2 | 2-1 | 1-0 | 2-3 | 2-0 | 1-2 | 1-2 | 4-2 | 2-0 | 1-3 | 1-1 | 4-1 |
| Colwyn Bay | 0-5 | 3-2 | 2-3 | 1-1 | 3-4 | — | 1-0 | 1-3 | 1-0 | 1-1 | 0-5 | 5-0 | 1-3 | 3-3 | 0-0 | 1-0 | 4-4 | 0-2 | 1-0 | 1-1 | 1-2 | 0-0 |
| Farsley Celtic | 1-1 | 2-2 | 4-0 | 2-2 | 1-0 | 5-0 | — | 3-3 | 5-3 | 1-3 | 2-1 | 1-1 | 0-0 | 2-2 | 1-2 | 5-0 | 2-1 | 0-2 | 1-0 | 3-1 | 1-0 | 2-1 |
| Gateshead | 2-1 | 2-1 | 0-3 | 2-3 | 1-0 | 1-2 | 3-4 | — | 1-5 | 2-1 | 2-1 | 2-1 | 4-2 | 1-0 | 1-3 | 3-2 | 0-2 | 1-1 | 2-0 | 4-1 | 1-0 | 2-3 |
| Guiseley | 1-1 | 3-0 | 1-1 | 2-1 | 1-3 | 1-2 | 2-0 | 4-2 | — | 0-1 | 4-0 | 2-0 | 1-1 | 1-2 | 3-1 | 1-2 | 1-1 | 0-1 | 2-1 | 0-0 | 2-2 | 3-1 |
| Hyde United | 4-0 | 3-1 | 1-1 | 3-1 | 0-0 | 4-0 | 1-1 | 0-2 | 1-0 | — | 1-0 | 1-0 | 0-1 | 2-0 | 2-1 | 4-0 | 5-2 | 4-1 | 2-0 | 1-1 | 0-1 | 3-1 |
| Kendal Town | 2-3 | 2-1 | 1-2 | 1-0 | 1-1 | 2-1 | 2-2 | 1-2 | 2-2 | 1-3 | — | 1-3 | 2-1 | 2-3 | 1-2 | 1-1 | 0-1 | 2-3 | 2-1 | 2-1 | 2-1 | 0-5 |
| Kidsgrove Athletic | 1-1 | 2-0 | 1-1 | 4-2 | 2-2 | 1-2 | 1-4 | 2-1 | 1-2 | 1-2 | 2-1 | — | 0-1 | 1-2 | 1-0 | 4-1 | 1-2 | 0-1 | 1-3 | 2-1 | 0-2 | 1-1 |
| Leek Town | 1-0 | 1-1 | 0-0 | 3-2 | 2-0 | 0-1 | 1-2 | 0-0 | 2-2 | 5-2 | 1-0 | 1-2 | — | 3-1 | 0-2 | 1-2 | 0-1 | 1-1 | 2-1 | 2-0 | 2-2 | 1-2 |
| Lincoln United | 1-1 | 0-0 | 0-0 | 2-0 | 4-1 | 2-1 | 0-1 | 0-1 | 2-2 | 2-0 | 4-3 | 2-1 | 1-1 | — | 5-2 | 3-3 | 0-0 | 1-0 | 4-0 | 0-0 | 4-1 | 1-0 |
| Matlock Town | 1-0 | 3-1 | 0-1 | 3-5 | 4-0 | 1-1 | 2-0 | 2-0 | 1-2 | 2-5 | 0-0 | 3-1 | 1-0 | 4-2 | — | 1-1 | 3-0 | 2-1 | 4-1 | 3-1 | 2-1 | 4-0 |
| North Ferriby United | 2-0 | 2-0 | 0-3 | 2-2 | 2-3 | 5-0 | 0-2 | 1-2 | 2-0 | 2-0 | 3-1 | 2-1 | 1-1 | 0-1 | 0-2 | — | 2-3 | 4-1 | 2-3 | 1-1 | 1-3 | 1-1 |
| Ossett Town | 2-3 | 2-0 | 0-0 | 0-1 | 1-0 | 4-1 | 1-2 | 4-0 | 1-2 | 2-2 | 0-2 | 1-1 | 0-2 | 3-1 | 0-4 | 2-2 | — | 2-2 | 0-0 | 3-0 | 2-3 | 1-2 |
| Prescot Cables | 2-3 | 1-0 | 4-2 | 1-1 | 4-1 | 0-2 | 0-1 | 2-0 | 1-0 | 0-1 | 2-1 | 2-1 | 1-3 | 1-0 | 0-2 | 3-1 | 5-3 | — | 0-1 | 2-3 | 3-0 | 0-2 |
| Rossendale United | 3-2 | 1-1 | 3-0 | 3-1 | 0-0 | 1-3 | 1-1 | 1-3 | 1-1 | 1-2 | 0-0 | 0-0 | 1-1 | 4-2 | 2-0 | 1-0 | 1-2 | 5-2 | — | 0-0 | 0-1 | 3-3 |
| Stocksbridge PS | 1-3 | 3-3 | 2-1 | 2-0 | 4-0 | 0-3 | 2-2 | 3-0 | 1-1 | 2-2 | 0-2 | 2-1 | 0-2 | 3-2 | 2-1 | 3-0 | 1-2 | 3-1 | 2-4 | — | 0-1 | 0-1 |
| Witton Albion | 0-0 | 2-0 | 2-0 | 2-1 | 3-1 | 0-1 | 2-2 | 0-2 | 1-2 | 4-3 | 3-1 | 0-0 | 1-1 | 1-3 | 1-1 | 1-1 | 3-1 | 2-2 | 5-0 | 1-3 | — | 1-2 |
| Workington | 1-2 | 1-1 | 4-2 | 1-2 | 4-0 | 2-1 | 2-2 | 0-2 | 2-2 | 1-1 | 0-1 | 0-1 | 3-0 | 0-5 | 2-1 | 2-1 | 7-0 | 0-0 | 0-1 | 2-0 | 4-0 | — |

## UNIBOND LEAGUE CHALLENGE CUP 2003–04

**FIRST ROUND**
Ashton United 1, Leek Town 1
*(aet; Ashton United won 6-5 on penalties.)*
Bamber Bridge 1, Lancaster City 2
Bishop Auckland 2, Blyth Spartans 0
Burscough 5, Colwyn Bay 0
Guiseley 4, Wakefield & Emley 1
Hyde United 0, Altrincham 1
Kidsgrove Athletic 0, Matlock Town 2
Lincoln United 2, Gainsborough Trinity 1
Marine 2, Runcorn FC Halton 1
Ossett Town 3, Farsley Celtic 1
Rossendale United 4, Kendal Town 1
Stocksbridge Park Steels 1, Frickley Athletic 3
Workington 2, Gateshead 1

**SECOND ROUND**
Ashton United 1, Southport 3
Bradford Park Avenue 1, Bishop Auckland 6
Droylsden 4, Chorley 1
Frickley Athletic 4, Hucknall Town 5
Guiseley 2, Harrogate Town 1
Lancaster City 1, Radcliffe Borough 2
Lincoln United 2, Alfreton Town 1
Marine 1, Burscough 2
Matlock Town 1, Belper Town 0
Spennymoor United 4, Ossett Town 2
Stalybridge Celtic 1, Prescot Cables 2
Vauxhall Motors 3, Rossendale United 0
Whitby Town 2, Bridlington Town 1
Witton Albion 4, Barrow 1
Workington 0, Altrincham 0
*(aet; Altrincham won 3-1 on penalties.)*
Worksop Town 3, North Ferriby United 4

**THIRD ROUND**
Altrincham 1, Vauxhall Motors 2
Bishop Auckland 4, Prescot Cables 0
Burscough 4, Spennymoor United 2
Hucknall Town 2, Lincoln United 1
Matlock Town 2, North Ferriby United 1
Southport 2, Guiseley 3
Whitby Town 6, Radcliffe Borough 2
Witton Albion 0, Droylsden 1

**FOURTH ROUND**
Bishop Auckland 2, Burscough 1 *aet*
Matlock Town 1, Guiseley 0
Vauxhall Motors 0, Hucknall Town 1
Whitby Town 1, Droylsden 2

**SEMI-FINALS**
Droylsden 3, Bishop Auckland 2
Hucknall Town 2, Matlock Town 1

**FINAL**
Droylsden 2, 2, Hucknall Town 0, 1

## PRESIDENT'S CUP

**FIRST ROUND**
Alfreton Town 0, Harrogate Town 2
Barrow 3, Bradford Park Avenue 1
Belper Town 1, Marine 3
Bridlington Town 3, Rossendale United 1
Chorley 1, Lancaster City 2
Ossett Town 0, Worksop Town 6
Stalybridge Celtic 3, Ashton United 4 *aet*
Workington 3, Frickley Athletic 1

**SECOND ROUND**
Ashton United 0, Barrow 0
*(aet; Barrow won 4-2 on penalties.)*
Bridlington Town 0, Harrogate Town 3
Marine 1, Worksop Town 0
Workington 1, Lancaster City 0

**SEMI-FINALS**
Marine 0, Barrow 2
Workington 4, Harrogate Town 4
*(aet; Workington won 4-3 on penalties.)*

**FINAL**
Barrow 3, 3, Workington 2, 4
*(aet; Barrow won on away goals.)*

## CHAIRMAN'S CUP

**FIRST ROUND**
Colwyn Bay 2, Kidsgrove Athletic 2
*(aet; Kidsgrove Athletic won 6-5 on penalties.)*
Farsley Celtic 2, Bamber Bridge 1
Hyde United 4, Kendal Town 2
Leek Town 2, Runcorn FC Halton 1
Wakefield & Emley 3, Gateshead 2 *aet*

**SECOND ROUND**
Blyth Spartans 0, Kidsgrove Athletic 1
Hyde United 2, Wakefield & Emley 1 *aet*
Leek Town 3, Farsley Celtic 2
Stocksbridge Park Steels 0, Gainsborough Trinity 3

**SEMI-FINALS**
Hyde United 3, Kidsgrove Athletic 1
Leek Town 2, Gainsborough Trinity 0

**FINAL**
Hyde United 1, 1, Leek Town 0, 0

## PETER SWALES MEMORIAL SHIELD

Hucknall Town 0, Droylsden 1

## UNIBOND LEAGUE PROMOTION PLAY-OFFS

**QUARTER-FINALS**
Ashton United 2, Hyde United 1 *aet*
Bradford Park Avenue 3, Spennymoor United 1
Marine 1, Burscough 3
Whitby Town 2, Radcliffe Borough 2
*(aet; Radcliffe Borough won 8-7 on penalties.)*

**SEMI-FINALS**
Ashton United 1, Bradford Park Avenue 2
Radcliffe Borough 0, Burscough 2

**FINAL**
Bradford Park Avenue 2, Burscough 0 *aet*

# DR MARTENS LEAGUE 2003–04

## PREMIER DIVISION

| | | | *Home* | | | | | *Away* | | | | | *Total* | | | | | | |
|---|---|---|---|---|---|---|---|---|---|---|---|---|---|---|---|---|---|---|---|
| | | *P* | *W* | *D* | *L* | *F* | *A* | *W* | *D* | *L* | *F* | *A* | *W* | *D* | *L* | *F* | *A* | *GD* | *Pts* |
| 1 | Crawley Town | 42 | 13 | 4 | 4 | 45 | 23 | 12 | 5 | 4 | 32 | 20 | 25 | 9 | 8 | 77 | 43 | 34 | 84 |
| 2 | Weymouth | 42 | 10 | 6 | 5 | 37 | 18 | 10 | 6 | 5 | 39 | 29 | 20 | 12 | 10 | 76 | 47 | 29 | 72 |
| 3 | Stafford Rangers | 42 | 12 | 3 | 6 | 34 | 21 | 7 | 8 | 6 | 21 | 22 | 19 | 11 | 12 | 55 | 43 | 12 | 68 |
| 4 | Nuneaton Borough | 42 | 11 | 6 | 4 | 34 | 19 | 6 | 9 | 6 | 31 | 30 | 17 | 15 | 10 | 65 | 49 | 16 | 66 |
| 5 | Worcester City | 42 | 12 | 3 | 6 | 42 | 19 | 6 | 6 | 9 | 29 | 31 | 18 | 9 | 15 | 71 | 50 | 21 | 63 |
| 6 | Hinckley United | 42 | 7 | 8 | 6 | 28 | 21 | 8 | 6 | 7 | 27 | 25 | 15 | 14 | 13 | 55 | 46 | 9 | 59 |
| 7 | Newport County | 42 | 6 | 9 | 6 | 23 | 30 | 9 | 5 | 7 | 29 | 20 | 15 | 14 | 13 | 52 | 50 | 2 | 59 |
| 8 | Cambridge City | 42 | 6 | 8 | 7 | 28 | 32 | 8 | 7 | 6 | 26 | 21 | 14 | 15 | 13 | 54 | 53 | 1 | 57 |
| 9 | Welling United | 42 | 10 | 2 | 9 | 32 | 29 | 6 | 6 | 9 | 24 | 29 | 16 | 8 | 18 | 56 | 58 | −2 | 56 |
| 10 | Weston Super Mare | 42 | 10 | 5 | 6 | 31 | 24 | 4 | 8 | 9 | 21 | 28 | 14 | 13 | 15 | 52 | 52 | 0 | 55 |
| 11 | Eastbourne Borough | 42 | 7 | 9 | 5 | 25 | 23 | 7 | 4 | 10 | 23 | 33 | 14 | 13 | 15 | 48 | 56 | −8 | 55 |
| 12 | Havant & Waterlooville | 42 | 8 | 5 | 8 | 35 | 38 | 7 | 5 | 9 | 24 | 32 | 15 | 10 | 17 | 59 | 70 | −11 | 55 |
| 13 | Moor Green | 42 | 7 | 6 | 8 | 21 | 24 | 7 | 6 | 8 | 21 | 30 | 14 | 12 | 16 | 42 | 54 | −12 | 54 |
| 14 | Merthyr Tydfil | 42 | 7 | 7 | 7 | 28 | 31 | 6 | 7 | 8 | 32 | 35 | 13 | 14 | 15 | 60 | 66 | −6 | 53 |
| 15 | Tiverton Town | 42 | 7 | 11 | 3 | 35 | 24 | 5 | 4 | 12 | 28 | 40 | 12 | 15 | 15 | 63 | 64 | −1 | 51 |
| 16 | Bath City | 42 | 10 | 4 | 7 | 27 | 20 | 3 | 8 | 10 | 22 | 37 | 13 | 12 | 17 | 49 | 57 | −8 | 51 |
| 17 | Dorchester Town | 42 | 9 | 5 | 7 | 30 | 23 | 5 | 4 | 12 | 26 | 46 | 14 | 9 | 19 | 56 | 69 | −13 | 51 |
| 18 | Chelmsford City | 42 | 5 | 9 | 7 | 22 | 27 | 6 | 7 | 8 | 24 | 26 | 11 | 16 | 15 | 46 | 53 | −7 | 49 |
| 19 | Dover Athletic | 42 | 9 | 7 | 5 | 33 | 26 | 3 | 6 | 12 | 17 | 33 | 12 | 13 | 17 | 50 | 59 | −9 | 49 |
| 20 | Hednesford Town | 42 | 7 | 7 | 7 | 35 | 28 | 5 | 5 | 11 | 21 | 41 | 12 | 12 | 18 | 56 | 69 | −13 | 48 |
| 21 | Chippenham Town | 42 | 4 | 9 | 8 | 23 | 31 | 6 | 8 | 7 | 28 | 32 | 10 | 17 | 15 | 51 | 63 | −12 | 47 |
| 22 | Grantham Town | 42 | 7 | 6 | 8 | 26 | 33 | 3 | 9 | 9 | 19 | 34 | 10 | 15 | 17 | 45 | 67 | −22 | 45 |

## EASTERN DIVISION

| | | | *Home* | | | | | *Away* | | | | | *Total* | | | | | | |
|---|---|---|---|---|---|---|---|---|---|---|---|---|---|---|---|---|---|---|---|
| | | *P* | *W* | *D* | *L* | *F* | *A* | *W* | *D* | *L* | *F* | *A* | *W* | *D* | *L* | *F* | *A* | *GD* | *Pts* |
| 1 | King's Lynn | 42 | 16 | 3 | 2 | 52 | 18 | 12 | 4 | 5 | 38 | 17 | 28 | 7 | 7 | 90 | 35 | 55 | 91 |
| 2 | Histon | 42 | 12 | 6 | 3 | 48 | 22 | 14 | 4 | 3 | 48 | 19 | 26 | 10 | 6 | 96 | 41 | 55 | 88 |
| 3 | Tonbridge Angels | 42 | 12 | 3 | 6 | 35 | 25 | 15 | 4 | 2 | 47 | 21 | 27 | 7 | 8 | 82 | 46 | 36 | 88 |
| 4 | Eastleigh* | 42 | 14 | 2 | 5 | 52 | 18 | 13 | 2 | 6 | 36 | 22 | 27 | 4 | 11 | 88 | 40 | 48 | 82 |
| 5 | Folkestone Invicta | 42 | 10 | 9 | 2 | 40 | 19 | 10 | 6 | 5 | 51 | 26 | 20 | 15 | 7 | 91 | 45 | 46 | 75 |
| 6 | Salisbury City | 42 | 10 | 8 | 3 | 33 | 21 | 11 | 3 | 7 | 40 | 24 | 21 | 11 | 10 | 73 | 45 | 28 | 74 |
| 7 | Stamford | 42 | 13 | 5 | 3 | 37 | 20 | 7 | 6 | 8 | 26 | 25 | 20 | 11 | 11 | 63 | 45 | 18 | 71 |
| 8 | Banbury United | 42 | 14 | 2 | 5 | 35 | 23 | 5 | 8 | 8 | 30 | 34 | 19 | 10 | 13 | 65 | 57 | 8 | 67 |
| 9 | Burgess Hill Town | 42 | 11 | 3 | 7 | 38 | 24 | 8 | 4 | 9 | 29 | 30 | 19 | 7 | 16 | 67 | 54 | 13 | 64 |
| 10 | Sittingbourne | 42 | 9 | 4 | 8 | 27 | 26 | 9 | 4 | 8 | 34 | 29 | 18 | 8 | 16 | 61 | 55 | 6 | 62 |
| 11 | Bashley | 42 | 9 | 5 | 7 | 38 | 29 | 9 | 2 | 10 | 28 | 29 | 18 | 7 | 17 | 66 | 58 | 8 | 61 |
| 12 | Ashford Town | 42 | 8 | 6 | 7 | 25 | 25 | 7 | 3 | 11 | 26 | 28 | 15 | 9 | 18 | 51 | 53 | −2 | 54 |
| 13 | Chatham Town | 42 | 6 | 5 | 10 | 23 | 31 | 7 | 5 | 9 | 26 | 36 | 13 | 10 | 19 | 49 | 67 | −18 | 49 |
| 14 | Fisher Athletic | 42 | 8 | 4 | 9 | 28 | 38 | 5 | 6 | 10 | 33 | 43 | 13 | 10 | 19 | 61 | 81 | −20 | 49 |
| 15 | Corby Town | 42 | 9 | 4 | 8 | 28 | 35 | 3 | 5 | 13 | 16 | 40 | 12 | 9 | 21 | 44 | 75 | −31 | 45 |
| 16 | Dartford | 42 | 9 | 2 | 10 | 28 | 38 | 4 | 4 | 13 | 20 | 43 | 13 | 6 | 23 | 48 | 81 | −33 | 45 |
| 17 | Burnham* | 42 | 5 | 4 | 12 | 26 | 46 | 7 | 7 | 7 | 26 | 30 | 12 | 11 | 19 | 52 | 76 | −24 | 44 |
| 18 | Hastings United | 42 | 7 | 4 | 10 | 33 | 38 | 5 | 3 | 13 | 27 | 53 | 12 | 7 | 23 | 60 | 91 | −31 | 43 |
| 19 | Newport (IW) | 42 | 7 | 5 | 9 | 24 | 30 | 4 | 2 | 15 | 18 | 39 | 11 | 7 | 24 | 42 | 69 | −27 | 40 |
| 20 | Rothwell Town | 42 | 3 | 5 | 13 | 15 | 30 | 6 | 6 | 9 | 15 | 17 | 9 | 11 | 22 | 30 | 47 | −17 | 38 |
| 21 | Erith & Belvedere | 42 | 5 | 4 | 12 | 23 | 42 | 2 | 6 | 13 | 22 | 42 | 7 | 10 | 25 | 45 | 84 | −39 | 31 |
| 22 | Fleet Town | 42 | 2 | 4 | 15 | 18 | 55 | 3 | 3 | 15 | 17 | 59 | 5 | 7 | 30 | 35 | 114 | −79 | 22 |

**3 points deducted for fielding ineligible player.*

## WESTERN DIVISION

| | | | *Home* | | | | | *Away* | | | | | *Total* | | | | | | |
|---|---|---|---|---|---|---|---|---|---|---|---|---|---|---|---|---|---|---|---|
| | | *P* | *W* | *D* | *L* | *F* | *A* | *W* | *D* | *L* | *F* | *A* | *W* | *D* | *L* | *F* | *A* | *GD* | *Pts* |
| 1 | Redditch United | 40 | 12 | 5 | 3 | 35 | 14 | 13 | 4 | 3 | 40 | 16 | 25 | 9 | 6 | 75 | 30 | 45 | 84 |
| 2 | Gloucester City | 40 | 12 | 5 | 3 | 44 | 25 | 12 | 2 | 6 | 33 | 21 | 24 | 7 | 9 | 77 | 46 | 31 | 79 |
| 3 | Cirencester Town | 40 | 13 | 1 | 6 | 36 | 20 | 11 | 3 | 6 | 37 | 20 | 24 | 4 | 12 | 73 | 40 | 33 | 76 |
| 4 | Halesowen Town | 40 | 12 | 7 | 1 | 39 | 13 | 8 | 6 | 6 | 25 | 27 | 20 | 13 | 7 | 64 | 40 | 24 | 73 |
| 5 | Rugby United | 40 | 11 | 4 | 5 | 30 | 24 | 10 | 4 | 6 | 27 | 16 | 21 | 8 | 11 | 57 | 40 | 17 | 71 |
| 6 | Team Bath | 40 | 11 | 1 | 8 | 32 | 19 | 10 | 5 | 5 | 30 | 22 | 21 | 6 | 13 | 62 | 41 | 21 | 69 |
| 7 | Solihull Borough | 40 | 9 | 4 | 7 | 27 | 16 | 10 | 5 | 5 | 23 | 15 | 19 | 9 | 12 | 50 | 31 | 19 | 66 |
| 8 | Sutton Coldfield | 40 | 8 | 9 | 3 | 28 | 19 | 8 | 6 | 6 | 24 | 19 | 16 | 15 | 9 | 52 | 38 | 14 | 63 |
| 9 | Bromsgrove Rovers | 40 | 9 | 5 | 6 | 36 | 25 | 7 | 6 | 7 | 24 | 23 | 16 | 11 | 13 | 60 | 48 | 12 | 59 |
| 10 | Ilkeston Town | 40 | 7 | 4 | 9 | 36 | 41 | 9 | 6 | 5 | 22 | 18 | 16 | 10 | 14 | 58 | 59 | −1 | 58 |
| 11 | Clevedon Town | 40 | 7 | 2 | 11 | 29 | 29 | 9 | 3 | 8 | 26 | 30 | 16 | 5 | 19 | 55 | 59 | −4 | 53 |
| 12 | Gresley Rovers | 40 | 8 | 3 | 9 | 29 | 31 | 7 | 4 | 9 | 23 | 29 | 15 | 7 | 18 | 52 | 60 | −8 | 52 |
| 13 | Mangotsfield United | 40 | 9 | 4 | 7 | 42 | 34 | 5 | 4 | 11 | 28 | 36 | 14 | 8 | 18 | 70 | 70 | 0 | 50 |
| 14 | Evesham United | 40 | 9 | 2 | 9 | 27 | 20 | 6 | 3 | 11 | 29 | 37 | 15 | 5 | 20 | 56 | 57 | −1 | 50 |
| 15 | Taunton Town | 40 | 9 | 3 | 8 | 29 | 20 | 5 | 5 | 10 | 21 | 35 | 14 | 8 | 18 | 50 | 55 | −5 | 50 |
| 16 | Yate Town | 40 | 7 | 6 | 7 | 30 | 35 | 4 | 3 | 13 | 21 | 44 | 11 | 9 | 20 | 51 | 79 | −28 | 42 |
| 17 | Swindon Supermarine | 40 | 8 | 7 | 5 | 24 | 22 | 2 | 2 | 16 | 17 | 47 | 10 | 9 | 21 | 41 | 69 | −28 | 39 |
| 18 | Stourport Swifts | 40 | 7 | 3 | 10 | 21 | 27 | 2 | 8 | 10 | 22 | 35 | 9 | 11 | 20 | 43 | 62 | −19 | 38 |
| 19 | Bedworth United | 40 | 4 | 7 | 9 | 12 | 18 | 4 | 5 | 11 | 27 | 43 | 8 | 12 | 20 | 39 | 61 | −22 | 36 |
| 20 | Cinderford Town | 40 | 4 | 3 | 13 | 23 | 47 | 3 | 6 | 11 | 27 | 47 | 7 | 9 | 24 | 50 | 94 | −44 | 30 |
| 21 | Shepshed Dynamo | 40 | 2 | 9 | 9 | 14 | 44 | 3 | 4 | 13 | 17 | 43 | 5 | 13 | 22 | 31 | 87 | −56 | 28 |

**DR MARTENS LEAGUE ATTENDANCES**

| | | |
|---|---|---|
| Premier Average | 673 | Division Highest: 4522 Crawley Town v Weymouth (6/3/2004) |
| Eastern Division Average | 273 | Division Highest: 1617 King's Lynn v Histon (12/4/2004) |
| Western Division Average | 241 | Division Highest: 1384 Redditch United v Bromsgrove Rovers (27/12/2003) |

## DR MARTENS LEADING GOALSCORERS

**PREMIER DIVISION**

| | |
|---|---|
| Allan Tait (Crawley Town) | 22 |
| *20 scored for Folkestone Invicta* | |
| Daniel Bloomfield (Cambridge City) | 20 |
| Steve Claridge (Weymouth) | 20 |
| Scott Partridge (Bath City) | 20 |
| Lee Phillips (Weymouth) | 20 |
| Daniel Davidson (Stafford Rangers) | 19 |
| Chukkie Eribenne (Havant & Waterlooville) | 19 |
| Charlie MacDonald (Crawley Town) | 19 |
| Scott Ramsay (Eastbourne Borough) | 18 |
| Cortez Belle (Merthyr Tydfil) | 17 |
| Darren Edwards (Tiverton Town) | 17 |
| *13 scored for Mangotsfield United* | |
| Charles Griffin (Chippenham Town) | 17 |
| Gerald Murphy (Nuneaton Borough) | 17 |
| Craig Wilkins (Dover Athletic) | 17 |
| Paul Booth (Welling United) | 16 |
| Mark Danks (Hednesford Town) | 16 |
| Leon Kelly (Worcester City) | 16 |
| Neil Davis (Moor Green) | 13 |
| James Mudge (Tiverton Town) | 13 |
| James Constable (Chippenham Town) | 12 |
| Kevin Wilkin (Nuneaton Borough) | 12 |

**WESTERN DIVISION**

| | |
|---|---|
| Andy Hoskins (Gloucester City) | 28 |
| David Seal (Mangotsfield United) | 25 |
| Gareth Hopkins (Cirencester Town) | 22 |
| Dean Perrow (Sutton Coldfield Town) | 19 |
| Richard Ball (Stourport Swifts) | 18 |
| Robert Beard (Rugby United) | 18 |
| Jason Moore (Ashby) (Halesowen Town) | 18 |
| Matthew Rawlins (Yate Town) | 18 |
| Jimmy Cox (Gloucester City) | 17 |
| Paul Szewczyk (Bromsgrove Rovers) | 17 |
| Chris Freestone (Ilkeston Town) | 16 |
| Anthony Lynch (Taunton Town) | 16 |
| Paul Hunter (Solihull Borough) | 15 |
| Richard Leadbeater (Redditch United) | 15 |
| Martin Myers (Redditch United) | 14 |
| Jack Pitcher (Mangotsfield United) | 14 |
| Jody Bevan (Cirencester Town) | 12 |
| Richard Kear (Cinderford Town) | 12 |
| Scott Griffin (Cirencester Town) | 11 |
| Justin Miller (Swindon Supermarine) | 11 |
| Craig Pountney (Evesham United) | 11 |
| Mark Shepherd (Redditch United) | 11 |

**EASTERN DIVISION**

| | |
|---|---|
| Paul Sales (Eastleigh) | 29 |
| Nicholas Sullivan (Burgess Hill Town) | 23 |
| Kevin Byrne (Stamford) | 22 |
| James Dryden (Folkestone Invicta) | 22 |
| Neil Kennedy (Histon) | 22 |
| Steven Harper (Burgess Hill Town) | 21 |
| David Staff (King's Lynn) | 20 |
| Matthew Tubbs (Salisbury City) | 19 |
| Carl Holmes (King's Lynn) | 18 |
| George Redknapp (Banbury United) | 18 |
| Akpol Sodje (Erith & Belvedere) | 18 |
| Richard Brady (Fisher Athletic) | 17 |
| Brendan Cass (Tonbridge Angels) | 17 |
| Carl Rook (Hastings United) | 16 |
| Nicholas Banger (Eastleigh) | 15 |
| Hamid Barr (Tonbridge Angels) | 15 |
| Joby Thorogood (Ashford Town) | 15 |
| Adrian Cambridge (Histon) | 14 |
| Shaun Hale (Fleet Town) | 14 |
| Tostao Kwashi (Dartford) | 14 |

## DR MARTENS LEAGUE CUP 2003–04

**FIRST ROUND**
Banbury 1, Kings Lynn 1
*(Kings Lynn won 3-2 on penalties).*
Bashley 1, Fleet Town 2
Erith & Belvedere 3, Ashford Town 1
Gloucester City 1, Solihull Borough 4
Gresley Rovers 2, Shepshed Dynamo 1
Hastings United 2, Folkestone Invicta 6
Mangotsfield United 1, Cinderford Town 2
Rugby United 2, Ilkeston Town 1
Sittingbourne 1, Chatham Town 2
Stamford 2, Corby Town 1
Stourport Swifts 1, Redditch United 1
*(Stourport Swifts won 4-2 on penalties).*
Sutton Coldfield Town 3, Evesham United 2
Tonbridge Angels 0, Fisher Athletic 3
Yate Town 0, Clevedon Town 3
Dartford 0, Burgess Hill Town 3
Eastleigh 3, Burnham 1
Swindon Supermarine 0, Taunton Town 3
Newport (IW) 3, Salisbury City 2
Bromsgrove Rovers 2, Halesowen Town 1
Rothwell Town 0, Histon 1
Team Bath 2, Cirencester Town 3

**SECOND ROUND**
Bedworth United 4, Solihull Borough 2
Cambridge City 4, Stamford 1
Cirencester Town 3, Clevedon Town 0
Erith & Belvedere 0, Fleet Town 2
Folkestone Invicta 3, Fisher Athletic 2
Gresley Rovers 3, Stourport Swifts 2
Kings Lynn 1, Histon 2
Sutton Coldfield Town 2, Rugby United 1
Weymouth 3, Taunton Town 1
Eastleigh 2, Newport (IW) 1
Chatham Town 1, Burgess Hill Town 0
Cinderford Town 3, Bromsgrove Rovers 3
*Replay:* Bromsgrove Rovers 3, Cinderford Town 1

**THIRD ROUND**
Worcester City 1, Sutton Coldfield Town 1
*(Worcester City won 5-4 on penalties).*
Bath City 3, Cirencester Town 0
Dover Athletic 4, Chatham Town 1
Dorchester Town 2, Weston-Super-Mare 0
Granthan Town 0, Cambridge City 2
Hednesford Town 3, Bedworth United 3
*(Hednesford Town won 4-2 on penalties).*
Folkestone Invicta 4, Chelmsford City 3
Hinckley United 3, Histon 0
Moor Green 5, Stafford Rangers 0
Weymouth 4, Merthyr Tydfil 2
Nuneaton Borough 1, Gresley Rovers 0
Havant & Waterlooville 2, Crawley Town 3
Eastleigh 4, Fleet Town 1
Newport County 0, Chippenham Town 4
Welling United 2, Eastbourne Borough 1
*(After match abandoned 0-0: fog).*
Tiverton Town 3, Bromsgrove Rovers 0

**FOURTH ROUND**
Crawley Town 1, Welling United 0
Hinckley United 0, Hednesford Town 1
Tiverton Town 1, Chippenham Town 4
Weymouth 2, Bath City 0
Cambridge City 2, Nuneaton Borough 1
Dorchester Town 1, Eastleigh 2
Dover Athletic 2, Folkestone Invicta 0
Worcester City 0, Moor Green 2

**FIFTH ROUND**
Eastleigh 5, Weymouth 2
Cambridge City 1, Hednesford Town 0
Crawley Town 1, Dover Athletic 0
Moor Green 3, Chippenham Town 1

**SEMI-FINALS**
Crawley Town 2, Eastleigh 0
Moor Green 3, Cambridge City 0

**FINAL FIRST LEG**
Moor Green 1, Crawley Town 2

**FINAL SECOND LEG**
Crawley Town 2, Moor Green 0

## DR MARTENS LEAGUE – PREMIER DIVISION RESULTS 2003–04

| | Bath City | Cambridge City | Chelmsford City | Chippenham Town | Crawley Town | Dorchester Town | Dover Athletic | Eastbourne Borough | Grantham Town | Havant & Waterlooville | Hednesford Town | Hinckley United | Merthyr Tydfil | Moor Green | Newport County | Nuneaton Borough | Stafford Rangers | Tiverton Town | Welling United | Weston Super Mare | Weymouth | Worcester City |
|---|---|---|---|---|---|---|---|---|---|---|---|---|---|---|---|---|---|---|---|---|---|---|
| Bath City | — | 1-2 | 0-1 | 2-2 | 0-0 | 0-0 | 2-1 | 2-0 | 5-1 | 2-0 | 2-0 | 0-2 | 0-2 | 0-1 | 1-0 | 1-3 | 1-0 | 2-1 | 2-0 | 3-1 | 0-2 | 1-1 |
| Cambridge City | 0-0 | — | 2-0 | 1-1 | 2-5 | 4-2 | 2-1 | 0-0 | 1-1 | 2-3 | 0-1 | 1-2 | 2-2 | 1-1 | 0-2 | 1-3 | 1-0 | 6-4 | 0-3 | 1-1 | 1-0 | 0-0 |
| Chelmsford City | 0-0 | 1-1 | — | 1-3 | 0-4 | 2-0 | 0-0 | 3-1 | 0-0 | 1-1 | 2-0 | 0-3 | 3-1 | 1-0 | 0-0 | 1-2 | 1-2 | 3-3 | 0-1 | 0-0 | 1-3 | 2-2 |
| Chippenham Town | 1-1 | 0-2 | 0-0 | — | 0-1 | 1-6 | 0-0 | 0-1 | 2-2 | 3-0 | 0-0 | 2-1 | 3-3 | 4-0 | 2-1 | 1-1 | 0-3 | 1-1 | 0-2 | 1-1 | 1-3 | 1-2 |
| Crawley Town | 2-0 | 2-0 | 0-0 | 3-2 | — | 2-3 | 2-0 | 3-1 | 4-2 | 3-1 | 6-1 | 0-3 | 1-2 | 2-2 | 1-2 | 2-2 | 2-0 | 2-1 | 0-0 | 2-0 | 2-1 | 4-0 |
| Dorchester Town | 1-0 | 0-2 | 4-1 | 3-1 | 2-0 | — | 0-2 | 0-1 | 2-2 | 1-2 | 3-4 | 1-1 | 1-0 | 0-1 | 1-2 | 0-0 | 0-0 | 1-0 | 2-0 | 3-2 | 2-2 | 3-0 |
| Dover Athletic | 3-3 | 0-1 | 2-2 | 0-0 | 2-2 | 1-2 | — | 2-0 | 2-0 | 0-2 | 2-1 | 1-1 | 2-2 | 2-0 | 2-0 | 3-2 | 0-0 | 2-1 | 3-1 | 0-2 | 2-3 | 2-1 |
| Eastbourne Borough | 1-1 | 1-1 | 1-1 | 1-2 | 1-1 | 2-1 | 3-1 | — | 1-0 | 2-0 | 2-2 | 0-2 | 1-1 | 0-1 | 1-2 | 0-0 | 1-1 | 2-1 | 1-1 | 1-0 | 2-1 | 1-3 |
| Grantham Town | 1-1 | 2-1 | 1-3 | 0-2 | 1-0 | 4-0 | 2-2 | 0-3 | — | 0-2 | 1-1 | 1-1 | 0-1 | 0-1 | 2-1 | 0-5 | 0-2 | 1-1 | 2-0 | 3-2 | 1-1 | 4-3 |
| Havant & Waterlooville | 1-4 | 2-3 | 0-2 | 1-1 | 1-3 | 3-2 | 2-2 | 1-0 | 2-1 | — | 1-2 | 2-0 | 4-2 | 0-0 | 0-3 | 5-1 | 2-2 | 3-2 | 1-1 | 0-1 | 4-1 | 0-5 |
| Hednesford Town | 4-0 | 2-2 | 2-1 | 4-1 | 0-0 | 2-4 | 0-1 | 1-2 | 2-0 | 1-0 | — | 1-1 | 1-2 | 4-4 | 1-2 | 0-0 | 1-2 | 3-1 | 1-2 | 2-2 | 0-0 | 3-1 |
| Hinckley United | 1-2 | 0-0 | 1-2 | 0-0 | 4-0 | 1-0 | 3-1 | 2-2 | 0-1 | 2-2 | 4-0 | — | 1-2 | 0-0 | 1-4 | 1-1 | 1-1 | 2-0 | 2-1 | 1-0 | 1-2 | 0-0 |
| Merthyr Tydfil | 2-0 | 1-3 | 1-3 | 3-1 | 2-1 | 1-0 | 0-0 | 2-2 | 2-2 | 1-1 | 2-0 | 1-1 | — | 1-2 | 1-1 | 4-3 | 1-1 | 0-2 | 2-0 | 1-2 | 0-4 | 0-2 |
| Moor Green | 0-3 | 1-1 | 1-0 | 3-2 | 1-2 | 1-3 | 1-0 | 0-1 | 0-0 | 2-1 | 2-1 | 0-1 | 1-1 | — | 1-1 | 2-0 | 1-2 | 2-0 | 0-2 | 0-0 | 1-2 | 1-1 |
| Newport County | 2-1 | 1-0 | 1-0 | 2-2 | 1-2 | 0-0 | 2-1 | 1-1 | 2-2 | 0-2 | 1-1 | 0-3 | 1-1 | 1-1 | — | 1-2 | 3-1 | 2-1 | 0-0 | 1-4 | 1-1 | 0-4 |
| Nuneaton Borough | 2-1 | 2-1 | 1-2 | 1-1 | 0-1 | 2-0 | 1-1 | 4-0 | 1-1 | 1-2 | 3-0 | 2-0 | 2-1 | 1-0 | 2-0 | — | 0-0 | 0-1 | 2-2 | 1-1 | 4-3 | 2-1 |
| Stafford Rangers | 2-0 | 1-1 | 2-1 | 2-0 | 0-1 | 3-0 | 2-1 | 4-1 | 0-1 | 2-1 | 1-1 | 2-0 | 3-1 | 1-2 | 1-0 | 0-3 | — | 1-2 | 3-2 | 1-1 | 1-2 | 2-0 |
| Tiverton Town | 1-1 | 1-1 | 3-3 | 3-1 | 2-2 | 1-1 | 1-0 | 2-3 | 1-1 | 5-1 | 2-3 | 3-0 | 2-1 | 2-1 | 0-0 | 0-0 | 0-0 | — | 2-2 | 2-0 | 1-2 | 1-1 |
| Welling United | 2-1 | 0-1 | 1-0 | 1-3 | 0-3 | 6-1 | 2-1 | 1-2 | 0-1 | 1-1 | 2-0 | 2-3 | 0-3 | 2-1 | 0-2 | 2-1 | 2-1 | 4-0 | — | 2-1 | 2-2 | 0-1 |
| Weston Super Mare | 1-0 | 1-0 | 0-0 | 1-2 | 1-2 | 1-1 | 0-1 | 2-1 | 2-0 | 2-0 | 3-2 | 2-2 | 3-2 | 2-3 | 0-0 | 1-1 | 5-1 | 1-3 | 2-1 | — | 0-2 | 1-0 |
| Weymouth | 3-3 | 2-1 | 2-2 | 0-1 | 0-1 | 8-0 | 3-0 | 1-0 | 1-0 | 0-1 | 2-0 | 2-0 | 2-2 | 3-0 | 2-1 | 1-1 | 0-1 | 1-1 | 1-2 | 0-0 | — | 3-1 |
| Worcester City | 7-0 | 0-2 | 1-0 | 0-0 | 0-1 | 1-0 | 5-1 | 2-1 | 4-1 | 1-1 | 0-1 | 2-0 | 2-0 | 3-0 | 1-5 | 4-0 | 0-1 | 1-2 | 3-1 | 3-0 | 2-2 | — |

# DR MARTENS LEAGUE – WESTERN DIVISION RESULTS 2003–04

| | Bedworth United | Bromsgrove Rovers | Cinderford Town | Cirencester Town | Clevedon Town | Evesham United | Gloucester City | Gresley Rovers | Halesowen Town | Ilkeston Town | Mangotsfield United | Redditch United | Rugby United | Shepshed Dynamo | Solihull Borough | Stourport Swifts | Sutton Coldfield | Swindon Supermarine | Taunton Town | Team Bath | Yate Town |
|---|---|---|---|---|---|---|---|---|---|---|---|---|---|---|---|---|---|---|---|---|---|
| Bedworth United | — | 0-0 | 1-0 | 0-1 | 0-0 | 1-2 | 1-2 | 0-0 | 0-1 | 2-1 | 2-1 | 0-1 | 0-0 | 0-1 | 0-0 | 0-0 | 0-1 | 3-1 | 1-2 | 1-1 | 0-3 |
| Bromsgrove Rovers | 1-2 | — | 2-2 | 0-0 | 3-0 | 2-1 | 0-1 | 0-2 | 3-3 | 3-0 | 1-1 | 0-1 | 1-3 | 5-1 | 0-1 | 2-0 | 2-1 | 3-0 | 2-1 | 3-3 | 3-2 |
| Cinderford Town | 4-1 | 1-2 | — | 1-8 | 0-1 | 0-3 | 0-2 | 0-4 | 1-2 | 1-0 | 1-3 | 2-0 | 1-5 | 1-1 | 1-3 | 0-1 | 0-2 | 4-3 | 2-2 | 3-3 | 0-1 |
| Cirencester Town | 2-3 | 2-0 | 5-0 | — | 0-0 | 2-0 | 2-1 | 2-0 | 0-1 | 2-1 | 1-2 | 0-3 | 3-0 | 4-1 | 1-2 | 3-2 | 0-2 | 3-1 | 2-1 | 1-0 | 1-0 |
| Clevedon Town | 3-1 | 0-0 | 1-1 | 2-3 | — | 2-4 | 0-2 | 2-0 | 2-0 | 2-3 | 3-0 | 0-3 | 0-2 | 2-1 | 1-2 | 2-0 | 1-2 | 0-1 | 2-3 | 0-1 | 4-0 |
| Evesham United | 3-0 | 0-1 | 2-1 | 0-0 | 2-3 | — | 4-2 | 1-1 | 1-2 | 0-1 | 0-1 | 2-0 | 0-1 | 0-2 | 1-0 | 3-0 | 1-3 | 1-0 | 4-0 | 0-1 | 2-1 |
| Gloucester City | 2-1 | 1-0 | 4-0 | 2-0 | 3-1 | 3-1 | — | 3-3 | 2-2 | 0-1 | 2-2 | 1-1 | 0-1 | 5-2 | 2-2 | 1-0 | 2-1 | 3-1 | 3-1 | 4-3 | 1-2 |
| Gresley Rovers | 2-0 | 0-3 | 1-2 | 0-3 | 0-2 | 2-0 | 1-2 | — | 1-0 | 0-2 | 2-0 | 2-3 | 2-3 | 3-0 | 1-0 | 3-3 | 1-1 | 2-1 | 1-4 | 1-1 | 4-1 |
| Halesowen Town | 6-3 | 0-0 | 1-1 | 2-1 | 3-0 | 0-2 | 0-0 | 2-0 | — | 2-2 | 6-0 | 0-0 | 1-0 | 1-1 | 1-0 | 2-2 | 1-0 | 6-0 | 3-1 | 1-0 | 1-0 |
| Ilkeston Town | 2-0 | 2-2 | 2-2 | 2-2 | 3-5 | 2-3 | 0-3 | 1-2 | 0-0 | — | 4-2 | 0-6 | 0-4 | 5-1 | 1-0 | 1-3 | 2-1 | 0-1 | 3-1 | 1-2 | 5-1 |
| Mangotsfield United | 2-1 | 4-3 | 6-2 | 1-5 | 1-2 | 3-1 | 3-2 | 1-2 | 4-0 | 2-4 | — | 2-3 | 0-3 | 0-1 | 0-0 | 3-1 | 0-0 | 5-2 | 0-0 | 1-1 | 4-1 |
| Redditch United | 1-1 | 4-0 | 5-2 | 2-1 | 1-0 | 3-1 | 0-1 | 2-0 | 0-2 | 1-1 | 3-0 | — | 1-0 | 1-0 | 1-2 | 1-1 | 1-1 | 2-0 | 0-0 | 2-1 | 4-0 |
| Rugby United | 4-1 | 1-5 | 2-1 | 2-1 | 1-1 | 3-2 | 1-0 | 2-1 | 1-0 | 0-1 | 1-0 | 2-3 | — | 1-0 | 1-2 | 1-1 | 1-1 | 2-1 | 2-0 | 0-1 | 2-2 |
| Shepshed Dynamo | 0-0 | 1-1 | 2-2 | 1-3 | 1-2 | 2-1 | 0-6 | 0-3 | 2-2 | 0-0 | 0-9 | 0-0 | 0-0 | — | 0-4 | 1-1 | 0-2 | 1-0 | 1-1 | 2-3 | 0-4 |
| Solihull Borough | 3-2 | 0-1 | 3-0 | 1-2 | 3-1 | 3-1 | 0-0 | 0-1 | 0-1 | 0-0 | 0-0 | 1-1 | 2-0 | 3-0 | — | 2-1 | 0-1 | 2-1 | 0-1 | 0-1 | 4-1 |
| Stourport Swifts | 1-1 | 1-2 | 1-4 | 0-1 | 2-0 | 0-1 | 1-2 | 1-1 | 0-2 | 0-1 | 2-1 | 0-4 | 3-0 | 2-1 | 2-0 | — | 0-3 | 1-1 | 2-0 | 0-2 | 2-0 |
| Sutton Coldfield | 2-2 | 1-1 | 1-0 | 2-0 | 1-0 | 2-1 | 0-1 | 2-0 | 3-1 | 1-1 | 3-1 | 1-0 | 0-0 | 2-2 | 1-1 | 2-2 | — | 0-0 | 2-3 | 1-2 | 1-1 |
| Swindon Supermarine | 0-3 | 1-0 | 2-2 | 1-0 | 3-1 | 1-1 | 0-2 | 2-1 | 4-2 | 0-1 | 3-2 | 1-2 | 0-0 | 1-1 | 0-1 | 2-1 | 1-1 | — | 0-0 | 1-0 | 1-1 |
| Taunton Town | 0-1 | 1-2 | 2-0 | 1-3 | 1-2 | 3-1 | 5-0 | 2-0 | 1-1 | 0-1 | 1-3 | 0-2 | 1-0 | 1-0 | 1-1 | 3-1 | 0-0 | 4-1 | — | 0-1 | 2-0 |
| Team Bath | 2-1 | 1-0 | 4-0 | 0-1 | 1-2 | 0-0 | 1-3 | 1-2 | 1-2 | 2-1 | 1-0 | 1-2 | 0-2 | 3-0 | 0-1 | 2-1 | 2-0 | 3-1 | 4-0 | — | 3-0 |
| Yate Town | 3-3 | 2-1 | 0-5 | 0-2 | 1-3 | 3-3 | 2-1 | 5-0 | 1-1 | 0-0 | 0-0 | 1-5 | 1-3 | 3-1 | 0-1 | 1-1 | 4-1 | 2-1 | 1-0 | 0-3 | — |

## DR MARTENS LEAGUE – EASTERN DIVISION RESULTS 2003–04

| | Ashford Town | Banbury United | Bashley | Burgess Hill Town | Burnham | Chatham Town | Corby Town | Dartford | Eastleigh | Erith & Belvedere | Fisher Athletic | Fleet Town | Folkestone Invicta | Hastings United | Histon | King's Lynn | Newport (IW) | Rothwell Town | Salisbury City | Sittingbourne | Stamford | Tonbridge Angels |
|---|---|---|---|---|---|---|---|---|---|---|---|---|---|---|---|---|---|---|---|---|---|---|
| Ashford Town | — | 1-1 | 2-1 | 2-2 | 1-2 | 1-1 | 2-1 | 2-1 | 0-1 | 1-1 | 0-2 | 1-1 | 2-1 | 3-1 | 1-2 | 3-1 | 1-0 | 0-0 | 0-2 | 1-2 | 1-0 | 0-2 |
| Banbury United | 1-0 | — | 1-0 | 4-1 | 1-1 | 3-1 | 4-0 | 1-1 | 1-2 | 2-1 | 3-0 | 1-0 | 4-3 | 1-0 | 0-4 | 0-3 | 2-1 | 1-0 | 0-1 | 3-1 | 1-0 | 1-3 |
| Bashley | 1-0 | 1-1 | — | 1-0 | 1-1 | 2-2 | 3-2 | 3-3 | 4-1 | 2-0 | 2-0 | 7-0 | 3-0 | 5-0 | 0-3 | 1-2 | 0-2 | 0-1 | 2-4 | 0-1 | 0-0 | 0-6 |
| Burgess Hill Town | 1-0 | 2-1 | 1-2 | — | 0-1 | 0-2 | 5-2 | 0-1 | 5-2 | 3-1 | 4-1 | 3-0 | 2-2 | 6-2 | 0-1 | 0-3 | 1-1 | 0-0 | 1-0 | 2-0 | 2-1 | 0-1 |
| Burnham | 2-2 | 0-4 | 0-1 | 1-2 | — | 0-2 | 1-1 | 0-3 | 1-2 | 2-2 | 2-2 | 3-0 | 0-4 | 3-1 | 0-2 | 0-3 | 4-3 | 2-0 | 2-1 | 2-5 | 0-4 | 1-2 |
| Chatham Town | 1-1 | 0-1 | 3-1 | 0-3 | 1-1 | — | 3-2 | 3-0 | 1-2 | 3-2 | 0-3 | 0-0 | 0-3 | 0-1 | 0-1 | 1-0 | 2-1 | 0-2 | 2-3 | 1-1 | 2-2 | 0-1 |
| Corby Town | 0-5 | 0-2 | 1-0 | 2-3 | 1-1 | 2-1 | — | 3-0 | 1-0 | 2-1 | 1-0 | 2-2 | 0-4 | 2-3 | 3-3 | 2-1 | 0-1 | 0-0 | 2-1 | 0-4 | 3-1 | 1-2 |
| Dartford | 0-2 | 2-2 | 1-3 | 2-1 | 2-1 | 1-1 | 0-1 | — | 1-5 | 1-3 | 3-1 | 3-0 | 1-6 | 3-0 | 0-5 | 1-0 | 2-0 | 2-0 | 0-3 | 1-0 | 0-1 | 2-3 |
| Eastleigh | 1-2 | 6-1 | 3-1 | 4-0 | 3-0 | 2-0 | 4-1 | 5-0 | — | 5-1 | 3-1 | 3-0 | 2-1 | 6-2 | 0-2 | 0-0 | 2-1 | 1-0 | 1-2 | 1-2 | 0-1 | 0-0 |
| Erith & Belvedere | 0-2 | 2-1 | 1-3 | 1-1 | 0-3 | 2-1 | 0-0 | 2-0 | 1-2 | — | 4-1 | 3-4 | 0-4 | 1-1 | 0-3 | 0-5 | 3-0 | 0-2 | 0-3 | 1-1 | 1-2 | 1-3 |
| Fisher Athletic | 1-2 | 1-2 | 3-1 | 1-3 | 1-0 | 1-0 | 2-0 | 2-1 | 2-1 | 1-1 | — | 1-2 | 1-1 | 2-2 | 2-1 | 0-2 | 0-3 | 0-0 | 2-1 | 1-4 | 1-4 | 3-7 |
| Fleet Town | 1-1 | 1-1 | 1-5 | 0-3 | 0-2 | 1-2 | 1-0 | 0-0 | 0-3 | 0-3 | 2-5 | — | 2-6 | 3-0 | 2-5 | 0-1 | 1-1 | 1-3 | 1-5 | 0-3 | 0-4 | 1-2 |
| Folkestone Invicta | 3-1 | 3-2 | 1-2 | 2-1 | 1-1 | 5-1 | 0-0 | 1-0 | 1-2 | 0-0 | 3-0 | 6-1 | — | 2-0 | 1-1 | 2-2 | 3-0 | 0-0 | 2-2 | 1-0 | 2-2 | 1-1 |
| Hastings United | 2-0 | 1-0 | 1-1 | 1-2 | 2-2 | 1-2 | 3-1 | 0-3 | 0-1 | 4-0 | 4-4 | 4-1 | 1-2 | — | 1-4 | 0-2 | 0-2 | 1-0 | 1-4 | 2-2 | 3-0 | 1-5 |
| Histon | 0-2 | 2-2 | 1-1 | 2-0 | 6-1 | 2-1 | 3-0 | 6-0 | 1-0 | 1-1 | 2-0 | 5-1 | 2-2 | 1-2 | — | 1-4 | 6-1 | 2-1 | 2-1 | 2-1 | 0-0 | 1-1 |
| King's Lynn | 1-0 | 4-1 | 1-0 | 2-1 | 1-2 | 6-0 | 2-0 | 4-1 | 1-1 | 1-0 | 2-2 | 4-1 | 1-1 | 4-2 | 1-0 | — | 4-0 | 1-0 | 0-2 | 5-2 | 3-1 | 4-1 |
| Newport (IW) | 3-2 | 0-4 | 0-2 | 1-1 | 1-0 | 1-2 | 0-1 | 3-0 | 0-3 | 3-1 | 2-2 | 2-1 | 0-3 | 1-2 | 1-1 | 0-0 | — | 0-2 | 1-1 | 1-2 | 2-0 | 2-0 |
| Rothwell Town | 2-0 | 1-0 | 0-1 | 2-2 | 0-1 | 0-2 | 0-1 | 2-2 | 0-1 | 1-1 | 0-3 | 0-1 | 1-4 | 2-3 | 1-2 | 1-1 | 2-0 | — | 0-2 | 0-0 | 0-2 | 0-1 |
| Salisbury City | 2-1 | 1-1 | 5-1 | 0-1 | 1-1 | 1-1 | 2-0 | 3-1 | 0-4 | 3-0 | 2-1 | 1-0 | 1-1 | 3-2 | 0-0 | 0-3 | 2-0 | 1-1 | — | 3-0 | 1-1 | 1-1 |
| Sittingbourne | 1-2 | 0-0 | 2-0 | 0-2 | 4-1 | 0-0 | 4-2 | 1-3 | 1-0 | 3-1 | 0-1 | 3-1 | 2-1 | 2-2 | 1-3 | 1-2 | 1-0 | 0-3 | 1-0 | — | 0-0 | 0-2 |
| Stamford | 4-1 | 3-3 | 1-0 | 1-0 | 2-1 | 5-3 | 0-0 | 1-0 | 1-1 | 2-1 | 2-2 | 5-0 | 0-0 | 1-0 | 1-2 | 2-3 | 1-0 | 1-0 | 2-0 | 1-0 | — | 1-3 |
| Tonbridge Angels | 1-0 | 3-0 | 0-2 | 1-0 | 1-3 | 0-1 | 1-1 | 1-0 | 0-2 | 2-1 | 2-2 | 2-1 | 1-2 | 2-1 | 4-3 | 2-0 | 2-1 | 4-0 | 2-2 | 1-3 | 3-0 | — |

# RYMAN LEAGUE 2003–04

## PREMIER DIVISION

| | | | Home | | | | | Away | | | | | Total | | | | | | |
|---|---|---|---|---|---|---|---|---|---|---|---|---|---|---|---|---|---|---|---|
| | | P | W | D | L | F | A | W | D | L | F | A | W | D | L | F | A | GD | Pts |
| 1 | Canvey Island | 46 | 17 | 4 | 2 | 62 | 23 | 15 | 4 | 4 | 44 | 19 | 32 | 8 | 6 | 106 | 42 | 64 | 104 |
| 2 | Sutton United | 46 | 11 | 6 | 6 | 46 | 30 | 14 | 4 | 5 | 48 | 26 | 25 | 10 | 11 | 94 | 56 | 38 | 85 |
| 3 | Thurrock | 46 | 12 | 5 | 6 | 43 | 18 | 12 | 6 | 5 | 44 | 27 | 24 | 11 | 11 | 87 | 45 | 42 | 83 |
| 4 | Hendon | 46 | 11 | 6 | 6 | 33 | 24 | 14 | 2 | 7 | 35 | 23 | 25 | 8 | 13 | 68 | 47 | 21 | 83 |
| 5 | Hornchurch* | 46 | 16 | 3 | 4 | 34 | 12 | 8 | 8 | 7 | 29 | 23 | 24 | 11 | 11 | 63 | 35 | 28 | 82 |
| 6 | Grays Athletic | 46 | 13 | 10 | 0 | 51 | 16 | 9 | 5 | 9 | 31 | 23 | 22 | 15 | 9 | 82 | 39 | 43 | 81 |
| 7 | Carshalton Athletic | 46 | 12 | 5 | 6 | 36 | 31 | 12 | 4 | 7 | 30 | 24 | 24 | 9 | 13 | 66 | 55 | 11 | 81 |
| 8 | Hayes | 46 | 11 | 8 | 4 | 29 | 15 | 10 | 3 | 10 | 27 | 31 | 21 | 11 | 14 | 56 | 46 | 10 | 74 |
| 9 | Kettering Town | 46 | 10 | 6 | 7 | 34 | 34 | 10 | 5 | 8 | 29 | 29 | 20 | 11 | 15 | 63 | 63 | 0 | 71 |
| 10 | Bognor Regis Town | 46 | 13 | 3 | 7 | 45 | 25 | 7 | 7 | 9 | 24 | 42 | 20 | 10 | 16 | 69 | 67 | 2 | 70 |
| 11 | Bishop's Stortford | 46 | 11 | 6 | 6 | 45 | 26 | 9 | 3 | 11 | 33 | 35 | 20 | 9 | 17 | 78 | 61 | 17 | 69 |
| 12 | Maidenhead United | 46 | 10 | 4 | 9 | 31 | 36 | 8 | 5 | 10 | 29 | 32 | 18 | 9 | 19 | 60 | 68 | –8 | 63 |
| 13 | Ford United | 46 | 11 | 6 | 6 | 42 | 26 | 5 | 8 | 10 | 27 | 37 | 16 | 14 | 16 | 69 | 63 | 6 | 62 |
| 14 | Basingstoke Town | 46 | 7 | 3 | 13 | 24 | 37 | 10 | 6 | 7 | 34 | 27 | 17 | 9 | 20 | 58 | 64 | –6 | 60 |
| 15 | Bedford Town | 46 | 11 | 3 | 9 | 41 | 34 | 3 | 10 | 10 | 21 | 29 | 14 | 13 | 19 | 62 | 63 | –1 | 55 |
| 16 | Heybridge Swifts | 46 | 7 | 5 | 11 | 31 | 37 | 7 | 6 | 10 | 26 | 41 | 14 | 11 | 21 | 57 | 78 | –21 | 53 |
| 17 | Harrow Borough | 46 | 5 | 8 | 10 | 21 | 28 | 7 | 6 | 10 | 26 | 35 | 12 | 14 | 20 | 47 | 63 | –16 | 50 |
| 18 | Kingstonian | 46 | 5 | 10 | 8 | 21 | 22 | 7 | 3 | 13 | 19 | 34 | 12 | 13 | 21 | 40 | 56 | –16 | 49 |
| 19 | St Albans City | 46 | 6 | 5 | 12 | 24 | 36 | 6 | 7 | 10 | 31 | 47 | 12 | 12 | 22 | 55 | 83 | –28 | 48 |
| 20 | Hitchin Town | 46 | 6 | 6 | 11 | 29 | 42 | 7 | 2 | 14 | 26 | 47 | 13 | 8 | 25 | 55 | 89 | –34 | 47 |
| 21 | Northwood | 46 | 6 | 4 | 13 | 34 | 45 | 6 | 5 | 12 | 31 | 50 | 12 | 9 | 25 | 65 | 95 | –30 | 45 |
| 22 | Billericay Town | 46 | 5 | 5 | 13 | 20 | 31 | 6 | 6 | 11 | 31 | 35 | 11 | 11 | 24 | 51 | 66 | –15 | 44 |
| 23 | Braintree Town | 46 | 4 | 1 | 18 | 19 | 48 | 7 | 5 | 11 | 22 | 40 | 11 | 6 | 29 | 41 | 88 | –47 | 39 |
| 24 | Aylesbury United | 46 | 3 | 6 | 14 | 17 | 45 | 2 | 8 | 13 | 24 | 56 | 5 | 14 | 27 | 41 | 101 | –60 | 29 |

**1 point deducted for fielding ineligible player.*

## DIVISION ONE NORTH

| | | P | W | D | L | F | A | W | D | L | F | A | W | D | L | F | A | GD | Pts |
|---|---|---|---|---|---|---|---|---|---|---|---|---|---|---|---|---|---|---|---|
| 1 | Yeading | 46 | 20 | 1 | 2 | 70 | 20 | 12 | 6 | 5 | 42 | 34 | 32 | 7 | 7 | 112 | 54 | 58 | 103 |
| 2 | Leyton | 46 | 14 | 6 | 3 | 46 | 28 | 15 | 3 | 5 | 44 | 25 | 29 | 9 | 8 | 90 | 53 | 37 | 96 |
| 3 | Cheshunt | 46 | 15 | 3 | 5 | 60 | 28 | 12 | 7 | 4 | 59 | 26 | 27 | 10 | 9 | 119 | 54 | 65 | 91 |
| 4 | Chesham United | 46 | 15 | 4 | 4 | 64 | 24 | 9 | 5 | 9 | 40 | 36 | 24 | 9 | 13 | 104 | 60 | 44 | 81 |
| 5 | Dunstable Town | 46 | 12 | 4 | 7 | 44 | 26 | 11 | 5 | 7 | 42 | 35 | 23 | 9 | 14 | 86 | 61 | 25 | 78 |
| 6 | Hemel Hempstead Town | 46 | 10 | 6 | 7 | 41 | 41 | 12 | 6 | 5 | 34 | 31 | 22 | 12 | 12 | 75 | 72 | 3 | 78 |
| 7 | Wealdstone | 46 | 12 | 3 | 8 | 39 | 26 | 11 | 4 | 8 | 42 | 25 | 23 | 7 | 16 | 81 | 51 | 30 | 76 |
| 8 | Arlesey Town | 46 | 16 | 2 | 5 | 54 | 26 | 7 | 5 | 11 | 41 | 44 | 23 | 7 | 16 | 95 | 70 | 25 | 76 |
| 9 | Boreham Wood | 46 | 13 | 4 | 6 | 49 | 27 | 7 | 9 | 7 | 33 | 32 | 20 | 13 | 13 | 82 | 59 | 23 | 73 |
| 10 | Harlow Town | 46 | 8 | 7 | 8 | 29 | 22 | 12 | 3 | 8 | 46 | 29 | 20 | 10 | 16 | 75 | 51 | 24 | 70 |
| 11 | Wingate & Finchley | 46 | 8 | 7 | 8 | 30 | 37 | 11 | 6 | 6 | 38 | 26 | 19 | 13 | 14 | 68 | 63 | 5 | 70 |
| 12 | East Thurrock United | 46 | 13 | 2 | 8 | 41 | 23 | 6 | 9 | 8 | 21 | 31 | 19 | 11 | 16 | 62 | 54 | 8 | 68 |
| 13 | Uxbridge | 46 | 10 | 8 | 5 | 29 | 21 | 5 | 6 | 12 | 30 | 36 | 15 | 14 | 17 | 59 | 57 | 2 | 59 |
| 14 | Aveley | 46 | 9 | 11 | 3 | 31 | 16 | 6 | 3 | 14 | 36 | 55 | 15 | 14 | 17 | 67 | 71 | –4 | 59 |
| 15 | Thame United | 46 | 11 | 4 | 8 | 42 | 32 | 5 | 5 | 13 | 30 | 51 | 16 | 9 | 21 | 72 | 83 | –11 | 57 |
| 16 | Waltham Forest* | 46 | 10 | 4 | 9 | 41 | 34 | 5 | 9 | 9 | 21 | 26 | 15 | 13 | 18 | 62 | 60 | 2 | 55 |
| 17 | Wivenhoe Town | 46 | 7 | 7 | 9 | 39 | 47 | 8 | 3 | 12 | 40 | 57 | 15 | 10 | 21 | 79 | 104 | –25 | 55 |
| 18 | Barton Rovers | 46 | 10 | 3 | 10 | 31 | 38 | 6 | 3 | 14 | 21 | 42 | 16 | 6 | 24 | 52 | 80 | –28 | 54 |
| 19 | Oxford City | 46 | 5 | 8 | 10 | 28 | 36 | 9 | 3 | 11 | 27 | 29 | 14 | 11 | 21 | 55 | 65 | –10 | 53 |
| 20 | Berkhamsted Town | 46 | 6 | 6 | 11 | 38 | 48 | 6 | 4 | 13 | 28 | 40 | 12 | 10 | 24 | 66 | 88 | –22 | 46 |
| 21 | Great Wakering Rovers | 46 | 5 | 8 | 10 | 27 | 38 | 5 | 5 | 13 | 20 | 59 | 10 | 13 | 23 | 47 | 97 | –50 | 43 |
| 22 | Tilbury | 46 | 4 | 5 | 14 | 22 | 46 | 6 | 4 | 13 | 34 | 54 | 10 | 9 | 27 | 56 | 100 | –44 | 39 |
| 23 | Barking & East Ham U | 46 | 4 | 4 | 15 | 18 | 44 | 4 | 3 | 16 | 19 | 56 | 8 | 7 | 31 | 37 | 100 | –63 | 31 |
| 24 | Enfield | 46 | 3 | 3 | 17 | 23 | 81 | 2 | 4 | 17 | 21 | 57 | 5 | 7 | 34 | 44 | 138 | –94 | 22 |

**3 points deducted for fielding ineligible player.*

## DIVISION ONE SOUTH

| | | P | W | D | L | F | A | W | D | L | F | A | W | D | L | F | A | GD | Pts |
|---|---|---|---|---|---|---|---|---|---|---|---|---|---|---|---|---|---|---|---|
| 1 | Lewes | 46 | 15 | 5 | 3 | 58 | 24 | 14 | 2 | 7 | 55 | 37 | 29 | 7 | 10 | 113 | 61 | 52 | 94 |
| 2 | Worthing | 46 | 15 | 4 | 4 | 46 | 23 | 11 | 10 | 2 | 41 | 23 | 26 | 14 | 6 | 87 | 46 | 41 | 92 |
| 3 | Windsor & Eton | 46 | 14 | 5 | 4 | 43 | 21 | 12 | 8 | 3 | 32 | 18 | 26 | 13 | 7 | 75 | 39 | 36 | 91 |
| 4 | Slough Town | 46 | 15 | 5 | 3 | 56 | 26 | 13 | 1 | 9 | 47 | 37 | 28 | 6 | 12 | 103 | 63 | 40 | 90 |
| 5 | Hampton & Richmond B | 46 | 13 | 5 | 5 | 39 | 24 | 13 | 6 | 4 | 43 | 21 | 26 | 11 | 9 | 82 | 45 | 37 | 89 |
| 6 | Staines Town | 46 | 15 | 5 | 3 | 47 | 24 | 11 | 4 | 8 | 38 | 28 | 26 | 9 | 11 | 85 | 52 | 33 | 87 |
| 7 | Dulwich Hamlet | 46 | 12 | 5 | 6 | 44 | 37 | 11 | 10 | 2 | 33 | 20 | 23 | 15 | 8 | 77 | 57 | 20 | 84 |
| 8 | Bromley | 46 | 10 | 6 | 7 | 36 | 28 | 12 | 4 | 7 | 44 | 30 | 22 | 10 | 14 | 80 | 58 | 22 | 76 |
| 9 | Walton & Hersham | 46 | 12 | 5 | 6 | 43 | 25 | 8 | 9 | 6 | 33 | 30 | 20 | 14 | 12 | 76 | 55 | 21 | 74 |
| 10 | Croydon Athletic | 46 | 13 | 3 | 7 | 41 | 28 | 7 | 7 | 9 | 29 | 26 | 20 | 10 | 16 | 70 | 54 | 16 | 70 |
| 11 | Tooting & Mitcham U | 46 | 11 | 4 | 8 | 41 | 35 | 9 | 5 | 9 | 41 | 33 | 20 | 9 | 17 | 82 | 68 | 14 | 69 |
| 12 | Ashford Town (Mx) | 46 | 9 | 7 | 7 | 38 | 29 | 9 | 6 | 8 | 31 | 33 | 18 | 13 | 15 | 69 | 62 | 7 | 67 |
| 13 | Leatherhead | 46 | 9 | 6 | 8 | 40 | 39 | 10 | 3 | 10 | 43 | 49 | 19 | 9 | 18 | 83 | 88 | –5 | 66 |
| 14 | Bracknell Town | 46 | 12 | 3 | 8 | 51 | 40 | 7 | 3 | 13 | 30 | 47 | 19 | 6 | 21 | 81 | 87 | –6 | 63 |
| 15 | Horsham | 46 | 8 | 4 | 11 | 39 | 34 | 8 | 7 | 8 | 32 | 35 | 16 | 11 | 19 | 71 | 69 | 2 | 59 |
| 16 | Marlow | 46 | 10 | 6 | 7 | 29 | 25 | 6 | 5 | 12 | 21 | 39 | 16 | 11 | 19 | 50 | 64 | –14 | 59 |
| 17 | Whyteleafe | 46 | 9 | 2 | 12 | 35 | 43 | 8 | 2 | 13 | 31 | 50 | 17 | 4 | 25 | 66 | 93 | –27 | 55 |
| 18 | Banstead Athletic | 46 | 7 | 4 | 12 | 30 | 31 | 8 | 4 | 11 | 26 | 42 | 15 | 8 | 23 | 56 | 73 | –17 | 53 |
| 19 | Molesey | 46 | 5 | 5 | 13 | 20 | 35 | 7 | 1 | 15 | 25 | 49 | 12 | 6 | 28 | 45 | 84 | –39 | 42 |
| 20 | Metropolitan Police | 46 | 4 | 8 | 11 | 29 | 39 | 5 | 6 | 12 | 29 | 45 | 9 | 14 | 23 | 58 | 84 | –26 | 41 |
| 21 | Croydon | 46 | 6 | 5 | 12 | 28 | 43 | 4 | 5 | 14 | 29 | 45 | 10 | 10 | 26 | 57 | 88 | –31 | 40 |
| 22 | Egham Town | 46 | 4 | 6 | 13 | 28 | 41 | 4 | 2 | 17 | 27 | 51 | 8 | 8 | 30 | 55 | 92 | –37 | 32 |
| 23 | Corinthian Casuals | 46 | 3 | 4 | 16 | 22 | 56 | 3 | 2 | 18 | 26 | 54 | 6 | 6 | 34 | 48 | 110 | –62 | 24 |
| 24 | Epsom & Ewell | 46 | 2 | 4 | 17 | 21 | 55 | 3 | 4 | 16 | 19 | 62 | 5 | 8 | 33 | 40 | 117 | –77 | 23 |

## DIVISION TWO

| | | | Home | | | | | Away | | | | | Total | | | | | | |
|---|---|---|---|---|---|---|---|---|---|---|---|---|---|---|---|---|---|---|---|
| | | P | W | D | L | F | A | W | D | L | F | A | W | D | L | F | A | GD | Pts |
| 1 | Leighton Town | 42 | 16 | 3 | 2 | 68 | 16 | 12 | 4 | 5 | 43 | 20 | 28 | 7 | 7 | 111 | 36 | 75 | 91 |
| 2 | Dorking | 42 | 18 | 0 | 3 | 48 | 19 | 9 | 8 | 4 | 39 | 28 | 27 | 8 | 7 | 87 | 47 | 40 | 89 |
| 3 | Hertford Town | 42 | 11 | 5 | 5 | 33 | 17 | 13 | 4 | 4 | 41 | 18 | 24 | 9 | 9 | 74 | 35 | 39 | 81 |
| 4 | Chertsey Town | 42 | 10 | 6 | 5 | 30 | 23 | 12 | 3 | 6 | 45 | 30 | 22 | 9 | 11 | 75 | 53 | 22 | 75 |
| 5 | Flackwell Heath | 42 | 12 | 3 | 6 | 39 | 29 | 10 | 2 | 9 | 32 | 24 | 22 | 5 | 15 | 71 | 53 | 18 | 71 |
| 6 | Witham Town | 42 | 12 | 7 | 2 | 48 | 18 | 8 | 3 | 10 | 27 | 36 | 20 | 10 | 12 | 75 | 54 | 21 | 70 |
| 7 | Kingsbury Town | 42 | 10 | 5 | 6 | 35 | 26 | 4 | 6 | 11 | 25 | 38 | 14 | 11 | 17 | 60 | 64 | -4 | 53 |
| 8 | Ware | 42 | 10 | 2 | 9 | 39 | 30 | 4 | 8 | 9 | 28 | 30 | 14 | 10 | 18 | 67 | 60 | 7 | 52 |
| 9 | Abingdon Town | 42 | 8 | 4 | 9 | 47 | 42 | 7 | 2 | 12 | 36 | 39 | 15 | 6 | 21 | 83 | 81 | 2 | 51 |
| 10 | Camberley Town | 42 | 8 | 3 | 10 | 24 | 25 | 7 | 3 | 11 | 27 | 46 | 15 | 6 | 21 | 51 | 71 | -20 | 51 |
| 11 | Wembley | 42 | 9 | 4 | 8 | 25 | 25 | 4 | 5 | 12 | 21 | 42 | 13 | 9 | 20 | 46 | 67 | -21 | 48 |
| 12 | Wokingham Town | 42 | 7 | 3 | 11 | 32 | 43 | 5 | 4 | 12 | 23 | 51 | 12 | 7 | 23 | 55 | 94 | -39 | 43 |
| 13 | Edgware Town | 42 | 5 | 4 | 12 | 37 | 43 | 7 | 2 | 12 | 25 | 45 | 12 | 6 | 24 | 62 | 88 | -26 | 42 |
| 14 | Chalfont St Peter | 42 | 4 | 5 | 12 | 33 | 46 | 8 | 1 | 12 | 24 | 43 | 12 | 6 | 24 | 57 | 89 | -32 | 42 |
| 15 | Clapton | 42 | 3 | 3 | 15 | 21 | 60 | 5 | 2 | 14 | 26 | 69 | 8 | 5 | 29 | 47 | 129 | -82 | 29 |

## RYMAN LEAGUE PLAY OFFS 2003–04

Yeading 0, Lewes 1
Dulwich Hamlet 2, Wealdstone 2
*Wealdstone won 5-4 on penalties and will compete in step 3 next season.*
Basingstoke Town 1, Lewes 4
Bedford Town 3, Hitchin Town 1

Heybridge Swifts 3, St Albans City 4
Harrow Borough 0, Kingstonian 0
*Kingstonian won 4-2 on penalties.*
Bedford Town 4, St Albans City 5
Lewes 1, Kingstonian 0
*St Albans City and Lewes compete in step 2 next season*

## RYMAN LEAGUE GOALSCORERS

**PREMIER DIVISION**

| | | | Lge | BC |
|---|---|---|---|---|
| 42 | Lee Boylan | Canvey Island | 42 | |
| 32 | Tresor Kandol | Thurrock | 27 | 5 |
| 30 | Freddie Eastwood | Grays Athletic | 29 | 1 |
| 27 | Drew Roberts | Bedford Town | 24 | |
| | *Includes 3 play-off goals* | | | |
| 26 | Cliff Akurang | Thurrock | 25 | 1 |
| 22 | Danny Hockton | Billericay Town | 22 | |
| 22 | Craig McAllister | Basingstoke Town | 21 | |
| | *Includes 1 play-off goal* | | | |
| 21 | Eugene Ofori | Hendon | 19 | 2 |
| 20 | Nick Bailey | Sutton United | 19 | 1 |

**DIVISION ONE NORTH**

| | | | Lge | BC |
|---|---|---|---|---|
| 37 | DJ Campbell | Yeading | 33 | 3 |
| | *Includes 1 Charity Shield Goal* | | | |
| 34 | Gary Sippetts | Chesham United | 30 | 4 |
| 32 | Sammy Winston | Boreham Wood | 31 | 1 |
| 30 | Grant Carney | Dunstable Town | 27 | 3 |
| 28 | Darrell Cox | Cheshunt | 24 | 4 |
| 27 | Leon Archer | Cheshunt | 18 | 9 |
| 27 | John Lawford | Chesham United | 27 | |
| | *Includes 1 league goal for Waltham Forest* | | | |
| 26 | Trevor Paul | Leyton | 22 | 4 |

**DIVISION ONE SOUTH**

| | | | Lge | BC |
|---|---|---|---|---|
| 34 | Ian Hodge | Slough Town | 34 | |
| 28 | Omari Coleman | Dulwich Hamlet | 28 | |
| 27 | Tony Boot | Slough Town | 27 | |
| 26 | Phil Ruggles | Leatherhead | 26 | |
| 26 | Mark Tompkins | Whyteleafe | 26 | |
| 23 | Craig Dundas | Dulwich Hamlet | 23 | |
| | *Includes 11 league goals for Croydon* | | | |
| 23 | Sam Francis | Worthing | 23 | |

**DIVISION TWO**

| | | | Lge | BC |
|---|---|---|---|---|
| 29 | John Frendo | Ware | 29 | |
| 29 | Matt Rawdon | Leighton Town | 29 | |
| 28 | Kevin Cooper | Hertford Town | 28 | |
| 24 | Kevin Hawes | Witham Town | 24 | |
| 23 | Craig Duffell | Dorking | 23 | |

## LEADING ATTENDANCES

**PREMIER DIVISION**
1260 Kettering Town v Bedford Town (12/4/2004)
1213 Sutton United v Carshalton Athletic (27/12/2003)
1174 Bedford Town v Kettering Town (26/12/2003)

**DIVISION ONE NORTH**
408 Wealdstone v Hemel Hempstead Town (24/4/2004)
408 Hemel Hempstead Town v Arlesey Town (1/5/2004)
404 Chesham United v Boreham Wood (26/12/2003)

**DIVISION ONE SOUTH**
932 Lewes v Worthing (12/4/2004)
872 Worthing v Lewes (20/4/2004)
727 Windsor & Eton v Slough Town (12/4/2004)

**DIVISION TWO**
389 Dorking v Hertford Town (1/5/2004)
328 Ware v Hertford Town (12/4/2004)
302 Hertford Town v Ware (26/12/2003)

## RYMAN LEAGUE – PREMIER DIVISION RESULTS 2003–04

| | Aylesbury United | Basingstoke Town | Bedford Town | Billericay Town | Bishop's Stortford | Bognor Regis Town | Braintree Town | Canvey Island | Carshalton Athletic | Ford United | Grays Athletic | Harrow Borough | Hayes | Hendon | Heybridge Swifts | Hitchin Town | Hornchurch | Kettering Town | Kingstonian | Maidenhead United | Northwood | St Albans City | Sutton United | Thurrock |
|---|---|---|---|---|---|---|---|---|---|---|---|---|---|---|---|---|---|---|---|---|---|---|---|---|
| Aylesbury United | — | 0-3 | 3-3 | 3-2 | 0-1 | 1-0 | 0-0 | 0-2 | 1-1 | 3-2 | 0-3 | 0-1 | 0-1 | 1-1 | 0-0 | 1-4 | 0-2 | 0-2 | 0-0 | 1-3 | 1-2 | 0-2 | 0-6 | 2-4 |
| Basingstoke Town | 2-0 | — | 2-0 | 0-1 | 1-2 | 0-1 | 3-0 | 1-2 | 1-2 | 1-0 | 0-2 | 0-1 | 0-2 | 1-4 | 1-1 | 2-3 | 0-3 | 2-2 | 2-1 | 2-1 | 2-0 | 1-1 | 0-5 | 0-3 |
| Bedford Town | 4-1 | 5-2 | — | 2-1 | 0-3 | 8-0 | 2-0 | 2-4 | 1-0 | 1-1 | 0-4 | 2-0 | 1-2 | 0-2 | 3-1 | 1-2 | 2-1 | 2-3 | 0-0 | 1-2 | 1-4 | 1-0 | 2-1 | 0-0 |
| Billericay Town | 2-2 | 3-1 | 0-0 | — | 1-0 | 1-1 | 0-1 | 0-3 | 0-1 | 1-0 | 0-1 | 0-1 | 0-2 | 1-2 | 1-2 | 1-3 | 2-0 | 3-1 | 1-2 | 0-1 | 1-4 | 1-1 | 0-1 | 1-1 |
| Bishop's Stortford | 4-4 | 0-1 | 3-1 | 3-0 | — | 0-0 | 2-3 | 2-0 | 0-3 | 4-0 | 1-2 | 1-1 | 0-0 | 2-0 | 0-1 | 3-0 | 2-1 | 4-1 | 2-1 | 2-1 | 6-0 | 2-2 | 1-1 | 1-3 |
| Bognor Regis Town | 4-0 | 1-3 | 0-0 | 2-0 | 0-1 | — | 4-1 | 0-0 | 0-1 | 3-2 | 2-1 | 3-1 | 4-0 | 1-2 | 2-0 | 2-0 | 1-3 | 1-0 | 2-0 | 0-3 | 5-2 | 2-2 | 0-2 | 6-1 |
| Braintree Town | 2-0 | 0-1 | 0-2 | 2-2 | 2-0 | 0-3 | — | 0-3 | 0-1 | 1-2 | 0-5 | 0-2 | 1-2 | 1-3 | 1-3 | 2-0 | 1-3 | 0-1 | 0-1 | 1-2 | 2-5 | 2-4 | 0-3 | 1-0 |
| Canvey Island | 4-0 | 3-1 | 3-1 | 0-2 | 5-1 | 3-1 | 4-1 | — | 3-0 | 3-1 | 1-1 | 1-1 | 2-1 | 1-0 | 2-0 | 4-0 | 3-2 | 1-1 | 6-1 | 3-1 | 1-1 | 4-0 | 1-3 | 4-3 |
| Carshalton Athletic | 3-0 | 0-2 | 2-1 | 2-1 | 1-2 | 1-1 | 2-1 | 0-2 | — | 1-1 | 0-2 | 3-2 | 2-0 | 1-3 | 4-1 | 2-1 | 0-0 | 3-2 | 2-1 | 3-2 | 1-0 | 1-1 | 2-2 | 0-3 |
| Ford United | 4-1 | 1-1 | 1-1 | 2-1 | 3-0 | 2-0 | 3-0 | 0-3 | 2-1 | — | 3-0 | 1-3 | 0-0 | 0-1 | 5-3 | 3-0 | 0-0 | 2-0 | 0-1 | 1-1 | 3-0 | 2-2 | 2-4 | 2-3 |
| Grays Athletic | 2-1 | 3-1 | 1-1 | 1-1 | 3-1 | 6-0 | 1-1 | 1-1 | 0-0 | 2-0 | — | 2-2 | 4-0 | 1-0 | 4-0 | 2-0 | 0-0 | 1-1 | 1-0 | 1-1 | 2-1 | 9-1 | 3-2 | 1-1 |
| Harrow Borough | 0-2 | 1-1 | 2-1 | 2-1 | 1-0 | 0-1 | 2-3 | 0-1 | 0-0 | 1-1 | 0-0 | — | 1-0 | 1-2 | 0-0 | 0-2 | 0-0 | 1-2 | 0-1 | 1-1 | 2-2 | 3-1 | 2-4 | 1-2 |
| Hayes | 3-0 | 2-1 | 1-0 | 1-1 | 1-0 | 0-1 | 0-0 | 2-1 | 1-0 | 1-1 | 1-1 | 1-1 | — | 3-1 | 2-0 | 5-1 | 1-1 | 0-1 | 1-0 | 0-1 | 1-1 | 1-0 | 0-0 | 1-2 |
| Hendon | 1-1 | 0-1 | 1-0 | 3-0 | 2-5 | 2-2 | 1-0 | 1-0 | 1-2 | 2-2 | 1-0 | 2-0 | 3-2 | — | 0-1 | 3-0 | 1-0 | 1-2 | 2-0 | 3-1 | 1-1 | 1-1 | 0-2 | 1-1 |
| Heybridge Swifts | 1-2 | 0-3 | 0-0 | 1-4 | 1-0 | 1-2 | 1-2 | 1-4 | 4-0 | 4-1 | 3-0 | 2-3 | 1-2 | 0-0 | — | 4-2 | 1-1 | 1-0 | 0-2 | 0-0 | 3-2 | 0-2 | 2-2 | 0-3 |
| Hitchin Town | 2-2 | 2-2 | 1-3 | 2-5 | 0-2 | 2-2 | 2-0 | 1-3 | 0-3 | 1-1 | 1-0 | 3-2 | 0-2 | 1-4 | 1-2 | — | 0-2 | 1-1 | 3-0 | 2-0 | 1-2 | 1-0 | 2-4 | 0-0 |
| Hornchurch | 1-0 | 2-0 | 1-0 | 1-1 | 2-0 | 3-0 | 2-1 | 0-0 | 2-0 | 1-0 | 2-0 | 2-1 | 0-2 | 0-2 | 0-2 | 4-0 | — | 1-1 | 1-0 | 1-0 | 3-1 | 0-1 | 3-0 | 2-0 |
| Kettering Town | 2-2 | 0-3 | 0-0 | 1-0 | 3-2 | 3-1 | 1-2 | 1-4 | 0-3 | 0-3 | 0-0 | 1-1 | 0-3 | 4-1 | 4-1 | 1-1 | 3-2 | — | 1-1 | 3-1 | 2-1 | 2-0 | 0-1 | 2-1 |
| Kingstonian | 0-0 | 2-0 | 0-0 | 0-0 | 1-1 | 1-1 | 2-2 | 1-2 | 0-1 | 0-2 | 3-1 | 1-1 | 1-0 | 0-1 | 1-1 | 1-1 | 0-1 | 1-0 | — | 3-1 | 0-1 | 1-2 | 1-2 | 1-1 |
| Maidenhead United | 4-2 | 0-2 | 2-1 | 1-0 | 0-4 | 0-2 | 4-0 | 0-0 | 0-0 | 1-1 | 1-4 | 1-0 | 1-0 | 0-1 | 2-4 | 2-1 | 1-1 | 1-2 | 0-4 | — | 3-1 | 4-2 | 2-0 | 1-4 |
| Northwood | 1-1 | 0-0 | 3-1 | 4-5 | 2-3 | 1-2 | 3-1 | 1-5 | 0-4 | 2-3 | 1-1 | 3-1 | 3-4 | 0-1 | 2-1 | 1-0 | 0-1 | 1-2 | 2-0 | 0-0 | — | 3-4 | 1-2 | 0-3 |
| St Albans City | 3-1 | 0-3 | 1-3 | 0-2 | 3-2 | 2-2 | 0-0 | 4-1 | 0-4 | 2-0 | 0-3 | 0-1 | 1-1 | 0-4 | 0-0 | 1-2 | 1-1 | 0-1 | 0-1 | 1-2 | 3-0 | — | 2-0 | 0-2 |
| Sutton United | 2-2 | 2-2 | 1-1 | 1-1 | 2-2 | 1-0 | 1-2 | 0-1 | 6-0 | 2-3 | 1-0 | 3-0 | 4-1 | 2-0 | 5-1 | 0-3 | 3-1 | 2-1 | 4-1 | 0-3 | 0-0 | 4-2 | — | 0-3 |
| Thurrock | 5-0 | 0-0 | 1-1 | 1-0 | 1-1 | 4-1 | 0-1 | 1-2 | 2-3 | 0-0 | 2-0 | 3-0 | 2-0 | 2-0 | 1-1 | 2-0 | 1-3 | 0-2 | 4-1 | 3-1 | 6-0 | 2-0 | 0-1 | — |

## RYMAN LEAGUE – DIVISION ONE NORTH RESULTS 2003–04

| | Arlesey Town | Aveley | Barking & East Ham U | Barton Rovers | Berkhamsted Town | Boreham Wood | Chesham United | Cheshunt | Dunstable Town | East Thurrock United | Enfield | Great Wakering Rovers | Harlow Town | Hemel Hempstead Town | Leyton | Oxford City | Thame United | Tilbury | Uxbridge | Waltham Forest | Wealdstone | Wingate & Finchley | Wivenhoe Town | Yeading |
|---|---|---|---|---|---|---|---|---|---|---|---|---|---|---|---|---|---|---|---|---|---|---|---|---|
| Arlesey Town | — | 4-2 | 4-2 | 0-1 | 1-4 | 1-0 | 3-2 | 2-2 | 2-1 | 1-0 | 1-2 | 9-0 | 0-1 | 1-0 | 4-1 | 1-0 | 4-2 | 3-1 | 2-0 | 2-0 | 0-2 | 1-1 | 3-2 | 5-0 |
| Aveley | 4-0 | — | 0-0 | 1-0 | 1-0 | 1-2 | 0-0 | 1-1 | 5-1 | 0-0 | 1-1 | 2-1 | 4-1 | 0-0 | 1-2 | 0-0 | 0-2 | 4-2 | 0-0 | 0-0 | 3-1 | 1-0 | 1-1 | 1-1 |
| Barking & East Ham U | 1-2 | 2-0 | — | 0-0 | 2-1 | 0-3 | 0-4 | 0-2 | 2-6 | 2-0 | 0-0 | 0-0 | 0-3 | 0-1 | 0-4 | 2-3 | 1-2 | 2-0 | 1-1 | 0-1 | 1-4 | 1-2 | 0-3 | 1-2 |
| Barton Rovers | 3-2 | 2-1 | 1-0 | — | 2-3 | 1-1 | 1-1 | 1-5 | 0-1 | 0-3 | 4-0 | 3-2 | 1-3 | 0-2 | 0-2 | 3-1 | 2-1 | 0-2 | 2-1 | 1-0 | 1-1 | 0-2 | 3-1 | 0-3 |
| Berkhamsted Town | 4-3 | 1-5 | 2-2 | 2-1 | — | 1-2 | 1-1 | 0-5 | 0-2 | 2-4 | 1-1 | 1-2 | 3-2 | 1-2 | 1-1 | 0-1 | 5-0 | 1-2 | 2-1 | 2-1 | 0-0 | 2-2 | 3-4 | 3-4 |
| Boreham Wood | 4-0 | 2-1 | 1-2 | 2-0 | 4-0 | — | 1-1 | 1-3 | 3-1 | 4-0 | 2-1 | 0-2 | 1-1 | 2-2 | 1-2 | 1-0 | 0-1 | 6-0 | 3-1 | 1-1 | 3-2 | 2-0 | 4-3 | 1-3 |
| Chesham United | 1-3 | 3-1 | 5-0 | 3-0 | 4-2 | 1-1 | — | 1-0 | 1-2 | 5-1 | 1-1 | 7-0 | 1-0 | 5-2 | 2-0 | 1-4 | 6-1 | 1-1 | 4-0 | 1-0 | 1-3 | 2-0 | 8-2 | 0-0 |
| Cheshunt | 3-0 | 2-3 | 5-0 | 3-0 | 0-2 | 2-0 | 1-2 | — | 2-2 | 4-1 | 4-2 | 4-0 | 1-3 | 5-0 | 3-1 | 2-0 | 1-1 | 1-0 | 4-2 | 1-1 | 3-2 | 1-2 | 6-3 | 2-1 |
| Dunstable Town | 1-1 | 4-0 | 5-0 | 1-2 | 2-1 | 0-2 | 2-1 | 2-2 | — | 1-1 | 2-1 | 2-3 | 1-3 | 0-1 | 3-1 | 1-0 | 2-1 | 3-1 | 0-0 | 1-2 | 2-0 | 4-1 | 5-1 | 0-1 |
| East Thurrock United | 1-1 | 3-1 | 5-0 | 2-1 | 0-1 | 3-3 | 4-0 | 1-3 | 0-1 | — | 3-0 | 2-0 | 1-0 | 1-0 | 1-0 | 1-2 | 3-1 | 2-0 | 0-1 | 3-0 | 0-2 | 0-1 | 2-3 | 3-2 |
| Enfield | 0-6 | 1-2 | 3-1 | 3-2 | 1-1 | 2-4 | 2-7 | 1-3 | 1-5 | 1-1 | — | 0-0 | 0-6 | 1-2 | 1-2 | 3-2 | 0-5 | 1-4 | 1-7 | 0-4 | 0-8 | 0-4 | 0-1 | 1-4 |
| Great Wakering Rovers | 0-1 | 2-2 | 4-0 | 3-3 | 4-1 | 0-2 | 0-0 | 1-4 | 1-3 | 0-3 | 2-1 | — | 2-1 | 0-3 | 1-1 | 0-3 | 1-1 | 1-2 | 2-1 | 0-0 | 0-0 | 1-1 | 0-2 | 2-3 |
| Harlow Town | 0-2 | 0-1 | 0-1 | 1-0 | 2-0 | 3-2 | 4-0 | 3-0 | 0-2 | 0-0 | 4-0 | 3-1 | — | 1-1 | 0-0 | 2-3 | 2-1 | 1-3 | 0-0 | 0-1 | 0-1 | 1-1 | 1-1 | 1-1 |
| Hemel Hempstead Town | 1-0 | 1-1 | 1-0 | 4-0 | 0-3 | 0-0 | 3-1 | 3-7 | 3-3 | 3-2 | 3-2 | 4-0 | 2-4 | — | 2-4 | 0-1 | 1-1 | 1-5 | 1-0 | 2-2 | 2-1 | 1-2 | 2-1 | 1-1 |
| Leyton | 4-3 | 1-0 | 3-2 | 0-1 | 3-1 | 1-0 | 2-4 | 2-1 | 0-0 | 1-1 | 2-1 | 3-3 | 3-3 | 1-1 | — | 2-1 | 3-0 | 3-2 | 4-1 | 1-0 | 1-0 | 0-0 | 5-1 | 1-2 |
| Oxford City | 1-0 | 2-3 | 2-1 | 0-1 | 0-0 | 2-1 | 1-2 | 1-1 | 2-2 | 0-1 | 3-1 | 0-1 | 2-4 | 1-2 | 1-3 | — | 2-1 | 2-2 | 1-1 | 1-1 | 1-3 | 1-3 | 1-1 | 1-1 |
| Thame United | 4-3 | 2-1 | 3-0 | 0-3 | 2-0 | 2-0 | 1-3 | 0-0 | 1-2 | 0-0 | 8-0 | 3-0 | 1-0 | 2-3 | 0-2 | 1-2 | — | 4-3 | 1-0 | 2-2 | 0-3 | 1-2 | 2-1 | 2-2 |
| Tilbury | 3-4 | 2-0 | 1-2 | 0-1 | 1-1 | 1-1 | 0-2 | 1-1 | 0-3 | 0-0 | 3-2 | 1-2 | 0-4 | 0-3 | 1-3 | 2-1 | 3-0 | — | 0-4 | 0-0 | 0-2 | 1-6 | 1-2 | 1-2 |
| Uxbridge | 0-0 | 3-2 | 1-1 | 2-0 | 2-1 | 1-1 | 1-0 | 0-5 | 1-0 | 0-0 | 3-0 | 0-0 | 1-0 | 1-1 | 0-1 | 0-1 | 2-2 | 6-1 | — | 0-0 | 1-3 | 2-0 | 2-0 | 0-2 |
| Waltham Forest | 1-6 | 4-1 | 3-1 | 2-0 | 3-0 | 3-0 | 2-4 | 0-2 | 1-1 | 0-1 | 3-2 | 3-0 | 0-1 | 0-1 | 1-2 | 2-0 | 1-1 | 2-2 | 1-2 | — | 1-1 | 0-3 | 5-2 | 3-1 |
| Wealdstone | 0-0 | 1-0 | 1-2 | 2-1 | 2-2 | 1-2 | 3-1 | 0-4 | 5-0 | 3-1 | 2-0 | 5-0 | 0-1 | 0-2 | 1-2 | 2-2 | 3-0 | 1-0 | 2-1 | 1-0 | — | 3-1 | 0-2 | 1-2 |
| Wingate & Finchley | 1-0 | 4-4 | 2-1 | 2-2 | 2-0 | 4-4 | 2-1 | 1-1 | 2-1 | 0-0 | 1-0 | 1-1 | 1-4 | 0-1 | 1-5 | 2-0 | 0-4 | 0-0 | 0-2 | 1-3 | 2-0 | — | 0-1 | 1-2 |
| Wivenhoe Town | 4-4 | 2-3 | 2-0 | 3-2 | 0-4 | 1-1 | 0-3 | 2-6 | 0-2 | 0-1 | 1-2 | 4-2 | 1-1 | 3-3 | 0-4 | 0-0 | 4-1 | 2-1 | 2-2 | 4-1 | 0-1 | 1-1 | — | 3-2 |
| Yeading | 3-0 | 7-2 | 2-1 | 6-0 | 2-0 | 1-1 | 2-0 | 2-1 | 3-1 | 4-0 | 3-1 | 2-0 | 3-0 | 6-1 | 0-1 | 1-0 | 5-1 | 7-0 | 3-2 | 2-1 | 3-2 | 0-3 | 3-2 | — |

## RYMAN LEAGUE – DIVISION ONE SOUTH RESULTS 2003–04

| | Ashford Town (Mx) | Banstead Athletic | Bracknell Town | Bromley | Corinthian Casuals | Croydon | Croydon Athletic | Dulwich Hamlet | Egham Town | Epsom & Ewell | Hampton & Richmond B | Horsham | Leatherhead | Lewes | Marlow | Metropolitan Police | Molesey | Slough Town | Staines Town | Tooting & Mitcham U | Walton & Hersham | Whyteleafe | Windsor & Eton | Worthing |
|---|---|---|---|---|---|---|---|---|---|---|---|---|---|---|---|---|---|---|---|---|---|---|---|---|
| Ashford Town (Mx) | — | 2-0 | 4-1 | 1-1 | 2-1 | 0-2 | 2-0 | 1-1 | 1-0 | 2-0 | 0-0 | 1-2 | 2-2 | 2-3 | 1-1 | 3-1 | 1-2 | 1-2 | 0-2 | 2-3 | 2-2 | 4-2 | 3-0 | 1-1 |
| Banstead Athletic | 0-1 | — | 1-0 | 1-2 | 0-1 | 1-4 | 1-1 | 1-1 | 5-1 | 4-1 | 0-1 | 1-2 | 1-3 | 6-1 | 1-0 | 1-1 | 0-2 | 1-2 | 0-1 | 2-1 | 0-1 | 2-0 | 0-3 | 1-1 |
| Bracknell Town | 0-0 | 3-0 | — | 0-1 | 5-0 | 5-4 | 1-0 | 1-2 | 3-2 | 2-0 | 0-4 | 2-1 | 1-3 | 0-3 | 1-1 | 0-3 | 4-0 | 4-2 | 3-4 | 0-6 | 2-1 | 10-1 | 0-0 | 4-2 |
| Bromley | 2-3 | 1-1 | 4-0 | — | 3-0 | 2-0 | 2-2 | 2-2 | 1-2 | 2-0 | 2-0 | 1-3 | 2-0 | 1-2 | 0-2 | 1-1 | 4-0 | 0-4 | 2-1 | 1-0 | 0-3 | 2-2 | 1-0 | 0-0 |
| Corinthian Casuals | 0-2 | 1-6 | 0-3 | 0-1 | — | 0-4 | 1-3 | 0-3 | 4-2 | 0-1 | 1-1 | 1-1 | 3-2 | 2-4 | 2-4 | 1-1 | 0-1 | 4-1 | 0-0 | 0-3 | 1-2 | 0-5 | 0-3 | 1-3 |
| Croydon | 2-2 | 3-1 | 0-2 | 0-1 | 4-3 | — | 0-2 | 2-2 | 0-2 | 0-2 | 0-3 | 4-2 | 3-1 | 0-4 | 2-4 | 0-1 | 3-1 | 1-0 | 0-4 | 2-2 | 1-1 | 0-1 | 0-1 | 1-1 |
| Croydon Athletic | 1-0 | 3-0 | 1-2 | 0-2 | 3-2 | 1-0 | — | 2-2 | 2-1 | 3-0 | 2-4 | 1-2 | 3-2 | 1-2 | 2-0 | 4-2 | 4-1 | 1-0 | 0-3 | 0-2 | 2-0 | 5-1 | 0-0 | 0-0 |
| Dulwich Hamlet | 4-0 | 1-2 | 2-2 | 0-4 | 3-2 | 2-0 | 1-0 | — | 1-0 | 3-1 | 2-1 | 1-0 | 4-2 | 4-1 | 3-1 | 1-1 | 1-3 | 2-4 | 2-2 | 1-1 | 1-4 | 1-3 | 2-2 | 2-1 |
| Egham Town | 2-2 | 1-2 | 1-2 | 1-4 | 1-1 | 3-2 | 1-3 | 0-0 | — | 1-0 | 2-2 | 0-2 | 2-3 | 2-4 | 0-0 | 3-0 | 1-2 | 2-3 | 2-1 | 1-1 | 0-1 | 2-3 | 0-1 | 0-2 |
| Epsom & Ewell | 0-5 | 1-1 | 0-2 | 1-1 | 4-1 | 1-2 | 1-1 | 0-2 | 1-2 | — | 0-2 | 0-3 | 1-2 | 0-4 | 0-3 | 2-5 | 2-0 | 1-4 | 0-2 | 2-3 | 0-3 | 0-1 | 2-4 | 2-2 |
| Hampton & Richmond B | 1-0 | 2-1 | 1-1 | 1-3 | 2-0 | 2-0 | 1-1 | 1-3 | 1-1 | 2-1 | — | 1-0 | 1-2 | 4-3 | 1-0 | 3-0 | 3-1 | 4-0 | 2-0 | 2-1 | 1-1 | 2-2 | 0-1 | 1-2 |
| Horsham | 1-0 | 3-1 | 4-1 | 1-2 | 1-1 | 2-2 | 1-2 | 0-1 | 1-3 | 5-0 | 3-1 | — | 2-3 | 0-2 | 3-0 | 2-2 | 5-0 | 1-4 | 0-3 | 2-3 | 0-0 | 1-0 | 0-1 | 1-2 |
| Leatherhead | 2-2 | 6-0 | 2-2 | 0-5 | 2-0 | 2-2 | 3-2 | 0-2 | 2-1 | 1-2 | 0-3 | 0-1 | — | 5-4 | 3-1 | 3-3 | 2-2 | 2-3 | 1-0 | 1-0 | 2-2 | 0-1 | 1-0 | 0-1 |
| Lewes | 2-0 | 2-2 | 4-0 | 3-1 | 3-2 | 2-0 | 1-2 | 4-0 | 4-1 | 2-0 | 2-2 | 6-1 | 2-2 | — | 3-0 | 2-1 | 3-0 | 3-2 | 1-1 | 1-2 | 3-0 | 2-1 | 1-2 | 2-2 |
| Marlow | 0-2 | 0-1 | 2-1 | 1-0 | 4-3 | 2-0 | 0-0 | 0-0 | 1-1 | 4-1 | 1-1 | 2-0 | 3-4 | 1-2 | — | 2-0 | 0-1 | 0-0 | 3-1 | 1-0 | 1-2 | 1-0 | 0-0 | 0-5 |
| Metropolitan Police | 0-1 | 0-2 | 1-2 | 1-3 | 2-0 | 1-1 | 1-1 | 0-0 | 2-0 | 2-2 | 1-3 | 1-1 | 1-2 | 1-4 | 1-1 | — | 1-0 | 1-3 | 1-3 | 2-2 | 1-2 | 6-2 | 2-2 | 0-2 |
| Molesey | 0-2 | 1-0 | 4-3 | 1-2 | 2-3 | 1-1 | 0-2 | 0-0 | 2-0 | 2-0 | 0-1 | 1-1 | 0-2 | 2-2 | 3-0 | 0-2 | — | 0-3 | 0-2 | 0-3 | 1-1 | 0-2 | 0-1 | 0-2 |
| Slough Town | 1-1 | 5-1 | 4-1 | 4-2 | 2-1 | 3-1 | 1-0 | 1-2 | 3-1 | 7-1 | 1-1 | 3-2 | 3-1 | 1-0 | 1-2 | 3-0 | 3-1 | — | 2-2 | 2-0 | 1-1 | 3-1 | 1-3 | 1-1 |
| Staines Town | 5-1 | 0-0 | 3-0 | 3-1 | 0-2 | 5-2 | 1-0 | 3-2 | 1-0 | 2-0 | 1-0 | 0-0 | 3-2 | 3-1 | 3-0 | 4-2 | 2-1 | 1-3 | — | 1-2 | 0-0 | 2-1 | 1-1 | 3-3 |
| Tooting & Mitcham U | 2-3 | 2-0 | 3-2 | 4-3 | 3-0 | 0-0 | 2-1 | 1-2 | 4-1 | 3-3 | 0-2 | 2-2 | 4-0 | 0-4 | 0-1 | 2-1 | 1-3 | 0-2 | 2-0 | — | 2-1 | 2-1 | 1-1 | 1-2 |
| Walton & Hersham | 0-0 | 0-1 | 2-0 | 3-3 | 3-2 | 2-1 | 2-1 | 0-1 | 3-1 | 8-0 | 1-3 | 1-1 | 1-1 | 1-0 | 3-0 | 2-0 | 2-1 | 3-1 | 2-4 | 1-1 | — | 3-0 | 0-1 | 0-2 |
| Whyteleafe | 1-2 | 1-3 | 0-2 | 1-1 | 2-1 | 2-1 | 1-4 | 0-3 | 3-2 | 5-2 | 1-4 | 2-3 | 1-2 | 0-0 | 2-0 | 0-1 | 3-2 | 2-0 | 1-2 | 3-2 | 2-0 | — | 1-3 | 1-3 |
| Windsor & Eton | 5-1 | 0-1 | 2-0 | 1-0 | 1-0 | 2-0 | 1-1 | 0-0 | 4-2 | 1-1 | 0-1 | 3-1 | 4-2 | 1-2 | 0-0 | 2-0 | 2-0 | 1-4 | 2-0 | 3-1 | 5-3 | 2-0 | — | 1-1 |
| Worthing | 2-1 | 4-0 | 2-1 | 2-1 | 2-0 | 4-0 | 1-0 | 1-2 | 2-1 | 1-1 | 1-3 | 1-1 | 2-0 | 0-3 | 4-0 | 4-1 | 2-1 | 2-0 | 2-0 | 3-2 | 2-2 | 0-1 | 2-2 | — |

## RYMAN LEAGUE – DIVISION TWO RESULTS 2003–04

| | Abingdon Town | Camberley Town | Chalfont St Peter | Chertsey Town | Clapton | Dorking | Edgware Town | Flackwell Heath | Hertford Town | Kingsbury Town | Leighton Town | Ware | Wembley | Witham Town | Wokingham Town |
|---|---|---|---|---|---|---|---|---|---|---|---|---|---|---|---|
| Abingdon Town | — | 3-2 | 3-0 | 0-1 | 7-1 | 1-2 | 2-4 | 1-2 | 2-3 | 5-5 | 2-7 | 1-2 | 5-3 | 4-1 | 0-0 |
| Camberley Town | 2-1 | — | 3-2 | 0-0 | 2-3 | 1-3 | 0-1 | 2-1 | 0-2 | 2-1 | 0-1 | 1-1 | 0-0 | 1-2 | 2-0 |
| Chalfont St Peter | 1-1 | 2-4 | — | 1-1 | 4-3 | 0-4 | 2-3 | 2-3 | 0-1 | 0-3 | 0-1 | 1-1 | 2-2 | 0-3 | 7-2 |
| Chertsey Town | 4-1 | 2-1 | 0-1 | — | 0-4 | 0-1 | 2-1 | 1-0 | 1-1 | 1-0 | 2-1 | 1-1 | 3-0 | 2-3 | 1-0 |
| Clapton | 1-1 | 1-2 | 3-0 | 0-6 | — | 1-1 | 0-2 | 2-4 | 1-6 | 0-2 | 0-4 | 1-7 | 0-1 | 0-1 | 1-2 |
| Dorking | 2-1 | 3-0 | 2-1 | 4-1 | 3-2 | — | 3-1 | 1-0 | 5-3 | 3-0 | 1-2 | 1-0 | 3-0 | 1-0 | 4-0 |
| Edgware Town | 6-3 | 0-1 | 1-2 | 2-6 | 2-1 | 2-2 | — | 0-1 | 0-4 | 1-1 | 0-3 | 0-0 | 0-1 | 3-1 | 1-2 |
| Flackwell Heath | 1-0 | 3-1 | 1-0 | 1-3 | 3-3 | 4-1 | 1-0 | — | 1-3 | 3-1 | 3-1 | 3-2 | 4-0 | 1-3 | 3-1 |
| Hertford Town | 0-3 | 0-1 | 1-2 | 1-0 | 0-2 | 1-1 | 3-0 | 2-1 | — | 4-1 | 0-1 | 1-1 | 2-0 | 2-0 | 2-1 |
| Kingsbury Town | 2-0 | 3-0 | 0-1 | 0-3 | 3-0 | 4-1 | 0-1 | 0-0 | 2-4 | — | 0-2 | 2-1 | 0-0 | 2-0 | 1-1 |
| Leighton Town | 3-2 | 8-0 | 3-0 | 3-1 | 9-0 | 2-1 | 2-0 | 1-0 | 1-1 | 1-2 | — | 3-2 | 3-2 | 2-0 | 9-0 |
| Ware | 0-1 | 2-4 | 1-2 | 0-1 | 1-2 | 1-1 | 2-1 | 0-1 | 0-1 | 5-1 | 1-0 | — | 3-1 | 2-3 | 4-1 |
| Wembley | 2-0 | 0-0 | 2-0 | 1-4 | 4-0 | 0-1 | 1-0 | 0-2 | 0-1 | 1-0 | 0-5 | 0-2 | — | 1-1 | 1-4 |
| Witham Town | 3-1 | 5-1 | 4-2 | 1-1 | 6-1 | 1-1 | 5-0 | 1-0 | 1-0 | 1-1 | 1-1 | 3-0 | 2-0 | — | 3-0 |
| Wokingham Town | 0-2 | 4-0 | 1-3 | 2-4 | 4-0 | 0-0 | 1-4 | 0-3 | 1-3 | 1-0 | 0-3 | 2-0 | 2-2 | 2-1 | — |

| | Abingdon Town | Camberley Town | Chalfont St Peter | Chertsey Town | Clapton | Dorking | Edgware Town | Flackwell Heath | Hertford Town | Kingsbury Town | Leighton Town | Ware | Wembley | Witham Town | Wokingham Town |
|---|---|---|---|---|---|---|---|---|---|---|---|---|---|---|---|
| Abingdon Town | — | 1-2 | - | 0-2 | - | 2-2 | - | 3-1 | - | 2-0 | - | 2-1 | - | 1-1 | - |
| Camberley Town | - | — | 2-0 | - | 4-0 | - | 0-1 | - | 0-2 | - | 1-0 | - | 0-1 | - | 1-3 |
| Chalfont St Peter | 0-3 | - | — | 6-1 | - | 1-3 | - | 0-2 | - | 2-2 | - | 2-1 | - | 0-2 | - |
| Chertsey Town | - | 2-0 | - | — | 1-1 | - | 2-2 | - | 1-0 | - | 2-2 | - | 1-1 | - | 1-2 |
| Clapton | 0-5 | - | 3-0 | - | — | 1-7 | - | 0-3 | - | 3-1 | - | 2-2 | - | 1-3 | - |
| Dorking | - | 1-0 | - | 3-2 | - | — | 6-1 | - | 0-3 | - | 0-2 | - | 1-0 | - | 1-0 |
| Edgware Town | 3-4 | - | 1-3 | - | 10-0 | - | — | 1-3 | - | 0-2 | - | 3-2 | - | 1-1 | - |
| Flackwell Heath | - | 0-4 | - | 0-1 | - | 0-1 | - | — | 1-0 | - | 2-2 | - | 3-1 | - | 1-1 |
| Hertford Town | 3-0 | - | 1-1 | - | 2-0 | - | 4-0 | - | — | 1-1 | - | 0-0 | - | 3-1 | - |
| Kingsbury Town | - | 2-2 | - | 1-4 | - | 2-2 | - | 2-1 | - | — | 3-2 | - | 3-0 | - | 3-1 |
| Leighton Town | 1-0 | - | 8-0 | - | 1-2 | - | 4-1 | - | 1-1 | - | — | 1-1 | - | 2-0 | - |
| Ware | - | 2-2 | - | 3-1 | - | 1-3 | - | 2-1 | - | 1-0 | - | — | 4-2 | - | 4-1 |
| Wembley | 1-0 | - | 3-2 | - | 1-0 | - | 1-1 | - | 0-0 | - | 1-2 | - | — | 5-0 | - |
| Witham Town | - | 2-0 | - | 1-2 | - | 3-1 | - | 3-3 | - | 1-1 | - | 0-1 | - | — | 1-1 |
| Wokingham Town | 4-7 | - | 0-2 | - | 2-1 | - | 4-1 | - | 0-2 | - | 1-1 | - | 1-4 | - | — |

# THE BRYCO CUP 2003–04

## FIRST ROUND
Arlesey Town 3, Abingdon Town 0
Chalfont St Peter 5, Ware 1
Clapton *v* Bracknell Town
*(Bracknell Town w.o. – Clapton withdrew).*
Dorking 0, Worthing 1
Dunstable Town 7, Wivenhoe Town 1
East Thurrock United 2, Croydon 1
Epsom & Ewell 0, Waltham Forest 1
Flackwell Heath 1, Egham Town 5
Great Wakering Rovers 2, Barton Rovers 1
Harlow Town 2, Hertford Town 0
Kingsbury Town 0, Wealdstone 8
Leatherhead 1, Croydon Athletic 4
Leighton Town 0, Ashford Town (Mx) 2
Marlow 2, Barking & East Ham United 2
*(Marlow won 5-4 on penalties).*
Metropolitan Police 2, Corinthian Casuals 1
Molesey 3, Windsor & Eton 1
Oxford City 1, Cheshunt 3
Staines Town 4, Witham Town 4
*(Witham Town won 5-4 on penalties).*
Tooting & Mitcham United 1, Leyton 2
Wembley 0, Camberley Town 1
Wingate & Finchley 2, Chertsey Town 0
Wokingham Town 2, Tilbury 4
Yeading 5, Edgware Town 1

## SECOND ROUND
Arlesey Town 0, Hornchurch 2
Basingstoke Town 2, Aylesbury United 0
Bedford Town 1, Bognor Regis Town 0
Berkhamsted Town 0, Ashford Town (Mx) 2
Billericay Town 1, East Thurrock United 2
Bracknell Town 5, Chalfont St Peter 0
Braintree Town 1, Thurrock 2
Camberley Town 0, Northwood 1
Canvey Island 0, Hendon 3
Carshalton Athletic 0, Harlow Town 1
Chesham United 1, Lewes 0
Dulwich Hamlet 3, Hampton & Richmond Borough 3
*(Hampton & Richmond Borough won 4-3 on penalties).*
Egham Town 4, Tilbury 2
Ford United 2, Bishop's Stortford 1
Great Wakering Rovers 2, Banstead Athletic 1
Harrow Borough 2, Bromley 0
Heybridge Swifts 2, St Albans City 1
Horsham 2, Witham Town 1
Kingstonian 2, Croydon Athletic 0
Leyton 4, Enfield 1
Maidenhead United 3, Hayes 2
Marlow 3, Boreham Wood 2
Molesey 0, Walton & Hersham 0
*(Molesey won 4-3 on penalties).*
Slough Town 1, Cheshunt 4
Sutton United 2, Metropolitan Police 0
Thame United 1, Hitchin Town 2
Uxbridge 1, Dunstable Town 2
Waltham Forest 0, Aveley 2
Whyteleafe 0, Grays Athletic 2
Wingate & Finchley 2, Wealdstone 0
Worthing 2, Kettering Town 0
Yeading 2, Hemel Hempstead Town 1

## THIRD ROUND
Aveley 0, Hornchurch 5
Basingstoke Town 0, Ashford Town (Mx) 0
*(Ashford Town (Mx) won 3-2 on penalties).*
Bracknell Town 4, Hendon 3
Chesham United 6, Molesey 1
East Thurrock United 1, Wingate & Finchley 2
Egham Town 0, Grays Athletic 1
Ford United 0, Northwood 1
Harlow Town 3, Great Wakering Rovers 1
Heybridge Swifts 3, Harrow Borough 2
Hitchin Town 1, Marlow 3
Horsham 0, Bedford Town 3
Leyton 1, Hampton & Richmond Borough 2
Sutton United 2, Dunstable Town 3
Thurrock 1, Kingstonian 0
Worthing 2, Maidenhead United 0
Yeading 4, Cheshunt 4
*(Cheshunt won 9-8 on penalties).*

## FOURTH ROUND
Bracknell Town 2, Worthing 1
Chesham United 2, Ashford Town (Mx) 0
Dunstable Town 1, Grays Athletic 0
Hampton & Richmond Borough 4, Wingate & Finchley 2
Heybridge Swifts 3, Cheshunt 4
Hornchurch 0, Harlow Town 0
*(Harlow Town won 4-2 on penalties).*
Marlow 2, Northwood 0
Thurrock 4, Bedford Town 1

## FIFTH ROUND
Bracknell Town 1, Hampton & Richmond Borough 2
Dunstable Town 4, Harlow Town 1
Marlow 1, Cheshunt 2
Thurrock 2, Chesham United 1

## SEMI-FINALS FIRST LEG
Cheshunt 0, Thurrock 2
Dunstable Town 2, Hampton & Richmond Borough 1

## SEMI-FINALS SECOND LEG
Hampton & Richmond Borough 1, Dunstable Town 3
Thurrock 1, Cheshunt 2

## FINAL
*Final due to be played on 3 May was postponed.*
*New date for final still to be arranged.*

# NON-LEAGUE PYRAMID

Considering the extreme complexities caused by the revolutionary restructuring of the non-league game and despite much heart-searching plus a little blood-letting, those involved in the operation deserve much credit for their diligence in arriving at the final solution.

With some clubs wanting to transfer from Ryman to Dr Martens influence and the obvious need for suitable pairing to achieve the switch, the alterations continued to the wire. One of the last changes came about as a result of Hendon deciding to decline a place in Conference South despite finishing fourth in the Ryman because of their impending move from Claremont Road to the Barnet Copthall Stadium. This meant an unexpected reprieve for Basingstoke Town who appeared to have been doomed by a comprehensive 4-1 defeat at the hands of Lewes, who were probably the least well served by the compact nature of the Ryman play-offs, conducted in less than a week.

Lewes began their marathon with a 1-0 win at Yeading. Two days later came the victory at Basingstoke. Three days on from that match they entertained Kingstonian in one of the two final games and again came through 1-0. Confusion over these last fixtures concerning the actual venues did not help keep nerves from fraying at the edges!

St Albans City involved in some high-scoring affairs accompanied Lewes after defeating Bedford Town 5-4. The successful Dr Martens pair proved to be Redditch United and Dorchester Town.

The top of the pyramid system will consist of three levels: Conference North and South; Northern and Southern Premier; Northern First, Southern, Eastern and Western plus Isthmian First. Each division will comprise 22 teams.

The rules which appear in the League tables for the Unibond, Dr Martens and Ryman Leagues on pages 976 to 991, was the original Basis for moving clubs into the new set-up. Because no clubs were relegated from the Conference, which is to be known as the Conference National from the start of the new season, there was a further alteration to the hoped for allocation. Obviously geographical location played its part in the final analysis. As far as the two North and South sections of the new Second Division Conference are concerned, the original idea was for two relegated clubs from the Conference itself to join with clubs finishing in the top 13 places in the three previously-mentioned Leagues, excluding those promoted to the Conference itself, plus five from the play-offs.

For the Premier Divisions of the Unibond, Dr Martens and Ryman Leagues, the next nine finishing in the Unibond, seven from the Dr Martens and nine from the Ryman would join with respectively the top 13 from the Unibond First Division, top seven from each of the two Dr Martens First Division sections and 12 from the regional First Divisions of the Ryman.

Completing the 66 clubs involved in the three new Premier Leagues would be winners of play-offs involving Dr Martens and Ryman First Division. The Unibond First, two regional Dr Martens Divisions and the remaining Ryman First Division totalling 88 clubs will be composed of the rest of the clubs featured in the tables.

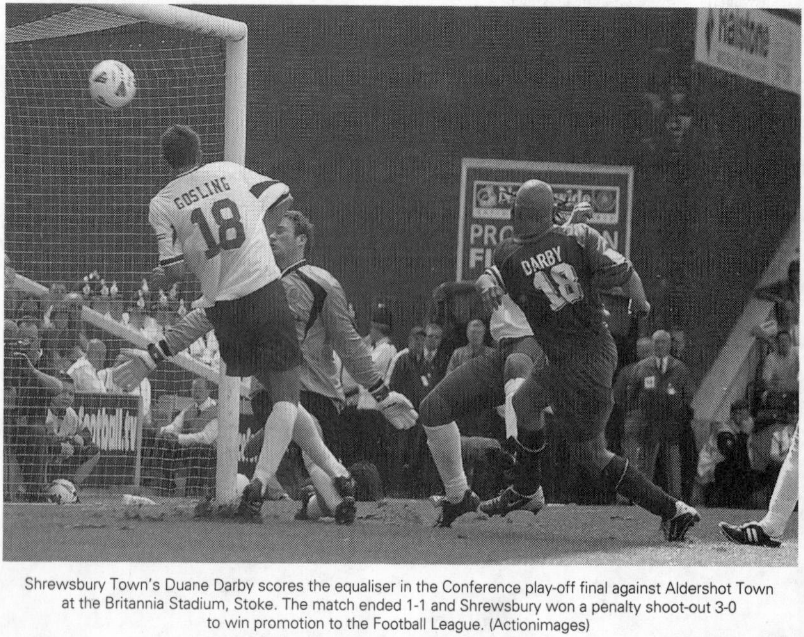


Shrewsbury Town's Duane Darby scores the equaliser in the Conference play-off final against Aldershot Town at the Britannia Stadium, Stoke. The match ended 1-1 and Shrewsbury won a penalty shoot-out 3-0 to win promotion to the Football League. (Actionimages)

# THE FA TROPHY 2003–04

## IN PARTNERSHIP WITH CARLSBERG

### PRELIMINARY ROUND

| | |
|---|---|
| Bamber Bridge v Witton Albion | 4-3 |
| Bishop Auckland v Farsley Celtic | 4-2 |
| North Ferriby United v Hyde United | 3-2 |
| Chorley v Gresley Rovers | 1-2 |
| Rossendale United v Colwyn Bay | 1-0 |
| Lincoln United v Workington | 0-0, 0-1 |
| Ilkeston Town v Bridlington Town | 1-2 |
| Gateshead v Kendal Town | 1-0 |
| Guiseley v Kidsgrove Athletic | 7-1 |
| Stocksbridge Park Steels v Leek Town | 3-1 |
| Prescot Cables v Belper Town | 2-1 |
| Matlock Town v Ossett Town | 2-0 |
| Cinderford Town v Yate Town | 1-1, 3-1 |
| Salisbury City v Clevedon Town | 0-1 |
| Team Bath v Banbury United | 2-0 |
| Gloucester City v Evesham United | 2-0 |
| Halesowen Town v Stourport Swifts | 4-3 |
| Mangotsfield United w.o. v Atherstone United removed. | |
| Bedworth United v Rugby United | 0-3 |
| Bromsgrove Rovers v Sutton Coldfield Town | 3-1 |
| Shepshed Dynamo v Solihull Borough | 0-0, 2-1 |
| Taunton Town v Corby Town | 3-1 |
| Arlesey Town v Fleet Town | 3-1 |
| Wivenhoe Town v Newport (IW) | 3-1 |
| Wingate & Finchley v Walton & Hersham | 2-1 |
| Hastings United v Yeading | 3-4 |
| Bracknell Town v Croydon | 4-2 |
| Eastleigh v Great Wakering Rovers | 3-0 |
| Hemel Hempstead Town v Metropolitan Police | 3-2 |
| Fisher Athletic v Horsham | 1-1, 3-1 |
| Dunstable Town v Lewes | 1-2 |
| Leyton v Molesey | 3-3, 4-3 |
| Dulwich Hamlet v Cheshunt | 2-0 |
| Chesham United v Worthing | 0-2 |
| Oxford City v Folkestone Invicta | 1-4 |
| Waltham Forest v Boreham Wood | 1-2 |
| Tooting & Mitcham United v Sittingbourne | 1-2 |
| Leatherhead v Wealdstone | 1-3 |
| Uxbridge v Harlow Town | 3-3, 1-0 |
| Whyteleafe v Egham Town | 2-1 |
| Corinthian Casuals v King's Lynn | 0-2 |
| Berkhamsted Town v Thame United | 0-3 |
| Staines Town v Barking & East Ham United | 3-0 |
| Enfield v Epsom & Ewell | 7-3 |
| Aveley v Burgess Hill Town | 1-2 |
| Burnham v Stamford | 1-2 |
| Bashley v Marlow | 2-2, 1-3 |
| Windsor & Eton v Chatham Town | 2-1 |

### FIRST ROUND

| | |
|---|---|
| Alfreton Town v Prescot Cables | 0-0, 4-1 |
| Ashton United v Lancaster City | 1-1, 2-3 |
| Workington v Spennymoor United | 0-3 |
| Frickley Athletic v Radcliffe Borough | 5-1 |
| Guiseley v Gainsborough Trinity | 2-0 |
| Gresley Rovers v Matlock Town | 1-0 |
| Wakefield & Emley v Blyth Spartans | 1-2 |
| Marine v Bamber Bridge | 1-0 |
| Runcorn FC Halton v Bishop Auckland | 7-0 |
| Stocksbridge Park Steels v North Ferriby United | 2-1 |
| Gateshead v Altrincham | 1-2 |
| Rossendale United v Bridlington Town | 2-0 |
| Redditch United v Cirencester Town | 6-2 |
| Rothwell Town v Gloucester City | 1-1, 1-4 |
| Mangotsfield United v Bath City | 1-2 |
| Rugby United v Hinckley United | 0-0, 2-3 |
| Swindon Supermarine v Grantham Town | 3-2 |
| Shepshed Dynamo v Hednesford Town | 0-1 |
| Clevedon Town v Taunton Town | 0-3 |
| Team Bath v Halesowen Town | 0-0, 2-3 |
| Weymouth v Merthyr Tydfil | 5-2 |
| Moor Green v Cinderford Town | 2-3 |
| Weston-Super-Mare v Bromsgrove Rovers | 1-1, 3-0 |
| Kingstonian v Stamford | 2-0 |
| Boreham Wood v Bracknell Town | 1-0 |
| Grays Athletic v Fisher Athletic | 2-2, 3-0 |
| Lewes v Northwood | 4-2 |
| Folkestone Invicta v Hemel Hempstead Town | 4-1 |
| Slough Town v Bishop's Stortford | 2-2, 1-2 |
| Whyteleafe v Ashford Town | 1-1, 2-1 |
| Staines Town v Croydon Athletic | 2-0 |
| Arlesey Town v Hampton & Richmond Borough | 1-1, 2-0 |
| Dulwich Hamlet v Yeading | 1-1, 0-5 |
| Dartford v Ashford Town (Mx) | 2-2, 1-2 |
| Burgess Hill Town v Sittingbourne | 2-0 |
| Wealdstone v East Thurrock United | 5-0 |
| Uxbridge v Bognor Regis Town | 0-1 |
| Barton Rovers v Ford United | 0-0, 0-1 |
| Worthing v Cambridge City | 0-0, 3-2 |
| King's Lynn v Thame United | 3-1 |
| Carshalton Athletic v Bromley | 3-1 |
| Billericay Town v Tilbury | 4-3 |
| Braintree Town v Harrow Borough | 0-3 |
| Wivenhoe Town v Hitchin Town | 0-0, 2-4 |
| Leyton v Dorchester Town | 1-5 |
| Aylesbury United v Banstead Athletic | 1-1, 1-0 |
| Heybridge Swifts v Histon | 0-1 |
| Windsor & Eton v Enfield | 2-2, 2-1 |
| *(abandoned 100 mins)* | 3-0 |
| Tonbridge Angels v Marlow | 1-3 |
| Eastbourne Borough v Welling United | 1-2 |
| Wingate & Finchley v Hornchurch | 0-2 |
| Erith & Belvedere v Eastleigh | 1-2 |

### SECOND ROUND

| | |
|---|---|
| Harrogate Town v Barrow | 2-2, 2-4 |
| Altrincham v Southport | 1-0 |
| Lancaster City v Hednesford Town | 1-1, 0-1 |
| Whitby Town v Bradford Park Avenue | 1-1, 0-1 |
| Rossendale United v Guiseley | 0-0, 1-1 |
| *(abandoned 35 minutes; fog)* | 0-2 |
| Gresley Rovers v Hinckley United | 3-2 |
| Marine v Worcester City | 2-0 |
| Stafford Rangers v Spennymoor United | 2-1 |
| Blyth Spartans v Stocksbridge Park Steels | 4-2 |
| Hucknall Town v Nuneaton Borough | 2-1 |
| Runcorn FC Halton v Frickley Athletic | 3-2 |
| Alfreton Town v Vauxhall Motors | 1-1, 4-2 |
| Worksop Town v Droylsden | 1-0 |
| Redditch United v Stalybridge Celtic | 0-3 |
| Marlow v Tiverton Town | 3-0 |
| Ford United v Chelmsford City | 4-1 |
| Wealdstone v Hitchin Town | 1-0 |
| Hornchurch v Newport County | 1-0 |
| Boreham Wood v Arlesey Town | 1-2 |
| Burgess Hill Town v Staines Town | 1-2 |
| Bath City v Gloucester City | 2-1 |
| Billericay Town v King's Lynn | 0-2 |
| Eastleigh v Histon | 1-4 |
| Whyteleafe v Worthing | 0-4 |
| St Albans City v Crawley Town | 0-0, 1-4 |
| Welling United v Dover Athletic | 0-1 |
| Weymouth v Ashford Town (Mx) | 3-3, 3-1 |
| Dorchester Town v Harrow Borough | 3-0 |
| Sutton United v Bedford Town | 2-0 |
| Hendon v Kettering Town | 1-1, 2-2 |
| *Kettering Town won 5-4 on penalties.* | |
| Swindon Supermarine v Maidenhead United | 3-3, 1-2 |
| Cinderford Town v Lewes | 3-3, 3-4 |
| Carshalton Athletic v Thurrock | 2-2, 0-1 |
| Kingstonian v Bishop's Stortford | 0-2 |
| Havant & Waterlooville v Folkestone Invicta | 2-2, 0-1 |
| Aylesbury United v Grays Athletic | 2-2, 1-0 |
| Weston-Super-Mare v Bognor Regis Town | 1-0 |
| Halesowen Town v Hayes | 1-3 |
| Chippenham Town v Basingstoke Town | 1-1, 0-1 |
| Windsor & Eton v Canvey Island | 1-3 |
| Taunton Town v Yeading | 3-3, 3-1 |

### THIRD ROUND

| | |
|---|---|
| Telford United v Alfreton Town | 2-0 |
| Shrewsbury Town v Morecambe | 2-0 |
| Altrincham v Runcorn FC Halton | 2-1 |
| Scarborough v Stafford Rangers | 1-2 |
| Hednesford Town v Gresley Rovers | 2-0 |
| Leigh RMI v Stalybridge Celtic | 1-1 |
| *Leigh RMI removed from competition; ineligible player. Stalybridge Celtic awarded the tie.* | |
| Blyth Spartans v Barrow | 1-0 |

| | |
|---|---|
| Chester City v Halifax Town | 1-2 |
| Burton Albion v Accrington Stanley | 4-2 |
| Marine v Northwich Victoria | 1-0 |
| Guiseley v Worksop Town | 0-2 |
| Hucknall Town v Bradford Park Avenue | 1-0 |
| Burscough v Tamworth | 0-1 |
| Bishop's Stortford v Aldershot Town | 2-4 |
| King's Lynn v Basingstoke Town | 3-1 |
| Gravesend & Northfleet v Weston-Super-Mare | 2-2, 0-1 |
| Dorchester Town v Margate | 2-2, 0-2 |
| Folkestone Invicta v Stevenage Borough | 1-3 |
| Hornchurch v Aylesbury United | 2-0 |
| Kettering Town v Woking | 0-0, 3-2 |
| Exeter City v Hereford United | 3-2 |
| Marlow v Ford United | 3-1 |
| Barnet v Dover Athletic | 3-2 |
| *Barnet removed from competition; ineligible player. Dover Athletic awarded the tie.* | |
| Forest Green Rovers v Sutton United | 4-0 |
| Histon v Maidenhead United | 1-3 |
| Lewes v Weymouth | 5-8 |
| Wealdstone v Thurrock | 3-2 |
| Canvey Island v Farnborough Town | 6-0 |
| Hayes v Arlesey Town | 2-2, 1-1 |
| *Arlesey Town won 4-3 on penalties.* | |
| Dagenham & Redbridge v Crawley Town | 0-0, 2-1 |
| Staines Town v Bath City | 1-0 |
| Worthing v Taunton Town | 3-0 |

**FOURTH ROUND**

| | |
|---|---|
| Shrewsbury Town v Hucknall Town | 2-1 |
| Margate v Worksop Town | 2-0 |
| Marlow v Tamworth | 0-4 |
| Forest Green Rovers v Dover Athletic | 3-3, 1-2 |
| Stalybridge Celtic v Marine | 1-1, 1-0 |
| Hornchurch v Stevenage Borough | 1-0 |
| Halifax Town v Staines Town | 1-1, 3-2 |
| Weymouth v Altrincham | 0-2 |
| Blyth Spartans v Aldershot Town | 1-3 |
| Maidenhead United v Wealdstone | 5-1 |
| Telford United v Weston-Super-Mare | 4-2 |
| Stafford Rangers v Canvey Island | 0-2 |
| Hednesford Town v Worthing | 1-1, 2-1 |
| Dagenham & Redbridge v Arlesey Town | 3-3, 2-4 |
| King's Lynn v Exeter City | 0-3 |
| Burton Albion v Kettering Town | 1-1, 2-1 |

**FIFTH ROUND**

| | |
|---|---|
| Altrincham v Shrewsbury Town | 0-1 |
| Halifax Town v Maidenhead United | 0-2 |
| Stalybridge Celtic v Canvey Island | 0-0, 0-4 |
| Exeter City v Arlesey Town | 3-0 |
| Hednesford Town v Dover Athletic | 1-0 |
| Aldershot Town v Tamworth | 1-1, 2-0 |
| Hornchurch v Burton Albion | 2-1 |
| Telford United v Margate | 3-0 |

**SIXTH ROUND**

| | |
|---|---|
| Aldershot Town v Exeter City | 2-1 |
| Hednesford Town v Hornchurch | 3-1 |
| Shrewsbury Town v Telford United | 1-1, 1-2 |
| Canvey Island v Maidenhead United | 4-0 |

**SEMI-FINALS** (two legs)

| | |
|---|---|
| Aldershot Town v Hednesford Town | 0-2, 1-1 |
| Telford United v Canvey Island | 0-0, 2-2 |
| *Canvey Island won 4-2 on penalties.* | |

**THE FA TROPHY FINAL**

Sunday, 23 May 2004
(at Villa Park)

**Hednesford Town (1) 3** *(Maguire 27, Hines 53, Brindley 86)*

**Canvey Island (0) 2** *(Boylan 46, Brindley 47 (og))* 6635

*Hednesford Town:* Young; Simkin, Hines, Brindley, Ryder (Barrow), Palmer, Maguire, King, Anthrobus, Danks (Piearce), Charie (Evans S).

*Canvey Island:* Potter; Kennedy, Midgley (Berquez), Chenery, Ward, Cowan, Gooden (Dobinson), Minton, Gregory (McDougald), Boylan, Duffy.

*Referee:* M. Dean (Wirral).

## THE FA TROPHY – PREVIOUS WINNERS

| *Year* | *Winners* | *Runners-up* | *Score* |
|---|---|---|---|
| 1970 | Macclesfield Town | Telford United | 2-0 |
| 1971 | Telford United | Hillingdon Borough | 3-2 |
| 1972 | Stafford Rangers | Barnet | 3-0 |
| 1973 | Scarborough | Wigan Athletic | 2-1 |
| 1974 | Morecambe | Dartford | 2-1 |
| 1975 | Matlock Town | Scarborough | 4-0 |
| 1976 | Scarborough | Stafford Rangers | 3-2 |
| 1977 | Scarborough | Dagenham | 2-1 |
| 1978 | Altrincham | Leatherhead | 3-1 |
| 1979 | Stafford Rangers | Kettering Town | 2-0 |
| 1980 | Dagenham | Mossley | 2-1 |
| 1981 | Bishop's Stortford | Sutton United | 1-0 |
| 1982 | Enfield | Altrincham | 1-0 |
| 1983 | Telford | Northwich Victoria | 2-0 |
| 1984 | Northwich Victoria | Bangor City | 1-1 |
| | *Replay* | | 2-1 |
| 1985 | Wealdstone | Boston United | 2-1 |
| 1986 | Altrincham | Runcorn | 1-0 |
| 1987 | Kidderminster Harriers | Burton Albion | 0-0 |
| | *Replay* | | 2-1 |
| 1988 | Enfield | Telford United | 0-0 |
| | *Replay* | | 3-2 |
| 1989 | Telford United | Macclesfield Town | 1-0 |
| 1990 | Barrow | Leek Town | 3-0 |
| 1991 | Wycombe Wanderers | Kidderminster Harriers | 2-1 |
| 1992 | Colchester United | Witton Albion | 3-1 |
| 1993 | Wycombe Wanderers | Runcorn | 4-1 |
| 1994 | Woking | Runcorn | 2-1 |
| 1995 | Woking | Kidderminster Harriers | 2-1 |
| 1996 | Macclesfield Town | Northwich Victoria | 3-1 |
| 1997 | Woking | Dagenham & Redbridge | 1-0 |
| 1998 | Cheltenham Town | Southport | 1-0 |
| 1999 | Kingstonian | Forest Green Rovers | 1-0 |
| 2000 | Kingstonian | Kettering Town | 3-2 |
| 2001 | Canvey Island | Forest Green Rovers | 1-0 |
| 2002 | Yeovil Town | Stevenage Borough | 2-0 |
| 2003 | Burscough | Tamworth | 2-1 |

## THE FA VASE – PREVIOUS WINNERS

| *Year* | *Winners* | *Runners-up* | *Score* |
|---|---|---|---|
| 1975 | Hoddesdon Town | Epsom & Ewell | 2-1 |
| 1976 | Billericay Town | Stamford | 1-0 |
| 1977 | Billericay Town | Sheffield | 1-1 |
| | *Replay* | | 2-1 |
| 1978 | Blue Star | Barton Rovers | 2-1 |
| 1979 | Billericay Town | Almondsbury Greenway | 4-1 |
| 1980 | Stamford | Guisborough Town | 2-0 |
| 1981 | Wickham | Willenhall Town | 3-2 |
| 1982 | Forest Green Rovers | Rainworth MW | 3-0 |
| 1983 | VS Rugby | Halesowen Town | 1-0 |
| 1984 | Stansted | Stamford | 3-2 |
| 1985 | Halesowen Town | Fleetwood Town | 3-1 |
| 1986 | Halesowen Town | Southall | 3-0 |
| 1987 | St Helens Town | Warrington Town | 3-2 |
| 1988 | Colne Dynamoes | Emley | 1-0 |
| 1989 | Tamworth | Sudbury Town | 1-1 |
| | *Replay* | | 3-0 |
| 1990 | Yeading | Bridlington Town | 0-0 |
| | *Replay* | | 1-0 |
| 1991 | Guiseley | Gresley Rovers | 4-4 |
| | *Replay* | | 3-1 |
| 1992 | Wimborne Town | Guiseley | 5-3 |
| 1993 | Bridlington Town | Tiverton Town | 1-0 |
| 1994 | Diss Town | Taunton Town | 2-1 |
| 1995 | Arlesey Town | Oxford City | 2-1 |
| 1996 | Brigg Town | Clitheroe | 3-0 |
| 1997 | Whitby Town | North Ferriby United | 3-0 |
| 1998 | Tiverton Town | Tow Law Town | 1-0 |
| 1999 | Tiverton Town | Bedlington Terriers | 1-0 |
| 2000 | Deal Town | Chippenham Town | 1-0 |
| 2001 | Taunton Town | Berkhamsted Town | 2-1 |
| 2002 | Whitley Bay | Tiptree United | 1-0 |
| 2003 | Brigg Town | AFC Sudbury | 2-1 |

# THE FA VASE 2003–04

**FIRST QUALIFYING ROUND**

Alsager Town v Rossington Main 5-0
Liversedge v Kennek Ryhope CA 3-1
Penrith v Flixton 3-2
Washington v Warrington Town 0-2
Squires Gate v Chadderton 5-2
Poulton Victoria v Ryton 4-1
Abbey Hey v Ramsbottom United 1-2
Evenwood Town v Ashington 2-4
Billingham Synthonia v Brodsworth MW 3-2
Hatfield Main removed v New Mills w.o.
Norton & Stockton Ancients v Tadcaster Albion 0-1
Retford United v Oldham Town 3-0
Chester-Le-Street Town v Marske United 2-1
Padiham v Armthorpe Welfare 2-1
Cammell Laird v Great Harwood Town 7-0
Skelmersdale United v Eccleshill United 3-3, 3-1
Guisborough Town v Maltby Main 2-1
Arnold Town v Coventry Sphinx 3-4
Friar Lane OB v Boldmere St Michaels 4-2
Rainworth MW v Dudley Town 2-0
Glapwell v Castle Vale KH 3-1
Oldbury United v Dudley Sports 8-0
Blaby & Whetstone Athletic v Deeping Rangers 3-0
Biddulph Victoria v Birstall United 1-0
Highgate United v Chasetown 0-3
Marconi v Pegasus Juniors 4-1
Causeway United v Barwell 0-2
Bolehall Swifts v Brierley & Hagley 0-2
Sandiacre Town v Teversal 4-0
Highfield Rangers v Shifnall Town 2-1
Ledbury Town v Blackstones 3-1
Willenhall Town v Buxton 1-2
Congleton Town v Leek CSOB 4-0
Heanor Town v Boston Town 3-1
Shirebrook Town v Sutton Town 2-1
Bedford United & Valerio v Raunds Town 2-1
Brackley Town v Great Yarmouth Town 0-1
Ford Sports Daventry v Ipswich Wanderers 0-0, 2-0
Bicester Town v Stanway Rovers 2-1
Eton Manor v Witham Town 0-1
Stansted v Harpenden Town 3-2
Brentwood w.o. v Saffron Walden Town removed.
Cornard United v Thetford Town 5-0
Stewarts & Lloyds v Southend Manor 3-3, 2-2
*Stewarts & Lloyds won 5-4 on penalties.*
Whitton United v Halstead Town 3-1
Clacton Town v Sawbridgeworth Town 1-2
Colney Heath v Wisbech Town 1-3
St Ives Town v Greenacres (Hemel Hempstead) 1-6
AFC Kempston Rovers v Ruislip Manor 3-0
Haverhill Rovers v Woodford United 3-2
Hoddesdon Town w.o. v Tring Town removed.
Edgware Town v Newport Pagnell Town 2-1
Broxbourne Borough V&E v Leverstock Green 1-3
Kingsbury Town v Eynesbury Rovers 3-1
Mildenhall Town v Tiptree United 3-1
Yaxley v Norwich United 4-0
Stowmarket Town v Coggenhoe Town 3-1
Steyning Town v Selsey 2-1
Lancing v Reading Town 0-4
Wantage Town v Alton Town 0-0, 2-1
Southwick v Littlehampton Town 2-6
Wick v Raynes Park Vale 0-1
Eastbourne Town v Dorking 6-3
Westfield v AFC Wimbledon 2-7
Tunbridge Wells v Chessington United 2-4
Blackfield & Langley v Ramsgate 1-3
Deal Town v Milton United 1-0
Thatcham Town v Ringmer 3-0
Didcot Town v Slade Green 2-0
Saltdean United v East Preston 2-1
AFC Newbury v East Grinstead Town 2-0
Hungerford Town v Bedfont 1-2
Moneyfields v Hassocks 4-2
Street v Odd Down 1-0
Bristol Manor Farm v Liskeard Athletic 2-3
Poole Town v Willand Rovers 0-4
Barnstaple Town v Ilfracombe Town 2-1
Clevedon United v Portland United 2-6
Bridgwater Town v Bournemouth 1-2
Bitton v Chipping Norton Town 4-2
Tuffley Rovers v Porthleven 1-2
Wimborne Town v Chard Town 4-1
Saltash United v Hamworthy United 1-4
Wellington Town v Shepton Mallet 4-2

**SECOND QUALIFYING ROUND**

Easington Colliery v Worsborough Bridge MW 0-1
Tow Law Town v Ossett Albion 0-1
Pontefract Collieries v Blackpool Mechanics 0-2
Poulton Victoria v Prudhoe Town 3-1
South Shields v Washington Nissan 0-2
Horden CW v West Allotment Celtic 1-2
Cammell Laird v Warrington Town 0-2
Newcastle Benfield Saints v Thornaby 1-1
*(abandoned; injury to match official)* 4-1
Alnwick Town v Peterlee Newtown 3-4
Woodleigh Sports v Parkgate 7-0
Billingham Synthonia v Penrith 4-1
Retford United v Yorkshire Amateur 3-1
Squires Gate v Whickham 2-1
Nelson v Maine Road 3-1
Guisborough Town v West Auckland Town 3-0
Tadcaster Albion v Esh Winning 0-3
Atherton LR v Ashington 0-1
Merton v Bacup Borough 0-1
Consett v Sheffield 0-2
Cheadle Town v New Mills 3-2
Colne v Chester-Le-Street Town 3-2
Louth United removed v Willington w.o.
Silsden v Thackley 2-0
Selby Town v Winsford United 5-2
Liversedge v Darwen 4-2
St Helen's Town v Hebburn Town 3-2
Holker Old Boys v Garforth Town 4-4, 0-4
Winterton Rangers v Skelmersdale United 2-0
Crook Town v Padiham 2-1
Curzon Ashton v Glasshoughton Welfare 2-1
Newcastle Blue Star v Hallam 1-3
Atherton Collieries v Dunston FB 1-2
Seaham Red Star v Alsager Town 3-9
Hall Road Rangers v North Shields 4-1
Harrogate Railway v Jarrow Roofing Boldon CA 1-4
Ramsbottom United v Shotton Comrades 5-1
Shildon v Salford City 4-2
Brierley & Hagley v Nuneaton Griff 0-2
Lincoln Moorlands v Blidworth Welfare 6-1
Nantwich Town v Kimberley Town 2-1
Long Eaton United v Loughborough Dynamo 2-0
Chasetown v Bourne Town 2-0
Nettleham v Ledbury Town 4-4
*(Nettleham withdrew Ledbury Town w.o.)*
Leamington v Highfield Rangers 4-1
Carlton Town v Blabey & Whetstone Athletic 2-4
Ellistown w.o. v Gornall Athletic removed.
Fernhill County Sports removed v Norton United w.o.
Cradley Town v Biddulph Victoria 3-3, 0-3
Rugby Town v Anstey Nomads 4-2
Studley v Wednesfield 6-1
Heanor Town v Alvechurch 1-0
Ludlow Town v Rolls Royce Leisure 2-0
Barrow Town v Malvern Town 3-0
Sandiacre Town v West Midlands Police 3-0
Wellington v Shirebrook Town 1-0
Quorn v Pelsall Villa
*(tie awarded to Quorn; Pelsall Villa failed to fulfil fixture)*
Marconi v Stafford Town 6-0
Tipton Town v Barwell 3-1
Coventry Sphinx v Downes Sports 2-0
Blackwell MW v Glapwell 1-4
Daventry Town v Friar Lane OB 1-0
Gedling Town v Shawbury United 3-1
Kirby Muxloe v Congleton Town 0-3
Tivedale v St Andrews 2-1
Rainworth MW v Glossop North End 2-1
Stapenhill v Oldbury United 3-0
Meir KA v Stone Dominoes 0-1
Lye Town v Mickleover Sports 0-2
Grosvenor Park v Graham St Prims 2-0
Buxton v Borrowash Victoria 4-0
Coalville Town v Westfields 3-2
Staveley MW v Dunkirk 2-3
Heath Hayes v Ibstock Welfare 1-4
Sawbridgeworth Town v March Town United 5-1
Haringey Borough v Barkingside 0-1
London Colney v Hadleigh United 1-0
Harwich & Parkeston v Henley Town 8-0
Cornard United v Biggleswade United 1-3
Long Buckby v AFC Kempston Rovers 2-2, 2-3
Harefield United v Greenacres (Hemel Hempstead) 3-2
Bowers United v Stansted 0-2
Chalfont St Peter v Desborough Town 1-2
Clapton v Long Melford 1-1, 1-0

Brook House v Brentwood 3-1
North Greenford United v Mildenhall Town 1-4
Somersham Town v St Neots Town 0-4
Edgware Town v Kingsbury Town 3-1
Holmer Green v Newmarket Town 1-7
Yaxley v Langford 3-0
Wisbech Town w.o. v Worboys Town withdrew.
Stotfold v Leverstock Green 4-1
Needham Market w.o. v Milton Keynes City removed.
Stewarts & Lloyds v Potton United 3-1
Southall Town v Whitton United 3-0
Bedford United & Valerio v Burnham Ramblers 2-2, 3-3
*Burnham Ramblers won 3-0 on penalties.*
Stowmarket Town v Bicester Town 3-0
Bugbrooke St Michaels v Great Yarmouth Town 0-1
Cockfosters v Northampton Spencer 0-0, 0-4
Hanwell Town v Hoddesdon Town 3-0
St Margaretsbury v Oxhey Jets 4-1
Ford Sports Daventry v Dereham Town 0-1
Romford v Witham Town 0-2
Leighton Town v Royston Town 1-0
Hullbridge Sports v Leiston 0-2
Fakenham Town v Ely City 1-0
Haverhill Rovers v Biggleswade Town 0-1
Brimsdown Rovers v Woodbridge Town 3-4
Rothwell Corinthians v Bury Town 1-4
Felixstowe & Walton United v Godmanchester Rovers 1-0
Camberley Town v Herne Bay 1-2
Farnham Town v Redhill 1-2
Three Bridges v Hythe Town 2-0
Saltdean United v Erith Town 1-1, 0-2
Sandhurst Town v Bedfont 0-3
Didcot Town v Petersfield Town 2-0
Lordswood v Beckenham Town 1-2
*Tie awarded to Lordswood; Beckenham Town included an ineligible player*
Eastbourne United v Wantage Town 1-2
Hillingdon Borough v Brockenhurst 3-2
Sidlesham v Andover 2-5
Littlehampton Town v Oakwood 3-1
Deal Town v Peacehaven & Telscombe 2-1
Chipstead v BAT Sports 1-2
Walton Casuals v Steyning Town 0-1
Cove v Fareham Town 0-2
Reading Town v Moneyfields 1-3
Raynes Park Vale v VCD Athletic 0-2
Godalming & Guildford v Whitstable Town 1-3
Sidley United v Ramsgate 2-2, 1-3
Chichester City United v Abingdon United 1-2
Chessington United v Whitchurch United 0-2
Chessington & Hook United v Cowes Sports 3-1
Cobham v Abingdon Town 1-2
Broadbridge Heath v Hartley Wintney 0-3
Greenwich Borough v Ash United 1-2
Mile Oak v Haywards Heath Town 1-0
Eastbourne Town v Wokingham Town 3-3, 3-5
AFC Newbury v Mertsham 6-0
Frimley Green v Thatcham Town 1-4
Hailsham Town v Rye & Iden United 0-1
*Tie awarded to Hailsham Town; Rye & Iden United withdrew.*
Pagham v AFC Wimbledon 0-1
Wimborne Town v Falmouth Town 5-1
Budleigh Salterton v Launceston 4-1
Hallen v Pershore Town 6-0
Liskeard Athletic v Keynsham Town 0-0, 2-5
Bridport v Fairford Town 1-1, 0-1
Harrow Hill v Torrington 2-5
Street v Almondsbury Town 2-3
Newquay v Barnstaple Town 0-2
Porthleven v Backwell United 2-4
Frome Town v Dawlish Town 4-1
Willand Rovers v Shortwood United 2-1
Cullompton Rangers v Bishop's Cleeve 0-1
Bemerton Heath Harlequins v Wootton Bassett Town 4-1
Minehead Town v Bishop Sutton 3-1
Downton v Calne Town 3-0
Westbury United v Melksham Town 2-1
Pewsey Vale v Wellington Town 3-2
Corsham Town v Highworth Town 1-3
Portland United v Welton Rovers 2-4
Newton Abbot v Amesbury Town 5-2
Bromyard Town v Elmore 2-2
*Bromyard Town won 5-3 on penalties.*
Hamworthy United v Bodmin Town 2-0
Bitton v Exmouth Town 5-1
Bournemouth v Paulton Rovers 0-1

**FIRST ROUND**

Goole v Liversedge 0-3
Curzon Ashton v Poulton Victoria 0-2
Crook Town v Ramsbottom United 2-3
St Helen's Town v Willington 2-1
Hall Road Rangers v Ashington 2-1
Woodleigh Sports v Hallam 2-3
Jarrow Roofing Boldon CA v Bedlington Terriers 2-1
Colne v Washington Nissan 3-1
Dunston FB v Brandon United 2-1
Shildon v Garforth Town 3-0
Warrington Town v Esh Winning 1-0
Selby Town v Newcastle Benfield Saints 4-1
Blackpool Mechanics v Sheffield 0-5
West Allotment Celtic v Ossett Albion 5-0
Guisborough Town v Peterlee Newtown 4-2
Trafford v Cheadle Town 2-1
Alsager Town v Silsden 1-0
Squires Gate v Nelson 2-1
Worsborough Bridge MW v Bacup Borough 0-1
Winterton Rangers v Billingham Synthonia 1-3
Stone Dominoes v Ellistown 2-1
Rainworth MW v Retford United 1-2
Nantwich Town v Tipton Town 1-0
Rocester v Rugby Town 3-1
Racing Club Warwick v Chasetown 1-0
Mickleover Sports v Ibstock Welfare 3-1
Quorn v Spalding United 3-3, 0-1
Buxton v Rushall Olympic 5-2
Biddulph Victoria v Gedling Town 1-3
Long Eaton United v Daventry Town 2-2, 1-2
Heanor Town v Stourbridge 1-2
Bromyard Town v Studley 1-3
Grosvenor Park v Holbeach United 2-0
Wellington v Dunkirk 2-0
Coventry Sphinx v Tivedale 5-3
Sandiacre Town v Lincoln Moorlands 2-3
Norton United v Nuneaton Griff 2-3
Leamington v Barrow Town 2-2, 1-0
Blaby & Whetstone Athletic v Ledbury Town 3-1
Stratford Town v Coalville Town 1-3
Marconi v Congleton Town 0-0, 0-2
Eastwood Town v Ludlow Town 2-0
Stapenhill v Glapwell 2-1
Soham Town Rangers v Leiston 2-0
Beaconsfield SYCOB v Wisbech Town 2-1
Biggleswade United v Dereham Town 2-3
Stewarts & Lloyds v Clapton 1-2
Southall Town v Ilford 5-2
Stowmarket Town v Mildenhall Town 1-2
Burnham Ramblers v Wembley 1-0
Flackwell Heath v Northampton Spencer 2-0
Brook House v Newmarket Town 0-1
St Neots Town v Needham Market 3-1
Hanwell Town v Harwich & Parkeston 3-7
Bury Town v Witham Town 1-0
Yaxley v Hertford Town 1-2
Enfield Town v Felixstowe & Walton United 2-0
St Margaretsbury v Great Yarmouth Town 0-2
Stansted v Desborough Town 0-2
Concord Rangers v Sawbridgeworth Town 1-0
Woodbridge Town v Harefield United 1-2
Barkingside v Fakenham Town 0-1
*FA ordered replay; Barkingside won 3-1*
Potters Bar Town v Stotfold 3-2
AFC Kempston Rovers v Leighton Town 2-3
Biggleswade Town v Edgware Town 0-2
London Colney v AFC Wallingford 1-3
Wokingham Town v Whitstable Town 1-0
BAT Sports v Ash United 3-0
Abingdon Town v Fareham Town 0-1
Maidstone United v Horsham YMCA 3-1
Deal Town v Cray Wanderers 1-2
Moneyfields v Steyning Town 1-0
Herne Bay v AFC Wimbledon 2-3
AFC Totton v Bedfont 2-2, 1-3
Carterton Town v Chessington & Hook United 1-2
Chertsey Town v Hartley Wintney 0-0, 4-1
AFC Newbury v Littlehampton Town 1-2
Whitchurch United v Three Bridges 1-1, 0-2
Andover v Hillingdon Borough 3-2
Abingdon United v Erith Town 1-3
Hailsham Town v Gosport Borough 0-4
Thamesmead Town v VCD Athletic 4-3
Wantage Town v Didcot Town 0-0, 0-4
Whitehawk v Mile Oak 6-1
Redhill v North Leigh 2-3
Thatcham Town v St Leonards 2-0
Lordswood v Ramsgate 0-1

| | |
|---|---|
| Minehead Town v Willand Rovers | 1-2 |
| Hallen v Hamworthy United | 1-2 |
| Bitton v Budleigh Salterton | 1-0 |
| Torrington v Pewsey Vale | 3-0 |
| Welton Rovers v Brislington | 2-1 |
| Wimborne Town v Bishop's Cleeve | 2-3 |
| Bemerton Heath Harlequins v Fairford Town | 2-3 |
| Westbury United v Almondsbury Town | 4-3 |
| Newton Abbot v Highworth Town | 1-3 |
| Keynsham Town v Downton | 6-0 |
| Barnstaple Town v Backwell United | 0-3 |
| Frome Town v Paulton Rovers | 4-1 |

**SECOND ROUND**

| | |
|---|---|
| Fleetwood Town v Ramsbottom United | 2-2, 1-3 |
| West Allotment Celtic v St Helen's Town | 1-0 |
| Northallerton Town v Warrington Town | 1-1, 0-2 |
| Jarrow Roofing Boldon CA v Hall Road Rangers | 2-1 |
| Morpeth Town v Poulton Victoria | 6-1 |
| Bacup Borough v Guisborough Town | 0-3 |
| Clitheroe v Whitley Bay | 0-2 |
| Shildon v Pickering Town | 2-0 |
| Dunston FB v Sheffield | 0-0, 0-0 |
| *Sheffield won 3-0 on penalties.* | |
| Billingham Town v Squires Gate | 3-3, 3-0 |
| Mossley v Trafford | 4-2 |
| Liversedge v Billingham Synthonia | 1-2 |
| Selby Town v Durham City | 0-2 |
| Hallam v Colne | 2-2, 0-1 |
| Alsager Town v Leamington | 1-2 |
| Desborough Town v Newcastle Town | 1-0 |
| Congleton Town v Rocester | 3-3, 2-1 |
| Blaby & Whetstone Athletic v Nuneaton Griff | 5-2 |
| Brigg Town v Buxton | 0-1 |
| Nantwich Town v Grosvenor Park | 5-1 |
| Stourbridge v Lincoln Moorlands | 4-4, 0-1 |
| Stone Dominoes v Coventry Sphinx | 4-0 |
| Eastwood Town v Spalding United | 6-1 |
| Retford United v Oadby Town | 0-1 |
| Studley v Mickleover Sports | 0-0, 2-0 |
| Stapenhill v Wellington | 1-2 |
| Daventry Town v Gedling Town | 1-3 |
| Racing Club Warwick v Coalville Town | 0-1 |
| Newmarket Town v Hertford Town | 2-4 |
| Ware v Thamesmead Town | 2-4 |
| St Neots Town v Beaconsfield SYCOB | 2-2, 1-1 |
| *St Neots Town won 5-4 on penalties.* | |
| Littlehampton Town v Great Yarmouth Town | 1-2 |
| North Leigh v Clapton | 11-0 |
| Three Bridges v Diss Town | 4-1 |
| Chertsey Town v Barkingside | 3-0 |
| Mildenhall Town v Bury Town | 1-3 |
| Maidstone United v AFC Wallingford | 3-0 |
| Whitehawk v Burnham Ramblers | 5-2 |
| Didcot Town v Ramsgate | 1-1, 1-2 |
| Edgware Town v Wroxham | 2-3 |
| Arundel v Concord Rangers | 1-3 |
| AFC Wimbledon v Wootton Blue Cross | 3-0 |
| Harwich & Parkeston v Erith Town | 2-0 |
| Wokingham Town v Soham Town Rangers | 0-4 |
| Dereham Town v Southall Town | 4-4, 0-2 |
| Withdean 2000 v Bedfont | 5-1 |
| Harefield United v Potters Bar Town | 1-1, 4-2 |
| Buckingham Town v Maldon Town | 4-1 |
| Cray Wanderers v Chessington & Hook United | 6-0 |
| Gorleston v Leighton Town | 2-7 |
| Flackwell Heath v Enfield Town | 0-1 |
| AFC Sudbury v Lowestoft Town | 5-1 |
| Bitton v Fairford Town | 3-1 |
| Westbury United v Devizes Town | 8-3 |
| Bideford v Welton Rovers | 7-0 |
| Torrington v Moneyfields | 3-0 |
| Gosport Borough v Highworth Town | 6-0 |
| Lymington & New Milton v Backwell United | 5-1 |
| Thatcham Town v Fareham Town | 2-3 |
| St Blazey v Willand Rovers | 4-1 |
| Winchester City v Hamworthy United | 2-0 |
| Christchurch v Andover | 0-2 |
| Bishop's Cleeve v Keynsham Town | 3-4 |
| BAT Sports v Frome Town | 3-2 |

**THIRD ROUND**

| | |
|---|---|
| Wellington v Billingham Synthonia | 1-2 |
| Studley v Blaby & Whetstone Athletic | 3-0 |
| Stone Dominoes v Sheffield | 3-2 |
| Desborough Town v Guisborough Town | 3-0 |
| Buxton v Congleton Town | 0-0, 1-1 |
| *Congleton Town won 5-4 on penalties.* | |
| Jarrow Roofing Boldon CA v Eastwood Town | 0-2 |
| Morpeth Town v Colne | 0-1 |
| Warrington Town v West Allotment Celtic | 1-2 |
| Gedling Town v Ramsbottom United | 2-1 |
| Mossley v Whitley Bay | 4-0 |
| Leamington v Durham City | 2-1 |
| Oadby Town v Shildon | 1-0 |
| Nantwich Town v Coalville Town | 6-0 |
| Billingham Town v Lincoln Moorlands | 5-2 |
| Bideford v Withdean 2000 | 6-0 |
| St Neots Town v Thamesmead Town | 2-1 |
| BAT Sports v AFC Wimbledon | 0-1 |
| Andover v Three Bridges | 4-3 |
| St Blazey v Soham Town Rangers | 2-0 |
| Fareham Town v Leighton Town | 0-1 |
| Gosport Borough v Bury Town | 1-0 |
| Westbury United v Wroxham | 2-6 |
| Whitehawk v Winchester City | 1-3 |
| Southall Town v North Leigh | 0-2 |
| Concord Rangers v Ramsgate | 1-0 |
| Cray Wanderers v Great Yarmouth Town | 3-2 |
| Chertsey Town v Harefield United | 1-0 |
| Lymington & New Milton v Buckingham Town | 0-0 |
| *abandoned after 88 minutes.* | 2-1 |
| Enfield Town v Torrington | 2-4 |
| AFC Sudbury v Harwich & Parkeston | 3-2 |
| Maidstone United v Bitton | 0-1 |
| Hertford Town v Keynsham Town | 3-3, 2-2 |
| *Keynsham Town won 3-0 on penalties.* | |

**FOURTH ROUND**

| | |
|---|---|
| Eastwood Town v St Blazey | 3-1 |
| Stone Dominoes v Concord Rangers | 5-1 |
| North Leigh v Andover | 0-1 |
| Billingham Town v Bideford | 2-4 |
| Keynsham Town v St Neots Town | 1-0 |
| Nantwich Town v Wroxham | 1-3 |
| AFC Sudbury v Desborough Town | 3-1 |
| Congleton Town v Billingham Synthonia | 2-1 |
| West Allotment Celtic v Cray Wanderers | 0-1 |
| Studley v Leamington | 2-1 |
| Gedling Town v Leighton Town | 2-3 |
| Lymington & New Milton v Bitton | 2-3 |
| Gosport Borough v Oadby Town | 2-1 |
| Chertsey Town v Torrington | 5-1 |
| Mossley v Winchester City | 1-2 |
| AFC Wimbledon v Colne | 1-2 |

**FIFTH ROUND**

| | |
|---|---|
| Congleton Town v AFC Sudbury | 0-2 |
| Studley v Gosport Borough | 1-1, 1-2 |
| Colne v Bitton | 2-0 |
| Andover v Leighton Town | 3-1 |
| Chertsey Town v Bideford | 0-1 |
| Wroxham v Winchester City | 0-3 |
| Eastwood Town v Stone Dominoes | 3-3, 3-1 |
| Keynsham Town v Cray Wanderers | 0-2 |

**SIXTH ROUND**

| | |
|---|---|
| Colne v Eastwood Town | 4-4, 2-1 |
| Winchester City v Andover | 5-1 |
| Cray Wanderers v AFC Sudbury | 0-2 |
| Bideford v Gosport Borough | 3-0 |

**SEMI-FINALS** (two legs)

| | |
|---|---|
| Bideford v Winchester City | 3-3, 0-4 |
| AFC Sudbury v Colne | 3-2, 1-1 |

**THE FA VASE FINAL**

Sunday, 16 May 2004

(at St Andrews, Birmingham)

**AFC Sudbury (0) 0**

**Winchester City (1) 2** *(Forbes 18, Dyke 77 (pen))* 5080

*AFC Sudbury:* Greygoose; Head, Betson (Francis 85), Girling, Tracey, Wardley, Hyde (Calver 56), Norfolk, Bennett, Claydon, Owen (Banya 62).

*Winchester City:* Arthur; Dyke (Tate 84), Bicknell, Blake, Redwood, Goss, Smith, Webber, Mancey, Forbes (Rogers 70), Green.

*Referee:* P. Crossley (Kent).

# THE FA YOUTH CUP 2003–04

## IN PARTNERSHIP WITH PEPSI

**PRELIMINARY ROUND**

| | |
|---|---|
| Southport v Ryton | 10-0 |
| Burscough v Penrith | 2-1 |
| Radcliffe Borough v Altrincham | 3-4 |
| Ossett Town v Northwich Victoria | 1-2 |
| Atherstone United v Boldmere St Michaels | 0-2 |
| Southend Manor v Diss Town | 2-0 |
| Thurrock v Hullbridge Sports | 5-1 |
| Leyton v Carterton Town | 2-2 |
| *Leyton won 7-6 on penalties.* | |
| Stansted v Uxbridge | 3-2 |
| Staines Town v Barton Rovers | 5-1 |
| Saltdean United v Folkestone Invicta | 2-3 |
| Chipstead v Maidenhead United | 3-2 |

**FIRST QUALIFYING ROUND**

| | |
|---|---|
| Lancaster City v Selby Town | 4-1 |
| Wakefield & Emley v Bradford Park Avenue | 1-1 |
| *Bradford Park Avenue won 3-0 on penalties.* | |
| Southport v Thackley | 1-3 |
| Retford United v Northwich Victoria | 0-3 |
| Barrow v Frickley Athletic | 4-2 |
| Guiseley v Workington | 6-2 |
| Yorkshire Amateur v Trafford | 1-3 |
| Stocksbridge Park Steels v Curzon Ashton | 1-2 |
| Morecambe v Chester-Le-Street Town | 3-4 |
| Glasshoughton Welfare v Seaham Red Star | 0-3 |
| Altrincham w.o. v Louth United removed. | |
| Harrogate Railway v Worksop Town | 3-4 |
| Whitley Bay v Darlington College | 0-3 |
| Chadderton v Pickering Town | 2-4 |
| Hallam v Pontefract Collieries | 5-0 |
| Chester City v Halifax Town | 1-0 |
| North Ferriby United v Consett | 2-0 |
| Witton Albion v Burscough | 0-2 |
| Vauxhall Motors v Marine | 0-2 |
| Farsley Celtic v Garforth Town | 6-1 |
| Belper Town v Arnold Town | 4-1 |
| Long Buckby v Alvechurch | 2-3 |
| Cradley Town v Dudley Sports | 6-3 |
| Hinckley United v Congleton Town | 6-0 |
| Hednesford Town w.o. v Grantham Town withdrew. | |
| Bloxwich Town v Boldmere St Michaels | 1-3 |
| Kettering Town v Lincoln United | 1-0 |
| Burton Albion v Nuneaton Borough | 1-2 |
| Northampton Spencer v Quorn | 1-2 |
| Gornal Athletic v Deeping Rangers | 1-2 |
| Wellington v Racing Club Warwick | 2-1 |
| Matlock Town v Coventry Sphinx | 5-4 |
| Stourbridge v Corby Town | 0-4 |
| Tamworth v Eastwood Town | 0-1 |
| Alfreton Town v Leamington | 3-0 |
| Barrow Town v Mickleover Sports | 1-3 |
| Hucknall Town v Stone Dominoes | 3-3 |
| *Hucknall Town won 4-3 on penalties.* | |
| Rugby United v Chasetown | 2-1 |
| Marconi v Stratford Town | 4-2 |
| Coggenhoe United v Lye Town | 3-4 |
| Malvern Town v Rushall Olympic | 2-1 |
| Bedworth United v Shrewsbury Town | 1-2 |
| Sutton Coldfield Town v Newcastle Town | 3-1 |
| Nantwich Town v Gresley Rovers | 7-2 |
| Bugbrooke St Michaels v Wealdstone | 0-6 |
| Wembley v Ford United | 2-3 |
| Grays Athletic v Heybridge Swifts | 1-6 |
| Broxbourne Borough v Lowestoft Town | 0-1 |
| Staines Town v Hoddesdon Town | 0-3 |
| Soham Town Rangers v Southend Manor | 0-2 |
| March Town United v Aylesbury United | 0-0 |
| *Aylesbury United won 2-1 on penalties.* | |
| Marlow v Bedford Town | 1-4 |
| Chesham United v AFC Kempston Rovers | 2-0 |
| Wisbech Town v Flackwell Heath | 2-2 |
| *Wisbech Town won 3-2 on penalties.* | |
| Royston Town v Ware | 2-0 |
| Boreham Wood v Sawbridgeworth Town | 9-0 |
| Witham Town v East Thurrock United | 1-2 |
| Wingate & Finchley v North Greenwood United | 3-2 |
| Canvey Island v Clapton | 5-1 |
| Ipswich Wanderers v Fakenham Town | 1-2 |
| Stevenage Borough v Hanley Town | 10-0 |
| Cheshunt v AFC Wallingford | 4-1 |
| Cambridge City v Great Yarmouth Town | 4-0 |
| Romford v Newmarket Town | 1-5 |
| St Margaretsbury v Hitchin Town | 2-3 |
| Bowers United v Brentwood | 3-0 |
| Chalfont St Peter v Leighton Town | 1-1 |
| *Chalfont St Peter won 5-4 on penalties.* | |
| Dereham Town v Leyton | 2-1 |
| Thurrock v Hemel Hempstead Town | 1-2 |
| Didcot Town v Hampton & Richmond Borough | 2-1 |
| Chelmsford City v Thame United | 3-1 |
| Hayes v Stansted | 1-1 |
| *Hayes won 6-5 on penalties.* | |
| Woodbridge Town v Great Wakering Rovers | 2-1 |
| Haringey Borough v Burnham Ramblers | 2-2 |
| *Burnham Ramblers won 5-3 on penalties.* | |
| Banbury United v Ilford | 1-2 |
| Buckingham Town v Beaconsfield SYCOB | 3-2 |
| Ruislip Manor v Northwood | 2-3 |
| Bishop's Stortford withdrew v Braintree Town w.o. | |
| Berkhamsted Town v Waltham Forest | 2-3 |
| Bury Town v Histon | 5-0 |
| Burnham v St Albans City | 1-3 |
| Brook House v Maldon Town | 3-4 |
| Hertford Town v Enfield | 1-5 |
| Hornchurch v Concord Rangers | 1-3 |
| Walton Casuals v Fleet Town | 2-1 |
| Eastbourne Borough v Bashley | 4-0 |
| Ashford Town v Thamesmead Town | 5-0 |
| Banstead Athletic v Sittingbourne | 2-1 |
| Hailsham Town v Littlehampton Town | 0-3 |
| Sutton United v Lordswood | 3-0 |
| Erith Town v Leatherhead | 4-1 |
| Whitstable Town v Tooting & Mitcham United | 0-3 |
| Farnborough Town v Whyteleafe | 2-0 |
| Dover Athletic v Thatcham Town | 3-4 |
| AFC Newbury v Arundel | 3-2 |
| Wick v Gravesend & Northfleet | 1-2 |
| Hillingdon Borough v Walton & Hersham | 4-0 |
| Lewes v Westfield | 4-1 |
| Dartford v Woking | 1-2 |
| Pagham v Carshalton Athletic | 3-4 |
| Ramsgate v Cobham | 2-1 |
| Chichester City United v Horndean | 1-2 |
| Crawley Town v Chipstead | 4-0 |
| Andover v Alton Town | 0-5 |
| Kingstonian withdrew v Chatham Town w.o. | |
| Sidlesham v Croydon Athletic | 1-2 |
| Havant & Waterlooville v Bromley | 1-0 |
| Ashford Town (Mx) v Chertsey Town | 0-1 |
| Horsham v Tonbridge Angels | 1-4 |
| Molesey v Epsom & Ewell | 1-2 |
| Camberley Town v Folkestone Invicta | 5-2 |
| Winchester City v Burgess Hill Town | 1-2 |
| Reading Town v Sandhurst Town | 6-0 |
| Aldershot Town v Bracknell Town | 11-1 |
| Whitehawk v Mile Oak | 2-1 |
| Wokingham Town v Three Bridges | 2-1 |
| Cirencester Town v Pershore Town | 5-2 |
| Bournemouth v Wootton Bassett Town | 1-5 |
| Bath City v Bemerton Heath Harlequins | 4-4 |
| *Bemerton Heath Harlequins won 6-5 on penalties.* | |
| Salisbury City v Mangotsfield United | 2-2 |
| *Salisbury City won 3-1 on penalties.* | |
| Frome Town v Bridgwater Town | 0-1 |
| Clevedon Town v Forest Green Rovers | 2-3 |
| Bitton v Christchurch | 2-2 |
| *Bitton won 6-5 on penalties.* | |
| Newport County v Evesham United | 6-0 |
| Yate Town v Worcester City | 2-3 |
| Hereford United v Cinderford Town | 8-1 |
| Paulton Rovers v Gloucester City | 0-2 |
| Exeter City v Brislington | 4-0 |

**SECOND QUALIFYING ROUND**

| | |
|---|---|
| Altrincham v Pickering Town | 3-2 |
| Marine v Farsley Celtic | 4-0 |
| Barrow v Hallam | 1-2 |
| Worksop Town v North Ferriby United | 4-1 |
| Seaham Red Star v Curzon Ashton | 2-1 |
| Chester-Le-Street Town v Burscough | 2-1 |

| | |
|---|---|
| Northwich Victoria v Trafford | 3-1 |
| Chester City v Darlington College | 1-2 |
| Lancaster City v Thackley | 0-6 |
| Guiseley v Bradford Park Avenue | 0-2 |
| Quorn v Lye Town | 1-3 |
| Hinckley United v Shrewsbury Town | 0-1 |
| Belper Town v Alvechurch | 1-2 |
| Malvern Town v Hucknall Town | 3-1 |
| Eastwood Town v Hednesford Town | 1-3 |
| Deeping Rangers v Corby Town | 1-1 |
| *Deeping Rangers won 3-1 on penalties.* | |
| Cradley Town v Kettering Town | 0-2 |
| Rugby United v Wellington | 1-0 |
| Nantwich Town v Sutton Coldfield Town | 2-3 |
| Mickleover Sports v Nuneaton Borough | 6-5 |
| Marconi v Alfreton Town | 1-2 |
| Matlock Town v Boldmere St Michaels | 3-4 |
| Hitchin Town v Burnham Ramblers | 3-0 |
| Waltham Forest v Southend Manor | 5-1 |
| Wealdstone v Buckingham Town | 5-1 |
| Hayes v Lowestoft Town | 2-1 |
| Hoddesdon Town v Wingate & Finchley | 2-0 |
| Stevenage Borough v Maldon Town | 6-1 |
| Concord Rangers v Northwood | 0-1 |
| Ilford v Royston Town | 0-2 |
| Dereham Town v Chesham United | 1-4 |
| Fakenham Town v Woodbridge Town | 2-4 |
| Heybridge Swifts v Bowers United | 3-5 |
| Newmarket Town v Enfield | 0-2 |
| Bury Town v Boreham Wood | 3-0 |
| Aylesbury United v Didcot Town | 0-2 |
| Cambridge City v Chelmsford City | 2-3 |
| Bedford Town v Cheshunt | 2-2 |
| *Bedford Town won 4-3 on penalties.* | |
| Hemel Hempstead Town v Wisbech Town | 2-1 |
| St Albans City v Ford United | 3-2 |
| Braintree Town v Chalfont St Peter | 1-2 |
| East Thurrock United v Canvey Island | 2-3 |
| Tonbridge Angels v Croydon Athletic | 1-2 |
| Aldershot Town v Crawley Town | 0-1 |
| Tooting & Mitcham United v Carshalton Athletic | 2-0 |
| *Carshalton Athletic awarded tie; Tooting & Mitcham United fielded ineligible player.* | |
| Reading Town v Walton Casuals | 0-4 |
| Camberley Town v Gravesend & Northfleet | 0-1 |
| Chertsey Town v Hillingdon Borough | 1-1 |
| *Hillingdon Borough won 3-2 on penalties.* | |
| Thatcham Town v Alton Town | 4-0 |
| Chatham Town v Littlehampton Town | 3-3 |
| *Chatham Town won 4-2 on penalties.* | |
| Burgess Hill Town v Ramsgate | 3-0 |
| Farnborough Town v Sutton United | 0-3 |
| Wokingham Town v Eastbourne Borough | 0-2 |
| Whitehawk v Horndean | 3-2 |
| Banstead Athletic v Epsom & Ewell | 1-2 |
| AFC Newbury v Lewes | 0-4 |
| Ashford Town v Woking | 4-2 |
| Havant & Waterlooville v Erith Town | 4-2 |
| Newport County v Bemerton Heath Harlequins | 5-1 |
| Bridgwater Town v Exeter City | 0-5 |
| Wootton Bassett Town v Bitton | 3-4 |
| Forest Green Rovers v Gloucester City | 1-0 |
| Salisbury City v Cirencester Town | 2-5 |
| Hereford United v Worcester City | 2-1 |

## THIRD QUALIFYING ROUND

| | |
|---|---|
| Thackley v Northwich Victoria | 4-2 |
| Seaham Red Star v Darlington College | 1-3 |
| Marine v Worksop Town | 0-1 |
| Chester-Le-Street Town v Bradford Park Avenue | 3-0 |
| Altrincham v Hallam | 3-1 |
| Rugby United v Alvechurch | 5-1 |
| Hednesford Town v Boldmere St Michaels | 3-0 |
| Shrewsbury Town v Kettering Town | 10-0 |
| Deeping Rangers v Alfreton Town | 1-0 |
| Malvern Town v Lye Town | 7-2 |
| Mickleover Sports v Sutton Coldfield Town | 2-1 |
| Bowers United v Didcot Town | 1-0 |
| Chalfont St Peter v Canvey Island | 4-2 |
| Hoddesdon Town v Chelmsford City | 0-4 |
| Enfield v Hemel Hempstead Town | 1-5 |
| Woodbridge Town v Royston Town | 0-5 |
| Chesham United v St Albans City | 0-3 |
| Hayes v Northwood | 3-1 |
| Bedford Town v Bury Town | 1-2 |
| Hitchin Town v Wealdstone | 3-4 |
| Stevenage Borough v Waltham Forest | 3-2 |
| Lewes v Thatcham Town | 2-1 |
| Crawley Town v Chatham Town | 6-2 |
| Whitehawk v Sutton United | 0-2 |
| Hillingdon Borough v Gravesend & Northfleet | 0-2 |
| Eastbourne Borough v Croydon Athletic | 3-6 |
| Burgess Hill Town v Epsom & Ewell | 5-0 |
| Ashford Town v Carshalton Athletic | 2-1 |
| Havant & Waterlooville v Walton Casuals | 2-1 |
| Bitton v Hereford United | 5-3 |
| Cirencester Town v Forest Green Rovers | 2-1 |
| Exeter City v Newport County | 1-1 |
| *Exeter City won 5-4 on penalties.* | |

## FIRST ROUND

| | |
|---|---|
| Hartlepool United v Chester-Le-Street Town | 0-2 |
| Macclesfield Town v Blackpool | 3-2 |
| Worksop Town v Oldham Athletic | 0-2 |
| Huddersfield Town v Grimsby Town | 0-0 |
| *Huddersfield Town won 4-2 on penalties.* | |
| Darlington College v Tranmere Rovers | 0-8 |
| Barnsley v Altrincham | 4-0 |
| Thackley v Darlington | 3-2 |
| Sheffield Wednesday v Rochdale | 3-0 |
| Wrexham v Scunthorpe United | 4-3 |
| Stockport County v Carlisle United | 2-0 |
| York City v Hull City | 1-0 |
| Deeping Rangers v Mansfield Town | 2-9 |
| Kidderminster Harriers v Oadby Town | 2-3 |
| Rugby United v Mickleover Sports | 1-2 |
| Notts County v Malvern Town | 3-0 |
| Shrewsbury Town v Lincoln City | 4-1 |
| Northampton Town v Rushden & Diamonds | 0-3 |
| Hednesford Town v Chesterfield | 0-3 |
| Gravesend & Northfleet v Oxford United | 1-4 |
| Crawley Town v Lewes | 1-0 |
| Brighton & Hove Albion v Luton Town | 2-0 |
| Havant & Waterlooville v Brentford | 0-3 |
| Dulwich Hamlet v Ashford Town | 1-0 |
| Bowers United v Cambridge United | 0-5 |
| Wealdstone v Royston Town | 4-2 |
| Chalfont St Peter v Wycombe Wanderers | 0-3 |
| Stevenage Borough v Hemel Hempstead Town | 2-1 |
| Hayes v Queens Park Rangers | 3-3 |
| *Hayes won 5-4 on penalties.* | |
| Chelmsford City v Colchester United | 1-0 |
| Burgess Hill Town v Croydon Athletic | 1-1 |
| *Croydon Athletic won 10-9 on penalties.* | |
| Southend United v Leyton Orient | 0-1 |
| Sutton United v Bury Town | 2-3 |
| Bristol Rovers v AFC Bournemouth | 0-0 |
| *Bristol Rovers won 5-4 on penalties.* | |
| Cirencester Town v Exeter City | 2-1 |
| Cheltenham Town v Bitton | 6-0 |
| Swindon Town v Yeovil Town | 5-0 |
| Torquay United v Swansea City | 2-1 |
| Bristol City v Plymouth Argyle | 4-2 |

*Byes:* Port Vale & St Albans City.

## SECOND ROUND

| | |
|---|---|
| Oadby Town v Shrewsbury Town | 0-1 |
| Notts County v Mansfield Town | 4-0 |
| Sheffield Wednesday v Tranmere Rovers | 2-4 |
| Barnsley v Oldham Athletic | 2-2 |
| *Barnsley won 5-4 on penalties.* | |
| Stockport County v Wrexham | 0-1 |
| Chester-Le-Street Town v Port Vale | 5-3 |
| York City v Macclesfield Town | 0-1 |
| Huddersfield Town v Thackley | 4-2 |
| Mickleover Sports v Chesterfield | 1-2 |
| Leyton Orient v Brentford | 0-3 |
| Bristol Rovers v Crawley Town | 2-3 |
| Wycombe Wanderers v Swindon Town | 2-4 |
| Oxford United v Stevenage Borough | 1-6 |
| Rushden & Diamonds v Hayes | 5-1 |
| Croydon Athletic v Cirencester Town | 2-5 |
| Brighton & Hove Albion v Dulwich Hamlet | 4-2 |
| Torquay United v Chelmsford City | 3-1 |
| Bristol City v Cheltenham Town | 7-2 |
| Bury Town v St Albans City | 2-2 |
| *Bury Town won 4-3 on penalties.* | |
| Cambridge United v Wealdstone | 3-1 |

## THIRD ROUND

| | |
|---|---|
| Brighton & Hove Albion v Stevenage Borough | 0-2 |
| Huddersfield Town v West Ham United | 0-1 |

| | |
|---|---|
| West Bromwich Albion v Tottenham Hotspur | 2-1 |
| Crewe Alexandra v Brentford | 1-0 |
| Bury Town v Blackburn Rovers | 0-2 |
| Charlton Athletic v Sunderland | 0-2 |
| Derby County v Chester-Le-Street Town | 1-2 |
| Leeds United v Ipswich Town | 1-2 |
| Portsmouth v Newcastle United | 1-2 |
| Macclesfield Town v Walsall | 1-2 |
| Cambridge United v Millwall | 2-0 |
| Leicester City v Birmingham City | 2-0 |
| Cirencester Town v Bradford City | 2-1 |
| Cardiff City v Notts County | 3-2 |
| Reading v Southampton | 0-3 |
| Nottingham Forest v Preston North End | 1-0 |
| Chelsea v Aston Villa | 0-2 |
| Norwich City v Bolton Wanderers | 1-0 |
| Crawley Town v Arsenal | 0-9 |
| Watford v Wrexham | 2-0 |
| Coventry City v Everton | 1-0 |
| Sheffield United v Burnley | 4-1 |
| Stoke City v Bristol City | 3-0 |
| Crystal Palace v Tranmere Rovers | 1-2 |
| Wigan Athletic v Manchester City | 1-2 |
| Wimbledon v Torquay United | 3-1 |
| Middlesbrough v Fulham | 3-0 |
| Swindon Town v Chesterfield | 4-1 |
| Barnsley v Wolverhampton Wanderers | 0-3 |
| Rushden & Diamonds v Manchester United | 1-2 |
| Rotherham United v Shrewsbury Town | 5-1 |
| Liverpool v Gillingham | 0-1 |

### FOURTH ROUND

| | |
|---|---|
| Aston Villa v Wimbledon | 4-0 |
| Swindon Town v Cardiff City | 1-0 |
| Manchester United v Manchester City | 2-0 |
| West Ham United v Chester-Le-Street Town | 2-0 |
| Leicester City v Cambridge United | 0-1 |
| Walsall v Middlesbrough | 1-2 |
| Arsenal v Southampton | 0-2 |
| Nottingham Forest v Coventry City | 1-1 |
| *Nottingham Forest won 4-3 on penalties.* | |
| Tranmere Rovers v Stevenage Borough | 2-1 |
| Wolverhampton Wanderers v Rotherham United | 0-2 |
| Blackburn Rovers v West Bromwich Albion | 6-2 |
| Cirencester Town v Crewe Alexandra | 1-1 |
| *Crewe Alexandra won 6-5 on penalties.* | |
| Ipswich Town v Sunderland | 1-2 |
| Gillingham v Watford | 1-0 |
| Stoke City v Newcastle United | 0-1 |
| Norwich City v Sheffield United | 2-0 |

### FIFTH ROUND

| | |
|---|---|
| Blackburn Rovers v Gillingham | 2-1 |
| Swindon Town v Cambridge United | 1-0 |
| Rotherham United v Aston Villa | 0-5 |
| Sunderland v Crewe Alexandra | 1-2 |
| Middlesbrough v Newcastle United | 2-1 |
| Tranmere Rovers v Southampton | 3-3 |
| *Tranmere Rovers won 6-5 on penalties.* | |
| West Ham United v Nottingham Forest | 2-2 |
| *West Ham United won 4-2 on penalties.* | |
| Manchester United v Norwich City | 4-2 |

### SIXTH ROUND

| | |
|---|---|
| Tranmere Rovers v Middlesbrough | 0-1 |
| Blackburn Rovers v Manchester United | 2-0 |
| West Ham United v Aston Villa | 0-2 |
| Crewe Alexandra v Swindon Town | 3-0 |

### SEMI-FINALS (two legs)

| | |
|---|---|
| Crewe Alexandra v Middlesbrough | 0-2, 0-1 |
| Aston Villa v Blackburn Rovers | 2-0, 2-2 |

### THE FA YOUTH CUP FINAL (First Leg)

Thursday, 15 April 2004

**Aston Villa (0) 0**

**Middlesbrough (0) 3** *(Wheater 47, Morrison 52, 78 (pen))* 6551

*Aston Villa:* Olejnik; Ward, Green (Grant 72), Gardner Troest, Cahill, Kabeya (Paul 68), Foley, Agbonlahor, Moore L, Nix.

*Middlesbrough:* Knight; McMahon, Masters, Kennedy, Bates, Wheater, Morrison (Johnson 90), Liddle, Craddock, Taylor, Peacock.

*Referee:* A. D'Urso (Essex).

### THE FA YOUTH CUP FINAL (Second Leg)

Monday, 19 April 2004

**Middlesbrough (0) 1** *(Kennedy 47)*

**Aston Villa (0) 0** 16,321

*Middlesbrough:* Knight; McMahon, Masters, Kennedy (Johnson 76), Bates, Wheater, Morrison, Liddle, Craddock (Reed 82), Taylor, Peacock.

*Aston Villa:* Olejnik; Ward (Kabeya 58), Green, Gardner, Troest, Cahill, Paul (Morgan 79), Foley, Agbonlahor, Moore L, Nix.

*Referee:* A. D'Urso (Essex).

## THE FA YOUTH CUP – PREVIOUS WINNERS
(Aggregate Scores)

| *Year* | *Winners* | *Runners-up* | *Score* |
|---|---|---|---|
| 1953 | Manchester United | Wolverhampton W | 9-3 |
| 1954 | Manchester United | Wolverhampton W | 5-4 |
| 1955 | Manchester United | West Bromwich Albion | 7-1 |
| 1956 | Manchester United | Chesterfield | 4-3 |
| 1957 | Manchester United | West Ham United | 8-2 |
| 1958 | Wolverhampton W | Chelsea | 7-6 |
| 1959 | Blackburn Rovers | West Ham United | 2-1 |
| 1960 | Chelsea | Preston North End | 5-2 |
| 1961 | Chelsea | Everton | 5-3 |
| 1962 | Newcastle United | Wolverhampton W | 2-1 |
| 1963 | West Ham United | Liverpool | 6-5 |
| 1964 | Manchester United | Swindon Town | 5-2 |
| 1965 | Everton | Arsenal | 3-2 |
| 1966 | Arsenal | Sunderland | 5-3 |
| 1967 | Sunderland | Birmingham City | 2-0 |
| 1968 | Burnley | Coventry City | 3-2 |
| 1969 | Sunderland | West Bromwich Albion | 6-3 |
| 1970 | Tottenham Hotspur | Coventry City | 4-3 |
| 1971 | Arsenal | Cardiff City | 2-0 |
| 1972 | Aston Villa | Liverpool | 5-2 |
| 1973 | Ipswich Town | Bristol City | 4-1 |
| 1974 | Tottenham Hotspur | Huddersfield Town | 2-1 |
| 1975 | Ipswich Town | West Ham United | 5-1 |
| 1976 | West Bromwich Albion | Wolverhampton W | 5-0 |
| 1977 | Crystal Palace | Everton | 1-0* |
| 1978 | Crystal Palace | Aston Villa | 1-0 |
| 1979 | Millwall | Manchester City | 2-0 |
| 1980 | Aston Villa | Manchester City | 3-2 |
| 1981 | West Ham United | Tottenham Hotspur | 2-1 |
| 1982 | Watford | Manchester United | 7-6 |
| 1983 | Norwich City | Everton | 6-5 |
| 1984 | Everton | Stoke City | 4-2 |
| 1985 | Newcastle United | Watford | 4-1 |
| 1986 | Manchester City | Manchester United | 3-1 |
| 1987 | Coventry City | Charlton Athletic | 2-1 |
| 1988 | Arsenal | Doncaster Rovers | 6-1 |
| 1989 | Watford | Manchester City | 2-1 |
| 1990 | Tottenham Hotspur | Middlesbrough | 3-2 |
| 1991 | Millwall | Sheffield Wednesday | 3-0 |
| 1992 | Manchester United | Crystal Palace | 6-3 |
| 1993 | Leeds United | Manchester United | 4-1 |
| 1994 | Arsenal | Millwall | 5-3 |
| 1995 | Manchester United | Tottenham Hotspur | 2-2 |
| | *Manchester United won 4-3 on penalties.* | | |
| 1996 | Liverpool | West Ham United | 4-1 |
| 1997 | Leeds United | Crystal Palace | 3-1 |
| 1998 | Everton | Blackburn Rovers | 5-3 |
| 1999 | West Ham United | Coventry City | 9-0 |
| 2000 | Arsenal | Coventry City | 5-1 |
| 2001 | Arsenal | Blackburn Rovers | 6-3 |
| 2002 | Aston Villa | Everton | 4-2 |
| 2003 | Manchester United | Middlesbrough | 3-1 |

* One match only

# THE FA SUNDAY CUP 2003–04

## IN PARTNERSHIP WITH CARLSBERG

**RST ROUND**

ast Bowling Unity v Clubmoor Nalgo 1-2
FC Bromborough v Britannia 0-0
*AFC Bromborough won 5-4 on penalties.*
: Aloysius E v Queensbury 3-1
obster v Orchard Park 1-2
eaton Sluice SC v Grey Bull 0-1
ltway Valentine w.o. v Fantail Manfast withdrew.
artlepool Lion Hillcarter v Canada 2-1
olton Woods v Bruce Ennis Square 3-5
hankhouse United v Seymour 2-2
*Seymour won 5-3 on penalties.*
restige Brighams v Hartlepool Supporters Athletic 3-1
lifton v Fairweather Green WMC 6-2
nith & Nephew v Oakenshaw 2-0
verstone v Casino Cars 2-1
C Sportsman v Bartley Green 1-2
ebeq v Celtic SC (Luton) 2-0
rosvenor Park (Sunday) v Queensmen 3-3
*Grosvenor Park (Sunday) won 3-2 on penalties.*
eadflex Rangers v Crawley Green (Sunday) 2-2
*Readflex Rangers won 4-3 on penalties.*
*Tie awarded to Crawley Green (Sunday); Readflex Rangers fielded an ineligible player.*
ittle Paxton v Travellers 3-5
oll End v St Joseph's Luton 0-3
tandens Barn v Walsall Wood Royal Exchange 0-0
*Walsall Wood Royal Exchange won 4-2 on penalties.*
orest Town Welfare v FC Houghton Centre 1-3
larden v Coopers Kensington 2-0
rooper v Grange Athletic 0-1
urley v Lewsey Social 0-3
edfont Sunday v VS Villa 1-1
*Bedfont Sunday won 4-3 on penalties.*
eading Irish v Lashings 5-0
AA Heathrow v Hexton 1-2
oneyfield Trailers v Galleon 5-3
ercival v London Colney BCH 1-2
apel Plough v Hammer 2-1
*yes:* Allerton, Duke of York

**ECOND ROUND**

FC Bromborough v Hessle Rangers 1-0
lubmoor Nalgo w.o. v Schofields withdrew
llerton v Dickie Lewis 2-1
rchard Park v Queens Park 2-1
Aloysius E v Western Approaches 2-1
ltway Valentine v Marske Ship Inn 6-1
rey Bull v Taxi Club 2-1
ruce Ennis Square v Clifton 2-0
artlepool Lion Hillcarter v Norcoast 2-0
3 (Canada) v Canon 3-2
eymour v Albion Sports 3-0
arry's v Nicosia 1-4
restige Brighams v Sandon Dock 2-0
reeze v Ford Motors 2-3
mith & Nephew v Hetton Lyons Cricket Club 2-3
artley Green v Belstone 5-3
verstone v Lodge Cottrell 0-5
C Houghton Centre v Austin Ex Apprentices 2-0
rosvenor Park (Sunday) v Gossoms End 1-4
St Joseph's (Luton) v UK Flooring 0-2
Travellers v Lebeq 6-1
Crawley Green (Sunday) v Mackadown Lane S&S 0-2
Marden v Linfield Yenton 0-4
Walsall Wood Royal Exchange v Grange Athletic 1-2
Bedfont Sunday v Duke of York 0-2
Lewsey Social v Quested 0-1
Hexton v Rainham Sports 4-0
Reading Irish v Sutton High 4-2
CB Hounslow United v Pioneer 2-3
Honeyfield Trailers v Poole Wanderers 4-1
Capel Plough v Moat 4-0
London Colney BCH v St Margarets 4-4
*St Margarets won 4-2 on penalties.*

**THIRD ROUND**

A3 (Canada) v Orchard Park 3-1
Seymour v Hartlepool Lion Hillcarter 0-1
St Aloysius E v Allerton 3-4
Travellers v AFC Bromborough 1-2
Nicosia v Altway Valentine 2-3
*Tie awarded to Nicosia; Altway Valentine fielded an ineligible player.*
Hetton Lyons Cricket Club v Grey Bull 3-1
Bruce Ennis Square v Prestige Brighams 3-4
Clubmoor Nalgo v Ford Motors 6-0
Quested v Gossoms End 3-0
Hexton v Duke of York 1-7
UK Flooring v FC Houghton Centre 4-3
St Margarets v Bartley Green 3-1
Reading Irish v Mackadown Lane S&S 3-0
Capel Plough v Linfield Yenton 3-3
*Capel Plough won 4-3 on penalties.*
Grange Athletic v Pioneer 2-1
Lodge Cottrell v Honeyfield Trailers 3-2

**FOURTH ROUND**

Hartlepool Lion Hillcarter v Prestige Brighams 0-1
Clubmoor Nalgo v Hetton Lyons Cricket Club 1-1
*Clubmoor Nalgo won 3-2 on penalties.*
AFC Bromborough v Nicosia 0-1
Allerton v A3 (Canada) 3-5
Duke of York v Grange Athletic 3-0
Lodge Cottrell v Capel Plough 0-1
St Margarets v Reading Irish 3-1
UK Flooring v Quested 1-0

**FIFTH ROUND**

Nicosia v Prestige Brighams 2-0
A3 (Canada) v Clubmoor Nalgo 4-2
Capel Plough v St Margarets 0-1
UK Flooring v Duke of York 1-0

**SEMI-FINALS**

Nicosia v A3 (Canada) 3-2
UK Flooring v St Margarets 4-1

**FINAL**

Nicosia (1) 3 *(Olu 25 (og), Gibiliru 50, Madin 88)*
UK Flooring (0) 1 *(Pritchard 90)* 1526
*(at Liverpool FC).*

## THE FA SUNDAY CUP – PREVIOUS WINNERS

| *'ear* | *Winners* | *Runners-up* | *Score* |
|---|---|---|---|
| 965 | London | Staffordshire | 6-2 |
| 966 | Ubique United | Aldridge Fabrications | 1-0 |
| 967 | Carlton United | Stoke Works | 2-0 |
| 968 | Drovers | Brook United | 2-0 |
| 969 | Leigh Park | Loke United | 3-1 |
| 970 | Vention United | Ubique United | 1-0 |
| 971 | Beacontree United | Saltley United | 2-0 |
| 972 | Newtown Unity | Springfield Colts | 4-0 |
| 973 | Carlton United | Wear Valley | 2-1 |
| 974 | Newtown Unity | Brentford East | 3-0 |
| 975 | Fareham Town Centipedes | Players Athletic Engineers | 1-0 |
| 976 | Brandon United | Evergreen | 2-1 |
| 977 | Langley Park Rams Head | Newtown Unity | 2-0 |
| 978 | Arras | Lion Rangers | 2-1 |
| 1979 | Lobster | Carlton United | 3-2 |
| 1980 | Fantail | Twin Foxes | 1-0 |
| 1981 | Fantail | Mackintosh | 1-0 |
| 1982 | Dingle Rail | Twin Foxes | 2-1 |
| 1983 | Eagle | Lee Chapel North | 1-1 |
| | *Replay* | | 2-1 |
| 1984 | Lee Chapel North | Eagle | 4-3 |
| 1985 | Hobbies United | Avenue | 2-2 |
| | *Replay* | | 1-1 |
| | *Second Replay* | | 2-1 |
| 1986 | Avenue | Glenn Sports | 1-0 |
| 1987 | Lodge Cottrell | Avenue | 1-0 |
| 1988 | Nexday | Humbledon Plains Farm | 2-0 |
| 1989 | Almithak | East Levenshulme | 3-1 |
| 1990 | Humbledon Plains Farm | Marston Sports | 2-1 |
| 1991 | Nicosia | Ouzavich | 3-2 |

## THE FA SUNDAY CUP – PREVIOUS WINNERS (cont.)

| | | | |
|---|---|---|---|
| 1992 | Theale | Marston Sports | 3-2 |
| 1993 | Seymour | Bedfont Sunday | 1-0 |
| 1994 | Ranelagh Sports | Hartlepool Lion Hotel | 2-0 |
| 1995 | St Joseph's (Luton) | B&A Scaffolding | 2-1 |
| 1996 | St Joseph's (Luton) | Croxteth & Gilmoss RBL | 2-1 |
| 1997 | Marston United | Northwood | 1-0 |
| 1998 | Olympic Star | St Joseph's (Luton) | 1-1 |
| | *Olympic Star won 5-3 on penalties.* | | |
| 1999 | Little Paxton | St Joseph's (Luton) | 2 |
| | *Little Paxton won 4-3 on penalties.* | | |
| 2000 | Prestige Brighams | Albion Sports | 1 |
| 2001 | Hartlepool Lion Hillcarter | FC Houghton Centre | 0 |
| | *Hartlepool Lion Hillcarter won 3-2 on penalties.* | | |
| 2002 | Britannia | Little Paxton | 2 |
| 2003 | Duke of York | Travellers | 3 |

# THE FA COUNTY YOUTH CUP 2003–04

IN PARTNERSHIP WITH PEPSI

**FIRST ROUND**

| | |
|---|---|
| Sheffield & Hallamshire v West Riding | 3-4 |
| North Riding v Leicestershire & Rutland | 5-1 |
| Durham v Lincolnshire | 8-1 |
| Manchester v Westmorland | 4-1 |
| Cheshire v Staffordshire | 2-0 |
| Cumberland v Nottinghamshire | 0-1 |
| Worcestershire v Surrey | 2-1 |
| Dorset v Jersey | 0-1 |
| Huntingdonshire v Essex | 1-3 |
| Northamptonshire v Guernsey | 2-4 |
| Cambridgeshire v Gloucestershire | 1-4 |
| Berks & Bucks v Somerset | 2-3 |
| Wiltshire v Army | 1-0 |
| Devon v Norfolk | 1-2 |
| Suffolk v Herefordshire | 1-0 |

**SECOND ROUND**

| | |
|---|---|
| Isle of Man v Shropshire | 2-0 |
| Manchester v Birmingham | 3-1 |
| Durham v Lancashire | 5-1 |
| Derbyshire v East Riding | 0-3 |
| Nottinghamshire v West Riding | 0-3 |
| North Riding v Liverpool | 3-1 |
| Northumberland v Cheshire | 0-1 |
| Bedfordshire v Worcestershire | 1-3 |
| Oxfordshire v Gloucestershire | 4-5 |
| Essex v Norfolk | 0-1 |
| Cornwall v Hampshire | 1-4 |
| Hertfordshire v Kent | 1 |
| Somerset v Sussex | 1 |
| Jersey v Suffolk | 0 |
| Middlesex v Guernsey | 2 |
| London v Wiltshire | 2 |

**THIRD ROUND**

| | |
|---|---|
| London v Worcestershire | 0 |
| West Riding v East Riding | 0 |
| Kent v Gloucestershire | 4 |
| Manchester v Durham | 1 |
| Hampshire v Isle of Man | 3 |
| Middlesex v Suffolk | 1 |
| North Riding v Sussex | 3 |
| Norfolk v Cheshire | 2 |

**FOURTH ROUND**

| | |
|---|---|
| Durham v Cheshire | 2 |
| Worcestershire v Middlesex | 1 |
| Kent v North Riding | 2 |
| Hampshire v East Riding | 2 |

**SEMI-FINALS**

| | |
|---|---|
| East Riding v North Riding | 0 |
| Durham v Middlesex | 3 |

**FINAL**

| | |
|---|---|
| North Riding v Durham | 0 |

att: 902.

## THE FA COUNTY YOUTH CUP – PREVIOUS WINNERS
### (Aggregate scores until 1970)

| *Year* | *Winners* | *Runners-up* | *Score* |
|---|---|---|---|
| 1945 | Staffordshire | Wiltshire | 3-2 |
| 1946 | Berks & Bucks | Durham | 4-3 |
| 1947 | Durham | Essex | 4-2 |
| 1948 | Essex | Liverpool | 5-3 |
| 1949 | Liverpool | Middlesex | 4-3 |
| 1950 | Essex | Middlesex | 4-3 |
| 1951 | Middlesex | Leicestershire & Rutland | 3-1 |
| 1952 | Sussex | Liverpool | 3-1 |
| 1953 | Sheffield & Hallamshire | Hampshire | 5-3 |
| 1954 | Liverpool | Gloucestershire | 4-1 |
| 1955 | Bedfordshire | Sheffield & Hallamshire | 2-0 |
| 1956 | Middlesex | Staffordshire | 3-2 |
| 1957 | Hampshire | Cheshire | 4-3 |
| 1958 | Staffordshire | London | 8-0 |
| 1959 | Birmingham | London | 7-5 |
| 1960 | London | Birmingham | 6-4 |
| 1961 | Lancashire | Nottinghamshire | 6-3 |
| 1962 | Middlesex | Nottinghamshire | 6-3 |
| 1963 | Durham | Essex | 3-2 |
| 1964 | Sheffield & Hallamshire | Birmingham | 1-0 |
| 1965 | Northumberland | Middlesex | 7-4 |
| 1966 | Leicestershire & Rutland | London | 6-5 |
| 1967 | Northamptonshire | Hertfordshire | 5-4 |
| 1968 | North Riding | Devon | 7-4 |
| 1969 | Northumberland | Sussex | 1-0 |
| 1970 | Hertfordshire | Cheshire | 2-1 |
| 1971 | Lancashire | Gloucestershire | 2-0 |
| 1972 | Middlesex | Liverpool | 2-0 |
| 1973 | Hertfordshire | Northumberland | 3-0 |
| 1974 | Nottinghamshire | London | 2-0 |
| 1975 | Durham | Bedfordshire | 2-1 |
| 1976 | Northamptonshire | Surrey | 7 |
| 1977 | Liverpool | Surrey | 3 |
| 1978 | Liverpool | Kent | 3 |
| 1979 | Hertfordshire | Liverpool | 4 |
| 1980 | Liverpool | Lancashire | 2 |
| 1981 | Lancashire | East Riding | 3 |
| 1982 | Devon | Kent | 0 |
| | *Replay* | | 3 |
| 1983 | London | Gloucestershire | 3 |
| 1984 | Cheshire | Manchester | 2 |
| 1985 | East Riding | Middlesex | 2 |
| 1986 | Hertfordshire | Manchester | 4 |
| 1987 | North Riding | Gloucestershire | 3 |
| 1988 | East Riding | Middlesex | 1 |
| | *Replay* | | 5 |
| 1989 | Liverpool | Hertfordshire | 2 |
| 1990 | Staffordshire | Hampshire | 1 |
| | *Replay* | | 2 |
| 1991 | Lancashire | Surrey | 6 |
| 1992 | Nottinghamshire | Surrey | 1 |
| 1993 | Durham | Liverpool | 4 |
| 1994 | West Riding | Sussex | 3 |
| 1995 | Liverpool | Essex | 3 |
| 1996 | Durham | Gloucestershire | 1 |
| 1997 | Cambridgeshire | Lancashire | 1 |
| 1998 | Northumberland | West Riding | 2 |
| 1999 | Durham | Sussex | 1 |
| 2000 | Birmingham | Surrey | 2 |
| 2001 | Northamptonshire | Birmingham | 3 |
| 2002 | Birmingham | Durham | 2 |
| 2003 | Northumberland | Liverpool | 1 |

# SCHOOLS FOOTBALL 2003–04

## BOODLE & DUNTHORNE INDEPENDENT SCHOOLS FA CUP 2003–04

**IRST ROUND**
.lleyn's 2, City of London 1
imbolton 3, Brentwood 4 *(aet)*
atymer Upper 4, St Edmund's, Cantab 1
alvern 7, Dover College 1
t Mary's College, Crosby 0, QEGS, Blackburn 3
illfield 3, Bradfield 0
'estminster 0, Shrewsbury 3
'inchester 2, Chigwell 1
'olverhampton GS 2, John Lyon 0

**ECOND ROUND**
ldenham 1, Grange 4
rdingly 1, Alleyn's 1
*et; Alleyn's won 3-1 on penalties).*
harterhouse 1, Manchester GS 0
ton 2, Wellingborough 0
orest 1, Wolverhampton GS 0
ampton 0, Bolton 2
ighgate 0, Brentwood 2
ing's School, Chester 0, Millfield 2
alvern 2, Haileybury 2
*et; Malvern won 4-2 on penalties)*
epton 9, Oswestry 0
ancing 1, Hulme GS, Oldham 1
*et; Lancing won 5-3 on penalties).*
atymer Upper 1, St Bede's College 2 *(aet)*
EGS, Blackburn 6, King's School, Ely 0
t Bede's School 2, Bury GS 1
hrewsbury 4, Birkdale 0
'inchester 6, KES, Whitley 0

**THIRD ROUND**
Bolton 0, QEGS, Blackburn 4
Eton 2, Charterhouse 1
Forest 4, Alleyn's 0
Grange 0, Brentwood 3
Malvern 2, Lancing 1
St Bede's College 3, St Bede's School 1
Shrewsbury 0, Millfield 2 *(aet)*
Winchester 1, Repton 6

**FOURTH ROUND**
Eton 1, QEGS, Blackburn 3
Repton 1, Forest 0
St Bede's College 1, Brentwood 2
Millfield 7, Malvern 0

**SEMI-FINALS**
Brentwood 0, Millfield 5
QEGS, Blackburn 4, Repton 0

**FINAL**
(at Leicester City FC)

**QEGS, Blackburn 2** *(Fletcher, Hawthornthwaite)*
**Millfield 2** *(Shaw, Follett) aet*

*QEGS, Blackburn:* F. Fielding; N. Fielding, M. Sharples, M. Fletcher, J. Dunne (O. Dent), N. Pearson (R. Benson), M. Grindrod, G. Jones (R. Hawthornthwaite), R. Woods, N. Nelson, J. O'Keefe.
*Millfield:* B. Brooke; L. Wilson, K. Follett, J. Cook, L. Shaw, A. Kirkham, A. Turner, A. Zaranis, J. Cinicola (S. Bird), J. Llewellyn, L. Irish.
*QEGS, Blackburn won 5-4 on penalties.*
*Referee:* S. Bennett (Kent).

# NATIONAL LEAGUE SYSTEM CUP 2003–04

## IN PARTNERSHIP WITH CARLSBERG

**IRST ROUND**

| | |
|---|---|
| iverpool County Combination v Northern Football Alliance | 1-0 |
| edford & District v Cambridgeshire County | 0-3 |
| idland Football Combination v Central Midlands | 5-2 |
| ssex Intermediate v Hertfordshire Senior County | 6-2 |
| iddlesex County v Kent County | 4-2 |
| orset Premier v Hampshire | 3-0 |

*yes:* Combined Counties Div 1, Gloucestershire County, Mid Cheshire, Northampton, North Berks, Peterborough & District, South Western, Wearside, West Cheshire, Wiltshire.

**ECOND ROUND**

| | |
|---|---|
| iverpool County Combination v Wearside | 3-1 |
| id Cheshire v West Cheshire | 2-0 |
| ambridgeshire County v Northampton | 4-1 |
| idland Football Combination v Peterborough & District | 3-1 |
| ssex Intermediate v North Berks | 5-0 |
| iddlesex County v Combined Counties Div 1 | 3-1 |
| Dorset Premier v South Western | 0-1 |
| Gloucestershire County v Wiltshire | 2-1 |

**THIRD ROUND**

| | |
|---|---|
| Mid Cheshire v Liverpool County Combination | 4-2 |
| Midland Football Combination v Cambridgeshire County | 1-2 |
| Essex Intermediate v Middlesex County | 6-1 |
| South Western v Gloucestershire County | 4-2 |

**SEMI-FINAL**

| | |
|---|---|
| South Western v Mid Cheshire | 1-2 |
| Essex Intermediate v Cambridgeshire County | 0-2 |

**FINAL**
Saturday, 8 May
(at Cambridge United FC)

**Mid Cheshire (1) 2** *(Gahgan 2, Towey 88)*
**Cambridgeshire County (0) 0** 500

# UNIVERSITY FOOTBALL 2003–04

## 120th UNIVERSITY MATCH

(at Upton Park, 13 March 2004)

**Oxford (0) 2, Cambridge (0) 0**

*Oxford:* A. Hill; R. Milburn, N. Light, C. Griffin, M. Addley, J. Cachel (D. McCourt 64), N. Armstrong, T. Batterbee (J. Perkins 90), M. Lowe, D. Walpole (A. Yentob 74), M. Elliot.
*Scorers:* Lowe 2.

*Cambridge:* J. Garrood; G. Devine (T. Hall 78), L. McNally, T. Cairnes, S. Lewis, J. Darby, J. Hughes (H. Hughes 74), D. Harding (M. Chalmers 74), M. Adams, C. Fairbairn, A. Hall.

*Referee:* P. Dowd (Staffordshire).

*Oxford drew level with their 46th win. 28 matches have been drawn.*

## UNIVERSITY OF LONDON UNION MEN'S COMPETITIONS

*(Limited to one game against each member)*

| **Premier Division One** | *P* | *W* | *D* | *L* | *F* | *A* |
|---|---|---|---|---|---|---|
| Queen Mary Westfield College | 11 | 9 | 0 | 2 | 41 | 22 |
| Imperial College | 11 | 8 | 1 | 2 | 34 | 10 |
| University College | 11 | 8 | 0 | 3 | 27 | 10 |
| London School of Economics | 11 | 7 | 1 | 3 | 20 | 14 |
| Royal Holloway College | 11 | 5 | 2 | 4 | 24 | 13 |
| King's College | 11 | 5 | 2 | 4 | 16 | 25 |
| Imperial College School of Medicine | 11 | 4 | 2 | 5 | 12 | 20 |
| R Free, UC & Middx Hospitals MS | 11 | 4 | 0 | 7 | 18 | 34 |
| School of Oriental & African Studies | 11 | 3 | 2 | 6 | 23 | 30 |
| St Barts & R. London Hospitals MC | 11 | 3 | 0 | 8 | 12 | 25 |
| Imperial College Res | 11 | 2 | 2 | 7 | 19 | 22 |
| Guy's, King's & St. Thomas's MS | 11 | 1 | 2 | 8 | 9 | 30 |

| **Premier Division Two** | *P* | *W* | *D* | *L* | *F* | *A* |
|---|---|---|---|---|---|---|
| London School of Economics Res | 11 | 10 | 1 | 0 | 43 | 6 |
| University College Res | 11 | 9 | 1 | 1 | 32 | 8 |
| Royal Holloway College 3rd | 11 | 6 | 2 | 3 | 25 | 19 |
| Royal Holloway College Res | 11 | 6 | 1 | 4 | 15 | 8 |
| St George's Hospital MS | 10 | 6 | 0 | 4 | 30 | 23 |
| Imperial College 3rd | 11 | 5 | 1 | 5 | 32 | 20 |
| Imperial College Sch of Med Res | 11 | 4 | 3 | 4 | 22 | 26 |
| University College 3rd | 11 | 3 | 1 | 7 | 13 | 23 |
| Queen Mary Westfeld College Res | 11 | 3 | 0 | 8 | 17 | 35 |
| St George's Hospital MS Res | 9 | 2 | 1 | 6 | 16 | 28 |
| Birkbeck College Students | 11 | 2 | 1 | 8 | 10 | 39 |
| King's College Res | 10 | 2 | 0 | 8 | 9 | 29 |

*(Played as conventional Leagues)*

| **Division 1** | *P* | *W* | *D* | *L* | *F* | *A* |
|---|---|---|---|---|---|---|
| Royal Holloway College 4th | 22 | 19 | 3 | 0 | 43 | 12 |
| Goldsmiths' College | 22 | 17 | 1 | 4 | 60 | 38 |
| Guy's, King's, St. Thomas's MS Res | 22 | 13 | 3 | 6 | 77 | 35 |
| London School of Economics 4th | 22 | 10 | 3 | 9 | 43 | 28 |
| University College 4th | 22 | 10 | 3 | 9 | 44 | 44 |
| Imperial College 4th | 22 | 10 | 2 | 10 | 48 | 36 |
| Guy's, King's, St. Thomas's MS 3rd | 22 | 9 | 3 | 10 | 32 | 45 |
| R Free, UC & Middx Hosp MS 3rd | 22 | 9 | 2 | 11 | 38 | 41 |
| London School of Economics 3rd | 22 | 7 | 3 | 12 | 61 | 54 |
| R Free, UC & Middx Hosp MS Res | 22 | 5 | 7 | 10 | 23 | 39 |
| King's College 3rd | 22 | 5 | 3 | 14 | 46 | 49 |
| Goldsmiths' College Res | 22 | 1 | 1 | 20 | 38 | 132 |

| **Division 2** | *P* | *W* | *D* | *L* | *F* | *A* |
|---|---|---|---|---|---|---|
| University College 5th | 22 | 18 | 3 | 1 | 92 | 29 |
| Royal Veterinary College | 22 | 16 | 4 | 2 | 78 | 27 |
| Royal Holloway College 5th | 22 | 15 | 3 | 4 | 59 | 30 |
| Imperial College 5th | 22 | 14 | 2 | 6 | 53 | 29 |
| Imperial College (R. School of Mines) | 22 | 13 | 3 | 6 | 66 | 37 |
| London School of Economics 5th | 22 | 9 | 5 | 8 | 42 | 35 |
| King's College 4th | 22 | 8 | 0 | 14 | 52 | 53 |
| Imperial College Sch of Med Res 3rd | 22 | 6 | 4 | 12 | 29 | 45 |
| St Barts & R. London Hosps MC Res | 22 | 5 | 3 | 14 | 35 | 64 |
| St Barts & R. London Hosps MC 3rd | 22 | 5 | 0 | 17 | 21 | 73 |
| R Free, UC & Middx Hosp MS 4th | 22 | 5 | 0 | 17 | 27 | 81 |
| Imperial College Sch of Med 4th | 22 | 4 | 1 | 17 | 23 | 74 |

**Division 3**
10 teams – Won by University College 7th

**Division 4**
11 teams – Won by London School of Economics 7th

**IALLENGE CUP**
ondon School of Economics 2 Royal Holloway College 1

**:SERVES' CHALLENGE CUP**
ng's College 6th 0 University College 2

**RESERVES' PLATE**
Goldsmiths' College 2 Royal Holloway College 4th 0

**VASE**
Royal Veterinary College 2 Royal Holloway College 5th 1

## UNIVERSITY OF LONDON UNION WOMEN'S LEAGUES

| emier Division | P | W | D | L | F | A | Pts |
|---|---|---|---|---|---|---|---|
| iiversity College | 10 | 9 | 1 | 0 | 42 | 11 | 28 |
| ondon School of Economics | 10 | 6 | 0 | 4 | 27 | 16 | 18 |
| ueen Mary Westfield College | 10 | 5 | 2 | 3 | 36 | 23 | 17 |
| iy's, King's & St.Thomas's MS | 10 | 5 | 0 | 5 | 33 | 29 | 15 |
| iperial College | 10 | 3 | 1 | 6 | 19 | 37 | 10 |
| ng's College | 10 | 0 | 0 | 10 | 8 | 49 | 0 |

**vision 1**
eams – Won by Royal Holloway College

**vision 2**
eams – Won by R Free, UC & Middx Hosp MS

## LONDON UNIVERSITY REPRESENTATIVE XI

| | | |
|---|---|---|
| Brunel University | Lost | 0–3 |
| Oxford University | Lost | 0–1 |
| Amateur Football Combination | Drawn | 0–0 |
| Amateur Football Alliance | Lost | 0–1 |
| v United Hospitals | Drawn | 1–1 |
| v Arthurian League | Lost | 0–3 |
| v Southern Amateur League | Won | 4–2 |

## BRITISH UNIVERSITIES SPORTS ASSOCIATION CHAMPIONSHIP

**EN'S QUARTER-FINALS**
ith 0 Edge Hill 1
W Swansea 2 Brunel W London 1
oughborough 6 Exeter 0
effield Hallam 1 Nottingham 1
*'ottingham won 5-4 on penalties)*

**:MI-FINALS**
lge Hill 1 UW Swansea 2
ottingham 0 Loughborough 2

**NAL (AT STEVENAGE BOROUGH)**
oughborough 1 UW Swansea 0

**ATE**
iester 4 Oxford Brookes 4
*'hester won 4-2 on penalties)*

**IIELD**
linburgh 0 Central Lancashire 1

**WOMEN'S FINAL (AT STEVENAGE BOROUGH)**
Loughborough 2 Bath 0

**PLATE**
Glasgow 4 Derby 1

**SHIELD**
St Mark & St John 3 Abertay 1

# FA PREMIER RESERVE LEAGUES 2003–04

## FA PREMIER RESERVE LEAGUE – NORTH SECTION

| | P | W | D | L | F | A | GD | Pts |
|---|---|---|---|---|---|---|---|---|
| Aston Villa | 26 | 17 | 5 | 4 | 55 | 31 | +24 | 56 |
| Liverpool | 26 | 14 | 8 | 4 | 41 | 21 | +20 | 50 |
| Manchester U | 26 | 13 | 8 | 5 | 55 | 39 | +16 | 47 |
| Newcastle U | 26 | 13 | 4 | 9 | 50 | 42 | +8 | 43 |
| Manchester C | 26 | 11 | 8 | 7 | 34 | 24 | +10 | 41 |
| Blackburn R | 26 | 11 | 6 | 9 | 49 | 45 | +4 | 39 |
| Everton | 26 | 10 | 8 | 8 | 37 | 33 | +4 | 38 |
| Leeds U | 26 | 10 | 7 | 9 | 40 | 40 | 0 | 37 |
| Middlesbrough | 26 | 8 | 10 | 8 | 33 | 33 | 0 | 34 |
| Sunderland | 26 | 8 | 7 | 11 | 37 | 46 | –9 | 31 |
| WBA | 26 | 8 | 6 | 12 | 36 | 48 | –12 | 30 |
| Birmingham C | 26 | 6 | 5 | 15 | 28 | 42 | –14 | 23 |
| Wolverhampton W | 26 | 4 | 6 | 16 | 27 | 49 | –22 | 18 |
| Bolton W | 26 | 3 | 4 | 19 | 22 | 51 | –29 | 13 |

| Leading Goalscorers | |
|---|---|
| Simon Johnson (Leeds U) | 15 |
| Proctor (Sunderland) | 13 |
| Mellor (Liverpool) | 10 |
| Johnson (Blackburn R) | 9 |
| Nardiello (Manchester U) | 9 |
| Chopra (Newcastle U) | 9 |
| Moore L (Aston Villa) | 8 |
| Chadwick (Everton) | 8 |
| Elliott (Manchester C) | 8 |
| Wright-Phillips, B (Manchester C) | 8 |
| Brown (WBA) | 8 |
| Moore S (Aston Villa) | 7 |
| Figueroa (Birmingham C) | 7 |
| Osman (Liverpool) | 7 |
| Guy (Newcastle U) | 7 |

**Aston Villa League appearances**
*(full appearances and substitutes):* Aaritalo 1 + 5; Agbonlohor 1 + 5; Allback 3; Amoo 21; Balaban 1; Bewers 19; Brazi + 2; Cahill 13 + 4; Cooke 15; Cormell 2 + 5; Crouch 5; Davis 16; De la Cruz 3; Delaney 3; Dublin 7; Edwards Enckelman 1; Foley-Sheridan 15 + 3; Gardner 0 + 2; Grant 1; Hadji 8; Henderson 6; Hitzlsperger 3; Hynes 12 + Jackman 10; Kachloul 1; Kinsella 11; Marshall 0 + 1; Moore L 18 + 4; Moore S 15; Morgan 0 + 1; Nix 3 + 6; O'Conn 12; Paul 0 + 4; Postma 19; Ridgewell 14 + 1; Troest 1 + 1; Tshimanga 1 + 2; Vassell 1; Ward 7 + 3; Whittingham 8.
**Goals:** Moore L 8, Moore S 7, Cooke 5, Hynes 5, Crouch 4, Hadji 4, Foley-Sheridan 3, Davis 2, Dublin 2, Kinsella Ridgewell 2, Ward 2, Whittingham 2, Aaritalo 1, Allback 1, Balaban 1, Vassell 1.

**North Section**
**Results**
**2003–2004**

| | Aston Villa | Birmingham C | Blackburn R | Bolton W | Everton | Leeds U | Liverpool | Manchester C | Manchester U | Middlesbrough | Newcastle U | Sunderland | WBA | |
|---|---|---|---|---|---|---|---|---|---|---|---|---|---|---|
| Aston Villa | — | 1-0 | 4-2 | 2-0 | 6-2 | 1-2 | 3-1 | 2-0 | 1-1 | 2-1 | 3-1 | 1-1 | 5-2 | 2 |
| Birmingham C | 2-2 | — | 0-4 | 2-1 | 1-1 | 3-1 | 0-1 | 1-2 | 1-2 | 1-3 | 3-1 | 0-2 | 3-0 | 2 |
| Blackburn R | 1-3 | 3-0 | — | 1-1 | 1-0 | 1-2 | 0-2 | 1-0 | 2-2 | 1-2 | 3-6 | 1-1 | 5-3 | 1 |
| Bolton W | 1-3 | 2-0 | 0-3 | — | 1-4 | 1-3 | 2-2 | 0-2 | 1-2 | 0-2 | 2-3 | 2-1 | 1-1 | 0 |
| Everton | 2-2 | 1-0 | 1-1 | 1-0 | — | 1-1 | 0-2 | 3-0 | 3-2 | 0-0 | 2-4 | 0-2 | 1-1 | 5 |
| Leeds U | 0-1 | 2-1 | 1-3 | 1-0 | 0-0 | — | 3-1 | 1-3 | 2-2 | 1-2 | 2-2 | 2-3 | 0-2 | 3 |
| Liverpool | 3-2 | 0-0 | 1-1 | 3-1 | 1-0 | 1-1 | — | 0-0 | 0-1 | 0-0 | 1-1 | 5-1 | 2-0 | 2 |
| Manchester C | 2-1 | 1-0 | 3-0 | 2-0 | 3-2 | 0-0 | 0-1 | — | 1-1 | 0-0 | 0-1 | 3-0 | 1-1 | 1 |
| Manchester U | 3-0 | 3-1 | 0-2 | 2-0 | 1-2 | 2-1 | 1-1 | 3-3 | — | 2-3 | 2-1 | 2-2 | 2-0 | 2 |
| Middlesbrough | 0-1 | 1-3 | 2-4 | 0-0 | 1-2 | 3-4 | 0-2 | 1-0 | 2-2 | — | 1-2 | 3-1 | 2-1 | 0 |
| Newcastle U | 1-2 | 3-1 | 4-0 | 2-3 | 0-0 | 3-1 | 1-0 | 1-3 | 0-4 | 2-2 | — | 3-1 | 3-0 | 1 |
| Sunderland | 1-1 | 3-0 | 3-3 | 1-0 | 1-2 | 0-2 | 0-2 | 1-0 | 5-3 | 1-1 | 1-3 | — | 1-2 | 0 |
| WBA | 0-1 | 0-0 | 1-2 | 3-1 | 1-0 | 1-2 | 2-6 | 2-2 | 2-4 | 0-0 | 3-1 | 4-1 | — | 2 |
| Wolverhampton W | 1-3 | 0-3 | 0-3 | 4-2 | 1-2 | 0-2 | 0-1 | 0-2 | 3-4 | 1-1 | 2-0 | 1-3 | 1-2 | [illegible] |

## FA PREMIER RESERVE LEAGUE – SOUTH SECTION

| | P | W | D | L | F | A | GD | Pts |
|---|---|---|---|---|---|---|---|---|
| Charlton Ath | 28 | 17 | 6 | 5 | 46 | 19 | +27 | 57 |
| Derby Co | 28 | 13 | 10 | 5 | 46 | 31 | +15 | 49 |
| Southampton | 28 | 14 | 6 | 8 | 43 | 28 | +15 | 48 |
| West Ham U | 28 | 12 | 8 | 8 | 37 | 35 | +2 | 44 |
| Tottenham H | 28 | 11 | 9 | 8 | 42 | 35 | +7 | 42 |
| Arsenal | 28 | 10 | 9 | 9 | 41 | 35 | +6 | 39 |
| Chelsea | 28 | 11 | 6 | 11 | 37 | 33 | +4 | 39 |
| Leicester C | 28 | 9 | 11 | 8 | 34 | 40 | –6 | 38 |
| Coventry C | 28 | 9 | 10 | 9 | 38 | 40 | –2 | 37 |
| Wimbledon | 28 | 9 | 5 | 14 | 35 | 47 | –12 | 32 |
| Watford | 28 | 6 | 12 | 10 | 32 | 40 | –8 | 30 |
| Portsmouth | 28 | 6 | 11 | 11 | 36 | 39 | –3 | 29 |
| Nottingham F | 28 | 6 | 11 | 11 | 33 | 41 | –8 | 29 |
| Ipswich T | 28 | 8 | 4 | 16 | 34 | 44 | –10 | 28 |
| Fulham | 28 | 6 | 8 | 14 | 27 | 54 | –27 | 26 |

| Leading Goalscorers | |
|---|---|
| Kneissl (Chelsea) | 12 |
| Bowditch (Ipswich T) | 9 |
| Aliadiere (Arsenal) | 8 |
| Labarthe (Derby Co) | 8 |
| Davies (Southampton) | 8 |
| Jephott (Coventry C) | 7 |
| Blackstock (Southampton) | 7 |
| Griffit (Southampton) | 7 |
| Junior (Derby Co) | 6 |
| McLeod (Derby Co) | 6 |
| Sava (Fulham) | 6 |
| Armstrong (Ipswich T) | 6 |
| Westcarr (Nottingham F) | 6 |
| Barnard (Tottenham H) | 6 |
| Pearson (West Ham U) | 6 |

**arlton Athletic League appearances**
*ll appearances and substitutes):* Ashton 7 + 2; Bailey 2; Bart-Williams 3; Bartlett 4; Beckford 6 + 7; Campbell-Ryce Cole 3 + 1; Cottrell 2; De Bolla 3 + 2; Deane 14 + 2; Di Canio 2; Eastwood 2; Elliot 0 + 1; Euell 1; Fish 3; Fortune 4; ller 4 + 5; Gross 17; Hughes 17 +1; Hunt 3; Jackson 3 + 5; Johansson 6; John 0 + 2; Kamara 0 + 2; Kiely 1; Kishishev 1; nchesky 2; Leite 16; Lisbie 4; Long 9 + 6; McCafferty 26; Ndombe 0 + 1; Perry 1; Phillips 0 + 2; Howell 7; Ricketts 15 ; Rowett 4; Royce 11; Rufus 4; Sam 11 + 1; Sankofa 20; Stuart 5; Svensson 2; Thanda 1 + 3; Thomas 6; Turner M 22; rner A 1; Varney 11 + 3; Walker 1 + 2; Ward 0 + 1; Wilson 1 + 3; Young 2.
**als:** Johansson 5, Bartlett 4, Varney 4, Campbell-Ryce 3, Di Canio 3, Stuart 3, Thomas 3, Deane 2, Hughes 2, Sam 2, kofa 2, Svensson 2, Turner M 2, Beckford 1, Cole 1, De Bolla 1, Fortune 1, Hunt 1, Lisbie 1, Long 1, Powell 1, Rowett 1.

**uth Section**

**sults**

**)3–2004**

| | Arsenal | Charlton Ath | Chelsea | Coventry C | Derby Co | Fulham | Ipswich T | Leicester C | Nottingham F | Portsmouth | Southampton | Tottenham H | Watford | West Ham U | Wimbledon |
|---|---|---|---|---|---|---|---|---|---|---|---|---|---|---|---|
| senal | — | 0-0 | 2-1 | 2-2 | 4-0 | 1-1 | 0-2 | 3-0 | 1-1 | 1-0 | 0-1 | 4-0 | 0-2 | 3-5 | 1-4 |
| arlton Ath | 0-0 | — | 2-0 | 2-1 | 1-2 | 4-0 | 3-1 | 5-0 | 3-2 | 0-3 | 1-0 | 1-2 | 0-0 | 0-0 | 4-1 |
| elsea | 3-2 | 0-1 | — | 1-1 | 1-2 | 1-0 | 4-0 | 1-1 | 0-0 | 3-1 | 0-1 | 2-0 | 1-0 | 1-2 | 0-2 |
| ventry C | 0-2 | 0-3 | 2-0 | — | 2-0 | 4-0 | 1-0 | 0-2 | 1-3 | 3-2 | 0-2 | 3-1 | 3-1 | 1-1 | 1-1 |
| rby Co | 2-0 | 0-1 | 0-0 | 2-0 | — | 5-5 | 2-2 | 1-1 | 1-1 | 1-1 | 2-2 | 2-2 | 1-1 | 3-0 | 5-0 |
| ham | 1-3 | 1-1 | 0-3 | 1-1 | 0-2 | — | 1-6 | 2-0 | 0-0 | 2-1 | 1-3 | 1-0 | 2-4 | 1-0 | 1-0 |
| wich T | 1-4 | 0-3 | 0-1 | 1-0 | 0-1 | 1-0 | — | 1-1 | 5-1 | 0-0 | 2-0 | 2-3 | 1-1 | 0-1 | 0-1 |
| cester C | 2-2 | 2-1 | 3-2 | 0-0 | 0-3 | 3-0 | 3-0 | — | 1-0 | 1-1 | 0-1 | 1-1 | 2-1 | 3-3 | 1-0 |
| ttingham F | 2-3 | 0-1 | 0-2 | 1-1 | 1-3 | 1-1 | 3-2 | 2-2 | — | 3-2 | 3-0 | 0-0 | 0-1 | 1-1 | 3-2 |
| tsmouth | 1-1 | 3-1 | 4-1 | 1-1 | 0-2 | 1-1 | 1-3 | 0-1 | 1-0 | — | 2-1 | 0-0 | 0-2 | 5-1 | 2-2 |
| uthampton | 2-0 | 0-2 | 3-3 | 1-1 | 3-0 | 3-0 | 2-0 | 3-1 | 3-0 | 1-1 | — | 1-1 | 4-0 | 2-1 | 0-1 |
| ttenham H | 0-2 | 0-1 | 1-1 | 5-0 | 1-2 | 1-2 | 3-0 | 2-1 | 1-1 | 2-0 | 3-1 | — | 3-3 | 2-1 | 3-0 |
| tford | 0-0 | 1-1 | 1-3 | 1-3 | 0-1 | 2-2 | 0-3 | 0-0 | 2-2 | 2-2 | 2-0 | 1-1 | — | 0-1 | 2-2 |
| st Ham U | 2-0 | 0-2 | 0-1 | 3-3 | 0-0 | 1-0 | 2-0 | 1-1 | 1-0 | 2-0 | 1-1 | 1-2 | 1-0 | — | 3-2 |
| mbledon | 0-0 | 0-2 | 2-1 | 1-3 | 2-1 | 2-1 | 2-1 | 4-1 | 0-2 | 1-1 | 0-2 | 1-2 | 1-2 | 1-2 | — |

# PONTIN'S RESERVE LEAGUES

## PONTIN'S HOLIDAYS LEAGUE

### EMIER DIVISION

| | *P* | *W* | *D* | *L* | *F* | *A* | *GD* | *Pts* |
|---|---|---|---|---|---|---|---|---|
| ke C | 22 | 13 | 4 | 5 | 45 | 31 | +14 | 43 |
| nmere R | 22 | 13 | 3 | 6 | 42 | 32 | +10 | 42 |
| lsall | 22 | 12 | 5 | 5 | 38 | 18 | +20 | 41 |
| effield U | 22 | 11 | 4 | 7 | 28 | 26 | +2 | 37 |
| ll C | 22 | 9 | 6 | 7 | 39 | 32 | +7 | 33 |
| dford C | 22 | 6 | 9 | 7 | 30 | 28 | +2 | 27 |
| effield W | 22 | 8 | 3 | 11 | 32 | 33 | −1 | 27 |
| ston NE | 22 | 6 | 7 | 9 | 39 | 34 | +5 | 25 |
| nsley | 22 | 6 | 7 | 9 | 31 | 37 | −6 | 25 |
| therham U | 22 | 7 | 4 | 11 | 35 | 56 | −21 | 25 |
| ddersfield T* | 22 | 6 | 6 | 10 | 28 | 34 | −6 | 24 |
| rnley* | 22 | 4 | 4 | 14 | 26 | 52 | −26 | 16 |

### VISION ONE WEST

| | *P* | *W* | *D* | *L* | *F* | *A* | *GD* | *Pts* |
|---|---|---|---|---|---|---|---|---|
| gan Ath | 18 | 11 | 3 | 4 | 43 | 25 | +18 | 36 |
| ckport Co | 18 | 10 | 3 | 5 | 31 | 23 | +8 | 33 |
| lisle U | 18 | 10 | 2 | 6 | 38 | 35 | +3 | 32 |
| ckpool | 18 | 7 | 5 | 6 | 29 | 25 | +4 | 26 |
| lham Ath | 18 | 7 | 5 | 6 | 24 | 24 | 0 | 26 |
| ry | 18 | 7 | 3 | 8 | 22 | 25 | −3 | 24 |
| rewsbury T | 18 | 6 | 2 | 10 | 36 | 31 | +5 | 20 |
| cclesfield T | 18 | 4 | 8 | 6 | 20 | 27 | −7 | 20 |
| exham | 18 | 5 | 4 | 9 | 36 | 46 | −10 | 19 |
| chdale | 18 | 5 | 1 | 12 | 25 | 43 | −18 | 16 |

### VISION ONE EAST

| | *P* | *W* | *D* | *L* | *F* | *A* | *GD* | *Pts* |
|---|---|---|---|---|---|---|---|---|
| rtlepool U | 18 | 12 | 4 | 2 | 41 | 18 | +23 | 40 |
| wcastle U | 18 | 9 | 3 | 6 | 38 | 28 | +10 | 30 |
| nthorpe U | 18 | 7 | 8 | 3 | 22 | 22 | 0 | 29 |
| ston U | 18 | 8 | 0 | 10 | 34 | 33 | +1 | 24 |
| imsby T | 18 | 5 | 7 | 6 | 28 | 27 | +1 | 22 |
| tts Co | 18 | 6 | 4 | 8 | 25 | 26 | −1 | 22 |
| lington | 18 | 6 | 4 | 8 | 29 | 35 | −5 | 22 |
| ncaster R | 18 | 4 | 8 | 6 | 20 | 25 | −5 | 20 |
| rk C | 18 | 4 | 7 | 7 | 24 | 34 | −10 | 19 |
| coln C | 18 | 3 | 7 | 8 | 23 | 37 | −14 | 16 |

## PONTIN'S HOLIDAYS COMBINATION

### CENTRAL AND EAST DIVISION

| | *P* | *W* | *D* | *L* | *F* | *A* | *GD* | *Pts* |
|---|---|---|---|---|---|---|---|---|
| Reading | 14 | 12 | 1 | 1 | 48 | 11 | +37 | 37 |
| Gillingham | 14 | 10 | 2 | 2 | 27 | 9 | +18 | 32 |
| Northampton T | 14 | 8 | 3 | 3 | 33 | 25 | +8 | 27 |
| Millwall | 14 | 8 | 3 | 3 | 31 | 25 | +6 | 27 |
| Cambridge U | 14 | 7 | 2 | 5 | 29 | 24 | +5 | 23 |
| Crystal Palace | 14 | 6 | 3 | 5 | 25 | 18 | +7 | 21 |
| Brighton & HA | 14 | 6 | 2 | 6 | 34 | 24 | +10 | 20 |
| QPR | 14 | 6 | 2 | 6 | 16 | 22 | −6 | 20 |
| Peterborough U | 14 | 4 | 7 | 3 | 31 | 25 | +6 | 19 |
| Colchester U | 14 | 5 | 2 | 7 | 15 | 13 | +2 | 17 |
| Norwich C | 14 | 5 | 2 | 7 | 21 | 23 | −2 | 17 |
| Wycombe W | 14 | 3 | 4 | 7 | 14 | 22 | −8 | 13 |
| Brentford | 14 | 1 | 7 | 6 | 22 | 33 | −11 | 10 |
| Aldershot T | 14 | 2 | 1 | 11 | 16 | 66 | −50 | 7 |
| Southend U | 14 | 1 | 1 | 12 | 7 | 29 | −22 | 4 |

*Southend U awarded 1-0 win v Aldershot T following late postponement.*

### WALES AND WEST DIVISION

| | *P* | *W* | *D* | *L* | *F* | *A* | *GD* | *Pts* |
|---|---|---|---|---|---|---|---|---|
| Cardiff C | 18 | 11 | 3 | 4 | 35 | 20 | +15 | 36 |
| Plymouth Arg | 18 | 11 | 2 | 5 | 49 | 21 | +28 | 35 |
| Yeovil T | 18 | 9 | 5 | 4 | 53 | 34 | +19 | 32 |
| Bristol C | 18 | 6 | 7 | 5 | 37 | 27 | +10 | 25 |
| Bournemouth | 18 | 5 | 7 | 6 | 22 | 34 | −12 | 22 |
| Bristol R | 18 | 6 | 3 | 9 | 33 | 37 | −4 | 21 |
| Swansea C | 18 | 5 | 5 | 8 | 24 | 36 | −12 | 20 |
| Swindon T | 18 | 4 | 7 | 7 | 25 | 34 | −9 | 19 |
| Cheltenham T | 18 | 4 | 6 | 8 | 30 | 36 | −6 | 18 |
| Oxford U | 18 | 5 | 3 | 10 | 31 | 60 | −29 | 18 |

*Swansea C awarded 1-0 win v Bristol C following late postponement.*

# FA ACADEMY UNDER-19 LEAGUE 2003–04

| GROUP A | P | W | D | L | F | A | GD | Pts |
|---|---|---|---|---|---|---|---|---|
| Manchester C | 26 | 20 | 2 | 4 | 58 | 24 | +34 | 62 |
| Blackburn R | 26 | 13 | 7 | 6 | 42 | 25 | +17 | 46 |
| Liverpool | 26 | 12 | 9 | 5 | 46 | 36 | +10 | 45 |
| Crewe Alex | 26 | 10 | 9 | 7 | 40 | 36 | +4 | 39 |
| Everton | 26 | 10 | 8 | 8 | 36 | 37 | –1 | 38 |
| Manchester U | 26 | 10 | 7 | 9 | 38 | 36 | +2 | 37 |
| Wolverhampton W | 26 | 9 | 8 | 9 | 38 | 32 | +6 | 35 |
| Bolton W | 26 | 8 | 4 | 14 | 39 | 52 | –13 | 28 |
| Stoke C | 26 | 4 | 7 | 15 | 37 | 63 | –26 | 19 |
| Sheffield W | 26 | 4 | 6 | 16 | 31 | 50 | –19 | 18 |

| GROUP B | P | W | D | L | F | A | GD | Pts |
|---|---|---|---|---|---|---|---|---|
| Sheffield U | 26 | 16 | 5 | 5 | 52 | 29 | +23 | 53 |
| Middlesbrough | 26 | 15 | 3 | 8 | 54 | 36 | +18 | 48 |
| Leeds U | 26 | 12 | 5 | 9 | 36 | 27 | +9 | 41 |
| Newcastle U | 26 | 13 | 2 | 11 | 49 | 45 | +4 | 41 |
| Sunderland | 26 | 12 | 5 | 9 | 46 | 42 | +4 | 41 |
| Nottingham F | 26 | 11 | 3 | 12 | 41 | 38 | +3 | 36 |
| Huddersfield T | 26 | 7 | 5 | 14 | 35 | 45 | –10 | 26 |
| Derby Co | 26 | 6 | 8 | 12 | 38 | 52 | –14 | 26 |
| Barnsley | 26 | 6 | 5 | 15 | 34 | 59 | –25 | 23 |

| GROUP C | P | W | D | L | F | A | GD |
|---|---|---|---|---|---|---|---|
| Arsenal | 26 | 16 | 4 | 6 | 58 | 29 | +29 |
| Chelsea | 26 | 12 | 3 | 11 | 40 | 33 | +7 |
| Aston Villa | 26 | 12 | 2 | 12 | 54 | 48 | +6 |
| Birmingham C | 26 | 10 | 7 | 9 | 30 | 24 | +6 |
| Leicester C | 26 | 10 | 5 | 11 | 40 | 43 | –3 |
| Watford | 26 | 10 | 5 | 11 | 38 | 51 | –13 |
| Reading | 26 | 9 | 4 | 13 | 36 | 40 | –4 |
| Fulham | 26 | 4 | 7 | 15 | 22 | 52 | –30 |
| Bristol C | 26 | 3 | 5 | 18 | 37 | 64 | –27 |

| GROUP D | P | W | D | L | F | A | GD |
|---|---|---|---|---|---|---|---|
| Southampton | 26 | 20 | 5 | 1 | 58 | 22 | +36 |
| Charlton Ath | 26 | 16 | 3 | 7 | 44 | 34 | +10 |
| West Ham U | 26 | 13 | 5 | 8 | 51 | 36 | +15 |
| Millwall | 26 | 9 | 8 | 9 | 48 | 44 | +4 |
| Tottenham H | 26 | 10 | 3 | 13 | 27 | 38 | –11 |
| Norwich C | 26 | 9 | 4 | 13 | 46 | 55 | –9 |
| Wimbledon | 26 | 9 | 3 | 14 | 23 | 40 | –17 |
| Ipswich T | 26 | 7 | 8 | 11 | 34 | 43 | –9 |
| Crystal Palace | 26 | 7 | 5 | 14 | 27 | 43 | –16 |

# FA ACADEMY UNDER-17 LEAGUE 2003–04

| GROUP A | P | W | D | L | F | A | GD | Pts |
|---|---|---|---|---|---|---|---|---|
| Everton | 26 | 17 | 5 | 4 | 52 | 24 | +28 | 56 |
| Blackburn R | 26 | 16 | 4 | 6 | 80 | 38 | +42 | 52 |
| Manchester U | 26 | 14 | 7 | 5 | 50 | 36 | +14 | 49 |
| Liverpool | 26 | 11 | 7 | 8 | 53 | 43 | +10 | 40 |
| Manchester C | 26 | 12 | 2 | 12 | 48 | 55 | –7 | 38 |
| Crewe Alex | 26 | 6 | 7 | 13 | 46 | 58 | –12 | 25 |

| GROUP B | P | W | D | L | F | A | GD | Pts |
|---|---|---|---|---|---|---|---|---|
| Leeds U | 26 | 12 | 7 | 7 | 45 | 30 | +15 | 43 |
| Sheffield U | 26 | 10 | 8 | 8 | 46 | 47 | –1 | 38 |
| Nottingham F | 26 | 9 | 6 | 11 | 42 | 41 | +1 | 33 |
| Middlesbrough | 26 | 8 | 6 | 12 | 45 | 52 | –7 | 30 |
| Wolverhampton W | 26 | 6 | 5 | 15 | 28 | 64 | –36 | 23 |
| Derby Co | 26 | 4 | 7 | 15 | 36 | 58 | –22 | 19 |

| GROUP C | P | W | D | L | F | A | GD |
|---|---|---|---|---|---|---|---|
| Aston Villa | 26 | 16 | 5 | 5 | 90 | 41 | +49 |
| Leicester C | 26 | 14 | 5 | 7 | 59 | 54 | +5 |
| Coventry C | 26 | 12 | 6 | 8 | 55 | 46 | +9 |
| Arsenal | 26 | 12 | 6 | 8 | 39 | 40 | –1 |
| Birmingham C | 26 | 11 | 7 | 8 | 52 | 47 | +5 |
| Bristol C | 26 | 9 | 3 | 14 | 55 | 62 | –7 |
| Fulham | 26 | 7 | 6 | 13 | 37 | 56 | –19 |
| Watford | 26 | 5 | 5 | 16 | 38 | 71 | –33 |

| GROUP D | P | W | D | L | F | A | GD |
|---|---|---|---|---|---|---|---|
| Southampton | 26 | 17 | 6 | 3 | 79 | 43 | +36 |
| Tottenham H | 26 | 13 | 6 | 7 | 59 | 44 | +15 |
| West Ham U | 26 | 13 | 5 | 8 | 57 | 38 | +19 |
| Charlton Ath | 26 | 10 | 6 | 10 | 48 | 48 | 0 |
| Millwall | 26 | 10 | 5 | 11 | 44 | 48 | –4 |
| Crystal Palace | 26 | 5 | 4 | 17 | 26 | 64 | –38 |
| Reading | 26 | 5 | 3 | 18 | 34 | 69 | –35 |
| Wimbledon | 26 | 3 | 5 | 18 | 29 | 55 | –26 |

# FOOTBALL LEAGUE YOUTH TABLES 2003–04

## THE UMBRO ISOTONIC UNDER-19s FOOTBALL LEAGUE

### DIVISION ONE NORTH

| | P | W | D | L | F | A | GD | Pts |
|---|---|---|---|---|---|---|---|---|
| Oldham Ath | 9 | 6 | 2 | 1 | 22 | 11 | +11 | 20 |
| Tranmere R | 9 | 6 | 1 | 2 | 25 | 11 | +14 | 19 |
| Bradford C | 9 | 5 | 2 | 2 | 20 | 11 | +9 | 17 |
| Port Vale | 9 | 4 | 2 | 3 | 16 | 15 | +1 | 14 |
| Preston NE | 9 | 3 | 1 | 5 | 14 | 13 | +1 | 10 |
| Grimsby T | 9 | 3 | 1 | 5 | 10 | 15 | –5 | 10 |
| Rotherham U | 9 | 3 | 1 | 5 | 16 | 23 | –7 | 10 |
| Wigan Ath | 9 | 2 | 3 | 4 | 10 | 14 | –4 | 9 |
| Lincoln C | 9 | 2 | 3 | 4 | 13 | 22 | –9 | 9 |
| Notts Co | 9 | 2 | 2 | 5 | 10 | 21 | –11 | 8 |

### DIVISION TWO NORTH

| | P | W | D | L | F | A | GD | Pts |
|---|---|---|---|---|---|---|---|---|
| Stockport Co | 8 | 6 | 2 | 0 | 21 | 7 | +14 | 20 |
| Chesterfield | 8 | 6 | 1 | 1 | 21 | 11 | +10 | 19 |
| Carlisle U | 8 | 4 | 2 | 2 | 14 | 14 | 0 | 14 |
| Blackpool | 8 | 4 | 1 | 3 | 12 | 11 | +1 | 13 |
| Scunthorpe U | 8 | 4 | 0 | 4 | 12 | 8 | +4 | 12 |
| Shrewsbury T | 8 | 3 | 0 | 5 | 13 | 16 | –3 | 9 |
| Hartlepool U | 8 | 2 | 2 | 4 | 15 | 19 | –4 | 8 |
| Hull C | 8 | 0 | 4 | 4 | 10 | 18 | –8 | 4 |
| Mansfield T | 8 | 0 | 2 | 6 | 7 | 21 | –14 | 2 |

### DIVISION THREE NORTH

| | P | W | D | L | F | A | GD | Pts |
|---|---|---|---|---|---|---|---|---|
| Bury | 8 | 6 | 1 | 1 | 15 | 5 | +10 | 19 |
| Burnley | 8 | 6 | 0 | 2 | 22 | 7 | +15 | 18 |
| York C | 8 | 6 | 0 | 2 | 21 | 7 | +14 | 18 |
| Rochdale | 8 | 4 | 0 | 4 | 10 | 11 | –1 | 12 |
| Macclesfield T | 7 | 3 | 1 | 3 | 9 | 9 | 0 | 10 |
| Wrexham | 8 | 3 | 0 | 5 | 11 | 11 | 0 | 9 |
| Chester C | 8 | 3 | 0 | 5 | 10 | 16 | –6 | 9 |
| Halifax T | 7 | 2 | 1 | 4 | 8 | 24 | –16 | 7 |
| Darlington | 8 | 0 | 1 | 7 | 5 | 21 | –16 | 1 |

### DIVISION ONE SOUTH

| | P | W | D | L | F | A | GD | Pts |
|---|---|---|---|---|---|---|---|---|
| Cambridge U | 8 | 5 | 2 | 1 | 16 | 7 | +9 | 17 |
| Colchester U | 8 | 5 | 1 | 2 | 16 | 6 | +10 | 16 |
| Walsall | 8 | 4 | 2 | 2 | 11 | 8 | +3 | 14 |
| WBA | 7 | 4 | 1 | 2 | 12 | 7 | +5 | 13 |
| Plymouth Arg | 8 | 3 | 2 | 3 | 10 | 11 | –1 | 11 |
| Cardiff C | 8 | 3 | 0 | 5 | 10 | 11 | –1 | 9 |
| Brighton & HA | 8 | 2 | 3 | 3 | 5 | 9 | –4 | 9 |
| AFC Bournemouth | 8 | 0 | 4 | 4 | 8 | 17 | –9 | 4 |
| Gillingham | 7 | 0 | 3 | 4 | 5 | 17 | –12 | 3 |

### DIVISION TWO SOUTH

| | P | W | D | L | F | A | GD | Pts |
|---|---|---|---|---|---|---|---|---|
| Portsmouth | 7 | 6 | 0 | 1 | 16 | 4 | +12 | 18 |
| Luton T | 7 | 6 | 0 | 1 | 18 | 7 | +11 | 18 |
| Cheltenham T | 7 | 5 | 1 | 1 | 9 | 4 | +5 | 16 |
| Torquay U | 7 | 2 | 1 | 4 | 14 | 11 | +3 | 7 |
| Swansea C | 6 | 2 | 0 | 4 | 8 | 19 | –11 | 6 |
| Swindon T | 7 | 1 | 2 | 4 | 10 | 14 | –4 | 5 |
| Oxford U | 6 | 1 | 1 | 4 | 5 | 12 | –7 | 4 |
| Brentford | 7 | 1 | 1 | 5 | 7 | 16 | –9 | 4 |

### DIVISION THREE SOUTH

| | P | W | D | L | F | A | GD | Pts |
|---|---|---|---|---|---|---|---|---|
| Leyton Orient | 8 | 4 | 3 | 1 | 13 | 5 | +8 | 15 |
| Southend U | 8 | 4 | 3 | 1 | 9 | 6 | +3 | 15 |
| Cirencester T | 8 | 3 | 3 | 2 | 13 | 11 | +2 | 12 |
| Rushden & D | 8 | 3 | 3 | 2 | 12 | 10 | +2 | 12 |
| Exeter C | 8 | 3 | 3 | 2 | 7 | 7 | 0 | 12 |
| Wycombe W | 8 | 3 | 2 | 3 | 10 | 9 | +1 | 11 |
| Kidderminster H | 8 | 3 | 1 | 4 | 11 | 15 | –4 | 10 |
| Northampton T | 8 | 2 | 1 | 5 | 9 | 17 | –8 | 7 |
| Bristol R | 8 | 1 | 1 | 6 | 8 | 12 | –4 | 4 |

## THE UMBRO ISOTONIC UNDER-17s FOOTBALL LEAGUE

### SOUTH WEST CONFERENCE

| | P | W | D | L | F | A | GD | Pts |
|---|---|---|---|---|---|---|---|---|
| AFC Bournemouth | 19 | 12 | 5 | 2 | 56 | 22 | +34 | 41 |
| Cardiff C | 19 | 11 | 2 | 6 | 49 | 29 | +20 | 35 |
| Yeovil T | 19 | 10 | 5 | 4 | 42 | 36 | +6 | 35 |
| Plymouth Arg | 19 | 9 | 4 | 6 | 44 | 40 | +4 | 31 |
| Swindon T | 20 | 9 | 3 | 8 | 37 | 38 | –1 | 30 |
| Cheltenham T | 20 | 8 | 5 | 7 | 33 | 37 | –4 | 29 |
| Swansea C | 20 | 7 | 4 | 9 | 33 | 41 | –8 | 25 |
| Exeter C | 20 | 6 | 6 | 8 | 47 | 59 | –12 | 24 |
| Cirencester T | 19 | 4 | 5 | 10 | 32 | 41 | –9 | 17 |
| Bristol R | 20 | 4 | 5 | 11 | 28 | 41 | –13 | 17 |
| Torquay U | 19 | 3 | 4 | 12 | 20 | 37 | –17 | 13 |

### SOUTH EAST CONFERENCE

| | P | W | D | L | F | A | GD | Pts |
|---|---|---|---|---|---|---|---|---|
| Brighton & HA | 26 | 20 | 1 | 5 | 74 | 28 | +46 | 61 |
| QPR | 26 | 18 | 6 | 2 | 88 | 27 | +61 | 60 |
| Cambridge U | 25 | 14 | 4 | 7 | 57 | 30 | +27 | 46 |
| Portsmouth | 26 | 12 | 7 | 7 | 53 | 39 | +14 | 43 |
| Luton T | 25 | 13 | 2 | 10 | 59 | 41 | +18 | 41 |
| Rushden & D | 26 | 11 | 8 | 7 | 59 | 51 | +8 | 41 |
| Colchester U | 26 | 11 | 7 | 8 | 56 | 45 | +11 | 40 |
| Southend U | 26 | 10 | 5 | 11 | 50 | 46 | +4 | 35 |
| Gillingham | 26 | 8 | 6 | 12 | 42 | 68 | –26 | 30 |
| Oxford U | 25 | 9 | 2 | 14 | 39 | 60 | –21 | 29 |
| Brentford | 25 | 7 | 7 | 11 | 36 | 48 | –12 | 28 |
| Wycombe W | 26 | 6 | 7 | 13 | 37 | 64 | –27 | 25 |
| Northampton T | 26 | 4 | 3 | 19 | 32 | 74 | –42 | 15 |
| Leyton Orient | 26 | 3 | 3 | 20 | 35 | 96 | –61 | 12 |

# NON-LEAGUE TABLES 2003–04

### SPARTAN SOUTH MIDLANDS PREMIER

| | P | W | D | L | F | A | GD | Pts |
|---|---|---|---|---|---|---|---|---|
| Beaconsfield SYCOB | 36 | 27 | 7 | 2 | 95 | 21 | 74 | 88 |
| Brook House | 36 | 26 | 2 | 8 | 82 | 35 | 47 | 80 |
| St Margaretsbury | 36 | 24 | 5 | 7 | 66 | 29 | 37 | 77 |
| Potters Bar Town | 36 | 22 | 8 | 6 | 86 | 35 | 51 | 74 |
| Harefield United | 36 | 22 | 5 | 9 | 87 | 50 | 37 | 71 |
| Hanwell Town | 36 | 22 | 4 | 10 | 86 | 49 | 37 | 70 |
| London Colney | 36 | 18 | 6 | 12 | 76 | 48 | 28 | 60 |
| Greenacres (Hemel) | 36 | 16 | 6 | 14 | 77 | 78 | –1 | 54 |
| Leverstock Green | 36 | 14 | 7 | 15 | 54 | 55 | –1 | 49 |
| Ruislip Manor | 36 | 14 | 6 | 16 | 60 | 62 | –2 | 48 |
| Hoddesdon Town | 36 | 13 | 7 | 16 | 53 | 53 | 0 | 46 |
| Hillingdon Borough | 36 | 13 | 7 | 16 | 56 | 67 | –11 | 46 |
| Royston Town | 36 | 11 | 7 | 18 | 63 | 78 | –15 | 40 |
| Harpenden Town | 36 | 9 | 9 | 18 | 47 | 81 | –34 | 36 |
| Biggleswade Town | 36 | 9 | 8 | 19 | 56 | 82 | –26 | 35 |
| Broxbourne B V&E | 36 | 9 | 3 | 24 | 36 | 93 | –57 | 30 |
| Bedford U & Valerio | 36 | 6 | 6 | 24 | 32 | 84 | –52 | 24 |
| Haringey Borough | 36 | 5 | 7 | 24 | 43 | 90 | –47 | 22 |
| Holmer Green | 36 | 5 | 4 | 27 | 41 | 106 | –65 | 19 |

### SPARTAN SOUTH MIDLANDS DIVISION ONE

| | P | W | D | L | F | A | GD | Pts |
|---|---|---|---|---|---|---|---|---|
| Haywood United | 34 | 23 | 7 | 4 | 91 | 32 | 59 | 76 |
| Langford | 34 | 21 | 6 | 7 | 92 | 43 | 49 | 69 |
| Welwyn Garden City | 34 | 19 | 9 | 6 | 62 | 26 | 36 | 66 |
| Tring Athletic | 34 | 19 | 6 | 9 | 67 | 37 | 30 | 63 |
| Buckingham Athletic | 34 | 18 | 7 | 9 | 67 | 38 | 29 | 61 |
| Colney Heath | 34 | 17 | 6 | 11 | 66 | 54 | 12 | 57 |
| Cockfosters | 34 | 17 | 5 | 12 | 63 | 56 | 7 | 56 |
| Biggleswade United | 34 | 16 | 7 | 11 | 55 | 50 | 5 | 55 |
| Sun Postal Sports | 34 | 14 | 5 | 15 | 64 | 62 | 2 | 47 |
| Brimsdown Rovers | 34 | 13 | 8 | 13 | 53 | 56 | –3 | 47 |
| Stony Stratford Town | 34 | 13 | 5 | 16 | 57 | 64 | –7 | 44 |
| Kings Langley | 34 | 8 | 14 | 12 | 42 | 64 | –22 | 38 |
| Brache Sparta | 34 | 9 | 8 | 17 | 52 | 69 | –17 | 35 |
| Pitstone & Ivinghoe | 34 | 9 | 6 | 19 | 40 | 60 | –20 | 33 |
| The 61 FC | 34 | 8 | 8 | 18 | 32 | 59 | –27 | 32 |
| New Bradwell St Peter | 34 | 8 | 6 | 20 | 41 | 79 | –38 | 30 |
| Shillington | 34 | 8 | 2 | 24 | 40 | 84 | –44 | 26 |
| Ampthill Town | 34 | 7 | 3 | 24 | 34 | 85 | –51 | 24 |

### COMBINED COUNTIES PREMIER

| | P | W | D | L | F | A | GD | Pts |
|---|---|---|---|---|---|---|---|---|
| AFC Wimbledon | 46 | 42 | 4 | 0 | 180 | 32 | 148 | 130 |
| AFC Wallingford | 46 | 32 | 7 | 7 | 115 | 43 | 72 | 103 |
| Reading Town | 46 | 28 | 10 | 8 | 79 | 46 | 33 | 94 |
| Southall | 46 | 29 | 5 | 12 | 121 | 55 | 66 | 92 |
| Sandhurst Town | 46 | 27 | 11 | 8 | 109 | 60 | 49 | 92 |
| Bedfont (+3) | 46 | 26 | 11 | 9 | 94 | 62 | 32 | 92 |
| Walton Casuals | 46 | 25 | 9 | 12 | 112 | 64 | 48 | 84 |
| Chipstead | 46 | 26 | 6 | 14 | 92 | 57 | 35 | 84 |
| Ash United | 46 | 23 | 11 | 12 | 103 | 68 | 35 | 80 |
| Chessington & Hook | 46 | 21 | 8 | 17 | 94 | 75 | 19 | 71 |
| Godalming & Guildford | 46 | 20 | 9 | 17 | 65 | 61 | 4 | 69 |
| Merstham | 46 | 20 | 9 | 17 | 63 | 67 | –4 | 69 |
| Feltham | 46 | 19 | 6 | 21 | 82 | 67 | 15 | 63 |
| North Greenford United | 46 | 18 | 6 | 22 | 80 | 91 | –11 | 60 |
| Hartley Wintney (–3) | 46 | 17 | 7 | 22 | 77 | 111 | –34 | 55 |
| Raynes Park Vale | 46 | 12 | 9 | 25 | 72 | 94 | –22 | 45 |
| Horley Town | 46 | 12 | 8 | 26 | 67 | 94 | –27 | 44 |
| Cobham | 46 | 12 | 8 | 26 | 57 | 114 | –57 | 44 |
| Westfield (–3) | 46 | 11 | 10 | 25 | 53 | 88 | –35 | 40 |
| Frimley Green | 46 | 9 | 10 | 27 | 53 | 109 | –56 | 37 |
| Withdean 2000 (+3) | 46 | 8 | 7 | 31 | 62 | 116 | –54 | 34 |
| Farnham Town | 46 | 8 | 4 | 34 | 44 | 125 | –81 | 28 |
| Chessington United | 46 | 7 | 6 | 33 | 52 | 140 | –88 | 27 |
| Cove | 46 | 7 | 5 | 34 | 50 | 137 | –87 | 26 |

### COMBINED COUNTIES DIVISION ONE

| | P | W | D | L | F | A | GD | Pts |
|---|---|---|---|---|---|---|---|---|
| AFC Guildford | 34 | 26 | 5 | 3 | 98 | 26 | 72 | 83 |
| Colliers Wood United | 34 | 25 | 3 | 6 | 93 | 27 | 66 | 78 |
| Bookham (+7) | 34 | 20 | 8 | 6 | 73 | 35 | 38 | 75 |
| Hersham RBL | 34 | 20 | 4 | 10 | 76 | 37 | 39 | 64 |
| Coney Hall | 34 | 19 | 7 | 8 | 81 | 43 | 38 | 64 |
| Merrow | 34 | 19 | 6 | 9 | 76 | 50 | 26 | 63 |
| Farleigh Rovers | 34 | 16 | 11 | 7 | 56 | 32 | 24 | 59 |
| Staines Lammas (–1) | 34 | 16 | 6 | 12 | 80 | 49 | 31 | 53 |
| Worcester Park | 34 | 17 | 2 | 15 | 63 | 53 | 10 | 53 |
| Ditton | 34 | 15 | 6 | 13 | 82 | 66 | 16 | 51 |
| Monotype | 34 | 13 | 8 | 13 | 59 | 65 | –6 | 47 |
| Crescent Rovers | 34 | 12 | 4 | 18 | 51 | 71 | –20 | 40 |
| Seelec Delta (–4) | 34 | 11 | 10 | 13 | 57 | 57 | 0 | 39 |
| Shottermill & Haslemere | 34 | 9 | 5 | 20 | 48 | 67 | –19 | 32 |
| Netherne Village | 34 | 9 | 4 | 21 | 40 | 72 | –32 | 31 |
| Chobham & Ottershaw | 34 | 4 | 6 | 24 | 26 | 105 | –79 | 18 |
| Sheerwater (–3) | 34 | 3 | 4 | 27 | 40 | 120 | –80 | 10 |
| Cranleigh (+3) | 34 | 2 | 1 | 31 | 29 | 153 | –124 | 10 |

### ESSEX SENIOR

| | P | W | D | L | F | A | GD | Pts |
|---|---|---|---|---|---|---|---|---|
| Concord Rangers | 30 | 22 | 4 | 4 | 75 | 26 | 49 | 70 |
| Ilford | 30 | 19 | 8 | 3 | 66 | 23 | 43 | 65 |
| Sawbridgeworth Town | 30 | 19 | 6 | 5 | 60 | 29 | 31 | 63 |
| Enfield Town | 30 | 18 | 9 | 3 | 60 | 35 | 25 | 63 |
| Romford | 30 | 18 | 4 | 8 | 66 | 39 | 27 | 58 |
| Waltham Abbey | 30 | 15 | 7 | 8 | 50 | 38 | 12 | 52 |
| Basildon United | 30 | 15 | 4 | 11 | 67 | 42 | 25 | 49 |
| Bowers United | 30 | 13 | 4 | 13 | 41 | 51 | –10 | 43 |
| Eton Manor | 30 | 9 | 8 | 13 | 43 | 52 | –9 | 35 |
| Southend Manor | 30 | 9 | 7 | 14 | 42 | 50 | –8 | 34 |
| Barkingside | 30 | 9 | 7 | 14 | 47 | 62 | –15 | 34 |
| Burnham Ramblers | 30 | 7 | 10 | 13 | 42 | 58 | –16 | 31 |
| Stansted | 30 | 7 | 5 | 18 | 33 | 72 | –39 | 26 |
| Brentwood | 30 | 5 | 5 | 20 | 31 | 60 | –29 | 20 |
| London APSA | 30 | 5 | 5 | 20 | 34 | 76 | –42 | 20 |
| Hullbridge Sports | 30 | 2 | 3 | 25 | 28 | 72 | –44 | 9 |

### ESSEX INTERMEDIATE

| | P | W | D | L | F | A | GD | Pts |
|---|---|---|---|---|---|---|---|---|
| White Ensigns (–1) | 22 | 16 | 3 | 3 | 49 | 18 | 31 | 50 |
| Manford Way | 22 | 12 | 9 | 1 | 36 | 9 | 27 | 45 |
| Harold Wood Ath (+5) | 22 | 10 | 5 | 7 | 40 | 27 | 13 | 40 |
| Frenford Senior (–6) | 22 | 12 | 8 | 2 | 45 | 22 | 23 | 38 |
| Bishop's Stortford Swifts | 22 | 8 | 7 | 7 | 31 | 25 | 6 | 31 |
| Takeley | 22 | 9 | 4 | 9 | 29 | 36 | –7 | 31 |
| Shenfield AFC (+3) | 22 | 6 | 7 | 9 | 29 | 34 | –5 | 28 |
| Epping | 22 | 5 | 7 | 10 | 21 | 41 | –20 | 22 |
| Rayleigh Town | 22 | 6 | 3 | 13 | 33 | 37 | –4 | 21 |
| Kelvedon Hatch | 22 | 4 | 9 | 9 | 28 | 38 | –10 | 21 |
| White Notley | 22 | 3 | 8 | 11 | 25 | 41 | –16 | 17 |
| Canning Town | 22 | 4 | 4 | 14 | 26 | 64 | –38 | 16 |

### HELLENIC PREMIER

| | P | W | D | L | F | A | GD | Pts |
|---|---|---|---|---|---|---|---|---|
| Brackley Town | 42 | 28 | 8 | 6 | 106 | 36 | 70 | 92 |
| Southall Town | 42 | 28 | 8 | 6 | 104 | 42 | 62 | 92 |
| Bishops Cleeve | 42 | 27 | 8 | 7 | 94 | 36 | 58 | 89 |
| Slimbridge | 42 | 26 | 11 | 5 | 85 | 29 | 56 | 89 |
| Didcot Town | 42 | 28 | 4 | 10 | 90 | 35 | 55 | 88 |
| Hungerford Town (–1) | 42 | 25 | 6 | 11 | 90 | 45 | 45 | 80 |
| Carterton Town | 42 | 22 | 9 | 11 | 63 | 45 | 18 | 75 |
| North Leigh | 42 | 21 | 6 | 15 | 70 | 51 | 19 | 69 |
| Highworth Town | 42 | 19 | 11 | 12 | 66 | 45 | 21 | 68 |
| Fairford Town (–3) | 42 | 21 | 8 | 13 | 74 | 63 | 11 | 68 |
| Abingdon United | 42 | 19 | 11 | 12 | 54 | 49 | 5 | 68 |
| Chipping Norton Town | 42 | 15 | 9 | 18 | 57 | 68 | –11 | 54 |
| Tuffley Rovers | 42 | 11 | 13 | 18 | 43 | 49 | –6 | 46 |
| Bicester Town | 42 | 11 | 6 | 25 | 32 | 64 | –32 | 39 |
| Henley Town | 42 | 11 | 6 | 25 | 44 | 82 | –38 | 39 |
| Wootton Bassett Town | 42 | 11 | 5 | 26 | 38 | 73 | –35 | 38 |
| Pegasus Juniors | 42 | 11 | 5 | 26 | 45 | 105 | –60 | 38 |
| Pewsey Vale | 42 | 10 | 7 | 25 | 58 | 99 | –41 | 37 |
| Shortwood United | 42 | 11 | 4 | 27 | 53 | 95 | –42 | 37 |
| Hook Norton | 42 | 8 | 12 | 22 | 42 | 76 | –34 | 36 |
| Almondsbury Town | 42 | 10 | 5 | 27 | 33 | 86 | –53 | 35 |
| Gloucester United | 42 | 4 | 8 | 30 | 40 | 108 | –68 | 20 |

### HELLENIC DIVISION ONE WEST

| | P | W | D | L | F | A | GD | Pts |
|---|---|---|---|---|---|---|---|---|
| Purton | 34 | 24 | 10 | 0 | 83 | 25 | 58 | 82 |
| Ross Town | 34 | 22 | 8 | 4 | 73 | 34 | 39 | 74 |
| Shrivenham | 34 | 22 | 6 | 6 | 78 | 26 | 52 | 72 |
| Witney United | 34 | 18 | 9 | 7 | 63 | 34 | 29 | 63 |
| Ardley United | 34 | 17 | 10 | 7 | 68 | 46 | 22 | 61 |
| Easington Sports | 34 | 12 | 16 | 6 | 49 | 40 | 9 | 52 |
| Quarry Nomads | 34 | 14 | 7 | 13 | 71 | 59 | 12 | 49 |
| Old Woodstock Town | 34 | 14 | 7 | 13 | 53 | 60 | –7 | 49 |
| Winterbourne United | 34 | 13 | 8 | 13 | 62 | 52 | 10 | 47 |
| Headington Amateurs | 34 | 12 | 8 | 14 | 59 | 66 | –7 | 44 |
| Harrow Hill | 34 | 12 | 6 | 16 | 45 | 61 | –16 | 4[illegible] |
| Kidlington | 34 | 10 | 11 | 13 | 66 | 69 | –3 | 4[illegible] |
| Cheltenham Saracens | 34 | 11 | 8 | 15 | 47 | 53 | –6 | 4[illegible] |
| Malmesbury Victoria | 34 | 11 | 6 | 17 | 41 | 52 | –11 | 3[illegible] |
| Cirencester United | 34 | 8 | 9 | 17 | 51 | 66 | –15 | 3[illegible] |
| Middle Barton | 34 | 7 | 5 | 22 | 34 | 81 | –47 | 2[illegible] |
| Adderbury Park | 34 | 5 | 3 | 26 | 34 | 95 | –61 | 1[illegible] |
| Clanfield | 34 | 3 | 5 | 26 | 37 | 95 | –58 | 1[illegible] |

## HELLENIC DIVISION ONE EAST

| | P | W | D | L | F | A | GD | Pts |
|---|---|---|---|---|---|---|---|---|
| ntage Town | 32 | 23 | 7 | 2 | 85 | 16 | 69 | 76 |
| combe | 32 | 19 | 10 | 3 | 60 | 27 | 33 | 67 |
| ton United | 32 | 16 | 11 | 5 | 71 | 45 | 26 | 59 |
| n Wick | 32 | 15 | 9 | 8 | 64 | 45 | 19 | 54 |
| field | 32 | 15 | 8 | 9 | 52 | 38 | 14 | 53 |
| yners Lane | 32 | 14 | 9 | 9 | 73 | 51 | 22 | 51 |
| alfont Wasps | 32 | 15 | 4 | 13 | 54 | 51 | 3 | 49 |
| champstead | 32 | 12 | 9 | 11 | 54 | 42 | 12 | 45 |
| rtin Baker Sports | 32 | 12 | 3 | 17 | 49 | 73 | –24 | 39 |
| n & Tylers Green | 32 | 9 | 11 | 12 | 46 | 54 | –8 | 38 |
| nnor | 32 | 10 | 5 | 17 | 46 | 57 | –11 | 35 |
| ley Sports | 32 | 9 | 8 | 15 | 38 | 52 | –14 | 35 |
| stwood | 32 | 9 | 6 | 17 | 63 | 75 | –12 | 33 |
| dshot Lea | 32 | 9 | 6 | 17 | 50 | 73 | –23 | 33 |
| glefield Green Rovers | 32 | 8 | 7 | 17 | 44 | 76 | –32 | 31 |
| unslow Borough (–1) | 32 | 8 | 5 | 19 | 45 | 80 | –35 | 28 |
| yport | 32 | 6 | 8 | 18 | 42 | 81 | –39 | 26 |

## MIDLAND ALLIANCE

| | P | W | D | L | F | A | GD | Pts |
|---|---|---|---|---|---|---|---|---|
| cester | 46 | 28 | 12 | 6 | 96 | 45 | 51 | 96 |
| lenhall Town | 46 | 27 | 13 | 6 | 114 | 49 | 65 | 94 |
| atford Town | 46 | 28 | 8 | 10 | 89 | 45 | 44 | 92 |
| orn | 46 | 26 | 12 | 8 | 84 | 47 | 37 | 90 |
| dley | 46 | 26 | 7 | 13 | 96 | 52 | 44 | 85 |
| dby Town | 46 | 23 | 8 | 15 | 90 | 56 | 34 | 77 |
| asetown | 46 | 22 | 11 | 13 | 68 | 50 | 18 | 77 |
| alville Town | 46 | 20 | 12 | 14 | 87 | 61 | 26 | 72 |
| urbridge | 46 | 19 | 15 | 12 | 74 | 52 | 22 | 72 |
| dgnorth Town | 46 | 20 | 12 | 14 | 76 | 66 | 10 | 72 |
| bury United | 46 | 19 | 14 | 13 | 72 | 55 | 17 | 71 |
| cing Club Warwick | 46 | 20 | 9 | 17 | 64 | 63 | 1 | 69 |
| stfields | 46 | 20 | 6 | 20 | 67 | 61 | 6 | 66 |
| shall Olympic | 46 | 15 | 16 | 15 | 58 | 55 | 3 | 61 |
| dmere St Michaels | 46 | 17 | 9 | 20 | 76 | 77 | –1 | 60 |
| dulph Victoria | 46 | 16 | 12 | 18 | 66 | 74 | –8 | 60 |
| useway United | 46 | 15 | 11 | 20 | 66 | 82 | –16 | 56 |
| well | 46 | 15 | 9 | 22 | 63 | 75 | –12 | 54 |
| vechurch | 46 | 12 | 14 | 20 | 67 | 87 | –20 | 50 |
| dlow Town | 46 | 12 | 11 | 23 | 56 | 84 | –28 | 47 |
| osvenor Park | 46 | 9 | 9 | 28 | 53 | 79 | –26 | 36 |
| adley Town | 46 | 8 | 12 | 26 | 60 | 92 | –32 | 36 |
| lsall Villa | 46 | 7 | 7 | 32 | 46 | 132 | –86 | 28 |
| afford Town | 46 | 1 | 5 | 40 | 27 | 176 | –149 | 8 |

## MIDLAND COMBINATION

| | P | W | D | L | F | A | GD | Pts |
|---|---|---|---|---|---|---|---|---|
| mulus | 40 | 31 | 2 | 7 | 128 | 44 | 84 | 95 |
| amington | 40 | 30 | 4 | 6 | 101 | 36 | 65 | 94 |
| gby Town | 40 | 25 | 5 | 10 | 80 | 55 | 25 | 80 |
| ventry Sphinx | 40 | 23 | 8 | 9 | 74 | 55 | 19 | 77 |
| ckenham | 40 | 21 | 8 | 11 | 79 | 63 | 16 | 71 |
| ventry Marconi | 40 | 22 | 4 | 14 | 84 | 53 | 31 | 70 |
| ir KA | 40 | 18 | 11 | 11 | 89 | 68 | 21 | 65 |
| neaton Griff | 40 | 15 | 15 | 10 | 74 | 62 | 12 | 60 |
| stle Vale K H | 40 | 17 | 8 | 15 | 76 | 72 | 4 | 59 |
| dley Sports | 40 | 16 | 9 | 15 | 84 | 64 | 20 | 57 |
| est Midlands Police | 40 | 16 | 9 | 15 | 67 | 78 | –11 | 57 |
| ghgate United | 40 | 15 | 11 | 14 | 62 | 52 | 10 | 56 |
| lehall Swifts | 40 | 16 | 8 | 16 | 67 | 77 | –10 | 56 |
| octon | 40 | 15 | 10 | 15 | 53 | 59 | –6 | 55 |
| rshore Town | 40 | 10 | 15 | 15 | 65 | 83 | –18 | 45 |
| ifnal Town | 40 | 11 | 10 | 19 | 44 | 52 | –8 | 43 |
| assey Ferguson | 40 | 12 | 5 | 23 | 65 | 93 | –28 | 41 |
| leshill Town | 40 | 11 | 5 | 24 | 49 | 83 | –34 | 38 |
| ntinental Star | 40 | 6 | 9 | 25 | 53 | 88 | –35 | 27 |
| utham United | 40 | 3 | 6 | 31 | 32 | 115 | –83 | 15 |
| veston | 40 | 2 | 8 | 30 | 29 | 103 | –74 | 14 |

## WEST MIDLANDS PREMIER

| | P | W | D | L | F | A | GD | Pts |
|---|---|---|---|---|---|---|---|---|
| alvern Town | 38 | 29 | 3 | 6 | 134 | 38 | 96 | 90 |
| oton Town | 38 | 26 | 8 | 4 | 105 | 36 | 69 | 86 |
| ngton Town | 38 | 26 | 2 | 10 | 100 | 62 | 38 | 80 |
| awbury United | 38 | 21 | 10 | 7 | 73 | 56 | 17 | 73 |
| dbury Town | 38 | 22 | 6 | 10 | 96 | 60 | 36 | 72 |
| ath Hayes | 38 | 20 | 6 | 12 | 81 | 48 | 33 | 66 |
| arket Drayton Town | 38 | 19 | 8 | 11 | 69 | 54 | 15 | 65 |
| vidale | 38 | 18 | 8 | 12 | 81 | 55 | 26 | 62 |
| ellington | 38 | 18 | 8 | 12 | 74 | 54 | 20 | 62 |
| e Town | 38 | 19 | 5 | 14 | 62 | 52 | 10 | 62 |
| omyard Town | 38 | 17 | 4 | 17 | 78 | 66 | 12 | 55 |
| ierley & Hagley All. | 38 | 14 | 7 | 17 | 59 | 68 | –9 | 49 |
| stleholme | 38 | 13 | 3 | 22 | 76 | 85 | –9 | 42 |
| adley Town | 38 | 11 | 9 | 18 | 65 | 81 | –16 | 42 |
| ingshall Holy Trinity | 38 | 12 | 4 | 22 | 58 | 90 | –32 | 40 |
| olverhampton United | 38 | 12 | 3 | 23 | 63 | 116 | –53 | 39 |
| nethwick Sikh Temple | 38 | 11 | 5 | 22 | 65 | 93 | –28 | 38 |
| ednesfield | 38 | 11 | 4 | 23 | 49 | 125 | –76 | 37 |
| olverhampton Casuals | 38 | 7 | 2 | 29 | 51 | 106 | –55 | 23 |
| seley Town | 38 | 0 | 3 | 35 | 23 | 117 | –94 | 3 |

## LEICESTERSHIRE SENIOR PREMIER

| | P | W | D | L | F | A | GD | Pts |
|---|---|---|---|---|---|---|---|---|
| Loughborough Dynamo | 34 | 28 | 4 | 2 | 114 | 24 | 90 | 88 |
| Kirby Muxloe SC | 34 | 19 | 9 | 6 | 58 | 32 | 26 | 66 |
| Friar Lane OB | 34 | 17 | 9 | 8 | 80 | 46 | 34 | 60 |
| Ellistown | 34 | 18 | 5 | 11 | 69 | 47 | 22 | 59 |
| Ratby Sports | 34 | 18 | 3 | 13 | 66 | 60 | 6 | 57 |
| Ibstock Welfare | 34 | 16 | 8 | 10 | 62 | 48 | 14 | 56 |
| Birstall United | 34 | 15 | 8 | 11 | 56 | 36 | 20 | 53 |
| Blaby & Whetstone Ath | 34 | 14 | 8 | 12 | 49 | 56 | –7 | 50 |
| Leicester YMCA | 34 | 14 | 5 | 15 | 59 | 71 | –12 | 47 |
| Stapenhill | 34 | 14 | 4 | 16 | 68 | 72 | –4 | 46 |
| Holwell Sports | 34 | 14 | 4 | 16 | 58 | 65 | –7 | 46 |
| St Andrews SC | 34 | 14 | 2 | 18 | 53 | 57 | –4 | 44 |
| Highfield Rangers (–3) | 34 | 12 | 9 | 13 | 61 | 61 | 0 | 42 |
| Barrow Town | 34 | 12 | 6 | 16 | 65 | 82 | –17 | 42 |
| Downes Sports | 34 | 8 | 9 | 17 | 58 | 76 | –18 | 33 |
| Thurmaston Town | 34 | 8 | 5 | 21 | 53 | 70 | –17 | 29 |
| Thurnby Rangers | 34 | 7 | 7 | 20 | 45 | 89 | –44 | 28 |
| Anstey Nomads | 34 | 4 | 3 | 27 | 35 | 117 | –82 | 15 |

## WESSEX

| | P | W | D | L | F | A | GD | Pts |
|---|---|---|---|---|---|---|---|---|
| Winchester City | 42 | 35 | 3 | 4 | 151 | 35 | 116 | 108 |
| Wimborne Town | 42 | 31 | 6 | 5 | 105 | 45 | 60 | 99 |
| Gosport Borough | 42 | 29 | 5 | 8 | 96 | 40 | 56 | 92 |
| Lymington & New Milton | 42 | 29 | 3 | 10 | 98 | 38 | 60 | 90 |
| AFC Newbury | 42 | 26 | 4 | 12 | 94 | 53 | 41 | 82 |
| Andover | 42 | 25 | 4 | 13 | 100 | 65 | 35 | 79 |
| Fareham Town | 42 | 24 | 6 | 12 | 71 | 38 | 33 | 78 |
| AFC Totton | 42 | 18 | 10 | 14 | 76 | 55 | 21 | 64 |
| Brockenhurst | 42 | 19 | 7 | 16 | 49 | 74 | –25 | 64 |
| Thatcham Town | 42 | 16 | 10 | 16 | 70 | 72 | –2 | 58 |
| Christchurch | 42 | 17 | 6 | 19 | 63 | 62 | 1 | 57 |
| Bemerton Heath H | 42 | 16 | 7 | 19 | 78 | 79 | –1 | 55 |
| Hamble ASSC | 42 | 16 | 7 | 19 | 51 | 76 | –25 | 55 |
| Cowes Sports | 42 | 15 | 8 | 19 | 51 | 59 | –8 | 53 |
| BAT Sports | 42 | 13 | 7 | 22 | 57 | 68 | –11 | 46 |
| Portland United | 42 | 14 | 4 | 24 | 58 | 86 | –28 | 46 |
| Moneyfields | 42 | 11 | 8 | 23 | 51 | 83 | –32 | 41 |
| Alton Town | 42 | 12 | 2 | 28 | 55 | 110 | –55 | 38 |
| Downton | 42 | 8 | 7 | 27 | 43 | 106 | –63 | 31 |
| Bournemouth | 42 | 8 | 6 | 28 | 41 | 86 | –45 | 30 |
| Blackfield & Langley | 42 | 7 | 7 | 28 | 51 | 99 | –48 | 28 |
| Whitchurch United | 42 | 7 | 5 | 30 | 37 | 117 | –80 | 26 |

## HAMPSHIRE PREMIER

| | P | W | D | L | F | A | GD | Pts |
|---|---|---|---|---|---|---|---|---|
| VT FC | 34 | 28 | 4 | 2 | 125 | 31 | 94 | 88 |
| Andover New Street | 34 | 26 | 4 | 4 | 97 | 40 | 57 | 82 |
| Poole Town | 34 | 23 | 6 | 5 | 107 | 46 | 61 | 75 |
| Liss Athletic | 34 | 18 | 9 | 7 | 96 | 47 | 49 | 63 |
| Horndean | 34 | 20 | 3 | 11 | 87 | 52 | 35 | 63 |
| Portsmouth Royal Navy | 34 | 20 | 1 | 13 | 94 | 65 | 29 | 61 |
| Lymington Town | 34 | 16 | 7 | 11 | 96 | 69 | 27 | 55 |
| Amesbury Town | 34 | 16 | 7 | 11 | 88 | 85 | 3 | 55 |
| East Cowes Vics | 34 | 15 | 9 | 10 | 81 | 58 | 23 | 54 |
| Ringwood Town | 34 | 12 | 10 | 12 | 60 | 62 | –2 | 46 |
| Bishops Waltham Town | 34 | 12 | 7 | 15 | 64 | 87 | –23 | 43 |
| Hythe & Dibden | 34 | 13 | 4 | 17 | 58 | 87 | –29 | 43 |
| Stockbridge | 34 | 11 | 9 | 14 | 54 | 59 | –5 | 42 |
| Petersfield Town | 34 | 8 | 6 | 20 | 57 | 81 | –24 | 30 |
| Locks Heath | 34 | 6 | 8 | 20 | 52 | 84 | –32 | 26 |
| Fawley | 34 | 4 | 6 | 24 | 51 | 125 | –74 | 18 |
| AFC Aldermaston | 34 | 3 | 4 | 27 | 33 | 121 | –88 | 13 |
| Brading Town | 34 | 1 | 4 | 29 | 23 | 124 | –101 | 7 |

## HAMPSHIRE DIVISION ONE

| | P | W | D | L | F | A | GD | Pts |
|---|---|---|---|---|---|---|---|---|
| Colden Common | 26 | 15 | 6 | 5 | 58 | 27 | 31 | 51 |
| Farnborough North End | 26 | 15 | 3 | 8 | 60 | 33 | 27 | 48 |
| Micheldever | 26 | 14 | 4 | 8 | 43 | 33 | 10 | 46 |
| Paulsgrove | 26 | 12 | 9 | 5 | 44 | 35 | 9 | 45 |
| Hayling United | 26 | 13 | 4 | 9 | 42 | 32 | 10 | 43 |
| Overton United | 26 | 11 | 9 | 6 | 48 | 41 | 7 | 42 |
| Clanfield | 26 | 10 | 6 | 10 | 43 | 42 | 1 | 36 |
| Alresford Town | 26 | 10 | 5 | 11 | 45 | 38 | 7 | 35 |
| Tadley Town | 26 | 9 | 6 | 11 | 40 | 40 | 0 | 33 |
| Fleet Spurs | 26 | 8 | 6 | 12 | 34 | 44 | –10 | 30 |
| Laverstock & Ford | 26 | 7 | 6 | 13 | 41 | 48 | –7 | 27 |
| Verwood Town | 26 | 7 | 5 | 14 | 35 | 56 | –21 | 26 |
| AFC Portchester | 26 | 7 | 3 | 16 | 30 | 51 | –21 | 24 |
| Fleetlands | 26 | 4 | 8 | 14 | 37 | 80 | –43 | 20 |

### DORSET PREMIER

| | P | W | D | L | F | A | GD | Pts |
|---|---|---|---|---|---|---|---|---|
| Hamworthy United | 32 | 26 | 3 | 3 | 89 | 25 | 64 | 81 |
| Dorchester Town Res | 32 | 23 | 7 | 2 | 76 | 17 | 59 | 76 |
| Hamworthy Recreation | 32 | 20 | 4 | 8 | 81 | 45 | 36 | 64 |
| Gillingham Town | 32 | 17 | 8 | 7 | 51 | 31 | 20 | 59 |
| Sherborne Town | 32 | 15 | 7 | 10 | 59 | 38 | 21 | 52 |
| Holt United | 32 | 15 | 6 | 11 | 65 | 44 | 21 | 51 |
| Westland Sports | 32 | 14 | 9 | 9 | 49 | 37 | 12 | 51 |
| Poole Borough | 32 | 15 | 5 | 12 | 59 | 43 | 16 | 50 |
| Bournemouth Sports | 32 | 11 | 9 | 12 | 54 | 47 | 7 | 42 |
| Shaftesbury (–3) | 32 | 11 | 9 | 12 | 56 | 62 | –6 | 39 |
| Dorchester United | 32 | 11 | 6 | 15 | 57 | 68 | –11 | 39 |
| Blandford United | 32 | 10 | 6 | 16 | 49 | 77 | –28 | 36 |
| Cobham Sports | 32 | 10 | 5 | 17 | 45 | 84 | –39 | 35 |
| Wareham Rangers | 32 | 9 | 6 | 17 | 52 | 68 | –16 | 33 |
| Bridport Reserves | 32 | 8 | 5 | 19 | 37 | 69 | –32 | 29 |
| Sturminster Newton | 32 | 3 | 7 | 22 | 31 | 73 | –42 | 16 |
| Stourpaine | 32 | 2 | 2 | 28 | 37 | 119 | –82 | 8 |

### WESTERN PREMIER

| | P | W | D | L | F | A | GD | Pts |
|---|---|---|---|---|---|---|---|---|
| Bideford | 34 | 25 | 7 | 2 | 110 | 30 | 80 | 82 |
| Paulton Rovers | 34 | 25 | 2 | 7 | 85 | 28 | 57 | 77 |
| Frome Town | 34 | 21 | 5 | 8 | 84 | 43 | 41 | 68 |
| Backwell United | 34 | 20 | 5 | 9 | 67 | 35 | 32 | 65 |
| Exmouth Town | 34 | 19 | 7 | 8 | 70 | 34 | 36 | 64 |
| Bridgwater Town | 34 | 19 | 3 | 12 | 67 | 47 | 20 | 60 |
| Brislington | 34 | 18 | 4 | 12 | 57 | 40 | 17 | 58 |
| Welton Rovers | 34 | 14 | 7 | 13 | 62 | 54 | 8 | 49 |
| Odd Down | 34 | 13 | 10 | 11 | 48 | 44 | 4 | 49 |
| Barnstaple Town | 34 | 12 | 11 | 11 | 47 | 42 | 5 | 47 |
| Torrington | 34 | 12 | 10 | 12 | 69 | 74 | –5 | 46 |
| Bridport | 34 | 12 | 6 | 16 | 52 | 52 | 0 | 42 |
| Devizes Town | 34 | 11 | 2 | 21 | 55 | 69 | –14 | 35 |
| Melksham Town | 34 | 9 | 6 | 19 | 38 | 61 | –23 | 33 |
| Keynsham Town | 34 | 8 | 5 | 21 | 45 | 84 | –39 | 29 |
| Bishop Sutton | 34 | 8 | 4 | 22 | 42 | 77 | –35 | 28 |
| Dawlish Town | 34 | 6 | 5 | 23 | 30 | 103 | –73 | 23 |
| Elmore | 34 | 4 | 1 | 29 | 26 | 137 | –111 | 13 |

### WESTERN DIVISION ONE

| | P | W | D | L | F | A | GD | Pts |
|---|---|---|---|---|---|---|---|---|
| Hallen | 36 | 24 | 7 | 5 | 75 | 26 | 49 | 79 |
| Bitton | 36 | 23 | 7 | 6 | 84 | 37 | 47 | 76 |
| Bristol Manor Farm | 36 | 20 | 14 | 2 | 74 | 38 | 36 | 74 |
| Clyst Rovers | 36 | 21 | 9 | 6 | 74 | 41 | 33 | 72 |
| Corsham Town | 36 | 19 | 9 | 8 | 70 | 41 | 29 | 66 |
| Willand Rovers | 36 | 17 | 8 | 11 | 72 | 50 | 22 | 59 |
| Shrewton United | 36 | 17 | 4 | 15 | 86 | 70 | 16 | 55 |
| Larkhall Athletic | 36 | 15 | 10 | 11 | 65 | 54 | 11 | 55 |
| Calne Town | 36 | 13 | 10 | 13 | 49 | 45 | 4 | 49 |
| Wellington | 36 | 14 | 7 | 15 | 54 | 55 | –1 | 49 |
| Westbury United | 36 | 14 | 6 | 16 | 52 | 56 | –4 | 48 |
| Street | 36 | 11 | 10 | 15 | 54 | 51 | 3 | 43 |
| Clevedon United | 36 | 11 | 9 | 16 | 60 | 75 | –15 | 42 |
| Weston St Johns | 36 | 11 | 9 | 16 | 72 | 95 | –23 | 42 |
| Cadbury Heath | 36 | 9 | 10 | 17 | 50 | 64 | –14 | 37 |
| Ilfracombe Town | 36 | 7 | 6 | 23 | 43 | 106 | –63 | 27 |
| Chard Town | 36 | 7 | 5 | 24 | 48 | 87 | –39 | 26 |
| Shepton Mallet | 36 | 5 | 9 | 22 | 49 | 82 | –33 | 24 |
| Minehead | 36 | 5 | 9 | 22 | 35 | 93 | –58 | 24 |

### DEVON

| | P | W | D | L | F | A | GD | Pts |
|---|---|---|---|---|---|---|---|---|
| Holsworthy | 40 | 26 | 11 | 3 | 100 | 40 | 60 | 89 |
| Ivybridge Town | 40 | 25 | 9 | 6 | 115 | 49 | 66 | 84 |
| Vospers Oak Villa | 40 | 25 | 6 | 9 | 105 | 53 | 52 | 81 |
| Elburton Villa | 40 | 23 | 7 | 10 | 93 | 65 | 28 | 76 |
| Dartington SC | 40 | 22 | 8 | 10 | 123 | 71 | 52 | 74 |
| Ottery St Mary (+3) | 40 | 20 | 8 | 12 | 87 | 64 | 23 | 71 |
| Newton Abbot | 40 | 22 | 4 | 14 | 79 | 63 | 16 | 70 |
| Buckland Athletic | 40 | 21 | 6 | 13 | 86 | 63 | 23 | 69 |
| Dartmouth | 40 | 16 | 10 | 14 | 88 | 64 | 24 | 58 |
| Crediton United | 40 | 15 | 12 | 13 | 78 | 70 | 8 | 57 |
| University of Exeter | 40 | 17 | 3 | 20 | 64 | 63 | 1 | 54 |
| Budleigh Salterton | 40 | 13 | 15 | 12 | 66 | 69 | –3 | 54 |
| Plymstock United | 40 | 13 | 13 | 14 | 61 | 63 | –2 | 52 |
| Alphington | 40 | 12 | 10 | 18 | 55 | 73 | –18 | 46 |
| Appledore | 40 | 13 | 6 | 21 | 54 | 79 | –25 | 45 |
| Cullompton Rangers | 40 | 10 | 14 | 16 | 71 | 71 | 0 | 44 |
| Stoke Gabriel | 40 | 12 | 7 | 21 | 53 | 92 | –39 | 43 |
| Newton Abbot Spurs | 40 | 9 | 10 | 21 | 55 | 103 | –48 | 37 |
| Exeter Civil Service | 40 | 5 | 12 | 23 | 37 | 79 | –42 | 27 |
| Heavitree United | 40 | 6 | 5 | 29 | 50 | 139 | –89 | 23 |
| Topsham Town (–5) | 40 | 4 | 6 | 30 | 28 | 115 | –87 | 13 |

### SOUTH WESTERN

| | P | W | D | L | F | A | GD |
|---|---|---|---|---|---|---|---|
| St Blazey | 34 | 27 | 5 | 2 | 90 | 26 | 64 |
| Bodmin Town | 34 | 26 | 4 | 4 | 88 | 29 | 59 |
| Porthleven | 34 | 19 | 5 | 10 | 68 | 46 | 22 |
| Millbrook | 34 | 14 | 14 | 6 | 75 | 42 | 33 |
| Saltash United | 34 | 16 | 8 | 10 | 62 | 58 | 4 |
| St Austell | 34 | 16 | 6 | 12 | 58 | 45 | 13 |
| Wadebridge Town | 34 | 14 | 11 | 9 | 57 | 39 | 18 |
| Penzance | 34 | 14 | 8 | 12 | 50 | 46 | 4 |
| Plymouth Parkway | 34 | 12 | 9 | 13 | 51 | 60 | –9 |
| Tavistock | 34 | 12 | 7 | 15 | 52 | 71 | –19 |
| Launceston | 34 | 11 | 8 | 15 | 52 | 67 | –15 |
| Liskeard Athletic | 34 | 11 | 6 | 17 | 43 | 50 | –7 |
| Falmouth Town | 34 | 11 | 5 | 18 | 52 | 72 | –20 |
| Torpoint Athletic | 34 | 10 | 6 | 18 | 53 | 72 | –19 |
| Truro City | 34 | 7 | 10 | 17 | 47 | 69 | –22 |
| Penryn Athletic | 34 | 9 | 4 | 21 | 67 | 90 | –23 |
| Newquay | 34 | 7 | 5 | 22 | 41 | 81 | –40 |
| Callington Town | 34 | 7 | 5 | 22 | 50 | 93 | –43 |

### EASTERN COUNTIES PREMIER

| | P | W | D | L | F | A | GD |
|---|---|---|---|---|---|---|---|
| AFC Sudbury | 42 | 32 | 5 | 5 | 123 | 30 | 93 |
| Maldon Town | 42 | 30 | 6 | 6 | 107 | 35 | 72 |
| Wroxham | 42 | 29 | 8 | 5 | 108 | 36 | 72 |
| Diss Town | 42 | 27 | 5 | 10 | 104 | 54 | 50 |
| Soham Town Rangers | 42 | 24 | 8 | 10 | 88 | 62 | 26 |
| Clacton Town | 42 | 19 | 14 | 9 | 65 | 54 | 11 |
| Halstead Town | 42 | 19 | 9 | 14 | 77 | 54 | 23 |
| Lowestoft Town | 42 | 19 | 8 | 15 | 66 | 68 | –2 |
| Bury Town | 42 | 17 | 11 | 14 | 86 | 82 | 4 |
| Newmarket Town | 42 | 18 | 7 | 17 | 76 | 78 | –2 |
| Norwich United | 42 | 17 | 10 | 15 | 51 | 58 | –7 |
| Mildenhall Town | 42 | 16 | 12 | 14 | 72 | 61 | 11 |
| Histon Reserves | 42 | 14 | 10 | 18 | 70 | 77 | –7 |
| Wisbech Town (–1) | 42 | 13 | 8 | 21 | 64 | 82 | –18 |
| King's Lynn Reserves | 42 | 11 | 11 | 20 | 63 | 71 | –8 |
| Great Yarmouth Town | 42 | 10 | 13 | 19 | 59 | 67 | –8 |
| Woodbridge Town | 42 | 12 | 6 | 24 | 52 | 78 | –26 |
| Dereham Town | 42 | 10 | 9 | 23 | 42 | 85 | –43 |
| Stowmarket Town | 42 | 11 | 6 | 25 | 42 | 88 | –46 |
| Gorleston | 42 | 9 | 10 | 23 | 56 | 86 | –30 |
| Tiptree United | 42 | 9 | 7 | 26 | 40 | 95 | –55 |
| Fakenham Town | 42 | 2 | 5 | 35 | 30 | 140 | –110 |

### EASTERN COUNTIES DIVISION ONE

| | P | W | D | L | F | A | GD |
|---|---|---|---|---|---|---|---|
| Cambridge City Res | 38 | 25 | 8 | 5 | 76 | 40 | 36 |
| Harwich & Parkeston | 38 | 24 | 8 | 6 | 89 | 48 | 41 |
| Leiston | 38 | 22 | 8 | 8 | 74 | 40 | 34 |
| Stanway Rovers | 38 | 20 | 10 | 8 | 69 | 43 | 26 |
| Kirkley | 38 | 18 | 10 | 10 | 84 | 60 | 24 |
| Whitton United | 38 | 19 | 5 | 14 | 85 | 57 | 28 |
| Godmanchester Rovers | 38 | 17 | 8 | 13 | 54 | 52 | 2 |
| Ipswich Wanderers (–2) | 38 | 17 | 9 | 12 | 51 | 36 | 15 |
| Swaffham Town | 38 | 15 | 13 | 10 | 62 | 54 | 8 |
| Ely City | 38 | 19 | 1 | 18 | 60 | 58 | 2 |
| Haverhill Rovers | 38 | 17 | 5 | 16 | 73 | 66 | 7 |
| Cornard United | 38 | 15 | 7 | 16 | 53 | 60 | –7 |
| Long Melford | 38 | 14 | 8 | 16 | 62 | 66 | –4 |
| Needham Market | 38 | 14 | 5 | 19 | 67 | 73 | –6 |
| Felixstowe & Walton | 38 | 12 | 9 | 17 | 52 | 63 | –11 |
| March Town United | 38 | 12 | 5 | 21 | 70 | 99 | –29 |
| Downham Town | 38 | 9 | 7 | 22 | 43 | 79 | –36 |
| Hadleigh United | 38 | 6 | 13 | 19 | 42 | 57 | –15 |
| Thetford Town | 38 | 6 | 6 | 26 | 38 | 85 | –47 |
| Somersham Town | 38 | 4 | 5 | 29 | 34 | 102 | –68 |

### KENT

| | P | W | D | L | F | A | GD |
|---|---|---|---|---|---|---|---|
| Cray Wanderers | 32 | 22 | 4 | 6 | 88 | 35 | 53 |
| Thamesmead Town | 32 | 22 | 3 | 7 | 72 | 38 | 34 |
| VCD Athletic | 32 | 21 | 5 | 6 | 65 | 29 | 36 |
| Maidstone United | 32 | 19 | 10 | 3 | 71 | 30 | 41 |
| Whitstable Town | 32 | 19 | 5 | 8 | 77 | 52 | 25 |
| Hythe Town | 32 | 17 | 7 | 8 | 51 | 41 | 10 |
| Erith Town | 32 | 17 | 2 | 13 | 53 | 45 | 8 |
| Greenwich Borough | 32 | 14 | 8 | 10 | 57 | 53 | 4 |
| Ramsgate | 32 | 11 | 11 | 10 | 49 | 46 | 3 |
| Herne Bay | 32 | 11 | 7 | 14 | 50 | 49 | 1 |
| Sevenoaks Town | 32 | 12 | 1 | 19 | 40 | 57 | –17 |
| Beckenham Town | 32 | 9 | 8 | 15 | 39 | 53 | –14 |
| Lordswood | 32 | 9 | 5 | 18 | 34 | 68 | –34 |
| Tunbridge Wells | 32 | 8 | 6 | 18 | 30 | 57 | –27 |
| Slade Green | 32 | 7 | 8 | 17 | 42 | 47 | –5 |
| Deal Town | 32 | 5 | 4 | 23 | 37 | 71 | –34 |
| Sporting Bengal United | 32 | 1 | 2 | 29 | 26 | 110 | –84 |

### KENT COUNTY PREMIER

| | P | W | D | L | F | A | GD | Pts |
|---|---|---|---|---|---|---|---|---|
| ockenhill | 26 | 19 | 4 | 3 | 58 | 24 | 34 | 61 |
| d Roan | 26 | 19 | 2 | 5 | 67 | 30 | 37 | 59 |
| 'dd Town | 26 | 17 | 5 | 4 | 61 | 27 | 34 | 56 |
| ay Valley PM | 26 | 16 | 5 | 5 | 67 | 27 | 40 | 53 |
| ansfield O&BC | 26 | 11 | 9 | 6 | 54 | 32 | 22 | 42 |
| eerness East | 26 | 10 | 11 | 5 | 43 | 24 | 19 | 41 |
| 'eenways | 26 | 10 | 6 | 10 | 38 | 43 | –5 | 36 |
| arsted | 26 | 11 | 2 | 13 | 36 | 41 | –5 | 35 |
| nterden Town | 26 | 10 | 3 | 13 | 51 | 67 | –16 | 33 |
| auwater | 26 | 8 | 4 | 14 | 31 | 53 | –22 | 28 |
| odland | 26 | 8 | 2 | 16 | 47 | 76 | –29 | 26 |
| ilton Athletic | 26 | 5 | 5 | 16 | 30 | 45 | –15 | 20 |
| ew Romney | 26 | 5 | 1 | 20 | 30 | 73 | –43 | 16 |
| ennington | 26 | 1 | 5 | 20 | 29 | 80 | –51 | 8 |

### SUSSEX COUNTY DIVISION ONE

| | P | W | D | L | F | A | GD | Pts |
|---|---|---|---|---|---|---|---|---|
| hichester City United | 36 | 23 | 8 | 5 | 87 | 40 | 47 | 77 |
| ye & Iden United | 36 | 20 | 11 | 5 | 75 | 37 | 38 | 71 |
| ast Preston | 36 | 22 | 5 | 9 | 72 | 36 | 36 | 71 |
| hree Bridges | 36 | 20 | 10 | 6 | 63 | 34 | 29 | 70 |
| astbourne Town | 36 | 21 | 3 | 12 | 85 | 53 | 32 | 66 |
| rundel | 36 | 18 | 7 | 11 | 77 | 61 | 16 | 61 |
| assocks | 36 | 16 | 11 | 9 | 74 | 54 | 20 | 59 |
| hitehawk | 36 | 17 | 8 | 11 | 59 | 48 | 11 | 59 |
| ast Grinstead Town | 36 | 17 | 4 | 15 | 64 | 60 | 4 | 55 |
| ngmer | 36 | 14 | 11 | 11 | 54 | 54 | 0 | 53 |
| edhill | 36 | 13 | 7 | 16 | 53 | 50 | 3 | 46 |
| ailsham Town | 36 | 13 | 7 | 16 | 55 | 58 | –3 | 46 |
| orsham YMCA | 36 | 11 | 9 | 16 | 55 | 62 | –7 | 42 |
| outhwick | 36 | 10 | 11 | 15 | 39 | 51 | –12 | 41 |
| dlesham | 36 | 10 | 8 | 18 | 50 | 71 | –21 | 38 |
| dley United | 36 | 10 | 8 | 18 | 42 | 63 | –21 | 38 |
| gham | 36 | 6 | 10 | 20 | 30 | 55 | –25 | 28 |
| elsey | 36 | 5 | 5 | 26 | 35 | 94 | –59 | 20 |
| horeham | 36 | 2 | 5 | 29 | 30 | 118 | –88 | 11 |

### SUSSEX COUNTY DIVISION TWO

| | P | W | D | L | F | A | GD | Pts |
|---|---|---|---|---|---|---|---|---|
| ttlehampton Town | 34 | 23 | 7 | 4 | 89 | 29 | 60 | 76 |
| astbourne United Ass | 34 | 18 | 12 | 4 | 78 | 39 | 39 | 66 |
| 'orthing United | 34 | 20 | 6 | 8 | 70 | 36 | 34 | 66 |
| 'ick | 34 | 17 | 8 | 9 | 57 | 38 | 19 | 59 |
| akwood | 34 | 18 | 4 | 12 | 77 | 50 | 27 | 58 |
| idhurst & Easebourne | 34 | 18 | 4 | 12 | 75 | 50 | 25 | 58 |
| ile Oak | 34 | 17 | 6 | 11 | 56 | 49 | 7 | 57 |
| teyning Town | 34 | 16 | 9 | 9 | 39 | 35 | 4 | 57 |
| 'estfield | 34 | 16 | 5 | 13 | 70 | 63 | 7 | 53 |
| roadbridge Heath | 34 | 15 | 5 | 14 | 51 | 54 | –3 | 50 |
| rawley Down Village | 34 | 14 | 5 | 15 | 51 | 48 | 3 | 47 |
| eacehaven & Telscombe | 34 | 14 | 4 | 16 | 54 | 52 | 2 | 46 |
| altdean United | 34 | 11 | 7 | 16 | 52 | 56 | –4 | 40 |
| 'ealden | 34 | 12 | 4 | 18 | 43 | 64 | –21 | 40 |
| eaford Town | 34 | 10 | 8 | 16 | 55 | 51 | 4 | 38 |
| ease Pottage Village | 34 | 5 | 5 | 24 | 43 | 121 | –78 | 20 |
| aywards Heath Town | 34 | 4 | 5 | 25 | 27 | 89 | –62 | 17 |
| ancing | 34 | 4 | 4 | 26 | 26 | 89 | –63 | 16 |

### UNITED COUNTIES PREMIER

| | P | W | D | L | F | A | GD | Pts |
|---|---|---|---|---|---|---|---|---|
| palding United | 42 | 28 | 6 | 8 | 97 | 44 | 53 | 90 |
| uckingham Town | 42 | 25 | 10 | 7 | 102 | 46 | 56 | 85 |
| arrowby United | 42 | 24 | 9 | 9 | 85 | 56 | 29 | 81 |
| t Neots Town | 42 | 24 | 8 | 10 | 85 | 44 | 41 | 80 |
| oston Town | 42 | 24 | 7 | 11 | 67 | 43 | 24 | 79 |
| ogenhoe United | 42 | 23 | 9 | 10 | 86 | 38 | 48 | 78 |
| olbeach United | 42 | 23 | 5 | 14 | 80 | 59 | 21 | 74 |
| axley | 42 | 22 | 4 | 16 | 99 | 64 | 35 | 70 |
| ord Sports Daventry | 42 | 19 | 11 | 12 | 83 | 56 | 27 | 68 |
| totfold | 42 | 19 | 8 | 15 | 73 | 59 | 14 | 65 |
| lackstone | 42 | 16 | 10 | 16 | 57 | 62 | –5 | 58 |
| 'oodford United | 42 | 14 | 13 | 15 | 61 | 53 | 8 | 55 |
| ewport Pagnell Town | 42 | 15 | 9 | 18 | 60 | 72 | –12 | 54 |
| 'ootton Blue Cross | 42 | 14 | 10 | 18 | 59 | 61 | –2 | 52 |
| ourne Town | 42 | 12 | 11 | 19 | 54 | 90 | –36 | 47 |
| esborough Town | 42 | 13 | 7 | 22 | 56 | 88 | –32 | 46 |
| eeping Rangers | 42 | 12 | 9 | 21 | 48 | 78 | –30 | 45 |
| orthampton Spencer | 42 | 11 | 10 | 21 | 47 | 75 | –28 | 43 |
| tewarts & Lloyds | 42 | 11 | 7 | 24 | 52 | 81 | –29 | 40 |
| aunds Town | 42 | 7 | 12 | 23 | 55 | 94 | –39 | 33 |
| ong Buckby | 42 | 8 | 4 | 30 | 46 | 134 | –88 | 28 |
| 'aventry Town | 42 | 5 | 7 | 30 | 40 | 95 | –55 | 22 |

### UNITED COUNTIES DIVISION ONE

| | P | W | D | L | F | A | GD | Pts |
|---|---|---|---|---|---|---|---|---|
| Potton United | 34 | 25 | 5 | 4 | 99 | 25 | 74 | 80 |
| Cottingham | 34 | 23 | 7 | 4 | 80 | 31 | 49 | 76 |
| Eye United | 34 | 23 | 5 | 6 | 93 | 33 | 60 | 74 |
| Thrapston Town | 34 | 20 | 10 | 4 | 86 | 30 | 56 | 70 |
| Eynesbury Rovers | 34 | 19 | 10 | 5 | 87 | 40 | 47 | 67 |
| Sileby Rangers | 34 | 17 | 10 | 7 | 78 | 62 | 16 | 61 |
| Wellingborough Whit. | 34 | 16 | 4 | 14 | 57 | 52 | 5 | 52 |
| Northampton ON Ch. | 34 | 15 | 5 | 14 | 72 | 82 | –10 | 50 |
| Blisworth | 34 | 11 | 12 | 11 | 56 | 59 | –3 | 45 |
| St Ives Town | 34 | 11 | 10 | 13 | 52 | 58 | –6 | 43 |
| Olney Town | 34 | 11 | 6 | 17 | 52 | 69 | –17 | 39 |
| Rothwell Corinthians | 34 | 10 | 5 | 19 | 45 | 74 | –29 | 35 |
| Bugbrooke St Michael | 34 | 9 | 5 | 20 | 46 | 71 | –25 | 32 |
| Irchester United | 34 | 8 | 5 | 21 | 46 | 76 | –30 | 29 |
| Higham Town | 34 | 6 | 9 | 19 | 52 | 93 | –41 | 27 |
| AFC Kempston | 34 | 5 | 11 | 18 | 48 | 87 | –39 | 26 |
| Huntingdon Town | 34 | 5 | 10 | 19 | 36 | 66 | –30 | 25 |
| Burton Park Wanderers | 34 | 6 | 3 | 25 | 32 | 109 | –77 | 21 |

### NORTHERN COUNTIES EAST PREMIER

| | P | W | D | L | F | A | GD | Pts |
|---|---|---|---|---|---|---|---|---|
| Ossett Albion | 38 | 22 | 10 | 6 | 76 | 37 | 39 | 76 |
| Eastwood Town | 38 | 23 | 7 | 8 | 73 | 34 | 39 | 76 |
| Brigg Town | 38 | 20 | 11 | 7 | 73 | 40 | 33 | 71 |
| Sheffield | 38 | 19 | 12 | 7 | 64 | 40 | 24 | 69 |
| Pickering Town | 38 | 19 | 10 | 9 | 67 | 44 | 23 | 67 |
| Goole | 38 | 18 | 10 | 10 | 67 | 44 | 23 | 64 |
| Buxton | 38 | 17 | 12 | 9 | 69 | 50 | 19 | 63 |
| Selby Town | 38 | 16 | 11 | 11 | 86 | 57 | 29 | 59 |
| Liversedge | 38 | 17 | 8 | 13 | 72 | 58 | 14 | 59 |
| Glapwell | 38 | 14 | 10 | 14 | 53 | 45 | 8 | 52 |
| Thackley | 38 | 14 | 9 | 15 | 61 | 67 | –6 | 51 |
| Harrogate Railway | 38 | 12 | 13 | 13 | 63 | 64 | –1 | 49 |
| Mickleover Sports | 38 | 14 | 5 | 19 | 52 | 66 | –14 | 47 |
| Armthorpe Welfare | 38 | 14 | 4 | 20 | 48 | 67 | –19 | 46 |
| Hallam | 38 | 13 | 5 | 20 | 56 | 76 | –20 | 44 |
| Eccleshill United | 38 | 12 | 8 | 18 | 52 | 74 | –22 | 44 |
| Glasshoughton Welfare | 38 | 10 | 7 | 21 | 58 | 83 | –25 | 37 |
| Arnold Town | 38 | 10 | 6 | 22 | 45 | 67 | –22 | 36 |
| Borrowash Victoria | 38 | 8 | 7 | 23 | 35 | 84 | –49 | 31 |
| Brodsworth Miners W | 38 | 3 | 5 | 30 | 38 | 111 | –73 | 14 |

### NORTHERN COUNTIES EAST DIVISION ONE

| | P | W | D | L | F | A | GD | Pts |
|---|---|---|---|---|---|---|---|---|
| Shirebrook Town | 34 | 22 | 5 | 7 | 59 | 26 | 33 | 71 |
| Long Eaton United | 34 | 22 | 2 | 10 | 63 | 40 | 23 | 68 |
| Maltby Main (–3) | 34 | 21 | 7 | 6 | 81 | 49 | 32 | 67 |
| Sutton Town | 34 | 19 | 8 | 7 | 79 | 37 | 42 | 65 |
| Gedling Town | 34 | 18 | 9 | 7 | 81 | 49 | 32 | 63 |
| Garforth Town | 34 | 17 | 7 | 10 | 60 | 47 | 13 | 58 |
| Yorkshire Amateur | 34 | 15 | 8 | 11 | 57 | 44 | 13 | 53 |
| Lincoln Moorlands | 34 | 14 | 10 | 10 | 53 | 40 | 13 | 52 |
| Carlton Town | 34 | 14 | 7 | 13 | 52 | 51 | 1 | 49 |
| Parkgate | 34 | 12 | 11 | 11 | 52 | 53 | –1 | 47 |
| Winterton Rangers | 34 | 13 | 8 | 13 | 52 | 56 | –4 | 47 |
| Rossington Main | 34 | 13 | 5 | 16 | 56 | 62 | –6 | 44 |
| South Normanton Ath | 34 | 11 | 3 | 20 | 49 | 62 | –13 | 36 |
| Hall Road Rangers | 34 | 9 | 5 | 20 | 43 | 70 | –27 | 32 |
| Worsborough Bridge | 34 | 9 | 2 | 23 | 31 | 75 | –44 | 29 |
| Staveley MW | 34 | 7 | 6 | 21 | 41 | 75 | –34 | 27 |
| Pontefract Collieries | 34 | 5 | 10 | 19 | 30 | 60 | –30 | 25 |
| Tadcaster Albion | 34 | 6 | 5 | 23 | 32 | 75 | –43 | 23 |

### CENTRAL MIDLANDS

| | P | W | D | L | F | A | GD | Pts |
|---|---|---|---|---|---|---|---|---|
| Retford United | 36 | 26 | 7 | 3 | 113 | 32 | 81 | 85 |
| Dinnington Town | 36 | 23 | 7 | 6 | 68 | 32 | 36 | 76 |
| Heanor Town | 36 | 22 | 8 | 6 | 78 | 46 | 32 | 74 |
| Sandiacre Town | 36 | 21 | 5 | 10 | 73 | 52 | 21 | 68 |
| Pelican | 36 | 20 | 6 | 10 | 81 | 51 | 30 | 66 |
| Dunkirk | 36 | 19 | 4 | 13 | 63 | 42 | 21 | 61 |
| Barton Town Old Boys | 36 | 18 | 7 | 11 | 62 | 47 | 15 | 61 |
| Teversal | 36 | 17 | 9 | 10 | 62 | 43 | 19 | 60 |
| Gedling Miners Welfare | 36 | 15 | 8 | 13 | 50 | 42 | 8 | 53 |
| Graham Street Prims | 36 | 16 | 5 | 15 | 60 | 58 | 2 | 53 |
| Radford | 36 | 14 | 7 | 15 | 54 | 62 | –8 | 49 |
| Kiveton Park | 36 | 9 | 15 | 12 | 48 | 62 | –14 | 42 |
| Holbrook | 36 | 11 | 7 | 18 | 49 | 60 | –11 | 40 |
| Clipstone Welfare | 36 | 11 | 4 | 21 | 53 | 78 | –25 | 37 |
| Nettleham | 36 | 9 | 7 | 20 | 41 | 61 | –20 | 34 |
| Askern Welfare | 36 | 8 | 3 | 25 | 35 | 90 | –55 | 27 |
| Greenwood Meadows | 36 | 6 | 8 | 22 | 36 | 69 | –33 | 26 |
| Rolls Royce Leisure | 36 | 6 | 6 | 24 | 32 | 75 | –43 | 24 |
| Blackwell Miners Wel | 36 | 5 | 9 | 22 | 33 | 89 | –56 | 24 |

### NORTHERN DIVISION ONE

| | P | W | D | L | F | A | GD | Pts |
|---|---|---|---|---|---|---|---|---|
| Dunston Fed Brewery | 40 | 25 | 9 | 6 | 76 | 32 | 44 | 84 |
| Durham City | 40 | 23 | 9 | 8 | 90 | 53 | 37 | 78 |
| Bedlington Terriers (–3) | 40 | 25 | 5 | 10 | 104 | 58 | 46 | 77 |
| Shildon (–3) | 40 | 21 | 11 | 8 | 82 | 52 | 30 | 71 |
| Billingham Town | 40 | 20 | 10 | 10 | 83 | 62 | 21 | 70 |
| Jarrow Roofing Boldon CA | 40 | 19 | 6 | 15 | 98 | 90 | 8 | 63 |
| Peterlee Newtown | 40 | 17 | 9 | 14 | 82 | 67 | 15 | 60 |
| Brandon United | 40 | 17 | 7 | 16 | 71 | 77 | –6 | 58 |
| Billingham Synthonia | 40 | 16 | 9 | 15 | 75 | 65 | 10 | 57 |
| Whitley Bay | 40 | 16 | 6 | 18 | 71 | 76 | –5 | 54 |
| Morpeth Town (–3) | 40 | 16 | 8 | 16 | 70 | 59 | 11 | 53 |
| Thornaby (–3) | 40 | 14 | 12 | 14 | 56 | 61 | –5 | 51 |
| West Auckland Town | 40 | 14 | 8 | 18 | 63 | 96 | –33 | 50 |
| Guisborough Town | 40 | 13 | 10 | 17 | 59 | 57 | 2 | 49 |
| Esh Winning | 40 | 13 | 9 | 18 | 52 | 68 | –16 | 48 |
| Tow Law Town | 40 | 13 | 8 | 19 | 63 | 78 | –15 | 47 |
| Chester Le Street Town | 40 | 14 | 4 | 22 | 74 | 85 | –11 | 46 |
| Horden CW | 40 | 11 | 11 | 18 | 58 | 81 | –23 | 44 |
| Washington | 40 | 10 | 6 | 24 | 55 | 97 | –42 | 36 |
| Marske United | 40 | 8 | 9 | 23 | 46 | 76 | –30 | 33 |
| Penrith | 40 | 8 | 8 | 24 | 45 | 83 | –38 | 32 |

### NORTHERN DIVISION TWO

| | P | W | D | L | F | A | GD | Pts |
|---|---|---|---|---|---|---|---|---|
| Ashington | 38 | 27 | 7 | 4 | 91 | 28 | 63 | 88 |
| Newcastle Benfield Saints | 38 | 26 | 7 | 5 | 106 | 42 | 64 | 85 |
| Consett | 38 | 25 | 8 | 5 | 84 | 35 | 49 | 83 |
| Newcastle Blue Star (–3) | 38 | 24 | 6 | 8 | 87 | 53 | 34 | 75 |
| Washington Nissan | 38 | 21 | 6 | 11 | 81 | 47 | 34 | 69 |
| Prudhoe Town | 38 | 18 | 4 | 16 | 73 | 70 | 3 | 58 |
| Northallerton Town | 38 | 15 | 12 | 11 | 73 | 57 | 16 | 57 |
| Hebburn Town | 38 | 16 | 6 | 16 | 64 | 58 | 6 | 54 |
| Kennek Ryhope CA | 38 | 15 | 8 | 15 | 65 | 55 | 10 | 53 |
| Whickham | 38 | 14 | 10 | 14 | 66 | 57 | 9 | 52 |
| Alnwick Town | 38 | 15 | 6 | 17 | 50 | 59 | –9 | 51 |
| South Shields | 38 | 14 | 8 | 16 | 61 | 68 | –7 | 50 |
| Seaham Red Star | 38 | 11 | 10 | 17 | 73 | 78 | –5 | 43 |
| Evenwood Town | 38 | 13 | 4 | 21 | 43 | 58 | –15 | 43 |
| Murton | 38 | 11 | 9 | 18 | 58 | 68 | –10 | 42 |
| Crook Town | 38 | 11 | 8 | 19 | 61 | 79 | –18 | 41 |
| Willington | 38 | 11 | 5 | 22 | 50 | 104 | –54 | 38 |
| Norton & Stockton An | 38 | 10 | 5 | 23 | 49 | 89 | –40 | 35 |
| Easington Colliery | 38 | 8 | 3 | 27 | 41 | 119 | –78 | 27 |
| Shotton Comrades | 38 | 6 | 6 | 26 | 47 | 99 | –52 | 24 |

### NORTH WEST COUNTIES DIVISION ONE

| | P | W | D | L | F | A | GD | Pts |
|---|---|---|---|---|---|---|---|---|
| Clitheroe | 42 | 29 | 5 | 8 | 88 | 55 | 33 | [illegible] |
| Mossley (–3) | 42 | 28 | 8 | 6 | 109 | 54 | 55 | [illegible] |
| Fleetwood Town | 42 | 26 | 8 | 8 | 84 | 51 | 33 | [illegible] |
| Woodley Sports | 42 | 26 | 5 | 11 | 99 | 56 | 43 | [illegible] |
| Warrington Town | 42 | 20 | 10 | 12 | 72 | 59 | 13 | [illegible] |
| Newcastle Town | 42 | 21 | 6 | 15 | 94 | 67 | 27 | [illegible] |
| Curzon Ashton (–3) | 42 | 19 | 10 | 13 | 84 | 79 | 5 | [illegible] |
| Skelmersdale United | 42 | 19 | 6 | 17 | 79 | 64 | 15 | [illegible] |
| Alsager Town | 42 | 16 | 15 | 11 | 54 | 47 | 7 | [illegible] |
| Stone Dominoes | 42 | 18 | 8 | 16 | 57 | 60 | –3 | [illegible] |
| Congleton Town | 42 | 15 | 16 | 11 | 62 | 50 | 12 | [illegible] |
| Atherton LR | 42 | 17 | 7 | 18 | 77 | 76 | 1 | [illegible] |
| Nantwich Town | 42 | 15 | 11 | 16 | 73 | 66 | 7 | [illegible] |
| Bacup Borough | 42 | 15 | 8 | 19 | 68 | 72 | –4 | [illegible] |
| Salford City | 42 | 14 | 11 | 17 | 62 | 66 | –4 | [illegible] |
| Trafford | 42 | 14 | 8 | 20 | 72 | 90 | –18 | [illegible] |
| Ramsbottom United | 42 | 12 | 12 | 18 | 71 | 92 | –21 | [illegible] |
| Glossop North End | 42 | 9 | 9 | 24 | 51 | 95 | –44 | [illegible] |
| St Helens Town (–3) | 42 | 10 | 6 | 26 | 51 | 81 | –30 | [illegible] |
| Squires Gate | 42 | 7 | 12 | 23 | 52 | 83 | –31 | [illegible] |
| Abbey Hey | 42 | 7 | 8 | 27 | 46 | 90 | –44 | [illegible] |
| Atherton Collieries (–4) | 42 | 6 | 9 | 27 | 47 | 99 | –52 | [illegible] |

### NORTH WEST COUNTIES DIVISION TWO

| | P | W | D | L | F | A | GD | Pts |
|---|---|---|---|---|---|---|---|---|
| Colne | 38 | 26 | 6 | 6 | 102 | 40 | 62 | [illegible] |
| Maine Road | 38 | 23 | 5 | 10 | 99 | 58 | 41 | [illegible] |
| Formby | 38 | 21 | 9 | 8 | 86 | 48 | 38 | [illegible] |
| Darwen | 38 | 17 | 11 | 10 | 81 | 67 | 14 | [illegible] |
| Great Harwood Town | 38 | 15 | 14 | 9 | 68 | 44 | 24 | [illegible] |
| Flixton | 38 | 16 | 11 | 11 | 76 | 60 | 16 | [illegible] |
| Ashton Town | 38 | 16 | 11 | 11 | 66 | 60 | 6 | [illegible] |
| Winsford United | 38 | 15 | 11 | 12 | 66 | 62 | 4 | [illegible] |
| Holker Old Boys | 38 | 15 | 8 | 15 | 82 | 76 | 6 | [illegible] |
| Nelson | 38 | 14 | 11 | 13 | 54 | 64 | –10 | [illegible] |
| Leek CSOB | 38 | 14 | 8 | 16 | 72 | 63 | 9 | [illegible] |
| Padiham | 38 | 14 | 8 | 16 | 63 | 80 | –17 | [illegible] |
| Oldham Town | 38 | 13 | 9 | 16 | 69 | 74 | –5 | [illegible] |
| Blackpool Mechanics | 38 | 13 | 7 | 18 | 45 | 59 | –14 | [illegible] |
| Norton United | 38 | 11 | 12 | 15 | 66 | 72 | –6 | [illegible] |
| Cheadle Town | 38 | 12 | 9 | 17 | 55 | 69 | –14 | [illegible] |
| Eccleshall | 38 | 10 | 14 | 14 | 56 | 65 | –9 | [illegible] |
| Chadderton | 38 | 7 | 11 | 20 | 42 | 63 | –21 | [illegible] |
| Daisy Hill | 38 | 7 | 10 | 21 | 33 | 82 | –49 | [illegible] |
| Castleton Gabriels | 38 | 6 | 5 | 27 | 53 | 128 | –75 | [illegible] |

# OLYMPIC FOOTBALL

**Previous medallists**

1896 Athens*
1 Denmark
2 Greece

1900 Paris*
1 Great Britain
2 France

1904 St Louis**
1 Canada
2 USA

1908 London
1 Great Britain
2 Denmark
3 Holland

1912 Stockholm
1 England
2 Denmark
3 Holland

1920 Antwerp
1 Belgium
2 Spain
3 Holland

1924 Paris
1 Uruguay
2 Switzerland
3 Sweden

1928 Amsterdam
1 Uruguay
2 Argentina
3 Italy

1932 Los Angeles
no tournament

1936 Berlin
1 Italy
2 Austria
3 Norway

1948 London
1 Sweden
2 Yugoslavia
3 Denmark

1952 Helsinki
1 Hungary
2 Yugoslavia
3 Sweden

1956 Melbourne
1 USSR
2 Yugoslavia
3 Bulgaria

1960 Rome
1 Yugoslavia
2 Denmark
3 Hungary

1964 Tokyo
1 Hungary
2 Czechoslovakia
3 East Germany

1968 Mexico City
1 Hungary
2 Bulgaria
3 Japan

1972 Munich
1 Poland
2 Hungary
3 E Germany/USSR

1976 Montreal
1 East Germany
2 Poland
3 USSR

1980 Moscow
1 Czechoslovakia
2 East Germany
3 USSR

1984 Los Angeles
1 France
2 Brazil
3 Yugoslavia

1988 Seoul
1 USSR
2 Brazil
3 West Germany

1992 Barcelona
1 Spain
2 Poland
3 Ghana

1996 Atlanta
1 Nigeria
2 Argentina
3 Brazil

2000 Sydney
1. Cameroon
2. Spain
3. Chile

* No official tournamen
** No official tournament but gold medal later awarded by IO

# AMATEUR FOOTBALL ALLIANCE 2003–04

## AFA SENIOR CUP

Sponsored by Ladbrokes

**1st ROUND PROPER**
Old Woodhouseians 4*:3p Clapham Old Xaverians 4*:0p
Southgate County 2 Old Minchendenians 0
Old Grammarians 9 William Fitt 3
Polytechnic 1 Kew Association 0
Hale End Athletic 2 Old Manorians 0
Pegasus 2* Old Parkonians 3*
HSBC 0 Old Owens 2
Mill Hill County Old Boys 0 Winchmore Hill 13
Albanian 4 South Bank Cuaco 2
Bromleian Sports 4 Old Cholmeleians 2
Old Finchleians 4* Old Bealonians 1*
Old Latymerians 2* Civil Service 4*
Kings Old Boys 1 Merton 3
Hon. Artillery Company 4 Old Hamptonians 3
Alleyn Old Boys 3 Wandsworth Borough 2
Crouch End Vampires 2 Bradfield Old Boys 0
Old Meadonians 6 Old Whitgiftians 0
Old Aloysians 3 Old Vaughanians 1
Wake Green 4 Old Tiffinians 1
Nottsborough 7 Old Westminster 1
Old Sedcopians 3 London Welsh 1
West Wickham 6 Southgate Olympic 0
Parkfield 2*:4p Old Salvatorians 2*:3p
Old Actonians Assn 6 Old Malvernian 0
Broomfield 2 Old Stationers 1
BB Eagles 1 Glynn Old Boys 0
Old Ignatians 3 Old Camdenians 4
Norsemen 3 Latymer Old Boys 1
E. Barnet Old Grammarians 3 UCL Academicals 5
Bank of England 1 Old Salesians 2
Lancing Old Boys 0 Old Parmiterians 1
Old Edmontonians 0 Old Esthameians 6

**2nd ROUND PROPER**
Southgate County 1 Alleyn Old Boys 2
Crouch End Vampires 0 Broomfield 6
Old Woodhouseians 0 Hale End Athletic 3
Old Aloysians 0 Old Parkonians 3
Wake Green 3 Old Finchleians 0
Old Meadonians 1 Old Grammarians 0
Parkfield 3 UCL Academicals 4
Old Actonians Assn 2 Civil Service 3
Nottsborough 2 West Wickham 0
Old Esthamians 4 Norsemen 2
Old Parmiterians 0 Polytechnic 1
Bromleian Sports 0 Old Salesians 2
Old Sedcopians 1 Old Camdenians 2
Winchmore Hill 2 BB Eagles 0
Albanian 2 Merton 0
Old Owens 1 Hon. Artillery Company 0

**3RD ROUND PROPER**
Old Esthameians 0 Broomfield 2
Old Meadonians 5 Wake Green 0
Old Owens 0 Civil Service 5
Old Parkonians 1* UCL Academicals 3*
Alleyn Old Boys 6 Old Camdenians 3
Hale End Athletic 1 Albanian 3
Winchmore Hill 1*:4p Polytechnic 1*:3p
Old Salesians 0 Nottsborough 1

**4TH ROUND PROPER**
Broomfield 2 Old Meadonians 7
Civil Service 1 UCL Academicals 2
Alleyn Old Boys 1 Albanian 0
Winchmore Hill 1 Nottsborough 2

**SEMI-FINALS**
Old Meadonians 7 UCL Academicals 1
Alleyn Old Boys 2 Nottsborough 4

**FINAL**
Old Meadonians 3 Nottsborough 0
**aet; p – penalties.*

## OTHER CUP FINALS

**ESSEX SENIOR**
Old Parkonians 2 Hale End Athletic 4
**MIDDLESEX SENIOR**
Polytechnic 2 Old Lyonian 1
**SURREY SENIOR**
Old Salesians 2 Kew Association 1
**INTERMEDIATE**
Old Meadonians Res 2*:2p Mt Pleasant PO 1st 2*:3p
**JUNIOR**
UCL Academicals 3rd 1*:4p Alexandra Park 3rd 1*:3p
**MINOR**
Old Esthameians 4th 2 Albanian 4th 1
**VETERANS**
Old Parmitarians A 5 William Fitt A 2
**OPEN VETERANS**
William Fitt A 5 Winchmore Hill A 0
**GREENLAND**
Winchmore Hill 2 Old Hamptonians 1
**ESSEX INTERMEDIATE**
Davenant Wanderers O B 1st 1 Old Buckwllians Res 5
**KENT INTERMEDIATE**
West Wickham Res 0 Old Addeyans 1st 2
**MIDDLESEX INTERMEDIATE**
Old Vaughanians Res 1 Alexandra Park Res 2
**SURREY INTERMEDIATE**
Royal Sun Alliance 1st 0 Old Thorntonians 1st 2
**SENIOR NOVETS**
Old Tiffinians 5th 0 Old Camdenians 4th 5
**INTERMEDIATE NOVETS**
Old Finchleians 6th 2 Old Actonians Assn 6th 0
**JUNIOR NOVETS**
Old Finchleians 7th 2 Old Salvatorians 7th 3

**SATURDAY YOUTH**
**U-18**
Deportivo Youth London 3 Devas 0
**U-17**
ParkView Rangers 1 Bethwin SE "B" 0
**U-16**
Santley United 3*:4p Providence House 3*:5p
**U-15**
Santley United 5 Enfield Youth 4
**U-14**
Bethwin SE "A" 0 Blue Diamonds 12
**U-13**
Bec United 2 Providence House 1
**U-12**
Santley United 2 Develop 5
**U-11**
West Essex Colts 0 Future Stars 1
**SUNDAY YOUTH**
**U-17**
Old Finchleians 3 Cheshunt 1
**U-16**
Young Parmiterians "A" 0 Potters Bar United "A" 3
**U-15**
Prohawks 2*:3p Southgate Olympic 2*:1p
**U-14**
Old Bealonians 3 Chase Side 6
**U-13**
Winchmore Hill 3 Minchenden 4
**U-12**
Leyton 1 Develop 8
**U-11**
Whitewebb Eagles "A" 4 Whitewebb Eagles "B" 2

## ARTHUR DUNN CUP

Old Salopians 3 Old Brentwoods 0

## ARTHURIAN LEAGUE

| PREMIER DIVISION | P | W | D | L | F | A | Pts |
|---|---|---|---|---|---|---|---|
| Old Harrovians | 18 | 12 | 3 | 3 | 63 | 35 | 39 |
| Lancing Old Boys | 18 | 10 | 3 | 5 | 31 | 19 | 33 |
| Old Carthusians | 18 | 9 | 2 | 7 | 40 | 37 | 29 |
| Old Foresters | 18 | 8 | 3 | 7 | 37 | 29 | 27 |
| Old Etonians | 18 | 8 | 3 | 7 | 39 | 32 | 27 |
| Old Brentwoods | 18 | 8 | 3 | 7 | 36 | 31 | 27 |
| Old Westminsters | 18 | 8 | 3 | 7 | 42 | 43 | 27 |
| Old Salopians | 18 | 7 | 2 | 9 | 37 | 48 | 23 |
| Old Cholmeleians | 18 | 3 | 4 | 11 | 40 | 57 | 13 |
| Old Bradfieldian* | 18 | 4 | 0 | 14 | 23 | 57 | 9 |

| DIVISION 1 | P | W | D | L | F | A | Pts |
|---|---|---|---|---|---|---|---|
| Old Reptonians | 14 | 9 | 1 | 4 | 43 | 20 | 28 |
| Old Wykehamists | 14 | 8 | 4 | 2 | 36 | 20 | 28 |
| Old Chigwellians | 14 | 6 | 6 | 2 | 28 | 23 | 24 |
| Old Malvernians | 14 | 5 | 5 | 4 | 28 | 33 | 20 |
| Old Aldenhamians | 14 | 5 | 4 | 5 | 23 | 27 | 19 |
| Old Haberdashers | 14 | 4 | 4 | 6 | 28 | 36 | 16 |
| Old Witleians | 14 | 4 | 0 | 10 | 19 | 30 | 12 |
| Old Tonbridgians | 14 | 2 | 2 | 10 | 19 | 35 | 8 |

| DIVISION 2 | P | W | D | L | F | A | Pts |
|---|---|---|---|---|---|---|---|
| Old Etonians Res | 14 | 11 | 1 | 2 | 36 | 11 | 34 |
| Old Chigwellians Res | 14 | 10 | 0 | 4 | 34 | 18 | 30 |
| Old Carthusians 3rd | 14 | 6 | 4 | 4 | 28 | 29 | 22 |
| Old Carthusians Res | 14 | 6 | 1 | 7 | 21 | 23 | 19 |
| Old Salopians Res* | 14 | 6 | 1 | 7 | 23 | 29 | 16 |
| Old Foresters Res | 14 | 4 | 3 | 7 | 27 | 30 | 15 |
| Old Cholmeleians Res | 14 | 4 | 2 | 8 | 31 | 36 | 14 |
| Lancing Old Boys Res | 14 | 2 | 2 | 10 | 16 | 40 | 8 |

| DIVISION 3 | P | W | D | L | F | A | Pts |
|---|---|---|---|---|---|---|---|
| Old Westminsters Res | 14 | 12 | 1 | 1 | 54 | 14 | 37 |
| Old Haileyburians | 14 | 11 | 1 | 2 | 50 | 17 | 34 |
| Old Etonians 3rd | 14 | 8 | 2 | 4 | 26 | 23 | 26 |
| Old Brentwoods Res | 14 | 7 | 3 | 4 | 52 | 31 | 24 |
| Old Foresters 3rd | 14 | 3 | 2 | 9 | 18 | 32 | 11 |
| Old Malvernians Res* | 14 | 5 | 0 | 9 | 23 | 45 | 9 |
| Old Bradfieldians Res | 14 | 1 | 4 | 9 | 20 | 41 | 7 |
| Old Cholmeleians 3rd* | 14 | 2 | 1 | 11 | 19 | 59 | 4 |

| DIVISION 4 | P | W | D | L | F | A | Pts |
|---|---|---|---|---|---|---|---|
| Old Bradfieldians 3rd | 14 | 11 | 2 | 1 | 63 | 17 | 32 |
| Old Aldenhameians Res | 14 | 6 | 5 | 3 | 30 | 30 | 23 |
| Old Foresters 4th | 14 | 6 | 3 | 5 | 33 | 26 | 21 |
| Old Brentwoods 3rd | 14 | 4 | 5 | 5 | 29 | 26 | 17 |
| Old Brentwoods 4th | 14 | 5 | 1 | 8 | 20 | 40 | 16 |
| Old Eastbournians | 14 | 4 | 5 | 5 | 27 | 32 | 14 |
| Old Harrovians Res | 14 | 2 | 5 | 7 | 17 | 33 | 11 |
| Old Reptonians Res | 14 | 4 | 2 | 8 | 20 | 35 | 8 |

| DIVISION 5 | P | W | D | L | F | A | Pts |
|---|---|---|---|---|---|---|---|
| Old Chigwellians 3rd | 15 | 10 | 3 | 2 | 52 | 16 | 33 |
| Old Chigwellians 4th | 15 | 7 | 5 | 3 | 32 | 31 | 26 |
| Old Oundelians | 15 | 8 | 1 | 6 | 37 | 24 | 25 |
| Old Westminsters 3rd | 15 | 6 | 2 | 7 | 22 | 27 | 20 |
| Old Berkhamstedians | 15 | 3 | 3 | 9 | 21 | 47 | 12 |
| Old Cholmeleians 4th | 15 | 2 | 4 | 9 | 15 | 34 | 1 |

** Points deducted for breach of rule*

**JUNIOR LEAGUE CUP**
Old Carthusians 3rd 3*:5p Old Chigwellians 3*:4p
**DERRIK MOORE VETERANS' CUP**
Old Carthusians 2* Old Cholmeleians 1*
**JIM DIXSON SIX-A-SIDE CUP**
Won by Old Cholmeleians

## LONDON FINANCIAL FOOTBALL ASSOCIATION

| DIVISION 1 | P | W | D | L | F | A | Pts |
|---|---|---|---|---|---|---|---|
| Dresdner Kleinwort Wasserstein | 14 | 11 | 1 | 2 | 44 | 13 | 34 |
| Granby | 14 | 8 | 3 | 3 | 32 | 22 | 27 |
| Mount Pleasant Post Office* | 14 | 7 | 6 | 1 | 37 | 16 | 26 |
| Royal Sun Alliance | 14 | 7 | 3 | 4 | 37 | 25 | 24 |
| Churchill Insurance | 14 | 5 | 2 | 7 | 36 | 39 | 17 |
| Marsh | 14 | 4 | 3 | 7 | 28 | 39 | 15 |
| Bank of America* | 14 | 2 | 3 | 9 | 20 | 51 | 8 |
| J P Morgan* | 14 | 0 | 3 | 11 | 8 | 37 | 2 |

National Westminster Bank *Withdrawn – record expunged*

| DIVISION 2 | P | W | D | L | F | A | Pts |
|---|---|---|---|---|---|---|---|
| Citigroup Res | 16 | 13 | 3 | 0 | 52 | 17 | 42 |
| Citigroup | 16 | 10 | 2 | 4 | 46 | 26 | 32 |
| Marsh 3rd | 16 | 9 | 2 | 5 | 47 | 35 | 29 |
| Granby Res | 16 | 7 | 4 | 5 | 35 | 30 | 25 |
| Coutts & Co* | 16 | 8 | 0 | 8 | 37 | 41 | 19 |
| Marsh Res | 16 | 4 | 4 | 8 | 26 | 39 | 16 |
| Fusion Allstars | 16 | 4 | 3 | 9 | 35 | 51 | 15 |
| Royal Sun Alliance Res | 16 | 3 | 2 | 11 | 27 | 52 | 11 |
| City Group CIB | 16 | 2 | 4 | 10 | 19 | 33 | 10 |

| DIVISION 3 | P | W | D | L | F | A | Pts |
|---|---|---|---|---|---|---|---|
| Royal Sun Alliance 3rd | 18 | 12 | 4 | 2 | 47 | 22 | 40 |
| National Westminster Bank Res* | 18 | 8 | 5 | 5 | 46 | 28 | 28 |
| National Westminster Bank 3rd | 18 | 8 | 3 | 7 | 42 | 31 | 27 |
| Royal Bank of Scotland | 18 | 7 | 3 | 8 | 21 | 32 | 24 |
| Granby 3rd | 18 | 6 | 4 | 8 | 31 | 41 | 22 |
| Temple Bar | 18 | 4 | 7 | 7 | 30 | 40 | 19 |
| Credit Suisse First Boston | 18 | 4 | 2 | 12 | 19 | 42 | 14 |

| DIVISION 4 | P | W | D | L | F | A | Pts |
|---|---|---|---|---|---|---|---|
| Zurich Eagle Star | 18 | 16 | 1 | 1 | 74 | 23 | 49 |
| National Westminster Bank 4th | 18 | 11 | 3 | 4 | 49 | 32 | 36 |
| South Bank Cuaco 6th | 18 | 7 | 5 | 6 | 52 | 29 | 26 |
| Royal Bank of Scotland Res | 18 | 6 | 4 | 8 | 35 | 51 | 22 |
| Marsh 4th | 18 | 5 | 4 | 9 | 30 | 48 | 19 |
| Foreign & Commonwealth Office | 18 | 3 | 6 | 9 | 33 | 53 | 15 |
| Temple Bar Res | 18 | 3 | 1 | 14 | 29 | 66 | 10 |

** Points deducted for breach of rule*

**CHALLENGE CUP**
Bank of England 6 Granby 1
**SENIOR CUP**
Dresdner Kleinwort Wasserstein 4 Mount Pleasant P O 0
**JUNIOR CUP**
Royal Sun Alliance 3rd 1 Zurich Eagle Star 1st 0

## LONDON LEGAL LEAGUE

| DIVISION I | P | W | D | L | F | A | Pts |
|---|---|---|---|---|---|---|---|
| KPMG ICE | 16 | 12 | 1 | 3 | 45 | 21 | 37 |
| Slaughter & May | 16 | 10 | 4 | 2 | 34 | 19 | 34 |
| Watson Farley & Williams | 16 | 9 | 1 | 6 | 26 | 17 | 28 |
| Baker & McKenzie | 16 | 9 | 0 | 7 | 45 | 35 | 27 |
| Linklaters & Alliance | 16 | 8 | 2 | 6 | 28 | 25 | 26 |
| Clifford Chance | 16 | 6 | 2 | 8 | 33 | 29 | 20 |
| Simmons & Simmons | 16 | 4 | 3 | 9 | 18 | 43 | 15 |
| Gray's Inn* | 16 | 5 | 1 | 10 | 16 | 22 | 14 |
| Eversheds* | 16 | 2 | 0 | 14 | 14 | 48 | 4 |

*Denton Wilde Sapte (A) – record expunged, programme not completed*

| DIVISION II | P | W | D | L | F | A | Pts |
|---|---|---|---|---|---|---|---|
| Richards Butler | 18 | 11 | 3 | 4 | 51 | 23 | 36 |
| Titmuss Sainer Dechert | 18 | 11 | 3 | 4 | 47 | 30 | 36 |
| Freshfields Bruckhaus Deringer | 18 | 11 | 2 | 5 | 42 | 24 | 35 |
| Norton Rose | 18 | 11 | 2 | 5 | 41 | 36 | 35 |
| CMS Cameron McKenna | 18 | 8 | 5 | 5 | 50 | 31 | 29 |
| Macfarlanes | 18 | 6 | 3 | 9 | 22 | 44 | 21 |
| Ashurst Morris Crisp* | 18 | 6 | 3 | 9 | 36 | 31 | 18 |
| Allen & Overy | 18 | 5 | 3 | 10 | 25 | 40 | 18 |
| Barlow Lyde & Gilbert | 18 | 4 | 2 | 12 | 36 | 60 | 14 |
| Lovells | 18 | 2 | 4 | 12 | 23 | 54 | 10 |

| DIVISION III | P | W | D | L | F | A | Pts |
|---|---|---|---|---|---|---|---|
| Mishcon de Reya | 16 | 13 | 0 | 3 | 55 | 19 | 39 |
| Financial Services A | 16 | 12 | 2 | 2 | 49 | 12 | 38 |
| Stephenson Harwood | 16 | 12 | 0 | 4 | 61 | 16 | 36 |
| Herbert Smith | 16 | 10 | 1 | 5 | 34 | 27 | 31 |
| Denton Wilde Sapte (B) | 16 | 6 | 2 | 8 | 28 | 40 | 20 |
| Hammonds Suddards Edge* | 16 | 6 | 1 | 9 | 19 | 14 | 16 |
| Pegasus (Inner Temple) | 16 | 4 | 4 | 8 | 26 | 38 | 16 |
| Farrer & Co | 16 | 3 | 2 | 11 | 18 | 67 | 11 |
| Taylor Wessing* | 16 | 0 | 0 | 16 | 14 | 71 | –2 |

*S J Berwin – Record expunged*
** Points deducted for breach of rule*

**LEAGUE CHALLENGE CUP**
Watson Farley & Williams 2 Linklaters 3 *(aet)*
**WEAVERS ARMS CUP**
Mishcon de Reya 0 Clifford Chance 4

**VITATION CUP**
erbert Smith 8 Farrar & Co 0

## LONDON OLD BOYS CUPS

**ENIOR**
lbanian 2* UCL Academicals 1*
**HALLENGE**
ld Paulines 2* Old Rutlishians 1*
**TERMEDIATE**
ld Meadonians Res 0*:5p UCL Academicals Res 0*:4p
**JNIOR**
CL Academicals 3rd 4 Old Wilsonians 3rd 1
**INOR**
ld Actonians Assn 5th 2 Albanian 4th 0
**RUMMOND (N)†**
ld Camdenians 4th 4 Old Chigwellians 4th 1
**EMEAN (W)†**
ld Kolsassians 4 Old Uffingtonians Res 3
**LYMPIAN (S)†**
ld Tiffinians 5th 4 Old Paulines 3rd 2
Entries now drawn regionally from former composition
the Drummond, Nemean and Novets competitions)
**ACK PERRY VETERANS**
ld Aloysians 2* Old Meadonians 4*

## OLD BOYS CUPS

**ENIOR**
ld Owens 2 Alleyn Old Boys 0
**UNIOR**
ld Owens Res 1 Old Salesians Res 0
**IINOR**
ld Finchleians 3rd 4 Old Bealonians 3rd 2
**OURTH XI**
ld Finchleians 4th 1 Old Westminster Citizens 4th 0
**FTH XI**
ld Minchendenians 5th 3 Old Stationers 5th 0
**IXTH XI**
lyn Old Boys 6th 3 Old Tenisonians 6th 0
**EVENTH XI**
ld Finchleians 7th 1 Old Parmiterians 7th 0
**ETERANS**
lyn Old Boys 2*:5p Old Finchleians 2*:4p

## MIDLAND AMATEUR ALLIANCE

| REMIER DIVISION | P | W | D | L | F | A | Pts |
|---|---|---|---|---|---|---|---|
| aribbean Cavaliers | 26 | 21 | 3 | 2 | 107 | 36 | 66 |
| adcliffe Olympic 3rd | 26 | 19 | 3 | 4 | 85 | 45 | 60 |
| eeston Old Boys Assn | 26 | 15 | 4 | 7 | 62 | 44 | 49 |
| erbyshire Amateurs Res | 26 | 14 | 2 | 10 | 72 | 65 | 44 |
| nderwood Villa | 26 | 12 | 6 | 8 | 74 | 60 | 42 |
| ady Bay | 26 | 12 | 2 | 12 | 70 | 80 | 38 |
| ottingham Trent University | 26 | 10 | 5 | 11 | 71 | 69 | 35 |
| ld Elizabethans | 26 | 9 | 6 | 11 | 71 | 74 | 33 |
| shland Rovers | 26 | 9 | 5 | 12 | 60 | 84 | 32 |
| irkby Autocentre | 26 | 9 | 4 | 13 | 51 | 54 | 31 |
| herwood Forest | 26 | 9 | 3 | 14 | 49 | 69 | 30 |
| quareform Stealers | 26 | 7 | 3 | 16 | 57 | 69 | 24 |
| assingfield | 26 | 6 | 4 | 16 | 46 | 80 | 22 |
| ld Bemrosians | 26 | 3 | 4 | 19 | 37 | 83 | 13 |

| IVISION 1 | P | W | D | L | F | A | Pts |
|---|---|---|---|---|---|---|---|
| Vollaton 3rd | 22 | 18 | 2 | 2 | 84 | 31 | 56 |
| outhwell Amateurs | 22 | 15 | 3 | 4 | 60 | 32 | 48 |
| runts Old Boys | 22 | 14 | 3 | 5 | 57 | 42 | 45 |
| lottinghamshire Res | 22 | 11 | 5 | 6 | 59 | 41 | 38 |
| acing Athletic | 22 | 9 | 5 | 8 | 52 | 45 | 32 |
| Vest Bridgford United | 22 | 9 | 1 | 12 | 45 | 57 | 28 |
| ounty Nalgo | 22 | 8 | 3 | 11 | 47 | 63 | 27 |
| adcliffe Olympic 4th | 22 | 7 | 5 | 10 | 57 | 61 | 26 |
| ld Elizabethans Res | 22 | 7 | 2 | 13 | 53 | 58 | 23 |
| irkby Autocentre Res | 22 | 5 | 7 | 10 | 42 | 59 | 22 |
| Voodburgh United | 22 | 4 | 4 | 14 | 46 | 69 | 16 |
| linphone | 22 | 4 | 2 | 16 | 34 | 78 | 14 |

| IVISION 2 | P | W | D | L | F | A | Pts |
|---|---|---|---|---|---|---|---|
| eyworth United 3rd | 24 | 21 | 2 | 1 | 94 | 17 | 65 |
| aribbean Cavaliers Res | 24 | 21 | 1 | 2 | 107 | 25 | 64 |
| ickling | 24 | 15 | 2 | 7 | 96 | 46 | 47 |
| ld Bemrosians Res | 24 | 12 | 5 | 7 | 70 | 55 | 41 |
| lottinghamshire 3rd | 24 | 12 | 1 | 11 | 43 | 34 | 37 |
| eeston Old Boys Assn Res | 24 | 11 | 4 | 9 | 37 | 43 | 37 |
| obbers Mill | 24 | 11 | 1 | 12 | 49 | 65 | 34 |
| Wollaton 4th | 24 | 9 | 4 | 11 | 74 | 72 | 31 |
| Ashland Rovers Res | 24 | 8 | 1 | 15 | 50 | 70 | 25 |
| Magdala Amateurs 3rd | 24 | 8 | 0 | 16 | 57 | 109 | 24 |
| EMTEC | 24 | 6 | 2 | 16 | 63 | 97 | 20 |
| Tibshelf Old Boys | 24 | 3 | 5 | 16 | 48 | 93 | 14 |
| Derbyshire Amateurs 3rd | 24 | 4 | 2 | 18 | 34 | 96 | 14 |

**LEAGUE SENIOR CUP**
Ashland Rovers 2 Old Elizabethans 0
**LEAGUE INTERMEDIATE CUP**
County Nalgo 3* Nottinghamshire Res 1*
**LEAGUE MINOR CUP**
Hickling 4* Nottinghamshire 3rd 2*

## SOUTHERN AMATEUR LEAGUE

**SENIOR SECTION**

| DIVISION 1 | P | W | D | L | F | A | Pts |
|---|---|---|---|---|---|---|---|
| Old Esthameians | 22 | 15 | 1 | 6 | 57 | 44 | 46 |
| Old Owens | 22 | 12 | 4 | 6 | 49 | 31 | 40 |
| Old Salesians | 22 | 12 | 2 | 8 | 52 | 39 | 38 |
| Winchmore Hill | 22 | 10 | 6 | 6 | 35 | 31 | 36 |
| Polytechnic | 22 | 11 | 1 | 10 | 49 | 41 | 34 |
| Norsemen | 22 | 11 | 1 | 10 | 44 | 41 | 34 |
| Civil Service | 22 | 9 | 5 | 8 | 35 | 33 | 32 |
| Broomfield | 22 | 8 | 4 | 10 | 36 | 43 | 28 |
| Old Actonians Association | 22 | 7 | 5 | 10 | 42 | 43 | 26 |
| West Wickham | 22 | 7 | 5 | 10 | 22 | 26 | 26 |
| Alleyn Old Boys | 22 | 7 | 4 | 11 | 27 | 42 | 25 |
| HSBC | 22 | 2 | 4 | 16 | 26 | 60 | 10 |

| DIVISION 2 | P | W | D | L | F | A | Pts |
|---|---|---|---|---|---|---|---|
| Nottsborough | 22 | 18 | 4 | 0 | 79 | 25 | 58 |
| Old Parmiterians | 22 | 11 | 4 | 7 | 49 | 39 | 37 |
| Old Finchleians | 22 | 10 | 5 | 7 | 50 | 42 | 35 |
| Bank of England | 22 | 10 | 4 | 8 | 37 | 31 | 34 |
| Weirside Rangers | 22 | 10 | 3 | 9 | 40 | 35 | 33 |
| Carshalton | 22 | 8 | 6 | 8 | 39 | 37 | 30 |
| South Bank Cuaco | 22 | 7 | 6 | 9 | 34 | 37 | 27 |
| Old Parkonians | 22 | 7 | 6 | 9 | 25 | 50 | 27 |
| East Barnet Old Grammarians | 22 | 7 | 4 | 11 | 41 | 37 | 25 |
| Old Lyonians | 22 | 7 | 2 | 13 | 32 | 59 | 23 |
| BB Eagles | 22 | 5 | 6 | 11 | 33 | 47 | 21 |
| Old Stationers | 22 | 4 | 6 | 12 | 21 | 41 | 18 |

| DIVISION 3 | P | W | D | L | F | A | Pts |
|---|---|---|---|---|---|---|---|
| Kew Association | 24 | 18 | 4 | 2 | 68 | 14 | 58 |
| Alexandra Park | 24 | 14 | 4 | 6 | 69 | 32 | 46 |
| Merton | 24 | 13 | 5 | 6 | 63 | 29 | 44 |
| Old Westminster Citizens | 24 | 11 | 5 | 8 | 50 | 43 | 38 |
| Old Latymerians | 24 | 7 | 7 | 10 | 39 | 55 | 28 |
| Crouch End Vampires | 24 | 8 | 3 | 13 | 43 | 61 | 27 |
| Southgate Olympic | 24 | 7 | 3 | 14 | 35 | 59 | 24 |
| Ibis | 24 | 5 | 5 | 14 | 44 | 75 | 20 |
| Lloyds TSB Bank | 24 | 5 | 4 | 15 | 40 | 83 | 19 |

**INTERMEDIATE SECTION**
**Division 1** – 12 teams
Won by Old Esthameians Res
**Division 2** – 12 teams
Won by Old Stationers Res
**Division 3** – 9 teams
Won by Alexandra Park Res

**THIRD TEAM SECTION**
**Division 1** – 12 teams
Won by Old Actonians Association 3rd
**Division 2** – 12 teams
Won by Alexandra Park 3rd
**Division 3** – 9 teams
Won by Old Parmiterians 3rd

**MINOR SECTION**
**Division 1** – 12 teams
Won by Old Actonians Association 4th

**NORTHERN**
**Division 2** – 10 teams
Won by Alexandra Park 4th
**Division 3** – 10 teams
Won by Old Esthameians 5th
**Division 4** – 10 teams
Won by Old Actonians Association 6th
**Division 5** – 10 teams
Won by Old Finchleians 7th
**Division 6** – 10 teams
Won by Old Parmiterians 8th

**SOUTHERN**
**Division 2** – 10 teams
Won by Nottsborough 4th
**Division 3** – 10 teams
Won by HSBC 5th
**Division 4** – 10 teams
Won by South Bank Cuaco 5th
**Division 5** – 10 teams
Won by Civil Service 7th
**Division 6** – 10 teams
Won by Polytechnic 8th

**CHALLENGE CUPS**
**JUNIOR**
Nottsborough 3rd 4 Norsemen 3rd 0
**MINOR**
Winchmore Hill 4th 3* Old Esthameians 4th 2*
**SENIOR NOVETS**
Norsemen 5th 2 Winchmore Hill 5th 0
**INTERMEDIATE NOVETS**
Carshalton 6th 1 Old Finchleians 6th 2
**JUNIOR NOVETS**
Old Finchleians 7th 5* Old Finchleians 8th 3*

## U-16 GIRLS CENTRE OF EXCELLENCE LEAGUE

Sponsored by Puma

| | *P* | *W* | *D* | *L* | *F* | *A* | *Pts* |
|---|---|---|---|---|---|---|---|
| Arsenal | 20 | 17 | 3 | 0 | 69 | 11 | 54 |
| Southampton | 20 | 13 | 3 | 4 | 52 | 21 | 42 |
| Fulham | 20 | 13 | 2 | 5 | 53 | 25 | 41 |
| Watford | 20 | 13 | 1 | 6 | 35 | 28 | 40 |
| Reading | 20 | 9 | 1 | 10 | 27 | 33 | 28 |
| Leyton Orient | 20 | 7 | 5 | 8 | 35 | 28 | 26 |
| Charlton Athletic | 20 | 7 | 5 | 8 | 38 | 32 | 26 |
| Chelsea | 20 | 7 | 4 | 9 | 32 | 35 | 25 |
| Colchester United | 20 | 6 | 2 | 12 | 26 | 46 | 20 |
| Millwall | 20 | 1 | 4 | 15 | 21 | 55 | 7 |
| Brighton & Hove Albion | 20 | 2 | 0 | 18 | 16 | 90 | 6 |

## AMATEUR FOOTBALL COMBINATION

| PREMIER DIVISION | *P* | *W* | *D* | *L* | *F* | *A* | *Pts* |
|---|---|---|---|---|---|---|---|
| Old Meadonians | 20 | 18 | 1 | 1 | 67 | 19 | 55 |
| Old Hamptonians | 20 | 14 | 3 | 3 | 49 | 36 | 45 |
| UCL Academicals | 20 | 11 | 4 | 5 | 50 | 43 | 37 |
| Old Wilsonians | 20 | 10 | 2 | 8 | 33 | 31 | 32 |
| Old Aloysians | 20 | 9 | 3 | 8 | 50 | 37 | 30 |
| Albanian | 20 | 8 | 4 | 8 | 44 | 40 | 28 |
| Hale End Athletic | 20 | 6 | 4 | 10 | 44 | 53 | 22 |
| Old Danes | 20 | 6 | 1 | 13 | 26 | 41 | 19 |
| Latymer Old Boys | 20 | 5 | 3 | 12 | 36 | 55 | 18 |
| Old Salvatorians | 20 | 4 | 3 | 13 | 29 | 44 | 15 |
| Old Ignatians | 20 | 3 | 4 | 13 | 24 | 53 | 13 |

| SENIOR DIVISION 1 | *P* | *W* | *D* | *L* | *F* | *A* | *Pts* |
|---|---|---|---|---|---|---|---|
| Parkfield | 16 | 11 | 4 | 1 | 38 | 11 | 37 |
| Old Wokingians | 16 | 9 | 3 | 4 | 23 | 18 | 30 |
| Old Isleworthians | 16 | 8 | 3 | 5 | 24 | 24 | 27 |
| Old Tenisonians | 16 | 7 | 3 | 6 | 20 | 21 | 24 |
| Old Bealonians | 16 | 6 | 4 | 6 | 30 | 23 | 22 |
| Honourable Artillery Company | 16 | 4 | 7 | 5 | 24 | 26 | 19 |
| Southgate County | 16 | 4 | 4 | 8 | 21 | 33 | 16 |
| Old Tiffinians | 16 | 2 | 6 | 8 | 19 | 27 | 12 |
| Old Vaughanians | 16 | 2 | 4 | 10 | 19 | 35 | 10 |

| SENIOR DIVISION 2 | *P* | *W* | *D* | *L* | *F* | *A* | *Pts* |
|---|---|---|---|---|---|---|---|
| Glyn Old Boys | 16 | 13 | 3 | 0 | 46 | 7 | 42 |
| Enfield Old Grammarians | 16 | 10 | 3 | 3 | 34 | 12 | 33 |
| Old Suttonians | 16 | 7 | 4 | 5 | 28 | 23 | 25 |
| Economicals | 16 | 6 | 5 | 5 | 31 | 30 | 23 |
| Old Grammarians | 16 | 4 | 7 | 5 | 33 | 30 | 19 |
| Old Buckwellians | 16 | 5 | 4 | 7 | 23 | 27 | 19 |
| Old Dorkinians | 16 | 5 | 3 | 8 | 28 | 33 | 18 |
| Old Manorians | 16 | 4 | 5 | 7 | 24 | 31 | 17 |
| Shene Old Grammarians | 16 | 1 | 0 | 15 | 17 | 71 | 3 |

| SENIOR DIVISION 3 | *P* | *W* | *D* | *L* | *F* | *A* | *Pts* |
|---|---|---|---|---|---|---|---|
| Wood Green Old Boys | 18 | 12 | 1 | 5 | 56 | 37 | 37 |
| Pegasus | 18 | 11 | 3 | 4 | 41 | 25 | 36 |
| Queen Mary College Old Boys | 18 | 10 | 5 | 3 | 36 | 25 | 35 |
| Old Reigatians | 18 | 10 | 3 | 5 | 39 | 25 | 33 |
| University of Hertfordshire | 18 | 8 | 4 | 6 | 46 | 35 | 2 |
| John Fisher Old Boys | 18 | 6 | 2 | 10 | 39 | 52 | 2 |
| Old Vaughians Res | 18 | 5 | 4 | 9 | 39 | 49 | 1 |
| Old Woodhouseians | 18 | 5 | 3 | 10 | 42 | 53 | 1 |
| King's Old Boys | 18 | 5 | 3 | 10 | 26 | 39 | 1 |
| Old Minchendenians | 18 | 3 | 2 | 13 | 29 | 53 | 1 |

| SENIOR DIVISION 4 | *P* | *W* | *D* | *L* | *F* | *A* | *Pt* |
|---|---|---|---|---|---|---|---|
| Old Challoners | 16 | 14 | 0 | 2 | 50 | 18 | 4 |
| Old Sedcopians | 16 | 12 | 2 | 2 | 59 | 24 | 3 |
| Clapham Old Xaverians | 16 | 11 | 1 | 4 | 50 | 20 | 3 |
| Parkfield Res | 16 | 7 | 2 | 7 | 34 | 35 | 2 |
| Centymca | 16 | 6 | 3 | 7 | 30 | 35 | 2 |
| Old Hamptonians Res | 16 | 5 | 3 | 8 | 18 | 34 | 1 |
| Old Wilsonians Res | 16 | 5 | 2 | 9 | 31 | 42 | 1 |
| Brent | 16 | 2 | 2 | 12 | 17 | 44 | [illegible] |
| Latymer Old Boys Res | 16 | 2 | 1 | 13 | 17 | 54 | [illegible] |

**INTERMEDIATE DIVISIONS**
**North** – 11 teams
Won by UCL Academicals Res
**South** – 12 teams
Won by Mickleham Old Boxhillians

**REGIONAL**
**North**
**Division 1** – 10 teams
Won by UCL Academicals 3rd
**Division 2** – 10 teams
Won by Enfield Old Grammarians Res
**Division 3** – 10 teams
Won by Albanian 4th
**Division 4** – 10 teams
Won by Egbertian 3rd
**Division 5** – 9 teams
Won by Old Aloysians 5th
**Division 6** – 10 teams
Won by UCL Academicals 5th
**Division 7** – 10 teams
Won by Wood Green Old Boys 4th
**Division 8** – 9 teams
Won by Old Minchendenians 5th
**Division 9** – 10 teams
Won by Old Minchendenians 6th

**South**
**Division 1** – 10 teams
Won by Wandsworth Borough
**Division 2** – 10 teams
Won by Old Rutlishians
**Division 3** – 10 teams
Won by Clapham Old Xaverians Res
**Division 4** – 10 teams
Won by Clapham Old Xaverians 3rd
**Division 5** – 10 teams
Won by Old Bromleians Res
**Division 6** – 10 teams
Won by Centymca 3rd
**Division 7** – 10 teams
Won by Old Tenisonians 4th
**Division 8** – 9 teams
Won by Clapham Old Xaverians 5th
**Division 9** – 10 teams
Won by Old Tiffinians 5th
**Division 10** – 10 teams
Won by Old Wokingians 7th
**Division 11** – 11 teams
Won by Old Wokingians 8th

**West**
**Division 1** – 10 teams
Won by Old Meadonians Res
**Division 2** – 11 teams
Won by Old Salvatorians 4th
**Division 3** – 10 teams
Won by Old Uxonians Res
**Division 4** – 9 teams
Won by Parkfield 5th
**Division 5** – 10 teams
Won by Phoenix Old Boys 3rd
**Division 6** – 8 teams
Won by Old Salvatorians 7th
**Division 7** – 8 teams
Won by Brent 3rd

# IMPORTANT ADDRESSES

**The Football Association:** The Secretary, 25 Soho Square, London W1D 4FA. *020 7745 4545*

**Scotland:** David Taylor, Hampden Park, Glasgow G42 9AY. *0141 616 6000*

**Northern Ireland** (Irish FA): D. I. Bowen, 20 Windsor Avenue, Belfast BT9 6EG. *028 9066 9458*

**Wales:** D. Collins, 3 Westgate Street, Cardiff, South Glamorgan CF10 1DP. *029 2037 2325*

**Republic of Ireland** B. Menton (FA of Ireland): 80 Merrion Square South, Dublin 2. *00353 16766864*

**International Federation** (FIFA): P. O. Box 85 8030 Zurich, Switzerland. *00 411 384 9595. Fax: 00 411 384 9696*

**Union of European Football Associations:** Secretary, Route de Geneve 46, Case Postale CH-1260 Nyon, Switzerland. *0041 22 994 44 44. Fax: 0041 22 994 44 88*

## THE LEAGUES

**The Premier League:** M. Foster, 11 Connaught Place, London W2 2ET. *020 7298 1600*

**The Football League:** Secretary, The Football League, Unit 5, Edward VII Quay, Navigation Way, Preston, Lancashire PR2 2YF. *01772 325800. Fax 01772 325801*

**Scottish Premier League:** R. Mitchell, Hampden Park, Somerville Drive, Glasgow G42 9BA. *0141 646 6962*

**The Scottish League:** P. Donald, Hampden Park, Glasgow G42 9AY. *0141 616 6000*

**The Irish League:** H. Wallace, 96 University Street, Belfast BT7 1HE. *028 9024 2888*

**Football League of Ireland:** D. Crowther, 80 Merrion Square, Dublin 2. *00353 16765120*

**Conference National:** Riverside House, 14b High Street, Crayford, DA1 4HG. *01322 411021*

**Central League:** A. Williamson, The Football League, Unit 5, Edward VII Quay, Navigation Way, Preston, Lancashire PR2 2YF. *01772 325800. Fax 01772 325801*

**Eastern Counties League:** B. A. Badcock, 41 The Copse, Southwood, Farnborough, Hampshire GU14 0QD. *01252 387588*

**Football Combination:** D. A. Daughtery, 3 Eastergate, Little Common, Bexhill-on-Sea, East Sussex TN31 4NU. *01424 848061*

**Hellenic League:** B. King, 83 Queens Road, Carterton, Oxon OX18 3YF. *01993 212738*

**Kent League:** R. Vinter, Bakery House, The Street, Chilham, Canterbury, Kent CT4 8BX. *01227 730457*

**Leicestershire Senior League:** R. J. Holmes, 8 Huntsmans Close, Markfield, Leics LE67 9XE. *01530 243093*

**Manchester League:** P. Platt, 26A Stalybridge Road, Mottram Hyde, Cheshire SK14 6NE. *01457 763821*

**Midland Combination:** N. Harvey, 115 Millfield Road, Handsworth Wood, Birmingham B20 1ED. *0121 357 4172*

**Northern Premier:** R. D. Bayley, 22 Woburn Drive, Hale, Altrincham, Cheshire WA15 8LZ. *0161 980 7007*

**Northern League:** T. Golightly, 85 Park Road North, Chester-le-Street, Co Durham DH3 3SA. *0191 3882056*

**Isthmian League:** Triumph House, Station Approach, Sanderstead Road, South Croydon, Surrey CR2 0PL. *020 8409 1978. Fax: 020 7639 5726*

**Southern League:** D. J. Strudwick, P.O. Box 90, Worcester, WR3 8XR. *01905 757509*

**Spartan South Midlands League:** M. Mitchell, 26 Leighton Court, Dunstable, Beds LU6 1EW. *01582 667291*

**United Counties League:** R. Gamble, 8 Bostock Avenue, Northampton NN1 4LW. *01604 637766*

**Western League:** K. A. Clarke, 32 Westmead Lane, Chippenham, Wilts SN15 3HZ. *01249 464467*

**West Midlands Regional League:** N. R. Juggins, 14 Badger Way, Blackwell, Bromsgrove, Worcs B60 1EX. *0121 445 2953*

**Northern Counties (East):** B. Wood, 6 Restmore Avenue, Guiseley, Leeds LS20 9DG. *01943 874558*

**Central Midlands Football League:** Frank Harwood, 103 Vestry Road, Oakwood, Derby, Derbyshire DE21 2BN. *01332 832372*

**Combined Counties League:** Clive R. Tidey, 22 Silo Road, Farncombe, Godalming, Surrey GU7 3PA. *01483 428453*

**Essex Senior League:** David Walls, Bramley Cottage, 2 Birch Street, Colchester CO2 0NW. *0207 587 4139*

**Lancashire Football League:** Barbara Howarth, 86 Windsor Road, Great Harwood, Blackburn, Lancs BB6 7RR. *01254 886267*

**Midland Football Alliance:** Peter Dagger, 32 Drysdale Close, Wickhamford, Worcs WR11 6RZ. *01386 831763*

**North West Counties Football League:** G. J. Wilkinson, 46 Oaklands Drive, Penwortham, Preston, Lancs PR1 0XY. *01772 746312*

**Wessex League:** Tom Lindon, 63 Downs Road, South Wonston, Winchester, Hants SO21 3EW. *01962 884760*

**South Western League:** R. Rowe, 5 Alverton Gardens, Truro, Cornwall TR1 1JA. *01872 242190*

## COUNTY FOOTBALL ASSOCIATIONS

**Bedfordshire:** P. D. Brown, Century House, Skimpot Road, Dunstable, Beds LU5 4JU. *01582 565111*

**Berks and Bucks:** B. G. Moore, 15a London Street, Faringdon, Oxon SN7 7HD. *01367 242099*

**Birmingham County:** D. Shelton, County FA Offices, Rayhall Lane, Great Barr, Birmingham B43 6JF. *0121 357 4278*

**Cambridgeshire:** R. K. Pawley, City Ground, Milton Road, Cambridge CB4 1FA. *01223 576770*

**Cheshire:** Ms M. Dunford, The Cottage, Hartford Moss Rec Centre, Winnington, Northwich CW8 4BG. *01606 871166*

**Cornwall:** B. Cudmore, 1 High Cross Street, St. Austell, Cornwall PL25 4AB. *01726 74080*

**Cumberland:** G. Turrell, 17 Oxford Street, Workington, Cumbria CA14 2AL. *01900 872310*

**Derbyshire:** K. Compton, No 8–9 Stadium, Business Court, Millenium Way, Pride Park, Derby DE24 8HZ *01332 361422*

**Devon County:** C. Davidson, County HQ, Coach Road, Newton Abbot, Devon TQ12 1EJ. *01626 332077*

**Dorset County:** P. Hough, County Ground, Blandford Close, Hamworthy, Poole, Dorset BH15 4BF. *01202 682375*

**Durham:** J. Topping, 'Codeslaw', Ferens Park, Durham DH1 1JZ. *0191 3848653*

**East Riding County:** D. R. Johnson, 50 Boulevard, Hull HU3 2TB. *01482 221158*

**Essex County:** P. Sammons, 31 Mildmay Road, Chelmsford, Essex CM2 0DN. *01245 357727*

**Gloucestershire:** P. Britton, Oaklands Park, Almondsbury, Bristol BS32 4AG. *01454 615888*

**Guernsey:** D. Dorey, Haut Regard, St. Clair Hill, St. Sampson's, Guernsey, GY2 4DT, CI. *01481 246231*

**Hampshire:** Neil Cassar, William Pickford House, 8 Ashwood Gardens, off Winchester Road, Southampton SO16 7PW. *023 8079 1110*

**Herefordshire:** J. S. Lambert, County Ground Offices, Widemarsh Common, Hereford HR4 9NA. *01432 342179*

**Hertfordshire:** E. King, County Ground, Baldock Road, Letchworth, Herts SG6 2EN. *01462 677622*

**Huntingdonshire:** M. M. Armstrong, Cromwell Chambers, 8 St Johns Street, Huntingdon, Cambs PE29 6DD. *01480 414422*

**Isle of Man:** Mrs A. Garrett, P.O. Box 53, The Bowl, Douglas IOM IM99 1GY. *01624 615576*

**Jersey:** Gill Morgan, Springfield Stadium, St Helier, Jersey JE2 4LF. *01534 500165*

**Kent County:** K. T. Masters, 69 Maidstone Road, Chatham, Kent ME4 6DT. *01634 843824*

**Lancashire:** J. Kenyon, The County Ground, Thurston Road, Leyland, Preston, Lancs PR5 1LF. *01772 624000*

**Leicestershire and Rutland:** P. Morrison, Holmes Park, Dog and Gun Lane, Whetstone, Leicester LE8 6FA. *0116 2867828*

**Lincolnshire:** J. Griffin, PO Box 26, 12 Dean Road, Lincoln LN2 4DP. *01522 524917*

**Liverpool County:** F. L. J. Hunter, Liverpool Soccer Centre, Walton Hall Park, Walton Hall Avenue, Liverpool L4 9XP. *0151 523 4488*

**London:** D. Fowkes, 6 Aldworth Grove, London SE13 6HY. *020 8690 9626*

**Manchester County:** John Dutton, Brantingham Road, Chorlton, Manchester M21 0TT. *0161 881 0299*

**Middlesex County:** P. J. Clayton, 39 Roxborough Road, Harrow, Middx HA1 1NS. *020 8424 8524*

**Norfolk County:** R. J. Howlett, Plantation Park, Blofield, Norwich, Norfolk, NR13 4PL. *01603 717177*

**Northamptonshire:** D. Payne, 2 Duncan Close, Moulton Park, Northampton NN3 6WL. *01604 670741*

**North Riding County:** M. Jarvis, Southlands Centre, Ormesby Road, Middlesbrough TS3 0HB. *01642 318603*

**Northumberland:** R. E. Maughan, Churchill Pavilion, Hartley Avenue, Whitley Bay NE26 3FA. *0191 2530656*

**Nottinghamshire:** M. Kilbee, 7 Clarendon Street Nottingham NG1 5HS. *0115 9418954*

**Oxfordshire:** I. Mason, P.O. Box 62, Witney, Oxon OX28 1HA. *01993 778586*

**Sheffield and Hallamshire:** J. Hope-Gill, Clegg House 69 Cornish Place, Cornish Street, Shalesmoor Sheffield S6 3AF. *0114 241 4999*

**Shropshire:** D. Rowe, Gay Meadow, Abbey Foregate Shrewsbury SY2 6AB. *01743 362769*

**Somerset & Avon (South):** Mrs H. Marchment, 30 North Road, Midsomer Norton, Radstock BA3 2QD. *01761 410280*

**Staffordshire:** B. J. Adshead, County Showground, Weston Road, Stafford ST18 0BD. *01785 256994*

**Suffolk County:** M. Head, The Buntings, Cedars Park, Stowmarket, Suffolk IP14 5GZ. *01449 616606*

**Surrey County:** R. Ward, 321 Kingston Road, Leatherhead, Surrey KT22 7TU. *01372 373543*

**Sussex County:** Ken Benham, County Office, Culver Road, Lancing, West Sussex BN15 9AX. *01903 753547*

**Westmorland:** P. G. Ducksbury, Unit 1, Angel Court, 21 Highgate, Kendal, Cumbria LA9 4DA. *01539 730946*

**West Riding County:** R. Carter, Fleet Lane, Woodlesford, Leeds LS26 8NX. *0113 2821222*

**Wiltshire:** M. G. Benson, Covingham Square, Covingham, Swindon SN3 5AA. *01793 525245*

**Worcestershire:** M. R. Leggett, Craftsman House, De Salis Drive, Hampton Lovett Industrial Estate, Droitwich WR9 0QE. *01905 827137*

## OTHER USEFUL ADDRESSES

**Amateur Football Alliance:** M. L. Brown, 55 Islington Park Street, London N1 1QB. *020 7359 3493*

**English Schools FA:** Ms A. Pritchard, 1/2 Eastgate Street, Stafford ST16 2NG. *01785 51142*

**Oxford University:** Richard Tur, Oriel College, Oriel Square, Oxford OX1 4EW. *01865 276648*

**Cambridge University:** Dr J. A. Little, St Catherine's College, Cambridge CB2 1RL. *01223 334376*

**Army:** Major W. T. E. Thomson ASCB (MOD), Clayton Barracks, Thornhill Road, Aldershot, Hants GU11 2BG. *01252 348571/4*

**Royal Air Force:** Sqn Ldr R. Moorehouse, OC PACS, RAF Coltishall, Norwich. *01603 737361 ext 7306*

**Royal Navy:** Lt-Cdr S. Vasey, RN Sports Office, HMS Temeraire, Portsmouth, Hants PO1 2HB. *023 9272 2671*

**British Universities Sports Association:** G. Gregory-Jones, Chief Executive: BUSA, 8 Union Street, London SE1 1SZ. *020 7357 8555*

**British Olympic Association:** 6 John Prince's Street, London W1M 0DH. *020 7408 2029*

**The Footbal Supporters Federation:** Chairman: Ian D. Todd MBE, 8 Wyke Close, Wyke Gardens, Isleworth, Middlesex TW7 5PE. *020 8847 2905 (and fax). Mobile: 0961 558908.* National Secretary: Mike Williamson, 2 Repton Avenue, Torrishome, Morecambe, Lancs LA4 6RZ. *01524 425242, 07729 906329 (mobile).* National Administrator: Mark Agate, 'The Stadium', 14 Coombe Close, Lordswood, Chatham, Kent ME5 8NU. *01634 319461 (and fax) 07931 635637 (mobile)*

**National Playing Fields Association:** Col. R. Satterthwaite, O.B.E., 578b Catherine Place, London, SW1.

**Professional Footballers' Association:** G. Taylor, 2 Oxford Court, Bishopsgate, Off Lower Mosley Street, Manchester M2 3WQ. *0161 236 0575*

**Referees' Association:** A. Smith, 1 Westhill Road, Coundon, Coventry CV6 2AD. *024 7660 1701*

**Women's Football Alliance:** Miss K. Doyle, The Football Association, 25 Soho Square, London W1D 4FA. *020 7745 4545*

**Institute of Football Management and Administration:** Camkin House, 8 Charles Court, Budbrooke Road, Warwick CV34 5LZ. *01926 411884. Fax: 01926 411041*

**Football Administrators Association:** as above.

**Commercial and Marketing Managers Association:** as above.

**Management Stats Association:** as above.

**League Managers Association:** as above.

**The Football Programme Directory:** David Stacey, 'The Beeches', 66 Southend Road, Wickford, Essex SS11 8EN. *01268 732041 (and fax)*

**England Football Supporters Association:** Publicity Officer, David Stacey, 'The Beeches', 66 Southend Road, Wickford, Essex SS11 8EN. *01268 732041 (and fax)*

**World Cup (1966) Association:** as above.

**The Ninety-Two Club:** 104 Gilda Crescent, Whitchurch, Bristol BS14 9LD.

**Scottish 38 Club:** Mark Byatt, 6 Greenfields Close, Loughton, Essex IG10 3HG. *0181 508 6088*

**The Football Trust:** Second Floor, Walkden House, 10 Melton Street, London NW1 2EJ. *020 7388 4504*

**Association of Provincial Football Supporters Clubs in London:** Stephen Moon, 32 Westminster Gardens, Barking, Essex IG11 0BJ. *020 8594 2367*

**World Association of Friends of English Football:** Carlisle Hill, Gluck, Habichthof 2, D24939 Flensburg, Germany. *0049 461 4700222*

**Football Postcard Collectors Club:** PRO: Bryan Horsnell, 275 Overdown Road, Tilehurst, Reading RG31 6NX. *0118 9424448 (and fax)*

**UK Programme Collectors Club:** Secretary, John Litster, 46 Milton Road, Kirkcaldy, Fife KY1 1TL. *01592 268718. Fax: 01592 595069*

**Programme Monthly:** as above.

**Scottish Football Historians Association:** as above.

**Phil Gould** (Licensed Football Agent), c/o Whoppit Management Ltd, P. O. Box 27204, London N11 2WS. *07071 732 468. Fax: 07070 732 469*

**The Scandinavian Union of Supporters of British Football:** Postboks, 15 Stovner, N-0913 Oslo, Norway.

**Football Writers' Association:** Executive Secretary, Ken Montgomery, 6 Chase Lane, Barkingside, Essex IG6 1BH. *0208 554 2455 (and fax)*

**Programme Promotions:** 47 The Beeches, Lampton Road, Hounslow, Middlesex TW3 4DF.
Web: www.footballprogrammes.com

# FOOTBALL CLUB CHAPLAINCY

'hey were both well into middle age and considerably experienced men. Yet this meeting was completely dif-erent from anything either of them had undertaken before. 'What do you deliver?' the chairman wanted to now. He'd heard a few of his co-chairmen mention chaplains with approval, but of course he wanted to hear or himself and make up his own mind.

'It's a fair enough question,' the other man thought. 'And on my reply will hang my future involvement here .. and that of anyone else for at least ten years.' He breathed a prayer for wisdom as he smiled at the chair-nan and the answer went something like this:

'Chaplaincy in any area of life is a challenging area of ministry, but in football, as in several other realms, it as become respected and established. Many Premier and Football League clubs enjoy the benefits of a chap-ain's services so the role-models are varied but several features are common to them all.

'Football chaplains offer loyalty to their club. They may or may not have grown up as one of its fans, but hey express loyalty in an ongoing, unpaid commitment that is demonstrated by regular visits to the club and s staff, plus an "on-call" availability.

'We provide experience linked with integrity. Our men are trained, gifted and knowledgeable in responding o pastoral needs (yet respectful of every person's attitude to life), and to spiritual ones for there is much more or example to a football club's receptionist than her telephone manner and to a footballer than his fitness and bility.

'Chaplains co-operate with other professionals at the club like the physiotherapist, the doctor, the adminis-rators, and whatever information is passed to them from any source is held in total confidentiality.

'By their vocations, chaplains are selfless – they don't force their views on unwilling listeners, are not inter-sted in status and do not seek publicity for themselves.

'So, in a nutshell, chairman, I suppose you could simply say that a chaplain offers a willingness to serve thers within your football club.'

That all took place some thirteen years ago. The chaplain has become a familiar, respected and accepted fig-re at the football club and the chairman knows that his friend is one of the best signings he's ever made.

**OBITUARY**
**REV MICHAEL CHANTRY**

'he Rev Michael Chantry (hon chaplain of Oxford United) died in September 2003.

Michael had been with the U's for over 41 years – in fact since they were elected to the Football League in 962. He was a football man through and through (though his ministry was distinguished and wide-ranging) nd had followed Sunderland, his local club, in his early boyhood days. He loved to tell how he had incorpo-ated a top-flight League match into his Ordination retreat while the Bishop had a post-prandial snooze! Aichael was hugely respected by the chaplains' fraternity and by generations of directors, players, staff and ans at Oxford United as well as by many men who had held senior positions at several leading football clubs.

THE REV

**)FFICIAL CHAPLAINS TO FA PREMIERSHIP AND FOOTBALL LEAGUE CLUBS**

Rev Steven Hawkins—Bristol R; Rev Catherine Bell—Luton T; Rev Peter Bye—Carlisle U; Rev Ken Iowles—Blackburn R; Rev David Langdon—QPR; Rev Andrew Taggart—Torquay U; Rev Gary Piper—'ulham; Rev David Jeans—Sheffield W; Rev Peter Amos—Barnsley; Rev Nigel Sands—Crystal Palace; Rev Barry Kirk—Reading; Rev Graham Spencer—Leicester C; Rev Martin Short and Very Rev John Richardson—Bradford C; Rev Kevan McCormack—Ipswich T; Rev John Boyers—Manchester U; Rev Allen Bagshawe—Hull C; Rev Martin Butt—Walsall; Rev David Tully—Newcastle U; Rev Derek Cleave—Bristol C; Rev Fr Alan Poulter and Fr Gerald Courell—Tranmere R; Rev Brian Rice—Hartlepool U; Rev Matt Baker nd Rev Jeffrey Heskins—Charlton Ath; Mr John Graham—Watford; Rev Owen Beament—Millwall; Rev Elwin Cockett—West Ham U; Rev Michael Futens—Derby Co; Rev Mick Woodhead—Sheffield U; Rev Ken Hawkins—Birmingham C; Rev Alan Comfort—Leyton Orient; Rev Simon Stevenette—Swindon T; Rev John Hall-Matthews—Wolverhampton W; Rev Steve Collis—Port Vale; Rev Chris Cullwick—York C; Rev Ken Baker—Northampton T; Rev Mark Hirst—Burnley; Rev Tony Porter—Manchester C; Rev Richard Hayton—Gillingham; Rev Clive Andrews—Notts Co; Fr Andrew McMahon—Southampton; Rev Chris Nelson—Preston North End; Rev Henry Corbett and Rev Harry Ross—Everton; Rev Paul Brown—Wrexham; Rev Jeff Howden—Plymouth Argyle; Rev Andy Rimmer and Mr Mick Mellows—Portsmouth; Rev Alan Hayday—Scunthorpe U; Rev James Booth—Southend U; Rev Philip Hearn—Kidderminster H; Rev David Ottley—Bury; Capt Nigel Tansley—Crewe Alex; Rev Billy Montgomery—Stockport Co; Rev Ken Hipkiss—WBA; Canon Roger Knight—Rushden & Diamonds; Rev Kevin Johns—Swansea C; Rev Anthony Wareham—Peterborough U; Revs David Male and Vaughan Pollard—Huddersfield T; Rev Jim Pearce—Yeovil T; Rev Brian Quow—Doncaster R.

*The chaplains hope that those who read this page will see the value and benefit of chaplaincy work in football and will take appropriate steps to spread the word where this is possible. They would also like to thank the edi-ors of the* Football Yearbook *for their continued support for this specialist and growing area of work.*

*The following addresses may be helpful: SCORE (Sports Chaplaincy Offering Resources and Encouragement), PO Box 123, Sale, Manchester M33 4ZA and Christians in Sport, Frampton House, Victoria Road, Bicester, OX26 6PB.*

# OBITUARIES

**Umberto Agnelli** (Born Lausanne, Switzerland, 1 November 1934. Died Turin, Italy, 27 May 2004.) Umbert Agnelli was president of Juventus for many years and was responsible for transforming the club into a major forc in the late 1950s with the signings of world-class players such as John Charles and Omar Sivori. At the time of hi death he was chairman of the Fiat motor company.

**Brian Albeson** (Born Oldham, 14 December 1946. Died October 2003.) Brian Albeson began his career at Bur before developing into a solid centre half with Darlington. He was an ever-present for Southend when they wo promotion from the old Fourth Division in 1971–72 and also played for Stockport, bringing his total of senic appearances to more than 300.

**Ron Ashman** (Born Whittlesey, Cambs, 19 May 1926. Died Scunthorpe, 21 June 2004.) Ron Ashman was one o Norwich City's greatest servants, making over 600 first-team appearances between 1947 and 1963, and skipperin the Canaries to the FA Cup semi-final in 1959. He later managed the club for three years before taking over a Scunthorpe United. He was in charge of the Irons from 1967 to 1973 and again from 1976 to 1981, with a spell a Grimsby Town in between.

**John Aston** (Born Prestwich, Manchester, 3 September 1921. Died 31 July 2003.) John Aston was one of the star of the Manchester United team in the immediate post-war period. Although initially an inside forward he eventu ally settled at left back, and he was a member of the side that defeated Blackpool to win the FA Cup in 1947–4 and then lifted the Football League championship in 1951–52. John represented England in the 1950 World Cu finals and won 17 full caps for his country.

**Harold Atkinson** (Born Bootle, 28 July 1925. Died Wirral, 4 September 2003.) Harold Atkinson was a centre fo ward who scored 104 goals in 197 appearances for Tranmere Rovers between 1945 and 1954. The highlight of hi career came in November 1952 when he netted six times in an 8-1 victory over non-league Ashington in the F Cup.

**Joe Baker** (Born Liverpool, 17 July 1940. Died Wishaw, Lanarkshire, 6 October 2003.) Joe Baker was one of th best strikers in Britain during the late 1950s and early 1960s. He once netted nine times for Hibernian in a Scottis Cup tie against Peebles Rovers, and after scoring 140 goals in 159 games for the Easter Road club he spent a sea son in Italy with Torino. He returned to play for Arsenal, for whom he also netted a century of goals, Nottinghar Forest, Sunderland and Raith Rovers. Joe later managed Albion Rovers. He won eight full caps for England an also appeared six times for the U23s.

**Bert Barlow** (Born Rotherham, 22 July 1916. Died Colchester, 19 March 2004.) Bert Barlow made almost 30 senior appearances for Barnsley, Wolves, Portsmouth, Leicester and Colchester during the years from 1936 t 1954. An effective inside forward, one of the highlights of his career was playing and scoring for Pompey in th 1939 FA Cup final when they defeated his former club Wolves by a 4-1 margin.

**Ted Bates, MBE** (Born Thetford, Norfolk, 3 May 1918. Died Southampton, 26 November 2003.) Ted Bates wa associated with Southampton for 66 years, after joining the club on a free transfer in May 1937. He made over 20 appearances as an inside forward for Saints and then joined the coaching staff, being promoted to manager in 195 Ted remained in post until 1973, taking the club into the First Division for the first time in their history. He subse quently held a number of positions, most recently as president.

**Orvar Bergmark** (Born Bureå, Sweden, 16 November 1930. Died Sweden, 10 May 2004.) Orvar Bergmark was full back who won 94 caps for Sweden and was a member of the team that was defeated by Brazil in the 195 World Cup final. At club level he played for Örebro SK, AIK and Roma, while he also coached the national tean for a while (1966 to 1970) and was a talented bandy player.

**John Bernard** (Born Bo'ness, West Lothian, 12 April 1908. Died Bo'ness, West Lothian, 3 November 2003.) Joh Bernard was a goalkeeper with Kilmarnock, East Fife and Bo'ness in the late 1920s and early 1930s. He was a ever-present for East Fife when they won promotion to the Scottish First Division in the 1929–30 season.

**Tom Berry** (Born Clayton-le-Moors, Lancashire, 31 March 1922. Died September 2003.) Tom Berry made almos 300 senior appearances for Hull City between 1947 and 1957. A versatile defender, he was a member of the Tigers Division Three North championship-winning team of 1948–49.

**Bigode** (Born Belo Horizonte, Brazil, 4 April 1922. Died Belo Horizonte, Brazil, 31 July 2003.) Bigode was the lef half for Brazil when they were surprisingly defeated by Uruguay in the game that decided the destiny of the 195 World Cup finals. He won a total of ten full caps and played at club level for Atletico Mineiro, Fluminense an Flamengo.

**John Birkbeck** (Born Lincoln, 1 October 1932. Died Australia, 29 February 2004.) John Birkbeck was a reserv forward at Lincoln City, where he made two senior appearances towards the end of the 1954–55 season. Later h was a member of the Boston United side that sensationally defeated Derby County 6-1 at the Baseball Ground i an FA Cup tie in 1955–56 before emigrating to Australia.

**Derek Birnage** (Born 13 June 1913. Died 18 January 2004). Derek Birnage was the first editor of the *Tiger* comi for boys, and the creator of the fictional Roy of the Rovers character.

**Tommy Blenkinsopp** (Born Bishop Auckland, 13 May 1920. Died 29 January 2004.) A tough and uncompromisin defender, Tommy Blenkinsopp played twice for the Football League representative side and made 190 senio appearances for Grimsby Town, Middlesbrough and Barnsley in the immediate post-war period.

**illy Bloomfield** (Born Kensington, London, 25 ugust 1939. Died September 2003.) As a promising oung forward for Brentford, Billy Bloomfield scored egularly for the reserves, but managed just two first-eam appearances in the late 1950s before an eye prob-em brought a premature end to his career

**ohn Bonnar** (Born West Calder, 11 January 1924. Died Glasgow, 14 January 2004.) A confident goal-eeper, John Bonnar joined Celtic from Arbroath in he summer of 1948 and went on to spend a decade at 'arkhead. He was a regular in the team that won a ouble of the Scottish League and Cup in 1953–54 and vound down his career with spells at Dumbarton and t Johnstone.

**ob Bryson** (Born circa 1919. Died September 2003.) centre half, Bob Bryson played for Shamrock overs when they won the FAI Cup in 1940 before ecoming a member of the successful Linfield team of he late 1940s.He was one of the few players to gain epresentative honours for both the League of Ireland nd the Irish League.

**Norman Bullock** (Born Nuneaton, Warwickshire, 26 March 1932. Died 2 October 2003.) After failing to nake the first team during a three-year spell at Aston Villa, Norman Bullock joined Chester in the summer f 1952 and quickly established himself in the line-up. predominantly left-footed player he was an xtremely versatile performer who made almost 200 ppearances during his spell at Sealand Road.

**Dick Burke** (Born Ashton-under-Lyne, Lancs, 28 October 1920. Died January 2004.) After making just a andful of appearances for Blackpool and Newcastle Jnited, Dick Burke forged a useful career as a efender with Carlisle United, for whom he was a reg-ılar in the 1947–48 and 1948–49 seasons.

John Charles

**ack Burkitt** (Born Wednesbury, Staffs, 19 January 1926. Died Brighouse, Yorkshire, 12 September 2003.) Jack Burkitt was a talented wing half and inspirational captain who led Nottingham Forest to victory over Luton Town n the 1959 FA Cup final. He was a stalwart figure in the Reds' line-up throughout the 1950s, amassing a total of 503 senior appearances. He later had a spell as manager of Notts County.

**Sean Byrne** (Born circa 1955. Died Melbourne, Australia, 11 August 2004.) Sean Byrne was a goalscoring midfield player with St Patrick's Athletic and Dundalk in the 1970s and early 1980s. He won representative honours for the League of Ireland and, after taking out citizenship, for New Zealand.

**Alex Cameron** (Born circa 1930. Died 23 July 2003.) Alex Cameron was one of the leading sports reporters in Scotland. After many years working for the *Scottish Daily Mail* he moved to the *Daily Record* where he became hief sports writer and sports editor. Alex also had a spell as presenter for the STV programme 'Scotsport'.

**Stewart Campbell** (Born Belfast, circa 1934. Died Belfast, 2003.) Stewart Campbell was a skilful inside forward for Glenavon in the late 1950s and early '60s. He was capped by Northern Ireland at amateur international level and also for the Irish League representative team.

**Willie Carver** (Born Broughty Ferry, Dundee, circa 1912. Died near Hereford, August 2003.) Willie Carver was a goal-scoring inside left for Arbroath in the 1930s. He also had brief spells with East Fife and Forfar Athletic.

**Clive Charles** (Born Bow, London, 3 October 1951. Died Portland, Oregon, USA, 26 August 2003.) Clive Charles appeared as a left back for West Ham and Cardiff City during the 1970s. He subsequently moved to the USA to play for Portland Timbers in the NASL and became a respected coach both in US college soccer and for the national Olympic team.

**John Charles** (Born Swansea, 27 December 1931. Died Wakefield, Yorkshire, 21 February 2004.) John Charles was one of the greatest British players of the post-war era. A giant of a man, he was equally effective at centre half or centre forward and alternated between the two roles throughout his career. He burst on the scene with Leeds United in the early 1950s and his total of 42 Football League goals in the 1953–54 season still stands as a club record. John moved to Italy in 1957 and was a huge success with Juventus, helping transform the team from also-rans to Serie A champions three times in four years. He later returned for a spell at Elland Road and also played for Roma and Cardiff City. He had spells in management at Hereford and Merthyr Tydfil and coached in Canada. John was also a key figure for Wales, helping the team reach the quarter-finals of the World Cup in 1958 and winning 38 caps in total.

**Tommy Cheetham** (Born Wavertree, Liverpool, 8 December 1950. Died Woolton, Liverpool, 5 October 2003.) A promising striker with the Liverpool Schools team, Tommy Cheetham graduated to play for Southport in the la 1960s, although he never managed to establish himself as a first-team regular during his spell at Haig Avenue.

**Kevin Clarke** (Born Drogheda, Ireland, 29 April 1923. Died Barrow-in-Furness, 16 March 2004.) Kevin Clark signed for Barrow shortly after the start of the 1945–46 season and established a reputation as a prolific centre fo ward. However, when peacetime football returned the goals dried up and he left Holker Street in the summer c 1947.

**Henry Cockburn** (Born Ashton-under-Lyne, Lancs, 14 September 1921. Died Ashton-under-Lyne, Lancs, February 2004.) Henry Cockburn was England's regular left half in the 1948–49 season and won 13 caps in total. A club level he was one of the stars of the Manchester United team of the immediate post-war era, gaining an F. Cup winners' medal in 1948 and helping his side to the Football League championship in 1951–52. He later ha spells with Bury and Peterborough United and subsequently coached Oldham Athletic and then Huddersfiel Town.

**Steve Cooper** (Born Birmingham, 22 June 1964. Died Birmingham, 15 February 2004.) Steve Cooper was a ta strong target man whose career peaked during his time at Airdrieonians, where he was a member of the team th lost out to Celtic in the 1995 Scottish Cup final. Earlier in his career he had played for a string of clubs in the low divisions in England including Newport County, Plymouth Argyle, Barnsley, Tranmere Rovers and York City.

**Ken Coote** (Born Paddington, London, 19 May 1928. Died August 2003) Ken Coote joined Brentford in the sum mer of 1949 and went on to become a fixture in the line-up at left half, establishing a club record of 514 Footba League appearances, a figure that has yet to be broken. Ken won representative honours for the London FA appearing in the team that took part in the Inter Cities Fairs Cup matches in the late 1950s.

**Graham Davies** (Born Swansea, 3 October 1921. Died November 2003.) Graham Davies made over 70 wartim appearances in goal for Swansea Town and subsequently spent two seasons on the books at Watford, for whom h made a handful of Football League appearances.

**Jimmy Davis** (Born Bromsgrove, 6 February 1982. Died Oxfordshire, 9 August 2003.) Jimmy Davis was a pac hard-running young midfielder, who had progressed through the ranks at Manchester United. He made a tremer dous impact on loan at Swindon during the 2002–03 campaign, and had been due to start the 2003–04 season o loan at Watford but was tragically killed in a car accident on his way to attend the Hornets' opening game agains Coventry City.

**Steve Death** (Born Elmswell, Suffolk, 19 September 1949. Died Reading, 26 October 2003.) A brave and agil 'keeper, Steve Death made just a single appearance for West Ham before moving on to join Reading. He becam one of the key figures in the Royals' line-up during the 1970s, making over 500 first-team appearances and featur ing in the defence that established a Football League record by not conceding a goal in 1,103 minutes of football.

**Ronnie Dicks** (Born Kennington, London, 13 April 1924. Died Middlesbrough, 30 January 2004.) Ronnie Dick joined Middlesbrough during the war and he went on to become a stalwart of the Boro' line-up for over a decad A speedy player who could kick with either foot, his early appearances were on the wing, but he later moved t wing half.

**Peter Dinsdale** (Born Bradford, 19 October 1938. Died British Columbia, Canada, 5 June 2004.) Peter Dinsdal was a tough-tackling half back who made over 200 appearances for Huddersfield Town in the 1960s. He late played for Vancouver Royals and Bradford Park Avenue, and after settling in Canada he coached the nationa team for a short while.

**George Dooley** (Born Chesterfield, 29 December 1922. Died Chesterfield, April 2004.) George Dooley was a inside left who played for Chesterfield during the war and made 11 appearances for Halifax Town during th second half of the 1946–47 campaign.

**Ray Dring** (Born Lincoln, 13 February 1924. Died Lincoln, 21 October 2003.) Goalkeeper Ray Dring was cappe by England Schools before the war and he later made four appearances as an amateur for Huddersfield Town dur ing the 1947–48 season.

**George Dryburgh** (Born 20 January 1940. Died 1 August 2003.) George Dryburgh was a big strong full back wh had a brief run in the Alloa Athletic first team during the late 1950s.

**Len Dudman** (Born Dundee, 4 August 1933. Died Perth, 12 February 2004.) Len Dudman was a talented all-roun sportsman who could claim to have represented Scotland at cricket, curling and football (albeit as a junior interna tionalist). His senior football was restricted to a single appearance for Falkirk and a season with Forfar Athletic i the late 1950s.

**John Duffy** (Born Dundee, 24 August 1929. Died Dundee, 4 May 2004.) John Duffy was a half back with Celti and Arbroath, before joining Southend United. He spent six seasons at Roots Hall, making over 100 Footbal League appearances.

**Alex Edmiston** (Born Kinghorn, Fife, circa 1930. Died Kirkcaldy, Fife, 3 May 2004.) Alex Edmiston was a goal keeper who made over 200 senior appearances for Dundee United and Brechin City during the period 1949 to 1963.

**Tommy Eggleston** (Born Consett, Co Durham, 21 February 1920. Died January 2004.) Tommy Eggleston was a solid but stylish left half with Derby County, Leicester City and Watford during the period 1946 to 1953. Afte injury brought his playing career to an end he served a number of clubs as trainer or coach, notably Sheffiel Wednesday, Everton and Ipswich Town. He also had a spell as manager of Mansfield Town in the late 1960s.

**Tommy Eglington** (Born Dublin, 15 January 1923. Died Dublin, 18 February 2004.) Tommy Eglington was alread a star with Shamrock Rovers when he signed for Everton along with his colleague Peter Farrell in the summer o 1946. He developed into a very talented winger during his time at Goodison, combining tremendous speed wit some fine close control and an ability to set up chances for his colleagues. He made over 500 senior appearance during his career, also playing for Tranmere Rovers and Cork Hibs. Tommy won 24 caps for the Republic o Ireland and six caps for Northern Ireland.

**Charlie Elliott, MBE** (Born Bolsover, Derbyshire, 4 April 1912. Died 1 January 2004.) Although best known for his achievements in the cricket world as a batsman for Derbyshire, and then a test umpire and England selector, Charlie Elliott was also a reliable defender who spent a decade on the books of Coventry City. He played 101 times for the Sky Blues between 1938 and 1948 and later served as caretaker-manager at Highfield Road during the 1954–55 season.

**Lothar Emmerich** (Born Dortmund, Germany, 29 November 1941. Died Germany, 13 August 2003.) Lothar Emmerich was a tall and powerful outside left who featured briefly for his country, four of his five caps coming during the 1966 World Cup finals when he scored a spectacular goal in the group match against Spain, and set up his country's last-minute equaliser in the final against England. He made his name playing for Borussia Dortmund before spending time with AC Beerschot (Belgium) and Klagenfurt (Austria).

**Johnny Evans** (Born Liverpool, 13 March 1938. Died 6 January 2004.) After unsuccessful spells at Liverpool and Bournemouth, Johnny Evans returned to play in non-league football before he was snapped up by Stockport County in October 1962. A strong and agile inside forward, he subsequently spent almost a decade in the lower divisions also appearing for Carlisle, Exeter and Barnsley.

**Miklos Feher** (Born Budapest, Hungary, 20 July 1979. Died Guimaraes, Portugal, 25 January 2004.) Miklos Feher was a talented Hungarian striker who died shortly after collapsing on the pitch whilst playing for Benfica against Vitoria Guimaraes. An international with over 20 full caps, his career began at Györ ETO and he later played for Porto before moving on to Benfica.

Redfern Froggatt

**Jack Fitzgerald** (Born Waterford, Republic of Ireland, 3 April 1930. Died Republic of Ireland, 23 November 2003.) Jack Fitzgerald was a tall and powerful centre forward with Waterford during the 1950s. He won two full caps for the Republic of Ireland and also appeared nine times for the League of Ireland representative side.

**Jack Flavell** (Born Wall Heath, Staffs, 15 May 1929. Died Barmouth, February 2004.) Jack Flavell spent six years on the books of West Bromwich Albion (1947–53) without making the first team, but made 22 first-team appearances at left back for Walsall in the 1953–54 season. He was better known as a right-arm fast bowler for Worcestershire between 1949 and 1967, winning four caps for England.

**Tony Freeman** (Born Melton Mowbray, 29 August 1928. Died Leicester, 1 February 2004.) Tony Freeman was a small and speedy outside right who spent four years on the books of Notts County in the late 1940s. He made 50 appearances for the Magpies before moving on to Midland League club Boston United.

**Redfern Froggatt** (Born Sheffield, 23 August 1924. Died Sheffield, 26 December 2003.) Redfern Froggatt spent almost 20 years on the books at Hillsborough and was one of the greatest of Sheffield Wednesday's post-war players. An intelligent inside forward, he made over 450 first-team appearances for the Owls, assisting the club to the Second Division title on three separate occasions (1951–52, 1955–56 and 1958–59). Redfern won four full England caps and also appeared once for the Football League representative side.

**Tommy Gemmell** (Born Mossblown, Ayrshire, 2 July 1930. Died Patna, Ayrshire, 8 January 2004.) Tommy Gemmell was a slightly built inside forward whose tally of 94 goals for St Mirren made him the club's leading post-war goal-scorer. Signed during the summer of 1951 he was a key player with the Paisley club for a decade and he also won two full caps for Scotland.

**Alex Gibson** (Born Kirkconnel, Ayrshire, 28 November 1939. Died 22 November 2003.) Alex Gibson was a powerful, hard-tackling centre half who made over 350 first-team appearances for Notts County during the 1960s when the club spent most of their time struggling in the lower divisions. He captained the team for a while, before dropping down to play for Boston United in the Northern Premier League.

**Jesús Gil** (Born Burgo de Osma, Soria, Spain, 11 March 1933. Died Madrid, 14 May 2004.) Jesús Gil was president of Atlético Madrid for 16 years from 1987. A controversial figure, he earned a reputation for hiring and firing coaches, going through a total of 39 during his spell in charge of the club.

**George Griffiths** (Born Warrington, 23 June 1924. Died January 2004.) George Griffiths was an effective and reliable full back who became a regular for Bury in the 1940s, making over 250 appearances in the post-war years before finishing his career with four seasons on the books at Halifax.

**George Hardwick** (Born Saltburn, 2 February 1920. Died 19 April 2004.) George Hardwick captained England in the immediate aftermath of the Second World War, by which time he had established a reputation as a formidable left back. He had begun his career at Middlesbrough, but blossomed during the war when he guested for Chelsea

George Hardwick

and appeared 17 times for England in unofficial internationals. He won 13 peacetime caps for England and also skippered the Great Britain side against a FIFA selection in May 1947. A knee injury brought his top-flight career to an end and he became player-manager of Oldham. George later coached PSV Eindhoven, the Netherlands national team for a six-month period (January to June 1957) and at Middlesbrough, subsequently having spells as manager of Sunderland and Gateshead.

**Ray Harford** (Born Halifax, 1 June 1945. Died 9 August 2003.) Ray Harford spent almost his entire playing career in the lower divisions where he proved a tall and extremely effective centre half, principally for Lincoln City and Colchester United. He achieved much greater success as a coach and manager, winning the Football League Cup with Luton (1988) and then coaching Blackburn Rovers under manager Kenny Dalglish when they won the Premiership title in 1994–95. Ray also had spells as manager or coach at Wimbledon, West Bromwich Albion, Queens Park Rangers and Millwall.

**Harry Harris** (Born Undy, South Wales, 2 November 1933. Died June 2004.) Harry Harris began his career as an inside left at Newport County, but after joining Portsmouth he became a no-nonsense left half. A key figure for Pompey throughout the 1960s, he made over 550 Football League appearances during a career which spanned the period 1954 to 1971.

**Alf Hobson** (Born Co Durham, 9 September 1913. Died 21 February 2004.) Alf Hobson was Liverpool's first-choice goalkeeper for the opening half of the 1936–37 season before losing his place. He later spent a season at Chester, but returned to Anfield during the war and made 172 appearances for the Reds during the hostilities. At the time of his death he was believed to have been the oldest surviving former Liverpool player.

**Bob Hodgkiss** (Born Little Hulton, Lancs, 22 March 1918. Died Worsley, Manchester, 3 December 2003.) Bob Hodgkiss was a powerful right back who had two spells for Southport either side of the war. He spent the 1946–47 season on the books at Everton, but failed to make the Toffees' first team during his time with them.

**Stewart Holden** (Born Grange Moor, Yorkshire, 21 April 1942. Died March 2004.) Stewart Holden was a utility player who could play at inside forward, wing half or in either full-back position. Although he failed to establish himself as a regular with Huddersfield Town or Oldham Athletic in the early 1960s, he enjoyed regular first-team action during a spell with Rochdale.

**Eddie Hopkinson** (Born Wheatley Hill, Co Durham, 29 October 1935. Died Royton, Lancs, 25 April 2004.) Although rather small for a goalkeeper, Eddie Hopkinson proved to be an exceptional performer, showing agility and great consistency in a career that spanned almost two decades. His total of 519 Football League appearances remains a record for Bolton Wanderers. An FA Cup winner with Bolton in 1958, he won 14 full and six U23 caps for England. As a youngster he played a handful of games for Oldham Athletic.

**Syd Howarth** (Born Bristol, 28 June 1923. Died Cardiff, 11 January 2004.) Syd Howarth was a talented inside forward for Merthyr Tydfil in the early post-war years. He subsequently joined Aston Villa for a then record fee paid to a non-league club, and later spent time with Swansea Town and Walsall.

**Billy Hughes** (Born Glasgow, 3 March 1929. Died West Knapton, nr. Malton, North Yorks, 17 October 2003.) A talented winger, Billy Hughes amassed almost 400 first-team appearances for York City between 1951 and 1962. A skilful, pacy player, he was one of the stars of the team that reached the FA Cup semi-final in the 1954–55 season.

**Alex Jamieson** (Born circa 1910. Died Glasgow, 5 March 2004.) Alex Jamieson was an inside forward with neat ball control and intelligent distribution who played for Arbroath, Montrose and Alloa Athletic during the 1930s.

**Fred Jarrie** (Born Hartlepool, 2 August 1922. Died 1 February 2004.) Fred Jarrie was Hartlepools' reserve goalkeeper in the period immediately after the war, managing just three first-team outings. He later spent many years with Crook Town, gaining an FA Amateur Cup winners' medal in 1954.

**Brian Jarvis** (Born Bangor-on-Dee, 26 August 1933. Died Shrewsbury, January 2004.) Brian Jarvis won youth international honours for Wales before going on to make over 150 senior appearances as a wing half for Wrexham and Oldham Athletic between 1954 and 1963.

**Alf Jeffries** (Born Bishop Auckland, 22 September 1915. Died Nottingham, 28 January 2004.) Outside right Alf Jeffries spent a year at Norwich City without breaking into the first team, then established himself at Bradford City in the mid-1930s before moving on to Derby. Generally a reserve during his time at the Baseball Ground, he joined Sheffield United in the summer of 1939 before the war brought his senior career to a close.

**Davie Johnston** (Born Nairn, 28 November 1942. Died Inverness, 7 April 2004.) Davie Johnston was perhaps the best-ever player produced by Nairn County and remains the holder of the record number of goals scored by a Highland League player in a single season. He also featured briefly at senior level for Hearts, and had a longer spell at Aberdeen, for whom he finished leading scorer in 1967–68.

**Harold Jones** (Born Liverpool, 22 May 1933. Died 6 September 2003.) Harold Jones spent two seasons on the books at Liverpool, making his only first-team appearance at centre half against Preston at the start of the 1953–54 season.

**Tommy ('TG') Jones** (Born Connah's Quay, Flintshire, 12 October 1917. Died Bangor, 3 January 2004.) Tommy Jones was a very skilful centre half who was equally comfortable playing the ball on the ground or in the air. He signed for Wrexham as a youngster, but was soon sold to Everton, where he was a member of the team that won the Football League championship in 1938–39. A key figure for the Toffees in the years either side of the war, he won 17 full caps for Wales between 1938 and 1949.

Tommy Jones

**Rory Keane** (Born Limerick, Ireland, 31 August 1922. Died Swansea, 13 February 2004.) Rory Keane was a tough-tackling full back with Swansea Town who made over 150 appearances during the period 1947 to 1955 before injury brought his career to a close. He won four caps for the Republic of Ireland and one for Northern Ireland.

**Arnold Kendall** (Born Halifax, 6 April 1925. Died December 2003.) Arnold Kendall made over 300 senior appearances for Bradford City, Rochdale and Bradford Park Avenue during the 1950s. He began his career as a centre forward, switching firstly to the inside-forward position and then to outside right.

**Allan Kennedy** (Born Arbroath, 11 March 1964. Died Arbroath, 3 February 2004.) Allan Kennedy won schoolboy caps at U18 level for Scotland, and subsequently forged a successful career as a forward in the lower divisions with Arbroath, Brechin City and Montrose.

**Jim Kennedy** (Born Johnstone, 31 January 1934. Died Paisley, 2 December 2003.) Jim Kennedy spent a decade on Celtic's books as a committed and hard-working full back before winding down his career at Morton. Although domestic honours eluded him, he won six full caps for Scotland holding his place briefly during the 1963–64 season.

**George Lackenby** (Born Newcastle upon Tyne, 22 May 1931. Died 3 April 2004.) George Lackenby was a tall, strong and versatile defender who began his career at Newcastle United, where he had a brief spell in the first team during the 1955–56 campaign. His subsequent career was spent in the lower divisions with Exeter, Carlisle, Gateshead and Hartlepools. He was a member of the Gateshead team when they lost their place in the Football League in 1960.

**Harry Lanham** (Born circa 1918. Died Southampton, September 2003.) Harry Lanham was capped by England at schoolboy level and played as a professional with Norwich City and Southampton without breaking into the first team prior to the outbreak of war. He subsequently made a handful of first-team appearances for the Saints during the hostilities.

**Frank Large** (Born Leeds, 26 January 1940. Died August 2003.) Although Frank Large began his career as a left half with Halifax, he quickly became known as a goalscoring centre forward. He netted 236 goals in over 600 senior appearances during a career that also saw him play for Queens Park Rangers, Northampton, Swindon, Carlisle, Oldham, Leicester, Fulham and Chesterfield. Frank won domestic honours on two occasions, helping both Northampton Town (1962–63) and Carlisle United (1964–65) to win the old Third Division title.

**Kit Lawlor** (Born Dublin, 3 December 1922. Died Dublin, 8 June 2004.) Kit Lawlor was a stylish inside forward who played for Drumcondra, Doncaster Rovers and Dundalk in the 1950s. He won three caps for the Republic of Ireland.

**Börje Leander** (Born Avesta, Sweden, 7 March 1918. Died Mora, Sweden, 30 October 2003.) Börje Leander won 23 caps as a defender for Sweden between 1941 and 1950 and was a member of the squad that won the Olympic gold medal at the 1948 games, although he did not appear in the final match. At club level he played for AIK and was instrumental in recruiting his brother-in-law Lennart Johansson into football management. Johansson, of course, eventually rose to become President of UEFA.

**Leônidas** (Born São Cristóvão, Rio de Janeiro, Brazil, 11 November 1913. Died Cotia, São Paulo, Brazil, 24 January 2004.) Leônidas was one of the greatest strikers in the history of Brazilian football and was widely credited as the first top-class player to employ the 'bicycle kick'. He was also the first player to score four times in a World Cup game when he achieved the feat in the 6-5 victory over Poland during the 1938 finals. Leônidas finished as the tournament's leading scorer with eight goals, but found himself rested for the semi-final against Italy and as a result his team were beaten 2-1.

**Ron 'Tot' Leverton** (Born Worksop, 8 May 1926. Died 19 August 2003.) Tot Leverton signed for Nottingham Forest during the war and went on to make over a century of appearances during his time at the City Ground. A goalscoring inside forward, he later played for Notts County and Walsall.

**Alf Liggins** (Born Aston, Birmingham, 23 April 1911. Died Southport, 14 December 2003.) Although Alf Liggins played as an amateur in the Central League for both Everton and Liverpool his only senior experience came at New Brighton for whom he proved to be an effective outside right, making 79 first-team appearances between 1931 and 1934.

**Alex Linwood** (Born Drumsmudden, Ayrshire, 13 March 1920. Died Renfrew, 26 October 2003.) Alex Linwood was a pacy centre forward with a great eye for goal who enjoyed the best years of his playing career with St Mirren netting over 150 goals for the Buddies during the hostilities. He later had spells with Middlesbrough, Hibernian, Clyde and Morton and won his only cap for Scotland against Wales in November 1949.

**Alex (Rennie) Logan** (Born 4 November 1928. Died December 2003.) Alex Logan was a hard-working inside forward who played for Falkirk and Hamilton Academical in the late 1940s and early '50s. He went on to achieve great success in the world of bowls, representing Scotland for many years. The highpoint of his bowls career came in the 1972 World Championships when he won a gold medal in the team event and silver in the fours.

**Tommy McCready** (Born Port Glasgow, 28 September 1923. Died 19 February 2004.) Tommy McCready was a skilful inside forward who was a regular with Cowdenbeath and Hartlepools in the late 1940s before concluding his career at Lincoln City in the 1950–51 season.

**Joe McDonald** (Born Blantyre, 10 February 1929. Died Australia, 7 September 2003.) Joe McDonald played at left back in the Nottingham Forest team that defeated Luton Town to win the 1959 FA Cup final. Earlier in his career he had played for Falkirk and Sunderland and was capped twice by Scotland.

**Danny McLennan** (Born Stirling, circa 1924. Died 11 May 2004.) Danny McLennan forged a useful career as a half back with East Fife, Stirling Albion, Falkirk, Dundee and Berwick Rangers in the immediate post-war period. He later had spells as manager of Berwick and Stirling before embarking on a coaching career that took him to all parts of the globe.

**Ally MacLeod** (Born Glasgow, 26 February 1931. Died Ayrshire, 1 February 2004.) Ally MacLeod is perhaps best known for his spell in charge of Scotland's national team during their disappointing 1978 World Cup finals campaign, but this was only a brief period in the career of a man who spent most of his life in football. A talented but unorthodox outside left, he played for Third Lanark, St Mirren, Blackburn Rovers (appearing in the 1960 FA Cup final), Hibernian and Ayr United. Then as a manager he served Ayr, Aberdeen, Motherwell, Airdrie and Queen of the South. Renowned for his enthusiasm, he was a popular figure at all his clubs.

**Ian McWilliams** (Born Malta, 19 March 1953. Died Glasgow, May 2004.) A giant defender who could also play up front, Ian McWilliams made around 50 senior appearances for Queen's Park and Celtic in the late 1970s.

**Joe Mallett** (Born Gateshead, 8 January 1916. Died St Leonard's-on-Sea, 8 February 2004.) Joe Mallett made almost 350 senior appearances with Charlton, Queens Park Rangers, Southampton and Leyton Orient between 1938 and 1945. Best known for his time with the Saints, for whom he was an intelligent wing half, he later enjoyed a successful career in coaching with Nottingham Forest and Birmingham City. In the USA from 1975 to 1983, he coached the likes of Pelé at New York Cosmos and George Best at San José Earthquakes.

**Roque Gaston Maspoli** (Born Montevideo, Uruguay, 12 October 1917. Died Montevideo, Uruguay, 22 February 2004.) Roque Maspoli was the Uruguay goalkeeper when they won the World Cup in 1950, and won 45 caps for his country. At club level he was mostly associated with Penarol and later became a respected coach, having two spells in charge of the Uruguay national team.

**Jack Maxfield** (Born Carlisle, 17 June 1919. Died 14 January 2004.) Jack Maxfield signed for Carlisle United in August 1939, and after wartime service in the Army he returned to the club. He spent the 1951–52 season at Workington, for whom he had the distinction of scoring the club's first-ever Football League goal (versus Halifax) and hat-trick (against Southport).

**Joe Melling** (Born circa 1946. Died 31 March 2004.) Joe Melling was one of the most respected football reporters of modern times. A former chairman of the Football Writers' Association, he began his career on the *Lancashire Evening Post* and later worked for the *Daily Express*. He subsequently spent 20 years with the *Mail on Sunday*, for whom he was the chief football writer.

**Jimmy Milne** (Born Arbroath, circa 1930. Died March 2004.) Jimmy Milne was a big strong centre half with plenty of skill on the ball who was a member of the Hearts team that won the Scottish League championship in 1957–58 and 1959–60. After beginning his career with Arbroath he spent a decade at Tynecastle before concluding his career with spells at Falkirk and Forfar Athletic.

**Jimmy Mitchell** (Born Glasgow, circa 1924. Died Glasgow, 11 March 2004.) A pacy right back who was strong in the tackle, Jimmy Mitchell made over 300 senior appearances for Queen's Park, Morton and Aberdeen between 1946 and 1958. He captained the Dons to their first-ever Scottish League title in 1954–55 and was 'capped' once by the Scottish League representative side. He also had a brief spell as manager of Cowdenbeath.

**Bob Moodie** (Born Fife, circa 1920. Died October 2003.) Bob Moodie was a versatile forward for Cowdenbeath in the immediate post-war period and also played for Dundee United and Montrose during his career.

**Amos Moss** (Born Birmingham, 28 August 1921. Died 8 April 2004.) Amos Moss was a tall and powerful half back who joined Aston Villa on leaving school, following in the footsteps of both his father, Frank, and brother, Frank junior. Although he never really established himself in the line-up, he made over 100 senior appearances and was a useful deputy.

**Gordon Neave** (Born Glasgow, 10 October 1924. Died 2 August 2003.) Gordon Neave was a wing half who failed to make the first team with Portsmouth, but later built a useful career in the lower divisions with Bournemouth and Aldershot. In 1959 he returned to Fratton Park and remained with Pompey for the next 40 years, performing a variety of backroom roles.

**Geoff Peach** (Born Torpoint, Cornwall, 11 October 1932. Died Torpoint, Cornwall, 11 December 2003.) Geoff Peach appeared regularly for Plymouth reserves in the mid-1950s, but made just a single first-team appearance for Argyle at inside right in the 1956–57 campaign. He subsequently enjoyed success as a goalscorer with non-league Falmouth Town for many seasons.

**.en Perry** (Born Walsall, 14 May 1930. Died January 2004.) Len Perry made a handful of appearances at left back or Walsall in the 1953–54 season before moving on to join Cheshire League club Wellington Town.

**Ernie Phillips** (Born North Shields, 29 November 1923. Died York, 10 January 2004.) Ernie Phillips was a reliable ull back who made over 300 senior appearances for Manchester City, Hull City and York City between 1949 and .958. The highlight of his career was captaining York to the FA Cup semi-final in the 1954–55 season.

**Don Pickwick** (Born Pen-y-graig, Rhondda, 7 February 1925. Died Queensland, Australia, 2004.) Don Pickwick pent almost a decade on the books of Norwich City in the immediate post-war period, proving to be a hard-working and effective wing half. After amassing almost 250 senior appearances he left the club to become player-manager of Spalding United and later emigrated to Australia.

**Tómas Pospíchal** (Born 26 June 1936. Died 21 October 2003.) Tómas Pospíchal was a pacy right winger who featured for Czechoslovakia in the 1962 World Cup final against Brazil. He played at club level for Baník Ostrava, Sparta Praha and Rouen, before becoming a successful coach with Bohemians Praha.

**Helmut Rahn** (Born Essen, Germany, 16 August 1929. Died Essen, Germany, 14 August 2003.) Helmut Rahn was a powerful outside right whose career peaked during the 1954 World Cup tournament when his two goals helped West Germany to a surprise victory over favourites Hungary in the final. He won a total of 40 international caps and played at club level for Rot-Weiss Essen, 1FC Köln, Twente Enschede and Meidericher SV Duisberg, eventually retiring in 1966.

**Gil Reece** (Born Cardiff, 2 July 1942. Died Cardiff, 20 December 2003.) Gil Reece impressed as a talented outside eft for Newport County before being sold to Sheffield United in April 1965. He made over 200 appearances for the Blades over the next seven years and won 29 full caps for Wales. Gil later wound down his career with spells at Cardiff and Swansea.

**Jocky Robertson** (Born Edinburgh, 21 May 1926. Died Edinburgh, 31 March 2004.) Jocky Robertson was a diminutive, but very agile goalkeeper who was a mainstay of the Third Lanark side throughout the 1950s, making 388 senior appearances for the Cathkin Park club. He concluded his career with a brief spell at Berwick Rangers.

**Derrick Robins** (Born Bexleyheath, Kent, 27 June 1914. Died South Africa, 9 May 2004.) Derrick Robins was chairman of Coventry City from 1960 to 1973, transforming the club from a perennial Third Division outfit to one of solid First Division status. He was also a useful cricketer and played two first-class matches for Warwickshire in 1947.

**John Robson** (Born Consett, Co Durham, 15 July 1950. Died Sutton Coldfield, 12 May 2004.) John Robson was a neat and effective left back who was a member of the Derby County team that won the Second Division title in 1968–69, going on to lift the Football League championship in 1971–72. He subsequently made around 150 appearances for Aston Villa before his career was ended by multiple sclerosis. He was capped by England at U23 level and also appeared for the Football League representative team.

**Willie Samson** (Born circa 1929. Died 19 January 2004.) Willie Samson was a half back who made two senior appearances for Arbroath between 1950 and 1952.

**Jim Sanders** (Born Holborn, London, 5 July 1920. Died 14 August 2003.) Goalkeeper Jim Sanders was briefly on the books of Charlton Athletic during the war, before making his name at West Bromwich Albion. He made a total of more than 350 senior appearances for the Baggies and gained an FA Cup winners' medal in 1954 after the 3-2 victory over Preston North End at Wembley.

**George Sang** (Born circa 1940. Died Aberdeen, 8 December 2003.) George Sang was a right back who made a handful of first-team appearances for Aberdeen during the 1959–60 season. The following campaign he was a regular in the Arbroath line-up before moving into Highland League soccer.

**Ken Shaw** (Born Dukinfield, 15 December 1920. Died Stockport, 15 February 2004.) Ken Shaw signed for Stockport County during the war and made over 100 appearances for the Hatters during the hostilities, retaining his place as a regular in the line-up during the 1946–47 season. A versatile forward, he appeared for Stockport in the famous wartime match against Doncaster Rovers in March 1946, which lasted some 203 minutes, finishing shortly before 7 pm.

**Jimmy Sheavills** (Born Eythorne, Kent, 28 July 1940. Died Barnsley, 4 September 2003.) A former Leeds United apprentice, Jimmy Sheavills was an outside right with Peterborough United at the time of their election to the Football League. He later spent two seasons as a regular with Barnsley before emigrating to South Africa where he played for a string of clubs.

**Chris Shyne** (Born Littleborough, Lancs, 10 December 1950. Died February 2004.) Chris Shyne was a goalkeeper who spent two-and-a-half seasons on the books with Rochdale and also played for Wigan Athletic in the late 1970s. He subsequently became a well-known figure in local football in the Rochdale area.

**Sidney Simmons** (Born circa 1923. Died 26 October 2003.) Sidney Simmons was an inside forward who scored 8 times in 17 appearances for Everton in the emergency wartime competitions. He was later a groundsman at Goodison Park.

**Ronnie Simpson** (Born Glasgow, 11 October 1930. Died Edinburgh, 19 April 2004.) Ronnie Simpson made his first-team debut for Queen's Park as a 14-year-old and went on to enjoy a career that spanned a quarter of a century. Perhaps best known for being Celtic's goalkeeper when they became the first British club to win the European Cup in 1967, he also played for Third Lanark, Newcastle United (where he won two FA Cup winners' medals) and Hibernian. An agile, efficient 'keeper, Ronnie became Scotland's oldest-ever debutant when assisting his country to a famous victory over England at Wembley, thus becoming the first team to defeat the World Cup holders following their success 12 months before. He later had a brief spell as manager of Hamilton Academical in the early 1970s.

**Gurra Sjöberg** (Born Stockholm, Sweden, 21 March 1913. Died Lidingö, Sweden, 3 October 2003.) Gurra Sjöberg made a record 321 league appearances as a goalkeeper for Swedish club AIK between 1932 and 1950. He made his international debut for Sweden against in England in 1937 and went on to win a total of 21 full caps.

**Audrius Slekys** (Born 2 April 1975. Died 27 July 2003.) Audrius Slekys was the star striker for FBK Kaunas and holder of one full cap for Lithuania. He died in a car accident shortly before his team were due to play Celtic in a European Champions' League qualifying tie.

**David Smith** (Born Fishponds, Bristol, 5 October 1934. Died December 2003.) David Smith was a left winger who spent several seasons on the books at Bristol City during the 1950s, although generally a reserve, and later had a spell at Millwall. He was better known for his exploits in the cricket world as a seam bowler for Gloucestershire and England, for whom he made five test appearances.

**Jimmy Smith** (Born Slamannan, Stirlingshire, 24 September 1911. Died 4 December 2003.) Jimmy Smith was a big powerful centre forward with a neat touch on the ball who made his name at East Stirlingshire. In December 1928 he moved on to Rangers for whom he averaged almost a goal a game throughout his senior career and held the club scoring record for half a century until Ally McCoist came along. He won five Scottish League championship medals at Ibrox and was also capped by Scotland on two occasions.

Bob Stokoe

**Reg Smith** (Born Battersea, London, 20 January 1912. Died Stevenage, Herts, 6 January 2004.) Reg Smith was a talented and pacy winger for Millwall in the years leading up to World War Two. He helped the Lions to win the Division Three South title in 1937–38 and won two full England caps in peacetime. Reg later joined Dundee, where he eventually became coach. He subsequently held managerial positions with Dundee United, Falkirk (leading the team to victory in the 1957 Scottish Cup final) and Millwall.

**Professor Sir Roland Smith** (Born 1 October 1928. Died 20 November 2003.) A successful academic and businessman, Roland Smith was chairman of Manchester United from 1991 to 2002, leading the club during their transition to plc status.

**Trevor Smith** (Born Brierley Hill, 13 April 1936. Died Essex, 9 August 2003.) Trevor Smith was a rugged centre half who excelled as a youngster before going on to establish himself in the Birmingham City line-up, making over 400 senior appearances. A member of the team that lost to Manchester City in the 1956 FA Cup final he was a regular for England U23s for several seasons and won two full caps.

**Tommy Southren** (Born Sunderland, 1 August 1927. Died Welwyn Garden City, Herts, 10 May 2004.) Tommy Southren was a speedy right winger who played for West Ham United, Aston Villa and Bournemouth, making around 200 senior appearances in the period between 1949 and 1960.

**Jackie Stewart** (Born Armadale, West Lothian, 23 January 1929. Died Edinburgh, 10 January 2004.) Jackie Stewart was a sprightly, menacing right winger for Dunfermline Athletic, East Fife and Walsall during the 1950s. He won two caps for the Scottish League representative side in 1952–53 and the following season was a member of the East Fife team that won the Scottish League Cup.

**Cecil Stirland** (Born Adwick-le-Street, Yorkshire, 15 July 1921. Died 2 February 2004.) Cecil Stirland was a wholehearted wing half who made almost 150 senior appearances for Doncaster Rovers, New Brighton and Scunthorpe United in the immediate post-war period. He was the regular right half for Doncaster when they won the Division Three North title in 1946–47.

**Bob Stokoe** (Born Mickley, nr Gateshead, 21 September 1930. Died Hartlepool, 1 February 2004.) Bob Stokoe was an effective centre half who made over 350 appearances for Newcastle United and Bury between 1950 and 1964, gaining an FA Cup winners' medal with the Magpies in 1955. He went on to a successful career in management, his greatest achievement coming when he led Sunderland to a remarkable victory over Leeds United in the 1973 FA Cup final. Bob also had spells as manager of Bury, Charlton Athletic, Rochdale, Carlisle United and Blackpool and was awarded the Football League Long Service Medal in 1984.

**Derek Stonehouse** (Born Skelton, 18 November 1932. Died Linthorpe, 9 April 2004.) Derek Stonehouse spent over a decade on the books at Ayresome Park, making close on 200 senior appearances as a reliable full back for Middlesbrough. He later had a couple of seasons at Hartlepools before joining the backroom staff at Darlington where he worked alongside manager Ray Yeoman.

**Eddie Thomas** (Born Newton-le-Willows, 23 October 1933. Died Allestree, Derby, 12 November 2003.) Eddie Thomas was a talented inside forward, known for his cool, accurate finishing. His career began at Everton and subsequently took in spells at Blackburn, Swansea, Derby and Leyton Orient. Eddie equalled a club record at Derby by scoring in six consecutive League games.

**George Thompson** (Born Maltby, Yorkshire, 15 September 1926. Died Blackburn, 7 March 2004.) George Thompson was the goalkeeper for Scunthorpe United in their first-ever Football League match against Shrewsbury Town in August 1950. He went on to make over 450 senior appearances in a career that saw him play for Preston North End, Manchester City and Carlisle United. He was a member of the North End side that was defeated by West Bromwich Albion in the 1954 FA Cup final and won one cap for England B.

**Guy Thys** (Born Antwerp, Belgium, 6 December 1922. Died 1 August 2003.) Guy Thys enjoyed a moderately successful playing career, winning two caps for Belgium as an outside left whilst on the books of Standard Liege. He later became a very successful coach, taking charge of the national team for over a decade during which time they were runners-up in the European Championships (1980) and semi-finalists in the World Cup (1986).

**Geoff Twentyman** (Born Brampton, Cumberland 19 January 1930. Died Southport, 16 February 2004.) Geoff Twentyman was best known for his work as a chief scout for Liverpool, a position he held for 20 years from 1967, during which time he discovered many of the club's future stars. As a player himself he had been an effective centre half with Carlisle, Liverpool and Ballymena, being capped nine times by the Irish League representative team. Geoff briefly managed Hartlepools before joining the staff at Anfield.

**Bobby Warrender** (Born Leven, Fife, 13 February 1929. Died Leven, Fife, 19 September 2003.) Bobby Warrender was a versatile forward who played for East Fife, York City, Brechin City and East Stirlingshire between 1947 and 1963.

**Paddy Waters** (Born Dublin, 31 January 1922. Died Carlisle, 2 March 2004.) Paddy Waters began his career in Ireland with Bohemians and then Glentoran, winning a wartime cap for Northern Ireland in May 1946. He subsequently played for Preston North End and then spent eight years at Carlisle United. A right half or centre half, he made a career total of around 350 senior appearances.

**Barry Watkins** (Born Merthyr Tydfil, 30 November 1921. Died June 2004.) Barry Watkins was a versatile player who was a regular for Bristol Rovers for the first two post-war seasons. He went on to play over 100 first-team games, spending much of his time at the club as a useful squad man.

**Willie Watson** (Born Bolton-on-Dearne, Yorkshire, 7 March 1920. Died Johannesburg, South Africa, 24 April 2004.) Willie Watson was one of a select group of sportsman to have represented England at both football and cricket. As a footballer he was initially an outside left before successfully switching to right half. Most of his career was spent at Sunderland, for whom he made over 200 appearances between 1946 and 1954, although he also played for Huddersfield Town and Halifax Town. He was later manager of Halifax Town and Bradford City. He won four caps for England at soccer. Willie was just as well known for his cricket exploits with Yorkshire, Leicestershire and England, winning 22 caps.

**Roland Wheatley** (Born Nottingham, 20 June 1924. Died Strelley, nr. Nottingham, July 2003.) Roland Wheatley was an inside forward who played for Nottingham Forest, Southampton and Grimsby Town in the years immediately after the war. He later acted as a scout for the Saints for a period of almost 20 years.

**George Whitelaw** (Born Paisley, 1 January 1937. Died Paisley, 8 January 2004.) George Whitelaw developed as a goal-scoring centre forward with St Johnstone during the 1950s. After an unsuccessful spell with Sunderland he continued his career in the lower divisions of the Football League with Queens Park Rangers, Halifax Town, Carlisle United, Stockport County and Barrow before injury brought on his retirement.

**Bob Whitfield** (Born Bywell, Northumberland, 30 June 1920. Died Hull, 20 January 2004.) Bob Whitfield was a defender who made 11 appearances for Torquay United in the late 1940s and later spent several years as a regular with Southern League club Bath City.

**Len Wilkins** (Born Southampton, 20 September 1925. Died: Richmond, British Columbia, Canada, 13 August 2003.) Len Wilkins was a versatile player who made over 250 first-team appearances for Southampton between 1945 and 1958. Able to play in any of the defensive positions, he had a spell as captain of the Saints before emigrating to Canada.

**Alvan Williams** (Born Penmon, Anglesey, 21 November 1932. Died Llandderfel, nr Bala, 22 December 2003.) Alvan Williams featured both at centre forward and centre half during his playing career, enjoying his best spell at Bradford PA where he earned a reputation as a successful penalty taker. He also played for Bury, Wrexham and Exeter City, and during the 1960s served Hartlepool, Southend United and Wrexham as manager.

**Dennis Wilshaw** (Born Stoke-on-Trent, 11 March 1926. Died Stoke-on-Trent, 10 May 2004.) Dennis Wilshaw was one of the stars of the great Wolves team of the 1950s and was the club's leading scorer in 1953–54 when the Football League title was won. A versatile forward who also played for Walsall and Stoke City, he scored 193 goals in 409 senior appearances between 1946 and 1961. He was capped 12 times for England, hitting four goals in the 7-2 win over Scotland at Wembley in 1955.

**Don Wilson** (Born Heywood, Lancs, 4 June 1930. Died Bury, 12 October 2003.) Don Wilson joined Bury in the summer of 1951 but although he spent 11 seasons on the club's books as a full back he never really established himself in the first team, making just 66 senior appearances. He subsequently became a successful manager of a number of non-league clubs in the North West, notably Mossley.

**Danny Winter** (Born Tonypandy, South Wales, 14 June 1918. Died Trealaw, South Wales, 22 March 2004.) Danny Winter was a full back who played for Bolton Wanderers and Chelsea in the years either side of the war. Like many of his era, the best years of his career coincided with the hostilities, during which time he was capped twice by Wales and was a member of the Chelsea team that won the Football League (South) Cup in 1945.

**Peter Wragg** (Born Rotherham, 12 January 1931. Died Plymouth, 24 June 2004.) Peter Wragg was a versatile player who made almost 300 senior appearances for York City between 1956 and 1963, captaining the 1958–59 promotion side. He also had spells with Rotherham United, Sheffield United and Bradford City during his career.

**Dick Wright** (Born Goldthorpe, nr. Rotherham, Yorks, 5 December 1931. Died October 2003.) Goalkeeper Dick Wright spent two seasons with Leeds United without making the first team, but after joining Chester in May 1951 he experienced regular first-team football. Injury then kept him out of action for some time and he later moved on to Bradford City, although he added no further senior appearances.

**Ray Yeoman** (Born Perth, 13 May 1934. Died 15 March 2004.) Ray Yeoman made his name as a right half with Northampton Town in the 1950s before joining Middlesbrough, for whom he played over 200 senior games between 1958 and 1964. He finished his career at Darlington and later managed the Quakers for a two-year spell from March 1968.

**Percy M. Young** (Born Northwich, Cheshire, 17 May 1912. Died York, 9 May 2004.) Percy Young was the author of a series of pioneering books on football history in the 1950s and 1960s, including club histories of Wolves, Manchester United and Bolton Wanderers. Away from soccer he was known for his scholarly work on classical music.

**Ia Nannestad, Soccer History Magazine**

# THE FA BARCLAYS PREMIERSHIP AND COCA-COLA FOOTBALL LEAGUE FIXTURES 2004–05



**Sky Sports; †PremPlus pay per view*

**Saturday, 7 August 2004**

**Coca-Cola Football League Championship**

Burnley v Sheffield U
Coventry C v Sunderland* (5:15)
Crewe Alex v Cardiff C
Ipswich T v Gillingham
Leeds U v Derby Co* (12:15)
Leicester C v West Ham U
Plymouth Arg v Millwall
Preston NE v Watford
QPR v Rotherham U
Reading v Brighton & HA
Wigan Ath v Nottingham F

**Coca-Cola Football League One**

Bristol C v Torquay U
Chesterfield v Brentford
Doncaster R v Blackpool
Hartlepool U v Bradford C
Hull C v Bournemouth
Luton T v Oldham Ath
Milton Keynes Dons v Barnsley
Peterborough U v Tranmere R
Sheffield W v Colchester U
Stockport Co v Huddersfield T
Walsall v Port Vale
Wrexham v Swindon T

**Coca-Cola Football League Two**

Boston U v Oxford U
Bury v Yeovil T
Darlington v Grimsby T
Leyton Orient v Macclesfield T
Mansfield T v Bristol R
Notts Co v Chester
Rushden & D'monds v Kidderminster H
Scunthorpe U v Rochdale
Shrewsbury v Lincoln C
Southend U v Cheltenham T
Swansea C v Northampton T
Wycombe W v Cambridge U

**Sunday, 8 August 2004**

**Coca-Cola Football League Championship**

Stoke C v Wolverhampton W*

**Monday, 9 August 2004**

**Coca-Cola Football League Championship**

Watford v QPR* (7:45)

**Tuesday, 10 August 2004**

**Coca-Cola Football League Championship**

Brighton & HA v Plymouth Arg
Cardiff C v Coventry C
Gillingham v Leeds U
Millwall v Wigan Ath
Rotherham U v Burnley
Sheffield U v Stoke C
Sunderland v Crewe Alex
West Ham U v Reading* (8:00)
Wolverhampton W v Preston NE

**Coca-Cola Football League One**

Barnsley v Bristol C
Blackpool v Sheffield W
Bournemouth v Walsall
Bradford C v Peterborough U
Brentford v Doncaster R
Colchester U v Stockport Co
Huddersfield T v Chesterfield
Oldham Ath v Wrexham
Port Vale v Milton Keynes Dons
Torquay U v Hull C
Tranmere R v Hartlepool U

**Coca-Cola Football League Two**

Bristol R v Bury
Cambridge U v Leyton Orient
Cheltenham T v Scunthorpe U
Chester v Wycombe W
Grimsby T v Boston U
Kidderminster H v Notts Co
Lincoln C v Southend U
Macclesfield T v Shrewsbury
Northampton T v Rushden & D'monds
Rochdale v Swansea C
Yeovil T v Darlington

**Wednesday, 11 August 2004**

**Coca-Cola Football League Championship**

Derby Co v Leicester C
Nottingham F v Ipswich T

**Coca-Cola Football League One**

Swindon T v Luton T

**Coca-Cola Football League Two**

Oxford U v Mansfield T

**Saturday, 14 August 2004**

**Barclays Premiership**

Aston Villa v Southampton
Blackburn R v WBA
Bolton W v Charlton Ath
Manchester C v Fulham
Middlesbrough v Newcastle U† (5:15)
Norwich C v Crystal Palace
Portsmouth v Bimingham C
Tottenham H v Liverpool† (12:45)

**Coca-Cola Football League Championship**

Brighton & HA v Coventry C
Cardiff C v Plymouth Arg
Derby Co v Ipswich T
Gillingham v Preston NE
Millwall v Leicester C
Nottingham F v Crewe Alex
Rotherham U v Stoke C
Sheffield U v Reading
Sunderland v QPR
Watford v Burnley
West Ham U v Wigan Ath
Wolverhampton W v Leeds U

**Coca-Cola Football League One**

Barnsley v Luton T
Blackpool v Stockport Co
Bournemouth v Bristol C
Bradford C v Doncaster R
Brentford v Wrexham
Colchester U v Peterborough U
Huddersfield T v Hartlepool U
Oldham Ath v Walsall
Port Vale v Hull C
Swindon T v Milton Keynes Dons
Torquay U v Sheffield W
Tranmere R v Chesterfield

**Coca-Cola Football League Two**

Bristol R v Notts Co
Cambridge U v Shrewsbury
Cheltenham T v Leyton Orient
Chester v Mansfield T
Grimsby T v Bury
Kidderminster H v Darlington
Lincoln C v Rushden & D'monds
Macclesfield T v Swansea C
Northampton T v Wycombe W
Oxford U v Scunthorpe U
Rochdale v Southend U
Yeovil T v Boston U

**Conference National**

Accrington Stanley v Burton Alb
Aldershot T v York C
Barnet v Forest Green R
Carlisle U v Canvey Island
Dagenham & Red v Stevenage B
Exeter C v Morecambe
Gravesend & N v Northwich Vic
Hereford U v Farnborough T
Leigh RMI v Crawley T
Scarborough v Woking
Tamworth v Halifax T

**Sunday, 15 August 2004**

**Barclays Premiership**

Chelsea v Manchester U* (4:05)
Everton v Arsenal* (2:00)

**Tuesday, 17 August 2004**

**Conference National**
Burton Alb v Leigh RMI
Canvey Island v Gravesend & N
Crawley T v Hereford U
Farnborough T v Barnet
Forest Green R v Dagenham & Red
Halifax T v Scarborough
Morecambe v Accrington Stanley
Northwich Vic v Carlisle U
Stevenage B v Aldershot T
Woking v Exeter C
York C v Tamworth

**Saturday, 21 August 2004**

**Barclays Premiership**
Bimingham C v Chelsea
Charlton Ath v Portsmouth
Crystal Palace v Everton
Fulham v Bolton W
Liverpool v Manchester C
Manchester U v Norwich C
Newcastle U v Tottenham H
Southampton v Blackburn R† (12:45)

**Coca-Cola Football League Championship**
Burnley v Wolverhampton W
Coventry C v Millwall
Crewe Alex v West Ham U
Ipswich T v Cardiff C
Leeds U v Nottingham F
Leicester C v Watford
Plymouth Arg v Sunderland
Preston NE v Sheffield U
QPR v Derby Co
Reading v Rotherham U
Stoke C v Gillingham
Wigan Ath v Brighton & HA

**Coca-Cola Football League One**
Bristol C v Swindon T
Chesterfield v Colchester U
Doncaster R v Tranmere R
Hartlepool U v Blackpool
Hull C v Oldham Ath
Luton T v Torquay U
Milton Keynes Dons v Bournemouth
Peterborough U v Brentford
Sheffield W v Huddersfield T
Stockport Co v Bradford C
Walsall v Barnsley
Wrexham v Port Vale

**Coca-Cola Football League Two**
Boston U v Macclesfield T
Bury v Chester
Darlington v Bristol R
Leyton Orient v Oxford U
Mansfield T v Kidderminster H
Notts Co v Yeovil T
Rushden & D'monds v Grimsby T
Scunthorpe U v Lincoln C
Shrewsbury v Northampton T
Southend U v Cambridge U
Swansea C v Cheltenham T
Wycombe W v Rochdale

**Conference National**
Burton Alb v Dagenham & Red
Canvey Island v Tamworth
Crawley T v Aldershot T
Farnborough T v Scarborough
Forest Green R v Carlisle U
Halifax T v Barnet
Morecambe v Gravesend & N
Northwich Vic v Exeter C
Stevenage B v Accrington Stanley
Woking v Leigh RMI
York C v Hereford U

**Sunday, 22 August 2004**

**Barclays Premiership**
Arsenal v Middlesbrough* (4:05)
WBA v Aston Villa* (1:00)

**Tuesday, 24 August 2004**

**Barclays Premiership**
Arsenal v Blackburn R
Bimingham C v Manchester C
Charlton Ath v Aston Villa
Crystal Palace v Chelsea* (8:00)
WBA v Tottenham H

**Wednesday, 25 August 2004**

**Barclays Premiership**
Fulham v Middlesbrough
Liverpool v Portsmouth
Manchester U v Everton
Newcastle U v Norwich C* (8:00)
Southampton v Bolton W

**Saturday, 28 August 2004**
Aston Villa v Newcastle U
Blackburn R v Manchester U† (12:45)
Chelsea v Southampton
Everton v WBA
Manchester C v Charlton Ath
Middlesbrough v Crystal Palace
Norwich C v Arsenal† (5:15)
Tottenham H v Bimingham C

**Coca-Cola Football League Championship**
Brighton & HA v Preston NE
Cardiff C v Stoke C
Derby Co v Crewe Alex
Gillingham v QPR
Millwall v Reading
Nottingham F v Coventry C
Rotherham U v Ipswich T
Sheffield U v Leeds U
Sunderland v Wigan Ath
Watford v Plymouth Arg
West Ham U v Burnley
Wolverhampton W v Leicester C

**Coca-Cola Football League One**
Barnsley v Hull C
Blackpool v Luton T
Bournemouth v Wrexham
Bradford C v Chesterfield
Brentford v Stockport Co
Colchester U v Doncaster R
Huddersfield T v Peterborough U
Oldham Ath v Milton Keynes Dons
Port Vale v Bristol C
Swindon T v Hartlepool U
Torquay U v Walsall
Tranmere R v Sheffield W

**Coca-Cola Football League Two**
Bristol R v Southend U
Cambridge U v Swansea C
Cheltenham T v Boston U
Chester v Darlington
Grimsby T v Mansfield T
Kidderminster H v Wycombe W
Lincoln C v Notts Co
Macclesfield T v Scunthorpe U
Northampton T v Leyton Orient
Oxford U v Shrewsbury
Rochdale v Bury
Yeovil T v Rushden & D'monds

**Conference National**
Accrington Stanley v Crawley T
Aldershot T v Burton Alb
Barnet v Northwich Vic
Carlisle U v Farnborough T
Dagenham & Red v Woking
Exeter C v Canvey Island
Gravesend & N v York C
Hereford U v Stevenage B
Leigh RMI v Halifax T
Scarborough v Morecambe
Tamworth v Forest Green R

**Sunday, 29 August 2004**

**Barclays Premiership**
Bolton W v Liverpool* (4:05)

**Monday, 30 August 2004**

**Barclays Premiership**
Portsmouth v Fulham* (8:00)

**Coca-Cola Football League Championship**
Burnley v Gillingham
Coventry C v West Ham U
Crewe Alex v Millwall
Ipswich T v Wolverhampton W
Leeds U v Watford
Leicester C v Brighton & HA
Plymouth Arg v Nottingham F
Preston NE v Rotherham U
QPR v Sheffield U
Reading v Sunderland
Stoke C v Derby Co
Wigan Ath v Cardiff C

**Coca-Cola Football League One**
Bristol C v Brentford
Chesterfield v Port Vale
Doncaster R v Huddersfield T
Hartlepool U v Colchester U
Hull C v Bradford C
Luton T v Bournemouth
Milton Keynes Dons v Torquay U
Peterborough U v Blackpool
Sheffield W v Oldham Ath
Stockport Co v Tranmere R
Walsall v Swindon T
Wrexham v Barnsley

**Coca-Cola Football League Two**
Boston U v Chester
Bury v Kidderminster H
Darlington v Cambridge U
Leyton Orient v Rochdale
Mansfield T v Yeovil T
Notts Co v Oxford U
Rushden & D'monds v Bristol R
Scunthorpe U v Northampton T
Shrewsbury v Cheltenham T
Southend U v Macclesfield T
Swansea C v Lincoln C
Wycombe W v Grimsby T

**Conference National**
Burton Alb v Scarborough
Canvey Island v Barnet

Crawley T v Dagenham & Red
Farnborough T v Exeter C
Forest Green R v Gravesend & N
Halifax T v Carlisle U
Morecambe v Leigh RMI
Northwich Vic v Hereford U
Stevenage B v Tamworth
Woking v Aldershot T
York C v Accrington Stanley

**Saturday, 4 September 2004**

**Coca-Cola Football League One**

Blackpool v Wrexham
Bradford C v Port Vale
Brentford v Bournemouth
Chesterfield v Milton Keynes Dons
Colchester U v Swindon T
Doncaster R v Walsall
Hartlepool U v Barnsley
Huddersfield T v Hull C
Peterborough U v Bristol C
Sheffield W v Luton T
Stockport Co v Torquay U
Tranmere R v Oldham Ath

**Coca-Cola Football League Two**

Boston U v Cambridge U
Bristol R v Shrewsbury
Bury v Lincoln C
Chester v Macclesfield T
Darlington v Scunthorpe U
Grimsby T v Rochdale
Kidderminster H v Leyton Orient
Mansfield T v Northampton T
Notts Co v Cheltenham T
Rushden & D'monds v Southend U
Wycombe W v Oxford U
Yeovil T v Swansea C

**Conference National**

Accrington Stanley v Woking
Aldershot T v Northwich Vic
Barnet v Morecambe
Carlisle U v Burton Alb
Dagenham & Red v York C
Exeter C v Crawley T
Gravesend & N v Stevenage B
Hereford U v Halifax T
Leigh RMI v Forest Green R
Scarborough v Canvey Island
Tamworth v Farnborough T

**Saturday, 11 September 2004**

**Barclays Premiership**

Aston Villa v Chelsea† (12:45)
Bolton W v Manchester U
Fulham v Arsenal
Liverpool v WBA
Manchester C v Everton
Middlesbrough v Bimingham C
Newcastle U v Blackburn R
Portsmouth v Crystal Palace* (5:15)

**Coca-Cola Football League Championship**

Burnley v Crewe Alex
Derby Co v Reading
Gillingham v Sunderland
Ipswich T v Millwall
Leeds U v Coventry C
Nottingham F v Cardiff C
Preston NE v Stoke C
QPR v Plymouth Arg
Rotherham U v Leicester C
Sheffield U v West Ham U
Watford v Brighton & HA
Wolverhampton W v Wigan Ath

**Coca-Cola Football League One**

Barnsley v Tranmere R
Bournemouth v Colchester U
Bristol C v Stockport Co
Hull C v Blackpool
Luton T v Chesterfield
Milton Keynes Dons v Doncaster R
Oldham Ath v Hartlepool U
Port Vale v Huddersfield T
Swindon T v Peterborough U
Torquay U v Brentford
Walsall v Sheffield W
Wrexham v Bradford C

**Coca-Cola Football League Two**

Cambridge U v Mansfield T
Cheltenham T v Yeovil T
Leyton Orient v Bristol R
Lincoln C v Boston U
Macclesfield T v Grimsby T
Northampton T v Notts Co
Oxford U v Rushden & D'monds
Rochdale v Darlington
Scunthorpe U v Chester
Shrewsbury v Bury
Southend U v Wycombe W
Swansea C v Kidderminster H

**Conference National**

Crawley T v York C
Dagenham & Red v Accrington Stanley
Farnborough T v Canvey Island
Gravesend & N v Hereford U
Halifax T v Forest Green R
Leigh RMI v Aldershot T
Northwich Vic v Morecambe
Scarborough v Exeter C
Stevenage B v Burton Alb
Tamworth v Barnet
Woking v Carlisle U

**Sunday, 12 September 2004**

**Barclays Premiership**

Tottenham H v Norwich C* (4:05)

**Monday, 13 September 2004**

**Barclays Premiership**

Charlton Ath v Southampton* (8:00)

**Tuesday, 14 September 2004**

**Coca-Cola Football League Championship**

Brighton & HA v Wolverhampton W
Cardiff C v Watford
Crewe Alex v QPR
Leicester C v Sheffield U
Millwall v Derby Co
Plymouth Arg v Leeds U
Reading v Preston NE
Stoke C v Ipswich T
Sunderland v Nottingham F
West Ham U v Rotherham U
Wigan Ath v Burnley

**Wednesday, 15 September 2004**

**Coca-Cola Football League Championship**

Coventry C v Gillingham

**Saturday, 18 September 2004**

**Barclays Premiership**

Arsenal v Bolton W† (12:45)
Bimingham C v Charlton Ath
Blackburn R v Portsmouth
Crystal Palace v Manchester C
Everton v Middlesbrough
Norwich C v Aston Villa
WBA v Fulham

**Coca-Cola Football League Championship**

Brighton & HA v QPR
Cardiff C v Derby Co
Coventry C v Rotherham U
Crewe Alex v Leeds U
Leicester C v Burnley
Millwall v Watford
Plymouth Arg v Wolverhampton W
Reading v Gillingham
Stoke C v Nottingham F
Sunderland v Preston NE
West Ham U v Ipswich T
Wigan Ath v Sheffield U

**Coca-Cola Football League One**

Blackpool v Swindon T
Bradford C v Bristol C
Brentford v Port Vale
Chesterfield v Walsall
Colchester U v Milton Keynes Dons
Doncaster R v Oldham Ath
Hartlepool U v Torquay U
Huddersfield T v Barnsley
Peterborough U v Hull C
Sheffield W v Bournemouth
Stockport Co v Luton T
Tranmere R v Wrexham

**Coca-Cola Football League Two**

Boston U v Shrewsbury
Bristol R v Lincoln C
Bury v Scunthorpe U
Chester v Cambridge U
Darlington v Northampton T
Grimsby T v Leyton Orient
Kidderminster H v Macclesfield T
Mansfield T v Rochdale
Notts Co v Southend U
Rushden & D'monds v Cheltenham T
Wycombe W v Swansea C
Yeovil T v Oxford U

**Conference National**

Accrington Stanley v Leigh RMI
Aldershot T v Dagenham & Red
Barnet v Gravesend & N
Burton Alb v Crawley T
Canvey Island v Halifax T
Carlisle U v Tamworth
Exeter C v Stevenage B
Forest Green R v Farnborough T
Hereford U v Scarborough
Morecambe v Woking
York C v Northwich Vic

**Sunday, 19 September 2004**

**Barclays Premiership**

Chelsea v Tottenham H* (4:05)
Southampton v Newcastle U* (2:00)

**Monday, 20 September 2004**

**Barclays Premiership**

Manchester U v Liverpool* (8:00)

**Tuesday, 21 September 2004**

**Conference National**

Barnet v Burton Alb
Canvey Island v Crawley T
Carlisle U v Scarborough
Farnborough T v Stevenage B
Forest Green R v Exeter C
Gravesend & N v Dagenham & Red
Halifax T v Morecambe
Hereford U v Aldershot T
Northwich Vic v Accrington Stanley
Tamworth v Woking
York C v Leigh RMI

**Saturday, 25 September 2004**

**Barclays Premiership**

Aston Villa v Crystal Palace
Bolton W v Bimingham C
Fulham v Southampton
Liverpool v Norwich C
Manchester C v Arsenal
Middlesbrough v Chelsea† (12:45)
Newcastle U v WBA
Tottenham H v Manchester U

**Coca-Cola Football League Championship**

Burnley v Stoke C
Derby Co v Wigan Ath
Gillingham v Brighton & HA
Ipswich T v Plymouth Arg
Leeds U v Sunderland
Nottingham F v West Ham U
Preston NE v Crewe Alex
QPR v Leicester C
Rotherham U v Millwall
Sheffield U v Coventry C
Watford v Reading
Wolverhampton W v Cardiff C

**Coca-Cola Football League One**

Barnsley v Chesterfield
Bournemouth v Doncaster R
Bristol C v Huddersfield T
Hull C v Stockport Co
Luton T v Peterborough U
Milton Keynes Dons v Hartlepool U
Oldham Ath v Colchester U
Port Vale v Blackpool
Swindon T v Bradford C
Torquay U v Tranmere R
Walsall v Brentford
Wrexham v Sheffield W

**Coca-Cola Football League Two**

Cambridge U v Grimsby T
Cheltenham T v Wycombe W
Leyton Orient v Boston U
Lincoln C v Chester
Macclesfield T v Darlington
Northampton T v Bristol R
Oxford U v Bury
Rochdale v Notts Co
Scunthorpe U v Mansfield T
Shrewsbury v Yeovil T
Southend U v Kidderminster H
Swansea C v Rushden & D'monds

**Conference National**

Accrington Stanley v Gravesend & N
Aldershot T v Carlisle U
Burton Alb v York C
Crawley T v Forest Green R
Dagenham & Red v Halifax T
Exeter C v Tamworth
Leigh RMI v Hereford U
Morecambe v Farnborough T
Scarborough v Barnet
Stevenage B v Northwich Vic
Woking v Canvey Island

**Sunday, 26 September 2004**

**Barclays Premiership**

Portsmouth v Everton* (4:05)

**Monday, 27 September 2004**

**Barclays Premiership**

Charlton Ath v Blackburn R* (8:00)

**Tuesday, 28 September 2004**

**Coca-Cola Football League Championship**

Burnley v Cardiff C
Gillingham v Leicester C
Ipswich T v Reading
Leeds U v Stoke C
Preston NE v Plymouth Arg
QPR v Coventry C
Rotherham U v Crewe Alex
Sheffield U v Sunderland
Watford v Wigan Ath
Wolverhampton W v Millwall

**Wednesday, 29 September 2004**

**Coca-Cola Football League Championship**

Derby Co v West Ham U
Nottingham F v Brighton & HA

**Saturday, 2 October 2004**

**Barclays Premiership**

Arsenal v Charlton Ath
Blackburn R v Aston Villa
Everton v Tottenham H
Manchester U v Middlesbrough
Norwich C v Portsmouth
Southampton v Manchester C† (12:45)
WBA v Bolton W† (5:15)

**Coca-Cola Football League Championship**

Brighton & HA v Sheffield U
Cardiff C v Leeds U
Coventry C v Ipswich T
Crewe Alex v Watford
Leicester C v Preston NE
Millwall v Nottingham F
Plymouth Arg v Gillingham
Reading v Burnley
Stoke C v QPR
Sunderland v Derby Co
West Ham U v Wolverhampton W
Wigan Ath v Rotherham U

**Coca-Cola Football League One**

Blackpool v Bournemouth
Bradford C v Barnsley
Brentford v Oldham Ath
Chesterfield v Bristol C
Colchester U v Port Vale
Doncaster R v Wrexham
Hartlepool U v Hull C
Huddersfield T v Walsall
Peterborough U v Torquay U
Sheffield W v Milton Keynes Dons
Stockport Co v Swindon T
Tranmere R v Luton T

**Coca-Cola Football League Two**

Boston U v Scunthorpe U
Bristol R v Oxford U
Bury v Macclesfield T
Chester v Swansea C
Darlington v Southend U
Grimsby T v Cheltenham T
Kidderminster H v Cambridge U
Mansfield T v Lincoln C
Notts Co v Leyton Orient
Rushden & D'monds v Rochdale
Wycombe W v Shrewsbury
Yeovil T v Northampton T

**Conference National**

Barnet v Woking
Canvey Island v Morecambe
Carlisle U v Crawley T
Farnborough T v Accrington Stanley
Forest Green R v Scarborough
Gravesend & N v Leigh RMI
Halifax T v Exeter C
Hereford U v Burton Alb
Northwich Vic v Dagenham & Red
Tamworth v Aldershot T
York C v Stevenage B

**Sunday, 3 October 2004**

**Barclays Premiership**

Bimingham C v Newcastle U (3:00)
Chelsea v Liverpool* (4:05)

**Monday, 4 October 2004**

**Barclays Premiership**

Crystal Palace v Fulham* (8:00)

**Tuesday, 5 October 2004**

**Conference National**

Accrington Stanley v Tamworth
Aldershot T v Gravesend & N
Burton Alb v Halifax T
Crawley T v Farnborough T
Dagenham & Red v Hereford U
Exeter C v Barnet
Leigh RMI v Carlisle U
Morecambe v York C
Scarborough v Northwich Vic
Stevenage B v Canvey Island
Woking v Forest Green R

**Saturday, 9 October 2004**

**Coca-Cola Football League One**

Barnsley v Brentford
Bournemouth v Stockport Co
Bristol C v Tranmere R
Hull C v Chesterfield
Luton T v Hartlepool U
Milton Keynes Dons v Bradford C
Oldham Ath v Blackpool
Port Vale v Doncaster R
Swindon T v Sheffield W
Torquay U v Huddersfield T
Walsall v Colchester U
Wrexham v Peterborough U

**Coca-Cola Football League Two**

Cambridge U v Bristol R
Cheltenham T v Chester
Leyton Orient v Bury
Lincoln C v Kidderminster H
Macclesfield T v Notts Co
Northampton T v Grimsby T
Oxford U v Darlington
Rochdale v Yeovil T
Scunthorpe U v Wycombe W

Shrewsbury v Rushden & D'monds
Southend U v Boston U
Swansea C v Mansfield T

**Conference National**
Accrington Stanley v Hereford U
Barnet v Dagenham & Red
Burton Alb v Gravesend & N
Canvey Island v Forest Green R
Crawley T v Northwich Vic
Exeter C v Carlisle U
Farnborough T v York C
Leigh RMI v Stevenage B
Morecambe v Tamworth
Scarborough v Aldershot T
Woking v Halifax T

**Saturday, 16 October 2004**
**Barclays Premiership**
Arsenal v Aston Villa
Bimingham C v Manchester U† (12:45)
Blackburn R v Middlesbrough
Bolton W v Crystal Palace
Everton v Southampton
Fulham v Liverpool
Manchester C v Chelsea
WBA v Norwich C

**Coca-Cola Football League Championship**
Cardiff C v Rotherham U
Coventry C v Leicester C
Crewe Alex v Brighton & HA
Derby Co v Watford
Gillingham v Sheffield U
Ipswich T v Burnley
Leeds U v Preston NE
Nottingham F v Wolverhampton W
Plymouth Arg v Wigan Ath
QPR v West Ham U
Stoke C v Reading
Sunderland v Millwall

**Coca-Cola Football League One**
Blackpool v Colchester U
Bournemouth v Port Vale
Bristol C v Hull C
Doncaster R v Torquay U
Hartlepool U v Chesterfield
Luton T v Huddersfield T
Milton Keynes Dons v Brentford
Sheffield W v Barnsley
Stockport Co v Peterborough U
Swindon T v Oldham Ath
Tranmere R v Bradford C
Wrexham v Walsall

**Coca-Cola Football League Two**
Boston U v Wycombe W
Cambridge U v Northampton T
Darlington v Bury
Grimsby T v Bristol R
Kidderminster H v Scunthorpe U
Leyton Orient v Shrewsbury
Mansfield T v Notts Co
Oxford U v Lincoln C
Rochdale v Cheltenham T
Rushden & D'monds v Chester
Southend U v Swansea C
Yeovil T v Macclesfield T

**Conference National**
Aldershot T v Accrington Stanley
Carlisle U v Barnet
Dagenham & Red v Leigh RMI
Forest Green R v Morecambe
Gravesend & N v Exeter C
Halifax T v Farnborough T
Hereford U v Woking
Northwich Vic v Burton Alb
Stevenage B v Crawley T
Tamworth v Scarborough
York C v Canvey Island

**Sunday, 17 October 2004**
**Barclays Premiership**
Charlton Ath v Newcastle U* (4:05)

**Monday, 18 October 2004**
**Barclays Premiership**
Portsmouth v Tottenham H* (8:00)

**Tuesday, 19 October 2004**
**Coca-Cola Football League Championship**
Brighton & HA v Cardiff C
Burnley v Coventry C
Leicester C v Ipswich T
Millwall v Gillingham
Preston NE v QPR
Reading v Leeds U
Rotherham U v Plymouth Arg
Sheffield U v Nottingham F
Watford v Sunderland
West Ham U v Stoke C
Wigan Ath v Crewe Alex
Wolverhampton W v Derby Co

**Coca-Cola Football League One**
Barnsley v Doncaster R
Bradford C v Blackpool
Brentford v Hartlepool U
Colchester U v Wrexham
Huddersfield T v Tranmere R
Hull C v Milton Keynes Dons
Oldham Ath v Bristol C
Peterborough U v Sheffield W
Port Vale v Swindon T
Torquay U v Bournemouth
Walsall v Luton T

**Coca-Cola Football League Two**
Bristol R v Yeovil T
Bury v Boston U
Cheltenham T v Mansfield T
Chester v Kidderminster H
Lincoln C v Rochdale
Macclesfield T v Cambridge U
Northampton T v Oxford U
Notts Co v Darlington
Scunthorpe U v Southend U
Shrewsbury v Grimsby T
Swansea C v Leyton Orient
Wycombe W v Rushden & D'monds

**Wednesday, 20 October 2004**
**Coca-Cola Football League One**
Chesterfield v Stockport Co

**Saturday, 23 October 2004**
**Barclays Premiership**
Aston Villa v Fulham
Chelsea v Blackburn R
Crystal Palace v WBA
Liverpool v Charlton Ath* (5:15)
Middlesbrough v Portsmouth
Newcastle U v Manchester C
Norwich C v Everton† (12:45)
Tottenham H v Bolton W

**Coca-Cola Football League Championship**
Brighton & HA v Leeds U
Burnley v Derby Co
Leicester C v Stoke C
Millwall v Cardiff C
Preston NE v Nottingham F
Reading v Crewe Alex
Rotherham U v Sunderland
Sheffield U v Plymouth Arg
Watford v Ipswich T
West Ham U v Gillingham
Wigan Ath v Coventry C
Wolverhampton W v QPR

**Coca-Cola Football League One**
Barnsley v Swindon T
Bradford C v Sheffield W
Brentford v Blackpool
Chesterfield v Doncaster R
Colchester U v Tranmere R
Huddersfield T v Milton Keynes Dons
Hull C v Luton T
Oldham Ath v Bournemouth
Peterborough U v Hartlepool U
Port Vale v Stockport Co
Torquay U v Wrexham
Walsall v Bristol C

**Coca-Cola Football League Two**
Bristol R v Kidderminster H
Bury v Rushden & D'monds
Cheltenham T v Cambridge U
Chester v Grimsby T
Lincoln C v Leyton Orient
Macclesfield T v Oxford U
Northampton T v Rochdale
Notts Co v Boston U
Scunthorpe U v Yeovil T
Shrewsbury v Southend U
Swansea C v Darlington
Wycombe W v Mansfield T

**Conference National**
Barnet v York C
Canvey Island v Leigh RMI
Carlisle U v Hereford U
Exeter C v Aldershot T
Farnborough T v Dagenham & Red
Forest Green R v Northwich Vic
Halifax T v Gravesend & N
Morecambe v Stevenage B
Scarborough v Accrington Stanley
Tamworth v Crawley T
Woking v Burton Alb

**Sunday, 24 October 2004**
**Barclays Premiership**
Manchester U v Arsenal* (4:05)
Southampton v Bimingham C* (2:00)

**Saturday, 30 October 2004**
**Barclays Premiership**
Arsenal v Southampton
Bimingham C v Crystal Palace† (12:45)
Blackburn R v Liverpool† (5:15)
Charlton Ath v Middlesbrough
Everton v Aston Villa
Fulham v Tottenham H
Portsmouth v Manchester U
WBA v Chelsea

**Coca-Cola Football League Championship**
Cardiff C v Leicester C
Coventry C v Reading
Crewe Alex v Sheffield U
Derby Co v Rotherham U
Gillingham v Wolverhampton W
Ipswich T v Preston NE
Leeds U v Wigan Ath
Nottingham F v Watford
Plymouth Arg v West Ham U
QPR v Burnley
Stoke C v Millwall
Sunderland v Brighton & HA

**Coca-Cola Football League One**
Blackpool v Huddersfield T
Bournemouth v Barnsley
Bristol C v Colchester U
Doncaster R v Peterborough U
Hartlepool U v Port Vale
Luton T v Bradford C
Milton Keynes Dons v Walsall
Sheffield W v Chesterfield
Stockport Co v Oldham Ath
Swindon T v Torquay U
Tranmere R v Brentford
Wrexham v Hull C

**Coca-Cola Football League Two**
Boston U v Bristol R
Cambridge U v Lincoln C
Darlington v Wycombe W
Grimsby T v Swansea C
Kidderminster H v Shrewsbury
Leyton Orient v Scunthorpe U
Mansfield T v Bury
Oxford U v Cheltenham T
Rochdale v Macclesfield T
Rushden & D'monds v Notts Co
Southend U v Northampton T
Yeovil T v Chester

**Sunday, 31 October 2004**
**Barclays Premiership**
Bolton W v Newcastle U* (4:05)

**Monday, 1 November 2004**
**Barclays Premiership**
Manchester C v Norwich C* (8:00)

**Tuesday, 2 November 2004**
**Coca-Cola Football League Championship**
Cardiff C v West Ham U
Crewe Alex v Leicester C
Gillingham v Watford
Ipswich T v Sheffield U
Leeds U v Burnley
Plymouth Arg v Reading
QPR v Millwall
Stoke C v Wigan Ath
Sunderland v Wolverhampton W

**Wednesday, 3 November 2004**
**Coca-Cola Football League Championship**
Coventry C v Preston NE
Derby Co v Brighton & HA
Nottingham F v Rotherham U

**Saturday, 6 November 2004**
**Barclays Premiership**
Aston Villa v Portsmouth† (12:45)
Chelsea v Everton
Crystal Palace v Arsenal* (5:15)
Liverpool v Bimingham C
Newcastle U v Fulham
Norwich C v Blackburn R
Southampton v WBA
Tottenham H v Charlton Ath

**Coca-Cola Football League Championship**
Brighton & HA v Crewe Alex
Burnley v Ipswich T
Leicester C v Coventry C
Millwall v Sunderland
Preston NE v Leeds U
Reading v Stoke C
Rotherham U v Cardiff C
Sheffield U v Gillingham
Watford v Derby Co
West Ham U v QPR
Wigan Ath v Plymouth Arg
Wolverhampton W v Nottingham F

**Coca-Cola Football League One**
Barnsley v Port Vale
Bradford C v Colchester U
Bristol C v Milton Keynes Dons
Chesterfield v Blackpool
Hartlepool U v Doncaster R
Huddersfield T v Brentford
Hull C v Walsall
Luton T v Wrexham
Peterborough U v Bournemouth
Stockport Co v Sheffield W
Torquay U v Oldham Ath
Tranmere R v Swindon T

**Coca-Cola Football League Two**
Cheltenham T v Bury
Chester v Leyton Orient
Kidderminster H v Boston U
Lincoln C v Northampton T
Mansfield T v Macclesfield T
Notts Co v Shrewsbury
Rochdale v Cambridge U
Rushden & D'monds v Darlington
Scunthorpe U v Grimsby T
Southend U v Oxford U
Swansea C v Bristol R
Wycombe W v Yeovil T

**Conference National**
Accrington Stanley v Exeter C
Aldershot T v Morecambe
Burton Alb v Farnborough T
Crawley T v Woking
Dagenham & Red v Scarborough
Gravesend & N v Carlisle U
Hereford U v Barnet
Leigh RMI v Tamworth
Northwich Vic v Canvey Island
Stevenage B v Halifax T
York C v Forest Green R

**Sunday, 7 November 2004**
**Barclays Premiership**
Manchester U v Manchester C* (4:05)
Middlesbrough v Bolton W* (2:00)

**Saturday, 13 November 2004**
**Barclays Premiership**
Bimingham C v Everton† (5:15)
Bolton W v Aston Villa
Charlton Ath v Norwich C
Fulham v Chelsea
Liverpool v Crystal Palace
Manchester C v Blackburn R
Southampton v Portsmouth
Tottenham H v Arsenal* (12:00)

**Coca-Cola Football League Championship**
Burnley v Nottingham F
Coventry C v Plymouth Arg
Gillingham v Derby Co
Ipswich T v Leeds U
Leicester C v Sunderland
Preston NE v Millwall
QPR v Wigan Ath
Reading v Cardiff C
Rotherham U v Wolverhampton W
Sheffield U v Watford
Stoke C v Crewe Alex
West Ham U v Brighton & HA

**Sunday, 14 November 2004**
**Barclays Premiership**
Newcastle U v Manchester U* (4:05)
WBA v Middlesbrough* (2:00)

**Saturday, 20 November 2004**
**Barclays Premiership**
Arsenal v WBA
Chelsea v Bolton W
Crystal Palace v Newcastle U
Everton v Fulham
Manchester U v Charlton Ath† (12:45)
Middlesbrough v Liverpool
Norwich C v Southampton
Portsmouth v Manchester C* (5:15)

**Coca-Cola Football League Championship**
Brighton & HA v Burnley
Cardiff C v Preston NE
Crewe Alex v Gillingham
Derby Co v Sheffield U
Leeds U v QPR
Millwall v West Ham U
Nottingham F v Reading
Plymouth Arg v Stoke C
Sunderland v Ipswich T
Watford v Rotherham U
Wigan Ath v Leicester C
Wolverhampton W v Coventry C

**Coca-Cola Football League One**
Blackpool v Tranmere R
Bournemouth v Chesterfield
Brentford v Bradford C
Colchester U v Huddersfield T
Doncaster R v Stockport Co
Milton Keynes Dons v Luton T
Oldham Ath v Barnsley
Port Vale v Torquay U
Sheffield W v Hartlepool U
Swindon T v Hull C
Walsall v Peterborough U
Wrexham v Bristol C

**Coca-Cola Football League Two**
Boston U v Mansfield T
Bristol R v Scunthorpe U
Bury v Notts Co
Cambridge U v Rushden & D'monds
Darlington v Lincoln C
Grimsby T v Kidderminster H
Leyton Orient v Wycombe W

Macclesfield T v Cheltenham T
Northampton T v Chester
Oxford U v Rochdale
Shrewsbury v Swansea C
Yeovil T v Southend U

**Conference National**
Barnet v Accrington Stanley
Canvey Island v Hereford U
Carlisle U v Dagenham & Red
Exeter C v Leigh RMI
Farnborough T v Northwich Vic
Forest Green R v Burton Alb
Halifax T v Aldershot T
Morecambe v Crawley T
Scarborough v Stevenage B
Tamworth v Gravesend & N
Woking v York C

**Sunday, 21 November 2004**
**Barclays Premiership**
Blackburn R v Bimingham C* (4:05)

**Monday, 22 November 2004**
**Barclays Premiership**
Aston Villa v Tottenham H* (8:00)

**Saturday, 27 November 2004**
**Barclays Premiership**
Bimingham C v Norwich C
Bolton W v Portsmouth
Charlton Ath v Chelsea
Fulham v Blackburn R† (12:45)
Manchester C v Aston Villa
Southampton v Crystal Palace
Tottenham H v Middlesbrough
WBA v Manchester U

**Coca-Cola Football League Championship**
Burnley v Millwall
Coventry C v Crewe Alex
Gillingham v Nottingham F
Ipswich T v Brighton & HA
Leicester C v Plymouth Arg
Preston NE v Derby Co
QPR v Cardiff C
Reading v Wigan Ath
Rotherham U v Leeds U
Sheffield U v Wolverhampton W
Stoke C v Sunderland
West Ham U v Watford

**Coca-Cola Football League One**
Barnsley v Blackpool
Bradford C v Oldham Ath
Bristol C v Sheffield W
Chesterfield v Swindon T
Hartlepool U v Bournemouth
Huddersfield T v Wrexham
Hull C v Brentford
Luton T v Doncaster R
Peterborough U v Port Vale
Stockport Co v Walsall
Torquay U v Colchester U
Tranmere R v Milton Keynes Dons

**Coca-Cola Football League Two**
Cheltenham T v Darlington
Chester v Oxford U
Kidderminster H v Northampton T
Lincoln C v Yeovil T
Mansfield T v Leyton Orient
Notts Co v Cambridge U
Rochdale v Boston U
Rushden & D'monds v Macclesfield T
Scunthorpe U v Shrewsbury
Southend U v Grimsby T
Swansea C v Bury
Wycombe W v Bristol R

**Conference National**
Accrington Stanley v Canvey Island
Aldershot T v Barnet
Burton Alb v Exeter C
Crawley T v Scarborough
Dagenham & Red v Morecambe
Gravesend & N v Woking
Hereford U v Tamworth
Leigh RMI v Farnborough T
Northwich Vic v Halifax T
Stevenage B v Forest Green R
York C v Carlisle U

**Sunday, 28 November 2004**
**Barclays Premiership**
Liverpool v Arsenal* (4:05)
Newcastle U v Everton* (2:00)

**Saturday, 4 December 2004**
**Barclays Premiership**
Arsenal v Bimingham C
Aston Villa v Liverpool
Blackburn R v Tottenham H* (5:15)
Chelsea v Newcastle U† (12:45)
Everton v Bolton W
Manchester U v Southampton
Norwich C v Fulham
Portsmouth v WBA

**Coca-Cola Football League Championship**
Brighton & HA v Rotherham U
Cardiff C v Gillingham
Crewe Alex v Ipswich T
Derby Co v Coventry C
Leeds U v Leicester C
Millwall v Sheffield U
Nottingham F v QPR
Plymouth Arg v Burnley
Sunderland v West Ham U
Watford v Stoke C
Wigan Ath v Preston NE
Wolverhampton W v Reading

**Conference National**
Barnet v Leigh RMI
Canvey Island v Burton Alb
Carlisle U v Stevenage B
Exeter C v York C
Farnborough T v Aldershot T
Forest Green R v Accrington Stanley
Halifax T v Crawley T
Morecambe v Hereford U
Scarborough v Gravesend & N
Tamworth v Dagenham & Red
Woking v Northwich Vic

**Sunday, 5 December 2004**
**Barclays Premiership**
Crystal Palace v Charlton Ath* (4:05)

**Monday, 6 December 2004**
**Barclays Premiership**
Middlesbrough v Manchester C* (8:00)

**Tuesday, 7 December 2004**
**Coca-Cola Football League One**
Blackpool v Torquay U
Bournemouth v Bradford C
Brentford v Luton T
Colchester U v Barnsley
Doncaster R v Bristol C
Milton Keynes Dons v Peterborough U
Oldham Ath v Chesterfield
Port Vale v Tranmere R
Walsall v Hartlepool U
Wrexham v Stockport Co

**Coca-Cola Football League Two**
Bristol R v Chester
Bury v Wycombe W
Cambridge U v Scunthorpe U
Darlington v Mansfield T
Grimsby T v Notts Co
Leyton Orient v Southend U
Macclesfield T v Lincoln C
Northampton T v Cheltenham T
Shrewsbury v Rochdale
Yeovil T v Kidderminster H

**Conference National**
Accrington Stanley v Carlisle U
Aldershot T v Canvey Island
Burton Alb v Morecambe
Crawley T v Barnet
Dagenham & Red v Exeter C
Gravesend & N v Farnborough T
Hereford U v Forest Green R
Leigh RMI v Scarborough
Northwich Vic v Tamworth
Stevenage B v Woking
York C v Halifax T

**Wednesday, 8 December 2004**
**Coca-Cola Football League One**
Sheffield W v Hull C
Swindon T v Huddersfield T

**Coca-Cola Football League Two**
Boston U v Rushden & D'monds
Oxford U v Swansea C

**Saturday, 11 December 2004**
**Barclays Premiership**
Crystal Palace v Blackburn R
Everton v Liverpool† (12:45)
Manchester C v Tottenham H
Newcastle U v Portsmouth
Norwich C v Bolton W
Southampton v Middlesbrough
WBA v Charlton Ath

**Coca-Cola Football League Championship**
Burnley v Preston NE
Cardiff C v Sunderland
Crewe Alex v Plymouth Arg
Derby Co v Nottingham F
Leicester C v Reading
Millwall v Brighton & HA
QPR v Ipswich T
Rotherham U v Sheffield U
Stoke C v Coventry C
Watford v Wolverhampton W
West Ham U v Leeds U
Wigan Ath v Gillingham

**Coca-Cola Football League One**
Blackpool v Bristol C
Bradford C v Walsall
Colchester U v Hull C
Hartlepool U v Stockport Co
Luton T v Port Vale
Milton Keynes Dons v Wrexham
Oldham Ath v Huddersfield T
Peterborough U v Chesterfield
Sheffield W v Brentford
Swindon T v Doncaster R
Torquay U v Barnsley
Tranmere R v Bournemouth

**Coca-Cola Football League Two**
Bristol R v Macclesfield T
Bury v Southend U
Chester v Shrewsbury
Darlington v Leyton Orient
Kidderminster H v Rochdale
Lincoln C v Cheltenham T
Mansfield T v Rushden & D'monds
Northampton T v Boston U
Notts Co v Wycombe W
Oxford U v Cambridge U
Scunthorpe U v Swansea C
Yeovil T v Grimsby T

**Conference National**
Crawley T v Burton Alb
Dagenham & Red v Aldershot T
Farnborough T v Forest Green R
Gravesend & N v Barnet
Halifax T v Canvey Island
Leigh RMI v Accrington Stanley
Northwich Vic v York C
Scarborough v Hereford U
Stevenage B v Exeter C
Tamworth v Carlisle U
Woking v Morecambe

**Sunday, 12 December 2004**
**Barclays Premiership**
Arsenal v Chelsea* (4:05)
Aston Villa v Bimingham C* (1:00)

**Monday, 13 December 2004**
**Barclays Premiership**
Fulham v Manchester U* (8:00)

**Saturday, 18 December 2004**
**Barclays Premiership**
Bimingham C v WBA
Blackburn R v Everton
Bolton W v Manchester C
Chelsea v Norwich C
Liverpool v Newcastle U† (12:45)
Manchester U v Crystal Palace
Middlesbrough v Aston Villa
Tottenham H v Southampton

**Coca-Cola Football League Championship**
Brighton & HA v Stoke C
Coventry C v Watford
Gillingham v Rotherham U
Ipswich T v Wigan Ath
Leeds U v Millwall
Nottingham F v Leicester C
Plymouth Arg v Derby Co
Preston NE v West Ham U
Reading v QPR
Sheffield U v Cardiff C
Sunderland v Burnley
Wolverhampton W v Crewe Alex

**Coca-Cola Football League One**
Barnsley v Peterborough U
Bournemouth v Swindon T
Brentford v Colchester U
Bristol C v Luton T
Chesterfield v Torquay U
Doncaster R v Sheffield W
Huddersfield T v Bradford C
Hull C v Tranmere R
Port Vale v Oldham Ath
Stockport Co v Milton Keynes Dons
Walsall v Blackpool
Wrexham v Hartlepool U

**Coca-Cola Football League Two**
Boston U v Darlington
Cambridge U v Bury
Cheltenham T v Kidderminster H
Grimsby T v Oxford U
Leyton Orient v Yeovil T
Macclesfield T v Northampton T
Rochdale v Bristol R
Rushden & D'monds v Scunthorpe U
Shrewsbury v Mansfield T
Southend U v Chester
Swansea C v Notts Co
Wycombe W v Lincoln C

**Conference National**
Accrington Stanley v Dagenham & Red
Aldershot T v Leigh RMI
Barnet v Tamworth
Burton Alb v Stevenage B
Canvey Island v Farnborough T
Carlisle U v Woking
Exeter C v Scarborough
Forest Green R v Halifax T
Hereford U v Gravesend & N
Morecambe v Northwich Vic
York C v Crawley T

**Sunday, 19 December 2004**
**Barclays Premiership**
Portsmouth v Arsenal* (4:05)

**Monday, 20 December 2004**
**Barclays Premiership**
Charlton Ath v Fulham* (8:00)

**Sunday, 26 December 2004**
**Barclays Premiership**
Arsenal v Fulham
Bimingham C v Middlesbrough* (3:30)
Blackburn R v Newcastle U
Chelsea v Aston Villa† (1:00)
Crystal Palace v Portsmouth
Everton v Manchester C
Manchester U v Bolton W
Norwich C v Tottenham H
Southampton v Charlton Ath
WBA v Liverpool* (6:00)

**Coca-Cola Football League Championship**
Brighton & HA v Gillingham
Cardiff C v Wolverhampton W
Coventry C v Sheffield U
Crewe Alex v Burnley
Leicester C v Rotherham U
Millwall v Ipswich T
Plymouth Arg v QPR
Reading v Watford
Stoke C v Preston NE
Sunderland v Leeds U
West Ham U v Nottingham F
Wigan Ath v Derby Co

**Coca-Cola Football League One**
Blackpool v Hull C
Bradford C v Wrexham
Brentford v Torquay U
Chesterfield v Luton T
Colchester U v Bournemouth
Doncaster R v Milton Keynes Dons
Hartlepool U v Oldham Ath
Huddersfield T v Port Vale
Peterborough U v Swindon T
Sheffield W v Walsall
Stockport Co v Bristol C
Tranmere R v Barnsley

**Coca-Cola Football League Two**
Boston U v Lincoln C
Bristol R v Leyton Orient
Bury v Shrewsbury
Chester v Scunthorpe U
Darlington v Rochdale
Grimsby T v Macclesfield T
Kidderminster H v Swansea C
Mansfield T v Cambridge U
Notts Co v Northampton T
Rushden & D'monds v Oxford U
Wycombe W v Southend U
Yeovil T v Cheltenham T

**Conference National**
Accrington Stanley v Halifax T
Aldershot T v Forest Green R
Burton Alb v Tamworth
Crawley T v Gravesend & N
Dagenham & Red v Canvey Island
Exeter C v Hereford U
Leigh RMI v Northwich Vic
Morecambe v Carlisle U
Scarborough v York C
Stevenage B v Barnet
Woking v Farnborough T

**Tuesday, 28 December 2004**
**Barclays Premiership**
Aston Villa v Manchester U* (8:00)
Bolton W v Blackburn R
Charlton Ath v Everton
Fulham v Bimingham C
Liverpool v Southampton* (4:30)
Manchester C v WBA
Middlesbrough v Norwich C
Portsmouth v Chelsea
Tottenham H v Crystal Palace

**Coca-Cola Football League Championship**
Burnley v Wigan Ath
Derby Co v Millwall
Gillingham v Coventry C
Ipswich T v Stoke C
Leeds U v Plymouth Arg
Nottingham F v Sunderland
Preston NE v Reading
QPR v Crewe Alex
Rotherham U v West Ham U
Sheffield U v Leicester C
Watford v Cardiff C
Wolverhampton W v Brighton & HA

**Coca-Cola Football League One**
Barnsley v Stockport Co
Bournemouth v Huddersfield T
Bristol C v Hartlepool U
Hull C v Doncaster R
Luton T v Colchester U
Milton Keynes Dons v Blackpool
Oldham Ath v Peterborough U
Port Vale v Sheffield W
Swindon T v Brentford
Torquay U v Bradford C
Walsall v Tranmere R
Wrexham v Chesterfield

**Coca-Cola Football League Two**
Cambridge U v Yeovil T
Cheltenham T v Bristol R
Leyton Orient v Rushden & D'monds
Lincoln C v Grimsby T
Macclesfield T v Wycombe W
Northampton T v Bury
Oxford U v Kidderminster H
Rochdale v Chester
Scunthorpe U v Notts Co
Shrewsbury v Darlington
Southend U v Mansfield T
Swansea C v Boston U

**Conference National**
Barnet v Scarborough
Canvey Island v Woking
Carlisle U v Aldershot T
Farnborough T v Morecambe
Forest Green R v Crawley T
Gravesend & N v Accrington Stanley
Halifax T v Dagenham & Red
Hereford U v Leigh RMI
Northwich Vic v Stevenage B
Tamworth v Exeter C
York C v Burton Alb

**Wednesday, 29 December 2004**
**Barclays Premiership**
Newcastle U v Arsenal* (8:00)

**Saturday, 1 January 2005**
**Barclays Premiership**
Aston Villa v Blackburn R
Bolton W v WBA
Charlton Ath v Arsenal
Fulham v Crystal Palace
Liverpool v Chelsea
Manchester C v Southampton
Middlesbrough v Manchester U
Newcastle U v Bimingham C
Portsmouth v Norwich C
Tottenham H v Everton

**Coca-Cola Football League Championship**
Burnley v Leicester C
Derby Co v Cardiff C
Gillingham v Reading
Ipswich T v West Ham U
Leeds U v Crewe Alex
Nottingham F v Stoke C
Preston NE v Sunderland
QPR v Brighton & HA
Rotherham U v Coyentry C
Sheffield U v Wigan Ath
Watford v Millwall
Wolverhampton W v Plymouth Arg

**Coca-Cola Football League One**
Barnsley v Hartlepool U
Bournemouth v Brentford
Bristol C v Peterborough U
Hull C v Huddersfield T
Luton T v Sheffield W
Milton Keynes Dons v Chesterfield
Oldham Ath v Tranmere R
Port Vale v Bradford C
Swindon T v Colchester U
Torquay U v Stockport Co
Walsall v Doncaster R
Wrexham v Blackpool

**Coca-Cola Football League Two**
Cambridge U v Boston U
Cheltenham T v Notts Co
Leyton Orient v Kidderminster H
Lincoln C v Bury
Macclesfield T v Chester
Northampton T v Mansfield T
Oxford U v Wycombe W
Rochdale v Grimsby T
Scunthorpe U v Darlington
Shrewsbury v Bristol R
Southend U v Rushden & D'monds
Swansea C v Yeovil T

**Conference National**
Barnet v Stevenage B
Canvey Island v Dagenham & Red
Carlisle U v Morecambe
Farnborough T v Woking
Forest Green R v Aldershot T
Gravesend & N v Crawley T
Halifax T v Accrington Stanley
Hereford U v Exeter C
Northwich Vic v Leigh RMI
Tamworth v Burton Alb
York C v Scarborough

**Monday, 3 January 2005**
**Barclays Premiership**
Arsenal v Manchester C
Bimingham C v Bolton W
Blackburn R v Charlton Ath
Chelsea v Middlesbrough
Crystal Palace v Aston Villa
Everton v Portsmouth
Manchester U v Tottenham H
Norwich C v Liverpool
Southampton v Fulham
WBA v Newcastle U

**Coca-Cola Football League Championship**
Brighton & HA v Watford
Cardiff C v Nottingham F
Coventry C v Leeds U
Crewe Alex v Preston NE
Leicester C v QPR
Millwall v Rotherham U
Plymouth Arg v Ipswich T
Reading v Derby Co
Stoke C v Burnley
Sunderland v Gillingham
West Ham U v Sheffield U
Wigan Ath v Wolverhampton W

**Coca-Cola Football League One**
Blackpool v Port Vale
Bradford C v Swindon T
Brentford v Walsall
Chesterfield v Barnsley
Colchester U v Oldham Ath
Doncaster R v Bournemouth
Hartlepool U v Milton Keynes Dons
Huddersfield T v Bristol C
Peterborough U v Luton T
Sheffield W v Wrexham
Stockport Co v Hull C
Tranmere R v Torquay U

**Coca-Cola Football League Two**
Boston U v Leyton Orient
Bristol R v Northampton T
Bury v Oxford U
Chester v Lincoln C
Darlington v Macclesfield T
Grimsby T v Cambridge U
Kidderminster H v Southend U
Mansfield T v Scunthorpe U
Notts Co v Rochdale
Rushden & D'monds v Swansea C
Wycombe W v Cheltenham T
Yeovil T v Shrewsbury

**Saturday, 8 January 2005**
**Coca-Cola Football League One**
Blackpool v Oldham Ath
Bradford C v Milton Keynes Dons
Brentford v Barnsley
Chesterfield v Hull C
Colchester U v Walsall
Doncaster R v Port Vale
Hartlepool U v Luton T
Huddersfield T v Torquay U
Peterborough U v Wrexham
Sheffield W v Swindon T
Stockport Co v Bournemouth
Tranmere R v Bristol C

**Coca-Cola Football League Two**
Boston U v Southend U
Bristol R v Cambridge U
Bury v Leyton Orient
Chester v Cheltenham T
Darlington v Oxford U
Grimsby T v Northampton T
Kidderminster H v Lincoln C
Mansfield T v Swansea C
Notts Co v Macclesfield T
Rushden & D'monds v Shrewsbury
Wycombe W v Scunthorpe U
Yeovil T v Rochdale

**Conference National**
Accrington Stanley v Farnborough T
Aldershot T v Tamworth
Burton Alb v Hereford U
Crawley T v Carlisle U
Dagenham & Red v Northwich Vic
Exeter C v Halifax T
Leigh RMI v Gravesend & N
Morecambe v Canvey Island
Scarborough v Forest Green R
Stevenage B v York C
Woking v Barnet

**Saturday, 15 January 2005**
**Barclays Premiership**
Aston Villa v Norwich C
Bolton W v Arsenal
Charlton Ath v Bimingham C
Fulham v WBA
Liverpool v Manchester U
Manchester C v Crystal Palace
Middlesbrough v Everton

Newcastle U v Southampton
Portsmouth v Blackburn R
Tottenham H v Chelsea

**Coca-Cola Football League Championship**
Burnley v Reading
Derby Co v Sunderland
Gillingham v Plymouth Arg
Ipswich T v Coventry C
Leeds U v Cardiff C
Nottingham F v Millwall
Preston NE v Leicester C
QPR v Stoke C
Rotherham U v Wigan Ath
Sheffield U v Brighton & HA
Watford v Crewe Alex
Wolverhampton W v West Ham U

**Coca-Cola Football League One**
Barnsley v Huddersfield T
Bournemouth v Sheffield W
Bristol C v Bradford C
Hull C v Peterborough U
Luton T v Stockport Co
Milton Keynes Dons v Colchester U
Oldham Ath v Doncaster R
Port Vale v Brentford
Swindon T v Blackpool
Torquay U v Hartlepool U
Walsall v Chesterfield
Wrexham v Tranmere R

**Coca-Cola Football League Two**
Cambridge U v Chester
Cheltenham T v Rushden & D'monds
Leyton Orient v Grimsby T
Lincoln C v Bristol R
Macclesfield T v Kidderminster H
Northampton T v Darlington
Oxford U v Yeovil T
Rochdale v Mansfield T
Scunthorpe U v Bury
Shrewsbury v Boston U
Southend U v Notts Co
Swansea C v Wycombe W

**Saturday, 22 January 2005**
**Barclays Premiership**
Arsenal v Newcastle U
Bimingham C v Fulham
Blackburn R v Bolton W
Chelsea v Portsmouth
Crystal Palace v Tottenham H
Everton v Charlton Ath
Manchester U v Aston Villa
Norwich C v Middlesbrough
Southampton v Liverpool
WBA v Manchester C

**Coca-Cola Football League Championship**
Brighton & HA v Nottingham F
Cardiff C v Burnley
Coventry C v QPR
Crewe Alex v Rotherham U
Leicester C v Gillingham
Millwall v Wolverhampton W
Plymouth Arg v Preston NE
Reading v Ipswich T
Stoke C v Leeds U
Sunderland v Sheffield U
West Ham U v Derby Co
Wigan Ath v Watford

**Coca-Cola Football League One**
Blackpool v Milton Keynes Dons
Bradford C v Torquay U
Brentford v Swindon T
Chesterfield v Wrexham
Colchester U v Luton T
Doncaster R v Hull C
Hartlepool U v Bristol C
Huddersfield T v Bournemouth
Peterborough U v Oldham Ath
Sheffield W v Port Vale
Stockport Co v Barnsley
Tranmere R v Walsall

**Coca-Cola Football League Two**
Boston U v Swansea C
Bristol R v Cheltenham T
Bury v Northampton T
Chester v Rochdale
Darlington v Shrewsbury
Grimsby T v Lincoln C
Kidderminster H v Oxford U
Mansfield T v Southend U
Notts Co v Scunthorpe U
Rushden & D'monds v Leyton Orient
Wycombe W v Macclesfield T
Yeovil T v Cambridge U

**Conference National**
Barnet v Exeter C
Canvey Island v Stevenage B
Carlisle U v Leigh RMI
Farnborough T v Crawley T
Forest Green R v Woking
Gravesend & N v Aldershot T
Halifax T v Burton Alb
Hereford U v Dagenham & Red
Northwich Vic v Scarborough
Tamworth v Accrington Stanley
York C v Morecambe

**Saturday, 29 January 2005**
**Coca-Cola Football League One**
Barnsley v Bradford C
Bournemouth v Blackpool
Bristol C v Chesterfield
Hull C v Hartlepool U
Luton T v Tranmere R
Milton Keynes Dons v Sheffield W
Oldham Ath v Brentford
Port Vale v Colchester U
Swindon T v Stockport Co
Torquay U v Peterborough U
Walsall v Huddersfield T
Wrexham v Doncaster R

**Coca-Cola Football League Two**
Cambridge U v Kidderminster H
Cheltenham T v Grimsby T
Leyton Orient v Notts Co
Lincoln C v Mansfield T
Macclesfield T v Bury
Northampton T v Yeovil T
Oxford U v Bristol R
Rochdale v Rushden & D'monds
Scunthorpe U v Boston U
Shrewsbury v Wycombe W
Southend U v Darlington
Swansea C v Chester

**Conference National**
Accrington Stanley v Northwich Vic
Aldershot T v Hereford U
Burton Alb v Barnet
Crawley T v Canvey Island
Dagenham & Red v Gravesend & N
Exeter C v Forest Green R
Leigh RMI v York C
Morecambe v Halifax T
Scarborough v Carlisle U
Stevenage B v Farnborough T
Woking v Tamworth

**Tuesday, 1 February 2005**
**Barclays Premiership**
Arsenal v Manchester U
Bimingham C v Southampton
Bolton W v Tottenham H
Charlton Ath v Liverpool
Portsmouth v Middlesbrough
WBA v Crystal Palace

**Wednesday, 2 February 2005**
**Barclays Premiership**
Blackburn R v Chelsea
Everton v Norwich C
Fulham v Aston Villa
Manchester C v Newcastle U

**Saturday, 5 February 2005**
**Barclays Premiership**
Aston Villa v Arsenal
Chelsea v Manchester C
Crystal Palace v Bolton W
Liverpool v Fulham
Manchester U v Bimingham C
Middlesbrough v Blackburn R
Newcastle U v Charlton Ath
Norwich C v WBA
Southampton v Everton
Tottenham H v Portsmouth

**Coca-Cola Football League Championship**
Brighton & HA v Derby Co
Burnley v Leeds U
Leicester C v Crewe Alex
Millwall v QPR
Preston NE v Coventry C
Reading v Plymouth Arg
Rotherham U v Nottingham F
Sheffield U v Ipswich T
Watford v Gillingham
West Ham U v Cardiff C
Wigan Ath v Stoke C
Wolverhampton W v Sunderland

**Coca-Cola Football League One**
Barnsley v Sheffield W
Bradford C v Tranmere R
Brentford v Milton Keynes Dons
Chesterfield v Hartlepool U
Colchester U v Blackpool
Huddersfield T v Luton T
Hull C v Bristol C
Oldham Ath v Swindon T
Peterborough U v Stockport Co
Port Vale v Bournemouth
Torquay U v Doncaster R
Walsall v Wrexham

**Coca-Cola Football League Two**
Bristol R v Grimsby T
Bury v Darlington
Cheltenham T v Rochdale
Chester v Rushden & D'monds
Lincoln C v Oxford U
Macclesfield T v Yeovil T

Northampton T v Cambridge U
Notts Co v Mansfield T
Scunthorpe U v Kidderminster H
Shrewsbury v Leyton Orient
Swansea C v Southend U
Wycombe W v Boston U

**Conference National**
Accrington Stanley v Scarborough
Aldershot T v Exeter C
Burton Alb v Woking
Crawley T v Tamworth
Dagenham & Red v Farnborough T
Gravesend & N v Halifax T
Hereford U v Carlisle U
Leigh RMI v Canvey Island
Northwich Vic v Forest Green R
Stevenage B v Morecambe
York C v Barnet

**Saturday, 12 February 2005**
**Barclays Premiership**
Arsenal v Crystal Palace
Bimingham C v Liverpool
Blackburn R v Norwich C
Bolton W v Middlesbrough
Charlton Ath v Tottenham H
Everton v Chelsea
Fulham v Newcastle U
Manchester C v Manchester U
Portsmouth v Aston Villa
WBA v Southampton

**Coca-Cola Football League Championship**
Cardiff C v Brighton & HA
Coventry C v Burnley
Crewe Alex v Wigan Ath
Derby Co v Wolverhampton W
Gillingham v Millwall
Ipswich T v Leicester C
Leeds U v Reading
Nottingham F v Sheffield U
Plymouth Arg v Rotherham U
QPR v Preston NE
Stoke C v West Ham U
Sunderland v Watford

**Coca-Cola Football League One**
Blackpool v Brentford
Bournemouth v Oldham Ath
Bristol C v Walsall
Doncaster R v Chesterfield
Hartlepool U v Peterborough U
Luton T v Hull C
Milton Keynes Dons v Huddersfield T
Sheffield W v Bradford C
Stockport Co v Port Vale
Swindon T v Barnsley
Tranmere R v Colchester U
Wrexham v Torquay U

**Coca-Cola Football League Two**
Boston U v Bury
Cambridge U v Macclesfield T
Darlington v Notts Co
Grimsby T v Shrewsbury
Kidderminster H v Chester
Leyton Orient v Swansea C
Mansfield T v Cheltenham T
Oxford U v Northampton T
Rochdale v Lincoln C
Rushden & D'monds v Wycombe W
Southend U v Scunthorpe U
Yeovil T v Bristol R

**Conference National**
Barnet v Hereford U
Canvey Island v Northwich Vic
Carlisle U v Gravesend & N
Exeter C v Accrington Stanley
Farnborough T v Burton Alb
Forest Green R v York C
Halifax T v Stevenage B
Morecambe v Aldershot T
Scarborough v Dagenham & Red
Tamworth v Leigh RMI
Woking v Crawley T

**Saturday, 19 February 2005**
**Coca-Cola Football League Championship**
Brighton & HA v Sunderland
Burnley v QPR
Leicester C v Cardiff C
Millwall v Stoke C
Preston NE v Ipswich T
Reading v Coventry C
Rotherham U v Derby Co
Sheffield U v Crewe Alex
Watford v Nottingham F
West Ham U v Plymouth Arg
Wigan Ath v Leeds U
Wolverhampton W v Gillingham

**Coca-Cola Football League One**
Barnsley v Bournemouth
Bradford C v Luton T
Brentford v Tranmere R
Chesterfield v Sheffield W
Colchester U v Bristol C
Huddersfield T v Blackpool
Hull C v Wrexham
Oldham Ath v Stockport Co
Peterborough U v Doncaster R
Port Vale v Hartlepool U
Torquay U v Swindon T
Walsall v Milton Keynes Dons

**Coca-Cola Football League Two**
Bristol R v Boston U
Bury v Mansfield T
Cheltenham T v Oxford U
Chester v Yeovil T
Lincoln C v Cambridge U
Macclesfield T v Rochdale
Northampton T v Southend U
Notts Co v Rushden & D'monds
Scunthorpe U v Leyton Orient
Shrewsbury v Kidderminster H
Swansea C v Grimsby T
Wycombe W v Darlington

**Conference National**
Accrington Stanley v Barnet
Aldershot T v Halifax T
Burton Alb v Forest Green R
Crawley T v Morecambe
Dagenham & Red v Carlisle U
Gravesend & N v Tamworth
Hereford U v Canvey Island
Leigh RMI v Exeter C
Northwich Vic v Farnborough T
Stevenage B v Scarborough
York C v Woking

**Tuesday, 22 February 2005**
**Coca-Cola Football League Championship**
Cardiff C v Millwall
Crewe Alex v Reading
Gillingham v West Ham U
Ipswich T v Watford
Leeds U v Brighton & HA
Plymouth Arg v Sheffield U
QPR v Wolverhampton W
Stoke C v Leicester C
Sunderland v Rotherham U

**Coca-Cola Football League One**
Blackpool v Bradford C
Bournemouth v Torquay U
Bristol C v Oldham Ath
Doncaster R v Barnsley
Hartlepool U v Brentford
Luton T v Walsall
Milton Keynes Dons v Hull C
Stockport Co v Chesterfield
Tranmere R v Huddersfield T
Wrexham v Colchester U

**Coca-Cola Football League Two**
Cambridge U v Cheltenham T
Darlington v Swansea C
Grimsby T v Chester
Kidderminster H v Bristol R
Leyton Orient v Lincoln C
Mansfield T v Wycombe W
Rochdale v Northampton T
Rushden & D'monds v Bury
Southend U v Shrewsbury
Yeovil T v Scunthorpe U

**Wednesday, 23 February 2005**
**Coca-Cola Football League Championship**
Coventry C v Wigan Ath
Derby Co v Burnley
Nottingham F v Preston NE

**Coca-Cola Football League One**
Sheffield W v Peterborough U
Swindon T v Port Vale

**Coca-Cola Football League Two**
Boston U v Notts Co
Oxford U v Macclesfield T

**Saturday, 26 February 2005**
**Barclays Premiership**
Aston Villa v Everton
Chelsea v WBA
Crystal Palace v Bimingham C
Liverpool v Blackburn R
Manchester U v Portsmouth
Middlesbrough v Charlton Ath
Newcastle U v Bolton W
Norwich C v Manchester C
Southampton v Arsenal
Tottenham H v Fulham

**Coca-Cola Football League Championship**
Brighton & HA v Millwall
Coventry C v Stoke C
Gillingham v Wigan Ath
Ipswich T v QPR
Leeds U v West Ham U
Nottingham F v Derby Co
Plymouth Arg v Crewe Alex

:eston NE v Burnley
.eading v Leicester C
heffield U v Rotherham U
underland v Cardiff C
'olverhampton W v Watford

**oca-Cola Football League One**
arnsley v Torquay U
ournemouth v Tranmere R
rentford v Sheffield W
ristol C v Blackpool
hesterfield v Peterborough U
oncaster R v Swindon T
luddersfield T v Oldham Ath
lull C v Colchester U
ort Vale v Luton T
tockport Co v Hartlepool U
'alsall v Bradford C
/rexham v Milton Keynes Dons

**oca-Cola Football League Two**
oston U v Northampton T
ambridge U v Oxford U
heltenham T v Lincoln C
rimsby T v Yeovil T
eyton Orient v Darlington
lacclesfield T v Bristol R
.ochdale v Kidderminster H
.ushden & D'monds v Mansfield T
nrewsbury v Chester
outhend U v Bury
wansea C v Scunthorpe U
/ycombe W v Notts Co

**onference National**
arnet v Aldershot T
'anvey Island v Accrington Stanley
'arlisle U v York C
xeter C v Burton Alb
arnborough T v Leigh RMI
orest Green R v Stevenage B
lalifax T v Northwich Vic
lorecambe v Dagenham & Red
carborough v Crawley T
amworth v Hereford U
/oking v Gravesend & N

**aturday, 5 March 2005**

**arclays Premiership**
.rsenal v Portsmouth
.ston Villa v Middlesbrough
rystal Palace v Manchester U
verton v Blackburn R
ulham v Charlton Ath
lanchester C v Bolton W
ewcastle U v Liverpool
orwich C v Chelsea
outhampton v Tottenham H
/BA v Bimingham C

**oca-Cola Football League hampionship**
urnley v Sunderland
:ardiff C v Sheffield U
rewe Alex v Wolverhampton W
erby Co v Plymouth Arg
eicester C v Nottingham F
lillwall v Leeds U
PR v Reading
:otherham U v Gillingham
toke C v Brighton & HA
/atford v Coventry C
Vest Ham U v Preston NE
Vigan Ath v Ipswich T

**Coca-Cola Football League One**
Blackpool v Walsall
Bradford C v Huddersfield T
Colchester U v Brentford
Hartlepool U v Wrexham
Luton T v Bristol C
Milton Keynes Dons v Stockport Co
Oldham Ath v Port Vale
Peterborough U v Barnsley
Sheffield W v Doncaster R
Swindon T v Bournemouth
Torquay U v Chesterfield
Tranmere R v Hull C

**Coca-Cola Football League Two**
Bristol R v Rochdale
Bury v Cambridge U
Chester v Southend U
Darlington v Boston U
Kidderminster H v Cheltenham T
Lincoln C v Wycombe W
Mansfield T v Shrewsbury
Northampton T v Macclesfield T
Notts Co v Swansea C
Oxford U v Grimsby T
Scunthorpe U v Rushden & D'monds
Yeovil T v Leyton Orient

**Conference National**
Accrington Stanley v Forest Green R
Aldershot T v Farnborough T
Burton Alb v Canvey Island
Crawley T v Halifax T
Dagenham & Red v Tamworth
Gravesend & N v Scarborough
Hereford U v Morecambe
Leigh RMI v Barnet
Northwich Vic v Woking
Stevenage B v Carlisle U
York C v Exeter C

**Saturday, 12 March 2005**

**Coca-Cola Football League Championship**
Burnley v Rotherham U
Coventry C v Cardiff C
Crewe Alex v Sunderland
Ipswich T v Nottingham F
Leeds U v Gillingham
Leicester C v Derby Co
Plymouth Arg v Brighton & HA
Preston NE v Wolverhampton W
QPR v Watford
Reading v West Ham U
Stoke C v Sheffield U
Wigan Ath v Millwall

**Coca-Cola Football League One**
Bristol C v Barnsley
Chesterfield v Huddersfield T
Doncaster R v Brentford
Hartlepool U v Tranmere R
Hull C v Torquay U
Luton T v Swindon T
Milton Keynes Dons v Port Vale
Peterborough U v Bradford C
Sheffield W v Blackpool
Stockport Co v Colchester U
Walsall v Bournemouth
Wrexham v Oldham Ath

**Coca-Cola Football League Two**
Boston U v Grimsby T
Bury v Bristol R
Darlington v Yeovil T
Leyton Orient v Cambridge U
Mansfield T v Oxford U
Notts Co v Kidderminster H
Rushden & D'monds v Northampton T
Scunthorpe U v Cheltenham T
Shrewsbury v Macclesfield T
Southend U v Lincoln C
Swansea C v Rochdale
Wycombe W v Chester

**Conference National**
Barnet v Crawley T
Canvey Island v Aldershot T
Carlisle U v Accrington Stanley
Exeter C v Dagenham & Red
Farnborough T v Gravesend & N
Forest Green R v Hereford U
Halifax T v York C
Morecambe v Burton Alb
Scarborough v Leigh RMI
Tamworth v Northwich Vic
Woking v Stevenage B

**Tuesday, 15 March 2005**

**Coca-Cola Football League Championship**
Brighton & HA v Wigan Ath
Cardiff C v Ipswich T
Gillingham v Stoke C
Millwall v Coventry C
Rotherham U v Reading
Sheffield U v Preston NE
Sunderland v Plymouth Arg
Watford v Leicester C
West Ham U v Crewe Alex
Wolverhampton W v Burnley

**Wednesday, 16 March 2005**

**Coca-Cola Football League Championship**
Derby Co v QPR
Nottingham F v Leeds U

**Saturday, 19 March 2005**

**Barclays Premiership**
Bimingham C v Aston Villa
Blackburn R v Arsenal
Bolton W v Norwich C
Charlton Ath v WBA
Chelsea v Crystal Palace
Liverpool v Everton
Manchester U v Fulham
Middlesbrough v Southampton
Portsmouth v Newcastle U
Tottenham H v Manchester C

**Coca-Cola Football League Championship**
Brighton & HA v Reading
Cardiff C v Crewe Alex
Derby Co v Leeds U
Gillingham v Ipswich T
Millwall v Plymouth Arg
Nottingham F v Wigan Ath
Rotherham U v QPR
Sheffield U v Burnley
Sunderland v Coventry C
Watford v Preston NE
West Ham U v Leicester C
Wolverhampton W v Stoke C

**Coca-Cola Football League One**
Barnsley v Milton Keynes Dons
Blackpool v Doncaster R
Bournemouth v Hull C
Bradford C v Hartlepool U
Brentford v Chesterfield
Colchester U v Sheffield W
Huddersfield T v Stockport Co
Oldham Ath v Luton T
Port Vale v Walsall
Swindon T v Wrexham
Torquay U v Bristol C
Tranmere R v Peterborough U

**Coca-Cola Football League Two**
Bristol R v Mansfield T
Cambridge U v Wycombe W
Cheltenham T v Southend U
Chester v Notts Co
Grimsby T v Darlington
Kidderminster H v Rushden & D'monds
Lincoln C v Shrewsbury
Macclesfield T v Leyton Orient
Northampton T v Swansea C
Oxford U v Boston U
Rochdale v Scunthorpe U
Yeovil T v Bury

**Conference National**
Accrington Stanley v Morecambe
Aldershot T v Stevenage B
Barnet v Farnborough T
Carlisle U v Northwich Vic
Dagenham & Red v Forest Green R
Exeter C v Woking
Gravesend & N v Canvey Island
Hereford U v Crawley T
Leigh RMI v Burton Alb
Scarborough v Halifax T
Tamworth v York C

**Friday, 25 March 2005**
**Conference National**
Burton Alb v Accrington Stanley
Canvey Island v Carlisle U
Crawley T v Leigh RMI
Farnborough T v Hereford U
Forest Green R v Barnet
Halifax T v Tamworth
Morecambe v Exeter C
Northwich Vic v Gravesend & N
Stevenage B v Dagenham & Red
Woking v Scarborough
York C v Aldershot T

**Saturday, 26 March 2005**
**Coca-Cola Football League One**
Bristol C v Bournemouth
Chesterfield v Tranmere R
Doncaster R v Bradford C
Hartlepool U v Huddersfield T
Hull C v Port Vale
Luton T v Barnsley
Milton Keynes Dons v Swindon T
Peterborough U v Colchester U
Sheffield W v Torquay U
Stockport Co v Blackpool
Walsall v Oldham Ath
Wrexham v Brentford

**Coca-Cola Football League Two**
Boston U v Yeovil T
Bury v Grimsby T
Darlington v Kidderminster H
Leyton Orient v Cheltenham T
Mansfield T v Chester
Notts Co v Bristol R
Rushden & D'monds v Lincoln C
Scunthorpe U v Oxford U
Shrewsbury v Cambridge U
Southend U v Rochdale
Swansea C v Macclesfield T
Wycombe W v Northampton T

**Monday, 28 March 2005**
**Coca-Cola Football League One**
Barnsley v Walsall
Blackpool v Hartlepool U
Bournemouth v Milton Keynes Dons
Bradford C v Stockport Co
Brentford v Peterborough U
Colchester U v Chesterfield
Huddersfield T v Sheffield W
Oldham Ath v Hull C
Port Vale v Wrexham
Swindon T v Bristol C
Torquay U v Luton T
Tranmere R v Doncaster R

**Coca-Cola Football League Two**
Bristol R v Darlington
Cambridge U v Southend U
Cheltenham T v Swansea C
Chester v Bury
Grimsby T v Rushden & D'monds
Kidderminster H v Mansfield T
Lincoln C v Scunthorpe U
Macclesfield T v Boston U
Northampton T v Shrewsbury
Oxford U v Leyton Orient
Rochdale v Wycombe W
Yeovil T v Notts Co

**Conference National**
Accrington Stanley v York C
Aldershot T v Woking
Barnet v Canvey Island
Carlisle U v Halifax T
Dagenham & Red v Crawley T
Exeter C v Farnborough T
Gravesend & N v Forest Green R
Hereford U v Northwich Vic
Leigh RMI v Morecambe
Scarborough v Burton Alb
Tamworth v Stevenage B

**Saturday, 2 April 2005**
**Barclays Premiership**
Arsenal v Norwich C
Bimingham C v Tottenham H
Charlton Ath v Manchester C
Crystal Palace v Middlesbrough
Fulham v Portsmouth
Liverpool v Bolton W
Manchester U v Blackburn R
Newcastle U v Aston Villa
Southampton v Chelsea
WBA v Everton

**Coca-Cola Football League Championship**
Burnley v Watford
Coventry C v Brighton & HA
Crewe Alex v Nottingham F
Ipswich T v Derby Co
Leeds U v Wolverhampton W
Leicester C v Millwall
Plymouth Arg v Cardiff C
Preston NE v Gillingham
QPR v Sunderland
Reading v Sheffield U
Stoke C v Rotherham U
Wigan Ath v West Ham U

**Coca-Cola Football League One**
Bristol C v Port Vale
Chesterfield v Bradford C
Doncaster R v Colchester U
Hartlepool U v Swindon T
Hull C v Barnsley
Luton T v Blackpool
Milton Keynes Dons v Oldham Ath
Peterborough U v Huddersfield T
Sheffield W v Tranmere R
Stockport Co v Brentford
Walsall v Torquay U
Wrexham v Bournemouth

**Coca-Cola Football League Two**
Boston U v Cheltenham T
Bury v Rochdale
Darlington v Chester
Leyton Orient v Northampton T
Mansfield T v Grimsby T
Notts Co v Lincoln C
Rushden & D'monds v Yeovil T
Scunthorpe U v Macclesfield T
Shrewsbury v Oxford U
Southend U v Bristol R
Swansea C v Cambridge U
Wycombe W v Kidderminster H

**Conference National**
Burton Alb v Aldershot T
Canvey Island v Exeter C
Crawley T v Accrington Stanley
Farnborough T v Carlisle U
Forest Green R v Tamworth
Halifax T v Leigh RMI
Morecambe v Scarborough
Northwich Vic v Barnet
Stevenage B v Hereford U
Woking v Dagenham & Red
York C v Gravesend & N

**Tuesday, 5 April 2005**
**Coca-Cola Football League Championship**
Burnley v West Ham U
Crewe Alex v Derby Co
Ipswich T v Rotherham U
Leeds U v Sheffield U
Leicester C v Wolverhampton W
Plymouth Arg v Watford
Preston NE v Brighton & HA
QPR v Gillingham
Reading v Millwall
Stoke C v Cardiff C
Wigan Ath v Sunderland

**Wednesday, 6 April 2005**
**Coca-Cola Football League Championship**
Coventry C v Nottingham F

**Saturday, 9 April 2005**
**Barclays Premiership**
Aston Villa v WBA
Blackburn R v Southampton
Bolton W v Fulham
Chelsea v Bimingham C

verton v Crystal Palace
anchester C v Liverpool
iddlesbrough v Arsenal
orwich C v Manchester U
ortsmouth v Charlton Ath
ottenham H v Newcastle U

**oca-Cola Football League hampionship**

righton & HA v Leicester C
ardiff C v Wigan Ath
erby Co v Stoke C
illingham v Burnley
illwall v Crewe Alex
ottingham F v Plymouth Arg
otherham U v Preston NE
heffield U v QPR
underland v Reading
/atford v Leeds U
/est Ham U v Coventry C
/olverhampton W v Ipswich T

**oca-Cola Football League One**

arnsley v Wrexham
lackpool v Peterborough U
ournemouth v Luton T
radford C v Hull C
rentford v Bristol C
olchester U v Hartlepool U
uddersfield T v Doncaster R
ldham Ath v Sheffield W
ort Vale v Chesterfield
windon T v Walsall
orquay U v Milton Keynes Dons
ranmere R v Stockport Co

**oca-Cola Football League Two**

ristol R v Rushden & D'monds
ambridge U v Darlington
heltenham T v Shrewsbury
hester v Boston U
rimsby T v Wycombe W
idderminster H v Bury
incoln C v Swansea C
acclesfield T v Southend U
orthampton T v Scunthorpe U
xford U v Notts Co
ochdale v Leyton Orient
eovil T v Mansfield T

**onference National**

ccrington Stanley v Stevenage B
ldershot T v Crawley T
arnet v Halifax T
arlisle U v Forest Green R
agenham & Red v Burton Alb
xeter C v Northwich Vic
ravesend & N v Morecambe
ereford U v York C
eigh RMI v Woking
carborough v Farnborough T
amworth v Canvey Island

**aturday, 16 April 2005**

**arclays Premiership**

rsenal v Everton
imingham C v Portsmouth
harlton Ath v Bolton W
rystal Palace v Norwich C
ulham v Manchester C
iverpool v Tottenham H
anchester U v Chelsea
ewcastle U v Middlesbrough
Southampton v Aston Villa
WBA v Blackburn R

**Coca-Cola Football League Championship**

Burnley v Brighton & HA
Coventry C v Wolverhampton W
Gillingham v Crewe Alex
Ipswich T v Sunderland
Leicester C v Wigan Ath
Preston NE v Cardiff C
QPR v Leeds U
Reading v Nottingham F
Rotherham U v Watford
Sheffield U v Derby Co
Stoke C v Plymouth Arg
West Ham U v Millwall

**Coca-Cola Football League One**

Barnsley v Oldham Ath
Bradford C v Brentford
Bristol C v Wrexham
Chesterfield v Bournemouth
Hartlepool U v Sheffield W
Huddersfield T v Colchester U
Hull C v Swindon T
Luton T v Milton Keynes Dons
Peterborough U v Walsall
Stockport Co v Doncaster R
Torquay U v Port Vale
Tranmere R v Blackpool

**Coca-Cola Football League Two**

Cheltenham T v Northampton T
Chester v Bristol R
Kidderminster H v Yeovil T
Lincoln C v Macclesfield T
Mansfield T v Darlington
Notts Co v Grimsby T
Rochdale v Shrewsbury
Rushden & D'monds v Boston U
Scunthorpe U v Cambridge U
Southend U v Leyton Orient
Swansea C v Oxford U
Wycombe W v Bury

**Conference National**

Burton Alb v Carlisle U
Canvey Island v Scarborough
Crawley T v Exeter C
Farnborough T v Tamworth
Forest Green R v Leigh RMI
Halifax T v Hereford U
Morecambe v Barnet
Northwich Vic v Aldershot T
Stevenage B v Gravesend & N
Woking v Accrington Stanley
York C v Dagenham & Red

**Tuesday, 19 April 2005**

**Barclays Premiership**

Bolton W v Southampton
Middlesbrough v Fulham
Norwich C v Newcastle U
Portsmouth v Liverpool

**Wednesday, 20 April 2005**

**Barclays Premiership**

Aston Villa v Charlton Ath
Blackburn R v Crystal Palace
Chelsea v Arsenal
Everton v Manchester U
Manchester C v Bimingham C
Tottenham H v WBA

**Saturday, 23 April 2005**

**Barclays Premiership**

Arsenal v Tottenham H
Aston Villa v Bolton W
Blackburn R v Manchester C
Chelsea v Fulham
Crystal Palace v Liverpool
Everton v Bimingham C
Manchester U v Newcastle U
Middlesbrough v WBA
Norwich C v Charlton Ath
Portsmouth v Southampton

**Coca-Cola Football League Championship**

Brighton & HA v West Ham U
Cardiff C v Reading
Crewe Alex v Stoke C
Derby Co v Gillingham
Leeds U v Ipswich T
Millwall v Preston NE
Nottingham F v Burnley
Plymouth Arg v Coventry C
Sunderland v Leicester C
Watford v Sheffield U
Wigan Ath v QPR
Wolverhampton W v Rotherham U

**Coca-Cola Football League One**

Blackpool v Chesterfield
Bournemouth v Peterborough U
Brentford v Huddersfield T
Colchester U v Bradford C
Doncaster R v Hartlepool U
Milton Keynes Dons v Bristol C
Oldham Ath v Torquay U
Port Vale v Barnsley
Sheffield W v Stockport Co
Swindon T v Tranmere R
Walsall v Hull C
Wrexham v Luton T

**Coca-Cola Football League Two**

Boston U v Kidderminster H
Bristol R v Swansea C
Bury v Cheltenham T
Cambridge U v Rochdale
Darlington v Rushden & D'monds
Grimsby T v Scunthorpe U
Leyton Orient v Chester
Macclesfield T v Mansfield T
Northampton T v Lincoln C
Oxford U v Southend U
Shrewsbury v Notts Co
Yeovil T v Wycombe W

**Conference National**

Aldershot T v Scarborough
Carlisle U v Exeter C
Dagenham & Red v Barnet
Forest Green R v Canvey Island
Gravesend & N v Burton Alb
Halifax T v Woking
Hereford U v Accrington Stanley
Northwich Vic v Crawley T
Stevenage B v Leigh RMI
Tamworth v Morecambe
York C v Farnborough T

**Saturday, 30 April 2005**

**Barclays Premiership**

Bimingham C v Blackburn R
Bolton W v Chelsea
Charlton Ath v Manchester U

Fulham v Everton
Liverpool v Middlesbrough
Manchester C v Portsmouth
Newcastle U v Crystal Palace
Southampton v Norwich C
Tottenham H v Aston Villa
WBA v Arsenal

**Coca-Cola Football League Championship**
Burnley v Plymouth Arg
Coventry C v Derby Co
Gillingham v Cardiff C
Ipswich T v Crewe Alex
Leicester C v Leeds U
Preston NE v Wigan Ath
QPR v Nottingham F
Reading v Wolverhampton W
Rotherham U v Brighton & HA
Sheffield U v Millwall
Stoke C v Watford
West Ham U v Sunderland

**Coca-Cola Football League One**
Barnsley v Colchester U
Bradford C v Bournemouth
Bristol C v Doncaster R
Chesterfield v Oldham Ath
Hartlepool U v Walsall
Huddersfield T v Swindon T
Hull C v Sheffield W
Luton T v Brentford
Peterborough U v Milton Keynes Dons
Stockport Co v Wrexham
Torquay U v Blackpool
Tranmere R v Port Vale

**Coca-Cola Football League Two**
Cheltenham T v Macclesfield T
Chester v Northampton T
Kidderminster H v Grimsby T
Lincoln C v Darlington
Mansfield T v Boston U
Notts Co v Bury
Rochdale v Oxford U
Rushden & D'monds v Cambridge U
Scunthorpe U v Bristol R
Southend U v Yeovil T
Swansea C v Shrewsbury
Wycombe W v Leyton Orient

**Conference National**
Accrington Stanley v Aldershot T
Barnet v Carlisle U
Burton Alb v Northwich Vic
Canvey Island v York C
Crawley T v Stevenage B
Exeter C v Gravesend & N
Farnborough T v Halifax T
Leigh RMI v Dagenham & Red
Morecambe v Forest Green R
Scarborough v Tamworth
Woking v Hereford U

**Saturday, 7 May 2005**
**Barclays Premiership**
Arsenal v Liverpool
Aston Villa v Manchester C
Blackburn R v Fulham
Chelsea v Charlton Ath
Crystal Palace v Southampton
Everton v Newcastle U
Manchester U v WBA
Middlesbrough v Tottenham H
Norwich C v Bimingham C
Portsmouth v Bolton W

**Coca-Cola Football League One**
Blackpool v Barnsley
Bournemouth v Hartlepool U
Brentford v Hull C
Colchester U v Torquay U
Doncaster R v Luton T
Milton Keynes Dons v Tranmere R
Oldham Ath v Bradford C
Port Vale v Peterborough U
Sheffield W v Bristol C
Swindon T v Chesterfield
Walsall v Stockport Co
Wrexham v Huddersfield T

**Coca-Cola Football League Two**
Boston U v Rochdale
Bristol R v Wycombe W
Bury v Swansea C
Cambridge U v Notts Co
Darlington v Cheltenham T
Grimsby T v Southend U
Leyton Orient v Mansfield T
Macclesfield T v Rushden & D'mond
Northampton T v Kidderminster H
Oxford U v Chester
Shrewsbury v Scunthorpe U
Yeovil T v Lincoln C

**Sunday, 8 May 2005**
**Coca-Cola Football League Championship**
Brighton & HA v Ipswich T
Cardiff C v QPR
Crewe Alex v Coventry C
Derby Co v Preston NE
Leeds U v Rotherham U
Millwall v Burnley
Nottingham F v Gillingham
Plymouth Arg v Leicester C
Sunderland v Stoke C
Watford v West Ham U
Wigan Ath v Reading
Wolverhampton W v Sheffield U

**Saturday, 14 May 2005**
**Barclays Premiership**
Bimingham C v Arsenal
Bolton W v Everton
Charlton Ath v Crystal Palace
Fulham v Norwich C
Liverpool v Aston Villa
Manchester C v Middlesbrough
Newcastle U v Chelsea
Southampton v Manchester U
Tottenham H v Blackburn R
WBA v Portsmouth

# THE SCOTTISH PREMIER LEAGUE AND FOOTBALL LEAGUE FIXTURES 2004–05



**Saturday, 7 August 2004**
**Bank of Scotland**
**Scottish Premier League**
Aberdeen v Rangers
Celtic v Motherwell
Dundee v Hearts
Dunfermline Ath v Dundee U
Hibernian v Kilmarnock
Livingston v Inverness CT

**Bell's Scottish First Division**
Airdrie U v St Johnstone
Clyde v Partick T
Hamilton A v Raith R
Queen of the S v Ross Co
St Mirren v Falkirk

**Bell's Scottish Second Division**
Berwick R v Morton
Dumbarton v Ayr U
Forfar Ath v Brechin C
Stirling Alb v Arbroath
Stranraer v Alloa Ath

**Bell's Scottish Third Division**
East Fife v Montrose
Gretna v Albion R
Peterhead v East Stirlingshire
Queen's Park v Cowdenbeath
Stenhousemuir v Elgin C

**Saturday, 14 August 2004**
**Bank of Scotland**
**Scottish Premier League**
Dundee U v Dundee
Hearts v Aberdeen
Kilmarnock v Celtic
Motherwell v Hibernian
Rangers v Livingston

**Bell's Scottish First Division**
Falkirk v Hamilton A
Partick T v Airdrie U
Raith R v Clyde
Ross Co v St Mirren
St Johnstone v Queen of the S

**Bell's Scottish Second Division**
Alloa Ath v Forfar Ath
Arbroath v Dumbarton
Ayr U v Berwick R
Brechin C v Stirling Alb
Morton v Stranraer

**Bell's Scottish Third Division**
Albion R v East Fife
Cowdenbeath v Stenhousemuir
East Stirlingshire v Gretna
Elgin C v Queen's Park
Montrose v Peterhead

**Sunday, 15 August 2004**
**Bank of Scotland**
**Scottish Premier League**
Inverness CT v Dunfermline Ath

**Saturday, 21 August 2004**
**Bank of Scotland**
**Scottish Premier League**
Dundee v Motherwell
Dunfermline Ath v Aberdeen
Hearts v Kilmarnock
Inverness CT v Celtic
Livingston v Dundee U
Rangers v Hibernian

**Bell's Scottish First Division**
Airdrie U v Raith R
Clyde v Ross Co
Hamilton A v Partick T
Queen of the S v Falkirk
St Mirren v St Johnstone

**Bell's Scottish Second Division**
Berwick R v Brechin C
Dumbarton v Morton
Forfar Ath v Arbroath
Stirling Alb v Alloa Ath
Stranraer v Ayr U

**Bell's Scottish Third Division**
East Fife v Cowdenbeath
Gretna v Montrose
Peterhead v Elgin C
Queen's Park v Albion R
Stenhousemuir v East Stirlingshire

**Saturday, 28 August 2004**
**Bank of Scotland**
**Scottish Premier League**
Aberdeen v Livingston
Celtic v Rangers
Dundee U v Inverness CT
Hibernian v Dundee
Motherwell v Hearts

**Bell's Scottish First Division**
Falkirk v Airdrie U
Queen of the S v Clyde
Ross Co v Partick T
St Johnstone v Raith R
St Mirren v Hamilton A

**Bell's Scottish Second Division**
Arbroath v Stranraer
Ayr U v Morton
Brechin C v Alloa Ath
Dumbarton v Forfar Ath
Stirling Alb v Berwick R

**Bell's Scottish Third Division**
Albion R v Peterhead
Cowdenbeath v East Stirlingshire
East Fife v Stenhousemuir
Elgin C v Montrose
Queen's Park v Gretna

**Sunday, 29 August 2004**
**Bank of Scotland**
**Scottish Premier League**
Kilmarnock v Dunfermline Ath

**Saturday, 4 September 2004**
**Bell's Scottish First Division**
Airdrie U v Queen of the S
Clyde v St Mirren
Hamilton A v St Johnstone
Partick T v Falkirk
Raith R v Ross Co

**Bell's Scottish Second Division**
Alloa Ath v Ayr U
Berwick R v Dumbarton
Forfar Ath v Stirling Alb
Morton v Arbroath
Stranraer v Brechin C

**Bell's Scottish Third Division**
East Stirlingshire v Elgin C
Gretna v Cowdenbeath
Montrose v Albion R
Peterhead v East Fife
Stenhousemuir v Queen's Park

**Saturday, 11 September 2004**
**Bank of Scotland**
**Scottish Premier League**
Celtic v Dundee
Dundee U v Aberdeen
Dunfermline Ath v Motherwell
Hearts v Rangers
Inverness CT v Hibernian
Livingston v Kilmarnock

**Bell's Scottish First Division**
Clyde v Airdrie U
Falkirk v Raith R
Queen of the S v Hamilton A
Ross Co v St Johnstone
St Mirren v Partick T

**Bell's Scottish Second Division**
Ayr U v Forfar Ath
Berwick R v Alloa Ath
Brechin C v Arbroath
Dumbarton v Stranraer
Stirling Alb v Morton

**Bell's Scottish Third Division**
Albion R v Stenhousemuir
Cowdenbeath v Elgin C
East Fife v East Stirlingshire
Peterhead v Gretna
Queen's Park v Montrose

**Saturday, 18 September 2004**
**Bank of Scotland**
**Scottish Premier League**
Dundee v Livingston
Hibernian v Celtic
Kilmarnock v Aberdeen
Motherwell v Dundee U
Rangers v Inverness CT

**Bell's Scottish First Division**
Airdrie U v Ross Co
Hamilton A v Clyde
Partick T v Queen of the S
Raith R v St Mirren
St Johnstone v Falkirk

**Bell's Scottish Second Division**
Alloa Ath v Dumbarton
Arbroath v Ayr U
Forfar Ath v Berwick R
Morton v Brechin C
Stranraer v Stirling Alb

**Bell's Scottish Third Division**
East Stirlingshire v Queen's Park
Elgin C v Albion R
Gretna v East Fife
Montrose v Cowdenbeath
Stenhousemuir v Peterhead

**Sunday, 19 September 2004**
**Bank of Scotland**
**Scottish Premier League**
Dunfermline Ath v Hearts

**Saturday, 25 September 2004**
**Bank of Scotland**
**Scottish Premier League**
Aberdeen v Hibernian
Celtic v Dunfermline Ath
Dundee v Rangers
Hearts v Inverness CT
Kilmarnock v Dundee U
Livingston v Motherwell

**Bell's Scottish First Division**
Falkirk v Clyde
Hamilton A v Ross Co
Raith R v Queen of the S
St Johnstone v Partick T
St Mirren v Airdrie U

**Bell's Scottish Second Division**
Alloa Ath v Morton
Ayr U v Brechin C
Berwick R v Arbroath
Dumbarton v Stirling Alb
Forfar Ath v Stranraer

**Bell's Scottish Third Division**
Albion R v East Stirlingshire
East Fife v Queen's Park
Gretna v Elgin C
Montrose v Stenhousemuir
Peterhead v Cowdenbeath

**Saturday, 2 October 2004**
**Bank of Scotland**
**Scottish Premier League**
Aberdeen v Dundee
Dundee U v Celtic
Dunfermline Ath v Hibernian
Inverness CT v Motherwell
Rangers v Kilmarnock

**Bell's Scottish First Division**
Airdrie U v Hamilton A
Clyde v St Johnstone
Partick T v Raith R
Queen of the S v St Mirren
Ross Co v Falkirk

**Bell's Scottish Second Division**
Arbroath v Alloa Ath
Brechin C v Dumbarton
Morton v Forfar Ath
Stirling Alb v Ayr U
Stranraer v Berwick R

**Bell's Scottish Third Division**
Cowdenbeath v Albion R
East Stirlingshire v Montrose
Elgin C v East Fife
Queen's Park v Peterhead
Stenhousemuir v Gretna

**Sunday, 3 October 2004**
**Bank of Scotland**
**Scottish Premier League**
Hearts v Livingston

**Saturday, 16 October 2004**
**Bank of Scotland**
**Scottish Premier League**
Celtic v Hearts
Dundee v Kilmarnock
Hibernian v Dundee U
Inverness CT v Aberdeen
Livingston v Dunfermline Ath
Motherwell v Rangers

**Bell's Scottish First Division**
Airdrie U v Partick T
Clyde v Raith R
Hamilton A v Falkirk
Queen of the S v St Johnstone
St Mirren v Ross Co

**Bell's Scottish Second Division**
Berwick R v Ayr U
Dumbarton v Arbroath
Forfar Ath v Alloa Ath
Stirling Alb v Brechin C
Stranraer v Morton

**Bell's Scottish Third Division**
East Fife v Albion R
Gretna v East Stirlingshire
Peterhead v Montrose
Queen's Park v Elgin C
Stenhousemuir v Cowdenbeath

**Saturday, 23 October 2004**
**Bank of Scotland**
**Scottish Premier League**
Aberdeen v Motherwell
Dundee v Dunfermline Ath
Hearts v Hibernian
Kilmarnock v Inverness CT
Livingston v Celtic
Rangers v Dundee U

**Bell's Scottish First Division**
Falkirk v St Mirren
Partick T v Clyde
Raith R v Hamilton A
Ross Co v Queen of the S
St Johnstone v Airdrie U

**Bell's Scottish Second Division**
Alloa Ath v Stranraer
Arbroath v Stirling Alb
Ayr U v Dumbarton
Brechin C v Forfar Ath
Morton v Berwick R

**Bell's Scottish Third Division**
Albion R v Gretna
Cowdenbeath v Queen's Park
East Stirlingshire v Peterhead
Elgin C v Stenhousemuir
Montrose v East Fife

**Tuesday, 26 October 2004**
**Bank of Scotland**
**Scottish Premier League**
Dundee U v Hearts

**Wednesday, 27 October 2004**
**Bank of Scotland**
**Scottish Premier League**
Celtic v Aberdeen
Dunfermline Ath v Rangers
Hibernian v Livingston
Inverness CT v Dundee
Motherwell v Kilmarnock

**Saturday, 30 October 2004**
**Bank of Scotland**
**Scottish Premier League**
Dundee U v Dunfermline Ath
Hearts v Dundee
Inverness CT v Livingston

lmarnock v Hibernian
otherwell v Celtic
angers v Aberdeen

**ell's Scottish First Division**
irdrie U v Falkirk
yde v Queen of the S
amilton A v St Mirren
rtick T v Ross Co
aith R v St Johnstone

**ell's Scottish Second Division**
loa Ath v Brechin C
erwick R v Stirling Alb
rfar Ath v Dumbarton
orton v Ayr U
ranraer v Arbroath

**ell's Scottish Third Division**
ast Stirlingshire v Cowdenbeath
retna v Queen's Park
ontrose v Elgin C
terhead v Albion R
enhousemuir v East Fife

**aturday, 6 November 2004**
**ank of Scotland**
**cottish Premier League**
berdeen v Hearts
eltic v Kilmarnock
undee v Dundee U
unfermline Ath v Inverness CT
ibernian v Motherwell
vingston v Rangers

**ell's Scottish First Division**
alkirk v Partick T
ueen of the S v Airdrie U
oss Co v Raith R
Johnstone v Hamilton A
Mirren v Clyde

**ell's Scottish Second Division**
rbroath v Morton
yr U v Alloa Ath
rechin C v Stranraer
umbarton v Berwick R
irling Alb v Forfar Ath

**ell's Scottish Third Division**
lbion R v Montrose
owdenbeath v Gretna
ast Fife v Peterhead
lgin C v East Stirlingshire
ueen's Park v Stenhousemuir

**aturday, 13 November 2004**
**ank of Scotland**
**cottish Premier League**
berdeen v Dunfermline Ath
eltic v Inverness CT
undee U v Livingston
ibernian v Rangers
ilmarnock v Hearts
otherwell v Dundee

**Bell's Scottish First Division**
Airdrie U v Clyde
Hamilton A v Queen of the S
Partick T v St Mirren
Raith R v Falkirk
St Johnstone v Ross Co

**Bell's Scottish Second Division**
Alloa Ath v Berwick R
Arbroath v Brechin C
Forfar Ath v Ayr U
Morton v Stirling Alb
Stranraer v Dumbarton

**Bell's Scottish Third Division**
East Stirlingshire v East Fife
Elgin C v Cowdenbeath
Gretna v Peterhead
Montrose v Queen's Park
Stenhousemuir v Albion R

**Saturday, 20 November 2004**
**Bank of Scotland**
**Scottish Premier League**
Dundee v Hibernian
Dunfermline Ath v Kilmarnock
Hearts v Motherwell
Inverness CT v Dundee U
Livingston v Aberdeen
Rangers v Celtic

**Bell's Scottish First Division**
Clyde v Hamilton A
Falkirk v St Johnstone
Queen of the S v Partick T
Ross Co v Airdrie U
St Mirren v Raith R

**Saturday, 27 November 2004**
**Bank of Scotland**
**Scottish Premier League**
Aberdeen v Dundee U
Dundee v Celtic
Hibernian v Inverness CT
Kilmarnock v Livingston
Motherwell v Dunfermline Ath
Rangers v Hearts

**Bell's Scottish First Division**
Falkirk v Ross Co
Hamilton A v Airdrie U
Raith R v Partick T
St Johnstone v Clyde
St Mirren v Queen of the S

**Bell's Scottish Second Division**
Ayr U v Arbroath
Berwick R v Forfar Ath
Brechin C v Morton
Dumbarton v Alloa Ath
Stirling Alb v Stranraer

**Bell's Scottish Third Division**
Albion R v Elgin C
Cowdenbeath v Montrose
East Fife v Gretna
Peterhead v Stenhousemuir
Queen's Park v East Stirlingshire

**Saturday, 4 December 2004**
**Bank of Scotland**
**Scottish Premier League**
Aberdeen v Kilmarnock
Celtic v Hibernian
Dundee U v Motherwell
Hearts v Dunfermline Ath
Inverness CT v Rangers
Livingston v Dundee

**Bell's Scottish First Division**
Airdrie U v St Mirren
Clyde v Falkirk
Partick T v St Johnstone
Queen of the S v Raith R
Ross Co v Hamilton A

**Bell's Scottish Second Division**
Arbroath v Berwick R
Brechin C v Ayr U
Morton v Alloa Ath
Stirling Alb v Dumbarton
Stranraer v Forfar Ath

**Bell's Scottish Third Division**
Cowdenbeath v Peterhead
East Stirlingshire v Albion R
Elgin C v Gretna
Queen's Park v East Fife
Stenhousemuir v Montrose

**Saturday, 11 December 2004**
**Bank of Scotland**
**Scottish Premier League**
Dundee U v Kilmarnock
Dunfermline Ath v Celtic
Hibernian v Aberdeen
Inverness CT v Hearts
Motherwell v Livingston
Rangers v Dundee

**Bell's Scottish First Division**
Airdrie U v St Johnstone
Clyde v Partick T
Hamilton A v Raith R
Queen of the S v Ross Co
St Mirren v Falkirk

**Saturday, 18 December 2004**
**Bank of Scotland**
**Scottish Premier League**
Celtic v Dundee U
Dundee v Aberdeen
Hibernian v Dunfermline Ath
Kilmarnock v Rangers
Livingston v Hearts
Motherwell v Inverness CT

**Bell's Scottish First Division**
Falkirk v Queen of the S
Partick T v Hamilton A
Raith R v Airdrie U

Ross Co v Clyde
St Johnstone v St Mirren

**Bell's Scottish Second Division**
Alloa Ath v Arbroath
Ayr U v Stirling Alb
Berwick R v Stranraer
Dumbarton v Brechin C
Forfar Ath v Morton

**Bell's Scottish Third Division**
Albion R v Cowdenbeath
East Fife v Elgin C
Gretna v Stenhousemuir
Montrose v East Stirlingshire
Peterhead v Queen's Park

**Sunday, 26 December 2004**
**Bell's Scottish First Division**
Falkirk v Airdrie U
Queen of the S v Clyde
Ross Co v Partick T
St Johnstone v Raith R
St Mirren v Hamilton A

**Monday, 27 December 2004**
**Bank of Scotland**
**Scottish Premier League**
Aberdeen v Inverness CT
Dundee U v Hibernian
Dunfermline Ath v Livingston
Hearts v Celtic
Kilmarnock v Dundee
Rangers v Motherwell

**Bell's Scottish Second Division**
Berwick R v Morton
Dumbarton v Ayr U
Forfar Ath v Brechin C
Stirling Alb v Arbroath
Stranraer v Alloa Ath

**Bell's Scottish Third Division**
East Fife v Montrose
Gretna v Albion R
Peterhead v East Stirlingshire
Queen's Park v Cowdenbeath
Stenhousemuir v Elgin C

**Wednesday, 29 December 2004**
**Bell's Scottish First Division**
Airdrie U v Queen of the S
Clyde v St Mirren
Hamilton A v St Johnstone
Partick T v Falkirk
Raith R v Ross Co

**Saturday, 1 January 2005**
**Bank of Scotland**
**Scottish Premier League**
Celtic v Livingston
Dundee U v Rangers
Dunfermline Ath v Dundee
Hibernian v Hearts
Inverness CT v Kilmarnock
Motherwell v Aberdeen

**Bell's Scottish First Division**
Clyde v Airdrie U
Falkirk v Raith R
Queen of the S v Hamilton A
Ross Co v St Johnstone
St Mirren v Partick T

**Bell's Scottish Second Division**
Alloa Ath v Stirling Alb
Arbroath v Forfar Ath
Ayr U v Stranraer
Brechin C v Berwick R
Morton v Dumbarton

**Bell's Scottish Third Division**
Albion R v Queen's Park
Cowdenbeath v East Fife
East Stirlingshire v Stenhousemuir
Elgin C v Peterhead
Montrose v Gretna

**Monday, 3 January 2005**
**Bell's Scottish Second Division**
Arbroath v Stranraer
Ayr U v Morton
Brechin C v Alloa Ath
Dumbarton v Forfar Ath
Stirling Alb v Berwick R

**Bell's Scottish Third Division**
Albion R v Peterhead
Cowdenbeath v East Stirlingshire
East Fife v Stenhousemuir
Elgin C v Montrose
Queen's Park v Gretna

**Saturday, 15 January 2005**
**Bank of Scotland**
**Scottish Premier League**
Aberdeen v Celtic
Dundee v Inverness CT
Hearts v Dundee U
Kilmarnock v Motherwell
Livingston v Hibernian
Rangers v Dunfermline Ath

**Bell's Scottish First Division**
Airdrie U v Ross Co
Hamilton A v Clyde
Partick T v Queen of the S
Raith R v St Mirren
St Johnstone v Falkirk

**Bell's Scottish Second Division**
Alloa Ath v Ayr U
Berwick R v Dumbarton
Forfar Ath v Stirling Alb
Morton v Arbroath
Stranraer v Brechin C

**Bell's Scottish Third Division**
East Stirlingshire v Elgin C
Gretna v Cowdenbeath
Montrose v Albion R
Peterhead v East Fife
Stenhousemuir v Queen's Park

**Saturday, 22 January 2005**
**Bank of Scotland**
**Scottish Premier League**
Aberdeen v Rangers
Celtic v Motherwell
Dundee v Hearts
Dunfermline Ath v Dundee U
Hibernian v Kilmarnock
Livingston v Inverness CT

**Bell's Scottish First Division**
Falkirk v Clyde
Hamilton A v Ross Co
Raith R v Queen of the S
St Johnstone v Partick T
St Mirren v Airdrie U

**Bell's Scottish Second Division**
Ayr U v Forfar Ath
Berwick R v Alloa Ath
Brechin C v Arbroath
Dumbarton v Stranraer
Stirling Alb v Morton

**Bell's Scottish Third Division**
Albion R v Stenhousemuir
Cowdenbeath v Elgin C
East Fife v East Stirlingshire
Peterhead v Gretna
Queen's Park v Montrose

**Saturday, 29 January 2005**
**Bank of Scotland**
**Scottish Premier League**
Dundee U v Dundee
Hearts v Aberdeen
Inverness CT v Dunfermline Ath
Kilmarnock v Celtic
Motherwell v Hibernian
Rangers v Livingston

**Bell's Scottish First Division**
Airdrie U v Hamilton A
Clyde v St Johnstone
Partick T v Raith R
Queen of the S v St Mirren
Ross Co v Falkirk

**Bell's Scottish Second Division**
Alloa Ath v Dumbarton
Arbroath v Ayr U
Forfar Ath v Berwick R
Morton v Brechin C
Stranraer v Stirling Alb

**Bell's Scottish Third Division**
East Stirlingshire v Queen's Park
Elgin C v Albion R
Gretna v East Fife
Montrose v Cowdenbeath
Stenhousemuir v Peterhead

**Saturday, 5 February 2005**
**Bell's Scottish Second Division**
Alloa Ath v Morton
Ayr U v Brechin C

rwick R v Arbroath
ımbarton v Stirling Alb
rfar Ath v Stranraer

**ll's Scottish Third Division**
bion R v East Stirlingshire
st Fife v Queen's Park
etna v Elgin C
ontrose v Stenhousemuir
terhead v Cowdenbeath

**turday, 12 February 2005**
**nk of Scotland**
**ottish Premier League**
ındee v Motherwell
ınfermline Ath v Aberdeen
earts v Kilmarnock
verness CT v Celtic
vingston v Dundee U
ıngers v Hibernian

**ll's Scottish First Division**
lkirk v Hamilton A
rtick T v Airdrie U
ith R v Clyde
oss Co v St Mirren
Johnstone v Queen of the S

**ll's Scottish Second Division**
rbroath v Alloa Ath
echin C v Dumbarton
orton v Forfar Ath
rling Alb v Ayr U
ranraer v Berwick R

**ll's Scottish Third Division**
wdenbeath v Albion R
st Stirlingshire v Montrose
gin C v East Fife
ueen's Park v Peterhead
enhousemuir v Gretna

**turday, 19 February 2005**
**nk of Scotland**
**ottish Premier League**
perdeen v Livingston
eltic v Rangers
ındee U v Inverness CT
bernian v Dundee
lmarnock v Dunfermline Ath
otherwell v Hearts

**ll's Scottish First Division**
rdrie U v Raith R
yde v Ross Co
amilton A v Partick T
ueen of the S v Falkirk
Mirren v St Johnstone

**ll's Scottish Second Division**
erwick R v Brechin C
ımbarton v Morton
rfar Ath v Arbroath
rling Alb v Alloa Ath
ranraer v Ayr U

**Bell's Scottish Third Division**
East Fife v Cowdenbeath
Gretna v Montrose
Peterhead v Elgin C
Queen's Park v Albion R
Stenhousemuir v East Stirlingshire

**Saturday, 26 February 2005**
**Bell's Scottish Second Division**
Alloa Ath v Forfar Ath
Arbroath v Dumbarton
Ayr U v Berwick R
Brechin C v Stirling Alb
Morton v Stranraer

**Bell's Scottish Third Division**
Albion R v East Fife
Cowdenbeath v Stenhousemuir
East Stirlingshire v Gretna
Elgin C v Queen's Park
Montrose v Peterhead

**Tuesday, 1 March 2005**
**Bank of Scotland**
**Scottish Premier League**
Dundee U v Aberdeen

**Wednesday, 2 March 2005**
**Bank of Scotland**
**Scottish Premier League**
Celtic v Dundee
Dunfermline Ath v Motherwell
Hearts v Rangers
Inverness CT v Hibernian
Livingston v Kilmarnock

**Saturday, 5 March 2005**
**Bank of Scotland**
**Scottish Premier League**
Dundee v Livingston
Dunfermline Ath v Hearts
Hibernian v Celtic
Kilmarnock v Aberdeen
Motherwell v Dundee U
Rangers v Inverness CT

**Bell's Scottish First Division**
Falkirk v Partick T
Queen of the S v Airdrie U
Ross Co v Raith R
St Johnstone v Hamilton A
St Mirren v Clyde

**Bell's Scottish Second Division**
Arbroath v Morton
Ayr U v Alloa Ath
Brechin C v Stranraer
Dumbarton v Berwick R
Stirling Alb v Forfar Ath

**Bell's Scottish Third Division**
Albion R v Montrose
Cowdenbeath v Gretna
East Fife v Peterhead
Elgin C v East Stirlingshire
Queen's Park v Stenhousemuir

**Saturday, 12 March 2005**
**Bank of Scotland**
**Scottish Premier League**
Aberdeen v Hibernian
Celtic v Dunfermline Ath
Dundee v Rangers
Hearts v Inverness CT
Kilmarnock v Dundee U
Livingston v Motherwell

**Bell's Scottish First Division**
Airdrie U v Falkirk
Clyde v Queen of the S
Hamilton A v St Mirren
Partick T v Ross Co
Raith R v St Johnstone

**Bell's Scottish Second Division**
Alloa Ath v Brechin C
Berwick R v Stirling Alb
Forfar Ath v Dumbarton
Morton v Ayr U
Stranraer v Arbroath

**Bell's Scottish Third Division**
East Stirlingshire v Cowdenbeath
Gretna v Queen's Park
Montrose v Elgin C
Peterhead v Albion R
Stenhousemuir v East Fife

**Saturday, 19 March 2005**
**Bank of Scotland**
**Scottish Premier League**
Aberdeen v Dundee
Dundee U v Celtic
Dunfermline Ath v Hibernian
Hearts v Livingston
Inverness CT v Motherwell
Rangers v Kilmarnock

**Bell's Scottish First Division**
Airdrie U v Clyde
Hamilton A v Queen of the S
Partick T v St Mirren
Raith R v Falkirk
St Johnstone v Ross Co

**Bell's Scottish Second Division**
Alloa Ath v Berwick R
Arbroath v Brechin C
Forfar Ath v Ayr U
Morton v Stirling Alb
Stranraer v Dumbarton

**Bell's Scottish Third Division**
East Stirlingshire v East Fife
Elgin C v Cowdenbeath
Gretna v Peterhead
Montrose v Queen's Park
Stenhousemuir v Albion R

**Saturday, 2 April 2005**
**Bank of Scotland**
**Scottish Premier League**
Celtic v Hearts
Dundee v Kilmarnock
Hibernian v Dundee U
Inverness CT v Aberdeen
Livingston v Dunfermline Ath
Motherwell v Rangers

**Bell's Scottish First Division**
Clyde v Hamilton A
Falkirk v St Johnstone
Queen of the S v Partick T
Ross Co v Airdrie U
St Mirren v Raith R

**Bell's Scottish Second Division**
Ayr U v Arbroath
Berwick R v Forfar Ath
Brechin C v Morton
Dumbarton v Alloa Ath
Stirling Alb v Stranraer

**Bell's Scottish Third Division**
Albion R v Elgin C
Cowdenbeath v Montrose
East Fife v Gretna
Peterhead v Stenhousemuir
Queen's Park v East Stirlingshire

**Saturday, 9 April 2005**
**Bank of Scotland**
**Scottish Premier League**
Aberdeen v Motherwell
Dundee v Dunfermline Ath
Hearts v Hibernian
Kilmarnock v Inverness CT
Livingston v Celtic
Rangers v Dundee U

**Bell's Scottish First Division**
Falkirk v Ross Co
Hamilton A v Airdrie U
Raith R v Partick T
St Johnstone v Clyde
St Mirren v Queen of the S

**Bell's Scottish Second Division**
Alloa Ath v Arbroath
Ayr U v Stirling Alb
Berwick R v Stranraer
Dumbarton v Brechin C
Forfar Ath v Morton

**Bell's Scottish Third Division**
Albion R v Cowdenbeath
East Fife v Elgin C
Gretna v Stenhousemuir
Montrose v East Stirlingshire
Peterhead v Queen's Park

**Saturday, 16 April 2005**
**Bank of Scotland**
**Scottish Premier League**
Celtic v Aberdeen
Dundee U v Hearts
Dunfermline Ath v Rangers
Hibernian v Livingston
Inverness CT v Dundee
Motherwell v Kilmarnock

**Bell's Scottish First Division**
Airdrie U v St Mirren
Clyde v Falkirk
Partick T v St Johnstone
Queen of the S v Raith R
Ross Co v Hamilton A

**Bell's Scottish Second Division**
Arbroath v Berwick R
Brechin C v Ayr U
Morton v Alloa Ath
Stirling Alb v Dumbarton
Stranraer v Forfar Ath

**Bell's Scottish Third Division**
Cowdenbeath v Peterhead
East Stirlingshire v Albion R
Elgin C v Gretna
Queen's Park v East Fife
Stenhousemuir v Montrose

**Saturday, 23 April 2005**
**Bell's Scottish First Division**
Falkirk v St Mirren
Partick T v Clyde
Raith R v Hamilton A
Ross Co v Queen of the S
St Johnstone v Airdrie U

**Bell's Scottish Second Division**
Alloa Ath v Stirling Alb
Arbroath v Forfar Ath
Ayr U v Stranraer
Brechin C v Berwick R
Morton v Dumbarton

**Bell's Scottish Third Division**
Albion R v Queen's Park
Cowdenbeath v East Fife
East Stirlingshire v Stenhousemuir
Elgin C v Peterhead
Montrose v Gretna

**Saturday, 30 April 2005**
**Bell's Scottish First Division**
Airdrie U v Partick T
Clyde v Raith R
Hamilton A v Falkirk
Queen of the S v St Johnstone
St Mirren v Ross Co

**Bell's Scottish Second Division**
Berwick R v Ayr U
Dumbarton v Arbroath
Forfar Ath v Alloa Ath
Stirling Alb v Brechin C
Stranraer v Morton

**Bell's Scottish Third Division**
East Fife v Albion R
Gretna v East Stirlingshire
Peterhead v Montrose
Queen's Park v Elgin C
Stenhousemuir v Cowdenbeath

**Saturday, 7 May 2005**
**Bell's Scottish First Division**
Falkirk v Queen of the S
Partick T v Hamilton A
Raith R v Airdrie U
Ross Co v Clyde
St Johnstone v St Mirren

**Bell's Scottish Second Division**
Alloa Ath v Stranraer
Arbroath v Stirling Alb
Ayr U v Dumbarton
Brechin C v Forfar Ath
Morton v Berwick R

**Bell's Scottish Third Division**
Albion R v Gretna
Cowdenbeath v Queen's Park
East Stirlingshire v Peterhead
Elgin C v Stenhousemuir
Montrose v East Fife

# OTHER FIXTURES 2004–05

## JULY 2004

1 Thur UEFA Championship Finals – Semi Final 2
3 Sat UEFA Intertoto Cup 2 (1)
4 Sun UEFA Intertoto Cup 2 (1)
UEFA Euro 2004 Championship Final
Luz Stadium, Lisbon – 8.45pm (local time)
7 Wed
10 Sat UEFA Intertoto Cup 2 (2)
11 Sun UEFA Intertoto Cup 2 (2)
14 Wed UEFA Champions League 1Q (1)
15 Thur UEFA Cup 1Q (1)
17 Sat UEFA Intertoto Cup 3 (1)
18 Sun UEFA Intertoto Cup 3 (1)
21 Wed UEFA Champions League 1Q (2)
24 Sat UEFA Intertoto Cup 3 (2)
28 Wed UEFA Champions League 2Q (1)
UEFA Intertoto Cup SF (1)
29 Thur UEFA Cup 1Q (2)
31 Sat

## AUGUST 2004

4 Wed UEFA Champions League 2Q (2)
UEFA Intertoto Cup SF (2)
7 Sat Start of Football League
8 Sun FA Community Shield
10 Tues UEFA Champions League 3Q (1)
UEFA Intertoto Cup Final (1)
11 Wed UEFA Champions League 3Q (1)
12 Thur UEFA Cup 2Q (1)
14 Sat Start of FA Premier League
18 Wed International (Friendly)
21 Sat
24 Tues UEFA Champions League 3Q (2)
UEFA Intertoto Cup Final (2)
25 Wed UEFA Champions League 3Q (2)
FL Carling Cup 1
26 Thur UEFA Cup 2Q (2)
27 Fri UEFA Super Cup
28 Sat FA Cup EP
30 Mon Bank Holiday

## SEPTEMBER 2004

1 Wed
4 Sat FA Cup P
FIFA World Cup – Austria v England
5 Sun FA Women's Cup 1Q
8 Wed FIFA World Cup – Poland v England
1 Sat FA Vase 1Q
3 Mon FA Youth Cup P**
4 Tues UEFA Champions League Match Day 1
5 Wed UEFA Champions League Match Day 1
6 Thur UEFA Cup (1)
8 Sat FA Cup 1Q
2 Wed FL Carling Cup 2
5 Sat FA Vase 2Q
6 Sun FA Women's Cup 2Q
7 Mon FA Youth Cup 1Q**
8 Tues UEFA Champions League Match Day 2
9 Wed UEFA Champions League Match Day 2
FL LDV Trophy 1
0 Thur UEFA Cup 1 (2)

## CTOBER 2004

2 Sat FA Cup 2Q
6 Wed
9 Sat FA Trophy P
FIFA World Cup – England v Wales
FA County Youth Cup 1*
10 Sun FA Sunday Cup 1
11 Mon FA Youth Cup 2Q**
13 Wed FIFA World Cup – Azerbaijan v England
16 Sat FA Cup 3Q
19 Tues UEFA Champions League Match Day 3
20 Wed UEFA Champions League Match Day 3
FL LDV Trophy 2
21 Thur UEFA Cup Match Day 1
23 Sat FA Vase 1P
24 Sun FA Women's Cup 1P
25 Mon FA Youth Cup 3Q**
27 Wed FL Carling Cup 3
30 Sat FA Cup 4Q

## NOVEMBER 2004

2 Tues UEFA Champions League Match Day 4
3 Wed UEFA Champions League Match Day 4
4 Thur UEFA Cup Match Day 2
6 Sat FA Trophy 1
FA County Youth Cup 2*
10 Wed FL Carling Cup 4
13 Sat FA Cup 1P
FA Youth Cup 1P**
14 Sun FA Women's Cup 2P
17 Wed International (Friendly)
20 Sat FA Vase 2P
21 Sun FA Sunday Cup 2
23 Tues UEFA Champions League Match Day 5
24 Wed UEFA Champions League Match Day 5
FA Cup 1P (replays)
25 Thur UEFA Cup Match Day 3
27 Sat FA Trophy 2
FA Youth Cup 2P*

## DECEMBER 2004

1 Wed UEFA Cup Match Day 4
FL Carling Cup 5
FL LDV Trophy AQF
2 Thur UEFA Cup Match Day 4
4 Sat FA Cup 2P
5 Sun FA Women's Cup 3P
7 Tues UEFA Champions League Match Day 6
8 Wed UEFA Champions League Match Day 6
11 Sat FA Vase 3P
FA County Youth Cup 3*
12 Sun FA Sunday Cup 3
15 Wed UEFA Cup Match Day 5
FA Cup 2P (replays)
16 Thur UEFA Cup Match Day 5
18 Sat FA Youth Cup 3P**
22 Wed
25 Sat Christmas Day
26 Sun Boxing Day
27 Mon Bank Holiday
28 Tues Bank Holiday

## JANUARY 2005

1 Sat New Year's Day
3 Mon Bank Holiday
5 Wed
8 Sat FA Cup 3P
9 Sun FA Sunday Cup 4P
12 Wed FL Carling Cup SF (1)
15 Sat FA Trophy 3
19 Wed FA Cup 3P (replays)
22 Sat FA Vase 4P
FA Youth Cup 4P*
23 Sun FA Sunday Cup 4

26 Wed FL Carling Cup SF (2)
FL LDV Trophy ASF
29 Sat FA Cup 4P
FA County Youth Cup 4*
30 Sun FA Women's Cup 5P

**FEBRUARY 2005**

5 Sat FA Trophy 4
9 Wed International Friendly
FA Cup 4P (replays)
12 Sat FA Vase 5P
13 Sun FA Sunday Cup 5
FA Women's Cup 6P
16 Wed UEFA Cup 32 (1)
FL LDV Trophy AF1
17 Thur UEFA Cup 32 (1)
19 Sat FA Cup 5P
FA Youth Cup 5P*
22 Tues UEFA Champions League 16 (1)
23 Wed UEFA Champions League 16 (1)
24 Thur UEFA Cup 32 (2)
26 Sat FA Trophy 5
27 Sun FL Carling Cup Final

**MARCH 2005**

2 Wed FA Cup 5P (replays)
5 Sat FA Vase 6P
FA County Youth Cup SF*
8 Tues UEFA Champions League 16 (2)
9 Wed UEFA Champions League 16 (2)
FL LDV Trophy AF2
10 Thur UEFA Cup 16 (1)
12 Sat FA Cup 6P
FA Trophy 6
13 Sun FA Women's Cup SF
16 Wed UEFA Cup 16 (2)
17 Thur UEFA Cup 16 (2)
19 Sat FA Vase SF (1)
FA Youth Cup 6P*
20 Sun FA Sunday Cup SF
22 Tues FA Cup 6P (replays)
25 Fri Good Friday
26 Sat FIFA World Cup – England v Northern Ireland
FA Vase SF (2)
28 Mon Easter Monday
30 Wed FIFA World Cup – England v Azerbaijan

**Closing date of round*
***Ties to be played week commencing*

**APRIL 2005**

2 Sat FA Trophy SF (1)
5 Tues UEFA Champions League QF (1)
6 Wed UEFA Champions League QF (1)
7 Thur UEFA Cup QF (1)
9 Sat FA Trophy SF (2)
FA Youth Cup SF (1)*
10 Sun FL LDV Trophy Final
12 Tues UEFA Champions League QF (2)
13 Wed UEFA Champions League QF (2)
14 Thur UEFA Cup QF (2)
16 Sat FA Cup SF
20 Wed
23 Sat FA Youth Cup SF (2)*
24 Sun FA Sunday Cup Final (prov)
26 Tues UEFA Champions League SF (1)
27 Wed UEFA Champions League SF (1)
28 Thur UEFA Cup SF (1)
30 Sat

**MAY 2005**

2 Mon Bank Holiday
FA Women's Cup Final
3 Tues UEFA Champions League SF (2)
4 Wed UEFA Champions League SF (2)
5 Thur UEFA Cup SF (2)
7 Sat End of Football League
11 Wed
14 Sat FA Vase Final
End of FA Premier League
FL Play Off SF (1)
18 Wed UEFA Cup Final
FL Play Off SF (2)
21 Sat FA Cup Final
22 Sun FA Trophy Final
25 Wed UEFA Champions League Final
28 Sat FL Division 3 Play Off Final
29 Sun FL Division 2 Play Off Final
30 Mon Bank Holiday
FL Division 1 Play Off Final

**JUNE 2005**

4 Sat FIFA World Cup – No England Fixture
8 Wed FIFA World Cup – No England Fixture

**TO BE DECIDED**

FA Youth Cup Final
FA County Youth Cup Final

# STOP PRESS

**Jo taxing problems for Arsenal except Vieira may go . . . Rooney wooed by Man Utd . . . Rom do for Chelsea vith Drogba club record breaking £24m capture . . .**

*Summer transfers completed and pending*

**PREMIER DIVISION**

**Arsenal:** Robin Van Persie (Feyenoord) Undisclosed; Manuel Almunia (Celta Vigo) Undisclosed; Arturo Lupoli (Parma) Undisclosed; **Aston Villa:** Martin Laursen (AC Milan) £3m; Carlton Cole (Chelsea) Loan; **Birmingham C:** Mikael Forssell (Chelsea) Loan; Emile Heskey (Liverpool) £6,250,000; Muzzy Izzet (Leicester C) Free; Julian Gray (Crystal Palace) Free; Mario Melchiot (Chelsea) Free; Jesper Gronkjaer (Chelsea) £2.2m; **Blackburn R:** Paul Dickov (Leicester C) £150,000; Javier De Pedro (Real Sociedad) Undisclosed; Dominic Matteo (Leeds U) Free; **Bolton W:** Michael Bridges (Leeds U) Free; Les Ferdinand (Leicester C) Free; Radhi Jaidi (Esperance Tunis) Free; **Charlton Ath:** Stephan Andersen (AB Copenhagen) £721,000; Bryan Hughes (Birmingham C) Free; Dennis Rommedahl (PSV Eindhoven) £2m; Talal El Karkouri (Paris St Germain) £1m; **Chelsea:** Peter Cech (Rennes) Undisclosed; Arjen Robben (PSV Eindhoven) £12m; Paulo Ferreira (Porto) £13.2m; Mateja Kezman (PSV Eindhoven) £5m; Tiago (Benfica) £10m; Didier Drogba (Marseille) £24m; **Crystal Palace:** Gabor Kiraly (Hertha Berlin) Free; Mark Hudson (Fulham) Undisclosed; Emmerson Boyce (Luton T) Free; Julian Speroni (Dundee) £500,000; **Everton:** Marcus Bent (Ipswich T) £450,000; Bjarni Vidarsson (Hafnarfjordur) Undisclosed; **Fulham:** Andy Cole (Blackburn R) Free; **Liverpool:** Djibril Cisse (Auxerre) £14m; **Manchester C:** Geert De Vlieger (Willem II) Free; Ben Thatcher (Leicester C) Undisclosed; Danny Mills (Leeds U) Free; **Manchester U:** Alan Smith (Leeds U) £7m; Gabriel Heinze (Paris St Germain) £6.9m; Liam Miller (Celtic) Free; Gerard Pique (Barcelona) Undisclosed; Giuseppe Rossi (Parma) Undisclosed; **Middlesbrough:** Michael Reiziger (Barcelona) Free; Mark Viduka (Leeds U) £4.5m; Jimmy Floyd Hasselbaink (Chelsea) Free; **Newcastle U:** James Milner (Leeds U) £5m; **Norwich C:** David Bentley (Arsenal) Loan; Paul Gallacher (Dundee U) Free; Youssef Safri (Coventry C) £500,000; Simon Charlton (Bolton W) £250,000; **Portsmouth:** Andy Griffin (Newcastle U) Free; Jamie Ashdown (Reading) Undisclosed; David Unsworth (Everton) Free; Lomana Lua-Lua (Newcastle U) £1.7m; **Southampton:** Mikael Nilsson (Halmstad) Undisclosed; Jelle Van Damme (Ajax) Undisclosed; Peter Crouch (Aston Villa) £2m; **Tottenham H:** Rodrigo Defendi (Cruzeiro) £600,000; Marton Fulop (MTK) Undisclosed; Paul Robinson (Leeds U) £2m; Sean Davis (Fulham) Undisclosed; Pedro Mendes (Porto) £2m; Leigh Mills (Swindon T) Undisclosed; **West Bromwich Albion:** Martin Albrechtsen (FC Copenhagen) £2.7m; Darren Purse (Birmingham C) £750,000; Riccardo Scimeca (Leicester C) Undisclosed; Tomasz Kuszcza (Hertha Berlin) Undisclosed.

**FOOTBALL LEAGUE CHAMPIONSHIP**

**Burnley:** Mike Duff (Cheltenham T) £30,000; Danny Coyne (Leicester C) £25,000; Micah Hyde (Watford) Free; **Coventry C:** Stephen Hughes (Charlton Ath) Free; Neil Wood (Manchester U) Free; Tim Sherwood (Portsmouth) Free; Louis Carey (Bristol C) Free; **Gillingham:** Iwan Roberts (Norwich C) Free; **Ipswich T:** Kevin Horlock (West Ham U) Free; **Leeds U:** Julian Joachim (Coventry C) Free; Matthew Spring (Luton T) Free; Paul Butler (Wolverhampton W) Free; Danny Pugh (Manchester U) Undisclosed; **Leicester C:** Jason Wilcox (Leeds U) Free; Dion Dublin (Aston Villa) Free; Kevin Pressman (Sheffield W) Free; **Nottingham F:** Chris Commons (Stoke C) Free; **Preston NE:** Callum Davidson (Leicester C) Free; **Rotherham U:** Paolo Vernazza (Watford) Free; Phil Gilchrist (WBA) Free; Julian Baudet (Notts Co) Free; **Stoke C:** Steve Simonsen (Everton) Free; **Sunderland:** Stephen Caldwell (Newcastle U) Free; Mark Lynch (Manchester U) Free; **Watford:** Andy Ferrell (Newcastle U) Free; **West Ham U:** Teddy Sheringham (Portsmouth) Free; **Wigan Ath:** David Wright (Crewe Alex) Undisclosed.

**FOOTBALL LEAGUE 1**

**Barnsley:** Stephen McPhail (Leeds U) Free; Nick Colgan (Hibernian) Free; Paul Reid (Northampton T) Free; **Bournemouth:** Dani Rodrigues (Ionikos) Free; **Brentford:** San Lee (West Ham U) Free; **Bristol C:** Bradley Orr (Newcastle U) Free; Paul Heffernan (Notts Co) £125,000; **Chesterfield:** Alex Bailey (Arsenal) Free; Shane Nicholson (Tranmere R) Free; **Colchester U:** Aidan Davison (Grimsby T) Free; Stephen Hunt (Southampton) Free; **Doncaster R:** Nick Fenton (Notts Co) Free; **Huddersfield T:** Junior Mendes (Mansfield T) Free; Chris Brandon (Chesterfield) Free; **Hull C:** Roland Edge (Hibernian) Free; Junior Lewis (Leicester C) Free; Nick Barmby (Leeds U) Free; Aaron Wilbraham (Stockport Co) £100,000; **Milton Keynes Dons:** Allan Smart (Crewe Alex) Free; **Oldham Ath:** Rodney Jack (Rushden & D) Free; **Port Vale:** Dean Smith (Sheffield W) Free; Robin Hulbert (Telford U) Free; **Sheffield W:** Steve MacLean (Rangers) Free; **Torquay U:** Martin Phillips (Plymouth Arg) Free; Gareth Owen (Stoke C) Free; **Tranmere R:** Jason McAteer (Sunderland) Free; **Wrexham:** Dean Bennett (Kidderminster H) Free; Andy Holt (Hull C) Free.

**FOOTBALL LEAGUE 2**

**Boston U:** Jason Lee (Falkirk) Free; **Bristol R:** Paul Trollope (Northampton T) Free; Robbie Ryan (Millwall) Free; **Bury:** Graeme Jones (Boston U) Free; Brian Barry-Murphy (Sheffield W) Free; **Cambridge U:** Abdu El Kholti (Yeovil T) Free; Ashley Nicholls (Darlington) Free; **Cheltenham T:** John Melligan (Wolverhampton W) £25,000; **Chester C:** Darren Edmondson (York C) Free; **Grimsby T:** Ashley Sestanovich (Sheffield U) Loan; Ronnie Bull (Millwall) Free; **Lincoln C:** Dean West (Burnley) Free; Michael Blackwood (Telford U) Free; **Macclesfield T:** Mark Bailey (Lincoln C) Free; **Mansfield T:** Derek Asamoah (Northampton T) Free; **Northampton T:** David Rowson (Partick T) Free; **Notts Co:** Glynn Hurst (Chesterfield) Free; Chris Palmer (Derby Co) Free; **Oxford U:** David Woozley (Torquay U) Free; Leo Roget (Rushden & D) Free; Tommy Mooney (Swindon T) Free; **Shrewsbury T:** John Grant (Telford U) Free; **Southend U:** Lewis Hunt (Derby Co) Free; **Wycombe W:** Clint Easton (Norwich C) Free.